FOUR COLOR COMICS
BUY
WHY YOU SHOULD CALL US BEFORE YOU SELL YOUR COLLECTION OF COMICS, ARTWORK OR MEMORABILIA:
SELL
We make it easy! No waiting for payment, No song and dance about grading. We'll come to you: Anywhere, Anytime! FOUR COLOR COMICS takes the risk out of selling. Treat yourself to an honest, straight-forward experience—Sell your collection to us and walk away with more money in your pocket and a smile on your face.
And if you're looking to buy comics, original artwork or memorabilia, give us a call first! We probably already have that elusive issue or object you've been searching for—and at a price you'll like!
CALL ROBERT ROGOVIN!
(914) 722-4696
THE JOKER © 2002, 1998 DC COMICS, ALL RIGHTS RESERVED
P.O.BOX 1399, Scarsdale, NY 10583 TEL: (914) 722-4696, FAX (914) 722-7656
NEW!
Visit our on-line
SEARCHABLE DATABASE!
1000's of Golden and Silver Age comics available without scrolling thru endless listings!
www.fourcolorcomics.com
ORIGINAL COMIC ART
SEARCH COMICS!
MOVIE POSTERS
W9-CCV-054

CGC UNIVERSAL GRADE
9.6
THE STRANGEST SUPER-HEROES OF ALL!
the X-MEN
FIRST ISSUE!
X-MEN VERSUS MAGNETO
SOLD

CGC UNIVERSAL GRADE
9.4
AMAZING FANTASY
SPIDER MAN
SOLD

CGC UNIVERSAL GRADE
9.4
JOURNEY INTO MYSTERY
INTRODUCING... THE MIGHTY THOR!
SOLD
BEGIN THE SAGA OF THOR IN THIS ISSUE!

CGC UNIVERSAL GRADE
9.4
JUSTICE LEAGUE of AMERICA
SOLD
NO RETURN!

CGC UNIVERSAL GRADE
9.4
The FLASH
NO USE, FLASH—YOU'LL NEVER....FIND....THE REAL ME... IN TIME...!
SOLD
"MASTER OF MIRRORS!"

CGC UNIVERSAL GRADE
9.0
No. 1
SPRING ISSUE
BATMAN
SOLD
ALL BRAND NEW ADVENTURES OF THE BATMAN AND ROBIN, THE BOY WONDER!

No. 1
JUNE, 1938
ACTION COMICS
10¢
© DC
No. 1
SPRING ISSUE
BATMAN
© DC
COMICS
GUARANTY, LLC
Charter
Member Dealer

CGC
It just makes sense.
CGC UNIVERSAL GRADE
9.6
7.5
9.6
9.4
HULK and SUB-MARINER
TALES TO ASTONISH
TALES OF HORROR AND SUSPENSE!
mister MYSTERY
CRISIS
HEADLINE COMICS
FOR THE AM AN BOY
9.6
9.4
7.0
9.4
ALAN MOORE
JOHN TOTLEBEN
Wonder Woman
ALL WINNERS
9.8
8.5
CRIME SUSPENSTORIES
MARVEL COMICS GROUP
Casper
VOTE
9.4
9.6
9.8
9.4
THE WORLD'S GREATEST COMIC MAGAZINE!
Fantastic Four
STOP HIM! IF THE SUB-MARINER REACHES THE WATER, HE'LL BECOME INVINCIBLE!
MARVEL COMICS GROUP.
GIANT-SIZE X-MEN
THE AMAZING SPIDER-MAN
WALT DISNEY
UNCLE SCROOGE
9.0
9.8
9.8
ILLUSTRATED TALES TO BEWITCH & BEDEVIL YOU
VAMPIRELLA
LOOK OUT! SHE'S WAITING INSIDE THIS FIRST COLLECTOR'S EDITION...FOR YOU!!
"THE EMPIRE STRIKES BACK"
A DUMB TV SHOW CALLED "QUINCY"
DON MARTIN
DAVE BERG
AL JAFFEE
...and the usual gang of idiots are all in this issue of...
MAD
75¢ CHEAP
THE SAVAGE SWORD OF CONAN

CGC UNIVERSAL GRADE
7.0
CAPTAIN AMERICA
COMICS
SOLD

CGC UNIVERSAL GRADE
9.2
THE INCREDIBLE
HULK
THE STRANGEST MAN OF ALL TIME!!
IS HE MAN OR MONSTER
FANTASY AS YOU LIKE IT!
SOLD

CGC UNIVERSAL GRADE
MARCH, 1937
Detective
COMICS
10¢
BRAND NEW! ACTION-PACKED STORIES IN COLOR!
SOLD

CGC UNIVERSAL GRADE
9.2
12¢
TALES OF SUSPENSE
WHO? OR WHAT, IS THE NEWEST, MOST BREATH-TAKING, MOST SENSATIONAL SUPER-HERO OF ALL...?
IRON MAN!
HE LIVES! HE WALKS! HE CONQUERS!
SOLD

CGC UNIVERSAL GRADE
9.6
MARVEL COMICS GROUP
MARVEL SPOTLIGHT ON...
GHOST RIDER
IS HE ALIVE OR DEAD?
A LEGEND IS BORN!
SOLD
THE MOST SUPERNATURAL SUPERHERO OF ALL!

CGC UNIVERSAL GRADE
9.9
THE UNCANNY
X-MEN
SOLD
ENTER THE MUTANT CALLED GAMBIT!

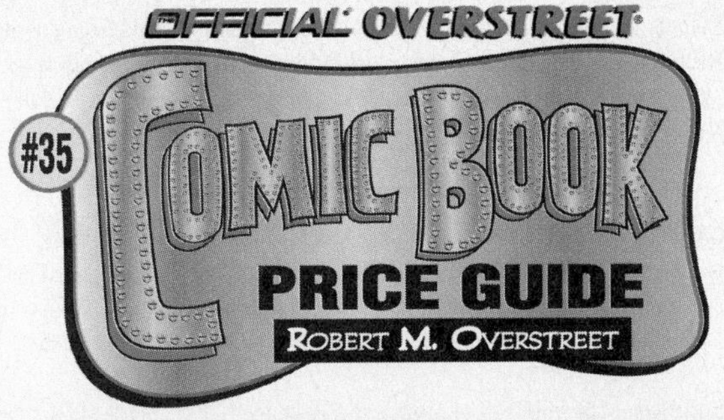

35th Edition

COMICS FROM 1828-PRESENT INCLUDED
FULLY ILLUSTRATED CATALOGUE & EVALUATION GUIDE

by ROBERT M. OVERSTREET

GEMSTONE PUBLISHING

J.C. Vaughn, **Executive Editor**
Arnold T. Blumberg, **Editor** • Brenda Busick, **Creative Director**
Mark Huesman, **Production Coordinator** • Tom Gordon III, **Managing Editor**
Jamie David, **Director of Marketing** • Sara Ortt, **Marketing Assistant**
Stacia Brown, **Editorial Coordinator** • Heather Winter, **Office Manager**

SPECIAL CONTRIBUTORS TO THIS EDITION

Weldon Adams • Robert L. Beerbohm • Arnold T. Blumberg • Steve Borock • Eric C. Caren
Douglas Gillock • Richard D. Olson, Ph.D. • J.C. Vaughn • Doug Wheeler

SENIOR OVERSTREET ADVISORS FOR OVER 25 YEARS

Dave Alexander • Steve Geppi • Bruce Hamilton • Paul Levitz • Michelle Nolan • Ron Pussell • Rick Sloane
John K. Snyder Jr. • Terry Stroud • Doug Sulipa • Harry B. Thomas • Raymond S. True

SENIOR OVERSTREET ADVISORS FOR OVER 20 YEARS

Gary M. Carter • Bill Cole • Stan Gold • M. Thomas Inge
Phil Levine • Richard Olson • Gene Seger • David R. Smith

SPECIAL ADVISORS

Tyler Alexander • Lon Allen • Dave Anderson • David J. Anderson, D.D.S. • Robert L. Beerbohm • Jon Berk • Brian Block
Steve Borock • Michael Browning • John Chruscinski • Gary Colabuono • Jack Copley • Carl De La Cruz • Peter Dixon
Gary Dolgoff • Joe Dungan • Bruce Ellsworth • Conrad Eschenberg • Michael Eury • Richard Evans • D'Arcy Farrell
Stephen Fishler • Dan Fogel • Chris Foss • Philip J. Gaudino • Steve Gentner • Michael Goldman • Tom Gordon III
Jamie Graham • Daniel Greenhalgh • Eric Groves • Gary Guzzo • John Grasse • Jim Halperin • Mark Haspel • John Hauser
Greg Holland • John Hone • George Huang • Bill Hughes • Rob Hughes • William Insignares • Ed Jaster • Paul Litch
Larry Lowery • Joe Mannarino • Nadia Mannarino • Rick Manzella • Patrick Marchbanks • Harry Matetsky • Jon McClure
Todd McDevitt • Mike McKenzie • Fred McSurley • Dale Moore • Steve Mortensen • Michael Naiman • Josh Nathanson
Matt Nelson • Terry O'Neill • George Pantela • James Payette • John Petty • Jim Pitts • Yolanda Ramirez • Jo Ann Reisler
Todd Reznik • Dave Robie • "Doc" Robinson • Israel Rodriguez • Robert Rogovin • Robert Roter
Chuck Rozanski • Matt Schiffman • Doug Schmell • Dave Smith • Laura Sperber • Tony Starks • Al Stoltz
Bob Storms • Ken Stribling • Joel Thingvall • Ted Van Liew • Joe Vereneault • Frank Verzyl • John Verzyl
Rose Verzyl • Bob Wayne • Jerry Weist • Mark Wilson • Anthony Yamada • Harley Yee • Vincent Zurzolo, Jr.

House of Collectibles
New York

Gemstone Publishing

Cover illustrations: *Tales of Suspense* #39 (Iron Man) re-created by John K. Snyder III; Little Lulu by John Stanley; *New Teen Titans* #1 25th anniversary re-creation by George Pérez, colored by Tom Smith.

THE OFFICIAL OVERSTREET COMIC BOOK PRICE GUIDE (35th Edition) is an original publication of Gemstone Publishing, Inc. and House of Collectibles. Distributed by Random House Information Group, a division of Random House, Inc., New York and simultaneously in Canada by Random House of Canada Limited, Toronto. This edition has never before appeared in book form.

House of Collectibles
Random House Information Group
1745 Broadway
New York, New York 10019

www.houseofcollectibles.com

Overstreet is a registered trademark of Gemstone Publishing, Inc.

House of Collectibles is a registered trademark and the H colophon is a trademark of Random House, Inc.

Published by arrangement with Gemstone Publishing, Inc.

ISBN: 0-375-72107-X
ISSN: 0891-8872

Printed in the United States of America

10 9 8 7 6 5 4 3 2 1

Thirty-Fifth Edition: May 2005

www.ComicCollectors.net
for high grade quality rare vintage comic books!!!
IT IS TIME, ONCE AGAIN, MY DEFENDERS OF FREEDOM, TO CRUSH THE EVILDOERS!!!

Table of Contents

Acknowledgements

Lon Allen (Golden Age data); Mark Arnold (Harvey data); Larry Bigman (Frazetta-Williamson data); Glenn Bray (Kurtzman data); Gary Carter (DC data); J. B. Clifford Jr. (EC data); Gary Coddington (Superman data); Wilt Conine (Fawcett data); Dr. S. M. Davidson (Cupples & Leon data); Al Dellinges (Kubert data); David Gerstein (Walt Disney Comics data); Kevin Hancer (Tarzan data); Charles Heffelfinger and Jim Ivey (March of Comics listing); R. C. Holland and Ron Pussell (Seduction and Parade of Pleasure data); Grant Irwin (Quality data); Richard Kravitz (Kelly data); Phil Levine (giveaway data); Paul Litch (Copper & Modern Age data); Dan Malan & Charles Heffelfinger (Classic Comics data); Jon McClure (Whitman data); Fred Nardelli (Frazetta data); Michelle Nolan (love comics); Mike Nolan (MLJ, Timely, Nedor data); George Olshevsky (Timely data); Chris Pedrin (DC War data); Scott Pell ('50s data); Greg Robertson (National data); Don Rosa (Late 1940s to 1950s data); Matt Schiffman (Bronze Age data); Frank Scigliano (Little Lulu data); Gene Seger (Buck Rogers data); Rick Sloane (Archie data); David R. Smith, Archivist, Walt Disney Productions (Disney data); Tony Starks (Silver and Bronze Age data); Al Stoltz (Golden Age & Promo data); Don and Maggie Thompson (Four Color listing); Mike Tiefenbacher & Jerry Sinkovec (Atlas and National data); Raymond True & Philip J. Gaudino (Classic Comics data); Jim Vadeboncoeur Jr. (Williamson and Atlas data); Kim Weston (Disney and Barks data); Cat Yronwode (Spirit data); Andrew Zerbe and Gary Behymer (M. E. data).

We thank John K. Snyder III for his "iron-willed" cover re-creation of *Tales of Suspense* #39. We're also pleased to present a Little Lulu cover by John Stanley, and thanks also to George Pérez for his 25th anniversary re-creation of *New Teen Titans* #1 for our bookstore edition cover.

Credit is due my two grading advisors, Steve Borock and Mark Haspel of Comics Guaranty Corp., for their ongoing input on grading. A special "thanks" is also given to Chuck Rozanski for his many years of support.

Thanks again to Doug Sulipa, Jon McClure, Fred McSurley and Tony Starks for continuing to provide detailed Bronze Age data. To Dave Alexander, Tyler Alexander, Dave Anderson (Oklahoma), Dave Anderson (Virginia), Stephen Barrington, Lauren Becker, Michael Browning, John Chruscinski, Gary Dolgoff, Conrad Eschenberg, D'Arcy Farrell, Dan Fogel, Stephen Gentner, Jamie Graham, Dan Greenhalgh, Eric Groves, John Hauser, Jef Hinds, Greg Holland, Bill Hughes, William Insignares, Nadia Mannarino, Joe Mannarino, Patrick Marchbanks, Todd McDevitt, Dale Moore, Steve Mortensen, Josh Nathanson, Terry O'Neill, Jim Payette, John Petty, Jim Pitts, Dave Robie, Ron Pussell, Israel Rodriguez, Rob Rogovin, Marnin Rosenberg, Matt Schiffman, Al Stoltz, Harry B. Thomas, Michael Tierney, John Verzyl, Frank Verzyl, Lon Webb and Vincent Zurzolo Jr., who supplied detailed pricing data, market reports or other material in this edition.

My gratitude is given to Chris Pedrin for his advice on DC war comics data; to Stephen Fishler for inspiring and helping develop the new 10 point grading system adopted in the 30th Edition; to Dr. Richard Olson for grading and Yellow Kid information; to Arnold T. Blumberg for his introduction to the Promotional Comics section; to Bill Blackbeard of the San Francisco Academy of Comic Art for his Platinum Age cover photos; to Bill Spicer and Zetta DeVoe (Western Publishing Co.) for their contribution of data; to Ted Hake for pricing the Big Little Book section; and especially to Bill for his kind permission to reprint portions of his and Jerry Bails' America's Four Color Pastime.

Special recognition is due Bob Beerbohm and Richard Olson who spent months researching the Victorian and Platinum sections in this edition. Thanks to Eric C. Caren for providing the Pioneer Age article and reproductions that appear in this edition. The "Boston Massacre" print that appears in our color gallery is courtesy of the Philip G. Straus collection.

Acknowledgement is also due to the following people who generously contributed much needed data for this edition: Nick Alfonso, Stephen Baer, Ron Ballard, Jonathan Bennett, Mike Bromberg, Richard M. Brown, Chris Boyko, Jonathan Calure, Jim Carper, Paul Howley, Bill Hutchison, John B. Jones, Jr., Joe Krolik, Michael Haller, Doug Ogle, Herb Patterson, Dennis Petilli, Ben Samuels, John Schmidt, Mark Squirek, Bob Wayne and Mike Wilbur.

Finally, special credit is due our talented production staff for their assistance with this edition; to Arnold T. Blumberg (Editor), Brenda Busick (Creative Director), Mark Huesman (Production Coordinator), Tom Gordon III (Managing Editor), Jamie David (Director of Marketing), Sara Ortt (Marketing Assistant), Stacia Brown (Editorial Coordinator), and Heather Winter (Office Manager), as well as to our Executive Editor, J.C. Vaughn, for their valuable contributions to this edition. Thanks to my wife, Caroline, for her encouragement and support on such a tremendous project, and to all who placed ads in this edition.

CGC UNIVERSAL GRADE
Daredevil #1
NM 9.4
HERE COMES...
DAREDEVIL
THE MAN WITHOUT FEAR!
SPIDER-MAN
CAN YOU GUESS WHY DAREDEVIL IS DIFFERENT FROM ALL OTHER CRIME-FIGHTERS...?

CGC UNIVERSAL GRADE
Batman #1
D.C. Comics, Spring 1940
9.0
CGC
SPRING ISSUE
No. 1
BATMAN
10¢
ALL BRAND NEW ADVENTURES

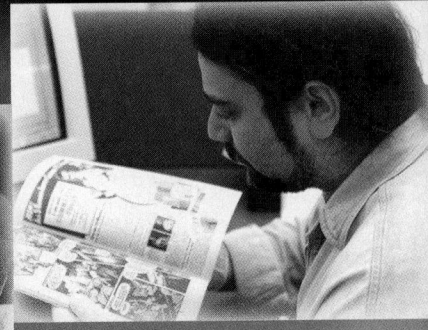

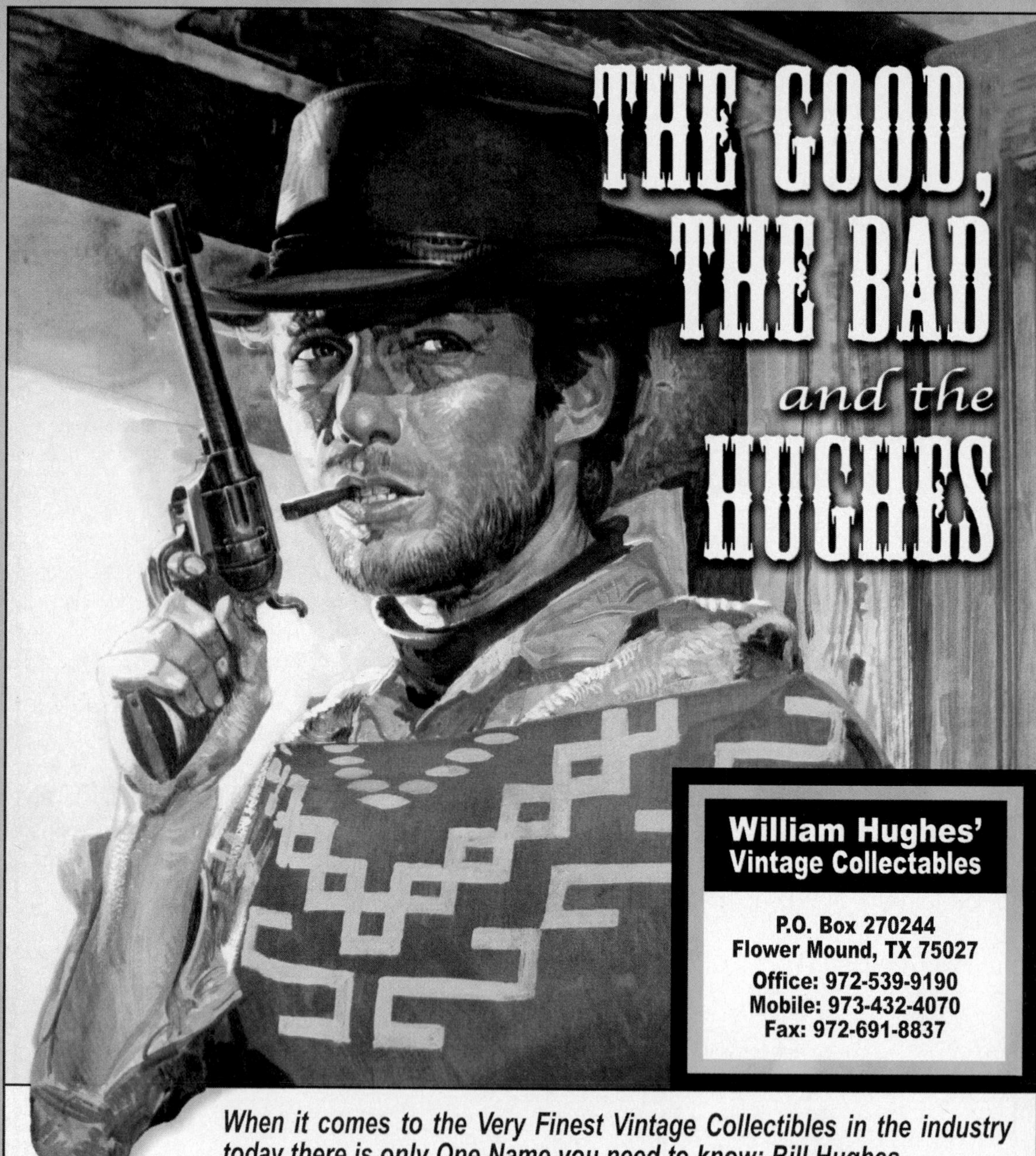

When it comes to the Very Finest Vintage Collectibles in the industry today there is only One Name you need to know: Bill Hughes

I have been instrumental is buying and selling some the largest, most valuable and note worthy collections and individual collectibles to ever surface into the marketplace. From the finest certified copy of **Marvel Comics #1** (*Publishers Pay Copy*) to the only known copy of the super-rare **Dracula Original One Sheet** to the **Original Artwork for the entire book to X-Men #1** to a **Cracker Jack Ty Cobb** Baseball Card. With over **30 Years** of experience **I have Seen and Done it All!**

Whether you are looking to Buy, Sell or Consign your collectibles, give me a call right away. With nearly **10,000 Active Buying Customers I can Afford to Pay the Most** because **I Get the Most** for **Top Quality items**. So **Why Wait**? If you want a **Few Dollars More**, give me a call right away to discuss what you have to offer, or, more importantly, what I have to offer you!

There is **No One** Quicker on the draw with **Fast Cash**! You will come away with a **Smile on your Face** and a **A Fistful of Dollars**.

Senior Advisor Overstreet Price Guide

CGC Comics Guaranty, LLC
CHARTER MEMBER DEALER

VintageCollectables.net • whughes199@yahoo.com

The Southeast's Coolest Shop
HEROES AND DRAGONS .COM
BUYING
LOTS OF COMICS
Woder Women©DC Comics 2004
Paying SUPER sums for Gold & Silver Age, ALL grades and titles, through 1970.
Now purchasing collections, store/convention stock, and bulk comics from 1970 to today.
Have cash, will travel anywhere to make offers on large and/or quality collections.
Be assured, all transactions are handled reliably and with the utmost professionalism.
1-803-731-4376
Batman symbol©DC Comics 2004
Spider-man©Marvel Comics 2004

In Person & Online
SELLING
LOTS OF COMICS
Human Torch©Marvel Comics 2004
Amazing variety from Gold to Modern Age comics available for sale.
Buy thousands of hand-picked comics from every genre at www.heroesanddragons.com
Visit us at most major national & regional conventions. Calendar online.
Drop by our 12,000 sq. ft. gallery showroom open 7 days a week to shop for comics, toys & tons of related cool stuff. Directions online.
Superman©DC Comics 2004
SUPERIOR SERVICE & PACKAGING
1563-B Broad River Road
Columbia, SC 29210
(803) 731-4376
HDweb@bellsouth.net
www.heroesanddragons.com
HEROES AND DRAGONS .COM

MOTOR CITY
COMICS
10¢
No. 1
Specializing in
GOLD &
SILVER AGE
ACTION
THE STRANGEST MAN OF ALL TIME!!
IS HE MAN OR MONSTER OR... IS HE BOTH
BUYING
• Top Prices Paid!!! •
• Senior Overstreet Advisor •
• We Pay 50% - 150% of Guide for pre-1970 Comics •
• We Pay up to 500% of Guide for GCC Graded Comics •
• Will Travel Anywhere to View Large Collections •
• Consignment Sales •
& SELLING
• Over 50,000 Gold & Silver Age Comics In Stock •
• Accurate Grading •
• Competitive Pricing •
• Pulps & Original Art • Want List Service •
• Free Catalogs: call or write for your copy •
MOTOR CITY COMICS
33228 W. 12 MILE RD. • PMB 286 • FARMINGTON HILLS, MI 48334
(248) 426-8059 • FAX 426-8064 • www.motorcitycomics.com
Buying & Selling Premium Comics & Collectibles Since 1986

Why Consign???

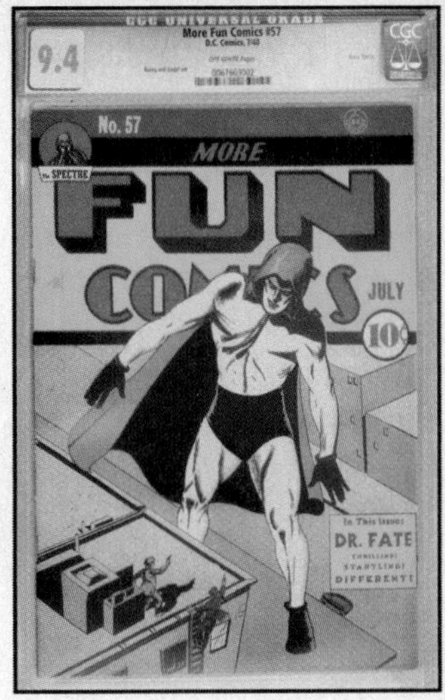

Why Consign to William Hughes' Vintage Collectables?

There are actually a number of sound reasons why consigning to W.H.V.C. may be the best way to maximize the value of your treasures. Here are a few:

Experience: I have been a regular face "on the scene" in at least eight of the hottest hobbies for many years now – ***Comic Books * Movie Posters * Baseball Cards * Sports Memorabilia * Non-Sports Cards *Disneyana * Music Memorabilia *Hollywood Memorabilia ***

I am a **"Senior Advisor"** to the **Official Comic Book Price Guide** by Robert Overstreet and still continue to gather and submit data for the new edition each year.

I am **"Charter Member #11"** of **CGC's (Comics Guaranty, LLC)** authorized group of dealers and have been one of their biggest submitters over the years.

I've been a guest columnist in various hobby publications over the years and have given too many television, radio and newspaper interviews to list (or even remember).

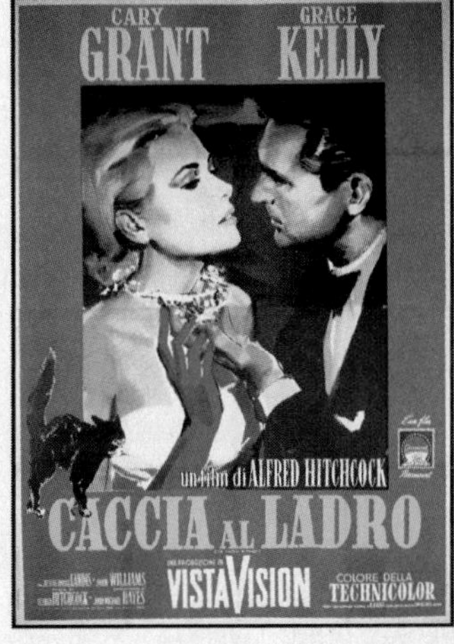

I was hired as the first consultant to **PSA** (Professional Sports Authentications), at an embryonic stage of the company's history, to define and implement their 10-point grading scale and to enlist collectors and dealers to the certified baseball card concept. I personally graded and encapsulated the **"Most Valuable Baseball Card in the World"**, ultra-rare 1909 T-206 Honus Wagner card that was once owned by **hockey Hall-of-Famer** *Wayne Gretzky*, presently valued at around **$2,000,000**.

I was instrumental in putting the deal together between **Greg Manning Auctions** & **Butterfields** auction houses and the 'Rock' band **"Kiss"** for the sale of the vast majority of their career-collected memorabilia. The 2001 Los Angeles auction did approximately **$1,600,000**.

I was also instrumental in the deal that brought the **Academy Award** winning actor, *Nicolas Cage's* comic book collection to the auction block. The October 2002 auction in Dallas brought nearly **$1,700,000**.

I put the deal together for the buyout of **World's Finest Comics** by **Greg Manning Auctions** and the subsequent sale of much of the same inventory to **'The Mint'** for approximately **$2,400,000**.

On behalf of GMAI, I bought the fabled collection of *Jack Kirby* original comic art from long-time collector *Tony Christopher*, which consisted of over 900 pages of *Kirby* art that included some of the earliest and most important known Silver-Age Marvel pages as well as other fabulous original art by *Steve Ditko, Neal Adams, Bill Everett* and others. Purchase price **$1,100,000**.

I've bought, sold and traded collectibles in every conceivable way, including through trade shows, my own auctions, live and telephone, and auctions that I've conducted for other "houses". In all, I have been involved in the retailing, wholesaling and auctioning of over **$30,000,000** worth of collectibles over a span of 31 years.

So Why Wait? Call Me Right Away to Discuss What You Have to Offer. Or, More Importantly, What I Have to Offer You!

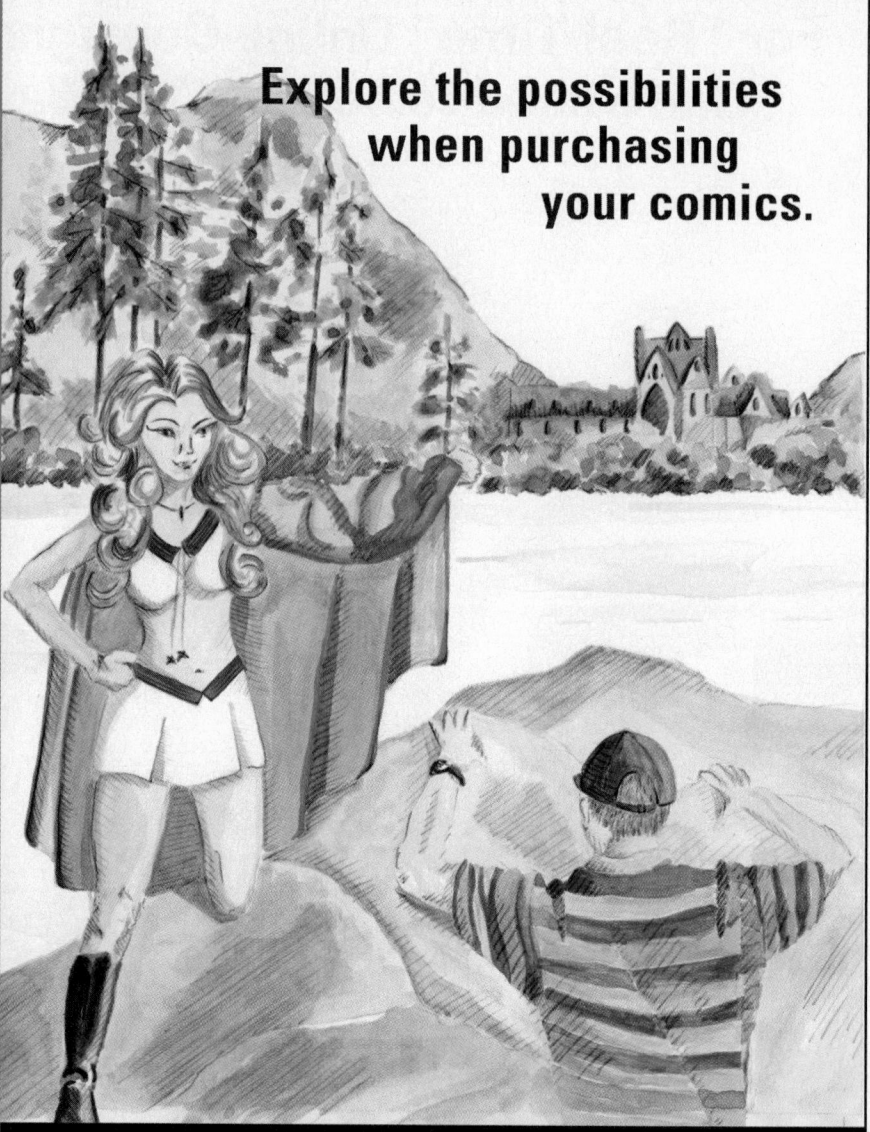

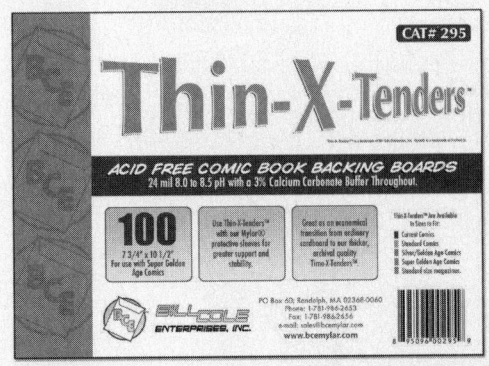

RUSS COCHRAN'S COMIC ART AUCTION

Russ Cochran's Comic Art Auction

started in 1973 with the publication of his illustrated art catalog, Graphic Gallery. Soon after that, it became the main source of comic strip and comic book art, as well as paintings by Carl Barks and Frank Frazetta. It is safe to say that Russ Cochran sold more Barks and Frazetta paintings than all the other dealers in comic art combined.

At the same time, auctions were being held for the EC original art, all of which passed through Russ's Comic Art Auction. Dozens of important originals by Hal Foster, Alex Raymond, George Herriman, George McManus, Milton Caniff, and virtually every comic artist have passed through the pages of this auction catalog, finding their way to comic art collections all over the western world.

In all, a total of 13 issues of Graphic Gallery were published, and to date, 67 issues of the Comic Art Auction.

If you are a collector of comic art, or if you have art to consign, contact

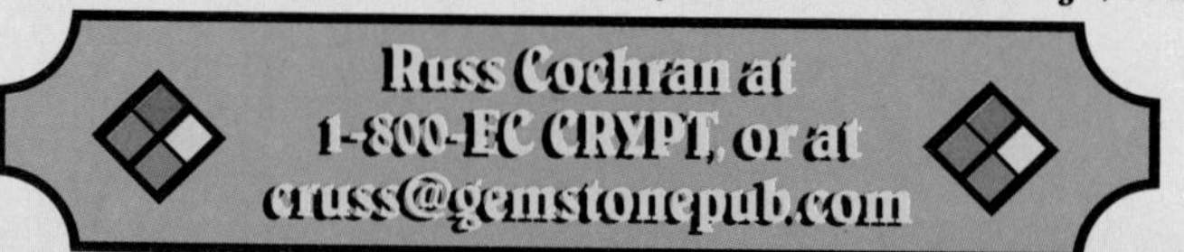

ACTION COMICS
10¢

AMAZING
12¢
FANTASY
15
SPIDER-MAN

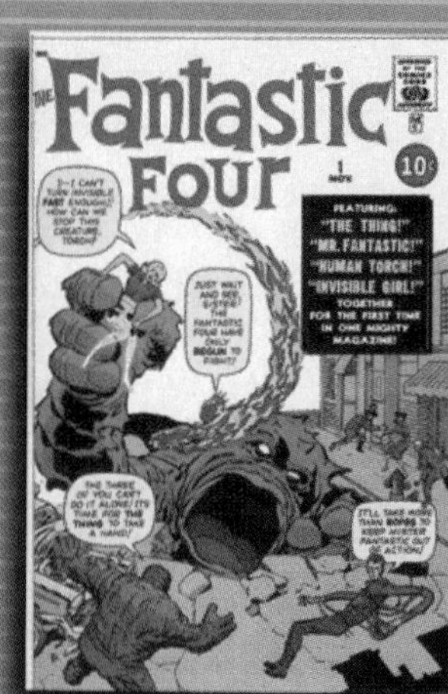

THE Fantastic Four
1
10¢
FEATURING:
"THE THING!"
"MR. FANTASTIC!"
"HUMAN TORCH!"
"INVISIBLE GIRL!"
TOGETHER FOR THE FIRST TIME IN ONE MIGHTY MAGAZINE!

CAPTAIN AMERICA
MARCH
COMICS
10¢
BUCKY

AMAZING
ALL NEW!
NOT A SINGLE REPRINT!
MARVEL COMICS GROUP
25¢
3
AUG

Planet Collector
MAGAZINE

Volume1, Number 2
Winter 2004
$5.95

Cashing In On Collectibles

Anthrax, "State of Euphoria"

A Brief History of Brownies

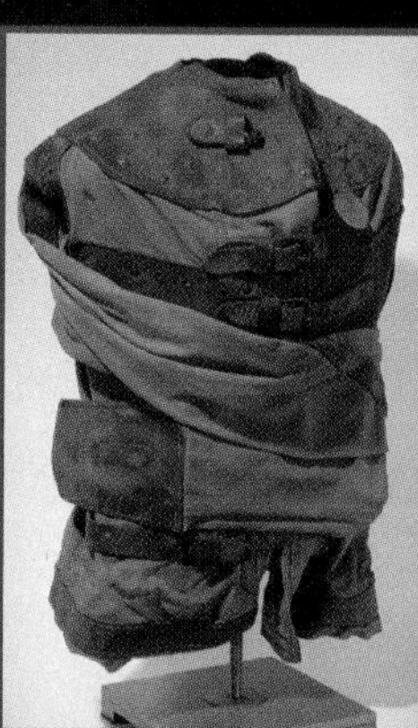

Houdini's Straight Jacket

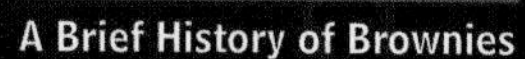

Lou Gehrig's Bat from 1932 "Batrite"

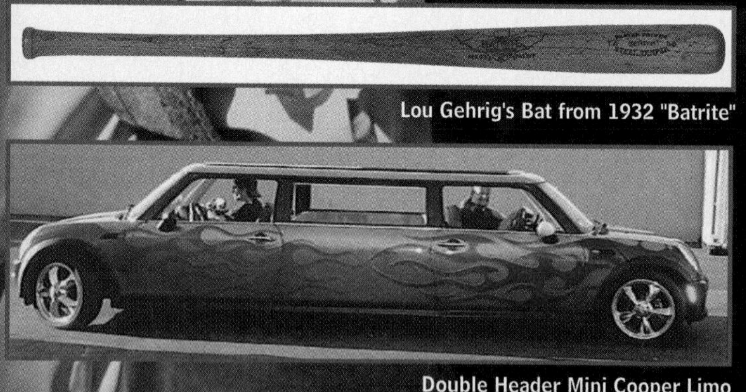

Double Header Mini Cooper Limo

Uncle Sam Poster

08 >
0 74470 05851 9

Introduction

About This Book

Welcome to the 35th edition of the most comprehensive reference work available on the history and pricing of American comic books! *The Official Overstreet Comic Book Price Guide* is respected and used by dealers and collectors throughout the world as their guide to American (and North American) comics. This is not a position we have earned easily or take lightly.

Documenting this rich avenue of American pop-culture history is clearly an organic, on-going process with many vital components. Just as we strive to record everything from major and minor trends to individual items, so do our advisors and regular readers. Such enthusiasts are the driving force behind the growth of this book. Whether supplying photos of rare comics or simply asking the question that gets us looking in the right direction, it is our fellow hobbyists and professionals who are our primary inspiration.

About Values

Values for items pictured in this book are based on the author's experience, consultations with a network of advisors including collectors specializing in various categories, and actual prices realized for specific items sold through private sales and auctions, sales catalogs, mail-, telephone-, and internet bid auctions. The values offered in this book are approximations influenced by many factors including condition, rarity and demand, and they should serve only as guidelines, presenting an average range of what one might expect to pay for the items. In the marketplace, knowledge and opinions held by both sellers and buyers determine prices asked and prices paid. This is not a price list of items for sale or items wanted by the author or publisher. The author and the publisher shall not be held responsible for losses that may occur in the purchase, sale or other transaction of property because of information contained herein. Efforts have been made to present accurate information, but the possibility of error exists. Readers who believe they have discovered an error are invited to mail corrective information to the author, Robert M. Overstreet, Gemstone Publishing, Inc., 1966 Greenspring Drive, Timonium, Maryland 21093 (or e-mail feedback@gemstonepub.com). Verified corrections will be incorporated into future editions of this book.

AGE	YEAR RANGE
Pioneer	1500s-1828
Victorian	1828-1883
Platinum	1883-1938
Golden	1938-1945
Atom	1946-1956
Silver	1956-1970
Bronze	1970-1984
Copper	1984-1992
Modern	1992-Present

How Comics Are Listed

Comic books are listed alphabetically by title, regardless of company. It is important to note that the true title of a comic book can usually be found listed with the publisher's information, or indicia, often found at the bottom of the first page. Titles that appear on the front cover can vary from the official title listed inside.

Comics are listed in the following sections: Big Little Books, Promotional Comics, Victorian Age, Platinum Age, and the main section, which is entitled Modern Age. This year, the *Guide* has added a new age, the Pioneer Age, which helps to more accurately define the progenitors of today's comics. (For some key dates and more insight into comic book Ages, see the chart below and the timeline that runs across the bottom of the next three pages.)

The listings include comic book titles, sequence of issues, dates of first and last issues, publishing companies, origin and special issues are listed when known. Prominent and collectible artists are also pointed out (usually in footnotes).

Prices listed are shown in a variety of grades, including 2.0, 4.0, 6.0, 8.0, 9.0, and 9.2 based on the 10-point scale outlined in this book and fully detailed in *The Official Overstreet Comic Book Grading Guide*. Some issues may not have prices listed in all categories if the author has not been able to determine if these particular books exist in a specific grade.

Many of the comic books are listed in groups, such as 11-20, 21-30, 31-50, and so on. The prices listed opposite these groupings represent the value of each issue in that group, not the group as a whole. More detailed information is given for individual comic books where warranted, such as publication dates, creators, and significant story and/or character notations.

Most comic books began with a #1, but occasionally many titles began with an odd number. There is a reason for this: publishers had to register new titles with the U.S. Post Office for 2nd Class permits, but the registration fee was comparatively expensive. To avoid this expense, many publishers would continue the numbering on new titles from older, defunct series. For instance, EC Comics' *Weird Science* #12 (1st issue) was continued from *Saddle Romances* #11 (the last issue). Captain America #100, for instance, followed Tales of Suspense #99. Sometimes this was done for creative reasons, but in most early instances publishers hoped to avoid the expense of registering new titles. However, the USPS would soon discover the new title and force the publisher to pay the registration fee as well as to list the correct number. As an example, Weird Science continued from #12 through #15. That was followed by #5 after the Post Office correction. Now the sequence of published issues (see the listings) is #12-15, #5-on. This sort of deviation created a problem in early fandom, but this *Guide* offers a roadmap to these sometimes confusing twists and turns in the publishing history of many comic book series.

New Comic Listings

Every effort is made to incorporate as many new comics into this Guide as possible during the course of a given year. Unfortunately, not all comics released each year may be listed in this book for reasons of space limitation or even the human error of simple oversight. We attempt to list complete information wherever possible, and we encourage readers to contact us with any information that may enhance the accuracy of our listings. We're also interested in review copies of any new comic books that are published.

In many cases, the market does not assess new comics at a value equal to their cover prices. In some cases, collectors may pay pennies on the dollar for copies of these issues. Nevertheless, since these comics have yet to establish themselves as collectors' items, they are listed at full cover price. Dealers and buyers alike should be aware the demand for many of the recent issues that do attract premium prices is highly volatile, and should act accordingly.

Regarding polybagged comics, it is the official policy of The Overstreet Comic Book Price Guide to grade comics regardless of whether they are still sealed in their polybag or not. If opened, the polybag and its contents should be preserved separately so that all components of the original package remain together. Most polybags degrade rapidly, so for collectors or dealers with large quantities of issues in polybags this is a concern.

Grading

About Grading

Before a comic book's true value can be assessed, its condition or state of preservation must be determined. In all cases, the better the condition of the comic, the more desirable and valuable the book will be. Comic book grading has evolved over the past several decades from a much looser interpretation of standards in the beginning to the very tight professional scrutiny in use by the market today. In recent years, grading criteria have become even tighter, especially in Silver and Bronze Age books, due to their higher survival rate.

Several events have impacted grading over the years. The first has to be the arrival of comic book conventions. Here, collectors could easily compare and discuss grading with dealers. The second major event was the discovery of the Mile High collection in 1977, which showed fandom truly high-grade Golden Age books.

Probably the most important event to date, however, was the arrival of comic book certification with Comics Guaranty, LLC (CGC), which has transformed much of the industry and introduced many die-hard and casual collectors alike to the subtle distinctions involved in grading comic books. For a profile of CGC, please turn to Page 995 in our article section.

The 2002 release of the second edition of *The Official Overstreet Comic Book Grading Guide* re-established Gemstone Publishing as the purveyors of a grading standard embraced by the vast majority of the comic book collecting community. The Overstreet standards, long relied upon by collectors from the professional to the casual level, describe a method for evaluating the condition of all comic books from the Victorian through the Modern Age.

For much more information on grading and restoration, as well as full-color photographs of many major defects and conditions, consult *The Official Overstreet Comic Book Grading Guide*. Copies are available through all normal distribution channels or can be ordered direct from Gemstone by sending $24 plus $5 postage and handling. You can also call Gemstone toll free at 1-888-375-9800, ext 249, or online at www.gemstonepub.com.

How To Grade

It is very important to be able to properly grade your books if you are trying to ascertain their value. Comics should be graded from the exterior (the covers) to the interior (the pages) and thoroughly examined before assigning a final grade.

Carefully remove the comic from its plastic bag or Mylar sleeve, if it is stored in one, and lay the comic down on a flat, clean surface. Under normal incandescent lighting, examine the exterior of the comic from front to back, identifying any defects, loss of cover reflectivity or other significant attributes. Check the spine for rusted staples, stress lines, tears, and spine roll.

Check to make sure that the centerfold and all interior pages are still present. The whiteness level of the pages is of major importance in determining the final grade as well. Locate and identify interior defects such as chipping, flaking, possible brittleness, and other flaws.

After all the above steps have been taken, the collector can then begin to consider an overall grade for his or her book, which may range from absolutely perfect Gem Mint condition to Poor, where a comic is extremely worn, dirty and even falling apart.

Numerous variables influence the evaluation of a comic book's condition and all must be considered in the final determination of a grade. Although the grade of a comic book is based upon an accumulation of defects, some defects may be more extreme for a particular grade as long as other acceptable listed defects are absent or less severe. As grading is the most subjective aspect of determining a comic's value - more of an art than a science - it is very important for the grader to take care not to allow wishful thinking to influence what the choice of grade. It is also very important to realize that older comics in high-grade condition are extremely scarce.

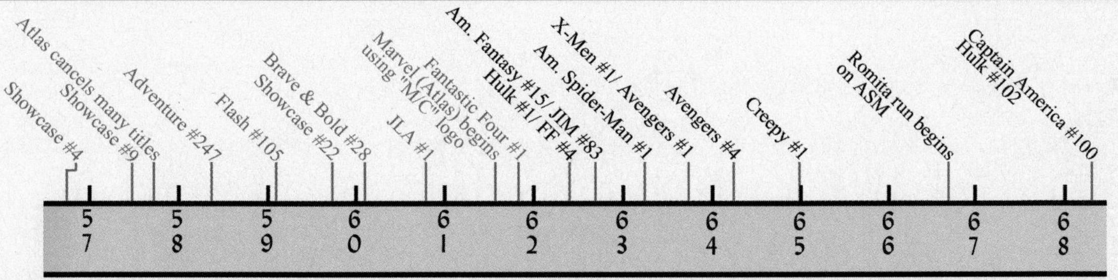

GRADING DEFINITIONS

10.0 GEM MINT (GM): An exceptional example of a given book - the best ever seen. Only the slightest bindery or printing defects are allowed. Cover is flat with no surface wear. Inks are bright with high reflectivity. Corners are cut square and sharp. Spine is tight and flat. Staples must be original, centered and clean with no rust. Paper is white, supple and fresh. No interior autographs or owner signatures.

9.9 MINT (MT): Near perfect in every way. Only subtle bindery or printing defects are allowed. Cover is flat with no surface wear. Inks are bright with high reflectivity and minimal fading. Corners are cut square and sharp. Small, inconspicuous, lightly penciled, stamped or inked arrival dates are acceptable as long as they are in an unobtrusive location. Spine is tight and flat. Staples must be original, generally centered and clean with no rust. Paper is white, supple and fresh.

9.8 NEAR MINT/MINT (NM/MT): Nearly perfect in every way with only minor imperfections that keep it from the next higher grade. Only subtle bindery or printing defects are allowed. Cover is flat with no surface wear. Inks are bright with high reflectivity and minimal fading. Corners are cut square and sharp. Small, inconspicuous, lightly penciled, stamped or inked arrival dates are acceptable as long as they are in an unobtrusive location. Spine is tight and flat. Staples must be original, generally centered and clean with no rust. Paper is white, supple and fresh. Only the slightest interior tears are allowed.

9.6 NEAR MINT+ (NM+): Nearly perfect with a minor additional virtue or virtues that raise it from Near Mint. Only subtle bindery or printing defects are allowed. No bindery tears are allowed, although on Golden Age books bindery tears of up to 1/8" have been noted. Cover is flat with no surface wear. Inks are bright with high reflectivity and a minimum of fading. One corner may be almost imperceptibly blunted, but still almost sharp and cut square. Almost imperceptible indentations are permissible, but no creases, bends, or color breaks. Small, inconspicuous, lightly penciled, stamped or inked arrival dates are acceptable as long as they are in an unobtrusive location. Spine is tight and flat. Staples must be original, generally centered, with only the slightest discoloration. Paper is off-white, supple and fresh. Only the slightest interior tears are allowed.

9.4 NEAR MINT (NM): Nearly perfect with only minor imperfections that keep it from the next higher grade. Subtle bindery/printing defects are allowed. Bindery tears must be less than 1/16" on Silver Age and later books, although on Golden Age books bindery tears of up to 1/4" have been noted. Cover is flat with no surface wear. Inks are bright with high reflectivity and a minimum of fading. Corners are cut square and sharp with ever-so-slight blunting permitted. A 1/16" bend is permitted with no color break. Small, inconspicuous, lightly penciled, stamped or inked arrival dates are acceptable as long as they are in an unobtrusive location. Slight foxing. Spine is tight and flat. Staples are generally centered; may have slight discoloration. Almost no stress lines. Paper is off-white to cream, supple and fresh. Slight interior tears are allowed.

9.2 NEAR MINT– (NM–): Nearly perfect with only a minor additional defect or defects that keep it from Near Mint. A limited number of minor bindery/printing defects are allowed. Cover is flat with no surface wear. Inks are bright with only the slightest dimming of reflectivity. Corners are cut square and sharp with ever-so-slight blunting permitted. A 1/16-1/8" bend is permitted with no color break. Small, inconspicuous, lightly penciled, stamped or inked arrival dates are acceptable as long as they are in an unobtrusive location. Slight foxing. Spine is tight and flat. Staples may show some discoloration. Almost no stress lines. Paper is off-white to cream, supple and fresh. Slight interior tears are allowed.

9.0 VERY FINE/NEAR MINT (VF/NM): Nearly perfect with outstanding eye appeal. A limited number of bindery/printing defects are allowed. Cover is almost flat with almost imperceptible wear. Inks are bright with slightly diminished reflectivity. An 1/8" bend is allowed if color is not broken. Corners are cut square and sharp with ever-so-slight blunting permitted but no creases. Several lightly penciled, stamped or inked arrival dates are acceptable. Very minor foxing. Spine is tight and flat. Staples may show some discoloration. Only the slightest staple tears are allowed. A very minor accumulation of stress lines may be present if they are nearly imperceptible. Paper is off-white to cream and supple. Very minor interior tears may be present.

8.5 VERY FINE+ (VF+): Fits the criteria for Very Fine but with an additional virtue or small accumulation of virtues that improves the book's appearance by a perceptible amount.

8.0 VERY FINE (VF): An excellent copy with outstanding eye appeal. A limited accumulation of minor bindery/printing defects is allowed. Cover is relatively flat with minimal surface wear beginning to show, possibly including some minute wear at corners. Inks are generally bright with moderate to high reflectivity. An unnoticeable 1/4" crease is acceptable if color is not broken. Stamped or inked arrival dates may be present. Minor foxing. Spine is almost completely flat with a possible minor color break. Staples may show some discoloration. Very slight staple tears and a few almost insignificant stress lines may be present. Paper is cream to tan and supple. Centerfold is mostly secure. Minor interior tears at the margin may be present.

7.5 VERY FINE– (VF–): Fits the criteria for Very Fine but with an additional defect or small accumulation of defects that detracts from the book's appearance by a perceptible amount.

7.0 FINE/VERY FINE (FN/VF): An above-average copy that shows minor wear but is still relatively flat and clean with outstanding eye appeal. A small accumulation of minor bindery/printing defects is allowed. Minor cover wear beginning to show, possibly

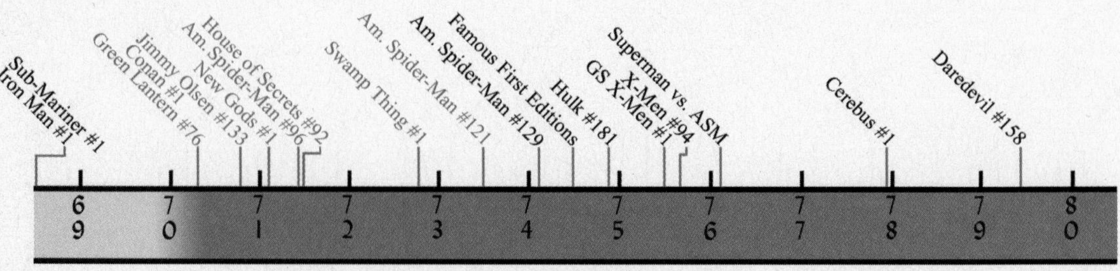

NO.	ABBREVIATION	NOMENCLATURE
10.0	GM	Gem Mint
9.9	MT	Mint
9.8	NM/MT	Near Mint/Mint
9.6	NM+	Near Mint+
9.4	NM	Near Mint
9.2	NM-	Near Mint-
9.0	VF/NM	Very Fine/Near Mint
8.5	VF+	Very Fine+
8.0	VF	Very Fine
7.5	VF-	Very Fine-
7.0	FN/VF	Fine/Very Fine
6.5	FN+	Fine+
6.0	FN	Fine
5.5	FN-	Fine-
5.0	VG/FN	Very Good/Fine
4.5	VG+	Very Good+
4.0	VG	Very Good
3.5	VG-	Very Good-
3.0	GD/VG	Good/Very Good
2.5	GD+	Good+
2.0	GD	Good
1.8	GD-	Good-
1.5	FR/GD	Fair/Good
1.0	FR	Fair

including minor creases. Corners may be blunted. Inks are generally bright with a moderate reduction in reflectivity. Stamped or inked arrival dates may be present. Minor foxing. The slightest spine roll may be present, as well as a possible moderate color break. Staples may show some discoloration. Slight staple tears and a small accumulation of light stress lines may be present. Slight rust migration. Paper is cream to tan. Centerfold is mostly secure. Minor interior tears at the margin may be present.

6.5 FINE+ (FN+): Fits the criteria for Fine but with an additional virtue or small accumulation of virtues that improves the book's appearance by a perceptible amount.

6.0 FINE (FN): An above-average copy that shows minor wear but is still relatively flat and clean with no significant creasing or other serious defects. Some accumulation of minor bindery/printing defects is allowed. Minor cover wear apparent, with minor to moderate creases. Inks show a significant reduction in reflectivity. Blunted corners are more common, as is minor staining, soiling, discoloration, and/or foxing. Stamped or inked arrival dates may be present. A minor spine roll is allowed. There can also be a 1/4" spine split or severe color break. Staples may show minor discoloration. Minor staple tears and a few slight stress lines may be present, as well as minor rust migration. Paper is tan to brown and fairly supple with no signs of brittleness. Minor interior tears at the margin may be present. Centerfold may be loose.

5.5 FINE– (FN–): Fits the criteria for Fine but with an additional defect or small accumulation of defects that detracts from the book's appearance by a perceptible amount.

5.0 VERY GOOD/FINE (VG/FN): An above-average but well-used comic book. An accumulation of bindery/printing defects is allowed. Minor to moderate cover wear apparent, with minor to moderate creases and/or dimples. Inks have moderate to low reflectivity. Blunted corners are increasingly common, as is minor to moderate staining, discoloration, and/or foxing. Stamped or inked arrival dates may be present. A minor to moderate spine roll is allowed. A spine split of up to 1/2" may be present. Staples may show minor discoloration. Minor staple tears and minor stress lines may also be present, as well as minor rust migration. Paper is tan to brown with no signs of brittleness. Centerfold may be loose. Minor interior tears may also be present.

4.5 VERY GOOD+ (VG): Fits the criteria for Very Good but with an additional virtue or small accumulation of virtues that improves the book's appearance by a perceptible amount.

4.0 VERY GOOD (VG): The average used comic book. Cover shows moderate to significant wear, and may be loose but not completely detached. Cover reflectivity is low. Can have moderate creases or dimples. Corners may be blunted. Store stamps, name stamps, arrival dates, initials, etc. have no effect on this grade. Some discoloration, fading, foxing, and even minor soiling is allowed. As much as a 1/4" triangle can be missing out of the corner or edge; a missing 1/8" square is also acceptable. Only minor unobtrusive tape and other amateur repair allowed on otherwise high grade copies. Moderate spine roll may be present and/or a 1" spine split. Staples may be discolored. Minor to moderate staple tears and stress lines may be present, as well as some rust migration. Paper is brown but not brittle. Minor to moderate interior tears may be present. Centerfold may be loose or detached at one staple.

3.5 VERY GOOD– (VG–): Fits the criteria for Very Good but with an additional defect or small accumulation of defects that detracts from the book's appearance by a perceptible amount.

3.0 GOOD/VERY GOOD (GD/VG): A used comic book showing some substantial wear. Cover shows significant wear, and may be loose or even detached at one staple. Cover reflectivity is very low. Can have a book-length crease and/or dimples. Corners may be blunted or even rounded. Discoloration, fading, foxing, and even minor to moderate soiling is allowed. A triangle from 1/4" to 1/2" can be missing out of the corner or edge; a missing 1/8" to 1/4" square is also acceptable. Tape and other amateur repair may be present. Moderate spine roll likely. May have a spine split of anywhere from 1" to 1-1/2". Staples may be rusted or replaced. Minor to moderate staple tears and moderate stress lines may be present, as well as some rust migration. Paper is brown but not brittle. Centerfold may be loose or detached at one staple. Minor

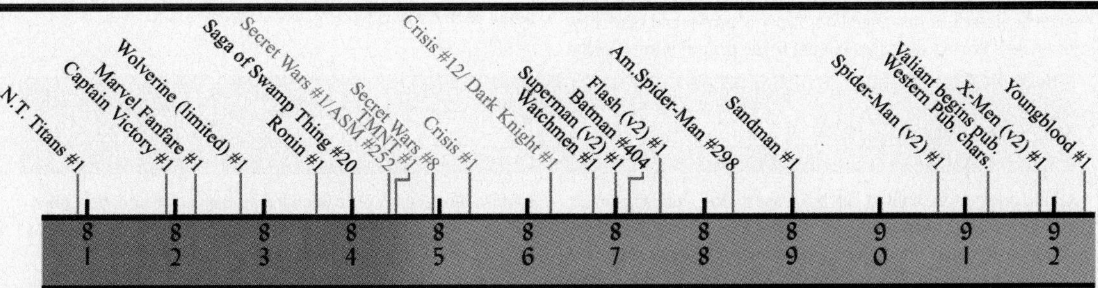

to moderate interior tears may be present.

2.5 GOOD+ (GD+): Fits the criteria for Good but with an additional virtue or small accumulation of virtues that improves the book's appearance by a perceptible amount.

2.0 GOOD (GD): Shows substantial wear; often considered a "reading copy." Cover shows significant wear and may even be detached. Cover reflectivity is low and in some cases completely absent. Book-length creases and dimples may be present. Rounded corners are more common. Moderate soiling, staining, discoloration and foxing may be present. The largest piece allowed missing from the front or back cover is usually a 1/2" triangle or a 1/4" square, although some Silver Age books such as 1960s Marvels have had the price corner box clipped from the top left front cover and may be considered Good if they would otherwise have graded higher. Tape and other forms of amateur repair are common in Silver Age and older books. Spine roll is likely. May have up to a 2" spine split. Staples may be degraded, replaced or missing. Moderate staple tears and stress lines may be present, as well as rust migration. Paper is brown but not brittle. Centerfold may be loose or detached. Moderate interior tears may be present.

1.8 GOOD– (GD–): Fits the criteria for Good but with an additional defect or small accumulation of defects that detracts from the book's appearance by a perceptible amount.

1.5 FAIR/GOOD (FR/GD): Shows substantial to heavy wear. Books in this grade are commonly creased, scuffed, abraded, soiled, and possibly unattractive, but still generally readable. Cover shows considerable wear and may be detached. Almost no cover reflectivity remaining. Book-length creases, tears and folds may be present. Rounded corners are increasingly common. Soiling, staining, discoloration and foxing is generally present. Up to 1/10 of the back cover may be missing. Tape and other forms of amateur repair are increasingly common in Silver Age and older books. Spine roll is common. May have a spine split between 2" and 2/3 the length of the book. Staples may be degraded, replaced or missing. Staple tears and stress lines are common, as well as rust migration. Paper is brown and may show brittleness around the edges. Acidic odor may be present. Centerfold may be loose or detached. Interior tears are common.

1.0 FAIR (FR): Shows heavy wear. Some collectors consider this the lowest collectible grade because comic books in lesser condition are usually incomplete and/or brittle. Cover may be detached, and inks have lost all reflectivity. Creases, tears and/or folds are prevalent. Corners are commonly rounded or absent. Soiling and staining is present. Books in this condition generally have all pages and most of the covers, although there may be up to 1/4 of the front cover missing or no back cover, but not both. Tape and other forms of amateur repair are more common. Spine roll is more common; spine split can extend up to 2/3 the length of the book. Staples may be missing or show rust and discoloration. An accumulation of staple tears and stress lines may be present, as well as rust migration. Paper is brown and may show brittleness around the edges but not in the central portion of the pages. Acidic odor may be present. Accumulation of interior tears. Chunks may be missing. The centerfold may be missing if readability is generally preserved. Coupons may be cut.

0.5 POOR (PR): Sufficiently degraded to the point where there is little or no collector value; easily identified by a complete absence of eye appeal. Brittle almost to the point of turning to dust with a touch, and usually incomplete. Extreme fading may render the cover almost indiscernible. May have extremely severe stains, mildew or heavy cover abrasion to the point that some cover inks are indistinct/absent. Covers may be detached with large chunks missing. Can have extremely ragged edges and extensive creasing. Corners are rounded or virtually absent. Covers may have been defaced with paints, varnishes, glues, oil, indelible markers or dyes, and may have suffered heavy water damage. Can also have extensive amateur repairs such as laminated covers. Extreme spine roll present; can have extremely ragged spines or a complete, book-length split. Staples can be missing or show extreme rust and discoloration. Extensive staple tears and stress lines may be present, as well as extreme rust migration. Paper exhibits moderate to severe brittleness (where the comic book literally falls apart when examined). Extreme acidic odor may be present. Extensive interior tears. Multiple pages, including the centerfold, may be missing that affect readability. Coupons may be cut.

Pedigrees

There are a group of special books, known as pedigrees, that have high cover gloss, brilliant cover inks and white, fresh, supple pages that place them far above other books that might receive the same technical grade. Books from these pedigree collections actually transcend their technical grade. Of these, many collectors and dealers agree that the most important collections are the Mile High (Edgar Church) collection, the San Francisco (Reilly) collection, and the Gaines file copies. They are the most sought after and generally the most well-documented, making it easier to ascertain identity or provenance. Books from these collections all exhibit the extra qualities mentioned above.

This striking difference becomes apparent when comparing two comic books of the same grade, one pedigree and one generic. In most cases, the pedigree book will far outshine the generic one. This is the reason why Mile Highs, San Franciscos and Gaines file copies bring multiples of *Guide*. Many also agree that a book from one of these collections could very well be one of, if not the, best surviving copies.

To the beginner, it may seem odd that a 9.2 Mile High will bring a higher price than a non-pedigree 9.4, but to the seasoned collector with a good understanding of the hobby and its historical background, it makes perfect sense. The novice collector should understand these facts and acquire as much knowledge as possible about all the other pedigree collections and their place in the market before paying large multiples of *Guide* for books that are not of pedigree quality.

Preservation & Storage

Comic books were built to last but a short time - utilizing acidic newsprint paper, thin covers, inconsistent inks, occasionally damaging bindery machinery - and bound not for a Mylar snug or a CGC slab but for a child's back pocket and eventually the nearest rubbish bin. Comics were intended as disposable fare, but collectors now apply the most stringent archival regulations on a class of collectible that was ephemeral at best.

Some of the best advice for preserving a comic is simply to handle it carefully. Most dealers and collectors hesitate to let anyone personally handle their rare comics, and it is common courtesy to ask permission before handling another person's comic book. Most dealers would prefer to remove the comic from its bag and show it to the customer themselves. In this way, if the book is damaged, it would be the dealer's responsibility and not the customer's.

When handling high grade comics, always wash your hands first, eliminating harmful oils from the skin before coming into contact with the books. Lay the comic on a flat surface or in the palm of your hand and slowly turn the pages. This will minimize the stress to the staples and spine. In basic handling situations:

Step 1: Remove the comic from its protective sleeve or bag very carefully (more detail can be found in "How to Grade").

Step 2: Gently lay the comic unopened in the palm of your hand so that it will stay relatively flat and secure.

Step 3: Leaf through the book by carefully rolling or flipping the pages with the thumb and forefinger of your other hand. Be sure the book always remains relatively flat or slightly rolled. Avoid creating stress points on the covers with your fingers and be particularly cautious in bending covers back too far.

Step 4: After examining the book, carefully insert it back into the bag or protective sleeve. Watch corners and edges for folds or tears as you replace the book. Always keep tape completely away while inserting a comic in a bag.

Careful handling of an exceptional book can go a long way to preserving its condition for some time to come, but careful storage is also a key element. Comic books must be protected from the elements, as well as the dangers of light, heat, and humidity. This can be accomplished with certain storage methods, but remember: improper storage methods will be detrimental to the "health" of your collection, and may even quicken its deterioration.

Store comic books away from direct light sources, especially florescent light, which contains high levels of ultraviolet (UV) radiation. UV lights are like sunlight, and will quickly fade the cover inks. Tungsten filament lighting is safer than florescent lighting, but should still be used at brief intervals. Remember, exposure to light accumulates damage, so store your collection in a cool, dark place away from windows.

Room temperature must also be carefully regulated. Fungus and mold thrives in higher temperatures, so the lower the temperature, the longer the life of your collection. Like UV, high relative humidity (rh) can also be damaging to paper. Maintaining a low and stable relative humidity, around 50%, is crucial. Varying humidity will only damage your collection.

Atmospheric pollution is another problem associated with long term storage of paper. Sulfuric dioxide, which can occur from automobile exhaust, will cause paper to turn yellow over a period of time. For this reason, it is best not to store your valuable comics close to a garage. Some of the best preserved comic books known were protected from exposure to the air, such as the Gaines EC collection. These books were carefully wrapped in paper at the time of publication and completely sealed from the air. Each package was then sealed in a box and stored in a closet in New York. After over 40 years of storage, when the packages were opened, you could instantly catch the odor of fresh newsprint; the paper was snow white and supple, and the cover inks were as brilliant as the day they were printed. This illustrates how important it is to protect your comics from the atmosphere.

Care must also be taken when choosing materials for storing your comics. Many common items such as plastic bags, boards, and boxes may not be as safe as they seem; some contain chemicals that will actually help to destroy your collection rather than save it. Always purchase materials designed for long-term storage, such as Mylar sleeves and acid-free backing boards and boxes. Polypropylene and polyethylene bags, while safe for temporary storage, should be changed every three to five years.

Comics are best stored vertically in boxes to preserve flatness and spine tightness. If you choose to store your comics on shelves, make sure that the books do not come into direct contact with the shelving surface. Use acid-free boards as a buffer between the shelves and the comics. Also, never store comics directly on the floor; elevate them 6-10 inches to allow for flooding. Similarly, never store your collection directly against a wall, particularly an outside wall. Condensation and poor air circulation will encourage mold and fungus growth.

Ultimately, nothing will prevent the deterioration of a comic book collection, but as examples like the Gaines collection have proven, there are occasions when even unintentionally well-stored comics can avoid the aging process for a considerable length of time. With some care in handling and attention to the materials used for comic book storage, your collection can enjoy a long life and maintain a reasonable condition for years to come.

Additional information about this book, comic collecting, and fandom is available online at www.gemstonepub.com.

Cover Bar Codes

Today's comic books are cover-coded for the direct sales (comic shop, newsstand, and foreign markets). They are all first printings, with the special coding being the only difference. The comics sold to the comic shops have to be coded differently, as they are sold on a no-return basis while newsstand comics are not. The *Guide* has not detected any price difference between these versions. Currently, the difference is easily detected by looking at the front cover bar code (a box located at the lower left). The bar code used to be filled in for newsstand sales and left blank or contain a character for comic shop sales. Now, as you can see below, direct sale editions are clearly marked, both versions containing the bar code.

Direct Sales (DC)

Direct Edition (Marvel)

Newsstand

Comic Book Reprints

Over the years, many publishers have reprinted comic books, from individual stories collected under new covers to entire issues published with facsimile covers that may be indistiguishable from the original. Some did not represent old material but were successive printings generated at the time of an original comic's release to satisfy demand for more copies. Whatever the reason for the reprint, distinguishing a reprint from an original edition can be tricky.

Many such reprints carry a notation somewhere in the indicia indicating that it is a "reprint," or "2nd printing," etc., and perhaps even a later copyright date. Still others even feature a variation in cover coloring or issue number information to distinguish it from the original. Fantastic Four #371, for example, featured an all-white embossed cover in its original printing, but the second printing changed to an all-red embossed cover. In the 1990s, many Marvel reprints sported a gold logo.

Unfortunately, many reprints were never marked as such. For example, a few of the Marvel movie books, such as *Star Wars*, the Marvel Treasury Editions, and tie-ins such as *G.I. Joe*, were reprinted and not identified as reprints. The *Star Wars* reprints have a large diamond with no date and a blank UPC symbol on the cover. Others had cover variations such as a date missing or different colors.

Gold Key and other comics were also sold with a Whitman label. Although collectors may prefer one label over the other, the *Guide* does not differentiate in price. Beginning in 1980, all comics produced by Western carried the Whitman label.

Recently, DC Comics reprinted many key issues with a gold foil "Millennium Edition" stamp. There is little difficulty in distinguishing the reprint, however, due to the distinctive modern trade dress and border surrounding the original cover art.

Publishers' Codes

The following abbreviations are used with cover reproductions throughout the book for copyright purposes:

ABC-America's Best Comics
AC-AC Comics
ACE-Ace Periodicals
ACG-American Comics Group
AJAX-Ajax-Farrell
AP-Archie Publications
ATLAS-Atlas Comics (see below)
AVON-Avon Periodicals
BP-Better Publications
C & L-Cupples & Leon
CC-Charlton Comics
CEN-Centaur Publications
CCG-Columbia Comics Group
CG-Catechetical Guild
CHES-Harry 'A' Chesler
CLDS-Classic Det. Stories
CM-Comics Magazine
CN-Condé Nast
DC-DC Comics, Inc.
DEF-Defiant Comics
DELL-Dell Publishing Co.
DH-Dark Horse
DMP-David McKay Publishing
DS-D. S. Publishing Co.
EAS-Eastern Color Printing Co.
EC-E. C. Comics
ECL-Eclipse Comics
ENWIL-Enwil Associates
EP-Elliott Publications
ERB-Edgar Rice Burroughs
FAW-Fawcett Publications
FC-First Comics
FF-Famous Funnies
FH-Fiction House Magazines
FOX-Fox Features Syndicate
GIL-Gilberton
GK-Gold Key
GP-Great Publications
HARV-Harvey Publications
H-B-Hanna-Barbera
HILL-Hillman Periodicals
HOKE-Holyoke Publishing Co.
IM-Image Comics
KING-King Features Syndicate
LEV-Lev Gleason Publications
MAL-Malibu Comics
MAR-Marvel Characters, Inc.
ME-Magazine Enterprises
MLJ-MLJ Magazines
MS-Mirage Studios
NOVP-Novelty Press
NYNS-New York News Syndicate
PG-Premier Group
PINE-Pines
PMI-Parents' Magazine Institute
PRIZE-Prize Publications
QUA-Quality Comics Group
REAL-Realistic Comics
RH-Rural Home
S & S-Street and Smith Publishers
SKY-Skywald Publications
STAR-Star Publications
STD-Standard Comics
STJ-St. John Publishing Co.
SUPR-Superior Comics
TC-Tower Comics
TM-Trojan Magazines
TMP-Todd McFarlane Prods.
TOBY-Toby Press
TOPS-Tops Comics
UFS-United Features Syndicate
VAL-Valiant
VITL-Vital Publications
WB-Warner Brothers.
WDC-The Walt Disney Company
WEST-Western Publishing Co.
WHIT-Whitman Publishing Co.
WHW-William H. Wise
WMG-William M. Gaines (E. C.)
WP-Warren Publishing Co.
YM-Youthful Magazines
Z-D-Ziff-Davis Publishing Co.

Timely/Marvel/Atlas Codes

"A Marvel Magazine" and "Marvel Group" were the designations used between December 1946 and May 1947 for the Timely/Marvel/Atlas group of comics during that period, although these taglines were not used on all of the titles/issues during that time. The Timely Comics symbol was used between July 1942 and September 1942, although again not on all titles/issues during the period. The round "Marvel Comic" symbol was used between February 1949 and June 1950. An early Comics Code symbol (star and bar) was used between April 1952 and February 1955. The Atlas globe symbol was used between December 1951 and September 1957. The M over C symbol (signifying the beginning of Marvel Comics as we know it today) was introduced in July 1961 and remained until the price increased to 12 cents in February 1962. We present here the publishers' codes for the Timely/Marvel/Atlas group of comics:

ACI-Animirth Comics, Inc.
AMI-Atlas Magazines, Inc.
ANC-Atlas News Co., Inc.
BPC-Bard Publishing Corp.
BFP-Broadcast Features Pubs.
CBS-Crime Bureau Stories
CLDS-Classic Detective Stories
CCC-Comic Combine Corp.
CDS-Current Detective Stories
CFI-Crime Files, Inc.
CmPI-Comedy Publications, Inc.
CmPS-Complete Photo Story
CnPC-Cornell Publishing Corp.
CPC-Chipiden Publishing Corp.
CPI-Crime Publications, Inc.
CPS-Canam Publishing Sales Corp.
CSI-Classics Syndicate, Inc.
DCI-Daring Comics, Inc.
EPC-Euclid Publishing Co.
EPI-Emgee Publications, Inc.
FCI-Fantasy Comics, Inc.
FPI-Foto Parade, Inc.
GPI-Gem Publishing, Inc.
HPC-Hercules Publishing Corp.
IPS-Interstate Publishing Corp.
JPI-Jaygee Publications, Inc.
LBI-Lion Books, Inc.
LCC-Leading Comic Corp.
LMC-Leading Magazine Corp.
MALE-Male Publishing Corp.
MAP-Miss America Publishing Corp.
MCI-Marvel Comics, Inc.
MgPC-Margood Publishing Corp.
MjMC-Marjean Magazine Corp.
MMC-Mutual Magazine Corp.
MPC-Medalion Publishing Corp.
MPI-Manvis Publications, Inc.
NPI-Newsstand Publications, Inc.
NPP-Non-Pareil Publishing Corp.
OCI-Official Comics, Inc.
OMC-Official Magazine Corp.
OPI-Olympia Publications, Inc.
PPI-Postal Publications, Inc.
PrPI-Prime Publications, Inc.
RCM-Red Circle Magazines, Inc.
SAI-Sports Actions, Inc.
SePI-Select Publications, Inc.
SnPC-Snap Publishing Co.
SPC-Select Publishing Co.
SPI-Sphere Publications, Inc.
TCI-Timely Comics, Inc.
TP-Timely Publications
20 CC-20th Century Comics Corp.
USA-U.S.A. Publications, Inc.
VPI-Vista Publications, Inc.
WFP-Western Fiction Publishing
WPI-Warwick Publications, Inc.
YAI-Young Allies, Inc.
ZPC-Zenith Publishing Co., Inc.

Comic Book Artists

Many of the more popular artists in the business are specially noted in the listings. When more than one artist worked on a story, their names are separated by a (/), with the penciler first and the inker second. When two or more artists worked on a story, only the most prominent will be noted in some cases. Due to space limitations, only the most popular artists can be listed.

The following artists are considered to be either the most collected in the comic field or otherwise historically significant. Artists designated below with an (*) indicate that only their most noted work will be listed. The rest will eventually have all their work shown as the information becomes available. This list could change from year to year as new artists come into prominence:

Adams, Arthur
Adams, Neal
Aragonés, Sergio
Anderson, Murphy
Aparo, Jim
Bachalo, Chris
Bagley, Mark
Baker, Matt
Barks, Carl
Beck, C. C.
*Brunner, Frank
*Buscema, John
Byrne, John
Campbell, J. Scott
Capullo, Greg
*Check, Sid
Colan, Gene
Cole, Jack
Cole, L. B.
Craig, Johnny
Crandall, Reed
Darrow, Geof
Davis, Jack
Disbrow, Jayson
*Ditko, Steve
Eisner, Will
*Elder, Bill
Evans, George
Everett, Bill
Feldstein, Al
Fine, Lou
Foster, Harold
Fox, Matt
Frazetta, Frank
Gibbons, Dave
*Giffen, Keith
Golden, Michael
Gottfredson, Floyd
*Guardineer, Fred
Gustavson, Paul
*Heath, Russ
Howard, Wayne
Hughes, Adam
*Infantino, Carmine
Ingels, Graham
Jones, Jeff
Kamen, Jack
Kane, Bob
*Kane, Gil
Kelly, Walt
Kieth, Sam
Kinstler, E. R.
Kirby, Jack
Krenkel, Roy
Krigstein, Bernie
Kubert, Adam
Kubert, Andy
*Kubert, Joe
Kurtzman, Harvey
Lapham, Dave
Larsen, Erik
Lee, Jae
Lee, Jim
Liefeld, Rob
Madureira, Joe
Manning, Russ
McFarlane, Todd
McWilliams, Al
Meskin, Mort
Mignola, Mike
Miller, Frank
Moreira, Ruben
*Morisi, Pete
*Newton, Don
Nostrand, Howard
Orlando, Joe
Pakula, Mac
*Palais, Rudy
*Perez, George
Portacio, Whilce
Powell, Bob
Quesada, Joe
Quitely, Frank
Raboy, Mac
Ramos, Humberto
Raymond, Alex
Ravielli, Louis
*Redondo, Nestor
Rogers, Marshall
Romita Sr., John
Ross, Alex
Schaffenberger, Kurt
Schomburg, Alex
Sears, Bart
Siegel & Shuster
Silvestri, Marc
Simon & Kirby (S&K)
*Simonson, Walt
Smith, Paul
Stanley, John
*Starlin, Jim
Steranko, Jim
Stevens, Dave
Swan, Curt
Texeira, Mark
Thibert, Art
Torres, Angelo
Toth, Alex
Turner, Michael
Tuska, George
Ward, Bill
Williamson, Al
Windsor-Smith, Barry
Woggon, Bill
Wolverton, Basil
Wood, Wallace
Wrightson, Bernie
Zeck, Mike

ARTISTS' FIRST WORK:

Adams, Neal - (1 pg.) **Archie's Jokebook Mag.** #41, 9/59; (1st on Batman, cvr only) **Detective Comics** #370, 12/67; (1st Warren art) **Creepy** #14
Aparo, Jim - **Go-Go** #1, 6/66
Balent, Jim - **Sgt. Rock** #393, 10/84
Barks, Carl - (art only) **Donald Duck Four Color** #9, 8/42; (scripts only) **Large Feature Comic** #7, ca. Spring 1942
Broderick, Pat - (cover & art) **Planet of Vampires** #1, 2/75
Brunner, Frank - (fan club sketch) **Creepy** #10, 1965
Buckler, Rich - **Flash Gordon** #10, 11/67
Burnley, Jack - (cover & art) **NY World's Fair** nn, '40
Buscema, John - (1st at Marvel) **Strange Tales** #150, 11/66
Byrne, John - **Nightmare** #20, 8/74; (1st at DC) **Untold Legend of the Batman** #1, 7/80; (1st at Marvel) **Giant-Size Dracula** #5, 6/75
Capullo, Greg - (1st on X-Force) **X-Force Annual** #1, '92
Colan, Gene - **Wings Comics** #53, 1/45
Cole, Jack - (1 pg.) **Star Comics** #11, 4/38
Crandall, Reed - **Hit Comics** #10, 4/41
Davis, Jack - (cartoon) **Tip Top Comics** #32, 12/38
Ditko, Steve - (1st publ.) **Black Magic** V4#3, 11-12/53 (1st drawn story), **Fantastic Fears** #5, 1-2/54
Everett, Bill - **Amazing Mystery Funnies** V1#2, 9/38
Fine, Lou - (1st cvr) **Wonder Comics** #2, 6/39; **Jumbo Comics** #4, 12/38
Frazetta, Frank - **Tally-Ho Comics** nn, 12/44
Garney, Ron - **G. I. Joe, A Real American Hero** #110, 3/91
Giffen, Keith - (1 pg.) **Deadly Hands of Kung-Fu** #17, 11/75; (1st story) **Deadly Hands of Kung-Fu** #22, 4?/76; (tied w/Deadly Hands) **Amazing Adventures** #35, 3/76
Golden, Michael - **Marvel Classics Comics** #28, '77
Grell, Mike - **Adventure Comics** #435, 9-10/74
Hamner, Cully - **Green Lantern: Mosaic** #1, 6/92
Hughes, Adam - **Blood of Dracula** #1, 11/87
Ingels, Graham art at E.C. - **Saddle Justice** #4, Sum '48
Jurgens, Dan - **Warlord** #53, 1/82
Kaluta, Michael - **Teen Confessions** #59, 12/69
Kelly, Walt - **New Comics** #1, 12/35
Keown, Dale - **Samurai** #13, 1987; **Nth Man the Ultimate Ninja** #8, 1/90; (1st at Marvel); (1st on Hulk) **Incredible Hulk** #367, 3/90
Kieth, Sam - **Primer** #5, 11?/83
Kirby, Jack - **Jumbo Comics** #1, 9/38;
Kubert, Adam/Andy/Joe art - **Sgt. Rock** #422, 7/88
Kurtzman, Harvey - **Tip Top Comics** #36, 4/39; (1st at E.C.) **Lucky Fights It Through** nn, 1949
Larsen, Erik - **Megaton** #1, 11/83
Lee, Jae - **Marvel Comics Presents** #85, '91
Lee, Jim - (1st at Marvel) **Alpha Flight** #51, 10/87; (1st on X-Men) **X-Men** #248?, ?/89; (art on Punisher) **Punisher War Journal** #1, 11/88
Liefeld, Rob - (1st at DC) **Warlord** #131, 9/88; (1st at Marvel) **X-Factor** #40, 4?/89; (1st full story) **Megaton** #8, 8/87; (inside front cover only) **Megaton** #5, 6/86
Lim, Ron - (art on Silver Surfer) **Silver Surfer Ann.** #1, '88
Matsuda, Jeff - **Brigade** #0, 9/93
Mayer, Sheldon - **New Comics** #1, 12/35
McFarlane, Todd - **Coyote** #11, ?/85; (1st full story) **All Star Squadron** #47, 7/85; (1st on Hulk) **Incredible Hulk** #330, 4/87
Medina, Angel - (pin-up only) **Megaton** #3, 2/86
Mignola, Mike - **Marvel Fanfare** #15, 5/83
Miller, Frank - (1st on Batman) **DC Special Series** #21, Spr '80; (1st on Daredevil) **Spectacular Spider-Man** #27, 2/79
Newton, Don - **Many Ghosts of Dr. Graves** #45, 5/74
Perez, George - (1st at DC) **Flash** #289, 9/80; (2 pgs.) **Astonishing Tales** #25, 8/74
Portacio, Whilce - (1st on X-Men) **X-Men** #201, 1/86
Pulido, Brian - **Evil Ernie** #1, 12/91
Quesada, Joe - (1st on X-Factor) **X-Factor Ann.** #7, '92
Raboy, Mac - (1st cover for Fawcett) **Master Comics** #21, 12/41
Ramos, Humberto - (1st U.S. work) **Hardwire** #15, 6/94
Romita, John - **Strange Tales** #4, 12/51; (1st at Marvel) **Daredevil** #12, 1/66
Romita, John Jr. - (1st complete story) **Iron Man** #115, 10/78
Ross, Alex - **The Terminator: The Burning Earth** V2#1, 3/90
Shuster, Joe - (cover) **New Adv. Comics** #16, 6/37
Siegel & Shuster - **New Fun Comics** #6, 10/35
Simon & Kirby - **Blue Bolt** #2, 7/40
Simonson, Walter - **Magnus, Robot Fighter** #10, 5/65
Smith, Paul - (1 pg. pin-up) **King Conan** #7, 9/81; (1st full story) **Marvel Fanfare** #1, 3/82
Steranko, Jim - **Spyman** #1, Sep '66; (1st at Marvel) **Strange Tales** #151, 12/66
Swan, Curt - **Dick Cole** #1, 12-1/48-49
Talbot, Bryan - (1st U.S. work) **Hellblazer Annual** #1, Summer '89
Thomas, Roy - (scripts) **Son of Vulcan** #50, 1/66
Torres, Angelo - **Crime Mysteries** #13, 5/54
Turner, Mike - **Cyberforce Origins-Stryker**, 2/95
Weeks, Lee - **Tales of Terror** #5, 11/85
Weiss, Alan - (illo) **Blue Beetle** #5, 3-4/65
Williamson, Al - (1st at E.C.) **Tales From the Crypt** #31, 9/52; (text illos) **Famous Funnies** #169, 8/48
Windsor-Smith, Barry - **X-Men** #53, 2/69
Wood, Wally - (1st at E.C.) **Saddle Romances** #10, 1-2/50
Wrightson, Bernie - **House of Mystery** #179, 4/68; (1st at Marvel) **Chamber of Darkness** #7, 10/70; (1st cover) **Web of Horror** #3, 4/70
Zeck, Mike - (illos) **Barney and Betty Rubble** #11, 2/75

Market Report 2005

With diminishing supplies...

WILL 2005 SET NEW RECORD PRICES?

by Robert M. Overstreet

The US economy remained steady the past twelve months with the stock market ending the year showing single digit growth. Predictions for 2005 are optimistic with the Dow increasing in the low double digits. Energy and precious metals enjoyed a rally during the year while the comic book market continued to show strong support from investors and collectors all year long. Collectibles of all types were sold through auction houses, from mail order and on the Internet, setting many record prices. As the year progressed, we began to notice a diminishing frequency of high quality comic books being offered for sale. Will this trend continue into 2005?

Superman #1 in VF- 7.5, $250,000!

© DC

Certified Comics: The newly certified magazine-size comics continued to pick up steam throughout the year with increased collector demand. Certified comics by Comics Guaranty, LLC continued to penetrate and influence the market. Many dealers now utilize the CGC population reports that point out books that are the highest grade copy; these books generally command premium prices.

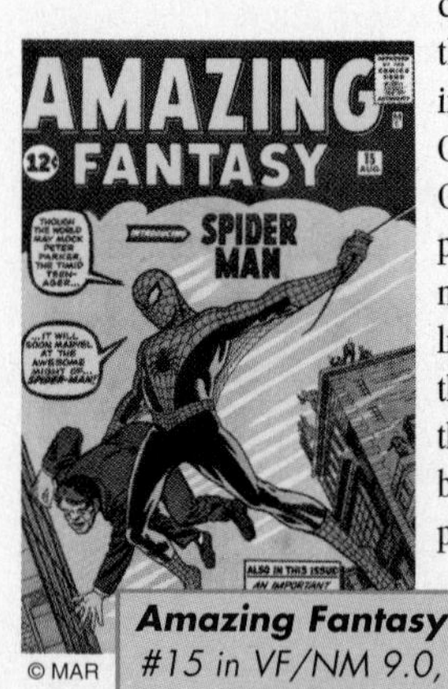

Amazing Fantasy #15 in VF/NM 9.0, $58,000!!

© MAR

Big Little Book Listings: These listings have been expanded as a result of research on our recently released, full color coffee-table book, *The Big Big Little Book Book: An Overstreet Photo-Journal Guide.* Our listings now include every variation known in this genre as well as many other related books.

Auction Houses: Last year, Hake's Americana Auctions of York, Pennsylvania was acquired by Diamond International Galleries, located in Timonium, Maryland. Hake's will now operate out of their Timonium offices. Heritage Comics Auctions continued to auction off millions of dollars in comic books, comic art and movie posters last year, giving our hobby more exposure than ever. There are now many dozens of auction houses selling collectibles of all types to anxious buyers throughout the world. What this means is liquidity! More than any time in the past, collectors have many venues for selling their collections quickly.

Record Certified Sales: The news for 2004 was the sale of a CGC certified 7.5 copy of *Superman* #1 which went for $250,000! Other important books that sold are: A CGC-certified *Walt Disney Comics & Stories* #1 in 8.5 brought

Batman #3 in VF/NM 9.0, $10,850!

© DC

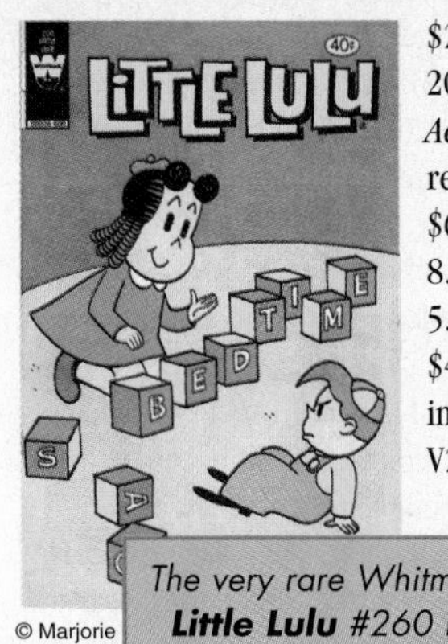

The very rare Whitman ***Little Lulu*** *#260 in NM/MT 9.8, $1805!*

© Marjorie Buell

$20,000! This was sold in 2003 and reported in 2004. *Action Comics* #1 in 6.5 restored - $45,100; #5 in 6.0 - $6037; *All-American* #17 in 8.5 - $13,225; *All Star* #8 in 5.5 - $5,175; #21 in 9.2 - $4,000; *All Star Western* #10 in 9.4 - $862; *All Winners* V2#1 in 8.5 - $2,645; *Amazing Fantasy* #15 in 9.0 - $58,000; in 9.0 - $32,500; in 6.0 - $7,187; in 4.0 - $3,000; *Amazing Spider-Man* #1 in 8.0 - $9,500; in 7.5 - $7,187; #11 in 9.6 - $10,500; #14 in 9.6 - $18,000; #28 in 9.4 - $5,013; #96 in 9.6 - $1,002; #101 in 9.6 - $1,322; #122 in 9.6 - $1,590; #129 in 9.6 - $2,237; #194 in 9.8 - $1,035; Annual #1 in 9.2 - $2,524; *America's Best* #10 Mile High in 9.2 - $2,300; *Batman* #3 in 9.0 - $10,850; #6 in 9.0 - $5,200; #11 in 9.0 - $8,750; #50 in 9.4 - 5,500; #100 in 9.0 - 5,500; *Blonde Phantom* #13 in 9.4 - $2,760; *Blue Ribbon* #1 in 8.5 - $3,105; *Captain Marvel* #24 Mile High in 9.4 - $3,220; *Captain Midnight* #14 Mile High in 9.4 - $2,760; *Comic Cavalcade* #1 in 8.5 - $8,050; *Detective Comics* #38 in 4.0 - $4,256; *Don Winslow* #1 in 9.2 - $2,632; Fa*ntastic Four* #1 in 1.8 - $900; *Flash Comics* #3 in 9.2 - $13,800; #5 in 9.0 - $5,462; *Giant-Size X-Men* #1 in 9.8 - $9,000; in 9.6 - $3,049; in 9.2 - $1,250; *Green Lantern* #82 in 9.8 - $1,150; *Haunt of Fear* #15/1 Gaines in 9.8 - $17,250; #7 Gaines in 9.8 - $3,220; *House Of Secrets* #92 in 9.6 - $4,400; *Human Torch* #2/1 in 6.5 restored - $3,680; *Incredible Hulk* #180 in 9.8 - $5,100; #181 in 9.6 - $4,310; in 9.4 - $2,425; *Journey Into Mystery* #83 in 7.5 - $4,400; *Little Lulu* (Whitman) #260 in 9.8 - $1,805; *MAD* #1 in 8.5 - $5,405; #2 Gaines in 9.4 - $4,025; *Marvel Mystery* #9 in 3.0 - $5,000; #16 in 8.0 - $2,150; *Marvel Spotlight* #5 in 9.4 - $1,600; *Mister Miracle* #1 in 9.8 - $850; *Moon Girl* #5 in 9.2 - $1,725; *Mystery In Space* #75 in 9.4 - $1,001; *New Adventure Comics* #19 Mile High in 9.6 - $12,650; *New Book of Comics* #1 in 8.0 - $11,500; *Nova* #1 in 9.8 - $304; *Planet Comics* #37 in 9.4 - $2,500; *Planet Of The Apes* #1 in 9.8 - $255; *Sandman* #1 ('74) in 9.8 - $529; *Sensation Comics* #1 in 9.4 restored - $5,000; *Shadow Comics* #3 in 9.2 - $3,000; *Showcase* #4 in 5.0 - $3,383; #22 in 8.5 - $4,153; *Silver Surfer* #1 in 9.6 - $4,600; #4 in 9.8 - $6,050; *Sub-Mariner Comics* #1 in 6.0 - $4,000; #11 in 8.5 - $2,530; *Superman* #1 in 4.5 restored - $16,500; #24 in 9.0 - $4,725; *Suspense* #3 in 4.0 $11,500; *Tales From The Crypt* #33 in 9.6 - $3,500; *Tales Of Suspense* #39 in 9.2 - $16,000; in 8.5 - $3,910; #48 in 9.4 - $1,500; *Tales To Astonish* #27 in 7.0 - $1,795; #44 in 9.6 - $6,250; *Teen Titans* #1 in 9.6 - $3,905; *Tom Mix Western* #1 in 9.2 - $1092; *Two-Fisted Tales* #19 Gaines in 9.6 - $3,450; *Vampirella* #7 in 9.6 - $898; *Vault Of Horror* #16 Gaines in 9.6 - $3,220; *War Against Crime* #11 Gaines in 9.8 - $10,062; *Weird Fantasy* #21 in 9.6 - $4,800; *Werewolf By Night* #1 in 9.6 - $1,500; *Wonder Woman* #1 in 5.0 - $4,140; *World's Finest* #18 Mile High in 9.6 - $8,711; *X-Men* #94 in 9.6 - $4,450; in 9.4 - $2,200; in 9.2 - $1,000.

Iron Man's debut in ***Tales of Suspense*** *#39 in NM- 9.2, $16,000!*

© MAR

RECORD SALES! RECORD SALES! RECORD SALES! RECORD SALES!

© DC

All-American Comics *#17 in VF+ 8.5, $13,225!*

© MAR

Amazing Spider-Man *#14 in NM+ 9.6, $18,000!*

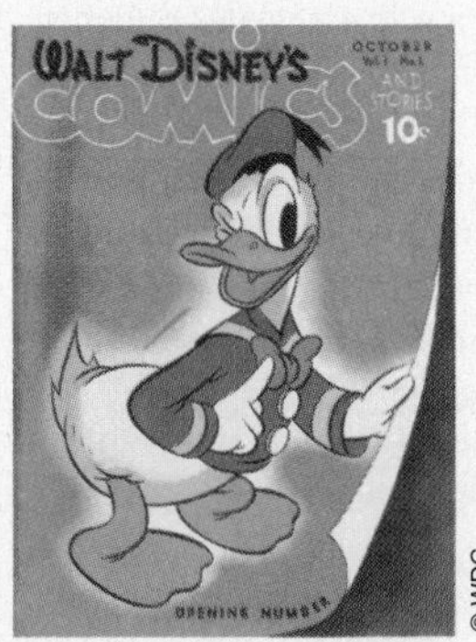

© WDC

Walt Disney's Comics & Stories *#1 in VF+ 8.5, $20,000!*

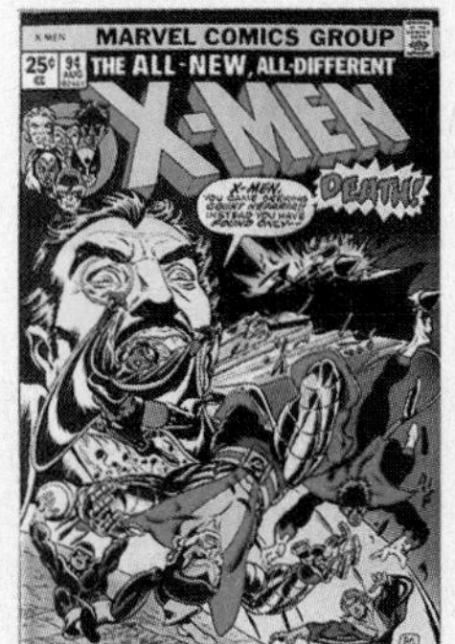

© MAR

X-Men *#94 in NM/MT 9.8, $9,000!!*

David T. Alexander & Tyler Alexander (Cultureandthrills.com)

2004 has been an absolutely fabulous year for selling old comic books. This was our 36th year of continuous operations and without a doubt has been the most spectacular for both buying and selling. The demand for comic books published prior to 1975 has been unceasing. We have noticed the trend of fewer full-time sellers exclusively providing vintage material has continued. The costs of maintaining a large inventory, plus the competition from the larger auction houses, has squeezed many marginal dealers to look for newer types of merchandise to offer their customers. Internet sales have continued to provide a way for collectors to buy and sell, and has placed additional pressure on many dealers. eBay, websites, and other Internet selling areas have hurt some dealers and some conventions.

For the first time in several years we made convention buying trips a priority area for acquisitions. We traveled close to 20,000 miles during the spring and summer and attended most of the major conventions. The overall trend seems to be placing less emphasis on older material at the conventions. A minority of dealers at most conventions are offering older material. Many of the collectors don't seem to want to take the time and expense to attend conventions and would rather buy from the comfort of home over the Internet. This has worked in our favor, as many convention dealers that we have seen this year have been very happy to offer material to us in large quantities at reasonable prices.

Acquisitions: Our buying appetite has not been quenched, although we have obtained many incredible collections during the past twelve months. The biggest group consisted of 70 large boxes of Golden Age comics. The owner had told me he wanted to sell five or six boxes of old comics with many being coverless. I was absolutely astounded to see over 70 boxes of original owner Golden Age comics by genre: superhero, horror, western, science fiction, war, romance, etc. It takes a lot to impress me after 36 years in the business, but this load did it. Exciting would be an understatement. There were even multiples of some very rare issues. The other collections that have come in this year have been pale next to this collection. This is not to say they have been bad, but none of them had the volume of the big load.

The other impressive fact from the year's acquisitions is geographical in nature. For years I could not find a decent original collection in Florida; this year was radically different. The year started out with a run of *Superman* #1-35 that had been in an Orlando garage for about 30 years; *Action* #2-60 were also part of this group. We were not all smiles with this one. Heartbreak prevailed as the original owner had disassembled the *Action* set, saving only the front covers and Superman stories, hoping to someday make them into a bound volume. That would have been a costly book.

A big surprise to us was that several other Golden Age collections were offered to us from Florida owners. Some of the books that came in were: *Flash* #92, *All-Winners* #19, *Namora* #1, *Sun Girl* #1, and various issues of *Phantom Lady, Black Cat, Crimes By Women, Captain America*, and other Timely, DC, Atlas, Avon, EC, Fox and Fawcett titles.

The other area of high volume acquisition was in the magazine field. Last year we took the position of Senior Advisor for the second edition of the *Old Magazines Identification And Value Guide*. This position allowed us to be in contact with many people who wanted to part with their magazine collections. We have obtained tons of material, and as we began to organize and research it, a connection with comic books became apparent. Many top comic artists worked on a variety of magazines. Some of this material has been highly collected for years, additional items have surfaced in the last year that would be of interest to comic collectors. Some of the top comic book artists to work in the magazine field are: Hal Foster, Frank Frazetta, Jack Davis, Matt Baker, George Gross, Jack Kirby, Carl Barks, Bill Ward, Basil Wolverton, Norman Saunders, and George Evans. Don't overlook this area when seeking the work of your favorite artist.

Here is a tip for the astute collector. In the early 1940s, *Radio And Television Mirror* magazine had a *Superman* feature each month related to the *Superman* radio series. Each issue had panels of art accompanying a text adventure story. I have been told that the first print appearance of Lois Lane was in an issue of *Radio And Television Mirror*. What would be the value of that issue?

Internet vs. Catalog Sales: The volume of people buying on the Internet is huge. Many people who never heard of a price guide, fanzine, or comic convention can now add to their collections from home with a minimum of effort. Thousands have become addicted collectors with the advent of eBay and websites. We have noticed that most dealers have given up on issuing catalogs. Even though Internet activity accounted for over 50% of our sales volume for the first time last year, we still hear from a surprising number of collectors who prefer to order from a catalog. Believe it or not, some people still don't have a computer and don't want one. We will still issue our catalogs several times annually.

Victorian and Platinum Age: We have experienced steady demand and sales in this area. The group of collectors who are actively seeking this material is not large, but it is big enough to absorb all available quality material. We feel that some collectors are hesitant to enter this area because sales data is often not readily available. Very little of this type of material will show up at conventions and it takes dedication to seek it out. Any time you have a chance to get copies of *Judge* or *Puck* magazine, do not hesitate, as these appear to have the most growth potential in the short term.

Golden Age: Always popular, fun to own, fun to find, fun to read. The top publisher remains Timely. All issues are in demand, with *Captain America* leading the way. It seems that every Timely publication will be on someone's want list. As prices increase, there are fewer collectors trying to complete runs; instead they're seeking special issues or popular covers. The most requested issues due to the outstanding cover concepts are *Marvel Mystery* #46 and #63. The majority of the superhero issues will sell at 100% to 150% of *Guide* in all grades. Even Timely funny animal and teenage comics are very popular. These types represent the area where many collectors are still trying to complete sets; relative to most Timely titles these appear to be bargains. *Millie the Model* and all related titles have additional demand from those who collect paper dolls. Atlas comics of the 1950s era were very popular. Horror, romance, western and war issues all were quick sellers at *Guide* and higher. The *Love Romance* and *Teen-Age Romance* titles from the Atlas/Marvel transition era in the early 1960s with Jack Kirby art all went for 5 to 8 times *Guide* in mid-grades.

© MAR

Amazing Spider-Man *is the leader of both the Silver and Bronze Ages. (#6 shown)*

DC comics will never see a slowdown in popularity. Many collectors are driven to pick and choose among their favorite issues as very few can afford to try to complete sets. Increased demand was seen for *Mr. District Attorney, Gangbusters, Sensation* and *Wonder Woman*. These all sell at above *Guide* in all grades. Some *Wonder Woman* issues have sold at 5 times *Guide* in mid-grades. Funny animal, teenage and romance all had increased demand. DC war comics were strong sellers at around *Guide*. A few key and minor key issues of *Our Army At War* constantly bring 3 to 5 times *Guide* in any grade.

Fiction House comics continue to be strong sellers, as do the pulps published by Fiction House. *Jumbo* is the strongest comic book followed closely by *Planet Comics*. In the pulp area, *Jungle Stories* and *Planet Stories* lead the way.

Western Comics: Demand has actually increased in the last year for cowboy material. We feel that this demand is fueled by nostalgia. A lot of previous non-collectors have discovered the road to finding their childhood treasures through Internet access. B-movie and TV-related comics have once again become hot items. Dell and Fawcett are the top sellers here. Prices are mostly above *Guide* levels as this Internet-driven collector is often unaware of any price guides; they buy based on what an item is worth to them. *Roy Rogers* and *Hopalong Cassidy* are the leaders here. Atlas westerns are very popular, particularly those with Joe Maneely covers. Joe did highly detailed western covers that almost have a surreal fantasy element to them. How did he come up with the concepts for all those outfits and gun belts?

Disney Comics: These have had a resurgent demand. The majority of Disney material that we ship now goes outside the US. Believe it or not, most of the issues we sold in the last year went for above *Guide* prices.

Archie Comics: Pre-Archie MLJ issues are good movers. The early Archie appearances are almost impossible to find. *Archie* #1 was the most requested Golden Age book last year. *Archie* comics have taken on a life of their own and many people want to live that life. Keep sending those want lists.

Harvey Comics: *Richie Rich* is king here; we received a huge collection of *Richie Rich* comics during the year. The previous owner was a fanatic collector and had kept his comics since childhood and added to the collection constantly up to the week of the sale. This impressive group had all the key issues and tons of multiple copies. The collector did not care how many multiples he had and bought any *Richie Rich* comic that he saw for sale.

Pulp Magazines: We were able to add substantially to our pulp library; we picked up nice runs of detective and aviation titles. We had an almost complete run of *Spider* pulps that sold as individual issues on eBay; most went in the first week they were offered. High grade *Shadow* pulps were the other highlight in the incoming pulp department.

Silver and Bronze Age: *Spider-Man* is the leader, closely followed by *X-Men*. Marvel volume tops DC. Certainly that is not a revelation to a seasoned collector. Bronze Age continues to impress us. We suggest that you buy any 20-cent cover price Marvels and any 52-page 25-cent cover price DC comics from this era.

Original Art: Demand has grown. We have trouble keeping significant or even mediocre pieces of DC or Marvel art. Our big surprise has been the demand for production art. We have sold tons of color guides, preliminary covers and comic story scripts. If it has anything to do with the production of a comic book, collectors want it. As most of these items are one of a kind pieces of art, we feel the values will escalate in coming years. Comic books are heavily computer generated now, so this past era hand done production art will continue to be sought after by collectors and historians alike.

Dave Anderson (Want List Comics)

Going Up: As I have mentioned in previous reports, pre-hero comics – specifically those published from 1933-38 – have risen very little if at all in the past few years. Although these Platinum Age books are extremely hard to find, especially above 6.0, they are consistently held at a static level. I don't expect an increase the size of *Gobbledygook* #1, but a little respect for the 'founding fathers' of an industry would seem appropriate.

Going Up, Part 2: No decreases come to mind in the area in which I specialize. Superhero Golden and Silver Age are still the places to be over all for the greatest percentage increases. Each year these books become rarer as they are buried forever in personal collections while at the same time the number of collectors and investors increases and demand seems unending.

Stephen Barrington (with Michael Haller and John Schmidt)

The 2003-04 fiscal year saw moderate gains across the board but didn't appear to reach any record levels locally. Even the 2004 San Diego International Comic Con had a different feel to it. The Mobile, Alabama area was adversely affected by Hurricane Ivan in September but comic sales still went on; some things are stronger than nature. This area also saw the loss of a major comic book store, causing the remaining two shops to see big increases in new sales.

New DC Comics: After starting this year surprisingly slow, DC has come on like a hurricane by blowing away the competition with what makes comics truly great: beautiful artwork and gripping stories. Sales have grown quietly but steadily throughout the year. DC has seen big gains overall with *Identity Crisis* and Jim Lee's run on *Superman* affecting all of the Man of Steel's titles. Michael Turner, the man behind *Aspen* and *Soulfire*, has joined Lee at the top with his unparalleled penciling of another huge title, *Superman/Batman*. The title has shot to the top in sales for DC with back issues hard to keep in stock. This, along with new teams, on *Action* and *Adventures of Superman* has brought Superman back into the fold with a vengeance. The biggest hit of this year is the seven-issue mini-series *Identity Crisis*. This is what I mean when I said gripping stories. Brad Meltzer and Rags Morales have combined to captivate comic readers and non-comic readers with his "whodunit" tale involving some of the greatest comic book icons of all time, while Morales adds a 'days gone by' style of artwork that reminds fans of the great artists such as Steranko and Kubert. These events, along with the long awaited comeback of Hal Jordan as the Green Lantern, have caused a major panic for their main competition.

Batman still enjoys solid sales but his supporting titles are a bit off. *JLA* and *JSA* continue to be strong, as well as *Teen Titans*. Their sales are beginning to rival Marvel's X-titles. Back issues of *Teen Titans* are very strong. Vertigo sales are hit and miss but have never been extremely big in this area. *Green Arrow, Smallville, Flash, Plastic Man, Wonder Woman, Losers, Losers, Human Target* and *Fallen Angel* are pretty much middle of the road sellers and in some cases just marginal.

© DC

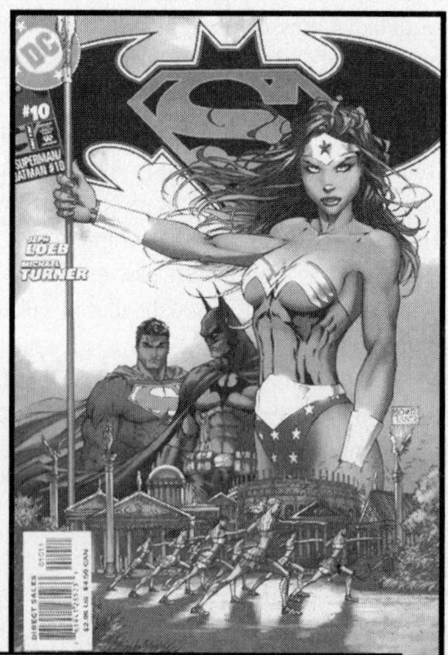

Superman/Batman *with covers and art by Michael Turner is a top seller. (#10 shown)*

New Marvel Comics: Marvel's X-titles still enjoy strong sales with *Uncanny, Astonishing, X-Men, New X-Men, X-Force* and *Ultimate X-Men* doing very well. *Wolverine* is still a super seller with *Cable/DeadPool* picking up steam after a slow start. The Spider-Man titles are a mixed bag with *Amazing, Spectacular* and *Ultimate* doing very well while the remainder – *Marvel Knights, Marvel Age* etc. – is marginal at best. *Fantastic Four* seems to be dragging but *Daredevil, Iron Man* and *Hulk* are steady. Other Marvel titles are rather stagnant, including *Punisher, Marvel Knights 4, Spider-Girl, Emma Frost, Alpha Flight* and *She Hulk*. *Captain America* and *Cap and the Falcon* are embarrassing when it comes to sales. *Mary Jane* was an out and out flop, as was *Identity Disc*. It's too early to tell what kind of impact Marvel's relaunch of its major titles will have on the market. *Iron Man* looks promising with Warren Ellis handling the scripts. Marvel's relaunches are getting to be tiresome.

Even though Marvel is out of bankruptcy, their status as one of the "big two" has become a little less intimidating and credible. Relaunches, returns, cancellations, and more X-titles have plagued them this year, and it's hard to see how they still take up basically half of the sales chart each month. The opinion of many comic fans is that this is the only way Marvel can compete with DC's success. Sales, though, still tell the tale, as though Marvel is trying to recapture the glory they enjoyed in the early 1990s by offering new overrated multiple covers again. Only time will tell whether their decisions will come back to haunt them or give them a boost.

Archie Comics: *Sonic The Hedgehog* is Archie's biggest seller, selling as well as DC's and Marvel's middle titles. Back issues are impossible to keep in stock. The rest of the Archie line is almost nonexistent when it comes to new sales.

IDW: Quickly becoming the new Chaos!, these guys have done quite well by producing good horror stories and selling out of these low print books, but fans will eventually get tired of the $3.99 price tag per issue. That aside, many of their properties, like *30 Days of Night* and some others, have been offered up for a shot at the big screen.

Image: While Image plods along with too many titles, *Spawn* still holds its own and could see an upsurge with its recent restructuring. *The Walking Dead* is the most talked-about book from Image, with this sleeper catching quite a few people off guard. Robert Kirkman's tale of the zombie holocaust and its survivors has a realistic feel to it.

Silver Age: *Batman, Detective, Justice League of America* and *Wonder Woman* lead the pack for DC when it comes to issues from the Silver Age. All *Superman* family titles are slow as are DC's other core books, including *Green Lantern, Atom, Flash* and *World's Finest* despite the success of the *Superman/Batman* series. Off-beat titles such as *Metal Men, Sea Devils, Challengers of the Unknown* and *Rip Hunter,*

Time Master are dead in the water. The "Dial H For Hero" *House of Mystery* issues don't even get a casual glance anymore. Some other fine books constantly overlooked are Gold Key's *Magnus Robot Fighter* and *Doctor Solar* as well as the Charlton Steve Ditko's *Captain Atom* and *Blue Beetle* issues. On the Marvel front, it's *Spider-Man* hogging all of the action. Anything from the 1960s is usually snapped up while the rest are hit and miss at best. *Tales of Suspense, Tales To Astonish, Fantastic Four, Avengers, Hulk* and *Captain America* don't even sell well in high grade. *X-Men* issues still sit around for months at a time. The exceptions are key issues and very early numbers. Dell Comics in low to mid-grade sell well at 50 percent of *Guide* as do other miscellaneous companies from the 1950s. Oddball 1940s comics in the same grades are steady movers. *Classics Illustrated* sell every now and then as do movie cowboy titles.

Bronze/Copper/Modern Age: Comics from these periods are still very plentiful in all grades. With the exception of a few key issues, these comics are very affordable with a lot of dealers willing to cut the prices to move them. *X-Men* from this period are for the most part still overpriced and difficult to sell at *Guide*. *X-Men* and *Spider-Man* issues sell very well in the dollar boxes due to the residual effects of the recent movies. As usual, quarter boxes are a big hit with issues going back to the early '70s winding up there. If the issue is not high grade, it'll wind up in the cheap section.

eBay: Today's view of eBay is ever changing. While there will always be high-priced CGG comics for the extremely wealthy to purchase as a comic collector or to invest, the common man has found eBay to be an excellent source of obtaining current issues. Has your local shop received too many damaged books for a certain title and you didn't obtain your copy? Get it on eBay. Did your local shop not receive that variant cover you have been waiting months for? Get it on eBay. The number of comic book dealers increases day by day, which means there are more dealers who have little or no experience in the business. Some do note they are not professional comic dealers or graders. Most of these Internet sellers grab Overstreet grading and price guides for reference and then try to start selling. When it comes to getting a decent price on comics, it's still a free-for-all. It always depends on who's looking for a certain book and always what somebody is willing to pay. All of us have experienced many comics that went for over *Guide* one week and for $5 the next.

San Diego: With 80,000 in attendance, the San Diego Con continues to grow; in 1999, there were 50,000 attending. As usual, the convention was jam-packed with excellent guests from every spectrum of the medium. Exhibits, panels and other features kept one scurrying throughout the show. The dealer room was somewhat different this year with many new small-time merchants setting up; unfortunately this was not a good thing for the most part. Many of these new dealers set up with the thought of getting top dollar for their middle-of-the-road books. 'Hey, this is the San Diego Con; we can make a fortune regardless of what we have.' Wrong. Even the well-established dealers were hurting while other big-name sellers showcased their wares with over *Guide* prices. But there were a lot of bargains to be found.

This was the first year I (MH) attended Comic Con in San Diego. I was blown away by the sheer size of this convention and the mass of humanity that comes along with it. By the end of the convention I was a little bit weary of the atmosphere. It didn't seem as upbeat as I would have expected. DC was its usual powerful self, bringing in all of their heavy hitters including Jim Lee, Brad Meltzer and Matt Wagner. Marvel was non-existent except for several panel discussions. Their major announcement for the convention was the exclusive contract signing of Robert Kirkman. IDW, TokyoPop, Image, Dreamwave, Devil's Due and of course *Star Wars* were all represented strongly.

As far as selling goes with dealers, it was fast and furious; alas the furious part came when collectors saw the prices for high grade comics. Nearly every core issue of any title including *Batman, Superman,* and *Spider-Man* were easily double to triple *Guide,* and by the end of the convention, dealers were scrambling to make sales on these items. There were also plenty of current issues to be obtained and even issues coming the week before were marked up by 50%. At the end of the convention, many dealers were offering anywhere from 50-75% off all their books except for key Silver Age issues.

The San Diego convention is the one every comic fan should attend at least once in their lifetime and I can guarantee if they go that first time, they will want to attend every year. This year's convention allowed me to meet new dealers, some of my favorite artists and writers, and make several friends in the comic book industry. I was even sitting against a wall reading a few Spider-Man comics when all of a sudden Stan Lee walks by and catches me reading and tells me "Thanks for reading, True Believer!" Now if that's not worth the price of admission, I don't know what is.

Michael Browning

The law of supply and demand ruled the market this year, which could be called the Year of the Comic Book Variant. If it was even a little bit tough to find, it was expensive to buy. Several retailer premium variants skyrocketed and made lots of dealers very happy – and made them lots of money, an *Amazing Spider-Man* printing error cover was discovered, and an old line of variants were unearthed. All in all, it amounted to a lot of cash spent by completists to get books that were tough to find and very hot.

An *Amazing Spider-Man* #149 red cover error edition was discovered. This variant was printed without the cyan part of the CMYK (cyan, magenta, yellow and black) printing process, causing several of the cover colors to be drastically different. The regular cover has a green Jackal standing atop a green-suited Ned Leeds, with Spider-Man fighting a look-alike

Spider-Man clone. The error edition has a yellow Jackal standing atop a yellow building overtop a yellow-suited Ned Leeds. The logo on the error edition is red on pink and the corner-box Spider-Man is standing in a red on pink costume in front of a yellow circle. The regular cover has the correct-colored Spider-Man with a green circle behind him. One Spider-Man's costume – the one swinging from above – has a purple look to it on the regular cover, while the variant edition is red on pink. The other Spider-Man, coming from the bottom of the page, is wearing a red and grey costume on the error edition. Also, lettering on the book that is done in green on the regular edition is yellow on this edition.

This is an error variant and not a sun-faded comic. Several collectors have looked at the book and confirmed that it is indeed a manufacturer's error edition that was probably done at the start of the print run, with most of the error copies probably thrown in the trash. This book is definitely rare and is similar to the *Fantastic Four* #110 color variant edition in that both have manufacturer's error covers.

Last year's completist craze started off with a couple of high-priced sales of two trade paperbacks. A *Man of Steel* raffle edition, given away by DC Comics as a contest prize in 1987 after the mini-series was released, sold for $750 on eBay. The closing price was $1,000, but the buyer convinced the seller to sell him the book for $250 less than the closing bid. Another copy was traded for $750 in original art not long after the first copy sold. About 10 copies of this book surfaced during the year. At first, no one knew a lot about them, because the *Guide* had two listings for the same book. Now, we know that this was a trade paperback collection of all six issues, rebound under one generic cover and given away to raffle winners and retailers written in on the winner's entry forms.

A similar trade paperback collection, the Diamond retailer seminar copy of *Blind Justice* reprinting *Detective Comics* #598-600, was sold for $500 cash and $250 in trade. This was given out in 1989 to retailers attending the Diamond seminar. Only three copies of that book surfaced online. Another give-away at that Diamond retailer seminar was a trade paperback collection of the Todd McFarlane *Spider-Man* "Torment" storyline. A copy of that book sold for nearly $50 online. All three of these trade paperbacks are very tough to find and almost never come up for sale online or in stores.

The big sellers of 2004 were the variant covers and retailer premiums from DC Comics. A white-cover *Ultimate Spider-Man* #1 graded at 9.8 sold for $1,325. Two other 9.8s of the same book sold for $1,050 and $700. Two DC Comics RRPs, *Superman* #204 and *Identity Crisis* #1, both in CGC 9.8, sold for $1,849.95 each. Raw copies of the *Superman* #204 RRP with the Jim Lee sketch cover sold for $409.87, $580.05, $495 and $409.87; all were NM. Raw copies of *Identity Crisis* #1 RRPs sold for $405, $500, $499.95, $495, $429.95 and $406.01; all were NM. An older variant, the Walmart-distributed, second print *Spider-Man* #1 Gold with the UPC symbol, sold in 9.6 for $325. A copy of the scarce *Ultimate Spider-Man* #3 pink manufacturer's error did not sell at $1,999. Last year, three copies of this book surfaced.

DC Comics, Marvel and Archie all produced a line of variants that were sold to card, specialty and novelty shops in 1987 under a licensing agreement with SoMuchFun! Inc., which produced "Classic" comics in bagged sets of three. These comics were second printings of random Archie, DC and Marvel comics that were reprinted with a "Classic" logo under the regular logo. Some had different covers altogether and all were pre-packed in bags of three and sold at a discounted price. The SoMuchFun! Inc. variants are much like the Whitman DCs of the 1970s in that they were, in many cases, the original covers and comics with only slight differences. But while the Whitmans were all first printings, the SoMuchFun! variants are all second prints. So far, a listing of the SoMuchFun! Inc. books has not been completed. There was no rhyme or reason to the comics that were printed. The books were randomly picked by each respective comic company and were reprinted with changes made to the original covers and packaged to sell to a non-comics audience through gift stores for only a year before the project was abandoned. The print runs were 5,000 copies each, according to the former owner of the company, Steve Lishansky. A *Justice League* #217 and a *Batman* #401 were traded for $100 each not long after the variant line's discovery. A *Superman* #161 in VG sold for $15.

Other SoMuchFun! Inc., variants that were found are a *G.I. Joe, A Real American Hero* #63 (Marvel), an *Uncanny X-Men* #221, a *Fantastic Four* #306, a *Man of Steel* #1, an *Amazing Spider-Man* #292, a *Star Trek* #6 (DC), a *Betty and Veronica* #289 and an *Archie* #282. Many of the comics had the same covers as their original printings with the exception of the word "Classic" located somewhere on the front cover, usually near the logo. The location of the word "Classic" is, on some of the comics, in different places. Some have the word under their front cover logo; others had "Classic" in the banner atop their covers. Unlike the Marvel and DC "Classic" editions whose indicias read the same as the regular editions with the exception of a note saying "Second Printing," the Archie indicia reads "Archie Classic Comics." The last line says "Distributed by SoMuchFun! Inc., Phoenix Street, Shirley, MA 01464."

The *Batman* and *Justice League of America* "Classic" editions have variations on their covers that go beyond just the addition of the "Classic" logo. DC "Classics" used a different style of lettering than did the Marvel and Archie "Classics." DC's reprints used yellow block-style lettering, where Marvel and Archie used solid black lettering. The *Justice League of America* Classic has a completely altered cover and "Classic" under the JLA's logo. Most have the logo of the company where the UPC symbol would have been.

Each comic apparently was priced at $1.25, an increase from their original cover price. The books are fairly scarce due to their low print runs. The remaining stock of pre-packaged SoMuchFun! variants were sold with other leftover inventory from SoMuchFun! Inc. after the company folded in 1992.

This year was also a big year for back issues of Valiant Comics, which keep getting hotter and hotter, thanks in large part to CGC and collectors who know these are truly great comics. Several VALIANT (spelled all in caps, as Jim Shooter told me) comics saw large price hikes this year. A *Chaos Effect Alpha Red*, which received a CGC grade of 9.8, was sold on eBay for $1,500. A raw copy in VF/NM sold for $31, while another raw NM copy sold for $102.50. A *Turok Dinosaur Hunter* #1 Gold CGC 9.8 sold for $161.50. *Rai* was hot as prices for CGCed copies soared in value. A #1 9.8 sold for $61.01, while two copies of #3 in 9.6 sold for $67 and $62 respectively. A *Shadowman Valiant Validated Signature Series* #0 in NM sold for $43. *Solar* was hot as the sun. A #1 in 9.8 sold for $91, while a #60, the last issue, graded at 9.6, sold for $39. These prices are much higher than they were during the boom of the mid-1990s. A *Magnus* #21 Gold in 9.8 sold for $139.01, while a #1 9.8 sold for $127.50. A #12 9.8 sold for $113.61 and two other copies of #1 sold for around $100 each. Crossovers were also heating up, as a *Predator Vs. Magnus Robot Fighter* Platinum #1 sold for $113.50. The *X-O Manowar* #1/2 Gold from *Wizard* is reportedly very scarce and three copies unslabbed sold for $76.51, $75.51 and $67 online. The *Shadowman* Vol. 3 #2 variant cover, with a print run of approximately 750, sold for $177.50.

As for current comics, *Nyx* slept for awhile before everyone realized that X-23 had some relation to Wolverine. Then the prices went through the roof. Slabbed 9.8 copies of *Nyx* #3 went for $217.50, $199.99, $199.95, and $189.99, while NM and unslabbed copies of #4 were selling for around $15. *Thor* #80, the first part of the "Avengers Disassembled" crossover, sold briskly at around $25 each unslabbed. Subsequent issues of *Thor*, which reportedly was under-ordered by retailers, saw large increases in back issue prices as well.

Another company that saw some increased interest was Broadway. While many of the Broadway Comics line can be found in quarter boxes or for cover price, *Fatale*'s trade paperback and hardcover collections, called *Inherit The Earth*, saw huge increases. The trade paperback sold easily at $50 a copy, while the trade paperback was commanding prices of up to $175 when they could be found. Both the trade paperback and the hardcover are elusive. While Ultraverse comics haven't been hot in a long time, their day may be coming soon. A copy of *Lord Pumpkin* #1 limited signed by Dan Danko and Aaron Lopresti with a certificate of authenticity sold for $23.

Giveaways, as usual, were hot. The Free Comic Book Day edition of *The Ballad of Sleeping Beauty* wasn't free for long. Readers of this comic snatched up all of the FCBD copies and there just wasn't enough to go around, so prices quickly escalated to $10 a copy online, while copies of #2 and 3 were scarce in supply and high in demand. The *Spider-Man Acme Dingo Boots* giveaway comic, which is reportedly hard to find, sold in VG for $90.99. A J.C. Penney *Ultimate Spider-Man* #8 reprint sold in NM for $20.50. A *Resident Evil* giveaway from Marvel Comics sold in NM for $29.95. Two copies of *Shazam! Visits Portland, Oregon* in 1943 sold, both in NM, for $25 and for $50 respectively.

Golden and Silver Age back issues are quite scarce in the southern West Virginia, eastern Kentucky, southwestern Virginia areas, and at least one shop owner says he almost never sees Golden and Silver Age back issues these days. We don't have an abundance of comic shops, and those that are still around don't sell a lot of older back issues. They mainly survive on new comics and those new issues that are hot.

The Batman "Hush" series with Jim Lee art sold well in my area, as did the Michael Turner Superman "Godfall" crossover. A copy of *Batman* #608, the start of Lee's art, sold for nearly $50 at one area shop. Other shops sold copies of #608, 612 and the second printings of those books for around $25 each. Turner's art on *Superman/Batman* caused issue #8-10 to increase in value. Prices on #8 rose to around $20, while the harder-to-find #9 was priced at around $15-20.

The "Avengers Disassembled" series was hot, as were all the titles with crossovers of that event. *Aquaman* got hot when new writer Will Pfeiffer and new artist Patrick Gleason took over with #15. The introduction of Carnage into *Ultimate Spider-Man* was well-received and issues sold out soon after their release and soon after were selling at a premium. *Identity Crisis* kept readers on the edge of their seats and also saw a slight increase in back issue prices after the first issue sold out and a new printing of #1 was announced.

Spider-Girl #75-76 was hot due to the heroine wearing the black costume. Geoff Johns' and Mike McKone's *Teen Titans* was one of the best sellers of the year. Issue #1 with its McKone cover and Michael Turner variant sold well, with the Turner cover increasing to around $25. Turner seems to have the Midas touch when it comes to variant covers; anything he touches turns to gold.

Astonishing X-Men was a big success here in the coalfields, with copies of #1 quickly selling out and then selling for a high premium. Copies of #1, when they could be found at comic shops here, sold upwards of $10 each. Copies of the variant editions sold for $150 and $45 for the first issue Cassaday cover and no one received any of the Gabriele Dell'Otto variant covers. The Colossus variant cover to #4 also sold quickly. As retailers caught on to the variant craze, copies of #4 were selling for $10 straight out of the Diamond Comics box and soon were selling for around $30 as they made their way to the back issues walls of area stores. *The Pulse* took some time to heat up, but #1 started selling for a premium around the same time as #3 was released. *Uncanny X-Men* started selling well again after Chris Claremont's return in #444. *Excalibur* Vol. 2 #1 was also hot and was selling for $5 not long after its release.

The Jim Lee *Superman* was heavily ordered and copies flew off the shelves. However, the slow pace of the story kept many people away and back issue prices never reached the level of the Jim Lee *Batman* series. Even a Michael Turner variant cover (50/50) on #205 didn't make it a sell-out at our area stores for several weeks.

Free Comic Book Day was a success in our area for the few comic shops that participated in the promotional event. Some retailers pulled out of the promotion because of the increasing cost of the "free" comics. Many believed the time was wrong because so many potential comic readers were on vacation; our area's small-shop retailers said they believe many of the bigger stores in larger areas benefited, but not the smaller shops, which were far away from the vacation crowds.

Trade paperbacks continued to be very popular as many comic shops sold large amounts of trades. *Watchmen* is always a fast seller here as are traditional favorites Batman: *The Dark Knight Returns, The Killing Joke, The Death of Superman, Secret Wars, Crisis on Infinite Earths, The Chronicles of Conan* and many others. The Marvel-published *Essential Conan* trade paperback is no longer available on their list of *Essential* black-and-white "phone book" reprint editions and gets about $50 when copies can be found.

The *Hellboy, Punisher* and *Alien vs. Predator* movies did little to increase sales at area stores in southern West Virginia and eastern Kentucky. A bump in sales was felt when *Spider-Man 2* was released, as back issues sold briskly. After the movie left the screens, copies of Spider-Man back issues remained on comic shop walls.

Back issue sales for *Transformers* and *G.I. Joe* all seemed to cool off as the 1980s nostalgia market died down considerably. Collectors in our area seemingly couldn't care less about back issues of the new versions *of G.I. Joe, Transformers, Micronauts, Thundercats* and *Ghostbusters*, as copies could be found in quarter bins not long after their release. Marvel's *Conan the Barbarian* was a good seller after the Dark Horse series debuted. The new *Conan* #1 by Dark Horse was a strong seller at $10 and one dealer had the 25 cent #0 on the back issue wall for $25. It was gone by the time I paid my next visit.

Nearly all of the Marvel Tsunami titles were hot at one time or another, but all cooled off quickly when they started getting cancelled. The Marvel Age titles suffered the same fate, although they weren't being cancelled as quickly. *Mary Jane* was the first to fall and only time will tell which Marvel Age comic will be next.

On the flipside, the Marvel Age digest-sized trade paperbacks sold fairly well here. *Miracleman*'s later issues climbed in value, also. Issues #23 and 24 are both tougher to find in NM than #15 and collectors finally started realizing that fact. The 2D version of *Miracleman* 3D is the hardest-to-find book in the collection, as only a couple hundred are believed to exist. One collector was offering $500 for a copy of the 2D edition, which was published for color-blind readers who could not see the 3D effects of the regular edition. Just about any issue of *Miracleman* sells immediately when shops get them. Demand was high here for the last two issues of the regular series and many *Miracleman* collectors were looking for the Gold and Blue #1s and the 2D, 3D edition.

Archie and Harvey comics, when dealers can find them, sell well here. Whitman pre-pack issues get hotter every year. Several low grade copies of Whitman pre-pack comics were found in a collection here in southern West Virginia, but those were purchased by a private collector and have not reached the back issue market.

John Chruscinski (Tropic Comics)

It has been a big year for us. We are selling a lot of higher-dollar books and we also made a big move from South Florida to Lyndora, Pennsylvania. It was tough, but it was well worth it, if not just for the extra space to better serve our web customers. Our web sales have been strong this year except for our three months downtime during our move. We are now back up and running with major plans and changes for our website (www.tropiccomics.com) in 2005.

Golden Age: Books are tough to get at a reasonable price, but easy to sell, especially in high grade. Some titles that sold well for us this year were: *Superman, Action, Adventure, Flash, Green Lantern, All American, Captain America, All Winners, All Star, Marvel Mystery*, and *Detective Comics*. *Wonder Woman* and *Sensations* still sell strong at over *Guide* in lower grades. We sold more restored Golden Age keys this year than in the last two years combined, proving that the stigma on restoration may be loosening up a bit.

There are three factors in determining a price on restored issues. First: What was done to the book? Second: How does it look (amateurish or professional)? Third: Who did the work? If you have the correct combination to these questions, a restored book may bring you more than you expected it to.

Collectors are seeing deals being had for CGC books with restored labels and filling up holes on their want list with slightly restored books that are very reasonably priced.

Some sales we had this year were: *Sensation Comics* #1 CGC 9.4 (rest.) $5,000; *Sensation Comics* #1 CGC 8.0 $3,000; *Sub-Mariner* #1 CGC 6.0 (SP rest.) $4,000; *Batman* #1 G/VG (rest.) $4,000; *All Star* #3 VG (rest.) trimmed $3,000; *All Star* #8 VF/NM (rest.) $3,000; *Detective Comics* #31 VF (rest.) $4,000; *Green Lantern* #1 VF/NM (rest.) $5,000; *Captain America* #10 VF/NM (cover cleaned) $1,500; *Human Torch* #1 G/VG (rest.) $1,900

Atom Age: Mixed sales and demand varied on title and condition. Avons, horror, and crime books lead the way for want lists we received. Dells and Gold Keys sell moderately with *Four Colors* and duck titles most requested. We cannot keep Atlas in stock. Horror, western, and Romance sell over *Guide* in the lower grades. ECs are starting to pick up again in the mid-grades as collectors are realizing they can be had at bargain prices.

Silver Age: The heartbeat of the comic market. Marvels outsell all other companies combined. Graded CGCs of 9.4 or better still sell at multiples of *Guide* with *Spider-Man* and *X-Men* leading the way. Low grade sell fairly fast at adjusted prices. We cannot keep high grade CGC-certified DCs in stock. Again, 9.4 or higher seem to be the grades most requested. We anticipate that after more time, collectors will begin to tire while waiting to find DCs in CGC 9.4 and higher and start buying CGC 9.0s and higher, perhaps even CGC 8.0 and higher on some harder-to-find books. Low and mid-grade issues still sell slower than their Marvel counterparts, even at adjusted prices. Gold Key TV photo covers sell well, with high grade being the most sought after.

Bronze Age: Hot! The 1970s seem to be the new playing field for the CGC investor. With *Hulk* #181 being the "Holy Grail," other '70s like *Marvel Spotlight* #5 and *Amazing Spider-Man* #129 are selling for multiples of *Guide*. Magazines have gone from 0 to 60 in sales for us when CGC started grading magazines – *Creepy, Eerie, Vampirella, Savage Sword of Conan*, and *Savage Tales* to name a few. With high grade copies of '70s keys bringing jaw-dropping prices, I believe this is a good investment area for years to come. Look for a lot of minor key issues to become bigger players in the future. Price variants sell well with 35¢ variants being the hottest of all. High prices are being paid in this underestimated part of the market, so take notice.

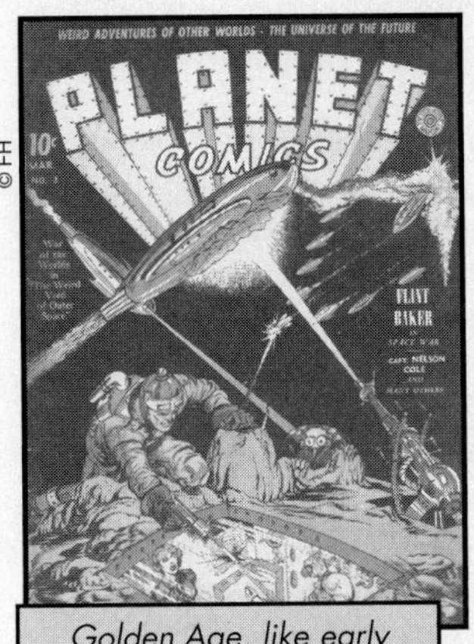

© FH

Golden Age, like early Fiction House, moves extremely well. (***Planet Comics*** *#3 shown)*

Modern Age: CGC graded books dominate this market. 9.8 is the starting point on most issues for the grade collector. Early 1980s independents like *Albedo, Cerebus, Teenage Mutant Ninja Turtles, Grendel*, and *Elfquest* are all rising from the dead to sell for unheard of prices in high grade. Even Valiants are making a comeback with pre-*Unity* and gold issues being some of our most requested titles. Printing errors are now being recognized; as in coins, these errors are now starting to sell for more then their counterparts. Before they weren't saleable to most consumers and sent to the distributor to be destroyed. Now have they are widely sought after.

All in all, I see a strong and healthy market in the next year and most of it due to the trust that CGC has brought back to this great hobby. As for us, we have many big plans in our new home in Pennsylvania, so please check in on us every now and then to see what's going on at www.tropiccomics.com.

Gary Dolgoff (Gary Dolgoff Comics)

2004 was a year that, due to the six prices now in the *Guide* plus other factors, saw an increase in hopeful sellers vastly over-grading and overvaluing their collections. Sales were very solid for a variety of grades. Some prefer high grade for investment, plus the joy of getting and viewing those beautiful, shiny copies (I define high grade as a nice FN to Mint). Others prefer a solid mid-grade comic that's sturdy and not tatty, as these can cost less than 25% of the price of a NM copy of the same book. It's a good way to build a strong, diverse, collection without breaking the bank, and they're books you can read as well without worrying about perfection.

There is a third group of collectors – those that want to buy nice and inexpensive (read: lower grade) oldies for their collections. It's amazing what Silver Age you can acquire for $2-5 a book, for instance. You can quickly develop a huge collection for the price of a few paychecks or less.

Golden Age: I've been lucky this year in getting a decent amount of Golden Age, including about 20 different *All Stars, Wonder Woman* #1, *Young Allies* #1, *More Fun* #17 in F/VF, *Batman* #9-11 in nice shape, early *Sensation Comics, Human Torch* #8, *Captain Midnight* #1, *Walt Disney Comics & Stories* #31 with a missing centerfold, and much more.

The better Golden Age still moves out extremely well–Timely, DC, MLJ, early Fiction House, Centaur, etc. However, with some of the miscellaneous early '40s books, I've been meeting with some surprising resistance here and there. How could someone not buy *Uncle Sam* #1? I've even got one in my collection – it's a great book.

I'll still buy them as they are true treasures, but I must admit that the better Silver Age – early '60s *AMZ* and *FF*, early *Showcase* and *Brave & the Bold* – now seem to sell to more briskly than some of the miscellaneous Golden Age. Of course Timelys, followed by '30s-'40s DCs, are still the kings of all collectibles. I'm always happy to pay 50-80% of *Guide* for these, as they sell in all grades. *Wonderworld* comics sell well as do *Master Comics*, particularly below #50. *Mary Marvel*, which is an inexpensive but not always available title, moves well, as do most issues of *Wow Comics* with Mary Marvel. Folks rightfully dig the very early *Capt. Marvel Jr*s. *Capt. Marvel* sells OK. *Whiz Comics* below #30 move quite solidly, especially the first 10 issues.

Fiction House: *Planet Comics* remains the best and a consistent seller. *Airboy*s, and *Capt. Midnight*s have slowed down somewhat. *Don Winslow*s sell somewhat slowly. Late '40s *Daredevil* and *Boy* comics aren't what one would call prime movers, although the early '40s *DD*s and to some extent the early *Boy* comics are desired.

Lev Gleason: The best are *Silver Streak* #6-7 with those awesome (DD Vs. Claw) covers. Also popular is #1 ('41) of *Daredevil*, in which he battles Hitler.

MLJ: The best sellers are *Hangman Comics* plus, of course, the early issues of *Archie Comics* and Archie's first two appearances in *Pep* #22 and *Jackpot* #4.

Restored: I'm finding more collections of '40s comics with amateur restoration on many of the books. Depending on the extent of the 'resto,' plus if the job is particularly ugly and unnatural–looking or not bad, I can get between 2/3 and 100% of Good *Guide* for these. Even professionally restored comics only go for so much. I have a beautiful-looking *All-*

Star #4 that has some innocuous-looking, relatively minor restoration. I offered it to folks for less than G/VG *Guide*, and despite its overall nice appearance, no one bought it! I happily buy restored books as long as I can sell them at a reasonable price.

1950s Superhero: Most 1950s superhero are DC, and they sell quite well, especially pre-Code across the board, #1s, and early *Showcase* Flash. In general, all early *Showcase* as well as *Brave & the Bold* #1-27 can be counted on to move out, particularly in Good or better shape. Early *Flash* #105-120 sell quite well.

Non-Superhero '50s DCs: Sci-fi and mystery (*House of Mystery, Mystery In Space, Strange Adventures*) sell very solidly. A small yet enthusiastic clientele seeks *Dean Martin* as well as *Jerry Lewis* comics. Later '50s DCs are also solid sellers. The pre-Code ones in general are just somewhat less around and sell faster. I never turn down a collection containing 1950s and earlier DCs!

Horror: These continue to sell great, especially if they have decapitated heads, tongues on cover, etc. EC horror sells the best. I've gotten in some EC collections in the last year, kept a few for my private collection, and sold the rest.

Sci-Fi: These sell well. I got in some EC Gaines File copies this year. I was happy to pay over *Guide* for these; they CGCed at 9.4 and 9.6 mostly! I sold three and kept one. Now I'm hoping for a big collection of high grade ECs to come my way. Lower grade sells decently as well.

Crime: These sell solidly but not brilliantly. Probably one of the best sellers here is EC's very own *Crime SuspenStories*.

Western: These sell OK but can't be counted on in general to move out quickly. Among these, *Red Ryder* is a leading seller, especially those early issues. I kept a #7 for myself – a great cover. The best western sellers are '50s Marvel westerns.

Romance: They sell well, especially the DC romance (10¢ cover) comics, followed by the Marvel romance books like *Millie* and *Patsy*. As with many '50s genres, the pre-Code comics sell more quickly and reliably than their post-Code counterparts.

War: Atlas war sells well with those gritty non-P.C. covers. Other war comics from the '50s sell decently. If the covers are crazy and violent, they'll sell better.

Classics: First printings below #44 sell best, although *Classics* in general are slow. Among the best sellers are #8 (*Arabian Nights*), #33 (*Sherlock Holmes*), and #43 (*Great Expectations*). Cheap *Classics* sell decently, especially at better comic book shows.

Archie: I have trouble keeping '50s Archies in stock. They sell well, although '40s issues sell better still, especially Archies below #20. *Katy Keene*s seem tougher to get and must be checked for completeness – they cut out those dresses in the '50s. I myself enjoy Archie comics and humor. Just don't try to sell them in England; the Brits just aren't into it where Archies are concerned.

Dells: Funny animal 1950s Dells are quite slow. It seems like everyone bought them and kept them. Many of them can be had quite cheaply, however, at $3-5 a book.

TV/Movie: *I Love Lucy* comics sell the best of these. In general, this genre sells OK.

Little Lulu: This is a '50s Dell exception. They are cool comics and well-drawn, many of them by John Stanley. I can't keep #1-10 and the Lulu *Four Color*s in stock. The covers of these early Lulus have some nice eye appeal.

Exotic '50s: They sell great. *Reform School Girl, Mask Of Dr. Fu Manchu, Blood Is The Harvest* – these late '40s/early '50s one-shots have fantastic covers and are truly a pleasure to own.

Famous Monsters: The early issues #1-30 sell quite well, especially #1-6.

Playboy: I don't have a great deal of experience with these, but I'm quite confident that #1-10 particularly are smart sellers, especially #1 and the rare #2.

MADs: They sell OK but not thrilling.

1960s DCs: The best '60s DC seller over all is *Batman*. I recently sold a new complete *Batman* #126-254 run. *Detective, Superman* family titles, *JLA, Flash,* and *Green Lantern* are all solid titles, as is *Brave & Bold.* The secondary JLA characters sell somewhat slower – *Aquaman, Hawkman, Atom* – as do the *HOM* "Dial H" and John J'onzz issues. I have sold, however, batches of these titles as an across-the-board deal for 20% off *Guide*. 1960s romance DCs always seem to find a new home. With war issues, though, it depends on the title. *Our Army at War* with Kubert's great art sells OK. 1960s *Our Fighting Forces*, however, are considerably slower. I do well on my occasional 1960s-'71 – 12 and 15¢ cover – blowouts at $3 each or less.

1960s Marvel: These are the kings of the Silver Age. For over three decades, they continue to fuel the fires of comic collecting. The higher grades – strict VG/F or better – sell really strongly, especially *AMZ*, *FF*, and *X-Men*. Marvels 1964 and earlier do especially well in higher grade as they are tougher to get in nice shape. In the old days, nice warehouse copies would surface from time to time, sometimes hundreds of an issue. I myself have bought huge warehouse deals over the years and continue to do so as they are offered to me. 1964 and before Marvels, in general, sell extra well, as they are around less than their 1965 and later counterparts. *AMZ* #1-50; *Avengers* #1-4; *DD* #1-7; *FF* #1-30; *JIM* (Thor) #83-110, 112; *Hulk* #1-6; *Sgt. Fury* #1; *TOS* (Iron Man) #39-50; *TTA* #27, 35; and *X-Men* #1-6 are some of the best sellers of the '60s Marvels. I love getting them in and re-reading many of them as I grade them. It's still an unmitigated pleasure. 1965-1971 Marvels also sell solidly for the most part, especially *AMZ, FF, Avengers* after #50, *X-Men* #50-66, *Silver Surfer* #1, 4, plus the first issues of *Iron Man,* and *Conan*. I find that it helps to sell *Strange Tales, Tales of Suspense, Tales To Astonish, Thor, Sgt. Fury*, and some others at discount if I want to sell them pretty well. By the way: '60s-'70s Marvels with a UK price are still originals and printed at the same time as their American counterparts. 1960s pre-superhero Marvels sell almost instantly in almost any grade. They're great reads!

1960s Other: '60s Charltons seem to be selling somewhat better in higher grades, especially Ghost and Mystery titles. I recently got in a small warehouse lot, and I've already sold five each across-the-board in VG/F or better to two different fellow dealers. Romance and war Charltons move slowly. The miscellaneous '60s stuff sells slower to moderate – *Flyman, Jaguar,* etc. *Magnus, Robot Fighter* sells OK, as does *Boris Karloff* and other mystery/horror stuff. 1960s romance DCs sell well. A couple years ago I had runs of many of these, but they're just about all gone. Marvel romance from the '60s aren't as brisk as the DCs, but at discount I move them OK.
1970s General: Early 1970s (20¢ cover) and 'giant size' (52 pgs, 100 pgs, etc.) sell better than later '70s books.
1970s DC: 100-pg. giants sell moderately to well. *Batman* in general – especially VG/F and better – move out pretty well. Neal Adams *Batman* and *Detective* sell very well, as do the early '70s horror comics liked *House Of Mystery,* and *House Of Secrets*. Many of them are loaded with good artists. In general, there aren't as many '70s DCs around as there are '70s Marvels. Some miscellaneous hero DCs move slowly: *Claw, Arak,* and *Rima* come to mind, and this despite the beautiful Nester Redondo art in *Rima, the Jungle Girl.*
1970s Marvel: 20¢ cover price and some other Marvels of the more popular titles are very popular and sell pretty briskly for the most part, especially *AMZ* #100-150; *DD* #61-100, 158-181; *FF* #100-150; *Hulk* #144-182; *Avengers* #93-140; *Iron Fist* #14, 15; *G.S. X-Men* #1; *X-Men* #94-142; and some of the early '70s #1s like *Ghost Rider, Tomb Of Dracula,* and *Werewolf by Night*. Many later '70s Marvels are more available in the marketplace, especially the discontinued titles like *Luke Cage, Marvel Team-Up, Marvel Two-In-One, Marvel Premiere,* and *Defenders*, etc. They sell slower, so I've taken to blowing them out at 50-75¢ each in larger batches. Sometimes the price makes the book more worthwhile. *Tomb Of Dracula* is a solid title and a great read throughout the run.
1970s Other: Miscellaneous early '70s Charlton, etc., seem to sell pretty well. Atlas-Seaboards are still pretty slow.
1980s-2000s: I like to blow these out, many at 50¢-$1 per book, with the more expensive '80s/'90s at 25%-1/3 of Near Mint *Guide.* Since there are tons of most of these around, I try to tempt folks by price. For instance, typical *X-Men* issues between #185-275 sell pretty well at $1-1.50 each in nice shape. I find that *X-Men* #266 (1st Gambit) is in some demand, and that the McFarlane *AMZ*s are decent sellers, with #298 and especially #300, selling very well. *Swamp Thing* #20-40 sell quite briskly to a smaller but no less enthusiastic clientele – they don't seem to show up nearly as much as many '80s/'90s do. '96-present comics sell much better in general than their earlier counterparts. I find that keeping these books within the sets I wholesale seems to help the entire set sell better. In the beginning of the 1990s, every other person would invest in these hyped, mass-produced, over-saturated comics. A few years later, most 'in' comics did the opposite, which resulted in a relative shortage of late '90s/early 2000s comics.
CGC: In general, I find the philosophy of encapsulating comics annoying as I generally believe that the essence of collecting is being able to open up the comic and read it, look at the art, and even – in the case of the '30s-'50s books – smell them! That being said, I must admit that CGC helps to preserve and recognize the value of super-high grade comics 9.4 and higher, and even 8.5, 9.0, and 9.2, with regards to '30s thru early '60s comics. Also, it helps buyers to trust the grading better when buying off relatively unknown sellers or those sellers that are normally known for looser grading.

I have found much to my surprise that I can typically get *Guide* or close to it for CGC-graded mainline Golden Age and better Silver Age. That's why I'm willing to pay 50-70%+ of *Guide* plus pay for encapsulation on more expensive oldies. I still think it's silly for someone to pay goodly sums for high grade CGC late '80s-2000s comic books. There exist many high-grade non-CGCed *Spawn* #1s, for instance.
Marvel Magazines: The 1970s horror mags sell pretty well. The superhero mags move slower, though they may pick up in sales.
Pulps: Generally I love them. They often have great covers, interestingly written titles on the spine, and a rich history. Shadow, Spider, G-8 & his Battle Birds, Operator 5, Weird Tales, Strange Tales, Dime Mystery, Horror Stories, Terror Tales, Wu Fang, Yen Sin, Zeppelin Stories. Whenever they're offered to me, I must try and buy them all.
Original Art: A great market; I love getting in almost any original art, especially '70s and back. 1960s art seems to sell the best, with Kirby and Ditko Marvel art leading the way, as well as DC and Marvel covers from the 1970s and back.
Website Sales/Catalogue: At long last website sales have started to pick up, aided no doubt by my first catalogue since 1997. Websites are good as they can be constantly updated; plus, one can always adjust their homepage as we did to also offer sets and discounted package deals. But remember folks: It's the grading more than the discounting that determines whether or not the comics for sale are worth it.

D'Arcy Farrell (Pendragon Comics)

What an amazing summer of 2004, or should I say, *Amazing Spider-Man* summer. Another blockbuster movie by Marvel has attracted new collectors and readers. Only the first *Spider-Man* and *Batman* have had a greater effect. I can predict Batman's upcoming
movie will draw even more fans out of the woodwork. All these great, well-made movies support everyone in the comic book industry, and it goes round and round. To the writers and artists, to the dealers/stores and the fans, everyone gains. Combined with the successful Free Comic Book Day that Diamond and publishers commit to every year just before school gets out – the best time, not in the midst of summer – we have a two-fold way of increasing our customer base as

well as encouraging children to read.

Conventions: I do a few in Canada, and I'm glad to say they are on the rise. One show in particular stands out among all the rest – the Canadian National Expo held in Toronto at the end of August. The organizer, Aman, has really accomplished something here. Every year the gate climbs to new records. The 2004 show had over 26,000 attendees. The main reason? A crossover of various collectibles and medias. Comics are just one aspect. It also has anime/manga, SF, gaming, TV and Hollywood. This is a smart way to introduce yet more non-comic fans to comics they would not normally be privy to. I always gain a few new comic collectors every year due to this show's success.

Golden Age: Anything superhero does well. Most in demand, as always, are Timely and DC; nothing else comes close. *Marvel Mystery, Human Torch,* and *Captain America* lead the way for Timely, and DC always has *Batman, Detective, Action,* and *Superman*. Other titles abound from these publishers that sell very well. I've begun noticing far less *Comic Cavalcade*s, and my collectors have mentioned the same. We are now 60+ years from the end of popular WWII issues. These are amazing books in low supply with paper quality getting poorer every year. In a few more years, these comics with Schomburg (et al) covers will most likely be in many collectors' bank vaults never to be seen by conventioneers again. Some will surface here and there, but at insane premiums. Not much happens fast in the non-superhero area. I notice high grade ECs do move well, and excellent westerns such as *Lone Ranger, Autry,* and *Red Ryder*. Anything Barks does well for Dells, but not much else. Crime is a bit better this year, but not great.

Silver Age: I cannot get enough *Amazing Spider-Man, X-Men* and Neal Adams anything. These items will sell forever and never lessen in popularity/demand. *Fantastic Four, Daredevil, TOS, TTA, Hulk, Batman, Detective*, and *Flash* sell best after *AMZ* and *X-Men*. I have noticed many collectors of superheroine issues are getting more and more rabid for issues such as *Action* #252 (first Supergirl), and *Detective* #359 (Batgirl).

Bronze Age: *Jonah Hex* and affiliated titles are selling fast, as are other DC oddball items like *Weird War Tales, Witching Hour,* and *Phantom Stranger*. Many of DC's non-mainstream titles, especially in the horror, war and western genres, have such great art and stories and are still so undervalued and under-appreciated that I suggest many investors should not ignore this area. Marvel has its own low print titles that are not on many investors' radar. *Werewolf By Night* and *Tomb Of Dracula* are the best examples.

Copper Age: Miller *Daredevil*s are particularly hotter than normal. All the lower print runs of DC from the early 1980s are in greater demand, especially *GL* and *Flash*. This is a future hotbed of investment; I give it less than five years to really explode.

Modern Age: Jim Lee went from *Batman* to *Superman*. It wasn't as successful, but it's still doing well. *Identity Crisis* and *Superman* are the best sellers for DC in 2004. Marvel has done shockingly well with *Secret Wars* and the *Avengers* storyline. The Avengers finale and new #1, along with DC's *Green Lantern Rebirth* #1, pre-dates this review, but I expect huge quantities of issues to be sold. Image still sells badly all around whereas TokyoPop manga titles still increase in sales every year. Dark Horse is doing somewhat better, especially since the *Hellboy* movie was well done and attracted new fans as well.

eBay and Internet Auctions: Everyone wants to be a dealer it seems. Buying is risky enough, but far too many unrealistic collectors who sell on eBay hurt this marketplace. Buyers be wary of bright fuzzy pictures or the lack thereof. Bright digital pictures hide dirt, soiling, mold and tanning. Only a close-up or 1:1 scans seem accurate enough to tell. But even then, with various art/digital programs, a picture/scan may still be manipulated. Buy from proven dealers or test others with some small articles first. Their service, speed and grading will determine if you spend the bigger money. Even then you are always at risk when buying something that you cannot see, touch, investigate – restored, touch up and so on – hold in your own two hands, and then buy on the spot. This can be done in a local store or convention, but never online.

Conclusion: Another banner year for our industry. Sales are still climbing in new and vintage books. I expect 2005-2006 to continue this trend. I also expect values to flatten for a year or two on these high-rising Marvels, bouncing the increase and demand towards DC and others, coinciding with the new Batman movie. Marvel has raised too far too fast, leaving others behind. It doesn't mean a decrease is expected, but the trend will go towards DC's flagship titles for a year or so. Marvel will always be in high demand as well; that will most likely never lessen.

Dan Fogel (Hippy Comix Inc./Comic Detectives)

Entering our 27th year in comics, we have merged our Comic Detectives retailing division with our publishing company, Hippy Comix, Inc. Along with forming this vertically integrated funny book Frankenstein, we've also switched from selling mainly at conventions to selling online with our revamped web store, hippycomix.com. We're also focusing on underground, adult, and alternative comix, an area due for vast growth following this year's long-awaited release of *Fogel's Underground Comic Book Price Guide.* Popular titles sold in this area include *Adult Star Stories: Felecia, Amazons Attack 3-D, American Splendor, Beer Nutz, Cheech Wizard, Cherry, Doll, D'Arc Tangent, Dr. Atomic, Exquisite Corpse, Felch Cumics, Fabulous Furry Freak Brothers, Illuminations, Inner City Romance, Junk Comix, Junkwaffel, Kieron Dwyer's Lowest Comic Denominator, Miami Mice, Quack!, Planet of the Geeks, Poizon, Pulp, Rip Off Comix, Smith Brown Jones, Star Reach, Subvert*, and *Superbitch*.

Other more mainstream-related sales include miscellaneous *Amazing Heroes, Comic Book Marketplace, Comics Reader, MAD, MAD Special,* Marvel Comics 1980 & 1981 Calendars, 1995 DC Power Chrome Cards Basic Set, both

Mayfair Games DC Role-playing *Watchmen* Modules, and the *Atlas of the DC Universe*.

Going Up: Black & white magazines, especially *MADs*, Warrens and Marvels; fanzines in general, especially *Alter Ego, RBCC, Comics Reader, Comics Journal, Amazing Heroes,* and *Comic Book Marketplace*; out-of-print Marvel and DC trades; Silver Age Marvel "split books:" *Tales of Suspense, Tales to Astonish, Strange Tales*; later Silver Age Marvels: *Iron Man, Captain America, Sub-Mariner, Doctor Strange, Silver Surfer, Incredible Hulk, Nick Fury*; DC Silver Age in general, but especially Superman and JLA-related titles and heroes; DC and Marvel digests and treasuries; *Cerebus*; DC and Marvel Silver and Bronze Age horror/mystery titles.

Going Down: None. No prisoners!

Stephen H. Gentner

As a comic book collector, I find that this is one of the best and strongest markets ever. Collections which were put together five to ten years ago have seen very nice gains, and in some instances astounding appreciation. Marvel Silver Age material, particularly in high grade, defies description in its growth and stability. DC Silver Age has enjoyed good growth and appreciation as well, albeit not quite as pronounced as Marvel. Lower grades of the popular titles for both publishers seem to sell quite well when priced fairly at *Guide* or *Guide* plus a premium for keys. Golden Age material by and large has plateaued, and the savvy collector may be able to find some favorites more reasonably priced. Bronze Age material has had excellent growth, and the hot titles and keys are becoming more well known by collectors. The window to catch these rising stars is closing quickly, and the collector and investor both should review their want lists to lock in.

As the market becomes more sophisticated, the availability, scarcity, and demand for key material plays out on eBay daily. Many of the sellers use CGC-graded material and census figures to justify high reserves. As time has passed and the CGC census figures stabilize, trends can be determined as to scarcity in given grades.

© MAR

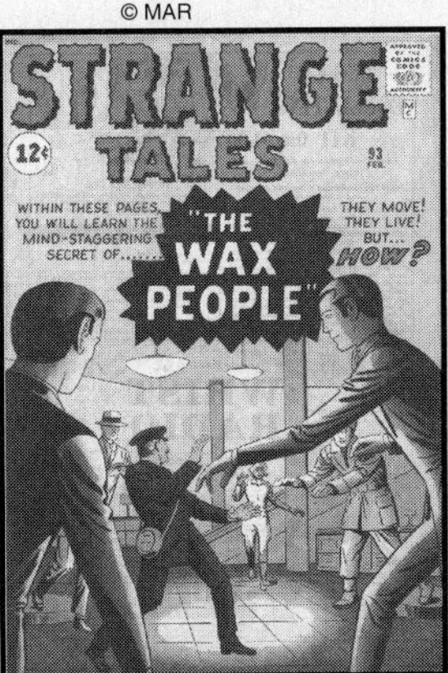

*Artists like Steve Ditko demand more attention. (**Strange Tales** #93 shown)*

I have been focusing on favorite artists more than individual titles of late. Tracking down nice copies of work by Neal Adams, Alex Schomburg, Matt Baker, Carmine Infantino, Joe Kubert, Russ Heath, and Murphy Anderson et al targets my dollars to keys and icons rather than long runs at the altar of completism. However, some artists make titles their own, which demands more attention from me, such as Russ Manning in *Magnus Robot Fighter,* Barry Smith and the first 23 *Conans*, Jack Kirby and Joe Simon in *The Fighting American*, Steve Ditko in *Strange Tales*, etc. The point is that artists rather than titles are influencing my sleuthing.

The last few years, the same trends seem to be holding my interest. I search for secret trends and confirm my findings and positions all the time. My reports may seem similar to previous efforts, but to me that only makes me more convinced how healthy the hobby is. Ho-hum, yawn – another banner year. Good hunting!

Going Up: Schomburg airbrush and war covers; 'Good Girl' art in standard Nedor; *Black Terror* #1; Fox 'Good Girl;' and 'Good Girl' post-WWII until 1949-50, which is scarce and cool.

Going Down: Golden Age DC post-WWII, particularly in lower grades; Fawcett, MLJ, Dell generally are flat; the same can be said for Quality, Centaur, *Classics Illustrated*, and Disney.

Daniel Greenhalgh (Showcase New England)

Most people familiar with my opinion of the market as an investment tool have known me to be decidedly bearish with respect to collecting comics, including Marvels, over the past decade. Three major events have occurred in the past five years to change this trend which had been spiraling downward and which, frankly, for a time I thought was irreversible. The first event was the introduction of Internet and online trading; the second event was the introduction of third party grading in comics. The third and most influential change, in my opinion, was the introduction and success of the Marvel movies. The impact these movies have had on expanding the collector base for comics cannot be emphasized sufficiently. The combination of these three events has created a change in the overall trend and a real opportunity for investors seeking alternative vehicles to make money. That doesn't mean you can just go out and buy anything; as an investor you still have to pick your spots.

Golden Age: Stable – that's the best word I can come up with to describe the mainstream Golden Age market. As a general rule you won't get the pop you might get with a high grade Marvel, but at least you are investing in a book in a relatively mature market. I would stay with the major DC and Timely titles where the books are more actively traded and prices can be more readily ascertained. I would avoid books from non-mainstream publishers like Fantastic Comics 3, for example, because values are not easily identified other than by a dealers representation...or misrepresentation. To sum up, stay with the books where values are more easily determined and avoid books that are thinly traded.

Silver Age: The theme hasn't changed in over a decade. Marvels have led the market, continue to lead the market and, unlike prior years, have accelerated in growth. Silver Age Marvels are the backbone of the market. This year has seen continued growth in CGC prices as well as a real strengthening in the price of raw, early Marvels. Investors should focus on buying high grade CGC marvels, particularly *Amazing*

Spider-Man and *Fantastic Four*, but almost all the major titles will fit the bill.

Apparent this year is just how difficult it is to find Silver Age DCs in 9.4. Many of the major runs have issues that lack any 9.4s. DCs from major runs, particularly *Showcase, Batman* and *Superman* prior to 1966 are also worthwhile investments. Unlike the early Marvels however, these books need to be certified to qualify as investment grade in most cases.

Bronze Age: Marvels and DCs from the major titles are also good investment vehicles as long as they are certified. However, anyone paying multiples of *Guide* – I don't care what it is – for anything published after 1980 will likely lose money on his or her books. As a rule of thumb, the higher the multiple, the more substantial you can expect your loss to be. Further, factoring the time value of money into the equation, the longer you keep these books, the greater your losses will be. In most cases, losses will be real regardless of when you sell your books.

CGC: Overall I think CGC does a pretty good job. It was not easy to come up with a system that would be widely accepted and that could quantify defects in comics, yet that is pretty much what CGC has done. That they have been an overwhelming success is reflected in the widespread acceptance of CGC by the community, as well as in the high prices CGC books command. I use CGC services extensively, and while I don't completely agree with their grading criteria –who does for that matter – I have come to accept them as an important member in the community.

John Hauser

Golden Age: Sells very well in any grade. Almost any popular title is a sure sale. Original owner collections of Golden Age are a thing of the past. Most of this material was stored at the parents' house. If you were buying comics for your kids in the '40s, there is a good chance you aren't storing their comics any longer. I expect this end of the market to strengthen over time as supplies dwindle.

Silver Age: Extremely strong in grade. Average copies still seem to be going down in value as they are plentiful and easy to get. People selling their collections of '60s comics will have to get used to the idea that the *Guide* is just a guide when you are selling average common material.

Bronze Age: Strong and growing stronger. These seem to sell in almost any grade. People trying to recapture their childhood are now after the comics of the '70s. It is a real surprise to me how nostalgic we are for those '70s comics. *Marvel Team-Up* is now one of my best-selling titles.

Modern Age: There seem to be lots of younger collectors after these comics. It's good to see new people coming into our hobby. Valiant comics are showing a comeback in the marketplace. These are coming out of the quarter boxes and are now worth real dollars.

CGC: Strong sales continue on any comic in grade and graded by a third party grader. This end of the market shows no sign of slowing down. They sell as fast as CGC can grade them.

Conventions: Attendance seemed down this year. More and more people are saving on gas and shopping on eBay. There is still a core group that likes to purchase their comics in person. Do yourself a favor and attend a convention this year. There are a lot of great items available at fair prices. The best part is that you don't have to spend anything on postage, leaving you more money for comics.

Greg Holland (ValiantComics.com)

The market for Valiant Comics has demonstrated some extreme prices in the past year. At one extreme, very high prices were paid for CGC 9.8 *Bloodshot* #0 Platinum Printing Error (no cover price) at $2,067, CGC 9.8 *Chaos Effect* Alpha Red Cover at $1,500, and CGC 9.8 *Harbinger* #1 at $969 in the first online auction for the book in nearly two years. In the other extreme, very low prices were common for nearly every 1993 Valiant book, with most auctions for the books ending under 25¢ per issue. Surprising sales have become a more frequent occurrence in the Valiant market, as some collectors appear to have no limit to the price they will pay for certain issues, while other Valiant books are destined to remain under $1 for decades to come. As usual, print runs are the key to determining demand. Books from 1993 were printed in such large quantities that they may sit unsold for another dozen years, while books from 1991-92 have mostly disappeared from back issue supplies.

Increase in demand for some Valiant books should not be interpreted as an increase in demand for all Valiant books. Over half of the eighty-million Valiant books in print were printed in 1993. As a result, issues from 1993 are nearly impossible to sell for more than a few cents each. Less than 10% of Valiant books in print sell consistently for even cover price. Fewer than 5% of the books are consistent sellers for $5 or more. While Valiant sales have demonstrated a very strong demand for particular issues, it is not enough to simply have the word 'Valiant' printed on the cover. Pre-*Unity* Valiant issues are among the most consistent sellers.

The term "Pre-*Unity*" has become standard for describing the earliest 1991-1992 Valiant books. Here's the list of the Pre-*Unity* issues: *Archer & Armstrong* #0, *Harbinger* #1-#7 (and #0 Pink cover), *Magnus* #0-#14, *Rai* #1-#5, *Shadowman* #1-#3, *Solar* #1-#11, *Vintage Magnus* #1-#4, and *X-O Manowar* #1-#6. These particular issues were printed before Valiant print runs skyrocketed in the early 1990s, though most would be among the top sellers if compared to today's sales figures. All are fantastic finds anywhere near cover price, and they are excellent examples of comics where the characters, art, story, and direction all come together nicely. To understand Valiant, one must know the Pre-*Unity* Valiant stories.

CGC grading popularity for Valiant issues has tripled in the twelve months prior to this writing, mainly because prices for CGC 9.8 copies of Valiant books have been strong, especially compared to other books printed in the 1990s. *Harbinger* #1 and *Solar* #10 have proven tougher to find in CGC 9.8 condition, though any significant increase in the number of CGC-graded copies available on the market would quickly have an effect on the prices being paid. Supplies do not have to be large to satisfy or outweigh the current demand for many of these books. While 2004 may have represented a peak in terms of prices paid for key Valiant issues, there are a number of Valiant collectors eager to buy the minute prices come back down.

Sales are far below cover price on 1993 regular issues, *Turok* #1, *Magnus* #25, and *Deathmate*. Issues that are cold – at or below cover price – include *Armorines, HARDCorps, Geomancer, Ninjak, PSI-Lords, Second Life of Dr. Mirage, Secret Weapons,* and *Timewalker.* Warming up are pre-*Unity* issues (1991-92), incentive variants, Valiant Validated Signature Series books (with certificate from Valiant, embossed seal on each book), and 1996 final issues. Hot issues include *Chaos Effect* Alpha Red cover, *Harbinger* #0 Pink cover, *Harbinger* #1 (with coupon), *Magnus* #0, *Predator vs. Magnus* 64-page TPB, *Solar* #0 Hardcover, *Unity* #0 Red cover, *X-O Manowar* #0 Gold, and *X-O Manowar* #1/2 Gold.

Nadia Mannarino (All Star Auctions)

For all prices realized for 2004 events and earlier, please visit our web site at allstarauc.com/asonline/realized.htm.

2004 was an exceptional year for comic character collectibles of all kinds. With Hollywood adapting comic books and their heroes for movies such as *Spider-Man 2*, there has been a heightened awareness of comic character collectibles in general. We ran thousands of eBay and Internet sales as well as catalogue sales throughout 2004 and we noticed the increased demand for CGC-graded comic books from the Silver and Bronze Ages. We also noticed that in the arena of comic and newspaper strip art, European buyers are certainly impacting prices once again, with their currency enjoying a healthy turn against the dollar. eBay continues to be a major force changing the landscape of our business. eBay is a convention a day – no matter what time or day one searches eBay, there is always something of interest, but with these opportunities, there are some serious consequences. In our opinion, there should be an 'eBay 101' course citing pluses and minuses. Frustrations abound, as do deals. 2005 promises to be another banner year as far as comic character-themed movies are concerned, with many movies scheduled for release.

We held our catalogue auction of 2004 on May 29-30. Results far exceeded expectations, with many lots surpassing pre-sale estimates. Following are some prices realized and highlights from 2004.

Golden Age: CGC-graded Golden Age comics in the 8.0-9.0 range continue their upward climb, with copies graded higher obviously realizing higher prices. It seems selling Golden Age comic books is not the problem but securing these individual books and collections is certainly the issue. Another category within Golden Age comics is the bound volume. These are copies bound by the publisher – File Copies – and in some instances by collectors. These bound volumes are a great resource and the books can be read and enjoyed and still maintain their condition. Dell, Harvey, and Timely bound volumes exist, and we are seeing an increased interest.

Silver Age: In 2004, we featured what is widely considered to be the finest square-bound collection of annuals, the Bill Howard collection. All were CGC-graded and over 80% realized a multiple of their *Guide* value. CGC-graded Silver Age comics in the 9.4 to 9.8 range continue to exceed expectations. The frenzy for high grade Silver Age books seems to have subsided a bit, but for the high grade 9.6-9.8 key Silver Age issues, demand is still strong.

Newspaper Strip Art: This uniquely American art form continues to gain in popularity. Europeans appreciate this art and continue their unabashed enthusiasm. The seminal artists: Raymond, Herriman, McCay, Foster, Frazetta, Caniff, Gould, Sickles, Capp, Schulz, and Kelly remain sought after and prices certainly reflect that. We are also seeing a rising trend in the newer comic strip artists: Jim Davis (*Garfield*), Russell Myers (*Broom Hilda*), Scott Adams (*Dilbert*), etc. While these artists have been toiling and producing their dailies and Sundays for years, we are now seeing more demand for their art.

Original Art: The DC Silver Age comic market has certainly been heating up, with prices steadily climbing as collectors realize how rare this art is and that in comparison to Marvel art – covers, splash pages and interior pages – DC art is under-priced. The mainstay artists are Kirby, Ditko, Steranko, Wood, and Infantino. Prices reflect that they are maintaining popularity. Covers and splash pages, whether DC or Marvel, continue to be items of interest for most collectors.

Animation Art: This market is enjoying resurgence, and with proper guidance and nurturing should once again become a dominant market in the 21st century. With the majority of studios going to computer generated animation, these hand-drawn examples by the masters should once again gain strength.

Toys and Premiums: Another area of comic character collectibles which seems to be enjoying a comeback. This is a great and educational way to link with the past while building a collection.

These are very exciting times to be in our business. Increased awareness along with integrity should be the focus in 2005.

Patrick Marchbanks (Golden Age Comics & Games)

Sales are up in all areas of the market, and as they usually do, Golden and Silver Age books lead the list. It has been amazing to see the prices that have been realized for high grade issues in both of these areas, and the fact that they have continuously risen over the last few years suggests there will be little downward motion to spending on Golden and Silver Age. It has also been refreshing to see many new and younger collectors getting into collecting and trying to put together entire runs of titles. Even the mass produced titles from the early 1990s have been selling much quicker than they ever have in the past. These sales covered all publishers, including Marvel, DC, Valiant, and Image.

CGC: It immensely aids the final selling price of a book if it is CGC encapsulated. With many individuals turning to the online world when searching for the next piece for their collection, CGC-graded books will almost always sell for a premium above a non-slabbed book. I am repeatedly told this is for the most part due to the restoration check that is performed on each book as it goes through the grading process.

For investment pieces I would lean my customers toward high grade Silver Age Marvel first editions, and you can never go wrong with pedigree Golden Age books. I welcome all to check out our website, www.GoldenAgeCollectibles.com, which includes updated market reports, online sales catalog and any interesting comic information that we can dig up that we feel may interest out customer base. We also look forward to your comic want lists and any information that you may have to share with us. Until next year we hope you continue to collect what you love and enjoy every page of every book you acquire.

Jon McClure

Rare and unusual comics are gaining ground fast. A 1977 35-cent variant of *Kid Colt Outlaw* #218 sold on eBay for $720 in VG, which is 180 times *Guide*! *AMZ* #169-173 sell for $500-1000 from VF 8.0 to NM- 9.2 on the rare occasion that one surfaces. *X-Men* #105-107 $115 in 9.2 and *Star Wars* #2-4 $75 in 9.2 range from $300-500 from VF 8.0 to NM- 9.2 when sold. This has been true for two years. All 1977 35-cent variants are much scarcer than their 1976 30-cent cousins and should be listed at least at eight times *Guide* for the least important copies.

DC horror is hot, with stupid money spent on late '60s to early '70s issues in 9.4 or higher. One recent example is *Witching Hour* #3 CGC 9.4 at $900. Golden Age Timelys, especially *Captain America*, come in at *Guide* or slightly higher, with the low grade selling quickly. *AMZ* #155-159 sell at $200-250 in NM- 9.2, which is 8-10 times *Guide*; they aren't common but infinitely harder to acquire than the #169-173 variants.

Going Up: All Marvel variants; *AMZ* #169-173; *Iron Fist* #14 (first Sabretooth), which recently sold for $1600 in VF 8.0.

Going Down: Dell Giants; common, over-printed Modern issues.

Todd McDevitt (New Dimension Comics)

2004/5 seems to be the year of extremes, from record-setting high grade pedigree Silver and Golden Age sales that seemed to prove there is no cap to the NM price of a rare treasure to the $1 bins at cons filled with 'readers' for the low-end collector. The trick is that this leaves a huge gap in the middle for mid-grade books that are tough sells. Take *Hulk* #181, for example. I can sell banged up copies – missing that darn Value Stamp – all the time for $25-40 to kids who just want to have one, or I could sell a sweet copy for $2000 or more. But a mid-range copy that would *Guide* at $300 will collect dust. Where are all the buyers for these types of books? They're not in Pennsylvania, where I have four locations to try and find them.

Modern Age: I have been buying and selling tons of books this year – lots of personal collections, store closeouts, even publisher warehouses. Selling online, I have seen premium prices for complete runs and sense that collectors do not want to mess around looking for missing issues but rather want to get the whole series in one gulp. All the blue chip titles are still sought after, like *X-Men, Spider-Man, JLA*, etc., but odd titles are ramping up as well. It seems that if you are the guy looking for a *Grimjack* #63, you don't have many options, and when you do, you don't mind spending a little extra for it. Classic supply and demand.

What's Hot: Yes, it's nice to say that comics are often hot again. DC has proven that 2+2=6 – that is, the whole is greater than the sum of its parts. Jim Lee Batman is hot. It's a trend we all like to see – top talent on top characters. On the value side, it's only a question of how well will they do that determines a quick rise in price or whether or not we will see them in quarter bins in the near future. Another classic supply and demand situation, but escalated by the heat factor.

Fred McSurley (Warehouse Auction Centers)

Quality material has no problem finding a home these days, and there's no bigger audience than on eBay. CGC remains the standard of the hobby and industry. If you're selling high-end material that is not CGC certified, you're selling your books short. If you're buying high-end material that is not CGC certified, well...be careful.

Sales of Bronze Age comics remain very strong as new record prices are realized on a consistent basis. Just a few short years ago, only a handful of '70s books could crack the hundred dollar mark; these days, it's not uncommon for high grade CGC-certified Bronze Age comics to realize four figures.

Hulk crossover appearances remain popular. *Fantastic Fours* are selling well across the board. Silver, Bronze, Copper, Modern – all *FFs* are in demand. Miller *Daredevils* and *Wolverines* have held up as staples, as have the rock-solid Byrne *X-Men* issues. Phoenix appearances are highly sought after right now. *Tomb Of Dracula* and *Werewolf By Night* sell frighteningly well.

Comics from the Modern Age are also faring well at auction, with new individual record prices being set almost daily. The term Copper Age is catching on. This area saw explosive growth throughout the year 2004, and this growth should continue for quite a while.

Dale Moore (with Damien Moore and Jerry Sims – Comics4Kids)

Hitting the ground running, we wanted to take this opportunity to suggest the 13 Essential Collector Tools of the 21st Century:

1) *The Overstreet Comic Book Price Guide*
2) eBay
3) www.artfact.com
4) Heritage Comics Auctions
5) *The Overstreet Comic Book Grading Guide*, second edition
6) *The Photo-Journal Guide to Comic Books* vols. 1-4
7) "Guide to Classics Illustrated" by Dan Malan in the *Guide*
8) *History of Comics* vols. 1-2 by Jim Steranko
9) *Comic Book Pedigrees: The 50 Greatest Collections Ever Discovered* by Matt Nelson
10) *Comic Effect* by Jim Kingman
11) Comics Guaranty, LLC (CGC)
12) *Comics Buyer's Guide*
13) GPAnalysis

Of course, none of these tools replace an experienced collector sharing insight in person. These tools are sources for information and corroboration of actual facts that allow competent navigation of the field to enhance buying, collecting and selling your prized possessions.

Golden Age: Activity is strong across the board with many titles difficult to stock in any depth. Low grade and even incomplete copies are selling, and the high grade specimens always migrate to the east coast. It is important to note that among the usual want lists, we have seen an increase in interest in the following, with very few turning up for sale: *Tiny Tot Comics* nn (#1)-10, *International Comics* #1-5, *Animal Fables* #1-11, *Dandy Comics* #1-7, *Picture Stories From Science* #1, 2 (1947), *Picture Stories From World History* #1, 2 (1947), *Picture Stories From the Bible* #1-4 (1942/3 only), *Land of Lost Comics* #1-9, and of course *Shock Illustrated* #1-3. Other EC comics move in any grade for popular horror.

Books like ***Pictures Stories from the Bible*** *#1 are increasingly popular on want lists.*

Additionally, some other Golden Age titles of interest, due to the paper reduction act of 1944/5, have made the short list possible. As the entire Timely/Marvel catalogue is intrinsically desirable, we'll focus on DC titles: *Action, Adventure, All American, Detective, Flash, More Fun, Sensation, Star Spangled,* all *Flash, All Star, Batman, Mutt & Jeff, Superman, Wonder Woman,* all funny comics, *Boy Commandos, Comic Cavalcade, Funny Stuff, Green Lantern, Leading, World's Finest.*

Silver Age: These met some price resistance on peripheral issues, but of course keys sell well in any grade. A useful tool to move Silver Age books on eBay is the eBay Store feature. This allows fixing the inaugural price at your wish, then discounting or adjusting price as you need to liquidate. A lot of times, accurately graded and described lots will allow for their price to catch up, or enough people who view it will ask questions or allow formulation of a stronger fair market value.

Additionally, the strongest and clearly far and away most liquid book anywhere is *Amazing Fantasy* #15. Regardless of grade or degree of restoration, these will sell consistently. Many entering the comic book field with an investment agenda see this as a blue chip benchmark and starting point.

A new trend has developed in the collecting field as the heavy metal generation comes into power – June 1966 "Triple Six" cover dated comics. Scooped up in higher grades and slabbed, this might be in contention for the new black in 2005. There are 72 confirmed issues with 29 unconfirmed but possible.

"Triple Six" confirmed: *Action Comics* #338, *Adventure Comics* #345, *Adventures into the Unknown* #164, *Adventures of Bob Hope* #99, *Amazing Spider-Man* #37, *Aquaman* #27, *Atom* #25, *Avengers* #29, *Batman* #181, *Beverly Hillbillies* #13, *Bewitched* #5, *Big Valley* #1, *Blackhawk* #221, *Brave & Bold* #66, *Captain Marvel* #2, *Cave Kids* #13, *Challengers of the Unknown* #50, *Daredevil* #17, *Detective Comics* #352, *Doctor Solar* #16, *Doom Patrol* #104, *Fantastic Four* #51, *Fantasy Masterpieces* #3, *Flash* #162, *Flintstones* #34, *Forbidden Worlds* #135, *G.I. Combat* #118, *Ghostly Tales* #56, *Girls' Romances* #121, *Go-Go* #1, *Green Lantern* #45, *Hawkman* #14, *Heart Throbs* #102, *Herbie* #18, *Hogan's Heroes* #1, *House of Mystery* #159, *House of Secrets* #78, *Jetsons* #21, *Josie* #19, *Judo Master* #87, *Justice League of America* #45, *Kid Colt Outlaw* #128, *Korak* #13, *Marvel Collector's Item Classics* #3, *Marvel Tales* #3, *Metal Men* #20, *Metamorpho* #6, *Mickey Mouse* #108, *Millie the Model* #139, *Munsters* #7, *Mystery in Space* #108, *Our Army at War* #168, *Porky Pig* #6, *Sea Devils* #29, *Sgt. Fury* #31, *Showcase* #62, *Star Spangled War Stories* #127, *Strange Adventures* #189, *Strange Tales* #145, *Sugar & Spike* #65, *Superboy* #130, *Superman* #187, *Superman's Pal Jimmy Olsen* #93, *Tales of Suspense* #78, *Tales To Astonish* #80, *Teen Titans* #3, *Thor* #129, *Thunder Agents* #5, *Two-Gun Kid* #81, *Unknown Worlds* #48, *Walt Disney's Comics & Stories* #309, *Wild Wild West* #1, *World's Finest* #158, *X-Men* #21.

"Triple Six" unconfirmed: *All American Men of War, Captain Atom, Daniel Boone, Donald Duck, Flyman, Huckleberry Hound, Life With Archie, Little Dot's Uncles, Man From U.N.C.L.E., March of Comics, Marge's Little Lulu, Patsy & Hedy, Phantom, Richie Rich Success, Shadows From*

Beyond, Space Adventures, Space Family Robinson, Summer Love, Superman's Girlfriend Lois Lane, Tarzan, Tippy Teen, Tomahawk, Turok, Uncle Scrooge, Voyage to the Bottom of the Sea, Wonder Woman, Zorro.

Within reason, there aren't the low print runs to contend with, and the key ratio is pretty limited. Quite a few people are building their own "Triple Six" collections, and we look forward to seeing the corroboration of information and new discoveries.

Bronze Age: Marvel sells well regardless of grade, and DC buyers are gravitating toward the high grade. The variant machines are still in full throttle with a few 30-cent Marvels slowing but still selling for multiples of *Guide*. Marvel 35-cent books are screaming hot. Our own *Mighty Marvel Western* #45 variant sold to a fellow advisor for $180 in VG; that's 45 times *Guide*! Whitman issues of former Gold Key titles are still insane, and the fan base is wider than for the Marvel variants. We have Doug Sulipa and Andrew Rathburn to thank for their extensive knowledge. DC Whitmans are still slow to catch with collectors at large; give it time. Window box Marvels are coming into play but to a lesser degree in the big picture.

Modern Age: A difficult animal to pen, foremost because of all the cool stories, innovative products and eye candy available. Museum editions as well as RRP books are still overpriced, like the Platinum *Spider-Man* #1 was in 1990. The retailer roundtable books are placing high in the CGC census while the museum editions won't be graded because of that nasty overhang, so authenticity becomes a factor trading there.

Astonishing X-Men, Superman/Batman, Teen Titans, 100 Bullets, Bite Club, Witches, and *Supreme Power* are cool reads with a few reaching benchmarks in the secondary market. Horror titles are doing well – *Night of the Living Dead, King of the Dead, Freddy's Nightmare, Jason Goes to Hell, Jason Vs. Leatherface, Leatherface, Nightmare on Elm Street* – with a range of prices but averaging about $6 an issue. The hardcover and softcover markets are also strong with lots of head and shoulder activity.

We weren't going to mention movies, but the announcement of *Sin City* at San Diego '04 raised the price of the first comic book appearance in *Dark Horse Fifth Anniversary Special* to double *Guide* with $19.99 confirmed sales. *Batman Begins* will spur international interest but it has lukewarm appeal on the domestic front. The same is true of *Superman* and its revolving cast/crew. *Constantine*, once bringing up *Swamp Thing* #37 and *Hellblazer* #1-10, 27, will falter due to producers changing John from the UK to LA. We probably won't even buy this on DVD. *Blade: Trinity* will rock as Wesley Snipes hangs up his fangs as the number one slayer – sorry, Buffy. Look for this film to raise the stakes for *Tomb of Dracula*, especially high grade magazines. Why don' t movie theaters sell comics?

Steve Mortensen (Colossus Comics)

2004 has been quite a ride for comic book collectors interested in the CGC market. The continued acceptance and use of CGC as the industry's standard third-party grading service has brought with it a surge in popularity of graded back issues and graded new comics. We at Colossus Comics are striving to meet the needs of collectors who are interested in buying their new comics already graded and archived in CGC's tamper-evident holder. Our clients are both speculators – those looking to profit from high grade books that quickly rise in value, and completists – those interested in maintaining high grade continuous runs of whichever title(s) they collect. We believe that over the long term, CGCed comics will hold their value and will be the preferred method of collecting high grade new comics. To encourage a love of reading comics and not just collecting, we include ungraded reading copies for all of our ongoing subscribers.

We started our CGC 9.8+ subscription service in November of 2003. For $33/month, which includes shipping, a collector receives a guaranteed CGC 9.8 plus a reading copy of their chosen title. Subscribers also receive first dibs on 9.9/10.0s and they can use their $33 as credit towards trading up. As many of you are aware, it is impossible to offer a 9.9/10.0 subscription due to the fact that some comics never grade that high. The trade-up option allows subscribers to fill in their runs with 9.8s and occasionally trade up for coveted 9.9/10.0s. As one of the top four modern submitters to CGC, we end up with a good portion of the 9.9/10.0s that are graded. We have seen steady growth and look forward to a banner year in 2005 as collectors continue to flock to CGC.

Looking back at 2004, it's interesting to see how the average CGC 9.8 new comic seems to have topped out at about $40/issue and settled into a consistent price of about $25/issue before shipping. I think it's good for all CGC modern buyers and sellers to have passed through most of the initial fad stage and to be settling into the real market, which I expect to remain steady through 2005. Here are some market report highlights from 2004 (as they appeared in *Overstreet's Comic Price Review*):

January: The international market is hot. UK collectors in particular are willing to pay a premium for high grade comics plus extra for the international shipping. Of particular international interest are Valiant titles such as *Solar Man of the Atom*, *X-O Manowar* and *Magnus Robot Fighter*. These have been great sellers in 9.6/9.8 conditions, at times reaching $300 each, and are hard to keep in stock.

March: We sold a CGC 10.0 *JLA/Avengers* #1 on eBay for an amazing $535; at the same time, you could still buy an ungraded copy of the comic at cover price. It was the only CGC 10.0 copy of the *JLA/Avengers* #1 in existence, which naturally added to its value. This sale demonstrates the new market that CGC has created. Before CGC, there was only one price for a hot comic in Mint condition. The lone Gem Mint comic was hidden among the Near Mint comics, and the average Joe Collector couldn't determine the difference. CGC has separated the Near Mint comics from the Gem Mint, essentially creating a new product category for collectors.

April: The market for graded Moderns remains strong. Ordinary issues command a $30-40 price, with many people picking them up to extend their runs in their collections. We are also seeing appreciation among graded Moderns, which is a very good sign for the overall graded market. CGC 9.8 copies of *Superman/Batman* #1 have gone from $40 to $60 over the past few months. I expect prices for graded comics to follow a similar supply/demand model as most collectibles. I think the best bet for buying graded comics that will increase in value is to stick with the tried and true characters and titles that have stood the test of time. When I started collecting 20 years ago, *Uncanny X-Men* was the book to collect. I remember picking up my NM copies of the Byrne issues for $20 each as well as the new issues. In both cases, the comics have done more than hold their own. They have become the cornerstone of my personal collection.

May: Our monthly subscriptions are continuing to grow at a strong pace. Many collectors and now comic book professionals are coming on board to subscribe to their favorite title. Last month we had a letterer in the comic book industry subscribe to the title he's working on because he wants to archive his professional work and thought our service was a perfect way to do it. By continuing to offer reading copies along with the CGC 9.8 copies, subscribers are able to enjoy all the benefits of reading plus all the benefits of collecting and preserving their comics for the future.

10.0s are going for record multiples. We received 110 times *Guide* for a CGC 10.0 *Spider-Man* #1 Silver edition and 77 times *Guide* for a 10.0 *Spider-Man* #1 Green edition. Our CGC 10.0 *Wolverine The End* #1 set a new record for its sale price at $375. We also sold a few *Secret War* #1 CGC 9.9s in the $200 range, with 9.8s selling in the $45 range.

July: As some CGC-graded books are settling into more predictable, or at least a bit less erratic price categories, we can take a look at the best grades to submit to CGC or purchase for a collection or investment. We are seeing the end of books like a CGC 9.4 *Batman* #617, whose value is currently less than the cost of grading that comic. Even a 9.6 CGC grade on a Modern comic has lost its value with the relatively affordable cost of ordering a CGC 9.8 – about $33 with shipping – from pre-order/subscription services like the one we offer.

Our CGC subscription service relies heavily on pre-screening, where we pick out the best of the comics each month from our Diamond order to help ensure that we're only paying for the grading costs of those that grade 9.8 or higher. CGC offers pre-screening for a fee, though a collector has to evaluate whether it's worth the cost. If you send in five copies of the same Modern comic and have CGC pre-screen for 9.8, you might get one 9.8 and pay pre-screening fees for the other four comics that turned out to be 9.6 or worse. For current books, this is likely to be more cost and hassle than if you had just ordered the one 9.8 grade book you wanted from a service like ours. But if you are looking at older comics that are higher in value, CGC's pre-screening cost may be worth the potential payoff.

August: Our subscribers' interests are across the board. Individual pre-order buyers tend to buy what is hot at the moment: *Avengers* #500, *Astonishing X-Men* #1 (various covers), Michael Turner covers. Our ongoing subscribers tend to buy what they like and what they collect, which are not always the books with the most hype surrounding them. The *Ultimate* titles have consistently placed in the top tiers each month since our service first began last November.

September: The modern CGC market is beginning to settle down. The initial novelty has passed and the days of being able to sell almost any CGC Modern comic are gone. While this dampens some initial profits for sellers, what's left is a more serious, long-term marketplace of buyers that will continue buying CGC Moderns in high grades for some time to come.

I'm noticing two types of consistent buyers. The first is someone who only buys key CGC books – i.e. first issues, first appearances, special artists, etc. This buyer is the speculator. He/she is not interested in completing long runs, but rather is buying the *Wanted* #1s, *Secret War* #1s, *Astonishing X-Men* #1 variants, *Wolverine The End* #1s and anything by Michael Turner or Jim Lee. The demand is high for these books and many will make money on their purchases, especially those buying in the 9.9/10.0 category. This is the type of buyer that will pick up single issues through our eBay auctions or from our online store, or who will call me each month to see what new high grade books I have in from CGC.

The second type of buyer is the completist. This is the collector who enjoys maintaining high grade runs of a chosen title, and who is buying monthly CGC 9.8 or higher copies of *Ultimate Spider-Man*, *Uncanny X-Men* and/or *Superman*. This is the individual that is the perfect fit for our CGC 9.8+ monthly subscription service.

2005 Forecast: I think the modern CGC market will settle into a more predictable price pattern, more or less developing "cover prices" for graded books. I see the prices settling into the $25-40 range for most books. Over the long-term, just like some ungraded new comics eventually fall into the quarter bins, some graded comics will likely lose their value and may end up in a new type of $5-$10 bin for CGC comics. The CGC 9.8 grade is not a magic cloak that can turn an undesirable comic into something of value, though this may have been the case in the early 2004 fad stage of CGC 9.8 books. Modern CGC 9.8 buyers are susceptible to the same risk as ungraded modern buyers, but there's the potential for greater appreciation and return on CGC 9.8 comics for those who choose well. I continue to believe that sticking with tried and true titles and characters is the best bet for values that will stand the test of time.

I also think that current CGC-graded comics will see an upsurge after they have passed the 1-2 year mark. After they have been sold out of the shelves and bins in comic stores – when the majority of the books have been handled – they will be hard to find in CGC 9.8. Actually, the common books – the ones without the popular draw – will become harder to find than the popular ones because too few of them were graded when they first came out. It will be more difficult to find books to grade CGC 9.8+ to fill holes and form runs in collections. So buy them while you have the chance.

In all, we expect exciting times for the hobby in 2005 and look forward to many great reads and collectibles.

Josh Nathanson (ComicLink)

ComicLink (www.comiclink.com) is a full service, automated exchange for investment-quality Golden Age, Silver Age, Bronze Age and CGC Graded comic books and original comic book art. It is important to note that this is the market I am specifically commenting on in this report.

2004 has been yet another banner year for the vintage comic book industry. Sellers are realizing record-setting prices on ComicLink.com and buyers are seeing more vintage product available than ever before. ComicLink has many buyers waiting in the wings and willing to pay retail prices for key Golden, Silver and Bronze Age books. I attribute this to the extremely high traffic being generated by the ComicLink web site, increased strength of CGC, and superhero movies establishing themselves in the film industry. Superhero movie franchises such as *Spider-Man* and *X-Men*, and the recent addition of *Daredevil, Hulk* and the *Punisher* to the Marvel movie circuit, have helped further the upswing in prices of this comic book market.

The exciting thing is that this seems to be a self-reinforcing cycle with no end in sight. Though it had taken a hiatus until the first *X-Men* movie a few years back, the enthusiasm that began with Christopher Reeve's hallmark debut in the first *Superman* movie appears to be here to stay. Let me also take this moment to extend a belated thank you to Christopher Reeve for the first *inspirational* superhero movie and for his heroic advocacy for the disabled and stem cell research. You will be missed! Those interested in giving to this worthwhile cause forwarded by Mr. Reeve can find out more and make a donation at www.christopherreeve.org.

©DC

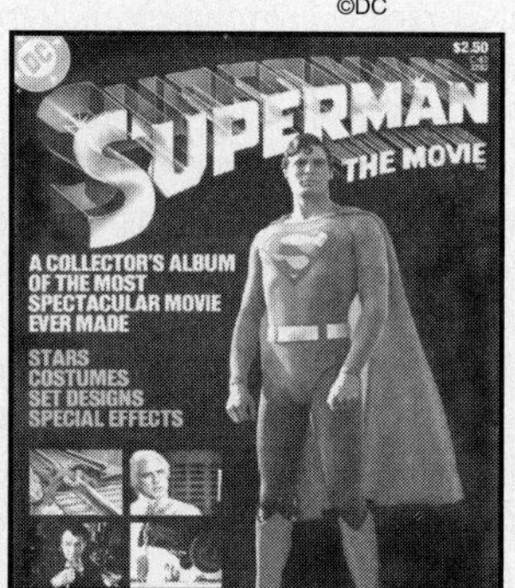

DC
$2.50
SUPERMAN
THE MOVIE
A COLLECTOR'S ALBUM OF THE MOST SPECTACULAR MOVIE EVER MADE
STARS
COSTUMES
SET DESIGNS
SPECIAL EFFECTS

Christopher Reeve's heroism on and off the screen will not be forgotten. ***(All-New Collectors' Edition*** *C-62 shown)*

New collectors continue to enter the market at higher prices and existing collectors are feeling more comfortable about the stability of the vintage comic book market. With such high consumer confidence, it's no surprise that more high dollar books sold on ComicLink.com in 2004 then in any previous year. A number of Silver Age books listed on ComicLink.com exceeded the $100,000 mark – a nice benchmark to set and a figure that previously had been largely unheard of for Silver Age comic books.

Not only has Silver and Bronze Age continued to exhibit strength, but Golden Age has experienced a long awaited revival in 2004. The Silver and Bronze Age market is still hot and will remain so, but buyers are waking up to the fact that Golden Age looks like a bargain in comparison. I have seen more interest in vintage Golden Age within the last year than I have seen in awhile.

ComicLink's new auction section has been well received by bidders and sellers alike. During the summer, the highest graded run of *Batman* issues between #2 and #100 ever offered to the public was auctioned on ComicLink.com. The auction was a resounding success. Seventy of the 87 Batman books in the auction (between #2 and #100) met or exceeded the reserve price. Most if not all are record prices realized at auction for these books in the corresponding conditions. Most of the remaining issues that did not sell at auction sold after the auction for prices that were within 10% of the reserves.

Along with *Batman* #2 through 100, the collection above also contained the finest known *Batman* #1 in existence. *Batman* #1 is one of the most desirable comic books ever published and the fact that one can still exist in this grade from 1940 is remarkable. Not only is the structure of this CGC 9.0 impeccable, but the color is newsstand fresh and the page quality is a pristine off-white to white. This breathtaking copy is currently listed for sale on ComicLink.com.

One other interesting development that has occurred in 2004 is that 1980s books have started to come of age. In the right grades, they are actually worth getting professionally graded. Interestingly enough, a lot of CGC-graded 1980s material has changed hands on ComicLink.com of late, and 9.4s and higher are moving better than expected. I never thought I would say this, but even a few Valiant issues have sold on ComicLink for a few hundred dollars (these came out in the 1990s).

What's ahead for 2005? High grade Silver and Bronze Age Marvel will lead the way in terms of dollar sales and will continue to set record prices. Popular Golden Age DC and Timely titles will continue to increase in price, and will look like bargains next to Silver Age. The highest grade 1980s material will continue to come into its own. Lastly, even more new collector-investors will enter the exciting vintage comic book market.

Terry O'Neill (Terry's Comics)

The best year ever! The end of 2003 and most of 2004 has been the best I have ever seen for comic sales. High grade Bronze and Silver Age comics are the most requested; this is especially true for early Marvel comics. High grade Warren magazines were also in very high demand.

Golden Age: Sales have been constant for Golden Age books. The exception would be odd titles and publishers that most collectors don't know even exist, like esoteric comics. I think a small adjustment downward on these may get collectors interested in them again. Timely comics are still steady sellers but they no longer command the over *Guide* prices they once did in lower grades. World War II covers by Schomburg are still the best sellers from this era. Some of the weakest selling books at most conventions were the lower grade Golden Age above $50. Some of the better selling titles were *Captain America, Spy Smasher*, early *Detective* and *Action Comics*, which I was able to sell above *Guide*. We picked up some Centaur titles like *Funny Pages, Funny Picture Stories* and *Amazing Man*. It's been a while since I had these titles, and I really enjoyed their fantastic artwork and content. I find it amazing that such a quality company could not survive through the Golden Age. I believe that overall Golden Age sales have not greatly increased because fewer collectors are entering this market. I hope this trend will reverse based on price corrections and building dealers' inventories with quality selections. With so much great artwork, stories and characters, it's no wonder these books are called Golden Age comics.

Atom Age: This group is my best seller in terms of material acquired to volume sold. Humor titles are doing quite well, with titles like *Dennis the Menace, Popeye* and *Felix the Cat* leading the way. Also *MAD* comic knock-offs like *Bughouse* are in high demand. Pre-Code horror has been cool, but classic covers still go fast if priced right. I think that the more common pre-Code horror books should have slight downward price corrections. An exception to this would be Atlas pre-Code horror in Fine or better condition; these books are very scarce and in high demand. ECs are doing quite well and are getting hard to acquire. Crime titles have remained steady, with the better titles like *Perfect Crime*, with good cover and graphic violence, selling best. Western comics have been doing well for the past few years; most of the Atlas western titles have been in greater demand and Dell westerns always seem to move at a steady pace. Some great westerns are the Avon titles with Kinstler covers, and Magazine Enterprise titles with Frazetta and Ayers covers. War comics are all constant sellers with a slight increase in DC titles like *Our Army at War* and *G.I. Combat*. All Atlas war titles like *Combat Casey*, with artwork by R.Q. Sale, sell very quickly at slightly above *Guide*. Science-fiction titles continue to sell well, with the highest demand for books with artists like Kirby, Ditko and Wood. Romance and teen comics are steady sellers with the most movement in the under $20 range. Many funny animal comics have slowed even when discounted; exceptions are Harvey titles in higher grade. Atom Age books are great bargains considering they are mostly more than 50 years old. If you don't already collect this era, then I recommend you check them out. I am sure that there are a few titles you will enjoy.

Silver Age: I believe that comic fandom as we know it today owes thanks to the great stories and art from this era. Once again *Amazing Spider-Man* leads the way as the top seller in price and demand. We had some nice early *AMZ*s that we brought to the San Diego Comic Convention and sold almost all of them before the first day was over. There is very high demand for almost every Marvel title from the early sixties; these books sell quickly in almost any grade. Some specific issues that are always in high demand are *Amazing Fantasy* #15, *Fantastic Four* #1, *Incredible Hulk* #1 and *Journey into Mystery* #83. DC Silver Age has increased in demand once again, especially in higher grade. An exception to this are some of the DC Silver Age keys in lower to mid-grade, such as *Brave and Bold* #28-30 and *Justice League* #1, both of which are hard to sell at *Guide*, and *Green Lantern* #1 and the associated *Showcase* issues. *Batman* and *Superman* titles as well as DC war titles are selling very well, and the romance titles sell fast in lower grade. Charlton comics have started to move again, with titles like *Phantom, Judo Master* and *Blue Beetle* selling best. Charlton romance comics also sell well, but they usually *Guide* for only $2-3 each in lower grades. Tower comics have slowed since they have started to be reprinted. Dell and Gold Key TV/movie titles continue to sell at *Guide* or slightly above. Some of the better selling titles are *Bewitched, Peanuts, Three Stooges* and *Twilight Zone*. It also seemed to be a good year for Silver Age humor comics, with good sales of *Herbie* and *Archie*s.

Bronze Age: Each year this era becomes a larger part of the collectibles market. Marvel comics sell best, but DC has been giving it a lot of competition. As usual, *Hulk* #181 is still the best seller, followed by *Spider-Man* #129. *Conan* #1 is making a comeback in popularity while the *X-Men* titles have slightly cooled. All the teams – *Champions, Defenders, Avengers, Fantastic Four* – from this era sell well at *Guide*. The DC mystery titles – *House of Secrets, House of Mystery, Unexpected* – are selling very well in high grade. Other good sellers in any grade are *Batman, Superman, Action* and *Detective*.

Magazines: Warren magazines are still top sellers in all grades, followed by Marvel titles and fanzines like *Foom* and *Amazing World of DC*. Some of the titles that were selling this year were *Love & Rockets, Epic, Howard the Duck, Comics Journal* and *Spirit* magazines. One title that is in very high demand is *Blazing Combat* by Warren. There are only four issues but the #1 issue is difficult to find in high grade.

Modern Age & Independents: Not a lot of change in this era. The supply of high grade books is still greater than the demand. *X-Men*, *Spider-Man* titles, *Hulk* and *Wolverine* are all steady sellers. There was a small bump in the *Punisher* and Dark Horse titles of *Aliens* and *Predator*; this was probably due to the movies associated with them. *Teenage Mutant Ninja Turtles* are still being sought after, with a first print of #1 always going over *Guide*.

CGC: This service is a boon to our industry. It also provides a way to have quality material protected and confirmed for condition and restoration check. They have been more consistent in the last few years with grading and their turnaround time has greatly improved. I highly recommend this service for expensive high grade material protection. I have seen the product from one of the new competitors and was not overly impressed. CGC will continue to be the leader unless a competitor can achieve collector confidence.

Internet Sales: I was happy with my website traffic and sales this past year. eBay is still a way to move material that you do not mind risking a loss on; occasionally you may even do better than at a convention. I usually keep my auctions to a minimum and only do them when there are no conventions or when I need to raise money for an extremely large collection.

In summary, comic book sales this year have been better than last year. Comic fan attendance at most conventions appears to have been up, and my last catalog was again my most successful. In short, the comic market seems to be healthy, and in many areas, expanding.

John E. Petty and Lon Allen (Heritage Comics Auctions)

Despite wars, rumors of wars, the uncertainty of an election year and a rollercoaster-like economy, 2004 has shaped up to be a strong year, at least as far as comics and collectibles are concerned.

It should come as no surprise to anyone that the growth of this hobby and the rise to prominence of CGC has happened concurrently. CGC continues to bring more and more people into the hobby, as it provides higher and higher levels of consumer confidence. We've certainly seen the spike in prices realized caused by third party grading, especially on formerly uncollectible titles. We've had a great deal of success with high grade Harvey File copies, for example. Who would ever have thought that a nice copy of *Richie Rich* or *Hot Stuff* could bring 10-12 times *Guide*? When they're CGC graded 9.6 and 9.8, they do!

However, it must also be said that the "CGC Feeding Frenzy" only applies to very high grade copies or to truly scarce books. Bronze Age titles, for example, CGC graded less than 9.4 just don't sell, as collectors are unwilling to pay a slabbing premium for books in lower grade. The threshold for Golden Age titles or for key books tends to be a bit lower, but it's still a strategy decision when it comes to what to grade and what to offer raw.

The CGC Registry is starting to make its presence known, with collectors competing for the highest graded copies of books so they can increase their registry scores. Look for this to become a much bigger part of our hobby over the next few years as CGC adds more sets to the registry and collectors become familiar with the service. As we have seen in the coin market, there can be a feeding frenzy for a relatively common book in extremely high grade that someone needs to complete their run. Even a fairly common run of late 1960s comics can be very difficult to complete in a specific grade. It can take a lot of searching, so when one comes up for sale, you'd better grab it now or you may not have a chance later.

Another area that's been surprising this year is the increased interest in high grade Silver Age DCs. Perhaps driven by the amazing scarcity of such Schwartz-era titles as *Superman, Batman, The Flash, Justice League of America,* etc., when these books do show up in 9.0 or above, they consistently bring record prices. A great example is the *Flash* #123 in CGC NM 9.4 with white pages that we sold in June 2004 for an amazing $23,000 – a whopping 11.5 times *Guide*! Likewise the copy of *Brave and the Bold* #28 we sold in April 2004 in CGC NM 9.4 with off-white pages for a record $60,375, or 8.1 time *Guide*! Clearly, these books are at the top of many collectors' want lists. The Pacific Coast pedigree copies, probably the nicest examples of these books on today's market, are particularly desirable.

Speaking of pedigrees, with a few notable exceptions, they don't seem to mean as much as they did in years past. Certainly, names like Mile High, Allentown, San Francisco and Larson still carry quite a bit of weight, but the second and third tier pedigrees seem to be leveling off in terms of desirability. Perhaps there are too many pedigrees for collectors to keep track of, or perhaps condition has become such a major issue that pedigree has become less important. Whatever the cause, we're seeing less of a spike in price due solely to provenance. Collectors are generally looking directly at the CGC number, and possibly the page quality, much more than any pedigree designation. Now may be an extremely good time to add some of these pedigrees to your collection as we have seen many Bethlehems, White Mountains and Bostons selling at *Guide* or a slight premium above *Guide*. After all of these books have been absorbed into the market, they could again be perceived as rare and a good long-term investment.

What this means more and more is that high grade, collectible books are harder and harder to come by as they find homes in permanent collections. Collectors of high grade books know what they want and they're willing to pay for it. The competition for the really nice books is becoming fierce, especially for key issues. Even as the census numbers continue to steadily increase for popular books like Silver Age Marvels, the demand continues to outweigh any supply. There has been no drop-off of interest in Spider-Man at all; we continue to sell mid-grade copies of *Amazing Spider-Man* #1 and *Amazing Fantasy* #15 for above *Guide* on an almost weekly basis.

All mainstream keys continue to perform very well in our auctions. We continue to receive literally dozens of requests for all Marvel keys, especially *Journey Into Mystery* #83, *Tales of Suspense* #39 and *X-Men* #1. The Silver Age DC keys are even rarer in grade, including, but not limited to *Action* #242 (first Brainiac), *Action* #252 (first Supergirl), *Adventure* #210 (first Krypto), *Adventure* #247 (first Legion), *Brave & the Bold* #28 (first JLA), *Detective* #225 (first Martian Manhunter), etc. If you have these books in VF or better condition, you can practically name your own price. At auction, it is difficult to estimate what these might go for. Three times *Guide*? Four? Five? We have had high grade DC keys sell for as much as 12 times *Guide* in 9.4!

Magazines have become more popular, especially now that CGC has started to certify them. Again, these are books that were considered junk not too long ago. Now collectors are starting to take magazines seriously, as we start to find out just how few of these oversized collectibles exist in grade. Early *MAD*s and *MAD Specials* (particularly the Gaines File Copies), most monster titles, and the Marvel titles from the 1970s lead the pack in bringing over-*Guide* prices, but this is still a very young field and definitely bears close watching. Again, condition here is the key element. When people think of Warren magazines, they should always realize that there were *tons* of warehouse copies of these books, but they have still proven to be very difficult to find in truly high grade. Most of these warehouse copies have been moved from location to location, shipped across the country, and ended up on dealer's tables in stacks. Because of this, 99% of them have acquired enough small bumps and rubs to keep them out of the 9.0 or better range. A 9.4 or better Warren magazine is a rare bird indeed, and we have been seeing the crazy multiples of *Guide* that other 1970s books were getting 3-4 years ago.

Overall, superhero books still rule the roost, although we're seeing strong interest in pre-hero Marvel titles like *Tales of Suspense* and *Strange Tales*. Unfortunately, other pre-Code horror titles continue to languish as do westerns for the most part. One area that is surprisingly hot right now (at least to some) are the mainstream Disney books. The market is very solid for *Walt Disney's Comics and Stories, Donald Duck* (*Four Color*), and other early *Four Colors*. To find these books in Fine or better condition is very rare. All pre-1945 *Comics and Stories* sell for *Guide* or above even in VG, and VF or better copies bring several multiples of *Guide*.

Early *Archie Comics* are as tough as ever. It would be a major accomplishment to put together a run of the first 50 issues, not even taking condition into consideration. Even the early cover appearance of Archie in *Pep Comics* rarely turns up for sale, and is snapped up quickly, or bid up to multiples of *Guide* when it's offered at auction.

Original art is as strong a category as ever. Major pieces continue to come out of the woodwork as record prices are set, with new treasures surfacing almost daily. Silver Age art is king here, eclipsing Golden Age art in popularity by a wide margin. Bronze Age art continues a steady climb as new collectors, driven by feelings of nostalgia, enter the hobby. We're starting to see Kirby originals, torpedoed by the sudden market glut after the sale of the Christopher collection several years ago, starting to rebound. As much of Christopher's material, which included great Kirby art from many early Marvel titles, finds good homes in permanent collections, the real prime material is becoming harder and harder to obtain once again. Other artists to watch include Steve Ditko, John Romita, Sr., Travis Charest, and John Buscema.

We're happy to report that interest in comic strip art, which seemed to have hit an all-time low several years ago, is definitely experiencing an upswing. Our sale of the Seashore Collection of newspaper strip art early in 2004 was an unqualified success, with many pieces in the collection setting record prices. Herriman, McCay, Raymond and Schulz are at the top of collectors' lists in terms of desirability, but even the more obscure artists and titles are realizing strong prices these days. It's ironic that at the same time comic strips are struggling to stay alive in the pages of our nation's newspapers, interest in collecting originals is on the rise.

An interesting aspect of original art collecting, and one to watch over the next few years, is the advent of original art restoration. This is becoming more and more prevalent in this hobby, and it will be interesting to see how it affects prices down the road. Will it follow the model of comics and negatively impact prices, or will collectors realize that original art is one-of-a-kind and accept restoration as conservation as many other hobbies have? Only time will tell.

Going Up: Early Harvey comics, especially in VF and above are almost impossible to find, and typically bring a premium when offered. Bronze Age keys, especially in high grade, seem for the most part to be undervalued right now. Carl Barks books are hot, as are John Stanley Little Lulus, Dell Giants, and 1960s cartoon and TV-related comics.

Going Down: For us, westerns are always a hard sell, as is virtually anything from 1980 and later. Non-Timely Golden Age titles typically sell at 20-60% of *Guide* routinely and have for years. Even 9.4 pedigreed books sell at only 80-125% of *Guide*.

Jim Halperin, Ed Jaster and Ben Samuels also contributed to this article.

Jim Pitts (Surf City Comix)

Comics ran very strong through the convention season ending last fall, but sales were soft through both last Christmas and winter, not really picking up until about March. This can most likely be attributed to the continuing war overseas and rising unemployment at the time. After March though, comics came back like gangbusters, making the 2004 conventions season exciting and busy. This is a continuing trend that we see running into 2005.

Adventure Comics *#210, the first appearance of TV's newest canine cartoon star, is heating up.*

Nobody can deny that Marvel Silver Age is one of the most collected areas in comics right now. During the last year, there continued to be very strong interest in *Amazing Spider-Man*. From the Ditko part of the run, issues are sellable in almost any grade, with high grade being the most desirable. As the release date of *Spidey 2* loomed closer, we were able to sell copies of *Amazing Spider-Man* #1 in G- ($800), G+ ($1100), and VG ($1750). A Fine copy of *AMZ* #3 went for $700, and a Fine copy of *AMZ* #4 sold for $650.

Issues of *Incredible Hulk* have been on fire. *Hulk* #2 in Good- sold for $250, *Hulk* #3 in Good+ sold for $200, and a couple copies of *Hulk* #6 in Good sold for $200 each. We also got $300 for a Very Fine copy of *Journey into Mystery* #89 (origin Thor).

Following Marvel Silver is the widely popular DC Silver Age titles. Chief amongst these are the first appearance titles – *Showcase, Brave and the Bold*, etc. People are also showing strong interest once again in *Adventure Comics, The Spectre, Hawkman, The Atom*, and others. Some sales of note in this category include *Adventure Comics* #210 (1st Krypto) in Fine for $1000, #214 (2nd Krypto) in Very Good for $125, #247 (1st Legion) in Good for $400, and #300 (Legion series begins) in Very Fine for $300. *Brave and the*

Bold #30 (JLA) in Fine sold for $500, #34 (1st Hawkman) in Fine fetched $600, and #52 (early Sgt. Rock) in Very Fine sold for $150.

Fawcett Golden Age remains popular. Copies in any condition are quick sellers. The most popular titles appear to be *Captain Midnight, Captain Marvel Adventures, Whiz Comics, Master Comics, Mary Marvel, Hoppy the Marvel Bunny*, and *Ibis*, just to name a few. Sales from here include *Captain Marvel Adventures* #9 Good + $180; #10 Very Good $250; #16 Very Good $250; #150 Very Fine $300; *Ibis* #1 Very Good $425; #3 Fine $225; *Marvel Family* #9 Fine $225; #14 Very Good $100.

ECs, as always, remain at the top of most collectors lists. Everybody seems to be collecting the main horror, war and sci-fi titles. The first 23 issues of *MAD* have been especially asked for lately, selling in almost any condition. Sales in this area include *Tales from the Crypt* #45 (last issue) Very Good $100; *MAD* #4 Fair $80; #5 Fine $500; #7 Very Good $150.

Other Golden Age sales of note include *Superman* #2 Fair $900; *World's Finest* #8 Good+ $250; *Wonder Woman* #34 (robot cover) Very Good $150; *All Flash* #8 Good+ (slight A) $200; *Christmas in Disneyland* #1 (Dell Giant) Very Fine $160; *Four Color* #178 (1st Uncle Scrooge) Fine $325; *Jackie Robinson* NN Very Fine $700; *Larry Doby* (Baseball Hero) G+ $110.

*MAD*s are my strongest sellers in the magazine department. *More Trash from MAD* #3 in FN/VF was a quick sell at $130. Undergrounds are a fast growing segment on the collecting horizon as more and more people discover the genius of Robert Crumb, Spain Rodriguez, Joel Beck, Rick Griffin, S. Clay Wilson, Gilbert Shelton, and others. In my dual role of both retailer and underground comix advisor to Heritage Auctions, it's exciting to see this segment of the market start to get the attention it so richly deserves. My sales in this area included *Zap Comix* #1 (Plymell) VG- $1000; #1 (Donahue) NM- $350; #1 (Donahue) NM $300; #1 (3rd) NM $100; *Zap* #3 (1st) NM $120; *Freak Brothers* #1 (1st) VF $90; *Tales From The Tube* (1st) NM $225; *Dr. Atomic* #4 (1st) NM $75; *Air Pirates* #1 NM $125, #2 NM $125; *Cherry Poptart* #1 (1st) NM $150.

There is no reason not to believe that if the economy continues to grow, and hopefully the war overseas concludes, that we will continue to see very steady growth in almost all areas of the hobby.

Ron Pussell (Redbeard's Book Den)

Led by a large increase in the Silver Age, prices continued to climb during the past year in the comic book marketplace. However, price increases varied within the marketplace. Golden Age prices were of a slower, more stable nature, whereas the Silver Age continued its torrid pace of increases.

Golden Age

1930s Titles: Slower sales as current prices continue to meet some resistance in the marketplace. DC titles remain the most requested. Renewed interest in early Dell titles continues.

1938-1945: Superhero titles are still leading the way. Timely is now the hottest seller. We remain very bullish in this area as Silver Age prices continue to skyrocket.

DC: Record prices for almost all books in 9.2 or higher. Sales on lower grade issues for most titles are still meeting resistance at current price levels. Key cover issues are still commanding above *Guide* prices in all grades. *Action, Superman, Wonder Woman, Detective, Flash* and Doctor Fate/Spectre *More Fun* cover issues sold well at above *Guide* prices in all grades. *Batman* and *All Star* in lesser grade have met some resistance due to current price levels. Slower sales for earlier issues of *Leading, Comic Cavalcade* and *Star Spangled*. Most other major superhero titles sold very well at or above current *Guide* levels. Offbeat titles sales were slower than superhero titles.

Timely: *Captain America, Marvel Mystery, Sub-Mariner* and *Human Torch* sold very quickly at prices well over *Guide* with record prices for 9.0 or higher. This is currently the hottest area in Golden Age comic books. Other superhero titles had good sales above current *Guide* levels. Slower sales for offbeat titles.

Fawcett: Good sales throughout. Best selling title is still *Captain Marvel* and his related titles. Good sales for *Wow, Master* and *Captain Marvel Jr.* Key covers brought higher prices on all titles. The Crowley collection has provided collectors with an opportunity to purchase many titles or issues that were previously unavailable. Many record prices for books from this collection.

Centaur: Sales are still slower for this publisher. Record prices continued for 9.4 or higher books. Key covers are still in demand at higher prices. Slower sales for their non-superhero titles.

Fox: Good sales at current *Guide* levels for most superhero titles. Lou Fine issues still the most demanded with 9.4 copies or higher bringing record prices. Offbeat titles sales slower.

Gleason: Slower sales overall continue for this publisher. Good sales on *Silver Streak* and earlier issues of *Daredevil*, but slower sales on earlier issues of *Boy*. Offbeat title sales slowed.

Fiction House: *Planet* sales remain strong at above *Guide* levels. Slight pickup in sales overall for the main titles the past year. Good girl art still helping this publisher's sales. Slow sales on offbeat titles.

Quality: Lou Fine titles are still the most popular. Slight pickup in sales for this publisher.

MLJ: Sales are still slower for this publisher. Record prices for 9.4 or better copies. Key covers are still in strong demand.

Nedor: Good sales as Schomburg covers remain very popular, including his work on offbeat titles.

Classic Comics: Slower sales continue for this publisher.

Funny Animal: Most requested publisher is still Dell with good sales at or above current *Guide* levels. Record prices for 9.2 or higher early Dells. Record prices for early high grade *Comics & Stories*. Timely and DC are also popular. Overall slow sales continue for this genre.

Misc. Publishers: Keys and first issues of superhero titles are still the most requested. Key covers are very important in determining demand. Slow sales overall continue for most publishers.

1946-1956: Mixed sales continue throughout. Demand varied as to titles or particular issues versus across the board as in previous years. Still, sales remained somewhat better than misc. Golden Age books.

Dell/Gold Key: Still looking for those high grade Duck one-shot file copies from yesteryear. 9.2 or better Duck one-shots bring record prices at auction. Barks remains very popular. Good sales continue in low grade. Still slow sales in mid-grade above Fine. 9.2 or higher copies continue to bring record prices.

Atlas: Mixed sales continue for this publisher. Record prices for 9.2 or higher copies. Key covers are very important. Good sales for crime, romance, war, western and horror/SF titles. Lesser demand for offbeat titles.

DC: This publisher has also had mixed sales. Most popular areas are still war and western titles followed by horror/SF titles.

TV/Movie: Lesser condition sales are still very good at current *Guide* levels. Medium grade titles remain slower. Photo covers are the most popular.

EC: Horror and SF titles are very good. Gaines File Copies continue to bring record prices, but not at the hefty multiples of *Guide* as in previous years. Good sales for *MAD* comic books. Very good sales for *Shock SS, Crime SS, Frontline* and *Two-Fisted. Picto-Fiction* magazine titles sell very well in all grades well above current *Guide* levels. Slower sales for *MAD* magazines.

Westerns: Good sales led by the photo cover issues. Key covers and issues very important in determining demand. Large pickup in demand for this area may force higher prices in the future.

Dell Giants: In lower grade, sales are good. Record prices for 9.4 or higher copies. Mid-grade sales in Fine and above remain slow.

Romance: Good sales continue across the board for most titles in this genre. Key covers bring record prices. 9.2 or higher copies are selling for record prices.

Humor/Funny Animal/Teenage/Strip Reprints: Slow sales at current *Guide* levels.

'Good Girl' Art: Solid demand continues for this genre in all grades. *Phantom Lady* is still very popular. Overall, Fox 'Good Girl' art titles had strong sales over current *Guide*. Key covers sell very well over current *Guide* levels. Record prices for *Phantom Lady* #17 and *Blue Beetle* #54.

Avon: Horror, science fiction, romance and crime titles continue to sell well. Good sales for western and war titles for this publisher. Offbeat titles sales slower.

Horror/SF: Good sales continue for this genre. Record prices for books in 9.2 or higher. Very strong sales for *Weird Mysteries, Weird Chills, Weird Tales of the Future, Weird Terror, Weird Horrors*, all Superior titles, *Mysterious Adventure, Thing, Horrific, Dark Mysteries, Beware, Voodoo, Mister Mystery* and *Chilling Tales*. Key covers range from strong demand to hot. Interior content also important in determining a titles demand.

Sports: Slower sales continue. Fawcett one-shots still sell well over current *Guide* levels.

Art Titles: Record prices for 9.2 or higher copies. Strong demand continues for Baker, with good sales over current *Guide* led by *Phantom Lady*. Good demand for LB Cole books, led by *Blue Bolt*. Strong sales for all Wolverton horror/science fiction titles, led by *Weird Tales of the Future* #2-3. Ditko and Kirby books still sell very well above current *Guide*. Frazetta is still very popular and continues to sell very well. Kubert, Krigstein, Toth and Williamson are still requested at a slower rate then those previously mentioned. Katz and Torres demand small in comparison to others.

Silver Age: How about those Silver Age DCs in 9.0 or higher? Staggering record prices at every auction. To say that this area is hot is still an understatement. Sales throughout the Silver Age has lead the comic book marketplace for two years. Top Marvel titles sell extremely well. Record prices for high grade copies. Good sales in all grades. Early *Spidey, FF, X-Men* and *Hulk* continue with very strong sales.

Bronze Age: Record prices are still being realized for very high-grade copies of mid-'70s books. Sales of better condition books from this period are strong at both conventions and Internet websites. The most popular are still new *X-Men* titles.

Dave Robie (www.bigscoreproductions.com/toys)

The Big Little Book market is growing. BLB and crossover collectors buying BLBs range from 20-year-olds to those in their later years who had BLBs as children. Many antique dealers complain about not being able to sell BLBs, but I've found them to be highly sought after when collectors have a reliable source with lots of inventory.

Condition: 50% of collectors seek VG and Fine books, 40% seek VF, and 10% are willing to pay a premium for NM and File copies. We're seeing under $50 for average books in VG to Fine condition. From here prices can go as high as $1500 and more.

Sought After Formats: BLBs with the :"Flip-It" feature, 3-color variant softcovers, rarities like the *Big Little Mother Goose* books, *Big Little Paint* books, etc. BLB-related premiums are on the rise but haven't yet reached the demand level of high end BLBs. Big Big Books are in average demand among BLB collectors although they appear to be in greater demand among comic book collectors. Whitman books are clearly in the greatest demand, but a select number of rarer Saalfield books are also highly sought after, like Popeye, Krazy Kat, and Katzenjammer Kids.

Sought After Characters / Categories: A List – Betty Boop, Buck Rogers, Felix, Flash Gordon, Green Hornet, John Carter, OZ, Phantom, Shadow. B List – Charlie Chan, Dick Tracy, Donald Duck, King of the Royal Mounted, Lone Ranger, Mickey Mouse, Nancy, Popeye, Roy Rogers, Smokey Stover.

Israel Rodriguez (Midgard Comic Den)

Sales are even higher this year than last. I have not seen this kind of interest in our industry since the '90s book. More and more investors are recognizing comic books as potential investment opportunities, and with blockbuster movies like *Spider-Man 2*, it's not hard to understand why.

Silver Age: Superheroes are led by Spider-Man with *AMZ* issues below #60, followed by *X-Men* below #15, *Avengers* below #50 with the exceptions of #53, 57, 58, 71 and 87 selling well. *TOS* #39, 46, 49, 52, 53, 57-65 are hot. *Brave & the Bold* #28-30, 34, 54, and 60 are hot in any grade. Silver Age war is led by *Our Army at War* and *G.I. Combat.*

Bronze Age: These are really picking up, with horror and war books leading the way. *Tomb of Dracula, Werewolf By Night, Swamp Thing, Man-Thing, Savage Tales, Adventures into Fear,* and anything with Blade move quickly. Surprisingly, *Doctor Strange* is gaining heat with heavy interest in issues #58-62. *G.I. Combat* leads the war books with the #201-259 "$1 size" stories, especially #201-202 with the Neal Adams covers. The runner-up in this category is *Weird War Tales*, which appeals to both horror and war collectors. Issue #1, 8, 64, 68, and 93 sell above *Guide.*

In superheroes, *AMZ* #101, 102, 120-122, 124, 127, 129, 134-136, 149 and 194 are on fire, with 129, 134, 124 and 101 the hottest. *X-Men* #94 and *GS* #1 are losing a little steam, but #101 is climbing. Superman and Batman are getting a little warm but nothing great. When the new movies come out, all of that will change. Wonder Woman books are getting more popular and easy to move. Of all the books that I can really sell, I would have to say that *Teen Titans* are number one, with the first appearance of Deathstroke the Terminator in *New Teen Titans* #2 selling at three times *Guide.*

Going Up: *Iron Man* #1, 55, *Avengers* #1-10, *Tomb of Dracula* #1, 10, 24, *Savage Tales* #1, *Werewolf By Night* all issues, *Jonny the Homicidal Maniac, Squee, Lenore, Superman/Batman, Teen Titans, Outsiders, Walking Dead,* Valiant comics like *Magnus Robot Fighter, Harbinger,* and *X-O Manowar, What If?*

Going Down: Jim Lee *Batman* #608-619, *Quasar, Guardians of the Galaxy, New Warriors.*

Marnin Rosenberg (ComicCollectors.net)

I've been in this hobby for so long, that I'm not even sure, but I think this is my 37th year of success in the comic book field. I'm grateful to all of you in that I've been able to do something I really enjoy for so long with this kind of success. Still very much the collector as well, I've continued to add some spectacular books to my own collection, some of which will be auctioned on ComicCollectors.net throughout 2005-2006.

It's become more and more difficult to find ultra-high grade investment books as each year flies by and comic book collecting has become big business with more and more collectors coming into the field, but I have been very lucky to continue to find these gems, and it's been a pleasure to bring these books to the hobby and into the hands of the true collectors.

I'm also very proud of the fact that most of my inventory is raw, and continues to go out the door as fast as it ever has. In 2005, it was my pleasure to have marketed two ultra-high grade runs of White Mountain *Strange Adventures* and *Mystery In Space*, most of which sold for record multiples. In addition, when you know how to consistently grade comic books, you get very few returns. In fact, thus far in 2004 – this is being written Sept. 28th – I have actually not had one returned book as yet.

2005 will be the year to remember at ComicCollectors.net. I can't reveal what I'm referring to now, but stay tuned, as I guarantee all of you will hear a great deal from us by the end of this year.

Matt Schiffman

Once again, the market beat and surpassed any expectations placed upon it, even when it was red hot in 2004. It certainly had no problems pushing past a lousy economy, those believing it had peaked, and a real lack of available material in the hottest segments of the market.

Heritage Auctions brought some stellar collections to the market as well as discoveries such as the Lost Valley Collection, the Vancouver Collection, and those found by Terry's Comics, Dave Alexander, and Ronnie Murry. One of the reasons why I believe that our hobby has done so well and persevered over time is the sheer diversity and continued expansion associated with it. Leading the way with a new horizon are the Bronze Age books and their continued growth and ability to pull in comic collectors previously not into this era, as well as new collectors that have hit the 25/30-year collecting factor. The interest in this segment has allowed a spark to be lit in the late '70s and early to mid-'80s books as well. The Silver Age continues to make headlines, news columns and sets records at each sale. Platinum Age comics and Big Little Books have solidified over the past few years and have found a renewed interest both inside the core group and with those new to the genre.

Big Little Books: There was a noticeable leap taken by the superhero tie-in characters, especially the Shadow, Green Hornet and the Phantom. It will be interesting to see how the market continues to shake up now that there is a continuing reference guide for this detailed segment of the hobby.

Golden Age: Just when there were those ready to claim all the great Golden Age books had been discovered, there was a record year for great, high grade books available on the marketplace. Many of them were new to the market and that drove prices to record levels. There still seems to be a softness in the VG-VF range for a good deal of the non-key Golden Age and that doesn't show any signs of really improving over the next year or so. It seems as if more Mile High pedigree issues were available to the overall marketplace than ever before, where previously most of these books would have traded privately.

Atom Age: The interest in this area of the hobby continues to grown and redefine itself with each passing year. High grade Matt Baker and horror continue to lead the way and no real signs of letting up. Out of the entire hobby, the Atom Age spreads are much, much closer than any other segment. With scarcity seemingly prevalent in a vast array of the titles and given issues, prices remain strong in almost all grades. Even many of the oddball and low-run funny animal books show signs of growth after years of disinterest. Westerns and TV/movie comics continue to find a welcome home outside of comics and those *Peanuts* comics set price records each year that they show up at BeagleFest.

Silver Age: Is there anything novel to say about Silver Age? The reports basically read the same, except by adding in a few much higher and higher phrases in front of high grade Marvel and DC. The DC books in high grade did make higher percentage gains last year than their Marvel counterparts, but that isn't saying much when we saw multiple Silver Age keys selling in the high five figures and even a few into six figures. There are a few titles that seem to break that trend and show strength in almost all grades – *Journey into Mystery* #83-120, *Amazing Spider-Man* #1-50, *TOS* #39-60, *X-Men* #1-25, and *FF* #1-50. The DC titles in lower grade continue to slide and have yet to show that stability in any of their titles, and the overall Silver in lower grade non-keys have shown no signs of slowing that disturbing trend.

Naughty books like **Reform School Girl** are bringing nice prices.

Bronze Age: An interesting trend is occurring here and we see it starting in the Silver Age but crossing over to Bronze and magnifying in intensity. Price levels for Marvel and Silver in 9.2 or better sets records on such a constant basis that it seems as if it is just a given that it will continue forever. But, the caveat is that those books in the lowest grades are difficult to sell for even minor fractions of their high grade counterparts. *Tomb of Dracula* #1 reportedly sold in CGC 9.8 for $4,000; an ungraded GD copy passed on eBay for $9.99 in the same three month window. We see this repeating itself across the board with these huge spreads. If history proves out, this will change over the years, but when we start so low, we have a long way to go to get back to historic normal spreads.

Modern Age: Just as everyone said over the years, it's those black and white small press independent books that are leading the market, and by a long, long way. Interestingly enough, the most desirable books have a quality story coupled with their high prices, a trend not seen too often anymore. *Grendel, Cerebus, TMNT, Mage* and *Love and Rockets* set the pace for the Modern Age. The low print run Valiants of the '90s in high grade are lighting up the record books and discussion boards. Getting a handle on these mid- to late '80s B&W independents is a true challenge, as there are so many hidden gems buried in their somewhere. They've been ignored and undocumented for so long that few understand the sheer depth of this area.

Al Stoltz (Basement Comics)

I would have to say that 2004 was a year that was not full of surprises for me; the same old items seemed to sell just like last year. High grade was the most asked-for item at the booth at every single show, and rare esoteric comics, keys and comics that are always on lists were demanded just like last year.

High grade comics just seem to have a limitless demand and the prices that people are willing to pay for the "best known copy" or "highest graded to date" have not peaked just yet. CGC-graded comics are so accepted that buyers pay for the comic based on that large grade number on the left and never really even look at the comic to confirm it themselves. The census is filling in nicely and a picture of what is rare and what is not is so easily illustrated now that picking and choosing those hard-to-get Marvel and DC issues to speculate on is very easy to do.

I still believe that just like in the stock market, insane prices for slabbed material will even out and the boom days of the last few years ma become just the stuff of legend. High grade will always be high grade and in demand, but is some of the stuff I have seen sell from the late '60s or '70s really worth far more than early *Batmans* or *Supermans*?

Raw or unslabbed material sells uncontested at multiples of *Guide* now at shows or online. True high grade material that we have been buying this year easily sells for two to three times *Guide* or more at shows as fast as I can slide it in a Mylar. I have tried to buy as much high grade as I can these days and build an inventory of it for the bigger shows, but it seems to only last a few hours and is depleted. However, as grading is in the eye of whoever seems to own the comic, material listed as high grade at shows or online many times seems to fall well short of what CGC or picky collectors call high grade; it sits at shows with large price tags and no takers.

Rare esoteric comics are also forever on lists of new and old collectors. *Teenage Dope Slaves, Reform School Girl,* and *Black Cat* #50 can be sold endlessly if you had a box of each. We sold three copies of *Teenage Dope Slaves* this year in all grades – a FN- sold for $600 and a G-VG sold for $345. We sold a CGC-graded 4.5 copy of *Reform School Girl* from the "Momma" collection for $2500 at San Diego this summer

– that's over eight times *Guide.* We also sold a GD-GD+ copy of *Black Cat* #50 for $350 with zero resistance from the customer. A set of *Babe* by Boody Rogers was bought out of our inventory at record speed at a show as well. *Spirit* sections also sold steadily throughout the entire year and it seemed I was able to replenish my inventory of them at a few lucky intervals during the year. Giveaway and oddball comics, something I have a fondness for, were also bought at a steady pace if presented to customers and it was explained how rare some of these items actually are. A copy of *Stories of Christmas*, a Walt Kelly giveaway graded 9.2 by CGC, was sold for $700. A serious price correction needs to be made for comics like *Teenage Dope* Slaves and *Reform School Girl* in the *Guide*. Recorded sales of these items on eBay alone offer evidence of their demand and prices that will be paid to own them.

Key issues and first editions are always going to sell and in any grade that you have them in. I honestly feel that Good *Guide* and even VG *Guide* prices are too low on many of the Marvel keys and dealers cannot buy them back at those prices to replace what has sold out of their inventories. Demand is so great for the first appearances of Marvel heroes that it has become a constant struggle to buy and offer them for sale at major conventions. Even the secondary keys like *Iron Fist* #14, *Iron Man* #55, *AMZ* #129, and *Giant Size X-Men* #1 just keep selling out and are always on my buy list. We sold a VG+ copy of *TMNT* #1 for $550 this year and struggled to find another to offer for sale. Marvel early issues such as *AMZ, FF,* and *Avengers* always seem to sell in lower grades when priced correctly out of our show boxes as well. Those who cannot play the big CGC graded game are always happy just to add books to their want lists and fill in with decent-looking G-VG copies.

Comics I see as needing serious price bumps due to rarity in high grade or just heavy demand are the following: *Blazing Combat* #1, *Albedo* #2, *TMNT* #1 first print, *Green Lantern* #76, *Strange Advs.* #205, *Hero For Hire* #1, *Reform School Girl, Teenage Dope Slaves*, *Sugar and Spike* #1, *Pussy Cat Magazine* #1, *Batman* #232, and *Charlton Bullseye Portfolio* just to name a few. *Blazing Combat* #1 has been sold by us when we have them in their typical VG condition for $250 each and we sell every copy we get. *Albedo* #2, the first appearance of Usagi Yojimbo with a print run of 2000, has been selling for well above $600 in any grade if you can find them. *TMNT* #1 first prints have been selling on eBay and at shows for heavy multiples of current *Guide*. *Green Lantern* #76 just seems to never show up in high grade, and even FN-VF copies bring a premium above Guide when found. *Strange Advs.* #205 seems impossible to find in grade due to its dark edges and cover and also sells for heavy multiples if located. *Hero For Hire* #1 is super-tough to find, also due to a dark cover and black edges. I just sold unslabbed copies that were FN-VF for four times *Guide* without a problem. *Pussy Cat Magazine*, a scarce Marvel mag with Bill Ward art, sells in all grades far above listed *Guide* prices and I can never keep one around for more than a month or so. *Charlton Bullseye Portfolio* is an unlisted item in the *Guide*, offered as a mail-in purchase item by Charlton. It had a print run of 500 and has a Steve Ditko Blue Beetle story inside it. I always sell this comic/fanzine at around $50-75 when I can find one. *Batman* #232 is exploding at the moment due to the upcoming movie; I just sold a VF+ copy for $350 at the Baltimore con and sales later for this comic in high grade may run higher.

eBay: This has been a steady source of income and I find it is a great place to weed out those books that just refuse to sell at shows after a few tries. Most of the better inventory seems to sell at 60-70% of sticker on eBay; that is well accepted on some items after never seeming to find interest in them from in person customers. While the cost of doing business on eBay has gone up, along with non-paying bidders, it still turns a decent profit for me and during those long winter months seems to be a great way to make a few extra dollars. Buying on eBay has been steady and some bargains happen now and then. Rare or undervalued books seem to be followed by everyone and they seldom sell at a steal; lots of last second activity runs up selling prices beyond retail at times.

Fanzines: These also seem to constantly sell for me since I try to keep a nice fresh supply of them with me at major shows. Interest in these early comic collecting items seems to be growing and I hope they end up in the *Guide* just like *FOOM* or *Amazing World of DC* or even *Charlton Bullseye*. I personally paid $6000 for a run of *Rocket's Blast Comic Collector* #1-20 this summer. Only four to five known copies were made of the first few issues and how many of them survive today? The desire to own these early publications that helped launch the comic market as it is may finally be gaining the recognition they deserve.

CGC: Graded comics are always a major part of my sales for the year. A few examples of what has sold this year would be: *Detective* #8 7.5 and #9 8.5 Lost Valley copies for $17,600, *Classic Comics* #1 Lost Valley 7.0 $2300, *Flash Comics* #17 Lost Valley 8.5 $1850, *DC Special* #1 9.4 $270, *Star Spangled War Stories* #151 9.8 $2100, *Detective* #400 9.4 $750, *Spooky Spooktown* #1 9.6 $1000, *Wendy* #2 9.6 $750, *Our Army at War* #269 9.6 $200, *Marvel Super-Heroes* #20 9.6 $250.

I think the market in general is far stronger than just a few years ago after 9/11. Collectibles have enjoyed a strong period of investment and it seems a new generation of buyers is coming on board looking for books from their childhood, such as *TMNT* and Valiants. Collections also seem to be on the market more often due to old-time collectors finally selling off. Tools such as eBay make it easier for the amateur to just put up their wares for sale and achieve a respectable sale price. 2005 will begin soon with me trying to hunt down all the same keys and grades that were easy to sell in 2004.

Doug Sulipa (Doug Sulipa's Comic World)

ACG: All the horror/mystery – *Adv. into Unknown, Forbidden Worlds, Unknown Worlds* – titles from all years were way up in demand, with VG to FN+ copies selling fastest at 110-120% *Guide.* Our pre-Code issues in low affordable grades have sold out. Requests have doubled for *Gasp, Herbie,* and *Magic Agent Midnight Mystery*, bringing 120-135% *Guide*; there was resistance to the VF and better copies. We had some FA/G thru VG/FN nice runs of the humor titles *Cookie, Funny Films, Giggle, Ha Ha,* and *Kilroys*, and sold about 90% of our stock at 120-150% *Guide*. The demand was not huge, but the collectors trying to complete their sets jumped at the opportunity to get large groups in one place. The 1960s superhero titles are in moderate steady demand and were the most requested in VF or better. The romance titles sold steadily, especially those priced at under $15 each. This year, as I identified them, the *Herbie* one-page original material – all different? – comic strips and cartoon ads were red hot – *Forbidden Worlds* #125, 126, *Unknown Worlds* #20, 31-39, etc. – at 120-135% *Guide*.

Alternative Comics: Many consider the alternative comics of 1975-1990 the unexplored "Last Frontier" in scarce comics. Small print runs under 10,000 abound, with hidden treasures everywhere. No one is sure what will be the hot titles in 5-10 years, but some are buying up some of the better known and popular titles. With many of the scarcer titles, you cannot be fussy about condition and should just grab them when you see them if they're reasonably priced. Record prices were set throughout the year for *Cerebus* #1 and *TMNT* #1 as investors see them as the best known and safest independents. That's understandable, but it might turn out to be a better buy to grab the many scarce issues that are still available at much smaller multiples of *Guide*. *Albedo Anthropomorphics* #2 – first Usagi Yojimbo – is still hot and very hard to find even in middle grades. An unread set of the very rare *Elflord* #1-15 (Nightwind Productions, Barry Blair, 6/1980-1982) surfaced this year, but is not yet for sale. #1 is easily worth $200 in VF, with others at $50 and up. Barry Blair has a strong fan following and many underestimate the long term potential. Blair also did the popular *Leather & Lace* series. *Blood of Dracula* #4, 16-19 with Wrightson are red hot and hard to keep in stock. Popular titles to consider include *Adventurers* (Aircel), *Albedo* #1-10 (hot), *Alien Encounters, Aliens* (1988 mini), *Alien Worlds*, all Alan Moore titles, *Armour, Army of Darkness* (red hot), *Authority, Berni Wrightson Master of Macabre, Big Apple, Black Kiss,* Blackthorne 3-D Series (especially *G.I. Joe, Star Wars, Transformers*), *Blood of Dracula* (hot), *Blazing Combat* (Apple), *Bone, Boris the Bear* (*Transformers* and many other parodies), *Caliber Presents* #1, *Captain Alcohol* (scarce), *Cerebus* #1-30, *Cody Starbuck*, many 1980s Continuity Comics (Adams etc.), *Cobalt Blue* (1977), *Crow* #1-3, *Critters* #1-5, 41-50 (48-50 are scarce), *Crow* (first series), *Crusaders* #1 (Southern Knights), *Dark Horse Insider, Deadworld, Dick Tracy* #91-99 (Blackthorne), *Dick Tracy Ruben Award* series, *Dirty Pair, Echo of Futurepast, Eddie Campbell's Bacchus, Eightball, Elflord* #1-15 (Nightwind, 1980/82), *Elfquest* (first prints) #1-10 in VFNM or better, *Fantasy Quarterly* #1, *Faust* and all other Tim Vigil titles, *Femforce, Fish Police, Flaming Carrot* #1-16, *Galaxia, Gasm, Gobbledygook* (1984), *Gore Shreik, Green Hornet* V2 #31-40 (Now, low print), *Grendel, Groo, Hate, Hobbit, Hot Stuf* (Sal Q), *How to Draw* series (especially *Transformers* and *G.I. Joe*), H.P. Lovecraft titles, *Imagine* (Star Reach), *John Byrne's Next Men* #21, *Judge Dredd, Justice Machine* #1-3 & Annual #1 (Noble), *Leather & Lace, Love & Rockets* #1-20, *Macross* #1 (1984), Mage #1-7 (1984), *Mangazine* #1-4, *Mechanics, Megalith, Megaton, Mr. A* series (Ditko), *Miracleman* #11-24 (red hot), *Mr. Monster, Mr. X, Ms. Mystic, Nexus* #1-3 (Capital), *Ninja High School* (1986/87), *Nucleus, Oktoberfest, Omaha Cat Dancer, Omen* (Vigil), *ORB*, all Paragon Pub. pre-1982 titles, *Femzine, Phantacea, Planet of the Apes* (Adventure), *Poison Elves, Power Comics* (1970s), *Primer* (Comico), *Pudge the Girl Blimp, Quadrant, Quack* (Star Reach), *Red Fox,* Robert E. Howard titles, *Rock Comics* (Adams-a), *Samuree,* Sherlock Holmes titles, *Skateman, Spicy Tales, Star Reach, Tales of Terror, Tank Girl, Tick, Teenage Mutant Ninja Turtles* (first prints) #1-10, *Thund'da* tales, *Tick, Toyboy, Transit, Twisted Tales, Untamed Love, Uncensored Mouse, Usagi Yojimbo*, Valiant titles, *Vietnam Journal* and other Apple Pub. war titles, *Voltron* (Modern, 1985), *Vortex, Wally Wood's Thunder Agents, Weird Romance, World of Wood, World's Worst Comic Awards, Xenozoic Tales, Yummy Fur, Zen* (1987), *Zero Patrol, Zot,* etc.

Archie: All in all, 2004 was our best year ever for old Archies; we sold 700 pre-1971 issues to one retail customer alone. Many dealers think Archies do not sell, but our 30,000 copy selection is the key to drawing many buyers. All issues of *Archie's Girls Betty & Veronica* remained our best sellers through the entire year, with #1-30 and #300-up remaining very elusive. *Betty & Veronica* #1 is very undervalued and could easily rise 50% in the *Guide*. All identified 1982-1993 appearances of Cheryl Blossom pre-"Love Showdown" remain in big demand and are not very difficult to keep in stock. Everything with Dan DeCarlo sells well, with some completionists even now collecting the original material DeCarlo covers on the 1980s and '90s digests. All 1941-1950 Archies are in big demand, mainly because so few different issues exist, thus causing excess demand. Typically the FA to VG copies sold best, but this year we had many request for VF or better copies that we could not supply. Demand for *Archie* #1, *Jackpot* #4 and *Pep* #22 is huge, among the hottest of all GA, commanding 150%+ *Guide* if you can find them in any grade. Even the 1950s issues where not numerous, thus demand often exceeded supply. The *Laugh* and *Pep* issues in particular were hard to find. The 1950s issues sell extremely well in FA, GD and VG because the current price/condition spreads make the low grade copies far too cheap. Ordinary non-key, non-hot titles from the 1950s in VF or better had resistance, but the hot '50s titles sold very well in FN/VF to VF+.

In 1982-1984, there was an Archie implosion, with titles cancelled and others dropping from monthly to bimonthly and quarterly. Many of these issues are in short supply, especially *Cheryl Blossom* and last issues. This is likely the era when the digests started to sell as well and even better than the regular comics. Since 1990, the standard comics must have mainly been produced as a future source of material for their best-selling digests, as the comics have low print runs and short supply. A complete set of 1990-2004 Archies would probably be more difficult to complete than a 1950-1960 set. *Archie Giant Series* #26 and #32 – for the DeCarlo pinups – plus the circa 1960 Archie titles with the SF/horror covers were red hot at 125-150% *Guide*. *Josie* and *Sabrina* remain in demand, with the last ten issues of each in very low supply. The 1960s MLJ revival superhero appearances in *Laugh* and *Pep* are in very high demand at 150% *Guide* if you can find them at all. The regular 1960s non-teen superhero issues – *Mighty Comics, Fly, Jaguar* – were slower but we had some demand for VF or better copies. The Red Circle and Archie adventure titles on the other hand sold quite well. The horror issues – *Sorcery, Madhouse* – were hot, especially in higher grades. The superhero issues sold well with the later Archie adventure issues in short supply. Many are just now realizing there are issues with art by Steranko, Morrow, Wood, Toth, Kaluta, Wrightson, Chaykin, etc. The Archie Gang as superheroes, while not hot, were good and steady sellers. Some of the later *TMNT* titles are quite scarce.

Best sellers bringing 120-150% *Guide* included all 1980 and newer low print Spire titles, *Archie* #1-30, 61-127, *Archie & Me* #1-10, *Archie at Riverdale* #1-5, 89-113, *Archie Giant Series* #1-35, 136-200, 600-up, *Archie's Girls Betty & Veronica* #1-347, *Archie's Madhouse* #1-30, 95-97, *Archie's Pal Jughead* #1-20, 77-101, *Archie's Pals N Gals* #1-54, 224, *Archie's TV Laughout* #1-23, 91-106, *Betty & Me* #1-16, *Cosmo* #1-6, *Ginger* #1-10, *Josie* #1-20, 45-75, 100-106, *Laugh* #20-144, 381-400, *Life with Archie* #1-66, *Little Archie* #1-60, *Chilling Adv./Red Circle Sorcery* #1-11, *Sabrina* #1-17, 71-77, *Scooby Doo* #1-21, *Sonic* #1-40, *That Wilkin Boy* #1-26, 50-52, *Veronica* #1-20, *Wilbur* #1-10, 71-90.

© AP

Early Archies are best sellers. (**Archie Comics** #5 shown).

Atlas/Marvel: The pre-hero horror/SF issues slowed this year, but we did sell most of our lowest graded reader copies. *Strange Tales* #97 is cheap at double current *Guide* and very hard to locate. The teenager titles were the best-selling this time around: *Cindy, Frankie, Georgie, Hedy, Jeannie, Millie the Model, Miss America, My Friend Irma, Nellie, Patsy, Rusty, Wendy Parker* and all others were in solid demand, especially anything with Dan DeCarlo, paper dolls and pinups. Romance, war and western titles sold steadily. Crime, sports, spy, and funny animal titles were still slower. *Kid Colt, Rawhide Kid, Ringo Kid* and *Two-Gun Kid* were the good sellers. Humor and parody titles were in short supply and sold fast. Most remain quite affordable in lower grades, especially when compared to the more common early 1960s Marvel hero comics.

Atlas/Seaboard: Never hot, but always solid and very affordable sellers. Many buyers want a set of all issues but *Gothic Romances* #1 remains rare with VF copies easily bringing $200+. *Vicki* #3 and #4 are the next scarcest, bringing around 200% *Guide* or more. *Devilina, Movie Monsters, Thrilling Adventure,* and *Weird Tales of the Macabre* sold better than usual, with #1s being more common but not in VF or better. All the Mag #2s are around in less than half the supply of #1s. This was the first year that we got a lot of requests for investment quality VF/NM or better copies of the regular color comic issues. Collectors are realizing they are about to reach 30 years old and are a real bargain in true high grades. There are low quantities of CGC copies in 9.4 or better. Those issues with art by Neal Adams, Chaykin, Ditko, Toth, Wood, and Wrightson are due for large price increases to high grade examples in the next few years.

Big Little Books: I managed to pick up two small collections of pre-1960 BLBs in G-FN average. We had a few requests for pre-1960 issues in VF or better, but could not supply them. The new listing in the *Guide* has raised awareness and we sold about double what we do in a normal year. The most requested was *Smokey Stover*; we sold out swiftly. The well known characters brought 125-150% *Guide* while the less popular character issues sold for 100-120% *Guide*. The 1977 Modern Promotion Pub. BLBs – four Flintstones titles, Huckleberry Hound, Yogi Bear, etc. – had smaller print runs and are scarcer. We sold a bunch in the VG $10 each range. The Whitman 2000 hardcover series books from #2001-2036 were our best sellers, with our minimum prices set at G $6, VG $10, FN $16, VF $24, with better titles at 25-50%. The best selling 2000 hardcover series books were *Aquaman, Batman, Dick Tracy, Fantastic Four, Frankenstein Jr., Lone Ranger, Tarzan, Hanna-Barbera's Shazzan* and *Space Ghost*.

The 1972-1980 softcover BLB 5700 series were decent sellers due to lower prices, with our minimum prices set at G $2, VG $4, FN $6, VF $9, with better titles about 1/3 higher. The best selling 5700s were *Batman, Donald Duck, Fantastic Four, Grimm's Ghost, Pink Panther, Popeye,* and *Spider-Man*. Merrigold Press has several scarce new material issues – *Superman, Hulk*, etc. – which bring 50% more than 5700 series issues. Most of the Merrigold Press are reprint titles, scarcer than the earlier printings, but they simply bring the same as the 5700 series editions. We sold several of the 1958 larger size TV 1600 series books in the G $12, VG $18, FN $26 range.

There are at least 20 titles in the Golden Star Library BLB 1965 hardcover 6000 series of 1966-1970, and they are not yet listed in the *Guide*. Golden Star Library BLBs are scarcer, especially in high grades, selling in the G $8, VG $12, FN $18 range. Better titles include *Fairy Tales by Hans Christian Andersen, Let's Go to the Moon, Peter Pan* (Disney), *Pinocchio* (Disney), *Richard Scarry's Mother Goose, Robinson Crusoe, Sleeping Beauty* and *Cinderella* (Disney),

Snow Queen by Hans Christian Andersen, Springtime Tales (Richard Scarry art), and *Treasure Island.*

The softcover *Illustrated Classics Editions* 4500 series by Moby Books, #4501-4536 (1977/83) sold well in the VF $14, FN $10, VG $7, G $5 range, especially to *Classics Illustrated* collectors. Best sellers included *Wizard of Oz, Sherlock Holmes, Tales of Mystery and Terror* by Poe, *War of the Worlds, Time Machine, Ben-Hur, Journey to the Center of the Earth, Dr. Jekyll and Mr. Hyde* and *Great Expectations.*

British/UK Items: Two of the all-time most important original material UK titles are *Warrior* and *2000 AD. Warrior* (1982/85) includes Bolland, Bolton, Alan Davis, Dillon, Dave Gibbons and Alan Moore script in #1-26, Grant Morrison, Parkhouse scripts, *Marvelman* (later *Miracleman*) by Alan Moore, *Laser Eraser* and *Pressbutton, Madman* by Paul Neary, and more, most in the $10-$20 range. *2000 AD* spawned most of the top UK talent and is probably their most important title, with #2 (1977) introducing *Judge Dredd.* #2 typically sells in the $100-$200 range, but high grade copies with the rare vionic stickers bonus have sold for in excess of $1000 at auction. *2000 AD* also contains Grant, Wagner, Dan Dare, Gibbons, Bolland, *Robo-Hunter, Strontium Dog, Stainless Steel Rat*, Leach, McMahon, Alan Moore, Dillon, Alan Davis, Bryan Talbot, Nemesis, *Rogue Trooper,* Slaine, Fabry, Bisley, Ridgway, and much more. Most issues from #100-1000 sell for $3-$6 each.

We have a bigger selection of UK comics than most British dealers, thus UK collectors are now ordering from us. Marvel UK editions are the most collected, ranging from early 1960s-present, with the bulk of the vintage material being from 1968-1983. They appear in different formats from weekly or monthly comics, magazines, digests, B&W, color, oblong, thick and thin, to the great hardcover annuals. US collectors like the reprints of their favorite characters and their favorite artists like Adams, Miller, Byrne, Kirby, Perez, Smith and others. There are even 1960s unidentified early new material covers by Barry Windsor-Smith. There are also early 1970s unidentified covers and art by Starlin. Hidden treasures include original UK comic stories of Hulk, Spider-Man, Ant-Man, Captain Britain, Nightraven and others. There are Alan Moore stories in *Doctor Who* and other issues. There are lots of new front and back cover and pinup art by UK artists as well as new art and pinups by US artists like Terry Austin. Most of the 1974-1985 issues go for $3-$6. We sold some nice larger runs, sets and near sets to several US buyers who enjoy oddball items and to UK completionists.

The horror issues of Alan Class, Miller and other B&W square bound giant 60-100 page reprints sold better than usual, with Alan Class (1950s-'80s) in the $7-$12 price range and early issues selling for higher. While Miller Pub issues (1960s) sold for $12-$30 as they had less titles/issues, they are scarcer and had more pre-Code reprints. They are a great way to buy cheaper reprints of many issues not reprinted in the US. They are loaded with '50s and '60s US horror and SF titles from Atlas/Marvel, Archie, ACG, DC, Charlton, and others.

The original material UK war comic digests – *Battle Picture Library, Commando, War Picture Library* – are in demand and still rising in value. Most 1970-'80s issues sell for $2-$6, with 1950s-'60s issues for $6-$20. War comics fans try them and find great stories and good art, virtually all never seen in the US. War fans like them as they contain many realistic stories of various wars, battles, campaigns, regiments, etc.

The UK hardcover annuals of the '50s-'90s were typically published in December and meant as Christmas gifts. Most saw little or no US distribution. They are packed with great covers, comics, art, text stories, photos, puzzles and games, much of which is new material not seen in the US. Most sold for $12-$25, with 1950-'60s at $20-$50. This year's best sellers included *Avengers* (TV), *Avengers* (Marvel), *Batman, Battlestar Galactica, Bionic Woman, Charlie's Angels, Cheyenne, Doctor Who, Dukes of Hazzard, Fantastic Four, Flintstones, Funky Phantom, Huckleberry Hound, Incredible Hulk, Laurel and Hardy, Lone Ranger,* Marvel Annuals, *Mighty World of Marvel, Planet of the Apes, Pow, Roy Rogers, Scooby Doo, Six Million Dollar Man, Space 1999, Spider-Man, Star Trek, Star Wars, Superadventure* (DC characters), *Superman & Batman, Tarzan, Thundercats, Transformers, 2000 A.D., Wagon Train, X-Men* and *Yogi Bear.* UK annual beginners should buy the price guide by Paul Green and Laura Taylor. Many of these beautiful annuals sell for less than similar vintage 36-page comics.

Canadian Comics: Golden Age "Canadian Whites" were still hot, but very difficult to restock this year; many less appeared on eBay. Demand is probably about 400% bigger than supply, thus the high current prices levels for low grade copies. Many have settled into permanent collections. The pre-1947 Canadian Whites of Fawcett hero titles with US comics redrawn by Canadian artists sold very well, but the most sought was the original material Canadian story and art titles. FA-VG sold for $35-$100 each, while FN-VF copies were very scarce, bringing $75-$250 each. Humor titles brought less than hero titles. The better #1s, key issues and one-shots brought $300-$1000 each in VG-FN/VF. The Canadian editions that are vintage variants of US comics are bringing 60-100% of their US equivalents depending on page count, rarity and condition. These GA Canadian variants survive in quantities of 1-20 copies each and are generally 10-50 times scarcer than the US editions. Canadian variants included issues from Archie, Atlas, Avon, Classics, DC, Dell, EC, Fawcett, Fiction House, Lev Gleason, Quality, Timely, Toby, and others. The Timely issues tend to bring higher percentages; the EC reprints bring lower percentages as they had the worst printing quality. The exception is *Weird SuspenStories*, with a nice mid-grade set of #1-3 in the $6000 range.

Our Canadian French language comics of Archie, DC and Marvel from the late 1960s-1990,again sold well to completionist collectors who like something different. These had very small print runs for newsstand comics, probably in the 2000-10,000 each range, with small survival rates of perhaps only 10-35% still existing on pre-1980 issues. There was perhaps

10 times the output of Marvel as opposed to DC, thus the Marvel issues always sell best as there are more to choose from. One buyer bought over 200 different reading copy DC issues. Most exist in G-FN, selling in the $3-$7 each range. Pre-1974 and key issues sell a bit higher. The new material French language comic digests from the '50s-'70s with western, war, adventure, jungle, and love themes brought $3-$7+ each.

We sold still more Canadian cover price newsstand edition variants to completionists and variant collectors at 150%+ of US copy prices. *Spider-Man* was most popular, but we also had buyers for *Avengers, Batman, Conan, Daredevil, Incredible Hulk, JLA, Jonah Hex, Vampirella, X-Men*, etc. For the record, known Canadian cover price variants eras include Archie Comics digests (1/1984-12/1997), Charlton (2/1983-8/1984), DC (10/1982-9/1988), Dell (random 1960-1962), Gold Key (5-8/1968 and 4/72-4/73), MAD (some 1964 and 7/1978-7/1979), Marvel (all newsstand comics, magazines and digests 10/1982-8/1986), Warren (3/1977-3/1983), and Whitman (4/1980-1984). The Canadian Archives has some original art for Golden Age Canadian comics, otherwise art is very rare on the market. In mid-2004 from the estate of one of the creators, about 30+ pages appeared that will be sold on the market. This includes some splash pages and covers. As there is no yardstick for prices, it will be interesting to see what these sell for.

Captain Canuck: *Unholy War* was released and sold out fast in most Canadian cities. They had a small print run, under 5000 copies each. February/2004 saw the release of *The New Original Captain Canuck Limited Edition* #1-A and #1-B, each limited to only 30 signed and serially numbered ashcan copies. A and B feature two different endings in the story and feature the return of Thomas Evans, the original Captain Canuck. But our single hottest comic of the entire year was *Captain Canuck* #15 (8/2004), finally printing the legendary complete unpublished issue #15, originally due to be published back in 1981 with art by Freeman and St. Aubin, story by Comely. It will be a limited edition of 150 signed and serially numbered copies, of which we bought and sold 50% of the print run in a two-month period. The original series #1-14 and *Special* #1 (1975-1981) remain rather plentiful, very affordable and among the cheapest of all mid- to Late '70s superhero comics. #1 is among the oldest comics to carry a CGC 10.0 grade, with the owner asking a lofty $5,000. *Captain Canuck* is about to become 30 years old and is now very nostalgic for many Canadian fans. These new limited editions, along with the first printing of the original oversized #4 (2/1977), should make good long-term investments. According to Richard Comely, *Captain Canuck Re-Born* (1993/1994) had these print runs for the English editions; #0 – 100,000 copies, #1 – 60,000, #2 – 30,000, #3 – 8,000, with much smaller print runs in French. Thus #3s are hard to keep in stock at US $10 each. We have stocked up on all of these, plus many related scarcer material such as memorabilia, portfolios, kid's books by Comely, t-shirts, promo items, autographs, the Canuck issue of *Time*, and original artwork items. This was our best year for *Captain Canuck* sales in over two decades. All the cover and story original art to #1-14 and *Special* #1 (1975-1981) was donated to the Canadian Archives. Small quantities of the non-Canuck pages, ad pages, etc. remain on the market, but in general, almost no pre-1982 art is available to the market. Comely has done paintings and sketches, and will do commissions, but these are all of the 1983-2004 era. George Freeman went on to do Marvel, DC, First, Pacific and comics for other publishers, with *Marvel Fanfare* #7 & the *Jack of Hearts* mini as his first non-Comely titles.

Cartoon and Comic Paperbacks: The mass market paperback format ceased to exist for cartoon and comic paperbacks in the early 1990s, now replaced by the higher-priced trade paperback, especially the oblong type as the new format of choice. Most were sold to the general public and not collectors, thus many are scarce in even FN or better. Luckily, most buyers want affordable reading copies. On most characters with over 10 titles, once you get 1/2 the set, the remaining titles – especially the newer/last titles, most with just one printing – often get scarcer to rare. The once fairly common 1966-1985 Marvel and DC paperbacks are now out of stock from most dealers, and given that many were bought by collectors, you would thing they would be easier to find in higher grades. But as they were read, not bagged and handled too often, most are only in the VG-FN range. VF/NM or better Marvel and DC paperbacks will likely become a hot commodity one day, but the most collected titles remain the newspaper strip reprint titles. The ultra-popular long-lasting titles like *Peanuts, Dennis the Menace*, and *MAD* tend to have lower values in the $2-$5 range, scarcer at $7-$15+, as more common. The popular but less common titles like *Beetle Bailey, Broom Hilda, Hagar,* and *Tumbleweeds* are bringing in the $4-$9 range, scarcer at $10-$25+. Older titles tend to have more multiple printings thus more common and lower values. Short-lived newspaper strips and characters with only 1-5 titles can often be quite scarce and can command $10-$25+ prices. We sold a few complete and near-complete runs, saving these buyers months to years of hunting.

Charlton: This was our best year ever for Charlton, with most titles selling quite well in all grades but mostly in G-FN, as not a lot of high grades are normally available. We did manage to locate a few nicer collections of horror/SF issues due to persistent customer demand. I thought we sold a lot of Charlton horror/SF titles comics in 2003, but we more than doubled those sales in 2004. Horror/SF titles were selling in all grades, but the demand for VF or better copies has almost tripled, especially for VF/NM or better copies. We got in a lot of nice copies in the Manitoba collection and found many anxious buyers paying 120-200% or more for 9.0 to 9.4 and higher copies. While the 1950-1965 titles had decent sales, the real demand has been for the issues from 1966-1986. The 1966-1972 issues are hard to find in even in strict FN/VF or better; these issues had huge demand at 130-175% *Guide* in all grades, but especially for strict FN-VF/NM examples: *Ghostly Tales* #55-120, *Ghostly Haunts* #20-40, *Ghost*

Manor #1-19 (1968/71) and #1-40 (1971/84), *Haunted* #1-30, *Many Ghosts of Dr. Graves* #1-50. Also hot at 115-135% *Guide* were all remaining issues of above titles, *Creepy Things, Doomsday+1, Fantastic Giants* #24, *Gorgo, Haunted Love, Konga, Midnight Tales, Monster Hunters, Out of This World, Outer Space, Professor Coffin, Reptisaurus, Scary Tales, Space Adventures, Space War,* and *Strange Suspense Stories.*

The 1984-1986 Charltons all had small print runs, which is the main reason buyers go beyond the 1980 mark. The late Silver and all Bronze issues are fast gaining demand. Especially popular are issues with Ditko, Sutton, Newton, Zeck, and Wayne Howard. Also popular are Aparo, Boyette, Giordano, Sanho Kim, Larson, Lopez, Morisi, Staton, etc. *Haunted* #21-up – the Baron Weirwulf issues – are fast growing in demand. *Haunted* #37 is the "Fiendish Females" issue, a cool oddball item. The all-Ditko specials are top sellers. One of the most under-appreciated artists in comics is Tom Sutton, and he did much of his best work in Bronze Age Charltons. As buyers gather Charltons, more are appreciating Sutton. *Charlton Bullseye*, the color comics series, had unpublished new material scheduled for #11-up that ended up being published in *Scary Tales* #37-up. *Many Ghosts of Dr. Graves* #54 has a early Byrne cover from 12/1975 and is one of his scarcest early issues. Popular and still undervalued titles which brought 120-130% *Guide* included pre-1970 war and western titles, *Abbott & Costello, Beetle Bailey, Bionic Woman, Blondie, Blue Beetle, Bobby Sherman, Bugaloos, Capt. Atom, Charlton Bullseye* (mag), *Cheyenne Kid, David Cassidy, Dudley Do-Right, E-Man, Emergency, Flash Gordon, Go-Go, Great Gazoo, Gunfighters, Hanna-Barbera Parade, Hercules, Hong Kong Phooey, Jetsons, Judo Master, Jungle Jim, Jungle Tales of Tarzan, Kid Montana, Mysterious Suspense, Outlaws of the West, Partridge Family, Phantom, Ponytail, Popeye, Ronald McDonald, Sarge Steel, Scooby Doo, Six Million Dollar Man,* soap opera love/romances, *Space: 1999, Speed Buggy, Static, Thane, Thunderbolt, Underdog, Wheelie & the Chopper Bunch.*

Christian and Religious: These continue to be good sellers. Spire is the most collected series. The toughest issues to keep in stock, at 150-200% *Guide,* include *Barney Bear Out of the Woods, Barney Bear Swamp Gang, Barney Bear Toyland, Hansi, Hello I'm Johnny Cash, In his Steps, Live it Up, Noah's Ark, On the Road with Andre Crouch, Prodigal Son, Tom Landy & Dallas Cowboys, Archie, ...and Big Ethyl, ...and Mr. Weatherbee, Circus, Date Book, Festival, Roller Coaster, Sports Scene,* and *Christmas with Archie*. There was a warehouse find on *God's Heroes in America,* thus they sell near *Guide*; otherwise all other Catechetical Guild titles are scarce and bring 125-150% Guide. We sold over 50% of *Sunday Pix* (David C. Cook) stock, with 1957-63 issues in the $4-12 range. We almost sold out of *Dennis the Menace and the Bible Kids* #1-6 at G $4, VG $6, FN $9, and were unable to find any copies of the scarce #7-9 VF $50 range and rare issue #10 VF $100 range. All the Marvel and DC Christian titles sold steady. The best sellers were *Francis, Limited Collectors Edition* C-36 (Bible), *Mother Theresa* and *Pope Paul.* We sold a lot of Crusaders – over-the-top 'fire and brimstone' comics by Jack Chick – at VF $8 each. These are actually well drawn and well worth collecting. We sold a good amount of the other assorted publisher religious comics, but are finding them more difficult to restock. We bought a few collections and now have a huge inventory of *Treasure Chest* comics, most in G-FN. This title had about 450+ issues, making it one of the biggest-ever series of the Golden to Silver Age. One day, the contents need to be better listed. Our current large selection has made this one of our best-ever years for sales on this title, as many buyers happily filled in their runs.

Classics Illustrated: For most of the last decade G and VG copies were the best sellers, but for two years now, we have had more requests for FN or better copies. Also, we typically sell 10 times the number of reprints as opposed to originals. This year, we had a great increase in demand for originals and actually sold several 100 of them. Also, demand for line-drawn covers and earlier reprint issues is up. In other words, there is a current wave of collectors, rather than just the usual readers, buying these little gems up. I think in part this is because the Golden Age issues are relatively cheap when compared to other desirable comics of the same vintage. The first appearance of new art or first new cover issues are a new type of original and also in big demand, with many harder to collect than originals due to modest prices. *Classics* collectors now want to have the line-drawn and painted cover versions, as both usually have different interior story/art as well. Those with only 1-2 printings of certain cover or art variations are getting to be in shorter supply; this may result in future price increases on those issues. Many buyers now have their cheaper copy painted cover sets and now need the earlier versions. As usual, these scarcer issues had endless demand at 120-135% *Guide*) – #8, 14, 20, 21, 33, 40, 43, 44, 53, 66, 71, 73, 74, 84, 110, 113-118, 129, 161-169. Canadian variant edition *Classics* exist on most issues #1-74; most are quite scarce and contain illustrated text stories on the inside cover not seen in any USA editions. Thus demand is good and we sold most of our selection.

*Classic Junior*s were strong sellers. Most buyers did not care about which printing and instead had preferred condition ranges. We did have a few buyers that did want better originals. About 20 of the 77 issues are common, especially due to the plentiful HRN #576 printings; about another 24 issues are uncommon. There are about 33 issues that had fewer printings and/or no HRN #576 printings, thus these are in very short supply. Some of the toughest *Junior*s include #506, 514, 525-529, 532-534, 537, 540, 542, 543, 547, 553, 555, 556, 558-565, 568, 571-573, 575-577, selling at FA-VG at 200-300% *Guide* and FN-VF at 150-200% *Guide.*

World Around Us and *Classics Special Series* were consistent sellers as per usual. We sold a bunch of miscellaneous *Classics*-related items, including Berkeley/First, UK/British, Moby Books-Big Little Books, Famous Authors, Golden Picture Classics, King Classics, Marvel Classics, Marcel-UK

Classic Digests, Pendulum, Pocket Classics, Power Records, and others. Once sold, many are difficult to restock. **Comic Digests:** Gold Key digests were solid sellers but are getting much harder to restock once gone. Golden, Mystery and Walt Disney Comics digests, along with the Story digest, brought 135-150% *Guide* for G-FN copies with 120-135% *Guide* for FN/VF to VF/NM copies. Normally these digest collections are rarely found in better than FN, but we located some 9.4 range copies and sold them in the 200% *Guide* range. All Harvey digests sold well with all issues scarce in high grades. The 1977-1985 digest brought 115-125% *Guide*. The Harvey digests from the 1986-1993 era had low print runs, especially the highest numbers, which are often found only in lower grades. The low numbers sell at 120-135% *Guide*, the high numbers at 150-200% *Guide*.

Dennis the Menace Pocket Full of Fun #1-50, and *Dennis & His Friends* #38-46 digests are disappearing from the market in all grades, with the early issues especially scarce. VF or better copies are nearly impossible to locate. *Pocket Full of Fun* #1 is from 1969 and would be a bargain at double current *Guide* if you can find it at all in any grade. The 1976 Archie digests are fast disappearing from the market and are difficult to replace. *Archie Comics Digest* #1-20 and *Jughead With Archie* #1-10 bring 150% to 200% *Guide* and are usually only found in FA/G to VG+ grades. Pre-1980 issues in even nice FN or better are getting scarcer, with VF/NM or better copies nearly non-existent. We now have 10,000 Archie digests in stock and sell many mid-grade issues to those who just want to complete their runs. We do get fairly frequent request for assorted #1-10 issues, usually wanting FN or better copies. *Katy Keene*, *Jokebook* and *Madhouse Comics* digests are getting difficult to restock. Be sure to count the pages on *Katy Keene* digests, as they are loaded with pinups that were often cut out of used copies.

Rare comic digests published by Charlton, and also variously by Xerox, Now Age Books, Ottenheimer and Pendulum Pub., but obviously all related and in the same format with 60 to 75 cent original cover prices, are now known to exist. They are *Barney & Betty*, *Bugs Bunny* (1971), *Flintstones*, *Jetsons* (1973), *Pebbles and Bamm-Bamm* (Teenage, Charlton, 1973), *Road Runner* #63-2970 (1971), *Scooby Doo* (1976), *Woody Woodpecker* #63-3020 (1971), and *Yogi Bear*. They are mostly around 100 pages in B&W and contain short one-page gag comics; all appear to be new material. They are scarce to rare with most having eluded *Guide* listing all these years. I have been selling G to FN/VF copies in the $15 to $50 range as I am able to locate them.

All DC digests sold extremely well this year, most in the VG to VF ranges, at 120-135% *Guide*. The set includes *Adventure* #491-503, *Best of DC* #1-71, with #41-71 low print, *DC Special Blue Ribbon* #20-24, *DC Special Series* #18, 19, 23, 24, *Jonah Hex and Other Western Tales* #1-3, and *Tarzan Digest* #1. It is still possible to get higher grade copies in the VF/NM range, but getting more difficult. These should be good long term item if you can locate investment grade copies. They are like small trade paperbacks, most with 100 pages and 6-10 stories each. This is a great way to get Golden and Silver Age classic reprints at affordable prices. Low grade copies of all titles by all publishers sold well, as many buyers just want to read them. Most digests sold to the general public and not to collectors, so strict VF or better pre-1980 issues are scarce, with strict NM copies being rare.

CGC and Condition: Most collectors and dealers still grade by 1980s and early 1990s standards. When CGC came along, this changed. Comics are now graded by the current much stricter standards. Prices in the *Guide* are based on the new standards, thus even 20-40 year veteran collectors are often misinformed about the grades of items they hold in their collections. Many people buy off eBay and assume the low standards are the current standards as bad grading is so widespread on eBay. The best way to get a grasp of the current strict standards is to dabble in a least a few CGC-graded books, examine them closely and compare them to books in your collection. Even well-meaning dealers are often mistaken about the current Overstreet and CGC standards, many getting an unwelcome surprise when they submit their first few items to CGC. Many buyers are paying 9.2 prices for over-graded VFs as they just do not know better. Every time someone asks for NM to NM/MT copies, I have to explain that 9.4-9.8 copies carry huge premiums. After explaining, we have found that many of them actually just wanted nice strictly graded VF books that are much more reasonably priced than actual 9.2 copies. Many have lowered their expectations to the strictly graded and beautiful VF copies, and this was our best year for selling unslabbed VF to VF/NM comics in over a decade.

DC digests like **Adventure Comics** #496 are selling well.

All year long, I ran into collectors with their original owner collection copies, many assuming they automatically held NM to NM/MT copies. Most collectors who bought comics new from 1970-1985 and read them once then bagged and stored them have in their possession comics in VF to VF/NM average. The main reasons for this include: 1) It was assumed that reading once would not lower the grade of the comic. Each comic was not treated as if it were a NM *Action* #1; 2) Strong and very stiff white backing boards were not in common use until the 1990s, while the thinner gray backing boards that only supplied minimal support and often stained the book and bags were used by perhaps under 25% of dealers and collectors in the 1980s; 3) Most collectors did not hand pick the absolute best copy available on the day of release before handling by too many others. Many stores held the new copies for their customers for them to pick up at a later date. Thus they received random copies often handled several times before they even bought them; 4) Even if one did manage to hand pick their own copies on the day of release, they usually did not have enough copies to select from, thus one often had for example 10 copies in VF thru NM- to pick from. Sometimes none of the 10 copies were above VF when new at the location where the collectors bought them; and 5) In the 1970s and 1980s the fussy collectors avoided factory flaws if possible, plus many selected copies that were as aligned as best possible at the spine. Copies with no factory flaws were considered the highest graded copies. This selection often meant picking copies with corner dings, hairline stress marks in the spine, and copies without razor sharp corners. Unfortunately the opposite is now true in the current high grade market. Factory flawed copies with no stress and razor sharp corners are now much more prized and valuable than copies with minor stress but no factory flaws.

We sold a large number of high grade raw – non-CGC graded – comics, magazines and treasuries from the Manitoba collection. Most of these were from 1975-1984 and had book values under $20, thus most were not worth slabbing. But there is a large group of collectors that want these comics in true strict high grade 9.0-9.6 or better while they are still affordable, and we sold most at 125-200% or more of *Guide*. The biggest difference between the CGC and raw market is that CGC buyers mostly prefer mainstream Marvel superheroes while the raw high grade market likes the same but especially all the other genres not commonly found in CGC copies, particularly horror. Selling comics raw cuts the cost per book by $15-$25 or more, saving CGC costs and leaving it up to the buyers if they want them graded. We sold a lot of high grade Charlton, Warren, Gold Key, Skywald, superhero Marvel/DC and non-superhero Marvel/DC. Most of the pre-1974 high grade Manitoba copies are sold, but the ones we still had did well. Many buyers are trying to complete large 50-100 book or more (especially 1975-1985) runs in 9.2 or better grades, like *Avengers, Conan, Hulk, Jonah Hex, Weird War*, etc. CGC magazine grading has so far been quite a success, with many amazing record prices. It can already be seen that in general, less copies of magazines exist in top grades than the same vintage standard comics. A lot of magazines remain very undervalued.

DC: All the superhero, SF, horror and good artist comics were in demand, with Bronze Age selling best followed by Silver Age, especially 1960s. This was the first year in over a decade that VF or better copies were the most requested. Collectors now realize that putting together a large runs of 9.0 to 9.4 and better copies is an near impossible task. Thus those who like high grade and actually want to finish runs bought VF 8.0 through VF/NM 9.0 copies along with any better we could find at a fast and furious pace. Low grade reading copies of all DCs sold well throughout the year, but higher grades sold best for the first time in quite some time.

Because we came across the Manitoba collection, we got in a lot of 9.0-9.8 DCs of 1975-1984. The late Bronze issues are now 20-25 years old and still have very low $2-$10 *Guide* values; they sold especially well in raw high grades. Contrary to popular belief, these issues are quite uncommon in strict 9.0 or better and are copies that would stand the test of CGC grading. Because of the low *Guide* values, not many CGC-graded copies are on the market, but high grade collectors still want these books. The Manitoba collection contains 1000s of these high grade books and many found very happy homes at good multiples of *Guide* for raw examples. This even included digests and treasuries that are rarely found in 9.0 or better. Currently my most requested high grade books of 1980-1985 include *Action, Adventure* #467-503, *All-Star Squadron* #1-67, *Batman, Brave & Bold, DC Comics Presents, Detective, Flash* #300-350, *G.I. Combat* #200-220, *Green Lantern* #116-150, all DC horror, *Jonah Hex* #81-92, *Justice League of America* #180-261, *Legion of Super-Heroes, New Teen Titans* #1-20, *Sgt. Rock* #302-320, *Superman* #400-423, *Swamp Thing* #20-64 (Alan Moore), *Weird Western, Wonder Woman* #290-329, and *World's Finest* #300-323.

For most of 2004, I saw the highest demand for DC horror comics from 1968-1983 ever. For the last ten years, they have always sold steadily in the normal G thru FN ranges, but not in the hot category. This year they reached the status as the single hottest group of comics for us. The biggest change is that the investors are buying them up in higher grades. There are not many found in CGC graded copies and there is a very short supply of strict high grade copies. Thus buyers have are not getting all they can before the expected big price increases of 1968-1972 in VF or better, 1973-1976 in VF+ or better, and 1977-1983 in VF/NM or better. I have bought and sold a lot of nice copies in these ranges this year and find them extremely difficult to restock in grade.

Some of the 1968-1972 issues might explode in price by late 2005. *House of Secrets* #81 and *House of Mystery* #174 are now viewed as major key issues, yet list at less than 1/3 the price of *Weird War* #1. All these DC horror issues are quite scarce in strict high grades and will not surface on the market at current low *Guide* values. Due for big price increases of 150% or more are *Ghosts* #1-10, *House of Mystery* #175-200, *House of Secrets* #82-100, *Phantom Stranger* #1-30, *Unexpected* #105-136, *Weird War* #5-20, 64, 68, 93-124, *Witching Hour* #1-20, especially those with covers and art by Adams, Wrightson, Toth and others. All the DC horror from any year with Wrightson covers, stories and even single splash pages, as well as Adams cover or art, are by far the most requested issues.

Very unusual is the sudden huge demand for 1977-1983 issues in the very difficult to find VF/NM or better copies. Many buyers have told me their local shops do not even have mid-grade copies of 1977-1983 issues any more as they are too low in the *Guide*. Anything in VF/NM or better in the $8-$12 range flies out the door by the stack. Last issues, giant issues, #1-10, 100s and any key issues are hottest, which tells us investors are buying these books. We sold literally many 100s of raw books at good multiples of 120-200% or more of *Guide*. Most earlier horror issues in CGC 9.4 would bring 300-600% *Guide* if you could find them. All issues from all DC horror titles are hot, including the later issues of the above and also including *Black Magic, Doorway to*

Nightmare, Forbidden Tales of Dark Mansion, From Beyond the Unknown, Madame Xanadu, Secrets of Haunted House, Secrets of Sinister House, Strange Adventures #217-244, *Tales of Ghost Castle, Time Warp, Weird Mystery,* and *Witching Hour. Ghosts* #97-99 have a Spectre story in each and are very fast sellers. *Weird War* has been the fastest growing in demand on the later issues, especially these issues, which can now be considered hot and are still very undervalued: #64 (Frank Miller's first work at DC), 68 (second Frank Miller), 93 (first app. and origin Creature Commandos), 94 (first return of "War that Time Forgot"-c/s with dinosaurs) 100 (Creature Commandos invade the War that Time Forgot), 101 (first app. and origin G.I. Robot-c/s by Kanigher), 124 (last issue; 6/1983).

Many collectors are trying to complete their DC special series sets as they like the odd combination of giants, digests and treasuries. All oddball material sold well to those filling in runs, usually in G-FN grades, with most at 120-135% *Guide*, including *Amazing World of DC,* cartoon, digests, fanzines, Fireside books, funny animal, giveaways, humor, magazines, paperbacks, parody, romance, teenage, treasuries, TV, war, and western. These still sell well and we filled in many runs for buyers. After horror and superhero, DC's big five war titles sold a strong third in all grades, with Sgt. Rock issues of *Our Army at War* by far the strongest in demand. The DC "Dollar" comic giants of 1979-1980 are round-bound rather than square-bound, causing excess stress at staples, thus many are now getting scarcer in strict VF/NM or better. Demand for *Fox & Crow* and *Real Screen* was strong this year and I sold 90% of our stock in all grades.

All pre-1975 Adams and Wrightson cover and/or art were in big demand. Many now have their interior art issue sets and now look to buy up the cover and splash pages issues they still lack. For example, we have a hard time keeping the Adams cover *Tomahawks* in stock in any grade, much less in the often asked for high grades. All 1960s appearances of Batgirl, Catwoman and Supergirl showed very strong demand, with even Black Canary and Zatanna appearances showing life. The 1960s Batgirl issues are especially hot and due for a 50% price increase. Minor key issues plus issues with popular villains sold 50%-100% better than regular issues in many titles. The hot Silver and Bronze issues that we got asked for all year long and are due for price increases include *Action* #347, 360, 373 (giants), 377-392 (Legion), *Adventure* #381, 397-400, all *New Collectors Edition* C-54-56, 58, *All Star Comics* #58-74, *Aquaman* #50-52, *Batman* #155, 164, 169, 171, 179, 181, 183, 189, 190, 197, 203, 210, 217, 219-222, 224-227, 229, 230, 232,234, 236-241, 243-246, 251, 255, *Batman Family* #11-20, *Beautiful Stories For Ugly Children* #21-30, *Brave & Bold* #51-100 (especially Adams), *Challengers* #74, *DC Special* #2-4, 6, 11, 28, 29, *DC Special Series* #1-16, *Detective* #355, 359, 363, 364, 369-372, 385, 387, 389, 391, 392, 394-422, *Fox & Crow, Freedom Fighters, G.I. Combat* #66-68, 83, 87-138, *Girls Love, Girls Romances, Green Lantern* #76-89, *Heart Throbs, Hot Wheels, Justice League of America* #91-117, 183-185, *Limited Collectors Edition* C#23-25, 32-34, 37, 39, 41, 43-46, 48-52, 57, *Men of War* (especially Enemy Ace issues), *Our Army at War* #83-301, *Our Fighting Forces* #123-162, *Plop* #1-5 in VF/NM or better, *Secret Society of Super Villains, Shazam* #8, 12-17, 25, 27-35, *Showcase* #55, 57, 60, 61, 64, 70, 79-81, 83, 84, *Spectre* #1-5, 9, *Strange Adv.* #205-216, *Star Spangled War* #84-163, *Superboy* #197-220, *Super DC Giant* #S-13-26, *Super Friends* #1-10, *Supergirl* (1972) #1-10, *Superman* #233-300, *Tarzan* #207-258, *Tarzan Family, Wonder Woman* #51-200, *World's Finest* #169, 173-177. The most requested DC CGC issues bringing 200% 9.2 *Guide* in 9.0, 500+% in 9.4, and sky high prices in 9.6, were *Batman* #232, *Detective* #400, and *Green Lantern* #76. All could double in raw grades in the *Guide* and still be a bit undervalued.

Dell: We sold a lot of ordinary G-FN range comics to 100s of buyers, most just attempting to complete their sets. Lowest available grade and cheapest copies were the most popular quantity-wise this year, but we also sold a lot of nice clean VG to FN/VF range books. There was resistance to the VF range copies we did have. We did not have the 9.4 copies that several buyers wanted. I found most will not pay the premiums needed to locate them in 9.4. Mostly only tough key issues are requested. *Four Color* comics continue to be in higher demand. Western comics were the bestsellers, with *Lone Ranger* and *Red Ryder* the most requested. The *Red Ryder* comics below #70 are getting harder to locate. The Harman #118-down issues far outsell the later painted cover issues. *Lone Ranger* #1-30 and 112-up were the bestsellers. *Smokey Stover* was impossible to keep in stock. *Tarzan* #1-30, 80-131 were top sellers and are still undervalued.

The best sellers at 115-135% *Guide* for FR-FN copies included: *Air War, Alvin, Andy Griffith, Beetle Bailey, Ben Bowie, Beverly Hillbillies, Bewitched, Big Valley, Brain Boy, Bugs Bunny* (especially *FC*s), *Cheyenne, Chilly Willy, Cisco Kid, Colt 45, Combat, Creature, Dracula, Felix the Cat, Flintstones, Flying Nun, Flying Saucers, Frankenstein, Fritzi Ritz* (with *Peanuts*), *F-Troop, Gene Autry, Get Smart, Ghost Stories, Have Gun Will Travel, Howdy Doody, Huckleberry Hound, Indian Chief, Jetsons, John Wayne, Jungle Jim, King of Royal Mounted, Kona, Little Beaver, Little Lulu, Lone Ranger, Looney Tunes, Maverick, Melvin Monster, Monkees, Mummy, Neutro, Nukla, Our Gang, Peanuts, Ponytail, Popeye, Rat Patrol, Rawhide, Red Ryder, Rifleman, Roy Rogers, Sgt. Preston, Smokey Stover, Tarzan, Thirteen, Toka, Tonto, Turok, Twilight Zone, Voyage to Bottom of Sea, Western Roundup, Yak Yak, Yogi Bear, Zane Grey* and *Zorro.*

Fanzines & Miscellaneous Comic Magazines: The pre-1970 ditto/mimeograph early fanzines had print runs of 100-500 copies or less, with perhaps 50-75% of those copies destroyed over the years, leaving tiny survival rates. These ditto 'zines are garnering a lot of interest of late, with most fetching $15-$50 each and some at up to $100 or more. Some of the better issues include Biljo White, Raymond Miller, SFCA publications, RBCC, Bill Black, Stalin (and Gemini pseudonym), Marvel and DC parodies, famous creator art and interviews, Saunders, Foss, Seuling, Love, Overstreet, Gene Klein (Gene Simmons of *Kiss*), Fagan, Newton, Fantucchio, and many more. Now that CGC is grading magazines, it will be interesting to see how many of the older magazines and fanzines surface in high grades. Typically, most older comics magazines are found in mid- to lower grades. There is no definitive price guide, although Jerry Weist made a good attempt at one, thus the market is quite erratic. Many 1960s and 1970s fanzines had small print runs of 100-2000 copies and contain early, obscure and scarce works of most of the greatest creators of the period.

Many Fanzines from the 1960s-'90s are loaded with great articles and art. Many are great sellers at $5-$20 each, with scarcer issues selling for $25-75. Titles to watch and some better selling titles include assorted Neal Adams fanzines, Alan Moore (*Big Numbers, Shocking Futures, Twisted Times, Warrior*, and anything else), *Ariel* book of fantasy (Frazetta, Jones, Smith, Corben, etc.), *Alter Ego, Amazing Heroes, Apple Pie, Art of Neal Adams, Asterix, Bananas, Barbarella, Basically Strange, Batfink & Rubin, Berford Seaman's Flabby Thighs & Butter, Blast, Buried Treasure, Capt. George's Comic World*, CFA-APA limited fanzines (Steranko, Byrne, Perez, etc.), *Collector's Dream* (Olshevski), *Comic Book Artist, Comic Book Marketplace, Comics Buyer's Guide*, assorted comics calendars, *Comics Feature, Comics Interview, Comics Journal, Comics Revue, Comic Reader, Comic Shop News, Comixscene*, convention programs (Seuling NY, Creation, etc.), *CPL, Cracked, Crazy, Diamond Previews, Doctor Weird* (Starlin), Dragon Lady Press magazines, *Dynamite, Electric Company* (Spider-Man comic strips in most), ERBdom, assorted Frazetta fanzines, *Flashback* (Alan Light), *Fuddle Duddle, Fun Comics* (Paragon), *Golden Age, Graphic Story, Harpoon* (Adams, Chaykin, Stalin, Simonson, etc.), *Hot Dog, Hot Stuf* (Sal Q.), *Humbug, International Insanity* (Adams, Heath, etc.), *Kosher Comics, Laugh-In, Le Beaver, Look-In, Lucky Luke, MAD, Masters of Universe, Mediascene, Menomonee Falls Gazette & Guardian, Monster Times, Myth Adventures, Neat Stuff, NEMO, Nostalgia Journal* (#32-up becomes *Comics Journal*), *Omniverse, Overstreet Advanced Collector* (combines with *CBM* at #22), Peterson's Mags (*CARtoons, CYCLEtoons, SURFtoons*, etc.), *Phantacea, RBCC, Sick, Sojourn* (1977), *Spa Fon, Squa Tront, Star Studded Comics* (Starlin, etc.), *Steve Canyon, Taboo, Tandra, Thimk, Tintin, Trump, Wacko, Weirdo, Witzend, Wizard,* assorted Wrightson fanzines, *Zany, Zippy*.

Gold Key: The horror titles have started to sell quite well, mostly in G-FN, including *Boris Karloff, Grimm's Ghost, Occult Files of Dr. Spector, Ripley's Believe it or Not, Spine Tingling Tales,* and *Twilight Zone*. We got in some nice high grade VF/NM up copies and most sold in short order. We could sell more if we could find them. *Black Hole* (Disney) #4 is a scarce and undervalued pre-pack only low print run Whitman. *Twilight Zone* #83-84 are 52-page giants, with lower print run and high demand. All the 52-page giants in the late '70s had low print runs and are getting a lot scarcer as more buyers try to complete their sets. *Twilight Zone* #84 is the first Frank Miller pro work in comics and is ready to explode in price. It currently brings 300% *Guide*, while #85 is very overlooked as the second pro Miller art.

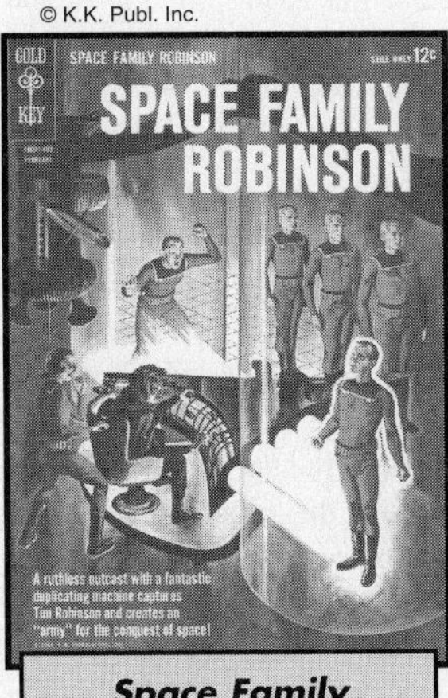

Space Family Robinson *is among the many strong Gold Key titles from the 1960s. (#6 shown)*

The key titles from Gold Key in the 1960s were very strong this year, especially in strict FN or better: *Boris Karloff, Dark Shadows, Dr. Solar, Magnus Robot Fighter, Mars Patrol, Mighty Samson, Phantom, Ripley's Believe it or Not, Scooby Doo, Space Family Robinson, Tarzan, Turok* and *Twilight Zone*. These are cheap when compared to similar vintage Marvel and DC counterparts. Very few CGC 9.2 or better issues of these titles ever hit the market. Most well known, long-running established characters seemed safe to buyers and enjoyed increased demand. Whitman Variant Editions are possible for all Gold Key comics and digests published from 11/1971-3/1980, but only exist on about 50% of all titles, with many of these variants being quite rare. These are 1968 Canadian newsstand variant cover price issues that are still selling to completionists and variant collectors at small premiums.

Other top-selling titles at 120-135% *Guide* included *Addams Family, Amazing Chan, Avengers* (TV), *Banana Splits, Battle of the Planets, Beetle Bailey* #39-53, *Beneath the Planet of Apes, Bugs Bunny* #86-120, *Bullwinkle, Dagar, Doc Savage, Fat Albert, Flash Gordon, Fun-In, Funky Phantom, Gomer Pyle, Green Hornet, Happy Days, Inspector, Jetsons, Korak, Krofft Supershow, Lancelot Link, Land of Giants, Little Monsters, Lone Ranger, Looney Tunes, Magnus, Mighty Mouse* #156-172 (especially *Mighty Heroes* issues), *Munsters, Nancy & Sluggo* (for the *Peanuts* strip), *Peanuts, Phantom, Pink* Panther, Popeye #66-80, *Space Ghost, Star Trek* #1-9, *Super TV Heroes, Three Stooges, UFO Flying Saucers, Underdog, Wacky Races, Wacky Witch, Wild Wild West* and *Zody the Mod Rob*.

Harvey: We had difficulty in restocking many titles, especially the hot titles and key issues. We still managed to get a few small collections and enjoyed great sales of Harvey comics again this year. Much of our stock is depleted, yet we still have one of the biggest selections around anywhere. Selection is what makes them sell. I noted that high grade pre-1960 key issues were in very short supply, and those that did appear got

CGC graded and auctioned at high multiples, even on some under 9.0. By far the most requested included *Devil Kids, Harvey Hits* key issues, *Hot Stuff* #1-100, *Richie Rich Poor Little Rich Boy* #1-50, *Wendy*, most pre-1975 #1-10, and key issues and giants. Others in big demand included *Baby Huey, Harvey Hits, Little Dot, Playful Little Audrey, Richie Rich Millions & Success,* 1970s Richie Rich titles, *Sad Sack* (all), *Spooky*, and *Stumbo*. The low print run comics and digests of 1988-1993, plus the Alfred Harvey titles circa 1990, are all consistent sellers at 150% *Guide*, with only the #1s being relatively common. Less requested but still good sellers include *Blondie, Bunny, Casper, Dagwood, Dick Tracy, Felix the Cat,* Hanna-Barbera titles, *Joe Palooka, Li'l Abner, Little Max, Mutt & Jeff,* and *Scooby Doo*.

This year we had many requests for VF or better copies from many who wish to avoid the high CGC multiples, but we were only able to find a few. Most of what we sold were for buyers filling gaps in sets who would take any grade available, with mid-grades the most popular. We cleared out a lot of our lowest grade reading copies.

The standard size Harveys should be 36 pages including covers, but many copies on the market are missing the ad page centerfolds. The 1970s Harvey #1s are a bit more findable and most of the sets that began in the 1970s can be completed with some legwork, thus this is attracting some new buyers. We have managed to find and sell some nice VF issues from these titles. The most popular of these 1970s titles are *Casper (& Ghostly Trio)* #1-10, *In Space, Space Ship, & Spooky, Strange Ghost Stories, Wendy, Harvey Collector's Comics* #1-16, *Hot Stuff Creepy Caves* #1-7, *Jackie Jokers, Richie Rich (& Casper, & Gloria, RR Bank Book, RR Cash, RR Diamonds, RR Fortunes, RR Gems, RR Inventions, RR Money World, RR Profits* #1-47, *RR Vault of Mystery, RR Zillionz), Sad Sack (Navy Gods 'n' Gals, With Sarge & Sadie, U.S.A.), Spooky Haunted House, Super Richie* #1-18. Finally, some of the near forgotten Harvey-related titles have shown some signs of life, including *Dotty Dripple, Flat-Top, Horace and Dotty Dripple, Mazie, Mortie, Nutty Comics, Rags Rabbit, & Stevie,* plus the assorted 1950s war and romance titles too.

IW & Super Reprints: These are undervalued as they are 40-50 years old and still have issues listed under $20 in *Guide* in high grade, with most under $10 in middle grades. We sell quite a few of these, and my minimum price is now set at G $4, VG $7, FN $10, VF $18. There are quite a number of completionists. About 20% of the 250-300 different issues are scarce to rare and if identified can easily bring 200% *Guide*. They published without the Code and many contain pre-Code reprints. Some of the better selling titles included *Avenger, Black Knight, Blazing Six-Guns, Brain* (hot for the DeCarlo-a), *Daring Adv., Dogface Dooley, Dream of Love, Dr. Fu Manchu, Fantastic Adv., Firehair* (GGA), *Foxhole, Jungle Adv., Malu, Master Detective, Meet Merton, Red Mask, Sheena, Strange Planets, US Paratroops,* and *Westerner*.

Marvel: This is the first year in which high grade Marvel magazines outsold low grade. There are still many readers buying them up, but investors are now getting in on a good thing. We had some top grade 9.0-9.6 copies from the Manitoba collection, with Marvel comics, treasuries and magazines in VF/NM-NM selling briskly at 125-200% *Guide* or more. *Tales of the Zombie* #1 had only one copy in CGC 9.2 or better at the time of writing; *Vampire Tales* #1 and *Dracula Lives* had only two each in CGC 9.2 or better; *Rampaging Hulk* #1 had 10 in CGC 9.2 or better; *Spectacular Spider-Man* magazine #2 had 108 copies in CGC 9.2 or better; *Savage Sword of Conan* #1 registered 50 copies in 9.2 or better, with CGC 9.6 copies selling at $500+ and 9.8 copies at $1000+. All CGC 9.2-up copies brought good premiums. The horror titles remain quite undervalued in *Guide*, especially in higher 9.0 or better grades. Magazines selling well in the 120-150% *Guide* range are *Bizarre Adv.* #25-28, 31, *Deadly Hands of Kung Fu* #1, 14, 17, 28, *Doc Savage* #1 and 8, *Dracula Lives* #1-13 and Annual, *Epic* #31-34, *Foom* #1-11, 22, *Haunt of Horror* #1-5, digest #1, 2, *Hulk* #10-18, *Marvel Preview* #3, 7, 8, 12, *Marvel Treasury* #1-20, *Monsters Unleashed* #1-11, *Planet of the Apes* #1, 21-29, *Rampaging Hulk* #1-9, *Tales of the Zombie* #1-10 and Annual, *Unknown Worlds of SF* #1-6 and Annual, *Vampire Tales* #1-11 and Annual. *Pussycat* #1 remains very scarce and sells instantly at 150%+ *Guide*. *Savage Tales* #1 is in high demand, especially in VF or better. *Gothic Tales of Love* #1-3 – yes, there is a #3 – are by far the scarcest Marvels with raw over-graded VF copies always selling at $200+ on eBay. CGC 9.4 copies would easily sell over $1000 each.

The Marvel adult cartoon magazines and digests – *Cartoons & Gags, Cartoon Capers/Laughs/Parade* – sell fast, especially with the "Pussycat" strip or Bill Ward art. It is not common knowledge, but Magazine Management (Marvel) and its many imprints produced hundreds of men's adventure adult magazines like *Action for Men, For Men Only, Ken for Men, Male, Men, Stag, True Action*. Most have nice to superb painted covers plus many illustrations and photos inside. Many of these magazines have interior art by comic artists. Many have great exploitative painted covers with Nazis, torture, whipping, 'Good Girl' art, etc. Early James Bama art appears in circa 1960 issues. Later issues turned into skin mags with more photos and less illustrations.

For the most of the year, all Conan and Robert E. Howard comics have had increased demand, probably due to the new Dark Horse series. In biggest demand are *Conan the Barbarian* #25-100, 250-275, all Conan graphic novels, *Creatures on the Loose* #10, *Kull* #1-5, *Kull & the Barbarians* #1-3, *Monsters on the Prowl* #16, *Savage Sword of Conan* #1-50, 200-235, *Conan Saga* #80-97, *Conan the King* #50-55, *Marvel Comics Super Special* #2, 9, *Marvel Feature* and the *Red Sonja* titles, *Savage Tales* #1-5, and the 1994-1998 *Conan* revival titles. *Savage Sword* #200-235 all had small print runs, especially #231-235, which are near impossible to keep in stock at 200-300% *Guide*. Many collections quit at #100, many more quit at #200, with few staying until #235. *Savage Sword* #235s in VF/NM bring $30+ each, and CGC 9.4s over $100. Although there are the high grade investors, they are not the main buyers; those who seek them out are mainly fans trying to complete their sets. here are a few high grade collectors beginning to look for the Howard titles before the prices start to rise. Many fans never got to the earlier issues just as many quit and never finished their sets. Most did not wander into the related Howard titles.

We had many high grade copies from 1975-1983 from the Manitoba collection. There was growing demand and we sold a lot of late Bronze (1981-pre-*Secret Wars*) and beyond in strict grade 9.0-9.6 copies at 120-200% and more of *Guide,* including *Amazing Spider-Man* #190-252, *Avengers* #180-230, *Capt. America* #230-282, *Conan the Barbarian, Daredevil* #182-233, *Defenders* #91-152, *Fantastic Four* #181-232, *Incredible Hulk* #201-300, *Iron Man* #118-200, *Man-Thing* (second series, 1979-1981) #1-11, *Red Sonja, Spectacular Spider-Man* #50-90, *Thor* #300-350, *Uncanny X-Men* #143-200. The 1981-1985 comics, now 20-25 years old, list on average at 25-35% of 1975-1977 comics, thus they are quite a bargain. They are much tougher in strict 9.0 and better than one would think.

The *Marvel Value Stamp Book*s (first series, 1974) and later second series have caused tens of thousands of Bronze Age comics to be incomplete as fans nationwide clipped the stamps out of the actual comics to complete the 100-stamp collections. Most completed books were sent in for apparently lame prizes. Completed books, even in lower grades, usually sell for $75 and up. This includes the notorious Stamp #54 – Shanna the She-Devil, which is scarce because you could only cut it out of *Incredible Hulk* #181. Most completed copies are badly warped with heavy waves through the book due to owners using too much glue. But even low grade copies are in high demand as many participated in the original stamp hunt and completed books are now scarce.

The most requested comics and those that bring high premiums for high grade copies include *Amazing Adventures* #11, *Amazing Spider-Man* #121, 122, 129, *Daredevil* #131, 158, 168, *Defenders* #1, 10, *Fear, Ghost Rider* #1-10, *Hero For Hire* #1-5, *Incredible Hulk* #122, 126, 140, 141, 161, 162, 180, 181, *Iron Man* #47-55, *Marvel Spotlight* #2, 5-11, *Marvel Team-Up* #1-4, *Sub-Mariner* #34, 35, *Tomb of Dracula* #1-10, *Werewolf by Night* #1-10, 32. These are red hot and even on eBay, unslabbed copies bring over *Guide* while CGC copies regularly bringing high multiples.

The Marvel horror magazines were hot. All the color comics in G-FN copies were selling excellent as per usual, but there was also a sharp rise in demand for any and all in VF or better, especially in 9.0 or better. These horror titles showed unusually strong demand: *Beware, Chamber of Chills, Dead of Night, Frankenstein*, all horror Giant Size titles, *Journey into Mystery* (1972), *Man-Thing, Marvel Chillers* #3-7, *Monsters on the Prowl, Supernatural Thrillers, Tomb of Dracula* (comic and magazine), *Uncanny Tales, Vault of Evil, War is Hell* #9-15, *Werewolf by Night, Where Creatures Roam* and *Where Monsters Dwell.*

Oddball titles are still top sellers but are too difficult to find in high grades, thus investors steer clear. Most copies are found and sell in G-FN with not a lot of requests for high grade copies. These brought 120%-135% *Guide*: cartoon, digests, fanzines, giveaway/promo items, magazines, memorabilia, paperbacks, reprint titles, romance, teenage, treasuries, TV/movie, war, western. The mass market paperbacks saw increased demand, with the 1966/67 Lancers being scarce in FN or better and the 1977 color paperbacks through the '80s B&W paperbacks all scarce in VF+ or better. With all the upcoming Marvel movies, it may be too much of a good thing and prices may not jump as anticipated every time a new movie hits the theaters. Low grade reading copies were again in big demand for both readers and those on modest budgets who just love comics (gotta love those fans that like the comic itself more than condition). Due to small print runs, many Marvels from 1996-2000 sell well, with many titles from 2000-2004 being hot. Due to very few dealers stocking up on anything in the last few years, many issues are sold out by most sellers, with many issues selling at 200-400% and more of cover price. Many of these Modern comics have less existing copies than still existing copies of most Bronze Age Marvels.

All superhero titles were in large demand as everyone wanted to complete everything from 1961-1985 in all grades, but especially for strict 9.0 and higher graded copies. The 1961-1964 Marvels are again hard to restock and selling fast, likely in part due to all the Hollywood movies. All these issues were in heavy demand and bringing 110%-135% *Guide*: *Amazing Adv.* #1-17, *Amazing Spider-Man* #1-30, 39, 40, 50, 91-200, *Astonishing Tales* #1-10, *Avengers* #1-11, 50-200, *Capt. America* #109-113, 117, 121-200, *Capt. Marvel* #1, 14, 21, 25-35, *Daredevil* #1-7, 16-18, 43, 50-181, *Defenders* #1-20, *Dr. Strange* #1-5, 14, 58-62, 81, *Fantastic Four* #1-30, 51-60, 100-200, Fireside books, most *Giant Size* titles, *G.I. Joe* #1-27, 93-120, 141-155, *Gunslinger* #1-3, *Hero For Hire, Human Torch* (1974/75), *Incredible Hulk* #1-6, 111-250, *Invaders* #1-20, 31-33, *Iron Fist, Iron Man* #1, 31-100, *Journey into Mystery* #83-112, *Jungle Action* #1-10, *Kid Colt* #91-156, *Marvel Feature* (first series) #1-12, *Marvel Fun & Games*, *Marvel Premiere* #3-28, *Marvel Tales* #1-10, *Marvel Superheroes* #12-20, *Marvel Team-Up* #1-50, *Marvel Two-in-One* #1-30 and Annual #2, *Masters of the Universe, Master of Kung Fu* #15-50, *Mighty Marvel Western* #1-15, all *Millie the Model, Ms. Marvel* #1, 4, 16-18, *My Love, Nick Fury* #1-15, *Night Nurse, Not Brand Echh, Night Rider* #1, *Nova* #1, 12, *Our Love Story, Powerman* #17-20, 48-50, 57, 66, 78, *Punisher* (1986 mini), *Rawhide Kid* #1-50, *Red Wolf, Savage She-Hulk* #1, 6, 8, 25, *Scooby Doo, Shanna, Silver Surfer* #14, *Spectacular Spider-Man* #26-28, 64, 81-83, *Spider-Woman* #6, 19, 32, 50, *Spidey Super Stories* #1-20, *Strange Tales* #101-135, 150-167 and Annuals, *Sub-Mariner* #1, 8, 21-50, *Tales of Suspense* #39-60, *Tales To Astonish* #40-60, *Thor* #150-230, 332, 333, 337, *Transformers* #61-80, *Western Gunfighters, Western Team-Up* #1, *What If* (first series) #1-31, *Wyatt Earp* #30-34, *X-Men* #1-15, 50-66, 94-121 and *GS* #1.

National Lampoon: We sold a lot of *National Lampoon* this year, with about 75% in G-FN but with now some growing demand for FN/VF to NM range copies. The regular pre-1980 copies issues are round-bound and have glossy stock covers, thus tending to split and fray easily, with many becoming detached at the staples. Thus examples in better than VF are getting tough to find. This is one of the most important titles in comics history, yet remains unlisted in the *Guide*, thus overlooked by most collectors. All were published with no Code. Artists include Adams, Bode, Frazetta, J. Jones, Kaluta, Morrow, Orlando, Rodrigues, Romita, A. Roth, Springer, Barry Windsor-Smith, G. Wilson, Wrightson, and more. Many nostalgic fans recall certain hilarious parodies, gags and stories, and want to get those issues back. They are loaded with great color comic strip parodies on many subjects. #1-10 bring $40-up, with #11-30 in the $10-$30 range and #31-100 and up at $4-$12 range. The 1986-1993 issues had low print runs and are difficult to restock, thus our minimum prices are now VF $9, FN $6, VG $4. The 1964 High School Yearbook parody has been reprinted, thus there is slow demand on the original. But collectors still want first printings. Many people are now collecting all the square-bound specials. Most were well read and typically show up in FA, G and VG, with FN copies being uncommon and VF or better being scarce. The stiff cardboard covers on the specials show creases easily, especially if read from cover to cover even once. Our minimum price on the specials is now G $5, VG $9, FN $14, VF $20.

Romance: Collectors like these as they are scarcer than most other genres, especially in higher grades, and they are filled with unintentionally funny stories. Many have great artwork and surprise, they are filled with girls, which appeal to a lot of guys. The pre-1960 assorted publisher issues are in low supply on the market, which means they have been selling. The better sellers at 115-135% *Guide* are titles by Atlas, Avon, Fox, Prize, St John's, Superior, and Ziff-Davis. The Matt Baker, Kirby, photo cover, minor key, 'Good Girl' art, and exploitation issues are in highest demand. We got in some nice collections of both DC and Marvel 1950s-'70s love comics, mostly in G-FN; we sold a lot of all titles. There are a lot of collectors that search all the major dealers trying to fill in holes in their collections. There are a surprising number of completionists for the DC and Marvel titles. Only a few have attempted to collect these in high grades as it is rather futile; high grade collectors mostly want just the key issues. *Gothic Tales of Love* #1-3 and *Gothic Romances* were impossible to find, often bringing 200-500% *Guide* on eBay on the rare occasions when they appeared. These would still be undervalued at double current *Guide*. Skywald's *Tender Love* and Warren's *Teen Love Stories* from 1969/70 sold well to completionists of those publishers. We sold a lot of Charlton love as well, with G-FN the most popular grades, and with resistance to VF or better copies.

Treasuries: Treasury Edition oversized comics sold better than usual this year. We actually sold out most of our lowest graded copies under VG, as they are too cheap in *Guide* in those grades. This year we finally turned up some high grade 9.0 to 9.6 copies from the Manitoba collection, and these sold swiftly at 120-200%+ *Guide*. These are normally quite scarce in better than strict VF. The hottest issues, bringing 115%-135% *Guide*, are *All-New Collectors Edition* C#53-56, and 58, *Annie* (scarce), *Captain America's Bicentennial Battles, Christmas with Archie* (rare), *DC Special Series* #27, *Famous First Edition* F-4 to F-8, *Funtastic World of Hanna-Barbera* #1-3, *G.I. Joe* (scarce), *Golden Picture Storybook* #1-4 (rare), *Jungle Book, King Kong, Limited Collectors Edition* C#21, 23-25, 32-34, 37-39, 41-52, *Marvel Special Edition (Spectacular Spider-Man)* #1 (1975), *Marvel Treasury* #1-28, *Superman vs. Spider-Man* #1, and the *Walt Disney Paint Book* series. In addition, we sold several of the scarce unlisted Modern Promotions 1972 B&W issues with newspaper strip reprints – *Beetle Bailey, Flash Gordon, Katzenjammer Kids, Mandrake the Magician*, etc. – at G $9, VG $15, and FN $22.

Tower: This year we saw increased demand for most titles. All grades sold well, but we got more requests than usual for FN or better copies. *Dynamo, Fight the Enemy, Noman, Thunder Agents*, and *Undersea Agents* are loaded with great art by Wood, Ditko, Crandall and others, and these great titles are due for a price increase. We had one high grade run of *Thunder Agents*, and most sold swiftly at about 120% *Guide*. The *Tippy Teen* titles still sell well, but more to readers who prefer low grade cheaper copies.

Valiant/Acclaim: The Scarcer Valiant titles are still gaining momentum, especially the hard to find premium editions. The low print regular editions from 1991-1992 are getting scarcer in strict VF/NM or better. Many of the later and last issues already regularly sell well over *Guide*. Most variants we were not able to stock, but had multiple customer requests. I tried to win some, usually without success, and followed many eBay prices for VF/NM or better. The key issues to grab while you still can include most Valiant Gold editions at $20-35+ each, with CGC copies much higher, most Valiant Signature Series issues at $50-75+ each, with CGC copies much higher, *Bloodshot* #50, 51 ($10+), *Chaos Effect Alpha* (Red cover $200+), *Harbinger* #0 (pink send-away $70), #1 ($40+), #2-10 ($6-$15 each), #41 ($10+); *Hard Corps* #30 ($7); *Magnus* #0 (with card $50+), #1 ($12), #2-10 ($6-10), 12 ($25), 64 ($12), *Ninjak* #26 ($7), *Predator vs. Magnus* #1 (Platinum $12), *Rai* #0 ($12), #1-2 ($12 each), #3-4 ($24 each), 5 ($10), 33 ($10), *Dr. Mirage* #18 ($6), *Shadowman* #1 ($10), #43 ($12), *Solar* #1-9 ($8-12 each), #10 ($20+), #58-59 ($7 each), #60 ($14), *Solar Alpha & Omega* #0 (HC $60), *Turok* #47 ($15), *Unity* #0 (Red variant $90), *Unity* Trade Paperback (Diamond Distributors $120), *Valiant Voice* #11-19 ($10-$20 each and up), *X-O Manowar* #68 ($15). CGC copies can often bring much higher multiples if you can find them. We have a hard time keeping the regular issues in stock, much less the premium issues. Plus many of the Acclaim revival issues had even smaller print runs of 5000 or less and should also be watched.

Variants and Premium Editions: The Marvel 30- and 35-cent variants showed strong demand. I had a hard time stocking anything of note. The *Guide* prices are perhaps more off on these than almost anything. *Spider-Man* is still the most requested. The western, war, horror and reprint title issues turn out to be some of the scarcest, with mid-grade unslabbed copies sometimes selling at over $200 on eBay. The Marvel 30-cent price variants brought 300%-1000%+ regular issue prices in grade. Our minimum price on these 30-cent variants is G $10, VG $15, FN $22, VF $35, NM $50. Minimum for 35-cent variants begins at double these prices.

© Skywald

Horror fans are requesting magazines like ***Nightmare****.*
(1974 Yearbook shown)

Canadian variants with higher cover prices were again popular but are often mistaken by Americans as rare variants. Newer variants like Gold, Platinum, Signed and Numbered, cover variants, etc., are normally fast sellers when new and become slow later. The exception seems to be long-proven characters like Vampirella. The Valiant premium editions are now hot. As some of these premium editions get older, if the character remains popular, they can begin to rise again in price. It will be interesting to see what they sell for in 10-20 years. Early Direct Distribution copies were mistaken for Whitman editions all year.

Warren, Skywald, Eerie/Stanley and other Horror Comic Magazines: Horror magazines were top sellers again this year. We had some top grade 9.0-9.6 copies from the Manitoba collection, with Skywald and Warren in VF/NM-NM selling briskly at 125-200% *Guide* or more. We also have solid demand for low graded reader copies too, selling several large 100-300 copy lots to eager buyers. The magazines from Eerie, Modern Day and Stanley still sold better to readers but garnered a few higher grade collectors recently too, especially pre-1971 and the low print 1979-1982 issues. *Creepy* and *Eerie* have less than five CGC-graded copies for most issues above #10 and not a lot for those under #10 – there goes the theory that they are common in high grades. Most higher grade Warren and Skywald magazines only grade in VF-VF+, with a big shortage of strict VF/NM or better copies. *Nightmare, Psycho* and *Scream* exist in much smaller quantities than Warrens, while demand grows stronger each year. Thus Skywalds should on average and often do bring 150-200% the price of the average Warren. We sold almost every VF or better Skywald I could get my hands on and also sold out on many issues in any grade.

Eerie #17 and *Blazing Combat* #1 easily bring 200% of *Guide* in any grade. *Eerie* #17 had a bad interior cutting factory flaw, thus the highest CGC-graded copy to date is a FN 6.0. If a CGC 9.4 *Eerie* #17 ever surfaces, it will bring $2000-$4000. We sold a good number of *Dracula* (magazine, New English Library Pub., 1971, full color, Estaban Maroto art) #1-12 at $5-$10 each in VG-VF+ as part of this run was reprinted to make the *Dracula* trade paperback for Warren. *Help*, Warren's classic Harvey Kurtzman humor magazine, badly needs to be listed in the *Guide* as one of the most important comics-related humor magazines in history. CGC is grading *Famous Monsters*, with the current highest grade at 9.0. If one ever surfaces in 9.4, it would likely break the $10,000 barrier. Most requested issues bringing 120-150% *Guide* or more include *Blazing Combat* #1, 2, and Anthology, *Comix International* #1, *Creepy* #9, 10, 14, 17-19, 29, 32, 50, 71, 76, 78, 113, 132-146, *Eerie* #5, 8, 17,18, 23-25, 28, 38-40, 45, 60, 81, 94, 95, 98, 108, 125, 128, 130-139, *Edgar Allan Poe's Fall of the House of Usher* HC, *Famous Monsters* #1-32 and paperbacks, *Ghoul Tales, Nightmare* #1-10, 20-23, *Odd World of Richard Corben, Psycho* #1-10, 20-24, *Scream* #1-3, 8-11, *Shock, Spacemen* (Warren), *Spirit Special, Teen Love Stories* #1-3, *Terrors of Dracula, Vampirella* #1-8, 12, 16, 19, 33, 36, 41, 45, 46, 48, 52, 61, 63, 64, 77, 78, 100-113, Annual #1, Special #1, UK magazines #1-4, paperbacks (UK and US) #1-6, *Web of Horror* #1-3, *Weird Vampire Tales, Wildest Westerns/Favorite Westerns of Filmland* #1-6.

Website/eBay: We did not sell much on eBay because prices were low on many unslabbed comics. But with large scans and being a known dealer, we did do some decent sales when we liquidated some Silver Age collections for clients. I did not buy much off eBay this year due to grading problems. I instead paid more but saved time and received properly graded comics by restocking from reliable well-known dealers. We ran into problems restocking many non-Marvel and non-DC items, especially Charlton, Harvey, Archie and 1966-1980 horror comics, as most dealers were sold out of the issues we required.

Our website – www.dougcomicworld.com – contains about 100 categories, many non-comic related, to choose from, with 10 to 150 pages of items listed in each category...and we have only listed 70% our inventory. If printed out, these listings would be about 5000 printed pages. Many of these categories have the biggest selection on the Internet. Many buyers do not like our website as they expect to see a shopping basket with everything graded and priced. They do not comprehend that we do not have a small 100,000 item inventory. We have perhaps 3 million items in stock, thus properly grading and pricing everything would take 10 or more years. By the time 25% were done, the first 10% would be obsolete. It has taken us four years to list the items currently listed on our website. We add 1000s of items each month to the lists. We make 1000s of updates each month for items sold, and all this on top of answering e-mails, phone calls and letters, as well as pulling, grading, pricing, processing, wrapping and shipping 100s of orders per month. All this is well under control by our current methods. Many buyers now prefer not to have to order single items one at a time in those annoying shopping baskets. A quick e-mail or phone call with most want lists is all that we need to go into action. The result – buyers often make orders for 50, 100, 300 and even 1000 items in a single order. I strongly feel that having most of my items catalogued for what is actually in stock is far better than having 10% of the items graded and priced in shopping baskets. We are extremely busy with returning customers, plus many new buyers that find those few things they need through search engines, with our third greatest customer source being referrals from happy buyers and even from other dealers. Some buyers expect us to compete with the lowest eBay prices, which we cannot do. Most of our buyers actually place a value on their time and appreciate our efforts to maintain our inventory levels with so many hard-to-find items. Most uncommon items under $10 are simply not worth the time, effort, expenses, aggravation and shipping charges to be worth bargain hunting. We excel at filling in gaps in collections at reasonable costs. Our customers prefer to buy many well-graded items all at once from one seller at reasonable market value prices over buying single items via auctions.

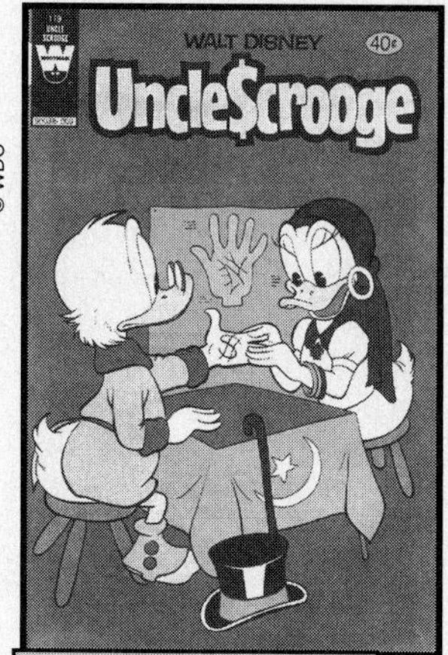

*The 8-12/1980 Whitmans continue to bring record prices. (**Uncle Scrooge** #179 shown)*

War and Western Misc. Pre-1960: There are many fans of both genres. Rather than collecting certain characters, these fans collect by genre. When they grow weary or jaded by Marvel, DC, Dell, Charlton, Fawcett and the other major publishers, they look for something different. The Fawcett westerns are rather high priced, thus some major resistance in grades above FN, but G and VG copies are affordable and selling well. There are a lot less war comics than western in the pre-1960 era, thus almost anything tends to sell well if in the $5-$35 price range. The EC war comics are beginning to sell again and remain some of the best comics ever. War comics from Ace, Farrell, Standard and Toby tend to sell faster than those by the more collectible publishers like Avon and Ziff-Davis, mainly because they are cheaper. The pre-Charlton St. John's are in double the demand, as Charlton collectors extend their sets back to the early issues. *G.I. Joe* and *Joe Yank* are extremely popular, especially those issues with Dan DeCarlo art. We sold a good number of *Wings* comics from Fiction House; they have exceptional art and good stories. In the oddball western comics, the 'Good Artist,' photo cover and known character issues sell first. The better selling publishers included Hillman, ME, St John's, and Toby. There was resistance to issues in better than FN and those priced over $50. Best selling titles were *Billy the Kid, Black Diamond Western, Bobby Benson, Bulls-Eye, Dead-Eye Western, Indians, Jesse James, John Wayne, Masked Ranger, Prize, Red Mask, Straight Arrow*, and *Tom Holt*.

Whitmans: The pre-pack only Whitman comics of August-December 1980 are still hot. After years of looking and through many collectors, we have determined that *Porky Pig* #99 was never printed and needs to be removed from the *Guide*. At least ten copies each exist of all the other 8-12/1980 Whitmans. This leaves *Super Goof* #61 as the rarest Whitman. eBay and other sales (not our sales) include *Battle of the Planets* #7 (CGC FN 6.0 $90), *Daffy Duck* #131 (CGC 6.5 $150), *Daisy & Donald* #47 (CGG 9.0 $122.50), *Little Lulu* #260 (CGC 9.2 $1535; CGC 3.0 $690; CGC 9.8 $1827), *Super Goof* #61 (rare; VG $399.04), *Uncle Scrooge* #179 (CGG 9.2 $800), *Winnie the Pooh* #22 (CGC 6.0 $400; CGC 7.5 $500), *WDC&S* #480 (CGC 9.2 $400).

Like it or not, the 8-12/1980 Whitmans have proven for over three years on eBay to be among the rarest comics of the last 50 years, and they continue to bring record prices, often for unslabbed copies. *Super Goof* #61 and *Winnie the Pooh* #22 are currently bringing $400 for mid-grade copies between a small number of buyers/sellers. These, along with *Daisy* #47, *Mickey* #208 and *BOP* #7, should all list at perhaps $120 each in the *Guide*. Once the rarity of 8-12/1980 Whitmans becomes more common knowledge and *Guide* price continue to rise, I expect more copies will surface and prices will settle into more realistic levels. *Lulu* #260 and *Scrooge* #179 remain the big two and should list in the $700+ range as those prices are now proven. *Donald Duck* #222 has cooled, but still needs to rise to $300+ in the *Guide*. *WDC&S* #480 should also list about 50% higher.

This rarity list was provided by top Whitman collector Andrew Rathburn. The rarest 8-12/1980 pre-pack only Whitmans, ranging from rarest to lesser scarcity issues, are as follows. With 10-50 copies of each issue currently known to exist: *Super Goof* #61, *Little Lulu* #260, *Tom and Jerry* #332, *Looney Tunes* #34, *Daffy Duck* #130, *Winnie the Pooh* #22, *Looney Tunes* #35, *Popeye* #158, *Woody Woodpecker* #190, 191, *Yosemite Sam* #70, *Chip and Dale* #69, *Beep Beep Road Runner* #93, *Pink Panther* #76, 77, *Tweety and Sylvester* #107, *Beep Beep Road Runner* #92, *Daisy and Donald* #47, *Mickey Mouse* #208, *Walt Disney's Comics and Stories* #480, *Battle of the Planets* #7, *Donald Duck* #222, and *Uncle Scrooge* #179. The rarest 1983-1984 no date, no date code issues ranging from rarest to lesser scarcity issues are as follows. With 50-200 copies of each issue currently known to exist: *Tweety and Sylvester* #118, *Woody Woodpecker* #199, 198, *Tweety and Sylvester* #117, *Popeye* #168, *Tweety and Sylvester* #119, *Beep Beep Road Runner* #103, 104, 102, *Popeye* #171, *Winnie the Pooh* #30, 31, 32, 29, 33. These 1983-1984 issues should guide for a minimum of $25, with top titles

– Disney duck, *Lulu*, etc. – and rarest titles closer to $50 each.

Whitman variants of Gold Keys 11/1971-2/1980 are possible and they sell to completionists for 150-300% of GK issue values. Collector Byron Glass has followed these for years and has determined that about 50% of all the possible issues do in fact exist as Whitmans, with many of the variants being quite rare. There are now about 170 known DC Whitman variants in 16 titles; all are scarce in VF or better. Completionists and variant collectors regularly pay $6-$15 for VG-VF copies. The treasury variants C-56 and C-61 are especially scarce and sell at 200-300% the regular edition prices.

This year we saw many sellers trying to pass off Whitman variants of Marvel comics. Some assume incorrectly that the early direct variants with black diamonds and no UPC codes must be Whitman variants. Take note: distributors were able to buy empty Whitman plastic bags and could fill them with random leftover comics and then heat seal them. This does not make them Whitman editions, but rather regular editions in Whitman bags. They carry no premium value except when sold to uniformed buyers. True Whitman variants must have the Whitman logo printed on the comic itself.

Harry B. Thomas

Overview: As healthy as it has ever been. It has been a great year for me on eBay and at the few shows I attend nowadays. I deal mostly in books from the Golden Age in the $35-500 range, none slabbed, and they have been as good to me this year as I ever remember. All grades have done exceptionally well. Some genres have faded but others have made great advances. The proliferation of the auction houses has not even begun to affect business down here in the trenches. Actually, I have yet to see the proof that slabbing and auctioneering have really had that big an effect on the hobby as a whole. They have their little slice of the market and we down here have the big slice of the pie. For all the hype and PR given out by the Powers That Be, the steady real sales continue with vim and vigor down here.

eBay is still the defining entity of the market and has been for some time now. Very few people in this hobby actually care what a 9.4 copy of *Action* #16 brought slabbed and sold at your favorite auction house. The anal retentives of grading, the "junkies" who live and die by grade, are thankfully a small but loud factor in our hobby. eBay puts it out there daily for all to see. As far as I have been able to see, slabbing has done very little for the hobby.

Dell: The reason I start with Dell is that they are consistently the best selling titles on eBay and at shows, maybe not the highest in value but certainly excellent sales potential. I never get stuck long with their books. They have the best product in terms of materials used – no better photo covers were ever done – writers and artists, and their titles were some of the most famous characters of the day.

Best sellers remain *Tarzan* – try to find a *Four Color* Tarzan #134 and 161. I had to bid on three listings of #134 to finally get a decent one on eBay, and I bid above *Guide* on all of them. Issues #1-12 with illustrated covers are tough to get and sell well. Every kid out there must have collected and kept *Roy Rogers* and *Gene Autry* as they are prolific in supply. I once saw six copies of *Roy Rogers* #1 for sale the same week on eBay. Both titles sell well in all grades but not at *Guide* unless it is a *Four Color*. *Little Lulu* remains hot and will always bring *Guide* in all grades, as will any Walt Disney book with Barks. All the *Four Color*s are collectible as there are many collectors of that series alone. The early issues with classic comic strip reprints are very hot. The two most sought-after of the late *Four Color* series are the two Andy Griffith issues. There is demand here that far, far outstrips the supply. I am not sure what high grade issues of these two books would bring, but certainly way above *Guide*.

Fawcett: All Fawcett titles sell well but at lower than *Guide* in most cases. *Captain Marvel, Whiz, Master*, and all the westerns sell well and are in high demand but rarely bring *Guide*. They sit on walls at shows because everyone knows they can get Fawcetts much cheaper on the Internet. Westerns have slowed down and will continue to do so as the base that remembers the characters pass on. The superheroes are still used by DC nowadays, but the cowboys are a thing of the past. The Fawcett movie adaptations of *Destination Moon, When Worlds Collide,* and especially *The Man From Planet X,* are very much in demand and in high grade will bring big bucks always.

EC: Gaines File Copies will bring as much unslabbed as slabbed. I see it on the Internet, I see it at shows – why slab something with this kind of reputation? Unslabbed books from Good to Fine always bring *Guide* for this legendary line of books. The horror titles are most sought after, then *MAD*, then the science fiction titles. However, all titles will not remain in stock very long.

DC: The most popular and famous of the Golden Age publishers, and all books in any grade with their superheroes bring decent prices. Of all their titles, however, the consistent best sellers remain *Action* and *Superman* from the Golden Age to the Silver Age. I have tracked them on the Internet, and the two titles almost always bring *Guide* or better when offered for sale and always bring multiple bids – more than the auction houses seem to get, I might add. *Batman* would be next, then *Detective* and the rest. The late Golden Age books from 1947 on are really sought after. The early Silver Age books bring decent money but are not nearly as popular as the Marvel Silver Age titles.

Timely/Marvel: It's hard to really put a value on the Timely books as they are so much in demand but there is so little product for sale. Without doubt, the Timely books always go high in any grade when offered for sale. No Golden Age company is represented with so few items on the Internet or at shows as is Timely. This is probably because collectors are not willing to sell or the company did not have that big a sell-through when they were publishing. *Captain America* remains the most popular of the Timely titles, very closely followed by the rest; *Marvel Mystery, Human Torch* and *Sub-Mariner*.

Marvel Silver Age books sell well, but not on the Internet. Rarely does a Silver Age book even approach *Guide* on the Internet, and slabbing does not help unless it is *AMZ* #1, *FF* #1, *AMZ Fantasy* #15 – you get the idea. Slabbing a Silver Age non-key below 9.4 or 9.2 will not help you one bit; check it out on eBay. You have probably paid more for the slabbing than you got for the book.

Going Up: Any Donald Duck *Four Color*, Tarzan *Four Color* #134 and 161, and *Tarzan* #1; Roy Rogers *Four Color* #34; *Action* and *Superman*, entire runs; *AMZ* #1 and *AMZ Fantasy* #15.

Going Down: For us, all the Fawcett western titles – the market is dying out, and they won't sell near *Guide* now. The same is true with Dell westerns and any other company that had them. There are some keys, however, that should not be changed here: the Ghost Rider issues both of his own title and the Tim Holt issues he is in; the Durango Kid issues with Frazetta art; and all the Frazetta western covers are still in demand.

Michael Tierney

The biggest news of 2004 was the failure of CrossGen. Before the collapse, CrossGen had ascended to being my third best-selling publisher. Their bankruptcy left a void on my shelves. CrossGen was a reliable publisher who understood that 'all ages comics' meant a comic that can be read by all ages, not a comic that has lowered its reading level to a younger audience. To lose a publisher who consistently supplied a high-quality product on time month in and year out is a blow to the entire industry. It also illustrates the difficulties that new publishers face.

A surprise for 2004 was the lack of effect from all the comics-related movies. Sales on *Hulk* were brisk until the movie debuted, then they hit the wall and dropped. While *Spider-Man 2* did increase awareness of comics, all the new customers it drew in were of grade school age. Once Marvel started making all ages material with the Marvel Age line, we had stuff to sell them, but before that, many parents were turned off by the PSR rating on all the other Marvel comics. Parents have been trained by the film industry to avoid exposing their children to anything with an 'R' in the rating.

The lack of new, older Spider-Man fans also reflects the problem in creating new *Star Wars* or *Star Trek* fans. For these heavily-saturated markets, new fans can't be made, they have to be born. If you're going to be a fan, it's likely that you already are.

Although no longer hot, Jim Lee's run on *Batman* is still holding its value. Azzarello's follow-up run on *Batman* never took off. Likewise, Azzarello's team-up with Jim Lee on *Superman*, while selling better than other recent issues, is still falling far short of Jim Lee's *Batman* numbers. Azzarello has a solid following on the crime noir title *100 Bullets*, but it doesn't seem to be translating into mainstream sales.

There were some brand-new series in 2004 that did see a good deal of success. DC had solid sellers with *Fables*, a contemporary reworking of childhood fairy tales, and *Y the Last Man*, which is a fulfillment of a juvenile fantasy about being the last available man in a world of women. A series that did very well with both established and lesser-known characters was *Identity Crisis*. While there were concerns over content that displayed violence to women, the story addressed the long-time superhero concern of protecting their families against reprisals by enemies. DC scored a huge hit by aggressively over-printing and then reprinting as news about the series spread. It's a great feeling as a retailer whenever a new customer enters or an old one returns and you can satisfy their demands.

Even with DC's over-printing policy, the print runs on modern comics are still ridiculously low when compared to books from the Silver Age. Circulation statements on the *Tarzan* comics from the early '60s regularly reported print runs in excess of 400,000 and 500,000. Print runs now average in the tens of thousands, with only a handful of major hits topping the 100,000 mark. Any titles made today, should they prove to have lasting power into the future, will be difficult to find. The old adage of supply and demand bodes well for future value. If you buy what you enjoy, you'll probably be ahead of the curve for collector demand.

Black and white comic magazines are a good example of strong demand that exceeds supply. *Vampirella, Creepy, Eerie, Savage Sword of Conan* and a host of other Marvel magazines like *Marvel Super Action*, which features a Punisher origin story, have all been in strong demand over the last few years. There is something very appealing to the eye about black and white artwork when accented with gray tones.

In the Silver and Golden Ages, as America's war on terrorism continues, war comics have been rebounding. *Sgt. Rock* has been hot. Western comics, on the other hand, are fading. Exceptions are series that featured still recognizable name stars like John Wayne and Annie Oakley.

2004 also saw the passing of long-time DC editor Julius Schwartz. Demand increased on his science fiction anthologies, *Strange Adventures* and *Tales of the Unexpected*, along with his weird tales anthologies, *House of Mystery* and *House of Secrets*. Values for all these were below *Guide*, especially on lower grades.

Many other areas of collector interest remained stable. Carl Barks' work on *Uncle Scrooge, Donald Duck*, and *Walt Disney's Comics and Stories* are undiminished in demand. *Classics Illustrated* and *Classic Comics* have also remained strong; in the last year we've sold a number of *Classic Comics* first printings. A mother once brought her daughter in and introduced her to *Classics Illustrated*, clearly explaining that these were the comics she used for cheating on book reports when she was her daughter's age – a tradition being passed on from one generation to the next!

What can I say? Comics hold something different for everyone.

Lon Webb
(Dark Adventure Comics)

Supply and demand is again the only consistent sales barometer in the 2004 marketplace. The principle of an item being worth only what someone is willing to pay for it has never been proven as true as in the current year. The demand for quality first tier collectible material in all investment areas has streamlined into such predictable patterns that items on many want lists are interchangeable. Supply is so short that prices hit record highs continuously while second and third tier interests rise steadily, creating growth in blooming tangent markets.

On the flipside, the marketplace has also been in a collecting flux for several years that is currently still playing out with the majority of material at hand cooling from the buyer's market created by the non-investment collector. Succinctly, buyers now fall almost by rote into the categories of deep pocket investor, window-shopping collector or tightly-budgeted reader with the spread on the continuum of monies spent among these three as wide as the distance between the price of Good and Near Mint in this *Guide.* And of course, everyone is playing dealer. The true wild cards are the buyers in mail order who silently defy all categorization.

Higher prices realized have brought many outstanding collections and prized material out into the marketplace to be snapped up by an anxious herd of investors and collectors while the lion's share of all printed comics languish in discounting, hoping to catch the flash in the eye of the collector or a CGC 9.8 for a momentary rescue from obscurity. The entire marketplace is as fickle and fee-ridden as eBay, but also as joyous as a good day on the trading floor or a good morning at a convention.

A thing to remember is that once upon a time everyone collected and bought comics because they loved them and the prices reflected that – a good book was in short supply so the prices naturally elevated. Strangely, this still holds true – the investor buys for the desired yearly percentages gained on paper, the collector out of almost obsessive-compulsive need, and the reader for the cheap thrill of it. The love of an item is again determining its overall worth. Investors cross over into the top one to three tiers of every age and ignore the rest while the budget collectors and readers form the prices on the bottom foundation market. One can argue this, but it is important to realize that investors and collector/investors supply 80% of the money in the marketplace for 20% of the books sold while budget collectors and readers supply 20% of the money for 80% of the books sold. What this means is that buyers each drive their own market segment and the dealer must drive his car to three different locations at the same time paying three different gas prices.

All is not lost in this era of love of money vs. love of possession vs. love of an art form. There is this *Guide,* chock full of the history and knowledge of graphic art in panels; there is you and your choices; and there are also all those comics with four color dreams glowing inside. There is something for everyone for today and tomorrow guaranteed. Pick your passion. Now on to the report.

Promotional Comics: These are so varied that there is truly something for everyone here. *Spirit* sections are the best kept secret, with high grades commanding many times *Guide*, especially for the tougher later volumes and the final classic Wally Wood issues. You can't go wrong with Eisner and Lou Fine. The full-size tabloid variants bring a huge premium. *March of Comics* titles are nice movers when they are popular characters or TV/movie tie-ins, and *Superman-Tims* are steady, though a niche. Let's not forget *Motion Picture Funnies Weekly* and *Is This Tomorrow?* No collection will ever be complete without a sweet stack of giveaways, so check out this section in the *Guide* and put at least five on your want list now.

Golden Age: A spastic and active giant. Key and iconic covers, issues and artists still drive the discerning collectors to distraction with an ever-dwindling supply in any grade. First appearance issues like *Detective* #27 and *More Fun* #52 lead the demand with more common fill-in issues of major title runs coming in second with Timely being our most popular. Obscure and artist-related titles bring up third place – the popularity of Schomburg, Everett, Cole and the cast of Golden Age greats always sell. It cannot be said enough that any grade hero titles sell if priced fairly and notable art or history within consistently raises the roof.

Having stated the obvious, there are many Golden Age books that have stalled, perhaps permanently, in sales anywhere near *Guide; Supersnipe* and the like head the pack. There is absolute waning interest in some titles, and I have noticed some genres, like westerns of the late '40s-'50s, falling severely by geographical region or age demographics – death of their true fans – of buyers. Crime and war still sell as a read over investment, and 'Good Girl' art and Disney will continue to sell in all forms and in upward prices. *Classics* are a small niche area but a worldwide niche market. The values on Golden Age material have narrowed the selling arena with all grades needed to the best of the best, widened it to include second and third-tier, but have almost killed substandard titles or companies with no important characters, artists or history and sent them to the bargain bins.

The truth is that Golden Age always sells, but a lot of these books sell at a fair discount and not grade specific. In today's market, value for the bigger money is keen. and we will see a lot of this type of material sit until it walks while iconic issues continue to stand and run. Hero memorabilia, especially Superman, is strong and actively sought.

Atom Age: There will never be enough '50s material to ever fill the demand. We quickly sell through all issues in any grade from this time period with the exception of higher priced mid-grade one-shots or genre markets that are slightly slow. All horror titles are still in high demand, along with most of the superhero titles in any and all grades. If there is ever a cover guide photo reference released for the '50s, DC and Atlas will see an explosion that will startle everyone as many collectors will actively hunt for scarce covers on issues that barely exist in even mid-grade.

Gaines file copies are commanding extravagant prices and EC horror in high grades are still following suit to fill in the demand, six years in a row now. ECs continue to be the blue chip Atom books behind key superhero issues. Lower interest genres such as crime and war sell well to a thriving reader market, mainly because of the exploitative content, and westerns are the main genre beginning to show a bottom while funny animal is consistent with Harvey humor rapidly escalating. Men's and science fiction pulps and magazines from this period are swiftly rising in value as notable comic artist content – Frazetta, Ward, etc. – are being popularized along with exploitation material and relatively unknown stories by writers such as Louis L'Amour and early sci-fi material. All memorabilia from this period is scarce and hot.

Silver Age: Boom and bust. High grade key issues are the market's forefront, with high grade fill-in superhero issues making the solid foundation. Marvel is king and DC the prince. There are so many keys that this Age is a varied and deeply sown goldmine. Harvey comics such as *Richie Rich, Hot Stuff, Little Dot* and *Lotta*, etc. are moving up to the interest level of superhero comics, and high grades – especially file copies – are commanding multiples with key issues in any grade selling well above *Guide*. As a matter of fact, a low to mid-grade Harvey key sells at a higher rate above *Guide* than a high grade Marvel or DC key by percentage. Gold Key & Dell, especially photo covers and TV tie-ins, are showing impressive movement in high grades for 2004. Disney, Archie, Warren and Tower are also showing strong demand.

The downside to the Silver market is mid-grade, which is aggressively discounted because of the buyer's perception of depreciative value below 9.0 and the commonality of most Silver Age issues. Readers buy up the cheaper, solid copy low grades because of the more affordable *Guide* spread and are happy to do it rather than spending many times that for a mid-grade. Third tier Marvel and DC titles like *Sea Devils, Sgt. Fury*, etc. are increasingly tougher to sell in any grade other than top-end investment grade or super-cheap low-end. Due to the excessive amount of lower grade Silver at this current time, it's a reader's market, much harsher than just a buyer's market.

Marvel fan club items are soaring and showing another leap in value, especially material having its original mailing envelope. Early fanzines are continuing to spread interest and as ever, are very difficult to locate. If these were more readily available and had a definitive reference book, we would see an even higher increase in demand. One of the coolest fan-related items I have ever seen is an unused promotional postcard I obtained from Julie Schwartz that was sent to *Showcase* letter writers advertising the soon-to-be published first issue of *Green Lantern*. It has nice Gil Kane art and I would never have known it even existed without Julie's knowledge, so a definitive fan-related and fanzine reference is sorely needed while the information can be obtained from still-living participants. For a Silver fan, that postcard rivals the coolness factor of the button National did to promote Wonder Woman in *Sensation Comics* for the early Golden Age fan.

Bronze Age: This is the era for the current crop of active reader/collectors. We sell far more reader copies of Bronze than any other era's books, both because of the lower prices and the fact that many of the current comic buyers and investors grew up during this time period, with the Silver boomers coming a close first. It took a while for the market to grow and even longer to gain any kind of momentum, but now it contains some of the most solid collectible issues with the most to gain in the long haul. *Hulk* #181, *New X-Men,* and *100 Page Spectaculars* are tops and the list grows longer as more people realize the characters introduced during this period are durable and many of this era's issues are extremely difficult to find in high-end grade, especially considering the commonality of most issues of this era.

©DC

DC 100 Page Super Spectaculars *are among the tops of the Bronze Age. (#17 shown)*

For mainstream comics, it's a high-end investment club and the rest of it is a reader's market. The only deviations are the key and scarce top 40 issues, and of course, those pesky three-pack-only Gold Key/Whitmans and price variant Marvels, which sell in all grades with some incredibly tough to locate. As more information is obtained about the three-pack-only and low print run later Gold Key/Whitmans, this market tangent will grow rapidly. *Uncle Scrooge* #179 is not the only rare book – there is way over a dozen others, perhaps more. I won't even go into the variations of the later run issues with no price, with price but no ads, etc., and how about the back cover variations?

Moving to the left are the Bronze Harveys, Archies and Disneys, which are the silent constant sellers. The digests of this period are moving – Marvel, DC, Harvey, Archie – as are the larger format Treasury Editions, though there is price resistance to Treasuries in high-end until CGC begins grading them. The *Rudolph* no number (C-20 implied) treasury is a rare gem and a must-have, and at any given time there is not even one for sale anywhere, whereas there is always an *Action* #1 or *Hulk* #181 on the market. For rarity, the DC in-house produced *Cancelled Comic Cavalcade* holds the distinction as the rarest of the rare – only 35 of these. We've only seen three and bought them all, with one verified by Vince Colletta as his personal copy set sold for over $2600. If you see a set for sale, buy it, because it is the ultimate Bronze item rather than the fluke.

Magazines are beginning to come into their own, as titles such as *Vampirella, Monsters Unleashed* and the rest of the Warren and Marvel line show rapid movement in *Guide* multiples for high-end grades and constant sales in the reader conditions at fair prices, though mid-grades are tough to sell at *Guide*. Superhero memorabilia is either a prize – Marvel black-lights – or an albatross – hero puffy stickers – due to the vast amount produced, and this era is a true blessing for all the strange and wonderful books, posters and cultural items produced that can keep one looking for another ten years.

Copper & Modern Age: There is a wealth of material here for the casual reader or investor, and these Ages contain some of the most literate and entertaining comics done to date. Some independent press books of note include *Teenage Mutant Ninja Turtles* #1 and the rarer precursor, *Gobbledygook* #1, *Cerebus* #1-30, early *Elfquest, Elflord* #1, the first couple of *Crow* issues, *Grendel* (especially *Comico Primer* #2 and the Comico series), *Love & Rockets* #1-20 and early *Flaming Carrot* (including the oversize #1, #2-16 and early appearances in *Visions* magazine). *Miracleman* #15 sells for way over *Guide* in any grade and is genuinely tough to locate along with the last issues of *Grendel*. Many Marvel last issues of the '80s are also on the move (*Conan* #275, *Sgt. Fury*, etc.) because of their low print runs.

Valiants have made a minor comeback and the scarcer issues are beginning to show force again along with the later issue numbers in the runs. The modern market is loaded with small press run issues from independent companies, and in the last few years, even Marvel and DC are printing ever fewer copies. I feel all the variants from the last decade have a long way to go before or if ever they approach investment status, but many people still avidly search them out. There is also a ton of one-shot and mini-series titles put out by the big two that are worth locating because of their interest and obscurity, like *Droids* and some giant movie issues. Attempt to find the two Blackthorne *Star Wars* 3-D issues – try to complete a run of Blackthorne 3-D issues and you'll go nuts – and you'll appreciate dealers.

The Gold Key/Whitman market is skyrocketing as the later issue print runs dwindled before the company rolled over. Dark Horse and other companies also have many books of note like *Hellboy*. One great market facet is the nice amount of hardcover editions produced that are truly collectible. *Miracleman* Book 1-4 are hot, commanding astronomical prices, as is the S/Ltd *Dark Knight, Elfquest,* and *Mage* limited editions. There are a wealth in futures here. There is so much memorabilia and promotional material tied to this market that it is a 'pick your poison' cornucopia.

eBay: The illegitimate son of car dealers? No, just what a world of sellers have made it – the end result of unschooled capitalism. What was once a collector's dream site has turned into the largest Third World garage sale of all time with a scant U.N. protectorate. We have noted that the truly scarce sells well, particularly fan-related merchandise and memorabilia. Third party graded comics were ready-made for this market and it is an excellent venue for buying or selling them, as what resembles truth enters into the auction descriptions on grade. Record prices are realized here for quality high grade slabbed comics. eBay is a wonderful area to find the unique, but be aware you can't trust the item descriptions of everyone selling there. There is a large amount of counterfeited and bootlegged memorabilia, especially Marvelmania items, so be prepared with knowledge before you search and bid. The downsides for sellers are the steadily rising fees with little in-house support and the garage sale mentality of the semi-anonymous community. The upside is that everything cool hits eBay once.

CGC & CGG: The market for third-party graded comics and comic-related material is as hot as ever. High-end Marvels lead the pack, with multiples of *Guide* routinely changing hands for the best of the best. Arguments abound on the concept of CGC-slabbed books to this day, but it is the needed future of mail order, online and sight-unseen sales, regardless of where one stands on the perception. The CGC census is helpful in determining scarcity and investment strategy, and the service, though flawed at times, is a must. There is some minor competition to CGC in the form of a new company, CGG, who offers a fine encapsulation holder and very conservative grading, but they must expand and become a competitive market force to be taken seriously across the board by collectors and investors.

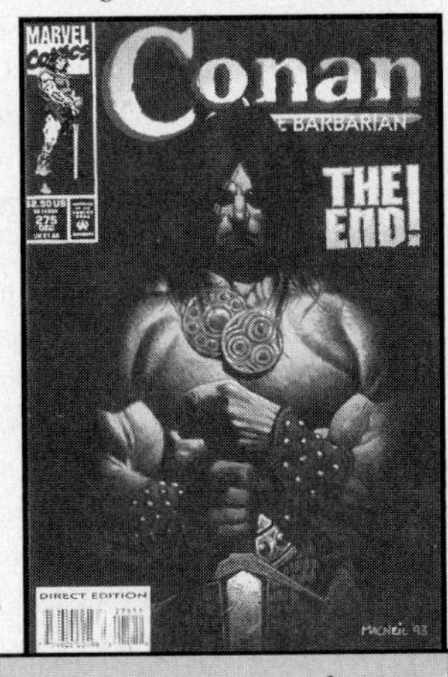

Marvel last issues from the '80s like **Conan the Barbarian** #275 are on the move.

With the cost of encapsulation and the proven demand on certain issues, we recommend all key, pricier and mid- to high grade Golden Age for the service along with all high grade Silver, especially Marvel and DC. In the Bronze Age we would suggest encapsulating only top 10 key issues in any grade and otherwise only extremely high grade issues. In Modern, we would say only key issues in extremely high grade to warrant the cost of the service. There is a market slowdown on general highly graded material from the last 20 years; one should do a closed auction eBay search from time to time to study the particulars of this market. Bear in mind that encapsulation is one of the best ways to preserve your comics.

Conventions: These are still gathering places for the comic lovers, but they have morphed into quite a different animal than the great shows of yesteryear. Nowhere is the split among buyers so evident than at a convention. We sell high-end investment material both encapsulated and unslabbed to one market segment and everything else is a hobbyist crapshoot. There is less disposable income in the dealer's room from the common fan due to show-related expenses, autograph fees and the like. Many attend just for freebies, socializing and the thrill of the venue. Impulse sales are rampant and I have seen more 50% off signs than ever before on more types of material than in the past. I find that if we balance our stock between high grade investment items and low-end hobby material, we do well – it's the in-between that kills. I suspect serious collectors pick one or two of the major shows to attend each year or just stay home and hit a dealer's catalog or go online while the bargain hunters roam the con aisles. Still, there is nothing like a convention for the hobby to be in one's face, and we've had an excellent show year.

Memorabilia and Weird Stuff: Anyone that knows us knows we love the mainstream, but we love the obscure even more. I would recommend looking for English-made *Triumph* magazines from the late '30s for the first British Superman appearances, printed just after the US comics and utilizing the same original artwork. One of those short comics sections may just be the closest you'll come to owning that *Action* #1, and it's from the same year of publication. There are also several *Family Circle* mags that contain articles on Superman and DC and contain art by early DC creators. For a special ride, leaf through *Esquire* magazines from 1968 – I won't tell you the month for the pleasure of the search – and find the great Jack Kirby JFK assassination comic story therein. Lastly, find that great *Movie Mirror* issue from the late '30s that has the first Disney Snow White appearance anywhere and marvel at that full color cover and interior insert.

More well-known is the pulp *Marvel Science Stories* with the super-early Kirby artwork and the rare Superman '40s comic puzzles, and even the *Radiocraft* mags of the wartime '40s that have those gorgeous painted Alex Schomburg normal scale war covers. As a final note, locate some '30s *Ken Magazines* and be pleasantly surprised at the comics and cultural oddities you'll find in some. Oh, and who painted those covers for *Mechanix Illustrated*?

Marvelmania items are probably the hottest '60s memorabilia around. The set of eight posters continually set price records in NM condition, mainly because of the fragile and thin paper they were printed on. The mail-away six foot wall posters of Spider-Man and the Hulk are the rarest Marvel posters and command high grade prices approaching a grand each. The 1971 black-light posters are a mixed bag, as five (we've had a couple dozen of the 2 Hulks, 2 Dr. Strange and Namor) of the 24 styles are almost common, while a full half of them are truly scarce. Speaking of scarce, try to locate the DC series of black-light posters from the same time that feature Superman, Aquaman, Hawkman and others, rendered in blown-up panel style, or the late '60s 45 rpm records that have great illustrated DC character covers with character songs, the rarest being Metamorpho.

The wealth of character memorabilia and limited supply of the truly classic makes this market a must-have add-on for investors, collectors and comic enthusiasts everywhere. In closing, we are always interested in any information on the obscure, so look us up in this *Guide* and drop us a line, especially if you know Millie the Model's last name – that's our secret password.

Vincent Zurzolo (Metropolis Comics)

The first quarter of 2004 was the best quarter Metropolis has had during my tenure as COO over the last five years. In fact, quarters 2-4 were exceptionally strong as well. The beginning of the year started where 2003 left off with very high demand on Silver Age Marvel keys. However, 2004 has seen its share of sales running the gamut from every decade of comic history. Sales were heavy on pedigrees from every era, Golden Age keys as well as non-key issues, 1950s comics, Silver, Bronze and the few Modern Age comics we sold. Grades also ranged very heavily with the only weak spots being mid-grade Golden and Silver Age comics; they are not priced cheap enough for collectors and do not hit the grade requirements for investors. Unlike previous years, this end of the market was not super slow; it just lagged behind the other grades. While not a huge surprise, later Disneys, most westerns, and *Classics* did not fare very well either.

Golden Age: Red hot this past year. Not unlike 2003, I was able to move many keys. In 2004, I sold three copies of *Detective* #27 ranging in grade from 2.5, 3.5 CGC and a raw, restored copy in 6.0. *Batman* #1s also moved well; I sold five copies of this perennial favorite, including the highest graded copy, a CGC graded 9.0 unrestored, a CGC graded 4.0, and three restored copies. I sold three copies of *Superman* #1, a FN- and two FR/GD copies, as well as a restored copy of *Action* #1 and an unrestored copy of *Marvel Comics* #1. My company is capable of achieving these types of sales due to our rock-solid reputation as an industry leader with over 40 years of experience combined, a vast

Detective Comics *#27 is selling well in lower grades.*

inventory of vintage comic books, a state of the art website and an intricate network of customer relationships allowing us to find and sell even the rarest comic book.

In general, *Pep Comics* sold very well; one sale in particular is quite memorable as a savvy, long time customer picked up a run from #1-34 in low grade. Other strong sellers were *Action, Batman, Captain America, Leading, Detectives, Young Allies* and *Archie Comics*. Sales included *All Star Comics* #8 CGC 7.5 VF- $19,500, *Batman* #9 CGC 9.4 NM $16,800, #11 CGC 9.0 VF/NM $9,250, *Captain America* #7 CGC 9.4 NM $16,000, *Catman* #1 CGC 9.4 NM Denver Copy $12,980, *Detective* #168 CGC 9.2 NM- $11,500, *Superworld* #1 VF++ $7,500 and a *Vault of Horror* #12 CGC 9.4 NM Northford Copy $27,500.

Silver Age: Although many people associate Metropolis with Golden Age, we do have the largest selection of low, mid- and high grade Silver Age comics on the market. Silver Age Marvel keys were fast movers the entire year. However, toward the end of 2004, they began to plateau; I expect this trend to continue into early 2005 until the new *Guide* you are holding in your hands debuts. Afterward, I expect many of the Marvels to continue to increase in value, although at a slower pace.

Spider-Man, the most popular character in the Marvel pantheon, is also the most highly collected title, making up almost 20% of CGC submissions. In April of 2004, I sold the Ohio Copy of *Amazing Fantasy* #15 CGC graded VF+ 8.5 for a record-breaking $29,500 and a few days later an *Amazing Spider-Man* #1 CGC graded NM- 9.2 for a record-breaking $33,000. A few weeks later, I sold an *Incredible Hulk* #1 CGC VF+ 8.5 for a record-breaking $31,000. Other record-breaking Silver Age Marvel sales included *Amazing Spider-Man* #3 CGC 9.4 NM $20,000, #16 CGC 9.6 NM+ $11,000, *Fantastic Four* #3 CGC 9.2 NM- $14,600, #12 CGC 9.4 NM $22,000, *Journey into Mystery* #83 CGC 9.0 VF/NM $18,500, *Tales of Suspense* #39 CGC 9.2 NM- $18,000, and *X-Men* #4 CGC 9.0 VF/NM $1,350.

© MAR

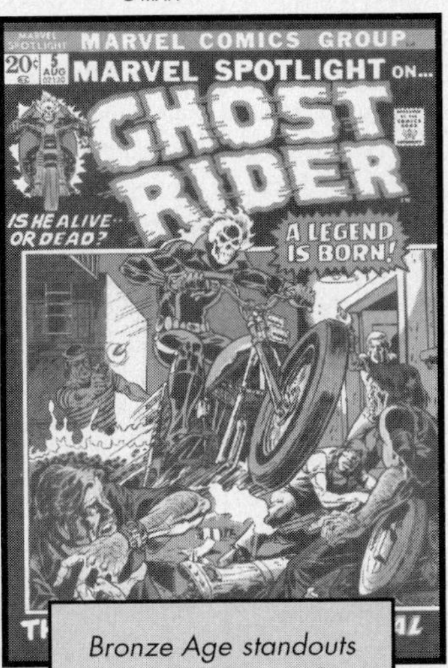

Bronze Age standouts include **Marvel Spotlight** #5, the debut of Ghost Rider.

DC Silver Age comics are scarcer than their Marvel counterparts yet more affordable. 2004 witnessed several record prices realized for DC keys, but I still believe everything goes in cycles and it is only a matter of time until DCs hit the same multiple levels as their Marvel counterparts. This may occur when DC launches its new superhero movies. With *Batman Begins* premiering this summer and *Superman* moving into pre-production, now might be the right time to purchase certain keys.

The Gold Key market is moving; this is the first year since the early '90s that I am seeing a very noticeable increase in demand for Gold Key titles. *Green Hornet, Doctor Solar, Magnus* and *Star Trek* are titles in which I have noticed the most interest. Grades desired vary from collector to collector, but I believe a lot of this has to do with the moderate pricing on these books even in high grade.

Bronze Age: The big three of the Bronze Age – *X-Men* #94, *Hulk* #181 and *Giant Size X-Men* #1 – are still doing well, but prices have leveled. Standouts from this time period are *Ghost Rider* #1, *Marvel Spotlight* #5, *Hero For Hire* #1, *Tomb of Dracula* #1 and #10, *Green Lantern* #76, *Batman* #232 and *Detective* #400.

I was very fortunate to purchase a large collection of Charlton comics this past year. It was quite a fun experience for me as there were many covers and titles I was not intimately familiar with. Some of the art was mediocre, but there were many downright impressive covers with interior art to match. Check out great art by Ditko, Sutton, Wood, Newton, Aparo, Staton, Montes, Giordano, Larson, Howard, Bache, Morisi and Glanzman on comics like *Haunted, Green Planet, Ghostly Haunts, Fightin' Air Force, Army Attack, Hot Rods and Racing Cars, Love Diary, Magilla Gorilla, Outer Space, Out of this World, Konga, Gorgo, Quick Draw McGraw, Teen-Age Love, Ghost Manor, Haunted Love* and *Blue Beetle*. My favorite cover is *Ghostly Haunts* #41 by Sutton – anybody know where this cover is?

Modern Age: I still love buying and reading new comic books. My favorite shop in NYC is Cosmic Comics, followed closely by Forbidden Planet. Both stores are situated near my gallery, well stocked, well lit and fun to hang out in. Many storeowners I have spoken to told me they have had a stellar year. This is extremely reassuring, as I do believe there is a connection between readers of new comics and collectors and investors of vintage comics.

My favorite comic book series this year were the *Loki* mini-series by writer Robert Rodi and painter extraordinaire Essad Ribic, and Kurt Busiek and Cary Nord's *Conan*. Ribic captures the visceral nature of Frazetta while infusing the lighting dynamics of Ross, bringing to life an Asgardian tale seldom seen. *Loki* is truly one of the prettiest painted books of the year. On *Conan*, Busiek masterfully spins tales of a young Conan, and Nord brings them to life in an exciting and pulse-pounding manner. The digital color enhances Nord's strong pencils, creating an almost oil painted effect that is visually captivating.

Avengers Disassembled, Marvel Knights *Spider-Man, Hard Time, Walking Dead, Books of Magic: Life During Wartime, Ultimates II, Secret War, Wanted, Superman/Batman, Identity Crisis, Astonishing X-Men* and *Ultimate Fantastic Four* were just several of the truly exceptional comics I had the opportunity to read. I must also mention I was dazzled by every cover Michael Turner rendered for DC this year.

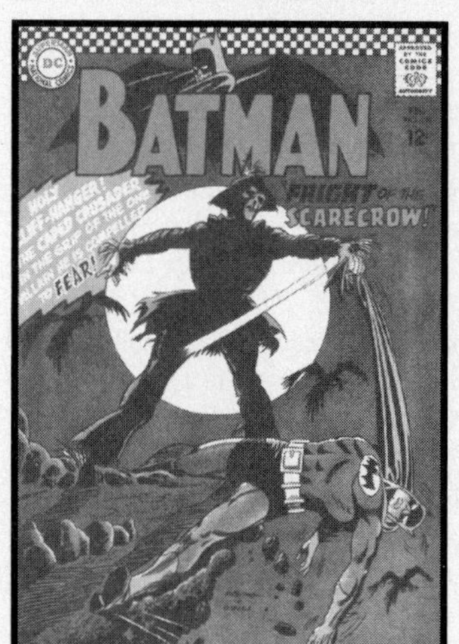

The Scarecrow comes to the big screen this summer in Batman Begins. (His Silver Age debut in **Batman** #189 shown)

© DC

As far as collecting goes, there are many really great comics being produced; read as many as you can. However, Modern Age investors must be very careful. Even with CGC's added value, sometimes buying a Modern book at the heights of its popularity can be a bad idea, as many can simply be the flavor of the month. *Ultimate Spider-Man*, however, is a tremendous exception to the rule; I still cannot believe the prices this book is trading at on a regular basis. Colossuscomics.com offers a very intriguing service for those of you who want a 9.8 CGC graded copy as well as a raw copy to read; check it out at their site.

Edgar Church/Mile High: 2004 was the year of Mile High madness. Over the last three years, I have made it a personal quest to amass a massive stockpile of Golden Age from the Edgar Church/Mile High Collection. This collection of approximately 20,000 Golden Age comics in ultra-high grade with exceptional page quality is the finest collection of comics ever known to exist. In most cases the copies I purchased were either the highest graded copies known or close to it. I always tell my customers there are comics, and then there are Mile Highs. Church copies that found their way into collectors' hands this past year include issues from these runs: *Blue Bolt, Detective, Exotic Romances, Fight, Girls in Love, Heroic, Jumbo, Jungle, Military, More Fun, Romantic Hearts, Smash, Speed, Terry Toons, Weird, Wings* and *Wow Comics*. Grades ranged from VF+ to NM/MT with multiples of 3-10x *Guide* realized depending on titles and conditions. If you collect Golden Age and you don't have a Church copy, you don't know what you are missing.

Movie-Related Comics: The upcoming *Fantastic Four* and *Batman Begins* movies will be premiering this summer. I truly expect an increase in interest in both titles. *FF* will have to be a really good movie, as the general public will make comparisons with the Pixar blockbuster, *The Incredibles*. *Fantastic Four*, already very popular amongst collectors and investors alike, will see increased demand on key issues and first appearances as the premiere date gets closer. In fact, at the time of this writing, I am down to my last two copies of *FF* #1; I usually have 5-10 copies in stock.

I have been screaming for years that Ra's al Ghul should be the villain of a Batman movie, and I think someone in Hollywood heard me. Only one problem – as with the previous three Batman movies, the powers that be seem to think one great villain is not enough, so they had to throw in the Scarecrow too. Now don't get me wrong, I think the Scarecrow is a cool villain, but unnecessary when you have such an iconic villain like Ra's al Ghul. Regardless, watch as there is a surge in demand for the first appearance of Ra's al Ghul (*Batman* #232) and Scarecrow (GA first appearance in *World's Finest* #3 and SA first appearance in *Batman* #189). The hype for this movie will not reach the heights of the 1989 Tim Burton/Jack Nicholson/Michael Keaton Classic, but it will be hot.

Conventions: The Metropolis convention circuit for 2004 was very rewarding and productive. The cons were not only successful for selling but also for buying. The highlight as usual was the San Diego Comic Convention, but the most exciting show of the year had to be the National Comic Convention in New York City; there was an energy in the room I have not felt in years at a convention. There were tons of great books on the dealer floor, as about a half dozen dealers had purchased brand new collections in the previous few weeks leading up to the National. I was pleased as punch to make several great purchases as well as sales. The coolest part of the convention had to be Frank Miller interviewing Neal Adams for over an hour and a half. There was also a very funny moment when a group of fans dressed up like *Star Wars* stormtroopers made their way out onto 7th Ave. across from the Garden and attempted to keep order with the huge line of fans trying to get into the con. It is really great to see the show Mike Carbonaro and I started in 1997 grow into what it is today. Keep up the great work, Carbo!

I am also impressed with the way *Wizard* shows keep sprouting up all over the country. Gareb Shamus and his staff started with the Chicago Con and have expanded to Philadelphia, Dallas/Ft. Worth, Long Beach (CA) and Boston. The shows have something for everybody, with a great line up of celebrities, super star artists and writers and of course a dealer line-up any promoter would die to have.

I am not trying to take anything away from conventions, but it does seem they continue to be less important for those collectors and investors trying to find really scarce or high grade books. Most really great comics are sold to want list customers over the phone or through the Internet. However, the one thing you can't beat by going to a con is actually being able to inspect each and every nook and cranny – love that term; thanks, Thomas' English Muffins – of a comic.

The Comic Zone: Every collector and investor should educate themselves and enjoy what they are doing. Over the last year I have hosted a radio show about comic books and pop culture on the Internet called *The Comic Zone*. Every Monday from 3-4pm EST, *The Comic Zone* is broadcast live onto your computer. I believe the show can be a valuable tool to better educate yourself about the state of the marketplace, learn about current trends, the history of our hobby, and of course to listen to creators from the past and the present. The show attracts thousands of listeners per week. The beauty of the show is that not only can people listen to it live, but in case you miss the live broadcast, every show can be listened to in the archives section. The live shows and the archives can be accessed by going to www.metropoliscomics.com and clicking on *The Comic Zone* icon at the top of the home page.

Past guests have included a veritable list of the who's who of the comic world including Stan Lee, Will Eisner, Neal Adams, Jim Steranko, John Byrne, Terry Austin, George Pérez, Gene Colan, John Romita Sr., Sal Buscema, Dick Ayers, Joe Kubert, Murphy Anderson, Irwin Hasen, Al Feldstein, Jack Kamen, Jack Davis, Alex Ross, Todd McFarlane, Mike Mignola, Billy Tucci, Erik Larsen, John Romita Jr., Howard Chaykin, Jim Starlin, James O'Barr, Jae Lee, Arthur Adams, Buzz, Darrick Robertson, Eric Shanower, Sean Chen, Mark Bagley, Walt Simonson, Marshall Rogers, Mark Bode, Frank Cho, Mike Mignola, Ron Garney, Howard Porter, Norm Breyfogle, Larry Hama, John Jackson Miller, writers Denny O'Neil, JC Vaughn, Danny Fingeroth, Brian Pulido, Roy Thomas, Jim Shooter, Peter David, Mike San Giacomo, sculptor Randy Bowen, comic historians Arlen Schumer and Jerry Weist, *Batman Dead End* director Sandy Collora, actors David Carradine and Thomas Jane, writer/director David Mandel (*Seinfeld, Euro Trip*), Producer Danny Simmons (*Def Poetry Jam*), Diamond Galleries President John Snyder, CGC President Steve Borock, CGC graders Mark Haspel and Paul Litch, restoration experts Matt Nelson and Susan Cicconi and GP Analysis President George Pantela. You can listen to all of these interviews and more for free on *The Comic Zone*.

Promoting the Hobby: Metropolis and the comic book market received a great deal of media attention during the course of the last year in financial publications and news services such as *Forbes Magazine, Barrons, Bloomberg, Institutional Investor*, Reuters, *CBS MarketWatch and Yahoo! Finance*, as well as traditional venues like *USA Today, The Chicago Tribune, The Seattle Times*, The Travel Channel, Bravo, MTV, ABC and CBS. Tie this in with the advent and overwhelming acceptance of CGC third party grading over the last five years, and the road is being paved for the comic book hobby to be a tremendous collectible investment market, though still in its infancy.

The Future: While my wife will not allow me to use her crystal ball, I will tell you this about the future – for collectors, the sky's the limit. There will continue to be great deals offered on low and mid-grade comics from the Golden, Silver and Bronze Age. On my website alone, there are over 39,000 discounted vintage comic books as well as thousands of group lot items at up to 50% off. For the avid investors I would advise you to look into certain segments of the comic market that are under-priced compared to others. Sure, it is still great to invest in high grade Silver Age Marvels and Timelys, but you don't need me to tell you that. Areas I would look into are less expensive Golden Age titles like *Captain Marvel Jr., Red Dragon, Ghost Rider, Green Lama, America's Best Comics, Exciting Comics, King Comics, Popular Comics* and *Target Comics*. Of particular note are MLJ Magazines (named after the founders Maurice Coyne, Louis Silberkleit and John Goldwater) titles like *Blue Ribbon, Pep, Top Notch, Archie* and *Zip Comics*. Not every issue in these runs is cheap but plenty of them are. Pick up a Gerber Photo-Journal and study it like you were getting ready for the SATs; you will find a multitude of comics with dynamic and incredible covers.

Another area I would invest in is high grade Bronze Age like any Archie title, Marvel, DC or Charlton super-hero, horror or war title. These comics are so cheap, even with the augmented values achieved by CGC graded copies. Remember these same titles were a fraction of the price just a few years ago. Even at their current values, a serious investor could put entire runs, a first issue or even a classic cover collection together without draining their bank accounts and having their spouses ready to throw them out the window.

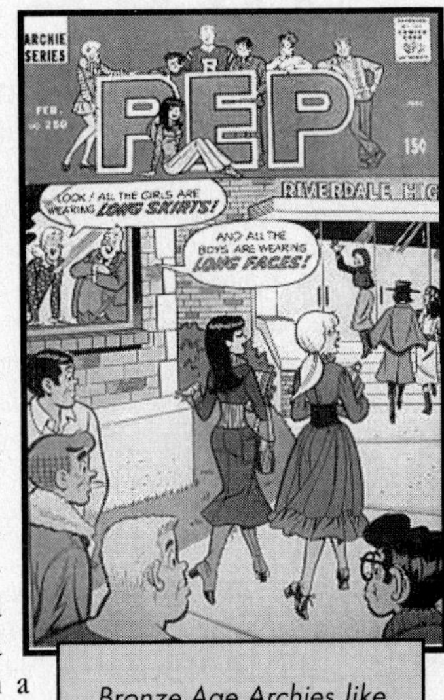

© AP

Bronze Age Archies like **Pep Comics #250** are attracting investors.

On the Harvey front, titles like *Hot Stuff, Casper, Dotty Dripple, Little Dot, Wendy the Witch, Little Lotta, Little Max, Little Audrey, Spooky*, and everybody's favorite poor little rich boy, *Richie Rich*, are in high demand. These issues are scarce and cheap in the *Guide*. Simply put, they have great upside investment potential.

With every movie made, and every article written in a newspaper, comic books draw themselves closer and closer into the mainstream consciousness as collectible and investment items. Furthermore, the general public doesn't see comic collecting solely as a hobby. Each and every day, more collectors are coming into the market seeking comic books as an investment vehicle for their finances. Do your research, find several titles you like, a dealer you trust, and get started.

Final Note: As I grow older, I have come to appreciate how much I have been blessed with. From my wife, family and friends, to my career, I really have a lot to feel good about and be grateful for. I thank all of you who have helped to make my life so fulfilling both personally and professionally. I wish you the best and hope 2005 is as good to you as 2004 was to me.

Market Comparison by Metropolis Collectibles

THE METROPOLIS INDEX

	1995	2005	CAGR	Total Return
DOW JONES IND. AVG.	3834.44	10783.01	13.09%	242.71%
METROPOLIS INDEX	$ 832,086	$ 2,835,600	13.04%	240.78%

* DJIA CAGR & Total Return assume dividends reinvested into the index, increasing the total return above simple price appreciation.

Due to the overwhelming response to **The Metropolis Index** in last year's 34th Edition (page 103), **Metropolis Collectibles** is proud to present this year's analysis. The Metropolis Index is a portfolio of 30 "blue-chip" vintage comics. Comics are selected based upon goodstanding reputation, sustainable growth and collector-driven demand. The index is diversified across a large number of comic industry market sectors, including superhero, humor, crime, horror and funny animal. Research is compiled using publicly available stock market data, and current and historical comic valuations as compiled by **Gemstone Publishing**.

While the rising values of vintage comics are known by hobbyists, it is only recently that they began to garner respect as credible investments by those outside the industry. The **"origin story"** of the index is a humble one. In late 2002, Metropolis' **Ben Smith** became intrigued by conversations heard over his cubicle wall in the dealership's NYC showroom. Some of Metropolis' clientele complained of stock market losses, and sought to increase their portfolio's diversification to include comics as a "safe equity." On a whim, Smith hypothesized that comics were emerging as "counter-cyclical" investments sought in times of a depressed economy. In conducting research, he found that comic investments thrived not only during times of economic downturn, but also demonstrated steady and stable growth over the long term.

Subequently, countless articles in financial publications and mainstream press have and continue to be published on the subject. In 2003, Metropolis' CEO **Stephen Fishler** and **Ben Smith** were asked by Bloomberg to conduct a seminar, and have been invited to present a follow-up study in 2005. Metropolis COO **Vincent Zurzolo** continues to be a comic book collecting and investing advocate, bringing new collectors into the fold each year.

On January 1, 2005, the **DJIA** stood at **10783.01.** Ten years prior in 1995, the **DJIA** was **3834.44.** If dividends paid are considered to have been reinvested into the index, an investor's **Total Return** was **242.71%**; implying a **Compound Annual Growth Rate (CAGR)** of **13.09%** over the 10 year period. Comparatively, the **Metropolis Index** total value in 1995 was **$832,086**, and is **$2,835,600** in 2005. The Total Return of the Metropolis Index is **13.04%** with a **CAGR** of **240.78%**.

Although numerous factors make an apples-to-apples comparison of comic books and stocks a difficult proposition, evidence lends itself to the long-term stability of the comic book market, and the security of comic book investments. Additional information can be found in the Press Section of **www.metropoliscomics.com**. Serious investors interested in consultation should contact **Vincent Zurzolo** of **Metropolis Collectibles** at **212.260.4147** or email **vincentz@metropolisent.com.**

THE METROPOLIS INDEX	30 Handpicked Blue Chip Comics		
	1995 9.2 NM-	2005 9.2 NM-	CAGR
ACTION COMICS #1	$ 118,750	$ 485,000	15.11%
ALL AMERICAN COMICS #16	$ 49,400	$ 180,000	13.80%
ALL STAR COMICS #3	$ 23,750	$ 60,000	9.71%
AMAZING FANTASY #15	$ 20,743	$ 42,500	7.44%
AMAZING SPIDER-MAN #1	$ 13,671	$ 32,500	9.05%
BATMAN #1	$ 39,900	$ 140,000	13.37%
BRAVE AND THE BOLD #28	$ 3,123	$ 8,800	10.91%
CAPTAIN AMERICA COMICS #1	$ 42,750	$ 140,000	12.60%
DETECTIVE COMICS #1*	$ 36,000	$ 60,000	5.24%
DETECTIVE COMICS #27	$ 109,250	$ 410,000	14.14%
FANTASTIC FOUR #1	$ 12,304	$ 35,000	11.02%
FLASH COMICS #1	$ 30,400	$ 110,000	13.72%
GIANT-SIZE X-MEN #1	$ 235	$ 1,100	16.68%
INCREDIBLE HULK #1	$ 8,045	$ 25,000	12.01%
INCREDIBLE HULK #181	$ 254	$ 1,300	17.73%
JOURNEY INTO MYSTERY #83	$ 2,803	$ 10,000	13.56%
MAD #1	$ 3,012	$ 6,700	8.32%
MARVEL COMICS #1	$ 80,952	$ 365,000	16.25%
MORE FUN COMICS #52	$ 30,400	$ 90,000	11.46%
NEW FUN COMICS #1*	$ 27,000	$ 46,000	5.47%
PEP #22	$ 4,777	$ 22,000	16.50%
SENSATION COMICS #1	$ 8,550	$ 44,000	17.80%
SHOWCASE #4	$ 19,800	$ 42,000	7.81%
SHOWCASE #22	$ 3,691	$ 7,500	7.35%
SUPERMAN #1	$ 76,000	$ 300,000	14.72%
VAULT OF HORROR #12	$ 2,635	$ 6,700	9.78%
WALT DISNEY COMICS & STORIES #1	$ 9,500	$ 25,000	10.16%
WHIZ COMICS #2 (1)	$ 43,700	$ 88,000	7.25%
WONDER WOMAN #1	$ 7,643	$ 37,500	17.24%
X-MEN #1	$ 3,048	$ 14,000	16.47%
TOTAL COMIC PORTFOLIO	$ 832,086	$ 2,835,600	13.04%

In instances where 8.0 prices weren't available in '95, 6.0 prices were used as the lower parameter for NM- calculation.
Detective #1 & New Fun Comics #1 are based on VF 8.0 values due to the believed non-existence in higher grade.

Sources: **Bloomberg; Official Overstreet Comic Book Price Guide.**
9.2 NM- values (or "top of guide" prices if lower) 1995 (adjusted), 2005

Editor's Note: *The above information was graciously provided by Metropolis Collectibles Inc.*

Key Comics Sold in 2004

The following lists of sales were reported to Gemstone during the year and represent only a small portion of the total amount of important books that have sold.

VICTORIAN AGE - PLATINUM AGE SALES

Adventures of Mickey Mouse (Soft cover ed.) FN $197.50
All the Funny Folks VG $147.50
Barker's "Komic" Picture Souvenir 1892 FN+ $400
Bringing Up Father #8 VF $252.52
Bringing Up Father #21 FN- $71
Bringing Up Father The Big Book 1 (w/dust jacket) GD $144.50
Brown's Blue Ribbon Book of Jokes and Jingles FN $465
Buster Brown And His Resolutions GD- $560.23
Buster Brown Funny Tricks VG+ $316.13
Buster Brown His Dog Tige And Their Troubles GD- $223.50
Buster Brown Pranks VG+ $900
Dreams Of The Rarebit Fiend GD/VG $2,045 (Now 5 Known)
F. Fox's Funny Folk FR $173.59
The Gumps Book No.1 (1918) GD- $153.91
History of Mr. Ogleby F/VF $1,200
How Dick Tracy And Dick Tracy Jr. Caught The Racketeers VG $245
How They Draw Prohibition VG+ $111.57
Jimmy And His Scrapes FN+ $540
Jimmy And His Scrapes GD- $275
The Latest Adventures of Foxy Grandpa FN $154.01
Little Sammy Sneeze GD- $1,535
Mickey Mouse Book 4 (1934) FN+ $413
Mickey Mouse Book 4 (1934) FN $400
Moon Mullins Series 3 FN $100
Moon Mullins Big Book 1 GD $105.59
Mutt and Jeff Book 5 (1916) VG $208.48
Pore Li'L Mose FR $600
Pore Li'L Mose GD- $999
Secret Agent X-9 Book 2 VG/FN $250
Smitty at the Ball Game (1929) FN $315
Thimble Theatre #1 VG+ $235
Thimble Theatre #1 GD- $152.53
The Trials of Lulu and Leander GD $203
The Yellow Kid In McFadden's Flats FR $2,901
The Yellow Kid Vol. 1 #3 FR $280

GOLDEN AGE - ATOM AGE SALES

Action Comics #11 GD/VG $585
Action Comics #23 GD/VG (restored) $450
Adventure Comics #53 VG $164.01
Adventure Comics #55 VF/NM (restored) $500
Adventure Comics #56 FN/VF $600
Adventure Comics #72 FN/VF (restored) $1,250
Adventure Comics #100 VG $285
Adventure Comics #210 GD $210
Airboy Comics V2#11 FN $150
Air Fighters Comics V1#8 GD $50
Air Fighters Comics V1#9 GD $75
Air Fighters Comics V2#2 GD $250
All-American Comics #18 VG $1065
All-American Comics #19 VF (restored) $1,080
All-American Comics #20 VG+ $470
All-American Comics #23 VG+ $304
All-American Comics #25 FN/VF (restored) $635
All-American Comics #26 FN- $407
All-American Comics #27 VG- (restored) $325
All-American Comics #43 VG $215
All-American Comics #100 VF (restored) $367
All-American Comics #102 FN $243.50
All-Flash Quarterly #1 VG- $805
All Star Comics #3 VF (restored) $3,000
All Star Comics #5 VF (restored) $521
All Star Comics #8 VF/NM (restored) $3,000
All Star Comics #28 FN (restored) $203.49
All Star Comics #36 VG $425
All Star Comics #36 GD/VG $200
All Star Comics #42, FN $312.50
All Star Comics #44 GD $127.50
All Star Comics #49 VG $177.50
All Star Comics #57 VF- $553
Atomic Bomb #1 FN/VF $100
Batman #1 VG- (restored) $7,000
Batman #1 GD+ $7,500
Batman #16 VG- $750
Batman #20 FN+ $875
Batman #21 GD/VG $76
Best of the West #3 NM- $125.50
Big All-American Comic Book #1 GD- $505
Buster Brown Comics Book 5 NM $60
Captain America Comics #10 VF/NM (cleaned) $1,500
Captain America Comics #67 VG- $300
Captain America Comics #70 FN $610
Captain America Comics #72 FN $613
Captain Marvel Adventures #85 FN+ $55
Captain Marvel Story Book #2 VF $150

Captain Midnight #4 GD/VG $100
Captain Midnight #13 VF/NM $144.50
Captain Midnight #19 VF $144.50
Captain Midnight #35 GD/VG $25
Century of Comics GD $2,500
Cisco Kid #1 VG+ $42.50
Classic Comics #2 (5th printing) VG $25
Classics Illustrated #55 (1st printing) VG $34
Comic Cavalcade #1 VG (restored) $554
Comics Calendar 1946 F/VF $152.50
Detective Comics #7 VF/NM (restored) $2,700
Detective Comics #9 VF/NM (restored) $2,700
Detective Comics #21 FN $1600
Detective Comics #25 VF/NM (restored) $1,625
Detective Comics #31 VF (restored) $4,000
Detective Comics #40 NM (restored) $698
Detective Comics #49 VF/NM (restored) $400
Detective Comics #163 VF $170
Don Winslow of the Navy #22 VG+ $28
Durango Kid #1 VG/FN $46
Durango Kid #7 NM $127.50
Durango Kid #11 VF/NM $73
Famous Funnies #82 (Buck Rogers cover) VG/FN $77.33
Flash Comics #72 VF/NM $875
Flash Comics #96 FN/VF $725
Flash Comics #104 VF- (restored) $611
Four Color Comics #62 (Donald Duck) VG/FN $400
Ghost Rider (1950) #1 VF $232.50
Ghost Rider (1950) #4 VG/FN $147.50
Ghost Rider (1950) #8 FN+ $96.05
Green Hornet Comics #1 FR/GD $311
Green Lantern #1 VF/NM (restored) $5,000
Human Torch #1 VG/FN (restored) $1,900
Jackpot Comics #1 GD $158.50
Jackpot Comics #4 VG $800
Jimmy Wakely #6 FN/VF $62.89
Kid Komics #1 FN- (restored) $338
March of Comics #62 (Roy Rogers) VF $62
Marvel Family #1 GD $100
More Fun Comics #30 (centerfold out) $113.50
More Fun Comics #45 VG- $400
New Adventure Comics #20 FN- $1,000
New York World's Fair 1940 VG $1,800
Pep Comics #22 GD+ $1,800
Picture Parade #1 FN $250
Planet Comics #1 VF (restored) $1,250
Silver Streak Comics #6 GD- $1,200
Smash Comics #1 GD/VG $375
Strange Adventures #1 FN+ $425
Strange Adventures #3 FN $137.50
Sub-Mariner Comics #32 VG/FN $750
Superman #53 FN+ $540.99
Victory Comics #1 FR/GD $200
Walt Disney Comics & Stories #21 VG $405
Wanted #33 FN $200
War Comics #1 FN $51.50
Weird Fantasy #16 VG+ $95
Whiz Comics #2 G+ $450
Whiz Comics #11 VG/FN $146.50
Wow Comics #2 FN (restored) $400
Young Men #24 VG- $500
Young Men #27 VG $315

SILVER AGE SALES

Action Comics #252 GD $80
Adventure Comics #300 FN $125
Adventures of the Big Boy #1 VG+ $315
Amazing Spider-Man #34 FN- $84
Amazing Spider-Man Annual #2 VG+ $74.75
Aquaman #5 VF $55
Avengers #4 VG/FN $400
Avengers #15 VG+ $30
Batman #197 FN+ $170
Brave and the Bold #25 FN $67.75
Brave and the Bold #26 VG+ $38.50
Brave and the Bold #28 FN+ $845
Brave and the Bold #28 VG+ $1,200
Brave and the Bold #30 VG+ $230
Challengers of the Unknown #16 VF $45
Daredevil #1 VG $375
Daredevil #2 GD/VG $75
Daredevil #3 FN/VF $168
Daredevil #4 VG/FN $78
Daredevil #8 VF $106
Detective Comics #229 GD+ $80
Detective Comics #265 FN $125
Doom Patrol #121 VG+ $50
Fantastic Four #1 VG+ $1,700
Fantastic Four #2 GD $250
Fantastic Four #3 GD $170
Fantastic Four #4 VG/FN $565
Fantastic Four #7 VG $125
Fantastic Four #24 VF/NM $96
Fantastic Four #45 VG+ $35
Fantastic Four #48 VG $180
Flash #109 GD- $35
Gene Autry Four Color #57 FN $123.71
Green Lantern #40 FN $85
House of Secrets #1 VG $115
House of Secrets #2 VG $90
Incredible Hulk #3 VG $195
Incredible Hulk #108 NM $47.75
Iron Man #12 FN+ $19.50
Jetsons #1 VF/NM #265

Journey into Mystery #61 FN/VF $215
Journey into Mystery #62 VF- $495
Journey into Mystery #82 VF $90
Justice League of America #1 GD/VG $300
Justice League of America #2 VF $199.75
Justice League of America #41 FN+ $22.50
Justice League of America #47 FN+ $27
Mystery in Space #53 VG $175
Sea Devils #1 VG+ $89.75
Showcase #22 FN- $450
Showcase #29 VG- $65.50
Showcase #34 VG+ $255.00
Silver Surfer #1 VF/NM $501
Silver Surfer #4 VG+ $90
Strange Tales #76 VF+ $400
Strange Tales #79 VF+ $400
Strange Tales #80 VF+ $200
Strange Tales #82 VF+ $275
Sub-Mariner #1 NM- $450
Sub-Mariner #2 NM- $180
Sub-Mariner #3 NM $120
Sugar & Spike #34 FN $37
Tales of Suspense #11 VF+ $475
X-Men #1 Fair $97
X-Men #2 VG+ $270
X-Men #6 VG $45
X-Men #9 FN $95
X-Men #12 VG $60
X-Men #15 VG+ $86
X-Men #40 VG $45.25

BRONZE AGE TO MODERN AGE SALES

Bronze Age Sales:

Amazing Spider-Man #129 VF/NM $350
Avengers #80 NM $18
Avengers #102 NM $50
Avengers #106 NM $60
Avengers #113 NM $40
Avengers #114 NM $40
Avengers #120 NM+ $50
Avengers #126 NM+ $50
Avengers #128 NM $40
Avengers #129 NM $40
Avengers #131 NM $28
Fantastic Four #126 NM $72
Fantastic Four #129 NM $50
Fantastic Four #133 NM- $40
Fantastic Four #134 NM- $40
Fantastic Four #137 NM- $35
Fantastic Four #140 NM- $40
Fantastic Four #143 NM $50
Fantastic Four #147 NM $35
Giant-Size Spider-Man #6 NM $16
Giant-Size X-Men #1 VG- $110
Incredible Hulk #181 VF $900
Incredible Hulk #181 VF $406
Incredible Hulk #181 VG $115
Iron Fist #14 VF $200
Iron Fist #14 VF $75
Marvel Super Action (magazine) #1 VG+ $22
Marvel Team-Up #1 VG- $28
Shadow, The #1 VF $29
Swamp Thing #2 VF $42
Vampirella #3 GD $35
X-Men #94 FN $275
X-Men #94 FN+ $319
X-Men #94 GD+ $65
X-Men #94 GD $60
X-Men #97 VF $29.75

Copper Age Sales:

Amazing Spider-Man #300 NM $79.95
G.I. Joe A Real American Hero #21 NM $40
Marvel Super-Heroes Secret Wars #8 NM $28
Teenage Mutant Ninja Turtles #2 NM $75
Teenage Mutant Ninja Turtles #3 NM $30
Uncanny X-Men #212 NM $22
Uncanny X-Men #212 NM $22
Uncanny X-Men #248 NM $24.75
Wolverine (1988) #1 VG $25

Modern Age Sales:

Astonishing X-Men #1 Cassaday Variant NM $95
Astonishing X-Men #4 Colossus Variant NM $20
Batman #608 Second Printing NM $55
Batman #612 Second Printing NM $40
Cerebus #300 NM $25
Green Lantern Rebirth #1 First Printing NM $9.95
Green Lantern Rebirth #2 First Printing NM $5.95
Identity Crisis #1 Diamond Retailer Summit Edition NM $595
John Byrne's Next Men #21 NM $55
NYX #1 NM $9.95
NYX #2 NM $9.95
NYX #3 NM $39.95
Superman #204 Diamond Retailer Summit Edition NM $495
Superman/Batman #1 Batman Cover First NM $29.95
Superman/Batman #1 Superman Cover NM $29.95
Superman/Batman #1 Second Printing NM $19.95
Superman/Batman #1 Third Printing NM $19.95
Teen Titans 1/2 VF $15
Ultimate Spider-Man #1 NM $175
Ultimate Spider-Man #2 NM $48
Ultimate Spider-Man #3 NM $35
Ultimate Spider-Man #4 NM $50
Ultimate Spider-Man #5 NM $50
Ultimate Spider-Man #6 NM $35
Wolverine Vol. 3 #20 Retailer Incentive NM $134.95
Wolverine: The End #1 Wizard World 2003 Ed. NM $65

BIG LITTLE BOOKS SALES

Bambi #1469 NM $127
Big Little Mother Goose HC VF/NM $899
Big Little Mother Goose CC VG/FN $1300
Big Little Paint Book (1st pr.) VF/NM $636
Buccaneer #1470 NM $228
Buck Rogers Vs. the Fiend of Space #1409 VF+ $309
Buck Rogers and the Super-Dwarf of Space #1490 FN $217
Bugs Bunny and His Pals #1496 NM/M $384
Dan Dunn Secret Operative 48 And The Gangsters' Frame-Up VG $356.50
Dick Tracy Detective (The Adventures of) #707 FN $299
Dick Tracy Detective (The Adventures of) #707 FN $126.50
Dick Tracy Out West #723 NM $862.50
Dick Tracy From Colorado to Nova Scotia #749 nn Premium Edition NM $603.75
Dick Tracy and the Racketeer Gang #1112 FN $57.50
Dick Tracy Solves the Penfield Mystery #1137 nn Premium Edition FN+ $460
Dick Tracy and the Boris Arson Gang #1163 VF $201.25
Dick Tracy and the Boris Arson Gang #1163 VG/FN $22
Dick Tracy in Chains of Crime #1185 NM $310.50
Dick Tracy and Yogee Yamma #1412 VF+ $92
Dick Tracy and the Hotel Murders #1420 NM $115
Dick Tracy and the Phantom Ship #1434 NM+ $97.75
Dick Tracy and His G-Men #1439 NM $132.25
Dick Tracy and the Bicycle Gang #1445 FN $31
Detective Dick Tracy and the Spider Gang #1446 VF/NM $126.50
Dick Tracy Special FBI Operative #1449 $36
Dick Tracy on the High Seas #1454 NM $356.50
Dick Tracy and the Tiger Lilly Gang #1460 VF+ $86.25
Dick Tracy on Voodoo Island #1478 NM $184
Dick Tracy and the Wreath Kidnaping Case #1482 NM $253
Dick Tracy the Super-Detective #1488 NM $322
Dick Tracy and the Man With No Face #1491 VF $92
Dick Tracy Encounters Facey #2001 VF/NM $16
Dick Tracy Returns #1495 NM $46
Donald Duck Headed for Trouble #1430 NM+ $949
Donald Duck Hunting for Trouble #1478 VF $149.50
Donald Duck is Here Again #1484 VF/NM $299
Donald Duck Off the Beam #1438 (352 pgs.) NM $690
Flaming Guns (Tom Mix) #22 VF/NM $355
Flash Gordon and the Monsters of Mongo (3-col) VF $637
Flash Gordon in the Water World of Mongo #1407 NM $367
The Green Hornet Strikes! #1453 FN/VF $70.15
Lone Ranger and the Black Shirt Highwayman #1450 VF/NM $158
Mickey Mouse #717 VG $460
Mickey Mouse in Blaggard Castle #726 VF/NM $345
Mickey Mouse the Mail Pilot #731 File Copy FN/VF $420
Mickey Mouse Sails for Treasure Island #750 NM $840
Mickey Mouse Presents A Walt Disney Silly Symphony #756 FN $115
Mickey Mouse Presents Walt Disney's Silly Symphony #1111 NM- $1,150
Mickey Mouse and Pluto the Racer #1128 NM $780
Mickey Mouse the Detective #1139 VF/NM $390
Mickey Mouse and the Bat Bandit #1153 NM- $920
Mickey Mouse and Bobo the Elephant #1160 NM $747.50
Mickey Mouse and the Sacred Jewel #1187 VF $127.65
Mickey Mouse Runs His Own Newspaper #1409 NM $805
Mickey Mouse in the Race for Riches #1476 NM- $120.75
Mickey Mouse on the Cave-Man Island #1499 NM $690
Mickey Mouse To Draw and Color #3061 VF $2,300
Mickey Mouse Waddle Book FN $1,200
"Pop-Up" Mickey Mouse in King Arthur's Court VF/NM $1,026
Red Ryder and Little Beaver on Hoofs on Thunder #1400 VF/NM $44
Red Ryder and Circus Luck #1466 VF $38
The Shadow and The Masters of Evil #1443 VG/FN $112.50
Silly Symphony Featuring Donald Duck #1169 NM $805
Silly Symphony Featuring Donald Duck and His (Mis)Adventures #1441 NM $1,150
Snow White and the Seven Dwarfs #1460 NM $517.50
Tarzan and the Ant Men #1444 NM $204
Tarzan and the Golden Lion #1448 FN/VF $153
Tarzan's Revenge #1488 VG $17
Thumper and the Seven Dwarfs #1409 VF/NM $127
Tom Swift and His Giant Telescope #1485 VG $60.99

GOLDEN AGE - SALES OF CGC GRADED COMICS

Ace Comics #1 FN+(6.5) $977.50
Action Comics #1 Appt. FN+ Slight (P) FN+(6.5) $45,100
Action Comics #5 FN(6.0) $6,037.50
Action Comics #15 VG-(3.5) $1,200
Action Comics #17 FN(6.0) $1,495
Action Comics #101 VF(8.0) $1,140
Adventure Comics #32 Qualified FN-(5.5) $358.80
Adventure Comics #43 FN+(6.5) $1,175
Adventure Comics #48 (restored) VF/NM(9.0) $3,000
Adventure Comics #67 VF(8.0) $1,350
Adventure Comics #81 VF/NM(9.0) $1,150
Adventure Into Fear Adventure Into #11 VF/NM(9.0) $20
Adventures into the Unknown #11 Northford VF/NM(9.0) $287.50
Air Fighters Comics #8 VG+(4.5) $103.50
Airboy Comics Vol.3 #5 VF(8.0) $126.50
All-American Comics #1 FN/VF(7.0) $609.99
All-American Comics #17 VF+(8.5) $13,225
All-American Comics #24 VF(8.0) $1,750
All Flash #14 FN-(5.5) $300

All Hero Comics #1 FN(6.0) $408.25
All Star Comics #3 FN+(6.5) Lost Valley $14,500
All Star Comics #8 FN-(5.5) $5,175
All Star Comics #14 FN-(5.5) $402.50
All Star Comics #21 NM-(9.2) $4,000
All Top Comics #10 VF+(8.5) $910
All Top Comics #17 VF+(8.5) $690
All Winners Comics #1 Apparent FN- FN-(5.5) $2,070
All Winners Comics #5 VF(8.0) $1,610
All Winners Comics Vol.2 #1 VF+(8.5) $2,645
America's Best Comics #10 Mile High NM-(9.2) $2,300
Archie Comics #5 VG/FN(5.0) $864.80
Archie's Pal Jughead #1 FN-(5.5) $900
Atomic Comics #2 VF+(8.5) $460
Atomic War! #3 Bethlehem VF/NM(9.0) $805
Baseball Heroes #nn Crowley VF+(8.5) $425.50
Batman #3 VF/NM(9.0) $10,850
Batman #6 VF/NM(9.0) $5,200
Batman #10 FN/VF(7.0) $1,195
Batman #11 VF/NM(9.0) $8,750
Batman #17 VF+(8.5) $1,650
Batman #18 FN/VF(7.0) $1,035
Batman #23 VF/NM(9.0) $3,999
Batman #26 VF/NM(9.0) $2,600
Batman #50 NM(9.4) $5,500
Batman #100 VF/NM(9.0) $5,500
Batman #120 Big Apple NM-(9.2) $1,121.25
Big All-American Comic Book #1 FN-(5.5) $1,725
Black Cat Mystery #32 NM(9.4) $431.25
Black Magic #1 FN(6.0) $114
Black Magic Vol. 2 #2 Bethlehem VF/NM(9.0) $264.50
Blackhawk #11 NM(9.4) $1,265
Blonde Phantom #13 NM(9.4) $2,760
Blue Beetle #1 Rockford VG+(4.5) $621
Blue Ribbon Comics #1 Larson VF+(8.5) $3,105
Boy Commandos #1 VF-(7.5) $2,070
Boy Commandos #16 NM(9.4) $561.20
Captain America Comics #1 Apparent VF/NM Moderate (P) VF/NM(9.0) $9,487.50
Captain America Comics #2 VG+(4.5) $2,760
Captain America Comics #8 FN/VF(7.0) $2,800
Captain Marvel Adventures #2 Crowley VG/FN(5.0) $977.50
Captain Marvel Adventures #10 Crowley VF/NM(9.0) $920
Captain Marvel Adventures #24 Mile High NM(9.4) $3,220
Captain Marvel Adventures #38 Mile High NM(9.4) $2,185
Captain Marvel and the Lieutenants of Safety #3 NM(9.4) $1,610
Captain Marvel Jr. #1 FN+(6.5) $1,076
Captain Midnight #14 Mile High NM(9.4) $2,760
Catman Comics #9 FN+(6.5) $563.50
Chamber of Chills #22 NM(9.4) $632.50
Chamber of Chills #23 (#3) Bethlehem VF/NM(9.0) $299
Classic Comics #1 First Edition FN-(5.5) $833.75
Classic Comics #9 VF/NM(9.0) $1,121.25
Comic Cavalcade #1 VF+(8.5) $8,050
Cowgirl Romances #1 Mile High VF/NM(9.0) $1,725
Crime SuspenStories #23 Gaines File NM-(9.2) $747.50
Daredevil Comics #38 Rockford NM-(9.2) $632.50
Detective Comics #6 FN/VF(7.0) Lost Valley $6,250
Detective Comics #34 VG+(4.5) $1,250
Detective Comics #38 VG(4.0) $4,256
Doll Man Quarterly #1 VG(4.0) $449
Don Winslow #1 Crowley NM-(9.2) $2632.50
Down with Crime #6 Crowley NM(9.4) $431.25
Extra! #5 Gaines File NM+(9.6) $747.50
F.B.I. #1 NM(9.4) $379.50
Famous Funnies #89 (Lost Valley) VF/NM(9.0) $300
Famous Funnies #211 VG/FN(5.0) $259.90
Famous Funnies #212 VF(8.0) $775
Flash Comics #1 Apparent FN/VF Extensive (P) FN/VF(7.0) $6,900
Flash Comics #3 NM-(9.2) $13,800
Flash Comics #5 Nova Scotia VF/NM(9.0) $5,462.50
Flash Comics #85 "D" Copy NM-(9.2) $1,840
Four Color #178 (Donald Duck) VF/NM(9.0) $1,399.95
Four Color #275 (Donald Duck) NM-(9.2) $1,725
Fox Giants Almanac of Crime #nn Aurora VF+(8.5) $488.75
Funny Picture Stories #1 Lost Valley VF-(7.5) $2,500
Gene Autry Comics #1 Crowley FN(6.0) $1,495
Gene Autry Comics #8 Mile High NM(9.4) $2,990
Green Hornet Comics #1 VF+(8.5) $4,500
Green Hornet Comics #2 Boston NM+(9.6) $862.50
Green Lantern #3 FN/VF(7.0) $1,782.50
Hansi, the Girl Who Loved the Swastika #1 NM+(9.6) $299.99
Haunt of Fear #7 Gaines File NM/MT(9.8) $3,220
Haunt of Fear #14 NM(9.4) $1,006.25
Haunt of Fear #15 Gaines File NM/MT(9.8) $17,250
Haunted Thrills #1 Bethlehem VF+(8.5) $402.50
Hopalong Cassidy #1 Crowley FN/VF(7.0) $1,610
House of Mystery #1 VG+(4.5) $356.50
Howdy Doody #3 NM-(9.2) $234.50
Human Torch #2 (#1) App. FN+ Slight (P) FN+(6.5) $3,680
If the Devil Would Talk VF/NM(9.0) $202.50
Impact #1 Gaines File VF/NM(9.0) $460
Jackie Gleason and the Honeymooners #3 VF(8.0) $276
Jackpot Comics #1 VG/FN(5.0) $690
Kid Movie Komics #11 VF+(8.5) $195.50
Killers #1 VF-(7.5) $448.50
King Comics #23 Mile High NM-(9.2) $1,265
MAD #1 Northford VF+(8.5) $5,405
MAD #2 Gaines File NM(9.4) $4,025
MAD #34 Gaines File NM(9.4) $1,035
MAD #40 Gaines File NM(9.4) $862.50
March of Comics #4 App. VG Moderate (P) VG(4.0) $920
Marvel Mystery Comics #9 GD/VG(3.0) $5,000
Marvel Mystery Comics #16 VF(8.0) $2,150
Marvel Mystery Comics #84 VF(8.0) $1,275
Master Comics #16 Crowley FN-(5.5) $253
M.D. #4 Gaines File NM-(9.2) $373.75
Military Comics #8 Pennsylvania VF/NM(9.0) $1,207.50
Military Comics #24 Rockford NM(9.4) $1,063.75

Moon Girl #5 NM-(9.2) $1,725
More Fun Comics #51 (restored) VF/NM(9.0) $1,200
More Fun Comics #62 VF(8.0) $2,070
More Fun Comics #71 VF/NM(9.0) $5,520
New Adventure Comics #19 Mile High NM+(9.6) $12,650
New Book of Comics #1 VF(8.0) $11,500
New Comics #1 (restored) FN/VF(7.0) $2,800
Our Gang #17 Dell File VF/NM(9.0) $264.50
Panic #1 Gaines File NM-(9.2) $920
Pep Comics #7 NM-(9.2) $1,667.50
Phantom Lady #13 FN(6.0) $920
Planet Comics #2 FN/VF(7.0) $1,999.99
Planet Comics #37 NM(9.4) $2,500
Police Comics #3 VG/FN(5.0) $345
Popular Comics #15 VF(8.0) $400
Popular Comics #79 Mile High NM(9.4) $1,035
Samson #1 VG/FN(5.0) $431.25
Sensation Comics #1 (restored) NM(9.4) $5,000
Sensation Comics #2 VG(4.0) $603.75
Sensation Comics #3 FN/VF(7.0) $1,265
Shadow Comics #3 NM-(9.2) $3,000
Shock SuspenStories #1 VF(8.0) $460
Shock SuspenStories #3 Gaines File NM+(9.6) $1,840
Silver Streak Comics #7 FN-(5.5) $1,425
Space Patrol #1 Bethlehem VF/NM(9.0) $1,063.75
Sparkler Comics Rockford #14 NM-(9.2) $603.75
Speed Comics #41 Mile High NM-(9.2) $1,121.25
Spy Smasher #2 Pennsylvania VF/NM(9.0) $1,782.50
Star Spangled Comics #25 FN+(6.5) $212.75
Strange Adventures #5 Bethlehem VF(8.0) $494.50
Sub-Mariner Comics #1 FN(6.0) $4,000
Sub-Mariner Comics #11 Pennsylvania VF+(8.5) $2,530
Sun Girl #1 VF-(7.5) $641.88
Superboy #1 Canadian VF/NM(9.0) $2,530
Superman #1 VF-(7.5) $250,000
Superman #1 (restored) VG+(4.5) $16,500
Superman #2 VG-(3.5) $2,300
Superman #10 FN+(6.5) $1,301
Superman #24 VF/NM(9.0) $4,725.55
Superman #36 VF/NM(9.0) $1,150
Superman #100 VG(4.0) $275
Suspense Comics #3 VG(4.0) $11,500
Suspense Comics #4 FN(6.0) $1,782.50
Tales From The Crypt #25 VF(8.0) $402.50
Tales From The Crypt #31 Gaines File NM(9.4) $1,840
Tales From The Crypt #33 NM+(9.6) $3,500
Target Comics Vol. 2 #10 Mile High VF/NM(9.0) $2,070
Terrific Comics #6 FN(6.0) $517.50
This Magazine Is Haunted #13 Crowley NM-(9.2) $632.50
Thrilling Comics #1 VG/FN(5.0) $575
Thun'da #1 VF(8.0) $891.25
Tom Mix Western #1 NM-(9.2) $1,092.50
Top-Notch Comics #1 VF-(7.5) $2,846.25
Top-Notch Comics #7 Big Apple VF+(8.5) $1,207.50
Two-Fisted Tales #19 Gaines File NM+(9.6) $3,450
Two-Fisted Tales #21 Gaines File NM(9.4) $1,322.50
Two-Fisted Tales #23 Gaines File NM+(9.6) $1,150
Uncle Sam Quarterly #1 FN/VF(7.0) $1,086.75
USA Comics #1 VF/NM(9.0) $1,207.50
USA Comics #7 VG+(4.5) $1,500
Vault of Horror #16 Gaines File NM+(9.6) $3,220
Vault of Horror #31 Gaines File NM+(9.6) $2,070
Vic Torry & His Flying Saucer nn Bethlehem NM-(9.2) $1,035
Walt Disney's Comics and Stories #86 VF-(7.5) $414
War Against Crime #11 Gaines File NM/MT(9.8) $10,062.50
Weird Fantasy #12 Al Williamson File VG(4.0) $448.50
Weird Fantasy #17 Gaines File NM(9.4) $1,782.50
Weird Fantasy #21 NM+(9.6) $4,800
Weird Science #5 Gaines File NM/MT(9.8) $3,220
Weird Science #7 Gaines File NM+(9.6) $2,185
Weird Science #13 (#2) Cosmic Aeroplane VF+(8.5) $1,035
Weird Science #29 Al Williamson File FN(6.0) $356.50
Weird Science-Fantasy #29 FN-(5.5) $218.50
Whiz Comics #3 (#2) Apparent VF Slight (P) VF-(7.5) $805
Whiz Comics #16 Crowley VF-(7.5) $632.50
Whiz Comics #61 Mile High NM(9.4) $1,150
Women Outlaws #1 VF/NM(9.0) $1,035
Wonder Comics #11 NM-(9.2) $1,092.50
Wonder Woman #1 VG/FN(5.0) $4,140
World's Finest Comics #3 VG(4.0) $448.50
World's Finest Comics #18 Mile High NM+(9.6) $8,711.25
Worlds of Fear #6 Crowley NM-(9.2) $747.50
World War III #1 NM-(9.2) $1,667.50
Wow Comics #3 Rockford VF+(8.5) $1,006.25
Young Allies Comics #2 Qualified VG/FN(5.0) $402.50
Young Men #28 VG/FN(5.0) $747.50
Zip Comics #1 FN/VF(7.0) $1,955

SILVER AGE - SALES OF CGC GRADED COMICS

Action Comics #252 VG(4.0) $149.50
Action Comics #267 NM(9.4) $1,600
Action Comics #267 VF/NM(9.0) $660
Action Comics #300 Pacific Coast NM-(9.2) $402.50
Action Comics #307 NM-(9.2) $150
Action Comics #315 NM(9.4) $250
Adventure Comics #300 VF+(8.5) $690
Adventure Comics #301 VF/NM(9.0) $201.25
Adventure Comics #347 VF/NM(9.0) $60
Adventures of Jerry Lewis #105 Curator NM+(9.6) $437
Adventures of Rex the Wonder Dog #2 VF/NM(9.0) $690
Adventures of The Jaguar #6 NM(9.4) $143.75
Amazing Adult Fantasy #10 VF/NM(9.0) $699.99
Amazing Adult Fantasy #10 VG-(3.5) $41

Amazing Fantasy #15 VF/NM(9.0) $58,000
Amazing Fantasy #15 VF/NM(9.0) $32,500
Amazing Fantasy #15 FN(6.0) $7,187.50
Amazing Fantasy #15 VG(4.0) $3,000
Amazing Spider-Man #1 VF(8.0) $9,500
Amazing Spider-Man #1 VF(8.0) $9,195
Amazing Spider-Man #1 VF-(7.5) $7,187.50
Amazing Spider-Man #1 FN/VF(7.0) $5,600
Amazing Spider-Man #1 Record Rep. NM+(9.6) $1,026.01
Amazing Spider-Man #2 VF+(8.5) $2,932.50
Amazing Spider-Man #2 FN(6.0) $1,050
Amazing Spider-Man #4 VF/NM(9.0) $3,499
Amazing Spider-Man #5 NM-(9.2) $3,910
Amazing Spider-Man #11 NM+(9.6) $10,500
Amazing Spider-Man #14 NM+(9.6) $18,000
Amazing Spider-Man #14 NM(9.4) $6,900
Amazing Spider-Man #14 NM-(9.2) $3,450
Amazing Spider-Man #17 NM+(9.6) $6,612.50
Amazing Spider-Man #19 NM/MT(9.8) $7,255
Amazing Spider-Man #28 NM(9.4) $5,013
Amazing Spider-Man #39 Curator NM+(9.6) $3,350
Amazing Spider-Man #39 NM(9.4) $1,650
Amazing Spider-Man #41 NM(9.4) $1,000
Amazing Spider-Man #42 VF/NM(9.0) $290
Amazing Spider-Man #43 NM+(9.6) $1,322.50
Amazing Spider-Man #50 NM(9.4) $4,500
Amazing Spider-Man Annual #1 NM-(9.2) $2,524
Amazing Spider-Man Annual #1 VF+(8.5) $1,035
Aquaman #1 VF(8.0) $485
Aquaman #25 NM(9.4) $172.50
Atom #16 Western Penn NM+(9.6) $517.50
Atom #29 NM-(9.2) $230
Atom and Hawkman #42 NM(9.4) $195
Avengers #1 VF-(7.5) $1,950
Avengers #1 VG/FN(5.0) $710
Avengers #2 NM(9.4) $4,250
Avengers #4 NM+(9.6) $17,500
Avengers #4 VF/NM(9.0) $1,782.50
Avengers #10 NM(9.4) $520
Avengers #15 Pacific Coast NM+(9.6) $1,500
Avengers #16 VF-(7.5) $86.25
Avengers Annual #1 NM+(9.6) $620
Batman #155 NM-(9.2) $320
Batman #171 VF/NM(9.0) $560
Batman #189 NM+(9.6) $4,070
Batman #200 Diamond Run VF-(7.5) $125
Brave and the Bold #28 FN-(5.5) $825
Brave and the Bold #34 VF-(7.5) $875
Captain Action #1 Boston NM+(9.6) $402.50
Captain America #100 NM/MT(9.8) $5,000
Captain America #106 NM/MT(9.8) $787
Captain America #113 NM/MT(9.8) $995
Captain Marvel #1 Western Penn NM/MT(9.8) $1,600
Captain Marvel #2 NM/MT(9.8) $345
Challengers of the Unknown #1 FN(6.0) $1,150
Chamber of Darkness #1 NM-(9.2) $67.85
Creepy #1 NM(9.4) $818
Creepy #3 NM+(9.6) $230.27
Creepy #10 NM+(9.6) $200
Daredevil #1 NM-(9.2) $5,100
Daredevil #1 VF+(8.5) $3,105
Daredevil #1 VG(4.0) $333.50
Daredevil #2 NM-(9.2) $1,475
Daredevil #4 Pacific Coast NM(9.4) $1,800
Daredevil #5 NM(9.4) $1,000
Daredevil #7 VF-(7.5) $322
Daredevil #8 NM-(9.2) $280
Detective Comics #359 VF/NM(9.0) $212.50
Doctor Strange #169 NM/MT(9.8) $1,000
Doctor Strange #170 NM+(9.6) $300
Doctor Strange #182 Pacific Coast NM+(9.6) $385
Eerie #7 Bethlehem VF(8.0) $345
Eerie #10 NM+(9.6) $202.50
Eerie #10 NM+(9.6) $158.05
80 Page Giant #8 NM(9.4) $1,249
Fantastic Four #1 VF+(8.5) $24,999.99
Fantastic Four #1 VF-(7.5) $10,815
Fantastic Four #1 GD-(1.8) $900
Fantastic Four #1 Record Reprint NM+(9.6) $1,432.07
Fantastic Four #2 VF-(7.5) $2,650
Fantastic Four #2 VF-(7.5) $2,500
Fantastic Four #4 NM(9.4) $2,150
Fantastic Four #5 VF/NM(9.0) $8,000
Fantastic Four #10 VF+(8.5) $1,207.50
Fantastic Four #28 VF/NM(9.0) $435.99
Fantastic Four #32 NM(9.4) $1,226
Fantastic Four #48 NM+(9.6) $3,150
Fantastic Four #48 NM(9.4) $1,680.43
Fantastic Four #49 NM-(9.2) $1,063.75
Fantastic Four #50 NM(9.4) $2,587.50
Fantastic Four #51 VF+(8.5) $77.05
Fantastic Four #94 NM+(9.6) $170
Fantastic Four Annual #1 VF+(8.5) $565
Flash #105 VF-(7.5) $2,760
Flash #105 VG/FN(5.0) $900
Flash #123 VF/NM(9.0) $3,400
Flash #167 NM/MT(9.8) $1,610
Flash #170 NM/MT(9.8) $1,725
Flash Annual #1 VF/NM(9.0) $350
Flash Gordon #4 (King) Curator NM/MT(9.8) $575
G.I. Combat #106 NM+(9.6) $330
Green Lantern #1 FN/VF(7.0) $1,062
Green Lantern #1 FN(6.0) $862.50
Green Lantern #7 NM+(9.6) $5,700
Green Lantern #23 NM+(9.6) $1,626
Green Lantern #40 NM-(9.2) $900
Green Lantern #42 NM/MT(9.8) $2,012.50
Hawkman #1 Diamond Run VF/NM(9.0) $517.50
Hot Stuff the Little Devil #1 FN(6.0) $450
Incredible Hulk #1 VF-(7.5) $7,495
Incredible Hulk #1 FN/VF(7.0) $4,750
Incredible Hulk #1 VG(4.0) $2,050

Incredible Hulk #2 White Mountain NM(9.4) $18,500
Incredible Hulk #2 GD(2.0) $93.15
Incredible Hulk #4 NM(9.4) $7,187.50
Incredible Hulk #6 NM(9.4) $9,500
Incredible Hulk #102 NM+(9.6) $985
Incredible Hulk #140 NM(9.4) $153.50
Iron Man #1 NM/MT(9.8) $5,000
Iron Man #1 NM+(9.6) $1,280
Iron Man #2 NM/MT(9.8) $800
Iron Man #3 Winnipeg NM(9.4) $425
Journey Into Mystery #83 VF/NM(9.0) $17,500
Journey Into Mystery #83 VF+(7.5) $5,500
Journey Into Mystery #84 FN/VF(7.0) $518
Journey Into Mystery #87 NM-(9.2) $2,000
Journey Into Mystery #87 NM-(9.2) $1,550
Journey Into Mystery #89 VF/NM(9.0) $1,495
Journey Into Mystery #91 NM-(9.2) $1,750
Journey Into Mystery #112 NM-(9.2) $1,750
Journey Into Mystery #121 NM+(9.6) $868.88
Justice League of America #1 FN+(6.5) $977.50
Justice League of America #1 VG(4.0) $517.50
Justice League of America #7 NM(9.4) $2,185
Justice League of America #9 NM-(9.2) $1,625
Justice League of America #22 NM-(9.2) $600
MAD #100 NM(9.4) $224.99
MAD #106 Gaines File NM+(9.6) $287.50
MAD #109 NM+(9.6) $120.75
Marvel Super-Heroes #12 NM/MT(9.8) $2,313.88
Metal Men #1 VF/NM(9.0) $960
Mystery in Space #75 NM(9.4) $1,001
Nick Fury Agent of SHIELD #1 NM+(9.6) $486
Nick Fury Agent of SHIELD #3 NM(9.4) $180
Nick Fury Agent of SHIELD #15 Winnipeg NM(9.4) $325
Showcase #4 VG/FN(5.0) $3,383
Showcase #17 VG/FN(5.0) $517.50
Showcase #22 VF+(8.5) $4,153.07
Showcase #22 VF-(7.5) $2,070
Showcase #30 VF/NM(9.0) $1,375
Showcase #31 VF(8.0) $345
Showcase #35 VF/NM(9.0) $925
Showcase #59 Mass Copy NM(9.4) $718.75
Showcase #60 Boston NM(9.4) $1,265
Silver Surfer #1 NM+(9.6) $4,600
Silver Surfer #2 NM+(9.6) $1,050
Silver Surfer #3 NM(9.4) $1,207.50
Silver Surfer #4 NM/MT(9.8) $6,050
Spectre #1 Boston NM(9.4) $663.55
Spirit, The (Harvey) #2 NM(9.4) $51
Star Trek #1 Gold Key VF-(7.5) $227.51
Star Trek #4 NM+(9.6) $860
Strange Tales #78 VF+(8.5) $399
Strange Tales #108 Pacific Coast NM-(9.2) $900
Strange Tales #109 NM(9.4) $1,200
Strange Tales #114 Pacific Coast NM(9.4) $2,800
Strange Tales #115 Pacific Coast NM(9.4) $3,500
Strange Tales #115 NM(9.4) $3,000
Sub-Mariner #1 NM/MT(9.8) $2,000
Sub-Mariner #1 Western Penn NM+(9.6) $711.98
Sub-Mariner #2 NM+(9.6) $310.50
Sub-Mariner #3 Boston NM+(9.6) $500
Tales of Suspense #39 NM-(9.2) $16,000
Tales of Suspense #39 VF+(8.5) $3,910
Tales of Suspense #39 VF(8.0) $3,565
Tales of Suspense #41 VF+(8.5) $700
Tales of Suspense #43 VF+(8.5) $300
Tales of Suspense #48 NM(9.4) $1,500
Tales of Suspense #48 Northland NM(9.4) $2,000
Tales of Suspense #49 VF/NM(9.0) $905
Tales of Suspense #52 VF+(8.5) $345
Tales of Suspense #53 NM(9.4) $1,050
Tales to Astonish #27 FN/VF(7.0) $1,795
Tales to Astonish #35 VF/NM(9.0) $2,226
Tales to Astonish #39 NM(9.4) $2,300
Tales to Astonish #44 Northland NM+(9.6) $6,250
Teen Titans #1 NM+(9.6) $3,905.55
Teen Titans #2 Pacific Coast NM+(9.6) $1,035
Teen Titans #8 (1967) Pacific Coast NM/MT(9.8) $805
Thor #146 NM(9.4) $122
X-Men #1 NM-(9.2) $23,000
X-Men #1 VF/NM(9.0) $11,500
X-Men #1 VF+(8.5) $7,950
X-Men #1 VG/FN(5.0) $1,501
X-Men #2 NM(9.4) $7,500
X-Men #2 VF(8.0) $800
X-Men #3 Massachusetts NM(9.4) $5,000
X-Men #3 VF/NM(9.0) $1,213.25
X-Men #20 NM+(9.6) $1,250
X-Men #10 NM-(9.2) $600
X-Men #12 VF+(8.5) $408
X-Men #14 NM(9.4) $1,699
X-Men #24 NM+(9.6) $900
X-Men #25 NM+(9.6) $948.75
X-Men #49 NM+(9.6) $705
X-Men #63 NM/MT(9.8) $1,132.07

BRONZE AGE - SALES OF CGC GRADED COMICS

Action Comics #408 NM+(9.6) $103.50
Adventure Comics #403 NM+(9.6) $288
Adventure Comics #428 NM+(9.6) $230
Adventure Comics #432 NM/MT(9.8) $235.75
All Star Western #10 NM(9.4) $862.50
All Star Western #11 NM(9.4) $250
Amazing Spider-Man #96 NM+(9.6) $1,002.99
Amazing Spider-Man #97 NM+(9.6) $760
Amazing Spider-Man #100 NM+(9.6) $950
Amazing Spider-Man #100 NM(9.4) $500

Amazing Spider-Man #101 NM+(9.6) $1,322.50
Amazing Spider-Man #121 NM+(9.6) $1,575
Amazing Spider-Man #121 NM-(9.2) $360.84
Amazing Spider-Man #122 NM+(9.6) $1,590
Amazing Spider-Man #122 NM(9.4) $600
Amazing Spider-Man #129 NM+(9.6) $2,237
Amazing Spider-Man #129 NM(9.4) $865
Amazing Spider-Man #129 VF/NM(9.0) $550
Amazing Spider-Man #200 NM/MT(9.8) $241.50
Amazing Spider-Man #203 NM/MT(9.8) $197.49
Amazing Spider-Man #238 MT(9.9) $2,695
Amazing Spider-Man #238 NM/MT(9.8) $677
Amazing Spider-Man #238 NM+(9.6) $155
Amazing Spider-Man #239 NM/MT(9.8) $175.48
Amazing Spider-Man #239 NM+(9.6) $150
Batman #232 NM/MT(9.8) $2,800
Batman #232 NM+(9.6) $910
Black Panther #1 NM/MT(9.8) $316.25
Conan the Barbarian #1 NM+(9.6) $1,100
Conan the Barbarian #1 NM(9.4) $862.50
Conan the Barbarian #23 NM(9.4) $59.80
Daredevil #168 NM+(9.6) $600
Daredevil #181 NM/MT(9.8) $149.50
Dark Mansion of Forbidden Love #1 NM(9.4) $461
DC Comics Presents #26 NM/MT(9.8) $500
DC 100 Page Super Spectacular #4 NM-(9.2) $359
DC 100 Page Super Spectacular #20 VF(8.0) $35
Defenders #1 NM+(9.6) $725
Detective Comics #400 VF/NM(9.0) $199.95
Detective Comics #423 NM/MT(9.8) $373.75
Evel Knievel #1 NM+(9.6) $153.50
Fantastic Four #109 NM+(9.6) $200
Fantastic Four #150 NM+(9.6) $81.65
Fantastic Four #155 NM/MT(9.8) $690
Fantastic Four #183 35¢ Price Variant VF+(8.5) $215.50
Flash #289 Mile High 2 NM-(9.2) $20
Forever People #1 NM/MT(9.8) $1,121.25
Forever People #1 NM+(9.6) $218.50
Forever People #2 NM+(9.6) $112.50
Frankenstein #1 NM+(9.6) $650
Ghost Rider #1 NM+(9.6) $2,450
Ghost Rider #1 NM(9.4) $561
Giant-Size Defenders #1 NM/MT(9.8) $310
Giant-Size Powerman #1 VF+(8.5) $20
Giant-Size Spider-Man #1 NM-(9.2) $77.05
Giant-Size Spider-Man #4 Winnipeg NM+(9.6) $750
Giant-Size Super-Heroes #1 NM+(9.6) $138
Giant-Size Super-Villain Team-Up #2 NM(9.4) $36
Giant-Size Thor #1 NM+(9.6) $155.25
Giant-Size X-Men #1 NM/MT(9.8) $9,000
Giant-Size X-Men #1 NM+(9.6) $3,049
Giant-Size X-Men #1 NM+(9.6) $3,301.98
Giant-Size X-Men #1 NM(9.4) $1,587.60
Giant-Size X-Men #1 NM-(9.2) $1,250
Giant-Size X-Men #1 VF/NM(9.0) $950
Giant-Size X-Men #1 VF(8.0) $510
Giant-Size X-Men #1 FN/VF(7.0) $300
Green Lantern #78 NM(9.4) $241.50
Green Lantern #81 NM/MT(9.8) $1,322.50
Green Lantern #82 NM/MT(9.8) $1,150
Green Lantern #82 NM+(9.6) $517.50
Green Lantern #85 NM+(9.6) $460
Green Lantern #86 NM+(9.6) $432
Green Lantern #89 NM+(9.6) $314
Green Lantern #89 NM(9.4) $175
House of Mystery #200 NM/MT(9.8) $393
House of Secrets #92 NM+(9.6) $4,400
House of Secrets #92 NM(9.4) $1,840
Howard the Duck #1 NM+(9.6) $70
Howard the Duck #13 NM/MT(9.8) $100
Incredible Hulk #180 NM/MT(9.8) $5,100
Incredible Hulk #180 NM(9.4) $610
Incredible Hulk #181 NM+(9.6) $4,310
Incredible Hulk #181 NM+(9.6) $4,205
Incredible Hulk #181 NM(9.4) $2,425
Incredible Hulk #181 NM(9.4) $2,075
Incredible Hulk #181 NM-(9.2) $1,600
Incredible Hulk #181 VF/NM(9.0) $1,075
Incredible Hulk #181 VF+(8.5) $850
Incredible Hulk #182 NM+(9.6) $750
Invaders Annual #1 NM(9.4) $100
Iron Fist #14 NM/MT(9.8) $1,500
Iron Fist #14 NM+(9.6) $455
Iron Fist #14 35¢ Variant FN/VF(7.0) $1,100
Justice League of America #114 NM/MT(9.8) $310
Justice League of America #116 NM+(9.6) $240
Ka-Zar #1 NM+(9.6) $305
Ka-Zar #1 Oakland NM+(9.6) $345
Legion of Monsters #1 NM+(9.6) $200.50
Little Lulu #260 (Whitman) NM/MT(9.8) $1,826.55
Little Lulu #260 (Whitman) NM/MT(9.8) $1,805
Man-Thing #1 NM/MT(9.8) $761
Marvel Double Feature #1 NM+(9.6) $150
Marvel Feature #1 NM+(9.6) $1,100
Marvel Spotlight #4 NM/MT(9.8) $1,000
Marvel Spotlight #5 NM(9.4) $1,600
Marvel Spotlight #5 VF/NM(9.0) $550
Marvel Spotlight #32 NM(9.4) $57.50
Marvel Super Action #1 NM+(9.6) $141.50
Marvel Team-Up #1 NM-(9.2) $227.50
Marvel Team-Up #2 NM/MT(9.8) $625
Marvel Triple Action #1 Oakland NM+(9.6) $250
Marvel Two-In-One #1 NM+(9.6) $550
Mister Miracle #1 NM/MT(9.8) $850
Mister Miracle #1 NM+(9.6) $264.99
Ms. Marvel #16 NM/MT(9.8) $248.27
Ms. Marvel #18 NM/MT(9.8) $1,199.99
Ms. Marvel #18 NM+(9.6) $545
New Gods #1 NM/MT(9.8) $529
New Gods #1 NM+(9.6) $143.75
New Teen Titans #1 NM+(9.6) $130.49
New Teen Titans #1 NM+(9.6) $110

New Teen Titans #2 NM+(9.6) $131.50
Night Nurse #1 NM(9.4) $306
Nova #1 NM/MT(9.8) $304
Omac #1 NM+(9.6) $62.50
Our Love Story #5 NM+(9.6) $609
Planet of the Apes #1 NM/MT(9.8) $255
Sandman #1 (1974) NM/MT(9.8) $529
Savage Sword of Conan #1 NM/MT(9.8) $2,026
Savage Sword of Conan #1 NM+(9.6) $445
Space: 1999 #6 NM(9.4) $24.95
Special Marvel Edition #15 NM/MT(9.8) $1,081.56
Spectacular Spider-Man #1 NM/MT(9.8) $1,045
Spectacular Spider-Man #1 NM+(9.6) $102.50
Star Wars #1 NM/MT(9.8) $400
Star Wars #1 NM+(9.6) $204
Star Wars #3 35 Cent Variant VF(8.0) $380
Superboy #203 Mile High 2 NM(9.4) $62.50
Superman #233 NM(9.4) $253.75
Superman's Pal Jimmy Olsen #137 NM/MT(9.8) $245
Swamp Thing #7 NM+(9.6) $132.25
Tomb of Dracula #10 NM-(9.2) $208.80
Tomb of Dracula #12 Mass Copy NM/MT(9.8) $1,000
Vampirella #7 NM+(9.6) $898
Wanted #2 (DC 1972) NM/MT(9.8) $165
Warlock #1 NM+(9.6) $337.50
Werewolf By Night #1 NM+(9.6) $1,500
Werewolf By Night #32 Mass Copy NM+(9.6) $1,500
Werewolf By Night #32 NM(9.4) $500
Wolverine: Limited Series #1 MT(9.9) $770
Wolverine Limited Series #1 NM/MT(9.8) $324
Wolverine Limited Series #1 NM+(9.6) $137.50
Wolverine Limited Series #4 NM/MT(9.8) $200
Wonder Woman #199 NM/MT(9.8) $730
X-Men #94 NM+(9.6) $4,450
X-Men #94 NM(9.4) $2,200
X-Men #94 NM-(9.2) $1,000
X-Men #94 VF(8.0) $450
X-Men #95 NM/MT(9.8) $2,026.98
X-Men #96 NM+(9.6) $460
X-Men #97 NM+(9.6) $610
X-Men #98 NM/MT(9.8) $1,147
X-Men #99 NM+(9.6) $450

COPPER AGE - SALES OF CGC GRADED COMICS

Albedo #2 NM-(9.2) $546.85
Amazing Spider-Man #252 NM/MT(9.8) $325
Amazing Spider-Man #252 NM+(9.6) $76
Amazing Spider-Man #265 MT(9.9) $471.50
Amazing Spider-Man #299 NM/MT(9.8) $200
Amazing Spider-Man #299 NM/MT(9.8) $168.50
Amazing Spider-Man #298 NM/MT(9.8) $308
Amazing Spider-Man #298 NM+(9.6) $125
Amazing Spider-Man #300 NM/MT(9.8) $995
Amazing Spider-Man #300 NM+(9.6) $250
Amazing Spider-Man #300 NM+(9.6) $200.05
Amazing Spider-Man #300 NM(9.4) $104.50
Batman #426 NM(9.4) $37.50
Batman: The Dark Knight Returns #1 NM/MT(9.8) $264
Batman: The Killing Joke MT(9.9) $75
Crisis on Infinite Earths #1 NM/MT(9.8) $75
Crow #1 NM/MT(9.8) $311.51
Daredevil #232 MT(9.9) $74.95
Daredevil #249 NM+(9.6) $90
Incredible Hulk #340 NM/MT(9.8) $212
Incredible Hulk #340 NM+(9.6) $75
Incredible Hulk #340 NM(9.4) $50
Kitty Pryde And Wolverine #5 NM+(9.6) $50
Kitty Pryde And Wolverine #6 NM/MT(9.8) $75
Marvel Super-Heroes Secret Wars #8 MT(9.9) $799.99
Marvel Super-Heroes Secret Wars #8 NM/MT(9.8) $153.50
Miracle Man #1 NM+(9.6) $138
Miracle Man #1 NM+(9.6) $62
New Mutants #87 NM/MT(9.8) $228.01
New Mutants #98 NM/MT(9.8) $175
Primer #2 NM/MT(9.8) $213.50
Primer #2 NM+(9.6) $100
Punisher Limited Series #1 NM/MT(9.8) $275
Punisher Limited Series #2 NM/MT(9.8) $175
Saga of the Swamp Thing #37 NM/MT(9.8) $375
Saga of the Swamp Thing #37 NM+(9.6) $95.33
Saga of the Swamp Thing #37 NM/MT(9.8) $277.50
Spectacular Spider-Man #101 MT(9.9) $85
Spider-Man #1 GM(10.0) $995
Spider-Man #1 Gold Edition UPC NM/MT(9.8) $690
Spider-Man #1 Gold Edition UPC NM+(9.6) $325
Spider-Man #1 Green Cover MT(9.9) $112.50
Spider-Man #1 Platinum GM(10.0) $810
Spider-Man #1 Platinum Edition NM/MT(9.8) $610
Spider-Man #1 Silver Cover GM(10.0) $361.51
Spider-Man #1 Silver Cover MT(9.9) $114.51
Star Wars #107 NM+(9.6) $232.50
Superman #1 (1987) MT(9.9) $175
Teenage Mutant Ninja Turtles #1 NM-(9.2) $1,713
Teenage Mutant Ninja Turtles #1 VF(8.0) $1,525
Teenage Mutant Ninja Turtles #2 NM/MT(9.8) $599.99
Teenage Mutant Ninja Turtles #2 NM+(9.6) $199.99
Transformers #1 NM+(9.6) $124.99
Web of Spider-Man #26 MT(9.9) $50
Wolverine #1 NM/MT(9.8) $162.50
Wolverine #10 NM/MT(9.8) $150.50
X-Men #248 NM/MT(9.8) $100
X-Men (Uncanny) #266 MT(9.9) $2,125.00
X-Men #266 NM/MT(9.8) $300
X-Men #266 NM+(9.6) $91

Action Comics #812 GM(10.0) $157.50
Action Comics #812 2nd Pr. Sketch-c GM(10.0) $334.95
Action Comics #812 MT(9.9) $94.95
Adventures of Superman #625 GM(10.0) $124.95
Amazing Spider-Man Vol.2 #30 MT(9.9) $92.51
Amazing Spider-Man Vol.2 #36 NM/MT(9.8) $145.50
Amazing Spider-Man Vol.2 #36 NM+(9.6) $65
Astonishing X-Men #1 MT(9.9) $174.95
Astonishing X-Men #1 Cassaday Var-c NM/MT(9.8) $227.50
Astonishing X-Men #1 Dell'Otto Variant NM/MT(9.8) $76
Astonishing X-Men #1 Director's Cut Ed. MT(9.9) $144.95
Astonishing X-Men #4 Variant Cover NM/MT(9.8) $124.95
Avengers/JLA #2 GM(10.0) $102.07
Avengers/JLA #4 GM(10.0) $86
Avengers/JLA #4 Signature Series GM(10.0) $202.50
Banzai Girl #1 NM/MT(9.8) $87.50
Batman #497 GM(10.0) $405
Batman #608 2nd Print NM/MT(9.8) $305
Batman #608 RRP NM/MT(9.8) $2,410.85
Batman #608 RRP NM+(9.6) $1,475
Batman #608 RRP NM(9.4) $1,175
Batman #608 RRP Qualified NM(9.4) $560
Batman #612 2nd Printing Sketch Cover MT(9.9) $399.95
Batman: The Long Halloween #1 NM+(9.6) $75
Birds of Prey #69 GM(10.0) $99.95
Bloodshot #0 Platinum NM/MT(9.8) $2,067.42
Born #2 GM(10.0) $99.99
Cerebus The Aardvark #300 NM/MT(9.8) $74.99
Chaos Effect: Alpha NM/MT(9.8) $1,500
Daredevil Vol. 2 #28 MT(9.9) $51.02
DC Presents: Green Lantern #1 GM(10.0) $199.95
Elektra Vol.2 #3 Nude Edition NM/MT(9.8) $203.51
Fables #1 NM/MT(9.8) $45
Fantastic Four #500 MT(9.9) $102.50
Harbinger #0 Pink NM/MT(9.8) $306
Harbinger #1 NM/MT(9.8) $969.60
Hulk: Grey #1 MT(9.9) $66.02
Identity Crisis #1 Diamond Summit Ed. NM/MT(9.8) $1,849.95
Identity Crisis #1 NM/MT(9.8) $40
Incredible Hulk: The End #1 NM/MT(9.8) $255
JLA/Avengers #1 MT(9.9) $79
JLA/Avengers #1 NM/MT(9.8) $30
JLA/Avengers #3 GM(10.0) $140.03
John Byrne's Next Men #21 NM/MT(9.8) $405
Magnus Robot Fighter #0 NM/MT(9.8) $270
Magnus Robot Fighter #1 NM/MT(9.8) $127.50
Magnus Robot Fighter #21 Gold NM/MT(9.8) $201.50
Marvel Age Fantastic Four #2 GM(10.0) $149.95
Marvel Knights Spider-Man #1 GM(10.0) $249.95
Marvel 1602 #8 Signature Series GM(10.0) $177.50
New X-Men #114 NM/MT(9.8) $32.02
Nightwing #1 NM+(9.6) $50
NYX #1 NM/MT(9.8) $59.95
NYX #3 NM/MT(9.8) $280
Punisher Kills the Marvel Universe #1 MT(9.9) $179.16
Secret War #1 Signature Series NM/MT(9.8) $229.16
Sojourn #1 NM/MT $74.98
Solar Man of the Atom #1 NM/MT(9.8) $111
Solar Man of the Atom #10 NM/MT(9.8) $382
Spawn #1 GM(10.0) $660
Spawn #1 MT(9.9) $139.95
Spawn #1 NM/MT(9.8) $100
Spawn #21 MT(9.9) $129.39
Superman #204 GM(10.0) $489
Superman #204 MT(9.9) $152.50
Superman #204 Diamond Summit Ed. NM/MT(9.8) $1,850
Superman #204 Diamond Summit Ed. NM/MT(9.8) $1,300
Superman #204 Diamond Summit Ed. NM+(9.6) $1,492
Superman/Batman #1 Retailer Edition NM/MT(9.8) $535
Superman/Batman #1 Superman Cover NM/MT(9.8) $112.50
Superman/Batman #8 NM/MT(9.8) $37.50
Superman/Batman #9 GM(10.0) $229.95
Teen Titans #1 Turner-c NM/MT(9.8) $46
Teen Titans #1 Turner-c NM+(9.6) $29.95
30 Days Of Night Annual #1 NM/MT(9.8) $75
24: One Shot GM(10.0) $151.95
Turok Dinosaur Hunter #1 Gold NM/MT(9.8) $161.50
Ultimate Fantastic Four #1 MT(9.9) $152.50
Ultimates #1 NM/MT (9.8) $39.95
Ultimates #2 NM/MT (9.8) $76.55
Ultimate Spider-Man #1 Red Cover NM/MT(9.8) $825
Ultimate Spider-Man #1 Red Cover NM+(9.6) $250
Ultimate Spider-Man #1 DF Edition NM/MT(9.8) $910
Ultimate Spider-Man #1 DF Edition NM/MT(9.8) $624.99
Ultimate Spider-Man #1 White Cover NM/MT(9.8) $1,325
Ultimate Spider-Man #1 White Cover NM+(9.6) $850.99
Ultimate Spider-Man #2 Car Cover NM/MT(9.8) $245
Ultimate Spider-Man #2 Swing Cover NM/MT(9.8) $200
Ultimate Spider-Man #63 MT(9.9) $257.45
Ultimate X-Men #1 NM/MT(9.8) $135
Ultimate X-Men #1 DF Edition NM/MT(9.8) $250
Unity #0 Red NM/MT(9.8) $447.42
Venom: Lethal Protector Black NM/MT(9.8) $444
Venom: Lethal Protector #1 Black Cover NM+(9.6) $610
Walt Disney's Uncle Scrooge #319 NM/MT(9.8) $142.50
Witchblade #1 NM/MT(9.8) $125
Wolverine #145 Nabisco Variant Cover NM+(9.6) $346.01
Wolverine: The End #1 MT(9.9) $99.90
Wolverine: The Origin #1 NM/MT(9.8) $275
Wolverine: The Origin #4 NM/MT(9.8) $152.50
X-O Manowar #0 Gold Sign. Series NM/MT(9.8) $128.72
X-O Manowar #1 NM/MT(9.8) $153.50
Y: The Last Man #1 NM/MT(9.8) $209.50
Y: The Last Man #2 NM/MT(9.8) $75

The following tables denote the rate of appreciation of the top Golden Age, Platinum Age, Silver Age and Bronze Age books, as well as selected genres over the past year. The retail value for a Near Mint- copy of each book (or VF where a Near Mint- copy is not known to exist) in 2005 is compared to its Near Mint- value in 2004. The rate of return for 2005 over 2004 is given. The place in rank is given for each comic by year, with its corresponding value in highest known grade. These tables can be very useful in forecasting trends in the market place. For instance, the investor might want to know which book is yielding the best dividend from one year to the next, or one might just be interested in seeing how the popularity of books changes from year to year. For instance, *Human Torch* #2 (#1) was in 21st place in 2004 and has increased to 18th place in 2005. Premium books are also included in these tables and are denoted with an asterisk(*).

The following tables are meant as a guide to the investor. However, it should be pointed out that trends may change at anytime and that some books can meet market resistance with a slowdown in price increases, while others can develop into real comers from a presently dormant state. In the long run, if the investor sticks to the books that are appreciating steadily each year, he shouldn't go very far wrong.

Top Golden Age Books

2005 over 2004 Guide Values

TITLE/ISSUE#	2005 RANK	2005 NM- PRICE	2004 RANK	2004 NM- PRICE	$ INCR.	% INCR.
Action Comics #1	1	$485,000	1	$440,000	$45,000	10%
Detective Comics #27	2	$410,000	2	$375,000	$35,000	9%
Marvel Comics #1	3	$365,000	3	$330,000	$35,000	11%
Superman #1	4	$300,000	4	$270,000	$30,000	11%
All-American Comics #16	5	$180,000	5	$160,000	$20,875	13%
Batman #1	6	$140,000	6	$125,000	$15,000	12%
Captain America Comics #1	6	$140,000	6	$125,000	$15,000	12%
Flash Comics #1	8	$110,000	8	$97,000	$13,000	13%
More Fun Comics #52	9	$90,000	9	$84,000	$6,000	7%
Whiz Comics #2 (#1)	10	$88,000	10	$84,000	$4,000	5%
Adventure Comics #40	11	$70,000	11	$64,000	$6,000	9%
Detective Comics #33	12	$65,000	12	$60,000	$5,000	8%
All Star Comics #3	13	$60,000	14	$55,000	$5,000	9%
Detective Comics #1	13	VF $60,000	13	VF $58,000	$2,000	3%
Detective Comics #38	13	$60,000	14	$55,000	$5,000	9%
Green Lantern #1	16	$55,000	16	$50,000	$5,000	10%
Action Comics #2	17	$51,000	17	$46,000	$5,000	11%
Detective Comics #29	18	$50,000	18	$45,000	$5,000	11%
Detective Comics #31	18	$50,000	18	$45,000	$5,000	11%
Human Torch #2 (#1)	18	$50,000	21	$44,000	$6,000	14%
Sub-Mariner Comics #1	18	$50,000	18	$45,000	$5,000	11%
All Star Comics #8	22	$48,000	21	$44,000	$4,000	9%
More Fun Comics #53	23	$46,000	24	$43,000	$3,000	7%
New Fun Comics #1	23	VF $46,000	23	VF $43,500	$2,500	6%
Captain Marvel Adventures #1	25	$45,000	25	$42,000	$3,000	7%
Sensation Comics #1	26	$44,000	26	$40,000	$4,000	10%
Marvel Mystery Comics #2	27	$43,000	27	$38,000	$5,000	13%
Action Comics #7	28	$40,000	29	$35,000	$5,000	14%
Marvel Mystery Comics #9	28	$40,000	28	$36,000	$4,000	11%
Adventure Comics #48	30	$38,000	29	$35,000	$3,000	9%
Wonder Woman #1	31	$37,500	31	$34,000	$3,500	10%
All Winners Comics #1	32	$35,000	32	$30,000	$5,000	17%
Marvel Mystery Comics #5	33	$34,000	32	$30,000	$4,000	13%
Action Comics #3	34	$32,000	36	$28,000	$4,000	14%
Daring Mystery Comics #1	35	$31,000	35	$29,000	$2,000	7%
Detective Comics #28	36	$30,000	38	$27,000	$3,000	11%
New York World's Fair 1939	36	VF/NM $30,000	32	VF/NM $30,000	$0	0%
Famous Funnies-Series 1 #1	38	VF $28,000	38	VF $27,000	$1,000	4%
* Motion Picture Funnies Weekly #1	38	$28,000	36	$28,000	$0	0%
** New Book of Comics #1	40	$27,000	-	$27,000	$0	0%

** The higest grade priced for New Book of Comics #1 was changed from VF to NM- with this edition.

TITLE/ISSUE#	2005 RANK	2005 NM- PRICE	2004 RANK	2004 NM- PRICE	$ INCR.	% INCR.
Action Comics #10	41	$26,000	43	$22,000	$4,000	18%
* Century Of Comics nn	42	VF $25,000	40	VF $24,000	$1,000	4%
Walt Disney's Comics & Stories #1 .	42	$25,000	41	$23,000	$2,000	9%
All-American Comics #19	44	$24,000	43	$22,000	$2,000	9%
All Flash #1	44	$24,000	43	$22,000	$2,000	9%
*Marvel Mystery Comics 132 pg. ...	44	VF $24,000	41	VF $23,000	$1,000	4%
Amazing Man Comics #5	47	$23,500	43	$22,000	$1,500	7%
Young Allies Comics #1	48	$23,000	48	$21,000	$2,000	10%
Wonder Comics #1	49	$22,500	48	$21,000	$1,500	7%
World's Best Comics #1	49	VF $22,500	47	VF $21,500	$1,000	5%
All-American Comics #17	51	$22,000	52	$20,500	$1,500	7%
Archie Comics #1	51	$22,000	52	$20,500	$1,500	7%
Captain America Comics 132 pg. ...	51	$22,000	48	$21,000	$1,000	5%
Marvel Mystery Comics #3	51	$22,000	62	$19,000	$3,000	16%
Mystic Comics #1	51	$22,000	52	$20,500	$1,500	7%
Pep Comics #22	51	$22,000	56	$20,000	$2,000	10%
Wow Comics #1	57	$21,500	56	$20,000	$1,500	8%
Batman #2	58	$21,000	59	$19,500	$3,750	24%
Captain America Comics #2	58	$21,000	62	$19,000	$2,000	11%
Famous Funnies #1	58	VF $21,000	56	VF $20,000	$1,000	5%
Jumbo Comics #1	58	VF $21,000	52	VF $20,500	$500	2%
More Fun Comics #55	58	$21,000	62	$19,000	$2,000	11%
New Fun Comics #6	58	VF $21,000	51	VF $20,700	$300	1%
Silver Streak Comics #6	58	$21,000	59	$19,500	$1,500	8%
Adventure Comics #73	65	$20,000	71	$17,500	$2,500	14%
Daredevil Comics #1	65	$20,000	66	$18,000	$2,000	11%
More Fun Comics #73	65	$20,000	66	$18,000	$2,000	11%
New Comics #1	65	VF $20,000	59	VF $19,500	$500	3%
Suspense Comics #3	65	$20,000	66	$18,000	$2,000	11%
All Star Comics #1	70	$19,500	66	$18,000	$1,500	8%
Superman #2	70	$19,500	71	$17,500	$2,000	11%
USA Comics #1	70	$19,500	66	$18,000	$1,500	8%
Action Comics #4	73	$19,000	71	$17,500	$1,500	9%
Action Comics #5	73	$19,000	71	$17,500	$1,500	9%
Action Comics #6	73	$19,000	71	$17,500	$1,500	9%
All-Select Comics #1	73	$19,000	76	$17,000	$2,000	12%
More Fun Comics #54	73	$19,000	76	$17,000	$2,000	12%
New Fun Comics #2	73	VF $19,000	65	VF $18,700	$300	2%
Adventure Comics #61	79	$18,500	76	$17,000	$1,500	9%
Marvel Mystery Comics #4	79	$18,500	81	$16,500	$2,000	12%
Planet Comics #1	79	$18,500	81	$16,500	$2,000	12%
Red Raven Comics #1	79	$18,500	76	$17,000	$1,500	9%
Adventure Comics #72	83	$17,500	85	$16,000	$1,500	9%
Detective Comics #35	83	$17,500	85	$16,000	$1,500	9%
Double Action Comics #2	83	$17,500	76	$17,000	$500	3%
Captain America Comics #3	86	$17,000	90	$15,500	$1,500	10%
Four Color Ser. 1 (Donald Duck) #4	86	$17,000	90	$15,500	$1,500	10%
Green Giant Comics #1	86	$17,000	85	$16,000	$1,000	6%
Looney Tunes and Merrie Melodies #1	86	$17,000	85	$16,000	$1,000	6%
New York World's Fair 1940	90	VF/NM $16,800	81	VF/NM $16,800	$0	0%
Detective Comics #2	91	VF $16,600	84	VF $16,300	$300	2%
Mickey Mouse Magazine #1	92	VF/NM $16,500	85	VF/NM $16,000	$500	3%
Silver Streak Comics #1	92	$16,500	90	$15,500	$1,000	6%
Marvel Mystery Comics #8	94	$16,000	93	$14,500	$1,500	10%
Mystery Men Comics #1	95	$15,500	93	$14,500	$1,000	7%
All-American Comics #18	96	$15,000	96	$14,000	$1,000	7%
* Funnies on Parade nn	96	$15,000	93	$14,500	$500	3%
Pep Comics #1	96	$15,000	96	$14,000	$1,000	7%
Tough Kid Squad Comics #1	96	$15,000	96	$14,000	$1,000	7%
Big All-American #1	100	$14,500	100	$13,500	$1,000	7%

Top 20 Silver Age Books

TITLE/ISSUE#	2005 RANK	2005 NM- PRICE	2004 RANK	2004 NM- PRICE	$ INCR.	% INCR.
Amazing Fantasy #15	1	$42,500	1	$42,500	$0	0%
Showcase #4 (The Flash)	2	$42,000	2	$41,000	$1,000	2%
Fantastic Four #1	3	$35,000	3	$34,000	$1,000	3%
Amazing Spider-Man #1	4	$32,500	4	$32,000	$500	2%
Incredible Hulk #1	5	$25,000	5	$23,000	$2,000	9%
Showcase #8 (The Flash)	6	$17,000	6	$16,800	$200	1%
X-Men #1	7	$14,000	7	$13,000	$1,000	8%
Showcase #9 (Lois Lane)	8	$11,000	8	$10,500	$500	5%
Journey Into Mystery #83 (Thor)	9	$10,000	9	$9,000	$1,000	11%
The Flash #105	10	$9,300	10	$8,500	$800	9%
Tales of Suspense #39 (Iron Man)	11	$9,000	11	$8,000	$1,000	13%
Brave and the Bold #28	12	$8,800	11	$8,000	$800	10%
Adventure Comics #247 (Legion)	13	$8,000	13	$7,500	$500	7%
Justice League of America #1	13	$8,000	14	$7,000	$1,000	14%
Showcase #22 (Green Lantern)	15	$7,500	14	$7,000	$500	7%
Fantastic Four #5	16	$7,200	16	$6,500	$700	11%
Green Lantern #1	16	$7,200	16	$6,500	$700	11%
Fantastic Four #2	18	$7,000	19	$6,250	$750	12%
Tales To Astonish #27 (Ant-Man)	18	$7,000	16	$6,500	$500	8%
Amazing Spider-Man #2	20	$6,700	20	$6,000	$700	12%

Top 10 Bronze Age Books

TITLE/ISSUE#	2005 RANK	2005 NM- PRICE	2004 RANK	2004 NM- PRICE	$ INCR.	% INCR.
Incredible Hulk #181	1	$1,300	1	$1,250	$50	4%
Giant-Size X-Men #1	2	$1,100	2	$1,200	-$100	-8%
X-Men #94	3	$1,000	3	$1,025	-$25	-2%
House of Secrets #92	4	$850	4	$800	$50	6%
DC 100 Page Super Spectacular #5	6	$750	6	$700	$50	7%
Cerebus #1	7	$650	10	$500	$150	30%
All-Star Western #10	8	$600	8	$560	$40	7%
Uncle Scrooge #179 (Whitman)	8	$600	7	$575	$25	4%
Vampirella Special HC	10	$560	9	$525	$35	7%
Green Lantern #76	10	$500	-	$425	$75	18%

***Star Wars #1 (35¢ price variant)** - Recent sales of this book include a CGC 9.2 for $4,050

Top 10 Copper Age Books

TITLE/ISSUE#	2005 RANK	2005 NM- PRICE	2004 RANK	2004 NM- PRICE	$ INCR.	% INCR.
Miracleman #1 Gold Edition	1	$1,500	1	$1,500	$0	0%
Miracleman #1 Blue Edition	2	$800	2	$800	$0	0%
Gobbledygook #1	2	$800	3	$450	$350	78%
Gobbledygook #2	4	$500	5	$350	$150	43%
Vampirella #113	5	$425	4	$410	$15	4%
Albedo #2	6	$250	6	$200	$50	25%
Grendel #1	7	$165	7	$140	$25	18%
Primer #2	8	$130	8	$125	$5	4%
Spider-Man #1 (2nd pr. w/Gold UPC)	9	$120	9	$120	$0	0%
Spider-Man #1 (Platinum)	9	$120	10	$100	$20	20%

***Teenage Mutant Ninja Turtles #1** - Recent sales of this book include a CGC 9.2 for $1,713

Top 20 Big Little Books

BOOK #	TITLE	2005 RANK	2005 VF/NM PRICE	2004 RANK	2004 VF/NM PRICE	$ INCR.	% INCR.
731	**Mickey Mouse the Mail Pilot** (variant version of Mickey Mouse #717) (Fine copy sold at auction for $5,090)						
nn	**Mickey Mouse and Minnie Mouse at Macy's**	2	$2,500	2	$2,200	$300	14%
717	**Mickey Mouse** (skinny Mickey on-c)	3	$2,400	(new to Guide)			
nn	**Mickey Mouse and Minnie March to Macy's**	4	$1,750	3	$1,600	$150	9%
W-707	**Dick Tracy The Detective**	4	$1,750	3	$1,600	$150	9%
725	**Big Little Mother Goose** HC	6	$1,650	6	$1,500	$150	10%
717	**Mickey Mouse** (reg. Mickey on-c)	7	$1,250	3	$1,600	-$350	-22%
4063	**Popeye Thimble Theater Starring...** (2nd printing)	8	$1,200	7	$1,200	$0	0%
725	**Big Little Mother Goose** SC	9	$1,150	8	$1,000	$150	15%
721	**Big Little Paint Book**	10	$1,100	8	$1,000	$100	11%
2070	**Big Big Paint Book**	11	$1,000	(new to Guide)			
nn	**Mickey Mouse** (Great Big Midget Book)	11	$1,000	(new to Guide)			
4062	**Mickey Mouse and the Smugglers**	11	$1,000	8	$1,000	$0	0%
4063	**Popeye Thimble Theater Starring...** (1st printing)	11	$1,000	8	$1,000	$0	0%
4062	**Mickey Mouse, The Story of...**	15	$900	8	$1,000	-$100	-10%
nn	**Buck Rogers**	15	$900	13	$850	$50	6%
nn	**Mickey Mouse Silly Symphonies**	15	$900	13	$850	$50	6%
nn	**Tarzan**	18	$875	15	$800	$75	9%
4071	**Dick Tracy and the Mystery of the Purple Cross**	19	$850	15	$800	$50	6%
4057	**Buck Rogers, The Adventures of...**	20	$800	17	$750	$50	7%

Top 10 Platinum Age Books

TITLE/ISSUE#	2005 RANK	2005 PRICE	2004 RANK	2004 PRICE	$ INCR.	% INCR.
Mickey Mouse Book (2nd printing)-variant	1	FN $12,000	1	FN $12,000	$0	0%
Mickey Mouse Book (1st printing)	2	VF $11,000	2	VF $11,000	$0	0%
Mickey Mouse Book (2nd printing)	3	VF $10,000	3	VF $10,000	$0	0%
Yellow Kid in McFadden Flats	4	FN $8,700	4	FN $8,700	$0	0%
Pore Li'l Mose	5	FN $5,500	5	FN $5,250	$250	5%
Buster Brown and His Resolutions 1903	6	FN $5,250	6	FN $5,000	$250	5%
Little Sammy Sneeze	7	FN $3,900	7	FN $3,900	$500	15%
Little Nemo 1906	8	FN $3,350	8	FN $3,200	$150	5%
Yellow Kid #1	9	FN $3,000	8	FN $3,000	$0	0%
Little Nemo 1909	10	FN $2,675	10	FN $2,600	$75	3%

Top 10 Crime Books

TITLE/ISSUE#	2005 RANK	2005 NM- PRICE	2004 RANK	2004 NM- PRICE	$ INCR.	% INCR.
Crime Does Not Pay #22	1	$3,400	1	$3,100	$300	10%
True Crime Comics #2	2	$1,900	2	$1,800	$100	6%
Crime Does Not Pay #23	3	$1,750	3	$1,650	$100	6%
Crimes By Women #1	4	$1,600	4	$1,540	$60	4%
The Killers #1	5	$1,400	5	$1,340	$60	4%
True Crime Comics #3	5	$1,400	5	$1,340	$60	4%
Crime Does Not Pay #24	7	$1,375	7	$1,300	$75	6%
True Crime Comics #4	8	$1,225	8	$1,175	$50	4%
The Killers #2	9	$1,150	9	$1,100	$50	5%
Crime Smashers #1	10	$1,125	10	$1,060	$65	6%

Top 10 Horror Books

TITLE/ISSUE#	2005 RANK	2005 NM- PRICE	2004 RANK	2004 NM- PRICE	$ INCR.	% INCR.
Vault of Horror #12	1	$6,700	1	$6,300	$400	6%
Eerie #1	2	$5,800	2	$5,000	$800	16%
Tales of Terror Annual #1	3	VF $4,600	3	VF $4,400	$200	5%
Journey into Mystery #1	4	$4,300	4	$4,000	$300	8%
Strange Tales #1	5	$4,200	5	$3,900	$300	8%
Crypt of Terror #17	6	$4,000	6	$3,800	$200	5%
Haunt of Fear #15	6	$4,000	6	$3,800	$200	5%
Crime Patrol #15	8	$3,700	8	$3,500	$200	6%
House of Mystery #1	9	$3,100	9	$2,850	$250	9%
Tales to Astonish #1	10	$2,600	10	$2,400	$200	8%

Top 10 Romance Books

TITLE/ISSUE#	2005 RANK	2005 NM- PRICE	2004 RANK	2004 NM- PRICE	$ INCR.	% INCR.
Giant Comics Edition #12	1	$1,450	1	$1,400	$50	4%
Intimate Confessions #1	2	$1,000	2	$950	$50	5%
Romance Trail #1	3	$785	3	$750	$35	5%
Young Lovers #18	3	$785	3	$750	$35	5%
DC 100 Page Super Spectacular #5	5	$750	5	$700	$50	7%
Secret Hearts #1	6	$700	8	$660	$40	6%
Giant Comics Edition #9	7	$685	6	$675	$10	1%
Giant Comics Edition #15	7	$685	6	$675	$10	1%
Personal Love #32	9	$675	9	$650	$25	4%
Women in Love - 1952	9	$675	10	$635	$40	6%

Top 10 Sci-Fi Books

TITLE/ISSUE#	2005 RANK	2005 NM- PRICE	2004 RANK	2004 NM- PRICE	$ INCR.	% INCR.
Mystery In Space #1	1	$4,800	2	$4,400	$400	9%
Strange Adventures #1	1	$4,800	1	$4,500	$300	7%
Showcase #17 (Adam Strange)	3	$3,800	3	$3,500	$300	9%
Showcase #15 (Space Ranger)	4	$3,150	6	$2,750	$400	15%
Journey Into Unknown Worlds #36	5	$3,100	4	$2,900	$200	7%
Fawcett Movie #15 (Man From Planet X)	6	$3,000	5	$2,850	$150	5%
Strange Adventures #9	7	$2,900	7	$2,700	$200	7%
Weird Fantasy #13 (#1)	8	$2,800	9	$2,600	$200	8%
Weird Science #12 (#1)	8	$2,800	9	$2,600	$200	8%
Weird Science-Fantasy Annual 1952	8	$2,800	8	$2,650	$150	6%

Top 10 Western Books

TITLE/ISSUE#	2005 RANK	2005 NM- PRICE	2004 RANK	2004 NM- PRICE	$ INCR.	% INCR.
Gene Autry Comics #1	1	$12,000	1	$11,000	$1,000	9%
Hopalong Cassidy #1	2	$7,300	3	$6,800	$500	7%
*Lone Ranger Ice Cream 1939 2nd	3	VF $7,200	2	VF $7,000	$200	3%
*Lone Ranger Ice Cream 1939	4	VF $6,700	4	VF $6,500	$200	3%
*Red Ryder Victory Patrol '42	5	$5,200	5	$5,000	$200	4%
*Red Ryder Victory Patrol '43	6	$4,800	6	$4,600	$200	4%
*Red Ryder Victory Patrol '44	6	$4,800	6	$4,600	$200	4%
Red Ryder Comics #1	8	$4,200	9	$3,800	$400	11%
*Tom Mix Ralston #1	8	$4,200	8	$4,000	$200	5%
Roy Rogers Four Color #38	10	$3,700	10	$3,500	$200	6%

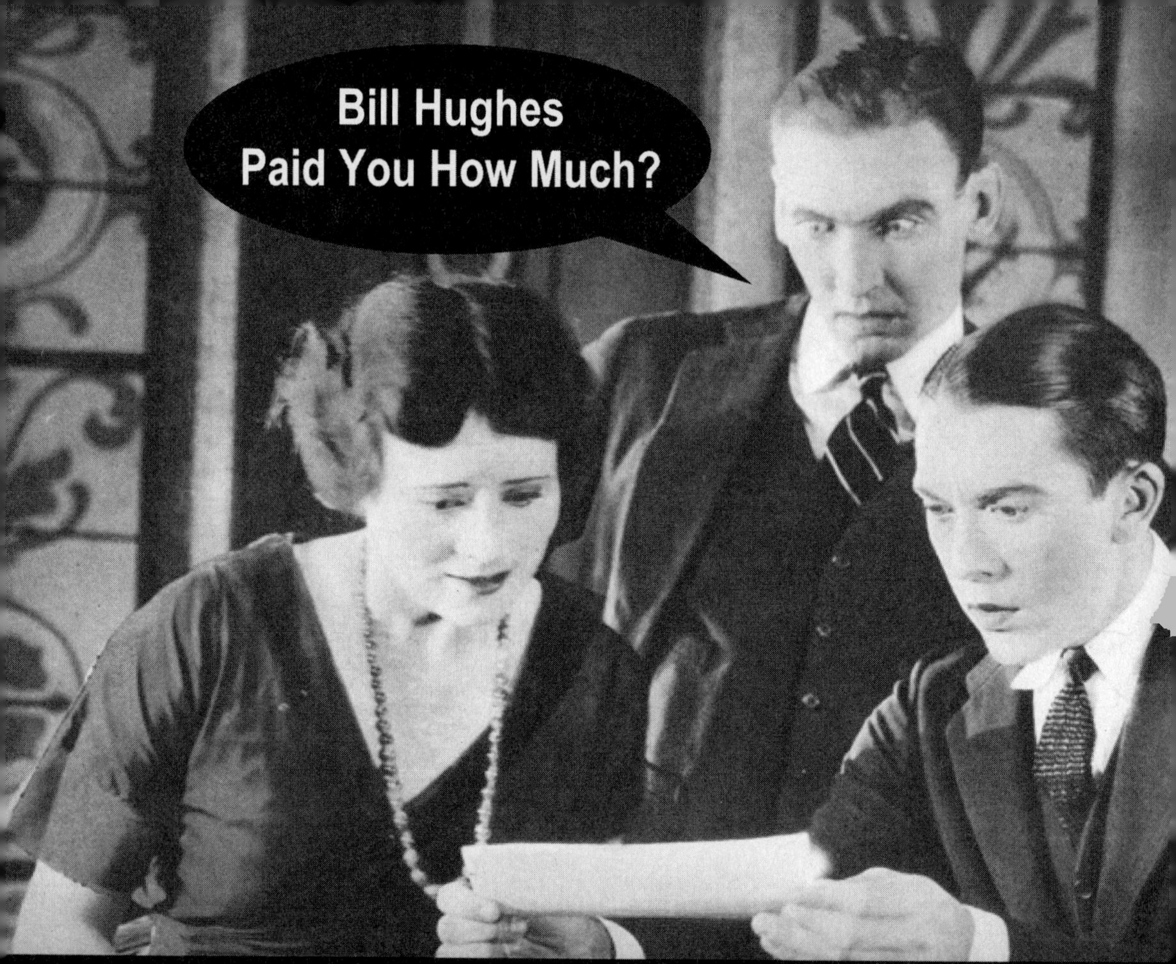

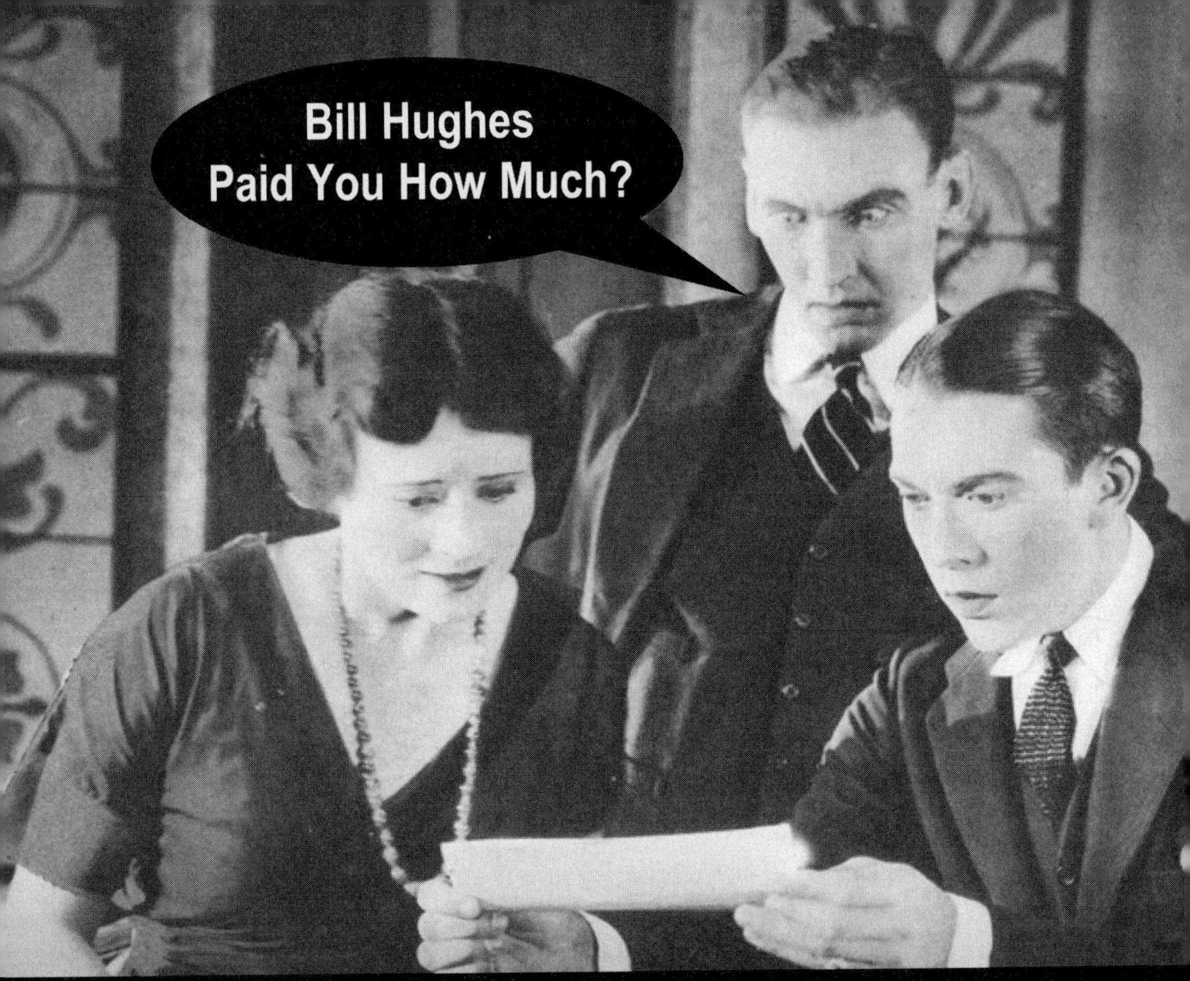

Senior Advisor
Overstreet
Price Guide
CGC
Comics Guaranty, LLC
CHARTER
MEMBER DEALER
COLOSSAL
Is My Desire for the Finest In Vintage Collectables
Why Sell Your Best Material to William Hughes?
I PAY THE MOST, BECAUSE I GET THE MOST!!
Yes, you read correctly, I will usually pay the most for quality vintage COMIC BOOKS, MOVIE POSTERS or BASEBALL CARDS because I can usually get the most for these items through my vast network of associates and customer list of thousands of active buyers. I also sell many items "outside the hobby" to people that don't care what price guides say and who don't want to bid in auctions.
I Am Up To The Challenge! I Will Do My Very Best To Pay Your Ultimate Desired Price, Just Try Me First.
William Hughes'
Vintage Collectables
P.O. Box 270244
Flower Mound, TX 75027
Office: 972-539-9190
Mobile: 973-432-4070
Fax: 972-691-8837

SIX CENTS PER COPY.

SERIES OF COMICAL DESIGNS,

D. C. JOHNSTON,

Chicago Daily Tribune

THE WORLD'S GREATEST NEWSPAPER

HOME

DEWEY DEFEATS TRUMAN

G.O.P. Sweep Indicated in State; Boyle Leads in City

REPUBLICAN TICKET AHEAD OF 1944 VOTE

Town Balloting Gives Trend

Tops Coghlan in Hot Race for Attorney

RECORD CITY VOTE SEEN IN LATE TALLIES

Suburban Ballot Near 375,000

BULLETINS ON ELECTIONS

Early Count Gives G.O.P. Senate Edge

PUTS G.O.P. BACK IN THE WHITE HOUSE

Sizable Electoral Margin Seen

WE'RE CONFUSED!

**THE FOLLOWING IS A TRUE STORY.
WE HOPE THAT SOMEONE WHO READS THIS
WILL BE ABLE TO EXPLAIN WHY THIS KIND OF
THING HAPPENS, BECAUSE WE DON'T GET IT !**

At one of the biggest conventions of the year, a dealer who traveled hundreds of miles to set up, sold a high-grade Fantastic Four #1 for roughly 1/2 the price that we would have paid. After that book passed through the hands of several dealers, we did in fact buy it. The fellow who initially sold it at the convention could easily have made ***Seven Thousand Dollars more*** if he had he sold it to us.

SHOULDN'T EVERYONE? IS IT STILL BETTER TO GET MORE MONEY FOR YOUR BOOKS THAN LESS? DOES THE EARTH STILL REVOLVE AROUND THE SUN? ARE THERE STILL PEOPLE OUT THERE WHO ARE NOT OFFERING THEIR BOOKS TO METROPOLIS AND LOSING MONEY SELLING TO THE WRONG GUY?

If anyone out there can shed any light on why this still happens in this day and age, could you please let us know?

COLLECTIBLES

**873 Broadway, Suite 201
New York, NY 10003
Call Toll Free: 1-800-229-6387
ph: (212) 260-4147 fax: (212) 260-4304
email: buying@metropoliscomics.com
web: www.metropoliscomics.com**

COMICS GUARANTY, LLC Charter Member Dealer

THE WORLD'S LARGEST VINTAGE COMIC BOOK DEALER

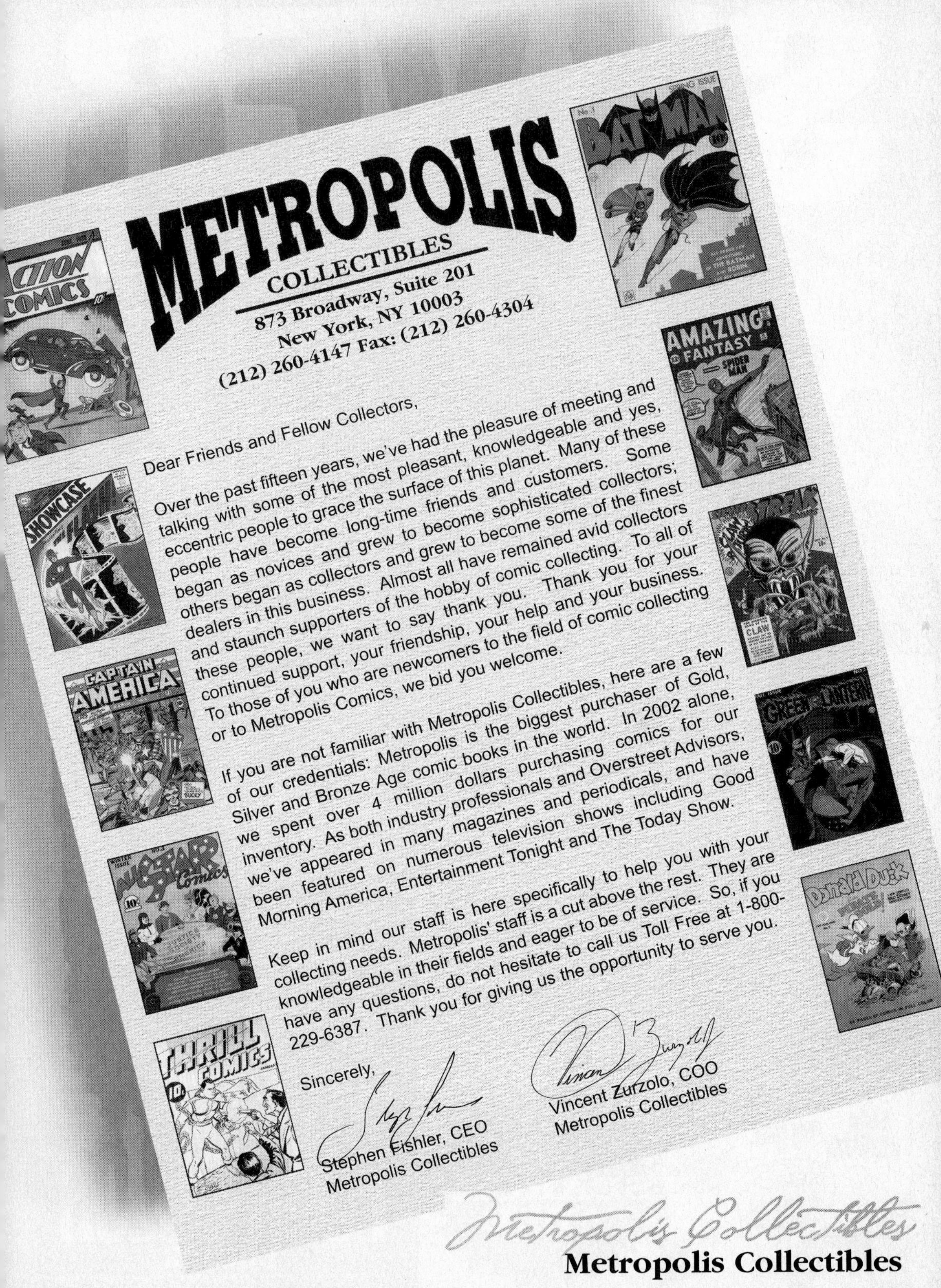

METROPOLIS

COLLECTIBLES

873 Broadway, Suite 201
New York, NY 10003
(212) 260-4147 Fax: (212) 260-4304

Dear Friends and Fellow Collectors,

Over the past fifteen years, we've had the pleasure of meeting and talking with some of the most pleasant, knowledgeable and yes, eccentric people to grace the surface of this planet. Many of these people have become long-time friends and customers. Some began as novices and grew to become sophisticated collectors; others began as collectors and grew to become some of the finest dealers in this business. Almost all have remained avid collectors and staunch supporters of the hobby of comic collecting. To all of these people, we want to say thank you. Thank you for your continued support, your friendship, your help and your business. To those of you who are newcomers to the field of comic collecting or to Metropolis Comics, we bid you welcome.

If you are not familiar with Metropolis Collectibles, here are a few of our credentials: Metropolis is the biggest purchaser of Gold, Silver and Bronze Age comic books in the world. In 2002 alone, we spent over 4 million dollars purchasing comics for our inventory. As both industry professionals and Overstreet Advisors, we've appeared in many magazines and periodicals, and have been featured on numerous television shows including Good Morning America, Entertainment Tonight and The Today Show.

Keep in mind our staff is here specifically to help you with your collecting needs. Metropolis' staff is a cut above the rest. They are knowledgeable in their fields and eager to be of service. So, if you have any questions, do not hesitate to call us Toll Free at 1-800-229-6387. Thank you for giving us the opportunity to serve you.

Sincerely,

Stephen Fishler, CEO
Metropolis Collectibles

Vincent Zurzolo, COO
Metropolis Collectibles

Metropolis Collectibles

FOUR COLOR
COMICS
BUYING PRE-1980 LINE-ART
I buy, sell, and collect original comic art. I can and will pay you the highest price for your art. Call me before you sell.
Of particular interest:
GOLDENAGE ART
DC SILVERAGE ART
MARVEL SILVERAGE ART
EC COVER ART
FRAZETTA, KIRBY, DITKO, BARKS
P.O. Box 1399
Scarsdale, NY 10583
Tel: (914) 722-4696
Fax: (914) 722-7656
www.fourcolorcomics.com

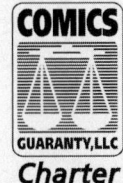

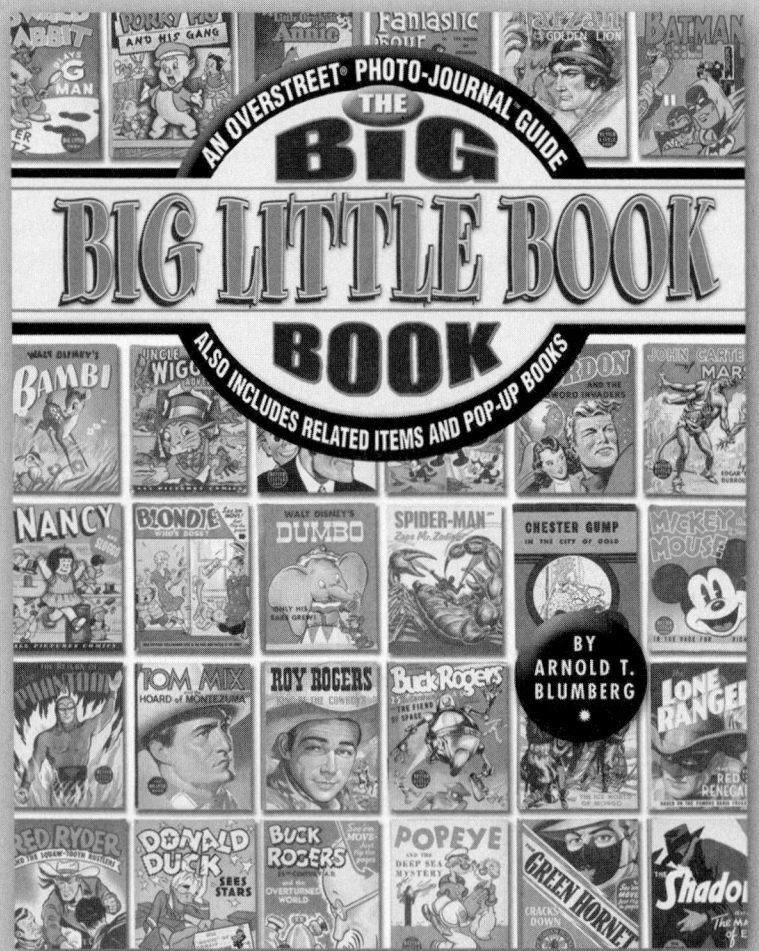

BUYING ALL COMICS

with 10 and 12¢ cover prices

TOP PRICES PAID!

IMMEDIATE CASH PAYMENT

**Stop Throwing Away
Those Old Comic Books!**

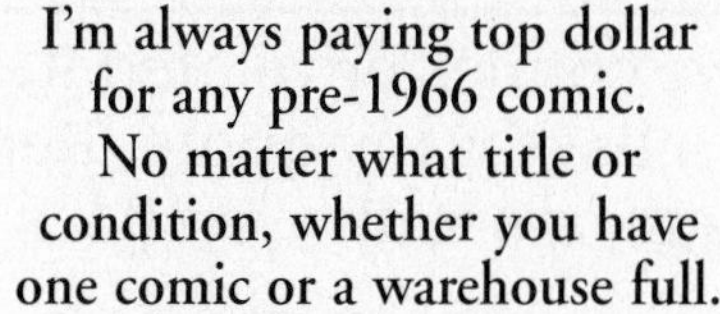

I'm always paying top dollar
for any pre-1966 comic.
No matter what title or
condition, whether you have
one comic or a warehouse full.

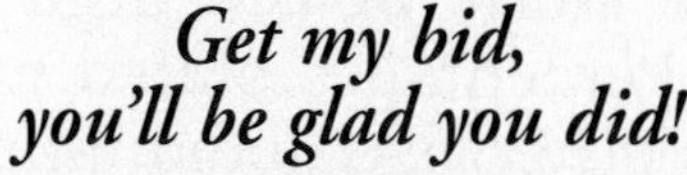

***Get my bid,
you'll be glad you did!***

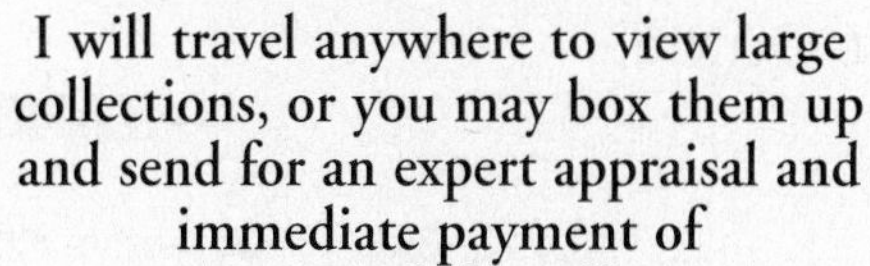

I will travel anywhere to view large
collections, or you may box them up
and send for an expert appraisal and
immediate payment of
my top dollar offer.
Satisfaction guaranteed.

**For a quick reply
Send a List
of What You Have
or Call Toll Free**

1-800-791-3037

or

1-608-277-8750

or write

Jef Hinds
P.O. Box 44803
Madison, WI 53744-4803

www.jhcomics.com

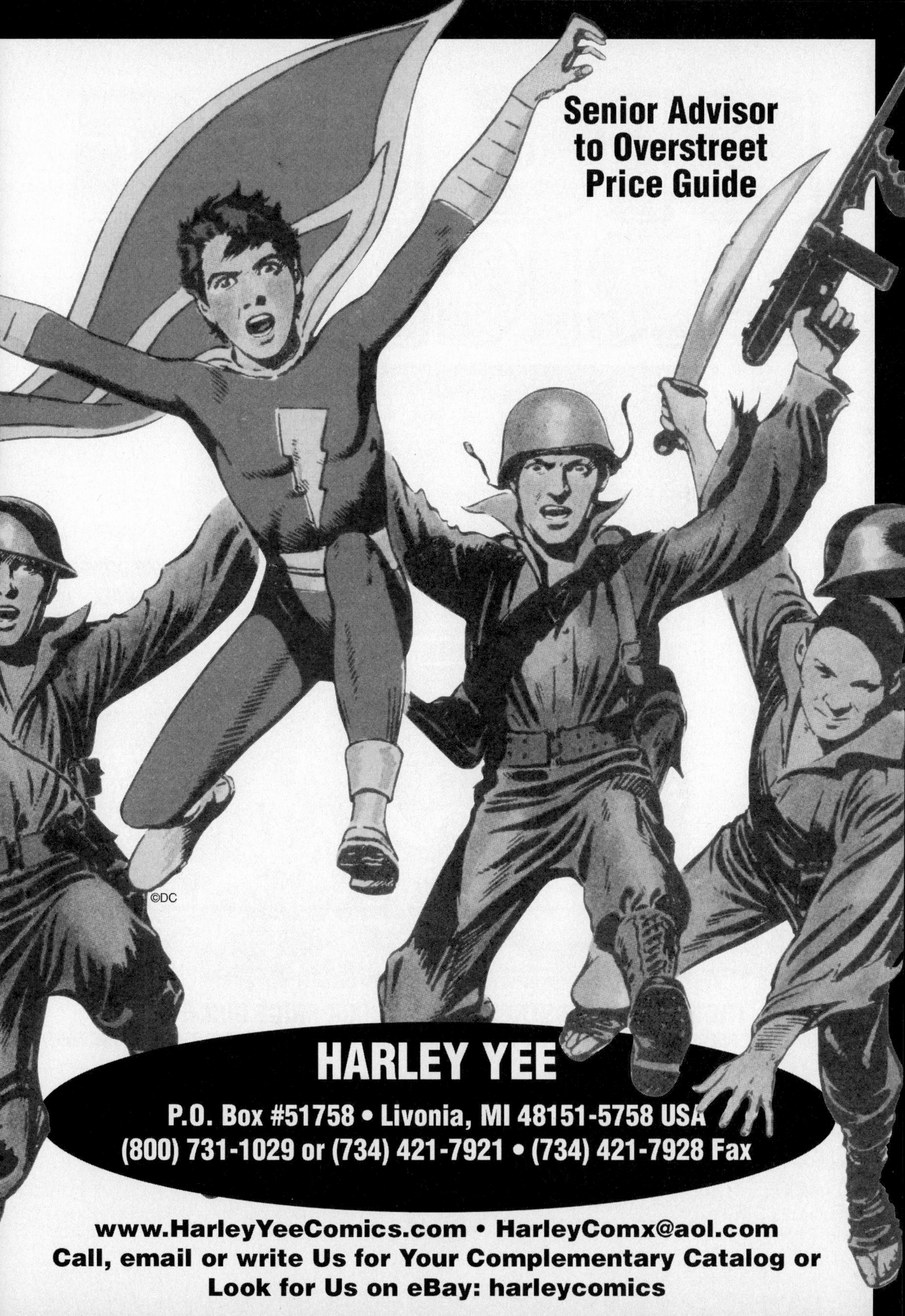

ROMITAMAN
ORIGINAL COMIC ART
www.romitaman.com
THE AMAZING SPIDER-MAN
HOW GREEN WAS MY GOBLIN!
GIANT-SIZED ANNUAL
THE AMAZING SPIDER-MAN
IF YOU LOVE COMICBOOKS, THEN YOU "MUST" CHECK OUT ONE OF THE LARGEST INTERNET WEBSITES FOR COMIC BOOK ART AND COMIC STRIP ART EVER PRODUCED! THIS MAY BE YOUR BEST ARTWORK INTERNET SOURCE!
CHECK OUT OVER 1000+ "PICTURED" PIECES OF COMICBOOK AND COMIC STRIP ART FOR SALE OR TRADE. ALSO CHECK OUT THE WORLD'S "LARGEST" SPIDER-MAN ORIGINAL ART GALLERY!
I BUY/SELL/AND TRADE "ALL" COMICBOOK/STRIP ARTWORK FROM THE 1930S TO PRESENT, SO LET ME KNOW YOUR WANTS, OR WHAT YOU HAVE FOR SALE OR TRADE!!
www.romitaman.com
Characters ©2003 Marvel Characters, Inc.

SILVER AGE
12¢
BUYING
COMICS
107
APR.
ALL COMICS, ALL GRADES
•WILL TRAVEL TO YOU!
•WILL PAY MORE!
•WILL PAY CASH!
SELLING
the LARGEST SELECTION of SILVER AGE in N.Y.C. WITHOUT APPOINTMENT
• COMPETITIVE PRICING!
• STRICT GRADING!
• MAIL ORDER ANYWHERE
• WANT LIST SERVICE
• FREE CATALOGUE
• OPEN 7 DAYS
©MARVEL COMICS

Explore the possibilities
when purchasing
your comics.

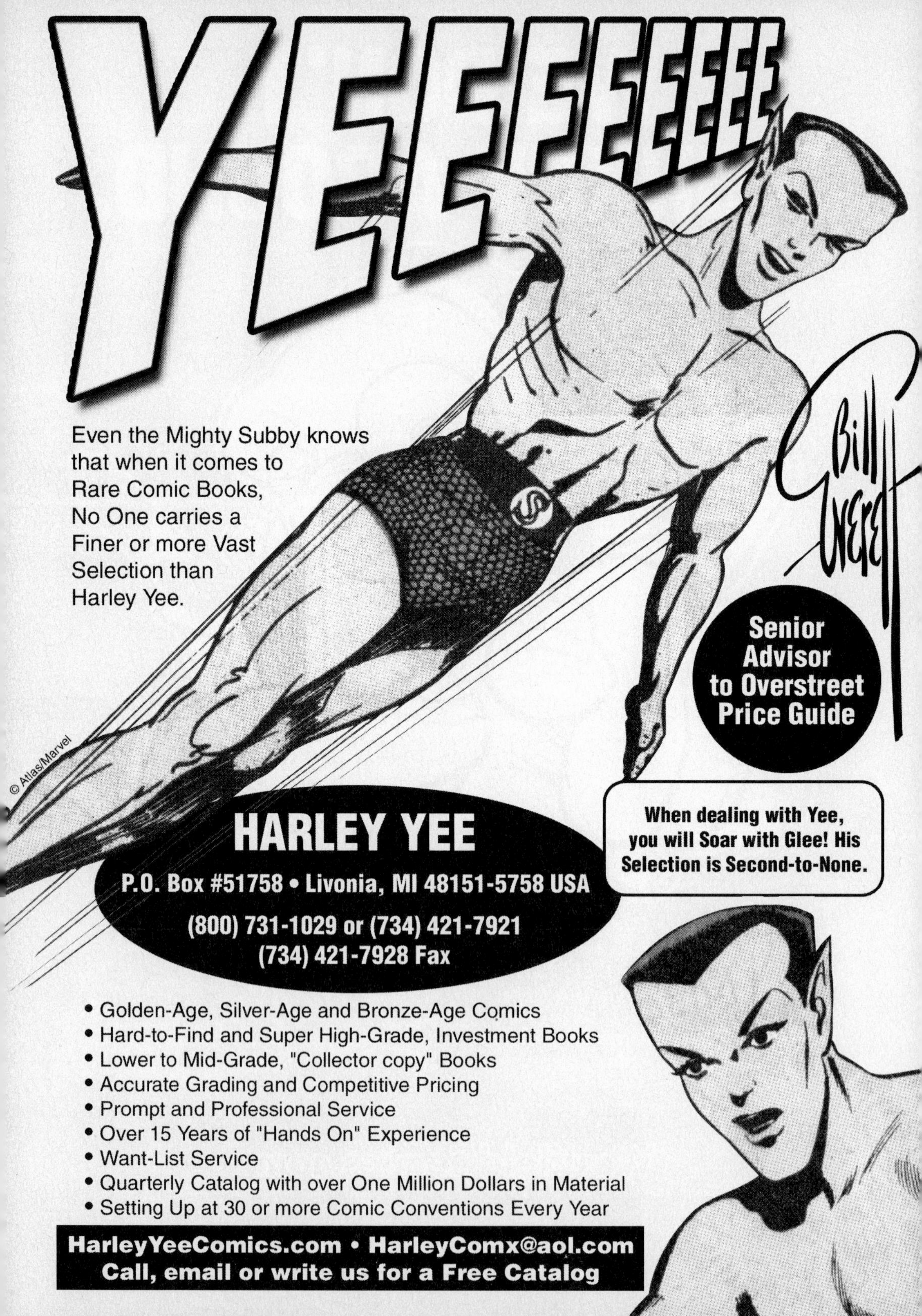
YEEEEEEEE
Even the Mighty Subby knows that when it comes to Rare Comic Books, No One carries a Finer or more Vast Selection than Harley Yee.
Bill Everett
© Atlas/Marvel
Senior Advisor to Overstreet Price Guide
When dealing with Yee, you will Soar with Glee! His Selection is Second-to-None.
HARLEY YEE
P.O. Box #51758 • Livonia, MI 48151-5758 USA
(800) 731-1029 or (734) 421-7921
(734) 421-7928 Fax
• Golden-Age, Silver-Age and Bronze-Age Comics
• Hard-to-Find and Super High-Grade, Investment Books
• Lower to Mid-Grade, "Collector copy" Books
• Accurate Grading and Competitive Pricing
• Prompt and Professional Service
• Over 15 Years of "Hands On" Experience
• Want-List Service
• Quarterly Catalog with over One Million Dollars in Material
• Setting Up at 30 or more Comic Conventions Every Year
HarleyYeeComics.com • HarleyComx@aol.com
Call, email or write us for a Free Catalog

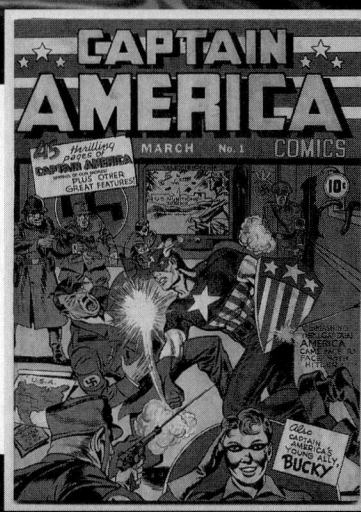

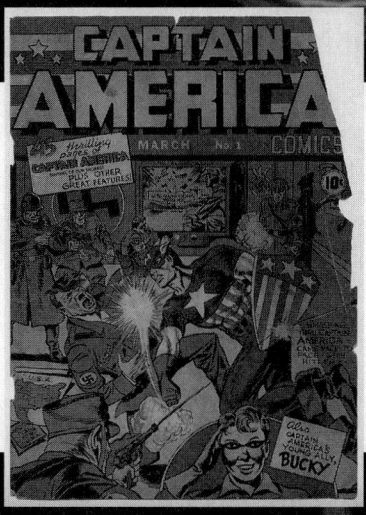

TROPIC COMICS
& COLLECTIBLES
MOVES TO PA!!!!

We Buy Collections!
Large & Small!
CAN'T FIND THAT RARE TITLE?... FEEL LIKE YOU'VE BEEN CONNED AT THE CON...?
WE GOT COMICS!
AT YOUR FRIENDLY
COMIC COLLECTOR SHOP
ALL KINDS "O" COMICS
OLD & NEW COMICS
COMIC COLLECTOR SHOP
167 E EL CAMINO REAL
MOUNTAIN VIEW, CA 94040
PHONE: 650-965-8272 FAX 650-965-9753
RIGHTIO!
RAID
IRA HARMON
www.comiccollectorshop.com
All characters ©2004 respective holders. All rights reserved.

DR. KOOP
NEEDS YOUR COMICS!

MY HISTORY IN COMICS:

If you are about to sell your Comic Book or Comic Art collection, above everything else seek an *experienced dealer whom you can trust.* I began with comics in the early 1960s, eventually publishing the EC fanzine *Squa Tront*. I attended conventions (even before there was *The Overstreet Comic Book Price Guide*), introducing people like Bruce Hamilton to fandom and becoming friends with *MAD Magazine* publisher Bill Gaines. By 1974 I had opened one of the first specialty comic stores in America, *The Million Year Picnic*.

Two partnerships and twenty years later, I inaugurated the first *Sotheby's Comic Book and Comic Art Auctions* in the fall of 1991. The auctions set the tone for the comics market with $12 million in sales and brought national press coverage and respect that comics had never before experienced. I recently have moved onto *eBay* with special "event" auctions that have sold over $1.5 million during the past two years and made me one of the leading *PowerSellers* in America for rare *Comic Art and Comic Books*.

I am also the author of *The Comic Art Price Guide*, 1st and 2nd editions, have recently finished Bradbury: An Illustrated Life for William Morrow, and also wrote The 100 Greatest Comic Books, just out this year from Whitman Press.

MY PROMISE TO YOU:

What all this means to you the seller is that in Jerry Weist you have one of the most experienced and capable people in comics at your disposal.

** Do you want to sell your comics?
I can give you the best price, and honestly appraise your collection before you sell.

** Do you want to bring your collection to auction, and possibly gain a better percentage of Guide value?
I have been bringing people to auction for the past fifteen years – with outstanding results!

** Do you want to consider a private sale of important comic artwork?

I have been working with the top buyers and VIP clients for over twenty years, and I wrote the book on comic art prices. My promise to you is that with my years of experience, I can honestly evaluate your collectibles and give you the assurance that you can choose the option that best fits your needs — Private Sales, Auction Sales or Individual Purchase. I have the flexibility to act as a consult, helping you decide how to best sell your collection and gain top dollar.

Photo credit: Photo by Glynn Crain. ©2005.

Jerry Weist, Ray Bradbury and Al Feldstein during filming for Tales From The Crypt: From Comic Books To Television, produced by Chip Selby in the fall of 2003. This photo was taken during the filming for the special DVD release interview where Bradbury and Feldstein met for the first time on film to discuss their experiences working together on EC's Bradbury adaptations.

You may contact me at jerryweist@adelphia.net, my home phone (978) 283-1419, or my home office at Jerry Weist, 18 Edgemoor Road, Gloucester, Massachusetts, 10930, USA.

Senior Overstreet Advisor since the 1970s, Charter CGC Member, Sotheby's Comic Art and Comic Book Consultant, eBay seller of the month and Power Seller with over 400 100% positive feedbacks, author of *The Comic Art Price Guide*, with over 40 years experience in the comic field.

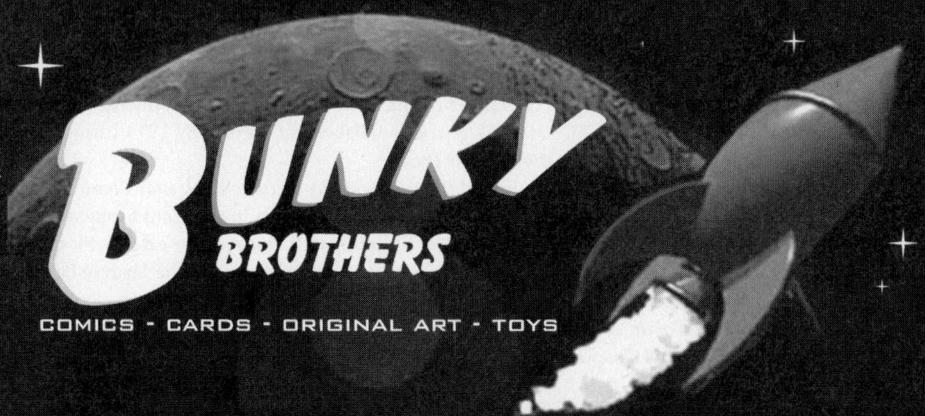
BUNKY
BROTHERS
COMICS - CARDS - ORIGINAL ART - TOYS

DAVE ROBIE

The #1 Big Little Book Dealer in the Country

• Specializing in Big Little Books •

www.bigscoreproductions.com/toys

BLB (Big Little Book) - Adventures of Dick Tracy (first Dick Tracy BLB)
BLB - Green Hornet Cracks Down
BLB - Tom Swift and the Magnetic Silencer
BLB - Alley Oop and Dinny (first one - #763)
BLB - Buck Rogers and the Fiend of Space
BLB - Flash Gordon and the Tyrant of Mongo
BLB - Big Little Mother Goose (hardcover)
BLB - Big Little Paint Book
Dime Action - Captain Marvel
Fast Action - John Carter
BBB (Big Big Book) - Skippy
BBB - Tom Mix
Tarzan Premium - Broncho Bill
Perkins Premium - Tarzan of the Apes
Pop-Up - Little Black Sambo
Pop-Up - Popeye/Among the White Savages

ALWAYS BUYING!!!
BIG LITTLE BOOKS AND RELATED BOOKS AND PREMIUMS

Dave Robie
1986 Pickering Trail
Lancaster, PA 17601
717-371-4491

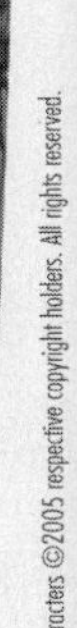

toys@bigscoreproductions.com • www.bigscoreproductions.com/toys

X-MEN
HERE COMES... DAREDEVIL
THE MAN WITHOUT FEAR!
CONAN THE BARBARIAN
the AMAZING SPIDER-MAN
THE CHAMELEON STRIKES!
Fantastic Four
AMAZING FANTASY
SPIDER MAN
the X-MEN
THE INCREDIBLE HULK
IS HE MAN OR MONSTER OR IS HE BOTH?
ALL HERO COMICS
SUPERMAN
THE COMPLETE STORY OF THE DARING EXPLOITS OF THE ONE AND ONLY SUPERMAN
WALT DISNEY'S MICKEY MOUSE OUTWITS THE PHANTOM BLOT
68 PAGES IN FULL COLOR
BATMAN
GOLDEN AGE COLLECTABLES
MARVELS, D.C.'S & INDEPENDENTS
STAR TREK & STAR WARS COLLECTABLES
SPORT & NON-SPORT TRADING CARDS
ROLE PLAYING GAMES & SUPPLIES
MOVIE STAR PHOTOS & AUTOGRAPHS
JAPANIMATION VIDEOS & BOOKS
THE NORTHWEST'S OLDEST & LARGEST
SEATTLE
WASHINGTON
1501 PIKE PLACE MARKET
401 LOWER LEVEL
SEATTLE, WA 98101
206-622-9799
VANCOUVER
CANADA
830 GRANVILLE STREET
VANCOUVER, B.C.
CANADA V6Z 1K3
604-683-2819

BEDROCK CITY
COMIC COMPANY
TM
Gold stars
MASTER COMICS
10¢
WALT DISNEY'S COMICS AND STORIES
10¢
SUPERMAN
No. 24
AMERICA'S FAVORITE ADVENTURE-STRIP CHARACTER
10¢
You'll find *united greats* of the *Golden Age* on-line at *www.bedrockcity.com*
Check out our *superpower* store at:
6517 Westheimer (at Hillcroft)
Houston, Texas 77057
Phone (713) 780-0675 Fax (713) 780-2366
And our other *star-spangled* stores:
4683 FM 1960 W.
Houston, Texas 77069
Phone (281) 444-9763
106 W. Bay Area Blvd.
Webster, Texas 77598
Phone (281) 557-2748

BIG APPLE CONVENTIONS PRESENTS
THE Big Apple Con
COMIC BOOK, ART, & TOY SHOW
THE EAST COAST'S PREMIER CONVENTIONS
2005 DATES
JUNE 17-18 FRI-SAT
SEPT 17-18 SAT-SUN
THE NATIONAL
COMIC BOOK, ART, & SCI-FI EXPO
NOV 18-19-20 FRI-SAT-SUN
CELEBRITIES!
ARTISTS!
GIVEAWAYS!
WW BY ADAM HUGHES. ©2005 DC COMICS. ALL RIGHTS RESESERVED.
BIG APPLE CON IS HELD @
PENN PLAZA PAVILION
7TH AVE AT 33RD ST
ACROSS FROM PENN STATION & MSG
NEW YORK, NY
the big apple con
comic book, art, & toy show
DEALER INQ: BIGAPPLECON@EARTHLINK.NET
BIG APPLE CONVENTIONS
75-34 METROPOLITAN AVE.
MIDDLE VILLAGE, NY 11379
OVER 300 TABLES BUYING, SELLING & TRADING!
BIGAPPLECON.COM/201-892-1212

The Numbers...

PRICE REALIZED: $120,750

Marvel Comics #1 (Timely, 1939)
CGC VF+ 8.5
Cream to off-white pages

All-Star Comics #3
Mile High pedigree (DC, 1940)
CGC NM+ 9.6
off-white to white pages

PRICE REALIZED: $126,500

PRICE REALIZED: $120,750

Detective Comics #38
Allentown pedigree (DC, 1940)
CGC NM 9.4,
Off-white pages

then it's in the HAKE!

Whether it shakes, quakes, rolls, rattles, cries, peeps, squawks, flies, jumps, or giggles, or can be found in this voluminous book that's jam-packed with pictures and pricing. From Superman to *Doctor Who*, from *Batman to I Dream of Jeannie, The Hake's Price and Photo Guide to Character Toys #5* from Gemstone Publishing is the comprehensive all-in-one guide that brings your favorite childhood characters back to life. *The Hake's Price and Photo Guide to Character Toys #5* - it gives new meaning to the words "shake, rattle, and roll!"

$35 +S&H

New England's Largest Dealer
is Looking to Buy Your
Comic Books & Original Comic Art
Over the Last 2 Years we've spent over
$1,000,000
We Can Provide Cash
OVERNIGHT!
If you're looking to sell
comic books from the 30's
to the 70's or original comic
art, contact us FIRST. You'll
be glad you did.
Nostalgic
Investments
PO Box 31
Marshfiled, MA 02059
1-800-229-9059
http://www.nostalgicinvestments.com
comics@nostalgicinvestments.com
CGC
CHARTER
MEMBER DEALER

Bridging the
Dealer or Collector,
Fan or Investor,
Vault Auctions links
America to Europe and
the rest of the world.
Discover why we are not just the
UK's leading auction company,
but Europe's #1 auction site
specializing in vintage
• American comics
(1920's-1980's)
• Toys, non-sports cards, TV &
comicbook related memorabilia
• Fanzines, Pulps & magazines
• Original Art
• British & Australian comics
(1900's-1980's)
visit: www.vaultauctions.com
SILVER SURFER
TO STEAL THE SURFER'S SOUL!
STRANGEST TALES OF FEAR AND SUPERSTITION!
BLACK CAT
SHOCKING HORROR RADIATES FROM... WHITE HEAT!
MAY, 1938
Detective COMICS
10¢
NOW IN FULL COLOR!
THE SPECTACULAR SPIDER-MAN
35¢
MARVEL FLYERS
FLY YOUR OWN COMIC BOOK HEROES!
OFFICIAL MEMBER
SUPERMAN CLUB
The New
DONALD DUCK
WRIST WATCH
The New
DONALD DUCK
WRIST WATCH

COMIC

- Timelys
- MLJs
- Golden Age DCs
- "Mile High" Copies (Church Collection)
- "San Francisco," "Bethlehem" and "Larson" Copies
- 1950s Horror and Sci-Fi Comics
- Fox/Quality/ECs
- Silver Age Marvels and DCs
- Most other brands and titles from the Golden and Silver Age

Specializing In Large Silver And Golden Age Collections

HEAVEN

I N G

JOHN VERZYL AND DAUGHTER ROSE, "HARD AT WORK."

John Verzyl started collecting comic books in 1965, and within ten years he had amassed thousands of Golden and Silver Age comic books. In 1979, with his wife Nanette, he opened "COMIC HEAVEN," a retail store devoted entirely to the buying and selling of comic books.

Over the years, John Verzyl has come to be recognized as an authority in the field of comic books. He has served as a special advisor to the "Overstreet Comic Book Price Guide" for the last ten years. Thousands of his "mint" comics were photographed for Ernst Gerber's newly-released "Photo-Journal Guide to Comic Books." His tables and displays at the annual San Diego Comic Convention and the Chicago Comic Convention draw customers from all over the country.

The first COMIC HEAVEN AUCTION was held in 1987, and today his Auction Catalogs are mailed out to more than ten thousand interested collectors and dealers.

Comic Heaven
John and Nanette Verzyl
P.O. Box 900
Big Sandy, TX 75755
1-903-636-5555

The Comic Book Price Guide
NO. 5
1875 Edgar Rice Burroughs 1975
NO. 6
The Comic Book Price Guide
$7.50
The Comic Book Price Guide
$9.95
Comic Book Price Guide
$9.95
I'M SITTING ON TOP OF THE WORLD! EVERYBODY'S CALLING TO CONGRATULATE ME FOR BEING ON THE COVER OF THE PRICE GUIDE!
SEE THE STARS CALLING KATY
The Confident Collector
The Overstreet Comic Book Price Guide
Robert M. Overstreet
22nd Edition
The Overstreet Comic Book Price Guide
The Overstreet Comic Book Price Guide
The No. 1 Guide
Robert M. Overstreet

Big Little Books

INTRODUCTION

In 1932, at the depths of the Great Depression, comic books were not selling despite their successes in the previous two decades. Desperate publishers had already reduced prices to 25¢, but this was still too much for many people to spend on entertainment. This necessitated a smaller, less expensive format.

Comic books evolved into two newer formats. The first was the comics magazine (today's term, comic book, remains an anachronism referring to the earlier sturdier publications) as represented by **Funnies on Parade**. The second was the format we now know as the Big Little Book. Both types retailed for 10¢. Very quickly, the traditionally successful characters we now identify as Classic Characters migrated to these formats.

Big Little Books began by reprinting the art (and adapting the stories) from newspaper comics. As their success grew and publishers began commissioning original material, movie adaptations and other entertainment-derived stories became commonplace.

GRADING

Before a Big Little Book's value can he assessed, its condition or state of preservation must be determined. A book in **Near Mint** condition will bring many times the price of the same book in **Poor** condition. Many variables influence the grading of a Big Little Book and all must be considered in the final evaluation. Due to the way they are constructed, damage occurs with very little use - usually to the spine, book edges and binding. Consequently, books in **Near Mint** or better are scarce. More important defects that affect grading are: Split spines, pages missing, page browning or brittleness, writing, crayoning, loose pages, color fading, chunks missing, and rolling or out of square. The following grading guide is given to aid the novice:

9.4 Near Mint: The overall look is as if it was just purchased and maybe opened once; only subtle defects are allowed; paper is cream to off-white, supple and fresh; cover is flat with no surface wear or creases; inks and colors are bright; small penciled or inked arrival dates are acceptable; very slight blunting of corners at top and bottom of spine are common; outside corners are cut square and sharp. Books in this grade could bring prices of guide and a half or more.

9.0 Very Fine/Near Mint: Limited number of defects; full cover gloss with only very slight wear on book corners and edges; very minor foxing; very minor tears allowed, binding still square and tight with no pages missing; paper quality still fresh from cream to off-white. Dates, stamps or initials allowed on cover or inside.

8.0 Very Fine: Most of the cover gloss retained with minor wear appearing at corners and around edges; spine tight with no pages missing; cream/tan paper allowed if still supple; up to 1/4" bend allowed on covers with no color break; cover relatively flat; minor tears allowed.

6.0 Fine: Slight wear beginning to show; cover gloss reduced but still clean, pages tan/brown but still supple (not brittle); up to 1/4" split or color break allowed; minor discoloration and/or foxing allowed.

4.0 Very Good: Obviously a read copy with original printing luster almost gone; some fading and discoloration, but not soiled; some signs of wear such as corner splits and spine rolling; paper can be brown but not brittle; a few pages can be loose but not missing; no chunks missing; blunted corners acceptable.

2.0 Good: An average used copy complete with only minor pieces missing from the spine, which may be partially split; slightly soiled or marked with spine rolling; color flaking and wear around edges, but perfectly sound and legible; could have minor tape repairs but otherwise complete.

1.0 Fair: Very heavily read and soiled with small chunks missing from cover; most or all of spine could be missing; multiple splits in spine and loose pages, but still sound and legible, bringing 50 to 70 percent of good price.

0.5 Poor: Damaged, heavily weathered, soiled or otherwise unsuited for collecting purposes.

IMPORTANT

Most BLBs on the market today will fall in the **Good** to **Fine** grade category. Rarely will **Very Fine** to **Near Mint** BLBs be offered for sale. When they are, they usually bring premium prices.

A WORD ON PRICING

The prices are given for **Good**, **Fine** and **Very Fine/ Near Mint** condition. A book in **Fair** would be 50-70% of the **Good** price. **Very Good** would be halfway between the **Good** and **Fine** price, and **Very Fine** would be halfway between the **Fine** and **Very Fine/ Near Mint** price. The prices listed were averaged from convention sales, dealers' lists, adzines, auctions, and by special contact with dealers and collectors from coast to coast. The prices and the spreads were determined from sales of copies in available condition or the highest grade known. Since most available copies are in the **Good** to **Fine** range, neither dealers nor collectors should let the **Very Fine/Near Mint** column influence the prices they are willing to charge or pay for books in less than near perfect condition.

In the past, the BLB market has lacked a point of focus due to the absence of an annual price guide that accurately reports sales and growth in the market. Due to this, current prices for BLBs still vary considerably from region to region. It is our hope that this section will contribute to the stability of the BLB market. The prices listed reflect a six times spread from **Good** to **Very Fine/ Near Mint** (1 - 3 - 6). We feel this spread accurately reflects the current market, especially when you consider the scarcity of books in **Very Fine/Near Mint** condition. When one or both end sheets are missing, the book's value would drop about a half grade.

Books with movie scenes are of double importance due to the high crossover demand by movie collectors.

Abbreviations: a-art; c-cover; nn-no number; p-pages; r-reprint.

Publisher Codes: BRP-Blue Ribbon Press; **ERB**-Edgar Rice Burroughs; **EVW**-Engel van Wiseman; **FAW**-Fawcett Publishing Co.; **Gold**-Goldsmith Publishing Co.; **Lynn**-Lynn Publishing Co.; **McKay**-David McKay Co.; **Whit**-Whitman Publishing Co.; **World**-World Syndicate Publishing Co.

Terminology: ***All Pictures Comics***-no text, all drawings; ***Fast-Action***-A special series of Dell books highly collected; ***Flip Pictures***-upper right corner of interior pages contain drawings that are put into motion when rifled; ***Movie Scenes***-book illustrated with scenes from the movie. ***Soft Cover***-A thin single sheet of cardboard used in binding most of the give-away versions.

"Big Little Book" and "Better Little Book" are registered trademarks of Whitman Publishing Co. "Little Big Book" is a registered trademark of the Saalfield Publishing Co.

"Pop-Up" is a registered trademark of Blue Ribbon Press. "Little Big Book" is a registered trademark of the Saalfield Co.

Top 20 Big Little Books and related size books*

Issue#	Rank	Title	Price
731	1	Mickey Mouse the Mail Pilot (variant version of Mickey Mouse #717) (Fine copy sold at auction for $5,090)	
nn	2	Mickey Mouse and Minnie Mouse at Macy's	$2,500
717	3	Mickey Mouse (skinny Mickey on-c)	$2,400
nn	4	Mickey Mouse and Minnie March to Macy's	$1,750
W-707	5	Dick Tracy The Detective	$1,750
725	6	Big Little Mother Goose HC	$1,650
717	7	Mickey Mouse (reg. Mickey on-c)	$1,250
4063	8	Popeye Thimble Theater Starring... (2nd printing)	$1,200
725	9	Big Little Mother Goose SC	$1,150
721	10	Big Little Paint Book	$1,100
2070	11	Big Big Paint Book	$1,000
nn	12	Mickey Mouse (Great Big Midget Book)	$1,000
4062	13	Mickey Mouse and the Smugglers	$1,000
4063	14	Popeye Thimble Theater Starring... (1st printing)	$1,000
4062	15	Mickey Mouse, The Story of...	$900
nn	16	Buck Rogers	$900
nn	17	Mickey Mouse Silly Symphonies	$900
nn	18	Tarzan	$875
4071	19	Dick Tracy and the Mystery of the Purple Cross	$850
4057	20	Buck Rogers, The Adventures of...	$800

*Includes only the various sized BLBs; no premiums, giveaways or other divergent forms are included.

1182 - Abbie an' Slats-and Becky © Saalfield

1403 - Apple Mary and Dennie's Lucky Apples © WHIT

2031 - Batman and Robin in the Cheetah Caper © DC

	GD	FN	VF/NM
1175-0- Abbie an' Slats, 1940, Saalfield, 400 pgs.	12.00	35.00	65.00
1182- Abbie an' Slats-and Becky, 1940, Saalfield, 400 pgs.	12.00	35.00	65.00
1177- Ace Drummond, 1935, Whitman, 432 pgs.	15.00	35.00	70.00
Admiral Byrd (See Paramount Newsreel ...)			
nn- Adventures of Charlie McCarthy and Edgar Bergen, The, 1938, Dell, 194 pgs., Fast-Action Story, soft-c	30.00	75.00	150.00
1422- Adventures of Huckleberry Finn, The, 1939, Whitman, 432 pgs., Henry E. Vallely-a	12.00	28.00	55.00
1648- Adventures of Jim Bowie (TV Series), 1958, Whitman, 280 pgs.	5.00	15.00	30.00
1056- Adventures of Krazy Kat and Ignatz Mouse in Koko Land, 1934, Saalfield, 160 pgs., oblong size, hard-c, Herriman-c/a	60.00	225.00	425.00
1306- Adventures of Krazy Kat and Ignatz Mouse in Koko Land, 1934, Saalfield, 164 pgs., oblong size, soft-c, Herriman-c/a	60.00	225.00	425.00
1082- Adventures of Pete the Tramp, The, 1935, Saalfield, hard-c, by C. D. Russell	10.00	30.00	60.00
1312- Adventures of Pete the Tramp, The, 1935, Saalfield, soft-c, by C. D. Russell	10.00	30.00	60.00
1053- Adventures of Tim Tyler, 1934, Saalfield, hard-c, oblong size, by Lyman Young	25.00	75.00	150.00
1303- Adventures of Tim Tyler, 1934, Saalfield, soft-c, oblong size, by Lyman Young	25.00	75.00	150.00
1058- Adventures of Tom Sawyer, The, 1934, Saalfield, 160 pgs., hard-c, Park Sumner-a	10.00	30.00	60.00
1308- Adventures of Tom Sawyer, The, 1934, Saalfield, 160 pgs., soft-c, Park Sumner-a	10.00	30.00	60.00
1448- Air Fighters of America, 1941, Whitman, 432 pgs., flip picture	12.00	35.00	70.00
Alexander Smart, ESQ. (See Top Line Comics)			
759- Alice in Wonderland, 1933, Whitman, 160 pgs., hard-c, photo-c, movie scenes	20.00	85.00	175.00
1481- Allen Pike of the Parachute Squad U.S.A., 1941, Whitman, 432 pgs.	12.00	35.00	70.00
763- Alley Oop and Dinny, 1935, Whitman, 384 pgs., V. T. Hamlin-a	18.00	55.00	115.00
1473- Alley Oop and Dinny in the Jungles of Moo, 1938, Whitman, 432 pgs., V. T. Hamlin-a	18.00	55.00	115.00
nn- Alley Oop and the Missing King of Moo, 1938, Whitman, 36 pgs., 2 1/2" x 3 1/2", Penny Book	12.00	35.00	70.00
nn- Alley Oop in the Kingdom of Foo, 1938, Whitman, 68 pgs., 3 1/4" x 3 1/2", Pan-Am premium	20.00	85.00	165.00
nn- "Alley Oop the Invasion of Moo," 1935, Whitman, 260 pgs., Cocomalt premium, soft-c; V. T. Hamlin-a	20.00	65.00	125.00
Andy Burnette (See Walt Disney's...)			
Andy Panda (Also see Walter Lantz ...)			
531- Andy Panda, 1943, Whitman, 3 3/4x8 3/4", Tall Comic Book, All Pictures Comics	25.00	75.00	150.00
1425- Andy Panda and Tiny Tom, 1944, Whitman, All Pictures Comics	12.00	35.00	70.00
1431- Andy Panda and the Mad Dog Mystery, 1947, Whitman, 288 pgs., by Walter Lantz	12.00	30.00	65.00
1441- Andy Panda in the City of Ice, 1948, Whitman, All Picture Comics, by Walter Lantz	12.00	35.00	70.00
1459- Andy Panda and the Pirate Ghosts, 1949, Whitman, 88 pgs., by Walter Lantz	12.00	30.00	65.00
1485- Andy Panda's Vacation, 1946, Whitman, All Pictures Comics, by Walter Lantz	15.00	35.00	70.00
15- Andy Panda (The Adventures of), 1942, Dell, Fast-Action Story	30.00	75.00	150.00
707-10 - Andy Panda and Presto the Pup, 1949, Whitman	12.00	30.00	65.00
1130- Apple Mary and Dennie Foil the Swindlers, 1936, Whitman, 432 pgs. (Forerunner to Mary Worth)	10.00	30.00	65.00
1403- Apple Mary and Dennie's Lucky Apples, 1939, Whitman, 432 pgs.	10.00	30.00	65.00
2017- (#17)-Aquaman-Scourge of the Sea, 1968, Whitman, 260 pgs., 39 cents, hard-c, color illos	5.00	15.00	30.00

	GD	FN	VF/NM
1192- Arizona Kid on the Bandit Trail, The, 1936, Whitman, 432 pgs.	10.00	25.00	55.00
1469- Bambi (Walt Disney's), 1942, Whitman, 432 pgs.	25.00	75.00	150.00
1497- Bambi's Children (Disney), 1943, Whitman, 432 pgs., Disney Studios-a	25.00	75.00	150.00
1138- Bandits at Bay, 1938, Saalfield, 400 pgs.	10.00	25.00	50.00
1459- Barney Baxter in the Air with the Eagle Squadron, 1938, Whitman, 432 pgs.	10.00	30.00	65.00
1083- Barney Google, 1935, Saalfield, hard-c	20.00	55.00	115.00
1313- Barney Google, 1935, Saalfield, soft-c	20.00	55.00	115.00
2031- Batman and Robin in the Cheetah Caper, 1969, Whitman, 258 pgs.	5.00	15.00	30.00
5771- Batman and Robin in the Cheetah Caper, 1974, Whitman, 258 pgs., 49 cents	2.00	5.00	10.00
5771-1- Batman and Robin in the Cheetah Caper, 1974, Whitman, 258 pgs., 69 cents	2.00	5.00	10.00
5771-2- Batman and Robin in the Cheetah Caper, 1975?, Whitman, 258 pgs.	2.00	5.00	10.00
nn- Beauty and the Beast, nd (1930s), np (Whitman), 36 pgs., 3" x 3 1/2" Penny Book	5.00	12.00	25.00
760- Believe It or Not!, 1933, Whitman, 160 pgs., by Ripley (c. 1931)	10.00	30.00	65.00
Betty Bear's Lesson (See Wee Little Books)			
1119- Betty Boop in Snow White, 1934, Whitman, 240 pgs., hard-c; adapted from Max Fleischer Paramount Talkartoon	50.00	175.00	350.00
1119- Betty Boop in Snow White, 1934, Whitman, 240 pgs., soft-c; same contents as hard-c	50.00	150.00	300.00
1158- Betty Boop in "Miss Gullivers Travels," 1935, Whitman, 288 pgs., hard-c	45.00	160.00	325.00
2070- Big Big Paint Book, 1936, Whitman, 432 pgs., 8 1/2" x 11 3/8", B&W pages to color	200.00	500.00	1000.00
1432- Big Chief Wahoo and the Lost Pioneers, 1942, Whitman, 432 pgs., Elmer Woggon-a	10.00	30.00	65.00
1443- Big Chief Wahoo and the Great Gusto, 1938, Whitman, 432 pgs., Elmer Woggon-a	10.00	30.00	65.00
1483- Big Chief Wahoo and the Magic Lamp, 1940, Whitman, 432 pgs., flip pictures, Woggon-c/a	10.00	30.00	65.00
725- Big Little Mother Goose, The, 1934, Whitman, 580 pgs. (Rare) Hardcover	175.00	800.00	1650.00
725- Big Little Mother Goose, The, 1934, Whitman, 580 pgs. (Rare) Softcover	115.00	550.00	1150.00
1005- Big Little Nickel Book, 1935, Whitman, 144 pgs., Blackie Bear stories and Donna the Donkey	10.00	25.00	55.00
1006- Big Little Nickel Book, 1935, Whitman, 144 pgs., Blackie Bear stories, folk tales in primer style	10.00	25.00	55.00
1007- Big Little Nickel Book, 1935, Whitman, 144 pgs., Wee Wee Woman, etc.	10.00	25.00	55.00
1008- Big Little Nickel Book, 1935, Whitman, 144 pgs., Peter Rabbit, etc.	10.00	25.00	55.00
721- Big Little Paint Book, The, 1933, Whitman, 336 pgs., 3 3/4" x 8 1/2", for crayoning (Rare)	155.00	550.00	1100.00
1178- Billy of Bar-Zero, 1940, Saalfield, 400 pgs.	10.00	25.00	55.00
773- Billy the Kid, 1935, Whitman, 432 pgs., Hal Arbo-a	10.00	30.00	65.00
1159- Billy the Kid on Tall Butte, 1939, Saalfield, 400 pgs.	10.00	25.00	55.00
1174- Billy the Kid's Pledge, 1940, Saalfield, 400 pgs.	10.00	25.00	55.00
nn- Billy the Kid, Western Outlaw, 1935, Whitman, 260 pgs., Cocomalt premium, Hal Arbo-a, soft-c	12.00	35.00	70.00
1057- Black Beauty, 1934, Saalfield, hard-c	10.00	25.00	50.00
1307- Black Beauty, 1934, Saalfield, soft-c	10.00	25.00	50.00
1414- Black Silver and His Pirate Crew, 1937, Whitman, 300 pgs.	10.00	30.00	60.00
1447- Blaze Brandon with the Foreign Legion, 1938, Whitman, 432 pgs.	10.00	30.00	60.00

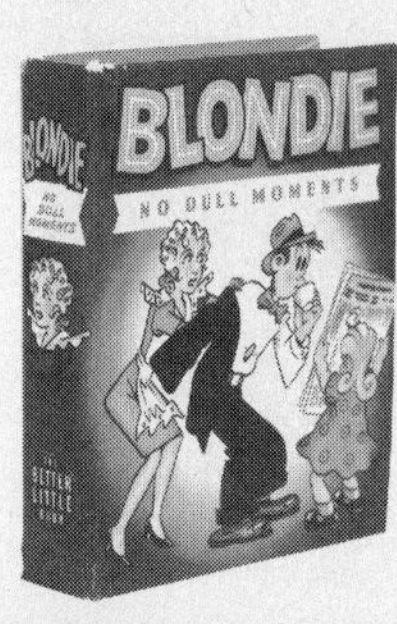

1450 - Blondie No Dull Moments © WHIT

The Brownies' Merry Adventures © Barefoot Books

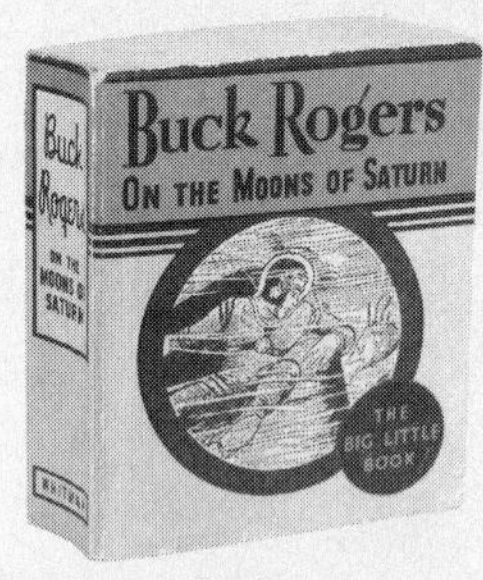

Buck Rogers on the Moons of Saturn (3-color premium) © KING

GD FN VF/NM

1410- **Blondie and Dagwood in Hot Water**, 1946, Whitman, 352 pgs., by Chic Young 10.00 30.00 65.00
1415- **Blondie and Baby Dumpling**, 1937, Whitman, 432 pgs., by Chic Young 12.00 35.00 70.00
1419- **Oh, Blondie the Bumsteads Carry On**, 1941, Whitman, 432 pgs., flip pictures, by Chic Young 12.00 35.00 70.00
1423- **Blondie Who's Boss?**, 1942, Whitman, 432 pgs., flip pictures, by Chic Young 12.00 35.00 70.00
1429- **Blondie with Baby Dumpling and Daisy**, 1939, Whitman, 432 pgs., by Chic Young 10.00 35.00 70.00
1430- **Blondie Count Cookie in Too!**, 1947, Whitman, 288 pgs., by Chic Young 10.00 30.00 65.00
1438- **Blondie and Dagwood Everybody's Happy**, 1948, Whitman, 288 pgs., by Chic Young 10.00 30.00 65.00
1450- **Blondie No Dull Moments**, 1948, Whitman, 288 pgs., by Chic Young 10.00 30.00 65.00
1463- **Blondie Fun For All**, 1949, Whitman, 288 pgs., by Chic Young 10.00 30.00 65.00
1466- **Blondie or Life Among the Bumsteads**, 1944, Whitman, 352 pgs., by Chic Young 12.00 35.00 70.00
1476- **Blondie and Bouncing Baby Dumpling**, 1940, Whitman, 432 pgs., by Chic Young 12.00 35.00 70.00
1487- **Blondie Baby Dumpling and All!**, 1941, Whitman, 432 pgs. flip pictures, by Chic Young 12.00 35.00 70.00
1490- **Blondie Papa Knows Best**, 1945, Whitman, 352 pgs., by Chic Young 10.00 30.00 65.00
1491- **Blondie-Cookie and Daisy's Pups**, 1943, Whitman, 1st printing, 432 pgs. 12.00 35.00 70.00
1491- **Blondie-Cookie and Daisy's Pups**, 1943, Whitman,. 2nd printing with different back-c & 352 pgs. 10.00 30.00 60.00
703-10- **Blondie and Dagwood Some Fun!**, 1949, Whitman, by Chic Young 10.00 25.00 50.00
21- **Blondie and Dagwood**, 194?, Lynn, by Chic Young 20.00 60.00 120.00
1108- **Bobby Benson on the H-Bar-O Ranch**, 1934, Whitman, 300 pgs., based on radio serial 12.00 40.00 80.00
Bobby Thatcher and the Samarang Emerald (See Top-Line Comics)
1432- **Bob Stone the Young Detective**, 1937, Whitman, 240 pgs., movie scenes 12.00 35.00 70.00
2002- **(#2)-Bonanza-The Bubble Gum Kid**, 1967, Whitman, 260 pgs., 39 cents, hard-c, color illos 5.00 15.00 30.00
1139- **Border Eagle, The**, 1938, Saalfield, 400 pgs. 10.00 25.00 50.00
1153- **Boss of the Chisholm Trail**, 1939, Saalfield, 400 pgs. 10.00 25.00 50.00
1425- **Brad Turner in Transatlantic Flight**, 1939, Whitman, 432 pgs. 12.00 28.00 55.00
1058- **Brave Little Tailor, The** (Disney), 1939, Whitman, 5" x 5 1/2", 68 pgs., hard-c (Mickey Mouse) 15.00 50.00 90.00
1427- **Brenda Starr and the Masked Impostor**, 1943, Whitman, 352 pgs., Dale Messick-a 12.00 40.00 80.00
1426- **Brer Rabbit** (Walt Disney's ...), 1947, Whitman, All Picture Comics, from "Song Of The South" movie 20.00 60.00 125.00
704-10- **Brer Rabbit**, 1949, Whitman 15.00 50.00 105.00
1059- **Brick Bradford in the City Beneath the Sea**, 1934, Saalfield, hard-c, by William Ritt & Clarence Gray 15.00 50.00 100.00
1309- **Brick Bradford in the City Beneath the Sea**, 1934, Saalfield, soft-c, by Ritt & Gray 15.00 50.00 100.00
1468- **Brick Bradford with Brocco the Modern Buccaneer**, 1938, Whitman, 432 pgs., by Wm. Ritt & Clarence Gray 10.00 32.00 65.00
1133- **Bringing Up Father**, 1936, Whitman, 432 pgs., by George McManus 15.00 45.00 90.00
1100- **Broadway Bill**, 1935, Saalfield, photo-c, 4 1/2" x 5 1/4", movie scenes (Columbia Pictures, horse racing) 12.00 35.00 70.00
1580- **Broadway Bill**, 1935, Saalfield, soft-c, photo-c, movie scenes 12.00 35.00 70.00
1181- **Broncho Bill**, 1940, Saalfield, 400 pgs. 10.00 28.00 55.00
nn- **Broncho Bill in Suicide Canyon** (See Top-Line Comics)
1417- **Bronc Peeler the Lone Cowboy**, 1937, Whitman, 432 pgs., by Fred Harman, forerunner of Red Ryder (also see Red Death on the Range) 10.00 30.00 65.00

GD FN VF/NM

nn- **Brownies' Merry Adventures, The**, 1993, Barefoot Books, 202 pgs., reprints from Palmer Cox's late 1800s books 5.00 10.00 15.00
1470- **Buccaneer, The**, 1938, Whitman, 240 pgs., photo-c, movie scenes 10.00 35.00 75.00
1646- **Buccaneers, The** (TV Series), 1958, Whitman, 4 1/2" x 5 1/4", 280 pgs., Russ Manning-a 5.00 15.00 30.00
1104- **Buck Jones in the Fighting Code**, 1934, Whitman, 160 pgs., hard-c, movie scenes 15.00 45.00 90.00
1116- **Buck Jones in Ride 'Em Cowboy** (Universal Presents), 1935, Whitman, 240 pgs., photo-c, movie scenes 15.00 45.00 90.00
1174- **Buck Jones in the Roaring West** (Universal Presents), 1935, Whitman, 240 pgs., movie scenes 15.00 45.00 90.00
1188- **Buck Jones in the Fighting Rangers** (Universal Presents), 1936, Whitman, 240 pgs., photo-c, movie scenes 15.00 45.00 90.00
1404- **Buck Jones and the Two-Gun Kid**, 1937, Whitman, 432 pgs. 12.00 35.00 65.00
1451- **Buck Jones and the Killers of Crooked Butte**, 1940, Whitman, 432 pgs. 12.00 35.00 65.00
1461- **Buck Jones and the Rock Creek Cattle War**, 1938, Whitman, 432 pgs. 12.00 35.00 65.00
1486- **Buck Jones and the Rough Riders in Forbidden Trails**, 1943, Whitman, flip pictures, based on movie; Tim McCoy app. 15.00 45.00 85.00
3- **Buck Jones in the Red Ryder**, 1934, EVW, 160 pgs., movie scenes 20.00 60.00 120.00
15- **Buck Jones in Rocky Rhodes**, 1935, EVW, 160 pgs., photo-c, movie scenes 20.00 60.00 120.00
4069- **Buck Jones and the Night Riders**, 1937, Whitman, 7" x 9", 320 pgs., Big Big Book 75.00 200.00 400.00
nn- **Buck Jones on the Six-Gun Trail**, 1939, Whitman, 36 pgs., 2 1/2" x 3 1/2", Penny Book 10.00 30.00 60.00
nn- **Buck Jones Big Thrill Chewing Gum**, 1934, Whitman, 8 pgs., 2 1/2" x 3 1/2" (6 diff.) each... 15.00 55.00 110.00
742- **Buck Rogers in the 25th Century A.D.**, 1933, Whitman, 320 pgs., Dick Calkins-a 40.00 150.00 325.00
nn- **Buck Rogers in the 25th Century A.D.**, 1933, Whitman, 204 pgs.,Cocomalt premium, Calkins-a 30.00 90.00 200.00
765- **Buck Rogers in the City Below the Sea**, 1934, Whitman, 320 pgs., Dick Calkins-a 30.00 90.00 190.00
765- **Buck Rogers in the City Below the Sea**, 1934, Whitman, 324 pgs., soft-c, Dick Calkins-c/a 45.00 165.00 350.00
1143- **Buck Rogers on the Moons of Saturn**, 1934, Whitman, 320 pgs., Dick Calkins-a 35.00 95.00 200.00
nn- **Buck Rogers on the Moons of Saturn**, 1934, Whitman, 324 pgs., premium w/no ads, soft 3-color-c, Dick Calkins-a 50.00 175.00 350.00
1169- **Buck Rogers and the Depth Men of Jupiter**, 1935, Whitman, 432 pgs., Calkins-a 35.00 95.00 190.00
1178- **Buck Rogers and the Doom Comet**, 1935, Whitman, 432 pgs., Calkins-a 30.00 90.00 180.00
1197- **Buck Rogers and the Planetoid Plot**, 1936, Whitman, 432 pgs., Calkins-a 30.00 90.00 180.00
1409- **Buck Rogers Vs. the Fiend of Space**, 1940, Whitman, 432 pgs., Calkins-a 30.00 90.00 180.00
1437- **Buck Rogers in the War with the Planet Venus**, 1938, Whitman, 432 pgs., Calkins-a 30.00 90.00 180.00
1474- **Buck Rogers and the Overturned World**, 1941, Whitman, 432 pgs., flip pictures, Calkins-a 30.00 90.00 185.00
1490- **Buck Rogers and the Super-Dwarf of Space**, 1943, Whitman, 11 Pictures Comics, Calkins-a 28.00 85.00 180.00
4057- **Buck Rogers, The Adventures of**, 1934, Whitman, 7" x 9 1/2", 320 pgs., Big Big Book, "The Story of Buck Rogers on the Planet Eros," Calkins-c/a 125.00 375.00 800.00
nn- **Buck Rogers**, 1935, Whitman, 4" x 3 1/2", Tarzan Ice Cream cup premium (Rare) 135.00 450.00 900.00
nn- **Buck Rogers in the City of Floating Globes**, 1935, Whitman, 258 pgs., Cocomalt premium, soft-c, Dick Calkins-a

2007 - Bugs Bunny-Double Trouble on Diamond Island © WB

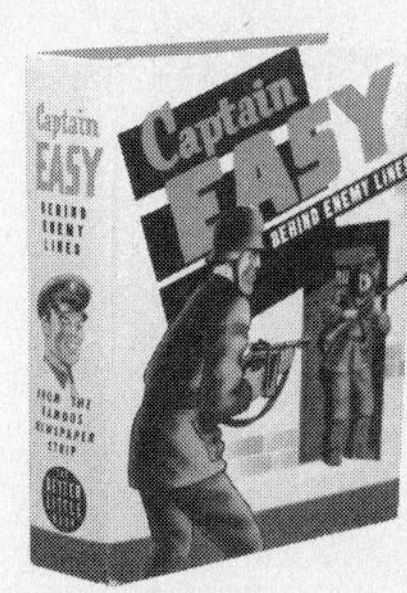

1474 - Captain Easy Behind Enemy Lines © WHIT

5 - Chester Gump and His Friends © WHIT

GD FN VF/NM

85.00 275.00 550.00

nn- **Buck Rogers Big Thrill Chewing Gum**, 1934, Whitman, 8 pgs., 2 1/2" x 3 " (6 diff.) each... 25.00 75.00 150.00

1135- **Buckskin and Bullets**, 1938, Saalfield, 400 pgs. 10.00 25.00 55.00

Buffalo Bill (See Wild West Adventures of ...)

nn- **Buffalo Bill**, 1934, World Syndicate, All pictures, by J. Carroll Mansfield 10.00 25.00 55.00

713- **Buffalo Bill and the Pony Express**, 1934, Whitman, hard-c, 384 pgs., Hal Arbo-a 10.00 30.00 65.00

nn- **Buffalo Bill and the Pony Express**, 1934, Whitman, soft-c, 384 pgs., Hal Arbo-a; three-color premium 30.00 100.00 200.00

1194- **Buffalo Bill Plays a Lone Hand**, 1936, Whitman, 432 pgs., Hal Arbo-a 10.00 25.00 55.00

530- **Bugs Bunny**, 1943, Whitman, All Pictures Comics, Tall Comic Book, 3 1/4" x 8 1/4", reprints/Looney Tunes 1 & 5 30.00 85.00 175.00

1403- **Bugs Bunny and the Pirate Loot**, 1947, Whitman, All Pictures Comics 12.00 30.00 65.00

1435- **Bugs Bunny**, 1944, Whitman, All Pictures Comics 12.00 35.00 70.00

1440- **Bugs Bunny in Risky Business**, 1948, Whitman, All Pictures & Comics 12.00 30.00 65.00

1455- **Bugs Bunny and Klondike Gold**, 1948, Whitman, 288 pgs. 12.00 30.00 65.00

1465- **Bugs Bunny The Masked Marvel**, 1949, Whitman, 288 pgs. 12.00 30.00 65.00

1496- **Bugs Bunny and His Pals**, 1945, Whitman, All Pictures Comics; r/Four Color Comics #33 12.00 35.00 75.00

13- **Bugs Bunny and the Secret of Storm Island**, 1942, Dell,194 pgs., Fast-Action Story 35.00 90.00 200.00

706-10- **Bugs Bunny and the Giant Brothers,** 1949, Whitman 10.00 25.00 55.00

2007- **(#7)-Bugs Bunny-Double Trouble on Diamond Island**, 1967, Whitman, 260 pgs., 39 cents, hard-c, color illos 5.00 15.00 30.00

2029-(#29)- **Bugs Bunny, Accidental Adventure,** 1969, Whitman, 256 pgs., hard-c, color illos. 4.00 10.00 20.00

2952- **Bugs Bunny's Mistake**, 1949, Whitman, 3 1/4" x 4", 24 pgs., Tiny Tales, full color (5 cents) 10.00 28.00 55.00

5757-2- **Bugs Bunny in Double Trouble on Diamond Island**,1967, (1980-reprints #2007), Whitman, 260 pgs., soft-c, 79 cents, B&W 4.00 10.00 20.00

5758- **Bugs Bunny, Accidental Adventure**, 1973, Whitman, 256 pgs., soft-c, B&W illos. 4.00 10.00 20.00

5772- **Bugs Bunny the Last Crusader**, 1975, Whitman, 49 cents, flip-it book 4.00 10.00 20.00

5772-2- **Bugs Bunny the Last Crusader**, 1975, Whitman, $1.50, flip-it book 1.00 3.00 8.00

1169- **Bullet Benton**, 1939, Saalfield, 400 pgs. 10.00 25.00 55.00

nn- **Bulletman and the Return of Mr. Murder**, 1941, Fawcett, 196 pgs., Dime Action Book 40.00 150.00 275.00

1142- **Bullets Across the Border** (A Billy The Kid story), 1938, Saalfield, 400 pgs. 10.00 25.00 55.00

Bunky (See Top-Line Comics)

837- **Bunty** (Punch and Judy), 1935, Whitman, 28 pgs., Magic-Action with 3 pop-ups 15.00 45.00 90.00

1091- **Burn 'Em Up Barnes**, 1935, Saalfield, hard-c, movie scenes 10.00 40.00 80.00

1321- **Burn 'Em Up Barnes**, 1935, Saalfield, soft-c, movie scenes 10.00 40.00 80.00

1415- **Buz Sawyer and Bomber 13**,1946, Whitman, 352 pgs., Roy Crane-a 10.00 40.00 80.00

1412- **Calling W-I-X-Y-Z, Jimmy Kean and the Radio Spies**, 1939, Whitman, 300 pgs. 10.00 32.00 65.00

Call of the Wild (See Jack London's...)

1107- **Camels are Coming**, 1935, Saalfield, movie scenes 10.00 30.00 60.00

1587- **Camels are Coming**, 1935, Saalfield, movie scene 10.00 30.00 60.00

GD FN VF/NM

nn- **Captain and the Kids, Boys Vill Be Boys, The**, 1938, 68 pgs., Pan-Am Oil premium, soft-c 12.00 40.00 80.00

1128- **Captain Easy Soldier of Fortune**, 1934, Whitman, 432 pgs., Roy Crane-a 12.00 40.00 80.00

nn- **Captain Easy Soldier of Fortune**, 1934, Whitman, 436 pgs., Premium, no ads, soft 3-color-c, Roy Crane-a 25.00 75.00 150.00

1474- **Captain Easy Behind Enemy Lines**, 1943, Whitman, 352 pgs., Roy Crane-a 10.00 35.00 75.00

nn- **Captain Easy and Wash Tubbs**, 1935, 260 pgs., Cocomalt premium, Roy Crane-a 10.00 35.00 75.00

1444- **Captain Frank Hawks Air Ace and the League of Twelve**, 1938, Whitman, 432 pgs. 10.00 30.00 65.00

nn- **Captain Marvel,** 1941, Fawcett, 196 pgs., Dime Action Book 50.00 200.00 375.00

1402- **Captain Midnight and Sheik Jomak Khan**, 1946, Whitman, 352 pgs. 20.00 65.00 150.00

1452- **Captain Midnight and the Moon Woman**, 1943, Whitman, 352 pgs. 25.00 80.00 160.00

1458- **Captain Midnight Vs. The Terror of the Orient**, 1942, Whitman, 432 pgs., flip pictures, Hess-a 25.00 80.00 160.00

1488- **Captain Midnight and the Secret Squadron**, 1941, Whitman, 432 pgs. 25.00 80.00 160.00

Captain Robb of.. (See Dirigible ZR90 ...)

nn- **Cauliflower Catnip Pearls of Peril**, 1981, Teacup Tales, 290 pgs., Joe Wehrle Jr.-s/a; deliberately printed on aged-looking paper to look like an old BLB 10.00 20.00 30.00

L20- **Ceiling Zero,** 1936, Lynn, 128 pgs., 7 1/2" x 5", hard-c, James Cagney, Pat O'Brien photos on-c, movie scenes, Warner Bros. Pictures 10.00 30.00 65.00

1093- **Chandu the Magician**, 1935, Saalfield, 5" x 5 1/4", 160 pgs., hard-c, Bela Lugosi photo-c, movie scenes 15.00 50.00 90.00

1323- **Chandu the Magician**, 1935, Saalfield, 5" x 5 1/4", 160 pgs., soft-c, Bela Lugosi photo-c 15.00 55.00 100.00

Charlie Chan (See Inspector ...)

1459- **Charlie Chan Solves a New Mystery** (See Inspector..), 1940, Whitman, 432 pgs., Alfred Andriola-a 12.00 40.00 85.00

1478- **Charlie Chan of the Honolulu Police, Inspector**, 1939, Whitman, 432 pgs., Andriola-a 12.00 40.00 85.00

Charlie McCarthy (See Story Of ...)

734- **Chester Gump at Silver Creek Ranch**, 1933, Whitman, 320 pgs., Sidney Smith-a 12.00 40.00 85.00

nn- **Chester Gump at Silver Creek Ranch**, 1933, Whitman, 204 pgs., Cocomalt premium, soft-c, Sidney Smith-a 15.00 50.00 100.00

nn- **Chester Gump at Silver Creek Ranch**, 1933, Whitman, 52 pgs., 4" x 5 1/2", premium-no ads, soft-c, Sidney Smith-a 25.00 75.00 150.00

766- **Chester Gump Finds the Hidden Treasure**, 1934, Whitman, 320 pgs., Sidney Smith-a 12.00 40.00 85.00

nn- **Chester Gump Finds the Hidden Treasure**, 1934, Whitman, 52 pgs., 3 1/2" x 5 3/4", premium-no ads, soft-c, Sidney Smith-a 25.00 75.00 150.00

nn- **Chester Gump Finds the Hidden Treasure**, 1934, Whitman, 52 pgs., 4" x 5 1/2", premium-no ads, Sidney Smith-a 25.00 75.00 150.00

1146- **Chester Gump in the City Of Gold**, 1935, Whitman, 432 pgs., Sidney Smith-a 12.00 40.00 85.00

nn- **Chester Gump in the City Of Gold**, 1935, Whitman, 436 pgs., premium-no ads, 3-color, soft-c, Sidney Smith-a 30.00 90.00 175.00

1402- **Chester Gump in the Pole to Pole Flight**, 1937, Whitman, 432 pgs. 12.00 40.00 75.00

5- **Chester Gump and His Friends,** 1934, Whitman, 132 pgs., 3 1/2" x 3 1/2", soft-c, Tarzan Ice Cream cup lid premium 25.00 85.00 165.00

nn- **Chester Gump at the North Pole**, 1938, Whitman, 68 pgs. soft-c, 3 3/4" x 3 1/2", Pan-Am giveaway 25.00 85.00 165.00

nn- **Chicken Greedy**, nd(1930s), np (Whitman), 36 pgs., 3" x 2 1/2", Penny Book 4.00 10.00 20.00

nn- **Chicken Licken**, nd (1930s), np (Whitman), 36 pgs., 3" x 2 1/2",

1446 - Convoy Patrol © WHIT

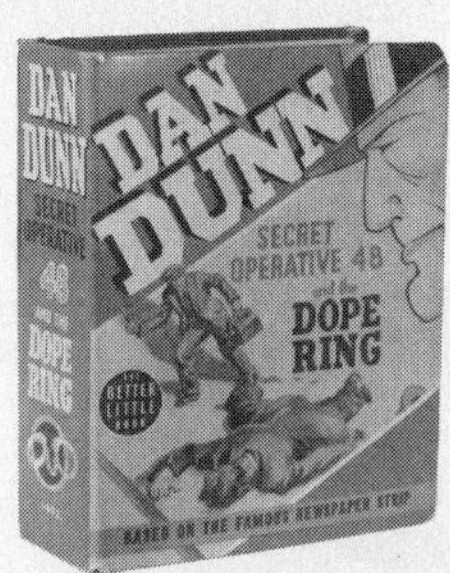

1492 - Dan Dunn and the Dope Ring © WHIT

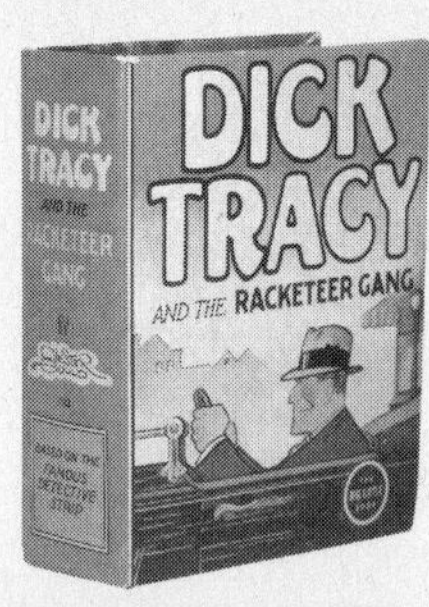

1112 - Dick Tracy and the Racketeer Gang © UFS

		GD	FN	VF/NM
	Penny Book	4.00	10.00	20.00
1101-	**Chief of the Rangers**, 1935, Saalfield, hard-c, Tom Mix photo-c, movie scenes from "The Miracle Rider"	20.00	60.00	120.00
1581-	**Chief of the Rangers**, 1935, Saalfield, soft-c, Tom Mix photo-c, movie scenes	20.00	60.00	120.00
	Child's Garden of Verses (See Wee Little Books)			
L14-	**Chip Collins'Adventures on Bat Island**, 1935, Lynn, 192 pgs.	10.00	35.00	70.00
2025-	**Chitty Chitty Bang Bang**, 1968, Whitman, movie photos	4.00	12.00	25.00
	Chubby Little Books, 1935, Whitman, 3" x 2 1/2", 200 pgs.			
W803-	**Golden Hours Story Book, The**	6.00	18.00	35.00
W803-	**Story Hours Story Book, The**	6.00	18.00	35.00
W804-	**Gay Book of Little Stories, The**	6.00	18.00	35.00
W804-	**Glad Book of Little Stories, The**	6.00	18.00	35.00
W804-	**Joy Book of Little Stories, The**	6.00	18.00	35.00
W804-	**Sunny Book of Little Stories, The**	6.00	18.00	35.00
1453-	**Chuck Malloy Railroad Detective on the Streamliner**, 1938, Whitman, 300 pgs.	10.00	25.00	55.00
	Cinderella (See Walt Disney's...)			
	Clyde Beatty (See The Steel Arena)			
1410-	**Clyde Beatty Daredevil Lion and Tiger Tamer**, 1939, Whitman, 300 pgs.	10.00	35.00	75.00
1480-	**Coach Bernie Bierman's Brick Barton and the Winning Eleven**, 1938, 300 pgs.	10.00	25.00	55.00
1446-	**Convoy Patrol** (A Thrilling U.S. Navy Story), 1942, Whitman, 432 pgs., flip pictures	10.00	25.00	55.00
1127-	**Corley of the Wilderness Trail**, 1937, Saalfield, hard-c	10.00	27.00	55.00
1607-	**Corley of the Wilderness Trail**, 1937, Saalfield, soft-c	10.00	27.00	55.00
1-	**Count of Monte Cristo**, 1934, EVW, 160 pgs., (Five Star Library), movie scenes, hard-c	20.00	55.00	110.00
1457-	**Cowboy Lingo Boys' Book of Western Facts**, 1938, Whitman, 300 pgs., Fred Harman-a	10.00	30.00	60.00
1171-	**Cowboy Malloy**, 1940, Saalfield, 400 pgs.	10.00	25.00	50.00
1106-	**Cowboy Millionaire**, 1935, Saalfield, movie scenes with George O'Brien, photo-c, hard-c	12.00	40.00	80.00
1586-	**Cowboy Millionaire**, 1935, Saalfield, movie scenes with George O'Brien, photo-c, soft-c	12.00	40.00	80.00
724-	**Cowboy Stories**, 1933, Whitman, 300 pgs., Hal Arbo-a	12.00	35.00	70.00
nn-	**Cowboy Stories**, 1933, Whitman, 52 pgs., soft-c, premium-no ads, 4" x 5 1/2" Hal Arbo-a	15.00	40.00	80.00
1161-	**Crimson Cloak, The**, 1939, Saalfield, 400 pgs.	10.00	25.00	55.00
L19-	**Curley Harper at Lakespur**, 1935, Lynn, 192 pgs.	10.00	25.00	55.00
5785-2-	**Daffy Duck in Twice the Trouble**, 1980, Whitman, 260 pgs., 79 cents soft-c	1.00	3.00	6.00
2018-(#18)-	**Daktari-Night of Terror**, 1968, Whitman, 260 pgs., 39 cents, hard-c, color illos	4.00	12.00	25.00
1010-	**Dan Dunn And The Gangsters' Frame-Up**, 1937, Whitman, 7 1/4" x 5 1/2", 64 pgs., Nickel Book	40.00	150.00	265.00
1116-	**Dan Dunn "Crime Never Pays,"** 1934, Whitman, 320 pgs., by Norman Marsh	12.00	40.00	75.00
1125-	**Dan Dunn on the Trail of the Counterfeiters**, 1936, Whitman, 432 pgs., by Norman Marsh	12.00	40.00	75.00
1171-	**Dan Dunn and the Crime Master**, 1937, Whitman, 432 pgs., by Norman Marsh	12.00	40.00	75.00
1417-	**Dan Dunn and the Underworld Gorillas,** 1941, Whitman, All Pictures Comics, flip pictures, by Norman Marsh	12.00	40.00	75.00
1454-	**Dan Dunn on the Trail of Wu Fang**, 1938, Whitman, 432 pgs., by Norman Marsh	15.00	45.00	90.00
1481-	**Dan Dunn and the Border Smugglers**, 1938, Whitman, 432 pgs., by Norman Marsh	12.00	40.00	75.00
1492-	**Dan Dunn and the Dope Ring**, 1940, Whitman, 432 pgs., by Norman Marsh	10.00	35.00	70.00

		GD	FN	VF/NM
nn-	**Dan Dunn and the Bank Hold-Up**, 1938, Whitman, 36 pgs., 2 1/2" x 3 1/2", Penny Book	12.00	30.00	55.00
nn-	**Dan Dunn and the Zeppelin Of Doom**, 1938, Dell, 196 pgs., Fast-Action Story, soft-c	35.00	90.00	185.00
nn-	**Dan Dunn Meets Chang Loo**, 1938, Whitman, 66 pgs., Pan-Am premium, by Norman Marsh	25.00	75.00	165.00
nn-	**Dan Dunn Plays a Lone Hand**, 1938, Whitman, 36 pgs., 2 1/2" x 3 1/2", Penny Book	12.00	30.00	60.00
	3 3/4" x 3 1/2", Buddy book	35.00	100.00	225.00
6-	**Dan Dunn Secret Operative 48 and the Counterfeiter Ring**, 1938, Whitman, 132 pgs., soft-c, 3 3/4" x 3 1/2", Buddy Book premium	35.00	110.00	225.00
9-	**Dan Dunn's Mysterious Ruse**, 1936, Whitman, 132 pgs., soft-c, 3 1/2" x 3 1/2", Tarzan Ice Cream cup lid premium	35.00	115.00	225.00
1177-	**Danger Trail North**, 1940, Saalfield, 400 pgs.	10.00	25.00	55.00
1151-	**Danger Trails in Africa**, 1935, Whitman, 432 pgs.	20.00	50.00	100.00
nn-	**Daniel Boone**, 1934, World Syndicate, High Lights of History Series, hard-c, All in Pictures	10.00	25.00	55.00
1160-	**Dan of the Lazy L**, 1939, Saalfield, 400 pgs.	10.00	25.00	55.00
1148-	**David Copperfield**, 1934, Whitman, hard-c, 160 pgs., photo-c, movie scenes (W. C. Fields)	15.00	60.00	110.00
nn-	**David Copperfield**, 1934, Whitman, soft-c, 164 pgs., movie scenes	15.00	60.00	110.00
1151-	**Death by Short Wave**, 1938, Saalfield	10.00	30.00	60.00
1156-	**Denny the Ace Detective**, 1938, Saalfield, 400 pgs.	10.00	25.00	50.00
1431-	**Desert Eagle and the Hidden Fortress, The**, 1941, Whitman, 432 pgs., flip pictures	12.00	30.00	60.00
1458-	**Desert Eagle Rides Again, The**, 1939, Whitman, 300 pgs.	12.00	30.00	60.00
1136-	**Desert Justice**, 1938, Saalfield, 400 pgs.	10.00	25.00	50.00
1484-	**Detective Higgins of the Racket Squad**, 1938, Whitman, 432 pgs.	12.00	30.00	60.00
1124-	**Dickie Moore in the Little Red School House**, 1936, Whitman, 240 pgs., photo-c, movie scenes (Chesterfield Motion Picts. Corp)	10.00	35.00	75.00
W-707-	**Dick Tracy the Detective, The Adventures of**, 1933, Whitman, 320 pgs. (The 1st Big Little Book), by Chester Gould (Scarce)	275.00	900.00	1750.00
nn-	**Dick Tracy Detective, The Adventures of**, 1933, Whitman, 52 pgs., 4" x 5 1/2", premium-no ads, soft-c, by Chester Gould	90.00	275.00	550.00
nn-	**Dick Tracy Detective, The Adventures of**, 1933, Whitman, 52 pgs., 4" x 5 1/2", inside back-c & back-c ads for Sundial Shoes, soft-c, by Chester Gould	100.00	300.00	600.00
710-	**Dick Tracy and Dick Tracy, Jr.** (The Advs. of ...), 1933, Whitman, 320 pgs., by Chester Gould	60.00	225.00	450.00
nn-	**Dick Tracy and Dick Tracy, Jr.** (The Advs. of ...), 1933, Whitman, 52 pgs., premium-no ads, soft-c, 4" x 5 1/2", by Chester Gould	60.00	225.00	450.00
nn-	**Dick Tracy the Detective and Dick Tracy, Jr.**, 1933, Whitman, 52 pgs., premium-no ads, 3 1/2"x 5 1/4", soft-c, by Chester Gould	60.00	225.00	450.00
723-	**Dick Tracy Out West**, 1933, Whitman, 300 pgs., by Chester Gould	35.00	135.00	275.00
749-	**Dick Tracy from Colorado to Nova Scotia**, 1933, Whitman, 320 pgs., by Chester Gould	35.00	125.00	240.00
nn-	**Dick Tracy from Colorado to Nova Scotia**, 1933, Whitman, 204 pgs., premium-no ads, soft-c, by Chester Gould	35.00	135.00	275.00
1105-	**Dick Tracy and the Stolen Bonds**, 1934, Whitman, 320 pgs., by Chester Gould	25.00	75.00	150.00
1112-	**Dick Tracy and the Racketeer Gang**, 1936, Whitman, 432 pgs., by Chester Gould	20.00	60.00	120.00
1137-	**Dick Tracy Solves the Penfield Mystery**, 1934, Whitman, 320 pgs., by Chester Gould	25.00	75.00	150.00
nn-	**Dick Tracy Solves the Penfield Mystery**, 1934, Whitman, 324 pgs., premium-no ads, 3-color, soft-c, by Chester Gould			

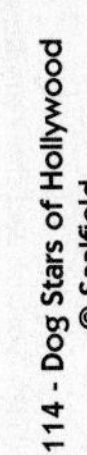
1445 - Dick Tracy and the Bicycle Gang © UFS

1114 - Dog Stars of Hollywood © Saalfield

1432 - Donald Duck and the Green Serpent © WDC

	GD	FN	VF/NM
	35.00	135.00	275.00
1163- **Dick Tracy and the Boris Arson Gang**, 1935, Whitman, 432 pgs., by Chester Gould	20.00	60.00	120.00
1170- **Dick Tracy on the Trail of Larceny Lu**, 1935, Whitman, 432 pgs., by Chester Gould	20.00	60.00	120.00
1185- **Dick Tracy in Chains of Crime**, 1936, Whitman, 432 pgs., by Chester Gould	20.00	60.00	120.00
1412- **Dick Tracy and Yogee Yamma**, 1946, Whitman, 352 pgs., by Chester Gould	20.00	60.00	120.00
1420- **Dick Tracy and the Hotel Murders**, 1937, Whitman, 432 pgs., by Chester Gould	20.00	60.00	120.00
1434- **Dick Tracy and the Phantom Ship**, 1940, Whitman, 432 pgs., by Chester Gould	20.00	60.00	120.00
1436- **Dick Tracy and the Mad Killer**, 1947, Whitman, 288 pgs., by Chester Gould	15.00	50.00	100.00
1439- **Dick Tracy and His G-Men**, 1941, Whitman, 432 pgs., flip pictures, by Chester Gould	20.00	60.00	120.00
1445- **Dick Tracy and the Bicycle Gang**, 1948, Whitman, 288 pgs., by Chester Gould	12.00	50.00	100.00
1446- **Detective Dick Tracy and the Spider Gang**, 1937, Whitman, 240 pgs., movie scenes from "Adventures of Dick Tracy" (Republic serial)	25.00	80.00	165.00
1449- **Dick Tracy Special F.B.I. Operative**, 1943, Whitman, 432 pgs. by Chester Gould	20.00	60.00	120.00
1454- **Dick Tracy on the High Seas**, 1939, Whitman, 432 pgs., by Chester Gould	20.00	60.00	120.00
1460- **Dick Tracy and the Tiger Lilly Gang**, 1949, Whitman, 288 pgs., by Chester Gould	15.00	50.00	95.00
1478- **Dick Tracy on Voodoo Island**, 1944, Whitman, 352 pgs., by Chester Gould	15.00	50.00	95.00
1479- **Detective Dick Tracy Vs. Crooks in Disguise**, 1939, Whitman, 432 pgs., flip pictures, by Chester Gould	20.00	60.00	120.00
1482- **Dick Tracy and the Wreath Kidnapping Case**, 1945, Whitman, 352 pgs.	15.00	50.00	100.00
1488- **Dick Tracy the Super-Detective**, 1939, Whitman, 432 pgs., by Chester Gould	20.00	60.00	120.00
1491- **Dick Tracy the Man with No Face**, 1938, Whitman, 432 pgs.	20.00	60.00	120.00
1495- **Dick Tracy Returns,** 1939, Whitman, 432 pgs., based on Republic Motion Picture serial, Chester Gould-a	20.00	60.00	120.00
2001- **(#1)-Dick Tracy-Encounters Facey,** 1967, Whitman, 260 pgs., 39 cents, hard-c, color illos	5.00	15.00	30.00
4055- **Dick Tracy, The Adventures of,** 1934, Whitman, 7" x 9 1/2", 320 pgs., Big Big Book, by Chester Gould	100.00	325.00	600.00
4071- **Dick Tracy and the Mystery of the Purple Cross,** 1938, 7" x 9 1/2", 320 pgs., Big Big Book, by Chester Gould (Scarce)	175.00	450.00	850.00
nn- **Dick Tracy and the Invisible Man,** 1939, Whitman, 3 1/4" x 3 3/4", 132 pgs., stapled, soft-c, Quaker Oats premium; NBC radio play script, Chester Gould-a	35.00	110.00	225.00
Vol. 2- **Dick Tracy's Ghost Ship,** 1939, Whitman, 3 1/2" x 3 1/2", 132 pgs., soft-c, stapled, Quaker Oats premium; NBC radio play script episode from actual radio show; Gould-a	35.00	110.00	225.00
3- **Dick Tracy Meets a New Gang,** 1934, Whitman, 3" x 3 1/2", 132 pgs., soft-c, Tarzan Ice Cream cup lid premium	50.00	200.00	400.00
11- **Dick Tracy in Smashing the Famon Racket,** 1938, Whitman, 3 3/4" x 3 1/2", Buddy Book-ice cream premium, by Chester Gould	50.00	200.00	400.00
nn- **Dick Tracy Gets His Man,** 1938, Whitman, 36 pgs., 2 1/2" x 3 1/2", Penny Book	10.00	30.00	65.00
nn- **Dick Tracy the Detective,** 1938, Whitman, 36 pgs., 2 1/2" x 3 1/2", Penny Book	10.00	30.00	65.00
9- **Dick Tracy and the Frozen Bullet Murders,** 1941, Dell, 196 pgs., Fast-Action Story, soft-c, by Gould	35.00	120.00	235.00
6833- **Dick Tracy Detective and Federal Agent,** 1936, Dell, 244 pgs., Cartoon Story Books, hard-c, by Gould	35.00	135.00	275.00
nn- **Dick Tracy Detective and Federal Agent,** 1936, Dell, 244 pgs., Fast-Action Story, soft-c, by Gould	35.00	120.00	260.00
nn- **Dick Tracy and the Blackmailers,** 1939, Dell, 196 pgs., Fast-Action Story, soft-c, by Gould	35.00	120.00	260.00
nn- **Dick Tracy and the Chain of Evidence, Detective**, 1938, Whitman, 196 pgs., Fast-Action Story, soft-c, by Chester Gould	35.00	130.00	260.00
nn- **Dick Tracy and the Crook Without a Face**, 1938, Whitman, 68 pgs., 3 1/4" x 3 1/2", Pan-Am giveaway, Gould-c/a	40.00	145.00	285.00
nn- **Dick Tracy and the Maroon Mask Gang**, 1938, Dell, 196 pgs., Fast-Action Story, soft-c, by Gould	35.00	130.00	260.00
nn- **Dick Tracy Cross-Country Race**, 1934, Whitman, 8 pgs., 2 1/2" x 3", Big Thrill chewing gum premium (6 diff.)	15.00	50.00	95.00
nn- **Dick Whittington and his Cat**, nd(1930s), np(Whitman), 36 pgs., Penny Book	5.00	15.00	30.00
Dinglehoofer und His Dog Adolph (See Top-Line Comics)			
Dinky (See Jackie Cooper in ...)			
1464- **Dirigible ZR90 and the Disappearing Zeppelin** (Captain Robb of ...), 1941, Whitman, 300 pgs., Al Lewin-a	18.00	55.00	110.00
1167- **Dixie Dugan Among the Cowboys**, 1939, Saalfield, 400 pgs.	12.00	30.00	60.00
1188- **Dixie Dugan and Cuddles**, 1940, Saalfield, 400 pgs., by Striebel & McEvoy	12.00	30.00	60.00
Doctor Doom (See Foreign Spies... & International Spy...)			
Dog of Flanders, A (See Frankie Thomas in ...)			
1114- **Dog Stars of Hollywood**, 1936, Saalfield, photo-c, photo-illos	15.00	45.00	90.00
1594- **Dog Stars of Hollywood**, 1936, Saalfield, photo-c, soft-c, photo-illos	15.00	45.00	90.00
Donald Duck (See Silly Symphony... & Walt Disney's ...)			
1404- **Donald Duck (Says Such a Life)** (Disney), 1939, Whitman, 432 pgs., Taliaferro-a	25.00	85.00	165.00
1411- **Donald Duck and Ghost Morgan's Treasure** (Disney), 1946, Whitman, All Pictures Comics, Barks-a; reprints Four Color #9	35.00	95.00	195.00
1422- **Donald Duck Sees Stars** (Disney), 1941, Whitman, 432 pgs., flip pictures, Taliaferro-a	25.00	80.00	160.00
1424- **Donald Duck Says Such Luck** (Disney), 1941, Whitman, 432 pgs., flip pictures, Taliaferro-a	25.00	80.00	160.00
1430- **Donald Duck Headed For Trouble** (Disney), 1942, Whitman, 432 pgs., flip pictures, Taliaferro-a	25.00	80.00	160.00
1432- **Donald Duck and the Green Serpent** (Disney), 1947, Whitman, All Pictures Comics, Barks-a; reprints Four Color #108	30.00	90.00	180.00
1434- **Donald Duck Forgets To Duck** (Disney), 1939, Whitman, 432 pgs., Taliaferro-a	25.00	80.00	160.00
1438- **Donald Duck Off the Beam** (Disney), 1943, Whitman, 352 pgs., flip pictures, Taliaferro-a	25.00	80.00	160.00
1438- **Donald Duck Off the Beam** (Disney), 1943, Whitman, 432 pgs., flip pictures, Taliaferro-a	25.00	80.00	160.00
1449- **Donald Duck Lays Down the Law**, 1948, Whitman, 288 pgs.,	25.00	80.00	160.00
1457- **Donald Duck in Volcano Valley** (Disney), 1949, Whitman, 288 pgs., Barks-a	25.00	80.00	160.00
1462- **Donald Duck Gets Fed Up** (Disney), 1940, Whitman, 432 pgs.,Taliaferro-a	25.00	80.00	160.00
1478- **Donald Duck-Hunting For Trouble** (Disney), 1938, Whitman, 432 pgs., Taliaferro-a	25.00	80.00	160.00
1484- **Donald Duck is Here Again!**, 1944, Whitman, All Pictures Comics, Taliaferro-a	25.00	80.00	160.00
1486- **Donald Duck Up in the Air** (Disney), 1945, Whitman, 352 pgs., Barks-a	30.00	90.00	180.00
705-10- **Donald Duck and the Mystery of the Double X,** (Disney), 1949, Whitman, Barks-a	15.00	40.00	80.00
2033-**(#33)- Donald Duck, Luck of the Ducks,** 1969, Whitman, 256 pgs., hard-c, 39 cents, color illos.	4.00	12.00	25.00
2009-**(#9)-Donald Duck-The Fabulous Diamond Fountain,** (Walt Disney), 1967, Whitman, 260 pgs., 39 cents, hard-c, color illos	5.00	15.00	30.00
5756- **Donald Duck-The Fabulous Diamond Fountain,** (Walt Disney), 1973, Whitman, 260 pgs., 79 cents, soft-c, color illos	5.00	12.00	20.00

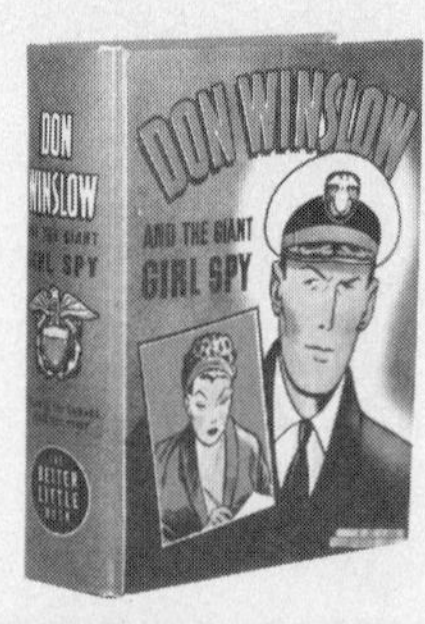

1408 - Don Winslow and the Giant Girl Spy © WHIT

11 - Ella Cinders' Exciting Experience © WHIT

1447 - Flash Gordon and the Fiery Desert of Mongo © KING

GD FN VF/NM

5756-1- Donald Duck-The Fabulous Diamond Fountain, (Walt Disney), 1973, Whitman, 260 pgs., 79 cents, soft-c, color illos 5.00 12.00 20.00
5756-2- Donald Duck-The Fabulous Diamond Fountain, (Walt Disney), 1973, Whitman, 260 pgs., 79 cents, soft-c, color illos 5.00 12.00 20.00
5760- Donald Duck in Volcano Valley (Disney), 1973, Whitman, 39 cents, flip-it book 5.00 12.00 20.00
5760-2- Donald Duck in Volcano Valley (Disney), 1973, Whitman, 79 cents, flip-it book 3.00 8.00 15.00
5764- Donald Duck, Luck of the Ducks, 1969, Whitman, 256 pgs., soft-c, 49 cents, color illos. 5.00 12.00 20.00
5773- Donald Duck - The Lost Jungle City, 1975, Whitman, 49 cents, flip-it book; 6 printings through 1980 3.00 6.00 12.00
nn- Donald Duck and the Ducklings, 1938, Whitman, 194 pgs., Fast-Action Story, soft-c, Taliaferro-a 50.00 160.00 325.00
nn- Donald Duck Out of Luck (Disney), 1940, Dell, 196 pgs., Fast-Action Story, has Four Color #4 on back-c, Taliaferro-a 50.00 160.00 325.00
8- Donald Duck Takes It on the Chin (Disney), 1941, Dell, 196 pgs., Fast-Action Story, soft-c, Taliaferro-a 50.00 160.00 325.00
L13- Donnie and the Pirates, 1935, Lynn, 192 pgs. 12.00 35.00 70.00
1438- Don O'Dare Finds War, 1940, Whitman, 432 pgs. 10.00 25.00 55.00
1107- Don Winslow, U.S.N., 1935, Whitman, 432 pgs. 15.00 45.00 90.00
nn- Don Winslow, U.S.N., 1935, Whitman, 436 pgs., premium-no ads, 3-color, soft-c 25.00 80.00 160.00
1408- Don Winslow and the Giant Girl Spy, 1946, Whitman, 352 pgs. 12.00 35.00 70.00
1418- Don Winslow Navy Intelligence Ace, 1942, Whitman, 432 pgs., flip pictures 15.00 50.00 90.00
1419- Don Winslow of the Navy Vs. the Scorpion Gang, 1938, Whitman, 432 pgs. 15.00 45.00 90.00
1453- Don Winslow of the Navy and the Secret Enemy Base, 1943, Whitman, 352 pgs. 15.00 45.00 90.00
1489- Don Winslow of the Navy and the Great War Plot, 1940, Whitman, 432 pgs. 15.00 45.00 90.00
nn- Don Winslow U.S. Navy and the Missing Admiral, 1938, Whitman, 36 pgs., 2 1/2" x 3 1/2", Penny Book 12.00 30.00 60.00
1137- Doomed To Die, 1938, Saalfield, 400 pgs. 10.00 25.00 55.00
1140- Down Cartridge Creek, 1938, Saalfield, 400 pgs. 10.00 25.00 55.00
1416- Draftie of the U.S. Army, 1943, Whitman, All Pictures Comics 12.00 30.00 60.00
1100B- Dreams (Your dreams & what they mean), 1938, Whitman, 36 pgs., 2 1/2" x 3 1/2", Penny Book 5.00 12.00 25.00
L24- Dumb Dora and Bing Brown, 1936, Lynn 12.00 40.00 80.00
1400- Dumbo, of the Circus - Only His Ears Grew! (Disney), 1941, Whitman, 432 pgs., based on Disney movie 25.00 80.00 160.00
10- Dumbo the Flying Elephant (Disney), 1944, Dell, 194 pgs., Fast-Action Story, soft-c 35.00 140.00 250.00
nn- East O' the Sun and West O' the Moon, nd (1930s), np (Whitman), 36 pgs., 3" x 2 1/2", Penny Book 5.00 12.00 25.00
774- Eddie Cantor in an Hour with You, 1934, Whitman, 154 pgs., 4 1/4" x 5 1/4", photo-c, movie scenes 15.00 45.00 90.00
nn- Eddie Cantor in Laughland, 1934, Goldsmith, 132 pgs., soft-c, photo-c, Vallely-a 15.00 45.00 90.00
1106- Ella Cinders and the Mysterious House, 1934, Whitman, 432 pgs. 12.00 40.00 80.00
nn- Ella Cinders and the Mysterious House, 1934, Whitman, 52 pgs., premium-no ads, soft-c, 3 1/2" x 5 3/4" 20.00 60.00 125.00
nn- Ella Cinders, 1935, Whitman, 148 pgs., 3 1/4" x 4", Tarzan Ice Cream cup lid premium 35.00 100.00 200.00
nn- Ella Cinders Plays Duchess, 1938, Whitman, 68 pgs., 3 3/4" x 3 1/2", Pan-Am Oil premium 15.00 50.00 90.00
nn- Ella Cinders Solves a Mystery, 1938, Whitman, 68 pgs., Pan-Am Oil premium, soft-c 15.00 50.00 90.00

GD FN VF/NM

11- Ella Cinders' Exciting Experience, 1934, Whitman, 3 1/2" x 3 1/2", 132 pgs., Tarzan Ice Cream cup lid giveaway 35.00 100.00 200.00
1406- Ellery Queen the Adventure of the Last Man Club, 1940, Whitman, 432 pgs. 12.00 40.00 75.00
1472- Ellery Queen the Master Detective, 1942, Whitman, 432 pgs., flip pictures 12.00 40.00 75.00
1081- Elmer and his Dog Spot, 1935, Saalfield, hard-c 10.00 25.00 55.00
1311- Elmer and his Dog Spot, 1935, Saalfield, soft-c 10.00 25.00 55.00
722- Erik Noble and the Forty-Niners, 1934, Whitman, 384 pgs. 12.00 30.00 60.00
nn- Erik Noble and the Forty-Niners, 1934, Whitman, 386 pgs., 3-color, soft-c 15.00 50.00 90.00
2019-(#19)- Fantastic Four in the House of Horrors, 1968, Whitman, 256 pgs., hard-c, color illos. 5.00 12.00 25.00
5775 - Fantastic Four in the House of Horrors, 1976, Whitman, 256 pgs., soft-c, color illos. 5.00 12.00 20.00
5775-1 - Fantastic Four in the House of Horrors, 1976, Whitman, 256 pgs., soft-c, color illos. 5.00 12.00 20.00
1058- Farmyard Symphony, The (Disney), 1939, 5" X 5 1/2", 68 pgs., hard-c 12.00 40.00 80.00
1129- Felix the Cat, 1936, Whitman, 432 pgs., Messmer-a 30.00 90.00 180.00
1439- Felix the Cat, 1943, Whitman, All Pictures Comics, Messmer-a 25.00 75.00 150.00
1465- Felix the Cat, 1945, Whitman, All Pictures Comics, Messmer-a 20.00 65.00 130.00
nn- Felix (Flip book), 1967, World Retrospective of Animation Cinema, 188 pgs., 2 1/2" x 4" by Otto Messmer 5.00 15.00 30.00
nn- Fighting Cowboy of Nugget Gulch, The, 1939, Whitman, 2 1/2" x 3 1/2", Penny Book 8.00 20.00 40.00
1401- Fighting Heroes Battle for Freedom, 1943, Whitman, All Pictures Comics, from "Heroes of Democracy" strip, by Stookie Allen 12.00 30.00 55.00
6- Fighting President, The, 1934, EVW (Five Star Library), 160 pgs., photo-c, photo ill., F. D. Roosevelt 12.00 35.00 70.00
nn- Fire Chief Ed Wynn and "His Old Fire Horse," 1934, Goldsmith, 132 pgs., H. Vallely-a, photo, soft-c 12.00 35.00 70.00
1464- Flame Boy and the Indians' Secret, 1938, Whitman, 300 pgs., Sekakuku-a (Hopi Indian) 10.00 25.00 55.00
22- Flaming Guns, 1935, EVW, with Tom Mix, movie scenes 20.00 55.00 110.00
1110- Flash Gordon on the Planet Mongo, 1934, Whitman, 320 pgs., by Alex Raymond 35.00 110.00 225.00
1166- Flash Gordon and the Monsters of Mongo, 1935, Whitman, 432 pgs., by Alex Raymond 30.00 105.00 215.00
nn- Flash Gordon and the Monsters of Mongo, 1935, Whitman, 436 pgs., premium-no ads, 3-color, soft-c, by Alex Raymond 50.00 165.00 325.00
1171- Flash Gordon and the Tournaments of Mongo, 1935, Whitman, 432 pgs., by Alex Raymond 35.00 110.00 220.00
1190- Flash Gordon and the Witch Queen of Mongo, 1936, Whitman, 432 pgs., by Alex Raymond 35.00 110.00 220.00
1407- Flash Gordon in the Water World of Mongo, 1937, Whitman, 432 pgs., by Alex Raymond 30.00 95.00 190.00
1423- Flash Gordon and the Perils of Mongo, 1940, Whitman, 432 pgs., by Alex Raymond 25.00 85.00 175.00
1424- Flash Gordon in the Jungles of Mongo, 1947, Whitman, 352 pgs., by Alex Raymond 20.00 60.00 120.00
1443- Flash Gordon in the Ice World of Mongo, 1942, Whitman, 432 pgs., flip pictures, by Alex Raymond 25.00 85.00 175.00
1447- Flash Gordon and the Fiery Desert of Mongo, 1948, Whitman, 288 pgs., Raymond-a 20.00 60.00 120.00
1469- Flash Gordon and the Power Men of Mongo, 1943, Whitman, 352 pgs., by Alex Raymond 25.00 85.00 175.00
1479- Flash Gordon and the Red Sword Invaders, 1945, Whitman, 352 pgs., by Alex Raymond 20.00 80.00 160.00

Flintstones: The Great Balloon Race © H-B

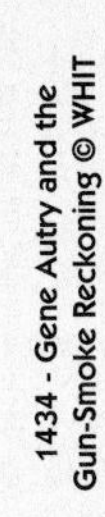

1434 - Gene Autry and the Gun-Smoke Reckoning © WHIT

1469 - G-Man and the Gun Runners © WHIT

	GD	FN	VF/NM
1484- Flash Gordon and the Tyrant of Mongo, 1941, Whitman, 432 pgs., flip pictures, by Alex Raymond	25.00	85.00	175.00
1492- Flash Gordon in the Forest Kingdom of Mongo, 1938, Whitman, 432 pgs., by Alex Raymond	35.00	110.00	225.00
12- Flash Gordon and the Ape Men of Mor, 1942, Dell, 196 pgs., Fast-Action Story, by Alex Raymond	50.00	165.00	325.00
6833- Flash Gordon Vs. the Emperor of Mongo, 1936, Dell, 244 pgs., Cartoon Story Books, hard-c, Alex Raymond-c/a	60.00	200.00	400.00
nn- Flash Gordon Vs. the Emperor of Mongo, 1936, Dell, 244 pgs., Fast-Action Story, soft-c, Alex Raymond-c/a	50.00	165.00	325.00
1467- Flint Roper and the Six-Gun Showdown, 1941, Whitman, 300 pgs.	10.00	25.00	55.00
2014-(#14)- Flintstones-The Case of the Many Missing Things, 1968, Whitman, 260 pgs., 39 cents, hard-c, color illos	4.00	12.00	25.00
nn- Flintstones: A Friend From the Past, 1977, Modern Promotions, 244 pgs., 49 cents, soft-c, flip pictures	3.00	6.00	12.00
nn- Flintstones: It's About Time, 1977, Modern Promotions, 244 pgs., 49 cents, soft-c, flip pictures	3.00	6.00	12.00
nn- Flintstones: Pebbles & Bamm-Bamm Met Santa Claus, 1977, Modern Promotions, 244 pgs., 49 cents, soft-c, flip pictures	3.00	6.00	12.00
nn- Flintstones: The Great Balloon Race, 1977, Modern Promotions, 244 pgs., 49 cents, soft-c, flip pictures	3.00	6.00	12.00
nn- Flintstones: The Mystery of the Many Missing Things, 1977, Modern Promotions, 244 pgs., 49 cents, soft-c, flip pictures	3.00	6.00	12.00
2003-(#3)- Flipper-Killer Whale Trouble, 1967, Whitman, 260 pgs., hard-c, 39 cents, color illos	4.00	10.00	20.00
2032-(#32)- Flipper, Deep-Sea Photographer, 1969, Whitman, 256 pgs., hard-c, color illos.	4.00	10.00	20.00
1108- Flying the Sky Clipper with Winsie Atkins, 1936, Whitman, 432 pgs.	10.00	25.00	55.00
1460- Foreign Spies Doctor Doom and the Ghost Submarine, 1939, Whitman, 432 pgs., Al McWilliams-a	12.00	35.00	70.00
1100B- Fortune Teller, 1938, Whitman, 36 pgs., 2 1/2" x 3 1/2", Penny Book	5.00	15.00	30.00
1175- Frank Buck Presents Ted Towers Animal Master, 1935, Whitman, 432 pgs.	12.00	30.00	60.00
2015-(#15)-Frankenstein, Jr. - The Menace of the Heartless Monster, 1968, Whitman, 260 pgs., 39 cents, hard-c, color illos.	4.00	12.00	25.00
16- Frankie Thomas in A Dog of Flanders, 1935, EVW, movie scenes	15.00	50.00	90.00
1121- Frank Merriwell at Yale, 1935, 432 pgs.	12.00	30.00	60.00
Freckles and His Friends in the North Woods (See Top-Line Comics)			
nn- Freckles and His Friends Stage a Play, 1938, Whitman, 36 pgs., 2 1/2" x 3 1/2", Penny Book	12.00	30.00	60.00
1164- Freckles and the Lost Diamond Mine, 1937, Whitman, 432 pgs., Merrill Blosser-a	12.00	35.00	70.00
nn- Freckles and the Mystery Ship, 1935, Whitman, 66 pgs., Pan-Am premium	15.00	50.00	90.00
1100B- Fun, Puzzles, Riddles, 1938, Whitman, 36 pgs., 2 1/2" x 3 1/2", Penny Book	4.00	12.00	25.00
1433- Gang Busters Step In, 1939, Whitman, 432 pgs., Henry E. Vallely-a	15.00	40.00	75.00
1437- Gang Busters Smash Through, 1942, Whitman, 432 pgs.	15.00	40.00	75.00
1451- Gang Busters in Action!, 1938, Whitman, 432 pgs.	15.00	40.00	75.00
nn- Gang Busters and Guns of the Law, 1940, Dell, 4" x 5", 194 pgs., Fast-Action Story, soft-c	40.00	115.00	225.00
nn- Gang Busters and the Radio Clues, 1938, Whitman, 36 pgs., 2 1/2" x 3 1/2", Penny Book	12.00	30.00	60.00
1409- Gene Autry and Raiders of the Range, 1946, Whitman, 352 pgs.	15.00	40.00	75.00
1425- Gene Autry and the Mystery of Paint Rock Canyon, 1947, Whitman, 288 pgs.	15.00	40.00	75.00
1428- Gene Autry Special Ranger, 1941, Whitman, 432 pgs., Erwin Hess-a	15.00	50.00	95.00
1433- Gene Autry in Public Cowboy No. 1, 1938, Whitman, 240 pgs., photo-c, movie scenes (1st Autry BLB)	30.00	90.00	175.00
1434- Gene Autry and the Gun-Smoke Reckoning, 1943, Whitman, 352 pgs.	15.00	45.00	90.00
1439- Gene Autry and the Land Grab Mystery, 1948, Whitman, 290 pgs.	12.00	35.00	70.00
1456- Gene Autry in Special Ranger Rule, 1945, Whitman, 352 pgs., Henry E. Vallely-a	15.00	45.00	90.00
1461- Gene Autry and the Red Bandit's Ghost, 1949, Whitman, 288 pgs.	12.00	35.00	65.00
1483- Gene Autry in Law of the Range, 1939, Whitman, 432 pgs.	15.00	45.00	90.00
1493- Gene Autry and the Hawk of the Hills, 1942, Whitman, 428 pgs., flip pictures, Vallely-a	15.00	45.00	90.00
1494- Gene Autry Cowboy Detective, 1940, Whitman, 432 pgs., Erwin Hess-a	15.00	45.00	90.00
700-10- Gene Autry and the Bandits of Silver Tip, 1949, Whitman	10.00	25.00	55.00
714-10- Gene Autry and the Range War, 1950, Whitman	10.00	25.00	55.00
nn- Gene Autry in Gun-Smoke, 1938, Dell, 196 pgs., Fast-Action story, soft-c	40.00	130.00	260.00
2035-(#35)- Gentle Ben, Mystery of the Everglades, 1969, Whitman, 256 pgs., hard-c, color illos.	4.00	10.00	20.00
1176- Gentleman Joe Palooka, 1940, Saalfield, 400 pgs.	15.00	45.00	90.00
George O'Brien (See The Cowboy Millionaire)			
1101- George O'Brien and the Arizona Badman, 1936?, Whitman	12.00	40.00	80.00
1418- George O'Brien in Gun Law, 1938, Whitman, 240 pgs., photo-c, movie scenes, RKO Radio Pictures	12.00	40.00	80.00
1457- George O'Brien and the Hooded Riders, 1940, Whitman, 432 pgs., Erwin Hess-a	12.00	30.00	60.00
nn- George O'Brien and the Arizona Bad Man, 1939, Whitman, 36 pgs., 2 1/2" x 3 1/2", Penny Book	12.00	30.00	60.00
1462- Ghost Avenger, 1943, Whitman, 432 pgs., flip pictures, Henry Vallely-a	10.00	25.00	55.00
nn- Ghost Gun Gang Meet Their Match, The, 1939. Whitman, 2 1/2" x 3 1/2", Penny Book	10.00	25.00	55.00
nn- Gingerbread Boy, The, nd(1930s), np(Whitman), 36 pgs., Penny Book	4.00	10.00	20.00
1118- G-Man on the Crime Trail, 1936, Whitman, 432 pgs.	12.00	35.00	70.00
1147- G-Man Vs. the Red X, 1936, Whitman, 432 pgs.	15.00	40.00	75.00
1162- G-Man Allen, 1939, Saalfield, 400 pgs.	10.00	25.00	55.00
1173- G-Man in Action, A, 1940, Saalfield, 400 pgs., J.R. White-a	10.00	25.00	55.00
1434- G-Man and the Radio Bank Robberies, 1937, Whitman, 432 pgs.	12.00	35.00	70.00
1469- G-Man and the Gun Runners, The, 1940, Whitman, 432 pgs.	12.00	35.00	70.00
1470- G-Man vs. the Fifth Column, 1941, Whitman, 432 pgs., flip pictures	12.00	35.00	70.00
1493- G-Man Breaking the Gambling Ring, 1938, Whitman, 432 pgs., James Gary-a	12.00	35.00	70.00
4- G-Men Foil the Kidnappers, 1936, Whitman, 132 pgs., 3 1/2" x 3 1/2", soft-c, Tarzan Ice Cream cup lid premium	35.00	100.00	200.00
nn- G-Man on Lightning Island, 1936, Dell, 244 pgs., Fast-Action Story, soft-c, Henry E. Vallely-a	30.00	90.00	175.00
6833- G-Man on Lightning Island, 1936, Dell, 244 pgs., Cartoon Story Book, hard-c, Henry E. Vallely-a	25.00	80.00	160.00
1157- G-Men on the Trail, 1938, Saalfield, 400 pgs.	10.00	25.00	55.00
1168- G Men on the Job, 1935, Whitman, 432 pgs.	12.00	35.00	70.00
nn- G-Men on the Job Again, 1938, Whitman, 36 pgs., 2 1/2" x 3 1/2", Penny Book	12.00	30.00	60.00
nn- G-Men and Kidnap Justice, 1938, Whitman, 68 pgs., Pan-Am premium, soft-c	12.00	35.00	70.00

5778 - Grimm's Ghost Stories © WHIT

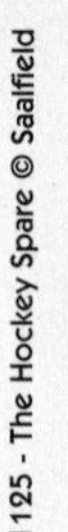

1125 - The Hockey Spare © Saalfield

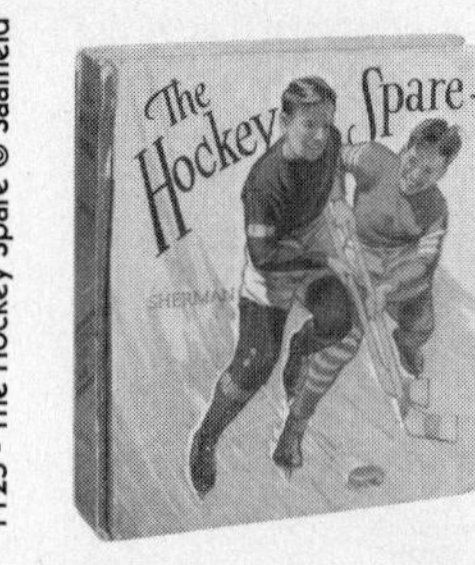

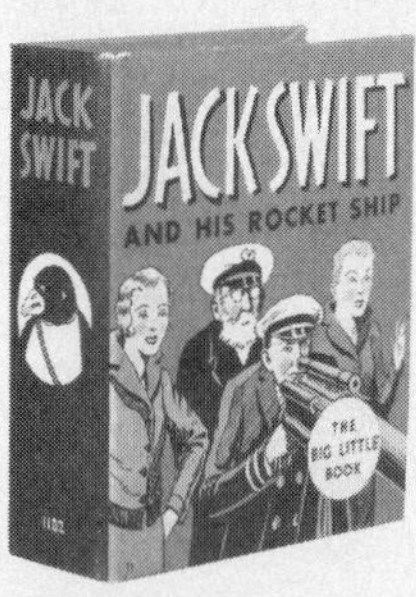

1102 - Jack Swift and His Rocket Ship © WHIT

GD FN VF/NM

nn- **G-Men and the Missing Clues**, 1938, Whitman, 36 pgs., 2 1/2"x 3 1/2", Penny Book 12.00 30.00 60.00

1097- **Go Into Your Dance**, 1935, Saalfield, 160 pgs.. photo-c, movie scenes with Al Jolson & Ruby Keeler 12.00 40.00 80.00

1577- **Go Into Your Dance**, 1935, Saalfield, 160 pgs., photo-c, movie scenes, soft-c 12.00 40.00 80.00

2021- **Goofy in Giant Trouble** (Walt Disney's ...), 1968, Whitman, hard-c, 260 pgs., 39 cents, color illos. 4.00 10.00 20.00

5751- **Goofy in Giant Trouble** (Walt Disney's ...), 1968, Whitman, soft-c, 260 pgs., 39 cents, color illos. 4.00 10.00 20.00

5751-2- **Goofy in Giant Trouble**, 1968 (1980-reprint of '67 version), Whitman, soft-c, 260 pgs., 79 cents, B&W 1.00 3.00 6.00

8- **Great Expectations**, 1934, EVW, (Five Star Library), 160 pgs., photo-c, movie scenes 20.00 55.00 110.00

1453- **Green Hornet Strikes!, The**, 1940, Whitman, 432 pgs., Robert Weisman-a 40.00 140.00 275.00

1480- **Green Hornet Cracks Down, The**, 1942, Whitman, 432 pgs., flip pictures, Henry Vallely-a 35.00 130.00 260.00

1496- **Green Hornet Returns, The**, 1941, Whitman, 432 pgs., flip pictures 35.00 130.00 260.00

5778- **Grimm's Ghost Stories**, 1976, Whitman, 256 pgs., Laura French-s adapted from fairy tales; blue spine & back-c 5.00 10.00 15.00

5778-1- **Grimm's Ghost Stories**, 1976, Whitman, 256 pgs., reprint of #5778; yellow spine & back-c 5.00 10.00 15.00

1172- **Gullivers' Travels**, 1939, Saalfield, 320 pgs., adapted from Paramount Pict. Cartoons 20.00 55.00 110.00

nn- **Gumps In Radio Land, The** (Andy Gump and the Chest of Gold), 1937, Lehn & Fink Prod. Corp., 100 pgs., 3 1/4" x 5 1/2", Pebeco Tooth Paste giveaway, by Gus Edson 20.00 70.00 130.00

nn- **Gunmen of Rustlers' Gulch, The**, 1939, Whitman, 36 pgs., 2 1/2" x 3 1/2", Penny Book 12.00 30.00 60.00

1426- **Guns in the Roaring West**, 1937, Whitman, 300 pgs. 10.00 25.00 55.00

1647- **Gunsmoke** (TV Series), 1958, Whitman, 280 pgs., 4 1/2" x 5 3/4" 8.00 20.00 40.00

1101- **Hairbreath Harry in Department QT**, 1935, Whitman, 384 pgs., by J. M. Alexander 12.00 35.00 70.00

1413- **Hal Hardy in the Lost Land of Giants**, 1938, Whitman, 300 pgs., "The World 1,000,000 Years Ago" 12.00 30.00 60.00

1159- **Hall of Fame of the Air**, 1936, Whitman, 432 pgs., by Capt. Eddie Rickenbacker 10.00 25.00 55.00

nn- **Hansel and Grethel, The Story of**, nd (1930s), no publ., 36 pgs., Penny Book 4.00 10.00 20.00

1145- **Hap Lee's Selection of Movie Gags**, 1935, Whitman, 160 pgs., photos of stars 12.00 40.00 80.00

Happy Prince, The (See Wee Little Books)

1111- **Hard Rock Harrigan-A Story of Boulder Dam**, 1935, Saalfield, hard-c, photo-c, photo illos. 10.00 25.00 55.00

1591- **Hard Rock Harrigan-A Story of Boulder Dam**, 1935, Saalfield, soft-c, photo-c, photo illos. 10.00 25.00 55.00

1418- **Harold Teen Swinging at the Sugar Bowl**, 1939, Whitman, 432 pgs., by Carl Ed 12.00 35.00 65.00

nn- **Hercules - The Legendary Journeys**, 1998, Chronicle Books, 310 pgs., based on TV series, 1-color (brown) illos 2.00 5.00 10.00

1100B- **Hobbies**, 1938, Whitman, 36 pgs., 2 1/2" x 3 1/2", Penny Book 4.00 10.00 20.00

1125- **Hockey Spare, The**, 1937, Saalfield, sports book 8.00 20.00 40.00

1605- **Hockey Spare, The**, 1937, Saalfield, soft-c 8.00 20.00 40.00

728- **Homeless Homer**, 1934, Whitman, by Dee Dobbin, for young kids 5.00 15.00 30.00

17- **Hoosier Schoolmaster, The**, 1935, EVW, movie scenes 15.00 45.00 85.00

715- **Houdini's Big Little Book of Magic**, 1927 (1933), 300 pgs. 12.00 45.00 90.00

nn- **Houdini's Big Little Book of Magic**, 1927 (1933), 196 pgs., American Oil Co. premium, soft-c 12.00 45.00 90.00

nn- **Houdini's Big Little Book of Magic**, 1927 (1933), 204 pgs., Cocomalt premium, soft-c 12.00 45.00 90.00

GD FN VF/NM

Huckleberry Finn (See The Adventures of...)

nn- **Huckleberry Hound Newspaper Reporter**, 1977, Modern Promotions, 244 pgs., 49 cents, soft-c, flip pictures 5.00 10.00 15.00

1644- **Hugh O'Brian TV's Wyatt Earp** (TV Series), 1958, Whitman, 280 pgs. 8.00 20.00 40.00

1424- **Inspector Charlie Chan Villainy on the High Seas**, 1942, Whitman, 432 pgs., flip pictures 15.00 45.00 90.00

1186- **Inspector Wade of Scotland Yard**, 1940, Saalfield, 400 pgs. 10.00 25.00 55.00

1448- **Inspector Wade Solves the Mystery of the Red Aces**, 1937, Whitman, 432 pgs. 10.00 25.00 55.00

1148- **International Spy Doctor Doom Faces Death at Dawn**, 1937, Whitman, 432 pgs., Arbo-a 12.00 35.00 70.00

1155- **In the Name of the Law**, 1937, Whitman, 432 pgs., Henry E. Vallely-a 10.00 25.00 55.00

2012-(#12)-**Invaders, The-Alien Missile Threat** (TV Series), 1967, Whitman, 260 pgs., hard-c, 39 cents, color illos. 4.00 12.00 25.00

1403- **Invisible Scarlet O'Neil**, 1942, Whitman, All Pictures Comics, flip pictures 12.00 35.00 70.00

1406- **Invisible Scarlet O'Neil Versus the King of the Slums**, 1946, Whitman, 352 pgs. 10.00 25.00 55.00

1098- **It Happened One Night**, 1935, Saalfield, 160 pgs., Little Big Book, Clark Gable, Claudette Colbert photo-c, movie scenes from Academy Award winner 20.00 60.00 120.00

1578- **It Happened One Night**, 1935, Saalfield, 160 pgs., soft-c 20.00 60.00 120.00

Jack and Jill (See Wee Little Books)

1432- **Jack Armstrong and the Mystery of the Iron Key**, 1939, Whitman, 432 pgs., Henry E. Vallely-a 12.00 35.00 70.00

1435- **Jack Armstrong and the Ivory Treasure**, 1937, Whitman, 432 pgs., Henry Vallely-a 12.00 35.00 70.00

Jackie Cooper (See Story Of..)

1084- **Jackie Cooper in Peck's Bad Boy**, 1934, Saalfield, 160 pgs., hard, photo-c, movie scenes 12.00 40.00 80.00

1314- **Jackie Cooper in Peck's Bad Boy**, 1934, Saalfield, 160 pgs., soft, photo-c, movie scenes 12.00 40.00 80.00

1402- **Jackie Cooper in "Gangster's Boy,"** 1939, Whitman, 240 pgs., photo-c, movie scenes 12.00 40.00 80.00

13- **Jackie Cooper in Dinky**, 1935, EVW, 160 pgs., movie scenes 12.00 40.00 85.00

nn- **Jack King of the Secret Service and the Counterfeiters**, 1939, Whitman, 36 pgs., 2 1/2" x 3 1/2", Penny Book, by John G. Gray 10.00 25.00 55.00

L11- **Jack London's Call of the Wild**, 1935, Lynn, 20th Cent. Pic., movie scenes with Clark Gable 15.00 45.00 90.00

nn- **Jack Pearl as Detective Baron Munchausen**, 1934, Goldsmith, 132 pgs., soft-c 12.00 35.00 70.00

1102- **Jack Swift and His Rocket Ship**, 1934, Whitman, 320 pgs. 20.00 55.00 115.00

1498- **Jane Arden the Vanished Princess**, Whitman, 300 pgs. 10.00 30.00 60.00

1179- **Jane Withers in This is the Life** (20th Century-Fox Presents...), 1935, Whitman, 240 pgs., photo-c, movie scenes 12.00 40.00 80.00

1463- **Jane Withers in Keep Smiling**, 1938, Whitman, 240 pgs., photo-c, movie scenes 12.00 40.00 80.00

Jaragu of the Jungle (See Rex Beach's ...)

1447- **Jerry Parker Police Reporter and the Candid Camera Clue**, 1941, Whitman, 300 pgs. 10.00 25.00 55.00

Jim Bowie (See Adventures of ...)

nn- **Jim Brant of the Highway Patrol and the Mysterious Accident**, 1939, Whitman, 36 pgs., 2 1/2" x 3 1/2", Penny Book 10.00 25.00 55.00

1466- **Jim Craig State Trooper and the Kidnapped Governor**, 1938, Whitman, 432 pgs. 10.00 25.00 55.00

nn- **Jim Doyle Private Detective and the Train Hold-Up**, 1939, Whitman, 36 pgs., 2 1/2" x 3 1/2", Penny Book 12.00 30.00 60.00

1180- **Jim Hardy Ace Reporter**, 1940, Saalfield, 400 pgs., Dick Moores-a 12.00 30.00 60.00

1143- **Jimmy Allen in the Air Mail Robbery**, 1936, Whitman, 432 pgs.

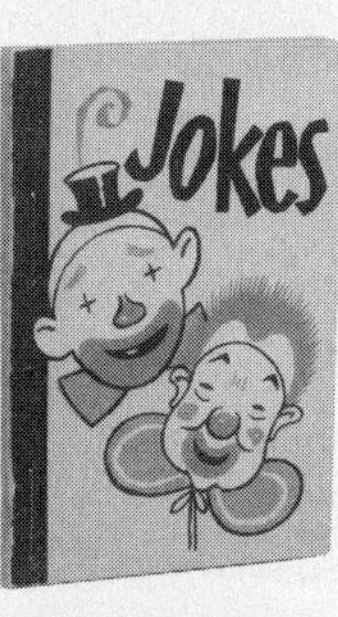

1100B - Jokes © WHIT

1411 - Kay Darcy and the Mystery Hideout © WHIT

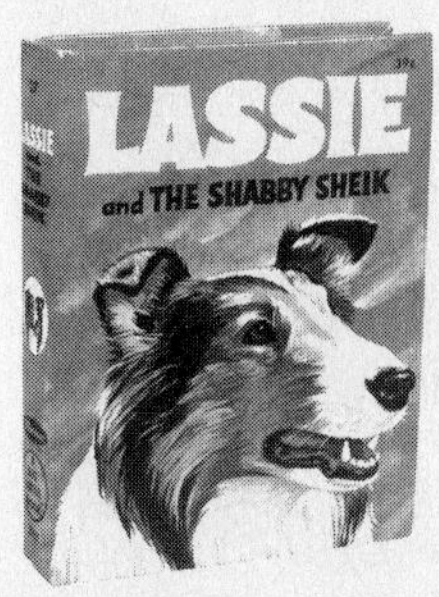

2027 - Lassie and the Shabby Sheik © WHIT

GD FN VF/NM

10.00 25.00 55.00
27- Jimmy Allen in The Sky Parade, 1936, Lynn, 130 pgs., 5 x 7 1/2", Paramount Pictures, movie scenes 15.00 35.00 75.00
L15- Jimmy and the Tiger, 1935, Lynn, 192 pgs. 12.00 30.00 60.00
Jimmy Skunk's Justice (See Wee Little Books)
1428- Jim Starr of the Border Patrol, 1937, Whitman, 432 pgs. 10.00 25.00 55.00
Joan of Arc (See Wee Little Books)
1105- Joe Louis the Brown Bomber, 1936, Whitman, 240 pgs., photo-c, photo-illos. 25.00 70.00 140.00
Joe Palooka (See Gentleman ...)
1123- Joe Palooka the Heavyweight Boxing Champ, 1934, Whitman, 320 pgs., Ham Fisher-a 20.00 80.00 125.00
1168- Joe Palooka's Great Adventure, 1939, Saalfield 15.00 75.00 100.00
nn- Joe Penner's Duck Farm, 1935, Goldsmith, Henry Vallely-a 12.00 35.00 70.00
1402- John Carter of Mars, 1940, Whitman, 432 pgs., John Coleman Burroughs-a 60.00 225.00 450.00
nn- John Carter of Mars, 1940, Dell, 194 pgs., Fast-Action Story, soft-c 60.00 225.00 450.00
1164- Johnny Forty Five, 1938, Saalfield, 400 pgs. 10.00 25.00 55.00
John Wayne (See Westward Ho!)
1100B- Jokes (A book of laughs galore), 1938, Whitman, 36 pgs., 2 1/2" x 3 1/2", Penny Book, laughing guy-c 4.00 10.00 20.00
1100B- Jokes (A book of side-splitting funny stories), 1938, Whitman, 36 pgs., 2 1/2" x 3 1/2", Penny Book, clowns on-c 4.00 10.00 20.00
2026- Journey to the Center of the Earth, The Fiery Foe, 1968, Whitman 4.00 12.00 24.00
Jungle Jim (See Top-Line Comics)
1138- Jungle Jim, 1936, Whitman, 432 pgs., Alex Raymond-a 20.00 60.00 120.00
1139- Jungle Jim and the Vampire Woman, 1937, Whitman, 432 pgs., Alex Raymond-a 20.00 60.00 120.00
1442- Junior G-Men, 1937, Whitman, 432 pgs., Henry E. Vallely-a 12.00 30.00 60.00
nn- Junior G-Men Solve a Crime, 1939, Whitman, 36 pgs., 2 1/2" x 3 1/2", Penny Book 12.00 30.00 60.00
1422- Junior Nebb on the Diamond Bar Ranch, 1938, Whitman, 300 pgs., by Sol Hess 12.00 30.00 60.00
1470- Junior Nebb Joins the Circus, 1939, Whitman, 300 pgs. by Sol Hess 12.00 30.00 60.00
nn- Junior Nebb Elephant Trainer, 1939, Whitman, 68 pgs., Pan-Am Oil premium, soft-c 12.00 40.00 80.00
1052- "Just Kids" (Adventures of ...), 1934, Saalfield, oblong size, by Ad Carter 20.00 65.00 125.00
1094- Just Kids and the Mysterious Stranger, 1935, Saalfield, 160 pgs., by Ad Carter 12.00 40.00 80.00
1184- Just Kids and Deep-Sea Dan, 1940, Saalfield, 400 pgs., by Ad Carter 12.00 35.00 70.00
1302- Just Kids, The Adventures of, 1934, Saalfield, oblong size, soft-c, by Ad Carter 20.00 65.00 125.00
1324- Just Kids and the Mysterious Stranger, 1935, Saalfield, 160 pgs., soft-c, by Ad Carter , 12.00 40.00 80.00
1401- Just Kids, 1937, Whitman, 432 pgs., by Ad Carter 12.00 40.00 80.00
1055- Katzenjammer Kids in the Mountains, 1934, Saalfield, hard-c, oblong, H. H. Knerr-a 20.00 60.00 120.00
1305- Katzenjammer Kids in the Mountains, 1934, Saalfield, soft-c, oblong, H. H. Knerr-a 20.00 60.00 120.00
14- Katzenjammer Kids, The, 1942, Dell, 194 pgs., Fast-Action Story, H. H. Knerr-a 25.00 65.00 130.00
1411- Kay Darcy and the Mystery Hideout, 1937, Whitman, 300 pgs., Charles Mueller-a 12.00 35.00 70.00
1180- Kayo in the Land of Sunshine (With Moon Mullins), 1937, Whitman, 432 pgs., by Willard 12.00 40.00 80.00
1415- Kayo and Moon Mullins and the One Man Gang, 1939, Whitman, 432 pgs., by Frank Willard 12.00 35.00 70.00
7- Kayo and Moon Mullins 'Way Down South, 1938, Whitman,

GD FN VF/NM

132 pgs., 3 1/2" x 3 1/2", Buddy Book 30.00 90.00 175.00
1105- Kazan in Revenge of the North (James Oliver Curwood's...), 1937, Whitman, 432 pgs., Henry E. Vallely-a 10.00 25.00 55.00
1471- Kazan, King of the Pack (James Oliver Curwood's...), 1940, Whitman, 432 pgs. 10.00 25.00 50.00
1420- Keep 'Em Flying! U.S.A. for America's Defense, 1943, Whitman, 432 pgs., Henry E. Vallely-a, flip pictures 10.00 25.00 55.00
1133- Kelly King at Yale Hall, 1937, Saalfield 10.00 25.00 50.00
Ken Maynard (See Strawberry Roan, Western Frontier & Wheels of Destiny)
776- Ken Maynard in "Gun Justice," 1934, Whitman, 160 pgs., hard-c, movie scenes (Universal Pic.) 20.00 60.00 120.00
776- Ken Maynard in "Gun Justice," 1934, Whitman, 160 pgs., soft-c, movie scenes (Universal Pic.) 20.00 60.00 120.00
1430- Ken Maynard in Western Justice, 1938, Whitman, 432 pgs., Irwin Myers-a 12.00 35.00 70.00
1442- Ken Maynard and the Gun Wolves of the Gila, 1939, Whitman, 432 pgs. 12.00 35.00 70.00
nn- Ken Maynard in Six-Gun Law, 1938, Whitman, 36 pgs., 2 1/2" x 3 1/2", Penny Book 10.00 25.00 55.00
1134- King of Crime, 1938, Saalfield, 400 pgs. 10.00 25.00 55.00
King of the Royal Mounted (See Zane Grey)
1010- King of the Royal Mounted in Arctic Law, 1937, Whitman, 7 1/4" x 5 1/2", 64 pgs., Nickel Book 12.00 40.00 80.00
nn- Kit Carson, 1933, World Syndicate, by J. Carroll Mansfield, High Lights Of History Series, hard-c 10.00 25.00 55.00
nn- Kit Carson, 1933, World Syndicate, same as hard-c above but with a black cloth-c 10.00 25.00 55.00
1105- Kit Carson and the Mystery Riders, 1935, Saalfield, hard-c, Johnny Mack Brown photo-c, movie scenes 15.00 50.00 100.00
1585- Kit Carson and the Mystery Riders, 1935, Saalfield, soft-c, Johnny Mack Brown photo-c, movie scenes 15.00 50.00 100.00
Krazy Kat (See Adventures of...)
2004- (#4)-Lassie-Adventure in Alaska (TV Series), 1967, Whitman, hard-c, 260 pgs., 39 cents, color illos 4.00 12.00 24.00
5754- Lassie-Adventure in Alaska (TV Series), 1973, Whitman, soft-c, 260 pgs., 49 cents, color illos 3.00 10.00 20.00
2027- Lassie and the Shabby Sheik (TV Series), 1968, Whitman, hard-c, 260 pgs., 39 cents 4.00 12.00 24.00
5762- Lassie and the Shabby Sheik (TV Series), 1972, Whitman, soft-c, 260 pgs., 39 cents 3.00 10.00 20.00
5769- Lassie, Old One-Eye (TV Series), 1975, Whitman, soft-c, 260 pgs., 49 cents, three printings 3.00 10.00 20.00
1132- Last Days of Pompeii, The, 1935, Whitman, 5 1/4" x 6 1/4", 260 pgs., photo-c, movie scenes 12.00 40.00 80.00
1128- Last Man Out (Baseball), 1937, Saalfield, hard-c 10.00 25.00 55.00
L30- Last of the Mohicans, The, 1936, Lynn, 192 pgs., movie scenes with Randolph Scott, United Artists Pictures 15.00 45.00 90.00
1126- Laughing Dragon of Oz, The, 1934, Whitman 432 pgs., by Frank Baum (scarce) 90.00 270.00 540.00
1086- Laurel and Hardy, 1934, Saalfield, 160 pgs., hard-c, photo-c, movie scenes 20.00 60.00 120.00
1316- Laurel and Hardy, 1934, Saalfield, 160 pgs. soft-c, photo-c, movie scenes 20.00 60.00 120.00
1092- Law of the Wild, The, 1935, Saalfield, 160 pgs., photo-c, movie scenes of Rex, The Wild Horse & Rin-Tin-Tin Jr. 12.00 35.00 70.00
1322- Law of the Wild, The, 1935, Saalfield, 160 pgs., photo-c, movie scenes, soft-c 12.00 35.00 70.00
1100B- Learn to be a Ventriloquist, 1938, Whitman, 36 pgs. 2 1/2" x 3 1/2", Penny Book 4.00 10.00 20.00
1149- Lee Brady Range Detective, 1938, Saalfield, 400 pgs. 10.00 25.00 50.00
L10- Les Miserables (Victor Hugo's ...), 1935, Lynn, 192 pgs., movie scenes 12.00 40.00 80.00
1441- Lightning Jim U.S. Marshall Brings Law to the West, 1940, Whitman, 432 pgs., based on radio program 12.00 35.00 70.00
nn- Lightning Jim Whipple U.S. Marshall in Indian Territory, 1939, Whitman, 36 pgs., 2 1/2" x 3 1/2", Penny Book 12.00 30.00 60.00

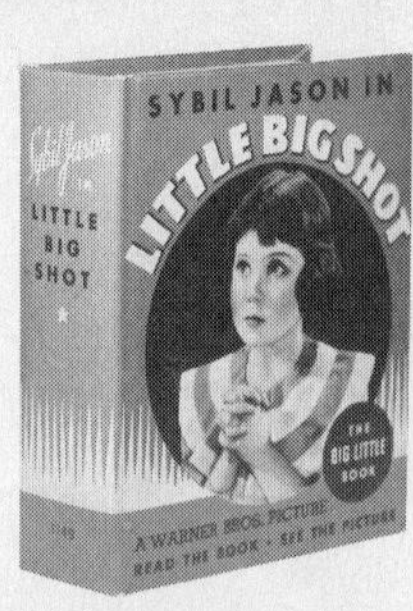

1149 - Little Big Shot © WHIT

1461 - Little Orphan Annie and the Underground Hide-Out © WHIT

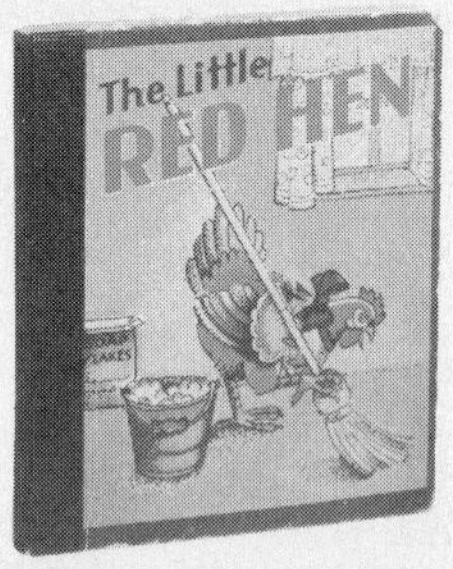

The Little Red Hen © WHIT

GD FN VF/NM

653- **Lions and Tigers** (With Clyde Beatty), 1934, Whitman, 160 pgs., photo-c movie scenes 15.00 45.00 90.00

1187- **Li'l Abner and the Ratfields**, 1940, Saalfield, 400 pgs., by Al Capp 15.00 50.00 100.00

1193- **Li'l Abner and Sadie Hawkins Day**, 1940, Saalfield, 400 pgs., by Al Capp 15.00 50.00 100.00

1198- **Li'l Abner in New York**, 1936, Whitman, 432 pgs., by Al Capp 20.00 55.00 110.00

1401- **Li'l Abner Among the Millionaires**, 1939, Whitman, 432 pgs., by Al Capp 20.00 55.00 110.00

1054- **Little Annie Rooney**, 1934, Saalfield, oblong - 4" x 8", All Pictures Comics, hard-c 15.00 55.00 110.00

1304- **Little Annie Rooney**, 1934, Saalfield, oblong - 4" x 8", All Pictures, soft-c 15.00 55.00 110.00

1117- **Little Annie Rooney and the Orphan House**, 1936, Whitman, 432 pgs. 10.00 30.00 65.00

1406- **Little Annie Rooney on the Highway to Adventure**, 1938, Whitman, 432 pgs. 10.00 30.00 65.00

1149- **Little Big Shot** (With Sybil Jason), 1935, Whitman, 240 pgs., photo-c, movie scenes 12.00 40.00 80.00

nn- **Little Black Sambo**, nd (1930s), np (Whitman), 36 pgs., 3" x 2 1/2", Penny Book 10.00 35.00 70.00

Little Bo-Peep (See Wee Little Books)

Little Colonel, The (See Shirley Temple)

1148- **Little Green Door, The**, 1938, Saalfield, 400 pgs. 10.00 30.00 60.00

1112- **Little Hollywood Stars**, 1935, Saalfield, movie scenes (Little Rascals, etc.), hard-c 12.00 40.00 80.00

1592- **Little Hollywood Stars**, 1935, Saalfield, movie scenes, soft-c 12.00 40.00 80.00

1087- **Little Jimmy's Gold Hunt**, 1935, Saalfield, 160 pgs., hard-c, Little Big Book, by Swinnerton 15.00 50.00 110.00

1317- **Little Jimmy's Gold Hunt**, 1935, Saalfield, 160 pgs., 4 1/4" x 5 3/4", soft-c, by Swinnerton 15.00 50.00 110.00

Little Joe and the City Gangsters (See Top-Line Comics)

Little Joe Otter's Slide (See Wee Little Books)

1118- **Little Lord Fauntleroy**, 1936, Saalfield, movie scenes, photo-c, 4 1/2" x 5 1/4", starring Mickey Rooney & Freddie Bartholomew, hard-c 12.00 35.00 70.00

1598- **Little Lord Fauntleroy**, 1936, Saalfield, photo-c, movie scenes, soft-c 12.00 35.00 70.00

1192- **Little Mary Mixup and the Grocery Robberies**, 1940, Saalfield 10.00 25.00 55.00

8- **Little Mary Mixup Wins A Prize**, 1936, Whitman, 132 pgs., 3 1/2" x 3 1/2", soft-c, Tarzan Ice Cream cup lid premium 35.00 100.00 200.00

1150- **Little Men**, 1934, Whitman, 4 3/4" x 5 1/4", movie scenes (Mascot Prod.), photo-c, hard-c 10.00 30.00 65.00

9- **Little Minister, The**,-Katharine Hepburn, 1935, 160 pgs., 4 1/4" x 5 1/2", EVW (Five Star Library), movie scenes (RKO) 15.00 45.00 90.00

1120- **Little Miss Muffet**, 1936, Whitman, 432 pgs., by Fanny Y. Cory 10.00 30.00 65.00

708- **Little Orphan Annie**, 1933, Whitman, 320 pgs., by Harold Gray, the 2nd Big Little Book 50.00 200.00 400.00

nn- **Little Orphan Annie**, 1928('33), Whitman, 52 pgs., 4" x 5 1/2", premium-no ads, soft-c, by Harold Gray 35.00 110.00 225.00

716- **Little Orphan Annie and Sandy**, 1933, Whitman, 320 pgs., by Harold Gray 30.00 90.00 180.00

716- **Little Orphan Annie and Sandy**, 1933, Whitman, 300 pgs., by Harold Gray 30.00 90.00 180.00

nn- **Little Orphan Annie and Sandy**, 1933, Whitman, 52 pgs., premium-no ads, 4" x 5 1/2", soft-c by Harold Gray 35.00 110.00 225.00

748- **Little Orphan Annie and Chizzler**, 1933, Whitman, 320 pgs., by Harold Gray 25.00 80.00 150.00

1010- **Little Orphan Annie and the Big Town Gunmen**, 1937, 7 1/4" x 5 1/2", 64 pgs., Nickel Book 12.00 40.00 80.00

GD FN VF/NM

nn- **Little Orphan Annie with the Circus**, 1934, Whitman, 320 pgs., same cover as L.O.A. 708 but with blue background, Ovaltine giveaway stamp inside front-c, by Harold Gray 100.00 200.00 300.00

1140- **Little Orphan Annie and the Big Train Robbery**, 1934, Whitman, 300 pgs., by Gray 15.00 45.00 100.00

1140- **Little Orphan Annie and the Big Train Robbery**, 1934, Whitman, 300 pgs., premium-no ads, soft-c, by Harold Gray 35.00 100.00 200.00

1154- **Little Orphan Annie and the Ghost Gang**, 1935, Whitman, 432 pgs. by Harold Gray 15.00 45.00 100.00

nn- **Little Orphan Annie and the Ghost Gang**, 1935, Whitman, 436 pgs., premium-no ads, 3-color, soft-c, by Harold Gray 35.00 100.00 200.00

1162- **Little Orphan Annie and Punjab the Wizard**, 1935, Whitman, 432 pgs., by Harold Gray 15.00 45.00 100.00

1186- **Little Orphan Annie and the $1,000,000 Formula**, 1936, Whitman, 432 pgs., by Gray 15.00 45.00 90.00

1414- **Little Orphan Annie and the Ancient Treasure of Am**, 1939, Whitman, 432 pgs., by Gray 12.00 40.00 80.00

1416- **Little Orphan Annie in the Movies**, 1937, Whitman, 432 pgs., by Harold Gray 12.00 40.00 80.00

1417- **Little Orphan Annie and the Secret of the Well**, 1947,Whitman, 352 pgs., by Gray 12.00 35.00 70.00

1435- **Little Orphan Annie and the Gooneyville Mystery**, 1947, Whitman, 288 pgs., by Gray 12.00 35.00 70.00

1446- **Little Orphan Annie in the Thieves' Den**, 1949, Whitman, 288 pgs., by Harold Gray 12.00 35.00 70.00

1449- **Little Orphan Annie and the Mysterious Shoemaker**, 1938, Whitman, 432 pgs., by Harold Gray 12.00 40.00 80.00

1457- **Little Orphan Annie and Her Junior Commandos**, 1943, Whitman, 352 pgs., by H. Gray 12.00 35.00 70.00

1461- **Little Orphan Annie and the Underground Hide-Out**, 1945, Whitman, 352 pgs., by Gray 12.00 35.00 70.00

1468- **Little Orphan Annie and the Ancient Treasure of Am**, 1949 (Misdated 1939), 288 pgs., by Gray 12.00 35.00 70.00

1482- **Little Orphan Annie and the Haunted Mansion**, 1941, Whitman, 432 pgs., flip pictures, by Harold Gray 15.00 45.00 90.00

3048- **Little Orphan Annie and Her Big Little Kit**, 1937, Whitman, 384 pgs., 4 1/2" x 6 1/2" box, includes miniature box of 4 crayons-red, yellow, blue and green 90.00 275.00 550.00

4054- **Little Orphan Annie, The Story of**, 1934, Whitman, 7" x 9 1/2", 320 pgs., Big Big Book, Harold Gray-c/a 100.00 300.00 600.00

nn- **Little Orphan Annie Gets into Trouble**, 1938, Whitman, 36 pgs., 2 1/2" x 3 1/2", Penny Book 12.00 30.00 60.00

nn- **Little Orphan Annie in Hollywood**, 1937, Whitman, 3 1/2" x 3 1/4", Pan-Am premium, soft-c 25.00 80.00 165.00

nn- **Little Orphan Annie in Rags to Riches**, 1939, Dell, 194 pgs., Fast-Action Story, soft-c 35.00 110.00 225.00

nn- **Little Orphan Annie Saves Sandy**, 1938, Whitman, 36 pgs., 2 1/2" x 3 1/2", Penny Book 12.00 30.00 60.00

nn- **Little Orphan Annie Under the Big Top**, 1938, Dell, 194 pgs., Fast-Action Story, soft-c 35.00 110.00 220.00

nn- **Little Orphan Annie Wee Little Books** (In open box) nn, 1934, Whitman, 44 pgs., by H. Gray

	GD	FN	VF/NM
L.O.A. And Daddy Warbucks	10.00	25.00	55.00
L.O.A. And Her Dog Sandy	10.00	25.00	55.00
L.O.A. And The Lucky Knife	10.00	25.00	55.00
L.O.A. And The Pinch-Pennys	10.00	25.00	55.00
L.O.A. At Happy Home	10.00	25.00	55.00
L.O.A. Finds Mickey	10.00	25.00	55.00
Complete set with box	45.00	175.00	350.00

nn- **Little Polly Flinders, The Story of**, nd (1930s), no publ., 36 pgs., 2 1/2" x 3", Penny Book 4.00 10.00 20.00

nn- **Little Red Hen, The**, nd(1930s), np(Whitman), 36 pgs., Penny Book 4.00 10.00 20.00

nn- **Little Red Riding Hood**, nd(1930s), np(Whitman), 36 pgs., 3" x 2 1/2", Penny Book 4.00 10.00 20.00

nn- **Little Red Riding Hood and the Big Bad Wolf** (Disney), 1934, McKay, 36 pgs., stiff-c, Disney Studio-a

1407 - Lone Ranger and Dead Men's Mine
© Lone Ranger Inc.

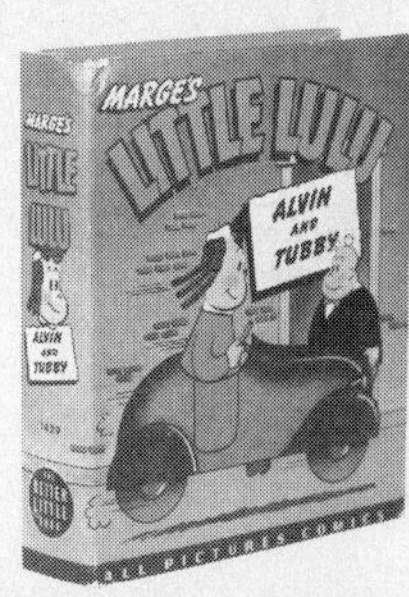
1429 - Marge's Little Lulu Alvin and Tubby
© Marjorie Buell

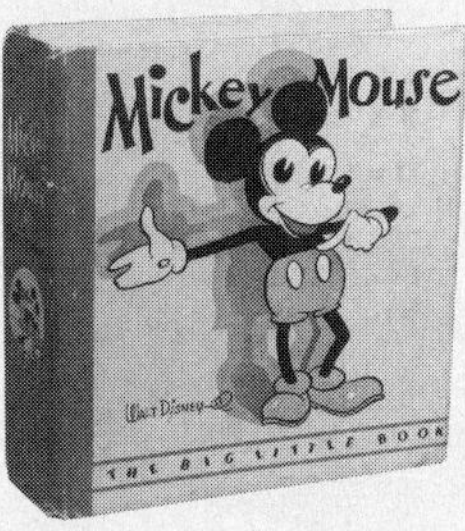
717 - Mickey Mouse (1st printing)
© WDC

	GD	FN	VF/NM
	30.00	90.00	180.00
757- Little Women, 1934, Whitman, 4 3/4" x 5 1/4", 160 pgs., photo-c, movie scenes, starring Katharine Hepburn	20.00	60.00	120.00
Littlest Rebel, The (See Shirley Temple)			
1181- Lone Ranger and his Horse Silver, 1935, Whitman, 432 pgs., Hal Arbo-a	25.00	75.00	160.00
1196- Lone Ranger and the Vanishing Herd, 1936, Whitman, 432 pgs.	20.00	60.00	120.00
1407- Lone Ranger and Dead Men's Mine, The, 1939, Whitman, 432 pgs.	15.00	50.00	110.00
1421- Lone Ranger on the Barbary Coast, The, 1944, Whitman, 352 pgs., Henry Vallely-a	15.00	45.00	90.00
1428- Lone Ranger and the Secret Weapon, The, 1943, Whitman,	15.00	45.00	90.00
1431- Lone Ranger and the Secret Killer, The, 1937, Whitman 432 pgs., H. Anderson-a	20.00	60.00	120.00
1450- Lone Ranger and the Black Shirt Highwayman, The, 1939, Whitman, 432 pgs.	15.00	50.00	110.00
1465- Lone Ranger and the Menace of Murder Valley, The, 1938, Whitman, 432 pgs., Robert Wiseman-a	15.00	50.00	110.00
1468- Lone Ranger Follows Through, The, 1941, Whitman, 432 pgs., H.E. Vallely-a	15.00	50.00	110.00
1477- Lone Ranger and the Great Western Span, The, 1942, Whitman, 424 pgs., H. E. Vallely-a	12.00	45.00	90.00
1489- Lone Ranger and the Red Renegades, The, 1939, Whitman, 432 pgs.	20.00	60.00	120.00
1498- Lone Ranger and the Silver Bullets, 1946, Whitman, 352 pgs., Henry E. Vallely-a	15.00	45.00	90.00
712-10- Lone Ranger and the Secret of Somber Cavern, The, 1950, Whitman	10.00	25.00	55.00
2013- (#13)-Lone Ranger Outwits Crazy Cougar, The, 1968, Whitman, 260 pgs., 39 cents, hard-c, color illos	4.00	12.00	24.00
5774- Lone Ranger Outwits Crazy Cougar, The, 1976, Whitman, 260 pgs., 49 cents, soft-c, color illos	4.00	11.00	22.00
5774-1- Lone Ranger Outwits Crazy Cougar, The, 1979, Whitman, 260 pgs., 69 cents, soft-c, color illos	4.00	10.00	20.00
nn- Lone Ranger and the Lost Valley, The, 1938, Dell, 196 pgs., Fast-Action Story, soft-c	35.00	110.00	225.00
1405- Lone Star Martin of the Texas Rangers, 1939, Whitman, 432 pgs.	15.00	50.00	100.00
19- Lost City, The, 1935, EVW, movie scenes	12.00	40.00	80.00
1103- Lost Jungle, The (With Clyde Beatty), 1936, Saalfield, movie scenes, hard-c	12.00	40.00	80.00
1583- Lost Jungle, The (With Clyde Beatty), 1936, Saalfield, movie scenes, soft -c	10.00	36.00	72.00
753- Lost Patrol, The, 1934, Whitman, 160 pgs., photo-c, movie scenes with Boris Karloff	12.00	40.00	80.00
nn- Lost World, The - Jurassic Park 2, 1997, Chronicle Books, 312 pgs., adapts movie, 1-color (green) illos	5.00	10.00	20.00
1189- Mac of the Marines in Africa, 1936, Whitman, 432 pgs.	10.00	30.00	60.00
1400- Mac of the Marines in China, 1938, Whitman, 432 pgs.	10.00	30.00	60.00
1100B- Magic Tricks (With explanations), 1938, Whitman, 36 pgs., 2 1/2" x 3 1/2", Penny Book, rabbit in hat-c	4.00	10.00	20.00
1100B- Magic Tricks (How to do them), 1938, Whitman, 36 pgs., 2 1/2" x 3 1/2", Penny Book, genie-c	4.00	10.00	20.00
Major Hoople (See Our Boarding House)			
2022-(#22)- Major Matt Mason, Moon Mission, 1968, Whitman, 256 pgs., hard-c, color illos.	5.00	15.00	30.00
1167- Mandrake the Magician, 1935, Whitman, 432 pgs., by Lee Falk & Phil Davis	20.00	65.00	130.00
1418- Mandrake the Magician and the Flame Pearls, 1946, Whitman, 352 pgs., by Lee Falk & Phil Davis	12.00	40.00	80.00
1431- Mandrake the Magician and the Midnight Monster, 1939, Whitman, 432 pgs., by Lee Falk & Phil Davis	15.00	45.00	90.00
1454- Mandrake the Magician Mighty Solver of Mysteries, 1941, Whitman, 432 pgs., by Lee Falk & Phil Davis, flip pictures	15.00	45.00	90.00

	GD	FN	VF/NM
2011-(#11)-Man From U.N.C.L.E., The-The Calcutta Affair (TV Series), 1967, Whitman, 260 pgs., 39 cents, hard-c, color illos	5.00	15.00	30.00
1429- Marge's Little Lulu Alvin and Tubby, 1947, Whitman, All Pictures Comics, Stanley-a	25.00	75.00	150.00
1438- Mary Lee and the Mystery of the Indian Beads, 1937, Whitman, 300 pgs.	10.00	25.00	55.00
1165- Masked Man of the Mesa, The, 1939, Saalfield, 400 pgs.	10.00	25.00	50.00
nn- Mask of Zorro, The, 1998, Chronicle Books, 312 pgs., adapts movie, 1-color (yellow-green) illos	2.00	5.00	10.00
1436- Maximo the Amazing Superman, 1940, Whitman, 432 pgs., Henry E. Vallely-a	12.00	40.00	80.00
1444- Maximo the Amazing Superman and the Crystals of Doom, 1941, Whitman,432 pgs., Henry E. Vallely-a	12.00	40.00	80.00
1445- Maximo the Amazing Superman and the Supermachine, 1941, Whitman, 432 pgs.	12.00	40.00	80.00
755- Men of the Mounted, 1934, Whitman, 320 pgs.	12.00	40.00	80.00
nn- Men of the Mounted, 1933, Whitman, 52 pgs., 3 1/2" x 5 3/4", premium-no ads; other versions with Poll Parrot & Perkins ad; soft-c	20.00	60.00	120.00
nn- Men of the Mounted, 1934, Whitman, Cocomalt premium, soft-c, by Ted McCall	12.00	35.00	70.00
1475- Men With Wings, 1938, Whitman, 240 pgs., photo-c, movie scenes (Paramount Pics.)	12.00	35.00	70.00
1170- Mickey Finn, 1940, Saalfield, 400 pgs., by Frank Leonard	12.00	35.00	70.00
717- Mickey Mouse (Disney), (1st printing) 1933, Whitman, 320 pgs., Gottfredson-a, skinny Mickey on cover	300.00	1000.00	2400.00
717- Mickey Mouse (Disney), (2nd printing)1933, Whitman, 320 pgs., Gottfredson-a, regular Mickey on cover	150.00	500.00	1250.00
nn- Mickey Mouse (Disney), 1933, Dean & Son, Great Big Midget Book, 320 pgs.	200.00	500.00	1000.00
731- Mickey Mouse the Mail Pilot (Disney), 1933, Whitman, (This is the same book as the 1st Mickey Mouse BLB #717(2nd printing) but with "The Mail Pilot" printed on the front. Lower left of back cover has a small box printed over the existing "No. 717." "No. 731" is printed next to it.) (sold at auction in 2001 in Fine condition for $5,090)			
726- Mickey Mouse in Blaggard Castle (Disney), 1934, Whitman, 320 pgs., Gottfredson-a	35.00	110.00	220.00
731- Mickey Mouse the Mail Pilot (Disney), 1933, Whitman, 300 pgs., Gottfredson-a	35.00	110.00	220.00
nn- Mickey Mouse the Mail Pilot (Disney), 1933, Whitman, 292 pgs., American Oil Co. premium, soft-c, Gottfredson-a; another version 3 1/2" x 4 3/4"	35.00	110.00	220.00
750- Mickey Mouse Sails for Treasure Island (Disney), 1933, Whitman, 320 pgs., Gottfredson-a	35.00	110.00	220.00
nn- Mickey Mouse Sails for Treasure Island (Disney), 1935, Whitman, 196 pgs., premium-no ads, soft-c, Gottfredson-a (Scarce)	50.00	150.00	300.00
nn- Mickey Mouse Sails for Treasure Island (Disney), 1935, Whitman, 196 pgs., Kolynos Dental Cream premium (Scarce)	50.00	150.00	300.00
nn- Mickey Mouse Sails for Treasure Island (Disney), 1933, Dean & Son, Great Big Midget Book, 320 pgs.	175.00	450.00	900.00
756- Mickey Mouse Presents a Walt Disney Silly Symphony (Disney), 1934, Whitman, 240 pgs., Bucky Bug app.	35.00	100.00	200.00
1111- Mickey Mouse Presents Walt Disney's Silly Symphonies Stories, 1936, Whitman, 432 pgs., Donald Duck app.	35.00	100.00	200.00
1128- Mickey Mouse and Pluto the Racer (Disney), 1936, Whitman, 432 pgs., Gottfredson-a	30.00	90.00	175.00
1139- Mickey Mouse the Detective (Disney), 1934, Whitman, 300 pgs., Gottfredson-a	35.00	100.00	200.00
1139- Mickey Mouse the Detective (Disney), 1934, Whitman, 304 pgs., premium-no ads, soft-c, Gottfredson-a (Scarce)	50.00	150.00	300.00
1153- Mickey Mouse and the Bat Bandit (Disney), 1935, Whitman, 432 pgs., Gottfredson-a	30.00	95.00	190.00

1451 - Mickey Mouse and the Desert Palace © WDC

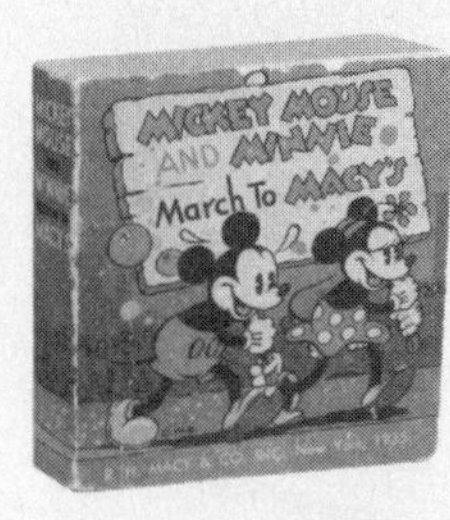

Mickey Mouse and Minnie March to Macy's © WDC

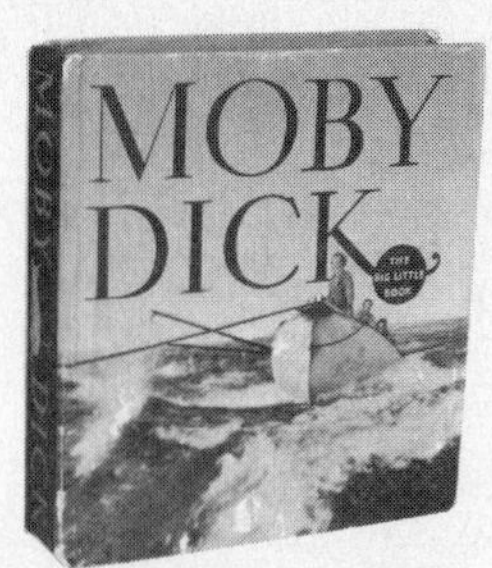

710 - Moby Dick the Great White Whale © WHIT

	GD	FN	VF/NM
nn- **Mickey Mouse and the Bat Bandit** (Disney), 1935, Whitman, 436 pgs., premium-no ads, 3-color, soft-c, Gottfredson-a (Scarce)	50.00	150.00	300.00
1160- **Mickey Mouse and Bobo the Elephant** (Disney), 1935, Whitman, 432 pgs., Gottfredson-a	30.00	95.00	190.00
1187- **Mickey Mouse and the Sacred Jewel** (Disney), 1936, Whitman, 432 pgs., Gottfredson-a	30.00	90.00	175.00
1401- **Mickey Mouse in the Treasure Hunt** (Disney), 1941, Whitman, 430 pgs., flip pictures of Pluto, Gottfredson-a	25.00	80.00	165.00
1409- **Mickey Mouse Runs His Own Newspaper** (Disney), 1937, Whitman, 432 pgs., Gottfredson-a	25.00	80.00	165.00
1413- **Mickey Mouse and the 'Lectro Box** (Disney), 1946, Whitman, 352 pgs., Gottfredson-a	20.00	55.00	110.00
1417- **Mickey Mouse on Sky Island** (Disney), 1941, Whitman, 432 pgs., flip pictures, Gottfredson-a; considered by Gottfredson to be his best Mickey story	25.00	85.00	165.00
1428- **Mickey Mouse in the Foreign Legion** (Disney), 1940, Whitman, 432 pgs., Gottfredson-a	25.00	85.00	165.00
1429- **Mickey Mouse and the Magic Lamp** (Disney), 1942, Whitman, 432 pgs., flip pictures	25.00	85.00	165.00
1433- **Mickey Mouse and the Lazy Daisy Mystery** (Disney), 1947, Whitman, 288 pgs.	20.00	55.00	110.00
1444- **Mickey Mouse in the World of Tomorrow** (Disney), 1948, Whitman, 288 pgs., Gottfredson-a	30.00	90.00	175.00
1451- **Mickey Mouse and the Desert Palace** (Disney), 1948, Whitman, 288 pgs.	20.00	55.00	110.00
1463- **Mickey Mouse and the Pirate Submarine** (Disney), 1939, Whitman, 432 pgs., Gottfredson-a	25.00	85.00	165.00
1464- **Mickey Mouse and the Stolen Jewels** (Disney), 1949, Whitman, 288 pgs.	20.00	75.00	150.00
1471- **Mickey Mouse and the Dude Ranch Bandit** (Disney), 1943, Whitman, 432 pgs., flip pictures	25.00	85.00	165.00
1475- **Mickey Mouse and the 7 Ghosts** (Disney), 1940, Whitman, 432 pgs., Gottfredson-a	25.00	85.00	165.00
1476- **Mickey Mouse in the Race for Riches** (Disney), 1938, Whitman, 432 pgs., Gottfredson-a	25.00	85.00	165.00
1483- **Mickey Mouse Bell Boy Detective** (Disney), 1945, Whitman, 352 pgs.	20.00	75.00	150.00
1499- **Mickey Mouse on the Cave-Man Island** (Disney), 1944, Whitman, 352 pgs.	20.00	75.00	150.00
2004- **Mickey Mouse, Here Comes** (Disney), 1936, Whitman, (Very Rare), 224 pgs., 12" x 8 1/4" box, with red, yellow and blue crayons, contains 224 loose pages to color, reprinted from early Mickey Mouse related movie and strip reprints	650.00	1500.00	3000.00
2020-(#20)- **Mickey Mouse, Adventure in Outer Space**, 1968, Whitman, 256 pgs.,hard-c, color illos.	4.00	12.00	25.00
5750- **Mickey Mouse, Adventure in Outer Space**, 1973, Whitman, 256 pgs.,soft-c, 39 cents, color illos.	4.00	10.00	20.00
3049- **Mickey Mouse and His Big Little Kit** (Disney), 1937, Whitman, 384 pgs., 4 1/2" x 6 1/2" box, includes miniature box of 4 crayons-red, yellow, blue and green	150.00	450.00	900.00
3061- **Mickey Mouse to Draw and Color** (The Big Little Set), nd (early 1930s), Whitman, with crayons; box contains 320 loose pages to color, reprinted from early Mickey Mouse BLBs	115.00	350.00	675.00
4062- **Mickey Mouse, The Story Of**, 1935, Whitman, 7" x 9 1/2", 320 pgs., Big Big Book, Gottfredson-a	150.00	450.00	900.00
4062- **Mickey Mouse and the Smugglers, The Story Of**, 1935, Whitman, (Scarce), 7" x 9 1/2", 320 pgs., Big Big Book, same contents as above version; Gottfredson-a	180.00	500.00	1000.00
708-10- **Mickey Mouse on the Haunted Island** (Disney), 1950, Whitman, Gottfredson-a	12.00	40.00	80.00
nn- **Mickey Mouse and Minnie at Macy's**, 1934 Whitman, 148 pgs., 3 1/4" x 3 1/2", soft-c, R. H. Macy & Co. Christmas giveaway (Rare, less than 20 known copies)	600.00	1200.00	2500.00
nn- **Mickey Mouse and Minnie March to Macy's**, 1935, Whitman, 148 pgs., 3 1/2" x 3 1/2", soft-c, R. H. Macy & Co. Christmas giveaway (scarce)	325.00	900.00	1750.00
nn- **Mickey Mouse and the Magic Carpet**, 1935, Whitman, 148 pgs., 3 1/2"x 4", soft-c, giveaway, Gottfredson-a, Donald Duck app.	90.00	275.00	550.00
nn- **Mickey Mouse Silly Symphonies**, 1934, Dean & Son, Ltd (England), 48 pgs., with 4 pop-ups, Babes In The Woods, King Neptune			
With dust jacket	135.00	450.00	900.00
Without dust jacket	110.00	350.00	675.00
nn- **Mickey Mouse the Sheriff of Nugget Gulch** (Disney) 1938, Dell, 196 pgs., Fast-Action Story, soft-c, Gottfredson-a	40.00	150.00	300.00
nn- **Mickey Mouse Waddle Book**, 1934, BRP, 20 pgs., 7 1/2" x 10", forerunner of the Blue Ribbon Pop-Up books; with 4 removable articulated cardboard characters (a file copy sold for $30,000 in 2004)			
nn- **Mickey Mouse with Goofy and Mickey's Nephews**, 1938, Dell, Fast-Action Story, Gottfredson-a	40.00	150.00	300.00
16- **Mickey Mouse and Pluto** (Disney), 1942, Dell, 196 pgs., Fast-Action story	40.00	150.00	300.00
512- **Mickey Mouse Wee Little Books** (In open box), nn, 1934, 44 pgs., small size, soft-c			
Mickey Mouse and Tanglefoot	10.00	38.00	75.00
Mickey Mouse at the Carnival	10.00	38.00	75.00
Mickey Mouse Will Not Quit!	10.00	38.00	75.00
Mickey Mouse Wins the Race!	10.00	38.00	75.00
Mickey Mouse's Misfortune	10.00	38.00	75.00
Mickey Mouse's Uphill Fight	10.00	38.00	75.00
Complete set with box	80.00	250.00	500.00
1493- **Mickey Rooney and Judy Garland and How They Got into the Movies**, 1941, Whitman, 432 pgs., photo-c	12.00	40.00	80.00
1427- **Mickey Rooney Himself**, 1939, Whitman, 240 pgs., photo-c, movie scenes, life story	12.00	40.00	80.00
532- **Mickey's Dog Pluto** (Disney), 1943, Whitman, All Picture Comics, A Tall Comic Book , 3 3/4" x 8 3/4"	35.00	100.00	200.00
2113- **Midget Jumbo Coloring Book**, 1935, Saalfield	35.00	100.00	200.00
21- **Midsummer Night's Dream**, 1935, EVW, movie scenes	12.00	40.00	80.00
nn- **Minute-Man** (Mystery of the Spy Ring), 1941, Fawcett, Dime Action Book	50.00	165.00	325.00
710- **Moby Dick the Great White Whale, The Story of**, 1934, Whitman, 160 pgs., photo-c, movie scenes from "The Sea Beast"	12.00	40.00	80.00
746- **Moon Mullins and Kayo** (Kayo and Moon Mullins-inside), 1933, Whitman, 320 pgs., Frank Willard-c/a	15.00	45.00	90.00
nn- **Moon Mullins and Kayo**, 1933, Whitman, Cocomalt premium, soft-c, by Willard	15.00	45.00	90.00
1134- **Moon Mullins and the Plushbottom Twins**, 1935, Whitman, 432 pgs., Willard-c/a	15.00	45.00	90.00
nn- **Moon Mullins and the Plushbottom Twins**, 1935, Whitman, 436 pgs., premium-no ads, 3-color, soft-c, by Willard	25.00	85.00	165.00
1058- **Mother Pluto** (Disney), 1939, Whitman, 68 pgs., hard-c	15.00	40.00	75.00
1100B- **Movie Jokes** (From the talkies), 1938, Whitman, 36 pgs., 2 1/2" x 3 1/2", Penny Book	4.00	10.00	20.00
1408- **Mr. District Attorney on the Job**, 1941, Whitman, 432 pgs., flip pictures	10.00	25.00	55.00
nn- **Musicians of Bremen, The**, nd (1930s), np (Whitman), 36 pgs., 3" x 2 1/2", Penny Book	4.00	10.00	20.00
1113- **Mutt and Jeff**, 1936, Whitman, 300 pgs., by Bud Fisher	25.00	75.00	150.00
1116- **My Life and Times** (By Shirley Temple), 1936, Saalfield, Little Big Book, hard-c, photo-c/illos	15.00	45.00	90.00
1596- **My Life and Times** (By Shirley Temple), 1936, Saalfield, Little Big Book, soft-c, photo-c/illos	15.00	45.00	90.00
1497- **Myra North Special Nurse and Foreign Spies**, 1938, Whitman, 432 pgs.	12.00	35.00	70.00
1400- **Nancy and Sluggo**, 1946, Whitman, All Pictures Comics, Ernie Bushmiller-a	12.00	35.00	70.00
1487- **Nancy Has Fun**, 1946, Whitman, All Pictures Comics	12.00	35.00	70.00

718 - Once Upon a Time © WHIT

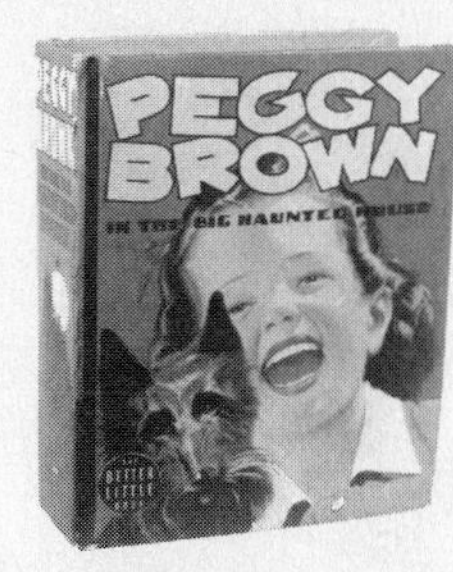

1491 - Peggy Brown in the Big Haunted House © WHIT

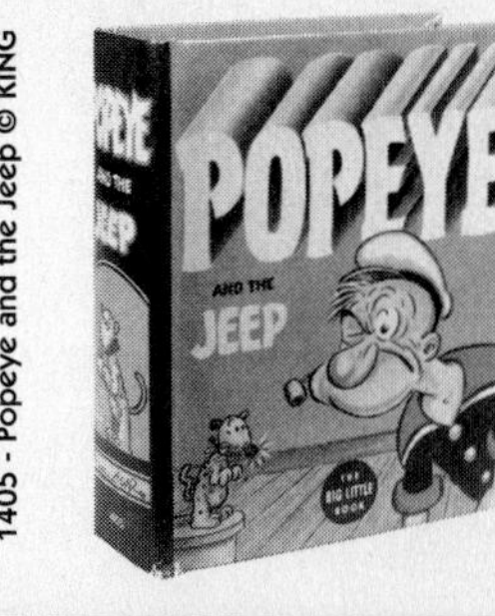

1405 - Popeye and the Jeep © KING

	GD	FN	VF/NM
1150- **Napoleon and Uncle Elby**, 1938, Saalfield, 400 pgs., by Clifford McBride	12.00	35.00	70.00
1166- **Napoleon Uncle Elby And Little Mary**, 1939, Saalfield, 400 pgs., by Clifford McBride	12.00	35.00	70.00
1179- **Ned Brant Adventure Bound**, 1940, Saalfield, 400 pgs.	10.00	25.00	55.00
1146- **Nevada Rides The Danger Trail**, 1938, Saalfield, 400 pgs., J.R. White-a	10.00	25.00	55.00
1147- **Nevada Whalen, Avenger**, 1938, Saalfield, 400 pgs.	10.00	25.00	55.00
Nicodemus O'Malley (See Top-Line Comics)			
1115- **Og Son of Fire**, 1936, Whitman, 432 pgs.	12.00	40.00	80.00
1419- **Oh, Blondie the Bumsteads** (See Blondie)			
11- **Oliver Twist**, 1935, EVW (Five Star Library), movie scenes, starring Dickie Moore (Monogram Pictures)	12.00	40.00	80.00
718- **Once Upon a Time**, 1933, Whitman, 364 pgs., soft-c	12.00	40.00	80.00
712- **100 Fairy Tales for Children, The**, 1933, Whitman, 288 pgs., Circle Library	10.00	25.00	55.00
1099- **One Night of Love**, 1935, Saalfield, 160 pgs., hard-c, photo-c, movie scenes, Columbia Pictures, starring Grace Moore	12.00	40.00	80.00
1579- **One Night of Love**, 1935, Sat, 160 pgs., soft-c, photo-c, movie scenes, Columbia Pictures, starring Grace Moore	12.00	40.00	80.00
1155- **$1000 Reward**, 1938, Saalfield, 400 pgs.	10.00	25.00	55.00
Orphan Annie (See Little Orphan ...)			
L17- **O'Shaughnessy's Boy**, 1935, Lynn, 192 pgs., movie scenes, w/Wallace Beery & Jackie Cooper (Metro-Goldwyn-Mayer)	12.00	35.00	70.00
1109- **Oswald the Lucky Rabbit**, 1934, Whitman, 288 pgs.	20.00	60.00	120.00
1403- **Oswald Rabbit Plays G-Man**, 1937, Whitman, 240 pgs., movie scenes by Walter Lantz	25.00	65.00	125.00
1190- **Our Boarding House, Major Hoople and his Horse**, 1940, Saalfield, 400 pgs.	12.00	35.00	70.00
1085- **Our Gang**, 1934, Saalfield, 160 pgs., photo-c, movie scenes, hard-c	12.00	40.00	80.00
1315- **Our Gang**, 1934, Saalfield, 160 pgs., photo-c, movie scenes, soft-c	12.00	40.00	80.00
1451- **"Our Gang" on the March**, 1942, Whitman, 432 pgs., flip pictures, Vallely-a	12.00	40.00	80.00
1456- **Our Gang Adventures**, 1948, Whitman, 288 pgs.	12.00	35.00	70.00
nn- **Paramount Newsreel Men with Admiral Byrd in Little America**, 1934, Whitman, 96 pgs., 6 1/4" x 6 1/4", photo-c, photo ill.	15.00	45.00	90.00
nn- **Patch**, nd (1930s), np (Whitman), 36 pgs., 3" x 2 1/2", Penny Book	4.00	10.00	20.00
1445- **Pat Nelson Ace of Test Pilots**, 1937, Whitman, 432 pgs.	10.00	25.00	55.00
1411- **Peggy Brown and the Mystery Basket**, 1941, Whitman, 432 pgs., flip pictures, Henry E. Vallely-a	12.00	30.00	60.00
1423- **Peggy Brown and the Secret Treasure**, 1947, Whitman, 288 pgs., Henry E. Vallely-a	12.00	30.00	60.00
1427- **Peggy Brown and the Runaway Auto Trailer**, 1937, Whitman, 300 pgs., Henry E. Vallely-a	12.00	30.00	60.00
1463- **Peggy Brown and the Jewel of Fire**, 1943, Whitman, 352 pgs., Henry E. Vallely-a	12.00	30.00	60.00
1491- **Peggy Brown in the Big Haunted House**, 1940, Whitman, 432 pgs., Vallely-a	12.00	30.00	60.00
1143- **Peril Afloat**, 1938, Saalfield, 400 pgs.	10.00	25.00	55.00
1199- **Perry Winkle and the Rinkeydinks**, 1937, Whitman, 432 pgs., by Martin Branner	12.00	40.00	80.00
1487- **Perry Winkle and the Rinkeydinks get a Horse**, 1938, Whitman, 432 pgs., by Martin Branner	12.00	40.00	80.00
Peter Pan (See Wee Little Books)			
nn- **Peter Rabbit**, nd(1930s), np(Whitman), 36 pgs., Penny Book, 3" x 2 1/2"	5.00	15.00	30.00
Peter Rabbit's Carrots (See Wee Little Books)			

	GD	FN	VF/NM
1100- **Phantom, The**, 1936, Whitman, 432 pgs., by Lee Falk & Ray Moore	40.00	115.00	240.00
1416- **Phantom and the Girl of Mystery, The**, 1947, Whitman, 352 pgs. by Falk & Moore	15.00	50.00	100.00
1421- **Phantom and Desert Justice, The**, 1941, Whitman, 432 pgs., flip pictures, by Falk & Moore	20.00	65.00	130.00
1468- **Phantom and the Sky Pirates, The**, 1945, Whitman, 352 pgs., by Falk & Moore	15.00	60.00	120.00
1474- **Phantom and the Sign of the Skull, The**, 1939, Whitman, 432 pgs., by Falk & Moore	25.00	75.00	145.00
1489- **Phantom, Return of the...**, 1942, Whitman, 432 pgs., flip pictures, by Falk & Moore	20.00	65.00	130.00
1130- **Phil Barton, Sleuth** (Scout Book), 1937, Saalfield, hard-c	10.00	20.00	45.00
Pied Piper of Hamlin (See Wee Little Books)			
1466- **Pilot Pete Dive Bomber**, 1941, Whitman, 432 pgs., flip pictures	10.00	25.00	55.00
5776- **Pink Panther Adventures in Z-Land, The**, 1976, Whitman, 260 pgs., soft-c, 49 cents, B&W	1.00	3.00	7.00
5776-2- **Pink Panther Adventures in Z-Land, The**, 1980, Whitman, 260 pgs., soft-c, 79 cents, B&W	1.00	3.00	6.00
5783-2- **Pink Panther at Castle Kreep, The**, 1980, Whitman, 260 pgs., soft-c, 79 cents, B&W	1.00	3.00	6.00
Pinocchio and Jiminy Cricket (See Walt Disney's ...)			
nn- **Pioneers of the Wild West** (Blue-c), 1933, World Syndicate, High Lights of History Series	10.00	25.00	50.00
nn- **Pioneers of the Wild West** (Red-c), 1933, World Syndicate, High Lights of History Series	10.00	25.00	50.00
1123- **Plainsman, The**, 1936, Whitman, 240 pgs., photo-c, movie scenes with Gary Cooper (Paramount Pics.)	15.00	75.00	150.00
Pluto (See Mickey's Dog ... & Walt Disney's ...)			
2114- **Pocket Coloring Book**, 1935, Saalfield	35.00	110.00	215.00
1060- **Polly and Her Pals on the Farm**, 1934, Saalfield, 164 pgs., hard-c, by Cliff Sterrett	12.00	40.00	80.00
1310- **Polly and Her Pals on the Farm**, 1934, Saalfield, soft-c	12.00	40.00	80.00
1051- **Popeye, Adventures of...**, 1934, Saalfield, oblong-size, E.C. Segar-a, hard-c	50.00	165.00	325.00
1088- **Popeye in Puddleburg**, 1934, Saalfield, 160 pgs., hard-c, E. C. Segar-a	20.00	65.00	125.00
1113- **Popeye Starring in Choose Your Weppins**, 1936, Saalfield, 160 pgs., hard-c, Segar-a	40.00	130.00	250.00
1117- **Popeye's Ark**, 1936, Saalfield, 4 1/2" x 5 1/2", hard-c, Segar-a	20.00	65.00	125.00
1163- **Popeye Sees the Sea**, 1936, Whitman, 432 pgs., Segar-a	20.00	70.00	135.00
1301- **Popeye, Adventures of...**, 1934, Saalfield, oblong-size, Segar-a	50.00	165.00	325.00
1318- **Popeye in Puddleburg**, 1934, Saalfield, 160 pgs., soft-c, Segar-a	20.00	65.00	125.00
1405- **Popeye and the Jeep**, 1937, Whitman, 432 pgs., Segar-a	25.00	70.00	135.00
1406- **Popeye the Super-Fighter**, 1939, Whitman, All Pictures Comics, flip pictures, Segar-a	20.00	65.00	125.00
1422- **Popeye the Sailor Man**, 1947, Whitman, All Pictures Comics	15.00	45.00	90.00
1450- **Popeye in Quest of His Poopdeck Pappy**, 1937, Whitman, 432 pgs., Segar-c/a	25.00	70.00	135.00
1458- **Popeye and Queen Olive Oyl**, 1949, Whitman, 288 pgs., Sagendorf-a	15.00	45.00	90.00
1459- **Popeye and the Quest for the Rainbird**, 1943, Whitman, Winner & Zaboly-a	15.00	50.00	100.00
1480- **Popeye the Spinach Eater**, 1945, Whitman, All Pictures Comics	15.00	45.00	90.00
1485- **Popeye in a Sock for Susan's Sake**, 1940, Whitman, 432 pgs., flip pictures	15.00	50.00	100.00
1497- **Popeye and Caster Oyl the Detective**, 1941, Whitman, 432 pgs. flip pictures, Segar-a	20.00	60.00	120.00
1499- **Popeye and the Deep Sea Mystery**, 1939, Whitman, 432 pgs.,			

103 - "Pop-Up" Buck Rogers in the Dangerous Mission © KING

1404 - Porky Pig and His Gang © WDC

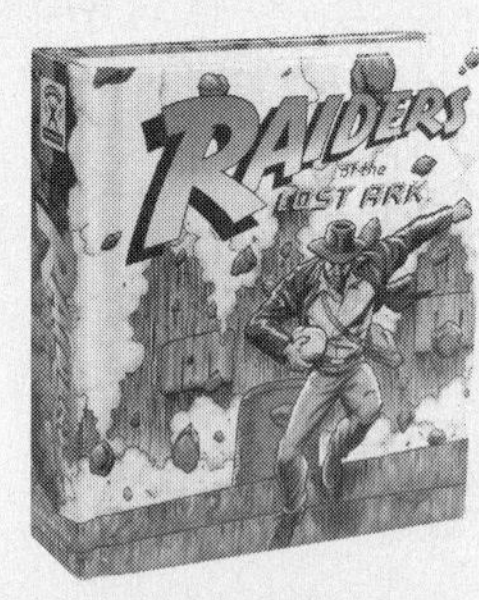
Raiders of the Lost Ark © 20th Century Fox

GD FN VF/NM

Segar-c/a 20.00 60.00 120.00

1593- Popeye Starring in Choose Your Weppins, 1936, Saalfield, 160 pgs., soft-c, Segar-a 20.00 60.00 120.00

1597- Popeye's Ark, 1936, Saalfield, 4 1/2" x 5 1/2", soft-c, Segar-a 20.00 60.00 120.00

2008-(#8)- Popeye-Ghost Ship to Treasure Island, 1967, Whitman, 260 pgs., 39 cents, hard-c, color illos 5.00 12.00 25.00

5755- Popeye-Ghost Ship to Treasure Island, 1973, Whitman, 260 pgs., soft-c, color illos 1.00 3.00 6.00

2034-(#34)- Popeye, Danger Ahoy!, 1969, Whitman, 256 pgs., hard-c, color illos. 5.00 12.00 25.00

5768- Popeye, Danger Ahoy!, 1975, Whitman, 256 pgs., soft-c, color illos. 1.00 3.00 6.00

4063- Popeye, Thimble Theatre Starring, 1935, Whitman, 7" x 9 1/2", 320 pgs., Big Big Book, Segar-c/a; (Cactus cover w/yellow logo) 180.00 500.00 1000.00

4063- Popeye, Thimble Theatre Starring, 1935, Whitman, 7" x 9 1/2", 320 pgs., Big Big Book, Segar-c/a; (Big Balloon-c with red logo), (2nd printing w/same contents as above) 200.00 600.00 1200.00

5761- Popeye and Queen Olive Oyl, 1973, 260 pgs., B&W, soft-c 4.00 12.00 24.00

5761-2- Popeye and Queen Olive Oyl, 1973 (1980-reprint of 1973 version), 260 pgs., 79 cents, B&W, soft-c 1.00 3.00 6.00

103- "Pop-Up" Buck Rogers in the Dangerous Mission (with Pop-Up picture), 1934, BRP, 62 pgs., The Midget Pop-Up Book w/Pop-Up in center of book, Calkins-a 200.00 600.00 1000.00

206- "Pop-Up" Buck Rogers - Strange Adventures in the Spider Ship, The, 1935, BRP, 24 pgs., 8" x 9", 3 Pop-Ups, hard-c, by Dick Calkins 150.00 600.00 1000.00

nn- "Pop-Up" Cinderella, 1933, BRP, 7 1/2" x 9 3/4", 4 Pop-Ups, hard-c
With dustjacket ($2.00) 100.00 300.00 600.00
Without dustjacket 80.00 250.00 500.00

207- "Pop-Up" Dick Tracy-Capture of Boris Arson, 1935, BRP, 24 pgs., 8" x 9", 3 Pop-Ups, hard-c, by Gould 115.00 325.00 650.00

210- "Pop-Up" Flash Gordon Tournament of Death, The, 1935, BRP, 24 pgs., 8" x 9", 3 Pop-Ups, hard-c, by Alex Raymond 200.00 600.00 1000.00

202- "Pop-Up" Goldilocks and the Three Bears, The, 1934, BRP, 24 pgs., 8" x 9", 3 Pop-Ups, hard-c 60.00 125.00 250.00

nn- "Pop-Up" Jack and the Beanstalk, 1933, BRP, hard-c (50 cents), 1 Pop-Up 60.00 125.00 250.00

nn- "Pop-Up" Jack the Giant Killer, 1933, BRP, hard-c (50 cents), 1 Pop-Up 60.00 125.00 250.00

nn- "Pop-Up" Jack the Giant Killer, 1933, BRP, 4 Pop-Ups, hard-c
With dustjacket ($2.00) 100.00 300.00 600.00
Without dust jacket 80.00 250.00 500.00

nn- "Pop-Up" Little Black Sambo, (with Pop-Up picture), 1934, BRP, 62 pgs., The Midget Pop-Up Book, one Pop-Up in center of book 50.00 200.00 400.00

208- "Pop-Up" Little Orphan Annie and Jumbo the Circus Elephant, 1935, BRP, 24 pgs., 8" x 9 1/2", 3 Pop-Ups, hard-c, by H. Gray 150.00 350.00 650.00

nn- "Pop-Up" Little Red Ridinghood, 1933, BRP, hard-c (50 cents), 1 Pop-Up 75.00 150.00 325.00

nn- "Pop-Up" Mickey Mouse, The, 1933, BRP, 34 pgs., 6 1/2" x 9", 3 Pop-Ups, hard-c, Gottfredson-a (75 cents) 100.00 300.00 600.00

nn- "Pop-Up" Mickey Mouse in King Arthur's Court, The,1933, BRP, 56 pgs., 7 1/2" x 9 1/4", 4 Pop-Ups, hard-c, Gottfredson-a
With dust jacket ($2.00) 400.00 750.00 1500.00
Without dustjacket 250.00 525.00 1100.00

101- "Pop-Up" Mickey Mouse in "Ye Olden Days" (with Pop-Up picture), 1934, 62 pgs., BRP, The Midget Pop-Up Book, one Pop-Up in center of book, Gottfredson-a 200.00 400.00 800.00

nn- "Pop-Up" Minnie Mouse, The, 1933, BRP, 36 pgs., 6 1/2" x 9", 3 Pop-Ups, hard-c (75 cents), Gottfredson-a 100.00 300.00 600.00

203- "Pop-Up" Mother Goose, The, 1934, BRP, 24 pgs., 8" x 9 1/4", 3 Pop-Ups, hard-c 100.00 225.00 425.00

nn- "Pop-Up" Mother Goose Rhymes, The, 1933, BRP, 96 pgs., 7 1/2" x 9 1/4", 4 Pop-Ups, hard-c
With dustjacket ($2.00) 100.00 275.00 550.00
Without dustjacket 75.00 225.00 450.00

209- "Pop-Up" New Adventures of Tarzan, 1935, BRP, 24 pgs., 8" x 9", 3 Pop-Ups, hard-c 200.00 600.00 850.00

104- "Pop-Up" Peter Rabbit, The (with Pop-Up picture), 1934, BRP, 62 pgs., The Midget Pop-Up Book, one Pop-Up in center of book 100.00 200.00 400.00

nn- "Pop-Up" Pinocchio, 1933, BRP, 7 1/2" x 9 3/4", 4 Pop-Ups, hard-c
With dustjacket ($2.00) 100.00 300.00 600.00
Without dust jacket 75.00 250.00 525.00

102- "Pop-Up" Popeye among the White Savages (with Pop-Up picture), 1934, BRP, 62 pgs., The Midget Pop-Up Book, one Pop-Up in center of book, E. C. Segar-a 150.00 325.00 600.00

205- "Pop-Up" Popeye with the Hag of the Seven Seas, The, 1935, BRP, 24 pgs., 8" x 9", 3 Pop-Ups, hard-c, Segar-a 150.00 450.00 750.00

201- "Pop-Up" Puss In Boots, The, 1934, BRP, 24 pgs., 3 Pop-Ups, hard-c 50.00 125.00 250.00

nn- "Pop-Up" Silly Symphonies, The (Mickey Mouse Presents His ...), 1933, BRP, 56 pgs., 9 3/4" x 7 1/2", 4 Pop-Ups, hard-c
With dust jacket ($2.00) 200.00 475.00 925.00
Without dust jacket 150.00 325.00 650.00

nn- "Pop-Up" Sleeping Beauty, 1933, BRP, hard-c, (50 cents), 1 Pop-up 50.00 150.00 275.00

212- "Pop-Up" Terry and the Pirates in Shipwrecked, The, 1935, BRP, 24 pgs., 8" x 9", 3 Pop-Ups, hard-c 100.00 300.00 600.00

211- "Pop-Up" Tim Tyler in the Jungle, The, 1935, BRP, 24 pgs., 8" x 9", 3 Pop-Ups, hard-c 100.00 250.00 450.00

1404- Porky Pig and His Gang, 1946, Whitman, All Pictures Comics, Barks-a, reprints Four Color #48 20.00 65.00 130.00

1408- Porky Pig and Petunia, 1942, Whitman, All Pictures Comics, flip pictures, reprints Four Color #16 & Famous Gang Book of Comics 15.00 45.00 90.00

1176- Powder Smoke Range, 1935, Whitman, 240 pgs., photo-c, movie scenes, Hoot Gibson, Harey Carey app. (RKO Radio Pict.) 12.00 40.00 80.00

1058- Practical Pig!, The (Disney), 1939, Whitman, 68 pgs., 5" x 5 1/2", hard-c 12.00 35.00 70.00

758- Prairie Bill and the Covered Wagon, 1934, Whitman, 384 pgs., Hal Arbo-a 12.00 35.00 70.00

nn- Prairie Bill and the Covered Wagon, 1934, Whitman, 390 pgs., premium-no ads, 3-color, soft-c, Hal Arbo-a 15.00 50.00 100.00

1440- Punch Davis of the U.S. Aircraft Carrier, 1945, Whitman, 352 pgs. 10.00 25.00 50.00

nn- Puss in Boots, nd(1930s), np(Whitman), 36 pgs., Penny Book 4.00 10.00 20.00

1100B- Puzzle Book, 1938, Whitman, 36 pgs., 2 1/2" x 3 1/2", Penny Book 4.00 12.00 24.00

1100B- Puzzles, 1938, Whitman, 36 pgs., 2 1/2" x 3 1/2", Penny Book 4.00 12.00 24.00

1100B- Quiz Book, The, 1938, Whitman, 36 pgs., 2 1/2" x 3 1/2", Penny Book 4.00 12.00 24.00

1142- Radio Patrol, 1935, Whitman, 432 pgs., by Eddie Sullivan & Charlie Schmidt (#1) 12.00 35.00 70.00

1173- Radio Patrol Trailing the Safeblowers, 1937, Whitman, 432 pgs. 10.00 25.00 55.00

1496- Radio Patrol Outwitting the Gang Chief, 1939, Whitman, 432 pgs. 10.00 25.00 55.00

1498- Radio Patrol and Big Dan's Mobsters, 1937, Whitman, 432 pgs. 10.00 25.00 55.00

nn- Raiders of the Lost Ark, 1998, Chronicle Books, 304 pgs., adapts movie, 1-color (green) illos 5.00 11.00 22.00

1441- Range Busters, The, 1942, Whitman, 432 pgs., Henry E. Vallely-a 10.00 25.00 55.00

1163- Ranger and the Cowboy, The, 1939, Saalfield, 400 pgs. 10.00 25.00 55.00

1154- Rangers on the Rio Grande, 1938, Saalfield, 400 pgs. 10.00 25.00 55.00

1447- Ray Land of the Tank Corps, U.S.A., 1942, Whitman, 432 pgs., flip pictures, Hess-a 10.00 25.00 55.00

1466 - Red Ryder and Circus Luck © WHIT

1494- Roy Rogers at Crossed Feathers Ranch © WHIT

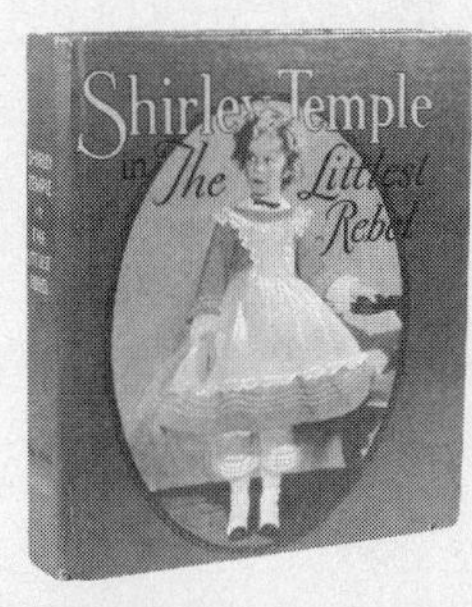

1115 - Shirley Temple in The Littlest Rebel © Saalfield

	GD	FN	VF/NM
1157- Red Barry Ace-Detective, 1935, Whitman, 432 pgs., by Will Gould	12.00	40.00	80.00
1426- Red Barry Undercover Man, 1939, Whitman, 432 pgs., by Will Gould	12.00	35.00	70.00
20- Red Davis, 1935, EVW, 160 pgs.	12.00	35.00	70.00
1449- Red Death on the Range, The, 1940, Whitman, 432 pgs., Fred Harman-a (Bronc Peeler)	12.00	35.00	70.00
nn- Red Falcon Adventures, The, 1937, Seal Right Ice Cream, 8 pgs., set of 50 books, circular in shape			
Issue #1	110.00	275.00	500.00
Issue #2-5	65.00	175.00	350.00
Issue #6-10	55.00	150.00	275.00
Issue #11-50	30.00	100.00	175.00
nn- Red Hen and the Fox, The, nd(1930s), np(Whitman), 36 pgs., 3" x 2 1/2", Penny Book	4.00	10.00	20.00
1145- Red-Hot Holsters, 1938, Saalfield, 400 pgs.	10.00	25.00	55.00
1400- Red Ryder and Little Beaver on Hoofs of Thunder, 1939, Whitman, 432 pgs., Harman-c/a	15.00	50.00	100.00
1414- Red Ryder and the Squaw-Tooth Rustlers, 1946, Whitman, 352 pgs., Fred Harman-a	12.00	40.00	80.00
1427- Red Ryder and the Code of the West, 1941, Whitman, 432 pgs., flip pictures, by Harman	15.00	45.00	90.00
1440- Red Ryder the Fighting Westerner, 1940, Whitman, Harman-a	15.00	45.00	90.00
1443- Red Ryder and the Rimrock Killer, 1948, Whitman, 288 pgs., Harman-a	12.00	35.00	70.00
1450- Red Ryder and Western Border Guns, 1942, Whitman, 432 pgs., flip pictures, by Harman	15.00	45.00	90.00
1454- Red Ryder and the Secret Canyon, 1948, Whitman, 288 pgs., Harman-a	12.00	35.00	70.00
1466- Red Ryder and Circus Luck, 1947, Whitman, 288 pgs., by Fred Harman	12.00	35.00	70.00
1473- Red Ryder in War on the Range, 1945, Whitman, 352 pgs., by Fred Harman	12.00	40.00	80.00
1475- Red Ryder and the Outlaw of Painted Valley, 1943, Whitman, 352 pgs., by Harman	12.00	35.00	70.00
702-10- Red Ryder Acting Sheriff, 1949, Whitman, by Fred Hannan	10.00	30.00	60.00
nn- Red Ryder Brings Law to Devil's Hole, 1939, Dell, 196 pgs., Fast-Action Story, Harman-c/a	30.00	110.00	225.00
nn- Red Ryder and the Highway Robbers, 1938, Whitman, 36 pgs., 2 1/2" x 3 1/2", Penny Book	12.00	35.00	70.00
754- Reg'lar Fellers, 1933, Whitman, 320 pgs., by Gene Byrnes	12.00	40.00	80.00
nn- Reg'lar Fellers, 1933, Whitman, 202 pgs., Cocomalt premium, by Gene Byrnes	12.00	40.00	80.00
1424- Rex Beach's Jaragu of the Jungle, 1937, Whitman, 432 pgs.	10.00	25.00	55.00
12- Rex, King of Wild Horses in "Stampede," 1935, EVW, 160 pgs., movie scenes, Columbia Pictures	10.00	30.00	60.00
1100B- Riddles for Fun, 1938, Whitman, 36 pgs., 2 1/2" x 3 1/2", Penny Book	4.00	12.00	24.00
1100B- Riddles to Guess, 1938, Whitman, 36 pgs., 2 1/2" x 3 1/2", Penny Book	4.00	12.00	24.00
1425- Riders of Lone Trails, 1937, Whitman, 300 pgs.	12.00	30.00	60.00
1141- Rio Raiders (A Billy The Kid Story), 1938, Saalfield, 400 pgs.	12.00	30.00	60.00
2023-(#23)- The Road Runner, The Super Beep Catcher, 1968, Whitman, 256 pgs., hard-c, color illos.	2.00	5.00	10.00
5759- The Road Runner, The Super Beep Catcher, 1973, Whitman, 256 pgs., soft-c, 39 cents, B&W illos., and flip pictures	1.00	3.00	6.00
5767-2- Road Runner, The Lost Road Runner Mine, The, 1974 (1980), 260 pgs., 79 cents, B&W, soft-c	1.00	3.00	6.00
5784- The Road Runner and the Unidentified Coyote, 1974, Whitman, 260 pgs., soft-c, flip pictures	1.00	3.00	6.00
nn- Road To Perdition, 2002, Dreamworks, screenplay from movie, hard-c (Dreamworks and 20th Century Fox)	2.00	5.00	10.00
Robin Hood (See Wee Little Books)			
10- Robin Hood, 1935, EVW, 160 pgs., movie scenes w/Douglas Fairbanks (United Artists), hard-c	15.00	50.00	100.00
719- Robinson Crusoe (The Story of...), nd (1933), Whitman, 364 pgs., soft-c	12.00	40.00	80.00
1421- Roy Rogers and the Dwarf-Cattle Ranch, 1947, Whitman, 352 pgs., Henry E. Vallely-a	15.00	45.00	90.00
1437- Roy Rogers and the Deadly Treasure, 1947, Whitman, 288 pgs.	15.00	45.00	90.00
1448- Roy Rogers and the Mystery of the Howling Mesa, 1948, Whitman, 288 pgs.	15.00	45.00	90.00
1452- Roy Rogers in Robbers' Roost, 1948, Whitman, 288 pgs.	15.00	45.00	90.00
1460- Roy Rogers Robinhood of the Range, 1942, Whitman, 432 pgs., Hess-a (1st)	20.00	50.00	100.00
1462- Roy Rogers and the Mystery of the Lazy M, 1949, Whitman	12.00	40.00	80.00
1476- Roy Rogers King of the Cowboys, 1943, Whitman, 352 pgs., Irwin Myers-a, based on movie	20.00	55.00	110.00
1494- Roy Rogers at Crossed Feathers Ranch, 1945, Whitman, 320 pgs., Erwin Hess-a , 3 1/4" x 5 1/2"	15.00	45.00	90.00
701-10- Roy Rogers and the Snowbound Outlaws, 1949, 3 1/4" x 5 1/2"	10.00	30.00	60.00
715-10- Roy Rogers Range Detective, 1950, Whitman, 2 1/2" x 5"	10.00	30.00	60.00
nn- Sandy Gregg Federal Agent on Special Assignment, 1939, Whitman, 36 pgs., 2 1/2" x 3 1/2", Penny Book	12.00	30.00	60.00
Sappo (See Top-Line Comics)			
1122- Scrappy, 1934, Whitman, 288 pgs.	20.00	55.00	110.00
L12- Scrappy (The Adventures of...), 1935, Lynn, 192 pgs., movie scenes	20.00	55.00	110.00
1191- Secret Agent K-7,1940, Saalfield, 400 pgs., based on radio show	10.00	25.00	55.00
1144- Secret Agent X-9, 1936, Whitman, 432 pgs., Charles Flanders-a	12.00	40.00	80.00
1472- Secret Agent X-9 and the Mad Assassin, 1938, Whitman, 432 pgs., Charles Flanders-a	12.00	40.00	80.00
1161- Sequoia, 1935, Whitman, 160 pgs., photo-c, movie scenes	12.00	35.00	70.00
1430- Shadow and the Living Death, The, 1940, Whitman, 432 pgs., Erwin Hess-a	50.00	200.00	400.00
1443- Shadow and the Master of Evil, The, 1941, Whitman, 432 pgs., flip pictures, Hess-a	50.00	200.00	400.00
1495- Shadow and the Ghost Makers, The, 1942, Whitman, 432 pgs., John Coleman Burroughs-c	50.00	200.00	400.00
2024- Shazzan, The Glass Princess, 1968, Whitman	4.00	12.00	24.00
Shirley Temple (See My Life and Times & Story of..)			
1095- Shirley Temple and Lionel Barrymore Starring In "The Little Colonel," 1935, Saalfield, photo hard-c, movie scenes	20.00	55.00	110.00
1115- Shirley Temple in "The Littlest Rebel," 1935, Saalfield, photo-c, movie scenes, hard-c	20.00	55.00	110.00
1575- Shirley Temple and Lionel Barrymore Starring In "The Little Colonel," 1935, Saalfield, photo soft-c, movie scenes	20.00	55.00	110.00
1595- Shirley Temple in "The Littlest Rebel," 1935, Saalfield, photo-c, movie scenes, soft-c	20.00	55.00	110.00
1195- Shooting Sheriffs of the Wild West, 1936, Whitman, 432 pgs.	10.00	25.00	55.00
1169- Silly Symphony Featuring Donald Duck (Disney), 1937, Whitman, 432 pgs., Taliaferro-a	35.00	90.00	175.00
1441- Silly Symphony Featuring Donald Duck and His (MIS) Adventures (Disney), 1937, Whitman, 432 pgs., Taliaferro-a	35.00	90.00	175.00
1155- Silver Streak, The, 1935, Whitman, 160 pgs., photo-c, movie scenes (RKO Radio Pict.)	10.00	30.00	60.00
Simple Simon (See Wee Little Books)			
1649- Sir Lancelot (TV Series), 1958, Whitman, 280 pgs.	8.00	20.00	40.00
1112- Skeezix in Africa, 1934, Whitman, 300 pgs., Frank King-a			

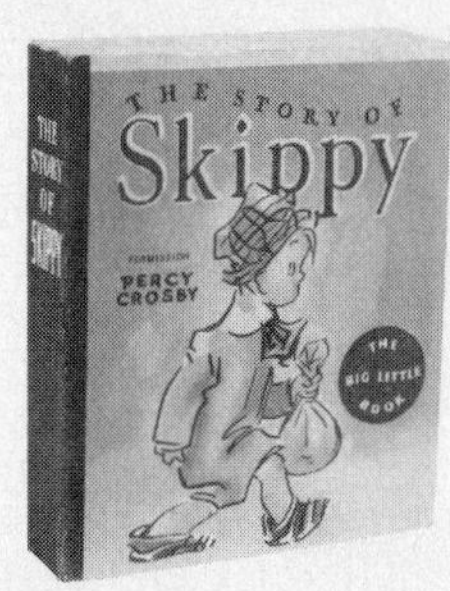

Skippy, The Story of © WHIT

2016 - Space Ghost-The Sorceress of Cyba-3 © H-B

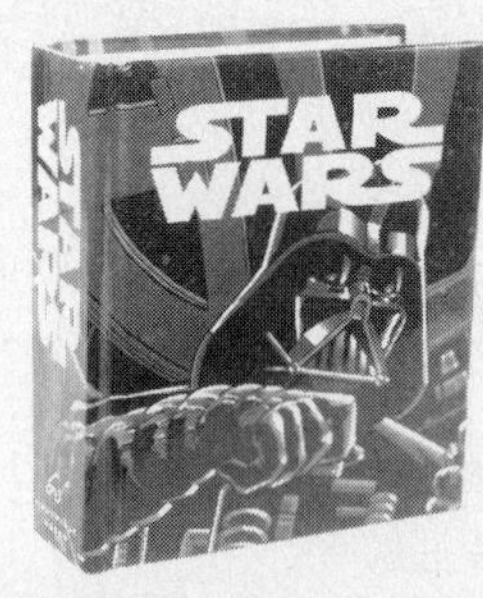

Star Wars - A New Hope © LucasFilm Ltd.

GD FN VF/NM

12.00 40.00 80.00

1408- **Skeezix at the Military Academy**, 1938, Whitman, 432 pgs., Frank King-a 12.00 40.00 80.00

1414- **Skeezix Goes to War**, 1944, Whitman, 352 pgs., Frank King-a 12.00 40.00 80.00

1419- **Skeezix on His Own in the Big City**, 1941, Whitman, All Pictures Comics, flip pictures, Frank King-a 12.00 40.00 80.00

761- **Skippy**, 1934, Whitman, 320 pgs., by Percy Crosby 12.00 40.00 80.00

4056- **Skippy, The Story of**, 1934, Whitman, 320 pgs., 7" x 9 1/2", Big Big Book, Percy Crosby-a 50.00 200.00 400.00

nn- **Skippy, The Story of**, 1934, Whitman, Phillips Dental Magnesia premium, soft-c, by Percy Crosby 12.00 40.00 80.00

1439- **Skyroads with Clipper Williams of the Flying Legion**, 1938, Whitman, 432 pgs., by Lt. Dick Calkins, Russell Keaton-a 12.00 35.00 70.00

1127- **Skyroads with Hurricane Hawk**, 1936, Whitman, 432 pgs., by Lt. Dick Calkins, Russell Keaton-a 12.00 35.00 70.00

Smilin' Jack and his Flivver Plane (See Top-Line Comics)

1152- **Smilin' Jack and the Stratosphere Ascent**, 1937, Whitman, 432 pgs., Zack Mosley-a 15.00 45.00 90.00

1412- **Smilin' Jack Flying High with "Downwind,"** 1942, Whitman, 432 pgs., Zack Mosley-a 12.00 40.00 80.00

1416- **Smilin' Jack in Wings over the Pacific**, 1939, Whitman, 432 pgs., Zack Mosley-a 12.00 40.00 80.00

1419- **Smilin' Jack and the Jungle Pipe Line**, 1947, Whitman, 352 pgs., Zack Mosley-a 12.00 35.00 70.00

1445- **Smilin' Jack and the Escape from Death Rock**, 1943, Whitman, 352 pgs., Mosley-a 12.00 35.00 70.00

1464- **Smilin' Jack and the Coral Princess**, 1945, Whitman, 352 pgs., Zack Mosley-a 12.00 35.00 70.00

1473- **Smilin' Jack Speed Pilot**, 1941, Whitman, 432 pgs., Zack Mosley-a 12.00 40.00 80.00

2- **Smilin' Jack and his Stratosphere Plane**, 1938, Whitman, 132 pgs., Buddy Book, soft-c, Zack Mosley-a 35.00 110.00 220.00

nn- **Smilin' Jack Grounded on a Tropical Shore**, 1938, Whitman, 36 pgs., 2 1/2" x 3 1/2", Penny Book 12.00 30.00 60.00

11- **Smilin' Jack and the Border Bandits**, 1941, Dell, 196 pgs., Fast-Action Story, soft-c, Zack Mosley-a 35.00 100.00 200.00

745- **Smitty Golden Gloves Tournament**, 1934, Whitman, 320 pgs., Walter Berndt-a 12.00 40.00 80.00

nn- **Smitty Golden Gloves Tournament**, 1934, Whitman, 204 pgs., Cocomalt premium, soft-c, Walter Berndt-a 15.00 45.00 90.00

1404- **Smitty and Herby Lost Among the Indians**, 1941, Whitman, All Pictures Comics 12.00 30.00 60.00

1477- **Smitty in Going Native**, 1938, Whitman, 300 pgs., Walter Berndt-a 12.00 30.00 60.00

2- **Smitty and Herby**, 1936, Whitman, 132 pgs., 3 1/2" x 3 1/2", soft-c, Tarzan Ice Cream cup lid premium 35.00 100.00 200.00

9- **Smitty's Brother Herby and the Police Horse**, 1938, Whitman, 132 pgs., 3 1/4" x 3 1/2", Buddy Book-ice cream premium, by Walter Berndt 35.00 100.00 200.00

1010- **Smokey Stover Firefighter of Foo**, 1937, Whitman, 7 1/4" x 5 1/2", 64 pgs., Nickel Book, Bill Holman-a 12.00 40.00 80.00

1413- **Smokey Stover**, 1942, Whitman, All Pictures Comics, flip pictures, Bill Holman-a 12.00 35.00 70.00

1421- **Smokey Stover the Foo Fighter**, 1938, Whitman, 432 pgs., Bill Holman-a 12.00 35.00 70.00

1481- **Smokey Stover the Foolish Foo Fighter**, 1942, Whitman, All Pictures Comics 12.00 35.00 70.00

1- **Smokey Stover the Fireman of Foo**, 1938, Whitman, 3 3/4" x 3 1/2", 132 pgs., Buddy Book-ice cream premium, by Bill Holman 35.00 100.00 200.00

1100A- **Smokey Stover**, 1938, Whitman, 36 pgs., 2 1/2" x 3 1/2", Penny Book 12.00 25.00 60.00

nn- **Smokey Stover and the Fire Chief of Foo**, 1938, Whitman, 36 pgs., 2 1/2" x 3 1/2", Penny Book, yellow shirt on-c 12.00 25.00 60.00

nn- **Smokey Stover and the Fire Chief of Foo**, 1938, Whitman, 36 pgs., Penny Book, green shirt on-c 12.00 25.00 60.00

GD FN VF/NM

1460- **Snow White and the Seven Dwarfs** (The Story of Walt Disney's ...), 1938, Whitman, 288 pgs. 30.00 85.00 165.00

1136- **Sombrero Pete**, 1936, Whitman, 432 pgs. 10.00 25.00 55.00

1152- **Son of Mystery**, 1939, Saalfield, 400 pgs. 10.00 25.00 55.00

1191- **SOS Coast Guard**, 1936, Whitman, 432 pgs., Henry E. Vallely-a 10.00 25.00 55.00

2016-(#16)-**Space Ghost-The Sorceress of Cyba-3** (TV Cartoon), 1968, Whitman, 260 pgs., 39¢-c, hard-c, color illos 10.00 25.00 50.00

1455- **Speed Douglas and the Mole Gang-The Great Sabotage Plot**, 1941, Whitman, 432 pgs., flip pictures 10.00 25.00 55.00

5779- **Spider-Man Zaps Mr. Zodiac**, 1976, 260 pgs., soft-c, B&W 2.00 5.00 10.00

5779-2- **Spider-Man Zaps Mr. Zodiac**, 1980, 260 pgs., 79¢-c, soft-c, B&W 1.00 3.00 6.00

1467- **Spike Kelly of the Commandos**, 1943, Whitman, 352 pgs. 10.00 25.00 55.00

1144- **Spook Riders on the Overland**, 1938, Saalfield, 400 pgs. 10.00 25.00 55.00

768- **Spy, The**, 1936, Whitman, 300 pgs. 12.00 35.00 70.00

nn- **Spy Smasher and the Red Death**, 1941, Fawcett, 4" x 5 1/2", Dime Action Book 50.00 165.00 325.00

1120- **Stan Kent Freshman Fullback**, 1936, Saalfield, 148 pgs., hard-c 8.00 25.00 50.00

1132- **Stan Kent, Captain**, 1937, Saalfield 8.00 25.00 50.00

1600- **Stan Kent Freshman Fullback**, 1936, Saalfield, 148 pgs., soft-c 8.00 25.00 50.00

1123- **Stan Kent Varsity Man**, 1936, Saalfield, 160 pgs., hard-c 8.00 25.00 50.00

1603- **Stan Kent Varsity Man**, 1936, Saalfield, 160 pgs., soft-c 8.00 25.00 50.00

nn- **Star Wars - A New Hope**, 1997, Chronicle Books, 320 pgs., adapts movie, 1-color (blue) illos 5.00 10.00 20.00

nn- **Star Wars - Empire Strikes Back, The**, 1997, Chronicle Books, 296 pgs., adapts movie, 1-color (blue) illos 5.00 10.00 20.00

nn- **Star Wars - Episode 1 - The Phantom Menace**, 1999, Chronicle Books, 344 pgs., adapts movie, 1-color (blue) illos 2.00 5.00 10.00

nn- **Star Wars - Episode 2 - Attack of the Clones**, 2002, Chronicle Books, 340 pgs., adapts movie, 1-color (blue) illos 2.00 5.00 10.00

nn- **Star Wars - Return of the Jedi**, 1997, Chronicle Books, 312 pgs., adapts movie, 1-color (blue) illos 5.00 10.00 20.00

1104- **Steel Arena, The** (With Clyde Beatty), 1936, Saalfield, hard-c, movie scenes adapted from "The Lost Jungle" 12.00 35.00 70.00

1584- **Steel Arena, The** (With Clyde Beatty), 1936, Saalfield, soft-c, movie scenes 12.00 35.00 70.00

1426- **Steve Hunter of the U.S. Coast Guard Under Secret Orders**, 1942, Whitman, 432 pgs. 10.00 25.00 55.00

1456- **Story of Charlie McCarthy and Edgar Bergen, The**, 1938, Whitman, 288 pgs. 12.00 40.00 80.00

Story of Daniel, The (See Wee Little Books)

Story of David, The (See Wee Little Books)

1110- **Story of Freddie Bartholomew, The**, 1935, Saalfield, 4 1/2" x 5 1/4", hard-c, movie scenes (MGM) 10.00 30.00 60.00

1590- **Story of Freddie Bartholomew, The**, 1935, Saalfield, 4 1/2" x 5 1/4", soft-c, movie scenes (MGM) 10.00 30.00 60.00

Story of Gideon, The (See Wee Little Books)

W714- **Story of Jackie Cooper, The**, 1933, Whitman, 240 pgs., photo-c, movie scenes, "Skippy" & "Sooky" movie 12.00 40.00 80.00

Story of Joseph, The (See Wee Little Books)

Story of Moses, The (See Wee Little Books)

Story of Ruth and Naomi (See Wee Little Books)

1089- **Story of Shirley Temple, The**, 1934, Saalfield, 160 pgs., hard-c, photo-c, movie scenes 12.00 40.00 80.00

1319- **Story of Shirley Temple, The**, 1934, Saalfield, 160 pgs., soft-c, photo-c, movie scenes 12.00 40.00 80.00

1090- **Strawberry-Roan**, 1934, Saalfield, 160 pgs., hard-c, Ken Maynard photo-c, movie scenes 12.00 40.00 80.00

1320- **Strawberry-Roan**, 1934, Saalfield, 160 pgs., soft-c, Ken Maynard photo-c, movie scenes 12.00 40.00 80.00

Streaky and the Football Signals (See Top-Line Comics)

Tailspin Tommy the Dirigible Flight to the North Pole (3-color premium) © WHIT

Tarzan and a Daring Rescue © ERB

1100B - Tell Your Fortune © WHIT

GD FN VF/NM

5780-2- Superman in the Phantom Zone Connection, 1980, 260 pgs., 79¢-c, soft-c, B&W 2.00 5.00 10.00

582- "Swap It" Book, The, 1949, Samuel Lowe Co., 260 pgs., 3 1/2" x 4 1/2"
1. Little Tex in the Midst of Trouble 5.00 20.00 40.00
2. Little Tex's Escape 5.00 20.00 40.00
3. Little Tex Comes to the XY Ranch 5.00 20.00 40.00
4. Get Them Cowboy 5.00 20.00 40.00
5. The Mail Must Go Through! A Story of the Pony Express 5.00 20.00 40.00
6. Nevada Jones, Trouble Shooter 5.00 20.00 40.00
7. Danny Meets the Cowboys 5.00 20.00 40.00
8. Flint Adams and the Stage Coach 5.00 20.00 40.00
9. Bud Shinners and the Oregon Trail 5.00 20.00 40.00
10. The Outlaws' Last Ride 5.00 20.00 40.00

Sybil Jason (See Little Big Shot)

747- Tailspin Tommy in the Famous Pay-Roll Mystery, 1933, Whitman, hard-c, 320 pgs., Hal Forrest-a (# 1) 12.00 40.00 80.00

747- Tailspin Tommy in the Famous Pay-Roll Mystery, 1933, Whitman, soft-c, 320 pgs., Hal Forrest-a (# 1) 12.00 40.00 80.00

nn- Tailspin Tommy the Pay-Roll Mystery, 1934, Whitman, 52 pgs., 3 1/2" x 5 1/4", premium-no ads, soft-c; another version with Perkins ad, Hal Forrest-a 25.00 75.00 150.00

1110- Tailspin Tommy and the Island in the Sky, 1936, Whitman, 432 pgs., Hal Forrest-a 12.00 35.00 70.00

1124- Tailspin Tommy the Dirigible Flight to the North Pole, 1934, Whitman, 432 pgs., H. Forrest-a 12.00 40.00 80.00

nn- Tailspin Tommy the Dirigible Flight to the North Pole, 1934, Whitman, 436 pgs., 3-color, soft-c, premium-no ads, Hal Forrest-a 35.00 95.00 200.00

1172- Tailspin Tommy Hunting for Pirate Gold, 1935, Whitman, 432 pgs., Hal Forrest-a 12.00 35.00 70.00

1183- Tailspin Tommy Air Racer, 1940, Saalfield, 400 pgs., hard-c 12.00 35.00 70.00

1184- Tailspin Tommy in the Great Air Mystery, 1936, Whitman, 240 pgs., photo-c, movie scenes 12.00 40.00 80.00

1410- Tailspin Tommy the Weasel and His "Skywaymen," 1941, Whitman, All Pictures Comics, flip pictures 10.00 30.00 60.00

1413- Tailspin Tommy and the Lost Transport, 1940, Whitman, 432 pgs., Hal Forrest-a 10.00 30.00 60.00

1423- Tailspin Tommy and the Hooded Flyer, 1937, Whitman, 432 pgs., Hal Forrest-a 12.00 35.00 70.00

1494- Tailspin Tommy and the Sky Bandits, 1938, Whitman 432 pgs., Hal Forrest-a 12.00 35.00 70.00

nn- Tailspin Tommy and the Airliner Mystery, 1938, Whitman, 196 pgs., Fast-Action Story, soft-c, Hal Forrest-a 40.00 130.00 260.00

nn- Tailspin Tommy in Flying Aces, 1938, Dell, 196 pgs., Fast-Action Story, soft-c, Hal Forrest-a 40.00 130.00 260.00

nn- Tailspin Tommy in Wings Over the Arctic, 1934, Whitman, Cocomalt premium, Forrest-a 20.00 55.00 110.00

nn- Tailspin Tommy Big Thrill Chewing Gum, 1934, Whitman, 8 pgs., 2 1/2" x 3 " (6 diff.) each.. 12.00 40.00 80.00

3- Tailspin Tommy on the Mountain of Human Sacrifice, 1938, Whitman, soft-c, Buddy Book 40.00 120.00 240.00

7- Tailspin Tommy's Perilous Adventure, 1934, Whitman, 132 pgs., 3 1/2" x 3 1/2" soft-c, Tarzan Ice Cream cup premium 40.00 120.00 240.00

nn- Tailspin Tommy, 1935, Whitman, 148 pgs., 3 1/2" x 4", Tarzan Ice Cream cup premium 50.00 150.00 300.00

L16- Tale of Two Cities, A, 1935, Lynn, movie scenes 12.00 40.00 80.00

744- Tarzan of the Apes, 1933, Whitman, 320 pgs., by Edgar Rice Burroughs (1st) 40.00 130.00 260.00

nn- Tarzan of the Apes, 1935, Whitman, 52 pgs., 3 1/2" x 5 1/4", soft-c, stapled, premium, no ad; another version with a Perkins ad 50.00 165.00 330.00

769- Tarzan the Fearless, 1934, Whitman, 240 pgs., Buster Crabbe photo-c, movie scenes, ERB 35.00 90.00 175.00

770- Tarzan Twins, The, 1934, Whitman, 432 pgs., ERB 110.00 325.00 650.00

770- Tarzan Twins, The, 1935, Whitman, 432 pgs., ERB 50.00 165.00 325.00

GD FN VF/NM

nn- Tarzan Twins, The, 1935, Whitman, 52 pgs., 3 1/2" x 5 3/4", premium-no ads, soft-c, ERB 50.00 200.00 425.00

nn- Tarzan Twins, The, 1935, Whitman, 436 pgs., 3-color, soft-c, premium-no ads, ERB 60.00 225.00 450.00

778- Tarzan of the Screen (The Story of Johnny Weissmuller), 1934, Whitman, 240 pgs., photo-c, movie scenes, ERB 40.00 100.00 190.00

1102- Tarzan, The Return of, 1936, Whitman, 432 pgs., Edgar Rice Burroughs 20.00 65.00 130.00

1180- Tarzan, The New Adventures of, 1935, Whitman, 160 pgs., Herman Brix photo-c, movie scenes, ERB 25.00 80.00 155.00

1182- Tarzan Escapes, 1936, Whitman, 240 pgs., Johnny Weissmuller photo-c, movie scenes, ERB 35.00 100.00 190.00

1407- Tarzan Lord of the Jungle, 1946, Whitman, 352 pgs., ERB 15.00 50.00 100.00

1410- Tarzan, The Beasts of, 1937, Whitman, 432 pgs., Edgar Rice Burroughs 20.00 60.00 120.00

1442- Tarzan and the Lost Empire, 1948, Whitman, 288 pgs., ERB 15.00 50.00 100.00

1444- Tarzan and the Ant Men, 1945, Whitman, 352 pgs., ERB 15.00 50.00 100.00

1448- Tarzan and the Golden Lion, 1943, Whitman, 432 pgs., ERB 20.00 60.00 120.00

1452- Tarzan the Untamed, 1941, Whitman, 432 pgs., flip pictures, ERB 20.00 60.00 120.00

1453- Tarzan the Terrible, 1942, Whitman, 432 pgs., flip pictures, ERB 20.00 60.00 120.00

1467- Tarzan in the Land of the Giant Apes, 1949, Whitman, ERB 15.00 50.00 100.00

1477- Tarzan, The Son of, 1939, Whitman, 432 pgs., ERB 20.00 60.00 120.00

1488- Tarzan's Revenge, 1938, Whitman, 432 pgs., ERB 20.00 60.00 120.00

1495- Tarzan and the Jewels of Opar, 1940, Whitman, 432 pgs. 20.00 60.00 120.00

4056- Tarzan and the Tarzan Twins with Jad-Bal-Ja the Golden Lion, 1936, Whitman, 7" x 9 1/2", 320 pgs., Big Big Book 115.00 325.00 650.00

709-10- Tarzan and the Journey of Terror, 1950, Whitman, 2 1/2" x 5", ERB, Marsh-a 12.00 30.00 60.00

2005- (#5)-Tarzan: The Mark of the Red Hyena, 1967, Whitman, 260 pgs., 39 cents, hard-c, color illos 5.00 15.00 30.00

nn- Tarzan, 1935, Whitman, 148 pgs., soft-c, 3 1/2" x 4", Tarzan Ice Cream cup premium, ERB (scarce) 130.00 450.00 875.00

nn- Tarzan and a Daring Rescue, 1938, Whitman, 68 pgs., Pan-Am premium, soft-c, ERB (blank back-c version also exists) 40.00 130.00 260.00

nn- Tarzan and his Jungle Friends, 1936, Whitman, 132 pgs., soft-c, 3 1/2" x 3 1/2", Tarzan Ice Cream cup premium, ERB (scarce) 100.00 300.00 600.00

nn- Tarzan in the Golden City, 1938, Whitman, 68 pgs., Pan-Am premium, soft-c, ERB 30.00 90.00 180.00

nn- Tarzan The Avenger, 1939, Dell, 194 pgs., Fast-Action Story, ERB, soft-c 40.00 130.00 250.00

nn- Tarzan with the Tarzan Twins in the Jungle, 1938, Dell, 194 pgs., Fast-Action Story, ERB 40.00 130.00 250.00

1100B- Tell Your Fortune, 1938, Whitman, 36 pgs., 2 1/2" x 3 1/2", Penny Book 5.00 15.00 30.00

nn- Terminator 2: Judgment Day, 1998, Chronicle Books, 310 pgs., adapts movie, 1-color (blue-gray) illos 2.00 5.00 10.00

1156- Terry and the Pirates, 1935, Whitman, 432 pgs., Milton Caniff-a (#1) 15.00 50.00 100.00

nn- Terry and the Pirates, 1935, Whitman, 52 pgs., 3 1/2" x 5 1/4", soft-c, premium, Milton Caniff-a; 3 versions: No ad, Sears ad & Perkins ad 30.00 90.00 175.00

1412- Terry and the Pirates Shipwrecked on a Desert Island, 1938, Whitman, 432 pgs., Milton Caniff-a 12.00 40.00 80.00

1420- Terry and War in the Jungle, 1946, Whitman, 352 pgs., Milton Caniff-a 12.00 35.00 70.00

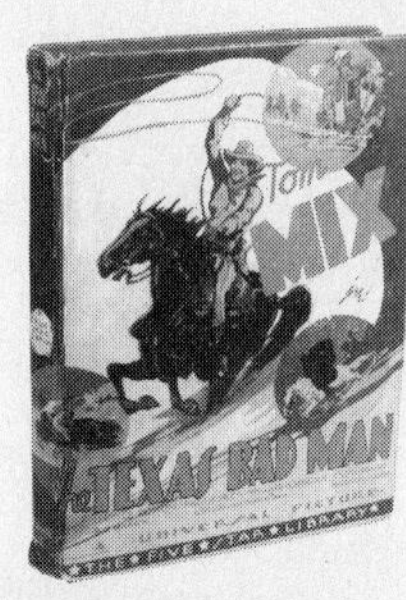
7 - Texas Bad Man © EVW

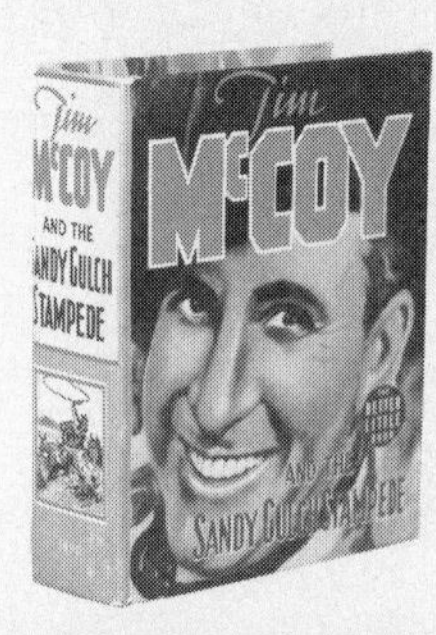
1490 - Tim McCoy and the Sandy Gulch Stampede © WHIT

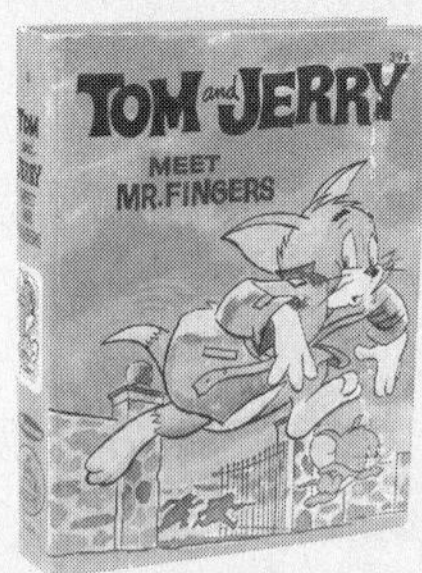
2006 - Tom and Jerry Meet Mr. Fingers © H-B

GD FN VF/NM

1436- Terry and the Pirates the Plantation Mystery, 1942, Whitman, 432 pgs., flip pictures, Milton Caniff-a 12.00 40.00 80.00
1446- Terry and the Pirates and the Giant's Vengeance, 1939, Whitman, 432 pgs., Caniff-a 12.00 40.00 80.00
1499- Terry and the Pirates in the Mountain Stronghold, 1941, Whitman, 432 pgs., Caniff-a 12.00 40.00 80.00
4073- Terry and the Pirates, The Adventures of, 1938, Whitman, 7" x 9 1/2", 320 pgs., Big Big Book, Milton Caniff-a 80.00 250.00 500.00
4- Terry and the Pirates Ashore in Singapore, 1938, Whitman, 132 pgs., 3 1/2" x 3 3/4", soft-c, Buddy Book premium 35.00 100.00 200.00
10- Terry and the Pirates Meet Again, 1936, Whitman, 132 pgs., 3 1/2" x 3 1/2", soft-c, Tarzan Ice Cream cup lid premium 50.00 165.00 325.00
nn- Terry and the Pirates, Adventures of, 1938, 36 pgs., 2 1/2" x 3 1/2", Penny Book, Caniff-a 10.00 30.00 60.00
nn- Terry and the Pirates and the Island Rescue, 1938, Whitman, 68 pgs., 3 1/4" x 3 1/2", Pan-Am premium 25.00 85.00 165.00
nn- Terry and the Pirates on Their Travels, 1938, 36 pgs., 2 1/2" x 3 1/2", Penny Book, Caniff-a 10.00 30.00 60.00
nn- Terry and the Pirates and the Mystery Ship, 1938, Dell, 194 pgs., Fast-Action Story, soft-c 35.00 110.00 220.00
1492- Terry Lee Flight Officer U.S.A., 1944, Whitman, 352 pgs., Milton Caniff-a 12.00 35.00 70.00
7- Texas Bad Man, The (Tom Mix), 1934, EVW, 160 pgs., (Five Star Library), movie scenes 20.00 65.00 130.00
1429- Texas Kid, The, 1937, Whitman, 432 pgs. 10.00 25.00 55.00
1135- Texas Ranger, The, 1936, Whitman, 432 pgs., Hal Arbo-a 10.00 25.00 55.00
nn- Texas Ranger, The, 1935, Whitman, 260 pgs., Cocomalt premium, soft-c, Hal Arbo-a 12.00 35.00 70.00
nn- Texas Ranger and the Rustler Gang, The, 1936, Whitman, Pan-Am giveaway 25.00 85.00 165.00
nn- Texas Ranger in the West, The, 1938, Whitman, 36 pgs., 2 1/2" x 3 1/2", Penny Book 12.00 30.00 55.00
nn- Texas Ranger to the Rescue, The, 1938, Whitman, 36 pgs., 2 1/2" x 3 1/2", Penny Book 12.00 30.00 55.00
12- Texas Ranger in Rustler Strategy, The, 1936, Whitman, 132 pgs., 3 1/2" x 3 1/2", soft-c, Tarzan Ice Cream cup lid premium 35.00 100.00 200.00
Tex Thorne (See Zane Grey)
Thimble Theatre (See Popeye)
L26- 13 Hours By Air, 1936, Lynn, 128 pgs., 5" x 7 1/2", photo-c, movie scenes (Paramount Pictures) 12.00 40.00 80.00
nn- Three Bears, The, nd (1930s), np (Whitman), 36 pgs., 3" x 2 1/2", Penny Book 4.00 10.00 20.00
1129- Three Finger Joe (Baseball), 1937, Saalfield, Robert A. Graef-a 10.00 25.00 55.00
nn- Three Little Pigs, The, nd (1930s), np (Whitman), 36 pgs., 3" x 2 1/2", Penny Book 4.00 10.00 20.00
1131- Three Musketeers, 1935, Whitman, 182 pgs., 5 1/4" x 6 1/4", photo-c, movie scenes 15.00 50.00 100.00
1409- Thumper and the Seven Dwarfs (Disney), 1944, Whitman, All Pictures Comics 20.00 60.00 120.00
1108- Tiger Lady, The (The life of Mabel Stark, animal trainer), 1935, Saalfield, photo-c, movie scenes, hard-c 10.00 30.00 60.00
1588- Tiger Lady, The, 1935, Saalfield, photo-c, movie scenes, soft-c 10.00 30.00 60.00
1442- Tillie the Toiler and the Wild Man of Desert Island, 1941, Whitman, 432 pgs., Russ Westover-a 12.00 35.00 70.00
1058- "Timid Elmer" (Disney), 1939, Whitman, 5" x 5 1/2", 68 pgs., hard-c 12.00 35.00 70.00
1152- Tim McCoy in the Prescott Kid, 1935, Whitman, 160 pgs., hard-c, photo-c, movie scenes 20.00 55.00 110.00
1193- Tim McCoy in the Westerner, 1936, Whitman, 240 pgs., photo-c, movie scenes 15.00 50.00 100.00
1436- Tim McCoy on the Tomahawk Trail, 1937, Whitman, 432 pgs., Robert Weisman-a 12.00 35.00 70.00
1490- Tim McCoy and the Sandy Gulch Stampede, 1939, Whitman, 424 pgs. 10.00 30.00 60.00
2- Tim McCoy in Beyond the Law, 1934, EVW, Five Star Library, photo-c, movie scenes (Columbia Pictures) 18.00 60.00 120.00
10- Tim McCoy in Fighting the Redskins, 1938, Whitman, 130 pgs., Buddy Book, soft-c 35.00 90.00 190.00
14- Tim McCoy in Speedwings, 1935, EVW, Five Star Library, 160 pgs., photo-c, movie scenes (Columbia Pictures) 20.00 65.00 130.00
nn- Tim the Builder, nd (1930s), np (Whitman), 36 pgs., 3" x 2 1/2", Penny Book 4.00 10.00 20.00
Tim Tyler (Also see Adventures of ...)
1140- Tim Tyler's Luck Adventures in the Ivory Patrol, 1937, Whitman, 432 pgs., by Lyman Young 12.00 35.00 70.00
1479- Tim Tyler's Luck and the Plot of the Exiled King, 1939, Whitman, 432 pgs., by Lyman Young 12.00 30.00 60.00
767- Tiny Tim, The Adventures of, 1935, Whitman, 384 pgs., by Stanley Link 12.00 40.00 80.00
1172- Tiny Tim and the Mechanical Men, 1937, Whitman, 432 pgs., by Stanley Link 12.00 35.00 70.00
1472- Tiny Tim in the Big, Big World, 1945, Whitman, 352 pgs., by Stanley Link 12.00 35.00 70.00
2006- (#6)-Tom and Jerry Meet Mr. Fingers, 1967, Whitman, 39¢-c 260 pgs., hard-c, color illos. 5.00 15.00 25.00
5752- Tom and Jerry Meet Mr. Fingers, 1973, Whitman, 39¢-c 260 pgs., soft-c, color illos., 5 printings 1.00 3.00 6.00
2030-(#30)- Tom and Jerry, The Astro-Nots, 1969, Whitman, 256 pgs., hard-c, color illos. 4.00 10.00 20.00
5765- Tom and Jerry, The Astro-Nots, 1974, Whitman, 256 pgs., soft-c, color illos. 1.00 3.00 6.00
5787-2- Tom and Jerry Under the Big Top, 1980, Whitman, 79¢-c, 260 pgs., soft-c, B&W 1.00 3.00 6.00
723- Tom Beatty Ace of the Service, 1934, Whitman, 256 pgs., George Taylor-a 12.00 35.00 70.00
nn- Tom Beatty Ace of the Service, 1934, Whitman, 260 pgs., soft-c 12.00 35.00 70.00
1165- Tom Beatty Ace of the Service Scores Again, 1937, Whitman, 432 pgs., Weisman-a 10.00 30.00 60.00
1420- Tom Beatty Ace of the Service and the Big Brain Gang, 1939, Whitman, 432 pgs. 10.00 30.00 60.00
nn- Tom Beatty Ace Detective and the Gorgon Gang, 1938?, Whitman, 36 pgs., 2 1/2" x 3 1/2", Penny Book 12.00 30.00 55.00
nn- Tom Beatty Ace of the Service and the Kidnapers, 1938?, Whitman, 36 pgs., 2 1/2" x 3 1/2", Penny Book 12.00 30.00 55.00
1102- Tom Mason on Top, 1935, Saalfield, 160 pgs., Tom Mix photo-c, from Mascot serial "The Miracle Rider," movie scenes, hard-c 15.00 50.00 110.00
1582- Tom Mason on Top, 1935, Saalfield, 160 pgs., Tom Mix photo-c, movie scenes, soft-c 15.00 50.00 110.00
Tom Mix (See Chief of the Rangers, Flaming Guns & Texas Bad Man)
762- Tom Mix and Tony Jr. in "Terror Trail," 1934, Whitman, 160 pgs., movie scenes 15.00 50.00 110.00
1144- Tom Mix in the Fighting Cowboy, 1935, Whitman, 432 pgs., Hal Arbo-a 12.00 40.00 80.00
nn- Tom Mix in the Fighting Cowboy, 1935, Whitman, 436 pgs., premium-no ads, 3 color, soft-c, Hal Arbo-a 30.00 85.00 165.00
1166- Tom Mix in the Range War, 1937, Whitman, 432 pgs., Hal Arbo-a 12.00 35.00 70.00
1173- Tom Mix Plays a Lone Hand, 1935, Whitman, 288 pgs., hard-c, Hal Arbo-a 12.00 35.00 70.00
1183- Tom Mix and the Stranger from the South, 1936, Whitman, 432 pgs. 12.00 35.00 70.00
1462- Tom Mix and the Hoard of Montezuma, 1937, Whitman, H. E. Vallely-a 12.00 35.00 70.00
1482- Tom Mix and His Circus on the Barbary Coast, 1940, Whitman, 432 pgs., James Gary-a 12.00 35.00 70.00
3047- Tom Mix and His Big Little Kit, 1937, Whitman, 384 pgs., 4 1/2" x 6 1/2" box, includes miniature box of 4 crayons-red, yellow, blue and green 100.00 275.00 550.00
4068- Tom Mix and the Scourge of Paradise Valley, 1937, Whitman, 7" x 9 1/2", 320 pgs., Big Big Book, Vallely-a 50.00 200.00 400.00
6833- Tom Mix in the Riding Avenger, 1936, Dell, 244 pgs., Cartoon Story Book, hard-c 30.00 90.00 175.00
nn- Tom Mix Rides to the Rescue, 1939, 36 pgs., 2 1/2" x 3",

1126 - Tommy of Troop Six © Saalfield

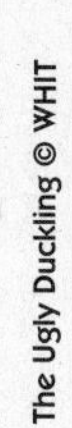
The Ugly Duckling © WHIT

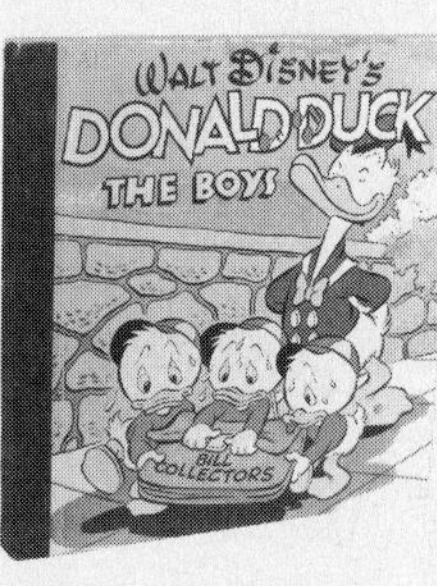

845 - Walt Disney's Donald Duck and the Boys © WDC

	GD	FN	VF/NM
Penny Book	12.00	30.00	60.00
nn- **Tom Mix Avenges the Dry Gulched Range King**, 1939, Dell, 196 pgs., Fast-Action Story, soft-c	30.00	90.00	180.00
nn- **Tom Mix in the Riding Avenger**, 1936, Dell, 244 pgs., Fast-Action Story	30.00	90.00	180.00
nn- **Tom Mix the Trail of the Terrible 6**, 1935, Ralston Purina Co., 84 pgs., 3" x 3 1/2", premium	20.00	60.00	125.00
4- **Tom Mix and Tony in the Rider of Death Valley**, 1934, EVW, Five Star Library, 160 pgs., movie scenes (Universal Pictures), hard-c	20.00	65.00	130.00
7- **Tom Mix in the Texas Bad Man**, 1934, EVW, Five Star Library, 160 pgs., movie scenes	20.00	65.00	130.00
10- **Tom Mix in the Tepee Ranch Mystery**, 1938, Whitman, 132 pgs., Buddy Book, soft-c	35.00	90.00	190.00
1126- **Tommy of Troop Six** (Scout Book), 1937, Saalfield, hard-c	10.00	25.00	55.00
1606- **Tommy of Troop Six** (Scout Book), 1937, Saalfield, soft-c	10.00	25.00	55.00
Tom Sawyer (See Adventures of ...)			
1437- **Tom Swift and His Magnetic Silencer**, 1941, Whitman, 432 pgs., flip pictures	15.00	45.00	90.00
1485- **Tom Swift and His Giant Telescope**, 1939, Whitman, 432 pgs., James Gary-a	15.00	45.00	90.00
540- **Top-Line Comics** (In Open Box), 1935, Whitman, 164 pgs., 3 1/2" x 3 1/2", 3 books in set, all soft-c:			
Bobby Thatcher and the Samarang Emerald	15.00	50.00	100.00
Broncho Bill in Suicide Canyon	15.00	50.00	100.00
Freckles and His Friends in the North Woods	15.00	50.00	100.00
Complete set with box	60.00	175.00	360.00
541- **Top-Line Comics** (In Open Box), 1935, Whitman, 164 pgs., 3 1/2" x 3 1/2", 3 books in set; all soft-c:			
Little Joe and the City Gangsters	15.00	50.00	100.00
Smilin' Jack and His Flivver Plane	15.00	50.00	100.00
Streaky and the Football Signals	15.00	50.00	100.00
Complete set with box	60.00	175.00	360.00
542- **Top-Line Comics** (In Open Box), 1935, Whitman, 164 pgs., 3 1/2" x 3 1/2", 3 books in set; all soft-c:			
Dinglehoofer Und His Dog Adolph by Knerr	15.00	50.00	100.00
Jungle Jim by Alex Raymond	20.00	65.00	130.00
Sappo by Segar	20.00	65.00	130.00
Complete set with box	70.00	210.00	450.00
543- **Top-Line Comics** (In Open Box), 1935, Whitman, 164 pgs., 3 1/2" x 3 1/2", 3 books in set; all soft-c:			
Alexander Smart, ESQ by Winner	15.00	50.00	100.00
Bunky by Billy de Beck	15.00	50.00	100.00
Nicodemus O'Malley by Carter	15.00	50.00	100.00
Complete set with box	60.00	175.00	360.00
1158- **Tracked by a G-Man**, 1939, Saalfield, 400 pgs.	10.00	25.00	55.00
L25- **Trail of the Lonesome Pine, The**, 1936, Lynn, movie scenes	15.00	45.00	90.00
nn- **Trail of the Terrible 6** (See Tom Mix ...)			
1185- **Trail to Squaw Gulch, The**, 1940, Saalfield, 400 pgs.	10.00	25.00	55.00
720- **Treasure Island**, 1933, Whitman, 362 pgs.	20.00	60.00	120.00
1141- **Treasure Island**, 1934, Whitman, 164 pgs., hard-c, 4 1/4" x 5 1/4", Jackie Cooper photo-c, movie scenes	15.00	45.00	90.00
1141- **Treasure Island**, 1934, Whitman, 164 pgs., soft-c, 4 1/4" x 5 1/4", Jackie Cooper photo-c, movie scenes	15.00	45.00	90.00
1018- **Trick and Puzzle Book**, 1939, Whitman, 100 pgs., soft-c	4.00	10.00	20.00
1100B-**Tricks Easy to Do** (Slight of hand & magic), 1938, Whitman, 36 pgs., 2 1/2" x 3 1/2", Penny Book	4.00	10.00	20.00
1100B- **Tricks You Can Do**, 1938, Whitman, 36 pgs., 2 1/2" x 3 1/2", Penny Book	4.00	10.00	20.00
5777- **Tweety and Sylvester, The Magic Voice**, 1976, Whitman, 260 pgs., soft-c, flip-it feature; 5 printings	3.00	6.00	12.00
1104- **Two-Gun Montana**, 1936, Whitman, 432 pgs., Henry E. Vallely-a	10.00	25.00	55.00
nn- **Two-Gun Montana Shoots it Out**, 1939, Whitman, 36 pgs.,			

	GD	FN	VF/NM
2 1/2" x 3 1/2", Penny Book	12.00	30.00	60.00
1058- **Ugly Duckling, The** (Disney), 1939, Whitman, 68 pgs., 5" x 5 1/2", hard-c	12.00	40.00	80.00
nn- **Ugly Duckling, The**, nd (1930s), np (Whitman), 36 pgs., 3" x 2 1/2", Penny Book	4.00	10.00	20.00
Unc' Billy Gets Even (See Wee Little Books)			
1114- **Uncle Don's Strange Adventures**, 1935, Whitman, 300 pgs., radio star-Uncle Don Carney	12.00	30.00	60.00
722- **Uncle Ray's Story of the United States**, 1934, Whitman, 300 pgs.	10.00	30.00	60.00
1461- **Uncle Sam's Sky Defenders**, 1941, Whitman, 432 pgs., flip pictures	10.00	25.00	55.00
1405- **Uncle Wiggily's Adventures**, 1946, Whitman, All Pictures Comics	15.00	45.00	90.00
1411- **Union Pacific**, 1939, Whitman, 240 pgs., photo-c, movie scenes	12.00	35.00	70.00
1189- **Up Dead Horse Canyon**, 1940, Saalfield, 400 pgs.	10.00	25.00	50.00
1455- **Vic Sands of the U.S. Flying Fortress Bomber Squadron**, 1944, Whitman, 352 pgs.	12.00	35.00	70.00
1645- **Walt Disney's Andy Burnett on the Trail** (TV Series), 1958, Whitman, 280 pgs.	5.00	15.00	25.00
711-10- **Walt Disney's Cinderella and the Magic Wand**, 1950, Whitman, 2 1/2" x 5", based on Disney movie	12.00	30.00	60.00
845- **Walt Disney's Donald Duck and his Cat Troubles** (Disney), 1948, Whitman, 100 pgs., 5" x 5 1/2", hard-c	12.00	35.00	70.00
845- **Walt Disney's Donald Duck and the Boys**, 1948, Whitman, 100 pgs., 5" x 5 1/2", hard-c, Barks-a	25.00	75.00	160.00
2952- **Walt Disney's Donald Duck in the Great Kite Maker**, 1949, Whitman, 24 pgs., 3 1/4" x 4", Tiny Tales, full color (5 cents)	10.00	25.00	55.00
804- **Walt Disney's Mickey and the Beanstalk**, 1948, Whitman, hard-c	12.00	35.00	70.00
845- **Walt Disney's Mickey Mouse and the Boy Thursday**, 194 pgs., Whitman, 5" x 5 1/2", 100 pgs.	12.00	35.00	70.00
845- **Walt Disney's Mickey Mouse the Miracle Maker**, 1948, Whitman, 5" x 5 1/2", 100 pgs.	12.00	35.00	70.00
2952- **Walt Disney's Mickey Mouse and the Night Prowlers**, Whitman, 1949, 24 pgs., 3 1/4" x 4", Tiny Tales, full color (5 ¢)	10.00	25.00	55.00
5770- **Walt Disney's Mickey Mouse - Mystery at Disneyland**, Whitman, 1975, 260 pgs., four printings	5.00	10.00	15.00
5781-2- **Walt Disney's Mickey Mouse - Mystery at Dead Man's Cove**, Whitman, 1980, 260 pgs., two printings	3.00	6.00	12.00
845- **Walt Disney's Minnie Mouse and the Antique Chair**, 1948, Whitman, 5" x 5 1/2", 100 pgs.	12.00	35.00	70.00
1435- **Walt Disney's Pinocchio and Jiminy Cricket**, 1940, Whitman, 432 pgs.	20.00	60.00	115.00
845- **Walt Disney's Poor Pluto**, 1948, Whitman, 5" x 5 1/2", 100 pgs., hard-c	12.00	35.00	70.00
1467- **Walt Disney's Pluto the Pup** (Disney), 1938, Whitman, 432 pgs., Gottfredson-a	15.00	50.00	100.00
1066- **Walt Disney's Story of Clarabelle Cow** (Disney), 1938, Whitman, 100 pgs.	12.00	35.00	70.00
66- **Walt Disney's Story of Dippy the Goof** (Disney), 1938, Whitman, 100 pgs.	12.00	35.00	70.00
1066- **Walt Disney's Story of Donald Duck** (Disney), 1938, Whitman, 100 pgs., hard-c, Taliaferro-a	12.00	35.00	70.00
1066- **Walt Disney's Story of Mickey Mouse** (Disney), 1938, Whitman, 100 pgs., hard-c, Gottfredson-a, Donald Duck app.	12.00	35.00	70.00
1066- **Walt Disney's Story of Minnie Mouse** (Disney), 1938, Whitman, 100 pgs., hard-c	12.00	35.00	70.00
1066- **Walt Disney's Story of Pluto the Pup**, (Disney), 1938, Whitman, 100 pgs., hard-c	12.00	35.00	70.00
2952- **Walter Lantz Presents Andy Panda's Rescue**, 1949, Whitman, Tiny Tales, full color (5 cents)	10.00	25.00	55.00
751- **Wash Tubbs in Pandemonia**, 1934, Whitman, 320 pgs., Roy Crane-a	12.00	35.00	70.00
1455- **Wash Tubbs and Captain Easy Hunting For Whales**, 1938, Whitman, 432 pgs., Roy Crane-a	12.00	35.00	70.00

1124 - The West Point Five © Saalfield

Xena - Warrior Princess © Universal Studios

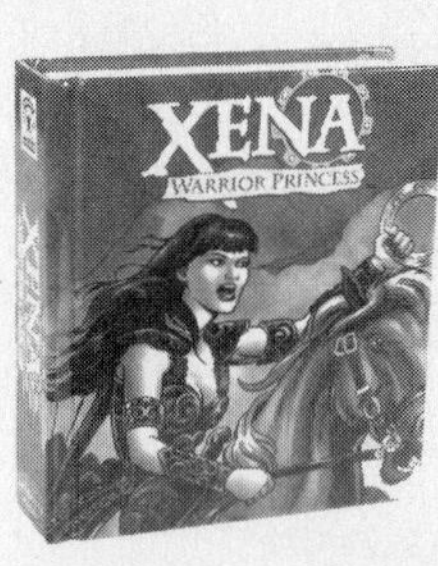

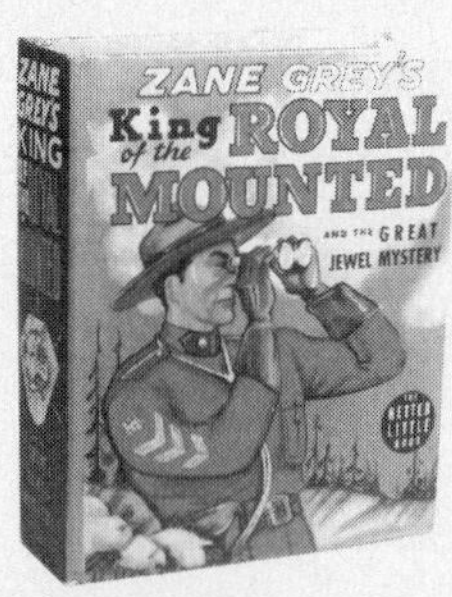

1486 - Zane Grey's King of the Royal Mounted and the Great Jewel Mystery © WHIT

GD FN VF/NM

6- **Wash Tubbs in Foreign Travel**, 1934, Whitman, soft-c, 3 1/2" x 3 1/2", Tarzan Ice Cream cup premium 35.00 90.00 190.00
nn- **Wash Tubbs**, 1934, Whitman, 52 pgs., 4" x 5 1/2", premium-no ads, soft-c, Roy Crane-a 20.00 55.00 110.00
513- **Wee Little Books** (In Open Box), 1934, Whitman, 44 pgs., small size, 6 books in set
Child's Garden of Verses 5.00 12.00 25.00
The Happy Prince (The Story of) 5.00 12.00 25.00
Joan of Arc (The Story of) 5.00 12.00 25.00
Peter Pan (The Story of) 5.00 12.00 25.00
Pied Piper Of Hamlin 5.00 12.00 25.00
Robin Hood (A Story of...) 5.00 12.00 25.00
Complete set with box 40.00 100.00 200.00
514- **Wee Little Books** (In Open Box), 1934, Whitman, 44 pgs., small size, 6 books in set
Jack And Jill 5.00 12.00 25.00
Little Bo-Peep 5.00 12.00 25.00
Little Tommy Tucker 5.00 12.00 25.00
Mother Goose 5.00 12.00 25.00
Old King Cole 5.00 12.00 25.00
Simple Simon 5.00 12.00 25.00
Complete set with box 40.00 100.00 200.00
518- **Wee Little Books** (In Open Box), 1933, Whitman, 44 pgs., small size, 6 books in set, written by Thornton Burgess
Betty Bear's Lesson-1930 5.00 12.00 25.00
Jimmy Skunk's Justice-1933 5.00 12.00 25.00
Little Joe Otter's Slide-1929 5.00 12.00 25.00
Peter Rabbit's Carrots-1933 5.00 12.00 25.00
Unc' Billy Gets Even-1930 5.00 12.00 25.00
Whitefoot's Secret-1933 5.00 12.00 25.00
Complete set with box 40.00 100.00 200.00
519- **Wee Little Books** (In Open Box) (Bible Stories), 1934, Whitman, 44 pgs., small size, 6 books in set, Helen Janes-a
The Story of David 5.00 12.00 25.00
The Story of Gideon 5.00 12.00 25.00
The Story of Daniel 5.00 12.00 25.00
The Story of Joseph 5.00 12.00 25.00
The Story of Ruth and Naorrii 5.00 12.00 25.00
The Story of Moses 5.00 12.00 25.00
Complete set with box 40.00 100.00 200.00
1471- **Wells Fargo**, 1938, Whitman, 240 pgs., photo-c, movie scenes 12.00 40.00 80.00
L18- **Western Frontier**, 1935, Lynn, 192 pgs., starring Ken Maynard, movie scenes 20.00 60.00 120.00
1121- **West Pointers on the Gridiron**, 1936, Saalfield, 148 pgs., hard-c, sports book 10.00 25.00 55.00
1601- **West Pointers on the Gridiron**, 1936, Saalfield, 148 pgs., soft-c, sports book 10.00 25.00 55.00
1124- **West Point Five, The**, 1937, Saalfield, 4 3/4" x 5 1/4", sports book, hard-c 10.00 25.00 55.00
1604- **West Point Five, The**, 1937, Saalfield, 4 1/4" x 5 1/4", sports book, soft-c 10.00 25.00 55.00
1164- **West Point of the Air**, 1935, Whitman, 160 pgs., photo-c, movie scenes 12.00 35.00 70.00
18- **Westward Ho!**, 1935, EVW, 160 pgs., movie scenes, starring John Wayne (Scarce) 40.00 145.00 285.00
1109- **We Three**, 1935, Saalfield, 160 pgs., photo-c, movie scenes, by John Barrymore, hard-c 12.00 30.00 60.00
1589- **We Three**, 1935, Saalfield, 160 pgs., photo-c, movie scenes, by John Barrymore, soft-c 12.00 30.00 60.00
5- **Wheels of Destiny**, 1934, EVW, 160 pgs., movie scenes, starring Ken Maynard 20.00 60.00 120.00
Whitefoot's Secret (See Wee Little Books)
nn- **Who's Afraid of the Big Bad Wolf**, "Three Little Pigs" (Disney), 1933, McKay, 36 pgs., 6" x 8 1/2", stiff-c, Disney studio-a 35.00 110.00 225.00
nn- **Wild West Adventures of Buffalo Bill**, 1935, Whitman, 260 pgs., Cocomalt premium, soft-c, Hal Arbo-a 12.00 40.00 80.00
1096- **Will Rogers, The Story of**, 1935, Saalfield, photo-hard-c 10.00 30.00 60.00

GD FN VF/NM

1576- **Will Rogers, The Story of**, 1935, Saalfield, photo-soft-c 10.00 30.00 60.00
1458- **Wimpy the Hamburger Eater**, 1938, Whitman, 432 pgs., E.C. Segar-a 20.00 60.00 120.00
1433- **Windy Wayne and His Flying Wing**, 1942, Whitman, 432 pgs., flip pictures 10.00 25.00 55.00
1131- **Winged Four, The**, 1937, Saalfield, sports book, hard-c 10.00 25.00 55.00
1407- **Wings of the U.S.A.**, 1940, Whitman, 432 pgs., Thomas Hickey-a 10.00 25.00 55.00
nn- **Winning of the Old Northwest, The**, 1934, World Syndicate, High Lights of History Series, full color-c 10.00 30.00 60.00
nn- **Winning of the Old Northwest, The**, 1934, World Syndicate, High Lights of History Series; red & silver-c 10.00 30.00 60.00
1122- **Winning Point, The**, 1936, Saalfield, (Football), hard-c 10.00 25.00 50.00
1602- **Winning Point, The**, 1936, Saalfield, soft-c 10.00 25.00 50.00
nn- **Wizard of Oz Waddle Book**, 1934, BRP, 20 pgs., 7 1/2" x 10", forerunner of the Blue Ribbon Pop-Up books; with 6 removable articulated cardboard characters. Book only 75.00 150.00 300.00
Dust jacket only 100.00 200.00 400.00
Near Mint Complete - $11,500
710-10-**Woody Woodpecker Big Game Hunter**, 1950, Whitman, by Walter Lantz 10.00 25.00 50.00
2010-(#10)-**Woody Woodpecker-The Meteor Menace**, 1967, Whitman, 260 pgs., 39¢-c, hard-c, color illos. 5.00 15.00 25.00
5753- **Woody Woodpecker-The Meteor Menace**, 1973, Whitman, 260 pgs., no price, soft-c, color illos. 1.00 3.00 6.00
2028- **Woody Woodpecker-The Sinister Signal**, 1969, Whitman 5.00 12.00 20.00
5763- **Woody Woodpecker-The Sinister Signal**, 1974, Whitman, 1st printing-no price; 2nd printing-39¢-c 1.00 3.00 6.00
23- **World of Monsters, The**, 1935, EVW, Five Star Library, movie scenes 15.00 50.00 95.00
779- **World War in Photographs, The**, 1934, Whitman, photo-c, photo illus. 10.00 25.00 55.00
Wyatt Earp (See Hugh O'Brian ...)
nn- **Xena - Warrior Princess**, 1998, Chronicle Books, 310 pgs., based on TV series, 1-color (purple) illos 2.00 5.00 10.00
nn- **Yogi Bear Goes Country & Western**, 1977, Modern Promotions, 244 pgs., 49 cents, soft-c, flip pictures 5.00 10.00 15.00
nn- **Yogi Bear Saves Jellystone Park**, 1977, Modern Promotions, 244 pgs., 49 cents, soft-c, flip pictures 5.00 10.00 15.00
nn- **Zane Grey's Cowboys of the West**, 1935, Whitman, 148 pgs., 3 3/4" x 4", Tarzan Ice Cream Cup premium, soft-c, Arbo-a 35.00 110.00 225.00
Zane Grey's King of the Royal Mounted (See Men of the Mounted)
1103- **Zane Grey's King of the Royal Mounted**, 1936, Whitman, 432 pgs. 12.00 40.00 80.00
nn- **Zane Grey's King of the Royal Mounted**, 1935, Whitman, 260 pgs., Cocomalt premium, soft-c 15.00 50.00 100.00
1179- **Zane Grey's King of the Royal Mounted and the Northern Treasure**, 1937, Whitman, 432 pgs. 12.00 40.00 80.00
1405- **Zane Grey's King of the Royal Mounted the Long Arm of the Law**, 1942, Whitman, All Pictures Comics 12.00 40.00 80.00
1452- **Zane Grey's King of the Royal Mounted Gets His Man**, 1938, Whitman, 432 pgs. 12.00 40.00 80.00
1486- **Zane Grey's King of the Royal Mounted and the Great Jewel Mystery**, 1939, Whitman, 432 pgs. 12.00 40.00 80.00
5- **Zane Grey's King of the Royal Mounted in the Far North**, 1938, Whitman, 132 pgs., Buddy Book, soft-c 35.00 100.00 200.00
nn- **Zane Grey's King of the Royal Mounted in Law of the North**, 1939, Whitman, 36 pgs., 2 1/2" x 3 1/2", Penny Book 10.00 25.00 50.00
nn- **Zane Grey's King of the Royal Mounted Policing the Frozen North**, 1938, Dell, 196 pgs., Fast-Action Story, soft-c 25.00 75.00 150.00
1440- **Zane Grey's Tex Thorne Comes Out of the West**, 1937, Whitman, 432 pgs. 10.00 25.00 55.00
1465- **Zip Saunders King of the Speedway**, 1939, 432 pgs., Weisman-a 10.00 25.00 55.00

THE MARKETING OF A MEDIUM

by Dr. Arnold T. Blumberg, DCD

with new material and additional research by Sol M. Davidson, PhD, and Robert L. Beerbohm

Starting with the 30th edition of ***The Official Overstreet Comic Book Price Guide****, we now list premium and giveaway comics (now collectively referred to as "promotional comics" in this edition) in their own section. This article has appeared in previous editions in a shorter form, but now contains even more detailed information on this often overlooked corner of the comic book collecting universe. We hope that by setting promotional comics apart, we can draw attention to this fertile but still poorly represented area of comic book history.*

A very rare piece indeed, this represents one of the few existing examples of Palmer Cox's signature, as Cox always printed his name on his art. The character depicted in the upper left, "The Dude," represents a typical New Yorker and was Cox's favorite. "Brownieland" was the name of Cox's studio.

Everyone wants something for free. It's in our nature to look for the quick fix, the good deal, the complimentary gift. We long to hit the lottery and quit our job, to win the trip around the world, or find that pot of gold at the end of the proverbial rainbow. Collectors in particular are certainly built to appreciate the notion of the "free gift," since it not only means a new item to collect and enjoy, but no risk or obligation in order to acquire it.

Ah, but there's the rub. Because things are not always what they seem, and "free gifts" usually come with a price. As the saying goes, "there's no such thing as a free lunch," so if it seems too good to be true, it probably is. This is the case even in the world of comics, where premiums and giveaways have a familiar agenda hidden behind the bright colors and fanciful stories. But where did it all begin?

EXTRA EXTRA

As we learn more about the early history of the comic book industry through continual investigation and the publishing of articles like those regularly featured in this book, we gain a much greater understanding of the financial and creative forces at work in shaping the medium, but perhaps one of the most intriguing and least recognized factors that influenced the dawn of comics is the concept of the premium or giveaway. (Note: Some of the historical information referenced in this article is derived from material also presented in Robert L. Beerbohm's introductory articles to the Platinum Age and Modern Age sections.)

The birth of the comic book as we know it today is intimately connected with the development of the comic strip in American newspapers and their use as an advertising and marketing tool for staple products such as bread, milk, and cereal. From the very beginning, comic characters have played several roles in pop culture, entertaining the youth of the country while also (sometimes none too subtly) acting as hucksters for whatever corporation foots the bill. From important staples to frivolous material produced simply to make a buck, these products have utilized the comics medium to sell, sell, sell. And what better way to hook a prospective customer than to give them "something for nothing?"

Starting in the 1850s, comics were being used in free almanacs such as **Elton's**, **Hostetter's** and **Wright's** to lure readers for the little booklets to sell patent medicine, farm products, tobacco, shoe polish, etc. Most of these are exceedingly rare today, hence it is difficult to compile an accurate history. More mention of these early precursors can be found in the Victorian Comics Era essay following this one. But although comic characters themselves were already being aggressively merchandised all around the world by the mid-1890s--as with, for example, Palmer Cox's **The Brownies**--the real starting point for the success of comics as a giveaway marketing mechanism can be traced to the introduction of **The Yellow Kid**, Richard Outcault's now legendary newspaper strip.

Newspaper publishers had already recognized that comic strips could boost circulation as well as please sponsors and advertisers by drawing more eyes to the page, so Sunday "supplements" were introduced to entice fans. Outcault's creation cemented the theory with proof of comic characters' marketing and merchandising power.

Soon after, Outcault (who had most likely been inspired by Cox's merchandising success with **The Brownies** in the first place) caught lightning in a bottle once more with **Buster Brown**, who has the distinction of being America's first nationally licensed comic strip character. Soon, comic strips proliferated throughout the nation's newspapers as tycoons like Hearst and Pulitzer recognized the drawing power of the new medium and fought circulation wars to capture the pennies of the nouveau readership. They paid exorbitant salaries to comic strip artists such as Rudolph Dirks (**Katzenjammer Kids**), and used the funnies as newspaper supplements and as premiums to attract readers. Corporations soon had the chance to license recognizable personas as their own personal pitchmen (or women or animals...). Comic character merchandise wasn't far behind, resulting in a boom of future collectibles now catalogued in volumes like **Hake's Price Guide to Character Toys**.

TWO BIRTHS FOR THE PRICE OF ONE

Comic books themselves were at the heart of this movement, and giveaway and premium collections of comic strips not only appealed to children and adults alike, but provided the impetus for the birth of the modern comic book format itself. It could be said that without the concept of the giveaway comic or the marketing push behind it, there would be no comic book industry as we have it today. Well-known now is the story of how in spring 1933 Harry Wildenberg of Eastern Color Printing Company convinced Proctor & Gamble to sponsor the first modern comic book, **Funnies on Parade**, as a premium. Its success led to the first continuing comic book, **Famous Funnies**, and the rest, as they say, is history.

One of the best examples of the Brownies' proliferation into all kinds of merchandise. This rare Luden's Cough Drop ad (1890s) is the earliest known character die-cut sign.

In 1935, while working on the printing presses of Eastern Color developing how modern comic books get printed, Juliun J. Proskauer came up with an idea for printing "Comic-Books-For-Industry." In July 1936 he made his first sale through his newly formed William C. Popper & Co. to David M. Davies, then advertising manager for Seagram's Distillers Corp. for three million copies of **Seagram's Merrymakers** in time for the 1936-37 Christmas season. "Thus was a new industry born," wrote **Printing News** in August 1945.

Even a casual perusal of the listings in this section of the Guide will dazzle the reader with the endless variety of purposes that this medium has served. Yes, promos have been used to hawk products from athletic equipment to zithers and zip codes, but comics are too versatile an art form to be confined to a few uses. They've swayed elections in cities (**The O'Dwyer Story**, 1949), in states (**Giant for a Day**: Jacob Javits, 1946) and nationwide (**The Story of Harry Truman**, 1948); solicited for charities (**Donald Duck and the Red Feather**, 1948); addressed health issues (**Blondie**, 1949, mental hygiene); discouraged kids from smoking (**Captain America Meets the Asthma Monster**, 1987); coached youngsters in sports skills (**Circling the Bases**, 1947, A.G. Spaulding); explained scientific complexities (**Adventures in Science**, 1946-61, GE); pleaded for social justice (**Consumer Comics**, 1975); espoused religious causes (**Oral Roberts' True Stories**, 1950s); protected the environment (**Our Spaceship Earth**, 1947); encouraged tourism (**Wyoming, The Cowboy State**, 1954); conveyed a sense of history (**Louisiana Purchase**, 1953); taught about computers (**Superman Radio Shack Giveaway**, 1980);

trained employees (**Dial Finance Dialogues**, 1961-70) and executives (**Beneficial Finance System, Managing New Employees**, 1950s); cautioned safety (**Willy Wing Flap**, 1944(?)); announced corporate annual results (**Motorola Annual Report**, 1952); defended free enterprise (**Steve Merritt**, 1949); hammered communism (**How Stalin Hopes to Destroy America**, 1951); fought discrimination (**Mammy Yokum & the Great Dogpatch Mystery**, 1956, B'nai Brith); aided young workers in job-hunting (**The Job Scene**, 1969); battled the scourge of sickle cell anemia (**Where's Herbie**, 1972, U.S. H.E.W.); inspired the overcoming of adversity (**Al Capp by Li'l Abner**, 1946); fostered reading (**Linus Gets a Library Card**, 1960); recruited for the armed forces (**Li'l Abner Joins the Navy**, 1950); beguiled readers into learning languages (**Blondie**, 1949, Philadelphia public schools); and even instructed in such delicate matters as birth control (**Escape from Fear**, 1950 (revised 1959, etc.), for Planned Parenthood).

READ ALL ABOUT IT

The impact of this new approach to advertising was not lost on the business world. Contrary to modern belief, comic books were hardly discounted by the adults of the time...at least not those who had the marketing savvy to recognize an opportunity - or a threat - when they saw one. In the April 1933 issue of **Fortune** magazine, an article titled "The Funny Papers" trumpeted the arrival of comics as a force to be reckoned with in the world of advertising and business, and what's more, a force to fear as well. At first providing a brief survey of the newspaper comic strip business (which for many of the magazine's readers must have seemed a foreign topic for serious discussion), the article goes on to examine the incredible financial draw of comics and their characters:

"Between 70 and 75 per cent {sic} of the readers of any newspaper follow its comic sections regularly...Even the advertiser has succumbed to the comic, and in 1932 spent well over $1,000,000 for comic-paper space."

"**Comic Weekly** is the comic section of seventeen Hearst Sunday papers...Advertisers who market their wares through balloon-speaking manikins {sic} may enjoy the proximity of Jiggs, Maggie, Barney Google, and other funny Hearst headliners."

Although the article continues to cast the notion of relying on comic strip material to sell product in a negative light, actually suggesting that advertisers who utilize comics are violating unspoken rules of "advertising decorum" and bringing themselves "down to the level" of comics (and since when have advertisers been stalwart preservers of good taste and high moral standards), there is no doubt that they are viewing comics in a new light. The comic characters have arrived by 1933...and they're ready to help sell your merchandise too.

Fortune wasn't the only one to take notice as World War II came and went. In 1948, Louis P. Birk, the head of Brevity, Inc., an important promotional comics publisher said, "Comics are serious business." In an article in **Printers' Ink** magazine, he estimated that more than 80 different "comic booklets" had been produced and more than 45,000,000 million copies distributed in the five years before 1948. But of course, comics were serious business long before businessman/historian Birk noted the fact for posterity.

THE MARCH OF WAR AND BEYOND

Through the relentless currents of time, comic strips, books, and the characters that starred in them became more and more an intrinsic part of American culture. During the turmoil of the Great Depression and World War II, comic characters in print and celluloid form entertained while informing and selling at the same time, and premium and giveaway comics came well and truly into their own, pushing everything from loaves of bread to war bonds.

In the 1950s and '60s, there was a shift in focus as the power of giveaway and premium comics was applied to more altruistic endeavors than simply selling something. Comic book format pamphlets, fully illustrated and often inventively written, taught children about banking, money, the dangers of poison and other household products, and even chronicled moments in American history. The comic book as giveaway was now not only a marketing gimmick--it was a tool for educating as well.

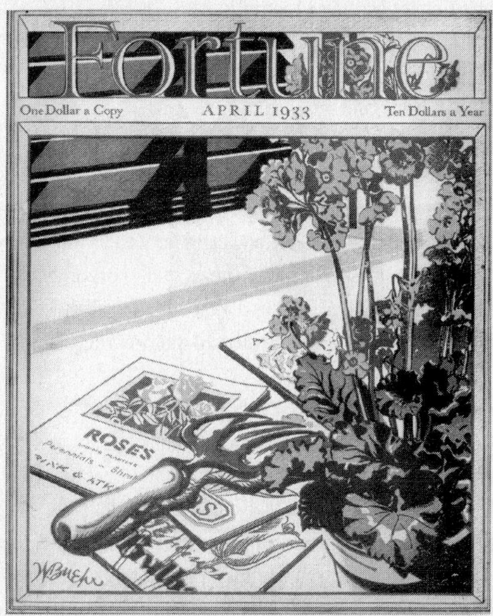

One of the earliest examples of the business world acknowledging and investigating the influence of the comic book on modern pop culture and American enterprise. ***FORTUNE Magazine****, April 1933.*

The 1970s and '80s saw another boom in premium and giveaway comics. Every product imaginable seemed to have a licensing deal with a comic book character, usually one of the prominent flag bearers of the Big Two, Marvel or DC. Spider-Man fought bravely against the Beetle for the benefit of All Detergent; Captain America allied himself with the Campbell Kids; and Superman helped a class of computer students beat a disaster-conjuring foe at his own game with the help of Radio Shack Tandy computers.

Newspapers rediscovered the power of comics, not just with enlarged strip supplements but with actual comic books. Spider-Man, the Hulk, and others turned up as giveaway comic extras in various American newspapers (including Chicago and Dallas publications), while a whole series of public information comics like those produced decades earlier used superheroes to caution children about the dangers of smoking, drugs, and child abuse.

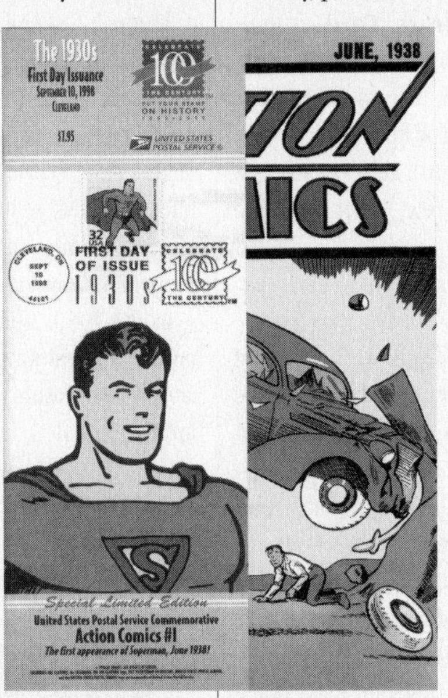

This 1998 U.S. Postal Service premium is one of the most recent examples of the continuing popularity of promotional comics.

Comics also turned up in a plethora of other toy products as the 1980s introduced kids to the joy of electronic games and action figures. Supplementary comics provided "free" with action figure and video game packages told the backstory about the product, adding depth to the play experience while providing an extra incentive to buy. Comics became an intrinsic part of the Atari line of video cartridges, for example, eventually spawning its own full-blown newsstand series as well.

As the twentieth century gave way to the twenty-first, giveaway comics were still being produced for inclusion in action figure and video game packages, as well as in conjunction with countless consumer items and corporations. It seems that the medium still has a lot to offer for all those companies desperate to make the most of their market share.

A COMIC BY ANY OTHER NAME

One of the earliest names for promotional comics was "special purpose comics." In their pursuit of superheroes, collectors have allowed promotional comics to lie fallow - underappreciated and uncollected. Without a legitimate name, these products were given sundry other appellations - industrial comics, promos, giveaways, premiums, promics - each accurate but only for a small segment of the unorganized but lusty and lively medium. Perhaps no one name can cover all the variations and purposes of this branch of comic art, but for practical reasons if we accept the general premise that these comics were created to promote an idea, a product or a person, then "Promotional Comics" is probably as convenient a catch-all title as we can come up with.

We used the phrase "for practical reasons" because the word "practical" goes to the heart of promotional comics more than it does for any other comics product. What greater testimony is there to the medium's impact on American culture than to note their use by hard-headed, profit-minded business people and corporations? They invest their money and they expect results.

Today, premium comics continue to thrive and are still utilized as a valuable marketing and promotional tool. "Free" comics are still packaged with action figures and video games, and offered as mail-away premiums from a variety of product manufacturers. The comic industry itself has expanded its use of giveaway comics to self-promote as well, with "ashcan" and other giveaway editions turning up at conventions and comic shops to advertise upcoming series and special events. Many of these function as old-fashioned premiums, with a coupon or other response required from the reader to receive the comic.

As for the supplements and giveaways printed all those years ago, they have spawned a collectible fervor all their own, thanks to their atypical distribution and frequent rarity. For that and the desire to delve deeper into comics history, we hope that by focusing more directly on this genre, we can enhance our understanding of this vital component in the development and history of the modern comic book.

Whether you're a collector or not, we're all motivated by that desire to get something for nothing. For as long as consumers are enticed by the notion of the "free gift," promotional comics will remain a vital marketing component in many business models, but they will also continue to fight the stigma that has long been associated with the industry as a whole. "Respectable" sources like **Fortune** may have taken notice of the power of comic-related advertising 71 years ago, but after all this time comics still fight an uphill battle to establish some measure of dignity for the medium. Perhaps the higher visibility of promotional comics will eventually prove to be a deciding factor in that intellectual war.

See ya in the funny papers.

Action Zone #1 © CBS

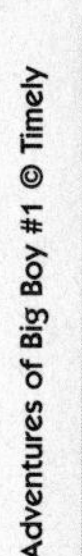
Adventures of Big Boy #1 © Timely

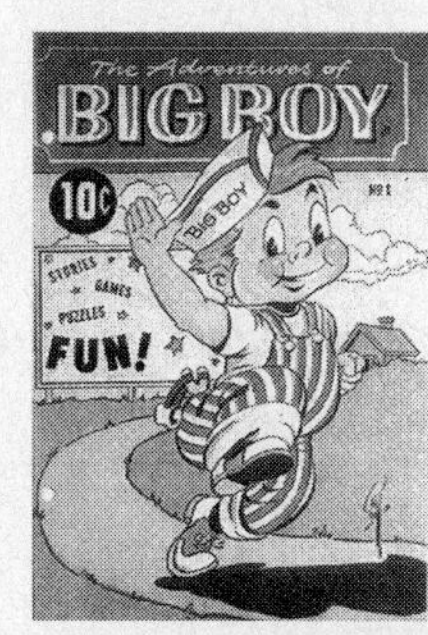

Amazing Spider-Man (Sony Pictures Edition) #50 © MAR

	GD	VG	FN	VF	VF/NM	NM-
	2.0	4.0	6.0	8.0	9.0	9.2

GD VG FN VF VF/NM NM- 2.0 4.0 6.0 8.0 9.0 9.2

ACTION COMICS
DC Comics: 1947 - 1998 (Giveaway)
1 (1976, 1983) paper cover w/10¢ price, 16 pgs. in color; reprints complete Superman story from #1 ('38) 3 6 9 16 20 25
1 (1976) Safeguard Giveaway; paper cover w/"free", 16 pgs. in color; reprints complete Superman story from #1 ('38) 3 6 9 18 23 28
1 (1987 Nestle Quik; 1988, 50¢) 1 2 3 5 7 9
1 (1993)-Came w/Reign of Superman packs 4.00
1 (1998 U.S. Postal Service, $7.95) Reprints entire issue; extra outer half-cover contains First Day Issuance of 32¢ Superman stamp with Sept. 10, 1998 Cleveland, OH postmark 1 2 3 5 6 8
Theater (1947, 32 pgs., 6-1/2 x 8-1/4", nn)-Vigilante story based on Columbia Vigilante serial; no Superman-c or story 66 132 198 413 635 855

ACTION ZONE
CBS Television: 1994 (Promotes CBS Saturday morning cartoons)
1-WildC.A.T.s, T.M.N.Turtles, Skeleton Warriors stories; Jim Lee-c 2.00

ADVENTURE COMICS
IGA: No date (early 1940s) (Paper-c, 32 pgs.)
Two diff. issues; Super-Mystery-r from 1941 25 50 75 144 207 270

ADVENTURE IN DISNEYLAND
Walt Disney Productions (Dist. by Richfield Oil): May, 1955 (Giveaway, soft-c., 16 pgs)
nn 10 20 30 58 77 95

ADVENTURES @ EBAY
eBay: 2000 (6 3/4" x 4 1/2", 16 pgs.)
1-Judd Winick-a/Rucka & Van Meter-s; intro to eBay comic buying 2.25

ADVENTURES OF BARRY WEEN, BOY GENIUS, THE
Oni Press: July, 2004 (Free Comic Book Day giveaway)
...: Secret Crisis Origin Files -Judd Winick-s/a 2.25

ADVENTURES OF BIG BOY
Timely Comics/Webs Adv. Corp./Illus. Features: 1956 - Present (Giveaway) (East & West editions of early issues)

	GD	VG	FN	VF	VF/NM	NM-
1-Everett-a	135	270	405	580	865	1150
2-Everett-a	35	70	105	201	293	385
3-5: 4-Robot-c	18	36	54	95	135	175
6-10: 6-Sci/fic issue	11	22	33	77	114	150
11-20	7	14	21	46	63	80
21-30	4	8	12	25	33	42
31-50	3	6	9	17	22	27
51-100	2	4	6	10	12	15
101-150	2	4	6	8	10	12
151-240	1	2	3	5	7	9
241-265,267-269,271-300:						6.00
266-Superman x-over	3	7	10	21	28	35
270-TV's Buck Rogers-c/s	3	6	9	16	20	25
301-400						4.00
401-500						3.00
1-(2nd series - '76-'84,Paragon Prod.) (...Shoney's Big Boy)	1	3	4	6	8	10
2-20						5.00
21-50						3.00
Summer, 1959 issue, large size	10	20	30	56	78	100

ADVENTURES OF G. I. JOE
1969 (3-1/4x7") (20 & 16 pgs.)
First Series: 1-Danger of the Depths. 2-Perilous Rescue. 3-Secret Mission to Spy Island. 4-Mysterious Explosion. 5-Fantastic Free Fall. 6-Eight Ropes of Danger. 7-Mouth of Doom. 8-Hidden Missile Discovery. 9-Space Walk Mystery. 10-Fight for Survival. 11-The Shark's Surprise.
Second Series: 2-Flying Space Adventure. 4-White Tiger Hunt. 7-Capture of the Pygmy Gorilla. 12-Secret of the Mummy's Tomb.
Third Series: Reprinted surviving titles of First Series. **Fourth Series:** 13-Adventure Team Headquarters. 14-Search For the Stolen Idol.
each.... 3 6 9 18 23 28

ADVENTURES OF KOOL-AID MAN
Marvel Comics: 1983; 1984 (Mail order giveaway)
1,2 1 2 3 4 5 7

ADVENTURES OF MARGARET O'BRIEN, THE
Bambury Fashions (Clothes): 1947 (20 pgs. in color, slick-c, regular size) (Premium)
In "The Big City" movie adaptation (scarce) 20 40 60 112 161 210

ADVENTURES OF QUIK BUNNY
Nestle's Quik: 1984 (Giveaway, 32 pgs.)
nn-Spider-Man app. 2 4 6 9 11 14

ADVENTURES OF STUBBY, SANTA'S SMALLEST REINDEER, THE
W. T. Grant Co.: nd (early 1940s) (Giveaway, 12 pgs.)
nn 6 12 18 33 41 48

ADVENTURES OF VOTEMAN, THE
Foundation For Citizen Education Inc.: 1968
nn 5 10 15 36 48 60

ADVENTURES WITH SANTA CLAUS
Promotional Publ. Co. (Murphy's Store): No date (early 50's) (9-3/4x 6-3/4", 24 pgs., giveaway, paper-c)
nn-Contains 8 pgs. ads 6 12 18 27 33 38
16 pg. version 6 12 18 29 36 42

AIR POWER (CBS TV & the U.S. Air Force Presents)
Prudential Insurance Co.: 1956 (5-1/4x7-1/4", 32 pgs., giveaway, soft-c)
nn-Toth-a? Based on 'You Are There' TV program by Walter Cronkite 10 20 30 58 77 95

ALICE IN BLUNDERLAND
Industrial Services: 1952 (Paper cover, 16 pgs. in color)
nn-Facts about government waste and inefficiency 14 28 42 79 110 140

ALICE IN WONDERLAND
Western Printing Company/Whitman Publ. Co.: 1965; 1969; 1982
Meets Santa Claus(1950s), nd, 16 pgs. 6 12 18 28 34 40
Rexall Giveaway(1965, 16 pgs., 5x7-1/4) Western Printing (TV, Hanna-Barbera) 3 6 9 18 24 30
Wonder Bakery Giveaway(1969, 16 pgs, color, nn, nd) (Continental Baking Company) 3 6 9 18 23 28

ALICE IN WONDERLAND MEETS SANTA
No publisher: nd (6-5/8x9-11/16", 16 pgs., giveaway, paper-c)
nn 9 18 27 52 66 80

ALL ABOARD, MR. LINCOLN
Assoc. of American Railroads: Jan, 1959 (16 pgs.)
nn-Abraham Lincoln and the Railroads 6 12 18 28 34 40

ALL NEW COMICS
Harvey Comics: Oct, 1993 (Giveaway, no cover price, 16 pgs.)(Hanna-Barbera)
1-Flintstones, Scooby Doo, Jetsons, Yogi Bear & Wacky Races previews for upcoming Harvey's new Hanna-Barbera line-up 5.00
NOTE: Material previewed in Harvey giveaway was eventually published by Archie.

AMAZING SPIDER-MAN, THE
Marvel Comics Group
Acme & Dingo Children's Boots (1980)-Spider-Woman app. 2 4 6 11 14 18
Adventures in Reading Starring... (1990,1991) Bogdanove & Romita-c/a 4.00
Aim Toothpaste Giveaway (36 pgs., reg. size)-1 pg. origin recap; Green Goblin-c/story 2 4 6 9 11 14
Aim Toothpaste Giveaway (16 pgs., reg. size)-Dr. Octopus app. 2 4 6 10 13 16
All Detergent Giveaway (1979, 36 pgs.), nn-Origin-r 2 4 6 10 13 16
Amazing Fantasy #15 (8/02) reprint included in Spider-Man DVD Collector's Gift Set 2.25
Amazing Spider-Man nn (1990, 6-1/8x9", 28 pgs.)-Shan-Lon giveaway; reprints Amazing Spider-Man #303 w/McFarlane-c/a 1 2 3 5 7 9
Amazing Spider-Man #3 Reprint (2004)-Best Buy/Sony giveaway 2.25
Amazing Spider-Man #50 (Sony Pictures Edition) (8/04)-mini-comic included in Spider-Man 2 movie DVD Collector's Gift Set; r/#50 & various ASM covers with Dr. Octopus 2.25
Amazing Spider-Man #129 (Lion Gate Films) (6/04)-promotional comic given away at movie theaters on opening night for The Punisher 2.25
...& Power Pack (1984, nn)(Nat'l Committee for Prevention of Child Abuse) (two versions, mail offer & store giveaway)-Mooney-a; Byrne-c
Mail offer 2 4 6 8 10 12
Store giveaway 4.00
...& The Hulk (Special Edition)(6/8/80; 20 pgs.)-Supplement to Chicago Tribune 2 4 6 10 13 16
...& The Incredible Hulk (1981, 1982; 36 pgs.)-Sanger Harris or May D&F supplement to Dallas Times, Dallas Herald, Denver Post, Kansas City Star, Tulsa World; Foley's supplement to Houston Chronicle (1982, 16 pgs.)- "Great Rodeo Robbery"; The Jones Store-giveaway (1983, 16 pgs.) 2 4 6 12 16 20
...and the New Mutants Featuring Skids nn (National Committee for Prevention of Child Abuse/K-Mart giveaway)-Williams-c(i) 5.00
... Battles Ignorance (1992)(Sylvan Learning Systems) giveaway; Mad Thinker app.

Spidey and the Mini-Marvels © MAR

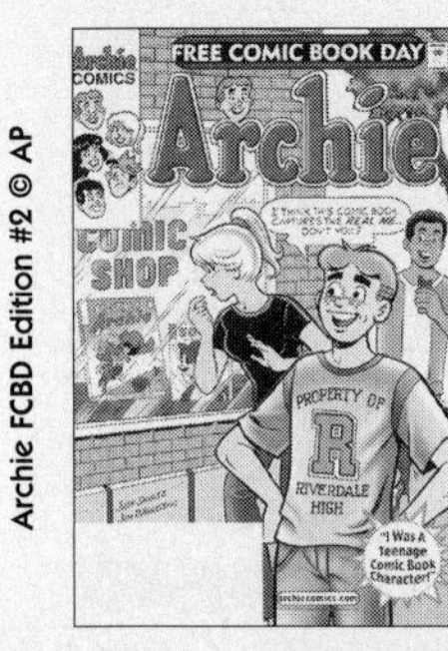

Archie FCBD Edition #2 © AP

Aurora Comic Scenes Instruction Booklet - Robin © DC

	GD 2.0	VG 4.0	FN 6.0	VF 8.0	VF/NM 9.0	NM- 9.2

Kupperberg-a 1 2 3 5 6 8
...Captain America, The Incredible Hulk, & Spider-Woman (1981)
(7-11 Stores giveaway; 36 pgs.) 2 4 6 10 12 15
...: Christmas in Dallas (1983) (Supplement to Dallas Times Herald)
giveaway 2 4 6 10 12 15
...: Danger in Dallas (1983) (Supplement to Dallas Times Herald)
giveaway 2 4 6 10 12 15
...: Danger in Denver (1983) (Supplement to Denver Post)
giveaway for May D&F stores 2 4 6 10 12 15
..., Fire-Star, And Ice-Man at the Dallas Ballet Nutcracker (1983; supplement to
Dallas Times Herald)-Mooney-p 2 4 6 10 12 15
Giveaway-Esquire Magazine (2/69)-Miniature-Still attached (scarce)
13 26 39 90 138 185
Giveaway-Eye Magazine (2/69)-Miniature-Still attached
10 20 30 72 104 135
...: Riot at Robotworld (1991; 16 pgs.)(National Action Council for Minorities in Engineering, Inc.)
giveaway; Saviuk-c 6.00
..., Storm & Powerman (1982; 20 pgs.)(American Cancer Society) giveaway;
also a 1991 2nd printing 1 2 3 5 6 8
...Vs. The Hulk (Special Edition; 1979, 20 pgs.)(Supplement to Columbus Dispatch)
2 4 6 12 16 20
...Vs. The Prodigy (Giveaway, 16 pgs. in color (1976, 5x6-1/2")-Sex education;
(1 million printed; 35-50¢) 3 6 9 16 20 24
Spidey & The Mini-Marvels Halloween 2003 Ashcan (12/03, 8 1/2"x 5 1/2") Giarusso-s/a;
Venom and Green Goblin app. 2.25

AMERICA MENACED!
Vital Publications: 1950 (Paper-c)

nn-Anti-communism 35 70 105 175 258 340

AMERICAN COMICS
Theatre Giveaways (Liberty Theatre, Grand Rapids, Mich. known): 1940's

Many possible combinations. "Golden Age" superhero comics with new cover added and given away at theaters. Following known: Superman #59, Capt. Marvel #20, Capt. Marvel Jr. #5, Action #33, Classics Comics #8, Whiz #39. Value would vary with book and should be 70-80 percent of the original.

ANDY HARDY COMICS
Western Printing Co.:

...& the New Automatic Gas Clothes Dryer (1952, 5x7-1/4", 16 pgs.)
Bendix Giveaway (soft-c) 6 12 18 31 38 45

ANIMANIACS EMERGENCY WORLD
DC Comics: 1995

nn-American Red Cross 4.00

APACHE HUNTER
Creative Pictorials: 1954 (18 pgs. in color) (promo copy) (saddle stitched)

nn-Severin, Heath stories 16 32 48 92 131 170

AQUATEERS MEET THE SUPER FRIENDS
DC Comics: 1979

nn 2 4 6 10 12 15

ARCHIE AND HIS GANG (Zeta Beta Tau Presents...)
Archie Publications: Dec. 1950 (St. Louis National Convention giveaway)

nn-Contains new cover stapled over Archie Comics #47 (11-12/50) on inside;
produced for Zeta Beta Tau 15 30 45 86 123 160

ARCHIE COMICS (Also see Sabrina)
Archie Publications

... And Friends and the Shield (10/02, 8 1/2"x 5 1/2") Diamond Comic Dist. 3.00
... And Friends - A Halloween Tale (10/98, 8 1/2"x 5 1/2") Diamond Comic Dist.;
Sabrina and Sonic app.; Dan DeCarlo-a 3.00
... And Friends - A Timely Tale (10/01, 8 1/2"x 5 1/2") Diamond Comic Dist. 3.00
... And Friends Monster Bash 2003 (8 1/2"x 5 1/2") Diamond Comic Dist. Halloween 3.00
...And His Friends Help Raise Literacy Awareness In Mississippi nn (3/94) 6.00
...And His Pals in the Peer Helping Program nn (2/91, 7"x4 1/2") produced by the FBI 6.00
...And the History of Electronics nn (5/90, 36 pgs.)-Radio Shack giveaway; Bender-c/a 6.00
Fairmont Potato Chips Giveaway-Mini comics 1970 (8 issues-nn's., 8 pgs. each)
3 6 9 18 23 28
Fairmont Potato Chips Giveaway-Mini comics 1970 (6 issues-nn's.,6 7/8" x 2 1/4", 8 pgs. each)
3 6 9 18 23 28
Fairmont Potato Chips Giveaway-Mini comics 1971 (4 issues-nn's.,6 7/8" x 5", 8 pgs. each)
3 6 9 18 23 28
... Free Comic Book Day Edition 1,2: 1-(7/03). 2-(9/04) 2.25
Official Boy Scout Outfitter (1946, 9-1/2x6-1/2, 16 pgs.)-B. R. Baker Co.
(Scarce) 47 94 141 287 436 585
Shoe Store giveaway (1948, Feb?) 17 34 51 95 135 175
...'s Ham Radio Adventure (1997) Morse code instruction; Goldberg-a 5.00
...'s Weird Mysteries (9/99, 8 1/2"x 5 1/2") Diamond Comic Dist. Halloween giveaway 2.25

ARCHIE SHOE-STORE GIVEAWAY
Archie Publications: 1944-49 (12-15 pgs. of games, puzzles, stories like Superman-Tim books, No nos. - came out monthly)

	GD	VG	FN	VF	VF/NM	NM-
(1944-47)-issues	14	28	42	79	110	140
2/48-Peggy Lee photo-c	14	28	42	79	110	140
3/48-Marylee Robb photo-c	12	24	36	71	98	125
4/48-Gloria De Haven photo-c	14	28	42	79	110	140
5/48,6/48,7/48	12	24	36	71	98	125
8/48-Story on Shirley Temple	14	28	42	81	113	145
10/48-Archie as Wolf on cover	13	26	39	76	106	135
5/49-Kathleen Hughes photo-c	11	22	33	62	84	105
7/49	10	20	30	60	80	100
8/49-Archie photo-c from radio show	16	32	48	92	131	170
10/49-Gloria Mann photo-c from radio show	13	26	39	76	106	135
11/49,12/49	10	20	30	60	80	100

ARCHIE'S JOKE BOOK MAGAZINE (See Joke Book ...)
Archie Publications

Drug Store Giveaway (No. 39 w/new-c) 6 12 18 33 41 48

ARCHIE'S TEN ISSUE COLLECTOR'S SET (Title inside of cover only)
Archie Publications: June, 1997 - No. 10, June, 1997 ($1.50, 20 pgs.)

1-10: 1,7-Archie. 2,8-Betty & Veronica. 3,9-Veronica. 4-Betty. 5-World of Archie. 6-Jughead.
10-Archie and Friends each... 4.00

ASTRO COMICS
American Airlines (Harvey): 1968 - 1979 (Giveaway)

Reprints of Harvey comics. 1968-Hot Stuff. 1969-Casper, Spooky, Hot Stuff, Stumbo the Giant, Little Audrey, Little Lotta, & Richie Rich reprints. 1970-r/Richie Rich #97
(all scarce) 3 7 10 21 28 36
1973-r/Richie Rich #122. 1975-Wendy. 1975-Richie Rich & Casper
3 6 9 16 21 26
1977-r/Richie Rich & Casper #20. 1978-r/Richie Rich & Casper #25. 1979-r/Richie Rich &
Casper #30 (scarce) 3 6 9 16 20 24

ATARI FORCE
DC Comics: 1982 - No. 5, 1983

1-3 (1982, 5X7", 52 pgs.)-Given away with Atari games
1 2 3 4 5 7
4,5 (1982-1983, 52 pgs.)-Given away with Atari games (scarcer)
2 4 6 8 10 12

AURORA COMIC SCENES INSTRUCTION BOOKLET (Included with superhero model kits)
Aurora Plastics Co.: 1974 (6-1/4x9-3/4," 8 pgs., slick paper)

181-140-Tarzan; Neal Adams-a 3 7 10 21 28 36
182-140-Spider-Man. 4 8 12 29 40 50
183-140-Tonto(Gil Kane art). 184-140-Hulk. 185-140-Superman. 186-140-Superboy.
187-140-Batman. 188-140-The Lone Ranger(1974-by Gil Kane). 192-140-Captain
America(1975). 193-140-Robin 3 6 9 18 24 30

BACK TO THE FUTURE
Harvey Comics

Special nn (1991, 20 pgs.)-Brunner-c; given away at Universal Studios in Florida 5.00

BALLAD OF SLEEPING BEAUTY
Beckett Entertainment Comics: July, 2004 (Free Comic Book Day giveaway)

1-Hawthorne-a/Amano-c/Benson-s; Fade From Grace preview 2.25

BALTIMORE COLTS
American Visuals Corp.: 1950 (Giveaway)

nn-Eisner-c 45 90 135 275 418 560

BAMBI (Disney)
K. K. Publications (Giveaways): 1941, 1942

1941-Horlick's Malted Milk & various toy stores; text & pictures; most copies mailed out with
store stickers on-c 45 90 135 240 357 475
1942-Same as 4-Color #12, but no price (Same as '41 issue?) (Scarce)
70 140 280 437 644 850

BATMAN
DC Comics: 1966 - Present

Act II Popcorn mini-comic(1998) 3.00
Batman #121 Toys R Us edition (1997) r/1st Mr. Freeze 3.00
Batman #362 Mervyn's edition (1989) 4.00
Batman Adventures #1 Free Comic Book Day edition (6/03) Timm-c 3.00
Batman Adventures #25 Best Western edition (1997) 3.00

Batman Onstar edition © DC

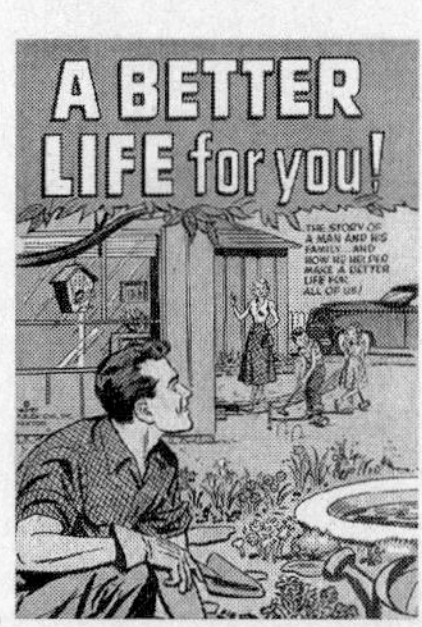
A Better Life For You! © HARV

Bob & Betty & Santa's Wishing Whistle © Sears

GD 2.0 | VG 4.0 | FN 6.0 | VF 8.0 | VF/NM 9.0 | NM- 9.2

Batman and Other DC Classics 1 (1989, giveaway)-DC Comics/Diamond Comic Distributors; Batman origin-r/Batman #47, Camelot 3000-r, Justice League-r('87), New Teen Titans-r 4.00
Batman Beyond Six Flags edition 6.00
Batman: Canadian Multiculturalism Custom (1992) 4.00
Batman Claritan edition (1999) 2.50
Kellogg's Poptarts comics (1966, Set of 6, 16 pgs.); All were folded and placed in Poptarts boxes. Infantino art on Catwoman and Joker issues.
"The Man in the Iron Mask", "The Penguin's Fowl Play", "The Joker's Happy Victims", "The Catwoman's Catnapping Caper", "The Mad Hatter's Hat Crimes", "The Case of the Batman II"
each.... 5 10 15 35 47 58
Mask of the Phantasm (1993) Mini-comic released w/video
1 2 3 4 5 7
Onstar - Auto Show Special Edition (OnStar Corp., 2001, 8 pgs.) Riddler app. 2.50
Pizza Hut giveaway (12/77)-exact-r of #122,123; Joker-c/story
2 4 6 8 10 12
Prell Shampoo giveaway (1966, 16 pgs.)- "The Joker's Practical Jokes" (6-7/8x3-3/8") 5 10 14 31 42 52
Revell in pack (1995) 3.00
...: The 10-Cent Adventure (3/02, 10¢) intro. to the "Bruce Wayne: Murderer" x-over; Rucka-s/ Burchett & Janson-a/Dave Johnson-c; these are alternate copies with special outer half-covers (at least 10 different) promoting comics, toys and games shops 2.50

BATMAN RECORD COMIC
National Periodical Publications: 1966 (one-shot)
1-With record (still sealed) 15 30 45 105 160 215
Comic only 9 18 27 60 85 110

BEETLE BAILEY
Charlton Comics: 1969-1970 (Giveaways)
Armed Forces ('69)-same as regular issue (#68) 2 4 6 11 14 18
Bold Detergent ('69)-same as regular issue (#67) 2 4 6 11 14 18
Cerebral Palsy Assn. V2#71('69) - V2#73(#1,1/70) 2 4 6 11 14 18
Red Cross (1969, 5x7", 16 pgs., paper-c) 2 4 6 11 14 18

BEST WESTERN GIVEAWAY
DC Comics: 1999
nn-Best Western hotels 2.25

BETTER LIFE FOR YOU, A
Harvey Publications Inc.: (16 pgs., paper cover)
nn-Better living through higher productivity 3 6 9 18 23 28

B-FORCE (Milwaukee Brewers and Wisconsin Dental Asso.)
Dark Horse Comics: 2001 (School and stadium giveaway)
nn-Brewers players combat the evils of smokeless tobacco 2.50

BIG BOY (see Adventures of...)

BIG JIM'S P.A.C.K.
Mattel, Inc. (Marvel Comics): No date (1975) (16 pgs.)
nn-Giveaway with Big Jim doll; Buscema/Sinnott-c/a 4 8 12 27 36 45

"BILL AND TED'S EXCELLENT ADVENTURE" MOVIE ADAPTATION
DC Comics: 1989 (No cover price)
nn-Torres-a 4.00

BIONICLE (LEGO robot toys)
DC Comics: Jun, 2001 - No. 18 ($2.25/$3.25, 16 pages, available to LEGO club members)
1 1 2 3 5 6 8
2-5 6.00
6-13 4.00
14-18 3.00
The Legend of Bionicle (McDonald's Mini-comic, 4-1/4 x 7") 4.00
Special Edition #0 (Six Heroes...One Destiny) '03 San Diego Comic Con; Ashley Wood-c 6.00

BLACK GOLD
Esso Service Station (Giveaway): 1945? (8 pgs. in color)
nn-Reprints from True Comics 6 12 18 27 33 38

BLAZING FOREST, THE (See Forest Fire and Smokey Bear)
Western Printing: 1962 (20 pgs., 5x7", slick-c)
nn-Smokey The Bear fire prevention 2 4 6 12 16 20

BLESSED PIUS X
Catechetical Guild (Giveaway): No date (Text/comics, 32 pgs., paper-c)
nn 5 10 15 25 31 36

BLIND JUSTICE (Also see Batman: Blind Justice)
DC Comics/Diamond Comic Distributors: 1989 (Giveaway, squarebound)
nn-Contains Detective #598-600 by Batman movie writer Sam Hamm, w/covers; published same time as originals? 6.00

BLONDIE COMICS
Harvey Publications: 1950-1964
1950 Giveaway 7 14 21 37 46 55
1962,1964 Giveaway 3 6 9 18 23 28
N. Y. State Dept. of Mental Hygiene Giveaway-(1950) Regular size; 16 pgs.; no # 4 8 12 27 36 45
N. Y. State Dept. of Mental Hygiene Giveaway-(1956) Regular size; 16 pgs.; no # 3 6 9 18 24 30
N. Y. State Dept. of Mental Hygiene Giveaway-(1961) Regular size; 16 pgs.; no # 3 6 9 16 21 26

BLOOD IS THE HARVEST
Catechetical Guild: 1950 (32 pgs., paper-c)
(Scarce)-Anti-communism (13 known copies) 138 276 414 863 1332 1800
Black & white version (5 known copies), saddle stitched
55 110 165 340 520 700
Untrimmed version (only one known copy); estimated value-$600
NOTE: *In 1979 nine copies of the color version surfaced from the old Guild's files plus the five black & white copies.*

BLUE BIRD CHILDREN'S MAGAZINE, THE
Graphic Information Service: V1#2, 1957 - No. 10 1958 (16 pgs., soft-c, regular size)
V1#2-10: Pat, Pete & Blue Bird app. 2 4 6 9 11 14

BLUE BIRD COMICS
Various Shoe Stores/Charlton Comics: Late 1940's - 1964 (Giveaway)
nn(1947-50)(36 pgs.)-Several issues; Human Torch, Sub-Mariner app. in some
18 36 54 102 146 190
1959-Li'l Genius, Timmy the Timid Ghost, Wild Bill Hickok (All #1)
3 6 9 17 21 26
1959-(6 titles; all #2) Black Fury #1,4,5, Freddy #4, Li'l Genius, Timmy the Timid Ghost #4, Masked Raider #4, Wild Bill Hickok (Charlton) 3 6 9 16 20 25
1959-(#5) Masked Raider #21 3 6 9 18 23 28
1960-(6 titles)(All #4) Black Fury #8,9, Masked Raider, Freddy #8,9, Timmy the Timid Ghost #9, Li'l Genius #7,9 (Charlt.) 3 6 9 16 20 24
1961,1962-(All #10's) Atomic Mouse #12,13,16, Black Fury #11,12, Freddy, Li'l Genius, Masked Raider, Six Gun Heroes, Texas Rangers in Action, Timmy the Ghost, Wild Bill Hickok, Wyatt Earp #3,11-13,16-18 (Charlton) 2 4 6 14 18 22
1963-Texas Rangers #17 (Charlton) 2 4 6 10 13 16
1964-Mysteries of Unexplored Worlds #18, Teenage Hotrodders #18, War Heroes #18 (Charlton) 2 4 6 10 13 16
1965-War Heroes #18 2 4 6 8 10 12
NOTE: *More than one issue of each character could have been published each year. Numbering is sporadic.*

BOB & BETTY & SANTA'S WISHING WHISTLE
Sears Roebuck & Co.: 1941 (Christmas giveaway, 12 pgs.)
nn 11 22 33 64 87 110

BOBBY BENSON'S B-BAR-B RIDERS (Radio)
Magazine Enterprises/AC Comics
...in the Tunnel of Gold-(1936, 5-1/4x8"; 100 pgs.) Radio giveaway by Hecker-H.O. Company (H.O. Oats); contains 22 color pgs. of comics, rest in novel form
10 20 30 60 80 100
...And The Lost Herd-same as above 10 20 30 60 80 100

BOBBY SHELBY COMICS
Shelby Cycle Co./Harvey Publications: 1949
nn 5 10 14 20 24 28

BOY SCOUT ADVENTURE
Boy Scouts of America: 1954 (16 pgs., paper cover)
nn 4 9 13 18 22 26

BOYS' RANCH
Harvey Publications: 1951
Shoe Store Giveaway #5,6 (Identical to regular issues except Simon & Kirby centerfold replaced with ad) 20 40 60 110 148 185

BOZO THE CLOWN (TV)
Dell Publishing Co.: 1961
Giveaway-1961, 16 pgs., 3-1/2x7-1/4", Apsco Products
6 12 18 38 52 65

BRER RABBIT IN "ICE CREAM FOR THE PARTY"
American Dairy Association: 1955 (5x7-1/4", 16 pgs., soft-c) (Walt Disney) (Premium)
nn-(Scarce) 45 90 135 230 335 440

BUCK ROGERS (In the 25th Century)
Kelloggs Corn Flakes Giveaway: 1933 (6x8", 36 pgs)

Buster Brown Comics #8 © Brown Shoe Co.

Captain America - Return of the Asthma Monster #2 © MAR

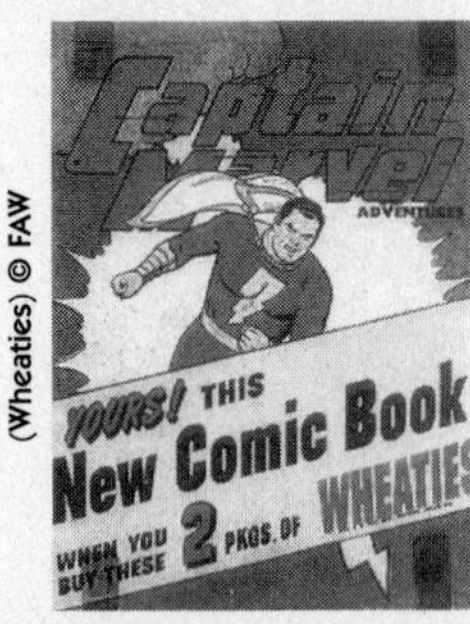

Captain Marvel Adventures (Wheaties) © FAW

	GD	VG	FN	VF	VF/NM	NM-
	2.0	4.0	6.0	8.0	9.0	9.2

GD VG FN VF VF/NM NM-
2.0 4.0 6.0 8.0 9.0 9.2

370A-By Phil Nowlan & Dick Calkins; 1st Buck Rogers radio premium & 1st app. in comics (tells origin) (Reissued in 1995) 100 200 350 750 - -
with envelope 175 350 500 850 - -

BUGS BUNNY (Puffed Rice Giveaway)
Quaker Cereals: 1949 (32 pgs. each, 3-1/8x6-7/8")

A1-Traps the Counterfeiters, A2-Aboard Mystery Submarine, A3- Rocket to the Moon, A4-Lion Tamer, A5-Rescues the Beautiful Princess, B1-Buried Treasure, B2-Outwits the Smugglers, B3-Joins the Marines, B4-Meets the Dwarf Ghost, B5-Finds Aladdin's Lamp, C1-Lost in the Frozen North, C2-Secret Agent, C3-Captured by Cannibals, C4-Fights the Man from Mars, C5-And the Haunted Cave
each.... 9 18 27 51 62 75
Mailing Envelope (has illo of Bugs on front)(Each envelope designates what set it contains, A,B or C on front) 9 18 27 51 62 75

BUGS BUNNY (3-D)
Cheerios Giveaway: 1953 (Pocket size) (15 titles)
each.... 10 20 30 60 80 100
Mailing Envelope (has Bugs drawn on front) 10 20 30 60 80 100

BUGS BUNNY
DC Comics: May, 1997 ($4.95, 24 pgs., comic-sized)
1-Numbered ed. of 100,000; "1st Day of Issue" stamp cancellation on-c 6.00

BUGS BUNNY POSTAL COMIC
DC Comics: 1997 (64 pgs., 7.5" x 5")
nn -Mail Fan; Daffy Duck app. 4.50

BULLETMAN
Fawcett Publications
Well Known Comics (1942)-Paper-c, glued binding; printed in red (Bestmaid/Samuel Lowe giveaway) 17 34 51 95 135 175

BULLS-EYE (Cody of The Pony Express No. 8 on)
Charlton: 1955
Great Scott Shoe Store giveaway-Reprints #2 with new cover 19 38 57 107 154 200

BUSTER BROWN COMICS (Radio)(Also see My Dog Tige in Promotional sec.)
Brown Shoe Co: 1945 - No. 43, 1959 (No. 5: paper-c)
nn, nd (#1,scarce)-Featuring Smilin' Ed McConnell & the Buster Brown gang "Midnight" the cat, "Squeaky" the mouse & "Froggy" the Gremlin; covers mention diff. shoe stores. Contains adventure stories 62 124 187 388 594 800
2 19 38 57 107 154 200
3,5-10 11 22 33 64 87 110
4 (Rare)-Low print run due to paper shortage 16 32 48 89 127 165
11-20 8 16 24 46 58 70
21-24,26-28 6 12 18 31 38 45
25,33-37,40,41-Crandall-a in all 10 20 30 58 77 95
29-32-"Interplanetary Police Vs. the Space Siren" by Crandall (pencils only #29) 10 20 30 58 77 95
38,39,42,43 6 12 18 31 38 45

BUSTER BROWN COMICS (Radio)
Brown Shoe Co: 1950s
...Goes to Mars (2/58-Western Printing), slick-c, 20 pgs., reg. size 11 22 33 66 91 115
...In "Buster Makes the Team!" (1959-Custom Comics) 8 16 24 45 57 68
...In The Jet Age (`50s), slick-c, 20 pgs., 5x7-1/4" 10 20 30 60 80 100
...Of the Safety Patrol ('60-Custom Comics) 3 7 10 21 28 35
...Out of This World ('59-Custom Comics) 7 14 21 35 43 50
...Safety Coloring Book ('58, 16 pgs.)-Slick paper 7 14 21 35 43 50

CALL FROM CHRIST
Catechetical Educational Society: 1952 (Giveaway, 36 pgs.)
nn 5 10 15 24 30 35

CANCELLED COMIC CAVALCADE
DC Comics, Inc.: Summer, 1978 - No. 2, Fall, 1978 (8-1/2x11", B&W)
(Xeroxed pgs. on one side only w/blue cover and taped spine)(Only 35 sets produced)
1-(412 pgs.) Contains xeroxed copies of art for: Black Lightning #12, cover to #13; Claw #13,14; The Deserter #1; Doorway to Nightmare #6; Firestorm #6; The Green Team #2,3.
2-(532 pgs.) Contains xeroxed copies of art for: Kamandi #60 (including Omac), #61; Prez #5; Shade #9 (including The Odd Man); Showcase #105 (Deadman), 106 (The Creeper); Secret Society of Super Villains #16 & 17; The Vixen #1; and covers to Army at War #2, Battle Classics #3, Demand Classics #1 & 2, Dynamic Classics #3, Mr. Miracle #26, Ragman #6, Weird Mystery #25 & 26, & Western Classics #1 & 2.
(A set of Number 1 & 2 was sold in 2002 for $2127.50, then resold for $2590 a month later)
NOTE: *In June, 1978, DC cancelled several of their titles. For copyright purposes, the unpublished original art for these titles was xeroxed, bound in the above books, published and distributed. Only 35 copies were made.*

Beware of bootleg copies.

CAP'N CRUNCH COMICS (See Quaker Oats)
Quaker Oats Co.: 1963; 1965 (16 pgs.; miniature giveaways; 2-1/2x6-1/2")
(1963 titles)- "The Picture Pirates", "The Fountain of Youth", "I'm Dreaming of a Wide Isthmus". (1965 titles)- "Bewitched, Betwitched, & Betweaked", "Seadog Meets the Witch Doctor", "A Witch in Time" 6 12 18 43 59 75

CAPTAIN ACTION (Toy)
National Periodical Publications
...& Action Boy('67)-Ideal Toy Co. giveaway (1st app. Captain Action) 14 28 42 100 153 205

CAPTAIN AMERICA
Marvel Comics Group
...& The Campbell Kids (1980, 36pg. giveaway, Campbell's Soup/U.S. Dept. of Energy) 2 4 6 8 10 12
...Goes To War Against Drugs(1990, no #, giveaway)-Distributed to direct sales shops; 2nd printing exists 6.00
...Meets The Asthma Monster (1987, no #, giveaway, Your Physician and Glaxo, Inc.) 6.00
Return of The Asthma Monster Vol. 1 #2 (1992, giveaway, Your Physician & Allen & Hanbury's) 6.00
...Vs. Asthma Monster (1990, no #, giveaway, Your Physician & Allen & Hanbury's) 6.00

CAPTAIN AMERICA COMICS
Timely/Marvel Comics: 1954
Shoestore Giveaway #77 65 130 195 406 628 850

CAPTAIN ATOM
Nationwide Publishers
...- Secret of the Columbian Jungle (16 pgs. in color, paper-c, 3-3/4x5-1/8")- Fireside Marshmallow giveaway 6 12 18 27 33 38

CAPTAIN BEN DIX
Bendix Aviation Corporation: 1943 (Small size)
nn 8 16 24 43 54 65

CAPTAIN BEN DIX IN ACTION WITH THE INVISIBLE CREW
Bendix Aviation Corp.: 1940s (nd), (20 pgs, 8-1/4"x11", heavy paper)
nn-WWII bomber-c; Jap app. 6 12 18 28 34 40

CAPTAIN FORTUNE PRESENTS
Vital Publications: 1955 - 1959 (Giveaway, 3-1/4x6-7/8", 16 pgs.)
"Davy Crockett in Episodes of the Creek War", "Davy Crockett at the Alamo", "In Sherwood Forest Tells Strange Tales of Robin Hood" ('57), "Meets Bolivar the Liberator" ('59), "Tells How Buffalo Bill Fights the Dog Soldiers" ('57), "Young Davy Crockett" 4 7 9 14 17 20

CAPTAIN GALLANT (...of the Foreign Legion) (TV)
Charlton Comics
Heinz Foods Premium (#1?)(1955; regular size)-U.S. Pictorial; contains Buster Crabbe photos; Don Heck-a 1 2 3 5 7 9
Mailing Envelope 20.00

CAPTAIN MARVEL ADVENTURES
Fawcett Publications
Bond Bread Giveaways-(24 pgs.; pocket size-7-1/4x3-1/2"; paper cover): "...& the Stolen City" ('48), "The Boy Who Never Heard of Capt. Marvel", "Meets the Weatherman" (1950) (reprint) each.... 30 60 90 165 228 290
...Well Known Comics (1944; 12 pgs.; 8-1/2x10-1/2")-printed in red & in blue; soft-c; glued binding - (Bestmaid/Samuel Lowe Co. giveaway) 20 40 60 110 155 200

CAPTAIN MARVEL ADVENTURES (Also see Flash and Funny Stuff)
Fawcett Publications (Wheaties Giveaway): 1945 (6x8", full color, paper-c)
nn- "Captain Marvel & the Threads of Life" plus 2 other stories (32 pgs.) 105 260 425 - - -
NOTE: *All copies were taped at each corner to a box of Wheaties and are never found in Fine or Mint condition. Prices listed for each grade include tape.*

CAPTAIN MARVEL AND THE LTS. OF SAFETY
Ebasco Services/Fawcett Publications: 1950 - 1951 (3 issues - no No.'s)
nn (#1) "Danger Flies a Kite" ('50, scarce), 233 466 700 1400 - -
nn (#2)"Danger Takes to Climbing" ('50), 183 366 550 1000 - -
nn (#3)"Danger Smashes Street Lights" ('51) 183 366 550 1000 - -

CAPTAIN MARVEL, JR.
Fawcett Publications: (1944; 12 pgs.; 8-1/2x10-1/2")
...Well Known Comics (Printed in blue; paper-c, glued binding)-Bestmaid/Samuel Lowe Co. giveaway 14 28 42 79 110 140

CARDINAL MINDSZENTY (The Truth Behind the Trial of...)

Carvel Comics #3 © Carvel Corp.

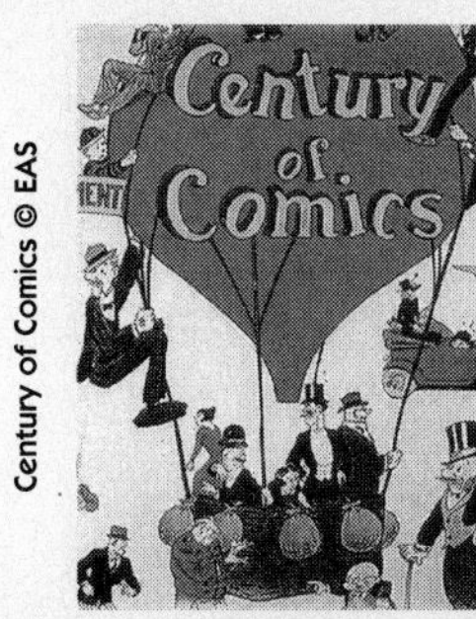

Century of Comics © EAS

Cheerios 3-D Giveaways © WDC

	GD 2.0	VG 4.0	FN 6.0	VF 8.0	VF/NM 9.0	NM- 9.2

Catechetical Guild Education Society: 1949 (24 pgs., paper cover)
nn-Anti-communism 8 16 24 46 58 70
Press Proof-(Very Rare)-(Full color, 7-1/2x11-3/4", untrimmed)
Only two known copies 195.00
Preview Copy (B&W, stapled), 18 pgs.; contains first 13 pgs. of Cardinal Mindszenty and was sent out as an advance promotion. Only one known copy 175.00 - 250.00
NOTE: *Regular edition also printed in French. There was also a movie released in 1949 called "Guilty of Treason" which is a fact-based account of the trial and imprisonment of Cardinal Mindszenty by the Communist regime in Hungary.*

CARNIVAL OF COMICS
Fleet-Air Shoes: 1954 (Giveaway)
nn-Contains a comic bound with new cover; several combinations possible; Charlton's Eh! known 5 10 14 20 24 28

CARTOON NETWORK
DC Comics: 1997 (Giveaway)
nn-reprints Cow and Chicken, Scooby-Doo, & Flintstones stories 4.00

CARVEL COMICS (Amazing Advs. of Capt. Carvel)
Carvel Corp. (Ice Cream): 1975 - No. 5, 1976 (25¢; #3-5: 35¢) (#4,5: 3-1/4x5")
1-3 1 2 3 5 6 8
4,5(1976)-Baseball theme 2 4 6 8 10 12

CASE OF THE WASTED WATER, THE
Rheem Water Heating: 1972? (Giveaway)
nn-Neal Adams-a 4 8 12 29 40 50

CASPER SPECIAL
Target Stores (Harvey): nd (Dec, 1990) (Giveaway with $1.00 cover)
Three issues-Given away with Casper video 6.00

CASPER, THE FRIENDLY GHOST (Paramount Picture Star...)(2nd Series)
Harvey Publications
American Dental Association (Giveaways):
...'s Dental Health Activity Book-1977 2 4 6 8 10 12
...Presents Space Age Dentistry-1972 2 4 6 9 11 14
..., His Den, & Their Dentist Fight the Tooth Demons-1974 2 4 6 9 11 14

CELEBRATE THE CENTURY SUPERHEROES STAMP ALBUM
DC Comics: 1998 - No. 5, 2000 (32 pgs.)
1-5: Historical stories hosted by DC heroes 3.00

CENTIPEDE
DC Comics: 1983
1-Based on Atari video game 1 3 4 6 8 10

CENTURY OF COMICS
Eastern Color Printing Co.: 1933 (100 pgs.)
Bought by Wheatena, Milk-O-Malt, John Wanamaker, Kinney Shoe Stores, & others to be used as premiums and radio giveaways. No publisher listed.
nn-Mutt & Jeff, Joe Palooka, etc. reprints 3670 7335 11,000 25,000 - -

CHEERIOS PREMIUMS (Disney)
Walt Disney Productions: 1947 (16 titles, pocket size, 32 pgs.)
Mailing Envelope for each set "W,X,Y & Z" (has Mickey illo on front)(each envelope designates the set it contains on the front) 10 20 30 60 80 100
Set "W"
W1-Donald Duck & the Pirates 10 20 30 60 80 100
W2-Bucky Bug & the Cannibal King 7 14 21 35 43 50
W3-Pluto Joins the F.B.I. 7 14 21 35 43 50
W4-Mickey Mouse & the Haunted House 8 16 24 40 50 60
Set "X"
X1-Donald Duck, Counter Spy 10 20 30 60 80 100
X2-Goofy Lost in the Desert 7 14 21 35 43 50
X3-Br'er Rabbit Outwits Br'er Fox 7 14 21 35 43 50
X4-Mickey Mouse at the Rodeo 8 16 24 40 50 60
Set "Y"
Y1-Donald Duck's Atom Bomb by Carl Barks. Disney has banned reprinting this book 85 170 255 531 816 1100
Y2-Br'er Rabbit's Secret 7 14 21 35 43 50
Y3-Dumbo & the Circus Mystery 7 14 21 35 43 50
Y4-Mickey Mouse Meets the Wizard 8 16 24 40 50 60
Set "Z"
Z1-Donald Duck Pilots a Jet Plane (not by Barks) 10 20 30 60 80 100
Z2-Pluto Turns Sleuth Hound 7 14 21 35 43 50
Z3-The Seven Dwarfs & the Enchanted Mtn. 8 16 24 40 50 60
Z4-Mickey Mouse's Secret Room 8 16 24 40 50 60

CHEERIOS 3-D GIVEAWAYS (Disney)
Walt Disney Productions: 1954 (24 titles, pocket size) (Glasses came in envelopes)
Glasses only... 7 14 21 37 46 55
Mailing Envelope (no art on front) 8 16 24 46 58 70
(Set 1)
1-Donald Duck & Uncle Scrooge, the Firefighters 9 18 27 54 70 85
2-Mickey Mouse & Goofy, Pirate Plunder 9 18 27 51 62 75
3-Donald Duck's Nephews, the Fabulous Inventors 9 18 27 54 70 85
4-Mickey Mouse, Secret of the Ming Vase 9 18 27 51 62 75
5-Donald Duck with Huey, Dewey, & Louie; ...the Seafarers (title on 2nd page) 9 18 27 54 70 85
6-Mickey Mouse, Moaning Mountain 9 18 27 51 62 75
7-Donald Duck, Apache Gold 9 18 27 54 70 85
8-Mickey Mouse, Flight to Nowhere 8 16 24 46 58 70
(Set 2)
1-Donald Duck, Treasure of Timbuktu 9 18 27 54 70 85
2-Mickey Mouse & Pluto, Operation China 8 16 24 46 58 70
3-Donald Duck in the Magic Cows 9 18 27 54 70 85
4-Mickey Mouse & Goofy, Kid Kokonut 8 16 24 46 58 70
5-Donald Duck, Mystery Ship 9 18 27 54 70 85
6-Mickey Mouse, Phantom Sheriff 9 18 27 51 62 75
7-Donald Duck, Circus Adventures 9 18 27 54 70 85
8-Mickey Mouse, Arctic Explorers 9 18 27 51 62 75
(Set 3)
1-Donald Duck & Witch Hazel 9 18 27 54 70 85
2-Mickey Mouse in Darkest Africa 9 18 27 51 62 75
3-Donald Duck & Uncle Scrooge, Timber Trouble 9 18 27 54 70 85
4-Mickey Mouse, Rajah's Rescue 9 18 27 51 62 75
5-Donald Duck in Robot Reporter 9 18 27 54 70 85
6-Mickey Mouse, Slumbering Sleuth 9 18 27 51 62 75
7-Donald Duck in the Foreign Legion 9 18 27 54 70 85
8-Mickey Mouse, Airwalking Wonder 9 18 27 51 62 75

CHESTY AND COPTIE (Disney)
Los Angeles Community Chest: 1946 (Giveaway, 4pgs.)
nn-(One known copy) by Floyd Gottfredson 85 170 255 525 763 1000

CHESTY AND HIS HELPERS (Disney)
Los Angeles War Chest: 1943 (Giveaway, 12 pgs., 5-1/2x7-1/4")
nn-Chesty & Coptie 55 110 165 350 488 650

CHOCOLATE THE FLAVOR OF FRIENDSHIP AROUND THE WORLD
The Nstle Company: 1955
nn 4 8 12 24 32 40

CHRISTMAS ADVENTURE, THE
S. Rose (H. L. Green Giveaway): 1963 (16 pgs.)
nn 2 4 6 10 13 16

CHRISTMAS AT THE ROTUNDA (Titled Ford Rotunda Christmas Book 1957 on) (Regular size)
Ford Motor Co. (Western Printing): 1954 - 1961 (Given away every Christmas at one location)
1954-56 issues (nn's) 5 10 15 24 30 35
1957-61 issues (nn's) 5 10 14 20 24 28

CHRISTMAS CAROL, A
Sears Roebuck & Co.: No date (1942-43) (Giveaway, 32 pgs., 8-1/4x10-3/4", paper cover)
nn-Comics & coloring book 18 36 54 104 150 195

CHRISTMAS CAROL, A
Sears Roebuck & Co.: 1940s ? (Christmas giveaway, 20 pgs.)
nn-Comic book & animated coloring book 16 32 48 92 131 170

CHRISTMAS CAROLS
Hot Shoppes Giveaway: 1959? (16 pgs.)
nn 4 8 11 16 19 22

CHRISTMAS COLORING FUN
H. Burnside: 1964 (20 pgs., slick-c, B&W)
nn 2 4 6 10 13 16

CHRISTMAS DREAM, A
Promotional Publishing Co.: 1950 (Kinney Shoe Store Giveaway, 16 pgs.)
nn 5 10 15 22 26 30

CHRISTMAS DREAM, A
J. J. Newberry Co.: 1952? (Giveaway, paper cover, 16 pgs.)
nn 4 8 12 18 22 25

CHRISTMAS DREAM, A

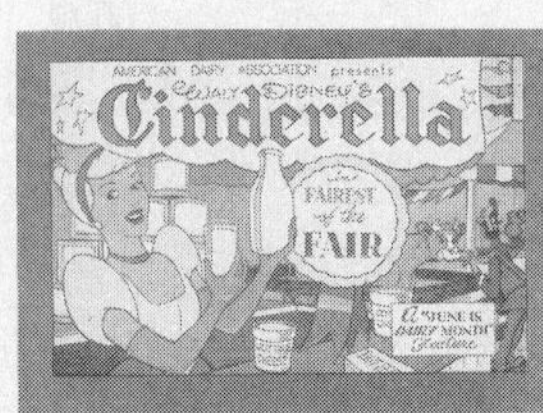

Cinderella in "Fairest of the Fair" © WDC

Classics Giveaways - Saks 34th St. © Saks

Cocomalt Big Book of Comics © CHES

	GD 2.0	VG 4.0	FN 6.0	VF 8.0	VF/NM 9.0	NM- 9.2

Promotional Publ. Co.: 1952 (Giveaway, 16 pgs., paper cover)
nn 4 8 12 18 22 25

CHRISTMAS FUN AROUND THE WORLD
No publisher: No date (early 50's) (16 pgs., paper cover)
nn 5 10 15 22 26 30

CHRISTMAS IS COMING!
No publisher: No date (early 50's?) (Store giveaway, 16 pgs.)
nn 4 8 12 18 22 25

CHRISTMAS JOURNEY THROUGH SPACE
Promotional Publishing Co.: 1960
nn-Reprints 1954 issue Jolly Christmas Book with new slick cover
3 6 9 18 24 30

CHRISTMAS ON THE MOON
W. T. Grant Co.: 1958 (Giveaway, 20 pgs., slick cover)
nn 8 16 24 46 58 70

CHRISTMAS PLAY BOOK
Gould-Stoner Co.: 1946 (Giveaway, 16 pgs., paper cover)
nn 8 16 24 46 58 70

CHRISTMAS ROUNDUP
Promotional Publishing Co.: 1960
nn-Marv Levy-c/a 2 4 6 10 13 16

CHRISTMAS STORY CUT-OUT BOOK, THE
Catechetical Guild: No. 393, 1951 (15¢, 36 pgs.)
393-Half text & half comics 7 14 21 37 46 55

CHRISTMAS USA (Through 300 Years) (Also see Uncle Sam's...)
Promotional Publ. Co.: 1956 (Giveaway)
nn-Marv Levy-c/a 3 6 8 12 14 16

CHRISTMAS WITH SNOW WHITE AND THE SEVEN DWARFS
Kobackers Giftstore of Buffalo, N.Y.: 1953 (16 pgs., paper-c)
nn 7 14 21 37 46 55

CHRISTOPHERS, THE
Catechetical Guild: 1951 (Giveaway, 36 pgs.) (Some copies have 15¢ sticker)
nn-Stalin as Satan in Hell 23 46 69 132 191 250

CINDERELLA IN "FAIREST OF THE FAIR"
American Dairy Association (Premium): 1955 (5x7-1/4", 16 pgs., soft-c) (Walt Disney)
nn 9 18 27 56 70 85

CINEMA COMICS HERALD
Paramount Pictures/Universal/RKO/20th Century Fox/Republic:
1941 - 1943 (4-pg. movie "trailers", paper-c, 7-1/2x10-1/2")(Giveaway)
"Mr. Bug Goes to Town" (1941) 11 22 33 64 87 110
"Bedtime Story" 9 18 27 51 62 75
"Lady For A Night", John Wayne, Joan Blondell ('42) 14 28 42 79 110 140
"Reap The Wild Wind" (1942) 9 18 27 52 66 80
"Thunder Birds" (1942) 9 18 27 51 62 75
"They All Kissed the Bride" 9 18 27 51 62 75
"Arabian Nights" (nd) 9 18 27 52 66 80
"Bombardie" (1943) 9 18 27 51 62 75
"Crash Dive" (1943)-Tyrone Power 9 18 27 52 66 80
NOTE: *The 1941-42 issues contain line art with color photos. 1943 issues are line art.*

CLASSICS GIVEAWAYS (Classic Comics reprints)
12/41–Walter Theatre Enterprises (Huntington, WV) giveaway containing #2 (orig.) w/new generic-c (only 1 known copy) 90 180 270 550 775 1000
1942–Double Comics containing CC#1 (orig.) (diff. cover) (not actually a giveaway) (very rare) (also see Double Comics) (only one known copy)
175 350 525 1100 1525 1950
12/42–Saks 34th St. Giveaway containing CC#7 (orig.) (diff. cover) (very rare; only 6 known copies) 640 1280 1920 2700 3850 5000
2/43–American Comics containing CC#8 (orig.) (Liberty Theatre giveaway) (different cover) (only one known copy) (see American Comics) 145 290 435 800 1100 1400
12/44–Robin Hood Flour Co. Giveaway - #7-CC(R) (diff. cover) (rare) (edition probably 5 [22]) 250 500 750 1300 1850 2400
NOTE: How are above editions determined without CC covers? 1942 is dated 1942, and CC#1-first reprint did not come out until 5/43. 12/42 and 2/43 are determined by blue note at bottom of first text page only in original edition. 12/44 is estimated from page width each reprint edition had progressively slightly smaller page width.
1951–Shelter Thru the Ages (C.I. Educational Series) (actually Giveaway by the Ruberoid Co.) (16 pgs.) (contains original artwork by H. C. Kiefer) (there are 5 diff. back cover ad variations: "Ranch" house ad, "Igloo" ad, "Doll House" ad, "Tree House" ad & blank) (scarce) 75 150 225 450 600 750
1952–George Daynor Biography Giveaway (CC logo) (partly comic book/pictures/newspaper articles) (story of man who built Palace Depression out of junkyard swamp in NJ) (64 pgs.) (very rare; only 3 known copies, one missing back-c)
800 1600 2400 3500 4900 6300
1953–Westinghouse/Dreams of a Man (C.I. Educational Series) (Westinghousebio./Westinghouse Co. giveaway) (contains original artwork by H. C. Kiefer) (16 pgs.) (also French/Spanish/Italian versions) (scarce) 70 140 210 430 565 700
NOTE: Reproductions of 1951, 1952, and 1953 exist with color photocopy covers and black & white photocopy interior ("W.C.N. Reprint") 2 4 5 7 8 10
1951-53–Coward Shoe Giveaways (all editions very rare); 2 variations of back-c ad exist:
With back-c photo ad: 5 (87), 12 (89), 22 (85), 32 (85), 49 (85), 69 (87), 72 (no HRN), 80 (0), 91 (0), 92 (0), 96 (0), 98 (0), 100 (0), 101 (0), 103-105 (all Os)
38 76 114 220 292 365
With back-c cartoon ad: 106-109 (all 0s), 110 (111), 112 (0)
40 80 120 240 320 400
1956–Ben Franklin 5-10 Store Giveaway (#65-PC with back cover ad) (scarce) 34 68 102 180 248 315
1956–Ben Franklin Insurance Co. Giveaway (#65-PC with diff. back cover ad) (very rare) 65 130 195 400 550 700
11/56–Sealtest Co. Edition - #4 (135) (identical to regular edition except for Sealtest logo printed, not stamped, on front cover) (only two copies known to exist)
40 80 120 225 300 375
1958–Get-Well Giveaway containing #15-CI (new cartoon-type cover) (Pressman Pharmacy) (only one copy known to exist) 35 70 105 200 263 325
1967-68–Twin Circle Giveaway Editions - all HRN 166, with back cover ad for National Catholic Press.
2(R68), 4(R67), 10(R68), 13(R68) 3 6 9 19 25 32
48(R67), 128(R68), 535(576-R68) 4 8 12 22 30 38
16(R68), 68(R67) 4 8 12 29 40 50
12/69–Christmas Giveaway ("A Christmas Adventure") (reprints Picture Parade #4-1953, new cover) (4 ad variations)
Stacey's Dept. Store 3 6 9 18 23 28
Anne & Hope Store 5 10 15 33 44 55
Gibson's Dept. Store (rare) 5 10 15 33 44 55
"Merry Christmas" & blank ad space 3 6 9 18 23 28

CLIFF MERRITT SETS THE RECORD STRAIGHT
Brotherhood of Railroad Trainsmen: Giveaway (2 different issues)
...and the Very Candid Candidate by Al Williamson 1 2 3 5 7 9
...Sets the Record Straight by Al Williamson (2 different-c: one by Williamson, the other by McWilliams) 1 2 3 5 7 9

CLYDE BEATTY COMICS (Also see Crackajack Funnies)
Commodore Productions & Artists, Inc.
...African Jungle Book('56)-Richfield Oil Co. 16 pg. giveaway, soft-c
10 20 30 56 73 90

C-M-O COMICS
Chicago Mail Order Co.(Centaur): 1942 - No. 2, 1942 (68 pgs., full color)
1-Invisible Terror, Super Ann, & Plymo the Rubber Man app. (all Centaur costume heroes)
92 184 276 575 888 1200
2-Invisible Terror, Super Ann app. 55 110 165 340 520 700

COCOMALT BIG BOOK OF COMICS
Harry 'A' Chesler (Cocomalt Premium): 1938 (Reg. size, full color, 52 pgs.)
1-(Scarce)-Biro-c/a; Little Nemo by Winsor McCay Jr., Dan Hastings; Jack Cole, Guardineer, Gustavson, Bob Wood-a 215 430 645 1344 2072 2800

COMIC BOOK (Also see Comics From Weatherbird)
American Juniors Shoe: 1954 (Giveaway)
Contains a comic rebound with new cover. Several combinations possible. Contents determine price.

COMIC BOOK MAGAZINE
Chicago Tribune & other newspapers: 1940 - 1943 (Similar to Spirit sections) (7-3/4x10-3/4"; full color; 16-24 pgs. ea.)
1940 issues 7 14 21 37 46 55
1941, 1942 issues 6 12 18 28 34 40
1943 issues 5 10 15 24 30 35
NOTE: *Published weekly. Texas Slim, Kit Carson, Spooky, Josie, Nuts & Jolts, Lew Loyal, Brenda Starr, Daniel Boone, Captain Storm, Rocky, Smokey Stover, Tiny Tim, Little Joe, Fu Manchu appear among others. Early issues had photo stories with pictures from the movies; later issues had comic art.*

COMIC BOOKS (Series 1)
Metropolitan Printing Co. (Giveaway): 1950 (16 pgs.; 5-1/4x8-1/2"; full color; bound at top; paper cover)
1-Boots and Saddles; intro The Masked Marshal 6 12 18 30 37 44
1-The Green Jet; Green Lama by Raboy 27 54 81 155 225 295

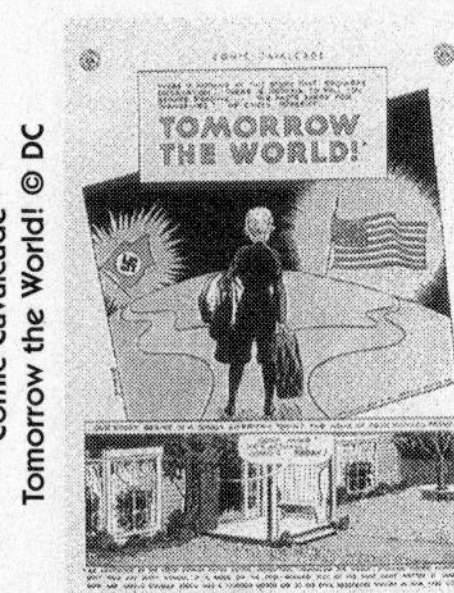

Comic Cavalcade - Tomorrow the World! © DC

Crackajack Funnies © DELL

DC Spotlight #1 © DC

	GD 2.0	VG 4.0	FN 6.0	VF 8.0	VF/NM 9.0	NM- 9.2
1-My Pal Dizzy (Teen-age)	5	10	15	20	24	28
1-New World; origin Atomaster (costumed hero)	10	20	30	58	77	95
1-Talullah (Teen-age)	4	9	13	18	22	30

COMIC CAVALCADE
All-American/National Periodical Publications

	GD 2.0	VG 4.0	FN 6.0	VF 8.0	VF/NM 9.0	NM- 9.2
Giveaway (1944, 8 pgs., paper-c, in color)-One Hundred Years of Co-operation-r/Comic Cavalcade #9	70	140	210	425	638	850
Giveaway (1945, 16 pgs., paper-c, in color)-Movie "Tomorrow The World" (Nazi theme); r/Comic Cavalcade #10	90	180	270	550	825	1100
Giveaway (c. 1944-45; 8 pgs, paper-c, in color)-The Twain Shall Meet-r/Comic Cavalcade #8	70	140	210	425	638	850

COMIC SELECTIONS (Shoe store giveaway)
Parents' Magazine Press: 1944-46 (Reprints from Calling All Girls, True Comics, True Aviation, & Real Heroes)

	GD 2.0	VG 4.0	FN 6.0	VF 8.0	VF/NM 9.0	NM- 9.2
1	5	10	15	22	26	30
2-5	4	8	11	16	19	22

COMICS FROM WEATHER BIRD (Also see Comic Book, Edward's Shoes, Free Comics to You & Weather Bird)
Weather Bird Shoes: 1954 - 1957 (Giveaway)
Contains a comic bound with new cover. Many combinations possible. Contents would determine price. Some issues do not contain complete comics, but only parts of comics. Value equals 40 to 60 percent of contents.

COMICS READING LIBRARIES (Educational Series)
King Features (Charlton Publ.): 1973, 1977, 1979 (36 pgs. in color) (Giveaways)

	GD 2.0	VG 4.0	FN 6.0	VF 8.0	VF/NM 9.0	NM- 9.2
R-01-Tiger, Quincy	2	4	6	8	10	12
R-02-Beetle Bailey, Blondie & Popeye	2	4	6	10	13	16
R-03-Blondie, Beetle Bailey	2	4	6	8	10	12
R-04-Tim Tyler's Luck, Felix the Cat	3	6	9	18	23	28
R-05-Quincy, Henry	2	4	6	8	10	12
R-06-The Phantom, Mandrake	3	6	9	18	23	28
1977 reprint(R-04)	2	4	6	9	11	14
R-07-Popeye, Little King	2	4	6	12	16	20
R-08-Prince Valiant (Foster), Flash Gordon	3	6	9	20	27	34
1977 reprint	2	4	6	11	14	18
R-09-Hagar the Horrible, Boner's Ark	2	4	6	10	13	16
R-10-Redeye, Tiger	2	4	6	8	10	12
R-11-Blondie, Hi & Lois	2	4	6	8	10	12
R-12-Popeye-Swee'pea, Brutus	2	4	6	12	16	20
R-13-Beetle Bailey, Little King	2	4	6	8	10	12
R-14-Quincy-Hamlet	2	4	6	8	10	12
R-15-The Phantom, The Genius	2	4	6	12	16	20
R-16-Flash Gordon, Mandrake	3	6	9	19	27	34
1977 reprint	2	4	6	10	13	16
Other 1977 editions....	1	2	3	5	7	9
1979 editions (68 pgs.)	1	2	3	5	7	9

NOTE: *Above giveaways available with purchase of $45.00 in merchandise. Used as a reading skills aid for small children.*

COMMANDMENTS OF GOD
Catechetical Guild: 1954, 1958

	GD 2.0	VG 4.0	FN 6.0	VF 8.0	VF/NM 9.0	NM- 9.2
300-Same contents in both editions; diff-c	5	10	14	20	24	28

COMPLIMENTARY COMICS
Sales Promotion Publ.: No date (1950's) (Giveaway)

	GD 2.0	VG 4.0	FN 6.0	VF 8.0	VF/NM 9.0	NM- 9.2
1-Strongman by Powell, 3 stories	8	16	24	40	50	60

COURTNEY CRUMRIN & THE NIGHT THINGS
Oni Press: 2003

	GD 2.0	VG 4.0	FN 6.0	VF 8.0	VF/NM 9.0	NM- 9.2
Free Comic Book Day Edition (5/03) Naifeh-s/a						2.25

CRACKAJACK FUNNIES (Giveaway)
Malto-Meal: 1937 (Full size, soft-c, full color, 32 pgs.)(Before No. 1?)

	GD 2.0	VG 4.0	FN 6.0	VF 8.0	VF/NM 9.0	NM- 9.2
nn-Features Dan Dunn, G-Man, Speed Bolton, Buck Jones, The Nebbs, Clyde Beatty, Freckles, Major Hoople, Wash Tubbs	92	184	276	575	888	1200

CROSLEY'S HOUSE OF FUN (Also see Tee and Vee Crosley...)
Crosley Div. AVCO Mfg. Corp.: 1950 (Giveaway, paper cover, 32 pgs.)

	GD 2.0	VG 4.0	FN 6.0	VF 8.0	VF/NM 9.0	NM- 9.2
nn-Strips revolve around Crosley appliances	5	10	15	22	26	30

CSI: CRIME SCENE INVESTIGATION
IDW Publishing: July, 2004 (Free Comic Book Day edition)

	GD 2.0	VG 4.0	FN 6.0	VF 8.0	VF/NM 9.0	NM- 9.2
Previews CSI: Bad Rap; The Shield: Spotlight; 24: One Shot; and 30 Days of Night						2.25

DAGWOOD SPLITS THE ATOM (Also see Topix V8#4)
King Features Syndicate: 1949 (Science comic with King Features characters) (Giveaway)

	GD 2.0	VG 4.0	FN 6.0	VF 8.0	VF/NM 9.0	NM- 9.2
nn-Half comic, half text; Popeye, Olive Oyl, Henry, Mandrake, Little King, Katzenjammer Kids app.	9	18	27	51	62	75

DAISY COMICS (Daisy Air Rifles)
Eastern Color Printing Co.: Dec, 1936 (5-1/4x7-1/2")

	GD 2.0	VG 4.0	FN 6.0	VF 8.0	VF/NM 9.0	NM- 9.2
nn-Joe Palooka, Buck Rogers (2 pgs. from Famous Funnies No. 18, 1st full cover app.), Napoleon Flying to Fame, Butty & Fally	30	60	90	170	245	320

DAISY LOW OF THE GIRL SCOUTS
Girl Scouts of America: 1954, 1965 (16 pgs., paper-c)

	GD 2.0	VG 4.0	FN 6.0	VF 8.0	VF/NM 9.0	NM- 9.2
1954-Story of Juliette Gordon Low	5	10	14	20	24	28
1965	2	4	6	9	11	14

DAN CURTIS GIVEAWAYS
Western Publishing Co.:1974 (3x6", 24 pgs., reprints)

	GD 2.0	VG 4.0	FN 6.0	VF 8.0	VF/NM 9.0	NM- 9.2
1-Dark Shadows	3	6	9	18	23	28
2,6-Star Trek	3	6	9	18	26	28
3,4,7-9: 3-The Twilight Zone. 4-Ripley's Believe It or Not! 7-The Occult Files of Dr. Spektor. 8-Dagar the Invincible. 9-Grimm's Ghost Stories	2	4	6	11	14	18
5-Turok, Son of Stone (partial-r/Turok #78)	3	6	9	18	23	28

DANNY KAYE'S BAND FUN BOOK
H & A Selmer: 1959 (Giveaway)

	GD 2.0	VG 4.0	FN 6.0	VF 8.0	VF/NM 9.0	NM- 9.2
nn	7	14	21	35	43	50

DAREDEVIL
Marvel Comics Group: 1993

	GD 2.0	VG 4.0	FN 6.0	VF 8.0	VF/NM 9.0	NM- 9.2
...Vs. Vapora 1 (Engineering Show Giveaway, 16 pg.) - Intro Vapora						6.00

DAVY CROCKETT (TV)
Dell Publishing Co.

	GD 2.0	VG 4.0	FN 6.0	VF 8.0	VF/NM 9.0	NM- 9.2
...Christmas Book (no date, 16 pgs., paper-c)-Sears giveaway	6	12	18	31	38	45
...Safety Trails (1955, 16pgs, 3-1/4x7")-Cities Service giveaway	8	16	24	40	50	60

DAVY CROCKETT
Charlton Comics

	GD 2.0	VG 4.0	FN 6.0	VF 8.0	VF/NM 9.0	NM- 9.2
Hunting With... nn ('55, 16 pgs.)-Ben Franklin Store giveaway (Publ.-S. Rose)	5	10	15	24	30	35

DAVY CROCKETT
Walt Disney Prod.: (1955, 16 pgs., 5x7-1/4", slick, photo-c)

	GD 2.0	VG 4.0	FN 6.0	VF 8.0	VF/NM 9.0	NM- 9.2
...In the Raid at Piney Creek-American Motors giveaway	8	16	24	40	50	60

DC SAMPLER
DC Comics : nn (#1) 1983 - No. 3, 1984 (36 pgs.; 6 1/2" x 10", giveaway)

	GD 2.0	VG 4.0	FN 6.0	VF 8.0	VF/NM 9.0	NM- 9.2
nn(#1) -3: nn-Wraparound-c, previews upcoming issues. 3-Kirby-a						6.00

DC SPOTLIGHT
DC Comics : 1985 (50th anniversary special) (giveaway)

	GD 2.0	VG 4.0	FN 6.0	VF 8.0	VF/NM 9.0	NM- 9.2
1-Includes profiles on Batman:The Dark Knight & Watchmen						5.00

DENNIS THE MENACE
Hallden (Fawcett)

	GD 2.0	VG 4.0	FN 6.0	VF 8.0	VF/NM 9.0	NM- 9.2
...& Dirt ('59)-Soil Conservation giveaway; r-# 36; Wiseman-c/a	2	4	6	14	18	22
...& Dirt ('68)-reprints '59 edition	2	4	6	8	10	12
...Away We Go('70)-Caladryl giveaway	1	3	4	6	8	10
...Coping with Family Stress-giveaway	1	3	4	6	8	10
...Takes a Poke at Poison('61)-Food & Drug Admin. giveaway; Wiseman-c/a	2	4	6	8	10	12
...Takes a Poke at Poison-Revised 1/66, 11/70	1	2	3	5	6	8
...Takes a Poke at Poison-Revised 1972, 1974, 1977, 1981	1	2	3	4	5	7

DETECTIVE COMICS (Also see other Batman titles)
National Periodical Publications/DC Comics

	GD 2.0	VG 4.0	FN 6.0	VF 8.0	VF/NM 9.0	NM- 9.2
27 (1984)-Oreo Cookies giveaway (32 pgs., paper-c) r-/Det. #27,#38 & Batman #1 (1st Joker)	5	10	15	33	44	55
38 (1995) Blockbuster Video edition; reprints 1st Robin app.						3.00
38 (1997) Toys R Us edition						3.00
359 (1997) Toys R Us edition; reprints 1st Batgirl app.						3.00

DICK TRACY GIVEAWAYS
1939 - 1958; 1990

	GD 2.0	VG 4.0	FN 6.0	VF 8.0	VF/NM 9.0	NM- 9.2
Buster Brown Shoes Giveaway (1940s?, 36 pgs. in color); 1938-39-r by Gould	33	66	99	190	283	375
Gillmore Giveaway (See Superbook)						
...Hatful of Fun (No date, 1950-52, 32pgs.; 8-1/2x10")-Dick Tracy hat promotion; Dick Tracy games, magic tricks. Miller Bros. premium	17	34	51	98	142	185
Motorola Giveaway (1953)-Reprints Harvey Comics Library #2; "The Case of the Sparkle						

Dick Tracy Service Station Giveaway © Tribune Media Services

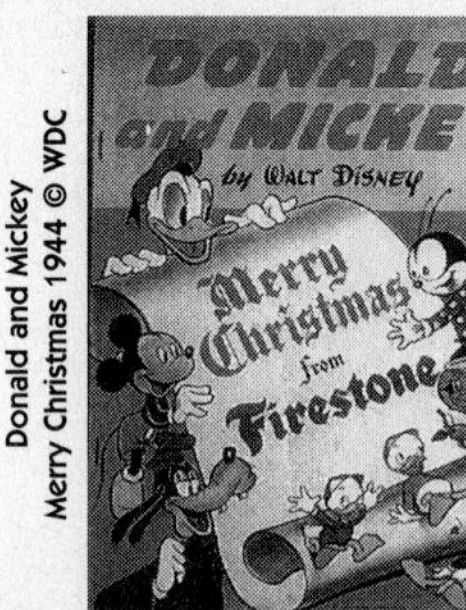

Donald and Mickey Merry Christmas 1944 © WDC

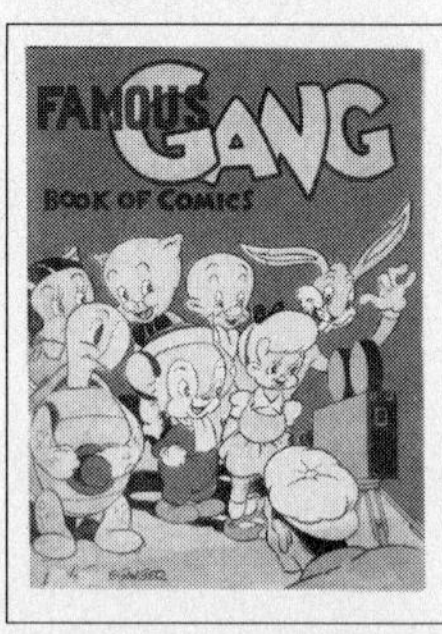

Famous Gang Book of Comics © Firestone/WB

	GD 2.0	VG 4.0	FN 6.0	VF 8.0	VF/NM 9.0	NM- 9.2
Plenty TV Mystery"	7	14	21	37	46	55
Original Dick Tracy by Chester Gould, The (Aug, 1990, 16 pgs., 5-1/2x8-1/2")-Gladstone Publ.; Bread Giveaway	1	3	4	6	8	10
Popped Wheat Giveaway (1947, 16 pgs. in color)-1940-r; Sig Feuchtwanger Publ.; Gould-a	4	8	12	17	21	24
...Presents the Family Fun Book; Tip Top Bread Giveaway, no date or number (1940, Fawcett Publ., 16 pgs. in color)-Spy Smasher, Ibis, Lance O'Casey app.	50	100	150	305	465	625
Same as above but without app. of heroes & Dick Tracy on cover only	15	30	45	83	117	150
Service Station Giveaway (1958, 16 pgs. in color)(regular size, slick cover)-Harvey Info. Press	5	10	14	20	24	28
Shoe Store Giveaway (Weatherbird)(1939, 16 pgs.)-Gould-a	14	28	42	79	110	140

DICK TRACY SHEDS LIGHT ON THE MOLE
Western Printing Co.: 1949 (16 pgs.) (Ray-O-Vac Flashlights giveaway)

	GD	VG	FN	VF	VF/NM	NM-
nn-Not by Gould	8	16	24	40	50	60

DICK WINGATE OF THE U.S. NAVY
Superior Publ./Toby Press: 1951; 1953 (no month)

	GD	VG	FN	VF	VF/NM	NM-
nn-U.S. Navy giveaway	5	10	15	24	30	35
1(1953, Toby)-Reprints nn issue? (same-c)	5	10	14	20	24	28

DIG 'EM
Kellogg's Sugar Smacks Giveaway: 1973 (2-3/8x6", 16 pgs.)

	GD	VG	FN	VF	VF/NM	NM-
nn-4 different issues	1	3	4	6	8	10

DOC CARTER VD COMICS
Health Publications Institute, Raleigh, N. C. (Giveaway): 1949 (16 pgs. in color) (Paper-c)

	GD	VG	FN	VF	VF/NM	NM-
nn	18	36	54	101	143	185

DONALD AND MICKEY MERRY CHRISTMAS (Formerly Famous Gang Book Of Comics)
K. K. Publ./Firestone Tire & Rubber Co.: 1943 - 1949 (Giveaway, 20 pgs.)
Put out each Christmas; 1943 issue titled "Firestone Presents Comics" (Disney)

	GD	VG	FN	VF	VF/NM	NM-
1943-Donald Duck-r/WDC&S #32 by Carl Barks	75	150	225	469	710	950
1944-Donald Duck-r/WDC&S #35 by Barks	70	140	210	438	669	900
1945- "Donald Duck's Best Christmas", 8 pgs. Carl Barks; intro. & 1st app. Grandma Duck in comic books	106	212	318	663	1019	1375
1946-Donald Duck in "Santa's Stormy Visit", 8 pgs. Carl Barks	73	146	219	455	690	925
1947-Donald Duck in "Three Good Little Ducks", 8 pgs. Carl Barks	73	146	219	455	690	925
1948-Donald Duck in "Toyland", 8 pgs. Carl Barks	73	146	219	455	690	925
1949-Donald Duck in "New Toys", 8 pgs. Barks	66	132	198	412	631	850

DONALD DUCK
K. K. Publications: 1944 (Christmas giveaway, paper-c, 16 pgs.)(2 versions)

	GD	VG	FN	VF	VF/NM	NM-
nn-Kelly cover reprint	83	166	249	519	797	1075

DONALD DUCK AND THE RED FEATHER
Red Feather Giveaway: 1948 (8-1/2x11", 4 pgs., B&W)

	GD	VG	FN	VF	VF/NM	NM-
nn	19	38	57	107	154	200

DONALD DUCK IN "THE LITTERBUG"
Keep America Beautiful: 1963 (5x7-1/4", 16 pgs., soft-c) (Disney giveaway)

	GD	VG	FN	VF	VF/NM	NM-
nn	4	8	12	27	36	45

DONALD DUCK "PLOTTING PICNICKERS" (See Frito-Lay Giveaway)

DONALD DUCK'S SURPRISE PARTY
Walt Disney Productions: 1948 (16 pgs.) (Giveaway for Icy Frost Twins Ice Cream Bars)

	GD	VG	FN	VF	VF/NM	NM-
nn-(Rare)-Kelly-c/a	314	628	943	1600	2550	3500

DOT AND DASH AND THE LUCKY JINGLE PIGGIE
Sears Roebuck Co.: 1942 (Christmas giveaway, 12 pgs.)

	GD	VG	FN	VF	VF/NM	NM-
nn-Contains a war stamp album and a punch out Jingle Piggie bank	10	20	30	56	77	95

DOUBLE TALK (Also see Two-Faces)
Feature Publications: No date (1962?) (32 pgs., full color, slick-c)
Christian Anti-Communism Crusade (Giveaway)

	GD	VG	FN	VF	VF/NM	NM-
nn-Sickle with blood-c	10	20	30	73	107	140

DUEL MASTERS (Based on a trading card game)
Dreamwave Productions: July, 2004 (Free Comic Book Day giveaway)

	GD	VG	FN	VF	VF/NM	NM-
1-Augustyn-s						2.25

DUMBO (Walt Disney's..., The Flying Elephant)
Weatherbird Shoes/Ernest Kern Co.(Detroit)/ Wieboldt's (Chicago): 1941
(K.K. Publ. Giveaway)

	GD 2.0	VG 4.0	FN 6.0	VF 8.0	VF/NM 9.0	NM- 9.2
nn-16 pgs., 9x10" (Rare)	48	96	144	293	447	600
nn-52 pgs., 5-1/2x8-1/2", slick cover in color; B&W interior; half text, half reprints 4-Color No. 17 (Dept. store)	27	54	81	155	225	295

DUMBO WEEKLY
Walt Disney Prod.: 1942 (Premium supplied by Diamond D-X Gas Stations)

	GD	VG	FN	VF	VF/NM	NM-
1	70	140	210	440	670	900
2-16	24	48	72	135	195	255
Binder only						475

NOTE: *A cover and binder came separate at gas stations. Came with membership card.*

EAT RIGHT TO WORK AND WIN
Swift & Company: 1942 (16 pgs.) (Giveaway)
Blondie, Henry, Flash Gordon by Alex Raymond, Toots & Casper, Thimble Theatre(Popeye), Tillie the Toiler, The Phantom, The Little King, & Bringing up Father - original strips just for this book -(in daily strip form which shows what foods we should eat and why)

	GD	VG	FN	VF	VF/NM	NM-
	50	100	150	260	368	475

EDWARD'S SHOES GIVEAWAY
Edward's Shoe Store: 1954 (Has clown on cover)
Contains comic with new cover. Many combinations possible. Contents determines price, 50-60 percent of original. (Similar to Comics From Weatherbird & Free Comics to You)

ELSIE THE COW
D. S. Publishing Co.

	GD	VG	FN	VF	VF/NM	NM-
Borden's cheese comic picture bk ("40, giveaway)	21	42	63	118	169	220
Borden Milk Giveaway-(16 pgs., nn) (3 ishs, 1957)	14	28	42	79	110	140
Elsie's Fun Book(1950; Borden Milk)	14	28	42	79	110	140
Everyday Birthday Fun With... (1957; 20 pgs.)(100th Anniversary); Kubert-a	14	28	42	79	110	140

ESCAPE FROM FEAR
Planned Parenthood of America: 1956, 1962, 1969 (Giveaway, 8 pgs., color) (On birth control)

	GD	VG	FN	VF	VF/NM	NM-
1956 edition	10	20	30	56	73	90
1962 edition	4	8	12	29	40	50
1969 edition	3	6	9	16	20	25

EVEL KNIEVEL
Marvel Comics Group (Ideal Toy Corp.): 1974 (Giveaway, 20 pgs.)

	GD	VG	FN	VF	VF/NM	NM-
nn-Contains photo on inside back-c	4	8	12	29	40	50

FAMOUS COMICS (Also see Favorite Comics)
Zain-Eppy/United Features Syndicate: No date; Mid 1930's (24 pgs., paper-c)

	GD	VG	FN	VF	VF/NM	NM-
nn-Reprinted from 1933 & 1934 newspaper strips in color; Joe Palooka, Hairbreadth Harry, Napoleon, The Nebbs, etc. (Many different versions known)	50	100	150	305	465	625

FAMOUS FAIRY TALES
K. K. Publ. Co.: 1942; 1943 (32 pgs.); 1944 (16 pgs.) (Giveaway, soft-c)

	GD	VG	FN	VF	VF/NM	NM-
1942-Kelly-a	40	80	120	238	354	470
1943-r-/Fairy Tale Parade No. 2,3; Kelly-a	30	60	90	170	245	320
1944-Kelly-a	27	54	81	152	219	285

FAMOUS FUNNIES -A CARNIVAL OF COMICS
Eastern Color: 1933
36 pgs., no date given, no publisher, no number; contains strip reprints of The Bungle Family, Dixie Dugan, Hairbreadth Harry, Joe Palooka, Keeping Up With the Jones, Mutt & Jeff, Reg'lar Fellers, S'Matter Pop, Strange As It Seems, and others. This book was sold by M. C. Gaines to Wheatena, Milk-O-Malt, John Wanamaker, Kinney Shoe Stores, & others to be given away as premiums and radio giveaways (1933). Originally came with a mailing envelope.

	GD	VG	FN	VF	VF/NM	NM-
	913	1816	2740	5480	9240	13,000

FAMOUS GANG BOOK OF COMICS (Becomes Donald & Mickey Merry Christmas 1943 on)
Firestone Tire & Rubber Co.: Dec, 1942 (Christmas giveaway, 32 pgs., paper-c)

	GD	VG	FN	VF	VF/NM	NM-
nn-(Rare)-Porky Pig, Bugs Bunny, Mary Jane & Sniffles, Elmer Fudd; r/Looney Tunes	65	130	195	406	628	850

FANTASTIC FOUR
Marvel Comics

	GD	VG	FN	VF	VF/NM	NM-
nn (1981, 32 pgs.) Young Model Builders Club	2	4	6	8	10	12
Vol. 3 #60 Baltimore Comic Book Show (10/02, newspaper supplement) 200,000 copies were distributed to Baltimore Sun home subscribers to promote Baltimore Comic Con						3.00

FATHER OF CHARITY
Catechetical Guild Giveaway: No date (32 pgs.; paper cover)

	GD	VG	FN	VF	VF/NM	NM-
nn	5	10	14	20	24	28

FAVORITE COMICS (Also see Famous Comics)
Grocery Store Giveaway (Diff. Corp.) (detergent): 1934 (36 pgs.)

	GD	VG	FN	VF	VF/NM	NM-
Book 1-The Nebbs, Strange As It Seems, Napoleon, Joe Palooka, Dixie Dugan, S'Matter Pop, Hairbreadth Harry, etc. reprints	85	170	255	531	810	1100
Book 2,3	55	110	165	340	520	700

Fearless Fosdick © Capp Ent.

Forest Fire © AFA

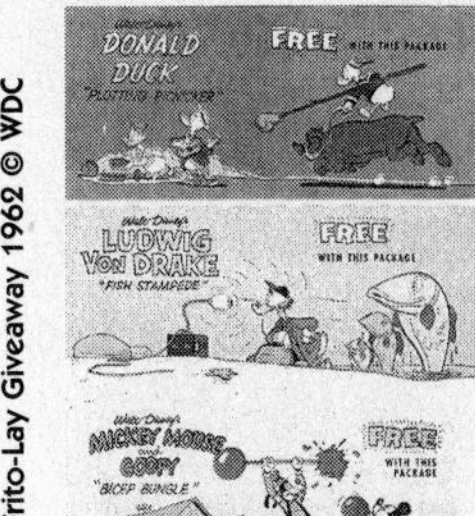

Frito-Lay Giveaway 1962 © WDC

	GD 2.0	VG 4.0	FN 6.0	VF 8.0	VF/NM 9.0	NM- 9.2

FAWCETT MINIATURES (See Mighty Midget)
Fawcett Publications: 1946 (3-3/4x5", 12-24 pgs.) (Wheaties giveaways)

Captain Marvel "And the Horn of Plenty"; Bulletman story 18 36 54 104 150 195
Captain Marvel "& the Raiders From Space"; Golden Arrow story 18 36 54 104 150 195
Captain Marvel Jr. "The Case of the Poison Press!" Bulletman story 18 36 54 104 150 195
Delecta of the Planets; C. C. Beck art; B&W inside; 12 pgs.; 3 printing variations (coloring) exist 25 50 75 144 207 270

FEARLESS FOSDICK
Capp Enterprises Inc.: 1951

...& The Case of The Red Feather 6 12 18 27 33 38

FIGHT FOR FREEDOM
National Assoc. of Mfgrs./General Comics: 1949, 1951 (Giveaway, 16 pgs.)

nn-Dan Barry-c/a; used in **POP**, pg. 102 6 12 18 31 38 45

FIRE AND BLAST
National Fire Protection Assoc.: 1952 (Giveaway, 16 pgs., paper-c)

nn-Mart Baily A-Bomb-c; about fire prevention 15 30 45 85 120 155

FIRE CHIEF AND THE SAFE OL' FIREFLY, THE
National Board of Fire Underwriters: 1952 (16 pgs.) (Safety brochure given away at schools) (produced by American Visuals Corp.)(Eisner)

nn-(Rare) Eisner-c/a 45 90 135 275 418 560

FLASH, THE
DC Comics

nn-(1990) Brochure for CBS TV series 4.00
The Flash Comes to a Standstill (1981, General Foods giveaway, 8 pages, 3-1/2 x 6-3/4", oblong) 2 4 6 10 12 15

FLASH COMICS (Also see Captain Marvel and Funny Stuff)
National Periodical Publications: 1946 (6-1/2x8-1/4", 32 pgs.) (Wheaties Giveaway)

nn-Johnny Thunder, Ghost Patrol, The Flash & Kubert Hawkman app.; Irwin Hasen-c/a 350 975 1600 - - -

NOTE: *All known copies were taped to Wheaties boxes and are never found in mint condition. Copies with light tape residue bring the listed prices in all grades*

FLASH FORCE 2000
DC Comics: 1984

1-5 5.00

FLASH GORDON
Dell Publishing Co.: 1943 (20 pgs.)

Macy's Giveaway-(Rare); not by Raymond 62 124 186 388 594 800

FLASH GORDON
Harvey Comics: 1951 (16 pgs. in color, regular size, paper-c) (Gordon Bread giveaway)

1,2: 1-r/strips 10/24/37 - 2/6/38. 2-r/strips 7/14/40 - 10/6/40; Reprints by Raymond each.... 2 4 6 11 14 18

NOTE: *Most copies have brittle edges.*

FLOOD RELIEF
Malibu Comics (Ultraverse): Jan, 1994 (36 pgs.)(Ordered thru mail w/$5.00 to Red Cross)

1-Hardcase, Prime & Prototype app. 6.00

FOREST FIRE (Also see The Blazing Forest and Smokey Bear)
American Forestry Assn.(Commerical Comics): 1949 (dated-1950) (16 pgs., paper-c)

nn-Intro/1st app. Smokey The Forest Fire Preventing Bear; created by Rudy Wendelein; Wendelein/Sparling-a; 'Carter Oil Co.' on back-c of original 17 34 51 95 135 175

FOREST RANGER HANDBOOK
Wrather Corp.: 1967 (5x7", 20 pgs., slick-c)

nn-WIth Corey Stuart & Lassie photo-c 2 4 6 14 18 22

FORGOTTEN STORY BEHIND NORTH BEACH, THE
Catechetical Guild: No date (8 pgs., paper-c)

nn 4 9 13 18 22 26

FORK IN THE ROAD
U.S. Army Recruiting Service: 1961 (16 pgs., paper-c)

nn 4 8 10 14 17 20

48 FAMOUS AMERICANS
J. C. Penney Co. (Cpr. Edwin H. Stroh): 1947 (Giveaway) (Half-size in color)

nn - Simon & Kirby-a 12 24 36 69 95 120

FOXHOLE ON YOUR LAWN
No Publisher: No date

nn-Charles Biro art 4 7 10 14 17 20

FRANKIE LUER'S SPACE ADVENTURES
Luer Packing Co.: 1955 (5x7", 36 pgs., slick-c)

nn - With Davey Rocket 4 8 12 17 21 24

FREDDY
Charlton Comics

Schiff's Shoes Presents... #1 (1959)-Giveaway 4 7 10 14 17 20

FREE COMICS TO YOU FROM... (name of shoe store) (Has clown on cover & another with a rabbit) (Like comics from Weather Bird & Edward's Shoes)
Shoe Store Giveaway: Circa 1956, 1960-61

Contains a comic bound with new cover - several combinations possible; some Harvey titles known. Contents determine price.

FREEDOM TRAIN
Street & Smith Publications: 1948 (Giveaway)

nn-Powell-c w/mailer 20 40 60 112 161 210

FREIHOFER'S COMIC BOOK
All-American Comics: 1940s (7 1/2 x 10 1/4")

2nd edition-(Scarce) Cover features All-American Comics characters Ultra-Man, Hop Harrigan, Red, White and Blue and others 60 120 180 375 575 775

FRIENDLY GHOST, CASPER, THE (Becomes Casper... #254 on)
Harvey Publications

American Dental Assoc. giveaway-Small size (1967, 16 pgs.) 3 6 9 19 25 32

FRITO-LAY GIVEAWAY
Frito-Lay: 1962 (3-1/4x7", soft-c, 16 pgs.) (Disney)

nn-Donald Duck "Plotting Picnickers" 6 12 18 40 55 70
nn-Ludwig Von Drake "Fish Stampede" 4 8 12 24 32 40
nn- Mickey Mouse & Goofy "Bicep Bungle" 4 8 12 27 36 45

FRONTIER DAYS
Robin Hood Shoe Store (Brown Shoe): 1956 (Giveaway)

1 4 7 10 14 17 20

FUNNIES ON PARADE (Premium)(See Toy World Funnies)
Eastern Color Printing Co.: 1933 (36 pgs., slick cover)
No date or publisher listed

nn-Contains Sunday page reprints of Mutt & Jeff, Joe Palooka, Hairbreadth Harry, Reg'lar Fellers, Skippy, & others (10,000 print run). This book was printed for Proctor & Gamble to be given away & came out before Famous Funnies or Century of Comics. 1160 2320 3480 6960 10,980 15,000

FUNNY PICTURE STORIES (Comic Pages V3#4 on)
Comics Magazine Co./Centaur Publications

Laundry giveaway (16-20 pgs., 1930s)-slick-c 30 60 100 155 228 300

FUNNY STUFF (Also see Captain Marvel & Flash Comics)
National Periodical Publications (Wheaties Giveaway): 1946 (6-1/2x8-1/4")

nn-(Scarce)-Dodo & the Frog, Three Mouseketeers, etc.; came taped to Wheaties box; never found in better than fine 170 340 500 – – –

FUTURE COP: L.A.P.D. (Electronic Arts video game)
DC Comics (WildStorm): 1998

nn-Ron Lim-a/Dave Johnson-c 2.25

GABBY HAYES WESTERN (Movie star)
Fawcett Publications

Quaker Oats Giveaway nn's(#1-5, 1951, 2-1/2x7") (Kagran Corp.)-...In Tracks of Guilt, ...In the Fence Post Mystery, ...In the Accidental Sherlock, ...In the Frame-Up, ...In the Double Cross Brand known 10 20 30 56 73 90
Mailing Envelope (has illo of Gabby on front) 10 20 30 56 73 90

GARY GIBSON COMICS (Donut club membership)
National Dunking Association: 1950 (Included in donut box with pin and card)

1-Western soft-c, 16 pgs.; folded into the box 5 10 14 20 24 28

GENE AUTRY COMICS
Dell Publishing Co.

...Adventure Comics And Play-Fun Book ('47)-32 pgs., 8x6-1/2"; games, comics, magic (Pillsbury premium) 40 80 120 233 342 450
Quaker Oats Giveaway(1950)-2-1/2x6-3/4"; 5 different versions; "Death Card Gang","Phantoms of the Cave", "Riddle of Laughing Mtn.", "Secret of Lost Valley", "Bond of the Broken Arrow" (came in wrapper) each... 15 30 45 85 120 155

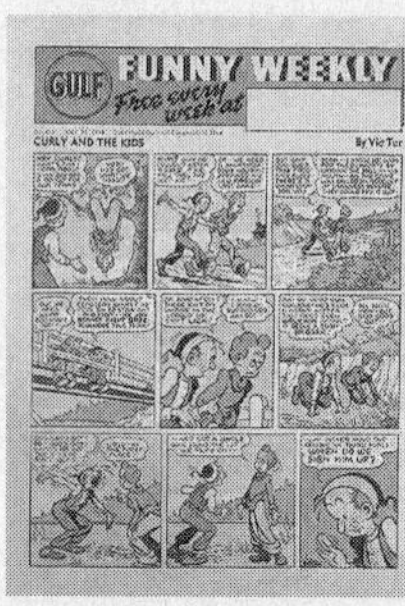

Gulf Funny Weekly #370 © Gulf Oil

History of Gas © AGA

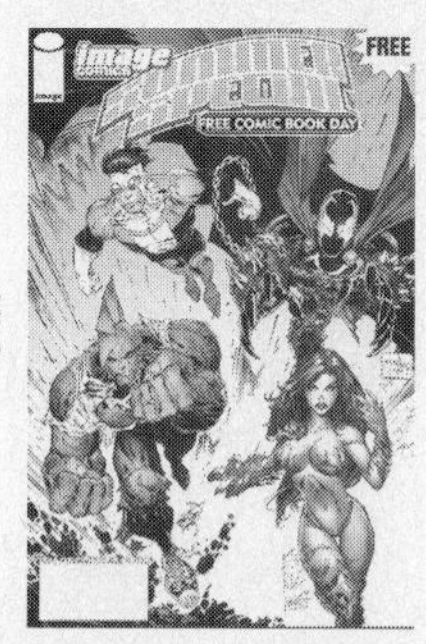

Image Comics Summer Special #1 © IM

	GD 2.0	VG 4.0	FN 6.0	VF 8.0	VF/NM 9.0	NM- 9.2
Mailing Envelope (has illo. of Gene on front)	15	30	45	85	120	155
3-D Giveaway(1953)-Pocket-size; 5 different	15	30	45	85	120	155
Mailing Envelope (no art on front)	10	20	30	60	80	100

GENE AUTRY TIM (Formerly Tim) (Becomes Tim in Space)
Tim Stores: 1950 (Half-size) (B&W Giveaway)

	GD	VG	FN	VF	VF/NM	NM-
nn-Several issues (All Scarce)	19	38	57	107	154	200

GENERAL FOODS SUPER-HEROES
DC Comics: 1979, 1980

1-4 (1979), 1-4 (1980) each... 12.00

G. I. COMICS (Also see Jeep & Overseas Comics)
Giveaways: 1945 - No. 73?, 1946 (Distributed to U. S. Armed Forces)

	GD	VG	FN	VF	VF/NM	NM-
1-73-Contains Prince Valiant by Foster, Blondie, Smilin' Jack, Mickey Finn, Terry & the Pirates, Donald Duck, Alley Oop, Moon Mullins & Capt. Easy strip reprints (at least 73 issues known to exist)	8	16	24	43	54	65

GOLDEN ARROW
Fawcett Publications

	GD	VG	FN	VF	VF/NM	NM-
...Well Known Comics (1944; 12 pgs.; 8-1/2x10-1/2"; paper-c; glued binding)- Bestmaid/ Samuel Lowe giveaway; printed in green	10	20	30	56	73	90

GOLDILOCKS & THE THREE BEARS
K. K. Publications: 1943 (Giveaway)

	GD	VG	FN	VF	VF/NM	NM-
nn	11	22	33	62	84	105

GREAT PEOPLE OF GENESIS, THE
David C. Cook Publ. Co.: No date (Religious giveaway, 64 pgs.)

	GD	VG	FN	VF	VF/NM	NM-
nn-Reprint/Sunday Pix Weekly	5	10	15	23	28	32

GREAT SACRAMENT, THE
Catechetical Guild: 1953 (Giveaway, 36 pgs.)

	GD	VG	FN	VF	VF/NM	NM-
nn	5	10	14	20	24	28

GRIT (YOU'VE GOT TO HAVE...)
GRIT Publishing Co.: 1959

	GD	VG	FN	VF	VF/NM	NM-
nn-GRIT newspaper sales recruitment comic; Schaffenberger-a. Later version has altered artwork	5	10	14	20	24	28

GULF FUNNY WEEKLY (Gulf Comic Weekly No. 1-4)(See Standard Oil Comics)
Gulf Oil Company (Giveaway): 1933 - No. 422, 5/23/41 (in full color; 4 pgs.; tabloid size to 2/3/39; 2/10/39 on, regular comic book size)(early issues undated)

	GD	VG	FN	VF	VF/NM	NM-
1	75	150	300	475	612	750
2-5	30	60	90	165	212	260
6-30	19	38	56	98	129	160
31-100	13	26	39	69	90	110
101-196	8	16	24	45	55	65
197-Wings Winfair begins(1/29/37); by Fred Meagher beginning in 1938	28	56	83	144	192	240
198-300 (Last tabloid size)	14	28	42	75	98	120
301-350 (Regular size)	8	16	24	42	51	60
351-422	6	12	18	32	39	45

GULLIVER'S TRAVELS
Macy's Department Store: 1939, small size

	GD	VG	FN	VF	VF/NM	NM-
nn-Christmas giveaway	14	28	42	79	110	140

GUN THAT WON THE WEST, THE
Winchester-Western Division & Olin Mathieson Chemical Corp.: 1956 (Giveaway, 24 pgs.)

	GD	VG	FN	VF	VF/NM	NM-
nn-Painted-c	5	10	15	24	30	35

HAPPINESS AND HEALING FOR YOU (Also see Oral Roberts'...)
Commercial Comics: 1955 (36 pgs., slick cover) (Oral Roberts Giveaway)

	GD	VG	FN	VF	VF/NM	NM-
nn	9	18	27	52	66	80

NOTE: *The success of this book prompted Oral Roberts to go into the publishing business himself to produce his own material.*

HAPPY TOOTH
DC Comics: 1996

1 3.00

HAWKMAN - THE SKY'S THE LIMIT
DC Comics: 1981 (General Foods giveaway, 8 pages, 3-1/2 x 6-3/4", oblong)

	GD	VG	FN	VF	VF/NM	NM-
nn	2	4	6	10	12	15

HAWTHORN-MELODY FARMS DAIRY COMICS
Everybody's Publishing Co.: No date (1950's) (Giveaway)

	GD	VG	FN	VF	VF/NM	NM-
nn-Cheerie Chick, Tuffy Turtle, Robin Koo Koo, Donald & Longhorn Legends	2	4	6	9	11	14

HENRY ALDRICH COMICS (TV)
Dell Publishing Co.

	GD	VG	FN	VF	VF/NM	NM-
Giveaway (16 pgs., soft-c, 1951)-Capehart radio	3	6	9	19	25	32

HERE IS SANTA CLAUS
Goldsmith Publishing Co. (Kann's in Washington, D.C.): 1930s (16 pgs., 8 in color) (stiff paper covers)

	GD	VG	FN	VF	VF/NM	NM-
nn	11	22	33	64	87	110

HERE'S HOW AMERICA'S CARTOONISTS HELP TO SELL U.S. SAVINGS BONDS
Harvey Comics: 1950? (16 pgs., giveaway, paper cover)

	GD	VG	FN	VF	VF/NM	NM-
Contains: Joe Palooka, Donald Duck, Archie, Kerry Drake, Red Ryder, Blondie & Steve Canyon	19	38	57	107	154	200

HISTORY OF GAS
American Gas Assoc.: Mar, 1947 (Giveaway, 16 pgs.)

	GD	VG	FN	VF	VF/NM	NM-
nn-Miss Flame narrates	6	12	18	29	36	42

HONEYBEE BIRDWHISTLE AND HER PET PEPI (Introducing...)
Newspaper Enterprise Assoc.: 1969 (Giveaway, 24 pgs., B&W, slick cover)

	GD	VG	FN	VF	VF/NM	NM-
nn-Contains Freckles newspaper strips with a short biography of Henry Fornhals (artist) & Fred Fox (writer) of the strip	5	10	15	36	48	60

HOPALONG CASSIDY
Fawcett Publications

	GD	VG	FN	VF	VF/NM	NM-
Grape Nuts Flakes giveaway (1950,9x6")	15	30	45	84	120	155
...& the Mad Barber (1951 Bond Bread giveaway)-7x5"; used in **SOTI**, pgs. 308,309	25	50	75	144	205	265
...Meets the Brend Brothers Bandits (1951 Bond Bread giveaway, color, paper-c, 16 pgs., 3-1/2x7")- Fawcett Publ.	12	24	36	69	95	120
...Strange Legacy (1951 Bond Bread giveaway)	12	24	36	69	95	120
White Tower Giveaway (1946, 16pgs., paper-c)	13	26	39	74	102	130

HOPELESS SAVAGES
Oni Press: May, 2002 (B&W)

Free Comic Book Day giveaway-Reprints #1 with "Free Comic Book Day" banner on-c 2.25

HOPPY THE MARVEL BUNNY (WELL KNOWN COMICS)
Fawcett Publications: 1944 (8-1/2x10-1/2", paper-c)

	GD	VG	FN	VF	VF/NM	NM-
Bestmaid/Samuel Lowe (printed in red or blue)	10	20	30	56	76	95

HOT STUFF, THE LITTLE DEVIL
Harvey Publications (Illustrated Humor):1963

	GD	VG	FN	VF	VF/NM	NM-
Shoestore Giveaway	4	8	12	27	36	45

HOW KIDS ENJOY NEW YORK
American Airlines: 1966 (Giveaway, 40 pgs., 4x9")

nn-Includes 8 color pages by Bob Kane featuring a tour of New York and his studio (a VG copy sold for $180 and a FN+ sold for $250 in 2004)

HOW STALIN HOPES WE WILL DESTROY AMERICA
Joe Lowe Co. (Pictorial Media): 1951 (Giveaway, 16 pgs.)

	GD	VG	FN	VF	VF/NM	NM-
nn	50	100	150	280	440	600

HURRICANE KIDS, THE (Also See Magic Morro, The Owl, Popular Comics #45)
R.S. Callender: 1941 (Giveaway, 7-1/2x5-1/4", soft-c)

	GD	VG	FN	VF	VF/NM	NM-
nn-Will Ely-a.	10	20	30	58	77	95

IF THE DEVIL WOULD TALK
Roman Catholic Catechetical Guild/Impact Publ.: 1950; 1958 (32 pgs.; paper cover; in full color)

	GD	VG	FN	VF	VF/NM	NM-
nn-(Scarce)-About secularism (20-30 copies known to exist); very low distribution	77	154	231	481	741	1000
1958 Edition-(Impact Publ.); art & script changed to meet church criticism of earlier edition; 80 plus copies known to exist	25	50	75	141	203	265
Black & White version of nn edition; small size; only 4 known copies exist	31	62	93	178	259	340

NOTE: *The original edition of this book was printed and killed by the Guild's board of directors. It is believed that a very limited number of copies were distributed. The 1958 version was a complete bomb with very limited, if any, circulation. In 1979, 11 original, 4 1958 reprints, and 4 B&W's surfaced from the Guild's old files in St. Paul, Minnesota.*

IMAGE COMICS SUMMER SPECIAL
Image Comics: July, 2004 (Free Comic Book Day giveaway)

1-New short stories of Spawn, Invincible, Savage Dragon and Witchblade 2.25

IN LOVE WITH JESUS
Catechetical Educational Society: 1952 (Giveaway, 36 pgs.)

	GD	VG	FN	VF	VF/NM	NM-
nn	6	12	18	27	33	38

INTERSTATE THEATRES' FUN CLUB COMICS
Interstate Theatres: Mid 1940's (10¢ on cover) (B&W cover) (Premium)

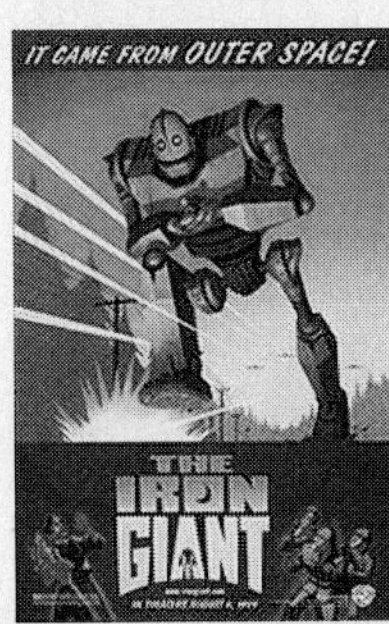

The Iron Giant #1 © WB

Jackie Joyner-Kersee in High Hurdles © DC

King James "The King of Basketball" © DC

Cover features MLJ characters looking at a copy of Top-Notch Comics, but contains an early Detective Comic on inside; many combinations possible 10 20 30 56 73 90

IN THE GOOD HANDS OF THE ROCKEFELLER TEAM
Country Art Studios: No date (paper cover, 8 pgs.)
nn-Joe Simon-a 8 16 24 43 54 65

IRON GIANT
DC Comics: 1999 (4 pages, theater giveaway)
1-Previews movie 3.00

IRON HORSE GOES TO WAR, THE
Association of American Railroads: 1960 (Giveaway, 16 pgs.)
nn-Civil War & railroads 3 6 9 16 20 25

IS THIS TOMORROW?
Catechetical Guild: 1947 (One Shot) (3 editions) (52 pgs.)
1-Theme of communists taking over the USA; (no price on cover) Used in **POP**, pg. 102 17 34 51 95 135 175
1-(10¢ on cover) 22 44 66 124 177 230
1-Has blank circle with no price on cover 23 46 69 130 188 245
Black & White advance copy titled "Confidential" (52 pgs.)-Contains script and art edited out of the color edition, including one page of extreme violence showing mob nailing a Cardinal to a door; (only two known copies) 65 130 195 406 628 850
NOTE: *The original color version first sold for 10 cents. Since sales were good, it was later printed as a giveaway. Approximately four million in total were printed. The two black and white copies listed plus two other versions as well as a full color untrimmed version surfaced in 1979 from the Guild's old files in St. Paul, Minnesota.*

IT'S FUN TO STAY ALIVE
National Automobile Dealers Association: 1948 (Giveaway, 16 pgs., heavy stock paper)
Featuring: Bugs Bunny, The Berrys, Dixie Dugan, Elmer, Henry, Tim Tyler, Bruce Gentry, Abbie & Slats, Joe Jinks, The Toodles, & Cokey; all art copyright 1946-48 drawn especially for this book 17 34 51 95 135 175

JACK & JILL VISIT TOYTOWN WITH ELMER THE ELF
Butler Brothers (Toytown Stores): 1949 (Giveaway, 16 pgs., paper cover)
nn 5 10 15 22 26 30

JACK ARMSTRONG (Radio)(See True Comics)
Parents' Institute: 1949
12-Premium version(distr. in Chicago only); Free printed on upper right-c; no price (Rare) 18 36 54 104 150 195

JACKIE JOYNER KERSEE IN HIGH HURDLES (Kellogg's Tony's Sports Comics)
DC Comics: 1992 (Sports Illustrated)
nn 3.00

JACKPOT OF FUN COMIC BOOK
DCA Food Ind.: 1957, giveaway
nn-Features Howdy Doody 11 22 33 64 87 110

JEEP COMICS
R. B. Leffingwell & Co.: 1945 - 1946
1-46 (Giveaways)-Strip reprints in all; Tarzan, Flash Gordon, Blondie, The Nebbs, Little Iodine, Red Ryder, Don Winslow, The Phantom, Johnny Hazard, Katzenjammer Kids; distr. to U.S. Armed Forces from 1945-1946 6 12 18 31 38 45

JINGLE BELLS CHRISTMAS BOOK
Montgomery Ward (Giveaway): 1971 (20 pgs., B&W inside, slick-c)
nn 6.00

JOAN OF ARC
Catechetical Guild (Topix) (Giveaway): No date (28 pgs.)
nn 10 20 30 56 73 90
NOTE: *Unpublished version exists which came from the Guild's files.*

JOE PALOOKA (2nd Series)
Harvey Publications
...Body Building Instruction Book (1958 B&M Sports Toy giveaway, 16pgs., 5-1/4x7")-Origin 9 18 27 49 62 75
...Fights His Way Back (1945 Giveaway, 24 pgs.) Family Comics 16 32 48 89 127 165
...in Hi There! (1949 Red Cross giveaway, 12 pgs., 4-3/4x6") 9 18 27 52 66 80
...in It's All in the Family (1945 Red Cross giveaway, 16 pgs., regular size) 10 20 30 58 77 95

JOE THE GENIE OF STEEL
U.S. Steel Corp., Pittsburgh, PA: 1950 (16 pgs.)
nn 5 10 15 22 26 30

JOHNNY JINGLE'S LUCKY DAY
American Dairy Assoc.: 1956 (16 pgs.; 7-1/4x5-1/8") (Giveaway) (Disney)
nn 5 10 15 24 30 35

JO-JOY (The Adventures of...)
W. T. Grant Dept. Stores: 1945 - 1953 (Christmas gift comic, 16 pgs., 7-1/16x10-1/4")
1945-53 issues 6 12 18 29 36 42

JOLLY CHRISTMAS BOOK (See Christmas Journey Through Space)
Promotional Publ. Co.: 1951; 1954; 1955 (36 pgs.; 24 pgs.)
1951-(Woolworth giveaway)-slightly oversized; no slick cover; Marv Levy-c/a 7 14 21 37 46 55
1954-(Hot Shoppes giveaway)-regular size-reprints 1951 issue; slick cover added; 24 pgs.; no ads 6 12 18 31 38 45
1955-(J. M. McDonald Co. giveaway)-reg. size 6 12 18 28 34 40

JOURNEY OF DISCOVERY WITH MARK STEEL (See Mark Steel)

JUMPING JACKS PRESENTS THE WHIZ KIDS
Jumping Jacks Stores giveaway: 1978 (In 3-D) with glasses (4 pgs.)
nn 6.00

JUNGLE BOOK FUN BOOK, THE (Disney)
Baskin Robbins: 1978
nn-Ice Cream giveaway 2 4 6 10 12 15

JUSTICE LEAGUE ADVENTURES (Based on Cartoon Network series)
DC Comics: May, 2002
Free Comic Book Day giveaway-Reprints #1 with "Free Comic Book Day" banner on-c 2.25

JUSTICE LEAGUE OF AMERICA
DC Comics: 1999 (included in Justice League of America Monopoly game)
nn - Reprints 1st app. in Brave and the Bold #28 2.50

KASCO KOMICS
Kasko Grainfeed (Giveaway): 1945; No. 2, 1949 (Regular size, paper-c)
1(1945)-Similar to Katy Keene; Bill Woggon-a; 28 pgs.; 6-7/8x9-7/8" 17 34 51 98 139 180
2(1949)-Woggon-c/a 13 26 39 76 106 135

KATY AND KEN VISIT SANTA WITH MISTER WISH
S. S. Kresge Co. : 1948 (Giveaway, 16 pgs., paper-c)
nn 6 12 18 29 36 42

KELLOGG'S CINNAMON MINI-BUNS SUPER-HEROES
DC Comics: 1993 (4 1/4" x 2 3/4")
4 editions: Flash, Justice League America, Superman, Wonder Woman and the Star Riders each..... 4.00

KERRY DRAKE DETECTIVE CASES
Publisher's Syndicate
...in the Case of the Sleeping City-(1951)-16 pg. giveaway for armed forces; paper cover 6 12 18 29 36 42

KEY COMICS
Key Clothing Co./Peterson Clothing: 1951 - 1956 (32 pgs.) (Giveaway)
Contains a comic from different publishers bound with new cover. Cover changed each year. Many combinations possible. Distributed in Nebraska, Iowa, & Kansas. Contents would determine price, 40-60 percent of original.

KING JAMES "THE KING OF BASKETBALL"
DC Comics: 2004 (Promo comic for LeBron James and Powerade Flava23 sports drink)
nn - Ten different covers by various artists; 4 covers for retail, 4 for mail-in, 1 for military commissaries, and 1 general market; Damion Scott-a/Gary Phillips-s 2.50

KIRBY'S SHOES COMICS
Kirby's Shoes: 1959 (8 pgs., soft-c)
nn-Features Kirby the Golden Bear 3 5 7 10 12 14

KITE FUN BOOK
Pacific, Gas & Electric/Sou. California Edison/Florida Power & Light/ Missouri Public Service Co.: 1952 - 1998 (16 pgs, 5x7-1/4", soft-c)
1952-Having Fun With Kites (P.G.&E.) 11 22 33 64 87 110
1953-Pinocchio Learns About Kites (Disney) 47 94 141 260 405 550
1954-Donald Duck Tells About Kites-Fla. Power, S.C.E. & version with label issues -Barks pencils-8 pgs.; inks-7 pgs. (Rare) 375 750 1125 1950 2775 3600
1954-Donald Duck Tells About Kites-P.G.&E. issue -7th page redrawn changing middle 3 panels to show P.G.&E. in story line; (All Barks-a) Scarce 235 470 705 1400 2150 2900
1955-Brer Rabbit in "A Kite Tail" (Disney) 32 64 96 175 253 330
1956-Woody Woodpecker (Lantz) 14 28 42 81 113 145
1957-Ruff and Reddy (exist?)

Kite Fun Book 1960 - Porky Pig © WB

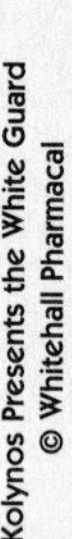
Kolynos Presents the White Guard © Whitehall Pharmacal

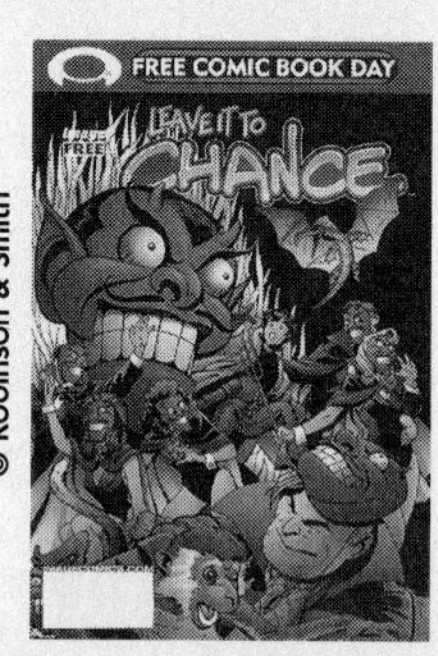

Leave It To Chance FCBD Edition © Robinson & Smith

	GD 2.0	VG 4.0	FN 6.0	VF 8.0	VF/NM 9.0	NM- 9.2
1958-Tom And Jerry (M.G.M.)	10	20	30	56	73	90
1959-Bugs Bunny (Warner Bros.)	6	12	18	38	52	65
1960-Porky Pig (Warner Bros.)	6	12	18	40	55	70
1960-Bugs Bunny (Warner Bros.)	6	12	18	40	55	70
1961-Huckleberry Hound (Hanna-Barbera)	7	14	21	48	63	80
1962-Yogi Bear (Hanna-Barbera)	5	10	15	36	48	60
1963-Rocky and Bullwinkle (TV)(Jay Ward)	10	20	30	73	107	140
1963-Top Cat (TV)(Hanna-Barbera)	6	12	18	40	55	70
1964-Magilla Gorilla (TV)(Hanna-Barbera)	6	12	18	38	52	65
1965-Jinks, Pixie and Dixie (TV)(Hanna-Barbera)	4	8	12	27	36	45
1965-Tweety and Sylvester (Warner); S.C.E. version with Reddy Kilowatt app.	3	6	9	18	23	28
1966-Secret Squirrel (Hanna-Barbera); S.C.E. version with Reddy Kilowatt app.	8	16	24	55	78	100
1967-Beep! Beep! The Road Runner (TV)(Warner)	3	6	9	19	25	32
1968-Bugs Bunny (Warner Bros.)	3	7	10	21	28	35
1969-Dastardly and Muttley (TV)(Hanna-Barbera)	6	12	18	38	52	65
1970-Rocky and Bullwinkle (TV)(Jay Ward)	8	16	24	53	74	95
1971-Beep! Beep! The Road Runner (TV)(Warner)	3	6	9	18	24	30
1972-The Pink Panther (TV)	3	6	9	16	21	26
1973-Lassie (TV)	4	8	12	27	36	45
1974-Underdog (TV)	3	6	9	19	25	32
1975-Ben Franklin	2	4	6	11	14	18
1976-The Brady Bunch (TV)	4	8	12	29	40	50
1977-Ben Franklin (exist?)	2	4	6	11	14	18
1977-Popeye	3	6	9	18	24	30
1978-Happy Days (TV)	3	7	10	21	28	35
1979-Eight is Enough (TV)	3	6	9	18	24	30
1980-The Waltons (TV, released in 1981)	3	6	9	18	24	30
1982-Tweety and Sylvester	2	4	6	14	18	22
1984-Smokey Bear	2	4	6	10	13	16
1986-Road Runner	2	4	6	8	10	13
1997-Thomas Edison						4.00
1998-Edison Field (Anaheim Stadium)						3.00

KNOW YOUR MASS
Catechetical Guild: No. 303, 1958 (35¢, 100 Pg. Giant) (Square binding)

	GD	VG	FN	VF	VF/NM	NM-
303-In color	7	14	21	35	43	50

KOLYNOS PRESENTS THE WHITE GUARD
Whitehall Pharmacal Co.: 1949 (paper cover, 8 pgs.)

	GD	VG	FN	VF	VF/NM	NM-
nn	6	12	18	27	33	38

K. O. PUNCH, THE (Also see Lucky Fights It Through)
E. C. Comics: 1948 (Educational giveaway)

	GD	VG	FN	VF	VF/NM	NM-
nn-Feldstein-splash; Kamen-a	85	170	255	531	816	1100

KOREA MY HOME (Also see Yalta to Korea)
Johnstone and Cushing: nd (1950s)

	GD	VG	FN	VF	VF/NM	NM-
nn-Anti-communist; Korean War	22	44	66	127	184	240

KRIM-KO KOMICS
Krim-ko Chocolate Drink: 5/18/35 - No. 6, 6/22/35; 1936 - 1939 (weekly)

	GD	VG	FN	VF	VF/NM	NM-
1-(16 pgs., soft-c, Dairy giveaways)-Tom, Mary & Sparky Advs. by Russell Keaton, Jim Hawkins by Dick Moores, Mystery Island! by Rick Yager begin	14	28	42	79	110	140
2-6 (6/22/35)	10	20	30	58	77	95
Lola, Secret Agent; 184 issues, 4 pg. giveaways - all original stories each....	7	14	21	37	46	55

LABOR IS A PARTNER
Catechetical Guild Educational Society: 1949 (32 pgs., paper-c)

	GD	VG	FN	VF	VF/NM	NM-
nn-Anti-communism	19	38	57	107	154	200
Confidential Preview-(8-1/2x11", B&W, saddle stitched)-only one known copy; text varies from color version, advertises next book on secularism (If the Devil Would Talk)	22	44	66	124	177	230

LADY AND THE TRAMP IN "BUTTER LATE THAN NEVER"
American Dairy Assoc. (Premium): 1955 (16 pgs., 5x7-1/4", soft-c) (Disney)

	GD	VG	FN	VF	VF/NM	NM-
nn	10	20	30	56	73	90

LASSIE (TV)
Dell Publ. Co

	GD	VG	FN	VF	VF/NM	NM-
The Adventures of... nn-(Red Heart Dog Food giveaway, 1949)-16 pgs, soft-c; 1st app. Lassie in comics	34	68	102	193	279	365

LEAVE IT TO CHANCE
Image Comics: 2003

	GD	VG	FN	VF	VF/NM	NM-
Free Comic Book Day Edition - James Robinson-s/Paul Smith-a						2.25

LIFE OF THE BLESSED VIRGIN
Catechetical Guild (Giveaway): 1950 (68pgs.) (square binding)

	GD	VG	FN	VF	VF/NM	NM-
nn-Contains "The Woman of the Promise" & "Mother of Us All" rebound	6	12	18	31	38	45

LIGHTNING RACERS
DC Comics: 1989

	GD	VG	FN	VF	VF/NM	NM-
1						4.50

LI'L ABNER (Al Capp's) (Also see Natural Disasters!)
Harvey Publ./Toby Press

	GD	VG	FN	VF	VF/NM	NM-
...& the Creatures from Drop-Outer Space-nn (Job Corps giveaway; 36 pgs., in color) (entire book by Frank Frazetta)	25	50	75	144	207	270
...Joins the Navy (1950) (Toby Press Premium)	11	22	33	64	87	110
Al Capp by Li'l Abner (Circa 1946, nd, giveaway) Al Capp bio and his life as an amputee	11	22	33	64	87	110

LITTLE ALONZO
Macy's Dept. Store: 1938 (B&W, 5-1/2x8-1/2")(Christmas giveaway)

	GD	VG	FN	VF	VF/NM	NM-
nn-By Ferdinand the Bull's Munro Leaf	9	18	27	52	66	80

LITTLE DOT
Harvey Publications

	GD	VG	FN	VF	VF/NM	NM-
Shoe store giveaway 2	5	10	14	31	42	52

LITTLE FIR TREE, THE
W. T. Grant Co. : nd (1942) (8-1/2x11") (12 pgs. with cover, color & B&W, heavy paper) (Christmas giveaway)

nn-Story by Hans Christian Anderson; 8 pg. Kelly-r/Santa Claus Funnies (not signed); X-Mas-c
(One copy in Mint sold for $1750.00 in 1986, another copy in VF sold for $1000.00 in 1991 and one copy in VG/FN sold for $1500 in 2002)

LITTLE KLINKER
Little Klinker Ventures: Nov, 1960 (20 pgs.) (slick cover) (Montgomery Ward Giveaway)

	GD	VG	FN	VF	VF/NM	NM-
nn	2	4	6	10	13	16

LITTLE MISS SUNBEAM COMICS
Magazine Enterprises/Quality Bakers of America

	GD	VG	FN	VF	VF/NM	NM-
Bread Giveaway 1-4(Quality Bakers, 1949-50)-14 pgs. each	6	12	18	31	38	45
Bread Giveaway (1957,61; 16pgs, reg. size)	5	10	15	24	30	35

LITTLE ORPHAN ANNIE
David McKay Publ./Dell Publishing Co.

	GD	VG	FN	VF	VF/NM	NM-
Junior Commandos Giveaway (same-c as 4-Color #18, K.K. Publ.)(Big Shoe Store); same back cover as '47 Popped Wheat giveaway; 16 pgs; flag-c; r/strips 9/7/42-10/10/42	31	62	93	178	259	340
Popped Wheat Giveaway ('47)-16 pgs. full color; reprints strips from 5/3/40 to 6/20/40	4	8	12	18	22	25
Quaker Sparkies Giveaway (1940)	20	40	60	112	161	210
Quaker Sparkies Giveaway (1941, full color, 20 pgs.); "LOA and the Rescue"; r/strips 4/13/39-6/21/39 & 7/6/39-7/17/39. "LOA and the Kidnappers"; r/strips 11/28/38-1/28/39	18	36	54	101	143	185
Quaker Sparkies Giveaway (1942, full color, 20 pgs.); "LOA and Mr. Gudge"; r/strips 2/13/38-3/21/38 & 4/18/37-5/30/37. "LOA and the Great Am"	17	34	51	95	135	175

LITTLE TREE THAT WASN'T WANTED, THE
W. T. Grant Co. (Giveaway): 1960, (Color, 28 pgs.)

	GD	VG	FN	VF	VF/NM	NM-
nn-Christmas story, puzzles and games	3	6	9	21	28	35

LOADED (Also see Re-Loaded)
DC Comics: 1995 (Interplay Productions)

	GD	VG	FN	VF	VF/NM	NM-
1-Garth Ennis-s; promotes video game						4.00

LONE RANGER, THE
Dell Publishing Co.

	GD	VG	FN	VF	VF/NM	NM-
Cheerios Giveaways (1954, 16 pgs., 2-1/2x7", soft-c) #1- "The Lone Ranger, His Mask & How He Met Tonto". #2- "The Lone Ranger & the Story of Silver" each....	20	40	60	92	131	170
Doll Giveaways (Gabriel Ind.)(1973, 3-1/4x5")- "The Story of The Lone Ranger," "The Carson City Bank Robbery" & "The Apache Buffalo Hunt"	2	4	6	11	16	20
How the Lone Ranger Captured Silver Book(1936)-Silvercup Bread giveaway	90	180	270	400	600	800
...In Milk for Big Mike (1955, Dairy Association giveaway), soft-c; 5x7-1/4", 16 pgs.	16	32	48	92	131	170
Legend of The Lone Ranger (1969, 16 pgs., giveaway)-Origin The Lone Ranger	4	8	12	27	36	45

Lone Ranger Comics Book 1 © Lone Ranger Inc.

March of Comics #4 © WDC

March of Comics #47 © Roy Rogers

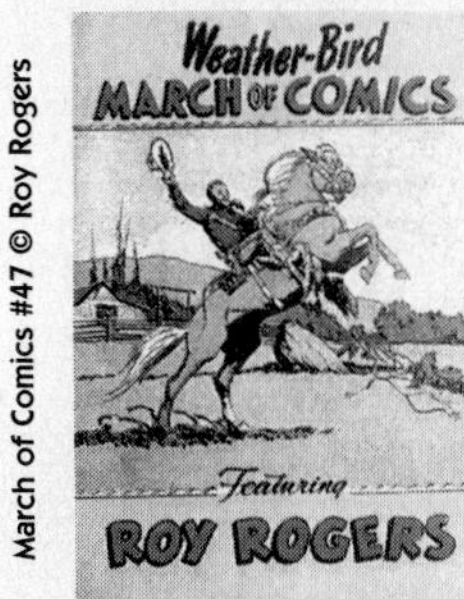

	GD 2.0	VG 4.0	FN 6.0	VF 8.0	VF/NM 9.0	NM- 9.2

Merita Bread giveaway (1954, 16 pgs., 5x7-1/4")- "How to Be a Lone Ranger Health & Safety Scout" 20 40 60 112 161 210

LONE RANGER COMICS, THE
Lone Ranger, Inc. : Book 1, 1939(inside) (shows 1938 on-c) (52 pgs. in color; regular size) (Ice cream mail order)

Book 1-(Scarce)-The first western comic devoted to a single character; not by Vallely 923 1961 3000 6700 - -
2nd version w/large full color promo poster pasted over centerfold & a smaller poster pasted over back cover; includes new additional premiums not originally offered (Rare) 1040 2120 3200 7200 - -

LOONEY TUNES
DC Comics: 1991, 1998

Claritan promotional issue (1998) 2.50
Colgate mini-comic (1998) 2.50
Tyson's 1-10 (1991) 4.00

LOVE FIGHTS
Oni Press: July, 2004 (Free Comic Book Day giveaway)

1-Flip book with r/Love Fights #1 and preview of Everest Facing the Goddess 2.25

LUCKY FIGHTS IT THROUGH (Also see The K. O. Punch)
Educational Comics: 1949 (Giveaway, 16 pgs. in color, paper-c)

nn-(Very Rare)-1st Kurtzman work for E. C.; V.D. prevention 120 240 360 650 975 1300
nn-Reprint in color (1977) 6.00

NOTE: *Subtitled "The Story of That Ignorant, Ignorant Cowboy". Prepared for Communications Materials Center, Columbia University.*

LUDWIG VON DRAKE (See Frito-Lay Giveaway)

MACO TOYS COMIC
Maco Toys/Charlton Comics: 1959 (Giveaway, 36 pgs.)

1-All military stories featuring Maco Toys 2 4 6 12 16 20

MAD MAGAZINE
DC Comics: 1997, 1999

Special Edition (1997, Tang giveaway) 2.50
Stocking Stuffer (1999) 2.50

MAGAZINELAND
DC Comics: 1977

nn-Kubert-c/a 3 6 9 16 20 24

MAGIC MORRO (Also see Super Comics #21, The Owl, & The Hurricane Kids)
K. K. Publications: 1941 (7-1/2 x 5-1/4", giveaway, soft-c)

nn-Ken Ernst-a. 13 26 39 74 102 130

MAGIC OF CHRISTMAS AT NEWBERRYS, THE
E. S. London: 1967 (Giveaway) (B&W, slick-c, 20 pgs.)

nn 1 3 4 6 8 10

MAJOR INAPAK THE SPACE ACE
Magazine Enterprises (Inapac Foods): 1951 (20 pgs.) (Giveaway)

1-Bob Powell-c/a 6.00

NOTE: *Many warehouse copies surfaced in 1973.*

MAMMY YOKUM & THE GREAT DOGPATCH MYSTERY
Toby Press: 1951 (Giveaway)

nn-Li'l Abner 17 34 51 95 135 175
nn-Reprint (1956) 5 10 15 22 26 30

MAN NAMED STEVENSON, A
Democratic National Committee: 1952 (20 pgs., 5 1/4 x 7")

nn 9 18 27 47 60 72

MAN OF PEACE, POPE PIUS XII
Catechetical Guild: 1950 (See Pope Pius XII... & To V2#8)

nn-All Powell-a 6 12 18 31 38 45

MAN OF STEEL BEST WESTERN
DC Comics: 1997

nn-Best Western hotels 4.00

MAN WHO WOULDN'T QUIT, THE
Harvey Publications Inc.: 1952 (16 pgs., paper cover)

nn-The value of voting 4 8 12 18 22 25

MARCH OF COMICS (Boys' and Girls'...#3-353)
K. K. Publications/Western Publishing Co.: 1946 - No. 488, April, 1982 (#1-4 are not numbered) (K.K. Giveaway) (Founded by Sig Feuchtwanger)

Early issues were full size, 32 pages, and were printed with and without an extra cover of slick stock, just for the advertiser. The binding was stapled if the slick cover was added; otherwise, the pages were glued together at the spine. Most 1948 - 1951 issues were full size,24 pages, pulp covers. Starting in 1952 they were half-size (with a few exceptions) and 32 pages with slick covers.1959 and later issues had only 16 pages plus covers. 1952 -1959 issues read oblong; 1960 and later issues read upright. All have new stories except where noted.

nn (#1, 1946)-Goldilocks; Kelly back-c (16 pgs., stapled) 31 62 93 175 253 330
nn (#2, 1946)-How Santa Got His Red Suit; Kelly-a (11 pgs., r/4-Color #61 from 1944) (16pgs., stapled) 29 58 87 167 241 315
nn (#3, 1947)-Our Gang (Walt Kelly) 40 80 120 230 335 440
nn (#4)-Donald Duck by Carl Barks, "Maharajah Donald", 28 pgs.; Kelly-c? (Disney) 800 1600 2400 4400 6100 7800
5-Andy Panda (Walter Lantz) 18 36 54 100 143 185
6-Popular Fairy Tales; Kelly-c; Noonan-a(2) 21 42 63 118 169 220
7-Oswald the Rabbit 19 38 57 107 154 200
8-Mickey Mouse, 32 pgs. (Disney) 55 110 165 300 438 575
9(nn)-The Story of the Gloomy Bunny 11 22 33 64 87 110
10-Out of Santa's Bag 10 20 30 60 80 100
11-Fun With Santa Claus 10 20 30 56 73 90
12-Santa's Toys 10 20 30 56 73 90
13-Santa's Surprise 10 20 30 56 73 90
14-Santa's Candy Kitchen 10 20 30 56 73 90
15-Hip-It-Ty Hop & the Big Bass Viol 9 18 27 52 66 80
16-Woody Woodpecker (1947)(Walter Lantz) 13 26 39 76 106 135
17-Roy Rogers (1948) 26 52 78 147 211 275
18-Popular Fairy Tales 11 22 33 64 87 110
19-Uncle Wiggily 10 20 30 58 77 95
20-Donald Duck by Carl Barks, "Darkest Africa", 22 pgs.; Kelly-c (Disney) 440 880 1320 2500 3550 4600
21-Tom and Jerry 11 22 33 66 91 115
22-Andy Panda (Lantz) 10 20 30 60 80 100
23-Raggedy Ann & Andy; Kerr-a 14 28 42 79 110 140
24-Felix the Cat, 1932 daily strip reprints by Otto Messmer 23 46 69 130 188 245
25-Gene Autry 23 46 69 130 188 245
26-Our Gang; Walt Kelly 21 43 63 118 169 220
27-Mickey Mouse; r/in M. M. #240 (Disney) 37 74 111 209 305 400
28-Gene Autry 22 44 66 123 177 230
29-Easter Bonnet Shop 7 14 21 37 46 55
30-Here Comes Santa 7 14 21 35 43 50
31-Santa's Busy Corner 7 14 21 35 43 50
32-No book produced
33-A Christmas Carol (12/48) 7 14 21 37 46 55
34-Woody Woodpecker 11 22 33 66 91 115
35-Roy Rogers (1948) 25 50 75 144 207 270
36-Felix the Cat(1949); by Messmer; '34 strip-r 19 38 57 107 154 200
37-Popeye 15 30 45 83 117 150
38-Oswald the Rabbit 9 18 27 52 66 80
39-Gene Autry 22 44 66 123 177 230
40-Andy and Woody 9 18 27 52 66 80
41-Donald Duck by Carl Barks, "Race to the South Seas", 22 pgs.; Kelly-c 325 650 975 1950 3075 4200
42-Porky Pig 9 18 27 54 70 85
43-Henry 9 18 27 51 62 75
44-Bugs Bunny 10 20 30 58 77 95
45-Mickey Mouse (Disney) 30 60 90 170 245 320
46-Tom and Jerry 10 20 30 58 77 95
47-Roy Rogers 21 42 63 121 173 225
48-Greetings from Santa 6 12 18 27 33 38
49-Santa Is Here 6 12 18 27 33 38
50-Santa Claus' Workshop (1949) 6 12 18 27 33 38
51-Felix the Cat (1950) by Messmer 17 34 51 95 135 175
52-Popeye 12 24 36 71 98 125
53-Oswald the Rabbit 9 18 27 51 62 75
54-Gene Autry 19 38 57 107 154 200
55-Andy and Woody 8 16 24 46 58 70
56-Donald Duck; not by Barks; Barks art on back-c (Disney) 27 54 81 154 222 290
57-Porky Pig 9 18 27 51 62 75
58-Henry 7 14 21 37 46 55
59-Bugs Bunny 9 18 27 54 70 85
60-Mickey Mouse (Disney) 27 54 81 152 219 285
61-Tom and Jerry 9 18 27 51 62 75
62-Roy Rogers 21 42 63 118 169 220
63-Welcome Santa (1/2-size, oblong) 6 12 18 27 33 38
64(nn)-Santa's Helpers (1/2-size, oblong) 6 12 18 27 33 38
65(nn)-Jingle Bells (1950) (1/2-size, oblong) 6 12 18 27 33 38

March of Comics #72 © KING

March of Comics #171 © Walter Lantz

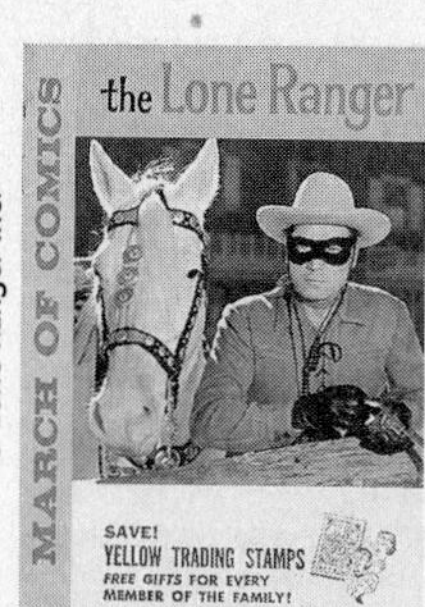

March of Comics #208 © Lone Ranger Inc.

	GD 2.0	VG 4.0	FN 6.0	VF 8.0	VF/NM 9.0	NM- 9.2
66-Popeye (1951)	11	22	33	64	87	110
67-Oswald the Rabbit	8	16	24	46	58	70
68-Roy Rogers	20	40	60	112	161	210
69-Donald Duck; Barks-a on back-c (Disney)	25	50	75	141	203	265
70-Tom and Jerry	8	16	24	43	54	65
71-Porky Pig	8	16	24	46	58	70
72-Krazy Kat	9	18	27	54	70	85
73-Roy Rogers	18	36	54	101	143	185
74-Mickey Mouse (1951)(Disney)	22	44	66	123	177	230
75-Bugs Bunny	8	16	24	46	58	70
76-Andy and Woody	8	16	24	43	54	65
77-Roy Rogers	17	34	51	95	135	175
78-Gene Autry (1951); last regular size issue	16	32	48	89	127	165

Note: All pre #79 issues came with or without a slick protective wrap-around cover over the regular cover which advertised Poll Parrot Shoes, Sears, etc. This outer cover protects the inside pages making them in nicer condition.
Issues with the outer cover are worth 15-25% more

	GD 2.0	VG 4.0	FN 6.0	VF 8.0	VF/NM 9.0	NM- 9.2
79-Andy Panda (1952, 5x7" size)	6	12	18	31	38	45
80-Popeye	10	20	30	58	77	95
81-Oswald the Rabbit	6	12	18	27	33	38
82-Tarzan; Lex Barker photo-c	17	34	51	95	135	175
83-Bugs Bunny	7	14	21	35	43	50
84-Henry	6	12	18	27	33	38
85-Woody Woodpecker	6	12	18	27	33	38
86-Roy Rogers	13	26	39	76	106	135
87-Krazy Kat	8	16	24	43	54	65
88-Tom and Jerry	6	12	18	29	36	42
89-Porky Pig	6	12	18	27	33	38
90-Gene Autry	12	24	36	69	95	120
91-Roy Rogers & Santa	13	26	39	74	102	130
92-Christmas with Santa	5	10	15	23	28	32
93-Woody Woodpecker (1953)	5	10	15	22	26	30
94-Indian Chief	9	18	27	54	70	85
95-Oswald the Rabbit	5	10	15	22	26	30
96-Popeye	9	18	27	54	70	85
97-Bugs Bunny	6	12	18	31	38	45
98-Tarzan; Lex Barker photo-c	16	32	48	92	131	170
99-Porky Pig	5	10	15	22	26	30
100-Roy Rogers	11	22	33	62	84	105
101-Henry	5	10	14	20	24	28
102-Tom Corbett (TV)('53, early app.); painted-c	13	26	39	76	106	135
103-Tom and Jerry	5	10	14	22	26	30
104-Gene Autry	10	20	30	60	80	100
105-Roy Rogers	10	20	30	60	80	100
106-Santa's Helpers	5	10	15	23	28	32
107-Santa's Christmas Book - not published						
108-Fun with Santa (1953)	5	10	15	23	28	32
109-Woody Woodpecker (1954)	5	10	15	23	28	32
110-Indian Chief	6	12	18	29	36	42
111-Oswald the Rabbit	5	10	14	20	24	28
112-Henry	4	8	12	17	21	24
113-Porky Pig	5	10	14	20	24	28
114-Tarzan; Russ Manning-a	16	32	48	92	131	170
115-Bugs Bunny	5	10	15	24	30	35
116-Roy Rogers	10	20	30	60	80	100
117-Popeye	9	18	27	54	70	85
118-Flash Gordon; painted-c	11	22	33	66	91	115
119-Tom and Jerry	5	10	14	20	24	28
120-Gene Autry	10	20	30	60	80	100
121-Roy Rogers	10	20	30	60	80	100
122-Santa's Surprise (1954)	5	10	14	20	24	28
123-Santa's Christmas Book	5	10	14	20	24	28
124-Woody Woodpecker (1955)	4	8	12	17	21	24
125-Tarzan; Lex Barker photo-c	15	30	45	86	123	160
126-Oswald the Rabbit	4	8	12	17	21	24
127-Indian Chief	6	12	18	33	41	48
128-Tom and Jerry	4	8	12	17	21	24
129-Henry	4	8	11	16	19	22
130-Porky Pig	4	8	12	17	21	24
131-Roy Rogers	10	20	30	60	80	100
132-Bugs Bunny	5	10	15	22	26	30
133-Flash Gordon; painted-c	10	20	30	60	80	100
134-Popeye	8	16	24	40	50	60
135-Gene Autry	10	20	30	56	73	90
136-Roy Rogers	10	20	30	56	73	90
137-Gifts from Santa	4	7	9	14	16	18

	GD 2.0	VG 4.0	FN 6.0	VF 8.0	VF/NM 9.0	NM- 9.2
138-Fun at Christmas (1955)	4	7	9	14	16	18
139-Woody Woodpecker (1956)	4	8	12	17	21	24
140-Indian Chief	6	12	18	33	41	48
141-Oswald the Rabbit	4	8	12	17	21	24
142-Flash Gordon	10	20	30	60	80	100
143-Porky Pig	4	8	12	17	21	24
144-Tarzan; Russ Manning-a; painted-c	14	28	42	81	113	145
145-Tom and Jerry	4	8	12	17	21	24
146-Roy Rogers; photo-c	10	20	30	56	73	90
147-Henry	4	7	10	14	17	20
148-Popeye	8	16	24	40	50	60
149-Bugs Bunny	5	10	14	20	24	28
150-Gene Autry	10	20	30	56	73	90
151-Roy Rogers	10	20	30	56	73	90
152-The Night Before Christmas	4	7	10	14	17	20
153-Merry Christmas (1956)	4	8	12	17	21	24
154-Tom and Jerry (1957)	4	8	12	17	21	24
155-Tarzan; photo-c	14	28	42	79	110	140
156-Oswald the Rabbit	4	8	12	17	21	24
157-Popeye	6	12	18	33	41	48
158-Woody Woodpecker	4	8	12	17	21	24
159-Indian Chief	6	12	18	33	41	48
160-Bugs Bunny	5	10	14	20	24	28
161-Roy Rogers	9	18	27	52	66	80
162-Henry	4	7	9	14	17	20
163-Rin Tin Tin (TV)	8	16	24	40	50	60
164-Porky Pig	4	8	12	17	21	24
165-The Lone Ranger	9	18	27	54	70	85
166-Santa and His Reindeer	4	7	9	14	16	18
167-Roy Rogers and Santa	9	18	27	52	66	80
168-Santa Claus' Workshop (1957, full size)	4	7	10	14	17	20
169-Popeye (1958)	6	12	18	33	41	48
170-Indian Chief	6	12	18	33	41	48
171-Oswald the Rabbit	4	8	11	16	19	22
172-Tarzan	11	22	33	64	87	110
173-Tom and Jerry	4	8	11	16	19	22
174-The Lone Ranger	9	18	27	54	70	85
175-Porky Pig	4	8	11	16	19	22
176-Roy Rogers	8	16	24	46	58	70
177-Woody Woodpecker	4	8	11	16	19	22
178-Henry	4	7	10	14	17	20
179-Bugs Bunny	4	8	11	16	19	22
180-Rin Tin Tin (TV)	7	14	21	37	46	55
181-Happy Holiday	3	6	8	12	14	16
182-Happi Tim	4	7	10	14	17	20
183-Welcome Santa (1958, full size)	3	6	8	12	14	16
184-Woody Woodpecker (1959)	4	7	10	14	17	20
185-Tarzan; photo-c	11	22	33	62	84	105
186-Oswald the Rabbit	4	7	10	14	17	20
187-Indian Chief	6	12	18	27	33	38
188-Bugs Bunny	4	7	10	14	17	20
189-Henry	4	7	9	14	16	18
190-Tom and Jerry	4	7	10	14	17	20
191-Roy Rogers	8	16	24	43	54	65
192-Porky Pig	4	7	10	14	17	20
193-The Lone Ranger	9	18	27	52	66	80
194-Popeye	6	12	18	29	36	42
195-Rin Tin Tin (TV)	6	12	18	33	41	48
196-Sears Special - not published						
197-Santa Is Coming	4	7	9	14	16	18
198-Santa's Helpers (1959)	4	7	9	14	16	18
199-Huckleberry Hound (TV)(1960, early app.)	8	16	24	40	50	60
200-Fury (TV)	6	12	18	27	33	38
201-Bugs Bunny	4	7	10	14	17	20
202-Space Explorer	8	16	24	43	54	65
203-Woody Woodpecker	4	7	9	14	16	18
204-Tarzan	9	18	27	54	70	85
205-Mighty Mouse	6	12	18	31	38	45
206-Roy Rogers; photo-c	8	16	24	43	54	65
207-Tom and Jerry	4	7	9	14	16	18
208-The Lone Ranger; Clayton Moore photo-c	11	22	33	62	84	105
209-Porky Pig	4	7	9	14	16	18
210-Lassie (TV)	6	12	18	31	38	45
211-Sears Special - not published						
212-Christmas Eve	4	7	9	14	16	18
213-Here Comes Santa (1960)	4	7	9	14	16	18

March of Comics #233 © Jay Ward

March of Comics #268 © WEST

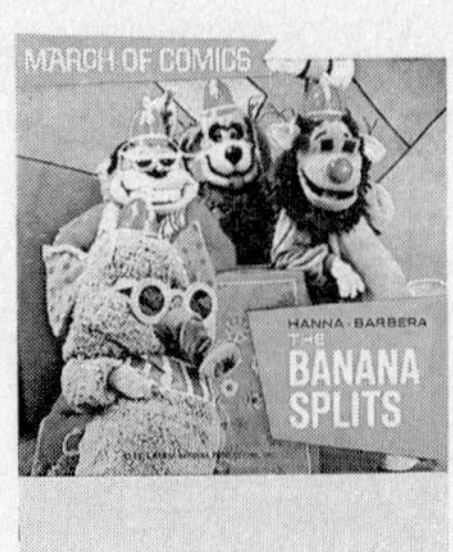

March of Comics #364 © H-B

	GD 2.0	VG 4.0	FN 6.0	VF 8.0	VF/NM 9.0	NM- 9.2
214-Huckleberry Hound (TV)(1961)	6	12	18	33	41	48
215-Hi Yo Silver	7	14	21	37	46	55
216-Rocky & His Friends (TV)(1961); predates Rocky and His Fiendish Friends #1 (see Four Color #1128)	10	20	30	56	73	90
217-Lassie (TV)	6	12	18	29	36	42
218-Porky Pig	4	7	9	14	16	18
219-Journey to the Sun	5	10	15	24	30	35
220-Bugs Bunny	4	7	10	14	17	20
221-Roy and Dale; photo-c	8	16	24	40	50	60
222-Woody Woodpecker	4	7	9	14	16	18
223-Tarzan	9	18	27	54	70	85
224-Tom and Jerry	4	7	9	14	16	18
225-The Lone Ranger	8	16	24	40	50	60
226-Christmas Treasury (1961)	4	7	9	14	16	18
227-Letters to Santa (1961)	4	7	9	14	16	18
228-Sears Special - not published?						
229-The Flintstones (TV)(1962); early app.; predates 1st Flintstones Gold Key issue (#7)	10	20	30	60	80	100
230-Lassie (TV)	5	10	15	24	30	35
231-Bugs Bunny	4	7	10	14	17	20
232-The Three Stooges	9	18	27	54	70	85
233-Bullwinkle (TV) (1962, very early app.)	10	20	30	58	77	95
234-Smokey the Bear	5	10	15	22	26	30
235-Huckleberry Hound (TV)	6	12	18	33	41	48
236-Roy and Dale	6	12	18	33	41	48
237-Mighty Mouse	5	10	15	24	30	35
238-The Lone Ranger	8	16	24	40	50	60
239-Woody Woodpecker	4	7	9	14	16	18
240-Tarzan	8	16	24	46	58	70
241-Santa Claus Around the World	3	6	8	12	14	16
242-Santa's Toyland (1962)	3	6	8	12	14	16
243-The Flintstones (TV)(1963)	8	16	24	46	58	70
244-Mister Ed (TV); early app.; photo-c	6	12	18	33	41	48
245-Bugs Bunny	4	7	10	14	17	20
246-Popeye	5	10	15	24	30	35
247-Mighty Mouse	5	10	15	24	30	35
248-The Three Stooges	9	18	27	54	70	85
249-Woody Woodpecker	4	7	9	14	16	18
250-Roy and Dale	6	12	18	33	41	48
251-Little Lulu & Witch Hazel	11	22	33	66	91	115
252-Tarzan; painted-c	8	16	24	43	54	65
253-Yogi Bear (TV)	8	16	24	40	50	60
254-Lassie (TV)	6	12	18	27	33	38
255-Santa's Christmas List	4	7	9	14	16	18
256-Christmas Party (1963)	4	7	9	14	16	18
257-Mighty Mouse	5	10	15	24	30	35
258-The Sword in the Stone (Disney)	8	16	24	43	54	65
259-Bugs Bunny	4	7	9	14	17	20
260-Mister Ed (TV)	6	12	18	29	36	42
261-Woody Woodpecker	4	7	9	14	16	18
262-Tarzan	8	16	24	40	50	60
263-Donald Duck; not by Barks (Disney)	9	18	27	52	66	80
264-Popeye	5	10	15	24	30	35
265-Yogi Bear (TV)	6	12	18	31	38	45
266-Lassie (TV)	5	10	15	22	26	30
267-Little Lulu; Irving Tripp-a	10	20	30	58	77	95
268-The Three Stooges	8	16	24	46	58	70
269-A Jolly Christmas	3	5	7	10	12	14
270-Santa's Little Helpers	3	5	7	10	12	14
271-The Flintstones (TV)(1965)	9	18	27	52	66	80
272-Tarzan	8	16	24	40	50	60
273-Bugs Bunny	4	7	10	14	17	20
274-Popeye	5	10	15	24	30	35
275-Little Lulu; Irving Tripp-a	9	18	27	52	66	80
276-The Jetsons (TV)	14	28	42	79	110	140
277-Daffy Duck	4	7	10	14	17	20
278-Lassie (TV)	5	10	15	22	26	30
279-Yogi Bear (TV)	6	12	18	31	38	45
280-The Three Stooges; photo-c	8	16	24	46	58	70
281-Tom and Jerry	3	6	8	12	14	16
282-Mister Ed (TV)	6	12	18	31	38	45
283-Santa's Visit	4	7	9	14	16	18
284-Christmas Parade (1965)	4	7	9	14	16	18
285-Astro Boy (TV); 2nd app. Astro Boy	31	62	93	178	259	340
286-Tarzan	7	14	21	37	46	55
287-Bugs Bunny	4	7	10	14	17	20
288-Daffy Duck	4	7	9	14	16	18
289-The Flintstones (TV)	9	18	27	52	66	80
290-Mister Ed (TV); photo-c	5	10	15	24	30	35
291-Yogi Bear (TV)	6	12	18	27	33	38
292-The Three Stooges; photo-c	8	16	24	46	58	70
293-Little Lulu; Irving Tripp-a	8	16	24	43	54	65
294-Popeye	5	10	15	24	30	35
295-Tom and Jerry	3	6	8	12	14	16
296-Lassie (TV); photo-c	5	10	14	20	24	28
297-Christmas Bells	3	6	8	12	14	16
298-Santa's Sleigh (1966)	3	6	8	12	14	16
299-The Flintstones (TV)(1967)	9	18	27	52	66	80
300-Tarzan	7	14	21	37	46	55
301-Bugs Bunny	4	7	9	14	16	18
302-Laurel and Hardy (TV); photo-c	6	12	18	27	33	38
303-Daffy Duck	3	5	7	10	12	14
304-The Three Stooges; photo-c	8	16	24	43	54	65
305-Tom and Jerry	3	5	7	10	12	14
306-Daniel Boone (TV); Fess Parker photo-c	6	12	18	33	41	48
307-Little Lulu; Irving Tripp-a	7	14	21	37	46	55
308-Lassie (TV); photo-c	5	10	14	20	24	28
309-Yogi Bear (TV)	5	10	15	24	30	35
310-The Lone Ranger; Clayton Moore photo-c	11	22	33	62	84	105
311-Santa's Show	4	7	9	14	16	18
312-Christmas Album (1967)	4	7	9	14	16	18
313-Daffy Duck (1968)	3	5	7	10	12	14
314-Laurel and Hardy (TV)	5	10	15	24	30	35
315-Bugs Bunny	4	7	9	14	16	18
316-The Three Stooges	7	14	21	37	46	55
317-The Flintstones (TV)	8	16	24	43	54	65
318-Tarzan	6	12	18	33	41	48
319-Yogi Bear (TV)	5	10	15	24	30	35
320-Space Family Robinson (TV); Spiegle-a	12	24	36	71	98	125
321-Tom and Jerry	3	5	7	10	12	14
322-The Lone Ranger	7	14	21	37	46	55
323-Little Lulu; not by Stanley	5	10	15	24	30	35
324-Lassie (TV); photo-c	5	10	14	20	24	28
325-Fun with Santa	4	7	9	14	16	18
326-Christmas Story (1968)	4	7	9	14	16	18
327-The Flintstones (TV)(1969)	8	16	24	43	54	65
328-Space Family Robinson (TV); Spiegle-a	12	24	36	71	98	125
329-Bugs Bunny	4	7	9	14	16	18
330-The Jetsons (TV)	10	20	30	58	77	95
331-Daffy Duck	3	5	7	10	12	14
332-Tarzan	6	12	18	27	33	38
333-Tom and Jerry	3	5	7	10	12	14
334-Lassie (TV)	4	8	12	17	21	24
335-Little Lulu	5	10	15	24	30	35
336-The Three Stooges	7	14	21	37	46	55
337-Yogi Bear (TV)	5	10	15	24	30	35
338-The Lone Ranger	7	14	21	37	46	55
339-(Was not published)						
340-Here Comes Santa (1969)	3	6	8	12	14	16
341-The Flintstones (TV)	8	16	24	43	54	65
342-Tarzan	4	8	12	22	30	38
343-Bugs Bunny	2	4	6	10	13	16
344-Yogi Bear (TV)	3	6	9	18	24	30
345-Tom and Jerry	2	4	6	9	11	14
346-Lassie (TV)	3	6	9	16	20	24
347-Daffy Duck	2	4	6	9	11	14
348-The Jetsons (TV)	7	14	21	50	68	85
349-Little Lulu; not by Stanley	3	6	9	18	23	28
350-The Lone Ranger	3	7	10	21	28	35
351-Beep-Beep, the Road Runner (TV)	2	4	6	11	14	18
352-Space Family Robinson (TV); Spiegle-a	10	20	30	67	96	125
353-Beep-Beep, the Road Runner (1971) (TV)	2	4	6	11	14	18
354-Tarzan (1971)	3	7	10	21	28	35
355-Little Lulu; not by Stanley	3	6	9	18	23	28
356-Scooby Doo, Where Are You? (TV)	7	14	21	50	68	85
357-Daffy Duck & Porky Pig	2	4	6	9	11	14
358-Lassie (TV)	3	6	9	16	20	24
359-Baby Snoots	2	4	6	11	14	18
360-H. R. Pufnstuf (TV); photo-c	7	14	21	50	68	85
361-Tom and Jerry	2	4	6	9	11	14
362-Smokey Bear (TV)	2	4	6	9	11	14
363-Bugs Bunny & Yosemite Sam	2	4	6	10	13	16

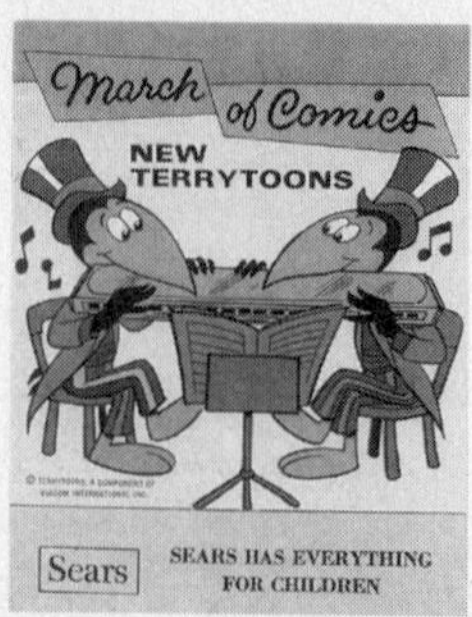

March of Comics #435 © Terrytoons

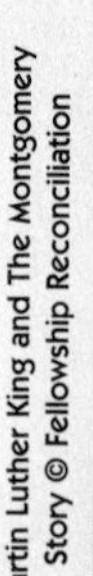
Martin Luther King and The Montgomery Story © Fellowship Reconciliation

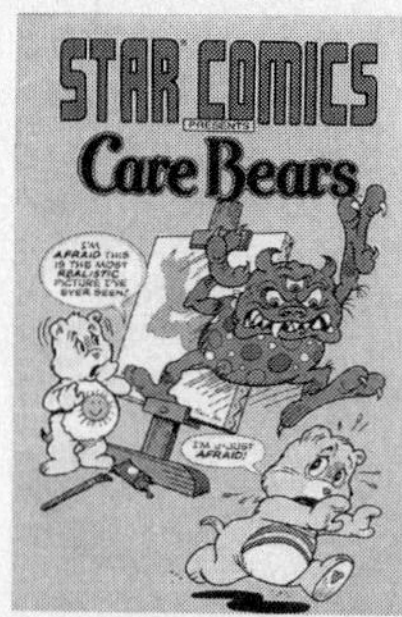

Marvel Comics Presents Care Bears © MAR

	GD 2.0	VG 4.0	FN 6.0	VF 8.0	VF/NM 9.0	NM- 9.2
364-The Banana Splits (TV); photo-c	6	12	18	40	55	70
365-Tom and Jerry (1972)	2	4	6	9	11	14
366-Tarzan	3	7	10	21	28	35
367-Bugs Bunny & Porky Pig	2	4	6	10	13	16
368-Scooby Doo (TV)(4/72)	6	12	18	40	55	70
369-Little Lulu; not by Stanley	2	4	6	14	18	22
370-Lassie (TV); photo-c	3	6	9	16	20	24
371-Baby Snoots	2	4	6	10	13	16
372-Smokey the Bear (TV)	2	4	6	9	11	14
373-The Three Stooges	4	8	12	28	38	48
374-Wacky Witch	2	4	6	9	11	14
375-Beep-Beep & Daffy Duck (TV)	2	4	6	9	11	14
376-The Pink Panther (1972) (TV)	2	4	6	11	14	18
377-Baby Snoots (1973)	2	4	6	10	13	16
378-Turok, Son of Stone; new-a	10	20	30	70	100	130
379-Heckle & Jeckle New Terrytoons (TV)	2	4	6	9	11	14
380-Bugs Bunny & Yosemite Sam	2	4	6	9	11	14
381-Lassie (TV)	2	4	6	12	16	20
382-Scooby Doo, Where Are You? (TV)	5	10	15	36	48	60
383-Smokey the Bear (TV)	2	4	6	9	11	14
384-Pink Panther (TV)	2	4	6	9	11	14
385-Little Lulu	2	4	6	12	16	20
386-Wacky Witch	2	4	6	9	11	14
387-Beep-Beep & Daffy Duck (TV)	2	4	6	9	11	14
388-Tom and Jerry (1973)	2	4	6	9	11	14
389-Little Lulu; not by Stanley	2	4	6	12	16	20
390-Pink Panther (TV)	2	4	6	9	11	14
391-Scooby Doo (TV)	4	8	12	28	38	48
392-Bugs Bunny & Yosemite Sam	2	4	6	8	10	12
393-New Terrytoons (Heckle & Jeckle) (TV)	2	4	6	8	10	12
394-Lassie (TV)	2	4	6	10	13	16
395-Woodsy Owl	2	4	6	8	10	12
396-Baby Snoots	2	4	6	9	11	14
397-Beep-Beep & Daffy Duck (TV)	2	4	6	8	10	12
398-Wacky Witch	2	4	6	8	10	12
399-Turok, Son of Stone; new-a	9	18	27	63	89	115
400-Tom and Jerry	2	4	6	8	10	12
401-Baby Snoots (1975) (r/#371)	2	4	6	9	11	14
402-Daffy Duck (r/#313)	1	3	4	6	8	10
403-Bugs Bunny (r/#343)	2	4	6	8	10	12
404-Space Family Robinson (TV)(r/#328)	7	14	21	51	71	90
405-Cracky	1	3	4	6	8	10
406-Little Lulu (r/#355)	2	4	6	11	14	18
407-Smokey the Bear (TV)(r/#362)	2	4	6	8	10	12
408-Turok, Son of Stone; c-r/Turok #20 w/changes; new-a	7	14	21	50	68	85
409-Pink Panther (TV)	1	3	4	6	8	10
410-Wacky Witch	1	2	3	5	6	8
411-Lassie (TV)(r/#324)	2	4	6	10	13	16
412-New Terrytoons (1975) (TV)	1	2	3	5	6	8
413-Daffy Duck (1976)(r/#331)	1	2	3	5	6	8
414-Space Family Robinson (r/#328)	7	14	21	50	68	85
415-Bugs Bunny (r/#329)	1	2	3	5	6	8
416-Beep-Beep, the Road Runner (r/#353)(TV)	1	2	3	5	6	8
417-Little Lulu (r/#323)	2	4	6	11	14	18
418-Pink Panther (r/#384) (TV)	1	2	3	5	6	8
419-Baby Snoots (r/#377)	1	3	4	6	8	10
420-Woody Woodpecker	1	2	3	5	6	8
421-Tweety & Sylvester	1	2	3	5	6	8
422-Wacky Witch (r/#386)	1	2	3	5	6	8
423-Little Monsters	1	3	4	6	8	10
424-Cracky (12/76)	1	2	3	5	6	8
425-Daffy Duck	1	2	3	5	6	8
426-Underdog (TV)	4	8	12	24	32	40
427-Little Lulu (r/#335)	2	4	6	9	11	14
428-Bugs Bunny	1	2	3	4	5	7
429-The Pink Panther (TV)	1	2	3	4	5	7
430-Beep-Beep, the Road Runner (TV)	1	2	3	4	5	7
431-Baby Snoots	1	2	3	5	6	8
432-Lassie (TV)	2	4	6	8	10	12
433-437: 433-Tweety & Sylvester. 434-Wacky Witch. 435-New Terrytoons (TV). 436-Wacky Advs. of Cracky. 437-Daffy Duck	1	2	3	4	5	7
438-Underdog (TV)	3	7	10	21	28	35
439-Little Lulu (r/#349)	2	4	6	9	11	14
440-442,444-446: 440-Bugs Bunny. 441-The Pink Panther (TV). 442-Beep-Beep, the Road Runner (TV). 444-Tom and Jerry. 445-Tweety and Sylvester. 446-Wacky Witch	1	2	3	5	6	8
443-Baby Snoots	1	2	3	5	6	8
447-Mighty Mouse	2	4	6	8	10	12
448-455,457,458: 448-Cracky. 449-Pink Panther (TV). 450-Baby Snoots. 451-Tom and Jerry. 452-Bugs Bunny. 453-Popeye. 454-Woody Woodpecker. 455-Beep-Beep, the Road Runner (TV). 457-Tweety & Sylvester. 458-Wacky Witch	1	2	3	5	6	8
456-Little Lulu (r/#369)	2	4	6	8	10	12
459-Mighty Mouse	2	4	6	8	10	12
460-466: 460-Daffy Duck. 461-The Pink Panther (TV). 462-Baby Snoots. 463-Tom and Jerry. 464-Bugs Bunny. 465-Popeye. 466-Woody Woodpecker	1	2	3	5	6	8
467-Underdog (TV)	3	6	9	18	24	30
468-Little Lulu (r/#385)	1	2	3	5	6	8
469-Tweety & Sylvester	1	2	3	5	6	8
470-Wacky Witch	1	2	3	5	6	8
471-Mighty Mouse	1	3	4	6	8	10
472-474,476-478: 472-Heckle & Jeckle(12/80). 473-Pink Panther(1/81)(TV). 474-Baby Snoots. 476-Bugs Bunny. 477-Popeye. 478-Woody Woodpecker	1	2	3	5	6	8
475-Little Lulu (r/#323)	1	3	4	6	8	10
479-Underdog (TV)	3	6	9	16	20	24
480-482: 480-Tom and Jerry. 481-Tweety and Sylvester. 482-Wacky Witch	1	2	3	4	5	8
483-Mighty Mouse	1	3	4	6	8	10
484-487: 484-Heckle & Jeckle. 485-Baby Snoots. 486-The Pink Panther (TV). 487-Bugs Bunny	1	2	3	4	5	8
488-Little Lulu (4/82) (r/#335) (Last issue)	2	4	6	11	14	18

MARGARET O'BRIEN (See The Adventures of...)

MARK STEEL
American Iron & Steel Institute: 1967, 1968, 1972 (Giveaway) (24 pgs.)

	GD 2.0	VG 4.0	FN 6.0	VF 8.0	VF/NM 9.0	NM- 9.2
1967,1968- "Journey of Discovery with..."; Neal Adams art	4	8	12	29	40	50
1972- "...Fights Pollution"; N. Adams-a	3	7	10	21	28	35

MARTIN LUTHER KING AND THE MONTGOMERY STORY
Fellowship Reconciliation: 1956 (Giveaway, 16 pgs.)

nn-In color with paper-c (a CGC 9.2 copy sold for $350 and a FN+ sold for $200 in 2004)

MARVEL AGE SPIDER-MAN
Marvel Comics: Aug, 2004 (Free Comic Book Day giveaway)

1-Spider-Man vs. The Vulture; Brooks-a 2.25

MARVEL COLLECTOR'S EDITION: X-MEN
Marvel Comics: 1993 (3-3/4x6-1/2")

1-4-Pizza Hut giveaways 5.00

MARVEL COMICS PRESENTS
Marvel Comics: 1987, 1988 (4 1/4 x 6 1/4, 20 pgs.)
...Mini Comic Giveaway

	GD 2.0	VG 4.0	FN 6.0	VF 8.0	VF/NM 9.0	NM- 9.2
nn-(1988) Alf	1	2	3	5	6	8
nn-(1987) Captain America r/ #250	1	2	3	4	5	7
nn-(1987) Care Bears (Star Comics...)	1	2	3	4	5	7
nn-(1988) Flintstone Kids	1	2	3	5	6	8
nn-(1987) Heathcliffe (Star Comics...)	1	2	3	4	5	7
nn-(1987) Spider-Man-r/Spect. Spider-Man #21	1	2	3	4	5	7
nn-(1988) Spider-Man-r/Amazing Spider-Man #1	1	2	3	4	5	7
nn-(1988) X-Men-reprints X-Men #53; B. Smith-a	1	2	3	4	5	7

MARVEL GUIDE TO COLLECTING COMICS, THE
Marvel Comics: 1982 (16 pgs., newsprint pages and cover)

	GD 2.0	VG 4.0	FN 6.0	VF 8.0	VF/NM 9.0	NM- 9.2
1-Simonson-c	1	2	3	4	5	7

MARVEL MINI-BOOKS
Marvel Comics Group: 1966 (50 pgs., B&W; 5/8x7/8") (6 different issues) (Smallest comics ever published) (Marvel Mania Giveaways)

	GD 2.0	VG 4.0	FN 6.0	VF 8.0	VF/NM 9.0	NM- 9.2
Captain America, Millie the Model, Sgt. Fury, Hulk, Thor each...	9	18	27	60	85	110
Spider-Man	9	18	27	65	93	120

NOTE: *Each came in six different color covers, usually one color: Pink, yellow, green, etc.*

MARVEL SUPER-HERO ISLAND ADVENTURES
Marvel Comics: 1999 (Sold at the park polybagged with Captain America V3 #19, one other comic, 5 trading cards and a cloisonné pin)

1-Promotes Universal Studios Islands of Adventures theme park 2.25

MARY'S GREATEST APOSTLE (St. Louis Grignion de Montfort)
Catechetical Guild (Topix) (Giveaway): No date (16 pgs.; paper cover)

	GD 2.0	VG 4.0	FN 6.0	VF 8.0	VF/NM 9.0	NM- 9.2
nn	5	10	14	20	24	28

Mickey Mouse Magazine V2#4 © WDC

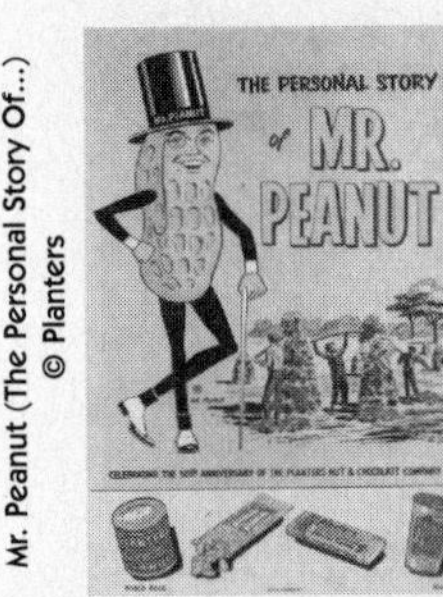

Mr. Peanut (The Personal Story Of...) © Planters

Motion Picture Funnies Weekly #4 © First Funnies Inc.

	GD 2.0	VG 4.0	FN 6.0	VF 8.0	VF/NM 9.0	NM- 9.2

MASK
DC Comics: 1985
1-3 5.00

MASKED PILOT, THE (See Popular Comics #43)
R.S. Callender: 1939 (7-1/2x5-1/4", 16 pgs., premium, non-slick-c)
nn-Bob Jenney-a 10 20 30 58 77 95

MASTERS OF THE UNIVERSE (He-Man)
DC Comics: 1982 (giveaways with action figures, at least 35 different issues, unnumbered)
nn 6.00

MATRIX, THE (1999 movie)
Warner Brothers: 1999 (Recalled by Warner Bros. over questionable content)
nn-Paul Chadwick-s/a (16 pgs.); Geof Darrow-c 6.00

McCRORY'S CHRISTMAS BOOK
Western Printing Co: 1955 (36 pgs., slick-c) (McCrory Stores Corp. giveaway)
nn-Painted-c 4 8 12 18 22 25

McCRORY'S TOYLAND BRINGS YOU SANTA'S PRIVATE EYES
Promotional Publ. Co.: 1956 (16 pgs.) (Giveaway)
nn-Has 9 pg. story plus 7 pgs. toy ads 4 8 11 16 19 22

McCRORY'S WONDERFUL CHRISTMAS
Promotional Publ. Co.: 1954 (20 pgs., slick-c) (Giveaway)
nn 4 8 12 18 22 25

McDONALDS COMMANDRONS
DC Comics: 1985
nn-Four editions 5.00

MEET HIYA A FRIEND OF SANTA CLAUS
Julian J. Proskauer/Sundial Shoe Stores, etc.: 1949 (18 pgs.?, paper-c)(Giveaway)
nn 6 12 18 31 38 45

MEET THE NEW POST GAZETTE SUNDAY FUNNIES
Pittsburgh Post Gazette: 3/12/49 (7-1/4x10-1/4", 16 pgs., paper-c)
Commercial Comics (insert in newspaper) (Rare)
Dick Tracy by Gould, Gasoline Alley, Terry & the Pirates, Brenda Starr, Buck Rogers by Yager, The Gumps, Peter Rabbit by Fago, Superman, Funnyman by Siegel & Shuster, The Saint, Archie, & others done especially for this book. A fine copy sold at auction in 1985 for $276.00.
550 1100 1650 4500 - -

MEN OF COURAGE
Catechetical Guild: 1949
Bound Topix comics-V7#2,4,6,8,10,16,18,20 6 12 18 31 38 45

MEN WHO MOVE THE NATION
Publisher unknown: (Giveaway) (B&W)
nn-Neal Adams-a 6 12 18 31 38 45

MERRY CHRISTMAS, A
K. K. Publications (Child Life Shoes): 1948 (Giveaway)
nn 6 12 18 33 41 48

MERRY CHRISTMAS
K. K. Publications (Blue Bird Shoes Giveaway): 1956 (7-1/4x5-1/4")
nn 4 8 12 18 22 25

MERRY CHRISTMAS FROM MICKEY MOUSE
K. K. Publications: 1939 (16 pgs.) (Color & B&W) (Shoe store giveaway)
nn-Donald Duck & Pluto app.; text with art (Rare); c-reprint/Mickey Mouse Mag. V3#3 (12/37)(Rare) 300 600 1200 1750 2475 3200

MERRY CHRISTMAS FROM SEARS TOYLAND (See Santa's Christmas Comic)
Sears Roebuck Giveaway: 1939 (16 pgs.) (Color)
nn-Dick Tracy, Little Orphan Annie, The Gumps, Terry & the Pirates
115 230 345 719 1110 1500

METALLIX
Future Comics: Apr, 2003
1-Free Comic Book Day Edition; Layton-c 2.25

MICKEY MOUSE (Also see Frito-Lay Giveaway)
Dell Publ. Co
...& Goofy Explore Business(1978) 1 3 4 6 8 10
...& Goofy Explore Energy(1976-1978, 36 pgs.); Exxon giveaway in color; regular size 1 3 4 6 8 10
...& Goofy Explore Energy Conservation(1976-1978)-Exxon
1 3 4 6 8 10
...& Goofy Explore The Universe of Energy(1985, 20 pgs.); Exxon giveaway in color; regular size 1 2 3 4 5 7
The Perils of Mickey nn (1993, 5-1/4x7-1/4", 16 pgs.)-Nabisco giveaway w/ games, Nabisco coupons & 6 pgs. of stories; Phantom Blot app. 5.00

MICKEY MOUSE MAGAZINE
Walt Disney Productions: V1#1, Jan, 1933 - V1#9, Sept, 1933 (5-1/4x7-1/4")
No. 1-3 published by Kamen-Blair (Kay Kamen, Inc.)
(Scarce)-Distributed by dairies and leading stores through their local theatres. First few issues had 5¢ listed on cover, later ones had no price.
V1#1 540 1080 2160 6400 - -
2-4 225 450 900 1700 - -
5-9 175 350 700 1300 - -

MICKEY MOUSE MAGAZINE
Walt Disney Productions: V1#1, 11/33 - V2#12, 10/35 (Mills giveaways issued by different dairies)
V1#1 240 600 960 1350 1975 2600
2-12: 2-X-Mas issue 80 200 320 475 663 850
V2#1-4,6-12: 2-X-Mas issue. 4-St. Valentine-c 55 124 192 310 443 575
V2#5 (3/35) 1st app. Donald Duck in sailor outfit on-c 96 192 288 600 950 1300

MICKEY MOUSE MAGAZINE
K.K. Publications: V4#1, Oct, 1938 (Giveaway)
V4#1 55 124 192 310 443 575

MIGHTY ATOM, THE
Whitman
Giveaway (1959, '63, Whitman)-Evans-a 3 6 9 16 20 24
Giveaway ('64r, '65r, '66r, '67r, '68r)-Evans-r? 2 4 6 9 11 14
Giveaway ('73r, '76r) 1 3 4 6 8 10

MILITARY COURTESY
Harvey Publications: (16 pgs.)
nn-Regulations and saluting instructions 5 10 14 20 24 28

MINUTE MAN
Sovereign Service Station giveaway: No date (16 pgs., B&W, paper-c blue & red)
nn-American history 3 6 8 12 14 16

MINUTE MAN ANSWERS THE CALL, THE
By M. C. Gaines: 1942,1943,1944,1945 (4 pgs.) (Giveaway inserted in Jr. JSA Membership Kit)
nn-Sheldon Moldoff-a 23 46 69 130 188 245

MIRACLE ON BROADWAY
Broadway Comics: Dec, 1995 (Giveaway)
1-Ernie Colon-c/a; Jim Shooter & Co. story; 1st known digitally printed comic book; 1st app. Spire & Knights on Broadway (1150 print run) 20.00
NOTE: *Miracle on Broadway was a limited edition comic given to 1100 VIPs in the entertainment industry for the 1995 Holiday Season.*

MISS SUNBEAM (See Little Miss Sunbeam Comics)

MR. BUG GOES TO TOWN (See Cinema Comics Herald)
K.K. Publications: 1941 (Giveaway, 52 pgs.)
nn-Cartoon movie (scarce) 75 150 225 469 722 975

MR. PEANUT, THE PERSONAL STORY OF
Planters Nut & Chocolate Co.: 1956
nn 4 8 12 25 33 42

MOTHER OF US ALL
Catechetical Guild Giveaway: 1950? (32 pgs.)
nn 5 10 15 22 26 30

MOTION PICTURE FUNNIES WEEKLY (Amazing Man #5 on?)
First Funnies, Inc.: 1939 (Giveaway)(B&W, 36 pgs.) No month given; last panel in Sub-Mariner story dated 4/39 (Also see Colossus, Green Giant & Invaders No. 20)
1-Origin & 1st printed app. Sub-Mariner by Bill Everett (8 pgs.); Fred Schwab-c; reprinted in Marvel Mystery #1 with color added over the craft tint which was used to shade the black & white version; Spy Ring, American Ace (reprinted in Marvel Mystery #3) app. (Rare)-only eight known copies, one near mint with white pages, the rest with brown pages.
4400 7700 11,000 16,500 22,250 28,000
Covers only to #2-4 (set) 1000
NOTE: The only eight known copies (with a ninth suspected) were discovered in 1974 in the estate of the deceased publisher. Covers only to issues No. 2-4 were also found which evidently were printed in advance along with #1. #1 was to be distributed only through motion picture movie houses. However, it is believed that only advanced copies were sent out and the motion picture houses not going for the idea. Possible distribution at local theaters in Boston suspected. The last panel of Sub-Mariner contains a rectangular box with "Continued Next Week" printed in it. When reprinted in Marvel Mystery, the box was left in with lettering omitted.

MY DOG TIGE (Buster Brown's Dog)
Buster Brown Shoes: 1957 (Giveaway)

New Teen Titans © DC

Overseas Comics

The Plot to Steal the World © Work & Unity Group

	GD 2.0	VG 4.0	FN 6.0	VF 8.0	VF/NM 9.0	NM- 9.2

nn 5 10 15 24 30 35

MY GREATEST THRILLS IN BASEBALL
Mission of California: Date? (16 pg. Giveaway)
nn-By Mickey Mantle 70 140 210 350 525 700

NATURAL DISASTERS!
Graphic Information Service/ Civil Defense: 1956 (16 pgs., soft-c)
nn-Al Capp Li'l Abner-c; Li'l Abner cameo (1 panel); narrated by Mr. Civil Defense
10 20 30 56 73 90

NAVY: HISTORY & TRADITION
Stokes Walesby Co./Dept. of Navy: 1958 - 1961 (nn) (Giveaway)
1772-1778, 1778-1782, 1782-1817, 1817-1865, 1865-1936, 1940-1945:
1772-1778-16 pg. in color 5 10 15 22 26 30
1861: Naval Actions of the Civil War: 1865-36 pg. in color; flag-c
5 10 15 22 26 30

NEW ADVENTURE OF WALT DISNEY'S SNOW WHITE AND THE SEVEN DWARFS, A
(See Snow White Bendix Giveaway)

NEW ADVENTURES OF PETER PAN (Disney)
Western Publishing Co.: 1953 (5x7-1/4", 36 pgs.) (Admiral giveaway)
nn 14 28 42 79 110 140

NEW FRONTIERS
Harvey Information Press (United States Steel Corp.) : 1958 (16 pgs., paper-c)
nn-History of barbed wire 2 4 6 14 18 22

NEW TEEN TITANS, THE
DC Comics: Nov. 1983
nn(11/83-Keebler Co. Giveaway)-In cooperation with "The President's Drug Awareness Campaign"; came in Presidential envelope w/letter from White House (Nancy Reagan)
1 2 3 4 5 7
nn-(re-issue of above on Mando paper for direct sales market); American Soft Drink Industry version; I.B.M. Corp. version 5.00

NOLAN RYAN IN THE WINNING PITCH (Kellogg's Tony's Sports Comics)
DC Comics: 1992 (Sports Illustrated)
nn 4.00

OLD GLORY COMICS
Chesapeake & Ohio Railway: 1944 (Giveaway)
nn-Capt. Fearless reprint 7 14 21 35 43 55

ON THE AIR
NBC Network Comic: 1947 (Giveaway, paper-c)
nn-(Rare) 26 52 78 147 211 275

OUT OF THE PAST A CLUE TO THE FUTURE
E. C. Comics (Public Affairs Comm.): 1946? (16 pgs.) (paper cover)
nn-Based on public affairs pamphlet "What Foreign Trade Means to You"
22 44 66 123 177 230

OUTSTANDING AMERICAN WAR HEROES
The Parents' Institute: 1944 (16 pgs., paper-c)
nn-Reprints from True Comics 5 10 15 22 26 30

OVERSEAS COMICS (Also see G.I. Comics & Jeep Comics)
Giveaway (Distributed to U.S. Armed Forces): 1944 - No. 105?, 1946 (7-1/4x10-1/4"; 16 pgs. in color)
23-105-Bringing Up Father (by McManus), Popeye, Joe Palooka, Dick Tracy, Superman, Gasoline Alley, Buz Sawyer, Li'l Abner, Blondie, Terry & the Pirates, Out Our Way
7 14 21 35 43 50

OWL, THE (See Crackajack Funnies #25 & Popular Comics #72)(Also see The Hurricane Kids & Magic Morro
Western Pub. Co./R.S. Callender: 1940 (Giveaway)(7-1/2x5-1/4")(Soft-c, color)
nn-Frank Thomas-a 22 44 66 123 177 230

OXYDOL-DREFT
Toby Press:1950 (Set of 6 pocket-size giveaways; distributed through the mail as a set) (Scarce)
1-3: 1-Li'l Abner. 2-Daisy Mae. 3-Shmoo 13 26 39 74 102 130
4-John Wayne; Williamson/Frazetta-c from John Wayne #3
17 34 51 95 135 175
5-Archie 16 32 48 89 127 165
6-Terrytoons Mighty Mouse 13 26 39 74 102 130
Mailing Envelope (has All Capp's Shmoo on front) 14 28 42 81 113 140

OZZIE SMITH IN THE KID WHO COULD (Kellogg's Tony's Sports Comics)
DC Comics: 1992 (Sports Illustrated)

	GD 2.0	VG 4.0	FN 6.0	VF 8.0	VF/NM 9.0	NM- 9.2

nn-Ozzie Smith app. 5.00

PADRE OF THE POOR
Catechetical Guild: nd (Giveaway) (16 pgs., paper-c)
nn 5 10 15 22 26 30

PAUL TERRY'S HOW TO DRAW FUNNY CARTOONS
Terrytoons, Inc. (Giveaway): 1940's (14 pgs.) (Black & White)
nn-Heckle & Jeckle, Mighty Mouse, etc. 12 24 36 69 95 120

PETER PAN (See New Adventures of Peter Pan)

PETER PENNY AND HIS MAGIC DOLLAR
American Bankers Association, N. Y. (Giveaway): 1947 (16 pgs.; paper-c; regular size)
nn-(Scarce)-Used in **SOTI**, pg. 310, 311 17 34 51 95 135 175
Diff. version (7-1/4x11")-redrawn, 16 pgs., paper-c 10 20 30 58 77 95

PETER WHEAT (The Adventures of...)
Bakers Associates Giveaway: 1948 - 1956? (16 pgs. in color) (paper covers)
nn(No.1)-States on last page, end of 1st Adventure of...; Kelly-a
31 62 93 173 249 325
nn(4 issues)-Kelly-a 18 36 54 100 143 185
6-10-All Kelly-a 14 28 42 81 113 145
11-20-All Kelly-a 12 24 36 71 98 125
21-35-All Kelly-a 11 22 33 62 84 105
36-66 9 18 27 51 62 75
...Artist's Workbook ('54, digest size) 9 18 27 51 62 75
...Four-In-One Fun Pack (Vol. 2, '54), oblong, comics w/puzzles
10 20 30 56 73 90
...Fun Book ('52, 32 pgs., paper-c, B&W & color, 8-1/2x10-3/4")-Contains cut-outs, puzzles, games, magic & pages to color 11 22 33 66 91 115
NOTE: *Al Hubbard art #36 on; written by Del Connell.*

PETER WHEAT NEWS
Bakers Associates: 1948 - No. 30, 1950 (4 pgs. in color)
Vol. 1-All have 2 pgs. Peter Wheat by Kelly 26 52 78 147 211 275
2-10 16 32 48 92 131 170
11-20 11 22 33 62 84 105
21-30 9 18 27 51 62 75
NOTE: *Early issues have no date & **Kelly** art.*

PINOCCHIO
Cocomalt/Montgomery Ward Co.: 1940 (10 pgs.; giveaway, linen-like paper)
nn-Cocomalt edition 46 92 138 281 428 575
nn-store edition 40 80 120 230 335 440

PIUS XII MAN OF PEACE
Catechetical Guild: No date (12 pgs.; 5-1/2x8-1/2") (B&W)
nn-Catechetical Guild Giveaway 6 12 18 27 33 38

PLOT TO STEAL THE WORLD, THE
Work & Unity Group: 1948, 16pgs., paper-c
nn-Anti communism 18 36 54 100 143 185

POCAHONTAS
Pocahontas Fuel Company (Coal): 1941 - No. 2, 1942
nn(#1), 2-Feat. life story of Indian princess Pocahontas & facts about Pocahontas coal, Pocahontas, VA. 16 32 48 89 127 165

POLL PARROT
Poll Parrot Shoe Store/International Shoe
K. K. Publications (Giveaway): 1950 - No. 4, 1951; No. 2, 1959 - No. 16, 1962
1 ('50)-Howdy Doody; small size 21 42 63 118 169 220
2-4('51)-Howdy Doody 17 34 51 95 135 175
2('59)-16('62): 2-The Secret of Crumbley Castle. 5-Bandit Busters. 7-The Make-Believe Mummy. 8-Mixed Up Mission('60). 10-The Frightful Flight. 11-Showdown at Sunup. 12-Maniac at Mubu Island. 13-...and the Runaway Genie. 14-Bully for You. 15-Trapped In Tall Timber. 16-...& the Rajah's Ruby('62) 3 6 9 18 23 28

POPEYE
Whitman
Bold Detergent giveaway (Same as regular issue #94) 2 4 6 9 11 14
Quaker Cereal premium (1989, 16pp, small size,4 diff.)(Popeye & the Time Machine, --On Safari, --& Big Foot, --vs. Bluto) 1 3 4 6 8 10

POPEYE
Charlton (King Features) (Giveaway): 1972 - 1974 (36 pgs. in color)
E-1 to E-15 (Educational comics) 2 4 6 9 11 14
nn-Popeye Gettin' Better Grades-4 pgs. used as intro. to above giveaways (in color) 2 4 6 9 11 14

Porky's Book of Tricks © WB

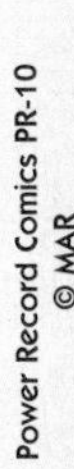
Power Record Comics PR-10 © MAR

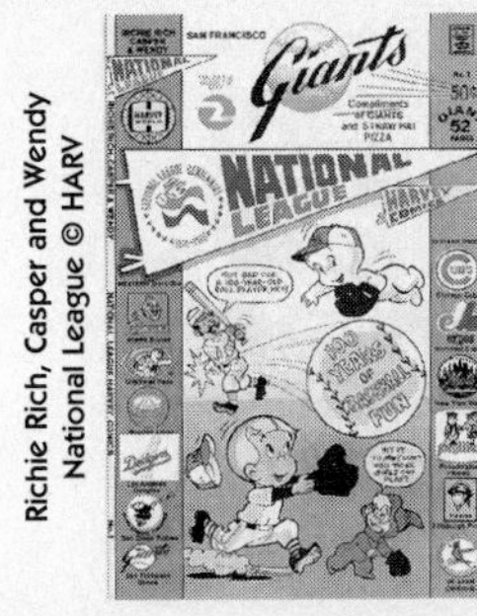

Richie Rich, Casper and Wendy National League © HARV

	GD	VG	FN	VF	VF/NM	NM-
	2.0	4.0	6.0	8.0	9.0	9.2

POPSICLE PETE FUN BOOK (See All-American Comics #6)
Joe Lowe Corp.: 1947, 1948

nn-36 pgs. in color; Sammy 'n' Claras, The King Who Couldn't Sleep & Popsicle Pete stories, games, cut-outs 11 22 33 66 91 115
Adventure Book ('48)-Has Classics ad with checklist to HRN #343 (Great Expectations #43) 10 20 30 58 77 95

PORKY'S BOOK OF TRICKS
K. K. Publications (Giveaway): 1942 (8-1/2x5-1/2", 48 pgs.)

nn-7 pg. comic story, text stories, plus games & puzzles 50 100 150 305 465 625

POST GAZETTE (See Meet the New...)

POWER RECORD COMICS
Marvel Comics/Power Records: 1974 - 1978 ($1.49, 7x10" comics, 20 pgs. with 45 R.P.M. record) (Clipped corners - reduce value 20%) (Comic alone - 50%; record alone - 50%)

PR10-Spider-Man-r/from #124,125; Man-Wolf app. PR18-Planet of the Apes-r. PR19-Escape From the Planet of the Apes-r. PR20-Beneath the Planet of the Apes-r. PR21-Battle for the Planet of the Apes-r. PR24-Spider-Man II-New-a begins. PR27-Batman "Stacked Cards"; N. Adams-a(p). PR30-Batman; N. Adams-r/Det.(7 pgs.).
With record; each... 5 10 15 36 48 60

PR11-Hulk-r. PR12-Captain America-r/#168. PR13-Fantastic Four-r/#126. PR14-Frankenstein-Ploog-r/#1. PR15-Tomb of Dracula-Colan-r/#2. PR16-Man-Thing-Ploog-r/#5. PR17-Werewolf By Night-Ploog-r/Marvel Spotlight #2. PR28-Superman "Alien Creatures". PR29-Space: 1999 "Breakaway". PR31-Conan-N. Adams-a; reprinted in Conan #116. PR32-Space: 1999 "Return to the Beginning". PR33-Superman-G.A. origin, Buckler-a(p). PR34-Superman. PR35-Wonder Woman-Buckler-a(p)
With record; each... 4 8 12 29 40 50

PR25-Star Trek "Passage to Moauv". PR26-Star Trek "Crier in Emptiness." PR36-Holo-Man. PR37-Robin Hood. PR39-Huckleberry Finn. PR40-Davy Crockett. PR41-Robinson Crusoe. PR42-20,000 Leagues Under the Sea. PR46-Star Trek "The Robot Masters". PR47-Little Women
With record; each... 4 8 12 24 32 40

PUNISHER: COUNTDOWN (Movie)
Marvel Comics: 2004 (7 1/4" X 4 3/4" mini-comic packaged with Punisher DVD)

nn-Prequel to 2004 movie; Ennis-s/Dillon-a/Bradstreet-c 2.25

PURE OIL COMICS (Also see Salerno Carnival of Comics, 24 Pages of Comics, & Vicks Comics)
Pure Oil Giveaway: Late 1930's (24 pgs., regular size, paper-c)

nn-Contains 1-2 pg. strips; i.e., Hairbreadth Harry, Skyroads, Buck Rogers by Calkins & Yager, Olly of the Movies, Napoleon, S'Matter Pop, etc. Also a 16 pg. 1938 giveaway with Buck Rogers 40 80 120 230 335 440

QUAKER OATS (Also see Cap'n Crunch)
Quaker Oats Co.: 1965 (Giveaway) (2-1/2x5-1/2") (16 pgs.)

"Plenty of Glutton", starring Quake & Quisp; 3 6 9 16 20 24
"Lava Come-Back", "Kite Tale" 1 3 4 6 8 10

QUEEN AND COUNTRY
Oni Press: May, 2002 (B&W)

Free Comic Book Day giveaway-Reprints #1 with "Free Comic Book Day" banner on-c 2.25

RAILROADS DELIVER THE GOODS!
Assoc. of American Railroads: Dec, 1954; Sept, 1957 (16 pgs.)

nn-The story of railway freight 6 12 18 28 34 40

RAILS ACROSS AMERICA!
Assoc. of American Railroads: nd (16 pgs.)

nn 6 12 18 28 34 40

REAL FUN OF DRIVING!!, THE
Chrysler Corp.: 1965, 1966, 1967 (Regular size, 16 pgs.)

nn-Schaffenberger-a (12 pgs.) 1 2 3 5 6 8

REAL HIT
Fox Features Publications: 1944 (Savings Bond premium)

1-Blue Beetle-r 18 36 54 100 143 185

NOTE: *Two versions exist, with and without covers. The coverless version has the title, No. 1 and price printed at top of splash page.*

RED BALL COMIC BOOK
Parents' Magazine Institute: 1947 (Red Ball Shoes giveaway)

nn-Reprints from True Comics 4 8 11 16 19 22

REDDY GOOSE
International Shoe Co. (Western Printing): No number, 1958?; No. 2, Jan, 1959 - No. 16, July, 1962 (Giveaway)

nn (#1) 6 12 18 36 48 65
2-16 3 7 10 21 28 35

REDDY KILOWATT (5¢) (Also see Story of Edison)
Educational Comics (E. C.): 1946 - No. 2, 1947; 1956 - 1965 (no month) (16 pgs., paper-c)

nn-Reddy Made Magic (1946, 5¢) 13 26 39 76 106 135
nn-Reddy Made Magic (1958) 9 18 27 51 65 78
2-Edison, the Man Who Changed the World (3/4" smaller than #1) (1947, 5¢) 13 26 39 76 106 135
...Comic Book 2 (1954)- "Light's Diamond Jubilee" 9 18 27 54 70 85
...Comic Book 2 (1958, 16 pgs.)- "Wizard of Light" 9 18 27 51 65 78
...Comic Book 2 (1965, 16 pgs.)- "Wizard of Light" 5 10 15 36 48 60
...Comic Book 3 (1956, 8 pgs.)- "The Space Kite"; Orlando story; regular size 9 18 27 49 62 75
...Comic Book 3 (1960, 8 pgs.)- "The Space Kite"; Orlando story; regular size 5 10 15 36 48 60

NOTE: *Several copies surfaced in 1979.*

REDDY MADE MAGIC
Educational Comics (E. C.): 1956, 1958 (16 pgs., paper-c)

1-Reddy Kilowatt-r (splash panel changed) 11 22 33 56 73 90
1 (1958 edition) 6 12 18 31 38 45

RED ICEBERG, THE
Impact Publ. (Catechetical Guild): 1960 (10¢, 16 pgs., Communist propaganda)

nn-(Rare)- "We The People" back-c 31 62 93 223 342 460
2nd version- "Impact Press" back-c 27 54 81 194 297 400
3rd version- "Explains comic" back-c 27 54 81 194 297 400
4th version- "Impact Press w/World Wide Secret Heart Program ad" 27 54 81 194 297 400
5th version- "Chicago Inter-Student Catholic Action" back-c 27 54 81 194 297 400

NOTE: *This book was the Guild's last anti-communist propaganda book and had very limited circulation. 3 - 4 copies surfaced in 1979 from the defunct publisher's files. Other copies do turn up.*

RED RYDER COMICS
Dell Publ. Co.

Buster Brown Shoes Giveaway (1941, color, soft-c, 32 pgs.) 27 54 81 152 219 285
Red Ryder Super Book of Comics (1944, paper-c, 32 pgs.; blank back-c) Magic Morro app. 29 58 87 167 241 315
Red Ryder Victory Patrol-nn(1942, 32 pgs.)(Langendorf bread; includes cut-out membership card and certificate, order blank and "Slide-Up" decoder, and a Super Book of Comics in color (same content as Super Book #4 w/diff. cover (Pan-Am)) (Rare) 463 1042 1621 3000 4100 5200
Red Ryder Victory Patrol-nn(1943, 32 pgs.)(Langendorf bread; includes cut-out "Rodeomatic" radio decoder, order coupon for "Magic V-Badge", cut-out membership card and certificate and a full color Super Book of comics comic book) (Rare) 421 948 1475 2700 3750 4800
Red Ryder Victory Patrol-nn(1944, 32 pgs.)-r-/#43,44; comic has a paper-c & is stapled inside a triple cardboard fold-out-c; contains membership card, decoder, map of R.R. home range, etc. Herky app. (Langendorf Bread giveaway; sub-titled 'Super Book of Comics') (Rare) 400 900 1400 2700 3750 4800
Wells Lamont Corp. giveaway (1950)-16 pgs. in color; regular size; paper-c; 1941-r 23 46 69 130 188 245

RELOADED (Also see Loaded)
DC Comics: 1996 (Interplay Productions, 16 pgs.)

1-Promotes video game; Alan Grrant-s/John Mueller-a 4.00

RICHIE RICH, CASPER & WENDY NATIONAL LEAGUE
Harvey Publications: June, 1976 (52 pgs.) (newsstand edition also exists)

1 (Released-3/76 with 6/76 date) 3 6 9 16 20 24
1 (6/76)-2nd version w/San Francisco Giants & KTVU 2 logos; has "Compliments of Giants and Straw Hat Pizza" on-c 3 6 9 16 20 24
1-Variants for other 11 NL teams, similar to Giants version but with different ad on inside front-c 3 6 9 16 20 24

RIDE THE HIGH IRON!
Assoc. of American Railroads: Jan, 1957 (16 pgs.)

nn-The Story of modern passenger trains 6 12 18 28 34 40

RIPLEY'S BELIEVE IT OR NOT!
Harvey Publications

J. C. Penney giveaway (1948) 9 18 27 52 66 80

ROBIN HOOD (New Adventures of...)
Walt Disney Productions: 1952 (Flour giveaways, 5x7-1/4", 36 pgs.)

"New Adventures of Robin Hood", "Ghosts of Waylea Castle", & "The Miller's Ransom" each.... 5 10 15 24 30 35

ROBIN HOOD'S FRONTIER DAYS (...Western Tales, Adventures of... #1)
Shoe Store Giveaway (Robin Hood Stores): 1956 (20 pgs., slick-c)(7 issues?)

nn 5 10 15 25 31 36

Rocket Comics: Ignite © DH

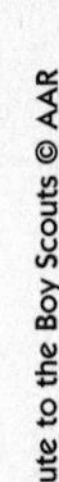

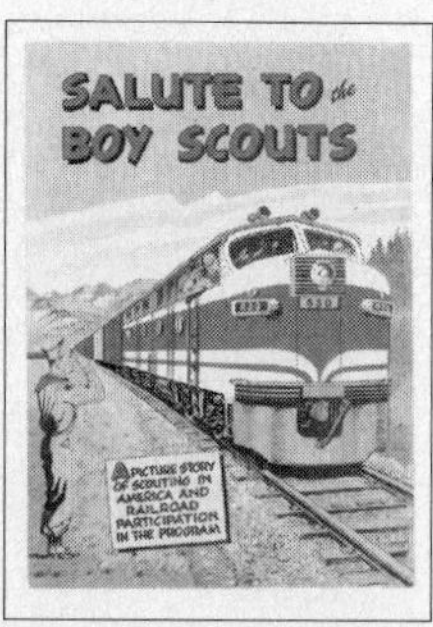

Salute to the Boy Scouts © AAR

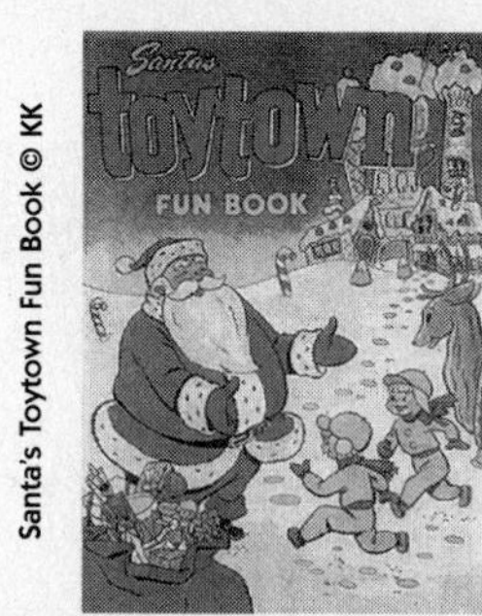

Santa's Toytown Fun Book © KK

	GD 2.0	VG 4.0	FN 6.0	VF 8.0	VF/NM 9.0	NM- 9.2
nn-Issues with Crandall-a	8	16	24	40	50	60
ROBOCOP (FRANK MILLER'S...)						
Avatar Press: Apr, 2003						
Free Comic Book Day Edition - Previews Robocop & Stargate SG•1; Busch-c						2.25
ROCKET COMICS: IGNITE						
Dark Horse Comics: Apr, 2003 (Free Comic Book Day giveaway)						
1-Previews Dark Horse series Syn, Lone, and Go Boy 7						2.25
ROCKETS AND RANGE RIDERS						
Richfield Oil Corp.: May, 1957 (Giveaway, 16 pgs., soft-c)						
nn-Toth-a	15	30	45	86	123	160
ROUND THE WORLD GIFT						
National War Fund (Giveaway): No date (mid 1940's) (4 pgs.)						
nn	11	22	33	66	91	115
ROY ROGERS COMICS						
Dell Publishing Co.						
...& the Man From Dodge City (Dodge giveaway, 16 pgs., 1954)-Frontier, Inc. (5x7-1/4")	14	28	42	81	113	145
Official Roy Rogers Riders Club Comics (1952; 16 pgs., reg. size, paper-c)	37	74	111	209	305	400
RUDOLPH, THE RED-NOSED REINDEER						
Montgomery Ward: 1939 (2,400,000 copies printed); Dec, 1951 (Giveaway)						
Paper cover-1st app. in print; written by Robert May; ill. by Denver Gillen	14	28	42	81	113	145
Hardcover version	19	38	57	109	157	205
1951 Edition (Has 1939 date)-36 pgs., slick-c printed in red & brown; pulp interior printed in four mixed-ink colors: red, green, blue & brown	10	20	30	58	77	95
1951 Edition with red-spiral promotional booklet printed on high quality stock, 8-1/2"x11", in red & brown, 25 pages composed of 4 fold outs, single sheets and the Rudolph comic book inserted (rare)	48	96	144	293	447	600
SABRINA THE TEENAGE WITCH						
Archie Comic Publications: (8 1/2"x 5 1/2", Diamond Comic Dist. Halloween giveaway)						
... And The Archies (2004)-Tania Del Rio-s/a; manga-style; Josie and the Pussycats app.						2.25
SAD CASE OF WAITING ROOM WILLIE, THE						
American Visuals Corp. (For Baltimore Medical Society): (nd, 1950?) (14 pgs. in color; paper covers; regular size)						
nn-By Will Eisner (Rare)	40	80	120	244	372	500
SAD SACK COMICS						
Harvey Publications: 1957-1962						
Armed Forces Complimentary copies, HD #1-40 (1957-1962)	3	6	9	16	20	24
SALERNO CARNIVAL OF COMICS (Also see Pure Oil Comics, 24 Pages of Comics, & Vicks Comics)						
Salerno Cookie Co.: Late 1930s (Giveaway, 16 pgs, paper-c)						
nn-Color reprints of Calkins' Buck Rogers & Skyroads, plus other strips from Famous Funnies	44	88	132	268	409	550
SALUTE TO THE BOY SCOUTS						
Association of American Railroads: 1960 (16 pgs.)						
nn-History of scouting and the railroad	3	6	9	16	20	24
SANTA AND POLLYANNA PLAY THE GLAD GAME						
Sales Promotion: Aug, 1960 (16 pgs.) (Disney giveaway)						
nn	2	4	6	14	18	22
SANTA & THE BUCCANEERS						
Promotional Publ. Co.: 1959 (Giveaway)						
nn-Reprints 1952 Santa & the Pirates	2	4	6	12	16	20
SANTA & THE CHRISTMAS CHICKADEE						
Murphy's: 1974 (Giveaway, 20 pgs.)						
nn	2	4	6	8	10	12
SANTA & THE PIRATES						
Promotional Publ. Co.: 1952 (Giveaway)						
nn-Marv Levy-c/a	4	8	11	16	19	22
SANTA CLAUS FUNNIES (Also see The Little Fir Tree)						
W. T. Grant Co./Whitman Publishing: nd; 1940 (Giveaway, 8x10"; 12 pgs., color & B&W, heavy paper)						
nn-(2 versions- no date and 1940)	14	28	42	79	110	140
SANTA ON THE JOLLY ROGER						

	GD 2.0	VG 4.0	FN 6.0	VF 8.0	VF/NM 9.0	NM- 9.2
Promotional Publ. Co. (Giveaway): 1965						
nn-Marv Levy-c/a	2	4	6	8	10	12
SANTA! SANTA!						
R. Jackson: 1974 (20 pgs.) (Montgomery Ward giveaway)						
nn	1	3	4	6	8	10
SANTA'S BUNDLE OF FUN						
Gimbels: 1969 (Giveaway, B&W, 20 pgs.)						
nn-Coloring book & games	2	4	6	8	10	12
SANTA'S CHRISTMAS COMIC VARIETY SHOW (See Merry Christmas From Sears Toyland)						
Sears Roebuck & Co.: 1943 (24 pgs.)						
Contains puzzles & new comics of Dick Tracy, Little Orphan Annie, Moon Mullins, Terry & the Pirates, etc.	58	116	174	363	557	750
SANTA'S CHRISTMAS TIME STORIES						
Premium Sales, Inc.: nd (Late 1940s) (16 pgs., paper-c) (Giveaway)						
nn	6	12	18	31	38	45
SANTA'S CIRCUS						
Promotional Publ. Co.: 1964 (Giveaway, half-size)						
nn-Marv Levy-c/a	2	4	6	9	11	14
SANTA'S FUN BOOK						
Promotional Publ. Co.: 1951, 1952 (Regular size, 16 pgs., paper-c) (Murphy's giveaway)						
nn	5	10	15	23	28	32
SANTA'S GIFT BOOK						
No Publisher: No date (16 pgs.)						
nn-Puzzles, games only	4	8	11	16	19	22
SANTA'S NEW STORY BOOK						
Wallace Hamilton Campbell: 1949 (16 pgs., paper-c) (Giveaway)						
nn	6	12	18	31	38	45
SANTA'S REAL STORY BOOK						
Wallace Hamilton Campbell/W. W. Orris: 1948, 1952 (Giveaway, 16 pgs.)						
nn	6	12	18	31	38	45
SANTA'S RIDE						
W. T. Grant Co.: 1959 (Giveaway)						
nn	3	6	9	16	20	24
SANTA'S RODEO						
Promotional Publ. Co.: 1964 (Giveaway, half-size)						
nn-Marv Levy-a	2	4	6	9	11	14
SANTA'S SECRET CAVE						
W.T. Grant Co.: 1960 (Giveaway, half-size)						
nn	2	4	6	12	16	20
SANTA'S SECRETS						
Sam B. Anson Christmas giveaway: 1951, 1952? (16 pgs., paper-c)						
nn-Has games, stories & pictures to color	4	8	12	17	21	24
SANTA'S STORIES						
K. K. Publications (Klines Dept. Store): 1953 (Regular size, paper-c)						
nn-Kelly-a	17	34	51	95	135	175
nn-Another version (1953, glossy-c, half-size, 7-1/4x5-1/4")-Kelly-a	11	22	33	63	87	110
SANTA'S SURPRISE						
K. K. Publications: 1947 (Giveaway, 36 pgs., slick-c)						
nn	7	14	21	39	49	58
SANTA'S TOYTOWN FUN BOOK						
Promotional Publ. Co.: 1953 (Giveaway)						
nn-Marv Levy-c	4	8	11	16	19	22
SANTA TAKES A TRIP TO MARS						
Bradshaw-Diehl Co., Huntington, W.VA.: 1950s (nd) (Giveaway, 16 pgs.)						
nn	4	8	11	16	19	22
SCIENCE FAIR STORY OF ELECTRONICS						
Radio Shack/Tandy Corp.: 1975 - 1987 (Giveaway)						
11 different issues (approx. 1 per year) each....						3.00
SERGEANT PRESTON OF THE YUKON						
Quaker Cereals: 1956 (4 comic booklets) (Soft-c, 16 pgs., 7x2-1/2" & 5x2-1/2") Giveaways						
"How He Found Yukon King", "The Case That Made Him A Sergeant", "How Yukon King Saved						

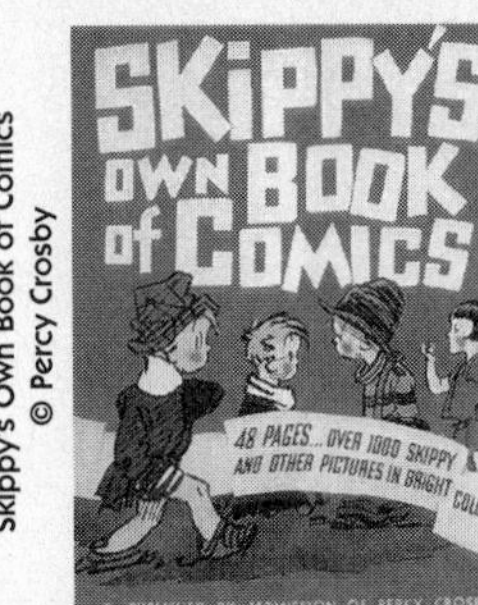
Skippy's Own Book of Comics © Percy Crosby

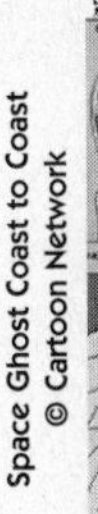
Space Ghost Coast to Coast © Cartoon Network

The Spirit 7/28/40 © Will Eisner

	GD 2.0	VG 4.0	FN 6.0	VF 8.0	VF/NM 9.0	NM- 9.2
Him From The Wolves", "How He Became A Mountie" each...	10	20	30	58	77	95
SHAZAM! (Visits Portland Oregon in 1943)						
DC Comics: 1989 (69¢ cover)						
nn-Promotes Super-Heroes exhibit at Oregon Museum of Science and Industry; reprints Golden Age Captain Marvel story	2	4	6	8	10	12
SHERIFF OF COCHISE, THE (TV)						
Mobil: 1957 (16 pgs.) Giveaway						
nn-Schaffenberger-a	4	8	12	17	21	24
SHIELD, THE (Based on the TV series)						
IDW Publishing: July, 2004 (Free Comic Book Day edition)						
Previews CSI: Bad Rap; The Shield: Spotlight; 24: One Shot; and 30 Days of Night						2.25
SILLY PUTTY MAN						
DC Comics: 1978						
1	2	4	6	9	11	14
SKATING SKILLS						
Custom Comics, Inc./Chicago Roller Skates: 1957 (36 & 12 pgs.; 5x7", two versions) (10¢)						
nn-Resembles old ACG cover plus interior art	4	7	10	14	17	20
SKINWALKER						
Oni Press: May, 2003 (Giveaway, B&W)						
1-Free Comic Book Day Edition						2.25
SKIPPY'S OWN BOOK OF COMICS (See Popular Comics)						
No publisher listed: 1934 (Giveaway, 52 pgs., strip reprints)						
nn-(Scarce)-By Percy Crosby	425	850	1275	2700	4100	5500

Published by Max C. Gaines for Phillip's Dental Magnesia to be advertised on the Skippy Radio Show and given away with the purchase of a tube of Phillip's Tooth Paste. This is the first four-color comic book of reprints about one character.

	GD 2.0	VG 4.0	FN 6.0	VF 8.0	VF/NM 9.0	NM- 9.2
SKY KING "RUNAWAY TRAIN" (TV)						
National Biscuit Co.: 1964 (Regular size, 16 pgs.)						
nn	8	16	24	51	71	90
SLAM BANG COMICS						
Post Cereal Giveaway: No. 9, No date						
9-Dynamic Man, Echo, Mr. E, Yankee Boy app.	9	18	27	52	66	80
SLAVE LABOR STORIES						
SLG Publishing: May, 2003 (Giveaway, B&W)						
1-Free Comic Book Day Edition; short stories by various; Dorkin Milk & Cheese-c						2.25
SMILIN' JACK						
Dell Publishing Co.						
Popped Wheat Giveaway (1947)-1938 strip reprints; 16 pgs. in full color	2	4	6	9	11	14
Shoe Store Giveaway-1938 strip reprints; 16 pgs.	5	10	15	24	30	35
Sparked Wheat Giveaway (1942)-16 pgs. in full color	5	10	15	24	30	35
SMOKEY BEAR (See Forest Fire for 1st app.)						
Dell Publ. Co.: 1959,1960						
True Story of..., The -U.S. Forest Service giveaway-Publ. by Western Printing Co.; reprints 1st 16 pgs. of Four Color #932. Inside front-c differs slightly in 1959 & 1960 editions	5	10	15	22	26	30
1964,1969 reprints	2	4	6	12	16	20
SMOKEY STOVER						
Dell Publishing Co.						
General Motors giveaway (1953)	8	16	24	40	50	60
National Fire Protection giveaway(1953 & 1954)-16 pgs., paper-c	8	16	24	40	50	60
SNOW FOR CHRISTMAS						
W. T. Grant Co.: 1957 (16 pgs.) (Giveaway)						
nn	4	8	12	18	22	25
SNOW WHITE AND THE SEVEN DWARFS						
Bendix Washing Machines: 1952 (32 pgs., 5x7-1/4", soft-c) (Disney)						
nn	12	24	36	69	95	120
SNOW WHITE AND THE SEVEN DWARFS						
Promotional Publ. Co.: 1957 (Small size)						
nn	6	12	18	28	34	40
SNOW WHITE AND THE SEVEN DWARFS						
Western Printing Co.: 1958 (16 pgs, 5x7-1/4", soft-c) (Disney premium)						
nn- "Mystery of the Missing Magic"	8	16	24	43	54	65
SNOW WHITE AND THE 7 DWARFS IN "MILKY WAY"						
American Dairy Assoc.: 1955 (16 pgs., soft-c, 5x7-1/4") (Disney premium)						
nn	12	24	36	69	95	120
SPACE GHOST COAST TO COAST						
Cartoon Network: Apr, 1994 (giveaway to Turner Broadcasting employees)						
1-(8 pgs.); origin of Space Ghost						6.00
SPACE PATROL (TV)						
Ziff-Davis Publishing Co. (Approved Comics)						
...'s Special Mission (8 pgs., B&W, Giveaway)	60	120	180	360	480	625
SPECIAL AGENT						
Assoc. of American Railroads: Oct, 1959 (16 pgs.)						
nn-The Story of the railroad police	8	16	24	40	50	60
SPECIAL DELIVERY						
Post Hall Synd.: 1951 (32 pgs.; B&W) (Giveaway)						
nn-Origin of Pogo, Swamp, etc.; 2 pg. biog. on Walt Kelly (One copy sold in 1980 for $150.00)						
SPECIAL EDITION (U. S. Navy Giveaways)						
National Periodical Publications: 1944 - 1945 (Regular comic format with wording simplified, 52 pgs.)						
1-Action (1944)-Reprints Action #80	59	118	177	365	520	700
2-Action (1944)-Reprints Action #81	59	118	177	365	520	700
3-Superman (1944)-Reprints Superman #33	59	118	177	365	520	700
4-Detective (1944)-Reprints Detective #97	59	118	177	365	520	700
5-Superman (1945)-Reprints Superman #34	59	118	177	365	520	700
6-Action (1945)-Reprints Action #84	59	118	177	365	520	700

NOTE: ***Wayne Boring** c-1, 2, 6. **Dick Sprang** c-4.*

SPIDER-MAN (See Amazing Spider-Man, The)

SPIRIT, THE (Weekly Comic Book)
Will Eisner: 6/2/40 - 10/5/52 (16 pgs.; 8 pgs.) (no cover) (in color)
(Distributed through various newspapers and other sources)
NOTE: **Eisner** script, pencils/inks for the most part from 6/2/40-4/26/42; a few stories assisted by Jack Cole, Fine, Powell and Kotsky.

	GD 2.0	VG 4.0	FN 6.0	VF 8.0	VF/NM 9.0	NM- 9.2
6/2/40(#1)-Origin/1st app. The Spirit; reprinted in Police #11; Lady Luck (Brenda Banks) (1st app.) by Chuck Mazoujian & Mr. Mystic (1st. app.) by S. R. (Bob) Powell begin	57	114	171	356	548	740
6/9/40(#2)	27	54	81	152	219	285
6/16/40(#3)-Black Queen app. in Spirit	17	34	51	98	139	180
6/23/40(#4)-Mr. Mystic receives magical necklace	14	28	42	81	113	145
6/30/40(#5)	14	28	42	81	113	145
7/7/40(#6)-1st app. Spirit carplane; Black Queen app. in Spirit	14	28	42	81	113	145
7/14/40(#7)-8/4/40(#10): 7/21/40-Spirit becomes fugitive wanted for murder	12	24	36	69	95	120
8/11/40-9/22/40	11	22	33	64	87	110
9/29/40-Ellen drops engagement with Homer Creep	10	20	30	58	77	95
10/6/40-11/3/40	10	20	30	58	77	95
11/10/40-The Black Queen app.	10	20	30	58	77	95
11/17/40, 11/24/40	10	20	30	58	77	95
12/1/40-Ellen spanking by Spirit on cover & inside; Eisner-1st 3 pgs., J. Cole rest	14	28	42	79	110	140
12/8/40-3/9/41	9	18	27	52	66	80
3/16/41-Intro. & 1st app. Silk Satin	12	24	36	69	95	120
3/23/41-6/1/41: 5/11/41-Last Lady Luck by Mazoujian; 5/18/41-Lady Luck by Nick Viscardi begins, ends 2/22/42	9	18	27	52	66	80
6/8/41-2nd app. Satin; Spirit learns Satin is also a British agent	10	20	30	60	80	100
6/15/41-1st app. Twilight	10	20	30	56	73	90
6/22/41-Hitler app. in Spirit	10	20	30	56	73	90
6/29/41-1/25/42,2/8/42	8	16	24	45	57	68
2/1/42-1st app. Duchess	10	20	30	56	73	90
2/15/42-4/26/42-Lady Luck by Klaus Nordling begins 3/1/42	9	18	27	51	62	75
5/3/42-8/16/42-Eisner/Fine/Quality staff assists on Spirit	7	14	21	37	46	55
8/23/42-Satin cover splash; Spirit by Eisner/Fine although signed by Fine	10	20	30	58	77	95
8/30/42,9/27/42-10/11/42,10/25/42-11/8/42-Eisner/Fine/Quality staff assists on Spirit	7	14	21	37	46	55
9/6/42-9/20/42,10/18/42-Fine/Belfi art on Spirit; scripts by Manly Wade Wellman	5	10	15	24	30	35
11/15/42-12/6/42,12/20/42,12/27/42,1/17/43-4/18/43,5/9/43-8/8/43-Wellman/						

The Spirit 2/19/50 © Will Eisner

Star Wars: Clone Wars Adventures © Lucasfilm Ltd

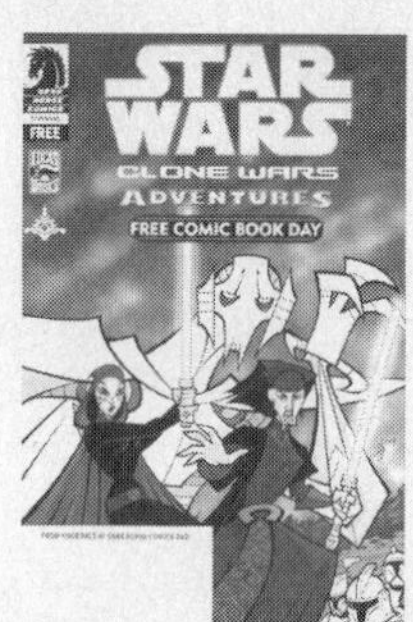

Steve Canyon - Strictly for the Smart Birds © HARV

	GD 2.0	VG 4.0	FN 6.0	VF 8.0	VF/NM 9.0	NM- 9.2
Woolfolk scripts, Fine pencils, Quality staff inks	5	10	15	24	30	35
12/13/42,1/3/43,1/10/43,4/25/43,5/2/43-Eisner scripts/layouts; Fine pencils, Quality staff inks	6	12	18	29	36	42
8/15/43-Eisner script/layout; pencils/inks by Quality staff; Jack Cole-a	5	10	15	22	26	30
8/22/43-12/12/43-Wellman/Woolfolk scripts, Fine pencils, Quality staff inks; Mr. Mystic by Guardineer-10/10/43-10/24/43	5	10	15	22	26	30
12/19/43-8/13/44-Wellman/Woolfolk/Jack Cole scripts; Cole, Fine & Robin King-a; Last Mr. Mystic-5/14/44	5	10	14	20	24	28
8/20/44-12/16/45-Wellman/Woolfolk scripts; Fine art with unknown staff assists	5	10	14	20	24	28
NOTE: *Scripts/layouts by Eisner, or Eisner/Nordling, Eisner/Mercer or Spranger/Eisner; inks by Eisner or Eisner/Spranger in issues 12/23/45-2/2/47.*						
12/23/45-1/6/46: 12/23/45-Christmas-c	6	12	18	29	36	42
1/13/46-Origin Spirit retold	8	16	24	45	57	68
1/20/46-1st postwar Satin app.	7	14	21	37	46	55
1/27/46-3/10/46: 3/3/46-Last Lady Luck by Nordling	6	12	18	29	36	42
3/17/46-Intro. & 1st app. Nylon	7	14	21	37	46	55
3/24/46,3/31/46,4/14/46	6	12	18	29	36	42
4/7/46-2nd app. Nylon	6	12	18	33	41	48
4/21/46-Intro. & 1st app. Mr. Carrion & His Pet Buzzard Julia	8	16	24	43	54	65
4/28/46-5/12/46,5/26/46-6/30/46: Lady Luck by Fred Schwab in issues 5/5/46-11/3/46	6	12	18	29	36	42
5/19/46-2nd app. Mr. Carrion	6	12	18	33	41	48
7/7/46-Intro. & 1st app. Dulcet Tone & Skinny	7	14	21	37	46	55
7/14/46-9/29/46	6	12	18	29	36	42
10/6/46-Intro. & 1st app. P'Gell	8	16	24	43	54	65
10/13/46-11/3/46,11/16/46-11/24/46	6	12	18	29	36	42
11/10/46-2nd app. P'Gell	6	12	18	33	41	48
12/1/46-3rd app. P'Gell	6	12	18	31	38	45
12/8/46-2/2/47	6	12	18	27	33	38
NOTE: *Scripts, pencils/inks by Eisner except where noted in issues 2/9/47-12/19/48.*						
2/9/47-7/6/47: 6/8/47-Eisner self satire	6	12	18	27	33	38
7/13/47- "Hansel & Gretel" fairy tales	7	14	21	37	46	55
7/20/47-Li'L Abner, Daddy Warbucks, Dick Tracy, Fearless Fosdick parody; A-Bomb blast-c	8	16	24	43	54	65
7/27/47-9/14/47	6	12	18	27	33	38
9/21/47-Pearl Harbor flashback	6	12	18	29	36	42
9/28/47-1st mention of Flying Saucers in comics-3 months after 1st sighting in Idaho on 6/25/47	10	20	30	58	77	95
10/5/47- "Cinderella" fairy tales	7	14	21	37	46	55
10/12/47-11/30/47	6	12	18	27	33	38
12/7/47-Intro. & 1st app. Powder Pouf	8	16	24	43	54	65
12/14/47-12/28/47	6	12	18	27	33	38
1/4/48-2nd app. Powder Pouf	6	12	18	33	41	48
1/11/48-1st app. Sparrow Fallon; Powder Pouf app.	6	12	18	33	41	48
1/18/48-He-Man ad cover; satire issue	6	12	18	33	41	48
1/25/48-Intro. & 1st app. Castanet	8	16	24	43	54	65
2/1/48-2nd app. Castanet	6	12	18	29	36	42
2/8/48-3/7/48	6	12	18	27	33	38
3/14/48-Only app. Kretchma	6	12	18	29	36	42
3/21/48,3/28/48,4/11/48-4/25/48	6	12	18	27	33	38
4/4/48-Only app. Wild Rice	6	12	18	29	36	42
5/2/48-2nd app. Sparrow	6	12	18	27	33	38
5/9/48-6/27/48,7/11/48,7/18/48: 6/13/48-TV issue	6	12	18	27	33	38
7/4/48-Spirit by Andre Le Blanc	5	10	15	22	26	30
7/25/48-Ambrose Bierce's "The Thing" adaptation classic by Eisner/Grandenetti	10	20	30	58	77	95
8/1/48-8/15/48,8/29/48-9/12/48	6	12	18	27	33	38
8/22/48-Poe's "Fall of the House of Usher" classic by Eisner/Grandenetti	10	20	30	58	77	95
9/19/48-Only app. Lorelei	6	12	18	33	41	48
9/26/48-10/31/48	6	12	18	27	33	38
11/7/48-Only app. Plaster of Paris	7	14	21	37	46	55
11/14/48-12/19/48	6	12	18	27	33	38
NOTE: *Scripts by Eisner or Feiffer or Eisner/Feiffer or Nordling. Art by Eisner with backgrounds by Eisner, Grandenetti, Le Blanc, Stallman, Nordling, Dixon and/or others in issues 12/26/48-1/4/51 except where noted.*						
12/26/48-Reprints some covers of 1948 with flashbacks	6	12	18	27	33	38
1/2/49-1/16/49	6	12	18	27	33	38
1/23/49,1/30/49-1st & 2nd app. Thorne	6	12	18	33	41	48
2/6/49-8/14/49	6	12	18	27	33	38
8/21/49,8/28/49-1st & 2nd app. Monica Veto	6	12	18	33	41	48
9/4/49,9/11/49	6	12	18	27	33	38
9/18/49-Love comic cover; has gag love comic ads on inside	6	12	18	33	41	48
9/25/49-Only app. Ice	6	12	18	29	36	42
10/2/49,10/9/49-Autumn News appears & dies in 10/9 issue	6	12	18	29	36	42
10/16/49-11/27/49,12/18/49,12/25/49	6	12	18	27	33	38
12/4/49,12/11/49-1st & 2nd app. Flaxen	6	12	18	29	36	42
1/1/50-Flashbacks to all of the Spirit girls-Thorne, Ellen, Satin, & Monica	9	18	27	51	62	75
1/8/50-Intro. & 1st app. Sand Saref	10	20	30	56	73	90
1/15/50-2nd app. Saref	8	16	24	43	54	65
1/22/50-2/5/50	6	12	18	27	33	38
2/12/50-Roller Derby issue	6	12	18	33	41	48
2/19/50-Half Dead Mr. Lox - Classic horror	7	14	21	37	46	55
2/26/50-4/23/50,5/14/50,5/28/50,7/23/50-9/3/50	6	12	18	27	33	38
4/30/50-Script/art by Le Blanc with Eisner framing	4	9	13	18	22	26
5/7/50,6/4/50-7/16/50-Abe Kanegson-a	4	9	13	18	22	26
5/21/50-Script by Feiffer/Eisner, art by Blaisdell, Eisner framing	4	9	13	18	22	26
9/10/50-P'Gell returns	6	12	18	33	41	48
9/17/50-1/7/51	6	12	18	27	33	38
1/14/51-Life Magazine cover; brief biography of Comm. Dolan, Sand Saref, Silk Satin, P'Gell, Sammy & Willum, Darling O'Shea, & Mr. Carrion & His Pet Buzzard Julia, with pin-ups by Eisner	7	14	21	37	46	55
1/21/51,2/4/51-4/1/51	6	12	18	27	33	38
1/28/51- "The Meanest Man in the World" classic by Eisner	7	14	21	37	46	55
4/8/51-7/29/51,8/12/51-Last Eisner issue	6	12	18	27	33	38
8/5/51,8/19/51-7/20/52-Not Eisner	4	8	12	17	21	24
7/27/52-(Rare)-Denny Colt in Outer Space by Wally Wood; 7 pg. S/F story of E.C. vintage	28	56	84	158	229	300
8/3/52-(Rare)- "Mission...The Moon" by Wood	28	56	84	158	229	300
8/10/52-(Rare)- "A DP On The Moon" by Wood	28	56	84	158	229	300
8/17/52-(Rare)- "Heart" by Wood/Eisner	23	46	69	132	191	250
8/24/52-(Rare)- "Rescue" by Wood	28	56	84	158	229	300
8/31/52-(Rare)- "The Last Man" by Wood	28	56	84	158	229	300
9/7/52-(Rare)- "The Man in The Moon" by Wood	28	56	84	158	229	300
9/14/52-(Rare)-Eisner/Wenzel-a	10	20	30	58	77	95
9/21/52-(Rare)- "Denny Colt, Alias The Spirit/Space Report" by Eisner/Wenzel	11	22	33	64	87	110
9/28/52-(Rare)- "Return From The Moon" by Wood	30	60	90	161	223	285
10/5/52-(Rare)- "The Last Story" by Eisner	12	24	36	69	95	120

Large Tabloid pages from 1946 on (Eisner) - Price 200 percent over listed prices.
NOTE: *Spirit sections came out in both large and small format. Some newspapers went to the 8-pg. format months before others. Some printed the pages so they cannot be folded into a small comic book section; these are worth less. (Also see Three Comics & Spiritman).*

SPY SMASHER
Fawcett Publications

	GD	VG	FN	VF	VF/NM	NM-
Well Known Comics (1944, 12 pgs., 8-1/2x10-1/2"), paper-c, glued binding, printed in green; Bestmaid/Samuel Lowe giveaway	16	32	48	89	127	165

STANDARD OIL COMICS (Also see Gulf Funny Weekly)
Standard Oil Co.: 1933 (Giveaway, tabloid size, 4 pgs. in color)

	GD	VG	FN	VF	VF/NM	NM-
1-Series has original art	52	104	156	317	484	650
2-5	24	48	72	135	195	255
6-14: 14-Fred Opper strip, 1 pg.	13	26	39	76	106	135

STAR TEAM
Marvel Comics Group: 1977 (6-1/2x5", 20 pgs.) (Ideal Toy Giveaway)

	GD	VG	FN	VF	VF/NM	NM-
nn	2	4	6	12	16	20

STAR WARS
Dark Horse Comics: May, 2002; July, 2004 (Free Comic Book Day giveaways)

	Price
...: Clone Wars Adventures (7/04) based on Cartoon Network series; Fillbach Bros. -a	2.25
...: Tales - A Jedi's Weapon (5/02, 16 pgs.) Anakin Skywalker Episode 2 photo-c	2.25

STEVE CANYON COMICS
Harvey Publications

	GD	VG	FN	VF	VF/NM	NM-
Dept. Store giveaway #3(6/48, 36pp)	10	20	30	56	73	90
...'s Secret Mission (1951, 16 pgs., Armed Forces giveaway); Caniff-a	9	18	27	54	70	85
Strictly for the Smart Birds (1951, 16 pgs.)-Information Comics Div. (Harvey) Premium	9	18	27	51	65	78

STORIES OF CHRISTMAS
K. K. Publications: 1942 (Giveaway, 32 pgs., paper cover)

	GD	VG	FN	VF	VF/NM	NM-
nn-Adaptation of "A Christmas Carol"; Kelly story "The Fir Tree"; Infinity-c	35	70	105	198	287	375

STORY HOUR SERIES (Disney)

The Story of Harry S. Truman © DNC

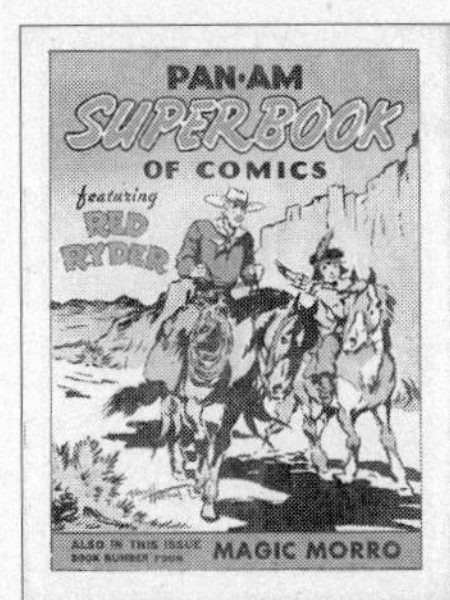

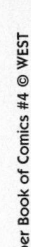

Super Book of Comics #4 © WEST

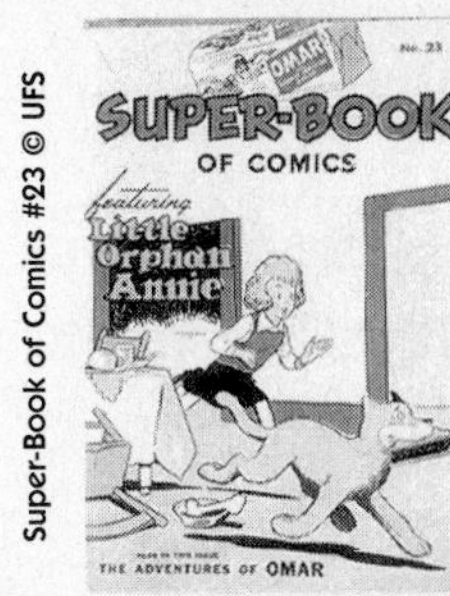

Super-Book of Comics #23 © UFS

Whitman Publ. Co.: 1948, 1949; 1951-1953 (36 pgs., paper-c) (4-3/4x6-1/2")
Given away with subscription to Walt Disney's Comics & Stories

	GD 2.0	VG 4.0	FN 6.0	VF 8.0	VF/NM 9.0	NM- 9.2
nn(1948)-Mickey Mouse and the Boy Thursday	11	22	33	66	91	115
nn(1948)-Mickey Mouse the Miracle Master	11	22	33	66	91	115
nn(1948)-Minnie Mouse and Antique Chair	11	22	33	66	91	115
nn(1949)-The Three Orphan Kittens(B&W & color)	8	16	24	46	58	70
nn(1949)-Danny-The Little Black Lamb	8	16	24	48	58	70
800(1948)-Donald Duck in "Bringing Up the Boys"	17	34	51	98	139	180
1953 edition	11	22	33	64	87	110
801(1948)-Mickey Mouse's Summer Vacation	10	20	30	56	73	90
1951, 1952 editions	6	12	18	31	38	45
802(1948)-Bugs Bunny's Adventures	9	18	27	51	62	75
803(1948)-Bongo	7	14	21	38	47	56
804(1948)-Mickey and the Beanstalk	8	16	24	46	58	70
805-15(1949)-Andy Panda and His Friends	7	14	21	39	49	58
806-15(1949)-Tom and Jerry	8	16	24	44	55	66
808-15(1949)-Johnny Appleseed	7	14	21	38	47	56

1948, 1949 Hard Cover Edition of each....30% - 40% more.

STORY OF EDISON, THE
Educational Comics: 1956 (16 pgs.) (Reddy Killowatt)

	GD 2.0	VG 4.0	FN 6.0	VF 8.0	VF/NM 9.0	NM- 9.2
nn-Reprint of Reddy Kilowatt #2(1947)	7	14	21	35	43	50

STORY OF HARRY S. TRUMAN, THE
Democratic National Committee: 1948 (Giveaway, regular size, soft-c, 16 pg.)

	GD 2.0	VG 4.0	FN 6.0	VF 8.0	VF/NM 9.0	NM- 9.2
nn-Gives biography on career of Truman; used in **SOTI**, pg. 311	14	28	42	79	110	140

STORY OF THE BALLET, THE
Selva and Sons, Inc.: 1954 (16 pgs., paper cover)

	GD 2.0	VG 4.0	FN 6.0	VF 8.0	VF/NM 9.0	NM- 9.2
nn	4	8	11	16	19	22

STRANGE AS IT SEEMS
McNaught Syndicate: 1936 (B&W, 5" x 7", 24 pgs.)

	GD 2.0	VG 4.0	FN 6.0	VF 8.0	VF/NM 9.0	NM- 9.2
nn-Ex-Lax giveaway	8	16	24	44	55	66

STRAY
Dark Horse Comics: 2004 (8 1/2"x 5 1/2", Diamond Comic Dist. Halloween giveaway)

	GD 2.0	VG 4.0	FN 6.0	VF 8.0	VF/NM 9.0	NM- 9.2
nn-Reprint from The Dark Horse Book of Hauntings; Evan Dorkin-s/Jill Thompson-a						2.25

STRAY BULLETS
El Capitan Books: May, 2002 (48 pgs., B&W, flip book)

	GD 2.0	VG 4.0	FN 6.0	VF 8.0	VF/NM 9.0	NM- 9.2
Free Comic Book Day giveaway-Reprints #2 with "Free Comic Book Day" banner on-c; flip book with The Matrix (printing of internet comic)						2.25

SUGAR BEAR
Post Cereal Giveaway: No date, circa 1975? (2 1/2" x 4 1/2", 16 pgs.)

	GD 2.0	VG 4.0	FN 6.0	VF 8.0	VF/NM 9.0	NM- 9.2
"The Almost Take Over of the Post Office", "The Race Across the Atlantic", "The Zoo Goes Wild" each...	1	2	3	5	6	8

SUNDAY WORLD'S EASTER EGG FULL OF EASTER MEAT FOR LITTLE PEOPLE
Supplement to the New York World: 3/27/1898 (soft-c, 16pg, 4"x8" approx., opens at top, color & B&W)(Giveaway)(shaped like an Easter egg)

	GD 2.0	VG 4.0	FN 6.0	VF 8.0	VF/NM 9.0	NM- 9.2
nn-By R.F. Outcault	19	38	57	107	154	200

SUPER BOOK OF COMICS
Western Publishing Co.: nd (1942-1943?) (Soft-c, 32 pgs.) (Pan-Am/Gilmore Oil/Kelloggs premiums)

	GD 2.0	VG 4.0	FN 6.0	VF 8.0	VF/NM 9.0	NM- 9.2
nn-Dick Tracy (Gilmore)-Magic Morro app.	37	74	111	209	305	400
1-Dick Tracy & The Smuggling Ring; Stratosphere Jim app. (Rare) (Pan-Am)	37	74	111	209	305	400
1-Smilin' Jack, Magic Morro (Pan-Am)	13	26	39	76	106	135
2-Smilin' Jack, Stratosphere Jim (Pan-Am)	13	26	39	76	106	135
2-Smitty, Magic Morro (Pan-Am)	13	26	39	76	106	135
3-Captain Midnight, Magic Morro (Pan-Am)	27	54	81	154	222	290
3-Moon Mullins?	13	26	39	76	106	135
4-Red Ryder, Magic Morro (Pan-Am). Same content as Red Ryder Victory Patrol comic w/diff. cover	16	32	48	89	127	165
4-Smitty, Stratosphere Jim (Pan-Am)	13	26	39	76	106	135
5-Don Winslow, Magic Morro (Gilmore)	16	32	48	89	127	165
5-Don Winslow, Stratosphere Jim (Pan-Am)	16	32	48	89	127	165
5-Terry & the Pirates	19	38	57	107	154	200
6-Don Winslow, Stratosphere Jim (Pan-Am)-McWilliams-a	16	32	48	89	127	165
6-King of the Royal Mounted, Magic Morro (Pan-Am)	16	32	48	89	127	165
7-Dick Tracy, Magic Morro (Pan-Am)	22	44	66	123	177	230
7-Little Orphan Annie	11	22	33	66	91	115
8-Dick Tracy, Stratosphere Jim (Pan-Am)	19	38	57	107	154	200
8-Dan Dunn, Magic Morro (Pan-Am)	11	22	33	66	91	115
9-Terry & the Pirates, Magic Morro (Pan-Am)	19	38	57	107	154	200
10-Red Ryder, Magic Morro (Pan-Am)	16	32	48	89	127	165

SUPER-BOOK OF COMICS
Western Publishing Co.: (Omar Bread & Hancock Oil Co. giveaways) 1944 - No. 30, 1947 (Omar); 1947 - 1948 (Hancock) (16 pgs.)

NOTE: The Hancock issues are all exact reprints of the earlier Omar issues. The issue numbers were removed in some of the reprints.

	GD 2.0	VG 4.0	FN 6.0	VF 8.0	VF/NM 9.0	NM- 9.2
1-Dick Tracy (Omar, 1944)	18	38	54	104	150	195
1-Dick Tracy (Hancock, 1947)	14	28	42	81	113	145
2-Bugs Bunny (Omar, 1944)	8	16	24	40	50	60
2-Bugs Bunny (Hancock, 1947)	6	12	18	32	39	46
3-Terry & the Pirates (Omar, 1944)	11	22	33	62	84	105
3-Terry & the Pirates (Hancock, 1947)	10	20	30	56	73	90
4-Andy Panda (Omar, 1944)	8	16	24	40	50	60
4-Andy Panda (Hancock, 1947)	6	12	18	32	39	46
5-Smokey Stover (Omar, 1945)	6	12	18	32	39	46
5-Smokey Stover (Hancock, 1947)	5	10	15	24	30	35
6-Porky Pig (Omar, 1945)	8	16	24	40	50	60
6-Porky Pig (Hancock, 1947)	6	12	18	32	39	46
7-Smilin' Jack (Omar, 1945)	8	16	24	40	50	60
7-Smilin' Jack (Hancock, 1947)	6	12	18	32	39	46
8-Oswald the Rabbit (Omar, 1945)	6	12	18	32	39	46
8-Oswald the Rabbit (Hancock, 1947)	5	10	15	24	30	35
9-Alley Oop (Omar, 1945)	11	22	33	66	91	115
9-Alley Oop (Hancock, 1947)	11	22	33	62	84	105
10-Elmer Fudd (Omar, 1945)	6	12	18	32	39	46
10-Elmer Fudd (Hancock, 1947)	5	10	15	24	30	35
11-Little Orphan Annie (Omar, 1945)	8	16	24	42	53	64
11-Little Orphan Annie (Hancock, 1947)	7	14	21	36	45	54
12-Woody Woodpecker (Omar, 1945)	6	12	18	32	39	46
12-Woody Woodpecker (Hancock, 1947)	5	10	15	24	30	35
13-Dick Tracy (Omar, 1945)	11	22	33	66	91	115
13-Dick Tracy (Hancock, 1947)	11	22	33	62	84	105
14-Bugs Bunny (Omar, 1945)	6	12	18	32	39	46
14-Bugs Bunny (Hancock, 1947)	5	10	15	24	30	35
15-Andy Panda (Omar, 1945)	6	12	18	28	34	40
15-Andy Panda (Hancock, 1947)	5	10	15	24	30	35
16-Terry & the Pirates (Omar, 1945)	11	22	33	62	84	105
16-Terry & the Pirates (Hancock, 1947)	9	18	27	51	62	75
17-Smokey Stover (Omar, 1946)	6	12	18	32	39	46
17-Smokey Stover (Hancock, 1948?)	5	10	15	24	30	35
18-Porky Pig (Omar, 1946)	6	12	18	28	34	40
18-Porky Pig (Hancock, 1948?)	5	10	15	24	30	35
19-Smilin' Jack (Omar, 1946)	6	12	18	32	39	46
nn-Smilin' Jack (Hancock, 1948)	5	10	15	24	30	35
20-Oswald the Rabbit (Omar, 1946)	6	12	18	28	34	40
nn-Oswald the Rabbit (Hancock, 1948)	5	10	15	24	30	35
21-Gasoline Alley (Omar, 1946)	8	16	24	42	53	64
nn-Gasoline Alley (Hancock, 1948)	7	14	21	36	45	54
22-Elmer Fudd (Omar, 1946)	6	12	18	28	34	40
nn-Elmer Fudd (Hancock, 1948)	5	10	15	24	30	35
23-Little Orphan Annie (Omar, 1946)	8	16	24	40	50	60
nn-Little Orphan Annie (Hancock, 1948)	6	12	18	32	39	46
24-Woody Woodpecker (Omar, 1946)	6	12	18	28	34	40
nn-Woody Woodpecker (Hancock, 1948)	5	10	15	24	30	35
25-Dick Tracy (Omar, 1946)	11	22	33	62	84	105
nn-Dick Tracy (Hancock, 1948)	9	18	27	52	66	80
26-Bugs Bunny (Omar, 1946))	6	12	18	28	34	40
nn-Bugs Bunny (Hancock, 1948)	5	10	15	24	30	35
27-Andy Panda (Omar, 1946)	6	12	18	28	34	40
27-Andy Panda (Hancock, 1948)	5	10	15	24	30	35
28-Terry & the Pirates (Omar, 1946)	11	22	33	62	84	105
28-Terry & the Pirates (Hancock, 1948)	9	18	27	51	62	75
29-Smokey Stover (Omar, 1947)	6	12	18	28	34	40
29-Smokey Stover (Hancock, 1948)	5	10	15	24	30	35
30-Porky Pig (Omar, 1947)	6	12	18	28	34	40
30-Porky Pig (Hancock, 1948)	5	10	15	24	30	35
nn-Bugs Bunny (Hancock, 1948)-Does not match any Omar book	6	12	18	28	34	40

SUPER CIRCUS (TV)
Cross Publishing Co.

	GD 2.0	VG 4.0	FN 6.0	VF 8.0	VF/NM 9.0	NM- 9.2
1-(1951, Weather Bird Shoes giveaway)	7	14	21	39	49	58

Super Friends Special #1 © DC

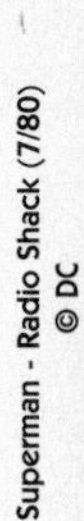
Superman - Radio Shack (7/80) © DC

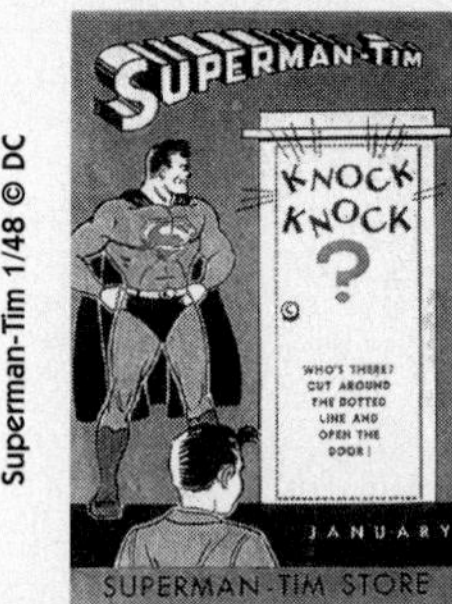

Superman-Tim 1/48 © DC

	GD 2.0	VG 4.0	FN 6.0	VF 8.0	VF/NM 9.0	NM- 9.2

SUPER FRIENDS
DC Comics: 1981 (Giveaway, no ads, no code or price)
...Special 1 -r/Super Friends #19 & 36 — 2 4 6 8 10 12

SUPERGEAR COMICS
Jacobs Corp.: 1976 (Giveaway, 4 pgs. in color, slick paper)
nn-(Rare)-Superman, Lois Lane; Steve Lombard app. (500 copies printed, over half destroyed?) — 24 48 72 170 260 350

SUPERGIRL
DC Comics: 1984, 1986 (Giveaway, Baxter paper)
nn-(American Honda/U.S. Dept. Transportation) Torres-c/a — 2 4 6 8 10 12

SUPER HEROES PUZZLES AND GAMES
General Mills Giveaway (Marvel Comics Group): 1979 (32 pgs., regular size)
nn-Four 2-pg. origin stories of Spider-Man, Captain America, The Hulk, & Spider-Woman — 3 6 9 16 20 24

SUPERMAN
National Periodical Publ./DC Comics
72-Giveaway(9-10/51)-(Rare)-Price blackened out; came with banner wrapped around book; without banner — 74 148 221 450 665 900
72-Giveaway with banner — 103 206 308 625 962 1300
Bradman birthday custom (1988)(extremely limited distribution) - no reported sales for 2004
... For the Animals (2000, Doris Day Animal Foundation, 30 pgs.) polybagged with Gotham Adventures #22, Hourman #12, Impulse #58, Looney Tunes #62, Stars and S.T.R.I.P.E. #8 and Superman Adventures #41 — 2.50
Kelloggs Giveaway-(2/3 normal size, 1954)-r-two stories/Superman #55 — 34 68 103 167 246 325
Kenner: Man of Steel (Doomsday is Coming) (1995, 16 pgs.) packaged with set of Superman and Doomsday action figures — 3.50
...Meets the Quik Bunny (1987, Nestles Quik premium, 36 pgs.) — 1 2 3 5 6 8
Pizza Hut Premiums (12/77)-Exact reprints of 1950s comics except for paid ads (set of 6 exist?); Vol. 1-r#97 (#113-r also known) — 1 3 4 6 8 10
Radio Shack Giveaway-36 pgs. (7/80) "The Computers That Saved Metropolis", Starlin/Giordano-a; advertising insert in Action #509, New Advs. of Superboy #7, Legion of Super-Heroes #265, & House of Mystery #282. (All comics were 68 pgs.) Cover of inserts printed on newsprint. Giveaway contains 4 extra pgs. of Radio Shack advertising that inserts do not have — 1 2 3 4 5 7
Radio Shack Giveaway-(7/81) "Victory by Computer" — 1 2 3 4 5 7
Radio Shack Giveaway-(7/82) "Computer Masters of Metropolis" — 1 2 3 4 5 7

SUPERMAN ADVENTURES, THE (TV)
DC Comics: 1996 (Based on animated series)
1-(1996) Preview issue distributed at Warner Bros. stores — 4.00
Titus Game Edition (1998) — 2.50

SUPERMAN AND THE GREAT CLEVELAND FIRE
National Periodical Publ.: 1948 (Giveaway, 4 pgs., no cover) (Hospital Fund)
nn-In full color — 85 170 255 400 575 750

SUPERMAN (Miniature)
National Periodical Publ.: 1942; 1955 - 1956 (3 issues, no #'s, 32 pgs.)
The pages are numbered in the 1st issue: 1-32; 2nd: 1A-32A, and 3rd: 1B-32B
No date-Py-Co-Pay Tooth Powder giveaway (8 pgs.; circa 1942) — 65 130 195 400 575 750
1-The Superman Time Capsule (Kellogg's Sugar Smacks)(1955) — 45 90 135 270 375 480
1A-Duel in Space (1955) — 40 80 120 250 338 425
1B-The Super Show of Metropolis (also #1-32, no B)(1955) — 40 80 120 250 338 425

NOTE: *Numbering variations exist. Each title could have any combination-#1, 1A, or 1B.*

SUPERMAN RECORD COMIC
National Periodical Publications: 1966 (Golden Records)
(With record)-Record reads origin of Superman from comic; came with iron-on patch, decoder, membership card & button; comic-r/Superman #125,146 — 20 40 60 116 171 230
Comic only — 10 20 30 66 93 120

SUPERMAN'S BUDDY (Costume Comic)
National Periodical Publications: 1954 (4 pgs., slick paper-c; one-shot) (Came in box w/costume)
1-With box & costume — 131 262 393 819 1260 1700
Comic only — 60 120 180 375 557 750
1-(1958 edition)-Printed in 2 colors — 18 36 54 102 146 190

SUPERMAN'S CHRISTMAS ADVENTURE
National Periodical Publications: 1940, 1944 (Giveaway, 16 pgs.)
Distributed by Nehi drinks, Bailey Store, Ivey-Keith Co., Kennedy's Boys Shop, Macy's Store, Boston Store
1(1940)-Burnley-a; F. Ray-c/r from Superman #6 (Scarce)-Superman saves Santa Claus. Santa makes real Superman Toys offered in 1940. 1st merchandising story — 575 1400 2200 3400 4600 5800
nn(1944) w/Santa Claus & X-mas tree-c — 110 250 400 680 1015 1350
nn(1944) w/Candy cane & Superman-c — 100 240 370 615 932 1250

SUPERMAN-TIM (Becomes Tim)
Superman-Tim Stores/National Periodical Publ.: Aug, 1942 - May, 1950 (Half size) (B&W Giveaway w/2 color covers) (Publ. monthly 2/43 on)
8/42 (#1)-All have Superman illos. — 130 260 390 812 1185 1600
1/43 (#2) — 40 80 120 244 372 500
2/43 (#3) — 40 80 120 239 357 475
3/43 (#4) — 40 80 120 239 357 475
4/43, 5/43, 6/43, 7/43, 8/43 — 39 78 117 222 324 425
9/43, 10/43, 11/43, 12/43 — 33 66 99 187 271 355
1/44-12/44 — 28 56 84 158 229 300
1/45-5/45, 10-12/45, 1/46-8/46 — 26 52 78 147 211 275
6/45-Classic Superman-c — 28 56 84 158 229 300
7/45-Classic Superman flag-c — 28 56 84 158 229 300
9/45-1st stamp album issue — 55 110 165 336 511 685
9/46-2nd stamp album issue — 46 92 138 281 428 575
10/46-1st Superman story — 34 68 102 196 283 370
11/46, 12/46, 1/47-8/47 issues-Superman story in each; 2/47-Infinity-c. All 36 pgs. — 34 68 102 196 283 370
9/47-Stamp album issue & Superman story — 44 88 132 268 409 550
10/47, 11/47, 12/47-Superman stories (24 pgs.) — 34 68 102 196 283 370
1/48-7/48,10/48, 11/48, 2/49, 4/49-11/49 — 28 56 84 158 229 300
8/48-Contains full page ad for Superman-Tim watch giveaway — 28 56 84 158 229 300
9/48-Stamp album issue — 37 74 111 209 305 400
1/49-Full page Superman bank cut-out — 28 56 84 158 229 300
3/49-Full page Superman boxing game cut-out — 28 56 84 158 229 300
12/49-3/50, 5/50-Superman stories — 30 60 90 173 249 325
4/50-Superman story, baseball stories; photo-c without Superman — 34 68 102 196 283 370

NOTE: *All issues have Superman illustrations throughout. The page count varies depending on whether a Superman-Tim comic story is inserted. If it is, the page count is either 36 or 24 pages. Otherwise all issues are 16 pages. Each issue has a special place for inserting a full color Superman stamp. The stamp album issues had spaces for the stamps given away the past year. The books were mailed as a subscription premium. The stamps were given away free (or when you made a purchase) only when you physically came into the store.*

SUPER SEAMAN SLOPPY
Allied Pristine Union Council, Buffalo, NY: 1940s, 8pg., reg. size (Soft-c)
nn — 4 8 12 17 21 24

SWAMP FOX, THE
Walt Disney Productions: 1960 (14 pgs, small size) (Canada Dry Premiums)
Titles: (A)-Tory Masquerade, (B)-Turnabout Tactics, (C)-Rindau Rampage; each came in paper sleeve, books 1,2 & 3;
Set with sleeves — 6 12 18 43 59 75
Comic only — 2 4 6 14 18 22

SWORDQUEST
DC Comics/Atari Pub.: 1982, 52pg., 5"x7" (Giveaway with video games)
1,2-Roy Thomas & Gerry Conway-s; George Pérez & Dick Giordano-c/a in all — 2 4 6 10 13 16
3-Low print — 3 6 9 16 20 25

SYNDICATE FEATURES (Sci/fi)
Harry A. Chesler Syndicate: V1#3, 11/15/37 (Tabloid size, 3 colors, 4 pgs.) (Editors premium) (Came folded)
V1#3-Dan Hastings daily strips-Guardineer-a — 450 900 1350 1800 2400 3000

TASTEE-FREEZ COMICS
Harvey Comics: 1957 (10¢, 36 pgs.)(6 different issues given away)
1-Little Dot — 7 14 21 51 71 90
2,4,5: 2-Rags Rabbit. 4-Sad Sack. 5-Mazie — 4 8 12 29 40 50
3-Casper — 6 12 18 40 55 70
6-Dick Tracy — 6 12 18 40 55 70

TAYLOR'S CHRISTMAS TABLOID
Dept. Store Giveaway: Mid 1930s, Cleveland, Ohio (Tabloid size; in color)
nn-(Very Rare)-Among the earliest pro work of Siegel & Shuster; one full color page called "The Battle in the Stratosphere", with a pre-Superman look; Shuster art thoughout. (Only 1 known copy) Estimated value... — 4000.00

Teen Titans Go! #1 FCBD Edition © DC

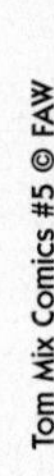

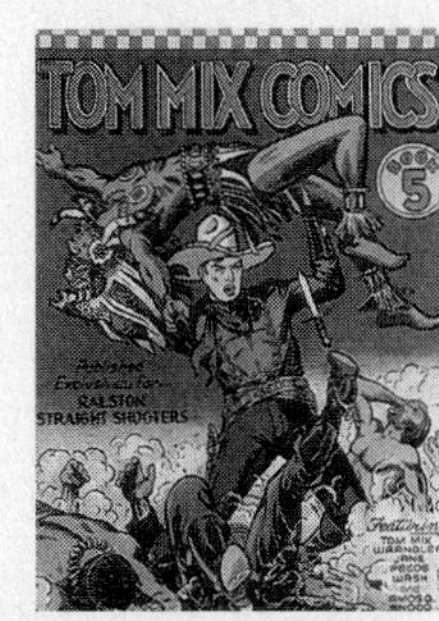

Tom Mix Comics #5 © FAW

24 IDW FCBD Edition © IDW

GD 2.0 | VG 4.0 | FN 6.0 | VF 8.0 | VF/NM 9.0 | NM- 9.2

TAZ'S 40TH BIRTHDAY BLOWOUT
DC Comics: 1994 (K-Mart giveaway, 16 pgs.)
nn-Six pg. story, games and puzzles 4.00

TEE AND VEE CROSLEY IN TELEVISION LAND COMICS (Also see Crosley's House of Fun)
Crosley Division, Avco Mfg. Corp. : 1951 (52 pgs.; 8x11"; paper cover; in color) (Giveaway)
Many stories, puzzles, cut-outs, games, etc. 6 12 18 33 41 48

TEEN TITANS GO!
DC Comics: Sept, 2004 (Free Comic Book Day giveaway)
1-Reprints Teen Titans Go! #1; 2 bound-in Wacky Packages stickers 2.25

TENNESSEE JED (Radio)
Fox Syndicate? (Wm. C. Popper & Co.): nd (1945) (16 pgs.; paper-c; regular size; giveaway)
nn 22 44 66 125 180 235

TENNIS (...For Speed, Stamina, Strength, Skill)
Tennis Educational Foundation: 1956 (16 pgs.; soft cover; 10¢)
Book 1-Endorsed by Gene Tunney, Ralph Kiner, etc. showing how tennis has helped them 6 12 18 27 33 38

TERRY AND THE PIRATES
Dell Publishing Co.: 1939 - 1953 (By Milton Caniff)
Buster Brown Shoes giveaway(1938)-32 pgs.; in color 25 50 75 141 203 265
Canada Dry Premiums-Books #1-3(1953, 36 pgs.; 2x5")-Harvey; #1-Hot Shot Charlie Flies Again; 2-In Forced Landing; 3-Dragon Lady in Distress) 15 30 45 86 123 160
Gambles Giveaway (1938, 16 pgs.) 10 20 30 56 73 90
Gillmore Giveaway (1938, 24 pgs.) 10 20 30 58 77 95
Popped Wheat Giveaway(1938)-Strip reprints in full color; Caniff-a 2 4 6 8 10 12
Shoe Store giveaway (Weatherbird)(1938, 16 pgs., soft-c)(2-diff.) 10 20 30 58 77 95
Sparked Wheat Giveaway(1942, 16 pgs.)-In color 10 20 30 58 77 95

TERRY AND THE PIRATES
Libby's Radio Premium: 1941 (16 pgs.; reg. size)(shipped folded in the mail)
"Adventure of the Ruby of Genghis Khan" - Each pg. is a puzzle that must be completed to read the story 400 875 1350 2600 - -

THAT THE WORLD MAY BELIEVE
Catechetical Guild Giveaway: No date (16 pgs.) (Graymoor Friars distr.)
nn 4 8 12 18 22 25

30 DAYS OF NIGHT
IDW Publishing: July, 2004 (Free Comic Book Day edition)
Previews CSI: Bad Rap; The Shield: Spotlight; 24: One Shot; and 30 Days of Night 2.25

3-D COLOR CLASSICS (Wendy's Kid's Club)
Wendy's Int'l Inc.: 1995 (5 1/2" x 8", comes with 3-D glasses)
The Elephant's Child, Gulliver's Travels, Peter Pan, The Time Machine, 20,000 Leagues Under the Sea: Neal Adams-a in all each.... 3.50

350 YEARS OF AMERICAN DAIRY FOODS
American Dairy Assoc.: 1957 (5x7", 16 pgs.)
nn-History of milk 3 6 8 12 14 16

THUMPER (Disney)
Grosset & Dunlap: 1942 (50¢, 32pgs., hardcover book, 7"x8-1/2" w/dust jacket)
nn-Given away (along with a copy of Bambi) for a $2.00, 2-year subscription to WDC&S in 1942. (Xmas offer). Book only 17 34 51 98 139 180
Dust jacket only 10 20 30 56 73 90

TILLY AND TED-TINKERTOTLAND
W. T. Grant Co.: 1945 (Giveaway, 20 pgs.)
nn-Christmas comic 7 14 21 37 46 55

TIM (Formerly Superman-Tim; becomes Gene Autry-Tim)
Tim Stores: June, 1950 - Oct, 1950 (B&W, half-size)
4 issues; 6/50, 9/50, 10/50 known 17 34 51 98 139 180

TIM AND SALLY'S ADVENTURES AT MARINELAND
Marineland Restaurant & Bar, Marineland, CA: 1957 (5x7", 16 pgs., soft-c)
nn-copyright Oceanarium, Inc. 2 4 6 8 10 12

TIME MACHINE, THE
DC Comics: 2002 (10 pgs.)
nn-Promotes the 2002 DreamWorks movie 5.00

TIME OF DECISION
Harvey Publications Inc.: (16 pgs., paper cover)
nn-ROTC recruitment 4 7 10 14 17 20

TIM IN SPACE (Formerly Gene Autry Tim; becomes Tim Tomorrow)
Tim Stores: 1950 (1/2 size giveaway) (B&W)
nn 12 24 36 71 98 125

TIM TOMORROW (Formerly Tim In Space)
Tim Stores: 8/51, 9/51, 10/51, Christmas, 1951 (5x7-3/4")
nn-Prof. Fumble & Captain Kit Comet in all 12 24 36 71 98 125

TITANS BEAT (Teen Titans)
DC Comics: Aug, 1996 (16 pgs., paper-c)
1-Intro./preview new Teen Titans members; Pérez-a 4.00

TOMB RAIDER: THE SERIES (Also see Witchblade/Tomb Raider)
Image Comics (Top Cow Prod.): May, 2002
Free Comic Book Day giveaway-Reprints #1 with "Free Comic Book Day" banner on-c 2.25

TOM MIX (...Commandos Comics #10-12)
Ralston-Purina Co.: Sept, 1940 - No. 12, Nov, 1942 (36 pgs.); 1983 (one-shot)
Given away for two Ralston box-tops; 1983 came in cereal box
1-Origin (life) Tom Mix; Fred Meagher-a 300 600 900 1925 3063 4200
2 92 184 276 575 888 1200
3-9 58 116 174 363 557 750
10-12: 10-Origin Tom Mix Commando Unit; Speed O'Dare begins; Japanese sub-c. 12-Sci/fi-c 52 104 156 317 484 650
1983- "Taking of Grizzly Grebb", Toth-a; 16 pg. miniature 2 4 6 10 12 15

TOM SAWYER COMICS
Giveaway: 1951? (Paper cover)
nn-Contains a coverless Hopalong Cassidy from 1951; other combinations known 3 6 9 16 20 25

TOPPS COMICS PRESENTS
Topps Comics: No. 0, 1993 (Giveaway, B&W, 36 pgs.)
0-Dracula vs. Zorro, Teenagents, Silver Star, & Bill the Galactic Hero 2.50

TOWN THAT FORGOT SANTA, THE
W. T. Grant Co.: 1961 (Giveaway, 24 pgs.)
nn 3 6 9 18 23 28

TOY LAND FUNNIES (See Funnies On Parade)
Eastern Color Printing Co.: 1934 (32 pgs., Hecht Co. store giveaway)
nn-Reprints Buck Rogers Sunday pages #199-201 from Famous Funnies #5. A rare variation of Funnies On Parade; same format, similar contents, same cover except for large Santa placed in center (value will be based on sale)

TOY WORLD FUNNIES (See Funnies On Parade)
Eastern Color Printing Co.: 1933 (36 pgs., slick cover, Golden Eagle and Wanamaker giveaway)
nn-Contains contents from Funnies On Parade/Century Of Comics. A rare variation of Funnies On Parade; same format, similar contents, same cover except for large Santa placed in center (value will be based on sale)

TRANSFORMERS ARMADA
Dreamwave Productions: May, 2003
Free Comic Book Day Edition 2.25

TRAPPED
Harvey Publications (Columbia Univ. Press): 1951 (Giveaway, soft-c, 16 pgs)
nn-Drug education comic (30,000 printed?) distributed to schools.; mentioned in **SOTI**, pgs. 256,350 2 4 6 8 10 12
NOTE: *Many copies surfaced in 1979 causing a setback in price; beware of trimmed edges, because many copies have a brittle edge.*

TRIP TO OUTER SPACE WITH SANTA
Sales Promotions, Inc/Peoria Dry Goods: 1950s (paper-c)
nn-Comics, games & puzzles 5 10 15 22 26 30

TRIP WITH SANTA ON CHRISTMAS EVE, A
Rockford Dry Goods Co.: No date (Early 1950s) (Giveaway, 16 pgs., paper-c)
nn 5 10 15 22 26 30

TRUTH BEHIND THE TRIAL OF CARDINAL MINDSZENTY, THE (See Cardinal Mindszenty)

24 (Based on the TV series)
IDW Publishing: July, 2004 (Free Comic Book Day edition)
Previews CSI: Bad Rap; The Shield: Spotlight; 24: One Shot; and 30 Days of Night 2.25

24 PAGES OF COMICS (No title) (Also see Pure Oil Comics, Salerno Carnival of Comics, & Vicks Comics)

Two Faces of Communism © CACC

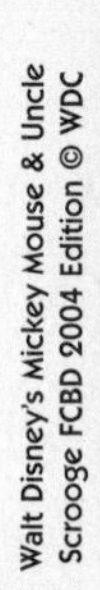
Walt Disney's Mickey Mouse & Uncle Scrooge FCBD 2004 Edition © WDC

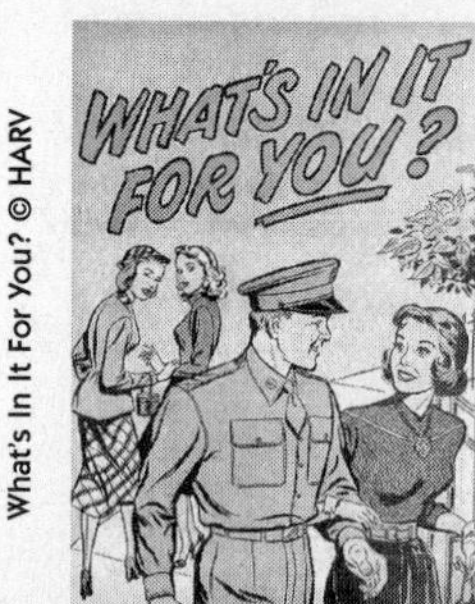

What's In It For You? © HARV

GD VG FN VF VF/NM NM-
2.0 4.0 6.0 8.0 9.0 9.2

Giveaway by various outlets including Sears: Late 1930s
nn-Contains strip reprints-Buck Rogers, Napoleon, Sky Roads, War on Crime
37 74 111 209 305 400

TWISTED METAL (Video game)
DC Comics: 1996
nn 3.00

TWO FACES OF COMMUNISM (Also see Double Talk)
Christian Anti-Communism Crusade, Houston, Texas: 1961 (Giveaway, paper-c, 36 pgs.)
nn 13 26 39 76 106 135

2001, A SPACE ODYSSEY (Movie)
Marvel Comics Group
Howard Johnson giveaway (1968, 8pp); 6 pg. movie adaptation, 2 pg. games, puzzles; McWilliams-a 2 4 6 10 12 15

ULTIMATE SPIDER-MAN
Marvel Comics: May, 2002
Free Comic Book Day giveaway - reprints #1 with "Free Comic Book Day" banner on-c 2.25
1-Kay Bee Toys variant edition 2 4 6 10 12 15

ULTIMATE X-MEN
Marvel Comics: July, 2003
1-Free Comic Book Day Edition - reprints #1 with "Free Comic Book Day" banner on-c 2.25

UNCLE SAM'S CHRISTMAS STORY
Promotional Publ. Co.: 1958 (Giveaway)
nn-Reprints 1956 Christmas USA 2 4 6 10 13 16

UNKEPT PROMISE
Legion of Truth: 1949 (Giveaway, 24 pgs.)
nn-Anti-alcohol 9 18 27 52 66 80

UNTOLD LEGEND OF THE BATMAN, THE
DC Comics: 1989 (28 pgs., 6X9", limited series of cereal premiums)
1-1st & 2nd printings known; Byrne-a 1 2 3 5 7 9
2,3: 1st & 2nd printings known 1 2 3 4 5 7

UNTOUCHABLES, THE (TV)
Leaf Brands, Inc.
Topps Bubblegum premiums produced by Leaf Brands, Inc.-2-1/2x4-1/2", 8 pgs. (3 diff. issues) "The Organization, Jamaica Ginger, The Otto Frick Story (drug), 3000 Suspects, The Antidote, Mexican Stakeout, Little Egypt, Purple Gang, Bugs Moran Story, & Lily Dallas Story" 3 6 9 18 24 30

VICKS COMICS (See Pure Oil Comics, Salerno Carnival of Comics & 24 Pages of Comics)
Eastern Color Printing Co. (Vicks Chemical Co.): nd (circa 1938) (Giveaway, 68 pgs. in color)
nn-Famous Funnies-r (before #40); contains 5 pgs. Buck Rogers (4 pgs. from F.F. #15, & 1 pg. from #16) Joe Palooka, Napoleon, etc. app. 62 124 186 388 594 800
nn-16 loose, untrimmed page giveaway; paper-c; r/Famous Funnies #14; Buck Rogers, Joe Palooka app. Has either "Vicks Comics" printed on cover or only a local store name as the logo. 23 46 69 132 191 250

WALT DISNEY'S COMICS & STORIES
K.K. Publications: 1942-1963 known (7-1/3"x10-1/4", 4 pgs. in color, slick paper) (folded horizontally once or twice as mailers) (Xmas subscription offer)
1942 mailer-r/Kelly cover to WDC&S 25; 2-year subscription + two Grosset & Dunlap hardcover books (32-pages each), of Bambi and of Thumper, offered for $2.00; came in an illustrated C&S envelope with an enclosed postage paid envelope
(Rare) Mailer only 26 52 78 147 211 275
with envelopes 32 64 96 184 267 350
1947,1948 mailer 19 38 57 107 154 200
1949 mailer-A rare Barks item: Same WDC&S cover as 1942 mailer, but with art changed so that nephew is handing teacher Donald a comic book rather than an apple, as originally drawn by Kelly. The tiny, 7/8"x1-1/4" cover shown was a rejected cover by Barks that was intended for C&S 110, but was redrawn by Kelly for C&S 111. The original art has been lost and this is its only app. (Rare) 40 80 120 244 372 500
1950 mailer-P.1 r/Kelly cover to Dell Xmas Parade 1 (without title); p.2 r/Kelly cover to C&S101 (w/o title), but with the art altered to show Donald reading C&S 122 (by Kelly); hardcover book, "Donald Duck in Bringing Up the Boys" given with a $1.00 one-year subscription; P.4 r/full Kelly Xmas cover to C&S 99 (Rare) 19 38 57 107 154 200
1952 mailer-P1 r/cover WDC&S #88 14 28 42 79 110 140
1953 mailer-P.1 r/cover Dell Xmas Parade 4 (w/o title); insides offer "Donald Duck Full Speed Ahead," a 28-page, color, 5-5/8"x6-5/8" book, not of the Story Hour series; P.4 r/full Barks C&S 148 cover (Rare) 14 28 42 79 110 140
1963 mailer-Pgs. 1,2 & 4 r/GK Xmas art; P.3 r/a 1963 C&S cover (Scarce) 10 20 30 58 77 95
NOTE: *It is assumed a different mailer was printed each Xmas for at least twenty years.*

WALT DISNEY'S COMICS & STORIES
Walt Disney Productions: 1943 (36 pgs.) (Dept. store Xmas giveaway)
nn-X-Mas-c with Donald & the Boys; Donald Duck by Jack Hannah; Thumper by Ken Hultgren 50 100 150 305 465 625

WALT DISNEY'S DONALD DUCK ADVENTURES
Gemstone Publishing: May, 2003 (giveaway promoting 2003 return of Disney Comics)
...Free Comic Book Day Edition - cover logo on red background; reprints "Maharajah Donald" & "The Peaceful Hills" from March of Comics #4; Barks-s/a; Kelly original-c on back-c 2.25
...San Diego Comic-Con 2003 Edition - cover logo on gold background 2.25
...ANA World's Fair of Money Baltimore Edition - cover logo on green background 2.25
...WizardWorld Chicago 2003 Edition - cover logo on blue background 2.25

WALT DISNEY'S MICKEY MOUSE AND UNCLE SCROOGE
Gemstone Publishing: June, 2004 (Free Comic Book Day giveaway)
nn-Flip book with r/Uncle Scrooge #15 and r/Mickey Mouse Four Color #79 (only Barks drawn Mickey Mouse story) 2.25

WATCH OUT FOR BIG TALK
Giveaway: 1950
nn-Dan Barry-a; about crooked politicians 7 14 21 37 46 55

WAY OF THE RAT
CrossGeneration Comics: Jun, 2003
Free Comic Book Day Special; reprints #1 w/features, interviews, CrossGen info 2.25

WEATHER-BIRD (See Comics From..., Dick Tracy, Free Comics to You..., Super Circus & Terry and the Pirates)
International Shoe Co./Western Printing Co.: 1958 - No. 16, July, 1962 (Shoe store giveaway)
1 4 8 12 29 40 50
2-16 2 4 6 14 18 22
NOTE: *The numbers are located in the lower bottom panel, pg. 1. All feature a character called Weather-Bird.*

WEATHER BIRD COMICS (See Comics From Weather Bird)
Weather Bird Shoes: 1957 (Giveaway)
nn-Contains a comic bound with new cover. Several combinations possible; contents determine price (40 - 60 percent of contents).

WEEKLY COMIC MAGAZINE
Fox Publications: May 12, 1940 (16 pgs.) (Others exist w/o super-heroes)
(1st Version)-8 pg. Blue Beetle story, 7 pg. Patty O'Day story; two copies known to exist. Estimated value... 625.00
(2nd Version)-7 two-pg. adventures of Blue Beetle, Patty O'Day, Yarko, Dr. Fung, Green Mask, Spark Stevens, & Rex Dexter; one copy known to exist. Estimated value... 525.00
(3rd version)-Captain Valor (only one known copy) 315.00
Discovered with business papers, letters and exploitation material promoting **Weekly Comic Magazine** for use by newspapers in the same manner of **The Spirit** weeklies. Interesting note: these are dated three weeks before the first Spirit comic. Letters indicate that samples may have been sent to a few newspapers. These sections were actually 15-1/2x22" pages which will fold down to an approximate 8x10" comic booklet. Other various comic sections were found with the above, but were more like the Sunday comic sections in format.

WHAT DO YOU KNOW ABOUT THIS COMICS SEAL OF APPROVAL?
No publisher listed (DC Comics Giveaway): nd (1955) (4 pgs., slick paper-c)
nn-(Rare) 62 124 186 388 594 800

WHAT'S BEHIND THESE HEADLINES
William C. Popper Co.: 1948 (16 pgs.)
nn-Comic insert "The Plot to Steal the World" 6 12 18 32 39 45

WHAT'S IN IT FOR YOU?
Harvey Publications Inc.: (16 pgs., paper cover)
nn-National Guard recruitment 4 7 10 14 17 20

WHEATIES (Premiums)
Walt Disney Productions: 1950 & 1951 (32 titles, pocket-size, 32 pgs.)
Mailing Envelope (no art on front)(Designates sets A,B,C or D on front) 9 18 27 51 62 75

(Set A-1 to A-8, 1950)

A-1-Mickey Mouse & the Disappearing Island, A-5-Mickey Mouse, Roving Reporter each... 7 14 21 37 46 55
A-2-Grandma Duck, Homespun Detective, A-6-Li'l Bad Wolf, Forest Ranger, A-7-Goofy, Tightrope Acrobat, A-8-Pluto & the Bogus Money each... 7 14 21 35 43 50
A-3-Donald Duck & the Haunted Jewels, A-4-Donald Duck & the Giant Ape each... 9 18 27 54 70 85

(Set B-1 to B-8, 1950)

B-1-Mickey Mouse & the Pharoah's Curse, B-4-Mickey Mouse & the Mystery Sea Monster each... 8 16 24 40 50 60
B-2-Pluto, Canine Cowpoke, B-5-Li'l Bad Wolf in the Hollow Tree Hideout,

Wisco - Tex Farnum, Frontiersman © Vital

Woody Woodpecker in Chevrolet Wonderland © Walter Lantz

X2 Presents The Ultimate X-Men #2 © MAR

	GD 2.0	VG 4.0	FN 6.0	VF 8.0	VF/NM 9.0	NM- 9.2
B-7-Goofy & the Gangsters each...	7	14	21	35	43	50
B-3-Donald Duck & the Buccaneers, B-6-Donald Duck,Trail Blazer, B-8 Donald Duck, Klondike Kid each...	9	18	27	54	70	85
(Set C-1 to C-8, 1951)						
C-1-Donald Duck & the Inca Idol, C-5-Donald Duck in the Lost Lakes, C-8-Donald Duck Deep-Sea Diver each...	9	18	27	54	70	85
C-2-Mickey Mouse & the Magic Mountain, C-6-Mickey Mouse & the Stagecoach Bandits each...	8	16	24	40	50	60
C-3-Li'l Bad Wolf, Fire Fighter, C-4-Gus & Jaq Save the Ship, C-7-Goofy, Big Game Hunter each...	7	14	21	35	43	50
(Set D-1 to D-8, 1951)						
D-1-Donald Duck in Indian Country, D-5-Donald Duck, Mighty Mystic each...	9	18	27	54	70	85
D-2-Mickey Mouse and the Abandoned Mine, D-6-Mickey Mouse & the Medicine Man each...	8	16	24	40	50	60
D-3-Pluto & the Mysterious Package, D-4-Bre'r Rabbit's Sunken Treasure, D-7-Li'l Bad Wolf and the Secret of the Woods, D-8-Minnie Mouse, Girl Explorer each...	7	14	21	35	43	50

NOTE: *Some copies lack the Wheaties ad.*

WHIZ COMICS (Formerly Flash Comics & Thrill Comics #1)
Fawcett Publications

	GD	VG	FN	VF	VF/NM	NM-
Wheaties Giveaway(1946, Miniature, 6-1/2x8-1/4", 32 pgs.); all copies were taped at each corner to a box of Wheaties and are never found in very fine or mint condition; "Capt. Marvel & the Water Thieves", plus Golden Arrow, Ibis, Crime Smasher stories	150	375	600	–	–	–

WILD KINGDOM (TV) (Mutual of Omaha's...)
Western Printing Co.: 1965, 1966 (Giveaway, regular size, slick-c, 16 pgs.)

	GD	VG	FN	VF	VF/NM	NM-
nn-Front & back-c are different on 1966 edition	2	4	6	10	12	15

WISCO/KLARER COMIC BOOK (Miniature)
Marvel Comics/Vital Publ./Fawcett Publ.: 1948 - 1964 (3-1/2x6-3/4", 24 pgs.)

Given away by Wisco "99" Service Stations, Carnation Malted Milk, Klarer Health Wieners, Fleers Dubble Bubble Gum, Rodeo All-Meat Wieners, Perfect Potato Chips, & others; see ad in Tom Mix #21

	GD	VG	FN	VF	VF/NM	NM-
Blackstone & the Gold Medal Mystery (1948)	9	18	27	51	62	75
Blackstone "Solves the Sealed Vault Mystery" (1950)	9	18	27	51	62	75
Blaze Carson in "The Sheriff Shoots It Out" (1950)	9	18	27	51	62	75
Captain Marvel & Billy's Big Game (r/Capt. Marvel Adv. #76)	29	58	87	167	241	315
(Prices vary widely on this book)						
China Boy in "A Trip to the Zoo" #10 (1948)	6	12	18	29	36	42
Indoors-Outdoors Game Book	4	8	12	18	22	25
Jim Solar Space Sheriff in "Battle for Mars", "Between Two Worlds", "Conquers Outer Space", "The Creatures on the Comet", "Defeats the Moon Missile Men", "Encounter Creatures on Comet", "Meet the Jupiter Jumpers", "Meets the Man From Mars", "On Traffic Duty", "Outlaws of the Spaceways", "Pirates of the Planet X", "Protects Space Lanes", "Raiders From the Sun", "Ring Around Saturn", "Robots of Rhea", "The Sky Ruby", "Spacetts of the Sky", "Spidermen of Venus", "Trouble on Mercury"	8	16	24	43	54	65
Johnny Starboard & the Underseas Pirates (1948)	6	12	18	27	33	38
Kid Colt in "He Lived by His Guns" (1950)	9	18	27	54	70	85
Little Aspirin as "Crook Catcher" #2 (1950)	5	10	14	20	24	28
Little Aspirin in "Naughty But Nice" #6 (1950)	5	10	14	20	24	28
Return of the Black Phantom (not M.E. character)(Roy Dare)(1948)	7	14	21	37	46	55
Secrets of Magic	5	10	15	22	26	30
Slim Morgan "Brings Justice to Mesa City" #3	5	10	15	22	26	30
Super Rabbit(1950)-Cuts Red Tape, Stops Crime Wave!	10	20	30	60	80	100
Tex Farnum, Frontiersman (1948)	5	10	15	24	30	35
Tex Taylor in "Draw or Die, Cowpoke!" (1950)	8	16	24	40	50	60
Tex Taylor in "An Exciting Adventure at the Gold Mine" (1950)	7	14	21	37	46	55
Wacky Quacky in "All-Aboard"	4	7	10	14	17	20
When School Is Out	4	7	10	14	17	20
Willie in a "Comic-Comic Book Fall" #1	4	8	12	17	21	24
Wonder Duck "An Adventure at the Rodeo of the Fearless Quacker!" (1950)	9	18	27	54	70	85
Rare uncut version of three; includes Capt. Marvel, Tex Farnum, Black Phantom Estimated value...						420.00
Rare uncut version of three; includes China Boy, Blackstone, Johnny Starboard & the Underseas Pirates Estimated value...						135.00

WOLVERINE
Marvel Comics

	GD	VG	FN	VF	VF/NM	NM-
145-(1999 Nabisco mail-in offer) Sienkiewicz-c	10	20	30	70	98	125
...Son of Canada (4/01, ed. of 65,000) Spider-Man & The Hulk app.; Lim-a						3.00

WOMAN OF THE PROMISE, THE
Catechetical Guild: 1950 (General Distr.) (Paper cover, 32 pgs.)

	GD	VG	FN	VF	VF/NM	NM-
nn	6	12	18	27	33	38

WONDERFUL WORLD OF DUCKS (See Golden Picture Story Book)
Colgate Palmolive Co.: 1975

	GD	VG	FN	VF	VF/NM	NM-
1-Mostly-r	1	3	4	6	8	10

WONDER WOMAN
DC Comics: 1977

	GD	VG	FN	VF	VF/NM	NM-
Pizza Hut Giveaways (12/77)-Reprints #60,62	2	4	6	10	12	15
... - The Minotaur (1981, General Foods giveaway, 8 pages, 3-1/2 x 6-3/4", oblong)	2	4	6	12	15	20

WONDER WORKER OF PERU
Catechetical Guild: No date (5x7", 16 pgs., B&W, giveaway)

	GD	VG	FN	VF	VF/NM	NM-
nn	5	10	15	24	30	35

WOODY WOODPECKER
Dell Publishing Co.

	GD	VG	FN	VF	VF/NM	NM-
Clover Stamp-Newspaper Boy Contest('56)-9 pg. story-(Giveaway)	7	14	21	35	43	50
In Chevrolet Wonderland(1954-Giveaway)(Western Publ.)-20 pgs., full story line; Chilly Willy app.	20	40	60	115	165	215
...Meets Scotty MacTape(1953-Scotch Tape giveaway)-16 pgs., full size	20	40	60	115	165	215

WOOLWORTH'S CHRISTMAS STORY BOOK
Promotional Publ. Co.(Western Printing Co.): 1952 - 1954 (16 pgs., paper-c) (See Jolly Christmas Book)

	GD	VG	FN	VF	VF/NM	NM-
nn	6	12	18	32	39	46

NOTE: *1952 issue-Marv Levy c/a.*

WOOLWORTH'S HAPPY TIME CHRISTMAS BOOK
F. W. Woolworth Co. (Western Printing Co.): 1952 (Christmas giveaway)

	GD	VG	FN	VF	VF/NM	NM-
nn-36 pgs.	6	12	18	29	36	42

WORLD'S FINEST COMICS
National Periodical Publ./DC Comics

	GD	VG	FN	VF	VF/NM	NM-
Giveaway (c. 1944-45, 8 pgs., in color, paper-c)-Johnny Everyman-r/World's Finest	24	48	72	138	199	260
Giveaway (c. 1949, 8 pgs., in color, paper-c)- "Make Way For Youth" r/World's Finest; based on film of same name	21	42	63	118	169	220
#176, #179- Best Western reprint edition (1997)						3.00

WORLD'S GREATEST SUPER HEROES
DC Comics (Nutra Comics) (Child Vitamins, Inc.): 1977 (Giveaway, 3-3/4x3-3/4", 24 pgs.)

	GD	VG	FN	VF	VF/NM	NM-
nn-Batman & Robin app.; health tips	2	4	6	10	13	16

XMAS FUNNIES
Kinney Shoes: No date (Giveaway, paper cover, 36 pgs.?)

	GD	VG	FN	VF	VF/NM	NM-
Contains 1933 color strip-r; Mutt & Jeff, etc.	35	70	105	198	287	375

X-MEN THE MOVIE
Marvel Comics/Toys R' Us: 2000

	GD	VG	FN	VF	VF/NM	NM-
Special Movie Prequel Edition						5.00

X2 PRESENTS THE ULTIMATE X-MEN #2
Marvel Comics/New York Post: July, 2003

	GD	VG	FN	VF	VF/NM	NM-
Reprint distributed inside issue of the New York Post						2.25

YALTA TO KOREA (Also see Korea My Home)
M. Phillip Corp. (Republican National Committee): 1952 (Giveaway, paper-c)

	GD	VG	FN	VF	VF/NM	NM-
nn-(8 pgs.)-Anti-communist propaganda book	20	40	60	115	165	215

YOGI BEAR (TV)
Dell Publishing Co.

	GD	VG	FN	VF	VF/NM	NM-
Giveaway ('84, '86)-City of Los Angeles, "Creative First Aid" & "Earthquake Preparedness for Children"	1	2	3	4	5	7

YOUR TRIP TO NEWSPAPERLAND
Philadelphia Evening Bulletin (Printed by Harvey Press): June, 1955 (14x11-1/2", 12 pgs.)

	GD	VG	FN	VF	VF/NM	NM-
nn-Joe Palooka takes kids on newspaper tour	5	10	15	24	30	35

YOUR VOTE IS VITAL!
Harvey Publications Inc.: 1952 (5" x 7", 16 pgs., paper cover)

	GD	VG	FN	VF	VF/NM	NM-
nn-The importance of voting	4	8	12	18	22	25

The Pioneer Age

The American Comic Book: 1500s-1828

by Eric C. Caren ©2005

Want to avoid an argument in social discourse? Steer clear of politics and religion. In the latter category, the most controversial subject is human evolution. Collectors can become just as squeamish when you start messing with the evolution of a particular collectible. In most cases, the origin of a particular comic character will be universally agreed upon, but try tackling the origin of printed comics and you are asking for trouble. Perhaps I will make more friends than enemies amongst comic collectors if I first admit that in my own field of expertise, rare newspapers and other news forms – broadsides, tracts, newsletters, periodicals, etc. – 35 years of experience has left me somewhat at a loss to tell you what the first newspaper was. Actually, to be fair to myself, I could give you a list of at least a dozen good candidates and then it would be subjective as to which item on the list qualified as the godfather. It so happens that journalism and comics are not such distant cousins, and because a picture paints a thousand words, I have provided you with a number of pictorial exhibits to accompany this treatise. First printed comic? Ancestors of my Silver Age companions growing up in the 1960s? Yes, centuries before there was a Spider-Man, an Incredible Hulk, and the Fantastic Four, there were comics and cartoons!

My friend and fellow newspaper collector, Dr. Stephen A. Goldman, has always lived by the old maxim, "Knowledge is Power," and to that end he keeps an enormous personal library of books relating to journalism, history, and collectibles. Many years ago, I was perusing through the spines of a myriad of reference books in his print library (pre-Internet) and hit upon a title that really intrigued me – *The Early Comic Strip* by David Kunzle, published by The University of California Press in 1973. The subtitle of the tome is *Narrative Strips and Picture Stories in the European Broadsheet from c. 1450 to 1825*. Kunzle gets down to business in the flap copy. He states that "because the 'comic strip' has never been adequately defined, no one has known where to look for its ancestors...In this book the 'comic strip' is defined as a mass produced series of narrative images printed either on a single sheet, or else strung across several sheets..." The Kunzle book opened a whole new world for me, and I started adding many early items to my news archive. These would share space in the comics division of the archive with more familiar friends like the Yellow Kid, Little Nemo, and the Brownies.

In this article, I would like to share some of our mutual cousins with you in the hopes that you will be inspired to

Figure 1. German broadsheet, dated 1569.

look back at what I am calling "The Pioneer Age" of comics. There are many things out there from the 16th to the 19th centuries that would be interesting for comic connoisseurs to collect. While some items illustrated within this article are virtually unobtainable, others *can* be found, and many other similar items are out there just waiting for inspired collectors to seek them out. All of the items pictured are taken from originals in my personal collection, with the exception of the Franklin snake cartoon which is proudly owned by Dr. Goldman. As far as I know, his example is the only one in private hands.

Figure 2. The Murder of King Henry III (1589).

Before we begin, a bit of terminology is imperative. The terms 'broadsheet' and 'broadside' regarding works of the 16th and 17th centuries are fairly interchangeable and they essentially refer to the modern equivalent of a poster. Today, technically speaking, a broadside is a single sheet of paper printed only on the recto and a broadsheet is a piece of paper with printing on both sides. The earliest comic item illustrated in Kunzle is a ten-panel religious broadside probably printed in Strasburg (then Germany) circa 1460. Ten panels, biblical – hmm, what could it possibly depict? Guttenberg had invented moveable type only a few years earlier and used his printing press to print a now famous bible in Mainz, Germany, so it is no surprise that this early comic would be religious in nature. Non-secular matter would dominate the printing arts for well over a century to come. However, Kunzle does present us with a satirical and rather racy comic broadsheet done by one Casper of Regensburg, with a title that roughly translates to "My Heart doth Smart." This piece is replete with a picture of an alluring half-clothed maiden just out of her German bathing-house being admired by a kneeling young male observer. Kunzle dates this piece to circa 1485.

The earliest comic piece in my archive is a German broadside dated 1569 [Figure 1]. It is an illustrated attack on the Spanish Catholics led by the notoriously cruel Duke of Alva (center) who had recently occupied the Low Countries (Belgium and The Netherlands) and committed atrocities on the resident Protestant populace. It is half-allegorical, with the foreground consisting of the Devil and a nun blowing ill wind into the ear of the Duke of Alva who has in turn chained up the women of the Low Countries, and half-journalistic, with the upper half depicting the execution of Egmont and Horn in Antwerp.

The next two exhibits are particularly interesting to me. They are the work of the Hogenberg family of Cologne, Germany. Franz Hogenberg, and later his son Abraham, issued approximately 500 current event illustrated news broadsides starting in the 1560s and ending around 1620. The father had already become famous for his extremely detailed and accurate city and town views that he had published with a partner named George Braun in atlas format. With correspondents all over Europe sending the Hogenberg family news and the city views already compiled, the Hogenbergs were able to have their news broadsides on the streets for sale within weeks of political and military events taking place in England and on the European Continent. In some cases, the news sheets were out of their print shop within days of the actual event, particularly when the event occurred in Germany. These sheets were of uniform size, approximately 10" x 13", sometimes numbered and interesting in that the graphics were always the dominant part of the broadside. Usually, text was relegated to a few lines of rhyming verse beneath the copperplate engravings. As literacy in this period was primarily confined to the nobility, this was a most pragmatic vehicle for dissemination of news – and often propaganda – to the populace at large. The picture told the story and the text could be read to groups of people who might remember it due to its catchy rhyming format.

A fair percentage of these news sheets were composed as strip narratives. One example of this is from 1589 [Figure 2] and shows the murder of King Henry III of France by the monk Jacques Clement near Paris. This four-panel broadside includes the stabbing of the king and concludes with Mr. Clement being drawn and quartered by four horses. The next work illustrated here is a 6-panel narrative strip with no text dating from 1617 [Figure 3]. The first panel depicts the shooting in Paris of the Italian Concini, who had ruled France while Louis XIII was still a young boy. The second panel shows the release of the birds from their cages to symbolize the new independence of the young King Louis, and the rest of the panels involve the common people attacking the corpse of Concini in various vicious ways.

The next piece is also the earliest English language piece in

Figure 3. The shooting of the Italian Concini (1617).

my collection to employ word balloons. It is a trompe l'oeil, or collage, caricature satirizing the catastrophic South Sea Bubble, which ruined many investors in a manner similar to our own Tech Stock "New Economy" bubble of the 1990s. It is titled "The Bubblers Medley, or a Sketch of the Times/Being Europe's Memorial from the Year 1720" [Figure 4]. The most interesting scene to comic historians would have to be the one in the upper right corner depicting a number of men in a London coffeehouse – where merchants would regularly gather to read and discuss the latest news – speaking with word balloons. One of the gentlemen seated at a table sarcastically announces "I was to have took S. Sea [stock] at 2000 but chose rather to live here like a Knave than go to Jayl [sic] like a Fool."

Figure 4. "The Bubblers Medley" (1720).

The first successful American newspaper was the *Boston News-Letter* begun in 1704. From that point until the French and Indian War, there were precious few illustrations in any colonial newspaper. Some of the best information on early illustration in colonial newspapers can be found in the book *Journals and Journeymen* by Clarence Brigham, author of the most important bibliography of colonial newspapers. In a chapter simply entitled "Illustration," Brigham points out that the first illustration in an American newspaper was a simple woodcut of a flag in an issue of the *Boston News-Letter* from January 26, 1708. Except for advertisements and title devices, Brigham could not find another illustration until 1733, when John Peter Zenger inserted a crude map of Louisburg into his *New York Weekly Journal*. Then, after perhaps one more map of Louisburg in 1745 came something in 1754 that was to have a lasting effect in the hearts and souls of the colonials right through the fight for independence.

Brigham tells us "Benjamin Franklin, in the *Pennsylvania Gazette* of May 9, 1754, published what may well be called the earliest American newspaper cartoon. That year, at a time when the prospect of a war with the French was imminent, a congress of the colonies was called at Albany to be held in June. Franklin, in a plea for united action, published an article on the situation on May 9. Accompanying the article was a cartoon woodcut engraving of a snake divided in eight parts [Figure 5]... Under the snake was the motto 'Join, Or Die...' The segmented snake device was of great importance in call-

Figure 5. "Join, or Die" from the Pennsylvania Gazette, May 9, 1754.

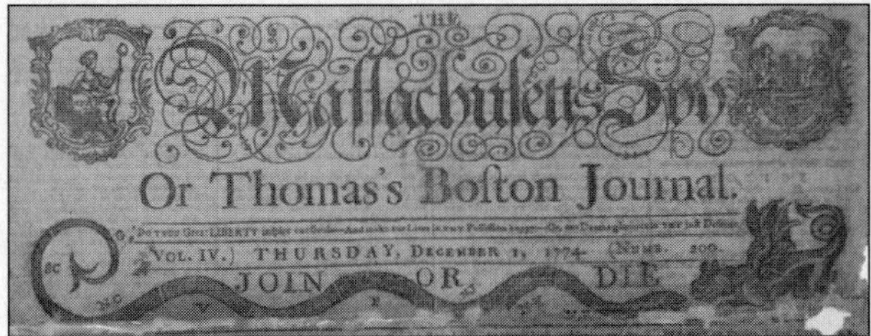
THE Massachusetts Spy
Or Thomas's Boston Journal.
VOL. IV.) THURSDAY, December 1, 1774 (NUMB. 200.
JOIN OR DIE

Figure 6. The snake meets a dragon in the Massachusetts Spy (1774).

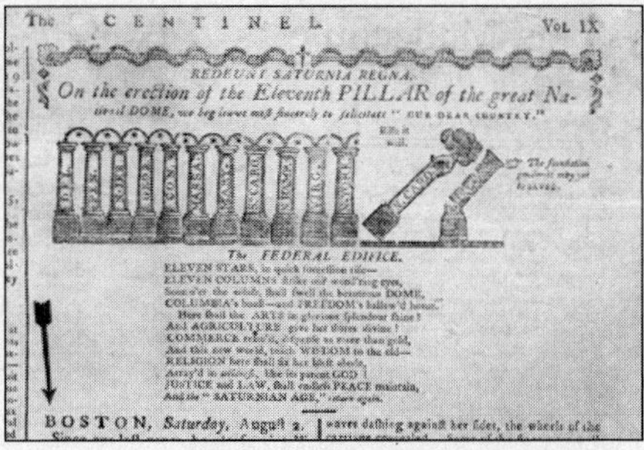
The CENTINEL Vol. IX
REDEUNT SATURNIA REGNA.
On the erection of the Eleventh PILLAR of the great National DOME, we beg leave most sincerely to felicitate "OUR DEAR COUNTRY."
The FEDERAL EDIFICE.
BOSTON, Saturday, August 2.

Figure 7. A "Federal Edifice Pillar" cartoon in the Massachusetts Centinel (1788).

ing the attention of the colonists to the necessity of union, and was revived at the time of the Stamp Act controversy in 1765 and again during the movement toward independence in 1774. That year, Isaiah Thomas used the snake cartoon device the full width of the first page in his *Massachusetts Spy*, and added a dragon, representing Great Britain, facing the snake..." [Figure 6]

The next time I find illustration in an American newspaper is at the time of our ratification process for the U.S. Constitution. *The Massachusetts Centinel* in 1787-1788 offered a series of what I call 'Federal Edifice Pillar' cartoons. Each time a state would ratify the Constitution, a new pillar would be added to the latest edifice cartoon. In Figure 7, we see the August 1788 cartoon with a headline reading "On the erection of the Eleventh Pillar of the great National Dome, we beg leave most sincerely to felicitate 'Our Dear Country.'" The cartoon thus shows that New York has ratified the Constitution. North Carolina's pillar is about to join New York according to the headline, which reads "Rise it Will," and lastly a fragmented Rhode Island Pillar is followed by a pointing hand which in turn is followed by the caption "The foundation Good – it may yet be SAVED." Under the cartoon can be found a dozen lines of verse called "The Federal Edifice." I have never seen any other illustrations in American newspapers dated before 1800. Therefore, it is safe to conclude that of the very few illustrations that were produced in American newspapers during the 18th century, the majority of them are cartoons!

Figure 8. "Florizel granting Independency to Perdita" from The Ramblers Magazine (1783).

Magazines of the 18th century offered more illustrations, perhaps because most of them were printed monthly, thereby giving the printer more time to produce an engraved plate or portrait to accompany the text of the periodical. Most of the illustrated magazines offered little in the way of cartoons; a notable exception was the *Royal American Magazine* printed in Boston. The famous silversmith and patriot, Paul Revere, produced the most famous cartoon of the era for this Boston magazine in June 1774 when he satirized the tea taxes and the closing down of Boston Harbor with a full page engraved cartoon entitled "The able Doctor or America Swallowing the Bitter Draught." This allegorical piece shows an Indian woman (representing colonials) having a pot of tea forced down her unwilling throat; a document labeled "Boston Port Bill" is thrown down at her simultaneously. The engraved cartoon was boldly signed in the lower right corner "P. Revere Sculp."

Figure 9. "Amusement for John Bull..." from The European Magazine (1783).

Much has been written about the icon "Bloody [Boston] Massacre..." by Paul Revere. It is claimed as an ancestor by

Figure 10. From The Anti-Jacobin Review and Magazine, January 1799.

collectors of newspapers, broadsides, printed Americana and, alas, comic/cartoon aficionados. I would add that nostalgia played a factor in my getting one for the collection many years ago (remembering it from history books as a young student). My friend Dr. Stephen A. Goldman says of Paul Revere's 1770 engraving of the Boston Massacre that it "has various elements common to early political cartoons. The piece has a distinct comic-like appearance, contains descriptive text (in verse), and is partly news, opinion, and propaganda. Revere in this work reveals himself to have much in common with later political cartoonists such as *Harper's Weekly*'s Thomas Nast (19th Century) and the *Washington Post*'s Herb Block (20th Century)" (for the image, see the color gallery later in this book).

I have the first volume of a bawdy London monthly entitled *The Ramblers Magazine* that dates from the year that the American Revolution was officially ended by the Treaty of

Figure 11. "The Whiskers" in The New Wits Magazine (1805), annotated by the son of the illlustrator, George Cruikshank.

CONNECTICUT MIRROR.

Figure 12. Cartoons satirizing Napoleon on the front page of the Connecticut Mirror, dated January 7, 1811.

Figure 13. Another Napoleon cartoon, this time dubbing him "The Corsican Munchausen, from the London Strand, December 4, 1813.

Paris (1783). The full title page contends that the magazine will be filled "With a Most Delicious Banquet of Amorous, Bacchanalian, Whimsical, Humorous, Theatrical and Polite [Not!] Entertainment." Almost every issue of this magazine contains a cartoon including word balloons. I have chosen one that is particularly delightful [Figure 8]. This is the first issue of the magazine, and it contains a plate entitled "Florizel granting Independency to Perdita." In it, a British aristocrat grabs the arm of a young maiden and his word balloon reads "Submit to my Royal Will." Seated on a sofa, the maiden responds "Declare me Independent and Then -----."

Another London periodical from April 1783, *The European Magazine*, contains a cartoon including a buffalo. It is believed that this is the first time that the buffalo was used to symbolize the young American nation. The plate is headed "Amusement for John Bull and his Cousin Paddy or, the Gambols of the American Buffalo, in St. James Street" [Figure 9]. An enormous 12" x 20" fold-out political cartoon was included in the January 1799 issue of *The Anti-Jacobin Review and Magazine* [Figure 10]. I am not familiar enough with the politics of the day to interpret the cartoon, but it is notable for its size and its extensive use of word balloons.

The earliest English language periodical identifying itself as a "Comic Work" which I have come across is *The New Wits Magazine* [Figure 11], printed in London. The printing on the very top of the outer wrapper reads "This Comic Work (which will be completed in Twenty-four Numbers, making three Volumes) may be had of every liberal bookseller in the United Kingdom – It is published regularly every fortnight without any interruption whatever." The comic plate inside the issue is entitled "The Whiskers" and is dated December 1805. This is a remarkable issue in many ways; first of all, the pages are uncut, the original outer wrapper is present, and best of all, the plate is annotated in pencil and signed by the

SALEM GAZ

VOLUME XXVII.] SALEM, TUESDAY, MARCH 30, 1

THE GERRY-MANDER, OR ESSEX SOUTH DISTRICT FORMED INTO A MONSTER!

Figure 14. "The Gerry-Mander" as seen in the Salem Gazette, dated March 30, 1813.

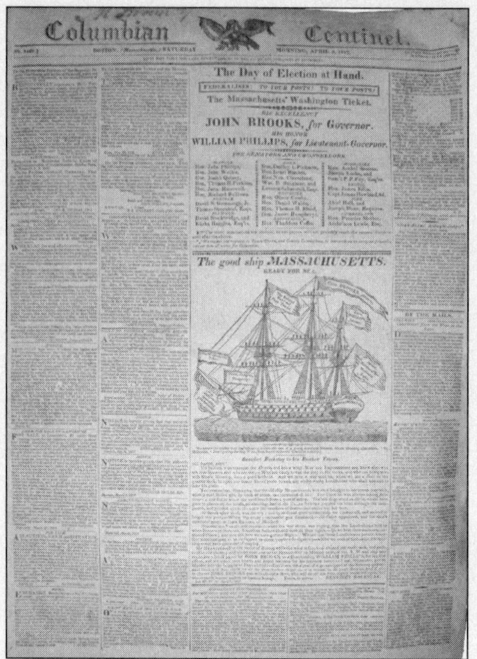

Columbian Centinel.

The Day of Election at Hand.

FEDERALISTS! TO YOUR POSTS! TO YOUR POSTS!

The Massachusetts' Washington Ticket.

HIS EXCELLENCY

JOHN BROOKS, for Governor.

HIS HONOR

WILLIAM PHILLIPS, for Lieutenant-Governor.

The good ship MASSACHUSETTS.

READY FOR SEA.

Figure 15. "The Good Ship Massachusetts Ready for Sea" in the Columbian Centinel (1817).

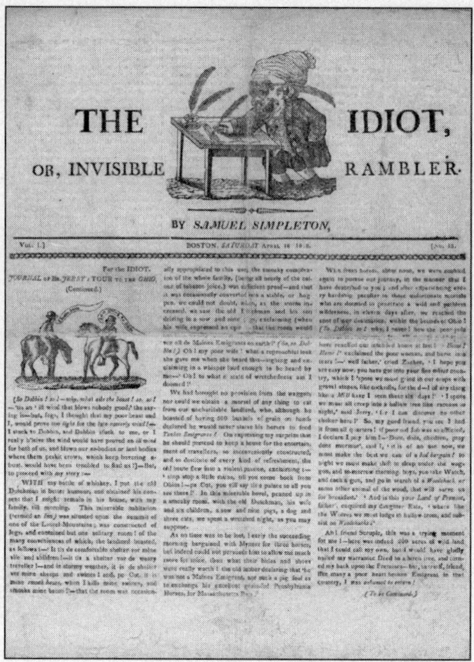

THE IDIOT,

OR, INVISIBLE RAMBLER.

BY SAMUEL SIMPLETON,

Figure 16. The comic paper, "The Idiot," printed in Boston in 1818.

most famous British illustrator of the 19th century – the illustrator for many of Charles Dickens' first editions, George Cruikshank. The blank space above the "Whisker" cartoon is filled with a pencil notation reading "engraved from a drawing by my father I. Cruikshank" and is signed in the same pencil with the initials "GCk." Isaac Cruikshank (c.1756-1811), father of George, was also a noted caricaturist. This then is George's own copy of a comic magazine illustrated by his father!

I have an issue of a Hartford, Connecticut newspaper entitled the *Connecticut Mirror* dated January 7, 1811. The front page contains what is known as a carrier's address. Newsboys would deliver a special issue either at Christmas or New Years, as in this case, with verse that would be specially prepared for that edition; to solicit tips, the newsboys used these carrier address issues. This particular title chose to grace the front page not only with verse but also three crude comic illustrations [Figure 12]. I am almost certain that the cartoons satirize Napoleon, as here is a sample of the accompanying comic verse: "...From deeds of bold and rash

Figure 17. "A Consultation at the Medical Board" from The Pasquin or General Satirist (1821).

THE NEW-HAMPSHIRE JOURNAL.

Monumental Inscriptions.

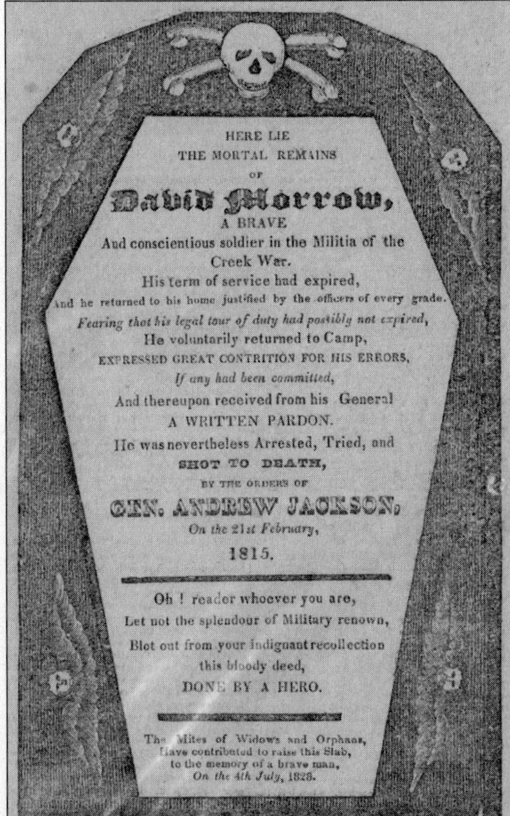

HERE LIE
THE MORTAL REMAINS
OF
David Morrow,
A BRAVE
And conscientious soldier in the Militia of the
Creek War.
His term of service had expired,
And he returned to his home justified by the officers of every grade.
Fearing that his legal tour of duty had possibly not expired,
He voluntarily returned to Camp,
EXPRESSED GREAT CONTRITION FOR HIS ERRORS,
If any had been committed,
And thereupon received from his General
A WRITTEN PARDON.
He was nevertheless Arrested, Tried, and
SHOT TO DEATH,
BY THE ORDERS OF
GEN. ANDREW JACKSON,
On the 21st February,
1815.

Oh ! reader whoever you are,
Let not the splendour of Military renown,
Blot out from your indignant recollection
this bloody deed,
DONE BY A HERO.

The Mites of Widows and Orphans,
Have contributed to raise this Slab,
to the memory of a brave man,
On the 4th July, 1828.

Figure 18. Above, the front page of The New Hampshire Journal, *dated October 20, 1828, with multiple tombstone "panels." Immediately above is a detail of the bottom right tombstone.*

emprize, to softer scenes we turn our eyes. Great Bonaparte's tender heart, Grows weary of his home-made queen, the mild, the beauteous Josephine..." It was not unusual to lampoon Napoleon, especially in Britain. "The Corsican Munchausen---Humming the Lads of Paris" [Figure 13] is a delightful hand-colored engraved cartoon "Published December 4, 1813" in the London *Strand*. Little Napoleon is spewing a multitude of word balloons ending with a particularly biting one that reads "Did I not burn Moscow – and leave 400,000 brave Soldiers to perish in the snow for the good of the French Nation?"

One of the most famous political cartoons in American history was first published in the *Salem Gazette* in Massachusetts on March 30, 1813. The front page contains "The Gerry-Mander, Essex South District Formed into a Monster!" [Figure 14] The expression gerrymandering has become famous when a geographical area is re-districted for the benefit of one political party over another. Elbridge Gerry, then Governor of Massachusetts, re-districted the state to get more Republican state senators than they otherwise would have netted. The cartoon puts the new district and the towns involved in a picture to resemble a winged dragon-like monster. Another Massachusetts newspaper called the *Columbian Centinel* issued a front-page endorsement in 1817 for John Brooks for Governor. Underneath this unabashed partisan endorsement is a cartoon of "The Good Ship Massachusetts Ready for Sea" [Figure 15] with all of the sails featuring either political slogans or the names of the candidates – Brooks, and his running mate for Lieutenant Governor, William Phillips.

Up until this point all of the American illustrations that I have discussed have been political cartoons of one sort or another. This would all change with the introduction of a comic paper called *The Idiot, or Invisible Rambler,* published under a pseudonym, "Samuel Simpleton." Printed in Boston in 1818, this publication was the earliest to present a recurring comic character that spoke with word balloons. This then is my choice for the 'Grandfather of all American Comics.' The comic is titled "Journal of Br. Jerry's Tour to the Ohio, (Continued)" [Figure 16]. The April 18, 1818 issue features the comic at the top of the first of the three columns on the front page of this four-page publication. It depicts two men on horses; one says to the other, "I am Going to Ohio." The other responds, "I have been." Ohio in 1818 was the Western frontier; it should be remembered that Lewis and Clark made their overland venture to the Pacific only about a dozen years earlier. Here, for the first time in American periodical publishing, do we encounter a secular and non-partisan comic of fictitious characters who speak with word balloons. Many of the elements that would later lead to familiar comic strip and comic book stylistic conventions are first found here.

Another really special publication in my holdings is an 1821 weekly British humor magazine in original green outer wrapper called *The Pasquin or General Satirist* [Figure 17]. I own issue #4, which has inserted into it a hand-colored word balloon cartoon relating to 'medical quackery.' One

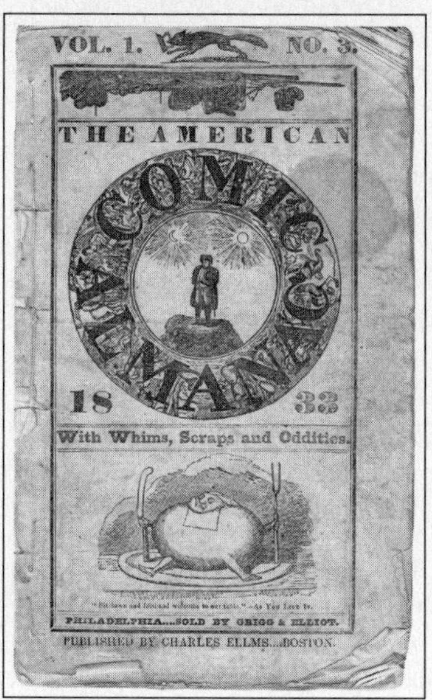

Figure 19. Front and back views of "The American Comic Almanac" (1833).

can only imagine the work that went into issuing a magazine with a hand-colored engraved cartoon. A poor patient stands before a doctor who is consulting with a mechanical robot made up of medical devices and tools. The consensus seems to be to "Bleed Him." The colored cartoon is titled "A Consultation at the Medical Board."

Did you know that the first full front-page illustration in an American newspaper was a cartoon? On Oct. 20, 1828, *The New Hampshire Journal* depicted a series of six coffins headed with skulls and bones. Each coffin has a biography describing various poor sods supposed to have been killed by General Andrew Jackson in duels, etc. Titled "Monumental Inscriptions" [Figure 18], who knows if it helped or hurt Jackson in his run for President. At any rate, he won the election and was re-elected President four years later.

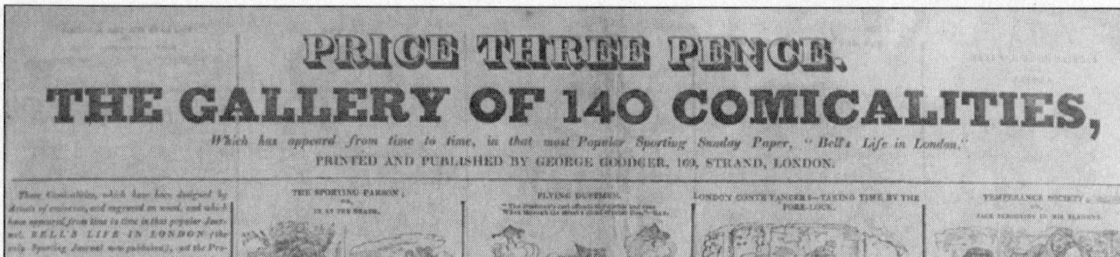

PRICE THREE PENCE.
THE GALLERY OF 140 COMICALITIES,
Which has appeared from time to time, in that most Popular Sporting Sunday Paper, "Bell's Life in London."
PRINTED AND PUBLISHED BY GEORGE GOODGER, 169, STRAND, LONDON.

Figure 20. The Gallery of 140 Comicalities, *a one-shot released by the newspaper* Bell's Life in London *on June 24, 1831.*

NOTION

THREE DOLLARS PER YEAR, PAYABLE IN ADVANCE.

17, 1841. SIX CENTS PER COPY.

SERIES OF COMICAL DESIGNS,

SALT BOX

Figure 21. One of the "Series of Comical Designs" regularly featured on the front page of The Boston Notion *(1841).*

An interesting sidelight to the history of comics as they relate to newspapers and periodicals would be something that we might consider a distant cousin of everything in this *Guide*. I have the third issue of a series called "The American Comic Almanac" [Figure 19], dated 1833 and published in Philadelphia "With Whims, Scraps and Oddities," and of course lots of comics.

Bell's Life in London, a popular British newspaper in the first half of the 19th century, issued a one-shot on June 24, 1831 called *The Gallery of 140 Comicalities* [Figure 20]. It is subtitled "Which has appeared from time to time, in the most Popular Sporting Sunday Paper, 'Bell's Life in London'." The first British comic book? Let the Brits fight that one out!

The Boston Notion of 1841 not only had a comic nameplate, called a masthead by some, but some front pages of this title carried a column headed "Series of Comical Designs, Executed for The Boston Notion" [Figure 21]. Later in the 1840s, we start to see the advent of comic magazines in America styled after the successful British humor magazine *Punch*. The Victorian Age of comics dawned with titles such as *Yankee Doodle,* and *John Donkey*. Books composed of comics like Obadiah Oldbuck have previously been discussed in articles on the Victorian Age like the one featured in this edition of the *Guide*. One last note: It has previously been asserted, quite correctly, that *Harper's Monthly Magazine* started reprinting British comics in the back pages of its magazines in the early 1850s. But what about a regular comic feature in an American newspaper? Take a look at the May 31, 1856 issue of *Frank Leslie's Illustrated Newspaper* and you will find a page titled "Comic Department" [Figure 22]!

Eric C. Caren was born (a collector) in 1959. By the age of 5 he had collected stamps, coins and baseball cards. He started collecting rare newspapers at the age of 11, after stumbling upon an abandoned house full of them in Rockland County, NY where he lived. In high school in the mid-1970s he apprenticed with a rare book dealer in Connecticut and actually set up as a dealer at a comic book convention in NYC sometime around 1975. He graduated from the University of Maryland with a Business degree in 1981. His first job was director of a gallery that dealt in rare newspapers in London in Covent Garden Market soon after it opened. He established The Caren Archive, a full-time business selling historical collectibles in 1983. He co-founded HCA Auctions with Dennis Holzman. He is a former Director of The Ephemera Society of America, a Member of The American Antiquarian Society, a Member of the Antiquarian Booksellers Association of America, and a Consultant to The Newseum, which will re-open in Washington DC on Pennsylvania Avenue in several years (his first newspaper collection will be the most substantial part of their permanent collection). He is a partner with Stephen A. Goldman in the business that bears his name as well as in OldNews, Inc. He has authored nine books using rare newspapers – The "Extra" series with Castle Books – and has recently co-authored his 10th book, "The Civil War" Smithsonian Institution Headliners Series with Dr. Stephen A. Goldman. Reprints of papers from his and Dr. Goldman's archive are sold at The Smithsonian Institution and The Holocaust Memorial Museum.

FRANK LESLIE'S ILLUSTRATED NEWSPAPER.

COMIC DEPARTMENT.

Figure 22. The "Comic Department" from the May 31, 1856 *issue of* Frank Leslie's Illustrated Newspaper.

Comic Strips and Book: 1828-1883

A Concise History Of The Field As Of 2005

ORIGINS OF AMERICAN COMIC STRIPS LONG BEFORE THE YELLOW KID

by Robert L. Beerbohm & Richard D. Olson, PhD ©2005

With special thanks to Richard Samuel West and Leonardo De Sá

(This article was originally created by Doug Wheeler, Robert Beerbohm and Richard D. Olson, PhD for OCBPG #32 2002 and continues to be revised annually by the current authors.)

We welcome any and all corrections and additions.

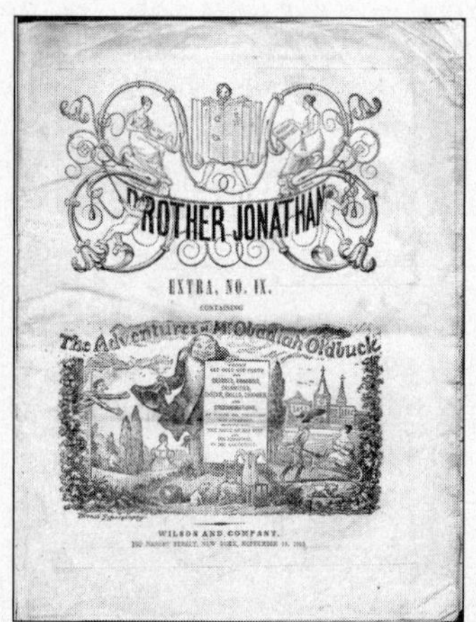

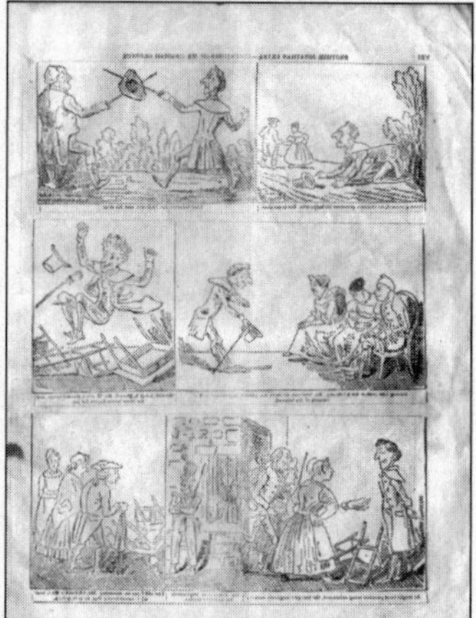

Left: Cover to the subscriber version of the earliest known sequential comic book published in America, ***The Adventures of Mr. Obadiah Oldbuck****, originally drawn by Swiss comics creator, Rodolphe Töpffer, Sept. 1842, Wilson & Co. New York. Right: Pages 8 and 28 from this 40-page 1842 graphic novel which launched the comic book business in America....the history books are being rewritten right here and once again we have more new information for you to learn of this medium which started centuries ago.*

Left: "The Burning of Mr. John Rogers," 1646 is the earliest-known North American cartoon printed on paper. Middle: The pamphlet ***Plain Truth*** *1747 contains Ben Franklin's earliest-known cartoon titled "Heaven Helps Only Those Who Help Themselves" depicting ancient "super hero" Hercules in the upper right corner. Right: "A Warm Place - Hell", one of two images definitely known to be drawn and engraved by Paul Revere, 1768. Word balloons had wide-spread usage in many cartoons in the 1700s.*

The comic strip originated across the Atlantic 100s of years before it was brought over to America by immigrants and imports. Title of this broadsheet example is ***A remarkable story of how Conchine Marquis d' Ancre was shot in Paris April 24 (1617), buried, disinterred and burned...*** *A man named Concini is arrested at the Louvre. His hair is pulled out along with his ears, fingers, genitals, heart, lips, nose, tongue and other body parts are cut off and thrust into a fire in front of the Bastille where the royalty can see.*

This Victorian Era section is devoted to comic strips and books published during the years the United States expanded across the North American continent, fought a Civil War, shifted from an agrarian to an industrial society, "welcomed" waves of immigrants, and struggled over race, class, religion, temperance, and suffrage - and all of it depicted and satirized by generations of mostly now long-forgotten cartoonists. The social attitudes, beliefs, and conventions of 19th century America, the good as well as the bad, are to be found in abundance. We can imagine the first question to pop into most readers' minds will be, "What, beyond the happenstance of publication date, are Victorian Era comics?"

The aspect we believe most distinguishes Victorian Era comic strips from those of later eras was the extremely rare use of word balloons within sequential (multi-picture) comic stories. When word balloons were used, it was nearly always within single-panel cartoons. On the occasions when they appeared inside a strip, with very few exceptions, the ballooned dialogue was non-essential to understanding the story. Nineteenth-century comics tended to place both narration and dialogue beneath comic panels rather than within the panel's borders. Many of these comics are to the word balloon-strewn post-**Yellow Kid** comics of the 20th Century as silent movies are to the later "talkies." Just as sound changed how stories were structured on film, so too did comic strips change when the words were moved from beneath panels to inside them, and dialogue rather than narration was made to forward a story in conjunction with the pictures.

The Victorian Era of comic books began on different dates in different nations, depending on when the first publication of a sequential comic book on their soil is known to have occurred. For the U.S.A. this happened when the American humor periodical **Brother Jonathan** printed the 40-page, 195-panel graphic novel **The Adventures of Mr. Obadiah Oldbuck** as a special extra dated September 14, 1842. Almost six decades later, America's Victorian comics came to their end, replaced by the onslaught of Platinum Age books reprinting newspaper strips from Bennett, Hearst & Pulitzer Sunday comic sections, among many others.

There is a lot of overlap between Victorian Era and Platinum Age comic books and strips. There has been a long slow-motion evolution of the comic strip. Those publications which continued from one century into the next, such as **Puck**, **Judge**, and **Life**, have their pre-1900 issues listed within the Victorian Age section, while their post-1899 issues can be found inside the Platinum Age. Some non-sequential (i.e., single panel) American comic items existing prior to 1842 are also listed herein, going back at present to 1795. These belong to what could tentatively be called the **Age of Caricature** (1770s through 1830s), during which Gillray, Rowlandson, Cruikshank, Heath, and Seymour were England's top cartoonists.

The earliest known cartoon-like woodcut printed on paper in North America was in a Puritan children's book first published in 1646. Titled simply "The Burning of Mr. John

The Tables Turned *by James Gillray, 1797 commenting on an "invasion" of England by 1400 French convicts. The use of word balloons was wide spread in many parts of the world long before the Yellow Kid's parrot uttered a few words in 1896.*

*Following a wave of anti-Catholic violence, the Protestant D.C. Johnston drew a series of cartoons decrying Protestant fanaticism in his self-published **Scraps** #6, 1835, and also converted to Catholicism himself. This pair of **Scraps** #6 cartoons contrasts nuns caring for Protestant cholera victims against a mob burning a Catholic church in Charlestown, Mass. Note use of word balloons, common to many cartoons .*

Rogers," it showed in flaming graphic detail what happens to those who stray from the flock and have to be burned at the stake. Wertham would have had a field day with that one as this was aimed directly at children!

Cartoon broadsheets and other single panel images, often using word balloons, appeared from Pre-Revolution days through the end of the 19th Century. The earliest known cartoon published by someone calling himself an "American" is generally credited as the Benjamin Franklin designed "Heaven Helps Only Those Who Help Themselves," which first appeared in his periodical **Plain Truth** in 1747.

The most popularly remembered 18th-Century American cartoons are likely Franklin's "Join or Die" in 1754, representing the American Colonies as severed snake parts, and "The Bloody Massacre Perpetrated in King Street" - Paul Revere's 1770 depiction of the Boston Massacre, whose design he likely pirated from the earlier Henry Pelham broadsheet cartoon "The Fruits of Arbitrary Power."

In September 1826, John Warner Barber, New Haven, Ct. (1798-1885) designed and self-published the broadside **The Drunkard's Progress, Or The Direct Road to Poverty, Wretchedness & Ruin** showing in four stages sequentially "The Morning Dram" which is "The Beginning of Sorrow, " "The Grog Shop" with its "Bad Company," "The Confirmed Drunkard" in a state of "Beastly Intoxication," and the "Concluding Scene" with the family being driven off to the alms house. It is an interesting set of cuts, faintly reminiscent

***Finn's Comic Sketch Book**, 1831 sample page.*

THE ADVENTURES OF MR. OBADIAH OLDBUCK. Wherein are duly set forth the Crosses, Chagrins, Calamities, Checks, Chills, Changes, and Circumgyrations, by which his Courtship was attended. Showing also the Issue of his Suit, and his Espousal to his Lady-Love. New York, Wilson & Company. (Jonathan Press.)

No child has ever encountered such a variety of adventures as fell to Mr. Oldbuck, and if the author has not drawn a little on his fancy for his facts in this relation, the eighth wonder of the world is at last revealed in this surprising history. The reader has undoubtedly heard graphic narrations spoken of, and will be compelled to acknowledge that this work comes entirely under that description, for a more exclusively as well as eloquently graphic production it was never any body's lot to see. In a word it is not a "story and picters to match" as Jack Downing says, but a story told entirely with the graver; being a series of over two hundred engravings of the most mirthmoving description. Their absurdity and grotesque wit—their depicture of the most ridiculous impossibilities challenge comparison.

The wildest fancy of the grotesque school could not conceive a series of adventures more laughably absurd than are here presented; and we can imagine no publication better devised to amuse children of all growths than Obadiah Oldbuck. Nor are the designs wanting in excellent keeping, and a whimsical regard for the rules of drawing. The canons are never departed from arbitrarily, or without an object; and we plead guilty to having lost more than one hour in mirth over this clever and bizarre performance. The price, like the other Jonathan extras, is only one shilling. Copies in any quantity are ready to answer orders—ten copies for one dollar.

***Brother Jonathan**, Sept 17, 1842, page 90 first known advertisement selling **The Adventures of Obadiah Oldbuck**, America's first comic book. Priced at one shilling each or ten for a dollar, the distribution systems were still being invented.*

of Hogarth. Barber began his cartooning career in 1819, age 21, engraving on wood. He worked on a multitude of varied art chores for books. As late as 1870 he was issuing **Barber's Temperance Tracts** which built upon his 1826 original plus four panels showing forward positive motion in living without alcohol.

The earliest-known American whose fame was based solely on his cartoons was David Claypool Johnston (1798-1865). Johnston provided illustrations for various almanacs, books, and periodicals, including the masthead for **Brother Jonathan**. This same masthead appears on the top half of the cover of the **Brother Jonathan** edition of **Obadiah Oldbuck**. Most notable of Johnston's comics work was his nine-issue series **Scraps**, which he self-published from 1828 to 1849, and his one-shot album **Outlines Illustrative of the Journal of F****** A*** K*****,** which parodies passages from the Journal of Frances A. Kemble. Johnston was widely known in his day as "the American Cruikshank." His **Scraps** series was highly influenced by George Cruikshank's series **Scraps and Sketches**, which first appeared in 1827. Each issue of Johnston's **Scraps** consists of four large folio-sized pages, printed on one side, with 9 to 12 single-panel cartoons per page, and each page often organized around a theme.

In 1831 Peabody & Co, 233 Broadway, New York City published a collection by D.C. Johnston's friend, actor Henry J. Finn, titled simply **Finn's Comic Sketch Book**, running 12 pages with upwards of half a dozen single-panel cartoons per page. Peabody was in business from 1831-1843, also publishing **Knickerbocker Magazine.**

But is fortunately rescued from immediate peril by the faithful elephant.

LIST of BOOKS for sale at the Brother Jonathan Office.

THE ADVENTURES OF OBADIAH OLDBUCK.—A Book of Pictures, which set forth, in a laughable manner, the Curious, Comical, Cunning, Extraordinary, Extravagant, Funny, Farcical, Lively, Pathetic, Perplexing, Quizzical, and Wonderful Incidents which attended the Courtship and Marriage of that unfortunate and perplexed old gentleman—showing likewise how he attempted to commit suicide on five different occasions, and each time was saved by "invidious fate." The story of Mr. Oldbuck's Love, as set forth by these pictures, is one of the most admirable satires and caricatures of a love-sick old bachelor that can be imagined. It is full of genuine, original, sparkling wit—nothing old or borrowed. It will amuse the most refined person, and cannot fail to please everybody. This book comprises 80 pages of pictures, well printed on fine hot-pressed paper. It is one of the cheapest pictorial works ever published. We send it free of postage for 25 cents per copy.

A DAY'S SPORT—Or, Hunting Adventures of S. Winks Wattles, a shopkeeper, Thomas Titt. Esq., a "legal gent.," and Major Nicholas Noggin, a jolly good fellow generally. This story is told by Pictures, and is really a witty and amusing book—the drawings by Henry L. Stevens of Philadelphia. It will make you laugh out loud to look over this book. It is handsomely printed, and put up in an illustrated cover, suitable for the centre table. We send it free of postage for 12½ cents per copy.

THE SEA-WITCH—A Story of Life and Adventure on board an African Slaver, and on the Coast. One of the best novels we have issued in a long time. Sent free of postage for 25 cents.

Send cash for the above books to B. H. Day, 48 Beekman-st., New York.

B. H. Day's ***Brother Jonathan Cheap Book Establishment*** *1855 catalog with 32-panel comic strip "Peter Piper in Bengal!" by John Tenniel (later Alice of Wonderland fame) with two comic books for sale on the above page:* ***Obadiah Oldbuck*** *by Töpffer and* ***A Day's Sport*** *by Henry L. Stevens of Philadelphia, a scarce newly-rediscovered original American comic book.*

Johnston was also involved in the theater, and he began collaborating with Finn in 1825 on various projects, including the 1831 **(American) Comic Annual**, with Finn as editor and Johnston as artist, published by Richardson, Lord and Holbrook, Boston. It has an inscription dated Dec. 26, 1830 on the front end-paper on one of the known copies which has almost 30 full-page copper engravings and woodcuts Johnston designed. Their collaborations ended when Finn died tragically in a steamboat accident on January 13, 1840.

The next step forward in the development of comics in America occurred when the weekly humor periodical **Brother Jonathan** published a parallel "Extra" series which reprinted mainly prose European novels. For example their eighth "extra" was the first American printing of a Charles Dickens novel. Becoming adventurous, the editors chose Rodolphe Töpffer's graphic novel, **The Adventures of Mr. Obadiah Oldbuck** for **Extra**, No. IX, reformatting it from its original small oblong strip shape to the side-stitched magazine shape in which the earlier Extras were published. This had the inadvertent prophetic effect of making this edition (alone) of **Obadiah Oldbuck** resemble a modern comic book. The arrival of this comic book on the shores of the New World would directly inspire a wave of American imitators, as happened earlier in European nations where Töpffer's comics had appeared. [This first Wilson printing of **Oldbuck** from 1842 was reprinted in same-size limited edition facsimile by the Naples Comicon in 2003.]

A translation by Leonardo De Sá of Töpffer's original draft is at leonardodesa.interdinamica.net/comics/lds/.

According to **The New York Times** (Sept. 3, 1904), the first American comic book was issued as a supplement to **Brother Jonathan** (New York, Sept. 14, 1842). Even so, by the beginning of the 20th century, this comics pioneer was largely forgotten in the New World. It is high time Töpffer received credit long overdue as the person who invented the modern comic strip, laying previously long-held myths to rest.

Töpffer (1799-1846) was a playwright, novelist, artist, and teacher from Geneva, Switzerland, who in 1827 had begun producing what he called "picture novels," sharing them with his friends and students. His earliest editions were published by him privately in Geneva via lithography on transfer paper as they use the word "autographie" in their imprints. The earliest printers were J. Freydig, Frutiger (1830s) and Schmidt (1840s). These first sequential comic books, scripted in Töpffer's native French language, found their way to Paris & became an instant hit. According to Gombrich in **Art and Illusion** (1960), "Töpffer recognized that he could rely on the reader to supplement from their own lives what was omitted between the panels. This is crucial in the development of the sequential comic strip."

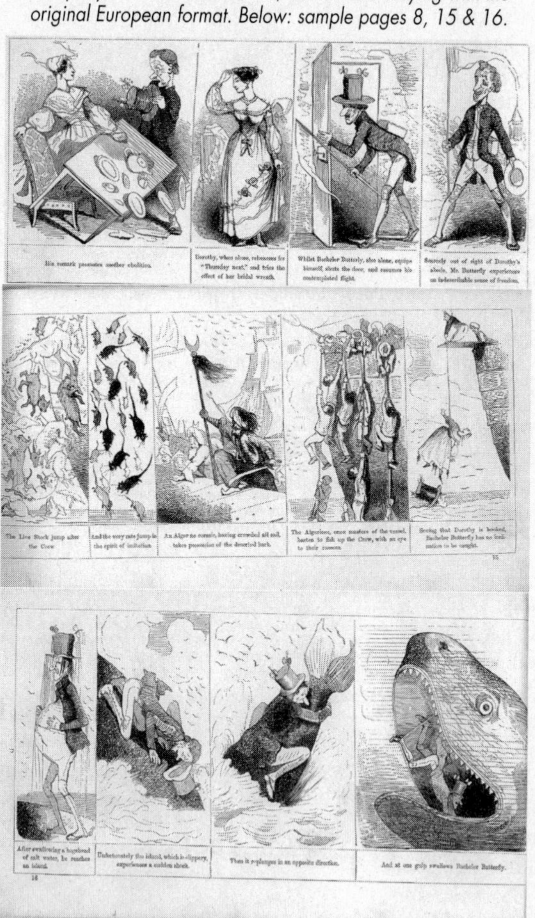

The Strange and Wonderful Adventures of Bachelor Butterfly *by Rodolphe Töpffer (New York, 1846) was Wilson & Company's second comic book, this time out staying with the original European format. Below: sample pages 8, 15 & 16.*

The demand for his comic books soon outstripped the supply, and pirated editions, redrawn by others, were created by Parisian publisher Aubert to capitalize on this. In a world where international copyright conventions did not exist, this was perfectly legal, if morally questionable. London publisher Tilt & Bogue struck a deal with George Cruikshank, resulting in the 1841 English version of Aubert's piracy of **Les Amours de M. Vieux Bois**.

This English translation was co-financed by George Cruikshank himself, and sported a new cover page by George's brother Robert, based on a montage of Töpffer's scenes. Confirmation came when George Cruikshank's personal copy surfaced in auction recently with the inscription "Copied from a French book by my Brother Robert" above the title page with the same scene. A still-unknown scenario led to America's Wilson and Company reprinting this translation.

Tilt & Bogue followed up their success by translating into English two additional stories of Töpffer's seven published graphic novels: **Beau Ogleby**, circa 1843 (originally **Histoire de M. Jabot**), and **Bachelor Butterfly** two years later (from **Histoire de M. Cryptogame**). David Bogue also published picture-story strip books by John Leighton using the pseudonym Luke Limner. He wrote and drew beautiful looking comic books titled **London Out of Town or The Adventures of the Browns At The Seaside**; **Comic Art-Manufactures**; and **The Ancient Story of the Old Dame and Her Pig** starting in 1847, but none of these seem to have had American editions discovered to date. They follow a definite Töpffer influence. This growing body of comic book production was made easier by the spreading understanding of transfer paper lithography, otherwise the panels would have to be drawn and lettered mirror reverse. Gombrich referred to Töpffer's comic books as "the innocent ancestors of today's manufactured dreams...everywhere in these countless episodes of almost surrealist inconsequence we find a mastery of physiognomic characterization which sets the standard for such influential humorous draftsmen in the 19th century as Wilhelm Busch in Germany."

A Register of The New York City Book Trades 1821-

1842 by Sidney F. & Elizabeth Stege Huttner (The Bibliographical Society of America, NYC, 1993) mentions Benjamin H. Day bought into **Brother Jonathan** in this year, becoming at some point some sort of equal partner with owner J. Gregg Wilson of Wilson & Company, who had been publishing since 1839. The **Register** lists them both at the address of 162 Nassau Street, and mentions them both as publishers with the same address as **Brother Jonathan**. Other historical artifacts state he eventually became sole-owner and publisher. Exactly when this happened remains open for debate.

This is the same Benjamin H. Day who in 1833 started the first successful penny newspaper, **The (New York) Sun**, transforming it in four short years into the largest circulation daily in the world, at the time. He sold out his ownership to his brother-in-law in that newspaper during the financial "panic" of 1837, a mistake he regretted his entire life. He re-emerged heavily involved in **Brother Jonathan** definitely by 1840 and as a partner by 1841. **Brother Jonathan** was right next door to Tamany Hall. (See the 2002 movie **Gangs of New York** to visualize the period atmosphere and their customer base.) According to **The Brothers Harper** by Eugene Exmen (Harper & Row, 1965), on page 125, "... **Brother Jonathan**... offered in its weekly edition and also in special supplements very cheap reprints of English novels. In effect, it began a price-cutting war against the older established 'pirates' among the book publishers..." This sounds perfect for Day to sink his teeth into and redeem himself.

With his own words as documented proof, along with the previous reference to them both listed in the New York City directories as working and living at the same address beginning in 1841, Benjamin H. Day and J. Gregg Wilson became the earliest-known comic book publishers in America. They were printers first, then became publishers who joined forces, but the exact relationship between these individuals in still dimly known. What we do know is that Wilson & Company picked up on **Bachelor Butterfly** in the States in 1846. In 1849, Wilson & Company reformatted **Obadiah Oldbuck** back into its original British shape using lithography, dropping a handful of comic panels and altering the text to hide these deletions. And soon thereafter published other comic books for a steadily growing market.

Back in Europe, perhaps inspired by his involvement with Töpffer's **Obadiah Oldbuck**, George Cruikshank soon created several sequential comic books of his own. These too found their way to America. **The Bachelor's Own Book**, published first in Britain in 1844, became the second known U.S. published sequential comic book when reprinted by Burgess, Stringer & Company the following year. Next was Cruikshank's masterpiece **The Bottle**, the Hogarthian-style tale of a man whose addiction to alcohol brings himself and his family to ruin. After debuting in London in 1847, it was reprinted the same year in a British-American co-publication between David Bogue and Americans Wiley and Putnam. Both printings were in huge folio form, available in either black & white or professionally hand-tinted versions. In 1848, the story saw American print again, this time in smaller form, placed at the front of the otherwise prose volume **Temperance Tales; Or, Six Nights with the Washingtonians**. It continued to be reprinted by a variety of publishers into the early 20th Century. **The Bottle** was popular in Revival and Temperance circles, made more so by its use in lectures, where the story was reproduced onto painted glass slides then projected for audiences by a magic lantern. **The Drunkard's Children**, Cruikshank's sequel to **The Bottle**, was issued July 1, 1848 as a British-American-Australian co-publishing venture, but was less successful, and had not nearly as many reprints.

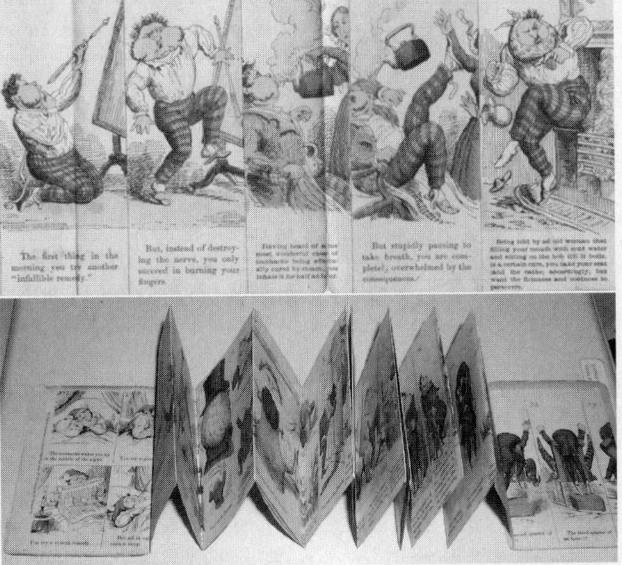

The Tooth-Ache *by George Cruikshank 1849 opens up accordion-like into a single strip 7 feet, 3 inches long!*

The most clearly sequential, as well as fun, of George Cruikshank's comic books was **The Tooth-Ache,** first issued in London in 1849. It was reprinted in the America later that same year by Philadelphia map maker J.L. Smith. An additional concurrent version was also issued from Boston.

When closed, this booklet appears an unassuming 5-1/4 inches tall by 3-1/4 inches wide. Its striking feature is that the book folds open accordian style, stretching the entire 43-panel story along one single strip of paper, which when fully extended is seven feet, three inches long! **The Tooth-Ache** was issued in both black & white and professionally hand-colored editions. Abridged editions of the story, printed in black & white and with a "normal" page-turning rather than

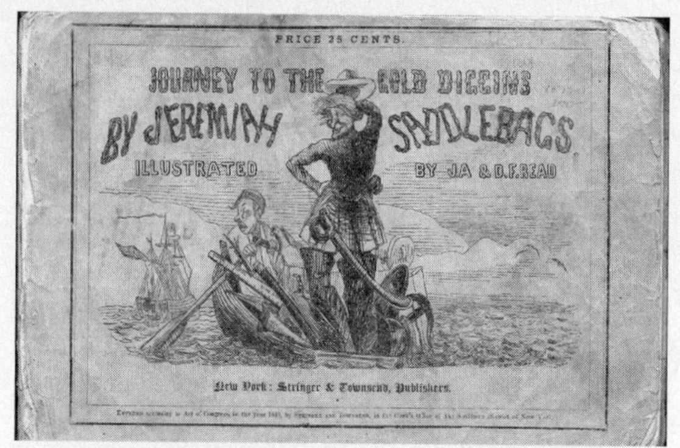

Cover of 1849's ***Journey to the Gold Diggins By Jeremiah Saddlebags****, the earliest known sequential comic book by American creators, J.A. and D.F. Read Below: a couple sample pages - note similarity to Töpffer's comics especially* ***Bachelor Butterfly****.*

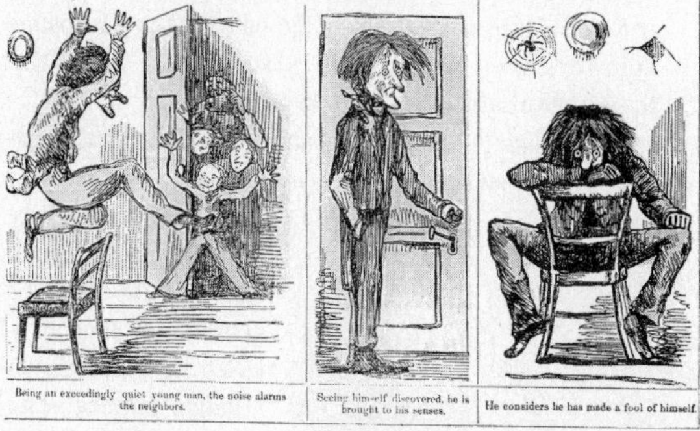

fold-out presentation, appeared inside promotional giveaway comics issued by American companies in the 1880s.

Between Töpffer and Cruikshank, 1842-1849 had seen six sequential European comic books reprinted in the U.S., not to mention additional comics imported directly without American reproduction. At that decade's end, this combined influence met with a national craze screaming for satirization - California's Gold Rush. The result was the earliest known American created sequential comic book.

Journey to the Gold Diggins by Jeremiah Saddlebags, by brothers James and Donald Read, was published in 1849, first in New York City by Stringer & Townsend, then soon after re-published in Cincinnati, Ohio, by U.P. James. This Töpffer-influenced comic book chronicles the adventures of its hero **Jeremiah Saddlebags** in his get-rich-quick quest for gold in California and is highly sought by collectors of Western Americana. Interestingly, the back cover of the Stringer & Townsend edition carries an advertisement for **Rose and Gertrude-a Genevese Story**, one of Rodolphe Töpffer's non-comics prose novels. Stringer was one of the 1845 participants in the American publication of **The Bachelor's Own Book**. One might speculate that his earlier involvement with Cruikshank's comic could have made Stringer more receptive to the Read brothers' **Jeremiah Saddlebags**.

Still other contemporary Gold Rush comics appeared. **The Adventures of Mr. Tom Plump** (a fat man who nearly starves to death in his failed attempt at California Gold riches) saw print in 1850. **The Adventures of Jeremiah Old-pot** was serialized across all twelve monthly issues of **Yankee Notions** in 1852. Gold Rush cartoons are found in the 1849 edition of David Claypool Johnston's **Scraps**, in comic almanacs, and in Currier & Ives broadsheets.

The circa 1850-51 booklet **The Clown, Or The Banquet of Wit**, includes a 13-page comic story "Moses Keyser the Bowery Bully's Trip to the California Gold Mines," reprinted from **Elton's Californian Comic All-My-Nack** for 1850. **The Clown** is also notable as the earliest known anthology of sequential comics, with the bonus that each multi-panel story is by a different artist. Many of the artists are as yet unidentified, and how much of it is original American material versus that reprinted from Europe is presently unknown. But verified are cartoons by George Cruikshank, Elton (American), the Read brothers, Grandville (French), and Richard Doyle (British). The Doyle contribution reprints the comics story "Brown, Jones and Robinson and How They Went to a Ball," which originally saw print in the August 24, 1850 issue of **Punch**. This is the first known American appearance of these Doyle characters, and was almost certainly pirated.

Richard Doyle's **The Foreign Tour of Messrs. Brown, Jones, and Robinson** is basically a travelogue in illustrated form, told via humorous episodes, part sequential cartoon sequences, and part snapshots of moments jumping forward in time. This halfway sequential format was ideal for most 19th Century cartoonists, who, with rare exception, had not quite grasped how to maintain a single sequential story for much longer than two dozen successive panels. Doyle had simplified Töpffer's formula in a manner most artists could attempt to emulate. Episodes of "Brown, Jones, and Robinson" originally appeared in **Punch** in 1850, until a dispute between the Roman Catholic Doyle and **Punch's** editors over an anti-Papal joke ended with Doyle quitting in particular because of a cartoon by John Tenniel. Doyle redrew and expanded the story into a single album, first seeing print in 1854 from British publisher Bradbury & Evans.

New York publisher D. Appleton brought the album to America, where he reprinted it in 1860, 1871, and 1877.

ADVENTURES OF MR. TOM PLUMP.
He thinks he will leave California.
He starts in a great hurry for the ship.
He turns sailor before starting.
He falls overboard from the ship into the sea.
He saves himself by swimming, and afterwards dances a hornpipe.

The Adventures of Tom Plump *story page 5, Huestis & Cozans, NYC c.1850-51 which also has similarities to Töpffer's and the Read Bros' comics.*

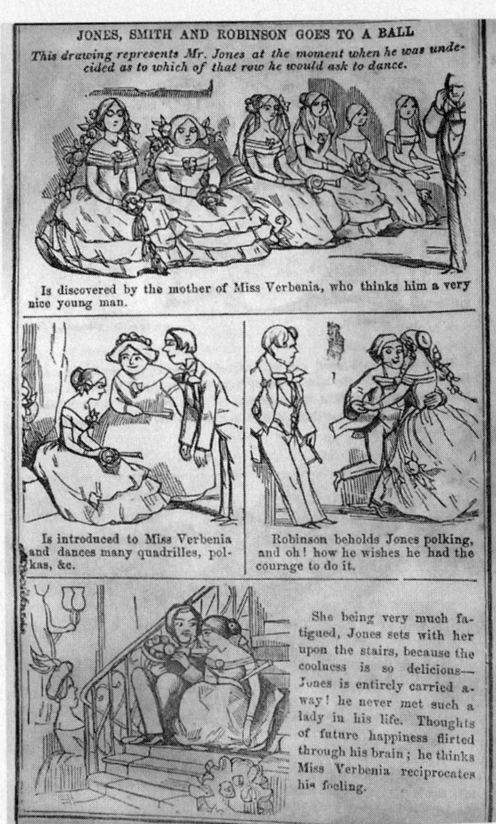

JONES, SMITH AND ROBINSON GOES TO A BALL
This drawing represents Mr. Jones at the moment when he was undecided as to which of that row he would ask to dance.
Is discovered by the mother of Miss Verbenia, who thinks him a very nice young man.
Is introduced to Miss Verbenia and dances many quadrilles, polkas, &c.
Robinson beholds Jones polking, and oh! how he wishes he had the courage to do it.
She being very much fatigued, Jones sets with her upon the stairs, because the coolness is so delicious—Jones is entirely carried away! he never met such a lady in his life. Thoughts of future happiness flirted through his brain; he thinks Miss Verbenia reciprocates his feeling.

Richard Doyle's ***Foreign Tour****, as it first appeared in America within* ***The Clown, or The Banquet of Wit*** *1850-51 pirated from Punch.*

Next, Dick & Fitzgerald (NY) pirated Doyle's story sometime in the early 1870s. Doyle's format from **Foreign Tour** was emulated again and again. Examples include: the 1857 **Mr. Hardy Lee, His Yacht**, by Charles Stedman; the 1860s to 1870s Carleton published **Our Artist In...** series, set in various Latin American countries; the Augustus Hoppin 1870s sketch novels **On the Nile, Crossing the Atlantic,** and **Ups and Downs on Land and Water**; and **Life** founder John Ames Mitchell's 1881 (pre-**Life**) **The Summer School of Philosophy at Mt. Desert**. D. Appleton, the official, authorized American publisher of **Foreign Tour**, even commissioned an American artist - Toby - to create a sequel comic album involving Doyle's characters visiting the U.S. and Canada, published in 1872 as **The American Tour of Messrs Brown, Jones and Robinson**. In terms of influencing the development of mid-19th Century American comics, Doyle's **Foreign Tour** ranks with the works of Töpffer, Cruikshank, and Busch.

Doyle additionally produced a second, earlier cartoon series for **Punch**, the popularity of which likewise exerted influence decades beyond its publication. In **Manners and Customs of Ye Englyshe, Mr. Pips Hys Diary**, gathered from **Punch** & reprinted in 1849, Doyle told his story using a deliberately primitive almost stick-figure art style, combined with the Hogarthian structure of large single panel cartoons leaping forward in time with each picture.

Manners and Customs of Ye Harvard Studente, which ran in the **Harvard Lampoon**, shows the clearest influence. The series by then student Francis Gilbert Attwood was collected in 1877 by Houghton Mifflin. Attwood followed it up with **Manners and Customs of Ye Bostonians**, again in the pages of the **Harvard Lampoon**, but it is unknown whether that series was ever reprinted in book form. Attwood later became one of the regular artists in **Life**.

The British humor periodical **Punch** additionally influenced American comics beyond Richard Doyle's series. Consisting of humorous text interspersed with (mostly) single panel cartoons, it began its weekly run in July 1841, and continued uninterrupted well into the 20th Century. A large subset of **Punch**'s subscriber base was located in the U.S., to which thousands of copies were exported on an ongoing basis. The result was that when American humor periodicals emerged, they invariably imitated **Punch**'s format and style.

The earliest known of these American imitators, **Yankee Doodle**, debuted on October 10, 1846, and lasted one year. **Punch in Canada** likewise appeared in the late 1840s, kicking off a smaller parallel comics evolution just north of the U.S. (The earliest known "illustrated" American humor peri-

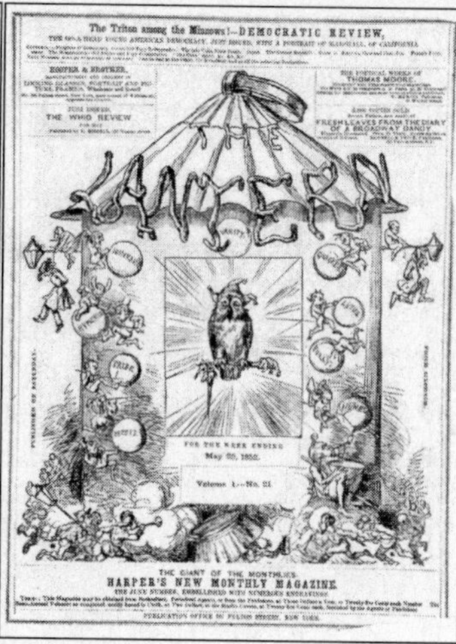

A few samples of the many humor magazines of the mid-1800s which ran cartoons. Wide-spread acceptance of the comic srtip slowly evolved over the decades. Left: ***Yankee Doodle*** *#30 title ran October 1846-October 1847; Middle:* ***The John-Donkey*** *#4 title ran January-October 1848; Right:* ***The Lantern*** *#21, May 29, 1851 title ran Jan. 10, 1852-July 1853*

odical, **The Humourist**, was published monthly in Baltimore from January 1829 to at least December of that same year, sans input from **Punch**. This monthly contained but one cartoon per issue, albeit hand-colored.)

Collections reprinting cartoons from **Punch** saw print in the U.S., such as **Merry Pictures by the Comic Hands**, imported for the 1859 Christmas Season, plus various John Leech, George Du Maurier, and Phil May books which appeared from the 1850s through 1910s. Finally, many American illustrated newspapers and periodicals, humorous and non-humorous, carried reprints of **Punch** cartoons. Such inclusions often became a prelude to switching to original material by American artists, should that publication's cartoon section become popular. Such was the case with **Harper's Monthly**. In the early 1850s, near the rear of each issue, it began to carry a few pages of single panel cartoons reprinted from **Punch**. This evolved into reprinting sequential comic pages from the British periodical **Town Talk**, and then, starting December 1853, original sequential comics by American artist Frank Bellew.

Bellew (1828-1888) could be regarded as the father of American sequential comics. Born in India, educated in France and England, he emigrated to America in 1850. His earliest work shows an influence from Doyle, but he rapidly developed his own unique art style. Bellew's comics, both sequential and single panel, graced numerous periodicals from the 1850s through the 1870s.

In the year prior to his **Harper's Monthly** appearances, in **The Lantern** volume one, Bellew had presented the 18-panel story "Mr. Blobb in Search of a Physician," serialized across six weekly issues. This was followed soon after by the 16-panel, three issue story "Mr. Bulbear's Dream", which concluded with the main character awakened from his dream by falling out of bed, in the exact same manner as would **Little Nemo** five decades later.

According to a 1923 article on famous cartoonists written by Charles Dana Gibson, it was Bellew's conception of **Uncle Sam** which "became the popular figure emblematic of the United States" starting with **The Lantern** issue published March 13, 1852. This was in a cartoon titled "Collins and Cunard - Raising the Wind; Or Both Sides of the Story." Gibson went on, "Thomas Nast (later) added whiskers and put stars on the vest, retaining Bellew's hat, high collar, and striped trousers."

Frank Bellew's son, Frank Bellew Jr., also became a cartoonist of note, which has caused confusion amongst those trying to identify the work of 19th century cartoonists. Bellew Sr. often signed his work by placing his name or initials within a triangle, with Bellew Jr. most frequently signing his using the nickname "Chips."

The Extraordinary and Mirth-provoking Adventures by Sea & Land of Oscar Shanghai, inspired by **Bachelor Butterfly**, was issued around the same time circa 1853 by Garrett & Co., Publishers, No. 18 Ann Street, New

Recently rediscovered USA printing of ***The Laughable Adventures of Messrs. Brown, Jones and Robinson*** *by Richard Doyle published by Garrett, Dick & Fitzgerald, circa 1856.*

***The Great Republication Reform Party**, 1855 has everybody talking with word balloons to John C. Fremont, first Republication Presidential hopeful, who is greeting new constituents: a black man, a Catholic church rep, a believer in Free Love, a communist, a woman's rights advocate, and a prohibitionist.*

York. **Oscar Shanghai** has many misadventures including being swallowed by a whale, making a trip in a flying machine which flies to Africa, where he is shot out of a huge bow by a "Black Prince" for not marrying a local princess of color. After more adventures, he makes it back home.

Oscar Shanghai's first publisher was confirmed this year with the discovery of a very rare 36-page catalog circa 1855 of books, pamphlets and prints handled by B.H. Day, owner & publisher of **Brother Jonathan** since the mid-1840s. The catalog has a few crossover advertisement pages from an associate publisher, Garrett. This newly rediscovered treasure, which sold for $750 in late 2002 itself, contains a sequential strip of one panel per page over 32 of those pages titled "Peter Piper in Bengal," by John Tenniel, reprinted from four 1853 issues of **Punch** to entice the reader to page through the entire booklet. Peter Piper tried his hand hunting all different kinds of wild game with many misadventures.

Amongst the many varied type of "Cheap Books" for sale in this rare catalog are the comic books **The Adventures of Obadiah Oldbuck**, **Bachelor Butterfly's Queer Love Adventures and Misfortunes** and **The Fortunes of Ferdinand Flipper** plus the aforementioned **Oscar Shanghai**. All priced at "25¢ per copy, postage free, refunds paid out in stamps."

There is also an advertisement for a comic book we have never heard of before titled **A Day's Sport - Or, Hunting Adventures of S. Winks Wattles, a Shopkeeper, Thomas Titt, a "legal gent," and Major Nicholas Noggin, a Jolly Good Fellow Generally** by Henry L. Stevens of Philadelphia. As we go to press again this year, we know of no existing complete copies and hope one still exists.

This catalog trumpets the concept that **Brother Jonathan** was for sale at the 1851 London World's Fair. Owner Benjamin H. Day was perhaps better known as the founder of **The New York Sun**, the very first successful "penny" newspaper in America begun in 1833, as well as having bought **Brother Jonathan** from Wilson sometime after selling out his interest in **The Sun**. Exactly when seems to be a matter open for debate amongst present-day historians.

Garrett & Co. was also responsible for the circa 1855 publication of **The Sad Tale of the Courtship of Chevalier Slyfox-Wikof, Showing His Heart-Rending Astounding & Most Wonderful Love Adventures with Fanny Elssler and Miss Gambol.** This book parodied the very public relationship between the then-famous wealthy American aristocrat Henry Wikoff, and the even more famous European actress/dancer Fanny Elssler. It is dated thusly because Wikoff's memoir is pictured in the comic book.

It appears circa 1855-56 Garrett & Co. formed a brief two-year partnership with Dick & Fitzgerald, becoming Garrett, Dick & Fitzgerald, while continuing to operate out of the same 18 Ann Street address in New York. During this time, they reprinted Richard Doyle's British published graphic novel **The Foreign Tour of Messrs. Brown, Jones, and Robinson**, reformatting it into the same oblong shape as Garrett's two prior comic books (which in turn were formatted in imitation of Töpffer's albums).

In 1858, Garrett appears to have dropped out, leaving Dick & Fitzgerald alone with the former's book stock, his place of business, and most importantly, the printing plates for his comic books. The Civil War was about to start, and for slightly more than a decade Dick & Fitzgerald steered away from reprinting his comic books. But in the 1870s they resumed publication - not only of the three albums published by Garrett, but also of **Obadiah Oldbuck** and **Bachelor Butterfly** from Wilson & Company, and **Ferdinand Flipper** from Brother Jonathan - all of them also making use of the original printing plates. The inclusion of books from Brother Jonathan, Wilson & Company, and Garrett & Co. all within the same promotional **Peter Piper** catalog from B.H. Day suggests (though not yet proven) that all these companies may have been part of Day's publishing empire, and that Dick &

***The Wonderful and Amusing Doings of Oscar Shanghai**, first published circa 1855 by Garrett & Co.; pictured here is a later Dick & Fitzgerald 1870's edition.*

Fitzgerald became the inheritor/acquirer of all of it. Dick & Fitzgerald became simply Fitzgerald Publishing in 1889, and are believed to have dropped out of the comic book business. Dick & Fitzgerald also reprinted in the 1870s the earlier William T. Peter published **Ichabod Academicus** (how that title might have connected, if at all, with B.H. Day's business remains unclear). We can now say, though, that an evolving group of a handful of publishers was responsible, over a span of 46 years, beginning with the very first graphic novel published in America in 1842, for keeping in print in America a cluster of slightly over half a dozen graphic novels.

While Bellew stood out for his sequential comics, Thomas Nast (1840-1902) brought a new style to American political cartoons, of which he is regarded the father. Even though he created several sequential strips early in his career, Nast made his name in the pages of the national news periodical **Harper's Weekly**, whose staff he joined a year into the Civil War. As Nast grew in prominence & success, American cartoonists increasingly emulated him. U.S. humor publications evolved towards an amalgamation of Nast and **Punch**, rather than sheer imitation of the latter.

While the northern **Vanity Fair** (December 31, 1859 - July 4, 1863) and the Confederate **Southern Punch** (August 15, 1863 - September, 1864) were both modeled after **Punch**, other Civil War era humor periodicals such as J.C. Haney's **Comic Monthly** and Frank Leslie's **Budget of Fun** were clearly absorbing lessons from Nast. These last two were issued in the same large folio size as **Harper's Weekly**, with a large front page cartoon, a larger double-page cartoon centerfold, and still more cartoons located on the back cover - a format approaching what eventually emerged in what **Puck** began doing.

The Sad Tale of the Courtship of Chevalier Slyfox-Wikof, *Garrett & Co, New York, c1855.*

"The Flight of Abraham Lincoln," first appeared in ***Harper's Weekly****, March 9, 1861.*

Sample panels from Frank Bellew Sr's ***The Flying Machine; And Professor High's Adventure therein in a Trip across the Ocean, Merryman's Monthly*** *V3#5, May 1865.*

After the War, with Nast's style of cartoons more entrenched in American readers' minds, efforts to launch **Punch**-like American periodicals floundered quickly. **Mrs. Grundy**, ironically most famous for its cover design by Nast, died after a mere twelve issues (running July 8 to September 23, 1865). **Punchinello** (April 2 to December 24, 1870) struggled nine months before its backers gave up. **Punchinello** had been financed by Tammany Hall politicians Tweed and Sweeney, as counter-propaganda against Nast's ongoing assault upon their corruption. They attempted to buy and threaten Nast into silence, to no avail.

American comics were also being pulled away from their initial Anglo-Franco imitation by the infusion of a third major source of European influence. Numerous European humor periodicals besides **Punch** found significant subscriber bases in America. The large German immigrant population imported their favorite humor periodicals into the U.S., including the popular **Fliegende Blätter** ("Flying Leaves") and **Münchener Bilderbogen**. As high in quality as these were, one German comic artist in particular excelled beyond the rest, his stories breaking out and crossing over into English language translations, the demand for which resulted in numerous printings. This artist, of course, was Heinrich Christian Wilhelm Busch (1832-1908).

Busch's work appeared in English in the 1860s in both British and American periodicals, often uncredited. For example, four of Busch's strips appeared in English in the pages of **Merryman's Monthly** in 1864, while in 1879 his graphic story "Fipps der Affe" was serialized across a 10-issue run of **Puck** as "Troddledums the Simian." The earliest known English language appearance of Busch in book form was **The Flying Dutchman, or The Wrath of Herr von Stoppelnoze**, in 1862, from New York publisher Carleton. Carleton not only pirated Busch's strip, but went so far as to credit the story to American poet John G. Saxe, with Busch's cartoons mere illustrations accompanying Saxe's prose!

MRS. GRUNDY.

MILITARY DENTISTRY;
OR, A SURE CURE FOR THE TOOTHACHE.

One! Two!!

Panels from ***Mrs. Grundy****, Saturday, July 15, 1865.*

The next known English language Busch book was **A Bushel of Merry Thoughts**, an 1868 London-published anthology collecting various Busch strips. Some of these same stories later appeared in the U.S.-published **The Mischief Book** (1880), newly translated and with a few more Busch tales added. One of these additions was "Hans Huckebein." A tale of a mischievous pet raven who in the end gets drunk and accidentally hangs himself, it became, at least in the States, Busch's 2nd most popular sequential comic story. The unrepentant bird was promoted to title character in two later collections: **Jack Huckaback, the Scapegrace Raven**, circa 1888, and the rarer **Hookeybeak the Raven and Other Tales** in 1878. There were also at least 3 trade card series in the 1870s & 1880s which reprinted the ending sequence, as **Fritz Spindle-Shanks-The Raven Black**.

Sample comics panels by Wilhelm Busch circa 1870.

The most popular Busch tale, though, was easily **Max und Moritz**, which in the U.S. saw print as **Max and Maurice - A Juvenile History in Seven Tricks**. Published in Boston in 1871, this English language version saw at minimum 60 reprintings by the century's end, plus countless more printings later. A separate British translation debuted in 1874, under the title **Max & Mortiz**. It is well known that the later Rudolph Dirks comic strip series, **Katzenjammer Kids** beginning in late 1897 was based on **Max und Moritz**.

According to documents found by Alfredo Castelli, **Katzenjammer Kids** was not yet another rip-off of Busch. Rather, William R. Hearst may have licensed the characters. Hearst's paper was published in different language editions for New York City's immigrant communities. In the German edition, the strip was published under its original name, **Max und Moritz**. Numerous other translations of Busch were published in America - too many to name in this article. Several can be found in the Victorian Age Index. There were many prominent talented artists in the incredibly scarce, still legendary (but now largely forgotten but to a few) 1870s humor periodicals, **Wild Oats** and **Schnedereddeng**, the German language companion publication to **Wild Oats**. In terms of the quality of their cartoons and comics, these two New York City publications were in 1872 at an artistic level **Puck** would not achieve until 1880.

Published by Winchell & Small and distributed through the New York News Company, **Schnedereddeng** and **Wild Oats** carried a crossroads of old and next generation comic artists, from the more established W. M. Avery, Thomas Francis "Frank" Beard, Frank Henry Temple Bellew, E.S. Bisbee, Michael Angelo Woolf, and Thomas Worth (remembered more these days for his Currier & Ives cartoon sheets), and up-and-comers such as Livingston Hopkins, Frederick Burr Opper, Palmer Cox and Wales.

Wild Oats began carrying sequential comic strips as early as #26, dated March 14, 1872, with the Livingston Hopkins strip pictured below (we do not know anything yet about the first 25 issues). The very next issue has a Worth double-page spread titled "The Political Humpty Dumpty... Horace Greeley" told in 11 panels plus the sequential fictional "Graphic Account of the Assassination of Queen Victoria" and "Love As the Angels Love." "The Doings of the Japanese Embasey At Washington" related in 12 panels by W. M. Avery follows up in #28 April 11, 1872. An unknown hand drew "The Physiology of Moving" in 6 panels in #30. Hopkins returns with a beautiful intense 28-panel double-page spread in #31 May 23. Hopkins and Worth alternated for many issues with sequential comic strips on baseball, horse racing and other pertinent subjects of the day. In #45 December 5, 1872, E.S. Bisbee contributed his first sequential in 17 panels and Worth showed up in "Humor & Pathos of a New England Thanksgiving" in 11 panels. Issue 47 expands the concept with a 12-panel job by Bisbee, 20-panel effort on one page by Hopkins and a 3-panel effort by Worth. And on it goes through 1873 as well - comic strip after comic strip. Issue 58 June 5, 1873, includes a particularly humorous 19-panel double-pager drawn by someone still unknown titled "The Terrible Adventures of Messrs. Buster & Stumps, with the Indians" which begins with two white men heading out west in an effort to exterminate Indians - and their misadventures of not quite getting the job done. It reads across both pages in a unique evolution similar to **Popeye** #2052 (found in the Platinum listings). Issue 65 contains two 9-panel Thomas Worth strips "Only a Mad Dog Scare - Another Lesson For Nervous People" and "Only a Cholera Scare - Something For Nervous People to Read and Ponder Over." Issue 66 Sept 18, 1873, has the very funny Hopkins 12-panel strip as well as two more 10-panel Worth strips on the delights of Hunting and Fishing plus one by Hopkins titled "The Adventures of Mr Old Party with Jersey Mosquitoes" in 12-panels. All told, four comic strips in this issue. They obviously liked what they were doing, judging from the exuberance of the work.

***Wild Oats** #26, 14 March 1872 Livingston Hopkins sequential comic strip. Hopkins later moved to Australia and became its premiere political cartoonist.*

The next issue has Worth's 9-panel report on "The Adventures of Young Muttonhead Among the Free Lovers" which was all about the "free sex" convention recently held in Chicago. Issue 68 has a 9-panel "An Adventure With a New Jersey Mosquito" which smacks of Winsor McCay in subject and even art style. Maybe McCay was inspired by this for his later animated cartoon as well as earlier **Rarebit Fiend**. We'll never know for sure. On through 1875, **Wild Oats** presented sequential comic strips issue after issue. With #148, October 27, 1875, Fredrick Opper has his very first **Wild Oats** cover, centering on inflation then rampant in the USA. He does covers through at least #161 before a short break and then comes right back with many more. By #158 January 5, 1876, Palmer Cox - some five years before inventing **The Brownies** - began a wonderful series of 24-panel double page spread comic strips, with a couple sample titles being "The Adventures of Mr & Mrs Sprowl And Their Christmas Turkey-A Crashing Chasing Tearful Tragedy But Happily Ending Well" and "Bachelor Broke & Widow Snuggi: A Pictorial Account of Their Sleigh Ride & What Became of It."

Even though he had been contributing many covers and interior single panel jobs to **Wild Oats** for years, by-then elderly Frank Bellew Sr. does not show up with his first comic strip until $190, August 16, 1876, with a 9-panel effort he titled, "Rodger's Patent Mosquito Armour." By this time the USA's "Father of the sequential comic strip" had inspired many other cartoonists to try their hand telling stories with words & pictures. Bellew Sr. had been making sequential comic strips for over a quarter century.

***Wild Oats** #163, Feb 9, 1876 last six panels by Palmer Cox who began doing sequential comic strips some years years before he created **The Brownies**.*

The seemingly disparate influences of Thomas Nast and German comics came together in Austrian immigrant Joseph Keppler (1838-1894). Like many cartoonists in America, Keppler's desire was to rival Nast. Unlike most, he possessed the talent and drive to accomplish it. Keppler first settled in St.

Louis, Missouri, where he took his first stab at starting a comic weekly, the German language **Die Vehme** (Aug 28, 1869 - Aug. 20, 1870). Seven months later, still in St. Louis, he tried again, launching another German language humor periodical, titled **Puck**. This German **Puck** began on March 18, 1871, joined by an English language version one year later, but both soon folded and ended on Aug. 24, 1872.

Wild Oats *#190 August 16, 1876 by Frank Bellew Sr., Father of American Comic Strips This one titled "Rodger's Patent Mosquito Armor."*

Keppler moved to New York City, doing cartoons primarily for Frank Leslie publications (including a one-shot, English language publication - **Centennial Fun** - which capitalized on the July, 1876 Centennial Exposition in Philadelphia). Four years after the first **Puck** died, Keppler was ready to try again. He re-launched the German language edition of **Puck** in New York City on September 27, 1876.

It was a Presidential Election year, with Republican candidate Hayes versus the Democrat Tilden. Keppler lucked out with material to satirize, when the election ended so close that each candidate needed only the electoral college votes of a few states in question - most notably Florida and Louisiana - and both parties were claiming to have won. Keppler depicted the two candidates as two trains on the same track, steaming towards each other, with the stability of the nation in the balance. After months of dispute, the victory was handed to the loser of the popular vote, the Republican Hayes. (Much later, scholars showed that Tilden, in truth, was the electoral as well as popular winner.)

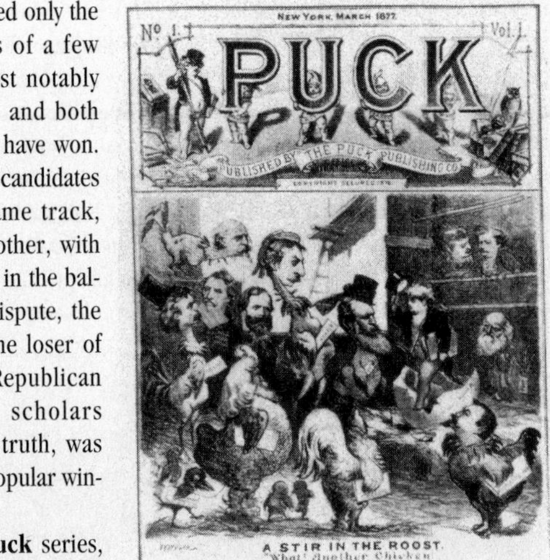

Puck *#1, March 14, 1877, NYC, was very important; but* ***Wild Oats*** *had been running sequential comic strips regularly for over six years.*

With his revamped **Puck** series, Keppler introduced a new element to American humor periodicals - color lithography. The color was initially limited, but it appeared, ambitiously, every week, and set **Puck** apart from anything else on American stands. The parallel English language edition of **Puck** was launched six months after the German version, on March 14, 1877. This English edition of **Puck** was a money-loser for several years, kept afloat by the German edition's profits and the determination of the English edition's literary editor, H.C. Bunner, not to give up. **Puck** became the new model for American humor publications. Keppler brought in other artists over time, most notably Opper, Zim and Howarth, and added black & white sequential comics and cartoons in the pages between the color front cover, back cover, and centerspread.

Puck was the model which William Randolph Hearst followed in 1895, adding a color comics section to his Sunday newspaper. He basically wanted to offer a "free" **Puck**-like supplement within his **New York Journal**. Further, **Puck** artist F.M. Howarth pointed the direction of those future newspaper comics pages, by creating full page sequential color comic strips on most **Puck** back covers starting in the early 1890s.

With the first issue dated October 29, 1881, **Puck's** chief rival, **Judge**, was born. Founded by **Puck** artist James A. Wales, **Judge** made several forays into **Puck's** talent pool over the years. Their best capture was Eugene Zimmerman (known popularly as "Zim"), who became for **Judge** the star artist that Frederick Burr Opper was for **Puck**

When Wales broke away to form **Judge**, it was from amongst his pre-**Puck** associates at the by-then defunct **Wild Oats** that he first recruited. One can speculate that having been a star artist in these earlier magazines may have driven Wales' desire to have more control of his cartoons rather than remain subordinate to Keppler, leading to Wales' creation of **Judge**.

Judge struggled financially for several years, and likely would have ceased publication if not for the Presidential Election of 1884, in which Republicans blamed Keppler and **Puck** for their loss.

By 1884 Frank Beard was the editor.

Republican backers had attempted to create a **Puck** rival titled **Jingo** in the last few months of that election, but it lacked the creative talent of **Puck** & **Judge**, and its backers let it die once the election results were known. Soon after, Republican backers bought and poured money into **Judge**, hoping to make the until-then politically neutral **Judge** their counterweight against Keppler's **Puck**. By this time, most of the ex-**Wild Oats** artists, save Wales, had moved elsewhere.

*Sample panels from **Quiddities of an Alaskan Trip**, 1873 - all about going to then-recently purchased Alaska.*

Numerous other **Puck** imitators emerged in the 1880s but quickly died. Note should be made of the **Puck**-like San Francisco **Wasp**, which debuted October 14, 1876 (too early for it to have been a mere **Puck** knockoff), and the black & white **Texas Siftings**, which debuted on May 9, 1881. Though neither approached **Puck** or **Judge** in circulation, both cut their own paths, managing to survive as cartoon humor magazines into the 1890s.

Published basically concurrent to **Wild Oats** during much of the latter's run was the New York City newspaper **The Daily Graphic** (March 4, 1873 to Sept 23, 1889), which has the claim to being the first regularly illustrated daily newspaper in the world. It was published every day except Sundays and holidays, with the vast majority of its illustrations being straight depictions of news events. (Not until the late 1890s could photographs be reproduced inexpensively enough for inclusion in mass publications, and so the norm was to send out photographers to record images of newsworthy events, but then have artists render those images into drawn engravings, which then were reproduced in newspapers.)

With so many artists needed for illustrated publications, the result was that virtually all 19th century periodicals which regularly featured illustrations, even if their primary aim was to provide realistic pictures, at some point in their runs included both single-panel cartoons, and sequential comics. At a publication rate of six days per week, unbroken over a 15-year run, **The Daily Graphic** had more than the usual hunger for illustrated material to fill its pages with.

Thus, **The Daily Graphic** became a rotating door for many circa 1870s and 1880s American cartoonists, usually those in the early parts of their careers (making one suspect that it was possibly not the best paying gig in town). Within its pages, like needles to be found in the haystack of its more than 4800 issues, is early work by Livingston Hopkins (who mysteriously ap-pears, vanishes, reappears, etc., for months to whole years at a time, right up to his 1884 departure to Australia), pre-**Life** work by Kemble, pre-Harper's appearances by A.B. Frost and W.A. Rogers, pre-**Puck** C.J. Taylor, Hamilton, and Gillam. Old hats, too, appear at times, such as Michael Woolf and Frank Bellew, Sr. Opper appears also.

Further, **The Daily Graphic** regularly plundered British periodicals for its back and sometimes center pages, not only perpetrating the usual swipes of single panel Punch cartoons, but also stealing sequential strips from **Punch**'s two main rival publications, **Judy** and **Fun**. This included occasionally reprinting (albeit at random) episodes of continuing British strips "The British Workman" by James Sullivan, and "McNab of that Ilk" by James Brown. Though, strangely enough, no episodes of Marie Duval's **Ally Sloper**, despite the fact that **The Daily Graphic** did reprint some of Duval's non-"Sloper" strips ("**Ally Sloper**" was a continuing sequential strip character who debuted in 1867, lasting into the 1920s, and had very successful solo British book collections of his strips published as early as 1873 - more than two decades prior to **Yellow Kid in McFadden's Flats**).

Livingston Hopkins, whose art style changed like a chameleon from one year to the next, exhibited a definite Duval influence in his work within a year following the publication of the first **Ally Sloper** collection. Given that Hopkins worked for **The Daily Graphic** during the same period in which **The Daily Graphic** was stealing cartoons from Sloper's home publication, **Judy**, this can hardly be considered coincidental. By the time Hopkins was about to emigrate to Australia to become lead cartoonist for the **Melbourne Punch**, his art style was imitating Kemble, who was working at **The Daily Graphic** just prior to his **Life** covers.

*Pre-**Puck** C.J. Taylor art, in the 1870s promo fold-out strip, "How Adolphus Slim-Jim Used Jackson's Best, and Was Happy." First panel has the small person talking with a word balloon.*

Another highly desirable American graphic novel, sought especially by collectors of Western lore, is **Quiddities of an Alaskan Trip** by William H. Bell which debuted in 1873. Bell was Timothy O'Sullivan's assistant photographer on the 1871-74 expeditions of Lt.

George Wheeler, surveying & mapping the western territories for the U.S. government. The story panels are laid out within ornate frames like those of stereograph cards, such as Bell was involved in creating on the expedition. It involves a parody of a trip from Washington, D.C. to survey the newly purchased territory of Alaska, which at the time was derisively referred to as "Seward's Folly." Bell published **Quiddities** in Portland, Oregon in 1873, a date which would have required that he drew it during the time he was on just such an expedition.

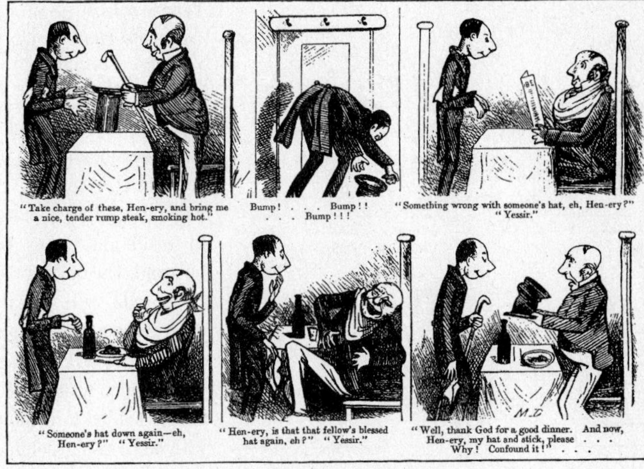

"Take charge of these, Hen-ery, and bring me a nice, tender rump steak, smoking hot."
Bump! . . . Bump!! . . . Bump!!!
"Something wrong with someone's hat, eh, Hen-ery?" "Yessir."
"Someone's hat down again—eh, Hen-ery?" "Yessir."
"Hen-ery, is that that fellow's blessed hat again, eh?" "Yessir."
"Well, thank God for a good dinner. And now, Hen-ery, my hat and stick, please . . . Why! Confound it!" . . .
M.D

A HAT OFF A PEG.

***The Daily Graphic** - In 1873 this newspaper began running comic strips for 15 years, and there are other places comic strips keep cropping up; sample comic strip might be by Marie Duval of **Alley Sloper** fame.*

Life debuted on January 4, 1883, founded by J.A. Mitchell, and modeled after the **Harvard Lampoon**. It quickly rose to become the third main pillar of late 1800s American humor periodicals. Smaller in size, black & white, and priced the same as **Puck** and **Judge**, it nevertheless succeeded by appealing to the more genteel, romantic and apolitical notions of the white upper class. Its earliest artists included Kemble and Palmer Cox, but its foremost artist would be Charles Dana Gibson, becoming world renowned as the hand behind the graceful, aristocratic "Gibson Girls."

Unlike **Judge**, which had to change format to survive in the next century, and **Puck**, which faded to a shadow of its former self, **Life** transitioned into the 20th century virtually unaltered, and thrived. By the mid-1880s, with **Puck**, **Judge**, and **Life** all solidly in place, American comics and cartoon humor had become very much their own, no longer looking first at Europe to take their cues.

Also very American in character were the country's promotional comics, which flourished throughout the latter half of the 19th century, starting first with comic almanacs in the mid-1850s. These free almanacs, usually created by medicine and farm product companies, initially killed off the more elaborate illustrated almanacs of the 1830s to early 1850s, which readers paid for. Competition amongst companies, whose goal was to get customers to read the almanacs and the advertisements contained therein again and again, meant that attention-getting humorous cartoons soon found their way back into these giveaway pamphlets. Initially their cartoons were done cheap, either poorly drawn or pirated from elsewhere, such as those found in the **Hostetter's** and **Wright's** almanac series. More elaborate promotional almanacs eventually did evolve, though, and amongst the best of these was **Barker's Illustrated Almanac**, first produced for the year 1878, and annually into the 1930s. Each **Barker's Almanac** contained ten to twelve full page cartoons, wonderful and bizarre in design, frequently racist, but also comically manic and crammed with details in a manner similar to Outcault's much later **Yellow Kid** pages. The cartoons in **Barker's Almanac** were so popular that in 1892, The Barker, Moore, and Mein Medicine Company published their first edition of **Barker's Komic Picture Souvenir**, reprinting nearly 150 pages of cartoons from their almanacs.

*Sequence by A.B. Frost, from the **MidSummer Puck** 1887.*

This first **Barker's Souvenir** features a wraparound color cover depicting people headed towards the Columbian World's Fair Exposition, which was to be held in Chicago the next year. It is the earliest confirmed "premium" comic book, sent to customers who mailed in a box label and outside wrapper from two different Barker's products. The **Souvenir** album was Barker's most in-demand premium. It was reprinted as a thick unnumbered booklet three more times in the 1890s, with the contents reorganized each time. Later, between

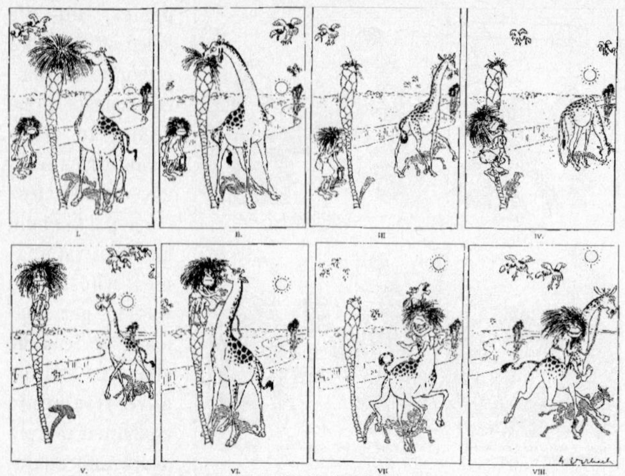
GIRAFFE HUNTING UP TO DATE.

***Truth** #438, page 11, Sept 7, 1895, NYC "Girraffe Hunting Up to Date" by immigrant Gustave Verbeek who went on to do **The Incredible Upside Downs** by 1903.*

1901 and 1903, Barker's broke the album into three separate "Parts," each of which required still more box labels and wrappers to obtain. The 3-part series of reprint albums expanded to four parts circa 1906 or 1907. Both the 3 and 4-part album series had multiple printings.

The first promotional comics which did not double as almanacs began to appear in the 1870s. They included the aforementioned reprints of Cruikshank and Busch strips, reprints of strips lifted from American sources (A.B. Frost's strip "The Bull Calf" was a particular favorite), and original material placing the product being promoted as the focus of the story. These original short cartoon dramas were in many ways similar in storyline to those found in modern television advertisements, except that the clothing is Victorian, and the claims, pre-F.D.A. and F.C.C., were unabashedly wild, over-the-top, and blunt. Chewing tobacco and snuff saved romances, calmed crying babies, and made the sick well. Stove polish that propelled you to wealth and power. Corsets that brought you a husband. The objective, of course, in an era before TV or radio, was to make each comic handout so entertaining that customers would want to keep and read the advertisement again and again.

The more wonderful graphics and outrageous claims tended to come from tobacco companies, who were using comic books and strips to sell their products more than a century before cries against "Joe Camel." The most elaborate of these were printed full color, and unfolded into a single long strip, just like Cruikshank's **The Tooth-Ache** from the 1840s, though usually limited to just the cover plus seven panels.

Examples are the Jackson Chewing Tobacco comics **How Adolphus Slim-Jim Used Jackson's Best** and **Ye Veracious Chronicle of Gruff & Pompey**, and Durham Smoking Tobacco's **Home Made Happy - A Romance for Married Men**. The artists of these comics are mostly unidentified, but their level of skill was equal to anything in **Puck** and **Judge**. The **Home Made Happy** comic, in fact, was produced for Durham by The Graphic Company -- the publisher of **The Daily Graphic**, the aforementioned 1870s illustrated newspaper which included cartoons.

In addition to the debut of **Puck** and the spread of non-almanac promotional comics, the 1870s saw a third major development. It was at this time that an unusually high number of full-length sequential comic book stories, or graphic novels, began to appear. A sort of mini-boom occurred in the U.S. following the 1840s appearances of Töpffer's and Cruikshank's comic books, but then largely died down for an approximate twenty year span. With the 1870s, graphic novels were back in even greater numbers.

A large part of this revival was brought about by New York City publisher Dick & Fitzgerald, infamous for their piracies after they evolved from Garrett and B.H. Day, who issued seven such comic books. These included Doyle's **Foreign Tour**, the reprints of the two Wilson and Company-printed Töpffer booklets and **Oscar Shangai** from Garrett retitled as **The Wonderful And Amusing Doings By Sea And Land of Oscar Shanghai**, **Sad Tale of the Courtship of Chevalier Slyfox-Wikof**; and the Yale-derived **College Experiences of Ichabod Academicus**. (**Ichabod Academicus**' original publication was in New Haven, CT in 1850, placing it right after **Jeremiah Saddlebags**).

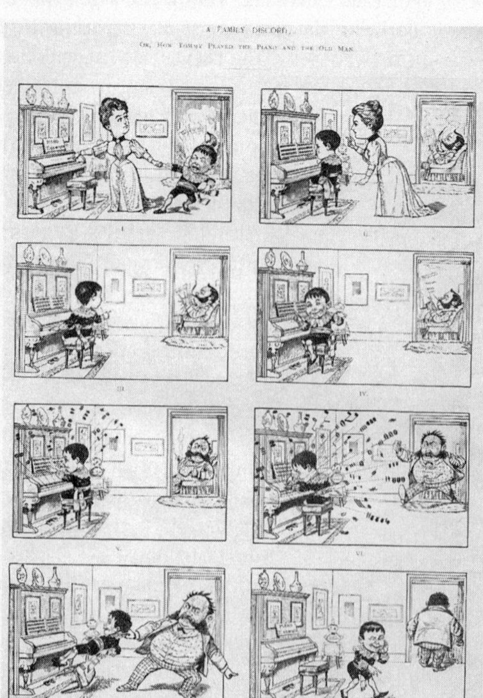
A FAMILY DISCORD,

*"A Family Discord" - One of many F.M. Howarth **Puck** back covers, this one later reprinted in **Pickings From Puck** #18 Dec 1895.*

***Judge** 1896 Eugene "ZIM" Zimmerman*
"A Sagacious Animal" is but one of hundreds by Zim who went on to run an early cartoonist training school.

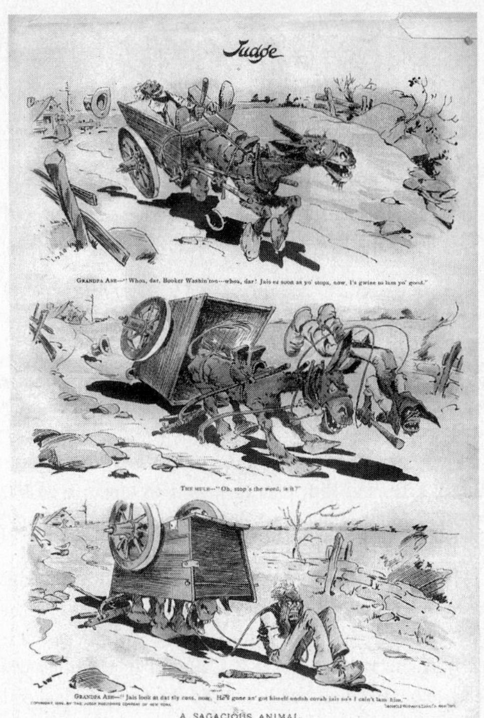

Other graphic novels also appeared during this period which have been mentioned earlier. The earliest known anthology devoted to collecting the comic strips of a single American artist was A.B. Frost's **Stuff and Nonsense** in 1884. The next known American collection came in 1888 - the very rare Frederick Burr Opper anthology, **Puck's Opper Book**. Both proved popular, so more Frost and Opper collections followed, to be joined within a few years by reprints collecting the cartoons and strips of American artists Kemble, Zim, Keppler, Gibson, Mayer, Taylor, "Chips," Howarth, Woolf, etc.

Puck, **Judge**, and **Texas Siftings** all began monthly **Library** series - smaller 8-1/2" x 11" magazines, mostly black & white, which organized previously published material around one theme or one artist. For example, the first **Puck's Library** (July 1887) was titled "The National Game," and gathered beneath one cover **Puck** material poking fun at the game of baseball.

Life tended more towards hardcover collections, such as its annual ten-issue series **The Good Things of Life** (1884-1893), which included cartoons and strips by Palmer Cox, T.S. Sullivant, Hy Mayer, and others.

The Good Things of Life was published initially by the firm of White, Stokes, and Allen, but by the fourth book, the reprint series was published by Frederick A. Stokes alone. Stokes published a number of other cartoon books in the 1880s and 1890s, the majority of them reprint collections. The experience he gained at this time with these reprint albums placed Stokes in the perfect position to pick up the wealth of material about to be created for the comics supplements of William R. Hearst's newspapers, making Stokes the first major publisher of the coming Platinum Age.

In 1892, Charles Scribner's Sons published A. B. Frost's **Bull Calf and Other Tales**. It contains sequential comic strip art on quite a few pages as well as single panel cartoons. By 1898, Charles Scribner's Sons also issued Kemble's **The Billy Goat and Other Comicalities** as a 112-page hardcover, which also has sequential comic strips.

In the early 1890s, the slum children cartoons of artist Michael Woolf (many of which were reprinted in the 1899 collection titled **Sketches of Lowly Life in a Great City**) were popular. **Truth** magazine, which followed **Puck**'s format of color front cover, back cover and centerspread cartoons, but in style was more akin to the aristocratic **Life**, was initially unable to secure Woolf's services, creating an opportunity for the young cartoonist Richard F. Outcault, who desired to break into one of the weekly comic periodicals.

It was in his Woolf-inspired slum children cartoons for **Truth** that Outcault's prototype of the **Yellow Kid** first emerged. The bald, sack-clothed youngster made four appearances in **Truth**, starting with #372 on June 2, 1894, prior to his newspaper debut.

During the rise of **Yellow Kid**'s popularity, he appeared in American comic magazines in parodies drawn by others, with politicians, even Hearst and Pulitzer, dressed up as the **Yellow Kid**. Such cartoons are known to have appeared in

***Time, One Minute** by Hy Mayer, **Truth**, 1896*
"Our artist-draws-a picture-before the kinetscope"
The last panel says "Thoz. A. Edizon," inventor of movies.

NERVE AND BONE INY
FOR 25 CENTS
The Big Nose Club is composed only of gentlemen that knows something that no body else knows, but they all know as everybody else should know that Barker's Nerve and Bone Liniment is the great pain reliever of rheumatism, sprains, cuts, bruises, lorns, etc. For man and beast. A large bottle for 25 cents; an extra large one for 50 cents.

Sample cartoon from the ***Barker's Illustrated Almanac for 1897*** *released in late 1896 reads "The Big Nose Club – Nosey People Telling What Each Knows About the Size of Some Other Fellow's Nose." Art by R.A. Williams.*

ALONE.
Susy: "What 's he cryin' for?"
Nelly (in a whisper): "That dead dog wuz his chum."

Michael Angelo Woolf cartoon ***Truth-r in 99 Truths From Woolf****. His many scenes from slum life in New York City was a major influence on Outcault's formulation of the Yellow Kid. Titled "Alone," caption reads Susy: "What's he cryin' for?" Nelly (in a whisper): "That dog was his chum."*

Judge, **Life**, and **Vim** plus various newspapers across the country. More about the Yellow Kid's importance can be found in the Platinum Age section of this book.

While comics definitely have their roots in Europe, and the earliest American comic books either reprinted or emulated those of Europe, the direction of influence was by no means one way. By at least the 1870s, American cartoons were being published and seen in the Old World, as evidenced by the arrest in Spain of the on-the-lamb corrupt Tammany Hall politician Boss Tweed by Spanish police who recognized Tweed from a Nast cartoon.

European piracy of American cartoons was just as lucrative as the American piracy of Europeans. In the 1880s and '90s, the comics of Zim, Chips Bellew, and Charles Dana Gibson all saw reprint in Europe. F.M. Howarth's domestic comedies from **Puck** were favorites in France. American Hy Mayer was commissioned to create original comics work for **Black and White** (Britain), **Le Rire** (France), and **Fliegende Blätter**. Michael Woolf's slum children cartoons saw print in the British periodical **Pick-Me-Up**, during the same years that top British artist Phil May's first published work debuted in that publication. May later became famous for his Woolf-inspired street children cartoons as well as his influence on the development of comics in Australia.

As the 19th Century ended, American comics were coming to the fore worldwide, soon to explode into a position of dominance with the Platinum Age revolution brought about by the emergence of the color comic supplement in America's newspapers and the arrival of Richard F. Outcault's **Yellow Kid.**

END NOTE: Victorian Era comics were issued in many relatively obscure formats compared to what most of us are used to today. The Victorian Era section can only grow as there are many more heretofore undiscovered comics from the 1800s which have fallen off the radar of history. Some may wonder why some of the earlier items listed contain as of yet no prices. The reason is simple. These books are part of a relatively "new" market which is still establishing itself. High-grade copies are almost unheard of in almost all instances. Some books may truly have only a handful left in existence. We are sure there are some known to have been published which no (as of yet) known copies have survived the ravages of time and neglect. Next year expect another quantum leap in our ever-expanding knowledge of the fascinating earliest origins of the comics as they relate to North America. Your input in helping this section of the Guide grow is most welcome. Happy Hunting!

Robert Beerbohm first sold comics through the legendary ***RBCC****, set up at his first comicon beginning in 1967, helped found the Comics & Comix chain stores in August 1972, co-hosted Berkeleycon 1973, the first UG creator-owned comix con; still buys & sells comics material for a living and has been compiling a detailed history book of the business of the comic book for some time now. Contact him at* **robert@blbcomics.com**

Richard Olson *is an Emeritus Research Professor at the University of New Orleans. He published the Richard Outcault Collector for years. Reach him directly at:* **redoak1@netdoor.com**

Both are life-long collectors and students of all forms of the comics who welcome corrections and additions to this concise compilation of our earliest American comics heritage dating back almost two centuries.

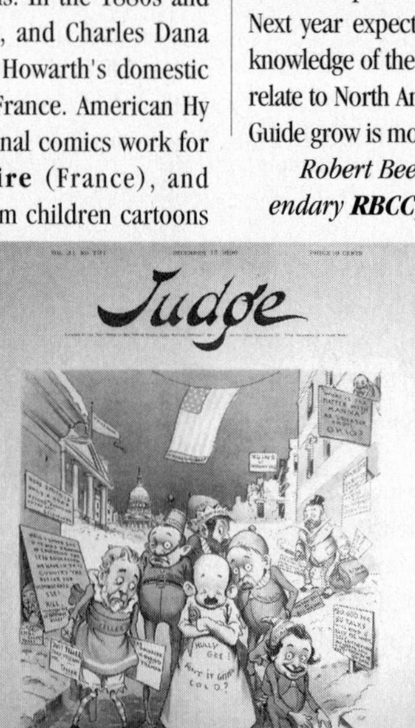

Judge
POLITICAL "KIDS" OUT IN THE COLD.

Judge *#791, Dec 12, 1896, depicting Tammany Hall politicians as RFO's Yellow Kid & Cox's Brownies. Art by Hamilton.*

The Strange and Wonderful Adventures of Bachelor Butterfly by Rodolphe Töpffer 1870s © Dick & Fitzgerald, New York

Bachelor's Own Book by Cruikshank 1845 © Burgess, Stringer & Co., NY

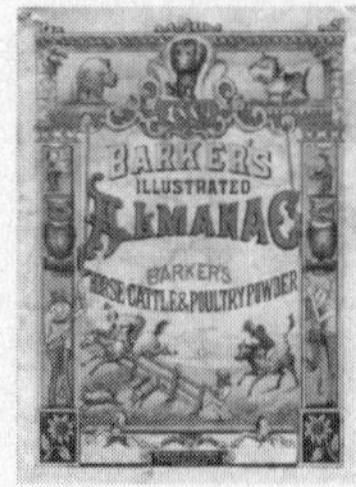

Barker's Illustrated Almanac 1889 © Barker, Moore & Mein Medicine Co.

FR1.0 GD2.0 FN6.0

COLLECTOR'S NOTE: Some of books listed in this section were published well over a century before organized comics fandom began archiving and helping to preserve these fragile popular culture artifacts. Consequently, copies of most all of these comics almost never surface in Fine+ or better shape. Most are in the Poor to VG range. If you want to collect these only in high grade, your collection will be extremely small. Each year we are filling in the price blanks on more items. The past few years we have been more concerned with simply establishing what is known to exist. The prices given for Fair, Good and Fine categories are for strictly graded editions. If you need help grading your item, we refer you to the grading section in this book or contact the authors of this essay. Items marked rare we are trying to figure out how many copies might still be in existence. We welcome help.

For ease ascertaining the contents of each item of this listing and the Platinum index list, we offer the following list of categories found immediately following most of the titles:

E - REPRINT OF EUROPEAN COMICS MATERIAL
G - GRAPHIC NOVEL (LONGER FORMAT COMIC TELLING A SINGLE STORY)
H - "HOW TO DRAW CARTOONS" BOOKS
I - ILLUSTRATED BOOKS NOTABLE FOR THE ARTIST, BUT NOT A COMIC.
M - REPRINT OF MAGAZINE / PERIODICAL COMICS MATERIAL
N - REPRINT OF NEWSPAPER COMICS MATERIAL
O - ORIGINAL COMIC MATERIAL NOT REPRINTED FROM ANOTHER SOURCE
P - PROMOTIONAL COMIC, EITHER GIVEN AWAY FOR FREE, OR A PREMIUM GIVEN IN CONJUNCTION WITH THE PURCHASE OF A PRODUCT.
S - SINGLE PANEL / NON-SEQUENTIAL CARTOONS (ENTIRELY OR PREDOMINANTLY)

Measurements are in inches. The first dimension given is Height and the second is Width. Some original British editions are included in the section, so as to better explain and differentiate their American counterparts. This section created, revised, and expanded by Robert Beerbohm, Doug Wheeler & Richard Olson with acknowledgment to Bill Blackbeard, Chris Brown, Alfredo Castelli, Darrell Coons, Leonardo De Sá, Scott Deschaine, Joe Evans, Ron Friggle, Tom Gordon, Michel Kempeneers, Andy Konkykru, Don Kurtz, Robert Quesinberry, Steve Rowe, Randy Scott, John Snyder, Art Spiegelman, Steve Thompson, Richard Samuel West and Richard Wright. Giant kudos to Gabriel Laderman.

ACROBATIC ANIMALS
R.H. Russell: 1899 (9x11-7/8", 72 pgs, B&W, hard-c)

nn 40.00 80.00 160.00
NOTE: *Animal strips by Gustave Verbeck, presented 1 panel per page.*

ALMY'S SANTA CLAUS (P,E)
Edward C. Almy & Co., Providence, R.I.: nd (1880's) (5-3/4x4-5/8", 20 pgs, B&W, paper cover)

nn - (Rare) 12.50 40.00 80.00
NOTE: *Department store Christmas giveaway containing an abbreviated 28-panel reprinting of George Cruikshank's* ***The Tooth-ache****. Santa Claus cover.*

AMERICANS (see **GIBSON'S PUBLISHED DRAWINGS**)

ATTWOOD'S PICTURES - AN ARTIST'S HISTORY OF THE LAST TEN YEARS OF THE NINETEENTH CENTURY (M,S)
Life Publishing Company, New York: 1900 (11-1/4x9-1/8", 156 pgs, B&W, gilted blue hard-c)

nn - By Attwood 40.00 80.00 160.00
NOTE: *Reprints monthly calendar cartoons which appeared in* ***LIFE****, for 1887 through 1899.*

BACHELOR BUTTERFLY, THE VERITABLE HISTORY OF MR. (E,G)
D. Bogue, London: 1845 (5-1/2x10-1/4", 74 pgs, B&W, gilted hardcover)

nn - By Rodolphe Töpffer (Scarce) 300.00 600.00 1320.00
nn - Hand colored edition (Very Rare) (no known sales)
NOTE: *This is the British Edition, translated from the re-engraved by Cham serialization found in* ***L'Illustration*** *- a periodical from Paris publisher Dubochet. Predates the first French collected edition. Third Töpffer comic book published in English. The first story page is numbered Page 3. Page 17 shows Bachelor Butterfly being swallowed by a whale.*

BACHELOR BUTTERFLY, THE STRANGE ADVENTURES OF (E,G)
Wilson & Co., New York: 1846 (5-3/8x10-1/8", 68 pgs, B&W, hardcover)

nn - By Rodolphe Töpffer (Very Rare) 300.00 600.00 1320.00
nn - At least one hand colored copy exists (Very Rare) (no known sales)
NOTE: *2nd Töpffer comic book printed in the U.S., 3rd earliest known sequential comic book in the USA. Reprinted from the British D. Bogue 1845 edition, itself from the earlier French language* ***Histoire de Mr. Cryptogame****. Released the same year as the French Dubochet edition. Two variations known, the earlier printing with Page number 17 placed on the inside (left) bottom corner in error, with slightly later printings corrected to place page number 17 on the outside (right) bottom corner of that page. For both printings: the first story page is numbered 2. Page 17 shows Bachelor Butterfly already in the whale. In most panels with 3 lines of text, the third line is indented further than the second, which is in turn indented further than the first.*

BACHELOR BUTTERFLY,THE STRANGE & WONDERFUL ADVENTURES OF
Dick & Fitzgerald, New York: 1870s-1888 (various printings 30 Cent cover price, 68 pgs, B&W, paper cover) (all versions Rare) (E,G)

nn - Black print on blue cover (5-1/2x10-1/2"); string bound 100.00 200.00 400.00
nn - Black print on green cover (5-1/2x10-1/2"); string bound 100.00 200.00 400.00
NOTE: *Reprints the earlier Wilson & Co. edition. Page 2 is the first story page. Page 17 shows Bachelor Butterfly already in the whale. In most panels with 3 lines of text, the second and third lines are equally indented in from the first. Unknown which cover (blue or green) is earlier.*

BACHELOR'S OWN BOOK. BEING THE PROGRESS OF MR. LAMBKIN, (GENT.) IN THE PURSUIT OF PLEASURE AND AMUSEMENT (E,O,G)
(See also PROGRESS OF MR. LAMBKIN)
D. Bogue, London: August 1, 1844 (5x8-1/4", 28 pgs printed one side only, cardboard cover & interior) (all versions Rare)

nn - First printing hand colored (no known sales)
nn - First printing black & white (no known sales)
NOTE: *First printing has misspellings in the title. "PURSUIT" is spelled "PERSUIT", and "AMUSEMENT" is spelled "AMUSEMEMT".*
nn - Second printing hand colored (no known sales)
nn - Second printing black & white (no known sales)
NOTE: Second printing. The misspelling of "PURSUIT" has been corrected, but "AMUSEMEMT" error is still present.
nn - Third printing hand colored No misspellings (no known sales)
nn - Third printing black & white (no known sales)
NOTE: *By George Cruikshank. This is the British Edition. Issued both in black & white, and professionally hand-colored editions. Hand-colored editions have survived in higher quantities than uncolored.*

BACHELOR'S OWN BOOK. BEING TWENTY-FOUR PASSAGES IN THE LIFE OF MR. LAMBKIN, GENT. (E,G)
Burgess, Stringer & Co., New York on cover; Carey & Hart, Philadelphia on title page: 1845 (31-1/4 cents, 7-1/2x4-5/8", 52 pgs, B&W, paper cover)

nn - By George Cruikshank (Very Rare) (no known sales)
NOTE: *This is the second known sequential comic book story published in America. Reprints the earlier British edition. Pages printed on one side only. New cover art by an unknown artist.*

BAD BOY'S FIRST READER (O,S)
G.W. Carleton & Co.: 1881 (5-3/4 x 4-1/8", 44 pgs, B&W, paper cover)

nn - By Frank Bellew (Senior) 50.00 100.00 200.00
NOTE: *Parody of a children's ABC primer, one cartoon illustration plus text per page. Includes one panel of Boss Tweed. Frank Bellew is considered the "Father of the American Sequential Comics."*

BARKER'S ILLUSTRATED ALMANAC (O,P,S)
Barker, Moore & Mein Medicine Co: 1878-1932+ (36 pgs, B&W, color paper-cr)

1878-1879 (Rare) 40.00 80.00 160.00
NOTE: *Not known what the cover art is.*
1880-1883 (Scarce, 7-3/4x6-1/8") 30.00 60.00 120.00
NOTE: *Cover art shows 4-mast ships & lighthouse.*
1884-1889 (8x6-1/4") 20.00 40.00 80.00
NOTE: *New cover art shows horse & rider jumping picket fence.*
1890-1897 (8-1/8x6-1/4") 20.00 40.00 80.00
1898-1899 (7-3/8x5-7/8") 20.00 40.00 80.00
1900+: see the Platinum Age Comics section (7x5-7/8")
NOTE: *Barker's Almanacs were actually issued in November of the year preceding the year which appears on the almanac. For example, the 1878 dated almanac was issued November 1877. They were given away to retailers of Barker's farm animal medicinal products, to in turn be given away to customers. Each Barker's almanac contains 10 full page cartoons. These frequently included racist stereotypes of blacks. Each cartoon contained advertisements for Barker's products. It is unknown whether the cartoons appeared only in the almanacs, or if they also ran as newspaper ads or flyers. Originally issued with a metal hook attached in the upper right hand corner, which could be used to hang the almanac.*

BARKER'S "KOMIC" PICTURE SOUVENIR (P,S)
Barker, Moore & Mein Medicine Co: nd (1892-94) (color cardboard cover, B&W interior) (all unnumbered editions Very Rare)

nn - (1892) (1st edition, 150 pgs) wraparound cover showing people headed towards Chicago for the 1893 World's Fair 80.00 160.00 350.00
nn - (1893) (2nd edition, ??? pgs) same cover as 1st edition 80.00 160.00 350.00
nn - (1894) (3rd edition, 180 pgs, 6-3/4x10-3/8") 80.00 160.00 350.00
NOTE: *New cover art showing crowd of people laughing with a copy of Barker's Almanac.The crowd picture is flanked on both sides by picture of a tall thin person.*
nn - (1894) (4th edition, 124 pgs, 6-3/8x9-3/8") same-c as 3rd edition 80.00 160.00 350.00
NOTE: *Essentially same-c as 3rd edition, except flanking picture on left edge is now gone. The 2nd through 4th editions state their printing on the first interior page, in the paragraph beneath the picture of the Barker's Building. These have been confirmed as premium comic books, predating the Buster Brown premiums. They reprint advertising cartoons from Barker's Illustrated Almanac. For the 50 page booklets by this same name, numbered as "Part"s, see the PLATINUM AGE SECTION. All "Editions in Parts", without exception, were published after 1900.*

BEAU OGLEBY, THE COMICAL ADVENTURES OF (E,G)
Tilt & Bogue: nd (c1843) (5-7/8x9-1/8", 72 pgs, printed one side only, green gilted hard-c, B&W)

nn - By Rodolphe Töpffer (Rare) 200.00 400.00 1100.00
nn - Hand coloured edition (Very Rare) (no known sales)
NOTE: *British Edition; no known American Edition. Second Töpffer comic book published in English. Translated from Paris publisher Aubert's unauthorized redrawn 1839 bootleg edition of Töpffer's* ***Histoire de Mr. Jabot****. The backmost interior page is an advertisement for* ***Obadiah Oldbuck****, showing the cover for that comic book.*

Barker's "Komic" Picture Souvenir,
Third Edition
1894 © Barker. Moore & Klein Medicine Co.

The Bottle by George Cruickshank
1871 © Geo. Gebbie, Philadelphia

The Story of The Man of Humanity
and The Bull Calf by A. B. Frost
1890 © C.H. Fargo & Co.

BEFORE AND AFTER. A LOCOFOCO CHRISTMAS PRESENT. (O, C)
D.C. Johnston, Boston: 1837 (4-3/4x3", 1 page, hand colored cardboard)

nn - (Very Rare) by David Claypool Johnston (sold at auction for $400 in GD)
NOTE: *Pull-tab cartoon envelope, parodying the 1836 New York City mayoral election, picturing the candidate of the Locofoco Party smiling "Before the N.York election", then, when the tab is pulled, picturing him with an angry sneer "After the N.York election".*

BILLY GOAT AND OTHER COMICALITIES, THE (M)
Charles Scribner's Sons: 1898 (6-3/4x8-1/2", 116 pgs., B&W, Hardcover)

nn - By E. W. Kemble 67.50 133.00 400.00

BLACKBERRIES, THE (N.S) (see Coontown's 400)
R. H. Russell: 1897 (9"x12", 76 pgs, hard-c, every other page in color, every other page in one color sepia tone)

nn - By E. W. Kemble 139.50 279.00 1100.00
NOTE: *Tastefully done comics about Black Americana during the USA's Jim Crow days.*

BOOK OF BUBBLES, YE (S)
Endicott & Co., New York: March 1864 (6-1/4 x 9-7/8",152 pgs?, guilt-illus. hard-c, B&W

nn - By unknown 40.00 80.00 160.00
NOTE: *Subtitle: A contribution to the New York Fair in aid of the Sanitary Commission; 68 single-sided pages of B&W cartoons, each with an accompanying limerick. A few are sequential.*

BOOK OF DRAWINGS BY FRED RICHARDSON (N,S)
Lakeside Press, Chicago: 1899 (13-5/8x10-1/2", 116 pgs, B&W, hard-c)

nn - (Scarce) 80.00 160.00 320.00
NOTE: *Reprinted from the **Chicago Daily News**. Mostly single panel. Includes one **Yellow Kid** parody, some Spanish-American War cartoons.*

BOTTLE, THE (E,O) (see also THE DRUNKARD'S CHILDREN, and TEA GARDEN TO TEA POT, and TEMPERANCE TALES; OR, SIX NIGHTS WITH THE WASHINGTONIANS)
D. Bogue, London, with others in later editions: nd (1846) (11-1/2x16-1/2", 16 pgs, printed one side only, paper cover)

D. Bogue, London (nd; 1846): first edition:
nn - Black & white (Scarce) 200.00 400.00 900.00
nn - Hand colored (Rare) (no known sales)
D. Bogue, London, and Wiley and Putnam, New York (nd; 1847) : second edition, misspells American publisher "Putnam" as "Putman":
nn - Black & white (Scarce) 150.00 300.00 600.00
nn - Hand colored (Rare) (no known sales)
D. Bogue, London, and Wiley and Putnam, New York (nd; 1847) : third edition has "Putnam" spelled correctly.
nn - Black & white (Scarce) 150.00 300.00 600.00
nn - Hand colored (Rare) (no known sales)
D. Bogue, London, Wiley and Putnam, New York, and J. Sands, Sydney, New South Wales: (nd; 1847) : fourth edition with no misspellings
nn - Black & white (Scarce) 150.00 300.00 600.00
nn - Hand colored (Rare) (no known sales)
NOTE: *By George Cruikshank. Temperance/anti-alcohol story. All editions are in precisely identical format. The only difference is to be found on the cover, where it lists who published it. Cover is text only - no cover art.*

BOTTLE, THE HISTORY OF THE
J.C. Becket, 22 Grea St James St, Montreal, Canada: 1851 (9-1/8x6", B&W)

nn - From Engravings by Cruikshank 150.00 300.00 600.00
NOTE: *As published in The Canada Temperance Advocate.*

BOTTLE, THE (E)
W. Tweedie, London: nd (1862) (11-1/2x17-1/3", 16 pgs, printed one side only, paper cover)

nn - Black & white; By George Cruikshank (Scarce) 100.00 200.00 400.00
nn - Hand colored (Scarce) (no known sales)

BOTTLE, THE (E)
Geo. Gebbie, Philadelphia: nd (c.1871) (11-3/8x17-1/8", 42 pgs, tinted interior, hard-c)

nn - By George Cruikshank 100.00 200.00 400.00
NOTE: *New cover art (cover not by Cruikshank).*

BOTTLE, THE (E)
National Temperance, London: nd (1881) (11-1/2x16-1/2", 16 pgs, printed one side only, paper-c, color)

nn - By George Cruikshank 100.00 200.00 400.00
NOTE: *See Platinum Age section for 1900s printings.*

BOTTLE, THE (E) (for the later Gowans & Gray, and the Frederick A. Stokes printings, see PLATINUM AGE section).

BULL CALF, THE (P,M)
Creme Oatmeal Toilet Soap: nd (c1890's) (3-7/8x4-1/8", 16 pgs, B&W, paper-c)

nn - By A.B. Frost 25.00 50.00 100.00
NOTE: *Reprints the popular strip story by Frost, with the art modified to place a sign for Creme Oatmeal Soap within each panel. The back cover advertises the specific merchant who gave this booklet away - multiple variations exist.*

BULL CALF AND OTHER TALES, THE (M)
Charles Scribner's Sons: 1892 (120 pgs., 6-3/4x8-7/8", B&W, illus. hard cover)

nn - By Arthur Burdett Frost 50.00 100.00 450.00
NOTE: *Blue, grey, tan hard covers known to exist.*

BULL CALF, THE STORY OF THE MAN OF HUMANITY AND THE (P,M)
C.H. Fargo & Co.: 1890 (5-1/4x6-1/4", 24 pgs, B&W, color paper-c)

nn - By A.B. Frost 42.50 85.00 185.00
NOTE: *Fargo shoe company giveaway; pages alternate between shoe advertisements and the strip story.*

BUSHEL OF MERRY THOUGHTS, A (see Mischief Book, The) (E)
Sampson Low Son & Marsten: 1868 (68 pgs, handcolored hardcover, B&W)

nn - (6-1/4 x 9-7/8", 138 pgs) red binding, publisher's name on title page only 200.00 400.00 800.00
nn - (6-1/2 x 10", 134 pgs) green binding, publisher's name on cover & title page 200.00 400.00 800.00
NOTE: *Cover plus story title pages designed by Leighton Brothers, based on Busch art. Translated by Harry Rogers (who is credited instead of Busch). This is a British publication, notable as the earliest known English language anthology collection of Wilhelm Busch comic strips. Page 13 of second story missing from all editions (panel dropped). Unknown which of the two editions was published first. Had a modern reprint, by Dover in 1971.*

BUTTON BURSTER, THE (M) (says on cover "ten cents hard cash")
M.J. Ivers & Co., 86 Nassau St., New York: 1873 (11x8-1/8", soft paper, B&W)

By various cartoonists 100.00 200.00 400.00
NOTE: *Reprints from various 1873 issues of Wild Oats; has (5) different sequential comic strips: (3) by Livingston Hopkins, (1) by Thomas Worth, other one creator presently unknown; Bellew, Sr. single panel cartoons.*

BUZZ A BUZZ OR THE BEES (E)
Griffith & Farran, London: September 1872 (8-1/2x5-1/2", 168 pgs, printed one side only, orange, black & white hardcover, B&W interior)

nn - By Wilhelm Busch (Scarce) 100.00 200.00 400.00
NOTE: *Reprint published by Phillipson & Golder, Chester; text written by English to accompany Busch art.*

BUZZ A BUZZ OR THE BEES (E)
Henry Holt & Company, New York: 1873 (9x6", 96 pgs, gilted hardcover, hand colored)

nn - By Wilhelm Busch (Scarce) 100.00 200.00 400.00
NOTE: *Completely different translation than the Griffith & Farran version. Also, contains 28 additional illustrations by Park Benjamin. The lower page count is because the Henry Holt edition prints on both sides of each page, and the Griffith & Farran edition is printed one side only.*

CALENDAR FOR THE MONTH; YE PICTORIAL LYSTE OF YE MATTERS OF INTEREST FOR SUMMER READING (P,M)
S.E. Bridgman & Company, Northampton, Mass: nd (c. late 1880's-1890's) (5-5/8x7-1/4", 64 pgs, paper-c, B&W)

nn - (Very Rare) T.S. Sullivant-c/a 100.00 200.00 400.00
NOTE: *Book seller's catalog, with every other page reprinting cartoons and strips (from Life??). Art by: Chips Bellew, Gibson, Howarth, Kemble, Sullivant, Townsend, Woolf.*

CARICATURE AND OTHER COMIC ART
Harper & Brothers, NY: 1877 (9-5/16x7-1/8", 360 pgs, B&W, green hard-c)

nn - By James Parton (over 200 illustrations) 25.00 75.00 150.00
NOTE: *This is the earliest known serious history of comics & related genre from around the world produced by an American. Parton was a cousin of Thomas Nast's wife Sarah. A large portion of this book was first serialized in **Harper's Monthly** in 1875.*

CARICATURE HISTORY OF CANADIAN POLITICS (M,S)
Grip, Toronto: 1886; 1886 (12-3/4x10-3/8", 440 pgs, hard-c, B&W)

nn (Vol. 1) - (blue gilted-c) cartoon-r from 1849-1878 67.50 125.00 250.00
NOTE: *The pages of Volume 1 are heavily interlaced with advertising sheets for Toronto businesses (these are not part of the page count), including a smaller sized 96-pg machinery catalog, all bound into the volume.*

Vol. 2 - (brown gilted-c) cartoon-r from 1879-1884 67.50 125.00 250.00
NOTE: *Chronologically organized reprinting of single panel Canadian political cartoons, taken from a variety of Canadian publications. Each right-hand page is a full page cartoon, while each left-hand page is text describing the political situation which was being satirized.*

CARROT-POMADE (O.G)
James G. Gregory, Publisher, New York: 1864 (9x6-7/8", 36 pgs, B&W)

nn - By Augustus Hoppin 70.00 140.00 280.00
NOTE: *The story of a quack remedy for baldness, sequentially told in the format parodying ABC primers. Has protective tissue pages (not part of page count).*

CARTOONS BY HOMER C. DAVENPORT (M,N,S)
De Witt Publishing House: 1898 (16-1/8x12", 102 pgs, hard-c, B&W)

nn 70.00 140.00 280.00
NOTE: *Reprinted from Harper's Weekly and the New York Journal. Includes cartoons about the Spanish-American War. Title page reads "Davenport's Cartoons".*

A Bushel of Merry Thoughts by Wilhelm Busch
1868 © Samuel Low Son & Marston

Buzz A Buzz Or The Bees by Wilhelm Busch
1872 © Griffith & Farran, London

The Clown, or The Banquet of Wit
1851 © Fisher & Brother

FR1.0 GD2.0 FN6.0

CARTOONS BY WILL E. CHAPIN (P,N,S)
The Times-Mirror Printing and Binding House, Los Angeles: 1899 (15-1/4x12", 98 pgs, hard-c, B&W)

nn 70.00 140.00 280.00
NOTE: *Premium item for subscribing to the Los-Angeles Times-Mirror newspaper, from which these cartoons were reprinted. Includes cartoons about the Spanish-American War.*

CARTOONS OF OUR WAR WITH SPAIN (N,S)
Frederick A. Stokes Company: 1898 (11-1/2x10", 72 pgs, hardcover, B&W)

nn - By Charles Nelan (r-New York Herald) 40.00 80.00 160.00
nn - 2nd printing noted on copy right page 30.00 60.00 120.00

CARTOONS OF THE WAR OF 1898 (E,M,N,S)
Belford, Middlebrook & Co., Chicago: 1898 (7x10-3/8",190 pgs, B&W, hard-c)

nn 50.00 100.00 200.00
NOTE: *Reprints single panel editorial cartoons on the Spanish-American War, from American, Spanish, Latino, and European newspapers and magazines, at rate of 2 to 6 cartoons per page. Art by Bart, Berryman, Bowman, Bradley, Chapin, Gillam, Nelan, Tenniel, others.*

CENTENNIAL FUN (O,S) (Rare)
Frank Leslie, Philadelphia: (July) 1876 (25¢, 11x8", 32 pgs, paper cover, B&W)

nn - By Joseph Keppler-c/a;Thomas Worth-a 50.00 100.00 200.00
NOTE: *Issued for the 1876 Centennial Exposition in Philadelphia. Exists with both black & white, and orange, black & white covers. One copy of the latter had an embossed newstand label from Partland, Maine, implying that the orange cover version, at least, was distributed and sold outside of Philadelphia.*

CHILDREN'S CHRISTMAS BOOK, THE
The New York Sunday World: 1897 (10-1/4x8-3/4", 16 pgs, full color)

Dec 12, 1897 - By George Luks, G.H. Grant, Will Crawford, others) (Rare)
50.00 100.00 280.00

CHIP'S DOGS (M)
R.H. Russell and Son Publishers: 1895 hardcover, B&W)

nn - By Frank P. W. "Chip" Bellew 25.00 50.00 100.00
Early printing 80 pgs, 8-7/8x11-7/8"; dark green border of hardcover surrounds all four sides of pasted on cover image; pages arranged in error -- see NOTE below. (more scarce)
nn - By Frank P. W. "Chip" Bellew 12.50 25.00 50.00
Later printing 72 pgs, 8-7/8x11-3/4";green border only on the binding side (one side) of the cover image.
NOTE: *Both are strip reprints from **LIFE**. The difference in page count is due to more blank pages in the first printing -- all printings have the same comics contents, but with the pages in the first printing arranged differently. This is noticeable particularly in the 2-page strip "Getting a Pointer", which appears on the 2nd & 3rd to last pages of the later printings, but in the early printing the first half of this strip is near the middle of the book, while the last half appears on the 2nd to last story page.*

CHIP'S OLD WOOD CUTS (M,S)
R.H. Russell & Son: 1895 (8-7/8x11-3/4", 72 pgs, hardcover, B&W)

nn - By Frank P. W. ("Chip") Bellew 25.00 50.00 100.00

CHIP'S UN-NATURAL HISTORY (O,S)
Frederick A. Stokes & Brother: 1888 (7x5-1/4", 64 pgs, hardcover, B&W)

nn - By Frank P. W. ("Chip") Bellew 12.50 25.00 50.00
NOTE: *Title page lists publisher as "Successors to White, Stokes & Allen."*

CLOWN, OR THE BANQUET OF WIT, THE (E,M,O)
Fisher & Brother, Philadelphia, Baltimore, New York, Boston: nd (c.1851) (7-3/8x4-1/2", 88 pgs, paper cover, B&W)

nn - (Very Rare; 2 known copies) 300.00 600.00 900.00
NOTE: *Earliest known multi-artist anthology of sequential comics; contains multiple sequential comics, plus numerous single panel cartoons. A mixture of reprinted and original material, involving both European and American artists. "Jones, Smith, and Robinson Goes to a Ball" by Richard Doyle (1st app. of Doyle's "Foreign Tour" in America, reprinted from PUNCH, August 24, 1850); "Moses Keyser The Bowery Bully's Trip to the Californian Gold Mines", by John H. Manning; "The Adventures of Mr. Gulp" (by the Read brothers?); more comics by artists unknown; cartoons by George Cruikshank, Grandville, Elton.*

COLD CUTS AND PICKLED EELS' FEET; DONE BROWN BY JOHN BROWN
P.J. Cozans, New York: nd (c1855-60) (B&W)

nn 50.00 100.00 200.00
NOTE: *Mostly a children's book. But, pages 87 to 110, and 111 to 122, contain narrative sequential stories.*

COLLEGE SCENES (O,G)
N. Hayward, Boston: 1850 (5x6-3/4", 72 pgs, printed one side only, B&W lithography)

nn - (Rare) by Nathan Hayward 200.00 400.00 600.00
NOTE: *This is the 2nd such production for an American University; the first issued at Yale circa 1845, decent funny art of story about life of a Harvard student from his entrance thru graduation entirely in caricature. Has art on back cover as well.*

COLLEGE CUTS Chosen From The Columbia Spectator 1880-81-82 (S)
White & Stokes, NY: 1882 (8x9-5/8", B&W)

By F. Benedict Herzog,H. McVickar,W. Bard McVickar,others 20.00 40.00 80.00

COMICAL COONS (M)
R.H. Russell: 1898 (8-7/8 x 11-7/8", 68 pgs, hardcover, B&W)

FR1.0 GD2.0 FN6.0

nn - By E. W. Kemble 150.00 300.00 770.00
NOTE: *Black Americana collection of 2-panel stories.*

COMIC ANNUAL, AMERICAN (O,I)
Richardson, Lord, & Holbrook, Boston: 1831 (6-7/8x4-3/8", 268 pgs, B&W, hard-c)

nn - (Very Rare) (no known sales)
NOTE: *Mostly text; front & back cover illustrations, 13 full page, and scattered smaller illustrations by David Claypool Johnston; edited by Henry J. Finn.*

COMIC HISTORY OF THE UNITED STATES, (I)
Carleton & Co., NY: 1876 (6-7/8x5-1/8", 336 pgs, hardcover, B&W)

nn - By Livingston Hopkins. 12.50 25.00 50.00
2nd printing: Cassell, Petter, Galpin & Co.: 1880 (6-7/8x5-1/8", 336 pgs, hardcover, B&W)
nn - By Livingston Hopkins. 12.50 25.00 50.00
NOTE: *Text with many B&W illustrations; some are multi-panel comics. Not to beconfused with **Bill Nye's Comic History Of The U.S.** which contains Frederick Opper illustrations.*

COMICS FROM SCRIBNER'S MAGAZINE (M)
Scribner's: nd (1891) (10 cents, 9-1/2x6-5/8", 24 pgs, paper cover, side stapled, B&W)

nn - (Rare) F.M.Howarth C&A 75.00 150.00 300.00
NOTE: *Advertised in SCRIBNER'S MAGAZINE in the June 1891 issue, page 793, as available by mail order for 10 cents. Collects together comics material which ran in the back pages of Scribner's Magazine. Art by Attwood, "Chip" Bellew, Döes, Frost, Gibson, Zim.*

COONTOWN'S 400 (M) (see **Blackberries**) (M)
The Life (Magazine) Co.: 1899 (10-15/16x8-7/8, 68 pgs, cloth light-brown hard-c, B&W

nn - By E.W. Kemble (scarce) 150.00 300.00 1100.00
NOTE: *Tastefully drawn depictions of Black Americana over one hundred years ago during Jim Crow days.*

CROSSING THE ATLANTIC (O,G)
James R. Osgood & Co., Boston: 1872 (68 pgs, hardcover, B&W); **Houghton, Osgood & Co., Boston:** 1880

1st printing - by Augustus Hoppin 45.00 90.00 180.00
2nd printing (1880; 66 pgs; 8-1/8x11-1/8") 32.50 65.00 150.00

CRUIKSHANK'S OMNIBUS: A VEHICLE FOR FUN AND FROLIC (E,S)
E. Ferrett & Co., Philadelphia: 1845 (25 cents, 7-1/2" x 4-5/8", 96 pgs, B&W, paper-c)

nn - By George Cruikshank c/a (Very Rare) 75.00 150.00 300.00
NOTE: *Mostly prose, with 10 plates of cartoons printed on one-side (about half the plates with multiple cartoons), plus illustrated cover, all by George Cruikshank. First (perhaps only) American printing of Cruikshank's Omnibus, which was published first in Britain. It is only a partial reprinting.*

CUBAN PICTURES (see OUR ARTIST IN CUBA) (O)

DAVENPORT'S CARTOONS (see CARTOONS BY HOMER C. DAVENPORT)

DAY'S SPORT - OR, HUNTING ADVENTURES OF S. WINKS WATTLES, A SHOPKEEPER, THOMAS TITT, A "LEGAL GENT," AND MAJOR NICHOLAS NOGGIN, A JOLLY GOOD FELLOW GENERALLY, A (O)
Brother Jonathan, NY: c1850s (???)

nn - By Henry L. Stevens, Philadelphia (no known sales)
NOTE: *Known only so far from a mid 1850s Brother Jonathan catalog - see Victorian Age essay. One partial copy turned by in late 2003 bound in with other 1800s material.*

DIE VEHME, ILLUSTRIRTES WOCHENBLATT FUR SCHERZ UND ERNEST (M,O)
Heinrich Binder, St. Louis: No.1 Aug 28, 1869 - No.?? Aug 20, 1870 (10 cents, 8 pgs, B&W, paper-c) (see also PUCK)

1-?? (Very Rare) by Joseph Keppler (no known sales)
NOTE: *Joseph Keppler's first attempt at a weekly American humor periodical. Entirely in German. The title translates into: **"The Star Chamber: An Illustrated Weekly Paper in Fun and Ernest"**.*

DRUNKARD'S CHILDREN, THE (see also THE BOTTLE) (E,O)
David Bogue, London; John Wiley and G.P. Putnam, New York; J. Sands, Sydney, New South Wales: July 1, 1848 (11x16", 16 pgs, printed on one side only, paper-c)

nn - Black & white edition (Rare) 300.00 600.00 900.00
nn - Hand colored edition (Rare) (no known sales)
NOTE: *Sequel story to THE BOTTLE, by George Cruikshank. Temperance/anti-alcohol story. British-American-Australian co-publication. Cover is text only - no cover art.*

DRUNKARD'S PROGRESS, OR THE DIRECT ROAD TO POVERTY, WRETCHEDNESS & RUIN, THE
J. W. Barber, New Haven, Conn.: Sept 1826 (single sheet)

nn - By John Warner Barber (no known sales)
NOTE: *Broadside designed and printed by barber contains four large wood engravings showing "The Morning Dram" which is "The Beginning of Sorrow"; "The Grog Shop" with its "Bad Company"; "The Confirmed Drunkard" in a state of "Beastly Intoxication"; and the "Concluding Scene" with the family being drive off to the alms house. It is an interesting set of cuts, faintly reminiscent of Hogarth.*

DUEL FOR LOVE, A (O,P)
E.C. DeWitt & Co., Chicago: nd (c1880's) (3-3/8" x 2-5/8", 12 pgs, B&W, paper-c)

nn - Art by F.M. Howarth 25.00 50.00 100.00
NOTE: *Advertising giveaway for DeWitt's Little Early Risers, featuring an 8-panel strip story, spread out 1 panel per page.*

Comics From Scribner's Magazine
1891 © Scribner's

Crossing the Atlantic by Augustus Heppin
1880 © Houghton, Osgood & Co., Boston

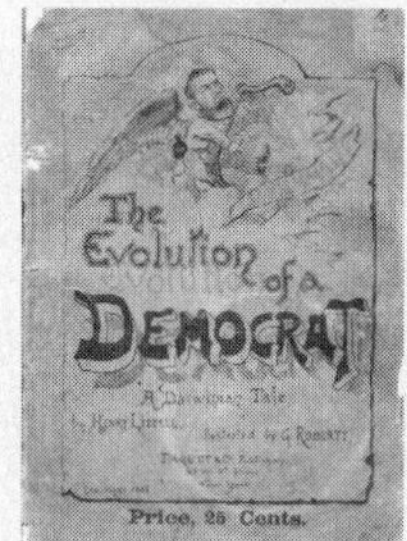

The Evolution of A Democrat
A Darwinian Tale
1888 © Paquet & Co., New York

EDUCATION OF MR. PIPP, THE (M) (see GIBSON'S PUBLISHED DRAWINGS)

ELTON'S COMIC ALL-MY-NACK (E,O.S)
Elton, Publisher, 18 Division & 90 Nassau St, NY: 1833-?? 1850s (7-1/2x4-1/2", 36 pgs, B&W)

	FR1.0	GD2.0	FN6.0
1-15 - 99% single panel cartoons	60.00	120.00	240.00
16 - contains 6 panel "A Tales of A Tayl-or" 1848-49	200.00	400.00	600.00
17 - contains "Moses Keyser, The Bowery Bully's Trip To the California Gold Mines" 1850 By John H. Manning, early comics creator told in 15 panels	200.00	400.00	600.00
18-up presently unknown contents	60.00	120.00	240.00

NOTE: *Contains both original American, and pirated European, cartoons. All single panel material, except where noted. Almanacs are published near the end of the year prior to that for which they are printed -- like calendars today. Thus, the 1833 No. 1 issue was really published in the last months of 1832. #17 has Elton's Californian Comic-All-My-Nack on the cover.*

ENTER: THE COMICS (E,G)
University of Nebraska Press: 1965

nn - By Ellen Weisse 25.00 50.00 100.00
NOTE: *Contains overview of Töpffer's life and career plus only published English translation of Töpffer's Monsieur Crepin (1837); appears to have been re-drawn by Weisse in the days before xerox machines.*

EVOLUTION OF A DEMOCRAT - A DARWINIAN TALE, THE (O,G)
Paquet & Co., New York: 1888 (25 cents, 7-7/8x5-1/2", 100 pgs, printed one side only, orange paper cover, B&W) (Very Rare)

nn - Written by Henry Liddell, art by G. Roberty 50.00 100.00 200.00
NOTE: *Political parody about the rise of an Irishman through Tammany Hall. Grover Cleveland appears as linked with Tammany. Ireland becomes the next state in the USA.*

FABLES FOR OUR TIMES (S, I)
R.H. Russell & Son, New York: 1896 (52 pgs, yellow hard-c)

nn - By H.W. Phillips and T.S. Sullivant 25.00 50.00 100.00

FERDINAND FLIPPER, ESQ., THE FORTUNES OF (O,G)
Brother Jonathan, Publisher, NY: nd (1851) (80 pgs, B&W, printed both sides)

nn - By Various (scarce) 300.00 600.00 900.00
NOTE: *Extended title: "...Commencing With A Period of Four Months And Anterior To His Birth Going Thru The Various Stages of His Infancy, Childhood, Verdant Years, Manhood, Middle Life, and Green and Ripe Old Age, And Ending A Short Time Subsequent to His Sudden Decease With His Final Exit, Funeral And Burial." Extremely unique comic book, put together by gathering 145 independent single illustrations and cartoons, by various artists, and stringing them together into a sequential story. The majority of panels are by Grandville. Also included are at least 19 signed Charles Martin, reprinted from 1847 issues of Yankee Doodle, 5 panels from D.C. Johnston, plus other panels by F.O.C. Darley, T.H. Matheson, and others. Printed by E.A. Alverds. The 1851 date is derived from an advertisement found in the Oct-Dec 1851 issue of the Brother Jonathan newspaper. It ispossible, however, that it actually came out even earlier.*

FERDINAND FLIPPER, ESQ., THE FORTUNES OF (G)
Dick & Fitzgerald, New York: nd (1870's to 1888) (30 Cents, 80 pgs, B&W, paper cover)

nn - (scarce reprint - several editions possible) 100.00 200.00 300.00

FINN'S COMIC SKETCHBOOK (S)
Peabody & Co., 223 Broadway, NY: 1831 (10-1/2x16", 12 pgs, B&W)

nn - By Henry J. Finn (no known sales)
NOTE: *Designs on copper plates; etched by J. Harris, NY; should have tissue paper in front of each plate.*

50 GREAT CARTOONS (M,P,S)
Ram's Horn Press: 1899

nn - By Frank Beard 30.00 60.00 120.00
NOTE: *Premium in return for a subscription to* ***The Ram's Horn*** *magazine.*

F**** A*** K*****, OUTLINES ILLUSTRATIVE OF THE JOURNAL OF** (O,S)
D.C. Johnston, Boston: 1835 (9-5/16 x 6", 12 pgs, printed one side only, blue paper cover, B&W interior) (see also **SCRAPS**)

nn - (Rare) by David Claypool Johnston 200.00 400.00 600.00
NOTE: *This is a series of 8 plates parodying passages from the Journal of Fanny (Frances) A. Kemble, a British woman who wrote a highly negative book about American Culture after returning from the U.S. Though remembered now for her campaign against slavery, she was prejudiced against most everything American culture, thus inspiring Johnston's satire. Contains 4 protective sheets (not part of page count.)*

FLY-ING DUTCHMAN; OR, THE WRATH OF HERR VON STOPPELNOZE, THE (E)
Carleton Publishing, New York: 1862 (7-5/8x5-1/4", 84 pgs, printed on one side only, gilted hardcover, B&W)

nn - By Wilhelm Busch (Scarce) 35.00 70.00 140.00
NOTE: *This is the earliest known English language book publication of a Wilhelm Busch work. The story is plagiarized by American poet John G. Saxe, who is credited with the text, while the uncredited Busch cartoons are described merely as accompanying illustrations.*

FLYING LEAVES (E)
E.R. Herrick & Company, New York: nd (c1889/1890's) (8-1/4" x 11-1/2", 76 pgs, B&W interior, orange, b&w hard-c)

nn- (Scarce) 80.00 160.00 240.00
NOTE: *Reprints strips and single panel cartoons from 1888 Fliegende Blatter issues, translated into English. Various artists, including Bechstein, Adolf Hengeler, Lothar Meggendorfer, Emil Reinicke.*

FR1.0 GD2.0 FN6.0

FOOLS PARADISE WITH THE MANY ADVENTURES THERE AS SEEN IN THE STRANGE SURPRISING PEEP SHOW OF PROFESSOR WOLLEY COBBLE, THE (E)
(see also THE COMICAL PEEP SHOW)
John Camden Hotten, London: Nov 1871 (1 crown, 9-7/8x7-3/8", 172 pgs, printed one side only, gilted green hardcover, hand colored interior)

nn - By Wilhelm Busch (Rare) 400.00 800.00 1750.00
NOTE: *Title on cover is:* ***WALK IN! WALK IN!! JUST ABOUT TO BEGIN!!! the FOOLS PARADISE****; below the above title page. Anthology of Wilhelm Busch comics, translated into English.*

FOOLS PARADISE WITH THE MANY WONDERFUL SIGHTS AS SEEN IN THE STRANGE SURPRISING PEEP SHOW OF PROFESSOR WOLLEY COBBLE, FURTHER ADVENTURES IN (E)
Chatto & Windus, London: 1873 (10x7-3/8", 128 pgs, printed one side only, brown hardcover, hand colored interior)

nn - By Wilhelm Busch (Rare) 300.00 600.00 1320.00
NOTE: *Sequel to the 1871* ***FOOLS PARADISE****, containing a completely different set of Busch stories, translated into English.*

FOOLS PARADISE MIRTH AND FUN FOR OLD & YOUNG (E)
Griffith & Farran, London: May 1883 (9-3/4x7-5/8", 78 pgs, color cover, color interior)

nn - By Wilhelm Busch (Rare) 100.00 200.00 420.00
NOTE: *Collection of selected stories reprinted from both the 1871 & 1873* ***FOOLS PARADISE****.*

FOREIGN TOUR OFMESSRS. BROWN, JONES, AND ROBINSON, THE (see Messrs....)

FUN BY RALL
Unknown: circa 1865 (11x7-7/8", 68 pgs, soft-c, B&W)

nn - By presently unknown 100.00 200.00 300.00
NOTE: *Wraparound soft cover like modern comic book; yellow paper cover with red & black ink.*

FUN FOR THE FAMILY IN PICTURES
D. Lothrop and Company: 1886 (3-3/4x6-3/4", 48 pgs, Silver & Red stiff-c; interior pages have various single color inks)

nn - By unknown hand 50.00 100.00 200.00
NOTE: *Single panel cartoons and sequential stories.*

FUNNY FOLK (M)
E. P. Dutton: 1899 (12x16-1/2", 90 pgs,14 strips in color-rest in b&w, hard-c)

	FR1.0	GD2.0	FN6.0
nn - By Franklin Morris Howarth	162.50	325.00	1350.00
nn - London: J.M. Dent, 1899 embossed-c; same interior	100.00	300.00	625.00

NOTE: *Reprints many sequential strips & single panel cartoons from* ***Puck****. This is considered by many to be yet another "missing link" between Victorian & Platinum Age comic books. Most comic books 1900-1917 reprinting Sunday newspaper comic strips follow this size format, except using cardboard-c rather than hard-c.*

GIBSON BOOK, THE (M,S)
Charles Scribner's Sons & R.H. Russell, New York: 1906 (11-3/8x17-5/8", gilted red hard-c, B&W)

Book I 50.00 100.00 200.00
NOTE: *Reprints in whole the books: Drawings, Pictures of People, London,Sketches and Cartoons, Education of Mr. Pipp, Americans. 414 pgs. 1907 2nd editions exist same value.*
Book II 50.00 100.00 200.00
NOTE: *Reprints in whole the books: A Widow and Her Friends, The Weaker Sex, Everyday People, Our Neighbors. 314 pgs 1907 second.edition for both also exists. Same value.*

GIBSON'S PUBLISHED DRAWINGS, MR. (M,S) (see Plat index for later issues post 1900)
R.H. Russell, New York: No.1 1894 - No. 9 1904 (11x17-3/4", hard-c, B&W)

	FR1.0	GD2.0	FN6.0
nn (No.1; 1894) Drawings 96 pgs	30.00	60.00	120.00
nn (No.2; 1896) Pictures of People 92 pgs	30.00	60.00	120.00
nn (No.3; 1898) Sketches and Cartoons 94 pgs	30.00	60.00	120.00
nn (No.4; 1899) The Education of Mr. Pipp 88 pgs	30.00	60.00	120.00
nn (No.5; 1900) Americans	30.00	60.00	120.00

NOTE: *By Charles Dana Gibson cartoons, reprinted from magazines, primarily* ***LIFE****. The Education of Mr. Pipp tells a story. Series continues how long after 1904?*

GIRL WHO WOULDN'T MIND GETTING MARRIED, THE (O)
Frederick Warne & Co., London & New York: nd (c1870's) (9-1/2x11-1/2", 28 pgs, printed 1 side, paper-c, B&W)

nn - By Harry Parkes 62.50 125.00 250.00
NOTE: *Published simultaneously with its companion volume,* ***The Man Who Would Like to Marry****.*

GOBLIN SNOB, THE (O)
DeWitt & Davenport, New York: nd (c1853-56) (24 x 17 cm, 96 pgs, B&W, color hard-c)

nn - (Rare) by H.L. Stephens (no known sales)

GREAT LOCOFOCO JUGGERNAUT, THE (S)
Imprint Society: 1971 (reprint)

nn - By David Claypool Johnston - 12.00 25.00

HALF A CENTURY OF ENGLISH HISTORY (S. M)
G.P. Putnam's Sons - The Knickerbocker Press, New York and London: 1884 (7-3/4 x 5-3/4", 316 pgs., illustrated hard-c)

Flying Leaves
1880s © E.R. Herrick & Company, New York

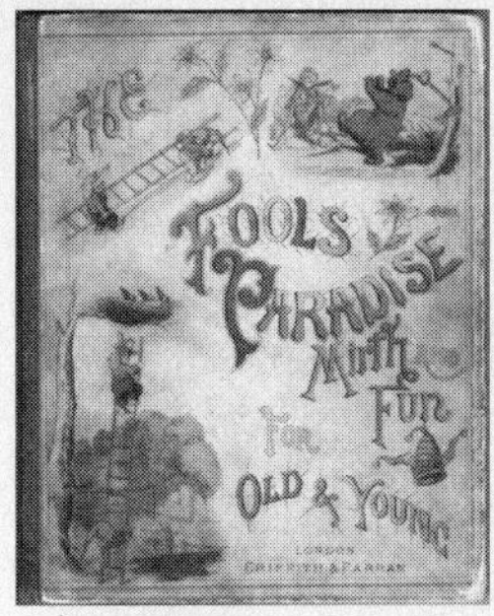

The Fools Paradise Mirth and Fun For Old and Young
1883 © Griffith & Farran, London

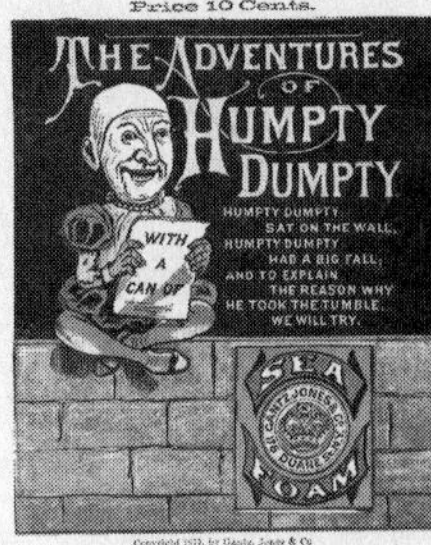

Humpty Dumpty, The Adventures of...
© Gantz, Jones and Co.

FR1.0 GD2.0 FN6.0

nn - By Various 25.00 50.00 175.00
NOTE: *Subtitle: Pictorially Presented in a Series of Cartoons from the Collection of Mr. Punch. Comprising 150 plates by Doyle, Leech, Tenniel, and others, in which are portrayed the political careers of Peel, Palmerston, Russell, Cobden, Bright, Beaconsfield, Derby, Salisbury, Gladstone and other English statesmen.*

HAIL COLUMBIA! HISTORICAL, COMICAL, AND CENTENNIAL (O,S)
The Graphic Co., New York & Walter F. Brown, Providence, RI: 1876 (10x11-3/8", 60 pgs, red gilted hard-c, B&W)

nn - (Rare) by Walter F. Brown 100.00 200.00 400.00

HEALTH GUYED (I)
Frederick A. Stokes Company: 1890 (5-3/8 x 8-3/8, 56 pgs, hardcover, B&W)

nn - By Frank P.W. ("Chip") Bellew (Junior) 25.00 50.00 175.00
NOTE: *Text & cartoon illustration parody of a health guide.*

HITS AT POLITICS (M,S)
R.H. Russell, New York: 1899 (15" x 12", 156 pgs, B&W, hard-c)

nn - W.A. Rogers c/a 100.00 200.00 300.00
NOTE: *Collection of W.A. Rogers cartoons, all reprinted from Harper's Weekly. Includes Spanish-American War cartoons.*

HOME MADE HAPPY. A ROMANCE FOR MARRIED MEN IN SEVEN CHAPTERS (O,P)
Genuine Durham Smoking Tobacco & The Graphic Co.: nd (c1870's) (5-1/4 tall x 3-3/8" wide folded, 27" wide unfolded, color cardboard)

nn - With all 8 panels attached (Scarce) 30.00 60.00 150.00
nn - Individual panels/cards 5.00 10.00 25.00
NOTE: *Consists of 8 attached cards, printed on one side, which unfold into a strip story of title card & 7 panels. Scrapbook hobbyists in the 19th Century tended to pull the panels apart to paste into their scrapbooks, making copies with all panels still attached scarce.*

HOME PICTURE BOOK FOR LITTLE CHILDREN (E,P)
Home Insurance Company, New York: July 1887 (8 x 6-1/8", 36 pgs, b&w, color paper-c)

nn 40.00 80.00 160.00
NOTE: *Contains an abbreviated 32-panel reprinting of "THE TOOTHACHE" by George Cruikshank. Remainder of booklet does not contain comics.*

HOOD'S COMICALITIES. COMICAL PICTURES FROM HIS WORKS (E,S)
Porter & Coates: nd (8-1/2x10-3/8", 104 pgs, printed one side, hard-c, B&W)

nn 20.00 40.00 80.00
NOTE: *Reprints 4 cartoon illustrations per page from the British Hood's Comic Annuals, which were poetry books by Thomas Hood.*

HOOKEYBEAK THE RAVEN, AND OTHER TALES (see also JACK HUCKABACK, THE SCAPEGRACE RAVEN) (E)
George Routledge and Sons, London & New York: nd (1878) (7-1/4x5-5/8", 104 pgs, hardcover, B&W)

nn - By Wilhelm Busch (Very Rare) 100.00 200.00 400.00

HOW ADOLPHUS SLIM-JIM USED JACKSON'S BEST, AND WAS HAPPY. A LENGTHY TALE IN 7 ACTS. (O,P)
Jackson's Best Chewing Tobacco & Donaldson Brothers: nd(c1870's) (5-1/8 tall x 3-3/8" wide folded, 27" wide unfolded, color cardboard)

nn - With all 8 panels attached (Scarce) 30.00 60.00 150.00
nn - Individual panels/cards 5.00 10.00 25.00
NOTE: *Consists of 8 attached cards, printed on one side, which unfold into a strip story of title card & 7 panels. Scrapbook hobbyists in the 19th Century tended to pull the panels apart topaste into their scrapbooks, making copies with all panels still attached scarce.*

HOW DAYS' DURHAM STANDARD OF THE WORLD SMOKING TOBACCO MADE TWO PAIRS OF TWINS HAPPY (O,P)
J.R. Day & Bro. Standard Durham Smoking Tobacco, Durham, NC: nd (c late 1870's/early 1880's) (3-5/8" x 5-1/2", folded, 21-3/4" tall unfolded, color cardboard)

nn- With all 6 panels attached (Scarce) 120.00 240.00 480.00
nn- Individual panels/cards 20.00 40.00 60.00
NOTE: *Highly sought by both Black Americana and Tobacciana collectors. Recurring mid-19th Century story about two African-American twin brothers who romance and marry a pair of African-American twin sisters. Although the text is racist at points, the art is not. Consists of 6 attached cards, printed on one side, which unfold downwards into a strip story of title card & 5 panels. Scrapbook hobbyists in the 19th Century tended to pull the panels apart and paste into their scrapbooks, making copies with all panels attached scarce. Note, there are numerous cartoon tellings of this same story, including several card series versions (with different art, and story variations, each time). But, the above is the only version which unfolds as a strip of attached cards. The cards from all the unattached versions are smaller sized, and thus distinguishable.*

HUGGINIANA; OR, HUGGINS' FANTASY, BEING A COLLECTION OF THE MOST ESTEEMED MODERN LITERARY PRODUCTIONS (I,S,P)
H.C. Southwick, New York: 1808 (18 pgs, printed one side, B&W)

nn - (Very Rare) (no known sales)
NOTE: *The earliest known surviving collected promotional cartoons in America. This is a booklet collecting 7 folded plus 1 full page flyer advertisements for barber John Richard Desborus Huggins, who hired American artists Elkanah Tisdale and William S. Leney to modify previously published illustrations into cartoons referring to his barber shop.*

FR1.0 GD2.0 FN6.0

HUMOROUS MASTERPIECES - PICTURES BY JOHN LEECH (E,M)
Frederick A. Stokes: nd (late 1900's - early 1910's) No.1-2 (5-5/8x3-7/8", 68 pgs, cardboard covers, B&W)

1- John Leech (single panel cartoon-r from **Punch**) 17.50 35.00 70.00
2- John Leech (single panel cartoon-r from **Punch**) 17.50 35.00 70.00

HUMOURIST, THE (E,I,S)
C.V. Nickerson and Lucas and Deaver, Baltimore: No.1 Jan 1829 - No.12 Dec 1829 (5-3/4x3-1/2", B&W text w/hand colored cartoon pg.)

Bound volume No.1-12 (Very Rare; 1 copy known; 270 pgs) (no known sales)
NOTE: *Earliest known American published periodical to contain a cartoon every issue. Surviving individual issues currently unknown -- all information comes from 1 surviving bound volume. Each issue is mostly text, with one full page hand-colored cartoon. Bound volume contains an additional hand-colored cartoons at front of each six month set (total of 14 cartoons in volume). Cartoons appear to be of British origin, possibly by George Cruikshank.*

HUMPTY DUMPTY, ADVENTURES OF...
1877 (Promotional chapbook from Gantz, Jones & Co, 10¢-c.)

nn-Promotes Gantz Sea Foam Baking Powder; early app. of a costumed character, dressed as Humpty Dumpty 50.00 100.00 300.00

HUSBAND AND WIFE, OR THE STORY OF A HAIR. (O,P)
Garland Stoves and Ranges, Michigan Stove Co.: 1883 (4-3/16 tall x 2-11/16" wide folded, 16" wide unfolded, color cardboard)

nn - With all 6 panels attached (Scarce) 25.00 50.00 125.00
nn - Individual panels/cards 5.00 10.00 25.00
NOTE: *Consists of 6 attached cards, printed on one side, which unfold into a strip story of title card & 5 panels. Scrapbook hobbyists in the 19th Century tended to pull the panels apart topaste into their scrapbooks, making copies with all panels still attached scarce.*

ICHABOD ACADEMICUS, THE COLLEGE EXPERIENCES OF (O,G)
William T. Peters, New Haven, CT: 1850 (5-1/2x9-3/4",108 pgs, B&W)

nn - By William T. Peters (Very Rare) 200.00 400.00 800.00
NOTE: *Pages are not uniform in size.*

ICHABOD ACADEMICUS, THE COLLEGE EXPERIENCES OF (O,G)
Dick & Fitzgerald, New York: nd (1870s-1888) (paper-c, B&W)

nn - By William T. Peters (Very Rare) 100.00 200.00 400.00
NOTE: *Pages are uniform in size.*

ILLUSTRATED SCRAP-BOOK OF HUMOR AND INTELLIGENCE (M)
John J. Dyer & Co.: nd (c1859-1860)

nn - Very Rare (no known sales)
NOTE: *A "printed scrapbook" of images culled from some unidentified periodical. About half of it is illustrations that would have accompanied prose pieces. There are pages of single panel cartoons (multiple per page). And there are roughly 8 to 12 pages of sequential comics (all different stories, but appears to all be by the same presently unidentified artist).*

IMAGERIE d'EPINAL (untrimmed individual sheets) (E)
Pellerin for Humoristic Publishing Co, Kansas City, Mo.: nd (1888) No.1-60 (15-7/8x11-3/4",single sheets, hand colored) (All are Rare)

1-14, 21, 22, 25-46, 49-60 - in the Album d'Images 25.00 50.00 100.00
15-20, 23,24, 47, 48 - not in the Album d'Images 40.00 80.00 160.00
NOTE: *Printed and hand colored in France expressly for the Humoristic Publishing Company . Printed on one side only. These are single sheets, sold separately. Reprints and translates the sheets from their original French.*

IMAGERIE d'EPINAL ALBUM d'IMAGES (E)
Pellerin for Humoristic Publishing Co., Kansas City. Mo: nd (1888) (15-1/2x11-1/2",108 pgs plus full color hard-c, hand colored interior)

nn - Various French artists (Rare) 300.00 600.00 1800.00
NOTE: *Printed and hand colored in France expressly for the Humoristic Publishing Company . Printed on one side only. This is supposedly a collection of sixty broadsheets, originally sold separately. All copies known only have fifty of the sixty known of these broadsheets (slightly bigger, before binding, trimming the margins in the process, down to 15-1/4x11-3/8".). Three slightly different covers known to exist, with or without the indication in French "Textes en Anglais" ("Texts in Englishi), with or without the general title "Contes de FEes" ("Fairy Tales"). All known copies were collected with sheets 15-20, 23,24, 47, and 48 missing.*

IN LAUGHLAND (M)
R.H. Russell, New York: 1899 (14-9/16x12", 72 pgs, hard-c)

nn - By Henry "Hy" Mayer (scarce) 100.00 200.00 400.00
NOTE: *Mostly strips plus single panel cartoon-r from various magazines. The majority are reprinted from Life, with the rest from: Truth, Dramatic Mirror, Black and White, Figaro Illustre, Le Rire, and Fliegende Blatter.*

IN THE "400" AND OUT (M,S) (see also **THE TAILOR-MADE GIRL**)
Keppler & Schwarzmann, New York: 1888 (8-1/4x12", 64 pgs, hardc, B&W)

nn - By C.J. Taylor 42.50 85.00 170.00
NOTE: *Cartoons reprinted from **Puck**. The "400" is a reference to New York City's aristocratic elite.*

IN VANITY FAIR (M,S)
R.H.Russell & Son, New York: 1896 (11-7/8x17-7/8", 80 pgs, hard-c, B&W)

Jingo No. 3, Sept 24
1884 © Art Newspaper Co, Boston & NYC

Judge, No. 1, October 29, 1881
1881 © Judge Publishing, NYC

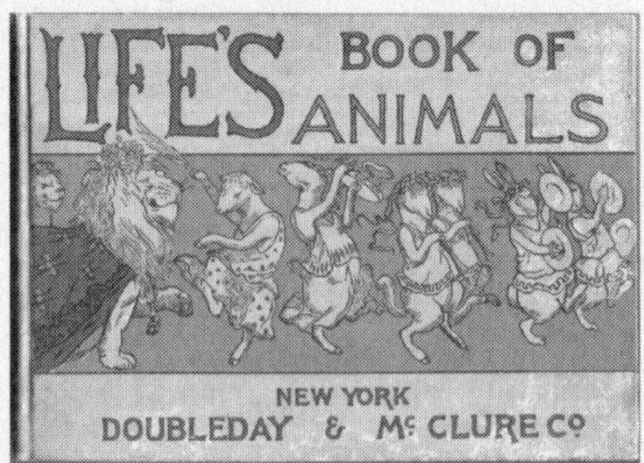

Life's Book of Animals
1888 © Doubleday & McClure Co.

nn - By A.B.Wenzell, r-LIFE and HARPER'S 45.00 90.00 180.00

JACK HUCKABACK, THE SCAPEGRACE RAVEN (see also HOOKEYBEAK THE RAVEN) (E)
Stroefer & Kirchner, New York: nd (c1888) (9-3/8x6-3/8", 56 pgs, printed one side only, hand colored hardcover, B&W interior)

nn - By Wilhelm Busch (Rare) 50.00 100.00 300.00
NOTE: *The 1888 date is derived from a gift signature on one known copy. The publication date might in truth be earlier.*

JINGO (M,O)
Art Newspaper Co., Boston & New York: No.1 Sept 10, 1884 - No.11 Nov 19, 1884 (10 cents, 13-7/8" x 10-1/4",16 pgs, color front/back-c and center, remainder B&W, paper-c)

1-11(Rare) 25.00 50.00 100.00
NOTE: *Satirical Republican propaganda magazine, modeled after **Puck** and **Judge**, which was published during the last couple months of the 1884 Presidential Election campaign. The Republicans lost, **Jingo** ceased publication, and Republican backers soon after purchased **Judge** magazine.*

JOURNEY TO THE GOLD DIGGINS BY JEREMIAH SADDLEBAGS (O,G)
Various publishers: 1849 (25 cents, 5-5/8 x 8-3/4", 68 pgs, green & black paper cover, B&W interior)

nn -- New York edition, Stringer & Townsend, Publishers
(Very Rare) 1000.00 2000.00 4200.00
nn -- Cincinnati, Ohio edition, published by U.P. James
(Very Rare) 1000.00 2000.00 4200.00
nn -- 1950 reprint, with introduction, published by William P. Wreden, Burlingame, California: 1950 (5-7/8 x 9", 92 pgs, hardcover, color interior)
(390 copies printed) 37.50 80.00 175.00
NOTE: *By J.A. and D.F. Read. Earliest known sequential comic book by an American creator; directly inspired by Töpffer's **Obadiah Oldbuck** and **Bachelor Butterfly** The New York and Cincinnati editions were both published in 1849, one soon after the other. Antiquarian Book sources have traditionally cited that the Cincinnati edition preceded the New York, but without referencing their evidence. Conflicting with this, the Cincinnati edition lists the New York publishers' 1849 copyright, while the New York edition makes no reference to the Cincinnati publishers. Such would indicate that the New York edition was first. Both are very rare, and until resolved both will be regarded as published simultaneously. A New York copy with missing back cover, detached front cover, and G/VG interior sold for $2000 in 2000.*

JUDGE (M,O)
Judge Publishing, New York: No.1 Oct 29, 1881 - No. 950, Dec ??, 1899 (10 cents, color front/back c and centerspread, remainder B&W, paper-c)

1 (Scarce) (no known sales)
2-26 (Volume 1; Scarce) 20.00 40.00 80.00
27-790,792-950 12.50 25.00 50.00
791 (12/12/1896; Vol.31) - satirical-c depicting Tammany Hall politicians as the Yellow Kid & Brownies 25.00 50.00 110.00
Bound Volumes (six month, 26 issue run each):
Vol. 1 (Scarce) (no known sales)
Vol. 2-30,32-37 140.00 280.00 600.00
Vol. 31 - includes issue 791 **YK/Brownies** parody 165.00 230.00 725.00
NOTE: *Rival publication to Puck. Purchased by Republican Party backers, following their loss in the 1884 Presidential Election, to become a Republican propaganda satire magazine.*

JUDGE'S LIBRARY (M)
Judge Publishing, New York: No.1, April 1890 - No. 141, Dec 1899 (10 cents, 11x8-1/8", 36 pgs, color paper-c, B&W)

1 8.50 17.00 33.00
2-141 8.50 17.00 33.00
151-??? (post-1900 issues; see Platinum Age section)
NOTE: ***Judge's Library** was a monthly magazine reprinting cartoons & prose from **Judge**, with each issue's material organized around the same subject. The cover art was often original. All issues were kept in print for the duration of the series, so later issues are more scarce than earlier ones.*

JUDGE'S QUARTERLY (M)
Judge Publishing Company/Arkell Publishing Company, New York: No.1 April 1892 - 31 Oct 1899 (25¢, 13-3/4x10-1/4", 64 pgs, color paper-c, B&W)

1-31 15.00 30.00 60.00
NOTE: *Similar to **Judge's Library**, except larger in size, and issued quarterly. All reprint material, except for the cover art.*

JUVENILE GEM, THE (see also THE ADVENTURES OF MR. TOM PLUMP, and OLD MOTHER MITTEN) (O,I)
Huestis & Cozans: nd (1850-1852) (6x3-7/8", 64 pgs, hand colored paper-c, B&W) (all versions Very Rare)

nn - First printing(s) publisher's address is 104 Nassau Street (1850-1851)(no known sales)
nn - 2nd printing(s) publisher's address is 116 Nassau Street (1851-1852) (no known sales)
nn - 3rd printing(s) publisher's address is 107 Nassau Street (1852+) (no known sales)
NOTE: *The JUVENILE GEM is a gathering of multiple booklets under a single, hand colored cover (none of the interior booklets have the covers which they were given when sold separately). The publisher appears to have gathered whichever printings of each booklet were available when copies of THE JUVENILE GEM was assembled, so that the booklets within, and the conglomerate cover, may be from a mixture of printings.*

FR1.0 GD2.0 FN6.0

*Contains two sequential comic booklets: THE ADVENTURES OF MR. TOM PLUMP, and OLD MOTHER MITTEN AND HER FUNNY KITTEN, plus five heavily illustrated children's booklets - **The Pretty Primer**, **The Funny Book**, **The Picture Book**, **The Two Sisters**, and **Story Of The Little Drummer**. Six of these -- including the two comic books -- were reprinted in the 1960's by Americana Review as a set of individual booklets, and included in a folder collectively titled "Six Children's Books of the 1850's".*

LATER PENCILLINGS FROM PUNCH (see also PICTURES OF LIFE AND CHARACTER) (M,S,E)
Bradbury and Evans, London: nd (13-1/4x11",272 pgs, red gilted hard-c, B&W)

nn - By John Leech; reprints from Punch 25.00 50.00 100.00

LIFE (miniature reprint of issue No.1) (M,P)
Mutual Life Insurance Company: falsely dated Jan 4, 1883 (actually published 1933) (3x2-1/2", 16 pgs, B&W, paper-c)

1 .25 2.00 5.00
NOTE: *Fiftieth Anniversary miniaturized reprint of **Life** No. 1, given away by the Mutual Life Insurance Company. This item is frequently misrepresented by sellers, knowingly or unknowingly, as the actual **Life** Number 1. It is an extremely common and near worthless item, listed here only to prevent further misrepresentation.*

LIFE (miniature reprint of issue No.1) (M,P)
Life Magazine: falsely dated Jan 4, 1883 (actually published 1958) (3x2-1/2", 16 pgs, B&W, paper-c) 1.25 2.00 5.00
NOTE: 1958 Life Magazine premium, sent to subscribers for renewing their subscriptions. Originally came in a small folder, along with a loose, folded flyer explaining what the booklet was. This item is frequently misrepresented by sellers, knowingly or unknowingly, as the actual Life Number 1. It is an extremely common and near worthless item, listed here only to prevent further misrepresentation.

LIFE (M,O) (continues with Vol.35 No. 894+ in the Platinum Age section)
J.A.Mitchell: Vol.1 No.1 Jan. 4, 1883 - Vol.1 No.26 June 29, 1883 (10-1/4x8", 16 pgs, B&W, paper cover); J.A. Mitchell: Vol. 2 No. 27, July 5, 1883 - Vol. 6 No.148, Oct 29, 1885 (10-1/4x8-1/4", 16 pgs., B&W, paper cover); Mitchell & Miller: Vol.6 No.149, Nov. 5, 1885 - Vol. 31, No. 796, March 17, 1898 (10-3/8x8-3/8", 16 pgs., B&W, paper cover); Life Publishing Company: Vol. 31 No. 797, March 24, 1898 - Vol. 34 No. 893, Dec 28, 1899 (10-3/8 x 8-1/2", 20 pgs., B&W, paper cover)

1-26 (Scarce) (no known sales)
27-799 5.00 10.00 20.00
800 (4/7/1898) parody Yellow Kid / Spanish-American War cover
(not by Outcault) 25.00 50.00 110.00
801-893 5.00 10.00 20.00
NOTE: *All covers for issues 1 - 26 are identical, apart from issue number & date.*
Hard bound collected volumes:
V. 1 (No.1-26) (Scarce) (no known sales)
V. 2-34 45.00 90.00 180.00
V. 31 YK #800 parody-c not by RFO 70.00 140.00 280.00
NOTE: *Because the covers of all issues in Volume 1 are identical, it was common practice to remove the covers before binding the issues together. This is not true of later volumes, though, in all volumes it was common to drop the advertising pages which appeared at the rear of each issue. Information on many more individual issues will expand next Guide.*

LIFE AND ADVENTURES OF JEFF DAVIS (I)
J.C. Haney & Co., NY: 1865 (10 cents, 7-1/2" x 4", 36 pgs, B&W, paper-c)

nn - By McArone 100.00 200.00 400.00
NOTE: *Humorous telling of the capture of Confederate President Jeff Davis in women's clothing, from the publisher of Merryman's Monthly. It contains an ad page for that publication; the material is perhaps reprinted from it. J.C. Haney licensed it to local printers, and so various publishers are found -- all printings currently regarded as simultaneous. (The Geo. H. Hees printing, Oswego, NY, contains an ad for the upcoming October 1865 issue of Merryman's Monthly, thus placing that printing in September 1865). Modern facsimile editions have been produced.*

LIFE IN PHILADELPHIA
W. Simpson, 66 Chestnut, Philadelphia; Siltart, No. 65 South Third St, Philadelphia: 1830 (7-3/4x6-7/8", 15 loose plates, hand colored copies exist, maybe B&W also)

nn - By Edward Williams Clay (1799-1857) (no known sales)
NOTE: *First 13 plates etched, with many word balloons; scenes of exaggerated Black Americana in Philadelphia viewed one by one as broadsides. Had several publishers over the years. Was also eventually collected into a book of same name but only with the first 13 plates used; the last two not used in book. Collected book not yet viewed to share info.*

LIFE'S BOOK OF ANIMALS (M,S)
Doubleday & McClure Co.: 1898 (7-1/4x10-1/8", 88 pgs, color hardcover, B&W)

nn 25.00 50.00 100.00
NOTE: *Reprints funny animal single panel and strip cartoons reprinted from LIFE. Art by Blaisdell, Chip Bellew, Kemble, Hy Mayer, Sullivant, Woolf.*

LIFE'S COMEDY (M,S)
Charles Scribner's Sons: Series 1 1897 - Series 3 1898 (12x9-3/8", hardcover, B&W)

1 (142 pgs). 2, 3 (138 pgs) 60.00 120.00 240.00
NOTE: *Gibson a-1-3; c-3. Hy Mayer a-1-3. Rose O'Neill a-2-3. Stanlaws a-2-3. Sullivant a-1-2. Verbeek a-2. Wenzell a-1-3; c(painted)-2.*

LIFE, THE GOOD THINGS OF (M,S)
White, Stokes, & Allen, NY: 1884 - No.3 1886 ; Frederick A. Stokes, NY: No.4

Max and Maurice by Wilhelm Busch
1871 © Roberts Brothers, Boston

Merryman's Monthly v3#5 with Bellew strip
May 1865 © J. C. Haney & Co., New York

Minneapolis Journal Cartoons Second Series
1895

1887; Frederick Stokes & Brother, NY: No.5 1888 - No.6 1889; Frederick A. Stokes Company, NY: No. 7 1890 - No.10 1893 (8-3/8x10-1/2", 74 pgs, gilted hardcover, B&W)

nn - 1884 (most common issue) 32.50 65.00 130.00
2 - 1885 32.50 65.00 130.00
3 - 1886 (76 pgs) 32.50 65.00 130.00
4 - 1887 (76 pgs) 32.50 65.00 130.00
5 - 1888 32.50 65.00 130.00
6 - 1889 32.50 65.00 130.00
7 - 1890 32.50 65.00 130.00
8 - 1891 32.50 65.00 130.00
9 - 1892 32.50 65.00 130.00
10 - 1893 32.50 65.00 130.00

NOTE: *Contains mostly single panel, and some sequential, comics reprinted from LIFE. Attwood a-1-4,10. Roswell Bacon a-5. Chip Bellew a-4-6. Frank Bellew a-4,6. Palmer Cox a-1. H. E. Dey a-5. C. D. Gibson a-4-10. F.M. Howarth a-5-6. Kemble a-1-3. Klapp a-5. Walt McDougall a-1-2. H. McVickar a-5; J. A. Mitchell a-5. Peter Newell a-2-3. Gray Parker a-4-5,7. J. Smith a-5. Albert E. Steiner a-5; T. S. Sullivant a-7-9. Wenzell a-8-10. Wilder a-3. Woolf a-3-6.*

LIFE, MINIATURE (see also LIFE (miniature reprint of of issue No. 1)) (M,P,S)
Life Publishing Co.: No. 1 ??? - No.2 1913 (5-3/4x4-5/8", 20 pgs, color paper cover, mostly B&W interior)

1- Exist? (no known sales)
2- (Rare) (no known sales)

NOTE: *Giveaway item from Life, to promote subscriptions. All reprint material. No.2: James Montgomery Flagg-c; a-Chip Bellew, Gus Dirks, Gibson, F.M.Howarth, Art Young.*

LIFE, THE SPICE OF (see SPICE OF LIFE, THE)

LIFE'S PICTURE GALLERY (becomes LIFE'S PRINTS) (M,S,P)
Life Publishing Company, New York: nd (1898-1899) (paper cover, B&W) (all are scarce)

nn - (nd; 1898, 100 pgs, 5-1/4x8-1/2") Gibson-c of a woman with closed umbrella; 1st interior page announcing that after January 1, 1899 Gibson will draw exclusively for LIFE; the word "SPECIMEN" is printed in red, diagonally, across every print; a-Gibson, Rose O'Neill, Sullivant 25.00 50.00 100.00
nn - (nd; 1899, 128 pgs, 4-7/8x7-3/8") Gibson-c of a woman golfer; 1st interior page announcing that Gibson & Hanna, Jr. draw exclusively for LIFE; the word "SPECIMEN" is printed in red, horizontally, across every print. Includes prints from Gibson's **THE EDUCATION OF MR. PIPP**; a-Gibson, Sullivant 25.00 50.00 100.00

NOTE: *Catalog of prints reprinted from **LIFE** covers & centerspreads. The first catalog was given away free to anyone requesting it, but after many people got the catalog without ordering anything, subsequent catalogs were sold at 10 cents.*

LOVING BALLADS OF LORD BATEMAN, THE (E,I)
G.W. Carleton & Co., Publishers, Madison Square, NY: 1871 (9x5-7/8", 6 cents)

nn - By George Cruikshank 50.00 100.00 200.00

MANNERS AND CUSTOMS OF YE HARVARD STUDENTE (M,S)
Houghton Mifflin & Co., Boston & Moses King, Cambridge: 1877 (7-7/8x11", 72 pgs, printed one side, hardc, B&W)

nn - by F.G. Attwood 175.00 350.00 700.00

NOTE: *Collection of cartoons originally serialized in the **Harvard Lampoon**. Attwood later became a major cartoonist for **Life**.*

MAN WHO WOULD LIKE TO MARRY, THE (O)
Frederick Warne & Co., London & New York: nd (c 1880's) (9-1/2x11-1/2", 28 pgs, printed 1 side, paper-c, B&W)

nn - By Harry Parkes 62.50 125.00 250.00

NOTE: *Published simultaneously with its companion volume, **The Girl Who Wouldn't Mind Getting Married**.*

MAX AND MAURICE: A JUVENILE HISTORY IN SEVEN TRICKS (E)
(see also Teasing Tom and Naughty Ned)
Roberts Brothers, Boston: 1871 first edition (8-1/8 x 5-1/2", 76 pgs, hard & soft-c B&W)

nn - By Wilhelm Busch (green or brown cloth hardbound) 200.00 400.00 800.00
nn - exactly the same, but soft paper cover 150.00 300.00 600.00

NOTE: *Page count includes 56 pgs of art, two blank endpapers at the front (one colored), 8 pgs of ads at the back, two blank endpapers at the end (one colored), and the covers. Green or brown illustrated hardcover. The name of the author is given on the title page as "William Busch." We assume this to be the 1st edition. Back side of title page states: Entered according to Act of Congress, in the year 1870, by Roberts Brothers, In the office of the Librarian of Congress at Washington.*

nn - By Wilhelm Busch (1872 edition) 150.00 300.00 600.00
nn - 1875 reprint 100.00 200.00 400.00
nn - 1882 reprint (76 pgs, hand colored- c/a, 75¢) 100.00 200.00 400.00

NOTE: *Each of the above contains 56 pages of art and text in a transitional format between a regular children's book and a comic book (the page count difference is ad pages in back). Seminal inspiration for William Randolph Hearst to acquire as a "new comic" (following the wild success of Outcault's Yellow Kid) to license M&M from Busch and hire Rudolph Dirks in late 1897 to create a New York American newspaper incarnation. In Hearst's English language newspapers it was called The Katzenjammer Kids and in his German language NYC newspaper it was titled Max & Moritz, Busch's original title. At least 50 other reprints versions are reputed to exist printed thru 1900. Translated from the 1865 German original. We are still sorting out the edition confusion.*

MAX AND MAURICE: A JUVENILE HISTORY IN SEVEN TRICKS (E)
(see also Teasing Tom and Naughty Ned)
Little, Brown, and Company, Boston: 1899 first edition(?) (8-1/8 x 5-5/8", 72 pgs, hardcover, black ink on orange paper)

nn - 1899 By Wilhelm Busch 50.00 100.00 200.00
nn - 1902 (64 pages, B&W) 10.00 30.00 90.00

MERRY MAPLE LEAVES Or A Summer In The Country (S)
E.P. Dutton And Company, New York: 1872 (9-3/8x7-3/8", 90 & 86 pgs pgs, hard-c)

nn - By Abner Perk 25.00 50.00 150.00

NOTE: *Each drawing contained in a maple leaf motif by Livingston Hopkins and others.*

MERRYMAN'S MONTHLY A COMIC MAGAZINE FOR THE FAMILY (M,O,E)
J.C. Haney & Co, NY: 1863-1877 (10-7/8x7-13/16", 30 pgs average, B&W)

Certain issues with short sequential comics 25.00 50.00 150.00

NOTE: *Sequential strips by Frank Bellew Sr, Wilhelm Busch found so far; others?*

MESSRS. BROWN, JONES, AND ROBINSON, THE FOREIGN TOUR OF
(see also **THE CLOWN, OR THE BANQUET OF WIT**) (E,M,O,G)
Bradbury & Evans, London: 1854 (11-5/8x9-1/2", 196 pgs, gilted hard-c, B&W)

nn - By Richard Doyle 35.00 70.00 140.00
nn - Bradbury & Evans 1900 reprint 20.00 40.00 80.00

NOTE: *Protective sheets between each page (not part of page count). Expanded and redrawn sequential comics story from the serialized episodes originally published in PUNCH. Also comes in a 174 pg 8-3/4x11" version.*

MESSRS. BROWN, JONES, AND ROBINSON, THE LAUGHABLE ADVENTURES OF (E,M,G)
Garrett, Dick & Fitzgerald, NY: nd (1856 or 1857) (5-3/4x9-1/4", 100 pgs, printed one side only, paper-c, B&W)

nn - (Very Rare) by Richard Doyle c/a 200.00 400.00 700.00

NOTE: *1st American reprinting of the "Foreign Tour"; reformatted into a small oblong format. Links the earlier Garrett & Co. to the later Dick & Fitzgerald. Back cover reprints full size the Garrett & Co. version cover for Oscar Shanghai. Interior front cover reprints full size the Garrett & Co. version cover for Slyfox-Wikof. Issued without a title page.*

MESSRS. BROWN, JONES, AND ROBINSON, THE FOREIGN TOUR OF (E,M,G)
D. Appleton & Co., New York: 1860 & 1877 (11-5/8x9-1/2", 196 pgs, gilted hard-c, B&W)

nn - (1860 printing) by Richard Doyle 30.00 60.00 120.00
nn - (1871 printing) by Richard Doyle 30.00 60.00 120.00
nn - (1877 printing) by Richard Doyle 30.00 60.00 120.00

NOTE: *Protective sheets between each page (not part of page count). Reprints the Bradbury & Evans edition.*

MESSRS BROWN JONES AND ROBINSON, THE AMERICAN TOUR OF (O,G)
D. Appleton & Co., New York: 1872 (11-5/8x9-1/2", 158 pgs, printed one side only, B&W, green gilted hard-c)

nn - By Toby 70.00 140.00 300.00

NOTE: *Original American graphic novel sequel to Richard Doyle's Foreign Tour of Brown, Jones, and Robinson, with the same characters visiting New York, Canada, and Cuba. Protective sheets between each page (not part of page count).*

MESSRS. BROWN, JONES, AND ROBINSON, THE LAUGHABLE ADVEN. OF (E,M,G)
Dick & Fitzgerald, NY: nd (late 1870's - 1888) (5-3/4x9-1/4", 100 pgs, printed one side only, green paper-c, B&W)

nn - (Scarce) by Richard Doyle 100.00 200.00 400.00

NOTE: *Reprints the Garrett, Dick & Fitzgerald printing, with the following changes: Takes what had been page 12 in the Garrett, D&F printing (art by M.H. Henry), and makes it a title page, which is numbered page 1. The first story page, "Go to the Races", is numbered 2 (whereas it is numbered 1 in the Garrett, Dick & Fitzgerald version). Numbering stays ahead of the G,D&F edition by 1 page up through page 12, after which the page numbering becomes identical.*

MINNEAPOLIS JOURNAL CARTOONS (N,S)
Minneapolis Journal: nn 1894 - No.2 1895 (7-3/4" x 10-7/8", 76 pgs, B&W, paper-c)

nn (1894) (Rare) 25.00 50.00 100.00
Second Series (1895) (Rare) 25.00 50.00 100.00
nn- "War Cartoons" Jan 1899 (9x8", 160 pgs, paperback, punched & string bound) 24.00 96.00 170.00

NOTE: *Reprints single panel cartoons from the prior year, by Charles "Bart" L. Bartholomew.*

MISCHIEF BOOK, THE (E)
R. Worthington, New York: 1880 (7-1/8 x 10-3/4", 176 pgs, hard-c, B&W)

nn - Green cloth binding; green on brown cover; cover art by R. Lewis based on Busch art by Wilhelm Busch 175.00 350.00 735.00
nn - Blue cloth binding; hand colored cover; completely different cover art based on Busch by Wilhelm Busch 175.00 350.00 735.00

NOTE: *Translated by Abby Langdon Alger. American published anthology collection of Wilhelm Busch comic strips. Includes two of the strips found in the British "Bushel of Merry-Thoughts" collection, translated better, and with the dropped panel restored. Unknown which cover version was first.*

MISSES BROWN, JONES AND ROBINSON, THE FOREIGN TOUR OF THE (E,O,G)

The Mischief Book by Wilhelm Busch
color cover art variation
1880 © R. Worthington, New York

Museum of Wonders by Opper
1894 © Routledge & Sons

99 "Woolf's" from Truth
1896 © Truth Company

Bickers & Sons, London: nd (c1850's) (12-1/4" x 9-7/8", 108 pgs, printed on one side, B&W, hard-c)

nn- "by Miss Brown" (Rare) 35.00 70.00 140.00
NOTE: *A female take on Doyle's Foreign Tour, by an unknown woman artist, using the pseudonym "Miss Brown."*

MISS MILLY MILLEFLEUR'S CAREER (S)
Sheldon & Co., NY: 1869 (10-3/4x9-7/8", 74 pgs, purple hard-c)

nn - Artist unknown 25.00 50.00 150.00

MUSEUM OF WONDERS, A (O,I)
Routledge & Sons: 1894 (13x10", 64 pgs, color-c, color thru out)

nn - By Frederick Opper 100.00 200.00 400.00

MY FRIEND WRIGGLES, A (Laughter) Moving Panorama, of His Fortunes And Misfortunes, Illustrated With Over 200 Engravings, of Most Comic Catastrophes And Side-Splitting Merriment) (O,G)
Stearn & Co, 202 Williams St, NY: 1850s (5-7/8x9-3/4", 100 pgs, B&W)

nn - By S. P. Avery (also the engraver) 200.00 400.00 800.00

MY SKETCHBOOK (E,S)
Dana Estes & Charles E. Lauriat, Boston; J. Sabins & Sons, New York: circa 1880s (9-3/8x12", brown hard-c)

nn - By George Cruikshank 25.00 50.00 150.00
NOTE: *Reprints British editions 1834-36; extensive usage of word balloons.*

NEW BOOK OF NONSENSE, THE: A Contribution To The Great Central Fair In Aid of the Sanitary Commission (O,S)
Ashmead & Evans, No. 724 Chestnut St, Philadelphia: June 1864 (red hard-c)

nn - Artists unknown 50.00 150.00 300.00

99 "WOOLFS" FROM TRUTH (see Sketches of Lowly Life in a Great City, Truth)
Truth Company, NY: 1896 (9x5-1/2", varnished paper-like cloth hard-c, 25 cents)

nn - By Michael Angelo Woolf 100.00 200.00 400.00
NOTE: *Woolf's cartoons are regarded as a primary influence on R.F. Outcault in the later development of The Yellow Kid newspaper strip. Copy sold in 2002 on eBay for $800.00.*

OBADIAH OLDBUCK, THE ADVENTURES OF MR. (E,G)
Tilt & Bogue, London: nd (1840-41) (5-15/16x9-3/16", 176 pgs,B&W, gilted hard-c)

nn - By Rodolphe Töpffer (Scarce) 300.00 600.00 1100.00
nn - Hand coloured edition (Very Rare) (no known sales)
NOTE: *This is the British edition, translating the unauthorized redrawn 1839 edition from Parisian publisher Aubert, adapted from Töpffer's "Les Amours de Mr. Vieux Bois" (aka "Histoire de Mr. Vieux Bois"), originally published in French in Switzerland, in 1837 (2nd ed. 1839). Early 19th century books are often found rebound, with original cover and/or title page gone. To distinguish editions having no cover or title page: the British oblong editions (published by Tilt & Bogue) use Roman Numerals to number pages. American oblong shaped editions use Arabic Numerals. British are printed on one side only. This is the earliest known English language sequential comic book. Has a new title page with art by Robert Cruikshank.*

OBADIAH OLDBUCK, THE ADVENTURES OF MR. (E,G)
Wilson and Company, New York: September 14, 1842 (11-3/4x9", 44 pgs, B&W, yellow paper-c on bookstand editions, hemp paper interior)

Brother Jonathan Extra No. IX - Very Rare bookstand edition 750.00 1500.00 4500.00
Brother Jonathan Extra No. IX Very Rare subscriber/mailorder 750.00 1500.00 4500.00
NOTE: *By Rodolphe Töpffer. Earliest known sequential American comic book, reprinting the 1841 British edition. Pages are numbered via Roman numerals. States "BROTHER JONATHAN EXTRA - ADVENTURES OF MR. OBADIAH OLDBUCK." at the top of each page. Prints 2 to 3 tiers of panels on both sides of each page. Copies could be had for ten cents according to adverts in* ***Brother Jonathan****. By Rodolphe Töpffer with cover masthead design by David Claypool Johnston, and cover art beneath the masthead reprinting Robert Cruikshank's title page art from the Tilt & Bogue edition. A special, additional cover was added for copies sold on stands (it was not issued with mail order or subscriber copies). Only 1 known copy possesses (partially) this very thin outer yellow cover. A decent (subscriber) copy sold on eBay in later October 2002 for over $3500.00.*

OBADIAH OLDBUCK, THE ADVENTURES OF MR. (E,G)
Wilson & Co, New York: nd (1849) (5-11/16x8-3/8", 92 pgs, B&W, hard-c)

nn - by Rodolphe Töpffer; title page by Robert Cruikshank (Very Rare)
300.00 700.00 1650.00
NOTE: *2nd Wilson & Co printing, reformatted into a small oblong format, with nine panels edited out, and text modified to smooth out this removal. Results in four less printed tiers/strips. Pages are numbered via Arabic numerals. Every panel on Pages 11, 14, 19, 21, 24, 34, 35 has one line of text. Reformatted to conform with British first edition.*

OBADIAH OLDBUCK, THE ADVENTURES OF MR. (E,G)
Dick & Fitzgerald, New York: nd (various printings; est. 1870s to 1888) (Thirty Cents, 84 pgs, B&W, paper-c) (all versions Rare)

nn - Black print on green cover(5-11/16x8-15/16"); string bound 200.00 400.00 650.00
nn - Black print on blue cover; same format as green-c 200.00 400.00 650.00
nn - Black print on white cover(5-13/16x9-3/16"); staple bound beneath cover);
this is a later printing than the blue or green-c 200.00 400.00 650.00
NOTE: *Reprints the abbreviated 1849 Wilson & Co. 2nd printing. Pages are numbered via Arabic numerals. Many of the panels on Pages 11, 14, 19, 21, 24, 34, 35 take two lines to print the same words found in the Wilson & Co version, which used only one text line for the same panels. Unknown whether the blue or green cover is earlier. White cover version has "thirty cents" line blackened out on the two copies known to exist. Robert Cruikshank's title page has been made the cover in the D&F editions.*

FR1.0 GD2.0 FN6.0

OLD MOTHER MITTEN AND HER FUNNY KITTEN (see also **The Juvenile Gem**) (O)
Huestis & Cozans: nd(1850-1852) (6x3-7/8"12pgs, hand colored paper-c, B&W)

nn - first printing(s) publisher's address is 104 Nassau Street (1850-1851)
(Very Rare) (no known sales)
NOTE: *A hand colored outer cover is highly rare, with only 1 recorded copy possessing it. Front cover image and text is repeated precisely on page 3 (albeit b&w), and only interior pages are numbered, together leading owners of coverless copies to believe they have the cover. The true back cover has ads for the publisher. Cover was issued only with copies which were sold separately - books which were bound together as part of THE JUVENILE GEM never had such covers.*

OLD MOTHER MITTEN AND HER FUNNY KITTEN (see JUVENILE GEM) (O)
Philip J. Cozans: nd (1850-1852) (6x3-7/8",12 pgs, hand colored paper-c, B&W)

nn - Second printing(s) publisher's address is 116 Nassau Street (1851-1852)
(Very Rare) (no known sales)
nn - Third printing(s) publisher's address is 107 Nassau Street (1852+)
(Very Rare) (no known sales)

OLD MOTHER MITTEN AND HER FUNNY KITTEN
Americana Review, Scotia, NY: nd (1960's) (6-1/4x4-1/8", 8 pgs, side-stapled, cardboard, B&W)

nn - Modern reprint 2.50 5.00 10.00
NOTE: *Issued within a folder titled SIX CHILDREN'S BOOKS OF THE 1850'S. States "Reprinted by American Review" at bottom of front cover. Reprints the 104 Nassau Street address.*

ON THE NILE (O,G)
James R. Osgood & Co., Boston: 1874 ; **Houghton, Osgood & Co., Boston:** 1880 (112 pgs, gilted green hardcover, B&W)

1st printing (1874; 10-3/4x16") - by Augustus Hoppin 45.00 90.00 180.00
2nd printing (1880; smaller sized) 32.50 65.00 130.00

OSCAR SHANGHAI, THE EXTRAORDINARY AND MIRTH-PROVKING ADVENTURES BY SEA & LAND OF (O, G)
Garrett & Co., Publishers, No. 18 Ann Street, New York: circa 1852-55 (5-3/4x9-1/4", 100 pgs, printed one side only, paper-c, 25¢, B&W)

nn - Samuel Avery-c; interior by ALC Very Rare) 400.00 800.00 1600.00
NOTE: *Not much is known of this first edition as the data comes from a recently rediscovered* ***Brother Jonathan*** *catalog issued circa 1853-55. No original known yet to exist.*

OSCAR SHANGHAI, THE WONDERFUL AND AMUSING DOINGS BY SEA AND LAND OF (G)
Dick & Fitzgerald, 10 Ann St, NY: nd (1870s-1888) (25 ¢, 5-3/4x9-1/4", 100 pgs, printed one side only, green paper c, B&W)

nn - Cover by Samuel Avery; interior by ALC (Rare) 200.00 300.00 600.00
NOTE: *Exact reprint of Garrett & Co original.*

OUR ARTIST IN CUBA (O)
Carleton, New York: 1865 (6-5/8x4-3/8", 120 pgs, printed one side only, gilted hard-c, B&W)

nn - By Geo. W. Carleton 37.50 75.00 150.00

OUR ARTIST IN CUBA, PERU, SPAIN, AND ALGIERS (O)
Carleton: 1877 (6-1/2x5-1/8", 156 pgs, hardcover, B&W)

nn - By Geo. W. Carleton 32.50 65.00 130.00
NOTE: *Reprints OUR ARTIST IN CUBA and OUR ARTIST IN PERU, then adds new section on Spain and Algiers.*

OUR ARTIST IN PERU (O)
Carleton, New York: 1866 (7-3/4x5-7/8", 68 pgs, gilted hardcover, B&W)

nn- By Geo. W. Carleton 37.50 75.00 150.00
NOTE: *Contains advertisement for the upcoming books* ***OUR ARTIST IN ITALY*** *and* ***OUR ARTIST IN FRANCE****, but no such publications have been found to date.*

PEN AND INK SKETCHES OF YALE NOTABLES (O,S)
Soule, Thomas and Winsor, St. Louis: 1872 (12-1/4x9-3/4", B&W)

By Squills 25.00 50.00 100.00
NOTE: *Printed by Steamlith Press, The R.P. Studley Company, St Louis.*

PETER PIPER IN BENGAL
Bengamin H Day.Publisher, Brother Jonathan Cheap Book Establishment, 48 Beekman, NY: 1953-55 (6-5/8x4-1/4, 36 pgs, yellow paper-c, B&W, 3 cents - two dollars per hundred)

nn - By John Tenniel - 32 panel comic strip Punch-r 500.00 1000.00 1500.00
NOTE: *Actually also a catalog of inexpensive books, prints, maps and half a dozen comic books for sale on separate pages from publishers Day and Garrett - see full story of this brand new find in the Victorian Era essay. A complete copy with split spine sold in November 2002 for $750.00. Published date most likely 1855.*

PHIL MAY'S SKETCH BOOK (E,S,M)
Chatto & Windus, London: 1897 (14-1/2x9-3/4", 64 pgs, red hard-c, B&W)

nn - By Phil May 42.50 85.00 170.00

The Wonderful and Amusing Doings by
Sea & Land of Oscar Shanghai
1870s © Dick & Fitzgerald, New York

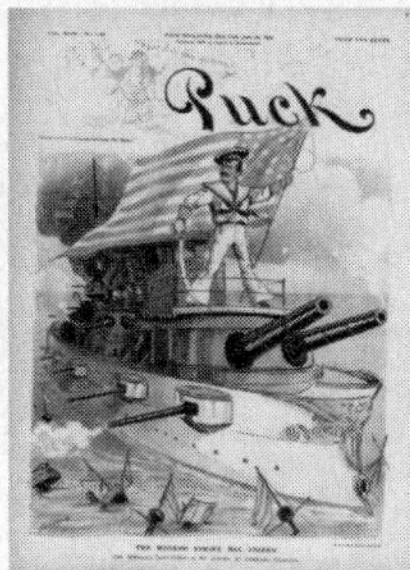

PUCK
© Keppler & Schwarzman, NY

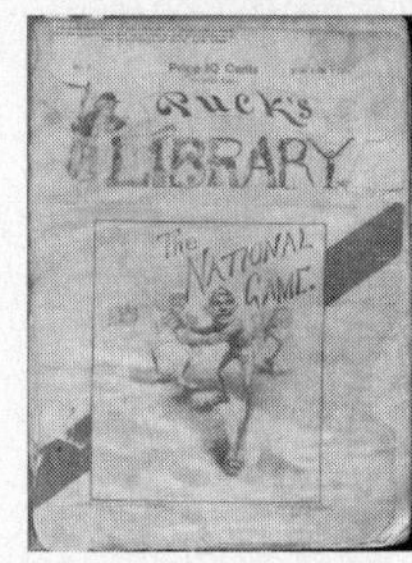

Puck's Library

FR1.0 GD2.0 FN6.0

PHIL MAY'S SKETCH BOOK (E,S,M)
R.H. Russell, New York: 1899 (14-5/8x10", 64 pgs, brown hard-c, B&W)

	FR1.0	GD2.0	FN6.0
nn - By Phil May	32.50	65.00	130.00

NOTE: *American reprint of the British edition.*

PICTURES OF ENGLISH SOCIETY (Parchment-Paper Series, No.4) (M,S,E)
D. Appleton & Co., New York: 1884 (5-5/8x4-3/8", 108 pgs, paper-c, B&W)

	FR1.0	GD2.0	FN6.0
4 - By George du Maurier; Punch-r	15.00	30.00	60.00

NOTE: *Every other page is a full page cartoon, with the opposite page containing the cartoon's caption.*

PICTURES OF LIFE AND CHARACTER (M,S,E)
Bradbury and Evans, London: No.1 1855 - No.5 c1864 (12-1/2x18", 100 pgs, illustrated hard-c, B&W)

	FR1.0	GD2.0	FN6.0
nn (No.1) (1855)	32.50	65.00	130.00
2 (1858), 3 (1860)	32.50	65.00	130.00
4 (nd; c1862) 5 (nd; c1864)	32.50	65.00	130.00
nn (nd (late 1860's)	32.50	65.00	130.00

NOTE: 2-1/2x18-1/4", 494 pgs, green gilted-c) reprints 1-5 in one book

	FR1.0	GD2.0	FN6.0
1-3 John Leech's... (nd; 12-3/8x10", ? pgs, red gilted-c).	25.00	50.00	100.00

NOTE: *Reprints John Leech cartoons from* ***Punch****. note that the Volume Number is mentioned only on the last page of these versions.*

PICTURES OF LIFE AND CHARACTER (E,M,S)
G.P. Putnam's Sons: 1880's (8-5/8x6-1/4", 218 pgs, hardcover, color-cr, B&W)

	FR1.0	GD2.0	FN6.0
nn - John Leech (single panel **Punch** cartoon-r)	20.00	40.00	160.00

NOTE: *Leech reprints which extend back to the 1850s.*

PICTURES OF LIFE AND CHARACTER (Parchment-Paper Series) (E,M,S)
(see also Humerous Masterpieces)
D. Appleton & Co., NY: 1884 (30¢, 5-3/4 x 4-1/2", 104 pgs, paper-c, B&W)

	FR1.0	GD2.0	FN6.0
nn - John Leech (single panel **Punch** cartoon-r)	20.00	40.00	160.00

NOTE: *An advertisment in the back refers to a cloth-bound edition for 50 cents.*

PICTURES OF PEOPLE (see Gibson's Published Drawings)

PIPPIN AMONG THE WIDE-AWAKES (O,S)
Werill & Chapin, 113 Nassau St, NYC, NY): 1860 (6x4-1/2", 36 pgs, 6 cents)

	FR1.0	GD2.0	FN6.0
nn - Artist unknown	100.00	200.00	400.00

PLISH AND PLUM (E.G)
Roberts Brothers, Boston: 1883 (8-1/8x5-3/4", 80 pgs, hardcover, B&W)

	FR1.0	GD2.0	FN6.0
nn - By Wilhelm Busch (Scarce)	40.00	80.00	160.00
nn - Reprint (Little, Brown & Co., 1899)	40.00	80.00	160.00

NOTE: *The adventures of two dogs.*

PROGRESS OF MR. LAMBKIN, (GENT) (E,G) (see also Bachelor's Own Book)
David Bryce and Son, Glasgow: 1884 (1 shilling, 7-7/8x5-3/4", 60 pgs, printed one side only, cardboard cover, B&W)

	FR1.0	GD2.0	FN6.0
nn	17.50	35.00	70.00

NOTE: *Reprint of George Cruikshank's* ***Bachelor's Own Book****.*

PUCK (German language edition, St. Louis) (M,O) (see also Die Vehme)
Publisher unknown, St. Louis: No.1, March 18, 1871 - No. ??, Aug. 24, 1872 (B&W, paper-c)

1-?? (Very Rare) by Joseph Keppler (no known sales)

NOTE: *Joseph Keppler's second attempt at a weekly humor periodical, following* ***Die Vehme*** *one year earlier. This was his first attempt to launch using the title* ***Puck****. This German language version ran for a full year before being joined by an English language version.*

PUCK (English language edition, St. Louis) (M,O)
Publisher unknown, St. Louis: No.1, March ?? 1872 - No. ??, Aug. 24, 1872 (B&W, paper c)

1-?? (Very Rare) by Joseph Keppler (no known sales)

NOTE: *Same material as in the German language edition, but in English.*

PUCK, ILLUSTRIRTES HUMORISTISCHES WOCHENBLATT (German language edition, NYC) (M,O)
Keppler & Schwarzmann, New York: No.1 Sept (27) 1876 - 1164 Dec ?? 1899 (10 cents, color front/back-c and centerspread, remainder B&W, paper-c)

1-26 (Volume 1; Rare) by Joseph Keppler - these issues precede the English language version, and contain cartoons not found in them. Includes cartoons on the controversial Tilden-Hayes 1876 Presidential Election debacle. (no known sales)
27-52 (Volume 2; Rare) by Joseph Keppler - contains some cartoon material not found in the English language editions. Particularly in the earlier issues. (no known sales)

	FR1.0	GD2.0	FN6.0
53-1164	7.50	15.00	30.00

Bound Volumes (six month, 26 issue run each):

	FR1.0	GD2.0	FN6.0
Vol. 1 (Rare)	(no known sales)		
Vol. 2-4 (Rare)	(no known sales)		
Vol. 5-47	62.50	125.00	250.00

NOTE: *Joseph Keppler's second, and successful, attempt to launch* ***Puck****. In German. The first six months precede the launch of the English language edition. Soon after (but not immediately after) the launch of the English edition, both editions began sharing the same cartoons, but, their prose material always remained different. The German language edition ceased publication at the end of 1899, while the English language edition continued into the early 20th Century. First American periodical to feature printed color every issue.*

PUCK (English language edition, NYC) (M,O)
Keppler & Schwarzmann, New York: No.1 March (14) 1877 - 1190 Dec ?? 1899 (10 cents, color front/back-c and centerspread, remainder B&W, paper-c)

	FR1.0	GD2.0	FN6.0
1 (Rare) by Joseph Keppler	(no known sales)		
2-26 (Rare) by Joseph Keppler	(no known sales)		
27-1190	12.50	25.00	50.00

(see Platinum Age section for year 1900+ issues)

Bound volumes (six month, 26 issue run each):

	FR1.0	GD2.0	FN6.0
Vol. 1 (Rare)	(no known sales)		
Vol. 2 (Scarce)	(no known sales)		
Vol. 3-6 (pre-1880 issues)	175.00	375.00	750.00
Vol. 7-46	140.00	300.00	600.00

NOTE: *The English language editions began six months after the German editions, and so the English edition numbering is always one volume number, and 26 issue numbers, behind its parallel German language edition. Pre-1880 & post-1900 issues are more scarce than 1880's & 1890's.*

PUCK (miniature) (M,P,I)
Keppler & Schwarzmann, New York: nd (c1895) (7x5-1/8", 12 pgs, color front & back paper-c, B&W interior)

	FR1.0	GD2.0	FN6.0
nn - Scarce	25.00	50.00	110.00

NOTE: *C.J.Taylor-c; F.M.Howarth-a; F.Opper-a; giveaway item promoting* ***Puck's*** *various publications. Mostly text, with art reprinted from* ***Puck****.*

PUCK, CARTOONS FROM (M,S)
Keppler & Schwarzmann, New York: 1893 (14-1/4x11-1/2", 244 pgs, hard-c, mostly B&W)

	FR1.0	GD2.0	FN6.0
nn - (Scarce) by Joseph Keppler (S/N)	25.00	50.00	100.00

NOTE: *Reprints Keppler cartoons from 1877 to 1893, mostly in B&W, though a few in color, with a text opposite each cartoon explaining the situation then being satirized. Issued only in an edition of 300 numbered issues, signed by Keppler. Only 1/4 of the pages are cartoons.*

PUCK'S LIBRARY (M)
Keppler & Schwarzmann, New York: No.1, July, 1887 - No. 174, Dec, 1899 (10 cents, 11-1/2x8-1/4", 36 pgs, color paper-c, B&W)

	FR1.0	GD2.0	FN6.0
1- "The National Game" (Baseball)	25.00	50.00	100.00
2-149	7.50	15.00	30.00

NOTE: ***Puck's Library*** *was a monthly magazine reprinting cartoons & prose from* ***Puck****, with each issue's material organized around the same subject. The cover art was often original. All issues were kept in print for the duration of the series, so later issues are more scarce than earlier ones.*

PUCK'S OPPER BOOK (M)
Keppler & Schwarzmann, New York: 1888 (30 cents, color paper-c, B&W)

	FR1.0	GD2.0	FN6.0
nn - (Very Rare) by F. Opper	50.00	100.00	300.00

NOTE: *Solidly strip and cartoon material by Opper, all of it reprinted from* ***Puck****.*

PUCK, PICKINGS FROM (M)
Keppler & Schwarzmann, New York: No.1, Sept, 1891 - No. 34, Dec, 1899 (25 cents, 13-1/4x10-1/4", 68 pgs, color paper-c, B&W)

	FR1.0	GD2.0	FN6.0
1-34	15.00	30.00	60.00

NOTE: *Similar to* ***Puck's Library****, except larger in size, and issued quarterly. All reprint material, except for the cover art. There also exist variations with "RAILROAD EDITION 30 CENTS" printed on the cover in place of the standard 25 cent price.*

PUCK PROOFS (M,P,S)
Keppler & Schwarzmann, New York: nd (1906-1909) (76 pgs, paper cover; B&W) (all are Scarce)

	FR1.0	GD2.0	FN6.0
nn - (c.1906, no price, 4-1/8x5-1/4") B&W painted -c of couple kissing over a chess board; 1905 & 1906-r	25.00	50.00	100.00
nn- (c.1909, 10 cents, 4-3/8x5-3/8") plain green paper-c; 1905-1909-r	25.00	50.00	100.00

NOTE: *Catalog of prints available from* ***Puck****, reprinting mostly cover & centerspread art from* ***Puck****. There likely exist more as yet unreported* ***Puck Proofs*** *catalogs. Art by Rose O'Neill.*

PUCK, THE TARIFF ?, CARTOONS AND COMMENTS FROM (M,S)
Keppler & Schwarzmann, New York: 1888 (10 cents, 6-7/8x10-3/8", 36 pgs, paper-c, B&W)

	FR1.0	GD2.0	FN6.0
nn - (Scarce)	25.00	50.00	100.00

NOTE: *Reprints both cartoons and commentary from* ***Puck****, concerning the issue of tariffs which were then being debated in Congress. Art by Gillam, Keppler, Opper, Taylor.*

PUCK, WORLD'S FAIR
Keppler & Schwarzmann, PUCK BUILDING, World's Fair Grounds, Chicago: No.1 May 1, 1893 - No.26 Oct 30, 1893 (10 cents, 11-1/4x8-3/4, 14 pgs, paper-c, color front/back/center pages, rest B&W)(All issues Scarce to Rare)

	FR1.0	GD2.0	FN6.0
1-26	30.00	60.00	130.00
1-26 bound volume:	500.00	1100.00	2200.00

Rays of Light
1886 © Morse Bros., Canton, Mass.

Scraps, New Series #1 by D.C. Johnston
1849 © D.C. Johnston, Boston

Shakespeare Would Ride the Bicycle If Alive Today. "The Reasons Why" by Opper
1896 © H. A. Lozier & Co.

FR1.0 GD2.0 FN6.0

NOTE: *Art by Joseph Keppler, F. Opper, F.M. Howarth, C.J. Taylor, W.A. Rogers. This was a separate, parallel run of* ***Puck****, published during the 1893 Chicago World's Fair from within the fairgrounds, and containing all new and different material than the regular weekly* ***Puck****. Smaller sized and priced the same, this originally sold poorly, and had not as wide distribution as* ***Puck****, and so consequently issues are much more rare than regular* ***Puck*** *issues from the same period. Not to be confused with the larger sized regular* ***Puck*** *issues from 1893 which sometimes also contained World's Fair related material, and sometimes had the words "World's Fair" appear on the cover. Can also be distinguished by the fact that* ***Puck's*** *issue numbering was in the 800's in 1893, while these issue number 1 through 26.*

QUIDDITIES OF AN ALASKAN TRIP (O,G)
G.A. Steel & Co., Portland, OR: 1873 (6-3/4x10-1/2", 80 pgs, gilted blue hard-c, B&W)

nn - By William H. Bell (Very Rare) 350.00 750.00 1200.00
NOTE: *Highly sought Western Americana collectors. Parody of a trip from Washington DC to Alaska, by a member of the team which went to survey Alaska, purchase commonly known then as "Seward's Folly".*

RARE CARTOONS OF CANADIAN HISTORY (see Caricature History of Canadian Politics)

"RAG TAGS" AND THEIR ADVENTURES, THE (N,S)
A. M. Robertson, San Francisco: 1899 (color hard-c, B&W interiors)

nn - By Arthur M. Lewis (SF Chronicle newspaper-r) 60.00 120.00 240.00

RAYS OF LIGHT (O,P)
Morse Bros., Canton, Mass.: No.1 1886 (7-1/8x5-1/8", 8 pgs, color paper-c, B&W)

1- (Rare) 50.00 100.00 200.00
NOTE: *Giveaway pamphlet in guise of an educational publication, consisting entirely of a sequential story in which a teacher instructs her classroom of young girls in the use of Rising Sun Stove Polish. Color front & back covers.*

RELIC OF THE ITALIAN REVOLUTION OF 1849, A
Gabici's Music Stores, New Orleans: 1849 (10-1/8x12-3/4", 144 pgs, hardcover)

nn - By G. Daelli 100.00 200.00 400.00
NOTE: *From the title page: "Album of fifty line engravings, executed on copper, by the most eminent artists at Rome in 1849; secreted from the papal police after the 'Restoration of Order,' And just imported into America."*

REMARKS ON THE JACOBINIAD (I,S)
Unknown, Boston: 1795 (8-1/4x5-1/8", 72 pgs, a number of B&W plates with text)

nn - Written by Rev. James Sylvester Gardner, artist unknown (no known sales)
NOTE: *Early comics-type characters. Not sequential comics, but uses word balloons. Satire directed against "The Jacobin Club," supporters of the French Revolution and Radical Republicans. Gardner came to America from England in 1783, was minister of Trinity Church, Boston.*

REV. MR. SOURBALL'S EUROPEAN TOUR, THE RECREATION OF A CITY, THE
Duffield Ashmead, Philadelphia: 1867 (7-5/8x6-1/4", 72 pgs, turquoise blue soft wrappers)

By Horace Cope 35.00 70.00 140.00

RHYMES OF NONSENSE TRUTH & FICTION (S)
G.W. Carleton & Co, Publishers, NY: 1874 (10x7-3/4", 44 pgs, hard-c, B&W)

nn - By Chaucer Jones and Michael Angelo Raphael Smith 25.00 50.00 100.00
NOTE: *Creator names obviously pseudonyms; looks like weak A.B. Frost.*

ROMANCE OF A HAMMOCK, THE - AS RECITED BY MR. GUS WILLIAMS IN "ONE OF THE FINEST" (O,P)
Unknown: 1880s (5-1/2x3-5/8" folded, 7 attached cardboard cards which fold out into a strip, color)

nn - By presently unknown 25.00 50.00 100.00
NOTE: *12-panel story, which one begins reading on one side of the folded-out strip, then flip to the other side to continue -- unlike the vast majority of folded strips, which are printed on only one side. This was a promotional handout, for a play titled "One of the Finest". The story pictured comes from a poem read in the play by then famous New York stage actor Gus Williams, who is pictured on the "cover"/title card."*

SAD TALE OF THE COURTSHIP OF CHEVALIER SLYFOX-WIKOF, SHOWING HIS HEART-RENDING ASTOUNDING & MOST WONDERFUL LOVE ADVENTURES WITH FANNY ELSSLER AND MISS GAMBOL, THE (O,G)
Garrett & Co., NY: nd (c1852-55) (25 ¢, 5-3/4x9-1/4", 100 pages, paper-c, B&W)

nn - (Very Rare) By T.C. Bond ?? 300.00 600.00 900.00
NOTE: *No surviving copies yet reported -- known via ads. Cover art by John McLenan and Samuel Avery. Graphic novel parodying the real-life romance between European actress/dancer Fanny Elssler and American aristocrat Henry Wikoff. The entire graphic novel is reprinted in the 1976 book "Fanny Elssler in America."*

SAD TALE OF THE COURTSHIP OF CHEVALIER SLYFOX-WIKOF, SHOWING HIS HEART-RENDING ASTOUNDING & MOST WONDERFUL LOVE ADVENTURES WITH FANNY ELSSLER AND MISS GUMBEL, THE (G) (25 cents printed on cover)
Dick And Fitzgerald, NY: 1870s-1888 (5-3/4x9-1/4", ??? pages, soft paper-c, B&W)

nn - By T.C. Bond ?? 100.00 200.00 300.00
NOTE: *Reprint of Garrett original printing before G,D&F partnership begins.*

SCRAPS (O,S) (see also **F****** A*** K*******)
D.C. Johnston, Boston: 1828 - No.8 1840; New Series No.1 1849 (12 pgs, printed one side only, paper-c, B&W)

1 - 1828 (9-1/4 x 11-3/4") (Very Rare) (no known sales)
2 - 1830 (9-3/4 x 12-3/4") (Very Rare) (no known sales)
3 - 1832 (10-7/8 x 13-1/8") (Very Rare) (no known sales)
4 - 1833 (11 x 13-5/8") (Very Rare) (no known sales)
5- 1834 (10-3/8 x 13-3/8") (Very Rare) (no known sales)

FR1.0 GD2.0 FN6.0

6 - 1835 (10-3/8 x 13-1/4") red lettering in title SCRAPS (Very Rare)
200.00 400.00 880.00
6 - 1835 (10-3/8 x 13-1/4") no red lettering in title (Very Rare)
200.00 400.00 880.00
7 - 1837 (10-3/4 x 13-7/8") 1st Edition (Very Rare) 200.00 400.00 880.00
7 - 1837 (10-3/4 x 13-3/4") 2nd Edition (so stated) (Scarce) 75.00 125.00 275.00
NOTE: *20 pgs. of text (double-sided), 4 pgs. of art (single-sided), plus the covers. There are no protective sheets between the art pages.*
8 - 1840 (10-1/2 x 13-7/8") (Very Rare) 200.00 400.00 880.00
New Series 1- 1849 (10-7/8 x 13-3/4") (Scarce) 75.00 125.00 275.00
NOTE: *By David Claypool Johnston. All issues consist of four one-sided sheets with 9 to 12 single panel cartoons per sheet. The other pages are blank or text. Contains 4 protective sheets (not part of page count) Only the 1849 New Series Number 1 has cover art along with 4 art pgs. (single sided) with 4 protective sheets and no text pages.New Series Number 1, and the second printing of issue 7, have survived in higher numbers due to a 1940s warehouse discovery.*

SHAKESPEARE WOULD RIDE THE BICYCLE IF ALIVE TODAY. "THE REASON WHY" (O,P,S)
Cleveland Bicycles H.A. Lozier & Co., Toledo, OH: 1896 (5-1/2x4",16 pgs, paper-c, color)

nn - By F. Opper (Rare) 70.00 140 .00 280.00
NOTE: *Original cartoons of Shakespearian characters riding bicycles; also popular amongst collectors of bicycle ephemera.*

SHAKINGS - ETCHINGS FROM THE NAVAL ACADEMY BY A MEMBER OF THE CLASS OF '67 (O.S)
Unknown: 1867 (7-7/8x10", 132 pages, blue hard-c)

By: Park Benjamin 35.00 70.00 140.00
NOTE: *Park Benjamin later became editor of Harper's Bazaar magazine.*

SHYS AT SHAKESPEARE
J.P. and T.C.P., Philadelphia: 1869 (9-1/4x6", 52 pgs)

nn - Artist unknown 35.00 70.00 140.00

SKETCHES AND CARTOONS (see Gibson's Published Drawings)

SKETCHES OF LOWLY LIFE IN A GREAT CITY (M,S) (See 99 "Woolfs" From Truth)
G. P. Puntam's Sons: 1899 (8-5/8x11-1/4", 200 pgs, hard-c, B&W)
(reprints from Life and Judge of Woolf's cartoons of NYC slum children)

nn - By Michael Angelo Woolf 75.00 150.00 300.00
NOTE: *Woolf's cartoons are regarded as a primary influence on R.F. Outcault in the later development of The Yellow Kid newspaper strip.*

SLOVENLY PETER; or, Cheerful Stories and Funny Pictures, For Good Little People. (E,I)
Porter & Coates, Philadelphia: 1880 (4to, 100 pgs, handcolored hard-c)

nn - By Heinrich Hoffman 50.00 100.00 400.00
NOTE: *The John C. Winston Co. did a number of reprints from at least 1901-1940 which range in price from $95 to $350 plus The Limited Editions Club, New York, published 1500 copies of a Samuel ("Mark Twain") Clemons translated version done in 1891 in Berlin but not printed until 1935, ranges in price from $285 to $450.*

SOCIAL LADDER, THE (see Gibson's Published Drawings)

SOCIETY PICTURES (M,S,E)
Charles H. Sergel Company, Chicago: 1895 (5-1/4x7-3/4", 168 pgs, printed 1 side, paper-c, B&W)

nn - By George du Maurier; reprints from **Punch**. 12.50 25.00 50.00

SOUVENIR OF SOHMER CARTOONS FROM PUCK, JUDGE, AND FRANK LESLIE'S (M,S,P)
Sohmer Piano Co.: nd(c.1893) (6x4-3/4", 16 pgs, paper-c, B&W)

nn 20.00 40.00 80.00
NOTE: *Reprints painted "cartoon" Sohmer Piano advertisements which appeared in the above publications. Artists include Keppler, Gillam, others.*

SPICE OF LIFE, THE (E,M,)
White and Allen: 1888 NY & London: 1888 (8-3/8x10-1/2",76 pgs, hard-c, B&W)

nn 50.00 100.00 200.00
NOTE: *Resembles* ***THE GOOD THINGS OF LIFE*** *in layout and format, and appears to be an attempt to compete with their former partner Frederick A. Stokes. However, the material is not from* ***LIFE****, but rather is reprinted and translated German sequential and single panel comics.*

STORY OF THE MAN OF HUMANITY AND THE BULL CALF, THE
(see Bull Calf, The Story of The Man Of Humanity And The)
NOTE: *Reprints of two of A. B. Frost's mostfamous sequential comic strips.*

STUFF AND NONSENSE (Harper's Monthly strip-r) (M)
Charles Scribner's Sons: 1884 (10-1/4x7-3/4", 100 pgs, hardcover, B&W)

nn - By Arthur Burdett Frost 60.00 120.00 240.00
nn - By A.B. Frost (1888 reprint, 104 pgs) 40.00 80.00 160.00
NOTE: *Earliest known anthology devoted to collecting the comic strips of a single American artist.*

SUMMER SCHOOL OF PHILOSOPHY AT MT. DESERT, THE
Henry Holt & Co.: 1881 (10-3/8x8-5/8", 60 pgs, illus. gilt hard-c, B&W)

nn - By J. A. Mitchell 60.00 120.00 240.00

Stuff and Nonsense by A.B. Frost
1884 © Charles Scribner's Sons

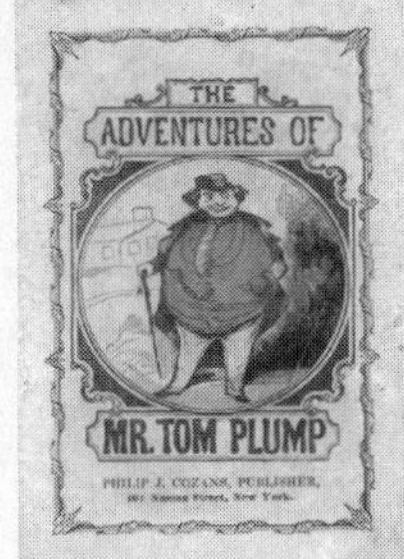
The Adventures of Mr. Tom Plump
1851 © Philip J. Cozans, New York

The Tooth-Ache by George Cruickshank
1849 © J. L. Smith, Philadelphia, PA

NOTE: *J.A.Mitchell went on to found **LIFE** two years later in 1883. Also, the long-running mascot for **LIFE** was Cupid - which you see multitudes of Cupids flying around in this story.*

TAILOR-MADE GIRL, HER FRIENDS, HER FASHIONS, AND HER FOLLIES, THE
(see also IN THE "400" AND OUT) (O,I)
Charles Scribner's Sons, New York: 1888 (8-3/8x10-1/2", 68 pgs, hard-c, B&W)

nn - Art by C.J. Taylor 17.50 35.00 70.00
NOTE: *Format is a full page cartoon on every other page, with a script style vignette, written by Philip H. Welch, on every page opposite the art.*

TALL STUDENT, THE
Roberts Brothers, Boston: 1873 (7x5", 48 pgs, printed one side only, gilted hard-c, B&W)

nn - By Wilhelm Busch (Scarce) 30.00 60.00 120.00

TARIFF ?, CARTOONS AND COMMENTS FROM PUCK, THE (see Puck, The Tariff...)

TEASING TOM AND NAUGHTY NED WITH A SPOOL OF CLARK'S COTTON, THE ADVENTURES OF (O,P)
Clark's O.N.T. Spool Cotton: nd (c1879-1880) (4-1/4x3", 12 pgs, B&W, paper-c)

nn 17.50 35.00 70.00
NOTE: *Knock-off of the "First Trick" in Wilhelm Busch's **Max and Maurice**, modified to involve Clark's Spool Cotton in the story, with similar but new art by an artist identified as "HB". The back cover advertises the specific merchant who gave this booklet away -- multiple variations of back cover suspected.*

TEMPERANCE TALES; OR, SIX NIGHTS WITH THE WASHINGTONIANS, VOL I & II
W.A. Leary & Co., Philadelphia: 1848 (50¢, 6-1/8x4", 328 pgs, B&W, hard-c)

nn (no known sales)
NOTE: *Mostly text. This edition gathers Volume I & II together. The first 8 pages reprints George Cruikshank's **THE BOTTLE**, re-drawn & re-engraved by Phil A. Pilliner. Later editions of this book do not include **THE BOTTLE** reprint and are therefore of little interest to comics collectors.*

THAT COMIC PRIMER (S)
G.W. Carleton & Co., Publishers: 1877 (6-5/8x5", 52 pgs, paper soft-c, B&W)

nn - By Frank Bellew Sr 35.00 70.00 140.00
NOTE: *Premium for the United States Life Insurance Company, New York.*

TOM PLUMP, THE ADVENTURES OF MR. (see also The Juvenile Gem) (O)
Huestis & Cozans, New York: nd (c1850-1851) (6x3-7/8", 12 pgs, hand colored paper-c, B&W)

nn- First printing(s) publisher's address is 104 Nassau Street (1850-1851)
(Very Rare) 200.00 400.00 700.00
NOTE: *California Gold Rush story. The hand colored outer cover is highly rare, with only 1 recorded copy possessing it. The front cover image and text is repeated precisely on page 3 (albeit b&w), and only interior pages are numbered, together leading owners of coverless copies to believe they have the cover. The true back cover contains ads for the publisher. The cover was issued only with copies which were sold separately - booklets which were bound together as part of **THE JUVENILE GEM** never had such covers.*

TOM PLUMP, THE ADVENTURES OF MR. (see also The Juvenile Gem) (O)
Philip J. Cozans: nd (1851-1852) (6x3-7/8", 12 pgs,hand colored paper-c, B&W)

nn- Second printing(s) publisher's address is 116 Nassau Street (1851-1852)
(Very Rare) 200.00 400.00 700.00
nn- Third printing(s) publisher's address is 107 Nassau Street (1852+)
(Very Rare) 200.00 400.00 700.00

TOM PLUMP, THE ADVENTURES OF MR.
Americana Review, Scotia, NY: nd(1960's) (6-1/4x4-1/8", 8 pgs, side-stapled, cardboard-c, B&W)

nn - Modern reprint - 12.00 24.00
NOTE: *Issued within a folder titled SIX CHILDREN'S BOOKS OF THE 1850'S. States "Reprinted by American Review" at bottom of front cover. Reprints the 104 Nassau Street address.*

TOM PLUMP, THE ADVENTURES OF MR.
Unknown: nd (1980's) (5-1/2x4-1/4", 8 pgs, side-stapled, black ink on colored paper)

nn - Modern reprint (Scarce) - 5.00 10.00
NOTE: *Photocopy reprint by a comix zine publisher, from an Americana Review copy, and available by mail order only.*

TOOTH-ACHE, THE (E,O)
D. Bogue, London: 1849 (???) --

nn - By Cruikshank, B&W (Very Rare) (no known sales)
nn - By Cruikshank, hand colored (Rare) (no known sales)
NOTE: *Scripted by Horace Mayhew, art by George Cruikshank. This is the British edition. Price 1/6 b&w, 3 hand colored. In British editions, the panels are not numbered. Publisher's name appears on cover. Booklet's "pages" unfold into a single, long, strip.*

TOOTH-ACHE, THE (E) (see also Almy's Santa Claus, and Home Picture Book for Little Children)
J.L. Smith, Philadelphia, PA: nd (1849) (15 cents, 5-1/8"x 3-3/4" folded, 86-7/8" wide unfolded, 26 pgs, cardboard-c, color)

nn - By Cruikshank, hand colored (Very Rare) (no known sales)
NOTE: *Reprints the D. Bogue edition. In American editions, the panels are numbered (43 panels, not counting front & back cover). Publisher's name stamped on inside front cover, plus printed along left-hand side of first interior page. Page 1 is pasted to inside back cover, and unfolds from there. Front cover not attached to back cover by design. Booklet's "pages" unfold into a single, long, strip (made from four individual strips pasted together on the blank back side).*

TOOTH-ACHE, THE (E)
Arts Council of Great Britain: nd (1974) (5-1/2x3-5/8", 28 pgs, B&W, cardboard-c, color interior)

nn - By Cruikshank, printed color - 15.00 30.00
NOTE: *Modern reprint of D. Bogue edition. 5000 copies printed, included in a catalogue issued with a show at the Victoria and Albert Museum, in London, 28 February-28 April 1974. Also included in the catalogue was a modern reprint of the Cruikshank booklet "A Comic Alphabet".*

TRUTH (See Platinum Age section for 1900-1906 issues)
Truth Company, NY: 1886-1906? (13-11/16x10-5/16", 16 pgs, process color-c & center-folds, rest B&W)

	FR1.0	GD2.0	FN6.0
1886-1887 issues	20.00	40.00	100.00
1888-1893 issues	15.00	30.00	80.00
1894-1895 non Outcault issues	10.00	20.00	55.00
Mar 10 1894 - precursor Yellow Kid RFO	50.00	150.00	330.00
#372 June 2 1894 - first app Yellow Kid RFO	150.00	450.00	1000.00
June 23 1894 - precursor Yellow Kid R. F. Outcault	50.00	150.00	330.00
July 14 1894 -2nd app Yellow Kid RFO	100.00	300.00	660.00
Sept 15 1894 - (2) 3rd app YK RFO plus YK precursor	100.00	300.00	660.00
Feb 9 1895 - 4th app Yellow Kid RFO	100.00	300.00	660.00
1896-1899 issues	10.00	20.00	55.00

NOTE: *This magazine contains the earliest known appearances of **The Yellow Kid** by Richard Felton Outcault. Feb 9 1895 issue's YK cartoon was reprinted one week later in the **New York World** Feb 17 1895 edition. We are still sorting out further Outcault appearances. Truth also contained full color sequential strips by Hy Mayer on the back plus Woolf, Verbeek, etc.*

TWO HUNDRED SKETCHES, HUMOROUS AND GROTESQUE, BY GUSTAVE DORE (E)
Frederick Warne & Co, London: 1867 (13-3/4x11-3/8, 94 pgs, hard-c, B&W)

	FR1.0	GD2.0	FN6.0
nn - (1867) by Gustave Dore	100.00	200.00	400.00
nn - (Second Edition; 1871)- by Gustave Dore	50.00	100.00	200.00
nn - (Third Edition; 1870's)- by Gustave Dore	50.00	100.00	200.00
nn - (Fourth Edition; 1870's- by Gustave Dore	50.00	100.00	200.00

NOTE: *Contains sequential comics stories, single panel cartoons, and sketches. Reprints and translates material which originally appeared in the French publications "Le Journal pour Rire", circa 1848-49. Although dated 1867, it was likely published & available for the 1866 Christmas Season, as has been confirmed for the American edition. Printed by Dalziel. The American & first British editions were printed simultaneously, the American edition is not a reprint of the British.*

TWO HUNDRED SKETCHES, HUMOROUS AND GROTESQUE, BY GUSTAVE DORE (E)
Roberts Brothers, Boston: 1867 (13-3/4x11-3/8", 96 pgs, hard-c, B&W)

nn - By Gustave Dore 100.00 200.00 400.00
NOTE: *Although dated 1867, it was published & available for the 1866 Christmas Season. Printed by Dalziel, in England, and imported to the USA expressly for a USA publisher.*

UNCLE BANTAM'S FUNNY BOOKS, FOR THE AMUSEMENT OF HIS LITTLE NEPHEWS AND NIECES. WITH SEVENTY-FIVE ILLUSTRATIONS. (I)
Davis Porter & Co., Philadelphia : 1865 (Quarto, 54 pgs, col. ill. ; pictorial paper covered boards) (See also Slovenly Peter)

nn - By Heinrich Hoffman 250.00 500.00 1000.00
NOTE: *Translation of "Der Struwwelpeter", first published in Germany in 1844. Hand-colored illustrations with lines of verse. This is a complete collection of six of the "Uncle Bantam's Funny Books" in one volume, each with 8 pgs.*

UNTIDY TOM & OTHER STORIES. (I)
Davis Porter & Co., Philadelphia: 1865 (8 pgs., color illustrations, 24 cm.)

nn - By Henrich Hoffman (no known sales)
NOTE: *Uncle Bantam's funny books for the amusement of his little nephews and nieces. Pub lisher's advertisement on back cover.(Contents: Untidy Tom -- Story of Johnny Look-in-the-Air -- Story of Augustus who would not have any soup -- Story of Little Suck-a-Thumb -- Story of Flying Robert.*

UPS AND DOWNS ON LAND AND WATER (O.G)
James R. Osgood & Co., Boston: 1871 ; **Houghton, Osgood & Co., Boston:** 1880 (108 pgs, gilted hard-c, B&W)

1st printing (1871; 10-3/4x16") - By Augustus Hoppin 45.00 90.00 180.00
2nd printing (1880; smaller sized) 32.50 65.00 130.00
NOTE: *Exists as blue or orange hard covers.*

VERY VERY FUNNY (M,S)
Dick & Fitzgerald, New York: nd(c1880's) (10¢, 7-1/2x5", 68 pgs, paper-c, B&W)

nn 22.50 45.00 90.00
NOTE: *Unauthorized reprints of prose and cartoons extracted from Puck, Texas Siftings, and other publications. Includes art by Chips Bellew, Bisbee, Graetz, Opper, Wales, Zim.*

WAR IN THE MIDST OF AMERICA. FROM A NEW POINT OF VIEW. (E,O,G)
Ackermann & Co., London: 1864 (4-3/8" x 5-7/8", folded, 36 feet wide unfolded, 80 pgs, hard-c, B&W)

nn- by Charles Dryden (rare) (no known sales)
NOTE: *British graphic novel about the American Civil War, with a pro-Confederate bent. Adventures of a British artist who decides to visually summarize the American Civil War for his countrymen, from newspaper accounts. Reaching current events, he finds he can not finish the story until the War ends, and so he travels to America, to end it. Book unfolds into a single long strip (binding was issued split, to enable the unfolding).*

WHAT I KNOW OF FARMING: Founded On The Experience of Horace Greeley (S)

Truth #372 (first app. The Yellow Kid)
June 2 1894 © Truth Company, NY

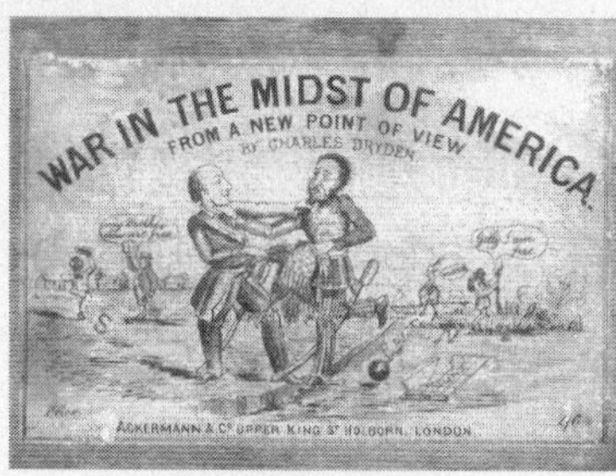

War in the Midst of America

Wild Oats Vol. XIV #181356
June 14, 1876 © Winchell & Small

FR1.0 GD2.0 FN6.0

The American News Company, New York: 1871 (7-1/4x4-1/2", paper-c, B&W)

nn - By Joseph Hull 35.00 70.00 140.00
NOTE: *Pay & Cox, Printers & Engravers, NY; political tract regarding Presidential elections.*

WIDOW AND HER FRIENDS, A (see Gibson's Published Drawings)

WILD OATS, An Illustrated Weekly Journal of Fun, Satire, Burlesque, and Nits at Persons and Events of the Day (O) (does anybody have any loose issues?)
Winchell & Small, 113 Fulton St /48 Ann St, NYC: Feb 1870-1881 (16-1/4x11", generally 16 pages, B&W, began as monthly, then bi-weekly, then weekly) (all loose issues scarce)

1-25 scarce, contents currently unknown (no known sales)
26 (3/14/72) Hopkins 16 panel sequential (no known sales)
27 (3/28/72) Worth 11 panel double pg sequential; Hopkins-c (no known sales)
28 (4/11/72) Avery double pg sequential; Howard-c (no known sales)
29 Worth-c; no sequential strips (no known sales)
30 Howard sequential "Physiology of Moving"; Hopkins-c (no known sales)
31 (5/23/72) beautiful Hopkins 28 panel sequential (no known sales)
32 (6/6/72) unknown sequential 12 panel (no known sales)
33 (6/20/72) Bellew; Bisbee-c (no known sales)
34 (7/4/72) two Hopikns sequential comic strips (no known sales)
35 (7/18/72) Worth sequential; Bellew-c (no known sales)
36 (8/1/72) Worth 10 panel baseball sequential; Worth-c (no known sales)
37 no sequentials (no known sales)
38 (8/29/72) Hopkins 20 panel sequential (no known sales)
39 Worth 13 panel horse racing sequential; Bellew-c (no known sales)
40 (9/26/72) Worth 12 panel sequential (no known sales)
41 (10/11/72) unknown 11 panel sequenial; F.R.-c (no known sales)
42 no sequenials (no known sales)
43 Worth 6 panel sequential; Worth-c (no known sales)
44 Worth 13 panel double page spread; F.J.-c (no known sales)
45 Bisbee 17 panel, Worth 11 panel double page; Bellew-c (no known sales)
46 Worth & Beard full pagers semi-sequential (no known sales)
47 Bisbee 12 panel, Hopkins 20 panel, Worth 3 panel sequentials; Worth-c (no known sales)
48 (1/16/73) Worth 13 panel sequential; first Woolf-c (no known sales)
49 (1/30/73) Worth 17 panel double page sequentials; Sears-c (no known sales)
50 (2/13/73) Bellew; Frenzeny-c (no known sales)
51 (Worth 18 panel double page spread, Woolf 9 panel (no known sales)
52 (3/13/73) no sequentials; Worth-c (no known sales)
53 (3/27/73) Worth 6 panel sequential; Worth-c (no known sales)
54 Beard double page spread (no known sales)
55 Hopkins 22 panel double page spread;unk 6 panel;Bellew-c (no known sales)
56, 59, 63 no sequentials (no known sales)
57 intense unknown 6 panel "Two Relics of Barbarism, or A Few Contrasted Pictures, Showing the origin of the North American Indian; Worth Hopkins single panel cartoons (no known sales)
58 (6/5/73) unknown 19 panel double pager "The Terrible Adventures of Messrs Buster & Stumps, About Exterminating the Indians" reads across both pages like Popeye #2095 (1933); Woolf-c (no known sales)
60 (7/3/73) Worth 17 panel "Life on Wall Street", unknown 13 panel job; Kappes first-c (no known sales)
61 (7/17/73) unknown 9 panel "Uncle Bumberton's 4th of July Visit to New York City";A.K.-c (no known sales)
62 (7/31/73) Worth 15 panel sequential' Woolf-c (no known sales)
64 unk. 6 panel, Worth 12 panel, Bisbee 6 panel sequentials (no known sales)
65 (9/4/73) two Worth 9 panel sequential comic strips titled "Only a Mad Dog Scare-Anothe Lesson for Nervous People" and "Only a Cholera Scare-Something for Nervous People to Read & Ponder Over" (no known sales)
66 (9/18/73) two Worth 10 panel "Hunting" & "Fishing"; unknown 6 panel;Hopkins 12 panel "Adv of Mr Old Portly with New Jersey Mosquitoes"; Beard-c (no known sales)
67 Shelton full pager;Worth 9 panel "Adv of Young Muttonhead Among the Free Lovers about "free sex" - convention in Chicago (no known sales)
68 (10/16/73) unknown 9 panel "Adv of New jersey Mosquito" looks like Winsor McCay type style: early inspiration for McCay's animated cartoon? (no known sales)
69 (10/30/73) unknown 6 panel; Bellew-c (no known sales)
70 unknown 6 panel; Hopkins 6 panel "Hopkins novel: A Tale of True Love, with all the variations"; Bellew-c (no known sales)
71 no sequentials; Woolf-c (no known sales)
72 (12/11/73) Worth 11 panel; Wales President Grant war-c (no known sales)
73 Hopkins 12 panel sequential comic strip (no known sales)
74 Hopkins 10 panel; Davenport comic like double page spread (no known sales)
75 (1/22/74) Hopkins 3 panel job; Hopkins first cover? (no known sales)
76 unknown 12 panel; Worth-c (no known sales)
77 unknown 7 panel; Worth-c (no known sales)
78 Bellew 5 panel double pager (no known sales)
79-105 (March 1874-Dec 1874) contents presently unknown (no known sales)
106 107 111 no sequentials; Bellew-c #106 110; Wales-c #107 (no known sales)
108 (1/20/75) Wales 12 panel double pg spread; Bellew-c (no known sales)
109 (1/27/75) unknown 6 panel; Wales-c (no known sales)
111 Busch 13 panel "The Conundrum of the Day - Is Lager Beer Intoxicating?"; Bellew-c (no known sales)
112 Wales 11 panel sequential comic strip (no known sales)
113 114 115 no sequentials Worth-c #114 (no known sales)
116 Wales 6 panel; Bellew full pager' Howard-c (no known sales)
117 intense Wales 6 panel "One of the Oppresions of the Civil Rights Laws"' Bellew-c (no known sales)
118-137 (3/31/75-8/4/75) no sequential comic strips (no known sales)
138 (8/18/75) both Bellew Sr & Bellew "Chips" Jr singles appear (no known sales)
139-143 145-147 154-157 159 no sequentials (no known sales)
144 (9/29/75) Hopkins 8 panel sequential; Wales-c (no known sales)
148 (10/27/75) Fred Opper's first cover; Opper singles (no known sales)
149 150 151 152 153 all Opper-c and much interior work (no known sales)
158 (1/5/76) Palmer Cox 1rst comic strip 24 panel double page spread "The Adv of Mr & Mrs Sprowl And Their Christmas Turkey - A Crashing Chasing Tearful Tragedy But Happily Ending Well"; Opper-c (no known sales)
159 160 162 167 Opper-c 165 Bellew-c no sequentials (no known sales)
161 Palmer Cox 11 panel sequential; unk 6 panel; Opper-c (no known sales)
163 (2/9/76) Palmer Cox 24 panel double pager (no known sales)
164 (2/16/76) Palmer Cox 12 panel double pager; Bellew-c (no known sales)
166 (3/1/76) Cox 12 panel sequential comic strip (no known sales)
168 (3/15/76) Palmer Cox 24 panel double page opus "Bachelor Boke & Widow Snugg: A Pictorial Account of Their Sleigh Ride And What Became of It" (no known sales)
169-173 no sequentials; Bellew-c #170 Opper-c #172 (no known sales)
174 (4/26/76) Cox 24 panel double pager "The Tramp's Progress; A Story of the West And the Union Pacific Railroad" (no known sales)
175-178 no sequentials; first Mann singles #170 (no known sales)
179 (5/31/76) Cox 3 panel "Story of a Collision"' Opper-c (no known sales)
180 (6/7/76) Beard & Opper work together; Woolf, Bellew singles (no known sales)
181 more Mann two panel jobs; Opper-c (no known sales)
182 (6/21/76) Cox 12 panel; Opper full page single; Opper-c (no known sales)
183-189 no sequentials (no known sales)
190 (8/16/76) Bellew 9 panel "Rodger's Patent Mosquito Armour" (no known sales)
191-end contents to be indexed by next year (no known sales)
NOTE: *There are no known loose issues. All issues are scarce. We present this index from the Library of Congress bound set. We would love to hear from any one who turns up loose copies. This scarce humor bi-weekly contains easily a couple hundred original first-time published sequential comic strips found in most issues plus innumerable single panel cartoons in every issue; distributed thru New York News Company, 8 Spruce St, NYC. Began as a monthly, at some point early on it became almost always bi-weekly (ie twice a month) till it died. Livingston Y. Hopkins, Thomas Worth, W.M. Avery, C.J. Howard, Frank Beard, Frank Bellew Sr & Jr, E.S. Bisbee, Michael Angelo Woolf, E. Sears, Paul Frenzeny, W.H. Shelton, Jae A. Wales, Kappes, Wilhelm Busch, Fredrick Opper and Palmer Cox are some of the cartoonists who graced its pages. Most of these cartoonists were doing sequentials and most likely interacting with each other as cartoonists were wont to do. Some cartoons carry double by-lines proving they were jamming together. Currently there is just one bound almost complete run (missing v1-2 (Feb 1870-Mar 1872, 7-8 (Mar 1874-Dec 1874) known to exist to the authors located at The Library of Congress. Any help locating further issues would be immensely appreciated. Please contact the authors of the Victorian & Platinum sections: Robert Beerbohm and Richard Olson whose e-mail addresses are at the end of each history essay.*

WOMAN IN SEARCH OF HER RIGHTS, THE ADVENTURES OF (G)
Lee & Shepard, Boston And New York: early 1850s (8-3/8x13", 40 pgs, hard-c)

By Florence Claxton (scarce) 300.00 600.00 900.00
NOTE: *Earliest known original comic book sequential story by a woman; contains "nearly 100 original drawings by the author, which have been reproduced in fac-simile by the graphotype process of engraving." Tinted two color lithography; orange tint printed first, thenprinted 2nd time with black ink; early women's sufferage.*

WORLD OVER, THE (I)
G. W. Dillingham Company, New York: 1897 (192 pgs, hardbound)

nn - By Joe Kerr; 80 illustrations by R.F. Outcault 30.00 90.00 300.00

WRECK-ELECTIONS OF BUSY LIFE (S)
Kellogg & Bulkeley: 1864? (9-1/4x11-3/4", ??? pages, soft-c)

nn - By J. Bowler 45.00 90.00 200.00
NOTE: *Says "Sold by American News Company, New York" on cover.*

YE VERACIOUS CHRONICLE OF GRUFF & POMPEY IN 7 TABLEAUX. (O,P)
Jackson's Best Chewing Tobacco & Donaldson Brothers: nd (c1870's) (5-1/8 tall x 3-3/8" wide folded, 27" wide unfolded, color cardboard)

nn - With all 8 panels attached (Scarce) 40.00 80.00 160.00
nn - Individual panels/cards 6.00 12.00 24.00
NOTE: *Black Americana interest. Consists of 8 attached cards, printed on one side, which unfold into a strip story of title card & 7 panels. Scrapbook hobbyists in the 19th Century tended to pull the panels apart and paste into their scrapbooks, making copies with all panels attached scarce.*

Read the introduction essays to learn more about the 160+ year history and origins of comics in America. For regular on-line discussions, go to:
PlatinumAgeComics@yahoogroups.com

The American Comic Book: 1883-1938

A Concise History Of The Field As Of 2005

A MULTITUDE OF VARIED FORMATS FIGHT IT OUT IN THE MARKETPLACE

by Robert L. Beerbohm and Richard D. Olson, PhD ©2005

(This article series was originally created by Robert L. Beerbohm and Richard D. Olson beginning in OCBPG #27 1997 and is revised annually as new information comes to light.)

The story of the success of the modern comic strip as we know it today is tied closely to the companies who sponsored them and bought licenses from the copyright holder for the purpose of advertising products. What mainly keeps the Platinum Age from being collected as much as later era comics is simply a general lack of awareness of these important historical books as well as the scarcity of many of these volumes, especially in any type of higher-grade condition. Many Platinum Age books are much rarer than so-called Golden Age comic books, yet despite this scarcity, **Mutt & Jeff**, **Bringing Up Father**, **The Katzenjammer Kids**, and many more were as popular, if not more so, than **Superman** and **Batman** when they were introduced. Recent research has come up with some more amazing rediscoveries. There is much that can be learned and applied to today's comics market by a simple historical examination of the medium's evolution over more than 160 years.

It should be noted that "ages" are applied to historical periods in the history of comics for convenience. In fact, ages typically overlap and there is no discrete beginning or ending for any given "age." This is the case with the Platinum Age, which clearly began with Palmer Cox's creation of The Brownies in 1883 even though it overlaps with the Victorian Age which ran through the end of the 19th Century. Cox introduced a qualitative change to the field, not an incremental quantitative change. Specifically he produced art and verse for children in children's magazines and then merchandised those characters. He published work for children not only in books but in magazines and newspapers, and he merchandised his creations to an extent that had never been done previously.

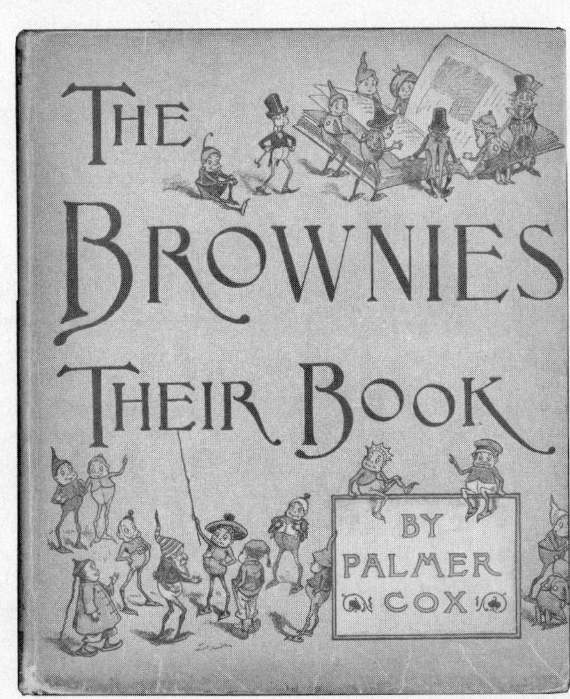

The Brownies' first book by Palmer Cox (from 1887) set the precedent for the Platinum Age by collecting and reprinting previously published material.

Palmer Cox was born in 1840 near Granby, Quebec. He journeyed to Oakland, California in 1863, and began publishing cartoon, prose and poems in the local press and media outlets such as **The San Francisco Examiner** wherein by 1867 it has been reported he also began creating sequential comic strips.

His first book, **Squibs of California,** was published in 1874. He subsequently moved to New York in 1875 and almost immediately began working for the magazine **Wild Oats**, of which more is written about in the preceding Victorian Age history introduction. He drew dozens of sequential comic strips for **Wild Oats**, a humor magazine so scarce no single copies have been offered on eBay yet in the past five years. And we're still dilegently looking.

Soon thereafter he became a major contributor to the Scribner publications, including **The St. Nicholas**, an illustrated magazine for young folk. His first cartoon for them was "The Wasp And The Bee," published in the March 1879 cover-date issue. While it is now clear that Cox used elves and brownie-like characters in his art for several different magazines as early as 1877 in **Harper's Young People** magazine as well as using Brownies-type characters beginning in the Feb

1881 issue of **Wide Awake**, the first true appearance of the Brownies in their own story using that title, a combination of art and verse was February, 1883, in **St. Nicholas.** Palmer Cox's **The Brownies** were the first North American comics-type characters to be internationally merchandised. Even though Cox was continuously doing sequential comic strips in magazines like **Wild Oats**, he left the medium of comics when he hit paydirt with The Brownies. For over a quarter of a century, Cox deftly combined the popular advertising motifs of animals and fairies into a wonderful, whimsical world of society at its best and worst.

The Brownies' first book was issued in 1887, titled **The Brownies: Their Book**; many more followed. Cox also added a run of his hugely popular characters in **Ladies Home Journal** from October 1891 through February 1895, as well as a special for December 1910. With the 1892-93 World's Fair, the merchandising exploded with a host of products, including pianos, paper dolls and other figurines, chairs, stoves, puzzles, cough drops, coffee, soap, boots, candy, and many more. **Brownies** material was being produced in Europe as well as the United States of America.

Cox tried out **The Brownies** as a newspaper strip in the **San Francisco Examiner** during 1898, where he had begun his newspaper career over 30 years before, and then in the **New York World** in 1900. It was syndicated from 1903 through 1907. He seems to have retired from regularly drawing **The Brownies** with the January 1914 issue of **St. Nicholas** when he was 74. A wealthy man, he lived to the ripe old age of 84, spending his last decade in his home he affectionately called Brownie Castle, back in Granby, Quebec.

By the mid-1890s, while keeping careful track of quickly rising circulations of magazines with graphic humor such as **Harper's**, **Puck**, **St. Nicholas**, **Judge**, **Life** and **Truth**, New York based newspaper publishers began to recognize that illustrated humor would sell extra papers. Thus was born the Sunday "comic supplement." Most of the regular favorites were under contract with these magazines. However, there was an artist working for **Truth** who wasn't. Roy L McCardell, then a staffer at **Puck**, informed Morrill Goddard, Sunday editor of **The New York World**, that he knew someone who could fit what was needed at the then-largest newspaper in America.

Richard F. Outcault (1863-1928) first introduced his street children strip in **Truth** #372, June 2, 1894, somewhat inspired by Michael Angelo Woolf's slum kids single panel cartoons in **Life** which had begun in the mid 1880s. The interested collector should seek out a copy of Woolf's **Sketches of Lowly Life In A Great City** (1899) listed in the Guide. It's also possible that Outcault's **Hogan's Alley** cast, including the Yellow Kid, was inspired by Charles W. Saalburg's **The Ting Ling Kids,** which began in the **Chicago Inter-Ocean** by May 1894. By 1895, Saalburg was Art Director in charge of coloring for the new color printing press at the **New York World**. Edward Harrigan's play "O'Reilly and the Four Hundred," which had a song beginning with the words "Down in Hogan's Alley..." likely provided direct inspiration.

By the November 18, 1894 issue of the **World**, Outcault was working for Goddard and Saalburg. Outcault produced a successful Sunday newspaper sequential comic strip in color with "The Origin of a New Species" on the back page in the World's first colored Sunday supplement. Long time pro Walt McDougall, a famous cartoonist reputed to have turned the 1884 Presidential race with a single cartoon that ran in the **World**, handled the cartoon art on the front page. Earlier, **The World** began running full page color single panels on May 21, 1893. McDougall did various other page panels during

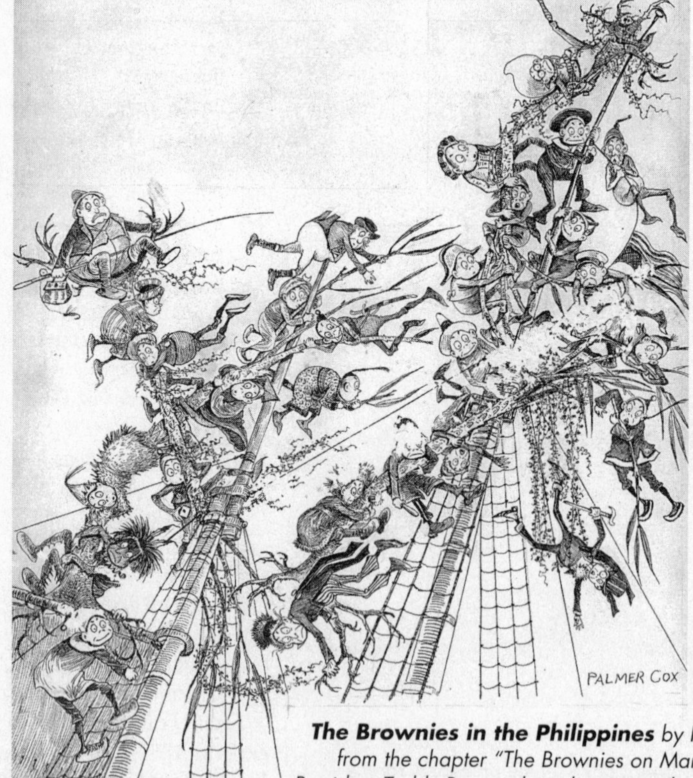

The Brownies in the Philippines *by Palmer Cox - scarce original artwork from the chapter "The Brownies on Marinduque," page 142, Oct 1904. President Teddy Roosevelt is also pictured within these multitudes of Brownie madness which was a Cox "signature trademark." His stories are comic strip-oriented in nature of time sequence as he boldly took his Brownies around the world.*

1893, but it was Jan. 28, 1894 when the first sequence of comic pictures in a newspaper appeared in panels in the same format as our comic strips today. It was a full page cut up into nine panels. This historic sequence was drawn entirely in pantomime, with no words, by Mark Fenderson.

The second page to appear in panels was an eight panel strip from February 4, 1894, also lacking words except for the title. This page was a collaboration between Walt McDougall and Mark Fenderson titled "The Unfortunate Fate of a Well-Intentioned Dog." From then on, many full page color strips by McDougall and Fenderson appeared; they were the first cartoonists to draw for the Sunday newspaper comic section. It was Outcault, however, who soon became the most famous cartoonist featured. After first appearing in black and white in Pulitzer's **The New York World** on February 17, 1895 and again on March 10, 1895, **The Yellow Kid** was introduced to the public in color on May 5, 1895.

Some have erroneously reported in scholarly journals that perhaps it was Frank Ladendorf's "Uncle Reuben," first introduced May 26, 1895, which became the first regularly recurring comics character in newspapers. This is wrong, as even Outcault's "Yellow Kid" began in Pulitzer's paper a good three months before **Uncle Reuben**. Until firm evidence to the contrary comes to light, that honor will forever be enshrined with Jimmy Swinnerton's **Little Bears** cartoon characters, found all over inside Hearst's **San Francisco Examiner** as early as 1892. Though never actually a comic strip, they nonetheless were the earliest presently known recurring comics characters in American newspapers. There never was a strip titled **Little Bears and Tigers**, as the Tigers portion was strictly for New York consumption when Hearst ordered Swinnerton to move to the Big Apple to compete better in the brewing comic strip wars.

The Yellow Kid's importance is widely recognized today as the first newspaper comic strip to demonstrate without a doubt that the general public was ready for full color comics. **The Yellow Kid** was the first in the USA to show that (1), comics could increase newspaper sales, and that (2), comic characters could be merchandised. **The Yellow Kid** was the headlining spark of what was soon dubbed by Hearst as "eight pages of polychromatic effulgence that makes the rainbow look like a lead pipe."

Ongoing research suggests that Palmer Cox's fabulous success with **The Brownies** was a direct inspiration for Richard Outcault's future merchandising work. The ultimate proof lies in the fourth Yellow Kid cartoon, which appeared in the February 9, 1895 issue of **Truth**. It was reprinted in the **New York World** eight days later on February 17, 1895,

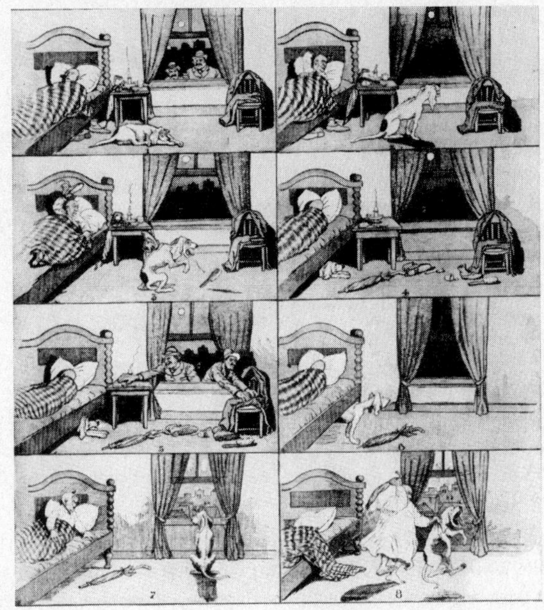

ORIGIN OF A NEW SPECIES, OR—
THE EVOLUTION OF THE CROCODILE EXPLAINED.

*Top: **Walt McDougall & Mark Fenderson**, the second American newspaper sequential comic strip, **New York World**, February 4, 1894, predates **Yellow Kid** in **The World** by over a year. Mark Fenderson drew the first real newspaper comic strip and we are still hunting down an example to display in future editions. Bottom: **New York World**, Nov. 18, 1894 predates YK "Origin of A New Species," Richard F. Outcault.*

R F Outcault
A FAIR CHAMPION.
LORREENA LAFFERTY (as a parting shot)—Remember dis, Issy Silberman may be a motzer. But de day will come when as a millionaire banker, an' me his bride, de dust his carriage wheels makes t'roo Forsythe street will not be able den to blind youz to his good qualities.

"A Fair Champion" artwork by Richard F. Outcault, ***Truth****, July 14 1894 (2nd Yellow Kid app.) Many of RFO's comics were fully integrated down around the corner of Hogan's Alley and Ryan's Arcade*

"Fourth Ward Brownies," artwork by Richard F. Outcault, Feb. 17, 1895, the 4th Yellow Kid app. and 1st in Pulitzer's ***New York World****. Note the Kid, second from left. This panel first saw print in* ***Truth****, Feb 9, 1895.*

becoming the first Yellow Kid cartoon in the newspapers. The caption read "FOURTH WARD BROWNIES. MICKEY, THE ARTIST (adding a finishing touch) Dere, Chimmy! If Palmer Cox wuz t' see yer, he'd git yer copyrighted in a minute." The Yellow Kid was widely licensed in the greater New York area for all kinds of products, including gum and cigarette cards, toys, pinbacks, cookies, postcards, tobacco products, and appliances. There was also a short-lived humor magazine from Street & Smith named **The Yellow Kid**, featuring exquisite Outcault covers, plus a 196-page comic book from Dillingham & Co. known as **The Yellow Kid in McFadden's Flats**, dated to early 1897. In addition, there were several Yellow Kid plays produced, spawning other collectibles like show posters, programs and illustrated sheet music. (For those interested in more information regarding the Yellow Kid, it is available on the Internet at www.neponset.com/yellowkid.)

Mickey Dugan burned brightly for a few years as Outcault secured a copyright on the character with the United States Government by Sept. 1896. By the time he completed the necessary paperwork, however, hundreds of business people nationwide had pirated the image of The Yellow Kid and plas-

Left: ***The Yellow Kid*** *#1, March 20, 1897, Street & Smith as Howard Ainslee, NY cover by Richard F. Outcault; lasted six issues with RFO YK covers. Right:* ***Yellow Kids On Parade*** *1897 part of Gilmore & Leonard's Hogan's Alley Company; one of at least half a dozen Yellow Kid productions performed with collectible sheet music generated.*

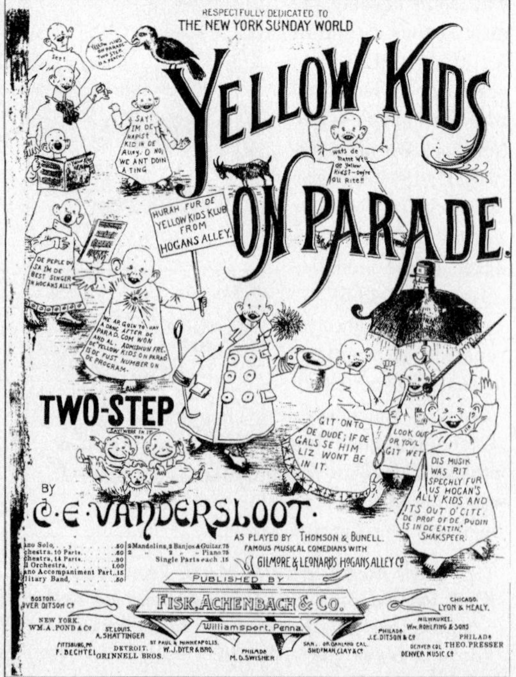

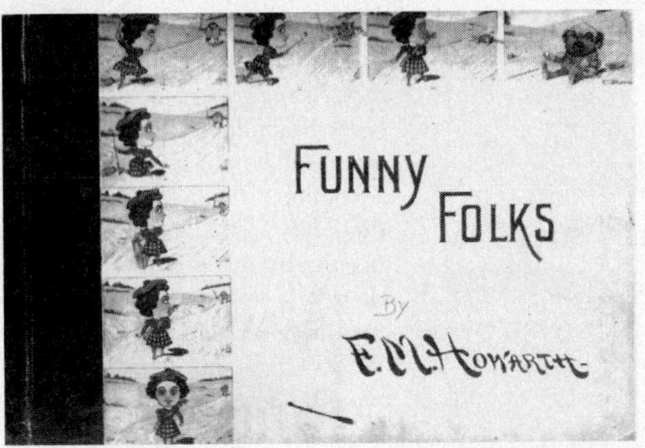

***Funny Folks**, F. M. Howarth, 1899, collected many early sequential comics from Puck; one of the titles many consider bridges the Victorian & Platinum Ages of comics.*

***The Adventures of Foxy Grandpa**, late 1900, newly re-discovered cover for the earliest known first edition of Carl "Bunny" Schultze's famous creation. He was one of the newspaper comics' first superstars.*

tered it all over every product imaginable; mothers were even dressing their newborns to look like Dugan. (Outcault, however, kept regularly utilizing images of **The Yellow Kid** in his comics style advertising work confirmed as late as 1915.) Outcault soon found himself in a maelstrom not of his choosing, which probably pushed him to eventually drop the character. Outcault's creation went back and forth between newspaper giants Pulitzer and Hearst until Bennett's New York Herald mercifully snatched the cartoonist away in 1900 to do what amounted to a few relatively short-run strips. Later, he did one particular strip for a year–a satire of rural Black America titled **Pore Li'l Mose**, and then his newer creation, **Buster Brown**, debuted May 4, 1902. Mose had a very rare comic book collection published in 1902 by Cupples & Leon, now highly sought after by today's savvy collectors. Outcault continued drawing him in the background of occasional **Buster Brown** strips for many years to come.

William Randolph Hearst loved the comic strip medium ever since he was a little boy growing up on **Max & Moritz** by Wilhelm Busch in American collected book editions translated from the original German (these collections were first published in book form in 1871, serving as the influence for **The Katzenjammer Kids**). One of the ways Hearst responded to losing Outcault in 1900 was by purchasing the highly successful 23-year-old humor magazine **Puck** from the heirs of founder Joseph Keppler. With **Puck** and its exclusive cartoonist contracts, he commanded, among others, the very popular F. M. Howarth and Frederick Burr Opper's undivided attention. Opper had first burst upon the comics scene in America back in 1880. Within a year Hearst had expanded this **National Lampoon** of its day into the colored Sunday comics section, **Puck-The Comic Weekly**. At first featuring Rudolph Dirk's **The Katzenjammer Kids** (1897), **Happy Hooligan** and other fine strips by the wildly popular Opper and a few others including Rudolph's brother Gus Dirks, the Hearst comic section steadily added more strips. For decades to come, there wasn't anything else that could compete with **Puck**. Hearst hired the best of the best and transformed **Puck** into the most popular comics section anywhere.

Outcault, meanwhile, followed in Palmer Cox's footprints a decade later by using the nexus of a World's Fair as a jumping off venue. **Buster Brown** was an instant sensation when he debuted as the new merchandising mascot of the Brown Shoe Company at the 1904 St. Louis World's Fair in a special Buster Brown Shoes pavilion. The character has the honor of being the first nationally licensed comic strip character in America. Many hundreds of different **Buster Brown** premiums have been issued. Comic books by Frederick A. Stokes Company featuring **Buster Brown & His Dog Tige** began as early as 1903 with **Buster Brown and His Resolutions**, simultaneously published in several different languages throughout the world.

After a few years, Buster and Outcault returned to Hearst in late 1905, joining what soon became the flagship of the comics world. Buster's popularity quickly spread all over the United States and then the world as he single-handedly spawned the first great comics licensing dynasty. For years, there were little people traveling from town to town performing as **Buster Brown** and selling shoes while accompanied by small dogs named Tige. Many other highly competitive licensed strips would soon follow. We suggest getting **Hake's Price Guide to Character Toys** for information on several hundred **Buster Brown** competitors, as well as several pages of the more fascinating **Buster Brown** material.

Soon there were many comic strip syndicates not only offering hundreds of various comic strips but also offering to license the characters for any company interested in paying the fee. The history of the comic strip with wide popularity

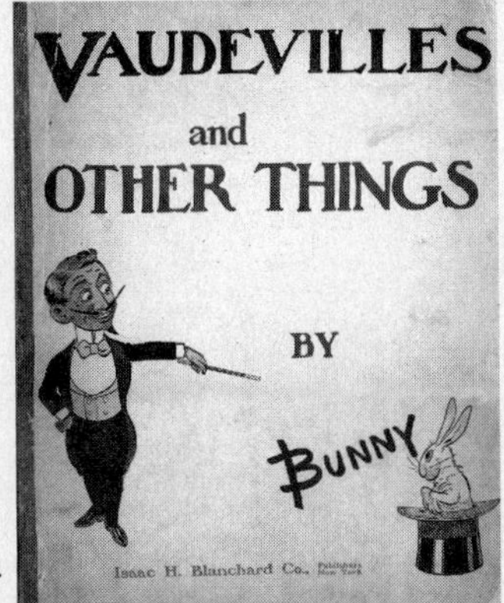

***Vaudevilles And Other Things**, 1900, first printing. Carl Schultze became famous creating **Foxy Grandpa**.*

HUGO HERCULES MISSES THE FOOTBALL, BUT—

*Beginning in late 1902, **The Chicago Tribune** introduced a straight super hero with obvious super strength called "Hugo Hercules" by the unknown artist J. Koerner. This Sunday strip ran until early 1903 and ran only in this one paper. It is entirely possible a very young Chicago-resident named Philip Wylie read "Hugo" since that was the same name he gave his super-heroic main character in his much-later book **The Gladiator** (1930). Other appearances have Hugo running with almost super speed.*

since **The Yellow Kid** has been intertwined with giveaway premiums and character-based, store-bought merchandise of all kinds. Since its infancy as a profitable art form unto itself with **The Yellow Kid**, the comic strip world has profited from selling all sorts of "stuff" to the public featuring their favorite character or strip as its motif. American business gladly responded to the desire for comic character memorabilia with thousands of fun items to enjoy and collect. Most of the early comics were not aimed specifically at kids, though children understandably enjoyed them as well.

Comic books have generally been associated with almost all of the licensed merchandise in this century. In the Platinum Age section beginning right after this essay, you will find a great many comic books in varied formats and sizes published before the advent of the first successful monthly newsstand comic magazine, **Famous Funnies**. What drove each of these evolutionary format changes was the need by their producers to make money so more books could be issued.

A very significant format was F. M. Howarth's **Funny Folks**, published in 1899 by E. P. Dutton and drawn from color as well as black and white pages of **Puck**. This rather large hardcover volume measured 16 1/2" wide by 12" tall. It contains numerous sequential comic strip pages as well as single gag illustrations. Howarth's art was a joy to behold and deserves wider recognition.

By Oct. 1900, Hearst had already caused Opper's **Folks In Funnyville** to be collected by publisher R. H. Russell, NY in a 12x9 hard cover format from his **New York Journal American Humorist** section. At the end of 1900, Carl Shultze had a first edition of **Vaudevilles and Other Things**

***Katzenjammer Kids** #1, 1902,*
by Rudolph Dirks was inspired by Wilhelm Busch.

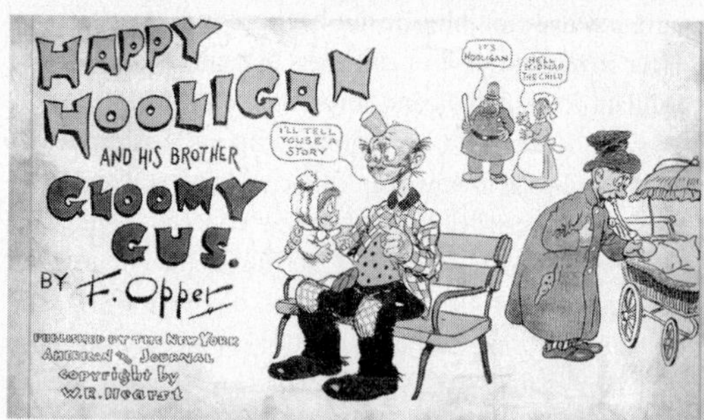

***Happy Hooligan Book** #1, 1902,*
by Frederick Opper, was wildly popular.

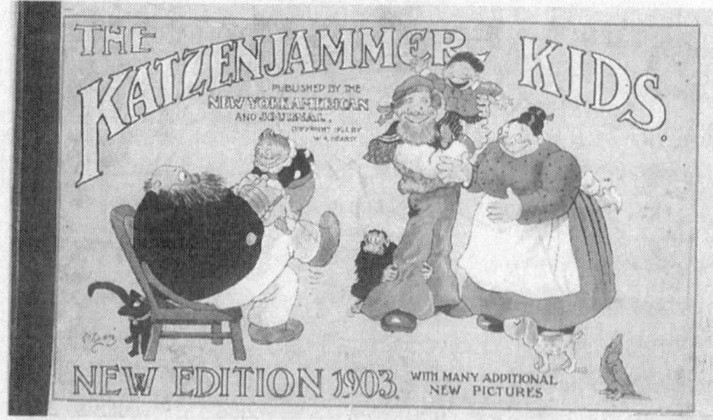

***Katzenjammer Kids** #2 by Rudolph Dirks. These*
Katz Kids have the longest running strip in America.

*The second **Happy Hooligan** comic book,*
1903, by Frederick Opper set a high standard.

Originally discovered listed for sale in a 1906 Lockwood Art School brochure, the existences of ***The Naughty Adventures of Vivacious Mr. Jack*** *and* ***Alphonse and Gaston New Edition 1903*** *were recently verified. So far only one copy of each is known to exist. We ask collectors who might have one of these to contact the authors.*

published by Isaac H. Blanchard Co., NY. It measures 10 1/2" wide by 13" tall with 22 pages including covers. Each interior page is a 2 to 7 panel comic strip with lots of color.

There were also recently unearthed format variation second and third printings of **Vaudevilles** with the inscription "From the Originator of the 'Foxy Grandpa' Series" at the bottom of its front cover of the third printing. This note is lacking on the earlier first two editions, and it also switches format size to 11" tall by 13" wide. Discovered last year was a heretofore undocumented **The Adventures of Foxy Grandpa** - also issued in 1900 - new to the Platinum listings. The second number dated 1901 drops the words "The Adventures of..." from the title.

E. W. Kemble's **The Blackberries** had a color collection by 1901, also published by R. H. Russell, NY, as well as a few other comic-related volumes by Kemble still to be unearthed and properly identified. An earlier one was titled **Coontown's 400** (1899) newly listed this year. While the title is definitely not "PC" by today's standards, Kemble's drawings are excellent slices of African-American life in the USA with some humor injected. Kemble did a good job documenting aspects of life.

Confirmed is the exact format of Hearst's 1902 **The Katzenjammer Kids** and **Happy Hooligan And His Brother Gloomy Gus**. They both measure 15 5/16" wide by 10" tall and contain 88 pages including covers. Confirmed also is the fact that there are two separate editions with different covers for the pictured 1902 first edition and a 1903 Frederick Stokes edition of **Katzenjammer Kids** and **Happy Hooligan** with differing contents. They both are two different books entirely, and what confuses many collectors is that they have identical indicia title pages, as does an entirely different **KK** from 1905.

Settling on a popular size of 17" wide by 11" tall, comic books were soon available that featured Charles "Bunny" Schultze's **Foxy Grandpa**, Rudolph Dirk's **The Katzenjammer Kids**, Winsor McCay's **Little Sammy Sneeze**, **Rarebit Fiend** and **Little Nemo**, and Fred Opper's **Happy Hooligan** and **Maud**, in addition to dozens of **Buster Brown** comic books. For well over a decade, these large-size, full-color volumes were the norm, retailing for 60¢. These collections offered full-size Sunday comics with the back side blank per page.

The very rare **Brainy Bowers and Drowsy Dugan** by R. W. Taylor is now crowned the first collection of strip reprints from daily newspapers published in America. There are now four different collections of Brainy Bower known to exist.

The Outbursts of Everett True by A. D. Condo and J. W. Raper was first published by Saalfield in 1907 in a 88-page hardcover collection. It qualifies as the second daily comic strip collection as it predates the first **Mutt & Jeff** collection from Ball by three years. Condo & Raper's creation began its regular run several times a week in 1905 daily newspapers and lasted until 1927, when Condo became too sick to continue. This same **Everett True** collection was later truncated a bit by Saalfield in

Little Sammy Sneeze*, 1905, by Winsor McCay is his best looking.*

The Three FunMakers*, 1908, the first anthology Platinum Age comic book.*

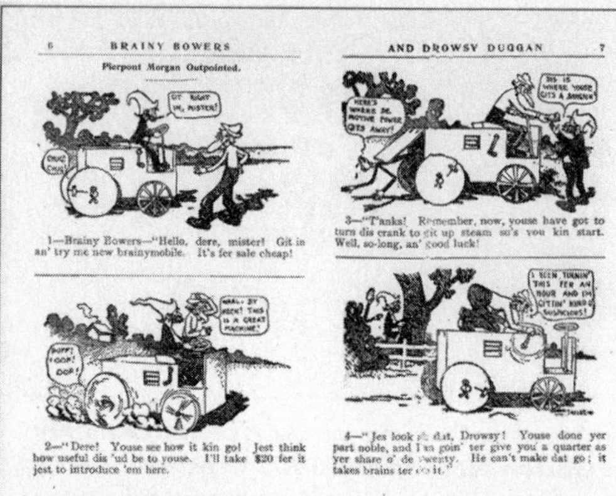

Brainy Bowers *appears to be the earliest known daily strip compilation; sample comic strip, 1905.*

1921 to 56 strips in just 32 pages measuring the standard 10"x10" Cupples & Leon size.

By 1908 Stokes had a large backlist of full color comic books for sale at 60¢ each. Some of these titles date back to 1903 and were reprinted over and over as demand warranted. Note the number of titles in the advertisement pulled from the back of **The Three Fun Makers** shown below.

With the ever-increasing popularity of Bud Fisher's new daily strip sensation, **Mutt & Jeff**, a new format was created for reprinting daily strips in black and white, a hardcover book about 15" wide by 5" tall, published by Ball starting in 1910 for five volumes. In 1912, Ball also branched out with at least the now-obscure **Doings of the Van Loons** by Fred I. Leipziger, a rare comic book in the same format as the **Mutt & Jeffs.**

Cartoons Magazine also began in 1912 and ran through 1921 before undergoing a radical format change. It is notable as a wonderful source for information on early comics and their creators. See also the Platinum index.

The next significant evolutionary change occurred in 1919, when Cupples & Leon began issuing their black and white daily strip reprint books in a new aforementioned format, about 10" wide by 10" tall, with four panels reprinted per page in a two by two matrix. These books were 52 pages for 25¢. The first ones featured **Bringing Up Father** and **Mutt & Jeff**; there were about 100 others.

By 1921, the last of the oblong (11"x15") color comic books were issued, with Cupples & Leon's **Jimmie Dugan** and **The Reg'lar Fellers** by Gene Byrne and EmBee's **The Trouble Of Bringing Up Father** by self publisher George McManus. Of special historical interest, Embee issued the first 10¢ monthly comic book, **Comic Monthly**, with a first issue dated January 1922. A dozen 8-1/2"x9" issues were published, each featuring solo adventures of popular King Features strips. The monthly 10¢ comic book concept had finally arrived, though it would be more than a decade before it became truly successful.

Skippy by Percy Crosby debuted in the long-running humor magazine **Life** in the March 22, 1923 issue. By 1924 the first hard cover collection, **Life Presents Skippy,** was published. The newspaper comic strip debuted June 23, 1925 with the McClure syndicate. Hearst soon picked up a

CIRCULATION

"America's Circulation Wow"

SKIPPY!

A New Sunday Comic Page in Colors by PERCY CROSBY

The most lovable kid comic page ever drawn

KING FEATURES SYNDICATE

Circulation *V5 #26 May 1926. The second Skippy solicitation ad from Hearst to sell this well-known strip by Percy L. Crosby to newspapers around the world via his King Feature Syndicate.*

Left, ***The Outbursts of Everett True****. This is the second daily strip collection, published 1907; reprinted in the '20s in the then-modern 10x10 format. Right: The earliest known display ad for comic books, found in the back of several 1908 Stokes comic books, with 27 titles then in print. Note cover prices are 60¢ for 80 pages of four color fun!*

Sunday page a year later in mid-1926, then added a daily strip in 1929. By the 1930s it was red hot - think **Calvin & Hobbes** or **Peanuts** in popularity. In its day, it was one of the most popular comic strips ever created. Read the Modern era essay for more on **Skippy**'s immense popularity.

Above, ***Mutt & Jeff*** *#5 by Bud Fisher, 1916, is fairly scarce as there was only one printing. Below,* ***Regular Fellers*** *by Gene Byrne, 1921, one of the very last large oblong comics.*

In 1926, Cupples & Leon added a new 7" wide by 9" tall format with **Little Orphan Annie**, **Smitty**, and others. These were issued in both softcover and hardcover editions with dust jackets, and became extremely popular at 60¢ per copy.

Dell began publishing all original material in **The Funnies** in late 1929 in a larger tabloid format. At least three dozen issues were published before Delacorte threw in the towel. Even the extremely popular **Big Little Book**, introduced in 1932, can be viewed as a smaller version of the existing formats. The competition amongst publishers now included Dell, McKay, Sonnet, Saalfield and Whitman. The 1930s saw a definite shift in merchandising comic strip material from adults to children. This was the decade when Kellogg's placed **Buck Rogers** on the map, and when Ovaltine issued tons of **Little Orphan Annie** material. Merchandising from such pioneers as Sam Gold and Kay Kamen spearheaded this next re-transformation of the comics biz beginning in the early 1930s.

Upwards of a thousand of these **Funnies On Parade** precursors, in all formats, were published through 1935 and were very popular. Towards the end of this era of once-popular comic book formats, beautiful collections of **Popeye**, **Mickey Mouse**, **Dick Tracy**, and many others were published which today command ever higher prices on the open market as they are rediscovered by the advanced collector who appreciates and enjoys truly great classic comics.

END NOTE: We are continuing to add many of the 1930s variant formats such as the **Little Lulu** series by Marjorie Henderson Buell reprinted from her **Saturday Evening Post** run. Each year, this Platinum Age section has grown as advanced collectors continue to report in with new finds. We encourage interested collectors and scholars to help with this section of the book, as each new data entry is very important for recovering our history.

For corrections and additions to next year's Guide of some treasures you may have uncovered, please feel free to contact Robert at this e-mail address, **robert@blbcomics.com,**
or Richard at **redoak1@netdoor.com**

For further information on this era of American comic books, read Robert L. Beerbohm's "The American Comic Book 1897-1932," originally printed in the 27th edition of **The Overstreet Comic Book Price Guide** and now available online at www.gemstonepub.com. Also see evolving comics history essays in Guides #29-#34.

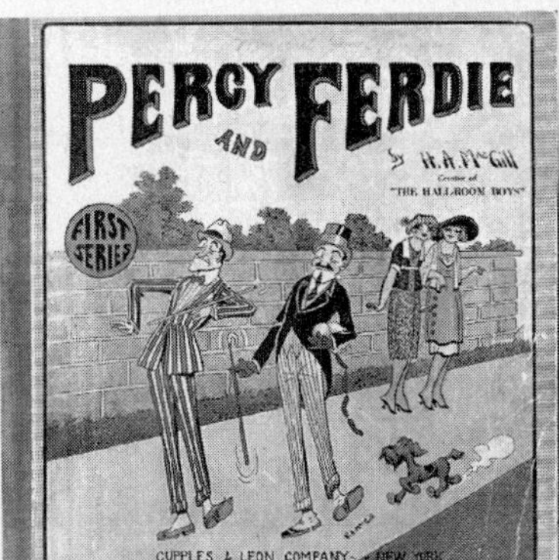

A 1921 example of Cupples & Leon's revolutionary new format.

Comic Monthly *#8 (top), #11 (bottom) 1922 the first 10¢ monthly newsstand comic book title.*

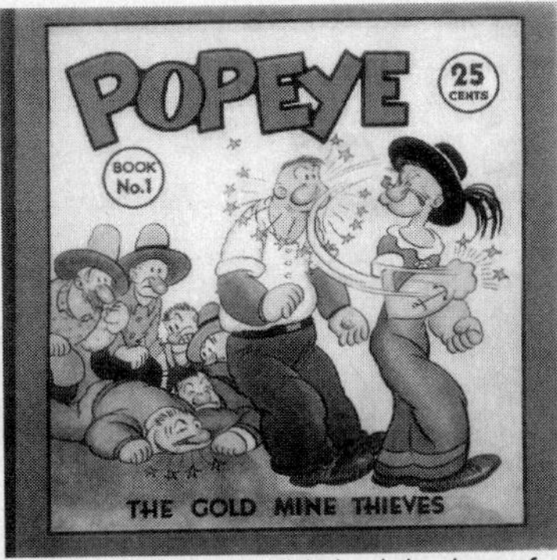

David McKay published the last of the 10x10 comic books in 1935 as ***Famous Funnies*** *grew.*

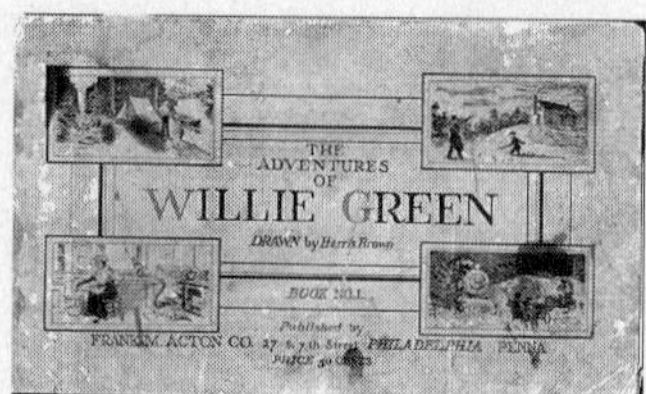

The Adventures of Willie Green
© Frank M. Acton

Alphonse and Gaston by Opper
1902 © Hearst's NY American & Journal

Banana Oil by Milt Gross
1924 © M.S. Publishing Company

GD2.0 FN6.0 VF8.0

COLLECTOR'S NOTE: The books listed in this section were published many decades before organized comics fandom began archiving and helping to preserve these fragile popular culture artifacts. Consequently, copies of most all of these comics do not often surface in Fine+ or better shape. eBay is proving that many items once considered rare actually are not, though they are in higher grades. Most Platinum Age comic books are in the Fair to VG range. If you want to collect these only in high grade, your collection will be extremely small. The prices given for Good, Fine and Very Fine categories are for strictly graded editions. If you need help grading your item, we refer you to the grading section in the front of book or contact the authors of the Platinum essay. Items marked scarce we are trying to ascertain how many copies might still be in existence. Your input is always welcome.

For ease of ascertaining the contents of each item of this listing, there is a code letter or two following most titles. A helpful list of categories pertaining to these codes can be found at the beginning of the Victorian Age pricing. Most measurements are in inches. A few measurements are in centimeters. The first dimension given is Height and the second is Width. This section created, revised, and expanded by Robert Beerbohm with Doug Wheeler & Richard Olson and able assistance from Ray Agricola, Bill Blackbeard, Roy Bonario, Ray Bottorff Jr., Chris Brown, Alfredo Castelli, Darrell Coons, Sol Davidson, Leonardo De Sá, Scott Deschaine, Mitchell Duval, Joe Evans, Tom Gordon, Bruce Hamilton, Andy Konkykru, Don Kurtz, Gabriel Laderman, Bruce Mason, Donald Puff, Robert Quesinberry, Steve Rowe, Randy Scott, John Snyder, Art Spiegelman, Steve Thompson, Joan Crosby Tibbets, Richard Samuel West, Richard Wright and Craig Yoe.

ADVENTURES OF EVA, PORA AND TED (M)
Evaporated Milk Association: 1932 (5x15", 16 pgs, B&W)

nn - By Steve 10.00 30.00 65.00
NOTE: *Appears to have had green, blue or white paper cover versions.*

ADVENTURES OF HAWKSHAW (N) (See Hawkshaw The Detective)
The Saalfield Publishing Co.: 1917 (9-3/4x13-1/2", 48 pgs., color & two-tone)

nn - By Gus Mager (only 24 pgs. of strips, reverse of each pg. is blank) 30.00 150.00 260.00
nn - 1927 Reprints 1917 issue 30.00 150.00 260.00
NOTE: *Started Feb 23, 1913-Sept 4, 1922, then begins again Dec 13, 1931-Feb 11, 1952.*

ADVENTURES OF SLIM AND SPUD, THE (M)
Prairie Farmer Publ. Co.: 1924 (3-3/4x 9-3/4", 104 pgs., B&W strip reprints)

nn 21.00 84.00 150.00
NOTE: *Illustrated mailing envelope exists postmarked out of Chicago, add 50%.*

ADVENTURES OF WILLIE WINTERS, THE (O,P)
Kelloggs Toasted Corn Flake Co.: 1912 (6-7/8x9-1/2", 20 pgs, full color)

nn - By Byron Williams & Dearborn Melvill 54.00 189.00 325.00

ADVENTURES OF WILLIE GREEN, THE (N) (see The Willie Green Comics)
Frank M. Acton Co.: 1915 (50¢, 52 pgs, 8-1/2X16", B&W, soft-c)

Book 1 - By Harris Brown; strip-r 54.00 189.00 325.00

A. E. F. IN CARTOONS BY WALLY, THE (N)
Don Sowers & Co.: 1933 (12x10-1/8", 88 pgs, hardcover B&W)

nn - By Wally Wallgren (WW One Stars & Stripes-r) 20.00 80.00 120.00

AFTER THE TOWN GOES DRY (I)
The Howell Publishing Co, Chicago: 1919 (48 pgs, 6-1/2x4", hardbound two color-c)

nn - By Henry C. Taylor; illus by Frank King 20.00 70.00 140.00

AIN'T IT A GRAND & GLORIOUS FEELING? (N) (Also see Mr. & Mrs.)
Whitman Publishing Co.: 1922 (9x9-3/4", 52 pgs., stiff cardboard-c)

nn - 1921 daily strip-r; B&W, color-c; Briggs-a 36.00 143.00 250.00
nn -(9x9-1/2", 28pgs., stiff cardboard-c)-Sunday strip-r in color (inside front-c says "More of the Married Life of Mr. & Mrs".) 36.00 143.00 250.00
NOTE: *Strip started in 1917; This is the 2nd Whitman comic book, after Brigg's MR. & MRS.*

ALL THE FUNNY FOLKS (I)
World Press Today, Inc.: 1926 (11-1/2x8-1/2", 112 pgs., color, hard-c)

nn-Barney Google, Spark Plug, Jiggs & Maggie, Tillie The Toiler, Happy Hooligan, Hans & Fritz, Toots & Casper, etc. 100.00 400.00 700.00
With Dust Jacket By Louis Biedermann 150.00 630.00 1260.00
NOTE: *Booklength race horse story masterfully enveloping all major King Features characters.*

ALPHONSE AND GASTON AND THEIR FRIEND LEON (N)
Hearst's New York American & Journal: 1902,1903 (10x15-1/4", Sunday strip reprints in color)

nn - (1902) - By Frederick Opper (scarce) 400.00 1400.00 -
nn - (1903) - By Frederick Opper (scarce) 400.00 1400.00 -
NOTE: *Strip ran Sept 22, 1901to at least July 17, 1904.*

ALWAYS BELITTLIN' (see Skippy; That Rookie From the 13th Squad; Between Shots)
Henry Holt & Co.: 1927 (6x8", hard-c with DJ,

nn -By Percy Crosby (text with cartoons) 43.00 172.00 300.00

ALWAYS BELITTLIN' (I) (see Skippy; That Rookie From the 13th Squad, Between Shots)
Percy Crosby, Publisher: 1933 (14 1/4 x 11", 72 pgs, hard-c, B&W)

nn - By Percy Crosby 43.00 172.00 300.00
NOTE: *Self-published; primarily political cartoons with text pages denouncing prohibition's gang warfare effects and cuts in the national defense budget as Crosby saw war looming in Europe and with Japan.*

GD2.0 FN6.0 VF8.0

AMERICAN-JOURNAL-EXAMINER JOKE BOOK SPECIAL SUPPLEMENT (O)
New York American: 1911-12 (12 x 9 3/4", 16 pgs) (known issues) (Very Rare)

1 Tom Powers Joke Book(12/10/11) 80.00 280.00 -
2 Mutt & Jeff Joke Book (Bud Fisher 12/17/11) 100.00 350.00 -
3 TAD's Joke Book (Thomas Dorgan 12/24/11) 80.00 280.00 -
4 F. Opper's Joke Book (Frederick Burr Opper 12/31/11) (contains Happy Hooligan) 100.00 350.00 -
5 not known to exist
6 Swinnerton's Joke Book (Jimmy Swinnerton 01/14/12) (contains Mr. Jack) 100.00 350.00 -
7 The Monkey's Joke Book (Gus Mager 01/21/12) (contains Sherlocko the Monk) 100.00 350.00 -
8 Joys And Glooms Joke Book (T. E. Powers 01/28/12) 80.00 280.00 -
9 The Dingbat Family's Joke Book (George Herriman 02/04/12) (contains early Krazy Kat & Ignatz) 200.00 700.00 -
10 Valentine Joke Book, A (Opper, Howarth, Mager, T. E. Powers 02/11/12) 80.00 280.00 -
11 Little Hatchet Joke Book (T. E. Powers 02/18/12) 80.00 280.00 -
12 Jungle Joke Book (Rudolph Dirks 02/25/12) 100.00 350.00 -
13 The Hayseeds Joke Book (03/03/12) 80.00 280.00 -
14 Married Life Joke Book (T.E. Powers 03/10/12) 80.00 280.00 -
NOTE: *These were insert newspaper supplements similar to Eisner's later Spirit sections. A Valentine Joke Book recently surfaced from Hearst's Boston Sunday American proving that other cities besides New York City had these special supplements. Each issue also contains work by other cartoonists besides the cover featured creator and those already listed above such as Sidney Smith, Winsor McCay, Hy Mayer, Grace Weiderseim (later Drayton), others.*

AMERICA'S BLACK & WHITE BOOK 100 Pictured Reasons Why We Are At War (N,S)
Cupples & Leon: 1917 (10 3/4 x 8", 216 pgs)

nn - W. A. Rogers (New York Herald-r) 32.00 114.00 195.00

AMONG THE FOLKS IN HISTORY
Rand McNally Print Guild: 1935 (192 pgs, 8-1/2x9-1/2", hard-c, B&W)

nn - By Gaar Williams 21.00 84.00 150.00

AMONG THE FOLKS IN HISTORY
The Book and Print Guild: 1935 (200 pgs, 8-1/2x9-1/2:,

nn - By Gaar Williams 21.00 84.00 150.00
NOTE: *Both the above are evidently different editions and contain largely full-page, single panel cartoons similar to Briggs' work of that sort. 8 or 10 pages are broken into panels, usually with a this is how it was in the old days, this is how it is today theme.*

ANGELIC ANGELINA (N)
Cupples & Leon Company: 1909 (11-1/2x17", 56 pgs., 2 colors)

nn - By Munson Paddock 67.00 233.00 400.00
NOTE: *Strip ran March 22, 1908-Feb 7, 1909.*

ANDY GUMP, HIS LIFE STORY (I)
The Reilly & Lee Co, Chicago: 1924 (192 pgs, hardbound)

nn - By Sidney Smith (over 100 illustrations) 20.00 80.00 140.00

ANIMAL CIRCUS, THE (from Puggery Wee)
Rand McNally + Company: 1908 (48 pgs, 11x8-1/2", color-c, 3-color insides)

nn - By unknown 20.00 80.00 140.00
NOTE: *Illustrated verse, many pages with multiple illustrations.*

ANIMAL SERIALS
T. Y. Crowell: 1906 (9x6-7/8", 214 pgs, hard-c, B&W)

nn - By E Warde Balisdell 20.00 80.00 140.00
NOTE: *Multi-page comic strip stories.*

A NOBODY'S SCRAP BOOK
Frederik A. Stokes Co., New York: 1900 (11" x 8-5/8", hard-c, color)

nn- (Scarce) 67.00 233.00 400.00
NOTE: *Designed in England, printed in Holland, on English paper -- which likely explains the mispelling of Frederick Stokes' name. Highly fragile paper. Strips and cartoons, all by the same unidentified artist, "A Nobody", almost certainly reprinted from somewhere, as they are very professional.*

AT THE BOTTOM OF THE LADDER (M)
J.P. Lippincott Company: 1926 (11x8-1/4", 296 pgs, hardcover, B&W)

nn - By Camillus Kessler 45.00 157.50 300.00
NOTE: *Hilarious single panel cartoons showing first jobs of then important "captains of industry."*

AUTO FUN, PICTURES AND COMMENTS FROM "LIFE"
Thomas Y. Crowell & Co.: 1905 (148 pgs, 9x7", hard-c, B&W)

nn -By various 45.00 157.00 300.00
NOTE: *The cover just has "Auto Fun" but the title page also has the subheading listed here. This is similar to other reprint books of Life cartoons printed in the guide. Largely single panel cartoons but also several sequential. One or more cartoons by Kemble, Levering, Dirks, Flagg, Sullivant. Sequential cartoons by Kemble, Levering, Sullivant, and the highpoint, a 2 pg 6 panel piece by Winsor McCay.*

BANANA OIL (N)
MS Publ. Co.: 1924 (9-7/8x10", 52 pgs., B&W)

nn - Milt Gross-a; not reprints 75.00 250.00 450.00

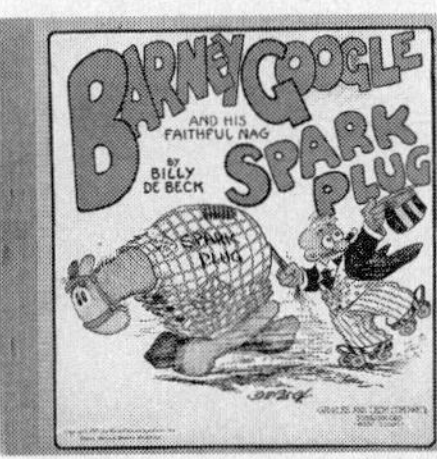
Barney Google and Spark Plug #1
© C&L

Bill the Boy Artist's Book by Ed Payne
1910 © C.M. Clark Publishing Co

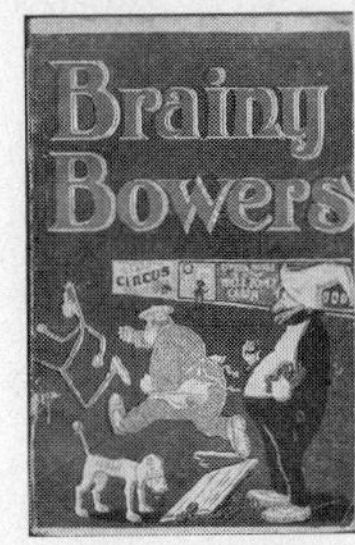
Brainy Bowers and Drowsy Duggan by R.W. Taylor
1905 © Star Publishing Co. - the first daily reprints

	GD2.0	FN6.0	VF8.0

BARKER'S ILLUSTRATED ALMANAC (O,P,S) (See Barkers in Victorian Era section)
Barker, Moore & Mein Medicine Co: 1900-1932+ (36 pgs, B&W, color paper-c)

1900-1932+ (7x5-7/8")	10.00	30.00	60.00

BARKER'S "KOMIC" PICTURE SOUVENIR (P,S) (see Barker's in Victorian)
Barker, Moore & Mein Medicine Co: nd (Parts 1-3, 1901-1903; Parts 1-4, 1906+) (color cardboard-c, B&W interior, 50 pages)

Parts 1-3 (Rare, earliest printing, nd (1901))	60.00	130.00	265.00

NOTE: *Same cover as 4th edition in Victorian Age Section, except has "Part 1", "Part 2", or "Part 3" printed in the blank space beneath the crate on which central figure is sitting. States "Edition in 3 Parts" on the first interior page, beneath the picture of the Barker's Building.*

Parts 1-3 (nd, c1901-1903)	30.00	60.00	135.00

NOTE: *New cover art on all Parts. States "Edition in 3 Parts" on the first interior page.*

Parts 1-4 (nd, c1906+)	25.00	50.00	85.00

NOTE: *States "Edition in 4 Parts" on the first interior page. Various printings known. These have been confirmed as premium comic books, predating the Buster Brown premiums. They reprint advertising cartoons from Barker's Illustrated Almanac. For the 50 page booklets by this same name, numbered as "Part"s, without exception, were published after 1900. Some editions are found to have 54 pages.*

BARNEY GOOGLE AND SPARK PLUG (N) (See **Comic Monthly**)
Cupples & Leon Co.: 1923 - No.6, 1928 (9-7/8x9-3/4"; 52 pgs., B&W, daily-r)

1 (nn)-By Billy DeBeck	57.00	229.00	400.00
2-4 (#5 & #6 do not exist)	46.00	186.00	325.00

NOTE: *Started June 17, 1919 as newspaper strip; Spark Plug introduced July 17, 1922; strip still running making it one of the oldest still in existence.*

BART'S CARTOONS FOR 1902 FROM THE MINNEAPOLIS JOURNAL (N,S)
Minneapolis Journal: 1903 (11x9", 102 pgs, paperback, B&W)

nn - By Charles L. Bartholomew	28.00	99.00	170.00

BELIEVE IT OR NOT! by Ripley (N,S)
Simon & Schuster: 1929 (8x 5-1/4", 68 pgs, red, B&W cover, B&W interior)

nn - By Robert Ripley (strip-r text & art)	40.00	120.00	240.00

NOTE: *1929 was the first printing of many reprintings . Strip began Dec 19, 1918 and is still running.*

BEN WEBSTER (N)
Standard Printing Company: 1928-1931 (13-3/4x4-7/16", 768 pgs, soft-c)

1 - "Bound to Win"	40.00	120.00	240.00
2 - "...in old Mexico	40.00	120.00	240.00
3 - "...At Wilderness Lake	40.00	120.00	240.00
4 - "...in the Oil Fields	40.00	120.00	240.00

NOTE: *Self Published by Edwin Alger, also contains fan's letter pages.*

BIG SMOKER
W.T. Blackwell & Co.: 1908 (16 pgs, 5-1/2x3-1/2", color-c & interior)

nn - By unknown	12.00	48.00	80.00

NOTE: *Stated reprint of 1878 version. no known copies of original printing.*

BILLY BOUNCE (I)
Donohue & Co.: 1906 (288 pgs, hardbound)

nn - By W.W. Denslow & Dudley Bragdon	150.00	525.00	900.00

NOTE: *Billy Bounce was created in 1901 as a comic strip by W. W. Denslow (strip ran from 1901 NOV 11 to 1905 DEC 3), but the series is best remembered in the C. W. Kahles version (from 1902 SEP 28). Denslow resumed his character in the above illustrated book.*

BILLY HON'S FAMOUS CARTOON BOOK (H)
Wasley Publishing Co.: 1927 (7-1/2x10", 68 pgs, softbound wraparound)

nn - By Billy Hon	12.00	48.00	80.00

BILLY THE BOY ARTIST'S BOOK OF FUNNY PICTURES (N)
C.M.Clark Publishing Co.: 1910 (9x12", hardcover-c, Boston Globe strip-r)

nn - By Ed Payne	79.00	316.00	550.00

NOTE: *This long lived strip ran in* ***The Boston Globe*** *from Nov 5 1899-Jan 7 1955; one of the longer run strips.*

BILLY THE BOY ARTIST'S PAINTING BOOK OF FUNNY PICTURES

(known to exist; more data required)	-	-	-

BIRD CENTER CARTOONS: A Chronicle of Social Happenings (N,S)
A. C. McClurg & Co.: 1904 (12-3/8x9-1/2", 216 pgs, hardcover, B&W)

nn - By John McCutcheon	40.00	140.00	240.00

NOTE: *Strip began in* ***The Chicago Tribune*** *in 1903. Satirical cartoons and text concerning a mythical town.*

BLASTS FROM THE RAM'S HORN
The Rams Horn Company: 1902 (330 pgs, 7x9", B&W)

nn - By various	20.00	70.00	120.00

NOTE: *Cartoons reprinted from what was, apparently, a religious newspaper. Many cartoons by Frank Beard. Mostly single panel but occasionally sequential. Allegorical cartoons similar to the Christian Cartoons book. This book mixes cartoons and text sort of like the Caricature books. One or more cartoons on every page.*

BOBBY THATCHER & TREASURE CAVE (N)
Altemus Co.: 1932 (9x7", 86 pgs., B&W, hard-c)

nn - Reprints; Storm-a	54.00	189.00	325.00

BOBBY THATCHER'S ROMANCE (N)
The Bell Syndicate/Henry Altemus Co.: 1931 (8-3/4x7", color cover, B&W)

nn - By Storm	54.00	189.00	325.00

BOOK OF CARTOONS, A (M,S)
Edward T. Miller: 1903 (12-1/4x9-1/4", 120 pgs, hardcover, B&W)

nn - By Harry J. Westerman (Ohio State Journal-r)	20.00	70.00	120.00

BOTTLE, THE (E) (see Victorian Age section for earlier printings)
Gowans & Gray, London & Glasgow: June 1905 (3-3/4x6", 72 pgs, printed one side only, paper cover, B&W)

nn - 1st printing (June 1905)	17.50	35.00	70.00
nn - 2nd printing (March 1906)	17.50	35.00	70.00
nn - 3rd printing (January 1911)	17.50	35.00	70.00

NOTE: *By George Cruikshank. Reprints both THE BOTTLE and THE DRUNKARD'S CHILDREN. Cover is text only - no cover art.*

BOTTLE, THE (E)
Frederick A. Stokes: nd (c1906) (3-3/4x6", 72 pgs, printed one side only, paper-c, B&W)

nn- by George Cruikshank	17.50	35.00	70.00

NOTE: *Reprint of the Gowans & Gray edition. Reprints both THE BOTTLE and THE DRUNKARD'S CHILDREN. Cover is text only - no cover art.*

BOYS AND FOLKS (N).
George H. Dornan Company: 1917 (10-1/4 x 8-1/4", 232 pgs. (single-sided), B&W strip-r.

nn - By Webster	21.00	64.00	150.00

NOTE: *Four sections: Life's Darkest Moments, Mostly About Folks, The Thrill That Comes Once in a Lifetime, and Our Boyhood Ambitions. Most are single-panel cartoons, but there are some sequential comic strips.*

BOY'S & GIRLS' BIG PAINTING BOOK OF INTERESTING COMIC PICTURES (N)
M. A. Donohue & Co.: 1914-16 (9x15, 70 pgs)

nn - By Carl "Bunny" Schultze (Foxy Grandpa-r)	81.00	284.00	-
#2 (1914)	81.00	284.00	-
#337 (1914) (sez "Big Painting & Drawing Book")	81.00	284.00	-
nn - (1916) (sez "Big Painting Book")(9-1/4x15")	81.00	284.00	-

NOTE: *These are all* ***Foxy Grandpa*** *items.*

BRAIN LEAKS: Dialogues of Mutt & Flea (N)
O. K. Printing Co. (Rochester Evening Times): 1911 (76 pgs, 6-5/8x4-5/8, hard-c, B&W)

nn - By Leo Edward O'Melia; newspaper strip-r	29.00	100.00	171.00

BRAINY BOWERS AND DROWSY DUGGAN (N)
Star Publishing: 1905 (7-1/4 x 4-9/16", 98 pgs., blue, brown & white color cover, B&W interior, 25¢) (daily strip-r 1902-04 Chicago Daily News)

#74 - By R. W. Taylor (Scarce)	400.00	1200.00	-

NOTE: *Part of a series of Atlantic Library Heart Series. Strip begins in 1901 and runs thru 1906. Taylor also created Yen the janitor for the* ***Chicago Daily News.***

BRAIN BOWERS AND DROWSY DUGAN (N)
Max Stein Pub. House, Chicago: 1905 (6-3/16x4-3/8", 64 pgs, B&W)

nn - By R.W. Taylor (Scarce)	400.00	1200.00	-

NOTE: *A coverless copy of this surfaced on eBay in 2002 selling for $700.00.;*

BRAINY BOWERS AND DROWSY DUGGAN GETTING ON IN THE WORLD WITH NO VISIBLE MEANS OF SUPPORT (STORIES TOLD IN PICTURES TO MAKE THEIR TELLING SHORT) (N)
Max Stein/Star Publishing: 1905 (7-3/8x5 1/8", 164 pgs, slick black, red & tan color cover, interior newsprint) (daily strip-r 1902-04 Chicago Daily News)

nn - By R. W. Taylor (Scarce)	400.00	1200.00	-
nn - Possible hard cover edition also?	-	-	-

NOTE: *These Brainy Bowers editions are the earliest known daily newspaper strip reprint books.*

BRINGING UP FATHER (N)
Star Co. (King Features): 1917 (5-1/2x16-1/2", 100 pgs., B&W, cardboard-c)

nn - (Scarcer)-Daily strip- by George McManus	158.00	553.00	950.00

BRINGING UP FATHER (N)
Cupples & Leon Co.: 1919 - No. 26, 1934 (10x10", 52 pgs., B&W, stiff cardboard-c) (No. 22 is 9-1/4x9-1/2")

1-Daily strip-r by George McManus in all	25.00	100.00	260.00
2-10	25.00	100.00	250.00
11-20	40.00	200.00	350.00
21-26 (Scarcer)	60.00	300.00	525.00

NOTE: Strip began Jan 2 1913-May 28 2000

The Big Book 1 (1926)-Thick book (hardcover; 10-1/4x10-1/4", 142 pgs.)	121.00	484.00	900.00
w/dust jacket (rare)	183.00	732.00	1325.00
The Big Book 2 (1929)	96.00	384.00	700.00
w/dust jacket (rare)	183.00	732.00	1325.00

NOTE: *The Big Books contain 3 regular issues rebound.*

BRINGING UP FATHER, THE TROUBLE OF (N)
Embee Publ. Co.: 1921 (9x15", 46 pgs, Sunday-r in color)

nn - (Rare)	75.00	300.00	525.00

NOTE: *Ties with Mutt & Jeff (EmBee) and Jimmie Dugan And The Reg'lar Fellers (C&L) as the last of the oblong size era. This was self published by George McManus.*

BRINGING UP FATHER (N) (see also SAGARA'S ENGLISH CARTOONS AND CARTOON STORIES)
Publisher unknown (actually, unreadable), Tokyo: October 1924 (9-7/8" x 7-1/2", 90

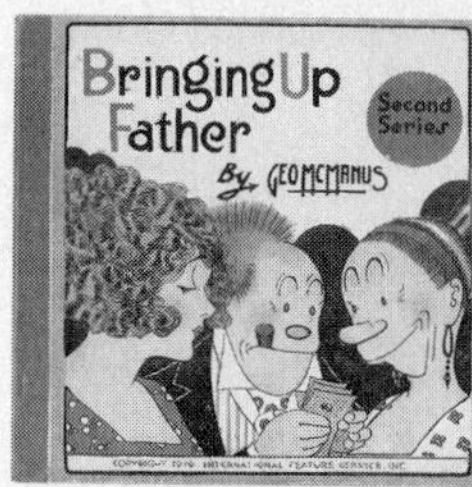

Bringing Up Father #2
© C&L

Brownie Clown of Brownie Town
© The Century Co.

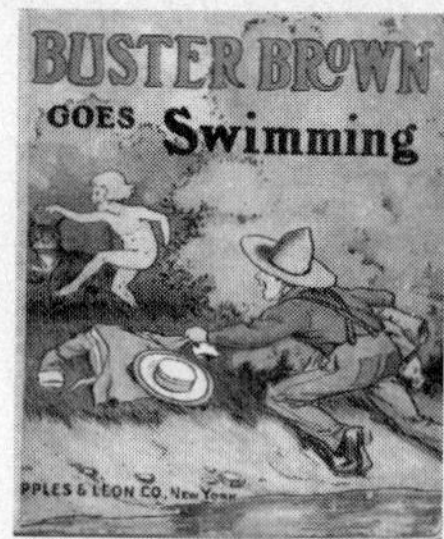

Buster Brown Nuggets - Goes Swimming
1907 © Cupples & Leon

GD2.0 FN6.0 VF8.0

pgs, color hard-c, B&W)
nn- (Scarce) by George McManus C&A - - -
NOTE: *Published in Tokyo, Japan, with all strips in both English and Japanese, to facilitate learning English. Introduction by George McManus. Scarce in USA.*

BRONX BALLADS (I)
Simon & Schuster, NY: 1927 (9-1/2x7-1/4", hard-c, B&W)
nn - By Robert Simon and Harry Hershfield 36.00 143.00 250.00

BROWNIES, THE
The Century Co.: 1887 - 1914 (all came with dust jackets; add $100-150 to value if original dust jacket is included and intact)
Book 1 - The Brownies: Their Book (1887) 200.00 850.00 1320.00
Book 2 - Another Brownies Book (1890) 150.00 635.00 1000.00
Book 3 - The Brownies at Home (1893) 125.00 530.00 825.00
Book 4 - The Brownies Around the World (1894) 100.00 425.00 660.00
Book 5 - The Brownies Through the Union (1895) 100.00 425.00 660.00
Book 6 - The Brownies Abroad (1899) 100.00 425.00 660.00
Book 7 - The Brownies in the Philippines (1904) 100.00 425.00 660.00
Book 8 - The Brownies' Latest Adventures (1910) 100.00 425.00 660.00
Book 9 - The Brownies Many More Nights (1914) 100.00 425.00 660.00

BROWNIE CLOWN OF BROWNIE TOWN (N)
The Century Co.: 1908 (6-7/8 x 9-3/8", 112 pgs, color hardcover & interior)
nn - By Palmer Cox (rare; 1907 newspaper strip-r) 250.00 800.00 1400.00
NOTE: *The Brownies created 1883 in* **St Nicholas Magazine.**

BUDDY TUCKER & HIS FRIENDS (N) (Also see **Buster Brown Nuggets**)
Cupples & Leon Co.: 1906 (11-5/8 x17", 58 pgs, color)
nn - 1905 Sunday strip-r by R. F. Outcault 300.00 950.00 1500.00
NOTE: *Strip began Apr 30, 1905 thru at least Oct 1908.*

BUFFALO BILL'S PICTURE STORIES
Street & Smith Publications: 1909 (Soft cardboard cover)
nn - Very rare 67.00 233.00 400.00

BUGHOUSE FABLES (N) (see also **Comic Monthly**)
Embee Distributing Co. (King Features): 1921 (10¢, 4x4-1/2", 48 pgs.)
1-By Barney Google (Billy DeBeck) 43.00 172.00 300.00

BUG MOVIES (O) (Also see Clancy The Cop & Deadwood Gulch)
Dell Publishing Co.: 1931 (9-13/16x9-7/8", 52 pgs., B&W)
nn - Original material; Stookie Allen-a 43.00 172.00 300.00

BULL
Bull Publishing Company, New York: No.1, March, 1916 - No.12, Feb, 1917 (10 cents, 10-3/4x8-3/4", 24 pgs, color paper-c, B&W)
1-12 (Very Rare) - - -
NOTE: *Pro-German, Anti-British cartoon/humor monthly, whose goal was to keep the U.S. neutral and out of World War I. We know of no copies which have sold in the past few years.*

BUNNY'S BLUE BOOK (see also Foxy Grandpa) (N)
Frederick A. Stokes Co.: 1911 (10x15, 60¢)
nn - By Carl "Bunny" Schultze strip-r 100.00 350.00 -

BUNNY'S RED BOOK (see also Foxy Grandpa) (N)
Frederick A. Stokes Co.: 1912 (10x15)
nn - By Carl "Bunny" Schultze strip-r 100.00 350.00 -

BUNNY'S GREEN BOOK (see also Foxy Grandpa) (N)
Frederick A. Stokes Co.: 1913 (10x15")
nn - By Carl "Bunny" Schultze 100.00 350.00 -

BUSTER BROWN (C) (Also see Brown's Blue Ribbon Book of Jokes and Jingles & Buddy Tucker & His Friends)
Frederick A. Stokes Co.: 1903 - 1916 (Daily strip-r in color)
1903...& His Resolutions (11-1/4x16", 66 pgs.) by R. F. Outcault (Rare)-1st nationally distributed comic. Distr. through Sears & Roebuck 1500.00 5250.00 -
1904...His Dog Tige & Their Troubles (11-1/4x16-1/4", 66 pgs.)(Rare) 600.00 1875.00 -
1905...Pranks (11-1/4x16-3/8", 66 pgs.) 400.00 1450.00 -
1906...Antics (11x16-3/8", 66 pgs.) 400.00 1450.00 -
1906...And Company (11x16-1/2", 66 pgs.) 300.00 1050.00 -
1906...Mary Jane & Tige (11-1/4x16, 66 pgs.) 300.00 1050.00 -
NOTE: ***Yellow Kid** pictured on two pages.*
1908 Collection of Buster Brown Comics 250.00 835.00 -
1909 Outcault's Real Buster and The Only Mary Jane (11x16, 66 pgs, Stokes) 250.00 835.00 -
1910...Up to Date (10-1/8x15-3/4", 66 pgs.) 208.00 729.00 1315.00
1911...Fun And Nonsense (10-1/8x15-3/4", 66 pgs.) 183.00 642.00 1150.00
1912...The Fun Maker (10-1/8x15-3/4", 66 pgs.) -Yellow Kid (4 pgs.) 183.00 642.00 1150.00
1913...At Home (10-1/8x15-3/4", 56 pgs.) 167.00 583.00 1050.00
1914...And Tige Here Again (10x16, 62 pgs, Stokes) 150.00 525.00 950.00
1915...And His Chum Tige (10x16, Stokes) 150.00 525.00 950.00
1916...The Little Rogue (10-1/8x15-3/4", 62 pgs.) 162.00 567.00 1025.00
1917...And the Cat (5-1/2x 6-1/2, 26 pgs, Stokes) 112.00 392.00 700.00
1917...Disturbs the Family (5-1/2x 6 1/2, 26 pgs, Stokes 112.00 392.00 700.00
NOTE: *Story featuring statue of "the Chinese Yellow Kid"*
1917...The Real Buster Brown (5-1/2x 6 -/2, 26 pgs, Stokes 112.00 392.00 700.00

Frederick A. Stokes Co. Hard Cover Series (I)
...Abroad (1904, 10-1/4x8", 86 pgs., B&W, hard-c)-R. F. Outcault-a (Rare) 200.00 700.00 1260.00
...Abroad (1904, B&W, 67 pgs.)-R. F. Outcault-a 200.00 700.00 1260.00
NOTE: *Not an actual comic book, but prose with illustrations.*
..."Tige" His Story 1905 (10x8", 63 pgs., B&W) (63 illos.)
nn-By RF Outcault 143.00 500.00 -
...My Resolutions 1906 (10x8", B&W, 68 pgs.)-R.F. Outcault-a (Rare) 233.00 817.00 1475.00
...Autobiography 1907 (10x8", B&W, 71 pgs.) (16 color plates & 36 B&W illos) 67.00 233.00 440.00
...And Mary Jane's Painting Book 1907 (10x13-1/4", 60 pgs, both card & hardcover versions exist
nn-RFO (first printing blank on top of cover) 67.00 233.00 440.00
First Series- this is a reprint if it says First Series 67.00 233.00 440.00
Volume Two - By RFO 67.00 233.00 440.00
... My Resolutions by Buster Brown (1907, 68 pgs, small size, cardboard covers) scarce 43.00 150.00 285.00
NOTE: *Not actual comic book per se, but a compilation of the Resolutions found at the end of Outcault's Buster Brown newspaper strips.*

BUSTER BROWN (N)
Cupples & Leon Co./N. Y. Herald Co.: 1906 - 1917 (11x17", color, strip-r)
NOTE: *Early issues by R. F. Outcault; most C&L editions are not by Outcault.*
1906...His Dog Tige And Their Jolly Times (11-3/8x16-5/8", 68 pgs.) 300.00 1100.00 1900.00
1906...His Dog Tige & Their Jolly Times (11x16, 46 pgs.) 163.00 600.00 1025.00
1907...Latest Frolics (11-3/8x16-5/8", 66 pgs., reprints 1905-06 strips) 163.00 600.00 1025.00
1908...Amusing Capers (58 pgs.) 129.00 475.00 815.00
1909...The Busy Body (11-3/8x16-5/8", 62 pgs.) 129.00 475.00 815.00
1910...On His Travels (11x16", 58 pgs.) 112.00 412.00 700.00
1911...Happy Days (11-3/8x16-5/8", 58 pgs.) 112.00 412.00 700.00
1912...In Foreign Lands (10x16", 58 pgs) 112.00 412.00 700.00
1913...And His Pets (11x16", 58 pgs.) STOKES???? 112.00 412.00 700.00
1913...And His Pets (26 pg partial reprint) - - -
1914...Funny Tricks (11-3/8x16-5/8", 58 pgs.) 112.00 412.00 700.00
1916...At Play (10x16, 58 pgs) 112.00 412.00 700.00

BUSTER BROWN NUGGETS (N)
Cupples & Leon Co./N.Y.Herald Co.: 1907 (1905, 7-1/2x6-1/2", 36 pgs., color, strip-r, hard-c)(By R. F. Outcault) (NOTE: books are all unnumbered)
Buster Brown Goes Fishing 39.00 137.00 250.00
Buster Brown Goes Swimming 39.00 137.00 250.00
Buster Brown Plays Indian 39.00 137.00 250.00
Buster Brown Goes Shooting 39.00 137.00 250.00
Buster Brown Plays Cowboy 39.00 137.00 250.00
Buster Brown On Uncle Jack's Farm 39.00 137.00 250.00
Buster Brown Tige And The Bull 39.00 137.00 250.00
Buster Brown And Uncle Buster 39.00 137.00 250.00
Buddy Tucker Meets Alice in Wonderland 50.00 175.00 315.00
Buddy Tucker Visits The House That Jack Built 39.00 137.00 250.00

BUSTER BROWN MUSLIN SERIES (N)
Saalfield: 1907 (also contain copyright Cupples & Leon)
...Goes Fishing (1907, 6-7/8x6-1/8", 24 pgs., color)-r/1905 Sunday comics page by Outcault (Rare) 50.00 175.00 315.00
...Plays Indian (1907, 6-7/8x6-1/8", 24 pgs., color)-r/1905 Sunday comics page by Outcault (Rare) 42.00 146.00 265.00
...Plays Cowboy (1907, 6-3/4x6", 10 pgs., color)-r/1905 Sunday comics page by Outcault (Rare) 42.00 146.00 265.00
...And The Donkey (1907, 6-7/8x6-1/8", 24 pgs., color)-r/1905 Sunday comics page by Outcault (Rare) 42.00 146.00 265.00
NOTE: *These are muslin versions of the C&L BB Nugget series.*
NOTE: *Muslin books are all cloth books, made to be washable so as not easily stained/destroyed by very young children. The Muslin books contain one strip each (the title strip), to the more common NUGGET's three strips.*

BUSTER BROWN PREMIUMS (Advertising premium booklets)
Various Publishers: 1904 - 1912 (3x5" to 5x7"; sizes vary)
American Fruit Product Company, Rochester, NY
Buster Brown Duffy's 1842 Cider (1904, 7x5". 12 pgs, C.E. Sherin Co, NYC)
nn - By R. F. Outcault (scarce) 100.00 350.00 600.00

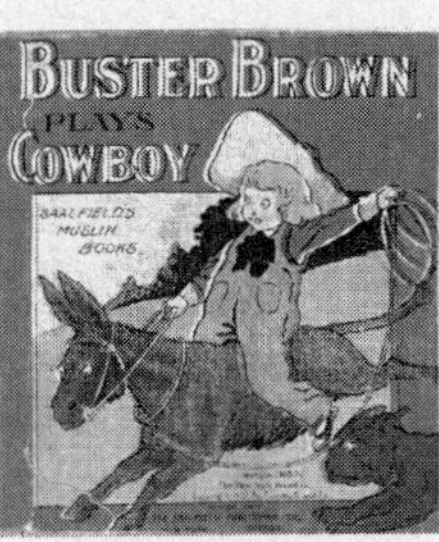
Buster Brown Nuggets -Buster Brown Plays Cowboy © C&L

Captain Easy and Wash Tubbs by Roy Crane 1934 © Whitman Famous Comics Cartoon Book

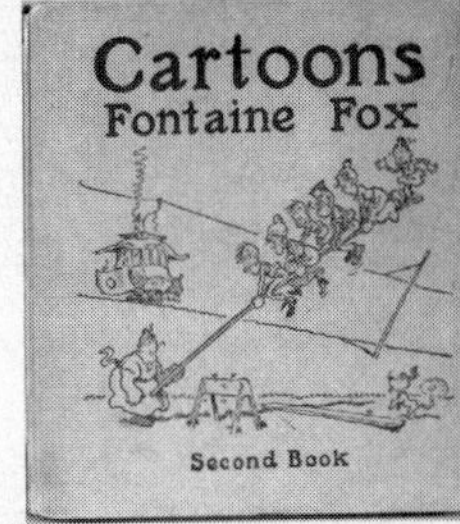
Cartoons Fontaine Fox Second Book early 1920s © Harper & Bros, NY

GD2.0 FN6.0 VF8.0

The Brown Shoe Company, St. Louis, USA
Set of five books (5x7", 16 pgs., color)
Brown's Blue Ribbon Book of Jokes and Jingles Book 1 (nn, 1904)-By R. F. Outcault; Buster Brown & Tige, Little Tommy Tucker, Jack & Jill, Little Boy Blue, Dainty Jane; The Yellow Kid app. on back-c (1st BB comic book premium) 300.00 1050.00 1900.00
Buster Brown's Blue Ribbon Book of Jokes and Jingles Book 2 (1905)- Original color art by Outcault 200.00 600.00 1260.00
Buster's Book of Jokes & Jingles Book 3 (1909) not by R.F. Outcault 150.00 400.00 840.00
NOTE: *Reprinted from the Blue Ribbon post cards with advert jingles added.*
Buster's Book of Instructive Jokes and Jingles Book 4 (1910)-Original color art not by R.F. Outcault 150.00 585.00 1050.00
...Book of Travels nn (1912, 3x5")-Original color art not signed by Outcault 117.00 408.00 735.00
NOTE: *Estimated 5 or 6 known copies exist of books #1-4.*

The Buster Brown Bread Company
"Buster Brown" Bread Book of Rhymes, The (1904, 4x6", 12 pgs., half color, half B&W)- Original color art not signed by RFO 158.00 553.00 1000.00

Buster Brown's Hosiery Mills
"How Buster Brown Got The Pie" nn (nd, 7x5-1/4". 16 pgs, color paper cover and color interior By R.F. Outcault 83.00 292.00 525.00
"The Autobiography of Buster Brown" nn (nd,9x6-1/8", 36 pgs, text story & art by R.F. Outcault 83.00 292.00 525.00
NOTE: *Similar to, but a distinctly different item than "Buster Brown's Autobiography."*

The Buster Brown Stocking Company
Buster Brown Drawing Book, The nn (nd, 5x6", 20 pgs.)-B&W reproductions of 1903 R.F. Outcault art to trace 50.00 150.00 315.00
NOTE: *Reprints a comic strip from Burr McIntosh Magazine, which includes Buster, Yellow Kid, and Pore Li'l Mose (only known story involving all three.)*
Buster Brown Stocking Magazine nn (Jan. 1906, 7-3/4x5-3/8", 36 pgs.) R.F. Outcault 35.00 70.00 125.00
NOTE: *This was actually a store bought item selling for 5 cents per copy.*

Collins Baking Company
Buster Brown Drawing Book nn (1904, 5x3", 12 pgs.)-Original B&W art to trace, not signed by R.F. Outcault 50.00 150.00 315.00

C. H. Morton, St. Albans, VT
Merry Antics of Buster Brown, Buddy Tucker & Tige nn (nd, 3-1/2x5-1/2", 16 pgs.) -Original B&W art by R.F. Outcault 83.00 292.00 525.00

Ivan Frank & Company
Buster Brown nn (1904, 3x5", 12 pgs.)-B&W repros of R. F. Outcault Sunday pages (First premium to actually reproduce Sunday comic pages – may be first premium comic strip-r book?) 125.00 438.00 785.00
Buster Brown's Pranks (1904, 3-1/2x5-1/8", 12 pgs.)-reprints intro of Buddy Tucker into the BB newspaper strip before he was spun off into his own short lived newspaper strip 125.00 438.00 785.00

Kaufmann & Strauss
Buster Brown Drawing Book (1906, 28 pages, 5x3-1/2") Color Cover, B+W original story signed by Outcault, tracing paper inserted as alternate pages. Back cover imprinted for Nox' Em All Shoes 50.00 150.00 315.00

Pond's Extract
Buster Brown's Experiences With Pond's Extract nn (1904, 6-3/4x4-1/2", 28 pgs.) Original color art by R.F. Outcault (may be the first BB premium comic book with original art) 100.00 250.00 525.00

C. A. Cross & Co.
Red Cross Drawing Book nn (1906, 4-7/8x3-1/2", color paper -c, B&W interior, 12 pgs.) 50.00 150.00 315.00
NOTE: *This is for Red Cross coffee; not the health organization.*

Ringen Stove Company
Quick Meal Steel Ranges nn (nd, 5x3", 16 pgs.)-Original B&W art not signed by R.F. Outcault 35.00 125.00 265.00

Steinwender Stoffregen Coffee Co.
"Buster Brown Coffee" (1905, 4-7/8x3", color paper cover, B&W interior, 12 printed pages, plus 1 tracing paper page above each interior image (total of 8 sheets) (Very Rare) 83.00 292.00 525.00
NOTE: *Part of a BB drawing contest. If instructions had been followed, most copies would have ended up destroyed.*

U. S. Playing Card Company
Buster Brown - My Own Playing Cards (1906, 2-1/2x1-3/4", full color)
nn - By R. F. Outcault 42.00 147.00 250.00
NOTE: *Series of full color panels tell stories, average about 5 cards per story.*

Publisher Unknown
The Drawing Book nn (1906, 3-9/16x5", 8 pgs.)-Original B&W art to trace not by R.F. Outcault 50.00 150.00 300.00

BUTLER BOOK A Series of Clever Cartoons of Yale Undergraduate Life
Yale Record: June 16, 1913 (10-3/4 x 17", 34 pgs, paper cover B&W)
nn - By Alban Bernard Butler 20.00 70.00 120.00
NOTE: *Cartoons and strips reprinted from The Yale Record student newspaper.*

BUTTONS & FATTY IN THE FUNNIES
Whitman Publishing Co.: nd 1927 (10-1/4x15-1/2", 28pg., color)
W936 - Signed "M.E.B.", probably Merrill Blosser; strips in color copyright The Brooklyn Daily Eagle; (very rare) 61.00 244.00 425.00

BY BRIGGS (M,N,P) (see also OLD GOLD THE SMOOTHER AND BETTER CIGARETTE)
Old Gold Cigarettes: nd (c1920's) (11" x 9-11/16", 44 pgs, cardboard-c, B&W)
nn- (Scarce) 20.00 70.00 120.00
NOTE: *Collection reprinting strip cartoons by Clare Briggs, advertising Old Gold Cigarettes. These strips originally appeared in various magazines, play program booklets, newspapers, etc. Some of the strips involve regular Briggs strip series. Contains all of the strips in the smaller, color "OLD GOLD" giveaways, plus more.*

CAMION CARTOONS
Marshall Jones Company: 1919 (7-1/2x5", 136 pgs, B&W)
nn - By Kirkland H. Day (W.W.One occupation) 20.00 70.00 120.00

CANYON COUNTRY KIDDIES (M)
Doubleday, Page & Co: 1923 (8x10-1/4", 88 pgs, hard-c, B&W)
nn - By James Swinnerton 39.00 137.00 235.00

CARLO (H)
Doubleday, Page & Co.: 1913 (8 x 9-5/8, 120 pgs, hardcover, B&W)
nn - By A.B. Frost 40.00 140.00 240.00
NOTE: *Original sequential strips about a dog. Became short lived newspaper comic strip in 1914. Originally published with a dust jacket which increases value 50%.*

CARTOON BOOK, THE
Bureau of Publicity, War Loan Organization, Treasury Department, Washington, D.C.: 1918 (6-1/2x4-7/8", 48 pgs, paper cover, B&W)
nn - By various artists 31.00 108.00 185.00
NOTE: *U.S. government issued booklet of WW I propaganda cartoons by 46 artists promoting the third sale of Liberty Loan bonds. The artists include: Berryman, Clare Briggs, Cesare, J. N. "Ding" Darling, Rube Goldberg, Kemble, McCutcheon, George McManus, F. Opper, T. E. Powers, Ripley, Satterfield, H. T. Webster, Gaar Williams.*

CARTOON CATALOGUE (S)
The Lockwood Art School, Kalamazoo, Mich.: 1919 (11-5/8x9, 52 pgs, B&W)
nn - Edited by Mr. Lockwood 20.00 60.00 100.00
NOTE: *Jammed with 100s of single panel cartoons and some sequential comics; Mr Lockwood began the very first cartoonist school back in 1892. Clare Briggs was one of his students.*

CARTOON COMICS
Lasco Publications, Detroit, Mich: #1, April 1930 - #2, May 1930 (8-3/6x5-1/5")
1 - By Lu Harris 20.00 60.00 100.00
2 - By Lu Harris 20.00 60.00 100.00
NOTE: *Contains recurring characters Hollywood Horace, Campus Charlie, Pair-A-Dice Alley and Jocko Monkey. Not much is presently known about the creator(s) or publisher.*

CARTOON HISTORY OF ROOSEVELT'S CAREER, A
The Review of Reviews Company: 1910 (276 pgs, 8-1/4x11",
nn - By various 40.00 120.00 240.00
NOTE: *Reprints editorial cartoons about Teddy Roosevelt from U.S. and international newspapers and cartoons from the humor magaines (Puck, Judge, etc.). A few cartoonists whose work is included are Dalrymple, Opper, McDougall, McCutcheon, Remington, Rogers, Kemble. Mostly single panel but 10 or so are sequential strips.*

CARTOON HUMOR
Collegian Press: 1938 (102 pgs, squarebound, B&W)
nn 20.00 70.00 120.00
NOTE: *Contains cartoons & strips by Otto Soglow, Syd Hoff, Peter Arno, Abner Dean, others.*

CARTOONIST'S PHILOSOPHY, A
Percy Crosby: 1931, HC, 252 pgs, 5-1/2x7-1/2", hard-c, celluloid dust wrapper
nn - By Percy Crosby (10 plates, 6 are of Skippy) 20.00 60.00 100.00
NOTE: *Crosby's partial autobiography regarding his return to France in 1929, and portrayals of Normandy, the "cliff dwellers" on Normandy cliffs (destroyed in WWII), his visit to London, comments on art, philosophy, several poems, and political dialogue. His description of his Cockney driver, " Harold" is amusing. Also describes his experience visiting Chicago to speak out against Capone, his concerns over the evils of Prohibition, and the economy prior to the 1929 crash. This book reveals he was aware of the dangers of his outspoken views, and is prophetic, re: his later years as political prisoner. Also reveals his religious beliefs.*

CARTOONS BY BRADLEY: CARTOONIST OF THE CHICAGO DAILY NEWS
Rand McNally & Company: 1917 (11-1/4x8-3/4", 112 pgs, hardcover, B&W)
nn - By Luther D. Bradley (editorial) 20.00 70.00 120.00

CARTOONS BY FONTAINE FOX (Toonerville Trolley) (S)
Harper & Brothers Publishers: nd early '20s (9x7-7/8",102 pgs., hard-c, B&W)
Second Book- By Fontaine Fox (Toonerville-r) 54.00 189.00 325.00

CARTOONS BY HALLADAY (N,S)
Providence Journal Co., Rhode Island: Dec 1914 (116 pgs, 10-1/2x 7-3/4", hard-c, B&W)
nn- (Scarce) 50.00 125.00 250.00
NOTE: *Cartoons on Rhode Island politics, plus some Teddy Roosevelt & WW I cartoons.*

CARTOONS BY McCUTCHEON (S)
A. C. McClurg & Co.: 1903 (12-3/8x9-3/4", 212 pgs., hardcover, B&W)
nn - By John McCutcheon 20.00 70.00 120.00

CARTOONS BY W. A. IRELAND (S)
The Columbus-Evening Dispatch: 1907 (13-3/4 x 10-1/2", 66 pgs, hardcover)

Cartoons Magazine v9 #5 by various creators
May 1916 © H. H. Windsor, Chicago

Charlie Chaplin in the Army by Segar
1917 © Essaney

Comic Monthly #2
© Embee Dist. Co.

GD2.0 FN6.0 VF8.0

nn - By W. A. Ireland (strip-r) 20.00 70.00 120.00

CARTOONS MAGAZINE (I,N,S)
H. H. Windsor, Publisher: Jan 1912-June 1921; July 1921-1923; 1923-1924; 1924-1927 (1912-July 1913 issues 12x9-1/4", 68-76 pgs; 1913-1921 issues 10x7", average 112 to 188 pgs, color covers)

1912-Jan-Dec 15.00 51.00 90.00
1913-1915 15.00 51.00 90.00
1916-1917 15.00 51.00 90.00
1917-(Apr) "How Comickers Regard Their Characters" 30.00 105.00 150.00
1917-(June) "A Genius of the Comic Page" - long article on George Herriman, Krazy Kat, etc with lots of Herriman art; "Cartoonists and Their Cars" 58.00 204.00 350.00
1918-1919 20.00 70.00 120.00
1920-June 1921 15.00 53.00 90.00
July 1921-1923 titled Wayside Tales & Cartoons Magazine 10.00 30.00 60.00
1923-1924 becomes Cartoons Magazine again 10.00 30.00 60.00
1924-1927 becomes Cartoons & Movie Magazine 10.00 30.00 60.00

NOTE: *Many issues contain a wealth of historical background on then current cartoonists of the day with an international slant; each issue profusely illustrated with many cartoons. We are unsure if this magazine continued after 1927.*

CARTOONS BY J. N. DARLING (S,N - some sequential strips)
The Register & Tribune Co., Des Moines, Iowa: 1909?-1920 (12x8-7/8",B&W)

Book 1 15.00 51.00 90.00
Book 2 Education of Alonzo Applegate (1910) 15.00 51.00 90.00
2nd printing 10.00 30.00 90.00
Book 3 Cartoons From The Files (1911) 15.00 51.00 90.00
Book 4 15.00 51.00 90.00
Book 5 In Peace And War (1916) 15.00 51.00 90.00
Book 6 Aces & Kings War Cartoons (Dec 1, 1918) 15.00 51.00 90.00
Book 7 The Jazz Era (Dec 1920) 15.00 51.00 90.00
Book 8 Our Own Outlines of History (1922) 15.00 51.00 90.00

NOTE: *Some of the most inspired hard hitting cartoons ever printed. Are there more?*

CARTOONS THAT MADE PRINCE HENRY FAMOUS, THE (N,S)
The Chicago Record-Herald: February 1902 (12-1/8" x 9", 32 pgs, paper-c, B&W)

nn- (Scarce) by McCutcheon 15.00 51.00 90.00

NOTE: *Cartoons about the visit of the British Prince Henry to the U.S.*

CAVALRY CARTOONS (O)
R. Montalboddi: nd (c1918) (14-1/4" x 11", 30 pgs, printed on one side, olive & black construction paper-c, B&W interior)

nn - By R.Montalboddi 15.00 51.00 90.00

NOTE: *Comics about life in the U.S.Cavalry during World War I, by a soldier who was in the 1st Cavalry.*

CHARLIE CHAPLIN (N)
Essanay/M. A. Donohue & Co.: 1917 (9x16", B&W, large size soft-c)

Series 1, #315-Comic Capers (9-3/4x15-3/4")-20 pgs. by Segar;
Series 1, #316-In the Movies 165.00 525.00 1200.00
#317-Up in the Air (20 pgs), #318-In the Army 165.00 525.00 1400.00
Funny Stunts-(12-1/2x16-3/8",16 color pgs) 165.00 525.00 1400.00

NOTE: *All contain pre-Thimble Theatre Segar art. The thin paper used makes high grade copies very scarce.*

CHASING THE BLUES
Doubleday Page: 1912 (7-1/2x10", 108 pgs., B&W, hard-c)

nn - By Rube Goldberg 150.00 525.00 900.00

NOTE: *Contains a dozen Foolish Questions, baseball, a few Goldberg poems and lots of sequential strips.*

CHRISTIAN CARTOONS (N,S)
The Sunday School Times Company: 1922 (7-1/4 x 6-1/8,104 pgs, brown hard-c, B&W)

nn - E.J. Pace 15.00 51.00 90.00

NOTE: *Religious cartoons reprinted from The Sunday School Times.*

CLANCY THE COP (O))
Dell Publishing Co.: 1930 - No. 2, 1931 (10x10", 52 pgs., B&W, cardboard-c)
(Also see Bug Movies & Deadwood Gulch)

1, 2-By Vep (original material; not reprints) 50.00 200.00 350.00

CLIFFORD MCBRIDE'S IMMORTAL NAPOLEON & UNCLE ELBY (N)
The Castle Press: 1932 (12x17"; soft-c cartoon book)

nn - Intro. by Don Herod 36.00 144.00 250.00

COLLECTED DRAWINGS OF BRUCE BAIRNSFATHER, THE
W. Colston Leigh: 1931 (11-1/4x8-1/4 ", 168 pages, hardcover, B&W)

nn - By Bruce Bairnsfather 24.00 96.00 165.00

COMICAL PEEP SHOW
McLoughlin Bros: 1902 (36 pgs, B&W)

nn 24.00 96.00 165.00

NOTE: *Comic stories of Wilhelm Busch redrawn; two versions with green or gold front cover logos; back covers different.*

COMIC ANIMALS (I)
Charles E. Graham & Co.: 1903 (9-3/4x7-1/4", 90 pgs, color cover)

nn - By Walt McDougall (not comic strips) 43.00 150.00 260.00

GD2.0 FN6.0 VF8.0

COMIC CUTS (O)
H. L. Baker Co., Inc.: 5/19/34-7/28/34 (Tabloid size 10-1/2x15-1/2", 24 pgs., 5¢)
(full color, not reprints; published weekly; created for news stand sales)

V1#1 - V1#7(6/30/34), V1#8(7/14/34), V1#9(7/28/34)-Idle Jack strips 50.00 150.00 300.00

NOTE: *According to a 1958 Lloyd Jacquet interview, this short-lived comics mag was the direct inspiration for Major Malcolm Wheeler-Nicholson's* ***New Fun Comics****, not* ***Famous Funnies****.*

COMIC MONTHLY (N)
Embee Dist. Co.: Jan, 1922 - No. 12, Dec, 1922 (10¢, 8-1/2"x9", 28 pgs., 2-color covers)
(1st monthly newsstand comic publication) (Reprints 1921 B&W dailies)

1-Polly & Her Pals by Cliff Sterrett 193.00 772.00 1350.00
2-Mike & Ike by Rube Goldberg 114.00 456.00 800.00
3-S'Matter, Pop? 114.00 456.00 800.00
4-Barney Google by Billy DeBeck 114.00 456.00 800.00
5-Tillie the Toiler by Russ Westover 114.00 456.00 800.00
6-Indoor Sports by Tad Dorgan 114.00 456.00 800.00

NOTE: *#6 contains more Judge Rummy than Indoor Sports.*

7-Little Jimmy by James Swinnerton 114.00 456.00 800.00
8-Toots and Casper by Jimmy Murphy 114.00 456.00 800.00
9-New Bughouse Fables by Barney Google 114.00 456.00 800.00
10-Foolish Questions by Rube Goldberg 114.00 456.00 800.00
11-Barney Google & Spark Plug by Billy DeBeck 114.00 456.00 800.00
12-Polly & Her Pals by Cliff Sterrett 193.00 772.00 1350.00

NOTE: *This series was published by George McManus (Bringing Up Father) as Em & Rudolph Block, Jr., son of Hearst's cartoon editor for many years, as "Bee." One would have thought this series would have done very well considering the tremendous amount of talent assembled. All issues are extremely hard to find these days and rarely show up in any type of higher grade.*

COMIC PAINTING AND CRAYONING BOOK (H)
Saalfield Publ. Co.: 1917 (13-1/2x10", 32 pgs.) (No price on-c)

nn - Tidy Teddy by F. M. Follett, Clarence the Cop, Mr. & Mrs. Butt-In; regular comic stories to read or color 50.00 175.00 300.00

COMPLETE TRIBUNE PRIMER, THE (I)
Mutual Book Company: 1901 (7 1/4 x 5", 152 pgs, red hard-c)

nn - By Frederick Opper; has 75 Opper cartoons 25.00 88.00 150.00

COURTSHIP OF TAGS, THE (N)
McCormick Press: pre-1910 (9x4", 88 pgs, red & B&W-c, B&W interior)

nn - By O. E. Wertz (strip-r Wichita Daily Beacon) 25.00 88.00 150.00

DAFFYDILS (N)
Cupples & Leon Co.: 1911 (5-3/4x7-7/8", 52 pgs., B&W, hard-c)

nn - By "Tad" Dorgan 58.00 204.00 350.00

NOTE: *Also exists in self-published TAD edition: The T.A. Dorgan Company; unknown which is first printing.*

DAN DUNN SECRET OPERATIVE 48 (Also See Detective Dan) (N)
Whitman Publishing: 1937 ((5 1/2 x 7 1/4", 68pgs., color cardboard-c, B&W)

1010 And The Gangsters' Frame-Up 36.00 144.00 250.00

NOTE: *There are two versions of the book the later printing has a 5 cent cover price. Dick Tracy look-alike character by Norman Marsh.*

DANGERS OF DOLLY DIMPLE, THE (N)
Penn Tobacco Co.: nd (1930's) (9-3/8x7-7/8", 28 pgs, red cardboard-c, B&W)

nn - (Rare) by Walter Enright 25.00 88.00 150.00

NOTE: *Reprints newspaper comic strip advertisements, in which in every episode, Dolly Dimple's life is saved by Penn's Smoking Tobacco. - how very un-P.C. by today's standards.*

DEADWOOD GULCH (O) (See The Funnies 1929)(also see Bug Movies & Clancy The Cop)
Dell Publishing Co.: 1931 (10x10", 52 pgs., B&W, color covers, B&W interior)

nn - By Charles "Boody" Rogers (original material) 50.00 200.00 350.00

DESTINY A Novel In Pictures (O)
Farrar & Rinehart: 1930 (8x7", 424 pgs, B&W, hard-c, dust jacket?)

nn - By Otto Nuckel (original graphic novel) 25.00 100.00 175.00

DICK TRACY & DICK TRACY JR. CAUGHT THE RACKETEERS, HOW
Cupples & Leon Co.: 1933 (8-1/2x7", 88 pgs., hard-c) (See Treasure Box of Famous Comics) (N)

2-(Numbered on pg. 84)-Continuation of Stooge Viller book (daily strip reprints from 8/3/33 thru 11/8/33)(Rarer than #1) 86.00 344.00 660.00
With dust jacket... 118.00 472.00 900.00

DICK TRACY & DICK TRACY JR. AND HOW THEY CAPTURED "STOOGE" VILLER (N)
Cupples & Leon Co.: 1933 (8-1/2x7", 100 pgs., hard-c, one-shot)
Reprints 1932 & 1933 Dick Tracy daily strips

nn(No.1)-1st app. of "Stooge" Viller 86.00 344.00 660.00
With dust jacket... 118.00 472.00 900.00

DIMPLES By Grace Drayton (N) (See Dolly Dimples)
Hearst's International Library Co.: 1915 (6 1/4 x 5 1/4, 12 pgs) (5 known)

nn-Puppy and Pussy; nn-She Goes For a Walk; nn-She Had A Sneeze; nn-She Has a Naughty Play Husband; nn-Wait Till Fido Comes Home 20.00 70.00 140.00

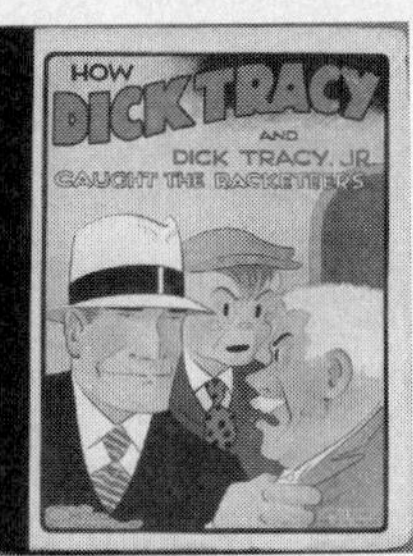

How Dick Tracy and Dick Tracy, Jr. Caught the Racketeers by Chester Gould 1933 © Cupples & Leon

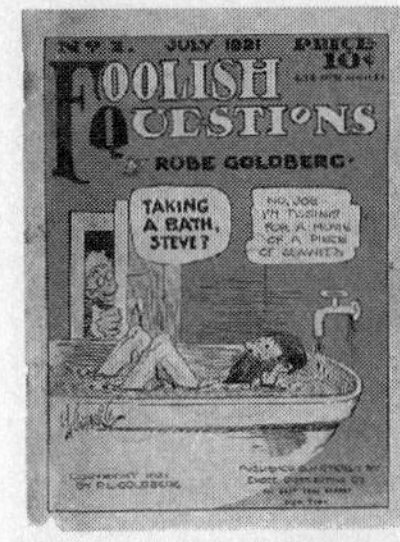

Foolish Questions by Rube Goldberg 1921 © EmBee Distributing Co., NY.

The Latest Adventures of Foxy Grandpa 1905 © Bunny Publ.

GD2.0 FN6.0 VF8.0

DOINGS OF THE DOO DADS, THE (N)
Detroit News (Universal Feat. & Specialty Co.): 1922 (50¢, 7-3/4x7-3/4", 34 pgs, B&W, red & white-c, square binding)

nn-Reprints 1921 newspaper strip "Text & Pictures" given away as prize in the Detroit News Doo Dads contest; by Arch Dale 43.00 173.00 300.00

DOINGS OF THE VAN-LOONS (N) (see Mutt & Jeff #1-#5)
Ball Publications: 1912 (5-3/4X15-1/2", 68pg., B&W, hard-c)

nn - By Fred I. Leipziger 88.00 306.00 525.00

DOLLY DIMPLES & BOBBY BOUNCE (See Dimples)
Cupples & Leon Co.: 1933 (8-3/4x7", color hardcover, B&W)

nn - Grace Drayton-a 24.00 96.00 165.00

DOO DADS, THE (Sleepy Sam and Tiny the Elephant)
Universal Feature * Specialty Co: 1922 (5-1/4x14", 36 pgs.,B&W, R&W-c,square binding)

nn - By Arch Dale 24.00 96.00 165.00

DREAMS OF THE RAREBIT FIEND (N)
Frederick A. Stokes Co.:1905 (10-1/4x7-1/2", 68 pgs, thin paper cover all B&W) newspaper reprints from the New York Evening Telegram printed on yellow paper

nn-By Winsor "Silas" McCay (Very Rare) (Five copies known to exist)
Estimated value.... 571.00 2000.00 -
NOTE: A G/VG copy sold for $2,045 in May 2004.

DRISCOLL'S BOOK OF PIRATES (O)
David McKay Publ.: 1934 (9x7", 124 pgs, B&W, hardcover)

nn - By Montford Amory (original material) 21.00 64.00 150.00

DUCKY DADDLES
Frederick A. Stokes Co: July 1911 (15x10")

nn - By Grace Weiderseim (later Drayton) strip-r 50.00 175.00 300.00

DUMBUNNIES AND THEIR FRIENDS IN RABBITBORO, THE (O)
Albertine Randall Wheelan: 1931 (8-3/4x7-1/8", 82 pgs, color hardcover, B&W)

nn - By Albertine Randall Wheelan (self-pub) 34.00 103.00 240.00

EDISON - INSPIRATION TO YOUTH (N)(Also see Life of Thomas---)
Thomas A. Edison, Incorporated: 1939 (9-1/2 x 6-1/2, paper cover, B&W)

nn - Photo-c 46.00 138.00 275.00
NOTE: *Reprints strip material found in the 1928 Life of Thomas A. Edison in Word and Picture.*

'ERBIE AND 'IS PLAYMATES
Democratic National Committee: 1932 (8x9-1/2, 16 pgs, B&W)

nn - By Frederick Opper (Rare) 34.00 103.00 240.00
NOTE: *Anti-Hoover/Pro-Roosevelt political comics.*

EXPANSION BEING BART'S BEST CARTOONS FOR 1899
Minneapolis Journal: 1900 (10-1/4x8-1/4", 124 pgs, paperback, B&W)

v2#1 - By Charles L. Bartholomew 24.00 84.00 145.00

FAMOUS COMICS (N)
King Features Synd. (Whitman Pub. Co.): 1934 (100 pgs., daily newspaper-r) (3-1/2x8-1/2"; paper cover)(came in an illustrated box)

684 (#1) - Little Jimmy, Katz Kids & Barney Google 34.00 103.00 240.00
684 (#2) - Polly, Little Jimmy, Katzenjammer Kids 34.00 103.00 240.00
684 (#3) - Little Annie Rooney, Polly and Her Pals, Katzenjammer Kids 34.00 103.00 240.00
Box price... 32.00 96.00 225.00

FAMOUS COMICS CARTOON BOOKS (N)
Whitman Publishing Co.: 1934 (8x7-1/4", 72 pgs, B&W hard-c, daily strip-r)

1200-The Captain & the Kids; Dirks reprints credited to Bernard Dibble 29.00 86.00 200.00
1202-Captain Easy & Wash Tubbs by Roy Crane; 2 slightly different versions of cover exist 34.00 103.00 240.00
1203-Ella Cinders By Conselman & Plumb 28.00 84.00 195.00
1204-Freckles & His Friends 25.00 75.00 175.00
NOTE: *Called Famous Funnies Cartoon Books inside back area sales advertisement.*

FANTASIES IN HA-HA (M)
Meyer Bros & Co.: 1900 (14 x 11-7/8", 64 pgs, color cover hardcover, B&W)

nn - By Hy Mayer 40.00 140.00 240.00

FELIX (N)
Henry Altemus Company: 1931 (6-1/2"x8-1/4", 52 pgs., color, hard-c w/dust jacket)

1-3-Sunday strip reprints of Felix the Cat by Otto Messmer. Book No. 2 r/1931 Sunday panels mostly two to a page in a continuity format oddly arranged so each tier of panels reads across two pages, then drops to the next tier. (Books 1 & 3 have not been documented.)(Rare)
Each 104.00 416.00 725.00
With dust jacket 150.00 600.00 1050.00

FELIX THE CAT BOOK (N)
McLoughlin Bros.: 1927 (8"x15-3/4", 52 pgs, half in color-half in B&W)

nn - Reprints 23 Sunday strips by Otto Messmer from 1926 & 1927, every other one in color, two pages per strip. (Rare) 200.00 800.00 1550.00
260-Reissued (1931), reformatted to 9-1/2"x10-1/4" (same color plates, but one strip per every three pages), retitled ("Book" dropped from title) and abridged (only eight strips repeated from first issue, 28 pgs.).(Rare) 79.00 316.00 600.00

F. FOX'S FUNNY FOLK (see Toonerville Trolley; Cartoons by Fontaine Fox) (C)
George H. Doran Company: 1917 (10-1/4x8-1/4", 228 pgs, red, B&W cover, B&W interior, hardcover; dust jacket?)

nn - By Fontaine Fox (Toonerville Trolley strip-r) 50.00 200.00 350.00

52 CAREY CARTOONS (O,S)
Carey Cartoon Service, NY: 1915 (25 cents, 6-3/4" x 10-1/2", 118 pgs, printed on one side, color cardboard-c, B&W)

nn - (1915) War - - -
NOTE: *The Carey Cartoon Service supplied a weekly, hand-colored single panel cartoon broadsheet, on current news events, starting in 1906 or 1907, for window display in Carey Fountain Pen chain stores. These broadsheets were 22-1/2" x 33" in size. Starting circa 1915, Carey Fountain Pens began offering subscriptions for the broadsheets to other merchants, for window display in their stores as well. This collects, in B&W, the cartoons for 1915. An "Edition Deluxe" was also advertised, with all cartoons hand colored. It is currently unknown whether a reprint collection was only issued in 1915, or if other editions exist.*

52 LETTERS TO SALESMEN
Steven-Davis Company: 1927 (???)

nn - (Rare) 21.00 64.00 128.00
NOTE: *52 motivational letters to salesmen, with page of comics for each week, bound into embossed leather binder.*

FOLKS IN FUNNYVILLE (S)
R.H. Russell: 1900 (12"x9-1/4", 48 pgs.)(cardboard-c)

nn - By Frederick Opper 271.00 950.00 -
NOTE: *Reprinted from Hearst's NY Journal American Humorist supplements.*

FOOLISH QUESTIONS (S)
Small, Maynard & Co.: 1909 (6-7/8 x 5-1/2", 174 pgs, hardcover, B&W)

nn - By Rube Goldberg (first Goldberg item) 75.00 263.00 450.00
NOTE: *Comic strip began Oct 23, 1908 running thru 1941. Also drawn by George Frinkin in 1909.*

FOOLISH QUESTIONS THAT ARE ASKED BY ALL
Levi Strauss & Co./Small, Maynard & Co.: 1909 (5-1/2x5-3/4", 24 pgs, paper-c, B&W)

nn- (Rare) by Rube Goldberg 46.00 160.00 275.00

FOOLISH QUESTIONS (Boxed card set) (S)
Wallie Dorr Co., N.Y.: 1919 (5-1/4x3-3/4")(box & card backs are red)

nn - Boxed set w/52 B&W comics on cards; each a single panel gag complete set w/box 75.00 263.00 450.00
NOTE: *There are two diff sets put out simultaneously with the first set, by the same company. One set continues/picks up the numbering of the cards from the other set.*

FOOLISH QUESTIONS (S)
EmBee Distributing Co.: 1921 (10¢, 4x5 1/2; 52 pgs, 3 color covers; B&W)

1-By Rube Goldberg 46.00 160.00 275.00

FOXY GRANDPA
Foxy Grandpa Company, 33 Wall St, NY : 1900 (9x15", 84 pgs, full color, cardboard-c)

nn - By Carl Schultze (By Permission of New York Herald) 271.00 950.00 -
NOTE: *This seminal comic strip began Jan 7, 1900 and was collected later that same year.*

FOXY GRANDPA (Also see The Funnies, 1st series) (N)
N. Y. Herald/Frederick A. Stokes Co./M. A. Donahue & Co./Bunny Publ. (L. R. Hammersly Co.): 1901 - 1916 (Strip-r in color, hard-c)

1901- 9x15" in color-N. Y. Herald 271.00 950.00 -
1902- "Latest Larks of…", 32 pgs., 9-1/2x15-1/2" 164.00 575.00 -
1902- "The Many Advs. of…", 9x12", 148 pgs., Hammersly Co. 179.00 625.00 -
1903- "Latest Advs.", 9x15", 24 pgs., Hammersly Co. 164.00 575.00 -
1903- "…'s New Advs.", 11x15", 66 pgs., Stokes 164.00 575.00 -
1904- "Up to Date", 10x15", 66 pgs., Stokes 146.00 510.00 950.00
1904- "The Many Adventures of…", 9x15, 144pgs, Donohue 146.00 510.00 950.00
1905- "& Flip-Flaps", 9-1/2x15-1/2", 52 pgs. 146.00 510.00 950.00
1905- "The Latest Advs. of…", 9x15", 28, 52, & 68 pgs, M.A. Donohue Co.; re-issue of 1902 issue 104.00 365.00 700.00
1905- "Latest Larks of…", 9-1/2x15-1/2", 52 pgs., Donahue; re-issue of 1902 issue with more pages added 104.00 365.00 700.00
1905- "Latest Larks of…", 9-1/2x15-1/2", 24 pgs. edition, Donahue; re-issue of 1902 issue 104.00 365.00 700.00
1905- "Merry Pranks of…", 9-1/2x15-1/2", 28, 52 & 62 pgs., Donahue 104.00 365.00 700.00
1905-"...Surprises",10x15", color, 64 pg,Stokes, 60¢ 104.00 365.00 700.00
1906- "Frolics", 10x15", 30 pgs., Stokes 104.00 365.00 700.00
1907?-"...& His Boys",10x15", 64 color pgs, Stokes 104.00 365.00 700.00
1907- "Triumphs", 10x15", 62 pgs, Stokes 104.00 365.00 700.00
1908-"...Mother Goose", Stokes 104.00 365.00 700.00
1909- "...& Little Brother", 10x15, 58 pgs, Stokes 104.00 365.00 700.00
1911- "Latest Tricks", r-1910,1911 Sundays-Stokes Co. 104.00 365.00 700.00

Giggles
© Pratt Food Co.

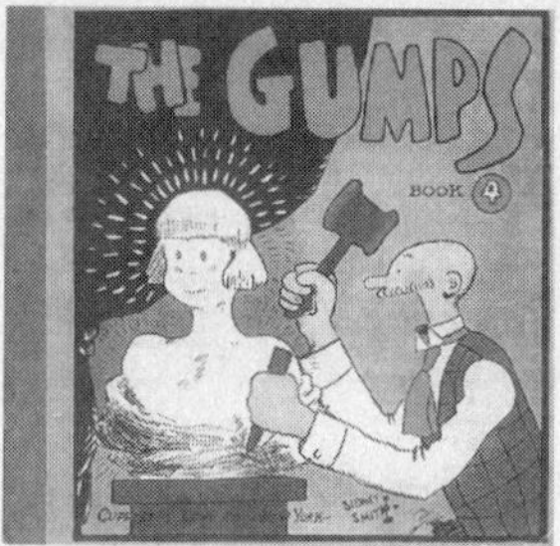

The Gumps by Sidney Smith
1927? © Cupples & Leon

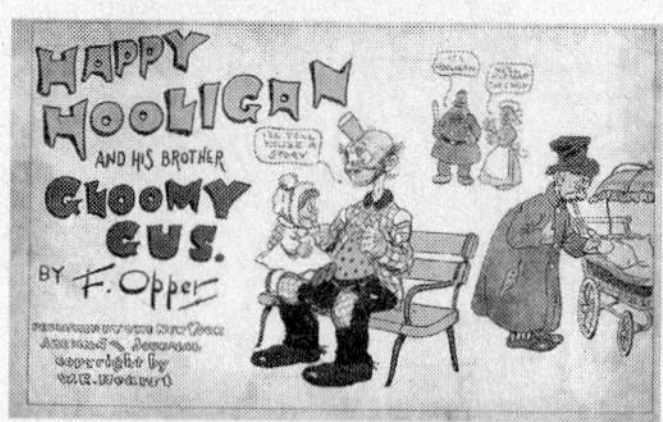

Happy Hooligan Book 1 1902
© Frederick A. Stokes

GD2.0 FN6.0 VF8.0

1914-(9-1/2x15-1/2", 24 pgs.)-6 color cartoons/page, Bunny Publ. Co. 88.00 306.00 575.00
1915 - ...Always Jolly (10x16, Stokes) 88.00 306.00 575.00
1916- "Merry Book", (10x15", 64 pgs, Stokes) 88.00 306.00 575.00
1917-"...Adventures (5 1/2 x 6 1/2, 26 pgs, Stokes) 52.00 184.00 350.00
1917-"...Frolics (5 1/2 x 6 1/2, 26 pgs, Stokes) 52.00 184.00 350.00
1917-"...Triumphs (5 1/2 x 6 1/2, 26 pgs, Stokes) 52.00 184.00 350.00

FOXY GRANDPA, FUNNY TRICKS OF (The Stump Books)
M.A. Donahue Co, Chicago: approx 1903 (1-7/8x6-3/8", 44 pgs, blue hardcover)
nn - By Carl Schultze 52.00 184.00 315.00
NOTE: *One of a series of ten "stump" books; the only comics one.*

FOXY GRANDPA'S MOTHER GOOSE (I)
Stokes: October 1903 (10-11/16x8-1/2", 86 pgs, hard-c)
nn - By Carl Schultze (not comics - illustrated book) 52.00 184.00 315.00

FOXY GRANDPA SPARKLETS SERIES (N)
M. A. Donahue & Co.: 1908 (7-3/4x6-1/2"; 24 pgs., color)
"... Rides the Goat", "...& His Boys", "...Playing Ball", "...Fun on the Farm", "...Fancy Shooting", "...Show His Boys Up-To-Date Sports", "...Plays Santa Claus" each.... 88.00 306.00 525.00
900- "Playing Ball"; Bunny illos; 8 pgs., linen like pgs., no date 73.00 254.00 435.00

FOXY GRANDPA VISITS RICHMOND (O,P)
Dietz Printing Co., Richmond, VA / Hotel Rueger: nd (c1920's) (5-7/8" x 4-1/2", 16 pgs, paper-c, B&W)
nn - (Scarce) By Bunny 25.00 88.00 150.00
NOTE: *Promotional comic given away to its guests by the Hotel Rueger, about Foxy Grandpa visiting and enjoying the Hotel. Originally came in an envelope, with the words "Foxy Grandpa Visits Richmond -- and Rueger's" printed on it.*

FOXY GRANDPA VISITS WASHINGTON, D.C. (P)
Dietz Printing Co., Richmond, VA / Hamilton Hotel: nd (c1920's) (5-7/8" x 4-1/2", 16 pgs, paper-c, B&W)
nn - (Scarce) By Bunny 25.00 88.00 150.00
NOTE: *Mostly reprints "... Visits Richmond", changing all references to Hotel Rueger, to Hamilton Hotel instead. Also, changes depictions of a waiter and a cook from black to white, plus incompletely erases the cover art on a book Foxy Grandpa falls asleep with (the latter is how we know that the Richmond version was first).*

FRAGMENTS FROM FRANCE (S)
G. P. Putnam & Sons: 1917 (9x6-1/4", 168 pgs, hardcover, $1.75)
nn - By Bruce Bairnsfather 25.00 88.00 150.00
NOTE: *WW1 trench warfare cartoons; color dust jacket.*

FUNNIES, THE (H) (See Clancy the Cop, Deadwood Gulch, Bug Movies)
Dell Publishing Co.: 1929 - No. 36, 10/18/30 (10¢; 5¢ No. 22 on) (16 pgs.)
Full tabloid size in color; not reprints; published every Saturday
1-My Big Brudder, Jonathan, Jazzbo & Jim, Foxy Grandpa, Sniffy, Jimmy Jams & other strips begin; first four-color comic newsstand publication; also contains magic, puzzles & stories 186.00 684.00 1300.00
2-21 (1930, 10¢) 54.00 214.00 375.00
22(nn-7/12/30-5¢) 43.00 171.00 300.00
23(nn-7/19/30-5¢), 24(nn-7/26/30-5¢), 25(nn-8/2/30), 26(nn-8/9/30), 27(nn-8/16/30), 28(nn-8/23/30), 29(nn-8/30/30), 30(nn-9/6/30), 31(nn-9/13/30), 32(nn-9/20/30), 33(nn-9/27/30), 34(nn-10/4/30), 35(nn-10/11/30), 36(nn, no date-10/18/30) each.... 43.00 171.00 300.00

GASOLINE ALLEY (Also see Popular Comics & Super Comics) (N)
Reilly & Lee Publishers: 1929 (8-3/4x7", B&W daily strip-r, hard-c)
nn - By King (96 pgs.) 57.00 228.00 400.00
Dust Wrapper - add 50% more
NOTE: *Of all the Frank King reprint books, this is the only one to reprint actual complete newspaper strips - all others are illustrated prose text stories.*

GIBSON'S PUBLISHED DRAWINGS, MR. (M,S) (see Victorian index for earlier issues)
R.H. Russell, New York: No.1 1894 - No. 9 1904 (11x17-3/4", hard-c, B&W)
nn (No.6; 1901) A Widow and her Friends (90 pgs.) 30.00 60.00 120.00
nn (No.7; 1902) The Social Ladder (88 pgs.) 30.00 60.00 120.00
8 - 1903 The Weaker Sex (88 pgs.) 30.00 60.00 120.00
9 - 1904 Everyday People (88 pgs.) 30.00 60.00 120.00
NOTE: *By Charles Dana Gibson cartoons, reprinted from magazines, primarily LIFE. The Education of Mr. Pipp tells a story. Series continues how long after 1904?*

GIGGLES
Pratt Food Co., Philadelphia, PA: 1908-09? (12x9", 8 pgs, color, 5 cents-c)
1-6: By Walt McDougall (#6 dated Jan 1909) 40.00 140.00 -
8 - Recently re-discovered dated March 1909 40.00 140.00 -
NOTE: *Appears to be monthly; almost tabloid size; yearly subscriptions was 25 cents.*

GOD'S MAN (H)
Jonathan Cape and Harrison Smith Inc.: 1929 (8-1/4x6", 298 pgs, B&W hardcover w/dust jacket) (original graphic novel in wood cuts)
nn - By Lynd Ward 43.00 171.00 300.00

GD2.0 FN6.0 VF8.0

GOLD DUST TWINS
N. K. Fairbank Co.: 1904 (4-5/8x6-3/4", 18 pgs, color and B&W)
nn - By E. W. Kemble (Rare) 30.00 60.00 120.00
NOTE: *Promo comic for Gold DustWashing Powder; includes page of watercolor paints.*

GOLF
Volland Co.: 1916 (9x12-3/4", 132 pgs, hard-c, B&W)
nn - By Clair Briggs 52.00 84.00 315.00

GUMPS, THE (N)
Landfield-Kupfer: No. 1, 1918 - No. 6, 1921; (B&W Daily strip-r)
Book No. 1(1918)(Rare)-cardboard-c, 5-1/4x13-1/3", 64 pgs., daily strip-r by Sidney Smith 67.00 233.00 400.00
Book No.2(1918)-(Rare); 5-1/4x13-1/3"; paper cover; 36 pgs. daily strip reprints by Sidney Smith 67.00 233.00 400.00
Book No. 3 121.00 423.00 725.00
Book No. 4 (1918) 5-3/8x13-7/8", 20 pgs. Color card-c 121.00 423.00 725.00
Book No. 5 10-1/4x13-1/2", 20 pgs. Color paper-c 121.00 423.00 725.00
Book No. 6 (Rare) 121.00 423.00 725.00

GUMPS, ANDY AND MIN, THE (N)
Landfield-Kupfer Printing Co., Chicago/Morrison Hotel: nd (1920s) (Giveaway, 5-1/2"x14", 20 pgs., B&W, soft-c)
nn - Strip-r by Sidney Smith; art & logo embossed on cover w/hotel restaurant menu on back-c or a hotel promo ad; 4 different contents of issues known 50.00 175.00 300.00

GUMPS, THE (N)
Cupples & Leon: 1924-1930 (10x10, 52 pgs, B&W)
nn (1924)-By Sidney Smith 61.00 244.00 425.00
2,3 39.00 154.00 270.00
4-7 33.00 131.00 230.00

GUMP'S CARTOON BOOK, THE (N)
The National Arts Company: 1931 (13-7/8x10", 36 pgs, color covers, B&W)
nn - By Sidney Smith 57.00 228.00 400.00

GUMPS PAINTING BOOK, THE (N)
The National Arts Company: 1931 (11 x 15 1/4", 20 pgs, half in full color)
nn - By Sidney Smith 57.00 228.00 400.00

HALT FRIENDS! (see also **HELLO BUDDY**)
???: 1918? (4-3/8x5-3/4", 36 pgs, color-c, B&W, no cover price listed)
nn - Unknown 10.00 30.00 70.00
NOTE: *Says on front cover: "Comics of War Facts of Service Sold on its merits by Unemployed or Disabled Ex-Service Men. Credentials Shown On Request. Price - Pay What You Please." These are very common; contents vary widely.*

HAMBONE'S MEDITATIONS
Jahl & Co.: no date 1920 (6-1/8 x 7-1/2, 108 pgs, paper cover, B&W)
nn - By J. P. Alley 33.00 132.00 230.00
NOTE: *Reprint of racist single panel newspaper series, 2 cartoons per page.*

HAN OLA OG PER (N)
Anundsen Publishing Co, Decorah, Iowa: 1927 (10-3/8 x 15-3/4", 54 pgs, paper cover, B&W)
nn - American origin Norwegian language strips-r 33.00 131.00 230.00
NOTE: *1940s and modern reprints exist.*

HANS UND FRITZ (N)
The Saalfield Publishing Co.: 1917, 1927-29 (10x13-1/2", 28 pgs., B&W)
nn - By R. Dirks (1917, r-1916 strips) 96.00 335.00 575.00
nn - By R. Dirks (1923 edition- reprint of 1917 edition) 58.00 204.00 350.00
nn - By R. Dirks (1926 edition- reprint of 1917 edition) 58.00 204.00 350.00
The Funny Larks Of... By R. Dirks (©1917 outside cover; ©1916 inside indicia) 96.00 335.00 575.00
The Funny Larks Of... (1927) reprints 1917 edition of 1916 strips Halloween-c 58.00 204.00 350.00
The Funny Larks Of... 2 (1929) 58.00 204.00 350.00
193 - By R. Dirks; contains 1916 Sunday strip reprints of Katzenjammer Kids & Hawkshaw the Detective - reprint of 1917 nn edition (1929) this edition is not rare 58.00 204.00 350.00

HAPPY DAYS (S)
Coward-McCann Inc.: 1929 (12-1/2x9-5/8", 110 pgs, hardcover B&W)
nn - By Alban Butler (WW 1 cartoons) 20.00 60.00 120.00

HAPPY HOOLIGAN (See Alphonse...) (N)
Hearst's New York American & Journal: 1902,1903
Book 1-(1902)-"And His Brother Gloomy Gus", By Fred Opper; has 1901-02-r; (yellow & black)(86 pgs.)(10x15-1/4") 400.00 1400.00 -
New Edition, 1903 -10x15" 82 pgs. in color 300.00 1100.00 -
NOTE: *Strip ran March 26, 1900-Aug 14, 1932 and is widely recognized as setting the format standard for all newspaper comic strips which came after it. Opper (1857-1937) was going blind towards the end.*

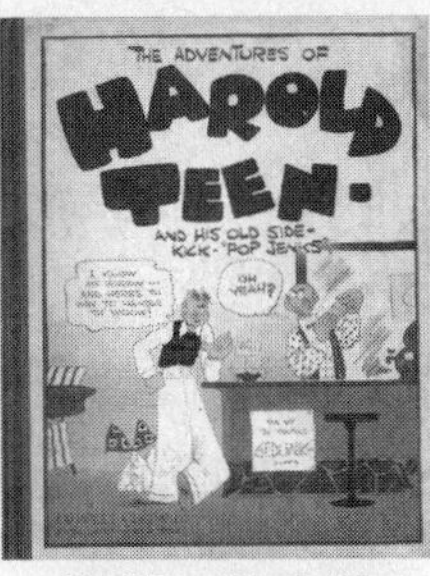

Harold Teen #2 by Carl Ed
1931 © Cupples & Leon

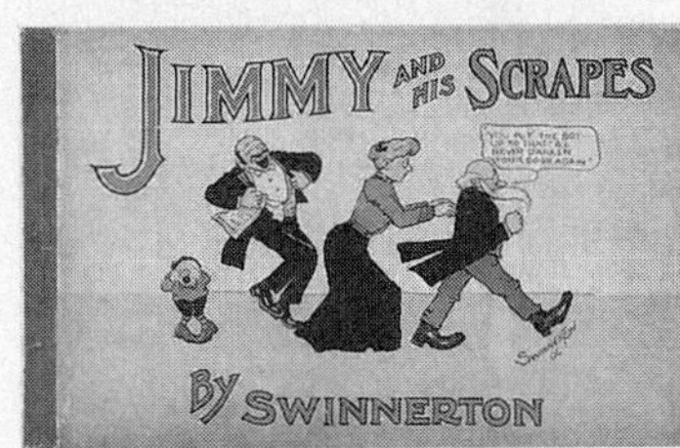

Jimmy and His Scrapes
© Frederick A. Stokes

Joys & Glooms By T.E. Powers
1912 © Reilly & Britton Co.

GD2.0 FN6.0 VF8.0

HAPPY HOOLIGAN (N) (By Fredrick Opper)
Frederick A. Stokes Co.: 1906-08 (10-1/4x15-3/4", cardboard color-c)
1906 - :Travels of...), 32 pgs,10-1/4x15-3/4", 1905-r 200.00 700.00 -
1907 - "--Home Again", 68 pgs., 10x15-3/4", 60¢; full color-c 200.00 700.00 -
1908 - "Handy--", 68 pgs, color 200.00 700.00 -

HAPPY HOOLIGAN (Story of...) (G)
McLoughlin Bros.: No. 281, 1932 (12x9-1/2", 16 pgs., soft-c)
281-Three-color text, pictures on heavy paper 57.00 228.00 400.00
NOTE: *An homage to Opper's creation on its 30th Anniversary in 1932.*

HAROLD HARDHIKE'S REJUVENATION
O'Sullivan Rubber: 1917 (6-1/4x3-1/2, 16 pgs, B&W)
nn 25.00 100.00 175.00
NOTE: *Comic book to promote rubber shoe heels.*

HAROLD TEEN (N)
Cupples & Leon Co.: 1929 (9-7/8x9-7/8", 52 pgs, cardboard covers)
nn - By Carl Ed 41.00 164.00 290.00
nn - (1931, 8-11/16x6-7/8", 96 pgs, hardcover w/dj) 41.00 164.00 290.00
NOTE: *Title 2nd book:* ***HAROLD TEEN AND HIS OLD SIDE-KICK– POP JENKINS,*** *(Adv. of...). Precursor for Archie Andrews & crew; strip began May 4, 1919 running into 1959.*

HAROLD TEEN PAINT AND COLOR BOOK (N)
McLoughlin Bros Inc.: 1932 (13x9-3/4, 28 pgs, B&W and color)
#2054 25.00 100.00 175.00

HAWKSHAW THE DETECTIVE (See Advs. of..., Hans Und Fritz & Okay) (N)
The Saalfield Publishing Co.: 1917 (10-1/2x13-1/2", 24 pgs., B&W)
nn - By Gus Mager (Sunday strip-r) 54.00 190.00 325.00
nn - By Gus Mayer (1923 reprint of 1917 edition) 25.00 100.00 175.00
nn - By Gus Mager (1926 reprint of 1917 edition) 25.00 100.00 175.00
NOTE: *Runs Feb 23, 1913-Sept 4, 1922, starts again from Dec 13, 1931-Feb 11, 1952; Sherlock Holmes spoof.*

HEALTH IN PICTURES
American Public Health Association, NYC: 1930 (6-1/2" x 5-3/16", 76 pgs, green & black paper-c, B&W interior)
nn - By various 15.00 51.00 90.00
NOTE: *Collection of strips and cartoons put out by the Public Health Association, on topics ranging from boating and food safety, to small pox and typhoid prevention.*

HE DONE HER WRONG (O)
Doubleday, Doran & Company: 1930 (8-1/4x 7-1/4", 276pgs, hardcover with dust jacket, B&W interiors)
nn - By Milt Gross 50.00 200.00 350.00
NOTE: *A seminal original-material wordless graphic novel, not reprints. Several modern reprints.*

HELLO BUDDY (see also **HALT FRIENDS**)
???: 1919? (4-3/8x5-3/4", 36 pgs, color-c, B&W, 15¢)
nn - Unknown 10.00 30.00 70.00
NOTE: *Says on front cover: "Comics of War Facts of Service Sold on its merits by Unemployed or Disabled Ex-Service Men." These are very common; contents vary widely.*

HENRY (N)
David McKay Co.: 1935 (25¢, soft-c)
Book 1 - By Carl Anderson 50.00 200.00 350.00
NOTE: *Strip began March 19 1932; this book ties with Popeye (David McKay) and Little Annie Rooney (David McKay) as the last of the 10x10" Platinum Age comic books.*

HENRY (M)
Greenberg Publishers Inc.: 1935 (11-1/4x 8-5/8", 72 pgs, red & blue color hardcover, dust jacket, B&W interiors) (strip-r from Saturday Evening Post)
nn - By Carl Anderson 50.00 200.00 350.00

HIGH KICKING KELLYS, THE (M)
Vaudeville News Corporation, NY: 1926 (5x11", B&W, two color soft-c)
nn - By Jack A. Ward (scarce) 40.00 160.00 280.00

HIGHLIGHTS OF HISTORY (N)
World Syndicate Publishing Co.: 1933-34 (4-1/2x4", 288 pgs)
nn - 5 different unnumbered issues; daily strip-r 10.00 40.00 70.00
NOTE: *Titles include Buffalo Bill, Daniel Boone, Kit Carson, Pioneers of the Old West, Winning of the Old Northwest. There are line drawing color covers and embossed hardcover versions. It is unknown which came out first.*

HOMER HOLCOMB AND MAY (N)
no publisher listed: 1920s (4 x 9-1/2", 40 pgs, paper cover, B&W)
nn - By Doc Bird Finch (strip-r) 10.00 40.00 70.00

HOME, SWEET HOME (N)
M.S. Publishing Co.: 1925 (10-1/4x10")
nn - By Tuthill 33.00 134.00 235.00

HOW THEY DRAW PROHIBITION (S)
Association Against Prohibition: 1930 (10x9", 100 pgs.)
nn - Single panel and multi-panel comics (rare) 71.00 285.00 500.00
NOTE: *Contains art by J.N. "Ding" Darling, James Flagg, Rollin Kirby, Winsor McCay, T.E. Powers, H.T. Webster, others. Also comes with a loose sheet listing all the newspapers where the cartoons originally appeared.*

HOW TO BE A CARTOONIST (H)
Saalfield Pub. Co: 1936 (10-3/8x12-1/2", 16 pgs, color-c, B&W)
nn - By Chas. H. Kuhn 10.00 40.00 70.00

HOW TO DRAW: A PRACTICAL BOOK OF INSTRUCTION (H)
Harper & Brothers: 1904 (9-1/4x12-3/8", 128 pgs, hardcover, B&W)
nn - Edited By Leon Barritt 57.00 228.00 400.00
NOTE: *Strips reprinted include: "Buster Brown" by Outcault, "Foxy Grandpa" by Bunny, "Happy Hooligan" by Opper, "Katzenjammer Kids" by Dirks, "Lady Bountiful" by Gene Carr, "Mr. Jack" by Swinnerton, "Panhandle Pete" by George McManus, "Mr E.Z. Mark" by F.M. Howarth others; non-character strips by Hy Mayer, Winsor McCay, T.E. Powers, others; single panel cartoons by Davenport, Frost, McDougall, Nast, W.A. Rogers, Sullivant, others.*

HOW TO DRAW CARTOONS (H)
Garden City Publishing Co.: 1926, 1937 (10 1/4 x 7 1/2, 150 pgs)
1926 first edition By Clare Briggs 25.00 75.00 150.00
1937 2nd edition By Clare Briggs 20.00 60.00 120.00
NOTE: *Seminal "how to" break into the comics syndicates with art by Briggs, Fisher, Goldberg, King, Webster, Opper, Tad, Hershfield, McCay, Ding, others. Came with Dust Jacket -add 50%.*

HOW TO DRAW FUNNY PICTURES: A Complete Course in Cartooning (H)
Frederick J. Drake & Co., Chicago: 1936 (10-3/8x6-7/8", 168 pgs, hardcover, B&W)
nn - By E.C. Matthews (200 illus by Eugene Zimmerman) 20.00 60.00 120.00

HY MAYER (M)
Puck Publishing: 1915 (13-1/2 x 20-3/4", 52 pgs, hardcover cover, color & B&W interiors) (reprints from Puck)
nn - By Hy Mayer 40.00 140.00 240.00

HYSTERICAL HISTORY OF THE CIVILIAN CONSERVATION CORPS
Peerless Engraving: 1934 (10-3/4x7-1/2", 104 pgs, soft-c, B&W)
nn - By various 20.00 60.00 120.00
NOTE: *Comics about CCC life, includes two color insert postcards in back.*

INDOOR SPORTS (N,S)
National Specials Co., New York: nd circa 1912 (25 cents, 6 x 9", 68 pgs, B&W)
nn - Tad 40.00 120.00 200.00
NOTE: *Cartoons reprinted from Hearst papers.*

IT HAPPENS IN THE BEST FAMILIES (N)
Powers Photo Engraving Co.: 1920 (52 pgs.)(9-1/2x10-3/4")
nn - By Briggs; B&W Sunday strips-r 29.00 114.00 200.00
Special Railroad Edition (30¢)-r/strips from 1914-1920 26.00 103.00 180.00

JIMMIE DUGAN AND THE REG'LAR FELLERS (N)
Cupples & Leon: 1921, 46 pgs. (11"x16")
nn - By Gene Byrne 71.00 284.00 500.00
NOTE: *Ties with EmBee's Mutt & Jeff and Trouble of Bringing Up Father as the last of this size.*

JIMMY (N)
N. Y. American & Journal: 1905 (10x15", 40 pgs., color)
nn - By Jimmy Swinnerton 200.00 700.00 1200.00
NOTE: *James Swinnerton was one of the original first pioneers of the American newspaper comic strip.*

JIMMY AND HIS SCRAPES (N)
Frederick A. Stokes: 1906, (10-1/4x15-1/4", 66 pgs, cardboard-c, color)
nn - By Jimmy Swinnerton 64.00 256.00 450.00

JIMMY, STORY OF (I)
McLoughlin Bros.:1932 (9-1/2"X12", 16 pgs., soft cover)
nn - By Jimmy Swinnerton and Mary Kinnaird 57.00 228.00 400.00

JOE PALOOKA (N)
Cupples & Leon Co.: 1933 (9-13/16x10", 52 pgs., B&W daily strip-r)
nn - By Ham Fisher (scarce) 114.00 456.00 800.00

JOLLY POLLY'S BOOK OF ENGLISH AND ETIQUETTE (S)
Jos. J. Frisch: 1931 (60 cents, 8 x 5-1/8, 88 pgs, paper-c, B&W)
nn - By Jos. J. Frisch 20.00 60.00 120.00
NOTE: *Reprint of single panel newspaper series, 4 per page, of English and etiquette lessons taught by a flapper.*

JOHN, JONATHAN, AND MR. OPPER (N,S)
Grant Richards, London: 1903 (2 shillings, 9-5/8" x 8-1/8", 100 pgs, hard-c, B&W)
nn- (Scarce) by F. Opper 20.00 60.00 120.00
NOTE: *Collection of single panel cartoons involving Uncle Sam (also known as Brother Jonathan), and John Bull (symbolic character for Britain), all reprinted from the* ***New York American and Journal.***

JOYS AND GLOOMS (N)
Reilly & Britton Co.: 1912 (11x8", 72 pgs, hard-c, B&W interior)
nn - By T. E. Powers (newspaper strip-r) 39.00 156.00 275.00

JUDGE - yet to be indexed

The Cruise of the Katzenjammer Kids
© NY American & Journal

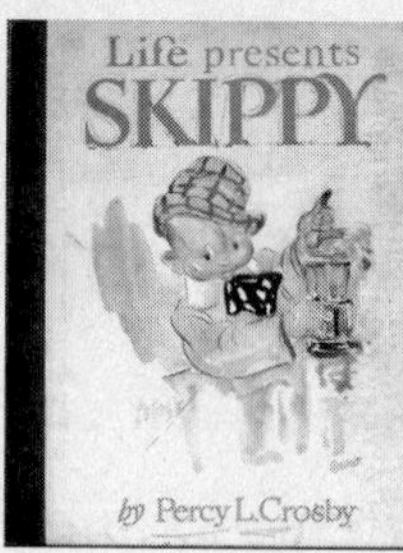

Life Presents Skippy by Percy L. Crosby
1924 © Life Publishing Company

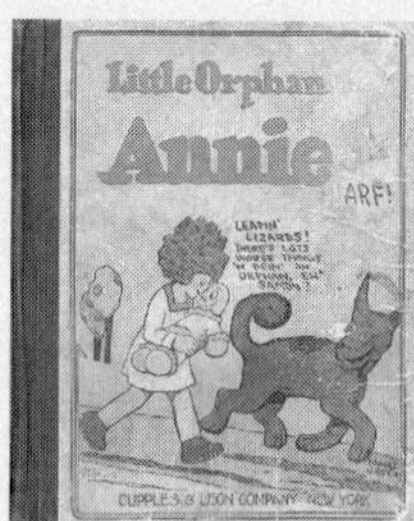

Little Orphan Annie 1926
© C&L

	GD2.0	FN6.0	VF8.0

JUDGE'S LIBRARY - yet to be indexed

JUST KIDS COMICS FOR CRAYON COLORING
King Features. NYC: 1928 (11x8-1/2, 16 pgs, soft-c)

nn - By Ad Carter 25.00 75.00 150.00
NOTE: *Porous better grade paper; top pics printed in color; lower in b&w to color.*

JUST KIDS, THE STORY OF (I)
McLoughlin Bros.: 1932 (12x9-1/2", 16 pgs., paper-c)

283-Three-color text, pictures on heavy paper 39.00 156.00 275.00

KAPTAIN KIDDO AND PUPPO (N)
Frederick A. Stokes Co.: 1910-1913 (11x16-1/2", 62 pgs)

1910-By Grace Wiederseim (later Drayton) 40.00 140.00 240.00
1910-Turr-ble Tales of... By Grace Wiederseim (Edward Stern & Co., 11x16-1/2", 64 pgs.) 40.00 140.00 240.00
1913- ...'Speriences By Grace Drayton 40.00 140.00 240.00
NOTE: *Strip ran approx. 1909-1912.*

KATZENJAMMER KIDS, THE (Also see Hans Und Fritz) (N)
New York American & Journal: 1902,1903 (10x15-1/4", 86 pgs., color)
(By Rudolph Dirks; strip first appeared in 1897) © W.R. Hearst
NOTE: *All KK books 1902-1905 all have the same exact title page with a 1902 copyright by W.R. Hearst; almost always look instead on the front cover.*

1902 (Rare) (red & black); has 1901-02 strips 500.00 1780.00 -
1903- **A New Edition** (Rare), 86 pgs 450.00 1575.00 -
1904- 10x15", 84 pgs 250.00 780.00 -
1905?-The Cruise of the, 10x15", 60¢, in color 250.00 780.00 -
1905-A Series of Comic Pictures, 10x15", 84 pgs. in color, possible reprint of 1904 edition 250.00 780.00 -
1905-Tricks of... (10x15", 66 pgs, Stokes) 250.00 780.00 -
1906-Stokes (10x16", 32 pgs. in color) 186.00 675.00 -
1907- The Cruise of the, 10x15", 62 pgs 1905-r? 186.00 675.00 -
1910-The Komical...(10x15) 108.00 400.00 700.00
1921-Embee Dist. Co., 10x16", 20 pgs. in color 100.00 375.00 650.00

KATZENJAMMER KIDS MAGIC DRAWING AND COLORING BOOK (N)
Sam L Gabriel Sons And Company: 1931 (8 1/2 x 12", 36 pages, stiff-c

838-By Knerr 50.00 200.00 350.00

KEEPING UP WITH THE JONESES (N)
Cupples & Leon Co.: 1920 - No. 2, 1921 (9-1/4x9-1/4",52 pgs.,B&W daily strip-r)

1,2-By Pop Momand 39.00 154.00 270.00

KID KARTOONS (N,S)
The Century Co.: 1922 (232 pgs, printed 1 side, 9-3/4 x 7-3/4", hard-c, B&W)

nn - By Gene Carr 60.00 240.00 -

KING OF THE ROYAL MOUNTED (Also See Dan Dunn) (N)
Whitman Publishing: 1937 (5 1/2 x 7 1/4", 68 pgs., color cardboard-c, B&W)

1010 36.00 144.00 250.00

LADY BOUNTIFUL (N)
Saalfield Publ. Co./Press Publ. Co.: 1917 (13-3/8x10", 36 pgs, color cardboard-c, B&W interiors)

nn - By Gene Carr; 2 panels per page 50.00 175.00 300.00
193S - 2nd printing (13-1/8x10",28 pgs color-c, B&W) 33.00 117.00 200.00

LAUGHS YOU MIGHT HAVE HAD From The Comic Pages of Six Week Day Issues of the Post-Dispatch (N)
St. Louis Post-Dispatch: 1921 (9 x 10 1/2", 28 pgs, B&W, red ink cover)

nn - Various comic strips 39.00 154.00 270.00

LIFE, DOGS FROM (M)
Doubleday, Page & Company: nn 1920 - No.2 1926 (130 pgs, 11-1/4 x 9", color painted-c, hard-c, B&W)

nn (No.1) 120.00 360.00 -
Second Litter 80.00 320.00 -
NOTE: *Reprints strips & cartoons featuring dogs, from Life Magazine. Edited by Thomas L. Masson. Highly sought by collectors of dog ephemera. Art in both books is mostly by Robert L. Dickey. Other art: Carl Anderson-1,2; Barbes-1; Chip Bellew-1; Lang Campbell-1,2; Percy Crosby-1,2; Edwina-2; Frueh-2; R.B. Fuller-1; Gibson-1,2; Don Herold-2; Gus Mager-2; Orr-1; J.R. Shaver-1,2; T.S. Sullivant-2; Russ Westover-1,2; Crawford Young-1.*

LIFE OF DAVY CROCKETT IN PICTURE AND STORY, THE
Cupples & Leon: 1935 (8-3/4x7", 64 pgs, B&W hardcover, dust jacket?)

nn - By C. Richard Schaare 28.00 112.00 195.00

LIFE OF THOMAS A. EDISON IN WORD AND PICTURE, THE (N)(Also see Edison...)
Thomas A. Edison Industries: 1928 (10x8", 56 pgs, paper cover, B&W)

nn - Photo-c 50.00 200.00 350.00
NOTE: *Reprints newspaper strip which ran August to November 1927.*

LIFE'S LITTLE JOKES (S)
M.S. Publ. Co.: No date (1924)(10-1/16x10", 52 pgs., B&W)

	GD2.0	FN6.0	VF8.0

nn - By Rube Goldberg 64.00 257.00 450.00

LIFE PRESENTS SKIPPY (see SKIPPY, LIFE PRESENTS)

LIFE'S PRINTS (was **LIFE'S PICTURE GALLERY** - See Victorian Age section) (M,S,P)
Life Publishing Company, New York: nd (c1907) (7x4-1/2", 132 pgs, paper cover, B&W) (all are Scarce)

nn - (nd; c1907) unillustrated black construction paper cover; reprints art from 1895-1907; art by J.M.Flagg, A.B.Frost, Gibson - - -
nn - (nd; c1908) b&w cardboard painted cover by Gibson, showing angel raising a champagne glass; reprints art from 1901-1908; art by J.M.Flagg, A.B.Frost, Gibson, Walt Kuhn, Art Young - - -
NOTE: *Catalog of prints reprinted from LIFE covers & centerspreads. There are likely more as yet unreported catalogs.*

LIFE, THE COMEDY OF LIFE
Life Publishing Company: 1907 (130 pgs, 11-3/4x9-1/4",embossed printed cloth covered board-c, B+W

nn - By various 20.00 80.00 120.00
NOTE: *Single cartoons and some sequential cartoons). Artists include Charles Dana Gibson, Harrison Cady, E.W. Kemble, James Montgomery Flagg.*

LILY OF THE ALLEY IN THE FUNNIES
Whitman Publishing Co.: No date (1927) (10-1/4x15-1/2"; 28 pgs., color)

W936 - By T. Burke (Rare) 57.00 228.00 400.00

LITTLE ANNIE ROONEY (N)
David McKay Co.: 1935 (25¢, soft-c)

Book 1 43.00 172.00 300.00
NOTE: *Ties with Henry & Popeye (David McKay) as the last of the 10x10" size Plat comic books.*

LITTLE ANNIE ROONEY WISHING BOOK (G) (See Happy Hooligan, Story of #281)
McLoughlin Bros.: 1932 (12x9-1/2", 16 pgs., soft-c, 3-color text, heavier paper)

282 - By Darrell McClure 38.00 134.00 230.00

LITTLE BIRD TOLD ME, A (E)
Life Publishing Co.: 1905? (96 pgs, hardbound)

nn - By Walt Kuhn (Life-r) 38.00 134.00 230.00

LITTLE FOLKS PAINTING BOOK (N)
The National Arts Company: 1931 (10-7/8 x 15-1/4", 20 pgs, half in full color)

nn - By "Tack" Knight (strip-r) 33.00 132.00 230.00

LITTLE JOHNNY & THE TEDDY BEARS (Judge-r) (M) (see Teddy Bear Books)
Reilly & Britton Co.: 1907 (10x14", 32 pgs.; green, red, black interior color)

nn - By J. R. Bray-a/Robert D. Towne-s 67.00 233.00 400.00

LITTLE JOURNEY TO THE HOME OF BRIGGS THE SKY-ROCKET, THE
Lockhart Art School: 1917 (10-3/4x7-7/8", 20 pgs, B&W) (I)

nn - About Clare Briggs (bio & lots of early art) 38.00 134.00 230.00

LITTLE KING, THE (see New Yorker Cartoon Albums for 1st appearance) (M)
Farrar & Reinhart, Inc: 1933 (10-1/4 x 8-3/4, 80 pgs, hardcover w/dust jacket

nn - By Otto Soglow (strip-r The New Yorker) 43.00 129.00 300.00
NOTE: *Copies with dust jacket are worth 50% more. Also exists in a 12x8-3/4 edition.*

LITTLE LULU BY MARGE (M)
Rand McNally & Company, Chicago: 1936 (6-9/16x6", 68 pgs, yellow hard-c, B&W)

nn - By Marjorie Henderson Buell 25.00 100.00 200.00
NOTE: *Begins reprinting single panel Little Lulu cartoons which began with Saturday Evening Post Feb. 23, 1935. This book was reprinted several times as late as 1940.*

LITTLE NAPOLEON
No publisher listed: 1924 , 50 pages, 10" by 10"; Color cardstock-c, B&W

nn - By Bud Counihan 25.00 100.00 200.00
NOTE: *Same format as Cupples and Leon books.*

LITTLE NEMO (...in Slumberland) (N)
Doffield & Co.(1906)/Cupples & Leon Co.(1909): 1906, 1909 (Sunday strip-r in color, cardboard covers)

1906-11x16-1/2" by Winsor McCay; 30 pgs. (scarce) 900.00 3350.00 -
1909-10x14" by Winsor McCay (scarce) 850.00 2675.00 -

LITTLE ORPHAN ANNIE (See Treasure Box of Famous Comics) (N)
Cupples & Leon Co.: 1926 - 1934 (8-3/4x7", 100 pgs., B&W daily strip-r, hard-c)

1 (1926)-Little Orphan Annie (softback see Treasure Box) 50.00 200.00 375.00
2 (1927)-In the Circus (softback see Wonder Box...) 36.00 144.00 275.00
3 (1928)-The Haunted House (softback see Wonder Box...) 36.00 144.00 275.00
4 (1929)-Bucking the World 36.00 144.00 275.00
5 (1930)-Never Say Die 30.00 120.00 225.00
6 (1931)-Shipwrecked 30.00 120.00 225.00
7 (1932)-A Willing Helper 24.00 96.00 190.00
8 (1933)-In Cosmic City 24.00 96.00 190.00
9 (1934)-Uncle Dan (not rare) 24.00 96.00 190.00
NOTE: *Each book reprints dailies from the previous year. Each hardcover came with a dust jacket. Books without dust jackets are worth 50% less. Many of copies of #9 Uncle Dan have been turning up on eBay recently.*

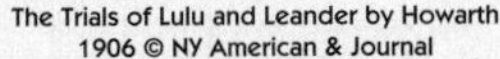
The Trials of Lulu and Leander by Howarth
1906 © NY American & Journal

Maud the Mirthful Mule by Opper
1908 © Frederick A. Stokes

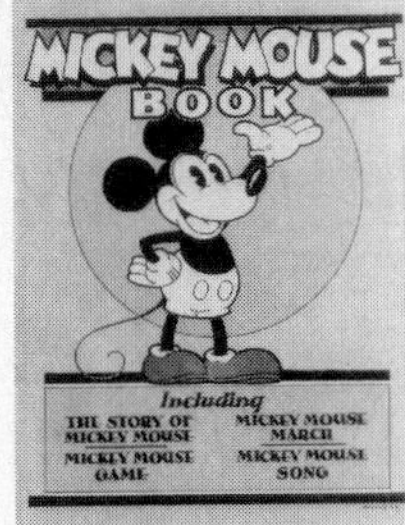

Mickey Mouse Book
1930 © Bibo & Lang

GD2.0 FN6.0 VF8.0

LITTLE ORPHAN ANNIE RUMMY CARDS (N)
Whitman Publishing Co., Racine: 1935 (box: 5 x 6 1/2" Cards: 3 1/2 x 2 1/4")

nn-Harold Gray 20.00 60.00 120.00
NOTE: *36 cards, including 1 instruction card, 5 character cards and 30 cards forming 5 sequential stories (6 cards each).*

LITTLE SAMMY SNEEZE (N)
New York Herald Co.: Dec 1905 (11x16-1/2", 72 pgs., color)

nn - By Winsor McCay (Very Rare) 1300.00 3900.00 -
NOTE: *Rarely found in fine to mint condition.*

LIVE AND LET LIVE
Travelers Insurance Co.: 1936 (5-3/4x7/3/4", 16 pgs. color and B&W)

nn - Bill Holman, Carl Anderson, etc 20.00 60.00 120.00

LULU AND LEANDER (N)
New York American & Journal: 1904 (76 pgs); **William A Stokes & Co:** 1906

nn - By F.M. Howarth 143.00 500.00 860.00
nn - The Trials of...(1906, 10x16", 68 pgs. in color) 143.00 500.00 860.00
NOTE: *F. M. Howarth helped pioneer the American comic strip in the pages of PUCK magazine in the early 1890s before the Yellow Kid.*

MADMAN'S DRUM (O)
Jonathan Cape and Harrison Smith Inc.: 1930 (8-1/4x6", 274 pgs, B&W hardcover w/dust jacket) (original graphic novel in wood cuts)

nn - By Lynd Ward 50.00 175.00 300.00

MAMA'S ANGEL CHILD IN TOYLAND (I)
Rand McNally, Chicago: 1915 (128 pgs, hardbound)

nn - By M.T. "Penny" Ross & Marie C, Sadler 40.00 140.00 240.00
NOTE: *Mamma's Angel Child published as a comic strip by the "Chicago Tribune" 1908 Mar 1 to 1920 Oct 17.This novel dedicated to Esther Starring Richartz, "the original Mamma's Angel Kid."*

MAUD (N) (see also **Happy Hooligan**)
Frederick A. Stokes Co.: 1906 - 1908? (10x15-1/2", cardboard-c)

1906-By Fred Opper (Scarce), 66 pgs. color 257.00 900.00 -
1907-The Matchless, 10x15" 70 pgs in color 200.00 700.00 -
1908-The Mirthful Mule, 10x15", 64 pgs in color 200.00 700.00 -
NOTE: *First run of strip began July 24, 1904 to at least Oct 6, 1907, spun out of* ***Happy Hooligan.***

MEMORIAL EDITION The Drawings of Clare Briggs (S)
Wm H. Wise & Company: 1930 (7-1/2x8-3/4", 284 pgs, pebbled false black leather, B&W) (posthumous boxed set of 7 books by Clare Briggs)

nn - The Days of Real Sport; nn-Golf; nn-Real Folks at Home; nn-Ain't it a Grand and Glorious Feeling?; nn-That Guiltiest Feeling; nn-Somebody's Always Taking the Joy Out of Life; nn-When a Feller Needs a Friend
Each book... 30.00 120.00 210.00
NOTE: *Also exists in a whitish cream colored paper back edition; first edition unknown presently.*

MENACE CARTOONS (M, S)
Menace Publishing Company, Aurora, Missouri: 1914 (10-3/8x8", 80 pgs, cardboard-c, B&W)

nn - (Rare) 50.00 150.00 450.00
NOTE: *Reprints anti-Catholic cartoons from K.K.K. related publication* ***The Menace.***

MEN OF DARING (N)
Cupples & Leon Co.: 1933 (8-3/4x7", 100 pgs)

nn - By Stookie Allen, intro by Lowell Thomas 30.00 90.00 180.00

MICKEY MOUSE BOOK
Bibo & Lang: 1930-1931 (12x9", stapled-c, 20 pgs., 4 printings)

nn - First Disney licensed publication (a magazine, not a book–see first book, Adventures of Mickey Mouse). Contains story of how Mickey met Walt and got his name; games, cartoons & song "Mickey Mouse (You Cute Little Feller)," written by Irving Bibo; Minnie, Clarabelle Cow, Horace Horsecollar & caricature of Walt shaking hands with Mickey. The changes made with the 2nd printing have been verified by billing affidavits in the Walt Disney Archives and include:Two Win Smith Mickey strips from 4/15/30 and 4/17/30 added to page 8 & back-c; "Printed in U.S.A." added to front cover; Bobette Bibo's age of 11 years added to title page; faulty type on the word "tail" corrected top of page 3; the word "start" added to bottom of page 7, removing the words "start 1 2 3 4" from the top of page 7; music and lyrics were rewritten on pages 12-14. A green ink border was added beginning with 2nd printing and some covers have inking variations. Art by Albert Barbelle, drawn in an Ub Iwerks style. Total circulation : 97,938 copies varying from 21,000 to 26,000 per printing.

1st printing. Contains the song lyrics **censored** in later printings, "When little Minnie's pursued by a big bad villain we feel so bad then we're glad when you up and kill him." Attached to the Nov. 15, 1930 issue of the Official Bulletin of the Mickey Mouse Club notes: "Attached to this Bulletin is a new Mickey Mouse Book that has just been published." This is thought to be the reason why a slightly disproportionate larger number of copies of the first printing still exist 1150.00 5400.00 11,000.00
2nd printing with a theater/advertising. Christmas greeting added to inside front cover (1 copy known with Dec. 27, 1930 date) – 12,000.00 –
2nd-4th printings 1050.00 5000.00 10,000.00
NOTE: *Theater/advertising copies do not qualify as separate printings. Most copies are missing pages 9 & 10 which had a puzzle to be cut out. Puzzle (pages 9 and 10) cut out or missing, subtract 60% to 75%.*

GD2.0 FN6.0 VF8.0

MICKEY MOUSE COLORING BOOK (S)
Saalfield Publishing Company:1931 (15-1/4x10-3/4", 32 pgs, color soft cover, half printed in full color interior, rest B&W, only Saalfield Mickey Mouse item known)

871 - By Ub Iwerks & Floyd Gottfredson (rare) 400.00 1200.00 2520.00
NOTE: *Contains reprints of first MM daily strip ever, including the "missing" speck the chicken is after found only on the original daily strip art by Iwerks plus other very early MM art.*

MICKEY MOUSE, THE ADVENTURES OF (I)
David McKay Co., Inc.: Book I, 1931 - Book II, 1932 (5-1/2"x8-1/2", 32 pgs.)

Book I-First Disney book, by strict definition (1st printing-50,000 copies)(see Mickey Mouse Book by Bibo & Lang). Illustrated text refers to Clarabelle Cow as "Carolyn" and Horace Horsecollar as "Henry". The name "Donald Duck" appears with a non-costumed generic duck on back cover & inside, not in the context of the character that later debuted in the Wise Little Hen.
Hardback w/characters on back-c 75.00 300.00 575.00
Softcover w/characters on back-c 38.00 151.00 290.00
Version without characters on back-c 45.00 180.00 350.00
Book II-Less common than Book I. Character development brought into conformity with the Mickey Mouse cartoon shorts and syndicated strips. Captain Church Mouse, Tanglefoot, Peg-Leg Pete and Pluto appear with Mickey & Minnie 46.00 186.00 360.00

MICKEY MOUSE COMIC (N)
David McKay Co.: 1931 - No. 4, 1934 (10"x9-3/4", 52 pgs., cardboard-c) (Later reprints exist)

1 (1931)-Reprints Floyd Gottfredson daily strips in black & white from 1930 & 1931, including the famous two week sequence in which Mickey tries to commit suicide 229.00 914.00 1680.00
2 (1932)-1st app. of Pluto reprinted from 7/8/31 daily. All pgs. from 1931 164.00 656.00 1200.00
3 (1933)-Reprints 1932 & 1933 Sunday pages in color, one strip per page, including the "Lair of Wolf Barker" continuity pencilled by Gottfredson and inked by Al Taliaferro & Ted Thwaites. First app. Mickey's nephews, Morty & Ferdie, one identified by name of Mortimer Fieldmouse, not to be confused with Uncle Mortimer Mouse who is introduced in the Wolf Barker story 214.00 856.00 1600.00
4 (1934)-1931 dailies, include the only known reprint of the infamous strip of 2/4/31 where the villainous Kat Nipp snips off the end of Mickey's tail with a pair of scissors 129.00 514.00 950.00

MICKEY MOUSE (N)
Whitman Publishing Co.: 1933-34 (10x8-3/4", 34 pgs, cardboard-c)

948-1932 & 1933 Sunday strips in color, printed from the same plates as Mickey Mouse Book #3 by David McKay, but only pages 5-17 & 32-48 (including all of the "Wolf Barker" continuity) 157.00 629.00 1100.00
NOTE: *Some copies bound with back cover upside down. Variance doesn't affect value. Same art appears on front and back covers of all copies. Height of Whitman reissue trimmed 1/2 inch.*

MILITARY WILLIE
J. I. Austen Co.: 1907 (7x9-1/2", 12 pgs., every other page in color, stapled)

nn - By F. R. Morgan 70.00 245.00 400.00

MINNEAPOLIS TRIBUNE CARTOON BOOK (S)
Minneapolis Tribune: 1899-1903 (11-3/8x9-3/8", B&W, paper cover)

nn (#1) (1899) 28.00 99.00 170.00
nn (#2) (1900) 28.00 99.00 170.00
nn (#3) (1901) (published Jan 01, 1901) 28.00 99.00 170.00
nn (#4) (1902) (114 pgs) 28.00 99.00 170.00
nn (#5) (1903) (9x10-3/4",110 pgs, B&W; color-c) 28.00 99.00 170.00
NOTE: *All by Roland C. Bowman (editorial-r).*

MINUTE BIOGRAPHIES: INTIMATE GLIMPSES INTO THE LIVES OF 150 FAMOUS MEN AND WOMEN
Grossett & Dunlap: 1931, 1933 (10-1/4x7-3/4", 168 pgs, hardcover, B&W)

nn - By Nisenson (art) & Parker(text) 20.00 60.00 120.00
More.... (1933) 20.00 60.00 120.00

MISCHIEVOUS MONKS OF CROCODILE ISLE, THE (N)
J. I. Austen Co., Chicago: 1908 (8-1/2x11-1/2", 12 pgs., 4 pgs. in color)

nn - By F. R. Morgan; reads longwise 96.00 335.00 575.00

MR. & MRS. (Also see Ain't It A Grand and Glorious Feeling?) (N)
Whitman Publishing Co.: 1922 (9x9-1/2", 52 & 28 pgs., cardboard-c)

nn - By Briggs (B&W, 52 pgs.) 37.00 149.00 260.00
nn - 28 pgs.-(9x9-1/2")-Sunday strips-r in color 41.00 163.00 285.00
NOTE: *The earliest presently-known Whitman comic books*

MR. BLOCK (N)
Industrial Workers of the World (IWW): 1913, 1919

nn - By Ernest Riebe (C) 50.00 150.00 -
...And The Profiteers (original material) (H) 50.00 150.00
NOTE: *Mr Block was a daily strip published from 1912 NOV 7 to 1913 SEP ? by the socialist newspaper "Industrial Worker"; Mr Block was a "square" guy (his head was in fact a block) who enthusiastically supported the same system that exploited him. The noted Joe Hill wrote a song about him (Mr Block,1913, on the air of*

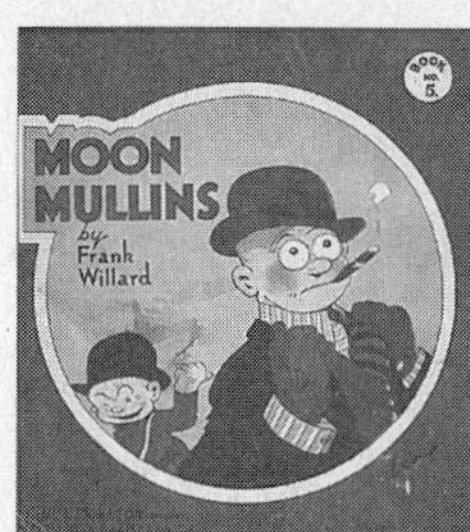

Moon Mullins #5 by Frank Willard
1931 @ Cupples & Leon

The Nebbs
© C&L

The Newlyweds by George McManus
1907 © Saalfield Publishing Co.

GD2.0 FN6.0 VF8.0

"It loooks me like a big time tonight") for the "Industrial Worker Songbook".

MR. TWEE-DEEDLE (N)
Cupples & Leon: 1913, 1917 (11-3/8 x 16-3/4" color strips-r from NY Herald)
nn - By John B. Gruelle (later of Raggedy Ann fame) 200.00 700.00 1300.00
nn - "Further Adventures of..." By Gruelle 200.00 700.00 1300.00
NOTE: *Strip ran Feb 5, 1911-March 10, 1918.*

MONKEY SHINES OF MARSELEEN AND SOME OF HIS ADVENTURES (C)
McLaughlin Bros. New York: 1906 (10 x 12-3/8", 36 pgs, full color hardcover)
nn - By Norman E. Jennett strip-r NY Evening Telegram 67.00 233.00 400.00
NOTE: *Strip began in 1906 until at least March 13, 1910.*

MONKEY SHINES OF MARSELEEN (N)
Cupples & Leon Co.: 1909 (11-1/2 x 17", 58 pgs. in two colors)
nn - By Norman E. Jennett (strip-r New York Herald) 63.00 219.00 375.00

MOON MULLINS (N)
Cupples & Leon Co.: 1927 - 1933 (52 pgs., B&W daily strip-r)
Series 1 ('27)-By Willard 57.00 228.00 400.00
Series 2 ('28), Series 3 ('29), Series 4 ('30) 39.00 156.00 275.00
Series 5 ('31), 6 ('32), 7 ('33) 36.00 144.00 250.00
Big Book 1 ('30)-B&W (scarce) 100.00 400.00 700.00
w/dust jacket (rare) 183.00 732.00 1275.00

MUTT & JEFF (...Cartoon, The) (N)
Ball Publications: 1911 - No. 5, 1916 (5-3/4 x 15-1/2", 68 pgs, B&W, hard-c)
1 (1910)(50¢) very common 71.00 286.00 500.00
2,3: 2 (1911)-Opium den panels; Jeff smokes opium (pipe dreams).
3 (1912) both very common 71.00 286.00 500.00
2-Reprint of 1913 edition with black ink cover 50.00 175.00 300.00
4 (1915) (50¢) (Scarce) 100.00 300.00 600.00
5 (1916) (Rare) -Photos of Fisher, 1st pg. (68 pages) 150.00 450.00 800.00
5-Scarce 84 page reprint edition 150.00 450.00 800.00
NOTE: *Mutt & Jeff first appeared in newspapers in 1907. Cover variations exist showing Mutt & Jeff reading various newspapers; i.e., The Oregon Journal, The American, and The Detroit News. Reprinting of each issue began soon after publication. No. 4 and 5 may not have been reprinted. Values listed include the reprints. Mutt & Jeff was the first successful American daily newspaper comic strip and as such remains one of the seminal strips of all time.*

MUTT & JEFF (N)
Cupples & Leon Co.: No. 6, 1919 - No. 22, 1934? (9-1/2x9-1/2", 52 pgs., B&W dailies, stiff-c)
6, 7 - By Bud Fisher (very common) 32.00 128.00 225.00
8-10 46.00 186.00 325.00
11-18 (Somewhat Scarcer) 60.00 240.00 420.00
19-22 (Rare) (do these #s even exist?) 71.00 286.00 500.00
nn (1920)-(Advs. of...) 11x16"; 44 pgs.; full color reprints of 1919 Sunday strips 93.00 372.00 650.00
Big Book nn (1926, 144 pgs., hardcovers) 114.00 456.00 800.00
w/dust jacket 193.00 772.00 1350.00
Big Book 1 (1928) - Thick book (hardcovers) 114.00 456.00 800.00
w/dust jacket (rare) 182.00 729.00 1275.00
Big Book 2 (1929) - Thick book (hardcovers) 114.00 456.00 800.00
w/dust jacket (rare) 182.00 729.00 1275.00
NOTE: *The Big Books contain three previous issues rebound.*

MUTT & JEFF (N)
Embee Publ. Co.: 1921 (9x15", color cardboard-c & interior)
nn - Sunday strips in color (Rare)- BY Bud Fisher 143.00 572.00 1000.00
NOTE: *Ties with The Trouble of Bringing Up Father (EmBee) and Jimmie Dugan & The Reg'lar Fellers (C&L) as the last of this size.*

MYSTERIOUS STRANGER AND OTHER CARTOONS, THE
McClure, Phillips & Co.: 1905 (12-3/8x9-3/4", 338 pgs, hardcover, B&W)
nn - By John McCutcheon 32.00 128.00 225.00

MY WAR - Szeged (Szuts)
Wm. Morrow Co.: 1932 (7x10-1/2", 210 pgs, hard-c, B&W)
nn - (All story panels, no words - powerful) 32.00 128.00 225.00

NAUGHTY ADVENTURES OF VIVACIOUS MR. JACK, THE
New York American & Journal: 1904 (15x10", color strips)
nn - By James Swinnerton; (1 known copy) (no known sales)

NEBBS, THE (N)
Cupples & Leon Co.: 1928 (52 pgs., B&W daily strip-r)
nn - By Sol Hess; Carlson-a 40.00 160.00 280.00

NERVY NAT'S ADVENTURES (E)
Leslie-Judge Co.: 1911 (90 pgs, 85¢, 1903 strip reprints from **Judge**)
nn - By James Montgomery Flagg 75.00 263.00 450.00

THE NEWLYWEDS AND THEIR BABY (N)
Saalfield Publ. Co.: 1907 (13x10", 52 pgs., hardcover)

GD2.0 FN6.0 VF8.0

...& Their Baby' by McManus; daily strips 50% color 200.00 700.00 -
NOTE: *Strip ran Apr 10, 1904 thru Jan 14, 1906 and then May 19, 1907-Dec 5, 1916; was a huge success with Baby Snookums long before McManus invented Bringing Up Father; Snookums brought back as a topper strip over BUF Nov 19, 1941-Dec 30, 1956.*

THE NEWLYWEDS AND THEIR BABY'S COMIC PICTURES FOR PAINTING AND CRAYONING (N)
Saalfield Publishign Company: 1916 (10-1/4x14-3/4", 52 pgs. Cardboard-c)
nn - 44 B&W pages, covers, and one color wrap glued to B&W title page.
Color wrap: color title pg. & 3 pgs of color strips 82.00 286.00 490.00
nn - (1917, 10x14", 20 pgs, oblong, cardboard-c) partial reprint of 1916 edition 30.00 120.00 240.00

THE NEWLYWEDS AND THEIR BABY (N)
Saalfield Publishing Company: 1917 (10-1/8x13-9/16", 52 pgs, full color cardstock-c, some pages full color, others two color (orange, blue))
nn 82.00 286.00 490.00

NEW YORKER CARTOON ALBUM, THE (M)
Doubleday, Doran & Company Inc.: (1928-1931); **Harper & Brothers.:** (1931-1933); **Random House** (1935-1937), 12x9", various pg counts, hardcovers w/dust jackets)
1928: nn-114 pgs Arno, Held, Soglow, Williams, etc 20.00 60.00 120.00
1928: SECOND-114 pgs Arno, Bairnsfather, Gross, Held, Soglow, Williams 10.00 30.00 60.00
1930: THIRD-172 pgs Arno, Bairnsfather, Held, Soglow, Art Young 10.00 30.00 60.00
1931: FOURTH-154 pgs Arno, Held, Soglow, Steig, Thurber, Williams, Art Young, "Little King" by Soglow begins 10.00 30.00 60.00
1932: FIFTH-156 pgs Arno, Bairnsfather, Held, Hoff, Soglow, Steig, Thurber, Williams 10.00 30.00 60.00
1933: SIXTH-156 pgs same as above 10.00 30.00 60.00
1935: SEVENTH-164 pgs 10.00 30.00 60.00
1937: 168 pgs; Charles Addams plus same as above but no Little King, two page "Gone With The Wind" parody strip 10.00 30.00 60.00
NOTE: *Some sequential strips but mostly single panel cartoons.*

NIPPY'S POP (N)
The Saalfield Publishing Co.: 1917 (10-1/2x13-1/2", 36 pgs., B&W, Sunday strip-r)
nn - 43.00 152.00 260.00

OH, MAN (A Bully Collection of Those Inimitable Humor Cartoons) (S)
P.F. Volland & Co.: 1919 (8-1/2x13"; 136 pgs.)
nn - By Briggs 43.00 152.00 260.00
NOTE: *Originally came in illustrated box with Briggs art (box is Rare - worth 50% more with box).*

OH SKIN-NAY! (S)
P.F. Volland & Co.: 1913 (8-1/2x13", 136 pgs.)
nn - The Days Of Real Sport by Briggs 43.00 152.00 260.00
NOTE: *Originally came in illustrated box with Briggs art (box is Rare - worth 50% more with box).*

OLD GOLD THE SMOOTHER AND BETTER CIGARETTE...NOT A COUGH IN A CARLOAD (M,N,P) (see also BY BRIGGS)
Old Gold Cigarettes: nd (c1920's) (16 pgs, paper-c, color) (both Scarce)
nn- (4-1/4" x 3-7/8") cover strip is "Oh, Man!"; also contains: "Real Folks at Home", "Ain't It a Grand and Glorious Feelin?", "It Happens in the Best Regulated Families", and "Mr. and Mrs." - - -
1440- (5-9/16" x 5-1/4") cover strip is "Frank and Ernest"; also contains: "That Guiltiest Feeling", "Real Folks at Home", "Oh, Man!", "When a Feller Needs a Friend". - - -
NOTE: *Collection reprinting strip cartoons by Clare Briggs, advertising Old Gold Cigarettes. These strips originally appeared in various magazines, play program booklets, newspapers, etc. Some of the strips involve regular Briggs strip series. The two booklets contain a completely different set of comics.*

ON AND OFF MOUNT ARARAT (also see **Tigers**) (N)
Hearst's New York American & Journal: 1902, 86pgs. 10x15-1/4"
nn - Noah's Ark satire by Jimmy Swinnerton (rare) 286.00 1000.00 -

ON THE LINKS (N)
Associated Feature Service: Dec, 1926 (9x10", 48 pgs.)
nn - Daily strip-r 25.00 100.00 175.00

ONE HUNDRED WAR CARTOONS (S)
Idaho Daily Statesman: 1918 (7-3/4x10", 102 pgs, paperback, B&W)
nn - By Villeneuve (WW I cartoons) 20.00 60.00 120.00

OUR ANTEDILUVIAN ANCESTORS (N,S)
New York Evening Journal, NY: 1903 (11-3/8x8-7/8", hardcover)
nn - By F Opper 25.00 100.00 175.00
NOTE: *There is a simultaneously published British edition, identical size and contents, from C. Arthur Pearson Ltd, London. A collection of single panel cartoons about cavemen. Similar to an earlier British cartoon book "Prehistoric Peeps from Punch", by E.T. Reed.*

OUTBURSTS OF EVERETT TRUE, THE (N)
Saalfield Publ. Co.(Werner Co.): 1907 (92 pgs, 9-7/16x5-1/4")
1907 (2-4 panel strips-r)-By Condo & Raper 75.00 300.00 525.00
1921-Full color-c; reprints 56 of 88 cartoons from 1907 ed. (10x10", 32 pgs B&W)

Oh Skin-nay! by Claire Briggs
1913 © P.F. Volland

The Adventures of Peck's Bad Boy With the Teddy Bear Show by McDougall
1907 © Charles C. Thompson, Co.

Roger Bean, R.G. #4
© C&L

GD2.0 FN6.0 VF8.0

37.00 148.00 260.00

OVER THERE COMEDY FROM FRANCE
Observer House Printing: nd (WW 1 era) (6x14", 60 pgs, paper cover)
nn - Artist(s) unknown 15.00 53.00 90.00

OWN YOUR OWN HOME (I)
Bobbs-Merrill Company, Indianapolis: 1919 (7-7/16x5-1/4")
nn - By Fontaine Fox - - -

PECKS BAD BOY (N)
Charles C. Thompson Co, Chicago (by Walt McDougal): 1906-1908 (strip-r)
...& His Country Cousin Cynthia (1907)-12x16-1/2," 34 pgs In color 100.00 400.00 700.00
Advs. of...And His Country Cousins (1907) 5-1/2x10 1/2", 18 pgs In color 50.00 175.00 300.00
...& Their Advs With The Teddy Bear (1907) 5-1/2x10-1/2", 18 pgs in color 50.00 175.00 300.00
...& Their Balloon Trip To the Country (1907) 5-1/2x 10-1/2, 18 pgs in color 50.00 175.00 300.00
...With the Teddy Bear Show (1907) 5-1/2x 10-1/2 50.00 175.00 300.00
...With The Billy Whiskers Goats (1907) 5-1/2 x 10-1/2, 18 pgs in color 50.00 175.00 300.00
...& His Chums (1908) - 11x16-3/8", 36 pgs. Stanton & Van Vliet Co 100.00 400.00 700.00
...& His Chums (1908)-Hardcover; full color;16 pgs. 100.00 350.00 600.00
Advs. of...in Pictures (1908) (11x17, 36 pgs)-In color; Stanton & Van V. Liet Co. 100.00 400.00 700.00

PERCY & FERDIE (N)
Cupples & Leon Co.: 1921 (10x10", 52 pgs., B&W dailies, cardboard-c)
nn - By H. A. MacGill (Rare) 61.00 244.00 425.00

PETER RABBIT (N)
John H. Eggers Co. The House of Little Books Publishers: 1922 - 1923
B1-B4-(Rare)-(Set of 4 books which came in a cardboard box)-Each book reprints half of a Sunday page per page and contains 8 B&W and 2 color pages; by Harrison Cady (9-1/4x6-1/4", paper-c) each.... 43.00 172.00 300.00
Box only 57.00 228.00 400.00

PHILATELIC CARTOONS (M)
Essex Publishing Company, Lynn, Mass.: 1916 (8-11/16" x 5-7/8", 40 pgs, light blue construction paper-c, B&W interior)
nn - By Leroy S. Bartlett 25.00 75.00 150.00
NOTE: *Comics reprinted from The New England Philatelist.*

PICTORIAL HISTORY OF THE DEPARTMENT OF COMMERCE UNDER HERBERT HOOVER (see Picture Life of a Great American) (O)
Hoover-Curtis Campaign Committee of New York State: no date, 1928 (3-1/4 x 5-1/4, 32 pgs, paper cover, B&W)
nn - By Satterfield (scarce) 40.00 120.00 240.00
NOTE: *1928 Presidential Campaign giveaway. Original material, contents completely different from Picture Life of a Great American.*

PICTURE LIFE OF A GREAT AMERICAN (see Pictorial History of the Department of Commerce under Herbert Hoover) (O)
Hoover-Curtis Campaign Committee of New York State: no date, 1928 (paper cover, B&W)
nn - (8-3/4 x 7, 20 pgs) Text cover, 2 page text introduction, 18 pgs of comics (scarcer first print) 40.00 120.00 240.00
nn - (9 x 6-3/4,24 pgs) Illustrated cover,5 page text introduction, 18 pgs of comics (scarce) 40.00 120.00 240.00
NOTE: *1928 Presidential Campaign giveaway. Unknown which above version was published first. Both contain the same original comics material by Satterfield.*

PINK LAFFIN (I)
Whitman Publishing Co.: 1922 (9x12")(Strip-r)
...the Lighter Side of Life, ...He Tells 'Em, ...and His Family, ...Knockouts; Ray Gleason-a (All rare) each... 26.00 104.00 185.00

POLLY (AND HER PALS) - (N)
Newspaper Feature Service: 1916 (3x2-1/2", color)
Altogether: Three Rahs and a Tiger! by Cliff Sterrett 20.00 60.00 120.00
There Is A Limit To Pa's Patience by Cliff Sterrett 20.00 60.00 120.00
NOTE: *Single sheet printed in full color on both sides, unfolds to show 12 panel story.*

POPEYE PAINT BOOK (N)
McLaughlin Bros, Inc., Springfield, Mass.: 1932 (9-7/8x13", 28 pgs, color-c)
2052 - By E. C. Segar 64.00 256.00 450.00
NOTE: *Contains a full color panel above and the exact same art in below panel n B&W which one was to color in; strip-r panels.*

POPEYE CARTOON BOOK (N)
The Saalfield Co.: 1934 (8-1/2x13", 40 pgs, cardboard-c)
2095-(scarce)-1933 strip reprints in color by Segar. Each page contains a vertical half of a Sunday strip, so the continuity reads row by row completely across each double page spread. If each page is read by itself, the continuity makes no sense. Each double page spread reprints one complete Sunday page from 1933 300.00 900.00 2525.00
12 Page Version 100.00 300.00 840.00

POPEYE (See Thimble Theatre for earlier Popeye-r from Sonnott) (N)
David McKay Publications: 1935 (25¢; 52 pgs, B&W) (By Segar)
1-Daily strip reprints- "The Gold Mine Thieves" 107.00 321.00 750.00
2-Daily strip-r (scarce) 100.00 300.00 700.00
NOTE: *Ties with Henry & Little Annie Rooney (David McKay) as the last of the 10x10" size books.*

PORE LI'L MOSE (N)
New York Herald Publ. by Grand Union Tea
Cupples & Leon Co.: 1902 (10-1/2x15", 78 pgs., color)
nn - By R. F. Outcault; Earliest known C&L comic book (scarce in high grade - very high demand) 1500.00 5500.00 -
NOTE: *Black Americana one page newspaper strips; falls in between Yellow Kid & Buster Brown. Complete copies have become scarce. Some have cut this book apart thinking that reselling individual pages will bring them more money.*

PRETTY PICTURES (M)
Farrar & Rinehart: 1931 (12 x 8-7/8", 104 pgs, color hardcover w/dust jacket, B&W; reprints from New Yorker, Judge, Life, Collier's Weekly)
nn - By Otto Soglow (contains "The Little King") 33.00 134.00 235.00

PUCK - to be indexed in next year's Guide

QUAINT OLD NEW ENGLAND (S)
Triton Syndicate: 1936 (5-1/4x6-1/4", 100 pgs, soft-c squarebound, B&W)
nn - By Jack Withycomb 36.00 144.00 250.00
NOTE: *Comics about weird doings in Old New England.*

RED CARTOONS (S)
Daily Worker Publishing Company: 1926 (12 x 9", 68 pgs,cardboard cover, B&W)
nn - By Various (scarce) 40.00 160.00 280.00
NOTE: *Reprint of American Communist Party editorial cartoons, from The Daily Worker, The Workers Monthly, and the Liberator. Art by Fred Ellis, William Gropper, Clive Weed, Art Young.*

REG'LAR FELLERS (See All-American Comics, Jimmie Dugan & The..., Popular Comics & Treasure Box of Famous Comics) (N)
Cupples & Leon Co./MS Publishing Co.: 1921-1929
1 (1921)-52 pgs. B&W dailies (Cupples & Leon, 10x10") 43.00 171.00 300.00
1925, 48 pgs. B&W dailies (MS Publ.) 39.00 157.00 275.00
Hardcover (1929, 8-3/4x7-1/2"; 96 pgs.)-B&W-r 54.00 214.00 375.00

REG'LAR FELLERS STORY PAINT BOOK
Whitman, Racine, Wisc.: 1932 (8-3/4x12-1/8", 132 pgs, red soft-c)
By Gene Byrnes 25.00 75.00 150.00

RIPLEY (See Believe It Or Not)

ROGER BEAN, R. G. (Regular Guy) (N)
The Indiana News Co, Distributers.: 1915 - No. 2, 1915 (5-3/8x17", 68 pgs., B&W, hardcovers); #3-#5 published by **Chas. B. Jackson:** 1916-1919
(No. 1 2 4 & 5 bound on side, No. 3 bound at top)
1-By Chas B. Jackson (68pgs.)(Scarce) 60.00 210.00 360.00
2- 5-5/8x17-1/8", 66 pgs (says 1913 inside - an obvious printing error) (red or green binding) 60.00 210.00 360.00
3-Along the Firing Line... (1916; 68 pgs, 6x17") 60.00 210.00 360.00
4-Into the Trenches and Out Again with... (1917, 68 pgs) 60.00 210.00 360.00
5 ...And The Reconstruction Period (1919, 5-3/8x15-1/2", 84 pgs) (Scarce) (has $1 printed on cover) 60.00 210.00 360.00
Baby Grand Editions 1-5 (10x10", cardboard-c) 60.00 210.00 360.00
NOTE: *No. 2 of the Twin Baby Grands (nd) 8-1/4x10-7/8", 52 pgs. Cardboard cover. B&W strip reprints. Cover also says "Politics Pickles People Police."*

ROGER BEAN PHILOSOPHER
Schnull & Co: 1917 (5-1/2x17", 36 pgs., B&W, brown & black paper-c, square binding)
nn - By Chic Jackson - - -

ROUND THE WORLD WITH THE DOO-DADS (see Doings of the Doo-Dads, Doo Dads)
Universal Feature And Specialty Co, Chicago: 1922 (12x10-1/2", 52 pgs, B&W, red & light blue-c, square binding)
nn - By Arch Dale newspaper strip-r 43.00 173.00 300.00
NOTE: *Intermixed single panel and sequential comic strips with scenes from Scotland, Ireland, England, Holland, Italy, Spain, Egypt, Africa, and Lions & Elephants along the Nile River, China, Australia & back home.*

RUBAIYKT OF THE EGG
The John C Winston Co, Philadelphia: 1905 (7x5/12", 64 pgs, purple-c, B&W)
nn - By Clare Victor Dwiggins 20.00 60.00 120.00
NOTE: *Book is printed & cut into the shape of an egg.*

RULING CLAWSS, THE (N,S)
The Daily Worker: 1935 (192 pgs, 10-1/4 x 7-3/8", hard-c, B&W)
nn - By Redfield 60.00 240.00 -
NOTE: *Reprints cartoons from the American Communist Party newspaper The Daily Worker.*

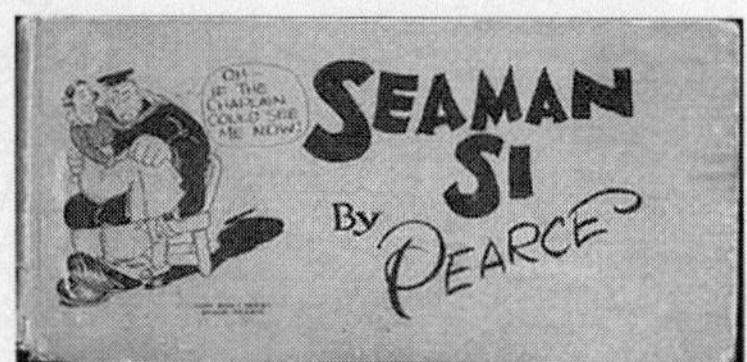

Seaman Si
© Pierce Publ. Co.

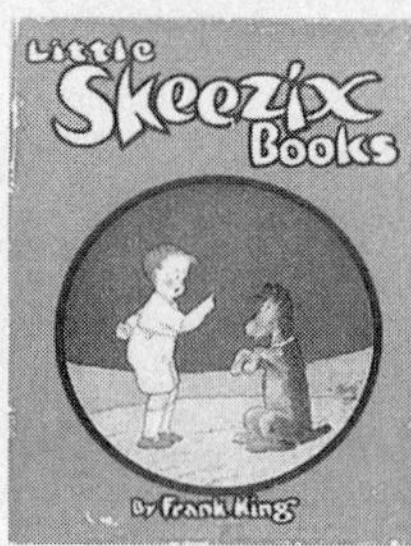

Little Skeezix Books by Frank King
1929 © Reilly & Lee

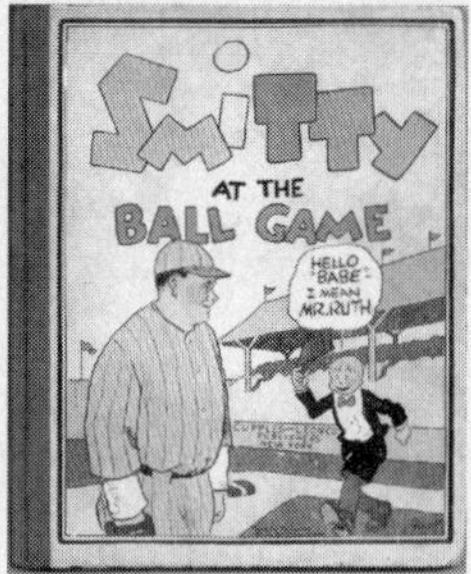

Smitty #2 By Walter Berndt
1929 © Cupples & Leon

GD2.0 FN6.0 VF8.0

SAGARA'S ENGLISH CARTOONS AND CARTOON STORIES (N)
Bunkosha, Tokyo: nd (c1925) (6-5/8" x 4-1/4", 272 pgs, hard-c, B&W)
nn- (Scarce) - - -
NOTE: *Published in Tokyo, Japan, with all strips in both English and Japanese, to facilitate learning English. Majority of book is Bringing Up Father by George McManus. Also contains Japanese strip Father Takes it Easy, by T. Sagara, reprinted from the Kokusai News Agency.*

SAM AND HIS LAUGH (N)
Frederick A. Stokes: 1906 (10x15", cardboard-c, Sunday strip-r in color)
nn - By Jimmy Swinnerton (scarce) 250.00 750.00 1350.00
NOTE: *Strip ran July 24, 1904 into 1906; its ethnic humor might be considered racist by today's standards.*

SCHOOL DAYS (N)
Harper & Bros.: 1919 (9x8", 104 pgs.)
nn - By Clare Victor Dwiggins 42.00 144.00 250.00

SEAMAN SI - A Book of Cartoons About the Funniest "Gob" in the Navy (N)
Pierce Publishing Co.: 1916 (4x8-1/2, 200 pgs, hardcover, B&W); 1918 (4-1/8x8-1/4, 104 pgs, hardcover, B&W)
nn - By Perce Pearce (1916) 43.00 150.00 260.00
nn - 1918 - (Reilly & Britton Co.) 26.00 90.00 156.00
NOTE: *There exists two different covers for the 1918 reprints. The earlier edition was self published by the artist. The newspaper strip is sometimes also known as "The American Sailor."*

SECRET AGENT X-9 (N)
David McKay Pbll.: 1934 (Book 1: 84 pgs; Book 2: 124 pgs.) (8x7-1/2")
Book 1-Contains reprints of the first 13 weeks of the strip by Dashiell Hammett & Alex Raymond, complete except for 2 dailies 83.00 250.00 600.00
Book 2-Contains reprints immediately following contents of Book 1, for 20 weeks by Dashiell Hammett & Alex Raymond; complete except for two dailies. 83.00 250.00 600.00
NOTE: *Raymond misdated the last 5 strips from 6/34, and while the dating sequence is confusing, the continuity is correct.*

SILK HAT HARRY'S DIVORCE SUIT (N)
M. A. Donoghue & Co.: 1912 (5-3/4x15-1/2", B&W)
nn - Newspaper-r by Tad (Thomas A. Dorgan) 33.00 117.00 200.00

SINBAD A DOG'S LIFE (M)
Coward - McCann, Inc.: 1930 (11x 8-3/4", 104 pgs., single-sided, illustrated hard-c, B&W
nn - By Edwina 11.00 33.00 100.00
Sinbad...Again (1932, 10-15/16x 8-9/16", 104 pgs.) 11.00 33.00 100.00
NOTE: *Wordless comic strips from LIFE.*

SIS HOPKINS OWN BOOK AND MAGAZINE OF FUN
Leslie-Judge Co.: 1899-July 1911 (36 pgs, color-c, B&W) (merged into Judge's Library, later titled Film Fun)
any issue - By various 11.00 33.00 100.00
NOTE: *Zim, Flagg, Young, Newell, Adams, etc.*

SKEEZIX (Also see Gasoline Alley & Little Skeezix Books listed below) (I)
Reilly & Lee Co.: 1925 - 1928 (Strip-r, soft covers) (pictures & text)
...and Uncle Walt (1924)-Origin 26.00 104.00 180.00
...and Pal (1925) 21.00 84.00 150.00
...at the Circus (1926) 21.00 84.00 150.00
...& Uncle Walt (1927) (does this actually exist?) - - -
...Out West (1928) 21.00 84.00 150.00
Hardback Editions... 34.00 136.00 235.00

SKEEZIX BOOKS, LITTLE (Also see Skeezix, Gasoline Alley) (G)
Reilly & Lee Co.: No date (1928, 1929) (Boxed set of three Skeezix books)
nn - Box with 3 issues of Skeezix. Skeezix & Pal, Skeezix at the Circus, Skeezix & Uncle Walt known. 1928 Set... 60.00 180.00 360.00
nn - Box with 4 issues of (3) above Skeezix plus "Out West" 80.00 330.00 550.00

SKEEZIX COLOR BOOK (N)
McLaughlin Bros. Inc, Springfield, Mass: 1929 (9-1/2x10-1/4", 28 pgs, one third in full color, rest in B&W)
2023 - By Frank King; strip-r to color 20.00 75.00 135.00

SKIPPY (see also Life Presents Skippy, Always Belittlin', That Rookie From 13th Squad)
No publisher listed: Circa 1920s (10x8", 16 pgs., color/B&W cartoons)
nn - By Percy Crosby 20.00 84.00 150.00

SKIPPY, LIFE PRESENTS (M)
Life Publishing Company & Henry Holt, NY: nd 1924 (134 pgs, 10-13/16x8-3/4", color hard-c, B&W
nn - By Percy L Crosby - - -
NOTE: *Many sequential & single panel reprints from Skippy's earliest appearances in Life Magazine.*

SKIPPY
Greenberg, Publisher, Inc, NY: 1925. (11-14x8-5/8, 72 pgs, hard-c, B&W and color
nn - By Percy L. Crosby - - -
NOTE: *Some but not all of these comics were also in Life Presents Skippy; issued with dust wrapper.*

SKIPPY AND OTHER HUMOR
Greenberg: Publisher, NY: 1929 (11-1/4x8-1/2",72 pgs,tan hard-c, B&W and color)
nn - By Percy L. Crosby 50.00 175.00 300.00
NOTE: *Came with a dust jacket.*

SKIPPY (I)
Grossett & Dunlap: 1929 (7-3/8x6, 370 pgs, hardcover text with some art)
nn - By Percy Crosby (issued with a dust jacket) 21.00 84.00 150.00
NOTE: *This is worth very little without the dust wrapper; very common without athe dust jacket.*

SKIPPY
Greenberg Press: 1930 (soft cover, ca. 16 pp.,
nn - By Percy Crosby (scarce) 50.00 175.00 300.00
NOTE: *Reprints from LIFE cartoons, color, b/w. Crosby told Greenberg to withdraw from the market as it cheapened the hard cover prior editions. Greenberg then stopped publishing per agreement, and sent Crosby all the copper & zinc bookplates, which were in Crosby estate until 1996.*

SKIPPY CRAYON AND COLORING BOOK (N)
McLoughlin Bros, Inc., Springfield, MA: 1931 (13x9-3/4", 28 pgs, color-c, color & B&W)
2050 - By Percy Crosby 28.00 84.00 195.00
NOTE: *This item says on the front cover: "Licensed by Percy Crosby" because he owned his creation. About half the pages have one panel pre-printed in full color with same one b&w below for person to copy the colors.*

SKIPPY RAMBLES (I)
G.P. Putnam's Sons: 1932 (7 1/8 x 5 1/8, 202 pgs)
nn - By Percy Crosby 21.00 84.00 150.00
NOTE: *Issued with a dustjacket. Has Skippy plates by Crosby every 4 or 5 pages.*

SKUDDABUD STARRY STORY SERIES - FOLK FROM THE FUTURE (O,G)
no publisher listed: 1936 (9" x 11-7/8", 48 pgs, cardboard-c, B&W)
Book One (Rare) "Parachuting" 21.00 84.00 150.00
NOTE: *By Columba Krebs. Top half of each page is a continuing strip story, while bottom half are different stories, in prose, about the same characters -- a race of aliens who have migrated to Earth, from their dying world.*

S'MATTER POP? (N)
Saalfield Publ. Co.: 1917 (10x14", 44 pgs., B&W, cardboard-c,)
nn - By Charlie Payne; in full color; pages printed on one side 48.00 169.00 290.00

S'MATTER POP? (N) (25 ¢ cover price)
E.I. Company, New York: 1927 (8-15/16x7-1/8", 52 pgs, yellow soft-c perfect bound
nn - By C.M. Payne (scarce) 24.00 84.00 145.00
NOTE: *First comic book published by Hugo Gernsback, noted for inventing Amazing Stories among other memorable science fiction pulps. The World Science Fiction Convention Award, The Hugo, is named for him.*

SMITTY (See Treasure Box of Famous Comics) (N)
Cupples & Leon Co.: 1928 - 1933 (9x7", 96 pgs., B&W strip-r, hardcover)
1928-(96 pgs. 7x8-3/4") By Walter Berndt 41.00 166.00 290.00
1929-At the Ball Game (Babe Ruth on cover) 57.00 229.00 400.00
1930-The Flying Office Boy, 1931-The Jockey, 1932-In the North Woods each... 31.00 126.00 220.00
1933-At Military School 31.00 126.00 220.00
NOTE: *Each hardbound was published with a dust jacket; worth 50% more with dust jacket. The 1923 edition is very popular with baseball collectors. Strip debuted Nov 27, 1922.*

SMOKEY STOVER (See Dan Dunn & King of the Royal Mounted) (N)
Whitman Publishing: 1937 (5 1/2 x 7 1/4", 68pgs., color cardboard-c, B&W)
1010 36.00 144.00 250.00

SOCIAL HELL, THE (O)
Rich Hill: 1902
nn - By Ryan Walker 20.00 70.00 120.00
NOTE: *"The conditions of workers and the corruption of a political system beholden to corporate interests have been a major focus of human rights concerns since the 19th century. This early graphic novel depicts the social evils of unreformed capitalism. Ryan Walker was a syndicate cartoonist for many mainstream newspapers as well as for the communist Daily Worker." This description comes from <http://www.lib.uconn.edu/DoddCenter/ascexh3.html>, where you can find also a reproduction of the cover. I add that Ryan Walker was the editor of "The Saint Louis Republic" comic section since its inception in 1897; the supplement published "Alma and Oliver", George McManus's first series.*

SPORT AND THE KID (see The Umbrella Man) (N)
Lowman & Hanford Co.: 1913 (6-1/4x6-5/8",114 pgs, hardcover, B&W&orange)
nn - By J.R. "Dok" Hager 20.00 70.00 120.00

STORY OF CONNECTICUT (N)
The Hartford Times: Vol.1 1935 - Vol.3 1936 (10-1/2" x 7-3/8",304 pgs,color hard-c, B&W)
Vol.1 - 3 20.00 70.00 120.00
NOTE: *Collects a newspaper strip on Connecticut State history, which ran in the Hartford Times. Strip is in a similar format to "Texas History Movies". Also published in a plain, blue hardcover.*

STORY OF JAPAN IN CHINA, THE (N,S)
Trans-Pacific News Service, NYC: Vol. 3, No.1 March 10, 1938 (9" x 6", 36 pgs, construction paper-c, B&W)
Vol.3 No.1 21.00 64.00 150.00
NOTE: *Part of the "China Reference Series" of booklets, detailing the Japanese occupation and brutalization of China. Consists entirely of cartoons. The other booklets in the series have no cartoons. Art by: Ding, Fitzpatrick, Herblock, Herman, Rollin Kirby, Knox, Low, Manning, Orr, Shoemaker, Talburt.*

STRANGE AS IT SEEMS (S)

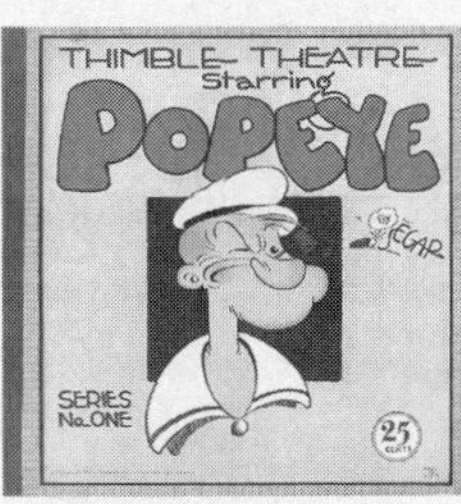

Thimble Theater #1 by E.C. Segar
1931 © Sonnet Publishing Co.

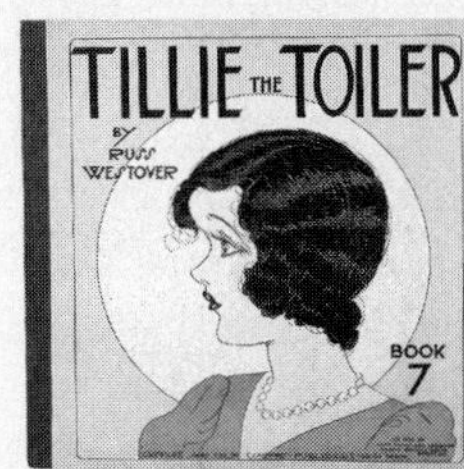

Tillie the Toiler #7 by Russ Westover
1932 © Cupples & Leon

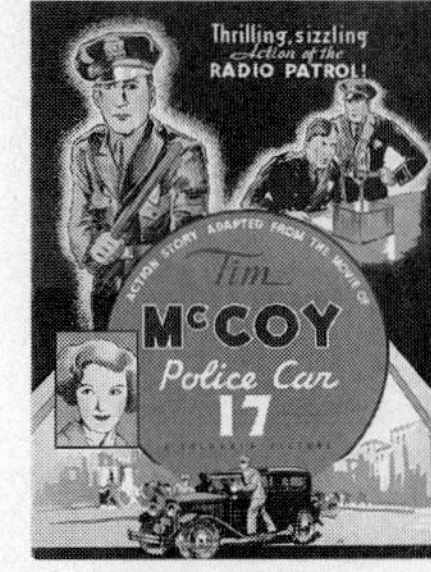

Tim McCoy, Police Car 17
© Whitman Publ. Co.

GD2.0 FN6.0 VF8.0

Blue-Star Publishing Co.: 1932 (64 pgs., B&W, square binding)

1-Newspaper-r 32.00 128.00 225.00
NOTE: *Published with and without No. 1 and price on cover.*
Ex-Lax giveaway (1936, B&W, 24 pgs., 5x7") - McNaught Synd. 13.00 52.00 90.00

SULLIVANT'S ABC ZOO (I)
The Old Wine Press: 1946 (11-3/4x9-3/8", hardcover)

nn - By T.S. Sullivant - - -
NOTE: *Reprints Mitchell & Miller material 1895-1898 and Life Publishing 1898-1926.*

TAILSPIN TOMMY STORY & PICTURE BOOK (N)
McLoughlin Bros.: No. 266, 1931? (nd) (10x10-1/2", color strip-r)

266 - By Forrest 43.00 172.00 300.00

TAILSPIN TOMMY (Also see Famous Feature Stories & The Funnies)(N)
Cupples & Leon Co.: 1932 (100 pgs., hard-c)

nn - (Scarce)-B&W strip reprints from 1930 by Hal Forrest & Glenn Claffin 50.00 150.00 300.00

TALES OF DEMON DICK AND BUNKER BILL (O)
Whitman Publishing Co.: 1934 (5-1/4x10-1/2", 80 pgs, color hardcover, B&W)

793 - By Spencer 33.00 100.00 225.00

TARZAN BOOK (The Illustrated...) (N)
Grosset & Dunlap: 1929 (9x7", 80 pgs.)

1(Rare)-Contains 1st B&W Tarzan newspaper comics from 1929. By Hal Foster Cloth reinforced spine & dust jacket (50¢); Foster-c
With dust jacket... 86.00 344.00 630.00
Without dust jacket... 43.00 172.00 315.00
2nd Printing(1934, 25¢, 76 pgs.)-4 Foster pgs. dropped; paper spine, circle in lower right cover with 25¢ price. The 25¢ is barely visible on some copies 34.00 136.00 250.00
1967-House of Greystoke reprint-7x10", using the complete 300 illustrations/text from the 1929 edition minus the original indicia, foreword, etc. Initial version bound in gold paper & sold for $5.00. Officially titled **Burroughs Bibliophile #2**. A very few additional copies were bound in heavier blue paper. Gold binding... 2.25 6.75 20.00
Blue binding... 2.50 7.50 27.00

TARZAN OF THE APES TO COLOR (N)
Saalfield Publishing Co.: No. 988, 1933 (15-1/4x10-3/4", 24 pgs)
(Coloring book)

988-(Very Rare)-Contains 1929 daily reprints with some new art by Hal Foster. Two panels blown up large on each page with one at the top of opposing pages on every other double-page spread. Believed to be the only time these panels appeared in color. Most color panels are reproduced a second time in B&W to be colored 271.00 1084.00 2000.00

TARZAN OF THE APES The Big Little Cartoon Book (N)
Whitman Publishing Company: 1933 (4-1/2x3 5/8", 320 pgs, color-c, B&W)

744 - By Hal Foster (comics on every page) 36.00 144.00 265.00

TECK HASKINS AT OHIO STATE (S)
Lea-Mar Press: 1908 (7-1/4x5-3/8", 84 pgs, B&W hardcover)

nn - By W.A. Ireland; football cartoons-r from Columbus Ohio Evening Dispatch 28.00 99.00 170.00
NOTE: *Small blue & white patch of cover art pasted atop a color cloth quilt patter; pasted patch can easily peel off some copies.*

TECK 1909 (S)
Lea-Mar Press: 1909 (8-5/8 x 8-1/8", 124 pgs., B&W hardcover, 25¢)

nn - By W.A. Ireland; Ohio State University baseball cartoons-r from Columbus Evening Dispatch 28.00 99.00 170.00

TEDDY BEAR BOOKS, THE (M) (see also LITTLE JOHNNY AND THE TEDDY BEARS)
Reilly & Britton Co., Chicago: 1907 (7-1/16" x 5-3/8", 24 pgs, hard-c, color

	GD2.0	FN6.0	VF8.0
The Teddy Bears Come to Life	20.00	60.00	120.00
The Teddy Bears at the Circus	20.00	60.00	120.00
The Teddy Bears in a Smashup	20.00	60.00	120.00
The Teddy Bears on a Lark	20.00	60.00	120.00
The Teddy Bears on a Toboggan	20.00	60.00	120.00
The Teddy Bears at School	20.00	60.00	120.00
The Teddy Bears Go Fishing	20.00	60.00	120.00
The Teddy Bears in Hot Water	20.00	60.00	120.00

NOTE: *Books are all unnumbered. C & A by J.R. Bray; s-Robert D. Towne. Reprints "Little Johnny & the Teddy Bears" strips, from Judge Magazine. Similar in format to the Buster Brown Nuggets series. All eight books debuted simultaneously.*

TEDDY BEARS IN FUN AND FROLIC (M) (see LITTLE JOHNNY & THE TEDDY BEARS)
Reilly & Britton Co., Chicago: 1908 (8-3/4" x 8-3/4", 50 pgs, cardboard-c, color)

nn - (Rare) by J.R. Bray-a; Robert D. Towne-s 100.00 400.00 700.00
NOTE: *Reprints "Little Johnny & the Teddy Bears" strips, from Judge Magazine. Unknown if there were any other "Teddy Bear" titles published in this format.*

THE TEENIE WEENIES
Reilly & Britton, Chicago: 1916 (16-3/8x10-1/2", 52 pgs, cardboard-c, full color)

nn - By Wm. Donahey (Chicago Tribune-r) 100.00 400.00 700.00

TEXAS HISTORY MOVIES (N)
Various editions, 1928 to 1986 (B&W)

Book I -1928 Southwest Press (7-1/4 x 5-3/8, 56 pgs, cardboard cover) for the Magnolia Petroleum Company 30.00 90.00 180.00
nn - 1928 Southwest Press (12-3/8 x 9-1/4, 232 pgs, hardcover) 50.00 150.00 300.00
nn - 1935 Magnolia Petroleum Company (6 x 9, 132 pgs, paper cover) 20.00 60.00 120.00
NOTE: *Exists with either Wagon Train or Texas Flag & Lafitte/pirate covers.*
nn - 1943 Magnolia Petroleum Company (132 pgs, paper cover) 15.00 45.00 90.00
nn - 1963 Graphic Ideas Inc (11 x 8-1/2, softcover) 10.00 30.00 60.00
NOTE: *Reprints daily newspaper strips from the Dallas News, on Texas history. 1935 editions onward distributed within the Texas Public School System. Prior to that they appear to be giveaway comic books for the Magnolia Petroleum Company. There are many more editions than the ones pointed out above.*

THAT ROOKIE FROM THE 13TH SQUAD (N) (also Between Shots; Always Belittlin'; Skippy)
Harper & Brothers Publishers: Feb. 1918 (8x9-1/4", 72 pgs, hardcover, B&W)

nn - By Lieut. P(ercy) L. Crosby 58.00 204.00 350.00
NOTE: *Strip began in 1917 at an Army base during basic training.*

THAT SON-IN-LAW OF PA'S! (N)
Newspaper Feature Service: 1914 (2-1/2 by 3", color)

nn - - -
NOTE: *Single sheet printed in full color on both sides, unfolds to show 12 panel story. Imprinted on back for THE LESTER SHOE STORE.*

THIMBLE THEATRE STARRING POPEYE (See also Popeye) (N)
Sonnet Publishing Co.: 1931 - No. 2, 1932 (25¢, B&W, 52 pgs.)(Rare)

1-Daily strip serial-r in both by Segar 157.00 650.00 1150.00
2 136.00 544.00 950.00
NOTE: *The very first Popeye reprint book. The first Thimble Theatre Sunday page appeared Dec 19, 1919. Popeye first entered Thimble Theatre on Jan 17, 1929.*

THREE FUN MAKERS, THE (N)
Stokes and Company: 1908 (10x15", 64 pgs., color) (1904-06 Sunday strip-r)

nn - Maud, Katzenjammer Kids, Happy Hooligan 314.00 1100.00 -
NOTE: *This is the first comic book to compile more than one newspaper strip together.*

TIGERS (Also see On and Off Mount Ararat) (N)
Hearst's New York American & Journal: 1902, 86 pgs. 10x15-1/4"

nn - Funny animal strip-r by Jimmy Swinnerton 286.00 1000.00 -
NOTE: *The strip began as The Journal Tigers in The New York Journal Dec 12, 1897-1902.*

TILLIE THE TOILER (N)
Cupples & Leon Co.: 1925 - No. 8, 1933 (52 pgs., B&W, daily strip-r)

nn (#1) By Russ Westover 54.00 216.00 375.00
2-8 50.00 175.00 300.00
NOTE: *First newspaper strip appearance was in January, 1921.*

TILLIE THE TOILER MAGIC DRAWING AND COLORING BOOK
Sam L Gabriel Sons And Company: 1931 (8-1/2 x 12", 36 pages, stiff-c)

838-By Russ Westover 39.00 156.00 275.00

TIMID SOUL, THE (N)
Simon & Schuster: 1931 (12-1/4x9", 136 pgs, B&W hardcover, dust jacket?)

nn - By H. T. Webster (newspaper strip-r) 40.00 120.00 240.00

TIM McCOY, POLICE CAR 17 (O)
Whitman Publishing Co.: 1934 (14-3/4x11", 32 pgs, stiff color covers)

674-1933 movie illustrated; first movie adaptation in comic books original material? 50.00 200.00 350.00

TOAST BOOK
John C. Winston Co: 1905 (7-1/4 x 6,104 pgs, skull-shaped book, feltcover, B&W)

nn - By Clare Dwiggins 50.00 175.00 300.00
NOTE: *Cartoon illustrations accompanying toasts/poems, most involving alcohol.*

TOM SAWYER & HUCK FINN (N)
Stoll & Edwards Co.:1925 (10x10-3/4", 52 pgs, stiff covers)

nn - By "Dwig" Dwiggins; 1923, 1924-r color Sunday strips 39.00 156.00 275.00
NOTE: *By Permission of the Estate of Samuel L. Clemons and the Mark Twain Company.*

TOONERVILLE TROLLEY AND OTHER CARTOONS (N) (See Cartoons by Fontaine Fox)
Cupples & Leon Co.: 1921 (10 x10", 52 pgs., B&W, daily strip-r)

1 - By Fontaine Fox 68.00 272.00 475.00

TRAINING FOR THE TRENCHES (M)
Palmer Publishing Company: 1917 (5-3/8 x 7", 20 pgs., paper-c, 10¢)

nn - By Lieut. Alban B. Butler, Jr. 21.00 84.00 150.00
NOTE: *Subtitle: "A book of humorous cartoons on a serious subject." Single-panels about military training.*

TREASURE BOX OF FAMOUS COMICS (N) (see Wonder Chest of Famous Comics)
Cupples & Leon Co.: 1934 8-1/2x(6-7/8", 36 pgs, soft covers) (Boxed set of 5 books)

When a Feller Needs a Friend
© P.F. Volland & Co.

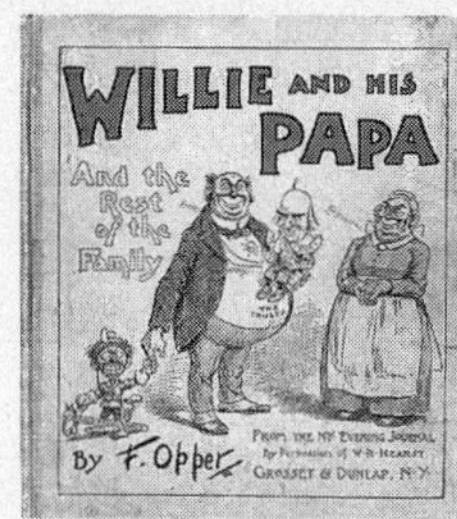

Willie and His Papa & the Rest of the Family by Opper
1901 © Grossett & Dunlap

The Yellow Kid #4 cover by Outcault
1897 © Howard Ainslee & Co.

	GD2.0	FN6.0	VF8.0
Little Orphan Annie (1926)	21.00	84.00	165.00
Reg'lar Fellers (1928)	19.00	76.00	145.00
Smitty (1928)	19.00	76.00	145.00
Harold Teen (1931)	19.00	76.00	145.00
How Dick Tracy & Dick Tracy Jr. Caught The Racketeers (1933)	26.00	104.00	205.00
Softcover set of five books in box	160.00	640.00	1250.00
Box only	57.00	228.00	450.00

NOTE: *Dates shown are copyright dates; all books actually came out in 1934 or later. The softcovers are abbreviated versions of the hardcover editions listed under each character.*

T.R. IN CARTOONS (N)
A.C. McClurg & Co., Chicago: June 13, 1910 (10-5/8" x 8", 104? pgs, paper-c, B&W)

nn - By McCutcheon - - -
NOTE: *Strips and cartoons about Teddy Roosevelt, all by McCutcheon.*

TRUTH (See Victorian section for earlier issues)
Truth Company, NY: 1886-1906? (13-11/16x10-5/16", 16 pgs, process color-c & center-folds, rest B&W)

1900-1906 issues 10.00 20.00 50.00

TRUTH SAVE IT FROM ABUSE & OVERWORK BEING THE EPISODE OF THE HIRED HAND & MRS. STIX PLASTER, CONCERTIST (N)
Radio Truth Society of WBAP: no date, 1924 (6-3/8 x 4-7/8, 40 pgs, paper cover, B&W)

nn - By V.T. Hamlin (Very Rare) 100.00 400.00 700.00
NOTE: *Radio station WBAP giveaway reprints strips from the Ft. Worth Texas Star-Telegram set at local radio station. 1st collected work by V.T. Hamlin, pre-Alley Oop.*

TWENTY FIVE YEARS AGO (see At The Bottom Of The Ladder) (M,S)
Coward-McCann: 1931 (5-3/4x8-1/4, 328 pgs, hardcover, B&W)

nn - By Camillus Kessler 32.00 128.00 225.00
NOTE: *Multi-image panel cartoons showing historical events for dates during the year.*

UMBRELLA MAN, THE (N) (See Sport And The Kid)
Lowman & Hanford Co.: 1911 (8-7/8x5-1/8",112 pgs, paperback, B&W&orange)

nn - By J.R. "Dok" Hager (Seattle Times-r) 20.00 70.00 120.00

UNCLE REMUS AND BRER RABBIT (N)
Frederick A. Stokes Co.: 1907 (64 pgs, hardbound, color)

nn - By Joel C Harris & J.M. Conde 50.00 175.00 300.00

UPSIDE DOWNS OF LITTLE LADY LOVEKINS AND OLD MAN MUFFAROO
New York Herald: 1905 (?) (N)

nn - By Gustav Verbeck 100.00 350.00 650.00

VAUDEVILLES AND OTHER THINGS (N)
Isaac H. Blandiard Co.: 1900 (13x10-1/2", 22 pgs., color) plus two reprints

nn - By Bunny (Scarce) 229.00 800.00 -
nn - 2nd print "By the Creator of Foxy Grandpa" on-c but only has copyright info of 1900 (10-1/2x15 1/2, 28 pgs, color) 171.00 600.00 -
nn - 3rd print. "By the creator of Foxy Grandpa" on-c; has both 1900 and 1901 copyright info (11x13") 171.00 600.00 -

WALLY - HIS CARTOONS OF THE A.E.F. (N)
Stars & Stripes: 1917 (96 and 108 pgs, B&W)

nn - By Abian A "Wally" Wallgren (7x18; 96 pgs) 20.00 70.00 120.00
nn - another edition (108 pgs, 7x17-1/2) 20.00 70.00 120.00
NOTE: *World War One cartoons reprints from Stars & Stripes; sold to U.S. servicemen with profits to go to French War Orphans Fund. various editions from 1917-1920; there might be more than what we list here.*

WAR CARTOONS (S)
Dallas News: 1918 (11x9", 112 pgs, hardcover, B&W)

nn - By John Knott (WWOne cartoons) 20.00 70.00 120.00

WAR CARTOONS FROM THE CHICAGO DAILY NEWS (N,S)
Chicago Daily News: 1914 (10 cents, 7-3/4x10-3/4", 68 pgs, paper-c, B&W)

nn - By L.D. Bradley 20.00 70.00 120.00

WEBER & FIELD'S FUNNYISMS (S,M,O)
Arkell Comoany, NY: 1904 (10-7/8x8", 112 pgs, color-c, B&W)

1 - By various (later issues?) 20.00 70.00 120.00
NOTE: *Contains some sequential & many single panel strips by Outcault, George Luks, CA David, Houston, L Smith, Hy Mayer, Verbeck, Woolf, Sydney Adams, Frank "Chip" Bellew, Eugene "ZIM" Zimmerman, Phil May, FT Richards, Billy Marriner, Grosvenor and many others.*

WE'RE NOT HEROES (O,S)
E.C. Wells and J.W. Moss: 1933 (8-11/16" x 5-7/8", 52 pgs, red & black paper-c, B&W interior)

nn - By Eddie Wells 10.00 30.00 60.00
NOTE: *Amateurish cartoons about World War I vets in the Walter Reed Veteran's Hospital.*

WHEN A FELLER NEEDS A FRIEND (S)
P. F. Volland & Co.: 1914 (11-11/16x8-7/8)

nn - By Clare Briggs 37.00 131.00 225.00
NOTE: *Originally came in box with Briggs art (box is Rare - worth more with box. There are also numerous more modern reprints)*

WILD PILGRIMAGE (O)
Harrison Smith & Robert Haas: 1932 (9-7/8x7", 210 pgs, B&W hardcover w/dust jacket)
(original wordless graphic novel in woodcuts)

nn - By Lynd Ward 50.00 175.00 300.00

WILLIE AND HIS PAPA AND THE REST OF THE FAMILY (I)
Grossett & Dunlap: 1901 (9-1/2x8", 200 pgs, hardcover from N.Y. Evening Journal by Permission of W. R. Hearst) (pictures & text)

nn - By Frederick Opper 50.00 200.00 340.00
NOTE: *Political satire series of single panel cartoons, involving whiny child Willie (President William McKinley), his rambunctious and uncontrollable cousin Teddy (Vice President Roosevelt), and Willie's Papa (trusts/monopolies) and their Maid (Senator) Hanna.*

WILLIE GREEN COMICS, THE (N) (see Adventures of Willie Green)
Frank M. Acton Co./Harris Brown: 1915 (8x15, 36 pgs); 1921 (6x10-1/8", 52 pgs, color paper cover, B&W interior, 25¢)

Book No. 1 By Harris Brown 45.00 158.00 270.00
Book 2 (#2 sold via mail order directly from the artist)(very rare) 45.00 172.00 300.00
NOTE: *Book No. 1 possible reprint of Adv. of Willie Green; definitely two different editions.*

WILLIE WESTINGHOUSE EDISON SMITH THE BOY INVENTOR (N)
William A. Stokes Co.: 1906 (10x16", 36 pgs. in color)

nn - By Frank Crane (Scarce) 214.00 750.00 -
NOTE: *Comic strip began May 27, 1900 and ran thru 1914. Parody of inventors Westinghouse and Edison.*

WINNIE WINKLE (N)
Cupples & Leon Co.: 1930 - No. 4, 1933 (52 pgs., B&W daily strip-r)

1 43.00 172.00 300.00
2-4 29.00 116.00 200.00
NOTE: *Strip began as a daily Sept 20, 1920.*

WISDOM OF CHING CHOW, THE (see also The Gumps)
R. J. Jefferson Printing Co.: 1928 (4x3", 100 pgs, red & B&W cardboard cover) (newspaper strip-r The Chicago Tribune)

nn - By Sidney Smith (scarce) 20.00 80.00 120.00

WONDER CHEST OF FAMOUS COMICS (N) see Treasure Chest of Famous Comics)
Cupples & Leon Co.: 1935? 8-1/2x(6-7/8", 36 pgs, soft covers) (Boxed set of 5 books)

	GD2.0	FN6.0	VF8.0
Little Orphan Annie #2 (1927) (Haunted House)	21.00	84.00	130.00
Little Orphan Annie #3 (1928) (in the Circus)	19.00	76.00	130.00
Smitty #2 (1929) (Babe Ruth app.)	19.00	76.00	130.00
Dolly Dimples and Bobby Bounce (1933) by Grace Drayton	19.00	76.00	130.00
How Dick Tracy & Dick Tracy Jr. Caught The Racketeers (1933)	26.00	104.00	185.00
Softcover set of five books in box	160.00	640.00	1125.00
Box only	57.00	228.00	400.00

NOTE: *Dates shown are original copyright dates of the first printings; all books actually came out in 1934 or later. The softcovers are extremely abbreviated versions of the hardcover editions listed under each character. It is suspected this new listing came out the Christmas season following the Teasure Chest of Famous Comics. which contains earlier editions of mainly the same poplulat titles.*

WORLD OF TROUBLE, A (S)
Minneapolis Journal: 1901 (10x8-3/4", 100 pgs, 40 pgs full color)

v3#1 - By Charles L. Bartholomew (editorial-r) 28.00 99.00 170.00

WORLD OVER, THE (I)
G. W. Dillingham Company, New York: 1897 (192 pgs, hardbound)

nn - By Joe Kerr; 80 illus by R.F. Outcault 200.00 700.00 -

WRIGLEY'S "MOTHER GOOSE"
Wm. Wrigley Jr. Company, Chicago: 1915 (6" x 4", 28 pgs, full color)

nn 20.00 70.00 120.00
NOTE: *Promotional comics for Wrigley's gum. Introduces Wrigley's "Spearmen."*

THE WRIGLEY SPEARMEN AT WORK AND PLAY - BOOK No. 2
Wm. Wrigley Jr. Company, Chicago: 1915 (6" x 4", 24 pgs, full color)

nn-Promotional comics for Wrigley's gum 20.00 70.00 120.00

YELLOW KID, THE (Magazine)(I) (becomes **The Yellow Book** #10 on)
Howard Ainslee & Co., N.Y.: Mar. 20, 1897 - #9, July 17, 1897 (5¢, B&W w/color covers, 52p., stapled) (not a comic book)

1-R.F. Outcault Yellow kid on-c only #1-6. The same Yellow Kid color ad app. on back-c #1-6 (advertising the New York Sunday Journal) 857.00 3000.00 -
2-6 (#2 4/3/97, #5 5/22/97, #6, 6/5/97) 743.00 2600.00 -
7-9 (Yellow Kid not on-c) 121.00 425.00 -
NOTE: *Richard Outcault's Yellow Kid from the Hearst New York American represents the very first successful newspaper comic strip in America. Listed here due to historical importance.*

YELLOW KID IN MCFADDEN'S FLATS, THE (N)
G. W. Dillingham Co., New York: 1897 (50¢, 7-1/2x5-1/2", 196 pgs., B&W, squarebound)

nn - The first "comic" book featuring The Yellow Kid; E. W. Townsend narrative w/R. F. Outcault Sunday comic page art-r & some original drawings 5000.00 8700.00 -
NOTE: A Fair condition copy sold for $2,901 in August 2004.

For a free, lively e-mail discussion group of Platinum Age comics collectors, fans, dealers, enthusiasts, and scholars you can join to look, listen, learn, and share by going to PlatinumAgeComics@Yahoogroups.com. Also go to The Grand Comics Database at www.comics.org. and www.bugpowder.com/andy/early for more resources always building. Any addititions or corrections to this section are always welcome.

The American Comic Book: 1938-Present

A Concise History Of The Field As Of 2005

THE MODERN COMICS MAGAZINE SUPPLANTS THE EARLIER FORMATS

by Robert L. Beerbohm & Richard D. Olson, PhD ©2005

(This article series was originally created by Robert Beerbohm and Richard Olson for OCBPG #27 1997 and is revised annually.)

Although somewhat similar in appearance to comic books of the Golden Age of the superhero, the varied formats that comic publishing pioneer Cupples & Leon popularized beginning in 1919 are quite different in appearance from today's comics. Even so, the books and those formats were consistently successful until the early 1930s, when they had to compete against The Great Depression; the Depression eventually won. One major reason for a format change was that at a cost of 25¢ per book for the 10" x 10" cardboard style and 60¢ for the 7" x 8 1/2" dustjacketed hardcovers, the price became increasingly prohibitive for most consumers already stifled by the crushed economy. As a result, all Cupples & Leon style books published between 1929-1935 are much rarer than their earlier counterparts because most Americans had little money to spend after paying for necessities like food and shelter.

By the early 1930s, the era of the Prestige Format black & white reprint comic book was over. In 1932-33 a lot of format variations arose, collecting such newspaper strips as **Bobby Thatcher, Bringing Up Father, Buck Rogers, Dick Tracy, Happy Hooligan, Joe Palooka, The Little King, Little Orphan Annie, Mickey Mouse, Moon Mullins, Mutt & Jeff, Smitty, Tailspin Tommy, Tarzan, Thimble Theater starring Popeye, Tillie the Toiler, Winnie Winkle**, and the **Highlights of History** series.

There had been Embee's **Comic Monthly**'s dozen issues in 1922, and several dozen of Dell & Eastern's **The Funnies** tabloid in 1929-30. It contained only original material and still failed.

It has been recently discovered that Eastern Color and Dell were also co-partners in **The Funnies**. It is possible that Eastern came up with the idea and Delecorte agreed to publish it for general standalone distribution. Similar format Sunday sections of the same material have been discovered by comics historian Ken Barker to be published at the same time in the **Montreal Standard**, a Canadian newspaper; it appears to have been an effort to get a new comics syndicate off the ground. The effort was not too successful as **The Standard** dropped the sections after just a few months. Allan Holtz went through the **E&P** yearbooks and found that this section (presumably a preprint) was advertised from 1930-34 by Eastern Color Printing out of New York City. This is a rediscovery of important magnitude as it pushes back the time known for Eastern Color Printing Company and Dell Publishing Company to be partners by four years into late 1928. They had almost discovered the winning formula which has ruled the format of comic books in America for the last 70 years. Unfortunately, it would be another four years before they successfully figured it out.

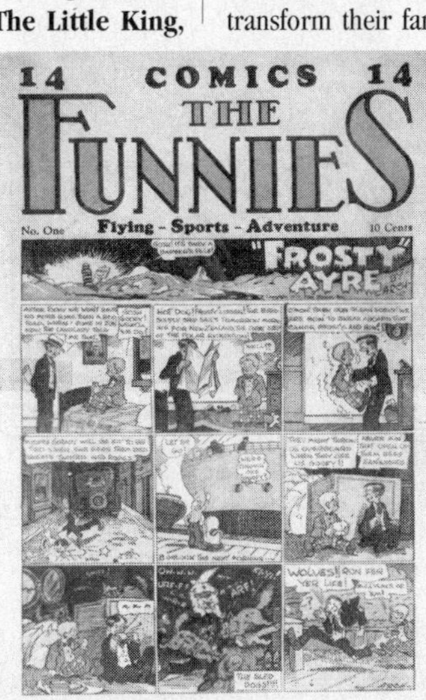

***The Funnies** #1, early 1929, Dell Publishing Company and Eastern Color. This was the very first original material newsstand comic book!*

With the 1933 newsstand appearance of Humor's **Detective Dan**, **Adventures of Detective Ace King**, **Bob Scully, Two Fisted Hick Detective**, and possibly the still unrediscovered but definitely advertised **Happy Mulligan**, these little understood original-material comic books were the direct inspiration for Jerry Siegel and Joe Shuster to transform their fanzine's evil character The Superman from **Science Fiction** #3 (January 1933) into a comic strip that would stand as a watershed heroic mark in American pop culture. The stage was set for a new frontier. With another format change including four colors, page counts beginning at 32 (soon hitting a whopping 68), and a hefty price reduction (starting for free as promotional premiums due to the nationwide numbing effects of worldwide deflation), the birthing pangs of the modern American comic book occurred in late 1932. Created out of desperation, to keep the printing presses rolling, the modern American comic book was born when a 45-year-old sales manager for Eastern Color Printing Company of New York reinvented the format from the failed tabloid **The Funnies**.

Harry I. Wildenberg's job was to come up with ideas that would sell color printing for Eastern, a company which also printed the comic sections for a score of newspapers along the eastern seaboard, including the **Boston Globe**, the **Brooklyn Times**, the **Providence Journal**, and the **Newark Ledger**. Downtime meant less take-home pay, so Wildenberg was always racking his brains for something to fit the color presses. He was fascinated by the miles of funny sheets which rolled off Eastern's presses each week, and he constantly sought new ways to exploit their commercial possibilities. If the funny papers were this popular, he reasoned, they should prove a good advertising medium. He decided to suggest a comics tabloid to a client.

Gulf Oil Company liked the idea and hired a few artists to create an original comic called **Gulf Comic Weekly**. The comic was dated April 1933 and was 10 1/2" x 15". It was the first comic to be advertised nationally on the radio beginning April 30th. Its first artists were Stan Schendel doing **The Uncovered Wagon**, Victor doing **Curly and the Kids**, and Svess on a strip named **Smileage**. All were full page, full color comic strips. Wildenberg promptly had Eastern print this four page comic, making it probably the first tabloid newsprint comic published for American distribution outside of a newspaper in the 20th Century. Wildenberg and Gulf were astonished when the tabloids were grabbed up as fast as Gulf service stations could offer them. Distribution shot up to 3,000,000 copies a week after Gulf changed the name to **Gulf Funny Weekly** with its 5th issue. The series remained a tabloid until early 1939 & ran for 422 issues until May 23, 1941.

Recent research has also turned up "new" rediscovered comics material from other oil companies from this same time span of 1933-34. Perhaps spurred by the runaway success of **Gulf Funny Weekly**, these other oil companies found they had to compete with licensed comic strip material of their own in order to remain profitable. The authors of this essay are actively soliciting help in uncovering more information regarding the following: There are at least 14 issues each of at least an A and a B series of a four page tabloid-size full color comics giveaway titled **Standard Oil Comics**, dating from 1933. The issues seen so far contain Fred Opper's **Si & Mirandi**, an older couple who interact with perennial favorites, **Happy Hooligan** & **Maud the Mule**, drawn by the grand old master himself, Frederick Opper, who had been a professional cartoonist for over 60 years by this time.

Detective Dan Secret Op. #48*, *Bob Scully The Two Fisted Hick Detective & The Adventures of Detective Ace King, *early 1933, Humor Publishing Co. Very rare from the 2nd original newsstand comic book publisher & the direct inspiration for Jerry Siegel & Joe Shuster's 1933 conversion of* ***The Superman*** *into a comic book due to a promise of publication. This earliest Superman was never published.*

Other strips include **Pesty And His Pop** & **Smiling Slim** by Sid Hicks. Considering the concept of **Gulf Funny Weekly** has been well known for decades while **Standard Oil Comics** remains virtually unknown, our guess is **Gulf Comic Weekly** began first and ran many years longer than Rockefeller's version.

Beginning with the March-April 1934 issue of **Shell Globe** (V4 #2), characters from Bud Fisher (**Mutt & Jeff**) and Fontaine Fox (**Toonerville Folks**) were licensed to sell gas & oil for this company. 52,000 eight foot standees were made for Fisher's **Mutt and Jeff** and Fox's **Powerful Katrinka** and **The Skipper** for placement around 13,000 Shell gas stations. Augmenting them was an army of 250,000 miniature figures of the same characters. In addition, more than 1,000,000 play masks were given away to children along with more than 285,000 window stickers. If that wasn't enough, hundreds of thousands of 3x5 foot posters featuring these characters were released in conjunction with twenty-four sheet outdoor billboards. Radio announcements of this promotion began running April 7th, 1934. It is presently unknown if Shell had a comics tabloid created to give away to customers.

The idea for creating an actual comic book as we know it today, however, did not occur to Wildenberg until later in 1933, when he said he was idly folding a newspaper in halves, then in quarters. As he looked at the twice-folded paper, it occurred to him that it was a convenient book size (actually it was late stage "Dime Novel" size, which companies like Street & Smith were pumping out). The format had its heyday from the 1880s through the 1910s, having been invented by the firm of Beadle and Adam in 1860 in more of a digest format. According to a 1942 article by Max Gaines (née Ginzberg), another contributing factor in the development of the format was an

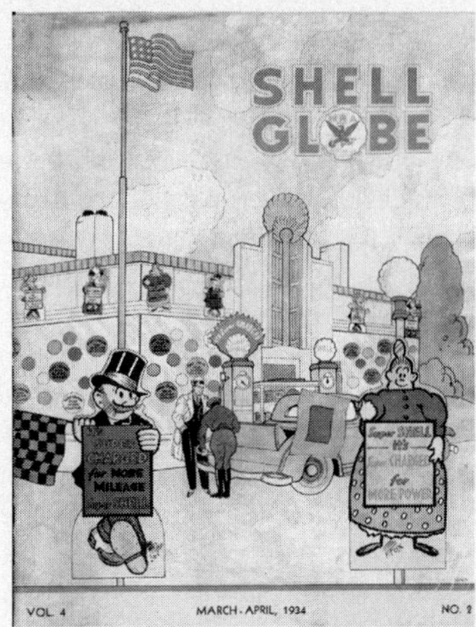

Left, ***Gulf Funny Weekly*** *#5, early 1933, Wildenberg's very first successful comics experiment. Middle,* ***Standard Oil Comics Weekly*** *#14, 1933. A recently discovered comics tabloid the same size as* ***Gulf Funny Weekly****. The oil companies recognized the power of comics early on!. Right, Not to be outdone, Shell Oil began a huge comics promotion in March 1934 to compete with Gulf and Standard Oil.*

inspection of a promotional folder published by the Ledger Syndicate, in which four-color Sunday comic pages were printed in 7"x9".

According to a 1949 interview with Wildenberg, he thought "why not a comic book? It would have 32 or 64 pages and make a fine item for concerns which distribute premiums." All they did at Eastern Color that one fateful day is fold a tabloid newspaper format down to "dime novel" size running full color throughout on most of the comic strips, then staple it, and they hit upon their winning formula.

But they did not yet know this...as we will find out.

Working for Eastern Color at this same time were quite a few future legends of the comics business, such as Max Gaines, Lev Gleason and a fellow named Harold Moore (all sales staff directly underneath the supervision of Wildenberg), Sol Harrison as a color separator, and George Dougherty Sr. as a printer.

Janosik, Wildenberg, Gaines, Gleason and crew obtained publishing rights to certain Associated, Bell, Fisher, McNaught and Public Ledger Syndicate comics, had an artist make up a few dummies by hand. The sales staff then walked them around to their biggest prospects. Wildenberg received a telegram from Proctor & Gamble for an order of a million copies for a 32-page color comic magazine called **Funnies on Parade**. The entire print run was given away in just a few weeks in the Spring of 1933. Most copies no longer exist and it is now hard to find. All of them worked on the **Funnies on Parade** project. Morris Margolis was brought in from Charlton in Derby, Connecticut to solve binding problems centered on getting the pages in proper numerical sequence on that last fold to "modern" comic book size. Most of them were infected with the comics bug for most of the rest of their lives.

The success of **Funnies on Parade** quickly led to Eastern publishing additional giveaway books in the same format by late 1933, including the 32-page **Famous Funnies A Carnival of Comics**, the 100-page **A Century of Comics** and the 52-page **Skippy's Own Book of Comics**.

The latter became the first "new" format comic book about a single character. Out of all the comic strips on the market in 1933, Eastern Color's growing comics market as devised by Harry Wildenberg, M.C. Gaines and Lev Gleason chose the Percy Crosby creation in **Skippy's Own Book of Comics** to be its first standalone title. This first solo effort in their new 52-page newsprint **Funnies On Parade** format had an initial print run of half a million, as did their 100-pager.

The idea that anyone would pay for them seemed fantastic to Wildenberg, so Max Gaines stickered ten cents on several dozen of the latest premium, **Famous Funnies A Carnival of Comics**, as a test, and talked a couple newsstands into participating in this experiment. The copies sold out over the weekend and newsies asked for more.

Eastern sales staffers then approached Woolworth's. The late Oscar Fitz-Alan Douglas, sales brains of Woolworth, showed some interest, but after several months of deliberation decided the book would not give enough value for ten cents. Kress, Kresge, McCrory, and several other dime stores turned them down even more abruptly. Wildenberg next went to George Hecht, editor of **Parents Magazine**, and tried to persuade him to run a comic supplement or publish a "higher level" comic magazine. Hecht also frowned on the idea.

In Wildenberg's 1949 interview, he noted that "even the comic syndicates couldn't see it. 'Who's going to read old comics?' they asked." With the failures of EmBee's **Comic Monthly** (1922) and Dell's **The Funnies** (1929) still fresh in some minds, no one could see why children would pay ten cents for a comic magazine when they could get all they wanted for free in a Sunday newspaper. But Wildenberg had become convinced that children as well as grown-ups were not getting all the comics they wanted in the Sunday papers; otherwise, the **Gulf Comic Weekly** and the premium comics would not have met with such success. Wildenberg said, "I decided that if boys and girls were willing to work for premium coupons to obtain comic books, they might be willing to pay ten cents on the newsstands." This conviction was also strengthened by Max Gaines' ten cent sticker experiment.

George Janosik, the president of Eastern Color, then called on George Delacorte to form another 50-50 joint venture to publish and market a comic book "magazine" for retail sales as they did with **The Funnies** just a few years previously, but this time American News turned them down cold. The magazine monopoly remembered the abortive **The Funnies** from just a few years before. After much discussion on how to proceed, Delacorte finally agreed to publish it and a partnership was formed. Feeling cautious, they printed 40,000 copies for distribution to a few chain stores who agreed to try it out. Known today as **Famous Funnies Series One**, it clocks in at 68 pages, with half its pages coming from reprints of the reprints in **Funnies on Parade** and half from **Famous Funnies A Carnival of Comics**. It is the scarcest issue.

With 68 full-color pages at only ten cents a piece, it sold out in thirty days with not a single returned copy. Delacorte refused to print a second edition. "Advertisers won't use it," he complained. "They say it's not dignified enough." The profit, however, was approximately $2,000. This particular edition is the rarest of all these early Eastern comic book experiments.

In early 1934, while riding the train, another Eastern Color employee named Harold A. Moore read an account from a prominent New York newspaper that indicated they owed much of their circulation success to their comics section. Mr. Moore went back to Harry Gold, President of American News, with the article in hand. He succeeded in acquiring a print order for 250,000 copies for a proposed monthly comics magazine. In May 1934, **Famous Funnies** #1 (with a July cover date) hit the newsstands with Steven O. Douglass as its only editor (even though Harold Moore was listed as such in #1) until it ceased publication some twenty years later. It was a 64-page version of the 32-page giveaways, and more importantly, it still sold for a dime! The first issue lost $4,150.60. Ninety percent of the copies sold out and a second issue dated September debuted in July. From then on, the comic book was published monthly. **Famous Funnies** also began carrying original material, apparently as early as the second issue. With #3, Buck Rogers took center stage and stayed there for the next twenty years, with covers by Frank Frazetta towards the end of the run–some of his best comics work ever.

***Funnies on Parade**, 1933 - what we recognize today as the first "modern" comic book.*

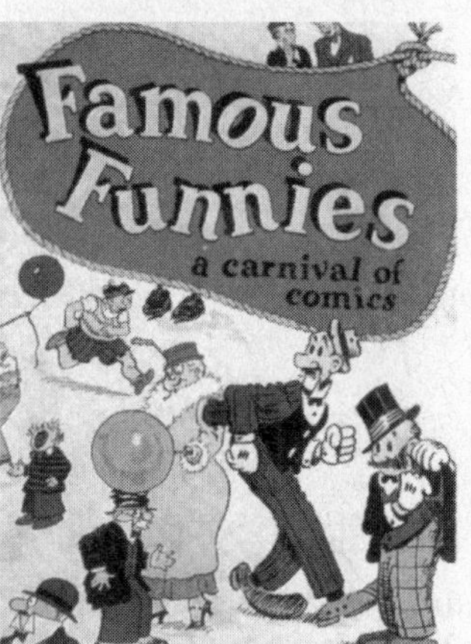

The fateful version Charlie Gaines stickered 10¢ a copy one weekend in late 1933.

***Famous Funnies Series One** is the rare one, as only 40,000 copies were printed.*

Delacorte got cold feet and sold back his interest to Eastern, even though the seventh issue cleared a profit of $2,664.25. Wildenberg emphasized that Eastern could make a manufacturer's profit by printing its own books as well as the publishing profits once it was distributed. Every issue showed greater sales than the preceding one, until within a year, close to a million 64-page books were being sold monthly at ten cents apiece; Eastern received the lion's share of the receipts, and soon found it was netting $30,000 per issue. The comic syndicates received $640 ($10 a page) for publishing rights. Original material could be obtained from budding professionals for just $5 a page. According to Will Eisner in R. C. Harvey's **The Art of the Comic Book**, the prices then paid for original material had a long range effect of keeping creator wages low for years.

Initially, Eastern's experiment was eyed with skepticism by the publishing world, but within a year or so after **Famous Funnies** was nonchalantly placed on sale alongside slicker magazines like **Atlantic Monthly** or **Harper's**, at least five other competitors tried this brand new format.

However, one other abortive periodical comics experiment was launched cover dated a full two months before the highly successful newsstand **Famous Funnies** format would have an important influence on a chain of events which led ultimately to **Superman** being published.

Comic Cuts #1, May 19, 1934, debuted published by H.L. Baker Co., Inc., 195 Main St, Buffalo, New York with editorial and executive offices at 381 Fourth St, NYC, same address as ULTEM (Centaur) would use just a couple years later - this address housed a number of publishers fighting to exist during the Great Depression. Indica says H. L. Baker was President &

Famous Funnies *#1, July 1934, was the first successful newsstand comic book, lasting until 1955.*

Treasurer and J. D. Geller was Vice President and Secretary. It lasted nine issues with the final one cover-dated July 28. It appears Jake Geller, Windsor, Ontario, Canada, acquired American rights to a number of comic strips from the publisher Amalgamated Press, publisher of **Comic Cuts** in England. He partnered in the publishing with H. L. Baker and they acquired the backing of S-M News Co., Inc. as their distributor. Most distributors back then functioned on many important levels. It was common practice for the distributor back then to front the funds to pay the paper company and the printer, collecting the revenue from the 900 I.D. distributors located around the country after months of on-sale time, then paying the publisher.

In late 1934, army officer/diplomat turned pulp writer turned publisher Major Wheeler-Nicholson (1890-1968) formed the under-funded National Allied Publishing which introduced **New Fun #1** (Feb 1935) at almost tabloid-size. **New Fun** was also distributed by S-M News. It is entirely possible Wheeler-Nicholson somehow convinced them he could produce a superior "home-grown" package as the imported strips were not selling well. **New Fun** was basically the same as **Comic Cuts** while also containing all original USA material such as carried in **The Funnies** (1929-30) from Dell/Eastern. With **New Fun,** what S-M News offered was more familiar American home grown. Coulton Waugh speculated in his 1947 history book **The Comics** on page 342: "...The Major had gone back to the 1929 idea of **The Funnies**, for the contents of **New Fun** were original material. (It should be recorded here that original art work had appeared in a one-color book called **Detective Dan**..."

Comic Cuts *#8, July 14, 1934, issued weekly by H.L. Baker Co. Inc., Buffalo, New York; editorial offices at 381 Fourth Ave, NYC; co-owner Jake D. Geller was Canadian. Title provided inspiration for* ***New Fun****.*

However, Lloyd Jacquet, a person definitely in a position to know better, wrote as Chapter One of a proposed "History of the Comic Book" in 1957, "When Major Malcolm Wheeler-Nicholson set up his card table and chair in an eleventh floor office of the Hathaway Building in New York that Fall of 1934, these most modest beginnings sparked off what can rightly be called the 'comic book era.' When he came back to the U.S. after his last stay abroad, he looked over the American newsstand, and thought that the European juvenile weekly papers, with their picture-story continuities, their colorful illustrations, and their low price would appeal to the American boys and girls in the same way. He knew that those European publications were made up of new material, specially drawn and produced for each little magazine. He also knew that the American presentation of such material would have to be different, and merely importing, or translating European produced features for republication here was not the answer. This was about the time I joined with him in his project. It was still embryonic, but beginning to take form under Nicholson's direction. We were in the depression then, & it was not too difficult to secure writers and artists - but it was a task to instruct them as to exactly what was wanted. We finally rounded up a small but gifted group of creative people, and we produced our first issue of a monthly magazine composed of original features and material, and which was called, simply, "**FUN**."

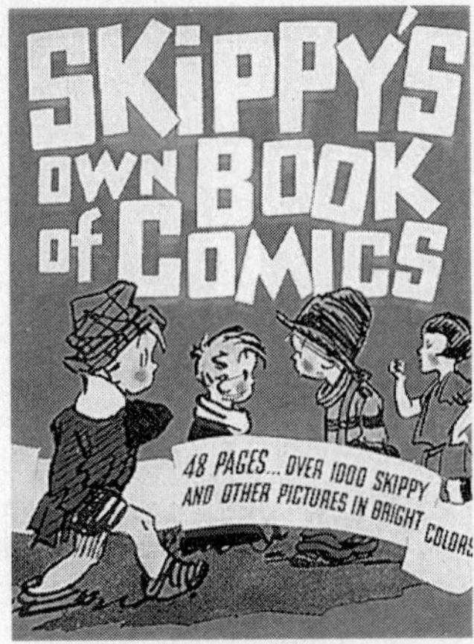

Skippy's Own Book of Comics*, 1934, had half a million issues printed and was the very first single character comic book in this "new" format.*

Around this same time in late 1934, M.C. Gaines left Eastern Color moving over to the McClure Newspaper Syndicate to become their manager of their Color Printing Department He immediately went to work convincing clients to

New Fun *#1, Feb 1935. According to first-employee Lloyd Jacquet, the format Major Malcolm Wheeler-Nicholson used was directly inspired by* ***Comic Cuts****. Many of the non-comics features were the same.*

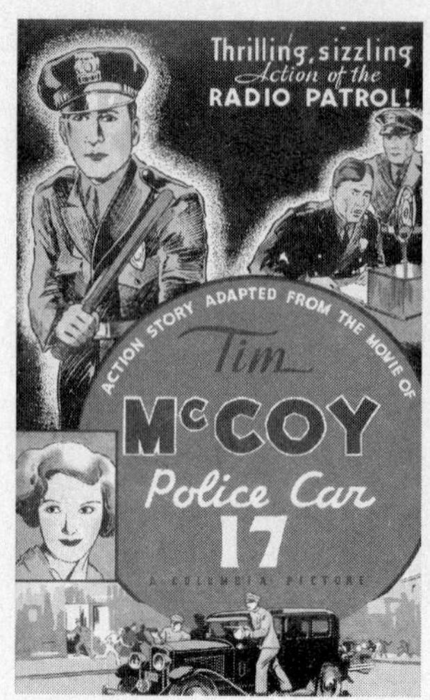

***Tim McCoy Police Car #17**, Whitman's first 1930s comic book (1934); the first movie adaptation*

issue promotional comics. Also, long-time comics publisher Whitman brought out the first original material movie adaptation, **Tim McCoy Police Car 17**, in the tabloid **New Fun** format with stiff card covers. A few years before, they had introduced the new comics formats known as the **Big Little Book** and the **Big Big Book**. The BLB and BBB formats would go toe-to-toe with Eastern's creation throughout the 1930s, but Eastern would win out with their new comics magazine format.

The very last 10" x 10" comic books pioneered by Cupples & Leon were published by the David McKay Publishing Company around mid-1935. Around this same time the Major published his 2nd comic book in which the editorial mentions amongst other exciting stories they were going to be showcasing the adventures of "hero supermen of the days to come."

By late 1935, Max Gaines (with his youthful assistant Sheldon Mayer) reached a business agreement with George Delacorte (who was re-entering the comic book business a third time) and McClure Syndicate (a growing newspaper comic strip enterprise) to be come editor of reprint newspaper comic strips in **Popular Comics**.

Also by late '35, Lev Gleason, another pioneer who participated in mercantiling **Funnies on Parade** and the early

__New Comics__ #1, Dec. 1935, was the Major's second entry into comic books, re-emphasizing the concept of "New!"

Famous Funnies, had become the first editor of United Feature's own **Tip Top Comics** with its first issue cover dated April 1936. In 1939 he would begin publishing his own titles starting with **Silver Streak**, created by the comics genius, Jack Cole, best known for Plastic Man. Gleason later created the crime comic book as a separate popular genre by 1942 with **Crime Does Not Pay** with a long run until 1955.

Wheeler-Nicholson introduced the concept of "the annual" into this new format with **Big Book of Fun Comics #1** cover dated March 1936. It featured reprints from his earlier efforts in **New Fun** #1-5 as he struggled to make a go of it.

Industry giant King Features introduced **King Comics #1** cover dated April 1936 through publisher David McKay, with Ruth Plumly Thompson as editor. McKay had already been issuing various format comic books with King Feature characters for a few years, including Mickey Mouse, Henry, Popeye and Secret Agent X-9, wherein Dashiell Hammett received cover billing and Alex Raymond was listed inside simply as "illustrator." McKay readily adapted to trying several formats. Soon many young comic book illustrators were copying Raymond.

The next month, William Cook & John Mahon, former disgruntled employees of Major Wheeler-Nicholson, issued their first issue of **Comics Magazine** #1 in May 1936.

This was followed by Henle Publishing issuing **Wow What**

*Left, Charlie Gaines & Sheldon Mayer packaged **Popular Comics** #1, Feb. 1936, for George Delecorte in late 1935 after the former left Eastern Color. Middle, **King Comics** #1, April 1936, marked King Features Syndicate's entry into the new 64-page color comic market with their new heavyweights, **Flash Gordon** and **Popeye**. By this point, Hearst had been involved in publishing comic books for close to 40 years. Right, Lev Gleason left Eastern & Wildenberg about the same time as Gaines to edit **Tip Top Comics** #1, April 1936, for United Features.*

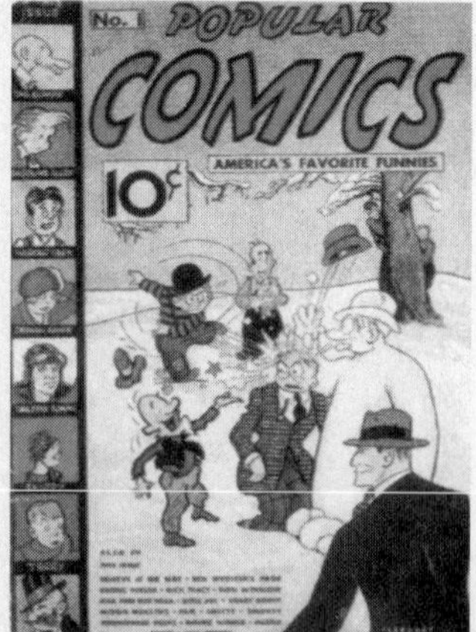

*Left, **The Comics Magazine** #2, June 1936, was the first title of what later became Centaur. Soon it had a name change and quickly made history. Middle, **Wow What A Magazine** is a rare title which ran four issues beginning in June 1936 with the first published work by youthful, eager Bernard Baily, Dick Briefer, Will Eisner & Bob Kane. Painted cover by Will Eisner. **Western Picture Stories** #1, Feb. 1937 has more art by Eisner, ties with **Star Ranger Funnies** #1 as first western comic book. Centaur also introduced the earliest crime comic book, **Detective Picture Stories #1** dated December 1936.*

A Magazine, which contained the earliest comic work of Will Eisner, Bob Kane, Dick Briefer & others. By the end of 1936, Cook and Mahon pioneered the first single theme comic books: **Funny Picture Stories** #1 in Nov. 1936 (adventure), **Detective Picture Stories** #1 in Feb. 1937 (crime), as well as **Western Picture Stories** #1 in Feb. 1937 (the Western). The company would eventually be known historically as Centaur Comics, and serve as the subject of endless debate among fan historians regarding their earliest origins as to who the owners were, where they came from and where they went.

Dell issued the second western genre comic book titled **Western Action Thrillers** #1 in April 1937. It was ten cents for one hundred pages as well as **100 Pages of Comics** 101, containing Big Little Book art reworked back into sequential comics.

Harry 'A' Chesler jumped ship from the Major, issuing his first comic books with **Star Comics** and **Star Ranger Funnies**, dated Feb 1937. Later that year, he sold these two titles to Ultem while remaining editor, and his newly set up art shop supplied contents. He then began **Feature Funnies** #1 in Oct. 1937, headlining Joe Palooka, at one time the #1 newspaper comic strip in America. Issue #2 sported a Rube Goldberg cover while #3 contains "Hawk of the Sea," Will Eisner's first work for what would soon become the Quality Comics Group when Everett "Busy" Arnold bought the company. **Feature Funnies** #3 also contains the first appearance of The Clock by George Brenner - the first costumed comic book hero.

Almost forty years after the first newspaper strip comic book compilations were issued at the dawn of international popularity for American comic strips, the race was on to get

*Left, **Feature Funnies #3**, Dec. 1937, contains George Brenner's The Clock, the first comic book costumed hero plus Eisner's first work for Quality Comics, when still owned by Chesler. **Circus the Comic Riot** #1, June 1938, contains Basil Wolverton's earliest professional comic book work plus more Will Eisner and Bob Kane. Right, **Action Comics** #1, June 1938, began revolutionizing the industry when Superman by Jerome Siegel & Joseph Shuster debuted. The publishers did not understand what they had at first as Superman does not appear on a cover again until #7. Nobody knew at first, it seemed, except book-keeper Victor Fox counting copies sold, who quit and formed his own comic book company.*

Left, ***Jumbo Comics*** *#1, Sept. 1938, debuts pulp publisher Fiction House's entry into the growing comic book industry. Middle,* ***Detective Comics*** *#27 introduced Batman created by Bob Kane and Bill Finger - need we say more? Right,* ***Wonder Comics*** *#1, May 1939, became Victor Fox's first entry into the comics biz when he fast-talked a youthful Will Eisner into creating a near-exact clone of the creation of Siegel & Shuster's brainchild, Superman. There was a quick lawsuit and #2 featured Yarko The Great instead. Bob Kane was busy that May as he is also in* ***Wonder*** *#1.*

titles out of the starting block. In late 1937 the Major began stumbling when he couldn't pay his printing bill to Harry Donenfeld. In recent interviews, Harry's son, Irwin, who as a 12-year old read the original art to the first issue of **Action Comics** #1 and **Detective Comics** #27 said "in 1932 my father and Paul Sampliner started Independent News with Liebowitz as the accountant. The company was begun with Paul Sampliner's mother's money. If it hadn't been for her investments into building the distribution as well as purchasing color printing presses, there might never have been a DC Comics....My father took over Wheeler-Nicholson's company with the Major's books literally on the printing presses. Harry had to absorb debt that could not otherwise be paid." Irwin told this writer " my dad did not originally willingly enter the comics business..."

Soon after the Major lost control of his company, **Action Comics** #1 was published with a cover date of June 1938, and the first Golden Age of superhero comics had begun. Early in 1938 at McClure Syndicate, Max Gaines and Shelly Mayer showed editor Vin Sullivan a many times rejected sample strip. Sullivan then talked Donenfeld, Paul Sampliner and Jack Liebowitz into publishing Jerry Siegel & Joe Shuster's creation of "The Last Son of Krypton." This was followed in 1939 by a lucrative partnership for Gaines beginning with Harry Donenfeld as the All-American Comics Group.

While there's a great deal of controversy surrounding such labeling, the "Golden Age" is viewed by many these days as beginning with **Action Comics** #1 and continuing through the end of World War II. There was a time not that long ago that the newspaper reprint comic book was collected with more fervor than the heroic comics of the '40s. **Prince Valiant FB** #26, **Flash Gordon 4C** #10 and **Tarzan SS** #20

Left, ***Marvel Comics*** *#1, Oct. 1939, was the first Martin Goodman comic book, introducing Human Torch by Carl Burgos and Sub-Mariner by Bill Everett. Middle,* ***Silver Streak*** *#1, Dec. 1939, Lev Gleason's first published comic book, introduced Jack Cole's classic, The Claw, running until #24, when the title changed to* ***Crime Does Not Pay****. Right,* ***Whiz Comics*** *#2 (#1), Feb. 1940, ushered Fawcett onto the comic book scene with yet another Superman clone - Captain Marvel, who was successful from the get-go. At one time his main title was issued every three weeks.*

Left, **Crime Does Not Pay** #43, Nov. 1945. Lev Gleason instigated a popular new genre which brought the industry unfairly under heavy fire from church and state. Middle, **My Date** #1, July 1947. Joe Simon and Jack Kirby created the romance genre when they developed the older female audience which lasted into the '70s. Right, **Atomic War** #1, Nov. 1952. Nuclear obliteration was heavy on the minds of most Americans. Due to the Korean War, there was a plethora of war titles and the genre survived well into the 1970s before being eventually marginalized by the super hero revival.

were some of the highest Holy Grails of collecting, but no more even though they contain fantastic art & story.

Today's marketplace dictates super heroes command the highest prices and are seemingly the most desirable. Maybe one day that pendulum will swing once again as there have been many years since they were introduced when super heroes almost disappeared completely from the racks.

The **Atomic/Romance** Age debuted with a bang by early 1946, revamping the industry once again as circulations soon hit their all-time highs with well over 1.3 billion periodical issues sold a year by the consignment honor system. By the early 1950s one in three periodicals sold in the USA was a comic book. 90% of all children admitted they read and enjoyed comics. There were dozens of genres being published. There were comic books for every taste and style. Hundreds of titles were being issued every month.

For many readers, the pinnacle was reached with the "New Trend" Entertaining Comics (E.C.) began delivering to the newsstands in 1950. The company still has a large following even today - a testament to its emphasis on quality art & story.

Comic book publishers glutted the market place by 1952-53. The attacks on comics begun the late 1940s came back anew in 1954 brought on by over-zealous church people and district attorneys with an agenda.

This continued until the advent of the self-censoring, industry-stifling Comics Code, created in response to a public outcry spearheaded by Dr. Frederic Wertham's tirade against the American comics industry, published as a book titled

Left, **Crime Detective** #9, July 1948. Some say the tied-up figure represents Dr. Fredric Wertham following his earliest attacks on the crime comic book. Hillman joined the first Code. Middle, **Justice Traps the Guilty** #56, Nov. 1953. The S&K studio placed themselves in the spotlight, with a pretty mother pointing out Joe Simon as the tall, dastardly ringleader. Jack Kirby is on the right end. Right, **Thing** #15, Apr. 1954. Ditko wreaks havoc on a world rising against comics as a giant worm eats Brooklyn in one of the most gruesome titles created. His early work is intense.

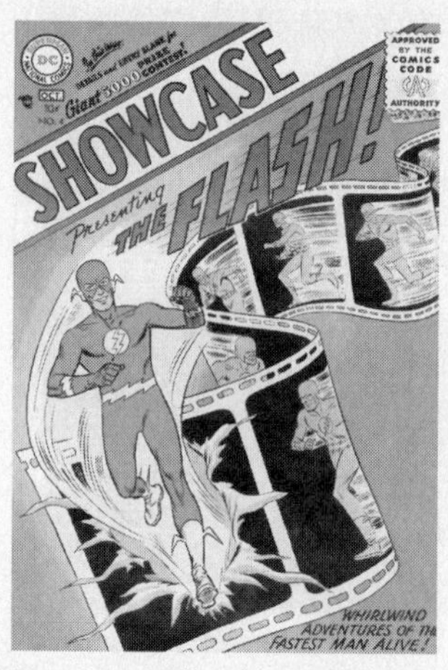

Left, By the early 1950s, Carl Barks increased the circulation of ***Walt Disney's C&S*** *to over 4 million per issue & in 1952 his creation, Uncle Scrooge, got his own book, selling over a million an issue through the '50s while superheroes slumbered. Middle, Harvey Kurtzman created* ***Mad Comics*** *#1, 1952, as the comics industry went in an entirely "New" Direction and has directly inspired countless comics creators for years. Right,* ***Showcase #4****, Sept. 1956, the superhero revival starts a year after the Code, though it was three years before the Flash earned his own title once again.*

Seduction of the Innocent, which removed crime and horror comic books from the marketplace. Some of them were quite gruesome; however in his last book, **The World of Fanzines**, Wertham exhonerated comics fans for misinterpreting his data more than 20 years previous.

It took a year or two to recover from that moralistic assault, with many historians speculating the Silver Age of Superheroes began with the publication of **Showcase** #4 in 1956. Others point to the 1952 successful releases of Kurtzman's **MAD** #1 and Bark's **Uncle Scrooge** 4C 386 as true Silver, since those titles soon broke the "million sold per issue" mark when the rest of the comic book industry was reeling from the effects of the public uproar fueled by Wertham. Within the Silver Era the term Bronze Age has been stated by some to begin when the Code approved newsstand comic book industry raised its standard cover price from 12 to 15 cents and Jack Kirby left Marvel for DC. As circulations plummeted after the Batman TV craze wore off by 1968 and the ensuing superhero glut withered on the stands, out in the Bay Area cartoonist Robert Crumb's creator-owned **Zap Comics** #1 appeared in Feb 1968, printed by Charles Plymell & Don Donahue on a small printing press. Soon after in Chicago, Jay Lynch and Skip Williamson brought out **Bijou Funnies**, Gilbert Shelton self-published **Feds 'N' Heads** while still in Austin, Texas, with Print Mint reprinting it almost immediately & Crumb let S. Clay Wilson, Victor Moscoso & Rick Griffin into **Zap #2.**

As originally published by the Print Mint beginning with #2 in 1968, **Zap Comics** almost single-handedly spawned an industry with tremendous growth in alternative comix running through the 1970s. During this decade the San

Left, ***Brave & Bold*** *#28, Feb/Mar. 1960, gathered together the revived DC heroes, further expanding the resurging super hero market DC Comics ushered in. Middle,* ***Fantastic Four*** *#1, Nov. 1962, began the revitalization of Martin Goodman's moribund Marvel Comics Group, directly inspired by the success of the JLA's own regular series begun 2 years earlier in late 1960. Right,* ***Amazing Fantasy*** *#15, Aug. 1962, introduced the Amazing Spider-Man, created almost completely by Steve Ditko with some assists from Stan Lee and Jack Kirby, which revolutionized the way comic book stories could be told.*

Left, ***Zap Comics*** *#1, Plymell first printing, Feb. 1968, was the "direct" inspiration for the earliest successful origins of the Direct Market and has sold over a million copies. Most issues have been continuously in print for over 30 years. High grade first printings have sold for over $4500. Middle, soon afterwards Gilbert Shelton brought* ***Feds 'N' Heads*** *to Print Mint and later joined* ***Zap****. It has sold for $1000. Right, famed poster artist Rick Griffin edited his own comic book,* ***Tales From the Tube*** *in 1973, with most of the* ***Zap*** *crew joining him. It currently brings over $200 in NM high grade.*

Francisco Bay Area was an intense hotbed of comix being issued without a comics code "seal of approval" from companies such as Rip Off Press, Last Gasp, San Francisco Comic Book Company, Company & Sons, Weirdom Publications, Star*Reach, and Comics & Comix. Kitchen Sink prospered for many years in Wisconsin and many small press comix publishers scattered across the USA and Canada - all of whom created the Direct Sales Market. There were hundreds of people involved with an independent mind producing & distributing alternative underground comix, creating the direct market. Phil Seuling introduced DC, Marvel and Warren to this already developed for five years, San Francisco Bay Area-based, comix business system as a "new" way of selling comics in late 1973, acknowedged by Phil himself in his last interview in **Will Eisner's Quarterly** #3, Summer 1984.

After DC and Marvel joined the DM in a serious way in 1979, the last 20 years have generally been called the "Modern Age", although there are hints of a new age emerging since the mid-'90s. The jury is still out on naming it.

The comic book store as an industry came into its own in the 1980s. Thousands of fans & entrepreneurs opened stores, fulfilling a life's dream for many of them - fueled by a vibrant speculator's market which lasted until the early 1990s, its last hurrah being when DC "killed" Superman in 1992. The comic book marketplace has been rebuilding ever since. Much of that growth has been outside the super hero genre.

In each of the preceding eras, however, the secret for collectors has remained the same: buy what you enjoy. We did, and we are still collectors today!

Portions excerpted from **Comics Archeology 101** *© 2005 Robert L. Beerbohm, a detailed, heavily researched book in progress covering the more than 160 year history of the American comic book business. His E-mail is:* **robert@blbcomics.com**.

Left, ***Conan*** *#1, Oct. 1970, by Roy Thomas and Barry Windsor-Smith introduced the sword & sorcery genre. Middle,* ***StarReach*** *#1, April 1974, published by Mike Friedrich, was the first comic book directed specifically at comic book stores. Right,* ***Giant-Size X-Men*** *#1, Summer, 1975, introduced the new X-team, which later on revolutionized the comic book store system with its phenomenal sales once Chris Claremont and John Byrne teamed up on the title.*

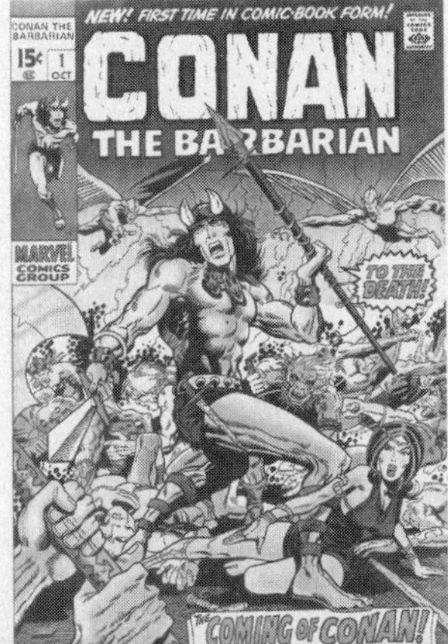

Abadazad #2 © DeMatteis & Ploog

Ace Comics #30 © DMP

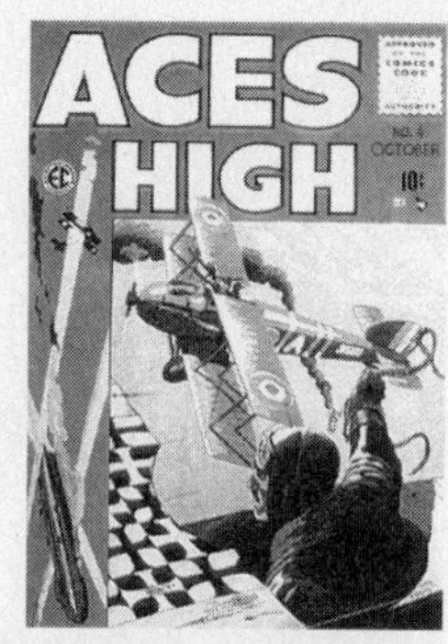

Aces High #4 © WMG

	GD	VG	FN	VF	VF/NM	NM-
	2.0	4.0	6.0	8.0	9.0	9.2

The correct title listing for each comic book can be determined by consulting the indicia (publication data) on the beginning interior pages of the comic. The official title is determined by those words of the title in capital letters only, and not by what is on the cover. Titles are listed in this book as if they were one word, ignoring spaces, hyphens, and apostrophes, to make finding titles easier. Exceptions are made in rare cases. Comic books listed should be assumed to be in color unless noted "B&W".

Comic publishers are invited to send us sample copies for possible inclusion in future guides.

PRICING IN THIS GUIDE: Prices for **GD 2.0** (Good), **VG 4.0** (Very Good), **FN 6.0** (Fine), **VF 8.0** (Very Fine), **VF/NM 9.0** (Very Fine/Near Mint),and **NM– 9.2** (Near Mint–) are listed in whole U.S. dollars except for prices below $7 which show dollars and cents. **The minimum price listed is $2.25**, the cover price for current new comics. Many books listed at this price can be found in $1.00 boxes at conventions and dealers stores.

A-1 (See A-One)

ABADAZAD
CrossGen (Code 6): Mar, 2004 - No. 3, May, 2004 ($2.95)

1-3-Ploog-a/c; DeMatteis-s 3.00
1-2nd printing with new cover 3.00

ABBIE AN' SLATS (...With Becky No. 1-4) (See Comics On Parade, Fight for Love, Giant Comics Edition 2, Giant Comics Editions #1, Sparkler Comics, Tip Topper, Treasury of Comics, & United Comics)
United Features Syndicate: 1940; March, 1948 - No. 4, Aug, 1948 (Reprints)

	GD	VG	FN	VF	VF/NM	NM-
Single Series 25 ('40)	40	80	120	230	325	440
Single Series 28	33	66	99	190	275	360
1 (1948)	19	38	57	107	154	200
2-4: 3-r/Sparkler #68-72	10	20	30	60	80	100

ABBOTT AND COSTELLO (...Comics)(See Giant Comics Editions #1 & Treasury of Comics)
St. John Publishing Co.: Feb, 1948 - No. 40, Sept, 1956 (Mort Drucker-a in most issues)

	GD	VG	FN	VF	VF/NM	NM-
1	58	116	174	363	562	760
2	34	68	102	193	279	365
3-9 (#8, 8/49; #9, 2/50)	21	42	63	121	173	225
10-Son of Sinbad story by Kubert (new)	25	50	75	144	207	270
11,13-20 (#11, 10/50; #13, 8/51; #15, 12/52)	16	32	48	92	131	170
12-Movie issue	17	34	51	98	139	180
21-30: 28-r/#8. 30-Painted-c	11	22	33	66	91	115
31-40: 33,38-Reprints	10	20	30	56	73	90
3-D #1 (11/53, 25¢)-Infinity-c	35	70	105	201	293	385

ABBOTT AND COSTELLO (TV)
Charlton Comics: Feb, 1968 - No. 22, Aug, 1971 (Hanna-Barbera)

	GD	VG	FN	VF	VF/NM	NM-
1	9	18	27	65	93	120
2	5	10	15	36	48	60
3-10	4	8	12	27	36	45
11-22	3	7	10	21	28	35

ABC (See America's Best TV Comics)

ABE SAPIEN: DRUMS OF THE DEAD
Dark Horse Comics: Mar, 1998 ($2.95, one-shot)

1-McDonald-s/Thompson-a. Hellboy back-up; Mignola-s/a/c 3.00

A. BIZARRO
DC Comics: Jul, 1999 - No. 4, Oct, 1999 (2.50, limited series)

1-4-Gerber-s/Bright-a 2.50

ABOMINATIONS (See Hulk)
Marvel Comics: Dec, 1996 - No. 3, Feb, 1997 (1.50, limited series)

1-3-Future Hulk storyline 2.25

ABRAHAM LINCOLN LIFE STORY (See Dell Giants)

ABRAHAM STONE
Marvel Comics (Epic): July, 1995 - No. 2, Aug, 1995 ($6.95, limited series)

1,2-Joe Kubert-s/a 7.00

ABSENT-MINDED PROFESSOR, THE
Dell Publishing Co.: Apr, 1961 (Disney)

	GD	VG	FN	VF	VF/NM	NM-
Four Color #1199-Movie, photo-c	9	18	27	63	89	115

ABSOLUTE VERTIGO
DC Comics (Vertigo): Winter, 1995 (99¢, mature)

nn-1st app. Preacher. Previews upcoming titles including Jonah Hex: Riders of the Worm, The Invisibles (King Mob), The Eaters, Ghostdancing & Preacher

	GD	VG	FN	VF	VF/NM	NM-
	2.0	4.0	6.0	8.0	9.0	9.2
	1	2	3	5	7	9

ABYSS, THE (Movie)
Dark Horse Comics: June, 1989 - No. 2, July, 1989 ($2.25, limited series)

1,2-Adaptation of film; Kaluta & Moebius-a 3.00

ACCELERATE
DC Comics (Vertigo): Aug, 2000 - No. 4, Nov, 2000 ($2.95, limited series)

1-4-Pander Bros.-a/Kadrey-s 3.00

ACCLAIM ADVENTURE ZONE
Acclaim Books: 1997 ($4.50, digest size)

1-Short stories of Turok, Troublemakers, Ninjak and others 4.50

ACE COMICS
David McKay Publications: Apr, 1937 - No. 151, Oct-Nov, 1949 (All contain some newspaper strip reprints)

	GD	VG	FN	VF	VF/NM	NM-
1-Jungle Jim by Alex Raymond, Blondie, Ripley's Believe It Or Not, Krazy Kat begin (1st app. of each)	317	634	951	2060	3330	4600
2	94	188	282	588	907	1225
3-5	63	126	189	394	610	825
6-10	46	92	138	281	431	580
11-The Phantom begins (1st app., 2/38) (in brown costume)	79	158	237	494	760	1025
12-20	40	80	120	230	335	440
21-25,27-30	36	72	108	204	297	390
26-Origin & 1st app. Prince Valiant (5/39); begins series?	102	204	306	638	982	1325
31-40: 37-Krazy Kat ends	26	52	78	147	211	275
41-60	19	38	57	107	154	200
61-64,66-76-(7/43; last 68 pgs.)	17	34	51	95	135	175
65-(8/42)-Flag-c	19	38	57	107	154	200
77-84 (3/44; all 60 pgs.)	14	28	42	79	110	140
85-99 (52 pgs.)	12	24	36	69	95	120
100 (7/45; last 52 pgs.)	14	28	42	81	113	145
101-134: 128-(11/47)-Brick Bradford begins. 134-Last Prince Valiant (all 36 pgs.)	10	20	30	58	77	95
135-151: 135-(6/48)-Lone Ranger begins	9	18	27	54	70	85

ACE KELLY (See Tops Comics & Tops In Humor)

ACE KING (See Adventures of Detective...)

ACES
Acme Press (Eclipse): Apr, 1988 - No. 5, Dec, 1988 ($2.95, B&W, magazine)

1-5 3.00

ACES HIGH
E.C. Comics: Mar-Apr, 1955 - No. 5, Nov-Dec, 1955

	GD	VG	FN	VF	VF/NM	NM-
1-Not approved by code	21	42	63	158	234	310
2	12	24	36	90	133	175
3-5	11	22	33	82	121	160

NOTE: *All have stories by **Davis**, **Evans**, **Krigstein**, and **Wood**. **Evans** c-1-5.*

ACES HIGH
Gemstone Publishing: Apr, 1999 - No. 5, Aug, 1999 ($2.50)

1-5-Reprints E.C. issues 2.50
Annual 1 ($13.50) r/#1-5 13.50

ACME NOVELTY LIBRARY, THE
Fantagraphics Books: Winter 1993-94 - Present (quarterly, various sizes)

1-Introduces Jimmy Corrigan; Chris Ware-s/a in all 7.00
1-2nd and later printings 4.00
2,3: 2-Quimby 5.00
4-Sparky's Best Comics & Stories 6.00
5-12: Jimmy Corrigan in all 5.00
13,15-($10.95-c) 11.00
14-($12.95-c) Concludes Jimmy Corrigan saga 13.00
Jimmy Corrigan, The Smartest Kid on Earth (2000, Pantheon Books, Hardcover, $27.50, 380 pgs.) Collects Jimmy Corrigan stories; folded dust jacket 27.50
Jimmy Corrigan, The Smartest Kid on Earth (2003, Softcover, $17.95) 18.00
NOTE: *Multiple printings exist for most issues.*

ACROSS THE UNIVERSE: THE DC UNIVERSE STORIES OF ALAN MOORE
DC Comics: 2003 ($19.95, TPB)

nn-Reprints selected Alan Moore written stories from '85-'87; Superman, Batman, Swamp Thing app. 20.00

ACTION ADVENTURE (War) (Formerly Real Adventure)

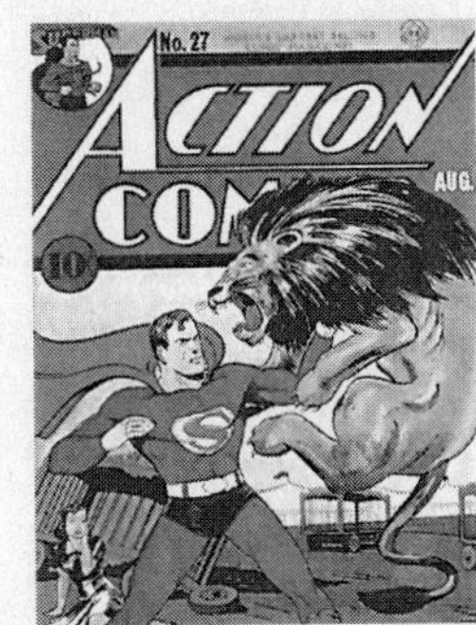

Action Comics #27 © DC

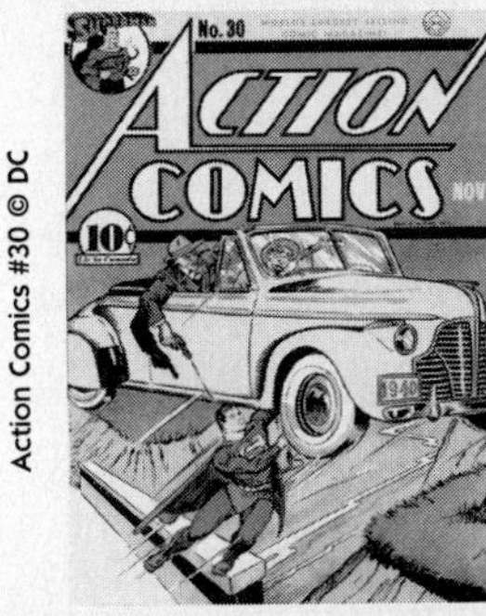

Action Comics #30 © DC

Action Comics #225 © DC

	GD 2.0	VG 4.0	FN 6.0	VF 8.0	VF/NM 9.0	NM- 9.2
Gillmor Magazines: V1#2, June, 1955 - No. 4, Oct, 1955						
V1#2-4	6	12	18	28	34	40
ACTION COMICS (...Weekly #601-642) (Also see The Comics Magazine #1, More Fun #14-17 & Special Edition) (Also see Promotional Comics section)						
National Periodical Publ./Detective Comics/DC Comics: 6/38 - No. 583, 9/86; No. 584, 1/87 - Present						
1-Origin & 1st app. Superman by Siegel & Shuster, Marco Polo, Tex Thompson, Pep Morgan, Chuck Dawson & Scoop Scanlon; 1st app. Zatara & Lois Lane; Superman story missing 4 pgs. which were included when reprinted in Superman #1; Clark Kent works for Daily Star; story continued in #2	38,500	77,000	115,500	231,000	358,000	485,000
1-Reprint, Oversize 13-1/2x10". **WARNING:** This comic is an exact reprint of the original except for its size. DC published it in 1974 with a second cover titling it as a Famous First Edition. There have been many reported cases of the outer cover being removed and the interior sold as the original edition. The reprint with the new outer cover removed is practically worthless. See Famous First Edition for value.						
2-O'Mealia non-Superman covers thru #6	3643	7286	10,930	25,500	38,250	51,000
3 (Scarce)-Superman apps. in costume in only one panel	2286	4572	6860	16,000	24,000	32,000
4-6: 6-1st Jimmy Olsen (called office boy)	1357	2714	4070	9500	14,250	19,000
7-2nd Superman cover	2857	5714	8570	20,000	30,000	40,000
8,9	929	1858	2790	6500	9750	13,000
10-3rd Superman cover by Siegel & Shuster; splash panel used as cover art for Superman #1	1733	3466	5200	12,130	19,065	26,000
11,14: 14-Clip Carson begins, ends #41; Zatara-c	439	878	1317	3073	4937	6800
12-Has 1 pg. Batman ad for Det. #27 (5/39); Zatara sci-fi cover	471	942	1413	3300	5300	7300
13-Shuster Superman-c; last Scoop Scanlon	839	1678	2517	5873	9437	13,000
15-Guardineer Superman-c; Detective Comics ad	645	1290	1935	4514	7258	10,000
16	324	648	972	2106	3403	4700
17-Superman cover; last Marco Polo	497	994	1490	3480	5590	7700
18-Origin 3 Aces; 1st X-Ray Vision?	324	648	972	2106	3403	4700
19-Superman covers begin; has full pg. ad for New York World's Fair 1939	471	942	1413	3300	5300	7300
20-The 'S' left off Superman's chest; Clark Kent works at 'Daily Star'	452	904	1356	3164	5082	7000
21-Has 2 ads for More Fun #52 (1st Spectre)	300	600	900	1925	3063	4100
22,24,25: 24-Kent at Daily Planet. 25-Last app. Gargantua T. Potts, Tex Thompson's sidekick	300	600	900	1892	2946	4000
23-1st app. Luthor (w/red hair) & Black Pirate; Black Pirate by Moldoff; 1st mention of The Daily Planet (4/40)-Has 1 panel ad for Spectre in More Fun	677	1355	2031	4740	7620	10,500
26-28,30	254	508	762	1588	2444	3300
29-1st Lois Lane-c (10/40)	292	584	876	1825	2813	3800
31,32: 32-Intro/1st app. Krypto Ray Gun in Superman story by Burnley	163	326	489	1018	1571	2125
33-Origin Mr. America; Superman by Burnley; has half page ad for All Star Comics #3	177	354	531	1106	1703	2300
34,35,38,39	156	312	468	975	1500	2025
36,37: 36-Classic robot-c. 37-Origin Congo Bill	163	326	489	1018	1571	2125
40-(9/41)-Intro/1st app. Star Spangled Kid & Stripesy; Jerry Siegel photo	169	338	507	1056	1628	2200
41	131	262	393	819	1260	1700
42-1st app./origin Vigilante; Bob Daley becomes Fat Man; origin Mr. America's magic flying carpet; The Queen Bee & Luthor app; Black Pirate ends; not in #41	177	354	531	1106	1703	2300
43-46,48-50: 44-Fat Man's i.d. revealed to Mr. America. 45-1st app. Stuff (Vigilante's oriental sidekick)	131	262	393	819	1260	1700
47-1st Luthor cover in comics (4/42)	200	400	600	1250	1925	2600
51-1st app. The Prankster	144	288	432	900	1388	1875
52-Fat Man & Mr. America become the Ameri-commandos; origin Vigilante retold; classic Superman and back-ups-c	158	316	474	988	1519	2050
53-56,59,60: 56-Last Fat Man. 59-Kubert Vigilante begins?, ends #70. 60-First app. Lois Lane as Super-woman	115	230	345	719	1110	1500
57-2nd Lois Lane-c in Action (3rd anywhere, 2/43)	127	254	381	794	1222	1650
58-"Slap a Jap-c"	129	258	387	806	1241	1675
61-Historic Atomic Radiation-c (6/43)	121	242	363	756	1166	1575
62,63-Japan war-c: 63-Last 3 Aces	115	230	345	719	1110	1500
64-Intro Toyman	121	242	363	756	1166	1575
65-70	96	192	288	600	925	1250
71-79: 74-Last Mr. America	81	162	243	506	778	1050
80-2nd app. & 1st Mr. Mxyztplk-c (1/45)	112	224	336	700	1075	1450
81-88,90: 83-Intro Hocus & Pocus	77	154	231	481	741	1000
89-Classic rainbow cover	81	162	243	506	778	1050
91-99: 93-X-Mas-c. 99-1st small logo (8/46)	71	142	213	444	685	925

	GD 2.0	VG 4.0	FN 6.0	VF 8.0	VF/NM 9.0	NM- 9.2
100	73	146	219	456	703	950
101-Nuclear explosion-c (10/46)	135	270	405	844	1297	1750
102-107,109-120: 102-Mxyztplk-c. 105,117-X-Mas-c	63	126	189	394	610	825
108-Classic molten metal-c	71	142	213	444	685	925
121,122,124-126,128-140: 135,136,138-Zatara by Kubert	58	116	174	363	561	760
123-(8/48) 1st time Superman flies rather than leaps	60	120	180	375	575	775
127-Vigilante by Kubert; Tommy Tomorrow begins (12/48, see Real Fact #6)	62	124	186	388	594	800
141-157,159-161: 151-Luthor/Mr. Mxyztplk/Prankster team-up. 156-Lois as Super Woman. 161- Last 52 pgs.	55	110	165	340	520	700
158-Origin Superman retold	123	246	369	769	1185	1600
162-180: 168,176-Used in **POP**, pg. 90. 173-Robot-c	50	100	150	305	465	625
181-201: 191-Intro. Janu in Congo Bill. 198-Last Vigilante. 201-Last pre-code issue	48	96	144	293	447	600
202-220,232: 212-(1/56)-Includes 1956 Superman calendar that is part of story. 232-1st Curt Swan-c in Action	42	84	126	256	391	525
221-231,233-240: 221-1st S.A. issue. 224-1st Golden Gorilla story. 228-(5/57)-Kongorilla in Congo Bill story (Congorilla try-out)	39	78	117	222	324	425
241,243-251: 241-Batman x-over. 248-Origin/1st app. Congorilla; Congo Bill renamed Congorilla. 251-Last Tommy Tomorrow	33	66	99	190	275	360
242-Origin & 1st app. Brainiac (7/58); 1st mention of Shrunken City of Kandor	139	278	417	1181	1915	2650
252-Origin & 1st app. Supergirl (5/59); intro new Metallo	147	294	441	1250	2025	2800
253-2nd app. Supergirl	52	104	156	317	484	650
254-1st meeting of Bizarro & Superman-c/story	40	80	120	240	358	475
255-1st Bizarro Lois Lane-c/story & both Bizarros leave Earth to make Bizarro World; 3rd app. Supergirl	35	70	105	201	293	385
256-260: 259-Red Kryptonite used	22	44	66	127	184	240
261-1st X-Kryptonite which gave Streaky his powers; last Congorilla in Action; origin & 1st app. Streaky The Super Cat	24	48	72	138	199	260
262,264-266,268-270	20	40	60	112	161	210
263-Origin Bizarro World	25	50	75	144	207	270
267(8/60)-3rd Legion app; 1st app. Chameleon Boy, Colossal Boy, & Invisible Kid, 1st app. of Supergirl as Superwoman.	50	100	150	305	465	625
271-275,277-282: 274-Lois Lane as Superwoman; 282-Last 10¢ issue	17	34	51	95	135	175
276(5/61)-6th Legion app; 1st app. Brainiac 5, Phantom Girl, Triplicate Girl, Bouncing Boy, Sun Boy, & Shrinking Violet; Supergirl joins Legion	30	60	90	170	245	320
283(12/61)-Legion of Super-Villains app. 1st 12¢	12	24	36	87	134	180
284(1/62)-Mon-el app.	12	24	36	87	134	180
285(2/62)-12th Legion app; Brainiac 5 cameo; Supergirl's existence revealed to world; JFK & Jackie cameos	15	30	45	109	167	225
286-287,289-292,294-299: 286(3/62)-Legion of Super Villains app. 287(4/62)-15th Legion app. (cameo). 289(6/62)-16th Legion app. (Adult); Lightning Man & Saturn Woman's marriage 1st revealed. 290(7/62)-Legion app. (cameo); Phantom Girl app. 1st Supergirl emergency squad. 291-1st meeting Supergirl & Mr. Mxyzptlk. 292-2nd app. Superhorse (see Adv.#293). 297-Mon-el app. 298-Legion cameo	10	20	30	73	107	140
288-Mon-el app.; r-origin Supergirl	11	22	33	77	114	150
293-Origin Comet (Superhorse)	13	26	39	90	138	185
300-(5/63)	12	24	36	84	127	170
301-303,305,307,308,310-312,315-320: 307-Saturn Girl app. 317-Death of Nor-Kan of Kandor. 319-Shrinking Violet app.	7	14	21	51	71	90
304,306,313: 304-Origin/1st app. Black Flame (9/63). 306-Brainiac 5, Mon-el app. 313-Batman app.	8	16	24	53	74	95
309-(2/64)-Legion app.; Batman & Robin-c & cameo; JFK app. (he died 11/22/63; on stands last week of Dec, 1963)	8	16	24	55	78	100
314-Retells origin Supergirl; J.L.A. x-over	8	16	24	53	74	95
321-333,335-339: 336-Origin Akvar (Flamebird)	6	12	18	43	59	75
334-Giant G-20; origin Supergirl, Streaky, Superhorse & Legion (all-r)	11	22	33	77	114	150
340-Origin, 1st app. of the Parasite	7	14	21	50	68	85
341,344,350,358: 341-Batman app. in Supergirl back-up story. 344-Batman x-over. 350-Batman, Green Arrow & Green Lantern app. in Supergirl back-up story. 358-Superboy meets Supergirl	5	10	15	36	48	60
342,343,345,346,348,349,351-357,359: 342-UFO story. 345-Allen Funt/Candid Camera story.	5	10	15	33	44	55
347,360-Giant Supergirl G-33,G-45; 347-Origin Comet-r plus Bizarro story. 360-Legion-r; r/origin Supergirl	8	16	24	53	74	95
361-364,367-372,374-378: 361-2nd app. Parasite. 363-366-Leper/Death story. 370-New facts about Superman's origin. 376-Last Supergirl in Action. 377-Legion begins (thru #392). 378-Last 12¢ issue	4	8	12	27	36	45

Action Comics #586 © DC

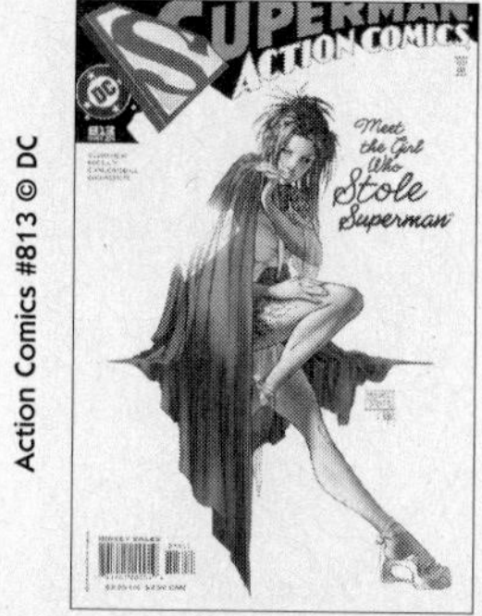

Action Comics #813 © DC

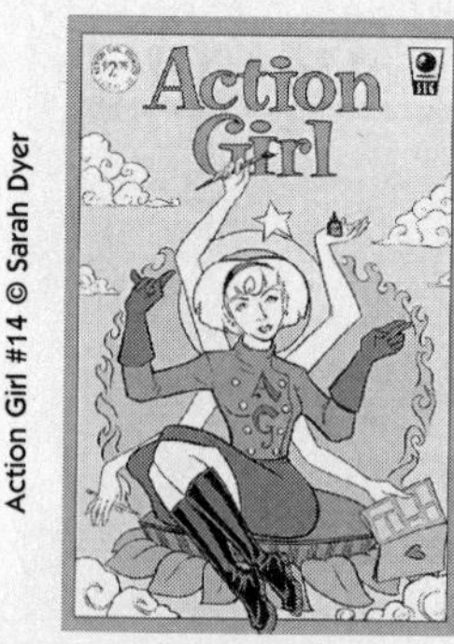

Action Girl #14 © Sarah Dyer

GD 2.0 · VG 4.0 · FN 6.0 · VF 8.0 · VF/NM 9.0 · NM- 9.2

365,366: 365-JLA & Legion app. 366-JLA app. 4 8 12 29 40 50
373-Giant Supergirl G-57; Legion-r 7 14 21 50 68 85
379-399,401: 388-Sgt. Rock app. 392-Batman-c/app.; last Legion in Action; Saturn Girl gets new costume. 393-401-All Superman issues 3 6 9 18 24 30
400 4 8 12 25 33 42
402-Last 15¢ issue; Superman vs. Supergirl duel 3 7 10 21 28 35
403-413: All 52 pg. issues. 411-Origin Eclipso-(r). 413-Metamorpho begins, ends #418 4 8 12 22 30 38
414-424: 419-Intro. Human Target. 421-Intro Capt. Strong; Green Arrow begins. 422,423-Origin Human Target 2 4 6 10 13 16
425-Neal Adams-a(p); The Atom begins 3 6 9 16 20 24
426-431,433-436,438,439 2 4 6 8 10 12
432-1st S.A. Toyman app (2/74). 2 4 6 14 18 22
437,443-(100 pg. Giants) 4 8 12 29 40 50
440-1st Grell-a on Green Arrow 2 4 6 10 13 16
441,442,444-448: 441-Grell-a on Green Arrow continues 1 3 4 6 8 10
449-(68 pgs.) 2 4 6 10 13 16
450-465,467-483,486,489-499: 454-Last Atom. 456-Grell Jaws-c. 458-Last Green Arrow. 1 2 3 4 5 7
466,485,487,488: 466-Batman, Flash app. 485-Adams-c. 487,488-(44 pgs.). 487-Origin & 1st app. Microwave Man; origin Atom retold 1 2 3 5 7 9
481-483,485-492,495-498,501-508-Whitman variants (low print run; none show issue # on cover) 1 2 3 4 5 7
484-Earth II Superman & Lois Lane wed; 40th anniversary issue(6/78) 1 3 4 6 8 10
484-Variant includes 3-D Superman punchout doll in cello. pack; 4 different inserts; Canadian promo?) 2 4 6 10 12 15
500-($1.00, 68 pgs.)-Infinity-c; Superman life story; shows Legion statues in museum 1 3 4 6 8 10
501-543,545,547-551: 511-514-Airwave II solo stories. 513-The Atom begins. 517-Aquaman begins; ends #541. 521-1st app. The Vixen. 532,536-New Teen Titans cameo. 535,536-Omega Men app. 551-Starfire becomes Red-Star 3.00
504,505,507,508-Whitman variants (no cover price) 6.00
544-(6/83, Mando paper, 68 pgs.)-45th Anniversary issue; origins new Luthor & Brainiac; Omega Men cameo; Shuster-a (pin-up); article by Siegel 1 2 3 4 5 7
546-J.L.A., New Teen Titans app. 1 2 3 5 6 8
552,553-Animal Man-c & app. (2/84 & 3/84) 5.00
554-582 3.00
583-Alan Moore scripts; last Earth 1 Superman story (cont'd from Superman #423) 1 3 4 6 8 10
584-Byrne-a begins; New Teen Titans app. 6.00
585-599: 586-Legends x-over. 596-Millennium x-over; Spectre app. 598-1st Checkmate 3.00
600-($2.50, 84 pgs., 5/88) 6.00
601-610,619-642: (#601-642 are weekly issues) ($1.50, 52 pgs.) 601-Re-intro The Secret Six; death of Katma Tui 3.00
611-618: 611-614-Catwoman stories (new costume in #611). 613-618-Nightwing stories 3.00
643-Superman & monthly issues begin again; Perez-c/a/scripts begin; swipes cover to Superman #1 4.00
644-649,651-661,663-673,675-683: 645-1st app. Maxima. 654-Part 3 of Batman storyline. 655-Free extra 8 pgs. 660-Death of Lex Luthor. 661-Begin $1.00-c. 667-($1.75, 52 pgs.). 675-Deathstroke cameo. 679-Last $1.00 issue. 683-Doomsday cameo 2.50
650-($1.50, 52 pgs.)-Lobo cameo (last panel) 3.00
662-Clark Kent reveals i.d. to Lois Lane; story cont'd in Superman #53 4.00
674-Supergirl logo & c/story (reintro) 5.00
683-685-2nd & 3rd printings 2.25
684-Doomsday battle issue 3.00
685,686-Funeral for a Friend issues; Supergirl app. 2.50
687-($1.95)-Collector's Ed.w/die-cut-c 2.50
687-($1.50)-Newsstand Edition with mini-poster 2.25
688-699,701-703-($1.50): 688-Guy Gardner-c/story. 697-Bizarro-c/story. 703-(9/94)-Zero Hour 2.25
695-($2.50)-Collector's Edition w/embossed foil-c 2.50
700-($2.95, 68 pgs.)-Fall of Metropolis Pt 1, Guice-a; Pete Ross marries Lana Lang and Smallville flashbacks with Curt Swan art & Murphy Anderson inks 3.00
700-Platinum 15.00
700-Gold 18.00
0(10/94), 704(11/94)-710-719,721-731: 710-Begin $1.95-c. 714-Joker app. 719-Batman-c/app. 721-Mr. Mxyzptlk app. 723-Dave Johnson-c. 727-Final Night x-over. 2.25
720-Lois breaks off engagement w/Clark 3.00
720-2nd print. 2.25
732-749,751-767: 732-New powers. 733-New costume, Ray app. 738-Immonen-s/a(p) begins. 741-Legion app. 744-Millennium Giants x-over. 745-747-70's-style Superman vs. Prankster. 753-JLA-c/app. 757-Hawkman-c. 760-1st Encantadora. 761-Wonder Woman app. 765-Joker & Harley-c/app. 766-Batman-c/app. 2.25
750-($2.95) 3.00
768,769,771-774: 768-Begin $2.25-c; Marvel Family-c/app. 771-Nightwing-c/app. 772,773-Ra's al Ghul app. 774-Martian Manhunter-c/app. 2.25
770-($3.50) Conclusion of Emperor Joker x-over 3.50
775-($3.75) Bradstreet-c; intro. The Elite 3.75
776-799: 776-Farewell to Krypton; Rivoche-c. 780-782-Our Worlds at War x-over. 781-Hippolyta and Major Lane killed. 782-War ends. 784-Joker: Last Laugh; Batman & Green Lantern app. 793-Return to Krypton. 795-The Elite app. 798-Van Fleet-c 2.25
800-(4/03, $3.95) Struzan painted-c; guest artists include Ross, Jim Lee, Jurgens, Sale 4.00
801-811: 801-Raney-a. 809-The Creeper app. 811-Mr. Majestic app. 2.25
812-Godfall part 1; Turner-c; Caldwell-a(p) 4.00
812-2nd printing; B&W sketch-c by Turner 3.00
813-Godfall pt. 4; Turner-c; Caldwell-a(p) 3.00
814-822: 814-Reis-a/Art Adams-c; Darkseid app.; begin $2.50-c. 815,816-Teen Titans-c/app. 820-Doomsday app. 2.50
#1,000,000 (11/98) Gene Ha-c; 853rd Century x-over 2.25
Annual 1-6('87-'94, $2.95)-1-Art Adams-c/a(p); Batman app. 2-Perez-c/a(i). 3-Armageddon 2001. 4-Eclipso vs. Shazam. 5-Bloodlines; 1st app. Loose Cannon. 6-Elseworlds story 3.00
Annual 7,9 ('95, '97, $3.95)-7-Year One story. 9-Pulp Heroes sty 4.00
Annual 8 (1996, $2.95)-Legends of the Dead Earth story 3.00

NOTE: ***Supergirl's*** *origin in 262, 280, 285, 291, 305, 309.* ***N. Adams*** *c-356, 358, 359, 361-364, 366, 367, 370-374, 377-379i, 398-400, 402, 404,405, 419p, 466, 468, 469, 473i, 485.* ***Aparo*** *a-642.* ***Austin*** *c/a-682i.* ***Baily*** *a-24, 25.* ***Boring*** *a-164, 194, 211, 223, 233, 241, 250, 261, 266-268, 346, 348, 352, 356, 357.* ***Burnley*** *a-28-33; c-48?, 53-55, 58, 59?, 60-63, 65, 66p, 67p, 70p, 71p, 79p, 82p, 84-86p, 90-92p, 93p?, 94p, 107p, 108p.* ***Byrne*** *a-584-598p, 599i, 600p; c-584-591, 596-600.* ***Ditko*** *a-642.* ***Giffen*** *a-560, 563, 565, 577, 579; c-539, 560, 563, 565, 577, 579.* ***Grell*** *a-440-442, 444-446, 450-452, 456-458; c-456.* ***Guardineer*** *a-24, 25; c-8, 11, 12, 14-16, 18. 25.* ***Guice*** *a(p)-676-681, 683-698, 700; c-683, 685, 686, 687(direct), 688-693i, 694-696, 697i, 698-700.* ***Infantino*** *a-642.* ***Kaluta*** *c-613.* ***Bob Kane's*** *Clip Carson-14-41.* ***Gil Kane*** *a-443r, 493r, 539-541, 544-546, 551-554, 601-605, 642; c-535p, 540, 541, 544p, 545-549, 551-554, 580, 627.* ***Kirby*** *c-638.* ***Meskin*** *a-42-121(most).* ***Mignola*** *a-600, Annual 2; c-c-614.* ***Moldoff*** *a-23-25, 443r.* ***Mooney*** *a-667p.* ***Mortimer*** *c-153, 154, 159-172, 174, 178-181, 184, 186-189, 191-193, 196, 200, 206.* ***Orlando*** *a-617p; c-621.* ***Perez*** *a-600i, 643-652p, Annual 2p; c-529p, 602, 643-651, Annual 2p.* ***Quesada*** *c-Annual 4p.* ***Fred Ray*** *c-34, 36-46, 50-52.* ***Siegel & Shuster*** *a-1-27.* ***Paul Smith*** *c-608.* ***Starlin*** *a-509; c-631.* ***Leonard Starr*** *a-597i(part),* ***Staton*** *a-525p, 526p, 531p, 535p, 536p.* ***Swan/Moldoff*** *c-281, 286, 287, 293, 298, 334.* ***Thibert*** *c-676, 677p, 678-681, 684.* ***Toth*** *a-406, 407, 413, 431; c-616.* ***Tuska*** *a-486p, 550.* ***Williamson*** *a-568i.* ***Zeck*** *c-Annual 5*

ACTION FORCE (Also see G.I. Joe European Missions)
Marvel Comics Ltd. (British): Mar, 1987 - No. 50, 1988 ($1.00, weekly, magazine)
1,3: British G.I. Joe series. 3-w/poster insert 6.00
2,4 4.00
5-10 3.00
11-50 2.50
...Special 1 (7/87) Summer holiday special; Snake Eyes-c/app. 6.00
...Special 2 (10/87) Winter special; 4.00

ACTION GIRL
Slave Labor Graphics: Oct, 1994 - Present ($2.50/$2.75/$2.95, B&W)
1-19: 4-Begin $2.75-c. 19-Begin $2.95-c 3.00
1-6 ($2.75, 2nd printings): All read 2nd Print in indicia. 1-(2/96). 2-(10/95). 3-(2/96). 4-(7/96). 5-(2/97). 6-(9/97) 2.75
1-4 ($2.75, 3rd printings): All read 3rd Print in indicia. 2.75

ACTION PLANET COMICS
Action Planet: 1996 - No. 3, Sept, 1997 ($3.95, B&W, 44 pgs.)
1-3: 1-Intro Monster Man by Mike Manley & other stories 4.00
Giant Size Action Planet Halloween Special (1998, $5.95, oversized) 6.00

ACTUAL CONFESSIONS (Formerly Love Adventures)
Atlas Comics (MPI): No. 13, Oct, 1952 - No. 14, Dec, 1952
13,14 8 16 24 40 50 60

ACTUAL ROMANCES (Becomes True Secrets #3 on?)
Marvel Comics (IPS): Oct, 1949 - No. 2, Jan, 1950 (52 pgs.)
1 12 24 36 69 95 120
2-Photo-c 8 16 24 46 58 70

ADAM AND EVE
Spire Christian Comics (Fleming H. Revell Co.): 1975,1978 (35¢/49¢)
nn-By Al Hartley 2 4 6 9 11 14

ADAM STRANGE (Also see Green Lantern #132, Mystery In Space #53 & Showcase #17)
DC Comics: 1990 - No. 3, 1990 ($3.95, 52 pgs, limited series, squarebound)
Book One - Three: Andy & Adam Kubert-c/a 4.00
...: The Man of Two Worlds (2003, $19.95, TPB) r/#1-3; sketch pages by Andy Kubert 20.00

ADAM STRANGE
DC Comics: Nov, 2004 - No. 8 ($2.95, limited series)

Adam-12 #2 © GK

Adventure Comics #59 © DC

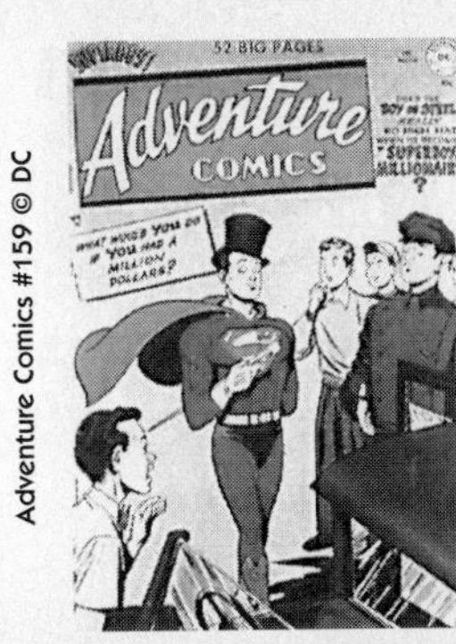

Adventure Comics #159 © DC

	GD 2.0	VG 4.0	FN 6.0	VF 8.0	VF/NM 9.0	NM- 9.2
1-3-Andy Diggle-s/Pascal Ferry-a/c. 1-Superman app.						3.00

ADAM-12 (TV)
Gold Key: Dec, 1973 - No. 10, Feb, 1976 (Photo-c)

	GD 2.0	VG 4.0	FN 6.0	VF 8.0	VF/NM 9.0	NM- 9.2
1	8	16	24	53	74	95
2-10	4	8	12	25	33	42

ADDAM OMEGA
Antarctic Press: Feb, 1997 - No. 4, Aug, 1997 ($2.95, B&W)

	GD 2.0	VG 4.0	FN 6.0	VF 8.0	VF/NM 9.0	NM- 9.2
1-4						3.00

ADDAMS FAMILY (TV cartoon)
Gold Key: Oct, 1974 - No. 3, Apr, 1975 (Hanna-Barbera)

	GD 2.0	VG 4.0	FN 6.0	VF 8.0	VF/NM 9.0	NM- 9.2
1	10	20	30	73	107	140
2,3	7	14	21	50	68	85

ADLAI STEVENSON
Dell Publishing Co.: Dec, 1966

	GD 2.0	VG 4.0	FN 6.0	VF 8.0	VF/NM 9.0	NM- 9.2
12-007-612-Life story; photo-c	4	8	12	25	33	42

ADOLESCENT RADIOACTIVE BLACK BELT HAMSTERS (See Clint)
Comic Castle/Eclipse Comics: 1986 - No. 9, Jan, 1988 ($1.50, B&W)

	GD 2.0	VG 4.0	FN 6.0	VF 8.0	VF/NM 9.0	NM- 9.2
1-9: 1st & 2nd printings exist						2.25
1-Limited Edition						3.00
1-In 3-D (7/86), 2-4 ($2.50)						2.50
Massacre The Japanese Invasion #1 (8/89, $2.00)						2.25

ADRENALYNN (See The Tenth)
Image Comics: Aug, 1999 - No. 4, Feb, 2000 ($2.50)

	GD 2.0	VG 4.0	FN 6.0	VF 8.0	VF/NM 9.0	NM- 9.2
1-4-Tony Daniel-s/Marty Egeland-a; origin of Adrenalynn						2.50

ADULT TALES OF TERROR ILLUSTRATED (See Terror Illustrated)

ADVANCED DUNGEONS & DRAGONS (Also see TSR Worlds)
DC Comics: Dec, 1988 - No. 36, Dec, 1991 (Newsstand #1 is Holiday, 1988-89) ($1.25-$1.75)

	GD 2.0	VG 4.0	FN 6.0	VF 8.0	VF/NM 9.0	NM- 9.2
1-Based on TSR role playing game						4.00
2-36: 25-$1.75-c begins						2.25
Annual 1 (1990, $3.95, 68 pgs.)						4.00

ADVENTURE BOUND
Dell Publishing Co.: Aug, 1949

	GD 2.0	VG 4.0	FN 6.0	VF 8.0	VF/NM 9.0	NM- 9.2
Four Color 239	6	12	18	43	59	75

ADVENTURE COMICS (Formerly New Adventure)(...Presents Dial H For Hero #479-490)
National Periodical Publications/DC Comics: No. 32, 11/38 - No. 490, 2/82; No. 491, 9/82 - No. 503, 9/83

	GD 2.0	VG 4.0	FN 6.0	VF 8.0	VF/NM 9.0	NM- 9.2
32-Anchors Aweigh (ends #52), Barry O'Neil (ends #60, not in #33), Captain Desmo (ends #47), Dale Daring (ends #47), Federal Men (ends #70), The Golden Dragon (ends #36), Rusty & His Pals (ends #52) by Bob Kane, Todd Hunter (ends #38) and Tom Brent (ends #39) begin	422	844	1266	2321	3161	4000
33-38: 37-Cover used on Double Action #2	200	400	600	1100	1500	1900
39(6/39)- Jack Wood begins, ends #42; 1st mention of Marijuana in comics	200	400	600	1100	1500	1900
40-(Rare, 7/39, on stands 6/10/39)-The Sandman begins by Bert Christman (who died in WWII); believed to be 1st conceived story (see N.Y. World's Fair for 1st published app.); Socko Strong begins, ends #54	4375	8750	13,125	31,000	50,500	70,000
41-O'Mealia shark-c	542	1084	1626	3794	6097	8400
42,44-Sandman-c by Flessel. 44-Opium story	677	1354	2031	4739	7620	10,500
43,45	310	620	930	2015	3258	4500
46,47-Sandman covers by Flessel. 47-Steve Conrad Adventurer begins, ends #76	477	954	1431	1340	4370	7400
48-Intro & 1st app. The Hourman by Bernard Baily; Baily-c (Hourman c-48,50,52-59)	2233	4466	6700	16,800	27,400	38,000
49,50: 50-Cotton Carver by Jack Lehti begins, ends #64	262	524	786	1638	2519	3400
51,60-Sandman-c: 51-Sandman-c by Flessel.	338	676	1014	2197	3549	4900
52-59: 53-1st app. Jimmy "Minuteman" Martin & the Minutemen of America in Hourman; ends #78. 58-Paul Kirk Manhunter begins (1st app.), ends #72	231	462	693	1444	2222	3000
61-1st app. Starman by Jack Burnley (4/41); Starman c-61-72; Starman by Burnley in #61-80	1088	2176	3264	8160	13,300	18,500
62-65,67,68,70: 67-Origin & 1st app. The Mist; classic Burnley-c. 70-Last Federal Men	192	384	576	1200	1850	2500
66-Origin/1st app. Shining Knight (9/41)	235	470	705	1470	2260	3050
69-1st app. Sandy the Golden Boy (Sandman's sidekick) by Paul Norris (in a Bob Kane style); Sandman dons new costume	200	400	600	1250	1925	2600
71-Jimmy Martin becomes costumed aide to the Hourman; 1st app. Hourman's Miracle Ray machine	185	370	555	1156	1778	2400
72-1st Simon & Kirby Sandman (3/42, 1st DC work)	1029	2058	3087	7718	12,609	17,500
73-Origin Manhunter by Simon & Kirby; begin new series; Manhunter-c (scarce)	1176	2352	3528	8820	14,410	20,000
74-78,80: 74-Thorndyke replaces Jimmy, Hourman's assistant; new Sandman-c begin by S&K. 75-Thor app. by Kirby; 1st Kirby Thor (see Tales of the Unexpected #16). 77-Origin Genius Jones; Mist story. 80-Last S&K Manhunter & Burnley Starman	185	370	555	1156	1778	2400
79-Classic Manhunter-c	246	492	738	1538	2369	3200
81-90: 83-Last Hourman. 84-Mike Gibbs begins, ends #102	119	238	357	744	1147	1550
91-Last Simon & Kirby Sandman	108	216	324	675	1038	1400
92-99,101,102: 92-Last Manhunter. 101-Shining Knight origin retold. 102-Last Starman, Sandman, & Genius Jones; most-S&K-c (Genius Jones cont'd in More Fun #108)	96	192	288	600	925	1250
100-S&K-c	129	258	387	806	1241	1675
103-Aquaman, Green Arrow, Johnny Quick & Superboy all move over from More Fun Comics #107; 8th app. Superboy; Superboy-c begin; 1st small logo (4/46)	312	624	936	1950	3075	4200
104	112	224	336	700	1075	1450
105-110	81	162	243	506	778	1050
111-120: 113-X-Mas-c	69	138	207	431	666	900
121,122-126,128-130: 128-1st meeting Superboy & Lois Lane	60	120	180	375	575	775
127-Brief origin Shining Knight retold	62	124	186	388	594	800
131-141,143-149: 132-Shining Knight 1st return to King Arthur time; origin aide Sir Butch	52	104	156	317	484	650
142-Origin Shining Knight & Johnny Quick retold	55	110	165	336	511	685
150,151,153,155,157,159,161,163-All have 6 pg. Shining Knight stories by Frank Frazetta. 159-Origin Johnny Quick	66	132	198	413	637	860
152,154,156,158,160,162,164-169: 166-Last Shining Knight. 168-Last 52 pg. issue	44	88	132	268	409	550
170-180	42	84	126	256	391	525
181-199: 189-B&W and color illo in **POP**	40	80	120	244	372	500
200 (5/54)	55	110	165	336	511	685
201-208: 207-Last Johnny Quick (not in 205)	40	80	120	230	335	440
209-Last pre-code issue; origin Speedy	40	80	120	235	348	460
210-1st app. Krypto (Superdog)-c/story (3/55)	294	588	882	2352	3826	5300
211-213,215-219	37	74	112	213	312	410
214-2nd app. Krypto	57	114	171	356	548	740
220-Krypto-c/sty	40	80	120	239	357	475
221-246: 229-1st S.A. issue. 237-1st Intergalactic Vigilante Squadron (6/57). 239-Krypto-c	32	64	96	184	267	350
247(4/58)-1st Legion of Super Heroes app.; 1st app. Cosmic Boy, Saturn Girl & Lightning Boy (later Lightning Lad in #267) (origin)	364	728	1092	3276	5638	8000
248-252,254,255-Green Arrow in all: 255-Intro. Red Kryptonite in Superboy (used in #252 but with no effect)	27	54	81	154	222	290
253-1st meeting of Superboy & Robin; Green Arrow by Kirby in #250-255 (also see World's Finest #96-99)	32	64	96	184	267	350
256-Origin Green Arrow by Kirby	65	130	195	406	628	850
257-259: 258-Green Arrow x-over in Superboy	22	44	66	127	184	240
260-1st Silver-Age origin Aquaman (5/59)	75	150	225	469	722	975
261-265,268,270: 262-Origin Speedy in Green Arrow. 270-Congorilla begins, ends #281,283	18	36	54	102	146	190
266-(11/59)-Origin & 1st app. Aquagirl (tryout, not same as later character)	19	38	57	107	154	200
267(12/59)-2nd Legion of Super Heroes; Lightning Boy now called Lightning Lad; new costumes for Legion	90	180	270	563	869	1175
269-Intro. Aqualad (2/60); last Green Arrow (not in #206)	31	62	93	178	259	340
271-Origin Luthor retold	35	70	105	198	287	375
272-274,277-280: 279-Intro White Kryptonite in Superboy. 280-1st meeting Superboy & Lori Lemaris	16	32	48	92	131	170
275-Origin Superman-Batman team retold (see World's Finest #94)	26	52	78	147	211	275
276-(9/60) Robinson Crusoe-like story	17	34	51	98	139	180
281,284,287-289: 281-Last Congorilla. 284-Last Aquaman in Adv.; Mooney-a. 287,288-Intro Dev-Em, the Knave from Krypton. 287-1st Bizarro Perry White & Jimmy Olsen. 288-Bizarro-c. 289-Legion cameo (statues)	15	30	45	85	120	155
282(3/61)-5th Legion app; intro/origin Star Boy	28	56	84	158	229	300
283-Intro. The Phantom Zone	25	50	75	144	207	270
285-1st Tales of the Bizarro World-c/story (ends #299) in Adv. (see Action #255)	21	42	63	121	173	225
286-1st Bizarro Mxyzptlk; Bizarro-c	20	40	60	112	161	210

Adventure Comics #368 © DC

Adventure Comics #466 © DC

Adventure is My Career © CN

GD 2.0 · VG 4.0 · FN 6.0 · VF 8.0 · VF/NM 9.0 · NM- 9.2

290(11/61)-9th Legion app; origin Sunboy in Legion (last 10¢ issue) 26 52 78 150 215 280
291,292,295-298: 291-1st 12¢ ish, (12/61). 292-1st Bizarro Lana Lang & Lucy Lane. 295-Bizarro-c; 1st Bizarro Titano 11 22 33 75 110 145
293(2/62)-13th Legion app; Mon-el & Legion of Super Pets (1st app./origin) app. (1st Superhorse). 1st Bizarro Luthor & Kandor 16 32 48 116 178 240
294-1st Bizarro Marilyn Monroe, Pres. Kennedy. 12 24 36 87 134 180
299-1st Gold Kryptonite (8/62) 11 22 33 77 114 150
300-Tales of the Legion of Super-Heroes series begins (9/62); Mon-el leaves Phantom Zone (temporarily), joins Legion 38 76 114 285 443 600
301-Origin Bouncing Boy 15 30 45 107 164 220
302-305: 303-1st app. Matter-Eater Lad. 304-Death of Lightning Lad in Legion 11 22 33 80 120 160
306-310: 306-Intro. Legion of Substitute Heroes. 307-1st app. Element Lad in Legion. 308-1st app. Lightning Lass in Legion 11 22 33 75 110 145
311-320: 312-Lightning Lad back in Legion. 315-Last new Superboy story; Colossal Boy app. 316-Origins & powers of Legion given. 317-Intro. Dream Girl in Legion; Lightning Lass becomes Light Lass; Hall of Fame series begins. 320-Dev-Em 2nd app. 9 18 27 65 93 120
321-Intro. Time Trapper 8 16 24 58 82 105
322-330: 327-Intro/1st app. Lone Wolf in Legion. 329-Intro The Bizarro Legionnaires; intro. Legion flight rings 7 14 21 51 71 90
331-340: 337-Chlorophyll Kid & Night Girl app. 340-Intro Computo in Legion 7 14 21 46 63 80
341-Triplicate Girl becomes Duo Damsel 6 12 18 40 55 70
342-345,347-351: 345-Last Hall of Fame; returns in 356,371. 348-Origin Sunboy; intro Dr. Regulus in Legion. 349-Intro Universo & Rond Vidar. 351-1st app. White Witch 6 12 18 38 52 65
346-1st app. Karate Kid, Princess Projectra, Ferro Lad, & Nemesis Kid. 8 16 24 53 74 95
352,354-360: 354,355-Superman meets the Adult Legion. 355-Insect Queen joins Legion (4/67) 5 10 15 36 48 60
353-Death of Ferro Lad in Legion 7 14 21 46 63 80
361-364,366,368-370: 369-Intro Mordru in Legion 4 8 12 29 40 50
365,367: 365-Intro Shadow Lass (memorial to Shadow Woman app. in #354's Adult Legion-s); lists origins & powers of L.S.H. 367-New Legion headquarters 5 10 15 33 44 55
371,372: 371-Intro. Chemical King (mentioned in #354's Adult Legion-s). 372-Timber Wolf & Chemical King join 5 10 15 33 44 55
373,374,376-380: 373-Intro. Tornado Twins (Barry Allen Flash descendants). 374-Article on comics fandom. 380-Last Legion in Adventure; last 12¢-c 4 8 12 28 38 48
375-Intro Quantum Queen & The Wanderers 5 10 15 33 44 55
381-Supergirl begins; 1st full length Supergirl story & her 1st solo book (6/69) 10 20 30 72 104 135
382-389 4 8 12 27 36 45
390-Giant Supergirl G-69 6 12 18 43 59 75
391-396,398 3 7 10 21 28 35
397-1st app. new Supergirl 4 8 12 29 40 50
399-Unpubbed G.A. Black Canary story 4 8 12 24 32 40
400-New costume for Supergirl (12/70) 4 8 12 29 40 50
401,402,404-408-(15¢-c) 3 6 9 16 20 25
403-68 pg. Giant G-81; Legion-r/#304,305,308,312 6 12 18 43 59 75
409-411,413-415,417-420-(52 pgs.): 413-Hawkman by Kubert r/B&B #44; G.A. Robotman-r/Det. #178; Zatanna by Morrow. 414-r-2nd Animal Man/Str. Advs. #184. 415-Animal Man-r/Str. Adv.#190 (origin recap). 417-Morrow Vigilante; Frazetta Shining Knight-r/Adv. #161; origin The Enchantress; no Zatanna. 418-Prev. unpub. Dr. Mid-Nite story from 1948; no Zatanna. 420-Animal Man-r/Str. Adv. #195 3 7 10 21 28 35
412-(52 pgs.) Reprints origin & 1st app. of Animal Man from Strange Adventures #180 3 7 10 21 28 35
416-Also listed as DC 100 Pg. Super Spectacular #10; Golden Age-r; r/1st app. Black Canary from Flash #86; no Zatanna

(see DC 100 Pg. Super Spectacular #10 for price)

421-424,427: 424-Last Supergirl in Adventure. 427-Last Vigilante 2 4 6 10 12 15
425-New look, content change to adventure; Kaluta-c; Toth-a, origin Capt. Fear 3 6 9 18 24 30
426-1st Adventurers Club 2 4 6 10 12 15
428-Origin/1st app. Black Orchid (c/story, 6-7/73) 6 12 18 40 55 70
429,430-Black Orchid-c/stories 3 7 10 21 28 35
431-Spectre by Aparo begins, ends #440. 6 12 18 43 59 75
432-439-Spectre app. 433-437-Cover title is Weird Adventure Comics. 436-Last 20¢ issue 4 8 12 22 30 38
440-New Spectre origin. 4 8 12 29 40 50
441-458: 441-452-Aquaman app. 443-Fisherman app. 445-447-The Creeper app. 446-Flag-c. 449-451-Martian Manhunter app. 450-Weather Wizard app. in Aquaman story. 453-458-Superboy app. 453-Intro. Mighty Girl. 457,458-Eclipso app. 1 2 3 5 7 9
459,460 (68 pgs.): 459-New Gods/Darkseid storyline concludes from New Gods #19 (#459 is dated 9-10/78) without missing a month. 459-Flash (ends #466), Deadman (ends #466), Wonder Woman (ends #464), Green Lantern (ends #460). 460-Aquaman (ends #478) 3 6 9 16 20 24
461,462 ($1.00, 68 pgs.): 461-Justice Society begins; ends 466. 461,462-Death Earth II Batman 3 7 10 21 28 35
463-466 ($1.00 size, 68 pgs.) 2 4 6 10 13 16
467-Starman by Ditko & Plastic Man begins; 1st app. Prince Gavyn (Starman). 2 4 6 8 10 12
468-490: 470-Origin Starman. 479-Dial 'H' For Hero begins, ends #490. 478-Last Starman & Plastic Man. 480-490: Dial 'H' For Hero 5.00
491-503: 491-100pg. Digest size begins; r/Legion of Super Heroes/Adv. #247, 267; Spectre, Aquaman, Superboy, S&K Sandman, Black Canary-r & new Shazam by Newton begin. 492,495,496,499-S&K Sandman-r/Adventure in all. 493-Challengers of the Unknown begins by Tuska w/brief origin. 493-495,497-499-G.A. Captain Marvel-r. 494-499-Spectre-r/Spectre 1-3, 5-7. 496-Capt. Marvel Jr. new-s, Cockrum-a. 498-Mary Marvel new-s; Plastic Man-r begin; origin Bouncing Boy-r/ #301. 500-Legion-r (Digest size, 148 pgs.). 501-503: G.A.-r 2 4 6 10 13 16
... 80 Page Giant (10/98, $4.95) Wonder Woman, Shazam, Superboy, Supergirl, Green Arrow, Legion, Bizarro World stories 5.00

NOTE: *Bizarro covers-285, 286, 288, 294, 295, 329. Vigilante app.-420, 426, 427.* **N. Adams** *a(r)-495i-498i; c-365-369, 371-373, 375-379, 381-383.* **Aparo** *a-431-433, 434i, 435, 436, 437i, 438i, 439-452, 503r; c-431-452.* **Austin** *a-449i 451i.* **Bernard Baily** *c-48, 50, 52-59.* **Bolland** *c-475.* **Burnley** *c-61-72, 116-120p.* **Chaykin** *a-438.* **Ditko** *a-467-478p; c-467p.* **Creig Flessel** *c-32, 33, 40, 42, 44, 46, 47, 51, 60.* **Giffen** *c-491p-494p, 500p.* **Grell** *a-435-437, 440.* **Guardineer** *c-34, 35, 45.* **Infantino** *a-416r.* **Kaluta** *c-425.* **Bob Kane** *a-38.* **G. Kane** *a-414r, 425; c-496-499, 537.* **Kirby** *a-250-256.* **Kubert** *a-413.* **Meskin** *a-81,127.* **Moldoff** *a-494i; c-49.* **Morrow** *a-413-415, 417, 422, 502r, 503r.* **Netzer/Nasser** *a-449-451.* **Newton** *a-459-461, 464-466, 491p, 492p.* **Paul Norris** *a-69.* **Orlando** *a-457p, 458p.* **Perez** *c-484-486, 490p.* **Simon/Kirby** *a-503r; c-73-97, 100-102.* **Starlin** *c-471.* **Staton** *a-445-447i, 456-458p, 459, 460, 461p-465p, 466,467p-478p, 502p(r); c-458, 461(back).* **Toth** *a-418, 419, 425, 431, 495p-497p.* **Tuska** *a-494p.*

ADVENTURE COMICS (Also see All Star Comics 1999 crossover titles)
DC Comics: May, 1999 ($1.99, one-shot)

1-Golden Age Starman and the Atom; Snejbjerg-a 2.25

ADVENTURE INTO MYSTERY
Atlas Comics (BFP No. 1/OPI No. 2-8): May, 1956 - No. 8, July, 1957

1-Powell s/f-a; Forte-a; Everett-c 40 80 120 230 335 440
2-Flying Saucer story 22 44 66 123 177 230
3,6-Everett-c 19 38 57 107 154 200
4-7: 4-Williamson-a, 4 pgs; Powell-a. 5-Everett-c/a, Orlando-a. 7-Torres-a; Everett-c 21 42 63 118 169 220
8-Moriera, Sale, Torres, Woodbridge-a, Severin-c 19 38 57 107 154 200

ADVENTURE IS MY CAREER
U.S. Coast Guard Academy/Street & Smith: 1945 (44 pgs.)

nn-Simon, Milt Gross-a 21 42 63 121 173 225

ADVENTURERS, THE
Aircel Comics/Adventure Publ.: Aug, 1986 - No. 10, 1987? ($1.50, B&W)
V2#1, 1987 - V2#9, 1988; V3#1, Oct, 1989 - V3#6, 1990

1-Peter Hsu-a 1 2 3 5 6 7
1-Cover variant, limited ed. 1 3 4 6 8 10
1-2nd print (1986); 1st app. Elf Warrior 3.00
2,3, 0 (#4, 12/86)-Origin, 5-10, Book II, reg. & Limited Ed. #1 3.50
Book II, #2,3,0,4-7 2.25
Book III, #1 (10/89, $2.25)-Reg. & limited-c, Book III, #2-6 2.25

ADVENTURES (No. 2 Spectacular... on cover)
St. John Publishing Co.: Nov, 1949 - No. 2, Feb, 1950 (No. 1 ...in Romance on cover) (Slightly larger size)

1(Scarce); Bolle, Starr-a(2) 28 56 84 158 229 300
2(Scarce)-Slave Girl; China Bombshell app.; Bolle, L. Starr-a 40 80 120 239 357 475

ADVENTURES FOR BOYS
Bailey Enterprises: Dec, 1954

nn-Comics, text, & photos 8 16 24 40 50 60

ADVENTURES IN PARADISE (TV)
Dell Publishing Co.: Feb-Apr, 1962

Four Color#1301 7 14 21 46 63 80

ADVENTURES IN ROMANCE (See Adventures)

ADVENTURES IN SCIENCE (See Classics Illustrated Special Issue)

Adventures in the DC Universe #19 © DC

Adventures Into Darkness #9 © STD

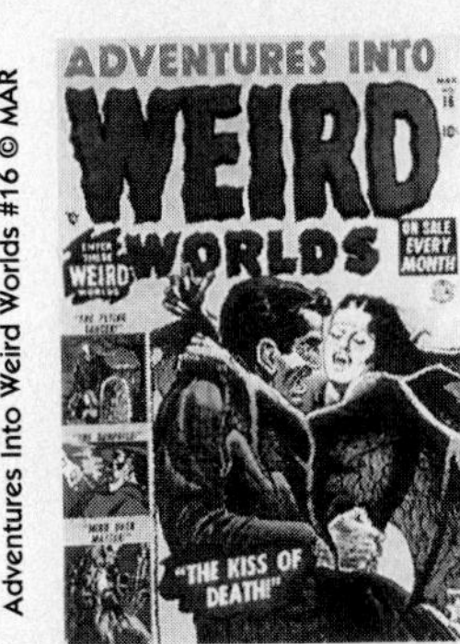

Adventures Into Weird Worlds #16 © MAR

ADVENTURES IN THE DC UNIVERSE
DC Comics: Apr, 1997 - No. 19, Oct, 1998 ($1.75/$1.95/$1.99)

	GD 2.0	VG 4.0	FN 6.0	VF 8.0	VF/NM 9.0	NM- 9.2
1-Animated style in all: JLA-c/app						5.00
2-11,13-17,19: 2-Flash app. 3-Wonder Woman. 4-Green Lantern. 6-Aquaman. 7-Shazam Family. 8-Blue Beetle & Booster Gold. 9-Flash. 10-Legion. 11-Green Lantern & Wonder Woman. 13-Impulse & Martian Manhunter. 14-Superboy/Flash race						3.50
12,18-JLA-c/app						3.50
Annual 1(1997, $3.95)-Dr. Fate, Impulse, Rose & Thorn, Superboy, Mister Miracle app.						4.50

ADVENTURES IN THE RIFLE BRIGADE
DC Comics (Vertigo): Oct, 2000 - No. 3, Dec, 2000 ($2.50, limited series)

	GD 2.0	VG 4.0	FN 6.0	VF 8.0	VF/NM 9.0	NM- 9.2
1-3-Ennis-s/Ezquerra-a/Bolland-c						2.50
TPB (2004, $14.95) r/series and Operation Bollock series						15.00

ADVENTURES IN THE RIFLE BRIGADE: OPERATION BOLLOCK
DC Comics (Vertigo): Oct, 2001 - No. 3, Jan, 2002 ($2.50, limited series)

	GD 2.0	VG 4.0	FN 6.0	VF 8.0	VF/NM 9.0	NM- 9.2
1-3-Ennis-s/Ezquerra-a/Fabry-c						2.50

ADVENTURES IN 3-D (With glasses)
Harvey Publications: Nov, 1953 - No. 2, Jan, 1954 (25¢)

	GD 2.0	VG 4.0	FN 6.0	VF 8.0	VF/NM 9.0	NM- 9.2
1-Nostrand, Powell-a, 2-Powell-a	19	38	57	107	154	200

ADVENTURES INTO DARKNESS (See Seduction of the Innocent 3-D)
Better-Standard Publications/Visual Editions: No. 5, Aug, 1952- No. 14, 1954

	GD 2.0	VG 4.0	FN 6.0	VF 8.0	VF/NM 9.0	NM- 9.2
5-Katz-c/a; Toth-a(p)	40	80	120	244	372	500
6-Tuska, Katz-a	29	58	87	164	237	310
7-9: 7-Katz-c/a. 8,9-Toth-a(p)	29	58	87	164	237	310
10-12: 10,11-Jack Katz-a. 12-Toth-a; lingerie panel	26	52	78	147	211	275
13-Toth-a(p); Cannibalism story cited by T. E. Murphy articles	31	62	93	178	259	340
14	19	38	57	107	154	200

NOTE: ***Fawcette*** *a-13.* ***Moriera*** *a-5.* ***Sekowsky*** *a-10, 11, 13(2).*

ADVENTURES INTO TERROR (Formerly Joker Comics)
Marvel/Atlas Comics (CDS): No. 43, Nov, 1950 - No. 31, May, 1954

	GD 2.0	VG 4.0	FN 6.0	VF 8.0	VF/NM 9.0	NM- 9.2
43(#1)	67	134	201	419	647	875
44(#2, 2/51)-Sol Brodsky-c	43	86	129	262	401	540
3(4/51), 4	31	62	93	175	253	330
5-Wolverton-c panel/Mystic #6; Rico-c panel also; Atom Bomb story	35	70	105	198	287	375
6,8: 8-Wolverton text illo r-/Marvel Tales #104	29	58	87	164	237	310
7-Wolverton-a "Where Monsters Dwell", 6 pgs.; Tuska-c; Maneely-c panels	58	116	174	363	562	760
9,10,12-Krigstein-a. 9-Decapitation panels	25	50	75	141	203	265
11,13-20	22	44	66	125	180	235
21-24,26-31	20	40	60	112	161	210
25-Matt Fox-a	26	52	78	147	211	275

NOTE: ***Ayers*** *a-21.* ***Colan*** *a-3, 5, 14, 21, 24, 25, 28, 29; c-27.* ***Colletta*** *a-30.* ***Everett*** *c-13, 21, 25.* ***Fass*** *a-28, 29.* ***Forte*** *a-28.* ***Heath*** *a-43, 44, 4-6, 22, 24, 26; c-43, 9, 11.* ***Lazarus*** *a-7.* ***Maneely*** *a-7(3 pg.), 10, 11, 21., 22 c-15, 29.* ***Don Rico*** *a-4, 5(3 pg.).* ***Sekowsky*** *a-43, 3, 4.* ***Sinnott*** *a-8, 9, 11, 28.* ***Tuska*** *a-14; c-7.*

ADVENTURES INTO THE UNKNOWN
American Comics Group: Fall, 1948 - No. 174, Aug, 1967 (No. 1-33: 52 pgs.)
(1st continuous series Supernatural comic; see Eerie #1)

	GD 2.0	VG 4.0	FN 6.0	VF 8.0	VF/NM 9.0	NM- 9.2
1-Guardineer-a; adapt. of 'Castle of Otranto' by Horace Walpole	215	430	645	1344	2072	2800
2,3: 3-Feldstein-a (9 pgs)	77	154	231	481	741	1000
4,5: 5- 'Spirit Of Frankenstein' series begins, ends #12 (except #11)	40	80	120	244	372	500
6-10	35	70	105	200	290	380
11-16,18-20: 13-Starr-a	29	58	87	164	237	310
17-Story similar to movie 'The Thing'	34	68	102	196	283	370
21-26,28-30	25	50	75	141	203	265
27-Williamson/Krenkel-a (8 pgs.)	32	64	96	184	267	350
31-50: 38-Atom bomb panels	20	40	60	112	161	210
51-(1/54)-(3-D effect-c/story)-Only white cover	38	76	114	219	320	420
52-58: (3-D effect-c/stories with black covers). 52-E.C. swipe/Haunt Of Fear #14	36	72	108	204	297	390
59-3-D effect story only; new logo	29	58	87	164	237	310
60-Wood*esque*-a by Landau	15	30	45	83	117	150
61-Last pre-code issue (1-2/55)	15	30	45	83	117	150
62-70	8	16	24	58	82	105
71-90	7	14	21	50	68	85
91,96(#95 on inside),107,116-All have Williamson-a	8	16	24	55	78	100
92-95,97-99,101-106,108-115,117-128: 109-113,118-Whitney painted-c. 128-Williamson/Krenkel/Torres-a(r)/Forbidden Worlds #63; last 10¢ issue	6	12	18	38	52	65
100	6	12	18	40	55	70
129-153,157: 153,157-Magic Agent app.	4	8	12	29	40	50
154-Nemesis series begins (origin), ends #170	6	12	18	38	52	65
155,156,158-167,170-174	4	8	12	28	38	48
168-Ditko-a(p)	5	10	15	36	48	60
169-Nemesis battles Hitler	5	10	15	36	48	60

NOTE: *"Spirit of Frankenstein" series in 5, 6, 8-10, 12, 16.* ***Buscema*** *a-100, 106, 108-110, 158r, 165r.* ***Cameron*** *a-34.* ***Craig*** *a-152, 160.* ***Goode*** *a-45, 47, 60.* ***Landau*** *a-51, 59-63.* ***Lazarus*** *a-34, 48, 51, 52, 56, 58, 79, 87; c-31-56, 58.* ***Reinman*** *a-102, 111, 112, 115-118, 124, 130, 137, 141, 145, 164.* ***Whitney*** *c-12-30, 57, 59-on (most.)* ***Torres/Williamson*** *a-116.*

ADVENTURES INTO WEIRD WORLDS
Marvel/Atlas Comics (ACI): Jan, 1952 - No. 30, June, 1954

	GD 2.0	VG 4.0	FN 6.0	VF 8.0	VF/NM 9.0	NM- 9.2
1-Atom bomb panels	67	134	201	419	647	875
2-Sci/fic stories (2); one by Maneely	40	80	120	230	335	440
3-10: 7-Tongue ripped out. 10-Krigstein, Everett-a	28	56	84	158	229	300
11-20	23	46	69	130	188	245
21-Hitler in Hell story	27	54	81	154	222	290
22-26: 24-Man holds hypo & splits in two	20	40	60	112	161	210
27-Matt Fox end of world story-a; severed head-c	38	76	114	219	320	420
28-Atom bomb story; decapitation panels	23	46	69	130	188	245
29,30	17	34	51	95	135	175

NOTE: ***Ayers*** *a-8, 26.* ***Everett*** *a-4, 5; c-6, 8, 10-13, 18, 19, 22, 24, 25; a-4, 25.* ***Fass*** *a-7.* ***Forte*** *a-21, 24.* ***Al Hartley*** *a-2.* ***Heath*** *a-1, 4, 17, 22; c-7, 9, 20.* ***Maneely*** *a-2, 3, 11, 20, 22, 23, 25; c-1, 3, 22, 25-27, 29.* ***Reinman*** *a-24, 28.* ***Rico*** *a-13.* ***Robinson*** *a-13.* ***Sinnott*** *a-25, 30.* ***Tuska*** *a-1, 2, 12, 15.* ***Whitney*** *a-7.* ***Wildey*** *a-28. Bondage c-22.*

ADVENTURES IN WONDERLAND
Lev Gleason Publications: April, 1955 - No. 5, Feb, 1956 (Jr. Readers Guild)

	GD 2.0	VG 4.0	FN 6.0	VF 8.0	VF/NM 9.0	NM- 9.2
1-Maurer-a	11	22	33	64	87	110
2-4	7	14	21	37	46	55
5-Christmas issue	8	16	24	40	50	60

ADVENTURES OF AARON
Image Comics: Mar, 1997 - No. 3, Sept, 1997 (2.95, B&W)

	GD 2.0	VG 4.0	FN 6.0	VF 8.0	VF/NM 9.0	NM- 9.2
1,2,100(#3),3(#4)						3.00

ADVENTURES OF ALAN LADD, THE
National Periodical Publ.: Oct-Nov, 1949 - No. 9, Feb-Mar, 1951 (All 52 pgs.)

	GD 2.0	VG 4.0	FN 6.0	VF 8.0	VF/NM 9.0	NM- 9.2
1-Photo-c	92	184	276	575	888	1200
2-Photo-c	48	96	144	293	447	600
3-6: Last photo-c	40	80	120	230	335	440
7-9	33	66	99	190	275	360

NOTE: ***Dan Barry*** *a-1.* ***Moreira*** *a-3-7.*

ADVENTURES OF ALICE (Also see Alice in Wonderland & ...at Monkey Island)
Civil Service Publ./Pentagon Publishing Co.: 1945

	GD 2.0	VG 4.0	FN 6.0	VF 8.0	VF/NM 9.0	NM- 9.2
1	15	30	45	83	117	150
2-Through the Magic Looking Glass	11	22	33	62	84	105

ADVENTURES OF BARON MUNCHAUSEN, THE
Now Comics: July, 1989 - No. 4, Oct, 1989 ($1.75, limited series)

	GD 2.0	VG 4.0	FN 6.0	VF 8.0	VF/NM 9.0	NM- 9.2
1-4: Movie adaptation						2.25

ADVENTURES OF BARRY WEEN, BOY GENIUS, THE (Also see Free Comic Book Day Edition in the Promotional Comics section)
Image Comics: Mar, 1999 - No. 3, May, 1999 ($2.95, B&W, limited series)

	GD 2.0	VG 4.0	FN 6.0	VF 8.0	VF/NM 9.0	NM- 9.2
1-3-Judd Winick-s/a						3.00
TPB (Oni Press, 11/99, $8.95)						9.00

ADVENTURES OF BARRY WEEN, BOY GENIUS 2.0, THE
Oni Press: Feb, 2000 - No. 3, Apr, 2000 ($2.95, B&W, limited series)

	GD 2.0	VG 4.0	FN 6.0	VF 8.0	VF/NM 9.0	NM- 9.2
1-3-Judd Winick-s/a						3.00
TPB (2000, $8.95)						9.00

ADVENTURES OF BARRY WEEN, BOY GENIUS 3, THE : MONKEY TALES
Oni Press: Feb, 2001 - No. 6, Feb, 2002 ($2.95, B&W, limited series)

	GD 2.0	VG 4.0	FN 6.0	VF 8.0	VF/NM 9.0	NM- 9.2
1-6-Judd Winick-s/a						3.00
TPB (2001, $8.95) r/#1-3; intro. by Peter David						9.00
...4 TPB (5/02, $8.95) r/#4-6						9.00

ADVENTURES OF BAYOU BILLY, THE (Based on video game)
Archie Comics: Sept, 1989 - No. 5, June, 1990 ($1.00)

	GD 2.0	VG 4.0	FN 6.0	VF 8.0	VF/NM 9.0	NM- 9.2
1-5: Esposito-c/a(i). 5-Kelley Jones-c						3.00

ADVENTURES OF BOB HOPE, THE (Also see True Comics #59)
National Per. Publ.: Feb-Mar, 1950 - No. 109, Feb-Mar, 1968 (#1-10: 52pgs.)

	GD 2.0	VG 4.0	FN 6.0	VF 8.0	VF/NM 9.0	NM- 9.2
1-Photo-c	185	370	555	1156	1778	2400
2-Photo-c	81	162	243	506	778	1050

Adventures of Homer Ghost #2 © MAR

Adventures of Dean Martin & Jerry Lewis #17 © DC

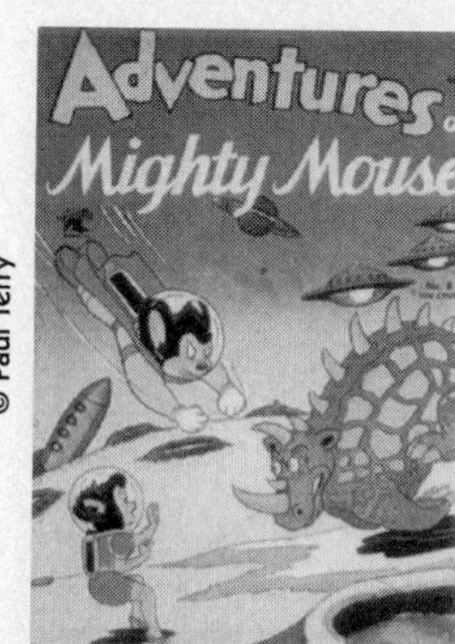

Adventures of Mighty Mouse #8 © Paul Terry

	GD 2.0	VG 4.0	FN 6.0	VF 8.0	VF/NM 9.0	NM- 9.2
3,4-Photo-c	50	100	150	305	465	625
5-10	40	80	120	244	372	500
11-20	28	56	84	158	229	300
21-31 (2-3/55; last precode)	19	38	57	107	154	200
32-40	11	22	33	77	114	150
41-50	9	18	27	65	93	120
51-70	7	14	21	51	71	90
71-93	5	10	15	36	48	60
94-Aquaman cameo	6	12	18	38	52	65
95-1st app. Super-Hip & 1st monster issue (11/65)	7	14	21	50	68	85
96-105: Super-Hip and monster stories in all. 103-Batman, Robin, Ringo Starr cameos	5	10	15	36	48	60
106-109-All monster-c/stories by N. Adams-c/a	7	14	21	51	71	90

NOTE: *Buzzy in #34. Kitty Karr of Hollywood in #15, 17-20, 23, 28. Liz in #26, 109. Miss Beverly Hills of Hollywood in #7, 8, 10, 13, 14. Miss Melody Lane of Broadway in #15. Rusty in #23, 25. Tommy in #24. No 2nd feature in #2-4, 6, 8, 11, 12, 28-108.*

ADVENTURES OF CAPTAIN AMERICA
Marvel Comics: Sept, 1991 - No. 4, Jan, 1992 ($4.95, 52 pgs., squarebound, limited series)

	GD	VG	FN	VF	VF/NM	NM-
1-4: 1-Origin in WW2; embossed-c; Nicieza scripts; Maguire-c/a(p) begins, ends #3. 2-4-Austin-c/a(i). 3,4-Red Skull app.						5.00

ADVENTURES OF CYCLOPS AND PHOENIX (Also See Askani'son & The Further Adventures of Cyclops And Phoenix)
Marvel Comics: May, 1994 - No. 4, Aug, 1994 ($2.95, limited series)

	GD	VG	FN	VF	VF/NM	NM-
1-4-Characters from X-Men; origin of Cable						4.00
Trade paperback ($14.95)-reprints #1-4						15.00

ADVENTURES OF DEAN MARTIN AND JERRY LEWIS, THE
(The Adventures of Jerry Lewis #41 on) (See Movie Love #12)
National Periodical Publications: July-Aug, 1952 - No. 40, Oct, 1957

	GD	VG	FN	VF	VF/NM	NM-
1	104	208	312	650	1000	1350
2-3 pg origin on how they became a team	51	102	153	311	476	640
3-10: 3- I Love Lucy text featurette	31	62	93	178	259	340
11-19: Last precode (2/55)	20	40	60	112	161	210
20-30	15	30	45	86	123	160
31-40	12	24	36	71	98	125

ADVENTURES OF DETECTIVE ACE KING, THE (Also see Bob Scully-- & Detective Dan)
Humor Publ. Corp.: No date (1933) (36 pgs., 9-1/2x12") (10¢, B&W, one-shot) (paper-c)

	GD	VG	FN	VF	VF/NM	NM-
Book 1-Along with Bob Scully & Detective Dan, the first comic w/original art & the first of a single theme.; Not reprints; Ace King by Martin Nadle (The American Sherlock Holmes). A Dick Tracy look-alike	375	750	1125	3000	-	-

ADVENTURES OF EVIL AND MALICE, THE
Image Comics: June, 1999 - No. 3, Nov, 1999 ($3.50/$3.95, limited series)

	GD	VG	FN	VF	VF/NM	NM-
1,2-Jimmie Robinson-s/a						3.50
3-(3.95)						4.00

ADVENTURES OF FELIX THE CAT, THE
Harvey Comics: May, 1992 ($1.25)

	GD	VG	FN	VF	VF/NM	NM-
1-Messmer-r						4.00

ADVENTURES OF FORD FAIRLANE, THE
DC Comics: May, 1990 - No. 4, Aug, 1990 ($1.50, limited series, mature)

	GD	VG	FN	VF	VF/NM	NM-
1-4: Andrew Dice Clay movie tie-in; Don Heck inks						3.00

ADVENTURES OF HOMER COBB, THE
Say/Bart Prod. : Sept, 1947 (Oversized) (Published in the U.S., but printed in Canada)

	GD	VG	FN	VF	VF/NM	NM-
1-(Scarce)-Feldstein-c/a	31	62	93	178	259	340

ADVENTURES OF HOMER GHOST (See Homer The Happy Ghost)
Atlas Comics: June, 1957 - No. 2, Aug, 1957

	GD	VG	FN	VF	VF/NM	NM-
V1#1,2: 2-Robot-c	10	20	30	56	73	90

ADVENTURES OF JERRY LEWIS, THE (Adventures of Dean Martin & Jerry Lewis No. 1-40) (See Super DC Giant)
National Periodical Publ.: No. 41, Nov, 1957 - No. 124, May-June, 1971

	GD	VG	FN	VF	VF/NM	NM-
41	9	18	27	65	93	120
42-60	7	14	21	51	71	90
61-67,69-73,75-80	6	12	18	43	59	75
68,74-Photo-c (movie)	8	16	24	55	78	100
81,82,85-87,90,91,94,96,98,99	5	10	15	36	48	60
83,84,88: 83-1st Monsters-c/s. 84-Jerry as a Super-hero-c/s. 88-1st Witch, Miss Kraft	6	12	18	40	55	70
89-Bob Hope app.; Wizard of Oz & Alfred E. Neuman in MAD parody	7	14	21	46	63	80
92-Superman cameo	7	14	21	46	63	80
93-Beatles parody as babies	6	12	18	40	55	70
95-1st Uncle Hal Wack-A-Boy Camp-c/s	6	12	18	40	55	70
97-Batman/Robin/Joker-c/story; Riddler & Penguin app; Dick Sprang-c.	10	20	30	70	100	130
100	6	12	18	43	59	75
101,103,104-Neal Adams-c/a	7	14	21	51	71	90
102-Beatles app.; Neal Adams c/a	9	18	27	65	93	120
105-Superman x-over	7	14	21	46	63	80
106-111,113-116	4	8	12	28	38	48
112,117: 112-Flash x-over. 117-W. Woman x-over	7	14	21	46	63	80
118-124	4	8	12	25	33	42

NOTE: *Monster-c/s-90,93,96,98,101. Wack-A-Buy Camp-c/s-96,99,102,107,108.*

ADVENTURES OF JO-JOY, THE (See Jo-Joy)

ADVENTURES OF LASSIE, THE (See Lassie)

ADVENTURES OF LUTHER ARKWRIGHT, THE
Valkyrie Press/Dark Horse Comics: Oct, 1987 - No. 9, Jan, 1989 ($2.00, B&W) V2, #1, Mar, 1990 - V2#9, 1990 ($1.95, B&W)

	GD	VG	FN	VF	VF/NM	NM-
1-9: 1-Alan Moore intro., V2#1-9 (Dark Horse): r-1st series; new-c						4.00
TPB (1997, $14.95) r/#1-9 w/Michael Moorcock intro.						15.00

ADVENTURES OF MIGHTY MOUSE (Mighty Mouse Adventures No. 1)
St. John Publishing Co.: No. 2, Jan, 1952 - No. 18, May, 1955

	GD	VG	FN	VF	VF/NM	NM-
2	25	50	75	144	207	270
3-5	14	28	42	79	110	140
6-18	10	20	30	58	77	95

ADVENTURES OF MIGHTY MOUSE (2nd Series) (Becomes Mighty Mouse #161 on)
(Two No. 144's; formerly Paul Terry's Comics; No. 129-137 have nn's)
St. John/Pines/Dell/Gold Key: No. 126, Aug, 1955 - No. 160, Oct, 1963

	GD	VG	FN	VF	VF/NM	NM-
126(8/55), 127(10/55), 128(11/55)-St. John	9	18	27	52	66	80
nn(129, 4/56)-144(8/59)-Pines	5	10	15	36	48	60
144(10-12/59)-155(7-9/62) Dell	5	10	15	33	44	55
156(10/62)-160(10/63) Gold Key	5	10	15	33	44	55

NOTE: *Early issues titled "Paul Terry's Adventures of ...."*

ADVENTURES OF MIGHTY MOUSE (Formerly Mighty Mouse)
Gold Key: No. 166, Mar, 1979 - No. 172, Jan, 1980

	GD	VG	FN	VF	VF/NM	NM-
166-172	1	2	3	5	6	8

ADVS. OF MR. FROG & MISS MOUSE (See Dell Junior Treasury No. 4)

ADVENTURES OF OZZIE & HARRIET, THE (See Ozzie & Harriet)

ADVENTURES OF PATORUZU
Green Publishing Co.: Aug, 1946 - Winter, 1946

	GD	VG	FN	VF	VF/NM	NM-
nn's-Contains Animal Crackers reprints	6	12	18	28	34	40

ADVENTURES OF PINKY LEE, THE (TV)
Atlas Comics: July, 1955 - No. 5, Dec, 1955

	GD	VG	FN	VF	VF/NM	NM-
1	28	56	84	158	229	300
2-5	17	34	51	95	135	175

ADVENTURES OF PIPSQUEAK, THE (Formerly Pat the Brat)
Archie Publications (Radio Comics): No. 34, Sept, 1959 - No. 39, July, 1960

	GD	VG	FN	VF	VF/NM	NM-
34	4	8	12	25	33	42
35-39	3	6	9	19	25	32

ADVENTURES OF QUAKE & QUISP, THE (See Quaker Oats "Plenty of Glutton")

ADVENTURES OF REX THE WONDER DOG, THE (Rex...No. 1)
National Periodical Publ.: Jan-Feb, 1952 - No. 45, May-June, 1959; No. 46, Nov-Dec, 1959

	GD	VG	FN	VF	VF/NM	NM-
1-(Scarce)-Toth-c/a	127	254	381	794	1222	1650
2-(Scarce)-Toth-c/a	58	116	174	363	557	750
3-(Scarce)-Toth-a	46	92	138	281	428	575
4,5	40	80	120	230	335	440
6-10	31	62	93	177	256	335
11-Atom bomb-c/story; dinosaur-c/sty	37	74	111	209	305	400
12-19: 19-Last precode (1-2/55)	19	38	57	107	154	200
20-46	14	28	42	79	110	140

NOTE: ***Infantino, Gil Kane** art in 5-19 (most)*

ADVENTURES OF RHEUMY PEEPERS AND CHUNKY HIGHLIGHTS, THE
Oni Press: Feb, 1999 ($2.95, B&W, one-shot)

	GD	VG	FN	VF	VF/NM	NM-
nn-Penn Jillette-s/Renée French-a						3.00

ADVENTURES OF ROBIN HOOD, THE (Formerly Robin Hood)
Magazine Enterprises (Sussex Publ. Co.): No. 7, 9/57 - No. 8, 11/57
(Based on Richard Greene TV Show)

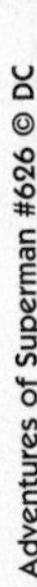
Adventures of Superman #626 © DC

Adventures of the Outsiders #36 © DC

Adventures on the Planet of the Apes #7 © MAR

GD 2.0 | VG 4.0 | FN 6.0 | VF 8.0 | VF/NM 9.0 | NM- 9.2

7,8-Richard Greene photo-c. 7-Powell-a 16 32 48 89 127 165

ADVENTURES OF ROBIN HOOD, THE
Gold Key: Mar, 1974 - No. 7, Jan, 1975 (Disney cartoon) (36 pgs.)

1(90291-403)-Part-r of $1.50 editions 2 4 6 12 16 20
2-7: 1-7 are part-r 2 4 6 8 10 12

ADVENTURES OF SNAKE PLISSKEN
Marvel Comics: Jan, 1997 ($2.50, one-shot)

1-Based on Escape From L.A. movie; Brereton-c 3.50

ADVENTURES OF SPIDER-MAN, THE (Based on animated TV series)
Marvel Comics: Apr, 1996 - No. 12, Mar, 1997 (99¢)

1-12: 1-Punisher app. 2-Venom cameo. 3-X-Men. 6-Fantastic Four 3.00

ADVENTURES OF SUPERBOY, THE (See Superboy, 2nd Series)

ADVENTURES OF SUPERMAN (Formerly Superman)
DC Comics: No. 424, Jan, 1987 - No. 499, Feb, 1993; No. 500, Early June, 1993 - Present

424-Ordway-c/a/Wolfman-s begin following Byrne's Superman revamp 3.00
425-435,437-462: 426-Legends x-over. 432-1st app. Jose Delgado who becomes Gangbuster in #434. 437-Millennium x-over. 438-New Brainiac app. 440-Batman app. 449-Invasion 3.00
436-Byrne scripts begin; Millennium x-over 3.50
463-Superman/Flash race; cover swipe/Superman #199 5.00
464-Lobo-c & app. (pre-dates Lobo #1) 4.00
465-495: 467-Part 2 of Batman story. 473-Hal Jordan, Guy Gardner x-over. 477-Legion app. 491-Last $1.00-c. 480-($1.75, 52 pgs.). 495-Forever People-c/story; Darkseid app. 2.50
496,497: 496-Doomsday cameo. 497-Doomsday battle issue 3.00
496,497-2nd printings 2.25
498,499-Funeral for a Friend; Supergirl app. 2.50
498-2nd & 3rd printings 2.25
500-($2.95, 68 pgs.)-Collector's edition w/card 3.50
500-($2.50, 68 pgs.)-Regular edition w/different-c 2.50
500-Platinum edition 30.00
501-($1.95)-Collector's edition with die-cut-c 2.25
501-($1.50)-Regular edition w/mini-poster & diff.-c 2.25
502-516: 502-Supergirl-c/story. 508-Challengers of the Unknown app. 510-Bizarro-c/story. 516-(9/94)-Zero Hour 2.25
505-($2.50)-Holo-grafx foil-c edition 2.50
0,517-523: 0-(10/94). 517-(11/94) 2.25
524-549,551-580: 524-Begin $1.95-c. 527-Return of Alpha Centurion (Zero Hour). 533-Impulse-c/app. 535-Luthor-c/app. 536-Brainiac app. 537-Parasite app. 540-Final Night x-over. 541-Superboy-c/app.; Lois & Clark honeymoon. 545-New powers. 546-New costume. 555-Red & Blue Supermen battle. 557-Millennium Giants x-over. 558-560: Superman Silver Age-style story; Krypto app. 561-Begin $1.99-c. 565-JLA app. 2.25
550-($3.50)-Double sized 3.50
581-588: 581-Begin $2.25-c. 583-Emperor Joker. 588-Casey-s 2.25
589-595: 589-Return to Krypton; Rivoche-c. 591-Wolfman-s. 593-595-Our Worlds at War x-over. 593-New Suicide Squad formed. 594-Doomsday-c/app. 2.25
596-Aftermath of "War" x-over has panel showing damaged World Trade Center buildings; issue went on sale the day after the Sept. 11 attack 5.00
597-599,601-624: 597-Joker: Last Laugh. 604,605-Ultraman, Owlman,Superwoman app. 606-Return to Krypton. 612-616,619-623-Nowlan-c. 624-Mr. Majestic app. 2.25
600-($3.95) Wieringo-a; painted-c by Adel; pin-ups by various 4.00
625,626-Godfall parts 2,5; Turner-c; Caldwell-a(p) 3.00
627-634: 627-Begin $2.50-c, Rucka-s/Clark-a/Ha-c begin. 628-Wagner-c. 631-Bagged with Sky Captain CD; Lois shot 634-Mxyzptlk visits DC offices 2.50
#1,000,000 (11/98) Gene Ha-c; 853rd Century x-over 3.00
Annual 1 (1987, $1.25, 52 pgs.)-Starlin-c & scripts 4.00
Annual 2,3 (1990, 1991, $2.00, 68 pgs.): 2-Byrne-c/a(i); Legion '90 (Lobo) app. 3-Armageddon 2001 x-over 3.00
Annual 4-6 ('92-'94, $2.50, 68 pgs.): 4-Guy Gardner/Lobo-c/story; Eclipso storyline; Quesada-c(p). 5-Bloodlines storyline. 6-Elseworlds sty. 3.00
Annual 7,9('95, '97, $3.95)-7-Year One story. 9-Pulp Heroes sty 4.00
Annual 8 (1996, $2.95)-Legends of the Dead Earth story 3.00
NOTE: ***Erik Larsen** a-431.*

ADVENTURES OF THE DOVER BOYS
Archie Comics (Close-up): September, 1950 - No. 2, 1950 (No month given)

1,2 9 18 27 54 70 85

ADVENTURES OF THE FLY (The Fly #1-6; Fly Man No. 32-39; See The Double Life of Private Strong, The Fly, Laugh Comics & Mighty Crusaders)
Archie Publications/Radio Comics: Aug, 1959 - No. 30, Oct, 1964; No. 31, May, 1965

1-Shield app.; origin The Fly; S&K-c/a 49 98 147 392 609 825
2-Williamson, S&K-a 29 58 87 206 316 425
3-Origin retold; Davis, Powell-a 24 48 72 170 260 350
4-Neal Adams-a(p)(1 panel); S&K-c; Powell-a; 2 pg. Shield story 14 28 42 102 156 210
5,6,9,10: 9-Shield app. 9-1st app. Cat Girl. 10-Black Hood app. 10 20 30 70 100 130
7,8: 7-1st S.A. app. Black Hood (7/60). 8-1st S.A. app. Shield (9/60) 11 22 33 80 120 160
11-13,15-20: 13-1st app. Fly Girl w/o costume. 16-Last 10¢ issue. 20-Origin Fly Girl retold 7 14 21 46 63 80
14-Origin & 1st app. Fly Girl in costume 8 16 24 55 78 100
21-30: 23-Jaguar cameo. 27-29-Black Hood 1 pg. strips. 30-Comet x-over (1st S.A. app.) in Fly Girl 5 10 15 33 44 55
31-Black Hood, Shield, Comet app. 5 10 15 36 48 60
Vol. 1 TPB ('04, $12.95) r/#1-4 & Double Life of Private Strong #1,2; foreward by Joe Simon 13.00
NOTE: ***Simon** c-2-4. **Tuska** a-1. Cover title to #31 is Flyman; Advs. of the Fly inside.*

ADVENTURES OF THE JAGUAR, THE (See Blue Ribbon Comics, Laugh Comics & Mighty Crusaders)
Archie Publications (Radio Comics): Sept, 1961 - No. 15, Nov, 1963

1-Origin Jaguar (1st app?) by J. Rosenberger 20 40 60 141 216 290
2,3: 3-Last 10¢ issue 10 20 30 73 107 140
4-6-Catgirl app. (#4's-c is same as splash pg.) 8 16 24 58 82 105
7-10 7 14 21 46 63 80
11-15: 13,14-Catgirl, Black Hood app. in both 6 12 18 38 52 65

ADVENTURES OF THE MASK (TV cartoon)
Dark Horse Comics: Jan, 1996 - No. 12, Dec, 1996 ($2.50)

1-12: Based on animated series 2.50

ADVENTURES OF THE NEW MEN (Formerly Newmen #1-21)
Maximum Press: No. 22, Nov, 1996; No. 23, March, 1997 ($2.50)

22,23-Sprouse-c/a 2.50

ADVENTURES OF THE OUTSIDERS, THE (Formerly Batman & The Outsiders; also see The Outsiders)
DC Comics: No. 33, May, 1986 - No. 46, June, 1987

33-46: 39-45-r/Outsiders #1-7 by Aparo 2.25

ADVENTURES OF THE SUPER MARIO BROTHERS (See Super Mario Bros.)
Valiant: 1990 - No. 9, Oct, 1991 ($1.50)

V2#1-9 5.00

ADVENTURES OF THE THING, THE (Also see The Thing)
Marvel Comics: Apr, 1992 - No. 4, July, 1992, ($1.25, limited series)

1-4: 1-r/Marvel Two-In-One #50 by Byrne; Kieth-c. 2-4-r/Marvel Two-In-One #80,51 & 77; 2-Ghost Rider-c/story; Quesada-c. 3-Miller-r/Quesada-c; new Perez-a (4 pgs.) 2.25

ADVENTURES OF THE X-MEN, THE (Based on animated TV series)
Marvel Comics: Apr, 1996 - No. 12, Mar, 1997 (99¢)

1-12: 1-Wolverine/Hulk battle. 3-Spider-Man-c. 5,6-Magneto-c/app. 3.00

ADVENTURES OF TINKER BELL (See Tinker Bell, 4-Color No. 896 & 982)

ADVENTURES OF TOM SAWYER (See Dell Junior Treasury No. 10)

ADVENTURES OF YOUNG DR. MASTERS, THE
Archie Comics (Radio Comics): Aug, 1964 - No. 2, Nov, 1964

1 3 7 10 21 28 35
2 3 6 9 16 20 24

ADVENTURES ON OTHER WORLDS (See Showcase #17 & 18)

ADVENTURES ON THE PLANET OF THE APES (Also see Planet of the Apes)
Marvel Comics Group: Oct, 1975 - No. 11, Dec, 1976

1-Planet of the Apes magazine-r in color; Starlin-c; adapts movie thru #6 3 6 9 18 24 30
2-5: 5-(25¢-c edition) 2 4 6 10 13 16
5-7-(30¢-c variants, limited distribution) 3 6 9 18 24 30
6-10: 6,7-(25¢-c edition). 7-Adapts 2nd movie (thru #11) 2 4 6 11 14 18
11-Last issue; concludes 2nd movie adaptation 2 4 6 14 18 22
NOTE: ***Alcala** a-6-11r. **Buckler** c-2p. **Nasser** c-7. **Ploog** a-1-9. **Starlin** c-6. **Tuska** a-1-5r.*

AFRICA
Magazine Enterprises: 1955

1(A-1 #137)-Cave Girl, Thun'da; Powell-c/a(4) 27 54 81 154 222 290

AFRICAN LION (Disney movie)
Dell Publishing Co.: Nov, 1955

Four Color #665 7 14 21 46 63 80

AFTER DARK

The Agents #1 © Gunstone & Dunn

Air Ace Comics #12 © S&S

Airboy Comics V8#7 © HILL

	GD 2.0	VG 4.0	FN 6.0	VF 8.0	VF/NM 9.0	NM- 9.2

Sterling Comics: No. 6, May, 1955 - No. 8, Sept, 1955

	GD 2.0	VG 4.0	FN 6.0	VF 8.0	VF/NM 9.0	NM- 9.2
6-8-Sekowsky-a in all	9	18	27	54	70	85

AFTERMATH (Leads into Lady Death: Dark Millennium)
Chaos! Comics: Feb, 2000 ($2.95, one-shot)

	NM- 9.2
1-Pulido & Kaminski-s/Luke Ross-a; Reis-c	3.00
1-($6.95) DF Edition; Brereton painted-c	7.00

AGAINST BLACKSHARD 3-D (Also see SoulQuest)
Sirius Comics: August, 1986 ($2.25)

	NM- 9.2
1	3.50

AGENCY, THE
Image Comics (Top Cow): August, 2001 - No. 6, Mar, 2002 ($2.50/$2.95/$4.95)

	NM- 9.2
1,2: 1-Jenkins-s/Hotz-a; three covers by Hotz, Turner, Silvestri	2.50
3-5 ($2.95)	3.00
6-($4.95) Flip-c preview of Jeremiah TV series	5.00
Preview (2001, 16 pgs.) B&W pages, cover previews, sketch pages	2.25

AGENT LIBERTY SPECIAL (See Superman, 2nd Series)
DC Comics: 1992 ($2.00, 52 pgs, one-shot)

	NM- 9.2
1-1st solo adventure; Guice-c/a(i)	2.50

AGENTS, THE
Image Comics: Apr, 2003 - No. 6, Sept, 2003 ($2.95, B&W)

	NM- 9.2
1-6-Ben Dunn-c/a	3.00

AGENTS OF LAW (Also see Comic's Greatest World)
Dark Horse Comics: Mar, 1995 - No. 6, Sept, 1995 ($2.50)

	NM- 9.2
1-6: 5-Predator app. 6-Predator app.; death of Law	2.50

AGENT X (Continued from Deadpool)
Marvel Comics: Sept. 2002 - No. 15, Dec, 2003 ($2.99/$2.25)

	NM- 9.2
1-($2.99) Simone-s/Udon Studios-a; Taskmaster app.	3.00
2-9-($2.25) 2-Punisher app.	2.25
10-15-($2.99) 10,11-Evan Dorkin-s. 12-Hotz-a	3.00

AGE OF APOCALYPSE: THE CHOSEN
Marvel Comics: Apr, 1995 ($2.50, one-shot)

	NM- 9.2
1-Wraparound-c	3.00

AGE OF BRONZE
Image Comics: Nov, 1998 - Present ($2.95/$3.50, B&W, limited series)

	NM- 9.2
1-6-Eric Shanower-c/s/a	3.00
7-19-($3.50)	3.50
...Behind the Scenes (5/02, $3.50) background info and creative process	3.50
...Special (6/99, $2.95) Story of Agamemnon and Menelaus	3.00
A Thousand Ships (7/01, $19.95, TPB) r/#1-9	20.00

AGE OF HEROES, THE
Halloween Comics/Image Comics #3 on: 1996 - No. 5, 1999 ($2.95, B&W)

	NM- 9.2
1-5: James Hudnall scripts; John Ridgway-c/a	3.00
...Special ($4.95) r/#1,2	5.00
...Special 2 ($6.95) r/#3,4	7.00
...Wex 1 ('98, $2.95) Hudnall-s/Angel Fernandez-a	3.00

AGE OF INNOCENCE: THE REBIRTH OF IRON MAN
Marvel Comics: Feb, 1996 ($2.50, one-shot)

	NM- 9.2
1-New origin of Tony Stark	3.00

AGE OF REPTILES
Dark Horse Comics: Nov, 1993 - No. 4, Feb, 1994 ($2.50, limited series)

	NM- 9.2
1-4: Delgado-c/a/scripts in all	3.00

AGE OF REPTILES: THE HUNT
Dark Horse Comics: May, 1996 - No. 5, Sept, 1996 ($2.95, limited series)

	NM- 9.2
1-5: Delgado-c/a/scripts in all; wraparound-c	3.00

AGGIE MACK
Four Star Comics Corp./Superior Comics Ltd.: Jan, 1948 - No. 8, Aug, 1949

	GD 2.0	VG 4.0	FN 6.0	VF 8.0	VF/NM 9.0	NM- 9.2
1-Feldstein-a, "Johnny Prep"	40	80	120	230	335	440
2,3-Kamen-c	21	42	63	118	169	220
4-Feldstein "Johnny Prep"; Kamen-c	28	56	84	158	229	300
5-8-Kamen-c/a	22	44	66	127	184	240

AGGIE MACK
Dell Publishing Co.: Apr - Jun, 1962

	GD 2.0	VG 4.0	FN 6.0	VF 8.0	VF/NM 9.0	NM- 9.2
Four Color #1335	4	8	12	29	40	50

AIR ACE (Formerly Bill Barnes No. 1-12)
Street & Smith Publications: V2#1, Jan, 1944 - V3#8(No. 20), Feb-Mar, 1947

	GD 2.0	VG 4.0	FN 6.0	VF 8.0	VF/NM 9.0	NM- 9.2
V2#1-Nazi concentration camp-c	40	80	120	239	357	475
V2#2-Classic-c	40	80	120	233	342	450
V2#3-12: 7-Powell-a	17	34	51	98	139	180
V3#1-6	14	28	42	79	110	140
V3#7-Powell bondage-c/a; all atomic issue	25	50	75	144	207	270
V3#8 (V5#8 on-c)-Powell-c/a	15	30	45	86	123	160

AIRBOY (Also see Airmaidens, Skywolf, Target: Airboy & Valkyrie)
Eclipse Comics: July, 1986 - No. 50, Oct, 1989 (#1-8, 50¢, 20 pgs., bi-weekly; #9-on, 36pgs.; #34-on monthly)

	NM- 9.2
1-4: 2-1st Marisa; Skywolf gets new costume. 3-The Heap begins	4.00
5-Valkyrie returns; Dave Stevens-c	6.00
6-49: 9-Begin $1.25-c; Skywolf begins. 11-Origin of G.A. Airboy & his plane Birdie. 28-Mr. Monster vs. The Heap. 33-Begin $1.75-c. 38-40-The Heap by Infantino. 41-r/1st app. Valkyrie from Air Fighters. 42-Begin $1.95-c. 46,47-part-r/Air Fighters. 48-Black Angel-r/A.F	3.00
50 ($4.95, 52 pgs.)-Kubert-c	5.00

NOTE: ***Evans*** c-21. ***Gulacy*** c-7, 20. ***Spiegle*** a-34, 35, 37. ***Ken Steacy*** painted c-17, 33.

AIRBOY COMICS (Air Fighters Comics No. 1-22)
Hillman Periodicals: V2#11, Dec, 1945 - V10#4, May, 1953 (No V3#3)

	GD 2.0	VG 4.0	FN 6.0	VF 8.0	VF/NM 9.0	NM- 9.2
V2#11	73	146	219	456	703	950
12-Valkyrie-c/app.	50	100	150	305	465	625
V3#1,2(no #3)	40	80	120	233	342	450
4-The Heap app. in Skywolf	37	74	112	213	312	410
5,7,8,10,11	32	64	96	184	267	350
6-Valkyrie-c/app.	35	70	105	200	290	380
9-Origin The Heap	37	74	112	213	312	410
12-Skywolf & Airboy x-over; Valkyrie-c/app.	40	80	120	233	342	450
V4#1-Iron Lady app.	35	70	105	200	290	380
2,3,12: 2-Rackman begins	25	50	75	144	207	270
4-Simon & Kirby-c	29	58	87	164	237	310
5-9,11-All S&K-a	28	56	84	158	229	300
10-Valkyrie-c/app.	30	60	90	170	245	320
V5#1-4,6-11: 4-Infantino Heap. 10-Origin The Heap	20	40	60	112	161	210
5-Skull-c.	22	44	66	127	184	240
12-Krigstein-a(p)	21	42	63	121	173	225
V6#1-3,5-12: 6,8-Origin The Heap	18	36	54	102	146	190
4-Origin retold	23	46	69	130	188	245
V7#1-12: 7,8,10-Origin The Heap	18	36	54	102	146	190
V8#1-3,5-12	17	34	51	95	135	175
4-Krigstein-a	18	36	54	100	143	185
V9#1,3,4,6-12: 7-One pg. Frazetta ad	14	28	42	81	113	145
2-Valkyrie app.	15	30	45	85	120	155
5(#100)	15	30	45	85	120	155
V10#1-4	13	26	39	74	102	130

NOTE: ***Barry*** a-V2#3, 7. ***Bolle*** a-V4#12. ***McWilliams*** a-V3#7, 9. ***Powell*** a-V7#2, 3, V8#1, 6. ***Starr*** a-V5#1, 12. ***Dick Wood*** a-V4#12. Bondage-c V5#8.

AIRBOY MEETS THE PROWLER
Eclipse Comics: Aug, 1987 ($1.95, one-shot)

	NM- 9.2
1-John Snyder, III-c/a	3.00

AIRBOY-MR. MONSTER SPECIAL
Eclipse Comics: Aug, 1987 ($1.75, one-shot)

	NM- 9.2
1	3.00

AIRBOY VERSUS THE AIR MAIDENS
Eclipse Comics: July, 1988 ($1.95)

	NM- 9.2
1	3.00

AIR FIGHTERS CLASSICS
Eclipse Comics: Nov, 1987 - No. 6, May, 1989 ($3.95, 68 pgs., B&W)

	NM- 9.2
1-6: Reprints G.A. Air Fighters #2-7. 1-Origin Airboy	4.00

AIR FIGHTERS COMICS (Airboy Comics #23 (V2#11) on)
Hillman Periodicals: Nov, 1941; No. 2, Nov, 1942 - V2#10, Fall, 1945

	GD 2.0	VG 4.0	FN 6.0	VF 8.0	VF/NM 9.0	NM- 9.2
V1#1-(Produced by Funnies, Inc.); Black Commander only app.	246	492	738	1538	2369	3200
2(11/42)-(Produced by Quality artists & Biro for Hillman); Origin & 1st app. Airboy & Iron Ace; Black Angel (1st app.), Flying Dutchman & Skywolf (1st app.) begin; Fuje-a; Biro-c/a	359	718	1077	2334	3767	5200
3-Origin/1st app. The Heap; origin Skywolf; 2nd Airboy app./c	185	370	555	1156	1778	2400
4-Japan war-c	135	270	405	844	1297	1750
5-Japanese octopus War-c	115	230	345	719	1110	1500

Akiko #29 © Mark Crilley

Albedo Anthropomorphics #2 © T&I

Aleister Arcane #1 © IDW

	GD 2.0	VG 4.0	FN 6.0	VF 8.0	VF/NM 9.0	NM- 9.2
6-Japanese soldiers as rats-c	131	262	393	819	1260	1700
7-Classic Nazi swastika-c	123	246	369	769	1185	1600
8-12: 8,10,11-War covers	83	166	249	519	797	1075
V2#1-Classic Nazi War-c	85	170	255	531	816	1100
2-Skywolf by Giunta; Flying Dutchman by Fuje; 1st meeting Valkyrie & Airboy (she worked for the Nazis in beginning); 1st app. Valkyrie (11/43); Valkyrie-c	108	216	324	675	1038	1400
3,4,6,8,9	63	126	189	394	610	825
5,7: 5-Flag-c; Fuje-a. 7-Valkyrie app.	67	134	201	419	647	875
10-Origin The Heap & Skywolf	72	144	216	450	695	940

NOTE: ***Fuje** a-V1#2, 5, 7, V2#2, 3, 5, 7-9. **Giunta** a-V2#2, 3, 7, 9.*

AIRFIGHTERS MEET SGT. STRIKE SPECIAL, THE
Eclipse Comics: Jan, 1988 ($1.95, one-shot, stiff-c)

	GD	VG	FN	VF	VF/NM	NM-
1-Airboy, Valkyrie, Skywolf app.						3.00

AIR FORCES (See American Air Forces)

AIRMAIDENS SPECIAL
Eclipse Comics: August, 1987 ($1.75, one-shot, Baxter paper)

	GD	VG	FN	VF	VF/NM	NM-
1-Marisa becomes La Lupina (origin)						3.00

AIR RAIDERS
Marvel Comics (Star Comics)/Marvel #3 on: Nov, 1987- No. 5, Mar, 1988 ($1.00)

	GD	VG	FN	VF	VF/NM	NM-
1,5: Kelley Jones-a in all						3.50
2-4: 2-Thunderhammer app.						2.50

AIRTIGHT GARAGE, THE (Also see Elsewhere Prince)
Marvel Comics (Epic Comics): July, 1993 - No. 4, Oct, 1993 ($2.50, lim. series, Baxter paper)

	GD	VG	FN	VF	VF/NM	NM-
1-4: Moebius-c/a/scripts						4.00

AIR WAR STORIES
Dell Publishing Co.: Sept-Nov, 1964 - No. 8, Aug, 1966

	GD	VG	FN	VF	VF/NM	NM-
1-Painted-c; Glanzman-c/a begins	5	10	15	33	44	55
2-8: 2,3-Painted-c	3	6	9	19	25	32

A.K.A. GOLDFISH
Caliber Comics: 1994 - 1995 (B&W, $3.50/$3.95)

	GD	VG	FN	VF	VF/NM	NM-
...:Ace; ...:Jack; ...:Queen; ...:Joker; ...:King -Brian Michael Bendis-s/a						4.00
TPB (1996, $17.95)						20.00
Goldfish: The Definitive Collection (Image, 2001, $19.95) r/series plus promo art and new prose story; intro. by Matt Wagner						20.00
10th Anniversary HC (Image, 2002, $49.95)						50.00

AKIKO
Sirius: Mar, 1996 - Present ($2.50/$2.95, B&W)

	GD	VG	FN	VF	VF/NM	NM-
1-Crilley-c/a/scripts in all						5.00
2						4.00
3-39: 25-($2.95, 32 pgs.)-w/Asala back-up pages						3.00
40-49,51,52: 40-Begin $2.95-c						3.00
50-($3.50)						3.50
Flights of Fancy TPB (5/02, $12.95) r/various features, pin-ups and gags						13.00
TPB Volume 1,4 ('97, 2/00, $14.95) 1-r/#1-7. 4-r/#19-25						15.00
TPB Volume 2,3 ('98, '99, $11.95) 2-r/#8-13. 3- r/#14-18						12.00
TPB Volume 5 (12/01, $12.95) r/#26-31						13.00
TPB Volume 6,7 (6/03, 4/04, $14.95) 6-r/#32-38. 7-r/#40-47						15.00

AKIKO ON THE PLANET SMOO
Sirius: Dec, 1995 ($3.95, B&W)

	GD	VG	FN	VF	VF/NM	NM-
V1#1-($3.95)-Crilley-c/a/scripts; gatefold-c						5.00
Ashcan ('95, mail offer)						3.00
Hardcover V1#1 (12/95, $19.95, B&W, 40 pgs.)						20.00
The Color Edition(2/00,$4.95)						5.00

AKIRA
Marvel Comics (Epic): Sept, 1988 - No. 38, Dec, 1995 ($3.50/$3.95/$6.95, deluxe, 68 pgs.)

	GD	VG	FN	VF	VF/NM	NM-
1-Manga by Katsuhiro Otomo	3	6	9	18	24	30
1,2-2nd printings (1989, $3.95)						5.00
2	2	4	6	10	12	15
3-5	2	4	6	8	10	12
6-16	1	2	3	5	7	9
17-33: 17-$3.95-c begins						6.00
34-37: 34-(1994)-$6.95-c begins. 35-37: 35-(1995). 37-Texeira back-up, Gibbons, Williams pin-ups	2	4	6	8	10	12
38-Moebius, Allred, Pratt, Toth, Romita, Van Fleet, O'Neill, Madureira pin-ups	2	4	6	9	11	14

ALADDIN & HIS WONDERFUL LAMP (See Dell Jr Treasury #2)

ALAN LADD (See The Adventures of...)

ALAN MOORE'S AWESOME UNIVERSE HANDBOOK (Also see Across the Universe:...)
Awesome Entertainment: Apr, 1999 ($2.95, B&W)

	GD	VG	FN	VF	VF/NM	NM-
1-Alan Moore-text/ Alex Ross-sketch pages and 2 covers						5.00

ALAN MOORE'S SONGBOOK
Caliber Comics: 1998 ($5.95, B&W)

	GD	VG	FN	VF	VF/NM	NM-
1-Alan Moore song lyrics w/illust. by various	1	2	3	4	5	7

ALARMING ADVENTURES
Harvey Publications: Oct, 1962 - No. 3, Feb, 1963

	GD	VG	FN	VF	VF/NM	NM-
1-Crandall/Williamson-a	10	20	30	67	96	125
2-Williamson/Crandall-a	6	12	18	43	59	75
3	6	12	18	38	52	65

NOTE: ***Bailey** a-1, 3. **Crandall** a-1p, 2i. **Powell** a-2(2). **Severin** c-1-3. **Torres** a-2? **Tuska** a-1. **Williamson** a-1i, 2p.*

ALARMING TALES
Harvey Publications (Western Tales): Sept, 1957 - No. 6, Nov, 1958

	GD	VG	FN	VF	VF/NM	NM-
1-Kirby-c/a(4); Kamandi prototype story by Kirby	28	56	84	158	229	300
2-Kirby-a(4)	20	40	60	112	161	210
3,4-Kirby-a. 4-Powell, Wildey-a	15	30	45	86	123	160
5-Kirby/Williamson-a; Wildey-a; Severin-c	16	32	48	92	131	170
6-Williamson-a?; Severin-c	13	26	39	74	102	130

ALBEDO
Thoughts And Images: Apr, 1985 - No. 14, Spring, 1989 (B&W)
Antarctic Press: (Vol. 2) Jun, 1991 - No. 10 ($2.50)

	GD	VG	FN	VF	VF/NM	NM-
0-Yellow cover; 50 copies	11	22	33	77	114	150
0-White cover, 450 copies	5	10	15	36	48	60
0-Blue, 1st printing, 500 copies	4	8	12	29	40	50
0-Blue, 2nd printing, 1000 copies	3	6	9	16	20	25
0-3rd & 4th printing	1	3	4	6	8	10
1-Dark red - low print run	4	8	12	27	36	45
1-Bright red - low print run	3	7	10	21	28	35
2 -1st app. Usagi Yojimbo by Stan Sakai; 2000 copies - no 2nd printing	17	34	51	121	186	250
3	2	4	6	12	16	20
4-Usagi Yojimbo-c	3	6	9	16	20	24
5-14						5.00
(Vol. 2) 1-10, Color Special						4.00

ALBEDO ANTHROPOMORPHICS
Antarctic Press: (Vol. 3) Spring, 1994 - No. 4, Jan, 1996 ($2.95, color);
(Vol. 4) Dec, 1999 - No. 2, Jan, 1999 ($2.95/$2.99, B&W)

	GD	VG	FN	VF	VF/NM	NM-
V3#1-4-Steve Gallacci-c/a. V4#1,2						3.00

ALBERTO (See The Crusaders)

ALBERT THE ALLIGATOR & POGO POSSUM (See Pogo Possum)

ALBUM OF CRIME (See Fox Giants)

ALBUM OF LOVE (See Fox Giants)

AL CAPP'S DOGPATCH (Also see Mammy Yokum)
Toby Press: No. 71, June, 1949 - No. 4, Dec, 1949

	GD	VG	FN	VF	VF/NM	NM-
71(#1)-Reprints from Tip Top #112-114	23	46	69	132	191	250
2-4: 4-Reprints from Li'l Abner #73	16	32	48	89	127	165

AL CAPP'S SHMOO (Also see Oxydol-Dreft & Washable Jones & Shmoo)
Toby Press: July, 1949 - No. 5, Apr, 1950 (None by Al Capp)

	GD	VG	FN	VF	VF/NM	NM-
1	40	80	120	233	342	450
2-5: 3-Sci-fi trip to moon. 4-X-Mas-c; origin/1st app. Super-Shmoo	28	56	84	158	229	300

AL CAPP'S WOLF GAL
Toby Press: 1951 - No. 2, 1952

	GD	VG	FN	VF	VF/NM	NM-
1,2-Edited-r from Li'l Abner #63,64	34	68	102	193	279	365

ALEISTER ARCANE
IDW Publishing: Apr, 2004 - No. 3, June, 2004 ($3.99, limited series)

	GD	VG	FN	VF	VF/NM	NM-
1-3-Steve Niles-s/Breehn Burns-a						4.00
TPB (10/04, $17.99) r/series; sketch pages						18.00

ALEXANDER THE GREAT (Movie)
Dell Publishing Co.: No. 688, May, 1956

	GD	VG	FN	VF	VF/NM	NM-
Four Color 688-Buscema-a; photo-c	9	18	27	60	85	110

ALF (TV) (See Star Comics Digest)
Marvel Comics: Mar, 1988 - No. 50, Feb, 1992 ($1.00)

Alias #25 © MAR

Alien Legion #2 © MAR

Aliens/Predator: The Deadliest of the Species #3 © 20th Century Fox

	GD 2.0	VG 4.0	FN 6.0	VF 8.0	VF/NM 9.0	NM- 9.2
1-Photo-c						4.00
1-2nd printing						2.50
2-19: 6-Photo-c						2.50
20-22: 20-Conan parody. 21-Marx Brothers. 22-X-Men parody						3.00
23-30: 24-Rhonda-c/app. 29-3-D cover						2.50
31-43,46-49						3.00
44,45: 44-X-Men parody. 45-Wolverine, Punisher, Capt. America-c						4.00
50-($1.75, 52 pgs.)-Final issue; photo-c						4.00
Annual 1-3: 1-Rocky & Bullwinkle app. 2-Sienkiewicz-c. 3-TMNT parody						3.00
...Comics Digest 1,2: 1-(1988)-Reprints Alf #1,2	1	2	3	5	6	8
Holiday Special 1,2 ('88, Wint. '89, 68 pgs.): 2-X-Men parody-c						3.00
Spring Special 1 (Spr/89, $1.75, 68 pgs.) Invisible Man parody						3.00
TPB (68 pgs.) r/#1-3; photo-c						5.00

ALFRED HARVEY'S BLACK CAT
Lorne-Harvey Productions: 1995 ($3.50, B&W/color)

	GD	VG	FN	VF	VF/NM	NM-
1-Origin by Mark Evanier & Murphy Anderson; contains history of Alfred Harvey & Harvey Publications; 5 pg. B&W Sad Sack story; Hildebrandts-c						5.00

ALGIE (LITTLE...)
Timor Publ. Co.: Dec, 1953 - No. 3, 1954

	GD	VG	FN	VF	VF/NM	NM-
1-Teenage	7	14	21	37	46	55
1-Misprint exists w/Secret Mysteries #19 inside	9	18	27	51	62	75
2,3	5	10	15	24	30	35
Accepted Reprint #2(nd)	3	6	8	12	14	16
Super Reprint #15	2	4	6	10	12	14

ALIAS:
Now Comics: July, 1990 - No. 5, Nov, 1990 ($1.75)

	GD	VG	FN	VF	VF/NM	NM-
1-5: 1-Sienkiewicz-c						2.25

ALIAS (Also see The Pulse)
Marvel Comics (MAX Comics): Nov, 2001 - No. 28, Jan, 2004 ($2.99)

	GD	VG	FN	VF	VF/NM	NM-
1-Bendis-s/Gaydos-a/Mack-c; intro Jessica Jones; Luke Cage app.	1	2	3	5	6	8
2-4						5.00
5-28: 7,8-Sienkiewicz-a (2 pgs.) 16-21-Spider-Woman app. 22,23-Jessica's origin. 24-28-Purple; Avengers app.; flashback-a by Bagley						3.00
HC (2002, $29.99) r/#1-9; intro. by Jeph Loeb						30.00
Vol. 1: TPB (2003, $19.99) r/#1-9						20.00
Vol. 2: Come Home TPB (2003, $13.99) r/#11-15						14.00
Vol. 3: The Underneath TPB (2003, $16.99) r/#10,16-21						17.00

ALICE (New Adventures in Wonderland)
Ziff-Davis Publ. Co.: No. 10, 7-8/51 - No. 11(#2), 11-12/51

	GD	VG	FN	VF	VF/NM	NM-
10-Painted-c; Berg-a	24	48	72	138	199	260
11-(#2 on inside) Dave Berg-a	14	28	42	81	113	145

ALICE AT MONKEY ISLAND (See The Adventures of Alice)
Pentagon Publ. Co. (Civil Service): No. 3, 1946

	GD	VG	FN	VF	VF/NM	NM-
3	9	18	27	54	70	85

ALICE IN WONDERLAND (Disney; see Advs. of Alice, Dell Jr. Treasury #1, The Dreamery, Movie Comics,Walt Disney Showcase #22, and World's Greatest Stories)
Dell Publishing Co.: No. 24, 1940; No. 331, 1951; No. 341, July, 1951

	GD	VG	FN	VF	VF/NM	NM-
Single Series 24 (#1)(1940)	46	92	138	281	428	575
Four Color 331, 341-"Unbirthday Party w/..."	16	32	48	112	171	230
1-(Whitman; 3/84)-r/4-Color #331						6.00

ALIEN ENCOUNTERS (Replaces Alien Worlds)
Eclipse Comics: June, 1985 - No. 14, Aug, 1987 ($1.75, Baxter paper, mature)

	GD	VG	FN	VF	VF/NM	NM-
1-10: Nudity, strong language in all. 9-Snyder-a						4.00
11-14-Low print run						5.00

ALIEN LEGION (See Epic & Marvel Graphic Novel #25)
Marvel Comics (Epic Comics): Apr, 1984 - No. 20, Sept, 1987

	GD	VG	FN	VF	VF/NM	NM-
nn-With bound-in trading card; Austin-i						4.00
2-20: 2-$1.50-c. 7,8-Portacio-i						3.00

ALIEN LEGION (2nd Series)
Marvel Comics (Epic): Aug, 1987(indicia)(10/87 on-c) - No. 18, Aug, 1990

	GD	VG	FN	VF	VF/NM	NM-
V2#1-18-Stroman-a in all. 7-18-Farmer-i						2.25
...: Force Nomad TPB (Checker Book Pub. Group, 2001, $24.95) r/#1-11						25.00
...: Piecemaker TPB (Checker Book Pub. Group, 2002, $19.95) r/#12-18						20.00

ALIEN LEGION: (Series of titles; all Marvel/Epic Comics)

	GD	VG	FN	VF	VF/NM	NM-
--BINARY DEEP, 1993 ($3.50, one-shot, 52 pgs.), nn-With bound-in trading card						3.50
--JUGGER GRIMROD, 8/92 ($5.95, one-shot, 52 pgs.) Book 1						6.00
--ONE PLANET AT A TIME, 5/93 - Book 3, 7/93 ($4.95, squarebound, 52 pgs.) Book 1-3: Hoang Nguyen-a						5.00
--ON THE EDGE (The... #2 & 3), 11/90 - No. 3, 1/91 ($4.50, 52 pgs.) 1-3-Stroman & Farmer-a						4.50
--TENANTS OF HELL, '91 - No. 2, '1 ($4.50, squarebound, 52 pgs.) Book 1,2-Stroman-c/a(p)						4.50

ALIEN NATION (Movie)
DC Comics: Dec, 1988 ($2.50; 68 pgs.)

	GD	VG	FN	VF	VF/NM	NM-
1-Adaptation of film; painted-c						4.00

ALIEN RESURRECTION (Movie)
Dark Horse Comics: Oct, 1997 - No. 2, Nov, 1997 ($2.50; limited series)

	GD	VG	FN	VF	VF/NM	NM-
1,2-Adaptation of film; Dave McKean-c						3.00

ALIENS, THE (Captain Johner and...)(Also see Magnus Robot Fighter...)
Gold Key: Sept-Dec, 1967; No. 2, May, 1982

	GD	VG	FN	VF	VF/NM	NM-
1-Reprints from Magnus #1,3,4,6-10; Russ Manning-a in all	4	8	12	24	32	40
2-(Whitman) Same contents as #1	1	2	3	5	6	8

ALIENS (Movie) (See Alien: The Illustrated..., Dark Horse Comics & Dark Horse Presents #24)
Dark Horse Comics: May, 1988 - No. 6, July, 1989 ($1.95, B&W, limited series)

	GD	VG	FN	VF	VF/NM	NM-
1-Based on movie sequel;1st app. Aliens in comics	2	4	6	12	16	20
1-2nd - 6th printings; 4th w/new inside front-c						3.00
2	1	2	3	5	7	9
2-2nd & 3rd printing, 3-6-2nd printings						3.00
3	1	2	3	4	5	7
4-6						5.00
Mini Comic #1 (2/89, 4x6")-Was included with Aliens Portfolio						4.00
Collection 1 ($10.95,)-r/#1-6 plus Dark Horse Presents #24 plus new-a						12.00
Collection 1-2nd printing (1991, $11.95)-On higher quality paper than 1st print; Dorman painted-c						12.00
Hardcover ('90, $24.95, B&W)-r/1-6, DHP #24						30.00
Platinum Edition - (See Dark Horse Presents: Aliens Platinum Edition)						-

ALIENS
Dark Horse Comics: V2#1, Aug, 1989 - No. 4, 1990 ($2.25, limited series)

	GD	VG	FN	VF	VF/NM	NM-
V2#1-Painted art by Denis Beauvais						5.00
1-2nd printing (1990), 2-4						3.00

ALIENS: (Series of titles, all Dark Horse)

	GD	VG	FN	VF	VF/NM	NM-
--ALCHEMY, 10/97 - No. 3, 11/97 ($2.95),1-3-Corben-c/a, Arcudi-s						3.00
--APOCALYPSE - THE DESTROYING ANGELS, 1/99 - No. 4, 4/99 ($2.95) 1-4-Doug Wheatly-a/Schultz-s						3.00
--BERSERKERS, 1/95 - No. 4, 4/95 ($2.50) 1-4						3.00
--COLONIAL MARINES, 1/93 - No. 10, 7/94 ($2.50) 1-10						3.00
--EARTH ANGEL, 8/94 ($2.95) 1-Byrne-a/story; wraparound-c						3.00
--EARTH WAR, 6/90 - No. 4, 10/90 ($2.50) 1-All have Sam Kieth-a & Bolton painted-c						5.00
1-2nd printing, 3,4						3.00
2						4.00
--GENOCIDE, 11/91 - No. 4, 2/92 ($2.50) 1-4-Suydam painted-c. 4-Wraparound-c, poster						3.00
--GLASS CORRIDOR, 6/98 ($2.95) 1-David Lloyd-s/a						3.00
--HARVEST (See Aliens: Hive)						
--HAVOC, 6/97 - No. 2, 7/97 ($2.95) 1,2: Schultz-s, Kent Williams-c, 40 artists including Art Adams, Kelley Jones, Duncan Fegredo, Kevin Nowlan						3.00
--HIVE, 2/92 - No. 4,5/92 ($2.50) 1-4: Kelley Jones-c/a in all						3.00
...Harvest TPB ('98, $16.95) r/series; Bolton-c						17.00
--KIDNAPPED, 12/97 - No. 3, 2/98 ($2.50) 1-3						3.00
--LABYRINTH, 9/93 - No. 4, 1/94 ($2.50)1-4: 1-Painted-c						3.00
--LOVESICK, 12/96 ($2.95) 1						3.00
--MONDO HEAT, 2/96 ($2.50) nn-Sequel to Mondo Pest						3.00
--MONDO PEST, 4/95 ($2.95, 44 pgs.)nn-r/Dark Horse Comics #22-24						3.00
--MUSIC OF THE SPEARS, 1/94 - No. 4, 4/94 ($2.50) 1-4						3.00
--NEWT'S TALE, 6/92 - No. 2, 7/92 ($4.95) 1,2-Bolton-c						5.00
--PIG, 3/97 ($2.95)1						3.00
--PREDATOR: THE DEADLIEST OF THE SPECIES, 7/93 - No. 12,8/95 ($2.50) 1-Bolton painted-c; Guice-a(p)						5.00
1-Embossed foil platinum edition						10.00

Aliens Vs. Predator: Eternal #4 © 20th Century Fox

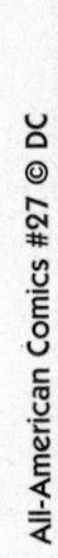
All-American Comics #27 © DC

All-American Men of War #13 © DC

GD VG FN VF VF/NM NM-
2.0 4.0 6.0 8.0 9.0 9.2

2-12: Bolton painted-c. 2,3-Guice-a(p) 3.00
--**PURGE,** 8/97 ($2.95) nn-Hester-a 3.00
--**ROGUE,** 4/993 - No. 4, 7/93 ($2.50)1-4: Painted-c 3.00
--**SACRIFICE,** 5/93 ($4.95, 52 pgs.) nn-P. Milligan scripts; painted-c/a 5.00
--**SALVATION,** 11/93 ($4.95, 52 pgs.) nn-Mignola-c/a(p); Gibbons script 5.00
--**SPECIAL,** 6/97 ($2.50) 1 3.00
--**STALKER,** 6/98 ($2.50)1-David Wenzel-s/a 3.00
--**STRONGHOLD,** 5/94 - No. 4, 9/94 ($2.50) 1-4 3.00
--**SURVIVAL,** 2/98 - No. 3, 4/98 ($2.95) 1-3-Tony Harris-c 3.00
--**TRIBES,** 1992 ($24.95, hardcover graphic novel) Bissette text-s with Dorman painted-a 25.00
...softcover ($9.95) 10.00

ALIENS VS. PREDATOR (See Dark Horse Presents #36)
Dark Horse Comics: June, 1990 - No. 4, Dec, 1990 ($2.50, limited series)

1-Painted-c 1 2 3 5 6 8
1-2nd printing 3.00
0-(7/90, $1.95, B&W)-r/Dark Horse Pres. #34-36 1 2 3 5 7 9
2,3 5.00
4-Dave Dorman painted-c 4.00
Annual (7/99, $4.95) Jae Lee-c 5.00
... : Booty (1/96, $2.50) painted-c 3.00
... : Thrill of the Hunt (9/04, $6.95, digest-size TPB) Based on 2004 movie 7.00
... Wraith 1 (7/98, $2.95) Jay Stephens-s 3.00
--**VS. PREDATOR: DUEL,** 3/95 - No. 2, 4/95 ($2.50) 1,2 3.00
--**VS. PREDATOR: ETERNAL,** 6/98 - No. 4, 9/98 ($2.50)1-4: Edginton-s/Maleev-a; Fabry-c 3.00
--**VS. PREDATOR VS. THE TERMINATOR,** 4/00 - No. 4, 7/00 ($2.95) 1-4: Ripley app. 3.00
--**VS. PREDATOR: WAR,** No. 0, 5/95 - No. 4, 8/95 ($2.50) 0-4: Corben painted-c 3.00
--**VS. PREDATOR: XENOGENESIS,** 12/99 - No. 4, 3/00 ($2.95) 1-4: Watson-s/Mel Rubi-a 3.00
--**XENOGENESIS,** 8/99 - No. 4, 11/99 ($2.95) 1-4: T&M Bierbaum-s 3.00

ALIEN TERROR (See 3-D Alien Terror)

ALIEN: THE ILLUSTRATED STORY (Also see Aliens)
Heavy Metal Books: 1980 ($3.95, soft-c, 8x11")

nn-Movie adaptation; Simonson-a 3 6 9 16 20 24

ALIEN ^{3} (Movie)
Dark Horse Comics: June, 1992 - No. 3, July, 1992 ($2.50, limited series)

1-3: Adapts 3rd movie; Suydam painted-c 3.00

ALIEN WORLDS (Also see Eclipse Graphic Album #22)
Pacific Comics/Eclipse: Dec, 1982 - No. 9, Jan, 1985

1,2,4: 2,4-Dave Stevens-c/a 6.00
3,5-7 4.00
8,9 1 2 3 4 5 7
3-D No. 1-Art Adams 1st published art 1 2 3 4 5 7

ALISON DARE, LITTLE MISS ADVENTURES (Also see Return of ...)
Oni Press: Sept, 2000 ($4.50, B&W, one-shot)

1-J. Torres-s/J.Bone-c/a 4.50

ALISON DARE & THE HEART OF THE MAIDEN
Oni Press: Jan, 2002 - No. 2, Feb, 2002 ($2.95, B&W, limited series)

1,2-J. Torres-s/J.Bone-c/a 3.00

ALISTER THE SLAYER
Midnight Press: Oct, 1995 ($2.50)

1-Boris-c 2.50

ALL-AMERICAN COMICS (...Western #103-126, ...Men of War #127 on; also see The Big All-American Comic Book)
All-American/National Periodical Publ.: April, 1939 - No. 102, Oct, 1948

1-Hop Harrigan (1st app.), Scribbly by Mayer (1st DC app.), Toonerville Folks, Ben Webster, Spot Savage, Mutt & Jeff, Red White & Blue (1st app.), Adventures in the Unknown, Tippie, Reg'lar Fellers, Skippy, Bobby Thatcher, Mystery Men of Mars, Daiseybelle, Wiley of West Point begin 700 1400 2100 4200 5800 7400
2-Ripley's Believe It or Not begins, ends #24 200 400 600 1200 1700 2200
3-5: 5-The American Way begins, ends #10 155 310 465 930 1290 1650
6,7: 6-Last Spot Savage; Popsicle Pete begins, ends #26, 28. 7-Last Bobby Thatcher
130 260 390 780 1065 1350
8-The Ultra Man begins & 1st-c app. 280 560 840 1680 2390 3100
9,10: 10-X-Mas-c 120 240 360 720 985 1250
11,15: 11-Ultra Man-c. 15-Last Tippie & Reg'lar Fellars; Ultra Man-c
130 260 390 780 1090 1400

GD VG FN VF VF/NM NM-
2.0 4.0 6.0 8.0 9.0 9.2

12-14: 12-Last Toonerville Folks 110 220 330 660 905 1150
16-(Rare)-Origin/1st app. Green Lantern by Sheldon Moldoff (c/a)(7/40) & begin series; appears in costume on-c & only one panel inside; created by Martin Nodell. Inspired in 1940 by a switchman's green lantern that would give trains the go ahead to proceed
9350 18,700 28,050 74,800 127,400 180,000
17-2nd Green Lantern 1294 2588 3882 9705 15,853 22,000
18-N.Y. World's Fair-c/story 968 1936 2904 6776 10,888 15,000
19-Origin/1st app. The Atom (10/40); last Ultra Man
1412 2824 4236 10,590 17,295 24,000
20-Atom dons costume; Ma Hunkle becomes Red Tornado (1st app.)(1st DC costumed heroine, before Wonder Woman, 11/40); Rescue on Mars begins, ends #25; 1 pg. origin Green Lantern 452 904 1356 3164 5082 7000
21-23: 21-Last Wiley of West Point & Skippy. 23-Last Daiseybelle; 3 Idiots begin, end #82
292 584 876 1825 2813 3800
24-Sisty & Dinky become the Cyclone Kids; Ben Webster ends; origin Dr. Mid-Nite & Sargon, The Sorcerer in text with app. 307 614 921 1996 3223 4450
25-Origin & 1st story app. Dr. Mid-Nite by Stan Asch; Hop Harrigan becomes Guardian Angel; last Adventure in the Unknown 903 1806 2709 6321 10,161 14,000
26-Origin/1st story app. Sargon, the Sorcerer 358 716 1074 2327 3764 5200
27: #27-32 are misnumbered in indicia with correct No. appearing on-c. Intro. Doiby Dickles, Green Lantern's sidekick 379 758 1137 2464 3982 5500
28-Hop Harrigan gives up costumed i.d. 181 362 543 1131 1741 2350
29,30 181 362 543 1131 1741 2350
31-40: 35-Doiby learns Green Lantern's i.d. 135 270 405 844 1297 1750
41-50: 50-Sargon ends 110 220 330 688 1057 1425
51-60: 59-Scribbly & the Red Tornado ends 94 188 282 588 907 1225
61-Origin/1st app. Solomon Grundy (11/44) 516 1032 1548 3612 5806 8000
62-70: 70-Kubert Sargon; intro Sargon's helper, Maximillian O'Leary
85 170 255 531 816 1100
71-88: 71-Last Red White & Blue. 72-Black Pirate begins (not in #74-82); last Atom. 73-Winky, Blinky & Noddy begins, ends #82. 79,83-Mutt & Jeff-c.
69 138 207 431 666 900
89-Origin & 1st app. Harlequin 112 224 336 700 1075 1450
90-99: 90-Origin/1st app. Icicle. 99-Last Hop Harrigan
108 216 324 675 1038 1400
100-1st app. Johnny Thunder by Alex Toth (8/48); western theme begins (Scarce) 196 392 588 1225 1888 2550
101-Last Mutt & Jeff (Scarce) 131 262 393 819 1260 1700
102-Last Green Lantern, Black Pirate & Dr. Mid-Nite (Scarce)
281 562 843 1756 2703 3650

NOTE: *No Atom in 47, 62-69.* ***Kinstler*** *Black Pirate-89.* ***Stan Aschmeier*** *a (Dr. Mid-Nite) 25-84; c-7.* ***Mayer*** *c-1, 2(part), 6, 10.* ***Moldoff*** *c-16-23.* ***Nodell*** *c-31.* ***Paul Reinman*** *a (Green Lantern)-53-55p, 56-84, 87; (Black Pirate)-83-88, 90; c-52, 55-76, 78, 80, 81, 87.* ***Toth*** *a-88, 92, 96, 98-102; c(p)-92, 96-102. Scribbly by* ***Mayer*** *in #1-59. Ultra Man by* ***Mayer*** *in #8-19.*

ALL-AMERICAN COMICS (Also see All Star Comics 1999 crossover titles)
DC Comics: May, 1999 ($1.99, one-shot)

1-Golden Age Green Lantern and Johnny Thunder; Barreto-a 2.25

ALL-AMERICAN MEN OF WAR (Previously All-American Western)
National Periodical Publ.: No. 127, Aug-Sept, 1952 - No. 117, Sept-Oct, 1966

127 (#1, 1952) 84 168 252 714 1157 1600
128 (1952) 51 102 153 413 657 900
2(12-1/'52-53)-5 44 88 132 352 551 750
6-Devil Dog story; Ghost Squadron story 35 70 105 263 412 560
7-10: 8-Sgt. Storm Cloud-s 35 70 105 263 412 560
11-16,18: 18-Last precode; 1st Kubert-c (2/55) 31 62 93 228 352 475
17-1st Frogman-s in this title 32 64 96 240 370 500
19,20,22-27 23 46 69 163 249 335
21-Easy Co. prototype 26 52 78 189 290 390
28 (12/55)-1st Sgt. Rock prototype; Kubert-a 33 66 99 245 387 525
29,30,32-Wood-a 24 48 72 170 260 350
31,33-38,40: 34-Gunner prototype-s. 35-Greytone-c. 36-Little Sure Shot prototype-s. 38-1st S.A. issue 19 38 57 134 205 275
39 (11/56)-2nd Sgt. Rock prototype; 1st Easy Co.? 29 58 87 206 316 425
41,43-47,49,50: 46-Tankbusters-c/s 15 30 45 109 167 225
42-Pre-Sgt. Rock Easy Co.-c/s 19 38 57 136 208 280
48-Easy Co.-c/s; Nick app.; Kubert-a 19 38 57 136 208 280
51-56,58-62,65,66: 61-Gunner-c/s 12 24 36 86 131 175
57(5/58),63,64 -Pre-Sgt. Rock Easy Co.-c/s 17 34 51 121 186 250
67-1st Gunner & Sarge by Andru & Esposito 33 66 99 248 392 535
68,69: 68-2nd app. Gunner & Sarge. 69-1st Tank Killer-c/s
15 30 45 109 167 225
70 12 24 36 82 124 165

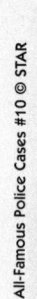

Alley Oop #17 © SYD

All-Famous Police Cases #10 © STAR

All-Flash #8 © DC

GD 2.0 | VG 4.0 | FN 6.0 | VF 8.0 | VF/NM 9.0 | NM- 9.2

71-80: 71,72,76-Tank Killer-c/s. 74-Minute Commandos-c/s
10 20 30 70 100 130
81,84-88: 88-Last 10¢ issue 8 16 24 58 82 105
82-Johnny Cloud begins(1st app.), ends #117 14 28 42 97 149 200
83-2nd Johnny Cloud 10 20 30 70 100 130
89-100: 89-Battle Aces of 3 Wars begins, ends #98 6 12 18 43 59 75
101-111,113-116: 111,114,115-Johnny Cloud 5 10 15 33 44 55
112-Balloon Buster series begins, ends #114,116 5 10 15 36 48 60
117-Johnny Cloud-c & 3-part story 5 10 15 36 48 60
NOTE: *Frogman stories in 17, 38, 44, 45, 50, 51, 53, 55-58, 63, 65, 66, 72, 76, 77.* ***Colan*** *a-112.* ***Drucker*** *a-47, 58, 61, 63, 65, 69, 71, 74, 77.* ***Grandenetti*** *c(p)-127, 128, 2-17(most).* ***Heath*** *a-14, 27, 32, 38, 41, 45, 47, 50, 51, 55-58, 62, 64, 71, 75, 76, 78, 95, 111-117; c-85, 91, 94-96, 100, 101, 110-112, others?* ***Infantino*** *a-8.* ***Kirby*** *a-29.* ***Krigstein*** *a-128('52), 2, 3, 5.* ***Kubert*** *a-22, 24, 28, 29, 33, 34, 36, 38, 39, 41-43, 47-50, 52, 53, 55, 56, 59, 60, 63-65, 69, 71-73, 76, 102, 103, 105, 106, 108, 114; c-41, 44, 52, 54, 55, 58, 64, 69, 76, 77, 79, 102-106, 108, 113-117, others? Tank Killer in 69, 71, 76 by* ***Kubert. P. Reinman*** *c-55, 57, 61, 62, 71, 72, 74-76, 80.* ***J. Severin*** *a-58.*

ALL-AMERICAN SPORTS
Charlton Comics: Oct, 1967

1 3 7 10 21 28 35

ALL-AMERICAN WESTERN (Formerly All-American Comics; Becomes All-American Men of War)
National Periodical Publ.: No. 103, Nov, 1948 - No. 126, June-July, 1952 (103-121: 52 pgs.)

103-Johnny Thunder & his horse Black Lightning continues by Toth, ends #126; Foley of The Fighting 5th, Minstrel Maverick, & Overland Coach begin; Captain Tootsie by Beck; mentioned in Love and Death 50 100 150 305 465 625
104-Kubert-a 39 78 117 222 324 425
105,107-Kubert-a 32 64 96 184 267 350
106,108-110,112: 112-Kurtzman's "Pot-Shot Pete" (1 pg.)
27 54 81 152 219 285
111,114-116-Kubert-a 28 56 84 158 229 300
113-Intro. Swift Deer, J. Thunder's new sidekick (4-5/50); classic Toth-c; Kubert-a 30 60 90 170 245 320
117-126: 121-Kubert-a; bondage-c 19 38 57 107 154 200
NOTE: ***G. Kane*** *c(p)-112, 119, 120, 123.* ***Kubert*** *a-103-105, 107, 111, 112(1 pg.), 113-116, 121.* ***Toth*** *a 103-125; c(p)-103-111,113-116, 121, 122, 124-126. Some copies of #125 have #12 on-c.*

ALL COMICS
Chicago Nite Life News: 1945

1 15 30 45 83 117 150

ALLEGRA
Image Comics (WildStorm): Aug, 1996 - No. 4, Dec, 1996 ($2.50)

1-4 2.50

ALLEY CAT (Alley Baggett)
Image Comics: July, 1999 - No. 6, Mar, 2000 ($2.50/$2.95)

Preview Edition 6.00
Prelude 5.00
Prelude w/variant-c 6.00
1-Photo-c 2.50
1-Painted-c by Dorian 3.50
1-Another Universe Edition, 1-Wizard World Edition 7.00
2-4: 4-Twin towers on-c 2.50
5,6-($2.95) 3.00
Lingerie Edition (10/99, $4.95) Photos, pin-ups, cover gallery 5.00
...Vs. Lady Pendragon ('99, $3.00) Stinsman-c 3.00

ALLEY OOP (See The Comics, The Funnies, Red Ryder and Super Book #9)
Dell Publishing Co.: No. 3, 1942

Four Color 3 (#1) 46 92 138 368 572 775

ALLEY OOP
Argo Publ.: Nov, 1955 - No. 3, Mar, 1956 (Newspaper reprints)

1 18 36 54 100 143 185
2,3 12 24 36 69 95 120

ALLEY OOP
Dell Publishing Co.: 12-2/62-63 - No. 2, 9-11/63

1 7 14 21 51 71 90
2 6 12 18 43 59 75

ALLEY OOP
Standard Comics: No. 10, Sept, 1947 - No. 18, Oct, 1949

10 25 50 75 141 203 265
11-18: 17,18-Schomburg-c 20 40 60 112 161 210

ALLEY OOP ADVENTURES
Antarctic Press: Aug, 1998 - No. 3, Dec, 1998 ($2.95)

1-3-Jack Bender-s/a 3.00

GD 2.0 | VG 4.0 | FN 6.0 | VF 8.0 | VF/NM 9.0 | NM- 9.2

ALLEY OOP ADVENTURES (Alley Oop Quarterly in indicia)
Antarctic Press: Sept, 1999 - No. 3, Mar, 2000 ($2.50/$2.99, B&W)

1-3-Jack Bender-s/a 3.00

ALL-FAMOUS CRIME (2nd series - Formerly Law Against Crime #1-3; becomes All-Famous Police Cases #6 on)
Star Publications: No. 8, 5/51 - No. 10, 11/51; No. 4, 2/52 - No. 5, 5/52;

8 (#1-1st series) 22 44 66 127 184 240
9 (#2)-Used in **SOTI**, illo- "The wish to hurt or kill couples in lovers' lanes is a not uncommon perversion;" L.B. Cole-c/a(r)/Law-Crime #3 36 72 108 204 297 390
10 (#3) 20 40 60 112 161 210
4 (#4-2nd series)-Formerly Law-Crime 19 38 57 107 154 200
5 (#5) Becomes All-Famous Police Cases #6 19 38 57 107 154 200
NOTE: *All have* ***L.B. Cole*** *covers.*

ALL FAMOUS CRIME STORIES (See Fox Giants)

ALL-FAMOUS POLICE CASES (Formerly All Famous Crime #5)
Star Publications: No. 6, Feb, 1952 - No. 16, Sept, 1954

6 20 40 60 112 161 210
7,8: 7-Baker story. 8-Marijuana story 19 38 57 107 154 200
9-16 17 34 51 95 135 175
NOTE: ***L. B. Cole*** *c-all; a-15, 1pg.* ***Hollingsworth*** *a-15.*

ALL-FLASH (...Quarterly No. 1-5)
National Per. Publ./All-American: Summer, 1941 - No. 32, Dec-Jan, 1947-48

1-Origin The Flash retold by E. E. Hibbard; Hibbard c-1-10,12-14,16,31p.
1412 2824 4236 10,590 17,295 24,000
2-Origin recap 345 690 1035 2243 3622 5000
3,4 177 354 531 1106 1703 2300
5-Winky, Blinky & Noddy begins (1st app.), ends #32
131 262 393 819 1260 1700
6-10 106 212 318 663 1019 1375
11-13: 12-Origin/1st The Thinker. 13-The King app. 90 180 270 563 869 1175
14-Green Lantern cameo 106 212 318 663 1019 1375
15-20: 18-Mutt & Jeff begins, ends #22 75 150 225 469 722 975
21-31 62 124 186 388 594 800
32-Origin/1st app. The Fiddler; 1st Star Sapphire 113 226 339 706 1091 1475
NOTE: *Book length stories in 2-13, 16. Bondage c-31, 32.* ***Martin Nodell*** *c-15, 17-28.*

ALL FOR LOVE (Young Love V3#5-on)
Prize Publications: Apr-May, 1957 - V3#4, Dec-Jan, 1959-60

V1#1 8 16 24 55 78 100
2-6: 5-Orlando-c 5 10 15 33 44 55
V2#1-5(1/59), 5(3/59) 4 8 12 22 30 38
V3#1(5/59), 1(7/59)-4: 2-Powell-a 3 6 9 18 23 28

ALL FUNNY COMICS
Tilsam Publ./National Periodical Publications (Detective): Winter, 1943-44 - No. 23, May-June, 1948

1-Genius Jones (1st app.), Buzzy (1st app., ends #4), Dover & Clover (see More Fun #93) begin; Bailey-a 48 96 144 293 447 600
2 24 48 72 135 195 255
3-10 15 30 45 85 120 155
11-13,15,18,19-Genius Jones app. 14 28 42 81 113 145
14,17,20-23 10 20 30 58 77 95
16-DC Super Heroes app. 33 66 99 190 275 360

ALL GOOD
St. John Publishing Co.: Oct, 1949 (50¢, 260 pgs.)

nn-(8 St. John comics bound together) 67 134 201 419 647 875
NOTE: *Also see Li'l Audrey Yearbook & Treasury of Comics.*

ALL GOOD COMICS (See Fox Giants)
Fox Features Syndicate: No.1, Spring, 1946 (36 pgs.)

1-Joy Family, Dick Transom, Rick Evans, One Round Hogan
27 54 81 154 222 290

ALL GREAT (See Fox Giants)
Fox Feature Syndicate: 1946 (36 pgs.)

1-Crazy House, Bertie Benson Boy Detective, Gussie the Gob
27 54 81 154 222 290

ALL GREAT
William H. Wise & Co.: nd (1945?) (132 pgs.)

nn-Capt. Jack Terry, Joan Mason, Girl Reporter, Baron Doomsday; Torture scenes
40 80 120 244 372 500

ALL GREAT COMICS (Formerly Phantom Lady #13? Dagar, Desert Hawk No. 14 on)

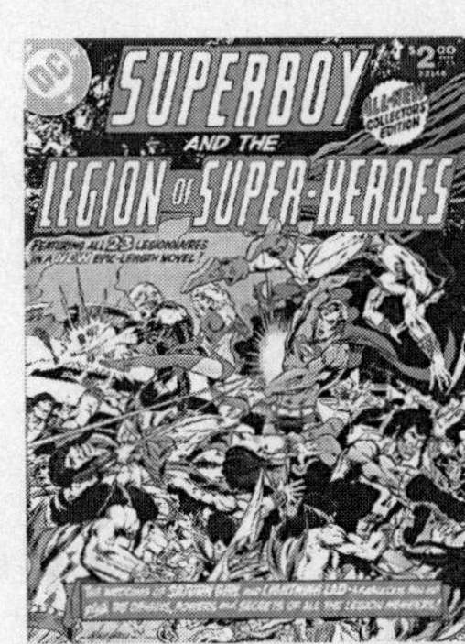

All New Collectors' Edition C-55 © DC

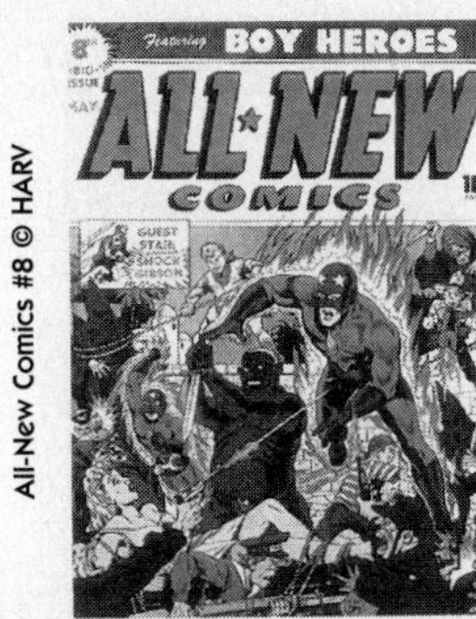

All-New Comics #8 © HARV

All Star Comics #4 © DC

	GD 2.0	VG 4.0	FN 6.0	VF 8.0	VF/NM 9.0	NM- 9.2

Fox Features Syndicate: No. 14, Oct, 1947 - No. 13, Dec, 1947 (Newspaper strip reprints)

14(#12)-Brenda Starr & Texas Slim-r (Scarce) 57 114 171 356 548 740
13-Origin Dagar, Desert Hawk; Brenda Starr (all-r); Kamen-c; Dagar covers begin 63 126 189 394 610 825

ALL-GREAT CONFESSIONS (See Fox Giants)

ALL GREAT CRIME STORIES (See Fox Giants)

ALL GREAT JUNGLE ADVENTURES (See Fox Giants)

ALL HALLOW'S EVE
Innovation Publishing: 1991 ($4.95, 52 pgs.)

1-Painted-c/a 1 2 3 4 5 7

ALL HERO COMICS
Fawcett Publications: Mar, 1943 (100 pgs., cardboard-c)

1-Capt. Marvel Jr., Capt. Midnight, Golden Arrow, Ibis the Invincible, Spy Smasher, Lance O'Casey; 1st Banshee O'Brien; Raboy-c 169 338 507 1056 1628 2200

ALL HUMOR COMICS
Quality Comics Group: Spring, 1946 - No. 17, December, 1949

1 21 42 63 118 169 220
2-Atomic Tot story; Gustavson-a 11 22 33 64 87 110
3-9: 3-Intro Kelly Poole who is cover feature #3 on. 5-1st app. Hickory? 8-Gustavson-a 8 16 24 40 50 60
10-17 7 14 21 35 43 50

ALLIANCE, THE
Image Comics (Shadowline Ink): Aug, 1995 - No. 3, Nov, 1995 ($2.50)

1-3: 2-(9/95) 2.50

ALL LOVE (...Romances No. 26)(Formerly Ernie Comics)
Ace Periodicals (Current Books): No. 26, May, 1949 - No. 32, May, 1950

26 (No. 1)-Ernie, Lily Belle app. 9 18 27 54 70 85
27-L. B. Cole-a 14 28 42 79 110 140
28-32 7 14 21 35 43 50

ALL-NEGRO COMICS
All-Negro Comics: June, 1947 (15¢)

1 (Rare) 684 1368 2052 3762 5131 6500

NOTE: *Seldom found in fine or mint condition; many copies have brown pages.*

ALL-NEW COLLECTORS' EDITION (Formerly Limited ...)
DC Comics, Inc.: Jan, 1978 - Vol. 8, No. C-62, 1979 (No. 54-58: 76 pgs.)

C-53-Rudolph the Red-Nosed Reindeer 5 10 15 33 44 55
C-54-Superman Vs. Wonder Woman 4 8 12 27 36 45
C-55-Superboy & the Legion of Super-Heroes; Wedding of Lightning Lad & Saturn Girl; Grell-c/a 4 8 12 27 36 45
C-56-Superman Vs. Muhammad Ali: story & wraparound N. Adams-c/a 6 12 18 43 59 75
C-56-Superman Vs. Muhammad Ali (Whitman variant)-low print 7 14 21 51 71 90
C-58-Superman Vs. Shazam 4 8 12 25 33 42
C-60-Rudolph's Summer Fun(8/78) 4 8 12 29 40 50
C-61-(See Famous First Edition-Superman #1)
C-62-Superman the Movie (68 pgs.; 1979)-Photo-c from movie plus photos inside (also see DC Special Series #25) 3 6 9 16 20 25

NOTE: ***Buckler** a-C-58; c-C-58*

ALL-NEW COMICS (...Short Story Comics No. 1-3)
Family Comics (Harvey Publications): Jan, 1943 - No. 14, Nov, 1946; No. 15, Mar-Apr, 1947 (10 x 13-1/2")

1-Steve Case, Crime Rover, Johnny Rebel, Kayo Kane, The Echo, Night Hawk, Ray O'Light, Detective Shane begin (all 1st app.?); Red Blazer on cover only; Sultan-a 300 600 900 1905 3003 4100
2-Origin Scarlet Phantom by Kubert 112 224 336 700 1075 1450
3-Nazi war-c 86 172 258 538 832 1125
4 69 138 207 431 666 900
5-11: 5-Schomburg-c thru #11. 6-The Boy Heroes & Red Blazer (text story) begin, end #12; Black Cat app.; intro. Sparky in Red Blazer. 7-Kubert, Powell-a; Black Cat & Zebra app. 8,9: 8-Shock Gibson app.; Kubert, Powell-a; Schomburg-c. 9-Black Cat app.; Kubert-a. 10-The Zebra app. (from Green Hornet Comics); Kubert-a(3). 11-Girl Commandos, Man In Black app. 83 166 249 519 797 1075
12,13: 12-Kubert-a. 13-Stuntman by Simon & Kirby; Green Hornet, Joe Palooka, Flying Fool app.; Green Hornet-c 63 126 189 394 610 825
14-The Green Hornet & The Man in Black Called Fate by Powell, Joe Flying Fool app.; Flying Fool app.; J. Palooka-c by Ham Fisher 58 116 174 363 562 760
15-(Rare)-Small size (5-1/2x8-1/2"; B&W; 32 pgs.). Distributed to mail subscribers only. Black Cat and Joe Palooka app. 100 200 300 625 963 1300

NOTE: *Also see Boy Explorers No. 2, Flash Gordon No. 5, and Stuntman No. 3.* ***Powell** a-11.* ***Schomburg** c-5-11. Captain Red Blazer & Spark on c-5-11 (w/Boy Heroes #12).*

ALL-OUT WAR
DC Comics: Sept-Oct, 1979 - No. 6, Aug, 1980 ($1.00, 68 pgs.)

1-The Viking Commando(origin), Force Three(origin), & Black Eagle Squadron begin 2 4 6 9 11 14
2-6 1 2 3 5 6 8

NOTE: ***Ayers** a(p)-1-6.* ***Elias** r-2.* ***Evans** a-1-6.* ***Kubert** c-16.*

ALL PICTURE ADVENTURE MAGAZINE
St. John Publishing Co.: Oct, 1952 - No. 2, Nov, 1952 (100 pg. Giants, 25¢, squarebound)

1-War comics 33 66 99 190 275 360
2-Horror-crime comics 46 92 138 281 428 575

NOTE: *Above books contain three St. John comics rebound; variations possible.* ***Baker** art known in both.*

ALL PICTURE ALL TRUE LOVE STORY
St. John Publishing Co.: Oct., 1952 - No. 2, Nov., 1952 (100 pgs., 25¢)

1-Canteen Kate by Matt Baker 48 96 144 293 447 600
2-Baker-c/a 35 70 105 198 287 375

ALL-PICTURE COMEDY CARNIVAL
St. John Publishing Co.: October, 1952 (100 pgs., 25¢)(Contains 4 rebound comics)

1-Contents can vary; Baker-a 43 86 129 262 401 540

ALL REAL CONFESSION MAGAZINE (See Fox Giants)

ALL ROMANCES (Mr. Risk No. 7 on)
A. A. Wyn (Ace Periodicals): Aug, 1949 - No. 6, June, 1950

1 10 20 30 60 80 100
2 6 12 18 31 38 45
3-6 6 12 18 28 34 40

ALL-SELECT COMICS (Blonde Phantom No. 12 on)
Timely Comics (Daring Comics): Fall, 1943 - No. 11, Fall, 1946

1-Capt. America (by Rico #1), Human Torch, Sub-Mariner begin; Black Widow story (4 pgs.); Classic Schomburg-c 1118 2236 3354 8385 13,693 19,000
2-Red Skull app. 379 758 1137 2464 3982 5500
3-The Whizzer begins 254 508 762 1588 2444 3300
4,5-Last Sub-Mariner 185 370 555 1156 1778 2400
6-9: 6-The Destroyer app. 8-No Whizzer 142 284 426 888 1369 1850
10-The Destroyer & Sub-Mariner app.; last Capt. America & Human Torch issue 142 284 426 888 1369 1850
11-1st app. Blonde Phantom; Miss America app.; all Blonde Phantom-c by Shores 269 538 807 1681 2591 3500

NOTE: ***Schomburg** c-1-10.* ***Sekowsky** a-7. #7 & 8 show 1944 in indicia, but should be 1945.*

ALL SPORTS COMICS (Formerly Real Sports Comics; becomes All Time Sports Comics No. 4 on)
Hillman Periodicals: No. 2, Dec-Jan, 1948-49; No. 3, Feb-Mar, 1949

2-Krigstein-a(p), Powell, Starr-a 37 74 111 209 305 400
3-Mort Lawrence-a 25 50 75 141 203 265

ALL STAR COMICS (All Star Western No. 58 on)
National Periodical Publ./All-American/DC Comics: Sum, '40 - No. 57, Feb-Mar, '51; No. 58, Jan-Feb, '76 -No. 74, Sept-Oct, '78

1-The Flash (#1 by E.E. Hibbard), Hawkman (by Shelly), Hourman (by Bernard Baily), The Sandman(by Creig Flessel), The Spectre(by Baily), Biff Bronson, Red White & Blue (ends #2) begin; Ultra Man's only app. (#1-3 are quarterly; #4 begins bi-monthly issues) 1147 2294 3441 8603 14,052 19,500
2-Green Lantern (by Martin Nodell), Johnny Thunder begin; Green Lantern figure swipe from the cover of All-American Comics #16; Flash figure swipe from cover of Flash Comics #8; Moldoff/Bailey-c (cut & paste-c.) 503 1006 1509 3521 5661 7800
3-Origin & 1st app. The Justice Society of America (Win/40); Dr. Fate & The Atom begin, Red Tornado cameo 3529 7058 10,587 27,000 43,500 60,000
3-Reprint, Oversize 13-1/2x10". **WARNING:** This comic is an exact reprint of the original except for its size. DC published it in 1974 with a second cover titling it as a Famous First Edition. There have been many reported cases of the outer cover being removed and the interior sold as the original edition. The reprint with the new outer cover removed is practically worthless. See Famous First Edition for value.
4-1st adventure for J.S.A. 523 1046 1569 3661 5881 8100
5-1st app. Shiera Sanders as Hawkgirl (1st costumed super-heroine, 6-7/41) 439 878 1317 3073 4937 6800
6-Johnny Thunder joins JSA 300 600 900 1892 2946 4000
7-Batman, Superman, Flash cameo; last Hourman; Doiby Dickles app. 328 656 984 2132 3441 4750
8-Origin & 1st app. Wonder Woman (12-1/41-42)(added as 9 pgs. making book 76 pgs.; origin cont'd in Sensation #1; see W.W. #1 for more detailed origin); Dr. Fate dons new helmet; Hop Harrigan text stories & Starman begin; Shiera app.; Hop Harrigan JSA guest;

All Star Comics #58 © DC

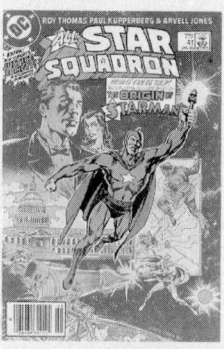

All Star Squadron #41 © DC

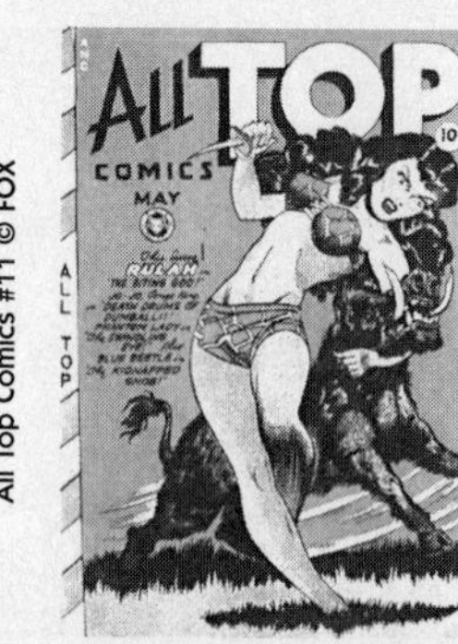

All Top Comics #11 © FOX

GD 2.0 | VG 4.0 | FN 6.0 | VF 8.0 | VF/NM 9.0 | NM- 9.2

Starman & Dr. Mid-Nite become members 2825 5650 8475 21,600 34,800 48,000
9-11: 9-JSA's girlfriends cameo; Shiera app.; J. Edgar Hoover of FBI made associate member of JSA. 10-Flash, Green Lantern cameo; Sandman new costume. 11-Wonder Woman begins; Spectre cameo; Shiera app.; Moldoff Hawkman-c 292 584 876 1825 2813 3800
12-Wonder Woman becomes JSA Secretary 262 524 786 1638 2519 3400
13,15: Sandman w/Sandy in #14 & 15. 15-Origin & 1st app. Brain Wave; Shiera app. 246 492 738 1538 2369 3200
14-(12/42) Junior JSA Club begins; w/membership offer & premiums 250 500 750 1563 2407 3250
16-20: 19-Sandman w/Sandy. 20-Dr. Fate & Sandman cameo 181 362 543 1131 1741 2350
21-23: 21-Spectre & Atom cameo; Dr. Fate by Kubert; Dr. Fate, Sandman end. 22-Last Hop Harrigan; Flag-c. 23-Origin/1st app. Psycho Pirate; last Spectre & Starman 158 316 474 988 1519 2050
24-Flash & Green Lantern cameo; Mr. Terrific only app.; Wildcat, JSA guest; Kubert Hawkman begins; Hitler-c 158 316 474 988 1519 2050
25-27: 25-Flash & Green Lantern start again. 26-Robot-c. 27-Wildcat, JSA guest (#24-26: only All-American imprint) 135 270 405 844 1297 1750
28-32 121 242 363 756 1166 1575
33-Solomon Grundy & Doiby Dickles app; classic Solomon Grundy cover & last G.A. app. 345 690 1035 2243 3622 5000
34,35-Johnny Thunder cameo in both 117 234 351 731 1128 1525
36-Batman & Superman JSA guests 277 554 831 1731 2666 3600
37-Johnny Thunder cameo; origin & 1st app. Injustice Society; last Kubert Hawkman 154 308 462 963 1482 2000
38-Black Canary begins; JSA Death issue 185 370 555 1156 1778 2400
39,40: 39-Last Johnny Thunder 113 226 339 706 1091 1475
41-Black Canary joins JSA; Injustice Society app. (2nd app.?) 113 226 339 706 1091 1475
42-Atom & the Hawkman don new costumes 113 226 339 706 1091 1475
43-49,51-56: 43-New logo; Robot-c. 55-Sci/Fi story. 56-Robot-c 113 226 339 706 1091 1475
50-Frazetta art, 3 pgs. 121 242 363 756 1166 1575
57-Kubert-a, 6 pgs. (Scarce); last app. G.A. Green Lantern, Flash & Dr. Mid-Nite 165 330 495 1031 1591 2150
V12 #58-(1976) JSA (Flash, Hawkman, Dr. Mid-Nite, Wildcat, Dr. Fate, Green Lantern, Robin & Star Spangled Kid) app.; intro. Power Girl 4 8 12 29 40 50
V12 #59,60: 59-Estrada & Wood-a 2 4 6 12 16 20
V12 #61-68: 62-65-Superman app. 64,65-Wood-c/a; Vandal Savage app. 66-Injustice Society app. 68-Psycho Pirate app. 2 4 6 12 16 20
V12 #69-1st Earth-2 Huntress (Helena Wayne) 3 7 10 21 28 35
V12 #70-73: 70-Full intro. of Huntress 2 4 6 12 16 20
V12 #74-(44 pgs.) Last issue, story continues in Adventure Comics #461 & 462 (death of Earth-2 Batman; Staton-c/a 3 6 9 18 23 28

NOTE: *No Atom-27, 36; no Dr. Fate-13; no Flash-8, 9, 11-23; no Green Lantern-8, 9,11-23; Hawkman in 1-57 (only one to app. in all 57 issues); no Johnny Thunder-5, 36; no Wonder Woman-9, 10, 23. Book length stories in 4-9, 11-14, 18-22, 25, 26, 29, 30, 32-36, 40, 42, 43. Johnny Peril in #42-46, 48, 49, 51, 52,54-57.* **Baily** *a-1-10, 12, 13, 14i, 15-20.* **Burnley** *Starman-8-13; c-12, 13.* **Grell** *c-58.* **E.E. Hibbard** *c-3, 4, 6-10.* **Infantino** *c-40.* **Kubert** *Hawkman-24-30, 33-37.* **Lampert/Baily/Flessel** *c-1, 2.* **Moldoff** *Hawkman-3-23; c-11.* **Mart Nodell** *c-25i, 26i, 27-32.* **Purcell** *c-5.* **Simon & Kirby** *Sandman 14-17, 19.* **Staton** *a-66-74p. c-74p.* **Toth** *a-37(2), 38(2), 40, 41; c-38, 41.* **Wood** *a-58i-63i, 64, 65; c-63i, 64, 65. Issues 1-7, 9-16 are 68 pgs.; #8 is 76 pgs.; #17-19 are 60 pgs.; #20-57 are 52 pgs.*

ALL STAR COMICS (Also see crossover 1999 editions of Adventure, All-American, National, Sensation, Smash, Star Spangled and Thrilling Comics)
DC Comics: May, 1999 - No. 2, May, 1999 ($2.95, bookends for JSA x-over)

1,2-Justice Society in World War 2; Robinson-s/Johnson-c 3.00
1-RRP Edition (price will be based on future sales)
...80-Page Giant (9/99, $4.95) Phantom Lady app. 5.00

ALL STAR INDEX, THE
Independent Comics Group (Eclipse): Feb, 1987 ($2.00, Baxter paper)

1 1 2 3 5 6 8

ALL-STAR SQUADRON (See Justice League of America #193)
DC Comics: Sept, 1981 - No. 67, Mar, 1987

1-Original Atom, Hawkman, Dr. Mid-Nite, Robotman (origin), Plastic Man, Johnny Quick, Liberty Belle, Shining Knight begin 1 2 3 4 5 7
2-10: 4,7-Spectre app. 8-Re-intro Steel, the Indestructable Man 5.00
11-46,48,49: 12-Origin G.A. Hawkman retold. 23-Origin/1st app. The Amazing Man. 24-Batman app. 25-1st app. Infinity, Inc. (9/83), 26-Origin Infinity, Inc.(2nd app.); Robin app. 27-Dr. Fate vs. The Spectre. 30-35-Spectre app. 33-Origin Freedom Fighters of Earth-X. 36,37-Superman vs. Capt. Marvel; Ordway-c. 41-Origin Starman 4.00
47-Origin Dr. Fate; McFarlane-a (1st full story)/part-c (7/85) 1 3 4 6 8 10
50-Double size; Crisis x-over 6.00
51-66: 51-56-Crisis x-over. 61-Origin Liberty Belle. 62-Origin The Shining Knight. 63-Origin Robotman. 65-Origin Johnny Quick. 66-Origin Tarantula 4.50
67-Last issue; retells first case of the Justice Society 6.00
Annual 1-3: 1(11/82)-Retells origin of G.A. Atom, Guardian & Wildcat; Jerry Ordway's 1st pencils for DC.(1st work was inking Carmine Infantino in Mystery in Space #94). 2(11/83)-Infinity, Inc. app. 3(9/84) 4.50

NOTE: **Buckler** *a-1-5; c-1, 3-5, 51.* **Kubert** *c-2, 7-18. JLA app. in 14, 15. JSA app. in 4, 14, 15, 19, 27, 28.*

GD 2.0 | VG 4.0 | FN 6.0 | VF 8.0 | VF/NM 9.0 | NM- 9.2

ALL-STAR STORY OF THE DODGERS, THE
Stadium Communications: Apr, 1979 ($1.00)

1 2 4 6 10 13 16

ALL STAR WESTERN (Formerly All Star Comics No. 1-57)
National Periodical Publ.: No. 58, Apr-May, 1951 - No. 119, June-July, 1961

58-Trigger Twins (ends #116), Strong Bow, The Roving Ranger & Don Caballero begin 44 88 132 268 409 550
59,60: Last 52 pgs. 27 54 81 152 219 285
61-66: 61-64-Toth-a 22 44 66 123 177 230
67-Johnny Thunder begins; Gil Kane-a 28 56 84 158 229 300
68-81: Last precode (2-3/55) 13 26 39 74 102 130
82-98: 97-1st S.A. issue 11 22 33 64 87 110
99-Frazetta-r/Jimmy Wakely #4 11 22 33 66 91 115
100 11 22 33 66 91 115
101-107,109-116,118,119 10 20 30 56 73 90
108-Origin J. Thunder; J. Thunder logo begins 22 44 66 123 177 230
117-Origin Super Chief 13 26 39 74 102 130

NOTE: **Gil Kane** *c(p)-58, 59, 61, 63, 64, 68, 69, 70-95(most), 97-199(most).* **Infantino** *art in most issues. Madame .44 app.-#117-119.*

ALL-STAR WESTERN (Weird Western Tales No. 12 on)
National Periodical Publications: Aug-Sept, 1970 - No. 11, Apr-May, 1972

1-Pow-Wow Smith-r; Infantino-a 5 10 15 36 48 60
2-Outlaw begins; El Diablo by Morrow begins; has cameos by Williamson, Torres, Kane, Giordano & Phil Seuling 4 8 12 29 40 50
3-Origin El Diablo 4 8 12 29 40 50
4-6: 5-Last Outlaw issue. 6-Billy the Kid begins, ends #8 3 7 10 21 28 35
7-9-(52 pgs.) 9-Frazetta-a, 3pgs.(r) 4 8 12 25 33 42
10-(52 pgs.) Jonah Hex begins (1st app., 2-3/72) 38 76 114 285 443 600
11-(52 pgs.) 2nd app. Jonah Hex; 1st cover 17 34 51 121 186 250

NOTE: **Neal Adams** *c-2-5;* **Aparo** *a-5.* **G. Kane a**-*3, 4, 6, 8.* **Kubert** *a-4r, 7-9r.* **Morrow** *a-2-4, 10, 11. No. 7-11 have 52 pgs..*

ALL SURPRISE (Becomes Jeanie #13 on) (Funny animal)
Timely/Marvel (CPC): Fall, 1943 - No. 12, Winter, 1946-47

1-Super Rabbit, Gandy & Sourpuss begin 37 74 111 209 305 400
2 17 34 51 98 139 180
3-10,12 13 26 39 74 102 130
11-Kurtzman "Pigtales" art 14 28 42 79 110 140

ALL TEEN (Formerly All Winners; All Winners & Teen Comics No. 21 on)
Marvel Comics (WFP): No. 20, January, 1947

20-Georgie, Mitzi, Patsy Walker, Willie app.; Syd Shores-c 15 30 45 83 117 150

ALL-TIME SPORTS COMICS (Formerly All Sports Comics)
Hillman Per.: V2No. 4, Apr-May, 1949 - V2No. 7, Oct-Nov, 1949 (All 52 pgs.)

V2#4 24 48 72 135 195 255
5-7: 5-(V1#5 inside)-Powell-a; Ty Cobb sty. 7-Krigstein-p; Walter Johnson & Knute Rockne sty 18 36 54 100 143 185

ALL TOP
William H. Wise Co.: 1944 (132 pgs.)

nn-Capt. V, Merciless the Sorceress, Red Robbins, One Round Hogan, Mike the M.P., Snooky, Pussy Katnip app. 33 66 99 190 275 360

ALL TOP COMICS (My Experience No. 19 on)
Fox Features Synd./Green Publ./Norlen Mag.: 1945; No. 2, Sum, 1946 - No. 18, Mar, 1949; 1957 - 1959

1-Cosmo Cat & Flash Rabbit begin (1st app.) 25 50 75 144 207 270
2 (#1-7 are funny animal) 12 24 36 71 98 125
3-7 9 18 27 54 70 85
8-Blue Beetle, Phantom Lady, & Rulah, Jungle Goddess begin (11/47); Kamen-c 254 508 762 1588 2444 3300
9-Kamen-c 131 262 393 819 1260 1700
10-Kamen bondage-c 140 280 420 875 1350 1825
11-13,15-17: 11-Rulah-c. 15-No Blue Beetle 113 226 339 706 1091 1475
14-No Blue Beetle; used in **SOTI**, illo- "Corpses of colored people strung up by their wrists"

All Western Winners #3 © MAR

All Winners Comics #10 © MAR

Alpha Flight ('04) #1 © MAR

GD 2.0 | VG 4.0 | FN 6.0 | VF 8.0 | VF/NM 9.0 | NM- 9.2

146 292 438 913 1407 1900
18-Dagar, Jo-Jo app; no Phantom Lady or Blue Beetle
71 142 213 444 685 925
6(1957-Green Publ.)-Patoruzu the Indian; Cosmo Cat on cover only. 6(1958-Literary Ent.)-Muggy Doo; Cosmo Cat on cover only. 6(1959-Norlen)-Atomic Mouse; Cosmo Cat on-c only.
6(1959)-Little Eva. 6(Cornell)-Supermouse on-c 5 10 15 24 30 35
NOTE: *Jo-Jo by Kamen-12,18.*

ALL TRUE ALL PICTURE POLICE CASES
St. John Publishing Co.: Oct, 1952 - No. 2, Nov, 1952 (100 pgs.)
1-Three rebound St. John crime comics 43 86 129 262 401 540
2-Three comics rebound 33 66 99 190 275 360
NOTE: *Contents may vary.*

ALL-TRUE CRIME (...Cases No. 26-35; formerly Official True Crime Cases)
Marvel/Atlas Comics: No. 26, Feb, 1948 - No. 52, Sept, 1952
(OFI #26,27/CFI #28,29/LCC #30-46/LMC #47-52)
26(#1)-Syd Shores-c 35 70 105 198 287 375
27(4/48)-Electric chair-c 27 54 81 152 219 285
28-41,43-48,50-52: 35-37-Photo-c 11 22 33 66 91 115
42,49-Krigstein-a. 49-Used in **POP**, Pg 79 12 24 36 71 98 125
NOTE: ***Robinson** a-47, 50. **Shores** c-26. **Tuska** a-48(3).*

ALL-TRUE DETECTIVE CASES (Kit Carson No. 5 on)
Avon Periodicals: #2, Apr-May, 1954 - No. 4, Aug-Sept, 1954
2(#1)-Wood-a 24 48 72 138 199 260
3-Kinstler-c 13 26 39 74 102 130
4-r/Gangsters And Gun Molls #2; Kamen-a 19 38 57 107 154 200
nn(100 pgs.)-7 pg. Kubert-a, Kinstler back-c 40 80 120 230 335 440

ALL TRUE ROMANCE (...Illustrated No. 3)
Artful Publ. #1-3/Harwell(Comic Media) #4-20?/Ajax-Farrell(Excellent Publ.) No. 22 on/Four Star Comic Corp.: 3/51 - No. 20, 12/54; No. 22, 3/55 - No. 30?, 7/57; No. 3(#31), 9/57;No. 4(#32), 11/57; No. 33, 2/58 - No. 34, 6/58
1 (3/51) 17 34 51 95 135 175
2 (10/51; 11/51 on-c) 9 18 27 54 70 85
3(12/51) - #5(5/52) 8 16 24 43 54 65
6-Wood-a, 9 pgs. (exceptional) 17 34 51 95 135 175
7-10 [two #7s: #7(11/52, 9/52 inside), #7(11/52, 11/52 inside)]
7 14 21 37 46 55
11-13,16-19(9/54),20(12/54) (no #21) 6 12 18 28 34 40
14-Marijuana story 6 12 18 31 38 45
22: Last precode issue (1st Ajax, 3/55) 6 12 18 28 34 40
23-27,29,30(7/57): 29-Disbrow-a 5 10 15 23 28 32
28 (9/56)-L. B. Cole, Disbrow-a 10 20 30 58 77 95
3(#31, 9/57),4(#32, 11/57),33,34 (Farrell, '57- '58) 5 10 15 22 26 30

ALL WESTERN WINNERS (Formerly All Winners; becomes Western Winners with No. 5; see Two-Gun Kid No. 5)
Marvel Comics(CDS): No. 2, Winter, 1948-49 - No. 4, April, 1949
2-Black Rider (origin/1st app.) & his horse Satan, Kid Colt & his horse Steel, & Two-Gun Kid & his horse Cyclone begin; Shores c-2-4 79 158 237 494 760 1025
3-Anti-Wertham editorial 40 80 120 230 335 440
4-Black Rider i.d. revealed; Heath, Shores-a 40 80 120 230 335 440

ALL WINNERS COMICS (All Teen #20) (Also see Timely Presents: ...)
USA No. 1-7/WFP No. 10-19/YAI No. 21: Summer, 1941 - No. 19, Fall, 1946; No. 21, Winter, 1946-47; (No #20) (No. 21 continued from Young Allies No. 20)
1-The Angel & Black Marvel only app.; Capt. America by Simon & Kirby, Human Torch & Sub-Mariner begin (#1 was advertised as All Aces); 1st app. All-Winners Squad in text story by Stan Lee 1944 3888 5832 14,600 24,800 35,000
2-The Destroyer & The Whizzer begin; Simon & Kirby Captain America
484 968 1452 3388 5444 7500
3 317 634 951 2061 3331 4600
4-Classic War-c by Al Avison 345 690 1035 2243 3622 5000
5 231 462 693 1444 2222 3000
6-The Black Avenger only app.; no Whizzer story; Hitler, Hirohito & Mussolini-c
277 554 831 1731 2666 3600
7-10 192 384 576 1200 1850 2500
11,13-18: 11-1st Atlas globe on-c (Winter, 1943-44; also see Human Torch #14).
14-16-No Human Torch 142 284 426 888 1369 1850
12-Red Skull story; last Destroyer; no Whizzer story
177 354 531 1106 1703 2300
19-(Scarce)-1st story app. & origin All Winners Squad (Capt. America & Bucky, Human Torch & Toro, Sub-Mariner, Whizzer, & Miss America; r-in Fantasy Masterpieces #10
439 878 1317 3073 4937 6800
21-(Scarce)-All Winners Squad; bondage-c 393 786 1179 2555 4128 5700

GD 2.0 | VG 4.0 | FN 6.0 | VF 8.0 | VF/NM 9.0 | NM- 9.2

NOTE: ***Everett** Sub-Mariner-1, 3, 4; **Burgos** Torch-1, 3, 4. **Schomburg** c-1, 7-18. **Shores** c-19p, 21.*
(2nd Series - August, 1948, Marvel Comics (CDS))
(Becomes All Western Winners with No. 2)
1-The Blonde Phantom, Capt. America, Human Torch, & Sub-Mariner app.
292 584 876 1825 2813 3800

ALL YOUR COMICS (See Fox Giants)
Fox Feature Syndicate (R. W. Voight): Spring, 1946 (36 pgs.)
1-Red Robbins, Merciless the Sorceress app. 22 44 66 124 172 230

ALMANAC OF CRIME (See Fox Giants)

AL OF FBI (See Little Al of the FBI)

ALONE IN THE DARK (Based on video game)
Image Comics: Feb, 2003 ($4.95)
1-Matt Haley-c/a; Jean-Marc & Randy Lofficier-s 5.00

ALPHA AND OMEGA
Spire Christian Comics (Fleming H. Revell): 1978 (49¢)
nn 1 3 4 6 8 11

ALPHA CENTURION (See Superman, 2nd Series & Zero Hour)
DC Comics: 1996 ($2.95, one-shot)
1 3.00

ALPHA FLIGHT (See X-Men #120,121 & X-Men/Alpha Flight)
Marvel Comics: Aug, 1983 - No. 130, Mar, 1994 (#52-on are direct sales only)
1-(52 pgs.) Byrne-a begins (thru #28) -Wolverine & Nightcrawler cameo 4.00
2-28: 2-Vindicator becomes Guardian; origin Marrina & Alpha Flight. 3-Concludes origin Alpha Flight. 6-Origin Shaman. 7-Origin Snowbird. 10,11-Origin Sasquatch. 12-(52 pgs.)-Death of Guardian. 13-Wolverine app. 16,17-Wolverine cameo. 17-X-Men x-over (mostly r-/X-Men #109); 20-New headquarters. 25-Return of Guardian. 28-Last Byrne issue 3.00
29-32,35-50: 39-47,49-Portacio-a(i). 50-Double size; Portacio-a(i) 2.50
33,34-1st & 2nd app. Lady Deathstrike; Wolverine app. 34-Origin Wolverine 3.00
51-Jim Lee's 1st work at Marvel (10/87); Wolverine cameo; 1st Lee Wolverine; Portacio-a(i) 5.00
52,53-Wolverine app.; Lee-a on Wolverine; Portacio-a(i); 53-Lee/Portacio-a 3.00
54-73,76-86,91-99,101-105: 54,63,64-No Jim Lee-a. 54-Portacio-a(i). 55-62-Jim Lee-a(p). 71-Intro The Sorcerer (villain). 91-Dr. Doom app. 94-F.F. x-over. 99-Galactus, Avengers app. 102-Intro Weapon Omega 2.25
74,75,87-90,100: 74-Wolverine, Spider-Man & The Avengers app. 75-Double size ($1.95, 52 pgs.). 87-90-Wolverine. 4 part story w/Jim Lee-c. 89-Original Guardian returns. 100-($2.00, 52 pgs.)-Avengers & Galactus app. 3.00
106-Northstar revelation issue 2.50
106-2nd printing (direct sale only) 2.25
107-109,112-119,121-129: 107-X-Factor x-over. 112-Infinity War x-overs 2.25
110,111: Infinity War x-overs, Wolverine app. (brief). 111-Thanos cameo 3.00
120-($2.25)-Polybagged w/Paranormal Registration Act poster 2.50
130-($2.25, 52 pgs.) 3.00
Annual 1,2 (9/86, 12/87) 3.00
Special V2#1(6/92, $2.50, 52 pgs.)-Wolverine-c/story 2.50
NOTE: ***Austin** c-1i, 2i, 53i. **Byrne** c-81, 82. **Guice** c-85, 91-99. **Jim Lee** a(p)-51, 53, 55-62, 64; c-53, 87-90. **Mignola** a-29-31p. **Whilce Portacio** a(i)-39-47, 49-54.*

ALPHA FLIGHT (2nd Series)
Marvel Comics: Aug, 1997 - No. 20, Mar, 1999 ($2.99/$1.99)
1-($2.99)-Wraparound cover 6.00
2,3: 2-Variant-c 4.00
4-11: 8,9-Wolverine-c/app. 3.00
12-($2.99) Death of Sasquatch; wraparound-c 4.00
13-20 3.00
.../Inhumans '98 Annual ($3.50) Raney-a 3.50

ALPHA FLIGHT (3rd Series)
Marvel Comics: May, 2004 - Present ($2.99)
1-10: 1-6-Lobdell-s/Henry-c/a 3.00
... Vol. 1: You Gotta Be Kiddin' Me (2004, $14.99) r/#1-6 15.00

ALPHA FLIGHT: IN THE BEGINNING
Marvel Comics: July, 1997 ($1.95, one-shot)
(-1)-Flashback w/Wolverine 2.25

ALPHA FLIGHT SPECIAL
Marvel Comics: July, 1991 - No. 4, Oct, 1991 ($1.50, limited series)
1-4: 1-3-r-A. Flight #97-99 w/covers. 4-r-A.Flight #100 2.25

ALPHA KORPS
Diversity Comics: Sept, 1996 ($2.50)
1-Origin/1st app. Alpha Korps 2.50

Amazing Adult Fantasy #7 © MAR

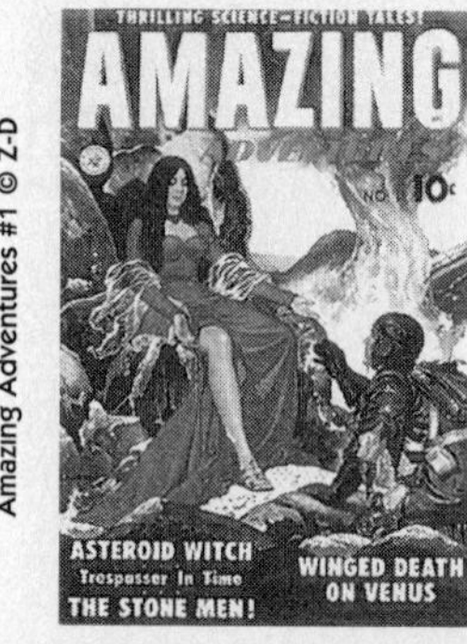

Amazing Adventures #1 © Z-D

Amazing Fantasy ('04) #1 © MAR

GD VG FN VF VF/NM NM-
2.0 4.0 6.0 8.0 9.0 9.2

ALTERED IMAGE
Image Comics: Apr, 1998 - No. 3, Sept, 1998 ($2.50, limited series)
1-3-Spawn, Witchblade, Savage Dragon; Valentino-s/a 3.00

ALTER EGO
First Comics: May, 1986 - No. 4, Nov, 1986 (Mini-series)
1-4 2.25

ALTER NATION
Image Comics: Feb, 2004 - No. 4, Jun, 2004 ($2.95, limited series)
1-4: 1-Two covers by Art Adams and Barberi; Barberi-a 3.00

ALVIN (TV) (See Four Color Comics No. 1042 or Three Chipmunks #1)
Dell Publishing Co.: Oct-Dec, 1962 - No. 28, Oct, 1973
12-021-212 (#1) 10 20 30 72 104 135
2 6 12 18 43 59 75
3-10 6 12 18 38 52 65
11-"Chipmunks sing the Beatles' Hits" 5 10 15 36 48 60
12-28 4 8 12 29 40 50
Alvin For President (10/64) 5 10 15 36 48 60
...& His Pals in Merry Christmas with Clyde Crashcup & Leonardo 1
(02-120-402)-(12-2/64) 9 18 27 63 89 115
Reprinted in 1966 (12-023-604) 6 12 18 40 55 70

ALVIN & THE CHIPMUNKS
Harvey Comics: July, 1992 - No. 5, May, 1994
1-5: 1-Richie Rich app. 4.00

AMALGAM AGE OF COMICS, THE: THE DC COMICS COLLECTION
DC Comics: 1996 ($12.95, trade paperback)
nn-r/Amazon, Assassins, Doctor Strangefate, JLX, Legends of the Dark Claw, & Super Soldier 13.00

AMANDA AND GUNN
Image Comics: Apr, 1997 - No. 4, Oct, 1997 ($2.95, B&W, limited series)
1-4 3.00

AMAZING ADULT FANTASY (Formerly Amazing Adventures #1-6; becomes Amazing Fantasy #15)
Marvel Comics Group (AMI): No. 7, Dec, 1961 - No. 14, July, 1962
7-Ditko-c/a begins, ends #14 50 100 150 400 625 850
8-Last 10¢ issue 41 82 123 485 573 660
9-13: 12-1st app. Mailbag. 13-Anti-communist sty 39 78 117 293 459 625
13-2nd printing (1994) 2 4 6 8 10 12
14-Prototype issue (Professor X) 41 82 123 318 497 675

AMAZING ADVENTURE FUNNIES (Fantoman No. 2 on)
Centaur Publications: June, 1940 - No. 2, Sept. 1940
1-The Fantom of the Fair by Gustavson (r/Amaz. Mystery Funnies V2#7,V2#8), The Arrow, Skyrocket Steele From the Year X by Everett (r/AMF #2); Burgos-a 185 370 555 1156 1778 2400
2-Reprints; Published after Fantoman #2 119 238 357 744 1147 1550
NOTE: *Burgos a-1(2). Everett a-1(3). Gustavson a-1(5), 2(3). Pinajian a-2.*

AMAZING ADVENTURES (Also see Boy Cowboy & Science Comics)
Ziff-Davis Publ. Co.: 1950; No. 1, Nov, 1950 - No. 6, Fall, 1952 (Painted covers)
1950 (no month given) (8-1/2x11) (8 pgs.) Has the front & back cover plus Schomburg story used in Amazing Advs. #1 (Sent to subscribers of Z-D s/f magazines & ordered through mail for 10¢. Used to test market) 52 104 156 317 484 650
1-Wood, Schomburg, Anderson, Whitney-a 77 154 231 481 741 1000
2-5: 2-Schomburg-a. 2,4,5-Anderson-a. 3,5-Starr-a 40 80 120 233 342 450
6-Krigstein-a 40 80 120 235 348 460

AMAZING ADVENTURES (Becomes Amazing Adult Fantasy #7 on)
Atlas Comics (AMI)/Marvel Comics No. 3 on: June, 1961 - No. 6, Nov, 1961
1-Origin Dr. Droom (1st Marvel-Age Superhero) by Kirby; Kirby/Ditko-a (5 pgs.) Ditko & Kirby-a in all; Kirby monster c-1-6 111 222 333 944 1522 2100
2 48 96 144 384 605 825
3-6: 6-Last Dr. Droom 41 82 123 330 515 700

AMAZING ADVENTURES
Marvel Comics Group: Aug, 1970 - No. 39, Nov, 1976
1-Inhumans by Kirby(p) & Black Widow (1st app. in Tales of Suspense #52) double feature begins 6 12 18 40 55 70
2-4: 2-F.F. brief app. 4-Last Inhumans by Kirby 3 6 9 19 25 32
5-8: Adams-a(p); 8-Last Black Widow; last 15¢-c 4 8 12 29 40 50
9,10: Magneto app. 10-Last Inhumans (origin-r by Kirby) 3 6 9 18 24 30

GD VG FN VF VF/NM NM-
2.0 4.0 6.0 8.0 9.0 9.2

11-New Beast begins(1st app. in mutated form; origin in flashback); X-Men cameo in flashback (#11-17 are X-Men tie-ins) 13 26 39 90 138 185
12-17: 12-Beast battles Iron Man. 13-Brotherhood of Evil Mutants x-over from X-Men. 15-X-Men app. 16-Rutland Vermont - Bald Mountain Halloween x-over; Juggernaut app. 17-Last Beast (origin); X-Men app. 5 10 15 33 44 55
18-War of the Worlds begins (5/73); 1st app. Killraven; Neal Adams-a(p) 3 6 9 18 24 30
19-35,38,39: 19-Chaykin-a. 25-Buckler-a. 35-Giffen's first published story (art), along with Deadly Hands of Kung-Fu #22 (3/76) 1 3 4 6 8 10
36,37-(Regular 25¢ edition)(7-8/76) 1 3 4 6 8 10
36,37-(30¢-c variants, limited distribution) 3 6 9 16 20 25
NOTE: *N. Adams c-6-8. Buscema a-1p, 2p. Colan a-3-5p, 26p. Ditko a-24r. Everett a(i)3-5, 7-9. Giffen a-35i, 38p. G. Kane c-11, 25p, 29p. Ploog a-12i. Russell a-27-32, 34-37, 39; c-28, 30-32, 33i, 34, 35, 37, 39i. Starlling a-17. Starlin c-15p, 16, 17, 27. Sutton a-11-15p.*

AMAZING ADVENTURES
Marvel Comics Group: Dec, 1979 - No. 14, Jan, 1981
V2#1-Reprints story/X-Men #1 & 38 (origins) 1 2 3 5 6 8
2-14: 2-6-Early X-Men-r. 7,8-Origin Iceman 6.00
NOTE: *Byrne c-6p, 9p. Kirby a-1-14r; c-7, 9. Steranko a-12r. Tuska a-7-9.*

AMAZING ADVENTURES
Marvel Comics: July, 1988 ($4.95, squarebound, one-shot, 80 pgs.)
1-Anthology; Austin, Golden-a 5.00

AMAZING ADVENTURES OF CAPTAIN CARVEL AND HIS CARVEL CRUSADERS, THE
(See Carvel Comics in the Promotional Comics section)

AMAZING CHAN & THE CHAN CLAN, THE (TV)
Gold Key: May, 1973 - No. 4, Feb, 1974 (Hanna-Barbera)
1-Warren Tufts-a in all 4 8 12 22 30 38
2-4 3 6 9 16 21 26

AMAZING COMICS (Complete Comics No. 2)
Timely Comics (EPC): Fall, 1944
1-The Destroyer, The Whizzer, The Young Allies (by Sekowsky), Sergeant Dix; Schomburg-c 231 462 693 1444 2222 3000

AMAZING DETECTIVE CASES (Formerly Suspense No. 2?)
Marvel/Atlas Comics (CCC): No. 3, Nov, 1950 - No. 14, Sept, 1952
3 30 60 90 170 245 320
4-6 17 34 51 95 135 175
7-10 15 30 45 86 123 160
11,12: 11-(3/52)-Horror format begins. 12-Krigstein-a 35 70 105 198 287 375
13-(Scarce)-Everett-a; electrocution-c/story 37 74 111 209 305 400
14 30 60 90 173 249 325
NOTE: *Colan a-9. Maneely c-13. Sekowsky a-12. Sinnott a-13. Tuska a-10.*

AMAZING FANTASY (Formerly Amazing Adult Fantasy #7-14)
Atlas Magazines/Marvel: #15, Aug, 1962 (Sept, 1962 shown in indicia); #16, Dec, 1995 - #18, Feb, 1996
15-Origin/1st app. of Spider-Man by Steve Ditko (11 pgs.); 1st app. Aunt May & Uncle Ben; Kirby/Ditko-c 1400 2800 4200 13,000 32,500 42,500
16-18 ('95-'96, $3.95): Kurt Busiek scripts; painted-c/a by Paul Lee 4.00

AMAZING FANTASY (Continues in Araña: The Heart of the Spider)
Marvel Comics: Aug, 2004 - No. 6, Jan, 2005 ($2.99)
1-Intro. Anya Corazon; Fiona Avery-s/Mark Brooks-c/a 4.00
2-6: 3,4-Roger Cruz-a 3.00

AMAZING GHOST STORIES (Formerly Nightmare)
St. John Publishing Co.: No. 14, Oct, 1954 - No. 16, Feb, 1955
14-Pit & the Pendulum story by Kinstler; Baker-c 34 68 102 196 283 370
15-r/Weird Thrillers #5; Baker-c, Powell-a 25 50 75 141 203 265
16-Kubert reprints of Weird Thrillers #4; Baker-c; Roussos, Tuska-a; Kinstler-a (1 pg.) 25 50 75 144 207 270

AMAZING HIGH ADVENTURE
Marvel Comics: 8/84; No. 2, 10/85; No. 3, 10/86 - No. 5, 1986 ($2.00)
1-5: Painted-c on all. 3,4-Baxter paper. 4-Bolton-c/a. 5-Bolton-a 3.50
NOTE: *Bissette a-4. Severin a-1, 3. Sienkiewicz a-1,2. Paul Smith a-2. Williamson a-2i.*

AMAZING-MAN COMICS (Formerly Motion Picture Funnies Weekly?)
(Also see Stars And Stripes Comics)
Centaur Publications: No. 5, Sept, 1939 - No. 26, Jan, 1942
5(#1)(Rare)-Origin/1st app. A-Man the Amazing Man by Bill Everett; The Cat-Man by Tarpe Mills (also #8), Mighty Man by Filchock, Minimidget & sidekick Ritty, & The Iron Skull by Burgos begins 1382 2764 4146 10,365 16,933 23,500
6-Origin The Amazing Man retold; The Shark begins; Ivy Menace by Tarpe Mills app.

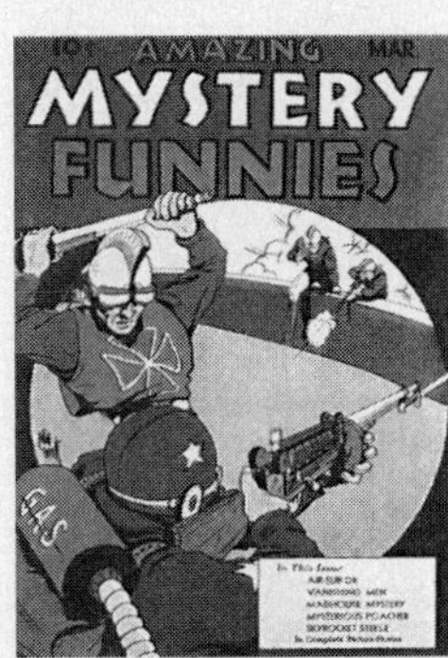

Amazing Mystery Funnies #12 © CEN

Amazing Spider-Man #33 © MAR

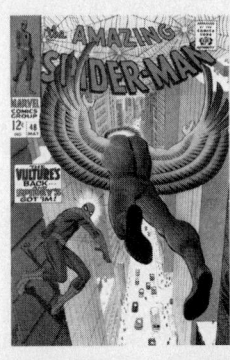

Amazing Spider-Man #48 © MAR

	GD 2.0	VG 4.0	FN 6.0	VF 8.0	VF/NM 9.0	NM- 9.2
	317	634	951	2061	3331	4600
7-Magician From Mars begins; ends #11	231	462	693	1444	2222	3000
8-Cat-Man dresses as woman	177	354	531	1106	1703	2300
9-Magician From Mars battles the 'Elemental Monster,' swiped into The Spectre in More Fun #54 & 55. Ties w/Marvel Mystery #4 for 1st Nazi War-c on a comic (2/40)	185	370	555	1156	1778	2400
10,11: 11-Zardi, the Eternal Man begins; ends #16; Amazing Man dons costume; last Everett issue	133	266	399	831	1278	1725
12,13	113	226	339	706	1091	1475
14-Reef Kinkaid, Rocke Wayburn (ends #20), & Dr. Hypno (ends #21) begin; no Zardi or Chuck Hardy	96	192	288	600	925	1250
15,17-20: 15-Zardi returns; no Rocke Wayburn. 17-Dr. Hypno returns; no Zardi	85	170	255	531	816	1100
16-Mighty Man's powers of super strength & ability to shrink & grow explained; Rocke Wayburn returns; no Dr. Hypno; Al Avison (a character) begins, ends #18 (a tribute to the famed artist)	86	172	258	538	832	1125
21-Origin Dash Dartwell (drug-use story); origin & only app. T.N.T.	86	172	258	538	832	1125
22-Dash Dartwell, the Human Meteor & The Voice app; last Iron Skull & The Shark; Silver Streak app. (classic-c)	123	246	369	769	1185	1600
23-Two Amazing Man stories; intro/origin Tommy the Amazing Kid; The Marksman only app.	77	154	231	481	741	1000
24-King of Darkness, Nightshade, & Blue Lady begin; end #26; 1st app. Super-Ann	77	154	231	481	741	1000
25,26 (Scarce): Meteor Martin by Wolverton in both; 26-Electric Ray app.	117	234	351	731	1128	1525

NOTE: ***Everett*** *a-5-11; c-5-11.* ***Gilman*** *a-14-20.* ***Giunta/Mirando*** *a-7-10.* ***Sam Glanzman*** *a-14-16, 18-21, 23.* ***Louis Glanzman*** *a-6, 9-11, 14-21; c-13-19, 21.* ***Robert Golden*** *a-9.* ***Gustavson*** *a-6; c-22, 23.* ***Lubbers*** *a-14-21.* ***Simon*** *a-10.* ***Frank Thomas*** *a-6, 9-11, 14, 15, 17-21.*

AMAZING MYSTERIES (Formerly Sub-Mariner Comics No. 31)
Marvel Comics (CCC): No. 32, May, 1949 - No. 35, Jan, 1950 (1st Marvel Horror Comic)

	GD	VG	FN	VF	VF/NM	NM-
32-The Witness app.	83	166	249	519	797	1075
33-Horror format	40	80	120	233	342	450
34,35: Changes to Crime. 34,35-Photo-c	21	42	63	118	169	220

AMAZING MYSTERY FUNNIES
Centaur Publications: Aug, 1938 - No. 24, Sept, 1940 (All 52 pgs.)

	GD	VG	FN	VF	VF/NM	NM-
V1#1-Everett-c(1st); Dick Kent Adv. story; Skyrocket Steele in the Year X on cover only	352	704	1056	2288	3694	5100
2-Everett 1st-a (Skyrocket Steele)	185	370	555	1156	1778	2400
3	94	188	282	588	907	1225
3(#4, 12/38)-nn on cover, #3 on inside; bondage-c	85	170	255	531	816	1100
V2#1-4,6: 2-Drug use story. 3-Air-Sub DX begins by Burgos. 4-Dan Hastings, Sand Hog begins (ends #5). 6-Last Skyrocket Steele	77	154	231	481	741	1000
5-Classic Everett-c	138	276	414	863	1332	1800
7 (Scarce)-Intro. The Fantom of the Fair & begins; Everett, Gustavson, Burgos-a	345	690	1035	2243	3622	5000
8-Origin & 1st app. Speed Centaur	142	284	426	888	1369	1850
9-11: 11-Self portrait and biog. of Everett; Jon Linton begins; early Robot cover (11/39)	77	154	231	481	741	1000
12 (Scarce)-1st Space Patrol; Wolverton-a (12/39); new costume Phantom of the Fair	192	384	576	1200	1850	2500
V3#1(#17, 1/40)-Intro. Bullet; Tippy Taylor serial begins, ends #24 (continued in The Arrow #2)	77	154	231	481	741	1000
18,20: 18-Fantom of the Fair by Gustavson	75	150	225	469	722	975
19,21-24: Space Patrol by Wolverton in all	92	184	276	575	888	1200

NOTE: ***Burgos*** *a-V2#3-9.* ***Eisner*** *a-V1#2, 3(2).* ***Everett*** *a-V1#2-4, V2#1, 3-6; c-V1#1-4,V2#3, 5, 18.* ***Filchock*** *a-V2#9.* ***Flessel*** *a-V2#6.* ***Guardineer*** *a-V1#4, V2#4-6;* ***Gustavson*** *a-V2#4, 5, 9-12, V3#1, 18, 19; c-V2#7, 9, 12, V3#1, 21, 22;* ***McWilliams*** *a-V2#9, 10.* ***TarpeMills*** *a-V2#2, 4-6, 9-12, V3#1.* ***Leo Morey****(Pulp artist) c-V2#10; text illo-V2#11.* ***FrankThomas*** *a-6-V2#11.* ***Webster*** *a-V2#4.*

AMAZING SAINTS
Logos International: 1974 (39¢)

	GD	VG	FN	VF	VF/NM	NM-
nn-True story of Phil Saint	2	4	6	8	10	12

AMAZING SCARLET SPIDER
Marvel Comics: Nov, 1995 - No. 2, Dec, 1995 ($1.95, limited series)

1,2: Replaces "Amazing Spider-Man" for two issues. 1-Venom/Carnage cameos. 2-Green Goblin & Joystick-c/app. 2.25

AMAZING SCREW-ON HEAD, THE
Dark Horse Comics (Maverick): May, 2002 ($2.99, one-shot)

1-Mike Mignola-s/a/c 3.00

AMAZING SPIDER-MAN, THE (See All Detergent Comics, Amazing Fantasy, America's Best TV Comics, Aurora, Deadly Foes of Spider-Man, Fireside Book Series, Giant-Size Spider-Man, Giant Size Super-Heroes Featuring..., Marvel Age..., Marvel Collectors Item Classics, Marvel Fanfare, Marvel Graphic Novel, Marvel Spec. Ed., Marvel Tales, Marvel Team-Up, Marvel Treasury Ed., Nothing Can Stop the Juggernaut, Official Marvel Index To..., Peter Parker..., Power Record Comics, Spectacular..., Spider-Man, Spider-Man Digest, Spider-Man Saga, Spider-Man 2099, Spider-Man Vs. Wolverine, Spidey Super Stories, Strange Tales Annual #2, Superman Vs. ..., Try-Out Winner Book, Ultimate Marvel Team-Up, Ultimate Spider-Man, Web of Spider- Man & Within Our Reach)

AMAZING SPIDER-MAN, THE
Marvel Comics Group: March, 1963 - No. 441, Nov, 1998

	GD	VG	FN	VF	VF/NM	NM-
1-Retells origin by Steve Ditko; 1st Fantastic Four x-over (ties with F.F. #12 as first Marvel x-over); intro. John Jameson & The Chameleon; Spider-Man's 2nd app.; Kirby/Ditko-c; Ditko-c/a #1-38	875	1750	2625	8750	20,625	32,500
1-Reprint from the Golden Record Comic set	14	28	42	97	149	200
With record (1966)	20	40	60	145	223	300
2-1st app. the Vulture & the Terrible Tinkerer	305	610	915	2790	4745	6700
3-1st app. Doc Octopus; 1st full-length story; Human Torch cameo; Spider-Man pin-up by Ditko	224	448	672	1960	3330	4700
4-Origin & 1st app. The Sandman (see Strange Tales #115 for 2nd app.); Intro. Betty Brant & Liz Allen	190	380	570	1663	2732	3800
5-Dr. Doom app.	160	320	480	1400	2300	3200
6-1st app. Lizard	153	306	459	1324	2162	3000
7,8,10: 7-Vs. The Vulture; 1st monthly issue. 8-Fantastic Four app. in back-up story by Kirby & Ditko. 10-1st app. Big Man & The Enforcers	100	200	300	850	1375	1900
9-Origin & 1st app. Electro (2/64)	106	212	318	1247	1636	2025
11,12: 11-1st app. Bennett Brant. 12-Doc Octopus unmasks Spider-Man-c/story	67	134	201	570	923	1275
13-1st app. Mysterio	92	184	276	782	1266	1750
14-(7/64)-1st app. The Green Goblin (c/story)(Norman Osborn); Hulk x-over	175	350	525	1531	2516	3500
15-1st app. Kraven the Hunter; 1st mention of Mary Jane Watson (not shown)	76	152	228	646	1048	1450
16-Spider-Man battles Daredevil (1st x-over 9/64); still in old yellow costume	58	116	174	493	797	1100
17-2nd app. Green Goblin (c/story); Human Torch x-over (also in #18 & #21)	72	144	216	612	994	1375
18-1st app. Ned Leeds who later becomes Hobgoblin; Fantastic Four cameo; 3rd app. Sandman	47	94	141	376	588	800
19-Sandman app.	41	82	123	305	478	650
20-Origin & 1st app. The Scorpion	54	108	162	459	742	1025
21-2nd app. The Beetle (see Strange Tales #123)	39	78	117	293	459	625
22-1st app. Princess Python	33	66	99	248	387	525
23-3rd app. The Green Goblin-c/story; Norman Osborn app.	45	90	135	360	568	775
24	31	62	93	228	352	475
25-(6/65)-1st brief app. Mary Jane Watson (face not shown); 1st app. Spencer Smythe; Norman Osborn app.	36	72	108	270	423	575
26-4th app. The Green Goblin-c/story; 1st app. Crime Master; dies in #27	39	78	117	293	457	620
27-5th app. The Green Goblin-c/story; Norman Osborn app.	36	72	108	270	423	575
28-Origin & 1st app. Molten Man (9/65, scarcer in high grade)	63	126	189	536	868	1200
29,30	25	50	75	181	278	375
31-1st app. Harry Osborn who later becomes 2nd Green Goblin, Gwen Stacy & Prof. Warren.	30	60	90	218	334	450
32-38: 34-4th app. Kraven the Hunter. 36-1st app. Looter. 37-Intro. Norman Osborn. 38-(7/66)-2nd brief app. Mary Jane Watson (face not shown); last Ditko issue	23	46	69	165	253	340
39-The Green Goblin-c/story; Green Goblin's i.d. revealed as Norman Osborn; Romita-a begins (8/66; see Daredevil #16 for 1st Romita-a on Spider-Man)	32	64	96	240	370	500
40-1st told origin The Green Goblin-c/story	39	78	117	293	459	625
41-1st app. Rhino	31	62	93	229	355	480
42-(11/66)-3rd app. Mary Jane Watson (cameo in last 2 panels); 1st time face is shown	20	40	60	141	216	290
43-49: 44,45-2nd & 3rd app. The Lizard. 46-Intro. Shocker. 47-M. J. Watson & Peter Parker 1st date. 47-Green Goblin cameo; Harry & Norman Osborn app. 47,49-5th & 6th app. Kraven the Hunter	15	30	45	107	164	220
50-1st app. Kingpin (7/67)	50	100	150	425	688	950
51-2nd app. Kingpin; Joe Robertson 1-panel cameo	22	44	66	155	238	320
52-58,60: 52-1st app. Joe Robertson & 3rd app. Kingpin. 56-1st app. Capt. George Stacy. 57,58-Ka-Zar app.	11	22	33	80	120	160
59-1st app. Brainwasher (alias Kingpin); 1st-c app. M. J. Watson	11	22	33	80	120	160
61-74: 67-1st app. Randy Robertson. 69-Kingpin-c. 69,70-Kingpin app. 73-1st app. Silvermane. 74-Last 12¢ issue	9	18	27	65	93	120

Amazing Spider-Man #90 © MAR

Amazing Spider-Man #129 © MAR

Amazing Spider-Man #330 © MAR

	GD 2.0	VG 4.0	FN 6.0	VF 8.0	VF/NM 9.0	NM- 9.2
75-83,87-89,91,92,95,99: 78,79-1st app. The Prowler. 83-1st app. Schemer & Vanessa (Kingpin's wife)	8	16	24	55	78	100
84-86,93: 84,85-Kingpin-c/story. 86-Re-intro & origin Black Widow in new costume. 93-1st app. Arthur Stacy	8	16	24	55	78	100
90-Death of Capt. Stacy	10	20	30	67	96	125
94-Origin retold	10	20	30	73	107	140
96-98-Green Goblin app. (97,98-Green Goblin-c); drug books not approved by CCA	11	22	33	75	110	145
100-Anniversary issue (9/71); Green Goblin cameo (2 pgs.)	17	34	51	121	186	250
101-1st app. Morbius the Living Vampire; Wizard cameo; last 15¢ issue (10/71)	17	34	51	121	186	250
101-Silver ink 2nd printing (9/92, $1.75)						2.25
102-Origin & 2nd app. Morbius (25¢, 52 pgs.)	11	22	33	79	117	155
103-118: 104,111-Kraven the Hunter-c/stories. 108-1st app. Sha-Shan. 109-Dr. Strange-c/story (6/72). 110-1st app. Gibbon. 113-1st app. Hammerhead. 116-118-reprints story from Spectacular Spider-Man Mag. in color with some changes	5	10	15	36	48	60
119,120-Spider-Man vs. Hulk (4 & 5/73)	8	16	24	55	78	100
121-Death of Gwen Stacy (6/73) (killed by Green Goblin) (reprinted in Marvel Tales #98 & 192)	19	38	57	134	205	275
122-Death of The Green Goblin-c/story (7/73) (reprinted in Marvel Tales #99 & 192)	20	40	60	141	216	290
123,126-128: 123-Cage app. 126-1st mention of Harry Osborn becoming Green Goblin	5	10	15	36	48	60
124-1st app. Man-Wolf (9/73)	6	12	18	43	59	75
125-Man-Wolf origin	6	12	18	38	52	65
129-1st app. The Punisher (2/74); 1st app. Jackal	31	62	93	233	364	495
130-133: 131-Last 20¢ issue	4	8	12	27	36	45
134-(7/74); 1st app. Tarantula; Harry Osborn discovers Spider-Man's ID; Punisher cameo	5	10	15	33	44	55
135-2nd full Punisher app. (8/74)	7	14	21	51	71	90
136-1st app. Harry Osborn Green Goblin in costume	8	16	24	53	74	95
137-Green Goblin-c/story (2nd Harry Osborn Goblin)	5	10	15	36	48	60
138-141: 139-1st Grizzly. 140-1st app. Glory Grant	3	7	10	21	28	35
142,143-Gwen Stacy clone cameos: 143-1st app. Cyclone	4	8	12	22	30	38
144-147: 144-Full app. of Gwen Stacy clone. 145,146-Gwen Stacy clone storyline continues. 147-Spider-Man learns Gwen Stacy is clone	4	8	12	22	30	38
148-Jackal revealed	4	8	12	27	36	45
149-Spider-Man clone story begins, clone dies (?); origin of Jackal	6	12	18	40	55	70
150-Spider-Man decides he is not the clone	4	8	12	25	33	42
151-Spider-Man disposes of clone body	4	8	12	25	33	42
152-160-(Regular 25¢ editions). 159-Last 25¢ issue(8/76)	3	6	9	18	23	28
155-159-(30¢-c variants, limited distribution)	4	8	12	24	32	42
161-Nightcrawler app. from X-Men; Punisher cameo; Wolverine & Colossus app.	3	7	10	21	28	35
162-Punisher, Nightcrawler app.; 1st Jigsaw	3	7	10	21	28	35
163-168,181-188: 167-1st app. Will O' The Wisp. 181-Origin retold; gives life history of Spidey; Punisher cameo in flashback (1 panel). 182-(7/78)-Peter's first proposal to Mary Jane, but she declines	2	4	6	14	18	22
169-173-(Regular 30¢ edition). 169-Clone story recapped. 171-Nova app.	2	4	6	14	18	22
169-173-(35¢-c variants, limited dist.)(6-10/77)	3	6	9	16	20	35
174,175-Punisher app.	3	6	9	16	20	25
176-180-Green Goblin app.	3	6	9	18	23	28
189,190-Byrne-a	3	6	9	16	20	24
191-193,195-199: 193-Peter & Mary Jane break up. 196-Faked death of Aunt May	2	4	6	11	14	18
NOTE: *Whitman 3-packs containing #192-194 exist.*						
194-1st app. Black Cat	4	8	12	24	32	40
200-Giant origin issue (1/80)	4	8	12	24	32	40
201,202-Punisher app.	2	4	6	11	14	18
203-205,207,208,210-219: 203-3rd app. Dazzler (4/80). 210-1st app. Madame Web. 212-1st app. Hydro Man; origin Sandman	2	4	6	8	10	12
206-Byrne-a	2	4	6	10	12	15
209-Origin & 1st app. Calypso (10/80)	2	4	6	12	16	20
220-237: 225-(2/82)-Foolkiller-c/story. 226,227-Black Cat returns. 236-Tarantula dies. 234-Free 16 pg. insert "Marvel Guide to Collecting Comics". 235-Origin Will-'O-The-Wisp	1	3	4	6	8	10
238-(3/83)-1st app. Hobgoblin (Ned Leeds); came with skin "Tattooz" decal. **NOTE:** The same decal appears in the more common Fantastic Four #252 which is being removed & placed in this issue as incentive to increase value (Value listed is with or without tattooz)	8	16	24	53	74	95
239-2nd app. Hobgoblin & 1st battle w/Spidey	4	8	12	29	40	50
240-243,246-248: 241-Origin The Vulture. 242-Mary Jane Watson cameo (last panel). 243-Reintro Mary Jane after 4 year absence	1	2	3	5	7	9
244-3rd app. Hobgoblin (cameo)	2	4	6	10	12	15
245-(10/83)-4th app. Hobgoblin (cameo); Lefty Donovan gains powers of Hobgoblin & battles Spider-Man	2	4	6	10	12	15
249-251: 3 part Hobgoblin/Spider-Man battle. 249-Retells origin & death of 1st Green Goblin. 251-Last old costume	2	4	6	10	13	16
252-Spider-Man dons new black costume (5/84); ties with Marvel Team-Up #141 & Spectacular Spider-Man #90 for 1st new costume in regular title (See Marvel Super-Heroes Secret Wars #8 for debut)	4	8	12	24	32	40
253-1st app. The Rose	2	4	6	8	10	12
254-258: 256-1st app. Puma. 257-Hobgoblin cameo; 2nd app. Puma; M.J. Watson reveals she knows Spidey's i.d. 258-Hobgoblin app.	1	2	3	5	7	9
259-Full Hobgoblin app.; Spidey back to old costume; origin Mary Jane Watson	2	4	6	9	11	14
260-Hobgoblin app.	1	3	4	6	8	11
261-Hobgoblin-c/story; painted-c by Vess	2	4	6	8	10	12
262-Spider-Man unmasked; photo-c	1	2	3	5	7	9
263,264,266-274,277-280,282,283: 274-Zarathos (The Spirit of Vengeance) app. 277-Vess back-up art. 279-Jack O'Lantern-c/story. 282-X-Factor x-over	1	2	3	4	5	7
265-1st app. Silver Sable (6/85)	2	4	6	10	13	16
265-Silver ink 2nd printing ($1.25)						2.25
275-($1.25, 52 pgs.)-Hobgoblin-c/story; origin-r by Ditko	2	4	6	12	16	20
276-Hobgoblin app.	1	3	4	6	8	10
281-Hobgoblin battles Jack O'Lantern	1	3	4	6	8	10
284,285: 284-Punisher cameo; Gang War story begins; Hobgoblin-c/story. 285-Punisher app.; minor Hobgoblin app.	1	3	4	6	8	10
286-288: 286-Hobgoblin-c & app. (minor). 287-Hobgoblin app. (minor). 288-Full Hobgoblin app.; last Gang War	1	3	4	6	8	10
289-(6/87, $1.25, 52 pgs.)-Hobgoblin's i.d. revealed as Ned Leeds; death of Ned Leeds; Macendale (Jack O'Lantern) becomes new Hobgoblin (1st app.)	3	6	9	16	20	24
290-292,295-297: 290-Peter proposes to Mary Jane. 292-She accepts; leads into wedding in Amazing Spider-Man Annual #21	1	2	3	4	5	7
293,294-Part 2 & 5 of Kraven story from Web of Spider-Man. 294-Death of Kraven	1	3	4	6	8	10
298-Todd McFarlane-c/a begins (3/88); 1st brief app. Eddie Brock who becomes Venom; (last pg.)	4	8	12	29	40	50
299-1st brief app. Venom with costume	3	6	9	18	24	30
300 ($1.50, 52 pgs.; 25th Anniversary)-1st full Venom app.; last black costume (5/88)	8.	16	24	53	74	95
301-305: 301 ($1.00 issues begin). 304-1st bi-weekly issue	2	4	6	10	13	16
306-311,313,314: 306-Swipes-c from Action #1	2	4	6	9	11	14
312-Hobgoblin battles Green Goblin	2	4	6	12	16	20
315-317-Venom app.	2	4	6	12	16	20
318-323,325: 319-Bi-weekly begins again	1	2	3	5	7	9
324-Sabretooth app.; McFarlane cover only	1	2	3	5	7	9
326,327,329: 327-Cosmic Spidey continues from Spectacular Spider-Man (no McFarlane-c/a)						5.00
328-Hulk x-over; last McFarlane issue	1	3	4	6	8	10
330,331-Punisher app. 331-Minor Venom app.						4.00
332,333-Venom-c/story	1	2	3	4	5	7
334-336,338-343: 341-Tarantula app.						4.00
337-Hobgoblin app.						4.00
344-1st app. Cletus Kasady (Carnage)	2	4	6	8	10	12
345-1st full app. Cletus Kasady; Venom cameo on last pg.	2	4	6	8	10	12
346,347-Venom app.	1	2	3	4	5	7
348,349,351-359: 348-Avengers x-over. 351,352-Nova of New Warriors app. 353-Darkhawk app.; brief Punisher app. 354-Punisher cameo & Nova, Night Thrasher (New Warriors), Darkhawk & Moon Knight app. 357,358-Punisher, Darkhawk, Moon Knight, Night Thrasher, Nova x-over. 358-3 part gatefold-c; last $1.00-c. 360-Carnage cameo						3.00
350-($1.50, 52pgs.)-Origin retold; Spidey vs. Dr. Doom; pin-ups; Uncle Ben app.						5.00
360-Carnage cameo						4.00
361-Intro Carnage (the Spawn of Venom); begin 3 part story; recap of how Spidey's alien costume became Venom	2	4	6	8	10	12
361-($1.25)-2nd printing; silver-c						2.50
362,363-Carnage & Venom-c/story	1	2	3	4	5	7

Amazing Spider-Man #435 © MAR

Amazing Spider-Man Annual #28 © MAR

Amazing Spider-Man V2#511 © MAR

GD VG FN VF VF/NM NM-
2.0 4.0 6.0 8.0 9.0 9.2

362-2nd printing 2.25

364,366-374,376-387: 364-The Shocker app. (old villain). 366-Peter's parents-c/story. 369-Harry Osborn back-up (Gr. Goblin II). 373-Venom back-up. 374-Venom-c/story. 376-Cardiac app. 378-Maximum Carnage part 3. 381,382-Hulk app. 383-The Jury app. 384-Venom/carnage app. 387-New costume Vulture 2.50

365-($3.95, 84 pgs.)-30th anniversary issue w/silver hologram on-c; Spidey/Venom/Carnage pull-out poster; contains 5 pg. preview of Spider-Man 2099 (1st app.); Spidey's origin retold; Lizard app.; reintro Peter's parents in Stan Lee 3 pg. text w/illo (story continues thru #370) 5.00

375-($3.95, 68 pgs.)-Holo-grafx foil-c; vs. Venom story; ties into Venom: Lethal Protector #1; Pat Olliffe-a. 5.00

388-($2.25, 68 pgs.)-Newsstand edition; Venom back-up & Cardiac & chance back-up 2.25

388-($2.95, 68 pgs.)-Collector's edition w/foil-c 3.00

389-396,398,399,401-420: 389-$1.50-c begins; bound-in trading card sheet; Green Goblin app. 394-Power & Responsibility Pt. 2. 396-Daredevil-c & app. 403-Carnage app. 406-1st New Doc Octopus. 407-Human Torch, Silver Sable, Sandman app. 409-Kaine, Rhino app. 410-Carnage app. 414-The Rose app. 415-Onslaught story; Spidey vs. Sentinels. 416-Epilogue to Onslaught; Garney-a(p); Williamson-a(i) 2.25

390-($2.95)-Collector's edition polybagged w/16 pg. insert of new animated Spidey TV show plus animation cel 3.00

394-($2.95, 48 pgs.)-Deluxe edition; flip book w/Birth of a Spider-Man Pt. 2; silver foil both-c; Power & Responsibility Pt. 2 3.00

397-($2.25)-Flip book w/Ultimate Spider-Man 2.25

400-($2.95)-Death of Aunt May 3.00

400-($3.95)-Death of Aunt May; embossed double-c 5.00

400-Collector's Edition; white-c 1 2 3 5 7 9

408-($2.95) Polybagged version with TV theme song cassette 8.00

421-424,426,428-433: 426-Begin $1.99-c. 432-Spiderhunt pt. 2 2.25

425-($2.99)-48 pgs., wraparound-c 3.00

427-($2.25) Return of Dr. Octopus; double gatefold-c 2.50

434-440: 434-Double-c with "Amazing Ricochet #1". 438-Daredevil app. 439-Avengers-c/app. 440-Byrne-s 2.25

441-Final issue; Byrne-s 4.00

#500-up (See Amazing Spider-Man Vol. 2; series resumed original numbering after Vol. 2 #58)

#(-1) Flashback issue (7/97, $1.95-c) 2.25

Annual 1 (1964, 72 pgs.)-Origin Spider-Man; 1st app. Sinister Six (Dr. Octopus, Electro, Kraven the Hunter, Mysterio, Sandman, Vulture) (new 41 pg. story); plus gallery of Spidey foes; early X-Men app. 82 164 246 697 1124 1550

Annual 2 (1965, 25¢, 72 pgs.)-Reprints from #1,2,5 plus new Doctor Strange story 34 68 102 255 403 550

Special 3 (11/66, 25¢, 72 pgs.)-New Avengers story & Hulk x-over; Doctor Octopus-r from #11,12; Romita-a 15 30 45 109 167 225

Special 4 (11/67, 25¢, 68 pgs.)-Spidey battles Human Torch (new 41 pg. story) 13 26 39 90 138 185

Special 5 (11/68, 25¢, 68 pgs.)-New 40 pg. Red Skull story; 1st app. Peter Parker's parents; last annual with new-a 12 24 36 86 131 175

Special 5-2nd printing (1994) 2 4 6 8 10 12

Special 6 (11/69, 25¢, 68 pgs.)-Reprints 41 pg. Sinister Six story from annual #1 plus 2 Kirby/Ditko stories (r) 6 12 18 38 52 65

Special 7 (12/70, 25¢, 68 pgs.)-All-r(#1,2) new Vulture-c 6 12 18 38 52 65

Special 8 (12/71)-All-r 6 12 18 38 52 65

King Size 9 ('73)-Reprints Spectacular Spider-Man (mag.) #2; 40 pg. Green Goblin-c/story (re-edited from 58 pgs.) 6 12 18 38 52 65

Annual 10 (1976)-Origin Human Fly (vs. Spidey); new-a begins 3 6 9 16 20 25

Annual 11-13 ('77-'79):12-Spidey vs. Hulk-r/#119,120. 13-New Byrne/Austin-a; Dr. Octopus x-over w/Spectacular S-M Ann. #1 2 4 6 10 12 15

Annual 14 (1980)-Miller-c/a(p); Dr. Strange app. 2 4 6 11 14 18

Annual 15 (1981)-Miller-c/a(p); Punisher app. 2 4 6 14 18 22

Annual 16-20:16 ('82)-Origin/1st app. new Capt. Marvel (female heroine). 17 ('83)-Kingpin app. 18 ('84)-Scorpion app.; JJJ weds. 19 ('85). 20 ('86)-Origin Iron Man of 2020 1 2 3 4 5 7

Annual 21 (1987)-Special wedding issue; newsstand & direct sale versions exist & are worth same 2 4 6 8 10 12

Annual 22 (1988, $1.75, 68 pgs.)-1st app. Speedball; Evolutionary War x-over; Daredevil app. 6.00

Annual 23 (1989, $2.00, 68 pgs.)-Atlantis Attacks; origin Spider-Man retold; She-Hulk app.; Byrne-c; Liefeld-a(p), 23 pgs. 4.00

Annual 24 (1990, $2.00, 68 pgs.)-Ant-Man app. 3.00

Annual 25 (1991, $2.00, 68 pgs.)-3 pg. origin recap; Iron Man app.; 1st Venom solo story; Ditko-a (6 pgs.) 5.00

Annual 26 (1992, $2.25, 68 pgs.)-New Warriors-c/story; Venom solo story cont'd in Spectacular Spider-Man Annual #12 4.00

Annual 27,28 ('93, '94, $2.95, 68 pgs.)-27-Bagged w/card; 1st app. Annex. 28-Carnage-c/story; Rhino & Cloak and Dagger back-ups 3.00

'96 Special-($2.95, 64 pgs.)-"Blast From The Past" 3.00

'97 Special-($2.99)-Wraparound-c,Sundown app. 3.00

Marvel Graphic Novel - Parallel Lives (3/89, $8.95) 2 4 6 8 10 12

Marvel Graphic Novel - Spirits of the Earth (1990, $18.95, HC) 3 6 9 18 23 28

Super Special 1 (4/95, $3.95)-Flip Book 4.00

...: Skating on Thin Ice 1(1990, $1.25, Canadian)-McFarlane-c; anti-drug issue; Electro app. 1 2 3 5 7 9

...: Skating on Thin Ice 1 (2/93, $1.50, American) 4.00

...: Double Trouble 2 (1990, $1.25, Canadian) 6.00

...: Double Trouble 2 (2/93, $1.50, American) 3.00

...: Hit and Run 3 (1990, $1.25, Canadian)-Ghost Rider-c/story 1 2 3 5 7 9

...: Hit and Run 3 (2/93. $1.50, American) 3.00

... : Carnage (6/93, $6.95)-r/ASM #344,345,359-363 1 2 3 4 5 7

...: Chaos in Calgary 4 (Canadian; part of 5 part series)-Turbine,Night Rider, Frightful app. 2 4 6 9 11 14

...: Chaos in Calgary 4 (2/93, $1.50, American) 3.00

...: Deadball 5 (1993, $1.60, Canadian)-Green Goblin-c/story; features Montreal Expos 2 4 6 11 14 18

Note: Prices listed above are for English Canadian editions. French editions are worth double.

....: Soul of the Hunter nn (8/92, $5.95, 52 pgs.)-Zeck-c/a(p) 6.00

Wizard #1 Ace Edition ($13.99) r/#1 w/ new Ramos acetate-c 14.00

Wizard #129 Ace Edition ($13.99) r/#129 w/ new Ramos acetate-c 14.00

NOTE: ***Austin*** *a(i)-248, 335, 337, Annual 13; c(i)-188, 241, 242, 248, 331, 334, 343, Annual 25.* ***J. Buscema*** *a(p)-72, 73, 76-81, 84, 85.* ***Byrne*** *a-189p, 190p, 206p, Annual 3r, 6r, 7r, 13p; c-189p, 268, 296, Annual 12.* ***Ditko*** *a-1-38, Annual 1, Special 3(r), 2, 24(2); c-1i, 2-38.* ***Guice*** *c/a-Annual 18i.* ***Gil Kane*** *a(p)-89-105, 120-124, 150, Annual 10, 12i, 24p; c-90p, 96, 98, 99, 101-105p, 129p, 131p, 132p, 137-140p, 143p, 148p, 149p, 151p, 153p, 160p, 161p, Annual 10p, 24.* ***Kirby*** *a-8.* ***Erik Larsen*** *a-324, 327, 329-350; c-327, 329-350, 354i, Annual 25.* ***McFarlane*** *a-298p, 299p, 300-303, 304-323p, 325p, 328; c-298-325, 328.* ***Miller*** *c-218, 219.* ***Mooney*** *a-65i, 67-82i, 84-88i, 173i, 178i, 189i, 190i, 192i, 193i, 196-202i, 207i, 211-219i, 221i, 222i, 226i, 227i, 229-233i, Annual 11i, 17i.* ***Nasser*** *c-228p.* ***Nebres*** *a-Annual 24i.* ***Russell*** *c-357i.* ***Simonson*** *c-222, 337i.* ***Starlin*** *a-113i, 114i, 187p.* ***Williamson*** *a-365i.*

AMAZING SPIDER-MAN (Volume 2) (Some issues reprinted in "Spider-Man, Best Of" hardcovers)
Marvel Comics: Jan, 1999 - Present ($2.99/$1.99/$2.25)

1-($2.99)-Byrne-a 6.00

1-($6.95) Dynamic Forces variant-c by the Romitas 1 3 4 6 8 10

2-($1.99) Two covers -by John Byrne and Andy Kubert 4.00

3-11: 4-Fantastic Four app. 5-Spider-Woman-c 2.25

12-($2.99) Sinister Six return (cont. in Peter Parker #12) 3.00

13-17: 13-Mary Jane's plane explodes 2.25

18,19,21-24,26-28: 18-Begin $2.25-c. 19-Venom-c. 24-Maximum Security 2.25

20-($2.99, 100 pgs.) Spider-Slayer issue; new story and reprints 3.00

25-($2.99) Regular cover; Peter Parker becomes the Green Goblin 3.00

25-($3.99) Holo-foil enhanced cover 4.00

29-Peter is reunited with Mary Jane 2.25

30-Straczynski-s/Campbell-c begin; intro. Ezekiel 6.00

31-35: Battles Morlun 4.00

36-Black cover; aftermath of the Sept. 11 tragedy in New York 6.00

37-49: 39-'Nuff Said issue 42-Dr. Strange app. 43-45-Doctor Octopus app. 46-48-Cho-c 2.25

50-Peter and MJ reunite; Captain America & Dr. Doom app.; Campbell-c 2.50

51-58: 51,52-Campbell-c. 55,56-Avery scripts. 57,58-Avengers, FF, Cyclops app. 2.25

(After #58 [Nov, 2003] numbering reverted back to original Vol. 1 with #500, Dec, 2003)

500-($3.50) J. Scott Campbell-c; Romita Jr. & Sr.-a; Uncle Ben app. 3.50

501-514: 501-Harris-c. 503-504-Loki app. 506-508-Ezekiel app. 509-514-Sins Past; intro. Gabriel and Sarah Osborn; Deodato-a 2.25

1999, 2000 Annual (6/99, '00, $3.50) 1999-Buscema-a 3.50

2001 Annual ($2.99) Follows Peter Parker: S-M #29; last Mackie-s 3.00

Collected Edition #30-32 ($3.95) reprints #30-32 w/cover #30 4.00

... 500 Covers HC (2004, $49.99) reprints covers for #1-500 & Annuals; yearly re-caps 50.00

...Vol. 1: Coming Home (2001, $15.95) r/#30-35; J. Scott Campbell-c 16.00

...Vol. 2: Revelations (2002, $8.99) r/#36-39; Kaare Andrews-c 9.00

...Vol. 3: Until the Stars Turn Cold (2002, $12.99) r/#40-45; Romita Jr.-c 13.00

...Vol. 4: The Life and Death of Spiders (2003, $11.99) r/#46-50; Campbell-c 12.00

...Vol. 5: Unintended Consequences (2003, $12.99) r/#51-56; Dodson-c 13.00

...Vol. 6: Happy Birthday (2003, $12.99) r/#57,58,500-502 13.00

...Vol. 7: The Book of Ezekiel (2004, $12.99) r/#503-508; Romita Jr.-c 13.00

AMAZING WILLIE MAYS, THE
Famous Funnies Publ.: No date (Sept, 1954)

nn 75 150 225 469 722 975

AMAZING WORLD OF DC COMICS
DC Comics: Jul, 1974 - No. 17, 1978 ($1.50, B&W, mail-order DC Pro-zine)

1-Kubert interview; unpublished Kirby-a; Infantino-c 7 14 21 50 68 85

Amazing World of DC Comics #3 © DC

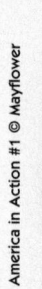

America in Action #1 © Mayflower

America's Best Comics #12 © Nedor

GD VG FN VF VF/NM NM-
2.0 4.0 6.0 8.0 9.0 9.2

2-4: 3-Julie Schwartz profile. 4-Batman; Robinson-c 5 10 15 33 44 55
5-Sheldon Mayer 4 8 12 27 36 45
6,8,13: 6-Joe Orlando; EC-r; Wrightson pin-up. 8-Infantino; Batman-r from Pop Tart giveaway. 13-Humor; Aragonés-c; Wood/Ditko-a; photos from serials of Superman, Batman, Captain Marvel 3 6 9 19 25 32
7,10-12: 7-Superman; r/1955 Pep comic giveaway. 10-Behind the scenes at DC; Showcase article. 11-Super-Villains; unpubl. Secret Society of S.V. story. 12-Legion; Grell-c/interview; 3 7 10 21 28 35
9-Legion of Super-Heroes; lengthy bios and history; Cockrum-c 8 16 24 53 74 95
14-Justice League 4 8 12 22 30 38
15-Wonder Woman; Nasser-c 4 8 12 28 38 48
16-Golden Age heroes 4 8 12 27 36 45
17-Shazam; G.A., 70s, TV and Fawcett heroes 4 8 12 22 30 38
Special 1 (Digest size) 3 6 9 19 25 32

AMAZING WORLD OF SUPERMAN (See Superman)

AMAZING X-MEN
Marvel Comics: Mar, 1995 - No. 4, July, 1995 ($1.95, limited series)
1-Age of Apocalypse; Andy Kubert-c/a 3.50
2-4 2.50

AMAZON
Comico: Mar, 1989 - No. 3, May, 1989 ($1.95, limited series)
1-3: Ecological theme 2.25

AMAZON (Also see Marvel Versus DC #3 & DC Versus Marvel #4)
DC Comics (Amalgam): Apr, 1996 ($1.95, one-shot)
1-John Byrne-c/a/scripts 2.25

AMAZON ATTACK 3-D
The 3-D Zone: Sept, 1990 ($3.95, 28 pgs.)
1-Chaykin-a 6.00

AMAZON WOMAN (1st Series)
FantaCo: Summer, 1994 - No. 2, Fall, 1994 ($2.95, B&W, limited series, mature)
1,2: Tom Simonton-c/a/scripts 3.00

AMAZON WOMAN (2nd Series)
FantaCo: Feb, 1996 - No. 4, May, 1996 ($2.95, B&W, limited series, mature)
1-4: Tom Simonton-a/scripts 3.00
...: Invaders of Terror ('96, $5.95) Simonton-a/s 6.00

AMBUSH (See Zane Grey, Four Color 314)

AMBUSH BUG (Also see Son of...)
DC Comics: June, 1985 - No. 4, Sept, 1985 (75¢, limited series)
1-4: Giffen-c/a in all 3.00
Nothing Special 1 (9/92, $2.50, 68pg.)-Giffen-c/a 3.00
Stocking Stuffer (2/86, $1.25)-Giffen-c/a 3.00

AMERICA AT WAR - THE BEST OF DC WAR COMICS (See Fireside Book Series)

AMERICA IN ACTION
Dell (Imp. Publ. Co.)/ Mayflower House Publ.: 1942; Winter, 1945 (36 pgs.)
1942-Dell-(68 pgs.) 19 38 57 107 154 200
1-(1945)-Has 3 adaptations from American history; Kiefer, Schrotter & Webb-a 13 26 39 74 102 130

AMERICAN, THE
Dark Horse Comics: July, 1987 - No. 8, 1989 ($1.50/$1.75, B&W)
1-8: ($1.50) 2.25
Collection ($5.95, B&W)-Reprints 6.00
Special 1 (1990, $2.25, B&W) 2.25

AMERICAN AIR FORCES, THE (See A-1 Comics)
William H. Wise(Flying Cadet Publ. Co./Hasan(No.1)/Life's Romances/ Magazine Ent. No. 5 on): Sept-Oct, 1944-No. 4, 1945; No. 5, 1951-No. 12, 1954
1-Article by Zack Mosley, creator of Smilin' Jack; Jap war-c 19 38 57 107 154 200
2-Classic-Jap war-c 28 56 84 158 229 300
3,4-Jap war-c 11 22 33 64 87 110
NOTE: *All part comic, part magazine. Art by* **Whitney, Chas. Quinlan, H. C. Kiefer,** *and* **Tony Dipreta.**
5(A-1 45)(Formerly Jet Powers), 6(A-1 54), 7(A-1 58), 8(A-1 65), 9(A-1 67), 10(A-1 74), 11(A-1 79), 12(A-1 91) 8 16 24 43 54 65
NOTE: **Powell** *c/a-5-12.*

AMERICAN CENTURY
DC Comics (Vertigo): May, 2001 - No. 27, Oct, 2003 ($2.50/$2.75)
1-Chaykin-s/painted-c; Tischman-a 4.00
2-27: 5-New story arc begins. 10-16,22-27-Orbik-c. 17-21-Silke-c. 18-$2.75-c begins 2.75
Hollywood Babylon (2002, $12.95, TPB) r/#5-9; w/sketch-to-art pages 13.00
Scars & Stripes (2001, $8.95, TPB) r/#1-4; Tischman intro. 9.00

AMERICAN FLAGG! (See First Comics Graphic Novel 3,9,12,21 & Howard Chaykin's..)
First Comics: Oct, 1983 - No. 50, Mar, 1988
1,21-27: 1-Chaykin-c/a begins. 21-27-Alan Moore scripts 4.00
2-20,28-49: 31-Origin Bob Violence 3.00
50-Last issue 4.00
Special 1 (11/86)-Introduces Chaykin's Time² 4.00

AMERICAN FREAK: A TALE OF THE UN-MEN
DC Comics (Vertigo): Feb, 1994 - No. 5, Jun, 1994 ($1.95, mini-series, mature)
1-5 2.25

AMERICAN GRAPHICS
Henry Stewart: No. 1, 1954; No. 2, 1957 (25¢)
1-The Maid of the Mist, The Last of the Eries (Indian Legends of Niagara) (sold at Niagara Falls) 11 22 33 62 84 105
2-Victory at Niagara & Laura Secord (Heroine of the War of 1812) 8 16 24 40 50 60

AMERICAN INDIAN, THE (See Picture Progress)

AMERICAN LIBRARY
David McKay Publ.: 1943 - No. 6, 1944 (15¢, 68 pgs., B&W, text & pictures)
nn (#1)-Thirty Seconds Over Tokyo (movie) 38 76 114 219 320 420
nn (#2)-Guadalcanal Diary; painted-c (only 10¢) 28 56 84 158 229 300
3-6: 3-Look to the Mountain. 4-Case of the Crooked Candle (Perry Mason). 5-Duel in the Sun. 6-Wingate's Raiders 15 30 45 83 117 150

AMERICAN: LOST IN AMERICA, THE
Dark Horse Comics: July, 1992 - No. 4, Oct, 1992 ($2.50, limited series)
1-4: 1-Dorman painted-c. 2-Phillips painted-c. 3-Mignola-c. 4-Jim Lee-c 2.50

AMERICAN SPLENDOR: (Series of titles)
Dark Horse Comics: Aug, 1996 - Present (B&W, all one-shots)
--**COMIC-CON COMICS** (8/96) 1-H. Pekar script. --**MUSIC COMICS** (11/97) nn-H. Pekar-s/ Sacco-a; r/Village Voice jazz strips. --**ODDS AND ENDS** (12/97) 1-Pekar-s. --**ON THE JOB** (5/97) 1-Pekar-s. --**A STEP OUT OF THE NEST** (8/94) 1-Pekar-s. --**TERMINAL** (9/99) 1-Pekar-s. --**TRANSATLANTIC** (7/98) 1-"American Splendour" on cover; Pekar-s 3.00
--**A PORTRAIT OF THE AUTHOR IN HIS DECLINING YEARS** (4/01, $3.99) 1-Photo-c. --**BEDTIME STORIES** (6/00, $3.95) 4.00

AMERICAN SPLENDOR: UNSUNG HERO
Dark Horse Comics: Aug, 2002 - No. 3, Oct, 2002 ($3.99, B&W, limited series)
1-3-Pekar script/Collier-a; biography of Robert McNeill 4.00
TPB (8/03, $11.95) r/#1-3 12.00

AMERICAN SPLENDOR: WINDFALL
Dark Horse Comics: Sept, 1995 - No. 2, Oct,1995 ($3.95, B&W, limited series)
1,2-Pekar script 4.00

AMERICAN TAIL: FIEVEL GOES WEST, AN
Marvel Comics: Early Jan, 1992 - No. 3, Early Feb, 1992 ($1.00, limited series)
1-3-Adapts Universal animated movie; Wildman-a 3.00
1-($2.95-c, 69 pgs.) Deluxe squarebound edition 5.00

AMERICA'S BEST COMICS
Nedor/Better/Standard Publications: Feb, 1942; No. 2, Sept, 1942 - No. 31, July, 1949 (New logo with #9)
1-The Woman in Red, Black Terror, Captain Future, Doc Strange, The Liberator, & Don Davis, Secret Ace begin 269 538 807 1681 2591 3500
2-Origin The American Eagle; The Woman in Red ends 100 200 300 625 963 1300
3-Pyroman begins (11/42, 1st app.; also see Startling Comics #18, 12/42) 75 150 225 469 722 975
4-6: 5-Last Capt. Future (not in #4); Lone Eagle app. 6-American Crusader app. 58 116 174 363 562 760
7-Hitler, Mussolini & Hirohito-c 100 200 300 625 963 1300
8-Last Liberator 57 114 171 356 548 740
9-The Fighting Yank begins; The Ghost app. 65 130 195 406 628 850
10,12-17,19-21: 10-Flag-c. 14-American Eagle ends. 21-Infinity-c. 54 108 162 329 502 675
11-Hirohito & Tojo-c. (10/44) 69 138 207 431 666 900
18-Classic-c 67 134 201 419 647 875
22-Capt. Future app. 47 94 141 287 436 585

America's Greatest Comics #3 © FAW

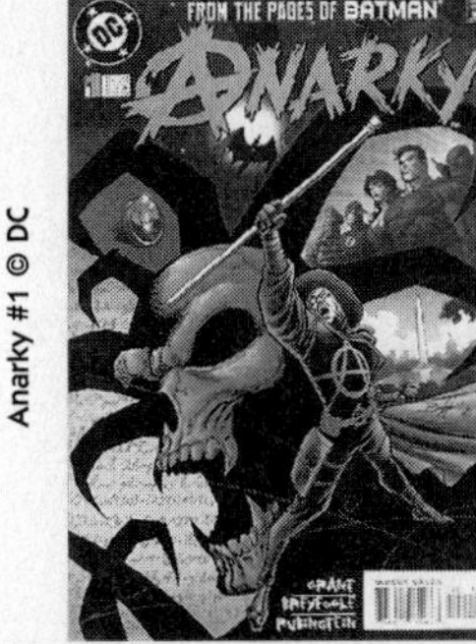

Anarky #1 © DC

A-Next #2 © MAR

GD VG FN VF VF/NM NM-
2.0 4.0 6.0 8.0 9.0 9.2

23-Miss Masque begins; last Doc Strange 55 110 165 340 520 700
24-Miss Masque bondage-c 54 108 162 329 502 675
25-Last Fighting Yank; Sea Eagle app. 40 80 120 240 363 485
26-31: 26-The Phantom Detective & The Silver Knight app.; Frazetta text illo & some panels in Miss Masque. 27,28-Commando Cubs. 27-Doc Strange. 28-Tuska Black Terror.
29-Last Pyroman 40 80 120 236 351 465

NOTE: *American Eagle not in 3, 8, 9, 13. Fighting Yank not in 10, 12. Liberator not in 2, 6, 7. Pyroman not in 9, 11, 14-16, 23, 25-27.* ***Schomburg (Xela)*** *c-5, 7-31. Bondage c-18, 24.*

AMERICA'S BEST COMICS
America's Best Comics: 1999 - Present

Preview (1999, Wizard magazine supplement) - Previews Tom Strong, Top Ten, Promethea, Tomorrow Stories 2.25
Sketchbook (2002, $5.95, square-bound)-Design sketches by Sprouse, Ross, Adams, Nowlan, Ha and others 6.00
Special 1 (2/01, $6.95)-Short stories of Alan Moore's characters; art by various; Ross-c 7.00
TPB (2004, $17.95) Reprints short stories and sketch pages from ABC titles 18.00

AMERICA'S BEST TV COMICS (TV)
American Broadcasting Co. (Prod. by Marvel Comics): 1967 (25¢, 68 pgs.)

1-Spider-Man, Fantastic Four (by Kirby/Ayers), Casper, King Kong, George of the Jungle, Journey to the Center of the Earth stories (promotes new TV cartoon show) 15 30 45 107 164 220

AMERICA'S BIGGEST COMICS BOOK
William H. Wise: 1944 (196 pgs., one-shot)

1-The Grim Reaper, The Silver Knight, Zudo, the Jungle Boy, Commando Cubs, Thunderhoof app. 40 80 120 240 363 485

AMERICA'S FUNNIEST COMICS
William H. Wise: 1944 - No. 2, 1944 (15¢, 80 pgs.)

nn(#1), 2 31 62 93 178 259 340

AMERICA'S GREATEST COMICS
Fawcett Publications: May?, 1941 - No. 8, Summer, 1943 (15¢, 100 pgs., soft cardboard-c)

1-Bulletman, Spy Smasher, Capt. Marvel, Minute Man & Mr. Scarlet begin; Classic Mac Raboy-c. 1st time that Fawcett's major super-heroes appear together as a group on a cover.
Fawcett's 1st squarebound comic 331 662 993 2152 3476 4800
2 146 292 438 913 1407 1900
3 106 212 318 663 1019 1375
4,5: 4-Commando Yank begins; Golden Arrow, Ibis the Invincible & Spy Smasher cameo in Captain Marvel 77 154 231 481 741 1000
6,7: 7-Balbo the Boy Magician app.; Captain Marvel, Bulletman cameo in Mr. Scarlet 71 142 213 444 685 925
8-Capt. Marvel Jr. & Golden Arrow app.; Spy Smasher x-over in Capt. Midnight; no Minute Man or Commando Yank 71 142 213 444 685 925

AMERICA'S SWEETHEART SUNNY (See Sunny, ...)

AMERICA VS. THE JUSTICE SOCIETY
DC Comics: Jan, 1985 - No. 4, Apr, 1985 ($1.00, limited series)

1-Double size; Alcala-a(i) in all 1 2 3 5 7 9
2-4: 3,4-Spectre cameo 1 2 3 4 5 7

AMERICOMICS
Americomics: April, 1983 - No. 6, Mar, 1984 ($2.00, Baxter paper/slick paper)

1-Intro/origin The Shade; Intro. The Slayer, Captain Freedom and The Liberty Corps; Perez-c 5.00
1,2-2nd printings ($2.00) 2.25
2-6: 2-Messenger app. & 1st app. Tara on Jungle Island. 3-New & old Blue Beetle battle. 4-Origin Dragonfly & Shade. 5-Origin Commando D. 6-Origin the Scarlet Scorpion 3.00
Special 1 (8/83, $2.00)-Sentinels of Justice (Blue Beetle, Captain Atom, Nightshade & The Question) 4.50

AMETHYST
DC Comics: Jan, 1985 - No. 16, Aug, 1986 (75¢)

1-16: 8-Fire Jade's i.d. revealed 2.25
Special 1 (10/86, $1.25), 1-4 (11/87 - 2/88)(Limited series) 2.25

AMETHYST, PRINCESS OF GEMWORLD (See Legion of Super-Heroes #298)
DC Comics: May, 1983 - No. 12, Apr, 1984 (Maxi-series)

1-(60¢) 2.25
1,2-(75¢): tested in Austin & Kansas City 3 6 9 16 20 25
2-12, Annual 1(9/84): 5-11-Pérez-c(p) 2.25

AMY RACECAR COLOR SPECIAL (See Stray Bullets)
El Capitán Books: July, 1997; Oct, 1999 ($2.95/$3.50)

1,2-David Lapham-a/scripts. 2-($3.50) 3.50

ANARCHO DICTATOR OF DEATH (See Comics Novel)

ANARKY (See Batman titles)
DC Comics: May, 1997 - No. 4, Aug, 1997 ($2.50, limited series)

1 3.50
2-4 2.50

ANARKY (See Batman titles)
DC Comics: May, 1999 - No. 8, Dec, 1999 ($2.50)

1-8: 1-JLA app.; Grant-s/Breyfogle-a. 3-Green Lantern app. 7-Day of Judgment; Haunted Tank app. 8-Joker-c/app. 2.50

ANCHORS ANDREWS (The Saltwater Daffy)
St. John Publishing Co.: Jan, 1953 - No. 4, July, 1953 (Anchors the Saltwater... No. 4)

1-Canteen Kate by Matt Baker (9 pgs.) 21 42 63 118 169 220
2-4 8 16 24 43 54 65

ANCIENT JOE
Dark Horse Comics: Oct, 2001 - No. 3, Dec, 2001 ($3.50, B&W, limited series)

1-3-C. Scott Morse-s/a 3.50

ANDY & WOODY (See March of Comics No. 40, 55, 76)

ANDY BURNETT (TV, Disney)
Dell Publishing Co.: Dec, 1957

Four Color 865-Photo-c 10 20 30 72 104 135

ANDY COMICS (Formerly Scream Comics; becomes Ernie Comics)
Current Publications (Ace Magazines): No. 20, June, 1948-No. 21, Aug, 1948

20,21: Archie-type comic 8 16 24 43 54 65

ANDY DEVINE WESTERN
Fawcett Publications: Dec, 1950 - No. 2, 1951

1 60 120 180 375 575 775
2 44 88 132 268 409 550

ANDY GRIFFITH SHOW, THE (TV)(1st show aired 10/3/60)
Dell Publishing Co.: #1252, Jan-Mar, 1962; #1341, Apr-Jun, 1962

Four Color 1252(#1) 38 76 114 285 443 600
Four Color 1341-Photo-c 35 70 105 263 412 560

ANDY HARDY COMICS (See Movie Comics #3 by Fiction House)
Dell Publishing Co.: April, 1952 - No. 6, Sept-Nov, 1954

Four Color 389(#1) 5 10 15 36 48 60
Four Color 447,480,515, #5,#6 4 8 12 24 32 40

ANDY PANDA (Also see Crackajack Funnies #39, The Funnies, New Funnies & Walter Lantz...)
Dell Publishing Co.: 1943 - No. 56, Nov-Jan, 1961-62 (Walter Lantz)

Four Color 25(#1, 1943) 54 108 162 405 628 850
Four Color 54(1944) 31 62 93 228 352 475
Four Color 85(1945) 18 36 54 126 193 260
Four Color 130(1946),154,198 12 24 36 84 127 170
Four Color 216,240,258,280,297 9 18 27 63 89 115
Four Color 326,345,358 7 14 21 46 63 80
Four Color 383,409 5 10 15 36 48 60
16(11-1/52-53) - 30 4 8 12 24 32 40
31-56 3 6 9 18 23 28

(See March of Comics #5, 22, 79, & Super Book #4, 15, 27.)

A-NEXT (See Avengers)
Marvel Comics: Oct, 1998 - No. 12, Sept, 1999 ($1.99)

1-Next generation of Avengers; Frenz-a 3.00
2-12: 2-Two covers. 3-Defenders app. 2.25

ANGEL
Dell Publishing Co.: Aug, 1954 - No. 16, Nov-Jan, 1958-59

Four Color 576(#1, 8/54) 4 8 12 24 32 40
2(5-7/55) - 16 3 6 9 16 20 25

ANGEL (TV) (Also see Buffy the Vampire Slayer)
Dark Horse Comics: Nov, 1999 - No. 17, Apr, 2001 ($2.95/$2.99)

1-17: 1-3,5-7,10-14-Zanier-a. 1-4,7,10-Matsuda & photo-c. 16-Buffy-c/app. 3.00
...: Earthly Possessions TPB (4/01, $9.95) r/#5-7, photo-c 10.00
...: Surrogates TPB (12/00, $9.95) r/#1-3; photo-c 10.00

ANGEL (Buffy the Vampire Slayer)
Dark Horse Comics: Sept, 2001 - No. 4, May, 2002 ($2.99, limited series)

1-4-Joss Whedon & Matthews-s/Rubi-a; photo-c and Rubi-c on each 3.00

ANGELA

Angel and the Ape (2nd) #1 © DC

Anima #10 © DC

Animal Man #13 © DC

Image Comics (Todd McFarlane Prod.): Dec, 1994 - No. 3, Feb, 1995 ($2.95, lim. series)

	GD 2.0	VG 4.0	FN 6.0	VF 8.0	VF/NM 9.0	NM- 9.2
1-Gaiman scripts & Capullo-c/a in all; Spawn app.	1	2	3	5	6	8
2						6.00
3						5.00
Special Edition (1995)-Pirate Spawn-c	3	6	9	16	20	25
Special Edition (1995)-Angela-c	3	6	9	16	20	25
TPB ($9.95, 1995) reprints #1-3 & Special Ed. w/additional pin-ups						10.00

ANGELA/GLORY: RAGE OF ANGELS (See Glory/Angela: Rage of Angels)
Image Comics (Todd McFarlane Productions): Mar, 1996 ($2.50, one-shot)

	GD 2.0	VG 4.0	FN 6.0	VF 8.0	VF/NM 9.0	NM- 9.2
1-Liefeld-c/Cruz-a(p); Darkchylde preview flip book						4.00
1-Variant-c						4.00

ANGEL AND THE APE (Meet Angel No. 7) (See Limited Collector's Edition C-34 & Showcase No. 77)
National Periodical Publications: Nov-Dec, 1968 - No. 6, Sept-Oct, 1969

	GD 2.0	VG 4.0	FN 6.0	VF 8.0	VF/NM 9.0	NM- 9.2
1-(11-12/68)-Not Wood-a	5	10	15	36	48	60
2-5-Wood inks in all. 4-Last 12¢ issue	4	8	12	22	30	38
6-Wood inks	4	8	12	27	36	45

ANGEL AND THE APE (2nd Series)
DC Comics: Mar, 1991 - No. 4, June, 1991 ($1.00, limited series)

	GD 2.0	VG 4.0	FN 6.0	VF 8.0	VF/NM 9.0	NM- 9.2
1-4						3.00

ANGEL AND THE APE (3rd Series)
DC Comics(Vertigo): Oct, 2001 - No. 4, Jan 2002 ($2.95, limited series)

	GD 2.0	VG 4.0	FN 6.0	VF 8.0	VF/NM 9.0	NM- 9.2
1-4-Chaykin & Tischman-s/Bond-a/Art Adams-c						3.00

ANGEL LOVE
DC Comics: Aug, 1986 - No. 8, Mar, 1987 (75¢, limited series)

	GD 2.0	VG 4.0	FN 6.0	VF 8.0	VF/NM 9.0	NM- 9.2
1-8, Special 1 (1987, $1.25, 52 pgs.)						2.25

ANGEL OF LIGHT, THE (See The Crusaders)

ANGELTOWN
DC Comics (Vertigo): Jan, 2005 - No. 5 ($2.95, limited series)

	GD 2.0	VG 4.0	FN 6.0	VF 8.0	VF/NM 9.0	NM- 9.2
1-Gary Phillips-s/Shawn Martinbrough-a						3.00

ANGRY CHRIST COMIX (See Cry For Dawn)

ANIMA
DC Comics: Mar, 1994 - No. 15, July, 1995 ($1.75/$1.95/$2.25)

	GD 2.0	VG 4.0	FN 6.0	VF 8.0	VF/NM 9.0	NM- 9.2
1-7,0,8-15: 7-(9/94)-Begin $1.95-c; Zero Hour x-over						2.50

ANIMAL ADVENTURES
Timor Publications/Accepted Publ. (reprints): Dec, 1953 - No. 3, May?, 1954

	GD 2.0	VG 4.0	FN 6.0	VF 8.0	VF/NM 9.0	NM- 9.2
1-Funny animal	8	16	24	40	50	60
2,3: 2-Featuring Soopermutt (2/54)	6	12	18	28	34	40
1-3 (reprints, nd)	3	6	8	11	13	15

ANIMAL ANTICS (Movietown... No. 24 on)
National Periodical Publ: Mar-Apr, 1946 - No. 23, Nov-Dec, 1949 (All 52 pgs.?)

	GD 2.0	VG 4.0	FN 6.0	VF 8.0	VF/NM 9.0	NM- 9.2
1-Raccoon Kids begins by Otto Feuer; many-c by Grossman; Seaman Sy Wheeler by Kelly in some issues; Grossman-a in most issues	44	88	132	268	409	550
2	26	52	78	147	211	275
3-10: 10-Post-c/a	16	32	48	89	127	165
11-23: 14,15,18,19-Post-a	11	22	33	64	87	110

ANIMAL COMICS
Dell Publishing Co.: Dec-Jan, 1941-42 - No. 30, Dec-Jan, 1947-48

	GD 2.0	VG 4.0	FN 6.0	VF 8.0	VF/NM 9.0	NM- 9.2
1-1st Pogo app. by Walt Kelly (Dan Noonan art in most issues)	90	180	270	630	952	1275
2-Uncle Wiggily begins	45	90	135	315	475	635
3,5	33	66	99	231	348	465
4,6,7-No Pogo	18	36	54	129	197	265
8-10	22	44	66	160	245	330
11-15	14	28	42	97	149	200
16-20	10	20	30	70	100	130
21-30: 24-30- "Jigger" by John Stanley	8	16	24	58	82	105

NOTE: *Dan Noonan a-18-30.* ***Gollub*** *art in most later issues; c-29, 30.* ***Kelly*** *c-7-26, part #27-30.*

ANIMAL CRACKERS (Also see Adventures of Patoruzu)
Green Publ. Co./Norlen/Fox Feat.(Hero Books): 1946; No. 31, July, 1950; No. 9, 1959

	GD 2.0	VG 4.0	FN 6.0	VF 8.0	VF/NM 9.0	NM- 9.2
1-Super Cat begins (1st app.)	19	38	57	107	154	200
2	10	20	30	58	77	95
31(Fox)-Formerly My Love Secret	8	16	24	40	50	60
9(1959-Norlen)-Infinity-c	5	10	14	20	24	28
nn, nd ('50s), no publ.; infinity-c	5	10	14	20	24	28

ANIMAL FABLES
E. C. Comics (Fables Publ. Co.): July-Aug, 1946 - No. 7, Nov-Dec, 1947

	GD 2.0	VG 4.0	FN 6.0	VF 8.0	VF/NM 9.0	NM- 9.2
1-Freddy Firefly (clone of Human Torch), Korky Kangaroo, Petey Pig, Danny Demon begin	48	96	144	293	447	600
2-Aesop Fables begin	31	62	93	175	253	330
3-6	25	50	75	144	207	270
7-Origin Moon Girl	63	126	189	394	610	825

ANIMAL FAIR (Fawcett's...)
Fawcett Publications: Mar, 1946 - No. 11, Feb, 1947

	GD 2.0	VG 4.0	FN 6.0	VF 8.0	VF/NM 9.0	NM- 9.2
1	28	56	84	158	229	300
2	14	28	42	79	110	140
3-6	11	22	33	62	84	105
7-11	9	18	27	52	66	80

ANIMAL FUN
Premier Magazines: 1953 (25¢, came w/glasses)

	GD 2.0	VG 4.0	FN 6.0	VF 8.0	VF/NM 9.0	NM- 9.2
1-(3-D)-Ziggy Pig, Silly Seal, Billy & Buggy Bear	37	74	111	209	305	400

ANIMAL MAN (See Action Comics #552, 553, DC Comics Presents #77, 78, Secret Origins #39, Strange Adventures #180 & Wonder Woman #267, 268)
DC Comics (Vertigo imprint #57 on): Sept, 1988 - No. 89, Nov, 1995 ($1.25/$1.50/$1.75/$1.95/$2.25, mature)

	GD 2.0	VG 4.0	FN 6.0	VF 8.0	VF/NM 9.0	NM- 9.2
1-Grant Morrison scripts begin, ends #26	1	3	4	6	8	10
2-10: 2-Superman cameo. 6-Invasion tie-in. 9-Manhunter-c/story						6.00
11-49,51-55,57-89: 24-Arkham Asylum story; Bizarro Superman app. 25-Inferior Five app. 26-Morrison apps. in story; part photo-c (of Morrison?)						3.00
50-($2.95, 52 pgs.)-Last issue w/Veitch scripts						5.00
56-($3.50, 68 pgs.)						5.00
Annual 1 (1993, $3.95, 68 pgs.)-Bolland-c; Children's Crusade Pt. 3						6.00
...: Deus Ex Machina TPB (2003, $19.95) r/#18-26; Morrison-a; new Bolland-c						20.00
...: Origin of the Species TPB (2002, $19.95) r/#10-17 & Secret Origins #39						20.00

NOTE: ***Bolland*** *c-1-63. 71-****Sutton****-a(i)*

ANIMAL MYSTIC (See Dark One...)
Cry For Dawn/Sirius: 1993 - No. 4, 1995 ($2.95?/$3.50, B&W)

	GD 2.0	VG 4.0	FN 6.0	VF 8.0	VF/NM 9.0	NM- 9.2
1	3	6	9	16	20	24
1-Alternate	4	8	12	27	36	45
1-2nd printing						5.00
2	2	4	6	11	14	18
2,3-2nd prints (Sirius)						3.50
3 ,4: 4-Color poster insert, Linsner-s	1	2	3	5	7	9
TPB ($14.95) r/series						18.00

ANIMAL MYSTIC WATER WARS
Sirius: 1996 - Present ($2.95, limited series)

	GD 2.0	VG 4.0	FN 6.0	VF 8.0	VF/NM 9.0	NM- 9.2
1-6-Dark One-c/a/scripts						5.00

ANIMAL WORLD, THE (Movie)
Dell Publishing Co.: No. 713, Aug, 1956

	GD 2.0	VG 4.0	FN 6.0	VF 8.0	VF/NM 9.0	NM- 9.2
Four Color 713	4	8	12	27	36	45

ANIMANIACS (TV)
DC Comics: May, 1995 - No. 59, Apr, 2000 ($1.50/$1.75/$1.95/$1.99)

	GD 2.0	VG 4.0	FN 6.0	VF 8.0	VF/NM 9.0	NM- 9.2
1	1	2	3	4	5	7
2-20: 13-Manga issue. 19-X-Files parody; Miran Kim-c; Adlard-a (4 pgs.)						4.00
21-59: 26-E.C. parody-c. 34-Xena parody. 43-Pinky & the Brain take over						3.00
A Christmas Special (12/94, $1.50, "1" on-c)						3.00

ANIMATED COMICS
E. C. Comics: No date given (Summer, 1947?)

	GD 2.0	VG 4.0	FN 6.0	VF 8.0	VF/NM 9.0	NM- 9.2
1 (Rare)	77	154	231	481	741	1000

ANIMATED FUNNY COMIC TUNES (See Funny Tunes)

ANIMATED MOVIE-TUNES (Movie Tunes No. 3)
Margood Publishing Corp. (Timely): Fall, 1945 - No. 2, Sum, 1946

	GD 2.0	VG 4.0	FN 6.0	VF 8.0	VF/NM 9.0	NM- 9.2
1,2-Super Rabbit, Ziggy Pig & Silly Seal	28	56	84	158	229	300

ANIMAX
Marvel Comics (Star Comics): Dec, 1986 - No. 4, June, 1987

	GD 2.0	VG 4.0	FN 6.0	VF 8.0	VF/NM 9.0	NM- 9.2
1-4: Based on toys; Simonson-a						3.00

ANNE RICE'S INTERVIEW WITH THE VAMPIRE
Innovation Books: 1991 - No. 12, Jan, 1994 ($2.50, limited series)

	GD 2.0	VG 4.0	FN 6.0	VF 8.0	VF/NM 9.0	NM- 9.2
1-12: Adapts novel; Moeller-a						3.00

ANNE RICE'S THE MASTER OF RAMPLING GATE
Innovation Books: 1991 ($6.95, one-shot)

Annie #1 © MAR

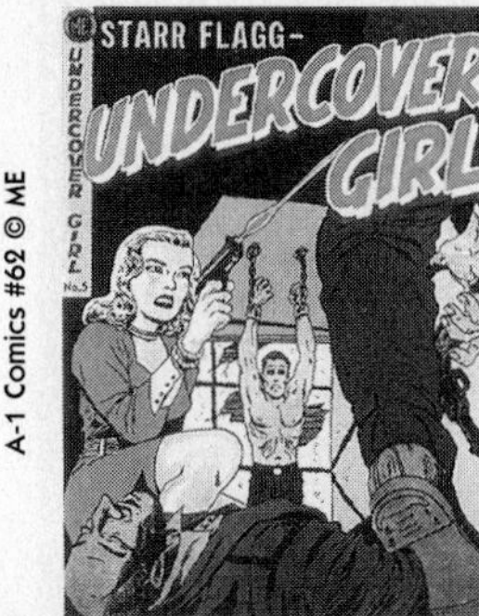

A-1 Comics #62 © ME

A-1 Comics #109 © ME

	GD 2.0	VG 4.0	FN 6.0	VF 8.0	VF/NM 9.0	NM- 9.2

1-Bolton painted-c; Colleen Doran painted-a 7.00

ANNE RICE'S THE MUMMY OR RAMSES THE DAMNED
Millennium Publications: Oct, 1990 - No. 12, Feb, 1992 ($2.50, limited series)

1-12: Adapts novel; Mooney-p in all 3.00

ANNE RICE'S THE WITCHING HOUR
Millennium Publ./Comico: 1992 - No. 13, Jan, 1993 ($2.50, limited series)

1-13 3.00

ANNETTE (Disney, TV)
Dell Publishing Co.: No. 905, May, 1958; No. 1100, May, 1960 (Mickey Mouse Club)

Four Color 905-Annette Funicello photo-c 31 62 93 223 342 460
Four Color 1100-...'s Life Story (Movie); A. Funicello photo-c 25 50 75 181 278 375

ANNEX (See Amazing Spider-Man Annual #27 for 1st app.)
Marvel Comics: Aug, 1994 - No. 4, Nov, 1994 ($1.75)

1-4: 1,4-Spider-Man app. 2.25

ANNIE
Marvel Comics Group: Oct, 1982 - No. 2, Nov, 1982 (60¢)

1,2-Movie adaptation 4.00
Treasury Edition ($2.00, tabloid size) 3 6 9 18 23 28

ANNIE OAKLEY (See Tessie The Typist #19, Two-Gun Kid & Wild Western)
Marvel/Atlas Comics(MPI No. 1-4/CDS No. 5 on): Spring, 1948 - No. 4, 11/48; No. 5, 6/55 - No. 11, 6/56

1 (1st Series, 1948)-Hedy Devine app. 45 90 135 275 418 560
2 (7/48, 52 pgs.)-Kurtzman-a, "Hey Look", 1 pg; Intro. Lana; Hedy Devine app; Captain Tootsie by Beck 28 56 84 158 229 300
3,4 23 46 69 132 191 250
5 (2nd Series, 1955)-Reinman-a ; Maneely-c 17 34 51 95 135 175
6-9: 6,8-Woodbridge-a. 9-Williamson-a (4 pgs.) 13 26 39 76 106 135
10,11: 11-Severin-c 12 24 36 71 98 125

ANNIE OAKLEY AND TAGG (TV)
Dell Publishing Co./Gold Key: 1953 - No. 18, Jan-Mar, 1959; July, 1965 (Gail Davis photo-c #3 on)

Four Color 438 (#1) 16 32 48 116 178 240
Four Color 481,575 (#2,3) 10 20 30 73 107 140
4(7-9/55)-10 9 18 27 65 93 120
11-18(1-3/59) 8 16 24 55 78 100
1(7/65-Gold Key)-Photo-c (c-r/#6) 6 12 18 43 59 75
NOTE: *Manning a-13. Photo back c-4, 9, 11.*

ANOTHER WORLD (See Strange Stories From...)

ANTHRO (See Showcase #74)
National Periodical Publications: July-Aug, 1968 - No. 6, July-Aug, 1969

1-(7-8/68)-Howie Post-a in all 6 12 18 43 59 75
2-5: 5-Last 12¢ issue 4 8 12 25 33 42
6-Wood-c/a (inks) 4 8 12 28 38 48

ANTI-HITLER COMICS
New England Comics Press: Summer, 1992 ($2.75, B&W, one-shot)

1-Reprints Hitler as Devil stories from wartime comics 5.00

ANT-MAN'S BIG CHRISTMAS
Marvel Comics: Feb, 2000 ($5.95, square-bound, one-shot)

1-Bob Gale-s/Phil Winslade-a; Avengers app. 6.00

ANTONY AND CLEOPATRA (See Ideal, a Classical Comic)

ANYTHING GOES
Fantagraphics Books: Oct, 1986 - No. 6, 1987 ($2.00, #1-5 color & B&W/#6 B&W, lim.series)

1-6: 1-Flaming Carrot app. (1st in color?); G. Kane-c. 2-6: 2-Miller-c(p); Alan Moore scripts; Kirby-a; early Sam Kieth-a (2 pgs.). 3-Capt. Jack, Cerebus app.; Cerebus-c by N. Adams. 4-Perez-c. 5-3rd color Teenage Mutant Ninja Turtles app. 3.50

A-1
Marvel Comics (Epic Comics): 1992 - No. 4, 1993 ($5.95, limited series, mature)

1-4: 1-Fabry-c/a, Russell-a, S. Hampton-a. 3-Bisley-c; Kent Williams-a. 4-McKean-a; Dorman-s/a 1 2 3 4 5 7

A-1 COMICS (A-1 appears on covers No. 1-17 only)(See individual title listings for #11-139) (1st two issues not numbered.)
Life's Romances Publ.-No. 1/Compix/Magazine Ent.: 1944 - No. 139, Sept-Oct, 1955 (No #2)

nn-(1944) (See Kerry Drake Detective Cases)

1-Dotty Dripple (1 pg.), Mr. Ex, Bush Berry, Rocky, Lew Loyal (20 pgs.) 13 26 39 74 102 130
3-8,10: Texas Slim & Dirty Dalton, The Corsair, Teddy Rich, Dotty Dripple, Inca Dinca, Tommy Tinker, Little Mexico & Tugboat Tim, The Masquerader & others. 7-Corsair-c/s. 8-Intro Rodeo Ryan 9 18 27 51 62 75
9-All Texas Slim 9 18 27 52 66 80

(See Individual Alphabetical listings for prices)

11-Teena; Ogden Whitney-c	12,15-Teena
13-Guns of Fact & Fiction (1948). Used in **SOTI**, pg. 19; Ingels & Johnny Craig-a	14-Tim Holt Western Adventures #1 16-Vacation Comics; The Pixies, Tom Tom, Flying Fredd, & Koko & Kola
17-Tim Holt #2; photo-c; last issue to carry A-1 on cover (9-10/48)	18,20-Jimmy Durante; photo covers on both
19-Tim Holt #3; photo-c	21-Joan of Arc (1949)-Movie adaptation; Ingrid Bergman photo-covers & interior photos; Whitney-a
22-Dick Powell (1949)-Photo-c	
23-Cowboys and Indians #6; Doc Holiday-c/story	24-Trail Colt #1-Frazetta-r in-Manhunt #13; Ingels-c; L. B. Cole-a
25-Fibber McGee & Molly (1949) (Radio)	
26-Trail Colt #2-Ingels-c	27-Ghost Rider #1(1950)-Origin
28-Christmas-(Koko & Kola #6) ('50)	29-Ghost Rider #2-Frazetta-c (1950)
30-Jet Powers #1-Powell-a	31-Ghost Rider #3-Frazetta-c & origin ('51)
32-Jet Powers #2	
33-Muggsy Mouse #1('51)	34-Ghost Rider #4-Frazetta-c (1951)
35-Jet Powers #3-Williamson/Evans-a	36-Muggsy Mouse #2; Racist-c
37-Ghost Rider #5-Frazetta-c (1951)	38-Jet Powers #4-Williamson/Wood-a
39-Muggsy Mouse #3	40-Dogface Dooley #1('51)
41-Cowboys 'N' Indians #7 (1951)	42-Best of the West #1-Powell-a
43-Dogface Dooley #2	44-Ghost Rider #6
45-American Air Forces #5-Powell-c/a	46-Best of the West #2
47-Thun'da, King of the Congo #1-Frazetta-c/a('52)	48-Cowboys 'N' Indians #8 49-Dogface Dooley #3
50-Danger Is Their Business #11 ('52)-Powell-a	51-Ghost Rider #7 ('52) 52-Best of the West #3
53-Dogface Dooley #4	54-American Air Forces #6(8/52)-Powell-a
55-U.S. Marines #5-Powell-a	
56-Thun'da #2-Powell-c/a	57-Ghost Rider #8
58-American Air Forces #7-Powell-a	59-Best of the West #4
60-The U.S. Marines #6-Powell-a	61-Space Ace #5('53)-Guardineer-a
62-Starr Flagg, Undercover Girl #5 (#1) reprinted from A-1 #24	63-Manhunt #13-Frazetta 64-Dogface Dooley #5
65-American Air Forces #8-Powell-a	66-Best of the West #5
67-American Air Forces #9-Powell-a	68-U.S. Marines #7-Powell-a
69-Ghost Rider #9(10/52)	70-Best of the West #6
71-Ghost Rider #10(12/52)-Vs. Frankenstein	72-U.S. Marines #8-Powell-a(3) 73-Thun'da #3-Powell-c/a
74-American Air Forces #10-Powell-a	75-Ghost Rider #11(3/52)
76-Best of the West #7	77-Manhunt #14
78-Thun'da #4-Powell-c/a	79-American Air Forces #11-Powell-a
80-Ghost Rider #12(6/52)-One-eyed Devil-c	81-Best of the West #8 82-Cave Girl #11(1953)-Powell-c/a; origin (#1)
83-Thun'da #5-Powell-c/a	
84-Ghost Rider #13(7-8/53)	85-Best of the West #9
86-Thun'da #6-Powell-c/a	87-Best of the West #10(9-10/53)
88-Bobby Benson's B-Bar-B Riders #20	89-Home Run #3-Powell-a; Stan Musial photo-c
90-Red Hawk #11(1953)-Powell-c/a	
91-American Air Forces #12-Powell-a	92-Dream Book of Romance #5-Photo-c; Guardineer-a
93-Great Western #8('54)-Origin The Ghost Rider; Powell-a	94-White Indian #11-Frazetta-a(r); Powell-c
95-Muggsy Mouse #4	
96-Cave Girl #12, with Thun'da; Powell-c/a	97-Best of the West #11 98-Undercover Girl #6-Powell-c
99-Muggsy Mouse #5	100-Badmen of the West #1-Meskin-a(?)
101-White Indian #12-Frazetta-a(r)	
101-Dream Book of Romance #6 (4-6/54); Marlon Brando photo-c; Powell, Bolle, Guardineer-a	103-Best of the West #12-Powell-a 104-White Indian #13-Frazetta-a(r) ('54)
105-Great Western #9-Ghost Rider app.; Powell-a, 6 pgs.; Bolle-c	106-Dream Book of Love #1 (6-7/54) -Powell, Bolle-a; Montgomery Clift, Donna Reed photo-c
107-Hot Dog #1	
108-Red Fox #15 (1954)-L.B. Cole-c/a; Powell-a	109-Dream Book of Romance #7 (7-8/54). Powell-a; movie photo-c
110-Dream Book of Romance #8 (10/54)-Movie photo-c	111-I'm a Cop #1 ('54); drug mention story; Powell-a
112-Ghost Rider #14 ('54)	113-Great Western #10; Powell-a

Apache Kid #14 © MAR

Approved Comics #11 © STJ

Aquaman #45 © DC

	GD 2.0	VG 4.0	FN 6.0	VF 8.0	VF/NM 9.0	NM- 9.2

114-Dream Book of Love #2- Guardineer, Bolle-a; Piper Laurie, Victor Mature photo-c
115-Hot Dog #3
116-Cave Girl #13-Powell-c/a
117-White Indian #14
118-Undercover Girl #7-Powell-c
119-Straight Arrow's Fury #1 (origin); Fred Meagher-c/a
120-Badmen of the West #2
121-Mysteries of Scotland Yard #1; reprinted from Manhunt (5 stories)
122-Black Phantom #1 (11/54)
123-Dream Book of Love #3 (10-11/54)-Movie photo-c
124-Dream Book of Romance #8 (10-11/54)
125-Cave Girl #14-Powell-c/a
126-I'm a Cop #2-Powell-a
127-Great Western #11('54)-Powell-a
128-I'm a Cop #3-Powell-a
129-The Avenger #1('55)-Powell-c
130-Strongman #1-Powell-a (2-3/55)
131-The Avenger #2('55)-Powell-c/a
132-Strongman #2
133-The Avenger #3-Powell-c/a
134-Strongman #3
135-White Indian #15
136-Hot Dog #4
137-Africa #1-Powell-c/a(4)
138-The Avenger #4-Powell-c/a
139-Strongman #4-Powell-a

NOTE: *Bolle a-110. Photo-c-17-22, 89, 92, 101, 106, 109, 110, 114, 123, 124.*

APACHE
Fiction House Magazines: 1951

	GD 2.0	VG 4.0	FN 6.0	VF 8.0	VF/NM 9.0	NM- 9.2
1	23	46	69	132	191	250
I.W. Reprint No. 1-r/#1 above	3	7	10	21	28	35

APACHE KID (Formerly Reno Browne; Western Gunfighters #20 on)
(Also see Two-Gun Western & Wild Western)
Marvel/Atlas Comics(MPC No. 53-10/CPS No. 11 on): No. 53, 12/50 - No. 10, 1/52; No. 11, 12/54 - No. 19, 4/56

	GD 2.0	VG 4.0	FN 6.0	VF 8.0	VF/NM 9.0	NM- 9.2
53(#1)-Apache Kid & his horse Nightwind (origin), Red Hawkins by Syd Shores begins	37	74	111	209	305	400
2(2/51)	18	36	54	102	146	190
3-5	12	24	36	71	98	125
6-10 (1951-52): 7-Russ Heath-a	10	20	30	60	80	100
11-19 (1954-56)	9	18	27	52	66	80

NOTE: ***Heath** a-7. c-11, 13. **Maneely** a-53; c-53(#1), 12, 14-16. **Powell** a-14. **Severin** c-17.*

APACHE MASSACRE (See Chief Victorio's...)

APACHE SKIES
Marvel Comics: Sept, 2002 - No. 4, Dec, 2002 ($2.99, limited series)

	GD 2.0	VG 4.0	FN 6.0	VF 8.0	VF/NM 9.0	NM- 9.2
1-4-Apache Kid app.; Ostrander-s/Manco-c/a						3.00
TPB (2003, $12.99) r/#1-4						13.00

APACHE TRAIL
Steinway/America's Best: Sept, 1957 - No. 4, June, 1958

	GD 2.0	VG 4.0	FN 6.0	VF 8.0	VF/NM 9.0	NM- 9.2
1	11	22	33	64	87	110
2-4: 2-Tuska-a	8	16	24	40	50	60

APE (Magazine)
Dell Publishing Co.: 1961 (52 pgs., B&W)

	GD 2.0	VG 4.0	FN 6.0	VF 8.0	VF/NM 9.0	NM- 9.2
1-Comics and humor	4	8	12	28	38	48

APHRODITE IX
Image Comics (Top Cow): Sept, 2000 - No. 4, Mar, 2002 ($2.50)

	GD 2.0	VG 4.0	FN 6.0	VF 8.0	VF/NM 9.0	NM- 9.2
1-3: 1-Four covers by Finch, Turner, Silvestri, Benitez						4.00
1-Tower Record Ed.; Finch-c						3.00
1-DF Chrome ($14.99)						15.00
4-($4.95) Double-sized issue; Finch-c						5.00
Convention Preview						10.00
...: Time Out of Mind TPB (6/04, $14.99) r/#1-4, & #0; cover gallery						15.00
Wizard #0 (4/00, bagged w/Tomb Raider magazine) Preview & sketchbook						5.00
#0-(6/01, $2.95) r/Wizard #0 with cover gallery						3.00

APOLLO SMILE
Eagle Wing Press: July, 1998 - No. 2 ($2.95)

	GD 2.0	VG 4.0	FN 6.0	VF 8.0	VF/NM 9.0	NM- 9.2
1,2-Manga						3.00

APPARITION
Caliber Comics: 1995 ($3.95, 52 pgs., B&W)

	GD 2.0	VG 4.0	FN 6.0	VF 8.0	VF/NM 9.0	NM- 9.2
1 ($3.95)						4.00
V2#1-6 ($2.95)						3.00
Visitations						4.00

APPLESEED
Eclipse Comics: Sept, 1988 - Book 4, Vol. 4, Aug, 1991 ($2.50/$2.75/$3.50, 52/68 pgs, B&W)

	GD 2.0	VG 4.0	FN 6.0	VF 8.0	VF/NM 9.0	NM- 9.2
Book One, Vol. 1-5: 5-(1/89), Book Two, Vol. 1(2/89) -5(7/89): Art Adams-c, Book Three, Vol. 1(8/89) -4 ($2.75), Book Three, Vol. 5 ($3.50), Book Four, Vol. 1 (1/91) - 4 (8/91) ($3.50, 68 pgs.)						6.00

APPLESEED DATABOOK
Dark Horse Comics: Apr, 1994 - No. 2, May, 1994 ($3.50, B&W, limited series)

	GD 2.0	VG 4.0	FN 6.0	VF 8.0	VF/NM 9.0	NM- 9.2
1,2: 1-Flip book format						3.50

APPROVED COMICS (Also see Blue Ribbon Comics)
St. John Publishing Co. (Most have no c-price): March, 1954 - No. 12, Aug, 1954 (Painted-c on #1-5,7,8,10)

	GD 2.0	VG 4.0	FN 6.0	VF 8.0	VF/NM 9.0	NM- 9.2
1-The Hawk #5-r	10	20	30	58	77	95
2-Invisible Boy (3/54)-Origin; Saunders-c	18	36	54	100	143	185
3-Wild Boy of the Congo #11-r (4/54)	10	20	30	58	77	95
4,5: 4-Kid Cowboy-r. 5-Fly Boy-r	10	20	30	58	77	95
6-Daring Adv.-r (5/54); Krigstein-a(2); Baker-c	13	26	39	74	102	130
7-The Hawk #6-r	10	20	30	58	77	95
8-Crime on the Run (6/54); Powell-a; Saunders-c	10	20	30	58	77	95
9-Western Bandit Trails #3-r, with new-c; Baker-c/a	13	26	39	74	102	130
10-Dinky Duck (Terrytoons)	6	12	18	31	38	45
11-Fightin' Marines #3-r (8/54); Canteen Kate app; Baker-c/a	14	28	42	79	110	140
12-Northwest Mounties #4-r(8/54); new Baker-c	14	28	42	79	110	140

AQUAMAN (See Adventure Comics #260, Brave & the Bold, DC Comics Presents #5, DC Special #28, DC Special Series #1, DC Super Stars #7, Detective Comics, JLA, Justice League of America, More Fun #73, Showcase #30-33, Super DC Giant, Super Friends, and World's Finest Comics)

AQUAMAN (1st Series)
National Periodical Publications/DC Comics: Jan-Feb, 1962 - #56, Mar-Apr, 1971; #57, Aug-Sept,1977 - #63, Aug-Sept, 1978

	GD 2.0	VG 4.0	FN 6.0	VF 8.0	VF/NM 9.0	NM- 9.2
1-(1-2/62)-Intro. Quisp	74	148	222	629	1015	1400
2	32	64	96	240	370	500
3-5	19	38	57	134	205	275
6-10	13	26	39	90	138	185
11,18: 11-1st app. Mera. 18-Aquaman weds Mera; JLA cameo	10	20	30	73	107	140
12-17,19,20	10	20	30	70	100	130
21-32: 23-Birth of Aquababy. 26-Huntress app.(3-4/66). 29-1st app. Ocean Master, Aquaman's step-brother. 30-Batman & Superman-c & cameo	7	14	21	46	63	80
33-1st app. Aqua-Girl (see Adventure #266)	7	14	21	51	71	90
34-40: 40-Jim Aparo's 1st DC work (8/68)	5	10	15	36	48	60
41-46,47,49: 45-Last 12¢-c	4	8	12	29	40	50
48-Origin reprinted	5	10	15	33	44	55
50-52-Deadman by Neal Adams	7	14	21	51	71	90
53-56('71): 56-1st app. Crusader; last 15¢-c	2	4	6	10	13	16
57('77)-63: 58-Origin retold	1	2	3	5	7	9

NOTE: ***Aparo** a-40-45, 46p, 47-59; c-58-63. **Nick Cardy** c-1-40. **Newton** a-60-63.*

AQUAMAN (1st limited series)
DC Comics: Feb, 1986 - No. 4, May, 1986 (75¢, limited series)

	GD 2.0	VG 4.0	FN 6.0	VF 8.0	VF/NM 9.0	NM- 9.2
1-New costume; 1st app. Nuada of Thierna Na Oge.						5.50
2-4: 3-Retelling of Aquaman & Ocean Master's origins.						4.00
Special 1 (1988, $1.50, 52 pgs.)						3.75

NOTE: ***Craig Hamilton** c/a-1-4p. **Russell** c-2-4i.*

AQUAMAN (2nd limited series)
DC Comics: June, 1989 - No. 5, Oct, 1989 ($1.00, limited series)

	GD 2.0	VG 4.0	FN 6.0	VF 8.0	VF/NM 9.0	NM- 9.2
1-5: Giffen plots/breakdowns; Swan-a(p).						3.00
Special 1 (Legend of..., $2.00, 1989, 52 pgs.)-Giffen plots/breakdowns; Swan-a(p)						3.00

AQUAMAN (2nd Series)
DC Comics: Dec, 1991 - No. 13, Dec, 1992 ($1.00/$1.25)

	GD 2.0	VG 4.0	FN 6.0	VF 8.0	VF/NM 9.0	NM- 9.2
1-5						2.50
6-13: 6-Begin $1.25-c. 9-Sea Devils app.						2.50

AQUAMAN (3rd Series)(Also see Atlantis Chronicles)
DC Comics: Aug, 1994 - No. 75, Jan, 2001 ($1.50/$1.75/$1.95/$1.99/$2.50)

	GD 2.0	VG 4.0	FN 6.0	VF 8.0	VF/NM 9.0	NM- 9.2
1-(8/94)-Peter David scripts begin; reintro Dolphin						6.00
2-(9/94)-Aquaman loses hand						6.50
0-(10/94)-Aquaman replaces lost hand with hook.						6.50
3-8: 3-(11/94)-Superboy-c/app. 4-Lobo app. 6-Deep Six app.						3.50
9-69: 9-Begin $1.75-c. 10-Green Lantern app. 11-Reintro Mera. 15-Re-intro Kordax. 16-vs. JLA. 18-Reintro Ocean Master & Atlan (Aquaman's father). 19-Reintro Garth (Aqualad). 23-1st app. Deep Blue (Neptune Perkins & Tsunami's daughter). 23,24-Neptune Perkins, Nuada, Tsunami, Arion, Power Girl, & The Sea Devils app. 26-Final Night. 28-Martian Manhunter-c/app. 29-Black Manta-c/app. 32-Swamp Thing-c/app. 37-Genesis x-over. 41-Maxima-c/app. 43-Millennium Giants x-over; Superman-c/app. 44-G.A. Flash & Sentinel app. 50-Larsen-s begins. 53-Superman app. 60-Tempest marries Dolphin; Teen Titans app. 63-Kaluta covers begin. 66-JLA app.						2.50
70-75: 70-Begin $2.50-c. 71-73-Warlord-c/app. 75-Final issue						2.50
#1,000,000 (11/98) 853rd Century x-over						3.00

Aquaman (4th) #15 © DC

Archer & Armstrong #25 © VAL

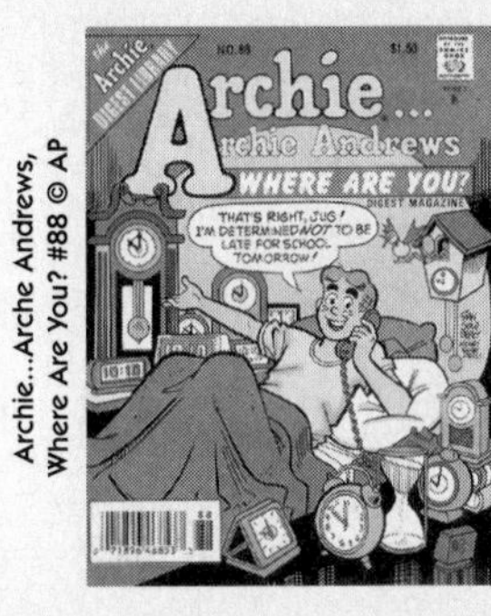

Archie...Arche Andrews, Where Are You? #88 © AP

	GD 2.0	VG 4.0	FN 6.0	VF 8.0	VF/NM 9.0	NM- 9.2
Annual 1 (1995, $3.50)-Year One story						3.50
Annual 2 (1996, $2.95)-Legends of the Dead Earth story						3.00
Annual 3 (1997, $3.95)-Pulp Heroes story						4.00
Annual 4,5 ('98, "99, $2.95)-4-Ghosts; Wrightson-c. 5-JLApe						3.00
...Secret Files 1 (12/98, $4.95) Origin-s and pin-ups						5.00

NOTE: ***Art Adams**-c, Annual 5. **Mignola** c-6. **Simonson** c-15.*

AQUAMAN (4th Series)(Also see JLA #69-75)
DC Comics: Feb, 2003 - Present ($2.50)

	GD	VG	FN	VF	VF/NM	NM-
1-Veitch-s/Guichet-a/Maleev-c						3.00
2-14: 2-Martian Manhunter app. 8-11-Black Manta app.						2.50
15-25: 15-San Diego flooded; Pfeifer-s/Davis-c begin. 23,24-Sea Devils app.						2.50
...Secret Files 2003 (5/03, $4.95) background on Aquaman's new powers; pin-ups						5.00
...: The Waterbearer TPB (2003, $12.95) r/#1-4, stories from Aquaman Secret Files and JLA/JSA Secret Files #1; JG Jones-c						13.00

AQUAMAN: TIME & TIDE (3rd limited series) (Also see Atlantis Chronicles)
DC Comics: Dec, 1993 - No. 4, Mar, 1994 ($1.50, limited series)

	GD	VG	FN	VF	VF/NM	NM-
1-4: Peter David scripts; origin retold.						3.00
Trade paperback ($9.95)						10.00

AQUANAUTS (TV)
Dell Publishing Co.: May - July, 1961

	GD	VG	FN	VF	VF/NM	NM-
Four Color 1197-Photo-c	8	16	24	58	82	105

ARABIAN NIGHTS (See Cinema Comics Herald)

ARACHNOPHOBIA (Movie)
Hollywood Comics (Disney Comics): 1990 ($5.95, 68 pg. graphic novel)

	GD	VG	FN	VF	VF/NM	NM-
nn-Adaptation of film; Spiegle-a						6.00
Comic edition ($2.95, 68 pgs.)						3.00

ARAK/SON OF THUNDER (See Warlord #48)
DC Comics: Sept, 1981 - No. 50, Nov, 1985

	GD	VG	FN	VF	VF/NM	NM-
1,24,50: 1-1st app. Angelica, Princess of White Cathay. 24,50-(52 pgs.)						3.00
2-23,25-49: 3-Intro Valda. 12-Origin Valda. 20-Origin Angelica						2.25
Annual 1(10/84)						3.00

ARCANA (Also see Books of Magic limited & ongoing series and Mister E)
DC Comics (Vertigo): 1994 ($3.95, 68 pgs., annual)

	GD	VG	FN	VF	VF/NM	NM-
1-Bolton painted-c; Children's Crusade/Tim Hunter story						4.00

ARCANUM
Image Comics (Top Cow Productions): Apr, 1997 - No. 8, Feb, 1998 ($2.50)

	GD	VG	FN	VF	VF/NM	NM-
1/2 Gold Edition						12.00
1-Brandon Peterson-s/a(p), 1-Variant-c, 4-American Ent. Ed.						3.00
2-8						2.50
3-Variant-c						4.00

ARCHANGEL (See Uncanny X-Men, X-Factor & X-Men)
Marvel Comics: Feb, 1996 ($2.50, B&W, one-shot)

	GD	VG	FN	VF	VF/NM	NM-
1-Milligan story						2.50

ARCHARD'S AGENTS (See Ruse)
CrossGeneration Comics: Jan, 2003; Nov, 2003; Apr, 2004 ($2.95)

	GD	VG	FN	VF	VF/NM	NM-
1-Dixon-s/Perkins-a						3.00
...: The Case of the Puzzled Pugilist (11/03) Dixon-s/Perkins-a						3.00
Vol. 3 - Deadly Dare (4/04) Dixon-s/McNiven-a; preview of Lady Death: The Wild Hunt						3.00

ARCHER & ARMSTRONG
Valiant: July (June inside), 1992 - No. 26, Oct, 1994 ($2.50)

	GD	VG	FN	VF	VF/NM	NM-
0-(7/92)-B. Smith-c/a; Reese-i assists						3.00
0-(Gold Logo)						6.00
1-7,9-26: 1-(8/92)-Origin & 1st app. Archer; Miller-c; B. Smith/Layton-a. 2-2nd app. Turok (c/story); Smith/Layton-a; Simonson-c. 3,4-Smith-c&a(p) & scripts. 10-2nd app. Ivar. 10,11-B. Smith-c. 21,22-Shadowman app. 22-w/bound-in trading card. 25-Eternal Warrior app. 26-Flip book w/Eternal Warrior #26						2.50
8-($4.50, 52 pgs.)-Combined with Eternal Warrior #8; B. Smith-c/a & scripts; 1st app. Ivar the Time Walker						4.50

ARCHIE (See Archie Comics) (Also see Christmas & Archie, Everything's..., Explorers of the Unknown, Jackpot, Little..., Oxydol-Dreft, Pep, Riverdale High, Teenage Mutant Ninja Turtles Adventures & To Riverdale and Back Again)

ARCHIE AMERICANA SERIES, BEST OF THE FORTIES
Archie Publications: 1991,2002 ($10.95, trade paperback)

	GD	VG	FN	VF	VF/NM	NM-
Vol. 1,2-r/early strips from 1940's 1-Intro. by Steven King. 2-Intro. by Paul Castiglia						11.00

ARCHIE AMERICANA SERIES, BEST OF THE FIFTIES
Archie Publications: 1991 ($8.95, trade paperback)

	GD	VG	FN	VF	VF/NM	NM-
V2-r/strips from 1950's;						9.00
2nd printing (1998, $9.95)						10.00
Book 2 (2003, $10.95)						11.00

ARCHIE AMERICANA SERIES, BEST OF THE SIXTIES
Archie Publications: 1995 ($9.95, trade paperback)

	GD	VG	FN	VF	VF/NM	NM-
V3-r/strips from 1960's; intro. by Frankie Avalon.						10.00

ARCHIE AMERICANA SERIES, BEST OF THE SEVENTIES
Archie Publications: 1997 ($9.95, trade paperback)

	GD	VG	FN	VF	VF/NM	NM-
V4-r/strips from 1970's						10.00

ARCHIE AMERICANA SERIES, BEST OF THE EIGHTIES
Archie Publications: 2001 ($10.95, trade paperback)

	GD	VG	FN	VF	VF/NM	NM-
V5-r/strips from 1980's; foreward by Steve Geppi						11.00

ARCHIE AND BIG ETHEL
Spire Christian Comics (Fleming H. Revell Co.): 1982 (69¢)

	GD	VG	FN	VF	VF/NM	NM-
nn-(Low print run)	2	4	6	11	14	18

ARCHIE & FRIENDS
Archie Comics: Dec, 1992 - Present ($1.25/$1.50/$1.75/$1.79/$1.99/$2.19, bi-monthly)

	GD	VG	FN	VF	VF/NM	NM-
1						5.00
2,4,10-14,17,18,20-Sabrina app. 20-Archie's Band-c						4.00
3,5-9,16						2.50
15-Babewatch-s with Sabrina app.						6.00
19-Josie and the Pussycats app.; E.T. parody-c/s						5.00
21-46						2.25
47-All Josie and the Pussycats issue; movie and actress profiles/photos						2.25
48-89: 48-56,58,60-Josie and the Pussycats-c/s. 79-Cheryl Blossom returns						2.25

ARCHIE AND ME (See Archie Giant Series Mag. #578, 591, 603, 616, 626)
Archie Publications: Oct, 1964 - No. 161, Feb, 1987

	GD	VG	FN	VF	VF/NM	NM-
1	17	34	51	121	186	250
2	10	20	30	67	96	125
3-5	6	12	18	43	59	75
6-10	4	8	12	27	36	45
11-20	3	6	9	18	24	30
21(6/68)-26,28-30: 21-UFO story. 26-X-Mas-c	3	6	9	16	20	24
27-Groovyman & Knowman superhero-s; UFO-sty	3	6	9	18	24	30
31-42: 37-Japan Expo '70-c/s	2	4	6	10	13	16
43-48,50-63-(All Giants): 43-(8/71) Mummy-s. 44-Mermaid-s. 62-Elvis cameo-c. 63-(2/74)	3	6	9	16	20	24
49-(Giant) Josie & the Pussycats-c/app.	3	6	9	19	25	32
64-66,68-99-(Regular size): 85-Bicentennial-s. 98-Collectors Comics	1	3	4	6	8	10
67-Sabrina app.(8/74)	2	4	6	10	13	16
100-(4/78)	2	4	6	8	10	12
101-120: 107-UFO-s						6.00
121(8/80)-159: 134-Riverdale 2001						5.00
160,161: 160-Origin Mr. Weatherbee. 161-Last issue						6.00

ARCHIE AND MR. WEATHERBEE
Spire Christian Comics (Fleming H. Revell Co.): 1980 (59¢)

	GD	VG	FN	VF	VF/NM	NM-
nn - (Low print run)	2	4	6	9	11	14

ARCHIE...ARCHIE ANDREWS, WHERE ARE YOU? (...Comics Digest #9, 10; ...Comics Digest Mag. No. 11 on)
Archie Publications: Feb, 1977 - No. 114, May, 1998 (Digest size, 160-128 pgs., quarterly)

	GD	VG	FN	VF	VF/NM	NM-
1	3	6	9	18	24	30
2,3,5,7-9-N. Adams-a; 8-r-/origin The Fly by S&K. 9-Steel Sterling-r	2	4	6	10	13	16
4,6,10 ($1.00/$1.50)	2	4	6	8	10	12
11-20: 17-Katy Keene story	1	2	3	5	7	9
21-50,100	1	2	3	4	5	7
51-70						4.00
71-114: 113-Begin $1.95-c						3.00

ARCHIE AS PUREHEART THE POWERFUL (Also see Archie Giant Series #142, Jughead as Captain Hero, Life With Archie & Little Archie)
Archie Publications (Radio Comics): Sept, 1966 - No. 6, Nov, 1967

	GD	VG	FN	VF	VF/NM	NM-
1-Super hero parody	10	20	30	73	107	140
2	6	12	18	43	59	75
3-6	5	10	15	36	48	60

NOTE: *Evilheart cameos in all. Title: Archie As Pureheart the Powerful #1-3; ...As Capt. Pureheart-#4-6.*

ARCHIE AT RIVERDALE HIGH (See Archie Giant Series Magazine #573, 586, 604 & Riverdale High)

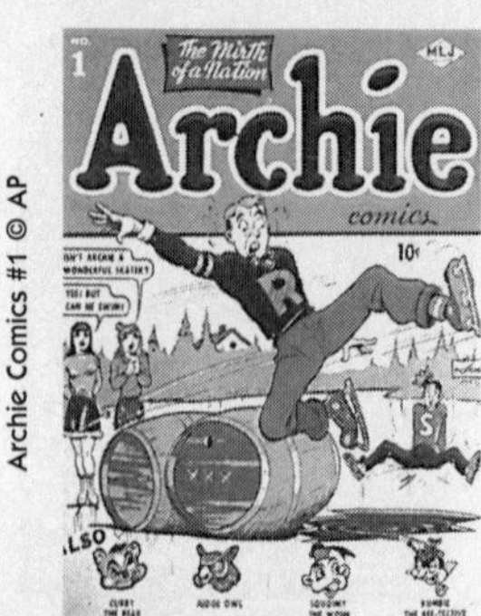

Archie Comics #1 © AP

Archie Comics #422 © AP

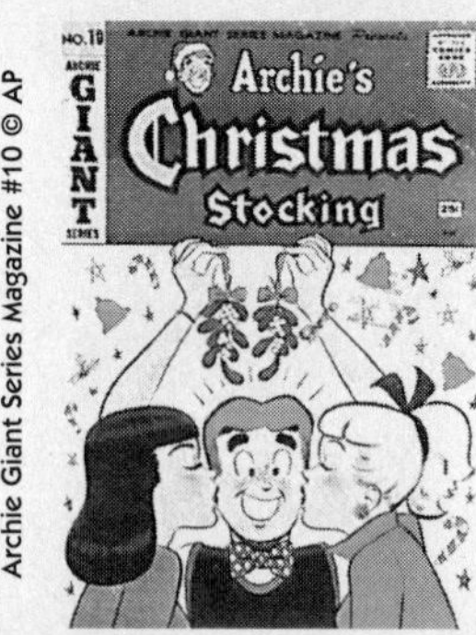

Archie Giant Series Magazine #10 © AP

Archie Publications: Aug, 1972 - No. 113, Feb, 1987

	GD 2.0	VG 4.0	FN 6.0	VF 8.0	VF/NM 9.0	NM- 9.2
1	7	14	21	50	68	85
2	4	8	12	24	32	40
3-5	3	6	9	18	24	30
6-10	2	4	6	12	16	20
11-30	2	4	6	8	10	12
31(12/75)-46,48-50(12/77)	1	2	3	5	7	9
47-Archie in drag-s; Betty mud wrestling-s	2	4	6	9	11	15
51-80,100 (12/84)						6.00
81(8/81)-88, 91,93-95,97,98: 96-Anti-smoking issue						5.00
89,90-Early Cheryl Blossom app. 90-Archies Band app.	2	4	6	9	11	14
92,96,99-Cheryl Blossom app.	1	3	4	6	8	10
101,102,104-109,111,112: 102-Ghost-c						4.00
103-Archie dates Cheryl Blossom-s	1	3	4	6	8	10
110,113: 110-Godzilla-s. 113-Last issue						6.00

ARCHIE COMICS (Archie #114 on; 1st Teen-age comic; Radio show aired 6/2/45 by NBC)
MLJ Magazines No. 1-19/Archie Publ. No. 20 on: Winter, 1942-43 - No. 19, 3-4/46; No. 20, 5-6/46 - Present

	GD 2.0	VG 4.0	FN 6.0	VF 8.0	VF/NM 9.0	NM- 9.2
1 (Scarce)-Jughead, Veronica app.; 1st app. Mrs. Andrews	1294	2588	3882	9705	15,853	22,000
2	317	634	951	2061	3331	4600
3 (60 pgs.)(scarce)	254	508	762	1588	2444	3300
4,5: 4-Article about Archie radio series	138	276	414	863	1332	1800
6,8-10: 6-X-Mas-c. 9-1st Miss Grundy cover	96	192	288	600	925	1250
7-1st definitive love triangle story	100	200	300	625	963	1300
11-20: 15,17,18-Dotty & Ditto by Woggon. 16,19-Woggon-a. 18-Halloween pumpkin-c.	63	126	189	394	610	825
21-30: 23-Betty & Veronica by Woggon. 25-Woggon-a. 30-Coach Piffle app., a Coach Kleets prototype. 34-Pre-Dilton try-out (named Dilbert)	40	80	120	244	372	500
31-40	29	58	87	164	237	310
41-50	20	40	60	112	161	210
51-60	11	22	33	77	114	150
61-70 (1954): 65-70, Katy Keene app.	9	18	27	65	93	120
71-80: 72-74-Katy Keene app.	7	14	21	51	71	90
81-99: 94-1st Coach Kleets	6	12	18	43	59	75
100	7	14	21	51	71	90
101-122,126,128-130 (1962)	4	8	12	29	40	50
123-125,127-Horror/SF covers. 123-UFO-c/s	5	10	15	36	48	60
131,132,134-157,159,160: 137-1st Caveman Archie gang story	3	6	9	18	24	30
133 (12/62)-1st app. Cricket O'Dell	4	8	12	25	33	42
158-Archie in drag story	3	7	10	21	28	35
161(2/66)-184,186-195,197-199: 168-Superhero gag-c. 176,178-Twiggy-c 183-Caveman Archie gang story	2	4	6	14	18	22
185-1st "The Archies" Band story	4	8	12	22	30	38
196 (12/69)-Early Cricket O'Dell app.	3	6	9	19	25	32
200 (6/70)	3	6	9	16	20	24
201-230(11/73): 213-Sabrina/Josie-c cameos. 229-Lost Child issue	2	4	6	9	11	14
231-260(3/77): 253-Tarzan parody	1	3	4	6	8	10
261-282, 284-299	1	2	3	5	6	8
283(8/79)-Cover/story plugs "International Children's Appeal" which was a fraudulent charity, according to TV's 20/20 news program broadcast July 20, 1979	1	2	3	5	7	9
300(1/81)-Anniversary issue	1	3	4	6	8	10
301-321,323-325,327-335,337-350: 323-Cheryl Blossom pin-up						5.00
322-E.T. story						6.00
326-Early Cheryl Blossom story	2	4	6	10	13	16
336-Michael Jackson/Boy George parody						6.00
351-399: 356-Calgary Olympics Special. 393-Infinity-c; 1st comic book printed on recycled paper						4.00
400 (6/92)-Shows 1st meeting of Little Archie and Veronica						6.00
401-428						3.00
429-Love Showdown part 1						5.00
430-555: 467- "A Storm Over Uniforms" x-over parts 3,4. 538-Comic-Con issue						2.25
Annual 1 ('50)-116 pgs. (Scarce)	169	338	507	1056	1628	2200
Annual 2 ('51)	85	170	255	531	816	1100
Annual 3 ('52)	50	100	150	305	465	625
Annual 4,5 (1953-54)	40	80	120	230	335	440
Annual 6-10 (1955-59): 8,9-(100 pgs.). 10-(84 pgs.) Elvis record on-c	15	30	45	107	164	220
Annual 11-15 (1960-65): 12,13-(84 pgs.) 14,15-(68 pgs.)	9	18	27	60	85	110
Annual 16-20 (1966-70)(all 68 pgs.): 20-Archie's band-c	5	10	15	33	44	55
Annual 21,22,24-26 (1971-75): 21,22-(68 pgs.). 22-Archie's band-s. 24-26-(52 pgs.). 25-Cavemen-s	3	6	9	18	23	28
Annual 23-Archie's band-c/s; Josie/Sabrina-c	3	6	9	19	25	32
Annual Digest 27 ('75)	4	8	12	24	32	40
...28-30	3	6	9	16	20	24
...31-34	2	4	6	10	13	16
...35-40 (...Magazine #35 on)	1	3	4	6	8	10
...41-65 ('94)						5.00
...66-69						3.00
...All-Star Specials(Winter '75, $1.25)-6 remaindered Archie comics rebound in each; titles: "The World of Giant Comics", "Giant Grab Bag of Comics", "Triple Giant Comics" & "Giant Spec. Comics	4	8	12	29	40	50
Special Edition-Christmas With Archie 1(1/75)-Treasury (rare)	6	12	18	40	55	70

NOTE: *Archies Band-s-185, 188-192, 197, 198, 201, 204, 205, 208, 209, 215, 329, 330; Band-c-191, 330. Cavemen Archie Gang-s-183, 192, 197, 208, 210, 220, 223, 282, 333, 335, 338, 340.* ***Al Fagly*** *c-17-35.* ***Bob Montana*** *c-38, 41-50, 58, Annual 1-4.* ***Bill Woggon*** *c-53, 54.*

ARCHIE COMICS DIGEST (...Magazine No. 37-95)
Archie Publications: Aug, 1973 - Present (Small size, 160-128 pgs.)

	GD 2.0	VG 4.0	FN 6.0	VF 8.0	VF/NM 9.0	NM- 9.2
1-1st Archie digest	10	20	30	72	104	135
2	6	12	18	38	52	65
3-5	4	8	12	27	36	45
6-10	3	6	9	16	20	25
11-33: 32,33-The Fly-r by S&K	2	4	6	10	12	15
34-60	1	3	4	6	8	10
61-80,100	1	2	3	5	6	8
81-99						5.00
101-140: 36-Katy Keene story						4.00
141-165						3.00
166-214: 194-Begin $2.39-c						2.50

NOTE: ***Neal Adams*** *a-1, 2, 4, 5, 19-21, 24, 25, 27, 29, 31, 33. X-mas c-88, 94, 100, 106.*

ARCHIE COMICS PRESENTS: THE LOVE SHOWDOWN COLLECTION
Archie Publications: 1994 ($4.95, squarebound)

	GD 2.0	VG 4.0	FN 6.0	VF 8.0	VF/NM 9.0	NM- 9.2
nn-r/Archie #429, Betty #19, Betty & Veronica #82, & Veronica #39	1	2	3	4	5	7

ARCHIE GETS A JOB
Spire Christian Comics (Fleming H. Revell Co.): 1977

	GD 2.0	VG 4.0	FN 6.0	VF 8.0	VF/NM 9.0	NM- 9.2
nn	2	4	6	9	11	14

ARCHIE GIANT SERIES MAGAZINE
Archie Publications: 1954 - No. 632, July, 1992 (No #36-135, no #252-451)
(#1 not code approved) (#1-233 are Giants; #12-184 are 68 pgs.,#185-194,197-233 are 52 pgs.; #195,196 are 84 pgs.; #234-up are 36 pgs.)

	GD 2.0	VG 4.0	FN 6.0	VF 8.0	VF/NM 9.0	NM- 9.2
1-Archie's Christmas Stocking	127	254	381	794	1222	1650
2-Archie's Christmas Stocking('55)	71	142	213	444	685	925
3-6-Archie's Christmas Stocking('56- '59)	48	96	144	293	447	600
7-10: 7-Katy Keene Holiday Fun(9/60); Bill Woggon-c. 8-Betty & Veronica Summer Fun (10/60); baseball story w/Babe Ruth & Lou Gehrig. 9-The World of Jughead (12/60); Neal Adams-a. 10-Archie's Christmas Stocking(1/61)	38	76	114	219	320	420
11,13,16,18: 11-Betty & Veronica Spectacular (6/61). 13-Betty & Veronica Summer Fun (10/61). 16-Betty & Veronica Spectacular (6/62). 18-Betty & Veronica Summer Fun (10/62)	26	52	78	147	211	275
12,14,15,17,19,20: 12-Katy Keene Holiday Fun (9/61). 14-The World of Jughead (12/61); Vampire-s. 15-Archie's Christmas Stocking (1/62). 17-Archie's Jokes (9/62); Katy Keene app. 19-The World of Jughead (12/62). 20-Archie's Christmas Stocking (1/63)	18	36	54	102	146	190
21,23,28: 21-Betty & Veronica Spectacular (6/63). 23-Betty & Veronica Summer Fun (10/63). 28-Betty & Veronica Summer Fun (9/64)	10	20	30	73	107	140
22,24,25,27,29,30: 22-Archie's Jokes (9/63). 24-The World of Jughead (12/63). 25-Archie's Christmas Stocking (1/64). 27-Archie's Jokes (8/64). 29-Around the World with Archie (10/64); Doris Day-s. 30-The World of Jughead (12/64)	9	18	27	65	93	120
26-Betty & Veronica Spectacular (6/64); all pin-ups; DeCarlo-c/a	11	22	33	77	114	150
31,33-35: 31-Archie's Christmas Stocking (1/65). 33-Archie's Jokes (8/65). 34-Betty & Veronica Summer Fun (9/65). 35-Around the World with Archie (10/65).	7	14	21	51	71	90
32-Betty & Veronica Spectacular (6/65); all pin-ups; DeCarlo-c/a	9	18	27	60	85	110
36-135-**Do not exist**						
136-141: 136-The World of Jughead (12/65). 137-Archie's Christmas Stocking (1/66). 138-Betty						

Archie Giant Series Magazine #140 © AP

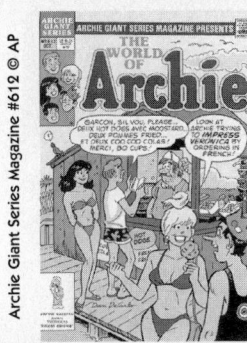

Archie Giant Series Magazine #612 © AP

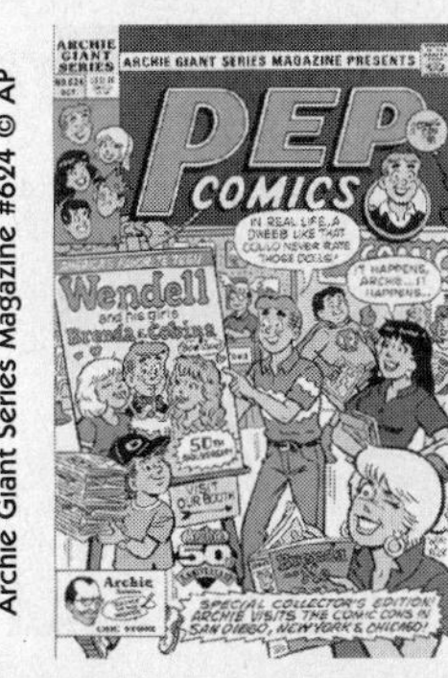

Archie Giant Series Magazine #624 © AP

GD 2.0 | VG 4.0 | FN 6.0 | VF 8.0 | VF/NM 9.0 | NM- 9.2

& Veronica Spectacular (6/66). 139-Archie's Jokes (6/66). 140-Betty & Veronica Summer Fun (8/66). 141-Around the World with Archie (9/66) 7 14 21 51 71 90

142-Archie's Super-Hero Special (10/66)-Origin Capt. Pureheart, Capt. Hero, and Evilheart 8 16 24 55 78 100

143-The World of Jughead(12/66); Capt. Hero-c/s; Man From R.I.V.E.R.D.A.L.E., Pureheart, Superteen app. 6 12 18 43 59 75

144-160: 144-Archie's Christmas Stocking (1/67). 145-Betty & Veronica Spectacular (6/67). 146-Archie's Jokes (6/67). 147-Betty & Veronica Summer Fun (8/67) 148-World of Archie (9/67). 149-World of Jughead (10/67). 150-Archie's Christmas Stocking (1/68). 151-World of Archie (2/68). 152-World of Jughead (2/68). 153-Betty & Veronica Spectacular (6/68). 154-Archie Jokes (6/68). 155-Betty & Veronica Summer Fun (8/68). 156-World of Archie (10/68). 157-World of Jughead (12/68). 158-Archie's Christmas Stocking (1/69). 159-Betty & Veronica Christmas Spectacular (1/69). 160-World of Archie (2/69); Frankenstein-s each... 4 8 12 25 33 42

161-World of Jughead (2/69); Super-Jughead-s; 11 pg.early Cricket O'Dell-s 4 8 12 27 36 45

162-183: 162-Betty & Veronica Spectacular (6/69). 163-Archie's Jokes(8/69). 164-Betty & Veronica Summer Fun (9/69). 165-World of Archie (9/69). 166-World of Jughead (9/69). 167-Archie's Christmas Stocking (1/70). 168-Betty & Veronica Christmas Spect. (1/70). 169-Archie's Christmas Love-In (1/70). 170-Jughead's Eat-Out Comic Book Mag. (12/69). 171-World of Archie (2/70). 172-World of Jughead (2/70). 173-Betty & Veronica Spectacular (6/70). 174-Archie's Jokes (8/70). 175-Betty & Veronica Summer Fun (9/70). 176-Li'l Jinx Giant Laugh-Out (8/70). 177-World of Archie (9/70). 178-World of Jughead (9/70). 179-Archie's Christmas Stocking(1/71). 180-Betty & Veronica Christmas Spect. (1/71). 181-Archie's Christmas Love-In (1/71). 182-World of Archie (2/71). 183-World of Jughead (2/71)-Last squarebound each... 3 6 9 18 24 30

184-189,193,194,197-199 (52 pgs.): 184-Betty & Veronica Spectacular (6/71). 185-Li'l Jinx Giant Laugh-Out (6/71). 186-Archie's Jokes (8/71). 187-Betty & Veronica Summer Fun (9/71). 188-World of Archie (9/71). 189-World of Jughead (9/71). 193-World of Archie (3/72).194-World of Jughead (4/72). 197-Betty & Veronica Spectacular (6/72). 198-Archie's Jokes (8/72). 199-Betty & Veronica Summer Fun (9/72) each... 3 6 9 16 20 25

190-192: 190-Archie's Christmas Stocking (12/71); Sabrina on-c. 191-Betty & Veronica Christmas Spect.(2/72); Sabrina app.. 192-Archie's Christmas Love-In (1/72); Archie Band-c/s 4 8 12 22 30 38

195-(84 pgs.)-Li'l Jinx Christmas Bag (1/72). 4 8 12 25 33 42

196-(84 pgs.)-Sabrina's Christmas Magic (1/72) 6 12 18 43 59 75

200-(52 pgs.)-World of Archie (10/72) 4 8 12 22 30 38

201-206,208-219,221-230,232,233 (All 52 pgs.): 201-Betty & Veronica Spectacular (10/72). 202-World of Jughead (11/72). 203-Archie's Christmas Stocking (12/72). 204-Betty & Veronica Christmas Spectacular (2/73). 205-Archie's Christmas Love-In (1/73). 206-Li'l Jinx Christmas Bag (12/72). 208-World of Archie (3/73). 209-World of Jughead (4/73). 210-Betty & Veronica Spectacular (6/73). 211-Archie's Jokes (8/73). 212-Betty & Veronica Summer Fun (9/73). 213-World of Archie (10/73). 214-Betty & Veronica Spectacular (10/73). 215-World of Jughead (11/73). 216-Archie's Christmas Stocking (12/73). 217-Betty & Veronica Christmas Spectacular (2/74). 218-Archie's Christmas Love-In (1/74). 219-Li'l Jinx Christmas Bag (12/73). 221-Betty & Veronica Spectacular (Advertised as World of Archie) (6/74). 222-Archie's Jokes (advertised as World of Jughead) (8/74). 223-Li'l Jinx (8/74). 224-Betty & Veronica Summer Fun (9/74). 225-World of Archie (9/74). 226-Betty & Veronica Spectacular (10/74). 227-World of Jughead (10/74). 228-Archie's Christmas Stocking (12/74). 229-Betty & Veronica Christmas Spectacular (12/74). 230-Archie's Christmas Love-In (1/75). 232-World of Archie (3/75). 233-World of Jughead (4/75) each... 2 4 6 10 13 16

207,220,231,243: Sabrina's Christmas Magic. 207-(12/72). 220-(12/73). 231-(1/75). 243-(1/76) each... 3 6 9 16 20 25

234-242,244-251 (36 pgs.): 234-Betty & Veronica Spectacular (6/75). 235-Archie's Jokes (8/75). 236-Betty & Veronica Summer Fun (9/75). 237-World of Archie (9/75) 238-Betty & Veronica Spectacular (10/75). 239-World of Jughead (10/75). 240-Archie's Christmas Stocking (12/75). 241-Betty & Veronica Christmas Spectacular (12/75). 242-Archie's Christmas Love-In (1/76). 244-World of Archie (3/76). 245-World of Jughead (4/76). 246-Betty & Veronica Spectacular (6/76). 247-Archie's Jokes (8/76). 248-Betty & Veronica Summer Fun (9/76). 249-World of Archie (9/76). 250-Betty & Veronica Spectacular (10/76). 251-World of Jughead each.... 2 4 6 9 11 14

252-451-Do not exist

452-454,456-466,468-478, 480-490,492-499: 452-Archie's Christmas Stocking (12/76). 453-Betty & Veronica Christmas Spectacular (12/76). 454-Archie's Christmas Love-In(1/77). 456-World of Archie (3/77). 457-World of Jughead (4/77). 458-Betty & Veronica Spectacular (6/77). 459-Archie's Jokes (8/77)-Shows 8/76 in error. 460-Betty & Veronica Summer Fun (9/77). 461-World of Archie (9/77). 462-Betty & Veronica Spectacular (10/77). 463-World of Jughead (10/77). 464-Archie's Christmas Stocking (12/77). 465-Betty & Veronica Christmas Spectacular (12/77). 466-Archie's Christmas Love-In (1/78). 468-World of Archie (2/78). 469-World of Jughead (2/78). 470-Betty & Veronica Spectacular(6/78). 471-Archie's Jokes (8/78). 472-Betty & Veronica Summer Fun (9/78). 473-World of Archie (9/78). 474-Betty & Veronica Spectacular (10/78). 475-World of Jughead (10/78). 476-Archie's Christmas Stocking (12/78). 477-Betty & Veronica Christmas Spectacular (12/78). 478-Archie's Christmas Love-In (1/79). 480-The World of Archie (3/79). 481-World of Jughead (4/79). 482-Betty & Veronica Spectacular (6/79). 483-Archie's Jokes (8/79). 484-Betty & Veronica Summer Fun(9/79). 485-The World of Archie (9/79). 486-Betty & Veronica Spectacular (10/79). 487-The World of Jughead (10/79). 488-Archie's Christmas Stocking (12/79). 489-Betty & Veronica Christmas Spectacular (1/80). 490-Archie's Christmas Love-in (1/80). 492-The World of Archie (2/80). 493-The World of Jughead (4/80). 494-Betty & Veronica Spectacular (6/80). 495-Archie's Jokes (8/80). 496-Betty & Veronica Summer Fun (9/80). 497-The World of Archie (9/80). 498-Betty & Veronica Spectacular (10/80). 499-The World of Jughead (10/80) each... 2 4 6 8 10 12

455,467,479,491,503-Sabrina's Christmas Magic: 455-(1/77). 467-(1/78). 479-(1/79) Dracula/ Werewolf-s. 491-(1/80), 503(1/81) 2 4 6 12 16 20

500-Archie's Christmas Stocking (12/80) 2 4 6 9 11 14

501-514,516-527,529-532,534-539,541-543,545-550: 501-Betty & Veronica Christmas Spectacular (12/80). 502-Archie's Christmas Love-in (1/81). 504-The World of Archie (3/81). 505-The World of Jughead (4/81). 506-Betty & Veronica Spectacular (6/81). 507-Archie's Jokes (8/81). 508-Betty & Veronica Summer Fun (9/81). 509-The World of Archie (9/81). 510-Betty & Vernonica Spectacular (9/81). 511-The World of Jughead (10/81). 512-Archie's Christmas Stocking (12/81). 513-Betty & Veronica Christmas Spectacular (12/81). 514-Archie's Christmas Love-in (1/82). 516-The World of Archie(3/82). 517-The World of Jughead (4/82). 518-Betty & Veronica Spectacular (6/82). 519-Archie's Jokes (8/82). 520-Betty & Veronica Summer Fun (9/82). 521-The World of Archie (9/82). 522-Betty & Veronica Spectacular (10/82). 523-The World of Jughead (10/82).524-Archie's Christmas Stocking (1/83). 525-Betty and Veronica Christmas Spectacular (1/83). 526-Betty and Veronica Spectacular (5/83). 527-Little Archie (8/83). 529-Betty and Veronica Summer Fun (8/83). 530-Betty and Veronica Spectacular (9/83). 531-The World of Jughead (9/83). 532-The World of Archie (10/83). 534-Little Archie (1/84). 535-Archie's Christmas Stocking (1/84). 536-Betty and Veronica Christmas Spectacular (1/84). 537-Betty and Veronica Spectacular (6/84). 538-Little Archie (8/84). 539-Betty and Veronica Summer Fun (8/84). 541-Betty and Veronica Spectacular (9/84). 542-The World of Jughead (9/84). 543-The World of Archie (10/84). 545-Little Archie (12/84). 546-Archie's Christmas Stocking (12/84). 547-Betty and Veronica Christmas Spectacular (12/84). 548-?. 549-Little Archie. 550-Betty and Veronica Summer Fun each... 1 2 3 5 7 9

515,528,533,540,544: 515-Sabrina's Christmas Magic (1/82). 528-Josie and the Pussycats (8/83). 533-Sabrina; Space Pirates by Frank Bolling (10/83). 540-Josie and the Pussycats (8/84). 544-Sabrina the Teen-Age Witch (10/84). each... 2 4 6 11 14 18

551,562,571,584,597-Josie and the Pussycats 2 4 6 8 10 12

552-561,563-570,572-583,585-596,598-600: 552-Betty & Veronica Spectacular. 553-The World of Jughead. 554-The World of Archie. 555-Betty's Diary. 556-Little Archie (1/86). 557-Archie's Christmas Stocking (1/86). 558-Betty & Veronica Christmas Spectacular(1/86). 559-Betty & Veronica Spectacular. 560-Little Archie. 561-Betty & Veronica Summer Fun. 563-Betty & Veronica Spectacular. 564-World of Jughead. 565-World of Archie. 566-Little Archie. 567-Archie's Christmas Stocking. 568-Betty & Veronica Christmas Spectacular. 569-Betty & Veronica Spring Spectacular. 570-Little Archie. 571-Dracula-c/s. 572-Betty & Veronica Summer Fun. 573-Archie At Riverdale High. 574-World of Archie. 575-Betty & Veronica Spectacular. 576-Pep. 577-World of Jughead. 578-Archie And Me. 579-Archie's Christmas Stocking. 580-Betty and Veronica Christmas Spectacular. 581-Little Archie Christmas Special. 582-Betty & Veronica Spring Spectacular. 583-Little Archie. 585-Betty & Veronica Summer Fun. 586-Archie At Riverdale High. 587-The World of Archie (10/88); 1st app. Explorers of the Unknown. 588-Betty & Veronica Spectacular. 589-Pep (10/88). 590-The World of Jughead. 591-Archie & Me. 592-Archie's Christmas Stocking. 593-Betty & Veronica Christmas Spectacular. 594-Little Archie. 595-Betty & Veronica Spring Spectacular. 596-Little Archie. 598-Betty & Veronica Summer Fun. 599-The World of Archie (10/89); 2nd app. Explorers of the Unknown. 600-Betty and Veronica Spectacular each.... 6.00

601,602,604-609,611-629: 601-Pep. 602-The World of Jughead. 604-Archie at Riverdale High. 605-Archie's Christmas Stocking. 606-Betty and Veronica Christmas Spectacular. 607-Little Archie. 608-Betty and Veronica Spectacular. 609-Little Archie. 611-Betty and Veronica Summer Fun. 612-The World of Archie. 613-Betty and Veronica Spectacular. 614-Pep (10/90). 615-Veronica's Summer Special. 616-Archie and Me. 617-Archie's Christmas Stocking. 618-Betty & Veronica Christmas Spectacular. 619-Little Archie. 620-Betty and Veronica Spectacular. 621-Betty and Veronica Summer Fun. 622-Josie & the Pussycats; not published. 623-Betty and Veronica Spectacular. 624-Pep Comics. 625-Veronica's Summer Special. 626-Archie and Me. 627-World of Archie. 628-Archie's Pals 'n' Gals Holiday Special. 629-Betty & Veronica Christmas Spectacular. each.... 4.00

603-Archie and Me; Titanic app. 5.00

610-Josie and the Pussycats 1 2 3 4 5 7

630-631: 630-Archie's Christmas Stocking. 631-Archie's Pals 'n' Gals 4.00

632-Last issue; Betty & Veronica Spectacular 1 2 3 4 5 7

NOTE: *Archies Band-c-173,180,192; s-189,192. Archie Cavemen-165,225,232,244,249. Little Sabrina-527,534, 538,545,556,566. UFO-s-178,487,594.*

ARCHIE MEETS THE PUNISHER (Same contents as The Punisher Meets Archie)

Archie's Double Digest #134 © AP

Archie's Girls Betty & Veronica #1 © AP

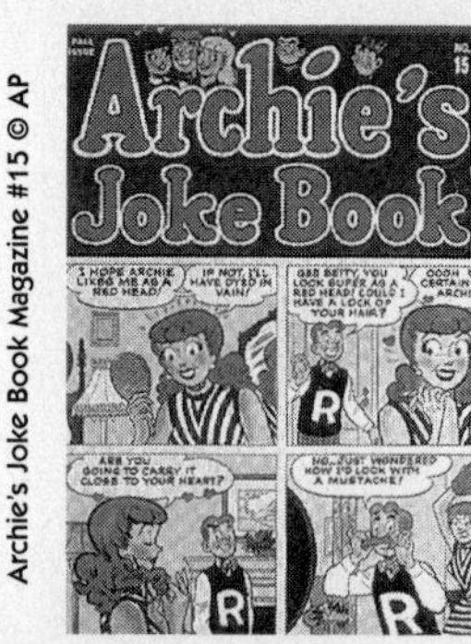

Archie's Joke Book Magazine #15 © AP

GD VG FN VF VF/NM NM-
2.0 4.0 6.0 8.0 9.0 9.2

Marvel Comics & Archie Comics Publ.: Aug, 1994 ($2.95, 52 pgs., one-shot)
1-Batton Lash story, J. Buscema-a on Punisher, S. Goldberg-a on Archie 6.00

ARCHIE'S ACTIVITY COMICS DIGEST MAGAZINE
Archie Enterprises: 1985 - No. 4 (Annual, 128 pgs., digest size)
1 (Most copies are marked) 2 4 6 9 11 14
2-4 1 2 3 5 6 8

ARCHIE'S CAR
Spire Christian Comics (Fleming H. Revell co.): 1979 (49¢)
nn 1 3 4 6 8 11

ARCHIE'S CHRISTMAS LOVE-IN (See Archie Giant Series Mag. No. 169, 181,192, 205, 218, 230, 242, 454, 466, 478, 490, 502, 514)

ARCHIE'S CHRISTMAS STOCKING (See Archie Giant Series Mag. No. 1-6,10, 15, 20, 25, 31, 137, 144, 150, 158, 167, 179, 190, 203, 216, 228, 240, 452, 464, 476, 488, 500, 512, 524, 535, 546, 557, 567, 579, 592, 605, 617, 630)

ARCHIE'S CHRISTMAS STOCKING
Archie Comics: 1993 - Present ($2.00, 52 pgs.)(Bound-in calendar poster in all)
1-Dan DeCarlo-c/a 5.00
2-5 4.00
6,7: 6-(1998, $2.25). 7-(1999, $2.29) 3.00

ARCHIE'S CLASSIC CHRISTMAS STORIES
Archie Comics: 2002 ($10.95, TPB)
Volume 1 - Reprints stories from 1955-1964 Archie's Christmas Stocking issues 11.00

ARCHIE'S CLEAN SLATE
Spire Christian Comics (Fleming H. Revell Co.): 1973 (35/49¢)
1-(35¢-c edition)(Some issues have nn) 2 4 6 10 13 16
1-(49¢-c edition) 2 4 6 9 11 14

ARCHIE'S DATE BOOK
Spire Christian comics (Fleming H. Revell Co.): 1981
nn-(Low print) 2 4 6 9 11 14

ARCHIE'S DOUBLE DIGEST QUARTERLY MAGAZINE
Archie Comics: 1981 - Present ($1.95/$2.75/$2.95/$3.19, 256 pgs.) (Archie's Double Digest Magazine No. 10 on)
1 3 6 9 18 24 30
2-10; 6-Katy Keene story. 2 4 6 11 14 18
11-30: 29-Pureheart story 2 4 6 8 10 12
31-50 1 2 3 4 5 7
51-70,100 5.00
71-99 4.00
101-158: 115-Begin $3.19-c. 123-Begin $3.29-c. 139-Begin $3.59-c 3.60

ARCHIE'S FAMILY ALBUM
Spire Christian Comics (Fleming H. Revell Co.): 1978 (39¢/49¢, 36 pgs.)
nn 1 3 4 6 8 11
nn (49¢-c edition) 1 2 3 5 6 8

ARCHIE'S FESTIVAL
Spire Christian Comics (Fleming H. Revell Co.): 1980 (49¢)
nn 2 4 6 8 10 12

ARCHIE'S GIRLS, BETTY AND VERONICA (Becomes Betty & Veronica)(Also see Veronica)
Archie Publications (Close-Up): 1950 - No. 347, Apr, 1987
1 192 384 576 1200 1850 2500
2 81 162 243 506 778 1050
3-5: 3-Betty's 1st ponytail. 4-Dan DeCarlo's 1st Archie work
48 96 144 293 447 600
6-10: 10-Katy Keene app. (2 pgs.) 40 80 120 239 357 475
11-20: 11,13,14,17-19-Katy Keene app. 17-Last pre-code issue (3/55). 20-Debbie's Diary (2 pgs.) 32 64 96 184 267 350
21-30: 27,30-Katy Keene app. 29-Tarzan 23 46 69 130 188 245
31-43,45-50: 41-Marilyn Monroe and Brigitte Bardot mentioned. 45-Fabian 1 pg. photo & bio. 46-Bobby Darin 1 pg. photo & bio 16 32 48 89 127 165
44-Elvis Presley 1 pg. photo & bio 18 36 54 100 143 185
51-55,57-74: 67-Jackie Kennedy homage. 73-Sci-fi-c8 16 24 58 82 105
56-Elvis and Bobby Darin records parody 10 20 30 67 96 125
75-Betty & Veronica sell souls to Devil 15 30 45 109 167 225
76-99: 82-Bobby Rydell 1 pg. illustrated bio; Elvis mentioned on-c. 84-Connie Francis 1 pg. illustrated bio 6 12 18 40 55 70
100 7 14 21 46 63 80
101-104, 106-117,120 (12/65): 113-Monsters-s 4 8 12 29 40 50
105-Beatles wig parody (5 pg. story)(9/64) 5 10 15 33 44 55
118-(10/65) 1st app./origin Superteen (also see Betty & Me #3)
6 12 18 43 59 75
119-2nd app./last Superteen story 5 10 15 33 44 55
121,122,124-126,128-140 (8/67): 135,140-Mod-c. 136-Slave Girl-s
3 6 9 18 24 30
123-"Jingo"-Ringo parody-c 3 7 10 21 28 35
127-Beatles Fan Club-s 4 8 12 28 38 48
141-156,158-163,165-180 (12/70) 2 4 6 14 18 22
157,164-Archies Band 3 6 9 18 24 30
181-193,195-199 2 4 6 10 12 15
194-Sabrina-c/s 3 6 9 18 24 30
200-(8/72) 2 4 6 11 14 18
201-205,207,209,211-215,217-240 1 3 4 6 8 10
206,208,216-Sabrina c/app. 206-Josie-c. 210-Sabrina app.
2 4 6 12 16 20
241 (1/76)-270 (6/78) 1 2 3 5 7 9
271-299: 281-UFO-s 1 2 3 5 6 8
300 (12/80)-Anniversary issue 1 2 3 5 7 9
301-309 6.00
310-John Travolta parody story 1 2 3 5 6 8
311-319 6.00
320 (10/82)-Intro. of Cheryl Blossom on cover and inside story (she also appears, but not on the cover, in Jughead #325 with same 10/82 publication date)
4 8 12 27 36 45
321,322-Cheryl Blossom app. 2 4 6 12 16 20
323,326,327,330,331,333-347: 333-Monsters-s 5.00
324,325-Crickett O'Dell app. 7.00
328-Cheryl Blossom app. 2 4 6 9 11 14
329,332: 329-Betty dressed as Madonna. 332-Superhero costume party
1 2 3 5 6 8
Annual 1 (1953) 90 180 270 563 869 1175
Annual 2 (1954) 42 84 126 256 391 525
Annual 3-5 (1955-1957) 37 74 111 209 305 400
Annual 6-8 (1958-1960) 24 48 72 138 199 260

ARCHIE'S HOLIDAY FUN DIGEST
Archie Comics: 1997 - Present ($1.75/$1.95/$1.99/$2.19/$2.39, annual)
1-9-Christmas stories 2.50

ARCHIE'S JOKEBOOK COMICS DIGEST ANNUAL (See Jokebook...)

ARCHIE'S JOKE BOOK MAGAZINE (See Joke Book ...)
Archie Publ: 1953 - No. 3, Sum, 1954; No. 15, Fall, 1954 - No. 288, 11/82 (subtitled...Laugh-In #127-140; ...Laugh-Out #141-194)
1953-One Shot (#1) 92 18 276 575 888 1200
2 47 94 141 287 436 585
3 (no #4-14) 40 80 120 233 342 450
15-20: 15-Formerly Archie's Rival Reggie #14; last pre-code issue (Fall/54). 15-17-Katy Keene app. 25 50 75 141 203 265
21-30 15 30 45 86 123 160
31-43: 42-Bio of Ed "Kookie" Byrnes. 43-story about guitarist Duane Eddy
11 22 33 62 84 105
44-1st professional comic work by Neal Adams, 4 pgs.
25 50 75 141 203 265
45-47-N. Adams-a in all, 2-6 pgs. 15 30 45 83 117 150
48-Four pgs. N. Adams-a 15 30 45 86 123 160
49,50 5 10 15 36 48 65
51-56,58-60 (1962): 58,59-Horror/Sci-Fi-c 4 8 12 28 38 48
57-Elvis mentioned; Marilyn Monroe cameo 5 10 15 36 48 60
61-80 (8/64): 66-(12¢ cover) 3 6 9 18 24 30
66-(15¢ cover variant) 3 7 10 21 28 35
81-89,91,92,94-99 2 4 6 14 18 22
90,93: 90-Beatles gag. 93-Beatles cameo 3 6 9 18 24 30
100 (5/66) 3 6 9 18 23 28
101,103-117,119-123,127,129,131-140 (9/69): 105-Superhero gag-c. 108-110-Archies Archers Band-s. 116-Beatles/Monkees/Bob Dylan cameos (posters)
2 4 6 11 14 18
102 (7/66) Archie Band prototype-c; Elvis parody panel, Rolling Stones mention
3 6 9 19 25 32
118,124,125,126,128,130: 118-Archie Band-c; Veronica & Groovers band-s. 124-Archies Band-c/app. 125-Beatles cameo (poster). 126,130-Monkees cameo. 128-Veronica/Archies Band app. 3 6 9 18 23 28
141-173,175-181,183-199 2 4 6 8 10 12
174-Sabrina-c. 182-Sabrina cameo 2 4 6 10 12 15
200 (9/74) 2 4 6 10 12 15
201-230 (3/77) 1 2 3 5 6 8

Archie's Pal Jughead #20 © AP

Archie's Pal Jughead #57 © AP

Archie's R/C Racers #3 © AP

	GD 2.0	VG 4.0	FN 6.0	VF 8.0	VF/NM 9.0	NM- 9.2
231-239,241-287						6.00
240-Elvis record-c	1	2	3	5	7	9
288-Last issue	1	2	3	4	5	7

NOTE: *Archies Band-c-118,124,147,172; 1 pg.-s-127,128,138,140,143,147,167; 2 pg.-s-124,131, 155. Sabrina app.-247,248,252-259,261,262,264,266-270,274,277,284-286.*

ARCHIE'S JOKES (See Archie Giant Series Mag. No. 17, 22, 27, 33, 139, 146, 154, 163, 174, 186, 198, 211, 222, 235, 247, 459, 471, 483, 495, 519)

ARCHIE'S LOVE SCENE
Spire Christian Comics (Fleming H. Revell Co.): 1973 (35¢/49¢/no price)

	GD 2.0	VG 4.0	FN 6.0	VF 8.0	VF/NM 9.0	NM- 9.2
1-(35¢ Edition)	2	4	6	10	13	16
1-(49¢ Edition/no price) (Some copies have nn)	2	4	6	8	10	12

ARCHIE'S LOVE SHOWDOWN SPECIAL
Archie Publications: 1994 ($2.00, one-shot)

	GD 2.0	VG 4.0	FN 6.0	VF 8.0	VF/NM 9.0	NM- 9.2
1-Concludes x-over from Archie #429, Betty #19, B&V #82, Veronica #39						3.00

ARCHIE'S MADHOUSE (Madhouse Ma-ad No. 67 on)
Archie Publications: Sept, 1959 - No. 66, Feb, 1969

	GD 2.0	VG 4.0	FN 6.0	VF 8.0	VF/NM 9.0	NM- 9.2
1-Archie begins	24	48	72	170	260	350
2	12	24	36	86	131	175
3-5	9	18	27	65	93	120
6-10	7	14	21	46	63	80
11-17 (Last w/regular characters)	6	12	18	38	52	65
18-21,23,29: 18-New format begins. 23-No Sabrina	4	8	12	29	40	50
22-1st app. Sabrina, the Teen-age Witch (10/62)	24	48	72	174	267	360
24-2nd app.Sabrina a	10	20	30	67	96	125
25,26,28-Sabrina app. 25-1st app. Captain Sprocket (4/63)	7	14	21	51	71	90
27-Sabrina-c; no story	6	12	18	40	55	70
30,34,38-40: No Sabrina. 34-Bordered-c begin.	3	6	9	18	24	30
31,33,37-Sabrina app.	6	12	18	38	52	65
32-Sabrina app.?	3	6	9	18	24	30
35-Beatles cameo. No Sabrina	3	7	10	21	28	35
36-1st Salem the Cat w/Sabrina story	7	14	21	51	71	90
41-48,51-57,60-62,64-66; No Sabrina 43-Mighty Crusaders cameo. 44-Swipes Mad #4 (Super-Duperman) in "Bird Monsters From Outer Space"	3	6	9	16	20	24
49,50,58,59,63-Sabrina stories	4	8	12	29	40	50
Annual 1 (1962-63) no Sabrina	8	16	24	55	78	100
Annual 2 (1964) no Sabrina	5	10	15	36	48	60
Annual 3 (1965)-Origin Sabrina the Teen-Age Witch	10	20	30	67	96	125
Annual 4,5('66-68)(Becomes Madhouse Ma-ad Annual #7 on); no Sabrina	3	6	9	19	25	32
Annual 6 (1969)-Sabrina the Teen-Age Witch-sty	6	12	18	40	55	70

NOTE: *Cover title to #61-65 is "Madhouse" and to #66 is "Madhouse Ma-ad Jokes". Sci-Fi/Horror covers 6, 8, 11, 13, 15-26, 29, 35, 36, 38, 42, 43, 48, 51, 58, 60.*

ARCHIE'S MECHANICS
Archie Publications: Sept, 1954 - No. 3, 1955

	GD 2.0	VG 4.0	FN 6.0	VF 8.0	VF/NM 9.0	NM- 9.2
1-(15¢; 52 pgs.)	79	158	237	494	760	1025
2-(10¢)-Last pre-code issue	48	96	144	293	447	600
3-(10¢)	40	80	120	240	363	485

ARCHIE'S MYSTERIES (Continued from Archie's Weird Mysteries)
Archie Comics: No. 25, Feb, 2003 - No. 34, June, 2004 ($2.19)

	GD 2.0	VG 4.0	FN 6.0	VF 8.0	VF/NM 9.0	NM- 9.2
25-34- Archie and gang as "Teen Scene Investigators"						2.25

ARCHIE'S ONE WAY
Spire Christian Comics (Fleming H. Revell Co.): 1972 (35¢/39¢/49¢, 36 pgs.)

	GD 2.0	VG 4.0	FN 6.0	VF 8.0	VF/NM 9.0	NM- 9.2
nn-(35¢ Edition)	2	4	6	10	12	15
nn-(39¢, 49¢, no price editions)	2	4	6	8	10	12

ARCHIE'S PAL, JUGHEAD (Jughead No. 127 on)
Archie Publications: 1949 - No. 126, Nov, 1965

	GD 2.0	VG 4.0	FN 6.0	VF 8.0	VF/NM 9.0	NM- 9.2
1 (1949)-1st app. Moose (see Pep #33)	146	292	438	913	1407	1900
2 (1950)	67	134	201	419	647	875
3-5	40	80	120	244	372	500
6-10: 7-Suzie app.	31	62	93	178	259	340
11-20: 20-Jughead as Sherlock Holmes parody	20	40	60	112	161	210
21-30: 23-25,28-30-Katy Keene app. 23-Early Dilton-s. 28-Debbie's Diary app.	15	30	45	83	117	150
31-50: 49-Archies Rock 'N' Rollers band-c	7	14	21	51	71	90
51-70: 58-Neal Adams-a. 59- Bio of Will Hutchins of TV's Sugarfoot. 67-Betty seducing Jughead-c. 68-Early Archie Gang Cavemen-s	5	10	15	36	48	60
71-76,83,84,89-99: 72-Jughead dates Betty & Veronica. 95-2nd app. Cricket O'Dell	3	7	10	21	28	35
77,78,80-82,85,86,88-Horror/Sci-Fi-c	4	8	12	29	40	50
79-Creature From the Black Lagoon-c	6	12	18	38	52	65
87-Early Big Ethel app.; UGAJ (United Girls Against Jughead)-s	4	8	12	29	40	50
100	4	8	12	27	36	45
101-Return of Big Ethyl	4	8	12	27	36	45
102-126	3	6	9	18	24	30
Annual 1 (1953, 25¢)	60	120	180	375	575	775
Annual 2 (1954, 25¢)-Last pre-code issue	40	80	120	235	348	460
Annual 3-5 (1955-57, 25¢)	29	58	87	164	237	310
Annual 6-8 (1958-60, 25¢)	18	36	54	102	146	190

ARCHIE'S PAL JUGHEAD COMICS (Formerly Jughead #1-45)
Archie Comic Publ.: No. 46, June, 1993 - Present ($1.25/$1.50/$1.75/$1.79/$1.99/$2.19)

	GD 2.0	VG 4.0	FN 6.0	VF 8.0	VF/NM 9.0	NM- 9.2
46-60						3.00
61-163: 100-"A Storm Over Uniforms" x-over part 1,2						2.25

ARCHIE'S PALS 'N' GALS (Also see Archie Giant Series Magazine #628)
Archie Publ: 1952-53 - No. 6, 1957-58; No. 7, 1958 - No. 224, Sept, 1991
(...All News Stories on-c #49-59)

	GD 2.0	VG 4.0	FN 6.0	VF 8.0	VF/NM 9.0	NM- 9.2
1-(116 pgs., 25¢)	77	154	231	481	741	1000
2(Annual)('54, 25¢)	40	80	120	244	372	500
3-5(Annual, '55-57, 25¢): 3-Last pre-code issue	31	62	93	178	259	340
6-10('58-'60)	19	38	57	107	154	200
11-18,20 (84 pgs.): 12-Harry Belafonte 2 pg. photos & bio. 12,15-Neal Adams-a. 17-B&V paper dolls. 18-Horror/Sci-Fi-c	11	22	33	62	84	105
19-Marilyn Monroe app.	15	30	45	83	117	150
21,22,24-28,30 (68 pgs.)	6	12	18	40	55	70
23-(Wint./62) 6 pg. Josie-s with Pepper and Melody (1st app.?); Betty in towel pin-up	11	22	33	77	114	150
29-Beatles satire (68 pgs.)	9	18	27	63	89	115
31(Wint. 64/65)-39 -(68 pgs.)	5	10	15	36	48	60
40-Early Superteen-s; with Pureheart	6	12	18	43	59	75
41(8/67)-43,45-50(2/69) (68 pgs.)	4	8	12	24	32	40
44-Archies Band-s; WEB cameo	4	8	12	29	40	50
51(4/69),52,55-64(6/71): 62-Last squarebound	3	6	9	19	25	32
53-Archies Band-c/s	4	8	12	24	32	40
54-Satan meets Veronica-s	5	10	15	33	44	55
65(8/70),67-70,73-81,83(6/74) (52 pgs.)	2	4	6	14	18	22
66,82-Sabrina-c	3	7	10	21	28	35
71,72-Two part drug story (8/72,9/72)	3	6	9	19	25	32
75-Archies Band-s	3	6	9	18	24	30
84-99	1	3	4	6	8	10
100 (12/75)	2	4	6	10	12	15
101-130(3/79): 125,126-Riverdale 2001-s	1	2	3	5	6	8
131-160,162-170 (7/84)						6.00
161 (11/82) 3rd app./1st solo Cheryl Blossom-s and pin-up; 2nd Jason Blossom	3	6	9	18	23	28
171-173,175,177-197,199: 197-G. Colan-a						4.00
174,176,198: 174-New Archies Band-s. 176-Cyndi Lauper-c. 198-Archie gang on strike at Archie Ent. offices						6.00
200(9/88)-Illiteracy-s						6.00
201,203-223: Later issues $1.00 cover						3.00
202-Explains end of Archie's jalopy; Dezerland-c/s; James Dean cameo						6.00
224-Last issue						5.00

NOTE: *Archies Band-c-45,47,49,53,56; s-44,53,75,174. UFO-s-50,63,209,220.*

ARCHIE'S PALS 'N' GALS DOUBLE DIGEST MAGAZINE
Archie Comic Publications: Nov, 1992 - Present ($2.50-$3.59)

	GD 2.0	VG 4.0	FN 6.0	VF 8.0	VF/NM 9.0	NM- 9.2
1-Capt. Hero story; Pureheart app.	1	3	4	6	8	10
2-10: 2-Superduck story; Little Jinx in all. 4-Begin $2.75-c						6.00
11-29						4.00
30-92: 40-Begin $2.99-c. 48-Begin $3.19-c. 56-Begin $3.29-c. 72-Begin $3.59-c						3.60

ARCHIE'S PARABLES
Spire Christian Comics (Fleming H. Revell Co.): 1973,1975 (39/49¢, 36 pgs.)

	GD 2.0	VG 4.0	FN 6.0	VF 8.0	VF/NM 9.0	NM- 9.2
nn-By Al Hartley; 39¢ Edition	2	4	6	10	12	15
49¢, no price editions	2	4	6	8	10	12

ARCHIE'S R/C RACERS (Radio controlled cars)
Archie Comics: Sept, 1989 - No. 10, Mar, 1991 (95¢/$1)

	GD 2.0	VG 4.0	FN 6.0	VF 8.0	VF/NM 9.0	NM- 9.2
1						6.00
2,5-7,10: 5-Elvis parody. 7-Supervillain-c/s. 10-UFO-c/s						4.00
3,4,8,9						3.00

ARCHIE'S RIVAL REGGIE (Reggie & Archie's Joke Book #15 on)
Archie Publications: 1950 - No. 14, Aug, 1954

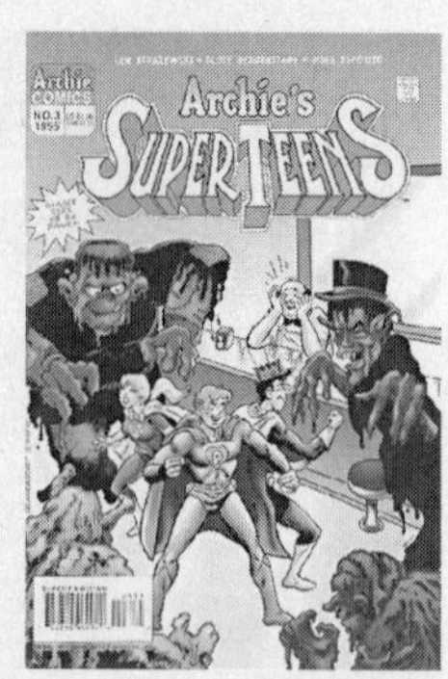

Archie's Super Teens #3 © AP

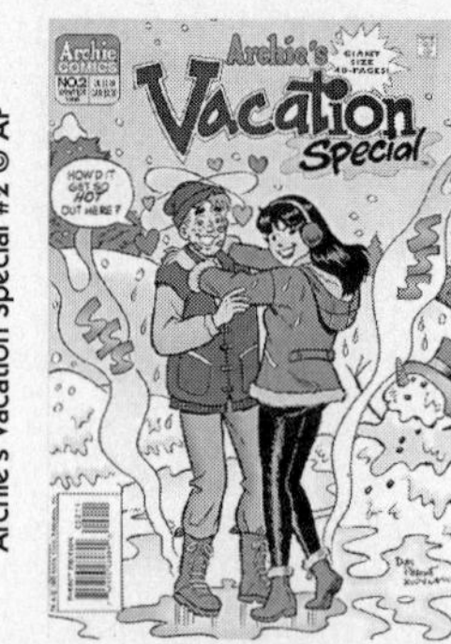

Archie's Vacation Special #2 © AP

Aria Preview © Haberlin & Holguin

	GD 2.0	VG 4.0	FN 6.0	VF 8.0	VF/NM 9.0	NM- 9.2
1-Reggie 1st app. in Jackpot Comics #5	81	162	243	506	778	1050
2	40	80	120	239	357	475
3-5	31	62	93	178	259	340
6-10	22	44	66	127	184	240
11-14: Katy Keene in No. 10-14, 1-2 pgs.	16	32	48	89	127	165

ARCHIE'S RIVERDALE HIGH (See Riverdale High)

ARCHIE'S ROLLER COASTER
Spire Christian Comics (Fleming H. Revell Co.): 1981 (69¢)

	GD	VG	FN	VF	VF/NM	NM-
nn-(Low print)	2	4	6	9	11	14

ARCHIE'S SOMETHING ELSE
Spire Christian Comics (Fleming H. Revell Co.): 1975 (39/49¢, 36 pgs.)

	GD	VG	FN	VF	VF/NM	NM-
nn-(39¢-c) Hell's Angels Biker on motorcycle-c	2	4	6	10	13	16
nn-(49¢-c)	2	4	6	8	10	12
Barbour Christian Comics Edition ('86, no price listed)	1	2	3	5	6	8

ARCHIE'S SONSHINE
Spire Christian Comics (Fleming H. Revell Co.): 1973, 1974 (39/49¢, 36 pgs.)

	GD	VG	FN	VF	VF/NM	NM-
39¢ Edition	2	4	6	10	12	15
49¢, no price editions	1	3	4	6	8	11

ARCHIE'S SPORTS SCENE
Spire Christian Comics (Fleming H. Revell Co.): 1983 (no cover price)

	GD	VG	FN	VF	VF/NM	NM-
nn-(Low print)	2	4	6	10	13	16

ARCHIE'S SPRING BREAK
Archie Comics: 1996 - Present ($2.00, 48 pgs., annual)

	GD	VG	FN	VF	VF/NM	NM-
1-Dan DeCarlo-c						3.00
2-4: 2-Dan DeCarlo-c						2.50

ARCHIE'S STORY & GAME COMICS DIGEST MAGAZINE
Archie Enterprises: Nov, 1986 - No. 39, Jan, 1998 ($1.25-$1.95, 128 pgs., digest-size)

	GD	VG	FN	VF	VF/NM	NM-
1: Marked-up copies are common	2	4	6	10	13	16
2-10	1	3	4	6	8	10
11-20						6.00
21-38						3.00
39-($1.95)						2.50

ARCHIE'S SUPER HERO SPECIAL (See Archie Giant Series Mag. No. 142)

ARCHIE'S SUPER HERO SPECIAL (...Comics Digest Mag. 2)
Archie Publications (Red Circle): Jan, 1979 - No. 2, Aug, 1979 (95¢, 148 pgs.)

	GD	VG	FN	VF	VF/NM	NM-
1-Simon & Kirby r-/Double Life of Pvt. Strong #1,2; Black Hood, The Fly, Jaguar, The Web app.	2	4	6	11	14	18
2-Contains contents to the never published Black Hood #1; origin Black Hood; N. Adams, Wood, McWilliams, Morrow, S&K-a(r); N. Adams-c. The Shield, The Fly, Jaguar, Hangman, Steel Sterling, The Web, The Fox-r	2	4	6	12	16	20

ARCHIE'S SUPER TEENS
Archie Comic Publications, Inc.: 1994 - No. 4, 1996 ($2.00, 52 pgs.)

	GD	VG	FN	VF	VF/NM	NM-
1-Staton/Esposito-c/a; pull-out poster						3.00
2-4: 2-Fred Hembeck script; Bret Blevins/Terry Austin-a						2.50

ARCHIE'S TV LAUGH-OUT ("...Starring Sabrina" on-c #1-50)
Archie Publications: Dec, 1969 - No. 106, Apr, 1986 (#1-7: 68 pgs.)

	GD	VG	FN	VF	VF/NM	NM-
1-Sabrina begins, thru #106	10	20	30	73	107	140
2 (68 pgs.)	6	12	18	40	55	70
3-6 (68 pgs.)	4	8	12	29	40	50
7-Josie begins, thru #105; Archie's & Josie's Bands cover logos begin	7	14	21	51	71	90
8-23 (52 pgs.): 10-1st Josie on-c. 12-1st Josie and Pussycats on-c. 14-Beatles cameo on poster	4	8	12	27	36	45
24-40: 37,39,40-Bicenntennial-c	2	4	6	14	18	24
41,47,56: 41-Alexandra rejoins J&P band. 47-Fonz cameo; voodoo-s. 56-Fonz parody; B&V with Farrah hair-c	3	6	9	16	20	25
42-46,48-55,57-60	2	4	6	10	12	15
61-68,70-80: 63-UFO-s. 79-Mummy-s	1	3	4	6	8	10
69-Sherlock Holmes parody	1	3	4	6	8	10
81-90,94,95,97-99: 84 Voodoo-s	1	2	3	5	6	8
91-Early Cheryl Blossom-s; Sabrina/Archies Band-c	2	4	6	11	14	18
92-A-Team parody	1	2	3	5	7	9
93-(2/84) Archie in drag-s; Hill Street Blues-s; Groucho Marx parody; cameo parody app. of Batman, Spider-Man, Wonder Woman and others	2	4	6	8	10	12
96-MASH parody-s; Jughead in drag; Archies Band-c	1	2	3	5	7	9
100-(4/85) Michael Jackson parody-c/s; J&P band and Archie band on-c	2	4	6	10	12	15
101-104-Lower print run. 104-Miami Vice parody-c	1	2	3	5	7	9
105-Wrestling/Hulk Hogan parody-c; J&P band-s	2	4	6	8	10	12
106-Last issue; low print run	2	4	6	8	10	12

NOTE: ***Dan DeCarlo-a*** *78-up(most),* ***c****-89-up(most).* ***Archies Band-s*** *2,7,9-11,15,20,25,37,64,65,67,68,70,73,76,78,79,83,84,86,90,96,100,101;* ***Archies Band-c*** *2,17,20,91,94,96,99-103.* ***Josie-s*** *12,21,26,35,52,78,80,90.* ***Josie-c*** *10,91,94.* ***Josie and the Pussycats (as a band in costume)-s*** *7,9,10,37,38,41,42,66,84,99-101,105.* ***Josie w/Pussycats member Valerie &/or Melody-s*** *17,20,22,25,27-29,31,33,36,39,40,43-51,53-65,67-77,79,81-83,85-89,92-94,102-104.* ***Josie w/Pussycats band-c*** *12,14,17,18,22,24.* ***Sabrina-s*** *1-9,11-86,88-106.* ***Sabrina-c*** *1-18,21,23,27,49,91,94.*

ARCHIE'S VACATION SPECIAL
Archie Publications: Winter, 1994 - Present ($2.00/$2.25/$2.29/$2.49, annual)

	GD	VG	FN	VF	VF/NM	NM-
1						4.00
2-8: 8-(2000, $2.49)						3.00

ARCHIE'S WEIRD MYSTERIES (Continues as Archie's Mysteries)
Archie Comics: Feb, 2000 - No. 24, Dec, 2002 ($1.79/$1.99)

	GD	VG	FN	VF	VF/NM	NM-
1						3.50
2-10: 3-Mighty Crusaders app.						3.00
11-24: 14-Super Teens-c/app.; Mighty Crusaders app.						2.50

ARCHIE'S WORLD
Spire Christian Comics (Fleming H. Revell Co.): 1973, 1976 (39/49¢)

	GD	VG	FN	VF	VF/NM	NM-
39¢ Edition	2	4	6	10	12	15
49¢ Edition, no price editions	1	3	4	6	8	11

ARCHIE 3000
Archie Comics: May, 1989 - No. 16, July, 1991 (75¢/95¢/$1.00)

	GD	VG	FN	VF	VF/NM	NM-
1,16: 16-Aliens-c/s						4.00
2-15: 6-Begin $1.00-c; X-Mas-c						3.00

ARCOMICS PREMIERE
Arcomics: July, 1993 ($2.95)

	GD	VG	FN	VF	VF/NM	NM-
1-1st lenticular-c on a comic (flicker-c)						3.00

AREA 52
Image Comics: Jan, 2001 - No. 4, June, 2001 ($2.95)

	GD	VG	FN	VF	VF/NM	NM-
1-4-Haberlin-s/Henry-a						3.00

AREA 88
Eclipse Comics/VIZ Comics #37 on: May 26, 1987 - No. 42, 1989 ($1.50/$1.75, B&W)

	GD	VG	FN	VF	VF/NM	NM-
1-42: 1,2-2nd printings exist						2.25

AREALA: ANGEL OF WAR (See Warrior Nun titles)
Antarctic Press: Sept, 1998 - No. 4, June, 1999 ($2.95/$2.99, color/B&W)

	GD	VG	FN	VF	VF/NM	NM-
1-4: 3,4-B&W. 4-($2.99-c)						3.00

ARENA
Alchemy Studios: Jan, 1990 ($1.50, 7x10-1/8", 20 pgs.)

	GD	VG	FN	VF	VF/NM	NM-
1-Science fiction						2.25
1-Signed & numbered ed. (500 copies)						3.00

ARGUS (See Flash, 2nd Series) (Also see Showcase '95 #1,2)
DC Comics: Apr, 1995 - No. 6, Oct, 1995 ($1.50, limited series)

	GD	VG	FN	VF	VF/NM	NM-
1-6: 4-Begin $1.75-c						2.25

ARIA
Image Comics (Avalon Studios): Jan, 1999 - Present ($2.50)

	GD	VG	FN	VF	VF/NM	NM-
Preview (11/98, $2.95)						5.00
1-Anacleto-c/a	1	2	3	5	6	8
1-Variant-c by Michael Turner	1	2	3	5	6	8
1-($10.00) Alternate-c by Turner	1	3	4	6	8	10
1,2-(Blanc & Noir) Black and white printing of pencil art						3.00
1-(Blanc & Noir) DF Edition						5.00
2-4: 2,4-Anacleto-c/a. 3-Martinez-a						3.00
4-($6.95) Glow in the Dark-c	1	3	4	6	8	10
Aria Angela 1 (2/00, $2.95) Anacleto-a; 4 covers by Anacleto, JG Jones, Portacio and Quesada						3.00
Aria Angela Blanc & Noir 1 (4/00, $2.95) Anacleto-c						3.00
Aria Angela European Ashcan						10.00
Aria Angela 2 (10/00, $2.95) Anacleto-a/c						3.00
...: A Midwinter's Dream 1 (1/02, $4.95, 7"x7") text-s w/Anacleto panels						5.00
...: The Enchanted Collection (5/04, $16.95) r/Summer's Spell & The Uses of Enchantment						17.00

ARIA: SUMMER'S SPELL
Image Comics (Avalon Studios): Mar, 2002 - No. 2, Jun, 2002 ($2.95)

	GD	VG	FN	VF	VF/NM	NM-
1,2-Anacleto-c/Holguin-s/Pajarillo & Medina-a						3.00

ARIA: THE SOUL MARKET
Image Comics (Avalon Studios): Mar, 2001 - No. 6, Dec, 2001 ($2.95)

Arizona Kid #1 © MAR

Armorines V2#1 © Acclaim

Army of Darkness: Ashes 2 Ashes #1 © Orion Picts.

	GD 2.0	VG 4.0	FN 6.0	VF 8.0	VF/NM 9.0	NM- 9.2
1-6-Anacleto-c/Holguin-s						3.00
HC (2002, $26.95, 8.25" x 12.25") oversized r/#1-6						27.00
SC (2004, $16.95, 8.25" x 12.25") oversized r/#1-6						17.00

ARIA: THE USES OF ENCHANTMENT
Image Comics (Avalon Studios): Feb, 2003 - No. 4, Sept, 2003 ($2.95)

	GD	VG	FN	VF	VF/NM	NM-
1-4-Anacleto-c/Holguin-s/Medina-a						3.00

ARIANE AND BLUEBEARD (See Night Music #8)

ARIEL & SEBASTIAN (See Cartoon Tales & The Little Mermaid)

ARION, LORD OF ATLANTIS (Also see Warlord #55)
DC Comics: Nov, 1982 - No. 35, Sept, 1985

	GD	VG	FN	VF	VF/NM	NM-
1-Story cont'd from Warlord #62						3.00
2-35, Special #1 (11/85)						2.25

ARION THE IMMORTAL (Also see Showcase '95 #7)
DC Comics: July, 1992 - No. 6, Dec, 1992 ($1.50, limited series)

	GD	VG	FN	VF	VF/NM	NM-
1						3.00
2-6: 4-Gustovich-a(i)						2.25

ARISTOCATS (See Movie Comics & Walt Disney Showcase No. 16)

ARISTOKITTENS, THE (...Meet Jiminy Cricket No. 1)(Disney)
Gold Key: Oct, 1971 - No. 9, Oct, 1975

	GD	VG	FN	VF	VF/NM	NM-
1	4	8	12	22	30	38
2-5,7-9	3	6	9	16	20	24
6-(52 pgs.)	3	6	9	18	23	28

ARIZONA KID, THE (Also see The Comics & Wild Western)
Marvel/Atlas Comics(CSI): Mar, 1951 - No. 6, Jan, 1952

	GD	VG	FN	VF	VF/NM	NM-
1	24	48	72	138	199	260
2-4: 2-Heath-a(3)	12	24	36	71	98	125
5,6	10	20	30	58	77	95

NOTE: ***Heath** a-1-3; c-1-3. **Maneely** c-4-6. **Morisi** a-4-6. **Sinnott** a-6.*

ARK, THE (See The Crusaders)

ARKAGA
Image Comics: Sept, 1997 ($2.95, one-shot)

	GD	VG	FN	VF	VF/NM	NM-
1-Jorgensen-s/a						3.00

ARKANIUM
Dreamwave Productions: Sept, 2002 - No. 5 ($2.95)

	GD	VG	FN	VF	VF/NM	NM-
1-5: 1-Gatefold wraparound-c						3.00

ARKHAM ASYLUM: LIVING HELL
DC Comics: July, 2003 - No. 6, Dec, 2003 ($2.50, limited series)

	GD	VG	FN	VF	VF/NM	NM-
1-6-Ryan Sook-a; Batman app. 3-Batgirl-c/app.						2.50

ARMAGEDDON
Chaos! Comics: Oct, 1999 - No. 4, Jan, 2000 ($2.95, limited series)

	GD	VG	FN	VF	VF/NM	NM-
Preview						5.00
1-4-Lady Death, Evil Ernie, Purgatori app.						3.00

ARMAGEDDON: ALIEN AGENDA
DC Comics: Nov, 1991 - No. 4, Feb, 1992 ($1.00, limited series)

	GD	VG	FN	VF	VF/NM	NM-
1-4						2.25

ARMAGEDDON FACTOR, THE
AC Comics: 1987 - No. 2, 1987; No. 3, 1990 ($1.95)

	GD	VG	FN	VF	VF/NM	NM-
1,2: Sentinels of Justice, Dragonfly, Femforce						2.25
3-($3.95, color)-Almost all AC characters app.						4.00

ARMAGEDDON: INFERNO
DC Comics: Apr, 1992 - No. 4, July, 1992 ($1.00, limited series)

	GD	VG	FN	VF	VF/NM	NM-
1-4: Many DC heroes app. 3-A. Adams/Austin-a						2.50

ARMAGEDDON 2001
DC Comics: May, 1991 - No. 2, Oct, 1991 ($2.00, squarebound, 68 pgs.)

	GD	VG	FN	VF	VF/NM	NM-
1-Features many DC heroes; intro Waverider						4.00
1-2nd & 3rd printings; 3rd has silver ink-c						2.25
2						3.00

ARMATURE
Olyoptics: Nov, 1996 - No. 2, ($2.95, limited series)

	GD	VG	FN	VF	VF/NM	NM-
1,2-Steve Oliff-c/s/a; Maxx app.						3.00

ARMED & DANGEROUS
Acclaim Comics (Armada): Apr, 1996 - No.4, July, 1996 ($2.95, B&W)

	GD	VG	FN	VF	VF/NM	NM-
1-4-Bob Hall-c/a & scripts						3.00
Special 1 (8/96, $2.95, B&W)-Hall-c/a & scripts.						3.00

ARMED & DANGEROUS HELL'S SLAUGHTERHOUSE
Acclaim Comics (Armada): Oct, 1996 - No. 4, Jan, 1997 ($2.95, B&W)

	GD	VG	FN	VF	VF/NM	NM-
1-4: Hall-c/a/scripts.						3.00

ARMOR (AND THE SILVER STREAK) (Revengers Featuring... in indicia for #1-3)
Continuity Comics: Sept, 1985 - No.13, Apr, 1992 ($2.00)

	GD	VG	FN	VF	VF/NM	NM-
1-13: 1-Intro/origin Armor & the Silver Streak; Neal Adams-c/a. 7-Origin Armor; Nebres-i						3.50

ARMOR (DEATHWATCH 2000)
Continuity Comics: Apr, 1993 - No. 6, Nov, 1993 ($2.50)

	GD	VG	FN	VF	VF/NM	NM-
1-6: 1-3-Deathwatch 2000 x-over						3.00

ARMORED TROOPER VOTOMS (Manga)
CPM Comics: July, 1996 ($2.95)

	GD	VG	FN	VF	VF/NM	NM-
1						3.00

ARMORINES (See X-O Manowar #25 for 16 pg. bound-in Armorines #0)
Valiant: June, 1994 - No. 12, June, 1995 ($2.25)

	GD	VG	FN	VF	VF/NM	NM-
0-Stand-alone edition with cardstock-c						25.00
0-Gold						10.00
1-12: 7-Wraparound-c. 12-Byrne-c/swipe (X-Men, 1st Series #138)						2.50

ARMORINES (Volume 2)
Acclaim Comics: Oct, 1999 - No. 4 ($3.95/$2.50, limited series)

	GD	VG	FN	VF	VF/NM	NM-
1-($3.95) Calafiore & P. Palmiotti-a						4.00
2,3-($2.50)						2.50

ARMY AND NAVY COMICS (Supersnipe No. 6 on)
Street & Smith Publications: May, 1941 - No. 5, July, 1942

	GD	VG	FN	VF	VF/NM	NM-
1-Cap Fury & Nick Carter	54	108	162	329	502	675
2-Cap Fury & Nick Carter	32	64	96	184	267	350
3,4: 4-Jack Farr-c/a	23	46	69	132	191	250
5-Supersnipe app.; see Shadow V2#3 for 1st app.; Story of Douglas MacArthur; George Marcoux-c/a	55	110	165	340	520	700

ARMY ATTACK
Charlton Comics: July, 1964 - No. 4, Feb, 1965; V2#38, July, 1965 - No. 47, Feb, 1967

	GD	VG	FN	VF	VF/NM	NM-
V1#1	5	10	15	33	44	55
2-4(2/65)	3	6	9	19	25	32
V2#38(7/65)-47 (formerly U.S. Air Force #1-37)	3	6	9	16	20	24

NOTE: ***Glanzman** a-1-3. **Montes/Bache** a-44.*

ARMY AT WAR (Also see Our Army at War & Cancelled Comic Cavalcade)
DC Comics: Oct-Nov, 1978

	GD	VG	FN	VF	VF/NM	NM-
1-Kubert-c; all new story and art	2	4	6	9	11	14

ARMY OF DARKNESS (Movie)
Dark Horse Comics: Nov, 1992 - No. 2, Dec, 1992; No. 3, Oct, 1993 ($2.50, limited series)

	GD	VG	FN	VF	VF/NM	NM-
1-3-Bolton painted-c/a						5.00

ARMY OF DARKNESS: ASHES 2 ASHES (Movie)
Devil's Due Publ.: July, 2004 - Present ($2.99, limited series)

	GD	VG	FN	VF	VF/NM	NM-
1-3-Four covers for each; Bradshaw-a						3.00

ARMY SURPLUS KOMIKZ FEATURING CUTEY BUNNY
Army Surplus Komikz/Eclipse Comics: 1982 - No. 5, 1985 ($1.50, B&W)

	GD	VG	FN	VF	VF/NM	NM-
1-Cutey Bunny begins	1	3	4	6	8	10
2-5: 5-(Eclipse)-JLA/X-Men/Batman parody						4.50

ARMY WAR HEROES (Also see Iron Corporal)
Charlton Comics: Dec, 1963 - No. 38, June, 1970

	GD	VG	FN	VF	VF/NM	NM-
1	5	10	15	36	48	60
2-10	3	6	9	21	28	35
11-21,23-30: 24-Intro. Archer & Corp. Jack series	3	6	9	16	20	25
22-Origin/1st app. Iron Corporal series by Glanzman	4	8	12	27	36	45
31-38	2	4	6	10	13	16
Modern Comics Reprint 36 ('78)						4.00

NOTE: ***Montes/Bache** a-1, 16, 17, 21, 23-25, 27-30.*

AROUND THE BLOCK WITH DUNC & LOO (See Dunc and Loo)

AROUND THE WORLD IN 80 DAYS (Movie) (See A Golden Picture Classic)
Dell Publishing Co.: Feb, 1957

	GD	VG	FN	VF	VF/NM	NM-
Four Color 784-Photo-c	8	16	24	55	78	100

AROUND THE WORLD UNDER THE SEA (See Movie Classics)

AROUND THE WORLD WITH ARCHIE (See Archie Giant Series Mag. #29, 35, 141)

AROUND THE WORLD WITH HUCKLEBERRY & HIS FRIENDS (See Dell Giant No. 44)

The Arrow #3 © CEN

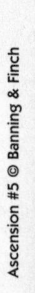

Ascension #5 © Banning & Finch

Aspen (Michael Turner's...) #2 © AspenMLT

	GD 2.0	VG 4.0	FN 6.0	VF 8.0	VF/NM 9.0	NM- 9.2

ARRGH! (Satire)
Marvel Comics Group: Dec, 1974 - No. 5, Sept, 1975 (25¢)

1-Dracula story; Sekowsky-a(p) 3 6 9 18 23 28
2-5: 2-Frankenstein. 3-Mummy. 4-Nightstalker(TV); Dracula-c/app., Hunchback. 5-Invisible Man, Dracula 2 4 6 11 14 18
NOTE *Alcala a-2; c-3. Everett a-1r, 2r. Grandenetti a-4. Maneely a-4r. Sutton a-1-3.*

ARROW (See Protectors)
Malibu Comics: Oct, 1992 ($1.95, one-shot)

1-Moder-a(p) 2.25

ARROW, THE (See Funny Pages)
Centaur Publications: Oct, 1940 - No. 2, Nov, 1940; No. 3, Oct, 1941

1-The Arrow begins(r/Funny Pages) 300 600 900 1940 3120 4300
2,3: 2-Tippy Taylor serial continues from Amazing Mystery Funnies #24. 3-Origin Dash Dartwell, the Human Meteor; origin The Rainbow-r; bondage-c 133 266 399 831 1278 1725
NOTE: *Gustavson a-1, 2; c-3.*

ARROWHEAD (See Black Rider and Wild Western)
Atlas Comics (CPS): April, 1954 - No. 4, Nov, 1954

1-Arrowhead & his horse Eagle begin 17 34 51 98 139 180
2-4: 4-Forte-a 10 20 30 56 73 90
NOTE: *Heath c-3. Jack Katz a-3. Maneely c-2. Pakula a-2. Sinnott a-1-4; c-1.*

ARROWSMITH (Also see Astro City/Arrowsmith flip book)
DC Comics (Cliffhanger): Sept, 2003 - No. 6, May, 2004 ($2.95)

1-6-Pacheco-a/Busiek-s 3.00
...: So Smart in Their Fine Uniforms TPB (2004, $14.95) r/#1-6 15.00

ARSENAL (Teen Titans' Speedy)
DC Comics: Oct, 1998 - No. 4, Jan, 1999 ($2.50, limited series)

1-4: Grayson-s. 1-Black Canary app. 2-Green Arrow app. 2.50

ARSENAL SPECIAL (See New Titans, Showcase '94 #7 & Showcase '95 #8)
DC Comics: 1996 ($2.95, one-shot)

1 3.00

ARTBABE
Fantagraphics Books: May, 1996 - Apr, 1999 ($2.50/$2.95/$3.50, B&W)

V1 #5, V2 #1-3 3.00
#4-($3.50) 3.50

ARTEMIS: REQUIEM (Also see Wonder Woman, 2nd Series #90)
DC Comics: June, 1996 - No. 6, Nov, 1996 ($1.75, limited series)

1-6: Messner-Loebs scripts & Benes-c/a in all. 1,2-Wonder Woman app. 3.00

ARTESIA
Sirius Entertainment: Jan, 1999 - No. 6, June, 1999 ($2.95, limited series)

1-6-Mark Smylie-s/a 3.00
Annual 1 (1999, $3.50) 3.50
Annual 2 (2001, $3.95) Crilley back-c 4.00
Annual 3 (2004, $4.95) Timeline of the Known World 5.00

ARTESIA AFIELD
Sirius Entertainment: Jul, 2000 - No. 6, Feb, 2001 ($2.95, limited series)

1-6-Mark Smylie-s/a 3.00

ARTESIA AFIRE
Archaia Studios Press: June, 2003 - No. 6, Feb, 2004 ($3.95, limited series)

1-6-Mark Smylie-s/a 4.00

ART OF HOMAGE STUDIOS, THE
Image Comics: Dec, 1993 ($4.95, one-shot)

1-Short stories and pin-ups by Jim Lee, Silvestri, Williams, Portacio & Chiodo 5.00

ART OF ZEN INTERGALACTIC NINJA, THE
Entity Comics: 1994 - No. 2, 1994 ($2.95)

1,2 3.00

ARZACH (See Moebius...)
Dark Horse Comics: 1996 ($6.95, one-shot)

nn-Moebius-c/a/scripts 1 2 3 4 5 7

ASCENSION
Image Comics (Top Cow Productions): Oct, 1997 - No. 22, Mar, 2000 ($2.50)

Preview 5.00
Preview Gold Edition 8.00
Preview San Diego Edition 2 4 6 8 10 12
0 4.00
1/2 6.00
1-David Finch-s/a(p)/Batt-s/a(i) 4.00
1-Variant-c w/Image logo at lower right 6.00
2-6 3.00
7-22 2.50
Fan Club Edition 5.00
...COLLECTED EDITION
1998 - No. 2 ($4.95, squarebound) 1,2: 1-r/#1,2. 2-r/#3,4 5.00

ASH
Event Comics: Nov, 1994 - No. 6, Dec, 1995; No. 0, May, 1996 ($2.50/$3.00)

0-Present & Future (Both 5/96, $3.00, foil logo-c)-w/pin-ups 3.00
0-Blue Foil logo-c (Present and Future) (1000 each) 4.00
0-Silver Prism logo-c (Present and Future) (500 each) 10.00
0-Red Prism logo-c (Present and Future) (250 each) 20.00
0-Gold Hologram logo-c (Present and Future) (1000 each) 8.00
1-Quesada-p/story; Palmiotti-i/story: Barry Windsor-Smith pin-up 2 4 6 8 10 12
2-Mignola Hellboy pin-up 1 2 3 4 5 7
3,4: 3-Big Guy pin-up by Geoff Darrow. 4-Jim Lee pin-up 4.00
4-Fahrenheit Gold 7.00
4-6-Fahrenheit Red (5,6-1000) 8.00
4-6-Fahrenheit White 12.00
5, 6-Double-c w/Hildebrandt Bros.-a, Quesada & Palmiotti. 6-Texeira-c 3.00
5,6-Fahrenheit Gold (2000) 4.00
6-Fahrenheit White (500)-Texeira-c 12.00
Volume 1 (1996, $14.95, TPB)-r/#1-5, intro by James Robinson 15.00
Wizard Mini-Comic (1996, magazine supplement) 2.25
Wizard #1/2 (1997, mail order) 4.00

ASH: CINDER & SMOKE
Event Comics: May, 1997 - No. 6, Oct, 1997 ($2.95, limited series)

1-6: Ramos-a/Waid, Augustyn-s in all. 2-6-variant covers by Ramos and Quesada 3.00

ASH: FILES
Event Comics: Mar, 1997 ($2.95, one-shot)

1-Comics w/text 3.00

ASH: FIRE AND CROSSFIRE
Event Comics: Jan, 1999 - No. 5 ($2.95, limited series)

1,2-Robinson-s/Quesada & Palmiotti-c/a 3.00

ASH: FIRE WITHIN, THE
Event Comics: Sept, 1996 - No. 2, Jan, 1997 ($2.95, unfinished limited series)

1,2: Quesada & Palmiotti-c/s/a 3.00

ASH/ 22 BRIDES
Event Comics: Dec, 1996 - No. 2, Apr, 1997 ($2.95, limited series)

1,2: Nicieza-s/Ramos-c/a 3.00

ASKANI'SON (See Adventures of Cyclops & Phoenix limited series)
Marvel Comics: Jan, 1996 - No. 4, May, 1996 ($2.95, limited series)

1-4: Story cont'd from Advs. of Cyclops & Phoenix; Lobdell/Loeb story; Gene Ha-c/a(p) 3.00
TPB (1997, $12.99) r/#1-4; Gene Ha painted-c 13.00

ASPEN (MICHAEL TURNER PRESENTS:...) (Also see Fathom)
Aspen MLT, Inc.: July, 2003 - Present ($2.99)

1-Fathom story; Turner-a/Johns-s; interviews w/Turner & Johns; two covers by Turner 3.00
2,3:2-Fathom story; Turner-a/Johns-s; two covers by Turner; pin-ups and interviews 3.00
Aspen Sketchbook 1 (2003, $2.99) sketch pages by Michael Turner and Talent Caldwell 3.00

ASSASSINETTE HARDCORE
Pocket Change Comics: 1995 - No. 2, 1995 ($2.50, B&W, limited series)

1,2 2.50

ASSASSINS
DC Comics (Amalgam): Apr, 1996 ($1.95)

1 2.25

ASTONISHING (Formerly Marvel Boy No. 1, 2)
Marvel/Atlas Comics(20CC): No. 3, Apr, 1951 - No. 63, Aug, 1957

3-Marvel Boy continues; 3-5-Marvel Boy-c 92 184 276 575 888 1200
4-6-Last Marvel Boy; 4-Stan Lee app. 65 130 195 406 628 850
7-10: 7-Maneely s/f story. 10-Sinnott s/f story 35 70 105 198 287 375
11,12,15,17,20 31 62 93 177 256 335
13,14,16,18,19-Krigstein-a. 18-Jack The Ripper sty 31 62 93 178 259 340

Astonishing X-Men #4 © MAR

Astro City A Visitor's Guide © Jukebox Prods.

Atari Force #13 © Atari

	GD 2.0	VG 4.0	FN 6.0	VF 8.0	VF/NM 9.0	NM- 9.2
21,22,24	26	52	78	150	215	280
23-E.C. swipe "The Hole In The Wall" from Vault Of Horror #16	27	54	81	152	219	285
25,29: 25-Crandall-a. 29-Decapitation-c	25	50	75	141	203	265
26-28	22	44	66	125	180	235
30-Tentacled eyeball-c/story; classic-c	34	68	102	193	279	365
31-37-Last pre-code issue	20	40	60	112	161	210
38-43,46,48-52,56,58,59,61	15	30	45	85	120	155
44,45,47,53-55,57,60: 44-Crandall swipe/Weird Fantasy #22. 45,47-Krigstein-a. 53-Ditko-a. 54-Torres-a, 55-Crandall, Torres-a. 57-Williamson/Krenkel-a (4 pgs.). 60-Williamson/Mayo-a (4 pgs.)	16	32	48	92	131	170
62,63: 62-Torres, Powell-a. 63-Woodbridge-a	16	32	48	89	127	165

NOTE: ***Ayers*** *a-16.* ***Berg*** *a-36, 53, 56.* ***Cameron*** *a-50.* ***Gene Colan*** *a-12, 20, 29, 56.* ***Ditko*** *a-53.* ***Drucker*** *a-41, 62.* ***Everett*** *a-3-6(3), 6, 10, 12, 37, 47, 48, 58; c-3-5, 13,15, 16, 18, 29, 47, 49, 51, 53-55, 57, 59-63.* ***Fass*** *a-11, 34.* ***Forte*** *a-53, 58, 60.* ***Fuje*** *a-11.* ***Heath*** *a-8, 29; c-8, 9, 19, 22, 25, 26.* ***Kirby*** *a-56.* ***Lawrence*** *a-28, 37, 38, 42.* ***Maneely*** *a-7(2); c-7, 31, 33, 34, 56.* ***Moldoff*** *a-33.* ***Morisi*** *a-10, 60.* ***Morrow*** *a-52, 61.* ***Orlando*** *a-47, 58, 61.* ***Pakula*** *a-10.* ***Powell*** *a-43, 44, 48.* ***Ravielli*** *a-28.* ***Reinman*** *a-32, 34, 38.* ***Robinson*** *a-20.* ***J. Romita*** *a-7, 18, 24, 43, 57,61.* ***Roussos*** *a-55.* ***Sale*** *a-28, 38, 59; c-32.* ***Sekowsky*** *a-13.* ***Severin*** *c-46.* ***Shores*** *a-16, 60.* ***Sinnott*** *a-11, 30.* ***Whitney*** *a-13.* ***Ed Win*** *a-20. Canadian reprints exist.*

ASTONISHING TALES (See Ka-Zar)
Marvel Comics Group: Aug, 1970 - No. 36, July, 1976 (#1-7: 15¢; #8: 25¢)

	GD 2.0	VG 4.0	FN 6.0	VF 8.0	VF/NM 9.0	NM- 9.2
1-Ka-Zar (by Kirby(p) #1,2; by B. Smith #3-6) & Dr. Doom (by Wood #1-4; by Tuska #5,6; by Colan #7,8; 1st Marvel villain solo series) double feature begins; Kraven the Hunter-c/story; Nixon cameo	6	12	18	40	55	70
2-Kraven the Hunter-c/story; Kirby, Wood-a	3	7	10	21	28	35
3-6: B. Smith-p; Wood-a-#3,4. 5,6-Red Skull 2-part story	4	8	12	25	33	42
7-Last 15¢ issue; Black Panther app.	3	6	9	16	20	24
8-(25¢, 52 pgs.)-Last Dr. Doom of series	4	8	12	22	30	38
9-All Ka-Zar issues begin; Lorna-r/Lorna #14	2	4	6	11	14	18
10-B. Smith/Sal Buscema-a.	3	6	9	16	20	24
11-Origin Ka-Zar & Zabu; death of Ka-Zar's father	2	4	6	12	16	20
12-2nd app.Man-Thing; by Neal Adams (see Savage Tales #1 for 1st app.)	4	8	12	24	32	40
13-3rd app.Man-Thing	3	6	9	18	24	30
14-20: 14-Jann of the Jungle-r (1950s); reprints censored Ka-Zar-s from Savage Tales #1. 17-S.H.I.E.L.D. begins. 19-Starlin-a(p). 20-Last Ka-Zar (continues into 1974 Ka-Zar series)	1	3	4	6	8	10
21-(12/73)-It! the Living Colossus begins, ends #24 (see Supernatural Thrillers #1)	3	6	9	19	25	32
22-24: 23,24-IT vs. Fin Fang Foom	2	4	6	14	18	22
25-1st app. Deathlok the Demolisher; full length stories begin, end #36; Perez's 1st work, 2 pgs. (8/74)	5	10	15	33	44	55
26-28,30	2	4	6	11	14	18
29-r/origin/1st app. Guardians of the Galaxy from Marvel Super-Heroes #18 plus-c w/4 pgs. omitted; no Deathlok story	1	3	4	6	8	10
31-34: 31-Watcher-r/Silver Surfer #3	2	4	6	9	11	14
35,36-(Regular 25¢ edition)(5,7/76)	2	4	6	9	11	14
35,36-(30¢-c, low distribution)	3	6	9	16	20	24

NOTE: ***Buckler*** *a-13i, 16p, 25, 26p, 27p, 28, 29p-36p; c-13, 25p, 26-30, 32-35p, 36.* ***John Buscema*** *a-9, 12p-14p, 16p; c-4-6p, 12p.* ***Colan*** *a-7p, 8p.* ***Ditko*** *a-21r.* ***Everett*** *a-6i.* ***G. Kane*** *a-11p, 15p; c-9, 10p, 11p, 14, 15p, 21p.* ***McWilliams*** *a-30i.* ***Starlin*** *a-19p; c-16p.* ***Sutton & Trimpe*** *a-8.* ***Tuska*** *a-5p, 6p, 8p.* ***Wood*** *a-1-4.* ***Wrightson*** *c-31i.*

ASTONISHING X-MEN
Marvel Comics: Mar, 1995 - No.4, July, 1995 ($1.95, limited series)

1-Age of Apocalypse; Magneto-c 4.00
2-4 3.00

ASTONISHING X-MEN
Marvel Comics: Sept, 1999 - No.3, Nov, 1999 ($2.50, limited series)

1-3-New team, Cable & X-Man app.; Peterson-a 2.50
TPB (11/00, $15.95) r/#1-3, X-Men #92 & #95, Uncanny X-Men #375 16.00

ASTONISHING X-MEN
Marvel Comics: July, 2004 - Present ($2.99)

1-Whedon-s/Cassaday-c/a; team of Cyclops, Beast, Wolverine, Emma Frost & Kitty Pryde 3.00
1-Director's Cut (2004, $3.99) different Cassaday partial sketch-c; cover gallery, sketch pages and script excerpt 4.00
1-Variant-c by Cassaday 5.00
1-Variant-c by Dell'Otto 5.00
2,3,5,6-X-Men battle Ord 3.00
4-Colossus returns 4.00
4-Variant Colossus cover by Cassaday 5.00

ASTOUNDING SPACE THRILLS: THE COMIC BOOK
Image Comics: Apr, 2000 - No. 4, Dec, 2000 ($2.95, limited series)

1-4-Steve Conley-s/a. 2,3-Flip book w/Crater Kid 3.00
Galaxy-Sized Astounding Space Thrills 1 (10/01, $4.95) 5.00

ASTRA
CPM Manga: 2001 - No. 8 ($2.95, B&W, limited series)

1-8: Created by Jerry Robinson; Tanaka-a. 1-Balent variant-c 3.00
TPB (2002, $15.95) r/#1-8; JH Williams III-c from #3 16.00

ASTRO BOY (TV) (See March of Comics #285 & The Original...)
Gold Key: August, 1965 (12¢)

	GD 2.0	VG 4.0	FN 6.0	VF 8.0	VF/NM 9.0	NM- 9.2
1(10151-508)-Scarce;1st app. Astro Boy in comics	44	88	132	324	500	675

ASTRO CITY / ARROWSMITH (Flip book)
DC Comics (WildStorm Productions): Jun, 2004 ($2.95, one-shot flip book)

1-Intro. Black Badge; Ross-c; Arrowsmith a/c by Pacheco 3.00

ASTRO CITY
DC Comics (WildStorm Productions): Dec, 2004 ($5.95, one-shot)

... A Visitor's Guide (12/04) short story, city guide and pin-ups by various; Ross-c 6.00

ASTRO CITY: LOCAL HEROES (Also see Kurt Busiek's Astro City)
DC Comics (WildStorm Productions): Apr, 2003 - No. 5, Feb, 2004 ($2.95, limited series)

1-5-Busiek-s/Anderson-a/Ross-c 3.00
HC (2005, $24.95) r/series; Kurt Busiek's Astro City V2 #21,22; stories from Astro City/ Arrowsmith #1; and 9-11, The World's Finest... Vol. 2; Alex Ross sketch pages 25.00

ASYLUM
Millennium Publications: 1993 ($2.50)

1-3: 1-Bolton-c/a; Russell 2-pg. illos 2.50

ASYLUM
Maximum Press: Dec, 1995 - No. 11, Jan, 1997 ($2.95/$2.99, anthology)
(#1-6 are flip books)

1-11: 1-Warchild by Art Adams, Beanworld, Avengelyne, Battlestar Galactica. 2-Intro Mike Deodato's Deathkiss; Cybrid story begins, ends #5. 4-1st app.Christian; painted Battlestar Galactica story begins. 5-Intro Black Seed (formerly Black Flag) by Dan Fraga; B&W Christian story. 6-Intro Bionix (Six Million Dollar Man & the Bionic Woman). 7-Begin $2.99-c; Don Simpson's Megaton Man; Black Seed pinup. 8-B&W-a. 9- Foot Soldiers & Kid Supreme 10-Lady Supreme by Terry Moore-c/app. 4.00

ATARI FORCE (Also see Promotional comics section)
DC Comics: Jan, 1984 - No. 20, Aug, 1985 (Mando paper)

1-(1/84)-Intro Tempest, Packrat, Babe, Morphea, & Dart 4.00
2-20 3.00
Special 1 (4/86) 3.00

NOTE: ***Byrne*** *c-Special 1i.* ***Giffen*** *a-12p, 13i.* ***Rogers*** *a-18p, Special 1p.*

A-TEAM, THE (TV) (Also see Marvel Graphic Novel)
Marvel Comics Group: Mar, 1984 - No. 3, May, 1984 (limited series)

	GD 2.0	VG 4.0	FN 6.0	VF 8.0	VF/NM 9.0	NM- 9.2
1-3						5.00
1,2-(Whitman bagged set) w/75¢-c	1	3	4	6	8	10
3-(Whitman, no bag) w/75¢-c	1	2	3	5	6	8

ATHENA INC. THE MANHUNTER PROJECT
Image Comics: Dec, 2001; Apr, 2002 - Present ($2.95/$4.95/$5.95)

...The Beginning (12/01, $5.95) Anacleto-c/a; Haberlin-s 6.00
1-5: 1-(4/02, $2.95) two covers by Anacleto 3.00
6-($4.95) 5.00
...: Agents Roster #1 (11/02, $5.95, 8 1/2 x 11") bios and sketch pages by Anacleto 6.00
Vol. 1 TPB (4/03, $19.95) r/#1-6 & Agents Roster; cover gallery 20.00

ATLANTIS CHRONICLES, THE (Also see Aquaman, 3rd Series & Aquaman: Time & Tide)
DC Comics: Mar, 1990 - No. 7, Sept, 1990 ($2.95, limited series, 52 pgs.)

1-7: 1-Peter David scripts. 7-True origin of Aquaman; nudity panels 3.25

ATLANTIS, THE LOST CONTINENT
Dell Publishing Co.: May, 1961

	GD 2.0	VG 4.0	FN 6.0	VF 8.0	VF/NM 9.0	NM- 9.2
Four Color #1188-Movie, photo-c	12	24	36	82	124	165

ATLAS (See 1st Issue Special)

ATLAS
Dark Horse Comics: Feb, 1994 - No. 4, 1994 ($2.50, limited series)

1-4 2.50

ATMOSPHERICS
Avatar Press: June, 2002 ($5.95, B&W, one-shot graphic novel)

1-Warren Ellis-s/Ken Meyer Jr.-painted-a/c 6.00

ATOM, THE (See Action #425, All-American #19, Brave & the Bold, D.C. Special Series #1, Detective Comics, Flash Comics #80, Hawkman, Identity Crisis, JLA, Power Of The Atom, Showcase #34 -36, Super Friends, Sword of The Atom, Teen Titans & World's Finest)

The Atom #4 © DC

Atom-Age Combat #3 © STJ

Atomic Comics #3 © Green Publ.

ATOM, THE (...& the Hawkman No. 39 on)
National Periodical Publ.: June-July, 1962 - No. 38, Aug-Sept, 1968

	GD 2.0	VG 4.0	FN 6.0	VF 8.0	VF/NM 9.0	NM- 9.2
1-(6-7/62)-Intro Plant-Master; 1st app. Maya	74	148	222	629	1015	1400
2	32	64	96	240	370	500
3-1st Time Pool story; 1st app. Chronos (origin)	22	44	66	160	245	330
4,5: 4-Snapper Carr x-over	17	34	51	121	186	250
6,9,10	12	24	36	87	134	180
7-Hawkman x-over (6-7/63; 1st Atom & Hawkman team-up); 1st app. Hawkman since Brave & the Bold tryouts	30	60	90	213	327	440
8-Justice League, Dr. Light app.	13	26	39	92	141	190
11-15: 13-Chronos-c/story	10	20	30	67	96	125
16-20: 19-Zatanna x-over	8	16	24	53	74	95
21-28,30: 28-Chronos-c/story	7	14	21	46	63	80
29-1st solo Golden Age Atom x-over in S.A.	15	30	45	107	164	220
31-35,37,38: 31-Hawkman x-over. 37-Intro. Major Mynah; Hawkman cameo	6	12	18	40	55	70
36-G.A. Atom x-over	7	14	21	51	71	90

NOTE: ***Anderson** a-1-11i, 13i; c-inks-1-25, 31-35, 37. **Sid Greene** a-8i-37i. **Gil Kane** a-1p-37p; c-1p-28p, 29, 33p, 34. **George Roussos** 38i **Mike Sekowsky** 38p Time Pool stories also in 6, 9,12, 17, 21, 27, 35.*

ATOM, THE (See Tangent Comics/ The Atom)

ATOM AGE (See Classics Illustrated Special Issue)

ATOM-AGE COMBAT
St. John Publishing Co.: June, 1952 - No. 5, Apr, 1953; Feb, 1958

	GD 2.0	VG 4.0	FN 6.0	VF 8.0	VF/NM 9.0	NM- 9.2
1-Buck Vinson in all	47	94	141	287	436	585
2-Flying saucer story	30	60	90	173	249	325
3,5: 3-Mayo-a (6 pgs.). 5-Flying saucer-c/story	26	52	78	147	211	275
4 (Scarce)	30	60	90	173	249	325
1(2/58-St. John)	22	44	66	125	180	235

ATOM-AGE COMBAT
Fago Magazines: No. 2, Jan, 1959 - No. 3, Mar, 1959

	GD 2.0	VG 4.0	FN 6.0	VF 8.0	VF/NM 9.0	NM- 9.2
2-A-Bomb explosion-c;	27	54	81	154	222	290
3	21	42	63	118	169	220

ATOMAN
Spark Publications: Feb, 1946 - No. 2, April, 1946

	GD 2.0	VG 4.0	FN 6.0	VF 8.0	VF/NM 9.0	NM- 9.2
1-Origin & 1st app. Atoman; Robinson/Meskin-a; Kidcrusaders, Wild Bill Hickok, Marvin the Great app.	67	134	201	419	647	875
2-Robinson/Meskin-a; Robinson c-1,2	43	86	129	262	401	540

ATOM & HAWKMAN, THE (Formerly The Atom)
National Periodical Publ: No. 39, Oct-Nov, 1968 - No. 45, Oct-Nov, 1969

	GD 2.0	VG 4.0	FN 6.0	VF 8.0	VF/NM 9.0	NM- 9.2
39-43: 40-41-Kubert/Anderson-a. 43-(7/69)-Last 12¢ issue; 1st app. Gentleman Ghost	6	12	18	38	52	65
44,45: 44-(9/69)-1st 15¢-c; origin Gentleman Ghost	6	12	18	38	52	65

NOTE: ***M. Anderson** a-39, 40i, 41i, 43, 44. **Sid Greene** a-40i-45i. **Kubert** a-40p, 41p; c-39-45.*

ATOM ANT (TV) (See Golden Comics Digest #2) (Hanna-Barbera)
Gold Key: January, 1966 (12¢)

	GD 2.0	VG 4.0	FN 6.0	VF 8.0	VF/NM 9.0	NM- 9.2
1(10170-601)-1st app. Atom Ant, Precious Pup, and Hillbilly Bears	31	62	93	231	358	485

ATOM ANT & SECRET SQUIRREL (See Hanna-Barbera Presents)

ATOMIC AGE
Marvel Comics (Epic Comics): Nov, 1990 - No. 4, Feb, 1991 ($4.50, limited series, square-bound, 52 pgs.)

	GD 2.0	VG 4.0	FN 6.0	VF 8.0	VF/NM 9.0	NM- 9.2
1-4: Williamson-a(i); sci-fi story set in 1957						4.50

ATOMIC ATTACK (True War Stories; formerly Attack, first series)
Youthful Magazines: No. 5, Jan, 1953 - No. 8, Oct, 1953 (1st story is sci/fi in all issues)

	GD 2.0	VG 4.0	FN 6.0	VF 8.0	VF/NM 9.0	NM- 9.2
5-Atomic bomb-c; science fiction stories in all	40	80	120	236	351	465
6-8	27	54	81	152	219	285

ATOMIC BOMB
Jay Burtis Publications: 1945 (36 pgs.)

	GD 2.0	VG 4.0	FN 6.0	VF 8.0	VF/NM 9.0	NM- 9.2
1-Airmale & Stampy (scarce)	69	138	207	431	666	900

ATOMIC BUNNY (Formerly Atomic Rabbit)
Charlton Comics: No. 12, Aug, 1958 - No. 19, Dec, 1959

	GD 2.0	VG 4.0	FN 6.0	VF 8.0	VF/NM 9.0	NM- 9.2
12	12	24	36	71	98	125
13-19	8	16	24	43	54	65

ATOMIC COMICS
Daniels Publications (Canadian): Jan, 1946 (Reprints, one-shot)

	GD 2.0	VG 4.0	FN 6.0	VF 8.0	VF/NM 9.0	NM- 9.2
1-Rocketman, Yankee Boy, Master Key app.	40	80	120	230	335	440

ATOMIC COMICS
Green Publishing Co.: Jan, 1946 - No. 4, July-Aug, 1946 (#1-4 were printed w/o cover gloss)

	GD 2.0	VG 4.0	FN 6.0	VF 8.0	VF/NM 9.0	NM- 9.2
1-Radio Squad by Siegel & Shuster; Barry O'Neal app.; Fang Gow cover-r/ Detective Comics (Classic-c)	131	262	393	819	1260	1700
2-Inspector Dayton; Kid Kane by Matt Baker; Lucky Wings, Congo King, Prop Powers (only app.) begin	62	124	186	388	594	800
3,4: 3-Zero Ghost Detective app.; Baker-a(2) each; 4-Baker-c	42	84	126	256	391	525

ATOMIC KNIGHTS (See Strange Adventures #117)

ATOMIC MOUSE (TV, Movies) (See Blue Bird, Funny Animals, Giant Comics Edition & Wotalife Comics)
Capitol Stories/Charlton Comics: 3/53 - No. 54, 6/63; No. 1, 12/84; V2#10, 19/85 - No. 12, 1/86

	GD 2.0	VG 4.0	FN 6.0	VF 8.0	VF/NM 9.0	NM- 9.2
1-Origin & 1st app.; Al Fago-c/a in most	35	70	105	198	287	375
2	15	30	45	83	117	150
3-10: 5-Timmy The Timid Ghost app.; see Zoo Funnies	10	20	30	60	80	100
11-13,16-25	8	16	24	40	50	60
14,15-Hoppy The Marvel Bunny app.	9	18	27	52	66	80
26-(68 pgs.)	11	22	33	66	91	115
27-40: 36,37-Atom The Cat app.	6	12	18	29	36	42
41-54	5	10	15	22	26	30
1 (1984)-Low print run; rep/#7-c w/diff. stories	2	4	6	8	10	12
V2#10 (9/85) -12(1/86)-Low print run	1	3	4	6	8	10

ATOMIC RABBIT (Atomic Bunny #12 on; see Giant Comics #3 & Wotalife)
Charlton Comics: Aug, 1955 - No. 11, Mar, 1958

	GD 2.0	VG 4.0	FN 6.0	VF 8.0	VF/NM 9.0	NM- 9.2
1-Origin & 1st app.; Al Fago-c/a in all?	31	62	93	175	253	330
2	14	28	42	79	110	140
3-10	10	20	30	56	73	90
11-(68 pgs.)	14	28	42	79	110	140

ATOMICS, THE
AAA Pop Comics: Jan, 2000 - No. 15, Nov, 2001 ($2.95)

	GD 2.0	VG 4.0	FN 6.0	VF 8.0	VF/NM 9.0	NM- 9.2
1-11-Mike Allred-s/a; 1-Madman-c/app.						3.00
12-15-($3.50): 13-15-Savage Dragon-c/app. 15-Afterword by Alex Ross; colored reprint of 1st Frank Einstein story						3.50
...King-Size Giant Spectacular: Jigsaw (2000, $10.00) r/#1-4						10.00
...King-Size Giant Spectacular: Lessons in Light, Lava, & Lasers (2000, $8.95) r/#5-8						9.00
...King-Size Giant Spectacular: Running With the Dragon ('02, $8.95) r/#13-15 and r/1st Frank Einstein app. in color						9.00
...King-Size Giant Spectacular: Worlds Within Worlds ('01, $8.95) r/#9-12						9.00
...: Spaced Out & Grounded in Snap City TPB (10/03, $12.95) r/one-shots - It Girl, Mr. Gum, Spaceman and Crash Metro & the Star Squad; sketch pages						13.00

ATOMIC SPY CASES
Avon Periodicals: Mar-Apr, 1950 (Painted-c)

	GD 2.0	VG 4.0	FN 6.0	VF 8.0	VF/NM 9.0	NM- 9.2
1-No Wood-a; A-bomb blast panels; Fass-a	35	70	105	198	287	375

ATOMIC THUNDERBOLT, THE
Regor Company: Feb, 1946 (one-shot) (scarce)

	GD 2.0	VG 4.0	FN 6.0	VF 8.0	VF/NM 9.0	NM- 9.2
1-Intro. Atomic Thunderbolt & Mr. Murdo	66	132	198	413	637	860

825

ATOMIC TOYBOX
Image Comics: Dec, 1999 ($2.95)

	GD 2.0	VG 4.0	FN 6.0	VF 8.0	VF/NM 9.0	NM- 9.2
1- Aaron Lopresti-c/s/a						3.00

ATOMIC WAR!
Ace Periodicals (Junior Books): Nov, 1952 - No. 4, Apr, 1953

	GD 2.0	VG 4.0	FN 6.0	VF 8.0	VF/NM 9.0	NM- 9.2
1-Atomic bomb-c	92	184	276	575	888	1200
2,3: 3-Atomic bomb-c	59	118	177	369	572	775
4-Used in **POP**, pg. 96 & illo.	59	118	177	369	572	775

ATOMIK ANGELS
Crusade Comics: May, 1996 - No. 4, Nov. 1996 ($2.50)

	GD 2.0	VG 4.0	FN 6.0	VF 8.0	VF/NM 9.0	NM- 9.2
1-4: 1-Freefall from Gen 13 app.						3.00
1-Variant-c						4.00
Intrep-Edition (2/96, B&W, giveaway at launch party)-Previews Atomik Angels #1; includes Billy Tucci interview.						4.00

ATOM SPECIAL (See Atom & Justice League of America)
DC Comics: 1993/1995 ($2.50/$2.95)(68pgs.)

	GD 2.0	VG 4.0	FN 6.0	VF 8.0	VF/NM 9.0	NM- 9.2
1,2: 1-Dillon-c/a. 2-McDonnell-a/Bolland-c/Peyer-s						3.00

ATOM THE CAT (Formerly Tom Cat; see Giant Comics #3)
Charlton Comics: No. 9, Oct, 1957 - No. 17, Aug, 1959

	GD 2.0	VG 4.0	FN 6.0	VF 8.0	VF/NM 9.0	NM- 9.2
9	9	18	27	54	70	85

Attack #3 © YM

Authentic Police Cases #10 © STJ

The Authority V2#1 © WSP

GD VG FN VF VF/NM NM-
2.0 4.0 6.0 8.0 9.0 9.2

10,13-17 6 12 18 33 41 48
11,12: 11(64 pgs)-Atomic Mouse app. 12(100 pgs.) 11 22 33 62 84 105

ATTACK
Youthful Mag./Trojan No. 5 on: May, 1952 - No. 4, Nov, 1952; No. 5, Jan, 1953 - No. 5, Sept, 1953

1-(1st series)-Extreme violence 32 64 96 184 267 350
2,3-Both Harrison-c/a; bondage, whipping 17 34 51 95 135 175
4-Krenkel-a (7 pgs.); Harrison-a (becomes Atomic Attack #5 on)
17 34 51 95 135 175
5-(#1, Trojan, 2nd series) 14 28 42 79 110 140
6-8 (#2-4), 5 10 20 30 58 77 95

ATTACK
Charlton Comics: No. 54, 1958 - No. 60, Nov, 1959

54 (25¢, 100 pgs.) 11 22 33 66 91 115
55-60 6 12 18 29 36 42

ATTACK!
Charlton Comics: 1962 - No. 15, 3/75; No. 16, 8/79 - No. 48, 10/84

nn(#1)-('62) Special Edition 5 10 15 36 48 60
2('63), 3(Fall, '64) 3 7 10 21 28 35
V4#3(10/66), 4(10/67)-(Formerly Special War Series #2; becomes Attack At Sea V4#5)
3 6 9 16 20 25
1(9/71) 3 6 9 16 20 25
2-5: 4-American Eagle app. 2 4 6 10 12 15
6-15(3/75): 1 3 4 6 8 10
16(8/79) - 40 5.00
41-47 Low print run 7.00
48(10/84)-Wood-r; S&K-c (low print) 1 3 4 6 8 10
Modern Comics 13('78)-r 4.00
NOTE: *Sutton a-9,10,13.*

ATTACK!
Spire Christian Comics (Fleming H. Revell Co.): 1975 (39¢/49¢, 36 pgs.)

nn 1 3 4 6 8 10

ATTACK AT SEA (Formerly Attack!, 1967)
Charlton Comics: V4#5, Oct, 1968 (one-shot)

V4#5 3 6 9 16 20 25

ATTACK ON PLANET MARS (See Strange Worlds #18)
Avon Periodicals: 1951

nn-Infantino, Fawcette, Kubert & Wood-a; adaptation of Tarrano the Conqueror by Ray Cummings 77 154 231 481 741 1000

ATTITUDE LAD
Slave Labor Graphics: Apr, 1994 - No. 3, Nov, 1994 ($2.95, B&W)

1-3 3.00

AUDREY & MELVIN (Formerly Little...)(See Little Audrey & Melvin)
Harvey Publications: No. 62, Sept, 1974

62 2 4 6 8 10 12

AUGIE DOGGIE (TV) (See Hanna-Barbera Band Wagon, Quick-Draw McGraw, Spotlight #2, Top Cat & Whitman Comic Books)
Gold Key: October, 1963 (12¢)

1-Hanna-Barbera character 20 40 60 141 216 290

AUTHENTIC POLICE CASES
St. John Publishing Co.: 2/48 - No. 6, 11/48; No. 7, 5/50 - No. 38, 3/55

1-Hale the Magician by Tuska begins 43 86 129 262 401 540
2-Lady Satan, Johnny Rebel app. 28 56 84 158 229 300
3-Veiled Avenger app.; blood drainage story plus 2 Lucky Coyne stories; used in **SOTI**, illo. from Red Seal #16 46 92 138 281 428 575
4,5: 4-Masked Black Jack app. 5-Late 1930s Jack Cole-a(r); transvestism story
28 56 84 158 229 300
6-Matt Baker-c; used in **SOTI**, illo- "An invitation to learning", r-in Fugitives From Justice #3; Jack Cole-a; also used by the N.Y. Legis. Comm. 48 96 144 293 447 600
7,8,10-14: 7-Jack Cole-a; Matt Baker-a begins #8, ends #?; Vic Flint in #10-14. 10-12-Baker-a(2 each) 24 48 72 135 195 255
9-No Vic Flint 19 38 57 107 154 200
15-Drug-c/story; Vic Flint app.; Baker-c 24 48 72 135 195 255
16,18,20,21,23: Baker-a(i) 15 30 45 85 120 155
17,19,22-Baker-c 17 34 51 95 135 175
24-28 (All 100 pgs.): 26-Transvestism 33 66 99 190 275 360
29,31,32-Baker-c 11 22 33 66 91 115
30 10 20 30 60 80 100
33-38: 33-Transvestism; Baker-c. 34-Baker-c; r/#9. 35-Baker-c/a(2); r/#10. 36-r/#11; Vic Flint strip-r; Baker-c/a(2) unsigned. 37-Baker-c; r/#17. 38- Baker-c/a; r/#18
14 28 42 79 110 140
NOTE: *Matt Baker c-6-16, 17, 19, 22, 27, 29, 31-38; a-13, 16. Bondage c-1, 3.*

AUTHORITY, THE (See Stormwatch and Jenny Sparks: The Secret History of...)
DC Comics (WildStorm): May, 1999 - No. 29, Jul, 2002 ($2.50)

1-Wraparound-c; Warren Ellis-s/Bryan Hitch and Paul Neary-a
2 4 6 9 11 14
2-4 1 3 4 6 8 10
5-12: 12-Death of Jenny Sparks; last Ellis-s 1 2 3 5 6 8
13-Mark Millar-s/Frank Quitely-c/a begins 2 4 6 8 10 12
14-16-Authority vs. Marvel-esque villains 1 2 3 4 5 7
17-22: 17,18-Weston-a. 19,20,22-Quitely-a. 21-McCrea-a 5.00
23-29: 23-26-Peyer-s/Nguyen-a; new Authority. 24-Preview of "The Establishment." 25,26-Jenny Sparks app. 27,28-Millar-s/Adams-a/c 4.00
Annual 2000 ($3.50) Devil's Night x-over; Hamner-a/Bermejo-c
1 2 3 4 5 7
Absolute Authority Slipcased Hardcover (2002, $49.95) oversized r/#1-12 plus script pages by Ellis and sketch pages by Hitch 50.00
...: Earth Inferno and Other Stories TPB (2002, $14.95) r/#17-20, Annual 2000, and Wildstorm Summer Special; new Quitely-c 15.00
...: Human on the Inside HC (2004, $24.95, dust jacket) Ridley-s/Oliver-a/c 25.00
...: Kev (10/02, $4.95) Ennis-s/Fabry-c/a 5.00
...: Relentless TPB (2000, $17.95) r/#1-8 18.00
...: Scorched Earth (2/03, $4.95) Robbie Morrison-s/Frazer Irving-a/Ashley Wood-c 5.00
...: Transfer of Power TPB (2002, $17.95) r/#22-29 18.00
...: Under New Management TPB (2000, $17.95) r/#9-16; new Quitely-c 18.00

AUTHORITY, THE (See previews in Sleeper, Stormwatch: Team Achilles and Wildcats Version 3.0)
DC Comics (WildStorm): Jul, 2003 - No. 14, Oct, 2004 ($2.95)

1-14: 1-Robbie Morrison-s/Dwayne Turner-a. 5-Huat-a. 14-Portacio-a 3.00
#0 (10/03, $2.95) r/preview back-up-s listed above; Turner sketch pages 3.00
...: Harsh Realities TPB (2004, $14.95) r/#0-5; cover gallery 15.00
.../Lobo: Jingle Hell (2/04, $4.95) Bisley-c/a; Giffen & Grant-s 5.00

AUTHORITY, THE: MORE KEV
DC Comics (WildStorm): Jul, 2004 - No. 4, Dec, 2004 ($2.95, limited series)

1-4-Garth Ennis-s/Glenn Fabry-c/a 3.00

AUTHORITY, THE: REVOLUTION
DC Comics (WildStorm): Dec, 2004 - Present ($2.95)

1,2-Brubaker-s/Nguyen-a 3.00

AUTOMATIC KAFKA
DC Comics (WildStorm): Sept, 2002 - No. 9, Jul, 2003 ($2.95)

1-9-Ashley Wood-c/a; Joe Casey-s 3.00

AUTOMATON
Image Comics (Flypaper Press): Sept, 1998 - No. 3, 1998 ($2.95, lim. series)

1-3-R.A. Jones-s/Peter Vale-a 3.00

AUTUMN
Caliber Comics: 1995 - No. 3, 1995 ($2.95, B&W)

1-3 3.00

AUTUMN ADVENTURES (Walt Disney's...)
Disney Comics: Autumn, 1990; No. 2, Autumn, 1991 ($2.95, 68 pgs.)

1-Donald Duck-r(2) by Barks, Pluto-r, & new-a 4.00
2-D. Duck-r by Barks; new Super Goof story 4.00

AVATAARS: COVENANT OF THE SHIELD
Marvel Comics: Sept, 2000 - No. 3, Nov, 2000 ($2.99, limited series)

1-3-Kaminski-s/Oscar Jimenez-a 3.00

AVATAR
DC Comics: Feb, 1991 - No. 3, Apr, 1991 ($5.95, limited series, 100 pgs.)

1-3: Based on TSR's Forgotten Realms 6.00

AVENGEBLADE
Maximum Press: July, 1996 - No. 2, Aug, 1996 ($2.99, limited series)

1,2: Bad Girls parody 3.00

AVENGELYNE
Maximum Press: May, 1995 - No. 3, July, 1995 ($2.50/$3.50, limited series)

1/2 2 4 6 8 10 12
1/2 Platinum 15.00
1-Newstand ($2.50)-Photo-c; poster insert 6.00

Avengers #23 © MAR

Avengers #42 © MAR

Avengers #189 © MAR

	GD 2.0	VG 4.0	FN 6.0	VF 8.0	VF/NM 9.0	NM- 9.2
1-Direct Market ($3.50)-Chromium-c; poster	1	2	3	4	5	7
1-Glossy edition	2	4	6	12	16	20
1-Gold						12.00
2-3: 2-Polybagged w/card						3.00
3-Variant-c; Deodato pin-up						5.00
...Bible (10/96, $3.50)						4.00
.../Glory (9/95, $3.95) 2 covers						4.00
.../Glory Swimsuit Special (6/96, $2.95) photo and illos. covers						3.00
.../Glory: The Godyssey (9/96, $2.99) 2 covers (1 photo)						3.00
...Revelation One (Avatar, 1/01, $3.50) 3 covers by Haley, Rio, Shaw; Shaw-a						3.50
.../Shi (Avatar, 11/01, $3.50) Eight covers; Waller-a						3.50
...Swimsuit (8/95, $2.95)-Pin-ups/photos. 3-Variant-c exist (2 photo, 1 Liefeld-a)						4.00
...Swimsuit (1/96, $3.50, 2nd printing)-photo-c						4.00
Trade paperback (12/95, $9.95)						10.00
.../Warrior Nun Areala 1 (11/96, $2.99) also see Warrior Nun/Avengelyne						3.00

AVENGELYNE
Maximum Press: V2#1, Apr, 1996 - No. 14, Apr, 1997 ($2.95/$2.50)

	GD 2.0	VG 4.0	FN 6.0	VF 8.0	VF/NM 9.0	NM- 9.2
V2#1-Four covers exist (2 photo-c).						4.00
V2#2-Three covers exist (1 photo-c); flip book w/Darkchylde						5.00
V2#0, 3-14: 0-(10/96).3-Flip book w/Priest preview. 5-Flip book w/Blindside						3.00

AVENGELYNE (Volume 3)
Awesome Comics: Mar, 1999 ($2.50)

	GD 2.0	VG 4.0	FN 6.0	VF 8.0	VF/NM 9.0	NM- 9.2
1-Fraga & Liefeld-a						3.00

AVENGELYNE: ARMAGEDDON
Maximum Press: Dec, 1996 - No. 3, Feb, 1997 ($2.99, limited series)

	GD 2.0	VG 4.0	FN 6.0	VF 8.0	VF/NM 9.0	NM- 9.2
1-3-Scott Clark-a(p)						3.00

AVENGELYNE: DEADLY SINS
Maximum Press: Feb, 1996 - No. 2, Mar, 1996 ($2.95, limited series)

	GD 2.0	VG 4.0	FN 6.0	VF 8.0	VF/NM 9.0	NM- 9.2
1,2: 1-Two-c exist (1 photo, 1 Liefeld-a). 2-Liefeld-c; Pop Mhan-a(p).						3.00

AVENGELYNE/POWER
Maximum Press: Nov, 1995 - No.3, Jan, 1996 ($2.95, limited series)

	GD 2.0	VG 4.0	FN 6.0	VF 8.0	VF/NM 9.0	NM- 9.2
1-3: 1,2-Liefeld-c. 3-Three variant-c. exist (1 photo-c)						3.00

AVENGELYNE • PROPHET
Maximum Press: May, 1996; No. 2, Feb. 1997 ($2.95, unfinished lim. series)

	GD 2.0	VG 4.0	FN 6.0	VF 8.0	VF/NM 9.0	NM- 9.2
1,2-Liefeld-c/a(p)						3.00

AVENGER, THE (See A-1 Comics)
Magazine Enterprises: Feb-Mar, 1955 - No. 4, Aug-Sept, 1955

	GD 2.0	VG 4.0	FN 6.0	VF 8.0	VF/NM 9.0	NM- 9.2
1(A-1 #129)-Origin	40	80	120	236	351	465
2(A-1 #131), 3(A-1 #133) Robot-c, 4(A-1 #138)	28	56	84	158	229	300
IW Reprint #9('64)-Reprints #1 (new cover)	4	8	12	22	30	38

NOTE: ***Powell*** *a-2-4; c-1-4.*

AVENGERS, THE (TV)(Also see Steed and Mrs. Peel)
Gold Key: Nov, 1968 ("John Steed & Emma Peel" cover title) (15¢)

	GD 2.0	VG 4.0	FN 6.0	VF 8.0	VF/NM 9.0	NM- 9.2
1-Photo-c	25	50	75	181	278	375
1-(Variant with photo back-c)	31	62	93	223	342	460

AVENGERS, THE (See Essential..., Giant-Size..., JLA/..., Kree/Skrull War Starring..., Marvel Graphic Novel #27, Marvel Super Action, Marvel Super Heroes('66), Marvel Treasury Ed., Marvel Triple Action, New Avengers, Solo Avengers, Tales Of Suspense #49, West Coast Avengers & X-Men Vs....)

AVENGERS, THE (The Mighty Avengers on cover only #63-69)
Marvel Comics Group: Sept, 1963 - No. 402, Sept, 1996

	GD 2.0	VG 4.0	FN 6.0	VF 8.0	VF/NM 9.0	NM- 9.2
1-Origin & 1st app. The Avengers (Thor, Iron Man, Hulk, Ant-Man, Wasp); Loki app.	257	514	771	2249	3825	5400
2-Hulk leaves Avengers	60	120	180	510	830	1150
3-2nd Sub-Mariner x-over outside the F.F. (see Strange Tales #107 for 1st); Sub-Mariner & Hulk team-up & battle Avengers; Spider-Man cameo (1/64)	41	82	123	330	515	700
4-Revival of Captain America who joins the Avengers; 1st Silver Age app. of Captain America & Bucky (3/64)	132	264	396	1122	1811	2500
4-Reprint from the Golden Record Comic set	11	22	33	77	114	150
With Record (1966)	16	32	48	112	171	230
5-Hulk app.	31	62	93	228	352	475
6,8: 6-Intro/1st app. original Zemo & his Masters of Evil. 8-Intro Kang	24	48	72	170	260	350
7-Rick Jones app. in Bucky costume	30	60	90	218	334	450
9-Intro Wonder Man who dies in same story	31	62	93	228	352	475
10-Intro/1st app. Immortus; early Hercules app. (11/64)	22	44	66	158	242	325
11-Spider-Man-c & x-over (12/64)	27	54	81	194	297	400
12-15: 15-Death of original Zemo	15	30	45	109	167	225
16-New Avengers line-up (Hawkeye, Quicksilver, Scarlet Witch join; Thor, Iron Man, Giant-Man, Wasp leave)	20	40	60	141	216	290
17,18	12	24	36	84	127	170
19-1st app. Swordsman; origin Hawkeye (8/65)	13	26	39	90	138	185
20-22: Wood inks	9	18	27	60	85	110
23-30: 23-Romita Sr. inks (1st Silver Age Marvel work). 25-Dr. Doom-c/story. 28-Giant-Man becomes Goliath (5/66)	7	14	21	50	68	85
31-40	6	12	18	38	52	65
41-46,49-52,54-56: 43,44-1st app. Red Guardian. 46-Ant-Man returns (re-intro, 11/67). 52-Black Panther joins; 1st app. The Grim Reaper. 54-1st app. new Masters of Evil. 56-Zemo app; story explains how Capt. America became imprisoned in ice during WWII, only to be rescued in Avengers #4	5	10	15	33	44	55
47-Magneto-c/story	5	10	15	36	48	60
48-Origin/1st app. new Black Knight (1/68)	5	10	15	36	48	60
53-X-Men app.	7	14	21	50	68	85
57-1st app. S.A. Vision (10/68)	13	26	39	92	141	190
58-Origin The Vision	8	16	24	55	78	100
59-65: 59-Intro. Yellowjacket. 60-Wasp & Yellowjacket wed. 63-Goliath becomes Yellowjacket; Hawkeye becomes the new Goliath. 65-Last 12¢ issue	5	10	15	33	44	55
66,67-B. Smith-a	5	10	15	36	48	60
68-70: 70-Nighthawk on cover	4	8	12	27	36	45
71-1st app. The Invaders (12/69); 1st app. Nighthawk; Black Knight joins	7	14	21	46	63	80
72-79,81,82,84-86,89-91: 82-Daredevil app	4	8	12	25	33	42
80-Intro. Red Wolf (9/70)	4	8	12	27	36	45
83-Intro. The Liberators (Wasp, Valkyrie, Scarlet Witch, Medusa & the Black Widow)	4	8	12	29	40	50
87-Origin The Black Panther	4	8	12	29	40	50
88-Written by Harlan Ellison	4	8	12	24	32	40
88-2nd printing (1994)	2	4	6	8	10	12
92-Last 15¢ issue; Neal Adams-c	4	8	12	29	40	50
93-(52 pgs.)-Neal Adams-c/a	12	24	36	84	127	170
94-96-Neal Adams-c/a	6	12	18	43	59	75
97-G.A. Capt. America, Sub-Mariner, Human Torch, Patriot, Vision, Blazing Skull, Fin, Angel, & new Capt. Marvel x-over	4	8	12	29	40	50
98,99: 98-Goliath becomes Hawkeye; Smith c/a(i). 99-Smith-c, Smith/Sutton-a	4	8	12	25	33	42
100-(6/72)-Smith-c/a; featuring everyone who was an Avenger	9	18	27	60	85	110
101-Harlan Ellison scripts	3	6	9	18	24	32
102-106,108,109	3	6	9	18	23	28
107-Starlin-a(p)	3	6	9	19	25	32
110,111-X-Men app.	4	8	12	25	33	42
112-1st app. Mantis	4	8	12	22	30	38
113-115,119-124,126-130: 123-Origin Mantis	2	4	6	14	18	22
116-118-Defenders/Silver Surfer app.	4	8	12	22	30	38
125-Thanos-c & brief app.	3	6	9	18	23	28
131-133,136-140: 136-Ploog-r/Amazing Advs. #12	2	4	6	10	12	15
134,135-Origin of the Vision revised (also see Avengers Forever mini-series)	2	4	6	14	18	22
141-143,145,152-163	1	3	4	6	8	11
144-Origin & 1st app. Hellcat	2	4	6	12	16	20
146-149-(Reg.25¢ editions)(4-7/76)	1	3	4	6	8	11
146-149-(30¢-c variants, limited distribution)	3	6	9	16	20	25
150-Kirby-a(r); new line-up: Capt. America, Scarlet Witch, Iron Man, Wasp, Yellowjacket, Vision & The Beast	2	4	6	9	11	14
150-(30¢-c variant, limited distribution)	3	6	9	18	23	28
151-Wonder Man returns w/new costume	2	4	6	8	10	12
160-164-(35¢-c variants, limited dist.)(6-10/77)	2	4	6	14	18	22
164-166: Byrne-a	2	4	6	8	10	12
167-180: 168-Guardians of the Galaxy app. 174-Thanos cameo. 176-Starhawk app.	1	2	3	4	5	7
181-191-Byrne-a: 181-New line-up: Capt. America, Scarlet Witch, Iron Man, Wasp, Vision, Beast & The Falcon. 183-Ms. Marvel joins. 185-Origin Quicksilver & Scarlet Witch	1	2	3	5	7	9
192-199: 195-1st Taskmaster						6.00
200-(10/80, 52 pgs.)-Ms. Marvel leaves.	1	3	4	6	8	10
201-213,217-238: 211-New line-up: Capt. America, Iron Man, Tigra, Thor, Wasp & Yellowjacket. 213-Yellowjacket leaves. 217-Yellowjacket & Wasp return. 221-Hawkeye & She-Hulk join. 227-Capt. Marvel (female) joins; origins of Ant-Man, Wasp, Giant-Man, Goliath, Yellowjacket, & Avengers. 230-Yellowjacket quits. 231-Iron Man leaves. 232-Starfox (Eros) joins. 234-Origin Quicksilver, Scarlet Witch. 238-Origin Blackout						4.50

Avengers V3#5 © MAR

Avengers V3#503 © MAR

Avengers Forever #4 © MAR

	GD 2.0	VG 4.0	FN 6.0	VF 8.0	VF/NM 9.0	NM- 9.2

214-Ghost Rider-c/story 6.00
215,216,239,240,250: 215,216-Silver Surfer app. 216-Tigra leaves. 239-(1/84) Avengers app. on David Letterman show. 240-Spider-Woman revived. 250-($1.00, 52 pgs.) 4.00
241-249, 251-262 3.50
263-1st app. X-Factor (1/86)(story continues in Fant. Four #286) 6.00
264-299: 272-Alpha Flight app. 291-$1.00 issues begin. 297-Black Knight, She-Hulk & Thor resign. 298-Inferno tie-in 3.00
300 (2/89, $1.75, 68 pgs.)-Thor joins; Simonson-a 4.00
301-304,306-313,319-325,327,329-343: 302-Re-intro Quasar. 320-324-Alpha Flight app. (320-cameo). 327-2nd app. Rage. 341,342-New Warriors app. 343-Last $1.00-c 3.00
305,314-318: 305-Byrne scripts begin. 314-318-Spider-Man x-over 3.50
326-1st app. Rage (11/90) 4.00
328,344-349,351-359,361,362,364,365,367: 328-Origin Rage. 365-Contains coupon for Hunt for Magneto contest 3.00
350-($2.50, 68 pgs.)-Double gatefold-c showing-c to #1; r/#53 w/cover in flip book format; vs. The Starjammers 3.50
360-($2.95, 52 pgs.)-Embossed all-foil-c; 30th ann. 4.00
363-($2.95, 52 pgs.)-All silver foil-c 4.00
366-($3.95, 68 pgs.)-Embossed all gold foil-c 4.00
368,370-374,376-399: 368-Bloodties part 1; Avengers/X-Men x-over. 374-bound-in trading card sheet. 380-Deodato-a. 390,391-"The Crossing." 395-Death of "old" Tony Stark; wraparound-c. 3.00
369-($2.95)-Foil embossed-c; Bloodties part 5 4.00
375-($2.00, 52 pgs.)-Regular ed.; Thunderstrike returns; leads into Malibu Comics' Black September. 3.00
375-($2.50, 52 pgs.)-Collector's ed. w/bound-in poster; leads into Malibu Comics' Black September. 3.50
400-402: Waid-s; 402-Deodato breakdowns; cont'd in X-Men #56 & Onslaught: Marvel Universe. 4.00
#500-503 (See Avengers Vol. 3; series resumed original numbering after Vol. 3 #84)
Special 1 (9/67, 25¢, 68 pgs.)-New-a; original & new Avengers team-up 10 20 30 70 100 130
Special 2 (9/68, 25¢, 68 pgs.)-New-a; original vs. new Avengers 6 12 18 40 55 70
Special 3 (9/69, 25¢, 68 pgs.)-r/Avengers #4 plus 3 Capt. America stories by Kirby (art); origin Red Skull 4 8 12 25 33 42
Special 4 (1/71, 25¢, 68 pgs.)-Kirby-r/Avengers #5,6 3 6 9 16 20 25
Special 5 (1/72, 52 pgs.)-Spider-Man x-over 3 6 9 16 20 25
Annual 6 (11/76) Peréz-a; Kirby-c 2 4 6 10 12 15
Annual 7 (11/77)-Starlin-c/a; Warlock dies; Thanos app. 4 8 12 27 36 45
Annual 8 (1978)-Dr. Strange, Ms. Marvel app. 1 3 4 6 8 10
Annual 9 (1979)-Newton-a(p) 1 2 3 5 6 8
Annual 10 (1981)-Golden-p; X-Men cameo; 1st app. Rogue & Madelyne Pryor 4 8 12 27 36 45
Annual 11-13: 11(1982)-Vs. The Defenders. 12('83), 13('84) 4.00
Annual 14-18: 14('85),15('86),16('87),17('88)-Evolutionary War x-over, 18('89)-Atlantis Attacks 4.00
Annual 19-23 (90-'94, 68 pgs.). 22-Bagged/card 3.00
...Kree-Skrull War ('00, $24.95, TPB) new Neal Adams-c 25.00
...: Legends Vol. 3: George Perez ('03, $16.99)-r/#161,162,194-196,201, Ann. #6&8 17.00
Marvel Double Feature...Avengers/Giant-Man #379 ($2.50, 52 pgs.)-Same as Avengers #379 w/Giant-Man flip book 2.50
Marvel Graphic Novel - Deathtrap: The Vault (1991, $9.95) Venom-c/app. 2 4 6 8 10 12
The Korvac Saga TPB (2003, $19.95)-r/#167,168,170-177; Perez-c 20.00
The Yesterday Quest ($6.95)-r/#181,182,185-187 1 2 3 4 5 7
Under Siege ('98, $16.95, TPB) r/#270,271,273-277 17.00
...: Visionaries ('99, $16.95)-r/early George Perez art 17.00

NOTE: ***Austin*** *c(i)-157, 167, 168, 170-177, 181, 183-188, 198-201, Annual 8.* ***John Buscema*** *a-41-44p, 46p, 47p, 49, 50, 51-62p, 74-77, 79-85, 87-91, 97, 105p, 121p, 124p,125p, 152, 153p, 255-279p, 281-302p; c-41-66, 68-71, 73-91, 97-99, 178, 256-259p, 261-279p, 281-302p.* ***Byrne*** *a-164-166p, 181-191p, 233p, Annual 13i, 14p; c-186-190p, 233p, 260, 305p; scripts-305-312.* ***Colan*** *a(p)-63-65, 111, 206-208, 210, 211; c(p)-65, 206-208, 210, 211.* ***Ditko*** *a-Annual 13.* ***Guice*** *a-Annual 12p.* ***Don Heck*** *a-9-15, 17-40, 157.* ***Kane*** *c-37p, 159p.* ***Kane/Everett*** *c-97.* ***Kirby*** *a-1-8p, Special 3r, 4r(p); c-1-30, 148, 151-158; layouts-14-16.* ***Ron Lim*** *c(p)-335-341.* ***Miller*** *c-193p.* ***Mooney*** *a-86i, 179p, 180p.* ***Nebres*** *a-178i; c-179i.* ***Newton*** *a-204p, Annual 9p.* ***Perez*** *a(p)-141, 143, 144, 148, 150, 154, 155, 160, 161, 162, 167,168, 170, 171, 194-196, 198-202, Annual 6, 8; c(p)-160-162, 164-166, 170-174, 181,183-185, 191, 192, 194-201, 379-382, Annual 8.* ***Starlin*** *c-121, 135.* ***Staton*** *a-127-134i.* ***Tuska*** *a-47i,48i, 51i, 53i, 54i, 106p, 107p, 135p, 137-140p, 163p. Guardians of the Galaxy app. in #167, 168, 170, 173, 175, 181.*

AVENGERS, THE (Volume Two)
Marvel Comics: V2#1, Nov, 1996 - No. 13, Nov, 1997 ($2.95/$1.95/$1.99) (Produced by Extreme Studios)

1-($2.95)-Heroes Reborn begins; intro new team (Captain America, Swordsman, Scarlet Witch, Vision, Thor, Hellcat & Hawkeye); 1st app. Avengers Island; Loki & Enchantress app.; Rob Liefeld-p & plot; Chap Yaep-p; Jim Valentino scripts; variant-c exists 5.00
1-($1.95)-Variant-c 6.00
2-13: 2,3-Jeph Loeb scripts begin, Kang app. 4-Hulk-c/app. 5-Thor/Hulk battle; 2 covers. 10,11,13-"World War 3"-pt. 2, x-over w/Image characters. 12-($2.99) "Heroes Reunited"-pt.2 4.00

AVENGERS, THE (Volume Three)
Marvel Comics: Feb, 1998 - No. 84, Aug, 2004; No. 500, Sept, 2004 - No. 503, Dec, 2004 ($2.99/$1.99/$2.25)

1-($2.99, 48 pgs.) Busiek-s/Perez-a/wraparound-c; Avengers reassemble after Heroes Return 5.00
1-Variant Heroes Return cover 1 2 3 4 5 7
1-Rough Cut-Features original script and pencil pages 3.00
2-($1.99)Perez-c, 2-Lago painted-c 4.00
3,4: 3-Wonder Man-c/app. 4-Final roster chosen; Perez poster 3.00
5-11: 5,6-Squadron Supreme-c/app. 8-Triathlon-c/app. 2.50
12-($2.99) Thunderbolts app. 3.00
12-Alternate-c of Avengers w/white background; no logo 15.00
13-24,26,28: 13-New Warriors app. 16-18-Ordway-s/a. 19-Ultron returns. 26-Immonen-a 2.25
16-Variant-c with purple background 5.00
25,27-($2.99) 25-vs. the Exemplars; Spider-Man app. 27-100 pgs. 3.00
29-33,35-47: 29-Begin $2.25-c. 35-Maximum Security x-over; Romita Jr.-a. 36-Epting-a; poster by Alan Davis. 38-Davis-a begins ($1.99-c) 2.25
34-($2.99) Last Pérez-a; Thunderbirds app. 3.00
48-($3.50, 100 pgs.) new story w/Dwyer-a & r/#98-100 3.50
49,51-59: 49-'Nuff Said story. 51-Anderson-a. 52-Reis-a. 57-Johns-s begin 2.25
50,60-($3.50): 50 Dwyer-a; Quasar app. 3.50
61-84: 61,62-Frank-a; new line-up. 63-Davis-a. 64-Reis-a. 65-70-Coipel-a. 75-Hulk app. 76-Jack of Hearts dies; Jae Lee-c. 77-(50¢-c) Coipel-a/Cassaday-c. 78,80,81Coipel-a 83,84-New Invaders app. 2.25
(After #84 [Aug, 2004] numbering reverted back to original Vol. 1 with #500, Sept, 2004)
500-($3.50) "Avengers Disassembled" begins; Bendis-s/Finch-a; Ant-Man (Scott Lang) killed, Vision destroyed 3.50
500-Director's Cut ($4.99) Cassaday foil variant-c plus interviews and galleries 5.00
501, 502-($2.25): 502-Hawkeye killed 2.25
503-($3.50) "Avengers Disassembled" ends; reprint pages from Avengers V1#16 3.50
#1 1/2 (12/99, $2.50) Timm-c/a/Stern-s; 1963-style issue 2.50
.../ Squadron Supreme '98 Annual ($2.99) 3.00
1999, 2000 Annual (7/99, '00, $3.50) 1999-Manco-a. 2000-Breyfogle-a 3.50
2001 Annual ($2.99) Reis-a; back-up-s art by Churchill 3.00
... Assemble HC ('04, $29.95, oversized) r/#1-11 & '98 Annual; Busiek intro.; Pérez pencil art and Busiek script from Avengers #1 30.00
...: Clear and Present Dangers TPB ('01, $19.95) r/#8-15 20.00
...Finale 1 (1/05, $3.50) Epilogue to Avengers Disassembled; Neal Adams-c; art by various incl. Peréz, Maleev, Oeming, Powell, Mayhew, Mack, McNiven, Cheung, Frank 3.50
...: Living Legends TPB ('04, $19.99) r/#23-30; last Busiek/Pérez arc 20.00
...Supreme Justice TPB (4/01, $17.95) r/Squadron Supreme appearances in Avengers #5-7, '98 Annual, Iron Man #7, Capt. America #8, Quicksilver #10; Pérez-c 18.00
The Kang Dynasty TPB ('02, $29.99) r/#41-55 & 2001 Annual 30.00
The Morgan Conquest TPB ('00, $14.95) r/#1-4 15.00
.../Thunderbolts Vol. 1: The Nefaria Protocols (2004, $19.99) r/#31-34, 42-44 20.00
Ultron Unleashed TPB (8/99, $3.50) reprints early app. 3.50
Ultron Unlimited TPB (4/01, $14.95) r/#19-22 & #0 prelude 15.00
Wizard #0-Ultron Unlimited prelude 2.50
Vol. 1: World Trust TPB ('03, $14.99) r/#57-62 & Marvel Double-Shot #2 15.00
Vol. 2: Red Zone TPB ('04, $14.99) r/#64-70 15.00
Vol. 3: The Search For She-Hulk TPB ('04, $12.99) r/#71-76 13.00
Vol. 4: The Lionheart of Avalon TPB ('04, $11.99) r/#77-81 12.00
Vol. 5: Once an Invader TPB ('04, $14.99) r/#82-84, V1 #71; Invaders #0 & Ann #1 ('77) 15.00

AVENGERS: CELESTIAL QUEST
Marvel Comics: Nov, 2001 - No. 8, June, 2002 ($2.50/$3.50, limited series)

1-7-Englehart-s/Santamaría-a; Thanos app. 2.50
8-($3.50) 3.50

AVENGERS COLLECTOR'S EDITION, THE
Marvel Comics: 1993 (Ordered through mail w/candy wrapper, 20 pgs.)

1-Contains 4 bound-in trading cards 5.00

AVENGERS: EARTH'S MIGHTIEST HEROES
Marvel Comics: Jan, 2005 - No. 8 ($3.50, limited series)

1,2-Retells origin; Casey-s/Kolins-a 3.50

AVENGERS FOREVER
Marvel Comics: Dec, 1998 - No. 12, Feb, 2000 ($2.99)

1-Busiek-s/Pacheco-a in all 4.00
2-12: 4-Four covers. 6-Two covers. 8-Vision origin revised. 12-Rick Jones becomes

	GD 2.0	VG 4.0	FN 6.0	VF 8.0	VF/NM 9.0	NM- 9.2

Avengers West Coast #69 © MAR

Azrael #60 © DC

Aztek: The Ultimate Man #10 © DC

GD VG FN VF VF/NM NM-
2.0 4.0 6.0 8.0 9.0 9.2

Capt. Marvel 3.00
TPB (1/01, $24.95) r/#1-12; Busiek intro.; new Pacheco-c 25.00

AVENGERS INFINITY
Marvel Comics: Sept, 2000 - No. 4, Dec, 2000 ($2.99, limited series)
1-4-Stern-s/Chen-a 3.00

AVENGERS/ JLA (See JLA/Avengers for #1 & #3)
DC Comics: No, 2, 2003; No. 4, 2003 ($5.95, limited series)
2-Busiek-s/Pérez-a; wraparound-c; Krona, Galactus app. 6.00
4-Busiek-s/Pérez-a; wraparound-c 6.00

AVENGERS LOG, THE
Marvel Comics: Feb, 1994 ($1.95)
1-Gives history of all members; Perez-c 2.25

AVENGERS SPOTLIGHT (Formerly Solo Avengers #1-20)
Marvel Comics: No. 21, Aug, 1989 - No. 40, Jan, 1991 (75¢/$1.00)
21-Byrne-c/a 3.00
22-40: 26-Acts of Vengeance story. 31-34-U.S. Agent series. 36-Heck-i. 37-Mortimer-i. 40-The Black Knight app. 2.25

AVENGERS STRIKEFILE
Marvel Comics: Jan, 1994 ($1.75, one-shot)
1 2.25

AVENGERS: THE CROSSING
Marvel Comics: July, 1995 ($4.95, one-shot)
1-Deodato-c/a; 1st app. Thor's new costume 5.00

AVENGERS: THE TERMINATRIX OBJECTIVE
Marvel Comics: Sept, 1993 - No. 4, Dec, 1993 ($1.25, limited series)
1 ($2.50)-Holo-grafx foil-c 3.00
2-4-Old vs. current Avengers 2.25

AVENGERS: THE ULTRON IMPERATIVE
Marvel Comics: Nov, 2001 ($5.99, one-shot)
1-Follow-up to the Ultron Unlimited ending in Avengers #42; BWS-c 6.00

AVENGERS/THUNDERBOLTS
Marvel Comics: May, 2004 - No. 6, Sept, 2004 ($2.99, limited series)
1-6: Busiek & Nicieza-s/Kitson-c. 1,2-Kitson-a. 3-6-Grummett-a 3.00
Vol. 2: Best Intentions (2004, $14.99) r/#1-6 15.00

AVENGERS: TIMESLIDE
Marvel Comics: Feb, 1996 ($4.95, one-shot)
1-Foil-c 5.00

AVENGERS TWO: WONDER MAN & BEAST
Marvel Comics: May, 2000 - No. 3, July, 2000 ($2.99, limited series)
1-3: Stern-s/Bagley-c/a 3.00

AVENGERS/ULTRAFORCE (See Ultraforce/Avengers)
Marvel Comics: Oct, 1995 ($3.95, one-shot)
1-Wraparound foil-c by Perez 4.00

AVENGERS UNITED THEY STAND
Marvel Comics: Nov, 1999 - No. 7, June, 2000 ($2.99/$1.99)
1-Based on the animated series 3.00
2-6-($1.99) 2-Avengers battle Hydra 2.25
7-($2.99) Devil Dinosaur-c/app.; reprints Avengers Action Figure Comic 3.00

AVENGERS UNIVERSE
Marvel Comics: Jun, 2000 - No. 3, Oct, 2000 ($3.99)
1-3-Reprints recent stories 4.00

AVENGERS UNPLUGGED
Marvel Comics: Oct, 1995 - No. 6, Aug, 1996 (99¢, bi-monthly)
1-6 2.25

AVENGERS WEST COAST (Formerly West Coast Avengers)
Marvel Comics: No. 48, Sept, 1989 - No. 102, Jan, 1994 ($1.00/$1.25)
48,49: 48-Byrne-c/a & scripts continue thru #57 3.00
50-Re-intro original Human Torch 4.00
51-69,71-74,76-83,85,86,89-99: 54-Cover swipe/F.F. #1. 78-Last $1.00-c. 79-Dr. Strange x-over. 93-95-Darkhawk app. 2.25
70,75,84,87,88: 70-Spider-Woman app. 75 (52 pgs.)-Fantastic Four x-over. 84-Origin Spider-Woman retold; Spider-Man app. (also in #85,86). 87,88-Wolverine-c/story 3.00
100-($3.95, 68 pgs.)-Embossed all red foil-c 4.00
101,102: 101-X-Men x-over 4.00

GD VG FN VF VF/NM NM-
2.0 4.0 6.0 8.0 9.0 9.2

Annual 5-8 ('90- '93, 68 pgs.)-5,6-West Coast Avengers in indicia. 7-Darkhawk app. 8-Polybagged w/card 3.00

AVIATION ADVENTURES AND MODEL BUILDING (True Aviation Advs. ...No. 15)
Parents' Magazine Institute: No. 16, Dec, 1946 - No. 17, Feb, 1947
16,17-Half comics and half pictures 8 16 24 43 54 65

AVIATION CADETS
Street & Smith Publications: 1943
nn 19 37 57 107 154 200

A-V IN 3-D
Aardvark-Vanaheim: Dec, 1984 ($2.00, 28 pgs. w/glasses)
1-Cerebus, Flaming Carrot, Normalman & Ms. Tree 4.00

AWAKENING, THE
Image Comics: Oct, 1997 - No. 4, Apr, 1998 ($2.95, B&W, limited series)
1-4-Stephen Blue-s/c/a 3.00

AWESOME ADVENTURES
Awesome Entertainment: Aug, 1999 ($2.50)
1-Alan Moore-s/ Steve Skroce-a; Youngblood story 3.00

AWESOME HOLIDAY SPECIAL
Awesome Entertainment: Dec, 1997 ($2.50, one-shot)
1-Flip book w/covers of Fighting American & Coven. Holiday stories also featuring Kaboom and Shaft by regular creators. 3.00
1-Gold Edition 5.00

AWFUL OSCAR (Formerly & becomes Oscar Comics with No. 13)
Marvel Comics: No. 11, June, 1949 - No. 12, Aug, 1949
11,12 11 22 33 66 91 115

AWKWARD UNIVERSE
Slave Labor Graphics: 12/95 ($9.95, graphic novel)
nn 10.00

AXA
Eclipse Comics: Apr, 1987 - No. 2, Aug, 1987 ($1.75)
1,2 2.25

AXEL PRESSBUTTON (Pressbutton No. 5; see Laser Eraser &...)
Eclipse Comics: Nov, 1984 - No. 6, July, 1985 ($1.50/$1.75, Baxter paper)
1-6: Reprints Warrior (British mag.). 1-Bolland-c; origin Laser Eraser & Pressbutton 3.00

AXIS ALPHA
Axis Comics: Feb, 1994 ($2.50, one-shot)
V1-Previews Axis titles including, Tribe, Dethgrip, B.E.A.S.T.I.E.S. & more; Pitt app. in Tribe story. 3.00

AZRAEL (...Agent of the Bat #47 on)(Also see Batman: Sword of Azrael)
DC Comics: Feb, 1995 - No. 100, May, 2003 ($1.95/$2.25/$2.50/$2.95)
1-Dennis O'Neil scripts begin 5.00
2,3 3.00
4-46,48-62: 5,6-Ras Al Ghul app. 13-Nightwing-c/app. 15-Contagion Pt. 5 (Pt. 4 on-c). 16-Contagion Pt. 10. 22-Batman-c/app. 23,27-Batman app. 27,28-Joker app. 35-Hitman app. 36-39-Batman, Bane app. 50-New costume. 53-Joker-c/app. 56,57,60-New Batgirl app. 2.50
47-($3.95) Flip book with Batman: Shadow of the Bat #80 4.00
63-74,76-92: 63-Huntress-c/app.; Azrael returns to old costume. 67-Begin $2.50-c. 70-79-Harris-c. 83-Joker x-over. 91-Bruce Wayne: Fugitive pt. 15 2.50
75-($3.95) New costume; Harris-c 4.00
93-100: 93-Begin $2.95-c. 95,96-Two-Face app. 100-Last issue; Zeck-c 3.00
#1,000,000 (11/98) Giarrano-a 2.50
Annual 1 (1995, $3.95)-Year One story 4.00
Annual 2 (1996, $2.95)-Legends of the Dead Earth story 3.00
Annual 3 (1997, $3.95)-Pulp Heroes story; Orbik-c 4.00
Plus (12/96, $2.95)-Question-c/app. 3.00

AZRAEL/ ASH
DC Comics: 1997 ($4.95, one-shot)
1-O'Neil-s/Quesada, Palmiotti-a 5.00

AZTEC ACE
Eclipse Comics: Mar, 1984 - No. 15, Sept, 1985 ($2.25/$1.50/$1.75, Baxter paper)
1-$2.25-c (52 pgs.) 3.00
2-15: 2-Begin 36 pgs. 2.25
NOTE: *N. Redondo a-1i-8i, 10i. c-6-8i.*

AZTEK: THE ULTIMATE MAN

Babe #2 © PRIZE

Baby Huey #4 © HARV

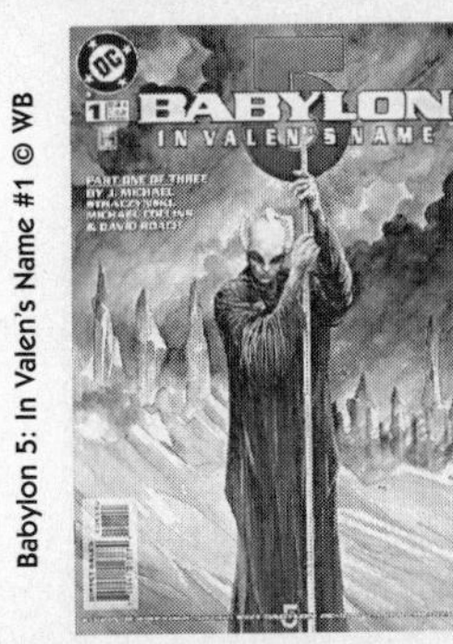

Babylon 5: In Valen's Name #1 © WB

	GD 2.0	VG 4.0	FN 6.0	VF 8.0	VF/NM 9.0	NM- 9.2

DC Comics: Aug, 1996 - No. 10, May 1997 ($1.75)

1-1st app. Aztek & Synth; Grant Morrison & Mark Millar scripts in all 6.00
2-9: 2-Green Lantern app. 3-1st app. Death-Doll. 4-Intro The Lizard King. 5-Origin. 6-Joker app.; Batman cameo. 7-Batman app. 8-Luthor app. 9-vs. Parasite-c/app. 4.00
10-JLA-c/app. 1 2 4 6 8 10
NOTE: *Breyfogle c-5p.* ***N. Steven Harris*** *a-1-5p.* ***Porter*** *c-1p.* ***Wieringo*** *c-2p.*

BABE (...Darling of the Hills, later issues)(See Big Shot and Sparky Watts)
Prize/Headline/Feature: June-July, 1948 - No. 11, Apr-May, 1950

1-Boody Rogers-a 26 52 78 150 215 280
2-Boody Rogers-a 15 30 45 86 123 160
3-11-All by Boody Rogers 13 26 39 76 106 135

BABE
Dark Horse Comics (Legend): July, 1994 - No. 4, Jan, 1994 ($2.50, lim. series)

1-4: John Byrne-c/a/scripts; ProtoTykes back-up story 2.50

BABE RUTH SPORTS COMICS (Becomes Rags Rabbit #11 on?)
Harvey Publications: April, 1949 - No. 11, Feb, 1951

1-Powell-a 40 80 120 244 372 500
2-Powell-a 30 60 90 170 245 320
3-11: Powell-a in most 24 48 72 138 199 260
NOTE: *Baseball c-2-4, 9. Basketball c-1, 6. Football c-5. Yogi Berra c/story-8. Joe DiMaggio c/story-3. Bob Feller c/story-4. Stan Musial c-9.*

BABES IN TOYLAND (Disney, Movie) (See Golden Pix Story Book ST-3)
Dell Publishing Co.: No. 1282, Feb-Apr, 1962

Four Color 1282-Annette Funicello photo-c 15 30 45 105 160 215

BABES OF BROADWAY
Broadway Comics: May, 1996 ($2.95, one-shot)

1-Pin-ups of Broadway Comics' female characters; Alan Davis, Michael Kaluta, J. G. Jones, Alan Weiss, Guy Davis & others-a; Giordano-c. 3.00

BABE 2
Dark Horse Comics (Legend): Mar, 1995 - No. 2, May, 1995 ($2.50, lim. series)

1,2: John Byrne-c/a/scripts 2.50

BABY HUEY
Harvey Comics: No. 1, Oct, 1991 - No. 9, June, 1994 ($1.00/$1.25/$1.50, quarterly)

1 ($1.00): 1-Cover says "Big Baby Huey" 5.00
2-9 ($1.25-$1.50) 3.00

BABY HUEY AND PAPA (See Paramount Animated...)
Harvey Publications: May, 1962 - No. 33, Jan, 1968 (Also see Casper The Friendly Ghost)

1 18 36 54 131 201 270
2 10 20 30 67 96 125
3-5 6 12 18 40 55 75
6-10 4 8 12 24 32 42
11-20 3 6 9 18 23 28
21-33 2 4 6 14 18 22

BABY HUEY DIGEST
Harvey Publications: June, 1992 (Digest-size, one-shot)

1-Reprints 1 2 3 4 5 7

BABY HUEY DUCKLAND
Harvey Publications: Nov, 1962 - No. 15, Nov, 1966 (25¢ Giants, 68 pgs.)

1 13 26 39 94 145 195
2-5 7 14 21 46 63 80
6-15 4 8 12 25 33 42

BABY HUEY, THE BABY GIANT (Also see Big Baby Huey, Casper, Harvey Hits #22, Harvey Comics Hits #60, & Paramount Animated Comics)
Harvey Publ: 9/56 - #97, 10/71; #98, 10/72; #99, 10/80; #100, 10/90; #101, 11/90

1-Infinity-c 47 94 141 376 588 800
2 24 48 72 170 260 350
3-Baby Huey takes anti-pep pills 15 30 45 109 167 225
4,5 11 22 33 77 114 150
6-10 7 14 21 51 71 90
11-20 6 12 18 40 55 70
21-40 4 8 12 28 38 48
41-60 3 6 9 18 24 30
61-79 (12/67) 2 4 6 14 18 22
80(12/68) - 95-All 68 pg. Giants 3 6 9 19 25 32
96,97-Both 52 pg. Giants 3 6 9 16 20 24
98-Regular size 2 4 6 10 12 15
99-Regular size 1 2 3 5 6 8
100,101 ($1.00) 4.00

BABYLON 5 (TV)
DC Comics: Jan, 1995 - No. 11, Dec, 1995 ($1.95/$2.50)

1 2 4 6 9 11 14
2-5 1 2 3 5 7 9
6-11: 7-Begin $2.50-c 1 2 3 4 5 7
... The Price of Peace (1998, $9.95, TPB) r/#1-4,11 10.00

BABYLON 5: IN VALEN'S NAME
DC Comics: Mar, 1998 - No. 3, May, 1998 ($2.50, limited series)

1-3 4.00

BABY SNOOTS (Also see March of Comics #359,371,396,401,419,431,443,450,462,474,485)
Gold Key: Aug, 1970 - No. 22, Nov, 1975

1 3 7 10 21 28 35
2-11 2 4 6 11 14 18
12-22: 22-Titled Snoots, the Forgetful Elefink 1 3 4 6 8 10

BACCHUS (Also see Eddie Campbell's ...)
Harrier Comics (New Wave): 1988 - No. 2, Aug, 1988 ($1.95, B&W)

1,2: Eddie Campbell-c/a/scripts. 2.25

BACHELOR FATHER (TV)
Dell Publishing Co.: No. 1332, 4-6/62 - No. 2, Sept.-Nov., 1962

Four Color 1332 (#1), 2-Written by Stanley 9 18 27 63 89 115

BACHELOR'S DIARY
Avon Periodicals: 1949 (15¢)

1(Scarce)-King Features panel cartoons & text-r; pin-up, girl wrestling photos; similar to Sideshow 42 84 126 256 391 525

BACKPACK MARVELS (B&W backpack-sized reprint collections)
Marvel Comics: Nov, 2000 - Present ($6.95, B&W, digest-size)

Avengers 1 -r/Avengers #181-189; profile pages 7.00
Spider-Man 1-r/ASM #234-240 7.00
X-Men 1-r/Uncanny X-Men #167-173 7.00
X-Men 2-r/Uncanny X-Men #174-179; new painted-c by Greg Horn 7.00

BACK DOWN THE LINE
Eclipse Books: 1991 (Mature adults, 8-1/2 x 11", 52 pgs.)

nn (Soft-c, $8.95)-Bolton-c/a 9.00
nn (Limited Hard-c, $29.95) 30.00

BACKLASH (Also see The Kindred)
Image Comics (WildStorm Prod.): Nov,1994 - No. 32, May, 1997 ($1.95/$2.50)

1-Double-c; variant-double-c 3.00
2-7,9-32: 5-Intro Mindscape; 2 pinups. 19-Fire From Heaven Pt 2. 20-Fire From Heaven Pt 10. 31-WildC.A.T.S app. 2.50
8-($1.95, newsstand)-Wildstorm Rising Pt. 8 2.50
8-($2.50, direct market)-Wildstorm Rising Pt. 8 2.50
25-($3.95)-Double-size 4.00
...& Taboo's African Holiday (9/99, $5.95) Booth-s/a(p) 6.00

BACKLASH/SPIDER-MAN
Image Comics (WildStorm Productions): Aug, 1996 - No. 2, Sept, 1996 ($2.50, lim. series)

1,2: Pike (villain from WildC.A.T.S) & Venom app. 3.00

BACK TO THE FUTURE (Movie, TV cartoon)
Harvey Comics: Nov, 1991 - No. 4, June, 1992 ($1.25)

1-4: 1,2-Gil Kane-c; based on animated cartoon 3.00

BACK TO THE FUTURE: FORWARD TO THE FUTURE
Harvey Comics: Oct, 1992 - No. 3, Feb, 1993 ($1.50, limited series)

1-3 3.00

BAD BOY
Oni Press: Dec, 1997 ($4.95, one-shot)

1-Frank Miller-s/Simon Bisley-a/painted-c 5.00

BAD COMPANY
Quality Comics/Fleetway Quality #15 on: Aug, 1988 - No. 19?, 1990 ($1.50/$1.75, high quality paper)

1-19: 5,6-Guice-c 2.25

BADGE OF JUSTICE (Formerly Crime And Justice #21)
Charlton Comics: No. 22, 1/55 - No. 2, 4/55 - No. 4, 10/55

22(#1)(1/55) 10 20 30 60 80 100
2-4 7 14 21 35 43 50

The Badger #10 © FPI

Baffling Mysteries #7 © ACE

Bambi Four Color #30 © WDC

GD 2.0 | VG 4.0 | FN 6.0 | VF 8.0 | VF/NM 9.0 | NM- 9.2

BADGER, THE
Capital Comics(#1-4)/First Comics: Dec, 1983 - No. 70, Apr, 1991; V2#1, Spring, 1991
1 5.00
2-70: 52-54-Tim Vigil-c/a 3.00
50-($3.95, 52 pgs.) 4.00
V2#1 (Spring, 1991, $4.95) 5.00

BADGER, THE
Image Comics: V3#78, May, 1997 - V3#88 ($2.95, B&W)
78-Cover lists #1, Baron-s 3.00
79/#2, 80/#3, 81(indicia lists #80)/#4,82-88/#5-11 3.00

BADGER GOES BERSERK
First Comics: Sept, 1989 - No. 4, Dec, 1989 ($1.95, lim. series, Baxter paper)
1-4: 2-Paul Chadwick-c/a(2pgs.) 3.00

BADGER: SHATTERED MIRROR
Dark Horse Comics: July, 1994 - No. Oct, 1994 ($2.50, limited series)
1-4 3.00

BADGER: ZEN POP FUNNY-ANIMAL VERSION
Dark Horse Comics: July, 1994 - No. 2, Aug, 1994 ($2.50, limited series)
1,2 3.00

BAD GIRLS
DC Comics: Oct, 2003 - No. 5, Feb, 2004 ($2.50, limited series)
1-5-Vance-s/Graves-a/Cook-c 2.50

BAD IDEAS
Image Comics: Apr, 2004 - No. 2, July, 2004 ($5.95, B&W, limited series)
1,2-Chinsang-s/Mahfood & Crosland-a 6.00

BAD KITTY
Chaos! Comics: Feb, 2001 - No. 3, Apr, 2001 ($2.99, limited series)
1-3-Pulido-s/Batista-a 3.00
1-Premium Edition ($9.99) Scott Lewis-c 10.00
...Mischief Night 1 (11/01, one-shot) Mota-a 3.00
...Reloaded 1-4 (10/01- No. 4, 2/02) Batista-a; Chastity app. 3.00

BADLANDS
Vortex Comics: May, 1990 ($3.00, glossy stock, mature)
1-Chaykin-c 3.00

BADLANDS
Dark Horse Comics: July, 1991 - No. 6, Dec, 1991 ($2.25, B&W, limited series)
1-6: 1-John F. Kennedy-c; reprints Vortex Comics issue 2.25

BADMEN OF THE WEST
Avon Periodicals: 1951 (Giant) (132 pgs., painted-c)
1-Contains rebound copies of Jesse James, King of the Bad Men of Deadwood, Badmen of Tombstone; other combinations possible.
Issues with Kubert-a... 40 80 120 236 351 465

BADMEN OF THE WEST! (See A-1 Comics)
Magazine Enterprises: 1953 - No. 3, 1954
1(A-1 100)-Meskin-a? 26 52 78 147 211 275
2(A-1 120), 3: 2-Larsen-a 16 32 48 89 127 165

BADMEN OF TOMBSTONE
Avon Periodicals: 1950
nn 17 34 51 95 135 175

BADROCK (Also see Youngblood)
Image Comics (Extreme Studios): Mar, 1995 - No. 2, Jan, 1996 ($1.75/$2.50)
1-Variant-c (3) 3.00
2-Liefeld-c/a & story; Savage Dragon app, flipbook w/Grifter/Badrock #2; variant-c exist 2.50
Annual 1(1995,$2.95)-Arthur Adams-c 3.00
Annual 1 Commemorative ($9.95)-3,000 printed 10.00
.../Wolverine (6/96, $4.95, squarebound)-Sauron app; pin-ups; variant-c exists 5.00
.../Wolverine (6/96)-Special Comicon Edition 5.00

BADROCK AND COMPANY (Also see Youngblood)
Image Comics (Extreme Studios): Sept, 1994 - No.6, Feb, 1995 ($2.50)
1-6 : 6-Indicia reads "October 1994"; story cont'd in Shadowhawk #17 2.50

BAFFLING MYSTERIES (Formerly Indian Braves No. 1-4; Heroes of the Wild Frontier No. 26 on)
Periodical House (Ace Magazines): No. 5, Nov, 1951 - No. 26, Oct, 1955
5 40 80 120 233 342 450
6-19,21-24: 8-Woodish-a by Cameron. 10-E.C. Crypt Keeper swipe on-c.
24-Last pre-code issue 25 50 75 144 207 270
20-Classic-c 32 64 96 184 267 350
25-Reprints; surrealistic-c 19 38 57 107 154 200
26-Reprints 17 34 51 95 135 175
NOTE: ***Cameron** a-8, 10, 16-18, 20-22. **Colan** a-5, 11, 25r/5. **Sekowsky** a-5, 6, 22. Bondage c-20, 23. Reprints in 18(1), 19(1), 24(3).*

BALBO (See Master Comics #33 & Mighty Midget Comics)

BALDER THE BRAVE
Marvel Comics Group: Nov, 1985 - No. 4, 1986 (Limited series)
1-4: Simonson-c/a; character from Thor 3.00

BALLAD OF HALO JONES, THE
Quality Comics: Sept, 1987 - No. 12, Aug, 1988 ($1.25/$1.50)
1-12: Alan Moore scripts in all 2.25

BALL AND CHAIN
DC Comics (Homage): Nov, 1999 - No. 4, Feb, 2000 ($2.50, limited series)
1-4-Lobdell-s/Garza-a 2.50

BALLISTIC (Also See Cyberforce)
Image Comics (Top Cow Productions): Sept, 1995 - No. 3, Dec, 1995 ($2.50, limited series)
1-3: Wetworks app, Turner-c/a 3.00

BALLISTIC ACTION
Image Comics (Top Cow Productions): May, 1996 ($2.95, one-shot)
1-Pin-ups of Top Cow characters participating in outdoor sports 3.00

BALLISTIC IMAGERY
Image Comics (Top Cow Productions): Jan, 1996 ($2.50, anthology, one-shot)
1-Cyberforce app. 2.50

BALLISTIC/ WOLVERINE
Image Comics (Top Cow Productions): Feb, 1997 ($2.95, one-shot)
1-Devil's Reign pt. 4; Witchblade cameo (1 page) 4.00

BALOO & LITTLE BRITCHES (Disney)
Gold Key: Apr, 1968
1-From the Jungle Book 4 8 12 27 36 45

BAMBI (Disney) (See Movie Classics, Movie Comics, and Walt Disney Showcase No. 31)
Dell Publishing Co.: No. 12, 1942; No. 30, 1943; No. 186, Apr, 1948; 1984
Four Color 12-Walt Disney's... 59 158 177 417 659 900
Four Color 30-Bambi's Children (1943) 56 112 168 400 620 840
Four Color 186-Walt Disney's...; reprinted as Movie Classic Bambi #3 (1956)
18 36 54 126 193 260
1-(Whitman, 1984; 60¢)-r/Four Color #186 (3-pack) 2 4 6 8 10 12

BAMBI (Disney)
Grosset & Dunlap: 1942 (50¢, 7"x8-1/2", 32pg, hard-c w/dust jacket)
nn-Given away w/a copy of Thumper for a $2.00, 2-yr. subscription to WDC&S in 1942 (Xmas offer).
Book only 22 44 66 127 184 240
w/dust jacket 40 80 120 233 342 450

BAMM BAMM & PEBBLES FLINTSTONE (TV)
Gold Key: Oct, 1964 (Hanna-Barbera)
1 10 20 30 72 104 135

BANANA SPLITS, THE (TV) (See Golden Comics Digest & March of Comics No. 364)
Gold Key: June, 1969 - No. 8, Oct, 1971 (Hanna-Barbera)
1-Photo-c on all 12 24 36 87 134 180
2-8 9 18 27 60 85 110

BAND WAGON (See Hanna-Barbera Band Wagon)

BANDY MAN, THE
Caliber: 1996 - No. 3, ($2.95, B&W, limited series)
1-3-Stephan Petrucha scripts; 1-Jill Thompson-a; Miran Kim-c 3.00

BANG-UP COMICS
Progressive Publishers: Dec, 1941 - No. 3, June, 1942
1-Cosmo Mann & Lady Fairplay begin; Buzz Balmer by Rick Yager in all (origin #1)
100 200 300 625 963 1300
2,3 50 100 150 305 465 625

BANISHED KNIGHTS (See Warlands)
Image Comics: Dec, 2001 - No. 4, June, 2002 ($2.95)
1-4-Two covers (Alvin Lee, Pat Lee) 3.00

BANNER COMICS (Becomes Captain Courageous No. 6)
Ace Magazines: No. 3, Sept, 1941 - No. 5, Jan, 1942

Barbie #59 © Mattel

Barbie Fashion #14 © Mattel

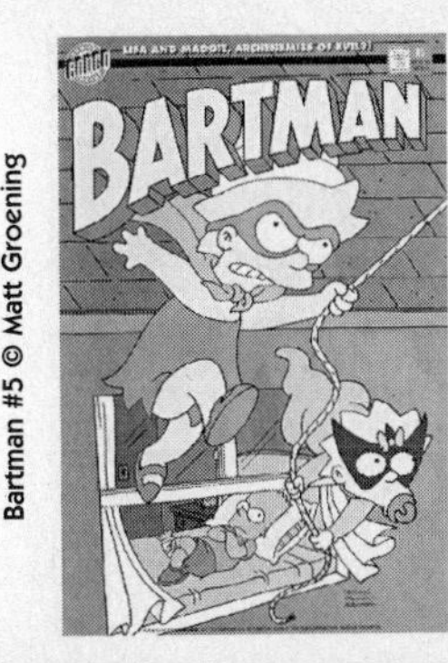

Bartman #5 © Matt Groening

	GD 2.0	VG 4.0	FN 6.0	VF 8.0	VF/NM 9.0	NM- 9.2
3-Captain Courageous (1st app.) & Lone Warrior & Sidekick Dicky begin; Jim Mooney-c	108	216	324	675	1038	1400
4,5: 4-Flag-c	66	132	198	413	637	860

BARABBAS
Slave Labor Graphics: Aug, 1986 - No. 2, Nov, 1986 ($1.50, B&W, lim. series)

	GD	VG	FN	VF	VF/NM	NM-
1,2						2.25

BARBARIANS, THE
Atlas Comics/Seaboard Periodicals: June, 1975

	GD	VG	FN	VF	VF/NM	NM-
1-Origin, only app. Andrax; Iron Jaw app.; Marcos-a	1	2	3	5	6	9

BARBIE
Marvel Comics: Jan, 1991 - No. 66, Apr, 1996 ($1.00/$1.25/$1.50)

	GD	VG	FN	VF	VF/NM	NM-
1-Polybagged w/Barbie Pink Card; Romita-c	2	4	6	10	12	15
2-49,51-65	1	2	3	5	7	9
50,66: 50-(Giant). 66-Last issue (lower print)	2	4	6	8	10	12

BARBIE & KEN
Dell Publishing Co.: May-July, 1962 - No. 5, Nov-Jan, 1963-64

	GD	VG	FN	VF	VF/NM	NM-
01-053-207(#1)-Based on Mattel toy dolls	39	78	117	293	459	625
2-4	31	62	93	225	355	485
5 (Rare)	33	66	99	248	387	525

BARBIE FASHION
Marvel Comics: Jan, 1991 - No. 63, Jan, 1996 ($1.00/$1.25/$1.50)

	GD	VG	FN	VF	VF/NM	NM-
1-Polybagged w/doorknob hanger	2	4	6	10	12	15
2-49,51-62: 4-Contains preview to Sweet XVI. 14-Begin $1.25-c	1	2	3	5	7	9
50,63: 50-(Giant). 63-Last issue (lower print)	2	4	6	8	10	12

BARBI TWINS, THE
Topps Comics: 1995 ($2.50/$5.00)

	GD	VG	FN	VF	VF/NM	NM-
1-Razor app.						2.50
Swimsuit Art Calendar ($5.00)-art by Linsner, Bradstreet, Hughes; Julie Bell-c						5.00

BARB WIRE (See Comics' Greatest World)
Dark Horse Comics: Apr, 1994 - No. 9, Feb, 1995 ($2.00/$2.50)

	GD	VG	FN	VF	VF/NM	NM-
1-9: 1-Foil logo						3.00
Trade paperback (1996, $8.95)-r/#2,3,5,6 w/Pamela Anderson bio						9.00

BARB WIRE: ACE OF SPADES
Dark Horse Comics: May, 1996 - No. 4, Sept, 1996 ($2.95, limited series)

	GD	VG	FN	VF	VF/NM	NM-
1-4: Chris Warner-c/a(p)/scripts; Tim Bradstreet-c/a(i) in all						3.00

BARB WIRE COMICS MAGAZINE SPECIAL
Dark Horse Comics: May, 1996 ($3.50, B&W, magazine, one-shot)

	GD	VG	FN	VF	VF/NM	NM-
nn-Adaptation of film; photo-c; poster insert.						3.50

BARB WIRE MOVIE SPECIAL
Dark Horse Comics: May, 1996 ($3.95, one-shot)

	GD	VG	FN	VF	VF/NM	NM-
nn-Adaptation of film; photo-c; 1st app. new look						4.00

BARKER, THE (Also see National Comics #42)
Quality Comics Group/Comic Magazine: Autumn, 1946 - No. 15, Dec, 1949

	GD	VG	FN	VF	VF/NM	NM-
1	22	44	66	123	177	230
2	11	22	33	66	91	115
3-10	9	18	27	52	66	80
11-14	7	14	21	37	46	55
15-Jack Cole-a(p)	8	16	24	40	50	60

NOTE: ***Jack Cole** art in some issues.*

BARNABY
Civil Service Publications Inc.: 1945 (25¢,102 pgs., digest size)

	GD	VG	FN	VF	VF/NM	NM-
V1#1-r/Crocket Johnson strips from 1942	5	10	14	20	24	28

BARNEY AND BETTY RUBBLE (TV) (Flintstones' Neighbors)
Charlton Comics: Jan, 1973 - No. 23, Dec, 1976 (Hanna-Barbera)

	GD	VG	FN	VF	VF/NM	NM-
1	4	8	12	29	40	50
2-11: 11(2/75)-1st Mike Zeck-a (illos)	3	6	9	16	20	25
12-23	2	4	6	11	14	18
Digest Annual (1972, B&W, 100 pgs.) (scarce)	3	7	10	21	28	35

BARNEY BAXTER (Also see Magic Comics)
David McKay/Dell Publishing Co./Argo: 1938 - No. 2, 1956

	GD	VG	FN	VF	VF/NM	NM-
Feature Books 15(McKay-1938)	40	80	120	236	351	465
Four Color 20(1942)	29	58	87	209	310	410
1,2 (1956-Argo)	9	18	27	52	66	80

BARNEY BEAR ...

Spire Christian Comics (Fleming H. Revell Co.): 1977-1981

	GD 2.0	VG 4.0	FN 6.0	VF 8.0	VF/NM 9.0	NM- 9.2
...Home Plate nn-(1979, 49¢), ...Lost and Found nn-(1979, 49¢), Out of The Woods nn-(1980, 49¢), Sunday School Picnic nn-(1981, 69¢, The Swamp Gang!-(1977, 39¢)	1	3	4	6	8	10

BARNEY GOOGLE & SNUFFY SMITH
Dell Publishing Co./Gold Key: 1942 - 1943; April, 1964

	GD	VG	FN	VF	VF/NM	NM-
Four Color 19(1942)	38	76	115	285	430	575
Four Color 40(1944)	24	48	72	170	260	350
Large Feature Comic 11(1943)	37	74	112	213	312	410
1(10113-404)-Gold Key (4/64)	5	10	15	33	44	55

BARNEY GOOGLE & SNUFFY SMITH
Toby Press: June, 1951 - No. 4, Feb, 1952 (Reprints)

	GD	VG	FN	VF	VF/NM	NM-
1	14	28	42	79	110	140
2,3	8	16	24	46	58	70
4-Kurtzman-a "Pot Shot Pete", 5 pgs.; reprints John Wayne #5	12	24	36	71	98	125

BARNEY GOOGLE AND SNUFFY SMITH
Charlton Comics: Mar, 1970 - No. 6, Jan, 1971

	GD	VG	FN	VF	VF/NM	NM-
1	3	6	9	18	24	30
2-6	2	4	6	11	14	18

BARNUM!
DC Comics (Vertigo): 2003 ($29.95, hardcover with dust jacket)

	GD	VG	FN	VF	VF/NM	NM-
Hardcover-Chaykin & Tischman-s/Henrichon-a						30.00

BARNYARD COMICS (Dizzy Duck No. 32 on)
Nedor/Polo Mag./Standard(Animated Cartoons): June, 1944 - No. 31, Sept, 1950; No. 10, 1957

	GD	VG	FN	VF	VF/NM	NM-
1 (nn, 52 pgs.)-Funny animal	21	42	63	118	169	220
2 (52 pgs.)	11	22	33	64	87	110
3-5	8	16	24	46	58	70
6-12,16	8	16	24	40	50	60
13-15,17,21,23,26,27,29-All contain Frazetta text illos	9	18	27	52	66	80
18-20,22,24,25-All contain Frazetta-a & text illos	11	22	33	66	91	115
28,30,31	6	12	18	31	38	45
10 (1957)(Exist?)	4	7	10	14	17	20

BARRY M. GOLDWATER
Dell Publishing Co.: Mar, 1965 (Complete life story)

	GD	VG	FN	VF	VF/NM	NM-
12-055-503-Photo-c	4	8	12	28	38	48

BARRY WINDSOR-SMITH: STORYTELLER
Dark Horse Comics: Oct, 1996 - No. 9, July, 1997 ($4.95, oversize)

	GD	VG	FN	VF	VF/NM	NM-
1-9: 1-Intro Young Gods, Paradox Man & the Freebooters; Barry Smith-c/a/scripts						5.00
Preview						4.00

BAR SINISTER (Also see Shaman's Tears)
Acclaim Comics (Windjammer): Jun, 1995 - No. 4, Sept, 1995 ($2.50, lim. series)

	GD	VG	FN	VF	VF/NM	NM-
1-4: Mike Grell-c/a/scripts						2.50

BARTMAN (Also see Simpson's Comics & Radioactive Man)
Bongo Comics: 1993 - No. 6, 1994 ($1.95/$2.25)

	GD	VG	FN	VF	VF/NM	NM-
1-($2.95)-Foil-c; bound-in jumbo Bartman poster						6.00
2-6: 3-w/trading card						4.00

BART SIMPSON (See Simpsons Comics Presents Bart Simpson)

BASEBALL COMICS
Will Eisner Productions: Spring, 1949 (Reprinted later as a Spirit section)

	GD	VG	FN	VF	VF/NM	NM-
1-Will Eisner-c/a	71	142	213	444	685	925

BASEBALL COMICS
Kitchen Sink Press: 1991 ($3.95, coated stock)

	GD	VG	FN	VF	VF/NM	NM-
1-r/1949 ish. by Eisner; contains trading cards						6.00

BASEBALL HEROES
Fawcett Publications: 1952 (one-shot)

	GD	VG	FN	VF	VF/NM	NM-
nn (Scarce)-Babe Ruth photo-c; baseball's Hall of Fame biographies	79	158	237	494	760	1025

BASEBALL'S GREATEST HEROES
Magnum Comics: Dec, 1991 - No. 2, May, 1992 ($1.75)

	GD	VG	FN	VF	VF/NM	NM-
1-Mickey Mantle #1; photo-c; Sinnott-a(p)						5.00
2-Brooks Robinson #1; photo-c; Sinnott-a(i)						4.00

BASEBALL THRILLS

Batgirl #41 © DC

Batman #14 © DC

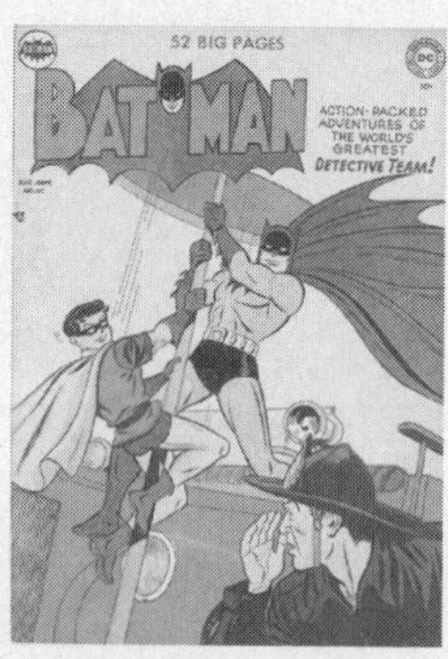

Batman #60 © DC

	GD	VG	FN	VF	VF/NM	NM-
	2.0	4.0	6.0	8.0	9.0	9.2

Ziff-Davis Publ. Co.: No. 10, Sum, 1951 - No. 3, Sum, 1952 (Saunders painted-c No.1,2)

10(#1)-Bob Feller, Musial, Newcombe & Boudreau stories
42 84 126 256 391 525

2-Powell-a(2)(Late Sum, '51); Feller, Berra & Mathewson stories
32 64 96 184 267 350

3-Kinstler-c/a; Joe DiMaggio story 32 64 96 184 267 350

BASEBALL THRILLS 3-D
The 3-D Zone: May, 1990 ($2.95, w/glasses)

1-New L.B. Cole-c; life stories of Ty Cobb & Ted Williams 6.00

BASICALLY STRANGE (Magazine)
John C. Comics (Archie Comics Group): Dec, 1982 ($1.95, B&W)

1-(21,000 printed; all but 1,000 destroyed; pgs. out of sequence)
3 6 9 18 23 28

1-Wood, Toth-a; Corben-c; reprints & new art 2 4 6 12 16 20

BASIC HISTORY OF AMERICA ILLUSTRATED
Pendulum Press: 1976 (B&W) (Soft-c $1.50; Hard-c $4.50)

07-1999-America Becomes a World Power 1890-1920. 07-2251-The Industrial Era 1865-1915. 07-226x-Before the Civil War 1830-1860. 07-2278-Americans Move Westward 1800-1850. 07-2286-The Civil War 1850-1876; Redondo-a. 07-2294-The Fight for Freedom 1750-1783. 07-2308-The New World 1500-1750. 07-2316-Problems of the New Nation 1800-1830. 07-2324-Roaring Twenties and the Great Depression 1920-1940. 07-2332-The United States Emerges 1783-1800. 07-2340-America Today 1945-1976. 07-2359-World War II 1940-1945

Softcover editions each 6.00
Hardcover editions each 12.00

BASIL (...the Royal Cat)
St. John Publishing Co.: Jan, 1953 - No. 4, Sept, 1953

1-Funny animal 7 14 21 37 46 55
2-4 5 10 15 22 26 30
I.W. Reprint 1 2 4 6 10 12 15

BASIL WOLVERTON'S FANTASTIC FABLES
Dark Horse Comics: Oct, 1993 - No. 2, Dec, 1993 ($2.50, B&W, limited series)

1,2-Wolverton-c/a(r) 6.00

BASIL WOLVERTON'S GATEWAY TO HORROR
Dark Horse Comics: June, 1988 ($1.75, B&W, one-shot)

1-Wolverton-r 6.00

BASIL WOLVERTON'S PLANET OF TERROR
Dark Horse Comics: Oct, 1987 ($1.75, B&W, one-shot)

1-Wolverton-r; Alan Moore-c 6.00

BASTARD SAMURAI
Image Comics: Apr, 2002 - No. 3, Aug, 2002 ($2.95)

1-3-Oeming & Gunter-s; Shannon-a/Oeming-i 3.00
TPB (2003, $12.95) r/#1-3; plus sketch pages and pin-ups 13.00

BATGIRL (See Batman: No Man's Land stories)
DC Comics: Apr, 2000 - Present ($2.50)

1-Scott & Campanella-a 6.00
1-(2nd printing) 2.50
2-10: 8-Lady Shiva app. 4.50
11-24: 12-"Officer Down" x-over. 15-Joker-c/app. 24-Bruce Wayne: Murderer pt. 2. 4.00
25-($3.25) Batgirl vs Lady Shiva 3.50
26-29: 27- Bruce Wayne: Fugitive pt. 5; Noto-a. 29-B.W.:F. pt. 13 3.50
30-49,51-58: 30-32-Connor Hawke app. 39-Intro. Black Wind. 41-Superboy-c/app. 53-Robin (Spoiler) app. 54-Bagged with Sky Captain CD. 55-57-War Games 2.50
50-($3.25) Batgirl vs Batman 3.25
Annual 1 ('00, $3.50) Planet DC; intro. Aruna 5.00
...: A Knight Alone (2001, $12.95, TPB) r/#7-11,13,14 13.00
...: Death Wish (2003, $14.95, TPB) r/#17-20,22,23,25 & Secret Files and Origins #1 15.00
...: Fists of Fury (2004, $14.95, TPB) r/#15,16,21,26-28 15.00
... Secret Files and Origins (8/02, $4.95) origin-s Noto-a; profile pages and pin-ups 5.00
...: Silent Running (2001, $12.95, TPB) r/#1-6 13.00

BATGIRL ADVENTURES (See Batman Adventures, The)
DC Comics: Feb, 1998 ($2.95, one-shot) (Based on animated series)

1-Harley Quinn and Poison Ivy app.; Timm-c 5.00

BATGIRL SPECIAL
DC Comics: 1988 ($1.50, one-shot, 52 pgs)

1-Kitson-a/Mignoia-c 1 2 3 5 7 9

BATGIRL: YEAR ONE
DC Comics: Feb, 2003 - No. 9, Oct, 2003 ($2.95, limited series)

	GD	VG	FN	VF	VF/NM	NM-
	2.0	4.0	6.0	8.0	9.0	9.2

1-9-Barbara Gordon becomes Batgirl; Killer Moth app.; Beatty & Dixon-s 3.00
TPB (2003, $17.95) r/#1-9 18.00

BAT LASH (See DC Special Series #16, Showcase #76, Weird Western Tales)
National Periodical Publications: Oct-Nov, 1968 - No. 7, Oct-Nov, 1969
(All 12¢ issues)

1-(10-11/68)-2nd app. Bat Lash 5 10 15 36 48 60
2-7 3 7 10 21 28 35

BATMAN (See Anarky, Aurora [in Promo. Comics section], Azrael, The Best of DC #2, Blind Justice, The Brave & the Bold, Cosmic Odyssey, DC 100-Page Super Spec. #14,20, DC Special, DC Special Series, Detective, Dynamic Classics, 80-Page Giants, Gotham By Gaslight, Gotham Nights, Greatest Batman Stories Ever Told, Greatest Joker Stories Ever Told, Heroes Against Hunger, JLA,The Joker, Justice League of America, Justice League Int., Legends of the Dark Knight, Limited Coll. Ed., Man-Bat, Nightwing, Power Record Comics, Real Fact #5, Robin, Saga of Ra's Al Ghul, Shadow of the..., Star Spangled, Super Friends, 3-D Batman, Untold Legend of..., Wanted... & World's Finest Comics)

BATMAN
National Per. Publ./Detective Comics/DC Comics: Spring, 1940 - Present
(#1-5 were quarterly)

1-Origin The Batman reprinted (2 pgs.) from Det. #33 w/splash from #34 by Bob Kane; see Detective #33 for 1st origin; 1st app. Joker (2 stories intended for 2 separate issues of Det. Comics which would have been 1st & 2nd app.); splash pg. to 2nd Joker story is similar to cover of Det. #40 (story intended for #40); 1st app. The Cat (Catwoman) (1st villainess in comics); has Batman story (w/Hugo Strange) without Robin originally planned for Det. #38; mentions location (Manhattan) where Batman lives (see Det. #31). This book was created entirely from the inventory of Det. Comics; 1st Batman/Robin pin-up on back-c; has text piece & photo of Bob Kane
7179 14,358 21,537 50,000 95,000 140,000

1-Reprint, oversize 13-1/2x10". **WARNING**: This comic is an exact duplicate reprint of the original except for its size. DC published it in 1974 with a second cover titling it as a Famous First Edition. There have been many reported cases of the outer cover being removed and the interior sold as the original edition. The reprint with the new outer cover removed is practically worthless. See Famous First Edition for value.

2-2nd app. The Joker; 2nd app. Catwoman (out of costume) in Joker story; 1st time called Catwoman (NOTE: A 15¢-c for Canadian distr. exists.)
1235 2470 3705 9263 15,132 21,000

3-3rd app Catwoman (1st in costume & 1st costumed villainess); 1st Puppet Master app.; classic Kane & Moldoff-c 839 1678 2517 5873 9437 13,000

4-3rd app. The Joker (see Det. #45 for 4th); 1st mention of Gotham City in a Batman comic (on newspaper)(Win/40) 677 1354 2031 4739 7620 10,500

5-1st app. the Batmobile with its bat-head front 484 968 1452 3388 5444 7500
6,7: 7-Bullseye-c; Joker app. 423 846 1269 2936 4718 6500
8-Infinity-c by Fred Ray; Joker app. 359 718 1077 2334 3767 5200

9-10:9-1st Batman x-mas story; Burnley-c. 10-Catwoman story (gets new costume)
345 690 1035 2243 3622 5000

11-Classic Joker-c by Ray/Robinson (3rd Joker-c, 6-7/42); Joker & Penguin app.
677 1354 2031 4739 7620 10,500

12,15: 12-Joker app. 15-New costume Catwoman 300 600 900 1892 2946 4000

13-Jerry Siegel (Superman's co-creator) appears in a Batman story.
300 600 900 1908 3004 4100

14-2nd Penguin-c; Penguin app. (12-1/42-43) 300 600 900 1925 3063 4200

16-Intro/origin Alfred (4-5/43); cover is a reverse of #9 cover by Burnley; 1st small logo
503 1006 1509 3521 5661 7800

17,20: 17-Classic war-c; Penguin app. 20-1st Batmobile-c (12-1/43-44); Joker app.
231 462 693 1444 2222 3000

18-Hitler, Hirohito, Mussolini-c. 292 584 876 1825 2813 3800
19-Joker app. 200 400 600 1250 1925 2600

21,22,24,26,28-30: 21-1st skinny Alfred in Batman (2-3/44). 21,30-Penguin app. 22-1st Alfred solo-c/story (Alfred solo stories in 22-32,36); Catwoman & The Cavalier app. 28-Joker story
154 308 462 963 1482 2000

23-Joker-c/story; classic black-c 246 492 738 1538 2369 3200

25-Only Joker/Penguin team-up; 1st team-up between two major villains
231 462 693 1444 2222 3000

27-Classic Burnley Christmas-c; Penguin app. 200 400 600 1250 1925 2600

31,32,34-36,39: 32-Origin Robin retold; Joker app. 35-Catwoman story (in new costume w/o cat head mask). 36-Penguin app. 114 228 342 713 1094 1475

33-Christmas-c 123 246 369 769 1185 1600
37,40,44-Joker-c/stories 154 308 462 963 1482 2000
38-Penguin-c/story 131 262 393 819 1260 1700

41,45,46: 41-1st Sci-fi cover/story in Batman; Penguin app.(6-7/47). 45-Christmas-c/story; Catwoman story. 46-Joker app. 83 166 249 519 797 1075

42-2nd Catwoman-c (1st in Batman)(8-9/47); Catwoman story also.
131 262 393 819 1260 1700

43-Penguin-c/story 112 224 336 700 1075 1450

47-1st detailed origin The Batman (6-7/48); 1st Bat-signal-c this title (see Detective #108); Batman tracks down his parent's killer and reveals i.d. to him
317 634 951 2061 3331 4600

Batman #189 © DC

Batman #245 © DC

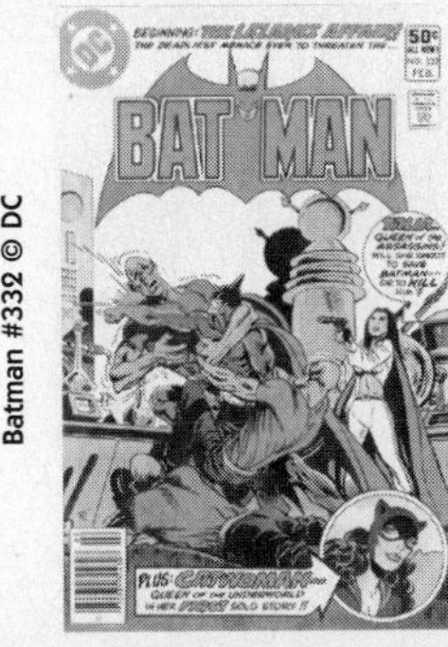

Batman #332 © DC

GD VG FN VF VF/NM NM-
2.0 4.0 6.0 8.0 9.0 9.2

48-1000 Secrets of the Batcave; r-in #203; Penguin story
110 220 330 688 1057 1425
49-Joker-c/story; 1st app. Mad Hatter; 1st app. Vicki Vale
173 346 519 1081 1666 2250
50-Two-Face impostor app. 92 184 276 575 88 1200
51,54,56,57,59,60: 57-Centerfold is a 1950 calendar; Joker app. 59-1st app. Deadshot; Batman in the future-c/story 79 158 237 494 760 1025
52,55-Joker-c/stories 106 212 318 663 1019 1375
53-Joker story 85 170 255 531 816 1100
58,61: 58-Penguin-c. 61-Origin Batman Plane II 87 174 261 544 835 1125
62-Origin Catwoman; Catwoman-c 121 242 363 756 1166 1575
63,80-Joker stories. 63-1st app. Killer Moth; flying saucer story(2-3/51)
75 150 225 469 872 975
64,67,70-72,74-77,79: 67-Joker story. 70-Robot-c. 72-Last 52 pg. issue. 74-Used in **POP**, Pg. 90. 76-Penguin story. 79-Vicki Vale in "The Bride of Batman"
62 124 186 388 594 800
65,69,84-Catwoman-c/stories. 84-Two-Face app. 75 150 225 469 872 975
66,73-Joker-c/stories. 66-Pre-2nd Batman & Robin team try-out. 73-Vicki Vale story
85 170 255 531 816 1100
68,81-Two-Face-c/stories 67 134 201 419 647 875
78-(8-9/53)-Roh Kar, The Man Hunter from Mars story-the 1st lawman of Mars to come to Earth (green skinned) 77 154 231 481 741 1000
82,83,85-89: 85,86-Joker story. 86-Intro Batmarine (Batman's submarine). 89-Last pre-code issue 59 118 177 369 565 760
90,91,93-99: 97-2nd app. Bat-Hound-c/story; Joker story. 99-(4/56)-Last G.A. Penguin app.
51 102 153 311 473 635
92-1st app. Bat-Hound-c/story 67 134 201 419 647 875
100-(6/56) 254 508 762 1588 2444 3300
101-(8/56)-Clark Kent x-over who protects Batman's i.d. (3rd story)
52 104 156 317 484 650
102-104,106-109: 103-1st S.A. issue; 3rd Bat-Hound-c/story
45 90 135 275 418 560
105-1st Batwoman in Batman (2nd anywhere) 57 114 171 356 546 735
110-Joker story 46 92 138 281 426 570
111-120: 112-1st app. Signalman (super villain). 113-1st app. Fatman; Batman meets his counterpart on Planet X w/a chest plate similar to S.A. Batman's design (yellow oval w/black design inside). 40 80 120 233 342 450
121- Origin/1st app. of Mr. Zero (Mr. Freeze). 47 94 141 287 436 585
122,124-126,128,130: 122,126-Batwoman-c/story. 124-2nd app. Signal Man. 128-Batwoman cameo. 130-Lex Luthor app. 30 60 90 173 249 325
123,127: 123-Joker story; Bat-Hound app. 127-(10/59)-Batman vs. Thor the Thunder God c/story; Joker story; Superman cameo 32 64 96 184 267 350
129-Origin Robin retold; bondage-c; Batwoman-c/story (reprinted in Batman Family #8)
34 68 102 193 279 365
131-135,137-139,141-143: 131-Intro 2nd Batman & Robin series (see #66; also in #135,145, 154,159,163). 133-1st Bat-Mite in Batman (3rd app. anywhere). 134-Origin The Dummy (not Vigilante's villain). 139-Intro 1st original Bat-Girl; only app. Signalman as the Blue Bowman. 141-2nd app. original Bat-Girl. 143-(10/61)-Last 10¢ issue
22 44 66 127 184 240
136-Joker-c/story 27 54 81 152 219 285
140-Joker story, Batwoman-c/s; Superman cameo 24 48 72 135 195 255
144-(12/61)-1st 12¢ issue; Joker story 17 34 51 121 186 250
145,148-Joker-c/stories 19 38 57 136 208 280
146,147,149,150 13 26 39 92 141 190
151-154,156-158,160-162,164-168,170: 152-Joker story. 156-Ant-Man/Robin team-up(6/63). 164-New Batmobile(6/64) new look & Mystery Analysts series begins
11 22 33 77 114 150
155-1st S.A. app. The Penguin (5/63) 31 62 93 230 358 485
159,163-Joker-c/stories. 159-Bat-Girl app. 13 26 39 92 141 190
169-2nd SA Penguin app. 14 28 42 97 149 200
171-1st Riddler app.(5/65) since Dec. 1948 38 76 114 285 448 610
172-175,177,178,180,184 9 18 27 63 89 115
176-(80-Pg. Giant G-17); Joker-c/story; Penguin app. in strip-r; Catwoman reprint
11 22 33 77 114 150
179-2nd app. Silver Age Riddler 15 30 45 107 164 220
181-Batman & Robin poster insert; intro. Poison Ivy 18 36 54 126 193 260
182,187-(80 Pg. Giants G-24, G-30); Joker-c/stories 10 20 30 67 96 125
183-2nd app. Poison Ivy 11 22 33 77 114 150
185-(80 Pg. Giant G-27) 9 18 27 65 93 120
186-Joker-c/story 9 18 27 65 93 120
188,191,192,194-196,199 6 12 18 43 59 75
189-1st S.A. app. Scarecrow; retells origin of G.A. Scarecrow from World's Finest #3(1st app.)
11 22 33 77 114 150
190-Penguin-c/app. 8 16 24 53 74 95

GD VG FN VF VF/NM NM-
2.0 4.0 6.0 8.0 9.0 9.2

193-(80-Pg. Giant G-37) 8 16 24 58 82 105
197-4th S.A. Catwoman app. cont'd from Det. #369; 1st new Batgirl app. in Batman (5th anywhere) 8 16 24 58 82 105
198-(80-Pg. Giant G-43); Joker-c/story-r/World's Finest #61; Catwoman-r/Det. #211; Penguin-r; origin-r/#47 9 18 27 63 89 115
200-(3/68)-Joker cameo; retells origin of Batman & Robin; 1st Neal Adams work this title (cover only) 12 24 36 84 127 170
201-Joker story 6 12 18 38 52 65
202,204-207,209-212: 210-Catwoman-c/app. 212-Last 12¢ issue
5 10 15 33 44 55
203-(80 Pg. Giant G-49); r/#48, 61, & Det. 185; Batcave Blueprints
7 14 21 46 63 80
208-(80 Pg. Giant G-55); New origin Batman by Gil Kane plus 3 G.A. Batman reprints w/Catwoman, Vicki Vale & Batwoman 7 14 21 46 63 80
213-(80-Pg. Giant G-61); 30th anniversary issue (7-8/69); origin Alfred (r/Batman #16), Joker(r/Det. #168), Clayface; new origin Robin with new facts
8 16 24 55 78 100
214-217: 214-Alfred given a new last name- "Pennyworth" (see Detective #96)
4 8 12 25 33 42
218-(80-Pg. Giant G-67) 6 12 18 40 55 70
219-Neal Adams-a 6 12 18 38 52 65
220,221,224-226,229-231 4 8 12 22 30 38
222-Beatles take-off; art lesson by Joe Kubert 5 10 15 35 47 58
223,228,233: 223,228-(80-Pg. Giants G-73,G-79). 233-G-85-(68 pgs., "64 pgs." on-c)
6 12 18 38 52 65
227-Neal Adams cover swipe of Detective #31 5 10 15 33 44 55
232-N. Adams-a. Intro/1st app. Ra's al Ghul; origin Batman & Robin retold; last 15¢ issue
13 26 39 90 138 185
234-(9/71)-1st modern app. of Harvey Dent/Two-Face; (see World's Finest #173 for Batman as Two-Face; only S.A. mention of character); N. Adams-a; 52 pg. issues begin, end #242
13 26 39 94 145 195
235,236,239-242: 239-XMas-c. 241-Reprint/#5 4 8 12 25 33 42
237-N. Adams-a. 1st Rutland Vermont - Bald Mountain Halloween x-over. G.A. Batman-r/ Det. #37; 1st app. The Reaper; Wrightson/Ellison plots
8 16 24 55 78 100
238-Also listed as DC 100 Page Super Spectacular #8; Batman, Legion, Aquaman-r; G.A. Atom, Sargon (r/Sensation #57), Plastic Man (r/Police #14) stories; Doom Patrol origin-r; N. Adams wraparound-c
(see DC 100 Pg. Super Spectacular #8 for price)
243-245-Neal Adams-a 6 12 18 38 52 65
246-250,252,253: 246-Scarecrow app. 253-Shadow-c & app.
3 7 10 21 28 35
251-(9/73)-N. Adams-c/a; Joker-c/story 8 16 24 53 74 95
254,256-259,261-All 100 pg. editions; part-r: 254-(2/74)-Man-Bat-c & app. 256-Catwoman app. 257-Joker & Penguin app. 258-The Cavalier-r. 259-Shadow-c/app.
5 10 15 36 48 60
255-(100 pgs.)-N. Adams-c/a; tells of Bruce Wayne's father who wore bat costume & fought crime (r/Det. #235); r/story Batman #22 6 12 18 43 59 75
260-Joker-c/story (100 pgs.) 6 12 18 43 59 75
262 (68pgs.) 4 8 12 22 30 38
263,264,266-285,287-290,292,293,295-299: 266-Catwoman back to old costume
2 4 6 11 14 18
265-Wrightson-a(i) 2 4 6 12 16 20
286,291,294: 294-Joker-c/stories 3 6 9 16 20 25
300-Double-size 3 6 9 16 20 25
301-(7/78)-310,312-315,317-320,325-331,333-352: 304-(44 pgs.). 306-3rd app. Black Spider. 308-Mr. Freeze app. 310-1st modern app. The Gentleman Ghost in Batman; Kubert-c. 312,314,346-Two-Face-c/stories. 313-2nd app. Calendar Man. 318-Intro Firebug. 319-2nd modern age app. The Gentleman Ghost; Kubert-c. 344-Poison Ivy app. 345-1st app. new Dr. Death. 345,346,351-Catwoman back-ups 2 4 6 8 10 12
306-308,311-317,319,320,323,324,326-(Whitman variants; low print run; none show issue # on cover) 2 4 6 10 12 15
311,316,322-324: 311-Batgirl-c/story; Batgirl reteams w/Batman. 316-Robin returns. 322-324-Catwoman (Selina Kyle) app. 322,323-Cat-Man cameos (1st in Batman, 1 panel each). 323-1st meeting Catwoman & Cat-Man. 324-1st full app. Cat-Man this title
2 4 6 10 12 15
321,353,359-Joker-c/stories 2 4 6 11 14 18
332-Catwoman's 1st solo 2 4 6 11 14 18
354-356,358,360-365,369,370: 361-1st app Harvey Bullock
1 2 3 5 7 9
357-1st app. Jason Todd (3/83); see Det. #524; 1st brief app. Croc
2 4 6 10 12 15
366-Jason Todd 1st in Robin costume; Joker-c/story 2 4 6 11 14 18
367-Jason in red & green costume (not as Robin) 2 4 6 8 10 12

Batman #408 © DC

Batman #558 © DC

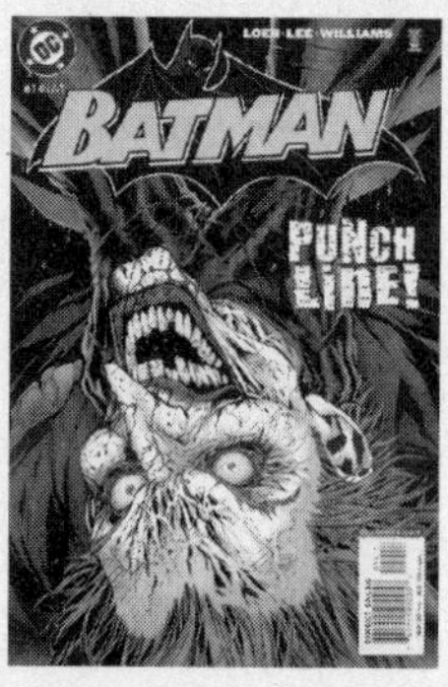

Batman #614 © DC

	GD 2.0	VG 4.0	FN 6.0	VF 8.0	VF/NM 9.0	NM- 9.2
368-1st new Robin in costume (Jason Todd)	2	4	6	10	12	15
371-399,401-403: 371-Cat-Man-c/story; brief origin Cat-Man (cont'd in Det. #538). 386,387-Intro Black Mask (villain). 380-391-Catwoman app. 398-Catwoman & Two-Face app. 401-2nd app. Magpie (see Man of Steel #3 for 1st). 403-Joker cameo						6.00

NOTE: *Most issues between 397 & 432 were reprinted in 1989 and sold in multi-packs. Some are not identified as reprints but have newer ads copyrighted after cover dates. 2nd and 3rd printings exist.*

	GD 2.0	VG 4.0	FN 6.0	VF 8.0	VF/NM 9.0	NM- 9.2
400 ($1.50, 68pgs.)-Dark Knight special; intro by Stephen King; Art Adams/Austin-a	3	6	9	16	20	25
404-Miller scripts begin (end 407); Year 1; 1st modern app. Catwoman (2/87)	2	4	6	14	18	22
405-407: 407-Year 1 ends (See Detective Comics #575-578 for Year 2)	2	4	6	10	13	16
408-410: New Origin Jason Todd (Robin)	2	4	6	11	14	18
411-416,421-425: 411-Two-face app. 412-Origin/1st app. Mime. 414-Starlin scripts begin, end #429. 416-Nightwing-c/story. 423-McFarlane-c						5.00
417-420: "Ten Nights of the Beast" storyline	2	4	6	8	10	12
426-($1.50, 52 pgs.)- "A Death In The Family" storyline begins, ends #429	2	4	6	12	16	20
427- "A Death In The Family" part 2.	2	4	6	10	12	15
428-Death of Robin (Jason Todd)	2	4	6	12	16	20
429-Joker-c/story; Superman app.	2	4	6	8	10	12
430-432						3.00
433-435-Many Deaths of the Batman story by John Byrne-c/scripts						3.00
436-Year 3 begins (ends #439); origin original Robin retold by Nightwing (Dick Grayson); 1st app. Timothy Drake (8/89)						4.00
436-441: 436-2nd printing. 437-Origin Robin cont. 440,441: "A Lonely Place of Dying" Parts 1 & 3						3.00
442-1st app. Timothy Drake in Robin costume						4.00
443-456,458,459,462-464: 445-447-Batman goes to Russia. 448,449-The Penguin Affair Pts 1 & 3. 450-Origin Joker. 450,451-Joker-c/stories. 452-454-Dark Knight Dark City storyline; Riddler app. 455-Alan Grant scripts begin, ends #466, 470. 464-Last solo Batman story; free 16 pg. preview of Impact Comics line						3.00
457-Timothy Drake officially becomes Robin & dons new costume						5.00
457-Direct sale edition (has #000 in indicia)						5.00
460,461,465-487: 460,461-Two part Catwoman story. 465-Robin returns to action with Batman. 470-War of the Gods x-over. 475,476-Return of Scarface-c/story. 476-Last $1.00-c. 477,478-Photo-c						3.00
488-Cont'd from Batman: Sword of Azrael #4; Azrael-c & app.	1	2	3	5	6	8
489-Bane-c/story; 1st app. Azrael in Bat-costume						5.00
490-Riddler-c/story; Azrael & Bane app.						6.00
491,492: 491-Knightfall lead-in; Joker-c/story; Azrael & Bane app.; Kelley Jones-c begin. 492-Knightfall part 1; Bane app.						4.00
492-Platinum edition (promo copy)						10.00
493-496: 493-Knightfall Pt. 3. 494-Knightfall Pt. 5; Joker-c & app. 495-Knightfall Pt. 7; brief Bane & Joker apps. 496-Knightfall Pt. 9, Joker-c/story; Bane cameo						3.00
497-(Late 7/93)-Knightfall Pt. 11; Bane breaks Batman's back; B&W outer-c; Aparo-a(p); Giordano-a(i)						5.00
497-499: 497-2nd printing. 497-Newsstand edition w/o outer cover. 498-Knightfall part 15; Bane & Catwoman-c & app. (see Showcase 93 #7 & 8) 499-Knightfall Pt. 17; Bane app.						3.00
500-($2.50, 68 pgs.)-Knightfall Pt. 19; Azrael in new Bat-costume; Bane-c/story						3.00
500-($3.95, 68 pgs.)-Collector's Edition w/die-cut double-c w/foil by Joe Quesada & 2 bound-in post cards						5.00
501-508,510,511: 501-Begin $1.50-c. 501-508-Knightquest. 503,504-Catwoman app. 507-Ballistic app.; Jim Balent-a(p). 510-KnightsEnd Pt. 7. 511-(9/94)-Zero Hour; Batgirl-c/story						2.50
509-($2.50, 52 pgs.)-KnightsEnd Pt. 1						3.00
512-514,516-518: 512-(11/94)-Dick Grayson assumes Batman role						2.50
515-Special Ed.($2.50)-Kelley Jones-a begins; all black embossed-c; Troika Pt. 1						3.00
515-Regular Edition						2.50
519-534,536-549: 519-Begin $1.95-c. 521-Return of Alfred, 522-Swamp Thing app. 525-Mr. Freeze app. 527,528-Two Face app. 529-Contagion Pt. 6. 530-532-Deadman app. 533-Legacy prelude. 534-Legacy Pt. 5. 536-Final Night x-over; Man-Bat-c/app. 540,541-Spectre-c-app. 544-546-Joker & The Demon. 548,549-Penguin-c/app.						2.50
530-532 ($2.50)-Enhanced edition; glow-in-the-dark-c.						3.00
535-(10/96, $2.95)-1st app. The Ogre						3.00
535-(10/96, $3.95)-1st app. The Ogre; variant, cardboard, foldout-c						4.00
550-($3.50)-Collector's Ed., includes 4 collector cards; intro. Chase, return of Clayface; Kelley Jones-c						3.50
550-($2.95)-Standard Ed.; Williams & Gray-c						3.00
551,552,554-562: 551,552-Ragman c/app. 554-Cataclysm pt. 12.						2.50
553-Cataclysm pt.3						4.00
563-No Man's Land; Joker-c by Campbell; Bob Gale-s						5.00
564-574: 569-New Batgirl-c/app. 572-Joker and Harley app.						2.50
575-579: 575-New look Batman begins; McDaniel-a						2.50
580-598: 580-Begin $2.25-c. 587-Gordon shot. 591,592-Deadshot-c/app.						2.50
599-Bruce Wayne: Murderer pt. 7						2.50
600-($3.95) Bruce Wayne: Fugitive pt. 1; back-up homage stories in '50s, 60's, & 70s styles; by Aragonés, Gaudiano, Shanower and others						5.00
600-(2nd printing)						4.00
601-604, 606,607: 601,603-Bruce Wayne: Fugitive pt.3,13. 606,607-Deadshot-c/app.						2.50
605-($2.95) Conclusion to Bruce Wayne: Fugitive x-over; Noto-c						3.00
608-(12/02) Jim Lee-a/c & Jeph Loeb-s begin; Poison Ivy & Catwoman app.						8.00
608-2nd printing; has different cover with Batman standing on gargoyle						12.00
608-Special Edition; has different cover; 200 printed; used for promotional purposes (one ungraded copy sold for $930, and a CGC graded 9.8 copy sold for $2,751)						
609-Huntress app.						9.00
610,611: 610-Killer Croc-c/app.; Batman & Catwoman kiss						8.00
612-Batman vs. Superman; 1st printing with full color cover						9.00
612-2nd printing with B&W sketch cover						15.00
613,614: 614-Joker-c/app.						7.00
615-617: 615-Reveals ID to Catwoman. 616-Ra's al Ghul app. 617-Scarecrow app.						5.00
618- Batman vs. "Jason Todd"						4.00
619-Newsstand cover; Hush story concludes; Riddler app.						5.00
619-Two variant tri-fold covers; one Heroes group , one Villains group						5.00
619-2nd printing with Riddler chess cover						5.00
620-Broken City pt. 1; Azzarello-s/Risso-a/c begin; Killer Croc app.						3.00
621-625-Azzarello-s/Risso-a/c						2.25
626-630,634-Winick-s/Nguyen-a/Wagner-c; Penguin & Scarecrow app.						2.25
631-633-War Games. 633-Conclusion to War Games x-over						3.00
#0 (10/94)-Zero Hour issue released between #511 & #512; Origin retold						2.50
#1,000,000 (11/98) 853rd Century x-over						2.50
Annual 1 (8-10/61)-Swan-c	57	114	171	485	785	1085
Annual 2	30	60	90	218	334	450
Annual 3 (Summer, '62)-Joker-c/story	31	62	93	223	342	460
Annual 4,5	14	28	42	102	156	210
Annual 6,7 (7/64, 25¢, 80 pgs.)	11	22	33	80	120	160
Annual V5#8 (1982)-Painted-c	1	2	3	5	6	8
Annual 9,10,12: 9(7/85). 10(1986). 12(1988, $1.50)						6.00
Annual 11 (1987, $1.25)-Penguin-c/story; Moore-s	1	2	3	5	6	8
Annual 13 (1989, $1.75, 68 pgs.)-Gives history of Bruce Wayne, Dick Grayson, Jason Todd, Alfred, Comm. Gordon, Barbara Gordon (Batgirl) & Vicki Vale; Morrow-i						5.00
Annual 14-17 ('90-'93, 68 pgs.)-14-Origin Two-Face. 15-Armageddon 2001 x-over; Joker app. 15 (2nd printing). 16-Joker-c/s; Kieth-c. 17 (1993, $2.50, 68 pgs.)-Azrael in Bat-costume; intro Ballistic						4.00
Annual 18 (1994, $2.95)						3.00
Annual 19 (1995, $3.95)-Year One story; retells Scarecrow's origin						4.00
Annual 20 (1996, $2.95)-Legends of the Dead Earth story; Giarrano-a						3.00
Annual 21 (1997, $3.95)-Pulp Heroes story						4.00
Annual 22,23 ('98, '99, $2.95)-22-Ghosts; Wrightson-c. 23-JLApe; Art Adams-c						3.00
Annual 24 ('00, $3.50) Planet DC; intro. The Boggart; Aparo-a						3.50

NOTE: ***Art Adams*** *a-400p.* ***Neal Adams*** *c-200, 203, 210, 217, 219-222, 224-227, 229, 230, 232, 234, 236-241, 243-246, 251, 255, Annual 14.* ***Aparo*** *a-414-420, 426-435, 440-448, 450, 451, 480-483, 486-491, 494-500; c-414-416, 481, 482, 463i, 486, 487i.* ***Bolland*** *a-400; c-445-447.* ***Burnley*** *a-10, 12-18, 20, 22, 25, 27; c-9, 15, 16, 27, 28p, 40p, 42p.* ***Byrne*** *c-401, 433-435, 533-535, Annual 11.* ***Travis Charest*** *c-488-490p.* ***Colan*** *a-340p, 343-345p, 348-351p, 373p, 383p; c-343p, 345p, 350p.* ***J. Cole*** *a-238r.* ***Cowan*** *a-Annual 10p.* ***Golden*** *a-295p, 303p, 484, 485.* ***Alan Grant*** *scripts-455-466, 470, 474-476, 479, 480, Annual 16(part).* ***Grell*** *a-287, 288p, 289p, 290; c-287-290.* ***Infantino/Anderson*** *c-167, 173, 175, 181, 186, 191, 192, 194, 195, 198, 199.* ***Kelley Jones*** *a-513-519, 521-525, 527; c-491-499, 500(newsstand), 501-510, 513.* ***Kaluta*** *c-242, 248, 253, Annual 12.* ***G. Kane/Anderson*** *c-178-180.* ***Bob Kane*** *a-1, 2, 5; c-1-5, 7, 17.* ***G. Kane*** *a-(r)-254, 255, 259, 261, 353i.* ***Kubert*** *a-238r, 400; c-310, 319p, 327, 328, 344.* ***McFarlane*** *c-423.* ***Mignola*** *c-426-429, 452-454, Annual 18.* ***Moldoff*** *c-101-140.* ***Moldoff/Giella*** *a-164-175, 177-181, 183, 184, 186.* ***Moldoff/Greene*** *a-169, 172-174, 177-179, 181, 184.* ***Mooney*** *a-255r.* ***Morrow*** *a-Annual 13i.* ***Newton*** *a-305, 306, 328p, 331p, 332p, 337p, 338p, 346p, 352-357p, 360-372p, 374-378p; c-374p, 378p.* ***Nino*** *a-Annual 9.* ***Irv Novick*** *c-201, 202.* ***Perez*** *a-400; c-436-442.* ***Fred Ray*** *c-8, 10; w/****Robinson****-11.* ***Robinson/Roussos*** *a-12-17, 20, 22, 24, 25, 27, 28, 31, 33, 37.* ***Robinson*** *a-12, 14, 18, 22-32,34, 36, 37, 255r, 260r, 261r; c-6, 10, 12-14, 18, 21, 24, 26, 30, 37, 39.* ***Simonson*** *a-300p, 312p, 321p; c-300p, 312p, 366, 413i.* ***P. Smith*** *a-Annual 9.* ***Dick Sprang*** *c-19, 20, 22, 23, 25, 29, 31-36, 38, 51, 55, 66, 73, 76.* ***Starlin*** *c/a-402.* ***Staton*** *a-334.* ***Sutton*** *a-400.* ***Wrightson*** *a-265i, 400; c-320r. Bat-Hound app. in 92, 97, 103, 123, 125, 133, 156, 158. Bat-Mite app. in 133, 136, 144, 146, 158, 161. Batwoman app. in 105, 116, 122, 125, 128, 129, 131, 133, 139, 140, 141, 144, 145, 150, 151, 153, 154, 157, 159, 162, 163.* ***Zeck*** *c-417-420. Catwoman back-ups in 332, 345, 346, 348-351. Joker app. in 1, 2, 4, 5, 7-9, 11-13, 19, 20, 23, 25, 28, 32 & many more. Robin solo back-up stories in 337-339, 341-343.*

BATMAN (Hardcover books and trade paperbacks)

	GD 2.0	VG 4.0	FN 6.0	VF 8.0	VF/NM 9.0	NM- 9.2
...: ABSOLUTION (2002, $24.95)-Hard-c.; DeMatteis-s/Ashmore painted-a						25.00
...: ABSOLUTION (2003, $17.95)-Soft-c.; DeMatteis-s/Ashmore painted-a						18.00
...: A LONELY PLACE OF DYING (1990, $3.95, 132 pgs.)-r/Batman #440-442 & New Titans #60,61; Perez-c						4.00
...: ANARKY TPB (1999, $12.95) r/early appearances						13.00
...AND DRACULA: RED RAIN nn (1991, $24.95)-Hard-c.; Elseworlds storyline						32.00
...AND DRACULA: Red Rain nn (1992, $9.95)-SC						12.00
ARKHAM ASYLUM Hard-c; Morrison-s/McKean-a (1989, $24.95)						30.00
ARKHAM ASYLUM Soft-c ($14.95)						15.00

Batman: Absolution SC © DC

Batman: Detective #27 © DC

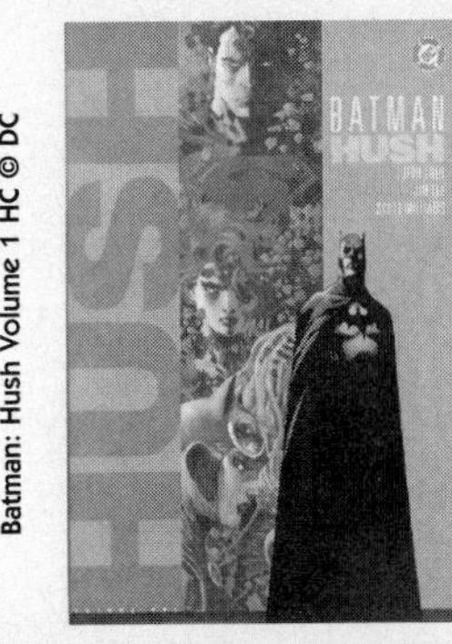

Batman: Hush Volume 1 HC © DC

	GD 2.0	VG 4.0	FN 6.0	VF 8.0	VF/NM 9.0	NM- 9.2

ARKHAM ASYLUM 15TH ANNIVERSARY EDITION Hard-c (2004, $29.95) reprint with Morrison's script and annotations, original page layouts; Karen Berger afterword 30.00
...: AS THE CROW FLIES-(2004, $12.95) r/#626-630; Nguyen sketch pages 13.00
BIRTH OF THE DEMON Hard-c (1992, $24.95)-Origin of Ra's al Ghul 25.00
BIRTH OF THE DEMON Soft-c (1993, $12.95) 13.00
BLIND JUSTICE nn (1992, $7.50)-r/Det. #598-600 7.50
BLOODSTORM (1994, $24.95,HC) Kelley Jones-c/a 28.00
BRIDE OF THE DEMON Hard-c (1990, $19.95) 20.00
BRIDE OF THE DEMON Soft-c ($12.95) 13.00
...: BROKEN CITY HC-(2004, $24.95) r/#620-625; new Johnson-c; intro by Schreck 25.00
...: BRUCE WAYNE: FUGITIVE Vol. 1 ('02, $12.95)-r/ story arc 13.00
...: BRUCE WAYNE: FUGITIVE Vol. 2 ('03, $12.95)-r/ story arc 13.00
...: BRUCE WAYNE: FUGITIVE Vol. 3 ('03, $12.95)-r/ story arc 13.00
...: BRUCE WAYNE-MURDERER? ('02, $19.95)-r/ story arc 20.00
...: CASTLE OF THE BAT ($5.95)-Elseworlds story 6.00
...: CATACLYSM ('99, $17.95)-r/ story arc 18.00
...: CHILD OF DREAMS (2003, $24.95, B&W, HC) Reprint of Japanese manga with Kia Asamiya-s/a/c; English adaptation by Max Allan Collins; Asamiya interview 25.00
...: CHILD OF DREAMS (2003, $19.95, B&W, SC) 20.00
...: COLLECTED LEGENDS OF THE DARK KNIGHT nn (1994, $12.95)-r/Legends of the Dark Knight #32-34,38,42,43 13.00
...: CRIMSON MIST (1999, $24.95,HC)-Vampire Batman Elseworlds story Doug Moench-s/Kelley Jones-c/a 25.00
...: CRIMSON MIST (2001, $14.95,SC) 25.00
...: DARK JOKER-THE WILD (1993, $24.95,HC)-Elseworlds story; Moench-s/Jones-c/a 25.00
...: DARK JOKER-THE WILD (1993, $9.95,SC) 10.00
...DARK KNIGHT DYNASTY nn (1997, $24.95)-Hard-c.; 3 Elseworlds stories; Barr-s/ S. Hampton painted-a, Gary Frank, McDaniel-a(p) 25.00
...DARK KNIGHT DYNASTY Softcover (2000, $14.95) Hampton-c 15.00
...DEADMAN: DEATH AND GLORY nn (1996, $24.95)-Hard-c.; Robinson-s/ Estes-c/a 25.00
...DEADMAN: DEATH AND GLORY ($12.95)-SC 13.00
DEATH IN THE FAMILY (1988, $3.95, trade paperback)-r/Batman #426-429 by Aparo 5.00
DEATH IN THE FAMILY: (2nd - 5th printings) 4.00
...: DETECTIVE #27 HC (2003, $19.95)-Elseworlds; Uslan-s/Snejbjerg-a 20.00
...: DETECTIVE #27 SC (2004, $12.95)-Elseworlds; Uslan-s/Snejbjerg-a 13.00
DIGITAL JUSTICE nn (1990, $24.95, Hard-c.)-Computer generated art 25.00
... :EVOLUTION (2001, $12.95, SC)-r/Detective Comics #743-750 13.00
... FACES (1995, $9.95, TPB) 10.00
...: FORTUNATE SON HC (1999, $24.95) Gene Ha-a 25.00
...: FORTUNATE SON SC (2000, $14.95) Gene Ha-a 15.00
FOUR OF A KIND TPB (1998, $14.95)-r/1995 Year One Annuals featuring Poison Ivy, Riddler, Scarecrow, & Man-Bat 15.00
...GOTHIC (1992, $12.95, TPB)-r/Legends of the Dark Knight #6-10 13.00
...: HARVEST BREED-(2000, $24.95) George Pratt-s/painted-a 25.00
...: HARVEST BREED-(2003, $17.95) George Pratt-s/painted-a 18.00
...: HAUNTED KNIGHT-(1997, $12.95) r/ Halloween specials 13.00
...: HONG KONG HC (2003, $24.95, with dustjacket) Doug Moench-s/Tony Wong-a 25.00
...: HONG KONG SC (2004, $17.95) Doug Moench-s/Tony Wong-a 18.00
...: HUSH DOUBLE FEATURE-(2003, $3.95) r/#608,609(1st 2 Jim Lee-a issues) 4.00
...: HUSH VOLUME 1 HC-(2003, $19.95) r/#608-612; & new 2 pg. origin w/Lee-a 20.00
...: HUSH VOLUME 1 SC-(2004, $12.95) r/#608-612; includes CD of DC GN art 13.00
...: HUSH VOLUME 2 HC-(2003, $19.95) r/#613-619; Lee intro & sketchpages 20.00
...: HUSH VOLUME 2 SC-(2004, $12.95) r/#613-619; Lee intro & sketchpages 13.00
...: ILLUSTRATED BY NEAL ADAMS VOLUME 1 HC-(2003, $49.95) r/Batman, Brave and the Bold, and Detective Comics stories and covers 50.00
...: ILLUSTRATED BY NEAL ADAMS VOLUME 2 HC-(2004, $49.95) r/Adams' Batman art from 1969-71; intro. by Dick Giordano 50.00
... IN THE FORTIES TPB ($19.95) Intro. by Bill Schelly 20.00
... IN THE FIFTIES TPB ($19.95) Intro. by Michael Uslan 20.00
... IN THE SIXTIES TPB ($19.95) Intro. by Adam West 20.00
... IN THE SEVENTIES TPB ($19.95) Intro. by Dennis O'Neil 20.00
... IN THE EIGHTIES TPB ($19.95) Intro. by John Wells 20.00
.../ JUDGE DREDD FILES (2004, $14.95) reprints cross-overs 15.00
... LEGACY-(1996,17.95) reprints Legacy 18.00
...: THE MANY DEATHS OF THE BATMAN (1992, $3.95, 84 pgs.)-r/Batman #433-435 w/new Byrne-c 4.00
...: THE MOVIES (1997, $19.95)-r/movie adaptations of Batman, Batman Returns, Batman Forever, Batman and Robin 20.00
...: NINE LIVES HC (2002, $24.95, sideways format) Motter-s/Lark-a 25.00
...: NINE LIVES SC (2003, $17.95, sideways format) Motter-s/Lark-a 18.00
...: OFFICER DOWN (2001, $12.95)-r/Commissioner shot x-over; Talon-c 13.00
...: PREY (1992, $12.95)-Gulacy/Austin-a 13.00
...: PRODIGAL (1997, $14.95)-Gulacy/Austin-a 15.00
SHAMAN (1993, $12.95)-r/Legends/D.K. #1-5 13.00

	GD 2.0	VG 4.0	FN 6.0	VF 8.0	VF/NM 9.0	NM- 9.2

...: SON OF THE DEMON Hard-c (9/87, $14.95) 30.00
...: SON OF THE DEMON limited signed & numbered Hard-c (1,700) 45.00
...: SON OF THE DEMON Soft-c w/new-c ($8.95) 10.00
...: SON OF THE DEMON Soft-c (1989, $9.95, 2nd printing - 5th printing) 10.00
... : STRANGE APPARITIONS ($12.95) r/'77-'78 Englehart/Rogers stories from Detective #469-479; also Simonson-a 13.00
...: TALES OF THE DEMON (1991, $17.95, 212 pgs.)-Intro by Sam Hamm; reprints by Neal Adams(3) & Golden; contains Saga of Ra's al Ghul #1 18.00
...: TEN NIGHTS OF THE BEAST (1994, $5.95)-r/Batman #417-420 6.00
...: TERROR (2003, $12.95, TPB)-r/Legends of the Dark Knight #137-141; Gulacy-c 13.00
...: THE CHALICE (HC, '99, $24.95) Van Fleet painted-a 25.00
...: THE CHALICE (SC, '00, $14.95) Van Fleet painted-a 15.00
...: THE LAST ANGEL (1994, $12.95, TPB) Lustbader-s 13.00
...: THE RING, THE ARROW AND THE BAT (2003, $19.95, TPB) r/Legends of the DCU #7-9 & Batman: Legends of the Dark Knight #127-131; Green Lantern & Green Arrow app. 20.00
...: THRILLKILLER (1998, $12.95, TPB)-r/series & Thrillkiller '62 13.00
...: VENOM (1993, $9.95, TPB)-r/Legends of the Dark Knight #16-20; embossed-c 10.00
... WAR DRUMS (2004, $17.95) r/Detective #790-796 & Robin #126-128 18.00
YEAR ONE Hard-c (1988, $12.95) 18.00
YEAR ONE (1988, $9.95, TPB)-r/Batman #404-407 by Miller; intro by Miller 10.00
YEAR ONE (TPB, 2nd & 3rd printings) 10.00
YEAR TWO (1990, $9.95, TPB)-r/Det. 575-578 by McFarlane; wraparound-c 10.00

BATMAN (one-shots)
... ABDUCTION, THE (1998, $5.95) 6.00
... & ROBIN (1997, $5.95)-Movie adaptation 6.00
...: ARKHAM ASYLUM - TALES OF MADNESS (5/98, $2.95) Cataclysm x-over pt. 16 3.00
... : BANE (1997, $4.95)-Dixon-s/Burchett-a; Stelfreeze-c; cover art interlocks w/Batman:(Batgirl, Mr. Freeze, Poison Ivy) 5.00
... : BATGIRL (1997, $4.95)-Puckett-s/Haley,Kesel-a; Stelfreeze-c; cover art interlocks w/Batman:(Bane, Mr. Freeze, Poison Ivy) 5.00
... : BATGIRL (6/98, $1.95)-Girlfrenzy; Balent-a 2.50
... : BLACKGATE (1/97, $3.95) Dixon-s 4.00
... : BLACKGATE - ISLE OF MEN (4/98, $2.95) Cataclysm x-over pt. 8; Moench-s/Aparo-a 3.00
... BOOK OF SHADOWS, THE (1999, $5.95) 6.00
BROTHERHOOD OF THE BAT (1995, $5.95)-Elseworlds-s 6.00
... BULLOCK'S LAW (8/99, $4.95) Dixon-s 5.00
.../CAPTAIN AMERICA (1996, $5.95, DC/Marvel) Elseworlds story; Byrne-c/s/a 6.00
... : CATWOMAN DEFIANT nn (1992, $4.95, prestige format)-Milligan scripts; cover art interlocks w/Batman: Penguin Triumphant; special foil logo 5.00
... /DAREDEVIL (2000, $5.95)-Barreto-a 6.00
...: DARK ALLEGIANCES (1996, $5.95)-Elseworlds story, Chaykin-c/a 6.00
...: DARK KNIGHT GALLERY (1/96, $3.50)-Pin-ups by Pratt, Balent, & others 3.50
...:DAY OF JUDGMENT (11/99, $3.95) 4.00
...:DEATH OF INNOCENTS (12/96, $3.95)-O'Neil-s/ Staton-a(p) 4.00
.../DEMON (1996, $4.95)-Alan Grant scripts 5.00
.../DEMON: A TRAGEDY (2000, $5.95)-Grant-s/Murray painted-a 6.00
...:D.O.A. (1999, $6.95)-Bob Hall-s/a 7.00
...:DREAMLAND (2000, $5.95)-Grant-s/Breyfogle-a 6.00
... : EGO (2000, $6.95)-Darwyn Cooke-s/a 7.00
... 80-PAGE GIANT (8/98, $4.95) Stelfreeze-c 6.00
... 80-PAGE GIANT 2 (10/99, $4.95) Luck of the Draw 6.00
... 80-PAGE GIANT 3 (7/00, $5.95) Calendar Man 6.00
... FOREVER (1995, $5.95, direct market) 6.00
... FOREVER (1995, $3.95, newsstand) 4.00
FULL CIRCLE nn (1991, $5.95, 68 pgs.)-Sequel to Batman: Year Two 6.00
...GALLERY, The 1 (1992, $2.95)-Pin-ups by Miller, N. Adams & others 3.00
...GOLDEN STREETS OF GOTHAM (2003, $6.95) Elseworlds in early 1900s 7.00
...GOTHAM BY GASLIGHT (1989, $3.95) 4.00
...GOTHAM CITY SECRET FILES 1 (4/00, $4.95) Batgirl app. 5.00
...: GOTHAM NOIR (2001, $6.95)-Elseworlds; Brubaker-s/Phillips-c/a 7.00
.../GREEN ARROW: THE POISON TOMORROW nn (1992, $5.95, square-bound, 68 pgs.) Netzer-c/a 6.00
HOLY TERROR nn (1991, $4.95, 52 pgs.)-Elseworlds story 5.00
.../HOUDINI: THE DEVIL'S WORKSHOP (1993, $5.95) 6.00
... :HUNTRESS/SPOILER - BLUNT TRAUMA (5/98, $2.95) Cataclysm pt. 13; Dixon-s/Barreto & Sienkiewicz-a 3.00
...: I, JOKER nn (1998, $4.95)-Elseworlds story; Bob Hall-s/a 5.00
...: IN DARKEST KNIGHT nn (1994, $4.95, 52 pgs.)-Elseworlds story; Batman w/Green Lantern's ring. 5.00
...:JOKER'S APPRENTICE (5/99, $3.95) Von Eeden-a 4.00
.../ JOKER: SWITCH (2003, $6.95)-Bolton-a/Grayson-s 7.00
...:JUDGE DREDD: JUDGEMENT ON GOTHAM nn (1991, $5.95, 68 pgs.) Simon Bisley-c/a; Grant/Wagner scripts 6.00
...:JUDGE DREDD: JUDGEMENT ON GOTHAM nn (2nd printing) 6.00

Batman: The 12¢ Adventure #1 © DC

Batman Adventures #2 © DC

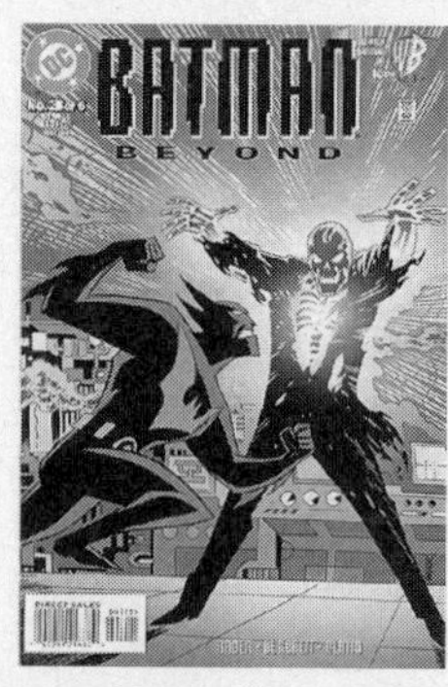
Batman Beyond #3 © DC

	GD 2.0	VG 4.0	FN 6.0	VF 8.0	VF/NM 9.0	NM- 9.2
...:JUDGE DREDD: THE ULTIMATE RIDDLE (1995, $4.95)						5.00
...:JUDGE DREDD: VENDETTA IN GOTHAM (1993, $5.95)						6.00
...: KNIGHTGALLERY (1995, $3.50)-Elseworlds sketchbook.						3.50
.../ LOBO (2000, $5.95)-Elseworlds; Joker app.; Bisley-a						6.00
...: MASK OF THE PHANTASM (1994, $2.95)-Movie adapt.						3.00
...: MASK OF THE PHANTASM (1994, $4.95)-Movie adapt.						5.00
...: MASQUE (1997, $6.95)-Elseworlds; Grell-c/s/a						7.00
...: MASTER OF THE FUTURE nn (1991, $5.95, 68 pgs.)-Elseworlds storyline; sequel to Gotham By Gaslight; embossed-c						6.00
...: MITEFALL (1995, $4.95)-Alan Grant script, Kevin O'Neill-a						5.00
... : MR. FREEZE (1997, $4.95)-Dini-s/Buckingham-a; Stelfreeze-c; cover art interlocks w/Batman:(Bane, Batgirl, Poison Ivy)						5.00
... /NIGHTWING: BLOODBORNE (2002, $5.95) Cypress-a; McKeever-c						6.00
...: NOSFERATU (1999, $5.95) McKeever-a						6.00
...: OF ARKHAM (2000, $5.95)-Elseworlds; Grant-s/Alcatena-a						6.00
...: OUR WORLDS AT WAR (8/01, $2.95)-Jae Lee-c						3.00
...: PENGUIN TRIUMPHANT nn (1992, $4.95)-Staton-a(p); foil logo						5.00
...•PHANTOM STRANGER nn (1997, $4.95) nn-Grant-s/Ransom-a						5.00
... : PLUS (2/97, $2.95) Arsenal-c/app.						3.00
... : POISON IVY (1997, $4.95)-J.F. Moore-s/Apthorp-a; Stelfreeze-c; cover art interlocks w/Batman:(Bane, Batgirl, Mr. Freeze)						5.00
.../POISON IVY: CAST SHADOWS (2004, $6.95) Van Fleet-c/a; Nocenti-s						7.00
.../PUNISHER: LAKE OF FIRE (1994, $4.95, DC/Marvel)						5.00
... :REIGN OF TERROR ('99, $4.95) Elseworlds						5.00
...RETURNS MOVIE SPECIAL (1992, $3.95)						4.00
...RETURNS MOVIE PRESTIGE (1992, $5.95, squarebound)-Dorman painted-c						6.00
...:RIDDLER-THE RIDDLE FACTORY (1995, $4.95)-Wagner script						5.00
...: ROOM FULL OF STRANGERS (2004, $5.95) Scott Morse-s/c/a						6.00
...: SCARECROW 3-D (12/98, $3.95) w/glasses						4.00
.../ SCARFACE: A PSYCHODRAMA (2001, $5.95)-Adlard-a/Sienkiewicz-c						6.00
...: SCAR OF THE BAT nn (1996, $4.95)-Elseworlds; Max Allan Collins script; Barreto-a						5.00
... :SCOTTISH CONNECTION (1998, $5.95) Quitely-a						6.00
... :SEDUCTION OF THE GUN nn (1992, $2.50, 68 pgs.)						3.00
.../SPAWN: WAR DEVIL nn (1994, $4.95, 52 pgs.)						5.00
... SPECIAL 1 (4/84)-Mike W. Barr story; Golden-c/a	1	2	3	5	6	8
.../SPIDER-MAN (1997, $4.95) Dematteis-s/Nolan & Kesel-a						5.00
... : THE ABDUCTION ('98, $5.95)						6.00
...: THE BLUE, THE GREY, & THE BAT (1992, $5.95)-Weiss/Lopez-a						6.00
... :THE HILL (5/00, $2.95)-Priest-s/Martinbrough-a						3.00
... :THE KILLING JOKE (1988, deluxe 52 pgs., mature readers)-Bolland-c/a; Alan Moore scripts; Joker cripples Barbara Gordon	2	4	6	10	12	15
...: THE KILLING JOKE (2nd thru 10th printings)						4.00
...: THE OFFICIAL COMIC ADAPTATION OF THE WARNER BROS. MOTION PICTURE (1989, $2.50, regular format, 68 pgs.)-Ordway-c						3.00
...: THE OFFICIAL COMIC ADAPTATION OF THE WARNER BROS. MOTION PICTURE (1989, $4.95, prestige format, 68 pgs.)-same interiors but different-c						5.00
...: THE ORDER OF BEASTS (2004, $5.95)-Elseworlds; Eddie Campbell-a						6.00
...: THE 10-CENT ADVENTURE (3/02, 10¢) intro. to the "Bruce Wayne: Murderer" x-over; Rucka-s/Burchett & Janson-a/Dave Johnson-c						2.25

NOTE: (Also see Promotional Comics section for alternate copies with special outer half-covers promoting local comic shops)

	GD 2.0	VG 4.0	FN 6.0	VF 8.0	VF/NM 9.0	NM- 9.2
...: THE 12-CENT ADVENTURE (10/04, 12¢) intro. to the "War Games" x-over; Grayson-s/Bachs-a; Catwoman & Spoiler app.						2.25
...: TWO-FACE-CRIME AND PUNISHMENT-(1995, $4.95)-McDaniel-a						5.00
... : TWO FACES (11/98, $4.95) Elseworlds						5.00
...: VENGEANCE OF BANE SPECIAL 1 (1992, $2.50, 68 pgs.)-Origin & 1st app. Bane (see Batman #491)	2	4	6	8	10	12
...: VENGEANCE OF BANE SPECIAL 1 (2nd printing)						3.00
....:VENGEANCE OF BANE II nn (1995, $3.95)-sequel						4.00
...Vs. THE INCREDIBLE HULK (1995, $3.95)-r/DC Special Series #27						4.00
...: VILLAINS SECRET FILES (10/98, $4.95) Origin-s						5.00

BATMAN ADVENTURES, THE (Based on animated series)
DC Comics: Oct, 1992 - No. 36, Oct, 1995 ($1.25/$1.50)

1-Penguin-c/story						4.00
1 ($1.95, Silver Edition)-2nd printing						2.25
2-6,8-19: 2,12-Catwoman-c/story. 3-Joker-c/story. 5-Scarecrow-c/story. 10-Riddler-c/story. 11-Man-Bat-c/story. 12-Batgirl & Catwoman-c/story. 16-Joker-c/story; begin $1.50-c. 18-Batgirl-c/story. 19-Scarecrow-c/story.						3.00
7-Special edition polybagged with Man-Bat trading card						5.00
20-24,26-32: 26-Batgirl app.						2.50
25-($2.50, 52 pgs.)-Superman app.						3.00
33-36: 33-Begin $1.75-c						2.25
Annual 1,2 ('94, '95): 2-Demon-c/story; Ra's al Ghul app.						3.50
...: Dangerous Dames & Demons (2003, $14.95, TPB) r/Annual 1,2, Mad Love & Adventures in the DC Universe #3; Bruce Timm painted-c						15.00
Holiday Special 1 (1995, $2.95)						4.00
The Collected Adventures Vol. 1,2 ('93, '95, $5.95)						6.00
TPB ('98, $7.95) r/#1-6; painted wraparound-c						8.00

BATMAN ADVENTURES (Based on animated series)
DC Comics: Jun, 2003 - No. 17, Oct, 2004 ($2.25)

1-Timm-c (2003 Free Comic Book Day edition is listed in Promotional Comics section)						2.25
2-17: 3,16-Joker-c/app. 4-Ra's al Ghul app. 6-8-Phantasm app. 14-Grey Ghost app.						2.25
Vol. 1: Rogues Gallery (2004, $6.95, digest size) r/#1-4 & Batman: Gotham Advs. #50						7.00
Vol. 2: Shadows & Masks (2004, $6.95, digest size) r/#5-9						7.00

BATMAN ADVENTURES, THE: MAD LOVE
DC Comics: Feb, 1994 ($3.95/$4.95)

1-Origin of Harley Quinn; Dini-s/Timm-c/a	2	4	6	8	10	12
1-($4.95, Prestige format) new Timm painted-c	1	2	3	5	6	8

BATMAN ADVENTURES, THE: THE LOST YEARS (TV)
DC Comics: Jan, 1998 - No. 5, May, 1998 ($1.95) (Based on animated series)

1-5-Leads into Fall '97's new animated episodes. 4-Tim Drake becomes Robin. 5-Dick becomes Nightwing						2.25
TPB-(1999, $9.95) r/series						10.00

BATMAN/ALIENS
DC Comics/Dark Horse: Mar, 1997 - No. 2, Apr, 1997 ($4.95, limited series)

1,2: Wrightson-c/a.						5.00
TPB-(1997, $14.95) w/prequel from DHP #101,102						15.00

BATMAN/ALIENS II
DC Comics/Dark Horse: 2003 - No. 3, 2003 ($5.95, limited series)

1-3-Edginton-s/Staz Johnson-a						6.00
TPB-(2003, $14.95) r/#1-3						15.00

BATMAN AND ROBIN ADVENTURES (TV)
DC Comics: Nov, 1995 - No. 25, Dec, 1997 ($1.75) (Based on animated series)

1-Dini-s.						3.00
2-24: 2-4-Dini script. 4-Penguin-c/story. 5-Joker-c/story; Poison Ivy, Harley Quinn-c/app. 9-Batgirl & Talia-c/story. 10-Ra's al Ghul-c/story. 11-Man-Bat app. 12-Bane-c/app. 13-Scarecrow-c/app. 15 Deadman-c/app. 16-Catwoman-c/app. 18-Joker-c/app. 24-Poison Ivy app.						2.25
25-($2.95, 48 pgs.)						3.00
Annual 1,2 (11/96, 11/97): 1-Phantasm-c/app. 2-Zatara & Zatanna-c/app.						4.00
...: Sub-Zero(1998, $3.95) Adaptation of animated video						4.00

BATMAN AND SUPERMAN ADVENTURES: WORLD'S FINEST
DC Comics: 1997 ($6.95, square-bound, one-shot) (Based on animated series)

1-Adaptation of animated crossover episode; Dini-s/Timm-c.						7.00

BATMAN AND SUPERMAN: WORLD'S FINEST
DC Comics: Apr, 1999 - No. 10, Jan, 2000 ($4.95/$1.99, limited series)

1,10-($4.95, squarebound) Taylor-a						5.00
2-9-($1.99) 5-Batgirl app. 8-Catwoman-c/app.						2.25
TPB (2003, $19.95) r/#1-10						20.00

BATMAN AND THE OUTSIDERS (The Adventures of the Outsiders #33 on)
(Also see Brave & The Bold #200 & The Outsiders) (Replaces The Brave and the Bold)
DC Comics: Aug, 1983 - No. 32, Apr, 1986 (Mando paper #5 on)

1-Batman, Halo, Geo-Force, Katana, Metamorpho & Black Lightning begin						4.00
2-32: 5-New Teen Titans x-over. 9-Halo begins. 11,12-Origin Katana. 18-More info on Metamorpho's origin. 28-31-Lookers origin. 32-Team disbands						2.50
Annual 1,2 (9/84, 9/85): 2-Metamorpho & Sapphire Stagg wed						3.00

NOTE: *Aparo a-1-9, 11-13p, 16-20; c-1-4, 5i, 6-21, Annual 1, 2.* ***B. Kane*** *a-3r.* ***Layton*** *a-19i, 20i.* ***Lopez*** *a-3p.* ***Miller*** *c-Annual 1.* ***Perez*** *c-5p.* ***B. Willingham*** *a-14p.*

BATMAN: BANE OF THE DEMON
DC Comics: Mar, 1998 - No. 4, June, 1998 ($1.95, limited series)

1-4-Dixon-s/Nolan-a; prelude to Legacy x-over						2.50

BATMAN BEYOND (Based on animated series)(Mini-series)
DC Comics: Mar, 1999 - No. 6, Aug, 1999 ($1.99)

1-6: 1,2-Adaptation of pilot episode, Timm-c						2.25
TPB (1999, $9.95) r/#1-6						10.00

BATMAN BEYOND (Based on animated series)(Continuing series)
DC Comics: Nov, 1999 - No. 24, Oct, 2001 ($1.99)

1-24: 1-Rousseau-a; Batman vs. Batman. 14-Demon-c/app. 21,22-Justice League Unlimited-c/app.						2.25
...: Return of the Joker (2/01, $2.95) adaptation of video release						3.00

Batman: Death and the Maidens #9 © DC

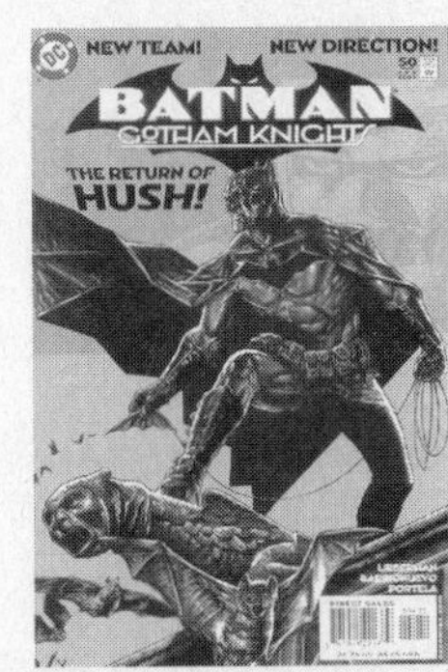

Batman: Gotham Knights #50 © DC

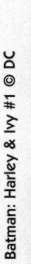

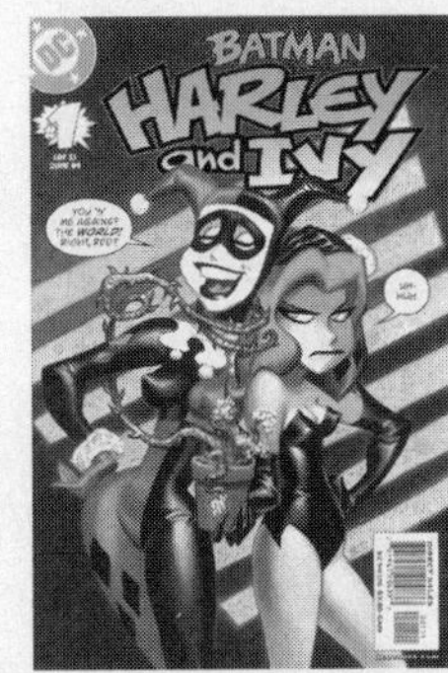

Batman: Harley & Ivy #1 © DC

GD 2.0 | VG 4.0 | FN 6.0 | VF 8.0 | VF/NM 9.0 | NM- 9.2

GD 2.0 | VG 4.0 | FN 6.0 | VF 8.0 | VF/NM 9.0 | NM- 9.2

BATMAN: BLACK & WHITE
DC Comics: June, 1996 - No. 4, Sept, 1996 ($2.95, B&W, limited series)

1-Stories by McKeever, Timm, Kubert, Chaykin, Goodwin; Jim Lee-c; Allred inside front-c; Moebius inside back-c 4.00
2-4: 2-Stories by Simonson, Corben, Bisley & Gaiman; Miller-c. 3-Stories by M. Wagner, Janson, Sienkiewicz, O'Neil & Kristiansen; B. Smith-c; Russell inside front-c; Silvestri inside back-c. 4-Stories by Bolland, Goodwin & Gianni, Strnad & Nowlan, O'Neil & Stelfreeze; Toth-c; pin-ups by Neal Adams & Alex Ross 3.00
Hardcover ('97, $39.95) r/series w/new art & cover plate 40.00
Softcover ('00, $19.95) r/series 20.00
Volume 2 HC ('02, $39.95, 7 3/4"x12") r/B&W back-up-s from Batman: Gotham Knights #1-16; stories and art by various incl. Ross, Buscema, Byrne, Ellison, Sale; Mignola-c 40.00
Volume 2 SC ('03, $19.95, 7 3/4"x12") same contents as HC 20.00

BATMAN: BOOK OF THE DEAD
DC Comics: Jun, 1999 - No. 2, July, 1999 ($4.95, limited series, prestige format)

1,2-Elseworlds; Kitson-a 5.00

BATMAN: CATWOMAN DEFIANT (See Batman one-shots)

BATMAN/ CATWOMAN: TRAIL OF THE GUN
DC Comics: 2004 - No. 2, 2004 ($5.95, limited series, prestige format)

1,2-Elseworlds; Van Sciver-a/Nocenti-s 6.00

BATMAN CHRONICLES, THE
DC Comics: Summer, 1995 - No. 23, Winter, 2001 ($2.95, quarterly)

1-3,5-19: 1-Dixon/Grant/Moench script. 3-Bolland-c. 5-Oracle Year One story, Richard Dragon app.,Chaykin-c. 6-Kaluta-c; Ra's al Ghul story. 7-Superman-c/app.11-Paul Pope-s/a. 12-Cataclysm pt. 10. 18-No Man's Land 3.50
4-Hitman story by Ennis, Contagion tie-in; Balent-c 2 4 6 8 10 12
20-23: 20-Catwoman and Relative Heroes-c/app. 21-Pander Bros.-a 3.00
...Gallery (3/97, $3.50) Pin-ups 3.50
...Gauntlet, The (1997, $4.95, one-shot) 5.00

BATMAN: CITY OF LIGHT
DC Comics: Dec, 2003 - No. 8, July, 2004 ($2.95, limited series)

1-8-Pander Brothers-a/s; Paniccia-s 3.00

BATMAN: DARK KNIGHT OF THE ROUND TABLE
DC Comics: 1999 - No. 2, 1999 ($4.95, limited series, prestige format)

1,2-Elseworlds; Giordano-a 5.00

BATMAN: DARK VICTORY
DC Comics: 1999 - No. 13, 2000 ($4.95/$2.95, limited series)

Wizard #0 Preview 2.25
1-($4.95) Loeb-s/Sale-c/a 5.00
2-12-($2.95) 3.00
13-($4.95) 5.00
Hardcover (2001, $29.95) with dust jacket; r/#0,1-13 30.00
Softcover (2002, $19.95) r/#0,1-13 20.00

BATMAN: DEATH AND THE MAIDENS
DC Comics: Oct, 2003 - No. 9, Aug, 2004 ($2.95, limited series)

1-Ra's al Ghul app.; Rucka-s/Janson-a 4.00
2-9: 9-Ra's al Ghul dies 3.00
TPB (2004, $19.95) r/#1-9 & Detective #783 20.00

BATMAN/ DEATHBLOW: AFTER THE FIRE
DC Comics/WildStorm: 2002 - No. 3, 2002 ($5.95, limited series)

1-3-Azzarello-s/Bermejo & Bradstreet-a 6.00
TPB (2003, $12.95) r/#1-3; plus concept art 13.00

BATMAN FAMILY, THE
National Periodical Pub./DC Comics: Sept-Oct, 1975 - No. 20, Oct-Nov, 1978 (#1-4, 17-on: 68 pgs.) (Combined with Detective Comics with No. 481)

1-Origin/2nd app. Batgirl-Robin team-up (The Dynamite Duo); reprints plus one new story begins; N. Adams-a(r); r/1st app. Man-Bat from Det. #400 3 6 9 19 25 32
2-5: 2-r/Det. #369. 3-Batgirl & Robin learn each's i.d.; r/Batwoman app. from Batman #105. 4-r/1st Fatman app. from Batman #113. 5-r/1st Bat-Hound app. from Batman #92 2 4 6 11 14 18
6,9-Joker's daughter on cover (1st app?) 2 4 6 14 18 22
7,8,14-16: 8-r/Batwoman app.14-Batwoman app. 15-3rd app. Killer Moth. 16-Bat-Girl cameo (last app. in costume until New Teen Titans #47) 2 4 6 10 12 15
10-1st revival Batwoman; Cavalier app.; Killer Moth app. 3 6 9 16 20 24
11-13,17-20: 11-13-Rogers-a(p): 11-New stories begin; Man-Bat begins. 13-Batwoman cameo. 17-($1.00 size)-Batman, Huntress begin; Batwoman & Catwoman 1st meet. 18-20: Huntress by Staton in all. 20-Origin Ragman retold 2 4 6 14 18 22

NOTE: ***Aparo** a-17; c-11-16. **Austin** a-12i. **Chaykin** a-14p. **Michael Golden** a-15-17,18-20p. **Grell** a-1; c-1. **Gil Kane** a-2r. **Kaluta** c-17, 19. **Newton** a-13. **Robinson** a-1r, 3i(r), 9r. **Russell** a-18i, 19i. **Starlin** a-17; c-18, 20.*

BATMAN: FAMILY
DC Comics: Dec, 2002 - No. 8, Feb, 2003 ($2.95/$2.25, weekly limited series)

1,8-($2.95). John Francis Moore-s/Hoberg & Gaudiano-a 3.00
2-7-($2.25). 3-Orpheus & Black Canary app. 2.25

BATMAN: GCPD
DC Comics: Aug, 1996 - No. 4, Nov, 1996 ($2.25, limited series)

1-4: Features Jim Gordon; Aparo/Sienkiewicz-a 2.50

BATMAN: GORDON OF GOTHAM
DC Comics: June, 1998 - No. 4, Sept, 1998 ($1.95, limited series)

1-4: Gordon's early days in Chicago 2.50

BATMAN: GORDON'S LAW
DC Comics: Dec, 1996 - No. 3, Feb, 1997 ($1.95, limited series)

1-3: Dixon-s/Janson-c/a 2.50

BATMAN: GOTHAM ADVENTURES (TV)
DC Comics: June, 1998 - No. 60, May, 2003 ($2.95/$1.95/$1.99/$2.25)

1-($2.95) Based on Kids WB Batman animated series 3.00
2-3-($1.95): 2-Two-Face-c/app. 2.50
4-22: 4-Begin $1.99-c. 5-Deadman-c. 13-MAD #1 cover swipe 2.50
23-60: 31,60-Joker-c/app. 50-Catwoman-c/app. 53-Begin $2.25-c. 58-Creeper-c/app. 2.25
TPB (2000, $9.95) r/#1-6 10.00

BATMAN: GOTHAM KNIGHTS
DC Comics: Mar, 2000 - Present ($2.50/$2.75)

1-Grayson-s; B&W back-up by Warren Ellis & Jim Lee 4.00
2-10-Grayson-s; B&W back-ups by various 2.75
11-($3.25) Bolland-c; Kyle Baker back-up story 3.25
12-24: 13-Officer Down x-over; Ellison back-up-s. 15-Colan back-up. 20-Superman-c/app. 2.75
25,26-Bruce Wayne: Murderer pt. 4,10 3.00
27-31: 28,30,31-Bruce Wayne: Fugitive pt. 7,14,17 2.75
32-49: 32-Begin $2.75-c; Kaluta-a back-up. 33,34-Bane-c/app. 35-Mahfood-a back-up. 38-Bolton-a back-up. 43-Jason Todd & Batgirl app. 44-Jason Todd flashback 2.75
50-54-Hush returns-Barrionuevo-a/Bermejo-c. 53,54-Green Arrow app. 3.00
55-($3.75) Batman vs. Hush; Joker & Riddler app. 4.00
56-60: 56-58-War Games; Jae Lee-c. 60-Hush app. 2.50

BATMAN: GOTHAM NIGHTS II (First series listed under Gotham Nights)
DC Comics: Mar, 1995 - No. 4, June, 1995 ($1.95, limited series)

1-4 2.50

BATMAN/GRENDEL (1st limited series)
DC Comics: 1993 - No. 2, 1993 ($4.95, limited series, squarebound; 52 pgs.)

1,2: Batman vs. Hunter Rose. 1-Devil's Riddle; Matt Wagner-c/a/scripts. 2-Devil's Masque; Matt Wagner-c/a/scripts 6.00

BATMAN/GRENDEL (2nd limited series)
DC Comics: June, 1996 - No. 2, July, 1996 ($4.95, limited series, squarebound)

1,2: Batman vs. Grendel Prime. 1-Devil's Bones. 2-Devil's Dance; Wagner-c/a/s 5.00

BATMAN: HARLEY & IVY
DC Comics: Jun, 2004 - No. 3, Aug, 2004 ($2.50, limited series)

1-3-Paul Dini-s/Bruce Timm-c/a 2.50

BATMAN: HARLEY QUINN
DC Comics: 1999 ($5.95, prestige format)

1-Intro. of Harley Quinn into regular DC continuity; Dini-s/Alex Ross-c 9.00
1-(2nd printing) 6.00

BATMAN: HAUNTED GOTHAM
DC Comics: 2000 - No. 4, 2000 ($4.95, limited series, squarebound)

1-4-Moench-s/Kelley Jones-c/a 5.00

BATMAN/ HELLBOY/STARMAN
DC Comics/Dark Horse: Jan, 1999 - No. 2, Feb, 1999 ($2.50, limited series)

1,2: Robinson-s/Mignola-a. 2-Harris-c 2.50

BATMAN: HOLLYWOOD KNIGHT
DC Comics: Apr, 2001 - No. 3, Jun, 2001 ($2.50, limited series)

1-3-Elseworlds Batman as a 1940's movie star; Giordano-a/Layton-s 2.50

BATMAN/ HUNTRESS: CRY FOR BLOOD
DC Comics: Jun, 2000 - No. 6, Nov, 2000 ($2.50, limited series)

Batman: Legends of the Dark Knight #121 © DC

The Batman Strikes! #1 © DC

Batman/Superman/Wonder Woman: Trinity HC © DC

GD 2.0 | VG 4.0 | FN 6.0 | VF 8.0 | VF/NM 9.0 | NM- 9.2

1-6: Rucka-s/Burchett-a; The Question app. 2.50
TPB (2002, $12.95) r/#1-6 13.00

BATMAN: JOKER TIME (...: It's Joker Time! on cover)
DC Comics: 2000 - No. 3 ($4.95, limited series, squarebound)
1-3-Bob Hall-s/a 5.00

BATMAN/ JUDGE DREDD "DIE LAUGHING"
DC Comics: 1998 - No. 2, 1999 ($4.95, limited series, squarebound)
1,2: 1-Fabry-c/a. 2-Jim Murray-c/a 5.00

BATMAN: KNIGHTGALLERY (See Batman one-shots)

BATMAN: LEAGUE OF BATMEN
DC Comics: 2001 - No. 2, 2001 ($5.95, limited series, squarebound)
1,2-Elseworlds; Moench-s/Bright & Tanghal-a/Van Fleet-c 6.00

BATMAN: LEGENDS OF THE DARK KNIGHT (Legends of the Dark...#1-36)
DC Comics: Nov, 1989 - Present ($1.50/$1.75/$1.95/$1.99/$2.25/$2.50)
1- "Shaman" begins, ends #5; outer cover has four different color variations, all worth same 4.00
2-10: 6-10- "Gothic" by Grant Morrison (scripts) 3.00
11-15: 11-15-Gulacy/Austin-a. 13-Catwoman app. 3.00
16-Intro drug Bane uses; begin Venom story 5.00
17-20 4.00
21-49,51-63: 38-Bat-Mite-c/story. 46-49-Catwoman app. w/Heath-c/a. 51-Ragman app.; Joe Kubert-c. 59,60,61-Knightquest x-over. 62,63-KnightsEnd Pt. 4 & 10 3.00
50-($3.95, 68 pgs.)-Bolland embossed gold foil-c; Joker-c/story; pin-ups by Chaykin, Simonson, Williamson, Kaluta, Russell, others 5.00
64-99: 64-(9/94)-Begin $1.95-c. 71-73-James Robinson-s,Watkiss-c/a. 74,75-McKeever-c/a/s. 76-78-Scott Hampton-c/a/s. 81-Card insert. 83,84-Ellis-s. 85-Robinson-s. 91-93-Ennis-s. 94-Michael T. Gilbert-s/a. 3.00
100-($3.95) Alex Ross painted-c; gallery by various 5.00
101-115: 101-Ezquerra-a. 102-104-Robinson-s 2.50
116-No Man's Land stories begin; Huntress-c 4.00
117-119,121-126: 122-Harris-c 2.50
120-ID of new Batgirl revealed 4.00
127-131: Return to Legends stories; Green Arrow app. 2.50
132-186: 132-136 ($2.25-c) Archie Goodwin-s/Rogers-a. 137-141-Gulacy-a. 142-145-Joker and Ra's al Ghul app. 146-148-Kitson-a. 158-Begin $2.50-c 169-171-Tony Harris-c/a. 182-184-War Games. 182-Bagged with Sky Captain CD 2.50
#0-(10/94)-Zero Hour; Quesada/Palmiotti-c; released between #64&65 3.00
Annual 1-7 ('91-'97, $3.50-$3.95, 68 pgs.): 1-Joker app. 2-Netzer-c/a. 3-New Batman (Azrael) app. 4-Elseworlds story. 5-Year One; Man-Bat app. 6-Legend of the Dead Earth story. 7-Pulp Heroes story 4.00
Halloween Special 1 (12/93, $6.95, 84 pgs.)-Embossed & foil stamped-c 1 2 3 4 5 7
Batman Madness-...Halloween Special (1994, $4.95) 5.00
Batman Ghosts-...Halloween Special (1995, $4.95) 5.00

NOTE: ***Aparo** a-Annual 1. **Chaykin** scripts-24-26. **Giffen** a-Annual 1. **Golden** a-Annual 1. **Alan Grant** scripts-38, 52, 53. **Gil Kane** c/a-24-26. **Mignola** a-54; c-54, 62. **Morrow** a-Annual 3i. **Quesada** a-Annual 1. **James Robinson** scripts- 71-73. **Russell** c/a-42, 43. **Sears** a-21, 23; c-21, 23. **Zeck** a-69, 70; c-69, 70.*

BATMAN-LEGENDS OF THE DARK KNIGHT: JAZZ
DC Comics: Apr, 1995 - No. 3, June, 1995 ($2.50, limited series)
1-3 2.50

BATMAN: MANBAT
DC Comics: Oct, 1995 - No. 3, Dec, 1995 ($4.95, limited series)
1-3-Elseworlds-Delano-script; Bolton-a. 5.00
TPB-(1997, $14.95) r/#1-3 15.00

BATMAN: MITEFALL (See Batman one-shots)

BATMAN MINIATURE (See Batman Kellogg's)

BATMAN: NEVERMORE
DC Comics: June, 2003 - No. 5, Oct, 2003 ($2.50, limited series)
1-5-Elseworlds Batman & Edgar Allan Poe; Wrightson-c/Guy Davis-a/Len Wein-s 2.50

BATMAN: NO MAN'S LAND (Also see 1999 Batman titles)
DC Comics: (one shots)
nn (3/99, $2.95) Alex Ross-c; Bob Gale-s; begins year-long story arc 3.00
Collector's Ed. (3/99, $3.95) Ross lenticular-c 5.00
#0 (: Ground Zero on cover) (12/99, $4.95) Orbik-c 5.00
...: Gallery (7/99, $3.95) Jim Lee-c 4.00
...: Secret Files (12/99, $4.95) Maleev-c 5.00
TPB ('99, $12.95) r/early No Man's Land stories; new Batgirl early app. 13.00
No Law and a New Order TPB(1999, $5.95) Ross-c 6.00
Volume 2 ('00, $12.95) r/later No Man's Land stories; Batgirl(Huntress) app.; Deodato-c 13.00
Volume 3-5 ('00,'01 $12.95) 3-Intro. new Batgirl. 4-('00). 5-('01) Land-c 13.00

BATMAN: ORPHEUS RISING
DC Comics: Oct, 2001 - No. 5, Feb, 2002 ($2.50, limited series)
1-5-Intro. Orpheus; Simmons-s/Turner & Miki-a 2.50

BATMAN: OUTLAWS
DC Comics: 2000 - No. 3, 2000 ($4.95, limited series)
1-3-Moench-s/Gulacy-a 5.00

BATMAN: PENGUIN TRIUMPHANT (See Batman one-shots)

BATMAN/PREDATOR III: BLOOD TIES
DC Comics/Dark Horse Comics: Nov, 1997 - No. 4, Feb, 1998 ($1.95, lim. series)
1-4: Dixon-s/Damaggio-c/a 2.50
TPB-(1998, $7.95) r/#1-4 8.00

BATMAN RETURNS MOVIE SPECIAL (See Batman one-shots)

BATMAN: RIDDLER-THE RIDDLE FACTORY (See Batman one-shots)

BATMAN: RUN, RIDDLER, RUN
DC Comics: 1992 - Book 3, 1992 ($4.95, limited series)
Book 1-3: Mark Badger-a & plot 5.00

BATMAN: SECRET FILES
DC Comics: Oct, 1997 ($4.95)
1-New origin-s and profiles 5.00

BATMAN: SHADOW OF THE BAT
DC Comics: June, 1992 - No. 94, Feb, 2000 ($1.50/$1.75/$1.95/$1.99)
1-The Last Arkham-c/story begins; Alan Grant scripts in all 4.00
1-($2.50)-Deluxe edition polybagged w/poster, pop-up & book mark 5.00
2-7: 4-The Last Arkham ends. 7-Last $1.50-c 3.00
8-28: 14,15-Staton-a(p). 16-18-Knightfall tie-ins. 19-28-Knightquest tie-ins w/Azrael as Batman. 25-Silver ink-c; anniversary issue 2.50
29-($2.95, 52 pgs.)-KnightsEnd Pt. 2 3.00
30-72: 30-KnightsEnd Pt. 8. 31-(9.94)-Begin $1.95-c; Zero Hour. 32-(11/94). 33-Robin-c. 35-Troika-Pt.2. 43,44-Cat-Man & Catwoman-c. 48-Contagion Pt. 1; card insert. 49-Contagion Pt.7. 56,57,58-Poison Ivy-c/app. 62-Two-Face app. 69,70-Fate app. 2.50
35-($2.95)-Variant embossed-c 3.00
73,74,76-78: Cataclysm x-over pts. 1,9. 76-78-Orbik-c 2.50
75-($2.95) Mr. Freeze & Clayface app.; Orbik-c 3.00
79,81,82: 79-Begin $1.99-c; Orbik-c 2.50
80-($3.95) Flip book with Azrael #47 4.00
83-No Man's Land; intro. new Batgirl (Huntress) 12.00
84,85-No Man's Land 4.00
86-94: 87-Deodato-a. 90-Harris-c. 92-Superman app. 93-Joker and Harley app. 94-No Man's Land ends 3.00
#0 (10/94) Zero Hour; released between #31&32 3.00
#1,000,000 (11/98) 853rd Century x-over; Orbik-c 2.50
Annual 1-5 ('93-'97 $2.95-$3.95, 68 pgs.): 3-Year One story; Poison Ivy app. 4-Legends of the Dead Earth story; Starman cameo. 5-Pulp Heroes story; Poison Ivy app. 4.00

BATMAN-SPAWN: WAR DEVIL (See Batman one-shots)

BATMAN SPECTACULAR (See DC Special Series No. 15)

BATMAN STRIKES!, THE (Based on the 2004 animated series)
DC Comics: Nov, 2004 - Present ($2.25)
1,2,4: 1-Penguin app. 2-Man-Bat app. 4-Bane app. 2.25
3-($2.95) Joker-c/app.; Catwoman & Wonder Woman-r from Advs. in the DCU 3.00

BATMAN/ SUPERMAN/WONDER WOMAN: TRINITY
DC Comics: 2003 - No. 3, 2003 ($6.95, limited series, squarebound)
1-3-Matt Wagner-s/a/c. 1-Ra's al Ghul & Bizarro app. 7.00
HC (2004, $24.95, with dust-jacket) r/series; intro. by Brad Meltzer 30.00

BATMAN: SWORD OF AZRAEL (Also see Azrael & Batman #488,489)
DC Comics: Oct, 1992 - No. 4, Jan, 1993 ($1.75, limited series)
1-Wraparound gatefold-c; Quesada-c/a(p) in all; 1st app. Azrael 2 4 6 8 10 12
2-4: 4-Cont'd in Batman #488 1 2 3 5 6 8
Silver Edition 1-4 (1993, $1.95)-Reprints #1-4 2.25
Trade Paperback (1993, $9.95)-Reprints #1-4 10.00
Trade Paperback Gold Edition 15.00

BATMAN/ TARZAN: CLAWS OF THE CAT-WOMAN
Dark Horse Comics/DC Comics: Sept, 1999 - No. 4, Dec, 1999 ($2.95, limited series)
1-4: Marz-s/Kordey-a 3.00

BATMAN: TENSES

Batman: The Dark Knight Returns #3 © DC

Battle #4 © MAR

Battle Action #3 © MAR

	GD 2.0	VG 4.0	FN 6.0	VF 8.0	VF/NM 9.0	NM- 9.2

DC Comics: 2003 - No. 2, 2003 ($6.95, limited series)

Issue	GD 2.0	VG 4.0	FN 6.0	VF 8.0	VF/NM 9.0	NM- 9.2
1,2-Joe Casey-s/Cully Hamner-a; Bruce Wayne's first year back in Gotham						7.00

BATMAN: THE ANKH
DC Comics: 2002 - No. 2, 2002 ($5.95, limited series)

Issue	GD 2.0	VG 4.0	FN 6.0	VF 8.0	VF/NM 9.0	NM- 9.2
1,2-Dixon-s/Van Fleet-a						6.00

BATMAN: THE CULT
DC Comics: 1988 - No. 4, Nov, 1988 ($3.50, deluxe limited series)

Issue	GD 2.0	VG 4.0	FN 6.0	VF 8.0	VF/NM 9.0	NM- 9.2
1-Wrightson-a/painted-c in all						6.00
2-4						5.00
Trade Paperback ('91, $14.95)-New Wrightson-c						15.00

BATMAN: THE DARK KNIGHT RETURNS (Also see Dark Knight Strikes Again)
DC Comics: Mar, 1986 - No. 4, 1986 ($2.95, squarebound, limited series)

Issue	GD 2.0	VG 4.0	FN 6.0	VF 8.0	VF/NM 9.0	NM- 9.2
1-Miller story & c/a(p); set in the future	5	10	15	33	44	55
1,2-2nd & 3rd printings, 3-2nd printing						6.00
2-Carrie Kelly becomes 1st female Robin	3	6	9	18	23	28
3-Death of Joker; Superman app.	2	4	6	14	18	22
4-Death of Alfred; Superman app.	2	4	6	11	14	18
Hardcover, signed & numbered edition ($40.00)(4000 copies)						250.00
Hardcover, trade edition						50.00
Softcover, trade edition (1st printing only)	2	4	6	11	14	18
Softcover, trade edition (2nd thru 8th printings)	1	2	3	5	7	9
10th Anniv. Slipcase set ('96, $100.00): Signed & numbered hard-c edition (10,000 copies), sketchbook, copy of script for #1, 2 color prints						100.00
10th Anniv. Hardcover ('96, $45.00)						45.00
10th Anniv. Softcover ('97, $14.95)						15.00
Hardcover 2nd printing ('02, $24.95) with 3 1/4" tall partial dustjacket						25.00

NOTE: *The #2 second printings can be identified by matching the grey background colors on the inside front cover and facing page. The inside front cover of the second printing has a dark grey background which does not match the lighter grey of the facing page. On the true 1st printings, the backgrounds are both light grey. All other issues are clearly marked.*

BATMAN: THE DOOM THAT CAME TO GOTHAM
DC Comics: 2000 - No. 3, 2001 ($4.95, limited series)

Issue	GD 2.0	VG 4.0	FN 6.0	VF 8.0	VF/NM 9.0	NM- 9.2
1-3-Elseworlds; Mignola-c/s; Nixey-a; Etrigan app.						5.00

BATMAN: THE KILLING JOKE (See Batman one-shots)

BATMAN: THE LONG HALLOWEEN
DC Comics: Oct, 1996 - No. 13, Oct, 1997 ($2.95/$4.95, limited series)

Issue	GD 2.0	VG 4.0	FN 6.0	VF 8.0	VF/NM 9.0	NM- 9.2
1-($4.95)-Loeb-s/Sale-c/a in all	1	2	3	5	6	8
2-5($2.95): 2-Solomon Grundy-c/app. 3-Joker-c/app., Catwoman, Poison Ivy app.						6.00
6-10: 6-Poison Ivy-c. 7-Riddler-c/app.						5.00
11,12						4.00
13-($4.95, 48 pgs.)-Killer revelations						5.00
HC-($29.95) r/series						30.00
SC-($19.95)						20.00

BATMAN: THE OFFICIAL COMIC ADAPTATION OF THE WARNER BROS. MOTION PICTURE (See Batman one-shots)

BATMAN: THE ULTIMATE EVIL
DC Comics: 1995 ($5.95, limited series, prestige format)

Issue	GD 2.0	VG 4.0	FN 6.0	VF 8.0	VF/NM 9.0	NM- 9.2
1,2-Barrett, Jr. adaptation of Vachss novel.						6.00

BATMAN 3-D (Also see 3-D Batman)
DC Comics: 1990 ($9.95, w/glasses, 8-1/8x10-3/4")

Issue	GD 2.0	VG 4.0	FN 6.0	VF 8.0	VF/NM 9.0	NM- 9.2
nn-Byrne-a/scripts; Riddler, Joker, Penguin & Two-Face app. plus r/1953 3-D Batman; pin-ups by many artists	2	4	6	8	10	12

BATMAN: TOYMAN
DC Comics: Nov, 1998 - No. 4, Feb, 1999 ($2.25, limited series)

Issue	GD 2.0	VG 4.0	FN 6.0	VF 8.0	VF/NM 9.0	NM- 9.2
1-4-Hama-s						2.50

BATMAN: TURNING POINTS
DC Comics: Jan, 2001 - No. 5, Jan, 2001 ($2.50, weekly limited series)

Issue	GD 2.0	VG 4.0	FN 6.0	VF 8.0	VF/NM 9.0	NM- 9.2
1-5: 2-Giella-a. 3-Kubert-c/Giordano-a. 4-Chaykin-c. 5-Pope-c/a						2.50

BATMAN: TWO-FACE-CRIME AND PUNISHMENT (See Batman one-shots)

BATMAN: TWO-FACE STRIKES TWICE
DC Comics: 1993 - No. 2, 1993 ($4.95, 52 pgs.)

Issue	GD 2.0	VG 4.0	FN 6.0	VF 8.0	VF/NM 9.0	NM- 9.2
1,2-Flip book format w/Staton-a (G.A. side)						5.00

BATMAN VERSUS PREDATOR
DC Comics/Dark Horse Comics: 1991 - No. 3, 1992 ($4.95/$1.95, limited series)
(1st DC/Dark Horse x-over)

Issue	GD 2.0	VG 4.0	FN 6.0	VF 8.0	VF/NM 9.0	NM- 9.2
1 (Prestige format, $4.95)-1 & 3 contain 8 Batman/Predator trading cards; Andy & Adam Kubert-a; Suydam painted-c						6.00
1-3 (Regular format, $1.95)-No trading cards						3.00
2,3-(Prestige)-2-Extra pin-ups inside; Suydam-c						5.00
TPB (1993, $5.95, 132 pgs.)-r/#1-3 w/new introductions & forward plus new wraparound-c by Dave Gibbons						6.00

BATMAN VERSUS PREDATOR II: BLOODMATCH
DC Comics: Late 1994 - No. 4, 1995 ($2.50, limited series)

Issue	GD 2.0	VG 4.0	FN 6.0	VF 8.0	VF/NM 9.0	NM- 9.2
1-4-Huntress app.; Moench scripts; Gulacy-a						3.00
TPB (1995, $6.95)-r/#1-4						7.00

BATMAN VS. THE INCREDIBLE HULK (See DC Special Series No. 27)

BATMAN: WAR ON CRIME
DC Comics: Nov, 1999 ($9.95, treasury size, one-shot)

Issue	GD 2.0	VG 4.0	FN 6.0	VF 8.0	VF/NM 9.0	NM- 9.2
nn-Painted art by Alex Ross; story by Alex Ross and Paul Dini						10.00

BATMAN/ WILDCAT
DC Comics: Apr, 1997 - No.3, June, 1997 ($2.25, mini-series)

Issue	GD 2.0	VG 4.0	FN 6.0	VF 8.0	VF/NM 9.0	NM- 9.2
1-3: Dixon/Smith-s: 1-Killer Croc app.						2.50

BAT MASTERSON (TV) (Also see Tim Holt #28)
Dell Publishing Co.: Aug-Oct, 1959; Feb-Apr, 1960 - No. 9, Nov-Jan, 1961-62

Issue	GD 2.0	VG 4.0	FN 6.0	VF 8.0	VF/NM 9.0	NM- 9.2
Four Color 1013 (#1) (8-10/59)	13	26	39	92	141	190
2-9: Gene Barry photo-c on all. 2-Two different back-c exist	8	16	24	53	74	95

BATS (See Tales Calculated to Drive You Bats)

BATS, CATS & CADILLACS
Now Comics: Oct, 1990 - No. 2, Nov, 1990 ($1.75)

Issue	GD 2.0	VG 4.0	FN 6.0	VF 8.0	VF/NM 9.0	NM- 9.2
1,2: 1-Gustovich-a(i); Snyder-c						2.25

BAT-THING
DC Comics (Amalgam): June, 1997 ($1.95, one-shot)

Issue	GD 2.0	VG 4.0	FN 6.0	VF 8.0	VF/NM 9.0	NM- 9.2
1-Hama-s/Damaggio & Sienkiewicz-a						2.25

BATTLE
Marvel/Atlas Comics(FPI #1-62/ Male #63 on): Mar, 1951 - No. 70, Jun, 1960

Issue	GD 2.0	VG 4.0	FN 6.0	VF 8.0	VF/NM 9.0	NM- 9.2
1	32	64	96	184	267	350
2	16	32	48	89	127	165
3-10: 4-1st Buck Pvt. O'Toole. 10-Pakula-a	12	24	36	69	95	120
11-20: 11-Check-a	10	20	30	56	73	90
21,23-Krigstein-a	10	20	30	60	80	100
22,24-36: 32-Tuska-a. 36-Everett-a	8	16	24	46	58	70
37-Kubert-a (Last precode, 2/55)	9	18	27	52	66	80
38-40,42-48	8	16	24	43	54	65
41,49: 41-Kubert/Moskowitz-a. 49-Davis-a	9	18	27	51	62	75
50-54,56-58	8	16	24	40	50	60
55-Williamson-a (5 pgs.)	9	18	27	51	62	75
59-Torres-a	8	16	24	43	54	65
60-62: 60,62-Combat Kelly app. 61-Combat Casey app.	8	16	24	40	50	60
63-Ditko-a	11	22	33	66	91	115
64-66-Kirby-a. 66-Davis-a; has story of Fidel Castro in pre-Communism days (an admiring profile)	14	28	42	81	113	145
67,68: 67-Williamson/Crandall-a (4 pgs.); Kirby, Davis-a. 68-Kirby/Williamson-a (4 pgs.); Kirby/Ditko-a	15	30	45	83	117	150
69,70: 69-Kirby-a. 70-Kirby/Ditko-a	14	28	42	81	113	145

NOTE: ***Andru** a-37. **Berg** a-38, 14, 60-62. **Colan** a-33, 55. **Everett** a-36, 50, 70; c-56, 57. **Heath** a-6, 9, 13, 31, 69; c-6, 9, 12, 26, 35, 37. **Kirby** c-64-69. **Maneely** a-4, 6, 31, 61; c-4, 33, 59, 61. **Orlando** a-47. **Powell** a-53, 55. **Reinman** a-8, 9, 26, 32. **Robinson** a-9, 39. **Romita** a-26. **Severin** a-28, 32-34, 66-69; c-36, 55. **Sinnott** a-33, 37. **Woodbridge** a-52, 55.*

BATTLE ACTION
Atlas Comics (NPI): Feb, 1952 - No. 12, 5/53; No. 13, 11/54 - No. 30, 8/57

Issue	GD 2.0	VG 4.0	FN 6.0	VF 8.0	VF/NM 9.0	NM- 9.2
1-Pakula-a	26	52	78	150	215	280
2	14	28	42	79	110	140
3,4,6,7,9,10: 6-Robinson-c/a. 7-Partial nudity	9	18	27	51	62	75
5-Used in **POP**, pg. 93,94	9	18	27	52	66	80
8-Krigstein-a	9	18	27	54	70	85
11-15 (Last precode, 2/55)	9	18	27	51	62	75
16-30: 27,30-Torres-a	8	16	24	46	58	70

NOTE: *Battle Brady app. 5-7, 10-12. **Berg** a-3. **Check** a-11. **Everett** a-7; c-13, 25. **Heath** a-3, 8, 18; c-3,15, 18, 21. **Maneely** a-1; c-5. **Reinman** a-1. **Robinson** a-6, 7; c-6. **Shores** a-7(2), 12. **Sinnott** a-3, 27. **Woodbridge** a-28, 30.*

BATTLE ATTACK
Stanmor Publications: Oct, 1952 - No. 8, Dec, 1955

Issue	GD 2.0	VG 4.0	FN 6.0	VF 8.0	VF/NM 9.0	NM- 9.2
1	11	22	33	66	91	115

Battle Chasers #4 © Joe Madureira

Battle Front #29 © MAR

Battle of the Planets #2 © Sandy Frank

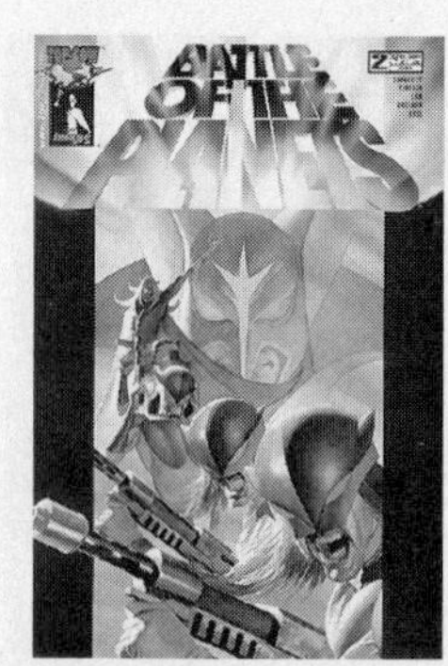

	GD 2.0	VG 4.0	FN 6.0	VF 8.0	VF/NM 9.0	NM- 9.2
2	8	16	24	40	50	60
3-8: 3-Hollingsworth-a	7	14	21	35	43	50

BATTLEAXES
DC Comics (Vertigo): May, 2000 - No. 4, Aug, 2000 ($2.50, limited series)

	GD 2.0	VG 4.0	FN 6.0	VF 8.0	VF/NM 9.0	NM- 9.2
1-4: Terry LaBan-s/Alex Horley-a						2.50

BATTLE BEASTS
Blackthorne Publishing: Feb, 1988 - No. 4, 1988 ($1.50/$1.75, B&W/color)

	GD 2.0	VG 4.0	FN 6.0	VF 8.0	VF/NM 9.0	NM- 9.2
1-4: 1-3- (B&W)-Based on Hasbro toys. 4-Color						2.50

BATTLE BRADY (Formerly Men in Action No. 1-9; see 3-D Action)
Atlas Comics (IPC): No. 10, Jan, 1953 - No. 14, June, 1953

	GD 2.0	VG 4.0	FN 6.0	VF 8.0	VF/NM 9.0	NM- 9.2
10: 10-12-Syd Shores-c	16	32	48	89	127	165
11-Used in **POP**, pg. 95 plus B&W & color illos	10	20	30	58	77	95
12-14	9	18	27	52	66	80

BATTLE CHASERS
Image Comics (Cliffhanger): Apr, 1998 - No. 4, Dec, 1998;
DC Comics (Cliffhanger): No. 5, May, 1999 - No. 8, May, 2001 ($2.50)
Image Comics: No. 9, Sept, 2001 ($3.50)

	GD 2.0	VG 4.0	FN 6.0	VF 8.0	VF/NM 9.0	NM- 9.2
Prelude (2/98)	1	3	4	6	8	10
Prelude Gold Ed.	1	3	4	6	8	10
1-Madureira & Sharrieff-s/Madureira-a(p)/Charest-c	1	2	3	5	7	9
1-American Ent. Ed. w/"racy" cover	1	3	4	6	8	10
1-Gold Edition						9.00
1-Chromium cover						40.00
1-2nd printing						3.00
2						5.00
2-Dynamic Forces BattleChrome cover	2	4	6	8	10	12
3-Red Monika cover by Madureira						4.00
4-8: 4-Four covers. 6-Back-up by Warren-s/a. 7-3 covers (Madureira, Ramos, Campbell)						3.00
9-($3.50, Image) Flip cover/story by Adam Warren						3.50
...: A Gathering of Heroes HC ('99, $24.95) r/#1-5, Prelude, Frank Frazetta Fantasy III.; cover gallery						25.00
...: A Gathering of Heroes SC ('99, $14.95)						15.00
...Collected Edition 1,2 (11/98, 5/99, $5.95) 1-r/#1,2. 2-r/#3,4						6.00

BATTLE CLASSICS (See Cancelled Comic Cavalcade)
DC Comics: Sept-Oct, 1978 (44 pgs.)

	GD 2.0	VG 4.0	FN 6.0	VF 8.0	VF/NM 9.0	NM- 9.2
1-Kubert-r; new Kubert-c	1	2	3	5	7	9

BATTLE CRY
Stanmor Publications: 1952 (May) - No. 20, Sept, 1955

	GD 2.0	VG 4.0	FN 6.0	VF 8.0	VF/NM 9.0	NM- 9.2
1	15	30	45	83	117	150
2	9	18	27	51	62	75
3,5-10: 8-Pvt. Ike begins, ends #13,17	7	14	21	35	43	50
4-Classic E.C. swipe	8	16	24	43	54	65
11-20	6	12	18	28	34	40

NOTE: ***Hollingsworth*** *a-9; c-20.*

BATTLEFIELD (War Adventures on the...)
Atlas Comics (ACI): April, 1952 - No. 11, May, 1953

	GD 2.0	VG 4.0	FN 6.0	VF 8.0	VF/NM 9.0	NM- 9.2
1-Pakula, Reinman-a	22	44	66	123	177	230
2-5: 2-Heath, Maneely, Pakula, Reinman-a	11	22	33	66	91	115
6-11	9	18	27	52	66	80

NOTE: ***Colan*** *a-11.* ***Everett*** *a-8.* ***Heath*** *a-1, 2, 5p; c-2, 8, 9, 11.* ***Ravielli*** *a-11.*

BATTLEFIELD ACTION (Formerly Foreign Intrigues)
Charlton Comics: No. 16, Nov, 1957 - No. 62, 2-3/66; No. 63, 7/80 - No. 89, 11/84

	GD 2.0	VG 4.0	FN 6.0	VF 8.0	VF/NM 9.0	NM- 9.2
V2#16	8	16	24	40	50	60
17,20-30	5	10	15	23	28	32
18,19-Check-a (2 stories in #18)	4	8	12	22	30	38
31-62(1966)	3	6	9	16	20	24
63-80(1983-84)						5.00
81-83,85-89 (Low print run)	1	2	3	4	5	7
84-Kirby reprints; 3 stories	1	3	4	6	8	10

NOTE: ***Montes/Bache*** *a-43, 55, 62.* ***Glanzman*** *a-87r.*

BATTLE FIRE
Aragon Magazine/Stanmor Publications: Apr, 1955 - No. 7, 1955

	GD 2.0	VG 4.0	FN 6.0	VF 8.0	VF/NM 9.0	NM- 9.2
1	10	20	30	58	77	95
2	6	12	18	33	41	48
3-7	5	10	15	24	30	35

BATTLE FOR A THREE DIMENSIONAL WORLD
3D Cosmic Publications: May, 1983 (20 pgs., slick paper w/stiff-c, $3.00)

	GD 2.0	VG 4.0	FN 6.0	VF 8.0	VF/NM 9.0	NM- 9.2
nn-Kirby c/a in 3-D; shows history of 3-D	2	4	6	8	10	12

BATTLEFORCE
Blackthorne Publishing: Nov, 1987 - No. 2, 1988 ($1.75, color/B&W)

	GD 2.0	VG 4.0	FN 6.0	VF 8.0	VF/NM 9.0	NM- 9.2
1,2: Based on game. 1-In color. 2-B&W						2.50

BATTLE FOR INDEPENDENTS, THE (Also See Cyblade/Shi & Shi/Cyblade: The Battle For Independents)
Image Comics (Top Cow Productions)/Crusade Comics: 1995 ($29.95)

	GD 2.0	VG 4.0	FN 6.0	VF 8.0	VF/NM 9.0	NM- 9.2
nn-boxed set of all editions of Shi/Cyblade & Cyblade/Shi plus new variant.	4	8	12	24	32	40

BATTLE FOR THE PLANET OF THE APES (See Power Record Comics)

BATTLEFRONT
Atlas Comics (PPI): June, 1952 - No. 48, Aug, 1957

	GD 2.0	VG 4.0	FN 6.0	VF 8.0	VF/NM 9.0	NM- 9.2
1-Heath-c	30	60	90	170	245	320
2-Robinson-a(4)	15	30	45	85	120	155
3-5	12	24	36	71	98	125
6-10: Combat Kelly in No. 6-10	10	20	30	60	80	100
11-22,24-28: 14,16-Battle Brady app. 22-Teddy Roosevelt & His Rough Riders story. 28-Last pre-code (2/55)	9	18	27	51	62	75
23,43-Check-a	9	18	27	52	66	80
29-39,41,44-47	8	16	24	43	54	65
40,42-Williamson-a	9	18	27	54	70	85
48-Crandall-a	9	18	27	51	62	75

NOTE: ***Ayers*** *a-19, 32.* ***Berg*** *a-44.* ***Colan*** *a-21, 22, 32, 33, 40.* ***Drucker*** *a-28, 29.* ***Everett*** *a-44.* ***Heath*** *c-23, 26, 27, 29, 32.* ***Maneely*** *a-22, 23; c-2, 7, 13, 22, 34, 35.* ***Morisi*** *a-42.* ***Morrow*** *a-41.* ***Orlando*** *a-47.* ***Powell*** *a-19, 21, 25, 29, 32, 40, 47.* ***Robinson*** *a-1-4, 5(4); c-4, 5.* ***Robert Sale*** *a-19.* ***Severin*** *a-32; c-40, 45.* ***Woodbridge*** *a-45, 46.*

BATTLEFRONT
Standard Comics: No. 5, June, 1952

	GD 2.0	VG 4.0	FN 6.0	VF 8.0	VF/NM 9.0	NM- 9.2
5-Toth-a	15	30	45	83	117	150

BATTLE GODS: WARRIORS OF THE CHAAK
Dark Horse Comics: Apr, 2000 - No. 4, July, 2000 ($2.95)

	GD 2.0	VG 4.0	FN 6.0	VF 8.0	VF/NM 9.0	NM- 9.2
1-4-Francisco Ruiz Velasco-s/a						3.00

BATTLE GROUND
Atlas Comics (OMC): Sept, 1954 - No. 20, Aug, 1957

	GD 2.0	VG 4.0	FN 6.0	VF 8.0	VF/NM 9.0	NM- 9.2
1	22	44	66	123	177	230
2-Jack Katz-a	11	22	33	66	91	115
3,4-Last precode (3/55)	9	18	27	54	70	85
5-8,10	9	18	27	51	62	75
9,11,13,18: 9-Krigstein-a. 11,13,18-Williamson-a in each	10	20	30	58	77	95
12,15-17,19,20	8	16	24	46	58	70
14-Kirby-a	11	22	33	64	87	110

NOTE: ***Ayers*** *a-4, 13, 16.* ***Colan*** *a-11, 13.* ***Drucker*** *a-7, 12, 13, 20.* ***Heath*** *c-2, 5, 13.* ***Maneely*** *a-14, 19; c-1, 18, 19.* ***Orlando*** *a-17.* ***Pakula*** *a-11.* ***Severin*** *a-4, 5, 12, 19. c-20.* ***Tuska*** *a-11.*

BATTLE HEROES
Stanley Publications: Sept, 1966 - No. 2, Nov, 1966 (25¢, squarebound giants)

	GD 2.0	VG 4.0	FN 6.0	VF 8.0	VF/NM 9.0	NM- 9.2
1	4	8	12	25	33	42
2	3	6	9	18	23	28

BATTLE OF THE BULGE (See Movie Classics)

BATTLE OF THE PLANETS (Based on syndicated cartoon by Sandy Frank)
Gold Key/Whitman No. 6 on: 6/79 - No. 10, 12/80

	GD 2.0	VG 4.0	FN 6.0	VF 8.0	VF/NM 9.0	NM- 9.2
1: Mortimer a-1-4,7-10	3	6	9	19	25	32
2-6,10	2	4	6	14	18	22
7-Low print run	4	8	12	27	36	45
8,9-Low print run: 8(11/80). 9-(3-pack only?)	4	8	12	24	32	40

BATTLE OF THE PLANETS (Also see Thundercats/...)
Image Comics (Top Cow): Aug, 2002 - No. 12, Sept, 2003 ($2.95/$2.99)

	GD 2.0	VG 4.0	FN 6.0	VF 8.0	VF/NM 9.0	NM- 9.2
1-($2.95) Alex Ross-c & art director; Tortosa-a(p); re-intro. G-Force						3.00
1-($5.95) Holofoil-c by Ross						6.00
2-11-($2.99) Ross-c on all						3.00
12-($4.99)						5.00
#1/2 (7/03, $2.99) Benitez-c; Alex Ross sketch pages						3.00
... Battle Book 1 (5/03, $4.99) background info on characters, equipment, stories						5.00
... : Jason 1 (7/03, $4.99) Ross-c; Erwin David-a; preview of Tomb Raider: Epiphany						5.00
... : Mark 1 (5/03, $4.99) Ross-c; Erwin David-a; preview of BotP: Jason						5.00
.../Thundercats 1 (Image/WildStorm, 5/03, $4.99) 2 covers by Ross & Campbell						5.00
.../Witchblade 1 (2/03, $5.95) Ross-c; Christina and Jo Chen-a						6.00
Vol.1: Trial By Fire (2003, $7.99) r/#1-3						8.00
Vol.2: Blood Red Sky (9/03, $16.95) r/#4-9						17.00
Vol.3: Destroy All Monsters (11/03, $19.95) r/#10-12, ...: Jason, ...: Mark, .../Witchblade						20.00
Vol.1: Digest (1/04, $9.99, 7-3/8x5", B&W) r/#1-9 & ...: Mark						10.00

Battle Report #1 © AJAX

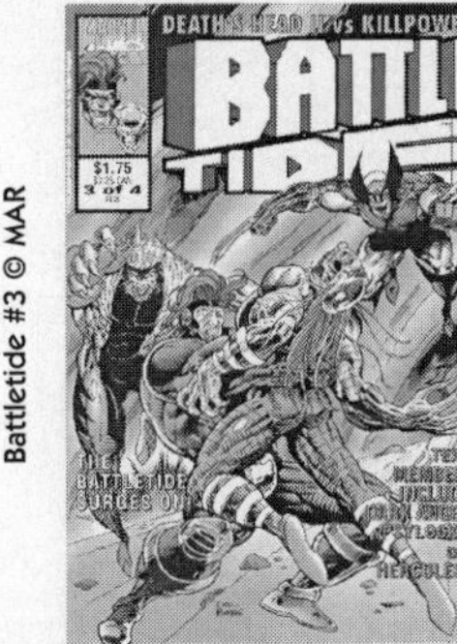

Battletide #3 © MAR

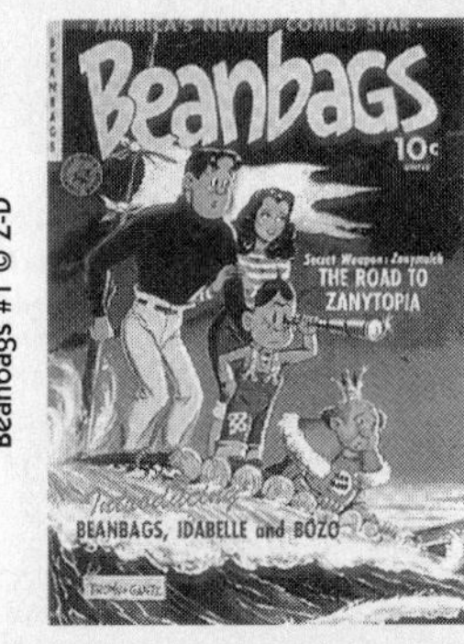

Beanbags #1 © Z-D

	GD 2.0	VG 4.0	FN 6.0	VF 8.0	VF/NM 9.0	NM- 9.2

Vol.2: Digest (8/04, $9.99, B&W) r/#10-12, ...: Jason, ...: Manga #1-3, .../Witchblade 10.00

BATTLE OF THE PLANETS: MANGA
Image Comics (Top Cow): Nov, 2003 - No. 3, Jan, 2004 ($2.99, B&W)

1-3-Edwin David-a/David Wohl-s; previews for Wanted & Tomb Raider #35 3.00

BATTLE OF THE PLANETS: PRINCESS
Image Comics (Top Cow): Nov, 2004 - No. 6 ($2.99, B&W, limited series)

1,2-Tortosa-a/Wohl-s. 1-Ross-c. 2-Tortosa-c 3.00

BATTLE REPORT
Ajax/Farrell Publications: Aug, 1952 - No. 6, June, 1953

1 10 20 30 58 77 95
2-6 7 14 21 35 43 50

BATTLE SQUADRON
Stanmor Publications: April, 1955 - No. 5, Dec, 1955

1 9 18 27 54 70 85
2-5: 3-Iwo Jima & flag-c 6 12 18 29 36 42

BATTLESTAR GALACTICA (TV) (Also see Marvel Comics Super Special #8)
Marvel Comics Group: Mar, 1979 - No. 23, Jan, 1981

1: 1-5 adapt TV episodes 1 3 4 6 8 10
2-23: 1-3-Partial-r 1 2 3 4 5 7

NOTE: ***Austin*** *c-9i, 10i.* ***Golden*** *c-18.* ***Simonson*** *a(p)-4, 5, 11-13, 15-20, 22, 23; c(p)-4, 5,11-17, 19, 20, 22, 23.*

BATTLESTAR GALACTICA (TV) (Also see Asylum)
Maximum Press: July, 1995 - No.4, Nov, 1995 ($2.50, limited series)

1-4: Continuation of TV series 4.00
Trade paperback (12/95, $12.95)-reprints series 13.00

BATTLESTAR GALACTICA (TV)
Realm Press: Dec, 1997 - No. 5, July, 1998 ($2.99)

1-5-Chris Scalf-s/painted-a/c 3.00
...Search For Sanctuary (9/98, $2.99) Scalf & Kuhoric-s 3.00
...Search For Sanctuary Special (4/00, $3.99) Kuhoric-s/Scalf & Scott-a 4.00

BATTLESTAR GALACTICA: APOLLO'S JOURNEY (TV)
Maximum Press: Apr, 1996 - No. 3, June, 1996 ($2.95, limited series)

1-3: Richard Hatch scripts 4.00

BATTLESTAR GALACTICA: JOURNEY'S END (TV)
Maximum Press: Aug, 1996 - No. 4, Nov, 1996 ($2.99, limited series)

1-4-Continuation of the T.V. series 4.00

BATTLESTAR GALACTICA: SEASON III
Realm Press: June/July, 1999 - No. 3, Sept, 1999 ($2.99)

1-3: 1-Kuhoric-s/Scalf & Scott-a; two covers by Scalf & Jae Lee. 2,3-Two covers 3.00
Gallery (4/00, $3.99) short story and pin-ups 4.00
1999 Tour Book (5/99, $2.99) 3.00
1999 Tour Book Convention Edition (6.99) 7.00
...Special: Centurion Prime (12/99, $3.99) Kuhoric-s 4.00

BATTLESTAR GALACTICA: SPECIAL EDITION (TV)
Maximum Press: Jan, 1997 ($2.99, one-shot)

1-Fully painted; Scalf-c/s/a; r/Asylum 3.00

BATTLESTAR GALACTICA: STARBUCK (TV)
Maximum Press: Dec, 1995 - No. 3, Mar, 1996 ($2.50, limited series)

1-3 4.00

BATTLESTAR GALACTICA: THE COMPENDIUM (TV)
Maximum Press: Feb, 1997 ($2.99, one-shot)

1 3.00

BATTLESTAR GALACTICA: THE ENEMY WITHIN (TV)
Maximum Press: Nov, 1995 - No. 3, Feb, 1996 ($2.50, limited series)

1-3: 3-Indicia reads Feb, 1995 in error. 4.00

BATTLESTONE (Also see Brigade & Youngblood)
Image Comics (Extreme): Nov, 1994 - No. 2, Dec, 1994 ($2.50, limited series)

1,2-Liefeld plots 2.50

BATTLE STORIES (See XMas Comics)
Fawcett Publications: Jan, 1952 - No. 11, Sept, 1953

1-Evans-a 16 32 48 89 127 165
2 9 18 27 52 66 80
3-11 8 16 24 43 54 65

BATTLE STORIES
Super Comics: 1963 - 1964

Reprints #10-12,15-18: 10-r/U.S Tank Commandos #? 11-r/? 11, 12,17-r/Monty Hall #?; 13-Kintsler-a (1pg).15-r/American Air Forces #7 by Powell; Bolle-r. 18-U.S. Fighting Air Force #? 2 4 6 10 13 16

BATTLETECH (See Blackthorne 3-D Series #41 for 3-D issue)
Blackthorne Publishing: Oct, 1987 - No. 6, 1988 ($1.75/$2.00)

1-6: Based on game. 1-Color. 2-Begin B&W 3.00
Annual 1 ($4.50, B&W) 5.00

BATTLETECH
Malibu Comics: Feb, 1995 ($2.95)

0 3.00

BATTLETECH FALLOUT
Malibu Comics: Dec, 1994 - No. 4, Mar, 1995 ($2.95)

1-4-Two edi. exist #1; normal logo 3.00
1-Gold version w/foil logo stamped "Gold Limited Edition 8.00
1-Full-c holographic limited edition 6.00

BATTLETIDE (Death's Head II & Killpower...)
Marvel Comics UK, Ltd.: Dec, 1992 - No. 4, Mar, 1993 ($1.75, mini-series)

1-4: Wolverine, Psylocke, Dark Angel app. 2.25

BATTLETIDE II (Death's Head II & Killpower...)
Marvel Comics UK, Ltd.: Aug, 1993 - No. 4, Nov, 1993 ($1.75, mini-series)

1-($2.95)-Foil embossed logo 3.00
2-4: 2-Hulk-c/story 2.25

BATTLEZONES: DREAM TEAM 2 (See Dream Team)
Malibu Comics (Ultraverse): Mar, 1996 ($3.95)

1-Pin-ups of Marvel & Malibu characters by Mike Wieringo, Phil Jimenez, Mike McKone, Cully Hamner, Gary Frank & others 4.00

BAY CITY JIVE
DC Comics (WildStorm): Jul, 2001 - No. 3, Sept, 2001 ($2.95, limited series)

1-3: Intro Sugah Rollins in 1970s San Francisco; Layman-s/Johnson-a 3.00

BAYWATCH COMIC STORIES (TV) (Magazine)
Acclaim Comics (Armada): May, 1996 - No. 4, 1997 ($4.95) (Photo-c on all)

1-4: Photo comics based on TV show 5.00

BEACH BLANKET BINGO (See Movie Classics)

BEAGLE BOYS, THE (Walt Disney)(See The Phantom Blot)
Gold Key: 11/64; No. 2, 11/65; No. 3, 8/66 - No. 47, 2/79 (See WDC&S #134)

1 6 12 18 38 52 65
2-5 3 6 9 19 25 32
6-10 3 6 9 17 21 26
11-20: 11,14,19-r 2 4 6 12 16 20
21-30: 27-r 2 4 6 9 11 14
31-47 1 3 4 6 8 10

BEAGLE BOYS VERSUS UNCLE SCROOGE
Gold Key: Mar, 1979 - No. 12, Feb, 1980

1 2 4 6 10 13 16
2-12: 9-r 1 2 3 5 6 8

BEANBAGS
Ziff-Davis Publ. Co. (Approved Comics): Winter, 1951 - No. 2, Spring, 1952

1,2 11 22 33 64 87 110

BEANIE THE MEANIE
Fago Publications: No. 3, May, 1959

3 5 10 15 24 30 35

BEANY AND CECIL (TV) (Bob Clampett's...)
Dell Publishing Co.: Jan, 1952 - 1955; July-Sept, 1962 - No. 5, July-Sept, 1963

Four Color 368 29 58 87 206 316 425
Four Color 414,448,477,530,570,635(1/55) 17 34 51 121 186 250
01-057-209 (#1) 16 32 48 112 171 230
2-5 11 22 33 79 117 155

BEAR COUNTRY (Disney)
Dell Publishing Co.: No. 758, Dec, 1956

Four Color 758-Movie 6 12 18 43 59 75

BEAST (See X-Men)
Marvel Comics: May, 1997 - No. 3, 1997 ($2.50, mini-series)

1-3-Giffen-s/Nocon-a 3.00

The Beatles #1 © DELL

Beautiful Killer #3 © Black Bull & Jimmy Palmiotti

Beetlejuice #1 © Geffen Film Co.

	GD 2.0	VG 4.0	FN 6.0	VF 8.0	VF/NM 9.0	NM- 9.2

BEAST BOY (See Titans)
DC Comics: Jan, 2000 - No. 4, Apr, 2000 ($2.95, mini-series)

1-4-Justiano-c/a; Raab & Johns-s 3.00

B.E.A.S.T.I.E.S. (Also see Axis Alpha)
Axis Comics: Apr, 1994 ($1.95)

1-Javier Saltares-c/a/scripts 2.25

BEATLES, THE (See Girls' Romances #109, Go-Go, Heart Throbs #101, Herbie #5, Howard the Duck Mag. #4, Laugh #166, Marvel Comics Super Special #4, My Little Margie #54, Not Brand Echh, Strange Tales #130, Summer Love, Superman's Pal Jimmy Olsen #79, Teen Confessions #37, Tippy's Friends & Tippy Teen)

BEATLES, THE (Life Story)
Dell Publishing Co.: Sept-Nov, 1964 (35¢)

	GD	VG	FN	VF	VF/NM	NM-
1-(Scarce)-Stories with color photo pin-ups; Paul S. Newman-s	42	84	126	336	526	715

BEATLES EXPERIENCE, THE
Revolutionary Comics: Mar, 1991 - No. 8, 1991 ($2.50, B&W, limited series)

1-8: 1-Gold logo 5.00

BEATLES YELLOW SUBMARINE (See Movie Comics under Yellow...)

BEAUTIFUL KILLER
Black Bull Comics: Sept., 2002 - No. 3, Jan, 2003 ($2.99, limited series)

...Limited Preview Edition (5/02, $5.00) preview pgs. & creator interviews 5.00
1-Noto-a/Palmiotti-s; Hughes-c; intro Brigit Cole 3.00
2,3: 2-Jusko-c. 3-Noto-c 3.00
TPB (5/03, $9.99) r/#1-3; cover gallery and Adam Hughes sketch pages 10.00

BEAUTIFUL PEOPLE
Slave Labor Graphics: Apr, 1994 ($4.95, 8-1/2x11", one-shot)

nn 5.00

BEAUTIFUL STORIES FOR UGLY CHILDREN
DC Comics (Piranha Press): 1989 - No. 30, 1991 ($2.00/$2.50, B&W, mature)

Vol. 1-20: 12-$2.50-c begins 3.50
21-25 4.50
26-30-(Lower print run) 5.00
A Cotton Candy Autopsy ($12.95, B&W)-Reprints 1st two volumes 13.00

BEAUTY AND THE BEAST, THE
Marvel Comics Group: Jan, 1985 - No. 4, Apr, 1985 (limited series)

1-4: Dazzler & the Beast from X-Men; Sienkiewicz-c on all 3.00

BEAUTY AND THE BEAST (Graphic novel)(Also see Cartoon Tales & Disney's New Adventures of...)
Disney Comics: 1992

nn-($4.95, prestige edition)-Adapts animated film 7.00
nn-($2.50, newsstand edition) 3.00

BEAUTY AND THE BEAST
Disney Comics: Sept., 1992 - No. 2, 1992 ($1.50, limited series)

1,2 3.00

BEAUTY AND THE BEAST: PORTRAIT OF LOVE (TV)
First Comics: May, 1989 - No. 2, Mar, 1990 ($5.95, 60 pgs., squarebound)

1,2: 1-Based on TV show, Wendy Pini-a/scripts. 2-...: Night of Beauty; by Wendy Pini 6.00

BEAVER VALLEY (Movie)(Disney)
Dell Publishing Co.: No. 625, Apr, 1955

	GD	VG	FN	VF	VF/NM	NM-
Four Color 625	7	14	21	51	71	90

BEAVIS AND BUTTHEAD (MTV's...)(TV cartoon)
Marvel Comics: Mar, 1994 - No. 28, June, 1996 ($1.95)

1-Silver ink-c. 1, 2-Punisher & Devil Dinosaur app. 4.00
1-2nd printing 2.25
2,3: 2-Wolverine app. 3-Man-Thing, Spider-Man, Venom, Carnage, Mary Jane & Stan Lee cameos; John Romita, Sr. art (2 pgs.) 2.50
4-28: 5-War Machine, Thor, Loki, Hulk, Captain America & Rhino cameos. 6-Psylocke, Polaris, Daredevil & Bullseye app. 7-Ghost Rider & Sub-Mariner app. 8-Quasar & Eon app. 9-Prowler & Nightwatch app. 11-Black Widow app. 12-Thunderstrike & Bloodaxe app. 13-Night Thrasher app. 14-Spider-Man 2099 app. 15-Warlock app. 16-X-Factor app. 25-Juggernaut app. 2.50

BECK & CAUL INVESTIGATIONS
Gauntlet Comics (Caliber): Jan, 1994 - No. 5, 1995? ($2.95, B&W)

1-5 3.00
Special 1 ($4.95) 5.00

BEDKNOBS AND BROOMSTICKS (See Walt Disney Showcase No. 6 & 50)

BEDLAM
Chaos! Comics: Sept, 2000 ($2.95, one-shot)

1-Steven Grant-s/David Brewer-a 3.00

BEDLAM!
Eclipse Comics: Sept, 1985 - No. 2, Sept, 1985 (B&W-r in color)

1,2: Bissette-a 3.00

BEDTIME STORY (See Cinema Comics Herald)

BEELZELVIS
Slave Labor Graphics: Feb, 1994 ($2.95, B&W, one-shot)

1 3.00

BEEP BEEP, THE ROAD RUNNER (TV)(See Daffy & Kite Fun Book)
Dell Publishing Co./Gold Key No. 1-88/Whitman No. 89 on: July, 1958 - No. 14, Aug-Oct, 1962; Oct, 1966 - No. 105, 1984

	GD	VG	FN	VF	VF/NM	NM-
Four Color 918 (#1, 7/58)	11	22	33	80	120	160
Four Color 1008,1046 (11-1/59-60)	7	14	21	46	63	80
4(2-4/60)-14(Dell)	6	12	18	40	55	70
1(10/66, Gold Key)	6	12	18	43	59	75
2-5	4	8	12	27	36	45
6-14	3	6	9	19	25	32
15-18,20-40	3	6	9	16	20	24
19-With pull-out poster	4	8	12	25	33	42
41-50	2	4	6	11	14	18
51-70	2	4	6	8	10	12
71-88	1	2	3	5	6	8
89,90,94-101: 100(3/82), 101(4/82)	1	2	3	5	7	9
91(8/80), 92(9/80), 93 (3-pack?) (low printing)	3	6	9	16	20	25
102-105 (All #90189 on-c; nd or date code; pre-pack) 102(6/83), 103(7/83), 104(5/84), 105(6/84)	2	4	6	11	14	18
#63-2970 (Now Age Books/Pendulum Pub. Comic Digest, 1971, 75¢, 100 pages, B&W) collection of one-page gags	3	6	9	18	24	36

NOTE: *See March of Comics #351, 353, 375, 387, 397, 416, 430, 442, 455. #5, 8-10, 35, 53, 59-62, 68-r; 96-102, 104 are 1/3-r.*

BEETLE BAILEY (See Giant Comic Album, Sarge Snorkel; also Comics Reading Libraries in the Promotional Comics section)
Dell Publishing Co./Gold Key #39-53/King #54-66/Charlton #67-119/Gold Key #120-131/ Whitman #132: #459, 5/53 - #38, 5-7/62; #39, 11/62 - #53, 5/66; #54, 8/66 - #65, 12/67;#67, 2/69 - #119, 11/76; #120, 4/78 - #132, 4/80

	GD	VG	FN	VF	VF/NM	NM-
Four Color 469 (#1)-By Mort Walker	11	22	33	80	120	160
Four Color 521,552,622	7	14	21	46	63	80
5(2-4/56)-10(5-7/57)	6	12	18	38	52	65
11-20(4-5/59)	4	8	12	27	36	45
21-38(5-7/62)	3	6	9	19	25	32
39-53(5/66)	3	6	9	16	21	26
54-65 (No. 66 publ. overseas only?)	2	4	6	14	18	22
67-69: 69-Last 12¢ issue	2	4	6	12	16	20
70-99	2	4	6	10	12	15
100	2	4	6	12	16	20
101-119	1	3	4	6	8	10
120-132						6.00

BEETLE BAILEY
Harvey Comics: V2#1, Sept, 1992 - V2#9, Aug, 1994 ($1.25/$1.50)

V2#1 4.00
2-9-($1.50) 3.00
Big Book 1(11/92),2(5/93)(Both $1.95, 52 pgs.) 3.50
Giant Size V2#1(10/92),2(3/93)(Both $2.25,68 pgs.) 3.50

BEETLEJUICE (TV)
Harvey Comics: Oct, 1991 ($1.25)

1 3.00

BEETLEJUICE CRIMEBUSTERS ON THE HAUNT
Harvey Comics: Sept, 1992 - No. 3, Jan, 1993 ($1.50, limited series)

1-3 3.00

BEE 29, THE BOMBARDIER
Neal Publications: Feb, 1945

	GD	VG	FN	VF	VF/NM	NM-
1-(Funny animal)	31	62	93	178	259	340

BEFORE THE FANTASTIC FOUR: BEN GRIMM AND LOGAN
Marvel Comics: July, 2000 - No. 3, Sept, 2000 ($2.99, limited series)

1-3-The Thing and Wolverine app.; Hama-s 3.00

BEFORE THE FANTASTIC FOUR: REED RICHARDS

Beowulf #1 © DC

Best Love #34 © MAR

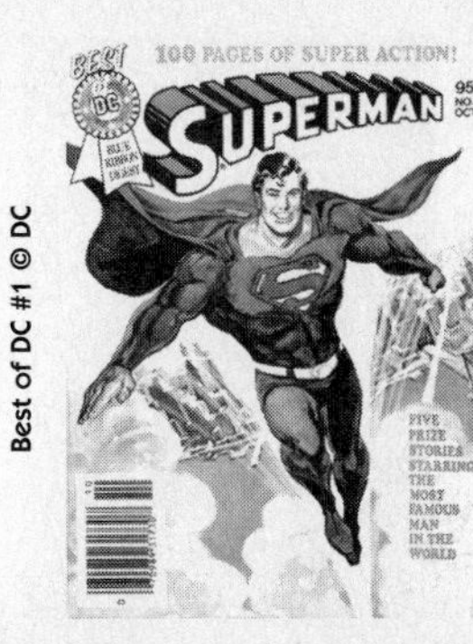

Best of DC #1 © DC

GD VG FN VF VF/NM NM-
2.0 4.0 6.0 8.0 9.0 9.2

Marvel Comics: Sept, 2000 - No. 3, Dec, 2000 ($2.99, limited series)
1-3-Peter David-s/Duncan Fegredo-c/a 3.00

BEFORE THE FANTASTIC FOUR: THE STORMS
Marvel Comics: Dec, 2000 - No. 3, Feb, 2001 ($2.99, limited series)
1-3-Adlard-a 3.00

BEHIND PRISON BARS
Realistic Comics (Avon): 1952
1-Kinstler-c 32 64 96 184 267 350

BEHOLD THE HANDMAID
George Pflaum: 1954 (Religious) (25¢ with a 20¢ sticker price)
nn 5 10 15 24 30 35

BELIEVE IT OR NOT (See Ripley's...)

BEN AND ME (Disney)
Dell Publishing Co.: No. 539, Mar, 1954
Four Color 539 4 8 12 29 40 50

BEN BOWIE AND HIS MOUNTAIN MEN
Dell Publishing Co.: 1952 - No. 17, Nov-Jan, 1958-59
Four Color 443 (#1) 9 18 27 60 85 110
Four Color 513,557,599,626,657 5 10 15 33 44 55
7(5-7/56)-11: 11-Intro/origin Yellow Hair 4 8 12 28 38 48
12-17 4 8 12 24 32 40

BEN CASEY (TV)
Dell Publishing Co.: June-July, 1962 - No. 10, June-Aug, 1965 (Photo-c)
12-063-207 (#1) 7 14 21 50 68 85
2(10/62),3,5-10 4 8 12 29 40 50
4-Marijuana & heroin use story 5 10 15 36 48 60

BEN CASEY FILM STORY (TV)
Gold Key: Nov, 1962 (25¢) (Photo-c)
30009-211-All photos 9 18 27 63 89 115

BENEATH THE PLANET OF THE APES (See Movie Comics & Power Record Comics)

BEN FRANKLIN (See Kite Fun Book)

BEN HUR
Dell Publishing Co.: No. 1052, Nov, 1959
Four Color 1052-Movie, Manning-a 11 22 33 77 114 150

BEN ISRAEL
Logos International: 1974 (39¢)
nn-Christian religious 2 4 6 9 11 14

BEOWULF (Also see First Comics Graphic Novel #1)
National Periodical Publications: Apr-May, 1975 - No. 6, Feb-Mar, 1976
1 2 4 6 9 11 14
2,3,5,6: 5-Flying saucer-c/story 1 2 3 5 6 8
4-Dracula-c/s 1 2 3 5 7 9

BERLIN
Black Eye Productions: Apr, 1996 - Present ($2.50/$2.95/$3.50, B&W)
1-8: Jason Lutes-c/a/scripts. 5-7-($2.95) 3.00
9,10-($3.50) 3.50
City of Stones TPB (2001, $15.95) r/#1-8 16.00

BERNI WRIGHTSON, MASTER OF THE MACABRE
Pacific Comics/Eclipse Comics No. 5: July, 1983 - No. 5, Nov, 1984 ($1.50, Baxter paper)
1-5: Wrightson-c/a(r). 4-Jeff Jones-r (11 pgs.) 5.00

BERRYS, THE (Also see Funny World)
Argo Publ.: May, 1956
1-Reprints daily & Sunday strips & daily Animal Antics by Ed Nofziger
6 12 18 29 36 42

BERZERKERS (See Youngblood V1#2)
Image Comics (Extreme Studios): Aug, 1995 - No. 3, Oct, 1995 ($2.50, limited series)
1-3: Beau Smith scripts, Fraga-a 2.50

BEST COMICS
Better Publications: Nov, 1939 - No. 4, Feb, 1940(Large size, reads sideways)
1-(Scarce)-Red Mask begins(1st app.) & c/s-all. Contains 6 pg. Boston Celtics photo story
87 174 261 544 835 1125
2-4: 4-Cannibalism story 50 100 150 305 465 625

BEST FROM BOY'S LIFE, THE

GD VG FN VF VF/NM NM-
2.0 4.0 6.0 8.0 9.0 9.2

Gilberton Company: Oct, 1957 - No. 5, Oct, 1958 (35¢)
1-Space Conquerors & Kam of the Ancient Ones begin, end #5; Bob Cousy photo/story
12 24 36 71 98 125
2,3,5 8 16 24 40 50 60
4-L.B. Cole-a 8 16 24 46 58 70

BEST LOVE (Formerly Sub-Mariner Comics No. 32)
Marvel Comics (MPI): No. 33, Aug, 1949 - No. 36, April, 1950 (Photo-c 33-36)
33-Kubert-a 13 26 39 74 102 130
34 8 16 24 43 54 65
35,36-Everett-a 9 18 27 54 70 85

BEST OF BUGS BUNNY, THE
Gold Key: Oct, 1966 - No. 2, Oct, 1968
1,2-Giants 6 12 18 40 55 70

BEST OF DC, THE (Blue Ribbon Digest) (See Limited Coll. Ed. C-52)
DC Comics: Sept-Oct, 1979 - No. 71, Apr, 1986 (100-148 pgs; mostly reprints)
1-Superman, w/"Death of Superman"-r 2 4 6 12 16 20
2,5-9: 2-Batman 40th Ann. Special. 5-Best of 1979. 6,8-Superman. 7-Superboy. 9-Batman, Creeper app. 2 4 6 8 10 12
3-Superfriends 2 4 6 10 12 15
4-Rudolph the Red Nosed Reindeer 2 4 6 10 13 16
10-Secret Origins of Super Villains; 1st ever Penguin origin-s
3 6 9 18 23 28
11-16,18-20: 11-The Year's Best Stories. 12-Superman Time and Space Stories.13-Best of DC Comics Presents. 14-New origin stories of Batman villains. 15-Superboy. 16-Superman Anniv. 18-Teen Titans new-s., Adams, Kane-a; Perez-c. 19-Superman. 20-World's Finest
1 2 3 5 7 9
17-Supergirl 2 4 6 8 10 12
21,22: 21-Justice Society. 22-Christmas; unpublished Sandman story w/Kirby-a
2 4 6 11 14 18
23-27: 23-(148 pgs.)-Best of 1981. 24 Legion, new story and 16 pgs. new costumes. 25-Superman. 26-Brave & Bold. 27-Superman vs. Luthor
2 4 6 10 12 15
28,29: 28-Binky, Sugar & Spike app. 29-Sugar & Spike, 3 new stories; new Stanley & his Monster story 2 4 6 10 13 16
30,32-36,38,40: 30-Detective Comics. 32-Superman. 33-Secret origins of Legion Heroes and Villains. 34-Metal Men; has #497 on-c from Adv. Comics. 35-The Year's Best Comics Stories(148 pgs.). 36-Superman vs. Kryptonite. 38-Superman. 40-World of Krypton
2 4 6 10 12 15
31-JLA 2 4 6 11 14 18
37,39: 37-"Funny Stuff", Mayer-a. 39-Binky 2 4 6 11 14 18
41,43,45,47,49,53,55,58,60,63,65,68,70: 41-Sugar & Spike new stories with Mayer-a. 43,49,55-Funny Stuff. 45,53,70-Binky. 47,58,65,68-Sugar & Spike. 60-Plop!; Wood-c(r) & Aragonés-r (5/85). 63-Plop!; Wrightson-a(r) 3 6 9 16 20 24
42,44,46,48,50-52,54,56,57,59,61,62,64,66,67,69,71: 42,56-Superman vs. Aliens. 44,57,67-Superboy & LSH. 46-Jimmy Olsen. 48-Superman Team-ups. 50-Year's best Superman. 51-Batman Family. 52 Best of 1984. 54,56,59-Superman. 61-(148 pgs.)Year's best. 62-Best of Batman 1985. 69-Year's best Team stories. 71-Year's best
2 4 6 11 14 18

NOTE: ***N. Adams** a-2r, 14r, 18r, 26, 51. **Aparo** a-9, 14, 26, 30; c-9, 14, 26. **Austin** a-51i. **Buckler** a-40p; c-16, 22. **Giffen** a-50, 52; c-33p. **Grell** a-33p. **Grossman** a-37. **Heath** a-26. **Infantino** a-10r, 18. **Kaluta** a-40. **G. Kane** a-10r, 18r; c-40, 44. **Kubert** a-10r, 21, 26. **Layton** a-21. **S. Mayer** c-29, 37, 41, 43, 47; a-28, 29, 37, 41, 43, 47, 58, 65, 68. **Moldoff** c-64p. **Morrow** a-40; c-40. **W. Mortimer** a-39p. **Newton** a-5, 51. **Perez** a-24, 50p; c-18, 21, 23. **Rogers** a-14, 51p. **Simonson** a-11r. **Spiegle** a-52. **Starlin** a-51. **Staton** a-5, 21. **Tuska** a-24. **Wolverton** a-60. **Wood** a-60, 63; c-60, 63. **Wrightson** a-60. New art in #14, 18, 24.*

BEST OF DENNIS THE MENACE, THE
Hallden/Fawcett Publications: Summer, 1959 - No. 5, Spring, 1961 (100 pgs.)
1-All reprints; Wiseman-a 8 16 24 55 78 100
2-5 5 10 15 36 48 60

BEST OF DONALD DUCK, THE
Gold Key: Nov, 1965 (12¢, 36 pgs.)(Lists 2nd printing in indicia)
1-Reprints Four Color #223 by Barks 9 18 27 60 85 110

BEST OF DONALD DUCK & UNCLE SCROOGE, THE
Gold Key: Nov, 1964 - No. 2, Sept, 1967 (25¢ Giants)
1(30022-411)('64)-Reprints 4-Color #189 & 408 by Carl Barks; cover of F.C. #189 redrawn by Barks 10 20 30 67 96 125
2(30022-709)('67)-Reprints 4-Color #256 & "Seven Cities of Cibola" & U.S. #8 by Barks
9 18 27 60 85 110

BEST OF HORROR AND SCIENCE FICTION COMICS
Bruce Webster: 1987 ($2.00)
1-Wolverton, Frazetta, Powell, Ditko-r 5.00

Best of Uncle Scrooge & Donald Duck © WDC

Best Western #58 © MAR

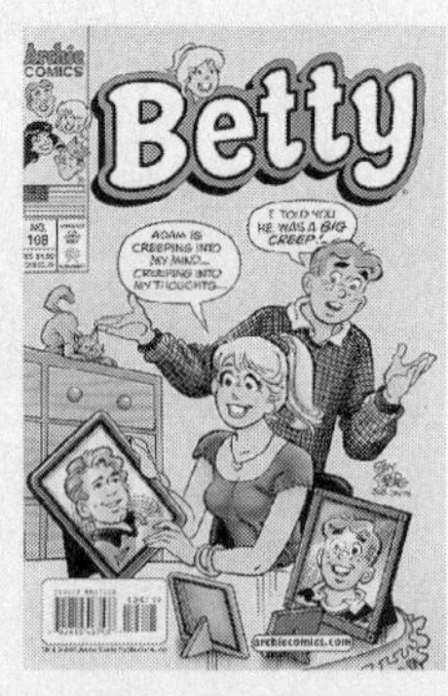

Betty #108 © AP

BEST OF JOSIE AND THE PUSSYCATS
Archie Comics: 2001 ($10.95, TPB)

	GD 2.0	VG 4.0	FN 6.0	VF 8.0	VF/NM 9.0	NM- 9.2
1-Reprints 1st app. and noteworthy stories						11.00

BEST OF MARMADUKE, THE
Charlton Comics: 1960

	GD 2.0	VG 4.0	FN 6.0	VF 8.0	VF/NM 9.0	NM- 9.2
1-Brad Anderson's strip reprints	3	7	10	21	28	35

BEST OF MS. TREE, THE
Pyramid Comics: 1987 - No. 4, 1988 ($2.00, B&W, limited series)

	GD 2.0	VG 4.0	FN 6.0	VF 8.0	VF/NM 9.0	NM- 9.2
1-4						2.50

BEST OF RAY BRADBURY, THE
ibooks: 2003 ($18.95, TPB)

	GD 2.0	VG 4.0	FN 6.0	VF 8.0	VF/NM 9.0	NM- 9.2
The Graphic Novel - Reprints from Ray Bradbury Comics; adaptations by various						19.00

BEST OF THE BRAVE AND THE BOLD, THE (See Super DC Giant)
DC Comics: Oct, 1988 - No. 6, Jan, 1989 ($2.50, limited series)

	GD 2.0	VG 4.0	FN 6.0	VF 8.0	VF/NM 9.0	NM- 9.2
1-6: Neal Adams-r, Kubert-r & Heath-r in all						4.00

BEST OF THE WEST (See A-1 Comics)
Magazine Enterprises: 1951 - No. 12, April-June, 1954

	GD 2.0	VG 4.0	FN 6.0	VF 8.0	VF/NM 9.0	NM- 9.2
1(A-1 42)-Ghost Rider, Durango Kid, Straight Arrow, Bobby Benson begin	40	80	120	244	372	500
2(A-1 46)	23	46	69	132	191	250
3(A-1 52), 4(A-1 59), 5(A-1 66)	19	38	57	107	154	200
6(A-1 70), 7(A-1 76), 8(A-1 81), 9(A-1 85), 10(A-1 87), 11(A-1 97), 12(A-1 103)	15	30	45	83	117	150

NOTE: ***Bolle** a-9. **Borth** a-12. **Guardineer** a-5, 12. **Powell** a-1, 12.*

BEST OF UNCLE SCROOGE & DONALD DUCK, THE
Gold Key: Nov, 1966 (25¢)

	GD 2.0	VG 4.0	FN 6.0	VF 8.0	VF/NM 9.0	NM- 9.2
1(30030-611)-Reprints part 4-Color #159 & 456 & Uncle Scrooge #6,7 by Carl Barks	9	18	27	60	85	110

BEST OF WALT DISNEY COMICS, THE
Western Publishing Co.: 1974 ($1.50, 52 pgs.) (Walt Disney)
(8-1/2x11" cardboard covers; 32,000 printed of each)

	GD 2.0	VG 4.0	FN 6.0	VF 8.0	VF/NM 9.0	NM- 9.2
96170-Reprints 1st two stories less 1 pg. each from 4-Color #62	4	8	12	29	40	50
96171-Reprints Mickey Mouse and the Bat Bandit of Inferno Gulch from 1934 (strips) by Gottfredson	4	8	12	29	40	50
96172-r/Uncle Scrooge #386 & two other stories	4	8	12	29	40	50
96173-Reprints "Ghost of the Grotto" (from 4-Color #159) & "Christmas on Bear Mountain" (from 4-Color #178)	4	8	12	29	40	50

BEST ROMANCE
Standard Comics (Visual Editions): No. 5, Feb-Mar, 1952 - No. 7, Aug, 1952

	GD 2.0	VG 4.0	FN 6.0	VF 8.0	VF/NM 9.0	NM- 9.2
5-Toth-a; photo-c	13	26	39	74	102	130
6,7-Photo-c	7	14	21	37	46	55

BEST SELLER COMICS (See Tailspin Tommy)

BEST WESTERN (Formerly Terry Toons? or Miss America Magazine
Marvel Comics (IPC): V7#24(#57)?; Western Outlaws & Sheriffs No. 60 on)
No. 58, June, 1949 - No. 59, Aug, 1949

	GD 2.0	VG 4.0	FN 6.0	VF 8.0	VF/NM 9.0	NM- 9.2
58,59-Black Rider, Kid Colt, Two-Gun Kid app.; both have Syd Shores-c	22	44	66	125	180	235

BETTIE PAGE COMICS
Dark Horse Comics: Mar, 1996 ($3.95)

	GD 2.0	VG 4.0	FN 6.0	VF 8.0	VF/NM 9.0	NM- 9.2
1-Dave Stevens-c; Blevins & Heath-a; Jaime Hernandez pin-up	1	2	3	4	5	7

BETTIE PAGE COMICS: QUEEN OF THE NILE
Dark Horse Comics: Dec, 1999 - No. 3, Apr, 2000 ($2.95, limited series)

	GD 2.0	VG 4.0	FN 6.0	VF 8.0	VF/NM 9.0	NM- 9.2
1-3-Silke-s/a; Stevens-c						3.00

BETTIE PAGE COMICS: SPICY ADVENTURE
Dark Horse Comics: Jan, 1997 ($2.95, one-shot, mature)

	GD 2.0	VG 4.0	FN 6.0	VF 8.0	VF/NM 9.0	NM- 9.2
nn-Silke-c/s/a						4.00

BETTY (See Pep Comics #22 for 1st app.)
Archie Comics: Sept, 1992 - Present ($1.25/$1.50/$1.75/$1.79/$1.99/$2.19)

	GD 2.0	VG 4.0	FN 6.0	VF 8.0	VF/NM 9.0	NM- 9.2
1						5.00
2-18,20-24: 20-1st Super Sleuther-s						3.00
19-Love Showdown part 2						5.00
25-Pin-up page of Betty as Marilyn Monroe, Madonna, Lady Di						5.00
26-50						3.00
51-145: 57- "A Storm Over Uniforms" x-over part 5,6						2.25

BETTY AND HER STEADY (Going Steady with Betty No. 1)
Avon Periodicals: No. 2, Mar-Apr, 1950

	GD 2.0	VG 4.0	FN 6.0	VF 8.0	VF/NM 9.0	NM- 9.2
2	10	20	30	56	73	90

BETTY AND ME
Archie Publications: Aug, 1965 - No. 200, Aug, 1992

	GD 2.0	VG 4.0	FN 6.0	VF 8.0	VF/NM 9.0	NM- 9.2
1	10	20	30	73	107	140
2,3: 3-Origin Superteen	6	12	18	40	55	70
4-8: Superteen in new costume #4-7; dons new helmet in #5, ends #8.	4	8	12	29	40	50
9,10: Girl from R.I.V.E.R.D.A.L.E. 9-UFO-s	4	8	12	22	30	38
11-15,17-20(4/69)	3	6	9	18	24	30
16-Classic cover; w/risqué cover dialogue	4	8	12	24	32	40
21,24-35: 33-Paper doll page	2	4	6	14	18	22
22-Archies Band-s	3	6	9	16	20	25
23-I Dream of Jeannie parody	3	6	9	18	24	30
36(8/71),37,41-55 (52 pgs.): 42-Betty as vamp-s	3	6	9	16	20	24
38-Sabrina app.	4	8	12	22	30	38
39-Josie and Sabrina cover cameos	3	6	9	19	25	32
40-Archie & Betty share a cabin	3	6	9	16	20	25
56(4/71)-80(12/76): 79 Betty Cooper mysteries thru #86. 79-81-Drago the Vampire-s	2	4	6	9	11	14
81-99: 83-Harem-c. 84-Jekyll & Hyde-c/s	1	3	4	6	8	10
100(3/79)	2	4	6	9	11	14
101,118: 101-Elvis mentioned. 118-Tarzan mentioned	1	2	3	5	6	8
102-117,119-130(9/82): 103,104-Space-s. 124-DeCarlo-c begins						6.00
131-138,140,142-147,149-154,156-158: 135,136-Jason Blossom app. 136-Cheryl Blossom cameo. 137-Space-s. 138-Tarzan parody						4.00
139,141,148: 139-Katy Keene collecting-s; Archie in drag-s. 141-Tarzan parody-s. 148-Cyndi Lauper parody-s						5.00
155,159,160(8/87): 155-Archie in drag-s. 159-Superhero gag-c. 160-Wheel of Fortune parody						5.00
161-169,171-199						3.00
170,200: 170-New Archie Superhero-s						5.00

BETTY AND VERONICA (Also see Archie's Girls...)
Archie Enterprises: June, 1987 - Present (75¢ /$1.25/$1.50/$1.75/$1.79/$1.99/$2.19)

	GD 2.0	VG 4.0	FN 6.0	VF 8.0	VF/NM 9.0	NM- 9.2
1	1	2	3	5	7	9
2-10						5.50
11-30						4.00
31-50						3.00
51-81						2.50
82-Love Showdown part 3						5.00
83-158						2.50
159-206						2.25
Summer Fun 1 (1994, $2.00, 52 pgs. plus poster)						3.00

BETTY & VERONICA ANNUAL DIGEST (...Digest Magazine #1-4, 44 on; ...Comics Digest Mag. #5-43)
Archie Publications: Nov, 1980 - Present ($1.00/$1.50/$1.75/$1.95/$1.99/$2.39, digest size)

	GD 2.0	VG 4.0	FN 6.0	VF 8.0	VF/NM 9.0	NM- 9.2
1	3	6	9	18	23	28
2-10: 2(11/81-Katy Keene story), 3(8/82)	2	4	6	10	13	16
11-30	1	3	4	6	8	10
31-50	1	2	3	4	5	7
51-70						4.00
71-154: 110-Begin $2.19-c. 135-Begin $2.39-c						2.40

BETTY & VERONICA ANNUAL DIGEST MAGAZINE
Archie Comics: Sept, 1989 - No. 16, Aug, 1997 ($1.50/$1.75/$1.79, 128 pgs.)

	GD 2.0	VG 4.0	FN 6.0	VF 8.0	VF/NM 9.0	NM- 9.2
1	1	2	3	5	7	9
2-10: 9-Neon ink logo						5.00
11-16: 16-Begin $1.79-c						3.00

BETTY & VERONICA CHRISTMAS SPECTACULAR (See Archie Giant Series Magazine #159, 168, 180, 191, 204, 217, 229, 241, 453, 465, 477, 489, 501, 513, 525, 536, 547, 558, 568, 580, 593, 606, 618)

BETTY & VERONICA DOUBLE DIGEST MAGAZINE
Archie Enterprises: 1987 - Present ($2.25-$2.99, digest size, 256 pgs.)(...Digest #12 on)

	GD 2.0	VG 4.0	FN 6.0	VF 8.0	VF/NM 9.0	NM- 9.2
1	2	4	6	8	10	12
2-10	1	2	3	4	5	7
11-25: 5,17-Xmas-c. 16-Capt. Hero story						5.00
26-50						4.00
51-131: 87-Begin $3.19-c. 95-Begin $3.29-c. 114-Begin $3.59-c						3.60

BETTY & VERONICA SPECTACULAR (See Archie Giant Series Mag. #11, 16, 21, 26, 32, 138, 145, 153, 162, 173, 184, 197, 201, 210, 214, 221, 226, 234, 238, 246, 250, 458, 462, 470, 482, 486, 494, 498, 506,

Beware the Creeper #2 © DC

Beyond #11 © ACE

Big Bang Comics V2#17 © Image

GD 2.0 | VG 4.0 | FN 6.0 | VF 8.0 | VF/NM 9.0 | NM- 9.2

510, 518, 522, 526, 530, 537, 552, 559, 563, 569, 575, 582, 588, 600, 608, 613, 620, 623, and Betty & Veronica)

BETTY AND VERONICA SPECTACULAR
Archie Comics: Oct, 1992 - Present ($1.25/$1.50/$1.75/$1.99/$2.19)
1-Dan DeCarlo-c/a 5.00
2-20 3.00
21-69: 48-Cheryl Blossom leaves Riverdale. 64-Cheryl Blossom returns 2.25

BETTY & VERONICA SPRING SPECTACULAR (See Archie Giant Series Magazine #569, 582, 595)

BETTY & VERONICA SUMMER FUN (See Archie Giant Series Mag. #8, 13, 18, 23, 28, 34, 140, 147, 155, 164, 175, 187, 199, 212, 224, 236, 248, 460, 484, 496, 508, 520, 529, 539, 550, 561, 572, 585, 598, 611, 621)
Archie Comics: 1994 - Present ($2.00/$2.25/$2.29)
1-6: 5-($2.25-c). 6-($2.29-c) 2.50
Vol. 1 (2003, $10.95) reprints stories from Archie Giant Series editions 11.00

BETTY BOOP'S BIG BREAK
First Publishing: 1990 ($5.95, 52 pgs.)
nn-By Joshua Quagmire; 60th anniversary ish. 6.00

BETTY PAGE 3-D COMICS
The 3-D Zone: 1991 ($3.95, "7-1/2x10-1/4," 28 pgs., no glasses)
1-Photo inside covers; back-c nudity 1 2 3 5 6 8

BETTY'S DIARY (See Archie Giant Series Magazine No. 555)
Archie Enterprises: April, 1986 - No. 40, Apr, 1991 (#1:65¢; 75¢/95¢)
1 6.00
2-10 4.00
11-40 2.50

BETTY'S DIGEST
Archie Enterprises: Nov, 1996 - No. 2 ($1.75/$1.79)
1,2 3.00

BEVERLY HILLBILLIES (TV)
Dell Publishing Co.: 4-6/63 - No. 18, 8/67; No. 19, 10/69; No. 20, 10/70; No. 21, Oct, 1971
1-Photo-c 18 36 54 126 193 260
2-Photo-c 10 20 30 70 100 130
3-9: All have photo covers 8 16 24 55 78 100
10: No photo cover 6 12 18 38 52 65
11-21: All have photo covers. 18-Last 12¢ issue. 19-21-Reprint #1-3 (covers and insides)
6 12 18 43 59 75
NOTE: *#1-9, 11-21 are photo covers.*

BEWARE (Formerly Fantastic; Chilling Tales No. 13 on)
Youthful Magazines: No. 10, June, 1952 - No. 12, Oct, 1952
10-E.A. Poe's Pit & the Pendulum adaptation by Wildey; Harrison/Bache-a; atom bomb and shrunken head-c 56 112 168 350 538 725
11-Harrison-a; Ambrose Bierce adapt. 39 78 117 222 324 425
12-Used in **SOTI**, pg. 388; Harrison-a 39 78 117 222 324 425

BEWARE
Trojan Magazines/Merit Publ. No. ?: No. 13, 1/53 - No. 16, 7/53; No. 5, 9/53 - No. 15, 5/55
13(#1)-Harrison-a 56 112 168 350 538 725
14(#2, 3/53)-Krenkel/Harrison-c; dismemberment, severed head panels
39 78 117 222 324 425
15,16(#3, 5/53; #4, 7/53)-Harrison-a 34 68 102 193 279 365
5,9,12,13 33 66 99 187 271 355
6-Ill. in **SOTI**- "Children are first shocked and then desensitized by all this brutality." Corpse on cover swipe/V.O.H. #26; girl on cover swipe/Advs. Into Darkness #10
59 118 177 369 565 760
7,8-Check-a 34 68 102 193 279 365
10-Frazetta/Check-c; Disbrow, Check-a 67 134 201 419 647 875
11-Disbrow-a; heart torn out, blood drainage 39 78 117 222 324 425
14,15: 14-Myron Fass-c. 15-Harrison-a 28 56 84 158 229 300
NOTE: ***Fass** a-5, 6, 8; c-6, 11, 14. **Forte** a-8. **Hollingsworth** a-15(#3), 16(#4), 9; c-16(#4), 8, 9. **Kiefer** a-16(#4), 5, 6, 10.*

BEWARE (Becomes Tomb of Darkness No. 9 on)
Marvel Comics Group: Mar, 1973 - No. 8, May, 1974 (All reprints)
1-Everett-c; Kirby & Sinnott-r ('54) 3 6 9 16 20 25
2-8: 2-Forte, Colan-r. 6-Tuska-a. 7-Torres-r/Mystical Tales #7
2 4 6 10 13 16
NOTE: ***Infantino** a-4r. **Gil Kane** c-4. **Wildey** a-7r.*

BEWARE TERROR TALES
Fawcett Publications: May, 1952 - No. 8, July, 1953
1-E.C. art swipe/Haunt of Fear #5 & Vault of Horror #26
47 94 141 287 436 585
2 32 64 96 184 267 350
3-7 26 52 78 150 215 280
8-Tothish-a; people being cooked-c 31 62 93 178 259 340
NOTE: ***Andru** a-2. **Bernard Bailey** a-1; c-1-5. **Powell** a-1, 2, 8. **Sekowsky** a-2.*

BEWARE THE CREEPER (See Adventure, Best of the Brave & the Bold, Brave & the Bold, 1st Issue Special, Flash #318-323, Showcase #73, World's Finest Comics #249)
National Periodical Publications: May-June, 1968 - No. 6, Mar-Apr, 1969 (All 12¢ issues)
1-(5-6/68)-Classic Ditko-c; Ditko-a in all 10 20 30 73 107 140
2-6: 2-5-Ditko-c. 2-Intro. Proteus. 6-Gil Kane-c 6 12 18 40 55 70

BEWARE THE CREEPER
DC Comics (Vertigo): June, 2003 - No. 5, Oct, 2003 ($2.95, limited series)
1-5-Female vigilante in 1920s Paris; Jason Hall-s/Cliff Chiang-a 3.00

BEWITCHED (TV)
Dell Publishing Co.: 4-6/65 - No. 11, 10/67; No. 12, 10/68 - No. 13, 1/69; No. 14, 10/69
1-Photo-c 17 34 51 121 186 250
2-No photo-c 9 18 27 63 89 115
3-13-All have photo-c. 12-Rep. #1. 13-Last 12¢-c 8 16 24 53 74 95
14-No photo-c; reprints #2 6 12 18 38 52 65

BEYOND, THE
Ace Magazines: Nov, 1950 - No. 30, Jan, 1955
1-Bakerish-a(p) 43 86 129 262 401 540
2-Bakerish-a(p) 30 60 90 170 245 320
3-10: 10-Woodish-a by Cameron 20 40 60 115 165 215
11-20: 18-Used in **POP**, pgs. 81,82 16 32 48 89 127 165
21-26,28-30 15 30 45 86 123 160
27-Used in **SOTI**, pg. 111 16 32 48 89 127 165
NOTE: ***Cameron** a-10, 11p, 12p, 15, 16, 21-27, 30; c-20. **Colan** a-6, 13, 17. **Sekowsky** a-2, 3, 5, 7, 11, 14, 27r. No. 1 was to appear as Challenge of the Unknown No. 7.*

BEYOND THE GRAVE
Charlton Comics: July, 1975 - No. 6, June, 1976; No. 7, Jan, 1983 - No. 17, Oct, 1984
1-Ditko-a (6 pgs.); Sutton painted-c 3 6 9 19 25 32
2-6: 2-5-Ditko-a; Ditko c-2,3,6 2 4 6 10 13 16
7-17: ('83-'84) Reprints. 13-Aparo-c(r). 15-Sutton-c (low print run) 6.00
Modern Comics Reprint 2('78) 4.00
NOTE: ***Howard** a-4. **Kim** a-1. **Larson** a-4, 6.*

BIBLE, THE: EDEN
IDW Publishing: 2003 ($21.99, hardcover graphic novel)
HC-Scott Hampton painted-a; adaptation of Genesis by Dave Elliot and Keith Giffen 22.00

BIBLE TALES FOR YOUNG FOLK (...Young People No. 3-5)
Atlas Comics (OMC): Aug, 1953 - No. 5, Mar, 1954
1 27 54 81 154 222 290
2-Everett, Krigstein-a 19 38 57 107 154 200
3-5: 4-Robinson-c 16 32 48 89 127 165

BIG (Movie)
Hit Comics (Dark Horse Comics): Mar, 1989 ($2.00)
1-Adaptation of film; Paul Chadwick-c 2.50

BIG ALL-AMERICAN COMIC BOOK, THE (See All-American Comics)
All-American/National Per. Publ.: 1944 (132 pgs., one-shot) (Early DC Annual)
1-Wonder Woman, Green Lantern, Flash, The Atom, Wildcat, Scribbly, The Whip, Ghost Patrol, Hawkman by Kubert (1st on Hawkman), Hop Harrigan, Johnny Thunder, Little Boy Blue, Mr. Terrific, Mutt & Jeff app.; Sargon on cover only; cover by Kubert/Hibbard/Mayer and others 935 1870 2805 6545 10,523 14,500

BIG BABY HUEY (See Baby Huey)

BIG BANG COMICS (Becomes Big Bang #4)
Caliber Press: Spring, 1994 - No. 4, Feb, 1995; No. 0, May, 1995 ($1.95, lim. series)
1-4-($1.95-c) 2.25
0-(5/95, $2.95) Alex Ross-c; color and B&W pages 3.00
Your Big Book of Big Bang Comics TPB ('98, $11.00) r/#0-2 11.00

BIG BANG COMICS (Volume 2)
Image Comics (Highbrow Ent.): V2#1, May, 1996 - No. 35, Jan, 2001 ($1.95-$3.95)
1-23,26: 1-Mighty Man app. 2-4-S.A. Shadowhawk app. 5-Begin $2.95-c. 6-Curt Swan/Murphy Anderson-c. 7-Begin B&W. 12-Savage Dragon-c/app. 16,17,21-Shadow Lady 3.00
24,25,27-35-($3.95): 24,27-History of Big Bang Comics Vol. 1,2. 35-Big Bang vs. Alan Moore's "1963" characters 4.00
...Round Table of America (2/04, $3.95) Don Thomas-a 4.00
...Summer Special (8/03, $4.95) World's Nastiest Nazis app. 5.00

BIG BLACK KISS
Vortex Comics: Sep, 1989 - No. 3, Nov, 1989 ($3.75, B&W, lim. series, mature)

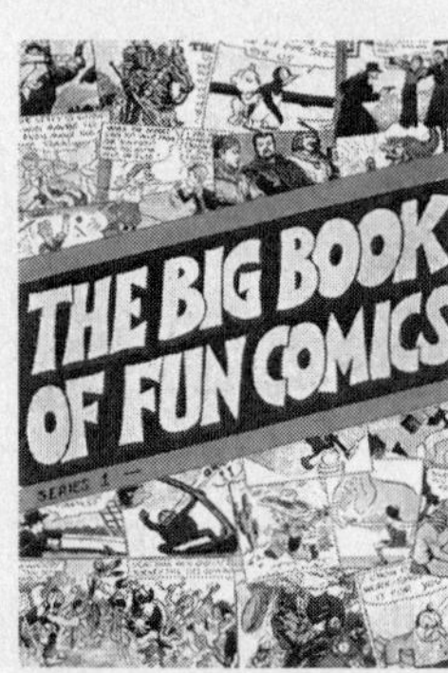

The Big Book of Fun Comics #1 © DC

Big Chief Wahoo #1 © EAS

Big Shot Comics #3 © DC

	GD 2.0	VG 4.0	FN 6.0	VF 8.0	VF/NM 9.0	NM- 9.2
1-3-Chaykin-s/a						4.00

BIG BLOWN BABY (Also see Dark Horse Presents)
Dark Horse Comics: Aug, 1996 - No. 4, Nov, 1996 ($2.95, lim. series, mature)

	GD	VG	FN	VF	VF/NM	NM-
1-4: Bill Wray-c/a/scripts						3.00

BIG BOOK OF ..., THE
DC Comics (Paradox Press): 1994 - Present (B&W)($12.95 - $14.95)
nn-...**BAD,** 1998 ($14.95),...**CONSPIRACIES,** 1995 ($12.95), ...**DEATH,** 1994 ($12.95), ...**FREAKS,** 1996 ($14.95), ...**GRIMM,** 1999 ($14.95), ...**HOAXES,** 1996 ($14.95), ...**LITTLE CRIMINALS,** 1996 ($14.95), ...**LOSERS,** 1997 ($14.95), **MARTYRS,** 1997 ($14.95), ...**SCANDAL,** 1997 ($14.95), ...**THE WEIRD WILD WEST,** 1998 ($14.95), ...**THUGS,** 1997 ($14.95), ...**UNEXPLAINED,** 1997 ($14.95), ...**URBAN LEGENDS,** 1994 ($12.95), ...**VICE,** 1999 ($14.95), ...**WEIRDOS,** 1995 ($12.95) cover price

BIG BOOK OF FUN COMICS (See New Book of Comics)
National Periodical Publications: Spring, 1936 (Large size, 52 pgs.)
(1st comic book annual & DC annual)

	GD	VG	FN	VF	VF/NM	NM-
1 (Very rare)-r/New Fun #1-5	2250	4500	6750	14,500	-	-

BIG BOOK ROMANCES
Fawcett Publications: Feb, 1950 (no date given) (148 pgs.)

	GD	VG	FN	VF	VF/NM	NM-
1-Contains remaindered Fawcett romance comics - several combinations possible	40	80	120	239	357	475

BIG BRUISERS
Image Comics (WildStorm Productions): July, 1996 ($3.50, one-shot)

	GD	VG	FN	VF	VF/NM	NM-
1-Features Maul from WildC.A.T.S, Impact from Cyberforce & Badrock from Youngblood						3.50

BIG CHIEF WAHOO
Eastern Color Printing/George Dougherty (distr. by Fawcett): July, 1942 - No. 7, Wint., 1943/44?(no year given)(Quarterly)

	GD	VG	FN	VF	VF/NM	NM-
1-Newspaper-r (on sale 6/15/42)	40	80	120	239	357	475
2-Steve Roper app.	23	46	69	132	191	250
3-5: 4-Chief is holding a Katy Keene comic	18	36	54	100	143	185
6-7	13	26	39	76	106	135

NOTE: *Kerry Drake in some issues.*

BIG CIRCUS, THE (Movie)
Dell Publishing Co.: No. 1036, Sept-Nov, 1959

	GD	VG	FN	VF	VF/NM	NM-
Four Color 1036-Photo-c	8	16	24	53	74	95

BIG COUNTRY, THE (Movie)
Dell Publishing Co.: No. 946, Oct, 1958

	GD	VG	FN	VF	VF/NM	NM-
Four Color 946-Photo-c	8	16	24	58	82	105

BIG DADDY DANGER
DC Comics: Oct, 2002 - No. 9, June, 2003 ($2.95, limited series)

	GD	VG	FN	VF	VF/NM	NM-
1-9-Adam Pollina-s/a/c						3.00

BIG DADDY ROTH (Magazine)
Millar Publications: Oct-Nov, 1964 - No. 4, Apr-May, 1965 (35¢)

	GD	VG	FN	VF	VF/NM	NM-
1-Toth-a	18	36	54	126	193	260
2-4-Toth-a	12	24	36	84	127	170

BIGG TIME
DC Comics (Vertigo): 2002 ($14.95, B&W, graphic novel)

	GD	VG	FN	VF	VF/NM	NM-
nn-Ty Templeton-s/c/a						15.00

BIG GUY AND RUSTY THE BOY ROBOT, THE (Also See Madman Comics #6,7 & Martha Washington Stranded In Space)
Dark Horse (Legend): July, 1995 - No. 2, Aug, 1995 ($4.95, oversize, limited series)

	GD	VG	FN	VF	VF/NM	NM-
1,2-Frank Miller scripts & Geoff Darrow-c/a	1	2	3	4	5	7
Trade paperback (10/96, $14.95)-r/1,2 w/cover gallery						15.00

BIG HERO ADVENTURES (See Jigsaw)

BIG HAIR PRODUCTIONS
Image Comics: Feb, 2000 - No. 2, Mar, 2000 ($3.50, B&W)

	GD	VG	FN	VF	VF/NM	NM-
1,2						3.50

BIG JON & SPARKIE (Radio)(Formerly Sparkie, Radio Pixie)
Ziff-Davis Publ. Co.: No. 4, Sept-Oct, 1952 (Painted-c)

	GD	VG	FN	VF	VF/NM	NM-
4-Based on children's radio program	21	42	63	118	169	220

BIG LAND, THE (Movie)
Dell Publishing Co.: No. 812, July, 1957

	GD	VG	FN	VF	VF/NM	NM-
Four Color 812-Alan Ladd photo-c	10	20	30	73	107	140

BIG RED (See Movie Comics)

BIG SHOT COMICS
Columbia Comics Group: May, 1940 - No. 104, Aug, 1949

	GD	VG	FN	VF	VF/NM	NM-
1-Intro. Skyman; The Face (1st app.; Tony Trent), The Cloak (Spy Master), Marvelo, Monarch of Magicians, Joe Palooka, Charlie Chan, Tom Kerry, Dixie Dugan, Rocky Ryan begin; Charlie Chan moves over from Feature Comics #31 (4/40)	238	476	714	1488	2294	3100
2	87	174	261	544	835	1125
3-The Cloak called Spy Chief; Skyman-c	77	154	231	481	741	1000
4,5	56	112	168	350	538	725
6-10: 8-Christmas-c	45	90	135	275	418	560
11-13	40	80	120	244	372	500
14-Origin & 1st app. Sparky Watts (6/41)	44	88	132	268	409	550
15-Origin The Cloak	45	90	135	275	418	560
16-20	35	70	105	201	293	385
21-23,26,27,29,30: 29-Intro. Capt. Yank; Bo (a dog) newspaper strip-r by Frank Beck begin, ends #104. 30-X-Mas-c	30	60	90	170	245	320
24-Classic Tojo-c.	42	84	126	256	391	525
25-Hitler-c	37	74	111	209	305	400
28-Hitler, Tojo & Mussolini-c	48	96	144	293	447	600
31,33-40	22	44	66	127	184	240
32-Vic Jordan newspaper strip reprints begin, ends #52; Hitler, Tojo & Mussolini-c	40	80	120	235	348	460
41,42,44,45,47-50: 42-No Skyman. 50-Origin The Face retold	19	38	57	107	154	200
43-Hitler-c	33	66	99	190	275	360
46-Hitler, Tojo-c (6/44)	31	62	93	178	259	340
51-56,58-60	16	32	48	89	127	165
57-Hitler, Tojo Halloween mask-c	23	46	69	132	191	250
61-70: 63 on-Tony Trent, the Face	13	26	39	76	106	135
71-80: 73-The Face cameo. 74-(2/47)-Mickey Finn begins. 74,80-The Face app. in Tony Trent. 78-Last Charlie Chan strip-r	12	24	36	71	98	125
81-90: 85-Tony Trent marries Babs Walsh. 86-Valentines-c	10	20	30	58	77	95
91-99,101-104: 69-94-Skyman in Outer Space. 96-Xmas-c	9	18	27	52	66	80
100	10	20	30	60	80	100

NOTE: ***Mart Bailey** art on "The Face" No. 1-104. **Guardineer** a-5. Sparky Watts by **Boody Rogers**-No. 14-42, 77-104, (by others No. 43-76). Others than Tony Trent wear "The Face" mask in No. 46-63, 93. Skyman by **Ogden Whitney**-No. 1, 2, 4, 12-37, 49, 70-101. Skyman covers-No. 1, 3, 7-12, 14, 16, 20, 27, 89, 95, 100.*

BIG SMASH BARGAIN COMICS
No publisher listed: Early 1950s (25¢, 160pgs., Canadian reprints)

	GD	VG	FN	VF	VF/NM	NM-
1-4: Contains 4 comics from various companies bundled with new cover (scarce)	28	56	84	158	229	300

BIG TEX
Toby Press: June, 1953

	GD	VG	FN	VF	VF/NM	NM-
1-Contains (3) John Wayne stories-r with name changed to Big Tex	10	20	30	60	80	100

BIG-3
Fox Features Syndicate: Fall, 1940 - No. 7, Jan, 1942

	GD	VG	FN	VF	VF/NM	NM-
1-Blue Beetle, The Flame, & Samson begin	231	462	693	1444	2222	3000
2	90	180	270	563	869	1175
3-5	64	128	192	400	613	825
6,7: 6-Last Samson. 7-V-Man app.	50	100	150	305	465	625

BIG TOP COMICS, THE (TV's Great Circus Show)
Toby Press: 1951 - No. 2, 1951 (No month)

	GD	VG	FN	VF	VF/NM	NM-
1	10	20	30	60	80	100
2	9	18	27	49	62	75

BIG TOWN (Radio/TV) (Also see Movie Comics, 1946)
National Periodical Publ: Jan, 1951 - No. 50, Mar-Apr, 1958 (No. 1-9: 52pgs.)

	GD	VG	FN	VF	VF/NM	NM-
1-Dan Barry-a begins	66	132	198	413	637	860
2	37	74	111	209	305	400
3-10	22	44	66	123	177	230
11-20	16	32	48	89	127	165
21-31: Last pre-code (1-2/55)	12	24	36	71	98	125
32-50	10	20	30	56	73	90

BIG VALLEY, THE (TV)
Dell Publishing Co.: June, 1966 - No. 5, Oct, 1967; No. 6, Oct, 1969

	GD	VG	FN	VF	VF/NM	NM-
1: Photo-c #1-5	6	12	18	43	59	75
2-6: 6-Reprints #1	4	8	12	25	33	42

Billy Bunny #1 © Excellent Prod.

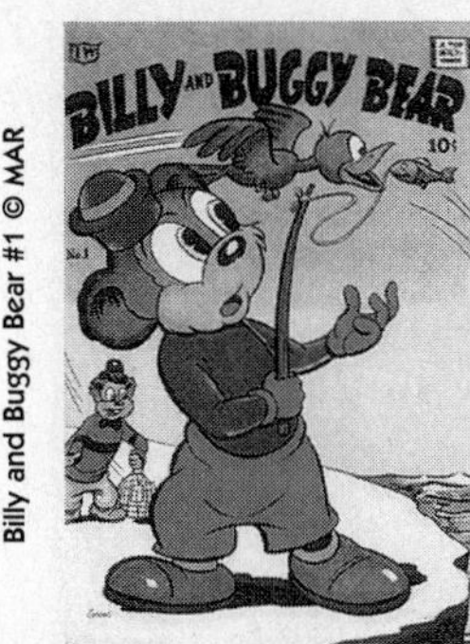

Billy and Buggy Bear #1 © MAR

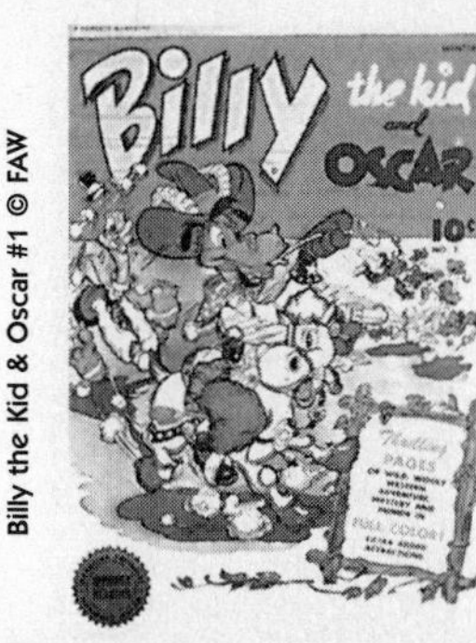

Billy the Kid & Oscar #1 © FAW

BIKER MICE FROM MARS (TV)
Marvel Comics: Nov, 1993 - No. 3, Jan, 1994 ($1.50, limited series)

	GD 2.0	VG 4.0	FN 6.0	VF 8.0	VF/NM 9.0	NM- 9.2
1-3: 1-Intro Vinnie, Modo & Throttle. 2-Origin						3.50

BILL & TED'S BOGUS JOURNEY
Marvel Comics: Sept, 1991 ($2.95, squarebound, 84 pgs.)

	GD 2.0	VG 4.0	FN 6.0	VF 8.0	VF/NM 9.0	NM- 9.2
1-Adapts movie sequel						3.00

BILL & TED'S EXCELLENT COMIC BOOK (Movie)
Marvel Comics: Dec, 1991 - No. 12, 1992 ($1.00/$1.25)

	GD 2.0	VG 4.0	FN 6.0	VF 8.0	VF/NM 9.0	NM- 9.2
1-12: 3-Begin $1.25-c						2.50

BILL BARNES COMICS (...America's Air Ace Comics No. 2 on) (Becomes Air Ace V2#1 on; also see Shadow Comics)
Street & Smith Publications: Oct, 1940(No. month given) - No. 12, Oct, 1943

	GD 2.0	VG 4.0	FN 6.0	VF 8.0	VF/NM 9.0	NM- 9.2
1-23 pgs.-comics; Rocket Rooney begins	85	170	255	531	816	1100
2-Barnes as The Phantom Flyer app.; Tuska-a	43	86	129	262	401	540
3-5	40	80	120	230	335	440
6-12	35	70	105	198	287	375

BILL BATTLE, THE ONE MAN ARMY (Also see Master Comics No. 133)
Fawcett Publications: Oct, 1952 - No. 4, Apr, 1953 (All photo-c)

	GD 2.0	VG 4.0	FN 6.0	VF 8.0	VF/NM 9.0	NM- 9.2
1	14	28	42	79	110	140
2	8	16	24	46	58	70
3,4	8	16	24	40	50	60

BILL BLACK'S FUN COMICS
Paragon #1-3/Americomics #4: Dec, 1982 - No. 4, Mar, 1983 ($1.75/$2.00, Baxter paper) (1st AC comic)

	GD 2.0	VG 4.0	FN 6.0	VF 8.0	VF/NM 9.0	NM- 9.2
1-(B&W fanzine; 7x8-1/2"; low print) Intro. Capt. Paragon, Phantom Lady & Commando D	2	4	6	14	18	22
2-4: 2,3-(B&W fanzines; 8-1/2x11"). 3-Kirby-c. 4-($2.00, color)-Origin Nightfall (formerly Phantom Lady); Nightveil app.; Kirby-a	1	3	4	6	8	10

BILL BOYD WESTERN (Movie star; see Hopalong Cassidy & Western Hero)
Fawcett Publ: Feb, 1950 - No. 23, June, 1952 (1-3,7,11,14-on: 36 pgs.)

	GD 2.0	VG 4.0	FN 6.0	VF 8.0	VF/NM 9.0	NM- 9.2
1-Bill Boyd & his horse Midnite begin; photo front/back-c	48	96	144	293	447	600
2-Painted-c	28	56	84	158	229	300
3-Photo-c begin, end #23; last photo back-c	21	42	63	118	169	220
4-6(52 pgs.)	17	34	51	98	139	180
7,11(36 pgs.)	14	28	42	79	110	140
8-10,12,13(52 pgs.)	14	28	42	81	113	145
14-22	13	26	39	74	102	130
23-Last issue	14	28	42	79	110	140

BILL BUMLIN (See Treasury of Comics No. 3)

BILL ELLIOTT (See Wild Bill Elliott)

BILLI 99
Dark Horse Comics: Sept, 1991 - No. 4, 1991 ($3.50, B&W, lim. series, 52 pgs.)

	GD 2.0	VG 4.0	FN 6.0	VF 8.0	VF/NM 9.0	NM- 9.2
1-4: Tim Sale-c/a						3.50

BILL STERN'S SPORTS BOOK
Ziff-Davis Publ. Co.(Approved Comics): Spring-Sum, 1951 - V2#2, Win, 1952

	GD 2.0	VG 4.0	FN 6.0	VF 8.0	VF/NM 9.0	NM- 9.2
V1#10-(1951)	22	44	66	127	184	240
2-(Sum/52; reg. size)	17	34	51	95	135	175
V2#2-(1952, 96 pgs.)-Krigstein, Kinstler-a	23	46	69	132	191	250

BILL THE BULL: ONE SHOT, ONE BOURBON, ONE BEER
Boneyard Press: Dec, 1994 ($2.95, B&W, mature)

	GD 2.0	VG 4.0	FN 6.0	VF 8.0	VF/NM 9.0	NM- 9.2
1						3.00

BILL THE CLOWN
Slave Labor Graphics: Feb, 1992 ($2.50, one-shot)

	GD 2.0	VG 4.0	FN 6.0	VF 8.0	VF/NM 9.0	NM- 9.2
1 ,1-(2nd printing, 4/93, $2.95)						3.00
Comedy Isn't Pretty 1 (11/92, $2.50)						3.00
Death & Clown White 1 (9/93, $2.95)						3.00

BILLY AND BUGGY BEAR (See Animal Fun)
I.W. Enterprises/Super: 1958; 1964

	GD 2.0	VG 4.0	FN 6.0	VF 8.0	VF/NM 9.0	NM- 9.2
I.W. Reprint #1, #7('58)-All Surprise Comics #?(Same issue-r for both)	2	4	6	11	14	18
Super Reprint #10(1964)	2	4	6	9	11	14

BILLY BUCKSKIN WESTERN (2-Gun Western No. 4)
Atlas Comics (IMC No. 1/MgPC No. 2,3): Nov, 1955 - No. 3, Mar, 1956

	GD 2.0	VG 4.0	FN 6.0	VF 8.0	VF/NM 9.0	NM- 9.2
1-Mort Drucker-a; Maneely-c/a	16	32	48	89	127	165
2-Mort Drucker-a	10	20	30	58	77	95
3-Williamson, Drucker-a	12	24	36	69	95	120

BILLY BUNNY (Black Cobra No. 6 on)
Excellent Publications: Feb-Mar, 1954 - No. 5, Oct-Nov, 1954

	GD 2.0	VG 4.0	FN 6.0	VF 8.0	VF/NM 9.0	NM- 9.2
1	9	18	27	51	62	75
2	6	12	18	27	33	38
3-5	5	10	15	23	28	32

BILLY BUNNY'S CHRISTMAS FROLICS
Farrell Publications: 1952 (25¢ Giant, 100 pgs.)

	GD 2.0	VG 4.0	FN 6.0	VF 8.0	VF/NM 9.0	NM- 9.2
1	21	42	63	118	169	220

BILLY COLE
Cult Press: May, 1994 - No. 4, Aug, 1994 ($2.75, B&W, limited series)

	GD 2.0	VG 4.0	FN 6.0	VF 8.0	VF/NM 9.0	NM- 9.2
1-4						2.75

BILLY MAKE BELIEVE
United Features Syndicate: No. 14, 1939

	GD 2.0	VG 4.0	FN 6.0	VF 8.0	VF/NM 9.0	NM- 9.2
Single Series 14	32	64	96	184	267	350

BILLY NGUYEN, PRIVATE EYE
Caliber Press: V2#1, 1990 ($2.50)

	GD 2.0	VG 4.0	FN 6.0	VF 8.0	VF/NM 9.0	NM- 9.2
V2#1						2.50

BILLY THE KID (Formerly The Masked Raider; also see Doc Savage Comics & Return of the Outlaw)
No. 9, Nov, 1957 - No. 121, Dec, 1976; No. 122, Sept, 1977 - No. 123,
Charlton Publ. Co.: Oct, 1977; No. 124, Feb, 1978 - No. 153, Mar, 1983

	GD 2.0	VG 4.0	FN 6.0	VF 8.0	VF/NM 9.0	NM- 9.2
9	10	20	30	58	77	95
10,12,14,17-19: 12-2 pg Check-sty	7	14	21	37	46	55
11-(68 pgs.)-Origin & 1st app. The Ghost Train	9	18	27	49	62	75
13-Williamson/Torres-a	8	16	24	43	54	65
15-Origin; 2 pgs. Williamson-a	8	16	24	43	54	65
16-Williamson-a, 2 pgs.	8	16	24	40	50	60
20-26-Severin-a(3-4 each)	8	16	24	43	54	65
27-30: 30-Masked Rider app.	3	7	10	21	28	35
31-40	3	6	9	16	20	25
41-60	2	4	6	12	16	20
61-65	2	4	6	10	12	15
66-Bounty Hunter series begins.	2	4	6	11	14	18
67-80: Bounty Hunter series; not in #79,82,84-86	2	4	6	9	11	14
81-90: 87-Last Bounty Hunter	1	2	3	5	7	9
91-123: 110-Dr. Young of Boothill app. 111-Origin The Ghost Train. 117-Gunsmith & Co., The Cheyenne Kid app.						6.00
124(2/78)-153						4.00
Modern Comics 109 (1977 reprint)						4.00

NOTE: ***Boyette*** *a-91-110.* ***Kim*** *a-73.* ***Morsi*** *a-12,14.* ***Sattler*** *a-118-123.* ***Severin*** *a(r)-121-129, 134; c-23, 25.* ***Sutton*** *a-111.*

BILLY THE KID ADVENTURE MAGAZINE
Toby Press: Oct, 1950 - No. 29, 1955

	GD 2.0	VG 4.0	FN 6.0	VF 8.0	VF/NM 9.0	NM- 9.2
1-Williamson/Frazetta-a (2 pgs) r/from John Wayne Adventure Comics #2; photo-c	31	62	93	178	259	340
2-Photo-c	11	22	33	64	87	110
3-Williamson/Frazetta "The Claws of Death", 4 pgs. plus Williamson art	35	70	105	200	290	380
4,5,7,8,10: 4,7-Photo-c	9	18	27	52	66	80
6-Frazetta assist on "Nightmare"; photo-c	15	30	45	86	123	160
9-Kurtzman Pot-Shot Pete; photo-c	11	22	33	66	91	115
11,12,15-20: 11-Photo-c	8	16	24	43	54	65
13-Kurtzman-r/John Wayne #12 (Genius)	9	18	27	51	62	75
14-Williamson/Frazetta; r-of #1 (2 pgs.)	10	20	30	58	77	95
21,23-29	7	14	21	37	46	55
22-Williamson/Frazetta-r(1pg.)/#1; photo-c	8	16	24	43	54	65

BILLY THE KID AND OSCAR (Also see Fawcett's Funny Animals)
Fawcett Publications: Winter, 1945 - No. 3, Summer, 1946 (Funny animal)

	GD 2.0	VG 4.0	FN 6.0	VF 8.0	VF/NM 9.0	NM- 9.2
1	15	30	45	86	123	160
2,3	10	20	30	58	77	95

BILLY WEST (Bill West No. 9,10)
Standard Comics (Visual Editions): 1949-No. 9, Feb, 1951; No. 10, Feb, 1952

	GD 2.0	VG 4.0	FN 6.0	VF 8.0	VF/NM 9.0	NM- 9.2
1	14	28	42	79	110	140
2	8	16	24	46	58	70
3-6,9,10	7	14	21	37	46	55
7,8-Schomburg-c	8	16	24	43	54	65

NOTE: ***Celardo*** *a-1-6, 9; c-1-3.* ***Moreira*** *a-3.* ***Roussos*** *a-2.*

Birds of Prey #59 © DC

Bishop The Last X-Man #1 © MAR

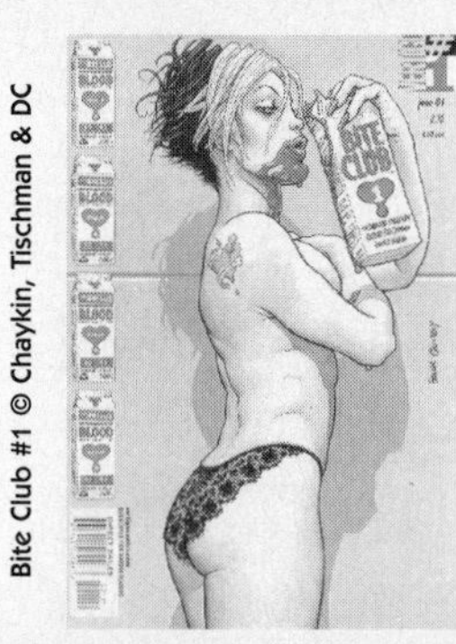

Bite Club #1 © Chaykin, Tischman & DC

GD 2.0 | VG 4.0 | FN 6.0 | VF 8.0 | VF/NM 9.0 | NM- 9.2

BING CROSBY (See Feature Films)

BINGO (...Comics) (H. C. Blackerby)
Howard Publ.: 1945 (Reprints National material)

1-L. B. Cole opium-c 37 74 111 209 305 400

BINGO, THE MONKEY DOODLE BOY
St. John Publishing Co.: Aug, 1951; Oct, 1953

1(8/51)-By Eric Peters 8 16 24 40 50 60
1(10/53) 6 12 18 28 34 40

BINKY (Formerly Leave It to...)
National Periodical Publ./DC Comics: No. 72, 4-5/70 - No. 81, 10-11/71; No. 82,Summer/77

72-76 3 6 9 18 24 30
77-79: (68pgs.). 77-Bobby Sherman 1pg. story w/photo. 78-1 pg. sty on Barry Williams of Brady Bunch. 79-Osmonds 1pg. story 5 10 15 33 44 55
80,81 (52pgs.)-Sweat Pain story 4 8 12 27 36 45
82 (1977, one-shot) 4 8 12 22 30 38

BINKY'S BUDDIES
National Periodical Publications: Jan-Feb, 1969 - No. 12, Nov-Dec, 1970

1 6 12 18 40 55 70
2-12: 3-Last 12¢ issue 3 7 10 21 28 35

BIONEERS
Mirage Publishing: Aug, 1994 ($2.75)

1-w/bound-in trading card 2.75

BIONIC WOMAN, THE (TV)
Charlton Publications: Oct, 1977 - No. 5, June, 1978

1 3 6 9 16 20 25
2-5 2 4 6 10 12 15

BIRDS OF PREY (Also see Black Canary/Oracle: Birds of Prey)
DC Comics: Jan, 1999 - Present ($1.99/$2.50)

1-Dixon-s/Land-c/a 1 3 4 6 8 10
2-4 6.00
6,7,9-15: 15-Guice-a begins. 4.00
8-Nightwing-c/app.; Barbara & Dick's circus date 2 4 6 10 12 15
16-38: 23-Grodd-c/app. 26-Bane app. 32-Noto-c begin 2.50
39,40-Bruce Wayne: Murderer pt. 5,12 3.00
41-Bruce Wayne: Fugitive pt. 2 4.00
42-46: 42-Fabry-a. 45-Deathstroke-c/app. 2.50
47-74,76,77: 47-49-Terry Moore-s/Conner & Palmiotti-a; Noto-c. 50-Gilbert Hernandez-s begin. 52,54-Metamorpho app. 56-Simone-s/Benes-a begin. 65,67,68,70-Land-c 2.50
75-($2.95) Pearson-c; back-up story of Lady Blackhawk 3.00
TPB (1999, $17.95) r/ previous series and one-shots 18.00
...: Batgirl 1 (2/98, $2.95) Dixon-s/Frank-c 5.00
...: Batgirl/Catwoman 1 ('03, $5.95) Robertson-a; cont'd in BOP: Catwoman/Oracle 1 6.00
...: Catwoman/Oracle 1 ('03, $5.95) Cont'd from BOP: Batgirl/Catwoman 1; David Ross-a 6.00
...: Of Like Minds TPB (2004, $14.95) r/#55-61 15.00
...: Old Friends, New Enemies TPB (2003, $17.95) r/#1-6, ...: Batgirl, ...: Wolves 18.00
...: Revolution 1 (1997, $2.95) Frank-c/Dixon-s 5.00
... Secret Files 2003 (8/03, $4.95) Short stories, pin-ups and profile pages; Noto-c 5.00
...: The Ravens 1 (6/98, $1.95)-Dixon-s; Girlfrenzy issue 4.00
...: Wolves 1 (10/97, $2.95) Dixon-s/Giordano & Faucher-a 5.00

BIRDS OF PREY: MANHUNT
DC Comics: Sept, 1996 - No. 4, Dec, 1996 ($1.95, limited series)

1-Features Black Canary, Oracle, Huntress, & Catwoman; Chuck Dixon scripts; Gary Frank-c on all. 1-Catwoman cameo only 1 2 3 5 6 8
2-4 6.00

NOTE: ***Gary Frank*** *c-1-4.* ***Matt Haley*** *a-1-4p.* ***Wade Von Grawbadger*** *a-1i.*

BIRTH CAUL, THE
Eddie Campbell Comics: 1999 ($5.95, B&W, one-shot)

1-Alan Moore-s/Eddie Campbell-a 6.00

BIRTH OF THE DEFIANT UNIVERSE, THE
Defiant Comics: May, 1993

nn-Contains promotional artwork & text; limited print run of 1000 copies. 2 4 6 8 10 12

BISHOP (See Uncanny X-Men & X-Men)
Marvel Comics: Dec, 1994 - No.4, Mar, 1995 ($2.95, limited series)

1-4: Foil-c; Shard & Mountjoy in all. 1-Storm app. 3.00

BISHOP THE LAST X-MAN
Marvel Comics: Oct, 1999 - No. 16, Jan, 2001 ($2.99/$1.99/$2.25)

1-($2.99)-Jeanty-a 3.50
2-8-($1.99): 2-Two covers 2.50
9-11,13-16: 9-Begin $2.25-c. 15-Maximum Security x-over; Xavier app. 2.50
12-($2.99) 3.00

BISHOP: XAVIER SECURITY ENFORCER
Marvel Comics: Jan, 1998 - No.3, Mar, 1998 ($2.50, limited series)

1-3: Ostrander-s 3.00

BITE CLUB
DC Comics (Vertigo): Jun, 2004 - No. 6, Nov, 2004 ($2.95, limited series)

1-4-Chaykin-s/Tischman-a/Quitely-c 3.00

BIZARRE ADVENTURES (Formerly Marvel Preview)
Marvel Comics Group: No. 25, 3/81 - No. 34, 2/83 (#25-33: Magazine-$1.50)

25,26: 25-Lethal Ladies. 26-King Kull; Bolton-c/a 1 3 4 6 8 10
27,28: 27-Phoenix, Iceman & Nightcrawler app. 28-The Unlikely Heroes; Elektra by Miller; Neal Adams-a 2 4 6 10 13 16
29,30,32,33: 29-Stephen King's Lawnmower Man. 30-Tomorrow; 1st app. Silhouette. 32-Gods; Thor-c/s. 33-Horror; Dracula app.; photo-c 1 2 3 5 7 9
31-After The Violence Stops; new Hangman story; Miller-a 1 3 4 6 8 10
34 ($2.00, Baxter paper, comic size)-Son of Santa; Christmas special; Howard the Duck by Paul Smith 1 2 3 5 6 8

NOTE: ***Alcala*** *a-27i.* ***Austin*** *a-25i, 28i.* ***Bolton*** *a-26, 32.* ***J. Buscema*** *a-27p, 29, 30p; c-26.* ***Byrne*** *a-31 (2 pg.).* ***Golden*** *a-25p, 28p.* ***Perez*** *a-27p.* ***Rogers*** *a-25p.* ***Simonson*** *a-29; c-29.* ***Paul Smith*** *a-34.*

BIZARRO COMICS!
DC Comics: 2001 ($29.95, hardcover, one-shot)

HC-Short stories by various alternative cartoonists including Dorkin, Pope, Fingerman, Abel Haspiel, Kidd, Kochalka, Millionaire, Stephens, Wray; includes "Superman's Babysitter" by Kyle Baker from Elseworlds 80-Page Giant recalled by DC; Groening-c 30.00
Softcover (2003, $19.95) 20.00

BLACK AND WHITE (See Large Feature Comic, Series I)

BLACK & WHITE (Also see Codename: Black & White)
Image Comics (Extreme): Oct,1994 - No. 3, Jan,1995 ($1.95, limited series)

1-3: Thibert-c/story 2.25

BLACK & WHITE MAGIC
Innovation Publishing: 1991 ($2.95, 98 pgs., B&W w/30 pgs. color, squarebound)

1-Contains rebound comics w/covers removed; contents may vary 3.00

BLACK AXE
Marvel Comics (UK): Apr, 1993 - No. 7, Oct, 1993 ($1.75)

1-4: 1-Romita Jr.-c. 2-Sunfire-c/s 3.00
5-7: 5-Janson-c; Black Panther app. 6,7-Black Panther-c/s 3.00

BLACKBALL COMICS
Blackball Comics: Mar, 1994 ($3.00)

1-Trencher-c/story by Giffen; John Pain by O'Neill 3.00

BLACKBEARD'S GHOST (See Movie Comics)

BLACK BEAUTY (See Son of Black Beauty)
Dell Publishing Co.: No. 440, Dec, 1952

Four Color 440 4 8 12 29 40 50

BLACKBURNE COVENANT, THE
Dark Horse Comics: Apr, 2003 - No. 4, July, 2003 ($2.99, limited series)

1-4-Nicieza-s/Raffaele-a 3.00
TPB (2003, $12.95) r/#1-4 13.00

BLACK CANARY (See All Star Comics #38, Flash Comics #86, Justice League of America #75 & World's Finest #244)
DC Comics: Nov, 1991 - No. 4, Feb, 1992 ($1.75, limited series)

1-4 2.50

BLACK CANARY
DC Comics: Jan, 1993 - No. 12, Dec, 1993 ($1.75)

1-7 2.50
8-12: 8-The Ray-c/story. 9,10-Huntress-c/story 3.00

BLACK CANARY/ORACLE: BIRDS OF PREY (Also see Showcase '96 #3)
DC Comics: 1996 ($3.95, one-shot)

1-Chuck Dixon scripts & Gary Frank-c/a. 1 2 3 5 7 9

BLACK CAT COMICS (...Western #16-19; ...Mystery #30 on)
(See All-New #7,9, The Original Black Cat, Pocket & Speed Comics)
Harvey Publications (Home Comics): June-July, 1946 - No. 29, June, 1951

Black Cobra #1 © Farrell

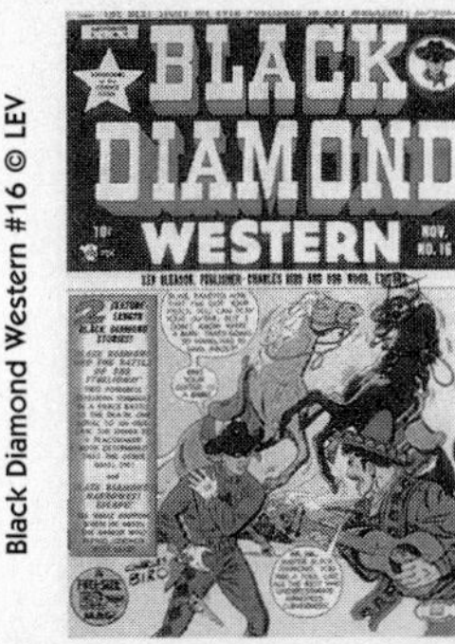

Black Diamond Western #16 © LEV

Blackhawk #12 © QUA

	GD 2.0	VG 4.0	FN 6.0	VF 8.0	VF/NM 9.0	NM- 9.2
1-Kubert-a; Joe Simon c-1-3	71	142	213	444	685	925
2-Kubert-a	40	80	120	233	342	450
3,4: 4-The Red Demons begin (The Demon #4 & 5)	32	64	96	184	267	350
5,6,7: 5,6-The Scarlet Arrow app. in ea. by Powell; S&K-a in both. 6-Origin Red Demon. 7-Vagabond Prince by S&K plus 1 more story	40	80	120	230	335	440
8-S&K-a; Kerry Drake begins, ends #13	35	70	105	200	290	380
9-Origin Stuntman (r/Stuntman #1)	39	78	117	227	331	435
10-20: 14,15,17-Mary Worth app. plus Invisible Scarlet O'Neil-#15,20,24	27	54	81	154	222	290
21-26	22	44	66	125	180	235
27,28: 27-Used in **SOTI**, pg. 193; X-Mas-c; 2 pg. John Wayne story. 28-Intro. Kit, Black Cat's new sidekick	23	46	69	132	191	250
29-Black Cat bondage-c; Black Cat stories	23	46	69	130	188	245

BLACK CAT MYSTERY (Formerly Black Cat; ...Western Mystery #54; ...Western #55,56; ...Mystery #57; ...Mystic #58-62; Black Cat #63-65)
Harvey Publications: No. 30, Aug, 1951 - No. 65, Apr, 1963

	GD 2.0	VG 4.0	FN 6.0	VF 8.0	VF/NM 9.0	NM- 9.2
30-Black Cat on cover only	31	62	93	178	259	340
31,32,34,37,38,40	24	48	72	138	199	260
33-Used in **POP**, pg. 89; electrocution-c	27	54	81	154	222	290
35-Atomic disaster cover/story	30	60	90	173	249	325
36,39-Used in **SOTI**: #36-Pgs. 270,271; #39-Pgs. 386-388	29	58	87	167	241	315
41-43	24	48	72	138	199	260
44-Eyes, ears, tongue cut out; Nostrand-a	26	52	78	147	211	275
45-Classic "Colorama" by Powell; Nostrand-a	40	80	120	239	357	475
46-49,51-Nostrand-a in all	25	50	75	144	207	270
50-Check-a; classic Warren Kremer-c showing a man's face & hands burning away	73	146	219	456	703	950
52,53 (r/#34 & 35)	16	32	48	89	127	165
54-Two Black Cat stories (2/55, last pre-code)	19	38	57	107	154	200
55,56-Black Cat app.	16	32	48	89	127	165
57(7/56)-Kirby-c	16	32	48	89	127	165
58-60-Kirby-a(4). 58,59-Kirby-c. 60,61-Simon-c	21	42	63	118	169	220
61-Nostrand-a; "Colorama" r/#45	19	38	57	107	154	200
62 (3/58)-E.C. story swipe	15	30	45	85	120	155
63-65: Giants(10/62,1/63, 4/63); Reprints; Black Cat app. 63-origin Black Kitten. 65-1 pg. Powell-a	19	38	57	107	154	200

NOTE: ***Kremer** a-37, 39, 43; c-36, 37, 47. **Meskin** a-51. **Palais** a-30, 31(2), 32(2), 33-35, 37-40. **Powell** a-32-35, 36(2), 40, 41, 43-53, 57. **Simon** c-63-65. **Sparling** a-44. Bondage c-32, 34, 43.*

BLACK COBRA (Bride's Diary No. 4 on) (See Captain Flight #8)
Ajax/Farrell Publications(Excellent Publ.): No. 1, 10-11/54; No. 6(No. 2), 12-1/54-55; No. 3, 2-3/55

	GD 2.0	VG 4.0	FN 6.0	VF 8.0	VF/NM 9.0	NM- 9.2
1-Re-intro Black Cobra & The Cobra Kid (costumed heroes)	35	70	105	198	287	375
6(#2)-Formerly Billy Bunny	19	38	57	107	154	200
3-(Pre-code)-Torpedoman app.	18	36	54	100	143	185

BLACK CONDOR (Also see Crack Comics, Freedom Fighters & Showcase '94 #10,11)
DC Comics: June, 1992 - No. 12, May, 1993 ($1.25)

	NM- 9.2
1-8-Heath-c	2.50
9-12: 9,10,12-Heath-c. 9,10-The Ray app. 12-Batman-c/app.	3.00

BLACK CROSS SPECIAL (See Dark Horse Presents)
Dark Horse Comics: Jan, 1988 ($1.75, B&W, one-shot)(Reprints & new-a)

	NM- 9.2
1-1st printing	3.00
1-(2nd printing) has 2 pgs. new-a	2.50

BLACK CROSS: DIRTY WORK (See Dark Horse Presents)
Dark Horse Comics: Apr, 1997 ($2.95, one-shot)

	NM- 9.2
1-Chris Warner-c/s/a	3.00

BLACK DIAMOND
Americomics: May, 1983 - No. 5, 1984 (no month)($2.00-$1.75, Baxter paper)

	NM- 9.2
1-3-Movie adapt.; 1-Colt back-up begins	4.00
4,5	3.00

NOTE: ***Bill Black** a-1i; c-1. **Gulacy** c-2-5. Sybil Danning photo back-c-1.*

BLACK DIAMOND WESTERN (Formerly Desperado No. 1-8)
Lev Gleason Publ: No. 9, Mar, 1949 - No. 60, Feb, 1956 (No. 9-28: 52 pgs.)

	GD 2.0	VG 4.0	FN 6.0	VF 8.0	VF/NM 9.0	NM- 9.2
9-Black Diamond & his horse Reliapon begin; origin & 1st app. Black Diamond	22	44	66	123	177	230
10	11	22	33	64	87	110
11-15	9	18	27	52	66	80
16-28(11/49-11/51)-Wolverton's Bing Bang Buster	12	24	36	69	95	120
29-40: 31-One pg. Frazetta anti-drug ad	8	16	24	40	50	60
41-50,53-59	7	14	21	35	43	50
51-3-D effect-c/story	15	30	45	86	123	160
52-3-D effect story	14	28	42	79	110	140
60-Last issue	8	16	24	40	50	60

NOTE: ***Biro** c-9-35?. **Fass** a-58, c-54-56, 58. **Guardineer** a-9, 15, 18. **Kida** a-9. **Maurer** a-10. **Ed Moore** a-16. **Morisi** a-55. **Tuska** a-10, 48.*

BLACK DRAGON, THE
Marvel Comics (Epic Comics): 5/85 - No. 6, 10/85 (Baxter paper, mature)

	NM- 9.2
1-6: 1-Chris Claremont story & John Bolton painted-c/a in all	3.00

BLACK DRAGON, THE
Dark Horse Comics: Apr, 1996 ($17.95, B&W, trade paperback)

	NM- 9.2
nn-Reprints Epic Comics limited series; intro by Anne McCaffrey	18.00

BLACK FLAG (See Asylum #5)
Maximum Press: Jan, 1995 - No.4, 1995; No. 0, July, 1995 ($2.50, B&W) (No. 0 in color)

	NM- 9.2
Preview Edition (6/94, $1.95, B&W)-Fraga/McFarlane-c.	3.00
0-4: 0-(7/95)-Liefeld/Fraga-c. 1-(1/95).	3.00
1-Variant cover	5.00
2,4-Variant covers	3.00

NOTE: ***Fraga** a-0-4, Preview Edition; c-1-4. **Liefeld/Fraga** c-0. **McFarlane/Fraga** c-Preview Edition.*

BLACK FOREST, THE
Image Comics: Mar, 2004 ($9.95, B&W, graphic novel)

	NM- 9.2
nn-Livingston & Tinnell-s/Vokes-a/Oeming-c	10.00

BLACK FURY (Becomes Wild West No. 58) (See Blue Bird)
Charlton Comics Group: May, 1955 - No. 57, Mar-Apr, 1966 (Horse stories)

	GD 2.0	VG 4.0	FN 6.0	VF 8.0	VF/NM 9.0	NM- 9.2
1	8	16	24	46	58	70
2	5	10	15	24	30	35
3-10	4	8	12	18	22	25
11-15,19,20	3	6	8	12	14	16
16-18-Ditko-a	8	16	24	46	58	70
21-30	2	4	6	9	11	14
31-57	1	3	4	6	8	10

BLACK GOLIATH (See Avengers #32-35,41,54)
Marvel Comics Group: Feb, 1976 - No. 5, Nov, 1976

	GD 2.0	VG 4.0	FN 6.0	VF 8.0	VF/NM 9.0	NM- 9.2
1-Tuska-a(p) thru #3	2	4	6	9	11	14
2-5: 2-4-(Regular 25¢ editions). 4-Kirby-c/Buckler-a	1	2	3	5	7	9
2-4-(30¢-c variants, limited distribution)(4,6,8/76)	2	4	6	9	11	14

BLACKHAWK (Formerly Uncle Sam #1-8; see Military & Modern Comics)
Comic Magazines(Quality)No. 9-107(12/56); National Periodical Publications No. 108 (1/57) -250; DC Comics No. 251 on: No. 9, Winter, 1944 - No. 243, 10-11/68; No. 244, 1-2/76 - No. 250, 1-2/77; No. 251, 10/82 - No. 273, 11/84

	GD 2.0	VG 4.0	FN 6.0	VF 8.0	VF/NM 9.0	NM- 9.2
9 (1944)	372	744	1116	2418	3909	5400
10 (1946)	127	254	381	794	1222	1650
11-15: 14-Ward-a; 13,14-Fear app.	87	174	261	544	835	1125
16-20: 20-Ward Blackhawk	69	138	207	431	666	900
21-30 (1950)	47	94	141	287	436	585
31-40: 31-Chop Chop by Jack Cole	39	78	117	227	331	435
41-49,51-60: 42-Robot-c	32	64	96	184	267	350
50-1st Killer Shark; origin in text	35	70	105	200	290	380
61,62: 61-Used in **POP**, pg. 91. 62-Used in **POP**, pg. 92 & color illo	28	56	84	158	229	300
63-70,72-80: 65-H-Bomb explosion panel. 66-B&W & color illos **POP**. 70-Return of Killer Shark; atomic explosion panel. 75-Intro. Blackie the Hawk	26	52	78	150	215	280
71-Origin retold; flying saucer-c; A-Bomb panels	30	60	90	173	249	325
81-86: Last precode (3/55)	23	46	69	132	191	250
87-92,94-99,101-107: 91-Robot-c. 105-1st S.A.	19	38	57	107	154	200
93-Origin in text	19	38	57	109	157	205
100	23	46	69	132	191	250
108-1st DC issue (1/57); re-intro. Blackie, the Hawk, their mascot; not in #115	41	82	123	318	497	675
109-117: 117-(10/57)-Mr. Freeze app.	16	32	48	114	175	235
118-(11/57)-Frazetta-r/Jimmy Wakely #4 (3 pgs.)	17	34	51	119	182	245
119-130 (11/58): 120-Robot-c	12	24	36	82	124	165
131-140 (9/59): 133-Intro. Lady Blackhawk	10	20	30	70	100	130
141-150,152-163,165,166: 141-Cat-Man returns-c/s. 143-Kurtzman-r/Jimmy Wakely #4. 150-(7/60)-King Condor returns. 166-Last 10¢ issue	8	16	24	53	74	95
151-Lady Blackhawk receives & loses super powers	8	16	24	55	78	100
164-Origin retold	8	16	24	58	82	105

Blackhawk #253 © DC

Black Hood #1 © DC

Black Magic #1 © Headline

	GD 2.0	VG 4.0	FN 6.0	VF 8.0	VF/NM 9.0	NM- 9.2
167-180	5	10	15	36	48	60
181-190	4	8	12	27	36	45
191-196,199,201,202,204-210: 196-Combat Diary series begins.	3	7	10	21	28	35
197,198,200: 197-New look for Blackhawks. 198-Origin retold	4	8	12	24	32	40
203-Origin Chop Chop (12/64)	4	8	12	27	36	45
211-227,229-243(1968): 230-Blackhawks become superheroes; JLA cameo 242-Return to old costumes	3	6	9	18	24	30
228-Batman, Green Lantern, Superman, The Flash cameos.	3	7	10	21	28	35
244 ('76) -250: 250-Chuck dies	1	2	3	4	5	7
251-273: 251-Origin retold; Black Knights return. 252-Intro Domino. 253-Part origin Hendrickson. 258-Blackhawk's Island destroyed. 259-Part origin Chop-Chop. 265-273 (75¢ cover price)						3.00

NOTE: ***Chaykin** a-260; c-257-260, 262. **Crandall** a-10, 11, 13, 16?, 18-20, 22-26, 30-33, 35p, 36(2), 37, 38?, 39-44, 46-50, 52-58, 60, 63, 64, 66, 67; c-14-20, 22-63(most except #28-33, 36, 37, 39). **Evans** a-244, 245,246i, 248-250i. **G. Kane** c-263, 264. **Kubert** c-244, 245. **Newton** a-266p. **Severin** a-257.**Spiegle** a-261-267, 269-273; c-265-272. **Toth** a-260p. **Ward** a-16-27(Chop Chop, 8pgs. ea.); pencilled stories-No. 17-63(approx.). **Wildey** a-268. Chop Chop solo stories in #10-95?*

BLACKHAWK
DC Comics: Mar, 1988 - No. 3, May, 1988 ($2.95, limited series, mature)

	GD 2.0	VG 4.0	FN 6.0	VF 8.0	VF/NM 9.0	NM- 9.2
1-3: Chaykin painted-c/a/scripts						4.00

BLACKHAWK (Also see Action Comics #601)
DC Comics: Mar, 1989 - No. 16, Aug, 1990 ($1.50, mature)

	GD 2.0	VG 4.0	FN 6.0	VF 8.0	VF/NM 9.0	NM- 9.2
1						3.50
2-6,8-16: 16-Crandall-c swipe						2.50
7-($2.50, 52 pgs.)-Story-r/Military #1						3.00
Annual 1 (1989, $2.95, 68 pgs.)-Recaps origin of Blackhawk, Lady Blackhawk, and others						3.50
Special 1 (1992, $3.50, 68 pgs.)-Mature readers						3.50

BLACKHAWK INDIAN TOMAHAWK WAR, THE
Avon Periodicals: 1951 (Also see Fighting Indians of the Wild West)

	GD 2.0	VG 4.0	FN 6.0	VF 8.0	VF/NM 9.0	NM- 9.2
nn-Kinstler-c; Kit West story	20	40	60	115	165	215

BLACK HEART ASSASSIN
Iguana Comics: Jan, 1994 ($2.95)

	GD 2.0	VG 4.0	FN 6.0	VF 8.0	VF/NM 9.0	NM- 9.2
1						3.00

BLACK HOLE (See Walt Disney Showcase #54) (Disney, movie)
Whitman Publishing Co.: Mar, 1980 - No. 4, Sept, 1980

	GD 2.0	VG 4.0	FN 6.0	VF 8.0	VF/NM 9.0	NM- 9.2
11295(#1) (1979, Golden, $1.50-c, 52 pgs., graphic novel; 8 1/2x11") Photo-c; Spiegle-a.	2	4	6	12	16	20
1-3: 1,2-Movie adaptation. 2,3-Spiegle-a. 3-McWilliams-a; photo-c. 3-New stories	1	3	4	6	8	10
4-Sold only in pre-packs; new story; Spiegle-a	3	6	9	16	20	25

BLACK HOOD, THE (See Blue Ribbon, Flyman & Mighty Comics)
Red Circle Comics (Archie): June, 1983 - No. 3, Oct, 1983 (Mandell paper)

	GD 2.0	VG 4.0	FN 6.0	VF 8.0	VF/NM 9.0	NM- 9.2
1-Morrow, McWilliams, Wildey-a; Toth-c						6.00
2,3: The Fox by Toth-c/a; Boyette-a. 3-Morrow-a; Toth wraparound-c						4.00

(Also see Archie's Super-Hero Special Digest #2)

BLACK HOOD
DC Comics (Impact Comics): Dec, 1991 - No. 12, Dec, 1992 ($1.00)

	GD 2.0	VG 4.0	FN 6.0	VF 8.0	VF/NM 9.0	NM- 9.2
1						3.50
2-12: 11-Intro The Fox. 12-Origin Black Hood						2.50
Annual 1 (1992, $2.50, 68 pgs.)-w/Trading card						3.00

BLACK HOOD COMICS (Formerly Hangman #2-8; Laugh Comics #20 on; also see Black Swan, Jackpot, Roly Poly & Top-Notch #9)
MLJ Magazines: No. 9, Wint., 1943-44 - No. 19, Sum., 1946 (on radio in 1943)

	GD 2.0	VG 4.0	FN 6.0	VF 8.0	VF/NM 9.0	NM- 9.2
9-The Hangman & The Boy Buddies cont'd	108	216	324	675	1038	1400
10-Hangman & Dusty, the Boy Detective app.	62	124	186	388	594	800
11-Dusty app.; no Hangman	48	96	144	293	447	600
12-18: 14-Kinstler blood-c. 17-Hal Foster swipe from Prince Valiant; 1st issue with "An Archie Magazine" on-c	42	84	126	256	388	520
19-I.D. exposed; last issue	52	104	156	317	484	650

NOTE: *Hangman by **Fuje** in 9, 10. **Kinstler** a-15, c-14-16.*

BLACK JACK (Rocky Lane's...; formerly Jim Bowie)
Charlton Comics: No. 20, Nov, 1957 - No. 30, Nov, 1959

	GD 2.0	VG 4.0	FN 6.0	VF 8.0	VF/NM 9.0	NM- 9.2
20	9	18	27	54	70	85
21,27,29,30	6	12	18	31	38	45
22,23: 22-(68 pgs.). 23-Williamson/Torres-a	8	16	24	43	54	65
24-26,28-Ditko-a	10	20	30	58	77	95

BLACK KNIGHT, THE
Toby Press: May, 1953; 1963

	GD 2.0	VG 4.0	FN 6.0	VF 8.0	VF/NM 9.0	NM- 9.2
1-Bondage-c	26	52	78	150	215	280
Super Reprint No. 11 (1963)-Reprints 1953 issue	3	6	9	19	25	32

BLACK KNIGHT, THE
Atlas Comics (MgPC): May, 1955 - No. 5, April, 1956

	GD 2.0	VG 4.0	FN 6.0	VF 8.0	VF/NM 9.0	NM- 9.2
1-Origin Crusader; Maneely-c/a	85	170	255	531	816	1100
2-Maneely-c/a(4)	60	120	180	375	575	775
3-5: 4-Maneely-c/a. 5-Maneely-c, Shores-a	46	92	138	281	428	575

BLACK KNIGHT (See The Avengers #48, Marvel Super Heroes & Tales To Astonish #52)
Marvel Comics: June, 1990 - No. 4, Sept, 1990 ($1.50, limited series)

	GD 2.0	VG 4.0	FN 6.0	VF 8.0	VF/NM 9.0	NM- 9.2
1-4: 1-Original Black Knight returns. 3,4-Dr. Strange app.						2.50

NOTE: ***Buckler** c-1-4p*

BLACK KNIGHT: EXODUS
Marvel Comics: Dec, 1996 ($2.50, one-shot)

	GD 2.0	VG 4.0	FN 6.0	VF 8.0	VF/NM 9.0	NM- 9.2
1-Raab-s; Apocalypse-c/app.						2.50

BLACK LAMB, THE
DC Comics (Helix): Nov, 1996 - No, 6, Apr, 1997 ($2.50, limited series)

	GD 2.0	VG 4.0	FN 6.0	VF 8.0	VF/NM 9.0	NM- 9.2
1-6: Tim Truman-c/a/scripts						2.50

BLACK LIGHTNING (See The Brave & The Bold, Cancelled Comic Cavalcade, DC Comics Presents #16, Detective #490 and World's Finest #257)
National Periodical Publ./DC Comics: Apr, 1977 - No. 11, Sept-Oct, 1978

	GD 2.0	VG 4.0	FN 6.0	VF 8.0	VF/NM 9.0	NM- 9.2
1-Origin Black Lightning	2	4	6	8	10	12
2,3,6-10						6.00
4,5-Superman-c/s. 4-Intro Cyclotronic Man	1	2	3	4	5	7
11-The Ray new solo story	1	2	3	5	7	9

NOTE: ***Buckler** c-1-3p, 6-11p. #11 is 44 pgs.*

BLACK LIGHTNING (2nd Series)
DC Comics: Feb, 1995 - No. 13, Feb, 1996 ($1.95/$2.25)

	GD 2.0	VG 4.0	FN 6.0	VF 8.0	VF/NM 9.0	NM- 9.2
1-5-Tony Isabella scripts begin, ends #8						3.00
6-13: 6-Begin $2.25-c. 13-Batman-c/app.						3.00

BLACK MAGIC (...Magazine) (Becomes Cool Cat V8#6 on)
Crestwood Publ. V1#1-4,V6#1-V7#5/Headline V1#5-V5#3,V7#6-V8#5: 10-11/50 - V4#1, 6-7/53: V4#2, 9-10/53 - V5#3, 11-12/54; V6#1, 9-10/57 - V7#2, 11-12/58: V7#3, 7-8/60 - V8#5, 11-12/61 (V1#1-5, 52pgs.; V1#6-V3#3, 44pgs.)

	GD 2.0	VG 4.0	FN 6.0	VF 8.0	VF/NM 9.0	NM- 9.2
V1#1-S&K-a, 10 pgs.; Meskin-a(2)	131	262	393	819	1260	1700
2-S&K-a, 17 pgs.; Meskin-a	58	116	174	363	557	750
3-6(8-9/51)-S&K, Roussos, Meskin-a	51	102	153	311	476	640
V2#1(10-11/51),4,5,7(#13),9(#15),12(#18)-S&K-a	37	74	111	209	305	400
2,3,6,8,10,11(#17)	28	56	84	158	229	300
V3#1(#19, 12/52) - 6(#24, 5/53)-S&K-a	29	58	87	167	241	315
V4#1(#25, 6-7/53), 2(#26, 9-10/53)-S&K-a(3-4)	30	60	90	173	249	325
3(#27, 11-12/53)-S&K-a; Ditko-a (2nd published-a); also see Captain 3-D, Daring Love #1, Strange Fantasy #9, & Fantastic Fears #5 (Fant. Fears was 1st drawn, but not 1st publ.)	48	96	144	293	447	600
4(#28)-Eyes ripped out/story-S&K, Ditko-a	40	80	120	236	351	465
5(#29, 3-4/54)-S&K, Ditko-a	31	62	93	178	259	340
6(#30, 5-6/54)-S&K, Powell?-a	24	48	72	135	195	255
V5#1(#31, 7-8/54 - 3(#33, 11-12/54)-S&K-a	18	36	54	102	146	190
V6#1(#34, 9-10/57), 2(#35, 11-12/57)	10	20	30	60	80	100
3(1-2/58) - 6(7-8/58)	10	20	30	60	80	100
V7#1(9-10/58) - 3(7-8/60)	10	20	30	56	73	90
4(9-10/60)	10	20	30	60	80	100
5(11-12/60)-Hitler-c; Torres-a	13	26	39	74	102	130
6(1-2/61)-Powell-a(2)	10	20	30	56	73	90
V8#1(3-4/61)-Powell-c/a	10	20	30	56	73	90
2(5-6/61)-E.C. story swipe/W.F. #22; Ditko, Powell-a	10	20	30	60	80	100
3(7-8/61)-E.C. story swipe/W.F. #22; Powell-a(2)	10	20	30	60	80	100
4(9-10/61)-Powell-a(5)	10	20	30	56	73	90
5-E.C. story swipe/W.S.F. #28; Powell-a(3)	10	20	30	60	80	100

NOTE: ***Bernard Baily** a-V4#6?, V5#3(2). **Grandenetti** a-V2#3, 11. **Kirby** c-V1#1-6, V2#1-12, V3#1-6, V4#1, 2, 4-6, V5#1-3. **McWilliams** a-V3#2i. **Meskin** a-V1#1(2), 2, 3, 4(2), 5(2), 6, V2/1, 2, 3(2), 4(3), 5, 6(2), 7-9, 11, 12i, V3#1(2), 5, 6, V5#1(2), 2. **Orlando** a-V6#1, 4, V7#2; c-V6/1-6. **Powell** a-V5#1?. **Roussos** a-V1#3-5, 6(2), V2#3(2), 4, 5(2), 6, 8, 9, 10(2), 11, 12p, V3#1(2), 2i, 5, V5#2. **Simon** a-V2#12, V3#2, V7#5? c-V4#3?, V7#3?, 4, 5?, 6?, V8#1-5. **Simon & Kirby** a-V1#1, 2(2), 3-6, V2#1, 4, 5, 7, 9, 12, V3#1-6, V4#1(3), 2(4), 3(2), 4(2), 5, 6, V5#1-3; c-V2#1. **Leonard Starr** a-V1#1. **Tuska** a-V6#3, 4. **Woodbridge** a-V7#4.*

BLACK MAGIC
National Periodical Publications: Oct-Nov, 1973 - No. 9, Apr-May, 1975

	GD 2.0	VG 4.0	FN 6.0	VF 8.0	VF/NM 9.0	NM- 9.2
1-S&K reprints	3	6	9	18	24	30

Black Orchid #10 © DC

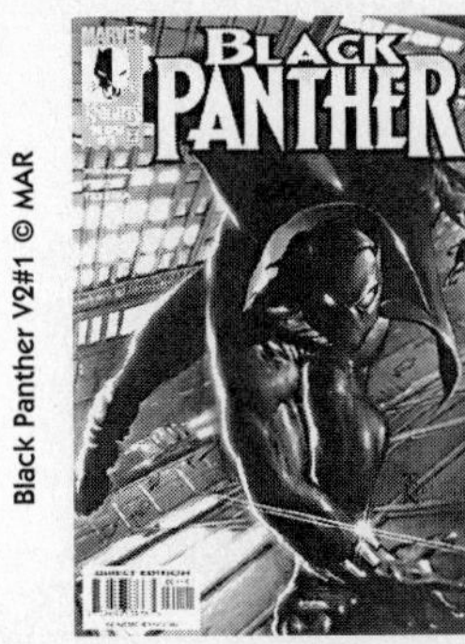

Black Panther V2#1 © MAR

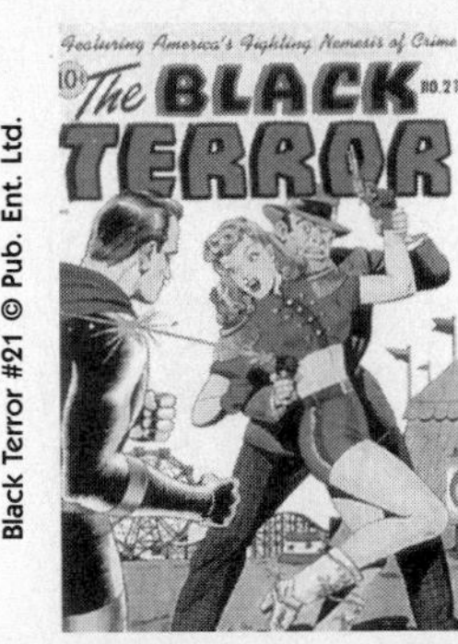

Black Terror #21 © Pub. Ent. Ltd.

	GD 2.0	VG 4.0	FN 6.0	VF 8.0	VF/NM 9.0	NM- 9.2
2-8-S&K reprints	2	4	6	10	13	16
9-S&K reprints	2	4	6	11	14	18

BLACK MAGIC
Eclipse International: Apr, 1990 - No. 4, Oct, 1990 ($2.75, B&W, mini-series)

1-($3.50, 68pgs.)-Japanese manga 4.00
2-4 ($2.75, 52 pgs.) 3.00

BLACKMAIL TERROR (See Harvey Comics Library)

BLACK MASK
DC Comics: 1993 - No. 3, 1994 ($4.95, limited series, 52 pgs.)

1-3 5.00

BLACK OPS
Image Comics (WildStorm): Jan, 1996 - No. 5, May, 1996 ($2.50, lim. series)

1-5 2.50

BLACK ORCHID (See Adventure Comics #428 & Phantom Stranger)
DC Comics: Holiday, 1988-89 - No. 3, 1989 ($3.50, lim. series, prestige format)

Book 1,3: Gaiman scripts & McKean painted-a in all 6.00
Book 2-Arkham Asylum story; Batman app. 1 2 3 5 6 8
TPB (1991, $19.95) r/#1-3; new McKean-c 20.00

BLACK ORCHID
DC Comics: Sept, 1993 - No. 22, June, 1995 ($1.95/$2.25)

1-22: Dave McKean-c all issues 2.50
1-Platinum Edition 12.00
Annual 1 (1993, $3.95, 68 pgs.)-Children's Crusade 4.00

BLACKOUTS (See Broadway Hollywood...)

BLACK PANTHER, THE (Also see Avengers #52, Fantastic Four #52, Jungle Action & Marvel Premiere #51-53)
Marvel Comics Group: Jan, 1977 - No. 15, May, 1979

	GD	VG	FN	VF	VF/NM	NM-
1	3	6	9	18	24	30
2-13: 4,5-(Regular 30¢ editions). 8-Origin	2	4	6	8	10	12
4,5-(35¢-c variants, limited dist.)(7,9/77)	3	6	9	18	23	28
14,15-Avengers x-over. 14-Origin	2	4	6	11	14	18

NOTE: *J. Buscema c-15p. Kirby c/a & scripts-1-12. Layton c-13i.*

BLACK PANTHER
Marvel Comics Group: July, 1988 - No. 4, Oct, 1988 ($1.25)

1-4-Gillis-s/Cowan & Delarosa-a 2.50

BLACK PANTHER (Marvel Knights)
Marvel Comics: Nov, 1998 - No. 62, Sept, 2003 ($2.50)

1-Texeira-a/c; Priest-s 6.00
1-($6.95) DF edition w/Quesada & Palmiotti-c 1 2 3 5 6 8
2-4: 2-Two covers by Texeira and Timm. 3-Fantastic Four app. 3.50
5-35,37-40: 5-Evans-a. 6-8-Jusko-a. 8-Avengers-c/app. 15-Hulk app. 22-Moon Knight app. 23-Avengers app. 25-Maximum Security x-over. 26-Storm-c/app. 28-Magneto & Sub-Mariner-c/app. 29-WWII flashback meeting w/Captain America. 35-Defenders-c/app. 37-Luke Cage and Falcon-c/app. 2.50
36-($3.50, 100 pgs.) 35th Anniversary issue incl. r/1st app. in FF #52 3.50
41-56: 41-44-Wolverine app. 47-Thor app. 48,49-Magneto app. 2.50
57-62: 57-Begin $2.99-c. 59-Falcon app. 3.00
...: The Client (6/01, $14.95, TPB) r/#1-5 15.00
... 2099 #1 (11/04, $2.99) Kirkman-s/Hotz-a/Pat Lee-c 3.00

BLACK PANTHER: PANTHER'S PREY
Marvel Comics: May, 1991 - No. 4, Oct, 1991 ($4.95, squarebound, lim. series, 52 pgs.)

1-4: McGregor-s/Turner-a 5.00

BLACK PEARL, THE
Dark Horse Comics: Sept, 1996 - No. 5, Jan, 1997 ($2.95, limited series)

1-5: Mark Hamill scripts 3.00

BLACK PHANTOM (See Tim Holt #25, 38)
Magazine Enterprises: Nov, 1954 (one-shot) (Female outlaw)

1 (A-1 #122)-The Ghost Rider story plus 3 Black Phantom stories; Headlight-c/a 39 78 117 222 324 425

BLACK PHANTOM
AC Comics: 1989 - No. 3, 1990 ($2.50, B&W; #2 color)(Reprints & new-a)

1-3: 1-Ayers-r, Bolle-r/B.P. #1-3-Redmask-r 2.75

BLACK PHANTOM, RETURN OF THE (See Wisco)

BLACK RIDER (Western Winners #1-7; Western Tales of Black Rider #28-31; Gunsmoke Western #32 on)(See All Western Winners, Best Western, Kid Colt, Outlaw Kid, Rex Hart, Two-Gun Kid, Two-Gun Western, Western Gunfighters, Western Winners, & Wild Western)
Marvel/Atlas Comics(CDS No. 8-17/CPS No. 19 on): No. 8, 3/50 - No. 18, 1/52; No. 19, 11/53 - No. 27, 3/55

	GD	VG	FN	VF	VF/NM	NM-
8 (#1)-Black Rider & his horse Satan begin; 36 pgs; Stan Lee photo-c as Black Rider)	43	86	129	262	401	540
9-52 pgs. begin, end #14	24	48	72	138	199	260
10-Origin Black Rider	29	58	87	164	237	310
11-14: 14-Last 52pgs.	18	36	54	102	146	190
15-19: 19-Two-Gun Kid app.	15	30	45	86	123	160
20-Classic-c; Two-Gun Kid app.	17	34	51	98	139	180
21-27: 21-23-Two-Gun Kid app. 24,25-Arrowhead app. 26-Kid Colt app. 27-Last issue; last precode. Kid Colt app. The Spider (a villain) burns to death	14	28	42	81	113	145

NOTE: *Ayers c-22. Jack Keller a-15, 26, 27. Maneely a-14; c-16, 17, 25, 27. Syd Shores a-19, 21, 22, 23(3), 24(3), 25-27; c-19, 21, 23. Sinnott a-24, 25. Tuska a-12, 19-21.*

BLACK RIDER RIDES AGAIN!, THE
Atlas Comics (CPS): Sept, 1957

1-Kirby-a(3); Powell-a; Severin-c 26 52 78 147 211 275

BLACK SEPTEMBER (Also see Avengers/Ultraforce, Ultraforce (1st series) #10 & Ultraforce/Avengers)
Malibu Comics (Ultraverse): 1995 ($1.50, one-shot)

Infinity-Intro to the newUltraverse; variant-c exists. 2.25

BLACKSTONE (See Super Magician Comics & Wisco Giveaways)

BLACKSTONE, MASTER MAGICIAN COMICS
Vital Publ./Street & Smith Publ.: Mar-Apr, 1946 - No. 3, July-Aug, 1946

	GD	VG	FN	VF	VF/NM	NM-
1	32	64	96	184	267	350
2,3	20	40	60	112	161	210

BLACKSTONE, THE MAGICIAN (...Detective on cover only #3 & 4)
Marvel Comics (CnPC): No. 2, May, 1948 - No. 4, Sept, 1948 (No #1) (Cont'd from E.C. #1?)

	GD	VG	FN	VF	VF/NM	NM-
2-The Blonde Phantom begins, ends #4	62	124	186	388	594	800
3,4: 3-Blonde Phantom by Sekowsky	40	80	120	236	351	465

BLACKSTONE, THE MAGICIAN DETECTIVE FIGHTS CRIME
E. C. Comics: Fall, 1947

1-1st app. Happy Houlihans 50 100 150 305 465 625

BLACK SUN (X-Men Black Sun on cover)
Marvel Comics: Nov, 2000 - No. 5, Nov, 2000 ($2.99, weekly limited series)

1-(...: X-Men), 2-(...: Storm), 3-(...: Banshee and Sunfire), 4-(...: Colossus and Nightcrawler), 5-(...: Wolverine and Thunderbird); Claremont-s in all; Evans interlocking painted covers; Magik returns 3.00

BLACK SUN
DC Comics (WildStorm): Nov, 2002 - No. 6, Jun, 2003 ($2.95, limited series)

1-6-Andreyko-s/Scott-a 3.00

BLACK SWAN COMICS
MLJ Magazines (Pershing Square Publ. Co.): 1945

1-The Black Hood reprints from Black Hood No. 14; Bill Woggon-a; Suzie app. 23 46 69 132 191 250

BLACK TARANTULA (See Feature Presentations No. 5)

BLACK TERROR (See America's Best Comics & Exciting Comics)
Better Publications/Standard: Winter, 1942-43 - No. 27, June, 1949

	GD	VG	FN	VF	VF/NM	NM-
1-Black Terror, Crime Crusader begin	300	600	900	1925	3063	4200
2	115	230	345	719	1110	1500
3	79	158	237	494	760	1025
4,5	67	134	201	419	647	875
6-10: 7-The Ghost app.	57	114	171	356	548	740
11-20: 20-The Scarab app.	50	100	150	305	465	625
21-Miss Masque app.	54	108	162	329	502	675
22-Part Frazetta-a on one Black Terror story	50	100	150	305	465	625
23,25-27	44	88	132	268	409	550
24-Frazetta-a (1/4 pg.)	45	90	135	275	418	560

NOTE: *Schomburg (Xela) c-2-27; bondage c-2, 17, 24. Meskin a-27. Moreira a-27. Robinson/Meskin a-23, 24(3), 25, 26. Roussos/Mayo a-24. Tuska a-26, 27.*

BLACK TERROR, THE (Also see Total Eclipse)
Eclipse Comics: Oct, 1989 - No. 3, June, 1990 ($4.95, 52 pgs., squarebound, limited series)

1-3: Beau Smith & Chuck Dixon scripts; Dan Brereton painted-c/a 5.00

BLACKTHORNE 3-D SERIES
Blackthorne Publishing Co.: May, 1985 - No. 80, 1989 ($2.25/$2.50)

1-Sheena in 3-D #1. D. Stevens-c/retouched-a 1 2 3 5 6 8

Black Widow ('04) #1 © MAR

Blade #3 © MAR

Blade of Kumori #1 © Devil's Due

GD 2.0 | VG 4.0 | FN 6.0 | VF 8.0 | VF/NM 9.0 | NM- 9.2

2-10: 2-MerlinRealm in 3-D #1. 3-3-D Heroes #1. Goldyn in 3-D #1. 5-Bizarre 3-D Zone #1. 6-Salimba in 3-D #1. 7-Twisted Tales in 3-D #1. 8-Dick Tracy in 3-D #1. 9-Salimba in 3-D #2. 10-Gumby in 3-D #1 — 6.00
11-19: 11-Betty Boop in 3-D #1. 12-Hamster Vice in 3-D #1. 13-Little Nemo in 3-D #1. 14-Gumby in 3-D #2. 15-Hamster Vice #6 in 3-D. 16-Laffin' Gas #6 in 3-D. 17-Gumby in 3-D #3. 18-Bullwinkle and Rocky in 3-D #1. 19-The Flintstones in 3-D #1 — 6.00
20(#1),26(#2),35(#3),39(#4),52(#5),62,71(#6)-G.I. Joe in 3-D. 62-G.I. Joe Annual — 2 4 6 9 11 14
21-24,27-28: 21-Gumby in 3-D #4. 22-The Flintstones in 3-D #2. 23-Laurel & Hardy in 3-D #1. 24-Bozo the Clown in 3-D #1. 27-Bravestarr in 3-D #1. 28- Gumby in 3-D #5 — 6.00
25,29,37-The Transformers in 3-D — 2 4 6 9 11 14
30-Star Wars in 3-D #1 — 3 6 9 16 20 24
31-34,36,38,40: 31-The California Raisins in 3-D #1. 32-Richie Rich & Casper in 3-D #1. 33-Gumby in 3-D #6. 34-Laurel & Hardy in 3-D #2. 36-The Flintstones in 3-D #3. 38-Gumby in 3-D #7. 40-Bravestarr in 3-D #2 — 6.00
41-46,49,50: 41-Battletech in 3-D #1. 42-The Flintstones in 3-D #4. 43-Underdog in 3-D #1 44-The California Raisins in 3-D #2. 45-Red Heat in 3-D #1 (movie adapt.). 46-The California Raisins in 3-D #3. 49-Rambo in 3-D #1. 49-Sad Sack in 3-D #1. 50-Bullwinkle For President in 3-D #1 — 6.00
47,48-Star Wars in 3-D #2,3 — 2 4 6 10 13 16
51,53-60: 51-Kull in 3-D #1. 53-Red Sonja in 3-D #1. 54-Bozo in 3-D #2. 55-Waxwork in 3-D #1 (movie adapt.). 57-Casper in 3-D #1. 58-Baby Huey in 3-D #1. 59-Little Dot in 3-D #1. 60-Solomon Kane in 3-D #1 — 6.00
61,63-70,72-80: 61-Werewolf in 3-D #1. 63-The California Raisins in 3-D #4. 64-To Die For in 3-D #1. 65-Capt. Holo in 3-D #1. 66-Playful Little Audrey in 3-D #1. 67-Kull in 3-D #2. 69-The California Raisins in 3-D #5. 70-Wendy in 3-D #1. 72-Sports Hall of Shame #1. 74-The Noid in 3-D #1. 75-Moonwalker in 3-D #1 (Michael Jackson movie adapt.). 76-79. 80-The Noid in 3-D #2 — 1 2 3 4 5 7

BLACK TIDE
Image Comics: Nov, 2001 - No. 4, May, 2002 ($2.95)
1-4-Bishop-s; Mike Miller-a. 1-Three covers by Miller, Park & Bachalo — 3.00

BLACK TIDE (Volume 2)
Avatar Press/Angel Gate: July, 2002 - Present ($3.50/$2.95)
1-4: 1-Bishop-s; Mike Miller-a. 1-Three covers by Miller, Park & Pajarillo — 3.50
5-10-($2.95) Breyfogle-a/c — 3.00

BLACK WIDOW (Marvel Knights) (Also see Marvel Graphic Novel)
Marvel Comics: May, 1999 - No. 3, Aug, 1999 ($2.99, limited series)
1-(June on-c) Devin Grayson-s/J.G. Jones-c/a; Daredevil app. — 5.00
1-Variant-c by J.G. Jones — 6.00
2,3 — 4.00
...Web of Intrigue (6/99, $3.50) r/origin & early appearances — 3.50
TPB (7/01, $15.95) r/Vol. 1 & 2; Jones-c — 16.00

BLACK WIDOW (Marvel Krfights) (Volume 2)
Marvel Comics: Jan, 2001 - No. 3, May, 2001 ($2.99, limited series)
1-3-Grayson & Rucka-s/Scott Hampton-c/a; Daredevil app. — 3.00

BLACK WIDOW (Marvel Knights)
Marvel Comics: Nov, 2004 - No. 6 ($2.99, limited series)
1-3-Sienkiewicz-a/Land-c — 3.00

BLACK WIDOW: PALE LITTLE SPIDER (Marvel Knights) (Volume 3)
Marvel Comics: Jun, 2002 - No. 3, Aug, 2002 ($2.99, limited series)
1-3-Rucka-s/Kordey-a/Horn-c — 3.00

BLACKWULF
Marvel Comics: June, 1994 - No. 10, Mar, 1995 ($1.50)
1-($2.50)-Embossed-c; Angel Medina-a — 3.00
2-10 — 2.25

BLADE (The Vampire Hunter)
Marvel Comics
1-(3/98, $3.50) Colan-a(p)/Christopher Golden-s — 3.50
... Black & White TPB (2004, $15.99, B&W) reprints from magazines Vampire Tales #8,9; Marvel Preview #3,6; Crescent City Blues #1 and Marvel Shadow and Light #1 — 16.00
San Diego Con Promo (6/97) Wesley Snipes photo-c — 3.00
...Sins of the Father (10/98, $5.99) Sears-a; movie adaption — 6.00
Blade 2: Movie Adaptation (5/02, $5.95) Ponticelli-a/Bradstreet-c — 6.00

BLADE (The Vampire Hunter)
Marvel Comics: Nov, 1998 - No. 3, Jan, 1999 ($3.50/$2.99)
1-($3.50) Contains Movie insider pages; McKean-a — 3.50
2,3-($2.99): 2-Two covers — 3.00

BLADE (Volume 2)
Marvel Comics (MAX): May, 2002 -No. 6, Oct, 2002 ($2.99)
1-6-Bradstreet-c/Hinz-s. 1-5-Pugh-a. 6-Homs-a — 3.00

BLADE OF KUMORI
Devil's Due Publ.: Nov, 2004 - Present ($2.95)
1-Ron Marz-s; two covers — 3.00

BLADE OF THE IMMORTAL (Manga)
Dark Horse Comics: June, 1996 - Present ($2.95/$2.99/$3.95, B&W)
1-Hiroaki Samura-s/a in all — 1 3 4 6 8 10
2-5: 2-#1 on cover in error — 6.00
6-10 — 5.00
11,19,20,34-($3.95, 48 pgs.): 34-Food one-shot — 4.00
12-18,21-33,35-41,43-92: 12-20-Dreamsong. 21-28-On Silent Wings. 29-33-Dark Shadow. 35-42-Heart of Darkness. 43-57-The Gathering — 3.00
42-($3.50) Ends Heart of Darkness — 3.50

BLADE RUNNER (Movie)
Marvel Comics Group: Oct, 1982 - No. 2, Nov, 1982
1,2-r/Marvel Super Special #22; 1-Williamson-c/a. 2-Williamson-a — 3.50

BLADESMEN UNDERSEA
Blue Comet Press: 1994 ($3.50, B&W)
1-Polybagged w/trading card — 3.50

BLADE: THE VAMPIRE-HUNTER
Marvel Comics: July, 1994 - No. 10, Apr, 1995 ($1.95)
1-($2.95)-Foil-c; Dracula returns; Wheatley-c/a — 3.50
2-10: 2,3,10-Dracula-c/app. 8-Morbius app. — 2.50

BLADE: VAMPIRE-HUNTER
Marvel Comics: Dec, 1999 - No. 6, May, 2000 ($3.50/$2.50)
1-($3.50)-Bart Sears-s; Sears and Smith-a — 3.50
2-6-($2.50): 2-Regular & Wesley Snipes photo-c — 2.50

BLAIR WITCH CHRONICLES, THE
Oni Press: Mar, 2000 - No. 4, July, 2000 ($2.95, B&W, limited series)
1-4-Van Meter-s.1-Guy Davis-a. 2-Mireault-a — 3.00
1-DF Alternate-c by John Estes — 7.00
TPB (9/00, $15.95) r/#1-4 & Blair Witch Project one-shot — 16.00

BLAIR WITCH: DARK TESTAMENTS
Image Comics: Oct, 2000 ($2.95, one-shot)
1-Edington-s/Adlard-a; story of murderer Rustin Parr — 3.00

BLAIR WITCH PROJECT, THE (Movie companion, not adaption)
Oni Press: July, 1999 ($2.95, B&W, one-shot)
1-(1st printing) History of the Blair Witch, art by Edwards, Mireault, and Davis; Van Meter-s; only the stick figure is red on the cover — 12.00
1-(2nd printing) Stick figure and title lettering are red on cover — 4.00
1-(3rd printing) Stick figure, title, and creator credits are red on cover — 3.00
DF Glow in the Dark variant-c ($10.00) — 10.00

BLAST (Satire Magazine)
G & D Publications: Feb, 1971 - No. 2, May, 1971
1-Wrightson & Kaluta-a/Everette-c — 7 14 21 51 71 90
2-Kaluta-c/a — 6 12 18 38 52 65

BLAST CORPS
Dark Horse Comics: Oct, 1998 ($2.50, one-shot, based on Nintendo game)
1-Reprints from Nintendo Power magazine; Mahn-a — 2.50

BLASTERS SPECIAL
DC Comics: 1989 ($2.00, one-shot)
1-Peter David scripts; Invasion spin-off — 2.50

BLAST-OFF (Three Rocketeers)
Harvey Publications (Fun Day Funnies): Oct, 1965 (12¢)
1-Kirby/Williamson-a(2); Williamson/Crandall-a; Williamson/Torres/Krenkel-a; Kirby/Simon-c — 7 14 21 46 63 80

BLAZE
Marvel Comics: Aug, 1994 - No. 12, July, 1995 ($1.95)
1-($2.95)-Foil embossed-c — 3.50
2-12: 2-Man-Thing-c/story. 11,12-Punisher app. — 2.50

BLAZE CARSON (Rex Hart #6 on)(See Kid Colt, Tex Taylor, Wild Western, Wisco)
Marvel Comics (USA): Sept, 1948 - No. 5, June, 1949
1: 1,2-Shores-c — 28 56 84 158 229 300

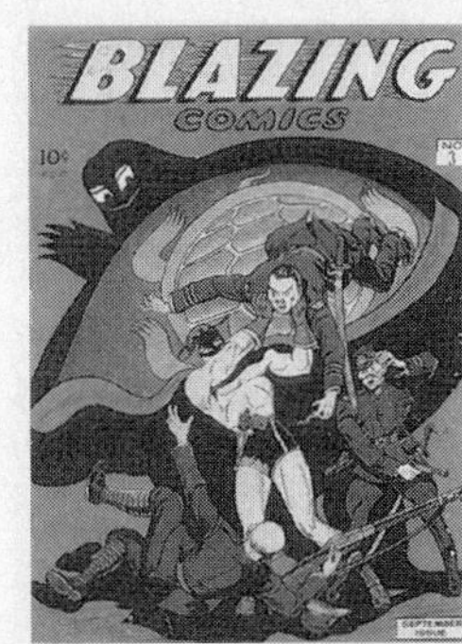

Blazing Comics #1 © Enwil

Blazing West #7 © ACG

Blitzkrieg #1 © DC

	GD 2.0	VG 4.0	FN 6.0	VF 8.0	VF/NM 9.0	NM- 9.2
2,4,5: 4-Two-Gun Kid app. 5-Tex Taylor app.	19	38	57	107	154	200
3-Used by N.Y. State Legis. Comm. (injury to eye splash); Tex Morgan app.	20	40	60	112	161	210

BLAZE: LEGACY OF BLOOD (See Ghost Rider & Ghost Rider/Blaze)
Marvel Comics (Midnight Sons imprint): Dec, 1993 - No. 4, Mar, 1994 ($1.75, limited series)

1-4 2.50

BLAZE OF GLORY
Marvel Comics: Feb, 2000 - No. 4, Mar, 2000 ($2.99, limited series)

1-4-Ostrander-s/Manco-a; Two-Gun Kid, Rawhide Kid, Red Wolf and Ghost Rider app. 3.00
TPB (7/02, $9.99) r/#1-4 10.00

BLAZE THE WONDER COLLIE (Formerly Molly Manton's Romances #1?)
Marvel Comics(SePI): No. 2, Oct, 1949 - No. 3, Feb, 1950 (Both have photo-c)

2(#1), 3-(Scarce) 24 48 72 138 199 260

BLAZING BATTLE TALES
Seaboard Periodicals (Atlas): July, 1975

1-Intro. Sgt. Hawk & the Sky Demon; Severin, McWilliams, Sparling-a; Nazi-c by Thorne
2 4 6 9 11 14

BLAZING COMBAT (Magazine)
Warren Publishing Co.: Oct, 1965 - No. 4, July, 1966 (35¢, B&W)

1-Frazetta painted-c on all 20 40 60 145 223 300
2 7 14 21 50 68 85
3,4: 4-Frazetta half pg. ad 6 12 18 43 59 75
nn-Anthology (reprints from No. 1-4) (low print) 7 14 21 50 68 85
NOTE: ***Adkins** a-4. **Colan** a-3,4,nn. **Crandall** a-all. **Evans** a-1,4. **Heath** a-4,nn. **Morrow** a-1-3,nn. **Orlando** a-1-3,nn. **J. Severin** a-all. **Torres** a-1-4. **Toth** a-all. **Williamson** a-2. and **Wood** a-3,4,nn.*

BLAZING COMBAT: WORLD WAR I AND WORLD WAR II
Apple Press: Mar, 1994 ($3.75, B&W)

1,2: 1-r/Colan, Toth, Goodwin, Severin, Wood-a. 2-r/Crandall, Evans, Severin, Torres, Williamson-a 4.00

BLAZING COMICS (Also see Blue Circle Comics and Red Circle Comics)
Enwil Associates/Rural Home: 6/44 - #3, 9/44; #4, 2/45; #5, 3/45; #5(V2#2), 3/55 - #6(V2#3), 1955?

1-The Green Turtle, Red Hawk, Black Buccaneer begin; origin Jun-Gal
50 100 150 305 465 625
2-5: 3-Briefer-a. 5-(V2#2 inside) 35 70 105 198 287 375
5(3/55, V2#2-inside)-Black Buccaneer-c, 6(V2#3-inside, 1955)-Indian/Japanese-c; cover is from Apr. 1945 18 36 54 102 146 190
NOTE: *No. 5 & 6 contain remaindered comics rebound and the contents can vary. Cloak & Daggar, Will Rogers, Superman 64, Star Spangled 130, Kaanga known. Value would be half of contents.*

BLAZING SIXGUNS
Avon Periodicals: Dec, 1952

1-Kinstler-c/a; Larsen/Alascia-a(2), Tuska?-a; Jesse James, Kit Carson, Wild Bill Hickok app. 17 34 51 95 135 175

BLAZING SIXGUNS
I.W./Super Comics: 1964

I.W. Reprint #1,8,9: 1-r/Wild Bill Hickok #26, Western True Crime #? & Blazing Sixguns #1 by Avon; Kinstler-c. 8-r/Blazing Western #?; Kinstler-c. 9-r/Blazing Western #1; Ditko-r; Kintsler-c reprinted from Dalton Boys #1 2 4 6 11 14 18
Super Reprint #10,11,15,16: 10,11-r/The Rider #2,1. 15-r/Silver Kid Western #?. 16-r/Buffalo Bill #?; Wildey-r; Severin-c. 17(1964)-r/Western True Crime #?
2 4 6 11 14 18
12-Reprints Bullseye #3; S&K-a 4 8 12 22 30 38
18-r/Straight Arrow #? by Powell; Severin-c 2 4 6 11 14 18

BLAZING SIX-GUNS (Also see Sundance Kid)
Skywald Comics: Feb, 1971 - No. 2, Apr, 1971 (52 pgs.)

1-The Red Mask (3-D), Sundance Kid begin (new-s), Avon's Geronimo reprint by Kinstler; Wyatt Earp app. 3 6 9 16 20 25
2-Wild Bill Hickok, Jesse James, Kit Carson-r plus M.E. Red Mask-r (3-D)
2 4 6 11 14 18

BLAZING WEST (The Hooded Horseman #21 on)
American Comics Group (B&I Publ./Michel Publ.): Fall, 1948 - No. 20, Nov-Dec, 1951

1-Origin & 1st app. Injun Jones, Tenderfoot & Buffalo Belle; Texas Tim & Ranger begins, ends #13 21 42 63 118 169 220
2,3 (1-2/49) 10 20 30 60 80 100
4-Origin & 1st app. Little Lobo; Starr-a (3-4/49) 9 18 27 54 70 85
5-10: 5-Starr-a 8 16 24 46 58 70
11-13 7 14 21 37 46 55
14(11-12/50)-Origin/1st app. The Hooded Horseman 12 24 36 71 98 125
15-20: 15,16,18,19-Starr-a 9 18 27 51 62 75

BLAZING WESTERN
Timor Publications: Jan, 1954 - No. 5, Sept, 1954

1-Ditko-a (1st Western-a?); text story by Bruce Hamilton
17 34 51 98 139 180
2-4 8 16 24 46 58 70
5-Disbrow-a 9 18 27 51 62 75

BLEAT
Slave Labor Graphics: Aug, 1995 ($2.95)

1 3.00

BLINDSIDE
Image Comics (Extreme Studios): Aug, 1996 ($2.50)

1-Variant-c exists 2.50

BLINK (See X-Men Age of Apocalypse storyline)
Marvel Comics: March, 2001 - No. 4, June, 2001 ($2.99, limited series)

1-4-Adam Kubert-c/Lobdell-s/Winick-script; leads into Exiles #1 3.00

BLIP
Marvel Comics Group: 2/1983 - 1983 (Video game mag. in comic format)

1-1st app. Donkey Kong & Mario Bros. in comics, 6pgs. comics; photo-c
1 2 3 5 6 8
2-Spider-Man photo-c; 6pgs. Spider-Man comics w/Green Goblin
1 3 4 6 8 10
3,4,6 5.00
5-E.T., Indiana Jones; Rocky-c 6.00
7-6pgs. Hulk comics; Pac-Man & Donkey Kong Jr. Hints 1 2 3 4 5 7

BLISS ALLEY
Image Comics: July, 1997 - No. 2, Sept, 1997 ($2.95, B&W)

1,2-Messner-Loebs-s/a 3.00

BLITZKRIEG
National Periodical Publications: Jan-Feb, 1976 - No. 5, Sept-Oct, 1976

1-Kubert-c on all 4 8 12 27 36 45
2-5 3 6 9 16 20 25

BLONDE PHANTOM (Formerly All-Select #1-11; Lovers #23 on)(Also see Blackstone, Marvel Mystery, Millie The Model #2, Sub-Mariner Comics #25 & Sun Girl)
Marvel Comics (MPC): No. 12, Winter, 1946-47 - No. 22, Mar, 1949

12-Miss America begins, ends #14 165 330 495 1031 1591 2150
13-Sub-Mariner begins (not in #16) 98 196 294 613 944 1275
14,15: 15-Kurtzman's "Hey Look" 90 180 270 563 869 1175
16-Captain America with Bucky story by Rico(p), 6 pgs.; Kurtzman's "Hey Look" (1 pg.)
121 242 363 756 1166 1575
17-22: 22-Anti Wertham editorial 77 154 231 481 741 1000
NOTE: ***Shores** c-12-18.*

BLONDIE (See Ace Comics, Comics Reading Libraries (Promotional Comics section), Dagwood, Daisy & Her Pups, Eat Right to Work..., King & Magic Comics)
David McKay Publications: 1942 - 1946

Feature Books 12 (Rare) 79 158 237 494 760 1025
Feature Books 27-29,31,34(1940) 22 44 66 127 184 240
Feature Books 36,38,40,42,43,45,47 21 42 63 121 173 225
...1944 (Hard-c, 1938, B&W, 128 pgs.)-1944 daily strip-r
17 34 51 98 139 180

BLONDIE & DAGWOOD FAMILY
Harvey Publ. (King Features Synd.): Oct, 1963 - No. 4, Dec, 1965 (68 pgs.)

1 4 8 12 29 40 50
2-4 3 6 9 18 24 30

BLONDIE COMICS (...Monthly No. 16-141)
David McKay #1-15/Harvey #16-163/King #164-175/Charlton #177 on:
Spring, 1947 - No. 163, Nov, 1965; No. 164, Aug, 1966 - No. 175, Dec, 1967; No. 177, Feb, 1969 - No. 222, Nov, 1976

1 28 56 84 158 229 300
2 15 30 45 83 117 150
3-5 11 22 33 64 87 110
6-10 9 18 27 54 70 85
11-15 8 16 24 43 54 65
16-(3/50; 1st Harvey issue) 9 18 27 54 70 85
17-20: 20-(3/51)-Becomes Daisy & Her Pups #21 & Chamber of Chills #21
5 10 15 36 48 60
21-30 4 8 12 29 40 50

Blood Legacy: The Young Ones #1 © TC

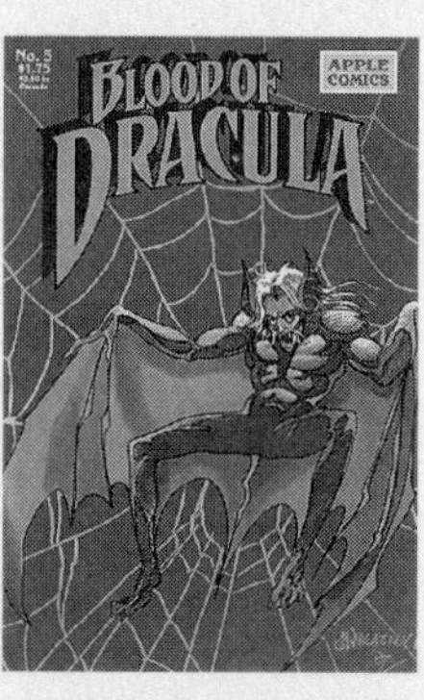

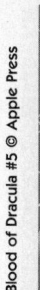

Blood of Dracula #5 © Apple Press

Bloodshot #5 © Voyager Comm.

	GD 2.0	VG 4.0	FN 6.0	VF 8.0	VF/NM 9.0	NM- 9.2
31-50	4	8	12	22	30	38
51-80	3	6	9	19	25	32
81-99	3	6	9	18	24	30
100	4	8	12	22	30	38
101-124,126-130	3	6	9	16	20	25
125 (80 pgs.)	4	8	12	27	36	45
131-136,138,139	2	4	6	12	16	20
137,140-(80 pgs.)	4	8	12	25	33	42
141-147,149-154,156,160,164-167	2	4	6	12	16	20
148,155,157-159,161-163 are 68 pgs.	3	6	9	19	25	32
168-175	2	4	6	10	13	16
177-199 (no #176)	2	4	6	8	10	12
200	2	4	6	9	11	14
201-210,213-222	1	2	3	5	7	9
211,212-1st & 2nd app. Super Dagwood	2	4	6	8	10	12
Blondie, Dagwood & Daisy by Chic Young #1(Harvey, 1953, 100 pg. squarebound giant) new stories; Popeye (1 pg.) and Felix (1pg.) app.	23	46	69	132	191	250

BLOOD
Marvel Comics (Epic Comics): Feb, 1988 - No. 4, Apr, 1988 ($3.25, mature)

1-4: DeMatteis scripts & Kent Williams-c/a 3.50

BLOOD AND GLORY (Punisher & Captain America)
Marvel Comics: Oct, 1992 - No. 3, Dec, 1992 ($5.95, limited series)

1-3: 1-Embossed wraparound-c by Janson; Chichester & Clarke-s 6.00

BLOOD & ROSES: FUTURE PAST TENSE (Bob Hickey's...)
Sky Comics: Dec, 1993 ($2.25)

1-Silver ink logo 2.50

BLOOD & ROSES: SEARCH FOR THE TIME-STONE (Bob Hickey's...)
Sky Comics: Apr, 1994 ($2.50)

1 2.50

BLOOD AND SHADOWS
DC Comics (Vertigo): 1996 - Book 4, 1996 ($5.95, squarebound, mature)

Books 1-4: Joe R. Lansdale scripts; Mark A. Nelson-c/a. 6.00

BLOOD AND WATER
DC Comics (Vertigo): May, 2003 - No. 5, Sept, 2003 ($2.95, limited series)

1-5-Judd Winick-s/Tomm Coker-a/Brian Bolland-c 3.00

BLOOD: A TALE
DC Comics (Vertigo): Nov, 1996 - No. 4, Feb, 1997 ($2.95, limited series)

1-4: Reprints Epic series w/new-c; DeMatteis scripts; Kent Williams-c/a 3.00

BLOODBATH
DC Comics: Early Dec, 1993 - No. 2, Late Dec, 1993 ($3.50, 68 pgs.)

1-Neon ink-c; Superman app.; new Batman-c /app. 3.50

	GD	VG	FN	VF	VF/NM	NM-
2-Hitman 2nd app.	1	2	3	4	5	7

BLOODHOUND
DC Comics: Sept, 2004 - Present ($2.95)

1-6: 1-Jolley-s/Kirk-a/Johnson-c. 5-Firestorm app. (cont. from Firestorm #7) 3.00

BLOOD LEGACY
Image Comics (Top Cow): May, 2000 - No. 4, Nov, 2000; Apr, 2003 ($2.50/$4.99)

...: The Story of Ryan 1-4-Kerri Hawkins-s. 1-Andy Park-a(p); 3 covers 2.50
...: The Young Ones 1 (4/03, $4.99, one-shot) Basaldua-c/a 5.00
Preview Special ('00, $4.95) B&W flip-book w/The Magdalena Preview 5.00

BLOODLINES: A TALE FROM THE HEART OF AFRICA (See Tales From the Heart of Africa)
Marvel Comics (Epic Comics): 1992 ($5.95, 52 pgs.)

1-Story cont'd from Tales From... 6.00

BLOOD OF DRACULA
Apple Comics: Nov, 1987 - No. 20?, 1990 ($1.75/$1.95, B&W)($2.25 #14,16 on)

1-3,5-14,20: 1-10-Chadwick-c 3.00
4,16-19-Lost Frankenstein pgs. by Wrightson 5.00
15-Contains stereo flexidisc ($3.75) 4.00

BLOOD OF THE INNOCENT (See Warp Graphics Annual)
WaRP Graphics: 1/7/86 - No. 4, 1/28/86 (Weekly mini-series, mature)

1-4 2.50

BLOODPACK
DC Comics: Mar, 1995 - No. 4, June,1995 ($1.50, limited series)

1-4 2.25

BLOODPOOL
Image Comics (Extreme): Aug, 1995 - No. 4, Nov, 1995 ($2.50, limited series)

1-4: Jo Duffy scripts in all 2.50
Special (3/96, $2.50)-Jo Duffy scripts 2.50
Trade Paperback (1996, $12.95)-r/#1-4 13.00

BLOODSCENT
Comico: Oct, 1988 ($2.00, one-shot, Baxter paper)

1-Colan-p 2.50

BLOODSEED
Marvel Comics (Frontier Comics): Oct, 1993 - No. 2, Nov, 1993 ($1.95)

1,2: Sharp/Cam Smith-a 3.00

BLOODSHOT (See Eternal Warrior #4 & Rai #0)
Valiant/Acclaim Comics (Valiant): Feb, 1993 - No. 51, Aug, 1996 ($2.25/$2.50)

0-(3/94, $3.50)-Wraparound chromium-c by Quesada(p); origin 3.50
0-Gold variant; no cover price 5.00
Note: There is a "Platinum variant" ; press run error of Gold ed. (25 copies exist) (A CGC certified 9.8 copy sold for $2,067 in 2004)
1-($3.50)-Chromium embossed-c by B. Smith w/poster 3.50
2-5,8-14: 3-$2.25-c begins; cont'd in Hard Corps #5. 4-Eternal Warrior-c/story. 5-Rai & Eternal Warrior app. 14-(3/94)-Reese-c(i) 2.25
6,7: 6-1st app. Ninjak (out of costume). 7-In costume 2.25
15(4/94)-51: 16-w/bound-in trading card. 51-Bloodshot dies? 2.25
Yearbook 1 (1994, $3.95) 4.00
Special 1 (3/94, $5.95)-Zeck-c/a(p); Last Stand 6.00

BLOODSHOT (Volume Two)
Acclaim Comics (Valiant): July, 1997 - No. 16, Oct, 1998 ($2.50)

1-16: 1-Two covers. 5-Copycat-c. X-O Manowar-c/app 2.50

BLOODSTONE
Marvel Comics: Dec, 2001 - No. 4, Mar, 2002 ($2.99)

1-4-Intro. Elsa Bloodstone; Abnett & Lanning-s/Lopez-a 3.00

BLOODSTREAM
Image Comics: Jan, 2004 - No. 4 ($2.95)

1-3-Adam Shaw painted-a 3.00

BLOODSTRIKE (See Supreme V2#3)
Image Comics (Extreme Studios): 1993 - No. 22, May, 1995; No. 25, May, 1994 ($1.95/$2.50)

1-22, 25: Liefeld layouts in early issues. 1-Blood Brothers prelude. 2-1st app. Lethal. 5-1st app. Noble. 9-Black and White part 6 by Art Thibert; Liefeld pin-up. 9,10-Have coupon #3 & 7 for Extreme Prejudice #0. 10-(4/94). 11-(7/94). 16:Platt-c; Prophet app. 17-19-polybagged w/card . 25-(5/94)-Liefeld/Fraga-c 3.00

NOTE: ***Giffen** story/layouts-4-6. **Jae Lee** c-7, 8. **Rob Liefeld** layouts-1-3. **Art Thibert** c-6i.*

BLOODSTRIKE ASSASSIN
Image Comics (Extreme Studios): June, 1995 - No. 3, Aug, 1995; No. 0, Oct, 1995 ($2.50, limited series)

0-3: 3-(8/95)-Quesada-c. 0-(10/95)-Battlestone app. 3.00

BLOOD SWORD, THE
Jademan Comics: Aug, 1988 - No. 53, Dec, 1992 ($1.50/$1.95, 68 pgs.)

1-53-Kung Fu stories in all 3.00

BLOOD SWORD DYNASTY
Jademan Comics: 1989 -No. 41, Jan, 1993 ($1.25, 36 pgs.)

1-Ties into Blood Sword 2.50
2-41: Ties into Blood Sword 2.50

BLOOD SYNDICATE
DC Comics (Milestone): Apr, 1993 - No. 35, Feb, 1996 ($1.50/-$3.50)

1-($2.95)-Collector's Edition; polybagged with poster, trading card, & acid-free backing board (direct sale only) 3.50
1-9,11-24,26,27,29,33-34: 8-Intro Kwai. 15-Byrne-c. 16-Worlds Collide Pt. 6; Superman-c/app. 17-Worlds Collide Pt. 13. 29-(99¢); Long Hot Summer x-over 2.25
10,28,30-32: 10-Simonson-c. 30-Long Hot Summer x-over 2.50
25-($2.95, 52 pgs.) 3.00
35-Kwai disappears; last issue 3.50

BLOODWULF
Image Comics (Extreme): Feb, 1995 - No. 4, May, 1995 ($2.50, limited series)

1-4: 1-Liefeld-c w/4 diferent captions & alternate-c. 2.50
Summer Special (8/95, $2.50)-Jeff Johnson-c/a; Supreme app; story takes place between Legend of Supreme #3 & Supreme #23. 2.50

BLOODY MARY
DC Comics (Helix): Oct, 1996 - No. 4, Jan, 1997 ($2.25, limited series)

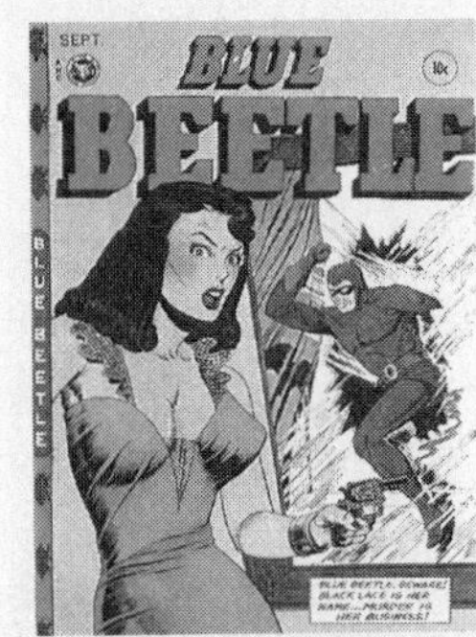

Blue Beetle #48 © FOX

Blue Bolt #2 © NOVP

Blue Bolt #115 © STAR

	GD 2.0	VG 4.0	FN 6.0	VF 8.0	VF/NM 9.0	NM- 9.2
1-4: Garth Ennis scripts; Ezquerra-c/a in all						3.50

BLOODY MARY: LADY LIBERTY
DC Comics (Helix): Sept, 1997 - No. 4, Dec, 1997 ($2.50, limited series)

	GD 2.0	VG 4.0	FN 6.0	VF 8.0	VF/NM 9.0	NM- 9.2
1-4: Garth Ennis scripts; Ezquerra-c/a in all						3.00

BLUE
Image Comics (Action Toys): Aug, 1999 - No. 2, Apr, 2000 ($2.50)

	GD 2.0	VG 4.0	FN 6.0	VF 8.0	VF/NM 9.0	NM- 9.2
1,2-Aronowitz-s/Struzan-c						2.50

BLUEBEARD
Slave Labor Graphics: Nov, 1993 - No. 3, Mar, 1994 ($2.95, B&W, lim. series)

	GD 2.0	VG 4.0	FN 6.0	VF 8.0	VF/NM 9.0	NM- 9.2
1-3: James Robinson scripts. 2-(12/93)						3.00
Trade paperback (6/94, $9.95)						13.00
Trade paperback (2nd printing, 7/96, $12.95)-New-c						13.00

BLUE BEETLE, THE (Also see All Top, Big-3, Mystery Men & Weekly Comic Magazine)
Fox Publ. No. 1-11, 31-60; Holyoke No. 12-30: Winter, 1939-40 - No. 57, 7/48; No. 58, 4/50 - No. 60, 8/50

	GD 2.0	VG 4.0	FN 6.0	VF 8.0	VF/NM 9.0	NM- 9.2
1-Reprints from Mystery Men #1-5; Blue Beetle origin; Yarko the Great-r/from Wonder Comics /Wonderworld #2-5 all by Eisner; Master Magician app.; (Blue Beetle in 4 different costumes)	452	904	1356	3164	5082	7000
2-K-51-r by Powell/Wonderworld #8,9	154	308	462	963	1482	2000
3-Simon-c	113	226	339	706	1091	1475
4-Marijuana drug mention story	75	150	225	469	722	975
5-Zanzibar The Magician by Tuska	66	132	198	413	637	860
6-Dynamite Thor begins (1st); origin Blue Beetle	62	124	186	388	594	800
7,8-Dynamo app. in both. 8-Last Thor	55	110	165	344	532	720
9-12: 9,10-The Blackbird & The Gorilla app. in both. 10-Bondage/hypo-c. 11(2/42)-The Gladiator app. 12(6/42)-The Black Fury app.	51	102	153	311	473	635
13-V-Man begins (1st app.), ends #18; Kubert-a; centerfold spread	60	120	180	375	580	785
14,15-Kubert-a in both. 14-Intro. side-kick (c/text only), Sparky (called Spunky #17-19)	53	106	159	323	492	660
16-18: 17-Brodsky-c	42	84	126	256	393	530
19-Kubert-a	43	86	129	262	401	450
20-Origin/1st app. Tiger Squadron; Arabian Nights begin	47	94	141	287	436	585
21-26: 24-Intro. & only app. The Halo. 26-General Patton story & photo	36	72	108	204	297	390
27-Tamaa, Jungle Prince app.	34	68	102	196	283	370
28-30(2/44)	30	60	90	170	245	320
31(6/44), 33,34,36-40: 34-38-"The Threat from Saturn" serial.	28	56	84	158	229	300
32-Hitler-c	42	84	126	256	391	525
35-Extreme violence	34	68	102	196	283	370
41-45 (#43 exist?)	26	52	78	147	211	275
46-The Puppeteer app.	29	58	87	167	241	315
47-Kamen & Baker-a begin	121	242	363	756	1166	1575
48-50	96	192	288	600	925	1250
51,53	81	162	243	506	778	1050
52-Kamen bondage-c; true crime stories begin	121	242	363	756	1166	1575
54-Used in **SOTI**. Illo, "Children call these 'headlights' comics"	129	258	387	806	1240	1675
55-57: 56-Used in **SOTI**, pg. 145. 57(7/48)-Last Kamen issue; becomes Western Killers?	79	158	237	494	760	1025
58(4/50)-60-No Kamen-a	17	34	51	98	139	180

NOTE: ***Kamen** a-47-51, 53, 55-57; c-47, 49-52. **Powell** a-4(2). Bondage-c 9-12, 46, 52.*

BLUE BEETLE (Formerly The Thing; becomes Mr. Muscles No. 22 on)
(See Charlton Bullseye & Space Adventures)
Charlton Comics: No. 18, Feb, 1955 - No. 21, Aug, 1955

	GD 2.0	VG 4.0	FN 6.0	VF 8.0	VF/NM 9.0	NM- 9.2
18,19-(Pre-1944-r). 18-Last pre-code issue. 19-Bouncer, Rocket Kelly-r	21	42	63	118	169	220
20-Joan Mason by Kamen	26	52	78	147	211	275
21-New material	20	40	60	112	161	210

BLUE BEETLE (Unusual Tales #1-49; Ghostly Tales #55 on)(See Captain Atom #83 & Charlton Bullseye)
Charlton Comics: V2#1, June, 1964 - V2#5, Mar-Apr, 1965; V3#50, July, 1965 - V3#54, Feb-Mar, 1966; #1, June, 1967 - #5, Nov, 1968

	GD 2.0	VG 4.0	FN 6.0	VF 8.0	VF/NM 9.0	NM- 9.2
V2#1-Origin/1st S.A. app. Dan Garrett-Blue Beetle	10	20	30	70	100	130
2-5: 5-Weiss illo; 1st published-a?	6	12	18	43	59	75
V3#50-54-Formerly Unusual Tales	6	12	18	40	55	70
1(1967)-Question series begins by Ditko	11	22	33	80	120	160
2-Origin Ted Kord-Blue Beetle (see Capt. Atom #83 for 1st Ted Kord Blue Beetle); Dan Garrett x-over	6	12	18	43	59	75
3-5 (All Ditko-c/a in #1-5)	6	12	18	38	52	65
1,3(Modern Comics-1977)-Reprints	1	2	3	4	5	7

NOTE: *#6 only appeared in the fanzine 'The Charlton Portfolio.'*

BLUE BEETLE (Also see Americomics, Crisis On Infinite Earths, Justice League & Showcase '94 #2-4)
DC Comics: June, 1986 - No. 24, May, 1988

	GD 2.0	VG 4.0	FN 6.0	VF 8.0	VF/NM 9.0	NM- 9.2
1-Origin retold; intro. Firefist						4.00
2-10,15-19,21-24: 2-Origin Firefist. 5-7-The Question app. 21-Millennium tie-in						2.25
11-14-New Teen Titans x-over						3.00
20-Justice League app.; Millennium tie-in						3.00

BLUEBERRY (See Lt. Blueberry & Marshal Blueberry)
Marvel Comics (Epic Comics): 1989 - No. 5, 1990 ($12.95/$14.95, graphic novel)

	GD 2.0	VG 4.0	FN 6.0	VF 8.0	VF/NM 9.0	NM- 9.2
1,3,4,5-($12.95)-Moebius-a in all						15.00
2-($14.95)						17.00

BLUE BOLT
Funnies, Inc. No. 1/Novelty Press/Premium Group of Comics: June, 1940 - No. 101 (V10#2), Sept-Oct, 1949

	GD 2.0	VG 4.0	FN 6.0	VF 8.0	VF/NM 9.0	NM- 9.2
V1#1-Origin Blue Bolt by Joe Simon, Sub-Zero Man, White Rider & Super Horse, Dick Cole, Wonder Boy & Sgt. Spook (1st app. of each)	310	620	930	2015	3258	4500
2-Simon & Kirby's 1st art & 1st super-hero (Blue Bolt)	169	338	507	1056	1628	2200
3-1 pg. Space Hawk by Wolverton; 2nd S&K-a on Blue Bolt (same cover date as Red Raven #1); 1st time S&K names app. in a comic; Simon-c	140	280	420	875	1350	1825
4,5-S&K-a in each; 5-Everett-a begins on Sub-Zero	127	254	381	794	1222	1650
6,8-10-S&K-a	119	238	357	744	1147	1550
7-S&K-c/a	133	266	399	831	1278	1725
11,12: 11-Robot-c	113	226	339	706	1091	1475
V2#1-Origin Dick Cole & The Twister; Twister x-over in Dick Cole, Sub-Zero, & Blue Bolt; origin Simba Karno who battles Dick Cole thru V2#5 & becomes main supporting character V2#6 on; battle-c	40	80	120	239	357	475
2-Origin The Twister retold in text	34	68	102	193	279	365
3-5: 5-Intro. Freezum	31	62	93	178	259	340
6-Origin Sgt. Spook retold	26	52	78	150	215	280
7-12: 7-Lois Blake becomes Blue Bolt's costume aide; last Twister. 12-Text-sty by Mickey Spillaine	22	44	66	127	184	240
V3#1-3	18	36	54	100	143	185
4-12: 4-Blue Bolt abandons costume	15	30	45	83	117	150
V4#1-Hitler, Tojo, Mussolini-c	37	74	111	209	305	400
V4#2-12: 3-Shows V4#3 on-c, V4#4 inside (9-10/43). 5-Infinity-c. 8-Last Sub-Zero	11	22	33	66	91	115
V5#1-8, V6#1-3,5-10, V7#1-12	11	22	33	64	87	110
V6#4-Racist cover	17	34	51	95	135	175
V8#1-6,8-12, V9#1-4,7,8, V10#1(#100),V10#2(#101)-Last Dick Cole, Blue Bolt	10	20	30	58	77	95
V8#7,V9#6,9-L. B. Cole-c	22	44	66	127	184	240
V9#5-Classic fish in the face-c	21	42	63	121	173	225

NOTE: ***Everett** c-V1#4, 11, V2#1, 2. **Gustavson** a-V1#1-12, V2#1-7. **Kiefer** c-V3#1. **Rico** a-V6#10, V7#4. Blue Bolt not in V9#8.*

BLUE BOLT (Becomes Ghostly Weird Stories #120 on; continuation of Novelty Blue Bolt)
(...Weird Tales of Terror #111,112,...Weird Tales #113-119)
Star Publications: No. 102, Nov-Dec, 1949 - No. 119, May-June, 1953

	GD 2.0	VG 4.0	FN 6.0	VF 8.0	VF/NM 9.0	NM- 9.2
102-The Chameleon, & Target app.	38	76	114	219	320	420
103,104-The Chameleon app. 104-Last Target	37	74	111	209	305	400
105-Origin Blue Bolt (from #1) retold by Simon; Chameleon & Target app.; opium den story	54	108	162	329	502	675
106-Blue Bolt by S&K begins; Spacehawk reprints from Target by Wolverton begin, ends #110; Sub-Zero begins; ends #109	52	104	156	317	484	650
107-110: 108-Last S&K Blue Bolt reprint. 109-Wolverton-c(r)/inside Spacehawk splash. 110-Target app.	50	100	150	305	465	625
111,112: 111-Red Rocket & The Mask-r; last Blue Bolt; 1pg. L. B. Cole-a. 112-Last Torpedo Man app.	45	90	135	275	418	560
113-Wolverton's Spacehawk-r/Target V3#7	47	94	141	287	436	585
114,116: 116-Jungle Jo-r	45	90	135	275	418	560
115-Sgt. Spook app.	47	94	141	287	436	585
117-Jo-Jo & Blue Bolt-r	46	92	138	281	426	570
118-"White Spirit" by Wood	47	94	141	287	436	585
119-Disbrow/Cole-c; Jungle Jo-r	46	92	138	281	426	570
Accepted Reprint #103(1957?, nd)	13	26	39	74	102	130

Blue Monday: Painted Moon #2 © Chynna Clugston-Major

Blue Ribbon Comics #4 © MLJ

Bob Colt #9 © FAW

GD VG FN VF VF/NM NM-
2.0 4.0 6.0 8.0 9.0 9.2

GD VG FN VF VF/NM NM-
2.0 4.0 6.0 8.0 9.0 9.2

NOTE: *L. B. Cole c-102-108, 110 on.* ***Disbrow*** *a-112(2), 113(3), 114(2), 115(2), 116-118.* ***Hollingsworth*** *a-117.* ***Palais*** *a-112r. Sci/Fi c-105-110. Horror c-111.*

BLUE BULLETEER, THE (Also see Femforce Special)
AC Comics: 1989 ($2.25, B&W, one-shot)
1-Origin by Bill Black; Bill Ward-a 4.00

BLUE BULLETEER (Also see Femforce Special)
AC Comics: 1996 ($5.95, B&W, one-shot)
1-Photo-c 6.00

BLUE CIRCLE COMICS (Also see Red Circle Comics, Blazing Comics & Roly Poly Comic Book)
Enwil Associates/Rural Home: June, 1944 - No. 6, Apr, 1945
1-The Blue Circle begins (1st app.); origin & 1st app. Steel Fist
32 64 96 184 267 350
2 20 40 60 112 161 210
3-Hitler parody-c 28 56 84 158 229 300
4-6: 5-Last Steel Fist. 16 32 48 92 131 170
6-(Dated 4/45, Vol. 2#3 inside)-Leftover covers to #6 were later restapled over early 1950's coverless comics; variations of the coverless comics exist.
Colossal Features known. 16 32 48 92 131 170

BLUE DEVIL (See Fury of Firestorm #24, Underworld Unleashed, Starman (2nd) #38)
DC Comics: June, 1984 - No. 31, Dec, 1986 (75¢/$1.25)
1 4.00
2-16,19-31: 4-Origin Nebiros. 7-Gil Kane-a. 8-Giffen-a 2.50
17,18-Crisis x-over 3.00
Annual 1 (11/85)-Team-ups w/Black Orchid, Creeper, Demon, Madame Xanadu, Man-Bat & Phantom Stranger 3.00

BLUE MONDAY: ... (one-shots)
Oni Press: Feb, 2002 - Present (B&W, Chynna Clugston-Major-s/a/c in all)
Dead Man's Party (10/02, $2.95) Dan Brereton painted back-c 3.00
Inbetween Days (9/03, $9.95, 8" x 5-1/2") r/Dead Man's Party, Lovecats, & Nobody's Fool 10.00
Lovecats (2/02, $2.95) Valentine's Day themed 3.00
Nobody's Fool (2/03, $2.95) April Fool's Day themed 3.00

BLUE MONDAY: ABSOLUTE BEGINNERS
Oni Press: Feb, 2001 - No. 4, Sept, 2001 ($2.95, B&W, limited series)
1-4-Chynna Clugston-Major-s/a/c 3.00
TPB (12/01, $11.95, 8" x 6") r/series 12.00

BLUE MONDAY: PAINTED MOON
Oni Press: Feb, 2004 - No. 4 ($2.99, B&W, limited series)
1-3-Chynna Clugston-Major-s/a/c 3.00

BLUE MONDAY: THE KIDS ARE ALRIGHT
Oni Press: Feb, 2000 - No. 3, May, 2000 ($2.95, B&W, limited series)
1-3-Chynna Clugston-Major-s/a/c. 1-Variant-c by Warren. 2-Dorkin-c 3.00
3-Variant cover by J. Scott Campbell 4.00
TPB (12/00, $10.95, digest-sized) r/#1-3 & earlier short stories 11.00

BLUE PHANTOM, THE
Dell Publishing Co.: June-Aug, 1962
1(01-066-208)-by Fred Fredericks 4 8 12 25 33 42

BLUE RIBBON COMICS (...Mystery Comics No. 9-18)
MLJ Magazines: Nov, 1939 - No. 22, Mar, 1942 (1st MLJ series)
1-Dan Hastings, Richy the Amazing Boy, Rang-A-Tang the Wonder Dog begin (1st app. of each); Little Nemo app. (not by W. McCay); Jack Cole-a(3) (1st MLJ comic) 379 758 1137 2464 3982 5500
2-Bob Phantom, Silver Fox (both in #3), Rang-A-Tang Club & Cpl. Collins begin (1st app. of each); Jack Cole-a 137 274 411 856 1316 1775
3-J. Cole-a 87 174 261 544 835 1125
4-Doc Strong, The Green Falcon, & Hercules begin (1st app. each); origin & 1st app. The Fox & Ty-Gor, Son of the Tiger 96 192 288 600 925 1250
5-8: 8-Last Hercules; 6,7-Biro, Meskin-a. 7-Fox app. on-c
65 130 195 406 623 840
9-(Scarce)-Origin & 1st app. Mr. Justice (2/41) 300 600 900 1892 2946 4000
10-13: 12-Last Doc Strong. 13-Inferno, the Flame Breather begins, ends #19; Devil-c
104 208 312 650 1000 1350
14,15,17,18: 15-Last Green Falcon 87 174 261 544 835 1125
16-Origin & 1st app. Captain Flag (9/41) 165 330 495 1031 1591 2150
19-22: 20-Last Ty-Gor. 22-Origin Mr. Justice retold 87 174 261 544 835 1125
NOTE: *Biro c-3-5; a-2 (Cpl. Collins & Scoop Cody).* ***S. Cooper*** *c-9-17. 20-22 contain "Tales From the Witch's Cauldron" (same strip as "Stories of the Black Witch" in Zip Comics). Mr. Justice c-9-18. Captain Flag c-16(w/Mr. Justice), 19-22.*

BLUE RIBBON COMICS (Becomes Teen-Age Diary Secrets #4)
(Also see Approved Comics, Blue Ribbon Comics and Heckle &Jeckle)
Blue Ribbon (St. John): Feb, 1949 - No. 6, Aug, 1949
1-Heckle & Jeckle (Terrytoons) 12 24 36 71 98 125
2(4/49)-Diary Secrets; Baker-c 24 48 72 138 199 260
3-Heckle & Jeckle (Terrytoons) 10 20 30 58 77 95
4(6/49)-Teen-Age Diary Secrets; Baker c/a(2) 24 48 72 138 199 260
5(8/49)-Teen-Age Diary Secrets; Oversize; photo-c; Baker-a(2)- Continues as Teen-Age Diary Secrets 30 60 90 173 249 325
6-Dinky Duck(8/49)(Terrytoons) 7 14 21 37 46 55

BLUE RIBBON COMICS
Red Circle Prod./Archie Ent. No. 5 on: Nov, 1983 - No. 14, Dec, 1984
1-S&K-r/Advs. of the Fly #1,2; Williamson/Torres-r/Fly #2; Ditko-c 6.00
2-7,9,10: 3-Origin Steel Sterling. 5-S&K Shield-r; new Kirby-c. 6,7-The Fox app. 5.00
8-Toth centerspread; Black Hood app.; Neal Adams-a(r) 6.00
11,13,14: 11-Black Hood. 13-Thunder Bunny. 14-Web & Jaguar 5.00
12-Thunder Agents; Noman new Ditko-a 6.00
NOTE: ***N. Adams*** *a(r)-8.* ***Buckler*** *a-4i.* ***Nino*** *a-2i.* ***McWilliams*** *a-8.* ***Morrow*** *a-8.*

BLUE STREAK (See Holyoke One-Shot No. 8)

BLUNTMAN AND CHRONIC TPB(Also see Jay and Silent Bob, Clerks, and Oni Double Feature)
Image Comics: Dec, 2001 ($14.95, TPB)
nn-Tie-in for "Jay & Silent Bob Strike Back" movie; new Kevin Smith-s/Michael Oeming-a; r/app. from Oni Double Feature #12 in color; Ben Affleck & Jason Lee afterwords 15.00

BLYTHE (Marge's)
Dell Publishing Co.: No. 1072, Jan-Mar, 1960
Four Color 1072 6 12 18 43 59 75

B-MAN (See Double-Dare Adventures)

BO (Tom Cat #4 on) (Also see Big Shot #29 & Dixie Dugan)
Charlton Comics Group: June, 1955 - No. 3, Oct, 1955 (A dog)
1-3: Newspaper reprints by Frank Beck 8 16 24 43 54 65

BOATNIKS, THE (See Walt Disney Showcase No. 1)

BOB BURDEN'S ORIGINAL MYSTERYMEN PRESENTS
Dark Horse Comics: 1999 - No. 4 ($2.95/$3.50)
1-3-Bob Burden-s/Sadowski-a(p) 3.50
4-($3.50) All Villain issue 3.50

BOBBY BENSON'S B-BAR-B RIDERS (Radio) (See Best of The West, The Lemonade Kid & Model Fun)
Magazine Enterprises/AC Comics: May-June, 1950 - No. 20, May-June, 1953
1-The Lemonade Kid begins; Powell-a (Scarce) 42 84 126 256 391 525
2 18 36 54 100 143 185
3-5: 4,5-Lemonade Kid-c (#4-Spider-c) 14 28 42 79 110 140
6-8,10 13 26 39 74 102 130
9,11,13-Frazetta-c; Ghost Rider in #13-15 by Ayers-a. 13-Ghost Rider-c
35 70 105 201 293 385
12,17-20: 20-(A-1 #88) 11 22 33 66 91 115
14-Decapitation/Bondage-c & story; classic horror-c 27 54 81 152 219 285
15-Ghost Rider-c 21 42 63 121 173 225
16-Photo-c 14 28 42 79 110 140
1 (1990, $2.75, B&W)-Reprints; photo-c & inside covers 3.00
NOTE: ***Ayers*** *a-13-15, 20.* ***Powell*** *a-1-12(4 ea.), 13(3), 14-16(Red Hawk only); c-1-8,1 0, 12. Lemonade Kid in most 1-13.*

BOBBY COMICS
Universal Phoenix Features: May, 1946
1-By S. M. Iger 9 18 27 51 62 75

BOBBY SHERMAN (TV)
Charlton Comics: Feb, 1972 - No. 7, Oct, 1972
1-Based on TV show "Getting Together" 5 10 15 36 48 60
2-7: 2,4-Photo-c 4 8 12 22 30 38

BOB COLT (Movie star)(See XMas Comics)
Fawcett Publications: Nov, 1950 - No. 10, May, 1952
1-Bob Colt, his horse Buckskin & sidekick Pablo begin; photo front/back-c begin 42 84 126 256 391 525
2 26 52 78 147 211 275
3-5 21 42 63 118 169 220
6-Flying Saucer story 18 36 54 100 143 185
7-10: 9-Last photo back-c 16 32 48 92 131 170

BOB HOPE (See Adventures of... & Calling All Boys #12)

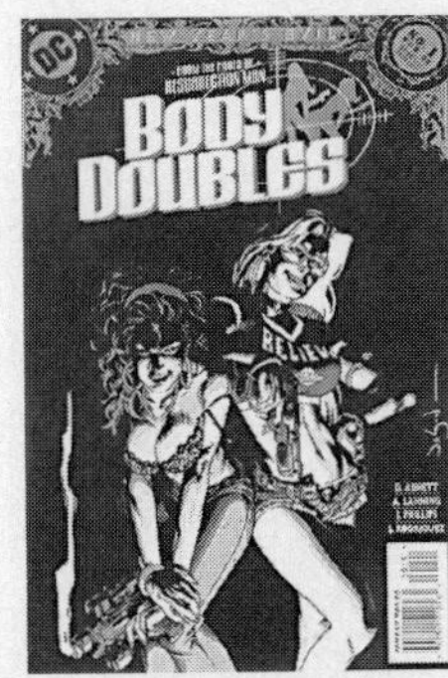

Body Doubles #1 © DC

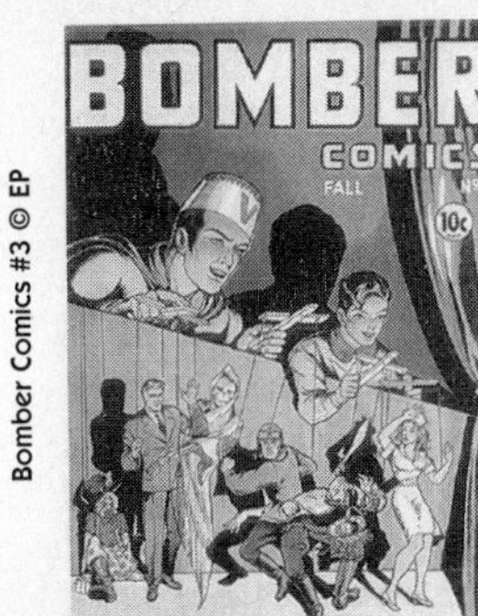

Bomber Comics #3 © EP

Bone #53 © Jeff Smith

BOB MARLEY, TALE OF THE TUFF GONG (Music star)
Marvel Comics: Aug, 1994 - No. 3, Nov, 1994 ($5.95, limited series)

	GD 2.0	VG 4.0	FN 6.0	VF 8.0	VF/NM 9.0	NM- 9.2
1-3						6.00

BOB POWELL'S TIMELESS TALES
Eclipse Comics: March, 1989 ($2.00, B&W)

	GD 2.0	VG 4.0	FN 6.0	VF 8.0	VF/NM 9.0	NM- 9.2
1-Powell-r/Black Cat #5 (Scarlet Arrow), 9 & Race for the Moon #1						3.00

BOB SCULLY, THE TWO-FISTED HICK DETECTIVE (Also see Advs. of Detective Ace King and Detective Dan)
Humor Publ. Co.: No date (1933) (36 pgs., 9-1/2x11", B&W, paper-c; 10¢-c)

	GD 2.0	VG 4.0	FN 6.0	VF 8.0	VF/NM 9.0	NM- 9.2
nn-By Howard Dell; not reprints; along with Advs. of Det. Ace King and Detective Dan, the first comic w/original art & the first of a single theme; has a blue 2-tone cover	375	750	1125	3000	-	-

BOB SON OF BATTLE
Dell Publishing Co.: No. 729, Nov, 1956

	GD 2.0	VG 4.0	FN 6.0	VF 8.0	VF/NM 9.0	NM- 9.2
Four Color 729	4	8	12	29	40	50

BOB STEELE WESTERN (Movie star)
Fawcett Publications/AC Comics: Dec, 1950 - No. 10, June, 1952; 1990

	GD 2.0	VG 4.0	FN 6.0	VF 8.0	VF/NM 9.0	NM- 9.2
1-Bob Steele & his horse Bullet begin; photo front/back-c begin	57	114	171	356	548	740
2	32	64	96	184	267	350
3-5: 4-Last photo back-c	23	46	69	132	191	250
6-10: 10-Last photo-c	19	38	57	107	154	200
1 (1990, $2.75, B&W)-Bob Steele & Rocky Lane reprints; photo-c & inside covers						3.00

BOB SWIFT (Boy Sportsman)
Fawcett Publications: May, 1951 - No. 5, Jan, 1952

	GD 2.0	VG 4.0	FN 6.0	VF 8.0	VF/NM 9.0	NM- 9.2
1	10	20	30	58	77	95
2-5: Saunders painted-c #1-5	6	12	18	33	41	48

BOB, THE GALACTIC BUM
DC Comics: Feb, 1995 - No. 4, June, 1995 ($1.95, limited series)

	GD 2.0	VG 4.0	FN 6.0	VF 8.0	VF/NM 9.0	NM- 9.2
1-4: 1-Lobo app.						2.50

BODY BAGS
Dark Horse Comics (Blanc Noir): Sept, 1996 - No. 4, Jan, 1997 ($2.95, mini-series, mature) (1st Blanc Noir series)

	GD 2.0	VG 4.0	FN 6.0	VF 8.0	VF/NM 9.0	NM- 9.2
1-Jason Pearson-c/a/scripts in all. 1-Intro Clownface & Panda.	1	2	3	5	6	8
2	1	3	4	6	8	10
3,4						6.00

BODYCOUNT (Also see Casey Jones & Raphael)
Image Comics (Highbrow Entertainment): Mar, 1996 - No. 4, July, 1996 ($2.50, lim. series)

	GD 2.0	VG 4.0	FN 6.0	VF 8.0	VF/NM 9.0	NM- 9.2
1-4: Kevin Eastman-a(p)/scripts; Simon Bisley-c/a(i); Turtles app.						2.50

BODY DOUBLES (See Resurrection Man)
DC Comics: Oct, 1999 - No. 4, Jan, 2000 ($2.50, limited series)

	GD 2.0	VG 4.0	FN 6.0	VF 8.0	VF/NM 9.0	NM- 9.2
1-4-Lanning & Abnett-s. 2-Black Canary app. 4-Wonder Woman app.						2.50
...(Villains) (2/98, $1.95, one-shot) 1-Pearson-c; Deadshot app.						2.50

BOFFO LAFFS
Paragraphics: 1986 - No. 5 ($2.50/$1.95)

	GD 2.0	VG 4.0	FN 6.0	VF 8.0	VF/NM 9.0	NM- 9.2
1-($2.50) First comic cover with hologram						3.00
2-5						2.25

BOHOS
Image Comics (Flypaper Press): June, 1998 - No. 3 ($2.95)

	GD 2.0	VG 4.0	FN 6.0	VF 8.0	VF/NM 9.0	NM- 9.2
1-3-Whorf-s/Penaranda-a						3.00

BOLD ADVENTURES
Pacific Comics: Oct, 1983 - No. 3, June, 1984 ($1.50)

	GD 2.0	VG 4.0	FN 6.0	VF 8.0	VF/NM 9.0	NM- 9.2
1-Time Force, Anaconda, & The Weirdling begin						3.00
2,3: 2-Soldiers of Fortune begins. 3-Spitfire						3.00

NOTE: *Kaluta c-3. Nebres a-1-3. Nino a-2, 3. Severin a-3.*

BOLD STORIES (Also see Candid Tales & It Rhymes With Lust)
Kirby Publishing Co.: Mar, 1950 - July, 1950 (Digest size, 144 pgs.)

	GD 2.0	VG 4.0	FN 6.0	VF 8.0	VF/NM 9.0	NM- 9.2
March issue (Very Rare) - Contains "The Ogre of Paris" by Wood	129	258	387	806	1241	1675
May issue (Very Rare) - Contains "The Cobra's Kiss" by Graham Ingels (21 pgs.)	112	224	336	700	1075	1450
July issue (Very Rare) - Contains "The Ogre of Paris" by Wood	98	196	294	613	944	1275

BOLT AND STAR FORCE SIX
Americomics: 1984 ($1.75)

	GD 2.0	VG 4.0	FN 6.0	VF 8.0	VF/NM 9.0	NM- 9.2
1-Origin Bolt & Star Force Six						3.00
Special 1 (1984, $2.00, 52pgs., B&W)						3.00

BOMBARDIER (See Bee 29, the Bombardier & Cinema Comics Herald)

BOMBAST
Topps Comics: 1993 ($2.95, one-shot) (Created by Jack Kirby)

	GD 2.0	VG 4.0	FN 6.0	VF 8.0	VF/NM 9.0	NM- 9.2
1-Polybagged w/Kirbychrome trading card; Savage Dragon app.; Kirby-c; has coupon for Amberchrome Secret City Saga #0						3.00

BOMBA THE JUNGLE BOY (TV)
National Periodical Publ.: Sept-Oct, 1967 - No. 7, Sept-Oct, 1968 (12¢)

	GD 2.0	VG 4.0	FN 6.0	VF 8.0	VF/NM 9.0	NM- 9.2
1-Intro. Bomba; Infantino/Anderson-c	4	8	12	27	36	45
2-7	3	6	9	16	20	25

BOMBER COMICS
Elliot Publ. Co./Melverne Herald/Farrell/Sunrise Times: Mar, 1944 - No. 4, Winter, 1944-45

	GD 2.0	VG 4.0	FN 6.0	VF 8.0	VF/NM 9.0	NM- 9.2
1-Wonder Boy, & Kismet, Man of Fate begin	77	154	231	481	741	1000
2-Hitler-c	62	124	186	388	594	800
3: 2-4-Have Classics Comics ad to HRN 20	42	84	126	256	391	525
4-Hitler, Tojo & Mussolini-c; Sensation Comics #13-c/swipe; has Classics Comics ad to HRN 20.	63	126	189	394	610	825

BONANZA (TV)
Dell/Gold Key: June-Aug, 1960 - No. 37, Aug, 1970 (All Photo-c)

	GD 2.0	VG 4.0	FN 6.0	VF 8.0	VF/NM 9.0	NM- 9.2
Four Color 1110 (6-8/60)	36	72	108	270	423	575
Four Color 1221,1283, & #01070-207, 01070-210	20	40	60	141	216	290
1(12/62-Gold Key)	21	42	63	148	227	305
2	11	22	33	80	120	160
3-10	10	20	30	67	96	125
11-20	8	16	24	53	74	95
21-37: 29-Reprints	7	14	21	46	63	80

BONE
Cartoon Books #1-20, 28 on/Image Comics #21-27: Jul, 1991 - No. 55, Jun, 2004 ($2.95, B&W)

	GD 2.0	VG 4.0	FN 6.0	VF 8.0	VF/NM 9.0	NM- 9.2
1-Jeff Smith-c/a in all	7	14	21	51	71	90
1-2nd printing	2	4	6	8	10	12
1-3rd thru 5th printings						4.00
2-1st printing	4	8	12	27	36	45
2-2nd & 3rd printings						4.00
3-1st printing	3	7	10	21	28	35
3-2nd thru 4th printings						4.00
4,5	2	4	6	11	14	18
6-10	1	2	3	5	7	9
11-37: 21-1st Image issue						4.00
13 1/2 (1/95, Wizard)	1	3	4	6	8	10
13 1/2 (Gold)	2	4	6	8	10	12
38-($4.95) Three covers by Miller, Ross, Smith						5.00
39-55-($2.95)						3.00
1-27-($2.95): 1-Image reprints begin w/new-c. 2-Allred pin-up.						3.00
... Holiday Special (1993, giveaway)						3.00
... Reader -($9.95) Behind the scenes info						10.00
... Sourcebook-San Diego Edition						3.00
...10th Anniversary Edition (8/01, $5.95) r/#1 in color; came with figure						6.00
Complete Bone Adventures Vol 1,2 ('93, '94, $12.95, r/#1-6 & #7-12)						13.00
...: One Volume Edition (2004, $39.95, 1300 pgs.) r/#1-54; extra material						40.00
Volume 1-($19.95, hard-c)-"Out From Boneville"						20.00
Volume 1-($12.95, soft-c)						13.00
Volume 2,5-($22.95, hard-c)-"The Great Cow Race" & "Rock Jaw"						23.00
Volume 2,5-($14.95, soft-c)						15.00
Volume 3,4-($24.95, hard-c)-"Eyes of the Storm" & "The Dragonslayer"						25.00
Volume 3,4,7-($16.95, soft-c)						17.00
Volume 6-($15.95, soft-c)-"Old Man's Cave"						16.00
Volume 7-($24.95, hard-c)-"Ghost Circles"						25.00
Volume 8-($23.95, hard-c)-"Treasure Hunters"						24.00

NOTE: *Printings not listed sell for cover price.*

BONGO (See Story Hour Series)

BONGO & LUMPJAW (Disney, see Walt Disney Showcase #3)
Dell Publishing Co.: No. 706, June, 1956; No. 886, Mar, 1958

	GD 2.0	VG 4.0	FN 6.0	VF 8.0	VF/NM 9.0	NM- 9.2
Four Color 706 (#1)	7	14	21	46	63	80
Four Color 886	6	12	18	38	52	65

BONGO COMICS PRESENTS RADIOACTIVE MAN (See Radioactive Man)

BON VOYAGE (See Movie Classics)

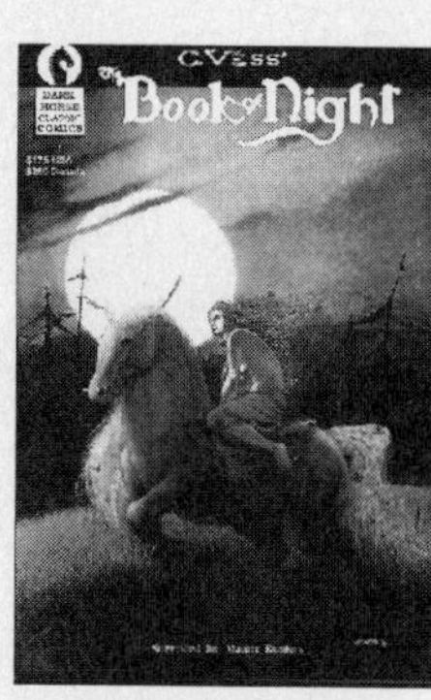

Book of Night #1 © DH

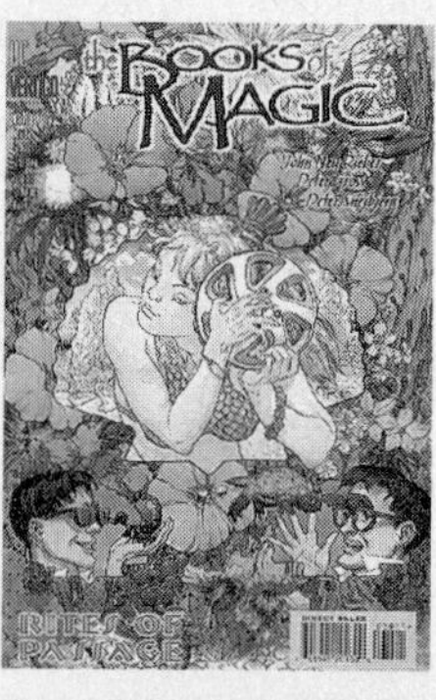

Books of Magic #30 © DC

Booster Gold #9 © DC

GD VG FN VF VF/NM NM-
2.0 4.0 6.0 8.0 9.0 9.2

GD VG FN VF VF/NM NM-
2.0 4.0 6.0 8.0 9.0 9.2

BOOF
Image Comics (Todd McFarlane Prod.): July, 1994 - No. 6, Dec, 1994 ($1.95)

	GD 2.0	VG 4.0	FN 6.0	VF 8.0	VF/NM 9.0	NM- 9.2
1-6						2.25

BOOF AND THE BRUISE CREW
Image Comics (Todd McFarlane Prod.): July, 1994 - No. 6, Dec, 1994 ($1.95)

	GD 2.0	VG 4.0	FN 6.0	VF 8.0	VF/NM 9.0	NM- 9.2
1-6						2.25

BOOK AND RECORD SET (See Power Record Comics)

BOOK OF ALL COMICS
William H. Wise: 1945 (196 pgs.)(Inside f/c has Green Publ. blacked out)

	GD 2.0	VG 4.0	FN 6.0	VF 8.0	VF/NM 9.0	NM- 9.2
nn-Green Mask, Puppeteer & The Bouncer	42	84	126	256	391	525

BOOK OF ANTS, THE
Artisan Entertainment: 1998 ($2.95, B&W)

	GD 2.0	VG 4.0	FN 6.0	VF 8.0	VF/NM 9.0	NM- 9.2
1-Based on the movie Pi; Aronofsky-s						3.00

BOOK OF BALLADS AND SAGAS, THE
Green Man Press: Oct, 1995 - No. 4 ($2.95/$3.50/$3.25, B&W)

	GD 2.0	VG 4.0	FN 6.0	VF 8.0	VF/NM 9.0	NM- 9.2
1-4: 1-Vess-c/a; Gaiman story.						3.50

BOOK OF COMICS, THE
William H. Wise: No date (1944) (25¢, 132 pgs.)

	GD 2.0	VG 4.0	FN 6.0	VF 8.0	VF/NM 9.0	NM- 9.2
nn-Captain V app.	40	80	120	239	357	475

BOOK OF FATE, THE (See Fate)
DC Comics: Feb, 1997 - No. 12, Jan, 1998 ($2.25/$2.50)

	GD 2.0	VG 4.0	FN 6.0	VF 8.0	VF/NM 9.0	NM- 9.2
1-12: 4-Two-Face-c/app. 6-Convergence. 11-Sentinel app.						3.00

BOOK OF LOVE (See Fox Giants)

BOOK OF NIGHT, THE
Dark Horse Comics: July, 1987 - No. 3, 1987 ($1.75, B&W)

	GD 2.0	VG 4.0	FN 6.0	VF 8.0	VF/NM 9.0	NM- 9.2
1-3: Reprints from Epic Illustrated; Vess-a						2.25
TPB-r/#1-3						15.00
Hardcover-Black-c with red crest						100.00
Hardcover w/slipcase (1991) signed and numbered						50.00

BOOK OF THE DEAD
Marvel Comics: Dec, 1993 - No. 4, Mar, 1994 ($1.75, limited series, 52 pgs.)

	GD 2.0	VG 4.0	FN 6.0	VF 8.0	VF/NM 9.0	NM- 9.2
1-4: 1-Ploog Frankenstein & Morrow Man-Thing-r begin; Wrightson-r/Chamber of Darkness #7. 2-Morrow new painted-c; Chaykin/Morrow Man-Thing; Krigstein-r/Uncanny Tales #54; r/Fear #10. 3-r/Astonishing Tales #10 & Starlin Man-Thing. 3,4-Painted-c						5.00

BOOKS OF FAERIE, THE
DC Comics (Vertigo): Mar, 1997 - No. 3, May,1997 ($2.50, limited series)

	GD 2.0	VG 4.0	FN 6.0	VF 8.0	VF/NM 9.0	NM- 9.2
1-3-Gross-a						3.00
TPB (1998, $14.95) r/#1-3 & Arcana Annual #1						15.00

BOOKS OF FAERIE, THE : AUBERON'S TALE
DC Comics (Vertigo): Aug, 1998 - No. 3, Oct,1998 ($2.50, limited series)

	GD 2.0	VG 4.0	FN 6.0	VF 8.0	VF/NM 9.0	NM- 9.2
1-3-Gross-a						3.00

BOOKS OF FAERIE, THE : MOLLY'S STORY
DC Comics (Vertigo): Sept, 1999 - No. 4, Dec,1999 ($2.50, limited series)

	GD 2.0	VG 4.0	FN 6.0	VF 8.0	VF/NM 9.0	NM- 9.2
1-4-Ney Rieber-s/Mejia-a						3.00

BOOKS OF MAGIC
DC Comics: 1990 - No. 4, 1991 ($3.95, 52 pgs., limited series, mature)

	GD 2.0	VG 4.0	FN 6.0	VF 8.0	VF/NM 9.0	NM- 9.2
1-Bolton painted-c/a; Phantom Stranger app.; Gaiman scripts in all	1	3	4	6	8	10
2,3: 2-John Constantine, Dr. Fate, Spectre, Deadman app. 3-Dr. Occult app.; minor Sandman app.	1	2	3	4	5	7
4-Early Death-c/app. (early 1991)	1	2	3	5	6	8
Trade paperback-($19.95)-Reprints limited series						20.00

BOOKS OF MAGIC (Also see Hunter: The Age of Magic and Names of Magic)
DC Comics (Vertigo): May, 1994 - No. 75, Aug, 2000 ($1.95/$2.50, mature)

	GD 2.0	VG 4.0	FN 6.0	VF 8.0	VF/NM 9.0	NM- 9.2
1-Charles Vess-c	2	4	6	8	10	12
1-Platinum	2	4	6	14	18	22
2-4: 4-Death app.	1	2	3	4	5	7
5-14; Charles Vess-c						4.00
15-50: 15-$2.50-c begins. 22-Kaluta-c. 25-Death-c/app; Bachalo-c						3.00
51-75: 51-Peter Gross-s/a begins. 55-Medley-a						2.50
Annual 1-3 (2/97, 2/98, '99, $3.95)						4.00
Bindings (1995, $12.95, TPB)-r/#1-4						13.00
Death After Death (2001, $19.95, TPB)-r/#42-50						20.00
Girl in the Box (1999, $14.95, TPB)-r/#26-32						15.00
Reckonings (1997, $12.95, TPB)-r/#14-20						13.00
Summonings (1996, $17.50, TPB)-r/#5-13, Vertigo Rave #1						17.50
The Burning Girl (2000, $17.95, TPB)-r/#33-41						18.00
Transformations (1998, $12.95, TPB)-r/#21-25						13.00

BOOKS OF MAGICK, THE : LIFE DURING WARTIME (See Books of Magic)
DC Comics (Vertigo): Sept, 2004 - Present ($2.50)

	GD 2.0	VG 4.0	FN 6.0	VF 8.0	VF/NM 9.0	NM- 9.2
1-5-Spencer-s/Ormston-a/Quitely-c; Constantine app. 2-Bagged with Sky Captain CD						2.50

BOONDOGGLE
Knight Press: Mar, 1995 - No. 4 ($2.95, B&W)

	GD 2.0	VG 4.0	FN 6.0	VF 8.0	VF/NM 9.0	NM- 9.2
1-4: Stegelin-c/a/scripts						3.00

BOONDOGGLE
Caliber Press: Jan, 1997 - No. 2 ($2.95, B&W)

	GD 2.0	VG 4.0	FN 6.0	VF 8.0	VF/NM 9.0	NM- 9.2
1,2: Stegelin-c/a/scripts						3.00

BOOSTER GOLD (See Justice League #4)
DC Comics: Feb, 1986 - No. 25, Feb, 1988 (75¢)

	GD 2.0	VG 4.0	FN 6.0	VF 8.0	VF/NM 9.0	NM- 9.2
1-Dan Jurgens-s/a(p)						3.00
2-25: 4-Rose & Thorn app. 6-Origin. 6,7,23-Superman app. 8,9-LSH app. 22-JLI app. 24,25-Millennium tie-ins						2.50

NOTE: *Austin c-22i. Byrne c-23i.*

BOOTS AND HER BUDDIES
Standard Comics/Visual Editions/Argo (NEA Service):
No. 5, 9/48 - No. 9, 9/49; 12/55 - No. 3, 1956

	GD 2.0	VG 4.0	FN 6.0	VF 8.0	VF/NM 9.0	NM- 9.2
5-Strip-r	17	34	51	95	135	175
6,8	11	22	33	64	87	110
7-(Scarce)	13	26	39	76	106	135
9-(Scarce)-Frazetta-a (2 pgs.)	26	52	78	147	211	275
1-3(Argo-1955-56)-Reprints	6	12	18	31	38	45

BOOTS & SADDLES (TV)
Dell Publ. Co.: No. 919, July, 1958; No. 1029, Sept, 1959; No. 1116, Aug, 1960

	GD 2.0	VG 4.0	FN 6.0	VF 8.0	VF/NM 9.0	NM- 9.2
Four Color 919 (#1)-Photo-c	9	18	27	63	89	115
Four Color 1029, 1116-Photo-c	6	12	18	43	59	75

BORDERLINE
Friction Press: June, 1992 ($2.25, B&W)

	GD 2.0	VG 4.0	FN 6.0	VF 8.0	VF/NM 9.0	NM- 9.2
0-Ashcan edition; 1st app. of Cliff Broadway						2.25
1-Painted-c						3.00
1-Special Edition (bagged w/ photo, S&N)						4.00

BORDER PATROL
P. L. Publishing Co.: May-June, 1951 - No. 3, Sept-Oct, 1951

	GD 2.0	VG 4.0	FN 6.0	VF 8.0	VF/NM 9.0	NM- 9.2
1	13	26	39	76	106	135
2,3	9	18	27	52	66	80

BORDER WORLDS (Also see Megaton Man)
Kitchen Sink Press: 7/86 - No. 7, 1987; V2#1, 1990 - No. 4, 1990 ($1.95-$2.00, B&W, mature)

	GD 2.0	VG 4.0	FN 6.0	VF 8.0	VF/NM 9.0	NM- 9.2
1-7, V2#1-4: Donald Simpson-c/a/scripts						3.00

BORIS KARLOFF TALES OF MYSTERY (TV) (...Thriller No. 1,2)
Gold Key: No. 3, April, 1963 - No. 97, Feb, 1980

	GD 2.0	VG 4.0	FN 6.0	VF 8.0	VF/NM 9.0	NM- 9.2
3-5-(Two #5's, 10/63,11/63): 5-(10/63)-11 pgs. Toth-a.	5	10	15	33	44	55
6-8,10: 10-Orlando-a	4	8	12	24	32	40
9-Wood-a	4	8	12	25	33	42
11-Williamson-a, 8 pgs.; Orlando-a, 5 pgs.	4	8	12	25	33	42
12-Torres, McWilliams-a; Orlando-a(2)	3	7	10	21	28	35
13,14,16-20	3	6	9	18	24	30
15-Crandall	3	6	9	19	25	32
21-Jeff Jones-a(3 pgs.) "The Screaming Skull"	3	6	9	19	25	32
22-Last 12¢ issue	3	6	9	16	20	24
23-30: 23-Reprint; photo-c	2	4	6	14	18	22
31-50: 36-Weiss-a	2	4	6	11	14	18
51-74: 74-Origin & 1st app. Taurus	2	4	6	9	11	14
75-79,87-97: 90-r/Torres, McWilliams-a/#12; Morrow-c	1	3	4	6	8	10
80-86-(52 pgs.)	2	4	6	9	11	14
Story Digest 1(7/70-Gold Key)-All text/illos.; 148pp.	5	10	15	36	48	60

(See Mystery Comics Digest No. 2, 5, 8, 11, 14, 17, 20, 23, 26)
NOTE: *Bolle a-51-54, 56, 58, 59. McWilliams a-12, 14, 18, 19, 72, 80, 81, 93. Orlando a-11-15, 21. Reprints: 78, 81-86, 88, 90, 92, 95, 97.*

BORIS KARLOFF THRILLER (TV) (Becomes Boris Karloff Tales...)
Gold Key: Oct, 1962 - No. 2, Jan, 1963 (84 pgs.)

	GD 2.0	VG 4.0	FN 6.0	VF 8.0	VF/NM 9.0	NM- 9.2
1-Photo-c	10	20	30	72	104	135

Boy Comics #9 © LEV

Boy Commandos #15 © DC

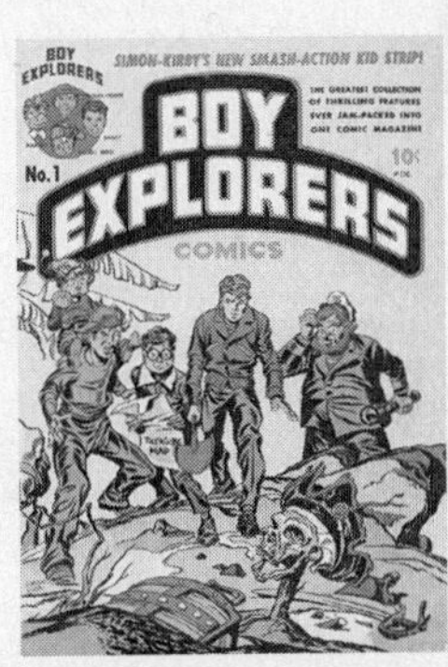
Boy Explorers Comics #1 © HARV

	GD 2.0	VG 4.0	FN 6.0	VF 8.0	VF/NM 9.0	NM- 9.2
2	7	14	21	46	63	80

BORIS THE BEAR
Dark Horse Comics/Nicotat Comics #13 on: Aug, 1986 - No. 34, 1990 ($1.50/$1.75/$1.95, B&W)

1 , Annual 1 (1988, $2.50) 3.00
1 (2nd printing),2,3,4A,4B,5-12, 14-34: 8-(44 pgs.) 2.25
13-1st Nicotat Comics issue 3.00

BORIS THE BEAR INSTANT COLOR CLASSICS
Dark Horse Comics: July, 1987 - No. 3, 1987 ($1.75/$1.95)

1-3 2.25

BORN
Marvel Comics: 2003 - No. 4, 2003 ($3.50, limited series)

1-4-Frank Castle (the Punisher) in 1971 Vietnam; Ennis-s/Robertson-a 3.50
HC (2004, $17.99) oversized reprint of series; proposal, layout pages 18.00
Punisher: Born SC (2004, $13.99) r/series; proposal, layout pages 14.00

BORN AGAIN
Spire Christian Comics (Fleming H. Revell Co.): 1978 (39¢)

	GD	VG	FN	VF	VF/NM	NM-
nn-Watergate, Nixon, etc.	2	4	6	8	10	12

BOUNCER, THE (Formerly Green Mask #9)
Fox Features Syndicate: 1944 - No. 14, Jan, 1945

	GD	VG	FN	VF	VF/NM	NM-
nn(1944, #10?)	31	62	93	178	259	340
11 (9/44)-Origin; Rocket Kelly, One Round Hogan app.	24	48	72	135	195	255
12-14: 14-Reprints no # issue	19	38	57	107	154	200

BOUNTY GUNS (See Luke Short's..., Four Color 739)

BOX OFFICE POISON
Antarctic Press: 1996 - No. 21, Sept, 2000 ($2.95, B&W)

	GD	VG	FN	VF	VF/NM	NM-
1-Alex Robinson-s/a in all	1	2	3	4	5	7

2-5 4.00
6-21, ...Kolor Karnival 1 (5/99, $2.99) 3.00
...Super Special 0 (5/97, $4.95) 5.00
Sherman's March: Collected BOP Vol. 1 (9/98, $14.95) r/#0-4 15.00
TPB (2002, $29.95, 608 pgs.) r/entire series 30.00

BOY AND HIS 'BOT, A
Now Comics: Jan, 1987 ($1.95)

1-A Holiday Special 3.00

BOY AND THE PIRATES, THE (Movie)
Dell Publishing Co.: No. 1117, Aug, 1960

	GD	VG	FN	VF	VF/NM	NM-
Four Color 1117-Photo-c	8	16	24	53	74	95

BOY COMICS (Captain Battle No. 1 & 2; Boy Illustories No. 43-108) (Stories by Charles Biro) (Also see Squeeks)
Lev Gleason Publ. (Comic House): No. 3, Apr, 1942 - No. 119, Mar, 1956

	GD	VG	FN	VF	VF/NM	NM-
3(No.1)-Origin Crimebuster, Bombshell & Young Robin Hood; Yankee Longago, Case 1001-1008, Swoop Storm, & Boy Movies begin; 1st app. Iron Jaw; Crimebuster's pet monkey Squeeks begins	300	600	900	1940	3120	4300
4-Hitler, Tojo, Mussolini-c	127	254	381	794	1222	1650
5	89	178	267	556	853	1150
6-Origin Iron Jaw; origin & death of Iron Jaw's son; Little Dynamite begins, ends #39; 1st Iron Jaw-c	300	600	900	1875	2888	3900
7-Flag & Hitler, Tojo, Mussolini-c	90	180	270	563	869	1175
8-Death of Iron Jaw; Iron Jaw-c	90	180	270	563	869	1175
9-Iron Jaw-c	79	158	237	494	760	1025
10-Return of Iron Jaw; classic Biro-c; Iron Jaw-c	121	242	363	756	1166	1575
11-Classic Iron Jaw-c	81	162	243	506	778	1050
12,13	55	110	165	340	520	700
14-Iron Jaw-c	63	126	189	394	610	825
15-Death of Iron Jaw	73	146	219	456	703	950
16,18-20	40	80	120	233	342	450
17-Flag-c	40	80	120	239	357	475
21-29,31,32-(All 68 pgs.). 28-Yankee Longago ends. 32-Swoop Storm & Young Robin Hood end	26	52	78	150	215	280
30-(68 pgs.)-Origin Crimebuster retold	37	74	111	209	305	400
33-40: 34-Crimebuster story(2); suicide-c/story	20	40	60	112	161	210
41-50	17	34	51	95	135	175
51-59: 57-Dilly Duncan begins, ends #71	15	30	45	83	117	150
60-Iron Jaw returns	16	32	48	89	127	165
61-Origin Crimebuster & Iron Jaw retold	18	36	54	102	146	190
62-Death of Iron Jaw explained	17	34	51	98	139	180
63-73: 63-McWilliams-a. 73-Frazetta 1-pg. ad	12	24	36	69	95	120
74-88: 80-1st app. Rocky X of the Rocketeers; becomes "Rocky X" #101; Iron Jaw, Sniffer & the Deadly Dozen in 80-118	10	20	30	56	73	90
89-92-The Claw serial app. in all	10	20	30	58	77	95
93-Claw cameo; Rocky X by Sid Check	10	20	30	56	73	90
94-97,99	9	18	27	54	70	85
98,100: 98-Rocky X by Sid Check	10	20	30	56	73	90
101-107,109,111,119: 101-Rocky X becomes spy strip. 106-RobinHood app. 119-Last Crimebuster. 111-Crimebuster becomes Chuck Chandler.	9	18	27	51	62	75
108,110,112-118-Kubert-a; 108-Ditko-a	9	18	27	54	70	85

(See Giant Boy Book of Comics)
NOTE: *Boy Movies in 3-5,40,41. Iron Jaw app.-3, 4, 6, 8, 10, 11, 13-15; returns-60-62, 68, 69, 72-79, 81-118.* ***Biro*** *c-all.* ***Briefer*** *a-5, 13, 14, 16-20 among others.* ***Fuje*** *a-55, 18 pgs.* ***Palais*** *a-14, 16, 17, 19, 20 among others.*

BOY COMMANDOS (See Detective #64 & World's Finest Comics #8)
National Periodical Publications: Winter, 1942-43 - No. 36, Nov-Dec, 1949

	GD	VG	FN	VF	VF/NM	NM-
1-Origin Liberty Belle; The Sandman & The Newsboy Legion x-over in Boy Commandos; S&K-a, 48 pgs.; S&K cameo? (classic WWII-c)	529	1058	1587	3703	5952	8200
2-Last Liberty Belle; Hitler-c; S&K-a, 46 pgs.; WWII-c	208	416	624	1300	2000	2700
3-S&K-a, 45 pgs.; WWII-c	112	224	336	700	1075	1450
4-6: All WWII-c. 6-S&K-a	83	166	249	519	797	1075
7-10: All WWII-c	54	108	162	329	502	675
11-13: All WWII-c. 11-Infinity-c	40	80	120	233	342	450
14,16,18-19-All have S&K-a. 18-2nd Crazy Quilt-c	31	62	93	178	259	340
15-1st app. Crazy Quilt, their arch nemesis	40	80	120	239	357	475
17,20-Sci/fi-c/stories	35	70	105	201	293	385
21,22,25: 22-3rd Crazy Quilt-c; Judy Canova x-over	24	48	72	138	199	260
23-S&K-c/a(all)	33	66	99	190	275	360
24-1st costumed superhero satire-c (11-12/47).	30	60	90	170	245	320
26-Flying Saucer story (3-4/48)-4th of this theme; see The Spirit 9/28/47(1st), Shadow Comics V7#10 (2nd, 1/48) & Captain Midnight #60 (3rd, 2/48)	29	58	87	164	237	310
27,28,30: 30-Cleveland Indians story	23	46	69	132	191	250
29-S&K story (1)	25	50	75	144	207	270
31-35: 32-Dale Evans app. on-c & in story. 33-Last Crazy Quilt-c. 34-Intro. Wolf, their mascot	22	44	66	125	180	235
36-Intro The Atomobile c/sci-fi story (Scarce)	40	80	120	233	342	450

NOTE: *Most issues signed by* ***Simon & Kirby*** *are not by them.* ***S&K*** *c-1-9, 13, 14, 17, 21, 23, 24, 30-32.* ***Feller*** *c-30.*

BOY COMMANDOS
National Per. Publ.: Sept-Oct, 1973 - No. 2, Nov-Dec, 1973 (G.A. S&K reprints)

	GD	VG	FN	VF	VF/NM	NM-
1,2: 1-Reprints story from Boy Commandos #1 plus-c & Detective #66 by S&K. 2-Infantino/Orlando-c	2	4	6	10	13	16

BOY COWBOY (Also see Amazing Adventures & Science Comics)
Ziff-Davis Publ. Co.: 1950 (8 pgs. in color)

	GD	VG	FN	VF	VF/NM	NM-
nn-Sent to subscribers of Ziff-Davis mags. & ordered through mail for 10¢; used to test market for Kid Cowboy	27	54	81	154	222	290

BOY DETECTIVE
Avon Periodicals: May-June, 1951 - No. 4, May, 1952

	GD	VG	FN	VF	VF/NM	NM-
1	20	40	60	112	161	210
2-4: 3,4-Kinstler-c	13	26	39	74	102	130

BOY EXPLORERS COMICS (Terry and The Pirates No. 3 on)
Family Comics (Harvey Publ.): May-June, 1946 - No. 2, Sept-Oct, 1946

	GD	VG	FN	VF	VF/NM	NM-
1-Intro The Explorers, Duke of Broadway, Calamity Jane & Danny Dixon...Cadet; S&K-c/a, 24 pgs.	67	134	201	419	647	875
2-(Scarce)-Small size (5-1/2x8-1/2"; B&W; 32 pgs.) Distributed to mail subscribers only; S&K-a	100	200	300	625	963	1300

(Also see All New No. 15, Flash Gordon No. 5, and Stuntman No. 3)

BOY ILLUSTORIES (See Boy Comics)

BOY LOVES GIRL (Boy Meets Girl No. 1-24)
Lev Gleason Publications: No. 25, July, 1952 - No. 57, June, 1956

	GD	VG	FN	VF	VF/NM	NM-
25(#1)	9	18	27	51	62	75
26,27,29-33: 30-33-Serial, 'Loves of My Life	6	12	18	31	38	45
34-42: 39-Lingerie panels	6	12	18	28	34	40
28-Drug propaganda story	7	14	21	35	43	50
43-Toth-a	7	14	21	37	46	55
44-50: 47-Toth-a? 50-Last pre-code (2/55)	5	10	15	24	30	35
51-57: 57-Ann Brewster-a	5	10	14	20	24	28

BOY MEETS GIRL (Boy Loves Girl No. 25 on)
Lev Gleason Publications: Feb, 1950 - No. 24, June, 1952 (No. 1-17: 52 pgs.)

Brady Bunch #2 © DELL

Brass #3 © WSP

Brave and the Bold #28 © DC

	GD 2.0	VG 4.0	FN 6.0	VF 8.0	VF/NM 9.0	NM- 9.2
1-Guardineer-a	13	26	39	74	102	130
2	8	16	24	46	58	70
3-10	8	16	24	40	50	60
11-24	7	14	21	37	46	55

NOTE: *Briefer a-24. Fuje c-3,7. Painted-c 1-17. Photo-c 19-21, 23.*

BOYS' AND GIRLS' MARCH OF COMICS (See March of Comics)

BOYS' RANCH (Also see Western Tales & Witches' Western Tales)
Harvey Publ.: Oct, 1950 - No. 6, Aug, 1951 (No.1-3, 52 pgs.; No. 4-6, 36 pgs.)

	GD	VG	FN	VF	VF/NM	NM-
1-S&K-c/a(3)	62	124	186	388	594	800
2-S&K-c/a(3)	42	84	126	256	391	525
3-S&K-c/a(2); Meskin-a	40	80	120	236	351	465
4-S&K-c/a, 5 pgs.	37	74	111	209	305	400
5,6-S&K-c, splashes & centerspread only; Meskin-a	21	42	63	121	173	225

BOZO (Larry Harmon's Bozo, the World's Most Famous Clown)
Innovation Publishing: 1992 ($6.95, 68 pgs.)

	GD	VG	FN	VF	VF/NM	NM-
1-Reprints Four Color #285(#1)	1	2	3	4	5	7

BOZO THE CLOWN (TV) (Bozo No. 7 on)
Dell Publishing Co.: July, 1950 - No. 4, Oct-Dec, 1963

	GD	VG	FN	VF	VF/NM	NM-
Four Color 285(#1)	21	42	63	150	230	310
2(7-9/51)-7(10-12/52)	12	24	36	84	127	170
Four Color 464,508,551,594(10/54)	10	20	30	73	107	140
1(nn, 5-7/62)	8	16	24	58	82	105
2 - 4(1963)	6	12	18	43	59	75

BOZZ CHRONICLES, THE
Marvel Comics (Epic Comics): Dec, 1985 - No. 6, 1986 (Lim. series, mature)

1-6-Logan/Wolverine look alike in 19th century. 1,3,5- Blevins-a 3.00

B.P.R.D.: HOLLOW EARTH (Mike Mignola's...)
Dark Horse Comics: Jan, 2002 - No. 3, June, 2002 ($2.99, limited series)

1-3-Mignola, Golden & Sniegoski-s/Sook-a/Mignola-c; Hellboy and Abe Sapien app. 3.00
... and Other Stories TPB (1/03; 7/04, $17.95) r/#1-3, Hellboy: Box Full of Evil, Abe Sapien: Drums of the Dead, and Dark Horse Extra; plus sketch pages 18.00
B.P.R.D Dark Waters (7/03, $2.99) Guy Davis-c/a; Augustyn-s 3.00
B.P.R.D Night Train (9/03, $2.99) Johns & Kolins-s; Kolins & Stewart-a 3.00
B.P.R.D There's Something Under My Bed (11/03, $2.99) Pollina-a/c 3.00
B.P.R.D The Soul of Venice (5/03, $2.99) Oeming-a/c; Gunter & Oeming-s 3.00
B.P.R.D The Soul of Venice and Other Stories TPB (8/04, $17.95) r/one-shots & new story by Mignola and Cam Stewart; sketch pages by various 18.00

B.P.R.D.: PLAGUE OF FROGS
Dark Horse Comics: Mar, 2004 - No. 5, July, 2004 ($2.99, limited series)

1-5-Mignola-s/Guy Davis-c/a 3.00

BRADLEYS, THE (Also see Hate)
Fantagraphics Books: Apr, 1999 - No. 6, Jan, 2000 ($2.95, B&W, limited series)

1-6-Reprints Peter Bagge's-s/a 3.00

BRADY BUNCH, THE (TV)(See Kite Fun Book and Binky #78)
Dell Publishing Co.: Feb, 1970 - No. 2, May, 1970

	GD	VG	FN	VF	VF/NM	NM-
1	12	24	36	86	131	175
2	9	18	27	63	89	115

BRAIN, THE
Sussex Publ. Co./Magazine Enterprises: Sept, 1956 - No. 7, 1958

	GD	VG	FN	VF	VF/NM	NM-
1-Dan DeCarlo-a in all including reprints	11	22	33	62	84	105
2,3	7	14	21	37	46	55
4-7	4	8	12	27	36	45
I.W. Reprints #1-4,8-10('63),14: 2-Reprints Sussex #2 with new cover added	2	4	6	10	13	16
Super Reprint #17,18(nd)	2	4	6	10	13	16

BRAINBANX
DC Comics (Helix): Mar, 1997 - No. 6, Aug, 1997 ($2.50, limited series)

1-6: Elaine Lee-s/Temujin-a 2.50

BRAIN BOY
Dell Publishing Co.: Apr-June, 1962 - No. 6, Sept-Nov, 1963 (Painted c-#1-6)

	GD	VG	FN	VF	VF/NM	NM-
Four Color 1330(#1)-Gil Kane-a; origin	14	28	42	97	149	200
2(7-9/62),3-6: 4-Origin retold	9	18	27	60	85	110

BRAM STOKER'S BURIAL OF THE RATS (Movie)
Roger Corman's Cosmic Comics: Apr, 1995 - No.3, June, 1995 ($2.50)

1-3: Adaptation of film; Jerry Prosser scripts 2.50

BRAM STOKER'S DRACULA (Movie)(Also see Dracula: Vlad the Impaler)
Topps Comics: Oct, 1992 - No. 4, Jan, 1993 ($2.95, limited series, polybagged)

1-(1st & 2nd printing)-Adaptation of film begins; Mignola-c/a in all; 4 trading cards & poster; photo scenes of movie 3.00
1-Crimson foil edition (limited to 500) 8.00
2-4: 2-Bound-in poster & cards. 4 trading cards in both. 3-Contains coupon to win 1 of 500 crimson foil-c edition of #1. 4-Contains coupon to win 1 of 500 uncut sheets of all 16 trading cards 3.00

BRAND ECHH (See Not Brand Echh)

BRAND NEW YORK: WHAT JUSTICE
Comic Box Inc.: July, 1997 ($3.95, B&W&Red)

1-Zoltan-s/a, Peter Avanti-s 4.00

BRAND OF EMPIRE (See Luke Short's...Four Color 771)

BRASS
Image Comics (WildStorm Productions): Aug, 1996 - No. 3, May, 1997 ($2.50, limited series)

1-($4.50) Folio Ed.; oversized 4.50
1-3: Wiesenfeld-s/Bennett-a. 3-Grunge & Roxy(Gen 13) cameo 2.50

BRASS
DC Comics (WildStorm): Aug, 2000 - No. 6 ($2.50, limited series)

1-5-Arcudi-s 2.50

BRATH
CrossGeneration Comics: Feb, 2003 - No. 14, June, 2004 ($2.95)

Prequel-Dixon-s/Di Vito-a 3.00
1-14: 1-(3/03)-Dixon-s/Di Vito-a 3.00
Vol. 1: Hammer of Vengeance (2003, $9.95) Digest-sized reprint of Prequel & #1-6 10.00

BRATPACK/MAXIMORTAL SUPER SPECIAL
King Hell Press: 1996 ($2.95, B&W, limited series)

1,2: Veitch-s/a 3.00

BRATS BIZARRE
Marvel Comics (Epic/Heavy Hitters): 1994 - No. 4, 1994 ($2.50, limited series)

1-4: All w/bound-in trading cards 2.50

BRAVADOS, THE (See Wild Western Action)
Skywald Publ. Corp.: Aug, 1971 (52 pgs., one-shot)

	GD	VG	FN	VF	VF/NM	NM-
1-Red Mask, The Durango Kid, Billy Nevada-r; Bolle-a; 3-D effect story	2	4	6	14	18	22

BRAVE AND THE BOLD, THE (See Best Of... & Super DC Giant) (Replaced by Batman & The Outsiders)
National Periodical Publ./DC Comics: Aug-Sept, 1955 - No. 200, July, 1983

	GD	VG	FN	VF	VF/NM	NM-
1-Viking Prince by Kubert, Silent Knight, Golden Gladiator begin; part Kubert-c	238	476	714	2083	3542	5000
2	105	210	315	893	1447	2000
3,4	58	116	174	493	797	1100
5-Robin Hood begins (4-5/56, 1st DC app.), ends #15; see Robin Hood Tales #7	61	122	183	519	835	1150
6-10: 6-Robin Hood by Kubert; last Golden Gladiator app.; Silent Knight; no Viking Prince. 8-1st S.A. issue	46	92	138	368	572	775
11-22,24: 12,14-Robin Hood-c. 18,21-23-Grey tone-c. 22-Last Silent Knight. 24-Last Viking Prince by Kubert (2nd solo book)	36	72	108	270	423	575
23-Viking Prince origin by Kubert; 1st B&B single theme issue & 1st Viking Prince solo book	46	92	138	368	572	775
25-1st app. Suicide Squad (8-9/59)	43	86	129	344	535	725
26,27-Suicide Squad	31	62	93	228	352	475
28-(2-3/60)-Justice League intro./1st app.; origin/1st app. Snapper Carr	400	800	1200	3660	6230	8800
29-Justice League (4-5/60)-2nd app. battle the Weapons Master; robot-c	175	350	525	1531	2516	3500
30-Justice League (6-7/60)-3rd app.; vs. Amazo	142	284	426	1207	1954	2700
31-1st app. Cave Carson (8-9/60); scarce in high grade; 1st try-out series	39	78	117	293	459	625
32,33-Cave Carson	24	48	72	174	267	360
34-Origin/1st app. Silver-Age Hawkman, Hawkgirl & Byth (2-3/61); Gardner Fox story, Kubert-c/a ; 1st S.A. Hawkman tryout series; 2nd in #42-44; both series predate Hawkman #1 (4-5/64)	185	370	555	1619	2660	3700
35-Hawkman by Kubert (4-5/61)-2nd app.	47	94	141	376	588	800
36-Hawkman by Kubert; origin & 1st app. Shadow Thief (6-7/61)-3rd app.	41	82	123	330	515	700
37-Suicide Squad (2nd tryout series)	24	48	72	170	260	350

Brave and the Bold #67 © DC

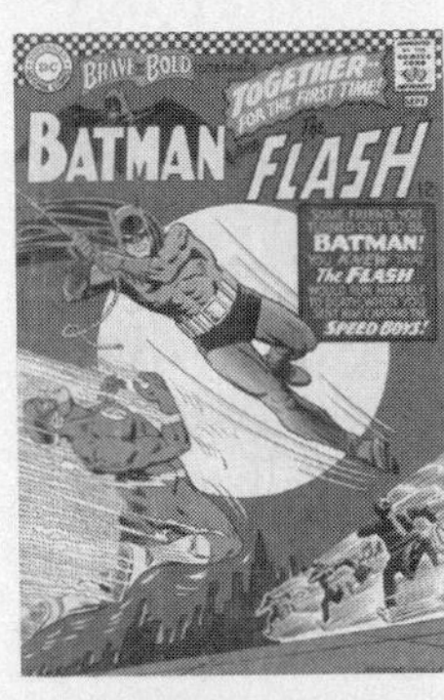

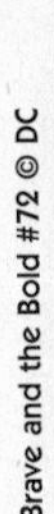
Brave and the Bold #72 © DC

Brave and the Bold #158 © DC

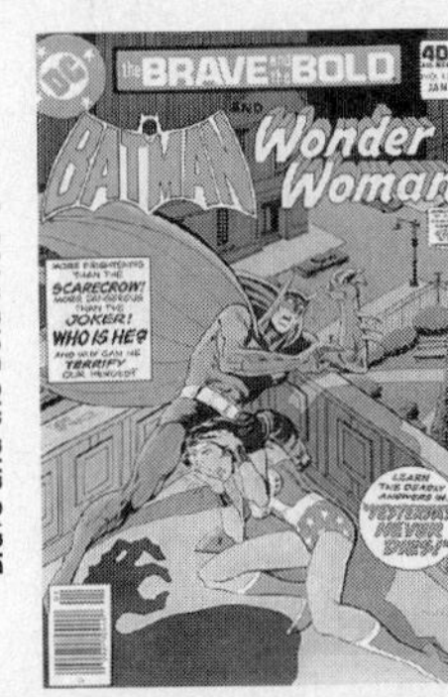

	GD 2.0	VG 4.0	FN 6.0	VF 8.0	VF/NM 9.0	NM- 9.2
38,39-Suicide Squad. 38-Last 10¢ issue	20	40	60	145	223	300
40,41-Cave Carson Inside Earth (2nd try-out series). 40-Kubert-a. 41-Meskin-a	15	30	45	109	167	225
42-Hawkman by Kubert (2nd tryout series); Hawkman earns helmet wings; Byth app.	31	62	93	223	342	460
43-Hawkman by Kubert; more detailed origin	35	70	105	263	412	560
44-Hawkman by Kubert; grey-tone-c	29	58	87	206	316	425
45-49-Strange Sports Stories by Infantino	10	20	30	67	96	125
50-The Green Arrow & Manhunter From Mars (10-11/63); 1st Manhunter x-over outside of Detective Comics (pre-dates House of Mystery #143); team-ups begin	19	38	57	136	208	280
51-Aquaman & Hawkman (12-1/63-64); pre-dates Hawkman #1	24	48	72	170	260	350
52-(2-3/64)-3 Battle Stars; Sgt. Rock, Haunted Tank, Johnny Cloud, & Mlle. Marie team-up for 1st time by Kubert (c/a)	20	40	60	145	223	300
53-Atom & The Flash by Toth	10	20	30	67	96	125
54-Kid Flash, Robin & Aqualad; 1st app./origin Teen Titans (6-7/64)	30	60	90	218	334	450
55-Metal Men & The Atom	8	16	24	55	78	100
56-The Flash & Manhunter From Mars	8	16	24	55	78	100
57-Origin & 1st app. Metamorpho (12-1/64-65)	18	36	54	131	201	270
58-2nd app. Metamorpho by Fradon	10	20	30	70	100	130
59-Batman & Green Lantern; 1st Batman team-up in Brave and the Bold	12	24	36	82	124	165
60-Teen Titans (2nd app.)-1st app. new Wonder Girl (Donna Troy), who joins Titans (6-7/65)	12	24	36	86	131	175
61-Origin Starman & Black Canary by Anderson	13	26	39	92	141	190
62-Origin Starman & Black Canary cont'd. 62-1st S.A. app. Wildcat (10-11/65); 1st S.A. app. of G.A. Huntress (W.W. villain)	11	22	33	80	120	160
63-Supergirl & Wonder Woman	8	16	24	55	78	100
64-Batman Versus Eclipso (see H.O.S. #61)	8	16	24	58	82	105
65-Flash & Doom Patrol (4-5/66)	6	12	18	38	52	65
66-Metamorpho & Metal Men (6-7/66)	6	12	18	38	52	65
67-Batman & The Flash by Infantino; Batman team-ups begin, end #200 (8-9/66)	7	14	21	50	68	85
68-Batman/Metamorpho/Joker/Riddler/Penguin-c/story; Batman as Bat-Hulk (Hulk parody)	9	18	27	65	93	120
69-Batman & Green Lantern	6	12	18	40	55	70
70-Batman & Hawkman; Craig-a(p)	6	12	18	40	55	70
71-Batman & Green Arrow	6	12	18	40	55	70
72-Spectre & Flash (6-7/67); 4th app. The Spectre; predates Spectre #1	6	12	18	43	59	75
73-Aquaman & The Atom	6	12	18	38	52	65
74-Batman & Metal Men	6	12	18	38	52	65
75-Batman & The Spectre (12-1/67-68); 6th app. Spectre; came out between Spectre #1 & #2	6	12	18	40	55	70
76-Batman & Plastic Man (2-3/68); came out between Plastic Man #8 & #9	6	12	18	38	52	65
77-Batman & The Atom	6	12	18	38	52	65
78-Batman, Wonder Woman & Batgirl	6	12	18	38	52	65
79-Batman & Deadman by Neal Adams (8-9/68); early Deadman app.	9	18	27	60	85	110
80-Batman & Creeper (10-11/68); N. Adams-a; early app. The Creeper; came out between Creeper #3 & #4	7	14	21	50	68	85
81-Batman & Flash; N. Adams-a	7	14	21	50	68	85
82-Batman & Aquaman; N. Adams-a; origin Ocean Master retold (2-3/69)	7	14	21	50	68	85
83-Batman & Teen Titans; N. Adams-a (4-5/69)	7	14	21	50	68	85
84-Batman (G.A., 1st S.A. app.) & Sgt. Rock; N. Adams-a; last 12¢ issue (6-7/69)	7	14	21	50	68	85
85-Batman & Green Arrow; 1st new costume for Green Arrow by Neal Adams (8-9/69)	7	14	21	51	71	90
86-Batman & Deadman (10-11/69); N. Adams-a; story concludes from Strange Adventures #216 (1-2/69)	7	14	21	50	68	85
87-Batman & Wonder Woman	4	8	12	28	38	48
88-Batman & Wildcat	4	8	12	28	38	48
89-Batman & Phantom Stranger (4-5/70); early Phantom Stranger app. (came out between Phantom Stranger #6 & 7	4	8	12	25	33	42
90-Batman & Adam Strange	4	8	12	25	33	42
91-Batman & Black Canary (8-9/70)	4	8	12	25	33	42
92-Batman; intro the Bat Squad	4	8	12	25	33	42
93-Batman-House of Mystery; N. Adams-a	6	12	18	43	59	75
94-Batman-Teen Titans	3	7	10	21	28	35
95-Batman & Plastic Man	3	7	10	21	28	35
96-Batman & Sgt. Rock; last 15¢ issue	4	8	12	22	30	38
97-Batman & Wildcat; 52 pg. issues begin, end #102; reprints origin & 1st app. Deadman from Strange Advs. #205	4	8	12	22	30	38
98-Batman & Phantom Stranger; 1st Jim Aparo Batman-a?	4	8	12	22	30	38
99-Batman & Flash	4	8	12	22	30	38
100-(2-3/72, 25¢, 52 pgs.)-Batman-Green Lantern-Green Arrow-Black Canary-Robin; Deadman-r by Adams/Str. Advs. #210	6	12	18	43	59	75
101-Batman & Metamorpho; Kubert Viking Prince	3	7	10	21	28	35
102-Batman-Teen Titans; N. Adams-a(p)	4	8	12	29	40	50
103-107,109,110: Batman team-ups: 103-Metal Men. 104-Deadman. 105-Wonder Woman. 106-Green Arrow. 107-Black Canary. 109-Demon. 110-Wildcat	2	4	6	14	18	22
108-Sgt. Rock	3	6	9	16	20	24
111-Batman/Joker-c/story	3	6	9	18	23	28
112-117: All 100 pgs.; Batman team-ups: 112-Mr. Miracle. 113-Metal Men; reprints origin/1st Hawkman from Brave and the Bold #34; r/origin Multi-Man/Challengers #14. 114-Aquaman. 115-Atom; r/origin Viking Prince from #23; r/Dr. Fate/Hourman/Solomon Grundy/Green Lantern from Showcase #55. 116-Spectre. 117-Sgt. Rock; last 100 pg. issue	4	8	12	29	40	50
118-Batman/Wildcat/Joker-c/story	3	6	9	18	23	28
119,121-123,125-128,132-140: Batman team-ups: 119-Man-Bat. 121-Metal Men. 122-Swamp Thing. 123-Plastic Man/Metamorpho. 125-Flash. 126-Aquaman. 127-Wildcat. 128-Mr. Miracle. 132-Kung-Fu Fighter. 133-Deadman. 134-Green Lantern. 135-Metal Men. 136-Metal Men/Green Arrow. 137-Demon. 138-Mr. Miracle. 139-Hawkman. 140-Wonder Woman	2	4	6	8	10	12
120-Kamandi (68 pgs.)	3	6	9	16	20	24
124-Sgt. Rock	2	4	6	10	12	15
129,130-Batman/Green Arrow/Atom parts 1 & 2; Joker & Two Face-c/stories	2	4	6	14	18	22
131-Batman & Wonder Woman vs. Catwoman-c/sty	2	4	6	10	13	16
141-Batman/Black Canary vs. Joker-c/story	2	4	6	14	18	22
142-160: Batman team-ups: 142-Aquaman. 143-Creeper; origin Human Target (44 pgs.). 144-Green Arrow; origin Human Target part 2 (44 pgs.). 145-Phantom Stranger. 146-G.A. Batman/Unknown Soldier. 147-Supergirl. 148-Plastic Man; X-Mas-c. 149-Teen Titans. 150-Anniversary issue; Superman. 151-Flash. 152-Atom. 153-Red Tornado. 154-Metamorpho. 155-Green Lantern. 156-Dr. Fate. 157-Batman vs. Kamandi (ties into Kamandi #59). 158-Wonder Woman. 159-Ra's Al Ghul. 160-Supergirl.	1	2	3	5	7	9
145(11/79)-147,150-159,165(8/80)-(Whitman variants; low print run; none show issue # on cover)	2	4	6	8	10	12
161-181,183-190,192-195,198,199: Batman team-ups: 161-Adam Strange. 162-G.A. Batman/Sgt. Rock. 163-Black Lightning. 164-Hawkman. 165-Man-Bat. 166-Black Canary; Nemesis (intro) back-up story begins, ends #192; Penguin-c/story. 167-G.A. Batman/Blackhawk; origin Nemesis. 168-Green Arrow. 169-Zatanna. 170-Nemesis. 171-Scalphunter. 172-Firestorm. 173-Guardians of the Universe. 174-Green Lantern. 175-Lois Lane. 176-Swamp Thing. 177-Elongated Man. 178-Creeper. 179-Legion. 180-Spectre. 181-Hawk & Dove. 183-Riddler. 184-Huntress. 185-Green Arrow. 186-Hawkman. 187-Metal Men. 188,189-Rose & the Thorn. 190-Adam Strange. 192-Superboy vs. Mr. I.Q. 193-Nemesis. 194-Flash. 195-I...Vampire. 198-Karate Kid. 199-Batman vs. The Spectre						6.00
182-G.A. Robin; G.A. Starman app.; 1st modern app. G.A. Batwoman	1	2	3	4	5	7
191-Batman/Joker-c/story; Nemesis app.	2	4	6	8	10	12
196-Ragman; origin Ragman retold.	1	2	3	5	6	8
197-Catwoman; Earth II Batman & Catwoman marry; 2nd modern app. of G.A. Batwoman	2	4	6	9	11	14
200-Double-sized (64 pgs.); printed on Mando paper; Earth One & Earth Two Batman app. in separate stories; intro/1st app. Batman & The Outsiders	1	3	4	6	8	10

NOTE: ***Neal Adams*** *a-79-86, 93, 100r, 102; c-75, 76, 79-86, 88-90, 93, 95, 99, 100r.* ***M. Anderson*** *a-115r; c-72i, 96i.* ***Andru/Esposito*** *c-25-27.* ***Aparo*** *a-98, 100-102, 104-125, 126i, 127-136, 138-145, 147, 148i, 149-152, 154, 155, 157-162, 168-170, 173-178, 180-182, 184, 186i-189i, 191i-193i, 195, 196, 200; c-105-109, 111-136, 137i, 138-175, 177, 180-184, 186-200.* ***Austin*** *a-166i.* ***Bernard Baily*** *c-32, 33, 58.* ***Buckler*** *a-185, 186p; c-137, 178p, 185p, 186p.* ***Giordano*** *a-143, 144.* ***Infantino*** *a-67p, 72p, 97r, 98r, 115r, 172p, 183p, 190p, 194p; c-45-49, 67p, 69p, 70p, 72p, 96p, 98r.* ***Kaluta*** *c-176.* ***Kane*** *a-115r; c-59, 64.* ***Kubert*** *&/or* ***Heath*** *a-1-24; reprints-101, 113, 115, 117.* ***Kubert*** *a-99r; c-22-24, 34-36, 40, 42-44, 52.* ***Mooney*** *a-114r.* ***Mortimer*** *a-64, 69.* ***Newton*** *a-153p, 156p, 165p.* ***Irv Novick*** *c-1(part), 2-21.* ***Fred Ray*** *a-78r.* ***Roussos*** *a-50, 76i, 114r.* ***Staton*** *148p. 52 pgs.-97, 100; 68 pgs.-120; 100 pgs.-112-117.*

BRAVE AND THE BOLD, THE
DC Comics: Dec, 1991 - No. 6, June, 1992 ($1.75, limited series)

1-6: Green Arrow, The Butcher, The Question in all; Grell scripts in all						2.50

NOTE: ***Grell*** *c-3, 4-6.*

BRAVE AND THE BOLD ANNUAL NO. 1 1969 ISSUE, THE
DC Comics: 2001 ($5.95, one-shot)

1-Reprints silver age team-ups in 1960s-style 80 pg. Giant format						6.00

Breakdown #1 © Devil's Due

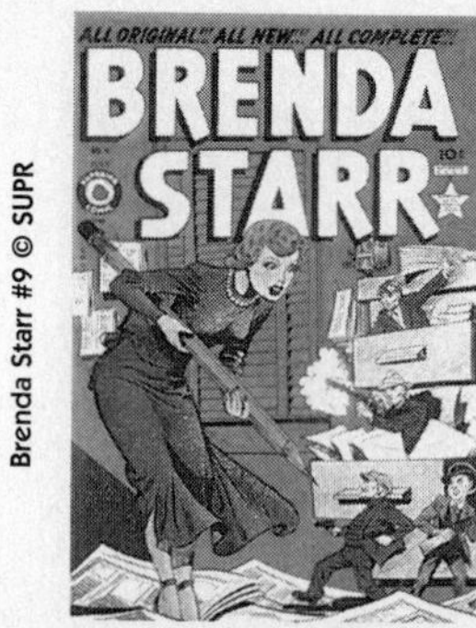

Brenda Starr #9 © SUPR

Brick Bradford #6 © STD

	GD 2.0	VG 4.0	FN 6.0	VF 8.0	VF/NM 9.0	NM- 9.2

BRAVE AND THE BOLD SPECIAL, THE (See DC Special Series No. 8)

BRAVE EAGLE (TV)
Dell Publishing Co.: No. 705, June, 1956 - No. 929, July, 1958

	GD	VG	FN	VF	VF/NM	NM-
Four Color 705 (#1)-Photo-c	8	16	24	53	74	95
Four Color 770, 816, 879 (2/58), 929-All photo-c	4	8	12	29	40	50

BRAVE OLD WORLD (V2K)
DC Comics (Vertigo): Feb, 2000 - No. 4, May, 2000 ($2.50, mini-series)

	GD	VG	FN	VF	VF/NM	NM-
1-4-Messner-Loeb-s/Guy Davis & Phil Hester-a						2.50

BRAVE ONE, THE (Movie)
Dell Publishing Co.: No. 773, Mar, 1957

	GD	VG	FN	VF	VF/NM	NM-
Four Color 773-Photo-c	6	12	18	43	59	75

BRAVURA
Malibu Comics (Bravura): 1995 (mail-in offer)

	GD	VG	FN	VF	VF/NM	NM-
0-wraparound holographic-c; short stories and promo pin-ups of Chaykin's Power & Glory, Gil Kane's & Steven Grant's Edge, Starlin's Breed, & Simonson's Star Slammers						5.00
1 1/2						7.00

BREAKDOWN
Devil's Due Publ.: Oct, 2004 - Present ($2.95)

	GD	VG	FN	VF	VF/NM	NM-
1,2: 1-Two covers by Dave Ross and Leinil Yu; Dixon-s/Ross-a						3.00

BREAKFAST AFTER NOON
Oni Press: May, 2000 - No. 6, Jan, 2001($2.95, B&W, limited series)

	GD	VG	FN	VF	VF/NM	NM-
1-6-Andi Watson-s/a						3.00
TPB (2001, $19.95) r/series						20.00

BREAKNECK BLVD.
MotioN Comics/Slave Labor Graphics Vol. 2: No. 0, Feb, 1994 - No. 2, Nov, 1994; Vol. 2#1, Jul, 1995 - #6, Dec., 1996 ($2.50/$2.95, B&W)

	GD	VG	FN	VF	VF/NM	NM-
0-2, V2#1-6: 0-Perez/Giordano-c						3.00

BREAK-THRU (Also see Exiles V1#4)
Malibu Comics (Ultraverse): Dec, 1993 - No. 2, Jan, 1994 ($2.50, 44 pgs.)

	GD	VG	FN	VF	VF/NM	NM-
1,2-Perez-c/a(p); has x-overs in Ultraverse titles						2.50

BREATHTAKER
DC Comics: 1990 - No. 4, 1990 ($4.95, 52 pgs., prestige format, mature)

	GD	VG	FN	VF	VF/NM	NM-
Book 1-4: Mark Wheatley-painted-c/a & scripts; Marc Hempel-a						5.00
TPB (1994, $14.95) r/#1-4; intro by Neil Gaiman						15.00

'BREED
Malibu Comics (Bravura): Jan, 1994 - No. 6, 1994 ($2.50, limited series)

	GD	VG	FN	VF	VF/NM	NM-
1-6: 1-(48 pgs.)-Origin/1st app. of 'Breed by Starlin; contains Bravura stamps; spot varnish-c. 2-5-contains Bravura stamps. 6-Death of Rachel						3.00
...:Book of Genesis (1994, $12.95)-reprints #1-6						13.00

'BREED II
Malibu Comics (Bravura): Nov, 1994 - No. 6, Apr, 1995 ($2.95, limited series)

	GD	VG	FN	VF	VF/NM	NM-
1-6: Starlin-c/a/scripts in all. 1-Gold edition						3.00

BREEZE LAWSON, SKY SHERIFF (See Sky Sheriff)

BRENDA LEE'S LIFE STORY
Dell Publishing Co.: July-Sept., 1962

	GD	VG	FN	VF	VF/NM	NM-
01-078-209	9	18	27	65	93	120

BRENDA STARR (Also see All Great)
Four Star Comics Corp./Superior Comics Ltd.: No. 13, 9/47; No. 14, 3/48; V2#3, 6/48 - V2#12, 12/49

	GD	VG	FN	VF	VF/NM	NM-
V1#13-By Dale Messick	81	162	243	506	778	1050
14-Kamen bondage-c	85	170	255	531	816	1100
V2#3-Baker-a?	67	134	201	419	647	875
4-Used in **SOTI**, pg. 21; Kamen bondage-c	81	162	243	506	778	1050
5-10	65	130	195	406	628	850
11,12 (Scarce)	66	132	198	413	637	860

NOTE: *Newspaper reprints plus original material through #6. All original #7 on.*

BRENDA STARR (...Reporter)(Young Lovers No. 16 on?)
Charlton Comics: No. 13, June, 1955 - No. 15, Oct, 1955

	GD	VG	FN	VF	VF/NM	NM-
13-15-Newspaper-r	39	78	117	222	324	425

BRENDA STARR REPORTER
Dell Publishing Co.: Oct, 1963

	GD	VG	FN	VF	VF/NM	NM-
1	16	32	48	116	178	240

BRER RABBIT (See Kite Fun Book, Walt Disney Showcase #28 and Wheaties)
Dell Publishing Co.: No. 129, 1946; No. 208, Jan, 1949; No. 693, 1956 (Disney)

	GD	VG	FN	VF	VF/NM	NM-
Four Color 129 (#1)-Adapted from Disney movie "Song of the South"	29	58	87	210	323	435
Four Color 208 (1/49)	12	24	36	86	131	175
Four Color 693-Part-r 129	10	20	30	70	100	130

BRIAN BOLLAND'S BLACK BOOK
Eclipse Comics: July, 1985 (one-shot)

	GD	VG	FN	VF	VF/NM	NM-
1-British B&W-r in color						3.00

BRIAN PULIDO'S LADY DEATH... (See Lady Death)

BRICK BRADFORD (Also see Ace Comics & King Comics)
King Features Syndicate/Standard: No. 5, July, 1948 - No. 8, July, 1949 (Ritt & Grey reprints)

	GD	VG	FN	VF	VF/NM	NM-
5	20	40	60	112	161	210
6-Robot-c (by Schomburg?).	32	64	96	184	267	350
7-Schomburg-c. 8-Says #7 inside, #8 on-c	17	34	51	95	135	175

BRIDE'S DIARY (Formerly Black Cobra No. 3)
Ajax/Farrell Publ.: No. 4, May, 1955 - No. 10, Aug, 1956

	GD	VG	FN	VF	VF/NM	NM-
4 (#1)	8	16	24	46	58	70
5-8	6	12	18	28	34	40
9,10-Disbrow-a	8	16	24	40	50	60

BRIDES IN LOVE (Hollywood Romances & Summer Love No. 46 on)
Charlton Comics: Aug, 1956 - No. 45, Feb, 1965

	GD	VG	FN	VF	VF/NM	NM-
1	10	20	30	60	80	100
2	7	14	21	35	43	50
3-6,8-10	4	8	12	22	30	38
7-(68 pgs.)	4	8	12	29	40	50
11-20	3	6	9	16	20	25
21-45	2	4	6	10	13	16

BRIDES ROMANCES
Quality Comics Group: Nov, 1953 - No. 23, Dec, 1956

	GD	VG	FN	VF	VF/NM	NM-
1	13	26	39	74	102	130
2	7	14	21	37	46	55
3-10: Last precode (3/55)	7	14	21	35	43	50
11-17,19-22: 15-Baker-a(p)?; Colan-a	6	12	18	31	38	45
18-Baker-a	7	14	21	37	46	55
23-Baker-c/a	10	20	30	58	77	95

BRIDE'S SECRETS
Ajax/Farrell(Excellent Publ.)/Four-Star: Apr-May, 1954 - No. 19, May, 1958

	GD	VG	FN	VF	VF/NM	NM-
1	10	20	30	60	80	100
2	7	14	21	35	43	50
3-6: Last precode (3/55)	6	12	18	28	34	40
7-11,13-19: 18-Hollingsworth-a	5	10	15	24	30	35
12-Disbrow-a	6	12	18	29	36	42

BRIDE-TO-BE ROMANCES (See True...)

BRIGADE
Image Comics (Extreme Studios): Aug, 1992 - No. 4, 1993 ($1.95, lim. series)

	GD	VG	FN	VF	VF/NM	NM-
1-Liefeld part plots/scripts in all, Liefeld-c(p); contains 2 Brigade trading cards						3.00
1-Gold foil stamped logo edition						8.00
2-Contains coupon for Image Comics #0 & 2 trading cards						3.00
2-With coupon missing						2.25
3,4: 3-Contains 2 trading cards; 1st Birds of Prey. 4-Flip book featuring Youngblood #5						2.50

BRIGADE
Image Comics (Extreme): V2#1, May, 1993 - V2#22, July, 1995, V2#25, May, 1996 ($1.95/$2.50)

	GD	VG	FN	VF	VF/NM	NM-
V2#1-22,25: 1-Gatefold-c; Liefeld co-plots; Blood Brothers part 1; Bloodstrike app. 2-(6/93, V2#1 on inside)-Foil merricote-c (newsstand ed. w/out foil-c exists). 3-Perez-c(i); Liefeld scripts. 8,9-Coupons #2 & 6 for Extreme Prejudice #0 bound-in. 11-(8/94, $2.50) WildC.A.T.S app. 16-Polybagged w/ trading card. 22-"Supreme Apocalypse" Pt. 4; w/ trading card						2.50
0-(9/93)-Liefeld scripts; 1st app. Warcry; Youngblood & Wildcats app.;						2.50
20-Variant-c. by Quesada & Palmiotti						2.50
Sourcebook 1 (8/94, $2.95)						3.00

BRIGADE
Awesome Entertainment: July, 2000 ($2.99)

	GD	VG	FN	VF	VF/NM	NM-
1-Flip book w/Century preview						3.00

BRIGAND, THE (See Fawcett Movie Comics No. 18)

BRINGING UP FATHER
Dell Publishing Co.: No. 9, 1942 - No. 37, 1944

	GD	VG	FN	VF	VF/NM	NM-
Large Feature Comic 9	30	60	90	170	245	320
Four Color 37	20	40	60	145	273	300

Broadway Romances #4 © QUA

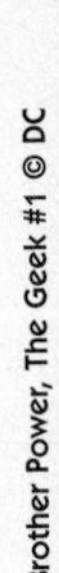

Brother Power, The Geek #1 © DC

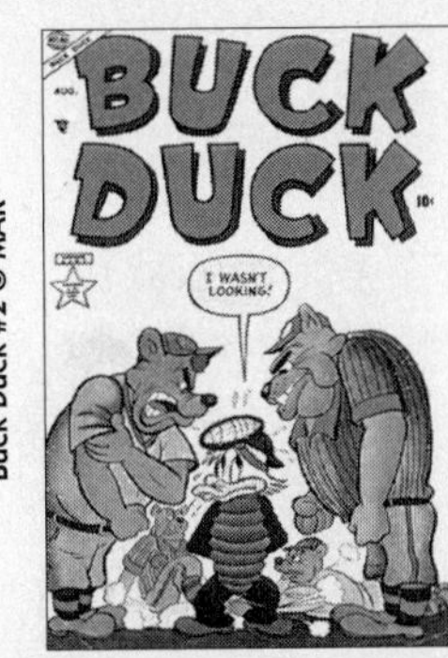

Buck Duck #2 © MAR

BRING BACK THE BAD GUYS
Marvel Comics: 1998($24.95, TPB)

	GD 2.0	VG 4.0	FN 6.0	VF 8.0	VF/NM 9.0	NM- 9.2
1-Reprints stories of Marvel villains' secrets						25.00

BRING ON THE BAD GUYS (See Fireside Book Series)

BRIT
Image Comics: July, 2003 - Present ($4.95, B&W)

	GD 2.0	VG 4.0	FN 6.0	VF 8.0	VF/NM 9.0	NM- 9.2
1-Robert Kirkman-s/Tony Moore-a						5.00
...Vol. 2 Cold Death, ...Vol. 3 Red White Black & Blue						5.00

BROADWAY HOLLYWOOD BLACKOUTS
Stanhall: Mar-Apr, 1954 - No. 3, July-Aug, 1954

	GD 2.0	VG 4.0	FN 6.0	VF 8.0	VF/NM 9.0	NM- 9.2
1	12	24	36	71	98	125
2,3	9	18	27	51	62	75

BROADWAY ROMANCES
Quality Comics Group: January, 1950 - No. 5, Sept, 1950

	GD 2.0	VG 4.0	FN 6.0	VF 8.0	VF/NM 9.0	NM- 9.2
1-Ward-c/a (9 pgs.); Gustavson-a	38	76	114	219	320	420
2-Ward-a (9 pgs.); photo-c	26	52	78	150	215	280
3-5: All-Photo-c	14	28	42	79	110	140

BROKEN ARROW (TV)
Dell Publishing Co.: No. 855, Oct, 1957 - No. 947, Nov, 1958

	GD 2.0	VG 4.0	FN 6.0	VF 8.0	VF/NM 9.0	NM- 9.2
Four Color 855 (#1)-Photo-c	7	14	21	46	63	80
Four Color 947-Photo-c	6	12	18	40	55	70

BROKEN CROSS, THE (See The Crusaders)

BRONCHO BILL (See Comics On Parade, Sparkler & Tip Top Comics)
United Features Syndicate/Standard(Visual Editions) No. 5-on: 1939 - 1940; No. 5, 1?/48 - No. 16, 8?/50

	GD 2.0	VG 4.0	FN 6.0	VF 8.0	VF/NM 9.0	NM- 9.2
Single Series 2 ('39)	52	104	156	317	484	650
Single Series 19 ('40)(#2 on cvr)	42	84	126	256	391	525
5	15	30	45	83	117	150
6(4/48)-10(4/49)	9	18	27	51	62	75
11(6/49)-16	8	16	24	40	50	60

NOTE: *Schomburg c-6, 7, 9-13, 16.*

BROOKLYN DREAMS
DC Comics (Paradox Press): 1994 ($4.95, B&W, limited series, mature)

	GD 2.0	VG 4.0	FN 6.0	VF 8.0	VF/NM 9.0	NM- 9.2
1-4						5.00

BROOKS ROBINSON (See Baseball's Greatest Heroes #2)

BROTHER BILLY THE PAIN FROM PLAINS
Marvel Comics Group: 1979 (68pgs.)

	GD 2.0	VG 4.0	FN 6.0	VF 8.0	VF/NM 9.0	NM- 9.2
1-B&W comics, satire, Jimmy Carter-c & x-over w/Brother Billy peanut jokes. Joey Adams-a (scarce)	3	7	10	21	28	35

BROTHERHOOD, THE (Also see X-Men titles)
Marvel Comics: July, 2001 - No. 9, Mar, 2002 ($2.25)

	GD 2.0	VG 4.0	FN 6.0	VF 8.0	VF/NM 9.0	NM- 9.2
1-Intro. Orwell & the Brotherhood; Ribic-a/X-s/Sienkiewicz-c						2.25
2-9: 2-Two covers (JG Jones & Sienkiewicz). 4-6-Fabry-c. 7-9-Phillips-c/a						2.25

BROTHER POWER, THE GEEK (See Saga of Swamp Thing Annual & Vertigo Visions)
National Periodical Publications: Sept-Oct, 1968 - No. 2, Nov-Dec, 1968

	GD 2.0	VG 4.0	FN 6.0	VF 8.0	VF/NM 9.0	NM- 9.2
1-Origin; Simon-c(i?)	6	12	18	43	59	75
2	4	8	12	22	30	38

BROTHERS, HANG IN THERE, THE
Spire Christian Comics (Fleming H. Revell Co.): 1979 (49¢)

	GD 2.0	VG 4.0	FN 6.0	VF 8.0	VF/NM 9.0	NM- 9.2
nn	2	4	6	8	10	12

BROTHERS OF THE SPEAR (Also see Tarzan)
Gold Key/Whitman No. 18: June, 1972 - No. 17, Feb, 1976; No. 18, May, 1982

	GD 2.0	VG 4.0	FN 6.0	VF 8.0	VF/NM 9.0	NM- 9.2
1	5	10	15	33	44	55
2-Painted-c begin, end #17	3	6	9	18	23	28
3-10	2	4	6	12	16	20
11-18: 12-Line drawn-c. 13-17-Spiegle-a. 18(5/82)-r/#2; Leopard Girl-r	2	4	6	9	11	14

BROTHERS, THE CULT ESCAPE, THE
Spire Christian Comics (Fleming H. Revell Co.): 1980 (49¢)

	GD 2.0	VG 4.0	FN 6.0	VF 8.0	VF/NM 9.0	NM- 9.2
nn	1	3	4	6	8	10

BROWNIES (See New Funnies)
Dell Publishing Co.: No. 192, July, 1948 - No. 605, Dec, 1954

	GD 2.0	VG 4.0	FN 6.0	VF 8.0	VF/NM 9.0	NM- 9.2
Four Color 192(#1)-Kelly-a	15	30	45	107	164	220
Four Color 244(9/49), 293 (9/50)-Last Kelly c/a	11	22	33	79	117	155
Four Color 337(7-8/51), 365(12-1/51-52), 398(5/52)	6	12	18	38	52	65
Four Color 436(11/52), 482(7/53), 522(12/53), 605	5	10	15	36	48	60

BRUCE GENTRY
Better/Standard/Four Star Publ./Superior No. 3: Jan, 1948 - No. 8, Jul, 1949

	GD 2.0	VG 4.0	FN 6.0	VF 8.0	VF/NM 9.0	NM- 9.2
1-Ray Bailey strip reprints begin, end #3; E. C. emblem appears as a monogram on stationery in story; negligee panels	50	100	150	305	465	625
2,3	37	74	112	213	312	410
4-8	26	52	78	147	211	275

NOTE: *Kamenish a-2-7; c-1-8.*

BRUCE LEE (Also see Deadly Hands of Kung Fu)
Malibu Comics: July, 1994 - No. 6, Dec, 1994 ($2.95, 36 pgs.)

	GD 2.0	VG 4.0	FN 6.0	VF 8.0	VF/NM 9.0	NM- 9.2
1-6: 1-(44 pgs.)-Mortal Kombat prev., 1st app. in comics. 2,6-(36 pgs.)						5.00

BRUCE JONES' OUTER EDGE
Innovation: 1993 ($2.50, B&W, one-shot)

	GD 2.0	VG 4.0	FN 6.0	VF 8.0	VF/NM 9.0	NM- 9.2
1-Bruce Jones-c/a/script						2.50

BRUCE WAYNE: AGENT OF S.H.I.E.L.D. (Also see Marvel Vs. DC #3 & DC Vs. Marvel #4)
Marvel Comics (Amalgam): Apr, 1996 ($1.95, one-shot)

	GD 2.0	VG 4.0	FN 6.0	VF 8.0	VF/NM 9.0	NM- 9.2
1-Chuck Dixon scripts & Cary Nord-c/a.						2.50

BRUISER
Anthem Publications: Feb, 1994 ($2.45)

	GD 2.0	VG 4.0	FN 6.0	VF 8.0	VF/NM 9.0	NM- 9.2
1						2.50

BRUTE, THE
Seaboard Publ. (Atlas): Feb, 1975 - No. 3, July, 1975

	GD 2.0	VG 4.0	FN 6.0	VF 8.0	VF/NM 9.0	NM- 9.2
1-Origin & 1st app; Sekowsky-a(p)	2	4	6	8	10	12
2-Sekowsky-a(p); Fleisher-s	1	2	3	5	6	8
3-Brunner/Starlin/Weiss-a(p)	1	2	3	5	7	9

BRUTE & BABE
Ominous Press: July, 1994 - No. 2, Aug, 1994

	GD 2.0	VG 4.0	FN 6.0	VF 8.0	VF/NM 9.0	NM- 9.2
1-($3.95, 8 tablets plus-c)-"...It Begins..."; tablet format						4.00
2-($2.50, 36 pgs.)-"Mael's Rage", 2-(40 pgs.)-Stiff additional variant-c						2.50

BRUTE FORCE
Marvel Comics: Aug, 1990 - No. 4, Nov, 1990 ($1.00, limited series)

	GD 2.0	VG 4.0	FN 6.0	VF 8.0	VF/NM 9.0	NM- 9.2
1-4: Animal super-heroes; Delbo & DeCarlo-a						2.50

B-SIDES (The Craptacular...)
Marvel Comics: Nov, 2002 - No. 3, Jan, 2003 ($2.99, limited series)

	GD 2.0	VG 4.0	FN 6.0	VF 8.0	VF/NM 9.0	NM- 9.2
1-3-Kieth-c/Weldele-a. 2-Dorkin-a (1 pg.) 2-FF cameo. 3-FF app.						3.00

BUBBLEGUM CRISIS: GRAND MAL
Dark Horse Comics: Mar, 1994 - No. 4, June, 1994 ($2.50, limited series)

	GD 2.0	VG 4.0	FN 6.0	VF 8.0	VF/NM 9.0	NM- 9.2
1-4-Japanese manga						2.50

BUCCANEER
I. W. Enterprises: No date (1963)

	GD 2.0	VG 4.0	FN 6.0	VF 8.0	VF/NM 9.0	NM- 9.2
I.W. Reprint #1(r-/Quality #20), #8(r-/#23): Crandall-a in each	3	6	9	19	25	32

BUCCANEERS (Formerly Kid Eternity)
Quality Comics: No. 19, Jan, 1950 - No. 27, May, 1951 (No. 24-27: 52 pgs.)

	GD 2.0	VG 4.0	FN 6.0	VF 8.0	VF/NM 9.0	NM- 9.2
19-Captain Daring, Black Roger, Eric Falcon & Spanish Main begin; Crandall-a	53	106	159	323	492	660
20,23-Crandall-a	40	80	120	230	335	440
21-Crandall-c/a	40	80	120	244	372	500
22-Bondage-c	32	64	96	184	267	350
24-26: 24-Adam Peril, U.S.N. begins. 25-Origin & 1st app. Corsair Queen. 26-last Spanish Main	28	56	84	158	229	300
27-Crandall-c/a	40	80	120	230	335	440
Super Reprint #12 (1964)-Crandall-r/#21	4	8	12	22	30	38

BUCCANEERS, THE (TV)
Dell Publishing Co.: No. 800, 1957

	GD 2.0	VG 4.0	FN 6.0	VF 8.0	VF/NM 9.0	NM- 9.2
Four Color 800-Photo-c	8	16	24	58	82	105

BUCKAROO BANZAI (Movie)
Marvel Comics Group: Dec, 1984 - No. 2, Feb, 1985

	GD 2.0	VG 4.0	FN 6.0	VF 8.0	VF/NM 9.0	NM- 9.2
1,2-Movie adaptation; r/Marvel Super Special #33; Texiera-c/a						3.00

BUCK DUCK
Atlas Comics (ANC): June, 1953 - No. 4, Dec, 1953

	GD 2.0	VG 4.0	FN 6.0	VF 8.0	VF/NM 9.0	NM- 9.2
1-Funny animal stories in all	14	28	42	81	113	145
2-4: 2-Ed Win-a(5)	8	16	24	46	58	70

Buddies in the U.S. Army #2 © AVON

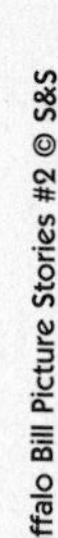

Buffalo Bill Picture Stories #2 © S&S

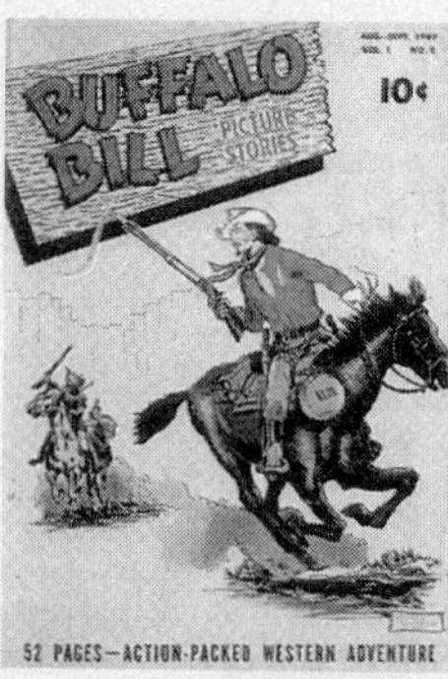

Buffy the Vampire Slayer #53 © 20th Century Fox

GD VG FN VF VF/NM NM-
2.0 4.0 6.0 8.0 9.0 9.2

GD VG FN VF VF/NM NM-
2.0 4.0 6.0 8.0 9.0 9.2

BUCK JONES (Also see Crackajack Funnies, Famous Feature Stories, Master Comics #7 & Wow Comics #1, 1936)
Dell Publishing Co.: No. 299, Oct, 1950 - No. 850, Oct, 1957 (All Painted-c)
Four Color 299(#1)-Buck Jones & his horse Silver-B begin; painted back-c begins, ends #5 14 28 42 97 149 200
2(4-6/51) 8 16 24 55 78 100
3-8(10-12/52) 7 14 21 46 63 80
Four Color 460,500,546,589 6 12 18 43 59 75
Four Color 652,733,850 5 10 15 33 44 55

BUCK ROGERS (Also see Famous Funnies, Pure Oil Comics, Salerno Carnival of Comics, 24 Pages of Comics, & Vicks Comics)
Famous Funnies: Winter, 1940-41 - No. 6, Sept, 1943
NOTE: Buck Rogers first appeared in the pulp magazine Amazing Stories Vol. 3 #5 in Aug, 1928.
1-Sunday strip reprints by Rick Yager; begins with strip #190; Calkins-c 310 620 930 2015 3258 4500
2 (7/41)-Calkins-c 131 262 393 819 1260 1700
3 (12/41), 4 (7/42) 113 226 339 706 1091 1475
5,6: 5-Story continues with Famous Funnies No. 80; Buck Rogers, Sky Roads. 6-Reprints of 1939 dailies; contains B.R. story "Crater of Doom" (2 pgs.) by Calkins not-r from Famous Funnies 96 192 288 600 925 1250

BUCK ROGERS
Toby Press: No. 100, Jan, 1951 - No. 9, May-June, 1951
100(#7)-All strip-r begin 31 62 93 175 253 330
101(#8), 9-All Anderson-a(1947-49-r/dailies) 24 48 72 138 199 260

BUCK ROGERS (...in the 25th Century No. 5 on) (TV)
Gold Key/Whitman No. 7 on: Oct, 1964; No. 2, July, 1979 - No. 16, May, 1982 (No #10; story was written but never released. #17 exists only as a press proof without covers and was never published)
1(10128-410, 12¢)-1st S.A. app. Buck Rogers & 1st new B. R. in comics since 1933 giveaway; painted-c; back-c pin-up 10 20 30 70 100 130
2(7/79)-6: 3,4,6-Movie adaptation; painted-c 2 4 6 9 11 14
7,11 (Whitman) 2 4 6 11 14 18
8,9 (prepack)(scarce) 3 6 9 18 23 28
12-16: 14(2/82), 15(3/82), 16(5/82) 1 3 4 6 8 10
Giant Movie Edition 11296(64pp, Whitman, $1.50), reprints GK #2-4 minus cover; tabloid size; photo-c (See Marvel Treasury) 3 6 9 18 24 30
Giant Movie Edition 02489(Western/Marvel, $1.50), reprints GK #2-4 minus cover 3 6 9 18 23 28
NOTE: *Bolle a-2p,3p, Movie Ed.(p).* ***McWilliams*** *a-2i,3i, 5-11, Movie Ed.(i). Painted c-1-9,11-13.*

BUCK ROGERS (Comics Module)
TSR, Inc.: 1990 - No. 10, 1991 ($2.95, 44 pgs.)
1-10 (1990): 1-Begin origin in 3 parts. 2-Indicia says #1. 2,3-Black Barney back-up story. 4-All Black Barney issue; B. B.-c. 5-Indicia says #6; Black Barney-c & lead story; Buck Rogers back-up story. 10-Flip book (72pgs.) 3.00

BUCKSKIN (TV)
Dell Publishing Co.: No. 1011, July, 1959 - No. 1107, June-Aug, 1960
Four Color 1011 (#1)-Photo-c 8 16 24 58 82 105
Four Color 1107-Photo-c 8 16 24 53 74 95

BUCKY O'HARE (Funny Animal)
Continuity Comics: 1988 ($5.95, graphic novel)
1-Golden-c/a(r); r/serial-Echo of Futurepast #1-6 1 2 3 4 5 7
Deluxe Hardcover ($40.00, 52 pg., 8 x 11") 40.00

BUCKY O'HARE
Continuity Comics: Jan, 1991 - No. 5, 1991 ($2.00)
1-6: 1-Michael Golden-c/a 2.50

BUDDIES IN THE U.S. ARMY
Avon Periodicals: Nov, 1952 - No. 2, 1953
1-Lawrence-c 14 28 42 79 110 140
2-Mort Lawrence-c/a 9 18 27 54 70 85

BUFFALO BEE (TV)
Dell Publishing Co.: No. 957, Nov, 1958 - No. 1061, Dec-Feb, 1959-60
Four Color 957 (#1) 10 20 30 72 104 135
Four Color 1002 (8-10/59), 1061 8 16 24 55 78 100

BUFFALO BILL (See Frontier Fighters, Super Western Comics & Western Action Thrillers)
Youthful Magazines: No. 2, Oct, 1950 - No. 9, Dec, 1951
2-Annie Oakley story 14 28 42 79 110 140
3-9: 2-4-Walter Johnson-c/a. 9-Wildey-a 9 18 27 54 70 85

BUFFALO BILL CODY (See Cody of the Pony Express)

BUFFALO BILL, JR. (TV) (See Western Roundup)
Dell/Gold Key: Jan, 1956 - No. 13, Aug-Oct, 1959; 1965 (All photo-c)
Four Color 673 (#1) 9 18 27 63 89 115
Four Color 742,766,798,828,856(11/57) 6 12 18 40 55 70
7(2-4/58)-13 5 10 15 36 48 60
1(6/65, Gold Key)-Photo-c(r/F.C. #798); photo-b/c 5 10 15 33 44 55

BUFFALO BILL PICTURE STORIES
Street & Smith Publications: June-July, 1949 - No. 2, Aug-Sept, 1949
1,2-Wildey, Powell-a in each 14 28 42 79 110 140

BUFFY THE VAMPIRE SLAYER (Based on the TV series)(Also see Tales of the Vampires)
Dark Horse Comics: 1998 - No. 63, Nov, 2003 ($2.95/$2.99)
1-Bennett-a/Watson-s; Art Adams-c 1 2 3 5 7 9
1-Variant photo-c 1 2 3 5 7 9
1-Gold foil logo Art Adams-c 15.00
1-Gold foil logo photo-c 20.00
2-15-Regular and photo-c. 4-7-Gomez-a. 5,8-Green-c 5.00
16-48: 29,30-Angel x-over. 43-45-Death of Buffy. 47-Lobdell-s begin. 48-Pike returns 3.00
50-($3.50) Scooby gang battles Adam; back-up story by Watson 3.50
51-63: 51-54-Viva Las Buffy; pre-Sunnydale Buffy & Pike in Vegas 3.00
Annual '99 ($4.95)-Two stories and pin-ups 1 2 3 4 5 7
...: A Stake to the Heart TPB (3/04, $12.95) r/#60-63 13.00
...: Chaos Bleeds (6/03, $2.99) Based on the video game; photo & Campbell-c 3.00
...: Creatures of Habit (3/02, $17.95) text with Horton & Paul Lee-a 18.00
...: Jonathan 1 (1/01, $2.99) two covers; Richards-a 3.00
...: Lost and Found 1 (3/02, $2.99) aftermath of Buffy's death; Richards-a 3.00
... Lovers Walk (2/01, $2.99) short stories by various; Richards & photo-c 3.00
...: Note From the Underground (3/03, $12.95) r/#47-50 13.00
...: Reunion (6/02, $3.50) Buffy & Angel's; Espenson-s; art by various 3.50
...: Slayer Interrupted TPB (2003, $14.95) r/#56-59 15.00
...: Tales of the Slayers (10/02, $3.50) art by Matsuda and Colan; art & photo-c 3.50
...: The Death of Buffy TPB (8/02, $15.95) r/#43-46 16.00
...: Viva Las Buffy TPB (7/03, $12.95) r/#51-54 13.00
Wizard #1/2 1 2 3 6 8 9

BUFFY THE VAMPIRE SLAYER: ANGEL
Dark Horse Comics: May, 1999 - No. 3, July, 1999 ($2.95, limited series)
1-3-Gomez-a; Matsuda-c & photo-c for each 3.00

BUFFY THE VAMPIRE SLAYER: GILES
Dark Horse Comics: Oct, 2000 ($2.95, one-shot)
1-Eric Powell-a; Powell & photo-c 3.00

BUFFY THE VAMPIRE SLAYER: HAUNTED
Dark Horse Comics: Dec, 2001 - No. 4, Mar, 2002 ($2.99, limited series)
1-4-Faith and the Mayor app.; Espenson-s/Richards-a 3.00
TPB (9/02, $12.95) r/series; photo-c 13.00

BUFFY THE VAMPIRE SLAYER: OZ
Dark Horse Comics: July, 2001 - No. 3, Sept, 2001 ($2.99, limited series)
1-3-Totleben & photo-c; Golden-s 3.00

BUFFY THE VAMPIRE SLAYER: SPIKE AND DRU
Dark Horse Comics: Apr, 1999; No. 2, Oct, 1999; No. 3, Dec, 2000 ($2.95)
1-3: 1,2-Photo-c. 3-Two covers (photo & Sook) 3.00

BUFFY THE VAMPIRE SLAYER: THE ORIGIN (Adapts movie screenplay)
Dark Horse Comics: Jan, 1999 - No. 3, Mar, 1999 ($2.95, limited series)
1-3-Brereton-s/Bennett-a; reg & photo-c for each 3.00

BUFFY THE VAMPIRE SLAYER: WILLOW & TARA
Dark Horse Comics: Apr, 2001 ($2.99, one-shot)
1-Terry Moore-a/Chris Golden & Amber Benson-s; Moore-c & photo-c 3.00
TPB (4/03, $9.95) r/#1 & W&T - Wilderness; photo-c 10.00

BUFFY THE VAMPIRE SLAYER: WILLOW & TARA - WILDERNESS
Dark Horse Comics: Jul, 2002 - No. 2, Sept, 2002 ($2.99, limited series)
1,2-Chris Golden & Amber Benson-s; Jothikaumar-c & photo-c 3.00

BUG
Marvel Comics: Mar, 1997 ($2.99, one-shot)
1-Micronauts character 3.00

BUGALOOS (TV)
Charlton Comics: Sept, 1971 - No. 4, Feb, 1972
1 5 10 15 33 44 55

Bugs Bunny Four Color #355 © WB

Bulls-Eye #4 © PRIZE

Bullseye: Greatest Hits #1 © MAR

	GD 2.0	VG 4.0	FN 6.0	VF 8.0	VF/NM 9.0	NM- 9.2
2-4	3	6	9	19	25	32

NOTE: *No. 3(1/72) went on sale late in 1972 (after No. 4) with the 1/73 issues.*

BUGBOY
Image Comics: June, 1998 ($3.95, B&W, one-shot)

1-Mark Lewis-s/a 4.00

BUGHOUSE (Satire)
Ajax/Farrell (Excellent Publ.): Mar-Apr, 1954 - No. 4, Sept-Oct, 1954

	GD	VG	FN	VF	VF/NM	NM-
V1#1	21	42	63	118	169	220
2-4	12	24	36	71	98	125

BUGS BUNNY (See The Best of..., Camp Comics, Comic Album #2, 6, 10, 14, Dell Giant #28, 32, 46, Dynabrite, Golden Comics Digest #1, 3, 5, 6, 8, 10, 14, 15, 17, 21, 26, 30, 34, 39, 42, 47, Kite Fun Book, Large Feature Comic #8, Looney Tunes and Merry Melodies, March of Comics #44, 59, 75, 83, 97, 115, 132, 149, 160, 179, 188, 201, 220, 231, 245, 259, 273, 287, 301, 315, 329, 343, 363, 367, 380, 392, 403, 415, 428, 440, 452, 464, 476, 487, Porky Pig, Puffed Wheat, Story Hour Series #802, Super Book #14, 26 and Whitman Comic Books)

BUGS BUNNY (See Dell Giants for annuals)
Dell Publishing Co./Gold Key No. 86-218/Whitman No. 219 on: 1942 - No. 245, April, 1984

	GD	VG	FN	VF	VF/NM	NM-
Large Feature Comic 8(1942)-(Rarely found in fine-mint condition)	128	256	384	896	1473	2050
Four Color 33 ('43)	115	230	345	805	1278	1750
Four Color 51	35	70	105	263	412	560
Four Color 88	24	48	72	170	260	350
Four Color 123('46),142,164	17	34	51	121	186	250
Four Color 187,200,217,233	12	24	36	87	134	180
Four Color 250-Used in **SOTI**, pg. 309	13	26	39	92	141	190
Four Color 266,274,281,289,298('50)	10	20	30	73	107	140
Four Color 307,317(#1),327(#2),338,347,355,366,376,393	10	20	30	67	96	125
Four Color 407,420,432(10/52)	8	16	24	58	82	105
Four Color 498(9/53),585(9/54), 647(9/55)	6	12	18	43	59	75
Four Color 724(9/56),838(9/57),1064(12/59)	6	12	18	38	52	65
28(12-1/52-53)-30	6	12	18	43	59	75
31-50	5	10	15	33	44	55
51-85(7-9/62)	4	8	12	22	30	38
86(10/62)-88-Bugs Bunny's Showtime-(25¢, 80pgs.)	7	14	21	51	71	90
89-99	3	6	9	18	24	30
100	3	6	9	19	25	32
101-118: 118-Last 12¢ issue	2	4	6	14	18	22
119-140	2	4	6	11	14	18
141-170	2	4	6	9	11	14
171-218	1	3	4	6	8	10
219,220,225-237(5/82): 229-Swipe of Barks story/WDC&S #223. 233(2/82)	1	3	4	6	8	11
221(9/80),222(11/80)-Pre-pack? (Scarce)	2	4	6	14	18	22
223 (1/81),224 (3/81)-Low distr.	2	4	6	11	14	18
238-245 (#90070 on-c, nd, nd code; pre-pack): 238(5/83), 239(6/83), 240(7/83), 241(7/83), 242(8/83), 243(8/83), 244(3/84), 245(4/84)	2	4	6	12	16	20

NOTE: *Reprints-100,102-104,110,115,123,143,144,147,167,173,175-177,179-185,187,190.*

	GD	VG	FN	VF	VF/NM	NM-
nn (Xerox Pub. Comic Digest, 1971, 100 pages, B&W) collection of one-page gags	3	6	9	18	24	30
...Comic-Go-Round 11196-(224 pgs.)($1.95)(Golden Press, 1979)	4	8	12	25	33	42
...Winter Fun 1(12/67-Gold Key)-Giant	6	12	18	38	52	65

BUGS BUNNY
DC Comics: June, 1990 - No. 3, Aug, 1990 ($1.00, limited series)

1-3: Daffy Duck, Elmer Fudd, others app. 4.00

BUGS BUNNY (...Monthly on-c)
DC Comics: 1993 - No. 3, 1994? ($1.95)

1-3-Bugs, Porky Pig, Daffy, Road Runner 3.50

BUGS BUNNY & PORKY PIG
Gold Key: Sept, 1965 (Paper-c, giant, 100 pgs.)

	GD	VG	FN	VF	VF/NM	NM-
1(30025-509)	9	18	27	65	93	120

BUGS BUNNY'S ALBUM (See Bugs Bunny, Four Color No. 498,585,647,724)

BUGS BUNNY LIFE STORY ALBUM (See Bugs Bunny, Four Color No. 838)

BUGS BUNNY MERRY CHRISTMAS (See Bugs Bunny, Four Color No. 1064)

BUILDING, THE
Kitchen Sink Press: 1987; 2000 (8 1/2" x 11" sepia toned graphic novel)

nn-Will Eisner-s/c/a 10.00
nn-(DC Comics, 9/00, $9.95) reprints 1987 edition 10.00

BULLET CROW, FOWL OF FORTUNE
Eclipse Comics: Mar, 1987 - No. 2, Apr, 1987 ($2.00, B&W, limited series)

1,2-The Comic Reader-r & new-a 2.50

BULLETMAN (See Fawcett Miniatures, Master Comics, Mighty Midget Comics, Nickel Comics & XMas Comics)
Fawcett Publications: Sum, 1941 - #12, 2/12/43; #14, Spr, 1946 - #16, Fall, 1946 (No #13)

	GD	VG	FN	VF	VF/NM	NM-
1-Silver metallic-c	372	744	1116	2418	3909	5400
2-Raboy-c	162	324	486	1013	1557	2100
3,5-Raboy-c each	110	220	330	688	1057	1425
4	96	192	288	600	925	1250
6-10: 7-Ghost Stories told by night watchman of cemetery begins; Eisnerish-a; hidden message "Chic Stone is a jerk". 10-Intro. Bulletdog	81	162	243	506	778	1050
11,12,14-16 (nn 13): 12-Robot-c	62	124	186	388	594	800

NOTE: ***Mac Raboy** c-1-3, 5, 6, 10. "Bulletman the Flying Detective" on cover #8 on.*

BULLETPROOF MONK (Inspired the 2003 film)
Image Comics (Flypaper Press): 1998 - No. 3, 1999 ($2.95, limited series)

1-3-Oeming-a 3.00
...: Tales of the BPM (3/03, $2.95) Flip book; 2 covers by Sale; art by Sale, Oeming, Dave Johnson; Seann William Scott afterword 3.00
TPB (2002, $9.95) r/#1-3; foreword by John Woo 10.00

BULLETS AND BRACELETS (Also see Marvel Versus DC #3 & DC Versus Marvel #4)
Marvel Comics (Amalgam): Apr, 1996 ($1.95)

1-John Ostrander script & Gary Frank-c/a 2.50

BULLSEYE: GREATEST HITS (Daredevil villain)
Marvel Comics: Nov, 2004 - No. 5 ($2.99)

1-3-Origin of Bullseye; Steve Dillon-a/Deodato-c. 3-Punisher app. 3.00

BULLS-EYE (Cody of The Pony Express No. 8 on)
Mainline No. 1-5/Charlton No. 6,7: 7-8/54-No. 5, 3-4/55; No. 6, 6/55; No. 7, 8/55

	GD	VG	FN	VF	VF/NM	NM-
1-S&K-c, 2 pgs.-a	55	110	165	340	520	700
2-S&K-c/a	46	92	138	281	428	575
3-5-S&K-c/a(2 each). 4-Last pre-code issue (1-2/55). 5-Censored issue with tomahawks removed in battle scene	40	80	120	236	351	465
6-S&K-c/a	35	70	105	198	287	375
7-S&K-c/a(3)	42	84	126	242	354	465

BULLS-EYE COMICS (Formerly Komik Pages #10; becomes Kayo #12)
Harry 'A' Chesler: No. 11, 1944

	GD	VG	FN	VF	VF/NM	NM-
11-Origin K-9, Green Knight's sidekick, Lance; The Green Knight, Lady Satan, Yankee Doodle Jones app.	42	84	126	256	391	525

BULLWHIP GRIFFIN (See Movie Comics)

BULLWINKLE (...and Rocky No. 22 on; See March of Comics #233 and Rocky & Bullwinkle) (TV) (Jay Ward)
Dell/Gold Key: 3-5/62 - #11, 4/74; #12, 6/76 - #19, 3/78; #20, 4/79 - #25, 2/80

	GD	VG	FN	VF	VF/NM	NM-
Four Color 1270 (3-5/62)	21	42	63	150	230	310
01-090-209 (Dell, 7-9/62)	17	34	51	119	182	245
1(11/62, Gold Key)	15	30	45	105	160	215
2(2/63)	10	20	30	70	100	130
3(4/72)-11(4/74-Gold Key)	6	12	18	40	55	70
12-14: 12(6/76)-Reprints. 13(9/76), 14-New stories	3	6	9	18	24	30
15-25	2	4	6	11	14	18
Mother Moose Nursery Pomes 01-530-207 (5-7/62, Dell)	19	38	57	134	205	275

NOTE: *Reprints: 6, 7, 20-24.*

BULLWINKLE (...& Rocky No. 2 on)(TV)
Charlton Comics: July, 1970 - No. 7, July, 1971

	GD	VG	FN	VF	VF/NM	NM-
1	7	14	21	51	71	90
2-7	5	10	15	36	48	60

BULLWINKLE AND ROCKY
Star Comics/Marvel Comics No. 3 on: Nov, 1987 - No. 9, Mar, 1989

1-9: Boris & Natasha in all. 3,5,8-Dudley Do-Right app. 4-Reagan-c 4.00

	GD	VG	FN	VF	VF/NM	NM-
Marvel Moosterworks (1/92, $4.95)	1	3	4	6	8	10

BUMMER
Fantagraphics Books: June, 1995 ($3.50, B&W, mature)

1 3.50

BUNNY (Also see Harvey Pop Comics)
Harvey Publications: Dec, 1966 - No. 20, Dec, 1971; No. 21, Nov, 1976

	GD	VG	FN	VF	VF/NM	NM-
1-68 pg. Giants begin	8	16	24	58	82	105
2-10	5	10	15	33	44	55

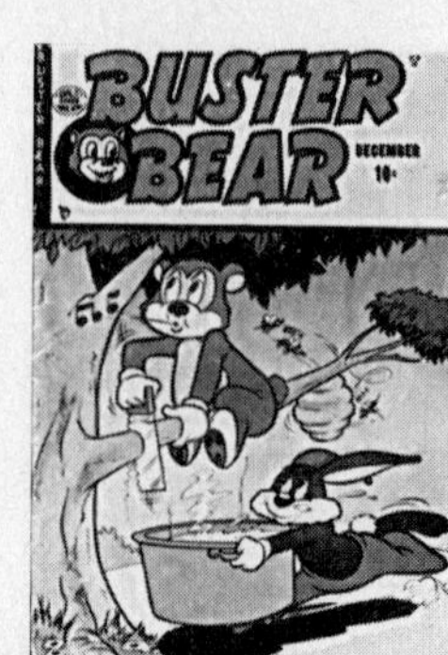

Buster Bear #1 © QUA

Buzzy #6 © DC

Cable #75 © MAR

	GD 2.0	VG 4.0	FN 6.0	VF 8.0	VF/NM 9.0	NM- 9.2
11-18: 18-Last 68 pg. Giant	4	8	12	29	40	50
19-21-52 pg. Giants: 21-Fruitman app.	4	8	12	27	36	45

BURKE'S LAW (TV)
Dell Publ.: 1-3/64; No. 2, 5-7/64; No. 3, 3-5/65 (All have Gene Barry photo-c)

	GD 2.0	VG 4.0	FN 6.0	VF 8.0	VF/NM 9.0	NM- 9.2
1-Photo-c	6	12	18	40	55	70
2,3-Photo-c	4	8	12	29	40	50

BURNING ROMANCES (See Fox Giants)

BUSTER BEAR
Quality Comics Group (Arnold Publ.): Dec, 1953 - No. 10, June, 1955

	GD 2.0	VG 4.0	FN 6.0	VF 8.0	VF/NM 9.0	NM- 9.2
1-Funny animal	10	20	30	60	80	100
2	7	14	21	35	43	50
3-10	6	12	18	28	34	40
I.W. Reprint #9,10 (Super on inside)	2	4	6	10	13	16

BUSTER BROWN COMICS (See Promotional Comics section)

BUSTER BUNNY
Standard Comics(Animated Cartoons)/Pines: Nov, 1949 - No. 16, Oct, 1953

	GD 2.0	VG 4.0	FN 6.0	VF 8.0	VF/NM 9.0	NM- 9.2
1-Frazetta 1 pg. text illo.	10	20	30	60	80	100
2	7	14	21	35	43	50
3-14,16	6	12	18	27	33	38
15-Racist-c	7	14	21	35	43	50

BUSTER CRABBE (TV)
Famous Funnies Publ.: Nov, 1951 - No. 12, 1953

	GD 2.0	VG 4.0	FN 6.0	VF 8.0	VF/NM 9.0	NM- 9.2
1-1st app.(?) Frazetta anti-drug ad; text story about Buster Crabbe & Billy the Kid	40	80	120	233	342	450
2-Williamson/Evans-c; text story about Wild Bill Hickok & Pecos Bill	39	78	117	222	324	425
3-Williamson/Evans-c/a	40	80	120	233	342	450
4-Frazetta-c/a, 1pg.; bondage-c	48	96	144	293	447	600
5-Frazetta-c; Williamson/Krenkel/Orlando-a, 11pgs. (per Mr. Williamson)	119	238	357	744	1147	1550
6,8	20	40	60	112	161	210
7-Frazetta one pg. ad	20	40	60	115	165	215
9-One pg. Frazetta Boy Scouts ad (1st?)	17	34	51	98	139	180
10-12	12	24	36	69	95	120

NOTE: Eastern Color sold 3 dozen each NM file copies of #s 9-12 a few years ago.

BUSTER CRABBE (The Amazing Adventures of...)(Movie star)
Lev Gleason Publications: Dec, 1953 - No. 4, June, 1954

	GD 2.0	VG 4.0	FN 6.0	VF 8.0	VF/NM 9.0	NM- 9.2
1,4: 1-Photo-c. 4-Flash Gordon-c	23	46	69	132	191	250
2,3-Toth-a	21	42	63	121	173	225

BUTCH CASSIDY
Skywald Comics: June, 1971 - No. 3, Oct, 1971 (52 pgs.)

	GD 2.0	VG 4.0	FN 6.0	VF 8.0	VF/NM 9.0	NM- 9.2
1-Pre-code reprints and new material; Red Mask reprint, retitled Maverick; Bolle-a; Sutton-a	3	6	9	16	20	24
2,3: 2-Whip Wilson-r. 3-Dead Canyon Days reprint/Crack Western No. 63; Sundance Kid app.; Crandall-a	2	4	6	10	13	16

BUTCH CASSIDY (...& the Wild Bunch)
Avon Periodicals: 1951

	GD 2.0	VG 4.0	FN 6.0	VF 8.0	VF/NM 9.0	NM- 9.2
1-Kinstler-c/a	19	38	57	107	154	200

NOTE: *Reinman story; Issue number on inside spine.*

BUTCH CASSIDY (See Fun-In No. 11 & Western Adventure Comics)

BUTCHER, THE (Also see Brave and the Bold, 2nd Series)
DC Comics: May, 1990 - No. 5, Sept, 1990 ($1.50, mature)

	NM- 9.2
1-5: 1-No indicia inside	2.50

BUTCHER KNIGHT
Image Comics (Top Cow): Jan, 2001 - No. 4, June, 2001 ($2.95, limited series)

	NM- 9.2
Preview (B&W, 16 pgs.) Dwayne Turner-c/a	2.25
1-4-Dwayne Turner-c/a	3.00

BUZ SAWYER (Sweeney No. 4 on)
Standard Comics: June, 1948 - No. 3, 1949

	GD 2.0	VG 4.0	FN 6.0	VF 8.0	VF/NM 9.0	NM- 9.2
1-Roy Crane-a	24	48	72	138	199	260
2-Intro his pal Sweeney	15	30	45	83	117	150
3	11	22	33	64	87	110

BUZ SAWYER'S PAL, ROSCOE SWEENEY (See Sweeney)

BUZZ, THE (Also see Spider-Girl)
Marvel Comics: July, 2000 - No. 3, Sept, 2000 ($2.99, limited series)

	NM- 9.2
1-3-Buscema-a/DeFalco & Frenz-s	3.00

BUZZ BUZZ COMICS MAGAZINE
Horse Press: May, 1996 ($4.95, B&W, over-sized magazine)

	NM- 9.2
1-Paul Pope-c/a/scripts; Moebius-a	5.00

BUZZY (See All Funny Comics)
National Periodical Publications/Detective Comics: Winter, 1944-45 - No. 75, 1-2/57; No. 76, 10/57; No. 77, 10/58

	GD 2.0	VG 4.0	FN 6.0	VF 8.0	VF/NM 9.0	NM- 9.2
1 (52 pgs. begin); "America's favorite teenster"	32	64	96	184	267	350
2 (Spr, 1945)	16	32	48	89	127	165
3-5	11	22	33	64	87	110
6-10	9	18	27	52	66	80
11-20	8	16	24	43	54	65
21-30	7	14	21	37	46	55
31,35-38	7	14	21	35	43	50
32-34,39-Last 52 pgs. Scribbly story by Mayer in each (these four stories were done for Scribbly #14 which was delayed for a year)	8	16	24	40	50	60
40-77: 62-Last precode (2/55)	6	12	18	31	38	45

BUZZY THE CROW (See Harvey Comics Hits #60 & 62, Harvey Hits #18 & Paramount Animated Comics #1)

BY BIZARRE HANDS
Dark Horse Comics: Apr, 1994 - No. 3, June, 1994 ($2.50, B&W, mature)

	NM- 9.2
1-3: Lansdale stories	2.50

CABBOT: BLOODHUNTER (Also see Bloodstrike & Bloodstrike: Assassin)
Maximum Press: Jan, 1997 ($2.50, one-shot)

	NM- 9.2
1-Rick Veitch-a/script; Platt-c; Thor, Chapel & Prophet cameos	2.50

CABLE (See Ghost Rider &..., & New Mutants #87) (Title becomes Soldier X)
Marvel Comics: May, 1993 - No. 107, Sept, 2002 ($3.50/$1.95/$1.50-$2.25)

	NM- 9.2
1-($3.50, 52 pgs.)-Gold foil & embossed-c; Thibert a-1-4p; c-1-3	5.00
2-15: 3-Extra 16 pg. X-Men/Avengers ann. preview. 4-Liefeld-a assist; last Thibert-a(p). 6-8-Reveals that Baby Nathan is Cable; gives background on Stryfe. 9-Omega Red-c/story. 11-Bound-in trading card sheet	3.50
16-Newsstand edition	2.50
16-Enhanced edition	5.00
17-20-($1.95)-Deluxe edition, 20-w/bound in '95 Fleer Ultra cards	3.00
17-20-($1.50)-Standard edition	2.50
21-24, 26-44, -1(7/97): 21-Begin $1.95-c; return from Age of Apocalyse. 24-Grizzly dies. 28-vs. Sugarman; Mr. Sinister app. 30-X-Man-c/app.; Exodus app. 31-vs. X-Man. 32-Post app. 33-Post-c/app; Mandarin app (flashback); includes "Onslaught Update". 34-Onslaught x-over; Hulk-c/app; Apocalypse app. (cont'd in Hulk #444). 35-Onslaught x-over; Apocalypse vs. Cable. 36-w/card insert. 38-Weapon X-c/app; Psycho Man & Micronauts app. 40-Scott Clark-a(p). 41-Bishop-c/app.	3.00
25 ($3.95)-Foil gatefold-c	4.00
45-49,51-74: 45-Operation Zero Tolerance. 51-1st Casey-s. 54-Black Panther. 55-Domino-c/app. 62-Nick Fury-c/app.63-Stryfe-c/app. 67,68-Avengers-c/app. 71,73-Liefeld-a	2.50
50-($2.99) Double sized w/wraparound-c	3.00
75 -($2.99) Liefeld-c/a; Apocalypse: The Twelve x-over	3.00
76-79: 76-Apocalypse: The Twelve x-over	2.50
80-96: 80-Begin $2.25-c. 87-Mystique-c/app.	2.50
97-99,101-107: 97-Tischman-s/Kordey-a/c begin	2.25
100($3.99) Dialogue-free 'Nuff Said back-up story	4.00
.../Machine Man '98 Annual ($2.99) Wraparound-c	3.00
.../X-Force '96 Annual ($2.95) Wraparound-c	3.00
...'99 Annual ($3.50) vs. Sinister; computer photo-c	3.50
...Second Genesis 1 (9/99, $3.99) r/New Mutants #99, 100 and X-Force #1; Liefeld-c	4.00
...: The End (2002, $14.99, TPB) r/#101-107	15.00

CABLE - BLOOD AND METAL (Also see New Mutants #87 & X-Force #8)
Marvel Comics: Oct, 1992 - No. 2, Nov, 1992 ($2.50, limited series, 52 pgs.)

	NM- 9.2
1-Fabian Nicieza scripts; John Romita, Jr.-c/a in both; Cable vs. Stryfe; 2nd app. of The Wild Pack (becomes The Six Pack); wraparound-c	4.00
2-Prelude to X-Cutioner's Song	3.00

CABLE/DEADPOOL ("Cable & Deadpool" on cover)
Marvel Comics: May, 2004 - Present ($2.99)

	NM- 9.2
1-9: 1-Nicieza-s/Liefeld-c. 7-9-X-Men app.	3.00
... Vol. 1: If Looks Could Kill TPB (2004, $14.99) r/#1-6	15.00

CADET GRAY OF WEST POINT (See Dell Giants)

CADILLACS & DINOSAURS (TV)
Marvel Comics (Epic Comics): Nov, 1990 - No. 6, Apr, 1991 ($2.50, limited series)

	NM- 9.2
1-6: r/Xenozoic Tales in color w/new-c	3.00
...In 3-D #1 (7/92, $3.95, Kitchen Sink)-With glasses	6.00

CADILLACS AND DINOSAURS (TV)

Cage #1 © MAR

The Call of Duty: The Precinct #1 © MAR

Calling All Boys #8 © PMI

GD VG FN VF VF/NM NM-
2.0 4.0 6.0 8.0 9.0 9.2

Topps Comics: V2#1, Feb, 1994 - V2#9, 1995 ($2.50, limited series)

V2#1-($2.95)-Collector's edition w/Stout-c & bound-in poster; Buckler-a; foil stamped logo; Giordano-a in all 6.00
V2#1-9: 1-Newsstand edition w/Giordano-c. 2,3-Collector's editions w/Stout-c & posters. 2,3-Newsstand ed. w/Giordano-c; w/o posters. 4-6-Collectors & Newsstand editions; Kieth-c. 7-9-Linsner-c 3.00

CAFFEINE
Slave Labor Graphics: Jan, 1996 - No. 10, 1999 ($2.95/$3.95, B&W)

1-9 3.00
10-($3.95) 4.00

CAGE (Also see Hero for Hire, Power Man & Punisher)
Marvel Comics: Apr, 1992 - No. 20, Nov, 1993 ($1.25)

1,3,10,12: 3-Punisher-c & minor app. 10-Rhino & Hulk-c/app. 12-(52 pgs.)-Iron Fist app. 3.00
2,4-9,11,13-20: 9-Rhino-c/story; Hulk cameo 2.50

CAGE (Volume 3)
Marvel Comics (MAX): Mar, 2002 - No. 5, Sept, 2002 ($2.99, mature)

1-5-Corben-c/a; Azzarello-s 3.00
HC (2002, $19.99, with dustjacket) r/#1-5; intro. by Darius James; sketch pages 20.00
SC (2003, $13.99) r/#1-5; intro. by Darius James 14.00

CAGED HEAT 3000 (Movie)
Roger Corman's Cosmic Comics: Nov, 1995 - No. 3, Jan, 1996 ($2.50)

1-3: Adaptation of film 2.50

CAGES
Tundra Publ.: 1991 - No. 10, May, 1996 ($3.50/$3.95/$4.95, limited series)

1-Dave McKean-c/a in all 2 4 6 8 10 12
2-Misprint exists 1 2 3 5 6 8
3-9: 5-$3.95-c begins 4.00
10-($4.95) 5.00

CAIN'S HUNDRED (TV)
Dell Publishing Co.: May-July, 1962 - No. 2, Sept-Nov, 1962

nn(01-094-207) 4 8 12 24 32 40
2 3 6 9 16 21 26

CAIN/VAMPIRELLA FLIP BOOK
Harris Comics: Oct, 1994 ($6.95, one-shot, squarebound)

nn-contains Cain #3 & #4; flip book is r/Vampirella story from 1993 Creepy Fearbook 1 2 3 5 7 9

CALIBER PRESENTS
Caliber Press: Jan, 1989 - No. 24, 1991 ($1.95/$2.50, B&W, 52 pgs.)

1-Anthology; 1st app. The Crow; Tim Vigil-c/a 6 12 18 43 59 75
2-Deadworld story; Tim Vigil-a 2 4 6 10 13 16
3-24: 15-24 ($3.50, 68 pgs.) 3.50

CALIBER PRESENTS: CINDERELLA ON FIRE
Caliber Press: 1994 ($2.95, B&W, mature)

1 3.00

CALIBER SPOTLIGHT
Caliber Press: May, 1995 ($2.95, B&W)

1-Kabuki app 3.50

CALIBRATIONS
Caliber: 1996 - No. 5 (99¢, anthology)

1-5: 1-Jill Thompson-c/a. 1,2-Atmospherics by Warren Ellis 2.50

CALIFORNIA GIRLS
Eclipse Comics: June, 1987 - No. 8, May, 1988 ($2.00, 40 pgs, B&W)

1-8: All contain color paper dolls 3.00

CALL, THE
Marvel Comics: June, 2003 - No. 4, Sept, 2003 ($2.25)

1-4-Austen-s/Olliffe-a 2.25

CALLING ALL BOYS (Tex Granger No. 18 on)
Parents' Magazine Institute: Jan, 1946 - No. 17, May, 1948 (Photo c-1-5,7,8)

1 13 26 39 74 102 130
2-Contains Roy Rogers article 8 16 24 40 50 60
3-7,9,11,14-17: 6-Painted-c. 11-Rin Tin Tin photo on-c; Tex Granger begins. 14-J. Edgar Hoover photo on-c. 15-Tex Granger-c begin 6 12 18 28 34 40
8-Milton Caniff story 8 16 24 46 58 70
10-Gary Cooper photo on-c 8 16 24 43 54 65
12-Bob Hope photo on-c 12 24 36 71 98 125

GD VG FN VF VF/NM NM-
2.0 4.0 6.0 8.0 9.0 9.2

13-Bing Crosby photo on-c 11 22 33 62 84 105

CALLING ALL GIRLS
Parents' Magazine Institute: Sept, 1941 - No. 89, Sept, 1949 (Part magazine, part comic)

1 17 34 51 95 135 175
2-Photo-c 9 18 27 54 70 85
3-Shirley Temple photo-c 12 24 36 69 95 120
4-10: 4,5,7,9-Photo-c. 9-Flag-c 8 16 24 40 50 60
11-Tina Thayer photo-c; Mickey Rooney photo-b/c; B&W photo inside of Gary Cooper as Lou Gehrig in "Pride of Yankees" 9 18 27 51 62 75
12-20 7 14 21 35 43 50
21-39,41-43(10-11/45)-Last issue with comics 6 12 18 31 38 45
40-Liz Taylor photo-c 17 34 51 98 139 180
44-51(7/46)-Last comic book size issue 5 10 15 24 30 35
52-89 5 10 15 22 26 30

NOTE: ***Jack Sparling*** *art in many issues; becomes a girls' magazine "Senior Prom" with #90.*

CALLING ALL KIDS (Also see True Comics)
Parents' Magazine Institute: Dec-Jan, 1945-46 - No. 26, Aug, 1949

1-Funny animal 13 26 39 74 102 130
2 8 16 24 40 50 60
3-10 6 12 18 31 38 45
11-26 6 12 18 28 34 40

CALL OF DUTY, THE : THE BROTHERHOOD
Marvel Comics: Aug, 2002 - No. 6, Jan, 2003 ($2.25)

1-Exploits of NYC Fire Dept.; Finch-c/a; Austen & Bruce Jones-s 4.00
2-6-Austen-s 2.50
...Vol 1: The Brotherhood & The Wagon TPB (2002, $14.99) r/#1-6 & ...The Wagon #1-4 15.00

CALL OF DUTY, THE : THE PRECINCT
Marvel Comics: Sept, 2002 - No. 5, Jan, 2003 ($2.25, limited series)

1-Exploits of NYC Police Dept.; Finch-c; Bruce Jones-s/Mandrake-a 3.00
2-4 2.25
...Vol 2: The Precinct TPB (2003, $9.99) r/#1-4 10.00

CALL OF DUTY, THE : THE WAGON
Marvel Comics: Oct, 2002 - No. 4, Jan, 2003 ($2.25, limited series)

1-4-Exploits of NYC EMS Dept.; Finch-c; Austen-s/Zelzej-a 2.25

CALVIN (See Li'l Kids)

CALVIN & THE COLONEL (TV)
Dell Publishing Co.: No. 1354, Apr-June, 1962 - No. 2, July-Sept, 1962

Four Color 1354(#1) 10 20 30 70 100 130
2 7 14 21 50 68 85

CAMBION
Slave Labor Graphics: Dec, 1995 - No. 2, Feb, 1996 ($2.95, B&W)

1,2 3.00

CAMELOT 3000
DC Comics: Dec, 1982 - No. 11, July, 1984; No. 12, Apr, 1985 (Direct sales, maxi series, Mando paper)

1-12: 1-Mike Barr scripts & Brian Bolland-c/a begin. 5-Intro Knights of New Camelot 3.00
TPB (1988, $12.95) r/#1-12 13.00

NOTE: ***Austin*** *a-7i-12i.* ***Bolland*** *a-1-12p; c-1-12.*

CAMERA COMICS
U.S. Camera Publishing Corp./ME: July, 1944 - No. 9, Summer, 1946

nn (7/44) 25 50 75 144 207 270
nn (9/44) 19 38 57 107 154 200
1(10/44)-The Grey Comet 19 38 57 107 154 200
2 14 28 42 79 110 140
3-Nazi WW II-c; photos 13 26 39 76 106 135
4-9: All half photos 11 22 33 66 91 115

CAMP CANDY (TV)
Marvel Comics: May, 1990 - No. 6, Oct, 1990 ($1.00, limited series)

1-6: Post-c/a(p); featuring John Candy 4.00

CAMP COMICS
Dell Publishing Co.: Feb, 1942 - No. 3, April, 1942 (All have photo-c)

1- "Seaman Sy Wheeler" by Kelly, 7 pgs.; Bugs Bunny app.; Mark Twain adaptation (scarce) 77 154 231 481 741 1000
2-Kelly-a, 12 pgs.; Bugs Bunny app.; classic-c 77 154 231 481 741 1000
3-(Scarce)-Dave Berg & Walt Kelly-a 62 124 186 388 594 800

CAMP RUNAMUCK (TV)
Dell Publishing Co.: Apr, 1966

Campus Romances #2 © AVON

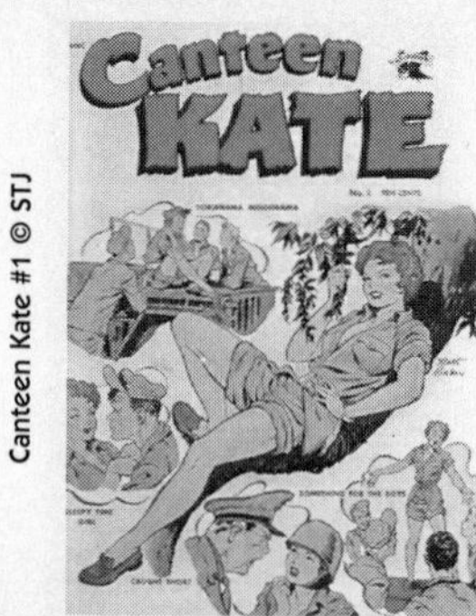

Canteen Kate #1 © STJ

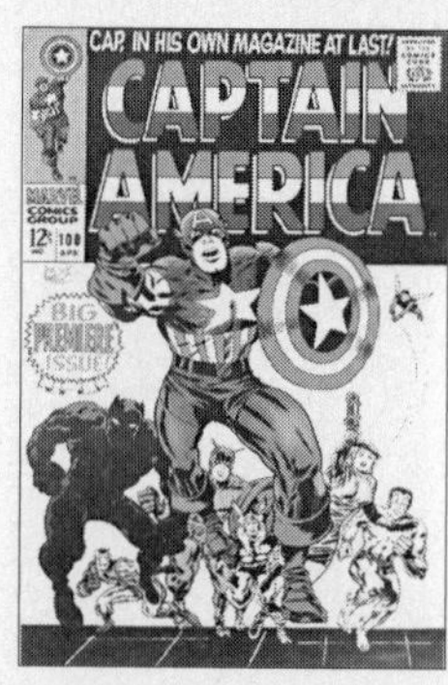

Captain America #100 © MAR

	GD 2.0	VG 4.0	FN 6.0	VF 8.0	VF/NM 9.0	NM- 9.2
1-Photo-c	4	8	12	25	33	42

CAMPUS LOVES
Quality Comics Group (Comic Magazines): Dec, 1949 - No. 5, Aug, 1950

	GD 2.0	VG 4.0	FN 6.0	VF 8.0	VF/NM 9.0	NM- 9.2
1-Ward-c/a (9 pgs.)	35	70	105	198	287	375
2-Ward-c/a	26	52	78	147	211	275
3-5	13	26	39	76	106	135

NOTE: *Gustavson a-1-5. Photo c-3-5.*

CAMPUS ROMANCE (...Romances on cover)
Avon Periodicals/Realistic: Sept-Oct, 1949 - No. 3, Feb-Mar, 1950

	GD 2.0	VG 4.0	FN 6.0	VF 8.0	VF/NM 9.0	NM- 9.2
1-Walter Johnson-a; c-/Avon paperback #348	25	50	75	141	203	265
2-Grandenetti-a; c-/Avon paperback #151	18	36	54	100	143	185
3-c-/Avon paperback #201	18	36	54	100	143	185
Realistic reprint	9	18	27	51	62	75

CANADA DRY PREMIUMS (See Swamp Fox, The & Terry & The Pirates in the Promotional Comics section)

CANCELLED COMIC CAVALCADE (See the Promotional Comics section)

CANDID TALES (Also see Bold Stories & It Rhymes With Lust)
Kirby Publ. Co.: April, 1950; June, 1950 (Digest size) (144 pgs.) (Full color)

	GD 2.0	VG 4.0	FN 6.0	VF 8.0	VF/NM 9.0	NM- 9.2
nn-(Scarce) Contains Wood female pirate story, 15 pgs., and 14 pgs. in June issue; Powell-a	96	192	288	600	925	1250

NOTE: *Another version exists with Dr. Kilmore by Wood; no female pirate story.*

CANDY
William H. Wise & Co.: Fall, 1944 - No. 3, Spring, 1945

	GD 2.0	VG 4.0	FN 6.0	VF 8.0	VF/NM 9.0	NM- 9.2
1-Two Scoop Scuttle stories by Wolverton	40	80	120	240	360	480
2,3-Scoop Scuttle by Wolverton, 2-4 pgs.	30	60	90	170	245	320

CANDY (Teen-age)(Also see Police Comics #37)
Quality Comics Group (Comic Magazines): Autumn, 1947 - No. 64, Jul, 1956

	GD 2.0	VG 4.0	FN 6.0	VF 8.0	VF/NM 9.0	NM- 9.2
1-Gustavson-a	24	48	72	138	199	260
2-Gustavson-a	13	26	39	74	102	130
3-10	9	18	27	52	66	80
11-30	7	14	21	37	46	55
31-64: 64-Ward-c(p)?	6	12	18	31	38	45
Super Reprint No. 2,10,12,16,17,18('63- '64):17-Candy #12	2	4	6	11	14	18

NOTE: *Jack Cole 1-2 pg. art in many issues.*

CANNON (See Heroes, Inc. Presents Cannon)

CANNON: DAWN OF WAR (Michael Turner's...)
Aspen MLT, Inc.: Nov, 2004 ($2.99)

	GD 2.0	VG 4.0	FN 6.0	VF 8.0	VF/NM 9.0	NM- 9.2
1-Turnbull-a; two covers by Turnbull and Turner						3.00

CANNONBALL COMICS
Rural Home Publishing Co.: Feb, 1945 - No. 2, Mar, 1945

	GD 2.0	VG 4.0	FN 6.0	VF 8.0	VF/NM 9.0	NM- 9.2
1-The Crash Kid, Thunderbrand, The Captive Prince & Crime Crusader begin; skull-c	88	176	264	550	850	1150
2-Devil-c	67	134	201	419	647	875

CANNON BUSTERS
Devil's Due Publ.: June, 2004

	GD 2.0	VG 4.0	FN 6.0	VF 8.0	VF/NM 9.0	NM- 9.2
Convention Preview Edition						2.25

CANNON GOD EXAXXION (Manga)
Dark Horse Comics: Nov, 2001 - Present ($2.99, B&W)

	GD 2.0	VG 4.0	FN 6.0	VF 8.0	VF/NM 9.0	NM- 9.2
1-8,15-20: 1-Kenichi Sonoda-s/a in all						3.00
9,12-($3.99, 48 pages)						4.00
10,11,13,14-($3.50)						3.50

CANTEEN KATE (See All Picture All True Love Story & Fightin' Marines)
St. John Publishing Co.: June, 1952 - No. 3, Nov, 1952

	GD 2.0	VG 4.0	FN 6.0	VF 8.0	VF/NM 9.0	NM- 9.2
1-Matt Baker-c/a	60	120	180	375	575	775
2-Matt Baker-c/a	42	84	126	256	391	525
3-(Rare)-Used in **POP**, pg. 75; Baker-c/a	50	100	150	305	465	625

CAPER
DC Comics: Dec, 2003 - No. 12, Nov, 2004 ($2.95, limited series)

	GD 2.0	VG 4.0	FN 6.0	VF 8.0	VF/NM 9.0	NM- 9.2
1-9: 1-4-Judd Winick-s/Farel Dalrymple-a. 5-8-John Severin-a. 9-12-Fowler-a						3.00

CAPES
Image Comics: Sept, 2003 - No. 3, Nov, 2003 ($3.50)

	GD 2.0	VG 4.0	FN 6.0	VF 8.0	VF/NM 9.0	NM- 9.2
1-3-Robert Kirkman-s/Mark Englert-a/c						3.50

CAP'N QUICK & A FOOZLE (Also see Eclipse Mag. & Monthly)
Eclipse Comics: July, 1984 - No. 3, Nov, 1985 ($1.50, color, Baxter paper)

	GD 2.0	VG 4.0	FN 6.0	VF 8.0	VF/NM 9.0	NM- 9.2
1-3-Rogers-c/a						3.00

CAPTAIN ACTION (Toy)
National Periodical Publications: Oct-Nov, 1968 - No. 5, June-July, 1969 (Based on Ideal toy)

	GD 2.0	VG 4.0	FN 6.0	VF 8.0	VF/NM 9.0	NM- 9.2
1-Origin; Wood-a; Superman-c app.	9	18	27	60	85	110
2,3,5-Kane/Wood-a	7	14	21	50	68	85
4	6	12	18	40	55	70

CAPTAIN AERO COMICS (Samson No. 1-6; also see Veri Best Sure Fire & Veri Best Sure Shot Comics)
Holyoke Publishing Co.: V1#7(#1), Dec, 1941 - V2#4(#10), Jan, 1943; V3#9(#11), Sept, 1943 -V4#3(#17), Oct, 1944; #21, Dec, 1944 - #26, Aug, 1946 (No #18-20)

	GD 2.0	VG 4.0	FN 6.0	VF 8.0	VF/NM 9.0	NM- 9.2
V1#7(#1)-Flag-Man & Solar, Master of Magic, Captain Aero, Cap Stone, Adventurer begin	165	330	495	1031	1591	2150
8-10: 8(#2)-Pals of Freedom app. 9(#3)-Alias X begins; Pals of Freedom app. 10(#4)-Origin The Gargoyle; Kubert-a	79	158	237	494	760	1025
11,12(#5,6)-Kubert-a; Miss Victory in #6	65	130	195	406	623	840
V2#1,2(#7,8): 8-Origin The Red Cross; Miss Victory app.; Brodsky-c(i)	40	80	120	240	363	485
3(#9)-Miss Victory app.	39	78	117	222	324	425
4(#10)-Miss Victory app.	31	62	93	178	259	340
V3#9 - V3#13(#11-15): 11,15-Miss Victory app.	26	52	78	147	211	275
V4#2(#16)	25	50	75	141	203	265
V4#3(#17), 21-25-L. B. Cole covers. 22-Intro/origin Mighty Mite.	45	90	135	275	418	560
26-L. B. Cole S/F-c; Palais-a(2) (scarce)	92	184	276	575	888	1200

NOTE: ***L.B. Cole** c-17. **Hollingsworth** a-23. **Infantino** a-23, 26. **Schomburg** c-15, 16.*

CAPTAIN AMERICA (See Adventures of..., All-Select, All Winners, Aurora, Avengers #4, Blood and Glory, Captain Britain 16-20, Giant-Size..., The Invaders, Marvel Double Feature, Marvel Fanfare, Marvel Mystery, Marvel Super-Action, Marvel Super Heroes V2#3, Marvel Team-Up, Marvel Treasury Special, Power Record Comics, Ultimates, USA Comics, Young Allies & Young Men)

CAPTAIN AMERICA (Formerly Tales of Suspense #1-99) (Captain America and the Falcon #134-223 & Steve Rogers: Captain America #444-454 appears on cover only)
Marvel Comics Group: No. 100, Apr, 1968 - No. 454, Aug, 1996

	GD 2.0	VG 4.0	FN 6.0	VF 8.0	VF/NM 9.0	NM- 9.2
100-Flashback on Cap's revival with Avengers & Sub-Mariner; story continued from Tales of Suspense #99; Kirby-c/a begins	28	56	84	203	312	420
101-The Sleeper-c/story; Red Skull app.	9	18	27	60	85	110
102-104: 102-Sleeper-c/s. 103,104-Red Skull-c/sty	7	14	21	46	63	80
105-108	6	12	18	38	52	65
109-Origin Capt. America retold	8	16	24	55	78	100
109-2nd printing (1994)	2	4	6	8	10	12
110-Rick becomes Cap's partner; Hulk x-over	10	20	30	70	100	130
111,113-Classic Steranko-c/a: 111-Death of Steve Rogers. 113-Cap's funeral	8	16	24	55	78	100
112-Origin retold; last Kirby-c/a	5	10	15	33	44	55
114-116,118-120: 115-Last 12¢ issue	4	8	12	22	30	38
117-1st app. The Falcon (9/69)	9	18	27	60	85	110
121-136,139,140: 121-Retells origin. 133-The Falcon becomes Cap's partner; origin Modok. 140-Origin Grey Gargoyle retold	3	6	9	16	20	25
137,138-Spider-Man x-over	3	6	9	19	25	32
141,142: 142-Last 15¢ issue	2	4	6	12	16	20
143-(52 pgs).	3	6	9	18	23	28
144-153: 144-New costume Falcon. 153-1st brief app. Jack Monroe	2	4	6	10	12	15
154-1st full app. Jack Monroe (Nomad)(10/72)	2	4	6	11	14	18
155-Origin; redrawn w/Falcon added; origin Jack Monroe	2	4	6	11	14	18
156-171,176-179: 155-158-Cap's strength increased. 160-1st app. Solarr. 164-1st app. Nightshade. 176-End of Capt. America.	1	3	4	6	8	10
172-175: X-Men x-over	2	4	6	11	14	18
180-Intro/origin of Nomad (Steve Rogers)	2	4	6	12	16	20
181-Intro/origin new Cap.	2	4	6	10	13	16
182,184-192: 186-True origin The Falcon	1	2	3	5	6	8
183-Death of new Cap; Nomad becomes Cap	2	4	6	8	10	12
193-Kirby-c/a begins	2	4	6	14	18	22
194-199-(Regular 25¢ edition)(4-7/76)	2	4	6	10	13	16
196-199-(30¢-c variants, limited distribution)	3	6	9	16	20	24
200-(Regular 25¢ edition)(8/76)	2	4	6	12	16	20
200-(30¢-c variant, limited distribution)	3	6	9	18	24	30
201-214-Kirby-c/a	2	4	6	9	11	14
210-214-(35¢-c variants, limited dist.)(6-10/77)	2	4	6	13	17	21
215,216,218-229,231-234,236-240,242-246: 215-Retells Cap's origin. 216-r/story from Strange Tales #114. 229-Marvel Man app. 233-Death of Sharon Carter. 234-Daredevil x-over. 244,245-Miller-c						5.00
217,230,235: 217-1st app. Marvel Man (later Quasar). 230-Battles Hulk-c/story cont'd in Hulk #232. 235-(7/79) Daredevil x-over; Miller-a(p)	1	2	3	4	5	7

Captain America V3#14 © MAR

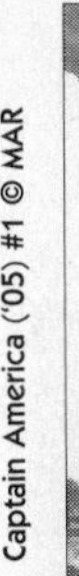

Captain America ('05) #1 © MAR

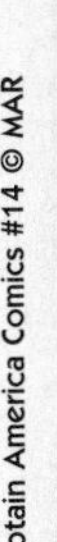

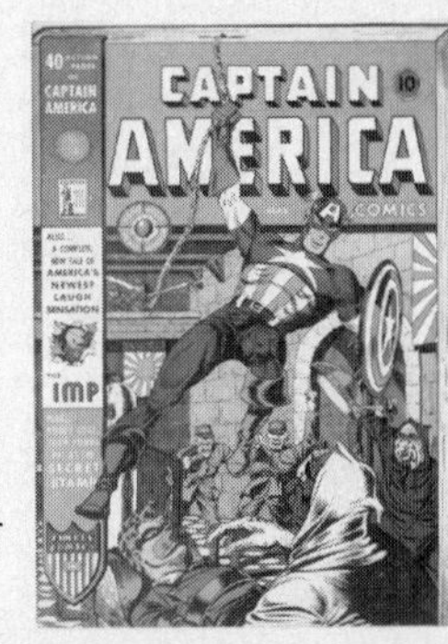

Captain America Comics #14 © MAR

	GD 2.0	VG 4.0	FN 6.0	VF 8.0	VF/NM 9.0	NM- 9.2

241-Punisher app.; Miller-c. 3 6 9 18 24 30
241-2nd print 3.00
247-255-Byrne-a. 255-Origin; Miller-c. 1 2 3 5 7 9
256-281,284,285,289-322,324-326,328-331: 264-Old X-Men cameo in flashback. 265,266-Nick Fury & Spider-Man app. 267-1st app. Everyman. 269-1st Team America. 279-(3/83)-Contains Tattooz skin decals. 281-1950s Bucky returns. 284-Patriot (Jack Mace) app. 285-Death of Patriot. 298-Origin Red Skull. 328-Origin & 1st app. D-Man 3.00
282-Bucky becomes new Nomad (Jack Monroe) 5.00
282-Silver ink 2nd print ($1.75) w/original date (6/83) 2.25
283,327,333-340: 283-2nd app. Nomad. 327-Capt. Amer. battles Super Patriot. 333-Intro & origin new Captain (Super Patriot). 339-Fall of the Mutants tie-in 4.00
286-288-Deathlok app. 4.00
323-1st app. new Super Patriot (see Nick Fury) 4.00
332-Old Cap resigns 6.00
341-343,345-349 3.00
344-($1.50, 52 pgs.)-Ronald Reagan cameo 4.00
350-($1.75, 68 pgs.)-Return of Steve Rogers (original Cap) to original costume 4.00
351-382,384-396: 351-Nick Fury app. 354-1st app. U.S. Agent (6/89, see Avengers West Coast). 373-Bullseye app. 375-Daredevil app. 386-U.S. Agent app. 387-389-Red Skull back-up stories. 396-Last $1.00-c. 396,397-1st app. all new Jack O'Lantern 2.50
383-($2.00, 68 pgs.)-50th anniversary issue; Red Skull story; Jim Lee-c(i) 4.00
397-399,401-424,425: 402-Begin 6 part Man-Wolf story w/Wolverine in #403-407. 405-410-New Jack O'Lantern app. in back-up story. 406-Cable & Shatterstar cameo. 407-Capwolf vs. Cable-c/story. 408-Infinity War x-over; Falcon solo back-up. 423-Vs. Namor-c/story 2.25
400-($2.25, 84 pgs.)-Flip book format w/double gatefold-c; r/Avengers #4 plus-c; contains cover pin-ups. 3.00
425-($2.95, 52 pgs.)-Embossed Foil-c ed.n; Fighting Chance Pt. 1 3.00
426-443,446,447,449-453: 427-Begin $1.50-c; bound-in trading card sheet. 449-Thor app. 450-"Man Without A Country" storyline begins, ends #453; Bill Clinton app; variant-c exists. 451-1st app.Cap's new costume. 453-Cap gets old costume back; Bill Clinton app. 2.25
444-Mark Waid scripts & Ron Garney-c/a(p) begins, ends #454; Avengers app. 5.00
445,454: 445-Sharon Carter & Red Skull return. 3.00
448-($2.95, double-sized issue)-Waid script & Garney-c/a; Red Skull "dies" 4.00
Special 1(1/71)-Origin retold 5 10 15 33 44 55
Special 2(1/72, 52 pgs.)-Colan-r/Not Brand Echh; all-r 3 6 9 18 24 30
Annual 3('76, 52 pgs.)-Kirby-c/a(new) 2 4 6 14 18 22
Annual 4('77, 34 pgs.)-Magneto-c/story 2 4 6 14 18 22
Annual 5-7: (52 pgs.)('81-'83) 5.00
Annual 8(9/86)-Wolverine-c/story 3 7 10 21 28 35
Annual 9-13('90-'94, 68 pgs.)-9-Nomad back-up. 10-Origin retold (2 pgs.). 11-Falcon solo story. 12-Bagged w/card. 13-Red Skull-c/story 3.00
...Ashcan Edition ('95, 75¢) 3.00
... and the Falcon: Madbomb TPB (2004, $16.99) r/#193-200; Kirby-s/a 17.00
...: Deathlok Lives! nn(10/93, $4.95)-r/#286-288 5.00
...Drug War 1-(1994, $2.00, 52 pgs.)-New Warriors app. 3.00
...Man Without a Country(1998, $12.99, TPB)-r/#450-453 13.00
...Medusa Effect 1 (1994, $2.95, 68 pgs.)-Origin Baron Zemo 3.00
...Operation Rebirth (1996, $9.95)-r/#445-448 10.00
...Streets of Poison ($15.95)-r/#372-378 16.00
...: The Movie Special nn (5/92, $3.50, 52 pgs.)-Adapts movie; printed on coated stock; The Red Skull app. 3.50

NOTE: **Austin** *c-225i, 239i, 246i.* **Buscema** *a-115p, 217p; c-136p, 217, 297.* **Byrne** *c-223(part), 238, 239, 247p-254p, 290, 291, 313p; a-247-254p, 255, 313p, 350.* **Colan** *a(p)-116-137, 256, Annual 5; c(p)-116-123, 126, 129.* **Everett** *a-136i, 137i; c-126i.* **Garney** *a(p)-444-454.* **Gil Kane** *a-145p; c-147p, 149p, 150p, 170p, 172-174, 180, 181p, 183-190p, 215, 216, 220, 221.* **Kirby** *a(p)-100-109, 112, 193-214, 216, Special 1, 2(layouts), Annual 3, 4; c-100-109, 112, 126p, 193-214.* **Ron Lim** *a(p)-366, 368-378, 380-386; c-366p, 368-378p, 379, 380-393p.* **Miller** *c-241p, 244p, 245p, 255p, Annual 5.* **Mooney** *a-149i.* **Morrow** *a-144.* **Perez** *c-243p, 246p.* **Robbins** *c(p)-183-187, 189-192, 225.* **Roussos** *a-140i, 168i.* **Starlin/Sinnott** *c-162.* **Sutton** *a-244i.* **Tuska** *a-112i, 215p, Special 2.* **Waid** *scripts-444-454.* **Williamson** *a-313i.* **Wood** *a-127i.* **Zeck** *a-263-289; c-300.*

CAPTAIN AMERICA (Volume Two)
Marvel Comics: V2#1, Nov, 1996 - No. 13, Nov, 1997($2.95/$1.95/$1.99)
(Produced by Extreme Studios)

1-($2.95)-Heroes Reborn begins; Liefeld-c/a; Loeb scripts; reintro Nick Fury 6.00
1-($2.95)-(Variant-c)-Liefeld-c/a 6.00
1-(7/96, $2.95)-(Exclusive Comicon Ed.)-Liefeld-c/a. 1 2 3 5 6 8
2-11,13: 5-Two-c. 6-Cable-c/app. 13-"World War 3"-pt. 4, x-over w/Image 3.00
12-($2.99) "Heroes Reunited"-pt. 4 4.00

CAPTAIN AMERICA (Vol. Three) (Also see Capt. America: Sentinel of Liberty)
Marvel Comics: Jan, 1998 - No. 50, Feb, 2002 ($2.99/$1.99/$2.25)

1-($2.99) Mark Waid-s/Ron Garney-a 4.00
1-Variant cover 6.00
2-($1.99): 2-Two covers 3.00
3-11: 3-Returns to old shield. 4-Hawkeye app. 5-Thor-c/app. 7-Andy Kubert-c/a begin. 9-New shield 2.50
12-($2.99) Battles Nightmare; Red Skull back-up story 3.50
13-17,19-Red Skull returns 2.25
18-($2.99) Cap vs. Korvac in the Future 3.00
20-24,26-29: 20,21-Sgt. Fury back-up story painted by Evans 2.25
25-($2.99) Cap & Falcon vs. Hatemonger 3.00
30-49: 30-Begin $2.25-c. 32-Ordway-a. 33-Jurgens-s/a begins; U.S. Agent app. 36-Maximum Security x-over. 41,46-Red Skull app. 2.25
.../Citizen V '98 Annual ($3.50) Busiek & Kesel-s 3.50
50-($5.95) Stories by various incl. Jurgens, Quitely, Immonen; Ha-c 6.00
1999 Annual ($3.50) Flag Smasher app. 3.50
2000 Annual ($3.50) Continued from #35 vs. Protocide; Jurgens-s 3.50
2001 Annual ($2.99) Golden Age flashback; Invaders app. 3.00
...: To Serve and Protect TPB (2/02, $17.95) r/Vol. 3 #1-7 18.00

CAPTAIN AMERICA (Volume 4)
Marvel Comics: Jun, 2002 - No. 32, Dec, 2004 ($3.99/$2.99)

1-Ney Rieber-s/Cassaday-c/a 4.00
2-9-($2.99) 3-Cap reveals Steve Rogers ID. 7-9-Hairsine-a 3.00
10-32: 10-16-Jae Lee-a. 17-20-Gibbons-s/Weeks-a. 21-26-Bachalo-a. 26-Bucky flashback. 27,28-Eddie Campbell-a. 29-32-Red Skull app. 3.00
...Vol. 1: The New Deal HC (2003, $22.99) r/#1-6; foreward by Max Allan Collins 23.00
...Vol. 2: The Extremists TPB (2003, $13.99) r/#7-11; Cassaday-c 14.00
...Vol. 3: Ice TPB (2003, $12.99) r/#12-16; Jae Lee-a; Cassaday-c 13.00
...Vol. 4: Cap Lives TPB (2004, $12.99) r/#17-22 & Tales of Suspense #66 13.00

CAPTAIN AMERICA
Marvel Comics: Jan, 2005 - Present ($2.99)

1-Brubaker-s/Epting-c/a; Red Skull app. 3.00

CAPTAIN AMERICA AND THE FALCON
Marvel Comics: May, 2004 - Present ($2.99, limited series)

1-4-Priest-s/Sears-a 3.00
5-7-Avengers Disassembled x-over. 6,7-Scarlet Witch app. 3.00
8-10-Modok app. 3.00

CAPTAIN AMERICA COMICS
Timely/Marvel Comics (TCI 1-20/CmPS 21-68/MjMC 69-75/Atlas Comics (PrPI 76-78): Mar, 1941 - No. 75, Feb, 1950; No. 76, 5/54 - No. 78, 9/54
(No. 74 & 75 titled Capt. America's Weird Tales)

1-Origin & 1st app. Captain America & Bucky by S&K; Hurricane, Tuk the Caveboy begin by S&K; 1st app. Red Skull; Hitler-c (by Simon?); intro of the "Capt. America Sentinels of Liberty Club" (advertised on inside front-c.); indicia reads Vol. 2, Number 1 7179 14,358 21,537 50,000 95,000 140,000
2-S&K Hurricane; Tuk by Avison (Kirby splash); classic Hitler-c 1235 2470 3705 9263 15,132 21,000
3-Classic Red Skull-c & app; Stan Lee's 1st text (1st work for Marvel) 1069 2138 3207 7500 12,250 17,000
4-Early use of full pg. panel in comic 710 1420 2130 4970 7985 11,000
5 645 1290 1935 4515 7258 10,000
6-Origin Father Time; Tuk the Caveboy ends 548 1096 1644 3836 6168 8500
7-Red Skull app.; classic-c 619 1238 1857 4333 6967 9600
8-10-Last S&K issue, (S&K centerfold #6-10) 439 878 1317 3073 4937 6800
11-Last Hurricane, Headline Hunter; Al Avison Captain America begins, ends #20; Avison-c(p) 386 772 1158 2509 4055 5600
12-The Imp begins, ends #16; last Father Time 366 732 1098 2379 3840 5300
13-Origin The Secret Stamp; classic-c 400 800 1200 2600 4200 5800
14,15 366 732 1098 2379 3840 5300
16-Red Skull unmasks Cap; Red Skull-c 423 846 1269 2970 4785 6600
17-The Fighting Fool only app. 310 620 930 2015 3258 4500
18-Classic-c 310 620 930 2015 3258 4500
19-Human Torch begins #19 277 554 831 1731 2666 3600
20-Sub-Mariner app.; no H. Torch 277 554 831 1731 2666 3600
21-25: 25-Cap drinks liquid opium 262 524 786 1638 2519 3400
26-30: 27-Last Secret Stamp; last 68 pg. issue. 28-60 pg. issues begin. 246 492 738 1538 2369 3200
31-35,38-40: 34-Centerfold poster of Cap 212 424 636 1325 2038 2750
36-Classic Hitler-c 300 600 900 1908 3004 4100
37-Red Skull app. 262 524 786 1638 2519 3400
41-45,47: 41-Last Jap War-c. 47-Last German War-c 181 362 543 1131 1741 2350
46-German Holocaust-c; classic 238 476 714 1488 2294 3100
48-58,60 138 276 414 863 1332 1800
59-Origin retold 303 606 909 1970 3185 4400
61-Red Skull-c/story 281 562 843 1756 2703 3650
62,64,65: 65-Kurtzman's "Hey Look" 181 362 543 1131 1741 2350

Captain America: Sentinel of Liberty #2 © MAR

Captain Atom #5 © Nationwide

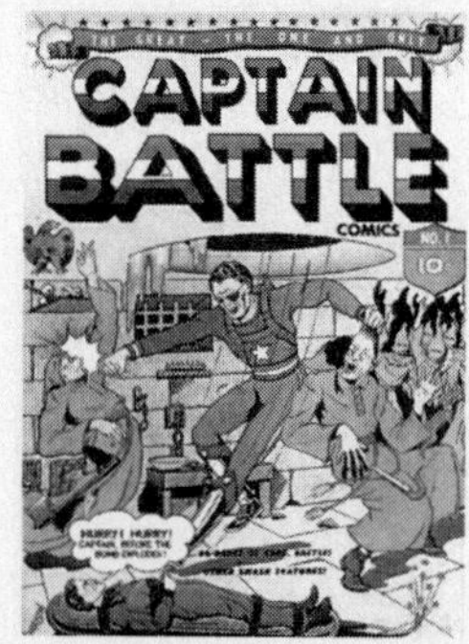

Captain Battle #1 © LEV

GD 2.0 | VG 4.0 | FN 6.0 | VF 8.0 | VF/NM 9.0 | NM- 9.2

63-Intro/origin Asbestos Lady 185 370 555 1156 1778 2400
66-Bucky is shot; Golden Girl teams up with Captain America & learns his i.d; origin Golden Girl 208 416 624 1300 2000 2700
67-73: 67-Captain America/Golden Girl team-up; Mxyztplk swipe; last Toro in Human Torch. 68,70-Sub-Mariner/Namora, and Captain America/Golden Girl team-up in each. 69-Human Torch/Sun Girl team-up. 70-Science fiction-c/story. 71-Anti Wertham editorial; The Witness, Bucky app. 196 392 588 1225 1888 2550
74-(Scarce)(10/49)-Titled "Captain America's Weird Tales"; Red Skull-c & app.; classic-c 548 1096 1644 3836 6168 8500
75(2/50)-Titled "C.A.'s Weird Tales"; no C.A. app.; horror cover/stories 196 392 588 1225 1888 2550
76-78(1954): Human Torch/Toro stories; all have communist-c/stories 104 208 312 650 1000 1350
132-Pg. Issue (B&W-1942)(Canadian)-Very rare. Has blank inside-c and back-c; contains Marvel Mystery #33 & Captain America #18 w/cover from Captain America #22; same contents as one version of the Marvel Mystery annuals 3500 7000 10,500 22,000 - -

NOTE: *Crandall a-2i, 3i, 9i, 10i.* ***Kirby*** *c-1, 2, 5-8p.* ***Rico*** *c-69-71.* ***Romita*** *c-77, 78.* ***Schomburg*** *c-3, 4, 26-29, 31, 33, 37-39, 41, 42, 45-54, 58.* ***Sekowsky*** *c-55, 56.* ***Shores*** *c-1i, 2i, 5-7i, 11i, 20-25, 30, 32, 34, 35, 40, 57, 59-67.* ***S&K*** *c-9, 10. Bondage c-3, 7, 15, 16, 34, 38.*

CAPTAIN AMERICA: DEAD MEN RUNNING
Marvel Comics: Mar, 2002 - No. 3, May, 2002 ($2.99, limited series)
1-3-Macan-s/Zezelj-a 3.00

CAPTAIN AMERICA/NICK FURY: BLOOD TRUCE
Marvel Comics: Feb, 1995 ($5.95, one-shot, squarebound)
nn-Chaykin story 6.00

CAPTAIN AMERICA/NICK FURY: THE OTHERWORLD WAR
Marvel Comics: Oct, 2001 ($6.95, one-shot, squarebound)
nn-Manco-a; Bucky and Red Skull app. 7.00

CAPTAIN AMERICA: RED, WHITE & BLUE
Marvel Comics: Sept, 2002 ($29.99, one-shot, hardcover with dustjacket)
nn-Reprints from Lee & Kirby, Steranko, Miller and others; and new short stories and pin-ups by various incl. Ross, Dini, Timm, Waid, Dorkin, Sienkiewicz, Miller, Bruce Jones, Collins, Piers-Rayner, Pope, Deodato, Quitely, Nino; Stelfreeze-c 30.00

CAPTAIN AMERICA, SENTINEL OF LIBERTY (See Fireside Book Series)

CAPTAIN AMERICA: SENTINEL OF LIBERTY
Marvel Comics: Sept, 1998 - No. 12, Aug, 1999 ($1.99)
1-Waid-s/Garney-a 3.00
1-Rough Cut ($2.99) Features original script and pencil pages 3.00
2-5: 2-Two-c; Invaders WW2 story 2.25
6-($2.99) Iron Man-c/app. 3.00
7-11: 8-Falcon-c/app. 9-Falcon poses as Cap 2.25
12-($2.99) Final issue; Bucky-c/app. 3.00

CAPTAIN AMERICA SPECIAL EDITION
Marvel Comics Group: Feb, 1984 - No. 2, Mar, 1984 ($2.00, Baxter paper)
1-Steranko-c/a(r) in both; r/ Captain America #110,111 6.00
2-Reprints the scarce Our Love Story #5, and C.A. #113 1 2 3 5 6 8

CAPTAIN AMERICA: THE CLASSIC YEARS
Marvel Comics: Jun, 1998 -No. 2 (trade paperbacks)
1-($19.95) Reprints Captain America Comics #1-5 25.00
2-($24.95) Reprints Captain America Comics #6-10 25.00

CAPTAIN AMERICA: THE LEGEND
Marvel Comics: Sept, 1996 ($3.95, one-shot)
1-Tribute issue; wraparound-c 4.00

CAPTAIN AMERICA: WHAT PRICE GLORY
Marvel Comics: May, 2003 - No. 4, May, 2003 ($2.99, weekly limited series)
1-4-Bruce Jones-s/Steve Rude & Mike Royer-a 3.00

CAPTAIN AND THE KIDS, THE (See Famous Comics Cartoon Books)

CAPTAIN AND THE KIDS, THE (See Comics on Parade, Katzenjammer Kids, Okay Comics & Sparkler Comics)
United Features Syndicate/Dell Publ. Co.: 1938 -12/39; Sum, 1947 - No. 32, 1955; Four Color No. 881, Feb, 1958
Single Series 1(1938) 92 184 276 575 888 1200
Single Series 1(Reprint)(12/39- "Reprint" on-c) 47 94 141 287 436 585
1(Summer, 1947-UFS)-Katzenjammer Kids 16 32 48 92 131 170
2 9 18 27 54 70 85
3-10 8 16 24 43 54 65
11-20 6 12 18 31 38 45
21-32 (1955) 6 12 18 28 34 40
50th Anniversary issue-(1948)-Contains a 2 pg. history of the strip, including an account of the famous Supreme Court decision allowing both Pulitzer & Hearst to run the same strip under different names 12 24 36 69 95 120
Special Summer issue, Fall issue (1948) 8 16 24 46 58 70
Four Color 881 (Dell) 4 8 12 29 40 50

CAPTAIN ATOM
Nationwide Publishers: 1950 - No. 7, 1951 (5¢, 5x7-1/4", 52 pgs.)
1-Science fiction 40 80 120 244 372 500
2-7 23 46 69 132 191 250

CAPTAIN ATOM (Formerly Strange Suspense Stories #77)(Also see Space Adventures)
Charlton Comics: V2#78, Dec, 1965 - V2#89, Dec, 1967
V2#78-Origin retold; Bache-a (3 pgs.) 10 20 30 67 96 125
79-82: 79-1st app. Dr. Spectro; 3 pg. Ditko cut & paste /Space Adventures #24. 82-Intro. Nightshade (9/66) 6 12 18 43 59 75
83-86: Ted Kord Blue Beetle in all. 83-(11/66)-1st app. Ted Kord. 84-1st app. new Captain Atom 6 12 18 40 55 70
87-89: Nightshade by Aparo in all 6 12 18 40 55 70
83-85(Modern Comics-1977)-reprints 1 2 3 4 5 7

NOTE: ***Aparo*** *a-87-89.* ***Ditko*** *c/a(p) 78-89. #90 only published in fanzine 'The Charlton Bullseye' #1, 2.*

CAPTAIN ATOM (Also see Americomics & Crisis On Infinite Earths)
DC Comics: Mar, 1987 - No. 57, Sept, 1991 (Direct sales only #35 on)
1-(44 pgs.)-Origin/1st app. with new costume 4.00
2-49: 5-Firestorm x-over. 6-Intro. new Dr. Spectro. 11-Millennium tie-in. 14-Nightshade app. 16-Justice League app. 17-$1.00-c begins; Swamp Thing app. 20-Blue Beetle x-over. 24,25-Invasion tie-in 2.50
51-57: 50-($2.00, 52 pgs.). 57-War of the Gods x-over 2.50
Annual 1,2 ('88, '89)-1-Intro Major Force 3.00

CAPTAIN BATTLE (Boy Comics #3 on) (See Silver Streak Comics)
New Friday Publ./Comic House: Summer, 1941 - No. 2, Fall, 1941
1-Origin Blackout by Rico; Captain Battle begins (1st appeared in Silver Streak #10, 5/41) 142 284 426 888 1369 1850
2 81 162 243 506 778 1050

CAPTAIN BATTLE (2nd Series)
Magazine Press/Picture Scoop No. 5: No. 3, Wint, 1942-43; No. 5, Sum, 1943 (No #4)
3-Origin Silver Streak-r/SS#3; origin Lance Hale-r/Silver Streak; Simon-a(r) (52 pgs., nd) 71 142 213 444 685 925
5-Origin Blackout retold (68 pgs.) 51 102 153 319 477 635

CAPTAIN BATTLE, JR.
Comic House (Lev Gleason): Fall, 1943 - No. 2, Winter, 1943-44
1-The Claw vs. The Ghost 135 270 405 844 1297 1750
2-Wolverton's Scoop Scuttle; Don Rico-c/a; The Green Claw story is reprinted from Silver Streak #6; bondage/torture-c 81 162 243 506 778 1050

CAPTAIN BEN DIX (See Promotional Comics section)

CAPTAIN BRITAIN (Also see Marvel Team-Up No. 65, 66)
Marvel Comics International: Oct. 13, 1976 - No. 39, July 6, 1977 (Weekly)
1-Origin; with Capt. Britain's face mask inside 2 4 6 10 13 16
2-Origin, part II; Capt. Britain's Boomerang inside 1 3 4 6 8 10
3-11: 3,8-Vs. Bank Robbers. 4-7-Vs. Hurricane. 9-11: Vs. Dr. Synne 5.00
12-23,25-27: (scarce)-12,13-Vs. Dr. Synne. 14,15-Vs. Mastermind. 16-23,25,26-With Captain America. 17 misprinted & color section reprinted in #18. 27-Origin retold 2 4 6 8 10 12
24-With C.B.'s Jet Plane inside 2 4 6 10 13 16
28-32,36-39: 28-32-Vs. Lord Hawk. 37-39-Vs. Highwayman & Munipulator 3.50
33-35-More on origin 4.00
Annual (1978, Hardback, 64 pgs.)-Reprints #1-7 with pin-ups of Marvel characters 2 4 6 9 11 14
Summer Special (1980, 52 pgs.)-Reprints 5.00

NOTE: *No. 1, 2, & 24 are rarer in mint due to inserts. Distributed in Great Britain only. Nick Fury-r by* ***Steranko*** *in 1-20, 24-31, 35-37. Fantastic Four-r by* ***J. Buscema*** *in all. New* ***Buscema****-a in 24-30. Story from No. 39 continues in Super Spider-Man (British weekly) No. 231-247. Following cancellation of his series, new Captain Britain stories appeared in "Super Spider-Man" (British weekly) No. 231-247. Captain Britain stories which appear in Super-Spider-Man No 248-253 are reprints of Marvel Team-Up No. 65&66. Capt. Britain stories also appeared in Hulk Comic (weekly) 1, 3-30, 42-55, 57-60, in Marvel Superheroes (monthly) 377-388, in Daredevils (monthly) 1-11, Mighty World of Marvel (monthly) 7-16 & Captain Britain (monthly) 1-14. Issues 1-23 have B&W & color, paper-c, & are 32 pgs. Issues 24 on are all B&W w/glossy-c & are 36 pgs.*

CAPTAIN CANUCK
Comely Comix (Canada) (All distr. in U. S.): 7/75 - No. 4, 7/77; No. 4, 7-8/79 - No. 14, 3-4/81

Captain Carrot and the Zoo Crew #4 © DC

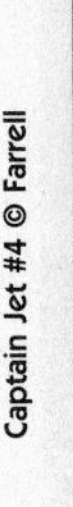
Captain Jet #4 © Farrell

Captain Johner & The Aliens #2 © VAL

	GD 2.0	VG 4.0	FN 6.0	VF 8.0	VF/NM 9.0	NM- 9.2

1-1st app. Bluefox 5.00
2,3(5-7/76)-2-1st app. Dr. Walker, Redcoat & Kebec. 3-1st app. Heather 4.00
4(1st printing-2/77)-10x14-1/2"; (5.00); B&W; 300 copies serially numbered and signed with one certificate of authenticity 8 16 24 55 78 100
4(2nd printing-7/77)-11x17", B&W; only 15 copies printed; signed by creator Richard Comely, serially #'d and two certificates of authenticity inserted; orange cardboard covers (Very Rare) 10 20 30 72 104 135
4-14: 4(7-8/79)-1st app. Tom Evans & Mr. Gold; origin The Catman. 5-Origin Capt. Canuck's powers; 1st app. Earth Patrol & Chaos Corps. 8-Jonn 'The Final Chapter'. 9-1st World Beyond. 11-1st 'Chariots of Fire' story 3.00
15-(8/04, $15.00) Limited edition of unpublished issue from 1981; serially #'d edition of 150; signed by creator Richard Comely 2 4 6 10 12 15
Special Collectors Pack (polybagged) 1 2 3 5 7 9
Summer Special 1(7-9/80, 95¢, 64 pgs.) 3.00
NOTE: *30,000 copies of No. 2 were destroyed in Winnipeg.*

CAPTAIN CANUCK: UNHOLY WAR
Comely Comix: Oct, 2004 - No. 3 ($2.50, limited series)
1-Riel Langlois-s/Drue Langlois-a 2.50

CAPTAIN CARROT AND HIS AMAZING ZOO CREW (Also see New Teen Titans & Oz-Wonderland War)
DC Comics: Mar, 1982 - No. 20, Nov, 1983
1-20: 1-Superman app. 3-Re-intro Dodo & The Frog. 9-Re-intro Three Mouseketeers, the Terrific Whatzit. 10,11- Pig Iron reverts back to Peter Porkchops. 20-Changeling app. 3.00

CAPTAIN CARVEL AND HIS CARVEL CRUSADERS (See Carvel Comics)

CAPTAIN CONFEDERACY
Marvel Comics (Epic Comics): Nov, 1991 - No. 4, Feb, 1992 ($1.95)
1-4: All new stories 2.25

CAPTAIN COURAGEOUS COMICS (Banner #3-5; see Four Favorites #5)
Periodical House (Ace Magazines): No. 6, March, 1942
6-Origin & 1st app. The Sword; Lone Warrior, Capt. Courageous app.; Capt. moves to Four Favorites #5 in May 75 150 225 469 722 975

CAPT'N CRUNCH COMICS (See Cap'n...)

CAPTAIN DAVY JONES
Dell Publishing Co.: No. 598, Nov, 1954
Four Color 598 6 12 18 38 52 65

CAPTAIN EASY (See The Funnies & Red Ryder #3-32)
Hawley/Dell Publ./Standard(Visual Editions)/Argo: 1939 - No. 17, Sept, 1949; April, 1956
nn-Hawley(1939)-Contains reprints from The Funnies & 1938 Sunday strips by Roy Crane 88 176 264 550 850 1150
Four Color 24 (1943) 40 80 120 300 468 635
Four Color 111(6/46) 15 30 45 107 164 220
10(Standard-10/47) 12 24 36 69 95 120
11,12,14,15,17: 11-17 all contain 1930s & '40s strip-r 10 20 30 56 73 90
13,16: Schomburg-c 11 22 33 62 84 105
Argo 1(4/56)-Reprints 7 14 21 37 46 55

CAPTAIN EASY & WASH TUBBS (See Famous Comics Cartoon Books)

CAPTAIN ELECTRON
Brick Computer Science Institute: Aug, 1986 ($2.25)
1-Disbrow-a 2.50

CAPTAIN EO 3-D (Disney)
Eclipse Comics: July, 1987 (Eclipse 3-D Special #18, $3.50, Baxter)
1-Adapts 3-D movie 4.00
1-2-D limited edition 1 2 3 4 5 7
1-Large size (11x17", 8/87)-Sold only at Disney Theme parks ($6.95) 2 4 6 11 14 18

CAPTAIN FEARLESS COMICS (Also see Holyoke One-Shot #6, Old Glory Comics & Silver Streak #1)
Helnit Publishing Co. (Holyoke Publ. Co.): Aug, 1941 - No. 2, Sept, 1941
1-Origin Mr. Miracle, Alias X, Captain Fearless, Citizen Smith Son of the Unknown Soldier; Miss Victory (1st app.) begins (1st patriotic heroine? before Wonder Woman) 85 170 255 531 816 1100
2-Grit Grady, Captain Stone app. 52 104 156 317 484 650

CAPTAIN FLAG (See Blue Ribbon Comics #16)

CAPTAIN FLASH
Sterling Comics: Nov, 1954 - No. 4, July, 1955
1-Origin; Sekowsky-a; Tomboy (female super hero) begins; only pre-code issue; atomic rocket-c 40 80 120 244 372 500
2-4: 4-Flying saucer invasion-c 24 48 72 138 199 260

CAPTAIN FLEET (Action Packed Tales of the Sea)
Ziff-Davis Publishing Co.: Fall, 1952
1-Painted-c 16 32 48 92 131 170

CAPTAIN FLIGHT COMICS
Four Star Publications: Mar, 1944 - No. 10, Dec, 1945; No. 11, Feb-Mar, 1947
nn 42 84 126 256 391 525
2-4: 4-Rock Raymond begins, ends #7 25 50 75 144 207 270
5-Bondage, classic torture-c; Red Rocket begins; the Grenade app. (scarce) 108 216 324 675 1038 1400
6 24 48 72 138 199 260
7-10: 7-L. B. Cole covers begin, end #11. 8-Yankee Girl begins; intro. Black Cobra & Cobra Kid & begins. 9-Torpedoman app.; last Yankee Girl; Kinstler-a. 10-Deep Sea Dawson, Zoom of the Jungle, Rock Raymond, Red Rocket, & Black Cobra app; bondage-c 51 102 153 311 476 640
11-Torpedoman, Blue Flame (Human Torch clone) app.; last Black Cobra, Red Rocket; classic L. B. Cole robot-c (scarce) 115 230 345 719 1110 1500

CAPTAIN GALLANT (...of the Foreign Legion) (TV) (Texas Rangers in Action No. 5 on?)
Charlton Comics: 1955; No. 2, Jan, 1956 - No. 4, Sept, 1956
Non-Heinz version (#1)-Buster Crabbe photo on-c; full page Buster Crabbe photo inside front-c 9 18 27 54 70 85
(Heinz version is listed in the Promotional Comics section)
2-4: Buster Crabbe in all 9 18 27 49 62 75

CAPTAIN GLORY
Topps Comics: Apr, 1993 ($2.95) (Created by Jack Kirby)
1-Polybagged w/Kirbychrome trading card; Ditko-a & Kirby-c; has coupon for Amberchrome Secret City Saga #0 3.00

CAPTAIN HERO (See Jughead as...)

CAPTAIN HERO COMICS DIGEST MAGAZINE
Archie Publications: Sept, 1981
1-Reprints of Jughead as Super-Guy 2 4 6 11 14 18

CAPTAIN HOBBY COMICS
Export Publication Ent. Ltd. (Dist. in U.S. by Kable News Co.): Feb, 1948 (Canadian)
1 8 16 24 40 50 60

CAPT. HOLO IN 3-D (See Blackthorne 3-D Series #65)

CAPTAIN HOOK & PETER PAN (Movie)(Disney)
Dell Publishing Co.: No. 446, Jan, 1953
Four Color 446 10 20 30 73 107 140

CAPTAIN JET (Fantastic Fears No. 7 on)
Four Star Publ./Farrell/Comic Media: May, 1952 - No. 5, Jan, 1953
1-Bakerish-a 23 46 69 132 191 250
2 12 24 36 71 98 125
3-5,6(?) 10 20 30 60 80 100

CAPTAIN JOHNER & THE ALIENS
Valiant: May, 1995 - No. 2, May, 1995 ($2.95, shipped in same month)
1,2: Reprints Magnus Robot Fighter 4000 A.D. back-up stories; new Paul Smith-c 3.00

CAPTAIN JUSTICE (TV)
Marvel Comics: Mar, 1988 - No. 2, Apr, 1988 (limited series)
1,2-Based on the 1987 "Once a Hero" television series 2.25

CAPTAIN KANGAROO (TV)
Dell Publishing Co.: No. 721, Aug, 1956 - No. 872, Jan, 1958
Four Color 721 (#1)-Photo-c 18 36 54 131 201 270
Four Color 780, 872-Photo-c 15 30 45 105 160 215

CAPTAIN KIDD (Formerly Dagar; My Secret Story #26 on)(Also see Comic Comics & Fantastic Comics)
Fox Feature Syndicate: No. 24, June, 1949 - No. 25, Aug, 1949
24,25: 24-Features Blackbeard the Pirate 15 30 45 85 120 155

CAPTAIN MARVEL (See All Hero, All-New Collectors' Ed., America's Greatest, Fawcett Miniature, Gift, JSA, Kingdom Come, Legends, Limited Collectors' Ed., Marvel Family, Master No. 21, Mighty Midget Comics, Power of Shazam!, Shazam, Special Edition Comics, Whiz, Wisco (in Promotional Comics section), World's Finest #253 and XMas Comics)

CAPTAIN MARVEL (Becomes ...Presents the Terrible 5 No. 5)
M. F. Enterprises: April, 1966 - No. 4, Nov, 1966 (25¢ Giants)
nn-(#1 on pg. 5)-Origin; created by Carl Burgos 5 10 15 33 44 55
2-4: 3-(#3 on pg. 4)-Fights the Bat 3 6 9 19 25 32

Captain Marvel #15 © MAR

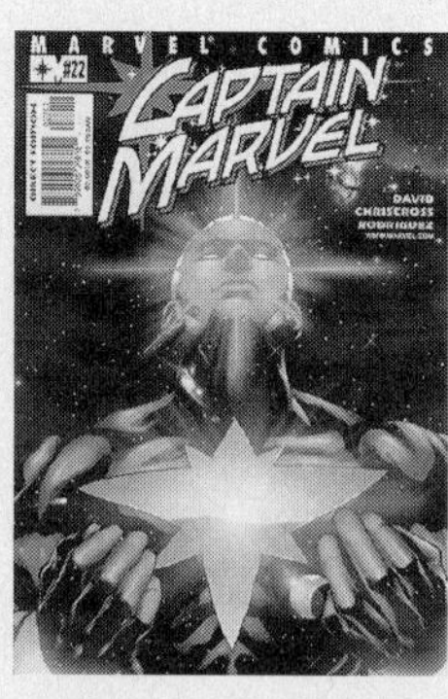

Captain Marvel V3#22 © MAR

Captain Marvel Adventures #17 © FAW

GD VG FN VF VF/NM NM-
2.0 4.0 6.0 8.0 9.0 9.2

CAPTAIN MARVEL (Marvel's Space-Born Super-Hero! Captain Marvel #1-6; see Giant-Size..., Life Of..., Marvel Graphic Novel #1, Marvel Spotlight V2#1 & Marvel Super-Heroes #12)
Marvel Comics Group: May, 1968 - No. 19, Dec, 1969; No. 20, June, 1970 - No. 21, Aug, 1970; No. 22, Sept, 1972 - No. 62, May, 1979

1 10 20 30 70 100 130
2-Super Skrull-c/story 4 8 12 29 40 50
3-5: 4-Captain Marvel battles Sub-Mariner 4 8 12 24 32 40
6-11: 11-Capt. Marvel given great power by Zo the Ruler; Smith/Trimpe-c; Death of Una 3 6 9 17 22 27
12,13,15-20: 16,17-New costume 2 4 6 11 14 18
14,21: 14-Capt. Marvel vs. Iron Man; last 12¢ issue. 21-Capt. Marvel battles Hulk; last 15¢ issue 3 6 9 18 24 30
22-24 2 4 6 10 13 16
25,26: 25-Starlin-c/a begins; Starlin's 1st Thanos saga begins (3/73), ends #34; Thanos cameo (5 panels). 26-Minor Thanos app. (see Iron Man #55); 1st Thanos-c 3 7 10 21 28 35
27,28-1st & 2nd full app. Thanos. 28-Thanos-c/s 3 6 9 18 24 30
29,30-Thanos cameos. 29-C.M. gains more powers 2 4 6 12 16 20
31,32: Thanos app. 31-Last 20¢ issue. 32-Thanos-c 2 4 6 14 18 22
33-Thanos-c & app.; Capt. Marvel battles Thanos; 1st origin Thanos 3 6 9 18 24 30
34-1st app. Nitro; C.M. contracts cancer which eventually kills him; last Starlin-c/a 2 4 6 12 16 20
35,37-40,42,46-48,50,53-56,58-62: 39-Origin Watcher. 58-Thanos cameo 1 2 3 5 6 8
36,41,43,49: 36-R-origin/1st app. Capt. Marvel from Marvel Super-Heroes #12. 41,43-Wrightson part inks; #43-c(i). 49-Starlin & Weiss-p assists 1 2 3 5 7 9
44,45-(Regular 25¢ editions)(5,7/76) 1 2 3 5 6 8
44,45-(30¢-c variants, limited distribution) 2 4 6 8 10 12
51,52-(Regular 30¢ editions)(7,9/77) 1 2 3 5 6 8
51,52-(35¢-c variants, limited distribution) 2 4 6 8 10 12
57-Thanos appears in flashback 1 3 4 6 8 10

NOTE: ***Alcala*** *a-35.* ***Austin*** *a-46i, 49-53i; c-52i.* ***Buscema*** *a-18p-21p.* ***Colan*** *a(p)-1-4; c(p)-1-4, 8, 9.* ***Heck*** *a-5-10p, 16p.* ***Gil Kane*** *a-17-21p; c-17-24p, 37p, 53.* ***Starlin*** *a-36.* ***McWilliams*** *a-40i. #25-34 were reprinted in The Life of Captain Marvel.*

CAPTAIN MARVEL
Marvel Comics: Nov, 1989 ($1.50, one-shot, 52 pgs.)

1-Super-hero from Avengers; new powers 3.00

CAPTAIN MARVEL
Marvel Comics: Feb, 1994 ($1.75, 52 pgs.)

1-(Indicia reads Vol 2 #2)-Minor Captain America app. 2.50

CAPTAIN MARVEL
Marvel Comics: Dec, 1995 - No. 6, May, 1996 ($2.95/$1.95)

1 ($2.95)-Advs. of Mar-Vell's son begins; Fabian Nicieza scripts; foil-c 3.50
2-6: 2-Begin $1.95-c 2.50

CAPTAIN MARVEL (Vol. 3) (See Avengers Forever)
Marvel Comics: Jan, 2000 - No. 35, Oct, 2002 ($2.50)

1-Peter David-s in all 4.00
2-10: 2-Two covers; Hulk app. 9-Silver Surfer app. 3.00
11-35: 12-Maximum Security x-over. 17,18-Starlin-a. 27-30-Spider-Man 2099 app. 2.50
Wizard #0-Preview and history of Rick Jones 4.00
...: First Contact (8/01, $16.95, TPB) r/#0,1-6 17.00

CAPTAIN MARVEL (Vol. 4) (See Avengers Forever)
Marvel Comics: Nov, 2002 - No. 25, Sept, 2004 ($2.25/$2.99)

1-Peter David-s/Chriscross-a ; 3 covers by Ross, Jusko & Chriscross 3.00
2-7: 2,3-Punisher app. 3-Alex Ross-c; new costume debuts. 4-Noto-c. 7-Thor app. 2.25
3-Sketchbook Edition-($3.50) includes Ross' concept design pages for new costume 3.50
8-25: 8-Begin $2.99-c; Thor app.; Manco-c. 10-Spider-Man-c/app. 15-Neal Adams-c 3.00
Vol. 1: Nothing To Lose (2003, $14.99, TPB) r/#1-6 15.00
Vol. 2: Coven (2003, $14.99, TPB) r/#7-12 15.00
Vol. 3: Crazy Like a Fox (2004, $14.99, TPB) r/#13-18 15.00
Vol. 4: Odyssey (2004, $16.99, TPB) r/#19-25 17.00

CAPTAIN MARVEL ADVENTURES (See Special Edition Comics for pre #1)
Fawcett Publications: 1941 (March) - No. 150, Nov, 1953 (#1 on stands 1/16/41)

nn(#1)-Captain Marvel & Sivana by Jack Kirby. The cover was printed on unstable paper stock and is rarely found in Fine or Mint condition; blank back inside-c 2650 5300 7950 20,000 32,500 45,000
2-(Advertised as #3, which was counting Special Edition Comics as the real #1); Tuska-a 423 846 1269 2740 4420 6100

GD VG FN VF VF/NM NM-
2.0 4.0 6.0 8.0 9.0 9.2

3-Metallic silver-c 285 570 855 1781 2741 3700
4-Three Lt. Marvels app. 200 400 600 1250 1925 2600
5 154 308 462 963 1482 2000
6-10: 9-1st Otto Binder scripts on Capt. Marvel 117 234 351 731 1128 1525
11-15: 12-Capt. Marvel joins the Army. 13-Two pg. Capt. Marvel pin-up. 15-Comic cards on back-c begin, end #26 92 184 276 575 888 1200
16,17: 17-Painted-c 86 172 258 538 832 1125
18-Origin & 1st app. Mary Marvel & Marvel Family (12/11/42); painted-c; Mary Marvel by Marcus Swayze 223 446 669 1394 2147 2900
19-Mary Marvel x-over; Christmas-c 73 146 219 456 703 950
20,21-Attached to the cover, each has a miniature comic just like the Mighty Midget Comics #11, except that each has a full color promo ad on the back cover. Most copies were circulated without the miniature comic. These issues with miniatures attached are very rare, and should not be mistaken for copies with the similar Mighty Midget glued in its place. The Mighty Midgets had blank back covers except for a small victory stamp seal. Only the Capt. Marvel, Captain Marvel Jr. and Golden Arrow No. 11 miniatures have been positively documented as having been affixed to these covers. Each miniature was only partially glued by its back cover to the Captain Marvel comic making it easy to see if it's the genuine miniature rather than a Mighty Midget.
with comic attached.... 352 704 1056 2288 3694 5100
20-Without miniature 69 138 207 431 666 900
21-Without miniature; Hitler-c 90 180 270 563 869 1175
22-Mr. Mind serial begins; 1st app. Mr. Mind 96 192 288 600 925 1250
23-25 67 134 201 419 647 875
26-28,30: 26-Flag-c. 27-1st Mr. Mind app. (his voice was heard over the radio before now) (9/43) 56 112 168 350 538 725
29-1st Mr. Mind-c (11/43) 59 118 177 369 565 760
31-35: 35-Origin Radar (5/44, see Master #50) 51 102 153 311 473 635
36-40: 37-Mary Marvel x-over 47 94 141 287 436 585
41-46: 42-Christmas-c. 43-Capt. Marvel 1st meets Uncle Marvel; Mary Batson cameo. 46-Mr. Mind serial ends 40 80 120 236 351 465
47-50 39 78 117 222 324 425
51-53,55-60: 51-63-Bi-weekly issues. 52-Origin & 1st app. Sivana Jr.; Capt. Marvel Jr. x-over 33 66 99 190 275 360
54-Special oversize 68 pg. issue 34 68 102 196 283 370
61-The Cult of the Curse serial begins 37 74 111 209 305 400
62-65-Serial cont.; Mary Marvel x-over in #65 33 66 99 190 275 360
66-Serial ends; Atomic War-c 37 74 111 209 305 400
67-77,79: 69-Billy Batson's Christmas; Uncle Marvel, Mary Marvel, Capt. Marvel Jr. x-over. 71-Three Lt. Marvels app. 79-Origin Mr. Tawny 29 58 87 164 237 310
78-Origin Mr. Atom 32 64 96 184 267 350
80-Origin Capt. Marvel retold 62 124 186 388 594 800
81-84,86-90: 81,90-Mr. Atom app. 82-Infinity-c. 82,86,88,90-Mr. Tawny app. 27 54 81 154 222 290
85-Freedom Train issue 32 64 96 184 267 350
91-99: 92-Mr. Tawny app. 96-Gets 1st name "Tawky" 26 52 78 150 215 280
100-Origin retold; silver metallic-c 46 92 138 281 428 575
101-115,117-120 25 50 75 144 207 270
116-Flying Saucer issue (1/51) 29 58 87 164 237 310
121-Origin retold 34 68 102 196 283 370
122-137,139-149: 141-Pre-code horror story "The Hideous Head-Hunter". 142-used in **POP**, pgs. 92,96 24 48 72 138 199 260
138-Flying Saucer issue (11/52) 29 58 87 164 237 310
150-(Low distribution) 42 84 126 256 391 525

NOTE: ***Swayze*** *a-12, 14, 15, 18, 19, 40; c-12, 15, 19.*

CAPTAIN MARVEL AND THE GOOD HUMOR MAN (Movie)
Fawcett Publications: 1950

nn-Partial photo-c w/Jack Carson & the Captain Marvel Club Boys 48 96 144 288 407 600

CAPTAIN MARVEL COMIC STORY PAINT BOOK (See Comic Story...)

CAPTAIN MARVEL, JR. (See Fawcett Miniatures, Marvel Family, Master Comics, Mighty Midget Comics, Shazam & Whiz Comics)

CAPTAIN MARVEL, JR.
Fawcett Publications: Nov, 1942 - No. 119, June, 1953 (No #34)

1-Origin Capt. Marvel Jr. retold (Whiz #25); Capt. Nazi app. Classic Raboy-c 529 1058 1587 3703 5952 8200
2-Vs. Capt. Nazi; origin Capt. Nippon 204 408 612 1275 1963 2650
3 113 226 339 706 1091 1475
4-Classic Raboy-c 119 238 357 744 1147 1550
5-Vs. Capt. Nazi 98 196 294 613 944 1275
6-8: 8-Vs. Capt. Nazi 79 158 237 494 760 1025
9-Classic flag-c 85 170 255 531 816 1100
10-Hitler-c 100 200 300 625 963 1300
11,12,15-Capt. Nazi app. 69 138 207 431 666 900
13-Classic Hitler, Tojo and Mussolini football-c 98 196 294 613 944 1275
14,16-20: 14-X-Mas-c. 16-Capt. Marvel & Sivana x-over. 19-Capt. Nazi & Capt. Nippon app.

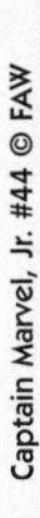
Captain Marvel, Jr. #44 © FAW

CAPTAIN MARVEL JR.
10¢
CAPT. MARVEL JR. and THE KEY TO THE MYSTERY!

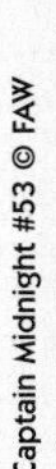
Captain Midnight #53 © FAW

Captain Science #3 © YM

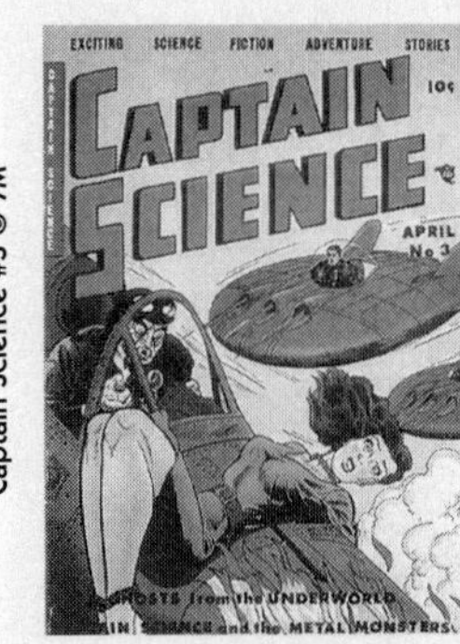

	GD 2.0	VG 4.0	FN 6.0	VF 8.0	VF/NM 9.0	NM- 9.2
	57	114	171	356	548	740
21-30: 25-Flag-c	47	94	141	287	436	585
31-33,36-40: 37-Infinity-c	34	68	102	196	283	370
35-#34 on inside; cover shows origin of Sivana Jr. which is not on inside. Evidently the cover to #35 was printed out of sequence and bound with contents to #34	34	68	102	196	283	370
41-70: 42-Robot-c. 53-Atomic Bomb-c/story	27	54	81	154	222	290
71-99,101-104: 87-Robot-c. 104-Used in **POP**, pg. 89	20	40	60	112	161	210
100	23	46	69	132	191	250
105-114,116-118: 116-Vampira, Queen of Terror app.	18	36	54	104	150	190
115-Injury to eye-c; Eyeball story w/injury-to-eye panels	40	80	120	233	342	450
119-Electric chair-c (scarce)	42	84	126	256	391	525

NOTE: ***Mac Raboy** c-1-28, 30-32, 57, 59 among others.*

CAPTAIN MARVEL PRESENTS THE TERRIBLE FIVE
M. F. Enterprises: Aug, 1966; V2#5, Sept, 1967 (No #2-4) (25¢)

	GD	VG	FN	VF	VF/NM	NM-
1	5	10	15	33	44	55
V2#5-(Formerly Captain Marvel)	3	6	9	19	25	32

CAPTAIN MARVEL'S FUN BOOK
Samuel Lowe Co.: 1944 (1/2" thick) (cardboard covers)(25¢)

	GD	VG	FN	VF	VF/NM	NM-
nn-Puzzles, games, magic, etc.; infinity-c	37	74	112	213	312	410

CAPTAIN MARVEL SPECIAL EDITION (See Special Edition)

CAPTAIN MARVEL STORY BOOK
Fawcett Publications: Summer, 1946 - No. 4, Summer?, 1948

	GD	VG	FN	VF	VF/NM	NM-
1-Half text	54	108	162	329	502	675
2-4	39	78	117	222	324	425

CAPTAIN MARVEL THRILL BOOK (Large-Size)
Fawcett Publications: 1941 (B&W w/color-c)

	GD	VG	FN	VF	VF/NM	NM-
1-Reprints from Whiz #8,10, & Special Edition #1 (Rare)	300	600	900	3000	-	-

NOTE: *Rarely found in Fine or Mint condition.*

CAPTAIN MIDNIGHT (TV, radio, films) (See The Funnies, Popular Comics & Super Book of Comics)(Becomes Sweethearts No. 68 on)
Fawcett Publications: Sept, 1942 - No. 67, Fall, 1948 (#1-14: 68 pgs.)

	GD	VG	FN	VF	VF/NM	NM-
1-Origin Captain Midnight, star of radio and movies; Captain Marvel cameo on cover	310	620	930	2015	3258	4500
2-Smashes the Jap Juggarnaut	146	292	438	913	1407	1900
3-Classic Nazi war-c	131	262	393	819	1260	1700
4,5: 4-Grapples the Gremlins	115	230	345	719	1110	1500
6-8	77	154	231	481	741	1000
9-Raboy-c	79	158	237	494	760	1025
10-Raboy Flag-c	81	162	243	506	778	1050
11-20: 11,17,18-Raboy-c. 16 (1/44)	56	112	168	350	538	725
21-23,25-30: 22-War savings stamp-c	45	90	135	275	418	560
24-Japan flag sunburst-c	47	94	141	287	436	585
31-40	34	68	102	196	283	370
41-59,61-67: 50-Sci/fi theme begins?	29	58	87	164	237	310
60-Flying Saucer issue (2/48)-3rd of this theme; see The Spirit 9/28/47(1st), Shadow Comics V7#10 (2nd, 1/48) & Boy Commandos #26 (4th, 3-4/48)	37	74	111	209	305	400

CAPTAIN NICE (TV)
Gold Key: Nov, 1967 (one-shot)

	GD	VG	FN	VF	VF/NM	NM-
1(10211-711)-Photo-c	8	16	24	55	78	100

CAPTAIN N: THE GAME MASTER (TV)
Valiant Comics: 1990 - No. 6? ($1.95, thick stock, coated-c)

	NM-
1-6: 4-6-Layton-c	3.00

CAPTAIN PARAGON (See Bill Black's Fun Comics)
Americomics: Dec, 1983 - No. 4, 1985

	NM-
1-Intro/1st app. Ms. Victory	4.00
2-4	3.00

CAPTAIN PARAGON AND THE SENTINELS OF JUSTICE
AC Comics: April, 1985 - No. 6, 1986 ($1.75)

	NM-
1-6: 1-Capt. Paragon, Commando D., Nightveil, Scarlet Scorpion, Stardust & Atoman	3.00

CAPTAIN PLANET AND THE PLANETEERS (TV cartoon)
Marvel Comics: Oct, 1991 - No. 12, Oct, 1992 ($1.00/$1.25)

	NM-
1-N. Adams painted-c	4.00
2-12: 3-Romita-c	3.00

CAPTAIN POWER AND THE SOLDIERS OF THE FUTURE (TV)
Continuity Comics: Aug, 1988 - No. 2, 1988 ($2.00)

	NM-
1,2: 1-Neal Adams-c/layouts/inks; variant-c exists.	3.00

CAPTAIN PUREHEART (See Archie as...)

CAPTAIN ROCKET
P. L. Publ. (Canada): Nov, 1951

	GD	VG	FN	VF	VF/NM	NM-
1	43	86	129	262	401	540

CAPT. SAVAGE AND HIS LEATHERNECK RAIDERS (...And His Battlefield Raiders #9 on)
Marvel Comics Group (Animated Timely Features): Jan, 1968 - No. 19, Mar, 1970 (See Sgt. Fury No. 10)

	GD	VG	FN	VF	VF/NM	NM-
1-Sgt. Fury & Howlers cameo	5	10	15	33	44	55
2,7,11: 2-Origin Hydra. 1-5,7-Ayers/Shores-a. 7-Pre-"Thing" Ben Grimm story. 11-Sgt. Fury app.	3	6	9	18	23	28
3-6,8-10,12-14: 14-Last 12¢ issue	3	6	9	16	20	25
15-19	2	4	6	14	18	22

CAPTAIN SCIENCE (Fantastic No. 8 on)
Youthful Magazines: Nov, 1950 - No. 7, Dec, 1951

	GD	VG	FN	VF	VF/NM	NM-
1-Wood-a; origin; 2 pg. text w/ photos of George Pal's "Destination Moon."	87	174	261	544	835	1125
2	45	90	115	275	418	560
3,6,7; 3,6-Bondage c-swipes/Wings #94,91	40	80	120	244	372	500
4,5-Wood/Orlando-c/a(2) each	81	162	243	506	778	1050

NOTE: ***Fass** a-4. Bondage c-3, 6, 7.*

CAPTAIN SILVER'S LOG OF SEA HOUND (See Sea Hound)

CAPTAIN SINBAD (Movie Adaptation) (See Fantastic Voyages of... & Movie Comics)

CAPTAIN STERNN: RUNNING OUT OF TIME
Kitchen Sink Press: Sept, 1993 - No. 5, 1994 ($4.95, limited series, coated stock, 52 pgs.)

	NM-
1-5: Berni Wrightson-c/a/scripts	6.00
1-Gold ink variant	10.00

CAPTAIN STEVE SAVAGE (...& His Jet Fighters, No. 2-13)
Avon Periodicals: 1950 - No. 8, 1/53; No. 5, 9-10/54 - No. 13, 5-6/56

	GD	VG	FN	VF	VF/NM	NM-
nn(1st series)-Wood art, 22 pgs. (titled "...Over Korea")	40	80	120	230	335	440
1(4/51)-Reprints nn issue (Canadian)	17	34	51	95	135	175
2-Kamen-a	11	22	33	66	91	115
3-11 (#6, 9-10/54, last precode)	9	18	27	51	62	75
12-Wood-a (6 pgs.)	12	24	36	69	95	120
13-Check, Lawrence-a	9	18	27	52	66	80

NOTE: ***Kinstler** c-2-5, 7-9, 11. **Lawrence** a-8. **Ravielli** a-5, 9.*

	GD	VG	FN	VF	VF/NM	NM-
5(9-10/54-2nd series)(Formerly Sensational Police Cases)	9	18	27	51	62	75
6-Reprints nn issue; Wood-a	10	20	30	58	77	95
7-13: 9,10-Kinstler-c. 10-r/cover #2 (1st series). 13-r/cover #8 (1st series)	7	14	21	37	46	55

CAPTAIN STONE (See Holyoke One-Shot No. 10)

CAPT. STORM (Also see G. I. Combat #138)
National Periodical Publications: May-June, 1964 - No. 18, Mar-Apr, 1967

	GD	VG	FN	VF	VF/NM	NM-
1-Origin	8	16	24	53	74	95
2-7,9-18: 3,6,13-Kubert-a. 4-Colan-a. 12-Kubert-c	5	10	15	33	44	55
8-Grey-tone-c	6	12	18	38	52	65

CAPTAIN 3-D (Super hero)
Harvey Publications: December, 1953 (25¢, came with 2 pairs of glasses)

	GD	VG	FN	VF	VF/NM	NM-
1-Kirby/Ditko-a (Ditko's 3rd published work tied with Strange Fantasy #9, see also Daring Love #1 & Black Magic V4 #3); shows cover in 3-D on inside; Kirby/Meskin-c	12	24	36	71	98	125

NOTE: *Half price without glasses*

CAPTAIN THUNDER AND BLUE BOLT
Hero Comics: Sept, 1987 - No. 10, 1988 ($1.95)

	NM-
1-10: 1-Origin Blue Bolt. 3-Origin Capt. Thunder. 6-1st app. Wicket. 8-Champions x-over	2.25

CAPTAIN TOOTSIE & THE SECRET LEGION (Advs. of...)(Also see Monte Hale #30,39 & Real Western Hero)
Toby Press: Oct, 1950 - No. 2, Dec, 1950

	GD	VG	FN	VF	VF/NM	NM-
1-Not Beck-a; both have sci/fi covers	33	66	99	190	275	360
2-The Rocketeer Patrol app.; not Beck-a	21	42	63	118	169	220

CAPTAIN TRIUMPH (See Crack Comics #27)

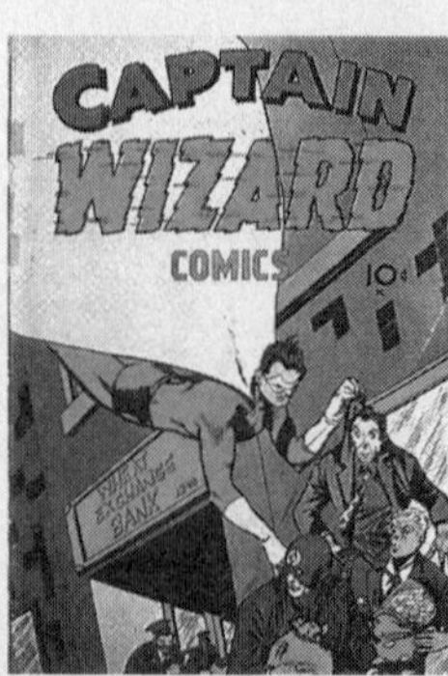
Captain Wizard Comics #1 © Rural Home

Cartoon Cartoons #13 © Cartoon Network

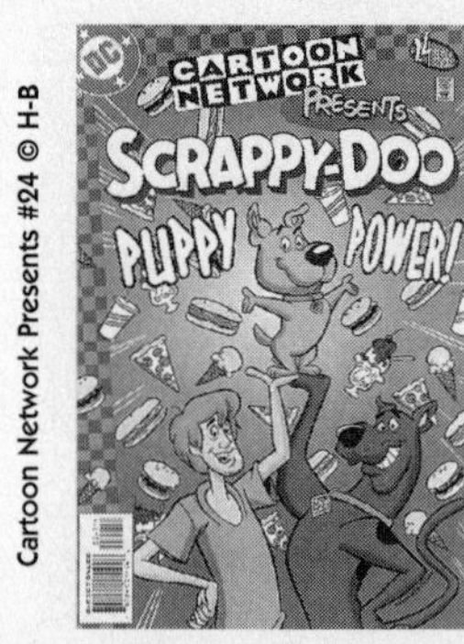

Cartoon Network Presents #24 © H-B

GD VG FN VF VF/NM NM-
2.0 4.0 6.0 8.0 9.0 9.2

GD VG FN VF VF/NM NM-
2.0 4.0 6.0 8.0 9.0 9.2

CAPTAIN VENTURE & THE LAND BENEATH THE SEA (See Space Family Robinson)
Gold Key: Oct, 1968 - No. 2, Oct, 1969

1-r/Space Family Robinson serial; Spiegle-a 6 12 18 38 52 65
2-Spiegle-a 5 10 15 33 44 55

CAPTAIN VICTORY AND THE GALACTIC RANGERS
Pacific Comics: Nov, 1981 - No. 13, Jan, 1984 ($1.00, direct sales, 36-48 pgs.)
(Created by Jack Kirby)

1-1st app. Mr. Mind 4.00
2-13: 3-N. Adams-a 3.00
Special 1-(10/83)-Kirby c/a(p) 4.00
*NOTE: **Conrad** a-10, 11. **Ditko** a-6. **Kirby** a-1-3p; c-1-13.*

CAPTAIN VICTORY AND THE GALACTIC RANGERS
Jack Kirby Comics: July, 2000 - No. 2, Sept, 2000 ($2.95, B&W)

1,2-New Jeremy Kirby-s with reprinted Jack Kirby-a; Liefeld pin-up art 3.00

CAPTAIN VIDEO (TV) (See XMas Comics)
Fawcett Publications: Feb, 1951 - No. 6, Dec, 1951 (No. 1,5,6-36pgs.; 2-4, 52pgs.) (All photo-c)

1-George Evans-a(2); 1st TV hero comic 117 234 351 731 1128 1525
2-Used in **SOTI**, pg. 382 77 154 231 481 741 1000
3-6-All Evans-a except #5 mostly Evans 65 130 195 406 623 840
*NOTE: Minor **Williamson** assists on most issues. Photo c-1, 5, 6; painted c-2-4.*

CAPTAIN WILLIE SCHULTZ (Also see Fightin' Army)
Charlton Comics: No. 76, Oct, 1985 - No. 77, Jan, 1986

76,77-Low print run 1 2 3 4 5 7

CAPTAIN WIZARD COMICS (See Meteor, Red Band & Three Ring Comics)
Rural Home: 1946

1-Capt. Wizard dons new costume; Impossible Man, Race Wilkins app.
33 66 99 190 275 360

CARE BEARS (TV, Movie)(See Star Comics Magazine)
Star Comics/Marvel Comics No. 15 on: Nov, 1985 - No. 20, Jan, 1989

1-20: Post-a begins. 11-$1.00-c begins. 13-Madballs app. 4.00

CAREER GIRL ROMANCES (Formerly Three Nurses)
Charlton Comics: June, 1964 - No. 78, Dec, 1973

V4#24-31 3 6 9 16 20 25
32-Elvis Presley, Herman's Hermits, Johnny Rivers line drawn-c
11 22 33 80 120 160
33-38,40-50 2 4 6 14 18 22
39-(4/67) 1st app. Tiffany Sinn, C.I.A. Sweetheart, Undercover Agent (also see Secret Agent #10; Dominguel-a 3 6 9 18 24 30
51-78 2 4 6 10 13 16

CAR 54, WHERE ARE YOU? (TV)
Dell Publishing Co.: Mar-May, 1962 - No. 7, Sept-Nov, 1963; 1964 - 1965 (All photo-c)

Four Color 1257(#1, 3-5/62) 10 20 30 70 100 130
2(6-8/62)-7 6 12 18 40 55 70
2,3(10-12/64), 4(1-3/65)-Reprints #2,3,&4 of 1st series
4 8 12 24 32 40

CARL BARKS LIBRARY OF WALT DISNEY'S GYRO GEARLOOSE COMICS AND FILLERS IN COLOR, THE
Gladstone: 1993 ($7.95, 8-1/2x11", limited series, 52 pgs.)

1-6: Carl Barks reprints 1 3 4 6 8 10

CARL BARKS LIBRARY OF WALT DISNEY'S COMICS AND STORIES IN COLOR, THE
Gladstone: Jan, 1992 - No. 51, Mar, 1996 ($8.95, 8-1/2x11", 60 pgs.)

1,2,6,8-51: 1-Barks Donald Duck-r/WDC&S #31-35; 2-r/#36,38-41; 6-r/#57-61; 8-r/#67-71; 9-r/#72-76; 10-r/#77-81; 11-r/#82-86; 12-r/#87-91; 13-r/#92-96; 14-r/#97-101; 15-r/#102-106; 16-r/#107-111; 17-r/#112,114,117,124,125; 18-r/#126-130; 19-r/#131,132(2),133,134; 20-r/#135-139; 21-r/#140-144; 22-r/#145-149; 23-r/#150-154; 24-r/#155-159; 25-r/#160-164; 26-r/#165-169; 27-r/#170-174;28-r/#175-179; 29-r/#180-184; 30-r/#185-189; 31-r/#190-194; 32-r/#195-199;33-r/#200-204; 34-r/#205-209; 35-r/#210-214; 36-r/#215-219; 37-r/#220-224; 38-r/#225-229; 39-r/#230-234; 40-r/#235-239; 41-r/#240-244; 42r/#245-249; 43-r/#250-254; 44-50; All contain one Heroes & Villains trading card each
1 3 4 6 8 10
3,4,7: 3-r/#42-46. 4-r/#47-51. 7-r/#62-66. 2 4 6 10 12 15
5-r/#52-56 2 4 6 12 16 20

CARL BARKS LIBRARY OF WALT DISNEY'S DONALD DUCK ADVENTURES IN COLOR, THE
Gladstone: Jan, 1994 - No. 25, Jan, 1996 ($7.95-$9.95, 44-68 pgs., 8-1/2"x11")
(all contain one Donald Duck trading card each)

1-5,7-25-Carl Barks-r: 1-r/FC #9; 2-r/FC #29; 3-r/FC #62; 4-r/FC #108; 5-r/FC #147 & #79(Mickey Mouse); 7-r/FC #159. 8-r/FC #178 & 189. 9-r/FC #199 & 203; 10-r/FC 223 & 238; 11-r/Christmas Parade #1 & 2; 12-r/FC #296; 13-r/FC #263; 14-r/MOC #20 & 41; 15-r/FC 275 & 282; 16-r/FC #291&300; 17-r/FC #308 & 318; 18-r/Vac. Parade #1 & Summer Fun #2; 19-r/FC #328 & 367 2 4 6 8 10 12
6-r/MOC #4, Cheerios "Atom Bomb," D.D. Tells About Kites
2 4 6 12 16 20

CARL BARKS LIBRARY OF WALT DISNEY'S DONALD DUCK CHRISTMAS STORIES IN COLOR, THE
Gladstone: 1992 ($7.95, 44pgs., one-shot)

nn-Reprints Firestone giveaways 1945-1949 2 4 6 10 12 15

CARL BARKS LIBRARY OF WALT DISNEY'S UNCLE SCROOGE COMICS ONE PAGERS IN COLOR, THE
Gladstone: 1992 - No. 2, 1993 ($8.95, limited series, 60 pgs., 8-1/2x11")

1-Carl Barks one pg. reprints 3 6 9 16 20 25
2-Carl Barks one pg. reprints 2 4 6 10 12 15

CARNAGE: IT'S A WONDERFUL LIFE
Marvel Comics: Oct, 1996 ($1.95, one-shot)

1-David Quinn scripts 3.00

CARNAGE: MIND BOMB
Marvel Comics: Feb, 1996 ($2.95, one-shot)

1-Warren Ellis script; Kyle Hotz-a 3.00

CARNATION MALTED MILK GIVEAWAYS (See Wisco)

CARNEYS, THE
Archie Comics: Summer, 1994 ($2.00, 52 pgs)

1-Bound-in pull-out poster 2.50

CARNIVAL COMICS (Formerly Kayo #12; becomes Red Seal Comics #14)
Harry 'A' Chesler/Pershing Square Publ. Co.: 1945

nn (#13)-Guardineer-a 18 36 54 100 143 185

CAROLINE KENNEDY
Charlton Comics: 1961 (one-shot)

nn-Interior photo covers of Kennedy family 10 20 30 67 96 125

CAROUSEL COMICS
F. E. Howard, Toronto: V1#8, April, 1948

V1#8 7 14 21 37 46 55

CARTOON CARTOONS (Anthology)
DC Comics: Mar, 2001 - No. 33, Oct, 2004 ($1.99/$2.25)

1-33-Short stories of Cartoon Network characters. 3,6,10,13,15-Space Ghost. 13-Begin $2.25-c. 17-Dexter's Laboratory begins 2.25

CARTOON KIDS
Atlas Comics (CPS): 1957 (no month)

1-Maneely-c/a; Dexter The Demon, Willie The Wise-Guy, Little Zelda app.
10 20 30 60 80 100

CARTOON NETWORK BLOCK PARTY (Anthology)
DC Comics: Nov, 2004 - Present ($2.25)

1,2-Short stories of Cartoon Network characters 2.25
3-($2.95) Bonus pages 3.00

CARTOON NETWORK PRESENTS
DC Comics: Aug, 1997 - No. 24, Aug, 1999 ($1.75-$1.99, anthology)

1-Dexter's Lab 5.00
1-Platinum Edition 1 2 3 5 7 9
2-10: 2-Space Ghost 3.50
11-24: 12-Bizarro World 2.25

CARTOON NETWORK PRESENTS SPACE GHOST
Archie Comics: Mar, 1997 ($1.50)

1-Scott Rosema-p 5.00

CARTOON NETWORK STARRING... (Anthology)
DC Comics: Sept, 1999 - No. 18, Feb, 2001 ($1.99)

1-Powerpuff Girls 5.00
2-18: 2,8,11,14,17-Johnny Bravo. 12,15,18-Space Ghost 3.00

CARTOON TALES (Disney's...)
W.D. Publications (Disney): nd, nn (1992) ($2.95, 6-5/8x9-1/2", 52 pgs.)

nn-Ariel & Sebastian-Serpent Teen; Beauty and the Beast; A Tale of Enchantment; Darkwing Duck - Just Us Justice Ducks; 101 Dalmatians - Canine Classics; Tale Spin - Surprise in the Skies; Uncle Scrooge - Blast to the Past 4.00

CARVERS

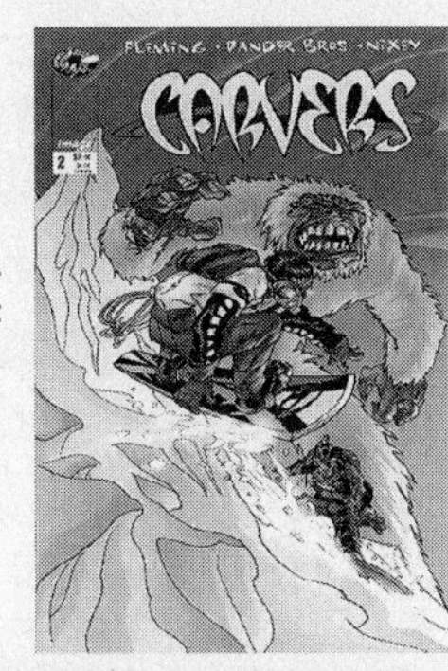

Carvers #2 © Flypaper Press

Casper and the Ghostly Trio #6 © Paramount

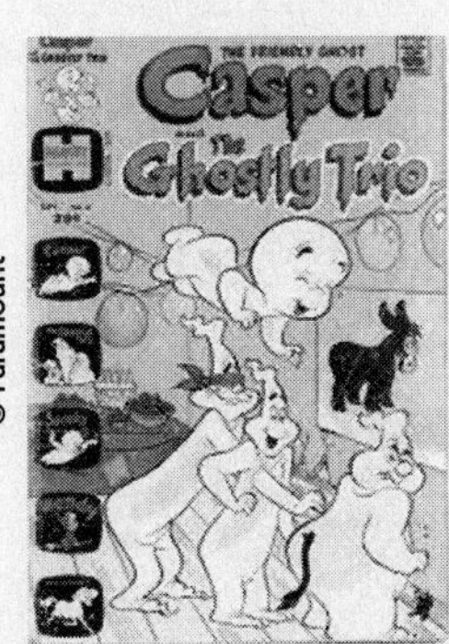

Casper's Ghostland #17 © Paramount

GD 2.0 | VG 4.0 | FN 6.0 | VF 8.0 | VF/NM 9.0 | NM- 9.2

Image Comics (Flypaper Press): 1998 - No. 3, 1999 ($2.95)
1-3-Pander Bros.-a/Fleming-s 3.00

CAR WARRIORS
Marvel Comics (Epic): June, 1991 - No. 4, Sept, 1991 ($2.25, lim. series)
1-4: 1-Says April in indicia 2.25

CASE FILES: SAM & TWITCH (Also see the Spawn titles)
Image Comics: May, 2003 - Present ($2.50, color #1-6/B&W #7-on)
1-11: 1-5-Scott Morse-a/Marc Andreyko-s. 7-11-Paul Lee-a 2.50

CASE OF THE SHOPLIFTER'S SHOE (See Perry Mason, Feature Book No.50)

CASE OF THE WINKING BUDDHA, THE
St. John Publ. Co.: 1950 (132 pgs.; 25¢; B&W; 5-1/2x7-5-1/2x8")
nn-Charles Raab-a; reprinted in Authentic Police Cases No. 25
29 58 87 164 237 310

CASEY-CRIME PHOTOGRAPHER (Two-Gun Western No. 5 on)(Radio)
Marvel Comics (BFP): Aug, 1949 - No. 4, Feb, 1950
1-Photo-c; 52 pgs. 25 50 75 144 207 270
2-4: Photo-c 17 34 51 98 139 180

CASEY JONES (TV)
Dell Publishing Co.: No. 915, July, 1958
Four Color 915-Alan Hale photo-c 6 12 18 43 59 75

CASEY JONES & RAPHAEL (See Bodycount)
Mirage Studios: Oct, 1994 ($2.75, unfinished limited series)
1-Bisley-c; Eastman story & pencils 2.75

CASEY JONES: NORTH BY DOWNEAST
Mirage Studios: May, 1994 - No. 2, July, 1994 ($2.75, limited series)
1,2-Rick Veitch script & pencils; Kevin Eastman story & inks 2.75

CASPER ADVENTURE DIGEST
Harvey Comics: V2#1, Oct, 1992 - V2#8, Apr, 1994 ($1.75/$1.95, digest-size)
V2#1: Casper, Richie Rich, Spooky, Wendy 5.00
2-8 3.50

CASPER AND...
Harvey Comics: Nov, 1987 - No. 12, June, 1990 (.75/$1.00, all reprints)
1-Ghostly Trio 5.00
2-12: 2-Spooky; begin $1.00-c. 3-Wendy. 4-Nightmare. 5-Ghostly Trio. 6-Spooky. 7-Wendy. 8-Hot Stuff. 9-Baby Huey. 10-Wendy.11-Ghostly Trio. 12-Spooky 3.00

CASPER AND FRIENDS
Harvey Comics: Oct, 1991 - No. 5, July, 1992 ($1.00/$1.25)
1-Nightmare, Ghostly Trio, Wendy, Spooky 4.00
2-5 3.00

CASPER AND FRIENDS MAGAZINE: Mar, 1997 - No. 3, July, 1997 ($3.99)
1-3 4.00

CASPER AND NIGHTMARE (See Harvey Hits# 37, 45, 52, 56, 59, 62, 65, 68,71, 75)

CASPER AND NIGHTMARE (Nightmare & Casper No. 1-5)
Harvey Publications: No. 6, 11/64 - No. 44, 10/73; No. 45, 6/74 - No. 46, 8/74 (25¢)
6: 68 pg. Giants begin, ends #32 5 10 15 36 48 60
7-10 4 8 12 24 32 40
11-20 3 6 9 18 24 30
21-37: 33-37-(52 pg. Giants) 3 6 9 16 20 24
38-46 2 4 6 10 12 15
NOTE: *Many issues contain reprints.*

CASPER AND SPOOKY (See Harvey Hits No. 20)
Harvey Publications: Oct, 1972 - No. 7, Oct, 1973
1 3 6 9 19 25 32
2-7 2 4 6 10 13 16

CASPER AND THE GHOSTLY TRIO
Harvey Pub.: Nov, 1972 - No. 7, Nov, 1973; No. 8, Aug, 1990 - No. 10, Dec, 1990
1 3 6 9 19 25 32
2-7 2 4 6 10 13 16
8-10 5.00

CASPER AND WENDY
Harvey Publications: Sept, 1972 - No. 8, Nov, 1973
1: 52 pg. Giant 3 6 9 19 25 32
2-8 2 4 6 10 13 16

CASPER BIG BOOK
Harvey Comics: V2#1, Aug, 1992 - No. 3, May, 1993 ($1.95, 52 pgs.)
V2#1-Spooky app. 4.00
2,3 3.00

CASPER CAT (See Dopey Duck)
I. W. Enterprises/Super: 1958; 1963
1,7:1-Wacky Duck #?.7-Reprint, Super No. 14('63) 2 4 6 10 13 16

CASPER DIGEST (...Magazine #?; ...Halloween Digest #8, 10)
Harvey Publications: Oct, 1986 - No. 18, Jan, 1991 ($1.25/$1.75, digest-size)
1 1 3 4 6 8 10
2-18: 11-Valentine-c. 18-Halloween-c 6.00

CASPER DIGEST (...Magazine #? on)
Harvey Comics: V2#1, Sept, 1991 - V2#14, Nov, 1994 ($1.75/$1.95, digest-size)
V2#1 5.00
2-14 3.50

CASPER DIGEST STORIES
Harvey Publications: Feb, 1980 - No. 4, Nov, 1980 (95¢, 132 pgs., digest size)
1 2 4 6 10 13 16
2-4 1 2 3 5 7 9

CASPER DIGEST WINNERS
Harvey Publications: Apr, 1980 - No. 3, Sept, 1980 (95¢, 132 pgs., digest size)
1 2 4 6 10 13 16
2,3 1 2 3 5 7 9

CASPER ENCHANTED TALES DIGEST
Harvey Comics: May, 1992 - No. 10, Oct, 1994 ($1.75, digest-size, 98 pgs.)
1-Casper, Spooky, Wendy stories 5.00
2-10 3.50

CASPER GHOSTLAND
Harvey Comics: May, 1992 ($1.25)
1 3.00

CASPER GIANT SIZE
Harvey Comics: Oct, 1992 - No. 4, Nov, 1993 ($2.25, 68 pgs.)
V2#1-Casper, Wendy, Spooky stories 5.00
2-4 4.00

CASPER HALLOWEEN TRICK OR TREAT
Harvey Publications: Jan, 1976 (52 pgs.)
1 3 6 9 19 25 32

CASPER IN SPACE (Formerly Casper Spaceship)
Harvey Publications: No. 6, June, 1973 - No. 8, Oct, 1973
6-8 2 4 6 10 13 16

CASPER'S GHOSTLAND
Harvey Publications: Winter, 1958-59 - No. 97, 12/77; No. 98, 12/79 (25¢)
1-84 pgs. begin, ends #10 20 40 60 141 216 290
2 11 22 33 75 110 145
3-10 8 16 24 58 82 105
11-20: 11-68 pgs. begin, ends #61. 13-X-Mas-c 7 14 21 46 63 80
21-40 5 10 15 33 49 55
41-61 3 6 9 19 25 32
62-77: 62-52 pgs. begin 2 4 6 10 13 16
78-98: 94-X-Mas-c 2 4 6 8 10 12
NOTE: *Most issues contain reprints w/new stories.*

CASPER SPACESHIP (Casper in Space No. 6 on)
Harvey Publications: Aug, 1972 - No. 5, April, 1973
1: 52 pg. Giant 3 7 10 21 28 35
2-5 2 4 6 11 14 18

CASPER STRANGE GHOST STORIES
Harvey Publications: October, 1974 - No. 14, Jan, 1977 (All 52 pgs.)
1 3 7 10 21 28 35
2-14 2 4 6 11 14 18

CASPER, THE FRIENDLY GHOST (See America's Best TV Comics, Famous TV Funday Funnies, The Friendly Ghost..., Nightmare &..., Richie Rich and..., Tastee-Freez, Treasury of Comics, Wendy the Good Little Witch & Wendy Witch World)

CASPER, THE FRIENDLY GHOST (Becomes Harvey Comics Hits No. 61 (No. 6), and then continued with Harvey issue No. 7)(1st Series)
St. John Publishing Co.: Sept, 1949 - No. 5, Aug, 1951

Casper the Friendly Ghost #15 © Paramount

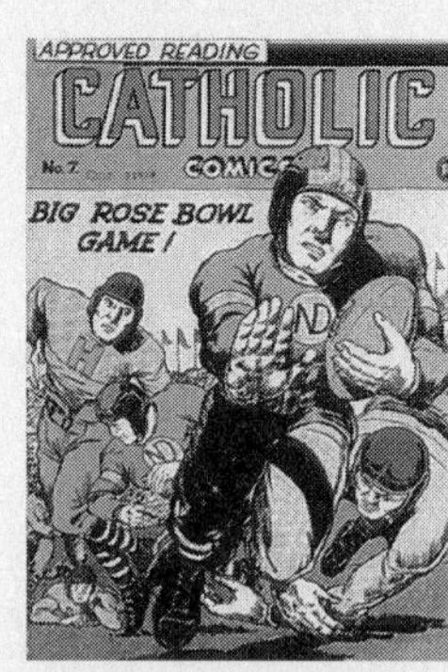

Catholic Comics #7 © Catholic Publ.

Catman Comics #8 © HOKE

GD VG FN VF VF/NM NM-
2.0 4.0 6.0 8.0 9.0 9.2

1(1949)-Origin & 1st app. Baby Huey & Herman the Mouse (1st time the name Casper app. in any media, even films) 192 384 576 1200 1850 2500
2,3 (2/50 & 8/50) 75 150 225 469 722 975
4,5 (3/51 & 8/51) 57 114 171 356 548 740

CASPER, THE FRIENDLY GHOST (Paramount Picture Star...)(2nd Series)
Harvey Publications (Family Comics): No. 7, Dec, 1952 - No. 70, July, 1958
Note: No. 6 is Harvey Comics Hits No. 61 (10/52)

7-Baby Huey begins, ends #9 34 68 102 255 398 540
8,9 20 40 60 145 223 300
10-Spooky begins (1st app., 6/53), ends #70? 24 48 72 174 267 360
11,12: 2nd & 3rd app. Spooky 14 28 42 97 149 200
13-18: Alfred Harvey app. in story 12 24 36 87 134 180
19-1st app. Nightmare (4/54) 19 38 57 138 212 285
20-Wendy the Witch begins (1st app., 5/54) 25 50 75 181 278 375
21-30: 24-Infinity-c 10 20 30 73 107 140
31-40: 38-Early Wendy app. 39-1st app. Samson Honeybun. 40-1st app. Dr. Brainstorm 8 16 24 55 78 100
41-1st Wendy app. on-c 7 14 21 51 71 90
42-50: 43-2nd Wendy-c. 46-1st app. Spooky's girl Pearl. 7 14 21 46 63 80
51-70 (Continues as Friendly Ghost... 8/58) 58-Early app. Bat Balfrey. 63-2nd app. Something the Baby Ghost. 66-1st app. Wildcat Witch 6 12 18 38 52 65

NOTE: *Baby Huey app. 7-9, 11, 121, 14, 16, 20. Buzzy app. 14, 16, 20. Nightmare app. 19, 27, 36, 37, 42, 46, 51, 53, 56, 70. Spooky app. 10-70. Wendy app. 20, 29-31, 35, 37, 38, 41-49, 51, 52, 54-58, 61, 64, 68.*

CASPER THE FRIENDLY GHOST (Formerly The Friendly Ghost...)(3rd Series)
Harvey Comics: No. 254, July, 1990 - No. 260, Jan, 1991 ($1.00)

254-260 3.00

CASPER THE FRIENDLY GHOST (4th Series)
Harvey Comics: Mar, 1991 - No. 28, Nov, 1994 ($1.00/$1.25/$1.50)

1-Casper becomes Mighty Ghost; Spooky & Wendy app. 5.00
2-10: 7,8-Post-a 3.00
11-28-($1.50) 2.50

CASPER T.V. SHOWTIME
Harvey Comics: Jan, 1980 - No. 5, Oct, 1980

1 2 4 6 10 12 15
2-5 1 2 3 5 6 8

CASSETTE BOOKS (Classics Illustrated)
Cassette Book Co./I.P.S. Publ.: 1984 (48 pgs, b&w comic with cassette tape)
NOTE: *This series was illegal. The artwork was illegally obtained, and the Classics Illustrated copyright owner, Twin Circle Publ. sued to get an injunction to prevent the continued sale of this series. Many C.I. collectors obtained copies before the 1987 injunction, but now they are already scarce. Here again the market is just developing, but sealed mint copies of com ic and tape should be worth at least $25.*

1001 (CI#1-A2)New-PC 1002(CI#3-A2)CI-PC 1003(CI#13-A2)CI-PC
1004(CI#25)CI-LDC 1005(CI#10-A2)New-PC 1006(CI#64)CI-LDC

CASTILIAN (See Movie Classics)

CASTLE WAITING
Olio: 1997 - No. 7, 1999 ($2.95, B&W)
Cartoon Books: Vol. 2, Aug, 2000 - Present ($2.95, B&W)

1-Linda Medley-s/a in all 1 2 3 5 6 8
2 4.00
3-7 3.00
The Lucky Road TPB r/#1-7 17.00
Hiatus Issue (1999) Crilley-c; short stories and previews 3.00
Vol. 2 #1-6,14-16 (#5&6 also have #12&13 on cover, for series numbering) 3.00

CASUAL HEROES
Image Comics (Motown Machineworks): Apr, 1996 ($2.25, unfinished lim. series)

1-Steve Rude-c 2.25

CAT, T.H.E. (TV) (See T.H.E. Cat)

CAT, THE (See Movie Classics)

CAT, THE (Female hero)
Marvel Comics Group: Nov, 1972 - No. 4, June, 1973

1-Origin & 1st app. The Cat (who later becomes Tigra); Mooney-a(i); Wood-c(i)/a(i) 4 8 12 27 36 45
2,3: 2-Marie Severin/Mooney-a. 3-Everett inks 2 4 6 14 18 22
4-Starlin/Weiss-a(p) 3 6 9 16 20 24

CATALYST: AGENTS OF CHANGE (Also see Comics' Greatest World)
Dark Horse Comics: Feb, 1994 - No.7, Nov, 1994 ($2.00, limited series)

1-7: 1-Foil stamped logo 2.50

GD VG FN VF VF/NM NM-
2.0 4.0 6.0 8.0 9.0 9.2

CAT & MOUSE
EF Graphics (Silverline): Dec, 1988 ($1.75, color w/part B&W)

1-1st printing (12/88, 32 pgs.), 1-2nd printing (5/89, 36 pgs.) 2.25

CAT FROM OUTER SPACE (See Walt Disney Showcase #46)

CATHOLIC COMICS (See Heroes All Catholic...)
Catholic Publications: June, 1946 - V3#10, July, 1949

1 31 62 93 178 259 340
2 16 32 48 89 127 165
3-13(7/47) 14 28 42 81 113 145
V2#1-10 10 20 30 60 80 100
V3#1-10: Reprints 10-part Treasure Island serial from Target V2#2-11 (see Key Comics #5) 11 22 33 62 84 105

CATHOLIC PICTORIAL
Catholic Guild: 1947

1-Toth-a(2) (Rare) 40 80 120 240 363 485

CATMAN COMICS (Formerly Crash Comics No. 1-5)
Holyoke Publishing Co./Continental Magazines V2#12, 7/44 on:
5/41 - No. 17, 1/43; No. 18, 7/43 - No. 22, 12/43; No. 23, 3/44 - No. 26, 11/44; No. 27, 4/45 - No. 30, 12/45; No. 31, 6/46 - No. 32, 8/46

1(V1#6)-Origin The Deacon & Sidekick Mickey, Dr. Diamond & Rag-Man; The Black Widow app.; The Catman by Chas. Quinlan & Blaze Baylor begin 372 744 1116 2418 3909 5400
2(V1#7) 135 270 405 844 1297 1750
3(V1#8)-The Pied Piper begins; classic Hitler, Stalin & Mussolini-c 117 234 351 731 1128 1525
4(V1#9) 96 192 288 600 925 1250
5(V2#10)-1st app. Kitten; The Hood begins (c-redated), 6,7(V2#11,12) 79 158 237 494 760 1025
8(V2#13,3/42)-Origin Little Leaders; Volton by Kubert begins (his 1st comic book work) 96 192 288 600 925 1250
9,10(V2#14,15): 10-Origin Blackout; Phantom Falcon begins 67 134 201 419 647 875
11 (V3#1)-Kubert-a 67 134 201 419 647 875
12 (V3#2), 14, 15, 17, 18(V3#8, 7/43). 12-Volton by Brodsky, not Kubert. 14-Brodsky-a 55 110 165 340 520 700
13-(scarce) 87 174 261 544 835 1125
16 (V3#5)-Hitler, Tojo, Mussolini, Goehring-c 79 158 237 494 760 1025
19,20: 19 (V2#6)-Hitler, Tojo, Mussolini-c. 20 (V2#7): Classic Hitler-c 83 166 249 519 797 1075
21-23 (V2#10, 3/44) 51 102 153 311 476 640
nn(V3#13, 5/44)-Rico-a; Schomburg bondage-c 51 102 153 311 476 640
nn(V2#12, 7/44, nn(V3#1, 9/44)-Origin The Golden Archer; Leatherface app. 47 94 141 287 436 585
nn(V3#2, 11/44)-L. B. Cole-c 81 162 243 506 778 1050
27-Origins Catman & Kitten retold; L. B. Cole Flag-c; Infantino-a 92 184 276 575 888 1200
28-Dr. Macabre app.; L. B. Cole-c/a 98 196 294 613 944 1275
29-32-L. B. Cole-c; bondage-#30 87 174 261 544 835 1125

NOTE: ***Fuje** a-11, 27, 28(2), 29(3), 30. **Palais** a-11, 16, 27, 28, 29(2), 30(2), 32; c-25(7/44). **Rico** a-11(2), 23, 27, 28.*

CATSEYE
Hyperwerks Comics: Dec, 1998 - No. 4, June, 1999 ($2.95)

1-4-Altstaetter-s/a 3.00

CAT TALES (3-D)
Eternity Comics: Apr, 1989 ($2.95)

1-Felix the Cat-r in 3-D 5.00

CATWOMAN (Also see Action Comics Weekly #611, Batman #404-407, Detective Comics, & Superman's Girlfriend Lois Lane #70, 71)
DC Comics: Feb, 1989 - No. 4, May, 1989 ($1.50, limited series, mature)

1 1 3 4 6 8 10
2-4: 3-Batman cameo. 4-Batman app. 1 2 3 5 7 9
Her Sister's Keeper (1991, $9.95, trade paperback)-r/#1-4 10.00

CATWOMAN (Also see Showcase '93, Showcase '95 #4, & Batman #404-407)
DC Comics: Aug, 1993 - No. 94, Jul, 2001 ($1.50-$2.25)

0-(10/94)-Zero Hour; origin retold. Released between #14&15 3.00
1-($1.95)-Embossed-c; Bane app.; Balent c-1-10; a-1-10p 4.00
2-20: 3-Bane flashback cameo. 4-Brief Bane app. 6,7-Knightquest tie-ins; Batman (Azrael) app. 8-1st app. Zephyr. 12-KnightsEnd pt. 6. 13-new Knights End Aftermath. 14-(9/94)-Zero Hour 3.00

Catwoman #94 © DC

Catwoman: The Movie #1 © DC

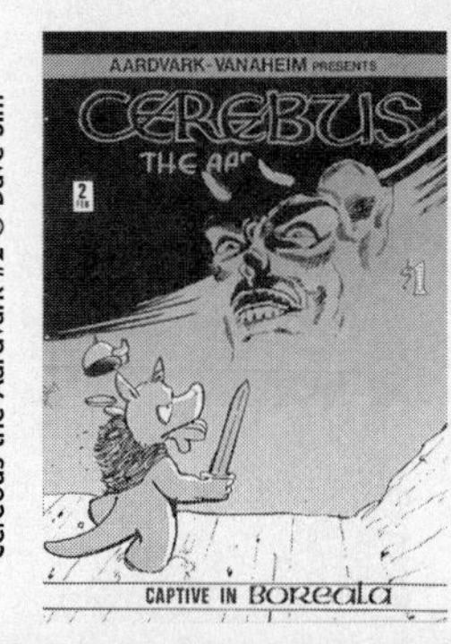

Cerebus the Aardvark #2 © Dave Sim

	GD 2.0	VG 4.0	FN 6.0	VF 8.0	VF/NM 9.0	NM- 9.2

21-24, 26-30, 33-49: 21-$1.95-c begins. 28,29-Penguin cameo app. 36-Legacy pt. 2. 38-40-Year Two; Batman, Joker, Penguin & Two-Face app. 46-Two-Face app. 2.50
25,31,32: 25-($2.95)-Robin app. 31,32-Contagion pt. 4 (Reads pt. 5 on-c) & pt. 9. 3.00
50-($2.95, 48 pgs.)-New armored costume 3.00
50-($2.95, 48 pgs.)-Collector's Ed.w/metallic ink-c 3.00
51-77: 51-Huntress-c/app. 54-Grayson-s begins. 56-Cataclysm pt.6. 57-Poison Ivy-c/app. 63-65-Joker-c/app. 72-No Man's Land; Ostrander-s begins 2.50
78-82: 80-Catwoman goes to jail 2.25
83-94: 83-Begin $2.25-c. 83,84,89-Harley Quinn-c/app. 2.25
#1,000,000 (11/98) 853rd Century x-over 2.25
Annual 1 (1994, $2.95, 68 pgs.)-Elseworlds story; Batman app.; no Balent-a 3.00
Annual 2,4 ('95, '97, $3.95) 2-Year One story. 4-Pulp Heroes 4.00
Annual 3 (1996, $2.95)-Legends of the Dead Earth story 3.00
...Plus 1 (11/97, $2.95) Screamqueen (Scare Tactics) app. 3.00
TPB ($9.95) r/#15-19, Balent-c 10.00

CATWOMAN (Also see Detective Comics #759-762)
DC Comics: Jan, 2002 - Present ($2.50)

1-Darwyn Cooke & Mike Allred-a; Ed Brubaker-s 6.00
2-4 3.00
5-37: 5-9-Rader-a/Paul Pope-c. 10-Morse-c. 16-JG Jones-c. 22-Batman-c/app. 34-36-War Games 2.50
...: Crooked Little Town TPB (2003, $14.95) r/#5-10 & Secret Files; Oeming-c 15.00
... Secret Files and Origins (10/02, $4.95) origin-s Oeming-a; profiles and pin-ups 5.00
...Selina's Big Score HC (2002, $24.95) Cooke-s/a; pin-ups by various 25.00
...Selina's Big Score SC (2003, $17.95) Cooke-s/a; pin-ups by various 18.00
...: The Dark End of the Street TPB (2002, $12.95) r/#1-4 & Slam Bradley back-up stories from Detective Comics #759-762 13.00

CATWOMAN/ GUARDIAN OF GOTHAM
DC Comics: 1999 - No. 2, 1999 ($5.95, limited series)

1,2-Elseworlds; Moench-s/Balent-a 6.00

CATWOMAN: NINE LIVES OF A FELINE FATALE
DC Comics: 2004 ($14.95, TPB)

nn-Reprints notable stories from Batman #1 to the present; pin-ups by various; Bolland-c 15.00

CATWOMAN: THE MOVIE (2004 Halle Berry movie)
DC Comics: 2004 ($4.95/$9.95)

1-($4.95) Movie adaptation; Jim Lee-c and sketch pages; Derenick-a 5.00
... & Other Cat Tales TPB (2004, $9.95)-r/Movie adaptation; Jim Lee sketch pages, r/Catwoman #0, Catwoman (2nd series) #11 & 25; photo-c 10.00

CATWOMAN/VAMPIRELLA: THE FURIES
DC Comics/Harris Publ.: Feb, 1997 ($4.95, squarebound, 46 pgs.) (1st DC/Harris x-over)

nn-Reintro Pantha; Chuck Dixon scripts; Jim Balent-c/a 5.00

CATWOMAN: WHEN IN ROME
DC Comics: Nov, 2004 - No. 6 ($3.50, limited series)

1,2-Jeph Loeb-s/Tim Sale-a/c; Riddler app. 3.50

CATWOMAN/WILDCAT
DC Comics: Aug, 1998 - No. 4, Nov, 1998 ($2.50, limited series)

1-4-Chuck Dixon & Beau Smith-s; Stelfreeze-c 3.00

CAUGHT
Atlas Comics (VPI): Aug, 1956 - No. 5, Apr, 1957

	GD	VG	FN	VF	VF/NM	NM-
1	23	46	69	132	191	250
2-4: 3-Maneely, Pakula, Torres-a. 4-Maneely-a	12	24	36	71	98	125
5-Crandall, Krigstein-a	13	26	39	76	106	135

NOTE: ***Drucker** a-2. **Heck** a-4. **Severin** c-1, 2, 4, 5. **Shores** a-4.*

CAVALIER COMICS
A. W. Nugent Publ. Co.: 1945; 1952 (Early DC reprints)

	GD	VG	FN	VF	VF/NM	NM-
2(1945)-Speed Saunders, Fang Gow	22	44	66	123	177	230
2(1952)	11	22	33	66	91	115

CAVE GIRL (Also see Africa)
Magazine Enterprises: No. 11, 1953 - No. 14, 1954

	GD	VG	FN	VF	VF/NM	NM-
11(A-1 82)-Origin; all Cave Girl stories	47	94	141	287	436	585
12(A-1 96), 13(A-1 116), 14(A-1 125)-Thunda by Powell in each	37	74	111	209	305	400

NOTE: ***Powell** c/a in all.*

CAVE GIRL
AC Comics: 1988 ($2.95, 44 pgs.) (16 pgs. of color, rest B&W)

1-Powell-r/Cave Girl #11; Nyoka photo back-c from movie; Powell/Bill Black-c; Special Limited Edition on-c 4.00

CAVE KIDS (TV) (See Comic Album #16)
Gold Key: Feb, 1963 - No. 16, Mar, 1967 (Hanna-Barbera)

	GD	VG	FN	VF	VF/NM	NM-
1	8	16	24	55	78	100
2-5	4	8	12	28	38	48
6-16: 7,12-Pebbles & Bamm Bamm app. 16-1st Space Kidettes	4	8	12	22	30	38

CAVEWOMAN
Basement Comics: Jan, 1994 - No. 6, 1995 ($2.95)

	GD	VG	FN	VF	VF/NM	NM-
1	3	6	9	18	24	30
2	2	4	6	10	12	15
3-6	1	2	3	5	6	8

...: Meets Explorers ('97, $2.95) 3.00
...: One-Shot Special (7/00, $2.95) Massey-s/a 3.00

CELESTINE (See Violator Vs. Badrock #1)
Image Comics (Extreme): May, 1996 - No. 2, June, 1996 ($2.50, limited series)

1,2: Warren Ellis scripts 2.50

CENTURION OF ANCIENT ROME, THE
Zondervan Publishing House: 1958 (no month listed) (B&W, 36 pgs.)

	GD	VG	FN	VF	VF/NM	NM-
(Rare) All by Jay Disbrow	48	96	144	293	447	600

CENTURIONS (TV)
DC Comics: June, 1987 - No. 4, Sept, 1987 (75¢, limited series)

1-4 2.50

CENTURY: DISTANT SONS
Marvel Comics: Feb, 1996 ($2.95, one-shot)

1-Wraparound-c 3.00

CENTURY OF COMICS (See Promotional Comics section)

CEREBUS BI-WEEKLY
Aardvark-Vanaheim: Dec. 2, 1988 - No. 26, Nov. 11, 1989 ($1.25, B&W)

Reprints Cerebus The Aardvark#1-26

	GD	VG	FN	VF	VF/NM	NM-
1-16, 18, 19, 21-26:						3.00
17-Hepcats app.	2	4	6	8	10	12
20-Milk & Cheese app.	2	4	6	10	12	15

CEREBUS: CHURCH & STATE
Aardvark-Vanaheim: Feb, 1991 - No. 30, Apr, 1992 ($2.00, B&W, bi-weekly)

1-30: r/Cerebus #51-80 3.00

CEREBUS: HIGH SOCIETY
Aardvark-Vanaheim: Feb, 1990 - No. 25, 1991 ($1.70, B&W)

1-25: r/Cerebus #26-50 3.00

CEREBUS JAM
Aardvark-Vanaheim: Apr, 1985

1-Eisner, Austin, Dave Sim-a (Cerebus vs. Spirit) 6.00

CEREBUS THE AARDVARK (See A-V in 3-D, Nucleus, Power Comics)
Aardvark-Vanaheim: Dec, 1977 - No. 300, March, 2004 ($1.70/$2.00/$2.25, B&W)

0 3.00
0-Gold 20.00

	GD	VG	FN	VF	VF/NM	NM-
1-1st app. Cerebus; 2000 print run; most copies poorly printed	41	82	123	305	478	650

Note: *There is a counterfeit version known to exist. It can be distinguished from the original in the following ways: inside cover is glossy instead of flat, black background on the front cover is blotted or spotty. Reports show that a counterfeit #2 also exists.*

	GD	VG	FN	VF	VF/NM	NM-
2-Dave Sim art in all	11	22	33	80	120	160
3-Origin Red Sophia	10	20	30	70	100	130
4-Origin Elrod the Albino	8	16	24	55	78	100
5,6	7	14	21	46	63	80
7-10	5	10	15	36	48	60
11,12: 11-Origin The Cockroach	4	8	12	24	32	40
13-15: 14-Origin Lord Julius	3	6	9	18	24	30
16-20	2	4	6	11	14	18
21-B. Smith letter in letter column	5	10	15	33	44	55
22-Low distribution; no cover price	3	6	9	18	23	28
23-30: 23-Preview of Wandering Star by Teri S. Wood. 26-High Society begins, ends #50	2	4	6	8	10	12
31-Origin Moonroach	2	4	6	10	12	15
32-40, 53-Intro. Wolveroach (brief app.)	1	2	3	5	7	9
41-50,52: 52-Church & State begins, ends #111; Cutey Bunny app.	1	2	3	5	6	8

51,54: 51-Cutey Bunny app. 54-1st full Wolveroach story

Challengers of the Unknown #4 © DC

Challengers of the Unknown ('04) #1 © DC

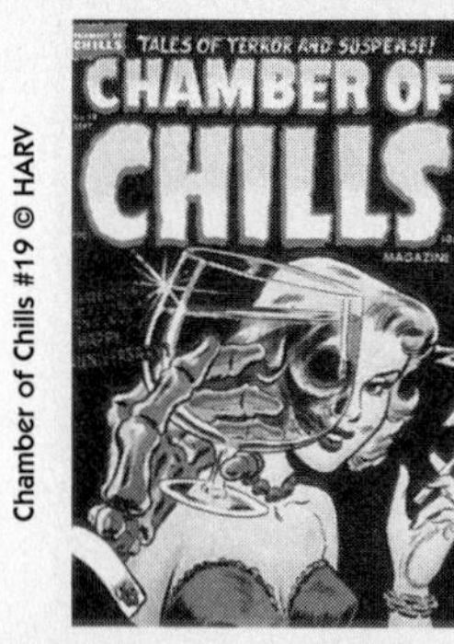

Chamber of Chills #19 © HARV

	GD 2.0	VG 4.0	FN 6.0	VF 8.0	VF/NM 9.0	NM- 9.2
	2	4	6	8	10	12
55,56-Wolveroach app.; Normalman back-ups by Valentino	1	2	3	5	7	9
57-100: 61,62: Flaming Carrot app. 65-Gerhard begins						4.00
101-160: 104-Flaming Carrot app. 112/113-Double issue. 114-Jaka's Story begins, ends #136. 139-Melmoth begins, ends #150. 151-Mothers & Daughters begins, ends #200						3.00
161-Bone app.	1	3	4	6	8	10
162-231: 175-($2.25, 44 pgs). 186-Strangers on Paradise cameo. 201-Guys storyline begins; Eddie Campbell's Bacchus app. 220-231-Rick's Story						2.50
232-265-Going Home						2.25
266-288,291-299-Latter Days: 267-Five-Bar Gate. 276-Spore (Spawn spoof)						2.25
289&290 ($4.50) Two issues combined						4.50
300-Final issue						2.25
Free Cerebus (Giveaway, 1991-92?, 36 pgs.)-All-r						4.00

CHAIN GANG WAR
DC Comics: July, 1993 - No. 12, June, 1994 ($1.75)

	GD 2.0	VG 4.0	FN 6.0	VF 8.0	VF/NM 9.0	NM- 9.2
1-($2.50)-Embossed silver foil-c, Dave Johnson-c/a						3.00
2-4,6-12: 3-Deathstroke app. 4-Brief Deathstroke app. 6-New Batman (Azrael) cameo. 11-New Batman-c/story. 12-New Batman app.						2.25
5-($2.50)-Foil-c; Deathstroke app; new Batman cameo (1 panel)						3.00

CHAINS OF CHAOS
Harris Comics: Nov, 1994 - No. 3, Jan, 1995 ($2.95, limited series)

	GD 2.0	VG 4.0	FN 6.0	VF 8.0	VF/NM 9.0	NM- 9.2
1-3-Re-Intro of The Rook w/ Vampirella						3.00

CHALLENGE OF THE UNKNOWN (Formerly Love Experiences)
Ace Magazines: No. 6, Sept, 1950 (See Web Of Mystery No. 19)

	GD 2.0	VG 4.0	FN 6.0	VF 8.0	VF/NM 9.0	NM- 9.2
6- "Villa of the Vampire" used in N.Y. Joint Legislative Comm. Publ; Sekowsky-a	35	70	105	198	287	375

CHALLENGER, THE
Interfaith Publications/T.C. Comics: 1945 - No. 4, Oct-Dec, 1946

	GD 2.0	VG 4.0	FN 6.0	VF 8.0	VF/NM 9.0	NM- 9.2
nn; nd; 32 pgs.; Origin the Challenger Club; Anti-Fascist with funny animal filler	46	92	138	281	428	575
2-4: Kubert-a; 4-Fuje-a	37	74	111	209	305	400

CHALLENGERS OF THE FANTASTIC
Marvel Comics (Amalgam): June 1997 ($1.95, one-shot)

	GD 2.0	VG 4.0	FN 6.0	VF 8.0	VF/NM 9.0	NM- 9.2
1-Karl Kesel-s/Tom Grummett-a						2.50

CHALLENGERS OF THE UNKNOWN (See Showcase #6, 7, 11, 12, Super DC Giant, and Super Team Family)
National Per. Publ./DC Comics: 4-5/58 - No. 77, 12-1/70-71; No. 78, 2/73 - No. 80, 6-7/73; No. 81, 6-7/77 - No. 87, 6-7/78

	GD 2.0	VG 4.0	FN 6.0	VF 8.0	VF/NM 9.0	NM- 9.2
1-(4-5/58)-Kirby/Stein-a(2); Kirby-c	190	380	570	1663	2732	3800
2-Kirby/Stein-a(2)	67	134	201	570	923	1275
3-Kirby/Stein-a(2)	58	116	174	493	797	1100
4-8-Kirby/Wood-a plus cover to #8	46	92	138	368	572	775
9,10	29	58	87	206	316	425
11-Grey tone-c	20	40	60	145	223	300
12-15: 14-Origin/1st app. Multi-Man (villain)	19	38	57	138	212	285
16-22: 18-Intro. Cosmo, the Challengers Spacepet. 22-Last 10¢ issue	13	26	39	92	141	190
23-30	8	16	24	55	78	100
31-Retells origin of the Challengers	8	16	24	58	82	105
32-40	5	10	15	36	48	60
41-47,49,50,52-60: 43-New look begins. 49-Intro. Challenger Corps. 55-Death of Red Ryan. 60-Red Ryan returns	4	8	12	27	36	45
48,51: 48-Doom Patrol app. 51-Sea Devils app.	4	8	12	29	40	50
61-68: 64,65-Kirby origin-r, parts 1 & 2. 66-New logo. 68-Last 12¢ issue.	3	6	9	18	23	28
69-73,75-80: 69-1st app. Corinna. 77-Last 15¢ issue	2	4	6	10	13	16
74-Deadman by Tuska/Adams; 1 pg. Wrightson-a	4	8	12	29	40	50
81,83-87: 81-(6-7/77). 83-87-Swamp Thing app. 84-87-Deadman app.	1	3	4	6	8	10
82-Swamp Thing begins (thru #87, c/s	2	4	6	9	11	14

NOTE: ***N. Adams*** *c-67, 68, 70, 72, 74i, 81i.* ***Buckler*** *c-83-86p.* ***Giffen*** *a-83-87p.* ***Kirby*** *a-75-80r; c-75, 77, 78.* ***Kubert*** *c-64, 66, 69, 76, 79.* ***Nasser*** *c/a-81p, 82p.* ***Tuska*** *a-73.* ***Wood*** *r-76.*

CHALLENGERS OF THE UNKNOWN
DC Comics: Mar, 1991 - No. 8, Oct, 1991 ($1.75, limited series)

	GD 2.0	VG 4.0	FN 6.0	VF 8.0	VF/NM 9.0	NM- 9.2
1-Jeph Loeb scripts & Tim Sale-a in all (1st work together); Bolland-c						3.00
2-8: 2-Superman app. 3-Dr. Fate app. 6-G. Kane-c(p). 7-Steranko-c/swipe by Art Adams						2.50
... Must Die! (2004, $19.95, TPB) r/series; intro by Bendis; Sale sketch pages						20.00

NOTE: ***Art Adams*** *c-7.* ***Hempel*** *c-5.* ***Gil Kane*** *c-6p.* ***Sale*** *a-1-8; c-3, 8.* ***Wagner*** *c-4.*

CHALLENGERS OF THE UNKNOWN
DC Comics: Feb, 1997 - No. 18, July, 1998 ($2.25)

	GD 2.0	VG 4.0	FN 6.0	VF 8.0	VF/NM 9.0	NM- 9.2
1-18: 1-Intro new team; Leon-c/a(p) begins. 4-Origin of new team. 11,12-Batman app. 15-Millennium Giants x-over; Superman-c/app.						2.50

CHALLENGERS OF THE UNKNOWN
DC Comics: Aug, 2004 - No. 6, Jan, 2005 ($2.95, limited series)

	GD 2.0	VG 4.0	FN 6.0	VF 8.0	VF/NM 9.0	NM- 9.2
1-6-Intro. new team; Howard Chaykin-s/a						3.00

CHALLENGE TO THE WORLD
Catechetical Guild: 1951 (10¢, 36 pgs.)

	GD 2.0	VG 4.0	FN 6.0	VF 8.0	VF/NM 9.0	NM- 9.2
nn	5	10	15	24	30	35

CHAMBER (See Generation X and Uncanny X-Men)
Marvel Comics: Oct, 2002 - No. 4, Jan, 2003 ($2.99, limited series)

	GD 2.0	VG 4.0	FN 6.0	VF 8.0	VF/NM 9.0	NM- 9.2
1-4-Bachalo-c/Vaughan-s/Ferguson-a. 1-Cyclops app.						3.00

CHAMBER OF CHILLS (Formerly Blondie Comics #20; ...of Clues No. 27 on)
Harvey Publications/Witches Tales: No. 21, June, 1951 - No. 26, Dec, 1954

	GD 2.0	VG 4.0	FN 6.0	VF 8.0	VF/NM 9.0	NM- 9.2
21 (#1)	47	94	141	287	436	585
22,24 (#2,4)	32	64	96	184	267	350
23 (#3)-Excessive violence; eyes torn out	35	70	105	201	293	385
5(2/52)-Decapitation, acid in face scene	35	70	105	201	293	385
6-Woman melted alive	34	68	102	196	283	370
7-Used in **SOTI**, pg. 389; decapitation/severed head panels	32	64	96	184	267	350
8-10: 8-Decapitation panels	27	54	81	154	222	290
11,12,14	21	42	63	121	173	225
13,15-24-Nostrand-a in all. 13,21-Decapitation panels. 18-Atom bomb panels. 20-Nostrand-c	27	54	81	154	222	290
25,26	17	34	51	95	135	175

NOTE: *About half the issues contain bondage, torture, sadism, perversion, gore, cannabalism, eyes ripped out, acid in face, etc.* ***Elias*** *c-4-11, 14-19, 21-26.* ***Kremer*** *a-12, 17.* ***Palais*** *a-21(1), 23.* ***Nostrand/Powell*** *a-13, 15, 16.* ***Powell*** *a-21, 23, 24('51), 5-8, 11, 13, 18-21, 23-25. Bondage-c-21, 24('51), 7. 25-r/#5; 26-r/#9.*

CHAMBER OF CHILLS
Marvel Comics Group: Nov, 1972 - No. 25, Nov, 1976

	GD 2.0	VG 4.0	FN 6.0	VF 8.0	VF/NM 9.0	NM- 9.2
1-Harlan Ellison adaptation	3	6	9	19	25	32
2-5: 2-1st app. John Jakes (Brak the Barbarian)	2	4	6	10	13	16
6-25: 22,23-(Regular 25¢ editions)	2	4	6	8	10	12
22,23-(30¢-c variants, limited distribution)(5,7/76)	2	4	6	11	14	18

NOTE: ***Adkins*** *a-1i, 2i.* ***Brunner*** *a-2-4; c-4.* ***Chaykin*** *a-4.* ***Ditko*** *r-14, 16, 19, 23, 24.* ***Everett*** *a-3i, 11r,21r.* ***Heath*** *a-1r.* ***Gil Kane*** *c-2p.* ***Kirby*** *r-11, 18, 19, 22.* ***Powell*** *a-13r.* ***Russell*** *a-1p, 2p.* ***Shores*** *a-5 .* ***Williamson/Mayo*** *a-13r.* ***Robert E. Howard*** *horror story adaptation-2, 3.*

CHAMBER OF CLUES (Formerly Chamber of Chills)
Harvey Publications: No. 27, Feb, 1955 - No. 28, April, 1955

	GD 2.0	VG 4.0	FN 6.0	VF 8.0	VF/NM 9.0	NM- 9.2
27-Kerry Drake-r/#19; Powell-a; last pre-code	8	16	24	40	50	60
28-Kerry Drake	7	14	21	35	43	50

CHAMBER OF DARKNESS (Monsters on the Prowl #9 on)
Marvel Comics Group: Oct, 1969 - No. 8, Dec, 1970

	GD 2.0	VG 4.0	FN 6.0	VF 8.0	VF/NM 9.0	NM- 9.2
1-Buscema-a(p)	6	12	18	43	59	75
2,3: 2-Neal Adams scripts. 3-Smith, Buscema-a	4	8	12	22	30	38
4-A Conan-esque tryout by Smith (4/70); reprinted in Conan #16; Marie Severin/Everett-c	7	14	21	51	71	90
5,8: 5-H.P. Lovecraft adaptation. 8-Wrightson-c	3	6	9	18	24	30
6	3	6	9	16	20	25
7-Wrightson-c/a, 7pgs. (his 1st work at Marvel); Wrightson draws himself in 1st & last panels; Kirby/Ditko-r; last 15¢-c	4	8	12	28	38	48
1-(1/72; 25¢ Special, 52 pgs.)	4	8	12	22	30	38

NOTE: ***Adkins/Everett*** *a-8.* ***Buscema*** *a-Special 1r.* ***Craig*** *a-5.* ***Ditko*** *a-6-8r.* ***Heck*** *a-1, 2, 8, Special 1r.* ***Kirby*** *a(p)-4, 5, 7r.* ***Kirby/Everett*** *c-5.* ***Severin/Everett*** *c-6.* ***Shores*** *a-2, 3i, Special 1r.* ***Sutton*** *a-1, 2i, 4, 7, Special 1r.* ***Wrightson*** *c-7, 8.*

CHAMP COMICS (Formerly Champion No. 1-10)
Worth Publ. Co./Champ Publ./Family Comics(Harvey Publ.): No. 11, Oct, 1940 - No. 24, Dec, 1942; No. 25, April, 1943

	GD 2.0	VG 4.0	FN 6.0	VF 8.0	VF/NM 9.0	NM- 9.2
11-Human Meteor cont'd. from Champion	89	178	267	556	853	1150
12-17,20: 14,15-Crandall-c. 20-The Green Ghost app.	69	138	207	431	666	900
18,19-Simon-c. 19-The Wasp app.	85	170	255	531	816	1100
21-23,25: 22-The White Mask app. 23-Flag-c	52	104	156	317	484	650
24-Hitler, Tojo & Mussolini-c	60	120	180	375	575	775

CHAMPION (See Gene Autry's...)

CHAMPION COMICS (Formerly Speed Comics #1?; Champ Comics No. 11 on)
Worth Publ. Co.(Harvey Publications): No. 2, Dec, 1939 - No. 10, Aug, 1940 (no No.1)

2-The Champ, The Blazing Scarab, Neptina, Liberty Lads, Jungleman, Bill

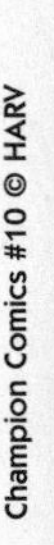
Champion Comics #10 © HARV

Chapel #1 © Awesome Ent.

Chase #9 © DC

GD VG FN VF VF/NM NM-
2.0 4.0 6.0 8.0 9.0 9.2

Handy, Swingtime Sweetie begin 177 354 531 1106 1703 2300
3-7: 7-The Human Meteor begins? 79 158 237 494 760 1025
8-10: 8-Simon-c. 9-1st S&K-c (1st collaboration together). 10-Bondage-c by
Kirby 142 284 426 888 1369 1850

CHAMPIONS, THE
Marvel Comics Group: Oct, 1975 - No. 17, Jan, 1978

1-Origin & 1st app. The Champions (The Angel, Black Widow, Ghost Rider, Hercules,
Iceman); Venus x-over 3 7 10 21 28 35
2-4,8-10,16: 2,3-Venus x-over 2 4 6 9 11 14
5-7-(Regular 25¢ edition)(4-8/76) 6-Kirby-c 2 4 6 9 11 14
5-7-(30¢-c variants, limited distribution) 2 4 6 12 16 20
11-14,17-Byrne-a. 14-(Regular 30¢ edition) 2 4 6 9 11 14
14,15-(35¢-c variant, limited distribution) 2 4 6 12 16 20
15-(Regular 30¢ edition)(9/77)-Byrne-a 2 4 6 9 11 14

NOTE: ***Buckler/Adkins** c-3. **Byrne** a-11-15, 17. **Kane/Adkins** c-1. **Kane/Layton** c-11. **Tuska** a-3p, 4p, 6p, 7p. Ghost Rider c-1-4, 7, 8, 10, 14, 16, 17 (4, 10, 14 are more prominent).*

CHAMPIONS (Game)
Eclipse Comics: June, 1986 - No. 6, Feb, 1987 (limited series)

1-6: 1-Intro Flare; based on game. 5-Origin Flare 2.50

CHAMPIONS (Also see The League of Champions)
Hero Comics: Sept, 1987 - No. 12, 1989 ($1.95)

1-12: 1-Intro The Marksman & The Rose. 14-Origin Malice 2.25
Annual 1(1988, $2.75, 52pgs.)-Origin of Giant 2.75

CHAMPION SPORTS
National Periodical Publications: Oct-Nov, 1973 - No. 3, Feb-Mar, 1974

1 3 6 9 18 24 30
2,3 2 4 6 10 12 15

CHANNEL ZERO
Image Comics: Feb, 1998 - No. 5 ($2.95, B&W, limited series)

1-5, ...Dupe (1/99) -Brian Wood-s/a 3.00

CHAOS (See The Crusaders)

CHAOS! BIBLE
Chaos! Comics: Nov, 1995 ($3.30, one-shot)

1-Profiles of characters & creators 3.50

CHAOS! CHRONICLES
Chaos! Comics: Feb, 2000 ($3.50, one-shot)

1-Profiles of characters, checklist of Chaos! comics and products 3.50

CHAOS EFFECT, THE
Valiant: 1994

Alpha (Giveaway w/trading card checklist) 2.25
Alpha-Gold variant, Alpha-Red variant, Omega-Gold variant 5.00
Omega (11/94, $2.25); Epilogue Pt. 1, 2 (12/94, 1/95; $2.95) 3.00

CHAOS! GALLERY
Chaos! Comics: Aug, 1997 ($2.95, one-shot)

1-Pin-ups of characters 3.00

CHAOS! QUARTERLY
Chaos! Comics: Oct, 1995 -No. 3, May, 1996 ($4.95, quarterly)

1-3: 1-anthology; Lady Death-c by Julie Bell. 2-Boris "Lady Demon"-c 5.00
1-Premium Edition (7,500) 25.00

CHAPEL (Also see Youngblood & Youngblood Strikefile #1-3)
Image Comics (Extreme Studios): No. 1 Feb, 1995 - No. 2, Mar, 1995 ($2.50, limited series)

1,2 2.50

CHAPEL (Also see Youngblood & Youngblood Strikefile #1-3)
Image Comics (Extreme Studios): V2 #1, Aug, 1995 - No. 7, Apr, 1996 ($2.50)

V2#1-7: 4-Babewatch x-over. 5-vs. Spawn. 7-Shadowhawk-c/app; Shadowhunt x-over 2.50
#1-Quesada & Palmiotti variant-c 2.50

CHAPEL (Also see Youngblood & Youngblood Strikefile #1-3)
Awesome Entertainment: Sept, 1997 ($2.99, one-shot)

1 (Reg. & alternate covers) 3.00

CHARLEMAGNE (Also see War Dancer)
Defiant Comics: Mar, 1994 - No. 5, July, 1994 ($2.50)

1/2 (Hero Illustrated giveaway)-Adam Pollina-c/a.
1-(3/94, $3.50, 52 pgs.)-Adam Pollina-c/a. 3.50
2,3,5: Adam Pollina-c/a. 2-War Dancer app. 5-Pre-Schism issue. 2.50
4-($3.25, 52 pgs.) 3.25

GD VG FN VF VF/NM NM-
2.0 4.0 6.0 8.0 9.0 9.2

CHARLIE CHAN (See Big Shot Comics, Columbia Comics, Feature Comics & The New Advs. of...)

CHARLIE CHAN (The Adventures of...) (Zaza The Mystic No. 10 on) (TV)
Crestwood(Prize) No. 1-5; Charlton No. 6(6/55) on: 6-7/48 - No. 5, 2-3/49; No.6, 6/55 - No. 9, 3/56

1-S&K-c, 2 pgs.; Infantino-a 79 158 237 494 760 1025
2-5-S&K-c: 3-S&K-c/a 50 100 150 305 465 625
6 (6/55-Charlton)-S&K-c 38 76 114 219 320 420
7-9 20 40 60 112 161 210

CHARLIE CHAN
Dell Publishing Co.: Oct-Dec, 1965 - No. 2, Mar, 1966

1-Springer-a 6 12 18 40 55 70
2 4 8 12 24 32 40

CHARLIE McCARTHY (See Edgar Bergen Presents...)
Dell Publishing Co.: No. 171, Nov, 1947 - No. 571, July, 1954 (See True Comics #14)

Four Color 171 28 56 84 199 305 410
Four Color 196-Part photo-c; photo back-c 18 36 54 129 197 265
1(3-5/49)-Part photo-c; photo back-c 16 32 48 112 171 230
2-9(7/52; #5,6-52 pgs.) 9 18 27 63 89 115
Four Color 445,478,527,571 6 12 18 43 59 75

CHARLTON BULLSEYE
CPL/Gang Publications: 1975 - No. 5, 1976 ($1.50, B&W, bi-monthly, magazine format)

1: 1 & 2 are last Capt. Atom by Ditko/Byrne intended for the never published
Capt. Atom #90; Nightshade app.; Jeff Jones-a 5 10 15 36 48 65
2-Part 2 Capt. Atom story by Ditko/Byrne 4 8 12 24 32 42
3-Wrong Country by Sanho Kim 2 4 6 12 16 22
4-Doomsday + 1 by John Byrne 3 6 9 18 24 32
5-Doomsday + 1 by Byrne, The Question by Toth; Neal Adams back-c; Toth-c
4 8 12 27 36 48

CHARLTON BULLSEYE
Charlton Publications: June, 1981 - No. 10, Dec, 1982; Nov, 1986

1-Blue Beetle, The Question app.; 1st app. Rocket Rabbit
1 2 3 5 7 9
2-5: 2-1st app. Neil The Horse; Rocket Rabbit app. 4-Vanguards 6.00
6-10: Low print run. 6-Origin & 1st app. Thunderbunny
1 2 3 5 7 9

NOTE: *Material intended for issue #11-up was published in **Scary Tales** #37-up.*

CHARLTON CLASSICS
Charlton Comics: Apr, 1980 - No. 9, Aug, 1981

1-Hercules-r by Glanzman in all 6.00
2-9 5.00

CHARLTON CLASSICS LIBRARY (1776)
Charlton Comics: V10 No.1, Mar, 1973 (one-shot)

1776 (title) - Adaptation of the film musical "1776"; given away at movie theatres;
also a newsstand version 2 4 6 14 18 22

CHARLTON PREMIERE (Formerly Marine War Heroes)
Charlton Comics: V1#19, July, 1967; V2#1, Sept, 1967 - No. 4, May, 1968

V1#19, V2#1,2,4: V1#19-Marine War Heroes. V2#1-Trio; intro. Shape, Tyro Team & Spookman.
2-Children of Doom; Boyette classic-a. 4-Unlikely Tales; Aparo, Ditko-a
3 6 9 18 23 28
V2#3-Sinistro Boy Fiend; Blue Beetle & Peacemaker x-over
3 7 10 21 28 35

CHARLTON SPORT LIBRARY - PROFESSIONAL FOOTBALL
Charlton Comics: Winter, 1969-70 (Jan. on cover) (68 pgs.)

1 4 8 12 24 32 40

CHARM SCHOOL (See Action Girl Comics #13)
Slave Labor Graphics: Apr, 2000 - Present ($2.95, B&W)

1-6-Elizabeth Watasin-s/a 3.00

CHASE (See Batman #550 for 1st app.)
DC Comics: Feb, 1998 - No. 9, Oct, 1998; #1,000,000 Nov, 1998 ($2.50)

1-9: Williams III & Gray-a. 1-Includes 4 Chase cards. 4-Teen Titans app. 7,8-Batman app.
9-GL Hal Jordan-c/app. 2.50
#1,000,000 (11/98) Final issue; 853rd Century x-over 2.50

CHASING DOGMA (See Jay and Silent Bob)

CHASSIS
Millenium Publications: 1996 - No. 3 ($2.95)

1-3: 1-Adam Hughes-c. 2-Conner var-c. 3.00

Chastity: Re-Imagined #1 © Chaos!

Cheryl Blossom #1 © AP

Child's Play 2 #1 © Universal

	GD 2.0	VG 4.0	FN 6.0	VF 8.0	VF/NM 9.0	NM- 9.2

CHASSIS
Hurricane Entertainment: 1998 - No. 3 ($2.95)

0,1-3: 1-Adam Hughes-c. 0-Green var-c. 3.00

CHASSIS (Vol. 3)
Image Comics: Nov, 1999 - No. 4 ($2.95, limited series)

1-4: 1-Two covers by O'Neil and Green. 2-Busch var-c. 3.00
1-($6.95) DF Edition alternate-c by Wieringo 7.00

CHASTITY
Chaos! Comics: (one-shots)

#1/2 (1/01, $2.95) Batista-a 3.00
Heartbreaker (3/02, $2.99) Adrian-a/Molenaar-c 3.00
Love Bites (3/01, $2.99) Vale-a/Romano-c 3.00
Reign of Terror 1 (10/00, $2.95) Grant-s/Ross-a/Rio-c 3.00
Re-Imagined 1 (7/02, $2.99) Conner-c; Toledo-a 3.00

CHASTITY: CRAZYTOWN
Chaos! Comics: Apr, 2002 - No. 3, June, 2002 ($2.99, limited series)

1-3-Nicieza-s/Batista-c/a 3.00

CHASTITY: LUST FOR LIFE
Chaos! Comics: May, 1999 - No. 3, July, 1999 ($2.95, limited series)

1-3-Nutman-s/Benes-c/a 3.00

CHASTITY: ROCKED
Chaos! Comics: Nov, 1998 - No. 4, Feb, 1999 ($2.95, limited series)

1-4-Nutman-s/Justiniano-c/a 3.00

CHASTITY: SHATTERED
Chaos! Comics: Jun, 2001 - No. 3, Sept, 2001 ($2.99, limited series)

1-3-Kaminski & Pulido-s/Batista-c/a 3.00

CHASTITY: THEATER OF PAIN
Chaos! Comics: Feb, 1997 - No. 3, June, 1997 ($2.95, limited series)

1-3-Pulido-s/Justiniano-c/a 3.00
TPB (1997, $9.95) r/#1-3 10.00

CHECKMATE (TV)
Gold Key: Oct, 1962 - No. 2, Dec, 1962

	GD	VG	FN	VF	VF/NM	NM-
1-Photo-c on both	7	14	21	46	63	80
2	6	12	18	40	55	70

CHECKMATE! (See Action Comics #598)
DC Comics: Apr, 1988 - No. 33, Jan, 1991 ($1.25)

1-33: 13: New format begins 2.50
NOTE: ***Gil Kane*** *c-2, 4, 7, 8, 10, 11, 15-19.*

CHERYL BLOSSOM (See Archie's Girls, Betty and Veronica #320 for 1st app.)
Archie Publications: Sept, 1995 - No. 3, Nov, 1995 ($1.50, limited series)

1-3 6.00
Special 1-4 ('95, '96, $2.00) 6.00

CHERYL BLOSSOM (Cheryl's Summer Job)
Archie Publications: July, 1996 - No. 3, Sept, 1996 ($1.50, limited series)

1-3 4.50

CHERYL BLOSSOM (...Goes Hollywood)
Archie Publications: Dec, 1996 - No. 3, Feb, 1997 ($1.50, limited series)

1-3 4.00

CHERYL BLOSSOM
Archie Publications: Apr, 1997 - No. 37, Mar, 2001 ($1.50/$1.75/$1.79/$1.99)

1-Dan DeCarlo-c/a 6.00
2-10: 2-7-Dan DeCarlo-c/a 3.50
11-37: 32-Begin $1.99-c. 34-Sabrina app. 2.25

CHESTY SANCHEZ
Antarctic Press: Nov, 1995 - No. 2, Mar, 1996 ($2.95, B&W)

1,2 3.00
...Super Special (2/99, $5.99) 6.00

CHEVAL NOIR
Dark Horse Comics: 1989 - No. 48, Nov, 1993 ($3.50, B&W, 68 pgs.)

1-8,10 ($3.50): 6-Moebius poster insert 3.50
9,11,13,15,17,20,22 ($4.50, 84 pgs.) 4.50
12,18,19,21,23,25,26 ($3.95): 12-Geary-a; Mignola-c. 26-Moebius-a begins 4.00
14 ($4.95, 76 pgs.)(7 pgs. color) 5.00
16,24 ($3.75): 16-19-Contain trading cards 3.75
27-48 ($2.95): 33-Snyder III-c 3.00
NOTE: ***Bolland*** *a-2, 6, 7, 13, 14.* ***Bolton*** *a-2, 4, 45; c-4, 20.* ***Chadwick*** *c-13.* ***Dorman*** *painted c-16.* ***Geary*** *a-13, 14.* ***Kelley Jones*** *c-27.* ***Kaluta*** *a-6; c-6, 18.* ***Moebius*** *c-5, 9, 26.* ***Dave Stevens*** *c-1, 7.* ***Sutton*** *painted c-36.*

CHEYENNE (TV)
Dell Publishing Co.: No. 734, Oct, 1956 - No. 25, Dec-Jan, 1961-62

	GD	VG	FN	VF	VF/NM	NM-
Four Color 734(#1)-Clint Walker photo-c	18	36	54	126	193	260
Four Color 772,803: Clint Walker photo-c	10	20	30	67	96	125
4(8-10/57) - 20: 4-9,13-20-Clint Walker photo-c. 10-12-Ty Hardin photo-c	7	14	21	46	63	80
21-25-Clint Walker photo-c on all	7	14	21	50	68	85

CHEYENNE AUTUMN (See Movie Classics)

CHEYENNE KID (Formerly Wild Frontier No. 1-7)
Charlton Comics: No. 8, July, 1957 - No. 99, Nov, 1973

	GD	VG	FN	VF	VF/NM	NM-
8 (#1)	8	16	24	43	54	65
9,15-19	6	12	18	29	36	42
10-Williamson/Torres-a(3); Ditko-c	11	22	33	62	84	105
11-(68 pgs.)-Cheyenne Kid meets Geronimo	10	20	30	60	80	100
12-Williamson/Torres-a(2)	10	20	30	60	80	100
13-Williamson/Torres-a (5 pgs.)	8	16	24	46	58	70
14-Williamson-a (5 pgs.?)	8	16	24	43	54	65
20-22,24,25-Severin c/a(3) each	4	8	12	25	33	42
23,27-29	3	6	9	16	20	25
26,30-Severin-a	3	6	9	19	25	32
31-59	2	4	6	10	13	16
60-65,67-80	2	4	6	8	10	12
66-Wander by Aparo begins, ends #87	2	4	6	9	11	14
81-99: Apache Red begins #88, origin in #89	1	2	3	5	7	9
Modern Comics Reprint 87,89(1978)						4.00

CHIAROSCURO (THE PRIVATE LIVES OF LEONARDO DA VINCI)
DC Comics (Vertigo): July, 1995 - No. 10, Apr, 1996 ($2.50/$2.95, limited series, mature)

1-9 2.50
10-($2.95) 3.00

CHICAGO MAIL ORDER (See C-M-O Comics)

CHI-CHIAN
Sirius Entertainment: 1997 - No. 6, 1998 ($2.95, limited series)

1-6-Voltaire-s/a 3.00

CHIEF, THE (Indian Chief No. 3 on)
Dell Publishing Co.: No. 290, Aug, 1950 - No. 2, Apr-June, 1951

	GD	VG	FN	VF	VF/NM	NM-
Four Color 290(#1)	7	14	21	51	71	90
2	6	12	18	43	59	75

CHIEF CRAZY HORSE (See Wild Bill Hickok #21)
Avon Periodicals: 1950 (Also see Fighting Indians of the Wild West!)

	GD	VG	FN	VF	VF/NM	NM-
nn-Fawcette-c	21	42	63	118	169	220

CHIEF VICTORIO'S APACHE MASSACRE (See Fight Indians of/Wild West!)
Avon Periodicals: 1951

	GD	VG	FN	VF	VF/NM	NM-
nn-Williamson/Frazetta-a (7 pgs.); Larsen-a; Kinstler-c	44	88	132	268	409	550

CHILDHOOD'S END
Image Comics: Oct, 1997 ($2.95, B&W)

1-Bourne-s/Calafiore-a 3.00

CHILDREN OF FIRE
Fantagor Press: Nov, 1987 - No. 3, 1988 ($2.00, limited series)

1-3: by Richard Corben 4.00

CHILDREN OF THE VOYAGER (See Marvel Frontier Comics Unlimited)
Marvel Frontier Comics: Sept, 1993 - No. 4, Dec, 1993 ($1.95, limited series)

1-($2.95)-Embossed glow-in-the-dark-c; Paul Johnson-c/a 3.00
2-4 2.25

CHILDREN'S BIG BOOK
Dorene Publ. Co.: 1945 (25¢, stiff-c, 68 pgs.)

	GD	VG	FN	VF	VF/NM	NM-
nn-Comics & fairy tales; David Icove-a	12	24	36	71	98	125

CHILDREN'S CRUSADE, THE
DC Comics (Vertigo): Dec, 1993 - No. 2, Jan, 1994 ($3.95, limited series)

1,2-Neil Gaiman scripts & Chris Bachalo-a; framing issues for Children's Crusade x-over 4.00

CHILD'S PLAY: THE SERIES (Movie)
Innovation Publishing: May, 1991 - #3, 1991 ($2.50, 28pgs.)

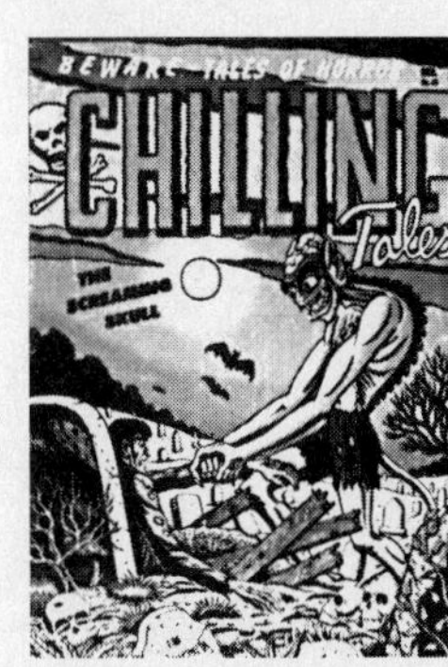

Chilling Tales #13 © YM

C.H.I.X. #1 © Studiosaurus

Chosen #1 © Mark Millar

GD VG FN VF VF/NM NM-
2.0 4.0 6.0 8.0 9.0 9.2

1-3 2.50

CHILD'S PLAY 2 THE OFFICIAL MOVIE ADAPTATION (Movie)
Innovation Publishing: 1990 - No. 3, 1990 ($2.50, bi-weekly limited series)
1-3: Adapts movie sequel 2.50

CHILI (Millie's Rival)
Marvel Comics Group: 5/69 - No. 17, 9/70; No. 18, 8/72 - No. 26, 12/73
1 7 14 21 51 71 90
2,4,5 4 8 12 27 36 45
3-Millie & Chili visit Marvel and meet Stan Lee & Stan Goldberg (6 pgs.)
4 8 12 29 40 50
6-17 3 6 9 19 25 32
18-26 3 6 9 16 20 25
Special 1(12/71, 52 pgs.) 4 8 12 29 40 50

CHILLER
Marvel Comics (Epic): Nov, 1993 - No. 2, Dec, 1993 ($7.95, lim. series)
1,2-(68 pgs.) 1 2 3 5 6 8

CHILLING ADVENTURES IN SORCERY (...as Told by Sabrina #1, 2)
(Red Circle Sorcery No. 6 on)
Archie Publications (Red Circle Productions): 9/72 - No. 2, 10/72; No. 3, 10/73 - No. 5, 2/74
1-Sabrina cameo as narrator 5 10 15 33 44 55
2-Sabrina cameo as narrator 3 6 9 18 23 28
3-5: Morrow-c/a, all. 4,5-Alcazar-a 2 4 6 10 13 16

CHILLING TALES (Formerly Beware)
Youthful Magazines: No. 13, Dec, 1952 - No. 17, Oct, 1953
13(No.1)-Harrison-a; Matt Fox-c/a 60 120 180 375 575 775
14-Harrison-a 40 80 120 240 363 485
15-Has #14 on-c; Matt Fox-c; Harrison-a 48 96 144 293 447 600
16-Poe adapt.-'Metzengerstein'; Rudyard Kipling adapt.- 'Mark of the Beast,'
by Kiefer; bondage-c 37 74 111 209 305 400
17-Matt Fox-c; Sir Walter Scott & Poe adapt. 40 80 120 244 372 500

CHILLING TALES OF HORROR (Magazine)
Stanley Publications: V1#1, 6/69 - V1#7, 12/70; V2#2, 2/71 - V2#6, 10/71(50¢, B&W, 52 pgs.)
V1#1 6 12 18 40 55 70
2-4,(no #5),6,7: 7-Cameron-a 4 8 12 27 36 45
V2#2-6: 2-Two different #2 issues exist (2/71 & 4/71). 2-(2/71) Spirit of Frankenstein -r/Adventures into the Unknown #16. 4-(8/71) different from other V2#4(6/71)
4 8 12 24 32 40
V2#4-(6/71) r/9 pg. Feldstein-a from Adventures into the Unknown #3
4 8 12 27 36 45
NOTE: *Two issues of V2#2 exist, Feb, 1971 and April, 1971. Two issues of V2#4 exist, Jun, 1971 and Aug, 1971.*

CHILLY WILLY (Also see New Funnies #211)
Dell Publ. Co.: No. 740, Oct, 1956 - No. 1281, Apr-June, 1962 (Walter Lantz)
Four Color 740 (#1) 7 14 21 50 68 85
Four Color 852 (2/58),967 (2/59),1017 (9/59),1074 (2-4/60),1122 (8/60),
1177 (4-6/61), 1212 (7-9/61), 1281 5 10 15 33 44 55

CHIMERA
CrossGeneration Comics: Mar, 2003 - No. 4, July, 2003 ($2.95, limited series)
1-4-Marz-s/Peterson-c/a 3.00
Vol. 1 TPB (2003, $15.95) r/#1-4 plus sketch pages, 3-D models, how-to guides 16.00

CHINA BOY (See Wisco in the Promotional Comics section)

CHIP 'N' DALE (Walt Disney)(See Walt Disney's C&S #204)
Dell Publishing Co./Gold Key/Whitman No. 65 on: Nov, 1953 - No. 30, June-Aug, 1962; Sept, 1967 - No. 83, July, 1984
Four Color 517(#1) 11 22 33 80 120 160
Four Color 581,636 7 14 21 46 63 80
4(12/55-2/56)-10 6 12 18 40 55 70
11-30 5 10 15 33 44 55
1(Gold Key, 1967)-Reprints 3 7 10 21 28 35
2-10 2 4 6 11 14 18
11-20 2 4 6 8 10 12
21-40 1 2 3 5 7 9
41-64,70-77: 75(2/82), 76(2-3/82), 77(3/82) 1 2 3 4 5 7
65,66 (Whitman) 1 3 4 6 8 10
67-69 (3-pack? 1980): 67(8/80), 68(10/80) (scarce) 3 6 9 16 20 25
78-83 (All #90214; 3-pack, nd, nd code): 78(4/83), 79(5/83), 80(7/83), 81(8/83),
82(5/84), 83(7/84) 2 4 6 10 13 16
NOTE: *All Gold Key/Whitman issues have reprints except No. 32-35, 38-41, 45-47. No. 23-28, 30-42, 45-47, 49 have new covers.*

CHIP 'N DALE RESCUE RANGERS
Disney Comics: June, 1990 - No. 19, Dec, 1991 ($1.50)
1-New stories; origin begins 3.00
2-19: 2-Origin continued 2.50

CHITTY CHITTY BANG BANG (See Movie Comics)

C.H.I.X.
Image Comics (Studiosaurus): Jan, 1998 ($2.50)
1-Dodson, Haley, Lopresti, Randall, and Warren-s/c/a 3.00
1-($5.00) "X-Ray Variant" cover 5.00
C.H.I.X. That Time Forgot 1 (8/98, $2.95) 3.00

CHOICE COMICS
Great Publications: Dec, 1941 - No. 3, Feb, 1942
1-Origin Secret Circle; Atlas the Mighty app.; Zomba, Jungle Fight,
Kangaroo Man, & Fire Eater begin 162 324 486 1013 1557 2100
2 85 170 255 531 816 1100
3-Double feature; Features movie "The Lost City" (classic cover); continued
from Great Comics #3 123 246 369 769 1185 1600

CHOLLY AND FLYTRAP (Arthur Suydam's...)
Image Comics: Nov, 2004 - No. 3 ($4.95, limited series)
1-Arthur Suydam-s/a/c 5.00

CHOO CHOO CHARLIE
Gold Key: Dec, 1969
1-John Stanley-a 10 20 30 73 107 140

CHOSEN
Dark Horse Comics: Jan, 2004 - No. 3, Aug, 2004 ($2.99, limited series)
1-3-Story of the second coming; Mark Millar-s/Peter Gross-a 3.00

CHRISTIAN (See Asylum)
Maximum Press: Jan, 1996 ($2.99, one-shot)
1-Pop Mhan-a 3.00

CHRISTIAN HEROES OF TODAY
David C. Cook: 1964 (36 pgs.)
nn 3 6 9 16 20 24

CHRISTMAS (Also see A-1 Comics)
Magazine Enterprises: No. 28, 1950
A-1 28 7 14 21 35 43 50

CHRISTMAS ADVENTURE, A (See Classics Comics Giveaways, 12/69)

CHRISTMAS ALBUM (See March of Comics No. 312)

CHRISTMAS ANNUAL
Golden Special: 1975 ($1.95, 100 pgs., stiff-c)
nn-Reprints Mother Goose stories with Walt Kelly-a 4 8 12 24 32 42

CHRISTMAS & ARCHIE
Archie Comics: Jan, 1975 ($1.00, 68 pgs., 10-1/4x13-1/4" treasury-sized)
1-(scarce) 6 12 18 40 55 70

CHRISTMAS BELLS (See March of Comics No. 297)

CHRISTMAS CARNIVAL
Ziff-Davis Publ. Co./St. John Publ. Co. No. 2: 1952 (25¢, one-shot, 100 pgs.)
nn 35 70 105 200 290 380
2-Reprints Ziff-Davis issue plus-c 18 36 54 100 143 185

CHRISTMAS CAROL, A (See March of Comics No. 33)

CHRISTMAS EVE, A (See March of Comics No. 212)

CHRISTMAS IN DISNEYLAND (See Dell Giants)

CHRISTMAS PARADE (See Dell Giant No. 26, Dell Giants, March of Comics No. 284, Walt Disney Christmas Parade & Walt Disney's...)

CHRISTMAS PARADE (Walt Disney's)
Gold Key: 1962 (no month listed) - No. 9, Jan, 1972 (#1,5: 80 pgs.; #2-4,7-9: 36 pgs.)
1 (30018-301)-Giant 10 20 30 70 100 130
2-6: 2-r/F.C. #367 by Barks. 3-r/F.C. #178 by Barks. 4-r/F.C. #203 by Barks. 5-r/Christmas Parade #1 (Dell) by Barks; giant. 6-r/Christmas Parade #2 (Dell) by Barks (64 pgs.); giant
8 16 24 53 74 95
7-Pull-out poster (half price w/o poster) 6 12 18 40 55 70
8-r/F.C. #367 by Barks; pull-out poster 8 16 24 53 74 95
9 5 10 15 33 44 55

CHRISTMAS PARTY (See March of Comics No. 256)

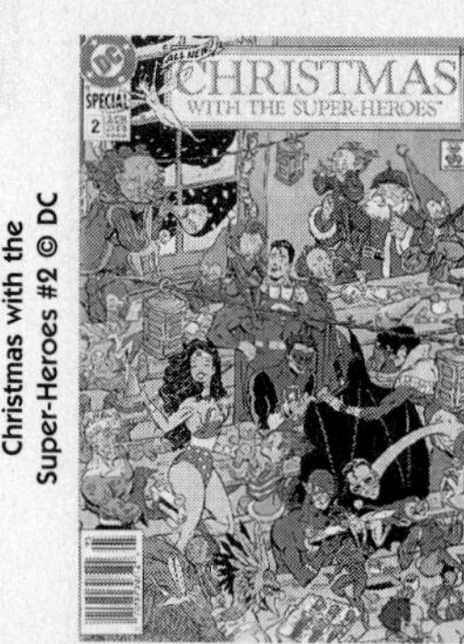

Christmas with the Super-Heroes #2 © DC

Chronos #4 © DC

Cinderella Love #29 © STJ

CHRISTMAS STORIES (See Little People No. 959, 1062)

CHRISTMAS STORY (See March of Comics No. 326 in the Promotional Comics section)

CHRISTMAS STORY BOOK (See Woolworth's Christmas Story Book)

CHRISTMAS TREASURY, A (See Dell Giants & March of Comics No. 227)

CHRISTMAS WITH ARCHIE
Spire Christian Comics (Fleming H. Revell Co.): 1973, 1974 (49¢, 52 pgs.)

	GD 2.0	VG 4.0	FN 6.0	VF 8.0	VF/NM 9.0	NM- 9.2
nn-Low print run	2	4	6	11	14	18

CHRISTMAS WITH MOTHER GOOSE
Dell Publishing Co.: No. 90, Nov, 1945 - No. 253, Nov, 1949

	GD 2.0	VG 4.0	FN 6.0	VF 8.0	VF/NM 9.0	NM- 9.2
Four Color 90 (#1)-Kelly-a	19	38	57	134	205	275
Four Color 126 ('46), 172 (11/47)-By Walt Kelly	14	28	42	102	156	210
Four Color 201 (10/48), 253-By Walt Kelly	13	26	39	90	138	185

CHRISTMAS WITH SANTA (See March of Comics No. 92)

CHRISTMAS WITH THE SUPER-HEROES (See Limited Collectors' Edition)
DC Comics: 1988; No. 2, 1989 ($2.95)

	GD 2.0	VG 4.0	FN 6.0	VF 8.0	VF/NM 9.0	NM- 9.2
1,2: 1-(100 pgs.)-All reprints; N. Adams-r, Byrne-c; Batman, Superman, JLA, LSH Christmas stories; r-Miller's 1st Batman/DC Special Series #21. 2-(68 pgs.)-Superman by Chadwick; Batman, Wonder Woman, Deadman, Green Lantern, Flash app.; Morrow-a; Enemy Ace by Byrne; all new-a						5.00

CHROMA-TICK, THE (...Special Edition, #1,2) (Also see The Tick)
New England Comics Press: Feb, 1992 - No. 8, Nov, 1993 ($3.95/$3.50, 44 pgs.)

	GD 2.0	VG 4.0	FN 6.0	VF 8.0	VF/NM 9.0	NM- 9.2
1,2-Includes serially numbered trading card set						5.00
3-8 ($3.50, 36 pgs.): 6-Bound-in card						4.00

CHROME
Hot Comics: 1986 - No. 3, 1986 ($1.50, limited series)

	GD 2.0	VG 4.0	FN 6.0	VF 8.0	VF/NM 9.0	NM- 9.2
1-3						2.25

CHROMIUM MAN, THE
Triumphant Comics: Aug, 1993 - No.10, May, 1994 ($2.50)

	GD 2.0	VG 4.0	FN 6.0	VF 8.0	VF/NM 9.0	NM- 9.2
1-1st app. Mr. Death; all serially numbered						2.50
2-10: 2-1st app. Prince Vandal. 3-1st app. Candi, Breaker & Coil. 4,5-Triumphant Unleashed x-over. 8,9-(3/94). 10-(5/94)						2.50
0-(4/94)-Four color-c, 0-All pink-c & all blue-c; no cover price						2.50

CHROMIUM MAN: VIOLENT PAST, THE
Triumphant Comics: Jan, 1994 - No. 2, Jan, 1994 ($2.50, limited series)

	GD 2.0	VG 4.0	FN 6.0	VF 8.0	VF/NM 9.0	NM- 9.2
1,2-Serially numbered to 22,000 each						2.50

CHRONICLES OF CONAN, THE (See Conan the Barbarian)

CHRONICLES OF CORUM, THE (Also see Corum...)
First Comics: Jan, 1987 - No. 12, Nov, 1988 ($1.75/$1.95, deluxe series)

	GD 2.0	VG 4.0	FN 6.0	VF 8.0	VF/NM 9.0	NM- 9.2
1-12: Adapts Michael Moorcock's novel						2.50

CHRONO MECHANICS
Image Comics: Oct, 2004 ($6.95, B&W, graphic novel)

	GD 2.0	VG 4.0	FN 6.0	VF 8.0	VF/NM 9.0	NM- 9.2
1-Art Thibert-s/a						7.00

CHRONOS
DC Comics: Mar, 1998 - No. 11, Feb. 1999 ($2.50)

	GD 2.0	VG 4.0	FN 6.0	VF 8.0	VF/NM 9.0	NM- 9.2
1-11-J.F. Moore-s/Guinan-a						2.50
#1,000,000 (11/98) 853rd Century x-over						2.50

CHRONOWAR (Manga)
Dark Horse Comics: Aug, 1996 - No. 9, Apr, 1997 ($2.95, limited series)

	GD 2.0	VG 4.0	FN 6.0	VF 8.0	VF/NM 9.0	NM- 9.2
1-9						3.00

CHUCKLE, THE GIGGLY BOOK OF COMIC ANIMALS
R. B. Leffingwell Co.: 1945 (132 pgs., one-shot)

	GD 2.0	VG 4.0	FN 6.0	VF 8.0	VF/NM 9.0	NM- 9.2
1-Funny animal	22	44	66	123	177	230

CHUCK NORRIS (TV)
Marvel Comics (Star Comics): Jan, 1987 - No. 4, July, 1987

	GD 2.0	VG 4.0	FN 6.0	VF 8.0	VF/NM 9.0	NM- 9.2
1-3: Ditko-a						3.50
4-No Ditko-a (low print run)						5.00

CHUCK WAGON (See Sheriff Bob Dixon's...)

CHYNA (WWF Wrestling)
Chaos! Comics: Sept, 2000; July, 2001 ($2.95/$2.99, one-shots)

	GD 2.0	VG 4.0	FN 6.0	VF 8.0	VF/NM 9.0	NM- 9.2
1-Grant-s/Barrows-a; photo-c						3.00
1-($9.95) Premium Edition; Cleavenger-c						10.00
II -(7/01, $2.99) Deodato-a; photo-c						3.00

CICERO'S CAT
Dell Publishing Co.: July-Aug, 1959 - No. 2, Sept-Oct, 1959

	GD 2.0	VG 4.0	FN 6.0	VF 8.0	VF/NM 9.0	NM- 9.2
1-Cat from Mutt & Jeff	6	12	18	38	52	65
2	5	10	15	33	44	55

CIMARRON STRIP (TV)
Dell Publishing Co.: Jan, 1968

	GD 2.0	VG 4.0	FN 6.0	VF 8.0	VF/NM 9.0	NM- 9.2
1-Stuart Whitman photo-c	4	8	12	29	40	50

CINDER AND ASHE
DC Comics: May, 1988 - No. 4, Aug, 1988 ($1.75, limited series)

	GD 2.0	VG 4.0	FN 6.0	VF 8.0	VF/NM 9.0	NM- 9.2
1-4: Mature readers						2.25

CINDERELLA (Disney) (See Movie Comics)
Dell Publishing Co.: No. 272, Apr, 1950 - No. 786, Apr, 1957

	GD 2.0	VG 4.0	FN 6.0	VF 8.0	VF/NM 9.0	NM- 9.2
Four Color 272	13	26	39	90	138	185
Four Color 786-Partial-r 272	8	16	24	55	78	100

CINDERELLA
Whitman Publishing Co.: Apr, 1982

	GD 2.0	VG 4.0	FN 6.0	VF 8.0	VF/NM 9.0	NM- 9.2
nn-Reprints 4-Color #272	1	2	3	4	5	7

CINDERELLA LOVE
Ziff-Davis/St. John Publ. Co. No. 12 on: No. 10, 1950; No. 11, 4-5/51; No. 12, 9/51; No. 4, 10-11/51 - No. 11, Fall, 1952; No. 12, 10/53 - No. 15, 8/54; No. 25, 12/54 - No. 29, 10/55 (No #16-24)

	GD 2.0	VG 4.0	FN 6.0	VF 8.0	VF/NM 9.0	NM- 9.2
10(#1)(1st Series, 1950)-Painted-c	15	30	45	86	123	160
11(#2, 4-5/51)-Crandall-a; Saunders painted-c	10	20	30	58	77	95
12(#3, 9/51)-Photo-c	9	18	27	51	62	75
4-8: 4,6,7-Photo-c	8	16	24	43	54	65
9-Kinstler-a; photo-c	9	18	27	52	66	80
10,11(Fall/'52), 14: 10,11-Photo-c. 14-Baker-a	9	18	27	51	62	75
12(St. John-10/53)-#13:13-Painted-c.	8	16	24	40	50	60
15(8/54)-Matt Baker-c	9	18	27	54	70	85
25(2nd Series)(Formerly Romantic Marriage) Baker-c	8	16	24	40	50	60
26-Baker-c; last precode (2/55)	9	18	27	54	70	85
27,29: Both Matt Baker-c	9	18	27	54	70	85
28	7	14	21	35	43	50

CINDY COMICS (...Smith No. 39, 40; Crime Can't Win No. 41 on)(Formerly Krazy Komics) (See Junior Miss & Teen Comics)
Timely Comics: No. 27, Fall, 1947 - No. 40, July, 1950

	GD 2.0	VG 4.0	FN 6.0	VF 8.0	VF/NM 9.0	NM- 9.2
27-Kurtzman-a, 3 pgs: Margie, Oscar begin	22	44	66	123	177	230
28-31-Kurtzman-a	13	26	39	76	106	135
32-40: 33-Georgie story; anti-Wertham editorial	10	20	30	56	73	90

NOTE: *Kurtzman's "Hey Look"-#27(3), 29(2), 30(2), 31; "Giggles 'n' Grins"-28.*

CINNAMON: EL CICLO
DC Comics: Oct, 2003 - No. 5, Feb, 2004 ($2.50, limited series)

	GD 2.0	VG 4.0	FN 6.0	VF 8.0	VF/NM 9.0	NM- 9.2
1-5-Van Meter-s/Chaykin-c/Paronzini-a						2.50

CIRCUS (...the Comic Riot)
Globe Syndicate: June, 1938 - No. 3, Aug, 1938

	GD 2.0	VG 4.0	FN 6.0	VF 8.0	VF/NM 9.0	NM- 9.2
1-(Scarce)-Spacehawks (2 pgs.), & Disk Eyes by Wolverton (2 pgs.), Pewee Throttle by Cole (2nd comic book work; see Star Comics V1#11), Beau Gus, Ken Craig & The Lords of Crillon, Jack Hinton by Eisner, Van Bragger by Kane	800	1600	2400	4800	6800	8800
2,3-(Scarce)-Eisner, Cole, Wolverton, Bob Kane-a in each	400	800	1200	2400	3400	4400

CIRCUS BOY (TV) (See Movie Classics)
Dell Publishing Co.: No. 759, Dec, 1956 - No. 813, July, 1957

	GD 2.0	VG 4.0	FN 6.0	VF 8.0	VF/NM 9.0	NM- 9.2
Four Color 759 (#1)-The Monkees' Mickey Dolenz photo-c	14	28	42	102	156	210
Four Color 785 (4/57),813-Mickey Dolenz photo-c	12	24	36	84	127	170

CIRCUS COMICS
Farm Women's Pub. Co./D. S. Publ.: 1945 - No. 2, Jun, 1945; Wint., 1948-49

	GD 2.0	VG 4.0	FN 6.0	VF 8.0	VF/NM 9.0	NM- 9.2
1-Funny animal	13	26	39	76	106	135
2	9	18	27	52	66	80
1(1948)-D.S. Publ.; 2 pgs. Frazetta	25	50	75	141	203	265

CIRCUS OF FUN COMICS
A. W. Nugent Publ. Co.: 1945 - No. 3, Dec, 1947 (A book of games & puzzles)

	GD 2.0	VG 4.0	FN 6.0	VF 8.0	VF/NM 9.0	NM- 9.2
1	15	30	45	83	117	150
2,3	9	18	27	54	70	85

CISCO KID, THE (TV)
Dell Publishing Co.: July, 1950 - No. 41, Oct-Dec, 1958

The Cisco Kid #4 © DELL

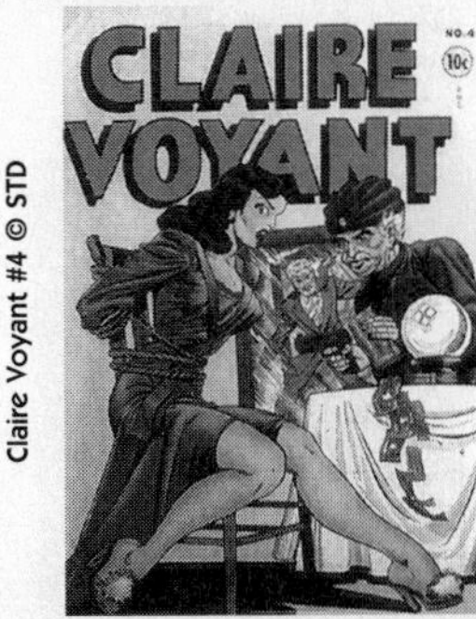

Claire Voyant #4 © STD

Clandestine #6 © MAR

	GD 2.0	VG 4.0	FN 6.0	VF 8.0	VF/NM 9.0	NM- 9.2
Four Color 292(#1)-Cisco Kid, his horse Diablo, & sidekick Pancho & his horse Loco begin; painted-c begin	26	52	78	189	290	390
2(1/51)	12	24	36	87	134	180
3-5	11	22	33	80	120	160
6-10	10	20	30	67	96	125
11-20	9	18	27	60	85	110
21-36-Last painted-c	7	14	21	51	71	90
37-41: All photo-c	10	20	30	73	107	140

NOTE: ***Buscema** a-40. **Ernest Nordli** painted c-5-16, 20, 35.*

CISCO KID COMICS
Bernard Bailey/Swappers Quarterly: Winter, 1944 (one-shot)

	GD	VG	FN	VF	VF/NM	NM-
1-Illustrated Stories of the Operas: Faust; Funnyman by Giunta; Cisco Kid (1st app.) & Superbaby begin; Giunta-c	43	86	129	262	401	540

CITIZEN SMITH (See Holyoke One-Shot No. 9)

CITIZEN V AND THE V-BATTALION (See Thunderbolts)
Marvel Comics: June, 2001 - No. 3, Aug, 2001 ($2.99, limited series)

1-3-Nicieza-a; Michael Ryan-c/a — 3.00
...: The Everlasting 1-4 (3/02 - No. 4, 7/02) Nicieza-s/LaRosa-a(p) — 3.00

CITY OF HEROES (Online game)
Dark Horse Comics/Blue King Studios: Sept, 2002; May, 2004 - Present ($2.95)

1-(no cover price) Dakan-s/Zombo-a — 2.25
1-7-($2.95) — 3.00

CITY OF SILENCE
Image Comics: May, 2000 - No. 3, July, 2000 ($2.50)

1-3-Ellis-s/Erskine-a — 2.50
TPB (6/04, $9.95) r/#1-3; pin-up gallery — 10.00

CITY OF THE LIVING DEAD (See Fantastic Tales No. 1)
Avon Periodicals: 1952

	GD	VG	FN	VF	VF/NM	NM-
nn-Hollingsworth-c/a	47	94	141	287	436	585

CITY PEOPLE NOTEBOOK
Kitchen Sink Press: 1989 ($9.95, B&W, magazine sized)

nn-Will Eisner-s/a — 10.00
nn-(DC Comics, 2000) Reprint — 10.00

CITY SURGEON (Blake Harper...)
Gold Key: August, 1963

	GD	VG	FN	VF	VF/NM	NM-
1(10075-308)-Painted-c	4	8	12	28	38	48

CIVIL WAR MUSKET, THE (Kadets of America Handbook)
Custom Comics, Inc.: 1960 (25¢, half-size, 36 pgs.)

	GD	VG	FN	VF	VF/NM	NM-
nn	3	6	9	18	23	28

CLAIRE VOYANT (Also see Keen Teens)
Leader Publ./Standard/Pentagon Publ.: 1946 - No. 4, 1947 (Sparling strip reprints)

	GD	VG	FN	VF	VF/NM	NM-
nn	62	124	186	388	594	800
2,4: 2-Kamen-c. 4-Kamen bondage-c	48	96	144	293	447	600
3-Kamen bridal-c; contents mentioned in Love and Death, a book by Gershom Legman(1949) referenced by Dr. Wertham in **SOTI**	55	110	165	340	520	700

CLANDESTINE (Also see Marvel Comics Presents & X-Men: ClanDestine)
Marvel Comics: Oct, 1994 - No.12, Sept, 1995 ($2.95/$2.50)

1-($2.95)-Alan Davis-c/a(p)/scripts & Mark Farmer-c/a(i) begin, ends #8; Modok app.; Silver Surfer cameo; gold foil-c — 3.00
2-12: 2-Wraparound-c. 2,3-Silver Surfer app. 5-Origin of ClanDestine. 6-Capt. America, Hulk, Spider-Man, Thing & Thor-c; Spider-Man cameo. 7-Spider-Man-c/app; Punisher cameo. 8-Invaders & Dr. Strange app. 10-Captain Britain-c/app. 11-Sub-Mariner app. — 2.50
Preview (10/94, $1.50) — 2.50

CLASH
DC Comics: 1991 - No. 3, 1991 ($4.95, limited series, 52 pgs.)

Book One - Three: Adam Kubert-c/a — 5.00

CLASSIC COMICS/ILLUSTRATED - INTRODUCTION
by Dan Malan

Since the first publication of this special introduction to the **Classics** section, a number of revisions have been made to further clarify the listings. **Classics** reprint editions prior to 1963 had either incorrect dates or no dates listed. Those reprint editions should be identified only by the highest number on the reorder list (HRN). Past *Guides* listed what were calculated to be approximately correct dates, but many people found it confusing for the *Guide* to list a date not listed in the comic itself.

We have also attempted to clear up confusion about edition variations, such as color, printer, etc. Such variations are identified by letters. Editions are determined by three categories. Original edition variations are designated as Edition 1A, 1B, etc. All reprint editions prior to 1963 are identified by HRN only. All reprint editions from 9/63 on are identified by the correct date listed in the comic.

Information is also included on four reprintings of **Classics**. From 1968-1976, Twin Circle, the Catholic newspaper, serialized over 100 **Classics** titles. That list can be found under non-series items at the end of this section. In 1972, twelve **Classics** were reissued as **Now Age Books Illustrated**. They are listed under **Pendulum Illustrated Classics**. In 1982, 20 **Classics** were reissued, adapted for teaching English as a second language. They are listed under **Regents Illustrated Classics**. Then in 1984, six **Classics** were reissued with cassette tapes. See the listing under **Cassette Books**.

UNDERSTANDING CLASSICS ILLUSTRATED
by Dan Malan

Since **Classics Illustrated** is the most complicated comic book series, with all its reprint editions and variations, changes in covers and artwork, a variety of means of identifying editions, and the most extensive worldwide distribution of any comic-book series, this introductory section is provided to assist you in gaining expertise about this series.

THE HISTORY OF CLASSICS
The **Classics** series was the brain child of Albert L. Kanter, who saw in the new comic-book medium a means of introducing children to the great classics of literature. In October of 1941 his Gilberton Co. began the **Classic Comics** series with **The Three Musketeers**, with 64 pages of storyline. In those early years, the struggling series saw irregular schedules and numerous printers, not to mention variable art quality and liberal story adaptations. With No.13 the page total was reduced to 56 (except for No. 33, originally scheduled to be No. 9), and with No. 15 the coming-next ad on the outside back cover moved inside. In 1945 the Jerry Iger Shop began producing all new CC titles, beginning with No. 23. In 1947 the search for a classier logo resulted in **Classics Illustrated**, beginning with No. 35, **Last Days of Pompeii**. With No. 45 the page total dropped again to 48, which was to become the standard.

Two new developments in 1951 had a profound effect upon the success of the series. One was the introduction of painted covers, instead of the old line drawn covers, beginning with No. 81, **The Odyssey**. The second was the switch to the major national distributor Curtis. They raised the cover price from 10 to 15 cents, making it the highest priced comic-book, but it did not slow the growth of the series, because they were marketed as books, not comics. Because of this higher quality image, **Classics** flourished during the fifties while other comic series were reeling from outside attacks. They diversified with their new **Juniors**, **Specials**, and **World Around Us** series.

Classics artwork can be divided into three distinct periods. The pre-Iger era (1941-44) was mentioned above for its variable art quality. The Iger era (1945-53) was a major improvement in art quality and adaptations. It came to be dominated by artists Henry Kiefer and Alex Blum, together accounting for some 50 titles. Their styles gave the first real personality to the series. The EC era (1954-62) resulted from the demise of the EC horror series, when many of their artists made the major switch to classical art.

But several factors brought the production of new CI titles to a complete halt in 1962. Gilberton lost its 2nd class mailing permit. External factors like television, cheap paperback books, and Cliff Notes were all eating away at their market. Production halted with No.167, **Faust**, even though many more titles were already in the works. Many of those found their way into foreign series, and are very desirable to collectors. In 1967, **Classics Illustrated** was sold to Patrick Frawley and his Catholic publication, Twin Circle. They issued two new titles in 1969 as part of an attempted revival, but succumbed to major distribution problems in 1971. In 1988, First Publishing acquired the rights to use the old CI series art, logo, and name from the Frawley Group, and released a short-lived series featuring contributions of modern creators. Acclaim Books and Twin Circles issued a series of **Classics** reprints from 1997-1998.

One of the unique aspects of the **Classics Illustrated** (CI) series was the proliferation of reprint variations. Some titles had as many as 25 editions. Reprinting began in 1943. Some **Classic Comics** (CC) reprints (r) had the logo format revised to a banner logo, and added a motto under the banner. In 1947 CC titles changed to the CI logo, but kept their line drawn covers (LDC). In 1948, Nos. 13, 18, 29 and 41 received second covers (LDC2), replacing covers considered too violent, and reprints of Nos. 13-44 had pages reduced to 48, except for No. 26, which had 48 pages to begin with.

Starting in the mid-1950s, 70 of the 80 LDC titles were reissued with new painted covers (PC). Thirty of them also received new interior artwork (A2). The new artwork was generally higher quality with larger art panels and more faithful but abbreviated storylines. Later on, there were 29 second painted covers (PC2), mostly by Twin Circle. Altogether there were 199 interior art variations (169 (O)s and 30 A2 editions) and 272 different covers (169 (O)s, four LDC2s, 70 new PCs of LDC (O)s, and 29 PC2s). It is mildly astounding to realize that there are nearly 1400 different editions in the U.S. CI series.

FOREIGN CLASSICS ILLUSTRATED
If U.S. Classics variations are mildly astounding, the veritable plethora of foreign CI variations will boggle your imagination. While we still anticipate additional discoveries, we presently know about series in 25 languages and 27 countries. There were 250 new CI titles in foreign series, and nearly 400 new foreign covers of U.S. titles. The 1400 U.S. CI editions pale in comparison

Classic Comics #1 © GIL

Classic Comics #2 © GIL

Classic Comics #3 © GIL

GD 2.0 VG 4.0 FN 6.0 VF 8.0 VF/NM 9.0 NM- 9.2

to the 4000 plus foreign editions. The very nature of CI lent itself to flourishing as an international series. Worldwide, they published over one billion copies! The first foreign CI series consisted of six Canadian Classic Comic reprints in 1946.

The following chart shows when CI series first began in each country:
1946: Canada. 1947: Australia. 1948: Brazil/The Netherlands. 1950: Italy. 1951: Greece/Japan/Hong Kong(?)/England/Argentina/Mexico. 1952: West Germany. 1954: Norway. 1955: New Zealand/South Africa. 1956: Denmark/Sweden/Iceland. 1957: Finland/France. 1962: Singapore(?). 1964: India (8 languages). 1971: Ireland (Gaelic). 1973: Belgium(?) /Philippines(?) & Malaysia(?).

Significant among the early series were Brazil and Greece. In 1950, Brazil was the first country to begin doing its own new titles. They issued nearly 80 new CI titles by Brazilian authors. In Greece in 1951 they actually had debates in parliament about the effects of Classics Illustrated on Greek culture, leading to the inclusion of 88 new Greek History & Mythology titles in the CI series.

But by far the most important foreign CI development was the joint European series which began in 1956 in 10 countries simultaneously. By 1960, CI had the largest European distribution of any American publication, not just comics! So when all the problems came up with U.S. distribution, they literally moved the CI operation to Europe in 1962, and continued producing new titles in all four CI series. Many of them were adapted and drawn in the U.S., the most famous of which was the British CI #158A. Dr. No, drawn by Norman Nodel. Unfortunately, the British CI series ended in late 1963, which limited the European CI titles available in English to 15. Altogether there were 82 new CI art titles in the joint European series, which ran until 1976.

IDENTIFYING CLASSICS EDITIONS

HRN: This is the highest number on the reorder list. It should be listed in ( ) after the title number. It is crucial to understanding various CI editions.

ORIGINALS (O): This is the all-important First Edition. To determine (O)s,there is one primary rule and two secondary rules (with exceptions):

Rule No. 1: All (O)s and only (O)s have coming-next ads for the next number. **Exceptions**: No. 14(15) (reprint) has an ad on the last inside text page only. No. 14(0) also has a full-page outside back cover ad (also rule 2). Nos.55(75) and 57(75) have coming-next ads. (Rules 2 and 3 apply here). Nos. 168(0) and 169(0) do not have coming-next ads. No.168 was never reprinted; No. 169(0) has HRN (166). No. 169(169) is the only reprint.

Rule No. 2: On nos.1-80, all (O)s and only (O)s list 10c on the front cover. **Exceptions**: Reprint variations of Nos. 37(62), 39(71), and 46(62) list 10c on the front cover. (Rules 1 and 3 apply here.)

Rule No. 3: All (O)s have HRN close to that title No. **Exceptions**: Some reprints also have HRNs close to that title number: a few CC(r)s, 58(62), 60(62), 149(149), 152(149) 153(149), and title nos. in the 160's. (Rules 1 and 2 apply here.)

DATES: Many reprint editions list either an incorrect date or no date. Since Gilberton apparently kept track of CI editions by HRN, they often left the (O) date on reprints. Often, someone with a CI collection for sale will swear that all their copies are originals. That is why we are so detailed in pointing out how to identify original editions. Except for original editions, which should have a coming-next ad, etc., all CI dates prior to 1963 are incorrect! So you want to go by HRN only if it is (165) or below, and go by listed date if it is 1963 or later. There are a few (167) editions with incorrect dates. They could be listed either as (167) or (62/3), which is meant to indicate that they were issued sometime between late 1962 and early 1963.

COVERS: A change from CC to LDC indicates a logo change, not a cover change; while a change from LDC to LDC2, LDC to PC, or from PC to PC2 does indicate a new cover. New PCs can be identified by HRN, and PC2s can be identified by HRN and date. Several covers had color changes, particularly from purple to blue.

Notes: If you see 15 cents in Canada on a front cover, it does not necessarily indicate a Canadian edition. Editions with an HRN between 44 and 75, with 15 cents on the cover are Canadian. Check the publisher's address. An HRN listing two numbers with a / between them indicates that there are two different reorder lists in the front and back covers. Official Twin Circle editions have a full-page back cover ad for their TC magazine, with no CI reorder list. Any CI with just a Twin Circle sticker on the front is not an official TC edition.

TIPS ON LISTING CLASSICS FOR SALE

It may be easy to just list Edition 17, but Classics collectors keep track of CI editions in terms of HRN and/or date, (O) or (r), CC or LDC, PC or PC2, A1 or A2, soft or stiff cover, etc. Try to help them out. For originals, just list (0), unless there are variations such as color (Nos. 10 and 61), printer (Nos. 18-22), HRN (Nos. 95, 108, 160), etc. For reprints, just list HRN if it's (165) or below. Above that, list HRN and date. Also, please list type of logo/cover/art for the convenience of buyers. They will appreciate it.

CLASSIC COMICS (Also see Best from Boys Life, Cassette Books, Famous Stories, Fast Fiction, Golden Picture Classics, King Classics, Marvel Classics Comics, Pendulum Illustrated Classics, Picture Parade, Picture Progress, Regents Ill. Classics, Spitfire, Stories by Famous Authors, Superior Stories, and World Around Us.)

CLASSIC COMICS (Classics Illustrated No. 35 on)
Elliot Publishing #1-3 (1941-1942)/Gilberton Publications #4-167 (1942-1967) /Twin Circle Pub. (Frawley) #168-169 (1968-1971):
10/41 - No. 34, 2/47; No. 35, 3/47 - No. 169, Spring 1969
(Reprint Editions of almost all titles 5/43 - Spring 1971)
(Painted Covers (0)s No. 81 on, and (r)s of most Nos. 1-80)

Abbreviations:
A–Art; C or c–Cover; CC–Classic Comics; CI–Classics Ill.; Ed–Edition; LDC–Line Drawn Cover; PC–Painted Cover; r–Reprint

1. The Three Musketeers

Ed	HRN	Date	Details	A	C	GD 2.0	VG 4.0	FN 6.0	VF 8.0	VF/NM 9.0	NM- 9.2
1	–	10/41	Date listed-1941; Elliot Pub; 68 pgs.	1	1	452	904	1356	3164	5082	7000
2	10	–	10¢ price removed on all (r)s; Elliot Pub; CC-r	1	1	37	74	111	209	305	400
3	15	–	Long Isl. Ind. Ed.; CC-r	1	1	27	54	81	152	219	285
4	18/20	–	Sunrise Times Ed.; CC-r	1	1	19	38	57	107	154	200
5	21	–	Richmond Courier Ed.; CC-r	1	1	17	34	51	95	135	175
6	28	1946	CC-r	1	1	14	28	42	79	110	140
7	36	–	LDC-r	1	1	8	16	24	43	54	65
8	60	–	LDC-r	1	1	6	12	18	27	33	38
9	64	–	LDC-r	1	1	5	10	15	22	26	30
10	78	–	C-price 15¢;LDC-r	1	1	4	9	13	18	22	26
11	93	–	LDC-r	1	1	4	9	13	18	22	26
12	114	–	Last LDC-r	1	1	4	8	11	16	19	22
13	134	–	New-c; old-a; 64 pg. PC-r	1	2	3	6	9	18	23	28
14	143	–	Old-a; PC-r; 64 pg.	1	2	2	4	6	12	16	20
15	150	–	New-a; PC-r; Evans/Crandall-a	2	2	3	6	9	17	21	26
16	149	–	PC-r	2	2	2	4	6	8	10	12
17	167	–	PC-r	2	2	2	4	6	8	10	12
18	167	4/64	PC-r	2	2	2	4	6	8	10	12
19	167	1/65	PC-r	2	2	2	4	6	8	10	12
20	167	3/66	PC-r	2	2	2	4	6	8	10	12
21	166	11/67	PC-r	2	2	2	4	6	8	10	12
22	166	Spr/69	C-price 25¢ ; stiff-c; PC-r	2	2	2	4	6	8	10	12
23	169	Spr/71	PC-r; stiff-c	2	2	2	4	6	8	10	12

2. Ivanhoe

Ed	HRN	Date	Details	A	C	GD 2.0	VG 4.0	FN 6.0	VF 8.0	VF/NM 9.0	NM- 9.2
1	(O)	12/41?	Date listed-1941; Elliot Pub; 68 pgs.	1	1	225	450	675	1406	2166	2925
2	10	–	Price & 'Presents' removed; Elliot Pub; CC-r	1	1	33	60	99	190	275	360
3	15	–	Long Isl. Ind. ed.; CC-r	1	1	21	42	63	121	173	225
4	18/20	–	Sunrise Times ed.; CC-r	1	1	19	38	57	107	154	200
5	21	–	Richmond Courier ed.; CC-r	1	1	17	34	51	95	135	175
6	28	1946	Last 'Comics'-r	1	1	14	28	42	79	110	140
7	36	–	1st LDC-r	1	1	9	18	27	49	62	75
8	60	–	LDC-r	1	1	6	12	18	27	33	38
9	64	–	LDC-r	1	1	5	10	15	22	26	30
10	78	–	C-price 15¢; LDC-r	1	1	4	9	13	18	22	26
11	89	–	LDC-r	1	1	4	8	12	17	21	24
12	106	–	LDC-r	1	1	4	7	10	14	17	20
13	121	–	Last LDC-r	1	1	4	7	10	14	17	20
14	136	–	New-c&a; PC-r	2	2	5	10	15	22	26	30
15	142	–	PC-r	2	2	2	4	6	9	11	14
16	153	–	PC-r	2	2	2	4	6	9	11	14
17	149	–	PC-r	2	2	2	4	6	9	11	14
18	167	–	PC-r	2	2	2	4	6	8	10	12
19	167	5/64	PC-r	2	2	2	4	6	8	10	12
20	167	1/65	PC-r	2	2	2	4	6	8	10	12
21	167	3/66	PC-r	2	2	2	4	6	8	10	12
22A	166	9/67	PC-r	2	2	2	4	6	8	10	12
22B	166	–	Center ad for Children's Digest & Young Miss; rare; PC-r	2	2	11	22	33	63	84	105

Classic Comics #4 © GIL

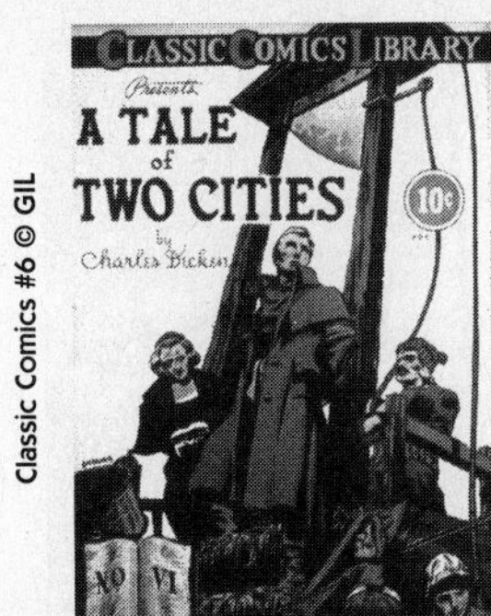

Classic Comics #6 © GIL

Classic Comics #7 © GIL

Ed	HRN	Date	Details	A	C	GD 2.0	VG 4.0	FN 6.0	VF 8.0	VF/NM 9.0	NM- 9.2
23	166	R/68	C-Price 25¢; PC-r	2	2	2	4	6	8	10	12
24	169	Win/69	Stiff-c	2	2	2	4	6	8	10	12
25	169	Win/71	PC-r; stiff-c	2	2	2	4	6	8	10	12

3. The Count of Monte Cristo

Ed	HRN	Date	Details	A	C	GD 2.0	VG 4.0	FN 6.0	VF 8.0	VF/NM 9.0	NM- 9.2
1	(O)	3/42	Elliot Pub; 68 pgs.	1	1	142	284	426	888	1369	1850
2	10	–	Conray Prods; CC-r	1	1	28	56	84	158	229	300
3	15	–	Long Isl. Ind. ed.; CC-r	1	1	22	44	66	123	177	230
4	18/20	–	Sunrise Times ed.; CC-r	1	1	20	40	60	112	161	210
5	20	–	Sunrise Times ed.; CC-r	1	1	18	36	54	100	143	185
6	21	–	Richmond Courier ed.; CC-r	1	1	17	34	51	95	135	175
7	28	1946	CC-r; new Banner logo	1	1	14	28	42	79	110	140
8	36	–	1st LDC-r	1	1	9	18	27	49	62	75
9	60	–	LDC-r	1	1	6	12	18	27	33	38
10	62	–	LDC-r	1	1	6	12	18	29	36	42
11	71	–	LDC-r	1	1	5	10	14	20	24	28
12	87	–	C-price 15¢; LDC-r	1	1	4	9	13	18	22	26
13	113	–	LDC-r	1	1	4	7	10	14	17	20
14	135	–	New-c&a; PC-r; Cameron-a	2	2	3	6	9	18	23	28
15	143	–	PC-r	2	2	2	4	6	9	11	14
16	153	–	PC-r	2	2	2	4	6	9	11	14
17	161	–	PC-r	2	2	2	4	6	9	11	14
18	167	–	PC-r	2	2	2	4	6	8	10	12
19	167	7/64	PC-r	2	2	2	4	6	8	10	12
20	167	7/65	PC-r	2	2	2	4	6	8	10	12
21	167	7/66	PC-r	2	2	2	4	6	8	10	12
22	166	R/68	C-price 25¢; PC-r	2	2	2	4	6	8	10	12
23	169	–	Win/69 Stiff-c; PC-r	2	2	2	4	6	8	10	12

4. The Last of the Mohicans

Ed	HRN	Date	Details	A	C	GD 2.0	VG 4.0	FN 6.0	VF 8.0	VF/NM 9.0	NM- 9.2
1	(O)	8/42	Date listed-1942; Gilberton #4(0) on; 68 pgs.	1	1	119	238	357	744	1147	1550
2	12	–	Elliot Pub; CC-r	1	1	28	56	84	158	229	300
3	15	–	Long Isl. Ind. ed.; CC-r	1	1	22	44	66	123	177	230
4	20	–	Long Isl. Ind. ed.; CC-r; banner logo	1	1	19	38	57	107	154	200
5	21	–	Queens Home News ed.; CC-r	1	1	17	34	51	95	135	175
6	28	1946	Last CC-r; new	1	1	14	28	42	79	110	140
7	36	–	1st LDC-r	1	1	9	18	27	49	62	75
8	60	–	LDC-r	1	1	6	12	18	27	33	38
9	64	–	LDC-r	1	1	5	10	14	20	24	28
10	78	–	C-price 15¢; LDC-r	1	1	4	9	13	18	22	26
11	89	–	LDC-r	1	1	4	8	12	17	21	24
12	117	–	Last LDC-r	1	1	4	7	10	14	17	20
13	135	–	New-c; PC-r	1	2	5	10	14	20	24	28
14	141	–	PC-r	1	2	3	6	8	12	14	16
15	150	–	New-a; PC-r; Severin, L.B. Cole-a	2	2	5	10	15	22	26	30
16	161	–	PC-r	2	2	2	4	6	8	10	12
17	167	–	PC-r	2	2	2	4	6	8	10	12
18	167	6/64	PC-r	2	2	2	4	6	8	10	12
19	167	8/65	PC-r	2	2	2	4	6	8	10	12
20	167	8/66	PC-r	2	2	2	4	6	8	10	12
21	166	R/67	C-price 25¢; PC-r	2	2	2	4	6	8	10	12
22	169	Spr/69	Stiff-c; PC-r	2	2	2	4	6	8	10	12

5. Moby Dick

Ed	HRN	Date	Details	A	C	GD 2.0	VG 4.0	FN 6.0	VF 8.0	VF/NM 9.0	NM- 9.2
1A	(O)	9/42	Date listed-1942; Gilberton; 68 pgs.	1	1	150	300	450	938	1444	1950
1B			inside-c, rare free promo			229	458	687	1431	2203	2975
2	10	–	Conray Prods; Pg. 64 changed from 105 title list to letter from Editor; CC-r	1	1	30	60	90	170	245	320
3	15	–	Long Isl. Ind. ed.; Pg. 64 changed from Letter to the Editor to Ill. poem-Concord Hymn; CC-r	1	1	25	50	75	141	203	265
4	18/20	–	Sunrise Times ed.; CC-r	1	1	20	40	60	112	161	210
5	20	–	Sunrise Times ed.; CC-r	1	1	19	38	57	107	154	200
6	21	–	Sunrise Times ed.; CC-r	1	1	17	34	51	95	135	175
7	28	1946	CC-r; new banner logo	1	1	15	30	45	83	117	150
8	36	–	1st LDC-r	1	1	9	18	27	49	62	75
9	60	–	LDC-r	1	1	6	12	18	27	33	38
10	62	–	LDC-r	1	1	6	12	18	29	36	42
11	71	–	LDC-r	1	1	5	10	15	22	26	30
12	87	–	C-price 15¢; LDC-r	1	1	5	10	14	20	24	28
13	118	–	LDC-r	1	1	4	8	12	17	21	24
14	131	–	New c&a; PC-r	2	2	5	10	15	22	26	30
15	138	–	PC-r	2	2	2	4	6	9	11	14
16	148	–	PC-r	2	2	2	4	6	9	11	14
17	158	–	PC-r	2	2	2	4	6	9	11	14
18	167	–	PC-r	2	2	2	4	6	8	10	12
19	167	6/64	PC-r	2	2	2	4	6	8	10	12
20	167	7/65	PC-r	2	2	2	4	6	8	10	12
21	167	3/66	PC-r	2	2	2	4	6	8	10	12
22	166	9/67	PC-r	2	2	2	4	6	8	10	12
23	166	Win/69	New-c & c-price 25¢; Stiff-c; PC-r	2	3	3	6	9	16	20	24
24	169	Win/71	PC-r	2	3	2	4	6	12	16	20

6. A Tale of Two Cities

Ed	HRN	Date	Details	A	C	GD 2.0	VG 4.0	FN 6.0	VF 8.0	VF/NM 9.0	NM- 9.2
1	(O)	10/42	Date listed-1942; 68 pgs. Zeckerberg c/a	1	1	119	238	357	744	1147	1550
2	14	–	Elliot Pub; CC-r	1	1	27	54	81	152	219	285
3	18	–	Long Isl. Ind. ed.; CC-r	1	1	21	42	63	118	169	220
4	20	–	Sunrise Times ed.; CC-r	1	1	19	38	57	107	154	200
5	28	1946	Last CC-r; new banner logo	1	1	14	28	42	79	110	140
6	51	–	1st LDC-r	1	1	8	16	24	43	54	65
7	64	–	LDC-r	1	1	5	10	15	23	28	32
8	78	–	C-price 15¢; LDC-r	1	1	5	10	14	20	24	28
9	89	–	LDC-r	1	1	4	7	10	14	17	20
10	117	–	LDC-r	1	1	4	7	10	14	17	20
11	132	–	New-c&a; PC-r; Joe Orlando-a	2	2	5	10	15	22	26	30
12	140	–	PC-r	2	2	2	4	6	8	10	12
13	147	–	PC-r	2	2	2	4	6	8	10	12
14	152	–	PC-r; very rare	2	2	19	38	57	107	154	200
15	153	–	PC-r	2	2	2	4	6	9	11	14
16	149	–	PC-r	2	2	2	4	6	9	11	14
17	167	–	PC-r	2	2	2	4	6	8	10	12
18	167	6/64	PC-r	2	2	2	4	6	8	10	12
19	167	8/65	PC-r	2	2	2	4	6	8	10	12
20	166	5/67	PC-r	2	2	2	4	6	8	10	12
21	166	Fall/68	New-c & 25¢; PC-r	2	3	3	6	9	17	21	26
22	169	Sum/70	Stiff-c; PC-r	2	3	2	4	6	12	16	20

7. Robin Hood

Ed	HRN	Date	Details	A	C	GD 2.0	VG 4.0	FN 6.0	VF 8.0	VF/NM 9.0	NM- 9.2
1	(O)	12/42	Date listed-1942; first Gift Box ad-bc; 68 pgs.	1	1	87	174	261	544	835	1125
2	12	–	Elliot Pub; CC-r	1	1	26	52	78	147	211	275
3	18	–	Long Isl. Ind. ed.; CC-r	1	1	20	40	60	112	161	210
4	20	–	Nassau Bulletin ed.; CC-r	1	1	19	38	57	107	154	200
5	22	–	Queens Cty. Times	1	1	17	34	51	95	135	175

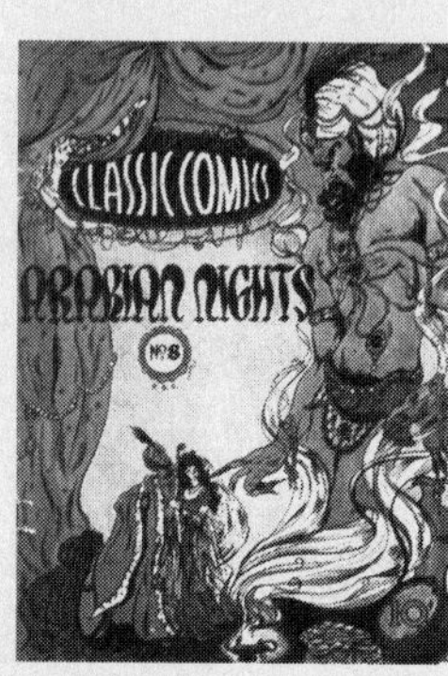

Classic Comics #8 © GIL

Classic Comics #11 © GIL

Classic Comics #12 © GIL

Ed	HRN	Date	Details	A	C	GD 2.0	VG 4.0	FN 6.0	VF 8.0	VF/NM 9.0	NM- 9.2
			ed.; CC-r								
6	28	–	CC-r	1	1	15	30	45	83	117	150
7	51	–	LDC-r	1	1	8	16	24	43	54	65
8	64	–	LDC-r	1	1	5	10	15	24	30	35
9	78	–	LDC-r	1	1	4	9	13	18	22	26
10	97	–	LDC-r	1	1	4	8	12	17	21	24
11	106	–	LDC-r	1	1	4	7	10	14	17	20
12	121	–	LDC-r	1	1	4	7	10	14	17	20
13	129	–	New-c; PC-r	1	2	5	10	15	22	26	30
14	136	–	New-a; PC-r	2	2	5	10	14	20	24	28
15	143	–	PC-r	2	2	2	4	6	9	11	14
16	153	–	PC-r	2	2	2	4	6	9	11	14
17	164	–	PC-r	2	2	2	4	6	8	10	12
18	167	–	PC-r	2	2	2	4	6	8	10	12
19	167	6/64	PC-r	2	2	2	4	6	8	10	12
20	167	5/65	PC-r	2	2	2	4	6	8	10	12
21	167	7/66	PC-r	2	2	2	4	6	8	10	12
22	166	12/67	PC-r	2	2	2	4	6	8	10	12
23	169	Sum/69	Stiff-c; c-price 25¢; PC-r	2	2	2	4	6	8	10	12

8. Arabian Nights

Ed	HRN	Date	Details	A	C	GD 2.0	VG 4.0	FN 6.0	VF 8.0	VF/NM 9.0	NM- 9.2
1	(O)	2/43	Original; 68 pgs. Lilian Chestney-c/a	1	1	148	296	444	925	1425	1925
2	17	–	Long Isl. ed.; pg. 64 changed from Gift Box ad to Letter from British Medical Worker; CC-r	1	1	55	110	165	336	511	685
3	20	–	Nassau Bulletin; Pg. 64 changed from letter to article-Three Men Named Smith; CC-r	1	1	44	88	132	268	409	550
4A	28	1946	CC-r; new banner logo, slick-c	1	1	34	68	102	193	279	365
4B	28	1946	Same, but w/stiff-c	1	1	34	68	102	193	279	365
5	51	–	LDC-r	1	1	24	48	72	135	195	255
6	64	–	LDC-r	1	1	20	40	60	112	161	210
7	78	–	LDC-r	1	1	19	38	57	107	154	200
8	164	–	New-c&a; PC-r	2	2	16	32	48	89	127	165

9. Les Miserables

Ed	HRN	Date	Details	A	C	GD 2.0	VG 4.0	FN 6.0	VF 8.0	VF/NM 9.0	NM- 9.2
1A	(O)	3/43	Original; slick paper cover; 68 pgs.	1	1	87	174	261	544	835	1125
1B	(O)	3/43	Original; rough, pulp type-c; 68 pgs.	1	1	108	216	324	675	1038	1400
2	14	–	Elliot Pub; CC-r	1	1	28	56	84	158	229	300
3	18	3/44	Nassau Bul. Pg. 64 changed from Gift Box ad to Bill of Rights article; CC-r	1	1	24	48	72	135	195	255
4	20	–	Richmond Courier ed.; CC-r	1	1	20	40	60	112	161	210
5	28	1946	Gilberton; pgs. 60-64 rearranged/ illos added; CC-r	1	1	15	30	45	83	117	150
6	51	–	LDC-r	1	1	9	18	27	49	62	75
7	71	–	LDC-r	1	1	6	12	18	29	36	42
8	87	–	C-price 15¢; LDC-r	1	1	6	12	18	27	33	38
9	161	–	New-c&a; PC-r	2	2	6	12	18	31	38	45
10	167	9/63	PC-r	2	2	2	4	6	12	16	20
11	167	12/65	PC-r	2	2	2	4	6	12	16	20
12	166	R/1968	New-c & price 25¢; PC-r	2	3	3	6	9	18	23	28

10. Robinson Crusoe (Used in **SOTI**, pg. 142)

Ed	HRN	Date	Details	A	C	GD 2.0	VG 4.0	FN 6.0	VF 8.0	VF/NM 9.0	NM- 9.2
1A	(O)	4/43	Original; Violet-c; 68 pgs; Zuckerberg c/a	1	1	75	150	225	469	722	975
1B	(O)	4/43	Original; blue-grey-c, 68 pgs.	1	1	85	170	255	531	816	1100
2A	14	–	Elliot Pub; violet-c; 68 pgs; CC-r	1	1	30	60	90	170	245	320
2B	14	–	Elliot Pub; blue-grey-c; CC-r	1	1	27	54	81	152	219	285
3	18	–	Nassau Bul. Pg. 64 changed from Gift Box ad to Bill of Rights article; CC-r	1	1	20	40	60	112	161	210
4	20	–	Queens Home News ed.; CC-r	1	1	17	34	51	95	135	175
5	28	1946	Gilberton; pg. 64 changes from Bill of Rights to WWII article-One Leg Shot Away; last CC-r	1	1	14	28	42	79	110	140
6	51	–	LDC-r	1	1	8	16	24	43	54	65
7	64	–	LDC-r	1	1	6	12	18	27	33	38
8	78	–	C-price 15¢; LDC-r	1	1	5	10	14	20	24	28
9	97	–	LDC-r	1	1	4	9	13	18	22	26
10	114	–	LDC-r	1	1	4	7	10	14	17	20
11	130	–	New-c; PC-r	1	2	5	10	15	22	26	30
12	140	–	New-a; PC-r	2	2	5	10	14	20	24	28
13	153	–	PC-r	2	2	2	4	6	8	10	12
14	164	–	PC-r	2	2	2	4	6	8	10	12
15	167	–	PC-r	2	2	2	4	6	8	10	12
16	167	7/64	PC-r	2	2	2	4	6	10	13	16
17	167	5/65	PC-r	2	2	2	4	6	10	13	16
18	167	6/66	PC-r	2	2	2	4	6	8	10	12
19	166	Fall/68	C-price 25¢; PC-r	2	2	2	4	6	8	10	12
20	166	R/68	(No Twin Circle ad)	2	2	2	4	6	9	11	14
21	169	Sm/70	Stiff-c; PC-r	2	2	2	4	6	9	11	14

11. Don Quixote

Ed	HRN	Date	Details	A	C	GD 2.0	VG 4.0	FN 6.0	VF 8.0	VF/NM 9.0	NM- 9.2
1	10	5/43	First (O) with HRN list; 68 pgs.	1	1	81	162	243	506	778	1050
2	18	–	Nassau Bulletin ed.; CC-r	1	1	25	50	75	141	203	265
3	21	–	Queens Home News ed.; CC-r	1	1	20	40	60	112	161	210
4	28	–	CC-r	1	1	15	30	45	83	117	150
5	110	–	New-PC; PC-r	1	2	6	12	18	29	36	42
6	156	–	Pgs. reduced 68 to 52; PC-r	1	2	4	7	10	14	17	20
7	165	–	PC-r	1	2	2	4	6	9	11	14
8	167	1/64	PC-r	1	2	2	4	6	9	11	14
9	167	11/65	PC-r	1	2	2	4	6	9	11	14
10	166	R/1968	New-c & price 25¢; PC-r	1	3	3	6	9	18	24	30

12. Rip Van Winkle and the Headless Horseman

Ed	HRN	Date	Details	A	C	GD 2.0	VG 4.0	FN 6.0	VF 8.0	VF/NM 9.0	NM- 9.2
1	11	6/43	Original; 68 pgs.	1	1	81	162	243	506	778	1050
2	15	–	Long Isl. Ind. ed.; CC-r	1	1	25	50	75	141	203	265
3	20	–	Long Isl. Ind. ed.;	1	1	20	40	60	112	161	210
4	22	–	Queens Cty. Times ed.; CC-r	1	1	17	34	51	95	135	175
5	28	–	CC-r	1	1	14	28	42	79	110	140
6	60	–	1st LDC-r	1	1	8	16	24	40	50	60
7	62	–	LDC-r	1	1	5	10	15	23	28	32
8	71	–	LDC-r	1	1	4	9	13	18	22	26
9	89	–	C-price 15¢; LDC-r	1	1	4	8	12	17	21	24
10	118	–	LDC-r	1	1	4	7	10	14	17	20
11	132	–	New-c; PC-r	1	2	5	10	15	22	26	30
12	150	–	New-a; PC-r	2	2	5	10	14	20	24	28
13	158	–	PC-r	2	2	2	4	6	9	11	14
14	167	–	PC-r	2	2	2	4	6	9	11	14
15	167	12/63	PC-r	2	2	2	4	6	8	10	12
16	167	4/65	PC-r	2	2	2	4	6	8	10	12
17	167	4/66	PC-r	2	2	2	4	6	8	10	12
18	166	R/1968	New-c&price 25¢; PC-r; stiff-c	2	3	2	4	6	14	18	22
19	169	Sm/70	PC-r; stiff-c	2	3	2	4	6	10	13	16

13. Dr. Jekyll and Mr. Hyde (Used in **SOTI**, pg. 143)(1st horror comic?)

Ed	HRN	Date	Details	A	C	GD 2.0	VG 4.0	FN 6.0	VF 8.0	VF/NM 9.0	NM- 9.2
1	12	8/43	Original 60 pgs.	1	1	123	246	369	769	1185	1600

Classic Comics #14 © GIL

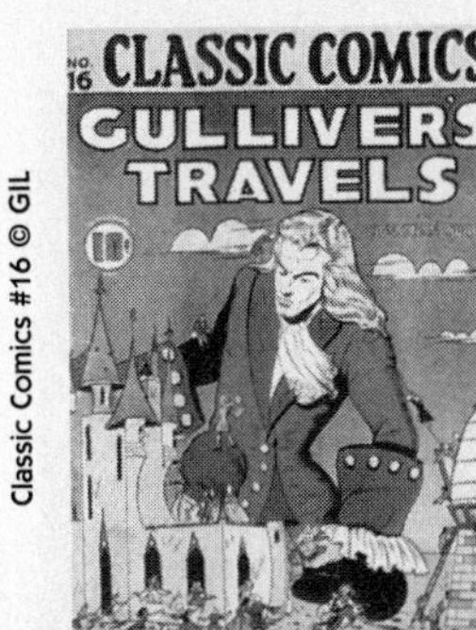

Classic Comics #16 © GIL

Classic Comics #18 © GIL

Ed	HRN	Date	Details	A	C	GD 2.0	VG 4.0	FN 6.0	VF 8.0	VF/NM 9.0	NM- 9.2
2	15	–	Long Isl. Ind. ed.; CC-r	1	1	35	70	105	200	290	380
3	20	–	Long Isl. Ind. ed.; CC-r	1	1	25	50	75	141	203	265
4	28	–	No c-price; CC-r	1	1	19	38	57	107	154	200
5	60	–	New-c; Pgs. reduced from 60 to 52; H.C. Kiefer-c; LDC-r	1	2	8	16	24	43	54	65
6	62	–	LDC-r	1	2	6	12	18	28	34	40
7	71	–	LDC-r	1	2	5	10	15	23	28	32
8	87	–	Date returns (erroneous); LDC-r	1	2	5	10	15	22	26	30
9	112	–	New-c&a; PC-r; Cameron-a	2	3	6	12	18	29	36	42
10	153	–	PC-r	2	3	2	4	6	10	12	15
11	161	–	PC-r	2	3	2	4	6	10	12	15
12	167	–	PC-r	2	3	2	4	6	8	10	12
13	167	8/64	PC-r	2	3	2	4	6	8	10	12
14	167	11/65	PC-r	2	3	2	4	6	8	10	12
15	166	R/68	C-price 25¢; PC-r	2	3	2	4	6	8	10	12
16	169	Wn/69	PC-r; stiff-c	2	3	2	4	6	8	10	12

14. Westward Ho!

Ed	HRN	Date	Details	A	C	GD 2.0	VG 4.0	FN 6.0	VF 8.0	VF/NM 9.0	NM- 9.2
1	13	9/43	Original; last outside bc coming-next ad; 60 pgs.	1	1	192	384	576	1200	1850	2500
2	15	–	Long Isl. Ind. ed.; CC-r	1	1	55	110	165	336	511	685
3	21	–	Queens Home News; Pg. 56 changed from coming-next ad to Three Men Named Smith; CC-r	1	1	44	88	132	268	409	550
4	28	1946	Gilberton; Pg. 56 changed again to WWII article-Speaking for America; last CC-r	1	1	40	80	120	230	335	440
5	53	–	Pgs. reduced from 60 to 52; LDC-r	1	1	35	70	105	201	293	385

15. Uncle Tom's Cabin (Used in **SOTI**, pgs. 102, 103)

Ed	HRN	Date	Details	A	C	GD 2.0	VG 4.0	FN 6.0	VF 8.0	VF/NM 9.0	NM- 9.2
1	14	11/43	Original; Outside-bc ad: 2 Gift Boxes; 60 pgs.; color var. on-c; green trunk,root on left & brown trunk, root on left	1	1	66	132	198	413	637	860
2	15	–	Long Isl. Ind. listed- bottom inside-fc; also Gilberton listed bottom-pg. 1; CC-r; green root vs. brown root var. occurs again	1	1	27	54	81	152	219	285
3	21	–	Nassau Bulletin ed.; CC-r	1	1	21	42	63	118	169	220
4	28	–	No c-price; CC-r	1	1	15	30	45	83	117	150
5	53	–	Pgs. reduced 60 to 52; LDC-r	1	1	8	16	24	43	54	65
6	71	–	LDC-r	1	1	6	12	18	27	33	38
7	89	–	C-price 15¢; LDC-r	1	1	5	10	15	24	30	35
8	117	–	New-c/lettering changes; PC-r	1	2	5	10	15	22	26	30
9	128	–	'Picture Progress' promo; PC-r	1	2	2	4	6	10	13	16
10	137	–	PC-r	1	2	2	4	6	9	11	14
11	146	–	PC-r	1	2	2	4	6	9	11	14
12	154	–	PC-r	1	2	2	4	6	9	11	14
13	161	–	PC-r	1	2	2	4	6	8	10	12
14	167	–	PC-r	1	2	2	4	6	8	10	12
15	167	6/64	PC-r	1	2	2	4	6	8	10	12
16	167	5/65	PC-r	1	2	2	4	6	8	10	12
17	166	5/67	PC-r	1	2	2	4	6	8	10	12
18	166	Wn/69	New-stiff-c; PC-r	1	3	2	4	6	14	18	22
19	169	Sm/70	PC-r; stiff-c	1	3	2	4	6	10	13	16

16. Gullivers Travels

Ed	HRN	Date	Details	A	C	GD 2.0	VG 4.0	FN 6.0	VF 8.0	VF/NM 9.0	NM- 9.2
1	15	12/43	Original-Lilian Chestney c/a; 60 pgs.	1	1	69	138	207	431	666	900
2	18/20	–	Price deleted; Queens Home News ed; CC-r	1	1	24	48	72	135	195	255
3	22	–	Queens Cty. Times ed.; CC-r	1	1	19	38	57	107	154	200
4	28	–	CC-r	1	1	14	28	42	79	110	140
5	60	–	Pgs. reduced to 48; LDC-r	1	1	6	12	18	31	38	45
6	62	–	LDC-r	1	1	5	10	15	23	28	32
7	78	–	C-price 15¢; LDC-r	1	1	5	10	14	20	24	28
8	89	–	LDC-r	1	1	4	8	12	17	21	24
9	155	–	New-c; PC-r	1	2	5	10	15	22	26	30
10	165	–	PC-r	1	2	2	4	6	8	10	12
11	167	5/64	PC-r	1	2	2	4	6	8	10	12
12	167	11/65	PC-r	1	2	2	4	6	8	10	12
13	166	R/1968	C-price 25¢; PC-r	1	2	2	4	6	8	10	12
14	169	Wn/69	PC-r; stiff-c	1	2	2	4	6	8	10	12

17. The Deerslayer

Ed	HRN	Date	Details	A	C	GD 2.0	VG 4.0	FN 6.0	VF 8.0	VF/NM 9.0	NM- 9.2
1	16	1/44	Original; Outside-bc ad: 3 Gift Boxes; 60 pgs.	1	1	60	120	180	375	575	775
2A	18	–	Queens Cty Times (inside-fc); CC-r	1	1	25	50	75	141	203	265
2B	18	–	Gilberton (bottom-pg. 1); CC-r; Scarce	1	1	35	70	105	200	290	380
3	22	–	Queens Cty. Times ed.; CC-r	1	1	20	40	60	112	161	210
4	28	–	CC-r	1	1	15	30	45	83	117	150
5	60	–	Pgs.reduced to 52; LDC-r	1	1	7	14	21	37	46	55
6	64	–	LDC-r	1	1	5	10	15	22	26	30
7	85	–	C-price 15¢; LDC-r	1	1	4	8	12	17	21	24
8	118	–	LDC-r	1	1	4	7	10	14	17	20
9	132	–	LDC-r	1	1	4	7	10	14	17	20
10	167	11/66	Last LDC-r	1	1	2	4	6	12	16	20
11	166	R/1968	New-c & price 25¢; PC-r	1	2	3	6	9	18	23	28
12	169	Spr/71	Stiff-c; letters from parents & educators; PC-r	1	2	2	4	6	11	14	18

18. The Hunchback of Notre Dame

Ed	HRN	Date	Details	A	C	GD 2.0	VG 4.0	FN 6.0	VF 8.0	VF/NM 9.0	NM- 9.2
1A	17	3/44	Orig.; Gilberton ed; 60 pgs.	1	1	79	158	237	494	760	1025
1B	17	3/44	Orig.; Island Pub. Ed.; 60 pgs.	1	1	69	138	207	431	666	900
2	18/20	–	Queens Home News ed.; CC-r	1	1	27	54	81	152	219	285
3	22	–	Queens Cty. Times ed.; CC-r	1	1	20	40	60	112	161	210
4	28	–	CC-r	1	1	17	34	51	95	135	175
5	60	–	New-c; 8pgs. deleted; Kiefer-c; LDC-r	1	2	8	16	24	43	54	65
6	62	–	LDC-r	1	2	5	10	15	22	26	30
7	78	–	C-price 15¢; LDC-r	1	2	5	10	14	20	24	28
8A	89	–	H.C.Kiefer on bottom right-fc; LDC-r	1	2	4	9	13	18	22	26
8B	89	–	Name omitted; LDC-r	1	2	5	10	15	24	30	35
9	118	–	LDC-r	1	2	4	8	12	17	21	24
10	140	–	New-c; PC-r	1	3	6	12	18	28	34	40
11	146	–	PC-r	1	3	4	9	13	18	22	26
12	158	–	New-c&a; PC-r; Evans/Crandall-a	2	4	5	10	15	22	26	30
13	165	–	PC-r	2	4	2	4	6	9	11	14
14	167	9/63	PC-r	2	4	2	4	6	9	11	14
15	167	10/64	PC-r	2	4	2	4	6	9	11	14

Classic Comics #19 © GIL

Classic Comics #20 © GIL

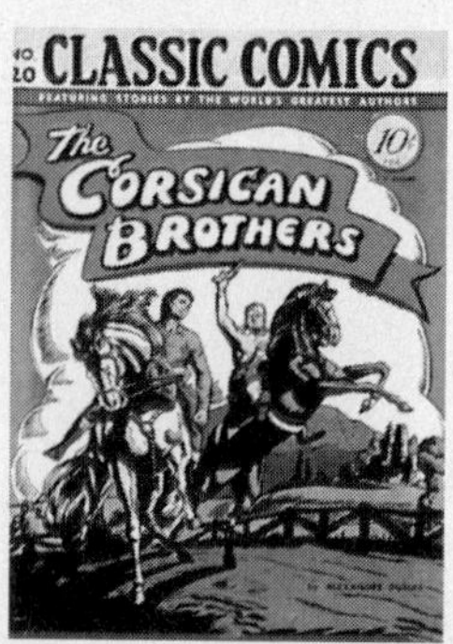

Classic Comics #23 © GIL

Ed	HRN	Date	Details	A	C	GD 2.0	VG 4.0	FN 6.0	VF 8.0	VF/NM 9.0	NM- 9.2
16	167	4/66	PC-r	2	4	2	4	6	8	10	12
17	166	R/1968	New price 25¢; PC-r	2	4	2	4	6	8	10	12
18	169	Sp/70	Stiff-c; PC-r	2	4	2	4	6	8	10	12

19. Huckleberry Finn

Ed	HRN	Date	Details	A	C	GD 2.0	VG 4.0	FN 6.0	VF 8.0	VF/NM 9.0	NM- 9.2
1A	18	4/44	Orig.; Gilberton ed.; 60 pgs.	1	1	50	100	150	305	465	625
1B	18	4/44	Orig.; Island Pub.; 60 pgs.	1	1	55	110	165	336	511	685
2	18	–	Nassau Bulletin ed.; fc-price 15¢-Canada; no coming-next ad; CC-r	1	1	25	50	75	141	203	265
3	22	–	Queens City Times ed.; CC-r	1	1	20	40	60	112	161	210
4	28	–	CC-r	1	1	14	28	42	79	110	140
5	60	–	Pgs. reduced to 48; LDC-r	1	1	6	12	18	31	38	45
6	62	–	LDC-r	1	1	5	10	15	23	28	32
7	78	–	LDC-r	1	1	4	9	13	18	22	26
8	89	–	LDC-r	1	1	4	8	12	17	21	24
9	117	–	LDC-r	1	1	4	7	10	14	17	20
10	131	–	New-c&a; PC-r	2	2	5	10	14	20	24	28
11	140	–	PC-r	2	2	2	4	6	9	11	14
12	150	–	PC-r	2	2	2	4	6	9	11	14
13	158	–	PC-r	2	2	2	4	6	9	11	14
14	165	–	PC-r (scarce)	2	2	3	6	9	16	20	24
15	167	–	PC-r	2	2	2	4	6	8	10	12
16	167	6/64	PC-r	2	2	2	4	6	8	10	12
17	167	6/65	PC-r	2	2	2	4	6	8	10	12
18	167	10/65	PC-r	2	2	2	4	6	8	10	12
19	166	9/67	PC-r	2	2	2	4	6	8	10	12
20	166	Win/69	C-price 25¢; PC-r; stiff-c	2	2	2	4	6	8	10	12
21	169	Sm/70	PC-r; stiff-c	2	2	2	4	6	9	11	12

20. The Corsican Brothers

Ed	HRN	Date	Details	A	C	GD 2.0	VG 4.0	FN 6.0	VF 8.0	VF/NM 9.0	NM- 9.2
1A	20	6/44	Orig.; Gilberton ed.; bc-ad: 4 Gift Boxes; 60 pgs.	1	1	43	86	129	262	401	540
1B	20	6/44	Orig.; Courier ed.; 60 pgs.	1	1	39	78	117	222	324	425
1C	20	6/44	Orig.; Long Island Ind. ed.; 60 pgs.	1	1	39	78	117	222	324	425
2	22	–	Queens Cty. Times ed.; white logo banner; CC-r	1	1	21	42	63	118	169	220
3	28	–	CC-r	1	1	20	40	60	112	161	210
4	60	–	Cl logo; no price; 48 pgs.; LDC-r	1	1	17	34	51	95	135	175
5A	62	–	LDC-r; Classics Ill. logo at top of pgs.	1	1	15	30	45	83	117	150
5B	62	–	w/o logo at top of pg. (scarcer)	1	1	16	32	48	89	127	165
6	78	–	C-price 15¢; LDC-r	1	1	14	28	42	79	110	140
7	97	–	LDC-r	1	1	13	26	39	74	102	130

21. 3 Famous Mysteries ("The Sign of the 4", "The Murders in the Rue Morgue", "The Flayed Hand")

Ed	HRN	Date	Details	A	C	GD 2.0	VG 4.0	FN 6.0	VF 8.0	VF/NM 9.0	NM- 9.2
1A	21	7/44	Orig.; Gilberton ed.; 60 pgs.	1	1	90	180	270	563	869	1175
1B	21	7/44	Orig. Island Pub. Co.; 60 pgs.	1	1	94	188	282	588	907	1225
1C	21	7/44	Original; Courier Ed.; 60 pgs.	1	1	79	158	237	494	760	1025
2	22	–	Nassau Bulletin ed.; CC-r	1	1	39	78	117	222	324	425
3	30	–	CC-r	1	1	30	60	90	170	245	320
4	62	–	LDC-r; 8 pgs. deleted; LDC-r	1	1	24	48	72	135	195	255
5	70	–	LDC-r	1	1	22	44	66	123	177	230
6	85	–	C-price 15¢; LDC-r	1	1	19	38	57	107	154	200
7	114	–	New-c; PC-r	1	2	19	38	57	107	154	200

22. The Pathfinder

Ed	HRN	Date	Details	A	C	GD 2.0	VG 4.0	FN 6.0	VF 8.0	VF/NM 9.0	NM- 9.2
1A	22	10/44	Orig.; No printer listed; ownership statement inside fc lists Gilberton & date; 60 pgs.	1	1	43	86	129	262	401	540
1B	22	10/44	Orig.; Island Pub. ed.; 60 pgs.	1	1	40	80	120	235	348	460
1C	22	10/44	Orig.; Queens Cty Times ed. 60 pgs.	1	1	40	80	120	235	348	460
2	30	–	C-price removed; CC-r	1	1	15	30	45	83	117	150
3	60	–	Pgs. reduced to 52; LDC-r	1	1	6	12	18	27	33	38
4	70	–	LDC-r	1	1	5	10	15	22	26	30
5	85	–	C-price 15¢; LDC-r	1	1	4	9	13	18	22	26
6	118	–	LDC-r	1	1	4	8	12	17	21	24
7	132	–	LDC-r	1	1	4	7	10	14	17	20
8	146	–	LDC-r	1	1	4	7	10	14	17	20
9	167	11/63	New-c; PC-r	1	2	4	8	12	24	32	40
10	167	12/65	PC-r	1	2	2	4	6	12	16	20
11	166	8/67	PC-r	1	2	2	4	6	12	16	20

23. Oliver Twist (1st Classic produced by the Iger Shop)

Ed	HRN	Date	Details	A	C	GD 2.0	VG 4.0	FN 6.0	VF 8.0	VF/NM 9.0	NM- 9.2
1	23	7/45	Original; 60 pgs.	1	1	42	84	126	256	391	525
2A	30	–	Printers Union logo on bottom left-fc same as 23(Orig.) (very rare); CC-r	1	1	33	66	99	190	275	360
2B	30	–	Union logo omitted; CC-r	1	1	14	28	42	79	110	140
3	60	–	Pgs. reduced to 48; LDC-r	1	1	6	12	18	29	36	42
4	62	–	LDC-r	1	1	5	10	15	23	28	32
5	71	–	LDC-r	1	1	5	10	14	20	24	28
6	85	–	C-price 15¢; LDC-r	1	1	4	9	13	18	22	26
7	94	–	LDC-r	1	1	4	7	10	14	17	20
8	118	–	LDC-r	1	1	4	7	10	14	17	20
9	136	–	New-PC, old-a; PC-r	1	2	5	10	14	20	24	28
10	150	–	Old-a; PC-r	1	2	4	7	10	14	17	20
11	164	–	Old-a; PC-r	1	2	4	8	11	16	19	22
12	164	–	New-a; PC-r; Evans/Crandall-a	2	2	4	8	12	24	32	40
13	167	–	PC-r	2	2	2	4	6	12	16	20
14	167	8/64	PC-r	2	2	2	4	6	8	10	12
15	167	12/65	PC-r	2	2	2	4	6	8	10	12
16	166	R/1968	New 25¢; PC-r	2	2	2	4	6	8	10	12
17	169	Win/69	Stiff-c; PC-r	2	2	2	4	6	8	10	12

24. A Connecticut Yankee in King Arthur's Court

Ed	HRN	Date	Details	A	C	GD 2.0	VG 4.0	FN 6.0	VF 8.0	VF/NM 9.0	NM- 9.2
1	–	9/45	Original	1	1	40	80	120	235	348	460
2	30	–	No price circle; CC-r	1	1	14	28	42	79	110	140
3	60	–	8 pgs. deleted; LDC-r	1	1	6	12	18	27	33	38
4	62	–	LDC-r	1	1	5	10	15	23	28	32
5	71	–	LDC-r	1	1	5	10	15	22	26	30
6	87	–	C-price 15¢; LDC-r	1	1	4	9	13	18	22	26
7	121	–	LDC-r	1	1	4	8	12	17	21	24
8	140	–	New-c&a; PC-r	2	2	5	10	15	22	26	30
9	153	–	PC-r	2	2	2	4	6	9	11	14
10	164	–	PC-r	2	2	2	4	6	8	10	12
11	167	–	PC-r	2	2	2	4	6	8	10	12
12	167	7/64	PC-r	2	2	2	4	6	8	10	12
13	167	6/66	PC-r	2	2	2	4	6	8	10	12
14	166	R/1968	C-price 25¢; PC-r	2	2	2	4	6	8	10	12
15	169	Spr/71	PC-r; stiff-c	2	2	2	4	6	8	10	12

25. Two Years Before the Mast

Ed	HRN	Date	Details	A	C	GD 2.0	VG 4.0	FN 6.0	VF 8.0	VF/NM 9.0	NM- 9.2
1	–	10/45	Original; Webb/	1	1	40	80	120	235	348	460

Classic Comics #28 © GIL

Classic Comics #32 © GIL

Classic Comics #33 © GIL

Ed	HRN	Date	Details	A	C	GD 2.0	VG 4.0	FN 6.0	VF 8.0	VF/NM 9.0	NM- 9.2
			Heames-a&c								
2	30	–	Price circle blank; CC-r	1	1	14	28	42	79	110	140
3	60	–	8 pgs. deleted; LDC-r	1	1	6	12	18	27	33	38
4	62	–	LDC-r	1	1	5	10	15	23	28	32
5	71	–	LDC-r	1	1	4	9	13	18	22	26
6	85	–	C-price 15¢; LDC-r	1	1	4	8	12	17	21	24
7	114	–	LDC-r	1	1	4	7	10	14	17	20
8	156	–	3 pgs. replaced by fillers; new-c; PC-r	1	2	5	10	15	22	26	30
9	167	12/63	PC-r	1	2	2	4	6	8	10	12
10	167	12/65	PC-r	1	2	2	4	6	8	10	12
11	166	9/67	PC-r	1	2	2	4	6	8	10	12
12	169	Win/69	C-price 25¢; stiff-c PC-r	1	2	2	4	6	8	10	12

26. Frankenstein (2nd horror comic?)

Ed	HRN	Date	Details	A	C	GD 2.0	VG 4.0	FN 6.0	VF 8.0	VF/NM 9.0	NM- 9.2
1	26	12/45	Orig.; Webb/Brewster a&c; 52 pgs.	1	1	96	192	288	600	925	1250
2A	30	–	Price circle blank; no indicia; CC-r	1	1	31	62	93	175	253	330
2B	30	–	With indicia; scarce; CC-r	1	1	36	72	108	204	297	390
3	60	–	LDC-r	1	1	17	34	51	95	135	175
4	62	–	LDC-r	1	1	15	30	45	83	117	150
5	71	–	LDC-r	1	1	7	14	21	35	43	50
6A	82	–	C-price 15¢; soft-c LDC-r	1	1	6	12	18	28	34	40
6B	82	–	Stiff-c; LDC-r	1	1	7	14	21	35	43	50
7	117	–	LDC-r	1	1	4	8	12	18	22	25
8	146	–	New Saunders-c; PC-r	1	2	5	10	15	24	30	35
9	152	–	Scarce; PC-r	1	2	7	14	21	37	46	55
10	153	–	PC-r	1	2	2	4	6	9	11	14
11	160	–	PC-r	1	2	2	4	6	9	11	14
12	165	–	PC-r	1	2	2	4	6	8	10	12
13	167	–	PC-r	1	2	2	4	6	8	10	12
14	167	6/64	PC-r	1	2	2	4	6	8	10	12
15	167	6/65	PC-r	1	2	2	4	6	8	10	12
16	167	10/65	PC-r	1	2	2	4	6	8	10	12
17	166	9/67	PC-r	1	2	2	4	6	8	10	12
18	169	Fall/69	C-price 25¢; stiff-c PC-r	1	2	2	4	6	8	10	12
19	169	Spr/71	PC-r; stiff-c	1	2	2	4	6	8	10	12

27. The Adventures of Marco Polo

Ed	HRN	Date	Details	A	C	GD 2.0	VG 4.0	FN 6.0	VF 8.0	VF/NM 9.0	NM- 9.2
1	–	4/46	Original	1	1	40	80	120	235	348	460
2	30	–	Last 'Comics' reprint; CC-r	1	1	14	28	42	79	110	140
3	70	–	8 pgs. deleted; no c-price; LDC-r	1	1	5	10	15	24	30	35
4	87	–	C-price 15¢; LDC-r	1	1	4	9	13	18	22	26
5	117	–	LDC-r	1	1	4	7	10	14	17	20
6	154	–	New-c; PC-r	1	2	5	10	14	20	24	28
7	165	–	PC-r	1	2	2	4	6	8	10	12
8	167	4/64	PC-r	1	2	2	4	6	8	10	12
9	167	6/66	PC-r	1	2	2	4	6	8	10	12
10	169	Spr/69	New price 25¢; stiff-c; PC-r	1	2	2	4	6	8	10	12

28. Michael Strogoff

Ed	HRN	Date	Details	A	C	GD 2.0	VG 4.0	FN 6.0	VF 8.0	VF/NM 9.0	NM- 9.2
1	–	6/46	Original	1	1	40	80	120	235	348	460
2	51	–	8 pgs. cut; LDC-r	1	1	14	28	42	79	110	140
3	115	–	New-c; PC-r	1	2	6	12	18	27	33	38
4	155	–	PC-r	1	2	4	7	10	14	17	20
5	167	11/63	PC-r	1	2	2	4	6	10	13	16
6	167	7/66	PC-r	1	2	2	4	6	10	13	16
7	169	Sm/69	C-price 25¢; stiff-c PC-r	1	3	3	6	9	16	20	24

29. The Prince and the Pauper

Ed	HRN	Date	Details	A	C	GD 2.0	VG 4.0	FN 6.0	VF 8.0	VF/NM 9.0	NM- 9.2
1	–	7/46	Orig.; "Horror"-c	1	1	55	110	165	340	520	700
2	60	–	8 pgs. cut; new-c by Kiefer; LDC-r	1	2	8	16	24	43	54	65
3	62	–	LDC-r	1	2	5	10	15	24	30	35
4	71	–	LDC-r	1	2	4	9	13	18	22	26
5	93	–	LDC-r	1	2	4	8	12	17	21	24
6	114	–	LDC-r	1	2	4	7	10	14	17	20
7	128	–	New-c; PC-r	1	3	5	10	14	20	24	28
8	138	–	PC-r	1	3	2	4	6	9	11	14
9	150	–	PC-r	1	3	2	4	6	9	11	14
10	164	–	PC-r	1	3	2	4	6	8	10	12
11	167	–	PC-r	1	3	2	4	6	8	10	12
12	167	7/64	PC-r	1	3	2	4	6	8	10	12
13	167	11/65	PC-r	1	3	2	4	6	8	10	12
14	166	R/68	C-price 25¢; PC-r	1	3	2	4	6	8	10	12
15	169	Sm/70	PC-r; stiff-c	1	3	2	4	6	8	10	12

30. The Moonstone

Ed	HRN	Date	Details	A	C	GD 2.0	VG 4.0	FN 6.0	VF 8.0	VF/NM 9.0	NM- 9.2
1	–	9/46	Original; Rico-c/a	1	1	40	80	120	235	348	460
2	60	–	LDC-r; 8pgs. cut	1	1	8	16	24	40	50	60
3	70	–	LDC-r	1	1	7	14	21	37	46	55
4	155	–	New L.B. Cole-c; PC-r	1	2	4	8	12	29	40	50
5	165	–	PC-r; L.B. Cole-c	1	2	3	6	9	18	24	30
6	167	1/64	PC-r; L.B. Cole-c	1	2	2	4	6	11	14	18
7	167	9/65	PC-r; L.B. Cole-c	1	2	2	4	6	10	13	16
8	166	R/1968	C-price 25¢; PC-r	1	2	2	4	6	9	11	14

31. The Black Arrow

Ed	HRN	Date	Details	A	C	GD 2.0	VG 4.0	FN 6.0	VF 8.0	VF/NM 9.0	NM- 9.2
1	30	10/46	Original	1	1	34	68	102	196	283	370
2	51	–	CI logo; LDC-r 8pgs. deleted	1	1	6	12	18	29	36	42
3	64	–	LDC-r	1	1	4	9	13	18	22	26
4	87	–	C-price 15¢; LDC-r	1	1	4	8	12	17	21	24
5	108	–	LDC-r	1	1	4	7	10	14	17	20
6	125	–	LDC-r	1	1	4	7	10	14	17	20
7	131	–	New-c; PC-r	1	2	5	10	14	20	24	28
8	140	–	PC-r	1	2	2	4	6	9	11	14
9	148	–	PC-r	1	2	2	4	6	9	11	14
10	161	–	PC-r	1	2	2	4	6	8	10	12
11	167	–	PC-r	1	2	2	4	6	8	10	12
12	167	7/64	PC-r	1	2	2	4	6	8	10	12
13	167	11/65	PC-r	1	2	2	4	6	8	10	12
14	166	R/1968	C-price 25¢; PC-r	1	2	2	4	6	8	10	12

32. Lorna Doone

Ed	HRN	Date	Details	A	C	GD 2.0	VG 4.0	FN 6.0	VF 8.0	VF/NM 9.0	NM- 9.2
1	–	12/46	Original; Matt Baker c&a	1	1	40	80	120	235	348	460
2	53/64	–	8 pgs. deleted; LDC-r	1	1	8	16	24	43	54	65
3	85	1951	C-price 15¢; LDC-r; Baker c&a	1	1	6	12	18	31	38	45
4	118	–	LDC-r	1	1	4	9	13	18	22	26
5	138	–	New-c; old-c becomes new title pg.; PC-r	1	2	5	10	15	23	28	32
6	150	–	PC-r	1	2	2	4	6	8	10	12
7	165	–	PC-r	1	2	2	4	6	8	10	12
8	167	1/64	PC-r	1	2	2	4	6	9	11	14
9	167	11/65	PC-r	1	2	2	4	6	9	11	14
10	166	R/1968	New-c; PC-r	1	3	3	6	9	18	24	30

33. The Adventures of Sherlock Holmes

Ed	HRN	Date	Details	A	C	GD 2.0	VG 4.0	FN 6.0	VF 8.0	VF/NM 9.0	NM- 9.2
1	33	1/47	Original; Kiefer-c; contains Study in Scarlet & Hound of the Baskervilles; 68 pgs.	1	1	119	238	357	744	1147	1550
2	53	–	"A Study in Scarlet" (17 pgs.) deleted; LDC-r	1	1	44	88	132	268	409	550
3	71	–	LDC-r	1	1	37	74	111	209	305	400
4A	89	–	C-price 15¢; LDC-r	1	1	30	60	90	170	245	320
4B	89	–	Kiefer's name	1	1	31	62	93	175	253	330

Classics Illustrated #36 © GIL

Classics Illustrated #38 © GIL

Classics Illustrated #42 © GIL

omitted from-c

34. Mysterious Island (Last "Classic Comic")

Ed	HRN	Date	Details	A	C	GD 2.0	VG 4.0	FN 6.0	VF 8.0	VF/NM 9.0	NM- 9.2
1	35	2/47	Original; Webb/Heames-c/a	1	1	40	80	120	235	348	460
2	60	–	8 pgs. deleted; LDC-r	1	1	6	12	18	31	38	45
3	62	–	LDC-r	1	1	5	10	15	23	28	32
4	71	–	LDC-r	1	1	6	12	18	31	38	45
5	78	–	C-price 15¢ in circle; LDC-r	1	1	5	10	14	20	24	28
6	92	–	LDC-r	1	1	4	9	13	18	22	26
7	117	–	LDC-r	1	1	4	7	10	14	17	20
8	140	–	New-c; PC-r	1	2	5	10	14	20	24	28
9	156	–	PC-r	1	2	2	4	6	9	11	14
10	167	10/63	PC-r	1	2	2	4	6	8	10	12
11	167	5/64	PC-r	1	2	2	4	6	8	10	12
12	167	6/66	PC-r	1	2	2	4	6	8	10	12
13	166	R/1968	C-price 25¢; PC-r	1	2	2	4	6	8	10	12

35. Last Days of Pompeii (First "Classics Illustrated")

Ed	HRN	Date	Details	A	C	GD 2.0	VG 4.0	FN 6.0	VF 8.0	VF/NM 9.0	NM- 9.2
1	35	3/47	Original; LDC; Kiefer-c/a	1	1	40	80	120	235	348	460
2	161	–	New c&a; 15¢; PC-r; Kirby/Ayers-a	2	2	4	8	12	29	40	50
3	167	1/64	PC-r	2	2	3	6	9	16	20	24
4	167	7/66	PC-r	2	2	3	6	9	16	20	24
5	169	Spr/70	New price 25¢; stiff-c; PC-r	2	2	3	6	9	16	20	24

36. Typee

Ed	HRN	Date	Details	A	C	GD 2.0	VG 4.0	FN 6.0	VF 8.0	VF/NM 9.0	NM- 9.2
1	36	4/47	Original	1	1	24	48	72	138	199	260
2	64	–	No c-price; 8 pg. ed.; LDC-r	1	1	6	12	18	31	38	45
3	155	–	New-c; PC-r	1	2	5	10	14	20	24	28
4	167	9/63	PC-r	1	2	2	4	6	10	12	15
5	167	7/65	PC-r	1	2	2	4	6	10	12	15
6	169	Sm/69	C-price 25¢; stiff-c PC-r	1	2	2	4	6	10	12	15

37. The Pioneers

Ed	HRN	Date	Details	A	C	GD 2.0	VG 4.0	FN 6.0	VF 8.0	VF/NM 9.0	NM- 9.2
1	37	5/47	Original; Palais-c/a	1	1	22	44	66	125	180	235
2A	62	–	8 pgs. cut; LDC-r; price circle blank	1	1	5	10	15	23	28	32
2B	62	–	10¢; LDC-r;	1	1	26	52	78	150	215	280
3	70	–	LDC-r	1	1	4	8	12	17	21	24
4	92	–	15¢; LDC-r	1	1	4	8	11	16	19	22
5	118	–	LDC-r	1	1	4	7	10	14	17	20
6	131	–	LDC-r	1	1	4	7	10	14	17	20
7	132	–	LDC-r	1	1	4	7	10	14	17	20
8	153	–	LDC-r	1	1	4	7	10	14	17	20
9	167	5/64	LDC-r	1	1	2	4	6	9	11	14
10	167	6/66	LDC-r	1	1	2	4	6	9	11	14
11	166	R/1968	New-c; 25¢; PC-r	1	2	3	6	9	18	24	30

38. Adventures of Cellini

Ed	HRN	Date	Details	A	C	GD 2.0	VG 4.0	FN 6.0	VF 8.0	VF/NM 9.0	NM- 9.2
1	–	6/47	Original; Froehlich c/a	1	1	30	60	90	173	249	325
2	164	–	New-c&a; PC-r	2	2	3	6	9	18	24	30
3	167	12/63	PC-r	2	2	2	4	6	10	12	15
4	167	7/66	PC-r	2	2	2	4	6	10	12	15
5	169	Spr/70	Stiff-c; new price 25¢; PC-r	2	2	2	4	6	10	13	16

39. Jane Eyre

Ed	HRN	Date	Details	A	C	GD 2.0	VG 4.0	FN 6.0	VF 8.0	VF/NM 9.0	NM- 9.2
1	–	7/47	Original	1	1	29	58	87	167	241	315
2	60	–	No c-price; 8 pgs. cut; LDC-r	1	1	6	12	18	28	34	40
3	62	–	LDC-r	1	1	5	10	15	24	30	35
4	71	–	LDC-r; c-price 10¢	1	1	5	10	15	22	26	30
5	92	–	C-price 15¢; LDC-r	1	1	4	9	13	18	22	26
6	118	–	LDC-r	1	1	4	8	12	17	21	24
7	142	–	New-c; old-a; PC-r	1	2	5	10	15	23	28	32
8	154	–	Old-a; PC-r	1	2	4	8	12	17	21	24
9	165	–	New-a; PC-r	2	2	3	6	9	18	23	28
10	167	12/63	PC-r	2	2	3	6	9	16	20	24
11	167	4/65	PC-r	2	2	2	4	6	14	18	22
12	167	8/66	PC-r	2	2	2	4	6	14	18	22
13	166	R/1968	New-c; PC-r	2	3	6	12	18	38	52	65

40. Mysteries ("The Pit and the Pendulum", "The Advs. of Hans Pfall" & "The Fall of the House of Usher")

Ed	HRN	Date	Details	A	C	GD 2.0	VG 4.0	FN 6.0	VF 8.0	VF/NM 9.0	NM- 9.2
1	40	8/47	Original; Kiefer-c/a, Froehlich, Griffiths-a	1	1	60	120	180	375	580	785
2	62	–	LDC-r; 8pgs. cut	1	1	26	52	78	147	211	275
3	75	–	LDC-r	1	1	22	44	66	123	177	230
4	92	–	C-price 15¢; LDC-r	1	1	19	38	57	107	154	200

41. Twenty Years After

Ed	HRN	Date	Details	A	C	GD 2.0	VG 4.0	FN 6.0	VF 8.0	VF/NM 9.0	NM- 9.2
1	–	9/47	Original; 'horror'-c	1	1	40	80	120	230	335	440
2	62	–	New-c; no c-price 8 pgs. cut; LDC-r; Kiefer-c	1	2	6	12	18	33	41	48
3	78	–	C-price 15¢; LDC-r	1	2	5	10	15	23	28	32
4	156	–	New-c; PC-r	1	3	5	10	14	20	24	28
5	167	12/63	PC-r	1	3	2	4	6	8	10	12
6	167	11/66	PC-r	1	3	2	4	6	8	10	12
7	169	Spr/70	New price 25¢; stiff-c; PC-r	1	3	2	4	6	8	10	12

42. Swiss Family Robinson

Ed	HRN	Date	Details	A	C	GD 2.0	VG 4.0	FN 6.0	VF 8.0	VF/NM 9.0	NM- 9.2
1	42	10/47	Orig.; Kiefer-c&a;	1	1	22	44	66	125	180	235
2A	62	–	8 pgs. cut; outside bc: Gift Box ad; LDC-r	1	1	6	12	18	29	36	42
2B	62	–	8 pgs. cut; outside-bc: Reorder list; scarce; LDC-r	1	1	10	20	30	56	73	90
3	75	–	LDC-r	1	1	5	10	14	20	24	28
4	93	–	LDC-r	1	1	4	9	13	18	22	26
5	117	–	LDC-r	1	1	3	6	9	16	20	24
6	131	–	New-c; old-a; PC-r	1	2	3	6	9	17	21	26
7	137	–	Old-a; PC-r	1	2	2	4	6	11	14	18
8	141	–	Old-a; PC-r	1	2	2	4	6	11	14	18
9	152	–	New-a; PC-r	2	2	3	6	9	17	21	26
10	158	–	PC-r	2	2	2	4	6	8	10	12
11	165	–	PC-r	2	2	3	6	9	17	21	26
12	167	12/63	PC-r	2	2	2	4	6	9	11	14
13	167	4/65	PC-r	2	2	2	4	6	8	10	12
14	167	5/66	PC-r	2	2	2	4	6	8	10	12
15	166	11/67	PC-r	2	2	2	4	6	8	10	12
16	169	Spr/69	PC-r; stiff-c	2	2	2	4	6	8	10	12

43. Great Expectations (Used in **SOTI**, pg. 311)

Ed	HRN	Date	Details	A	C	GD 2.0	VG 4.0	FN 6.0	VF 8.0	VF/NM 9.0	NM- 9.2
1	43	11/47	Original; Kiefer-a/c	1	1	89	178	267	556	853	1150
2	62	–	No c-price; 8 pgs. cut; LDC-r	1	1	59	118	177	369	565	760

44. Mysteries of Paris (Used in **SOTI**, pg. 323)

Ed	HRN	Date	Details	A	C	GD 2.0	VG 4.0	FN 6.0	VF 8.0	VF/NM 9.0	NM- 9.2
1A	44	12/47	Original; 56 pgs.; Kiefer-c/a	1	1	65	130	195	406	623	840
1B	44	12/47	Orig.; printed on white/heavier paper; (rare)	1	1	75	150	225	469	722	975
2A	62	–	8 pgs. cut; outside-bc: Gift Box ad; LDC-r	1	1	30	60	90	170	245	320
2B	62	–	8 pgs. cut; outside-bc: reorder list; LDC-r	1	1	30	60	90	170	245	320
3	78	–	C-price 15¢; LDC-r	1	1	25	50	75	141	203	265

45. Tom Brown's School Days

Ed	HRN	Date	Details	A	C

Classics Illustrated #46 © GIL

Classics Illustrated #48 © GIL

Classics Illustrated #51 © GIL

Ed	HRN	Date	Details	A	C	GD 2.0	VG 4.0	FN 6.0	VF 8.0	VF/NM 9.0	NM- 9.2
1	44	1/48	Original; 1st 48pg. issue	1	1	16	32	48	89	127	165
2	64	–	No c-price; LDC-r	1	1	6	12	18	31	38	45
3	161	–	New-c&a; PC-r	2	2	3	6	9	17	21	26
4	167	2/64	PC-r	2	2	2	4	6	9	11	14
5	167	8/66	PC-r	2	2	2	4	6	9	11	14
6	166	R/1968	C-price 25¢; PC-r	2	2	2	4	6	9	11	14

46. Kidnapped

Ed	HRN	Date	Details	A	C	GD 2.0	VG 4.0	FN 6.0	VF 8.0	VF/NM 9.0	NM- 9.2
1	47	4/48	Original; Webb-c/a	1	1	16	32	48	89	127	165
2A	62	–	Price circle blank; LDC-r	1	1	5	10	15	24	30	35
2B	62	–	C-price 10¢; rare; LDC-r	1	1	30	60	90	170	245	320
3	78	–	C-price 15¢; LDC-r	1	1	5	10	14	20	24	28
4	87	–	LDC-r	1	1	4	9	13	18	22	26
5	118	–	LDC-r	1	1	4	7	10	14	17	20
6	131	–	New-c; PC-r	1	2	4	9	13	18	22	26
7	140	–	PC-r	1	2	2	4	6	9	11	14
8	150	–	PC-r	1	2	2	4	6	9	11	14
9	164	–	Reduced pg.width; PC-r	1	2	2	4	6	8	10	12
10	167	–	PC-r	1	2	2	4	6	8	10	12
11	167	3/64	PC-r	1	2	2	4	6	8	10	12
12	167	6/65	PC-r	1	2	2	4	6	8	10	12
13	167	12/65	PC-r	1	2	2	4	6	8	10	12
14	166	9/67	PC-r	1	2	2	4	6	8	10	12
15	166	Win/69	New price 25¢; PC-r; stiff-c	1	2	2	4	6	8	10	12
16	169	Sm/70	PC-r; stiff-c	1	2	2	4	6	8	10	12

47. Twenty Thousand Leagues Under the Sea

Ed	HRN	Date	Details	A	C	GD 2.0	VG 4.0	FN 6.0	VF 8.0	VF/NM 9.0	NM- 9.2
1	47	5/48	Orig.; Kiefer-a&c;	1	1	17	34	51	95	135	175
2	64	–	No c-price; LDC-r	1	1	5	10	15	24	30	35
3	78	–	C-price 15¢; LDC-r	1	1	4	9	13	18	22	26
4	94	–	LDC-r	1	1	4	8	12	17	21	24
5	118	–	LDC-r	1	1	4	7	10	14	17	20
6	128	–	New-c; PC-r	1	2	5	10	14	20	24	28
7	133	–	PC-r	1	2	2	4	6	10	13	16
8	140	–	PC-r	1	2	2	4	6	9	11	14
9	148	–	PC-r	1	2	2	4	6	9	11	14
10	156	–	PC-r	1	2	2	4	6	9	11	14
11	165	–	PC-r	1	2	2	4	6	9	11	14
12	167	–	PC-r	1	2	2	4	6	9	11	14
13	167	3/64	PC-r	1	2	2	4	6	9	11	14
14	167	8/65	PC-r	1	2	2	4	6	9	11	14
15	167	10/66	PC-r	1	2	2	4	6	9	11	14
16	166	R/1968	C-price 25¢; new-c PC-r	1	3	2	4	6	11	14	18
17	169	Spr/70	Stiff-c; PC-r	1	3	2	4	6	12	16	20

48. David Copperfield

Ed	HRN	Date	Details	A	C	GD 2.0	VG 4.0	FN 6.0	VF 8.0	VF/NM 9.0	NM- 9.2
1	47	6/48	Original; Kiefer-c/a	1	1	16	32	48	89	127	165
2	64	–	Price circle replaced by motif of boy reading; LDC-r	1	1	5	10	15	24	30	35
3	87	–	C-price 15¢; LDC-r	1	1	4	8	12	17	21	24
4	121	–	New-c; PC-r	1	2	4	8	12	17	21	24
5	130	–	PC-r	1	2	2	4	6	9	11	14
6	140	–	PC-r	1	2	2	4	6	9	11	14
7	148	–	PC-r	1	2	2	4	6	9	11	14
8	156	–	PC-r	1	2	2	4	6	9	11	14
9	167	–	PC-r	1	2	2	4	6	8	10	12
10	167	4/64	PC-r	1	2	2	4	6	8	10	12
11	167	6/65	PC-r	1	2	2	4	6	8	10	12
12	166	5/67	PC-r	1	2	2	4	6	8	10	12
13	166	R/67	PC-r; C-price 25¢	1	2	2	4	6	10	13	16
14	166	Spr/69	C-price 25¢; stiff-c PC-r	1	2	2	4	6	8	10	12
15	169	Win/69	Stiff-c; PC-r	1	2	2	4	6	8	10	12

49. Alice in Wonderland

Ed	HRN	Date	Details	A	C	GD 2.0	VG 4.0	FN 6.0	VF 8.0	VF/NM 9.0	NM- 9.2
1	47	7/48	Original; 1st Blum a & c	1	1	20	40	60	112	161	210
2	64	–	No c-price; LDC-r	1	1	7	14	21	35	43	50
3A	85	–	C-price 15¢; soft-c LDC-r	1	1	6	12	18	28	34	40
3B	85	–	Stiff-c; LDC-r	1	1	6	12	18	31	38	45
4	155	–	New PC, similar to orig.; PC-r	1	2	4	8	12	25	33	42
5	165	–	PC-r	1	2	3	6	9	18	23	28
6	167	3/64	PC-r	1	2	3	6	9	16	20	24
7	167	6/66	PC-r	1	2	3	6	9	16	20	24
8A	166	Fall/68	New-c; soft-c; 25¢ c-price; PC-r	1	3	4	8	12	25	33	42
8B	166	Fall/68	New-c; stiff-c; 25¢ c-price; PC-r	1	3	7	14	21	51	71	90

50. Adventures of Tom Sawyer (Used in **SOTI**, pg. 37)

Ed	HRN	Date	Details	A	C	GD 2.0	VG 4.0	FN 6.0	VF 8.0	VF/NM 9.0	NM- 9.2
1A	51	8/48	Orig.; Aldo Rubano a&c	1	1	16	32	48	89	127	165
1B	51	9/48	Orig.; Rubano c&a	1	1	16	32	48	89	127	165
1C	51	9/48	Orig.; outside-bc: blue & yellow only; rare	1	1	22	44	66	123	177	230
2	64	–	No c-price; LDC-r	1	1	5	10	15	22	26	30
3	78	–	C-price 15¢; LDC-r	1	1	4	8	12	17	21	24
4	94	–	LDC-r	1	1	4	7	10	14	17	20
5	117	–	LDC-r	1	1	2	4	6	11	14	18
6	132	–	LDC-r	1	1	2	4	6	11	14	18
7	140	–	New-c; PC-r	1	2	3	6	9	18	23	28
8	150	–	PC-r	1	2	2	4	6	9	11	14
9	164	–	New-a; PC-r	2	2	3	6	9	18	23	28
10	167	–	PC-r	2	2	2	4	6	9	11	14
11	167	1/65	PC-r	2	2	2	4	6	8	10	12
12	167	5/66	PC-r	2	2	2	4	6	8	10	12
13	166	12/67	PC-r	2	2	2	4	6	8	10	12
14	169	Fall/69	C-price 25¢; stiff-c; PC-r	2	2	2	4	6	8	10	12
15	169	Win/71	PC-r	2	2	2	4	6	8	10	12

51. The Spy

Ed	HRN	Date	Details	A	C	GD 2.0	VG 4.0	FN 6.0	VF 8.0	VF/NM 9.0	NM- 9.2
1A	51	9/48	Original; inside-bc illo: Christmas Carol	1	1	15	30	45	85	120	155
1B	51	9/48	Original; inside-bc illo: Man in Iron Mask	1	1	15	30	45	85	120	155
1C	51	8/48	Original; outside-bc: full color	1	1	15	30	45	85	120	155
1D	51	8/48	Original; outside-bc: blue & yellow only; scarce	1	1	17	34	51	95	135	175
2	89	–	C-price 15¢; LDC-r	1	1	5	10	14	20	24	28
3	121	–	LDC-r	1	1	4	8	12	17	21	24
4	139	–	New-c; PC-r	1	2	3	6	9	18	23	28
5	156	–	PC-r	1	2	2	4	6	9	11	14
6	167	11/63	PC-r	1	2	2	4	6	8	10	12
7	167	7/66	PC-r	1	2	2	4	6	8	10	12
8A	166	Win/69	C-price 25¢; soft-c; scarce; PC-r	1	2	3	6	9	17	21	26
8B	166	Win/69	C-price 25¢; stiff-c; PC-r	1	2	2	4	6	8	10	12

52. The House of the Seven Gables

Ed	HRN	Date	Details	A	C	GD 2.0	VG 4.0	FN 6.0	VF 8.0	VF/NM 9.0	NM- 9.2
1	53	10/48	Orig.; Griffiths a&c	1	1	15	30	45	85	120	155
2	89	–	C-price 15¢; LDC-r	1	1	5	10	14	20	24	28
3	121	–	LDC-r	1	1	4	8	12	17	21	24
4	142	–	New-c&a; PC-r; Woodbridge-a	2	2	5	10	15	22	26	30
5	156	–	PC-r	2	2	2	4	6	9	11	14
6	165	–	PC-r	2	2	2	4	6	8	10	12
7	167	5/64	PC-r	2	2	2	4	6	9	11	14
8	167	3/66	PC-r	2	2	2	4	6	8	10	12
9	166	R/1968	C-price 25¢; PC-r	2	2	2	4	6	8	10	12
10	169	Spr/70	Stiff-c; PC-r	2	2	2	4	6	8	10	12

53. A Christmas Carol

Classics Illustrated #55 © GIL

Classics Illustrated #59 © GIL

Classics Illustrated #65 © GIL

Ed	HRN	Date	Details	A	C	GD 2.0	VG 4.0	FN 6.0	VF 8.0	VF/NM 9.0	NM- 9.2
1	53	11/48	Original & only ed; Kiefer-c/a	1	1	20	40	60	112	161	210

54. Man in the Iron Mask

Ed	HRN	Date	Details	A	C	GD 2.0	VG 4.0	FN 6.0	VF 8.0	VF/NM 9.0	NM- 9.2
1	55	12/48	Original; Froehlich-a, Kiefer-c	1	1	15	30	45	85	120	155
2	93	–	C-price 15¢; LDC-r	1	1	5	10	15	23	28	32
3A	111	–	(O) logo lettering; scarce; LDC-r	1	1	6	12	18	31	38	45
3B	111	–	New logo as PC; LDC-r	1	1	5	10	15	22	26	30
4	142	–	New-c&a; PC-r	2	2	5	10	15	22	26	30
5	154	–	PC-r	2	2	2	4	6	9	11	14
6	165	–	PC-r	2	2	2	4	6	8	10	12
7	167	5/64	PC-r	2	2	2	4	6	8	10	12
8	167	4/66	PC-r	2	2	2	4	6	8	10	12
9A	166	Win/69	C-price 25¢; soft-c PC-r	2	2	3	6	9	17	21	26
9B	166	Win/69	Stiff-c	2	2	2	4	6	8	10	12

55. Silas Marner (Used in **SOTI**, pgs. 311, 312)

Ed	HRN	Date	Details	A	C	GD 2.0	VG 4.0	FN 6.0	VF 8.0	VF/NM 9.0	NM- 9.2
1	55	1/49	Original-Kiefer-c	1	1	15	30	45	85	120	155
2	75	–	Price circle blank; 'Coming Next' ad; LDC-r	1	1	5	10	15	24	30	35
3	97	–	LDC-r	1	1	3	6	9	16	20	24
4	121	–	New-c; PC-r	1	2	3	6	9	18	23	28
5	130	–	PC-r	1	2	2	4	6	9	11	14
6	140	–	PC-r	1	2	2	4	6	9	11	14
7	154	–	PC-r	1	2	2	4	6	9	11	14
8	165	–	PC-r	1	2	2	4	6	8	10	12
9	167	2/64	PC-r	1	2	2	4	6	8	10	12
10	167	6/65	PC-r	1	2	2	4	6	8	10	12
11	166	5/67	PC-r	1	2	2	4	6	8	10	12
12A	166	Win/69	C-price 25¢; soft-c PC-r	1	2	3	6	9	18	21	26
12B	166	Win/69	C-price 25¢; stiff-c PC-r	1	2	2	4	6	8	10	12

56. The Toilers of the Sea

Ed	HRN	Date	Details	A	C	GD 2.0	VG 4.0	FN 6.0	VF 8.0	VF/NM 9.0	NM- 9.2
1	55	2/49	Original; A.M. Froehlich-c/a	1	1	24	48	72	135	195	255
2	165	–	New-c&a; PC-r; Angelo Torres-a	2	2	6	12	18	33	41	48
3	167	3/64	PC-r	2	2	3	6	9	17	21	26
4	167	10/66	PC-r	2	2	3	6	9	17	21	26

57. The Song of Hiawatha

Ed	HRN	Date	Details	A	C	GD 2.0	VG 4.0	FN 6.0	VF 8.0	VF/NM 9.0	NM- 9.2
1	55	3/49	Original; Alex Blum-c/a	1	1	14	28	42	81	133	145
2	75	–	No c-price w/15¢ sticker; 'Coming Next' ad; LDC-r	1	1	5	10	15	24	30	35
3	94	–	C-price 15¢; LDC-r	1	1	5	10	14	20	24	28
4	118	–	LDC-r	1	1	3	6	9	16	20	24
5	134	–	New-c; PC-r	1	2	3	6	9	18	23	28
6	139	–	PC-r	1	2	2	4	6	9	11	14
7	154	–	PC-r	1	2	2	4	6	9	11	14
8	167	–	Has orig.date; PC-r	1	2	2	4	6	8	10	12
9	167	9/64	PC-r	1	2	2	4	6	8	10	12
10	167	10/65	PC-r	1	2	2	4	6	8	10	12
11	166	F/1968	C-price 25¢; PC-r	1	2	2	4	6	8	10	12

58. The Prairie

Ed	HRN	Date	Details	A	C	GD 2.0	VG 4.0	FN 6.0	VF 8.0	VF/NM 9.0	NM- 9.2
1	60	4/49	Original; Palais c/a	1	1	14	28	42	81	113	145
2A	62	–	No c-price; no coming-next ad; LDC-r	1	1	8	16	24	43	55	65
2B	62		10¢ (rare)	1	1	17	34	51	95	135	175
3	78	–	C-price 15¢ in dbl. circle; LDC-r	1	1	5	10	14	20	24	28
4	114	–	LDC-r	1	1	4	8	12	17	21	24
5	131	–	LDC-r	1	1	4	7	10	14	17	20
6	132	–	LDC-r	1	1	4	7	10	14	17	20
7	146	–	New-c; PC-r	1	2	5	10	14	20	24	28
8	155	–	PC-r	1	2	2	4	6	9	11	14
9	167	5/64	PC-r	1	2	2	4	6	8	10	12
10	167	4/66	PC-r	1	2	2	4	6	8	10	12
11	169	Sm/69	New price 25¢; stiff-c; PC-r	1	2	2	4	6	8	10	12

59. Wuthering Heights

Ed	HRN	Date	Details	A	C	GD 2.0	VG 4.0	FN 6.0	VF 8.0	VF/NM 9.0	NM- 9.2
1	60	5/49	Original; Kiefer-c/a	1	1	15	30	45	85	120	155
2	85	–	C-price 15¢; LDC-r	1	1	6	12	18	28	34	40
3	156	–	New-c; PC-r	1	2	5	10	15	22	26	30
4	167	1/64	PC-r	1	2	2	4	6	9	11	14
5	167	10/66	PC-r	1	2	2	4	6	9	11	14
6	169	Sm/69	C-price 25¢; stiff-c; PC-r	1	2	2	4	6	9	11	14

60. Black Beauty

Ed	HRN	Date	Details	A	C	GD 2.0	VG 4.0	FN 6.0	VF 8.0	VF/NM 9.0	NM- 9.2
1	62	6/49	Original; Froehlich-c/a	1	1	14	28	42	81	113	145
2	62	–	No c-price; no coming-next ad; LDC-r (rare)	1	1	16	32	48	92	131	170
3	85	–	C-price 15¢; LDC-r	1	1	5	10	15	23	28	32
4	158	–	New L.B. Cole-c/a; PC-r	2	2	6	12	18	28	34	40
5	167	2/64	PC-r	2	2	2	4	6	12	16	20
6	167	3/66	PC-r	2	2	2	4	6	12	16	20
7	166	R/1968	New-c&price, 25¢; PC-r	2	3	5	10	15	36	48	60

61. The Woman in White

Ed	HRN	Date	Details	A	C	GD 2.0	VG 4.0	FN 6.0	VF 8.0	VF/NM 9.0	NM- 9.2
1A	62	7/49	Original; Blum-c/a fc-purple; bc: top illos light blue	1	1	15	30	45	85	120	155
1B	62	7/49	Original; Blum-c/a fc-pink; bc: top illos light violet	1	1	15	30	45	85	120	155
2	156	–	New-c; PC-r	1	2	5	10	15	23	28	32
3	167	1/64	PC-r	1	2	2	4	6	12	16	20
4	166	R/1968	C-price 25¢; PC-r	1	2	2	4	6	12	16	20

62. Western Stories ("The Luck of Roaring Camp" and "The Outcasts of Poker Flat")

Ed	HRN	Date	Details	A	C	GD 2.0	VG 4.0	FN 6.0	VF 8.0	VF/NM 9.0	NM- 9.2
1	62	8/49	Original; Kiefer-c/a	1	1	13	26	39	76	106	135
2	89	–	C-price 15¢; LDC-r	1	1	5	10	15	23	28	32
3	121	–	LDC-r	1	1	3	6	9	17	21	26
4	137	–	New-c; PC-r	1	2	3	6	9	18	23	28
5	152	–	PC-r	1	2	2	4	6	8	10	12
6	167	10/63	PC-r	1	2	2	4	6	8	10	12
7	167	6/64	PC-r	1	2	2	4	6	8	10	12
8	167	11/66	PC-r	1	2	2	4	6	8	10	12
9	166	R/1968	New-c&price 25¢; PC-r	1	3	3	6	9	17	21	26

63. The Man Without a Country

Ed	HRN	Date	Details	A	C	GD 2.0	VG 4.0	FN 6.0	VF 8.0	VF/NM 9.0	NM- 9.2
1	62	9/49	Original; Kiefer-c/a	1	1	14	28	42	81	113	145
2	78	–	C-price 15¢ in double circle; LDC-r	1	1	5	10	15	23	28	32
3	156	–	New-c, old-a; PC-r	1	2	5	10	15	23	28	32
4	165	–	New-a & text pgs.; PC-r; A. Torres-a	2	2	5	10	14	20	24	28
5	167	3/64	PC-r	2	2	2	4	6	8	10	12
6	167	8/66	PC-r	2	2	2	4	6	8	10	12
7	169	Sm/69	New price 25¢; stiff-c; PC-r	2	2	2	4	6	8	10	12

64. Treasure Island

Ed	HRN	Date	Details	A	C	GD 2.0	VG 4.0	FN 6.0	VF 8.0	VF/NM 9.0	NM- 9.2
1	62	10/49	Original; Blum-c/a	1	1	15	30	45	85	120	155
2A	82	–	C-price 15¢; soft-c LDC-r	1	1	5	10	15	22	26	30

Classics Illustrated #67 © GIL

Classics Illustrated #71 © GIL

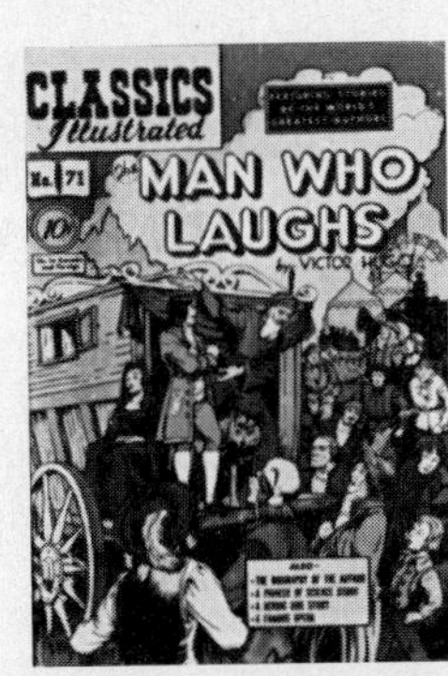

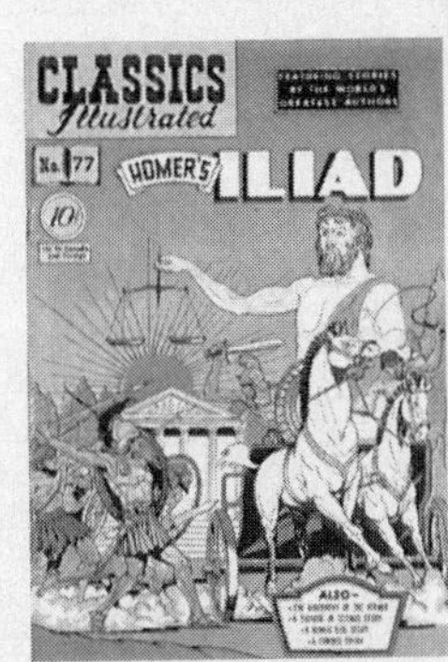

Classics Illustrated #77 © GIL

Ed	HRN	Date	Details	A	C	GD 2.0	VG 4.0	FN 6.0	VF 8.0	VF/NM 9.0	NM- 9.2
2B	82	–	Stiff-c; LDC-r	1	1	5	10	15	23	28	32
3	117	–	LDC-r	1	1	3	6	9	17	21	26
4	131	–	New-c; PC-r	1	2	3	6	9	18	23	28
5	138	–	PC-r	1	2	2	4	6	9	11	14
6	146	–	PC-r	1	2	2	4	6	9	11	14
7	158	–	PC-r	1	2	2	4	6	9	11	14
8	165	–	PC-r	1	2	2	4	6	8	10	12
9	167	–	PC-r	1	2	2	4	6	8	10	12
10	167	6/64	PC-r	1	2	2	4	6	8	10	12
11	167	12/65	PC-r	1	2	2	4	6	8	10	12
12A	166	10/67	PC-r	1	2	2	4	6	8	10	12
12B	166	10/67	w/Grit ad stapled in book	1	2	14	28	42	81	113	145
13	169	Spr/69	New price 25¢; stiff-c; PC-r	1	2	2	4	6	9	11	14
14	–	1989	Long John Silver's Seafood Shoppes; $1.95, First/Berkley Publ.; Blum-r	1	2						5.00

65. Benjamin Franklin

Ed	HRN	Date	Details	A	C	GD 2.0	VG 4.0	FN 6.0	VF 8.0	VF/NM 9.0	NM- 9.2
1	64	11/49	Original; Kiefer-c; Iger Shop-a	1	1	14	28	42	81	113	145
2	131	–	New-c; PC-r	1	2	5	10	15	22	26	30
3	154	–	PC-r	1	2	2	4	6	10	12	15
4	167	2/64	PC-r	1	2	2	4	6	9	11	14
5	167	4/66	PC-r	1	2	2	4	6	9	11	14
6	169	Fall/69	New price 25¢; stiff-c; PC-r	1	2	2	4	6	9	11	14

66. The Cloister and the Hearth

Ed	HRN	Date	Details	A	C	GD 2.0	VG 4.0	FN 6.0	VF 8.0	VF/NM 9.0	NM- 9.2
1	67	12/49	Original & only ed; Kiefer-a & c	1	1	29	58	87	164	237	310

67. The Scottish Chiefs

Ed	HRN	Date	Details	A	C	GD 2.0	VG 4.0	FN 6.0	VF 8.0	VF/NM 9.0	NM- 9.2
1	67	1/50	Original; Blum-a&c	1	1	12	24	36	71	98	125
2	85	–	C-price 15¢; LDC-r	1	1	5	10	15	23	28	32
3	118	–	LDC-r	1	1	3	6	9	17	21	26
4	136	–	New-c; PC-r	1	2	3	6	9	18	24	30
5	154	–	PC-r	1	2	2	4	6	9	11	14
6	167	11/63	PC-r	1	2	2	4	6	10	13	16
7	167	8/65	PC-r	1	2	2	4	6	9	11	14

68. Julius Caesar (Used in **SOTI**, pgs. 36, 37)

Ed	HRN	Date	Details	A	C	GD 2.0	VG 4.0	FN 6.0	VF 8.0	VF/NM 9.0	NM- 9.2
1	70	2/50	Original; Kiefer-c/a	1	1	12	24	36	71	98	125
2	85	–	C-price 15¢; LDC-r	1	1	5	10	15	22	26	30
3	108	–	LDC-r	1	1	4	9	13	18	22	26
4	156	–	New L.B. Cole-c; PC-r	1	2	5	10	15	23	28	32
5	165	–	New-a by Evans, Crandall; PC-r	2	2	5	10	15	22	26	30
6	167	2/64	PC-r	2	2	2	4	6	8	10	12
7	167	10/65	Tarzan books inside cover; PC-r	2	2	2	4	6	8	10	12
8	166	R/1967	PC-r	2	2	2	4	6	8	10	12
9	169	Win/69	PC-r; stiff-c	2	2	2	4	6	8	10	12

69. Around the World in 80 Days

Ed	HRN	Date	Details	A	C	GD 2.0	VG 4.0	FN 6.0	VF 8.0	VF/NM 9.0	NM- 9.2
1	70	3/50	Original; Kiefer-c/a	1	1	12	24	36	71	98	125
2	87	–	C-price 15¢; LDC-r	1	1	5	10	15	22	26	30
3	125	–	LDC-r	1	1	4	9	13	18	22	26
4	136	–	New-c; PC-r	1	2	5	10	15	22	26	30
5	146	–	PC-r	1	2	2	4	6	9	11	14
6	152	–	PC-r	1	2	2	4	6	9	11	14
7	164	–	PC-r	1	2	2	4	6	8	10	12
8	167	–	PC-r	1	2	2	4	6	8	10	12
9	167	7/64	PC-r	1	2	2	4	6	8	10	12
10	167	11/65	PC-r	1	2	2	4	6	8	10	12
11	166	7/67	PC-r	1	2	2	4	6	8	10	12
12	169	Spr/69	C-price 25¢; stiff-c; PC-r	1	2	2	4	6	8	10	12

70. The Pilot

Ed	HRN	Date	Details	A	C	GD 2.0	VG 4.0	FN 6.0	VF 8.0	VF/NM 9.0	NM- 9.2
1	71	4/50	Original; Blum-c/a	1	1	10	20	30	58	77	95
2	92	–	C-price 15¢; LDC-r	1	1	5	10	15	23	28	32
3	125	–	LDC-r	1	1	4	9	13	18	22	26
4	156	–	New-c; PC-r	1	2	5	10	15	23	28	32
5	167	2/64	PC-r	1	2	2	4	6	12	16	20
6	167	5/66	PC-r	1	2	2	4	6	10	13	16

71. The Man Who Laughs

Ed	HRN	Date	Details	A	C	GD 2.0	VG 4.0	FN 6.0	VF 8.0	VF/NM 9.0	NM- 9.2
1	71	5/50	Original; Blum-c/a	1	1	17	34	51	95	135	175
2	165	–	New-c&a; PC-r	2	2	11	22	33	66	91	115
3	167	4/64	PC-r	2	2	10	20	30	58	77	90

72. The Oregon Trail

Ed	HRN	Date	Details	A	C	GD 2.0	VG 4.0	FN 6.0	VF 8.0	VF/NM 9.0	NM- 9.2
1	73	6/50	Original; Kiefer-c/a	1	1	10	20	30	55	77	95
2	89	–	C-price 15¢; LDC-r	1	1	5	10	15	23	28	32
3	121	–	LDC-r	1	1	4	9	13	18	22	26
4	131	–	New-c; PC-r	1	2	5	10	15	22	26	30
5	140	–	PC-r	1	2	2	4	6	9	11	14
6	150	–	PC-r	1	2	2	4	6	9	11	14
7	164	–	PC-r	1	2	2	4	6	8	10	12
8	167	–	PC-r	1	2	2	4	6	8	10	12
9	167	8/64	PC-r	1	2	2	4	6	8	10	12
10	167	10/65	PC-r	1	2	2	4	6	8	10	12
11	166	R/1968	C-price 25¢; PC-r	1	2	2	4	6	8	10	12

73. The Black Tulip

Ed	HRN	Date	Details	A	C	GD 2.0	VG 4.0	FN 6.0	VF 8.0	VF/NM 9.0	NM- 9.2
1	75	7/50	1st & only ed.; Alex Blum-c/a	1	1	36	72	108	204	297	390

74. Mr. Midshipman Easy

Ed	HRN	Date	Details	A	C	GD 2.0	VG 4.0	FN 6.0	VF 8.0	VF/NM 9.0	NM- 9.2
1	75	8/50	1st & only edition	1	1	36	72	108	204	297	390

75. The Lady of the Lake

Ed	HRN	Date	Details	A	C	GD 2.0	VG 4.0	FN 6.0	VF 8.0	VF/NM 9.0	NM- 9.2
1	75	9/50	Original; Kiefer-c/a	1	1	10	20	30	58	77	95
2	85	–	C-price 15¢; LDC-r	1	1	5	10	15	24	30	35
3	118	–	LDC-r	1	1	5	10	14	20	24	28
4	139	–	New-c; PC-r	1	2	5	10	15	22	26	30
5	154	–	PC-r	1	2	2	4	6	9	11	14
6	165	–	PC-r	1	2	2	4	6	8	10	12
7	167	4/64	PC-r	1	2	2	4	6	8	10	12
8	167	5/66	PC-r	1	2	2	4	6	8	10	12
9	169	Spr/69	New price 25¢; stiff-c; PC-r	1	2	2	4	6	8	10	12

76. The Prisoner of Zenda

Ed	HRN	Date	Details	A	C	GD 2.0	VG 4.0	FN 6.0	VF 8.0	VF/NM 9.0	NM- 9.2
1	75	10/50	Original; Kiefer-c/a	1	1	10	20	30	58	77	95
2	85	–	C-price 15¢; LDC-r	1	1	5	10	15	23	28	32
3	111	–	LDC-r	1	1	3	6	9	17	21	26
4	128	–	New-c; PC-r	1	2	3	6	9	18	23	28
5	152	–	PC-r	1	2	2	4	6	9	11	14
6	165	–	PC-r	1	2	2	4	6	8	10	12
7	167	4/64	PC-r	1	2	2	4	6	8	10	12
8	167	9/66	PC-r	1	2	2	4	6	8	10	12
9	169	Fall/69	New price 25¢; stiff-c; PC-r	1	2	2	4	6	8	10	12

77. The Iliad

Ed	HRN	Date	Details	A	C	GD 2.0	VG 4.0	FN 6.0	VF 8.0	VF/NM 9.0	NM- 9.2
1	78	11/50	Original; Blum-c/a	1	1	10	20	30	58	77	95
2	87	–	C-price 15¢; LDC-r	1	1	5	10	15	24	30	35
3	121	–	LDC-r	1	1	3	6	9	18	21	26
4	139	–	New-c; PC-r	1	2	3	6	9	18	22	26
5	150	–	PC-r	1	2	2	4	6	9	11	14
6	165	–	PC-r	1	2	2	4	6	8	10	12
7	167	10/63	PC-r	1	2	2	4	6	8	10	12
8	167	7/64	PC-r	1	2	2	4	6	8	10	12
9	167	5/66	PC-r	1	2	2	4	6	8	10	12
10	166	R/1968	C-price 25¢; PC-r	1	2	2	4	6	8	10	12

78. Joan of Arc

Ed	HRN	Date	Details	A	C	GD 2.0	VG 4.0	FN 6.0	VF 8.0	VF/NM 9.0	NM- 9.2
1	78	12/50	Original; Kiefer-c/a	1	1	10	20	30	58	77	95
2	87	–	C-price 15¢; LDC-r	1	1	5	10	15	23	28	32

Classics Illustrated #79 © GIL

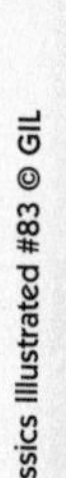

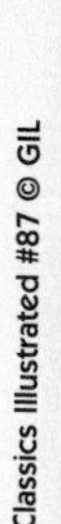

Ed	HRN	Date	Details	A	C	GD 2.0	VG 4.0	FN 6.0	VF 8.0	VF/NM 9.0	NM- 9.2
3	113	–	LDC-r	1	1	3	6	9	17	22	26
4	128	–	New-c; PC-r	1	2	3	6	9	18	23	28
5	140	–	PC-r	1	2	2	4	6	9	11	14
6	150	–	PC-r	1	2	2	4	6	9	11	14
7	159	–	PC-r	1	2	2	4	6	9	11	14
8	167	–	PC-r	1	2	2	4	6	9	11	14
9	167	12/63	PC-r	1	2	2	4	6	8	10	12
10	167	6/65	PC-r	1	2	2	4	6	8	10	12
11	166	6/67	PC-r	1	2	2	4	6	8	10	12
12	166	Win/69	New-c&price, 25¢; PC-r; stiff-c	1	3	3	6	9	18	23	28

79. Cyrano de Bergerac

Ed	HRN	Date	Details	A	C	GD 2.0	VG 4.0	FN 6.0	VF 8.0	VF/NM 9.0	NM- 9.2
1	78	1/51	Orig.; movie promo inside front-c; Blum-c/a	1	1	10	20	30	58	77	95
2	85	–	C-price 15¢; LDC-r	1	1	5	10	15	23	28	32
3	118	–	LDC-r	1	1	3	6	9	18	23	28
4	133	–	New-c; PC-r	1	2	3	6	9	17	21	26
5	156	–	PC-r	1	2	2	4	6	12	16	20
6	167	8/64	PC-r	1	2	2	4	6	12	16	20

80. White Fang (Last line drawn cover)

Ed	HRN	Date	Details	A	C	GD 2.0	VG 4.0	FN 6.0	VF 8.0	VF/NM 9.0	NM- 9.2
1	79	2/51	Orig.; Blum-c/a	1	1	10	20	30	58	77	95
2	87	–	C-price 15¢; LDC-r	1	1	5	10	15	24	30	35
3	125	–	LDC-r	1	1	3	6	9	17	22	26
4	132	–	New-c; PC-r	1	2	3	6	9	17	21	26
5	140	–	PC-r	1	2	2	4	6	9	11	14
6	153	–	PC-r	1	2	2	4	6	9	11	14
7	167	–	PC-r	1	2	2	4	6	8	10	12
8	167	9/64	PC-r	1	2	2	4	6	8	10	12
9	167	7/65	PC-r	1	2	2	4	6	8	10	12
10	166	6/67	PC-r	1	2	2	4	6	8	10	12
11	169	Fall/69	New price 25¢; PC-r; stiff-c	1	2	2	4	6	8	10	12

81. The Odyssey (1st painted cover)

Ed	HRN	Date	Details	A	C	GD 2.0	VG 4.0	FN 6.0	VF 8.0	VF/NM 9.0	NM- 9.2
1	82	3/51	First 15¢ Original; Blum-c	1	1	10	20	30	58	77	95
2	167	8/64	PC-r	1	1	2	4	6	12	16	20
3	167	10/66	PC-r	1	1	2	4	6	12	16	20
4	169	Spr/69	New, stiff-c; PC-r	1	2	3	6	9	18	24	30

82. The Master of Ballantrae

Ed	HRN	Date	Details	A	C	GD 2.0	VG 4.0	FN 6.0	VF 8.0	VF/NM 9.0	NM- 9.2
1	82	4/51	Original; Blum-c	1	1	9	18	27	51	62	75
2	167	8/64	PC-r	1	1	3	6	9	16	20	24
3	166	Fall/68	New, stiff-c; PC-r	1	2	3	6	9	18	24	30

83. The Jungle Book

Ed	HRN	Date	Details	A	C	GD 2.0	VG 4.0	FN 6.0	VF 8.0	VF/NM 9.0	NM- 9.2
1	85	5/51	Original; Blum-c Bossert/Blum-a	1	1	9	18	27	51	62	75
2	110	–	PC-r	1	1	2	4	6	10	13	16
3	125	–	PC-r	1	1	2	4	6	9	11	14
4	134	–	PC-r	1	1	2	4	6	9	11	14
5	142	–	PC-r	1	1	2	4	6	9	11	14
6	150	–	PC-r	1	1	2	4	6	9	11	14
7	159	–	PC-r	1	1	2	4	6	9	11	14
8	167	–	PC-r	1	1	2	4	6	8	10	12
9	167	3/65	PC-r	1	1	2	4	6	8	10	12
10	167	11/65	PC-r	1	1	2	4	6	8	10	12
11	167	5/66	PC-r	1	1	2	4	6	8	10	12
12	166	R/1968	New c&a; stiff-c; PC-r	2	2	3	6	9	18	24	30

84. The Gold Bug and Other Stories ("The Gold Bug", "The Tell-Tale Heart", "The Cask of Amontillado")

Ed	HRN	Date	Details	A	C	GD 2.0	VG 4.0	FN 6.0	VF 8.0	VF/NM 9.0	NM- 9.2
1	85	6/51	Original; Blum-c/a; Palais, Laverly-a	1	1	12	24	36	69	95	120
2	167	7/64	PC-r	1	1	10	20	30	56	73	90

85. The Sea Wolf

Ed	HRN	Date	Details	A	C	GD 2.0	VG 4.0	FN 6.0	VF 8.0	VF/NM 9.0	NM- 9.2
1	85	7/51	Original; Blum-c/a	1	1	8	16	24	43	54	65
2	121	–	PC-r	1	1	2	4	6	9	11	14
3	132	–	PC-r	1	1	2	4	6	9	11	14
4	141	–	PC-r	1	1	2	4	6	9	11	14
5	161	–	PC-r	1	1	2	4	6	8	10	12
6	167	2/64	PC-r	1	1	2	4	6	8	10	12
7	167	11/65	PC-r	1	1	2	4	6	8	10	12
8	169	Fall/69	New price 25¢; stiff-c; PC-r	1	1	2	4	6	8	10	12

86. Under Two Flags

Ed	HRN	Date	Details	A	C	GD 2.0	VG 4.0	FN 6.0	VF 8.0	VF/NM 9.0	NM- 9.2
1	87	8/51	Original; first delBourgo-a	1	1	8	16	24	40	50	60
2	117	–	PC-r	1	1	2	4	6	10	13	16
3	139	–	PC-r	1	1	2	4	6	9	11	14
4	158	–	PC-r	1	1	2	4	6	9	11	14
5	167	2/64	PC-r	1	1	2	4	6	8	10	12
6	167	8/66	PC-r	1	1	2	4	6	8	10	12
7	169	Sm/69	New price 25¢; stiff-c; PC-r	1	1	2	4	6	8	10	12

87. A Midsummer Nights Dream

Ed	HRN	Date	Details	A	C	GD 2.0	VG 4.0	FN 6.0	VF 8.0	VF/NM 9.0	NM- 9.2
1	87	9/51	Original; Blum c/a	1	1	8	16	24	43	54	65
2	161	–	PC-r	1	1	2	4	6	9	11	14
3	167	4/64	PC-r	1	1	2	4	6	8	10	12
4	167	5/66	PC-r	1	1	2	4	6	8	10	12
5	169	Sm/69	New price 25¢; stiff-c; PC-r	1	1	2	4	6	8	10	12

88. Men of Iron

Ed	HRN	Date	Details	A	C	GD 2.0	VG 4.0	FN 6.0	VF 8.0	VF/NM 9.0	NM- 9.2
1	89	10/51	Original	1	1	8	16	24	43	54	65
2	154	–	PC-r	1	1	2	4	6	9	11	14
3	167	1/64	PC-r	1	1	2	4	6	8	10	12
4	166	R/1968	C-price 25¢; PC-r	1	1	2	4	6	8	10	12

89. Crime and Punishment (Cover illo. in **POP**)

Ed	HRN	Date	Details	A	C	GD 2.0	VG 4.0	FN 6.0	VF 8.0	VF/NM 9.0	NM- 9.2
1	89	11/51	Original; Palais-a	1	1	8	16	24	43	54	65
2	152	–	PC-r	1	1	2	4	6	9	11	14
3	167	4/64	PC-r	1	1	2	4	6	8	10	12
4	167	5/66	PC-r	1	1	2	4	6	8	10	12
5	169	Fall/69	New price 25¢ stiff-c; PC-r	1	1	2	4	6	8	10	12

90. Green Mansions

Ed	HRN	Date	Details	A	C	GD 2.0	VG 4.0	FN 6.0	VF 8.0	VF/NM 9.0	NM- 9.2
1	89	12/51	Original; Blum-c/a	1	1	8	16	24	43	54	65
2	148	–	New L.B. Cole-c; PC-r	1	2	4	8	12	17	21	24
3	165	–	PC-r	1	2	2	4	6	8	10	12
4	167	4/64	PC-r	1	2	2	4	6	8	10	12
5	167	9/66	PC-r	1	2	2	4	6	8	10	12
6	169	Sm/69	New price 25¢; stiff-c; PC-r	1	2	2	4	6	8	10	12

91. The Call of the Wild

Ed	HRN	Date	Details	A	C	GD 2.0	VG 4.0	FN 6.0	VF 8.0	VF/NM 9.0	NM- 9.2
1	92	1/52	Orig.; delBourgo-a	1	1	8	16	24	43	54	65
2	112	–	PC-r	1	1	2	4	6	9	11	14
3	125	–	'Picture Progress' on back-c; PC-r	1	1	2	4	6	9	11	14
4	134	–	PC-r	1	1	2	4	6	9	11	14
5	143	–	PC-r	1	1	2	4	6	9	11	14
6	165	–	PC-r	1	1	2	4	6	9	11	14
7	167	–	PC-r	1	1	2	4	6	8	10	12
8	167	4/65	PC-r	1	1	2	4	6	8	10	12
9	167	3/66	PC-r	1	1	2	4	6	8	10	12
10	166	11/67	PC-r	1	1	2	4	6	8	10	12
11	169	Spr/70	New price 25¢; stiff-c; PC-r	1	1	2	4	6	8	10	12

92. The Courtship of Miles Standish

Ed	HRN	Date	Details	A	C	GD 2.0	VG 4.0	FN 6.0	VF 8.0	VF/NM 9.0	NM- 9.2
1	92	2/52	Original; Blum-c/a	1	1	8	16	24	40	50	60
2	165	–	PC-r	1	1	2	4	6	9	11	14
3	167	3/64	PC-r	1	1	2	4	6	9	11	14
4	166	5/67	PC-r	1	1	2	4	6	9	11	14

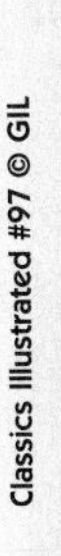
Classics Illustrated #97 © GIL

Classics Illustrated #101 © GIL

Classics Illustrated #104 © GIL

Ed	HRN	Date	Details	A	C	GD 2.0	VG 4.0	FN 6.0	VF 8.0	VF/NM 9.0	NM- 9.2
5	169	Win/69	New price 25¢ stiff-c; PC-r	1	1	2	4	6	9	11	14

93. Pudd'nhead Wilson

Ed	HRN	Date	Details	A	C	GD 2.0	VG 4.0	FN 6.0	VF 8.0	VF/NM 9.0	NM- 9.2
1	94	3/52	Orig.; Kiefer-c/a;	1	1	8	16	24	43	54	65
2	165	–	New-c; PC-r	1	2	2	4	6	12	16	20
3	167	3/64	PC-r	1	2	2	4	6	9	11	14
4	166	R/1968	New price 25¢; soft-c; PC-r	1	2	2	4	6	10	12	15

94. David Balfour

Ed	HRN	Date	Details	A	C	GD 2.0	VG 4.0	FN 6.0	VF 8.0	VF/NM 9.0	NM- 9.2
1	94	4/52	Original; Palais-a	1	1	8	16	24	43	54	65
2	167	5/64	PC-r	1	1	2	4	6	12	16	20
3	166	R/1968	C-price 25¢; PC-r	1	1	2	4	6	14	18	22

95. All Quiet on the Western Front

Ed	HRN	Date	Details	A	C	GD 2.0	VG 4.0	FN 6.0	VF 8.0	VF/NM 9.0	NM- 9.2
1A	96	5/52	Orig.; del Bourgo-a	1	1	11	22	33	64	87	110
1B	99	5/52	Orig.; del Bourgo-a	1	1	9	18	27	54	70	85
2	167	10/64	PC-r	1	1	3	6	9	17	22	26
3	167	11/66	PC-r	1	1	3	6	9	17	22	26

96. Daniel Boone

Ed	HRN	Date	Details	A	C	GD 2.0	VG 4.0	FN 6.0	VF 8.0	VF/NM 9.0	NM- 9.2
1	97	6/52	Original; Blum-a	1	1	8	16	24	40	50	60
2	117	–	PC-r	1	1	2	4	6	9	11	14
3	128	–	PC-r	1	1	2	4	6	9	11	14
4	132	–	PC-r	1	1	2	4	6	9	11	14
5	134	–	"Story of Jesus" on back-c; PC-r	1	1	2	4	6	9	11	14
6	158	–	PC-r	1	1	2	4	6	9	11	14
7	167	1/64	PC-r	1	1	2	4	6	8	10	12
8	167	5/65	PC-r	1	1	2	4	6	8	10	12
9	167	11/66	PC-r	1	1	2	4	6	8	10	12
10	166	Win/69	New-c; price 25¢; PC-r; stiff-c	1	2	3	6	9	16	20	24

97. King Solomon's Mines

Ed	HRN	Date	Details	A	C	GD 2.0	VG 4.0	FN 6.0	VF 8.0	VF/NM 9.0	NM- 9.2
1	96	7/52	Orig.; Kiefer-a	1	1	8	16	24	40	50	60
2	118	–	PC-r	1	1	2	4	6	9	11	14
3	131	–	PC-r	1	1	2	4	6	9	11	14
4	141	–	PC-r	1	1	2	4	6	9	11	14
5	158	–	PC-r	1	1	2	4	6	9	11	14
6	167	2/64	PC-r	1	1	2	4	6	8	10	12
7	167	9/65	PC-r	1	1	2	4	6	8	10	12
8	169	Sm/69	New price 25¢; stiff-c; PC-r	1	1	2	4	6	8	10	12

98. The Red Badge of Courage

Ed	HRN	Date	Details	A	C	GD 2.0	VG 4.0	FN 6.0	VF 8.0	VF/NM 9.0	NM- 9.2
1	98	8/52	Original	1	1	8	16	24	40	50	60
2	118	–	PC-r	1	1	2	4	6	9	11	14
3	132	–	PC-r	1	1	2	4	6	9	11	14
4	142	–	PC-r	1	1	2	4	6	9	11	14
5	152	–	PC-r	1	1	2	4	6	9	11	14
6	161	–	PC-r	1	1	2	4	6	9	11	14
7	167	–	Has orig.date; PC-r	1	1	2	4	6	9	11	14
8	167	9/64	PC-r	1	1	2	4	6	9	11	14
9	167	10/65	PC-r	1	1	2	4	6	9	11	14
10	166	R/1968	New-c&price 25¢; PC-r; stiff-c	1	2	3	6	9	17	21	26

99. Hamlet (Used in **POP**, pg. 102)

Ed	HRN	Date	Details	A	C	GD 2.0	VG 4.0	FN 6.0	VF 8.0	VF/NM 9.0	NM- 9.2
1	98	9/52	Original; Blum-a	1	1	8	16	24	43	54	65
2	121	–	PC-r	1	1	2	4	6	9	11	14
3	141	–	PC-r	1	1	2	4	6	9	11	14
4	158	–	PC-r	1	1	2	4	6	9	11	14
5	167	–	Has orig.date; PC-r	1	1	2	4	6	8	10	12
6	167	7/65	PC-r	1	1	2	4	6	8	10	12
7	166	4/67	PC-r	1	1	2	4	6	8	10	12
8	169	Spr/69	New-c&price 25¢; PC-r; stiff-c	1	2	3	6	9	17	21	26

100. Mutiny on the Bounty

Ed	HRN	Date	Details	A	C	GD 2.0	VG 4.0	FN 6.0	VF 8.0	VF/NM 9.0	NM- 9.2
1	100	10/52	Original	1	1	8	16	24	40	50	60
2	117	–	PC-r	1	1	2	4	6	9	11	14
3	132	–	PC-r	1	1	2	4	6	9	11	14
4	142	–	PC-r	1	1	2	4	6	9	11	14
5	155	–	PC-r	1	1	2	4	6	9	11	14
6	167	–	Has orig. date;PC-r	1	1	2	4	6	8	10	12
7	167	5/64	PC-r	1	1	2	4	6	8	10	12
8	167	3/66	PC-r	1	1	2	4	6	8	10	12
9	169	Spr/70	PC-r; stiff-c	1	1	2	4	6	8	10	12

101. William Tell

Ed	HRN	Date	Details	A	C	GD 2.0	VG 4.0	FN 6.0	VF 8.0	VF/NM 9.0	NM- 9.2
1	101	11/52	Original; Kiefer-c delBourgo-a	1	1	8	16	24	40	50	60
2	118	–	PC-r	1	1	2	4	6	9	11	14
3	141	–	PC-r	1	1	2	4	6	9	11	14
4	158	–	PC-r	1	1	2	4	6	9	11	14
5	167	–	Has orig.date; PC-r	1	1	2	4	6	8	10	12
6	167	11/64	PC-r	1	1	2	4	6	8	10	12
7	166	4/67	PC-r	1	1	2	4	6	8	10	12
8	169	Win/69	New price 25¢; stiff-c; PC-r	1	1	2	4	6	8	10	12

102. The White Company

Ed	HRN	Date	Details	A	C	GD 2.0	VG 4.0	FN 6.0	VF 8.0	VF/NM 9.0	NM- 9.2
1	101	12/52	Original; Blum-a	1	1	10	20	30	58	77	95
2	165	–	PC-r	1	1	3	6	9	18	23	28
3	167	4/64	PC-r	1	1	3	6	9	18	23	28

103. Men Against the Sea

Ed	HRN	Date	Details	A	C	GD 2.0	VG 4.0	FN 6.0	VF 8.0	VF/NM 9.0	NM- 9.2
1	104	1/53	Original; Kiefer-c; Palais-a	1	1	8	16	24	43	54	65
2	114	–	PC-r	1	1	4	8	11	16	19	22
3	131	–	New-c; PC-r	1	2	5	10	15	22	26	30
4	158	–	PC-r	1	2	4	7	10	14	17	20
5	149	–	White reorder list; came after HRN-158; PC-r	1	2	5	10	15	22	26	30
6	167	3/64	PC-r	1	2	2	4	6	9	11	14

104. Bring 'Em Back Alive

Ed	HRN	Date	Details	A	C	GD 2.0	VG 4.0	FN 6.0	VF 8.0	VF/NM 9.0	NM- 9.2
1	105	2/53	Original; Kiefer-c/a	1	1	8	16	24	40	50	60
2	118	–	PC-r	1	1	2	4	6	9	11	14
3	133	–	PC-r	1	1	2	4	6	9	11	14
4	150	–	PC-r	1	1	2	4	6	9	11	14
5	158	–	PC-r	1	1	2	4	6	9	11	14
6	167	10/63	PC-r	1	1	2	4	6	8	10	12
7	167	9/65	PC-r	1	1	2	4	6	8	10	12
8	169	Win/69	New price 25¢; stiff-c; PC-r	1	1	2	4	6	8	10	12

105. From the Earth to the Moon

Ed	HRN	Date	Details	A	C	GD 2.0	VG 4.0	FN 6.0	VF 8.0	VF/NM 9.0	NM- 9.2
1	106	3/53	Original; Blum-a	1	1	8	16	24	40	50	60
2	118	–	PC-r	1	1	2	4	6	9	11	14
3	132	–	PC-r	1	1	2	4	6	9	11	14
4	141	–	PC-r	1	1	2	4	6	9	11	14
5	146	–	PC-r	1	1	2	4	6	9	11	14
6	156	–	PC-r	1	1	2	4	6	9	11	14
7	167	–	Has orig. date; PC-r	1	1	2	4	6	8	10	12
8	167	5/64	PC-r	1	1	2	4	6	8	10	12
9	167	5/65	PC-r	1	1	2	4	6	8	10	12
10A	166	10/67	PC-r	1	1	2	4	6	8	10	12
10B	166	10/67	w/Grit ad stapled in book	1	1	9	18	27	63	89	115
11	169	Sm/69	New price 25¢; stiff-c; PC-r	1	1	2	4	6	8	10	12
12	169	Spr/71	PC-r	1	1	2	4	6	8	10	12

106. Buffalo Bill

Ed	HRN	Date	Details	A	C	GD 2.0	VG 4.0	FN 6.0	VF 8.0	VF/NM 9.0	NM- 9.2
1	107	4/53	Orig.; delBourgo-a	1	1	7	14	21	37	46	55
2	118	–	PC-r	1	1	2	4	6	9	11	14
3	132	–	PC-r	1	1	2	4	6	9	11	14
4	142	–	PC-r	1	1	2	4	6	9	11	14
5	161	–	PC-r	1	1	2	4	6	8	10	12

Classics Illustrated #108 © GIL

Classics Illustrated #115 © GIL

Classics Illustrated #123 © GIL

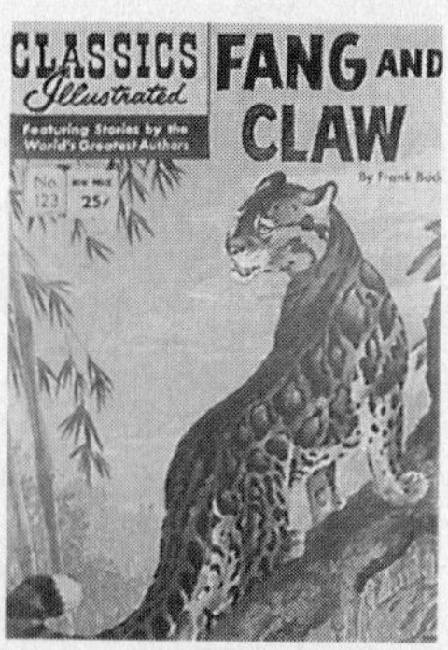

Ed	HRN	Date	Details	A	C	GD 2.0	VG 4.0	FN 6.0	VF 8.0	VF/NM 9.0	NM- 9.2
6	167	3/64	PC-r	1	1	2	4	6	8	10	12
7	166	7/67	PC-r	1	1	2	4	6	8	10	12
8	169	Fall/69	PC-r; stiff-c	1	1	2	4	6	8	10	12

107. King of the Khyber Rifles

Ed	HRN	Date	Details	A	C	GD 2.0	VG 4.0	FN 6.0	VF 8.0	VF/NM 9.0	NM- 9.2
1	108	5/53	Original	1	1	7	14	21	37	46	55
2	118	–	PC-r	1	1	2	4	6	9	11	14
3	146	–	PC-r	1	1	2	4	6	9	11	14
4	158	–	PC-r	1	1	2	4	6	9	11	14
5	167	–	Has orig.date; PC-r	1	1	2	4	6	8	10	12
6	167	–	PC-r	1	1	2	4	6	8	10	12
7	167	10/66	PC-r	1	1	2	4	6	8	10	12

108. Knights of the Round Table

Ed	HRN	Date	Details	A	C	GD 2.0	VG 4.0	FN 6.0	VF 8.0	VF/NM 9.0	NM- 9.2
1A	108	6/53	Original; Blum-a	1	1	8	16	24	43	54	65
1B	109	6/53	Original; scarce	1	1	8	16	24	46	58	70
2	117	–	PC-r	1	1	2	4	6	9	11	14
3	165	–	PC-r	1	1	2	4	6	8	10	12
4	167	4/64	PC-r	1	1	2	4	6	8	10	12
5	166	4/67	PC-r	1	1	2	4	6	8	10	12
6	169	Sm/69	New price 25¢; stiff-c; PC-r	1	1	2	4	6	8	10	12

109. Pitcairn's Island

Ed	HRN	Date	Details	A	C	GD 2.0	VG 4.0	FN 6.0	VF 8.0	VF/NM 9.0	NM- 9.2
1	110	7/53	Original; Palais-a	1	1	8	16	24	43	54	65
2	165	–	PC-r	1	1	2	4	6	9	11	14
3	167	3/64	PC-r	1	1	2	4	6	9	11	14
4	166	6/67	PC-r	1	1	2	4	6	9	11	14

110. A Study in Scarlet

Ed	HRN	Date	Details	A	C	GD 2.0	VG 4.0	FN 6.0	VF 8.0	VF/NM 9.0	NM- 9.2
1	111	8/53	Original	1	1	12	24	36	69	95	120
2	165	–	PC-r	1	1	10	20	30	56	73	90

111. The Talisman

Ed	HRN	Date	Details	A	C	GD 2.0	VG 4.0	FN 6.0	VF 8.0	VF/NM 9.0	NM- 9.2
1	112	9/53	Original; last H.C. Kiefer-a	1	1	8	16	24	43	54	65
2	165	–	PC-r	1	1	2	4	6	9	11	14
3	167	5/64	PC-r	1	1	2	4	6	9	11	14
4	166	Fall/68	C-price 25¢; PC-r	1	1	2	4	6	9	11	14

112. Adventures of Kit Carson

Ed	HRN	Date	Details	A	C	GD 2.0	VG 4.0	FN 6.0	VF 8.0	VF/NM 9.0	NM- 9.2
1	113	10/53	Original; Palais-a	1	1	8	16	24	40	50	60
2	129	–	PC-r	1	1	2	4	6	9	11	14
3	141	–	PC-r	1	1	2	4	6	9	11	14
4	152	–	PC-r	1	1	2	4	6	9	11	14
5	161	–	PC-r	1	1	2	4	6	8	10	12
6	167	–	PC-r	1	1	2	4	6	8	10	12
7	167	2/65	PC-r	1	1	2	4	6	8	10	12
8	167	5/66	PC-r	1	1	2	4	6	8	10	12
9	166	Win/69	New-c&price 25¢; PC-r; stiff-c	1	2	2	4	6	12	16	20

113. The Forty-Five Guardsmen

Ed	HRN	Date	Details	A	C	GD 2.0	VG 4.0	FN 6.0	VF 8.0	VF/NM 9.0	NM- 9.2
1	114	11/53	Orig.; delBourgo-a	1	1	9	18	27	54	70	85
2	166	7/67	PC-r	1	1	3	6	9	19	25	32

114. The Red Rover

Ed	HRN	Date	Details	A	C	GD 2.0	VG 4.0	FN 6.0	VF 8.0	VF/NM 9.0	NM- 9.2
1	115	12/53	Original	1	1	9	18	27	54	70	85
2	166	7/67	PC-r	1	1	3	6	9	19	25	32

115. How I Found Livingstone

Ed	HRN	Date	Details	A	C	GD 2.0	VG 4.0	FN 6.0	VF 8.0	VF/NM 9.0	NM- 9.2
1	116	1/54	Original	1	1	10	20	30	58	77	95
2	167	1/67	PC-r	1	1	4	8	12	27	36	45

116. The Bottle Imp

Ed	HRN	Date	Details	A	C	GD 2.0	VG 4.0	FN 6.0	VF 8.0	VF/NM 9.0	NM- 9.2
1	117	2/54	Orig.; Cameron-a	1	1	10	20	30	58	77	95
2	167	1/67	PC-r	1	1	4	8	12	27	36	45

117. Captains Courageous

Ed	HRN	Date	Details	A	C	GD 2.0	VG 4.0	FN 6.0	VF 8.0	VF/NM 9.0	NM- 9.2
1	118	3/54	Orig.; Costanza-a	1	1	9	18	27	54	70	85
2	167	2/67	PC-r	1	1	3	6	9	16	20	24
3	169	Fall/69	New price 25¢; stiff-c; PC-r	1	1	3	6	9	16	20	24

118. Rob Roy

Ed	HRN	Date	Details	A	C	GD 2.0	VG 4.0	FN 6.0	VF 8.0	VF/NM 9.0	NM- 9.2
1	119	4/54	Original; Rudy & Walter Palais-a	1	1	10	20	30	58	77	95
2	167	2/67	PC-r	1	1	4	8	12	27	36	45

119. Soldiers of Fortune

Ed	HRN	Date	Details	A	C	GD 2.0	VG 4.0	FN 6.0	VF 8.0	VF/NM 9.0	NM- 9.2
1	120	5/54	Schaffenberger-a	1	1	9	18	27	51	62	75
2	166	3/67	PC-r	1	1	3	6	9	16	20	24
3	169	Spr/70	New price 25¢; stiff-c; PC-r	1	1	3	6	9	16	20	24

120. The Hurricane

Ed	HRN	Date	Details	A	C	GD 2.0	VG 4.0	FN 6.0	VF 8.0	VF/NM 9.0	NM- 9.2
1	121	6/54	Orig.; Cameron-a	1	1	9	18	27	51	62	75
2	166	3/67	PC-r	1	1	3	6	9	19	25	32

121. Wild Bill Hickok

Ed	HRN	Date	Details	A	C	GD 2.0	VG 4.0	FN 6.0	VF 8.0	VF/NM 9.0	NM- 9.2
1	122	7/54	Original	1	1	7	14	21	37	46	55
2	132	–	PC-r	1	1	2	4	6	9	11	14
3	141	–	PC-r	1	1	2	4	6	9	11	14
4	154	–	PC-r	1	1	2	4	6	9	11	14
5	167	–	PC-r	1	1	2	4	6	8	10	12
6	167	8/64	PC-r	1	1	2	4	6	8	10	12
7	166	4/67	PC-r	1	1	2	4	6	8	10	12
8	169	Win/69	PC-r; stiff-c	1	1	2	4	6	8	10	12

122. The Mutineers

Ed	HRN	Date	Details	A	C	GD 2.0	VG 4.0	FN 6.0	VF 8.0	VF/NM 9.0	NM- 9.2
1	123	9/54	Original	1	1	8	16	24	43	54	65
2	136	–	PC-r	1	1	2	4	6	9	11	14
3	146	–	PC-r	1	1	2	4	6	9	11	14
4	158	–	PC-r	1	1	2	4	6	9	11	14
5	167	11/63	PC-r	1	1	2	4	6	8	10	12
6	167	3/65	PC-r	1	1	2	4	6	8	10	12
7	166	8/67	PC-r	1	1	2	4	6	8	10	12

123. Fang and Claw

Ed	HRN	Date	Details	A	C	GD 2.0	VG 4.0	FN 6.0	VF 8.0	VF/NM 9.0	NM- 9.2
1	124	11/54	Original	1	1	8	16	24	43	54	65
2	133	–	PC-r	1	1	2	4	6	9	11	14
3	143	–	PC-r	1	1	2	4	6	9	11	14
4	154	–	PC-r	1	1	2	4	6	9	11	14
5	167	–	Has orig.date; PC-r	1	1	2	4	6	8	10	12
6	167	9/65	PC-r	1	1	2	4	6	8	10	12

124. The War of the Worlds

Ed	HRN	Date	Details	A	C	GD 2.0	VG 4.0	FN 6.0	VF 8.0	VF/NM 9.0	NM- 9.2
1	125	1/55	Original; Cameron-c/a	1	1	10	20	30	56	73	90
2	131	–	PC-r	1	1	2	4	6	10	13	16
3	141	–	PC-r	1	1	2	4	6	10	13	16
4	148	–	PC-r	1	1	2	4	6	10	13	16
5	156	–	PC-r	1	1	2	4	6	10	13	16
6	165	–	PC-r	1	1	2	4	6	12	16	20
7	167	–	PC-r	1	1	2	4	6	9	11	14
8	167	11/64	PC-r	1	1	2	4	6	10	13	16
9	167	11/65	PC-r	1	1	2	4	6	9	11	14
10	166	R/1968	C-price 25¢; PC-r	1	1	2	4	6	9	11	14
11	169	Sm/70	PC-r; stiff-c	1	1	2	4	6	9	11	14

125. The Ox Bow Incident

Ed	HRN	Date	Details	A	C	GD 2.0	VG 4.0	FN 6.0	VF 8.0	VF/NM 9.0	NM- 9.2
1	–	3/55	Original; Picture Progress replaces reorder list	1	1	7	14	21	37	46	55
2	143	–	PC-r	1	1	2	4	6	9	11	14
3	152	–	PC-r	1	1	2	4	6	9	11	14
4	149	–	PC-r	1	1	2	4	6	9	11	14
5	167	–	PC-r	1	1	2	4	6	8	10	12
6	167	11/64	PC-r	1	1	2	4	6	8	10	12
7	166	4/67	PC-r	1	1	2	4	6	8	10	12
8	169	Win/69	New price 25¢; stiff-c; PC-r	1	1	2	4	6	8	10	12

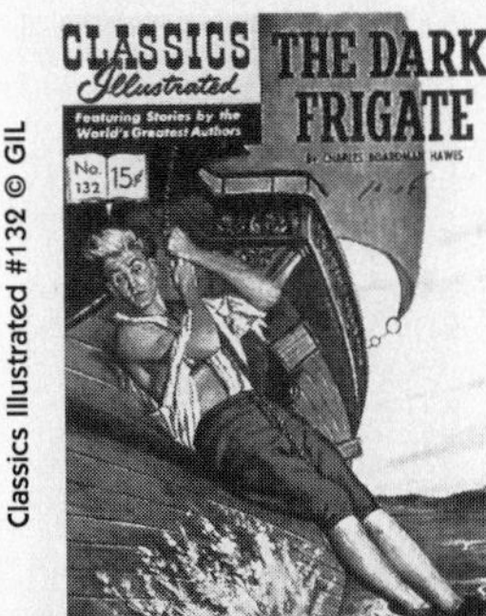

Classics Illustrated #132 © GIL

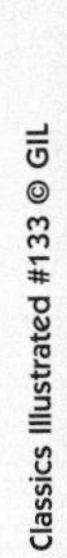

Classics Illustrated #133 © GIL

Classics Illustrated #138 © GIL

126. The Downfall

Ed	HRN	Date	Details	A	C	GD 2.0	VG 4.0	FN 6.0	VF 8.0	VF/NM 9.0	NM- 9.2
1	5/55	–	Orig.; 'Picture Progress' replaces reorder list; Cameron-c/a	1	1	8	16	24	43	54	65
2	167	8/64	PC-r	1	1	2	4	6	12	16	20
3	166	R/1968	C-price 25¢; PC-r	1	1	2	4	6	12	16	20

127. The King of the Mountains

Ed	HRN	Date	Details	A	C	GD 2.0	VG 4.0	FN 6.0	VF 8.0	VF/NM 9.0	NM- 9.2
1	128	7/55	Original	1	1	8	16	24	43	54	65
2	167	6/64	PC-r	1	1	2	4	6	10	13	16
3	166	F/1968	C-price 25¢; PC-r	1	1	2	4	6	10	13	16

128. Macbeth (Used in **POP**, pg. 102)

Ed	HRN	Date	Details	A	C	GD 2.0	VG 4.0	FN 6.0	VF 8.0	VF/NM 9.0	NM- 9.2
1	128	9/55	Orig.; last Blum-a	1	1	8	16	24	43	54	65
2	143	–	PC-r	1	1	2	4	6	9	11	14
3	158	–	PC-r	1	1	2	4	6	9	11	14
4	167	–	PC-r	1	1	2	4	6	8	10	12
5	167	6/64	PC-r	1	1	2	4	6	8	10	12
6	166	4/67	PC-r	1	1	2	4	6	8	10	12
7	166	R/1968	C-Price 25¢; PC-r	1	1	2	4	6	8	10	12
8	169	Spr/70	Stiff-c; PC-r	1	1	2	4	6	8	10	12

129. Davy Crockett

Ed	HRN	Date	Details	A	C	GD 2.0	VG 4.0	FN 6.0	VF 8.0	VF/NM 9.0	NM- 9.2
1	129	11/55	Orig.; Cameron-a	1	1	12	24	36	69	95	120
2	167	9/66	PC-r	1	1	10	20	30	56	73	90

130. Caesar's Conquests

Ed	HRN	Date	Details	A	C	GD 2.0	VG 4.0	FN 6.0	VF 8.0	VF/NM 9.0	NM- 9.2
1	130	1/56	Original; Orlando-a	1	1	8	16	24	43	54	65
2	142	–	PC-r	1	1	2	4	6	9	11	14
3	152	–	PC-r	1	1	2	4	6	9	11	14
4	149	–	PC-r	1	1	2	4	6	9	11	14
5	167	–	PC-r	1	1	2	4	6	8	10	12
6	167	10/64	PC-r	1	1	2	4	6	8	10	12
7	167	4/66	PC-r	1	1	2	4	6	8	10	12

131. The Covered Wagon

Ed	HRN	Date	Details	A	C	GD 2.0	VG 4.0	FN 6.0	VF 8.0	VF/NM 9.0	NM- 9.2
1	131	3/56	Original	1	1	5	10	15	33	44	55
2	143	–	PC-r	1	1	2	4	6	9	11	14
3	152	–	PC-r	1	1	2	4	6	9	11	14
4	158	–	PC-r	1	1	2	4	6	9	11	14
5	167	–	PC-r	1	1	2	4	6	8	10	12
6	167	11/64	PC-r	1	1	2	4	6	8	10	12
7	167	4/66	PC-r	1	1	2	4	6	8	10	12
8	169	Win/69	New price 25¢; stiff-c; PC-r	1	1	2	4	6	8	10	12

132. The Dark Frigate

Ed	HRN	Date	Details	A	C	GD 2.0	VG 4.0	FN 6.0	VF 8.0	VF/NM 9.0	NM- 9.2
1	132	5/56	Original	1	1	6	12	18	38	52	65
2	150	–	PC-r	1	1	2	4	6	10	12	15
3	167	1/64	PC-r	1	1	2	4	6	9	11	14
4	166	5/67	PC-r	1	1	2	4	6	9	11	14

133. The Time Machine

Ed	HRN	Date	Details	A	C	GD 2.0	VG 4.0	FN 6.0	VF 8.0	VF/NM 9.0	NM- 9.2
1	132	7/56	Orig.; Cameron-a	1	1	6	12	18	43	59	75
2	142	–	PC-r	1	1	2	4	6	10	13	16
3	152	–	PC-r	1	1	2	4	6	10	13	16
4	158	–	PC-r	1	1	2	4	6	10	13	16
5	167	–	PC-r	1	1	2	4	6	9	11	14
6	167	6/64	PC-r	1	1	2	4	6	10	13	16
7	167	3/66	PC-r	1	1	2	4	6	9	11	14
8	166	12/67	PC-r	1	1	2	4	6	9	11	14
9	169	Win/71	New price 25¢; stiff-c; PC-r	1	1	2	4	6	9	11	14

134. Romeo and Juliet

Ed	HRN	Date	Details	A	C	GD 2.0	VG 4.0	FN 6.0	VF 8.0	VF/NM 9.0	NM- 9.2
1	134	9/56	Original; Evans-a	1	1	6	12	18	38	52	65
2	161	–	PC-r	1	1	2	4	6	9	11	14
3	167	9/63	PC-r	1	1	2	4	6	8	10	12
4	167	5/65	PC-r	1	1	2	4	6	8	10	12
5	166	6/67	PC-r	1	1	2	4	6	8	10	12
6	166	Win/69	New c&price 25¢; stiff-c; PC-r	1	2	3	6	9	18	23	28

135. Waterloo

Ed	HRN	Date	Details	A	C	GD 2.0	VG 4.0	FN 6.0	VF 8.0	VF/NM 9.0	NM- 9.2
1	135	11/56	Orig.; G. Ingels-a	1	1	6	12	18	38	52	65
2	153	–	PC-r	1	1	2	4	6	9	11	14
3	167	–	PC-r	1	1	2	4	6	8	10	12
4	167	9/64	PC-r	1	1	2	4	6	8	10	12
5	166	R/1968	C-price 25¢; PC-r	1	1	2	4	6	8	10	12

136. Lord Jim

Ed	HRN	Date	Details	A	C	GD 2.0	VG 4.0	FN 6.0	VF 8.0	VF/NM 9.0	NM- 9.2
1	136	1/57	Original; Evans-a	1	1	6	12	18	38	52	65
2	165	–	PC-r	1	1	2	4	6	8	10	12
3	167	3/64	PC-r	1	1	2	4	6	8	10	12
4	167	9/66	PC-r	1	1	2	4	6	8	10	12
5	169	Sm/69	New price 25 ¢; stiff-c; PC-r	1	1	2	4	6	8	10	12

137. The Little Savage

Ed	HRN	Date	Details	A	C	GD 2.0	VG 4.0	FN 6.0	VF 8.0	VF/NM 9.0	NM- 9.2
1	136	3/57	Original; Evans-a	1	1	6	12	18	38	52	65
2	148	–	PC-r	1	1	2	4	6	9	11	14
3	156	–	PC-r	1	1	2	4	6	9	11	14
4	167	–	PC-r	1	1	2	4	6	8	10	12
5	167	10/64	PC-r	1	1	2	4	6	8	10	12
6	166	8/67	PC-r	1	1	2	4	6	8	10	12
7	169	Spr/70	New price 25¢; stiff-c; PC-r	1	1	2	4	6	8	10	12

138. A Journey to the Center of the Earth

Ed	HRN	Date	Details	A	C	GD 2.0	VG 4.0	FN 6.0	VF 8.0	VF/NM 9.0	NM- 9.2
1	136	5/57	Original	1	1	7	14	21	51	71	90
2	146	–	PC-r	1	1	2	4	6	11	14	18
3	156	–	PC-r	1	1	2	4	6	11	14	18
4	158	–	PC-r	1	1	2	4	6	11	14	18
5	167	–	PC-r	1	1	2	4	6	11	14	14
6	167	6/64	PC-r	1	1	2	4	6	12	16	20
7	167	4/66	PC-r	1	1	2	4	6	12	16	20
8	166	R/68	C-price 25¢; PC-r	1	1	2	4	6	10	13	16

139. In the Reign of Terror

Ed	HRN	Date	Details	A	C	GD 2.0	VG 4.0	FN 6.0	VF 8.0	VF/NM 9.0	NM- 9.2
1	139	7/57	Original; Evans-a	1	1	5	10	15	33	44	55
2	154	–	PC-r	1	1	2	4	6	9	11	14
3	167	–	Has orig.date; PC-r	1	1	2	4	6	8	10	12
4	167	7/64	PC-r	1	1	2	4	6	8	10	12
5	166	R/1968	C-price 25¢; PC-r	1	1	2	4	6	8	10	12

140. On Jungle Trails

Ed	HRN	Date	Details	A	C	GD 2.0	VG 4.0	FN 6.0	VF 8.0	VF/NM 9.0	NM- 9.2
1	140	9/57	Original	1	1	5	10	15	33	44	55
2	150	–	PC-r	1	1	2	4	6	9	11	14
3	160	–	PC-r	1	1	2	4	6	9	11	14
4	167	9/63	PC-r	1	1	2	4	6	8	10	12
5	167	9/65	PC-r	1	1	2	4	6	8	10	12

141. Castle Dangerous

Ed	HRN	Date	Details	A	C	GD 2.0	VG 4.0	FN 6.0	VF 8.0	VF/NM 9.0	NM- 9.2
1	141	11/57	Original	1	1	6	12	18	40	55	70
2	152	–	PC-r	1	1	2	4	6	9	11	14
3	167	–	PC-r	1	1	2	4	6	9	11	14
4	166	7/67	PC-r	1	1	2	4	6	9	11	14

142. Abraham Lincoln

Ed	HRN	Date	Details	A	C	GD 2.0	VG 4.0	FN 6.0	VF 8.0	VF/NM 9.0	NM- 9.2
1	142	1/58	Original	1	1	6	12	18	38	52	65
2	154	–	PC-r	1	1	2	4	6	9	11	14
3	158	–	PC-r	1	1	2	4	6	9	11	14
4	167	10/63	PC-r	1	1	2	4	6	8	10	12
5	167	7/65	PC-r	1	1	2	4	6	8	10	12
6	166	11/67	PC-r	1	1	2	4	6	8	10	12
7	169	Fall/69	New price 25¢; stiff-c; PC-r	1	1	2	4	6	8	10	12

143. Kim

Ed	HRN	Date	Details	A	C	GD 2.0	VG 4.0	FN 6.0	VF 8.0	VF/NM 9.0	NM- 9.2
1	143	3/58	Original; Orlando-a	1	1	5	10	15	33	44	55
2	165	–	PC-r	1	1	2	4	6	8	10	12

Classics Illustrated #145 © GIL

Classics Illustrated #148 © GIL

Classics Illustrated #152 © GIL

Ed	HRN	Date	Details	A	C	GD 2.0	VG 4.0	FN 6.0	VF 8.0	VF/NM 9.0	NM- 9.2
3	167	11/63	PC-r	1	1	2	4	6	8	10	12
4	167	8/65	PC-r	1	1	2	4	6	8	10	12
5	169	Win/69	New price 25¢; stiff-c; PC-r	1	1	2	4	6	8	10	12

144. The First Men in the Moon

Ed	HRN	Date	Details	A	C	GD 2.0	VG 4.0	FN 6.0	VF 8.0	VF/NM 9.0	NM- 9.2
1	143	5/58	Original; Woodbridge/Williamson/Torres-a	1	1	6	12	18	43	59	75
2	152	–	(Rare)-PC-r	1	1	7	14	21	51	71	90
3	153	–	PC-r	1	1	2	4	6	9	11	14
4	161	–	PC-r	1	1	2	4	6	8	10	12
5	167	–	PC-r	1	1	2	4	6	8	10	12
6	167	12/65	PC-r	1	1	2	4	6	8	10	12
7	166	Fall/68	New-c&price 25¢; PC-r; stiff-c	1	2	3	6	9	16	20	24
8	169	Win/69	Stiff-c; PC-r	1	2	2	4	6	11	14	18

145. The Crisis

Ed	HRN	Date	Details	A	C	GD 2.0	VG 4.0	FN 6.0	VF 8.0	VF/NM 9.0	NM- 9.2
1	143	7/58	Original; Evans-a	1	1	6	12	18	38	52	65
2	156	–	PC-r	1	1	2	4	6	9	11	14
3	167	10/63	PC-r	1	1	2	4	6	8	10	12
4	167	3/65	PC-r	1	1	2	4	6	8	10	12
5	166	R/68	C-price 25¢; PC-r	1	1	2	4	6	8	10	12

146. With Fire and Sword

Ed	HRN	Date	Details	A	C	GD 2.0	VG 4.0	FN 6.0	VF 8.0	VF/NM 9.0	NM- 9.2
1	143	9/58	Original; Woodbridge-a	1	1	6	12	18	38	52	65
2	156	–	PC-r	1	1	2	4	6	10	13	16
3	167	11/63	PC-r	1	1	2	4	6	9	11	14
4	167	3/65	PC-r	1	1	2	4	6	9	11	14

147. Ben-Hur

Ed	HRN	Date	Details	A	C	GD 2.0	VG 4.0	FN 6.0	VF 8.0	VF/NM 9.0	NM- 9.2
1	147	11/58	Original; Orlando-a	1	1	5	10	15	36	48	60
2	152	–	Scarce; PC-r	1	1	6	12	18	38	52	65
3	153	–	PC-r	1	1	2	4	6	9	11	14
4	158	–	PC-r	1	1	2	4	6	9	11	14
5	167	–	Orig.date; but PC-r	1	1	2	4	6	8	10	12
6	167	2/65	PC-r	1	1	2	4	6	8	10	12
7	167	9/66	PC-r	1	1	2	4	6	8	10	12
8A	166	Fall/68	New-c&price 25¢; PC-r; soft-c	1	2	3	6	9	18	23	28
8B	166	Fall/68	New-c&price 25¢; PC-r; stiff-c; scarce	1	2	4	8	12	27	36	45

148. The Buccaneer

Ed	HRN	Date	Details	A	C	GD 2.0	VG 4.0	FN 6.0	VF 8.0	VF/NM 9.0	NM- 9.2
1	148	1/59	Orig.; Evans/Jenny-a; Saunders-c	1	1	5	10	15	33	44	55
2	568	–	Juniors list only PC-r	1	1	2	4	6	9	11	14
3	167	–	PC-r	1	1	2	4	6	8	10	12
4	167	9/65	PC-r	1	1	2	4	6	8	10	12
5	169	Sm/69	New price 25¢; PC-r; stiff-c	1	1	2	4	6	8	10	12

149. Off on a Comet

Ed	HRN	Date	Details	A	C	GD 2.0	VG 4.0	FN 6.0	VF 8.0	VF/NM 9.0	NM- 9.2
1	149	3/59	Orig.;G.McCann-a; blue reorder list	1	1	6	12	18	38	52	65
2	155	–	PC-r	1	1	2	4	6	9	11	14
3	149	–	PC-r; white reorder list; no coming-next ad	1	1	2	4	6	9	11	14
4	167	12/63	PC-r	1	1	2	4	6	8	10	12
5	167	2/65	PC-r	1	1	2	4	6	8	10	12
6	167	10/66	PC-r	1	1	2	4	6	8	10	12
7	166	Fall/68	New-c & price 25¢; PC-r	1	2	3	6	9	17	21	26

150. The Virginian

Ed	HRN	Date	Details	A	C	GD 2.0	VG 4.0	FN 6.0	VF 8.0	VF/NM 9.0	NM- 9.2
1	150	5/59	Original	1	1	6	12	18	40	55	70
2	164	–	PC-r	1	1	2	4	6	12	16	20
3	167	10/63	PC-r	1	1	3	6	9	17	21	26
4	167	12/65	PC-r	1	1	2	4	6	12	16	20

151. Won By the Sword

Ed	HRN	Date	Details	A	C	GD 2.0	VG 4.0	FN 6.0	VF 8.0	VF/NM 9.0	NM- 9.2
1	150	7/59	Original	1	1	6	12	18	38	52	65
2	164	–	PC-r	1	1	2	4	6	10	13	16
3	167	10/63	PC-r	1	1	2	4	6	10	13	16
4	166	7/67	PC-r	1	1	2	4	6	10	13	16

152. Wild Animals I Have Known

Ed	HRN	Date	Details	A	C	GD 2.0	VG 4.0	FN 6.0	VF 8.0	VF/NM 9.0	NM- 9.2
1	152	9/59	Orig.; L.B. Cole c/a	1	1	6	12	18	43	59	75
2A	149	–	PC-r; white reorder list; no coming-next ad; IBC: Jr. list #572	1	1	2	4	6	9	11	14
2B	149	–	PC-r; inside-bc: Jr. list to #555	1	1	2	4	6	10	12	15
2C	149	–	PC-r; inside-bc: has World Around Us ad; scarce	1	1	3	6	9	17	21	26
3	167	9/63	PC-r	1	1	2	4	6	8	10	12
4	167	8/65	PC-r	1	1	2	4	6	8	10	12
5	169	Fall/69	New price 25¢; stiff-c; PC-r	1	1	2	4	6	8	10	12

153. The Invisible Man

Ed	HRN	Date	Details	A	C	GD 2.0	VG 4.0	FN 6.0	VF 8.0	VF/NM 9.0	NM- 9.2
1	153	11/59	Original	1	1	7	14	21	50	68	85
2A	149	–	PC-r; white reorder list; no coming-next ad; inside-bc: Jr. list to #572	1	1	2	4	6	11	14	18
2B	149	–	PC-r; inside-bc: Jr. list to #555	1	1	2	4	6	12	16	20
3	167	–	PC-r	1	1	2	4	6	10	12	15
4	167	2/65	PC-r	1	1	2	4	6	10	12	15
5	167	9/66	PC-r	1	1	2	4	6	10	12	15
6	166	Win/69	New price 25¢; PC-r; stiff-c	1	1	2	4	6	10	12	15
7	169	Spr/71	Stiff-c; letters spelling 'Invisible Man' are 'solid' not 'invisible;' PC-r	1	1	2	4	6	10	12	15

154. The Conspiracy of Pontiac

Ed	HRN	Date	Details	A	C	GD 2.0	VG 4.0	FN 6.0	VF 8.0	VF/NM 9.0	NM- 9.2
1	154	1/60	Original	1	1	6	12	18	40	55	70
2	167	11/63	PC-r	1	1	2	4	6	12	16	20
3	167	7/64	PC-r	1	1	2	4	6	12	16	20
4	166	12/67	PC-r	1	1	2	4	6	12	16	20

155. The Lion of the North

Ed	HRN	Date	Details	A	C	GD 2.0	VG 4.0	FN 6.0	VF 8.0	VF/NM 9.0	NM- 9.2
1	154	3/60	Original	1	1	6	12	18	38	52	65
2	167	1/64	PC-r	1	1	2	4	6	11	14	18
3	166	R/1967	C-price 25¢; PC-r	1	1	2	4	6	10	12	15

156. The Conquest of Mexico

Ed	HRN	Date	Details	A	C	GD 2.0	VG 4.0	FN 6.0	VF 8.0	VF/NM 9.0	NM- 9.2
1	156	5/60	Orig.; Bruno Premiani-c/a	1	1	6	12	18	38	52	65
2	167	1/64	PC-r	1	1	2	4	6	10	12	15
3	166	8/67	PC-r	1	1	2	4	6	10	12	15
4	169	Spr/70	New price 25¢; stiff-c; PC-r	1	1	2	4	6	8	10	12

157. Lives of the Hunted

Ed	HRN	Date	Details	A	C	GD 2.0	VG 4.0	FN 6.0	VF 8.0	VF/NM 9.0	NM- 9.2
1	156	7/60	Orig.; L.B. Cole-c	1	1	6	12	18	40	55	70
2	167	2/64	PC-r	1	1	2	4	6	12	16	20
3	166	10/67	PC-r	1	1	2	4	6	12	16	20

158. The Conspirators

Ed	HRN	Date	Details	A	C	GD 2.0	VG 4.0	FN 6.0	VF 8.0	VF/NM 9.0	NM- 9.2
1	156	9/60	Original	1	1	6	12	18	40	55	70
2	167	7/64	PC-r	1	1	2	4	6	12	16	20
3	166	10/67	PC-r	1	1	2	4	6	12	16	20

159. The Octopus

Ed	HRN	Date	Details	A	C

Classics Illustrated #162 © GIL

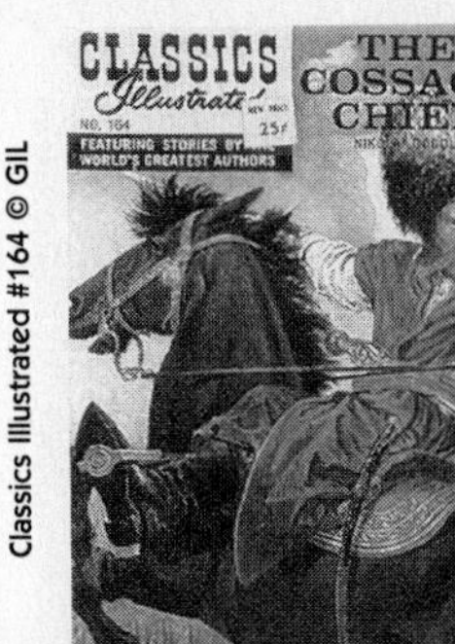

Classics Illustrated #164 © GIL

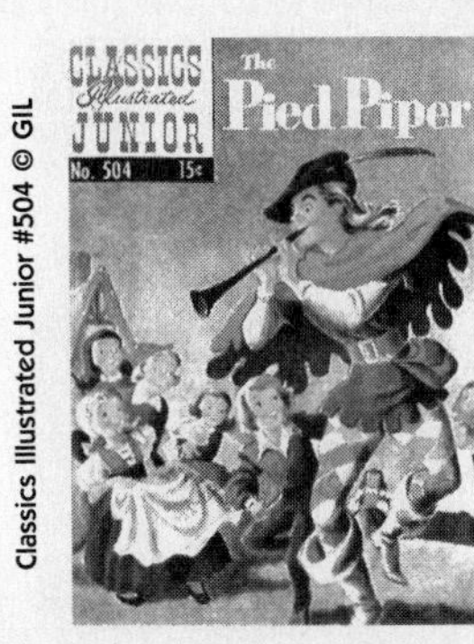

Classics Illustrated Junior #504 © GIL

Ed	HRN	Date	Details	A	C	GD 2.0	VG 4.0	FN 6.0	VF 8.0	VF/NM 9.0	NM- 9.2
1	159	11/60	Orig.; Gray Morrow-a; L.B. Cole-c	1	1	6	12	18	40	55	70
2	167	2/64	PC-r	1	1	2	4	6	12	16	20
3	166	R/1967	C-price 25¢; PC-r	1	1	2	4	6	12	16	20

160. The Food of the Gods

Ed	HRN	Date	Details	A	C	GD	VG	FN	VF	VF/NM	NM-
1A	159	1/61	Original	1	1	6	12	18	43	59	75
1B	160	1/61	Original; same, except for HRN	1	1	6	12	18	40	55	70
2	167	1/64	PC-r	1	1	2	4	6	12	16	20
3	166	6/67	PC-r	1	1	2	4	6	12	16	20

161. Cleopatra

Ed	HRN	Date	Details	A	C	GD	VG	FN	VF	VF/NM	NM-
1	161	3/61	Original	1	1	6	12	18	40	55	70
2	167	1/64	PC-r	1	1	2	4	6	14	18	22
3	166	8/67	PC-r	1	1	2	4	6	14	18	22

162. Robur the Conqueror

Ed	HRN	Date	Details	A	C	GD	VG	FN	VF	VF/NM	NM-
1	162	5/61	Original	1	1	6	12	18	40	55	70
2	167	7/64	PC-r	1	1	2	4	6	12	16	20
3	166	8/67	PC-r	1	1	2	4	6	12	16	20

163. Master of the World

Ed	HRN	Date	Details	A	C	GD	VG	FN	VF	VF/NM	NM-
1	163	7/61	Original; Gray Morrow-a	1	1	6	12	18	40	55	70
2	167	1/65	PC-r	1	1	2	4	6	12	16	20
3	166	R/1968	C-price 25¢; PC-r	1	1	2	4	6	12	16	20

164. The Cossack Chief

Ed	HRN	Date	Details	A	C	GD	VG	FN	VF	VF/NM	NM-
1	164	(1961)	Orig.; nd(10/61?)	1	1	6	12	18	40	55	70
2	167	4/65	PC-r	1	1	2	4	6	12	16	20
3	166	Fall/68	C-price 25¢; PC-r	1	1	2	4	6	12	16	20

165. The Queen's Necklace

Ed	HRN	Date	Details	A	C	GD	VG	FN	VF	VF/NM	NM-
1	164	1/62	Original; Morrow-a	1	1	6	12	18	40	55	70
2	167	4/65	PC-r	1	1	2	4	6	12	16	20
3	166	Fall/68	C-price 25¢; PC-r	1	1	2	4	6	12	16	20

166. Tigers and Traitors

Ed	HRN	Date	Details	A	C	GD	VG	FN	VF	VF/NM	NM-
1	165	5/62	Original	1	1	8	16	24	58	82	105
2	167	2/64	PC-r	1	1	3	7	10	21	28	35
3	167	11/66	PC-r	1	1	3	7	10	21	28	35

167. Faust

Ed	HRN	Date	Details	A	C	GD	VG	FN	VF	VF/NM	NM-
1	165	8/62	Original	1	1	13	26	39	90	138	185
2	167	2/64	PC-r	1	1	6	12	18	40	55	70
3	166	6/67	PC-r	1	1	6	12	18	40	55	70

168. In Freedom's Cause

Ed	HRN	Date	Details	A	C	GD	VG	FN	VF	VF/NM	NM-
1	169	Win/69	Original; Evans/ Crandall-a; stiff-c; 25¢; no coming-next ad;	1	1	14	28	42	102	156	210

169. Negro Americans The Early Years

Ed	HRN	Date	Details	A	C	GD	VG	FN	VF	VF/NM	NM-
1	166	Spr/69	Orig. & last issue; 25¢; Stiff-c; no coming-next ad; other sources indicate publication date of 5/69	1	1	13	26	39	92	141	190
2	169	Spr/69	Stiff-c	1	1	7	14	21	51	70	90

NOTE: *Many other titles were prepared or planned but were only issued in British/European series.*

CLASSIC PUNISHER (Also see Punisher)
Marvel Comics: Dec, 1989 ($4.95, B&W, deluxe format, 68 pgs.)

1-Reprints Marvel Super Action #1 & Marvel Preview #2 plus new story 5.00

CLASSICS ILLUSTRATED
First Publishing/Berkley Publishing: Feb, 1990 - No. 27, July, 1991 ($3.75/$3.95, 52 pgs.)

1-27: 1-Gahan Wilson-c/a. 4-Sienkiewicz painted-c/a. 6-Russell scripts/layouts. 7-Spiegle-a. 9-Ploog-c/a. 16-Staton-a. 18-Gahan Wilson-c/a; 20-Geary-a. 26-Aesop's Fables (6/91). 26,27-Direct sale only 5.00

CLASSICS ILLUSTRATED
Acclaim Books/Twin Circle PublishingCo.: Feb, 1997 - Present ($4.99, digest-size) (Each book contains study notes)

A Christmas Carol-(12/97), A Connecticut Yankee in King Arthur's Court-(5/97), All Quiet on the Western Front-(1/98), A Midsummer's Night Dream-(4/97) Around the World in 80 Days-(1/98), A Tale of Two Cities-(2/97)Joe Orlando-r, Captains Courageous-(11/97), Crime and Punishment-(3/97), Dr. Jekyll and Mr. Hyde-(10/97), Don Quixote-(12/97), Frankenstein-(10/97), Great Expectations-(4/97), Hamlet-(3/97), Huckleberry Finn-(3/97), Jane Eyre-(2/97), Kidnapped-(1/98), Les Miserables-(5/97), Lord Jim-(9/97),Macbeth-(5/97), Moby Dick-(4/97), Oliver Twist-(5/97), Robinson Crusoe-(9/97), Romeo & Juliet-(2/97), Silas Marner-(11/97), The Call of the Wild-(9/97), The Count of Monte Cristo-(1/98), The House of the Seven Gables-(9/97), The Iliad-(12/97), The Invisible Man-(10/97), The Last of the Mohicans-(12/97), The Master of Ballantrae-(11/97), The Odyssey-(3/97), The Prince and the Pauper-(4/97), The Red Badge Of Courage-(9/97), Tom Sawyer-(2/97) Wuthering Heights-(11/97) 5.00

NOTE: *Stories reprinted from the original Gilberton Classic Comics and Classics Illustrated.*

CLASSICS ILLUSTRATED GIANTS
Gilberton Publications: Oct, 1949 (One-Shots - "OS")

These Giant Editions, all with new front and back covers, were advertised from 10/49 to 2/52. They were 50¢ on the newsstand and 60¢ by mail. They are actually four Classics in one volume. All the stories are reprints of the Classics Illustrated Series.
NOTE: There were also British hardback Adventure & Indian Giants in 1952, with the same covers but different contents: Adventure - 2, 7, 10; Indian - 17, 22, 37, 58. They are also rare.

Title	GD	VG	FN	VF	VF/NM	NM-
"An Illustrated Library of Great Adventure Stories" - reprints of No. 6,7,8,10 (Rare); Kiefer-c	140	280	420	875	1350	1825
"An Illustrated Library of Exciting Mystery Stories" - reprints of No. 30,21,40, 13 (Rare); Blum-c	154	308	462	963	1482	2000
"An Illustrated Library of Great Indian Stories" - reprints of No. 4,17,22,37 (Rare); Blum-c	140	280	420	869	1350	1825

INTRODUCTION TO CLASSICS ILLUSTRATED JUNIOR

Collectors of Juniors can be put into one of two categories: those who want any copy of each title, and those who want all the originals. Those seeking every original and reprint edition are a limited group, primarily because Juniors have no changes in art or covers to spark interest, and because reprints are so low in value it is difficult to get dealers to look for specific reprint editions.

In recent years it has become apparent that most serious Classics collectors seek Junior originals. Those seeking reprints seek them for low cost. This has made the previous note about the comparative market value of reprints inadequate. Three particular reprint editions are worth even more. For the 535-Twin Circle edition, see Giveaways. There are also reprint editions of 501 and 503 which have a full-page bc ad for the very rare Junior record. Those may sell as high as $10-$15 in mint. Original editions of 557 and 558 also have that ad.

There are no reprint editions of 577. The only edition, from 1969, is a 25 cent stiff-cover edition with no ad for the next issue. All other original editions have coming-next ad. But 577, like C.I. #168, was prepared in 1962 but not issued. Copies of 577 can be found in 1963 British/European series, which then continued with dozens of additional new Junior titles.

PRICES LISTED BELOW ARE FOR ORIGINAL EDITIONS, WHICH HAVE AN AD FOR THE NEXT ISSUE.

NOTE: *Non HRN 576 copies- many are written on or colored . Reprints with 576 HRN are worth about 1/3 original prices. All other HRN #'s are 1/2 original price*

CLASSICS ILLUSTRATED JUNIOR
Famous Authors Ltd. (Gilberton Publications): Oct, 1953 - Spring, 1971

Title	GD	VG	FN	VF	VF/NM	NM-
501-Snow White & the Seven Dwarfs; Alex Blum-a	11	22	33	66	91	115
502-The Ugly Duckling	8	16	24	46	58	70
503-Cinderella	7	14	21	35	43	50
504-512: 504-The Pied Piper. 505-The Sleeping Beauty. 506-The Three Little Pigs. 507-Jack & the Beanstalk. 508-Goldilocks & the Three Bears. 509-Beauty and the Beast. 510-Little Red Riding Hood. 511-Puss-N Boots. 512-Rumpelstiltskin	5	10	15	24	30	35
513-Pinocchio	7	14	21	35	43	50
514-The Steadfast Tin Soldier	8	16	24	46	58	70
515-Johnny Appleseed	5	10	15	24	30	35
516-Aladdin and His Lamp	6	12	18	28	34	40
517-519: 517-The Emperor's New Clothes. 518-The Golden Goose. 519-Paul Bunyan	5	10	15	24	30	35
520-Thumbelina	6	12	18	29	36	42
521-King of the Golden River	5	10	15	24	30	35
522,523,530: 522-The Nightingale. 523-The Gallant Tailor. 530-The Golden Bird	5	10	15	23	28	32
524-The Wild Swans	6	12	18	28	34	40
525,526: 525-The Little Mermaid. 526-The Frog Prince	6	12	18	28	34	40
527-The Golden-Haired Giant	5	10	15	24	30	35

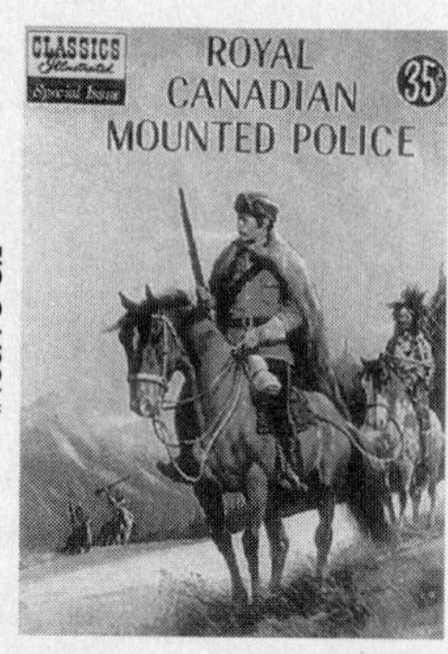

Classics Illustrated Special Issue #150A © GIL

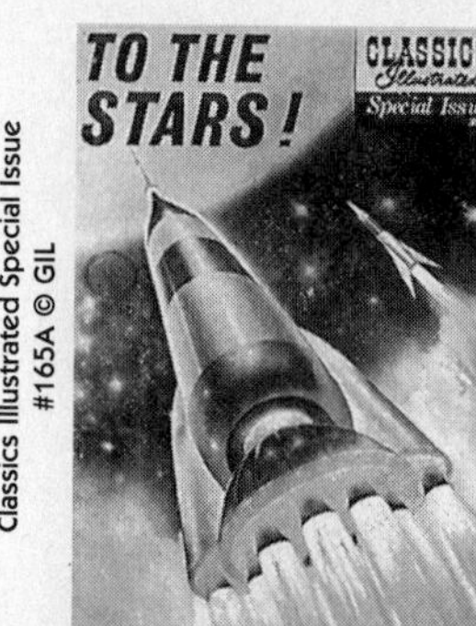

Classics Illustrated Special Issue #165A © GIL

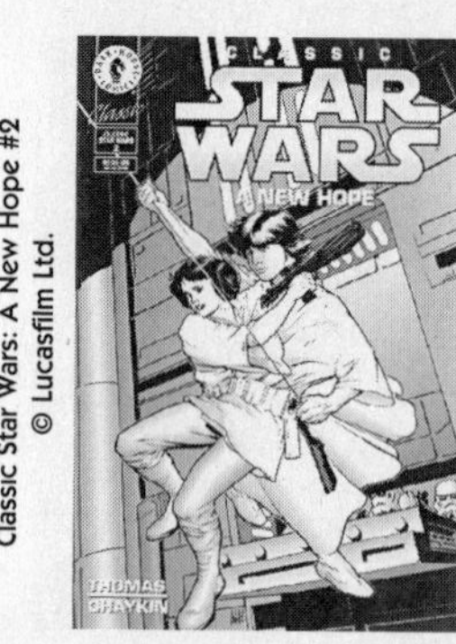

Classic Star Wars: A New Hope #2 © Lucasfilm Ltd.

	GD 2.0	VG 4.0	FN 6.0	VF 8.0	VF/NM 9.0	NM- 9.2
528-The Penny Prince	5	10	15	24	30	35
529-The Magic Servants	5	10	15	24	30	35
531-Rapunzel	5	10	15	24	30	35
532-534: 532-The Dancing Princesses. 533-The Magic Fountain. 534-The Golden Touch	5	10	15	22	26	30
535-The Wizard of Oz	8	16	24	43	54	65
536-The Chimney Sweep	5	10	15	24	30	35
537-The Three Fairies	6	12	18	27	33	38
538-Silly Hans	5	10	15	22	26	30
539-The Enchanted Fish	6	12	18	29	36	42
540-The Tinder-Box	6	12	18	29	36	42
541-Snow White & Rose Red	5	10	15	23	28	32
542-The Donkey's Tale	5	10	15	23	28	32
543-The House in the Woods	5	10	15	24	30	35
544-The Golden Fleece	6	12	18	31	38	45
545-The Glass Mountain	5	10	15	23	28	32
546-The Elves & the Shoemaker	5	10	15	23	28	32
547-The Wishing Table	5	10	15	24	30	35
548-551: 548-The Magic Pitcher. 549-Simple Kate. 550-The Singing Donkey. 551-The Queen Bee	5	10	15	22	26	30
552-The Three Little Dwarfs	5	10	15	24	30	35
553,556: 553-King Thrushbeard. 556-The Elf Mound	5	10	15	22	26	30
554-The Enchanted Deer	6	12	18	28	34	40
555-The Three Golden Apples	5	10	15	23	28	32
557-Silly Willy	6	12	18	27	33	38
558-The Magic Dish; L.B. Cole-c; soft and stiff-c exist on original	7	14	21	35	43	50
559-The Japanese Lantern; 1 pg. Ingels-a; L.B. Cole-c	7	14	21	35	43	50
560-The Doll Princess; L.B. Cole-c	7	14	21	35	43	50
561-Hans Humdrum; L.B. Cole-c	6	12	18	28	34	40
562-The Enchanted Pony; L.B. Cole-c	7	14	21	35	43	50
563,565-567,570: 563-The Wishing Well; L.B. Cole-c. 565-The Silly Princess; L.B. Cole-c. 566-Clumsy Hans; L.B. Cole-c. 567-The Bearskin Soldier; L.B. Cole-c. 570-The Pearl Princess	5	10	15	24	30	35
564-The Salt Mountain; L.B.Cole-c. 568-The Happy Hedgehog; L.B. Cole-c.	6	12	18	27	33	38
569,573: 569-The Three Giants.573-The Crystal Ball	5	10	15	23	28	32
571,572: 571-How Fire Came to the Indians. 572-The Drummer Boy	6	12	18	29	36	42
574-Brightboots	5	10	15	23	28	32
575-The Fearless Prince	6	12	18	27	33	38
576-The Princess Who Saw Everything	6	12	18	33	41	48
577-The Runaway Dumpling	8	16	24	43	54	65

NOTE: *Prices are for original editions. Last reprint - Spring, 1971.* ***Costanza*** *&* ***Schaffenberger*** *art in many issues.*

CLASSICS ILLUSTRATED SPECIAL ISSUE
Gilberton Co.: (Came out semi-annually) Dec, 1955 - Jul, 1962 (35¢, 100 pgs.)

	GD	VG	FN	VF	VF/NM	NM-
129-The Story of Jesus (titled ...Special Edition) "Jesus on Mountain" cover	11	22	33	62	84	105
"Three Camels" cover (12/58)	12	24	36	71	98	125
"Mountain" cover (no date)-Has checklist on inside b/c to HRN #161 & different testimonial on back-c	9	18	27	52	66	80
"Mountain" cover (1968 re-issue; has white 50¢ circle)	8	16	24	40	50	60
132A-The Story of America (6/56); Cameron-a	9	18	27	52	66	80
135A-The Ten Commandments(12/56)	8	16	24	46	58	70
138A-Adventures in Science(6/57); HRN to 137	8	16	24	43	54	65
138A-(6/57)-2nd version w/HRN to 149	6	12	18	28	34	40
138A-(12/61)-3rd version w/HRN to 149	7	14	21	35	43	50
141A-The Rough Rider (Teddy Roosevelt)(12/57); Evans-a	8	16	24	46	58	70
144A-Blazing the Trails West(6/58)- 73 pgs. of Crandall/Evans plus Severin-a	9	18	27	51	62	75
147A-Crossing the Rockies(12/58)-Crandall/Evans-a	8	16	24	46	58	70
150A-Royal Canadian Police(6/59)-Ingels, Sid Check-a	8	16	24	46	58	70
153A-Men, Guns & Cattle(12/59)-Evans-a (26 pgs.); Kinstler-a	8	16	24	46	58	70
156A-The Atomic Age(6/60)-Crandall/Evans, Torres-a	8	16	24	46	58	70
159A-Rockets, Jets and Missiles(12/60)-Evans, Morrow-a	8	16	24	46	58	70
162A-War Between the States(6/61)-Kirby & Crandall/Evans-a; Ingels-a	15	30	45	85	120	155
165A-To the Stars(12/61)-Torres, Crandall/Evans, Kirby-a	9	18	27	54	70	85
166A-World War II('62)-Torres, Crandall/Evans, Kirby-a	11	22	33	64	87	110
167A-Prehistoric World(7/62)-Torres & Crandall/Evans-a; two versions exist (HRN to 165 & HRN to 167)	11	22	33	64	87	110
nn Special Issue-The United Nations (1964; 50¢; scarce); this is actually part of the European Special Series, which cont'd on after the U.S. series stopped issuing new titles in 1962. This English edition was prepared specifically for sale at the U.N. It was printed in Norway	35	70	105	198	287	375

NOTE: *There was another U.S. Special Issue prepared in 1962 with artwork by* ***Torres*** *entitled World War I. Unfortunately, it was never issued in any English-language edition. It was issued in 1964 in West Germany, The Netherlands, and some Scandanavian countries, with another edition in 1974 with a new cover.*

CLASSICS LIBRARY (See King Classics)

CLASSIC STAR WARS (Also see Star Wars)
Dark Horse Comics: Aug, 1992 - No. 20, June, 1994 ($2.50)

	GD	VG	FN	VF	VF/NM	NM-
1-Begin Star Wars strip-r by Williamson; Williamson redrew portions of the panels to fit comic book format						6.00
2-10: 8-Polybagged w/Star Wars Galaxy trading card. 8-M. Schultz-c						4.00
11-19: 13-Yeates-c. 17-M. Schultz-c. 19-Evans-c						3.00
20-($3.50, 52 pgs.)-Polybagged w/trading card						3.50
Escape To Hoth TPB ($16.95) r/#15-20						17.00
The Rebel Storm TPB - r/#8-14						17.00
Trade paperback ($29.95, slip-cased)-Reprints all movie adaptations						30.00

NOTE: *Williamson c-1-5,7,9,10,14,15,20.*

CLASSIC STAR WARS: (Title series). **Dark Horse Comics**

	GD	VG	FN	VF	VF/NM	NM-
--A NEW HOPE, 6/94 - No. 2, 7/94 ($3.95) 1,2: 1-r/Star Wars #1-3, 7-9 publ; 2-r/Star Wars #4-6, 10-12 publ. by Marvel Comics						4.00
--DEVILWORLDS, 8/96 - No.2, 9/96 ($2.50s)1,2: r/Alan Moore-s						2.50
--HAN SOLO AT STARS' END, 3/97 - No. 3, 5/97 ($2.95) 1-3: r/strips by Alfredo Alcala						3.00
--RETURN OF THE JEDI, 10/94 - No.2, 11/94 ($3.50) 1,2: 1-r/1983-84 Marvel series; polybagged with w/trading card						3.50
--THE EARLY ADVENTURES, 8/94 - No. 9, 4/95 ($2.50)1-9						2.50
--THE EMPIRE STRIKES BACK, 8/94 - No. 2, 9/94 ($3.95) 1-r/Star Wars #39-44 published by Marvel Comics						4.00

CLASSIC X-MEN (Becomes X-Men Classic #46 on)
Marvel Comics Group: Sept, 1986 - No. 45, Mar, 1990

	GD	VG	FN	VF	VF/NM	NM-
1-Begins-r of New X-Men						5.00
2-10: 10-Sabretooth app.						4.00
11-45: 11-1st origin of Magneto in back-up story. 17-Wolverine-c. 27-r/X-Men #121. 26-r/X-Men #120; Wolverine-c/app. 35-r/X-Men #129. 39-New Jim Lee back-up story (2nd-a on X-Men). 43-Byrne-c/a(r); $1.75, double-size						3.00

NOTE: ***Art Adams*** *c(p)-1-10, 12-16, 18-23.* ***Austin*** *c-10,15-21,24-28i.* ***Bolton*** *back up stories in 1-28,30-35.* ***Williamson*** *c-12-14i.*

CLAW (See Capt. Battle, Jr., Daredevil Comics & Silver Streak Comics)

CLAW THE UNCONQUERED (See Cancelled Comic Cavalcade)
National Periodical Publications/DC Comics: 5-6/75 - No. 9, 9-10/76; No. 10, 4-5/78 - No. 12, 8-9/78

	GD	VG	FN	VF	VF/NM	NM-
1-1st app. Claw	1	3	4	6	8	10
2-12: 3-Nudity panel. 9-Origin						6.00

NOTE: ***Giffen*** *a-8-12p.* ***Kubert*** *c-10-12.* ***Layton*** *a-9i, 12i.*

CLAY CODY, GUNSLINGER
Pines Comics: Fall, 1957

	GD	VG	FN	VF	VF/NM	NM-
1-Painted-c	6	12	18	31	38	45

CLEAN FUN, STARRING "SHOOGAFOOTS JONES"
Specialty Book Co.: 1944 (10¢, B&W, oversized covers, 24 pgs.)

	GD	VG	FN	VF	VF/NM	NM-
nn-Humorous situations involving Negroes in the Deep South: White cover issue...	12	24	36	71	98	125
Dark grey cover issue...	13	26	39	76	106	135

CLEMENTINA THE FLYING PIG (See Dell Jr. Treasury)

CLEOPATRA (See Ideal, a Classical Comic No. 1)

CLERKS: THE COMIC BOOK (Also see Oni Double Feature #1)
Oni Press: Feb, 1998 ($2.95, B&W, one-shot)

	GD	VG	FN	VF	VF/NM	NM-
1-Kevin Smith-s	2	4	6	8	10	12
1-Second printing						4.00
...Holiday Special (12/98, $2.95) Smith-s						5.00
...The Lost Scene (12/99, $2.95) Smith-s/Hester-a						5.00

Climax! #1 © Gilmore Publ.

Cloak and Dagger #3 © MAR

Clue Comics V2#1 © HP

	GD 2.0	VG 4.0	FN 6.0	VF 8.0	VF/NM 9.0	NM- 9.2
CLIFFHANGER (See Battle Chasers, Crimson, and Danger Girl)						
WildStorm Prod./Wizard Press: 1997 (Wizard supplement)						
0-Sketchbook preview of Cliffhanger titles						6.00
CLIMAX! (Mystery)						
Gillmor Magazines: July, 1955 - No. 2, Sept, 1955						
1	17	34	51	95	135	175
2	14	28	42	79	110	140
CLINT (Also see Adolescent Radioactive Black Belt Hamsters)						
Eclipse Comics: Sept, 1986 - No. 2, Jan, 1987 ($1.50, B&W)						
1,2						2.25
CLINT & MAC (TV, Disney)						
Dell Publishing Co.: No. 889, Mar, 1958						
Four Color 889-Alex Toth-a, photo-c	14	28	42	97	149	200
CLIVE BARKER'S BOOK OF THE DAMNED: A HELLRAISER COMPANION						
Marvel Comics (Epic): Oct, 1991 - No. 3, Nov, 1992 ($4.95, semi-annual)						
Volume 1-3-(52 pgs.): 1-Simon Bisley-c. 2-(4/92). 3-(11/92)-McKean-a (1 pg.)						5.00
CLIVE BARKER'S HELLRAISER (Also see Epic, Hellraiser Nightbreed –Jihad, Revelations, Son of Celluloid, Tapping the Vein & Weaveworld)						
Marvel Comics (Epic Comics): 1989 - No. 20, 1993 ($4.50-6.95, mature, quarterly, 68 pgs.)						
Book 1-4,10-16,18,19: Based on Hellraiser & Hellbound movies; Bolton-c/a; Spiegle & Wrightson-a (graphic album). 10-Foil-c. 12-Sam Kieth-a						6.00
Book 5-9 ($5.95): 7-Bolton-a. 8-Morrow-a						6.00
Book 17-Alex Ross-a, 34 pgs.	2	4	6	8	10	12
Book 20-By Gaiman/McKean	1	2	3	5	6	8
...Collected Best (Checker Books, '02, $21.95)-r/by various incl. Ross, Gaiman, Mignola						22.00
...Collected Best II ('03, $19.95)-r/by various incl. Bolton, L. Wachowski, Dorman						20.00
...Collected Best III ('04, $26.95)-r/by various incl. Bolton, L. Wachowski, Wrightson						27.00
...Dark Holiday Special ('92, $4.95)-Conrad-a						6.00
...Spring Slaughter 1 ('94, $6.95, 52 pgs.)-Painted-c						7.00
...Summer Special 1 ('92, $5.95, 68 pgs.)						6.00
CLIVE BARKER'S NIGHTBREED (Also see Epic)						
Marvel Comics (Epic Comics): Apr, 1990 - No. 25, Mar, 1993 ($1.95/$2.25/$2.50, mature readers)						
1-25: 1-4-Adapt horror movie. 5-New stories; Guice-a(p)						2.50
CLIVE BARKER'S THE HARROWERS						
Marvel Comics (Epic Comics): Dec, 1993 - No. 6, May, 1994 ($2.50)						
1-($2.95)-Glow-in-the-dark-c; Colan-c/a in all						3.00
2-6						2.50
NOTE: *Colan a(p)-1-6; c-1-3, 4p, 5p. Williamson a(i)-2, 4, 5(part).*						
CLOAK AND DAGGER						
Ziff-Davis Publishing Co.: Fall, 1952						
1-Saunders painted-c	28	56	84	158	229	300
CLOAK AND DAGGER (Also see Marvel Fanfare)						
Marvel Comics Group: Oct, 1983 - No. 4, Jan, 1984 (Mini-series) (See Spectacular Spider-Man #64)						
1-4-Austin-c/a(i) in all. 4-Origin						3.00
CLOAK AND DAGGER (2nd Series)(Also see Marvel Graphic Novel #34 & Strange Tales)						
Marvel Comics Group: July, 1985 - No. 11, Jan, 1987						
1-11: 9-Art Adams-p						2.50
...And Power Pack (1990, $7.95, 68 pgs.)						8.00
NOTE: *Mignola c-7, 8.*						
CLOAK AND DAGGER (3rd Series listed as Mutant Misadventures Of...)						
CLOBBERIN' TIME						
Marvel Comics: Sept, 1995 ($1.95) (Based on card game)						
nn-Overpower game guide; Ben Grimm story						2.25
CLOCK MAKER, THE						
Image Comics: Jan, 2003 - No. 4, May, 2003 ($2.50, comic unfolds to 10"x13" pages)						
1-4-Krueger-s						2.50
... Act Two (4/04, $4.95, standard format) Krueger-s/Matt Smith-c						5.00
CLONEZONE SPECIAL						
Dark Horse Comics/First Comics: 1989 ($2.00, B&W)						
1-Back-up series from Badger & Nexus						2.25
CLOSE ENCOUNTERS (See Marvel Comics Super Special & Marvel Special Edition)						
CLOSER						
Oni Press: May, 2004 ($14.95, B&W, digest size, graphic novel)						
nn-Antony Johnston-s/Mike Norton-a						15.00
CLOSE SHAVES OF PAULINE PERIL, THE (TV cartoon)						
Gold Key: June, 1970 - No. 4, March, 1971						
1	4	8	12	24	32	40
2-4	3	6	9	16	21	26
CLOWN COMICS (No. 1 titled Clown Comic Book)						
Clown Comics/Home Comics/Harvey Publ.: 1945 - No. 3, Win, 1946						
nn (#1)	12	24	36	71	98	125
2,3	9	18	27	51	62	75
CLOUDBURST						
Image Comics: June, 2004 ($7.95, squarebound)						
1-Gray & Palmiotti-s/Shy & Gouveia-a						8.00
CLOUDFALL						
Image Comics: Nov, 2003 ($4.95, B&W, squarebound)						
1-Kirkman-s/Su-a/c						5.00
CLOWNS, THE (I Pagliacci)						
Dark Horse Comics: 1998 ($2.95, B&W, one-shot)						
1-Adaption of the opera; P. Craig Russell-script						3.00
CLUBHOUSE RASCALS (#1 titled ...Presents?) (Also see Three Rascals)						
Sussex Publ. Co. (Magazine Enterprises): June, 1956 - No. 2, Oct, 1956						
1-The Brain app. in both; DeCarlo-a	8	16	24	46	58	70
2	7	14	21	36	43	50
CLUB "16"						
Famous Funnies: June, 1948 - No. 4, Dec, 1948						
1-Teen-age humor	13	26	39	74	102	130
2-4	8	16	24	46	58	70
CLUE COMICS (Real Clue Crime V2#4 on)						
Hillman Periodicals: Jan, 1943 - No. 15(V2#3), May, 1947						
1-Origin The Boy King, Nightmare, Micro-Face, Twilight, & Zippo	135	270	405	844	1297	1750
2 (scarce)	77	154	231	481	741	1000
3-5 (9/43)	42	84	126	256	391	525
6,8,9: 8-Palais-c/a(2)	32	64	96	184	267	350
7-Classic torture-c (3/44)	48	96	144	293	447	600
10-Origin/1st app. The Gun Master & begin series; content changes to crime (10/46)	32	64	96	184	267	350
11 (12/46)	24	48	72	138	199	260
12-Origin Rackman; McWilliams-a, Guardineer-a(2)	30	60	90	170	245	320
V2#1-Nightmare new origin; Iron Lady app.; Simon & Kirby-a (3/47)	50	100	150	305	465	625
V2#2-S&K-a(2)-Bondage/torture-c; man attacks & kills people with electric iron. Infantino-a	67	134	201	419	647	875
V2#3-S&K-a(3)	52	104	156	317	484	650
CLUELESS SPRING SPECIAL (TV)						
Marvel Comics: May, 1997 ($3.99, magazine sized, one-shot)						
1-Photo-c from TV show						4.00
CLUTCHING HAND, THE						
American Comics Group: July-Aug, 1954						
1	40	80	120	230	335	440
CLYDE BEATTY COMICS (Also see Crackajack Funnies)						
Commodore Productions & Artists, Inc.: October, 1953 (84 pgs.)						
1-Photo front/back-c; movie scenes and comics	27	54	81	154	222	290
CLYDE CRASHCUP (TV)						
Dell Publishing Co.: Aug-Oct, 1963 - No. 5, Sept-Nov, 1964						
1-All written by John Stanley	14	28	42	97	149	200
2-5	12	24	36	86	131	175
COBALT BLUE (Also see Power Comics)						
Innovation Publishing: Sept, 1989 - No. 2, Oct, 1989 ($1.95, 28 pgs.)						
1,2-Gustovich-c/a/scripts						2.25
The Graphic Novel ($6.95, color, 52 pgs.)-r/1,2						7.00
CODE BLUE						
Image Comics (Jet-Black): Apr, 1998 ($2.95, B&W)						
1-Jimmie Robinson-s/a						3.00

Codename: Stryke Force #8 © TCOW

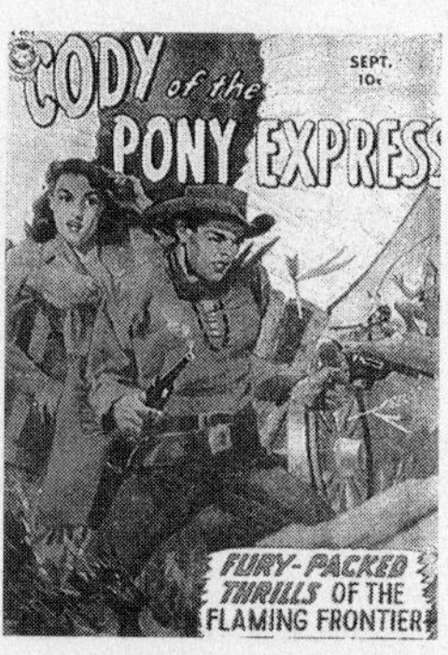

Cody of the Pony Express #1 © FOX

Combat #2 © ATLAS

	GD 2.0	VG 4.0	FN 6.0	VF 8.0	VF/NM 9.0	NM- 9.2

CODE NAME: ASSASSIN (See 1st Issue Special)

CODENAME: DANGER
Lodestone Publishing: Aug, 1985 - No. 4, May, 1986 ($1.50)
1-4 2.25

CODENAME: FIREARM (Also see Firearm)
Malibu Comics (Ultraverse): June, 1995 - No. 5, Sept, 1995 ($2.95, bimonthly limited series)
0-5: 0-2-Alec Swan back-up story by James Robinson 3.00
NOTE: *Perez c-0.*

CODENAME: GENETIX
Marvel Comics UK: Jan, 1993 - No. 4, May, 1993 ($1.75, limited series)
1-4: Wolverine in all 3.00

CODENAME: KNOCKOUT
DC Comics (Vertigo): No. 0, Jun, 2001 - No. 23, June, 2003 ($2.50/$2.75)
0-15: Rodi-s in all. 0-6-Small Jr. -a. 1-Two covers by Chiodo & Cho. 7,8,10,11,12-Paquette-a. 9,13,14-Conner-a 2.50
16-23: 16-Begin $2.75-c. 23-Last issue; JG Jones-c 2.75

CODENAME SPITFIRE (Formerly Spitfire And The Troubleshooters)
Marvel Comics Group: No. 10, July, 1987 - No. 13, Oct, 1987
10-13: 10-Rogers-c/a (low printing) 3.50

CODENAME: STRYKE FORCE (Also See Cyberforce V1#4 & Cyberforce/Stryke Force: Opposing Forces
Image Comics (Top Cow Productions): Jan, 1994 - No. 14, Sept, 1995 ($1.95-$2.25)
0,1-14: 1-12-Silvestri stories, Peterson-a. 4-Stormwatch app. 14-Story continues in Cyberforce/Stryke Force: Opposing Forces; Turner-a 2.25
1-Gold, 1-Blue 4.00

CODE NAME: TOMAHAWK
Fantasy General Comics: Sept, 1986 ($1.75, high quality paper)
1-Sci/fi 2.25

CODE OF HONOR
Marvel Comics: Feb, 1997 - No. 4, May, 1997 ($5.95, limited series)
1-4-Fully painted by various; Dixon-s 6.00

CODY OF THE PONY EXPRESS (See Colossal Features Magazine)
Fox Features Syndicate: Sept, 1950 (See Women Outlaws)(One shot)
1-Painted-c 15 30 45 83 117 150

CODY OF THE PONY EXPRESS (Buffalo Bill...) (Outlaws of the West #11 on; Formerly Bullseye)
Charlton Comics: No. 8, Oct, 1955; No. 9, Jan, 1956; No. 10, June, 1956
8-Bullseye on splash pg; not S&K-a 8 16 24 46 58 70
9,10: Buffalo Bill app. in all 6 12 18 29 36 42

CODY STARBUCK (1st app. in Star Reach #1)
Star Reach Productions: July, 1978
nn-Howard Chaykin-c/a 2 4 6 8 10 12
2nd printing 1 2 3 5 6 8
NOTE: *Both printings say First Printing. True first printing is on lower-grade paper, somewhat off-register, and snow in snow sequence has green tint.*

CO-ED ROMANCES
P. L. Publishing Co.: November, 1951
1 8 16 24 43 54 65

COFFEE WORLD
World Comics: Oct, 1995 ($1.50, B&W, anthology)
1-Shannon Wheeler's Too Much Coffee Man story 3.00

COFFIN, THE
Oni Press: Sept, 2000 - No. 4, May, 2001 ($2.95, B&W, limited series)
1-4-Hester-s/Huddleston-a 3.00
TPB (8/01, $11.95, TPB) r/#1-4 12.00

COLLECTORS DRACULA, THE
Millennium Publications: 1994 - No. 2, 1994 ($3.95, color/B&W, 52 pgs., limited series)
1,2-Bolton-a (7 pgs.) 4.00

COLLECTORS ITEM CLASSICS (See Marvel Collectors Item Classics)

COLONIA
Colonia Press: 1998 ($2.95, B&W)
1-5-Jeff Nicholson-s/a 3.00

COLORS IN BLACK
Dark Horse Comics: Mar, 1995 - No. 4, June, 1995 ($2.95, limited series)
1-4 3.00

COLOSSAL FEATURES MAGAZINE (Formerly I Loved) (See Cody of the Pony Express)
Fox Features Syndicate: No. 33, 5/50 - No. 34, 7/50; No. 3, 9/50 (Based on Columbia serial)
33,34: Cody of the Pony Express begins. 33-Painted-c. 34-Photo-c 15 30 45 83 117 150
3-Authentic criminal cases 15 30 45 83 117 150

COLOSSAL SHOW, THE (TV)
Gold Key: Oct, 1969
1 6 12 18 40 55 70

COLOSSUS (See X-Men)
Marvel Comics: Oct, 1997 ($2.99, 48 pgs., one-shot)
1-Raab-s/Hitch & Neary-a, wraparound-c 3.00

COLOSSUS COMICS (See Green Giant & Motion Picture Funnies Weekly)
Sun Publications (Funnies, Inc.?): March, 1940
1-(Scarce)-Tulpa of Tsang(hero); Colossus app. 548 1096 1644 3836 6168 8500
NOTE: *Cover by artist that drew Colossus in Green Giant Comics.*

COLOUR OF MAGIC, THE (Terry Pratchett's...)
Innovation Publishing: 1991 - No. 4, 1991 ($2.50, limited series)
1-4: Adapts 1st novel of the Discworld series 3.00

COLT .45 (TV)
Dell Publishing Co.: No. 924, 8/58 - No. 1058, 11-1/59-60; No. 4, 2-4/60 - No. 9, 5-7/61
Four Color 924(#1)-Wayde Preston photo-c on all 11 22 33 80 120 160
Four Color 1004,1058, #4,5,7-9: 1004-Photo-b/c 9 18 27 65 93 120
6-Toth-a 10 20 30 70 100 130

COLUMBIA COMICS
William H. Wise Co.: 1943
1-Joe Palooka, Charlie Chan, Capt. Yank, Sparky Watts, Dixie Dugan app. 30 60 90 170 245 320

COLUMBUS
Dark Horse Comics: Sept, 1992 ($2.50, B&W, one-shot)
1-Yeates painted-c 2.50

COMANCHE
Dell Publishing Co.: No. 1350, Apr-Jun, 1962
Four Color 1350-Disney movie; reprints FC #966 with title change from "Tonka" to "Comanche"; Sal Mineo photo-c 6 12 18 43 59 75

COMANCHEROS, THE
Dell Publishing Co.: No. 1300, Mar-May, 1962
Four Color 1300-Movie, John Wayne photo-c 17 34 51 121 186 250

COMBAT
Atlas Comics (ANC): June, 1952 - No. 11, April, 1953
1 25 50 75 144 207 270
2-Heath-c/a 13 26 39 76 106 135
3,5-9,11: 9-Robert Q. Sale-a 10 20 30 58 77 95
4-Krigstein-a 10 20 30 60 80 100
10-B&W and color illos. in **POP** 10 20 30 58 77 95
NOTE: *Combat Casey in 7-11.* ***Heath*** *c-1, 2, 9.* ***Maneely*** *a-1; c-3.* ***Pakula*** *a-1.* ***Reinman*** *a-1.*

COMBAT
Dell Publishing Co.: Oct-Nov, 1961 - No. 40, Oct, 1973 (No #9)
1 6 12 18 43 59 75
2,3,5: 4 8 12 25 33 42
4-John F. Kennedy c/story (P.T. 109) 5 10 15 33 44 55
6,7,8(4-6/63), 8(7-9/63) 4 8 12 22 30 38
10-26: 26-Last 12¢ issue 3 6 9 18 23 28
27-40(reprints #1-14). 30-r/#4 2 4 6 14 18 22

COMBAT CASEY (Formerly War Combat)
Atlas Comics (SAI): No. 6, Jan, 1953 - No. 34, July, 1957
6 (Indicia shows 1/52 in error) 15 30 45 86 123 160
7 9 18 27 54 70 85
8-Used in **POP**, pg. 94 9 18 27 51 62 75
9 8 16 24 46 58 70
10,13-19-Violent art by R. Q. Sale; Battle Brady x-over #10 11 22 33 64 87 110
11,12,20-Last Precode (2/55) 8 16 24 46 58 70

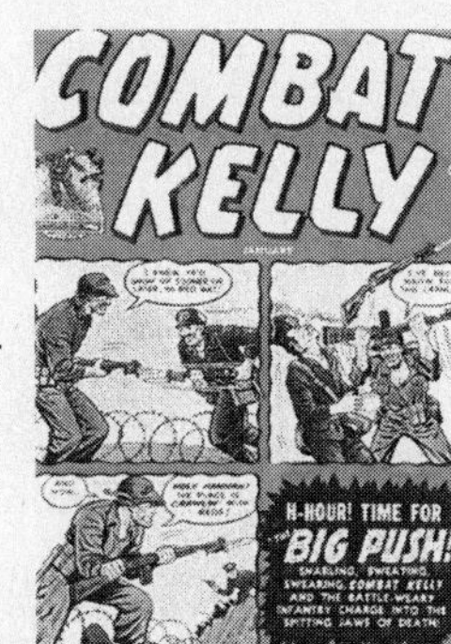

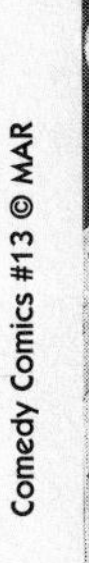
Combat Kelly #2 © ATLAS

Comedy Comics #13 © MAR

Comic Cavalcade #8 © DC

21-34 8 16 24 43 54 65
NOTE: *Everett a-6. Heath c-10, 17, 19, 23, 30. Maneely c-6, 8. Powell a-29(5), 30(5), 34. Severin c-26, 33.*

COMBAT KELLY
Atlas Comics (SPI): Nov, 1951 - No. 44, Aug, 1957
1-1st app. Combat Kelly; Heath-a 31 62 93 175 253 330
2 15 30 45 86 123 160
3-10 11 22 33 64 87 110
11-Used in **POP**, pgs. 94,95 plus color illo. 9 18 27 54 70 85
12-Color illo. in **POP** 9 18 27 54 70 85
13-16 9 18 27 51 62 75
17-Violent art by R. Q. Sale; Combat Casey app. 11 22 33 64 87 110
18-20,22-44: 18-Battle Brady app. 28-Last precode (1/55). 38-Green Berets story (8/56)
8 16 24 43 54 65
21-Transvestism-c 8 16 24 46 58 70
NOTE: *Berg a-8, 12-14, 16, 17, 19-23, 25, 26, 28, 31-36, 42-44; c-2. Colan a-42. Heath a-4; c-31. Lawrence a-23. Maneely a-4(2), 6, 7(3), 8; c-4, 5, 7, 8, 10, 25. R.Q. Sale a-17, 25. Severin c-41, 42. Whitney a-5.*

COMBAT KELLY (...and the Deadly Dozen)
Marvel Comics Group: June, 1972 - No. 9, Oct, 1973
1-Intro & origin new Combat Kelly; Ayers/Mooney-a; Severin-c (20¢)
3 6 9 18 23 28
2,5-8 2 4 6 10 12 15
3,4: 3-Origin. 4-Sgt. Fury-c/s 2 4 6 12 16 20
9-Death of the Deadly Dozen 2 4 6 14 18 22

COMBINED OPERATIONS (See The Story of the Commandos)

COMEBACK (See Zane Grey 4-Color 357)

COMEDY CARNIVAL
St. John Publishing Co.: no date (1950's) (100 pgs.)
nn-Contains rebound St. John comics 37 74 111 209 305 400

COMEDY COMICS (1st Series) (Daring Mystery #1-8) (Becomes Margie Comics #35 on)
Timely Comics (TCI 9,10): No. 9, April, 1942 - No. 34, Fall, 1946
9-(Scarce)-The Fin by Everett, Capt. Dash, Citizen V, & The Silver Scorpion app.; Wolverton-a; 1st app. Comedy Kid; satire on Hitler & Stalin; The Fin, Citizen V & Silver Scorpion cont. from Daring Mystery 289 578 867 1806 2778 3750
10-(Scarce)-Origin The Fourth Musketeer, Victory Boys; Monstro, the Mighty app.
219 438 657 1369 2110 2850
11-Vagabond, Stuporman app. 52 104 157 317 484 650
12,13 15 30 45 86 123 160
14-Origin/1st app. Super Rabbit (3/43) plus-c 52 104 157 317 484 650
15-20 14 28 42 81 113 145
21-32 11 22 33 62 84 105
33-Kurtzman-a (5 pgs.) 13 26 39 76 106 135
34-Intro Margie; Wolverton-a (5 pgs.) 21 42 63 118 169 220

COMEDY COMICS (2nd Series)
Marvel Comics (ACI): May, 1948 - No. 10, Jan, 1950
1-Hedy, Tessie, Millie begin; Kurtzman's "Hey Look" (he draws himself)
35 70 105 198 287 375
2 15 30 45 83 117 150
3,4-Kurtzman's "Hey Look" (?&3) 15 30 45 85 120 155
5-10 9 18 27 54 70 85

COMET, THE (See The Mighty Crusaders & Pep Comics #1)
Red Circle Comics (Archie): Oct, 1983 - No. 2, Dec, 1983
1-Re-intro & origin The Comet; The American Shield begins. Nino & Infantino art in both. Hangman in both 5.00
2-Origin continues. 4.00

COMET, THE
DC Comics (Impact Comics): July, 1991 - No. 18, Dec, 1992 ($1.00/$1.25)
1 3.00
2-18: 4-Black Hood app. 6-Re-intro Hangman. 8-Web x-over. 10-Contains Crusaders trading card. 4-Origin. Netzer(Nasser) c(p)-11,14-17 2.50
Annual 1 (1992, $2.50, 68 pgs.)-Contains Impact trading card; Shield back-up story 2.50

COMET MAN, THE (Movie)
Marvel Comics Group: Feb, 1987 - No. 6, July, 1987 (limited series)
1-6: 3-Hulk app. 4-She-Hulk shower scene c/s. Fantastic 4 app. 5-Fantastic 4 app. 2.50
NOTE: *Kelley Jones a-1-6p.*

COMIC ALBUM (Also see Disney Comic Album)
Dell Publishing Co.: Mar-May, 1958 - No. 18, June-Aug, 1962
1-Donald Duck 10 20 30 70 100 130
2-Bugs Bunny 6 12 18 38 52 65
3-Donald Duck 8 16 24 55 78 100
4-6,8-10: 4-Tom & Jerry. 5-Woody Woodpecker. 6,10-Bugs Bunny. 8-Tom & Jerry. 9-Woody Woodpecker 5 10 15 33 44 55
7,11,15: Popeye. 11-(9-11/60) 6 12 18 38 52 65
12-14: 12-Tom & Jerry. 13-Woody Woodpecker. 14-Bugs Bunny
5 10 15 33 44 55
16-Flintstones (12-2/61-62)-3rd app. Early Cave Kids app.
9 18 27 65 93 120
17-Space Mouse (3rd app.) 6 12 18 38 52 65
18-Three Stooges; photo-c 9 18 27 65 93 120

COMIC BOOK
Marvel Comics-#1/Dark Horse Comics-#2: 1995 ($5.95, oversize)
1-Spumco characters by John K. 1 2 3 4 5 7
2-(Dark Horse) 6.00

COMIC CAPERS
Red Circle Mag./Marvel Comics: Fall, 1944 - No. 6, Summer, 1946
1-Super Rabbit, The Creeper, Silly Seal, Ziggy Pig, Sharpy Fox begin
28 56 84 158 229 300
2 15 30 45 83 117 150
3-6 12 24 36 69 95 120

COMIC CAVALCADE
All-American/National Periodical Publications: Winter, 1942-43 - No. 63, June-July, 1954
(Contents change with No. 30, Dec-Jan, 1948-49 on)
1-The Flash, Green Lantern, Wonder Woman, Wildcat, The Black Pirate by Moldoff (also #2), Ghost Patrol, and Red White & Blue begin; Scribbly app.; Minute Movie
935 1870 2805 6545 10,523 14,500
2-Mutt & Jeff begin; last Ghost Patrol & Black Pirate; Minute Movies
254 508 762 1588 2444 3300
3-Hop Harrigan & Sargon, the Sorcerer begin; The King app.
173 346 519 1081 1666 2250
4,5: 4-The Gay Ghost, The King, Scribbly, & Red Tornado app. 5-Christmas-c. 5-Prints ad for Jr. JSA membership kit that includes "The Minute Man Answers The Call"
158 316 474 988 1519 2050
6-10: 7-Red Tornado & Black Pirate app.; last Scribbly. 9-Fat & Slat app.; X-Mas-c
123 246 369 769 1185 1600
11,12,14: 12-Last Red White & Blue 104 208 312 650 1000 1350
13-Solomon Grundy app.; X-Mas-c 162 324 486 1013 1557 2100
15-Just a Story begins 108 216 324 675 1038 1400
16-20: 19-Christmas-c 92 184 276 575 888 1200
21-23: 22-Johnny Peril begins. 23-Harry Lampert-c (Toth swipes)
87 174 261 544 835 1125
24-Solomon Grundy x-over in Green Lantern 115 230 345 719 1110 1500
25-28: 25-Black Canary app.; X-Mas-c. 26-28-Johnny Peril app. 28-Last Mutt & Jeff
77 154 231 481 741 1000
29-(10-11/48)-Last Flash, Wonder Woman, Green Lantern & Johnny Peril; Wonder Woman invents "Thinking Machine"; 2nd computer in comics (after Flash Comics #52); Leave It to Binky story (early app.) 87 174 261 544 835 1125
30-(12-1/48-49)-The Fox & the Crow, Dodo & the Frog & Nutsy Squirrel begin
40 80 120 239 357 475
31-35 24 48 72 138 199 260
36-49: 41-Last squarebound issue 18 36 54 100 143 185
50-62(Scarce) 22 44 66 123 177 230
63(Rare) 35 70 105 198 287 375
NOTE: *Grossman a-30-63. E.E. Hibbard c-(Flash only)-1-4, 7-14, 16-19, 21. Sheldon Mayer a(2-3)-40-63. Moulson c(G.L.)-7, 15. Nodell c(G.L.)-9. H.G. Peter c(W. Woman only)-1, 3-21, 24. Post a-31, 36. Purcell c(G.L.)-2-5, 10. Reinman a(Green Lantern)-4-6, 8, 9, 13, 15-21; c(Gr. Lantern)-6, 8, 19. Toth a(Green Lantern)-26-28; c-27. Atom app.-22, 23.*

COMIC COMICS
Fawcett Publications: Apr, 1946 - No. 10, Feb, 1947
1-Captain Kid; Nutty Comics #1 in indicia 15 30 45 83 117 150
2-10-Wolverton-a, 4 pgs. each. 5-Captain Kidd app. Mystic Moot by Wolverton in #2-10? 15 30 45 86 123 160

COMIC LAND
Fact and Fiction Publ.: March, 1946
1-Sandusky & the Senator, Sam Stupor, Sleuth, Marvin the Great, Sir Passer, Phineas Gruff app.; Irv Tirman & Perry Williams art 15 30 45 86 123 160

COMICO CHRISTMAS SPECIAL
Comico: Dec, 1988 ($2.50, 44pgs.)
1-Rude/Williamson-a; Dave Stevens-c 4.00

COMICO COLLECTION (Also see Grendel)
Comico: 1987 ($9.95, slipcased collection)

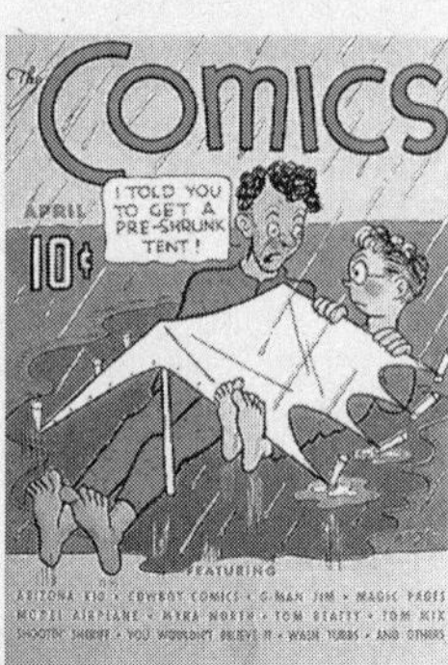

The Comics #2 © DELL

Comics On Parade #13 © UFS

Commander Battle and the Atomic Sub #3 © ACG

GD VG FN VF VF/NM NM-
2.0 4.0 6.0 8.0 9.0 9.2

nn-Contains exclusive Grendel: Devil's Vagary, 9 random Comico comics, a poster and newsletter in black slipcase w/silver ink 25.00

COMICO PRIMER (See Primer)

COMIC PAGES (Formerly Funny Picture Stories)
Centaur Publications: V3#4, July, 1939 - V3#6, Dec, 1939
V3#4-Bob Wood-a 54 108 162 329 502 675
5,6: 6-Schwab-c 42 84 126 256 391 525

COMICS (See All Good)

COMICS, THE
Dell Publ. Co.: Mar, 1937 - No. 11, Nov, 1938 (Newspaper strip-r; bi-monthly)
1-1st app. Tom Mix in comics; Wash Tubbs, Tom Beatty, Myra North, Arizona Kid, Erik Noble & International Spy w/Doctor Doom begin 177 354 531 1106 1703 2300
2 81 162 243 506 778 1050
3-11: 3-Alley Oop begins 66 132 198 413 637 860

COMICS AND STORIES (See Walt Disney's Comics and Stories)

COMICS & STORIES (Also see Wolf & Red)
Dark Horse Comics: Apr, 1996 - No. 4, July, 1996 ($2.95, lim. series) (Created by Tex Avery)
1-4: Wolf & Red app; reads Comics and Stories on-c. 1-Terry Moore-a. 2-Reed Waller-a 3.00

COMICS CALENDAR, THE (The 1946...)
True Comics Press (ordered through the mail): 1946 (25¢, 116 pgs.) (Stapled at top)
nn-(Rare) Has a "strip" story for every day of the year in color 40 80 120 239 357 475

COMICS DIGEST (Pocket size)
Parents' Magazine Institute: Winter, 1942-43 (B&W, 100 pgs)
1-Reprints from True Comics (non-fiction World War II stories) 10 20 30 56 73 90

COMICS EXPRESS
Eclipse Comics: Nov, 1989 - No. 2, Jan, 1990 ($2.95, B&W, 68pgs.)
1,2: Collection of strip-r; 2(12/89-c, 1/90 inside) 3.00

COMICS FOR KIDS
London Publ. Co./Timely: 1945 (no month); No. 2, Sum, 1945 (Funny animal)
1,2-Puffy Pig, Sharpy Fox 15 30 45 86 123 160

COMICS' GREATEST WORLD
Dark Horse Comics: Jun, 1993 - V4#4, Sept, 1993 ($1.00, weekly, lim. series)
Arcadia (Wk 1): V1#1,2,4: 1-X: Frank Miller-c. 2-Pit Bulls. 4-Monster. 2.25
1-B&W Press Proof Edition (1500 copies) 1 3 4 6 8 10
1-Silver-c; distr. retailer bonus w/print & cards 1 2 3 5 6 8
3-Ghost, Dorman-c; Hughes-a 4.00
Retailer's Prem. Emb. Silver Foil Logo-r/V1#1-4 1 3 4 6 8 10
Golden City (Wk 2: V2#1-4: 1-Rebel; Ordway-c. 2-Mecha; Dave Johnson-c.
3-Titan; Walt Simonson-c. 4-Catalyst; Perez-c. 2.25
1-Gold-c; distr. retailer bonus w/print & cards. 6.00
Retailer's Prem. Embos. Gold Foil Logo-r/V2#1-4 1 2 3 5 6 8
Steel Harbor (Week 3): V3#1-Barb Wire; Dorman-c; Gulacy-a(p) 4.00
2-4: 2-The Machine. 3-Wolfgang. 4-Motorhead 2.25
1-Silver-c; distr. retailer bonus w/print & cards 1 2 3 5 6 8
Retailer's Prem. Emb. Red Foil Logo-r/V3#1-4. 1 3 4 6 8 10
Vortex (Week 4): V4#1-4: 1-Division 13; Dorman-c. 2-Hero Zero; Art Adams-c.
3-King Tiger; Chadwick-a(p); Darrow-c. 4-Vortex; Miller-c. 2.25
1-Gold-c; distr. retailer bonus w/print & cards. 6.00
Retailer's Prem. Emb. Blue Foil Logo-r/V4#1-4. 1 2 3 5 6 8

COMICS' GREATEST WORLD: OUT OF THE VORTEX (See Out of The Vortex)

COMICS HITS (See Harvey Comics Hits)

COMICS MAGAZINE, THE (...Funny Pages #3)(Funny Pages #6 on)
Comics Magazine Co. (1st Comics Mag./Centaur Publ.): May, 1936 - No. 5, Sept, 1936 (Paper covers)
1-1st app. Dr. Mystic (a.k.a. Dr. Occult) by Siegel & Shuster (the 1st app. of a Superman prototype in comics). Dr. Mystic is not in costume but later appears in costume as a more pronounced prototype in More Fun #14-17. (1st episode of "The Koth and the Seven"; continues in More Fun #14; originally scheduled for publication at DC). 1 pg. Kelly-a; Sheldon Mayer-a 1550 3100 4650 12,400 - -
2-Federal Agent (a.k.a. Federal Men) by Siegel & Shuster; 1 pg. Kelly-a 280 560 840 1610 2205 2800
3-5 230 460 690 1320 1810 2300

COMICS NOVEL (Anarcho, Dictator of Death)
Fawcett Publications: 1947
1-All Radar; 51 pg anti-fascism story 31 62 93 178 259 340

COMICS ON PARADE (No. 30 on are a continuation of Single Series)
United Features Syndicate: Apr, 1938 - No. 104, Feb, 1955
1-Tarzan by Foster; Captain & the Kids, Little Mary Mixup, Abbie & Slats, Ella Cinders, Broncho Bill, Li'l Abner begin 352 704 1056 2288 3694 5100
2 (Tarzan & others app. on-c of #1-3,17) 125 250 375 781 1203 1625
3 98 196 294 613 944 1275
4,5 75 150 225 469 722 975
6-10 53 106 159 323 492 660
11-16,18-20 43 86 129 262 399 535
17-Tarzan-c 49 98 147 299 455 610
21-29: 22-Son of Tarzan begins. 22,24,28-Tailspin Tommy-c. 29-Last Tarzan issue 39 78 117 222 324 425
30-Li'l Abner 23 46 69 132 191 250
31-The Captain & the Kids 17 34 51 95 135 175
32-Nancy & Fritzi Ritz 14 28 42 81 113 145
33,36,39,42-Li'l Abner 19 38 57 107 154 200
34,37,40-The Captain & the Kids (10/41,6/42,3/43) 16 32 48 89 127 165
35,38-Nancy & Fritzi Ritz. 38-Infinity-c 14 28 42 79 110 140
41-Nancy & Fritzi Ritz 11 22 33 62 84 105
43-The Captain & the Kids 16 32 48 89 127 165
44 (3/44),47,50: Nancy & Fritzi Ritz 11 22 33 62 84 105
45-Li'l Abner 16 32 48 89 127 165
46,49-The Captain & the Kids 13 26 39 76 106 135
48-Li'l Abner (3/45) 16 32 48 89 127 165
51,54-Li'l Abner 13 26 39 76 106 135
52-The Captain & the Kids (3/46) 10 20 30 58 77 95
53,55,57-Nancy & Fritzi Ritz 10 20 30 58 77 95
56-The Captain & the Kids (r/Sparkler) 10 20 30 58 77 95
58-Li'l Abner; continues as Li'l Abner #61? 13 26 39 76 106 135
59-The Captain & the Kids 9 18 27 51 62 75
60-70-Nancy & Fritzi Ritz 8 16 24 46 58 70
71-99,101-104-Nancy & Sluggo: 71-76-Nancy only 8 16 24 40 50 60
100-Nancy & Sluggo 13 26 39 76 106 135
Special Issue, 7/46; Summer, 1948 - The Captain & the Kids app. 9 18 27 51 62 75
NOTE: Bound Volume (Very Rare) includes No. 1-12; bound by publisher in pictorial comic boards & distributed at the 1939 World's Fair and through mail order from ads in comic books (also see Tip Top) 262 524 786 1638 2519 3400
NOTE: *Li'l Abner reprinted from Tip Top.*

COMICS READING LIBRARIES (See the Promotional Comics section)

COMICS REVUE
St. John Publ. Co. (United Features Synd.): June, 1947 - No. 5, Jan, 1948
1-Ella Cinders & Blackie 11 22 33 66 91 115
2,4: 2-Hap Hopper (7/47). 4-Ella Cinders (9/47) 9 18 27 51 62 75
3,5: 3-Iron Vic (8/47). 5-Gordo No. 1 (1/48) 8 16 24 46 58 70

COMIC STORY PAINT BOOK
Samuel Lowe Co.: 1943 (Large size, 68 pgs.)
1055-Captain Marvel & a Captain Marvel Jr. story to read & color; 3 panels in color per pg. (reprints) 77 154 231 481 741 1000

COMIX BOOK
Marvel Comics Group/Krupp Comics Works No. 4,5: 1974 - No. 5, 1976 ($1.00, B&W, magazine)
1-Underground comic artists; 2 pgs. Wolverton-a 3 6 9 18 23 28
2,3: 2-Wolverton-a (1 pg.) 3 6 9 16 20 24
4(2/76), 4(5/76), 5 (Low distribution) 3 6 9 16 21 26
NOTE: *Print run No. 1-3: 200-250M; No. 4&5: 10M each.*

COMIX INTERNATIONAL
Warren Magazines: Jul, 1974 - No. 5, Spring, 1977 (Full color, stiff-c, mail only)
1-Low distribution; all Corben story remainders from Warren; Corben-c on all 9 18 27 60 85 110
2,4: 2-Two Dracula stories; Wood, Wrightson-r; Crandall-a; Maroto-a.
4-Printing w/ 3 Corben sty 4 8 12 29 40 50
3-5: 3-Dax story. 4-(printing without Corben story). 4-Crandall-a. 4,5-Vampirella stories.
5-Spirit story; Eisner-a 4 8 12 24 32 40
NOTE: *No. 4 had two printings with extra* ***Corben*** *story in one. No. 3 may also have a variation. No. 3 has two Jeff Jones reprints from Vampirella.*

COMMANDER BATTLE AND THE ATOMIC SUB
Amer. Comics Group (Titan Publ. Co.): Jul-Aug, 1954 - No. 7, Aug-Sep, 1955
1 (3-D effect)-Moldoff flying saucer-c 48 96 144 293 447 600
2,4-7: 2-Moldoff-c. 4-(1-2/55)-Last pre-code; Landau-a. 5-3-D effect story

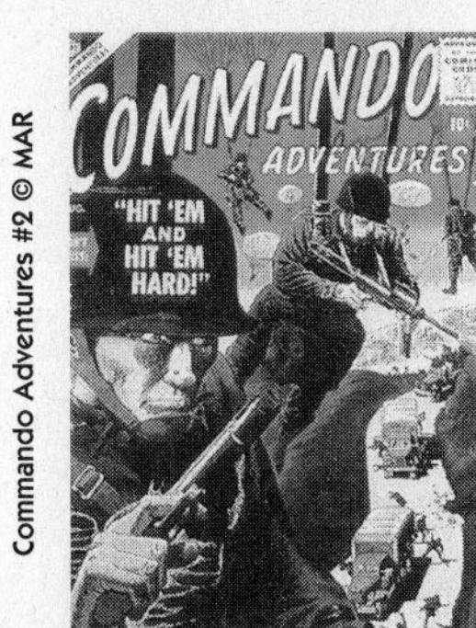

Commando Adventures #2 © MAR

Conan ('04) #1 (3rd printing) © Conan Prod.

Conan the Barbarian #9 © Conan Prod.

GD VG FN VF VF/NM NM-
2.0 4.0 6.0 8.0 9.0 9.2

(2 pgs.). 6,7-Landau-a. 7-Flying saucer-c 33 66 99 190 275 360
3-H-Bomb-c; Atomic Sub becomes Atomic Spaceship
35 70 105 198 287 375

COMMANDO ADVENTURES
Atlas Comics (MMC): June, 1957 - No. 2, Aug, 1957
1-Severin-c 12 24 36 71 98 125
2-Severin-c; Drucker-a? 10 20 30 56 73 90

COMMANDO YANK (See The Mighty Midget Comics & Wow Comics)

COMMON GROUNDS
Image Comics (Top Cow): Feb, 2004 - No. 6, July, 2004 ($2.99)
1-6: 1-Two covers; art by Jurgens and Oeming. 3-Bachalo, Jurgens-a. 4-Peréz-a 3.00
...: Baker's Dozen TPB (12/04, $14.99) r/#1-6; cover gallery; Holey Crullers pages 15.00

COMPLETE BOOK OF COMICS AND FUNNIES
William H. Wise & Co.: 1944 (25¢, one-shot, 196 pgs.)
1-Origin Brad Spencer, Wonderman; The Magnet, The Silver Knight by Kinstler, & Zudo the Jungle Boy app. 42 84 126 256 391 525

COMPLETE BOOK OF TRUE CRIME COMICS
William H. Wise & Co.: No date (Mid 1940's) (25¢, 132 pgs.)
nn-Contains Crime Does Not Pay rebound (includes #22)
115 230 345 719 1110 1500

COMPLETE COMICS (Formerly Amazing Comics No. 1)
Timely Comics (EPC): No. 2, Winter, 1944-45
2-The Destroyer, The Whizzer, The Young Allies & Sergeant Dix; Schomburg-c
162 324 486 1013 1557 2100

COMPLETE GUIDE TO THE DEADLY ARTS OF KUNG FU AND KARATE
Marvel Comics: 1974 (68 pgs., B&W magazine)
V1#1-Bruce Lee-c and 5 pg. story (scarce) 5 10 15 36 48 60

COMPLETE LOVE MAGAZINE (Formerly a pulp with same title)
Ace Periodicals (Periodical House): V26#2, May-June, 1951 - V32#4(#191), Sept, 1956
V26#2-Painted-c (52 pgs.) 8 16 24 46 58 70
V26#3-6(2/52), V27#1(4/52)-6(1/53) 7 14 21 35 43 50
V28#1(3/53), V28#2(5/53), V29#3(7/53)-6(12/53) 6 12 18 31 38 45
V30#1(2/54), V30#1(#176, 4/54),2,4-6(#181, 1/55) 6 12 18 31 38 45
V30#3(#178)-Rock Hudson photo-c 7 14 21 35 43 50
V31#1(#182, 3/55)-Last precode 6 12 18 28 34 40
V31#2(5/55)-6(#187, 1/56) 5 10 15 24 30 35
V32#1(#188, 3/56)-4(#191, 9/56) 5 10 15 24 30 35
NOTE: *(34 total issues). Photo-c V27#5-on. Painted-c V26#3.*

COMPLETE MYSTERY (True Complete Mystery No. 5 on)
Marvel Comics (PrPl): Aug, 1948 - No. 4, Feb, 1949 (Full length stories)
1-Seven Dead Men 45 90 135 275 418 560
2-4: 2-Jigsaw of Doom! 3-Fear in the Night; Burgos-c/a (28 pgs.). 4-A Squealer Dies Fast
40 80 120 230 335 440

COMPLETE ROMANCE
Avon Periodicals: 1949
1-(Scarce)-Reprinted as Women to Love 40 80 120 239 357 475

CONAN (See Chamber of Darkness #4, Giant-Size..., Handbook of..., King Conan, Marvel Graphic Novel #19, 28, Marvel Treasury Ed., Power Record Comics, Robert E. Howard's.., Savage Sword of Conan, and Savage Tales)

CONAN
Dark Horse Comics: Feb, 2004 - Present ($2.99)
1-Linsner-c/Busiek-s/Nord-a 5.00
1-(2nd printing) J. Scott Campell-c 3.00
1-(3rd printing) Nord-c 3.00
2-6 3.00
Vol. 1: The Frost Giant's Daughter and Other Stories (2005, $15.95) r/#1-6, partial #7 16.00

CONAN: (Title Series): Marvel Comics
CONAN, 8/95 - No. 11, 6/96 ($2.95), 1-11: 4-Malibu Comic's Rune app. 3.00
...CLASSIC, 6/94 - No. 11, 4/95 ($1.50), 1-11: 1-r/Conan #1 by B. Smith, r/covers w/changes. 2-11-r/Conan #2-11 by Smith. 2-Bound w/cover to Conan The Adventurer #2 by mistake 2.25
...DEATH COVERED IN GOLD, 9/99 - No. 3, 11/99 ($2.99), 1-3-Roy Thomas-s/ John Buscema-a 3.00
...FLAME AND THE FIEND, 8/00 - No. 3, 10/00 ($2.99), 1-3-Thomas-s 3.00
...RETURN OF STYRM, 9/98 - No. 3, 11/98 ($2.99), 1-3-Parente & Soresina-a; painted-c 3.00
...RIVER OF BLOOD, 6/98 - No. 3, 8/98 ($2.50), 1-3 2.50
...SCARLET SWORD, 12/98 - No. 3, 2/99 ($2.99), 1-3-Thomas-s/Raffaele-a 3.00

CONAN SAGA, THE
Marvel Comics: June, 1987 - No. 97, Apr, 1995 ($2.00/$2.25, B&W, magazine)
1-Barry Smith-r; new Smith-c 1 2 3 4 5 7
2-27: 2-9,11-new Barry Smith-c. 13,15-Boris-c. 17-Adams-r.18,25-Chaykin-r. 22-r/Giant-Size Conan 1,2 4.00
28-90: 28-Begin $2.25-c. 31-Red Sonja-r by N. Adams/SSOC #1; 1 pg. Jeff Jones-r. 32-Newspaper strip-r begin by Buscema. 33-Smith/Conrad-a. 39-r/Kull #1('71) by Andru & Wood. 44-Swipes-c/Savage Tales #1. 57-Brunner-r/SSOC #30. 66-r/Conan Annual #2 by Buscema. 79-r/Conan #43-45 w/Red Sonja. 85-Based on Conan #57-63 3.00
91-96 4.00
97-Last issue 5.00
NOTE: ***J. Buscema** r-32-on; c-86. **Chaykin** r-34. **Chiodo** painted c-63, 65, 66, 82. **G. Colan** a-47p. **Jusko** painted c-64, 83. **Kaluta** c-84. **Nino** a-37. **Ploog** a-50. **N. Redondo** painted c-48, 50, 51, 53, 57, 62. **Simonson** r-50-54, 56. **B. Smith** r-51. **Starlin** c-34. **Williamson** r-50i.*

CONAN THE ADVENTURER
Marvel Comics: June, 1994 - No. 14, July, 1995 ($1.50)
1-($2.50)-Embossed foil-c; Kayaran-a 3.00
2-14 2.50
2-Contents are Conan Classics #2 by mistake 2.50

CONAN THE BARBARIAN
Marvel Comics: Oct, 1970 - No. 275, Dec, 1993
1-Origin/1st app. Conan (in comics) by Barry Smith; 1st brief app. Kull; #1-9 are 15¢ issues 18 36 54 131 201 270
2 7 14 21 46 63 80
3-(Low distribution in some areas) 11 22 33 77 114 150
4,5 6 12 18 43 59 75
6-9: 8-Hidden panel message, pg. 14. 9-Last 15¢-c 4 8 12 29 40 50
10,11 (25¢ 52 pg. giants): 10-Black Knight-r; Kull story by Severin
6 12 18 40 55 70
12,13: 12-Wrightson-c(i) 4 8 12 24 32 40
14,15-Elric app. 5 10 15 33 44 55
16,19,20: 16-Conan-r/Savage Tales #1 4 8 12 24 32 40
17,18-No Barry Smith-a 3 6 9 16 20 25
21,22: 22-Has reprint from #1 3 6 9 18 24 30
23-1st app. Red Sonja (2/73) 4 8 12 24 32 40
24-1st full Red Sonja story; last Smith-a 4 8 12 22 30 38
25-John Buscema-c/a begins 2 4 6 14 18 22
26-30 2 4 6 10 13 16
31-36,38-40 1 3 4 6 8 10
37-Neal Adams-c/a; last 20¢ issue; contains pull-out subscription form
2 4 6 12 16 20
41-43,46-50: 48-Origin retold 1 2 3 5 6 8
44,45-N. Adams-i(Crusty Bunkers). 45-Adams-c 2 4 6 8 10 12
51-57,59,60: 59-Origin Belit 6.00
58-2nd Belit app. (see Giant-Size Conan #1) 1 2 3 5 6 8
61-65-(Regular 25¢ editions)(4-8/76) 5.00
61-65-(30¢-c variants, limited distribution) 1 2 3 4 5 7
66-99: 68-Red Sonja story cont'd from Marvel Feature #7. 75-79-(Reg. 30¢-c). 84-Intro. Zula. 85-Origin Zula. 87-r/Savage Sword of Conan #3 in color 4.00
75-79-(35¢-c variants, limited distribution) 6.00
100-(52 pg. Giant)-Death of Belit 6.00
101-114 2.25
115-Double size 3.00
116-199,201-231,233-249: 116-r/Power Record Comic PR31. 244-Zula returns 2.25
200,232: 200-(52 pgs.). 232-Young Conan storyline begins; Conan is born 4.00
250-(60 pgs.) 3.00
251-270: 262-Adapted from R.E. Howard story 3.00
271-274 5.00
275-($2.50, 68 pgs.)-Final issue; painted-c (low print) 1 2 3 5 6 8
King Size 1(1973, 35¢)-Smith-r/#2,4; Smith-c 3 6 9 16 20 25
Annual 2(1976, 50¢)-New full length story 2 4 6 8 10 12
Annual 3,4: 3('78)-Chaykin/N. Adams-r/SSOC #2. 4('78)-New full length story
1 2 3 5 6 8
Annual 5,6: 5(1979)-New full length Buscema story & part-c, 6(1981)-Kane-c/a 5.00
Annual 7-12: 7('82)-Based on novel "Conan of the Isles" (new-a). 8(1984). 9(1984). 10(1986). 11(1986). 12(1987) 4.00
Special Edition 1 (Red Nails) 4.00
The Chronicles of Conan Vol. 1: Tower of the Elephant and Other Stories (Dark Horse, 2003, $15.95) r/#1-8; afterword by Roy Thomas 16.00
The Chronicles of Conan Vol. 2: Rogues in the House and Other Stories (Dark Horse, 2003,

Conan the King #21 © Conan Prod.

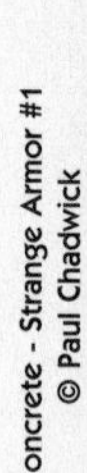
Concrete - Strange Armor #1 © Paul Chadwick

Congorilla #1 © DC

	GD 2.0	VG 4.0	FN 6.0	VF 8.0	VF/NM 9.0	NM- 9.2

$15.95) r/#9-13,16; afterword by Roy Thomas 16.00
The Chronicles of Conan Vol. 3: The Monster of the Monoliths and Other Stories (Dark Horse, 2003, $15.95) r/#14,15,17-21; afterword by Roy Thomas 16.00
The Chronicles of Conan Vol. 4: The Song of Red Sonja and Other Stories (Dark Horse, 2004, $15.95) r/#23-26 & "Red Nails" from Savage Tales; afterword by Roy Thomas 16.00
The Chronicles of Conan Vol. 5: The Shadow in the Tomb and Other Stories (Dark Horse, 2004, $15.95) r/#27-34; afterword by Roy Thomas 16.00
The Chronicles of Conan Vol. 6: The Curse of the Skull and Other Stories (Dark Horse, 2004, $15.95) r/#35-42; afterword by Roy Thomas 16.00

NOTE: ***Arthur Adams** c-248, 249. **Neal Adams** a-116r(i); c-49i. **Austin** a-125, 126; c-125i, 126i. **Brunner** c-17i. c-40. **Buscema** a-25-36p, 38, 39, 41-56p, 58-63p, 65-67p, 68, 70-78p, 84-86p, 88-91p, 93-126p, 136p, 140, 141-144p, 146-158p, 159, 161, 162, 163p, 165-185p, 187-190p, Annual 2(3pgs.). 3-5p, 7p; c(p)-26, 36, 44, 46, 52, 56, 58, 59, 64, 65, 72, 78-80, 83-91, 93-103, 105-126, 136-151, 155-159, 161, 162, 168, 169, 171, 172, 174, 175, 178-185, 188, 189, Annual 4, 5, 7. **Chaykin** a-79-83. **Golden** c-152. **Kaluta** c-167. **Gil Kane** a-12p, 17p, 18p, 127-130, 131-134p; c-12p, 17p, 18p, 23, 25, 27-32, 34, 35, 38, 39, 41-43, 45-51, 53-55, 57, 60-63, 65-71, 73p, 76p, 127-134. **Jim Lee** c-242. **McFarlane** c-241p. **Ploog** a-57. **Russell** a-21; c-251i. **Simonson** c-135. **B. Smith** a-1-11p, 12, 13-15p, 16, 19-21, 23, 24; c-1-11, 13-16, 19-24p. **Starlin** a-64. **Wood** a-47r. Issue Nos. 3-5, 7-9, 11, 16-18, 21, 23, 25, 27-30, 35, 37, 38, 42, 45, 52, 57, 58, 65, 69-71, 73, 79-83, 99, 100, 104, 114, Annual 2 have original Robert E. Howard stories adapted. Issues #32-34 adapted from Norvell Page's novel **Flame Winds**.*

CONAN THE BARBARIAN (Volume 2)
Marvel Comics: July, 1997 - No. 3, Oct, 1997 ($2.50, limited series)

1-3-Castellini-a 2.50

CONAN THE BARBARIAN MOVIE SPECIAL (Movie)
Marvel Comics Group: Oct, 1982 - No. 2, Nov, 1982

1,2-Movie adaptation; Buscema-a 3.00

CONAN THE BARBARIAN: THE USURPER
Marvel Comics: Dec, 1997 - No. 3, Feb, 1998 ($2.50, limited series)

1-3-Dixon-s 2.50

CONAN THE DESTROYER (Movie)
Marvel Comics Group: Jan, 1985 - No. 2, Mar, 1985

1,2-r/Marvel Super Special 2.50

CONAN THE KING (Formerly King Conan)
Marvel Comics Group: No. 20, Jan, 1984 - No. 55, Nov, 1989

20-49 3.00
50-54 4.00
55-Last issue 6.00

NOTE: ***Kaluta** c-20-23, 24i, 26, 27, 30, 50, 52. **Williamson** a-37i; c-37i, 38i.*

CONAN: THE LEGEND
Dark Horse Comics: No. 0, Nov, 2003 - Present (25¢/$2.99)

0-(25¢-c) Busiek-s/Nord-a 2.25
1-($2.99) Busiek-s/Nord-a/Linsner-c 3.00

CONAN: THE LORD OF THE SPIDERS
Marvel Comics: Mar, 1998 - No. 3, May, 1998 ($2.50, limited series)

1-3-Roy Thomas-s/Raffaele-a 2.50

CONAN THE SAVAGE
Marvel Comics: Aug, 1995 - No. 10, May, 1996 ($2.95, B&W, Magazine)

1-10: 1-Bisley-c. 4-vs. Malibu Comic's Rune. 5,10-Brereton-c 3.00

CONAN VS. RUNE (Also See Conan #4)
Marvel Comics: Nov, 1995 ($2.95, one-shot)

1-Barry Smith-c/a/scripts 3.00

CONCRETE (Also see Dark Horse Presents & Within Our Reach)
Dark Horse Comics: March, 1987 - No. 10, Nov, 1988 ($1.50, B&W)

	GD	VG	FN	VF	VF/NM	NM-
1-Paul Chadwick-c/a in all	1	3	4	6	8	10

1-2nd print 3.00
2 6.00
3-Origin 5.00
4-10 4.00
A New Life 1 (1989, $2.95, B&W)-r/#3,4 plus new-a (11 pgs.) 3.00
Celebrates Earth Day 1990 ($3.50, 52 pgs.) 6.00
Color Special 1 (2/89, $2.95, 44 pgs.)-r/1st two Concrete apps. from Dark Horse Presents #1,2 plus new-a 6.00
Land And Sea 1 (2/89, $2.95, B&W)-r/#1,2 6.00
Odd Jobs 1 (7/90, $3.50)-r/5,6 plus new-a 3.50

CONCRETE: (Title series), **Dark Horse Comics**

--ECLECTICA, 4/93 - No. 2, 5/93 ($2.95) 1,2 3.00
--FRAGILE CREATURE, 6/91 - No. 4, 2/92 ($2.50) 1-4 3.00
--KILLER SMILE, (Legend), 7/94 - No. 4, 10/94 ($2.9) 1-4 3.00
--STRANGE ARMOR, 12/97 - No. 5, 5/98 ($2.95, color) 1-5-Chadwick-s/c/a; retells origin 3.00
--THINK LIKE A MOUNTAIN, (Legend), 3/96 - No. 6, 8/96 ($2.95)

1-6: Chadwick-a/scripts & Darrow-c in all 3.00

CONDORMAN (Walt Disney)
Whitman Publishing: Oct, 1981 - No. 3, Jan, 1982

	GD	VG	FN	VF	VF/NM	NM-
1-3: 1,2-Movie adaptation; photo-c	1	3	4	6	8	10

CONEHEADS
Marvel Comics: June, 1994 - No. 4, 1994 ($1.75, limited series)

1-4 2.50

CONFESSIONS ILLUSTRATED (Magazine)
E. C. Comics: Jan-Feb, 1956 - No. 2, Spring, 1956

	GD	VG	FN	VF	VF/NM	NM-
1-Craig, Kamen, Wood, Orlando-a	26	52	78	147	211	275
2-Craig, Crandall, Kamen, Orlando-a	19	38	57	107	154	200

CONFESSIONS OF LOVE
Artful Publ.: Apr, 1950 - No. 2, July, 1950 (25¢, 7-1/4x5-1/4", 132 pgs.)

	GD	VG	FN	VF	VF/NM	NM-
1-Bakerish-a	28	56	84	158	229	300
2-Art & text; Bakerish-a	16	32	48	89	127	165

CONFESSIONS OF LOVE (Formerly Startling Terror Tales #10; becomes Confessions of Romance No. 7 on)
Star Publications: No. 11, 7/52 - No. 14, 1/53; No. 4, 3/53- No. 6, 8/53

	GD	VG	FN	VF	VF/NM	NM-
11-13: 12,13-Disbrow-a	16	32	48	92	131	170
14,5,6	13	26	39	74	102	130
4-Disbrow-a	14	28	42	79	110	140

NOTE: *All have **L. B. Cole** covers.*

CONFESSIONS OF ROMANCE (Formerly Confessions of Love)
Star Publications: No. 7, Nov, 1953 - No. 11, Nov, 1954

	GD	VG	FN	VF	VF/NM	NM-
7	16	32	48	92	131	170
8	13	26	39	74	102	130
9-Wood-a	15	30	45	83	117	150
10,11-Disbrow-a	14	28	42	79	110	140

NOTE: *All have **L. B. Cole** covers.*

CONFESSIONS OF THE LOVELORN (Formerly Lovelorn)
American Comics Group (Regis Publ./Best Synd. Features): No. 52, Aug, 1954 - No. 114, June-July, 1960

	GD	VG	FN	VF	VF/NM	NM-
52 (3-D effect)	29	58	87	164	237	310
53,55	9	18	27	54	70	85
54 (3-D effect)	29	58	87	164	237	310
56-Anti-communist propaganda story, 10 pgs; last pre-code (2/55)	12	24	36	69	95	120
57-90,100	7	14	21	37	46	55
91-Williamson-a	9	18	27	54	70	85
92-99,101-114	6	12	18	31	38	45

NOTE: ***Whitney** a-most issues; c-52, 53. Painted c-106, 107.*

CONFIDENTIAL DIARY (Formerly High School Confidential Diary; Three Nurses #18 on)
Charlton Comics: No. 12, May, 1962 - No. 17, Mar, 1963

	GD	VG	FN	VF	VF/NM	NM-
12-17	3	6	9	16	21	26

CONGO BILL (See Action Comics & More Fun Comics #56)
National Periodical Publication: Aug-Sept, 1954 - No. 7, Aug-Sept, 1955

	GD	VG	FN	VF	VF/NM	NM-
1 (Scarce)	150	300	450	1200	-	-
2,7 (Scarce)	110	220	330	880	-	-
3-6 (Scarce). 4-Last pre-code issue	85	170	255	680	-	-

NOTE: *(Rarely found in fine to mint condition.) **Nick Cardy** c-1-7.*

CONGO BILL
DC Comics (Vertigo): Oct, 1999 - No. 4, Jan, 2000 ($2.95, limited series)

1-4-Corben-c 3.00

CONGORILLA (Also see Actions Comics #224)
DC Comics: Nov, 1992 - No. 4, Feb, 1993 ($1.75, limited series)

1-4: 1,2-Brian Bolland-c 3.00

CONJURORS
DC Comics: Apr, 1999 - No. 3, Jun, 1999 ($2.95, limited series)

1-3-Elseworlds; Phantom Stranger app.; Barreto-c/a 3.00

CONNECTICUT YANKEE, A (See King Classics)

CONQUEROR, THE
Dell Publishing Co.: No., 690, Mar, 1956

	GD	VG	FN	VF	VF/NM	NM-
Four Color 690-Movie, John Wayne photo-c	18	36	54	129	197	265

CONQUEROR COMICS

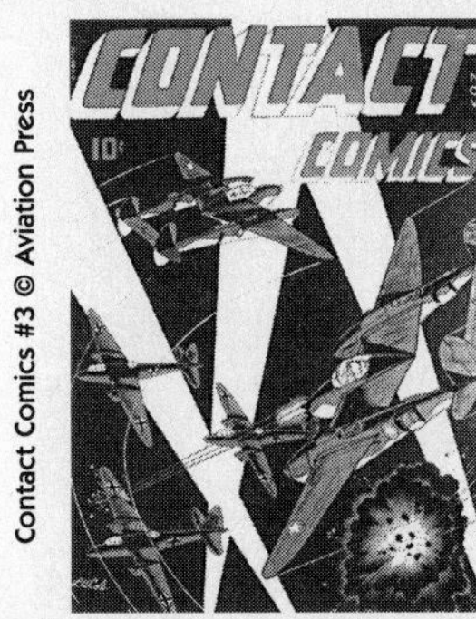

Contact Comics #3 © Aviation Press

Coo Coo Comics #42 © STD

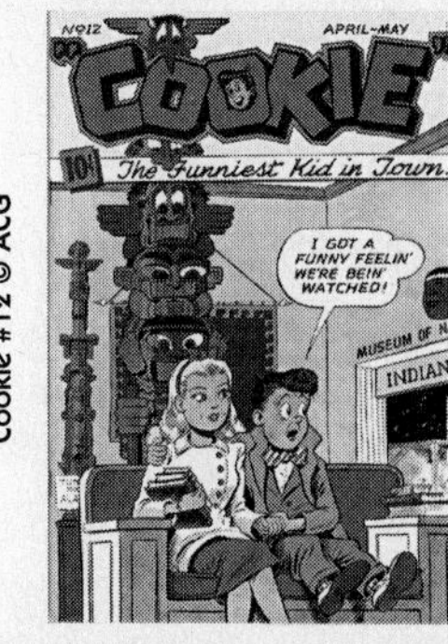

Cookie #12 © ACG

Albrecht Publishing Co.: Winter, 1945

	GD 2.0	VG 4.0	FN 6.0	VF 8.0	VF/NM 9.0	NM- 9.2
nn	21	42	63	121	173	225

CONQUEROR OF THE BARREN EARTH (See The Warlord #63)
DC Comics: Feb, 1985 - No. 4, May, 1985 (Limited series)

	GD 2.0	VG 4.0	FN 6.0	VF 8.0	VF/NM 9.0	NM- 9.2
1-4: Back-up series from Warlord						2.50

CONQUEST
Store Comics: 1953 (6¢)

	GD 2.0	VG 4.0	FN 6.0	VF 8.0	VF/NM 9.0	NM- 9.2
1-Richard the Lion Hearted, Beowulf, Swamp Fox	7	14	21	35	43	50

CONQUEST
Famous Funnies: Spring, 1955

	GD 2.0	VG 4.0	FN 6.0	VF 8.0	VF/NM 9.0	NM- 9.2
1-Crandall-a, 1 pg.; contains contents of 1953 ish.	5	10	15	22	26	30

CONSPIRACY
Marvel Comics: Feb, 1998 - No. 2, Mar, 1998 ($2.99, limited series)

	GD 2.0	VG 4.0	FN 6.0	VF 8.0	VF/NM 9.0	NM- 9.2
1,2-Painted art by Korday/Abnett-s						3.00

CONSTANTINE, JOHN (See Hellblazer)

CONSTRUCT
Caliber (New Worlds): 1996 - No. 6, 1997 ($2.95, B&W, limited series)

	GD 2.0	VG 4.0	FN 6.0	VF 8.0	VF/NM 9.0	NM- 9.2
1-6: Paul Jenkins scripts						3.00

CONTACT COMICS
Aviation Press: July, 1944 - No. 12, May, 1946

	GD 2.0	VG 4.0	FN 6.0	VF 8.0	VF/NM 9.0	NM- 9.2
nn-Black Venus, Flamingo, Golden Eagle, Tommy Tomahawk begin	54	108	162	329	502	675
2-5: 3-Last Flamingo. 3,4-Black Venus by L. B. Cole. 5-The Phantom Flyer app.	40	80	120	241	363	485
6,11-Kurtzman's Black Venus; 11-Last Golden Eagle, last Tommy Tomahawk; Feldstein-a	46	92	138	281	428	575
7-10	40	80	120	236	351	465
12-Sky Rangers, Air Kids, Ace Diamond app.; L.B. Cole sci-fi cover	85	170	255	531	816	1100

NOTE: ***L. B. Cole** a-3, 9; c-1-12. **Giunta** a-3. **Hollingsworth** a-5, 7, 10. **Palais** a-11, 12.*

CONTEMPORARY MOTIVATORS
Pendelum Press: 1977 - 1978 ($1.45, 5-3/8x8", 31 pgs., B&W)

	GD 2.0	VG 4.0	FN 6.0	VF 8.0	VF/NM 9.0	NM- 9.2
14-3002 The Caine Mutiny; 14-3010 Banner in the Sky; 14-3029 God Is My Co-Pilot; 14-3037 Guadalcanal Diary; 14-3045 Hiroshima; 14-3053 Hot Rod; 14-3061 Just Dial a Number; 14-3088 The Diary of Anne Frank; 14-3096 Lost Horizon	1	3	4	6	8	10

NOTE: *Also see Pendulum Illustrated Classics. Above may have been distributed the same.*

CONTEST OF CHAMPIONS (See Marvel Super-Hero...)

CONTEST OF CHAMPIONS II
Marvel Comics: Sept, 1999 - No. 5 ($2.50, limited series)

	GD 2.0	VG 4.0	FN 6.0	VF 8.0	VF/NM 9.0	NM- 9.2
1-5-Claremont-s/Jimenez-a						2.50

CONTRACTORS
Eclipse Comics: June, 1987 ($2.00, B&W, one-shot)

	GD 2.0	VG 4.0	FN 6.0	VF 8.0	VF/NM 9.0	NM- 9.2
1-Funny animal						2.25

CONTRACT WITH GOD, A
Baronet Publishing Co./Kitchen Sink Press: 1978 ($7.95, B&W, graphic novel)

	GD 2.0	VG 4.0	FN 6.0	VF 8.0	VF/NM 9.0	NM- 9.2
nn-Will Eisner-s/a	2	4	6	14	18	22
Reprint (DC Comics, 2000, $12.95)						13.00

CONVOCATIONS: A MAGIC THE GATHERING GALLERY
Acclaim Comics (Armada): Jan, 1996 ($2.50, one-shot)

	GD 2.0	VG 4.0	FN 6.0	VF 8.0	VF/NM 9.0	NM- 9.2
1-pin-ups by various artists including Kaluta, Vess, and Dringenberg						2.50

COO COO COMICS (...the Bird Brain No. 57 on)
Nedor Publ. Co./Standard (Animated Cartoons): Oct, 1942 - No. 62, Apr, 1952

	GD 2.0	VG 4.0	FN 6.0	VF 8.0	VF/NM 9.0	NM- 9.2
1-Origin/1st app. Super Mouse & begin series (cloned from Superman); the first funny animal super hero series (see Looney Tunes #5 for 1st funny animal super hero)	31	62	93	178	259	340
2	15	30	45	83	117	150
3-10: 10-(3/44)	10	20	30	56	73	90
11-33: 33-1 pg. Ingels-a	8	16	24	43	54	65
34-40,43-46,48-Text illos by Frazetta in all. 36-Super Mouse covers begin	10	20	30	60	80	100
41-Frazetta-a (6-pg. story & 3 text illos)	20	40	60	112	161	210
42,47-Frazetta-a & text illos.	15	30	45	83	117	150
49-(1/50)-3-D effect story; Frazetta text illo	11	22	33	66	91	115
50,51-3-D effect-c only. 50-Frazetta text illo	11	22	33	62	84	105
52-62: 56-Last Supermouse?	7	14	21	37	46	55

"COOKIE" (Also see Topsy-Turvy)
Michel Publ./American Comics Group(Regis Publ.): Apr, 1946 - No. 55, Aug-Sept, 1955

	GD 2.0	VG 4.0	FN 6.0	VF 8.0	VF/NM 9.0	NM- 9.2
1-Teen-age humor	21	42	63	118	169	220
2	11	22	33	64	87	110
3-10	9	18	27	51	62	75
11-20	8	16	24	43	54	65
21-23,26,28-30	6	12	18	31	38	45
24,25,27-Starlett O'Hara stories	7	14	21	35	43	50
31-34,37-50,52-55	6	12	18	28	34	40
35,36-Starlett O'Hara stories	6	12	18	31	38	45
51-(10-11/54) 8pg. TrueVision 3-D effect story	10	20	30	58	77	95

COOL CAT (Formerly Black Magic)
Prize Publications: V8#6, Mar-Apr, 1962 - V9#2, July-Aug, 1962

	GD 2.0	VG 4.0	FN 6.0	VF 8.0	VF/NM 9.0	NM- 9.2
V8#6, nn(V9#1, 5-6/62), V9#2	3	6	9	18	24	30

COOL WORLD (Movie by Ralph Bakshi)
DC Comics: Apr, 1992 - No. 4, Sept, 1992 ($1.75, limited series)

	GD 2.0	VG 4.0	FN 6.0	VF 8.0	VF/NM 9.0	NM- 9.2
1-4: Prequel to animated/live action movie. 1-Bakshi-c. Bill Wray inks in all						2.25
Movie Adaptation nn ('92, $3.50, 68pg.)-Bakshi-c						3.50

COPPER CANYON (See Fawcett Movie Comics)

COPS (TV)
DC Comics: Aug, 1988 - No. 15, Aug, 1989 ($1.00)

	GD 2.0	VG 4.0	FN 6.0	VF 8.0	VF/NM 9.0	NM- 9.2
1 ($1.50, 52 pgs.)-Based on Hasbro Toys						3.00
2-15: 14-Orlando-c(p)						2.25

COPS: THE JOB
Marvel Comics: June, 1992 - No. 4, Sept, 1992 ($1.25, limited series)

	GD 2.0	VG 4.0	FN 6.0	VF 8.0	VF/NM 9.0	NM- 9.2
1-4: All have Jusko scripts & Golden-c						2.25

CORBEN SPECIAL, A
Pacific Comics: May, 1984 (one-shot)

	GD 2.0	VG 4.0	FN 6.0	VF 8.0	VF/NM 9.0	NM- 9.2
1-Corben-c/a; E.A. Poe adaptation						5.00

CORKY & WHITE SHADOW (Disney, TV)
Dell Publishing Co.: No. 707, May, 1956 (Mickey Mouse Club)

	GD 2.0	VG 4.0	FN 6.0	VF 8.0	VF/NM 9.0	NM- 9.2
Four Color 707-Photo-c	8	16	24	58	82	105

CORLISS ARCHER (See Meet Corliss Archer)

CORMAC MAC ART (Robert E. Howard's...)
Dark Horse Comics: 1990 - No. 4, 1990 ($1.95, B&W, mini-series)

	GD 2.0	VG 4.0	FN 6.0	VF 8.0	VF/NM 9.0	NM- 9.2
1-4: All have Bolton painted-c; Howard adapts.						3.00

CORNY'S FETISH
Dark Horse Comics: Apr, 1998 ($4.95, B&W, one-shot)

	GD 2.0	VG 4.0	FN 6.0	VF 8.0	VF/NM 9.0	NM- 9.2
1-Renée French-s/a; Bolland-c						5.00

CORPORAL RUSTY DUGAN (See Holyoke One-Shot #2)

CORPSES OF DR. SACOTTI, THE (See Ideal a Classical Comic)

CORSAIR, THE (See A-1 Comics No. 5, 7, 10 under Texas Slim)

CORTEZ AND THE FALL OF THE AZTECS
Tome Press: 1993 ($2.95, B&W, limited series)

	GD 2.0	VG 4.0	FN 6.0	VF 8.0	VF/NM 9.0	NM- 9.2
1,2						3.00

CORUM: THE BULL AND THE SPEAR (See Chronicles Of Corum)
First Comics: Jan, 1989 - No. 4, July, 1989 ($1.95)

	GD 2.0	VG 4.0	FN 6.0	VF 8.0	VF/NM 9.0	NM- 9.2
1-4: Adapts Michael Moorcock's novel						2.50

COSMIC BOOK, THE
Ace Comics: Dec, 1986 - No. 1, 1987 ($1.95)

	GD 2.0	VG 4.0	FN 6.0	VF 8.0	VF/NM 9.0	NM- 9.2
1,2: 1-(44pgs.)-Wood, Toth-a. 2-(B&W)						2.25

COSMIC BOY (Also see The Legion of Super-Heroes)
DC Comics: Dec, 1986 - No. 4, Mar, 1987 (limited series)

	GD 2.0	VG 4.0	FN 6.0	VF 8.0	VF/NM 9.0	NM- 9.2
1-4: Legends tie-ins all issues						2.50

COSMIC GUARD
Devil's Due Publ.: Aug, 2004 - Present ($2.99)

	GD 2.0	VG 4.0	FN 6.0	VF 8.0	VF/NM 9.0	NM- 9.2
1-4-Jim Starlin-s/a						3.00

COSMIC HEROES
Eternity/Malibu Graphics: Oct, 1988 - No. 11, Dec, 1989 ($1.95, B&W)

	GD 2.0	VG 4.0	FN 6.0	VF 8.0	VF/NM 9.0	NM- 9.2
1-11: Reprints 1934-1936's Buck Rogers newspaper strips #1-728						2.25

COSMIC ODYSSEY
DC Comics: 1988 - No. 4, 1988 ($3.50, limited series, squarebound)

Cosmo Cat #4 © FOX

Coup D'Etat: Stormwatch #1 © WSP

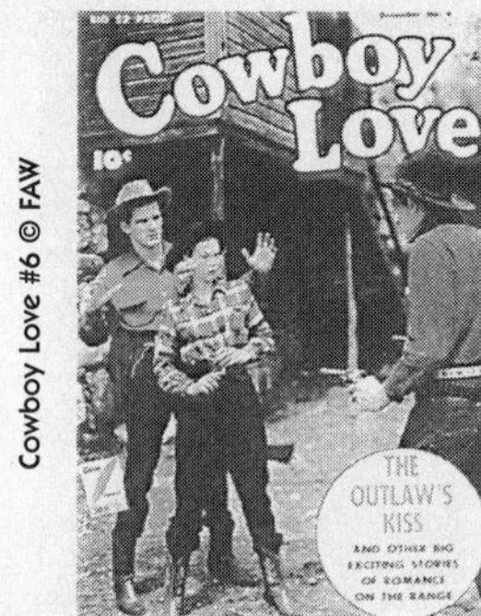

Cowboy Love #6 © FAW

	GD 2.0	VG 4.0	FN 6.0	VF 8.0	VF/NM 9.0	NM- 9.2

1-4: Reintro. New Gods into DC continuity; Superman, Batman, Green Lantern (John Stewart) app; Starlin scripts, Mignola-c/a in all. 2-Darkseid merges Demon & Jason Blood (separated in Demon limited series #4); John Stewart responsible for the death of a star system 5.00
Trade paperback-r/#1-4. 20.00

COSMIC POWERS
Marvel Comics: Mar, 1994 - No. 6, Aug, 1994 ($2.50, limited series)
1-6: 1-Ron Lim-c/a(p). 1,2-Thanos app. 2-Terrax. 3-Ganymede & Jack of Hearts app. 2.50

COSMIC POWERS UNLIMITED
Marvel Comics: May, 1995 - No. 5, May, 1996 ($3.95, quarterly)
1-5 4.00

COSMIC RAY
Image Comics: June, 1999 - No. 2 ($2.95, B&W)
1,2-Steven Blue-s/a 3.00

COSMIC SLAM
Ultimate Sports Entertainment: 1999 ($3.95, one-shot)
1-McGwire, Sosa, Bagwell, Justice battle aliens; Sienkiewicz-c 4.00

COSMO CAT (Becomes Sunny #11 on; also see All Top & Wotalife Comics)
Fox Publications/Green Publ. Co./Norlen Mag.: July-Aug, 1946 - No. 10, Oct, 1947; 1957; 1959

	GD	VG	FN	VF	VF/NM	NM-
1	28	56	84	158	229	300
2	15	30	45	83	117	150
3-Origin (11-12/46)	19	38	57	107	154	200
4-Robot-c	11	22	33	66	91	115
5-10	10	20	30	58	77	95
2-4(1957-Green Publ. Co.)	6	12	18	27	33	38
2-4(1959-Norlen Mag.)	5	10	15	23	28	32
I.W. Reprint #1	2	4	6	12	16	20

COSMO THE MERRY MARTIAN
Archie Publications (Radio Comics): Sept, 1958 - No. 6, Oct, 1959

	GD	VG	FN	VF	VF/NM	NM-
1-Bob White-a in all	15	30	45	86	123	160
2-6	10	20	30	60	80	100

COTTON WOODS
Dell Publishing Co.: No. 837, Sept, 1957

	GD	VG	FN	VF	VF/NM	NM-
Four Color 837	4	8	12	27	36	45

COUGAR, THE (Cougar No. 2)
Seaboard Periodicals (Atlas): April, 1975 - No. 2, July, 1975
1,2: 1-Vampire; Adkins-a(p). 2-Cougar origin; werewolf-s; Buckler-c(p)
1 2 3 5 7 9

COUNTDOWN (See Movie Classics)

COUNTDOWN
DC Comics (WildStorm): June, 2000 - No. 8, Jan, 2001 ($2.95)
1-8-Mariotte-s/Lopresti-a 3.00

COUNT DUCKULA (TV)
Marvel Comics: Nov, 1988 - No. 15, Jan, 1991 ($1.00)
1,8: 1-Dangermouse back-up. 8-Geraldo Rivera photo-c/& app.; Sienkiewicz-a(i) 5.00
2-7,9-15: Dangermouse back-ups in all 4.00

COUNT OF MONTE CRISTO, THE
Dell Publishing Co.: No. 794, May, 1957

	GD	VG	FN	VF	VF/NM	NM-
Four Color 794-Movie, Buscema-a	10	20	30	70	100	130

COUP D'ETAT (Oneshots)
DC Comics (WildStorm): April, 2004 ($2.95, weekly limited series)
...: Sleeper 1 (part 1 of 4) Jim Lee-a; 2 covers by Lee and Bermejo 3.00
...: Stormwatch 1 (part 2 of 4) D'Anda-a; 2 covers by D'Anda and Bermejo 3.00
...: Wildcats Version 3.0 1 (part 3 of 4) Garza-a; 2 covers by Garza and Bermejo 3.00
...: The Authority 1 (part 4 of 4) Portacio-a; 2 covers by Portacio and Bermejo 3.00
...: Afterword 1 (5/04) Profile pages and prelude stories for Sleeper & Wetworks 3.00
TPB (2004, $12.95) r/series and profile pages from Afterword 13.00

COURAGE COMICS
J. Edward Slavin: 1945

	GD	VG	FN	VF	VF/NM	NM-
1,2,77	14	28	42	79	110	140

COURTNEY CRUMRIN & THE COVEN OF MYSTICS
Oni Press: Dec, 2002 - No. 4, March, 2003 ($2.95, B&W, limited series)
1-4-Ted Naifeh-s/a 3.00
TPB (9/03, $11.95, 8" x 5-1/2") r/#1-4 12.00

COURTNEY CRUMRIN & THE NIGHT THINGS (Also see Promotional Section for FCBD Ed.)
Oni Press: Mar, 2002 - No. 4, June, 2002 ($2.95, B&W, limited series)
1-4-Ted Naifeh-s/a 3.00
TPB (12/02, $11.95) r/#1-4 12.00

COURTNEY CRUMRIN IN THE TWILIGHT KINGDOM
Oni Press: Dec, 2003 - No. 4, May, 2004 ($2.99, B&W, limited series)
1-4-Ted Naifeh-s/a 3.00
TPB (9/04, $11.95, digest-size) r/#1-4 12.00

COURTSHIP OF EDDIE'S FATHER (TV)
Dell Publishing Co.: Jan, 1970 - No. 2, May, 1970

	GD	VG	FN	VF	VF/NM	NM-
1-Bill Bixby photo-c on both	6	12	18	40	55	70
2	4	8	12	29	40	50

COVEN
Awesome Entertainment: Aug, 1997 - No. 5, Mar, 1998 ($2.50)

	GD	VG	FN	VF	VF/NM	NM-
Preview	1	2	3	5	6	8
1-Loeb-s/Churchill-a; three covers by Churchill, Liefeld, Pollina	1	2	3	5	6	8
1-Fan Appreciation Ed.(3/98); new Churchill-c						3.00
1+ :Includes B&W art from Kaboom	1	3	4	6	8	10
2-Regular-c w/leaping Fantom						6.00
2-Variant-c w/circle of candles	1	2	3	5	6	8
3-6-Contains flip book preview of ReGex						3.00
3-White variant-c	1	2	3	4	5	7
3,4: 3-Halloween wraparound-c. 4-Purple variant-c						3.00
...Black & White (9/98) Short stories						3.00
...Fantom Special (2/98) w/sketch pages						5.00

COVEN
Awesome Entertainment: Jan, 1999 - No. 3, June, 1999 ($2.50)
1-3: 1-Loeb-s/Churchill-a; 6 covers by various. 2-Supreme-c/app. 3-Flip book w/Kaboom preview 2.50
... Dark Origins (7/99, 2.50) w/Lionheart gallery 2.50

COVERED WAGONS, HO (Disney, TV)
Dell Publishing Co.: No. 814, June, 1957 (Donald Duck)

	GD	VG	FN	VF	VF/NM	NM-
Four Color 814-Mickey Mouse app.	6	12	18	43	59	75

COWBOY ACTION (Formerly Western Thrillers No. 1-4; Becomes Quick-Trigger Western No. 12 on)
Atlas Comics (ACI): No. 5, March, 1955 - No. 11, March, 1956

	GD	VG	FN	VF	VF/NM	NM-
5	14	28	42	79	110	140
6-10: 6-8-Heath-c	10	20	30	56	73	90
11-Williamson-a (4 pgs.); Baker-a	11	22	33	62	84	105

NOTE: ***Ayers** a-8. **Drucker** a-6. **Maneely** c/a-5, 6. **Severin** c-10. **Shores** a-7.*

COWBOY COMICS (Star Ranger #12, Stories #14)(Star Ranger Funnies #15)
Centaur Publishing Co.: No. 13, July, 1938 - No. 14, Aug, 1938

	GD	VG	FN	VF	VF/NM	NM-
13-(Rare)-Ace and Deuce, Lyin Lou, Air Patrol, Aces High, Lee Trent, Trouble Hunters begin	125	250	375	781	1203	1625
14-Filchock-c	87	174	261	544	835	1125

NOTE: ***Guardineer** a-13, 14. **Gustavson** a-13, 14.*

COWBOY IN AFRICA (TV)
Gold Key: Mar, 1968

	GD	VG	FN	VF	VF/NM	NM-
1(10219-803)-Chuck Connors photo-c	6	12	18	38	52	65

COWBOY LOVE (Becomes Range Busters?)
Fawcett Publications/Charlton Comics No. 28 on: 7/49 - V2#10, 6/50; No. 11, 1951; No. 28, 2/55 - No. 31, 8/55

	GD	VG	FN	VF	VF/NM	NM-
V1#1-Rocky Lane photo back-c	20	40	60	112	161	210
2	9	18	27	51	62	75
V1#3,4,6 (12/49)	8	16	24	42	54	65
5-Bill Boyd photo back-c (11/49)	9	18	27	52	66	80
V2#7-Williamson/Evans-a	10	20	30	60	80	100
V2#8-11	7	14	21	37	46	55
V1#28 (Charlton)-Last precode (2/55) (Formerly Romantic Story?)	7	14	21	35	43	50
V1#29-31 (Charlton; becomes Sweetheart Diary #32 on)	6	12	18	31	38	45

NOTE: ***Powell** a-10. **Marcus Swayze** a-2, 3. Photo c-1-11. No. 1-3, 5-7, 9, 10 are 52 pgs.*

COWBOY ROMANCES (Young Men No. 4 on)
Marvel Comics (IPC): Oct, 1949 - No. 3, Mar, 1950 (All photo-c & 52 pgs.)

	GD	VG	FN	VF	VF/NM	NM-
1-Photo-c	24	48	72	138	199	260

2-William Holden, Mona Freeman "Streets of Laredo" photo-c

Cowgirl Romances #8 © FH

Crackajack Funnies #20 © DELL

Crack Comics #18 © QUA

GD VG FN VF VF/NM NM-
2.0 4.0 6.0 8.0 9.0 9.2

17 34 51 95 135 175
3-Photo-c 15 30 45 83 117 150

COWBOYS 'N' INJUNS (...and Indians No. 6 on)
Com No. 1-5/Magazine Enterprises No. 6 on: 1946 - No. 5, 1947; No. 6, 1949 - No. 8, 1952

1 14 28 42 79 110 140
2-5-All funny animal western 9 18 27 54 70 85
6(A-1 23)-Half violent, half funny; Ayers-a 12 24 36 69 95 120
7(A-1 41, 1950), 8(A-1 48)-All funny 8 16 24 51 62 75
I.W. Reprint No. 1,7 (Reprinted in Canada by Superior, No. 7)
2 4 6 12 16 20
Super Reprint #10 (1963) 2 4 6 12 16 20

COWBOY WESTERN COMICS (TV)(Formerly Jack In The Box; Becomes Space Western No. 40-45 & Wild Bill Hickok & Jingles No. 68 on; title:Cowboy Western Heroes No. 47 & 48; Cowboy Western No. 49 on)
Charlton (Capitol Stories): No. 17, 7/48 - No. 39, 8/52; No. 46, 10/53; No. 47, 12/53; No. 48, Spr, '54; No. 49, 5-6/54 - No. 67, 3/58 (nn 40-45)

17-Jesse James, Annie Oakley, Wild Bill Hickok begin; Texas Rangers app.
22 44 66 123 177 230
18,19-Orlando-c/a. 18-Paul Bunyan begins. 19-Wyatt Earp story
13 26 39 74 102 130
20-25: 21-Buffalo Bill story. 22-Texas Rangers-c/story. 24-Joel McCrea photo-c & adaptation from movie "Three Faces West". 25-James Craig photo-c & adaptation from movie "Northwest Stampede" 11 22 33 62 84 105
26-George Montgomery photo-c and adaptation from movie "Indian Scout"; 1 pg. bio on Will Rogers 13 26 39 74 102 130
27-Sunset Carson photo-c & adapts movie "Sunset Carson Rides Again" plus 1 other Sunset Carson story 60 120 180 375 575 775
28-Sunset Carson line drawn-c; adapts movies "Battling Marshal" & "Fighting Mustangs" starring Sunset Carson 33 66 99 190 275 360
29-Sunset Carson line drawn-c; adapts movies "Rio Grande" with Sunset Carson & "Winchester '73" w/James Stewart plus 5 pg. life history of Sunset Carson featuring Tom Mix 33 66 99 190 275 360
30-Sunset Carson photo-c; adapts movie "Deadline" starring Sunset Carson plus 1 other Sunset Carson story 58 116 174 363 557 750
31-34,38,39,47-50 (no #40-45): 50-Golden Arrow, Rocky Lane & Blackjack (r?) stories
10 20 30 56 73 90
35,36-Sunset Carson-c/stories (2 in each). 35-Inside front-c photo of Sunset Carson plus photo on-c 33 66 99 190 275 360
37-Sunset Carson stories (2) 22 44 66 127 184 240
46-(Formerly Space Western)-Space western story 22 44 66 127 184 240
51-57,59-66: 51-Golden Arrow(r?) & Monte Hale-r renamed Rusty Hall. 53,54-Tom Mix-r. 55-Monte Hale story(r?). 66-Young Eagle story. 67-Wild Bill Hickok and Jingles-c/story
8 16 24 43 54 65
58-(1/56, 15¢, 68 pgs.)-Wild Bill Hickok, Annie Oakley & Jesse James stories; Forgione-a
9 18 27 54 70 85
67-(15¢, 68 pgs.)-Williamson/Torres-a, 5 pgs. 10 20 30 60 80 100
NOTE: *Many issues trimmed 1" shorter.* ***Maneely*** *a-67(5). Inside front/back photo c-29.*

COWGIRL ROMANCES
Marvel Comics (CCC): No. 28, Jan, 1950 (52 pgs.)

28(#1)-Photo-c 22 44 66 123 177 230

COWGIRL ROMANCES
Fiction House Magazines: 1950 - No. 12, Winter, 1952-53 (No. 1-3: 52 pgs.)

1-Kamen-a 40 80 120 233 342 450
2 20 40 60 112 161 210
3-5: 5-12-Whitman-c (most) 17 34 51 95 135 175
6-9,11,12 16 32 48 89 127 165
10-Frazetta?/Williamson?-a; Kamen?/Baker-a; r/Mitzi story from Movie Comics #4 w/all new dialogue 32 64 96 184 267 350

COW PUNCHER (...Comics)
Avon Periodicals: Jan, 1947; No. 2, Sept, 1947 - No. 7, 1949

1-Clint Cortland, Texas Ranger, Kit West, Pioneer Queen begin; Kubert-a; Alabam stories begin 42 84 126 256 391 525
2-Kubert, Kamen/Feldstein-a; Kamen-c 38 76 114 219 320 420
3-5,7: 3-Kiefer story 27 54 81 154 222 290
6-Opium drug mention story; bondage, headlight-c; Reinman-a
34 68 102 196 283 370

COWPUNCHER
Realistic Publications: 1953 (nn) (Reprints Avon's No. 2)

nn-Kubert-a 11 22 33 64 87 110

COWSILLS, THE (See Harvey Pop Comics)

COW SPECIAL, THE
Image Comics (Top Cow): Spring-Summer 2000; 2001 ($2.95)

1-Previews upcoming Top Cow projects; Yancy Butler photo-c 3.00
Vol. 2 #1-Witchblade-c; previews and interviews 3.00

COYOTE
Marvel Comics (Epic Comics): June, 1983 - No. 16, Mar, 1986

1-10,15: 7-10-Ditko-a 2.50
11-1st McFarlane-a. 6.00
12-14,16: 12-14-McFarlane-a. 14-Badger x-over. 16-Reagan c/app. 4.00

CRACKAJACK FUNNIES (Also see The Owl)
Dell Publishing Co.: June, 1938 - No. 43, Jan, 1942

1-Dan Dunn, Freckles, Myra North, Wash Tubbs, Apple Mary, The Nebbs, Don Winslow, Tom Mix, Buck Jones, Major Hoople, Clyde Beatty, Boots begin
246 492 738 1538 2369 3200
2 98 196 294 613 944 1275
3 71 142 213 444 685 925
4 54 108 162 329 502 675
5-Nude woman on cover 55 110 165 340 520 700
6-8,10: 8-Speed Bolton begins (1st app.) 43 86 129 262 399 535
9-(3/39)-Red Ryder strip-r begin by Harman; 1st app. in comics & 1st cover app.
177 354 531 1106 1703 2300
11-14 40 80 120 241 363 485
15-Tarzan text feature begins by Burroughs (9/39); not in #26,35
43 86 129 262 401 540
16-24: 18-Stratosphere Jim begins (1st app., 12/39). 23-Ellery Queen begins plus-c (1st comic book app., 5/40) 35 70 105 200 290 380
25-The Owl begins (1st app., 7/40); in new costume #26 by Frank Thomas (also see Popular Comics #72) 77 154 231 481 741 1000
26-30: 28-Part Owl-c 54 108 162 329 502 675
31-Owl covers begin, end #42 55 110 165 340 520 700
32-Origin Owl Girl 59 118 177 369 565 760
33-38: 36-Last Tarzan issue. 37-Cyclone & Midge begin (1st app.)
52 104 156 317 484 650
39-Andy Panda begins (intro/1st app., 9/41) 60 120 180 375 575 775
40-42: 42-Last Owl-c. 40 80 120 236 351 465
43-Terry & the Pirates-r 36 72 108 204 297 390
NOTE: ***McWilliams*** *art in most issues.*

CRACK COMICS (Crack Western No. 63 on)
Quality Comics Group: May, 1940 - No. 62, Sept, 1949

1-Origin & 1st app. The Black Condor by Lou Fine, Madame Fatal, Red Torpedo, Rock Bradden & The Space Legion; The Clock, Alias the Spider (by Gustavson), Wizard Wells, & Ned Brant begin; Powell-a; Note: Madame Fatal is a man dressed as a woman
470 940 1410 3290 5295 7300
2 235 470 705 1469 2260 3050
3 162 324 486 1013 1557 2100
4 133 266 399 831 1278 1725
5-10: 5-Molly The Model begins. 10-Tor, the Magic Master begins
102 204 306 638 982 1325
11-20: 13-1 pg. J. Cole-a. 15-1st app. Spitfire 89 178 267 556 853 1150
21-24: 23-Pen Miller begins; continued from National Comics #22. 24-Last Fine Black Condor
66 132 198 413 637 860
25,26: 26-Flag-c 55 110 165 336 511 685
27-(1/43)-Intro & origin Captain Triumph by Alfred Andriola (Kerry Drake artist) & begin series 102 204 306 638 982 1325
28-30 46 92 138 281 428 575
31-39: 31-Last Black Condor 30 60 90 170 245 320
40-46 22 44 66 125 180 235
47-57,59,60-Capt. Triumph by Crandall 23 46 69 132 191 250
58,61,62-Last Captain Triumph 16 32 48 92 131 170
NOTE: *Black Condor by* ***Fine:*** *No. 1, 2, 5, 6, 8, 10-24; by* ***Sultan:*** *No. 3, 7; by* ***Fugitani:*** *No. 9.* ***Cole*** *a-34.* ***Crandall*** *a-61(unsigned); c-48, 49, 51-61.* ***Guardineer*** *a-17.* ***Gustavson*** *a-1, 2, 4, 7, 13, 17, 23.* ***McWilliams*** *a-15-27. Black Condor c-2, 4, 6, 8, 10, 12, 14, 16, 18, 20-26. Capt. Triumph c-27-62. The Clock c-1, 3, 5, 7, 9, 11, 13, 15, 17, 19.*

CRACKED (Magazine) (Satire) (Also see The 3-D Zone #19)
Major Magazines(#1-212)/Globe Communications(#213-346/American Media #347 on): Feb-Mar, 1958 - Present

1-One pg. Williamson-a; Everett-c; Gunsmoke-s 16 32 48 116 178 240
2-1st Shut-Ups & Bonus Cut-Outs; Superman parody-c by Severin (his 1st cover on the title) Frankenstein-s 9 18 27 63 89 115
3-5 7 14 21 50 68 85
6-10: 7-Reprints 1st 6 covers on-c. 8-Frankenstein-c. 10-Wolverton-a
6 12 18 38 52 65

Cracked #14 © Major Mags.

Cracked #226 © Global Comm. Corp.

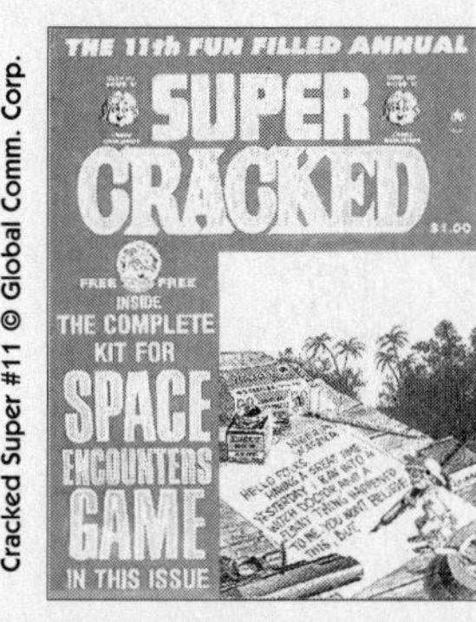

Cracked Super #11 © Global Comm. Corp.

GD VG FN VF VF/NM NM-
2.0 4.0 6.0 8.0 9.0 9.2

11-12, 13(nn,3/60), 5 10 15 33 44 55
14-Kirby-a 6 12 18 38 52 65
15-17, 18(nn,2/61), 19,20 4 8 12 29 40 50
21-27(11/62), 27(No.28, 2/63; mis-#d), 29(5/63) 4 8 12 27 36 45
30-40(11/64): 37-Beatles and Superman cameos 4 8 12 24 32 40
41-45,47-56,59,60: 47,49,52-Munsters. 51-Beatles inside-c. 59-Laurel and Hardy photos 3 7 10 21 28 35
46,57,58: 46,58-Man From U.N.C.L.E. 46-Beatles. 57-Rolling Stones 4 8 12 22 30 38
61-80: 62-Beatles cameo. 69-Batman, Superman app. 70-(8/68) Elvis cameo. 71-Garrison's Gorillas; W.C. Fields photos 3 6 9 16 21 26
81-99: 99-Alfred E. Neuman on-c 2 4 6 14 18 22
100 3 6 9 19 25 32
101-119: 104-Godfather-c/s. 108-Archie Bunker-s. 112,119-Kung Fu (TV). 113-Tarzan-s. 115-MASH. 117-Cannon. 118-The Sting-c/s 2 4 6 10 13 16
120(12/74) Six Million Dollar Man-c/s; Ward-a 2 4 6 12 16 20
121,122,124-126,128-133,136-140: 121-American Graffiti. 122-Korak-c/s. 124,131-Godfather-c/s. 128-Capone-c. 129,131-Jaws. 132-Baretta-c/s. 133-Space 1999. 136-Laverne and Shirley/Fonz-c. 137-Travolta/Kotter-c/s. 138-Travolta/Laverne and Shirley/ Fonz-c. 139-Barney Miller-c/s. 140-King Kong-c/s; Fonz-s 2 4 6 10 13 16
123-Planet of the Apes-c/s; Six Million Dollar Man 2 4 6 12 16 20
127,134,135: 127-Star Trek-c/s; Ward-a. 134-Fonz-c/s; Starsky and Hutch. 135-Bionic Woman-c/s; Ward-a 2 4 6 11 14 18
141,151-Charlie's Angels-c/s. 151-Frankenstein 2 4 6 11 14 18
142,143,150,152-155,157: 142-MASH-c/s. 143-Rocky-c/s; King Kong-s. 150-(5/78) Close Encounters-c/s. 152-Close Enc./Star Wars-c/s. 153-Close Enc./Fonz-c/s. 154-Jaws II-c/s; Star Wars-s. 155-Star Wars/Fonz-c 2 4 6 10 12 15
144,149,156,158-160: 144-Fonz/Happy Days-c. 149-Star Wars/Six Mil.$ Man-c/s. 156-Grease/Travolta-c. 158-Mork & Mindy. 159-Battlestar Galactica-c/s; MASH-s. 160-Superman-c/s 2 4 6 11 14 18
145,147-Both have insert postcards: 145-Fonz/Rocky/L&S-c/s. 147-Star Wars-s; Farrah photo page (missing postcards-1/2 price) 3 6 9 16 20 24
146,148: 46-Star Wars-c/s with stickers insert (missing stickers-1/2 price). 148-Star Wars-c/s with inside-c color poster 3 6 9 18 23 28
161,170-Ward-a: 161-Mork & Mindy-c/s. 170-Dukes of Hazzard-c/s 2 4 6 8 10 12
162,165-168,171,172,175-178,180-Ward-a: 162-Sherlock Holmes-s. 165-Dracula-c/s. 167-Mork-c/s. 168,175-MASH-c/s. 168-Mork-s. 172-Dukes of Hazzard/CHiPs-c/s. 176-Barney Miller-c/s 1 3 4 6 8 10
163,179:163-Postcard insert; Mork & Mindy-c/s. 179-Insult cards insert; Popeye, Dukes of Hazzard-c/s 2 4 6 14 18 22
164,169,173,174: 164-Alien movie-c/s; Mork & Mindy-s. 169-Star Trek. 173,174-Star Wars-Empire Strikes Back. 173-SW poster 2 4 6 10 12 15
181,182,185-191,193,194,196-198-most Ward-a: 182-MASH-c/s. 185-Dukes of Hazzard-c/s; Jefferson-s. 187-Love Boat. 188-Fall Guy-s. 189-Fonz/Happy Days-c. 190,194-MASH-c/s. 191-Magnum P.I./Rocky-c; Magnum-s. 193-Knight Rider-s. 196-Dukes of Hazzard/Knight Rider-c/s. 198-Jaws III-c/s; Fall Guy-s 1 2 3 5 7 9
183,184,192,195,199,200-Ward-a in all: 183-Superman-c/s. 184-Star Trek-c/s. 192-E.T.-c/s; Rocky-s. 195-E.T.-c/s. 199-Jabba-c; Star Wars-s. 200-(12/83) 1 3 4 6 8 10
201,203,210-A-Team-c/s 6.00
202,204-206,211-224,226,227,230-233: 202-Knight Rider-s. 204-Magnum P.I.; A-Team-s. 206-Michael Jackson/Mr. T-c/s. 212-Prince-s; Cosby-s. 213-Monsters issue-c/s. 215-Hulk Hogan/Mr. T-c/s. 216-Miami Vice-s; James Bond-s. 217-Rambo-s; Cosby-s; A-Team-s. 218-Rocky-c/s. 219-Arnold/Commando-c/s; Rocky-s; Godzilla. 220-Rocky-c/s. 221-Stephen King app. 223-Miami Vice-s. 224-Cosby-s. 226-29th Anniv.; Tarzan-s; Aliens-s; Family Ties-s. 227-Cosby, Family Ties, Miami Vice-s. 230-Monkees-c/s; Elvis on-c; Gumby-s. 232-Alf, Cheers, StarTrek-s. 233-Superman/James Bond-c/s; Robocop, Predator-s 5.00
207-209,225,234: 207-Michael Jackson-c/s. 208-Indiana Jones-c/s. 209-MichaelJackson/ Gremlins-c/s; Star Trek III-s. 225-Schwarzenegger/Stallone/G.I. Joe-c/s. 234-Don Martin-a begins; Batman/Robocop/Clint Eastwood-c/s 6.00
228,229: 228-Star Trek-c/s; Alf, Pee Wee Herman-s. 229-Monsters issue-c/s; centerfold with many superheroes 6.00
235,239,243,249: 235-1st Martin-c; Star Trek:TNG-s; Alf-s. 239-Beetlejuice-c/s; Mike Tyson-s. 243-X-Men and other heroes app. 249-Batman/Indiana Jones/Ghostbusters-c/s 6.00
236,244,245,248: 236-Madonna/Stallone-c/s; Twilight Zone-s. 244-Elvis-c/s; Martin-c. 245-Roger Rabbit-c/s. 248-Batman issue 6.00
237,238,240-242,246,247,250: 237-Robocop-s. 238-Rambo-c/s; Star Trek-s. 242-Dirty Harry-s, Ward-a. 246-Alf-s; Star Trek-s., Ward-a. 247-Star Trek-s. 250-Batman/Ghostbusters-s 4.00
251-253,255,256,259,261-265,275-278,281,284,286-297,299: 252-Star Trek-s. 253-Back to the Future-c/s. 255-TMNT-c/s. 256-TMNT-c/s; Batman, Bart Simpson on-c. 259-Die Hard II, Robocop-s. 261-TMNT, Twin Peaks-s. 262-Rocky-c/s; Rocky Horror-s. 265-TMNT-s. 276-Aliens III, Batman-s. 277-Clinton-c. 284-Bart Simpson-c; 90210-s. 297-Van Damme-s/photo-c. 299-Dumb & Dumber-c/s 4.00

GD VG FN VF VF/NM NM-
2.0 4.0 6.0 8.0 9.0 9.2

254,257,266,267,272,280,282,285,298,300: 254-Back to the Future, Punisher-s; Wolverton-a, Batman-s, Ward-a. 257-Batman, Simpsons-s; Spider-Man and other heroes app. 266-Terminator-c/s. 267-Toons-c/s. 272-Star Trek VI-s. 280-Swimsuit issue. 282-Cheers-c/s. 285-Jurassic Park-c/s. 298-Swimsuit issue; Martin-c. 300-(8/95) Brady Bunch-c/s 5.00
258,260,274,279,283: 258-Simpsons-c/s; Back to the Future-s. 260-Spider-Man-c/s; Simpsons-s. 274-Batman-c/s. 279-Madonna-c/s. 283-Jurassic Park-c/s; Wolverine app. inside back-c 5.00
301-305,307-348 2.50
306-Toy Story-c/s 4.00
Biggest... (Winter, 1977) 2 4 6 12 16 20
Biggest, Greatest... nn('65) 5 10 15 33 44 55
Biggest, Greatest... 2('66) - #5('69) 3 6 9 19 25 32
Biggest, Greatest... 6('70) - #12('76) 2 4 6 14 18 22
Biggest, Greatest...13('77) - #21(Wint. '86) 2 4 6 8 10 12
...Blockbuster 1(Sum '87), 2('88) 1 2 3 5 7 9
...Digest 1(Fall, '86, 148 pgs.) - #5 1 2 3 5 7 9
...Collectors' Edition 4 ('73; formerly ...Special) 2 4 6 12 16 20
5-10 2 4 6 11 14 18
11-30: 23-Ward-a 2 4 6 8 10 12
31-50 1 2 3 5 7 9
51-70 6.00
71-84: 83-Elvis, Batman parodies 4.00
...Party Pack 1,2('88) 4.00
...Shut-Ups (2/72-'72; Cracked Spec. #3) 1 3 6 9 19 25 32
2 2 4 6 14 18 22
...Special 3('73; formerly Cracked Shut-Ups; ...Collectors' Edition#4 on) 2 4 6 12 16 20
Extra Special... 1('76) 2 4 6 11 14 18
Extra Special... 2('76) 2 4 6 10 12 15
Giant... nn('65) 5 10 15 36 48 60
Giant... 2('66)-5('69) 3 7 10 21 28 35
Giant...6('70)-12('76) 3 6 9 18 23 28
Giant...nn(9/77)-24 2 4 6 11 14 18
Giant...25-35 2 4 6 8 10 12
Giant...36-48('87) 1 2 3 5 6 8
King Sized... 1('67) 4 8 12 29 40 50
King Sized... 2('68)-5('71) 3 6 9 19 25 32
King Sized... 6('72)-11('77) 3 6 9 16 20 24
King Sized... 12-17 2 4 6 8 10 12
King Sized... 18-22 (Sum/'86) 1 2 3 5 7 9
Super... 1('68) 4 8 12 27 36 45
Super... 2('69)-5 3 6 9 19 25 32
Super... 6-10 3 6 9 16 20 25
Super... 11-16 2 4 6 11 14 18
Super... 17-24('84): #23 mis-numbered as #24 2 4 6 8 10 12
Super... 1('87, 100 pgs.)-Severin & Elder-a 1 2 3 5 7 9

NOTE: ***Burgos*** *a-1-10.* ***Colan*** *a-257.* ***Davis*** *a-5, 11-17, 24, 40, 80; c-12-14, 16.* ***Elder*** *a-5, 6, 10-13; c-10.* ***Everett*** *a-1-10, 23-25, 61; c-1.* ***Heath*** *a-1-3, 6, 13, 14, 17, 110; c-6.* ***Jaffee*** *a-5, 6.* ***Don Martin*** *c-235, 244, 247, 259, 261, 264.* ***Morrow*** *a-8-10.* ***Reinman*** *a-1-4.* ***Severin*** *c/a-in most all issues.* ***Shores*** *a-3-7.* ***Torres*** *a-7-10.* ***Ward*** *a-22-24, 27, 35, 40, 120-193, 195, 197-205, 242, 244, 246, 247, 250, 252-257.* ***Williamson*** *a-1 (1 pg.).* ***Wolverton*** *a-10 (2 pgs.), Giant nn('65).* ***Wood*** *a-27, 35, 40. Alfred E. Neuman c-177, 200, 202. Batman c-234, 248, 249, 256, 274. Captain America c-256. Christmas c-234, 243. Spider-Man c-260. Star Trek c-127, 169, 207, 228. Star Wars c-145, 146, 148, 149, 152, 155, 173, 174, 199. Superman c-183, 233. #144, 146 have free full-color pre-glued stickers. #145, 147, 155, 163 have free full-color postcards. #123, 137, 154, 157 have free iron-ons.*

CRACKED MONSTER PARTY
Globe Communications: July, 1988 - No. 27, Spr, 1995

1 2 4 6 10 12 15
2-10 1 3 4 6 8 10
11-26 6.00
27-Interview with a Vampire-c/s 1 3 4 6 8 10

CRACKED'S FOR MONSTERS ONLY
Major Magazines: Sept, 1969 - No. 9, Sept, 1969

1 4 8 12 29 40 50
2-9 3 6 9 16 20 25

CRACKED SPACED OUT
Globe Communications: Fall, 1993 - No. 4, 1994?

1-4 3.00

CRACK WESTERN (Formerly Crack Comics; Jonesy No. 85 on)
Quality Comics Group: No. 63, Nov, 1949 - No. 84, May, 1953 (36 pgs., 63-68,74-on)

63(#1)-Ward-c; Two-Gun Lil (origin & 1st app.)(ends #84), Arizona Ames, his horse Thunder (with sidekick Spurs & his horse Calico), Frontier Marshal (ends #70), & Dead Canyon Days (ends #69) begin; Crandall-a 23 46 69 132 191 250

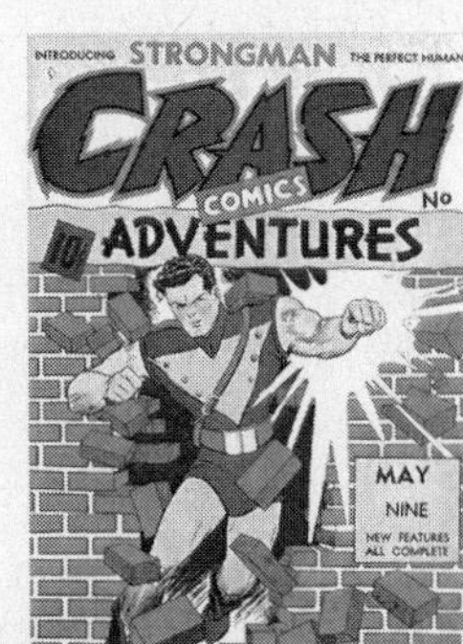

Crash Comics #1 © Tem Pub. Co.

Crash Ryan #1 © MAR

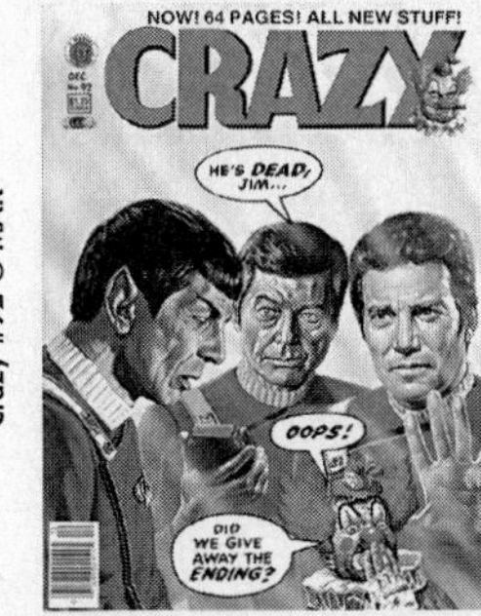

Crazy #92 © MAR

	GD 2.0	VG 4.0	FN 6.0	VF 8.0	VF/NM 9.0	NM- 9.2
64,65: 64-Ward-c. Crandall-a in both.	18	36	54	100	143	185
66,68-Photo-c. 66-Arizona Ames becomes A. Raines (ends #84)	15	30	45	85	120	155
67-Randolph Scott photo-c; Crandall-a	17	34	51	95	135	175
69(52pgs.)-Crandall-a	15	30	45	85	120	155
70(52pgs.)-The Whip (origin & 1st app.) & his horse Diablo begin (ends #84); Crandall-a	15	30	45	85	120	155
71(52pgs.)-Frontier Marshal becomes Bob Allen F. Marshal (ends #84); Crandall-c/a	17	34	51	95	135	175
72(52pgs.)-Tim Holt photo-c	14	28	42	81	113	145
73(52pgs.)-Photo-c	10	20	30	60	80	120
74-76,78,79,81,83-Crandall-c. 83-Crandall-a(p)	13	26	39	76	106	135
77,80,82	9	18	27	54	70	85
84-Crandall-c/a	14	28	42	81	113	145

NOTE: ***Crandall** c-71p, 74-81, 83p(w/**Cuidera**-i).*

CRASH COMICS (Catman Comics No. 6 on)
Tem Publishing Co.: May, 1940 - No. 5, Nov, 1940

	GD	VG	FN	VF	VF/NM	NM-
1-The Blue Streak, Strongman (origin), The Perfect Human, Shangra begin (1st app. of each); Kirby-a	310	620	930	2015	3258	4500
2-Simon & Kirby-a	154	308	462	963	1482	2000
3,5-Simon & Kirby-a	129	258	387	806	1241	1675
4-Origin & 1st app. The Catman; S&K-a	310	620	930	2015	3258	4500

NOTE: *Solar Legion by **Kirby** No. 1-5 (5 pgs. each). Strongman c-1-4. Catman c-5.*

CRASH DIVE (See Cinema Comics Herald)

CRASH METRO AND THE STAR SQUAD
Oni Press: May, 1999 ($2.95, B&W, one-shot)

1-Allred-s/Ontiveros-a — 3.00

CRASH RYAN (Also see Dark Horse Presents #44)
Marvel Comics (Epic): Oct, 1984 - No. 4, Jan, 1985 (Baxter paper, lim. series)

1-4 — 2.25

CRAZY (Also see This Magazine is Crazy)
Atlas Comics (CSI): Dec, 1953 - No. 7, July, 1954

	GD	VG	FN	VF	VF/NM	NM-
1-Everett-c/a	30	60	90	170	245	320
2	20	40	60	112	161	210
3-7: 4-I Love Lucy satire. 5-Satire on censorship	16	32	48	92	131	170

NOTE: ***Ayers** a-5. **Berg** a-1, 2. **Burgos** c-5, 6. **Drucker** a-6. **Everett** a-1-4. **Al Hartley** a-4. **Heath** a-3, 7; c-7. **Maneely** a-1-7, c-3, 4. **Post** a-3-6. Funny monster c-1-4.*

CRAZY (Satire)
Marvel Comics Group: Feb, 1973 - No. 3, June, 1973

	GD	VG	FN	VF	VF/NM	NM-
1-Not Brand Echh-r; Beatles cameo (r)	3	6	9	16	20	25
2,3-Not Brand Echh-r; Kirby-a	2	4	6	10	13	16

CRAZY MAGAZINE (Satire)
Oct, 1973 - No. 94, Apr, 1983 (40-90¢, B&W magazine)
Marvel Comics: (#1, 44 pgs; #2-90, reg. issues, 52 pgs; #92-95, 68 pgs)'

	GD	VG	FN	VF	VF/NM	NM-
1-Wolverton(1 pg.), Bode-a; 3 pg. photo story of Neal Adams & Dick Giordano; Harlan Ellison story; TV Kung Fu sty.	4	8	12	29	40	50
2-"Live & Let Die" c/s; 8pgs; Adams/Buscema-a; McCloud w5 pgs. Adams-a; Kurtzman's "Hey Look" 2 pg.-r	3	6	9	119	25	32
3-5: 3-"High Plains Drifter" w/Clint Eastwood c/s; Waltons app; Drucker, Reese-a. 4-Shaft-c/s; Ploog-a; Nixon 3 pg. app; Freas-a. 5-Michael Crichton's "Westworld" c/s; Nixon app.	3	6	9	16	21	26
6,7,18: 6-Exorcist c/s; Nixon app. 7-TV's Kung Fu c/s; Nixon app.; Ploog & Freas-a. 18-Six Million Dollar Man/Bionic Woman c/s; Welcome Back Kotter story	2	4	6	14	18	22
8-10: 8-Serpico c/s; Casper parody; TV's Police Story. 9-Joker cameo; Chinatown story; Eisner s/a begins; Has 1st 8 covers on-c. 10-Playboy Bunny-c; M. Severin-a; Lee Marrs-a begins; "Deathwish" story	2	4	6	12	16	20
11-17,19: 11-Towering Inferno. 12-Rhoda. 13-"Tommy" the Who Rock Opera. 14-Mandingo. 15-Jaws story. 16-Santa/Xmas-c; "Good Times" TV story; Jaws. 17-Bicentennial issue; Baretta; Woody Allen. 19-King Kong c/s; Reagan, J. Carter, Howard the Duck cameos, "Laverne & Shirley"	2	4	6	10	13	16
20,24,27: 20-Bicentennial-c; Space 1999 sty; Superheroes song sheet, 4pgs. 24-Charlie's Angels. 27-Charlie's Angels/Travolta/Fonz-c; Bionic Woman sty	2	4	6	12	16	20
21-23,25,26,28-30: 21-Starsky & Hutch. 22-Mount Rushmore/J. Carter-c; TV's Barney Miller; Superheroes spoof. 23-Santa/Xmas-c; "Happy Days" sty; "Omen" sty. 25-J. Carter-c/s; Grandenetti-a begins; TV's Alice; Logan's Run. 26-TV Stars-c; Mary Hartman, King Kong. 28-Donny & Marie Osmond-c/s; Marathon Man. 29-Travolta/Kotter-c; "One Day at a Time", Gong Show. 30-1977, 84 pgs. w/bonus; Jaws, Baretta, King Kong, Happy Days	2	4	6	9	11	14
31,33-35,38,40: 31-"Rocky"-c/s; TV game shows. 33-Peter Benchley's "Deep". 34-J. Carter-c; TV's "Fish". 35-Xmas-c with Fonz/Six Million Dollar Man/Wonder Woman/Darth Vader/ Travolta, TV's "Mash" & "Family Matters". 38-Close Encounters of the Third Kind-c/s. 40-"Three's Company-c/s	1	3	4	6	8	10
32-Star Wars/Darth Vader-c/s; "Black Sunday"	2	4	6	14	18	22
36,42,47,49: 36-Farrah Fawcett/Six Million Dollar Man-c; TV's Nancy Drew & Hardy Boys; 1st app. Howard The Duck in Crazy, 2 pgs. 42-84 pgs. w/bonus; TV Hulk/Spider-Man-c; Mash, Gong Show, One Day at a Time, Disco, Alice. 47-Battlestar Galactica xmas-c; movie "Foul Play". 49-1979, 84 pgs. w/bonus; Mork & Mindy-c; Jaws, Saturday Night Fever, Three's Company	2	4	6	9	11	14
37-1978, 84 pgs. w/bonus. Darth Vader-c; Barney Miller, Laverne & Shirley, Good Times, Rocky, Donny & Marie Osmond, Bionic Woman	2	4	6	12	16	20
39,44: 39-Saturday Night Fever-c/s. 44-"Grease"-c w/Travolta/O. Newton-John	2	4	6	11	14	18
41-Kiss-c & 1pg. photos; Disaster movies, TV's "Family", Annie Hall	4	8	12	27	36	45
43,45,46,48,51: 43-Jaws-c; Saturday Night Fever. 43-E.C. swipe from Mad #131. 45-Travolta/O. Newton-John/J. Carter-c; Eight is Enough. 46-TV Hulk-c/s; Punk Rock. 48-"Wiz"-c, Battlestar Galactica-s. 51-Grease/Mork & Mindy/D&M Osmond-c, Mork & Mindy-sty. "Boys from Brazil"	1	3	4	6	8	10
50,58: 50-Superman movie-c/sty, Playboy Mag., TV Hulk, Fonz; Howard the Duck, 1 pg. 58-1980, 84 pgs. w/32 pg. color comic bonus insert-Full reprint of Crazy Comic #1, Battlestar Galactica, Charlie's Angels, Starsky & Hutch	2	4	6	11	14	18
52,59,60,64: 52-1979, 84 pgs. w/bonus. Marlon Brando-c; TV Hulk, Grease. Kiss, 1 pg. photos. 59-Santa Ptd-c by Larkin; "Alien"; "Moonraker", Rocky-2, Howard the Duck, 1 pg. 60-Star Trek w/Muppets-c; Star Trek sty; 1st app/origin Teen Hulk; Severin-a. 64-84 pgs. w/bonus Monopoly game satire. "Empire Strikes Back", 8 pgs., One Day at a Time	2	4	6	11	14	18
53,54,65,67-70: 53-"Animal House"-c/sty; TV's "Vegas", Howard the Duck, 1 pg. 54-Love at First Bite-c/sty, Fantasy Island sty, Howard the Duck 1 pg. 65-(Has #66 on-c, Aug/'80). "Black Hole" w/Janson-a; Kirby,Wood/Severin-a(r), 5 pgs. Howard the Duck, 3 pgs.; Broderick-a; Buck Rogers, Mr. Rogers. 67-84 pgs. w/bonus; TV's Kung Fu, Exorcist; Ploog-a(r). 68-American Gigolo, Dukes of Hazzard, Teen Hulk; Howard the Duck, 3 pgs. Broderick-a; Monster sty/5 pg. Ditko-a(r). 69-Obnoxio the Clown-c/sty; Stephen King's "Shining", Teen Hulk, Richie Rich, Howard the Duck, 3pgs; Broderick-a. 70-84 pgs. Towering Inferno, Daytime TV; Trina Robbins-a	1	2	3	5	7	9
55-57,61,63: 55-84 pgs. w/bonus; Love Boat, Mork & Mindy, Fonz, TV Hulk. 56-Mork/Rocky/ J. Carter-c; China Syndrome. 57-TV Hulk with Miss Piggy-c, Dracula, Taxi, Muppets. 61-1980, 84 pgs. Adams-a(r), McCloud, Pro wrestling, Casper, TV's Police Story. 63-Apocalypse Now-Coppola's cult movie; 3rd app. Teen Hulk, Howard the Duck, 3 pgs.	2	4	6	8	10	12
62-Kiss-c & 2 pg. app; Quincy, 2nd app. Teen Hulk	4	8	12	22	30	38
66-Sept/'80, Empire Strikes Back-c/sty; Teen Hulk by Severin, Howard the Duck, 3pgs. by Broderick	2	4	6	10	13	16
71,72,75-77,79: 71-Blues Brothers parody, Teen Hulk, Superheroes parody, WKRP in Cincinnati, Howard the Duck, 3pgs. by Broderick. 72-Jackie Gleason/Smokey & the Bandit II-c/sty, Shogun, Teen Hulk. Howard the Duck, 3pgs. by Broderick. 75-Flash Gordon movie c/sty; Teen Hulk, Cat in the Hat, Howard the Duck 3pgs. by Broderick. 76-84 pgs. w/bonus; Monster-sty w/ Crandall-a(r), Monster-stys(2) w/Kirby-a(r), 5pgs. ea; Mash, TV Hulk, Chinatown. 77-Popeye movie/R. Williams-c/sty; Teen Hulk, Love Boat, Howard the Duck 3 pgs. 79-84 pgs. w/bonus color stickers; has new material; "9 to 5" w/Dolly Parton, Teen Hulk, Magnum P.I., Monster-sty w/5pgs, Ditko-a(r), "Rat" w/Sutton-a(r), Everett-a, 4 pgs.(r)	1	2	3	5	7	9
73,74,78,80: 73-84 pgs. w/bonus Hulk/Spiderman Finger Puppets-c & bonus; "Live & Let Die", Jaws, Fantasy Island. 74-Dallas/"Who Shot J.R."-c/sty; Elephant Man, Howard the Duck 3pgs. by Broderick. 78-Clint Eastwood-c/sty; Teen Hulk, Superheroes parody, Lou Grant. 80-Star Wars, 2 pg. app; "Howling", TV's "Greatest American Hero"	2	4	6	8	10	12
81,84,86,87,89: 81-.Superman Movie II-c/sty; Wolverine cameo, Mash, Teen Hulk. 84-American Werewolf in London, Johnny Carson app; Teen Hulk. 86-Time Bandits-c/sty; Private Benjamin. 87-Rubix Cube-c; Hill Street Blues, "Ragtime", Origin Obnoxio the Clown; Teen Hulk. 89-Burt Reynolds "Sharkey's Machine", Teen Hulk	1	2	3	5	7	9
82-X-Men-c w/new Byrne-a, 84 pgs. w/new material; Fantasy Island, Teen Hulk, "For Your Eyes Only", Spiderman/Human Torch-r by Kirby/Ditko; Sutton-a(r); Rogers-a; Hunchback of Notre Dame, 5 pgs.	2	4	6	11	14	18
83-Raiders of the Lost Ark-c/sty; Hart to Hart; Reese-a; Teen Hulk	2	4	6	9	11	14
85,88: 85-84 pgs; Escape from New York, Teen Hulk; Kirby-a(r), 5 pgs, Posiedon Adventure, Flintstones, Sesame Street. 88-84 pgs. w/bonus Dr. Strange Game; some new material; Jeffersons, X-Men/Wolverine, 10 pgs.; Byrne-a; Apocalypse Now, Teen Hulk	1	3	4	6	8	10

90-94: 90-Conan-c/sty; M. Severin-a; Teen Hulk. 91-84 pgs, some new material; Bladerunner-c/sty, "Deathwish-II, Teen Hulk, Black Knight, 10 pgs.-'50s-r w/Maneely-a.

Crazyman #3 © Continuity Pub.

The Creeper #5 © DC

Creepy #4 © WP

GD 2.0 | VG 4.0 | FN 6.0 | VF 8.0 | VF/NM 9.0 | NM- 9.2

92-Wrath of Khan Star Trek-c/sty; Joanie & Chachi, Teen Hulk. 93-"E.T."-c/sty, Teen Hulk, Archie Bunkers Place, Dr. Doom Game. 94-Poltergeist, Smurfs, Teen Hulk, Casper, Avengers parody-8pgs. Adams-a 2 4 6 10 13 16

Crazy Summer Special #1 (Sum, '75, 100 pgs.)-Nixon, TV Kung Fu, Babe Ruth, Joe Namath, Waltons, McCloud, Chariots of the Gods 2 4 6 14 18 22

NOTE: ***N. Adams*** *a-2, 61r, 94p.* ***Austin*** *a-82i.* ***Buscema*** *a-2, 82.* ***Byrne*** *c-82p.* ***Nick Cardy*** *c-7, 8, 10, 12-16, Super Special 1.* ***Crandall*** *a-76r.* ***Ditko*** *a-68r, 79r, 82r.* ***Drucker*** *a-3.* ***Eisner*** *a-9-16.* ***Kelly Freas*** *c-1-6, 9, 11; a-7.* ***Kirby/Wood*** *a-66r.* ***Ploog*** *a-1, 4, 7, 67r, 73r.* ***Rogers*** *a-82.* ***Sparling*** *a-92.* ***Wood*** *a-65r. Howard the Duck in 36, 50, 51, 53, 54, 59, 63, 65, 66, 68, 69, 71, 72, 74, 75, 77. Hulk in 46, c-42, 46, 57, 73. Star Wars in 32, 66; c-37.*

CRAZYMAN
Continuity Comics: Apr, 1992 - No. 3, 1992 ($2.50, high quality paper)

1-($3.95, 52 pgs.)-Embossed-c; N. Adams part-i 4.00
2,3 ($2.50): 2-N. Adams/Bolland-c 2.50

CRAZYMAN
Continuity Comics: V2#1, 5/93 - No. 4, 1/94 ($2.50, high quality paper)

V2#1-4: 1-Entire book is die-cut. 2-(12/93)-Adams-c(p) & part scripts. 3-(12/93). 4-Indicia says #3, Jan. 1993 2.50

CRAZY, MAN, CRAZY (Magazine) (Becomes This Magazine is...?)
(Formerly From Here to Insanity)
Humor Magazines (Charlton): V2#1, Dec, 1955 - V2#2, June, 1956

V2#1,V2#2-Satire; Wolverton-a, 3 pgs. 15 30 45 83 117 150

CREATURE, THE (See Movie Classics)

CREATURE COMMANDOS (See Weird War Tales #93 for 1st app.)
DC Comics: May, 2000 - No. 8, Dec, 2000 ($2.50, limited series)

1-8: Truman-s/Eaton-a 2.50

CREATURES OF THE ID
Caliber Press: 1990 ($2.95, B&W)

1-Frank Einstein (Madman) app.; Allred-a 3 6 9 18 24 30

CREATURES ON THE LOOSE (Formerly Tower of Shadows No. 1-9)(See Kull)
Marvel Comics: No. 10, March, 1971 - No. 37, Sept, 1975 (New-a & reprints)

10-(15¢)-1st full app. King Kull; see Kull the Conqueror; Wrightson-a 6 12 18 43 59 75
11-15: 15-Last 15¢ issue 3 6 9 16 20 24
16-Origin Warrior of Mars (begins, ends #21) 2 4 6 11 14 18
17-20 2 4 6 8 10 12
21-Steranko-c 2 4 6 11 14 18
22-Steranko-c; Thongor stories begin 2 4 6 12 16 20
23-29-Thongor-c/stories 1 2 3 5 7 9
30-Manwolf begins 3 6 9 16 20 25
31-33 2 4 6 9 11 14
34-37 2 4 6 8 10 12

NOTE: ***Crandall*** *a-13.* ***Ditko*** *r-15, 17, 18, 20, 22, 24, 27, 28.* ***Everett*** *a-16i(new).* ***Matt Fox*** *r-21i.* ***Howard*** *a-26i.* ***Gil Kane*** *a-16p, 17p, 19i; c-16, 17, 19, 20, 25, 29, 33p, 35p, 36p.* ***Kirby*** *a-10-15r, 16(2)r, 17r, 19r.* ***Morrow*** *a-20, 21.* ***Perez*** *a-33-37; c-34p.* ***Shores*** *a-11.* ***innott*** *r-21.* ***Sutton*** *c-10.* ***Tuska*** *a-31p, 32p.*

CREECH, THE
Image Comics: Oct, 1997 - No. 3, Dec, 1997 ($1.95/$2.50, limited series)

1-3: 1-Capullo-s/c/a(p) 2.50
TPB (1999, $9.95) r/#1-3, McFarlane intro. 10.00
Out for Blood 1-3 (7/01 - No. 3, 11/01; $4.95) Capullo-s/c/a 5.00

CREED
Hall of Heroes Comics: Dec, 1994 - No. 2, Jan, 1995 ($2.50, B&W)

1 2 4 6 10 12 15
2 2 4 6 8 10 12

CREED
Lightning Comics: June, 1995 - Present ($2.75/$3.00, B&W/color)

1-($2.75) 4.00
1-($3.00, color) 5.00
1-($9.95)-Commemorative Edition 10.00
1-TwinVariant Edition (1250? print run) 10.00
1-Special Edition; polybagged w/certificate 4.00
1 Gold Collectors Edition; polybagged w/certificate 3.00
2,3-($3.00, color)-Butt Naked Edition & regular-c 3.00
3-($9.95)-Commemorative Edition; polybagged w/certificate & card 10.00

CREED: APPLE TREE
Gearbox Press: Dec, 2000 - No. 2 ($2.95, B&W)

1,2-Kaniuga-s/c/a 3.00

CREED: CRANIAL DISORDER
Lightning Comics: Oct, 1996 ($3.00, limited series)

1-3-Two covers 3.00
1-($5.95)-Platinum Edition 6.00
2,3-($9.95)Ltd.l Edition 10.00

CREED: MECHANICAL EVOLUTION
Gearbox Press: Sept, 2000 - No. 2, Oct, 2000 ($2.95, B&W)

1,2-Kaniuga-s/c/a 3.00

CREED/TEENAGE MUTANT NINJA TURTLES
Lightning Comics: May, 1996 ($3.00, one-shot)

1-Kaniuga-a(p)/scripts; Laird-c; variant-c exists 3.00
1-($9.95)-Platinum Edition 10.00
1-Special Edition; polybagged w/certificate 5.00

CREED: USE YOUR DELUSION
Avatar Press: Jan, 1998 - No. 2, Feb, 1998 ($3.00, B&W)

1,2-Kaniuga-s/c/a 3.00
1,2-($4.95) Foil cover 5.00

CREED: UTOPIATE
Image Comics: Feb, 2002 - No. 3, Aug, 2002 ($2.95/$4.95, color)

1,2-Kaniuga-c/a/Christina Z-s 3.00
3-($4.95) 5.00

CREEPER, THE (See Beware... , Showcase #73 & 1st Issue Special #7)
DC Comics: Dec, 1997 - No. 11; #1,000,000 Nov, 1998 ($2.50)

1-11-Kaminski-s/Martinbrough-a(p). 7,8-Joker-c/app. 3.00
#1,000,000 (11/98) 853rd Century x-over 3.00

CREEPS
Image Comics: Oct, 2001 - No. 4, May, 2002 ($2.95)

1-4-Mandrake-a/Mishkin-s 3.00

CREEPSHOW
Plume/New American Library Pub.: July, 1982 (softcover graphic novel)

1st edition-nn-(68 pgs.) Kamen-c/Wrightson-a; screenplay by Stephen King for the George Romero movie 3 6 9 19 25 32
2nd-7th printings 2 4 6 12 16 20

CREEPSVILLE
Laughing Reindeer Press: V2#1, Winter, 1995 ($4.95)

V2#1-Comics w/text 5.00

CREEPY (See Warren Presents)
Warren Publishing Co./Harris Publ. #146: 1964 - No. 145, Feb, 1983; No. 146, 1985 (B&W, magazine)

1-Frazetta-a (his last story in comics?); Jack Davis-c; 1st Warren all comics magazine; 1st app. Uncle Creepy 11 22 33 80 120 160
2-Frazetta-c & 1 pg. strip 7 14 21 50 68 85
3-8,11-13,15-17: 3-7,9-11,15-17-Frazetta-c. 7-Frazetta 1 pg. strip. 15,16-Adams-a. 16-Jeff Jones-a 4 8 12 27 36 45
9-Creepy fan club sketch by Wrightson (1st published-a); has 1/2 pg. anti-smoking strip by Frazetta; Frazetta-c; 1st Wood and Ditko art on this title; Toth-a (low print) 7 14 21 46 63 80
10-Brunner fan club sketch (1st published work) 4 8 12 29 40 50
14-Neal Adams 1st Warren work 4 8 12 29 40 50
18-28,30,31: 27-Frazetta-c 3 7 10 21 28 35
29,34: 29-Jones-a 4 8 12 22 30 38
32-(scarce) Frazetta-c; Harlan Ellison sty 6 12 18 38 52 65
33,35,37,39,40,42-47,49: 35-Hitler/Nazi-s. 39-1st Uncle Creepy solo-s, Cousin Eerie app.; early Brunner-a. 42-1st San Julian-c. 44-1st Ploog-a. 46-Corben-a 3 6 9 18 24 30
36-(11/70)1st Corben art at Warren 4 8 12 24 32 40
38,41-(scarce): 38-1st Kelly-c. 41-Corben-a 4 8 12 27 36 45
48,55,65-(1972, 1973, 1974 Annuals) #55 & 65 contain an 8 pg. slick comic insert. 48-(84 pgs.). 55-Color poster bonus (1/2 price if missing). 65-(100 pgs.) Summer Giant 4 8 12 24 32 40
50-Vampirella/Eerie/Creepy-c 4 8 12 27 36 45
51,54,56-61,64: All contain an 8 pg. slick comic insert in middle. 59-Xmas horror. 54,64-Chaykin-a 3 7 10 21 28 35
52,53,66,71,72,75,76,78-80: 71-All Bermejo-a; Space & Time issue. 72-Gual-a. 78-Fantasy issue. 79,80-Monsters issue 2 4 6 14 18 22
62,63-1st & 2nd full Wrightson story art; Corben-a; 8 pg. color comic insert 3 7 10 21 28 35
67,68,73 3 6 9 16 21 26
69,70-Edgar Allan Poe issues; Corben-a 3 6 9 16 20 24
74,77: 74-All Crandell-a. 77-Xmas Horror issue; Corben-a,Wrightson-a

The Crew #1 © MAR

Crime Clinic #3 © Z-D

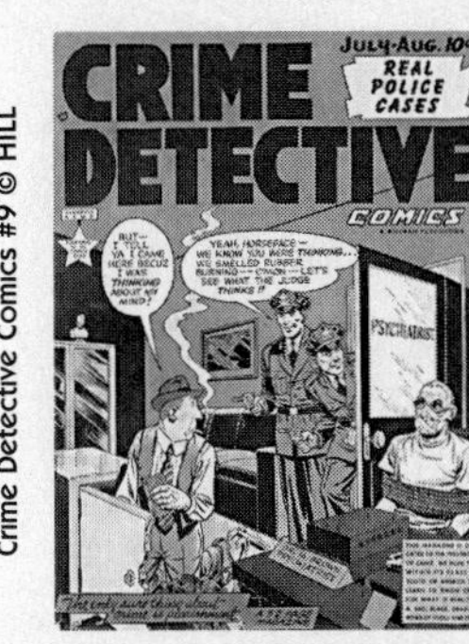

Crime Detective Comics #9 © HILL

	GD 2.0	VG 4.0	FN 6.0	VF 8.0	VF/NM 9.0	NM- 9.2
	3	6	9	18	24	30
81,84,85,88-90,92-94,96-99,102,104-112,114-118,120,122-130: 84,93-Sports issue. 85,97,102-Monster issue. 89-All war issue; Nino-a. 94-Weird Children issue. 96,109-Aliens issue. 99-Disasters. 103-Corben-a. 104-Robots issue. 106-Sword & Sorcery.107-Sci-fi. 116-End of Man. 125-Xmas Horror	2	4	6	8	10	12
82,100,101: 82-All Maroto issue. 100-(8/78) Anniversary. 101-Corben-a	2	4	6	11	14	18
83,95-Wrightson-a. 83-Corben-a. 95-Gorilla/Apes.	2	4	6	9	11	14
86,87,91,103-Wrightson-a. 86-Xmas Horror	2	4	6	9	11	14
113-All Wrightson-r issue	3	6	9	16	20	24
119,121: 119-All Nino issue.121-All Severin-r issue	2	4	6	9	11	14
131,133-136,138,140: 135-Xmas issue	2	4	6	9	11	14
132,137,139: 132-Corben. 137-All Williamson-r issue. 139-All Toth-r issue	2	4	6	11	14	18
141,143,144 (low dist.): 144-Giant, $2.25; Frazetta-c	2	4	6	14	18	22
142,145 (low dist.): 142-(10/82, 100 pgs.) All Torres issue. 145-(2/83) last Warren issue	2	4	6	14	18	22
146 ($2.95)-1st from Harris; resurrection issue	7	14	21	50	68	85
Year Book '68-'70: '70-Neal Adams, Ditko-a(r)	4	8	12	29	40	50
Annual 1971,1972	4	8	12	27	36	45
1993 Fearbook ($3.95)-Harris Publ.; Brereton-c; Vampirella by Busiek-s/Art Adams-a; David-s; Paquette-a	4	8	12	24	32	40
....:The Classic Years TPB (Harris/Dark Horse,'91, $12.95) Kaluta-c; art by Frazetta,Torres, Crandall, Ditko, Morrow, Williamson, Wrightson						25.00

NOTE: *All issues contain many good artists works:* ***Neal Adams, Brunner, Corben, Craig (Taycee), Crandall, Ditko, Evans, Frazetta, Heath, Jeff Jones, Krenkel, McWilliams, Morrow, Nino, Orlando, Ploog, Severin, Torres, Toth, Williamson, Wood, & Wrightson****; covers by* ***Crandall, Davis, Frazetta, Morrow, San Julian, Todd/Bode****; Otto Binder's "Adam Link" stories in No. 2, 4, 6, 8, 9, 12, 13, 15 with* ***Orlando*** *art.* ***Frazetta*** *c-2-7, 9-11, 15-17, 27, 32, 83r, 89r, 91r.* ***E.A. Poe*** *adaptations in 66, 69, 70.*

CREEPY (Mini-series)
Harris Comics/Dark Horse: 1992 - Book 4, 1992 (48 pgs, B&W, squarebound)

	GD	VG	FN	VF	VF/NM	NM-
Book 1-4: Brereton painted-c on all. Stories and art by various incl. David (all), Busiek(2), Infantino(2), Guice(3), Colan(1)	2	4	6	8	10	12

CREEPY THINGS
Charlton Comics: July, 1975 - No. 6, June, 1976

	GD	VG	FN	VF	VF/NM	NM-
1-Sutton-c/a	2	4	6	12	16	20
2-6: Ditko-a in 3,5. Sutton c-3,4. 6-Zeck-c	1	3	4	6	8	10
Modern Comics Reprint 2-6(1977)						4.00

NOTE: ***Larson*** *a-2,6.* ***Sutton*** *a-1,2,4,6.* ***Zeck*** *a-2.*

CREMATOR
Chaos! Comics: Dec, 1998 - No. 5, May, 1999 ($2.95, limited series)

	GD	VG	FN	VF	VF/NM	NM-
1-5-Leonardo Jimenez-s/a						3.00

CREW, THE
Marvel Comics: July, 2003 - No. 7, Jan, 2004 ($2.50)

	GD	VG	FN	VF	VF/NM	NM-
1-7-Priest-s/Bennett-a; James Rhodes(War Machine) app.						2.50

CRIME AND JUSTICE (Badge Of Justice #22 on; Rookie Cop? No. 27 on)
Capitol Stories/Charlton Comics: March, 1951 - No. 21; No. 23 - No. 26, Sept, 1955 (No #22)

	GD	VG	FN	VF	VF/NM	NM-
1	33	66	99	190	275	360
2	13	26	39	76	106	135
3-8,10-13: 6-Negligee panels	11	22	33	62	84	105
9-Classic story "Comics Vs. Crime"	24	48	72	138	199	260
14-Color illos in **POP**; gory story of man who beheads women	19	38	57	107	154	200
15-17,19-21,23-26; 15-Negligee panels. 23,25,26 (exist?)	8	16	24	46	58	70
18-Ditko-a	25	50	75	144	207	270

NOTE: ***Alascia*** *c-20.* ***Ayers*** *a-17.* ***Shuster*** *a-19-21; c-19. Bondage c-11, 12.*

CRIME AND PUNISHMENT (Title inspired by 1935 film)
Lev Gleason Publications: April, 1948 - No. 74, Aug, 1955

	GD	VG	FN	VF	VF/NM	NM-
1-Mr. Crime app. on-c	35	70	105	198	287	375
2	18	36	54	100	143	185
3-Used in **SOTI**, pg. 112; injury-to-eye panel; Fuje-a	20	40	60	112	161	210
4,5	14	28	42	79	110	140
6-10	11	22	33	64	87	110
11-20	10	20	30	58	77	95
21-30	9	18	27	51	62	75
31-38,40-44,46: 46-One pg. Frazetta-a	8	16	24	43	54	65
39-Drug mention story "The 5 Dopes"	11	22	33	62	84	105
45- "Hophead Killer" drug story	11	22	33	62	84	105
47-57,60-65,70-74:	8	16	24	40	50	60
58-Used in **POP**, pg. 79	8	16	24	43	54	65
59-Used in **SOTI**, illo "What comic-book America stands for"	30	60	90	170	245	320
66-Toth-c/a(4); 3-D effect issue (3/54); 1st "Deep Dimension" process	40	80	120	230	335	440
67- "Monkey on His Back" heroin story; 3-D effect issue	35	70	105	200	290	380
68-3-D effect issue; Toth-c (7/54)	30	60	90	170	245	320
69- "The Hot Rod Gang" dope crazy kids	11	22	33	62	84	105

NOTE: ***Biro*** *c-most.* ***Everett*** *a-31.* ***Fuje*** *a-3, 4, 12, 13, 17, 18, 20, 26, 27.* ***Guardineer*** *a-2-4, 10, 14, 17, 18, 20, 26-28, 32, 38-44,54.* ***Kinstler*** *c-69.* ***McWilliams*** *a-41, 48, 49.* ***Tuska*** *a-28, 30, 51, 64, 70.*

CRIME AND PUNISHMENT: MARSHALL LAW TAKES MANHATTAN
Marvel Comics (Epic Comics): 1989 ($4.95, 52 pgs., direct sales only, mature)

	GD	VG	FN	VF	VF/NM	NM-
nn-Graphic album featuring Marshall Law						5.00

CRIME CAN'T WIN (Formerly Cindy Smith)
Marvel/Atlas Comics (TCI 41/CCC 42,43,4-12): No. 41, 9/50 - No. 43, 2/51; No. 4, 4/51 - No. 12, 9/53

	GD	VG	FN	VF	VF/NM	NM-
41(#1)	26	52	78	150	215	280
42(#2)	15	30	45	85	120	155
43(#3)-Horror story	18	36	54	100	143	185
4(4/51),5-12: 10-Possible use in **SOTI**, pg. 161	12	24	36	71	98	125

NOTE: ***Robinson*** *a-9-11.* ***Tuska*** *a-43.*

CRIME CASES COMICS (Formerly Willie Comics)
Marvel/Atlas Comics(CnPC No.24-8/MJMC No.9-12): No. 24, 8/50 - No. 27, 3/51; No. 5, 5/51 - No. 12, 7/52

	GD	VG	FN	VF	VF/NM	NM-
24 (#1, 52 pgs.)-True police cases	18	36	54	102	146	190
25-27(#2-4): 27-Morisi-a	12	24	36	71	98	125
5-12: 11-Robinson-a. 12-Tuska-a	11	22	33	62	84	105

CRIME CLINIC
Ziff-Davis Publishing Co.: No. 10, July-Aug, 1951 - No. 5, Summer, 1952

	GD	VG	FN	VF	VF/NM	NM-
10(#1)-Painted-c; origin Dr. Tom Rogers	30	60	90	170	245	320
11(#2),4,5: 4,5-Painted-c	20	40	60	112	161	210
3-Used in **SOTI**, pg. 18	21	42	63	118	169	220

NOTE: *All have painted covers by* ***Saunders. Starr*** *a-10.*

CRIME CLINIC
Slave Labor Graphics: May, 1995 - No. 2, Oct, 1995 ($2.95, B&W, limited series)

	GD	VG	FN	VF	VF/NM	NM-
1,2						3.00

CRIME DETECTIVE COMICS
Hillman Periodicals: Mar-Apr, 1948 - V3#8, May-June, 1953

	GD	VG	FN	VF	VF/NM	NM-
V1#1-The Invisible 6, costumed villains app; Fuje-c/a, 15 pgs.	30	60	90	170	245	320
2,5: 5-Krigstein-a	13	26	39	76	106	135
3,4,6,7,10-12: 6-McWilliams-a	11	22	33	62	84	105
8-Kirbyish-a by McCann	11	22	33	62	84	105
9-Used in **SOTI**, pg. 16 & "Caricature of the author in a position comic book publishers wish he were in permanently" illo.	37	74	111	209	305	400
V2#1,4,7-Krigstein-a: 1-Tuska-a	10	20	30	60	80	100
2,3,5,6,8-12 (1-2/52)	9	18	27	51	62	75
V3#1-Drug use-c	9	18	27	52	66	80
2-8	8	16	24	40	50	60

NOTE: ***Briefer*** *a-11, V3#1.* ***Kinstlerish***-*a by* ***McCann***-*V2#7, V3#2.* ***Powell*** *a-10, 11.* ***Starr*** *a-10.*

CRIME DETECTOR
Timor Publications: Jan, 1954 - No. 5, Sept, 1954

	GD	VG	FN	VF	VF/NM	NM-
1	21	42	63	118	169	220
2	11	22	33	64	87	110
3,4	10	20	30	58	77	95
5-Disbrow-a (classic)	22	44	66	125	180	235

CRIME DOES NOT PAY (Formerly Silver Streak Comics No. 1-21)
Comic House/Lev Gleason/Golfing: No. 22, June, 1942 - No. 147, July, 1955
(1st crime comic)(Title inspired by film)

	GD	VG	FN	VF	VF/NM	NM-
22 (23 on cover, 22 on indicia)-Origin The War Eagle & only app.; Chip Gardner begins; #22 was rebound in Complete Book of True Crime (Scarce)	262	524	786	1638	2519	3400
23 (Scarce)	135	270	405	844	1297	1750
24-Intro. & 1st app. Mr. Crime (Scarce).	106	212	318	663	1019	1375
25,26,28-30: 30-Wood and Biro app.	60	120	180	375	575	775
27-Classic Biro-c	67	134	201	419	647	875
31,32,34-40	40	80	120	240	360	480
33-Classic Biro Hanging & hatchet-c	45	90	135	275	418	560
41-Origin & 1st app. Officer Common Sense	32	64	96	184	267	350

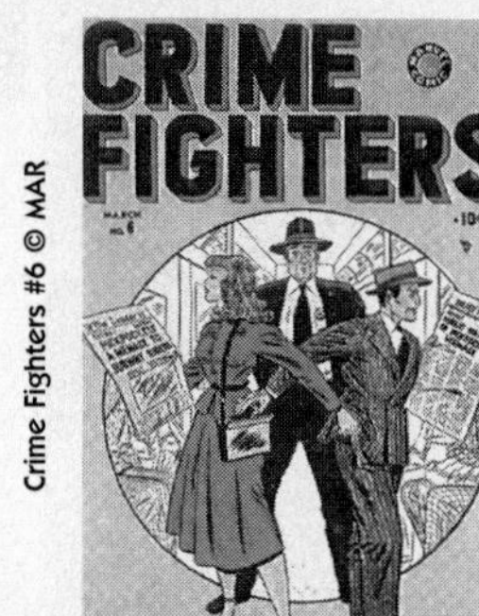

Crime Fighters #6 © MAR

Crime Must Lose #7 © MAR

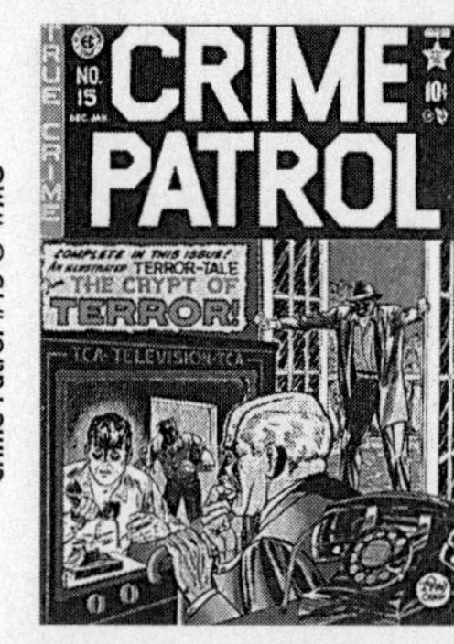

Crime Patrol #15 © WMG

	GD 2.0	VG 4.0	FN 6.0	VF 8.0	VF/NM 9.0	NM- 9.2
42-Electrocution-c	37	74	111	209	305	400
43-46,48-50: 44,45,50 are 68 pg. issues; 44-"legs" diamond story	21	42	63	121	173	225
47-Electric chair-c	35	70	105	201	293	385
51-70: 63,64-Possible use in **SOTI**, pg. 306. 63-Contains Biro & Gleason's self censorship code of 12 listed restrictions (5/48)	17	34	51	98	139	180
71-99: 87-Chip Gardner begins, ends #100	15	30	45	85	120	155
100	16	32	48	92	131	170
101-104,107-110: 102-Chip Gardner app	11	22	33	64	87	110
105-Used in **POP**, pg. 84	12	24	36	69	95	120
106,114-Frazetta-a, 1 pg.	11	22	33	64	87	110
111-Used in **POP**, pgs. 80 & 81; injury-to-eye sty illo	12	24	36	69	95	120
112,113,115-130	9	18	27	52	66	80
131-140	8	16	24	43	54	65
141,142-Last pre-code issue; Kubert-a(1)	10	20	30	58	77	95
143-Kubert-a in one story	10	20	30	58	77	95
144-146	8	16	24	43	54	65
147-Last issue (scarce); Kubert-a	14	28	42	81	113	145
1(Golfing-1945)	8	16	24	43	54	65
The Best of...(1944, 128 pgs.)-Series contains 4 rebound issues	79	158	237	494	760	1025
...1945 issue	60	120	180	375	575	775
...1946-48 issues	45	90	135	275	418	560
...1949-50 issues	40	80	120	240	360	480
...1951-53 issues	35	70	105	201	293	385

NOTE: *Many issues contain violent covers and stories. Who Dunnit by **Guardineer**-39-42, 44-105, 108-110; Chip Gardner by **Bob Fujitani (Fuje)**-88-103. **Alderman** a-29, 41-44, 49. **Dan Barry** a-67, 75. **Biro** c-1-76, 122, 142. **Briefer** a-29(2), 30, 31, 33, 37, 39. **G. Colan** a-105. **Fuje** c-88, 89, 91-94, 96, 98, 99, 102, 103. **Guardineer** a-57, 67, 68, 71, 74. **Kubert** c-143. **Landau** a-118. **Maurer** a-29, 39, 41, 42. **McWilliams** a-91, 93, 95, 100-103. **Palais** a-30, 33, 37, 39, 41-43, 44(2), 46, 49. **Powell** a-146, 147. **Tuska** a-48, 50(2), 51, 52, 56, 57(2), 60-64, 66, 67, 68, 71, 74. Painted c-87-102. Bondage c-43, 62, 98.*

CRIME EXPOSED
Marvel Comics (PPI)/Marvel Atlas Comics (PrPI): June, 1948; Dec, 1950 - No. 14, June, 1952

	GD 2.0	VG 4.0	FN 6.0	VF 8.0	VF/NM 9.0	NM- 9.2
1(6/48)	35	70	105	198	287	375
1(12/50)	20	40	60	112	161	210
2	14	28	42	79	110	140
3-9,11,14	11	22	33	64	87	110
10-Used in **POP**, pg. 81	12	24	36	69	95	120
12-Krigstein & Robinson-a	12	24	36	69	95	120
13-Used in **POP**, pg. 81; Krigstein-a	12	24	36	71	98	125

NOTE: ***Maneely** c-8. **Robinson** a-11, 12. **Tuska** a-3, 4.*

CRIMEFIGHTERS
Marvel Comics (CmPS 1-3/CCC 4-10): Apr, 1948 - No. 10, Nov, 1949

	GD 2.0	VG 4.0	FN 6.0	VF 8.0	VF/NM 9.0	NM- 9.2
1-Some copies are undated & could be reprints	25	50	75	144	207	270
2,3: 3-Morphine addict story	14	28	42	79	110	140
4-10: 6-Anti-Wertham editorial. 9,10-Photo-c	12	24	36	69	95	120

CRIME FIGHTERS (...Always Win)
Atlas Comics (CnPC): No. 11, Sept, 1954 - No. 13, Jan, 1955

	GD 2.0	VG 4.0	FN 6.0	VF 8.0	VF/NM 9.0	NM- 9.2
11-13: 11-Maneely-a,13-Pakula, Reinman, Severin-a	12	24	36	69	95	120

CRIME-FIGHTING DETECTIVE (Shock Detective Cases No. 20 on; formerly Criminals on the Run)
Star Publications: No. 11, Apr-May, 1950 - No. 19, June, 1952 (Based on true crime cases)

	GD 2.0	VG 4.0	FN 6.0	VF 8.0	VF/NM 9.0	NM- 9.2
11-L. B. Cole-c/a (2 pgs.); L. B. Cole-c on all	20	40	60	112	161	210
12,13,15-19: 17-Young King Cole & Dr. Doom app.	15	30	45	85	120	155
14-L. B. Cole-c/a, r/Law-Crime #2	17	34	51	95	135	175

CRIME FILES
Standard Comics: No. 5, Sept, 1952 - No. 6, Nov, 1952

	GD 2.0	VG 4.0	FN 6.0	VF 8.0	VF/NM 9.0	NM- 9.2
5-1pg. Alex Toth-a; used in **SOTI**, pg. 4 (text)	25	50	75	141	203	265
6-Sekowsky-a	13	26	39	74	102	130

CRIME ILLUSTRATED (Magazine)
E. C. Comics: Nov-Dec, 1955 - No. 2, Spring, 1956 (25¢, Adult Suspense Stories on-c)

	GD 2.0	VG 4.0	FN 6.0	VF 8.0	VF/NM 9.0	NM- 9.2
1-Ingels & Crandall-a	17	34	51	95	135	175
2-Ingels & Crandall-a	13	26	39	76	106	135

NOTE: ***Craig** a-2. **Crandall** a-1, 2; c-2. **Evans** a-1. **Davis** a-2. **Ingels** a-1, 2. **Krigstein/Crandall** a-1. **Orlando** a-1, 2; c-1.*

CRIME INCORPORATED (Formerly Crimes Incorporated)
Fox Features Syndicate: No. 2, Aug, 1950; No. 3, Aug, 1951

	GD 2.0	VG 4.0	FN 6.0	VF 8.0	VF/NM 9.0	NM- 9.2
2	27	54	81	152	219	285
3(1951)-Hollingsworth-a	19	38	57	107	154	200

CRIME MACHINE (Magazine reprints pre-code crime and gangster comics)
Skywald Publications: Feb, 1971 - No. 2, May, 1971 (B&W, 68 pgs., roundbound)

	GD 2.0	VG 4.0	FN 6.0	VF 8.0	VF/NM 9.0	NM- 9.2
1-Kubert-a(2)(r)(Avon); bikini girl in cake-c	6	12	18	43	59	75
2-Torres, Wildey-a; violent-c/a	4	8	12	27	36	45

CRIME MUST LOSE! (Formerly Sports Action?)
Sports Action (Atlas Comics): No. 4, Oct, 1950 - No. 12, April, 1952

	GD 2.0	VG 4.0	FN 6.0	VF 8.0	VF/NM 9.0	NM- 9.2
4-Ann Brewster-a in all; c-used in N.Y. Legis. Comm. documents	19	38	57	107	154	200
5-12: 9-Robinson-a. 11-Used in **POP**, pg. 89	13	26	39	74	102	130

CRIME MUST PAY THE PENALTY (Formerly Four Favorites; Penalty #47, 48)
Ace Magazines (Current Books): No. 33, Feb, 1948; No. 2, Jun, 1948 - No. 48, Jan, 1956

	GD 2.0	VG 4.0	FN 6.0	VF 8.0	VF/NM 9.0	NM- 9.2
33(#1, 2/48)-Becomes Four Teeners #34?	35	70	105	198	287	375
2(6/48)-Extreme violence; Palais-a?	22	44	66	123	177	230
3,4,8: 3- "Frisco Mary" story used in Senate Investigation report, pg. 7. 4,8-Transvestism stories	16	32	48	89	127	165
5-7,9,10	11	22	33	64	87	110
11-19	10	20	30	60	80	100
20-Drug story "Dealers in White Death"	14	28	42	79	110	140
21-32,34-40,42-48: 44-Last pre-code	8	16	24	43	54	65
33(7/53)- "Dell Fabry-Junk King" drug story; mentioned in Love and Death	11	22	33	62	84	105
41-reprints "Dealers in White Death"	9	18	27	51	62	75

NOTE: ***Cameron** a-29-31, 34, 35, 39-41. **Colan** a-20, 31. **Kremer** a-3, 37r. **Larsen** a-32. **Palais** a-5?,37.*

CRIME MUST STOP
Hillman Periodicals: October, 1952 (52 pgs.)

	GD 2.0	VG 4.0	FN 6.0	VF 8.0	VF/NM 9.0	NM- 9.2
V1#1(Scarce)-Similar to Monster Crime; Mort Lawrence, Krigstein-a	69	138	207	431	666	900

CRIME MYSTERIES (Secret Mysteries #16 on; combined with Crime Smashers #7 on)
Ribage Publ. Corp. (Trojan Magazines): May, 1952 - No. 15, Sept, 1954

	GD 2.0	VG 4.0	FN 6.0	VF 8.0	VF/NM 9.0	NM- 9.2
1-Transvestism story; crime & terror stories begin	56	112	168	350	538	725
2-Marijuana story (7/52)	40	80	120	236	351	465
3-One pg. Frazetta-a	37	74	111	213	312	410
4-Cover shows girl in bondage having her blood drained; 1 pg. Frazetta-a	56	112	168	350	538	725
5-10	31	62	93	178	259	340
11,12,14	30	60	90	170	245	320
13-(5/54)-Angelo Torres 1st comic work (inks over Check's pencils); Check-a	35	70	105	200	290	380
15-Acid in face-c	40	80	120	241	363	485

NOTE: ***Fass** a-13; c-4, 10. **Hollingsworth** a-10-13, 15; c-2, 12, 13, 15. **Kiefer** a-4. **Woodbridge** a-13? Bondage-c-1, 8, 12.*

CRIME ON THE RUN (See Approved Comics #8)

CRIME ON THE WATERFRONT (Formerly Famous Gangsters)
Realistic Publications: No. 4, May, 1952 (Painted cover)

	GD 2.0	VG 4.0	FN 6.0	VF 8.0	VF/NM 9.0	NM- 9.2
4	30	60	90	170	245	320

CRIME PATROL (Formerly International #1-5; International Crime Patrol #6; becomes Crypt of Terror #17 on)
E. C. Comics: No. 7, Summer, 1948 - No. 16, Feb-Mar, 1950

	GD 2.0	VG 4.0	FN 6.0	VF 8.0	VF/NM 9.0	NM- 9.2
7-Intro. Captain Crime	67	134	201	419	647	875
8-14: 12-Ingels-a	59	118	177	369	565	760
15-Intro. of Crypt Keeper (inspired by Witches Tales radio show) & Crypt of Terror (see Tales From the Crypt #33 for origin); used by N.Y. Legis. Comm.; last pg. Feldstein-a	255	510	765	1913	2807	3700
16-2nd Crypt Keeper app.; Roussos-a	166	332	498	1245	1823	2400

NOTE: ***Craig** c/a in most issues. **Feldstein** a-9-16. **Kiefer** a-8, 10, 11. **Moldoff** a-7.*

CRIME PATROL
Gemstone Publishing: Apr, 2000 - No. 10, Jan, 2001 ($2.50)

	NM- 9.2
1-10: E.C. reprints	2.50
Volume 1,2 (2000, $13.50) 1-r/#1-5. 2-r/#6-10	14.00

CRIME PHOTOGRAPHER (See Casey...)

CRIME REPORTER
St. John Publ. Co.: Aug, 1948 - No. 3, Dec, 1948 (Indicia shows Oct.)

	GD 2.0	VG 4.0	FN 6.0	VF 8.0	VF/NM 9.0	NM- 9.2
1-Drug club story	51	102	153	311	473	635
2-Used in **SOTI**: illo- "Children told me what the man was going to do with the red-hot poker;" r/Dynamic #17 with editing; Baker-c; Tuska-a	71	142	213	444	685	925
3-Baker-c; Tuska-a	40	80	120	241	363	485

CRIMES BY WOMEN
Fox Features Syndicate: June, 1948 - No. 15, Aug, 1951; 1954 (True crime cases)

Crime SuspenStories #6 © WMG

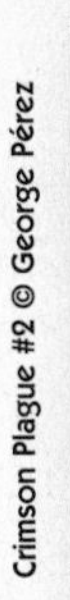

Crimson Plague #2 © George Pérez

Crisis on Multiple Earths Vol. 2 © DC

	GD 2.0	VG 4.0	FN 6.0	VF 8.0	VF/NM 9.0	NM- 9.2
1-True story of Bonnie Parker	123	246	369	769	1185	1600
2,3: 3-Used in **SOTI**, pg. 234	65	130	195	406	623	840
4,5,7-9,11-15: 8-Used in **POP**	59	118	177	369	565	760
6-Classic girl fight-c; acid-in-face panel	63	126	189	394	610	825
10-Used in **SOTI**, pg. 72; girl fight-c	60	120	180	375	575	775
54(M.S. Publ.-'54)-Reprint; (formerly My Love Secret)	27	54	81	154	222	290

CRIMES INCORPORATED (Formerly My Past)
Fox Features Syndicate: No. 12, June, 1950 (Crime Incorporated No. 2 on)

	GD 2.0	VG 4.0	FN 6.0	VF 8.0	VF/NM 9.0	NM- 9.2
12	21	42	63	121	173	225

CRIMES INCORPORATED (See Fox Giants)

CRIME SMASHER (See Whiz #76)
Fawcett Publications: Summer, 1948 (one-shot)

	GD 2.0	VG 4.0	FN 6.0	VF 8.0	VF/NM 9.0	NM- 9.2
1-Formerly Spy Smasher	44	88	132	268	409	550

CRIME SMASHERS (Becomes Secret Mysteries No. 16 on)
Ribage Publishing Corp.(Trojan Magazines): Oct, 1950 - No. 15, Mar, 1953

	GD 2.0	VG 4.0	FN 6.0	VF 8.0	VF/NM 9.0	NM- 9.2
1-Used in **SOTI**, pg. 19,20, & illo "A girl raped and murdered;" Sally the Sleuth begins	87	174	261	544	835	1125
2-Kubert-c	46	92	138	281	428	575
3,4	38	76	114	219	320	420
5-Wood-a	44	88	132	268	409	550
6,8-11: 8-Lingerie panel	30	60	90	170	245	320
7-Female heroin junkie story	32	64	96	184	267	350
12-Injury to eye panel; 1 pg. Frazetta-a	32	64	96	184	267	350
13-Used in **POP**, pgs. 79,80; 1 pg. Frazetta-a	32	64	96	184	267	350
14,15	26	52	78	147	211	275

NOTE: ***Hollingsworth** a-14. **Kiefer** a-15. Bondage c-7, 9.*

CRIME SUSPENSTORIES (Formerly Vault of Horror No. 12-14)
E. C. Comics: No. 15, Oct-Nov, 1950 - No. 27, Feb-Mar, 1955

	GD 2.0	VG 4.0	FN 6.0	VF 8.0	VF/NM 9.0	NM- 9.2
15-Identical to #1 in content; #1 printed on outside front cover. #15 (formerly "The Vault of Horror") printed and blackened out on inside front cover with Vol. 1, No. 1 printed over it. Evidently, several of No. 15 were printed before a decision was made not to drop the Vault of Horror and Haunt of Fear series. The print run was stopped on No. 15 and continued on No. 1. All of the No. 15 issues were changed as described above.	145	290	435	1088	1594	2100
1	107	214	321	803	1177	1550
2	58	116	174	435	638	840
3-5: 3-Poe adaptation. 3-Old Witch stories begin	40	80	120	300	438	575
6-10	33	66	99	248	367	485
11,12,14,15: 15-The Old Witch guest stars	26	52	78	195	283	370
13,16-Williamson-a	28	56	84	210	305	400
17-Williamson/Frazetta-a (6 pgs.)	33	66	99	248	362	475
18,19: 19-Used in **SOTI**, pg. 235	22	44	66	165	243	320
20-Cover used in **SOTI**, illo "Cover of a children's comic book"	28	56	84	210	305	400
21,24-26: 24- "Food For Thought" similar to "Cave In" in Amazing Detective Cases #13 (1952)	16	32	48	120	178	235
22,23-Used in Senate investigation on juvenile delinquency. 22-Ax decapitation-c	22	44	66	165	243	320
27-Last issue (Low distribution)	20	40	60	150	220	290

NOTE: ***Craig** a-1-21; c-1-18, 20-22. **Crandall** a-18-26. **Davis** a-4, 5, 7, 9-12, 20. **Elder** a-17,18. **Evans** a-15, 19, 21, 23, 25, 27; c-23, 24. **Feldstein** c-19. **Ingels** a-1-12, 14, 15, 27. **Kamen** a-2, 4-18, 20-27; c-25-27. **Krigstein** a-22, 24, 25, 27. **Kurtzman** a-1, 3. **Orlando** a-16, 22, 24, 26. **Wood** a-1, 3. Issues No. 1-3 were printed in Canada as "Weird Suspenstories." Issues No. 11-15 have E. C. "quickie" stories. No. 25 contains the famous "Are You a Red Dupe?" editorial. Ray Bradbury adaptations-15, 17.*

CRIME SUSPENSTORIES
Russ Cochran/Gemstone Publ.: Nov, 1992 - No. 24 ($1.50/$2.00/$2.50)

	GD 2.0	VG 4.0	FN 6.0	VF 8.0	VF/NM 9.0	NM- 9.2
1-24: Reprints Crime SuspenStories series						3.00

CRIMINALS ON THE RUN (Formerly Young King Cole) (Crime Fighting Detective No. 11 on)
Premium Group (Novelty Press): V4#1, Aug-Sep, 1948-#10, Dec-Jan, 1949-50

	GD 2.0	VG 4.0	FN 6.0	VF 8.0	VF/NM 9.0	NM- 9.2
V4#1-Young King Cole continues	31	62	93	175	253	330
2-6: 6-Dr. Doom app.	27	54	81	152	219	285
7-Classic "Fish in the Face" c by L. B. Cole	55	110	165	336	511	685
V5#1,2 (#8,9),10: 9,10-L. B. Cole-c	25	50	75	141	203	265

NOTE: *Most issues have **L. B. Cole** covers. **McWilliams** a-V4#6, 7, V5#2; c-V4#5.*

CRIMINAL MACABRE: A CAL MCDONALD MYSTERY
Dark Horse Comics: May, 2003 - No. 5, Sept, 2003 ($2.99)

	GD 2.0	VG 4.0	FN 6.0	VF 8.0	VF/NM 9.0	NM- 9.2
1-5-Niles-s/Templesmith-a						3.00

CRIMSON (Also see Cliffhanger #0)
Image Comics (Cliffhanger Productions): May, 1998 - No. 7, Dec, 1998;
DC Comics (Cliffhanger Prod.): No. 8, Mar, 1999 - No. 24, Apr, 2001 ($2.50)

	GD 2.0	VG 4.0	FN 6.0	VF 8.0	VF/NM 9.0	NM- 9.2
1-Humberto Ramos-a/Augustyn-s						5.00
1-Variant-c by Warren						8.00
1-Chromium-c						20.00
2-Ramos-c with street crowd, 2-Variant-c by Art Adams						3.00
2-Dynamic Forces CrimsonChrome cover						15.00
3-7: 3-Ramos Moon background-c. 7-3 covers by Ramos, Madureira, & Campbell						3.50
8-23: 8-First DC issue						2.50
24-($3.50) Final issue; wraparound-c						3.50
DF Premiere Ed. 1998 ($6.95) covers by Ramos and Jae Lee						7.00
Crimson: Scarlet X Blood on the Moon (10/99, $3.95)						4.00
Crimson Sourcebook (11/99, $2.95) Pin-ups and info						3.00
Earth Angel TPB (2001, $14.95) r/#13-18						15.00
Heaven and Earth TPB (1/00, $14.95) r/#7-12						15.00
Loyalty and Loss TPB ('99, $12.95) r/#1-6						13.00
Redemption TPB ('01, $14.95) r/#19-24						15.00

CRIMSON AVENGER, THE (See Detective Comics #20 for 1st app.)(Also see Leading Comics #1 & World's Best/Finest Comics)
DC Comics: June, 1988 - No. 4, Sept, 1988 ($1.00, limited series)

	GD 2.0	VG 4.0	FN 6.0	VF 8.0	VF/NM 9.0	NM- 9.2
1-4						2.50

CRIMSON DYNAMO
Marvel Comics (Epic): Oct, 2003 - No. 6, Apr, 2004 ($2.50/$2.99)

	GD 2.0	VG 4.0	FN 6.0	VF 8.0	VF/NM 9.0	NM- 9.2
1-4,6: 1-John Jackson Miller-s/Steve Ellis-a/c						2.50
5-($2.99) Iron Man-c/app.						3.00

CRIMSON NUN
Antarctic Press: May, 1997 - No. 4, Nov, 1997 ($2.95, limited series)

	GD 2.0	VG 4.0	FN 6.0	VF 8.0	VF/NM 9.0	NM- 9.2
1-4						3.00

CRIMSON PLAGUE
Event Comics: June, 1997 ($2.95, unfinished mini-series)

	GD 2.0	VG 4.0	FN 6.0	VF 8.0	VF/NM 9.0	NM- 9.2
1-George Perez-a						3.00

CRIMSON PLAGUE (George Pérez's...)
Image Comics (Gorilla): June, 2000 - No. 2, Aug, 2000 ($2.95, mini-series)

	GD 2.0	VG 4.0	FN 6.0	VF 8.0	VF/NM 9.0	NM- 9.2
1-George Perez-a; reprints 6/97 issue with 16 new pages						3.00
2-($2.50)						2.50

CRIMSON SKIES
Image Comics (Top Cow): Winter, 2000

	GD 2.0	VG 4.0	FN 6.0	VF 8.0	VF/NM 9.0	NM- 9.2
Preview-Comic and Microsoft video game preview						3.00

CRISIS ON INFINITE EARTHS (Also see Official... Index and Legends of the DC Universe)
DC Comics: Apr, 1985 - No. 12, Mar, 1986 (maxi-series)

	GD 2.0	VG 4.0	FN 6.0	VF 8.0	VF/NM 9.0	NM- 9.2
1-1st DC app. Blue Beetle & Detective Karp from Charlton; Pérez-c on all	2	4	6	10	13	16
2-6: 6-Intro Charlton's Capt. Atom, Nightshade, Question, Judomaster, Peacemaker & Thunderbolt into DC Universe	1	3	4	6	8	10
7-Double size; death of Supergirl	2	4	6	14	18	22
8-Death of the Flash (Barry Allen)	2	4	6	12	16	20
9-11: 9-Intro. Charlton's Ghost into DC Universe. 10-Intro. Charlton's Banshee, Dr. Spectro, Image, Punch & Jewellee into DC Universe; Starman (Prince Gavyn) dies	1	3	4	6	8	10
12-(52 pgs.)-Deaths of Dove, Kole, Lori Lemaris, Sunburst, G.A. Robin &Huntress; Kid Flash becomes new Flash; 3rd & final DC app. of the 3 Lt. Marvels; Green Fury gets new look (becomes Green Flame in Infinity, Inc. #32)	2	4	6	9	11	14
Slipcased Hardcover (1998, $99.95) Wraparound dust-jacket cover by Pérez and Alex Ross; sketch pages by Pérez; intro by Wolfman						125.00
TPB (2000, $29.95) Wraparound-c by Pérez and Ross						30.00

NOTE: *Crossover issues: All Star Squadron 50-56,60; Amethyst 13; Blue Devil 17,18; DC Comics Presents 78,86-88,95; Detective Comics 558; Fury of Firestorm 41,42; G.I. Combat 274; Green Lantern 194-196,198; Infinity, Inc. 18-25 & Annual 1, Justice League of America 244,245 & Annual 3; Legion of Super-Heroes 16,18; Losers Special 1; New Teen Titans 13,14; Omega Men 31,33; Superman 413-415; Swamp Thing 44,46; Wonder Woman 327-329.*

CRISIS ON MULTIPLE EARTHS
DC Comics: 2002, 2003, 2004 ($14.95, trade paperbacks)

	GD 2.0	VG 4.0	FN 6.0	VF 8.0	VF/NM 9.0	NM- 9.2
TPB-(2003) Reprints 1st 4 Silver Age JLA/JSA crossovers from J.L.ofA. #21,22; 29,30; 37,38; 46,47; new painted-c by Alex Ross; intro. by Mark Waid						15.00
Volume 2 (2003, $14.95) r/J.L.ofA. #55,56; 64,65; 73,74; 82,83; new Ordway-c						15.00
Volume 3 (2004, $14.95) r/J.L.ofA. #91,92; 100-102; 107-108; 113; Wein intro., Ross-c						15.00

CRITICAL MASS (See A Shadowline Saga: Critical Mass)

CRITTERS (Also see Usagi Yojimbo Summer Special)
Fantagraphics Books: 1986 - No. 50, 1990 ($1.70/$2.00, B&W)

	GD 2.0	VG 4.0	FN 6.0	VF 8.0	VF/NM 9.0	NM- 9.2
1-Cutey Bunny, Usagi Yojimbo app.	1	3	4	6	8	10
2,4,5,8,9						6.00
3,6,7,10-Usagi Yojimbo app.	1	2	3	4	5	7

Cross #4 © Andrew Vachss

The Crow #1 © Crowvision Inc.

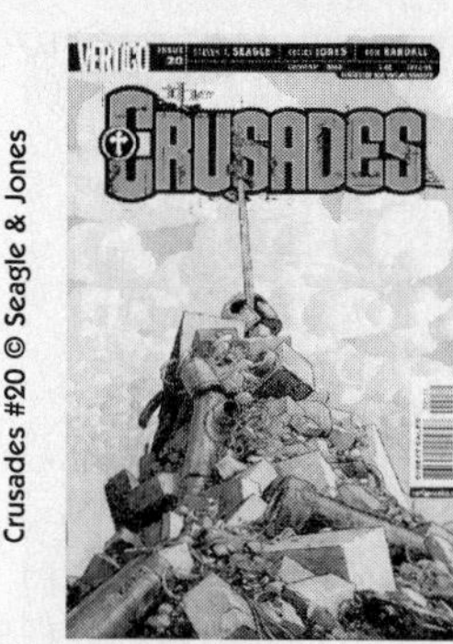

Crusades #20 © Seagle & Jones

GD 2.0 | VG 4.0 | FN 6.0 | VF 8.0 | VF/NM 9.0 | NM- 9.2

11-22,24-37,39,40: 11,14-Usagi Yojimbo app. 11-Christmas Special (68 pgs.); Usagi Yojimbo. 22-Watchmen parody; two diff. covers exist 2.50
23-With Alan Moore Flexi-disc ($3.95) 5.00
38-($2.75-c) Usagi Yojimbo app. 3.00
41-49 4.00
50 ($4.95, 84 pgs.)-Neil the Horse, Capt. Jack, Sam & Max & Usagi Yojimbo app.; Quagmire, Shaw-a 1 2 3 4 5 7
Special 1 (1/88, $2.00) 3.00

CROSS
Dark Horse Comics: No. 0, Oct, 1995 - No. 6, Apr, 1995 ($2.95, limited series, mature)
0-6: Darrow-c & Vachss scripts in all 3.00

CROSS AND THE SWITCHBLADE, THE
Spire Christian Comics (Fleming H. Revell Co.): 1972 (35-49¢)
1-Some issues have nn 2 4 6 8 10 12

CROSSFIRE
Spire Christian Comics (Fleming H. Revell Co.): 1973 (39/49¢)
nn 2 4 6 8 10 12

CROSSFIRE (Also see DNAgents)
Eclipse Comics: 5/84 - No. 17, 3/86; No. 18, 1/87 - No. 26, 2/88 ($1.50, Baxter paper) (#18-26 are B&W)
1-11,14-26: 1-DNAgents x-over; Spiegle-c/a begins 2.50
12,13-Death of Marilyn Monroe. 12-Dave Stevens-c 4.00

CROSSFIRE AND RAINBOW (Also see DNAgents)
Eclipse Comics: June, 1986 - No. 4, Sept, 1986 ($1.25, deluxe format)
1-3: Spiegle-a. 4-Dave Stevens-c 2.25

CROSSGEN...
CrossGeneration Comics
CrossGenesis (1/00) Previews CrossGen universe; cover gallery 3.00
...Primer (1/00) Wizard supplement; intro. to the CrossGen universe 2.25
...Sampler (2/00) Retailer preview book 3.00

CROSSGEN CHRONICLES
CrossGeneration Comics: June, 2000 - No. 8 ($3.95)
1-Intro. to CrossGen characters & company 4.00
1-(no cover price) same contents, customer preview 4.00
2-(3/01) George Pérez-c/a 10.00
3-8: 3-5-Pérez-a/Waid-s. 6,7-Nebres-c/a 4.00

CROSSING THE ROCKIES (See Classics Illustrated Special Issue)

CROSSOVERS, THE
CrossGeneration Comics: Feb, 2003 - Present ($2.95)
1-12-Robert Rodi-s. 1-6-Mauricet & Ernie Colon-a. 7-Staton-a begins 3.00
Vol. 1: Cross Currents (2003, $9.95) digest-sized reprints #1-6 10.00

CROSSROADS
First Comics: July, 1988 - No. 5, Nov, 1988 ($3.25, lim. series, deluxe format)
1-5 3.25

CROW, THE (Also see Caliber Presents)
Caliber Press: Feb, 1989 - No. 4, 1989 ($1.95, B&W, limited series)
1-James O'Barr-c/a/scripts 5 10 15 36 48 60
1-3-2nd printing 6.00
2-4 3 6 9 19 25 32
2-3rd printing 4.00

CROW, THE
Tundra Publishing, Ltd.: Jan, 1992 - No. 3, 1992 ($4.95, B&W, 68 pgs.)
1-3: 1-r/#1,2 of Caliber series. 2-r/#3 of Caliber series w/new material. 3-All new material 1 2 3 5 6 8

CROW, THE
Kitchen Sink Press: 1/96 - No. 3, 3/96 ($2.95, B&W)
1-3: James O'Barr-c/scripts 5.00
#0-A Cycle of Shattered Lives (12/98, $3.50) new story by O'Barr 4.00

CROW, THE
Image Comics (Todd McFarlane Prod.): Feb, 1999 - No. 10, Nov, 1999 ($2.50)
1-10: 1-Two covers by McFarlane and Kent Williams; Muth-s in all. 2-6,10-Paul Lee-a 3.00
Book 1 - Vengeance (2000, $10.95, TPB) r/#1-3,5,6 11.00
Book 2 - Evil Beyond Reach (2000, $10.95, TPB) r/#4,7-10 11.00
Todd McFarlane Presents The Crow Magazine 1 (3/00, $4.95) 5.00

CROW, THE: CITY OF ANGELS (Movie)
Kitchen Sink Press: July, 1996 - No. 3, Sept, 1996 ($2.95, limited series)
1-3: Adaptation of film; two-c (photo & illos.). 1-Vincent Perez interview 3.00

CROW, THE: FLESH AND BLOOD
Kitchen Sink Press: May, 1996 - No. 3, July, 1996 ($2.95, limited series)
1-3: O'Barr-c 3.00

CROW, THE: RAZOR - KILL THE PAIN
London Night Studios: Apr, 1998 - No. 3, July, 1998 ($2.95, B&W, lim. series)
1-3-Hartsoe-s/O'Barr-painted-c 3.00
0(10/98) Dorien painted-c, Finale (2/99) 3.00
The Lost Chapter (2/99, $4.95), Tour Book-(12/97) pin-ups; 4 diff.-c 5.00

CROW, THE: WAKING NIGHTMARES
Kitchen Sink Press: Jan, 1997 - No. 4, 1998 ($2.95, B&W, limited series)
1-4-Miran Kim-c 5.00

CROW, THE: WILD JUSTICE
Kitchen Sink Press: Oct, 1996 - No. 3, Dec, 1996 ($2.95, B&W, limited series)
1-3-Prosser-s/Adlard-a 3.00

CROWN COMICS
Golfing/McCombs Publ.: Wint, 1944-45; No. 2, Sum, 1945 - No. 19, July, 1949
1- "The Oblong Box" E.A. Poe adaptation 38 76 114 219 320 420
2,3-Baker-a; 3-Voodah by Baker 26 52 78 147 211 275
4-6-Baker-c/a; Voodah app. #4,5 29 58 87 164 237 310
7-Feldstein, Baker, Kamen-a; Baker-c 29 58 87 167 241 315
8-Baker-a; Voodah app. 24 48 72 138 199 260
9-11,13-19: Voodah in #10-19. 13-New logo 16 32 48 89 127 165
12-Master Marvin by Feldstein, Starr-a; Voodah-c 17 34 51 95 135 175
NOTE: *Bolle a-11, 13-16, 18, 19; c-11p, 15.* ***Powell*** *a-19.* ***Starr*** *a-11-13; c-11i.*

CRUCIBLE
DC Comics (Impact): Feb, 1993 - No. 6, July, 1993 ($1.25, limited series)
1-6: 1-(99¢)-Neon ink-c. 1,2-Quesada-c(p). 1-4-Quesada layouts 2.50

CRUEL AND UNUSUAL
DC Comics (Vertigo): June, 1999 - No. 4, Sept, 1999 ($2.95, limited series)
1-4-Delano & Peyer-s/McCrea-c/a 3.00

CRUSADER FROM MARS (See Tops in Adventure)
Ziff-Davis Publ. Co.: Jan-Mar, 1952 - No. 2, Fall, 1952 (Painted-c)
1-Cover is dated Spring 75 150 225 469 722 975
2-Bondage-c 55 110 165 340 520 700

CRUSADER RABBIT (TV)
Dell Publishing Co.: No. 735, Oct, 1956 - No. 805, May, 1957
Four Color 735 (#1) 32 64 96 232 361 490
Four Color 805 26 52 78 184 282 380

CRUSADERS, THE (Religious)
Chick Publications: 1974 - Vol. 17, 1988 (39/69¢, 36 pgs.)
Vol.1-Operation Bucharest ('74). Vol.2-The Broken Cross ('74). Vol.3-Scarface ('74). Vol.4-Exorcists ('75). Vol.5-Chaos ('75) 2 4 6 8 10 12
Vol.6-Primal Man? ('76)-(Disputes evolution theory). Vol.7-The Ark-(claims proof of existence, destroyed by Bolsheviks). Vol.8-The Gift-(Life story of Christ). Vol.9-Angel of Light-(Story of the Devil). Vol.10-Spellbound?-(Tells how rock music is Satanic & produced by witches). 11-Sabotage?. 12-Alberto. 13-Double Cross. 14-The Godfathers. (No. 6-14 low in distribution; loaded with religious propaganda.). 15-The Force. 16-The Four Horsemen 2 4 6 8 10 12
Vol. 17-The Prophet (low print run) 2 4 6 9 11 14

CRUSADERS (Southern Knights No. 2 on)
Guild Publications: 1982 (B&W, magazine size)
1-1st app. Southern Knights 1 3 4 6 8 10

CRUSADERS, THE (Also see Black Hood, The Jaguar, The Comet, The Fly, Legend of the Shield, The Mighty... & The Web)
DC Comics (Impact): May, 1992 - No. 8, Dec, 1992 ($1.00/$1.25)
1-8-Contains 3 Impact trading cards 2.50

CRUSADES, THE
DC Comics (Vertigo): 2001 - No. 20, Dec, 2002 ($3.95/$2.50)
...: Urban Decree ('01, $3.95) Intro. the Knight; Seagle-s/Kelley Jones-c/a 4.00
1-(5/01, $2.50) Sienkiewicz-c 3.00
2-20: 2-Moeller-c. 18-Begin $2.95-c 3.00

CRUSH
Dark Horse Comics: Oct, 2003 - No. 4, Jan, 2004 ($2.99, limited series)

Crux #18 © CRO

CSI: Crime Scene Investigation #5 © CBS Worldwide

Curse of the Spawn #12 © TMP

	GD 2.0	VG 4.0	FN 6.0	VF 8.0	VF/NM 9.0	NM- 9.2
1-4-Jason Hall-s/Sean Murphy-a						3.00

CRUSH, THE
Image Comics (Motown Machineworks): Jan, 1996 - No. 5, July, 1996 ($2.25, limited series)

1-5: Baron scripts 3.00

CRUX
CrossGeneration Comics: May, 2001 - Present ($2.95)

1-23: 1-Waid-s/Epting & Magyar-a/c. 6-Pelletier-a. 13-Dixon-s begin. 25-Cover has fake creases and other aging 3.00
Atlantis Rising Vol. 1 TPB (2002, $15.95) r/#1-6 16.00
Test of Time Vol. 2 TPB (12/02, $15.95) r/#7-12 16.00
Vol. 3: Strangers in Atlantis (2003, $15.95) r/#13-18 16.00
Vol. 4: Chaos Reborn (2003, $15.95) r/#19-24 16.00

CRY FOR DAWN
Cry For Dawn Pub.: 1989 - No. 9 ($2.25, B&W, mature)

	GD 2.0	VG 4.0	FN 6.0	VF 8.0	VF/NM 9.0	NM- 9.2
1	8	16	24	55	78	100
1-2nd printing	3	7	10	21	28	35
1-3rd printing	3	6	9	16	20	25
2	5	10	15	36	48	60
2-2nd printing	2	4	6	12	16	20
3	4	8	12	24	32	40
3a-HorrorCon Edition (1990, less than 400 printed, signed inside-c)						200.00
4-6	2	4	6	12	16	20
5-2nd printing	1	2	3	5	6	8
7-9	2	4	6	9	11	14
4-9-Signed & numbered editions	3	6	9	16	20	25
Angry Christ Comix HC (4/03, $29.99) reprints various stories; and 30pgs. new material						30.00
...Calendar (1993)						35.00

CRYIN' LION COMICS
William H. Wise Co.: Fall, 1944 - No. 3, Spring, 1945

	GD 2.0	VG 4.0	FN 6.0	VF 8.0	VF/NM 9.0	NM- 9.2
1-Funny animal	15	30	45	86	123	160
2-Hitler app.	13	26	39	76	106	135
3	10	20	30	58	77	95

CRYPT
Image Comics (Extreme): Aug, 1995 - No.2, Oct. 1995 ($2.50, limited series)

1,2-Prophet app. 2.50

CRYPTIC WRITINGS OF MEGADETH
Chaos! Comics: Sept, 1997 - No. 4, Jun, 1998 ($2.95, quarterly)

1-4-Stories based on song lyrics by Dave Mustaine 3.00

CRYPT OF DAWN (see Dawn)
Sirius: 1996 ($2.95, B&W, limited series)

1-Linsner-c/s; anthology. 5.00
2, 3 (2/98) 4.00
4,5: 4- (6/98), 5-(11/98) 3.00
Ltd. Edition 20.00

CRYPT OF SHADOWS
Marvel Comics Group: Jan, 1973 - No. 21, Nov, 1975 (#1-9 are 20¢)

	GD 2.0	VG 4.0	FN 6.0	VF 8.0	VF/NM 9.0	NM- 9.2
1-Wolverton-r/Advs. Into Terror #7	3	6	9	16	20	25
2-10: 2-Starlin/Everett-c	2	4	6	10	13	16
11-21: 18,20-Kirby-a	2	4	6	9	11	14

NOTE: ***Briefer** a-2r. **Ditko** a-13r, 18-20r. **Everett** a-6, 14r; c-2i. **Heath** a-1r. **Gil Kane** c-1, 6. **Mort Lawrence** a-1r, 8r. **Maneely** a-2r. **Moldoff** a-8. **Powell** a-12r, 14r. **Tuska** a-2r.*

CRYPT OF TERROR (Formerly Crime Patrol; Tales From the Crypt No. 20 on)
E. C. Comics: No. 17, Apr-May, 1950 - No. 19, Aug-Sept, 1950

	GD 2.0	VG 4.0	FN 6.0	VF 8.0	VF/NM 9.0	NM- 9.2
17-1st New Trend to hit stands	276	552	828	2070	3035	4000
18,19	159	318	477	1193	1747	2300

NOTE: ***Craig** c/a-17-19. **Feldstein** a-17-19. **Ingels** a-19. **Kurtzman** a-18. **Wood** a-18. Canadian reprints known; see Table of Contents.*

CSI: CRIME SCENE INVESTIGATION (Based on TV series)
IDW Publishing: Jan, 2003 - No. 5, May, 2003 ($3.99, limited series)

1-Two covers (photo & Ashley Wood); Max Allan Collins-s 4.00
2-5 4.00
...: Serial TPB (2003, $19.99) r/#1-5; bonus short story by Collins/Wood 20.00
...: Thicker Than Blood (7/03, $6.99) Mariotte-s/Rodriguez-a 7.00

CSI: CRIME SCENE INVESTIGATION - BAD RAP
IDW Publishing: Aug, 2003 - No. 5, Dec, 2003 ($3.99, limited series)

1-5-Two photo covers; Max Allan Collins-s/Rodriguez-a 4.00
TPB (3/04, $19.99) r/#1-5 20.00

CSI: CRIME SCENE INVESTIGATION - DEMON HOUSE
IDW Publishing: Feb, 2004 - No. 5, Jun, 2004 ($3.99, limited series)

1-5-Photo covers on all; Max Allan Collins-s/Rodriguez-a 4.00
TPB (10/04, $19.99) r/#1-5 20.00

CSI: CRIME SCENE INVESTIGATION - DOMINOS
IDW Publishing: Aug, 2004 - No. 5 ($3.99, limited series)

1-3-Photo covers on all; Oprisko-s/Rodriguez-a 4.00

CSI: MIAMI
IDW Publishing: Oct, 2003; Apr, 2004 ($6.99, one-shots)

... - Blood Money (9/04)-Oprisko-s/Guedes & Perkins-a 7.00
... - Smoking Gun (10/03)-Mariotte-s/Avilés & Wood-a 7.00
... - Thou Shalt Not... (4/04)-Oprisko-s/Guedes & Wood-a 7.00

C•23 (Jim Lee's...) (Based on Wizards of the Coast card game)
Image Comics: Apr, 1998 - No. 8, Nov, 1998 ($2.50)

1-8: 1,2-Choi & Mariotte-s/ Charest-c. 2-Variant-c by Jim Lee. 4-Ryan Benjamin-c. 5,8-Corben var-c. 6-Flip book with Planetary preview; Corben-c 3.00

CUD
Fantagraphics Books: 8/92 - No. 8, 12/94 ($2.25-$2.75, B&W, mature)

1-8: Terry LaBan scripts & art in all. 6-1st Eno & Plum 3.00

CUD COMICS
Dark Horse Comics: Jan, 1995 - No. 8, Sept, 1997 ($2.95, B&W)

1-8: Terry LaBan-c/a/scripts. 5-Nudity; marijuana story 3.00
Eno and Plum TPB (1997, $12.95) r/#1-4, DHP #93-95 13.00

CUPID
Marvel Comics (U.S.A.): Dec, 1949 - No. 2, Mar, 1950

	GD 2.0	VG 4.0	FN 6.0	VF 8.0	VF/NM 9.0	NM- 9.2
1-Photo-c	15	30	45	86	123	160
2-Bettie Page ('50s pin-up queen) photo-c; Powell-a (see My Love #4)	35	70	105	200	290	380

CURIO
Harry 'A' Chesler: 1930's(?) (Tabloid size, 16-20 pgs.)

	GD 2.0	VG 4.0	FN 6.0	VF 8.0	VF/NM 9.0	NM- 9.2
nn	21	42	63	118	169	220

CURLY KAYOE COMICS (Boxing)
United Features Syndicate/Dell Publ. Co.: 1946 - No. 8, 1950; Jan, 1958

	GD 2.0	VG 4.0	FN 6.0	VF 8.0	VF/NM 9.0	NM- 9.2
1 (1946)-Strip-r (Fritzi Ritz); biography of Sam Leff, Kayoe's artist	19	38	57	107	154	200
2	10	20	30	60	80	100
3-8	9	18	27	52	66	80
United Presents...(Fall, 1948)	9	18	27	52	66	80
Four Color 871 (Dell, 1/58)	4	8	12	27	36	45

CURSED
Image Comics (Top Cow): Oct, 2003 - No. 4, Feb, 2004 ($2.99)

1-4-Avery & Blevins-s/Molenaar-a 3.00

CURSE OF DRACULA, THE
Dark Horse Comics: July, 1998 - No. 3, Sept, 1998 ($2.95, limited series)

1-3-Wolfman-s/Colan-a 3.00

CURSE OF DREADWOLF
Lightning Comics: Sept, 1994 ($2.75, B&W)

1 2.75

CURSE OF RUNE (Becomes Rune, 2nd Series)
Malibu Comics (Ultraverse): May, 1995 - No. 4, Aug, 1995 ($2.50, lim. series)

1-4: 1-Two covers form one image 2.50

CURSE OF THE SPAWN
Image Comics (Todd McFarlane Prod.): Sept, 1996 - No. 29, Mar, 1999 ($1.95)

	GD 2.0	VG 4.0	FN 6.0	VF 8.0	VF/NM 9.0	NM- 9.2
1-Dwayne Turner-a(p)						6.00
1-B&W Edition	2	4	6	10	13	16
2-3						4.00
4-29: 12-Movie photo-c of Melinda Clarke (Priest)						2.50
Blood and Sutures ('99, $9.95, TPB) r/#5-8						10.00
Lost Values ('00, $10.95, TPB) r/#12-14,22; Ashley Wood-c						11.00
Sacrifice of the Soul ('99, $9.95, TPB) r/#1-4						10.00
Shades of Gray ('00, $9.95, TPB) r/#9-11,29						10.00

CURSE OF THE WEIRD
Marvel Comics: Dec, 1993 - No. 4, Mar, 1994 ($1.25, limited series)
(Pre-code horror-r)

1-4: 1,3,4-Wolverton-r(1-Eye of Doom; 3-Where Monsters Dwell; 4-The End of the World).

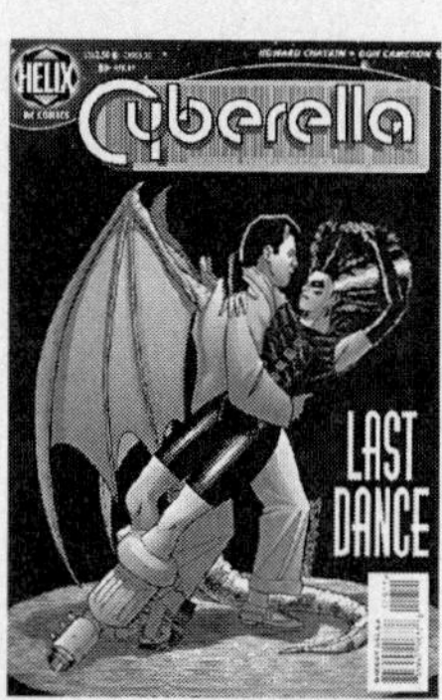

Cyberella #8 © Chaykin & Cameron

Cyberforce #24 © TCOW

Cyclone Comics #2 © Bilbara Pub.

	GD 2.0	VG 4.0	FN 6.0	VF 8.0	VF/NM 9.0	NM- 9.2

2-Orlando-r. 4-Zombie-r by Everett; painted-c 5.00
NOTE: *Briefer r-2.* ***Davis*** *a-4r.* ***Ditko*** *a-1r, 2r, 4r; c-1r.* ***Everett*** *r-1.* ***Heath*** *r-1-3.* ***Kubert*** *r-3.* ***Wolverton*** *a-1r, 3r, 4r.*

CUSTER'S LAST FIGHT
Avon Periodicals: 1950

	GD	VG	FN	VF	VF/NM	NM-
nn-Partial reprint of Cowpuncher #1	18	36	54	100	143	185

CUTEY BUNNY (See Army Surplus Komikz Featuring...)

CUTIE PIE
Junior Reader's Guild (Lev Gleason): May, 1955 - No. 3, Dec, 1955; No. 4, Feb, 1956; No. 5, Aug, 1956

	GD	VG	FN	VF	VF/NM	NM-
1	8	16	24	43	54	65
2-5: 4-Misdated 2/55	6	12	18	27	33	38

CUTTING EDGE
Marvel Comics: Dec, 1995 ($2.95)
1-Hulk-c/story; Messner-Loebs scripts 3.00

CVO: COVERT VAMPIRIC OPERATIONS
IDW Publishing: June, 2003 ($5.99, one-shot)
1-Alex Garner-s/Mindy Lee-a(p) 6.00
... - Human Touch 1 (8/04, $3.99, one-shot) Hernandez & Garner-a 4.00
TPB (9/04, $19.99) r/#1 and ... - Artifact #1-3; intro. by Garner 20.00

CVO: COVERT VAMPIRIC OPERATIONS - ARTIFACT
IDW Publishing: Oct, 2003 - No. 3, Dec, 2003 ($3.99, limited series)
1-3-Jeff Mariotte-s/Gabriel Hernandez-a/Alex Garner-c 4.00

CVO: COVERT VAMPIRIC OPERATIONS - ROGUE STATE
IDW Publishing: Nov, 2004 - Present ($3.99)
1-Jeff Mariotte-s/Vazquez-a 4.00

CYBERELLA
DC Comics (Helix): Sept, 1996 - No. 12, Aug, 1997 ($2.25/$2.50)(1st Helix series)
1-12: 1-5-Chaykin & Cameron-a. 1,2-Chaykin-c. 3-5-Cameron-c 2.50

CYBERFORCE
Image Comics (Top Cow Productions): Oct, 1992 - No. 4, 1993; No. 0, Sept, 1993 ($1.95, limited series)
1-Silvestri-c/a in all; coupon for Image Comics #0; 1st Top Cow Productions title 6.00
1-With coupon missing 2.25
2-4,0: 2-(3/93). 3-Pitt-c/story. 4-Codename: Stryke Force back-up (1st app.); foil-c. 0-(9/93)-Walt Simonson-c/a/scripts 3.00

CYBERFORCE
Image Comics (Top Cow Productions)/Top Cow Comics No. 28 on:
V2#1, Nov, 1993 - No. 35, Sept. 1997 ($1.95)
V2#1-24: 1-7-Marc Silvestri/Keith Williams-c/a. 8-McFarlane-c/a. 10-Painted variant-c exists. 18-Variant-c exists. 23-Velocity-c. 2.50
1-3: 1-Gold Logo-c. 2-Silver embossed-c. 3-Gold embossed-c 10.00
1-(99¢, 3/96, 2nd printing) 2.25
25-($3.95)-Wraparound, foil-c 4.00
26-35: 28-(11/96)-1st Top Cow Comics iss. Quesada & Palmiotti's Gabriel app. 27-Quesada & Palmiotti's Ash app. 2.50
Annual 1,2 (3/95, 8/96, $2.50, $2.95) 3.00
NOTE: *Annuals read Volume One in the indica.*

CYBERFORCE ORIGINS
Image Comics (Top Cow Productions): Jan, 1995 - No. 3, Nov, 1995 ($2.50)
1-Cyblade (1/95) 5.00
1-Cyblade (3/96, 99¢, 2nd printing) 2.25
1A-Exclusive Ed.; Tucci-c 4.00
2,3: 2-Stryker (2/95)-1st Mike Turner-a. 3-Impact 2.50
(#4) Misery (12/95, $2.95) 3.00

CYBERFORCE/STRYKEFORCE: OPPOSING FORCES (See Codename: Stryke Force #15)
Image Comics (Top Cow Productions): Sept, 1995 - No.2, Oct, 1995 ($2.50, limited series)
1,2: 2-Stryker disbands Strykeforce. 2.50

CYBERFORCE UNIVERSE SOURCEBOOK
Image Comics (Top Cow Productions): Aug, 1994/Feb, 1995 ($2.50)
1,2-Silvestri-c 2.50

CYBERFROG
Hall of Heroes: June, 1994 - No. 2, Dec, 1994 ($2.50, B&W, limited series)
1,2 3.00

CYBERFROG
Harris Comics: Feb, 1996 - No. 3, Apr, 1996 ($2.95)
0-3: Van Sciver-c/a/scripts. 2-Variant-c exists 5.00

CYBERFROG: (Title series), **Harris Comics**
--RESERVOIR FROG, 9/96 - No. 2, 10/96 ($2.95) 1,2: Van Sciver-c/a/scripts; wraparound-c 3.00
--3RD ANNIVERSARY SPECIAL, 1/97 - #2, ($2.50, B&W) 1,2 3.00
--VS. CREED, 7/97 ($2.95, B&W)1 3.00

CYBERNARY (See Deathblow #1)
Image Comics (WildStorm Productions): Nov, 1995 - No.5, Mar, 1996 ($2.50)
1-5 2.50

CYBERNARY 2.0
DC Comics (WildStorm): Sept, 2001 - No. 6, Apr, 2002 ($2.95, limited series)
1-6: Joe Harris-s/Eric Canete-a. 6-The Authority app. 3.00

CYBERPUNK
Innovation Publishing: Sept, 1989 - No. 2, Oct, 1989 ($1.95, 28 pgs.) Book 2, #1, May, 1990 - No. 2, 1990 ($2.25, 28 pgs.)
1,2, Book 2 #1,2:1,2-Ken Steacy painted-covers (Adults) 2.25

CYBERPUNK: THE SERAPHIM FILES
Innovation Publishing: Nov, 1990 - No. 2, Dec, 1990 ($2.50, 28 pgs., mature)
1,2: 1-Painted-c; story cont'd from Seraphim 2.50

CYBERPUNX
Image Comics (Extreme Studios): Mar, 1996 ($2.50)
1 3.00

CYBERRAD
Continuity Comics: 1991 - No. 7, 1992 ($2.00)(Direct sale & newsstand-c variations) V2#1, 1993 ($2.50)
1-7: 5-Glow-in-the-dark-c by N. Adams (direct sale only). 6-Contains 4 pg. fold-out poster; N. Adams layouts 2.50
V2#1-($2.95, direct sale ed.)-Die-cut-c w/B&W hologram on-c; Neal Adams sketches 3.00
V2#1-($2.50, newsstand ed.)-Without sketches 2.50

CYBERRAD DEATHWATCH 2000 (Becomes CyberRad w/#2, 7/93)
Continuity Comics: Apr, 1993 - No. 2, 1993 ($2.50)
1,2: 1-Bagged w/2 cards; Adams-c & layouts & plots. 2-Bagged w/card; Adams scripts 2.50

CYBER 7
Eclipse Comics: Mar, 1989 - #7, Sept, 1989; V2#1, Oct, 1989 - #10, 1990 ($2.00, B&W)
1-7, Book 2 #1-10: Stories translated from Japanese 2.50

CYBLADE/ GHOST RIDER
Marvel Comics /Top Cow Productions: Jan 1997 ($2.95, one-shot)
1-Devil's Reign pt. 2 4.00

CYBLADE/SHI (Also see Battle For The Independents & Shi/Cyblade: The Battle For The Independents)
Image Comics (Top Cow Productions): 1995 ($2.95, one-shot)

	GD	VG	FN	VF	VF/NM	NM-
San Diego Preview	3	6	9	16	20	25
1-($2.95)-1st app. Witchblade	2	4	6	12	16	20
1-($2.95)-variant-c; Tucci-a	2	4	6	10	12	15

CYBRID
Maximum Press: July, 1995; No. 0, Jan, 1997 ($2.95/$3.50)
1-(7/95) 3.50
0-(1/97)-Liefeld-a/script; story cont'd in Avengelyne #4 3.50

CYCLONE COMICS (Also see Whirlwind Comics)
Bilbara Publishing Co.: June, 1940 - No. 5, Nov, 1940

	GD	VG	FN	VF	VF/NM	NM-
1-Origin Tornado Tom; Volton (the human generator), Tornado Tom, Kingdom of the Moon, Mister Q begin (1st app. of each)	154	308	462	963	1482	2000
2	77	154	231	481	741	1000
3-Classic-c (scarce)	110	220	330	688	1057	1425
4	65	130	198	406	628	850
5-(Scarce)	83	166	249	519	797	1075

CYCLOPS (X-Men)
Marvel Comics: Oct, 2001 - No. 4, Jan, 2002 ($2.50, limited series)
1-4-Texeira-c/a. 1,2-Black Tom and Juggernaut app. 2.50

CYCLOPS: RETRIBUTION
Marvel Comics: 1994 ($5.95, trade paperback)
nn-r/Marvel Comics Presents #17-24 6.00

CY-GOR (See Spawn #38 for 1st app.)

Dagar, Desert Hawk #14 © FOX

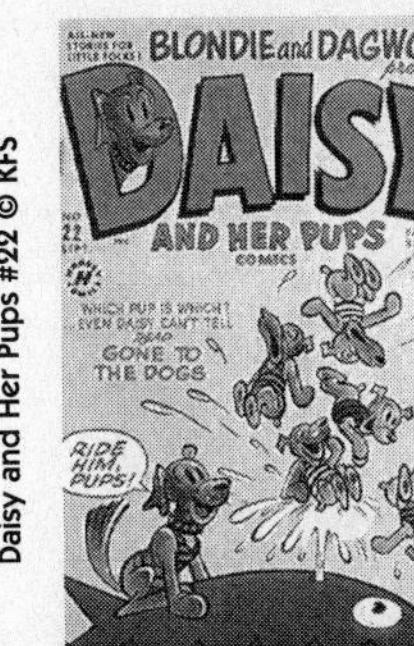

Daisy and Her Pups #22 © KFS

Dale Evans Comics #7 © DC

	GD 2.0	VG 4.0	FN 6.0	VF 8.0	VF/NM 9.0	NM- 9.2

Image Comics (Todd McFarlane Prod.): July, 1999 - No. 6, Dec, 1999 ($2.50)
1-6-Veitch-s 2.50

CYNTHIA DOYLE, NURSE IN LOVE (Formerly Sweetheart Diary)
Charlton Publications: No. 66, Oct, 1962 - No. 74, Feb, 1964
66-74 3 6 9 16 20 24

DAEMONSTORM
Caliber Comics: 1997 ($3.95, one-shot)
1-McFarlane-c 4.00

DAEMONSTORM: STORMWALKER
Caliber Comics: 1997 ($3.95, B&W, one-shot)
nn 4.00

DAFFY (Daffy Duck No. 18 on)(See Looney Tunes)
Dell Publishing Co./Gold Key No. 31-127/Whitman No. 128 on: #457, 3/53 - #30, 7-9/62; #31, 10-12/62 - #145, 6/84 (No #132,133)
Four Color 457(#1)-Elmer Fudd x-overs begin 10 20 30 73 107 140
Four Color 536,615('55) 6 12 18 40 55 70
4(1-3/56)-11('57) 5 10 15 33 44 55
12-19(1958-59) 4 8 12 22 30 38
20-40(1960-64) 3 6 9 18 23 28
41-60(1964-68) 2 4 6 14 18 22
61-90(1969-74)-Road Runner in most. 76-82-"Daffy Duck and the Road Runner" on-c
2 4 6 10 13 16
91-110 1 3 4 6 8 10
111-127 1 2 3 5 6 8
128,134-141: 139(2/82), 140(2-3/82), 141(4/82) 1 2 3 5 7 9
129(8/80),130,131 (pre-pack?) (scarce). 129-Sherlock Holmes parody-s
3 6 9 16 21 26
142-145(#90029 on-c; nd, nd code, pre-pack): 142(6/83), 143(8/83), 144(3/84), 145(6/84) 2 4 6 12 16 20
Mini-Comic 1 (1976; 3-1/4x6-1/2") 1 2 3 5 6 8
NOTE: *Reprint issues-No.41-46, 48, 50, 53-55, 58, 59, 65, 67, 69, 73, 81, 96, 103-108; 136-142, 144, 145(1/3-2/3-r). (See March of Comics No. 277, 288, 303, 313, 331, 347, 357,375, 387, 397, 402, 413, 425, 437, 460).*

DAFFY TUNES COMICS
Four-Star Publications: June, 1947; No. 12, Aug, 1947
nn 9 18 27 52 66 80
12-Al Fago-c/a; funny animal 8 16 24 46 58 70

DAGAR, DESERT HAWK (Captain Kidd No. 24 on; formerly All Great)
Fox Features Syndicate: No. 14, Feb, 1948 - No. 23, Apr, 1949 (No #17,18)
14-Tangi & Safari Cary begin; Good bondage-c/a 75 150 225 469 722 975
15,16-E. Good-a; 15-Bondage-c 46 92 138 281 428 575
19,20,22: 19-Used in **SOTI**, pg. 180 (Tangi) 40 80 120 241 363 485
21,23: 21- "Bombs & Bums Away" panel in "Flood of Death" story used in **SOTI.** 23-Bondage-c 44 88 132 268 409 550
NOTE: *Tangi by* **Kamen**-*14-16, 19, 20; c-20, 21.*

DAGAR THE INVINCIBLE (Tales of Sword & Sorcery...) (Also see Dan Curtis Giveaways & Gold Key Spotlight)
Gold Key: Oct, 1972 - No. 18, Dec, 1976; No. 19, Apr, 1982
1-Origin; intro. Villains Olstellon & Scor 4 8 12 22 30 38
2-5: 3-Intro. Graylin, Dagar's woman; Jarn x-over 2 4 6 11 14 18
6-1st Dark Gods story 2 4 6 9 11 14
7-10: 9-Intro. Torgus. 10-1st Three Witches story 2 4 6 9 11 14
11-18: 13-Durak & Torgus x-over; story continues in Dr. Spektor #15. 14-Dagar's origin retold. 18-Origin retold 1 3 4 6 8 10
19(4/82)-Origin-r/#18 6.00
NOTE: *Durak app. in 7, 12, 13. Tragg app. in 5, 11.*

DAGWOOD (Chic Young's) (Also see Blondie Comics)
Harvey Publications: Sept, 1950 - No. 140, Nov, 1965
1 15 30 45 107 164 220
2 9 18 27 60 85 110
3-10 7 14 21 46 63 80
11-20 6 12 18 38 52 65
21-30 5 10 15 36 48 60
31-50 4 8 12 29 40 50
51-70 3 7 10 21 28 35
71-100 3 6 9 16 21 26
101-128,130,135: 122-Square-bound 68 pg. giant 2 4 6 14 18 22
129,131-134,136-140-All are 68-pg. issues 3 7 10 21 28 35
NOTE: *Popeye and other one page strips appeared in early issues.*

DAI KAMIKAZE!
Now Comics: June, 1987 - No. 12, Aug, 1988 ($1.75)
1-1st app. Speed Racer; 2nd print exists 4.00
2-12 2.50

DAILY BUGLE (See Spider-Man)
Marvel Comics: Dec, 1996 - No. 3, Feb, 1997 ($2.50, B&W, limited series)
1-3-Paul Grist-s 2.50

DAISY AND DONALD (See Walt Disney Showcase No. 8)
Gold Key/Whitman No. 42 on: May, 1973 - No. 59, July, 1984 (no No. 48)
1-Barks-r/WDC&S #280,308 4 8 12 24 32 40
2-5: 4-Barks-r/WDC&S #224 2 4 6 12 16 20
6-10 2 4 6 10 12 15
11-20 1 3 4 6 8 10
21-41: 32-r/WDC&S #308 1 2 3 5 6 8
42-44 (Whitman) 2 4 6 9 11 14
45 (8/80),46-(pre-pack?)(scarce) 4 8 12 24 32 40
47-(12/80)-Only distr. in Whitman 3-pack (scarce) 6 12 18 40 55 70
48(3/81)-50(8/81): 50-r/#3 2 4 6 11 14 18
51-54: 51-Barks-r/4-Color #1150. 52-r/#2. 53(2/82), 54(4/82)
2 4 6 10 13 16
55-59-(all #90284 on-c, nd, nd code, pre-pack): 55(5/83), 56(7/83), 57(8/83), 58(8/83), 59(7/84) 2 4 6 14 18 22

DAISY & HER PUPS (Dagwood & Blondie's Dogs)(Formerly Blondie Comics #20)
Harvey Publications: No. 21, 7/51 - No. 27, 7/52; No. 8, 9/52 - No. 18, 5/54
21 (#1)-Blondie's dog Daisy and her 5 pups led by Elmer begin. Rags Rabbit app.
6 12 18 43 59 75
22-27 (#2-7): 26 has No. 6 on cover but No. 26 on inside. 23,25-The Little King app. 24-Bringing Up Father by McManus app. 25-27-Rags Rabbit app.
4 8 12 27 36 45
8-18: 8,9-Rags Rabbit app. 8,17-The Little King app. 11-The Flop Family Swan begins. 22-Cookie app. 11-Felix The Cat app. by 17,18-Popeye app.
4 8 12 24 32 40

DAISY DUCK & UNCLE SCROOGE PICNIC TIME (See Dell Giant #33)

DAISY DUCK & UNCLE SCROOGE SHOW BOAT (See Dell Giant #55)

DAISY DUCK'S DIARY (See Dynabrite Comics, & Walt Disney's C&S #298)
Dell Publishing Co.: No. 600, Nov, 1954 - No. 1247, Dec-Fef, 1961-62 (Disney)
Four Color 600 (#1) 8 16 24 55 78 100
Four Color 659, 743 (11/56) 7 14 21 46 63 80
Four Color 858 (11/57), 948 (11/58), 1247 (12-2/61-62)
6 12 18 40 55 70
Four Color 1055 (11-1/59-60), 1150 (12-1/60-61)-By Carl Barks)
10 20 30 72 104 135

DAISY HANDBOOK
Daisy Manufacturing Co.: 1946; No. 2, 1948 (10¢, pocket-size, 132 pgs.)
1-Buck Rogers, Red Ryder; Wolverton-a (2 pgs.) 39 78 117 222 324 425
2-Captain Marvel & Ibis the Invincible, Red Ryder, Boy Commandos & Robotman; Wolverton-a (2 pgs.); contains 8 pg. color catalog 39 78 117 222 324 425

DAISY MAE (See Oxydol-Dreft)

DAISY'S RED RYDER GUN BOOK
Daisy Manufacturing Co.: 1955 (25¢, pocket-size, 132 pgs.)
nn-Boy Commandos, Red Ryder; 1pg. Wolverton-a 27 54 81 152 219 285

DAKKON BLACKBLADE ON THE WORLD OF MAGIC: THE GATHERING
Acclaim Comics (Armada): June, 1996 ($5.95, one-shot)
1-Jerry Prosser scripts; Rags Morales-c/a. 6.00

DAKOTA LIL (See Fawcett Movie Comics)

DAKOTA NORTH
Marvel Comics Group: June, 1986 - No. 5, Feb, 1987
1-5 2.25

DAKTARI (Ivan Tors) (TV)
Dell Publishing Co.: July, 1967 - No. 3, Oct, 1968; No. 4, Oct, 1969
1-Marshall Thompson photo-c on all 4 8 12 29 40 50
2-4 3 7 10 21 28 35

DALE EVANS COMICS (Also see Queen of the West...)(See Boy Commandos #32)
National Periodical Publications: Sept-Oct, 1948 - No. 24, Jul-Aug, 1952 (No. 1-19: 52 pgs.)
1-Dale Evans & her horse Buttermilk begin; Sierra Smith begins by Alex Toth
96 192 288 600 925 1250
2-Alex Toth-a 46 92 138 281 428 575

Damage #4 © DC

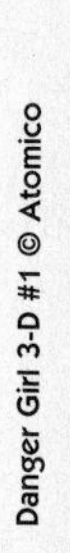
Danger Girl 3-D #1 © Atomico

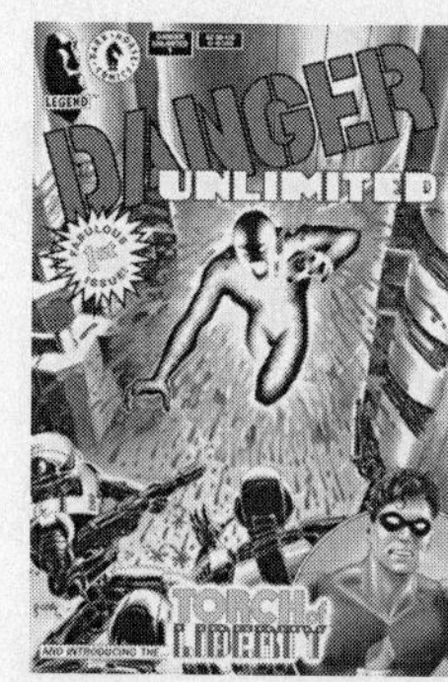

Danger Unlimited #1 © DH

	GD 2.0	VG 4.0	FN 6.0	VF 8.0	VF/NM 9.0	NM- 9.2
3-11-Alex Toth-a	32	64	96	184	267	350
12-20: 12-Target-c	18	36	54	102	146	190
21-24	19	38	57	107	154	200

NOTE: *Photo-c-1, 2, 4-14.*

DALGODA
Fantagraphics Books: Aug, 1984 - No. 8, Feb, 1986 (High quality paper)

	GD 2.0	VG 4.0	FN 6.0	VF 8.0	VF/NM 9.0	NM- 9.2
1,8: 1- Fujitake-c/a in all. 8-Alan Moore story						4.00
2-7: 2,3-Debut Grimwood's Daughter.						2.25

DALTON BOYS, THE
Avon Periodicals: 1951

	GD 2.0	VG 4.0	FN 6.0	VF 8.0	VF/NM 9.0	NM- 9.2
1-(Number on spine)-Kinstler-c	18	36	54	100	143	185

DAMAGE
DC Comics: Apr, 1994 - No. 20, Jan, 1996 ($1.75/$1.95/$2.25)

	GD 2.0	VG 4.0	FN 6.0	VF 8.0	VF/NM 9.0	NM- 9.2
1-20: 6-(9/94)-Zero Hour. 0-(10/94). 7-(11/94). 14-Ray app.						3.00

DAMAGE CONTROL (See Marvel Comics Presents #19)
Marvel Comics: 5/89 - No. 4, 8/89; V2#1, 12/89 - No. 4, 2/90 ($1.00)
V3#1, 6/91 - No. 4, 9/91 ($1.25, all are limited series)

	GD 2.0	VG 4.0	FN 6.0	VF 8.0	VF/NM 9.0	NM- 9.2
V1#1-4,V2#1-4,V3#1-4: V1#4-Wolverine app. V2#2,4-Punisher app. 1-Spider-Man app. 2-New Warriors app. 3,4-Silver Surfer app. 4-Infinity Gauntlet parody						2.50

DAMNED
Image Comics (Homage Comics): June, 1997 - No. 4, Sept, 1997 ($2.50, limited series)

	GD 2.0	VG 4.0	FN 6.0	VF 8.0	VF/NM 9.0	NM- 9.2
1-4-Steven Grant-s/Mike Zeck-c/a in all						2.50

DANCES WITH DEMONS (See Marvel Frontier Comics Unlimited)
Marvel Frontier Comics: Sept, 1993 - No. 4, Dec, 1993 ($1.95, limited series)

	GD 2.0	VG 4.0	FN 6.0	VF 8.0	VF/NM 9.0	NM- 9.2
1-($2.95)-Foil embossed-c; Charlie Adlard & Rod Ramos-a						3.00
2-4						2.25

DANDEE: Four Star Publications: 1947 (Advertised, not published)

DAN DUNN (See Crackajack Funnies, Detective Dan, Famous Feature Stories & Red Ryder)

DANDY COMICS (Also see Happy Jack Howard)
E. C. Comics: Spring, 1947 - No. 7, Spring, 1948

	GD 2.0	VG 4.0	FN 6.0	VF 8.0	VF/NM 9.0	NM- 9.2
1-Funny animal; Vince Fago-a in all; Dandy in all	38	76	114	219	320	420
2	27	54	81	152	219	285
3-7: 3-Intro Handy Andy who is c-feature #3 on	21	42	63	118	169	220

DANGER
Comic Media/Allen Hardy Assoc.: Jan, 1953 - No. 11, Aug, 1954

	GD 2.0	VG 4.0	FN 6.0	VF 8.0	VF/NM 9.0	NM- 9.2
1-Heck-c/a	23	46	69	132	191	250
2,3,5,7,9-11:	12	24	36	71	98	125
4-Marijuana cover/story	16	32	48	89	127	165
6- "Narcotics" story; begin spy theme	14	28	42	81	113	145
8-Bondage/torture/headlights panels	17	34	51	98	139	180

NOTE: *Morisi a-2, 5, 6(3), 10; c-2. Contains some reprints from Danger & Dynamite.*

DANGER (Formerly Comic Media title)
Charlton Comics Group: No. 12, June, 1955 - No. 14, Oct, 1955

	GD 2.0	VG 4.0	FN 6.0	VF 8.0	VF/NM 9.0	NM- 9.2
12(#1)	11	22	33	64	87	110
13,14: 14-r/#12	9	18	27	52	66	80

DANGER
Super Comics: 1964

	GD 2.0	VG 4.0	FN 6.0	VF 8.0	VF/NM 9.0	NM- 9.2
Super Reprint #10-12 (Black Dwarf; #10-r/Great Comics #1 by Novack. #11-r/Johnny Danger #1. #12-r/Red Seal #14), #15-r/Spy Cases #26. #16-Unpublished Chesler material (Yankee Girl), #17-r/Scoop #8 (Capt. Courage & Enchanted Dagger), #18(nd)-r/Guns Against Gangsters #5 (Gun-Master, Annie Oakley, The Chameleon; L.B. Cole-r)	2	4	6	12	16	20

DANGER AND ADVENTURE (Formerly This Magazine Is Haunted; Robin Hood and His Merry Men No. 28 on)
Charlton Comics: No. 22, Feb, 1955 - No. 27, Feb, 1956

	GD 2.0	VG 4.0	FN 6.0	VF 8.0	VF/NM 9.0	NM- 9.2
22-Ibis the Invincible-c/story; Nyoka app.; last pre-code issue	11	22	33	64	87	110
23-Lance O'Casey-c/sty; Nyoka app.; Ditko-a thru #27	13	26	39	74	102	130
24-27: 24-Mike Danger & Johnny Adventure begin	9	18	27	52	66	80

DANGER GIRL (Also see Cliffhanger #0)
Image Comics (Cliffhanger Productions): Mar, 1998 - No. 4, Dec, 1998;
DC Comics (Cliffhanger Prod.): No. 5, July, 1999 - No. 7, Feb, 2001

	GD 2.0	VG 4.0	FN 6.0	VF 8.0	VF/NM 9.0	NM- 9.2
Preview-Bagged in DV8 #14 Voyager Pack						4.00
Preview Gold Edition						8.00
1-($2.95) Hartnell & Campbell-s/Campbell/Garner-a	1	2	3	5	6	8
1-($4.95) Chromium cover						45.00
1-American Entertainment Ed.						8.00
1-American Entertainment Gold Ed., 1-Tourbook edition						10.00
1-"Danger-sized" ed.; over-sized format	3	6	9	18	24	30
2-($2.50)						4.00
2-Smoking Gun variant cover, 2-Platinum Ed., 2-Dynamic Forces Omnichrome variant-c	2	4	6	10	13	16
2-Gold foil cover						9.00
2-Ruby red foil cover						90.00
3,4: 3-c by Campbell, Charest and Adam Hughes. 4-Big knife variant-c						3.00
3,5: 3-Gold foil cover. 5-DF Bikini variant-c						5.00
4-6						3.00
7-($5.95) Wraparound gatefold-c; Last issue						6.00
...: Hawaiian Punch (5/03, $4.95) Campbell-c; Phil Noto-a						5.00
San Diego Preview (8/98, B&W) flip book w/Wildcats preview						5.00
Sketchbook (2001, $6.95) Campbell-a; sketches for comics, toys, games						7.00
...Special (2/00, $3.50) art by Campbell, Chiodo, and Art Adams						3.50
... 3-D #1 (4/03, $4.95, bagged with 3-D glasses) r/ Preview & #1 in 3-D						5.00
...: Viva Las Danger (1/04, $4.95) Noto-a/Campbell-c						5.00
... :The Dangerous Collection nn(8/98; r-#1)						6.00
... :The Dangerous Collection 2,3: 2-(11/98, $5.95) r/#2,3. 3-('99) r/#4,5						6.00
... :The Dangerous Collection nn, 2-($10.00) Gold foil logo						10.00
... :The Ultimate Collection HC ($29.95) r/#1-7; intro by Bruce Campbell						30.00
... :The Ultimate Collection SC ($19.95) r/#1-7; intro by Bruce Campbell						20.00

DANGER GIRL KAMIKAZE
DC Comics (Cliffhanger): Nov, 2001 - No. 2, Dec., 2001 ($2.95, lim. series)

	GD 2.0	VG 4.0	FN 6.0	VF 8.0	VF/NM 9.0	NM- 9.2
1,2-Tommy Yune-s/a						3.00

DANGER IS OUR BUSINESS!
Toby Press: 1953(Dec.) - No. 10, June, 1955

	GD 2.0	VG 4.0	FN 6.0	VF 8.0	VF/NM 9.0	NM- 9.2
1-Captain Comet by Williamson/Frazetta-a, 6 pgs. (science fiction)	44	88	132	268	409	550
2	14	28	42	79	110	140
3-10	11	22	33	64	87	110
I.W. Reprint #9('64)-Williamson/Frazetta-r/#1; Kinstler-c	9	18	27	65	93	120

DANGER IS THEIR BUSINESS (Also see A-1 Comic)
Magazine Enterprises: No. 50, 1952

	GD 2.0	VG 4.0	FN 6.0	VF 8.0	VF/NM 9.0	NM- 9.2
A-1 50-Powell-a	14	28	42	79	110	140

DANGER MAN (TV)
Dell Publishing Co.: No. 1231, Sept-Nov, 1961

	GD 2.0	VG 4.0	FN 6.0	VF 8.0	VF/NM 9.0	NM- 9.2
Four Color 1231-Patrick McGoohan photo-c	12	24	36	86	131	175

DANGER TRAIL (Also see Showcase #50, 51)
National Periodical Publ.: July-Aug, 1950 - No. 5, Mar-Apr, 1951 (52 pgs.)

	GD 2.0	VG 4.0	FN 6.0	VF 8.0	VF/NM 9.0	NM- 9.2
1-King Faraday begins, ends #4; Toth-a in all	123	246	369	769	1185	1600
2	87	174	261	544	835	1125
3-(Rare) one of the rarest early '50s DCs	123	246	369	769	1185	1600
4,5: 5-Johnny Peril-c/story (moves to Sensation Comics #107); new logo (also see Comic Cavalcade #15-29)	69	138	207	431	666	900

DANGER TRAIL
DC Comics: Apr, 1993 - No. 4, July, 1993 ($1.50, limited series)

	GD 2.0	VG 4.0	FN 6.0	VF 8.0	VF/NM 9.0	NM- 9.2
1-4: Gulacy-c on all						2.25

DANGER UNLIMITED (See San Diego Comic Con Comics #2 & Torch of Liberty Special)
Dark Horse (Legend): Feb, 1994 - No. 4, May, 1994 ($2.00, limited series)

	GD 2.0	VG 4.0	FN 6.0	VF 8.0	VF/NM 9.0	NM- 9.2
1-4: Byrne-c/a/scripts in all; origin stories of both original team (Doc Danger, Thermal, Miss Mirage, & Hunk) & future team (Thermal, Belebet, & Caucus). 1-Intro Torch of Liberty & Golgotha (cameo) in back-up story. 4-Hellboy & Torch of Liberty cameo in lead story						2.50
TPB (1995, $14.95)-r/#1-4; includes last pg. originally cut from #4						15.00

DAN HASTINGS (See Syndicate Features)

DANIEL BOONE (See The Exploits of..., Fighting... Frontier Scout...,The Legends of... & March of Comics No. 306)
Dell Publishing Co.: No. 1163, Mar-May, 1961

	GD 2.0	VG 4.0	FN 6.0	VF 8.0	VF/NM 9.0	NM- 9.2
Four Color 1163-Marsh-a	6	12	18	43	59	75

DANIEL BOONE (TV) (See March of Comics No. 306)
Gold Key: Jan, 1965 - No. 15, Apr, 1969 (All have Fess Parker photo-c)

	GD 2.0	VG 4.0	FN 6.0	VF 8.0	VF/NM 9.0	NM- 9.2
1	10	20	30	70	100	130
2	6	12	18	40	55	70
3-5	5	10	15	33	44	55

Daredevil #50 © MAR

Daredevil #181 © MAR

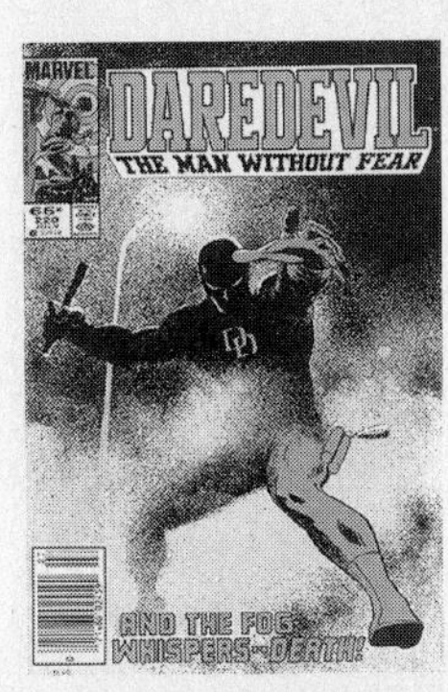

Daredevil #220 © MAR

	GD 2.0	VG 4.0	FN 6.0	VF 8.0	VF/NM 9.0	NM- 9.2
6-15	4	8	12	22	30	38

DAN'L BOONE
Sussex Publ. Co.: Sept, 1955 - No. 8, Sept, 1957

	GD 2.0	VG 4.0	FN 6.0	VF 8.0	VF/NM 9.0	NM- 9.2
1	15	30	45	83	117	150
2	10	20	30	56	73	90
3-8	8	16	24	40	50	60

DANNY BLAZE (...Firefighter) (Nature Boy No. 3 on)
Charlton Comics: Aug, 1955 - No. 2, Oct, 1955

	GD 2.0	VG 4.0	FN 6.0	VF 8.0	VF/NM 9.0	NM- 9.2
1	12	24	36	69	95	120
2	9	18	27	52	66	80

DANNY DINGLE (See Sparkler Comics)
United Features Syndicate: No. 17, 1940

	GD 2.0	VG 4.0	FN 6.0	VF 8.0	VF/NM 9.0	NM- 9.2
Single Series 17	27	54	81	154	222	290

DANNY THOMAS SHOW, THE (TV)
Dell Publishing Co.: No. 1180, Apr-June, 1961 - No. 1249, Dec-Feb, 1961-62

	GD 2.0	VG 4.0	FN 6.0	VF 8.0	VF/NM 9.0	NM- 9.2
Four Color 1180-Toth-a, photo-c	18	36	54	129	197	265
Four Color 1249-Manning-a, photo-c	17	34	51	121	186	250

DARBY O'GILL & THE LITTLE PEOPLE (Movie)(See Movie Comics)
Dell Publishing Co.: 1959 (Disney)

	GD 2.0	VG 4.0	FN 6.0	VF 8.0	VF/NM 9.0	NM- 9.2
Four Color 1024-Toth-a; photo-c.	11	22	33	80	120	160

DAREDEVIL (...& the Black Widow #92-107 on-c only; see Giant-Size...,Marvel Advs., Marvel Graphic Novel #24, Marvel Super Heroes, '66 & Spider-Man &...)
Marvel Comics Group: Apr, 1964 - No. 380, Oct, 1998

	GD 2.0	VG 4.0	FN 6.0	VF 8.0	VF/NM 9.0	NM- 9.2
1-Origin/1st app. Daredevil; intro Foggy Nelson & Karen Page; death of Battling Murdock; Bill Everett-c/a; reprinted in Marvel Super Heroes #1 (1966)	229	458	687	2004	3402	4800
2-Fantastic Four cameo; 2nd app. Electro (Spidey villain); Thing guest star	66	132	198	561	906	1250
3-Origin & 1st app. The Owl (villain)	43	86	129	344	535	725
4-Origin & 1st app. The Purple Man	36	72	108	270	423	575
5-Minor costume change; Wood-a begins	28	56	84	203	312	420
6-Mr. Fear app.	19	38	57	134	205	275
7-Daredevil battles Sub-Mariner & dons red costume for 1st time (4/65)	63	126	189	536	868	1200
8-10: 8-Origin/1st app. Stilt-Man	16	32	48	112	171	230
11-15: 12-1st app. Plunderer; Ka-Zar app. 13-Facts about Ka-Zar's origin; Kirby-a	10	20	30	73	107	140
16,17-Spider-Man x-over. 16-1st Romita-a on Spider-Man (5/66)	14	28	42	102	156	210
18-Origin & 1st app. Gladiator	10	20	30	67	96	125
19,20	8	16	24	53	74	95
21-26,28-30: 24-Ka-Zar app.	6	12	18	43	59	75
27-Spider-Man x-over	7	14	21	51	71	90
31-40: 38-Fantastic Four x-over; cont'd in F.F. #73. 39-1st Exterminator (later becomes Death-Stalker)	5	10	15	36	48	60
41,42,44-49: 41-Death Mike Murdock. 42-1st app. Jester. 45-Statue of Liberty photo-c	4	8	12	27	36	45
43-Daredevil battles Captain America; origin partially retold	6	12	18	40	55	70
50-53: 50-52-B. Smith-a. 53-Origin retold; last 12¢ issue	4	8	12	29	40	50
54-56,58-60: 54-Spider-Man cameo. 56-1st app. Death's Head (9/69); story cont'd in #57 (not same as new Death's Head)	3	6	9	18	24	30
57-Reveals i.d. to Karen Page; Death's Head app.	4	8	12	22	30	38
61-76,78-80: 79-Stan Lee cameo. 80-Last 15¢ issue	3	6	9	18	23	28
77-Spider-Man x-over	4	8	12	24	32	40
81-(52 pgs.) Black Widow begins (11/71).	4	8	12	24	32	40
82,84-99: 87-Electro-c/story	2	4	6	14	18	22
83-B. Smith layouts/Weiss-p	3	6	9	16	20	25
100-Origin retold	3	6	9	19	25	32
101-104,106-120: 107-Starlin-c; Thanos cameo. 113-1st brief app. Deathstalker. 114-1st full app. Deathstalker	2	4	6	11	14	18
105-Origin Moondragon by Starlin (12/73); Thanos cameo in flashback (early app.)	2	4	6	14	18	22
121-130,137: 124-1st app. Copperhead; Black Widow leaves. 126-1st new Torpedo	2	4	6	9	11	14
131-Origin/1st app. new Bullseye (see Nick Fury #15)	6	12	18	38	52	65
132-2nd app. new Bullseye (Regular 25¢ edition)	4	8	12	24	32	40
132-(30¢-c variant, limited distribution)(4/76)	5	10	15	36	48	60
133-136-(Regular 25¢ editions)	2	4	6	8	10	12
133-136-(30¢-c variants, limited distribution)(5-8/76)	2	4	6	11	14	18
138-Ghost Rider-c/story; Death's Head is reincarnated; Byrne-a	2	4	6	11	14	18
139,140,142-145,147-157: 142-Nova cameo. 147,148-(Reg. 30¢-c). 150-1st app. Paladin. 151-Reveals i.d. to Heather Glenn. 155-Black Widow returns. 156-The '60s Daredevil app.	2	4	6	8	10	12
141,146-Bullseye app.	3	6	9	16	20	25
146-(35¢-c variant, limited distribution)	4	8	12	22	30	38
147,148-(35¢-c variants, limited distribution)	2	4	6	11	14	18
158-Frank Miller art begins (5/79); origin/death of Deathstalker (see Captain America #235 & Spectacular Spider-Man #27	7	14	21	51	71	90
159	4	8	12	25	33	42
160,161-Bullseye app.	3	7	10	21	28	35
162-Ditko-a; no Miller-a	1	3	4	6	8	10
163,164: 163-Hulk cameo. 164-Origin retold	3	6	9	16	20	24
165-167,170	2	4	6	12	16	20
168-Origin/1st app. Elektra; 1st Miller scripts	9	18	27	60	85	110
169-2nd Electra app.	4	8	12	24	32	40
171-173	2	4	6	11	14	18
174,175-Elektra app.	2	4	6	12	16	20
176-180-Elektra app. 178-Cage app. 179-Anti-smoking issue mentioned in the Congressional Record	2	4	6	11	14	18
181-(52 pgs.)-Death of Elektra; Punisher cameo out of costume	3	7	10	21	28	35
182-184-Punisher app. by Miller (drug issues)	2	4	6	10	12	15
185-191: 187-New Black Widow. 189-Death of Stick. 190-($1.00, 52 pgs.)-Elektra returns, part origin. 191-Last Miller Daredevil	1	3	4	6	8	10
192-195,198,199,201-207,209-218,220-226,234-237: 226-Frank Miller plots begin						3.50
196-Wolverine-c/app.	2	4	6	9	11	14
197-Bullseye-c/app.; 1st app. Yuriko Oyama (who becomes Lady Deathstrike)						5.00
200,238: 200-Bullseye app. 238-Mutant Massacre; Sabretooth app.						6.00
208,219,228-233: 208-Harlan Ellison scripts borrowed from Avengers TV episode "House that Jack Built". 219-Miller-c/script. 228-233-Last Miller scripts						4.00
227-Miller scripts begin						6.00
239,240,242-247						3.00
241-Todd McFarlane-a(p)						5.00
248,249-Wolverine app.						6.00
250,251,253,258: 250-1st app. Bullet. 258-Intro The Bengal (a villain)						3.00
252,260 (52 pgs.): 252-Fall of the Mutants. 260-Typhoid Mary app.						5.00
254-Origin & 1st app. Typhoid Mary (5/88)	1	2	3	4	5	8
255,256,258: 255,256-2nd/3rd app. Typhoid Mary. 259-Typhoid Mary app.						5.00
257-Punisher app. (x-over w/Punisher #10)	1	3	4	6	8	10
261-281,283-294,296-299,301-304,307-318: 270-1st app. Black Heart. 272-Intro Shotgun (villain). 281-Silver Surfer cameo. 283-Capt. America app. 297-Typhoid Mary app.; Kingpin storyline begins. 292-D.G. Chichester scripts begin. 293-Punisher app. 303-Re-intro the Owl. 304-Garney-c/a. 309-Punisher-c.; Terror app. 310-Calypso-c						2.50
282,295,300,305,306: 282-Silver Surfer app. 295-Ghost Rider app. 300-($2.00, 52 pgs.) Kingpin story ends. 305,306-Spider-Man-c						3.00
319-Prologue to Fall From Grace; Elektra returns						6.00
319-2nd printing w/black-c						2.50
320-Fall From Grace Pt 1						5.00
321-Fall From Grace regular ed.; Pt 2; new costume; Venom app.						3.00
321-($2.00)-Wraparound Glow-in-the-dark-c ed.						5.00
322-Fall From Grace Pt 3; Eddie Brock app.						4.00
323,324-Fall From Grace Pt. 4 & 5: 323-Vs. Venom-c/story. 324-Morbius-c/story						4.00
325-($2.50, 52 pgs.)-Fall From Grace ends; contains bound-in poster						4.00
326-349,351-353: 326-New logo. 328-Bound-in trading card sheet. 330-Gambit app. 348-1st Cary Nord art in DD (1/96);"Dec" on-c. 353-Karl Kesel scripts; Nord-c/a begins; Mr. Hyde-c/app.						2.50
350-($2.95)-Double-sized						3.00
350-($3.50)-Double-sized; gold ink-c						3.50
354-374,376-379: Kesel scripts, Nord-c/a in all. 354-$1.50-c begins. 355-Larry Hama layouts; Pyro app. 358-Mysterio-c/app. 359-Absorbing Man cameo. 360-Absorbing Man-c/app. 361-Black Widow-c/app. 363,366-370-Gene Colan-a(p). 368-Omega Red-c/app. 372-Ghost Rider-c/app. 376-379-"Flying Blind", DD goes undercover for S.H.I.E.L.D.						2.50
375-($2.99) Wraparound-c; Mr. Fear-c/app.						3.00
380-($2.99) Final issue; flashback story						4.00
Special 1(9/67, 25¢, 68 pgs.)-New art/story	6	12	18	40	55	70
Special 2,3: 2(2/71, 25¢, 52 pgs.)-Entire book has Powell/Wood-r; Wood-c. 3(1/72, 52 pgs.)-Reprints	3	6	9	16	20	25
Annual 4(10/76)	1	3	4	6	8	10
Annual 4(#5)-10: ('89-94 68 pgs.)-5-Atlantis Attacks. 6-Sutton-a. 7-Guice-a (7 pgs.). 8-Deathlok-c/story. 9-Polybagged w/card						3.00
... :Born Again TPB ($17.95)-r/#227-233; Miller-s/Mazzucchelli-a & new-c						20.00

Daredevil V2#56 © MAR

Daredevil: Father #1 © MAR

Daredevil Comics #17 © LEV

GD VG FN VF VF/NM NM-
2.0 4.0 6.0 8.0 9.0 9.2

GD VG FN VF VF/NM NM-
2.0 4.0 6.0 8.0 9.0 9.2

.../Deadpool- (Annual '97, $2.99)-Wraparound-c 3.00
...:Fall From Grace TPB ($19.95)-r/#319-325 20.00
... :Gang War TPB ($15.95)-r/#169-172,180; Miller-s/a(p) 16.00
...Legends: (Vol. 4) Typhoid Mary TPB (2003, $19.95) r/#254-257,259-263 20.00
... :Love's Labors Lost TPB ($19.99)-r/#215-217,219-222,225,226; Mazzucchelli-c 20.00
.../Punisher TPB (1988, $4.95)-r/D.D. #182-184 (all printings) 5.00
...Visionaries: Frank Miller Vol. 1 TPB ($17.95) r/#158-161,163-167 18.00
...Visionaries: Frank Miller Vol. 2 TPB ($24.95) r/#168-182; new Miller-c 25.00
...Visionaries: Frank Miller Vol. 3 TPB ($24.95) r/#183-191, What If? #28,35 & Bizarre Adventures #28; new Miller-c 25.00
... Vs. Bullseye Vol. 1 TPB (2004, $15.99) r/#131-132,146,169,181,191 16.00
Wizard Ace Edition: Daredevil (Vol. 1) #1 (4/03, $13.99) Acetate Campbell-c 14.00

NOTE: ***Art Adams** c-238p, 239.* ***Austin** a-191i; c-151i, 200i.* ***John Buscema** a-136, 137p, 234p, 235p; c-86p, 136i, 137p, 142, 219.* ***Byrne** c-200p, 201, 203, 223.* ***Capullo** a-286p.* ***Colan** a(p)-20-49, 53-82, 84-98, 100, 110, 112, 124, 153, 154, 156, 157, 363, 366-370, Spec. 1p; c(p)-20-42, 44-49, 53-60, 71, 92, 98, 138, 153, 154, 156, 157, Annual 1.* ***Craig** a-50i, 52i.* ***Ditko** a-162, 234p, 235p, 264p; c-162.* ***Everett** c/a-1; inks-21, 83.* ***Garney** c/a-304.* ***Gil Kane** a-141p, 146-148p, 151p; c(p)-85, 90, 91, 93, 94, 115, 116, 119, 120, 125-128, 133, 139, 147, 152.* ***Kirby** c-2-4, 5p, 12p, 13p, 43, 136p.* ***Layton** c-202.* ***Miller** scripts-168-182, 183(part), 184-191, 219, 227-233; a-158-161p, 163-184p, 191p; c-158-161p, 163-184p, 185-189, 190p, 191.* ***Orlando** a-2-4p.* ***Powell** a-9p, 11p, Special 1r, 2r.* ***Simonson** c-199, 236p.* ***B. Smith** a-236p; c-51p, 52p, 217.* ***Starlin** a-105p.* ***Steranko** c-44i.* ***Tuska** a-39i, 145p.* ***Williamson** a(i)-237, 239, 240, 243, 248-257, 259-282, 283(part), 284, 285, 287, 288(part), 289(part), 293-300; c(i)-237, 243, 244, 248-257, 259-263, 265-278, 280-289, Annual 8.* ***Wood** a-5-8, 9i, 10, 11i, Spec. 2i; c-5i, 6-11, 164i.*

DAREDEVIL (Volume 2) (Marvel Knights)
Marvel Comics: Nov, 1998 - Present ($2.50)

1-Kevin Smith-s/Quesada & Palmiotti-a 12.00
1-($6.95) DF Edition w/Quesada & Palmiotti var.-c 15.00
1-($6.00) DF Sketch Ed. w/B&W-c 10.00
2-Two covers by Campbell and Quesada/Palmiotti 9.00
3-8: 4,5-Bullseye app. 8-Spider-Man-c/app.; last Smith-s 6.00
9-15: 9-11-David Mack-s; intro Echo. 12-Begin $2.99-c; Haynes-a. 13,14-Quesada-a 3.00
16-19-Direct editions; Bendis-s/Mack-c/painted-a 3.00
18,19,21,22-Newsstand editions with variant cover logo "Marvel Unlimited Featuring..." 3.00
20-($3.50) Gale-s/Winslade-a; back-up by Stan Lee-s/Colan-a; Mack-c 3.50
21-40: 21-25-Gale-s. 26-38-Bendis-s/Maleev-a. 32-Daredevil's ID revealed. 35-Spider-Man-c/app. 38-Iron Fist & Luke Cage app. 40-Dodson-a 3.50
41-(25¢-c) Begins "Lowlife" arc; Maleev-a; intro Milla Donovan 2.25
41-(Newsstand edition with 2.99¢-c) 4.00
42-45-"Lowlife" arc; Maleev-a 2.25
46-50-($2.99). 46-Typhoid Mary returns. 49-Bullseye app. 50-Art panels by various incl. Romita, Colan, Mack, Janson, Oeming, Quesada 3.00
51-64,66,67: 51-55-Mack-s/a; Echo app. 54-Wolverine-c/app. 61-64-Black Widow app. 3.00
65-($3.99) 40th Anniversary issue; Land-c; art by Maleev, Horn, Bachalo and others 4.00
...2099 #1 (11/04, $2.99) Kirkman-s/Moline-a 3.00
TPB ($9.95) r/#1-3 10.00
...Vol. 1 HC (2001, $29.99, with dustjacket) r/#1-11,13-15 30.00
...Vol. 1 HC (2003, $29.99, with dustjacket) r/#1-11,13-15; larger page size 30.00
...Vol. 2 HC (2002, $29.99, with dustjacket) r/#26-37; afterword by Bendis 30.00
...Vol. 3 HC (2004, $29.99, with dustjacket) r/#38-50; Maleev sketch pages 30.00
(Vol. 1) Visionaries TPB ($19.95) r/#1-8; Ben Affleck intro. 20.00
(Vol. 2) Parts of a Hole TPB (1/02, $17.95) r/#9-15; David Mack intro. 18.00
(Vol. 3) Wake Up TPB (7/02, $9.99) r/#16-19 10.00
...Vol. 4: Underboss TPB (8/02, $14.99) r/#26-31 15.00
...Vol. 5: Out TPB (2003, $19.99) r/#32-40 20.00
...Vol. 6: Lowlife TPB (2003, $13.99) r/#41-45 14.00
...Vol. 7: Hardcore TPB (2003, $13.99) r/#46-50 14.00
...Vol. 8: Echo - Vision Quest TPB (2004, $13.99) r/#51-55; David Mack-s/a 14.00
...Vol. 9: King of Hell's Kitchen TPB (2004, $13.99) r/#56-60 14.00
...Vol. 10: The Widow TPB (2004, $16.99) r/#61-65 & Vol. 1 #81 17.00

DAREDEVIL/ BATMAN (Also see Batman/Daredevil)
Marvel Comics/ DC Comics: 1997 ($5.99, one-shot)

nn-McDaniel-c/a 6.00

DAREDEVIL/ ELEKTRA: LOVE AND WAR
Marvel Comics: 2003 ($29.99, hardcover with dust jacket)

HC-Larger-size reprints of Daredevil: Love and War (Marvel Graphic Novel #24) & Elektra: Assassin; Frank Miller-s; Bill Sienkiewicz-a 30.00

DAREDEVIL: FATHER
Marvel Comics: June, 2004 - No. 5 ($3.50, limited series)

1-Quesada-s/a; Isanove-painted color 3.50

DAREDEVIL: NINJA
Marvel Comics: Dec, 2000 - No. 3, Feb, 2001 ($2.99, limited series)

1-3: Bendis-s/Haynes-a 3.00
1-Dynamic Forces foil-c 10.00
TPB (7/01, $12.95) r/#1-3 with cover and sketch gallery 13.00

DAREDEVIL/ SHI (See Shi/ Daredevil)
Marvel Comics/ Crusade Comics: Feb,1997 ($2.95, limited series)

1 3.00

DAREDEVIL/ SPIDER-MAN
Marvel Comics: Jan, 2001 - No. 4, Apr, 2001 ($2.99, limited series)

1-4-Jenkins-s/Winslade-a/Alex Ross-c; Stilt Man app. 3.00
TPB (8/01, $12.95) r/#1-4; Ross-c 13.00

DAREDEVIL THE MAN WITHOUT FEAR
Marvel Comics: Oct, 1993 - No. 5, Feb, 1994 ($2.95, limited series) (foil embossed covers)

1-Miller scripts; Romita, Jr./Williamson-c/a 6.00
2-5 5.00
Hardcover 100.00
Trade paperback 20.00

DAREDEVIL: THE MOVIE (2003 movie adaptation)
Marvel Comics: March, 2003 ($3.50/$12.95, one-shot)

1-Photo-c of Ben Affleck; Bruce Jones-s/Manuel Garcia-a 3.50
TPB ($12.95) r/movie adaptation; Daredevil #32; Ultimate Daredevil & Elektra #1 and Spider-Man's Tangled Web #4; photo-c of Ben Affleck 13.00

DAREDEVIL: THE TARGET (Daredevil Bullseye on cover)
Marvel Comics: Jan, 2003 - No. 4, ($3.50, limited series)

1-Kevin Smith-s/Glenn Fabry-c/a 3.50

DAREDEVIL: YELLOW
Marvel Comics: Aug, 2001 - No. 6, Jan, 2002 ($3.50, limited series)

1-6-Jeph Loeb-s/Tim Sale-a/c; origin & yellow costume days retold 3.50
HC (5/02, $29.95) r/#1-6 with dustjacket; intro by Stan Lee; sketch pages 30.00
Daredevil Legends Vol. 1: Daredevil Yellow (2002, $14.99, TPB) r/#1-6 15.00

DAREDEVIL COMICS (See Silver Streak Comics)
Lev Gleason Publications (Funnies, Inc. No. 1): July, 1941 - No. 134, Sept, 1956
(Charles Biro stories)

	GD 2.0	VG 4.0	FN 6.0	VF 8.0	VF/NM 9.0	NM- 9.2
1-No. 1 titled "Daredevil Battles Hitler"; The Silver Streak, Lance Hale, Cloud Curtis, Dickey Dean, Pirate Prince team up w/Daredevil and battle Hitler; Daredevil battles the Claw; Origin of Hitler feature story. Hitler photo app. on-c	1176	2352	3524	8820	14,410	20,000
2-London, Pat Patriot (by Reed Crandall), Nightro, Real American No. 1 (by Briefer #2-11), Dickie Dean, Pirate Prince, & Times Square begin; intro. & only app. The Pioneer, Champion of America	303	606	909	1970	3185	4400
3-Origin of 13	200	400	600	1250	1925	2600
4	173	346	519	1081	1666	2250
5-Intro. Sniffer & Jinx; Ghost vs. Claw begins by Bob Wood, ends #20	131	262	393	819	1260	1700
6-(#7 in indicia)	112	224	336	700	1075	1450
7-10: 8-Nightro ends	92	184	276	575	888	1200
11-London, Pat Patriot end; classic bondage/torture-c	123	246	369	769	1185	1600
12-Origin of The Claw; Scoop Scuttle by Wolverton begins (2-4 pgs.), ends #22, not in #21	142	284	426	888	1369	1850
13-Intro. of Little Wise Guys (10/42)	119	238	357	744	1147	1550
14	65	130	195	406	623	840
15-Death of Meatball	94	188	282	588	907	1225
16,17	60	120	180	375	580	785
18-New origin of Daredevil (not same as Silver Streak #6). Hitler, Mussolini Tojo and Mickey Mouse app. on-c	129	258	387	806	1241	1675
19,20	51	102	153	311	473	635
21-Reprints cover of Silver Streak #6 (on inside) plus intro. of The Claw from Silver Streak #1	90	180	270	563	869	1175
22-30: 27-Bondage/torture-c	40	80	120	244	372	500
31-Death of The Claw	81	162	243	506	778	1050
32-37,39-41: 35-Two Daredevil stories begin, end #68 (35-41 are 64 pgs.)	31	62	93	178	257	340
38-Origin Daredevil retold from #18	44	88	132	268	409	550
42-50: 42-Intro. Kilroy in Daredevil	26	52	78	147	211	275
51-69-Last Daredevil issue (12/50)	18	36	54	102	146	190
70-Little Wise Guys take over book; McWilliams-a; Hot Rock Flanagan begins, ends #80	11	22	33	66	91	115
71-78,81	9	18	27	52	66	80
79,80: 79-Daredevil returns. 80-Daredevil x-over	9	18	27	54	70	85
82,90,100: 82,90-One pg. Frazetta ad in both	9	18	27	52	66	80
83-89,91-99,101-134	8	16	24	46	58	70

NOTE: ***Biro** c/a-all?* ***Bolle** a-125.* ***Maurer** a-75.* ***McWilliams** a-73, 75, 79, 80.*

DARIA JONTAK

Daring Mystery Comics #1 © MAR

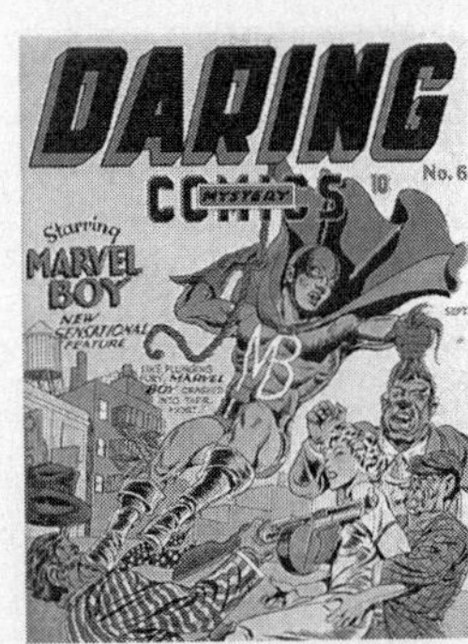

Daring Mystery Comics #6 © MAR

Darkchylde The Diary #1 © Randy Queen

	GD 2.0	VG 4.0	FN 6.0	VF 8.0	VF/NM 9.0	NM- 9.2

JMJ Media Group: Jan, 2001 ($4.99)
1-Matt Busch-s/a 5.00

DARING ADVENTURES (Also see Approved Comics)
St. John Publishing Co.: Nov, 1953 (25¢, 3-D, came w/glasses)
1 (3-D)-Reprints lead story from Son of Sinbad #1 by Kubert 35 70 105 200 290 380

DARING ADVENTURES
I.W. Enterprises/Super Comics: 1963 - 1964
I. W. Reprint #8-r/Fight Comics #53; Matt Baker-a 6 12 18 38 52 65
I.W. Reprint #9-r/Blue Bolt #115; Disbrow-a(3) 6 12 18 40 55 70
Super Reprint #10,11('63)-r/Dynamic #24,16; 11-Marijuana story; Yankee Boy app.; Mac Raboy-a 4 8 12 27 36 45
Super Reprint #12('64)-Phantom Lady from Fox (r/#14 only? w/splash pg. omitted); Matt Baker-a 12 24 36 82 124 165
Super Reprint #15('64)-r/Hooded Menace #1 8 16 24 53 74 95
Super Reprint #16('64)-r/Dynamic #12 4 8 12 24 32 40
Super Reprint #17('64)-r/Green Lama #3 by Raboy 5 10 15 33 44 55
Super Reprint #18-Origin Atlas from unpublished Atlas Comics #1 4 8 12 29 40 50

DARING COMICS (Formerly Daring Mystery) (Jeanie Comics No. 13 on)
Timely Comics (HPC): No. 9, Fall, 1944 - No. 12, Fall, 1945
9-Human Torch, Toro & Sub-Mariner begin 131 262 393 819 1260 1700
10-12: 10-The Angel only app. 11,12-The Destroyer app. 106 212 318 663 1019 1375
NOTE: ***Schomburg** c-9-11. **Sekowsky** c-12? Human Torch, Toro & Sub-Mariner c-9-12.*

DARING CONFESSIONS (Formerly Youthful Hearts)
Youthful Magazines: No. 4, 11/52 - No. 7, 5/53; No. 8, 10/53
4-Doug Wildey-a; Tony Curtis story 16 32 48 89 127 165
5-8: 5-Ray Anthony photo on-c. 6,8-Wildey-a 12 24 36 69 95 120

DARING ESCAPES
Image Comics: Sept, 1998 - No. 4, Mar, 1999 ($2.95/$2.50, mini-series)
1-Houdini; following app. in Spawn #19,20 3.00
2-4-($2.50) 2.50

DARING LOVE (Radiant Love No. 2 on)
Gilmor Magazines: Sept-Oct, 1953
1–Steve Ditko's 1st published work (1st drawn was Fantastic Fears #5)(Also see Black Magic #27)(scarce) 52 104 156 317 484 650

DARING LOVE (Formerly Youthful Romances)
Ribage/Pix: No. 15, 12/52; No. 16, 2/53-c, 4/53-Indicia; No. 17-4/53-c & indicia
15 11 22 33 64 87 110
16,17: 17-Photo-c 10 20 30 58 77 95
NOTE: ***Colletta** a-15. **Wildey** a-17.*

DARING LOVE STORIES (See Fox Giants)

DARING MYSTERY COMICS (Comedy Comics No. 9 on; title changed to Daring Comics with No. 9)
Timely Comics (TPI 1-6/TCI 7,8): 1/40 - No. 5, 6/40; No. 6, 9/40; No. 7, 4/41 - No. 8, 1/42
1-Origin The Fiery Mask (1st app.) by Joe Simon; Monako, Prince of Magic (1st app.), John Steele, Soldier of Fortune (1st app.), Doc Denton (1st app.) begin; Flash Foster & Barney Mullen, Sea Rover only app; bondage-c 1825 3650 5475 13,800 22,400 31,000
2-(Rare)-Origin The Phantom Bullet (1st & only app.); The Laughing Mask & Mr. E only app.; Trojak the Tiger Man begins, ends #6; Zephyr Jones & K-4 & His Sky Devils app., also #4 1000 2000 3000 7000 11,250 15,500
3-The Phantom Reporter, Dale of FBI, Captain Strong only app.; Breeze Barton, Marvex the Super-Robot, The Purple Mask begin 497 994 1491 3479 5590 7700
4,5: 4-Last Purple Mask; Whirlwind Carter begins; Dan Gorman, G-Man app. 5-The Falcon begins (1st app.); The Fiery Mask, Little Hercules app. by Sagendorf in the Segar style; bondage-c 331 662 993 2152 3476 4800
6-Origin & only app. Marvel Boy by S&K; Flying Flame, Dynaman, & Stuporman only app.; The Fiery Mask by S&K; S&K-c 423 846 1269 2790 4495 6200
7-Origin The Blue Diamond, Captain Daring by S&K, The Fin by Everett, The Challenger, The Silver Scorpion & The Thunderer by Burgos; Mr. Millions app 345 690 1035 2243 3622 5000
8-Origin Citizen V; Last Fin, Silver Scorpion, Capt. Daring by Borth, Blue Diamond & The Thunderer; Kirby & part solo Simon-c; Rudy the Robot only app.; Citizen V, Fin & Silver Scorpion continue in Comedy #9 300 600 900 1875 2888 3900
NOTE: ***Schomburg** c-1-4, 7. **Simon** a-2, 3, 5. Cover features: 1-Fiery Mask; 2-Phantom Bullet; 3-Purple Mask; 4-G-Man; 5-The Falcon; 6-Marvel Boy; 7, 8-Multiple characters.*

DARING NEW ADVENTURES OF SUPERGIRL, THE
DC Comics: Nov, 1982 - No. 13, Nov, 1983 (Supergirl No. 14 on)
1-Origin retold; Lois Lane back-ups in #2-12 1 2 3 5 6 8
2-13: 8,9-Doom Patrol app. 13-New costume; flag-c 4.00
NOTE: ***Buckler** c-1p, 2p. **Giffen** c-3p, 4p. **Gil Kane** c-6, ,8, 9, 11-13.*

DARK, THE
Continum Comics: Nov, 1990 - No. 4, Feb, 1993; V2#1, May, 1993 - V2#7, Apr?, 1994 ($1.95)
1-4: 1-Bright-p; Panosian, Hanna-i; Stroman-c. 2-(1/92)-Stroman-c/a(p). 4-Perez-c & part-i 3.00
V2#1,V2#2-6: V2#1-Red foil Bart Sears-c. V2#1-Red non-foil variant-c. V2#1-2nd printing w/blue foil Bart Sears-c. V2#2-Stroman/Bryant-a. 3-Perez-c(i). 3-6-Foil-c. 4-Perez-c & part-i; bound-in trading cards. 5,6-(2,3/94)-Perez-c(i). 7-(B&W)-Perez-c(i) 2.25
Convention Book 1 ,2(Fall/94, 10/94)-Perez-c 2.25

DARK ANGEL (Formerly Hell's Angel)
Marvel Comics UK, Ltd.: No. 6, Dec, 1992 - No. 16, Dec, 1993 ($1.75)
6-8,13-16: 6-Excalibur-c/story. 8-Psylocke app. 2.25
9-12-Wolverine/X-Men app. 3.00

DARK ANGEL: PHOENIX RESURRECTION (Kia Asamiya's...)
Image Comics: May, 2000 - No. 4, Oct, 2001 ($2.95)
1-4-Kia Asamiya-s/a. 3-Van Fleet variant-c 3.00

DARKCHYLDE (Also see Dreams of the Darkchylde)
Maximum Press #1-3/ Image Comics #4 on: June, 1996 - No. 5, Sept, 1997 ($2.95/ $2.50)
1-Randy Queen-c/a/scripts; "Roses" cover 6.00
1-American Entertainment Edition-wraparound-c 6.00
1-"Fashion magazine-style" variant-c 1 2 3 4 5 7
1-Special Comicon Edition (contents of #1) Winged devil variant-c 5.00
1-($2.50)-Remastered Ed.-wraparound-c 4.00
2(Reg-c),2-Spiderweb and Moon variant-c 6.00
3(Reg-c),3-"Kalvin Clein" variant-c by Drew 3.00
4,5(Reg-c), 4-Variant-c 4.00
5-B&W Edition, 5-Dynamic Forces Gold Ed. 8.00
0-(3/98, $2.50) 2.50
0-Remastered (1/01, $2.95) includes Darkchylde: Redemption preview 3.00
1/2-WIzard offer 4.00
1/2 Variant-c 6.00
... The Descent TPB ('98, $19.95) r/#1-5; bagged with Darkchylde The Legacy Preview Special 1998; listed price is for TPB only 20.00

DARKCHYLDE LAST ISSUE SPECIAL
Darkchylde Entertainment: June, 2002 ($3.95)
1-Wraparound-c; cover gallery 4.00

DARKCHYLDE REDEMPTION
Darkchylde Entertainment: Feb, 2001 - No. 2, Dec, 2001 ($2.95)
1,2: 1-Wraparound-c 3.00
1-Dynamic Forces alternate-c 6.00
1-Dynamic Forces chrome-c 16.00

DARKCHYLDE SKETCH BOOK
Image Comics (Dynamic Forces): 1998
1-Regular-c 8.00
1-DarkChrome cover 16.00

DARKCHYLDE SUMMER SWIMSUIT SPECTACULAR
DC Comics (WildStorm): Aug, 1999 ($3.95, one-shot)
1-Pin-up art by various 4.00

DARKCHYLDE SWIMSUIT ILLUSTRATED
Image Comics: 1998 ($2.50, one-shot)
1-Pin-up art by various 2.50
1-(6.95) Variant cover 7.00
1-Chromium cover 15.00

DARKCHYLDE THE DIARY
Image Comics: June, 1997 ($2.50, one-shot)
1-Queen-c/s/ art by various 2.50
1-Variant-c 5.00
1-Holochrome variant-c 8.00

DARKCHYLDE THE LEGACY
Image Comics/DC (WildStorm) #3 on: Aug, 1998 - No. 3, June, 1999 ($2.50)
1-3: 1-Queen-c. 2-Two covers by Queen and Art Adams 2.50

DARK CLAW ADVENTURES
DC Comics (Amalgam): June, 1997 ($1.95, one-shot)

Dark Days #2 © Niles & Templesmith

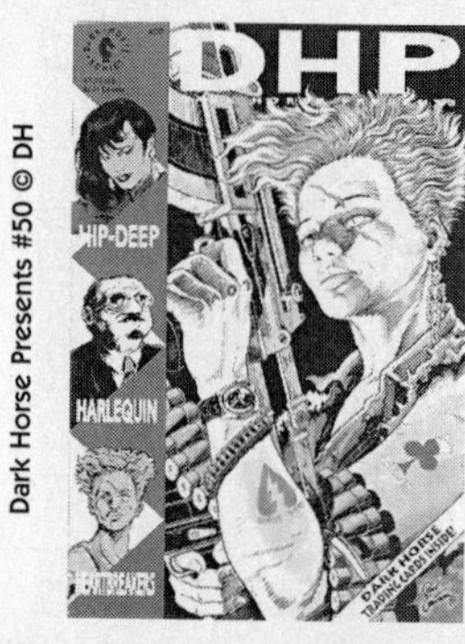

Dark Horse Presents #50 © DH

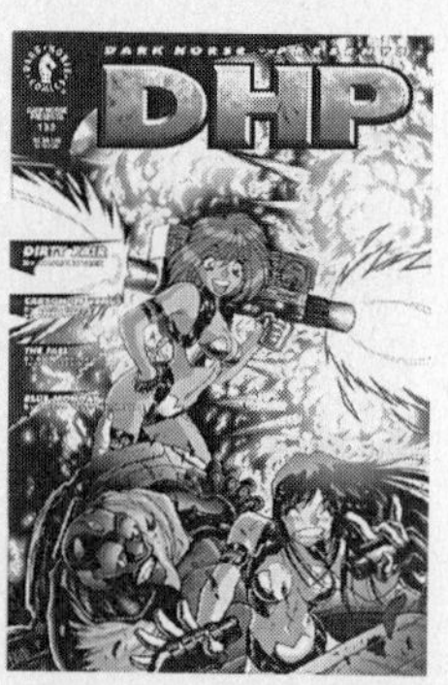

Dark Horse Presents #133 © DH

GD 2.0 | VG 4.0 | FN 6.0 | VF 8.0 | VF/NM 9.0 | NM- 9.2

1-Templeton-c/s/a & Burchett-a 2.50

DARK CROSSINGS: DARK CLOUDS RISING
Image Comics (Top Cow): June, 2000; Oct, 2000 ($5.95, limited series)

1-Witchblade, Darkness, Tomb Raider crossover; Dwayne Turner-a 6.00
1-(Dark Clouds Overhead) 6.00

DARK CRYSTAL, THE (Movie)
Marvel Comics Group: April, 1983 - No. 2, May, 1983

1,2-Adaptation of film 3.00

DARK DAYS (See 30 Days of Night)
IDW Publishing: June, 2003 - No. 6, Dec, 2003 ($3.99, limited series)

1-6-Sequel to 30 Days of Night; Niles-s/Templesmith-a 4.00
1-Retailer variant (Diamond/Alliance Fort Wayne 5/03 summit) 15.00
TPB (2004, $19.99) r/#1-6; cover gallery; intro. by Eric Red 20.00

DARKDEVIL (See Spider-Girl)
Marvel Comics: Nov, 2000 - No. 3, Jan, 2001 ($2.99, limited series)

1-3: 1-Origin of Darkdevil; Kingpin-c/app. 3.00

DARK DOMINION
Defiant: Oct, 1993 - No. 10, July, 1994 ($2.50)

1-10-Len Wein scripts begin. 4-Free extra 16 pgs. 7-9-J.G. Jones-c/a. 10-Pre-Schism issue; Shooter/Wein script; John Ridgway-a 2.50

DARKER IMAGE (Also see Deathblow, The Maxx, & Bloodwulf)
Image Comics: Mar, 1993 ($1.95, one-shot)

1-The Maxx by Sam Kieth begins; Bloodwulf by Rob Liefeld & Deathblow by Jim Lee begin (both 1st app.); polybagged w/1 of 3 cards by Kieth, Lee or Liefeld 2.50
1-B&W interior pgs. w/silver foil logo 6.00

DARKEWOOD
Aircel Publishing: 1987 - No. 5, 1988 ($2.00, 28pgs, limited series)

1-5 2.25

DARK FANTASIES
Dark Fantasy: 1994 - No. 8, 1995 ($2.95)

1-Test print Run (3,000)-Linsner-c 1 2 3 5 6 8
1-Linsner-c 5.00
2-8: 2-4 (Deluxe), 2-4 (Regular), 5-8 (Deluxe; $3.95) 4.00
5-8 (Regular; $3.50) 3.50

DARK GUARD
Marvel Comics UK: Oct, 1993 - No. 4, Jan, 1994 ($1.75)

1-($2.95)-Foil stamped-c 3.00
2-4 2.25

DARKHAWK
Marvel Comics: Mar, 1991 - No. 50, Apr, 1995 ($1.00/$1.25/$1.50)

1-Origin/1st app. Darkhawk; Hobgoblin cameo 4.00
2,3,13,14: 2-Spider-Man & Hobgoblin app. 3-Spider-Man & Hobgoblin app. 13,14-Venom-c/story 3.00
4-12,15-24,26-49: 6-Capt. America & Daredevil x-over. 9-Punisher app. 11,12-Tombstone app. 19-Spider-Man & Brotherhood of Evil Mutants-c/story. 20-Spider-Man app. 22-Ghost Rider-c/story. 23-Origin begins, ends #25. 27-New Warriors-c/story. 35-Begin 3 part Venom story. 39-Bound-in trading card sheet 2.25
25,50: (52 pgs.)-Red holo-grafx foil-c w/double gatefold poster; origin of Darkhawk armor 3.00
Annual 1-3 ('92-'94,68 pgs.)-1-Vs. Iron Man. 2 -Polybagged w/card 3.00

DARKHOLD: PAGES FROM THE BOOK OF SINS (See Midnight Sons Unlimited)
Marvel Comics (Midnight Sons imprint #15 on): Oct, 1992 - No. 16, Jan, 1994

1-($2.75, 52 pgs.)-Polybagged w/poster by Andy & Adam Kubert; part 4 of Rise of the Midnight Sons storyline 3.00
2-10,12-16: 3-Reintro Modred the Mystic (see Marvel Chillers #1). 4-Sabertooth-c/sty. 5-Punisher & Ghost Rider app. 15-Spot varnish-c. 15,16-Siege of Darkness pt. 4&12 2.25
11-($2.25)-Outer-c is a Darkhold envelope made of black parchment w/gold ink 2.50

DARK HORSE BOOK OF HAUNTINGS, THE
Dark Horse Comics: Aug, 2003 ($14.95, hardcover, 9 1/4" x 6 1/4")

nn-Short stories by various incl. Mignola (Hellboy), Thompson, Dorkin, Russell; Gianni-c 15.00

DARK HORSE BOOK OF WITCHCRAFT, THE
Dark Horse Comics: June, 2004 ($14.95, hardcover, 9 1/4" x 6 1/4")

nn-Short stories by various incl. Mignola (Hellboy), Thompson, Dorkin, Millionaire; Gianni-c 15.00

DARK HORSE CLASSICS (Title series), **Dark Horse Comics**

1992 ($3.95, B&W, 52 pgs. nn's): The Last of the Mohicans. 20,000 Leagues Under the Sea 4.00

DARK HORSE CLASSICS, 5/96 ($2.95) 1-r/Predator: Jungle Tales 3.00
--ALIENS VERSUS PREDATOR, 2/97 - No. 6, 7/97 ($2.95,) 1-6: r/Aliens Versus Predator 3.00
--GODZILLA: KING OF THE MONSTERS, 4/98 ($2.95) 1-6: 1-r/Godzilla: Color Special; Art Adams-a 3.00
--STAR WARS: DARK EMPIRE, 3/97 - No. 6, 8/97 ($2.95) 1-6: r/Star Wars: Dark Empire 3.00
--TERROR OF GODZILLA, 8/98 - No. 6, 1/99 ($2.95) 1-6-r/manga Godzilla in color; Art Adams-c 3.00

DARK HORSE COMICS
Dark Horse Comics: Aug, 1992 - No. 25, Sept, 1994 ($2.50)

1-Dorman double gategold painted-c; Predator, Robocop, Timecop (3-part) & Renegade stories begin 3.00
2-6,11-25: 2-Mignola-c. 3-Begin 3-part Aliens story; Aliens-c. 4-Predator-c. 6-Begin 4 part Robocop story. 12-Begin 2-part Aliens & 3-part Predator stories. 13-Thing From Another World begins w/Nino-a(i). 15-Begin 2-part Aliens: Cargo story. 16-Begin 3-part Predator story. 17-Begin 3-part StarWars: Droids story & 3-part Aliens: Alien story; Droids-c. 19-Begin 2-part X story; X cover 2.50
7-Begin Star Wars: Tales of the Jedi 3-part story 1 2 3 4 5 7
8-1st app. X and begins; begin 4-part James Bond 6.00
9,10: 9-Star Wars ends. 10-X ends; Begin 3-part Predator & Godzilla stories 4.00
NOTE: *Art Adams c-11.*

DARK HORSE DOWN UNDER
Dark Horse Comics: June, 1994 - No. 3, Oct, 1994 ($2.50, B&W, limited series)

1-3 2.50

DARK HORSE MAVERICK
Dark Horse Comics: July, 2000; July, 2001; Sept, 2002 (B&W, annual)

2000-($3.95) Short stories by Miller, Chadwick, Sakai, Pearson 4.00
2001-($4.99) Short stories by Sakai, Wagner and others; Miller-c 5.00
...: Happy Endings (9/02, $9.95) Short stories by Bendis, Oeming, Mahfood, Mignola, Miller, Kieth and others; Miller-c 10.00

DARK HORSE MONSTERS
Dark Horse Comics: Feb, 1997 ($2.95, one-shot)

1-reprints 3.00

DARK HORSE PRESENTS
Dark Horse Comics: July, 1986 - No. 157, Sept, 2000 ($1.50-$2.95, B&W)

1-1st app. Concrete by Paul Chadwick 2 4 6 9 11 14
1-2nd printing (1988, $1.50) 2.25
1-Silver ink 3rd printing (1992, $2.25)-Says 2nd printing inside 2.25
2-9: 2-6,9-Concrete app. 6.00
10-1st app. The Mask; Concrete app. 2 4 6 10 12 15
11-19,21-23: 11-19,21-Mask stories. 12,14,16,18,22-Concrete app. 15(2/88). 17-All Roachmill issue 6.00
20-(68 pgs.)-Concrete, Flaming Carrot, Mask 1 3 4 6 8 10
24-Origin Aliens-c/story (11/88); Mr. Monster app. 2 4 6 11 14 18
25-31,33,37-41,44,45,47-49: 28-(52 pgs.)-Concrete app.; Mr. Monster story (homage to Graham Ingels). 33-(44 pgs.). 38-Concrete. 40-(52 pgs.)-1st Argosy story. 44-Crash Ryan. 48,49-Contain 2 trading cards 3.00
32,34,35: 32-(68 pgs.)-Annual; Concrete, American. 34-Aliens-c/story. 35-Predator-c/app. 4.00
36-1st Aliens Vs. Predator story; painted-c, 36-Variant line drawn-c 5.00
42,43,46: 42,43-Aliens-c/stories. 46-Prequel to new Predator II mini-series 3.00
50-S/F story by Perez; contains 2 trading cards 4.00
51-53-Sin City by Frank Miller, parts 2-4; 51,53-Miller-c (see D.H.P. Fifth Anniversary Special for pt. 1) 4.00
54-62: 54-(9/91) The Next Men begins (1st app.) by Byrne; Miller-a/Morrow-c. Homocide by Morrow (also in #55). 55-2nd app. The Next Men; parts 5 & 6 of Sin City by Miller; Miller-c. 56-(68 pg. annual)-part 7 of Sin City by Miller; part prologue to Aliens: Genocide; Next Men by Byrne. 57-(52 pgs.)-Part 8 of Sin City by Miller; Next Men by Byrne; Byrne & Miller-c; Alien Fire story; swipes cover to Daredevil #1. 58,59-Alien Fire stories.58-61- Part 9-12 Sin City by Miller. 62-Last Sin City (entire book by Miller, c/a; 52 pgs.) 5.00
63-66,68-79,81-84-($2.25): 64-Dr. Giggles begins (1st app.), ends #66; Boris the Bear story. 66-New Concrete-c/story by Chadwick. 71-Begin 3 part Dominque story by Jim Balent; Balent-c. 72-(3/93)-Begin 3-part Eudaemon (1st app.) story by Nelson 3.00
67-($3.95, 68 pgs.)-Begin 3-part prelude to Predator: Race War mini-series; Oscar Wilde adapt. by Russell 4.00
80-Art Adams-c/a (Monkeyman & O'Brien) 4.00
85-87,92-99: 85-Begin $2.50-c. 92, 93, 95-Too Much Coffee Man 3.00
88-91-Hellboy by Mignola. 4.00
NOTE: *There are 5 different Dark Horse Presents #100 issues*
100-1-Intro Lance Blastoff by Miller; Milk & Cheese by Evan Dorkin 4.00
100-2-100-5: 100-2-Hellboy-c by Wrightson; Hellboy story by Mignola; includes Roberta Gregory & Paul Pope stories. 100-3-Darrow-c, Concrete by Chadwick; Pekar story.

Dark Knight Strikes Again #2 © DC

Dark Minds #1 © Dreamwave Prods.

The Darkness #9 © TCOW

GD 2.0 | VG 4.0 | FN 6.0 | VF 8.0 | VF/NM 9.0 | NM- 9.2

100-4-Gibbons-c: Miller story, Geary story/a. 100-5-Allred-c, Adams, Dorkin, Pope 3.00
101-125: 101-Aliens c/a by Wrightson, story by Paul Pope. 103-Kirby gatefold-c. 106-Big Blown Baby by Bill Wray. 107-Mignola-c/a. 109-Begin $2.95-c; Paul Pope-c. 110-Ed Brubaker-a/s. 114-Flip books begin; Lance Blastoff by Miller; Star Slammers by Simonson. 115-Miller-c. 117-Aliens-c/app. 118-Evan Dorkin-c/a. 119-Monkeyman & O'Brien. 124-Predator. 125-Nocturnals 3.00
126-($3.95, 48 pgs.)-Flip book: Nocturnals, Starship Troopers 4.00
127-134,136-140: 127-Nocturnals. 129-The Hammer. 132-134-Warren-a 3.00
135-($3.50) The Mark 3.50
141-All Buffy the Vampire Slayer issue 4.00
142-149: 142-Mignola-c. 143-Tarzan. 146,147-Aliens vs. Predator. 148-Xena 3.00
150-($4.50) Buffy-c by Green; Buffy, Concrete, Fish Police app. 4.50
151-157: 151-Hellboy-c/app. 153-155-Angel flip-c. 156,157-Witch's Son 3.00
Annual 1997 ($4.95, 64 pgs.)-Flip book; Body Bags, Aliens. Pearson-c; stories by Allred & Stephens, Pope, Smith & Morrow 1 2 3 5 6 8
Annual 1998 ($4.95, 64 pgs.) 1st Buffy the Vampire Slayer comic app.; Hellboy story and cover by Mignola 1 2 3 4 5 7
Annual 1999 (7/99, $4.95) Stories of Xena, Hellboy, Ghost, Luke Skywalker, Groo, Concrete, the Mask and Usagi Yojimbo in their youth. 5.00
Annual 2000 ($4.95) Girl sidekicks; Chiodo-c and flip photo Buffy-c 5.00
...Aliens Platinum Edition (1992)-r/DHP #24,43,43,56 & Special 11.00
...Fifth Anniversary Special nn (4/91, $9.95)-Part 1 of Sin City by Frank Miller (c/a); Aliens, Aliens vs. Predator, Concrete, Roachmill, Give Me Liberty & The American stories 10.00
The One Trick Rip-off (1997, $12.95, TPB)-r/stories from #101-112 13.00
NOTE: ***Geary*** *a-59, 60.* ***Miller*** *a-Special, 51-53, 55-62; c-59-62, 100-1; c-51, 53, 55, 59-62, 100-1.* ***Moebius*** *a-63; c-63, 70.* ***Vess*** *a-78; c-75, 78.*

DARK KNIGHT (See Batman: The Dark Knight Returns & Legends of the...)

DARK KNIGHT STRIKES AGAIN, THE (Also see Batman: The Dark Knight Returns)
DC Comics: 2001 - No. 3, 2002 ($7.95, prestige format, limited series)
1-Frank Miller-s/a/c; sequel 3 years after Dark Knight Returns; 2 covers 8.00
2,3 8.00
HC (2002, $29.95) intro. by Miller; sketch pages and exclusive artwork; cover has 3 1/4" tall partial dustjacket 30.00
SC (2002, $19.95) intro. by Miller; sketch pages 20.00

DARKLON THE MYSTIC (Also see Eerie Magazine #79,80)
Pacific Comics: Oct, 1983 (one-shot)
1-Starlin-c/a(r) 4.00

DARKMAN (Movie)
Marvel Comics: Sept, 1990; Oct, 1990 - No. 3, Dec, 1990 ($1.50)
1 (9/90, $2.25, B&W mag., 68 pgs.)-Adaptation of film 3.00
1-3: Reprints B&W magazine 2.25

DARKMAN
Marvel Comics: V2#1, Apr, 1993 -No. 6, Sept, 1993 ($2.95, limited series)
V2#1 ($3.95, 52 pgs.) 4.00
2-6 3.00

DARK MANSION OF FORBIDDEN LOVE, THE (Becomes Forbidden Tales of Dark Mansion No. 5 on)
National Periodical Publ.: Sept-Oct, 1971 - No. 4, Mar-Apr, 1972 (52 pgs.)
1 17 34 51 121 186 250
2-4: 2-Adams-c. 3-Jeff Jones-c 8 16 24 55 78 100

DARKMINDS
Image Comics (Dreamwave Prod.): July, 1998 - No. 8, Apr, 1999 ($2.50)
1-Manga; Pat Lee-s/a; 2 covers 1 3 4 6 8 10
1-2nd printing 2.50
2, 0-(1/99, $5.00) Story and sketch pages 5.00
3-8, 1/2-(5/99, $2.50) Story and sketch pages 2.50
... Collected 1,2 (1/99,3/99; $7.95) 1-r/#1-3. 2-r/#4-6 8.00
... Collected 3 (5/99; $5.95) r/#7,8 6.00

DARKMINDS (Volume 2)
Image Comics (Dreamwave Prod.): Feb, 2000 - No. 10, Apr, 2001 ($2.50)
1-10-Pat Lee-c 2.50
0-(7/00) Origin of Mai Murasaki; sketchbook 2.50

DARKMINDS: MACROPOLIS
Image Comics (Dreamwave Prod.): Jan, 2002 - No. 4, Dec, 2002 ($2.95)
Preview (8/01) Flip book w/Banished Knights preview 2.25
1-4-Jo Chen-a 3.00

DARKMINDS: MACROPOLIS (Volume 2)
Dreamwave Prod.: Sept, 2003 - No. 4, Jul, 2004 ($2.95)
1-4-Chris Sarracini-s/Kwang Mook Lim-a 3.00

DARKMINDS / WITCHBLADE (Also see Witchblade/Dark Minds)
Image Comics (Top Cow/Dreamwave Prod.): Aug, 2000 ($5.95, one-shot)
1-Wohl-s/Pat Lee-a; two covers by Silvestri and Lee 6.00

DARK MYSTERIES (Thrilling Tales of Horror & Suspense)
"Master" - "Merit" Publications: June-July, 1951 - No. 24, July, 1955
1-Wood-c/a (8 pgs.) 113 226 339 706 1091 1475
2-Wood/Harrison-c/a (8 pgs.) 77 154 231 481 741 1000
3-9: 7-Dismemberment, hypo blood drainage stys 43 86 129 262 399 535
10-Cannibalism story; witch burning-c 47 94 141 287 436 585
11-13,15-18: 11-Severed head panels. 13-Dismemberment-c/story. 17-The Old Gravedigger host 39 78 117 222 324 425
14-Several E.C. Craig swipes 39 78 117 227 331 435
19-Injury-to-eye panel; E.C. swipe; torture-c 45 90 135 275 418 560
20-Female bondage, blood drainage story 40 80 120 244 372 500
21,22: 21-Devil-c. 22-Last pre-code issue, misdated 3/54 instead of 3/55 27 54 81 154 222 290
23,24 21 42 63 121 173 225
NOTE: ***Cameron*** *a-1, 2.* ***Myron Fass*** *c/a-21.* ***Harrison*** *a-3, 7; c-3.* ***Hollingsworth*** *a-7-17, 20, 21, 23.* ***Wildey*** *a-5. Woodish art by* ***Fleishman****-9; c-10, 14-17. Bondage c-10, 18, 19.*

DARK NEMESIS (VILLAINS) (See Teen Titans)
DC Comics: Feb, 1998 ($1.95, one-shot)
1-Jurgens-s/Pearson-c 2.25

DARKNESS, THE (See Witchblade #10)
Image Comics (Top Cow Productions): Dec, 1996 - No. 40, Aug, 2001 ($2.50)
Special Preview Edition-(7/96, B&W)-Ennis script; Silvestri-a(p) 2 4 6 10 13 16
0 2 4 6 8 10 12
0-Gold Edition 16.00
1/2 1 3 4 6 8 10
1/2-Christmas-c 3 6 9 16 20 24
1/2-(3/01, $2.95) r/#1/2 w/new 6 pg. story & Silvestri-c 3.00
1-Ennis-s/Silvestri-a, 1-Black variant-c 2 4 6 10 12 15
1-Platinum variant-c 20.00
1-DF Green variant-c 12.00
1,2: 1-Fan Club Ed. 1 3 4 6 8 10
3-5 6.00
6-10: 9,10-Witchblade "Family Ties" x-over pt. 2,3 4.00
7-Variant-c w/concubine 1 2 3 5 7 9
8-American Entertainment 6.00
8-10-American Entertainment Gold Ed. 7.00
11-Regular Ed.; Ennis-s/Silverstri & D-Tron-c 3.00
11-Nine (non-chromium) variant-c (Benitez, Cabrera, the Hildebrandts, Finch, Keown, Peterson, Portacio, Tan, Turner 4.50
11-Chromium-c by Silvestri & Batt 20.00
12-19: 13-Begin Benitez-a(p) 3.00
20-24,26-40: 34-Ripclaw app. 2.50
25-($3.99) Two covers (Benitez, Silvestri) 4.00
25-Chromium-c variant by Silvestri 8.00
Holiday Pin-up-American Entertainment 5.00
Holiday Pin-up Gold Ed.-American Entertainment 7.00
Infinity #1 (8/99, $3.50) Lobdell-s 3.50
Prelude-American Entertainment 4.00
Prelude Gold Ed.-American Entertainment 9.00
Wizard ACE Ed.- Reprints #1 2 4 6 8 10 12
...Collected Editions #1-4 ($4.95,TPB) 1-r/#1,2. 2-r/#3,4. 3- r/#5,6. 4- r/#7,8 6.00
...Collected Editions #5,6 ($5.95, TPB)5- r/#11,12. 6-r/#13,14 6.00
Deluxe Collected Editions #1 (12/98, $14.95, TPB) r/#1-6 & Preview 15.00
...: Heart of Darkness (2001, $14.95, TPB) r/ #7,8, 11-14 15.00
...: Wanted Dead 1 (8/03, $2.99) Texiera-a/Tieri-s 3.00

DARKNESS (Volume 2)
Image Comics (Top Cow Productions): Dec, 2002 - Present ($2.99)
1-17: 1-6-Jenkins-s/Keown-a 3.00
...: Resurrection TPB (2/04, $16.99) r/#1-6 & Vol. 1 #40 17.00
.../ The Incredible Hulk (7/04, $2.99) Keown-a/Jenkins-s 3.00

DARKNESS/ BATMAN
Image Comics (Top Cow Productions): Aug, 1999 ($5.95, one-shot)
1-Silvestri, Finch, Lansing-a(p) 6.00

DARKNESS FALLS, THE TRAGIC LIFE OF MATILDA DIXON
Dark Horse Comics: 2003 ($2.99, one-shot)

Darkseid #1 © DC

Darling Romance #1 © AP

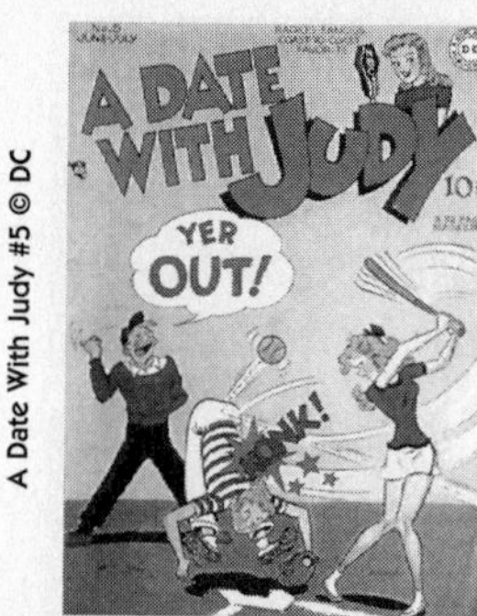

A Date With Judy #5 © DC

	GD 2.0	VG 4.0	FN 6.0	VF 8.0	VF/NM 9.0	NM- 9.2
1-Based on the 2003 movie "Darkness Falls"; Adlard-a						3.00

DARK ONE'S THIRD EYE
Sirius Entertainment: 1996; Dec, 1998 ($4.95, B&W)

	GD	VG	FN	VF	VF/NM	NM-
nn-Dark One-a; squarebound; pinups, Vol. 2-(12/98)						5.00

DARK OZ
Arrow Comics: 1997 - No. 5 ($2.75, B&W, limited series)

	GD	VG	FN	VF	VF/NM	NM-
1-5-Bill Bryan-a						2.75

DARK REALM
Image Comics: Oct, 2000 - No. 4, June, 2001 ($2.95, limited series)

	GD	VG	FN	VF	VF/NM	NM-
1-4-Taeson Chang-a. 3-Flip book w/Mech Destroyer prequel						3.00

DARKSEID (VILLAINS) (See Jack Kirby's New Gods and New Gods)
DC Comics: Feb, 1998 ($1.95, one-shot)

	GD	VG	FN	VF	VF/NM	NM-
1-Byrne-s/Pearson-c						2.25

DARKSEID VS. GALACTUS: THE HUNGER
DC Comics: 1995 ($4.95, one-shot) (1st DC/Marvel x-over by John Byrne)

	GD	VG	FN	VF	VF/NM	NM-
nn-John Byrne-c/a/script						5.00

DARK SHADOWS
Steinway Comic Publ. (Ajax)(America's Best): Oct, 1957 - No. 3, May, 1958

	GD	VG	FN	VF	VF/NM	NM-
1	26	52	78	150	215	280
2,3	19	38	57	107	154	200

DARK SHADOWS (TV) (See Dan Curtis Giveaways)
Gold Key: Mar, 1969 - No. 35, Feb, 1976 (Photo-c: 1-7)

	GD	VG	FN	VF	VF/NM	NM-
1(30039-903)-With pull-out poster (25¢)	28	56	84	199	305	410
1-With poster missing	11	22	33	75	110	145
2	10	20	30	67	96	125
3-With pull-out poster	14	28	42	102	156	210
3-With poster missing	8	16	24	53	74	95
4-7: 7-Last photo-c	8	16	24	58	82	105
8-10	7	14	21	46	63	80
11-20	6	12	18	40	55	70
21-35: 30-Last painted-c	5	10	15	36	48	60
Story Digest 1 (6/70, 148pp.)-Photo-c (low print)	10	20	30	67	96	125

DARK SHADOWS (TV) (See Nightmare on Elm Street)
Innovation Publishing: June, 1992 - No. 4, Spring, 1993 ($2.50, limited series, coated stock)

	GD	VG	FN	VF	VF/NM	NM-
1-Based on 1991 NBC TV mini-series; painted-c						5.00
2-4						4.00

DARK SHADOWS: BOOK TWO
Innovation Publishing: 1993 - No. 4, July, 1993 ($2.50, limited series)

	GD	VG	FN	VF	VF/NM	NM-
1-4-Painted-c. 4-Maggie Thompson scripts						4.00

DARK SHADOWS: BOOK THREE
Innovation Publishing: Nov, 1993 ($2.50)

	GD	VG	FN	VF	VF/NM	NM-
1-(Whole #9)						4.00

DARKSIDE
Maximum Press: Oct, 1996 ($2.99, one-shot)

	GD	VG	FN	VF	VF/NM	NM-
1-Avengelyne-c/app.						3.00

DARKSTARS, THE
DC Comics: Oct, 1992 - No. 38, Jan, 1996 ($1.75/$1.95)

	GD	VG	FN	VF	VF/NM	NM-
1-1st app. The Darkstars						3.00
2-24,0,25-38: 5-Hawkman & Hawkwoman app. 18-20-Flash app. 24-(9/94)-Zero Hour. 0-(10/94). 25-(11/94). 30-Green Lantern app. 31-...vs. Darkseid. 32-Green Lantern app.						2.50

NOTE: *Travis Charest a(p)-4-7; c(p)-2-5; c-6-11. **Stroman** a-1-3; c-1.*

DARK TOWN
Mad Monkey Press: 1995 ($3.95, magazine-size, quarterly)

	GD	VG	FN	VF	VF/NM	NM-
1-Kaja Blackley scripts; Vanessa Chong-a						4.00

DARKWING DUCK (TV cartoon) (Also see Cartoon Tales)
Disney Comics: Nov, 1991 - No. 4, Feb, 1992 ($1.50, limited series)

	GD	VG	FN	VF	VF/NM	NM-
1-4: Adapts hour-long premiere TV episode						3.00

DARLING LOVE
Close Up/Archie Publ. (A Darling Magazine): Oct-Nov, 1949 - No. 11, 1952 (no month) (52 pgs.)(Most photo-c)

	GD	VG	FN	VF	VF/NM	NM-
1-Photo-c	18	36	54	100	143	185
2-Photo-c	11	22	33	64	87	110
3-8,10,11: 3-6-photo-c	9	18	27	54	70	85
9-Krigstein-a	10	20	30	58	77	95

DARLING ROMANCE
Close Up (MLJ Publications): Sept-Oct, 1949 - No. 7, 1951 (All photo-c)

	GD	VG	FN	VF	VF/NM	NM-
1-(52 pgs.)-Photo-c	24	48	72	135	195	255
2	11	22	33	64	87	110
3-7	10	20	30	58	77	95

DARQUE PASSAGES (See Master Darque)
Acclaim (Valiant): April, 1998 ($2.50)

	GD	VG	FN	VF	VF/NM	NM-
1-Christina Z.-s/Manco-c/a						2.50

DART (Also see Freak Force & Savage Dragon)
Image Comics (Highbrow Entertainment): Feb, 1996 - No. 3, May, 1996 ($2.50, lim. series)

	GD	VG	FN	VF	VF/NM	NM-
1-3						3.00

DASTARDLY & MUTTLEY (See Fun-In No. 1-4, 6 and Kite Fun Book)

DATE WITH DANGER
Standard Comics: No. 5, Dec, 1952 - No. 6, Feb, 1953

	GD	VG	FN	VF	VF/NM	NM-
5,6-Secret agent stories: 6-Atom bomb story	9	18	27	54	70	85

DATE WITH DEBBI (Also see Debbi's Dates)
National Periodical Publ.: Jan-Feb, 1969 - No. 17, Sept-Oct, 1971; No. 18, Oct-Nov, 1972

	GD	VG	FN	VF	VF/NM	NM-
1-Teenage	6	12	18	38	52	65
2-5,17-(52 pgs) James Taylor sty.	3	6	9	19	25	32
6-12,18-Last issue	3	6	9	18	24	30
13-16-(68 pgs.): 14-1 pg. story on Jack Wild. 15-Marlo Thomas/"That Girl" story	4	8	12	22	30	38

DATE WITH JUDY, A (Radio/TV, and 1948 movie)
National Periodical Publications: Oct-Nov, 1947 - No. 79, Oct-Nov, 1960 (No. 1-25: 52 pgs.)

	GD	VG	FN	VF	VF/NM	NM-
1-Teenage	30	60	90	170	245	320
2	14	28	42	81	113	145
3-10	11	22	33	64	87	110
11-20	9	18	27	51	62	75
21-40	8	16	24	43	54	65
41-45: 45-Last pre-code (2-3/55)	7	14	21	37	46	55
46-79: 79-Drucker-c/a	7	14	21	35	43	50

DATE WITH MILLIE, A (Life With Millie No. 8 on)(Teenage)
Atlas/Marvel Comics (MPC): Oct, 1956 - No. 7, Aug, 1957; Oct, 1959 - No. 7, Oct, 1960

	GD	VG	FN	VF	VF/NM	NM-
1(10/56)-(1st Series)-Dan DeCarlo-a in #1-7	27	54	81	154	222	290
2	14	28	42	81	113	145
3-7	10	20	30	60	80	100
1(10/59)-(2nd Series)	15	30	45	83	117	150
2-7	10	20	30	58	77	95

DATE WITH PATSY, A (Also see Patsy Walker)
Atlas Comics: Sept, 1957 (One-shot)

	GD	VG	FN	VF	VF/NM	NM-
1-Starring Patsy Walker	11	22	33	66	91	115

DAVID AND GOLIATH (Movie)
Dell Publishing Co.: No. 1205, July, 1961

	GD	VG	FN	VF	VF/NM	NM-
Four Color 1205-Photo-c	8	16	24	53	74	95

DAVID AND GOLIATH
Image Comics: Sept, 2003 - Present ($2.95)

	GD	VG	FN	VF	VF/NM	NM-
1-3-Jay Ju-s/Leonel Castellani-a						3.00

DAVID BORING (See Eightball)
Pantheon Books: 2000 ($24.95, hardcover w/dust jacket)

	GD	VG	FN	VF	VF/NM	NM-
Hardcover - reprints David Boring stories from Eightball; Clowes-s/a						25.00

DAVID CASSIDY (TV)(See Partridge Family, Swing With Scooter #33 & Time For Love #30)
Charlton Comics: Feb, 1972 - No. 14, Sept, 1973

	GD	VG	FN	VF	VF/NM	NM-
1-Most have photo covers	7	14	21	46	63	80
2-5	4	8	12	28	38	48
6-14	4	8	12	25	33	42

DAVID LADD'S LIFE STORY (See Movie Classics)

DAVY CROCKETT (See Dell Giants, Fightin..., Frontier Fighters, It's Game Time, Power Record Comics, Western Tales & Wild Frontier)

DAVY CROCKETT (Frontier Fighter...)
Avon Periodicals: 1951

	GD	VG	FN	VF	VF/NM	NM-
nn-Tuska?, Reinman-a; Fawcette-c	19	38	57	107	154	200

DAVY CROCKETT (...King of the Wild Frontier No. 1,2)(TV)
Dell Publishing Co./Gold Key: 5/55 - No. 671, 12/55; No. 1, 12/63; No. 2, 11/69 (Walt Disney)

	GD	VG	FN	VF	VF/NM	NM-
Four Color 631(#1)-Fess Parker photo-c	21	42	63	148	227	305

Day of Judgment #1 © DC

Dazzler #32 © MAR

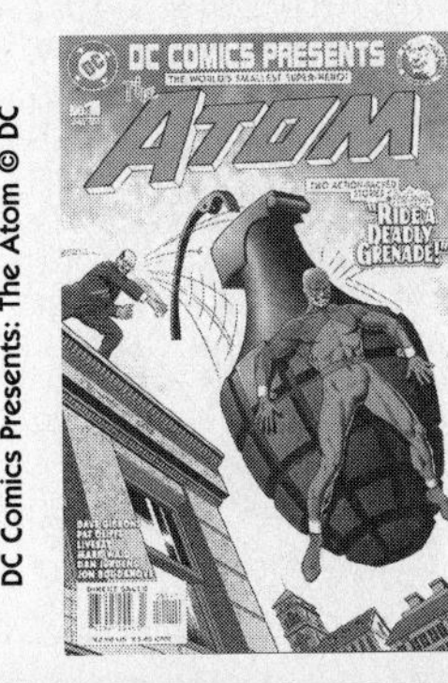

DC Comics Presents: The Atom © DC

GD 2.0 | VG 4.0 | FN 6.0 | VF 8.0 | VF/NM 9.0 | NM- 9.2

Four Color 639-Photo-c 17 34 51 119 182 245
Four Color 664,671(Marsh-a)-Photo-c 16 32 48 112 171 230
1(12/63-Gold Key)-Fess Parker photo-c; reprints 16 32 48 112 171 230
2(11/69)-Fess Parker photo-c; reprints 6 12 18 40 55 70

DAVY CROCKETT (...Frontier Fighter #1,2; Kid Montana #9 on)
Charlton Comics: Aug, 1955 - No. 8, Jan, 1957

1 10 20 30 58 77 95
2 7 14 21 35 43 50
3-8 5 10 15 24 30 35

DAWN
Sirius Entertainment/Image Comics: June, 1995 - No. 6, 1996 ($2.95)

1/2-w/certificate 1 2 3 5 6 8
1/2-Variant-c 2 4 6 11 14 18
1-Linsner-c/a 1 2 3 5 6 8
1-Black Light Edition 2 4 6 10 13 16
1-White Trash Edition 3 6 9 18 24 30
1-Look Sharp Edition 4 8 12 22 30 38
2-4: Linsner-c/a 4.50
2-Variant-c, 3-Limited Edition 2 4 6 14 18 22
4-6-Vibrato-c 3.50
4, 5-Limited Edition 2 4 6 8 10 12
6-Limited Edition 2 4 6 8 10 12
...Convention Sketchbook (Image Comics, 2002, $2.95) pin-ups 3.00
...2003 Convention Sketchbook (Image Comics, 3/03, $2.95) pin-ups 3.00
...2004 Convention Sketchbook (Image Comics, 4/04, $2.95) pin-ups 3.00
Genesis Edition ('99, Wizard supplement) previews Return of the Goddess 2.25
Lucifer's Halo TPB (11/97, $19.95) r/Drama, Dawn #1-6 plus 12 pages of new artwork 20.00
...: Tenth Anniversary Special (9/99, $2.95) Interviews 3.00
The Portable Dawn ($9.95, 5"x4", 64 pgs.) Pocket-sized cover gallery 10.00

DAWN OF THE DEAD (George A. Romaro's...)
IDW Publishing: Apr, 2004 - No. 3, Jun, 2004 ($3.99, limited series)

1-3-Adaptation of the 2004 movie; Niles-s 4.00
TPB (9/04, $17.99) r/#1-3; intro. by George A. Romero 18.00

DAWN: THE RETURN OF THE GODDESS
Sirius Entertainment: Apr, 1999 - No. 4, July, 2000 ($2.95, limited series)

1-4-Linsner-s/a 3.00
TPB (4/02, $12.95) r/#1-4; intro. by Linsner 13.00

DAWN: THREE TIERS
Image Comics: Jun, 2003 - No. 6 ($2.95, limited series)

1-4-Linsner-s/a. 2-Preview of Vampire's Christmas 3.00

DAYDREAMERS (See Generation X)
Marvel Comics: Aug, 1997 - No. 3, Oct, 1997 ($2.50, limited series)

1-3-Franklin Richards, Howard the Duck, Man-Thing app. 2.50

DAY OF JUDGMENT
DC Comics: Nov, 1999 - No. 5, Nov, 1999 ($2.95/$2.50, limited series)

1-($2.95) Spectre possessed; Matt Smith-a 3.00
2-5: Parallax returns. 5-Hal Jordan becomes the Spectre 3.00
...Secret Files 1 (11/99, $4.95) Harris-c 5.00

DAYS OF THE DEFENDERS (See Defenders, The)
Marvel Comics: Mar, 2001 ($3.50, one-shot)

1-Reprints early team-ups of members, incl. Marvel Feature #1; Larsen-c 3.50

DAYS OF THE MOB (See In the Days of the Mob)

DAZEY'S DIARY
Dell Publishing Co.: June-Aug, 1962

01-174-208: Bill Woggon-c/a 5 10 15 33 44 55

DAZZLER, THE (Also see Marvel Graphic Novel & X-Men #130)
Marvel Comics Group: Mar, 1981 - No. 42, Mar, 1986

1,22,24,27,28,38,42: 1-X-Men app. 22 (12/82)-vs. Rogue Battle-c/sty. 24-Full app. Rogue w/Powerman (Iron Fist). 27-Rogue app. 28-Full app. Rogue; Mystique app. 38-Wolverine-c/app.; X-Men app. 42-Beast-c/app. 4.00
2-21,23,25,26,29-37,39-41: 2-X-Men app. 10,11-Galactus app. 21-Double size; photo-c. 23-Rogue/Mystique 1 pg. app. 26-Jusko-c. 33-Michael Jackson thriller swipe-c/sty. 40-Secret Wars II 3.00

NOTE: *No. 1 distributed only through comic shops.* **Alcala** *a-1i, 2i.* **Chadwick** *a-38-42p; c(p)-39, 41, 42.* **Guice** *a-38i, 42i; c-38, 40.*

DC CHALLENGE (Most DC superheroes appear)
DC Comics: Nov, 1985 - No. 12, Oct, 1986 ($1.25/$2.00, maxi-series)

GD 2.0 | VG 4.0 | FN 6.0 | VF 8.0 | VF/NM 9.0 | NM- 9.2

1-11: 1-Colan-a. 2,8-Batman-c/app. 4-Gil Kane-c/a 2.50
12-($2.00-c) Giant; low print 3.00

NOTE: *Batman app. in 1-4, 6-12. Joker app. in 7.* **Infantino** *a-3.* **Ordway** *c-12.* **Swan/Austin** *c-10.*

DC COMICS PRESENTS
DC Comics: July-Aug, 1978 - No. 97, Sept, 1986 (Superman team-ups in all)

1-4th Superman/Flash race 2 4 6 14 18 22
1-(Whitman variant) 3 6 9 16 21 26
2-Part 2 of Superman/Flash race 2 4 6 10 12 15
2-4,10-12,14-16,19,21,22-(Whitman variants, low print run, none have issue # on cover) 2 4 6 10 12 15
3-10: 4-Metal Men. 6-Green Lantern. 8-Swamp Thing. 9-Wonder Woman 1 2 3 5 6 8
11-25,27-40: 13-Legion of Super-Heroes. 19-Batgirl. 31-Robin. 35-Man-Bat 6.00
26-(10/80)-Green Lantern; intro Cyborg, Starfire, Raven (1st app. New Teen Titans in 16 pg. preview); Starlin-c/a; Sargon the Sorcerer back-up 3 6 9 18 24 30
41,72,77,78,97: 41-Superman/Joker-c/story. 72-Joker/Phantom Stranger-c/story. 77,78-Animal Man app. (77-c also). 97-Phantom Zone 5.00
42-46,48-50,52-71,73-76,79-83: 42-Sandman. 43,80-Legion of Super-Heroes. 52-Doom Patrol. 58-Robin. 82-Adam Strange. 83-Batman & Outsiders 4.00
47-He-Man-c/s (1st app. in comics) 2 4 6 10 12 15
51,84: 51-Preview insert (16 pgs.) of He-Man (2nd app.). 84-Challengers of the Unknown; Kirby-c/s. 6.00
85-Swamp Thing; Alan Moore scripts 6.00
86-96: 86-88-Crisis x-over. 88-Creeper 4.00
Annual 1,4: 1(9/82)-G.A. Superman. 4(10/85)-Superwoman 4.00
Annual 2,3: 2(7/83)-Intro/origin Superwoman. 3(9/84)-Shazam 4.00

NOTE: **Adkins** *a-2, 54; c-2.* **Buckler** *a-33, 34; c-30, 33, 34.* **Giffen** *a-39; c-59.* **Gil Kane** *a-28, 35, Annual 3; c-48p, 56, 58, 60, 62, 64, 68, Annual 2, 3.* **Kirby** *c/a-84.* **Kubert** *c/a-66.* **Morrow** *c/a-65.* **Newton** *c/a-54p.* **Orlando** *c-53i.* **Perez** *a-26p, 61p; c-38, 61, 94.* **Starlin** *a-26-29p, 36p, 37p; c-26-29, 36, 37, 93.* **Toth** *a-84.* **Williamson** *i-79, 85, 87.*

DC COMICS PRESENTS: ...(Julie Schwartz tribute series of one-shots based on classic covers)
DC Comics: Sept, 2004 - Oct, 2004 ($2.50)

The Atom -(Based on cover of Atom #10) Gibbons-s/Oliffe-a; Waid-s/Jurgens-a; Bolland-c 2.50
Batman -(Batman #183) Johns-s/Infantino-a; Wein-s/Kuhn-a; Hughes-c 2.50
The Flash -(Flash #163) Loeb-s/McGuinness-a; O'Neil-s/Mahnke-a; Ross-c 2.50
Green Lantern -(Green Lantern #31) Azzarello-s/Breyfogle-a; Pasko-s/McDaniel-a; Bolland-c 2.50
Hawkman -(Hawkman #6) Bates-s/Byrne-a; Busiek-s/Simonson-a; Garcia-Lopez-c 2.50
Justice League of America -(J.L. of A. #53) Ellison & David-s/Giella-a; Wolfman-s/Nguyen-a; Garcia-Lopez-c 2.50
Mystery in Space -(M.I.S. #82) Maggin-s/Williams-a; Morrison-s/Ordway-a; Ross-c 2.50
Superman -(Superman #264) Stan Lee-s/Cooke-a; Levitz-s/Giffen-a; Hughes-c 2.50

DC FIRST: ...(series of one-shots)
DC Comics: July, 2002 ($3.50)

Batgirl/Joker 1-Sienkiewicz & Terry Moore-a; Nowlan-c 3.50
Green Lantern/Green Lantern 1-Alan Scott & Hal Jordan vs. Krona 3.50
Flash/Superman 1-Superman races Jay Garrick; Abra Kadabra app. 3.50
Superman/Lobo 1-Giffen-s; Nowlan-c 3.50

DC GRAPHIC NOVEL (Also see DC Science Fiction...)
DC Comics: Nov, 1983 - No. 7, 1986 ($5.95, 68 pgs.)

1-3,5,7: 1-Star Raiders. 2-Warlords; not from regular Warlord series. 3-The Medusa Chain; Ernie Colon story/a. 5-Me and Joe Priest; Chaykin-c. 7-Space Clusters; Nino-c/a 2 4 6 10 12 15
4-The Hunger Dogs by Kirby; Darkseid kills Himon from Mister Miracle & destroys New Genesis 4 8 12 29 40 50
6-Metalzoic; Sienkiewicz-c ($6.95) 2 4 6 10 12 15

DC/MARVEL: ALL ACCESS (Also see DC Versus Marvel & Marvel Versus DC)
DC Comics: 1996 - No. 4, 1997 ($2.95, limited series)

1-4: 1-Superman & Spider-Man app. 2-Robin & Jubilee app. 3-Dr. Strange & Batman-c/app., X-Men, JLA app. 4-X-Men vs. JLA-c/app. rebirth of Amalgam 3.00

DC/MARVEL: CROSSOVER CLASSICS
DC Comics: 1998; 2003 ($14.95, TPB)

Vol. II-Reprints Batman/Punisher: Lake of Fire, Punisher/Batman: Deadly Knights, Silver Surfer/Superman, Batman & Capt. America 15.00
Vol. 4 (2003, $14.95) Reprints Green Lantern/Silver Surfer: Unholy Alliances, Darkseid/ Galactus: The Hunger, Batman & Spider-Man, and Superman/Fantastic Four 15.00

DC 100 PAGE SUPER SPECTACULAR
(Title is 100 Page... No. 14 on)(Square bound) (Reprints, 50¢)
National Periodical Publications: No. 4, Summer, 1971 - No. 13, 6/72; No. 14, 2/73 - No. 22, 11/73 (No #1-3)

4-Weird Mystery Tales; Johnny Peril & Phantom Stranger; cover & splashes by Wrightson; origin Jungle Boy of Jupiter 18 36 54 126 193 260

DC 100 Page Super Spectacular #5 © DC

DC Special #1 © DC

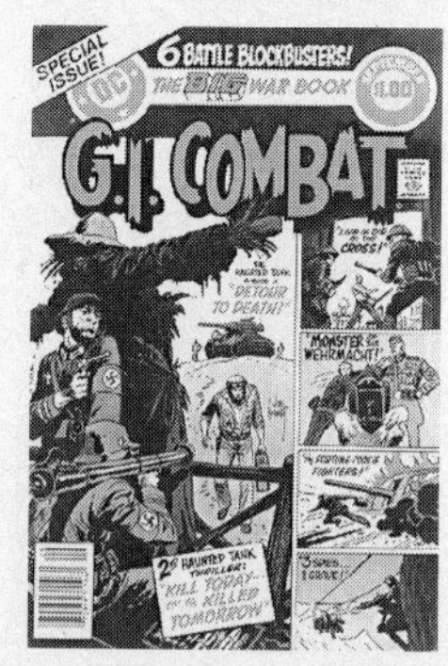

DC Special Series #22 © DC

GD 2.0 | VG 4.0 | FN 6.0 | VF 8.0 | VF/NM 9.0 | NM- 9.2

5-Love Stories; Wood inks (7 pgs.)(scarcer) 44 88 132 352 551 750
6- "World's Greatest Super-Heroes"; JLA, JSA, Spectre, Johnny Quick, Vigilante & Hawkman; contains unpublished Wildcat story; N. Adams wrap-around-c; r/JLA #21,22 18 36 54 126 193 260
6-Replica Edition (2004, $6.95) complete reprint w/wraparound-c 7.00
7-(Also listed as Superman #245) Air Wave, Kid Eternity, Hawkman-r; Atom-r/Atom #3 9 18 27 63 89 115
8-(Also listed as Batman #238) Batman, Legion, Aquaman-r; G.A. Atom, Sargon (r/Sensation #57), Plastic Man (r/Police #14) stories; Doom Patrol origin-r; Neal Adams wraparound-c 11 22 33 77 114 150
9-(Also listed as Our Army at War #242) Kubert-c 9 18 27 65 93 120
10-(Also listed as Adventure Comics #416) Golden Age-reprints; r/1st app. Black Canary from Flash #86; no Zatanna 11 22 33 75 110 145
11-(Also listed as Flash #214) origin Metal Men-r/Showcase #37; never before published G.A. Flash story. 8 16 24 55 78 100
12,14: 12-(Also listed as Superboy #185) Legion-c/story; Teen Titans, Kid Eternity (r/Hit #46), Star Spangled Kid-r(S.S. #55). 14-Batman-r/Detective #31,32,156; Atom-r/Showcase #34 7 14 21 51 71 90
13-(Also listed as Superman #252) Ray(r/Smash #17), Black Condor, (r/Crack #18), Hawkman(r/Flash #24); Starman-r/Adv. #67; Dr. Fate & Spectre-r/More Fun #57; Neal Adams-c 9 18 27 65 93 120
15,16,18,19,21,22: 15-r/2nd Boy Commandos/Det. #64. 21-Superboy; r/Brave & the Bold #54. 22-r/All-Flash #13. 5 10 15 36 48 60
17,20: 17-JSA-r/All Star #37 (10-11/47, 38 pgs.), Sandman-r/Adv. #65 (8/41), JLA #23 (11/63) & JLA #43 (3/66). 20-Batman-r/Det. #66,68, Spectre; origin Two-Face 6 12 18 38 52 65
... : Love Stories Replica Edition (2000, $6.95) reprints #5 7.00
NOTE: ***Anderson*** *r-11, 14, 18i, 22.* ***B. Baily*** *r-18, 20.* ***Burnley*** *r-18, 20.* ***Crandall*** *r-14p, 20.* ***Drucker*** *r-4.* ***Grandenetti*** *a-22(2)r.* ***Heath*** *a-22r.* ***Infantino*** *r-17, 20, 22.* ***G. Kane*** *r-18.* ***Kirby*** *r-15.* ***Kubert*** *r-6, 7, 16, 17; c-16, 19.* ***Manning*** *a-19r.* ***Meskin*** *r-4, 22.* ***Mooney*** *r-15, 21.* ***Toth*** *r-17, 20.*

DC ONE MILLION (Also see crossover #1,000,000 issues and JLA One Million TPB)
DC Comics: Nov, 1998 - No. 4, Nov, 1998 ($2.95/$1.99, weekly lim. series)

1-($2.95) JLA travels to the 853rd century; Morrison-s 3.00
2-4-($1.99) 2.25
... Eighty-Page Giant (8/99, $4.95) 5.00
TPB ('99, $14.95) r/#1-4 and several x-over stories 15.00

DC SCIENCE FICTION GRAPHIC NOVEL
DC Comics: 1985 - No. 7, 1987 ($5.95)

SF1-SF7: SF1-Hell on Earth by Robert Bloch; Giffen-p. SF2-Nightwings by Robert Silverberg; G. Colan-p. SF3-Frost & Fire by Bradbury. SF4-Merchants of Venus. SF5-Demon With A Glass Hand by Ellison; M. Rogers-a. SF6-The Magic Goes Away by Niven. SF7-Sandkings by George R.R. Martin 2 4 6 9 11 14

DC SILVER AGE CLASSICS
DC Comics: 1992 ($1.00, all reprints)

...Action Comics #252-r/1st Supergirl. Adventure Comics #247-r/1st Legion of Super-Heroes. The Brave and the Bold #28-r/1st JLA. Detective Comics #225-r/1st Martian Manhunter. Detective Comics #327-r/1st new look Batman. Green Lantern #76-r/1st Green Lantern/Green Arrow. House of Secrets #92-r/1st Swamp Thing. Showcase #4-r/1st S.A. Flash. Showcase #22-r/1st S.A. Green Lantern 2.50
...Sugar and Spike #99; includes 2 unpublished stories 4.00

DC SPECIAL (Also see Super DC Giant)
National Per. Publ.: 10-12/68 - No. 15, 11-12/71; No. 16, Spr/75 - No. 29, 8-9/77

1-All Infantino issue; Flash, Batman, Adam Strange-r; begin 68 pg. issues, end #21 8 16 24 55 78 100
2-Teen humor; Binky, Buzzy, Harvey app. 10 20 30 72 104 135
3-All-Girl issue; unpubl. GA Wonder Woman story 9 18 27 60 85 110
4,11: 4-Horror (1st Abel, brief). 11-Monsters 4 8 12 29 40 50
5-10,12-15: 5-All Kubert issue; Viking Prince, Sgt. Rock-r. 6-Western. 7,9,13-Strangest Sports. 12-Viking Prince; Kubert-c/a (r/B&B almost entirely). 15-G.A. Plastic Man origin-r/Police #1; origin Woozy by Cole; 14,15-(52 pgs.) 4 8 12 29 40 50
16-27: 16-Super Heroes Battle Super Gorillas; r/Capt. Storm #1, 1st Johnny Cloud/All-Amer. Men of War #82. 17-Early S.A. Green Lantern-r. 22-Origin Robin Hood. 26-Enemy Ace. 27-Captain Comet story 3 6 9 16 20 25
28,29: 28-Earth Shattering Disaster Stories; Legion of Super-Heroes story. 29-New "The Untold Origin of the Justice Society"; Staton-a 3 6 9 18 23 28
NOTE: ***N. Adams*** *c-3, 4, 6, 11, 29.* ***Grell*** *a-20; c-17, 20.* ***Heath*** *a-12r.* ***G. Kane*** *a-6p, 13r, 17r, 19-21r.* ***Kirby*** *a-4,11.* ***Kubert*** *a-6r, 12r, 22.* ***Meskin*** *a-10.* ***Moreira*** *a-10.* ***Staton*** *a-29p.* ***Toth*** *a-13, 20r. #1-15: 25¢; 16-27: 50¢; 28, 29: 60¢. #1-13, 16-21: 68 pgs.; 14, 15: 52 pgs.; 25-27: oversized.*

DC SPECIAL BLUE RIBBON DIGEST
DC Comics: Mar-Apr, 1980 - No. 24, Aug, 1982

1,2,4,5: 1-Legion reprints. 2-Flash. 4-Green Lantern. 5-Secret Origins; new Zatara and Zatanna 2 4 6 8 10 12
3-Justice Society 2 4 6 10 13 16
6,8-10: 6-Ghosts. 8-Legion. 9-Secret Origins. 10-Warlord-"The Deimos Saga"-Grell-s/c/a 2 4 6 8 10 12
7-Sgt. Rock's Prize Battle Tales 2 4 6 12 16 20
11,16: 11-Justice League. 16-Green Lantern/Green Arrow-r; all Adams-a 2 4 6 11 14 18
12-Haunted Tank; reprints 1st app. 2 4 6 12 16 20
13-15,17-19: 13-Strange Sports Stories. 14-UFO Invaders; Adam Strange app. 15-Secret Origins of Super Villains; JLA app. 17-Ghosts. 18-Sgt. Rock; Kubert front & back-c. 19-Doom Patrol; new Perez-c 2 4 6 10 12 15
20-Dark Mansion of Forbidden Love (scarce) 5 10 15 33 44 55
21-Our Army at War 3 6 9 16 20 25
22-24: 22-Secret Origins. 23-Green Arrow, w/new 7 pg. story. 24-House of Mystery; new Kubert wraparound-c 2 4 6 12 16 20
NOTE: ***N. Adams*** *a-16(6)r, 17r, 23r; c-16.* ***Aparo*** *a-6r, 24r; c-23.* ***Grell*** *a-8, 10; c-10.* ***Heath*** *a-14.* ***Infantino*** *a-15r.* ***Kaluta*** *a-17r.* ***Gil Kane*** *a-15r, 22r.* ***Kirby*** *a-5, 9, 23r.* ***Kubert*** *a-3, 18r, 21r; c-7, 12, 14, 17, 18, 21, 24.* ***Morrow*** *a-24r.* ***Orlando*** *a-17r, 22r; c-1, 20.* ***Toth*** *a-21r, 24r.* ***Wood*** *a-3, 17r, 24r.* ***Wrightson*** *a-16r, 17r, 24r.*

DC SPECIAL SERIES
National Periodical Publications/DC Comics: 9/77 - No. 16, Fall, 1978; No. 17, 8/79 - No. 27, Fall, 1981 (No. 18, 19, 23, 24 - digest size, 100 pgs.; No. 25-27 - Treasury sized)

1-"5-Star Super-Hero Spectacular 1977"; Batman, Atom, Flash, Green Lantern, Aquaman, in solo stories, Kobra app.; N. Adams-c 3 7 10 21 28 35
2(#1)-"The Original Swamp Thing Saga 1977"-r/Swamp Thing #1&2 by Wrightson; new Wrightson wraparound-c. 2 4 6 9 11 14
3,4,6-8: 3-Sgt Rock. 4-Unexpected. 6-Secret Society of Super Villains, Jones-a. 7-Ghosts Special. 8-Brave and Bold w/ new Batman, Deadman & Sgt Rock team-up 2 4 6 10 13 16
5-"Superman Spectacular 1977"-(84 pg, $1.00)-Superman vs. Brainiac & Lex Luthor, new 63 pg. story 2 4 6 14 18 22
9-Wonder Woman; Ditko-a (11 pgs.) 2 4 6 14 18 22
10-"Secret Origins of Superheroes Special 1978"-(52 pgs.)-Dr. Fate, Lightray & Black Canary on-c/new origin stories; Staton, Newton-a 2 4 6 12 16 20
11-"Flash Spectacular 1978"-(84 pgs.) Flash, Kid Flash, GA Flash & Johnny Quick vs. Grodd; Wood-i on Kid Flash chapter 2 4 6 10 13 16
12-"Secrets of Haunted House Special Spring 1978" 2 4 6 10 13 16
13-"Sgt. Rock Special Spring 1978", 50 pg new story 2 4 6 11 14 18
14,17,20-"Original Swamp Thing Saga", Wrightson-a: 14-Sum '78, r/#3,4. 17-Sum '79 r/#5-7. 20-Jan/Feb '80, r/#8-10 1 3 4 6 8 10
15-"Batman Spectacular Summer 1978", Ra's Al Ghul-app.; Golden-a. Rogers-a/front & back-c 3 6 9 16 20 25
16-"Jonah Hex Spectacular Fall 1978"; death of Jonah Hex, Heath-a; Bat Lash and Scalphunter stories 6 12 18 40 55 70
18,19-Digest size: 18-"Sgt. Rock's Prize Battle Tales Fall 1979". 19-"Secret Origins of Super-Heroes Fall 1979"; origins Wonder Woman (new-a),r/Robin, Batman-Superman team, Aquaman, Hawkman and others 2 4 6 10 13 16
21-"Super-Star Holiday Special Spring 1980", Frank Miller-a in "Batman--Wanted Dead or Alive" (1st Batman story); Jonah Hex, Sgt. Rock, Superboy & LSH and House of Mystery/Witching Hour-c/stories 3 7 10 21 28 35
22-"G.I. Combat Sept. 1980", Kubert-c. Haunted Tank-s 2 4 6 11 14 18
23,24-Digest size: 23-World's Finest-r. 24-Flash 2 4 6 10 13 16
V5#25-($2.95)-"Superman II, the Adventure Continues Summer 1981"; photos from movie & photo-c (see All-New Coll. Ed. C-62) 2 4 6 12 16 20
26-($2.50)-"Superman and His Incredible Fortress of Solitude Summer 1981" 2 4 6 12 16 20
27-($2.50)-"Batman vs. The Incredible Hulk Fall 1981" 3 7 10 21 28 35
NOTE: ***Aparo*** *c-8.* ***Heath*** *a-12i, 16.* ***Infantino*** *a-19r.* ***Kirby*** *a-23, 19r.* ***Kubert*** *c-13, 19r.* ***Nasser/Netzer*** *a-1, 10i, 15.* ***Newton*** *a-10.* ***Nino*** *a-4, 7.* ***Starlin*** *c-12.* ***Staton*** *a-1.* ***Tuska*** *a-19r. #25 & 26. were advertised as All-New Collectors' Edition C-63, C-64. #26 was originally planned as All-New Collectors' Ed. C-30?; has C-630 & A.N.C.E. on cover.*

DC SUPER-STARS
National Periodical Publications/DC Comics: March, 1976 - No. 18, Winter, 1978 (No.3-18: 52 pgs.)

1-(68 pgs.)-Re-intro Teen Titans (predates T. T. #44 (11/76); tryout iss.) plus r/Teen Titans; W.W. as girl was original Wonder Girl 3 6 9 16 20 25
2-7,9,11,12,16: 2,4,6,8-Adam Strange; 2-(68 pgs.)-r/1st Adam Strange/Hawkman team-up from Mystery in Space #90 plus Atomic Knights origin-r. 3-Legion issue. 4-r/Tales/Unexpected #45 1 3 4 6 8 10
8-r/1st Space Ranger from Showcase #15, Adam Strange-r/Mystery in Space #89 & Star Rovers-r/M.I.S. #80 2 4 6 8 10 12
10-Strange Sports Stories; Batman/Joker-c/story 2 4 6 9 11 14
13-Sergio Aragonés Special 2 4 6 14 18 22
14,15,18: 15-Sgt. Rock 2 4 6 8 10 12
17-Secret Origins of Super-Heroes (origin of The Huntress); origin Green Arrow by Grell; Legion app.; Earth II Batman & Catwoman marry (1st revealed; also see B&B #197 &

DC: The New Frontier #1 © DC

Dead King #1 © Chaos!

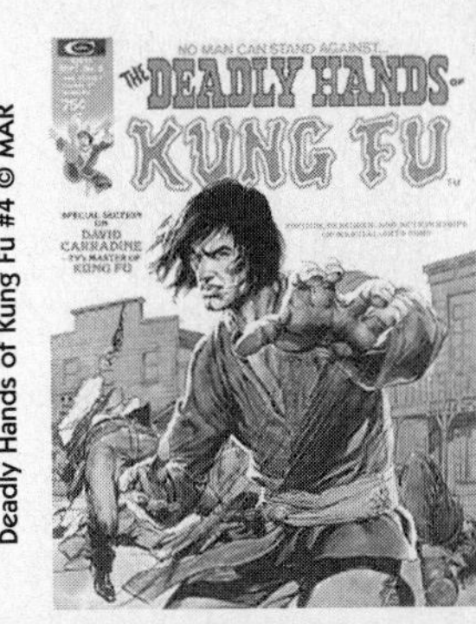

Deadly Hands of Kung Fu #4 © MAR

GD 2.0 | VG 4.0 | FN 6.0 | VF 8.0 | VF/NM 9.0 | NM- 9.2

Superman Family #211) 4 8 12 29 40 50

NOTE: ***M. Anderson*** *r-2, 4, 6.* ***Aparo*** *c-7, 14, 18.* ***Austin*** *a-11i.* ***Buckler*** *a-14p; c-10.* ***Grell*** *a-17.* ***G. Kane*** *a-1r, 10r.* ***Kubert*** *c-15.* ***Layton*** *c/a-16i, 17i.* ***Mooney*** *a-4r, 6r.* ***Morrow*** *c/a-11r.* ***Nasser*** *a-11.* ***Newton*** *c/a-16p.* ***Staton*** *a-17; c-17. No. 10, 12-18 contain all new material; the rest are reprints. #1 contains new and reprint material.*

DC: THE NEW FRONTIER
DC Comics: Mar, 2004 - No. 6, Nov, 2004 ($6.95, limited series)

1-6-DCU in the 1940s-60s; Darwyn Cooke-c/s/a in all. 1-Hal Jordan and The Losers app. 2-Origin Martian Manhunter; Barry Allen app. 3-Challengers of the Unknown 7.00

DC 2000
DC Comics: 2000 - No. 2, 2000 ($6.95, limited series)

1,2-JLA visit 1941 JSA; Semeiks-a 7.00

DCU HEROES SECRET FILES
DC Comics: Feb, 1999 ($4.95, one-shot)

1-Origin-s and pin-ups; new Star Spangled Kid app. 5.00

DC UNIVERSE CHRISTMAS, A
DC Comics: 2000 ($19.95)

TPB-Reprints DC Christmas stories by various 20.00

DC UNIVERSE HOLIDAY BASH
DC Comics: 1997- 1999 ($3.95)

I,II-(X-mas '96,'97) Christmas stories by various 5.00
III (1999, for Christmas '98, $4.95) 5.00

DC UNIVERSE: TRINITY
DC Comics: Aug, 1993 - No. 2, Sept, 1993 ($2.95, 52 pgs, limited series)

1,2-Foil-c; Green Lantern, Darkstars, Legion app. 3.50

DCU VILLAINS SECRET FILES
DC Comics: Apr, 1999 ($4.95, one-shot)

1-Origin-s and profile pages 5.00

DC VERSUS MARVEL (See Marvel Versus DC) (Also see Amazon, Assassins, Bruce Wayne: Agent of S.H.I. E. L.D., Bullets & Bracelets, Doctor Strangefate, JLX, Legend of the Dark Claw, Magneto & The Magnetic Men, Speed Demon, Spider-Boy, Super Soldier, X-Patrol)
DC Comics: No. 1, 1996, No. 4, 1996 ($3.95, limited series)

1,4: 1-Marz script, Jurgens-a(p); 1st app. of Access. 4.00
.../Marvel Versus DC ($12.95, trade paperback) r/1-4 13.00

D-DAY (Also see Special War Series)
Charlton Comics (no No. 3): Sum/63; No. 2, Fall/64; No. 4, 9/66; No. 5, 10/67; No. 6, 11/68

1,2: 1(1963)-Montes/Bache-c. 2(Fall '64)-Wood-a(4) 4 8 12 27 36 45
4-6('66-'68)-Montes/Bache-a #5 3 6 9 16 20 25

DEAD AIR
Slave Labor Graphics: July, 1989 ($5.95, graphic novel)

nn-Mike Allred's 1st published work 6.00

DEAD CORPSE
DC Comics (Helix): Sept, 1998 - No. 4, Dec, 1998 ($2.50, limited series)

1-4-Pugh-a/Hinz-s 2.50

DEAD END CRIME STORIES
Kirby Publishing Co.: April, 1949 (52 pgs.)

nn-(Scarce)-Powell, Roussos-a; painted-c 50 100 150 305 465 625

DEAD ENDERS
DC Comics (Vertigo): Mar, 2000 - No. 16, June, 2001 ($2.50)

1-16-Brubaker-s/Pleece & Case-a 2.50
Stealing the Sun (2000, $9.95, TPB) r/#1-4, Vertigo Winter's Edge #3 10.00

DEAD-EYE WESTERN COMICS
Hillman Periodicals: Nov-Dec, 1948 - V3#1, Apr-May, 1953

V1#1-(52 pgs.)-Krigstein, Roussos-a 20 40 60 112 161 210
V1#2,3-(52 pgs.) 11 22 33 62 84 105
V1#4-12-(52 pgs.) 8 16 24 46 58 70
V2#1,2,5-8,10-12: 1-7-(52 pgs.) 7 14 21 37 46 55
3,4-Krigstein-a 8 16 24 43 54 65
9-One pg. Frazetta ad 7 14 21 37 46 55
V3#1 7 14 21 37 46 55

NOTE: ***Briefer*** *a-V1#8. Kinstleresque stories by* ***McCann****-12, V2#1, 2, V3#1.* ***McWilliams*** *a-V1#5.* ***Ed Moore*** *a-V1#4.*

DEADFACE: DOING THE ISLANDS WITH BACCHUS
Dark Horse Comics: July, 1991 - No. 3, Sept, 1991 ($2.95, B&W, lim. series)

1-3: By Eddie Campbell 3.00

DEADFACE: EARTH, WATER, AIR, AND FIRE
Dark Horse Comics: July, 1992 - No. 4, Oct, 1992 ($2.50, B&W, limited series; British-r)

1-4: By Eddie Campbell 3.00

DEAD IN THE WEST
Dark Horse Comics: Oct, 1993 - No. 2, Mar, 1994 ($3.95, B&W, 52 pgs.)

1,2-Timothy Truman-c 4.00

DEAD KING (See Evil Ernie)
Chaos! Comics: May, 1998 - No. 4, Aug, 1998, ($2.95, limited series)

1-4-Fisher-s 3.00

DEADLIEST HEROES OF KUNG FU (Magazine)
Marvel Comics Group: Summer, 1975 (B&W)(76 pgs.)

1-Bruce Lee vs. Carradine painted-c; TV Kung Fu, 4pgs. photos/article; Enter the Dragon, 24 pgs. photos/article w/ Bruce Lee; Bruce Lee photo pinup 3 6 9 19 25 32

DEADLINE
Marvel Comics: June, 2002 - No. 4, Sept, 2002 ($2.99, limited series)

1-4: 1-Intro. Kat Farrell; Bill Rosemann-s/Guy Davis-a; Horn painted-c 3.00
TPB (2002. $9.99) r/#1-4 10.00

DEADLINE USA
Dark Horse Comics: Apr, 1992 - No. 8, Nov, 1992 ($3.95, B&W, 52 pgs.)

1-8: Johnny Nemo w/Milligan scripts in all 4.00

DEADLY DUO, THE
Image Comics (Highbrow Entertainment): Nov, 1994 - No. 3, Jan, 1995 ($2.50, lim. series)

1-3: 1-1st app. of Kill Cat 2.50

DEADLY DUO, THE
Image Comics (Highbrow Entertainment): June, 1995 - No. 4, Oct, 1995 ($2.50, lim. series)

1-4: 1-Spawn app. 2-Savage Dragon app. 3-Gen 13 app. 2.50

DEADLY FOES OF SPIDER-MAN (See Lethal Foes of...)
Marvel Comics: May, 1991 - No. 4, Aug, 1991 ($1.00, limited series)

1-4: 1-Punisher, Kingpin, Rhino app. 2.50

DEADLY HANDS OF KUNG FU, THE (See Master of Kung Fu)
Marvel Comics Group: April, 1974 - No. 33, Feb, 1977 (75¢) (B&W, magazine)

1(V1#4 listed in error)-Origin Sons of the Tiger; Shang-Chi, Master of Kung Fu begins (ties w/Master of Kung Fu #17 as 3rd app. Shang-Chi); Bruce Lee painted-c by Neal Adams; 2pg. memorial photo pinup w/8 pgs. photos/articles; TV Kung Fu, 9 pgs. photos/articles; 15 pgs. Starlin-a 4 8 12 29 40 50
2-Adams painted-c; 1st time origin of Shang-Chi, 34 pgs. by Starlin. TV Kung Fu, 6 pgs. photos & article w/2 pg. pinup. Bruce Lee, 11 pgs. ph/a 4 8 12 22 30 38
3,4,7,10: 3-Adams painted-c; Gulacy-a. Enter the Dragon, photos/articles, 8 pgs. 4-TV Kung Fu painted-c by Neal Adams; TV Kung Fu 7 pg. article/art; Fu Manchu; Enter the Dragon, 10 pg. photos/article w/Bruce Lee. 7-Bruce Lee painted-c & 9 pgs. photos/articles-Return of Dragon plus 1 pg. photo pinup. 10-(3/75)-Iron Fist painted-c & 34 pg. sty-Early app. 3 6 9 16 21 26
5,6: 5-1st app. Manchurian, 6 pgs. Gulacy-a. TV Kung Fu, 4 pg. article; reprints books w/Barry Smith-a. Capt. America-sty, 10 pgs. Kirby-a(r). 6-Bruce Lee photos/article, 6 pgs.; 15 pgs. early Perez-a 3 6 9 16 20 24
8,9,11: 9-Iron Fist, 2 pg. Preview pinup; Nebres-a. 11-Billy Jack painted-c by Adams; 17 pgs. photos/article 2 4 6 14 18 22
12,13: 12-James Bond painted-c by Adams; 14 pg. photos/article. 13-16 pgs. early Perez-a; Piers Anthony, 7 pgs. photos/article 2 4 7 12 16 20
14-Classic Bruce Lee painted-c by Adams. Lee pinup by Chaykin. Lee 16 pg. photos/article w/2 pgs. Green Hornet TV 5 10 15 36 48 60
15,19: 15-Sum, '75 Giant Annual #1. 20pgs. Starlin-a. Bruce Lee photo pinup & 3 pg. photos/ article re book; Man-Thing app. Iron Fist-c/sty; Gulacy-a 18pgs. 19-Iron Fist painted-c & series begins; 1st White Tiger 2 4 6 14 18 22
16,18,20: 16-1st app. Corpse Rider, a Samurai w/Sanho Kim-a. 20-Chuck Norris painted-c & 16 pgs. interview w/photos/article; Bruce Lee vs. C. Norris pinup by Ken Barr. Origin The White Tiger, Perez-a 2 4 6 11 14 18
17-Bruce Lee painted-c by Adams; interview w/R. Clouse, director Enter Dragon 7 pgs. w/B. Lee app. 1st Giffen-a (1pg. 11/75) 3 7 10 21 28 35
21-Bruce Lee 1pg. photos/article 2 4 6 11 14 18
22,30-32: 22-1st brief app. Jack of Hearts. 1st Giffen sty-a (along w/Amazing Adv. #35, 3/76). 30-Swordquest-c/sty & conclusion; Jack of Hearts app. 31-Jack of Hearts app; Staton-a. 32-1st Daughters of the Dragon-c/sty, 21 pgs. M. Rogers-a/Claremont-sty; Iron Fist pinup 2 4 6 11 14 18
23-26,29: 23-1st full app. Jack of Hearts. 24-Iron Fist-c & centerfold pinup. early Zeck-a; Shang Chi pinup; 6 pgs. Piers Anthony text sty w/Perez/Austin-a; Jack of Hearts app. early Giffen-a. 25-1st app. Shimuru, "Samurai", 20 pgs. Mantlo-sty/Broderick-a; "Swordquest"-c &

Deadman: Love After Death #2 © DC

Deadpool #51 © MAR

Deathblow #7 © WSP

GD 2.0 | VG 4.0 | FN 6.0 | VF 8.0 | VF/NM 9.0 | NM- 9.2

GD 2.0 | VG 4.0 | FN 6.0 | VF 8.0 | VF/NM 9.0 | NM- 9.2

begins 17 pg. sty by Sanho Kim; 11 pg. photos/article; partly Bruce Lee. 26-Bruce Lee painted-c & pinup; 16 pgs. interviews w/Kwon & Clouse; talk about Bruce Lee re-filming of Lee legend. 29-Ironfist vs. Shang Chi battle-c/sty; Jack of Hearts app.
3 6 9 16 20 24

27 2 4 6 10 13 16

28-All Bruce Lee Special Issue; (1st time in comics). Bruce Lee painted-c by Ken Barr & pinup. 36 pgs. comics chronicaling Bruce Lee's life; 15 pgs. B. Lee photos/article (Rare in high grade) 7 14 21 46 63 80

33-Shang Chi-c/sty; Classic Daughters of the Dragon, 21 pgs. M. Rogers-a/Claremont-story with nudity; Bob Wall interview, photos/article, 14 pgs.
3 6 9 16 20 24

...Special Album Edition 1(Summer, '74)-Iron Fist-c/story (early app., 3rd?); 10 pgs. Adams-i; Shang Chi/Fu Manchu, 10 pgs.; Sons of Tiger, 11 pgs.; TV Kung Fu, 6 pgs. photos/article
3 6 9 18 23 28

NOTE: ***Bruce Lee:*** *1-7, 14, 15, 17, 25, 26, 28.* ***Kung Fu (TV):*** *1, 2, 4.* ***Jack of Hearts:*** *22, 23, 29-33.* ***Shang Chi Master of Kung Fu:*** *1-9, 11-18, 29, 31, 33.* ***Sons of Tiger:*** *1, 3, 4, 6-14, 16-19.* ***Swordquest:*** *25-27, 29-33.* ***White Tiger:*** *19-24, 26, 27, 29-33.* ***N. Adams*** *a-1i(part), 27i; c-1, 2-4, 11, 12, 14, 17.* ***Giffen*** *a-22p, 24p.* ***G. Kane*** *a-23p.* ***Kirby*** *a-5r.* ***Nasser*** *a-27p, 28.* ***Perez*** *a(p)-6-14, 16, 17, 19, 21.* ***Rogers*** *a-26, 32, 33.* ***Starlin*** *a-1, 2r, 15r.* ***Staton*** *a-28p, 31, 32.*

DEADMAN (See The Brave and the Bold & Phantom Stranger #39)
DC Comics: May, 1985 - No. 7, Nov, 1985 ($1.75, Baxter paper)

1-7: 1-Deadman-r by Infantino, N. Adams in all. 5-Batman-c/story-r/Strange Adventures. 7-Batman-r 3.00

DEADMAN
DC Comics: Mar, 1986 - No. 4, June, 1986 (75¢, limited series)

1-4: Lopez-c/a. 4-Byrne-c(p) 3.00

DEADMAN
DC Comics: Feb, 2002 - No. 9, Oct, 2002 ($2.50)

1-9: 1-4-Vance-s/Beroy-a. 3,4-Mignola-c. 5,6-Garcia-Lopez-a 2.50

DEADMAN: DEAD AGAIN (Leads into 2002 series)
DC Comics: Oct, 2001 - No. 5, Oct, 2001 ($2.50, weekly limited series)

1-5: Deadman at the deaths of the Flash, Robin, Superman, Hal Jordan 2.50

DEADMAN: EXORCISM
DC Comics: 1992 - No. 2, 1992 ($4.95, limited series, 52 pgs.)

1,2: Kelley Jones-c/a in both 5.00

DEADMAN: LOVE AFTER DEATH
DC Comics: 1989 - No. 2, 1990 ($3.95, 52 pgs., limited series, mature)

Book One, Two: Kelley Jones-c/a in both. 1-contains nudity 4.00

DEAD OF NIGHT
Marvel Comics Group: Dec, 1973 - No. 11, Aug, 1975

1-Horror reprints 3 6 9 18 23 28
2-10: 10-Kirby-a. 6-Jack the Ripper-c/s 2 4 6 10 13 16
11-Intro Scarecrow; Kane/Wrightson-c 3 7 10 21 28 35

NOTE: ***Ditko*** *r-7, 10.* ***Everett*** *c-2.* ***Sinnott*** *r-1.*

DEAD OR ALIVE - A CYBERPUNK WESTERN
Image Comics (Shok Studio): Apr, 1998 - No. 4, July, 1998 ($2.50, lim. series)

1-4 3.00

DEADPOOL (See New Mutants #98)
Marvel Comics: Aug, 1994 - No. 4, Nov, 1994 ($2.50, limited series)

1-4: Mark Waid's 1st Marvel work; Ian Churchill-c/a 4.00

DEADPOOL (... : Agent of Weapon X on cover #57-60) (title becomes Agent X)
Marvel Comics: Jan, 1997 - No. 69, Sept, 2002 ($2.95/$1.95/$1.99)

1-($2.95)-Wraparound-c 1 2 3 4 5 7
2-Begin-$1.95-c. 5.00
3-10,12-22,24: 4-Hulk-c/app. 12-Variant-c. 14-Begin McDaniel-a. 22-Cable app. 5.00
11-($3.99)-Deadpool replaces Spider-Man from Amazing Spider-Man #47; Kraven, Gwen Stacy app. 6.00
23,25-($2.99); 23-Dead Reckoning pt. 1; wraparound-c 4.00
26-40: 27-Wolverine-c/app. 37-Thor app. 3.00
41-53,56-60: 41-Begin $2.25-c. 44-Black Panther-c/app. 46-49-Chadwick-a 51-Cover swipe of Detective #38. 57-60-BWS-c 3.00
54,55-Punisher-c/app. 54-Dillon-c. 55-Bradstreet-c 3.00
61-69: 61-64-Funeral For a Freak on cover. 65-69-Udon Studios-a. 67-Dazzler-c/app. 2.50
#(-1) Flashback (7/97) Lopresti-a; Wade Wilson's early days 3.00
.../Death '98 Annual ($2.99) Kelly-s, ... Team-Up (12/98, $2.99) Widdle Wade-c/app., Baby's First Deadpool Book (12/98, $2.99), Encyclopædia Deadpoolica (12/98, $2.99) Synopses 3.00
Mission Improbable TPB (9/98, $14.95) r/#1-5 15.00
Wizard #0 ('98, bagged with Wizard #87) 2.25

DEADPOOL: THE CIRCLE CHASE (See New Mutants #98)
Marvel Comics: Aug, 1993 - No. 4, Nov, 1993 ($2.00, limited series)

1-($2.50)-Embossed-c 4.00
2-4 3.00

DEADSHOT (See Batman #59, Detective Comics #474, & Showcase '93 #8)
DC Comics: Nov, 1988 - No. 4, Feb, 1989 ($1.00, limited series)

1-4 2.50

DEADSHOT
DC Comics: Feb, 2005 - No. 5 ($2.95, limited series)

1-Zeck-c/Gage-s/Cummings-a 3.00

DEADSIDE (See Shadowman)
Acclaim Comics: Feb, 1999 - No. 4, ($2.50, limited series)

1-3-Jenkins-s/Haselden-Wood-a 2.50

DEAD WHO WALK, THE (See Strange Mysteries, Super Reprint #15, 16)
Realistic Comics: 1952 (one-shot)

nn 53 106 159 323 492 660

DEADWORLD (Also see The Realm)
Arrow Comics/Caliber Comics: Dec, 1986 - No. 26 ($1.50/$1.95/#15-28: $2.50, B&W)

1-4 4.00
5-26-Graphic cover version 4.00
5-26-Tame cover version 3.00
...Archives 1-3 (1992, $2.50) 3.00

DEAN MARTIN & JERRY LEWIS (See Adventures of...)

DEAR BEATRICE FAIRFAX
Best/Standard Comics (King Features): No. 5, Nov, 1950 - No. 9, Sept, 1951 (Vern Greene art)

5-All have Schomburg air brush-c 11 22 33 64 87 110
6-9 8 16 24 40 50 60

DEAR HEART (Formerly Lonely Heart)
Ajax: No. 15, July, 1956 - No. 16, Sept, 1956

15,16 6 12 18 33 41 48

DEAR LONELY HEART (...Illustrated No. 1-6)
Artful Publications: Mar, 1951; No. 2, Oct, 1951 - No. 8, Oct, 1952

1 17 34 51 98 139 180
2 9 18 27 52 66 80
3-Matt Baker Jungle Girl story 20 40 60 112 161 210
4-8 8 16 24 46 58 70

DEAR LONELY HEARTS (Lonely Heart #9 on)
Harwell Publ./Mystery Publ. Co. (Comic Media): Aug, 1953 -No. 8, Oct, 1954

1 11 22 33 64 87 110
2-8 8 16 24 43 54 65

DEARLY BELOVED
Ziff-Davis Publishing Co.: Fall, 1952

1-Photo-c 17 34 51 95 135 175

DEAR NANCY PARKER
Gold Key: June, 1963 - No. 2, Sept, 1963

1-Painted-c on both 4 8 12 28 38 48
2 3 6 9 19 25 32

DEATH: AT DEATH'S DOOR (See Sandman: The Season of Mists)
DC Comics: 2003 ($9.95, graphic novel one-shot, B&W, 7-1/2" x 5")

1-Jill Thompson-s/a/c; manga-style; Morpheus and the Endless app. 10.00

DEATHBLOW (Also see Batman/Deathblow and Darker Image)
Image Comics (WildStorm Productions): May (Apr. inside), 1993 - No. 29, Aug, 1996 ($1.75/$1.95/$2.50)

0-(8/96, $2.95, 32 pgs.)-r/Darker Image w/new story & art; Jim Lee & Trevor Scott-a; new Jim Lee-c 3.00
1-($2.50)-Red foil stamped logo on black varnish-c; Jim Lee-c/a; flip-book side has Cybernary -c/story (#2 also) 3.00
1-($1.95)-Newsstand version w/o foil-c & varnish 2.25
2-29: 2-(8/93)-Lee-a; with bound-in poster. 2-($1.75)-Newsstand version w/o poster. 4-Jim Lee-c/Tim Sale-a begin. 13-W/pinup poster by Tim Sale & Jim Lee. 16-($1.95 Newsstand & $2.50 Direct Market editions)-Wildstorm Rising Pt. 6. 17-Variant "Chicago Comicon" edition exists. 20,21-Gen 13 app. 23-Backlash-c/app. 24,25-Grifter-c/app; Gen 13 & Dane from Wetworks app. 28-Deathblow dies. 29-Memorial issue 2.50

Deathmask #2 © Michelinie & Layton

Deathlok #1 © MAR

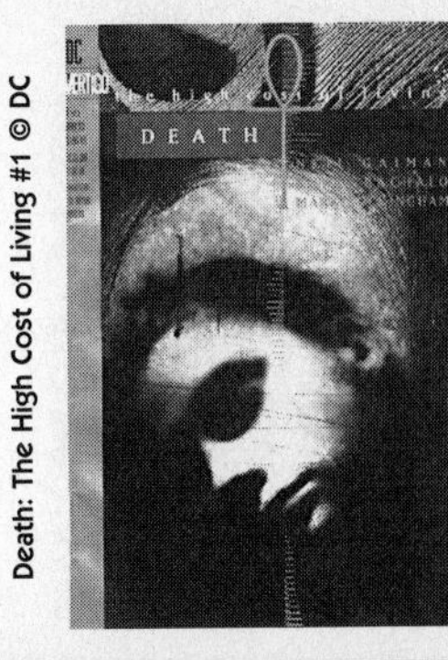

Death: The High Cost of Living #1 © DC

	GD 2.0	VG 4.0	FN 6.0	VF 8.0	VF/NM 9.0	NM- 9.2

5-Alternate Portacio-c (Forms larger picture when combined with alternate-c for Gen 13 #5, Kindred #3, Stormwatch #10, Team 7 #1, Union #0, Wetworks #2 & WildC.A.T.S #11) 6.00
...:Sinners and Saints TPB ('99, $19.95) r/#1-12; Sale-c 20.00

DEATHBLOW BY BLOWS
DC Comics (WildStorm): Nov, 1999 - No. 3, Jan, 2000 ($2.95, limited series)

1-3-Alan Moore-s/Jim Baikie-a 3.00

DEATHBLOW/WOLVERINE
Image Comics (WildStorm Productions)/ Marvel Comics: Sept, 1996 - No. 2, Feb, 1997 ($2.50, limited series)

1,2: Wiesenfeld-s/Bennett-a 2.50
TPB (1997, $8.95) r/#1,2 9.00

DEATHDEALER
Verotik: July, 1995 - No. 4, July, 1997 ($5.95)

1-Frazetta-c; Bisley-a	1	2	3	5	6	8
1-2nd print, 2-4-($6.95)-Frazetta-c; embossed logo	1	2	3	4	5	7

DEATHLOK (Also see Astonishing Tales #25)
Marvel Comics: July, 1990 - No. 4, Oct, 1990 ($3.95, limited series, 52 pgs.)

1-4: 1,2-Guice-a(p). 3,4-Denys Cowan-a, c-4 4.00

DEATHLOK
Marvel Comics: July, 1991 - No. 34, Apr, 1994 ($1.75)

1-Silver ink cover; Denys Cowan-c/a(p) begins 3.00
2-18,20-24,26-34: 2-Forge (X-Men) app. 3-Vs. Dr. Doom. 5-X-Men & F.F. x-over. 6,7-Punisher x-over. 9,10-Ghost Rider-c/story. 16-Infinity War x-over. 17-Jae Lee-c. 22-Black Panther app. 27-Siege app. 2.25
19-($2.25)-Foil-c 2.50
25-($2.95, 52 pgs.)-Holo-grafx foil-c 3.00
Annual 1 (1992, $2.25, 68 pgs.)-Guice-p; Quesada-c(p) 3.00
Annual 2 (1993, $2.95, 68 pgs.)-Bagged w/card; intro Tracer 3.00
NOTE: ***Denys Cowan** a(p)-9-13, 15, Annual 1; c-9-12, 13p, 14. **Guice/Cowan** c-8.*

DEATHLOK
Marvel Comics: Sept, 1999 - No. 11, June, 2000 ($1.99)

1-11: 1-Casey-s/Manco-a. 2-Two covers. 4-Canete-a 2.25

DEATHLOK SPECIAL
Marvel Comics: May, 1991 - No. 4, June, 1991 ($2.00, bi-weekly lim. series)

1-4: r/1-4(1990) w/new Guice-c #1,2; Cowan c-3,4 2.50
1-2nd printing w/white-c 2.25

DEATHMASK
Future Comics: Mar, 2003 - No. 3, June, 2003 ($2.99)

1-3-Giordano-a(p)/Michelinie & Layton-s 3.00

DEATHMATE
Valiant (Prologue/Yellow/Blue)/Image Comics (Black/Red/Epilogue):
Sept, 1993 - Epilogue (#6), Feb, 1994 ($2.95/$4.95, limited series)

Preview-(7/93, 8 pgs.) 2.25
Prologue (#1)–Silver foil; Jim Lee/Layton-c; B. Smith/Lee-a; Liefeld-a(p) 3.00
Prologue–Special gold foil ed. of silver ed. 4.00
Black (#2)-(9/93, $4.95, 52 pgs.)-Silvestri/Jim Lee-c; pencils by Peterson/Silvestri/Capullo/ Jim Lee/Portacio; 1st story app. Gen 13 telling their rebellion against the Troika (see WildC.A.T.S. Trilogy) 6.00
Black-Special gold foil edition 7.00
Yellow (#3)-(10/93, $4.95, 52 pgs)-Yellow foil-c; Indicia says Prologue Sept 1993 by mistake; 3rd app. Ninjak; Thibert-c(i) 5.00
Yellow-Special gold foil edition 6.00
Blue (#4)-(10/93, $4.95, 52 pgs.)-Thibert blue foil-c(i); Reese-a(i) 5.00
Blue-Special gold foil edition 6.00
Red (#5), Epilogue (#6)-(2/94, $2.95)-Silver foil Quesada/Silvestri-c; Silvestri-a(p) 3.00

DEATH METAL
Marvel Comics UK: Jan, 1994 - No. 4, Apr, 1994 ($1.95, limited series)

1-4: 1-Silver ink-c. Alpha Flight app. 2.25

DEATH METAL VS. GENETIX
Marvel Comics UK: Dec, 1993 - No. 2, Jan, 1994 (Limited series)

1-($2.95)-Polybagged w/2 trading cards 3.00
2-($2.50)-Polybagged w/2 trading cards 2.50

DEATH OF CAPTAIN MARVEL (See Marvel Graphic Novel #1)

DEATH OF MR. MONSTER, THE (See Mr. Monster #8)

DEATH OF SUPERMAN (See Superman, 2nd Series)

DEATH RACE 2020
Roger Corman's Cosmic Comics: Apr, 1995 - No. 8, Nov, 1995 ($2.50)

1-8: Sequel to the Movie 2.50

DEATH RATTLE (Formerly an Underground)
Kitchen Sink Press: V2#1, 10/85 - No. 18, 1988, 1994 ($1.95, Baxter paper, mature); V3#1, 11/95 - No. 5, 6/96 ($2.95, B&W)

V2#1-7,9-18: 1-Corben-c. 2-Unpubbed Spirit story by Eisner. 5-Robot Woman-r by Wolverton. 6-B&W issues begin. 10-Savage World-r by by Williamson/Torres/ Krenkel/Frazetta from Witzend #1. 16-Wolverton Spacehawk-r 4.00

8-(12/86)-1st app. Mark Schultz's Xenozoic Tales/Cadillacs & Dinosaurs	1	3	4	6	8	10

8-(1994)-r plus interview w/Mark Schultz 3.00
V3#1-5 ($2.95-c) 3.00

DEATH'S HEAD (See Daredevil #56, Dragon's Claws #5 & Incomplete...)
Marvel Comics: Dec, 1988 - No. 10, Sept, 1989 ($1.75)

1-Dragon's Claws spin-off 3.00
2-Fantastic Four app.; Dragon's Claws x-over 2.50
3-10: 8-Dr. Who app. 9-F. F. x-over; Simonson-c(p) 2.25

DEATH'S HEAD II (Also see Battletide)
Marvel Comics UK, Ltd.: Mar, 1992 - No. 4, June (May inside), 1992 ($1.75, color, lim. series)

1-4: 2-Fantastic Four app. 4-Punisher, Spider-Man, Daredevil, Dr. Strange, Capt. America & Wolverine in the year 2020 2.25
1,2-Silver ink 2nd printiings 2.25

DEATH'S HEAD II (Also see Battletide)
Marvel Comics UK, Ltd.: Dec, 1992 - No. 16, Mar, 1994 ($1.75/$1.95)

V2#1-13,15,16: 1-Gatefold-c. 1-4-X-Men app.15-Capt. America & Wolverine app. 2.25
14-($2.95)-Foil flip-c w/Death's Head II Gold #0 3.00
...Gold 1 (1/94, $3.95, 68 pgs.)-Gold foil-c 4.00

DEATH'S HEAD II & THE ORIGIN OF DIE CUT
Marvel Comics UK, Ltd.: Aug, 1993 - No. 2, Sept, 1993 (limited series)

1-($2.95)-Embossed-c 3.00
2 ($1.75) 2.25

DEATHSTROKE: THE TERMINATOR (Deathstroke: The Hunted #0-47; Deathstroke #48-60) (Also see Marvel & DC Present, New Teen Titans #2, New Titans, Showcase '93 #7,9 & Tales of the Teen Titans #42-44)
DC Comics: Aug, 1991 - No. 60, June, 1996 ($1.75-$2.25)

1-New Titans spin-off; Mike Zeck c-1-28 4.00
1-Gold ink 2nd printing ($1.75) 2.25
2 3.00
3-40,0(10/94),41(11/94)-49,51-60: 6,8-Batman cameo. 7,9-Batman-c/story. 9-1st brief app. new Vigilante (female). 10-1st full app. new Vigilante; Perez-i. 13-Vs. Justice League; Team Titans cameo on last pg. 14-Total Chaos, part 1; TeamTitans-c/story cont'd in New Titans #90. 15-Total Chaos, part 4. 40-(9/94). 0-(10/94)-Begin Deathstroke, The Hunted, ends #47. 2.50
50 ($3.50) 3.50
Annual 1-4 ('92-'95, 68 pgs.): 1-Nightwing & Vigilante app.; minor Eclipso app. 2-Bloodlines Deathstorm; 1st app. Gunfire. 3-Elseworlds story. 4-Year One story 4.00
NOTE: ***Golden** a-12. **Perez** a-11i. **Zeck** c-Annual 1, 2.*

DEATH: THE HIGH COST OF LIVING (See Sandman #8) (Also see the Books of Magic limited & ongoing series)
DC Comics (Vertigo): Mar, 1993 - No. 3, May, 1993 ($1.95, limited series)

1-Bachalo/Buckingham-a; Dave McKean-c; Neil Gaiman scripts in all 6.00
1-Platinum edition 40.00
2 3.50
3-Pgs. 19 & 20 had wrong placement 3.00
3-Corrected version w/pgs. 19 & 20 facing each other; has no-c & ads for Sebastion O & The Geek added 4.00
Death Talks About Life-giveaway about AIDS prevention 5.00
Hardcover (1994, $19.95)-r/#1-3 & Death Talks About Life; intro. by Tori Amos 20.00
Trade paperback (6/94, $12.95, Titan Books)-r/#1-3 & Death Talks About Life; prism-c 13.00

DEATH: THE TIME OF YOUR LIFE (See Sandman #8)
DC Comics (Vertigo): Apr, 1996 - No. 3, July, 1996 ($2.95, limited series)

1-3: Neil Gaiman story & Bachalo/Buckingham-a; Dave McKean-c. 2-(5/96) 3.00
Hardcover (1997, $19.95)-r/#1-3 w/3 new pages & gallery art by various 20.00
TPB (1997, $12.95)-r/#1-3 & Visions of Death gallery; Intro. by Claire Danes 13.00

DEATH 3
Marvel Comics UK: Sept, 1993 - No. 4, Dec, 1993 ($1.75, limited series)

1-($2.95)-Embossed-c 3.00
2-4 2.25

Death Valley #1 © CC

The Defenders #10 © MAR

Defiance #1 © Powerhouse Inc.

GD 2.0 | VG 4.0 | FN 6.0 | VF 8.0 | VF/NM 9.0 | NM- 9.2

GD 2.0 | VG 4.0 | FN 6.0 | VF 8.0 | VF/NM 9.0 | NM- 9.2

DEATH VALLEY (Cowboys and Indians)
Comic Media: Oct, 1953 - No. 6, Aug, 1954

1-Billy the Kid; Morisi-a; Andru/Esposito-c/a 15 30 45 83 117 150
2-Don Heck-c 9 18 27 52 66 80
3-6: 3,5-Morisi-a. 5-Discount-a 9 18 27 51 62 75

DEATH VALLEY (Becomes Frontier Scout, Daniel Boone No.10-13)
Charlton Comics: No. 7, 6/55 - No. 9, 10/55 (Cont'd from Comic Media series)

7-9: 8-Wolverton-a (half pg.) 8 16 24 40 50 60

DEATHWISH
DC Comics (Milestone Media): Dec, 1994 - No. 4, Mar, 1995 (2.50, lim. series)

1-4 2.50

DEATH WRECK
Marvel Comics UK: Jan, 1994 - No. 4, Apr, 1994 ($1.95, limited series)

1-4: 1-Metallic ink logo; Death's Head II app. 2.25

DEBBIE DEAN, CAREER GIRL
Civil Service Publ.: April, 1945 - No. 2, July, 1945

1,2-Newspaper reprints by Bert Whitman 14 28 42 79 110 140

DEBBI'S DATES (Also see Date With Debbi)
National Periodical Publications: Apr-May, 1969 - No. 11, Dec-Jan, 1970-71

1 6 12 18 38 52 65
2,3,5,7-11: 2-Last 12¢ issue 3 6 9 18 24 30
4-Neal Adams text illo 4 8 12 24 32 40
6-Superman cameo 6 12 18 38 52 65

DECADE OF DARK HORSE, A
Dark Horse Comics: Jul, 1996 - No. 4, Oct, 1996 ($2.95, B&W/color, lim. series)

1-4: 1-Sin City-c/story by Miller; Grendel by Wagner; Predator. 2-Star Wars wraparound-c. 3-Aliens-c/story; Nexus, Mask stories 3.00

DECAPITATOR (Randy Bowen's...)
Dark Horse Comics: Jun, 1998 - No. 4, ($2.95)

1-4-Bowen-s/art by various. 1-Mahnke-c. 3-Jones-c 4.00

DECEPTION, THE
Image Comics (Flypaper Press): 1999 - No. 3, 1999 ($2.95, B&W, mini-series)

1-3-Horley painted-c 3.00

DEEP, THE (Movie)
Marvel Comics Group: Nov, 1977 (Giant)

1-Infantino-c/a 1 2 3 5 7 9

DEEP SLEEPER
Oni Press/Image Comics: Feb, 2004 - No. 4, Sept, 2004 ($3.50/$2.95, B&W, limited series)

1,2-(Oni Press, $3.50)-Hester-s/Huddleston-a 3.50
3,4-(Image Comics, $2.95) 3.00
... Omnibus (Image, 8/04, $5.95) r/#1,2 6.00

DEFCON 4
Image Comics (WildStorm Productions): Feb, 1996 - No. 4, Sept, 1996 ($2.50, lim. series)

1/2 1 2 3 5 7 9
1/2 Gold-(1000 printed) 14.00
1-Main Cover by Mat Broome & Edwin Rosell 3.00
1-Hordes of Cymulants variant-c by Michael Golden 5.00
1-Backs to the Wall variant-c by Humberto Ramos & Alex Garner 5.00
1-Defcon 4-Way variant-c by Jim Lee 1 2 3 4 5 7
2-4 2.50

DEFENDERS, THE (TV)
Dell Publishing Co.: Sept-Nov, 1962 - No. 2, Feb-Apr, 1963

12-176-211(#1) 5 10 15 33 44 55
12-176-304(#2) 4 8 12 25 33 42

DEFENDERS, THE (Also see Giant-Size..., Marvel Feature, Marvel Treasury Edition, Secret Defenders & Sub-Mariner #34, 35; The New...#140-on)
Marvel Comics Group: Aug, 1972 - No. 152, Feb, 1986

1-The Hulk, Doctor Strange, Sub-Mariner begin 11 22 33 77 114 150
2-Silver Surfer x-over 6 12 18 38 52 65
3-5: 3-Silver Surfer x-over. 4-Valkyrie joins 4 8 12 24 32 40
6,7: 6-Silver Surfer x-over 3 6 9 16 20 25
8,9,11: 8-11-Defenders vs. the Avengers (Crossover with Avengers #115-118) 8,11-Silver Surfer x-over 3 6 9 18 24 30
10-Hulk vs. Thor battle 7 14 21 46 63 80
12-14: 12-Last 20¢ issue 2 4 6 10 12 15
15,16-Magneto & Brotherhood of Evil Mutants app. from X-Men 2 4 6 10 13 16
17-20: 17-Power Man x-over (11/74) 1 3 4 6 8 10
21-25: 24,25-Son of Satan app. 1 2 3 4 5 7
26-29-Guardians of the Galaxy app. (#26 is 8/75; pre-dates Marvel Presents #3): 28-1st full app. Starhawk (1st brief app. #27). 29-Starhawk joins Guardians 1 2 3 5 7 9
30-33,39-50: 31,32-Origin Nighthawk. 44-Hellcat joins. 45-Dr. Strange leaves. 47-49-Early Moon Knight app. (5/77). 48-50-(Reg. 30¢-c) 5.00
34-38-(Regular 25¢ editions): 35-Intro New Red Guardian 5.00
34-38-(30¢-c variants, limited distribution)(4-8/76) 1 2 3 4 5 7
48-52-(35¢-c variants, limited distribution)(6-10/77) 1 2 3 4 5 7
51-60: 51,52-(Reg. 30¢-c). 53-1st brief app. Lunatik (Lobo lookalike). 55-Origin Red Guardian; Lunatik cameo. 56-1st full Lunatik story 4.00
61-75: 61-Lunatik & Spider-Man app. 70-73-Lunatik (origin #71). 73-75-Foolkiller II app. (Greg Salinger). 74-Nighthawk resigns 3.00
76-93,95,97-99,102-119,123,124,126-149,151: 77-Origin Omega. 78-Original Defenders return thru #101. 104-The Beast joins. 105-Son of Satan joins. 106-Death of Nighthawk. 129-New Mutants cameo (3/84, early x-over) 2.50
94,101,120-122: 94-1st Gargoyle. 101-Silver Surfer-c & app. 120,121-Son of Satan-c/stories. 122-Final app. Son of Satan (2 pgs.) 4.00
96-Ghost Rider app. 4.00
100-(52 pgs.)-Hellcat (Patsy Walker) revealed as Satan's daughter 5.00
125,150: 125-(52 pgs.)-Intro new Defenders. 150-(52 pgs.)-Origin Cloud 4.00
152-(52 pgs.)-Ties in with X-Factor & Secret Wars II 4.00
Annual 1 (1976, 52 pgs.)-New book-length story 3 6 9 16 20 25

NOTE: ***Art Adams*** *c-142p.* ***Austin*** *a-53i; c-65i, 119i, 145i.* ***Frank Bolle*** *a-7i, 10i, 11i.* ***Buckler*** *c(p)-34, 38, 76, 77, 79-86, 90, 91.* ***J. Buscema*** *c-66.* ***Giffen*** *a-42-49p, 50, 51-54p.* ***Golden*** *a-53p, 54p; c-94, 96.* ***Guice*** *c-129.* ***G. Kane*** *c(p)-13, 16, 18, 19, 21-26, 31-33, 35-37, 40, 41, 52, 55.* ***Kirby*** *c-42-45.* ***Mooney*** *a-3i, 31-34i, 62i, 63i, 85i.* ***Nasser*** *c-88p.* ***Perez*** *c(p)-51, 53, 54.* ***Rogers*** *c-98.* ***Starlin*** *c-110.* ***Tuska*** *a-57p. Silver Surfer in No. 2, 3, 6, 8-11, 92, 98-101, 107, 112-115, 122-125.*

DEFENDERS, THE (Volume 2) (Continues in The Order)
Marvel Comics: Mar, 2001 - No. 12, Feb, 2002 ($2.99/$2.25)

1-Busiek & Larsen-s/Larsen & Janson-a/c 3.00
2-11: 2-Two covers by Larsen & Art Adams; Valkyrie app. 4-Frenz-a 2.25
12-($3.50) 'Nuff Said issue; back-up-s Reis-a 3.50

DEFENDERS OF DYNATRON CITY
Marvel Comics: Feb, 1992 - No. 6, July, 1992 ($1.25, limited series)

1-6-Lucasarts characters. 2-Origin 3.00

DEFENDERS OF THE EARTH (TV)
Marvel Comics (Star Comics): Jan, 1987 - No. 4, July, 1987

1-4: The Phantom, Mandrake The Magician, Flash Gordon begin. 3-Origin Phantom. 4-Origin Mandrake 4.00

DEFEX
Devil's Due Publ.: Oct, 2004 - Present ($2.95)

1,2-Wolfman-s/Caselli-a 3.00

DEFIANCE
Image Comics: Feb, 2002 - No. 8, Jun, 2003 ($2.95)

Preview Edition (12/01) 2.25
1-8-Barré-s/Kang & Suh-a 3.00

DEFINITIVE DIRECTORY OF THE DC UNIVERSE, THE (See Who's Who...)

DEITY (Also see Kosmic Kat)
Hyperwerks Comics: Sept, 1997 - No. 6, Apr, 1998, ($2.95, limited series)

1-6, 0(5/98) 4.00
1-Variant-c 5.00
2-6,0-Variant covers 4.00
0-NDC Edition 4.00
0-NDC Silver Ed. 8.00
0-NDC Gold Ed. 12.00

DEITY (Volume 2)
Hyperwerks Comics: Sept, 1998 - No. 5 ($2.95)

Preview (6/98) Flip book with Lady Pendragon preview 3.00
1-5: 1-Flip book w/Catseye preview 3.00

DEITY: REVELATIONS (Volume 3)
Hyperwerks Comics: July, 1999 - No. 4, Dec, 1999 ($2.95)

1-4-Alstaetter and Napton-s/a 3.00

DELECTA OF THE PLANETS (See Don Fortune & Fawcett Miniatures)

DELICATE CREATURES
Image Comics (Top Cow): 2001 ($16.95, hardcover with dust jacket)

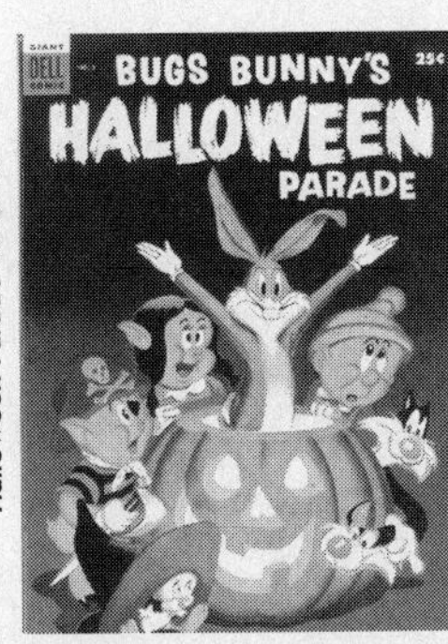

Dell Giant - Bugs Bunny Halloween Parade #2 © DC

Dell Giant - Lady and the Tramp #1 © WDC

Dell Giant - Vacation Parade #1 © WDC

	GD	VG	FN	VF	VF/NM	NM-
	2.0	4.0	6.0	8.0	9.0	9.2

nn-Fairy tale storybook; J. Michael Straczynski-s; Michael Zulli-a 17.00

DELLA VISION (...The Television Queen) (Patty Powers #4 on)
Atlas Comics: April, 1955 - No. 3, Aug, 1955

1-Al Hartley-c 16 32 48 92 131 170
2,3 11 22 33 64 87 110

DELL GIANT COMICS

Dell Publishing began to release square bound comics in 1949 with a 132-page issue called Christmas Parade #1. The covers were of a heavier stock to accommodate the increased number of pages. The books proved profitable at 25 cents, but the average number of pages was quickly reduced to 100. Ten years later they were converted to a numbering system similar to the Four Color Comics, for greater ease in distribution and the page counts cut back to mostly 84 pages. The label "Dell Giant" began to appear on the covers in 1954. Because of the size of the books and the heavier, less pliant cover stock, they are rarely found in high grade condition, and with the exception of a small quantity of copies released from Western Publishing's warehouse–are almost never found in near mint.

Abraham Lincoln Life Story 1(3/58) 7 14 21 56 96 135
Bugs Bunny Christmas Funnies 1(11/50, 116pp) 17 34 51 136 238 340
...Christmas Funnies 2(11/51, 116pp) 10 20 30 80 145 210
...Christmas Funnies 3-5(11/52-11/54,)-Becomes Christmas Party #6 9 18 27 72 129 185
...Christmas Funnies 7-9(12/56-12/58) 8 16 24 64 115 165
...Christmas Party 6(11/55)-Formerly Bugs Bunny Christmas Funnies 8 16 24 64 115 165
...County Fair 1(9/57) 9 18 27 72 131 190
...Halloween Parade 1(10/53) 10 20 30 80 145 210
...Halloween Parade 2(10/54)-Trick 'N' Treat Halloween Fun #3 on 9 18 27 72 124 175
...Trick 'N' Treat Halloween Fun 3,4(10/55-10/56)-Formerly Halloween Parade #2 9 18 27 72 124 175
...Vacation Funnies 1(7/51, 112pp) 16 32 48 128 229 330
...Vacation Funnies 2('52) 12 24 36 96 168 240
...Vacation Funnies 3-5('53-'55) 9 18 27 72 129 185
...Vacation Funnies 6-9('56-'59) 8 16 24 64 115 165
Cadet Gray of West Point 1(4/58)-Williamson-a, 10pgs.; Buscema-a; photo-c 7 14 21 56 96 135
Christmas In Disneyland 1(12/57)-Barks-a, 18 pgs. 24 48 72 192 334 475
Christmas Parade 1(11/49)(132 pgs.)(1st Dell Giant)-Donald Duck (25pgs. by Barks, r-in G.K. Christmas Parade #5); Mickey Mouse & other film oriented stories; Cinderella (prior to movie), 7 Dwarfs, Bambi & Thumper, So Dear To My Heart, Flying Mouse, Dumbo, Cookieland & others 55 110 165 440 770 1100
Christmas Parade 2('50)-Donald Duck (132 pgs.)(25 pgs. by Barks, r-in Gold Key's Christmas Parade #6). Mickey, Pluto, Chip & Dale, etc. Contents shift to a holiday expansion of W.D. C&S type format 40 80 120 320 560 800
Christmas Parade 3-7('51-'55, #3-116pgs; #4-7, 100 pgs.) 13 26 39 104 182 260
Christmas Parade 8(12/56)-Barks-a, 8 pgs. 20 40 60 160 285 410
Christmas Parade 9(12/58)-Barks-a, 20 pgs. 24 48 72 192 334 475
Christmas Treasury, A 1(11/54) 8 16 24 64 115 165
Davy Crockett, King Of The Wild Frontier 1(9/55)-Fess Parker photo-c; Marsh-a 18 36 54 144 252 360
Disneyland Birthday Party 1(10/58)-Barks-a, 16 pgs. r-by Gladstone 24 48 72 192 334 475
Donald and Mickey In Disneyland 1(5/58) 10 20 30 80 145 210
Donald Duck Beach Party 1(7/54)-Has an Uncle Scrooge story (not by Barks) that prefigures the later rivalry with Flintheart Glomgold and tells of Scrooge's wild rivalry with another millionaire 14 28 42 112 201 290
...Beach Party 2(1955)-Lady & Tramp 10 20 30 80 145 210
...Beach Party 3-5(1956-58) 10 20 30 80 140 200
...Beach Party 6(8/59, 84pp)-Stapled 7 14 21 56 103 150
Donald Duck Fun Book 1,2(1953 & 10/54)-Games, puzzles, comics & cut-outs (very rare in unused condition)(most copies commonly have defaced interior pgs.) 55 110 165 440 770 1100
Donald Duck In Disneyland 1(9/55)-1st Disneyland Dell Giant 14 28 42 112 194 275
Golden West Rodeo Treasury 1(10/57) 9 18 27 72 124 175
Huey, Dewey and Louie Back To School 1(9/58) 8 16 24 64 115 165
Lady and The Tramp 1(6/55) 15 30 45 120 215 310
Life Stories of American Presidents 1(11/57)-Buscema-a 6 12 18 48 89 130
Lone Ranger Golden West 3(8/55)-Formerly Lone Ranger Western Treasury 17 34 51 136 238 340
Lone Ranger Movie Story nn(3/56)-Origin Lone Ranger in text; Clayton Moore photo-c 34 68 102 272 474 675

	GD	VG	FN	VF	VF/NM	NM-
	2.0	4.0	6.0	8.0	9.0	9.2

...Western Treasury 1(9/53)-Origin Lone Ranger, Silver, & Tonto; painted cover 22 44 66 176 308 440
...Western Treasury 2(8/54)-Becomes Lone Ranger Golden West #3 17 34 51 136 238 340
Marge's Little Lulu & Alvin Story Telling Time 1(3/59)-r/#2,5,3,11,30,10,21,17,8, 14,16; Stanley-a 12 24 36 96 173 250
...& Her Friends 4(3/56)-Tripp-a 12 24 36 96 168 240
...& Her Special Friends 3(3/55)-Tripp-a 13 26 39 104 187 270
...& Tubby At Summer Camp 5,2: 5(10/57)-Tripp-a. 2(10/58)-Tripp-a 11 22 33 88 159 230
...& Tubby Halloween Fun 6,2: 6(10/57)-Tripp-a. 2(10/58)-Tripp-a 11 22 33 88 159 230
...& Tubby In Alaska 1(7/59)-Tripp-a 11 22 33 88 154 220
...On Vacation 1(7/54)-r/4C-110,14,4C-146,5,4C-97,4,4C-158,3,1;Stanley-a 23 46 69 184 327 470
...& Tubby Annual 1(3/53)-r/4C-165,4C-74,4C-146,4C-97,4C-158, 4C-139, 4C-131; Stanley-a (1st Lulu Dell Giant) 28 56 84 224 392 560
...& Tubby Annual 2('54)-r/4C-139,6,4C-115,4C-74,5,4C-97,3,4C-146,18; Stanley-a 23 46 69 184 327 470
Marge's Tubby & His Clubhouse Pals 1(10/56)-1st app. Gran'pa Feeb;1st app. Janie; written by Stanley; Tripp-a 13 26 39 104 187 270
Mickey Mouse Almanac 1(12/57)-Barks-a, 8pgs. 25 50 75 200 350 500
...Birthday Party 1(9/53)-r/entire 48pgs. of Gottfredson's "Mickey Mouse in Love Trouble" from WDC&S 36-39. Quality equal to original. Also reprints one story each from Four Color 27, 79, & 181 plus 6 panels of highlights in the career of Mickey Mouse 29 58 87 232 409 585
...Club Parade 1(12/55)-r/4-Color 16 with some death trap scenes redrawn by Paul Murry & recolored with night turned into day; quality less than original 21 42 63 168 297 425
...In Fantasy Land 1(5/57) 12 24 36 96 168 240
...In Frontier Land 1(5/56)-Mickey Mouse Club iss. 12 24 36 96 168 240
...Summer Fun 1(8/58)-Mobile cut-outs on back-c; becomes Summer Fun with #2 12 24 36 96 168 240
Moses & The Ten Commandments 1(8/57)-Not based on movie; Dell's adaptation; Sekowsky-a 6 12 18 48 84 120
Nancy & Sluggo Travel Time 1(9/58) 7 14 21 56 103 150
Peter Pan Treasure Chest 1(1/53, 212pp)-Disney; contains 54-page movie adaptation & other Peter Pan stories; plus Donald & Mickey stories w/P. Pan; a 32-page retelling of "D. Duck Finds Pirate Gold" with yellow beak, called "Capt. Hook & the Buried Treasure" 105 210 315 840 1470 2100
Picnic Party 6,7(7/55-6/56)(Formerly Vacation Parade)-Uncle Scrooge, Mickey & Donald 11 22 33 88 154 220
Picnic Party 8(7/57)-Barks-a, 6pgs 20 40 60 160 280 400
Pogo Parade 1(9/53)-Kelly-a(r-/Pogo from Animal Comics in this order: #11,13,21,14,27,16,23,9,18,15,17) 25 50 75 200 350 500
Raggedy Ann & Andy 1(2/55) 15 30 45 120 210 300
Santa Claus Funnies 1(11/52)-Dan Noonan -A Christmas Carol adaptation 8 16 24 64 115 165
Silly Symphonies 1(9/52)-Redrawing of Gotfredson's Mickey Mouse strip of "The Brave Little Tailor;" 2 Good Housekeeping pages (from 1943); Lady and the Two Siamese Cats, three years before "Lady & the Tramp;" a retelling of Donald Duck's first app. in "The Wise Little Hen" & other stories based on 1930's Silly Symphony cartoons 27 54 81 216 383 550
Silly Symphonies 2(9/53)-M. Mouse in "The Sorcerer's Apprentice", 2 Good Housekeeping pages (from 1944); The Pelican & the Snipe, Elmer Elephant, Peculiar Penguins, Little Hiawatha, & others 23 46 69 184 322 460
Silly Symphonies 3(2/54)-r/Mickey & The Beanstalk (4-Color #157, 39pgs.), Little Minnehaha, Pablo, The Flying Gauchito, Pluto, & Bongo, & 2 Good Housekeeping pages (1944) 19 38 57 152 264 375
Silly Symphonies 4(8/54)-r/Dumbo (4-Color 234), Morris The Midget Moose, The Country Cousin, Bongo, & Clara Cluck 19 38 57 152 264 375
Silly Symphonies 5-8: 5(2/55)-r/Cinderella (4-Color 272), Bucky Bug, Pluto, Little Hiawatha, The 7 Dwarfs & Dumbo, Pinocchio. 6(8/55)-r/Pinocchio (WDC&S 63), The 7 Dwarfs & Thumper (WDC&S 45), M. Mouse "Adventures With Robin Hood" (40 pgs.), Johnny Appleseed, Pluto & Peter Pan, & Bucky Bug; Cut-out on back-c. 7(2/57)-r/Reluctant Dragon, Ugly Duckling, M. Mouse & Peter Pan, Jiminy Cricket, Peter & The Wolf, Brer Rabbit, Bucky Bug; Cut-out on back-c. 8(2/58)-r/Thumper Meets The 7 Dwarfs (4-Color #19), Jiminy Cricket, Niok, Brer Rabbit; Cut-out on back-c 15 30 45 120 215 310
Silly Symphonies 9(2/59)-r/Paul Bunyan, Humphrey Bear, Jiminy Cricket, The Social Lion, Goliath II; cut-out on back-c 14 28 42 112 201 290
Sleeping Beauty 1(4/59) 25 50 75 200 350 500
Summer Fun 2(8/59, 84pp, stapled binding)(Formerly Mickey Mouse...)-Barks-a(2), 24 pgs. 24 48 144 192 334 475
Tarzan's Jungle Annual 1(8/52)-Lex Barker photo on-c of #1,2

Dell Giant #23 - Marge's Little Lulu and Tubby Halloween Fun © Marjorie Buell

Dell Giant #29 - Marge's Little Lulu and Tubby in Hawaii © Marjorie Buell

Dell Giant #43 - Mighty Mouse in Outer Space © DELL

	GD 2.0	VG 4.0	FN 6.0	VF 8.0	VF/NM 9.0	NM- 9.2
	13	26	39	104	187	270
...Annual 2(8/53)	10	20	30	80	140	200
...Annual 3-7('54-9/58)(two No. 5s)-Manning-a-No. 3,5-7; Marsh-a in No. 1-7 plus painted-c 1-7	8	16	24	64	115	165
Tom And Jerry Back To School 1(9/56)	11	22	33	88	159	230
...Picnic Time 1(7/58)	9	18	27	72	126	180
...Summer Fun 1(7/54)-Droopy written by Barks	14	28	42	112	196	280
...Summer Fun 2-4(7/55-7/57)	7	14	21	56	98	140
...Toy Fair 1(6/58)	8	16	24	64	117	170
...Winter Carnival 1(12/52)-Droopy written by Barks	19	38	57	152	266	380
...Winter Carnival 2(12/53)-Droopy written by Barks	15	30	45	120	215	310
...Winter Fun 3(12/54)	8	16	24	64	110	155
...Winter Fun 4-7(12/55-11/58)	6	12	18	48	89	130
Treasury of Dogs, A 1(10/56)	6	12	18	48	87	125
Treasury of Horses, A (9/55)	6	12	18	48	87	125
Uncle Scrooge Goes To Disneyland 1(8/57p)-Barks-a, 20pgs.r-by Gladstone	24	48	144	192	334	475
Vacation In Disneyland 1(8/58)	10	20	30	80	145	210
Vacation Parade 1(7/50, 132pp)-Donald Duck & Mickey Mouse; Barks-a, 55 pgs.	82	164	246	656	1153	1650
Vacation Parade 2(7/51,116pp)	24	48	72	192	334	475
Vacation Parade 3-5(7/52-7/54)-Becomes Picnic Party No. 6 on. #4-Robin Hood Advs.	13	26	39	104	182	260
Western Roundup 1(6/52)-Photo-c; Gene Autry, Roy Rogers, Johnny Mack Brown, Rex Allen, & Bill Elliott begin; photo back-c begin, end No. 14,16,18	23	46	69	184	322	460
Western Roundup 2(2/53)-Photo-c	13	26	39	104	182	260
Western Roundup 3-5(7-9/53 - 1-3/54)-Photo-c	10	20	30	80	145	210
Western Roundup 6-10(4-6/54 - 4-6/55)-Photo-c	9	18	27	72	131	190
Western Roundup 11-17,25-Photo-c; 11-13,16,17-Manning-a. 11-Flying A's Range Rider, Dale Evans begin	8	16	24	64	117	170
Western Roundup 18-Toth-a; last photo-c; Gene Autry ends	9	18	27	72	131	190
Western Roundup 19-24-Manning-a. 19-Buffalo Bill Jr. begins (7-9/57; early app.). 19,20,22-Toth-a. 21-Rex Allen, Johnny Mack Brown end. 22-Jace Pearson's Texas Rangers, Rin Tin Tin, Tales of Wells Fargo (2nd app., 4-6/58) & Wagon Train (2nd app.) begin	8	16	24	64	117	170
Woody Woodpecker Back To School 1(10/52)	9	18	27	72	131	190
...Back To School 2-4,6('53-10/57)-County Fair No. 5	7	14	21	56	103	150
...County Fair 5(9/56)-Formerly Back To School	7	14	21	56	103	150
...County Fair 2(11/58)	6	12	18	48	89	130

DELL GIANTS (Consecutive numbering)
Dell Publishing Co.: No. 21, Sept, 1959 - No. 55, Sept, 1961 (Most 84 pgs., 25¢)

	GD 2.0	VG 4.0	FN 6.0	VF 8.0	VF/NM 9.0	NM- 9.2
21-(#1)-M.G.M.'s Tom & Jerry Picnic Time (84pp, stapled binding)-Painted-c	10	20	30	80	140	200
22-Huey, Dewey & Louie Back to School (Disney; 10/59, 84pp, square binding begins)	8	16	24	64	115	165
23-Marge's Little Lulu & Tubby Halloween Fun (10/59)-Tripp-a	10	20	30	80	145	210
24-Woody Woodpecker's Family Fun (11/59)(Walter Lantz)	8	16	24	64	110	155
25-Tarzan's Jungle World(11/59)-Marsh-a; painted-c	10	20	30	80	140	200
26-Christmas Parade(Disney; 12/59)-Barks-a, 16pgs.; Barks draws himself on wanted poster on pg. 13	19	38	57	152	266	380
27-Walt Disney's Man in Space (10/59) r-/4-Color 716,866, & 954 (100 pgs., 35¢)(TV)	9	18	27	72	124	175
28-Bugs Bunny's Winter Fun (2/60)	9	18	27	72	124	175
29-Marge's Little Lulu & Tubby in Hawaii (4/60)-Tripp-a	10	20	30	80	145	210
30-Disneyland USA(Disney; 6/60)	8	16	24	64	115	165
31-Huckleberry Hound Summer Fun (7/60)(TV)(HannaBarbera)-Yogi Bear & Pixie & Dixie app.	12	24	36	96	166	235
32-Bugs Bunny Beach Party	7	14	21	56	96	135
33-Daisy Duck & Uncle Scrooge Picnic Time (Disney; 9/60)	8	16	24	64	115	165
34-Nancy & Sluggo Summer Camp (8/60)	7	14	21	56	96	135
35-Huey, Dewey & Louie Back to School (Disney; 10/60)-1st app. Daisy Duck's Nieces, April, May & June	10	20	30	80	145	210
36-Marge's Little Lulu & Witch Hazel Halloween Fun (10/60)-Tripp-a	10	20	30	80	140	200
37-Tarzan, King of the Jungle (11/60)-Marsh-a; painted-c	9	18	27	72	124	175
38-Uncle Donald & His Nephews Family Fun (Disney; 11/60)-Cover painting based on a pencil sketch by Barks	12	24	36	96	166	235
39-Walt Disney's Merry Christmas (Disney; 12/60)-Cover painting based on a pencil sketch by Barks	12	24	36	96	166	235
40-Woody Woodpecker Christmas Parade (12/60)(Walter Lantz)	6	12	18	48	82	115
41-Yogi Bear's Winter Sports (12/60)(TV)(Hanna-Barbera)-Huckleberry Hound, Pixie & Dixie, Augie Doggie app.	12	24	36	96	166	235
42-Marge's Little Lulu & Tubby in Australia (4/61)	10	20	30	80	145	210
43-Mighty Mouse in Outer Space (5/61)	17	34	51	136	243	350
44-Around the World with Huckleberry and His Friends (7/61)(TV)(Hanna-Barbera)-Yogi Bear, Pixie & Dixie, Quick Draw McGraw, Augie Doggie app.; 1st app. Yakky Doodle	12	24	36	96	171	245
45-Nancy & Sluggo Summer Camp (8/61)	6	12	18	48	87	125
46-Bugs Bunny Beach Party (8/61)	6	12	18	48	87	125
47-Mickey & Donald in Vacationland (Disney; 8/61)	8	16	24	64	110	155
48-The Flintstones (No. 1)(Bedrock Bedlam)(7/61)(TV)(Hanna-Barbera) 1st app. in comics	18	36	54	144	257	370
49-Huey, Dewey & Louie Back to School (Disney; 9/61)	8	16	24	64	115	165
50-Marge's Little Lulu & Witch Hazel Trick 'N' Treat (10/61)	10	20	30	80	140	200
51-Tarzan, King of the Jungle by Jesse Marsh (11/61)-Painted-c	7	14	21	56	101	145
52-Uncle Donald & His Nephews Dude Ranch (Disney; 11/61)	7	14	21	56	101	145
53-Donald Duck Merry Christmas (Disney; 12/61)	7	14	21	56	101	145
54-Woody Woodpecker's Christmas Party (12/61)-Issued after No. 55	7	14	21	56	96	135
55-Daisy Duck & Uncle Scrooge Showboat (Disney; 9/61)	8	16	24	64	115	165

NOTE: All issues printed with & without ad on back cover.

DELL JUNIOR TREASURY
Dell Publishing Co.: June, 1955 - No. 10, Oct, 1957 (15¢) (All painted-c)

	GD 2.0	VG 4.0	FN 6.0	VF 8.0	VF/NM 9.0	NM- 9.2
1-Alice in Wonderland; r/4-Color #331 (52 pgs.)	10	20	30	73	107	140
2-Aladdin & the Wonderful Lamp	8	16	24	58	82	105
3-Gulliver's Travels (1/56)	8	16	24	53	74	95
4-Adventures of Mr. Frog & Miss Mouse	8	16	24	55	78	100
5-The Wizard of Oz (7/56)	8	16	24	58	82	105
6-10: 6-Heidi (10/56). 7-Santa and the Angel. 8-Raggedy Ann and the Came with the Wrinkled Knees. 9-Clementina the Flying Pig. 10-Adventures of Tom Sawyer	8	16	24	53	74	95

DEMOLITION MAN
DC Comics: Nov, 1993 - No. 4, Feb, 1994 ($1.75, color, limited series)

	GD 2.0	VG 4.0	FN 6.0	VF 8.0	VF/NM 9.0	NM- 9.2
1-4-Movie adaptation						2.25

DEMON, THE (See Detective Comics No. 482-485)
National Periodical Publications: Aug-Sept, 1972 - V3#16, Jan, 1974

	GD 2.0	VG 4.0	FN 6.0	VF 8.0	VF/NM 9.0	NM- 9.2
1-Origin; Kirby-c/a in all	6	12	18	40	55	70
2-5	3	7	10	21	28	35
6-16	2	4	6	14	18	22

DEMON, THE (1st limited series)(Also see Cosmic Odyssey #2)
DC Comics: Nov, 1986 - No. 4, Feb, 1987 (75¢, limited series)(#2 has #4 of 4 on-c)

	GD 2.0	VG 4.0	FN 6.0	VF 8.0	VF/NM 9.0	NM- 9.2
1-4: Matt Wagner-a(p) & scripts in all. 4-Demon & Jason Blood become separate entities.						3.00

DEMON, THE (2nd Series)
DC Comics: July, 1990 - No. 58, May, 1995 ($1.50/$1.75/$1.95)

	GD 2.0	VG 4.0	FN 6.0	VF 8.0	VF/NM 9.0	NM- 9.2
1-Grant scripts begin, ends #39: 1-4-Painted-c						4.00
2-18,20-27,29-39,41,42,46,47: 3,8-Batman app. (cameo #4). 12-Bisley painted-c. 12-15,21-Lobo app. (1 pg. cameo #11). 23-Robin app. 29-Superman app. 31,33-39-Lobo app.						2.50
19,28,40: 19-($2.50, 44 pgs.)-Lobo poster stapled inside. 28-Superman-c/story; begin $1.75-c. 40-Garth Ennis scripts begin						4.00
43-45-Hitman app.	1	2	3	5	6	8
46-48 Return of The Haunted Tank-c/s. 48-Begin $1.95-c.						5.00
49,51,0-(10/94),55-58: 51-(9/94)						2.50
50 ($2.95, 52 pgs.)						3.00
52-54-Hitman-s						5.00
Annual 1 (1992, $3.00, 68 pgs.)-Eclipso-c/story						3.00
Annual 2 (1993, $3.50, 68 pgs.)-1st app. of Hitman	2	4	6	10	13	16

NOTE: *Alan Grant scripts in #1-16, 20, 21, 23-25, 30-39, Annual 1.* ***Wagner*** *a/scripts-22.*

DEMON DREAMS
Pacific Comics: Feb, 1984 - No. 2, May, 1984

	GD 2.0	VG 4.0	FN 6.0	VF 8.0	VF/NM 9.0	NM- 9.2
1,2-Mostly r-/Heavy Metal						2.25

The Demon (2nd series) #18 © DC

Dennis the Menace #9 © FAW

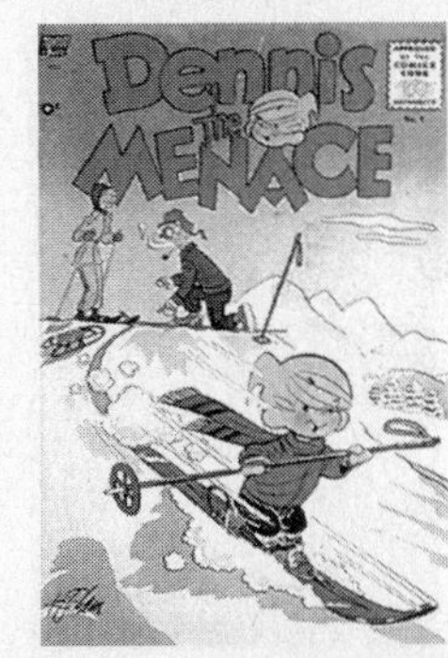

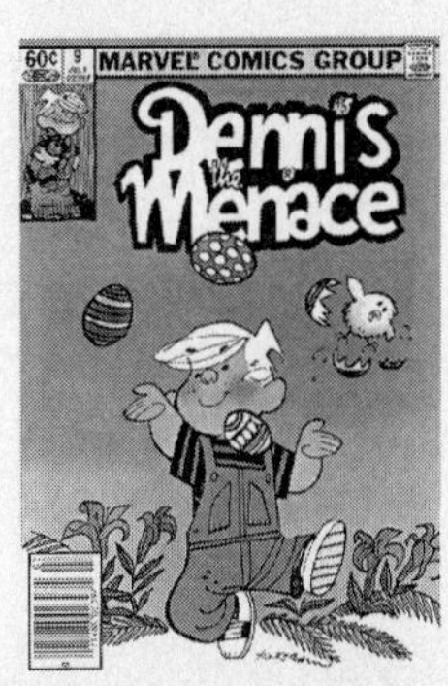

Dennis the Menace #9 © MAR

GD 2.0 | VG 4.0 | FN 6.0 | VF 8.0 | VF/NM 9.0 | NM- 9.2

DEMON: DRIVEN OUT
DC Comics: Nov, 2003 - No. 6, Apr, 2004 ($2.50, limited series)
1-6-Dysart-s/Mhan-a 2.50

DEMON-HUNTER
Seaboard Periodicals (Atlas): Sept, 1975
1-Origin/1st app. Demon-Hunter; Buckler-c/a 1 2 3 5 6 8

DEMON KNIGHT: A GRIMJACK GRAPHIC NOVEL
First Publishing: 1990 ($8.95, 52 pgs.)
nn-Flint Henry-a 9.00

DEMONSLAYER
Image Comics: Nov, 1999 - No. 3, Jan, 2000 ($2.95)
1-3-Story & art by Mychaels & Mendoza 3.00

DEMONSLAYER: INTO HELL (Volume 2)
Image Comics: Apr, 2000 - No. 3, Aug, 2000 ($2.95)
1-3-Story & art by Mychaels 3.00
1-3 ($5.00) Variant cover editions 5.00

DEMONWARS: EYE FOR AN EYE (R.A. Salvatore's...)
CrossGeneration Comics (Code 6 Comics): Jun, 2003 - No. 5, Nov, 2003 ($2.95, lim. series)
1-5-Ciencin-s/Tocchini-a 3.00

DEMONWARS: TRIAL BY FIRE (R.A. Salvatore's...)
CrossGeneration Comics (Code 6 Comics): Jan, 2003 - No. 5, May, 2003 ($2.95, lim. series)
1-5-Ciencin-s/Wagner-a 3.00
TPB (2003, $9.95) r/#1-5; new short story by Salvatore 10.00

DENNIS THE MENACE (TV with 1959 issues) (Becomes ...Fun Fest Series; See The Best of... & The Very Best of...)(...Fun Fest on-c only to #156-166)
Standard Comics/Pines No.15-31/Hallden (Fawcett) No.32 on: 8/53 - #14, 1/56; #15, 3/56 - #31, 11/58; #32, 1/59 - #166, 11/79

1-1st app. Dennis, Mr. & Mrs. Wilson, Ruff & Dennis' mom & dad; Wiseman-a, written by Fred Toole-most issues 62 124 186 388 594 800
2 30 60 90 170 245 320
3-10: 8-Last pre-code issue 16 32 48 92 131 170
11-20 12 24 36 71 98 125
21,23-30 10 20 30 56 73 90
22-1st app. Margaret w/blonde hair 11 22 33 62 84 105
31-1st app. Joey 11 22 33 62 84 105
32-38,40(1/60): 37-A-Bomb blast panel 7 14 21 37 46 55
39-1st app. Gina (11/59) 8 16 24 40 50 60
41-60(7/62) 4 8 12 22 30 38
61-80(9/65),100(1/69) 3 6 9 16 20 24
81-99 2 4 6 12 16 20
101-117: 102-Last 12¢ issue 2 4 6 10 12 15
118(1/72)-131 (All 52 pages) 2 4 6 11 14 18
132(1/74)-142,144-160 1 2 3 5 7 9
143(3/76) Olympic-c/s; low print 2 4 6 11 14 18
161-166 1 3 4 6 8 10
NOTE: *Wiseman c/a-1-46, 53, 68, 69.*

DENNIS THE MENACE (Giants) (No. 1 titled Giant Vacation Special; becomes Dennis the Menace Bonus Magazine No. 76 on)
(#1-8,18,23,25,30,38: 100 pgs.; rest to #41: 84 pgs.; #42-75: 68 pgs.)
Standard/Pines/Hallden(Fawcett): Summer, 1955 - No. 75, Dec, 1969

nn-Giant Vacation Special(Summ/55-Standard) 18 36 54 102 146 190
nn-Christmas issue (Winter '55) 16 32 48 92 131 170
2-Giant Vacation Special (Summer '56-Pines) 14 28 42 79 110 140
3-Giant Christmas issue (Winter '56-Pines) 13 26 39 74 102 130
4-Giant Vacation Special (Summer '57-Pines) 12 24 36 69 95 120
5-Giant Christmas issue (Winter '57-Pines) 12 24 36 69 95 120
6-In Hawaii (Giant Vacation Special)(Summer '58-Pines) 11 22 33 64 87 110
6-In Hawaii (Summer '59-Hallden)-2nd printing; says 3rd large printing on-c
6-In Hawaii (Summer '60)-3rd printing; says 4th large printing on-c
6-In Hawaii (Summer '62)-4th printing; says 5th large printing on-c each.... 8 16 24 43 54 65
6-Giant Christmas issue (Winter '58) 11 22 33 64 87 110
7-In Hollywood (Winter '59-Hallden) 6 12 18 40 55 70
7-In Hollywood (Summer '61)-2nd printing 4 8 12 25 33 42
8-In Mexico (Winter '60, 100 pgs.-Hallden/Fawcett) 6 12 18 40 55 70
8-In Mexico (Summer '62, 2nd printing) 4 8 12 25 33 42
9-Goes to Camp (Summer '61, 84 pgs.)-1st CCA approved issue 6 12 18 40 55 70
9-Goes to Camp (Summer '62)-2nd printing 4 8 12 25 33 42
10-12: 10-X-Mas issue (Winter '61), 11-Giant Christmas issue (Winter '62), 12-Triple Feature (Winter '62) 6 12 18 43 59 75
13-17: 13-Best of Dennis the Menace (Spring '63)-Reprints, 14-And His Dog Ruff (Summer '63), 15-In Washington, D.C. (Summer '63), 16-Goes to Camp (Summer '63)-Reprints No. 9, 17-& His Pal Joey (Winter '63) 4 8 12 27 36 45
18-In Hawaii (Reprints No. 6) 3 7 10 21 28 35
19-Giant Christmas issue (Winter '63) 4 8 12 27 36 45
20-Spring Special (Spring '64) 4 8 12 27 36 45
21-40 (Summer '66): 30-r/#6. #35-Xmas spec.Wint,'65 3 6 9 19 25 32
41-60 (Fall '68) 2 4 6 14 18 22
61-75 (12/69): 68-Partial-r/#6 2 4 6 11 14 18
NOTE: *Wiseman c/a-1-8, 12, 14, 15, 17, 20, 22, 27, 28, 31, 35, 36, 41, 49.*

DENNIS THE MENACE
Marvel Comics Group: Nov, 1981 - No. 13, Nov, 1982
1-New-a 2 4 6 8 10 12
2-13: 2-New art. 3-Part-r. 4,5-r. 5-X-Mas-c & issue, 7-Spider Kid-c/sty 1 2 3 4 5 7
NOTE: *Hank Ketcham c-most; a-3, 12. Wiseman a-4, 5.*

DENNIS THE MENACE AND HIS DOG RUFF
Hallden/Fawcett: Summer, 1961
1-Wiseman-c/a 6 12 18 40 55 70

DENNIS THE MENACE AND HIS FRIENDS
Fawcett Publ.: 1969; No. 5, Jan, 1970 - No. 46, April, 1980 (All reprints)
Dennis the Menace & Joey No. 2 (7/69) 2 4 6 14 18 22
Dennis the Menace & Ruff No. 2 (9/69) 2 4 6 14 18 22
Dennis the Menace & Mr. Wilson No. 1 (10/69) 3 6 9 18 23 28
Dennis & Margaret No. 1 (Winter '69) 3 6 9 18 23 28
5-12: 5-Dennis the Menace & Margaret. 6-...& Joey. 7-...& Ruff. 8-...& Mr. Wilson 2 4 6 9 11 14
13-21-(52 pg Giants): 13-(1/72). 21-(1/74) 2 4 6 11 14 18
22-37 1 3 4 6 8 10
38-46 (Digest size, 148 pgs., 4/78, 95¢) 2 4 6 9 11 14
NOTE: *Titles rotate every four issues, beginning with No. 5. Joey issues: #2(7/69),6,10,14,18,22,26,30,34. Ruff issues: #2(9/69), 7,11,15,19,23,27,31,35. Mr. Wilson issues: #1(10/69),8,12,16,20,24,28,32,36. Margaret issues: #1(Wint./69),5,9,13,17,21,25,29,33,37.*

DENNIS THE MENACE AND HIS PAL JOEY
Fawcett Publ.: Summer, 1961 (10¢) (See Dennis the Menace Giants No. 45)
1-Wiseman-c/a 6 12 18 40 55 70

DENNIS THE MENACE AND THE BIBLE KIDS
Word Books: 1977 (36 pgs.)
1-6: 1-Jesus. 2-Joseph. 3-David. 4-The Bible Girls. 5-Moses. 6-More About Jesus 2 4 6 8 10 12
7-9-Low print run: 7-The Lord's Prayer. 8-Stories Jesus told. 9-Paul, God's Traveller 2 4 6 11 14 18
10-Low print run; In the Beginning 2 4 6 14 18 22
NOTE: *Ketcham c/a in all.*

DENNIS THE MENACE BIG BONUS SERIES
Fawcett Publications: No. 10, Feb, 1980 - No. 11, Apr, 1980
10,11 1 2 3 5 6 8

DENNIS THE MENACE BONUS MAGAZINE (Formerly Dennis the Menace Giants Nos. 1-75) (...Big Bonus Series on-c for #174-194)
Fawcett Publications: No. 76, 1/70 - No. 95, 7/71; No. 95, 7/71; No. 97, '71; No. 194, 10/79; (No. 76-124: 68 pgs.; No. 125-163: 52 pgs.; No. 164 on: 36 pgs.)
76-90(3/71) 2 4 6 10 14 18
91-95, 97-110(10/72): Two #95's with same date(7/71) A-Summer Games, and B-That's Our Boy. No #96 2 4 6 10 13 16
111-124 2 4 6 8 10 12
125-163-(52 pgs.) 2 4 6 8 10 12
164-194: 166-Indicia printed backwards 1 2 3 4 5 7

DENNIS THE MENACE COMICS DIGEST
Marvel Comics Group: April, 1982 - No. 3, Aug, 1982 ($1.25, digest-size)
1-3-Reprints 1 3 4 6 8 10
1-Mistakenly printed with DC emblem on cover 2 4 6 10 12 15
NOTE: *Ketcham c-all. Wiseman a-all. A few thousand #1's were published with a DC emblem on cover.*

DENNIS THE MENACE FUN BOOK
Fawcett Publications/Standard Comics: 1960 (100 pgs.)
1-Part Wiseman-a 7 14 21 50 68 85

Desperado #3 © LEV

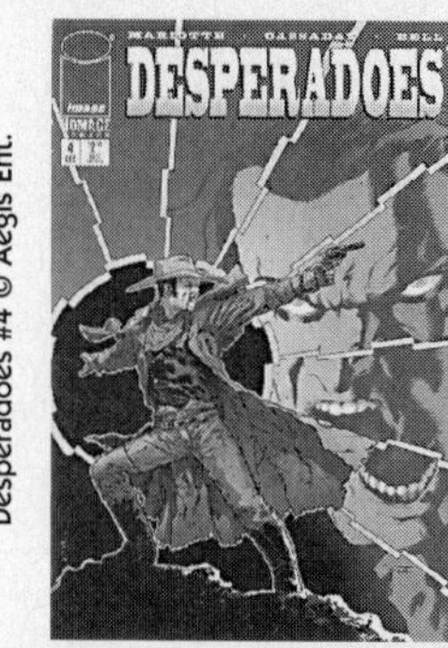

Desperadoes #4 © Aegis Ent.

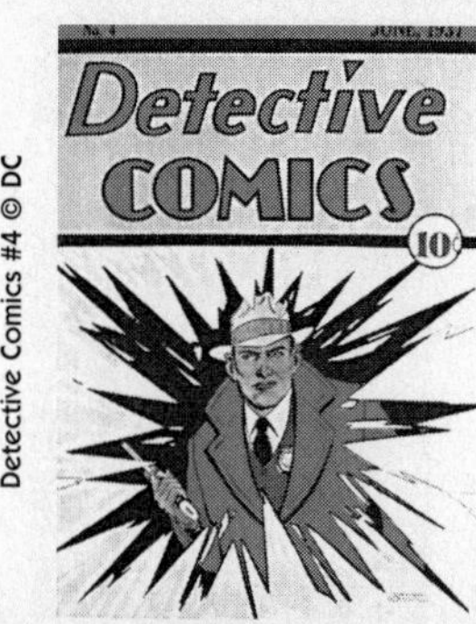

Detective Comics #4 © DC

	GD 2.0	VG 4.0	FN 6.0	VF 8.0	VF/NM 9.0	NM- 9.2

DENNIS THE MENACE FUN FEST SERIES (Formerly Dennis the Menace #166)
Hallden (Fawcett): No. 16, Jan, 1980 - No. 17, Mar, 1980 (40¢)
16,17-By Hank Ketcham 1 2 3 4 5 7

DENNIS THE MENACE POCKET FULL OF FUN!
Fawcett Publications (Hallden): Spring, 1969 - No. 50, March, 1980 (196 pgs.) (Digest size)
1-Reprints in all issues 6 12 18 40 55 70
2-10 4 8 12 27 36 45
11-20 3 6 9 16 20 25
21-28 2 4 6 11 14 18
29-50: 35,40,46-Sunday strip-r 2 4 6 8 10 12
NOTE: *No. 1-28 are 196 pgs.; No. 29-36: 164 pgs.; No. 37: 148 pgs.; No. 38 on: 132 pgs. No. 8, 11, 15, 21, 25, 29 all contain strip reprints.*

DENNIS THE MENACE TELEVISION SPECIAL
Fawcett Publ. (Hallden Div.): Summer, 1961 - No. 2, Spring, 1962 (Giant)
1 7 14 21 46 63 80
2 4 8 12 25 33 42

DENNIS THE MENACE TRIPLE FEATURE
Fawcett Publications: Winter, 1961 (Giant)
1-Wiseman-c/a 7 14 21 46 63 80

DEPUTY, THE (TV)
Dell Publishing Co.: No. 1077, Feb-Apr, 1960 - No. 1225, Oct-Dec, 1961 (all-Henry Fonda photo-c)
Four Color 1077 (#1)-Buscema-a 14 28 42 97 149 200
Four Color 1130 (9-11/60)-Buscema-a,1225 11 22 33 75 110 145

DEPUTY DAWG (TV) (Also see New Terrytoons)
Dell Publishing Co./Gold Key: Oct-Dec, 1961 - No. 1299, 1962; No. 1, Aug, 1965
Four Color 1238,1299 12 24 36 87 134 180
1(10164-508)(8/65)-Gold Key 12 24 36 87 134 180

DEPUTY DAWG PRESENTS DINKY DUCK AND HASHIMOTO-SAN (TV)
Gold Key: August, 1965
1(10159-508) 11 22 33 77 114 150

DESERT GOLD (See Zane Grey 4-Color 467)

DESIGN FOR SURVIVAL (Gen. Thomas S. Power's...)
American Security Council Press: 1968 (36 pgs. in color) (25¢)
nn-Propaganda against the Threat of Communism-Aircraft cover; H-Bomb panel
3 6 9 19 25 32
Twin Circle Edition-Cover shows panels from inside 2 4 6 12 16 20

DESPERADO (Becomes Black Diamond Western No. 9 on)
Lev Gleason Publications: June, 1948 - No. 8, Feb, 1949 (All 52 pgs.)
1-Biro-c on all; contains inside photo-c of Charles Biro, Lev Gleason & Bob Wood
15 30 45 86 123 160
2 9 18 27 52 66 80
3-Story with over 20 killings 9 18 27 54 70 85
4-8 7 14 21 37 46 55
NOTE: ***Barry** a-2. **Fuje** a-4, 8. **Guardineer** a-5-7. **Kida** a-3-7. **Ed Moore** a-4, 6.*

DESPERADOES
Image Comics (Homage): Sept, 1997 - No. 5, June, 1998 ($2.50/$2.95)
1-5-Mariotte-s/Cassaday-c/a: 1-($2.50-c). 2-5-($2.95) 3.00
...: A Moment's Sunlight TPB ('98, $16.95) r/#1-5 17.00
...: Epidemic! (11/99, $5.95) Mariotte-s 6.00

DESPERADOES: QUIET OF THE GRAVE
DC Comics (Homage): Jul, 2001 - No. 5, Nov, 2001 ($2.95)
1-5-Jeff Mariotte-s/John Severin-c/a 3.00
TPB (2002, $14.95) r/#1-5; intro. by Brian Keene 15.00

DESPERATE TIMES (See Savage Dragon)
Image Comics: Jun, 1998 - No. 4, Dec, 1998; Nov, 2000 - No. 4, July, 2001 ($2.95, B&W)
1-4-Chris Eliopoulos-s/a 3.00
(Vol. 2) 1-4 3.00
(Vol. 3) 0-(1/04, $3.50) Pages read sideways 3.50
(Vol. 3) 1-Pages read sideways 3.00

DESTINATION MOON (See Fawcett Movie Comics, Space Adventures #20, 23, & Strange Adventures #1)

DESTINY: A CHRONICLE OF DEATHS FORETOLD (See Sandman)
DC Comics (Vertigo): 1997 - No.3, 1998 ($5.95, limited series)
1-3-Alisa Kwitney-s in all: 1-Kent Williams & Michael Zulli-a, Williams painted-c. 2-Williams & Scott Hampton-painted-c/a. 3-Williams & Guay-a 6.00
TPB (2000, $14.95) r/series 15.00

DESTROY!!
Eclipse Comics: 1986 ($4.95, B&W, magazine-size, one-shot)
1 5.00
3-D Special 1-r-/#1 ($2.50) 5.00

DESTROYER, THE
Marvel Comics: Nov, 1989 - No. 9, Jun, 1990 ($2.25, B&W, magazine, 52 pgs.)
1-Based on Remo Williams movie, paperbacks 4.00
2-9: 2-Williamson part inks. 4-Ditko-a 3.00

DESTROYER, THE
Marvel Comics: V2#1, March, 1991 ($1.95, 52 pgs.)
V3#1, Dec, 1991 - No. 4, Mar, 1992 ($1.95, mini-series)
V2#1,V3#1-4: Based on Remo Williams paperbacks. V3#1-4-Simonson-c. 3-Morrow-a 2.50

DESTROYER, THE (Also see Solar, Man of the Atom)
Valiant: Apr, 1995 ($2.95, color, one-shot)
0-Indicia indicates #1 3.00

DESTROYER DUCK
Eclipse Comics: Feb, 1982 - No. 7, May, 1984 (#2-7: Baxter paper) ($1.50)
1-Origin Destroyer Duck; 1st app. Groo; Kirby-c/a(p) 1 3 4 6 8 10
2-5: 2-Starling back-up begins; Kirby-c/a(p) thru #5 5.00
6,7 4.00
NOTE: ***Neal Adams** c-1i. **Kirby** c/a-1-5p. **Miller** c-7.*

DESTRUCTOR, THE
Atlas/Seaboard: February, 1975 - No. 4, Aug, 1975
1-Origin/1st app.; Ditko/Wood-a; Wood-c(i) 1 3 4 6 8 10
2-4: 2-Ditko/Wood-a. 3,4-Ditko-a(p) 1 2 3 5 6 8

DETECTIVE COMICS (Also see other Batman titles)
National Periodical Publications/DC Comics: Mar, 1937 - Present
1-(Scarce)-Slam Bradley & Spy by Siegel & Shuster, Speed Saunders by Guardineer, Flat Foot Flannigan by Gustavson, Cosmo, the Phantom of Disguise, Buck Marshall, Bruce Nelson begin; Chin Lung in 'Claws of the Red Dragon' serial begins; Vincent Sullivan-c
8,500 17,000 25,500 60,000 - -
2 (Rare)-Creig Flessel-c begin; new logo 2350 4700 7050 16,600 - -
3 (Rare) 1675 3350 5025 11,700 - -
4,5: 5-Larry Steele begins 950 1900 2850 4750 6425 8100
6,7,9,10 688 1376 2064 3440 4620 5800
8-Mister Chang-c; classic-c 1025 2050 3075 5125 6913 8700
11-17,19: 16-Has interior ad for Action Comics #1. 17-1st app. Fu Manchu in Detective
525 1050 1575 2625 3538 4450
18-Fu Manchu-c; last Flessel-c 850 1700 2550 4250 5725 7200
20-The Crimson Avenger begins (1st app.) 788 1576 2364 3940 5320 6700
21,23-25 412 824 1236 2060 2780 3500
22-1st Crimson Avenger-c by Chambers (12/38) 538 1076 1614 2690 3620 4550
26 375 750 1125 1875 2563 3250
27-The Bat-Man & Commissioner Gordon begin (1st app.), created by Bill Finger & Bob Kane (5/39); Batman-c (1st)(by Kane). Bat-Man's secret identity revealed as Bruce Wayne in 6pg. sty. Signed Rob't Kane (also see Det. PIcture Stories #5 & Funny Pages V3#1)
31,500 63,000 94,500 190,000 300,000 410,000
27-Reprint, Oversize 13-1/2x10". WARNING: This comic is an exact duplicate reprint of the original except for its size. DC published it in 1974 with a second cover titling it as Famous First Edition. There have been many reported cases of the outer cover being removed and the interior sold as the original edition. The reprint with the new outer cover removed is practically worthless; see Famous First Edition for value.
28-2nd app. The Batman (6 pg. story); non-Bat-Man-c; signed Rob't Kane
1765 3530 5295 13,400 21,700 30,000
29-1st app. Doctor Death-c/story, Batman's 1st name villain. 1st 2 part story (10 pgs.).
2nd Batman-c by Kane 2941 5882 8823 22,000 36,000 50,000
30-Dr. Death app. Story concludes from issue #29. Classic Batman splash panel by Kane.
710 1420 2130 4970 7985 11,000
31-Classic Batman over castle cover; 1st app. The Monk & 1st Julie Madison (Bruce Wayne's 1st love interest); 1st Batplane (Bat-Gyro) and Batarang; 2nd 2-part Batman adventure. Gardner Fox takes over script from Bill Finger. 1st mention of locale (New York City) where Batman lives 2941 5882 8823 22,000 36,000 50,000
32-Batman story concludes from issue #31. 1st app. Dala (Monk's assistant). Batman uses gun for 1st time to slay The Monk and Dala. This was the 1st time a costumed hero used a gun in comic books. 1st Batman head logo on cover
619 1238 1857 4333 6967 9600
33-Origin The Batman (2 pgs.)(1st told origin); Batman gun holster-c; Batman w/smoking gun panel at end of story. Batman story now 12 pgs. Classic Batman-c
3825 7650 11,475 29,000 47,000 65,000
34-2nd Crimson Avenger-c by Creig Flessel and last non Batman-c. Story from issue #32 x-over as Bruce Wayne sees Julie Madison off to America from Paris. Classic Batman

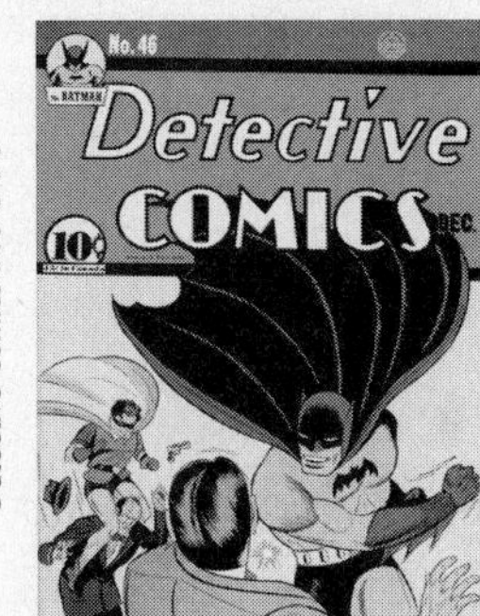

Detective Comics #46 © DC

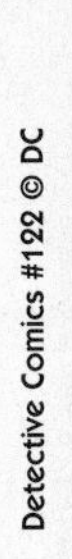

Detective Comics #122 © DC

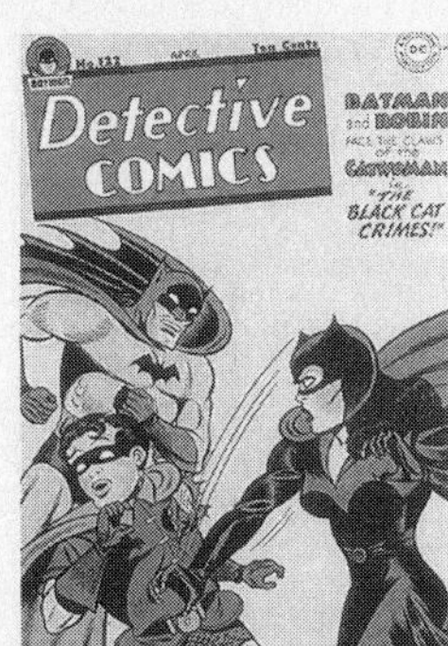

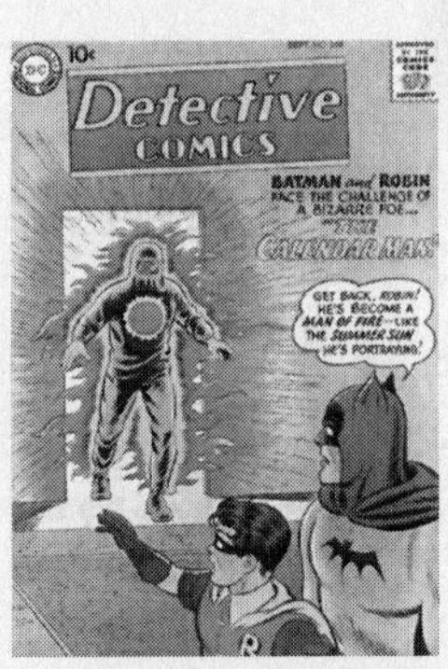

Detective Comics #259 © DC

	GD 2.0	VG 4.0	FN 6.0	VF 8.0	VF/NM 9.0	NM- 9.2
splash panel used later in Batman #1 for origin story. Steve Malone begins	484	968	1452	3388	5444	7500
35-Classic Batman hypodermic needle-c that reflects story in issue #34. Classic Batman with smoking .45 automatic splash panel. Batman-c begin	1029	2058	3087	7718	12,609	17,500
36-Batman-c that reflects adventure in issue #35. Origin/1st app. of Dr. Hugo Strange (1st major villain, 2/40). 1st finned-gloves worn by Batman	774	1548	2322	5418	8709	12,000
37-Last solo Golden-Age Batman adventure in Detective Comics. Panel at end of story reflects solo Batman adventure in Batman #1 that was originally planned for Detective #38. Cliff Crosby begins	677	1354	2031	4739	7620	10,500
38-Origin/1st app. Robin the Boy Wonder (4/40); Batman and Robin-c begin; cover by Kane & Robinson taken from splash page	3525	7050	10,575	26,600	43,300	60,000
39-Opium story	581	1162	1743	4067	6534	9000
40-Origin & 1st app. Clay Face (Basil Karlo); 1st Joker cover app. (6/40); Joker story intended for this issue was used in Batman #1 instead; cover is similar to splash page in 2nd Joker story in Batman #1	677	1354	2031	4739	7620	10,500
41-Robin's 1st solo	345	690	1035	2243	3622	5000
42-44: 44-Crimson Avenger-new costume	250	500	750	1563	2407	3250
45-1st Joker story in Det. (3rd book app. & 4th story app. over all, 11/40)	345	690	1035	2243	3622	5000
46-50: 46-Death of Hugo Strange. 48-1st time car called Batmobile (2/41); Gotham City 1st mention in Detective (1st mentioned in Wow #1; also see Batman #4). 49-Last Clay Face	231	462	693	1444	2222	3000
51-57	154	308	462	963	1482	2000
58-1st Penguin app. (12/41); last Speed Saunders; Fred Ray-c	423	846	1269	2790	4495	6200
59,60: 59-Last Steve Malone; 2nd Penguin; Wing becomes Crimson Avenger's aide. 60-Intro. Air Wave; Joker app. (2nd in Det.)	169	338	507	1056	1628	2200
61,63: 63-Last Cliff Crosby; 1st app. Mr. Baffle	150	300	450	938	1444	1950
62-Joker-c/story (2nd Joker-c, 4/42)	262	524	786	1638	2519	3400
64-Origin & 1st app. Boy Commandos by Simon & Kirby (6/42); Joker app.	386	772	1158	2509	4055	5600
65-1st Boy Commandos-c (S&K-a on Boy Commandos & Ray/Robinson-a on Batman & Robin on-c; 4 artists on one-c)	300	600	900	1925	3063	4200
66-Origin & 1st app. Two-Face	372	744	1116	2418	3909	5400
67-1st Penguin-c (9/42)	246	492	738	1538	2369	3200
68-Two-Face-c/story; 1st Two-Face-c	169	338	507	1056	1628	2200
69-Joker-c/story	169	338	507	1056	1628	2200
70	123	246	369	769	1185	1600
71-Joker-c/story	146	292	438	913	1407	1900
72,74,75: 74-1st Tweedledum & Tweedledee plus-c; S&K-a	110	220	330	688	1057	1425
73-Scarecrow-c/story (1st Scarecrow-c)	135	270	405	844	1297	1750
76-Newsboy Legion & The Sandman x-over in Boy Commandos; S&K-a; Joker-c/story	167	334	501	1044	1610	2175
77-79: All S&K-a	115	230	345	719	1110	1500
80-Two-Face app.; S&K-a	125	250	375	781	1203	1625
81,82,84,86-90: 81-1st Cavalier-c & app. 89-Last Crimson Avenger; 2nd Cavalier-c & app.	92	184	276	575	888	1200
83-1st "skinny" Alfred (1/44)(see Batman #21; last S&K Boy Commandos (also #92,128); most issues #84 on signed S&K are not by them	100	200	300	625	963	1300
85-Joker-c/story; last Spy; Kirby/Klech Boy Commandos	121	242	363	756	1166	1575
91,102-Joker-c/story	115	230	345	719	1110	1500
92-98: 96-Alfred's last name 'Beagle' revealed, later changed to 'Pennyworth' in #214	77	154	231	481	741	1000
99-Penguin-c	115	230	345	719	1110	1500
100 (6/45)	125	250	375	781	1203	1625
101,103-108,110-113,115-117,119: 108-1st Bat-signal-c (2/46). 114-1st small logo (8/46)	73	146	219	456	703	950
109,114,118-Joker-c/stories	100	200	300	625	963	1300
120-Penguin-c (white-c, rare above fine)	169	338	507	1056	1628	2200
121,123,125,127,129,130	69	138	207	431	666	900
122-1st Catwoman-c (4/47)	142	284	426	888	1369	1850
124,128-Joker-c/stories	96	192	288	600	925	1250
126-Penguin-c	96	192	288	600	925	1250
131-134,136,139	62	124	186	388	594	800
135-Frankenstein-c/story	79	158	237	494	760	1025
137-Joker-c/story; last Air Wave	81	162	243	506	778	1050
138-Origin Robotman (see Star Spangled #7 for 1st app.); series ends #202	113	226	339	706	1091	1475
140-The Riddler-c/story (1st app., 10/48)	439	878	1317	3073	4937	6800

	GD 2.0	VG 4.0	FN 6.0	VF 8.0	VF/NM 9.0	NM- 9.2
141,143-148,150: 150-Last Boy Commandos	62	124	186	388	594	800
142-2nd Riddler-c/story	119	238	357	744	1147	1550
149-Joker-c/story	83	166	249	519	797	1075
151-Origin & 1st app. Pow Wow Smith, Indian lawman (9/49) & begins series	75	150	225	469	722	975
152,154,155,157-160: 152-Last Slam Bradley	62	124	186	388	594	800
153-1st app. Roy Raymond TV Detective (11/49) ; origin The Human Fly	69	138	207	431	666	900
156(2/50)-The new classic Batmobile	87	174	261	544	835	1125
161-167,169,170,172-176: Last 52 pg. issue	56	112	168	350	538	725
168-Origin the Joker	345	690	1035	2243	3622	5000
171-Penguin-c	89	178	267	556	853	1150
177-179,181-186,188,189,191,192,194-199,201,202,204,206-210,212,214-216: 184-1st app. Fire Fly. 185-Secret of Batman's utility belt. 187-Two-Face app. 202-Last Robotman & Pow Wow Smith. 215-1st app. of Batmen of all Nations. 216-Last precode (2/55)	52	104	156	317	484	650
180,193-Joker-c/story	58	116	174	363	557	750
187-Two-Face-c/story	55	110	165	340	520	700
190-Origin Batman retold	75	150	225	469	722	975
200(10/53), 205: 205-Origin Batcave	69	138	207	431	666	900
203,211-Catwoman-c/stories	58	116	174	363	557	750
213-Origin & 1st app. Mirror Man	62	124	186	388	594	800
217-224: 218-Batman Jr. & Robin Sr. app.	45	90	135	275	418	560
225-(11/55)-1st app. Martian Manhunter, John Jones; later changed to J'onn J'onzz; origin begins; also see Batman #78	364	728	1092	3331	5666	8000
226-Origin Martian Manhunter cont'd (2nd app.)	138	276	414	863	1332	1800
227-229: Martian Manhunter stories in all	55	110	165	340	520	700
230-1st app. Mad Hatter; brief recap origin of Martian Manhunter	56	112	168	350	538	725
231-Brief origin recap Martian Manhunter	40	80	120	244	372	500
232,234,237-240: 239-Early DC grey tone-c	40	80	120	239	357	475
233-Origin & 1st app. Batwoman (7/56)	135	270	405	844	1297	1750
235-Origin Batman & his costume; tells how Bruce Wayne's father (Thomas Wayne) wore Bat costume & fought crime (reprinted in Batman #255)	65	130	195	406	623	840
236-1st S.A. issue; J'onn J'onzz talks to parents and Mars-1st since being stranded on Earth; 1st app. Bat-Tank?	43	86	129	262	399	535
241-260: 246-Intro. Diane Meade, John Jones' girl. 249-Batwoman-c/app. 253-1st app. The Terrible Trio. 254-Bat-Hound-c/story. 257-Intro. & 1st app. Whirly Bats. 259-1st app. The Calendar Man	35	70	105	198	287	375
261-264,266,268-271: 261-J. Jones tie-in to sci/fi movie "Incredible Shrinking Man"; 1st app. Dr. Double X. 262-Origin Jackal. 268,271-Manhunter origin recap	27	54	81	154	222	290
265-Batman's origin retold with new facts	40	80	120	230	335	440
267-Origin & 1st app. Bat-Mite (5/59)	40	80	120	241	363	485
272,274,275,277-280	22	44	66	127	184	240
273-J'onn J'onzz i.d. revealed for 1st time	23	46	69	132	191	250
276-2nd app. Bat-Mite	25	50	75	144	207	270
281-292, 294-297: 285,286,292-Batwoman-c/app. 287-Origin J'onn J'onzz retold. 289-Bat-Mite-c/story. 292-Last Roy Raymond. 297-Last 10¢ issue (11/61)	18	36	54	102	146	190
293-(7/61)-Aquaman begins (pre #1); ends #300	19	38	57	107	154	200
298-(12/61)-1st modern Clayface (Matt Hagen)	25	50	75	181	278	375
299, 300-(2/62)-Aquaman ends	12	24	36	82	124	165
301-(3/62)-J'onn J'onzz returns to Mars (1st time since stranded on Earth six years before)	10	20	30	73	107	140
302-317,319-321,323,324,326,329,330: 302,307,311,321-Batwoman-c/app. 311-Intro. Zook in John Jones; 1st app. Cat-Man. 321-2nd Terrible Trio. 326-Last J'onn J'onzz, story cont'd in House of Mystery #143; intro. Idol-Head of Diabolu	9	18	27	63	89	115
318,322,325: 318,325-Cat-Man-c/story (2nd & 3rd app.); also 1st & 2nd app. Batwoman as the Cat-Woman. 322-Bat-Girl's 1st/only app. in Det. (6th in all); Batman cameo in J'onn J'onzz (only hero to app. in series)	9	18	27	63	89	115
327-(5/64)-Elongated Man begins, ends #383; 1st new look Batman with new costume; Infantino/Giella new look-a begins; Batman with gun	12	24	36	86	131	175
328-Death of Alfred; Bob Kane biog, 2 pgs.	11	22	33	80	120	160
331,333-340: 334-1st app. The Outsider	7	14	21	51	71	90
342-358,360,361,366-368: 345-Intro Block Buster. 347-"What If" theme story (1/66). 351-Elongated Man new costume. 355-Zatanna x-over in Elongated Man. 356-Alfred brought back in Batman, early SA app.	6	12	18	43	59	75
332,341,365-Joker-c/stories	8	16	24	58	82	105
359-Intro/origin Batgirl (Barbara Gordon)-c/story (1/67); 1st Silver Age app. Killer Moth	13	26	39	92	141	190

Detective Comics #432 © DC

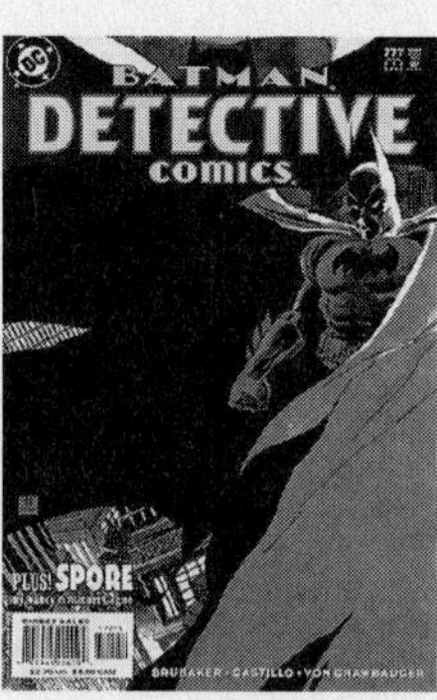

Detective Comics #777 © DC

Detective Comics #800 © DC

	GD 2.0	VG 4.0	FN 6.0	VF 8.0	VF/NM 9.0	NM- 9.2
362-364: 362,364-S.A. Riddler app. (early). 363-2nd app. new Batgirl	7	14	21	46	63	80
369(11/67)-N. Adams-a (Elongated Man); 3rd app. S.A. Catwoman (cameo; leads into Batman #197); 4th app. new Batgirl	8	16	24	58	82	105
370-1st Neal Adams-a on Batman (cover only, 12/67)	7	14	21	46	63	80
371-(1/68) 1st new Batmobile from TV show; classic Batgirl-c	8	16	24	53	74	95
372-376,378-386,389,390: 375-New Batmobile-c	6	12	18	38	52	65
377-S.A. Riddler-c/sty	6	12	18	40	55	70
387-r/1st Batman story from #27 (30th anniversary, 5/69); Joker-c;	7	14	21	51	71	90
388-Joker-c/story; last 12¢ issue	7	14	21	46	63	80
391-394,396,398,399,401,403,405,406,409: 392-1st app. Jason Bard. 401-2nd Batgirl/Robin team-up	4	8	12	29	40	50
395,397,402,404,407,408,410-Neal Adams-a. 404-Tribute to Enemy Ace	6	12	18	40	55	70
400-(6/70)-Origin & 1st app. Man-Bat; 1st Batgirl/Robin team-up (cont'd in #401); Neal Adams-a	13	26	39	92	141	190
411-413: 413-Last 15¢ issue	4	8	12	24	32	40
414-424: All-25¢, 52 pgs. 418-Creeper x-over. 424-Last Batgirl.	4	8	12	27	36	45
425-436: 426,430,436-Elongated Man app. 428,434-Hawkman begins, ends #467	3	6	9	18	23	28
437-New Manhunter begins (10-11/73, 1st app.) by Simonson, ends #443	4	8	12	29	40	50
438-445 (All 100 Page Super Spectaculars): 438-Kubert Hawkman-r. 439-Origin Manhunter. 440-G.A. Manhunter(Adv. #79) by S&K, Hawkman, Dollman, Green Lantern; Toth-a. 441-G.A. Plastic Man, Batman, Ibis-r. 442-G.A. Newsboy Legion, Black Canary, Elongated Man, Dr. Fate-r. 443-Origin The Creeper-r; death of Manhunter; G.A. Green Lantern, Spectre-r; Batman-r/Batman #18. 444-G.A. Kid Eternity-r. 445-G.A. Dr. Midnite-r	6	12	18	40	55	70
446-460: 457-Origin retold & updated	2	4	6	12	16	20
461-465,470,480: 480-(44 pgs.). 463-1st app. Black Spider. 464-2nd app. Black Spider	2	4	6	10	13	16
466-468,471-474,478,479-Rogers-a in all: 466-1st app. Signalman since Batman #139. 470,471-1st modern app. Hugo Strange. 474-1st app. new Deadshot. 478-1st app. 3rd Clayface (Preston Payne). 479-(44 pgs.)	3	7	10	21	28	35
469-Intro/origin Dr. Phosphorous; Simonson-a	3	6	9	19	25	32
475,476-Joker-c/stories; Rogers-a	6	12	18	40	55	70
477-Neal Adams-a(r); Rogers-a (3 pgs.)	3	6	9	19	25	32
481-(Combined with Batman Family, 12-1/78-79, begin $1.00, 68 pg. issues, ends #495); 481-495-Batgirl, Robin solo stories	2	4	6	12	16	20
482-Starlin/Russell, Golden-a; The Demon begins (origin-r), ends #485 (by Ditko #483-485)	2	4	6	10	13	16
483-40th Anniversary issue; origin retold; Newton Batman begins	2	4	6	12	16	20
484-495 (68 pgs): 484-Origin Robin. 485-Death of Batwoman. 487-The Odd Man by Ditko. 489-Robin/Batgirl team-up. 490-Black Lightning begins. 491-(#492 on inside)	2	4	6	8	10	12
496-499	1	2	3	5	7	9
500-($1.50, 52 pgs.)-Batman/Deadman team-up; new Hawkman story by Joe Kubert; incorrectly says 500th anniv. of Det.	2	4	6	10	13	16
501-503,505-523: 512-2nd app. new Dr. Death. 519-Last Batgirl. 521-Green Arrow series begins. 523-Solomon Grundy app.						6.00
504-Joker-c/story	2	4	6	8	10	12
524-2nd app. Jason Todd (cameo)(3/83)	1	2	3	5	6	8
525-3rd app. Jason Todd (See Batman #357)	1	2	3	5	6	8
526-Batman's 500th app. in Detective Comics ($1.50, 68 pgs.); Death of Jason Todd's parents, Joker-c/story (55 pgs.); Bob Kane pin-up	2	4	6	12	16	20
527-531,533,534,536-568,571,573: 538-Cat-Man-c/story cont'd from Batman #371. 542-Jason Todd quits as Robin (becomes Robin again #547). 549,550-Alan Moore scripts (Green Arrow). 554-1st new Black Canary (9/85). 566-Batman villains profiled. 567-Harlan Ellison scripts.						5.00
532,569,570-Joker-c/stories	1	3	4	6	8	10
535-Intro new Robin (JasonTodd)-1st appeared in Batman.						6.00
572-(3/87, $1.25, 60 pgs.)-50th Anniv. of Det. Comics						6.00
574-Origin Batman & Jason Todd retold						6.00
575-Year 2 begins, ends #578	2	4	6	12	16	20
576-578: McFarlane-c/a. 578-Clay Face app.	2	4	6	12	16	20
579-597,599,601-610: 579-New bat wing logo. 583-1st app. villains Scarface & Ventriloquist. 589-595-(52 pgs.)-Each contain free 16 pg. Batman stories. 604-607-Mudpack storyline; 604,607-Contain Batman mini-posters. 610-Faked death of Penguin; artists names app. on tombstone on-c						3.00
598-($2.95, 84 pgs.)- "Blind Justice" storyline begins by Batman movie writer Sam Hamm, ends #600						4.00
600-(5/89, $2.95, 84 pgs.)-50th Anniv. of Batman in Det.; 1 pg. Neal Adams pin-up, among other artists						4.00
611-626,628-658: 612-1st new look Cat-Man; Catwoman app. 615- "The Penguin Affair" part 2 (See Batman #448,449). 617-Joker-c/story. 624-1st new Catwoman (w/death) & 1st new Batwoman. 626-Batman's 600th app. in Detective. 642-Return of Scarface, part 2. 644-Last $1.00-c. 652,653-Huntress-c/story w/new costume plus Charest-c on both						3.00
627-($2.95, 84 pgs.)-Batman's 601st app. in Det.; reprints 1st story/#27 plus 3 versions (2 new) of same story						4.00
659-664: 659-Knightfall part 2; Kelley Jones-c. 660-Knightfall part 4; Bane-c by Sam Kieth. 661-Knightfall part 6; brief Joker & Riddler app. 662-Knightfall part 8; Riddler app.; Sam Kieth-c. 663-Knightfall part 10; Kelley Jones-c. 664-Knightfall part 12; Bane-c/story; Joker app.; continued in Showcase 93 #7 & 8; Jones-c						3.00
665-675: 665,666-Knightfall parts 16 & 18; 666-Bane-c/story. 667-Knightquest: The Crusade & new Batman begins (1st app. in Batman #500). 669-Begin $1.50-c; Knightquest, cont'd in Robin #1. 671,673-Joker app.						2.75
675-($2.95)-Collectors edition w/foil-c						3.50
676-($2.50, 52 pgs.)-KnightsEnd pt. 3						3.00
677,678: 677-KnightsEnd pt. 9. 678-(9/94)-Zero Hour tie-in.						2.75
679-685: 679-(11/94). 682-Troika pt. 3						2.75
682-($2.50) Embossed-c Troika pt. 3						3.00
686-699,701-719: 686-Begin $1.95-c. 693,694-Poison Ivy-c/app. 695-Contagion pt. 2; Catwoman, Penguin app. 696-Contagion pt. 8. 698-Two-Face-c/app. 701-Legacy pt. 6; Batman vs. Bane-c/app. 702-Legacy Epilogue. 703-Final Night x-over. 705-707-Riddler-app. 714,715-Martian Manhunter-app.						2.75
700-($4.95, Collectors Edition)-Legacy pt. 1; Ra's Al Ghul-c/app; Talia & Bane app; book displayed at shops in envelope						5.00
700-($2.95, Regular Edition)-Different-c						3.00
720-740: 720,721-Cataclysm pts. 5,14. 723-Green Arrow app. 730-740-No Man's Land stories						2.75
741-($2.50) Endgame; Joker-c/app.						3.00
742-749,751-765: 742-New look Batman begins. 751,752-Poison Ivy app. 756-Superman-c/app. 759-762-Catwoman back-up; Cooke-a						2.75
750-($4.95, 64 pgs.) Ra's al Ghul-c						5.00
766-772: 766,767-Bruce Wayne: Murderer pt. 1,8. 769-772-Bruce Wayne: Fugitive pts. 4,8,12,16						3.00
773,774,776-799,801: 773-Begin $2.75-c; Sienkiewicz-c. 777-784-Sale-c. 784-786-Alan Scott app. 787-Mad Hatter app. 793-Begin $2.95-c. 797-799-War Games. 801-Lapham-s						3.00
775-($3.50) Sienkiewicz-c						3.50
800-($3.50) Jock-c; aftermath of War Games; back-up by Lapham						3.50
#0-(10/94) Zero Hour tie-in						2.75
#1,000,000 (11/98) 853rd Century x-over						2.75
Annual 1 (1988, $1.50)						5.00
Annual 2-7,9 ('89-'94, '96, 68 pgs.)-4-Painted-c. 5-Joker-c/story (54 pgs.) continued in Robin Annual #1; Sam Kieth-c; Eclipso app. 6-Azrael as Batman in new costume; intro Geist the Twilight Man; Bloodlines storyline. 7-Elseworlds story. 9-Legends of the Dead Earth story						3.00
Annual 8 (1995, $3.95, 68 pgs.)-Year One story						4.00
Annual 10 (1997, $3.95)-Pulp Heroes story						4.00

NOTE: ***Neal Adams*** *c-370, 372, 385, 389, 391, 392, 394-422, 439.* ***Aparo*** *a-437, 438, 444-446, 500, 625-632p, 638-643p; c-430, 437, 440-446, 448, 468-470, 480, 484(back), 492-502,508, 509, 515, 518-522, 641, 716, 719, 722, 724.* ***Austin*** *a(i)-450, 451, 463-468, 471-476; c(i)-474-476, 478.* ***Baily*** *a-443r.* ***Buckler*** *a-434, 446p, 479p; c(p)-467, 482, 505-507, 511, 513-516, 518.* ***Burnley*** *a(Batman)-65, 75, 78, 83, 100, 103, 125; c-62i, 63i, 64, 73i, 78, 83p, 96p, 103p, 105p, 106, 108, 121p, 123p, 125p.* ***Chaykin*** *a-441.* ***Colan*** *a(p)-510, 512, 517, 523, 528-538, 540-546, 555-567; c(p)-510, 512, 528, 530-535, 537, 538, 540, 541, 543-545, 556-558, 560-564.* ***J. Craig*** *a-488.* ***Ditko*** *a-443r, 483-485, 487.* ***Golden*** *a-482p; c-625, 626, 628-631, 633, 644-646.* ***Alan Grant*** *scripts-584-597, 601-621, 641, 642, Annual 5.* ***Grell*** *a-445, 455, 463p, 464p; c-455.* ***Guardineer*** *c-23, 24, 26, 28, 30, 32.* ***Gustavson*** *a-441r.* ***Infantino*** *a-442(2)r, 500, 572.* ***Infantino/Anderson*** *c-333, 337-340, 343, 344, 347, 351, 352, 359, 361-368, 371.* ***Kelley Jones*** *c-651, 657i, 658i, 659, 661, 663-675.* ***Kaluta*** *c-423, 424, 426-428, 431, 434, 438, 484, 486, 572.* ***Bob Kane*** *a-Most early issues #27 on, 297r, 356r, 438-440r, 442r, 443r.* ***Kane/Robinson*** *c-33.* ***Gil Kane*** *a(p)-368, 370-374, 384, 385, 388-407, 438r, 439r, 520.* ***Kane/Anderson*** *c-369.* ***Sam Kieth*** *c-654-656 (657, 658 w/**Kelley Jones**), 660, 662, Annual #5.* ***Kubert*** *a-438r, 439r, 500; c-348, 350.* ***McFarlane*** *c/a(p)-576-578.* ***Meskin*** *a-420r.* ***Mignola*** *c-583.* ***Moldoff*** *c-233-354, 259, 266, 267, 275, 287, 289, 290, 297, 300.* ***Moldoff/Giella*** *a-328, 330, 332, 334, 336, 338, 340, 342, 344, 346, 348, 350, 352, 354, 356.* ***Mooney*** *a-444r.* ***Moreira*** *a-153-300, 419r, 444r, 445r.* ***Nasser/Netzer*** *a-654, 655, 657, 658.* ***Newton*** *a(p)-480, 481, 483-499, 501-509, 511, 513-516, 518-520, 524, 526, 539; c-526p.* ***Irv Novick*** *c-375-377, 383.* ***Robbins*** *a-426p, 429p.* ***Robinson*** *a-part: 66, 68, 71-73; all: 74-76, 79, 80; c-62, 64, 66, 68-74, 76, 79, 82, 86, 88, 442r, 443r.* ***Rogers*** *a-466-468, 471-479p, 481p; c-471p, 472p, 473, 474-479p.* ***Roussos*** *Airwave-76-105(most); c(i)-71, 72, 74-76, 79, 107.* ***Russell*** *a-481i, 482i.* ***Simon/Kirby*** *a-440r, 442r.* ***Simonson*** *a-437-443, 450, 469, 470, 500.* ***Dick Sprang*** *c-77, 82, 84, 85, 87, 89-93, 95-100, 102, 103i, 104i, 106, 108, 114, 117, 118, 122, 123, 128, 129, 131, 133, 135, 141, 148, 149, 168, 622-624.* ***Starlin*** *a-481p, 482p; c-503, 504, 567p.* ***Starr*** *a-444r.* ***Toth*** *a-442; r-414, 416, 418, 424, 440-441, 443, 444.* ***Tuska*** *a-486p, 490p.* ***Matt Wagner*** *c-647-649.* ***Wrightson*** *c-425.*

DETECTIVE DAN, SECRET OP. 48 (Also see Adventures of Detective Ace King and Bob Scully, The Two-Fisted Hick Detective)

Humor Publ. Co. (Norman Marsh): 1933 (10¢, 10x13", 36 pgs., B&W, one-shot) (3 color, cardboard-c)

nn-By Norman Marsh, 1st comic w/ original-a; 1st newsstand-c; Dick Tracy look-alike;

Devil Dinosaur #1 © MAR

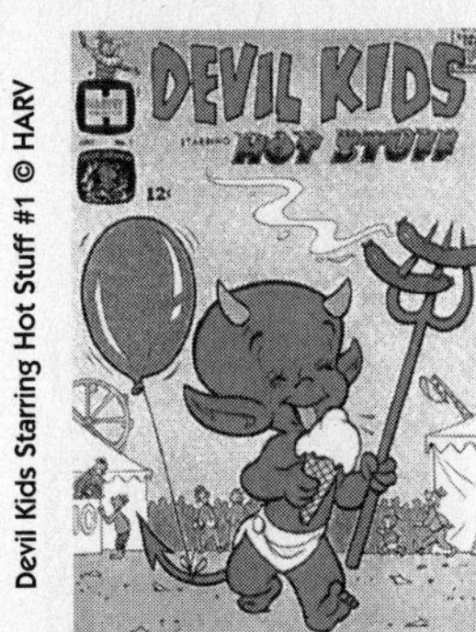

Devil Kids Starring Hot Stuff #1 © HARV

Diary Loves #5 © QUA

GD VG FN VF VF/NM NM-
2.0 4.0 6.0 8.0 9.0 9.2

forerunner of Dan Dunn. (Title and Wu Fang character inspired Detective Comics #1 four years later.) (1st comic of a single theme) 1500 3000 4500 9000 - -

DETECTIVE EYE (See Keen Detective Funnies)
Centaur Publications: Nov, 1940 - No. 2, Dec, 1940

1-Air Man (see Keen Detective) & The Eye Sees begins; The Masked Marvel & Dean Denton app. 215 430 645 1344 2072 2800
2-Origin Don Rance and the Mysticape; Binder-a; Frank Thomas-c 121 242 363 756 1166 1575

DETECTIVE PICTURE STORIES (Keen Detective Funnies No. 8 on?)
Comics Magazine Company: Dec, 1936 - No. 5, Apr, 1937
(1st comic of a single theme)

1 (all issues are very scarce) 550 1100 1650 2800 3800 4800
2-The Clock app. (1/37, early app.) 233 466 699 1200 1650 2100
3,4: 4-Eisner-a 150 300 450 800 1075 1350
5-The Clock-c/story (4/37); 1st detective/adventure art by Bob Kane; Bruce Wayne prototype app.(see Funny Pages V3/1) 166 332 500 900 1250 1600

DETECTIVES, THE (TV)
Dell Publishing Co.: No. 1168, Mar-May, 1961 - No. 1240, Oct-Dec, 1961

Four Color 1168 (#1)-Robert Taylor photo-c 11 22 33 80 120 160
Four Color 1219-Robert Taylor, Adam West photo-c 10 20 30 70 100 130
Four Color 1240-Tufts-a; Robert Taylor photo-c 10 20 30 70 100 130

DETECTIVES, INC. (See Eclipse Graphic Album Series)
Eclipse Comics: Apr, 1985 - No. 2, Apr, 1985 ($1.75, both w/April dates)

1,2: 2-Nudity 2.25

DETECTIVES, INC.: A TERROR OF DYING DREAMS
Eclipse Comics: Jun, 1987 - No. 3, Dec, 1987 ($1.75, B&W& sepia)

1-3: Colan-a 2.25
TPB ('99, $19.95) r/series 20.00

DETENTION COMICS
DC Comics: Oct, 1996 ($3.50, 56 pgs., one-shot)

1-Robin story by Dennis O'Neil & Norm Breyfogle; Superboy story by Ron Marz & Ron Lim; Warrior story by Ruben Diaz & Joe Phillips; Phillips-c 5.00

DETONATOR (Mike Baron's...)
Image Comics: Nov, 2004 - Present ($2.50)

1-Mike Baron-s/Mel Rubi-a 2.50

DEVASTATOR
Image Comics/Halloween: 1998 - No. 3 ($2.95, B&W, limited series)

1,2-Hudnall-s/Horn-c/a 3.00

DEVIL CHEF
Dark Horse Comics: July, 1994 ($2.50, B&W, one-shot)

nn 2.50

DEVIL DINOSAUR
Marvel Comics Group: Apr, 1978 - No. 9, Dec, 1978

1-Kirby/Royer-a in all; all have Kirby-c 2 4 6 12 16 20
2-9: 4-7-UFO/sci. fic. 8-Dinoriders-c/sty 1 3 4 6 8 10

DEVIL DINOSAUR SPRING FLING
Marvel Comics: June, 1997 ($2.99. one-shot)

1-(48pgs.) Moon-Boy-c/app. 3.00

DEVIL-DOG DUGAN (Tales of the Marines No. 4 on)
Atlas Comics (OPI): July, 1956 - No. 3, Nov, 1956

1-Severin-c 13 26 39 74 102 130
2-Iron Mike McGraw x-over; Severin-c 8 16 24 43 54 65
3 7 14 21 37 46 55

DEVIL DOGS
Street & Smith Publishers: 1942

1-Boy Rangers, U.S. Marines 29 58 87 164 237 310

DEVILINA (Magazine)
Atlas/Seaboard: Feb, 1975 - No. 2, May, 1975 (B&W)

1-Art by Reese, Marcos; "The Tempest" adapt. 3 6 9 16 20 25
2 (Low printing) 3 6 9 18 24 30

DEVIL KIDS STARRING HOT STUFF
Harvey Publications (Illustrated Humor): July, 1962 - No. 107, Oct, 1981 (Giant-Size #41-55)

1 (12¢ cover price #1-#41-9/69) 18 36 54 126 193 260
2 10 20 30 67 96 125
3-10 (1/64) 7 14 21 51 71 90
11-20 5 10 15 33 44 55
21-30 4 8 12 22 30 38
31-40: 40-(6/69) 3 6 9 18 23 28
41-50: All 68 pg. Giants 3 6 9 19 25 32
51-55: All 52 pg. Giants 3 6 9 18 23 28
56-70 2 4 6 10 12 15
71-90 1 2 3 5 7 9
91-107 6.00

DEVIL MAY CRY (Based on the video game)
Dreamwave Productions: March, 2004 - No. 4 ($3.95)

1-3: 1-Pat Lee-a/Brad Mick-s 4.00

DEVIL'S DUE STUDIOS MIX TAPE
Image Comics(Devil's Due): March, 2003 ($1.00)

1-Previews of upcoming titles like Voltron, Micronauts, G.I. Joe 2.00

DEVIL'S FOOTPRINTS, THE
Dark Horse Comics: March, 2003 - No. 4, June, 2003 ($2.99, limited series)

1-4-Paul Lee-c/a; Scott Allie-s 3.00

DEXTER COMICS
Dearfield Publ.: Summer, 1948 - No. 5, July, 1949

1-Teen-age humor 10 20 30 60 80 100
2-Junie Prom app. 8 16 24 43 54 65
3-5 7 14 21 35 43 50

DEXTER'S LABORATORY (Cartoon Network)
DC Comics: Sept, 1999 - No. 34, Apr, 2003 ($1.99/$2.25)

1 4.00
2-10: 2-McCracken-s 3.00
11-24 2.25
25-(50¢-c) Tartakovsky-s/a; Action Hank-c/app. 2.25
26-34: 31-Begin $2.25-c. 32-34-Wray-c 2.25

DEXTER THE DEMON (Formerly Melvin The Monster)(See Cartoon Kids & Peter the Little Pest)
Atlas Comics (HPC): No. 7, Sept, 1957

7 8 16 24 40 50 60

DHAMPIRE: STILLBORN
DC Comics (Vertigo): 1996 ($5.95, one-shot, mature)

1-Nancy Collins script; Paul Lee-c/a 6.00

DIABLO: TALES OF SANCTUARY (From the computer game)
Dark Horse Comics (Blizzard): Nov, 2001 ($5.95, 6.5 x 9", one-shot)

1-Francisco Ruiz-c/a 6.00

DIARY CONFESSIONS (Formerly Ideal Romance)
Stanmor/Key Publ.(Medal Comics): No. 9, May, 1955 - No. 14, Apr, 1955

9 8 16 24 43 54 65
10-14 6 12 18 29 36 42

DIARY LOVES (Formerly Love Diary #1; G. I. Sweethearts #32 on)
Quality Comics Group: No. 2, Nov, 1949 - No. 31, April, 1953

2-Ward-c/a, 9 pgs. 17 34 51 98 139 180
3 (1/50)-Photo-c begin, end #27? 8 16 24 46 58 70
4-Crandall-a 9 18 27 54 70 85
5-7,10 7 14 21 37 46 55
8,9-Ward-a 6,8 pgs. 8-Gustavson-a; Esther Williams photo-c 12 24 36 69 95 120
11,13,14,17-20 7 14 21 35 43 50
12,15,16-Ward-a 9,7,8 pgs. 11 22 33 62 84 105
21-Ward-a, 7 pgs. 10 20 30 56 73 90
22-31: 31-Whitney-a 6 12 18 31 38 45
NOTE: *Photo c-3-10, 12-27.*

DIARY OF HORROR
Avon Periodicals: December, 1952

1-Hollingsworth-c/a; bondage-c 42 84 126 256 391 525

DIARY SECRETS (Formerly Teen-Age Diary Secrets)(See Giant Comics Ed.)
St. John Publishing Co.: No. 10, Feb, 1952 - No. 30, Sept, 1955

10-Baker-c/a most issues 19 38 57 107 154 200
11-16,18,19 14 28 42 79 110 140
17,20: Kubert-r/Hollywood Confessions #1. 17-r/Teen Age Romances #9 14 28 42 79 110 140
21-30: 22,27-Signed stories by Estrada. 28-Last precode (3/55)

Dick Cole #2 © STAR

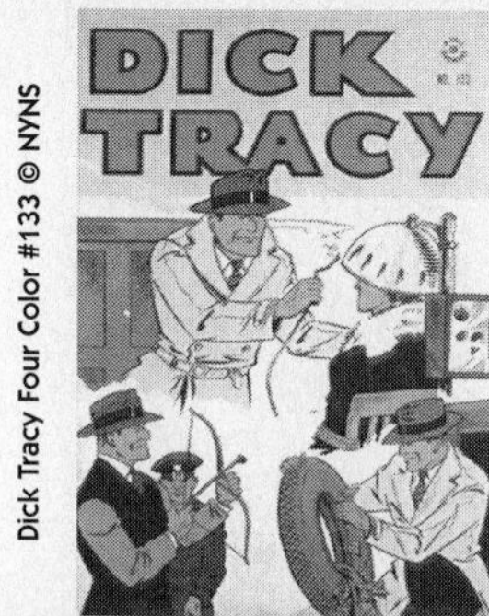

Dick Tracy Four Color #133 © NYNS

Die Cut #4 © MAR

GD VG FN VF VF/NM NM-
2.0 4.0 6.0 8.0 9.0 9.2

10 20 30 58 77 95
nn-(25¢ giant, nd (1950?)-Baker-c & rebound St. John comics
48 96 144 293 447 600

DICK COLE (Sport Thrills No. 11 on)(See Blue Bolt & Four Most #1)
Curtis Publ./Star Publications: Dec-Jan, 1948-49 - No. 10, June-July, 1950

1-Sgt. Spook; L. B. Cole-c; McWilliams-a; Curt Swan's 1st work
35 70 105 200 290 380
2,5 16 32 48 92 131 170
3,4,6-10: All-L.B. Cole-c. 10-Joe Louis story 24 48 72 135 195 255
Accepted Reprint #7(V1#6 on-c)(1950's)-Reprints #7; L.B. Cole-c
8 16 24 43 54 65
Accepted Reprint #9(nd)-(Reprints #9 & #8-c) 8 16 24 43 54 65

NOTE: ***L. B. Cole** c-1, 3, 4, 6-10. **Al McWilliams** a-6. Dick Cole in 1-9. Baseball c-10. Basketball c-9. Football c-8.*

DICKIE DARE
Eastern Color Printing Co.: 1941 - No. 4, 1942 (#3 on sale 6/15/42)

1-Caniff-a, bondage-c by Everett 65 130 195 406 628 850
2 32 64 96 184 267 350
3,4-Half Scorchy Smith by Noel Sickles who was very influential in Milton
Caniff's development 37 74 111 209 305 400

DICK POWELL (Also see A-1 Comics)
Magazine Enterprises: No. 22, 1949 (one shot)

A-1 22-Photo-c 26 52 78 147 211 275

DICK QUICK, ACE REPORTER (See Picture News #10)

DICKS
Caliber Comics: 1997 - No. 4, 1998 ($2.95, B&W)

1-4-Ennis-s/McCrea-c/a; r/Fleetway 3.00
TPB ('98, $12.95) r/series 13.00

DICK'S ADVENTURES
Dell Publishing Co.: No. 245, Sept, 1949

Four Color 245 7 14 21 46 63 80

DICK TRACY (See Famous Feature Stories, Harvey Comics Library, Limited Collectors' Ed., Mammoth Comics, Merry Christmas, The Original..., Popular Comics, Super Book No. 1, 7, 13, 25, Super Comics & Tastee-Freez)

DICK TRACY
David McKay Publications: May, 1937 - Jan, 1938

Feature Books nn - 100 pgs., partially reprinted as 4-Color No. 1 (appeared before Large Feature Comics, 1st Dick Tracy comic book) (Very Rare-five known copies; two incomplete) 774 1548 2322 5418 8709 12,000
Feature Books 4 - Reprints nn issue w/new-c 131 262 393 819 1260 1700
Feature Books 6,9 96 192 288 600 925 1250

DICK TRACY (...Monthly #1-24)
Dell Publishing Co.: 1939 - No. 24, Dec, 1949

Large Feature Comic 1 (1939) -Dick Tracy Meets The Blank
177 354 531 1106 1703 2300
Large Feature Comic 4,8 92 184 276 575 888 1200
Large Feature Comic 11,13,15 81 162 243 506 778 1050
Four Color 1(1939)('35-r) 718 1436 2154 5026 8263 11,500
Four Color 6(1940)('37-r)-(Scarce) 135 270 405 1071 1736 2400
Four Color 8(1940)('38-'39-r) 68 136 204 536 868 1200
Large Feature Comic 3(1941, Series II) 79 158 237 494 760 1025
Four Color 21('41)('38-r) 55 110 165 425 688 950
Four Color 34('43)('39-'40-r) 41 82 123 318 497 675
Four Color 56('44)('40-r) 36 72 108 270 423 575
Four Color 96('46)('40-r) 28 56 84 199 305 410
Four Color 133('47)('40-'41-r) 23 46 69 163 249 335
Four Color 163('47)('41-r) 19 38 57 136 208 280
Four Color 215('48)-Titled "Sparkle Plenty", Dick Tracy-r
12 24 36 86 131 175
1(1/48)('34-r) 41 82 123 305 478 650
2,3 24 48 72 174 267 360
4-10 22 44 66 155 238 320
11-18: 13-Bondage-c 16 32 48 116 178 240
19-1st app. Sparkle Plenty, B.O. Plenty & Gravel Gertie in a 3-pg. strip not by Gould 17 34 51 123 189 255
20-1st app. Sam Catchem; c/a not by Gould 16 32 48 112 171 230
21-24-Only 2 pg. Gould-a in each 15 30 45 107 164 220

NOTE: *No. 19-24 have a 2 pg. biography of a famous villain illustrated by **Gould**: 19-Little Face; 20-Flattop; 21-Breathless Mahoney; 22-Measles; 23-Itchy; 24-The Brow.*

DICK TRACY (Continued from Dell series)(...Comics Monthly #25-140)
Harvey Publications: No. 25, Mar, 1950 - No. 145, April, 1961

25-Flat Top-c/story (also #26,27) 18 36 54 129 197 265
26-28,30: 28-Bondage-c. 28,29-The Brow-c/stories 14 28 42 97 149 200
29-1st app. Gravel Gertie in a Gould-r 17 34 51 119 182 245
31,32,34,35,37-40: 40-Intro/origin 2-way wrist radio (6/51)
12 24 36 86 131 175
33- "Measles the Teen-Age Dope Pusher" 14 28 42 97 149 200
36-1st app. B.O. Plenty in a Gould-r 14 28 42 97 149 200
41-50 11 22 33 77 114 150
51-56,58-80: 51-2pgs Powell-a 10 20 30 70 100 130
57-1st app. Sam Catchem in a Gould-r 11 22 33 77 114 150
81-99,101-140: 99-109-Painted-c 9 18 27 65 93 120
100, 141-145 (25¢)(titled "Dick Tracy") 10 20 30 70 100 130

NOTE: ***Powell** a(1-2pgs.)-43, 44, 104, 108, 109, 145. No. 110-120, 141-145 are all reprints from earlier issues.*

DICK TRACY
Blackthorne Publishing: 12/84 - No. 24, 6/89 (1-12: $5.95; 13-24: $6.95, B&W, 76 pgs.)

1-8-1st printings; hard-c ed. ($14.95) 15.00
1-3-2nd printings, 1986; hard-c ed. 15.00
1-12-1st & 2nd printings; squarebound. thick-c 7.00
13-24 ($6.95): 21,22-Regular-c & stapled 7.00

NOTE: **Gould** daily & Sunday strip-r in all. 1-12 r-12/31/45-4/5/49; 13-24 r-7/13/41-2/20/44.

DICK TRACY (Disney)
WD Publications: 1990 - No. 3, 1990 (color) (Book 3 adapts 1990 movie)

Book One ($3.95, 52pgs.)-Kyle Baker-c/a 6.00
Book Two, Three ($5.95, 68pgs.)-Direct sale 6.00
Book Two, Three ($2.95, 68pgs.)-Newsstand 3.00

DICK TRACY ADVENTURES
Gladstone Publishing: May, 1991 ($4.95, 76 pgs.)

1-Reprints strips 2/1/42-4/18/42 5.00

DICK TRACY, EXPLOITS OF
Rosdon Books, Inc.: 1946 ($1.00, hard-c strip reprints)

1-Reprints the near complete case of "The Brow" from 6/12/44 to 9/24/44
(story starts a few weeks late) 27 54 81 152 219 285
with dust jacket... 40 80 120 239 357 475

DICK TRACY MONTHLY/WEEKLY
Blackthorne Publishing: May, 1986 - No. 99, 1989 ($2.00, B&W)
(Becomes Weekly #26 on)

1-60: Gould-r. 30,31-Mr. Crime app. 3.00
61-90 4.00
91-95 6.00
96-99-Low print 1 2 3 5 7 9

NOTE: *#1-10 reprint strips 3/10/40-7/13/41; #10(pg.8)-51 reprint strips 4/6/49-12/31/55; #52-99 reprint strips 12/26/56-4/26/64.*

DICK TRACY SPECIAL
Blackthorne Publ.: Jan, 1988 - No. 3, Aug. (no month), 1989 ($2.95, B&W)

1-3: 1-Origin D. Tracy; 4/strips 10/12/31-3/30/32 3.00

DICK TRACY: THE EARLY YEARS
Blackthorne Publishing: Aug, 1987 - No. 4, Aug (no month) 1989 ($6.95, B&W, 76 pgs.)

1-3: 1-4-r/strips 10/12/31(1st daily)-8/31/32 & Sunday strips 6/12/32-8/28/32;
Big Boy apps. in #1-3 1 2 3 4 5 7
4 ($2.95, 52pgs.) 3.00

DICK TRACY UNPRINTED STORIES
Blackthorne Publishing: Sept, 1987 - No. 4, June, 1988 ($2.95, B&W)

1-4: Reprints strips 1/1/56-12/25/56 3.00

DICK TURPIN (See Legend of Young...)

DIE-CUT
Marvel Comics UK, Ltd: Nov, 1993 - No. 4, Feb, 1994 ($1.75, limited series)

1-4: 1-Die-cut-c; The Beast app. 2.25

DIE-CUT VS. G-FORCE
Marvel Comics UK, Ltd: Nov, 1993 - No. 2, Dec, 1993 ($2.75, limited series)

1,2-($2.75)-Gold foil-c on both 2.75

DIE, MONSTER, DIE (See Movie Classics)

DIGIMON DIGITAL MONSTERS (TV)
Dark Horse Comics: May, 2000 - No. 12, Nov, 2000 ($2.95/$2.99)

1-12 3.00

DIGITEK
Marvel UK, Ltd: Dec, 1992 - No. 4, Mar, 1993 ($1.95/$2.25, mini-series)

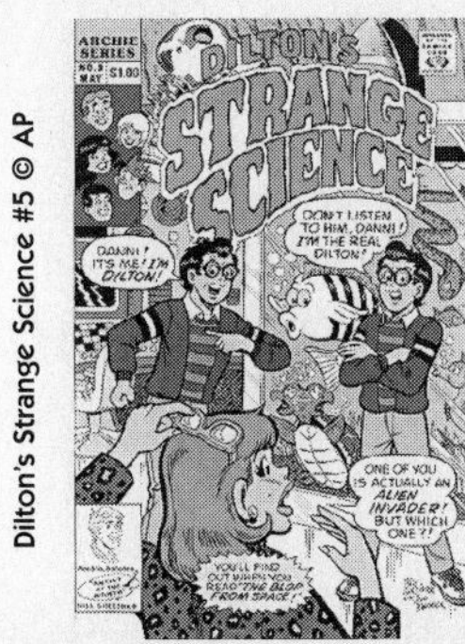

Dilton's Strange Science #5 © AP

Dirty Pair #3 © Studio Proteus

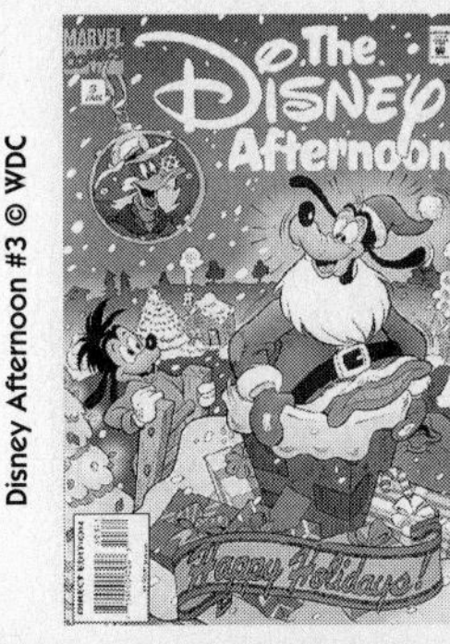

Disney Afternoon #3 © WDC

	GD 2.0	VG 4.0	FN 6.0	VF 8.0	VF/NM 9.0	NM- 9.2
1-4: 3-Deathlock-c/story						2.25

DILLY (Dilly Duncan from Daredevil Comics; see Boy Comics #57)
Lev Gleason Publications: May, 1953 - No. 3, Sept, 1953

	GD 2.0	VG 4.0	FN 6.0	VF 8.0	VF/NM 9.0	NM- 9.2
1-Teenage; Biro-c	7	14	21	35	43	50
2,3-Biro-c	5	10	15	22	26	30

DILTON'S STRANGE SCIENCE (See Pep Comics #78)
Archie Comics: May, 1989 - No. 5, May, 1990 (75¢/$1.00)

	GD 2.0	VG 4.0	FN 6.0	VF 8.0	VF/NM 9.0	NM- 9.2
1-5						3.00

DIME COMICS
Newsbook Publ. Corp.: 1945; 1951

	GD 2.0	VG 4.0	FN 6.0	VF 8.0	VF/NM 9.0	NM- 9.2
1-Silver Streak-c/story; L. B. Cole-c	69	138	207	431	666	900
1(1951)	9	18	27	51	62	75

DINGBATS (See 1st Issue Special)

DING DONG
Compix/Magazine Enterprises: Summer?, 1946 - No. 5, 1947 (52 pgs.)

	GD 2.0	VG 4.0	FN 6.0	VF 8.0	VF/NM 9.0	NM- 9.2
1-Funny animal	27	54	81	154	222	290
2 (9/46)	13	26	39	74	102	130
3 (Wint '46-'47) - 5	10	20	30	58	77	95

DINKY DUCK (Paul Terry's...) (See Approved Comics, Blue Ribbon, Giant Comics Edition #5A & New Terrytoons)
St. John Publishing Co./Pines No. 16 on: Nov, 1951 - No. 16, Sept, 1955; No. 16, Fall, 1956; No. 17, May, 1957 - No. 19, Summer, 1958

	GD 2.0	VG 4.0	FN 6.0	VF 8.0	VF/NM 9.0	NM- 9.2
1-Funny animal	13	26	39	74	102	130
2	8	16	24	43	54	65
3-10	6	12	18	28	34	40
11-16(9/55)	5	10	15	24	30	35
16(Fall,'56) - 19	5	10	14	20	24	28

DINKY DUCK & HASHIMOTO-SAN (See Deputy Dawg Presents...)

DINO (TV)(The Flintstones)
Charlton Publications: Aug, 1973 - No. 20, Jan, 1977 (Hanna-Barbera)

	GD 2.0	VG 4.0	FN 6.0	VF 8.0	VF/NM 9.0	NM- 9.2
1	3	7	10	21	28	35
2-10	2	4	6	11	14	18
11-20	2	4	6	8	10	12

DINO ISLAND
Mirage Studios: Feb, 1994 - No. 2, Mar, 1994 ($2.75, limited series)

	GD 2.0	VG 4.0	FN 6.0	VF 8.0	VF/NM 9.0	NM- 9.2
1,2-By Jim Lawson						2.75

DINO RIDERS
Marvel Comics: Feb, 1989 - No. 3, 1989 ($1.00)

	GD 2.0	VG 4.0	FN 6.0	VF 8.0	VF/NM 9.0	NM- 9.2
1-3: Based on toys						3.00

DINOSAUR REX
Upshot Graphics (Fantagraphics): 1986 - No. 3, 1986 ($2.00, limited series)

	GD 2.0	VG 4.0	FN 6.0	VF 8.0	VF/NM 9.0	NM- 9.2
1-3						2.25

DINOSAURS, A CELEBRATION
Marvel Comics (Epic): Oct, 1992 - No. 4, Oct, 1992 ($4.95, lim. series, 52 pgs.)

	GD 2.0	VG 4.0	FN 6.0	VF 8.0	VF/NM 9.0	NM- 9.2
1-4: 2-Bolton painted-c						5.00

DINOSAURS ATTACK! THE GRAPHIC NOVEL
Eclipse Comics: 1991 ($3.95, coated stock, stiff-c)

	GD 2.0	VG 4.0	FN 6.0	VF 8.0	VF/NM 9.0	NM- 9.2
Book One- Based on Topps trading cards						4.00

DINOSAURS FOR HIRE
Malibu Comics: Feb, 1993 - No. 12, Feb, 1994 ($1.95/$2.50)

	GD 2.0	VG 4.0	FN 6.0	VF 8.0	VF/NM 9.0	NM- 9.2
1-12: 1,10-Flip bk. 8-Bagged w/Skycap; Staton-c. 10-Flip book						2.50

DINOSAURS GRAPHIC NOVEL (TV)
Disney Comics: 1992 - No. 2, 1993 ($2.95, 52 pgs.)

	GD 2.0	VG 4.0	FN 6.0	VF 8.0	VF/NM 9.0	NM- 9.2
1,2-Staton-a; based on Dinosaurs TV show						3.00

DINOSAURUS
Dell Publishing Co.: No. 1120, Aug, 1960

	GD 2.0	VG 4.0	FN 6.0	VF 8.0	VF/NM 9.0	NM- 9.2
Four Color 1120-Movie, painted-c	9	18	27	63	89	115

DIPPY DUCK
Atlas Comics (OPI): October, 1957

	GD 2.0	VG 4.0	FN 6.0	VF 8.0	VF/NM 9.0	NM- 9.2
1-Maneely-a; code approved	9	18	27	54	70	85

DIRECTORY TO A NONEXISTENT UNIVERSE
Eclipse Comics: Dec, 1987 ($2.00, B&W)

	GD 2.0	VG 4.0	FN 6.0	VF 8.0	VF/NM 9.0	NM- 9.2
1						2.25

DIRTY DOZEN (See Movie Classics)

DIRTY PAIR (Manga)
Eclipse Comics: Dec, 1988 - No. 4, Apr, 1989 ($2.00, B&W, limited series)

	GD 2.0	VG 4.0	FN 6.0	VF 8.0	VF/NM 9.0	NM- 9.2
1-4: Japanese manga with original stories						3.00
...: Start the Violence (Dark Horse, 9/99, $2.95) r/B&W stories in color from Dark Horse Presents #132-134; covers by Warren & Pearson						3.00

DIRTY PAIR: FATAL BUT NOT SERIOUS (Manga)
Dark Horse Comics: July, 1995 - No. 5, Nov, 1995 ($2.95, limited series)

	GD 2.0	VG 4.0	FN 6.0	VF 8.0	VF/NM 9.0	NM- 9.2
1-5						3.00

DIRTY PAIR: RUN FROM THE FUTURE (Manga)
Dark Horse Comics: Jan, 2000 - No. 4, Mar, 2000 ($2.95, limited series)

	GD 2.0	VG 4.0	FN 6.0	VF 8.0	VF/NM 9.0	NM- 9.2
1-4-Warren-s/c/a. Var.-c by Hughes(1), Stelfreeze(2), Timm(3), Ramos(4)						3.00

DIRTY PAIR: SIM HELL (Manga)
Dark Horse Comics: May, 1993 - No. 4, Aug, 1993 ($2.50, B&W, limited series)

	GD 2.0	VG 4.0	FN 6.0	VF 8.0	VF/NM 9.0	NM- 9.2
1-4						3.00
...Remastered #1-4 (5/01 - 8/01) reprints in color, with pin-up gallery						3.00

DIRTY PAIR II (Manga)
Eclipse Comics: June, 1989 - No. 5, Mar, 1990 ($2.00, B&W, limited series)

	GD 2.0	VG 4.0	FN 6.0	VF 8.0	VF/NM 9.0	NM- 9.2
1-5: 3-Cover is misnumbered as #1						3.00

DIRTY PAIR III, THE (A Plague of Angels) (Manga)
Eclipse Comics: Aug, 1990 - No. 5, Aug, 1991 ($2.00/$2.25, B&W, lim. series)

	GD 2.0	VG 4.0	FN 6.0	VF 8.0	VF/NM 9.0	NM- 9.2
1-5						3.00

DISAVOWED
DC Comics (Homage): Mar, 2000 - No. 6, Sept, 2000 ($2.50)

	GD 2.0	VG 4.0	FN 6.0	VF 8.0	VF/NM 9.0	NM- 9.2
1-6: 1-3-Choi & Heisler-s/Edwards-a. 4,5-Lucas-a						2.50

DISCIPLES
Image Comics: Apr, 2001 - Present ($2.95)

	GD 2.0	VG 4.0	FN 6.0	VF 8.0	VF/NM 9.0	NM- 9.2
1,2: 1-Wraparound-c						3.00
...: Wheel of Fortune (12/01, $4.95)						5.00

DISHMAN
Eclipse Comics: Sept, 1988 ($2.50, B&W, 52 pgs.)

	GD 2.0	VG 4.0	FN 6.0	VF 8.0	VF/NM 9.0	NM- 9.2
1						2.50

DISNEY AFTERNOON, THE (TV)
Marvel Comics: Nov, 1994 - No. 10?, Aug, 1995 ($1.50)

	GD 2.0	VG 4.0	FN 6.0	VF 8.0	VF/NM 9.0	NM- 9.2
1-10: 3-w/bound-in Power Ranger Barcode Card						3.00

DISNEY COMIC ALBUM
Disney Comics: 1990(no month, year) - No. 8, 1991 ($6.95/$7.95)

	GD 2.0	VG 4.0	FN 6.0	VF 8.0	VF/NM 9.0	NM- 9.2
1,2 ($6.95): 1-Donald Duck and Gyro Gearloose by Barks(r). 2-Uncle Scrooge by Barks(r); Jr. Woodchucks app.						9.00
3-8: 3-Donald Duck-r/F.C. 308 by Barks; begin $7.95-c. 4-Mickey Mouse Meets the Phantom Blot; r/M.M Club Parade (censored 1956 version of story). 5-Chip 'n' Dale Rescue Rangers; new-a. 6-Uncle Scrooge. 7-Donald Duck in Too Many Pets; Barks-r(4) including F.C. #29. 8-Super Goof; r/S.G. #1, D.D. #102						9.00

DISNEY COMIC HITS
Marvel Comics: Oct, 1995 - No. 16, Jan, 1997 ($1.50/$2.50)

	GD 2.0	VG 4.0	FN 6.0	VF 8.0	VF/NM 9.0	NM- 9.2
1-16: 4-Toy Story. 6-Aladdin. 7-Pocahontas. 10-The Hunchback of Notre Dame (Same story in Disney's The Hunchback of Notre Dame). 13-Aladdin and the Forty Thieves						4.00

DISNEY COMICS
Disney Comics: June, 1990

	GD 2.0	VG 4.0	FN 6.0	VF 8.0	VF/NM 9.0	NM- 9.2
Boxed set of #1 issues includes Donald Duck Advs., Ducktales, Chip 'n Dale Rescue Rangers, Roger Rabbit, Mickey Mouse Advs. & Goofy Advs.; limited to 10,000 sets	2	4	6	10	12	15

DISNEYLAND BIRTHDAY PARTY (Also see Dell Giants)
Gladstone Publishing Co.: Aug, 1985 ($2.50)

	GD 2.0	VG 4.0	FN 6.0	VF 8.0	VF/NM 9.0	NM- 9.2
1-Reprints Dell Giant with new-photo-c	2	4	6	8	10	12
...Comics Digest #1-(Digest)	2	4	6	9	11	14

DISNEYLAND MAGAZINE
Fawcett Publications: Feb. 15, 1972 - ? (10-1/4"x12-5/8", 20 pgs, weekly)

	GD 2.0	VG 4.0	FN 6.0	VF 8.0	VF/NM 9.0	NM- 9.2
1-One or two page painted art features on Dumbo, Snow White, Lady & the Tramp, the Aristocats, Brer Rabbit, Peter Pan, Cinderella, Jungle Book, Alice & Pinocchio. Most standard characters app.	3	6	9	18	24	30

DISNEYLAND, USA (See Dell Giant No. 30)

DISNEY MOVIE BOOK
Walt Disney Productions (Gladstone): 1990 ($7.95, 8-1/2"x11", 52 pgs.) (w/pull-out poster)

Disney's The Lion King #1 © WDC

A Distant Soil #21 © Colleen Doran

District X #1 © MAR

GD VG FN VF VF/NM NM-
2.0 4.0 6.0 8.0 9.0 9.2

1-Roger Rabbit in Tummy Trouble; from the cartoon film strips adapted to the comic format. Ron Dias-c 2 4 6 8 10 12

DISNEY'S ACTION CLUB
Acclaim Books: 1997 - No. 4 ($4.50, digest size)
1-4: 1-Hercules. 4-Mighty Ducks 4.50

DISNEY'S ALADDIN (Movie)
Marvel Comics: Oct, 1994 - No. 11, 1995 ($1.50)
1-11 3.00

DISNEY'S BEAUTY AND THE BEAST (Movie)
Marvel Comics: Sept, 1994 - No. 13, 1995 ($1.50)
1-13 3.00

DISNEY'S BEAUTY AND THE BEAST HOLIDAY SPECIAL
Acclaim Books: 1997 ($4.50, digest size, one-shot)
1-Based on The Enchanted Christmas video 4.50

DISNEY'S COLOSSAL COMICS COLLECTION
Disney Comics: 1991 - No. 10, 1993 ($1.95, digest-size, 96/132 pgs.)
1-10: Ducktales, Talespin, Chip 'n Dale's Rescue Rangers. 4-r/Darkwing Duck #1-4. 6-Goofy begins. 8-Little Mermaid 5.00

DISNEY'S COMICS IN 3-D
Disney Comics: 1992 ($2.95, w/glasses, polybagged)
1-Infinity-c; Barks, Rosa, Gottfredson-r 5.00

DISNEY'S ENCHANTING STORIES
Acclaim Books: 1997 - No. 5 ($4.50, digest size)
1-5: 1-Hercules. 2-Pocahontas 4.50

DISNEY'S NEW ADVENTURES OF BEAUTY AND THE BEAST (Also see Beauty and the Beast & Disney's Beauty and the Beast)
Disney Comics: 1992 - No. 2, 1992 ($1.50, limited series)
1,2-New stories based on movie 3.00

DISNEY'S POCAHONTAS (Movie)
Marvel Comics: 1995 ($4.95, one-shot)
1-Movie adaptation 1 2 3 4 5 7

DISNEY'S TALESPIN LIMITED SERIES: "TAKE OFF" (TV) (See Talespin)
W. D. Publications (Disney Comics): Jan, 1991 - No. 4, Apr, 1991 ($1.50, lim. series, 52 pgs.)
1-4: Based on animated series; 4 part origin 2.50

DISNEY'S TARZAN (Movie)
Dark Horse Comics: June, 1999 - No. 2, July, 1999 ($2.95, limited series)
1,2: Movie adaptation 3.00

DISNEY'S THE LION KING (Movie)
Marvel Comics: July, 1994 - No. 2, July, 1994 ($1.50, limited series)
1,2: 2-part movie adaptation 3.00
1-($2.50, 52 pgs.)-Complete story 5.00

DISNEY'S THE LITTLE MERMAID (Movie)
Marvel Comics: Sept, 1994 - No. 12, 1995 ($1.50)
1-12 4.00

DISNEY'S THE LITTLE MERMAID LIMITED SERIES (Movie)
Disney Comics: Feb, 1992 - No. 4, May, 1992 ($1.50, limited series)
1-4: Peter David scripts 3.00

DISNEY'S THE LITTLE MERMAID: UNDERWATER ENGAGEMENTS
Acclaim Books: 1997 ($4.50, digest size)
1-Flip book 4.50

DISNEY'S THE HUNCHBACK OF NOTRE DAME (Movie)(See Disney's Comic Hits #10)
Marvel Comics: July, 1996 ($4.95, squarebound, one-shot)
1-Movie adaptation. 1 2 3 4 5 7
NOTE: *A different edition of this series was sold at Wal-Mart stores with new covers depicting scenes from the 1989 feature film. Inside contents and price were identical.*

DISNEY'S THE THREE MUSKETEERS (Movie)
Marvel Comics: Jan, 1994 - No. 2, Feb, 1994 ($1.50, limited series)
1,2-Morrow-c; Spiegle-a; Movie adaptation 2.25

DISNEY'S TOY STORY (Movie)
Marvel Comics: Dec, 1995 ($4.95, one-shot)
nn-Adaptation of film 1 2 3 4 5 7

DISTANT SOIL, A (1st Series)
WaRP Graphics: Dec, 1983 - No. 9, Mar 1986 ($1.50, B&W)
1-Magazine size 4.00
2-9: 2-4 are magazine size 3.00
NOTE: Second printings exist of #1, 2, 3 & 6.

DISTANT SOIL, A
Donning (Star Blaze): Mar, 1989 ($12.95, trade paperback)
nn-new material 13.00

DISTANT SOIL, A (2nd Series)
Aria Press/Image Comics (Highbrow Entertainment) #15 on: June, 1991 - Present ($1.75/$2.50/$2.95/$3.95, B&W)
1-27: 13-$2.95-c begins. 14-Sketchbook. 15-(8/96)-1st Image issue 3.00
29-33,35,37-($3.95) 4.00
34-($4.95, 64 pages) includes sketchbook pages 5.00
36-($4.50) Back-up story by Darnall & Doran 5.00
The Aria ('01, $16.95,TPB) r/#26-31 17.00
The Ascendant ('98, $18.95,TPB) r/#13-25 19.00
The Gathering ('97, $18.95,TPB) r/#1-13; intro. Neil Gaiman 19.00
NOTE: Four separate printings exist for #1 and are clearly marked. Second printings exist of #2-4 and are also clearly marked.

DISTANT SOIL, A: IMMIGRANT SONG
Donning (Star Blaze): Aug, 1987 ($6.95, trade paperback)
nn-new material 7.00

DISTRICT X (Also see X-Men titles)
Marvel Comics: July, 2004 - Present ($2.99)
1-7: 1-3-Bishop app.; Yardin-a/Hine-s 3.00

DIVER DAN (TV)
Dell Publishing Co.: Feb-Apr, 1962 - No. 2, June-Aug, 1962
Four Color 1254(#1), 2 6 12 18 40 55 75

DIVINE RIGHT
Image Comics (WildStorm Prod.): Sept, 1997 - No. 12, Nov, 1999 ($2.50)
Preview 5.00
1,2: 1-Jim Lee-s/a(p)/c, 1-Variant-c by Charest 4.00
1-($3.50)-Voyager Pack w/Stormwatch preview 3.50
1-American Entertainment Ed. 6.00
2-Variant-c of Exotica & Blaze 5.00
3-Chromium-c by Jim Lee 5.00
3-12: 3-5-Fairchild & Lynch app. 4-American Entertainment Ed. 8-Two covers. 9-1st DC issue. 11,12-Divine Intervention pt. 1,4 3.00
5-Pacific Comicon Ed. 6.00
6-Glow in the dark variant-c, European Tour Edition 20.00
...Book One TPB (2002, $17.95) r/#1-7 18.00
...Book Two TPB (2002, $17.95) r/#8-12 & Divine Intervention Gen13, ...Wildcats 18.00
...Collected Edition #1-3 ($5.95, TPB) 1-r/#1,2. 2-r/#3,4. 3-r/#5,6 6.00
Divine Intervention/Gen 13 (11/99, $2.50) Part 3; D'Anda-a 2.50
Divine Intervention/Wildcats (11/99, $2.50) Part 2; D'Anda-a 2.50

DIVISION 13 (See Comic's Greatest World)
Dark Horse Comics: Sept, 1994 - Jan, 1995 ($2.50, color)
1-4: Giffen story in all. 1-Art Adams-c 2.50

DIXIE DUGAN (See Big Shot, Columbia Comics & Feature Funnies)
McNaught Syndicate/Columbia/Publication Ent.: July, 1942 - No. 13, 1949 (Strip reprints in all)
1-Joe Palooka x-over by Ham Fisher 29 58 87 164 237 310
2 16 32 48 89 127 165
3 12 24 36 69 95 120
4,5(1945-46)-Bo strip-r 9 18 27 54 70 85
6-13(1/47-49): 6-Paperdoll cut-outs 8 16 24 46 58 70

DIXIE DUGAN
Prize Publications (Headline): V3#1, Nov, 1951 - V4#4, Feb, 1954
V3#1 9 18 27 54 70 85
2-4 7 14 21 35 43 50
V4#1-4(#5-8) 6 12 18 28 34 40

DIZZY DAMES
American Comics Group (B&M Distr. Co.): Sept-Oct, 1952 - No. 6, Jul-Aug, 1953
1-Whitney-c 15 30 45 85 120 155
2 9 18 27 52 66 80
3-6 8 16 24 40 50 60

DIZZY DON COMICS

Doc Savage #5 © CN

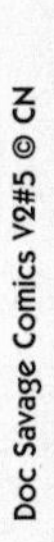

Doc Savage Comics V2#5 © CN

Dr. Fate #8 © DC

	GD 2.0	VG 4.0	FN 6.0	VF 8.0	VF/NM 9.0	NM- 9.2

F. E. Howard Publications/Dizzy Don Ent. Ltd (Canada): 1942 - No. 22, Oct, 1946; No. 3, Apr, 1947 (Most B&W)

	GD	VG	FN	VF	VF/NM	NM-
1 (B&W)	13	26	39	76	106	135
2 (B&W)	8	16	24	43	54	65
4-21 (B&W)	8	16	24	40	50	60
22-Full color, 52 pgs.	16	32	48	92	131	170
3 (4/47)-Full color, 52 pgs.	16	32	48	92	131	170

DIZZY DUCK (Formerly Barnyard Comics)
Standard Comics: No. 32, Nov, 1950 - No. 39, Mar, 1952

	GD	VG	FN	VF	VF/NM	NM-
32-Funny animal	10	20	30	56	73	90
33-39	6	12	18	29	36	42

DNAGENTS (The New DNAgents V2/1 on)(Also see Surge)
Eclipse Comics: March, 1983 - No. 24, July, 1985 ($1.50, Baxter paper)

1,24: 1-Origin. 4-Amber app. 24-Dave Stevens-c 3.00
2-23: 8-Infinity-c 2.25

DOBERMAN (See Sgt. Bilko's Private...)

DOBIE GILLIS (See The Many Loves of...)

DOC CHAOS: THE STRANGE ATTRACTOR
Vortex Comics: Apr, 1990 - No. 3, 1990 ($3.00, 32 pgs.)

1-3: The Lust For Order 3.00

DOC SAMSON (Also see Incredible Hulk)
Marvel Comics: Jan, 1996 - No. 4, Apr, 1996 ($1.95, limited series)

1-4: 1-Hulk c/app. 2-She-Hulk-c/app. 3-Punisher-c/app. 4-Polaris-c/app. 2.25

DOC SAVAGE
Gold Key: Nov, 1966

1-Adaptation of the Thousand-Headed Man; James Bama c-r/1964 Doc Savage paperback
11 22 33 79 117 155

DOC SAVAGE (Also see Giant-Size...)
Marvel Comics Group: Oct, 1972 - No. 8, Jan, 1974

	GD	VG	FN	VF	VF/NM	NM-
1	3	6	9	18	23	28
2,3-Steranko-c	2	4	6	10	13	16
4-8	2	4	6	8	10	12

NOTE: ***Gil Kane** c-5, 6. **Mooney** a-1i. No. 1, 2 adapts pulp story "The Man of Bronze"; No. 3, 4 adapts "Death in Silver"; No. 5, 6 adapts "The Monsters"; No. 7, 8 adapts "The Brand of The Werewolf".*

DOC SAVAGE (Magazine)
Marvel Comics Group: Aug, 1975 - No. 8, Spring, 1977 ($1.00, B&W)

	GD	VG	FN	VF	VF/NM	NM-
1-Cover from movie poster; Ron Ely photo-c	2	4	6	11	14	18
2-5: 3-Buscema-a. 5-Adams-a(1 pg.), Rogers-a(1 pg)	1	3	4	6	8	10
6-8	2	4	6	8	10	12

DOC SAVAGE
DC Comics: Nov, 1987 - No. 4, Feb, 1988 ($1.75, limited series)

1-4 3.00

DOC SAVAGE
DC Comics: Nov, 1988 - No. 24, Oct, 1990 ($1.75/$2.00: #13-24)

1-16,19-24 3.00
17,18-Shadow x-over 4.00
Annual 1 (1989, $3.50, 68 pgs.) 4.00

DOC SAVAGE COMICS (Also see Shadow Comics)
Street & Smith Publ.: May, 1940 - No. 20, Oct, 1943 (1st app. in Doc Savage pulp, 3/33)

	GD	VG	FN	VF	VF/NM	NM-
1-Doc Savage, Cap Fury, Danny Garrett, Mark Mallory, The Whisperer, Captain Death, Billy the Kid, Sheriff Pete & Treasure Island begin; Norgil, the Magician app.	484	968	1452	3388	5444	7500
2-Origin & 1st app. Ajax, the Sun Man; Danny Garrett, The Whisperer end; classic sci-fi cover	192	384	576	1200	1850	2500
3	127	254	381	794	1222	1650
4-Treasure Island ends; Tuska-a	102	204	306	638	982	1325
5-Origin & 1st app. Astron, the Crocodile Queen, not in #9 & 11; Norgi the Magician app.; classic-c	92	184	276	575	888	1200
6-10: 6-Cap Fury ends; origin & only app. Red Falcon in Astron story. 8-Mark Mallory ends; Charlie McCarthy app. on-c plus true life story. 9-Supersnipe app. 10-Origin & only app. The Thunderbolt	62	124	186	388	594	800
11,12	54	108	162	329	502	675
V2#1-8(#13-20): 15-Origin of Ajax the Sun Man; Jack Benny on-c; Hitler app. 16-The Pulp Hero, The Avenger app.; Fanny Brice story. 17-Sun Man ends; Nick Carter begins; Duffy's Tavern part photo-c & story. 18-Huckleberry Finn part-c/story. 19-Henny Youngman part photo-c & life story. 20-Only all funny-c w/Huckleberry Finn	52	104	156	317	484	650

DOC SAVAGE: CURSE OF THE FIRE GOD
Dark Horse Comics: Sept, 1995 - No, 4, Dec, 1995 ($2.95, limited series)

1-4 3.00

DOC SAVAGE: THE MAN OF BRONZE
Skylark Pub: Mar, 1979, 68pgs. (B&W comic digest, 5-1/4x7-5/8")(low print)

15406-0: Whitman-a, 60 pgs., new comics 4 8 12 22 30 38

DOC SAVAGE: THE MAN OF BRONZE
Millennium Publications: 1991 - No. 4, 1991 ($2.50, limited series)

1-4: 1-Bronze logo 3.00
...: The Manual of Bronze 1 ($2.50, B&W, color, one-shot)-Unpublished proposed Doc Savage strip in color, B&W strip-r 3.00

DOC SAVAGE: THE MAN OF BRONZE, DOOM DYNASTY
Millennium Publ.: 1992 (Says 1991) - No. 2, 1992 ($2.50, limited series)

1,2 3.00

DOC SAVAGE: THE MAN OF BRONZE - REPEL
Innovation Publishing: 1992 ($2.50)

1-Dave Dorman painted-c 3.00

DOC SAVAGE: THE MAN OF BRONZE THE DEVIL'S THOUGHTS
Millennium Publ.: 1992 (Says 1991) - No. 3, 1992 ($2.50, limited series)

1-3 3.00

DOC STEARN...MR. MONSTER (See Mr. Monster)

DR. ANTHONY KING, HOLLYWOOD LOVE DOCTOR
Minoan Publishing Corp./Harvey Publications No. 4: 1952(Jan) - No. 3, May, 1953; No. 4, May, 1954

	GD	VG	FN	VF	VF/NM	NM-
1	14	28	42	79	110	140
2-4: 4-Powell-a	9	18	27	51	62	75

DR. ANTHONY'S LOVE CLINIC (See Mr. Anthony's...)

DR. BOBBS
Dell Publishing Co.: No. 212, Jan, 1949

Four Color 212 6 12 18 38 52 65

DOCTOR BOOGIE
Media Arts Publishing: 1987 ($1.75)

1-Airbrush wraparound-c; Nick Cuti-i 2.25

DOCTOR CHAOS
Triumphant Comics: Nov, 1993 - No. 6, Mar, 1994 ($2.50)

1-6: 1,2-Triumphant Unleashed x-over. 2-1st app. War Dancer in pin-up. 3-Intro The Cry 2.50

DOCTOR CYBORG
Attention! Publishing: 1996 - No. 5 ($2.95, B&W)

1-5 3.00
The Clone Conspiracy TPB (1998, $14.95) r/#1-5 15.00

DR. DOOM'S REVENGE
Marvel Comics: 1989 (Came w/computer game from Paragon Software)

V1#1-Spider-Man & Captain America fight Dr. Doom 3.00

DR. FATE (See 1st Issue Special, The Immortal..., Justice League, More Fun #55, & Showcase)

DOCTOR FATE
DC Comics: July, 1987 - No. 4, Oct, 1987 ($1.50, limited series, Baxter paper)

1-4: Giffen-c/a in all 3.00

DOCTOR FATE
DC Comics: Winter, 1988-'89 - No. 41, June, 1992 ($1.25/$1.50 #5 on)

1,15: 15-Justice League app. 3.50
2-14 3.00
16-41: 25-1st new Dr. Fate. 36-Original Dr. Fate returns 2.50
Annual 1(1989, $2.95, 68 pgs.)-Sutton-a 3.50

DOCTOR FATE
DC Comics: Oct, 2003 - No. 5, Feb, 2004 ($2.50, limited series)

1-5-Golden-s/Kramer-a 2.50

DR. FU MANCHU (See The Mask of...)
I.W. Enterprises: 1964

1-r/Avon's "Mask of Dr. Fu Manchu"; Wood-a 9 18 27 60 85 110

DR. GIGGLES (See Dark Horse Presents #64-66)
Dark Horse Comics: Oct, 1992 - No. 2, Oct, 1992 ($2.50, limited series)

Doctor Solar #9 © GK

Doctor Strange #171 © MAR

Doctor Spectrum #1 © MAR

GD VG FN VF VF/NM NM-
2.0 4.0 6.0 8.0 9.0 9.2

1,2-Based on movie 2.50

DOCTOR GRAVES (Formerly The Many Ghosts of...)
Charlton Comics: No. 73, Sept, 1985 - No. 75, Jan, 1986

73-75-Low print run 1 2 3 4 5 7

DR. JEKYLL AND MR. HYDE (See A Star Presentation & Supernatural Thrillers #4)

DR. KILDARE (TV)
Dell Publishing Co.: No. 1337, 4-6/62 - No. 9, 4-6/65 (All Richard Chamberlain photo-c)

Four Color 1337(#1, 1962) 10 20 30 72 104 135
2-9 8 16 24 53 74 95

DR. MASTERS (See The Adventures of Young...)

DOCTOR MID-NITE (Also see All-American #25)
DC Comics: 1999 - No. 3, 1999 ($5.95, square-bound, limited series)

1-3-Matt Wagner-s/John K. Snyder III-painted art 6.00
TPB (2000, $19.95) r/series 20.00

DOCTOR OCTOPUS: NEGATIVE EXPOSURE
Marvel Comics: Dec, 2003 - No. 5, Apr, 2004 ($2.99, limited series)

1-5-Vaughan-s/Staz Johnson-a; Spider-Man app. 3.00
Spider-Man/Doctor Octopus: Negative Exposure TPB (2004, $13.99) r/series 14.00

DR. ROBOT SPECIAL
Dark Horse Comics: Apr, 2000 ($2.95, one-shot)

1-Bernie Mireault-s/a; some reprints from Madman Comics #12-15 3.00

DOCTOR SOLAR, MAN OF THE ATOM (See The Occult Files of Dr. Spektor #14 & Solar)
Gold Key/Whitman No. 28 on: 10/62 - No. 27, 4/69; No. 28, 4/81 - No. 31, 3/82 (1-27 have painted-c)

1-(#10000-210)-Origin/1st app. Dr. Solar (1st original Gold Key character)
21 42 63 148 227 305
2-Prof. Harbinger begins 10 20 30 67 96 125
3,4 7 14 21 46 63 80
5-Intro. Man of the Atom in costume 7 14 21 50 68 85
6-10 5 10 15 36 48 60
11-14,16-20 4 8 12 25 33 42
15-Origin retold 4 8 12 28 38 48
21-23: 23-Last 12¢ issue 3 7 10 21 28 35
24-27 3 6 9 19 25 32
28-31: 29-Magnus Robot Fighter begins. 31-(3/82)The Sentinel app.
2 4 6 12 16 20

NOTE: ***Frank Bolle*** *a-6-19, 29-31; c-29i, 30i.* ***Bob Fugitani*** *a-1-5.* ***Spiegle*** *a-29-31.* ***Al McWilliams*** *a-20-23.*

DOCTOR SOLAR, MAN OF THE ATOM
Valiant Comics: 1990 - No. 2, 1991 ($7.95, card stock-c, high quality, 96 pgs.)

1,2: Reprints Gold Key series 1 2 3 5 7 9

DOCTOR SPECTRUM (See Supreme Power)
Marvel Comics: Oct, 2004 - No. 6 ($2.99, limited series)

1-3-Origin; Sara Barnes-s/Travel Foreman-a 3.00

DOCTOR SPEKTOR (See The Occult Files of..., & Spine-Tingling Tales)

DOCTOR STRANGE (Formerly Strange Tales #1-168) (Also see The Defenders, Giant-Size..., Marvel Fanfare, Marvel Graphic Novel, Marvel Premiere, Marvel Treasury Edition, Strange & Strange Tales, 2nd Series)
Marvel Comics Group: No. 169, 6/68 - No. 183, 11/69; 6/74 - No. 81, 2/87

169(#1)-Origin retold; panel swipe/M.D. #1-c 13 26 39 92 141 190
170-177: 177-New costume 4 8 12 27 36 45
178-183: 178-Black Knight app. 179-Spider-Man story-r. 180-Photo montage-c.
181-Brunner-c(part-i), last 12¢ issue 4 8 12 24 32 40
1(6/74, 2nd series)-Brunner-c/a 7 14 21 46 63 80
2 3 7 10 21 28 35
3-5 2 4 6 14 18 22
6-10 2 4 6 8 10 12
11-13,15-20: 13,15-17-(Regular 25¢ editions) 1 2 3 4 5 7
13-17-(30¢-c variants, limited distribution) 1 3 4 6 8 10
14-(5/76) Dracula app.; (regular 25¢ edition) 1 3 4 6 8 10
21-40: 21-Origin-r/Doctor Strange #169. 23-25-(Regular 30¢ editions). 31-Sub-Mariner-c/story 4.00
23-25-(35¢-c variants, limited distribution)(6,8,10/77) 1 2 3 5 6 8
41-57,63-77,79-81: 56-Origin retold 3.50
58-62: 58-Re-intro Hannibal King (cameo). 59-Hannibal King full app. 59-62-Dracula app. (Darkhold storyline). 61,62-Doctor Strange, Blade, Hannibal King & Frank Drake team-up to battle. Dracula. 62-Death of Dracula & Lilith 5.00
78-New costume 3.00

GD VG FN VF VF/NM NM-
2.0 4.0 6.0 8.0 9.0 9.2

Annual 1(1976, 52 pgs.)-New Russell-a (35 pgs.) 2 4 6 10 13 16
.../Silver Dagger Special Edition 1 (3/83, $2.50)-r/#1,2,4,5; Wrightson-c 3.00
...What Is It That Disturbs You, Stephen? #1 (10/97, $5.99, 48 pgs.) Russell-a/Andreyko & Russell-s, retelling of Annual #1 story 6.00

NOTE: ***Adkins*** *a-169, 170, 171i; c-169-171, 172i, 173.* ***Adams*** *a-4i.* ***Austin*** *a(i)-48-60, 66, 68, 70, 73; c(i)-38, 47-53, 55, 58-60, 70.* ***Brunner*** *a-1-5p; c-1-6, 22, 28-30, 33.* ***Colan*** *a(p)-172-178, 180-183, 6-18, 36-45, 47; c(p)-172, 174-183, 11-21, 23, 27, 35, 36, 47.* ***Ditko*** *a-179r, 3r.* ***Everett*** *c-183i.* ***Golden*** *a-46p, 55p; c-42-44, 46, 55p.* ***G. Kane*** *c(p)-8-10.* ***Miller*** *c-46p.* ***Nebres*** *a-20, 22, 23, 24i, 26i, 32i; c-32i, 34.* ***Rogers*** *a-48-53p; c-47p-53p.* ***Russell*** *a-34i, 46i, Annual 1.* ***B. Smith*** *c-179.* ***Paul Smith*** *a-54p, 56p, 65, 66p, 68p, 69, 71-73; c-56, 65, 66, 68, 71.* ***Starlin*** *a-23p, 26; c-25, 26.* ***Sutton*** *a-27-29p, 31i, 33, 34p. Painted c-62, 63.*

DOCTOR STRANGE (Volume 2)
Marvel Comics: Feb, 1999 - No. 4, May, 1999 ($2.99, limited series)

1-4: 1,2-Tony Harris-a/painted cover. 3,4-Chadwick-a 3.00

DOCTOR STRANGE CLASSICS
Marvel Comics Group: Mar, 1984 - No. 4, June, 1984 ($1.50, Baxter paper)

1-4: Ditko-r; Byrne-c. 4-New Golden pin-up 3.00

NOTE: ***Byrne*** *c-1i, 2-4.*

DOCTOR STRANGEFATE (See Marvel Versus DC #3 & DC Versus Marvel #4)
DC Comics (Amalgam): Apr, 1996 ($1.95)

1-Ron Marz script w/Jose Garcia-Lopez-(p) & Kevin Nowlan-(i). Access & Charles Xavier app. 2.50

DOCTOR STRANGE MASTER OF THE MYSTIC ARTS (See Fireside Book Series)

DOCTOR STRANGE, SORCERER SUPREME
Marvel Comics (Midnight Sons imprint #60 on): Nov, 1988 - No. 90, June, 1996 ($1.25/$1.50/$1.75/$1.95, direct sales only, Mando paper)

1 ($1.25) 4.00
2-9,12-14,16-25,27,29-40,42-49,51-64: 3-New Defenders app. 5-Guice-c/a begins. 14-18-Morbius story line. 31-36-Infinity Gauntlet x-overs. 31-Silver Surfer app. 33-Thanos-c & cameo. 36-Warlock app. 37-Silver Surfer app. 40-Daredevil x-over. 41-Wolverine-c/story. 42-47-Infinity War x-overs. 47-Gamora app. 52,53-Morbius-c/stories. 60,61-Siege of Darkness pt. 7 & 15. 60-Spot varnish-c. 61-New Doctor Strange begins (cameo, 1st app.). 62-Dr. Doom & Morbius app. 2.50
10,11,26,28,41: 10-Re-intro Morbius w/new costume (11/89). 11-Hobgoblin app. 26-Werewolf by Night app. 28-Ghost Rider-s cont'd from G.R. #12; published at same time as Doctor Strange/Ghost Rider Special #1(4/91) 3.00
15-Unauthorized Amy Grant photo-c 4.00
50-($2.95, 52 pgs.)-Holo-grafx foil-c; Hulk, Ghost Rider & Silver Surfer app.; leads into new Secret Defenders series 3.00
65-74, 76-90: 65-Begin $1.95-c; bound-in card sheet. 72-Silver ink-c. 80-82- Ellis-s. 84-DeMatteis story begins. 87-Death of Baron Mordo 2.50
75 ($2.50) 3.00
75 ($3.50)-Foil-c 4.00
Annual 2-4 ('92-'94, 68 pgs.)-2-Defenders app. 3-Polybagged w/card 3.00
Ashcan (1995, 75¢) 2.25
.../Ghost Rider Special 1 (4/91, $1.50)-Same book as D.S.S.S. #28 2.50
...Vs. Dracula 1 (3/94, $1.75, 52 pgs.)-r/Tomb of Dracula #44 & Dr. Strange #14 2.50

NOTE: ***Colan*** *c/a-19.* ***Golden*** *c-28.* ***Guice*** *a-5-16, 18, 20-24; c-5-12, 20-24. See 1st series for Annual #1.*

DR. TOM BRENT, YOUNG INTERN
Charlton Publications: Feb, 1963 - No. 5, Oct, 1963

1 3 6 9 16 20 25
2-5 2 4 6 10 12 15

DR. TOMORROW
Acclaim Comics (Valiant): Sept, 1997 - No. 12 ($2.50)

1-12: 1-Mignola-c 2.50

DR. VOLTZ (See Mighty Midget Comics)

DR. WEIRD
Big Bang Comics: Oct, 1994 - No. 2, May, 1995 ($2.95, B&W)

1,2: 1-Frank Brunner-c 4.00

DR. WEIRD SPECIAL
Big Bang Comics: Feb, 1994 ($3.95, B&W, 68 pgs.)

1-Origin-r by Starlin; Starlin-c. 4.00

DOCTOR WHO (Also see Marvel Premiere #57-60)
Marvel Comics Group: Oct, 1984 - No. 23, Aug, 1986 ($1.50, direct sales, Baxter paper)

1-15-British-r 4.00
16-23 5.00
Graphic Novel Voyager (1985, $8.95) color reprints of B&W comic pages from Doctor Who Magazine #88-99; Colin Baker afterword 12.00

DR. WHO & THE DALEKS (See Movie Classics)

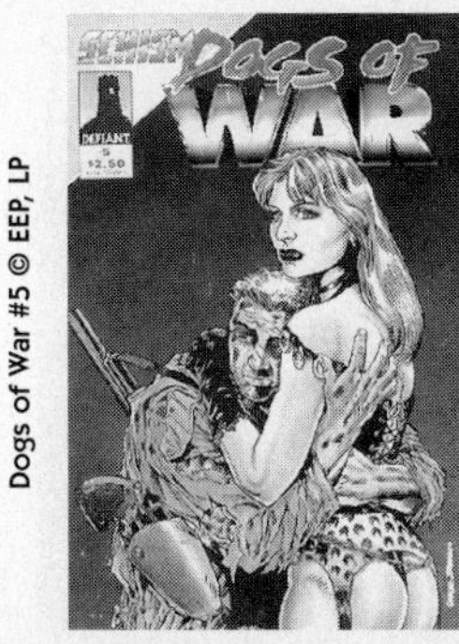

Dogs of War #5 © EEP, LP

Doll Man Quarterly #30 © QUA

Domino #2 © MAR

GD VG FN VF VF/NM NM-
2.0 4.0 6.0 8.0 9.0 9.2

DR. WONDER
Old Town Publishing: June, 1996 - No. 5 ($2.95, B&W)
1-5: 1-Intro & origin of Dr. Wonder; Dick Ayers-c/a; Irwin Hasen-a 3.00

DOCTOR ZERO
Marvel Comics (Epic Comics): Apr, 1988 - No. 8, Aug, 1989 ($1.25/$1.50)
1-8: 1-Sienkiewicz-c. 6,7-Spiegle-a 2.25
NOTE: ***Sienkiewicz*** *a-3i, 4i; c-1.* ***Spiegle*** *a-6, 7.*

DO-DO (Funny Animal Circus Stories)
Nation-Wide Publishers: 1950 - No. 7, 1951 (5¢, 5x7-1/4" Miniature)
1 (52 pgs.) 27 54 81 152 219 285
2-7 14 28 42 79 110 140

DODO & THE FROG, THE (Formerly Funny Stuff; also see It's Game Time #2)
National Periodical Publications: No. 80, 9-10/54 - No. 88, 1-2/56; No. 89, 8-9/56; No. 90, 10-11/56; No. 91, 9/57; No. 92, 11/57 (See Comic Cavalcade)
80-1st app. Doodles Duck by Sheldon Mayer 21 42 63 121 173 225
81-91: Doodles Duck by Mayer in #81,83-90 14 28 42 79 110 140
92-(Scarce)-Doodles Duck by S. Mayer 19 38 57 107 154 200

DOGFACE DOOLEY
Magazine Enterprises: 1951 - No. 5, 1953
1(A-1 40) 8 16 24 40 50 60
2(A-1 43), 3(A-1 49), 4(A-1 53), 5(A-1 64) 6 12 18 28 34 40
I.W. Reprint #1('64), Super Reprint #17 2 4 6 10 13 16

DOG MOON
DC Comics (Vertigo): 1996 ($6.95, one-shot)
1-Robert Hunter-scripts; Tim Truman-c/a. 7.00

DOG OF FLANDERS, A
Dell Publishing Co.: No. 1088, Mar, 1960
Four Color 1088-Movie, photo-c 6 12 18 38 52 65

DOGPATCH (See Al Capp's... & Mammy Yokum)

DOGS OF WAR (Also see Warriors of Plasm)
Defiant: Apr, 1994 - No. 5, Aug, 1994 ($2.50)
1-5 2.50

DOGS-O-WAR
Crusade Comics: June, 1996 - No. 3, Jan, 1997 ($2.95, B&W, limited series)
1-3: 1,2-Photo-c 3.00

DOLLFACE & HER GANG (Betty Betz'...)
Dell Publishing Co.: No. 309, Jan, 1951
Four Color 309 6 12 18 43 59 75

DOLLMAN (Movie)
Eternity Comics: Sept, 1991 - No. 4, Dec, 1991 ($2.50, limited series)
1-4: Adaptation of film 2.50

DOLL MAN QUARTERLY, THE (Doll Man #17 on; also see Feature Comics #27 & Freedom Fighters)
Quality Comics: Fall, 1941 - No. 7, Fall, '43; No. 8, Spr, '46 - No. 47, Oct, 1953
1-Dollman (by Cassone), Justin Wright begin 317 634 951 2061 3331 4600
2-The Dragon begins; Crandall-a(5) 135 270 405 844 1297 1750
3,4 89 178 267 556 853 1150
5-Crandall-a 77 154 231 481 741 1000
6,7(1943) 55 110 165 340 520 700
8(1946)-1st app. Torchy by Bill Ward 162 324 486 1013 1557 2100
9 55 110 165 340 520 700
10-20 43 86 129 262 399 535
21-30: 28-Vs. The Flame 39 78 117 222 324 425
31-36,38,40: 31-(12/50)-Intro Elmo, the wonder dog (Dollman's faithful dog).
32-34-Jeb Rivers app.; 34 by Crandall(p) 33 66 99 190 275 360
37-Origin & 1st app. Dollgirl; Dollgirl bondage-c 43 86 129 267 399 535
39- "Narcotics...the Death Drug" c-/story 35 70 105 200 290 380
41-47 23 43 69 130 188 245
Super Reprint #11('64, r/#20),15(r/#23),17(r/#28): 15,17-Torchy app.; Andru/Esposito-c
4 8 12 24 32 40
NOTE: ***Ward*** *Torchy in 8, 9, 11, 12, 14-24, 27; by Fox-#26, 30, 35-47.* ***Crandall*** *a-2, 5, 10, 13 & Super #11, 17, 18.* ***Crandall/Cuidera*** *c-40-42.* ***Guardineer*** *a-3. Bondage c-27, 37, 38, 39.*

DOLLS
Sirius: June, 1996 ($2.95, B&W, one-shot)
1 3.00

DOLLY
Ziff-Davis Publ. Co.: No. 10, July-Aug, 1951 (Funny animal)
10-Painted-c 8 16 24 40 50 60

DOLLY DILL
Marvel Comics/Newsstand Publ.: 1945
1 17 34 51 95 135 175

DOLLZ, THE
Image Comics: Apr, 2001 - No. 2, June, 2001 ($2.95)
1,2: 1-Four covers; Sniegoski & Green-s/Green-a 3.00

DOMINATION FACTOR
Marvel Comics: Nov, 1999 - 4.8, Feb, 2000 ($2.50, interconnected mini- series)
1.1, 2.3, 3.5, 4.7-Fantastic Four; Jurgens-s/a 2.50
1.2, 2.4, 3.6, 4.8-Avengers; Ordway-s/a 2.50

DOMINION
Image Comics: Jan, 2003 - No. 2 ($2.95)
1,2-Keith Giffen-s/a 3.00

DOMINION (Manga)
Eclipse Comics: Dec, 1990 - No. 6., July, 1990 ($2.00, B&W, limited series)
1-6 3.00

DOMINION: CONFLICT 1 (Manga)
Dark Horse Comics: Mar, 1996 - No. 6, Aug, 1996 ($2.95, B&W, limited series)
1-6: Shirow-c/a/scripts 3.00

DOMINIQUE: KILLZONE
Caliber Comics: May, 1995 ($2.95, B&W)
1 3.00

DOMINO (See X-Force)
Marvel Comics: Jan, 1997 - No. 3, Mar, 1997 ($1.95, limited series)
1-3: 2-Deathstrike-c/app. 2.25

DOMINO (See X-Force)
Marvel Comics: June, 2003 - No. 4, Aug, 2003 ($2.50, limited series)
1-4-Stelfreeze-c/a; Pruett-s. 2.50

DOMINO CHANCE
Chance Enterprises: May-June, 1982 - No. 9, May, 1985 (B&W)
1-9: 7-1st app. Gizmo, 2 pgs. 8-1st full Gizmo story. 1-Reprint, May, 1985 2.50

DONALD AND MICKEY IN DISNEYLAND (See Dell Giants)

DONALD AND SCROOGE
Disney Comics: 1992 ($8.95, squarebound, 100 pgs.)
nn-Don Rosa reprint special; r/U.S., D.D. Advs. 1 3 4 6 8 10
1-3 (1992, $1.50)-r/D.D. Advs. (Disney) #1,22,24 & U.S. #261-263,269 3.00

DONALD AND THE WHEEL (Disney)
Dell Publishing Co.: No. 1190, Nov, 1961
Four Color 1190-Movie, Barks-c 9 18 27 60 85 110

DONALD DUCK (See Adventures of Mickey Mouse, Cheerios, Donald & Mickey, Ducktales, Dynabrite Comics, Gladstone Comic Album, Mickey & Donald, Mickey Mouse Mag., Story Hour Series, Uncle Scrooge, Walt Disney's Comics & Stories, W. D.'s Donald Duck, Wheaties & Whitman Comic Books, Wise Little Hen, The)

DONALD DUCK
Whitman Publishing Co./Grosset & Dunlap/K.K.: 1935, 1936 (All pages on heavy linen-like finish cover stock in color;1st book ever devoted to Donald Duck; see Advs. of Mickey Mouse for 1st app.) (9-1/2x13")
978(1935)-16 pgs.; Illustrated text story book 380 760 1140 2090 3095 4100
nn(1936)-36 pgs.plus hard cover & dust jacket. Story completely rewritten with B&W illos added. Mickey appears and his nephews are named Morty & Monty
Book only 360 720 1080 1980 2940 3900
Dust jacket only.... 90 180 270 495 735 975

DONALD DUCK (Walt Disney's) (10¢)
Whitman/K.K. Publications: 1938 (8-1/2x11-1/2", B&W, cardboard-c)
(Has D. Duck with bubble pipe on-c)
nn-The first Donald Duck & Walt Disney comic book; 1936 & 1937 Sunday strip-r(in B&W); same format as the Feature Books; 1st strips with Huey, Dewey & Louie from 10/17/37
360 720 1080 1980 2940 3900

DONALD DUCK (Walt Disney's...#262 on; see 4-Color listings for titles & Four Color No. 1109 for origin story)
Dell Publ. Co./Gold Key #85-216/Whitman #217-245/Gladstone #246 on: 1940 - No. 84, Sept-Nov, 1962; No. 85, Dec, 1962 - No. 245, July, 1984; No. 246, Oct, 1986 - No. 279, May, 1990; No. 280, Sept, 1993 - No. 307, Mar,1998

Donald Duck Four Color #29 © WDC

Donald Duck #46 © WDC

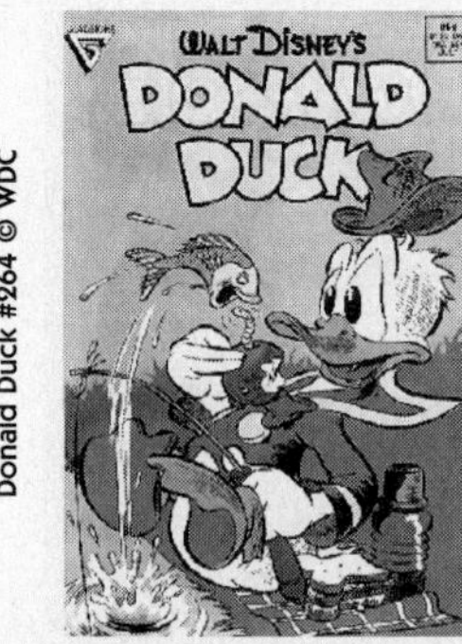

Donald Duck #264 © WDC

	GD 2.0	VG 4.0	FN 6.0	VF 8.0	VF/NM 9.0	NM- 9.2
Four Color 4(1940)-Daily 1939 strip-r by Al Taliaferro	875	1750	2625	6800	11,900	17,000
Large Feature Comic 16(1/41?)-1940 Sunday strips-r in B&W	484	968	1452	3388	5444	7500
Large Feature Comic 20('41)-Comic Paint Book, r-single panels from Large Feature #16 at top of each pg. to color; daily strip-r across bottom of each pg.	516	1032	1548	3612	5806	8000
Four Color 9('42)- "Finds Pirate Gold"; 64 pgs. by Carl Barks & Jack Hannah (pgs. 1,2,5,12-40 are by Barks, his 1st Donald Duck comic book art work; © 8/17/42)	750	1500	2250	5800	9813	14,000
Four Color 29(9/43)- "Mummy's Ring" by Barks; reprinted in Uncle Scrooge & Donald Duck #1('65), W. D. Comics Digest #44('73) & Donald Duck Advs. #14	513	1026	1539	4000	6750	9500
Four Color 62(1/45)- "Frozen Gold"; 52 pgs. by Barks, reprinted in The Best of W.D. Comics & Donald Duck Advs. #4	162	332	498	1365	2233	3100
Four Color 108(1946)- "Terror of the River"; 52 pgs. by Carl Barks; reprinted in Gladstone Comic Album #2	125	250	375	1063	1719	2375
Four Color 147(5/47)-in "Volcano Valley" by Barks	84	168	252	714	1155	1515
Four Color 159(8/47)-in "The Ghost of the Grotto";52 pgs. by Carl Barks; reprinted in Best of Uncle Scrooge & Donald Duck #1 ('66) & The Best of W.D. Comics & D.D. Advs. #9; two Barks stories	72	144	216	612	994	1375
Four Color 178(12/47)-1st app. Uncle Scrooge by Carl Barks; reprinted in Gold Key Christmas Parade #3 & The Best of Walt Disney Comics	100	200	300	850	1375	1900
Four Color 189(6/48)-by Carl Barks; reprinted in Best of Donald Duck & Uncle Scrooge #1('64) & D.D. Advs. #19	61	122	183	519	835	1150
Four Color 199(10/48)-by Carl Barks; mentioned in Love and Death; r/in Gladstone Comic Album #5	67	134	201	570	920	1270
Four Color 203(12/48)-by Barks; reprinted as Gold Key Christmas Parade #4	50	100	150	407	641	875
Four Color 223(4/49)-by Barks; reprinted as Best of Donald Duck #1 & Donald Duck Advs. #3.	64	128	192	544	868	1215
Four Color 238(8/49)-in "Voodoo Hoodoo" by Barks	50	100	150	407	641	875
Four Color 256(12/49)-by Barks; reprinted in Best of Donald Duck & Uncle Scrooge #2('67), Gladstone Comic Album #16 & W.D. Comics Digest 44('73)	41	82	123	318	497	675
Four Color 263(2/50)-Two Barks stories; r-in D.D. #278	41	82	123	305	478	650
Four Color 275(5/50), 282(7/50), 291(9/50), 300(11/50)-All by Carl Barks; 275, 282 reprinted in W.D. Comics Digest #44('73). #275 r/in Gladstone Comic Album #10. #291 r/in D. Duck Advs. #16	39	78	117	293	459	625
Four Color 308(1/51), 318(3/51)-by Barks; #318-reprinted in W.D. Comics Digest #34 & D.D. Advs. #2,19	36	72	108	270	423	575
Four Color 328(5/51)-by Carl Barks	37	56	84	210	398	585
Four Color 339(7-8/51), 379-2nd Uncle Scrooge-c; art not by Barks.	10	20	30	73	107	140
Four Color 348(9-10/51), 356,394-Barks-c only	19	38	57	134	205	275
Four Color 367(1-2/52)-by Barks; reprinted as Gold Key Christmas Parade #2 & #8	31	62	93	230	358	485
Four Color 408(7-8/52), 422(9-10/52)-All by Carl Barks. #408-r-in Best of Donald Duck & Uncle Scrooge #1('64) & Gladstone Comic Album #13	31	63	93	230	358	485
26(11-12/52)-In "Trick or Treat" (Barks-a, 36pgs.) 1st story r-in Walt Disney Digest #16 & Gladstone C.A. #23	31	62	93	230	358	485
27-30-Barks-c only	12	24	36	86	131	175
31-44,47-50	7	14	21	50	68	85
45-Barks-a (6 pgs.)	14	28	42	97	149	200
46- "Secret of Hondorica" by Barks, 24 pgs.; reprinted in Donald Duck #98 & 154	20	40	60	141	216	290
51-Barks-a,1/2 pg.	7	14	21	51	71	90
52- "Lost Peg-Leg Mine" by Barks, 10 pgs.	14	28	42	102	156	210
53,55-59	6	12	18	43	59	75
54- "Forbidden Valley" by Barks, 26 pgs. (10¢ & 15¢ versions exist)	17	34	51	121	186	250
60- "Donald Duck & the Titanic Ants" by Barks, 20 pgs. plus 6 more pgs.	17	34	51	121	186	250
61-67,69,70	5	10	15	36	48	60
68-Barks-a, 5 pgs.	11	22	33	77	114	150
71-Barks-r, 1/2 pg.	6	12	18	38	52	65
72-78,80,82-97,99,100: 96-Donald Duck Album	5	10	15	36	48	60
79,81-Barks-a, 1pg.	6	12	18	38	52	65
98-Reprints #46 (Barks)	6	12	18	38	52	65
101,103-111,113-135: 120-Last 12¢ issue. 134-Barks-r/#52 & WDC&S 194. 135-Barks-r/WDC&S 198, 19 pgs.	4	8	12	24	32	40
102-Super Goof. 112-1st Moby Duck	4	8	12	25	33	42
136-153,155,156,158: 149-20¢-c begin	3	6	9	16	20	24
154-Barks-r(#46)	3	6	9	18	24	30
157,159,160,164: 157-Barks-r(#45); 25¢-c begin. 159-Reprints/WDC&S #192 (10 pgs.). 160-Barks-r(#26). 164-Barks-r(#79)	3	6	9	16	20	24
161-163,165-173,175-187,189-191: 175-30¢-c begin. 187-Barks r/#68.	2	4	6	12	16	20
174,188: 174-r/4-Color #394.	2	4	6	14	18	22
192-Barks-r(40 pgs.) from Donald Duck #60 & WDC&S #226,234 (52 pgs.)	3	6	9	16	21	26
193-200,202-207,209-211,213-216	2	4	6	10	13	16
201,208,212: 201-Barks-r/Christmas Parade #26, 16pgs. 208-Barks-r/#60 (6 pgs.). 212-Barks-r/WDC&S #130	2	4	6	10	13	16
217-219: 217 has 216 on-c. 219-Barks-r/WDC&S #106,107, 10 pgs. ea.	2	4	6	11	14	18
220,225-228: 228-Barks-r/F.C. #275	2	4	6	14	18	22
221,223,224: Scarce; only sold in pre-packs. 221(8/80), 223(11/80), 224(12/80)	4	8	12	29	40	50
222-(9-10/80)-(Very low distribution)	17	34	51	121	186	250
229-240: 229-Barks-r/F.C. #282. 230-Barks-r/ #52 & WDC&S #194. 236(2/82), 237(2-3/82), 238(3/82), 239(4/82), 240(5/82)	2	4	6	10	13	16
241-245: 241(4/83), 242(5/83), 243(3/84), 244(4/84), 245(7/84)(low print)	3	6	9	16	20	24
246-(1st Gladstone issue)-Barks-r/FC #422	3	6	9	16	20	25
247-249,251: 248,249-Barks-r/DD #54 & 26. 251-Barks-r/1945 Firestone	2	4	6	10	13	16
250-($1.50, 68 pgs.)-Barks-r/4-Color #9	2	4	6	11	14	18
252-277,280: 254-Barks-r/FC #328. 256-Barks-r/FC #147. 257-($1.50, 52 pgs.)-Barks-r/ Vacaction Parade #1. 261-Barks-r/FC #300. 275-Kelly-r/FC #92. 280 (#1, 2nd Series)	1	2	3	5	6	8
278,279,286: 278,279 ($1.95, 68 pgs.): 278-Rosa-a; Barks-r/FC #263. 279-Rosa-c; Barks-r/MOC #4. 286-Rosa-a	1	2	3	5	7	9
281,282,284	1	2	3	4	5	7
283-Don Rosa-a, part-c & scripts	1	2	3	5	6	8
285,287-307						5.00
286 ($2.95, 68 pgs.)-Happy Birthday, Donald						6.00
Mini-Comic #1(1976)-(3-1/4x6-1/2"); r/D.D. #150	2	4	6	9	11	14

NOTE: ***Carl Barks** wrote all issues he illustrated, but #117, 126, 138 contain his script only. Issues 4-Color #189, 199, 203, 223, 238, 256, 263, 275, 282, 308, 348, 356, 367, 394, 408, 422, 26-30, 35, 44, 46, 52, 55, 57, 60, 65, 70-73, 77-80, 83, 101, 103, 105, 106, 111, 126, 246r, 266r, 268r, 271r, 275r, 278r(F.C. 263) all have **Barks** covers. **Barks** r-263-267, 269-278-282, 284, 285. #96 titled "Comic Album", #99-"Christmas Album". New art issues (not reprints)-106-46, 148-63, 167, 169, 170, 172, 173, 175, 178, 179, 196, 209, 223, 225, 236. **Taliaferro** daily newspaper strips #258-260, 264, 284, 285; Sunday strips #247, 280-283.*

DONALD DUCK ADVENTURES (See Walt Disney's Donald Duck Adventures)

DONALD DUCK ALBUM (See Comic Album No. 1,3 & Duck Album)
Dell Publishing Co./Gold Key: 5-7/59 - F.C. No. 1239, 10-12/61; 1962; 8/63 - No. 2, Oct, 1963

	GD 2.0	VG 4.0	FN 6.0	VF 8.0	VF/NM 9.0	NM- 9.2
Four Color 995 (#1)	7	14	21	50	68	85
Four Color 1182, 01204-207 (1962-Dell)	6	12	18	38	52	65
Four Color 1099,1140,1239-Barks-c	8	16	24	53	74	95
1(8/63-Gold Key)-Barks-c	7	14	21	46	63	80
2(10/63)	6	12	18	38	52	65

DONALD DUCK AND THE BOYS (Also see Story Hour Series)
Whitman Publishing Co.: 1948 (5-1/4x5-1/2", 100pgs., hard-c; art & text)

	GD 2.0	VG 4.0	FN 6.0	VF 8.0	VF/NM 9.0	NM- 9.2
845-(49) new illos by Barks based on his Donald Duck 10-pager in WDC&S #74, Expanded text not written by Barks; Cover not by Barks	50	100	150	350	575	800

(Prices vary widely on this book)

DONALD DUCK AND THE CHRISTMAS CAROL
Whitman Publishing Co.: 1960 (A Little Golden Book, 6-3/8"x7-5/8", 28 pgs.)

	GD 2.0	VG 4.0	FN 6.0	VF 8.0	VF/NM 9.0	NM- 9.2
nn-Story book pencilled by Carl Barks with the intended title "Uncle Scrooge's Christmas Carol." Finished art adapted by Norman McGary. (Rare)-Reprinted in Uncle Scrooge in Color.	30	60	90	150	210	270

DONALD DUCK BEACH PARTY (Also see Dell Giants)
Gold Key: Sept, 1965 (12¢)

	GD 2.0	VG 4.0	FN 6.0	VF 8.0	VF/NM 9.0	NM- 9.2
1(#10158-509)-Barks-r/WDC&S #45; painted-c	8	16	24	53	74	95

DONALD DUCK BOOK (See Story Hour Series)

DONALD DUCK COMICS DIGEST
Gladstone Publishing: Nov, 1986 - No. 5, July, 1987 ($1.25/$1.50, 96 pgs.)

	GD 2.0	VG 4.0	FN 6.0	VF 8.0	VF/NM 9.0	NM- 9.2
1,3: 1-Barks-c/a-r	1	3	4	6	8	10
2,4,5: 4,5-$1.50-c						6.00

DONALD DUCK FUN BOOK (See Dell Giants)

Don Fortune #5 © Don Fortune Publ.

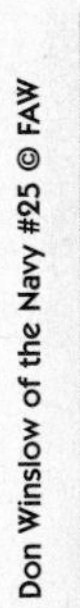
Don Winslow of the Navy #25 © FAW

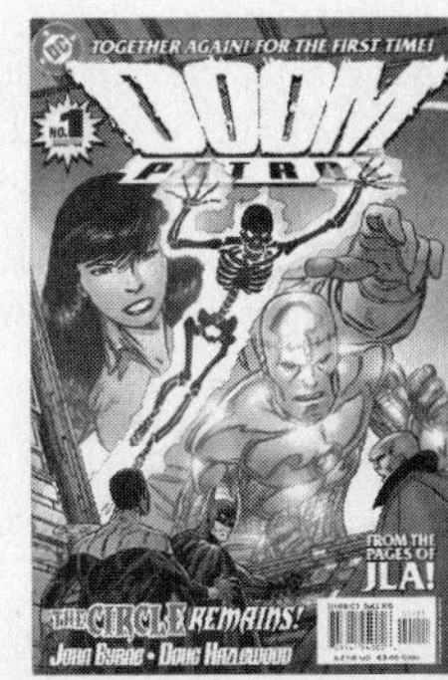
Doom Patrol ('04) #1 © DC

	GD	VG	FN	VF	VF/NM	NM-
	2.0	4.0	6.0	8.0	9.0	9.2

DONALD DUCK IN DISNEYLAND (See Dell Giants)

DONALD DUCK MARCH OF COMICS (See March of Comics #4,20,41,56,69,263)

DONALD DUCK MERRY CHRISTMAS (See Dell Giant No. 53)

DONALD DUCK PICNIC PARTY (See Picnic Party listed under Dell Giants)

DONALD DUCK TELLS ABOUT KITES (See Kite Fun Book)

DONALD DUCK, THIS IS YOUR LIFE (Disney, TV)
Dell Publishing Co.: No. 1109, Aug-Oct, 1960

Four Color 1109-Gyro flashback to WDC&S #141; origin Donald Duck (1st told) 15 30 45 105 160 215

DONALD DUCK XMAS ALBUM (See regular Donald Duck No. 99)

DONALD IN MATHMAGIC LAND (Disney)
Dell Publishing Co.: No. 1051, Oct-Dec, 1959 - No. 1198, May-July, 1961

Four Color 1051 (#1)-Movie 10 20 30 70 100 130
Four Color 1198-Reprint of above 8 16 24 53 74 95

DONATELLO, TEENAGE MUTANT NINJA TURTLE
Mirage Studios: Aug, 1986 ($1.50, B&W, one-shot, 44 pgs.)

1 1 2 3 5 7 9

DONDI
Dell Publishing Co.: No. 1176, Mar-May, 1961 - No. 1276, Dec, 1961

Four Color 1176 (#1)-Movie; origin, photo-c 6 12 18 38 52 65
Four Color 1276 4 8 12 22 30 38

DON FORTUNE MAGAZINE
Don Fortune Publishing Co.: Aug, 1946 - No. 6, Feb, 1947

1-Delecta of the Planets by C. C. Beck in all 26 52 78 150 215 280
2 15 30 45 83 117 150
3-6: 3-Bondage-c 12 24 36 71 98 125

DONKEY KONG (See Blip #1)

DONNA MATRIX
Reactor, Inc.: Aug, 1993 ($2.95, 52 pgs.)

1-Computer generated-c/a by Mike Saenz; 3-D effects 3.00

DON NEWCOMBE
Fawcett Publications: 1950 (Baseball)

nn-Photo-c 42 84 126 256 391 525

DON ROSA'S COMICS AND STORIES
Fantagraphics Books (CX Comics): 1983 ($2.95)

1,2: 1-(68 pgs.) Reprints Rosa's The Pertwillaby Papers episodes #128-133. 2-(60 pgs.) Reprints episodes #134-138 2 4 6 11 14 18

DON SIMPSON'S BIZARRE HEROES (Also see Megaton Man)
Fiasco Comics: May, 1990 - No. 17, Sept, 1996 ($2.50/$2.95, B&W)

1-10,0,11-17: 0-Begin $2.95-c; r/Bizarre Heroes #1. 17-(9/96)-Indicia also reads Megaton Man #0; intro Megaton Man and the Fiascoverse to new readers 3.00

DON'T GIVE UP THE SHIP
Dell Publishing Co.: No. 1049, Aug, 1959

Four Color 1049-Movie, Jerry Lewis photo-c 10 20 30 70 100 130

DON WINSLOW OF THE NAVY
Merwil Publishing Co.: Apr, 1937 - No. 2, May, 1937 (96 pgs.)(A pulp/comic book cross; stapled spine)

V1#1-Has 16 pgs. comics in color. Captain Colorful & Jupiter Jones by Sheldon Mayer; complete Don Winslow novel 629 1258 1887 4700 - -
2-Sheldon Mayer-a 171 342 513 1275 - -

DON WINSLOW OF THE NAVY (See Crackajack Funnies, Famous Feature Stories, Popular Comics & Super Book #5,6)
Dell Publishing Co.: No. 2, Nov, 1939 - No. 22, 1941

Four Color 2 (#1)-Rare 138 276 414 1035 1618 2200
Four Color 22 32 64 96 240 370 500

DON WINSLOW OF THE NAVY (See TV Teens; Movie, Radio, TV) (Fightin' Navy No. 74 on)
Fawcett Publications/Charlton No. 70 on: 2/43 - #64, 12/48; #65, 1/51 - #69, 9/51; #70, 3/55 - #73, 9/55

1-(68 pgs.)-Captain Marvel on cover 115 230 345 719 1110 1500
2 53 106 159 323 492 660
3 40 80 120 240 360 480
4-6: 6-Flag-c 35 70 105 201 293 385
7-10: 8-Last 68 pg. issue? 26 52 78 147 211 275
11-20 20 40 60 112 161 210
21-40 14 28 42 79 110 140
41-43,45-64: 51,60-Singapore Sal (villain) app. 64-(12/48) 11 22 33 66 91 115
44-Classic spider-c 18 36 54 100 143 185
65(1/51)-Flying Saucer attack; photo-c 16 32 48 92 131 170
66 - 69(9/51): All photo-c. 66-sci-fi story 15 30 45 83 117 150
70(3/55)-73: 70-73 r-/#26,58 & 59 10 20 30 56 73 90

DOOM
Marvel Comics: Oct, 2000 - No. 3, Dec, 2000 ($2.99, limited series)

1-3-Dr. Doom; Dixon-s/Manco-a 3.00

DOOM FORCE SPECIAL
DC Comics: July, 1992 ($2.95, 68 pgs., one-shot, mature) (X-Force parody)

1-Morrison scripts; Simonson, Steacy, & others-a; Giffen/Mignola-c 3.00

DOOM PATROL, THE (Formerly My Greatest Adventure No. 1-85; see Brave and the Bold, DC Special Blue Ribbon Digest 19, Official... Index & Showcase No. 94-96)
National Periodical Publ.: No. 86, 3/64 - No. 121, 9-10/68; No. 122, 2/73 - No. 124, 6-7/73

86-1 pg. origin (#86-121 are 12¢ issues) 11 22 33 77 114 150
87-98: 88-Origin The Chief. 91-Intro. Mento 8 16 24 58 82 105
99-Intro. Beast Boy (later becomes the Changeling in New Teen Titans 10 20 30. 67 96 125
100-Origin Beast Boy; Robot-Maniac series begins (12/65) 10 20 30 67 96 125
101-110: 102-Challengers of the Unknown app. 105-Robot-Maniac series ends. 106-Negative Man begins (origin) 6 12 18 40 55 70
111-120 5 10 15 33 44 55
121-Death of Doom Patrol; Orlando-c. 10 20 30 73 107 140
122-124: All reprints 2 4 6 8 10 12

DOOM PATROL
DC Comics (Vertigo imprint #64 on): Oct, 1987 - No, 87, Feb, 1995 (75¢-$1.95, new format)

1-Wraparound-c; Lightle-a 5.00
2-18: 3-1st app. Lodestone. 4-1st app. Karma. 8,15,16-Art Adams-c(i). 18-Invasion tie-in 3.00
19-(2/89)-Grant Morrison scripts begin, ends #63; 1st app Crazy Jane; $1.50-c & new format begins. 1 2 3 5 6 8
20-30: 29-Superman app. 30-Night Breed fold-out 5.00
31-49,51-56,58-60: 35-1st brief app. of Flex Mentallo. 36-1st full app. of Flex Mentallo. 39-World Without End preview.42-Origin of Flex Mentallo 2.50
50,57 ($2.50, 52 pgs.) 2.50
61-87: 61,70-Photo-c. 73-Death cameo (2 panels) 3.00
...And Suicide Squad 1 (3/88, $1.50, 52 pgs.)-Wraparound-c 2.50
Annual 1 (1988, $1.50, 52 pgs.) 2.50
Annual 2 (1994, $3.95, 68 pgs.)-Children's Crusade tie-in. 4.00
...: Crawling From the Wreckage TPB (2004, $19.95) r/#19-25; Morrison-s 20.00
...: The Painting That Ate Paris TPB (2004, $19.95) r/#26-34; Morrison-s 20.00

NOTE: ***Bisley*** *painted c-26-48, 55-58.* ***Bolland*** *c-64, 75.* ***Dringenberg*** *a-42(p).* ***Steacy*** *a-53.*

DOOM PATROL
DC Comics: Dec, 2001 - No. 22, Sept, 2003 ($2.50)

1-Intro. new team with Robotman; Tan Eng Huat-c/a; John Arcudi-s 3.00
2-22: 4,5-Metamorpho & Elongated Man app. 13,14-Fisher-a. 20-Geary-a 2.50

DOOM PATROL (see JLA #94-99)
DC Comics: Aug, 2004 - Present ($2.50)

1-6-John Byrne-s/a. 1-Green Lantern, Batman app. 2.50

DOOM PATROL (See Tangent Comics/ Doom Patrol)

DOOMSDAY
DC Comics: 1995 ($3.95, one-shot)

1-Year One story by Jurgens, L. Simonson, Ordway, and Gil Kane; Superman app. 4.00

DOOMSDAY + 1 (Also see Charlton Bullseye)
Charlton Comics: July, 1975 - No. 6, June, 1976; No. 7, June, 1978 - No. 12, May, 1979

1: #1-5 are 25¢ issues 3 6 9 16 20 25
2-6: 4-Intro Lor. 5-Ditko-a(1 pg.) 6-Begin 30¢-c 2 4 6 10 13 16
V3#7-12 (reprints #1-6) 6.00
5 (Modern Comics reprint, 1977) 4.00

NOTE: ***Byrne*** *c/a-1-12; Painted covers-2-7.*

DOOMSDAY SQUAD, THE
Fantagraphics Books: Aug, 1986 - No. 7, 1987 ($2.00)

1-7: Byrne-a in all. 1-3-New Byrne-c. 3-Usagi Yojimbo app. (1st in color).4-Neal Adams-c. 5-7-Gil Kane-c 3.00

DOOM'S IV
Image Comics (Extreme): July, 1994 - No.4, Oct, 1994 ($2.50, limited series)

Dopey Duck #1 © MAR

Double Comics 1941 © EP

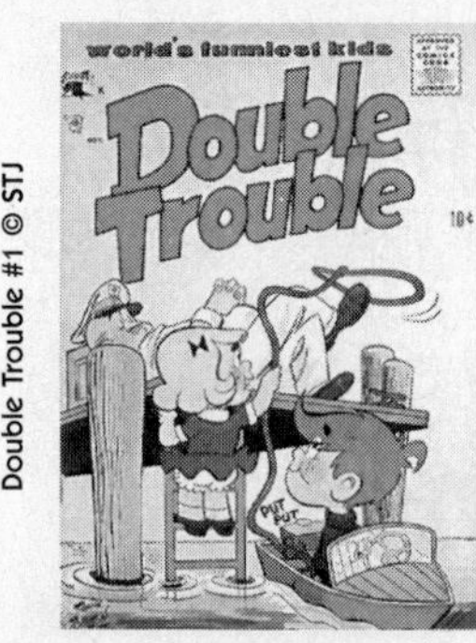

Double Trouble #1 © STJ

GD 2.0 | VG 4.0 | FN 6.0 | VF 8.0 | VF/NM 9.0 | NM- 9.2

1-4-Liefeld story 2.50
1,2-Two alternate Liefeld-c each, 4 covers form 1 picture 5.00

DOOM: THE EMPEROR RETURNS
Marvel Comics: Jan, 2002 - No. 3, Mar, 2002 ($2.50, limited series)
1-3-Dixon-s/Manco-a; Franklin Richards app. 2.50

DOOM 2099 (See Marvel Comics Presents #118 & 2099: World of Tomorrow)
Marvel Comics: Jan, 1993 - No. 44, Aug, 1996 ($1.25/$1.50/$1.95)
1-24,26-44: 1-Metallic foil stamped-c. 4-Ron Lim-c(p). 17-bound-in trading card sheet. 40-Namor & Doctor Strange app. 41-Daredevil app., Namor-c/app. 44-Intro The Emissary; story contin'd in 2099: World of Tomorrow 2.25
1-2nd printing 2.25
18-Variant polybagged with Sega Sub-Terrania poster 4.00
25 ($2.25, 52 pgs.) 2.50
25 ($2.95, 52pgs.) Foil embossed cover 3.00
29 ($3.50)-acetate-c. 3.50

DOORWAY TO NIGHTMARE (See Cancelled Comic Cavalcade)
DC Comics: Jan-Feb, 1978 - No. 5, Sept-Oct, 1978
1-Madame Xanadu in all 2 4 6 10 13 16
2-5: 4-Craig-a 1 3 4 6 8 10
NOTE: *Kaluta covers on all. Merged into The Unexpected with No. 190.*

DOPEY DUCK COMICS (Wacky Duck No. 3) (See Super Funnies)
Timely Comics (NPP): Fall, 1945 - No. 2, Apr, 1946
1,2-Casper Cat, Krazy Krow 22 44 66 123 177 230

DORK
Slave Labor: June, 1993 - Present ($2.50-$2.95, B&W, mature)
1-7,9,10: Evan Dorkin-c/a/scripts in all. 1(8/95),2(1/96)-(2nd printings). 1(3/97) (3rd printing). 1-Milk & Cheese app. 3-Eltingville Club starts. 6-Reprints 1st Eltingville Club app. from Instant Piano #1 3.00
8-($3.50) 3.50
Who's Laughing Now? TPB (2001, $11.95) reprints most of #1-5 12.00
The Collected Dork, Vol. 2: Circling the Drain (6/03, $13.95) r/most of #7-10 & other-s 14.00

DOROTHY LAMOUR (Formerly Jungle Lil)(Stage, screen, radio)
Fox Features Syndicate: No. 2, June, 1950 - No. 3, Aug, 1950
2,3-Wood-a(3) each, photo-c 28 56 84 158 229 300

DOT DOTLAND (Formerly Little Dot Dotland)
Harvey Publications: No. 62, Sept, 1974 - No. 63, Nov, 1974
62,63 2 4 6 10 12 15

DOTTY (...& Her Boy Friends)(Formerly Four Teeners; Glamorous Romances No. 41 on)
Ace Magazines (A. A. Wyn): No. 35, June, 1948 - No. 40, May, 1949
35-Teen-age 8 16 24 43 54 65
36-40: 37-Transvestism story 6 12 18 27 33 38

DOTTY DRIPPLE (Horace & Dotty Dripple No. 25 on)
Magazine Ent.(Life's Romances)/Harvey No. 3 on: 1946 - No. 24, June, 1952 (Also see A-1 No. 1, 3-8, 10)
1 (nd) (10¢) 10 20 30 56 73 90
2 6 12 18 31 38 45
3-10: 3,4-Powell-a 5 10 15 24 30 35
11-24 4 8 12 18 22 25

DOTTY DRIPPLE AND TAFFY
Dell Publishing Co.: No. 646, Sept, 1955 - No. 903, May, 1958
Four Color 646 (#1) 5 10 15 33 44 55
Four Color 691,718,746,801,903 4 8 12 22 30 38

DOUBLE ACTION COMICS
National Periodical Publications: No. 2, Jan, 1940 (68 pgs., B&W)
2-Contains original stories(?); pre-hero DC contents; same cover as Adventure No. 37. (seven known copies, five in high grade) (not an ashcan) 1445 2890 4335 9000 13,250 17,500
NOTE: *The cover to this book was probably reprinted from Adventure #37. #1 exists as an ash can copy with B&W cover; contains a coverless comic on inside with 1st & last page missing. Two copies exist in fair & fine condition proving at least limited newsstand distribution.*

DOUBLE COMICS
Elliot Publications: 1940 - 1944 (132 pgs.)
1940 issues; Masked Marvel-c & The Mad Mong vs. The White Flash covers known 238 476 714 1488 2294 3100
1941 issues; Tornado Tim-c, Nordac-c, & Green Light covers known 158 316 474 988 1519 2050
1942 issues 115 230 345 719 1110 1500
1943,1944 issues 94 188 282 588 907 1225
NOTE: *Double Comics consisted of an almost endless combination of pairs of remaindered, unsold issues of comics representing most publishers and usually mixed publishers in the same book; e.g., a Captain America with a Silver Streak, or a Feature with a Detective, etc., could appear inside the same cover. The actual contents would have to determine its price. Prices listed are for average contents. Any containing rare origin or first issues are worth much more. Covers also vary in same year. Value would be approximately 50 percent of contents.*

DOUBLE-CROSS (See The Crusaders)

DOUBLE-DARE ADVENTURES
Harvey Publications: Dec, 1966 - No. 2, Mar, 1967 (35¢/25¢, 68 pgs.)
1-Origin Bee-Man, Glowing Gladiator, & Magic-Master; Simon/Kirby-a (last S&K art as a team?) 7 14 21 51 71 90
2-Williamson/Crandall-a; r/Alarming Adv. #3('63) 5 10 15 36 48 60
NOTE: ***Powell** a-1. **Simon/Sparling** c-1, 2.*

DOUBLE DRAGON
Marvel Comics: July, 1991 - No. 6, Dec, 1991 ($1.00, limited series)
1-6: Based on video game. 2-Art Adams-c 2.50

DOUBLE EDGE
Marvel Comics: Alpha, 1995; Omega, 1995 ($4.95, limited series)
Alpha ($4.95)- Punisher story, Nick Fury app. 5.00
Omega ($4.95)-Punisher, Daredevil, Ghost Rider app. Death of Nick Fury 5.00

DOUBLE IMAGE
Image Comics: Feb, 2001 - No. 5, July, 2001 ($2.95)
1-5: 1-Flip covers of Codeflesh (Casey-s/Adlard-a) and The Bod (Young-s). 2-Two covers. 5-"Trust in Me" begins; Chaudhary-a 3.00

DOUBLE LIFE OF PRIVATE STRONG, THE
Archie Publications/Radio Comics: June, 1959 - No. 2, Aug, 1959
1-Origin & re-intro The Shield; Simon & Kirby-c/a, their re-entry into the super-hero genre; intro./1st app. The Fly; 1st S.A. super-hero for Archie Publ. 50 100 150 413 657 900
2-S&K-c/a; Tuska-a; The Fly app. (2nd or 3rd?) 33 66 99 248 392 535

DOUBLE TROUBLE
St. John Publishing Co.: Nov, 1957 - No. 2, Jan-Feb, 1958
1,2: Tuffy & Snuffy by Frank Johnson; dubbed "World's Funniest Kids" 6 12 18 31 38 45

DOUBLE TROUBLE WITH GOOBER
Dell Publishing Co.: No. 417, Aug, 1952 - No. 556, May, 1954
Four Color 417 4 8 12 29 40 50
Four Color 471,516,556 3 6 9 18 24 30

DOUBLE UP
Elliott Publications: 1941 (Pocket size, 200 pgs.)
1-Contains rebound copies of digest sized issues of Pocket Comics, Speed Comics, & Spitfire Comics 77 154 231 481 741 1000

DOVER & CLOVER (See All Funny & More Fun Comics #93)

DOVER BOYS (See Adventures of the...)

DOVER THE BIRD
Famous Funnies Publishing Co.: Spring, 1955
1-Funny animal; code approved 7 14 21 35 43 50

DOWN WITH CRIME
Fawcett Publications: Nov, 1952 - No. 7, Nov, 1953
1 34 68 102 196 283 370
2,4,5: 2,4-Powell-a in each. 5-Bondage-c 17 34 51 98 139 180
3-Used in **POP**, pg. 106; "H is for Heroin" drug story 19 38 57 107 154 200
6,7: 6-Used in **POP**, pg. 80 14 28 42 79 110 140

DO YOU BELIEVE IN NIGHTMARES?
St. John Publishing Co.: Nov, 1957 - No. 2, Jan, 1958
1-Mostly Ditko-c/a 50 100 150 305 465 625
2-Ayers-a 30 60 90 170 245 320

D.P. 7
Marvel Comics Group (New Universe): Nov, 1986 - No. 32, June, 1989
1-20, Annual #1 (11/87)-Intro. The Witness 2.25
21-32-Low print 4.00
NOTE: ***Williamson** a-9i, 11i; c-9i.*

DRACULA (See Bram Stoker's Dracula, Giant-Size..., Little Dracula, Marvel Graphic Novel, Requiem for Dracula, Spider-Man Vs...., Stoker's..., Tomb of... & Wedding of...; also see Movie Classics under Universal Presents as well as Dracula)

Dracula Lives! #1 © MAR

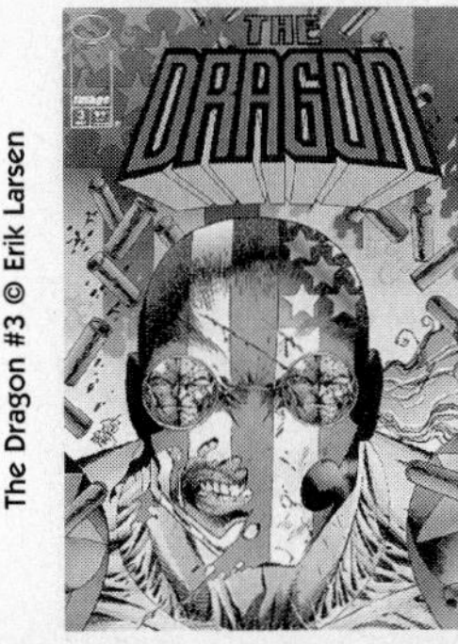

The Dragon #3 © Erik Larsen

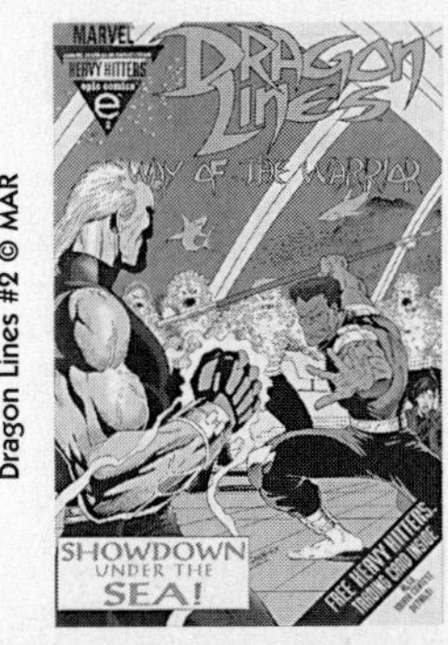

Dragon Lines #2 © MAR

DRACULA (See Movie Classics for #1)(Also see Frankenstein & Werewolf)
Dell Publ. Co.: No. 2, 11/66 - No. 4, 3/67; No. 6, 7/72 - No. 8, 7/73 (No #5)

	GD 2.0	VG 4.0	FN 6.0	VF 8.0	VF/NM 9.0	NM- 9.2
2-Origin & 1st app. Dracula (11/66) (super hero)	4	8	12	29	40	50
3,4: 4-Intro. Fleeta ('67)	3	6	9	19	25	32
6-('72)-r/#2 w/origin	3	6	9	16	21	26
7,8-r/#3, #4	2	4	6	12	16	20

DRACULA (Magazine)
Warren Publishing Co.: 1979 (120 pgs., full color)

	GD 2.0	VG 4.0	FN 6.0	VF 8.0	VF/NM 9.0	NM- 9.2
Book 1-Maroto art; Spanish material translated into English (mail order only)	6	12	18	40	55	70

DRACULA CHRONICLES
Topps Comics: Apr, 1995 - No. 3, June, 1995 ($2.50, limited series)

1-3-Linsner-c 3.00

DRACULA LIVES! (Magazine)(Also see Tomb of Dracula) (Reprinted in Stoker's Dracula)
Marvel Comics Group: 1973(no month) - No. 13, July, 1975 (75¢, B&W) (76 pgs.)

	GD 2.0	VG 4.0	FN 6.0	VF 8.0	VF/NM 9.0	NM- 9.2
1-Boris painted-c	6	12	18	40	55	70
2 (7/73)-1st time origin Dracula; Adams, Starlin-a	4	8	12	27	36	45
3-1st app. Robert E. Howard's Soloman Kane; Adams-c/a	4	8	12	27	36	45
4,5: 4-Ploog-a. 5(V2#1)-Bram Stoker's Classic Dracula adapt. begins	3	6	9	18	24	30
6-9: 6-8-Bram Stoker adapt. 9-Bondage-c	3	6	9	18	24	30
10 (1/75)-16 pg. Lilith solo (1st?)	4	8	12	24	32	40
11-13: 11-21 pg. Lilith solo sty. 12-31 pg. Dracula sty	3	6	9	19	25	32
Annual 1(Summer, 1975, $1.25, 92 pgs.)-Morrow painted-c; 6 Dracula stys. 25 pgs. Adams-a(r)	3	7	10	21	28	35

NOTE: ***N. Adams** a-2, 3i, 10i, Annual 1r(2, 3i). **Alcala** a-9. **Buscema** a-3p, 6p, Annual 1p. **Colan** a(p)-1, 2, 5, 6, 8. **Evans** a-7. **Gulacy** a-9. **Heath** a-1r, 13. **Pakula** a-6r. Sutton a-13.**Weiss** r-Annual 1p. 4 **Dracula** stories each in 1, 609; 3 **Dracula** stories each in 2, 4, 5,, 13.*

DRACULA: LORD OF THE UNDEAD
Marvel Comics: Dec, 1998 - No. 3, Dec, 1998 ($2.99, limited series)

1-3-Olliffe & Palmer-a 3.00

DRACULA: RETURN OF THE IMPALER
Slave Labor Graphics: July, 1993 - No. 4, Oct, 1994 ($2.95, limited series)

1-4 3.00

DRACULA'S REVENGE
IDW Publishing: Apr, 2004 - No. 3 ($3.99, limited series)

1,2-Forbeck-s/Kudranski-a 4.00

DRACULA VERSUS ZORRO
Topps Comics: Oct, 1993 - No. 2, Nov, 1993 ($2.95, limited series)

1,2: 1-Spot varnish & red foil-c. 2-Polybagged w/16 pg. Zorro #0 3.00

DRACULA VERSUS ZORRO
Dark Horse Comics: Sept, 1998 - No. 2, Oct, 1998 ($2.95, limited series)

1,2 3.00

DRACULA: VLAD THE IMPALER (Also see Bram Stoker's Dracula)
Topps Comics: Feb, 1993 - No. 3, Apr, 1993 ($2.95, limited series)

1-3-Polybagged with 3 trading cards each; Maroto-c/a 3.00

DRAFT, THE
Marvel Comics: 1988 ($3.50, one-shot, squarebound)

1-Sequel to "The Pitt" 3.50

DRAG 'N' WHEELS (Formerly Top Eliminator)
Charlton Comics: No. 30, Sept, 1968 - No. 59, May, 1973

	GD 2.0	VG 4.0	FN 6.0	VF 8.0	VF/NM 9.0	NM- 9.2
30	5	10	15	36	48	60
31-40-Scot Jackson begins	4	8	12	22	30	38
41-50	3	6	9	19	25	32
51-59: Scot Jackson	2	4	6	14	18	22
Modern Comics Reprint 58('78)						5.00

DRAGON, THE (Also see The Savage Dragon)
Image Comics (Highbrow Ent.): Mar, 1996 - No. 5, July, 1996 (99¢, lim. series)

1-5: Reprints Savage Dragon limited series w/new story & art. 5-Youngblood app; includes 5 pg. Savage Dragon story from 1984 2.25

DRAGON ARCHIVES, THE (Also see The Savage Dragon)
Image Comics: Jun, 1998 - No. 4, Jan, 1999 ($2.95, B&W)

1-4: Reprints early Savage Dragon app. 3.00

DRAGON, THE: BLOOD & GUTS (Also see The Savage Dragon)
Image Comics (Highbrow Entertainment): Mar, 1995 - No. 3, May, 1995 ($2.50, lim. series)

1-3: Jason Pearson-c/a/scripts 2.50

DRAGON BALL
Viz Comics: 1998 - Present ($2.95, B&W, Manga reprints read right to left)

	GD 2.0	VG 4.0	FN 6.0	VF 8.0	VF/NM 9.0	NM- 9.2
Part 1: 1-Akira Toriyama-s/a	1	2	3	5	6	8
2-12						5.00
1-12 (2nd & 3rd printings)						3.00
Part 2: 1-15: 15-($3.50-c)						4.00
Part 3: 1-14						3.00
Part 4: 1-10						3.00
Part 5: 1-7						3.00
Part 6: 1,2						3.50

DRAGON BALL Z
Viz Comics: 1998 - Present ($2.95, B&W, Manga reprints read right to left)

	GD 2.0	VG 4.0	FN 6.0	VF 8.0	VF/NM 9.0	NM- 9.2
Part 1: 1-Akira Toriyama-s/a	2	4	6	8	10	12
2-9						5.00
1-9 (2nd & 3rd printings)						3.00
Part 2: 1-14						4.00
Part 3: 1-10						3.00
Part 4: 1-15						3.00
Part 5: 1-10						3.00

DRAGON CHIANG
Eclipse Books: 1991 ($3.95, B&W, squarebound, 52 pgs.)

nn-Timothy Truman-c/a(p) 4.00

DRAGONFLIGHT
Eclipse Books: Feb, 1991 - No. 3, 1991 ($4.95, 52 pgs.)

Book One - Three: Adapts 1968 novel 5.00

DRAGONFLY (See Americomics #4)
Americomics: Sum, 1985 - No. 8, 1986 ($1.75/$1.95)

1 3.50
2-8 2.50

DRAGONFORCE
Aircel Publishing: 1988 - No. 13, 1989 ($2.00)

1-Dale Keown-c/a/scripts in #1-12 3.00
2-13: 13-No Keown-a 2.25
...Chronicles Book 1-5 ($2.95, B&W, 60 pgs.): Dale Keown-r/Dragonring & Dragonforce 3.00

DRAGONHEART (Movie)
Topps Comics: May, 1996 - No. 2, June, 1996 ($2.95/$4.95, limited series)

1-($2.95, 24 pgs.)-Adaptation of the film; Hildebrandt Bros-c; Lim-a. 3.00
2-($4.95, 64 pgs.) 5.00

DRAGONLANCE (Also see TSR Worlds)
DC Comics: Dec, 1988 - No. 34, Sept, 1991 ($1.25/$1.50, Mando paper)

1-Based on TSR game 4.00
2-34: Based on TSR game. 30-32-Kaluta-c 3.00

DRAGONLANCE: THE LEGEND OF HUMA
Devil's Due Publ.: Jan, 2004 - Present ($2.95)

1-5-Mike Miller & Rael-a 3.00

DRAGON LINES
Marvel Comics (Epic Comics/Heavy Hitters): May, 1993 - No. 4, Aug, 1993 ($1.95, limited series)

1-($2.50)-Embossed-c; Ron Lim-c/a in all 3.00
2-4 2.25

DRAGON LINES: WAY OF THE WARRIOR
Marvel Comics (Epic Comics/ Heavy Hitters): Nov, 1993 - No. 2, Jan, 1994 ($2.25, limited series)

1,2-Ron Lim-c/a(p) 2.25

DRAGONQUEST
Silverwolf Comics: Dec, 1986 - No. 2, 1987 ($1.50, B&W, 28 pgs.)

1,2-Tim Vigil-c/a in all 5.00

DRAGONRING
Aircel Publishing: 1986 - V2#15, 1988 ($1.70/$2.00, B&W/color)

1-6: 6-Last B&W issue, V2#1-15($2.00, color) 2.25

DRAGON'S CLAWS
Marvel UK, Ltd.: July, 1988 - No. 10, Apr, 1989 ($1.25/$1.50/$1.75, British)

Drakuun #19 © DH

Dreadstar #56 © FC

Dreaming #24 © DC

	GD 2.0	VG 4.0	FN 6.0	VF 8.0	VF/NM 9.0	NM- 9.2

1-10: 3-Death's Head 1 pg. strip on back-c (1st app.). 4-Silhouette of Death's Head on last pg. 5-1st full app. new Death's Head — 2.25

DRAGON'S LAIR: SINGE'S REVENGE (Based on the Don Bluth video game)
CrossGen Comics: Sept, 2003 - No. 6 ($2.95, limited series)

1-3-Mangels-s/Laguna-a — 3.00

DRAGONSLAYER (Movie)
Marvel Comics Group: October, 1981 - No. 2, Nov, 1981

1,2-Paramount Disney movie adaptation — 3.00

DRAGON'S STAR 2
Caliber Press: 1994 ($2.95, B&W)

1 — 3.00

DRAGON STRIKE
Marvel Comics: Feb, 1994 ($1.25)

1-Based on TSR role playing game — 2.25

DRAGOON WELLS MASSACRE
Dell Publishing Co.: No. 815, June, 1957

	GD	VG	FN	VF	VF/NM	NM-
Four Color 815-Movie, photo-c	9	18	27	63	89	115

DRAGSTRIP HOTRODDERS (World of Wheels No. 17 on)
Charlton Comics: Sum, 1963; No. 2, Jan, 1965 - No. 16, Aug, 1967

	GD	VG	FN	VF	VF/NM	NM-
1	8	16	24	55	78	100
2-5	5	10	15	33	44	55
6-16	4	8	12	27	36	45

DRAKUUN
Dark Horse Comics: Feb, 1997 - No. 25, Mar, 1999 ($2.95, B&W, manga)

1-25; 1-6- Johji Manabe-s/a in all. Rise of the Dragon Princess series. 7-12-Revenge of Gustav. 13-18-Shadow of the Warlock. 19-25-The Hidden War — 3.00

DRAMA
Sirius: June, 1994 ($2.95, mature)

	GD	VG	FN	VF	VF/NM	NM-
1-1st full color Dawn app. in comics	2	4	6	12	16	20
1-Limited edition (1400 copies); signed & numbered; fingerprint authenticity	4	8	12	29	40	50

NOTE: *Dawn's 1st full color app. was a pin-up in Amazing Heroes' Swimsuit Special #5.*

DRAMA OF AMERICA, THE
Action Text: 1973 ($1.95, 224 pgs.)

1- "Students' Supplement to History" — 5.00

DRAWING ON YOUR NIGHTMARES
Dark Horse Comics: Oct, 2003 ($2.99, one-shot)

1-Short stories; The Goon, Criminal Macabre, Tales of the Vampires; Templesmith-c — 3.00

DREADLANDS (Also see Epic)
Marvel Comics (Epic Comics): 1992 - No. 4, 1992 ($3.95, lim. series, 52 pgs.)

1-4: Stiff-c — 4.00

DREADSTAR
Marvel Comics (Epic Comics)/First Comics No. 27 on: Nov, 1982 - No. 64, Mar, 1991

1 — 4.00
2-5,8-49 — 3.00
6,7,51-64: 6,7-1st app. Interstellar Toybox; 8pgs. ea.; Wrightson-a. 51-67-Loer print run — 4.00
50 — 5.00
Annual 1 (12/83)-r/The Price — 4.00

DREADSTAR
Malibu Comics (Bravura): Apr, 1994 - No.6, Jan, 1995 ($2.50, limited series)

1-6-Peter David scripts: 1,2-Starlin-c — 2.50
NOTE: *Issues 1-6 contain Bravura stamps.*

DREADSTAR AND COMPANY
Marvel Comics (Epic Comics): July, 1985 - No. 6, Dec, 1985

1-6: 1,3,6-New Starlin-a: 2-New Wrightson-c; reprints of Dreadstar series — 2.25

DREAM BOOK OF LOVE (Also see A-1 Comics)
Magazine Enterprises: No. 106, June-July, 1954 - No. 123, Oct-Nov, 1954

	GD	VG	FN	VF	VF/NM	NM-
A-1 106 (#1)-Powell, Bolle-a; Montgomery Clift, Donna Reed photo-c	13	26	39	74	102	130
A-1-114 (#2)-Guardineer, Bolle-a; Piper Laurie, Victor Mature photo-c	10	20	30	58	77	95
A-1 123 (#3)-Movie photo-c	9	18	27	54	70	85

DREAM BOOK OF ROMANCE (Also see A-1 Comics)
Magazine Enterprises: No. 92, 1954 - No. 124, Oct-Nov, 1954

	GD	VG	FN	VF	VF/NM	NM-
A-1 92 (#5)-Guardineer-a; photo-c	12	24	36	69	95	120
A-1 101 (#6)(4-6/54)-Marlon Brando photo-c; Powell, Bolle, Guardineer-a	20	40	60	112	161	210
A-1 109,110,124: 109 (#7)(7-8/54)-Powell-a; movie photo-c. 110 (#8)(1/54)-Movie photo-c. 124 (#8)(10-11/54)	10	20	30	56	73	90

DREAMER, THE
Kitchen Sink Press: 1986 ($6.95, B&W, graphic novel)

nn-Will Eisner-s/a — 12.00
DC Comics Reprint ($7.95, 6/00) — 8.00

DREAMERY, THE
Eclipse Comics: Dec, 1986 - No. 14, Feb, 1989 ($2.00, B&W, Baxter paper)

1-14: 2-7-Alice In Wonderland adapt. — 2.25

DREAMING, THE (See Sandman, 2nd Series)
DC Comics (Vertigo): June, 1996 - No. 60, May, 2001 ($2.50)

1-McKean-c on all.; LaBan scripts & Snejbjerg-a — 4.00
2-30,32-60: 2,3-LaBan scripts & Snejbjerg-a. 4-7-Hogan scripts; Parkhouse-a. 8-Zulli-a. 9-11-Talbot-s/Taylor-a(p). 41-Previews Sandman: The Dream Hunters. 50-Hempel, Fegredo, McManus, Totleben-a — 2.50
31-($3.95) Art by various — 4.00
...Beyond The Shores of Night TPB ('97, $19.95) r/#1-8 — 20.00
...Special (7/98, $5.95, one-shot) Trial of Cain — 6.00
...Through The Gates of Horn and Ivory TPB ('99, $19.95) r/#15-19,22-25 — 20.00

DREAM OF LOVE
I. W. Enterprises: 1958 (Reprints)

	GD	VG	FN	VF	VF/NM	NM-
1,2,8: 1-r/Dream Book of Love #1; Bob Powell-a. 2-r/Great Lover's Romances #10. 8-Great Lover's Romances #1; also contains 2 Jon Juan stories by Siegel & Schomburg; Kinstler-c.	2	4	6	11	14	18
9-Kinstler-c; 1pg. John Wayne interview & Frazetta illo from John Wayne Adv. Comics #2	2	4	6	11	14	18

DREAMS OF THE DARKCHYLDE
Darkchylde Entertainment: Oct, 2000 - No. 6, Sept, 2001 ($2.95)

1-6-Randy Queen-s in all. 1-Brandon Peterson-c/a — 3.00

DREAM TEAM (See Battlezones: Dream Team 2)
Malibu Comics (Ultraverse): July, 1995 ($4.95, one-shot)

1-Pin-ups teaming up Marvel & Ultraverse characters by various artists including Allred, Romita, Darrow, Balent, Quesada & Palmiotti — 5.00

DREAMWALKER
Dreamwalker Press: 1996 - No. 5, 1996 ($2.95, B&W)

1-5-Jenni Gregory-c/s/a — 3.00

DREAMWALKER (Volume 2)
Caliber Comics (Tapestry): Dec, 1996 - No. 6, Jul, 1998 ($2.95, B&W)

1-6-Jenni Gregory-c/s/a — 3.00

DREAMWALKER
Avatar Press: Jenni Gregory-c/s/a in all

#0 (11/98, $3.00) — 3.00
--AUTUMN LEAVES, 9/99 - No. 2, 10/99 ($3.00) 1,2-wraparound-c — 3.00
--CAROUSEL, 3/99 - No. 2, 4/99 ($3.00) 1,2 — 3.00
--SUMMER RAIN, 7/99 ($3.00, one-shot) 1 — 3.00

DREAMWAVE PRODUCTIONS PREVIEW
Dreamwave Productions: May, 2002 ($1.00, one-shot)

nn-Previews Arkanium, Transformers: The War Within and other series — 2.25

DRIFT FENCE (See Zane Grey 4-Color 270)

DRIFT MARLO
Dell Publishing Co.: May-July, 1962 - No. 2, Oct-Dec, 1962

	GD	VG	FN	VF	VF/NM	NM-
01-232-207 (#1)	6	12	18	38	52	65
2 (12-232-212)	5	10	15	36	48	60

DRISCOLL'S BOOK OF PIRATES
David McKay Publ. (Not reprints): 1934 (B&W, hardcover; 124 pgs, 7x9")

	GD	VG	FN	VF	VF/NM	NM-
nn-By Montford Amory	25	50	75	141	203	265

DROIDS (Based on Saturday morning cartoon) (Also see Dark Horse Comics)
Marvel Comics (Star Comics): April, 1986 - No. 8, June, 1987

	GD	VG	FN	VF	VF/NM	NM-
1-R2D2 & C-3PO from Star Wars app. in all	2	4	6	12	16	20
2-8: 2,5,7,8-Williamson-a(i)	2	4	6	8	10	12

NOTE: ***Romita** a-3p. **Sinnott** a-3i.*

DROOPY (see Tom & Jerry #60)

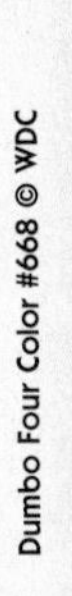
Duck Album Four Color #450 © WDC

Dumbo Four Color #668 © WDC

DV8 #14 © WSP

GD 2.0 | VG 4.0 | FN 6.0 | VF 8.0 | VF/NM 9.0 | NM- 9.2

DROOPY (Tex Avery's...)
Dark Horse Comics: Oct, 1995 - No. 3, Dec, 1995 ($2.50, limited series)
1-3: Characters created by Tex Avery; painted-c 2.50

DROPSIE AVENUE: THE NEIGHBORHOOD
Kitchen Sink Press: June, 1995 ($15.95/$24.95, B&W)
nn-Will Eisner (softcover) 16.00
nn-Will Eisner (hardcover) 25.00

DROWNED GIRL, THE
DC Comics (Piranha Press): 1990 ($5.95, 52 pgs, mature)
nn 6.00

DRUG WARS
Pioneer Comics: 1989 ($1.95)
1-Grell-c 2.25

DRUID
Marvel Comics: May, 1995 - No. 4, Aug, 1995 ($2.50, limited series)
1-4: Warren Ellis scripts. 3.00

DRUM BEAT
Dell Publishing Co.: No. 610, Jan, 1955
Four Color 610-Movie, Alan Ladd photo-c 10 20 30 70 100 130

DRUMS OF DOOM
United Features Syndicate: 1937 (25¢)(Indian)(Text w/color illos.)
nn-By Lt. F.A. Methot; Golden Thunder app.; Tip Top Comics ad in comic; nice-c
35 70 105 198 287 375

DRUNKEN FIST
Jademan Comics: Aug, 1988 - No. 54, Jan, 1993 ($1.50/$1.95, 68 pgs.)
1 4.00
2-50 3.00
51-54 2.50

DUCK ALBUM (See Donald Duck Album)
Dell Publishing Co.: No. 353, Oct, 1951 - No. 840, Sept, 1957
Four Color 353 (#1)-Barks-c; 1st Uncle Scrooge-c (also appears on back-c).
10 20 30 72 104 135
Four Color 450-Barks-c 8 16 24 55 78 100
Four Color 492,531,560,586,611,649,686, 6 12 18 43 59 75
Four Color 726,782,840 6 12 18 43 59 75

DUCKMAN
Dark Horse Comics: Sept, 1990 ($1.95, B&W, one-shot)
1-Story & art by Everett Peck 4.00

DUCKMAN
Topps Comics: Nov, 1994 - No. 5, May, 1995; No. 0, Feb, 1996 ($2.50)
0 (2/96, $2.95, B&W)-r/Duckman #1 from Dark Horse Comics 4.00
1-5: 1-w/ coupon #A for Duckman trading card. 2-w/Duckman 1st season episode guide 3.00

DUCKMAN: THE MOB FROG SAGA
Topps Comics: Nov, 1994 - No. 3, Feb, 1995 ($2.50, limited series)
1-3: 1-w/coupon #B for Duckman trading card, S. Shaw!-c 2.50

DUCKTALES
Gladstone Publ.: Oct, 1988 - No. 13, May, 1990 (1,2,9-11: $1.50; 3-8: 95¢)
1-Barks-r 6.00
2-11: 2-7,9-11-Barks-r 4.00
12,13 ($1.95, 68 pgs.)-Barks-r; 12-r/F.C. #495 5.00

DUCKTALES (TV)
Disney Comics: June, 1990 - No. 18, Nov, 1991 ($1.50)
1-All new stories 3.00
2-18 2.50
The Movie nn (1990, $7.95, 68 pgs.)-Graphic novel adapting animated movie 9.00

DUDLEY (Teen-age)
Feature/Prize Publications: Nov-Dec, 1949 - No. 3, Mar-Apr, 1950
1-By Boody Rogers 15 30 45 86 118 150
2,3 10 20 30 56 73 90

DUDLEY DO-RIGHT (TV)
Charlton Comics: Aug, 1970 - No. 7, Aug, 1971 (Jay Ward)
1 10 20 30 72 104 135
2-7 7 14 21 51 71 90

DUEL MASTERS (Based on a trading card game) (Also see Free Comic Book Day Edition in the Promotional Comics section)
Dreamwave Productions: Nov, 2003 - Present ($2.95)
1-8: 1-Bagged with card; Augustyn-s 3.00

DUKE OF THE K-9 PATROL
Gold Key: Apr, 1963
1 (10052-304) 4 8 12 29 40 50

DUMBO (Disney; see Movie Comics, & Walt Disney Showcase #12)
Dell Publishing Co.: No. 17, 1941 - No. 668, Jan, 1958
Four Color 17 (#1)-Mickey Mouse, Donald Duck, Pluto app.
185 370 555 1388 2194 3000
Large Feature Comic 19 ('41)-Part-r 4-Color 17 265 530 795 1920 2803 3700
Four Color 234 ('49) 13 26 39 92 141 190
Four Color 668 (12/55)-1st of two printings. Dumbo on-c with starry sky. Same-c as #234
11 22 33 77 114 150
Four Color 668 (1/58)-2nd printing. Same cover altered with Timothy Mouse added. Same contents 8 16 24 55 78 100

DUMBO COMIC PAINT BOOK (See Dumbo, Large Feature Comic No. 19)

DUMPED
Oni Press: 2002 ($5.95, B&W, 9"x 6", one-shot)
nn-Andi Watson-s/a 6.00

DUNC AND LOO (#1-3 titled "Around the Block with Dunc and Loo")
Dell Publishing Co.: Oct-Dec, 1961 - No. 8, Oct-Dec, 1963
1 10 20 30 73 107 140
2 8 16 24 53 74 95
3-8 6 12 18 43 59 75
NOTE: *Written by* ***John Stanley; Bill Williams*** *art.*

DUNCAN'S KINGDOM
Image Comics: 1999 - No. 2, 1999 ($2.95, B&W, limited series)
1,2-Gene Yang-s/Derek Kirk-a 3.00

DUNE (Movie)
Marvel Comics: Apr, 1985 - No. 3, June, 1985
1-3-r/Marvel Super Special; movie adaptation 3.00

DURANGO KID, THE (Also see Best of the West, Great Western & White Indian)
(Charles Starrett starred in Columbia's Durango Kid movies)
Magazine Enterprises: Oct-Nov, 1949 - No. 41, Oct-Nov, 1955 (All 36 pgs.)
1-Charles Starrett photo-c; Durango Kid & his horse Raider begin; Dan Brand & Tipi (origin) begin by Frazetta & continue through #16 73 146 219 456 703 950
2-Starrett photo-c. 39 78 117 222 324 425
3-5-All have Starrett photo-c. 35 70 105 201 293 385
6-10: 7-Atomic weapon-c/story 20 40 60 112 161 210
11-16-Last Frazetta issue 15 30 45 83 117 150
17-Origin Durango Kid 20 40 60 112 161 210
18-30: 18-Fred Meagher-a on Dan Brand begins.19-Guardineer-c/a(3) begins, end #41. 23-Intro. The Red Scorpion 11 22 33 62 84 105
31-Red Scorpion returns 10 20 30 60 80 100
32-41-Bolle/Frazetta*ish*-a (Dan Brand; true in later issues?)
10 20 30 58 77 95
NOTE: *#6, 8, 14, 15 contain* ***Frazetta*** *art not reprinted in White Indian.* ***Ayers*** *c-18.* ***Guardineer*** *a(3)-19-41; c-19-41.* ***Fred Meagher*** *a-18-29 at least.*

DURANGO KID, THE
AC Comics: 1990 - #2, 1990 ($2.50,$2.75, half-color)
1,2: 1-Starrett photo front/back-c; Guardineer-r. 2-B&W)-Starrett photo-c; White Indian-r by Frazetta; Guardineer-r (50th anniversary of films) 3.00

DUSTCOVERS: THE COLLECTED SANDMAN COVERS 1989-1997
DC Comics (Vertigo): 1997 ($39.95, Hardcover)
Reprints Dave McKean's Sandman covers with Gaiman text 40.00
Softcover (1998, $24.95) 25.00

DUSTY STAR
Image Comics (Desperado Studios): Apr, 1997 - No. 1 ($2.95, B&W)
0,1-Pruett-s/Robinson-a 3.00

DV8 (See Gen 13)
Image Comics (WildStorm Productions): Aug, 1996 - No. 25, Dec, 1998;
DC Comics (WildStorm Prod.): No. 0, Apr, 1999 - No. 32, Nov, 1999 ($2.50)
1/2 6.00
1-Warren Ellis scripts & Humberto Ramos-c/a(p) 4.00
1-(7-variant covers, w/1 by Jim Lee) ...each 4.00
2-4: 3-No Ramos-a 3.00

Dynamic Comics #9 © CHES

Dynamo #3 © TC

Easter with Mother Goose Four Color #103 © DELL

GD VG FN VF VF/NM NM-
2.0 4.0 6.0 8.0 9.0 9.2

5-32: 14-Regular-c, 14-Variant-c by Charest. 26-(5/99)-McGuinness-c 2.50
14-($3.50) Voyager Pack w/Danger Girl preview 5.00
0-(4/99, $2.95) Two covers (Rio and McGuinness) 3.00
Annual 1 (1/98, $2.95) 3.00
Annual 1999 ($3.50) Slipstream x-over with Gen13 3.50
Rave-(7/96, $1.75)-Ramos-c; pinups & interviews 3.00
...: Neighborhood Threat TPB (2002, $14.95) r/#1-6 & #1/2; Ellis intro.; Ramos-c 15.00

DV8 VS. BLACK OPS
Image Comics (WildStorm): Oct, 1997 - No. 3, Dec, 1997 ($2.50, lim. series)
1-3-Bury-s/Norton-a 3.00

DWIGHT D. EISENHOWER
Dell Publishing Co.: December, 1969
01-237-912 - Life story 6 12 18 38 52 65

DYLAN DOG
Dark Horse (Bonelli Comics): Mar, 1999 - No. 6, Aug, 1999 ($4.95, B&W, digest size)
1-6-Reprints Italian series in English; Mignola-c 5.00

DYNABRITE COMICS
Whitman Publishing Co.: 1978 - 1979 (69¢, 10x7-1/8", 48 pgs., cardboard-c)
(Blank inside covers)
11350 - Walt Disney's Mickey Mouse & the Beanstalk (4-C 157). 11350-1 - Mickey Mouse Album (4-C 1057, 1151,1246). 11351 - Mickey Mouse & His Sky Adventure (4-C 214, 343). 11354 - Goofy: A Gaggle of Giggles. 11354-1 - Super Goof Meets Super Thief. 11356 - (?). 11359 - Bugs Bunny-r. 11360 - Winnie the Pooh Fun and Fantasy (Disney-r).
each.... 2 4 6 8 10 12
11352 - Donald Duck (4-C 408, Donald Duck 45,52)-Barks-a. 11352-1 - Donald Duck (4-C 318, 10 pg. Barks/ WDC&S 125,128)-Barks-c(r). 11353 - Daisy Duck's Diary (4-C 1055,1150) Barks-a. 11355 - Uncle Scrooge (Barks-a/U.S. 12,33). 11355-1 - Uncle Scrooge (Barks-a/U.S. 13,16) - Barks-c(r). 11357 - Star Trek (r/-Star Trek 33,41). 11358 - Star Trek (r/-Star Trek 34,36). 11361 - Gyro Gearloose & the Disney Ducks (r/4-C 1047,1184)-Barks-c(r)
each.... 2 4 6 9 11 14

DYNAMIC ADVENTURES
I. W. Enterprises: No. 8, 1964 - No. 9, 1964
8-Kayo Kirby-r by Baker?/Fight Comics 53. 3 6 9 16 20 25
9-Reprints Avon's "Escape From Devil's Island"; Kinstler-c
3 6 9 18 24 30
nn (no date)-Reprints Risks Unlimited with Rip Carson, Senorita Rio; r/Fight #53
3 6 9 18 23 28

DYNAMIC CLASSICS (See Cancelled Comic Cavalcade)
DC Comics: Sept-Oct, 1978 (44 pgs.)
1-Neal Adams Batman, Simonson Manhunter-r 2 4 6 8 10 12

DYNAMIC COMICS (No #4-7)
Harry 'A' Chesler: Oct, 1941 - No. 3, Feb, 1942; No. 8, Mar, 1944 - No. 25, May, 1948
1-Origin Major Victory by Charles Sultan (reprinted in Major Victory #1), Dynamic Man & Hale the Magician; The Black Cobra only app.; Major Victory & Dynamic Man begin
177 354 531 1106 1703 2300
2-Origin Dynamic Boy & Lady Satan; intro. The Green Knight & sidekick Lance Cooper
81 162 243 506 778 1050
3-1st small logo, resumes with #10 71 142 213 444 685 925
8-Classic-c; Dan Hastings, The Echo, The Master Key, Yankee Boy begin; Yankee Doodle Jones app.; hypo story 81 162 243 506 778 1050
9-Mr. E begins; Mac Raboy-c 71 142 213 444 685 925
10-Small logo begins 55 110 165 340 520 700
11-16: 15-The Sky Chief app. 16-Marijuana story 47 94 141 287 436 585
17(1/46)-Illustrated in **SOTI**, "The children told me what the man was going to do with the hot poker," but Wertham saw this in Crime Reporter #2
65 130 195 406 623 840
18,19,21,22,25: 21-Dinosaur-c; new logo 40 80 120 239 357 475
20-Bare-breasted woman-c 69 138 207 431 666 900
23,24-(68 pgs.): 23-Yankee Girl app. 40 80 120 236 351 465
I.W. Reprint #1,8('64): 1-r/#23. 8-Exist? 3 7 10 21 28 35
NOTE: ***Kinstler** c-IW #1. **Tuska** art in many issues, #3, 9, 11, 12, 16, 19. Bondage c-16.*

DYNAMITE (Becomes Johnny Dynamite No. 10 on)
Comic Media/Allen Hardy Publ.: May, 1953 - No. 9, Sept, 1954
1-Pete Morisi-a; Don Heck-c; r-as Danger #6 28 56 84 158 229 300
2 15 30 45 83 117 150
3-Marijuana story; Johnny Dynamite (1st app.) begins by Pete Morisi(c/a); Heck text-a; man shot in face at close range 19 38 57 107 154 200
4-Injury-to-eye, prostitution; Morisi-c/a 18 36 54 102 146 190
5-9-Morisi-c/a in all. 7-Prostitute story & reprints 13 26 39 76 106 135

GD VG FN VF VF/NM NM-
2.0 4.0 6.0 8.0 9.0 9.2

DYNAMO (Also see Tales of Thunder & T.H.U.N.D.E.R. Agents)
Tower Comics: Aug, 1966 - No. 4, June, 1967 (25¢)
1-Crandall/Wood, Ditko/Wood-a; Weed series begins; NoMan & Lightning cameos; Wood-c/a 10 20 30 70 100 130
2-4: Wood-c/a in all 6 12 18 43 59 75
NOTE: ***Adkins/Wood** a-2. **Ditko** a-4?. **Tuska** a-2, 3.*

DYNAMO JOE (Also see First Adventures & Mars)
First Comics: May, 1986 - No. 15, Jan, 1988 (#12-15: $1.75)
1-15: 4-Cargonauts begin, Special 1(1/87)-Mostly-r/Mars 2.25

DYNOMUTT (TV)(See Scooby-Doo (3rd series))
Marvel Comics Group: Nov, 1977 - No. 6, Sept, 1978 (Hanna-Barbera)
1-The Blue Falcon, Scooby Doo in all 4 8 12 25 33 42
2-6-All newsstand only 3 6 9 18 23 28

EAGLE, THE (1st Series) (See Science Comics & Weird Comics #8)
Fox Features Syndicate: July, 1941 - No. 4, Jan, 1942
1-The Eagle begins; Rex Dexter of Mars app. by Briefer; all issues feature German war covers 177 354 531 1106 1703 2300
2-The Spider Queen begins (origin) 83 166 249 519 797 1075
3,4: 3-Joe Spook begins (origin) 66 132 198 413 637 860

EAGLE (2nd Series)
Rural Home Publ.: Feb-Mar, 1945 - No. 2, Apr-May, 1945
1-Aviation stories 47 94 141 287 436 585
2-Lucky Aces 27 54 81 154 222 290
NOTE: *L. B. Cole c/a in each.*

EAGLE
Crystal Comics/Apple Comics #17 on: Sept, 1986 - No. 23, 1989 ($1.50/1.75/1.95, B&W)
1-23: 12-Double size origin issue ($2.50) 2.50
1-Signed and limited 4.00

EARTH 4 (Also see Urth 4)
Continuity Comics: Dec, 1993 - No. 4, Jan, 1994 ($2.50)
1-4: 1-3 all listed as Dec, 1993 in indicia 2.50

EARTH 4 DEATHWATCH 2000
Continuity Comics: Apr, 1993 - No. 3, Aug, 1993 ($2.50)
1-3 2.50

EARTH MAN ON VENUS (An...) (Also see Strange Planets)
Avon Periodicals: 1951
nn-Wood-a (26 pgs.); Fawcette-c 131 262 393 819 1260 1700

EARTHWORM JIM (TV, cartoon)
Marvel Comics: Dec, 1995 - No. 3, Feb, 1996 ($2.25)
1-3: Based on video game and toys 3.00

EARTH X
Marvel Comics: No. 0, Mar, 1999 - No. 12, Apr, 2000 ($3.99/$2.99, lim. series)
nn- (Wizard supplement) Alex Ross sketchbook; painted-c
1 3 4 6 8 10
Sketchbook (2/99) New sketches and previews 6.00
0-(3/99)-Prelude; Leon-a(p)/Ross-c 1 2 3 4 5 7
1-(4/99)-Leon-a(p)/Ross-c 1 2 3 4 5 7
1-2nd printing 3.00
2-12 3.50
#X (6/00, $3.99) 4.00
TPB (12/00, $24.95) r/#0,1-12, X; foreward by Joss Whedon 25.00

EASTER BONNET SHOP (See March of Comics No. 29)

EASTER WITH MOTHER GOOSE
Dell Publishing Co.: No. 103, 1946 - No. 220, Mar, 1949
Four Color 103 (#1)-Walt Kelly-a 19 38 57 134 205 275
Four Color 140 ('47)-Kelly-a 15 30 45 109 167 225
Four Color 185 ('48),220-Kelly-a 14 28 42 97 149 200

EAST MEETS WEST
Innovation Publishing: Apr, 1990 - No. 2, 1990 ($2.50, limited series, mature)
1,2: 1-Stevens part-i; Redondo-c(i). 2-Stevens-c(i); 1st app. Cheech & Chong in comics 2.50

E. C. CLASSIC REPRINTS
East Coast Comix Co.: May, 1973 - No. 12, 1976 (E. C. Comics reprinted in color minus ads)
1-The Crypt of Terror #1 (Tales from the Crypt #46) 2 4 6 11 14 18
2-12: 2-Weird Science #15('52). 3-Shock SuspenStories #12. 4-Haunt of Fear #12. 5-Weird Fantasy #13('52). 6-Crime SuspenStories #25. 7-Vault of Horror #26. 8-Shock

Eclipso #11 © DC

Eddie Campbell's Bacchus #35 © Eddie Campbell

Edgar Rice Burrough's The Return of Tarzan #1 © ERB

GD 2.0 | VG 4.0 | FN 6.0 | VF 8.0 | VF/NM 9.0 | NM- 9.2

SuspenStories #6. 9-Two-Fisted Tales #34. 10-Haunt of Fear #23. 11-Weird Science 12(#1). 12-Shock SuspenStories #2 2 4 6 8 10 12

EC CLASSICS
Russ Cochran: Aug, 1985 - No. 12, 1986? (High quality paper; each-r 8 stories in color) (#2-12 were resolicited in 1990)($4.95, 56 pgs., 8x11")

1-12: 1-Tales From the Crypt. 2-Weird Science. 3-Two-Fisted Tales (r/31); Frontline Combat (r/9). 4-Shock SuspenStories. 5-Weird Fantasy. 6-Vault of Horror. 7-Weird Science-Fantasy (r/23,24). 8-Crime SuspenStories (r/17,18). 9-Haunt of Fear (r/14,15). 10-Panic (r/1,2). 11-Tales From the Crypt (r/23,24). 12-Weird Science (r/20,22) 1 2 3 4 5 7

ECHO
Image Comics (Dreamwave Prod.): Mar, 2000 - No. 5, Sept, 2000 ($2.50)

1-5: 1-3-Pat Lee-c 2.50
0-(7/00) 2.50

ECHO OF FUTUREPAST
Pacific Comics/Continuity Com.: May, 1984 - No. 9, Jan, 1986 ($2.95, 52 pgs.)

1-9: Neal Adams-c/a in all? 6.00
NOTE: ***N. Adams*** *a-1-6,7i,9i; c-1-3, 5p,7i,8,9i.* ***Golden*** *a-1-6 (Bucky O'Hare); c-6.* ***Toth*** *a-6,7.*

ECLIPSE GRAPHIC ALBUM SERIES
Eclipse Comics: Oct, 1978 - 1989 (8-1/2x11") (B&W #1-5)

1-Sabre (10/78, B&W, 1st print.); Gulacy-a; 1st direct sale graphic novel 16.00
1-Sabre (2nd printing, 1/79) 8.00
1-Sabre (3rd printing, $5.95) 6.00
3,4: 3-Detectives, Inc. (5/80, B&W, $6.95)-Rogers-a. 4-Stewart The Rat (1980, B&W) -G. Colan-a 10.00
5-The Price (10/81, B&W)-Starlin-a 16.00
2,6,7,13: 2-Night Music (11/79, B&W)-Russell-a. 6-I Am Coyote (11/84, color)-Rogers-c/a. 7-The Rocketeer (2nd print, $7.95). 7-The Rocketeer (3rd print, 1991, $8.95). 13-The Sisterhood of Steel ('87, $8.95, color) 10.00
7-The Rocketeer (9/85, color)-Dave Stevens-a (r/chapters 1-5)(see Pacific Presents & Starslayer); has 7 pgs. new-a 14.00
7-The Rocketeer, signed & limited HC 60.00
7-The Rocketeer, hardcover (1986, $19.95) 20.00
7-The Rocketeer, unsigned HC (3rd, $32.95) 33.00
8-Zorro In Old California ('86, color) 14.00
8,12-Hardcover 18.00
9,10: 9-Sacred And The Profane ('86)-Steacy-a. 10-Somerset Holmes ('86, $15.95)-Adults, soft-c 16.00
9,10,12-Hardcover ($24.95). 12-signed & #'d 25.00
11,14,16,18,20,23,24: 11-Floyd Farland, Citizen of the Future ('87, $3.95, B&W). 14-Samurai, Son of Death ('87, $4.95, B&W). 16,18,20,23-See Airfighters Classics #1-4. 24-Heartbreak ($4.95, B&W) 7.00
12,28,31,35: 12-Silverheels ('87, $7.95, color). 28-Miracleman Book I ($5.95). 31-Pigeons From Hell by R. E. Howard (11/88). 35-Rael: Into The Shadow of the Sun ('88, $7.95) 10.00
14,17,21,14-Samurai, Son of Death ($3.95, 2nd printing). 17-Valkyrie, Prisoner of the Past SC ('88, $3.95, color). 21-XYR-Multiple ending comic ('88, $3.95, B&W) 6.00
15,22,27: 15-Twisted Tales (11/87, color)-Dave Stevens-c. 22-Alien Worlds #1 (5/88, $3.95, 52 pgs.)-Nudity. 27-Fast Fiction (She) ($5.95, B&W) 8.00
17-Valkyrie, Prisoner of the Past S&N Hardcover ('88, $19.95) 20.00
19-Scout: The Four Monsters ('88, $14.95, color)-r/Scout #1-7; soft-c 15.00
25,30,32-34: 25-Alex Toth's Zorro Vol. 1 ,2($10.95, B&W). 30-Brought To Light; Alan Moore scripts ('89). 32-Teenaged Dope Slaves and Reform School Girls. 33-Bogie. 34-Air Fighters Classics #5 12.00
29-Real Love: Best of Simon & Kirby Romance Comics(10/88, $12.95) 15.00
30,31: Limited hardcover ed. ($29.95). 31-signed 30.00
36-Dr. Watchstop: Adventures in Time and Space ('89, $8.95) 10.00

ECLIPSE MAGAZINE (Becomes Eclipse Monthly)
Eclipse Publishing: May, 1981 - No. 8, Jan, 1983 ($2.95, B&W, magazine)

1-8: 1-1st app. Cap'n Quick and a Foozle by Rogers, Ms. Tree by Beatty, and Dope by Trina Robbins. 2-1st app. I Am Coyote by Rogers. 7-1st app. Masked Man by Boyer 3.00
NOTE: ***Colan*** *a-3, 5, 8.* ***Golden*** *c/a-2.* ***Gulacy*** *a-6, c-1, 6.* ***Kaluta*** *c/a-5.* ***Mayerik*** *a-2, 3.* ***Rogers*** *a-1-8.* ***Starlin*** *a-1.* ***Sutton*** *a-6.*

ECLIPSE MONTHLY
Eclipse Comics: Aug, 1983 - No. 10, Jul, 1984 (Baxter paper, $2.00/$1.50/$1.75)

1-10: ($2.00, 52 pgs.)-Cap'n Quick and a Foozle by Rogers, Static by Ditko, Dope by Trina Robbins, Rio by Wildey, The Masked Man by Boyer begin. 3-Ragamuffins begins 2.25
NOTE: ***Boyer*** *c-6.* ***Ditko*** *a-1-3.* ***Rogers*** *a-1-4; c-2, 4, 7.* ***Wildey*** *a-1, 2, 5, 9, 10; c-5, 10.*

ECLIPSO (See Brave and the Bold #64, House of Secrets #61 & Phantom Stranger, 1987)
DC Comics: Nov, 1992 - No. 18, Apr, 1994 ($1.25)

1-18: 1-Giffen plots/breakdowns begin. 10-Darkseid app. Creeper in #3-6,9,11-13. 18-Spectre-c/s 2.25
Annual 1 (1993, $2.50, 68 pgs.)-Intro Prism 2.50

ECLIPSO: THE DARKNESS WITHIN
DC Comics: July, 1992 - No. 2, Oct, 1992 ($2.50, 68 pgs.)

1,2: 1-With purple gem attached to-c, 1-Without gem; Superman, Creeper app., 2-Concludes Eclipso storyline from annuals 2.50

E. C. 3-D CLASSICS (See Three Dimensional...)

ECTOKID (See Razorline)
Marvel Comics: Sept, 1993 - No. 9, May, 1994 ($1.75/$1.95)

1-($2.50)-Foil embossed-c; created by C. Barker 3.00
2-9: 2-Origin. 5-Saint Sinner x-over 2.25
...: Unleashed! 1 (10/94, $2.95, 52 pgs.) 3.00

ED "BIG DADDY" ROTH'S RATFINK COMIX (Also see Ratfink)
World of Fandom/ Ed Roth: 1991 - No. 3, 1991 ($2.50)

1-3: Regular Ed., 1-Limited double cover 1 3 4 6 8 10

EDDIE CAMPBELL'S BACCHUS
Eddie Campbell Comics: May, 1995 - Present ($2.95, B&W)

1-Cerebus app. 1 2 3 5 6 8
1-2nd printing (5/97) 3.00
2-10: 9-Alex Ross back-c 5.00
11-60 3.00
Doing The Islands With Bacchus ('97, $17.95) 18.00
Earth, Water, Air & Fire ('98, $9.95) 10.00
King Bacchus ('99, $12.95) 13.00
The Eyeball Kid ('98, $8.50) 8.50

EDDIE STANKY (Baseball Hero)
Fawcett Publications: 1951 (New York Giants)

nn-Photo-c 37 74 111 209 305 400

EDEN MATRIX, THE
Adhesive Comics: 1994 ($2.95)

1,2-Two variant-c; alternate-c on inside back-c 3.00

EDEN'S TRAIL
Marvel Comics: Jan, 2003 - No. 6 ($2.99, limited series, Marvelscope-printed sideways)

1-5-Chuck Austen-s/Steve Uy-a 3.00

EDGAR ALLAN POE'S - THE FALL OF THE HOUSE OF USHER AND OTHER TALES OF HORROR
Catlan Communications Pub.: Sept. 1985 (hardcover graphic novel)

nn-Reprints of Poe story issues from Warren comic mags; all Richard Corben-a; numbered edition of 350 signed by Corben 110.00

EDGAR BERGEN PRESENTS CHARLIE McCARTHY
Whitman Publishing Co. (Charlie McCarthy Co.): No. 764, 1938 (36 pgs.; 15x10-1/2"; color)

764 75 150 225 469 722 975

EDGAR RICE BURROUGHS' TARZAN: A TALE OF MUGAMBI
Dark Horse Comics: 1995 ($2.95, one-shot)

1 3.00

EDGAR RICE BURROUGHS' TARZAN: IN THE LAND THAT TIME FORGOT AND THE POOL OF TIME
Dark Horse Comics: 1996 ($12.95, trade paperback)

nn-r/Russ Manning-a 13.00

EDGAR RICE BURROUGHS' TARZAN OF THE APES
Dark Horse Comics: May, 1999 ($12.95, trade paperback)

nn-reprints 13.00

EDGAR RICE BURROUGHS' TARZAN: THE LOST ADVENTURE
Dark Horse Comics: Jan, 1995 - No. 4, Apr, 1995 ($2.95, B&W, limited series)

1-4: ERB's last Tarzan story, adapted by Joe Lansdale 3.00
Hardcover (12/95, $19.95) 20.00
Limited Edition Hardcover ($99.95)-signed & numbered 100.00

EDGAR RICE BURROUGHS' TARZAN: THE RETURN OF TARZAN
Dark Horse Comics: May, 1997 - No. 3, July, 1997 ($2.95, limited series)

1-3 3.00

EDGAR RICE BURROUGHS' TARZAN: THE RIVERS OF BLOOD
Dark Horse Comics: Nov, 1999 - No. 4, Feb, 2000 ($2.95, limited series)

1-4-Kordey-c/a 3.00

EDGE

Eerie #14 © AVON

Eerie #16 © WP

Eerie #60 © WP

GD 2.0 | VG 4.0 | FN 6.0 | VF 8.0 | VF/NM 9.0 | NM- 9.2

Malibu Comics (Bravura): July, 1994 - No. 3, Apr, 1995 ($2.50/$2.95, unfinished lim.series)
1,2-S. Grant-story & Gil Kane-c/a; w/Bravura stamp 2.50
3-($2.95-c) 3.00

EDGE (Re-titled as Vector starting with #13)
CrossGeneration Comics: May, 2002 - No. 12, Apr, 2003 ($9.95/$11.95/$7.95, TPB)
1-3: Reprints from various CrossGen titles 10.00
4-8-($11.95) 12.00
9-12-($7.95, 8-1/4" x 5-1/2") digest-sized reprints 8.00

EDGE OF CHAOS
Pacific Comics: July, 1983 - No. 3, Jan, 1984 (Limited series)
1-3-Morrow c/a; all contain nudity 2.25

ED WHEELAN'S JOKE BOOK STARRING FAT & SLAT (See Fat & Slat)

EERIE (Strange Worlds No. 18 on)
Avon Per.: No. 1, Jan, 1947; No. 1, May-June, 1951 - No. 17, Aug-Sept, 1954
1(1947)-1st supernatural comic; Kubert, Fugitani-a; bondage-c (scarce)
400 800 1200 2600 4200 5800
1(1951)-Reprints story from 1947 #1 67 134 201 419 647 875
2-Wood-c/a; bondage-c 71 142 213 444 685 925
3-Wood-c; Kubert, Wood/Orlando-a 71 142 213 444 685 925
4,5-Wood-c 58 116 174 363 557 750
6,8,13,14: 8-Kinstler-a; bondage-c; Phantom Witch Doctor story
35 70 105 198 284 375
7-Wood/Orlando-c; Kubert-a 45 90 135 275 418 560
9-Kubert-a; Check-c 38 76 114 219 320 420
10,11: 10-Kinstler-a. 11-Kinstlerish-a by McCann 35 70 105 198 287 375
12-Dracula story from novel, 25 pgs. 40 80 120 230 335 440
15-Reprints No. 1('51) minus-c(bondage) 25 50 75 141 203 265
16-Wood-a r-/No. 2 25 50 75 141 203 265
17-Wood/Orlando & Kubert-a; reprints #3 minus inside & outside Wood-c
25 50 75 141 203 265

NOTE: ***Hollingsworth*** *a-9-11; c-10, 11.*

EERIE
I. W. Enterprises: 1964
I.W. Reprint #1('64)-Wood-c(r); r-story/Spook #1 4 8 12 27 36 45
I.W. Reprint #2,6,8: 8-Dr. Drew by Grandenetti from Ghost #9
4 8 12 24 32 40
I.W. Reprint #9-r/Tales of Terror #1(Toby); Wood-c 4 8 12 29 40 50

EERIE (Magazine)(See Warren Presents)
Warren Publ. Co.: No. 1, Sept, 1965; No. 2, Mar, 1966 - No. 139, Feb, 1983
1-24 pgs., black & white, small size (5-1/4x7-1/4"), low distribution; cover from inside back cover of Creepy No. 2; stories reprinted from Creepy No. 7, 8. At least three different versions exist.
First Printing - B&W, 5-1/4" wide x 7-1/4" high, evenly trimmed. On page 18, panel 5, in the upper left-hand corner, the large rear view of a bald headed man blends into solid black and is unrecognizable. Overall printing quality is poor.
32 64 96 240 370 500
Second Printing - B&W, 5-1/4x7-1/4", with uneven, untrimmed edges (if one of these were trimmed evenly, the size would be less than as indicated). The figure of the bald headed man on page 18, panel 5 is clear and discernible. The staples have a 1/4" blue stripe.
15 30 45 109 167 225
Other unauthorized reproductions for comparison's sake would be practically worthless. One known version was probably shot off a first printing copy with some loss of detail; the finer lines tend to disappear in this version which can be determined by looking at the lower right-hand corner of page one, first story. The roof of the house is shaded with straight lines. These lines are sharp and distinct on original, but broken on this version.
NOTE: ***The Overstreet Comic Book Price Guide*** *recommends that, before buying a 1st issue, you consult an expert.*
2-Frazetta-c; Toth-a; 1st app. host Cousin Eerie 10 20 30 67 96 125
3-Frazetta-c & half pg. ad (rerun in #4); Toth, Williamson, Ditko-a
7 14 21 51 71 90
4-7: 4-Frazetta-a (1/2 pg. ad). 5,7-Frazetta-c. Ditko-a in all.
5 10 15 33 44 55
8-Frazetta-c; Ditko-a 6 12 18 38 52 65
9-11,25: 9,10-Neal Adams-a, Ditko-a. 11-Karloff Mummy adapt.-Wood-s/a. 25-Steranko-c
5 10 15 36 48 60
12-16,18-22,24,32-35,40,45: 12,13,20-Poe-s. 12-Bloch-s. 12,15-Jones-a. 13-Lovecraft-s. 14,16-Toth-a. 16,19,24-Stoker-s. 16,32,33,43-Corben-a. 34-Early Boris-c. 35-Early Brunner-a. 35,40-Early Ploog-a. 40-Frankestein; Ploog-a (6/72, 6 months before Marvel's series) 4 8 12 24 32 40
17-(low distribution) 10 20 30 73 107 140
23-Frazetta-c; Adams-a(reprint) 6 12 18 40 55 70
26-31,36-38,43,44 3 7 10 21 28 35
39,41: 39-1st Dax the Warrior; Maroto-a. 41-(low distribution)
4 8 12 28 38 48
42,51: 42-('73 Annual, 84 pgs.) Spooktacular; Williamson-a. 51-('74 Annual, 76 pgs.) Color poster insert; Toth-a 4 8 12 27 36 45
46,48: 46-Dracula series by Sutton begins; 2pgs. Vampirella. 48-Begin "Mummy Walks" and "Curse of the Werewolf" series (both continue in #49,50,52,53)
4 8 12 22 30 38
47,49,50,52,53: 47-Lilith. 49-Marvin the Dead Thing. 50-Satanna, Daughter of Satan. 52-Hunter by Neary begins. 53-Adams-a 3 7 10 21 28 35
54,55-Color insert Spirit story by Eisner, reprints sections 12/21/47 & 6/16/46
54-Dr. Archaeus series begins 3 6 9 18 24 30
56,57,59,63,69,77,78: All have 8 pg. slick color insert. 56,57,77-Corben-a. 59-(100 pgs.) Summer Special, all Dax issue. 69-Summer Special, all Hunter issue, Neary-a. 78-All Mummy issue 3 6 9 18 24 30
58,60,62,68,72,: 8 pg. slick color insert & Wrightson-a in all. 58,60,62-Corben-a. 60-Summer Giant (9/74, $1.25) 1st Exterminator One; Wood-a. 62-Mummies Walk. 68-Summer Special (84 pgs.) 3 7 10 21 28 35
61,64-67,71: 61-Mummies Walk-s, Wood-a. 64-Corben-a. 64,65,67-Toth-a. 65,66-El Cid. 67-Hunter II. 71-Goblin-c/1st app. 3 6 9 16 20 25
70,73-75 2 4 6 11 14 18
76-1st app. Darklon the Mystic by Starlin-s/a 3 6 9 19 25 32
79,80-Origin Darklon the Mystic by Starlin 3 6 9 16 21 26
81,86,97: 81-Frazetta-c, King Kong; Corben-a. 86-(92 pgs.) All Corben issue. 97-Time Travel/ Dinosaur issue; Corben,Adams-a 3 6 9 16 20 24
82-Origin/1st app. The Rook 3 6 9 18 24 30
83,85,88,89,91-93,98,99: 98-Rook (31 pgs.). 99-1st Horizon Seekers.
2 4 6 9 11 14
84,87,90,96,100: 84,100-Starlin-a. 87-Hunter 3; Nino-a. 87,90-Corben-a. 96-Summer Special (92 pgs.). 100-(92 pgs.) Anniversary issue; Rook (30 pgs.)
2 4 6 11 14 18
94,95-The Rook & Vampirella team-up. 95-Vampirella-c; 1st MacTavish
3 6 9 18 23 28
101,106,112,115,118,120,121,128: 101-Return of Hunter II, Starlin-a. 106-Hard John Nuclear Hit Parade Special, Corben-a. 112-All Maroto issue, Luana-s. 115-All José Ortiz issues. 118-1st Haggarth. 120-1st Zud Kamish. 121-Hunter/Darklon. 128-Starlin-a, Hsu-a
2 4 6 10 13 16
102-105,107-111,113,114,116,117,119,122-124,126,127,129: 104-Beast World. 103-105,109-111-Gulacy-a 2 4 6 9 11 14
125-(10/81, 84 pgs.) all Neal Adams issue 2 4 6 14 18 22
130-(76 pgs.) Vampirella-c/sty (54 pgs.); Pantha, Van Helsing, Huntress, Dax, Schreck, Hunter, Exterminator One, Rook app. 3 6 9 18 23 28
131-(Lower distr.); all Wood issue 3 6 9 16 20 24
132-134,136: 132-Rook returns. 133-All Ramon Torrents-a issue. 134,136-Color comic insert
2 4 6 10 13 16
135-(Lower distr., 10/82, 100 pgs.) All Ditko issue 3 6 9 16 20 24
137-139 (lower distr.):137-All Super-Hero issue. 138-Sherlock Holmes. 138,139-Color comic insert 2 4 6 12 16 20
Yearbook '70-Frazetta-c 5 10 15 36 48 60
Annual '71, '72-Reprints in both 4 8 12 27 36 45
NOTE: *The above books contain art by many good artists:* ***N. Adams, Brunner, Corben, Craig (Taycee), Crandall, Ditko, Eisner, Evans, Jeff Jones, Krenkel, McWilliams, Morrow, Orlando, Ploog, Severin, Starlin, Torres, Toth, Williamson, Wood,*** *and* ***Wrightson****; covers by* ***Bode', Corben, Davis, Frazetta, Morrow****, and* ***Orlando****.* ***Frazetta*** *c-2, 3, 7, 8, 23. Annuals from 1973-on are included in regular numbering. 1970-74 Annuals are complete reprints. Annuals from 1975-on are in the format of the regular issues.*

EERIE ADVENTURES (Also see Weird Adventures)
Ziff-Davis Publ. Co.: Winter, 1951 (Painted-c)
1-Powell-a(2), McCann-a; used in **SOTI;** bondage-c; Krigstein back-c
40 80 120 244 372 500
NOTE: *Title dropped due to similarity to Avon's Eerie & legal action.*

EERIE TALES (Magazine)
Hastings Associates: 1959 (Black & White)
1-Williamson, Torres, Tuska-a, Powell(2), & Morrow(2)-a
14 28 42 79 110 140

EERIE TALES
Super Comics: 1963-1964
Super Reprint No. 10,11,12,18: 10('63)-r/Spook #27. Purple Claw in #11,12 ('63); #12-r/Avon's Eerie #1('51)-Kida-r 3 6 9 19 25 32
15-Wolverton-a, Spacehawk-r/Blue Bolt Weird Tales #113; Disbrow-a
6 12 18 38 52 65

EGBERT
Arnold Publications/Quality Comics Group: Spring, 1946 - No. 20, 1950
1-Funny animal; intro Egbert & The Count 20 40 60 112 161 210
2 10 20 30 60 80 100
3-10 8 16 24 43 54 65
11-20 6 12 18 31 38 45

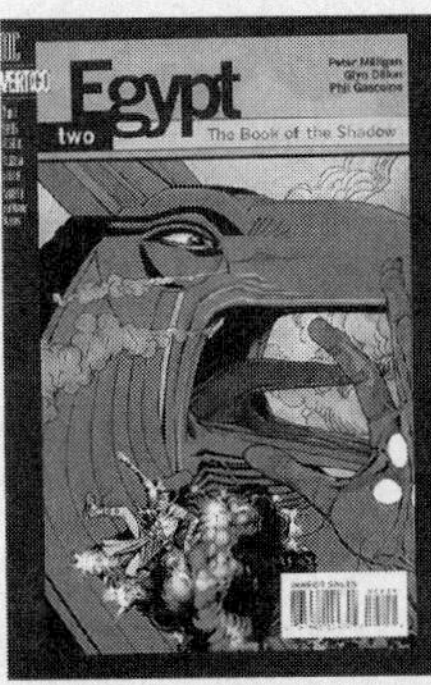

Egypt #2 © Milligan & Dillon

Eightball #23 © Daniel G. Clowes

Elektra V2#1 © MAR

GD VG FN VF VF/NM NM-
2.0 4.0 6.0 8.0 9.0 9.2

EGON
Dark Horse Comics: Jan, 1998 - No.2, Feb, 1998 ($2.95, limited series)
1,2-Horley-painted-c 3.00

EGYPT
DC Comics (Vertigo): Aug, 1995 - No.7, Feb, 1996 ($2.50, lim. series, mature)
1-7: Milligan scripts in all. 3.00

EH! (...Dig This Crazy Comic) (From Here to Insanity No. 8 on)
Charlton Comics: Dec, 1953 - No. 7, Nov-Dec, 1954 (Satire)
1-Davis-*ish*-c/a by Ayers, Wood-*ish*-a by Giordano; Atomic Mouse app.
37 74 111 209 305 400
2-Ayers-c/a 21 42 63 121 173 225
3,5,7 19 38 57 107 154 200
4,6: Sexual innuendo-c. 6-Ayers-a 20 40 60 115 165 215

EIGHTBALL (Also see David Boring)
Fantagraphics Books: Oct, 1989 - Present ($2.75/$2.95/$3.95, semi-annually, mature)
1 (1st printing) Daniel Clowes-s/a in all 2 4 6 8 10 12
2,3 1 2 3 5 6 8
4-8 6.00
9-19: 17-(8/96) 4.00
20-($4.50) 4.50
21-($4.95) Concludes David Boring 3-parter 5.00
22-($5.95) 29 short stories 6.00
23-($7.00, 9" x 12") The Death Ray 7.00
Twentieth Century Eightball (2002, $19.00) r/Clowes strips 19.00

EIGHTH WONDER, THE
Dark Horse Comics: Nov, 1997 ($2.95, one-shot)
nn-Reprints stories from Dark Horse Presents #85-87 3.00

EIGHT IS ENOUGH KITE FUN BOOK (See Kite Fun Book)

EIGHT LEGGED FREAKS
DC Comics (WildStorm): 2002 ($6.95, one-shot, squarebound)
nn-Adaptation of 2002 mutant spider movie; Joe Phillips-a; intro by Dean Devlin 7.00

80 PAGE GIANT (...Magazine No. 2-15)
National Periodical Publications: 8/64 - No. 15, 10/65; No. 16, 11/65 - No. 89, 7/71 (25¢)
(All reprints) (#1-56: 84 pgs.; #57-89: 68 pgs.)
1-Superman Annual; originally planned as Superman Annual #9 (8/64)
41 82 123 330 515 700
2-Jimmy Olsen 25 50 75 179 275 370
3,4: 3-Lois Lane. 4-Flash-G.A.-r; Infantino-a 20 40 60 141 216 290
5-Batman; has Sunday newspaper strip; Catwoman-r; Batman's Life Story-r (25th anniversary special) 20 40 60 141 216 290
6-Superman 17 34 51 123 189 255
7-Sgt. Rock's Prize Battle Tales; Kubert-c/a 23 46 69 165 253 340
8-More Secret Origins-origins of JLA, Aquaman, Robin, Atom, & Superman; Infantino-a 35 70 105 263 412 560
9-15: 9-Flash (r/Flash #106,117,123 & Showcase #14); Infantino-a. 10-Superboy. 11-Superman; all Luthor issue. 12-Batman; has Sunday newspaper strip. 13-Jimmy Olsen. 14-Lois Lane. 15-Superman and Batman; Joker-c/story
17 34 51 119 182 245

Continued as part of regular series under each title in which that particular book came out, a Giant being published instead of the regular size. Issues No. 16 to No. 89 are listed for your information. See individual titles for prices. 16-JLA #39 (11/65), 17-Batman #176, 18-Superman #183, 19-Our Army at War #164, 20-Action #334, 21-Flash #160, 22-Superboy #129, 23-Superman #187, 24-Batman #182, 25-Jimmy Olsen #95, 26-Lois Lane #68, 27-Batman #185, 28-World's Finest #161, 29-JLA #48, 30-Batman #187, 31-Superman #193, 32-Our Army at War #177, 33-Action #347, 34-Flash #169, 35-Superboy #138, 36-Superman #197, 37-Batman #193, 38-Jimmy Olsen #104, 39-Lois Lane #77, 40-World's Finest #170, 41-JLA #58, 42-Superman #202, 43-Batman #198, 44-Our Army at War #190, 45-Action #360, 46-Flash #178, 47-Superboy #147, 48-Superman #207, 49-Batman #203, 50-Jimmy Olsen #113, 51-Lois Lane #86, 52-World's Finest #179, 53-JLA #67, 54-Superman #212, 55-Batman #208, 56-Our Army at War #203, 57-Action #373, 58-Flash #187, 59-Superboy #156, 60-Superman #217, 61-Batman #213, 62-Jimmy Olsen #122, 63-Lois Lane #95, 64-World's Finest #188, 65-JLA #76, 66-Superman #222, 67-Batman #218, 68-Our Army at War #216, 69-Adventure #390, 70-Flash #196, 71-Superboy #165, 72-Superman #227, 73-Batman #223, 74-Jimmy Olsen #131, 75-Lois Lane #104, 76-World's Finest #197, 77-JLA #85, 78-Superman #232, 79-Batman #228, 80-Our Army at War #229, 81-Adventure #403, 82-Flash #205, 83-Superboy #174, 84-Superman #239, 85-Batman #233, 86-Jimmy Olsen #140, 87-Lois Lane #113, 88-World's Finest #206, 89-JLA #93.

87TH PRECINCT (TV) (Based on the Ed McBain novels)
Dell Publishing Co.: Apr-June, 1962 - No. 2, July-Sept, 1962
Four Color 1309(#1)-Krigstein-a 11 22 33 80 120 160
2 10 20 30 70 100 130

EL BOMBO COMICS
Standard Comics/Frances M. McQueeny: 1946
nn(1946), 1(no date) 11 22 33 64 87 110

GD VG FN VF VF/NM NM-
2.0 4.0 6.0 8.0 9.0 9.2

EL CAZADOR
CrossGen Comics: Oct, 2003 - No. 6, Jun, 2004 ($2.95)
1-Dixon-s/Epting-a 5.00
2-6: 5-Lady Death preview 3.00
Collected Edition (2003, $5.95) r/#1-3 6.00
...: The Bloody Ballad of Blackjack Tom 1 (4/04, $2.95, one-shot) Cariello-a 3.00

EL CID
Dell Publishing Co.: No. 1259, 1961
Four Color 1259-Movie, photo-c 8 16 24 58 82 105

EL DIABLO (See All-Star Western #2 & Weird Western Tales #12)
DC Comics: Aug, 1989 - No. 16, Jan, 1991 ($1.50-$1.75, color)
1 ($2.50, 52pgs.)-Masked hero 3.00
2-16 2.50

EL DIABLO
DC Comics (Vertigo): Mar, 2001 - No. 4, Jun, 2001 ($2.50, limited series)
1-4-Azzarello-s/Zezelj-a/Sale-c 2.50

EL DORADO (See Movie Classics)

ELECTRIC UNDERTOW (See Strikeforce Morituri: Electric Undertow)

ELECTRIC WARRIOR
DC Comics: May, 1986 - No. 18, Oct, 1987 ($1.50, Baxter paper)
1-18 2.25

ELECTROPOLIS
Image Comics: May, 2001 - No. 4, Jan, 2003 ($2.95/$5.95)
1-3-Dean Motter-s/a. 3-(12/01) 3.00
4-(1/03, $5.95, 72 pages) The Infernal Machine pts. 4-6 6.00

ELEKTRA (Also see Daredevil #319-325)
Marvel Comics: Mar, 1995 - No. 4, June, 1995 ($2.95, limited series)
1-4-Embossed-c; Scott McDaniel-a 3.00

ELEKTRA (Also see Daredevil)
Marvel Comics: Nov, 1996 - No. 19, Jun, 1998 ($1.95)
1-Peter Milligan scripts; Deodato-c/a 3.00
1-Variant-c 5.00
2-19: 4-Dr. Strange-c/app. 10-Logan-c/app. 2.50
#(-1) Flashback (7/97) Matt Murdock-c/app.; Deodato-c/a 2.50
.../Cyblade (Image, 3/97,$2.95) Devil's Reign pt. 7 3.00

ELEKTRA (Vol. 2) (Marvel Knights)
Marvel Comics: Sept, 2001 - No. 35, Jun, 2004 ($3.50/$2.99)
1-Bendis-s/Austen-a/Horn-c 4.00
2-6: 2-Two covers (Sienkiewicz and Horn) 3,4-Silver Samurai app. 3.00
3-Initial printing with panel of nudity; most copies pulped 18.00
7-35: 7-Rucka-s begin. 9,10,17-Bennett-a. 19-Meglia-a. 23-25-Chen-a; Sienkiewicz-c 3.00
...Vol. 1: Introspect TPB (2002, $16.99) r/#10-15; Marvel Knights: Double Shot #3 17.00
...Vol. 2: Everything Old is New Again TPB (2003, $16.99) r/#16-22 17.00
...Vol. 3: Relentless TPB (2004, $14.99) r/#23-28 15.00
...Vol. 4: Frenzy TPB (2004, $17.99) r/#29-35 18.00

ELEKTRA & WOLVERINE: THE REDEEMER
Marvel Comics: Jan, 2002 - No. 3, Mar, 2002 ($5.95, square-bound, lim. series)
1-3-Greg Rucka-s/Yoshitaka Amano-a/c 6.00
HC (5/02, $29.95, with dustjacket) r/#1-3, interview with Greg Rucka 30.00

ELEKTRA: ASSASSIN (Also see Daredevil)
Marvel Comics (Epic Comics): Aug, 1986 - No. 8, June, 1987 (Limited series, mature)
1,8-Miller scripts in all; Sienkiewicz-c/a. 6.00
2-7 5.00
Signed & numbered hardcover (Graphitti Designs, $39.95, 2000 print run)- reprints 1-8 50.00
TPB (2000, $24.95) 25.00

ELEKTRA: GLIMPSE & ECHO
Marvel Comics: Sept, 2002 - No. 4, Dec, 2002 ($2.99, limited series)
1-4-Scott Morse-s/painted-a 3.00

ELEKTRA LIVES AGAIN (Also see Daredevil)
Marvel Comics (Epic Comics): 1990 ($24.95, oversize, hardcover, 76 pgs.)
(Produced by Graphitti Designs)
nn-Frank Miller-c/a/scripts; Lynn Varley painted-a; Matt Murdock & Bullseye app. 35.00
2nd printing (9/02, $24.99) 25.00

ELEKTRA MEGAZINE
Marvel Comics: Nov, 1996 - No. 2, Dec, 1996 ($3.95, 96 pgs., reprints, limited series)

Elementals #6 © Comico

Elflord V1#1 © Warp Graphics

ElfQuest V2#18 © Warp Graphics

GD VG FN VF VF/NM NM-
2.0 4.0 6.0 8.0 9.0 9.2

1,2: Reprints Frank Miller's Elektra stories in Daredevil 4.00

ELEKTRA SAGA, THE
Marvel Comics Group: Feb, 1984 - No. 4, June, 1984 ($2.00, limited series, Baxter paper)
1-4-r/Daredevil 168-190; Miller-c/a 4.00

ELEKTRA: THE HAND
Marvel Comics: Nov, 2004 - No. 5 ($2.99, limited series)
1-4-Gossett-a/Sienkiewicz-c/Yoshida-s; origin of the Hand in the 16th century 3.00

ELEMENTALS, THE (See The Justice Machine & Morningstar Spec.)
Comico The Comic Co. : June, 1984 - No. 29, Sept, 1988; V2#1, Mar, 1989 - No. 28, 1994? ($1.50/$2.50, Baxter paper); V3#1, Dec, 1995 - No. 3 ($2.95)
1-Willingham-c/a, 1-8 5.00
2-29, V2#1-28: 9-Bissette-a(p). 10-Photo-c. V2#6-1st app. Strike Force America. 18-Prelude to Avalon mini-series. 27-Prequel to Strike Force America series 3.00
V3#1-3: 1-Daniel-a(p), bagged w/gaming card 3.00
Lingerie (5/96, $2.95) 3.00
Special 1,2 (3/86, 1/89)-1-Willingham-a(p) 3.00

ELEMENTALS: (Title series), **Comico**
--GHOST OF A CHANCE, 12/95 ($5.95)-graphic novel, nn-Ross-c. 6.00
--HOW THE WAR WAS WON, 6/96 - No. 2, 8/96 ($2.95) 1,2-Tony Daniel-a, & 1-Variant-c; no logo 3.00
--SEX SPECIAL, 1991 - No. 4, Feb, 1993 ($2.95, color) 2 covers for each 3.00
--SEX SPECIAL, 5/97 - No. 2, 6/97 ($2.95, B&W) 1-Tony Daniel, Jeff Moy-a, 2-Robb Phipps, Adam McDaniel-a 3.00
--SWIMSUIT SPECTACULAR 1996, 6/96 ($2.95), 1-pin-ups, 1-Variant-c; no logo 3.00
--THE VAMPIRE'S REVENGE, 6/96 - No. 2 8/96 ($2.95) 1,2-Willingham-s, 1-Variant-c; no logo 3.00

1111 (ELEVEN ELEVEN)
Crusade Entertainment: Oct, 1996 ($2.95, B&W, one-shot)
1-Wrightson-c/a 4.00

ELEVEN OR ONE
Sirius: Apr, 1995 ($2.95)
1-Linsner-c/a 1 3 4 6 8 10
1-(6/96) 2nd printing 3.50

ELFLORD
Nightwind Productions: Jun, 1980 - Vol. 2 #1, 1982 (B&W, magazine-size)
1-1st Barry Blair-s/c/a in comics; B&W-c; limited print run for all 200.00
2-5-B&W-c 75.00
6-14: 9-14-Color-c 60.00
Vol. 2 #1 (1982) 50.00

ELFLORD
Aircel Publ.: 1986 - No. 6, Oct, 1989 ($1.70, B&W); V2#1- V2#31, 1995 ($2.00)
1 3.00
2-4,V2#1-20,22-30: 4-6: Last B&W issue. V2#1-Color-a begin. 22-New cast. 25-Begin B&W 2.50
1,2-2nd printings 2.50
21-Double size ($4.95) 5.00

ELFLORD
Warp Graphics: Jan, 1997-No.4, Apr, 1997 ($2.95, B&W, mini-series)
1-4 3.00

ELFLORD (CUTS LOOSE) (Vol. 2)
Warp Graphics: Sept, 1997 - No. 7, Apr, 1998 ($2.95, B&W, mini-series)
1-7 3.00

ELFLORD: DRAGON'S EYE
Night Wynd Enterprises: 1993 ($2.50, B&W)
1 2.50

ELFLORD: THE RETURN
Mad Monkey Press: 1996 ($6.95, magazine size)
1 7.00

ELFQUEST (Also see Fantasy Quarterly & Warp Graphics Annual)
Warp Graphics, Inc.: No. 2, Aug, 1978 - No. 21, Feb, 1985 (All magazine size)
No. 1, Apr, 1979
NOTE: ***Elfquest*** was originally published as one of the stories in **Fantasy Quarterly** #1. When the publisher went out of business, the creative team, Wendy and Richard Pini, formed WaRP Graphics and continued the series, beginning with **Elfquest** #2. **Elfquest** #1, which reprinted the story from **Fantasy Quarterly**, was published about the same time **Elfquest** #4 was released. Thereafter, most issues were reprinted as demand warranted, until Marvel announced it would reprint the entire series under its Epic imprint (Aug., 1985).

GD VG FN VF VF/NM NM-
2.0 4.0 6.0 8.0 9.0 9.2

1(4/79)-Reprints Elfquest story from Fantasy Quarterly No. 1
1st printing ($1.00-c) 3 7 10 21 28 35
2nd printing ($1.25-c) 1 2 3 5 7 9
3rd printings ($1.50-c) 3.00
4th printing; different-c ($1.50-c) 2.50
2(8/78)-5: 1st printings ($1.00-c) 2 4 6 12 16 20
2nd printings ($1.25-c) 4.00
3rd & 4th printings ($1.50-c)(all 4th prints 1989) 2.50
6-9: 1st printings ($1.25-c) 1 3 4 6 8 10
2nd printings ($1.50-c) 3.00
3rd printings ($1.50-c) 2.50
10-21: ($1.50-c); 16-8pg. preview of A Distant Soil 6.00
10-14: 2nd printings ($1.50) 2.50

ELFQUEST
Marvel Comics (Epic Comics): Aug, 1985 - No. 32, Mar, 1988
1-Reprints in color the Elfquest epic by Warp Graphics 3.00
2-32 2.50

ELFQUEST
DC Comics: 2003 - Present
Archives Vol. 1 (2003, $49.95, HC) r/#1-5 50.00
25th Anniversary Special (2003, $2.95) r/Elfquest #1 (Apr, 1979); interview w/Pinis 3.00

ELFQUEST (Title series), Warp Graphics
'89 - No. 4, '89 ($1.50, B&W) 1-4: R-original Elfquest series 2.50

ELFQUEST (Volume 2),**Warp Graphics:** V2#1, 5/96 - No. 33, 2/99 ($4.95/$2.95, B&W)
V2#1-31: 1,3,5,8,10,12,13,18,21,23,25-Wendy Pini-c 5.00
32,33-($2.95-c) 3.00
--BLOOD OF TEN CHIEFS, 7/93 - No. 20, 9/95 ($2.00/$2.50) 1-20-By Richard & Wendy Pini 3.00
--HIDDEN YEARS, 5/92 - No. 29, 3/96 ($2.00/$2.25)1-9,9 1/2, 10-29 3.00
--JINK, 11/94 - No. 12, 2/6 ($2.25/$2.50) 1-12-W. Pini/John Byrne-back-c 3.00
--KAHVI, 10/95 - No. 6,3/96 ($2.25, B&W) 1-6 3.00
--KINGS CROSS, 11/97 - No. 2, 12/97 ($2.95, B&W) 1,2 3.00
--KINGS OF THE BROKEN WHEEL, 6/90 - No. 9, 2/92 ($2.00, B&W) (3rd Elfquest saga) 1-9: By R. & W. Pini; 1-Color insert 3.00
1-2nd printing 2.50
--METAMORPHOSIS, 4/96 ($2.95, B&W) 1 3.00
--NEW BLOOD (...Summer Special on-c #1 only), 8/92 - No. 35, 1/96 ($2.00-$2.50, color/ B&W) 1-($3.95, 68 pgs.,...Summer Special on-c)-Byrne-a/scripts (16 pgs.) 4.00
2-35: Barry Blair-a in all 3.00
1993 Summer Special ($3.95) Byrne-a/scripts 4.00
--SHARDS, 8/94 - No. 16, 3/96 ($2.25/$2.50) 1-16 3.00
--SIEGE AT BLUE MOUNTAIN, WaRP Graphics/Apple 3/87 - No. 8, 12/88 (1.75/ $1.95, B&W) 1-Staton-a(i) in all; 2nd Elfquest saga 4.00
1-3-2nd printing, 3-8 2.50
2 3.00
--THE REBELS, 11/94 - No. 12, 3/96 ($2.25/$2.50, B&W/color) 1-12 3.00
--TWO-SPEAR, 10/95 - No. 5, 2/96 ($2.25, B&W) 1-5 3.00
--WAVE DANCERS, 12/93 - No. 6, 3/96, 1-6: 1-Foil-c & poster 3.00
Special 1 ($2.95) 3.00
--WORLDPOOL, 7/97 ($2.95, B&W) 1-Richard Pini-s/Barry Blair-a 3.00

ELFQUEST: THE GRAND QUEST
DC Comics: 2004 - Present ($9.95, B&W, digest-size)
Vol. 1-5 ('04)1-r/Elfquest #1-5; new W. Pini-c. 2-r/#5-8. 3-r/#8-11. 4-r/#11-15. 5-r/#15-18 10.00

ELFQUEST: THE SEARCHER AND THE SWORD
DC Comics: 2004 ($24.95, hardcover with dust jacket)
HC-Wendy and Richard Pini-s/a/c 25.00

ELFQUEST: WOLFRIDER
DC Comics: 2003 - Present ($9.95, digest-size)
Volume 1 ('03, $9.95, digest-size) r/Elfquest V2#19,21,23,25,27,29,31; Blood of Ten Chiefs #2; Hidden Years #5; New Blood Special #1; New Blood 1993 Special #1; new W. Pini-c 10.00
Volume 2 ('03, $9.95, digest-size) r/Elfquest V2#33; Blood of Ten Chiefs #10,11,19; Warp Graphics Annual #1 10.00

ELF-THING
Eclipse Comics: March, 1987 ($1.50, B&W, one-shot)

Elric, Stormbringer #7 © Michael Moorcock

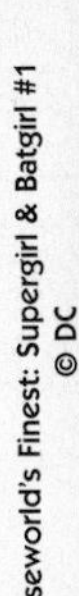
Elseworld's Finest: Supergirl & Batgirl #1 © DC

E-Man #2 © CC

	GD 2.0	VG 4.0	FN 6.0	VF 8.0	VF/NM 9.0	NM- 9.2

1 — 2.25

ELIMINATOR (Also see The Solution #16 & The Night Man #16)
Malibu Comics (Ultraverse): Apr, 1995 - No. 3, Jul, 1995 ($2.95/$2.50, lim. series)

0-Mike Zeck-a in all — 3.00
1-3-($2.50): 1-1st app. Siren — 2.50
1-($3.95)-Black cover edition — 4.00

ELIMINATOR FULL COLOR SPECIAL
Eternity Comics: Oct, 1991 ($2.95, one-shot)

1-Dave Dorman painted-c — 3.00

ELLA CINDERS (See Comics On Parade, Comics Revue #1,4, Famous Comics Cartoon Book, Giant Comics Editions, Sparkler Comics, Tip Top & Treasury of Comics)

ELLA CINDERS
United Features Syndicate: 1938 - 1940

	GD	VG	FN	VF	VF/NM	NM-
Single Series 3(1938)	40	80	120	240	360	480
Single Series 21(#2 on-c, #21 on inside), 28('40)	36	72	108	204	297	390

ELLA CINDERS
United Features Syndicate: Mar, 1948 - No. 5, Mar, 1949

	GD	VG	FN	VF	VF/NM	NM-
1-(#2 on cover)	14	28	42	81	113	145
2	9	18	27	54	70	85
3-5	8	16	24	40	50	60

ELLERY QUEEN
Superior Comics Ltd.: May, 1949 - No. 4, Nov, 1949

	GD	VG	FN	VF	VF/NM	NM-
1-Kamen-c; L.B. Cole-a; r-in Haunted Thrills	52	104	156	317	484	650
2-4: 3-Drug use stories(2)	40	80	120	233	342	450

NOTE: *Iger shop art in all issues.*

ELLERY QUEEN (TV)
Ziff-Davis Publishing Co.: 1-3/52 (Spring on-c) - No. 2, Summer/52 (Saunders painted-c)

	GD	VG	FN	VF	VF/NM	NM-
1-Saunders-c	46	92	138	281	428	575
2-Saunders bondage, torture-c	40	80	120	233	342	450

ELLERY QUEEN (Also see Crackajack Funnies No. 23)
Dell Publishing Co.: No. 1165, Mar-May, 1961 - No.1289, Apr, 1962

	GD	VG	FN	VF	VF/NM	NM-
Four Color 1165 (#1)	12	24	36	86	131	175
Four Color 1243 (11-1/61-61), 1289	10	20	30	70	100	130

ELMER FUDD (Also see Camp Comics, Daffy, Looney Tunes #1 & Super Book #10, 22)
Dell Publishing Co.: No. 470, May, 1953 - No. 1293, Mar-May, 1962

	GD	VG	FN	VF	VF/NM	NM-
Four Color 470 (#1)	7	14	21	51	71	90
Four Color 558,628,689('56)	5	10	15	33	44	55
Four Color 725,783,841,888,938,977,1032,1081,1131,1171,1222,1293('62)	4	8	12	27	36	45

ELMO COMICS
St. John Publishing Co.: Jan, 1948 (Daily strip-r)

	GD	VG	FN	VF	VF/NM	NM-
1-By Cecil Jensen	10	20	30	56	73	90

ELONGATED MAN (See Flash #112 & Justice League of America #105)
DC Comics: Jan, 1992 - No. 4, Apr, 1992 ($1.00, limited series)

1-4: 3-The Flash app. — 2.25

ELRIC (Of Melnibone)(See First Comics Graphic Novel #6 & Marvel Graphic Novel #2)
Pacific Comics: Apr, 1983 - No. 6, Apr, 1984 ($1.50, Baxter paper)

1-6: Russell-c/a(i) in all — 3.00

ELRIC
Topps Comics: 1996 ($2.95, one-shot)

0--One Life: Russell-c/a; adapts Neil Gaiman's short story "One Life--Furnished in Early Moorcock." — 3.00

ELRIC, SAILOR ON THE SEAS OF FATE
First Comics: June, 1985 - No. 7, June, 1986 ($1.75, limited series)

1-7: Adapts Michael Moorcock's novel — 3.00

ELRIC, STORMBRINGER
Dark Horse Comics/Topps Comics: 1997 - No. 7, 1997($2.95, limited series)

1-7: Russell-c/s/a; adapts Michael Moorcock's novel — 3.00

ELRIC: THE BANE OF THE BLACK SWORD
First Comics: Aug, 1988 - No. 6, June, 1989 ($1.75/$1.95, limited series)

1-6: Adapts Michael Moorcock's novel — 3.00

ELRIC: THE VANISHING TOWER
First Comics: Aug, 1987 - No. 6, June, 1988 ($1.75, limited series)

1-6: Adapts Michael Moorcock's novel — 3.00

ELRIC: WEIRD OF THE WHITE WOLF
First Comics: Oct, 1986 - No. 5, June, 1987 ($1.75, limited series)

1-5: Adapts Michael Moorcock's novel — 3.00

EL SALVADOR - A HOUSE DIVIDED
Eclipse Comics: March, 1989 ($2.50, B&W, Baxter paper, stiff-c, 52 pgs.)

1-Gives history of El Salvador — 2.50

ELSEWHERE PRINCE, THE (Moebius' Airtight Garage)
Marvel Comics (Epic): May, 1990 - No. 6, Oct, 1990 ($1.95, limited series)

1-6: Moebius scripts & back-up-a in all — 3.00

ELSEWORLDS 80-PAGE GIANT
DC Comics: Aug, 1999 ($5.95, one-shot)

1-Most copies destroyed by DC over content of the "Superman's Babysitter" story; some UK shipments sold before recall — 175.00

ELSEWORLD'S FINEST
DC Comics: 1997 - No. 2, 1997 ($4.95, limited series)

1,2: Elseworld's story-Superman & Batman in the 1920's — 5.00

ELSEWORLD'S FINEST: SUPERGIRL & BATGIRL
DC Comics: 1998 ($5.95, one-shot)

1-Haley-a — 6.00

ELSIE THE COW
D. S. Publishing Co.: Oct-Nov, 1949 - No. 3, July-Aug, 1950

	GD	VG	FN	VF	VF/NM	NM-
1-(36 pgs.)	26	52	78	150	215	280
2,3	19	38	57	107	154	200

ELSON'S PRESENTS
DC Comics: 1981 (100 pgs., no cover price)

	GD	VG	FN	VF	VF/NM	NM-
Series 1-6: Repackaged 1981 DC comics; 1-DC Comics Presents #29, Flash #303, Batman #331. 2-Superman #335, Ghosts #96, Justice League of America #186. 3-New Teen Titans #3, Secrets of Haunted House #32, Wonder Woman #275. 4-Secrets of the LSH #1, Brave & the Bold #170, New Adv. of Superboy #13. 5-LSH #271, Green Lantern #136, Super Friends #40. 6-Action #515, Mystery in Space #115, Detective #498	2	4	6	11	14	18

ELVEN (Also see Prime)
Malibu Comics (Ultraverse): Oct, 1994 - No. 4, Feb, 1995 ($2.50, lim. series)

0 ($2.95)-Prime app. — 3.00
1-4: 2,4-Prime app. 3-Primevil app. — 2.50
1-Limited Foil Edition- no price on cover — 3.00

ELVIRA MISTRESS OF THE DARK
Marvel Comics: Oct, 1988 ($2.00, B&W, magazine size)

1-Movie adaptation — 5.00

ELVIRA MISTRESS OF THE DARK
Claypool Comics (Eclipse): May, 1993 - Present ($2.50, B&W)

1-Austin-a(i). Spiegle-a — 6.00
2-6: Spiegle-a — 4.00
7-99,101-142-Photo-c: — 2.50
100-(8/01) Kurt Busiek back-up-s; art by DeCarlo and others — 2.50
TPB ($12.95) — 13.00

ELVIRA'S HOUSE OF MYSTERY
DC Comics: Jan, 1986 - No. 11, Jan, 1987

1,11: 11-Dave Stevens-c — 6.00
2-10: 9-Photo-c, Special 1 (3/87, $1.25) — 4.00

ELVIS MANDIBLE, THE
DC Comics (Piranha Press): 1990 ($3.50, 52 pgs., B&W, mature)

nn — 3.50

ELVIS PRESLEY (See Career Girl Romances #32, Go-Go, Howard Chaykin's American Flagg #10, Humbug #8, I Love You #60 & Young Lovers #18)

EL ZOMBO FANTASMA
Dark Horse Comics (Rocket Comics): Apr, 2004 - No. 3, June, 2004 ($2.99)

1-3-Wilkins-s&a/Munroe-s — 3.00

E-MAN
Charlton Comics: Oct, 1973 - No. 10, Sept, 1975 (Painted-c No. 7-10)

	GD	VG	FN	VF	VF/NM	NM-
1-Origin & 1st app. E-Man; Staton c/a in all	3	6	9	18	23	28
2-4: 2,4-Ditko-a. 3-Howard-a	2	4	6	9	11	14
5-Miss Liberty Belle app. by Ditko	2	4	6	8	10	12

6-10: 6,7,9,10-Early Byrne-a (#6 is 1/75). 6-Disney parody. 8-Full-length story; Nova begins

Emma Frost #1 © MAR

Empire #1 © Waid & Kitson

Enginehead #1 © DC

	GD	VG	FN	VF	VF/NM	NM-
	2.0	4.0	6.0	8.0	9.0	9.2

as E-Man's partner 2 4 6 11 14 18
1-4,9,10 (Modern Comics reprints, '77) 4.00
NOTE: *Killjoy app.-No. 2, 4. Liberty Belle app.-No. 5. Rog 2000 app.-No. 6, 7, 9, 10. Travis app.-No. 3.* ***Sutton*** *a-1.*

E-MAN
Comico: Sept, 1989 ($2.75, one-shot, no ads, high quality paper)
1-Staton-c/a; Michael Mauser story 2.75

E-MAN
Comico: V4#1, Jan, 1990 - No. 3, Mar, 1990 ($2.50, limited series)
1-3: Staton-c/a 2.50

E-MAN
Alpha Productions: Oct, 1993 ($2.75)
V5#1-Staton-c/a; 20th anniversary issue 2.75

E-MAN COMICS (Also see Michael Mauser & The Original E-Man)
First Comics: Apr, 1983 - No. 25, Aug, 1985 ($1.00/$1.25, direct sales only)
1-25: 2-X-Men satire. 3-X-Men/Phoenix satire. 6-Origin retold. 8-Cutey Bunny app. 10-Origin Nova Kane. 24-Origin Michael Mauser 2.50
NOTE: ***Staton*** *a-1-5, 6-25p; c-1-25.*

E-MAN RETURNS
Alpha Productions: 1994 ($2.75, B&W)
1-Joe Staton-c/a(p) 2.75

EMERALD DAWN
DC Comics: 1991 ($4.95, trade paperback)
nn-Reprints Green Lantern: Emerald Dawn #1-6 5.00

EMERALD DAWN II (See Green Lantern...)

EMERGENCY (Magazine)
Charlton Comics: June, 1976 - No. 4, Jan, 1977 (B&W)
1-Neal Adams-c/a; Heath, Austin-a 4 8 12 24 32 40
2,3: 2-N. Adams-c. 3-N. Adams-a. 3 7 10 21 28 35
4-Alcala-a 3 6 9 16 20 25

EMERGENCY (TV)
Charlton Comics: June, 1976 - No. 4, Dec, 1976
1-Staton-c; early Byrne-a (22 pages) 3 7 10 21 28 35
2-4: 2-Staton-c. 2,3-Byrne text illos. 3 6 9 16 20 24

EMERGENCY DOCTOR
Charlton Comics: Summer, 1963 (one-shot)
1 4 8 12 22 30 38

EMIL & THE DETECTIVES (See Movie Comics)

EMMA FROST
Marvel Comics: Aug, 2003 - Present ($2.50/$2.99)
1-7-Emma in high school; Bollers-s/Green-a/Horn-c 2.50
8-17-($2.99) 3.00
... Vol. 1: Higher Learning TPB (2004, $7.99, digest size) r/#1-6 8.00

EMMA PEEL & JOHN STEED (See The Avengers)

EMPEROR'S NEW CLOTHES, THE
Dell Publishing Co.: 1950 (10¢, 68 pgs., 1/2 size, oblong)
nn - (Surprise Books series) 6 12 18 27 33 38

EMPIRE
Image Comics (Gorilla): May, 2000 - No. 2, Sept, 2000 ($2.50)
DC Comics: No. 0, Aug, 2003; Sept, 2003 - No. 6, Feb, 2004 ($4.95/$2.50, limited series)
1,2: 1 (5/00)-Waid-s/Kitson-a; w/Crimson Plague prologue 2.50
0-(8/03) reprints #1,2 5.00
1-6: 1-(9/03) new Waid-s/Kitson-a/c 2.50
TPB (DC, 2004, $14.95) r/series; Kitson sketch pages; Waid intro. 15.00

EMPIRE STRIKES BACK, THE (See Marvel Comics Super Special #16 & Marvel Special Edition)

EMPTY LOVE STORIES
Slave Labor #1 & 2/Funny Valentine Press: Nov, 1994 - Present ($2.95, B&W)
1,2: Steve Darnall scripts in all. 1-Alex Ross-c. 2-(8/96)-Mike Allred-c 4.00
1,2-2nd printing (Funny Valentine Press) 3.00
... 1999-Jeff Smith-c; Doran-a 3.00
..."Special" (2.95) Ty Templeton-c 3.00

ENCHANTED
Sirius Entertainment: 1997 - No. 3 ($2.50, B&W, limited series)
1-3-Robert Chang-s/a 2.50

ENCHANTED (Volume 2)
Sirius Entertainment: 1998 - No. 3 ($2.95, limited series)
1-Robert Chang-s/a 3.00

ENCHANTED APPLES OF OZ, THE (See First Comics Graphic Novel #5)

ENCHANTER
Eclipse Comics: Apr, 1987 - No. 3, Aug. 1987 ($2.00, B&W, limited series)
1-3 2.25

ENCHANTING LOVE
Kirby Publishing Co.: Oct, 1949 - No. 6, July, 1950 (All 52 pgs.)
1-Photo-c 15 30 45 83 117 150
2-Photo-c; Powell-a 9 18 27 51 62 75
3,4,6: 3-Jimmy Stewart photo-c 8 16 24 46 58 70
5-Ingels-a, 9 pgs.; photo-c 15 30 45 86 123 160

ENCHANTMENT VISUALETTES (Magazine)
World Editions: Dec, 1949 - No. 5, Apr, 1950 (Painted c-1)
1-Contains two romance comic strips each 15 30 45 83 117 150
2 11 22 33 62 84 105
3-5 10 20 30 56 73 90

ENEMY
Dark Horse Comics: May, 1994 - No. 5, Sept, 1994 ($2.50, limited series)
1-5 2.50

ENEMY ACE SPECIAL (Also see Our Army at War #151, Showcase #57, 58 & Star Spangled War Stories #138)
DC Comics: 1990 ($1.00, one-shot)
1-Kubert-r/Our Army #151,153; c-r/Showcase 57 5.00

ENEMY ACE: WAR IDYLL
DC Comics: 1990 (Graphic novel)
Hardcover-George Pratt-s/painted-a/c 30.00
Softcover (1991, $14.95) 15.00

ENEMY ACE: WAR IN HEAVEN
DC Comics: 2001 - No. 2, 2001 ($5.95, squarebound, limited series)
1,2-Ennis-s; Von Hammer in WW2. 1-Weston & Alamy-a. 2-Heath-a 6.00
TPB (2003, $14.95) r/#1,2 & Star Spangled War Stories #139; Jim Dietz-painted-c 15.00

ENGINEHEAD
DC Comics: June, 2004 - No. 6, Nov, 2004 ($2.50, limited series)
1-6-Joe Kelly-s/Ted McKeever-a/c. 6-Metal Men app. 2.50

ENIGMA
DC Comics (Vertigo): Mar, 1993 - No. 8, Oct, 1993 ($2.50, limited series)
1-8: Milligan scripts 2.50
Trade paperback ($19.95)-reprints 20.00

ENO AND PLUM (Also see Cud Comics)
Oni Press: Mar, 1998 ($2.95, B&W)
1-Terry LaBan-s/c/a 3.00

ENSIGN O'TOOLE (TV)
Dell Publishing Co.: Aug-Oct, 1963 - No. 2, 1964
1 4 8 12 22 30 38
2 3 6 9 18 24 30

ENSIGN PULVER (See Movie Classics)

EPIC
Marvel Comics (Epic Comics): 1992 - Book 4, 1992 ($4.95, lim. series, 52 pgs.)
Book One-Four: 2-Dorman painted-c 5.00
NOTE: *Alien Legion in #3. Cholly & Flytrap by* ***Burden****(scripts) &* ***Suydam****(art) in 3, 4. Dinosaurs in #4. Dreadlands in #1. Hellraiser in #1. Nightbreed in #2. Sleeze Brothers in #2. Stalkers in #1-4. Wild Cards in #1-4.*

EPIC ANTHOLOGY
Marvel Comics (Epic Comics): Apr, 2004 - Present ($5.99)
1-Short stories by various 6.00

EPIC ILLUSTRATED (Magazine)
Marvel Comics Group: Spring, 1980 - No. 34, Feb, 1986 ($2.00/$2.50, B&W/color, mature)
1-Frazetta-c; Silver Surfer/Galactus-sty; Wendy Pini-s/a; Suydam-s/a; Metamorphosis Odyssey begins (thru #9) Starlin-a 2 4 6 8 10 12
2-10: 2-Bissette/Veitch-a; Goodwin-s. 3-Goodwin-s. 4-Ellison 15 pg. story w/art by Steacy; Hempel-s/a; Veitch-s/a. 5-Hildebrandts-c/interview; Jusko-a; Vess-s/a. 6-Ellison-s (26 pgs). 7-Adams-s/a(16 pgs.); BWS interview. 8-Suydam-s/a; Vess-s/a. 9-Conrad-c. 10-Marada the She-Wolf-c/sty(21 pgs.) by Claremont/Bolton 1 2 3 4 5 7

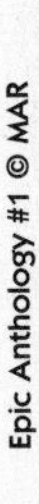
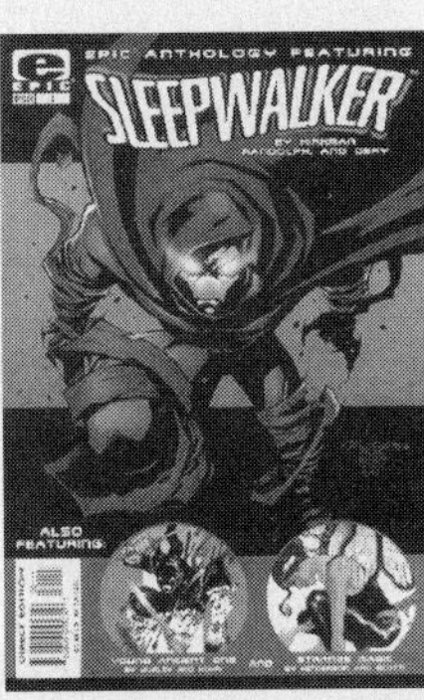

Epic Anthology #1 © MAR

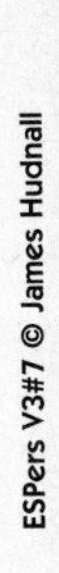

ESPers V3#7 © James Hudnall

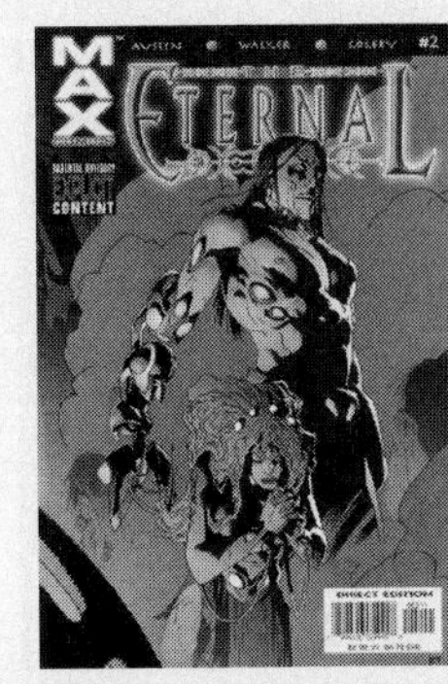

The Eternal #2 © MAR

	GD	VG	FN	VF	VF/NM	NM-
	2.0	4.0	6.0	8.0	9.0	9.2

GD VG FN VF VF/NM NM- 2.0 4.0 6.0 8.0 9.0 9.2

11-20: 11-Wood-a; Jusko-a. 12-Wolverton Spacehawk-r edited & recolored w/article on him; Muth-a. 13-Blade Runner preview by Williamson. 14-Elric of Melnibone by Russell; Revenge of the Jedi preview. 15-Vallejo-c & interview; 1st Dreadstar story (cont'd in Dreadstar #1). 16-B. Smith-c/a(2); Sim-s/a. 17-Starslammers preview. 18-Go Nagai; Williams-a. 19-Jabberwocky w/Hampton-a; Cheech Wizard-s. 20-The Sacred & the Profane begins by Ken Steacy; Elric by Gould; Williams-a 1 2 3 5 6 8

21-30: 21-Vess-s/a. 22-Frankenstein w/Wrightson-a. 26-Galactus series begins (thru #34); Cerebus the Aardvark story by Dave Sim. 27-Groo. 28-Cerebus. 29-1st Sheeva. 30-Cerebus; History of Dreadstar, Starlin-s/a; Williams-a; Vess-a 1 3 4 6 8 10

31-33: 31-Bolton-c/a. 32-Cerebus portfolio. 2 4 6 8 10 12

34-R.E.Howard tribute by Thomas-s/Plunkett-a; Moore-s/Veitch-a; Cerebus; Cholly & Flytrap w/Suydam-a; BWS-a 2 4 6 11 14 18

NOTE: ***N. Adams*** *a-7; c-6.* ***Austin*** *a-15-20i.* ***Bode*** *a-19, 23, 27r.* ***Bolton*** *a-7, 10-12, 15, 18, 22-25; c-10, 18, 22, 23.* ***Boris*** *c/a-15.* ***Brunner*** *c-12.* ***Buscema*** *a-1p, 9p, 11-13p.* ***Byrne/Austin*** *a-26-34.* ***Chaykin*** *a-2; c-8.* ***Conrad*** *a-2-5, 7-9, 25-34; c-17.* ***Corben*** *a-15; c-2.* ***Frazetta*** *c-1.* ***Golden*** *a-3r.* ***Gulacy*** *c/a-3.* ***Jeff Jones*** *c-25.* ***Kaluta*** *a-17r, 21, 24r, 26; c-4, 28.* ***Nebres*** *a-1.* ***Reese*** *a-12.* ***Russell*** *a-2-4, 9, 14, 33; c-14.* ***Simonson*** *a-17.* ***B. Smith*** *c/a-7, 16.* ***Starlin*** *a-1-9, 14, 15, 34.* ***Steranko*** *c-19.* ***Williamson*** *a-13, 27, 34.* ***Wrightson*** *a-13p, 22, 25, 27, 34; c-30.*

EPIC LITE
Marvel Comics (Epic Comics): Sept, 1991 ($3.95, 52 pgs., one-shot)

1-Bob the Alien, Normalman by Valentino 4.00

EPICURUS THE SAGE
DC Comics (Piranha Press): Vol. 1, 1991 - Vol. 2, 1991 ($9.95, 8-1/8x10-7/8")

Volume 1,2-Sam Kieth-c/a; Messner-Loebs-s 10.00
TPB (2003, $19.95) r/ #1,2, Fast Forward Rising the Sun; new story 20.00

EPSILON WAVE
Independent Comics/Elite Comics No. 5 on: Oct, 1985 - V2#2, 1987 ($1.50/$1.25/$1.75)

1-8,V2#1,2: 1-3,6-Seadragon app. V2 (B&W) 2.25

ERADICATOR
DC Comics: Aug, 1996 - No. 3, Oct, 1996 ($1.75, limited series)

1-3: Superman app. 3.00

ERNIE COMICS (Formerly Andy Comics #21; All Love Romances #26 on)
Current Books/Ace Periodicals: No. 22, Sept, 1948 - No. 25, Mar, 1949

nn (9/48,11/48; #22,23)-Teenage humor 8 16 24 40 50 60
24,25 6 12 18 28 34 40

ESCAPADE IN FLORENCE (See Movie Comics)

ESCAPE FROM DEVIL'S ISLAND
Avon Periodicals: 1952

1-Kinstler-c; r/as Dynamic Adventures #9 40 80 120 230 335 440

ESCAPE FROM THE PLANET OF THE APES (See Power Record Comics)

ESCAPE TO WITCH MOUNTAIN (See Walt Disney Showcase No. 29)

ESCAPIST (See Michael Chabon Presents The Amazing Adventures of the Escapist)

ESPERS (Also see Interface)
Eclipse Comics: July, 1986 - No. 5, Apr, 1987 ($1.25/$1.75, Mando paper)

1-5-James Hudnall story & David Lloyd-a. 3.00

ESPERS
Halloween Comics: V2#1, 1996 - No. 6, 1997 ($2.95, B&W)
(1st Halloween Comics series)

V2#1-6: James D. Hudnall scripts 3.00
Undertow TPB ('98, $14.95) r/#1-6 15.00

ESPERS
Image Comics: V3#1, 1997 - Present ($2.95, B&W, limited series)

V3#1-7: James D. Hudnall scripts 3.00
Black Magic TPB ('98, $14.95) r/#1-4 15.00

ESPIONAGE (TV)
Dell Publishing Co.: May-July, 1964 - No. 2, Aug-Oct, 1964

1,2 4 8 12 24 32 40

ESSENTIAL (Title series), **Marvel Comics**

--ANT-MAN, '02 (B&W- r) V1-Reprints app. from Tales To Astonish #27, #35-69; Kirby-c 15.00

--AVENGERS, '98 (B&W- r) V1-R-Avengers #1-24; new Immonen-c 15.00
V2(6/00)-Reprints Avengers #25-46, King-Size Special #1; Immonen-c 15.00
V3(3/01)-Reprints Avengers #47-68, Annual #2; Immonen-c 15.00
V4('04)-Reprints Avengers #69-97, Incredible Hulk #140; Neal Adams-c 17.00

--CAPTAIN AMERICA, '00 (B&W- r) V1-Reprints stories from Tales of Suspense #59-99, Captain America #100-102; new Romita & Milgrom-c 15.00
V2(1/02)-Reprints #103-126; Steranko-c 15.00

--CONAN, '00 (B&W- r) V1-R-Conan the Barbarian#1-25; new Buscema-c 15.00

--DAREDEVIL, '02 - Present (B&W-r)
V1-R-Daredevil #1-25 15.00
V2-($16.99) R-Daredevil #26-48, Special #1, Fantastic Four #73 17.00

--FANTASTIC FOUR, '98 - Present (B&W-r)
V1-Reprints FF #1-20, Annual #1; new Alan Davis-c 15.00
V2-Reprints FF #21-40, Annual #2; Davis and Farmer-c 15.00
V3-Reprints FF #41-63, Annual #3,4; Davis-c 15.00

--HOWARD THE DUCK, '02 (B&W- r) V1-Reprints #1-27, Annual #1; plus stories from Marvel Treasury Ed. #12, Man-Thing #1, Giant-Size Man-Thing #4,5, Fear #19; Bolland-c 15.00

--HULK, '99 (B&W-r) V1-R-Incred. Hulk #1-6, Tales To Astonish stories; new Timm-c 15.00
V2-Reprints Tales To Astonish #102-117, Annual #1 15.00

--HUMAN TORCH, '03 (B&W-r) V1-Strange Tales #101-134 & Ann. 2; Kirby-c 15.00

--IRON MAN, '00 - Present (B&W-r)
V1-Tales Of Suspense #39-72; new Timm-c and back-c 15.00
V2-Tales Of Suspense #73-99, Tales To Astonish #82 & Iron Man #1-11 17.00

--MARVEL TEAM-UP, '02 (B&W-r) V1-R/#1-24 15.00

--MONSTER OF FRANKENSTEIN, '04 (B&W-r) V1-Reprints Monster of Frankenstein #1-5, Frankenstein Monster #6-18, Giant-Size Werewolf #2, Monsters Unleashed #2,4-10 & Legion of Monsters #1 17.00

--PUNISHER, '04 (B&W-r) V1-Reprints early app. in Amazing Spider-Man, Captain America, Daredevil, Marvel Preview and Punisher #1-5 15.00

--SILVER SURFER, '98 (B&W-r) V1-R-material from SS#1-18 and Fantastic Four Ann. #5 15.00

--SPIDER-MAN, '96 - Present (B&W-r)
V1-R-AF #15, Amaz. S-M #1-20, Ann. #1 (2 printings) 15.00
V2-R-Amaz. Spider-Man #21-43, Annual #2,3 15.00
V3-R-Amaz. Spider-Man #44-68 15.00
V4-R-Amaz. Spider-Man #69-89; Annual #4,5; new Timm-f&b-c 15.00
V5-R-Amaz. Spider-Man #90-113; new Romita-c 15.00
V6-R-Amaz. Spider-Man #114-137, Giant-Size Super-Heroes #1 G-S S-M #1,2 17.00

--SUPER-VILLAIN TEAM-UP, '04 (B&W-r) V1-r/S-V T-U #1-14 & 16-17, Giant-Size S-V T-U #1,2; Avengers #154-156; Champions #16, & Astonishing Tales #1-8 17.00

--THOR, '01 (B&W-r) V1-R-Journey Into Mystery #83-112 15.00

--TOMB OF DRACULA, '03 - Present (B&W-r) V1-R-Tomb of Dracula #1-25, Werewolf By Night #15, Giant-Size Chillers #1 15.00
V2-($16.99) R-Tomb of Dracula #26-49, Giant-Size Dracula #2-5, Dr. Strange #14 17.00
V3-($16.99) R-Tomb of Dracula #50-70, Tomb of Dracula Magazine #1-4 17.00

--UNCANNY X-MEN, '99 - Present (B&W reprints)
V1-Reprints X-Men (1st series) #1-24; Timm-c 15.00

ESSENTIAL VERTIGO: THE SANDMAN
DC Comics (Vertigo): Aug, 1996 - No. 32, Mar, 1999 ($1.95/$2.25, reprints)

1-13,15-31: Reprints Sandman, 2nd series 3.00
14-($2.95) 3.50
32-($4.50) Reprints Sandman Special #1 4.50

ESSENTIAL VERTIGO: SWAMP THING
DC Comics: Nov, 1996 - No. 24, Oct, 1998 ($1.95/$2.25,B&W, reprints)

1-11,13-24: 1-9-Reprints Alan Moore's Swamp Thing stories 3.00
12-($3.50) r/Annual #2 3.50

ESSENTIAL WOLVERINE
Marvel Comics: 1999 - Present (B&W reprints)

V1-r/#1-23, V2-r/#24-47, V3-R/#48-69 15.00

ESSENTIAL X-MEN
Marvel Comics: 1996 - Present (B&W reprints)

V1-V4: V1-R/Giant Size X-Men #1, X-Men #94-119. V2-R-X-Men #120-144. V3-R-Uncanny X-Men #145-161, Ann. #3-5. V4-Uncanny X-Men #162-179, Ann. #6 15.00
V5-($16.99) R/Uncanny X-Men #180-198, Ann. #7-8 17.00

ESTABLISHMENT, THE (Also see The Authority and The Monarchy)
DC Comics (WildStorm): Nov, 2001 - No. 13, Nov, 2002 ($2.50)

1-13-Edginton-s/Adlard-a 2.50

ETC
DC Comics (Piranha Press): 1989 - No. 5, 1990 ($4.50, 60 pgs., mature)

Book 1-5: Conrad scripts/layouts in all 4.50

ETERNAL, THE
Marvel Comics (MAX): Aug, 2003 - No. 6, Jan, 2004 ($2.99, mature)

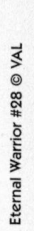

The Eternals #17 © MAR

Eternal Warrior #28 © VAL

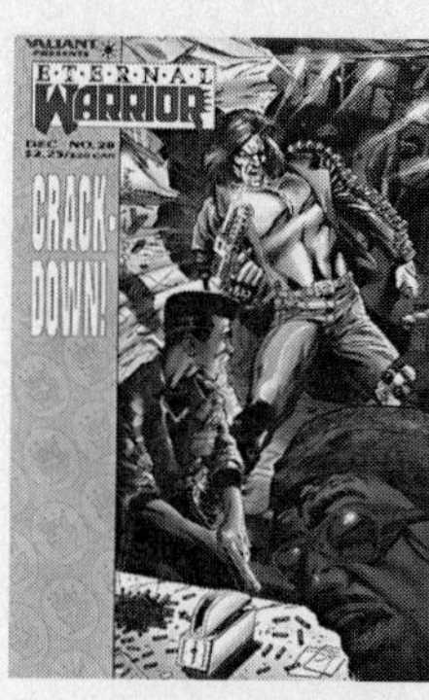

Even More Fund Comics 2004 © Sky Dog Press

1-6-Austen-s/Walker-a 3.00

ETERNAL BIBLE, THE
Authentic Publications: 1946 (Large size) (16 pgs. in color)

1 15 30 45 86 123 160

ETERNALS, THE
Marvel Comics Group: July, 1976 - No. 19, Jan, 1978

1-(Regular 25¢ edition)-Origin & 1st app. Eternals 2 4 6 14 18 22
1-(30¢-c variant, limited distribution) 3 6 9 19 26 33
2-(Reg. 25¢ edition)-1st app. Ajak & The Celestials 1 3 4 6 8 10
2-(30¢-c variant, limited distribution) 2 4 6 10 12 15
3-19: 14,15-Cosmic powered Hulk-c/story 1 2 3 5 7 9
12-16-(35¢-c variants, limited distribution) 2 4 6 9 11 14
Annual 1(10/77) 1 2 3 5 7 9
NOTE: *Kirby c/a(p) in all.*

ETERNALS, THE
Marvel Comics: Oct, 1985 - No. 12, Sept, 1986 (Maxi-series, mando paper)

1,12 (52 pgs.): 12-Williamson-a(i) 3.00
2-11 2.50

ETERNALS: THE HEROD FACTOR
Marvel Comics: Nov, 1991 ($2.50, 68 pgs.)

1 2.50

ETERNAL WARRIOR (See Solar #10 & 11)
Valiant/Acclaim Comics (Valiant): Aug, 1992 - No. 50, Mar, 1996 ($2.25/$2.50)

1-Unity x-over; Miller-c; origin Eternal Warrior & Aram (Armstrong) 4.00
1-($2.25-c) Gold logo 5.00
1-Gold foil logo on embossed cover; no cover price 6.00
2-8: 2-Unity x-over; Simonson-c. 3-Archer & Armstrong x-over. 4-1st brief app. Bloodshot (last pg.); see Rai #0 for 1st full app.; Cowan-c. 5-2nd full app. Bloodshot (12/92; see Rai #0). 6,7: 6-2nd app. Master Darque. 8-Flip book w/Archer & Armstrong #8 3.00
9-25,27-34: 9-1st Book of Geomancer. 14-16-Bloodshot app. 18-Doctor Mirage cameo. 19-Doctor Mirage app. 22-W/bound-in trading card. 25-Archer & Armstrong app.; cont'd from A&A #25 2.50
26-($2.75, 44 pgs.)-Flip book w/Archer & Armstrong 2.75
35-50: 35-Double-c; $2.50-c begins. 50-Geomancer app. 2.50
Special 1 (2/96, $2.50)-Wings of Justice; Art Holcomb script 2.50
Yearbook 1 (1993, $3.95), 2(1994, $3.95) 4.00

ETERNAL WARRIORS: BLACKWORKS
Acclaim Comics (Valiant Heroes): Mar, 1998 ($3.50, one-shot)

1 3.50

ETERNAL WARRIORS: DIGITAL ALCHEMY
Acclaim Comics (Valiant Heroes): Vol. 2, Sep, 1997 ($3.95, one-shot, 64 pgs.)

Vol. 2-Holcomb-s/Eaglesham-a(p) 4.00

ETERNAL WARRIORS: FIST AND STEEL
Acclaim Comics (Valiant): May, 1996 - No. 2, June, 1996 ($2.50, lim. series)

1,2: Geomancer app. in both. 1-Indicia reads "June." 2-Bo Hampton-a 2.50

ETERNAL WARRIORS: TIME AND TREACHERY
Acclaim Comics (Valiant Heroes): Vol. 1, Jun, 1997 ($3.95, one-shot, 48 pgs.)

Vol. 1-Reintro Aram, Archer, Ivar the Timewalker, & Gilad the Warmaster; 1st app. Shalla Redburn; Art Holcomb script 4.00

ETERNITY SMITH
Renegade Press: Sept, 1986 - No. 5, May, 1987 ($1.25/$1.50, 36 pgs.)

1-5: 1st app. Eternity Smith. 5-Death of Jasmine 2.25

ETERNITY SMITH
Hero Comics: Sept, 1987 - No. 9, 1988 ($1.95)

V2#1-9: 8-Indigo begins 2.25

ETTA KETT
King Features Syndicate/Standard: No. 11, Dec, 1948 - No. 14, Sept, 1949

11-Teenage 10 20 30 56 73 90
12-14 7 14 21 37 46 55

EUDAEMON, THE (See Dark Horse Presents #72-74)
Dark Horse Comics: Aug, 1993 - No. 3, Nov, 1993 ($2.50, limited series)

1-3: Nelson-a, painted-c & scripts 2.50

EUROPA AND THE PIRATE TWINS
Powder Monkey Productions: Oct, 1996 - No. 2, ($2.50, B&W, limited series)

1,2: Two covers 2.50

EVANGELINE (Also see Primer)
Comico/First Comics V2#1 on/Lodestone Publ.: 1984 - #2, 6/84; V2#1, 5/87 - V2#12, Mar, 1989 (Baxter paper)

1,2, V2#1 (5/87) - 12, Special #1 (1986, $2.00)-Lodestone Publ. 2.25

EVA THE IMP
Red Top Comic/Decker: 1957 - No. 2, Nov, 1957

1,2 5 10 14 20 24 28

EVEN MORE FUND COMICS (Benefit book for the Comic Book Legal Defense Fund) (Also see More Fund Comics)
Sky Dog Press: Sept, 2004 ($10.00, B&W, trade paperback)

nn-Anthology of short stories and pin-ups by various; Spider-Man-c by Cho 10.00

E.V.E. PROTOMECHA
Image Comics (Top Cow): Mar, 2000 - No. 6, Sept, 2000 ($2.50)

Preview ($5.95) Flip book w/Soul Saga preview 2 4 6 8 10 12
1-6: 1-Covers by Finch, Madureira, Garza. 2-Turner var-c 3.00
1-Another Universe variant-c 5.00
TPB (5/01, $17.95) r/#1-6 plus cover galley and sketch pages 18.00

EVERQUEST: ... (Based on online role-playing game)
DC Comics (WildStorm): 2002 ($5.95, one-shots)

The Ruins of Kunark - Jim Lee & Dan Norton-a; McQuaid & Lee-s; Lee-c 6.00
Transformations - Philip Tan-a; Devin Grayson-s; Portacio-c 6.00

EVERYBODY'S COMICS (See Fox Giants)

EVERYMAN, THE
Marvel Comics (Epic Comics): Nov, 1991 ($4.50, one-shot, 52 pgs.)

1-Mike Allred-a 1 2 3 4 5 7

EVERYTHING HAPPENS TO HARVEY
National Periodical Publications: Sept-Oct, 1953 - No. 7, Sept-Oct, 1954

1 28 56 84 158 229 300
2 15 30 45 86 123 160
3-7 12 24 36 71 98 125

EVERYTHING'S ARCHIE
Archie Publications: May, 1969 - No. 157, Sept, 1991 (Giant issues No. 1-20)

1-(68 pages) 9 18 27 60 85 110
2-(68 pages) 6 12 18 38 52 65
3-5-(68 pages) 4 8 12 29 40 50
6-13-(68 pages) 3 6 9 19 25 32
14-31-(52 pages) 2 4 6 12 16 20
32 (7/74)-50 (8/76) 1 3 4 6 8 10
51-80 (12/79),100 (4/82) 1 2 3 5 6 8
81-99 6.00
101-120 5.00
121-156: 142,148-Gene Colan-a 4.00
157-Last issue 5.00

EVERYTHING'S DUCKY (Movie)
Dell Publishing Co.: No. 1251, 1961

Four Color 1251 6 12 18 38 52 65

EVIL ERNIE
Eternity Comics: Dec, 1991 - No. 5, 1992 ($2.50, B&W, limited series)

1-1st app. Lady Death by Steven Hughes (12,000 print run); Lady Death app. in all issues 4 8 12 29 40 50
2,3: 2-1st Lady Death-c. 2,3-(7,000 print run) 3 6 9 16 20 25
4-(8,000 print run) 2 4 6 12 16 20
5 2 4 6 10 13 16
Special Edition 1 3 6 9 16 20 25
Youth Gone Wild! ($9.95, trade paperback)-r/#1-5 1 3 4 6 8 10
Youth Gone Wild! Director's Cut ($4.95)-Limited to 15,000, shows the making of the comic 5.00

EVIL ERNIE (Monthly series)
Chaos! Comics: July, 1998 - No. 10, Apr, 1999 ($2.95)

1-10-Pulido & Nutman-s/Brewer-a 3.00
1-($10.00) Premium Ed. 10.00

EVIL ERNIE: BADDEST BATTLES
Chaos! Comics: Jan, 1997 ($1.50, one-shot)

1-Pin-ups, 1-Variant-c 3.00

EVIL ERNIE: DEPRAVED
Chaos! Comics: Jul, 1999 - No. 3, Sept, 1999 ($2.95, limited series)

1-3-Pulido-s/Brewer-a 3.00

Evil Ernie #1 © Chaos!

Excalibur #2 © MAR

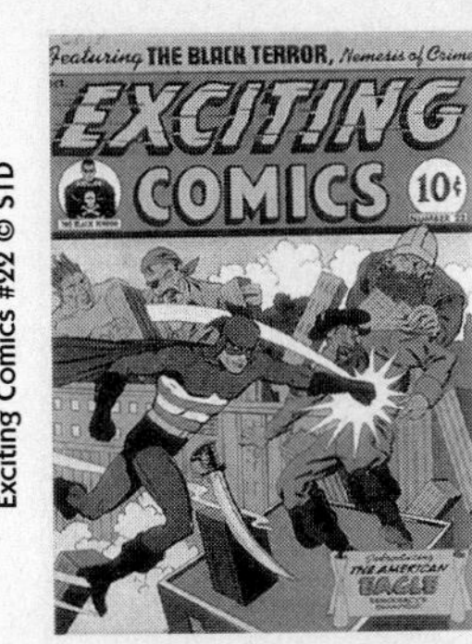

Exciting Comics #22 © STD

EVIL ERNIE: DESTROYER
Chaos! Comics: Oct, 1997 - No. 9, Jun, 1998 ($2.95, limited series)

	GD 2.0	VG 4.0	FN 6.0	VF 8.0	VF/NM 9.0	NM- 9.2
Preview ($2.50), 1-9-Flip cover						3.00

EVIL ERNIE: PIECES OF ME
Chaos! Comics: Nov, 2000 ($2.95, B&W, one-shot)

	GD	VG	FN	VF	VF/NM	NM-
1-Flashback story; Pulido-s/Beck-a						3.00

EVIL ERNIE: RELENTLESS
Chaos! Comics (Black Label Graphics): May, 2002 ($4.99, B&W, one-shot)

	GD	VG	FN	VF	VF/NM	NM-
1-Pulido-s/Beck, Bonk, & Brewer-a						5.00

EVIL ERNIE: RETURNS
Chaos! Comics (Black Label Graphics): Oct, 2001 ($3.99, B&W, one-shot)

	GD	VG	FN	VF	VF/NM	NM-
1-Pulido-s/Beck-a						4.00

EVIL ERNIE: REVENGE
Chaos! Comics: Oct, 1994 - No.4, Feb, 1995 ($2.95, limited series)

	GD	VG	FN	VF	VF/NM	NM-
1-Glow-in-the-dark-c; Lady Death app. 1-3-flip book w. Kilzone Preview (series of 3)						5.00
1-Commemorative-(4000 print run)	1	3	4	6	8	10
2-4						4.00
Trade paperback (10/95, $12.95)						13.00

EVIL ERNIE: STRAIGHT TO HELL
Chaos! Comics: Oct, 1995 - No. 5, May, 1996 ($2.95, limited series)

	GD	VG	FN	VF	VF/NM	NM-
1-5: 1-fold-out-c						3.00
1,3:1-($19.95) Chromium Ed. 3-Chastity Chase-c-(4000 printed)						20.00
Special Edition (10,000)						20.00

EVIL ERNIE: THE RESURRECTION
Chaos! Comics: 1993 - No. 4, 1994 (Limited series)

	GD	VG	FN	VF	VF/NM	NM-
0						5.00
1	2	4	6	8	10	12
1A-Gold	3	6	9	18	24	30
2-4	1	2	3	5	6	8

EVIL ERNIE VS. THE MOVIE MONSTERS
Chaos! Comics: Mar, 1997 ($2.95, one-shot)

	GD	VG	FN	VF	VF/NM	NM-
1						3.00
1-Variant-"Chaos-Scope•Terror Vision" card stock-c						5.00

EVIL ERNIE VS. THE SUPER HEROES
Chaos! Comics: Aug, 1995; Sept, 1998 ($2.95)

	GD	VG	FN	VF	VF/NM	NM-
1-Lady Death poster						3.00
1-Foil-c variant (limited to 10,000)	2	4	6	12	16	20
1-Limited Edition (1000)	2	4	6	12	16	20
2-(9/98) Ernie vs. JLA and Marvel parodies						3.00

EVIL ERNIE: WAR OF THE DEAD
Chaos! Comics: Nov, 1999 - No. 3, Jan, 2000 ($2.95, limited series)

	GD	VG	FN	VF	VF/NM	NM-
1-3-Pulido & Kaminski-s/Brewer-a. 3-End of Evil Ernie						3.00

EVIL EYE
Fantagraphics Books: June, 1998 - Present ($2.95/$3.50/$3.95, B&W)

	GD	VG	FN	VF	VF/NM	NM-
1-7-Richard Sala-s/a						3.00
8-10-($3.50)						3.50
11,12-($3.95)						4.00

EVO (Crossover from Tomb Raider #25 & Witchblade #60)
Image Comics (Top Cow): Feb, 2003 ($2.99, one-shot)

	GD	VG	FN	VF	VF/NM	NM-
1-Silvestri-c/a(p); Endgame x-over pt. 3; Sara Pezzini & Lara Croft app.						3.00

EWOKS (Star Wars) (TV) (See Star Comics Magazine)
Marvel Comics (Star Comics): June, 1985 - No. 14, Jul, 1987 (75¢/$1.00)

	GD	VG	FN	VF	VF/NM	NM-
1,10: 10-Williamson-a (From Star Wars)	2	4	6	10	12	15
2-9	2	4	6	8	10	12
11-14: 14-($1.00-c)	2	4	6	9	11	14

EXCALIBUR (Also see Marvel Comics Presents #31)
Marvel Comics: Apr, 1988; Oct, 1988 - No. 125, Oct, 1998 ($1.50/$1.75/$1.99)

	GD	VG	FN	VF	VF/NM	NM-
Special Edition nn (The Sword is Drawn)(4/88, $3.25)-1st Excalibur comic						6.00
Special Edition nn (4/88)-no price on-c	1	3	4	6	8	10
Special Edition nn (2nd & print, 10/88, 12/89)						3.00
...The Sword is Drawn (Apr, 1992, $4.95)						5.00
1($1.50, 10/88)-X-Men spin-off; Nightcrawler, Shadowcat(Kitty Pryde), Capt. Britain, Phoenix & Meggan begin						5.00
2-4						4.00
5-10						3.00
11-49,51-70,72-74,76: 10,11-Rogers/Austin-a. 21-Intro Crusader X. 22-Iron Man x-over. 24-John Byrne app. in story. 26-Ron Lim-c/a. 27-B. Smith-a(p). 37-Dr. Doom & Iron Man app. 41-X-Men (Wolverine) app.; Cable cameo. 49-Neal Adams c-swipe. 52,57-X-Men (Cyclops, Wolverine) app. 53-Spider-Man-c/story. 58-X-Men (Wolverine, Gambit, Cyclops, etc.)-c/story. 61-Phoenix returns. 68-Starjammers-c/story						2.50
50-($2.75, 56 pgs.)-New logo						3.00
71-($3.95, 52 pgs.)-Hologram on-c; 30th anniversary						5.00
75-($3.50, 52 pgs.)-Holo-grafx foil-c						4.00
75-($2.25, 52 pgs.)-Regular edition						2.50
77-81,83-86: 77-Begin $1.95-c; bound-in trading card sheet. 83-86-Deluxe Editions and Standard Editions. 86-1st app. Pete Wisdom						2.50
82-($2.50)-Newsstand edition						3.00
82-($3.50)-Enhanced edition						4.00
87-89,91-99,101-110: 87-Return from Age of Apocalypse. 92-Colossus-c/app. 94-Days of Future Tense 95-X-Man-c/app. 96-Sebastian Shaw & the Hellfire Club app. 99-Onslaught app. 101-Onslaught tie-in. 102-w/card insert. 103-Last Warren Ellis scripts; Belasco app. 104,105-Hitch & Neary-c/a. 109-Spiral-c/app.						2.50
90,100-($2.95)-double-sized. 100-Onslaught tie-in; wraparound-c						4.00
111-124: 111-Begin $1.99-c, wraparound-c. 119-Calafiore-a						2.50
125-($2.99) Wedding of Capt. Britain and Meggan						4.00
Annual 1,2 ('93, '94, 68 pgs.)-1st app. Khaos. 2-X-Men & Psylocke app.						3.00
#(-1) Flashback (7/97)						2.50
...Air Apparent nn (12/91, $4.95)-Simonson-c						5.00
...Mojo Mayhem nn (12/89, $4.50)-Art Adams/Austin-c/a						5.00
...: The Possession nn (7/91, $2.95, 52 pgs.)						3.00
...: XX Crossing (7/92, 5/92-inside, $2.50)-vs. The X-Men						2.50

EXCALIBUR
Marvel Comics: Feb, 2001 - No. 4, May, 2001 ($2.99)

	GD	VG	FN	VF	VF/NM	NM-
1-4-Return of Captain Britain; Raimondi-a						3.00

EXCALIBUR (X-Men Reloaded title)
Marvel Comics: July, 2004 - Present ($2.99)

	GD	VG	FN	VF	VF/NM	NM-
1-7-Claremont-s/Lopresti-a/Park-c; Magneto returns. 6,7-Beast app.						3.00
... Vol. 1: Forging the Sword (2004, $9.99) r/#1-4						10.00

EXCITING COMICS
Nedor/Better Publications/Standard Comics: Apr, 1940 - No. 69, Sept, 1949

	GD	VG	FN	VF	VF/NM	NM-
1-Origin & 1st app. The Mask, Jim Hatfield, Sgt. Bill King, Dan Williams begin; early Robot-c (see Smash #1)	393	786	1179	2555	4128	5700
2-The Sphinx begins; The Masked Rider app.; Son of the Gods begins, ends #8	173	346	519	1081	1666	2250
3-Robot-c	119	238	357	744	1147	1550
4-6	77	154	231	481	741	1000
7,8	62	124	186	388	594	800
9-Origin/1st app. of The Black Terror & sidekick Tim, begin series (5/41) (Black Terror c-9-21,23-52,54,55)	903	1806	2709	6321	10,161	14,000
10-2nd app. Black Terror	289	578	867	1806	2778	3750
11	146	292	438	913	1407	1900
12,13	96	192	288	600	925	1250
14-Last Sphinx, Dan Williams	67	134	201	419	642	865
15-The Liberator begins (origin)	69	138	207	431	666	900
16-20: 20-The Mask ends	56	112	168	350	538	725
21,23-25: 25-Robot-c	48	96	144	293	447	600
22-Origin The Eaglet; The American Eagle begins	56	112	168	350	538	725
26-Schomburg-c begin	65	130	195	406	628	850
27,29,30	60	120	180	375	580	785
28-(Scarce) Crime Crusader begins, ends #58	92	184	276	575	888	1200
31-38: 35-Liberator ends, not in 31-33	55	110	165	336	511	685
39-Origin Kara, Jungle Princess	65	130	195	406	623	840
40-50: 42-The Scarab begins. 45-Schomburg Robot-c. 49-Last Kara, Jungle Princess. 50-Last American Eagle	57	114	171	356	548	740
51-Miss Masque begins (1st app.)	62	124	186	388	594	800
52-54: Miss Masque ends. 53-Miss Masque-c	55	110	165	336	511	685
55-58: 55-Judy of the Jungle begins (origin), ends #69; 1 pg. Ingels-a; Judy of the Jungle c-56-66. 57,58-Airbrush-c	55	110	165	336	511	685
59-Frazetta art in Caniff style; signed Frank Frazeta (one t), 9 pgs.	55	110	165	340	520	700
60-66: 60-Rick Howard, the Mystery Rider begins. 66-Robinson/Meskin-a	50	100	150	305	465	625
67-69-All western covers	22	44	66	123	177	230

NOTE: ***Schomburg (Xela)** c-26-68; airbrush c-57-66. Black Terror by **R. Moreira**-#65. **Roussos** a-62. Bondage-c 9, 12, 13, 20, 23, 25, 30, 59.*

EXCITING ROMANCES
Fawcett Publications: 1949 (nd); No. 2, Spring, 1950 - No. 5, 10/50; No. 6 (1951, nd); No. 7,

Exiles #22 © MAR

Ex Machina #1 © Vaughan & Harris

Exposed #4 © DS

	GD 2.0	VG 4.0	FN 6.0	VF 8.0	VF/NM 9.0	NM- 9.2

9/51 -No. 12, 1/53

1,3: 1(1949). 3-Wood-a	14	28	42	79	110	140
2,4,5-(1950)	9	18	27	54	70	85
6-12	8	16	24	46	58	70

NOTE: ***Powell** a-8-10. **Marcus Swayze** a-5, 6, 9. Photo c-1-7, 10-12.*

EXCITING ROMANCE STORIES (See Fox Giants)

EXCITING WAR (Korean War)
Standard Comics (Better Publ.): No. 5, Sept, 1952 - No. 8, May, 1953; No. 9, Nov, 1953

5	9	18	27	54	70	85
6,7,9	7	14	21	35	43	50
8-Toth-a	8	16	24	46	58	70

EXCITING X-PATROL
Marvel Comics (Amalgam): June, 1997 ($1.95, one-shot)

1-Barbara Kesel-s/ Bryan Hitch-a 2.50

EXILES (Also see Break-Thru)
Malibu Comics (Ultraverse): Aug, 1993 - No. 4, Nov, 1993 ($1.95)

1,2,4: 1,2-Bagged copies of each exist. 2-Gustovich-c. 4-Team dies; story cont'd in Break-Thru #1 2.25
3-($2.50, 40 pgs.)-Rune flip-c/story by B. Smith (3 pgs.) 2.50

1-Holographic-c edition	1	2	3	5	6	8

EXILES (All New, The) (2nd Series) (Also see Black September)
Malibu Comics (Ultraverse): Sept, 1995 - V2#11, Aug, 1996 ($1.50)

Infinity (9/95, $1.50)-Intro new team including Marvel's Juggernaut & Reaper 2.25

Infinity (2000 signed), V2#1 (2000 signed)	1	3	4	6	8	10

V2#1-4,6-11: 1-(10/95, 64 pgs.)-Reprint of Ultraforce V2#1 follows lead story. 2-1st app. Hellblade. 8-Intro Maxis. 11-Vs. Maxis; Ripfire app.; cont'd in Ultraforce #12 2.25
V2#5-($2.50) Juggernaut returns to the Marvel Universe. 2.50

EXILES (Also see X-Men titles)
Marvel Comics: Aug, 2001 - Present ($2.99/$2.25)

1-($2.99) Blink and parallel world X-Men; Winick-s/McKone & McKenna-a	1	2	3	4	5	7

2-10-($2.25) 2-Two covers (McKone & JH Williams III). 5-Alpha Flight app. 3.00
11-24: 22-Blink leaves; Magik joins. 23,24-Walker-a; alternate Weapon-X app. 2.25
25-55: 25-Begin $2.99-c; Inhumans app.; Walker-a. 26-30-Austen-s. 33-Wolverine app. 35-37-Fantastic Four app. 37-Sunfire dies, Blink returns. 38-40-Hyperion app. 3.00
TPB (3/02, $12.95) r/#1-4 13.00
...: A World Apart TPB (7/02, $14.99) r/#5-11 15.00
...: Vol. 3: Out of Time TPB (2003, $17.99) r/#12-19 18.00
...: Vol. 4: Legacy TPB (2003, $12.99) r/#20-25 13.00
...: Vol. 5: Unnatural Instinct TPB (2003, $14.99) r/#26-30 15.00
...: Vol. 6: Fantastic Voyage TPB (2004, $17.99) r/#31-37 18.00
...: Vol. 7: A Blink in Time TPB (2004, $19.99) r/#38-45 20.00
...: Vol. 8: Earn Your Wings TPB (2004, $14.99) r/#46-51 15.00

EXILES VS. THE X-MEN
Malibu Comics (Ultraverse): Oct, 1995 (one-shot)

0-Limited Super Premium Edition; signed w/certificate; gold foil logo, 0-Limited Premium Edition	1	3	4	6	8	10

EX MACHINA
DC Comics: Aug, 2004 - Present ($2.95)

1-Intro. Mitchell Hundred; Vaughan-s/Harris-a/c 4.00
2-7 3.00

EX-MUTANTS
Malibu Comics: Nov, 1992 - No. 18, Apr, 1994 ($1.95/$2.25/$2.50)

1-18: 1-Polybagged w/Skycap; prismatic cover 2.50

EXORCISTS (See The Crusaders)

EXOSQUAD (TV)
Topps Comics: No. 0, Jan, 1994 ($1.25)

0-($1.00, 20 pgs.)-1st app.; Staton-a(p); wraparound-c 2.25

EXOTIC ROMANCES (Formerly True War Romances)
Quality Comics Group (Comic Magazines): No. 22, Oct, 1955-No. 31, Nov, 1956

22	11	22	33	62	84	105
23-26,29	7	14	21	37	46	55
27,31-Baker-c/a	14	28	42	79	110	140
28,30-Baker-a	11	22	33	64	87	110

EXPLOITS OF DANIEL BOONE
Quality Comics Group: Nov, 1955 - No. 6, Oct, 1956

1-All have Cuidera-c(i)	28	56	84	158	229	300
2	19	38	57	107	154	200
3-6	16	32	48	89	127	165

EXPLOITS OF DICK TRACY (See Dick Tracy)

EXPLORER JOE
Ziff-Davis Comic Group (Approved Comics): Win, 1951 - No. 2, Oct-Nov, 1952

1-2: Saunders painted covers; 2-Krigstein-a	14	28	42	79	110	140

EXPLORERS OF THE UNKNOWN (See Archie Giant Series #587, 599)
Archie Comics: June, 1990 - No. 6, Apr, 1991 ($1.00)

1-6: Featuring Archie and the gang 3.00

EXPOSED (...True Crime Cases; ...Cases in the Crusade Against Crime #5-9)
D. S. Publishing Co.: Mar-Apr, 1948 - No. 9, July-Aug, 1949

1	24	48	72	138	199	260
2-Giggling killer story with excessive blood; two injury-to-eye panels; electrocution panel	30	60	90	170	245	320
3,8,9	12	24	36	71	98	125
4-Orlando-a	13	26	39	76	103	135
5-Breeze Lawson, Sky Sheriff by E. Good	13	26	39	76	103	135
6,7: 6-Ingels-a; used in **SOTI**, illo. "How to prepare an alibi" 7-Illo. in **SOTI**, "Diagram for housebreakers;" used by N.Y. Legis. Committee	37	74	111	209	305	400

EXPOSURE
Image Comics: 1999 - No. 4, 2000 ($2.50)

1-4: Al Rio-a/David Campiti-s. 1-Wraparound & photo covers 2.50
1-Variant-c 10.00
Prelude ($5.00) 5.00

EXPOSURE SECOND COMING
Avatar Press: Sept, 2000 ($3.50)

1-Al Rio-a/David Campiti-s; wraparound & photo covers 3.50

EXTINCT!
New England Comics Press: Wint, 1991-92 - No. 2, Fall, 1992 ($3.50, B&W)

1,2-Reprints and background info of "perfectly awful" Golden Age stories 3.50

EXTINCTION EVENT
DC Comics (WildStorm): Sept, 2003 - No. 5, Jan, 2004 ($2.50, limited series)

1-5-Booth-a/Weinberg-s 2.50

EXTRA!
E. C. Comics: Mar-Apr, 1955 - No. 5, Nov-Dec, 1955

1-Not code approved	19	38	57	143	212	280
2-5	12	24	36	90	135	180

NOTE: ***Craig, Crandall, Severin** art in all.*

EXTRA!
Gemstone Publishing: Jan, 2000 - No. 5, May, 2000 ($2.50)

1-5-Reprints E.C. series 2.50

EXTRA COMICS
Magazine Enterprises: 1948 (25¢, 3 comics in one)

1-Giant; consisting of rebound ME comics. Two versions known; (1)-Funnyman by Siegel & Shuster, Space Ace, Undercover Girl, Red Fox by L.B. Cole, Trail Colt & (2)-All Funnyman	55	110	165	336	511	685

EXTREME
Image Comics (Extreme Studios): Aug, 1993 (Giveaway)

0 3.00

EXTREME DESTROYER
Image Comics (Extreme Studios): Jan, 1996 ($2.50)

Prologue 1-Polybagged w/card; Liefeld-c, Epilogue 1-Liefeld-c 2.50

EXTREME JUSTICE
DC Comics: No. 0, Jan, 1995 - No. 18, July, 1996 ($1.50/$1.75)

0-18 3.00

EXTREMELY YOUNGBLOOD
Image Comics (Extreme Studios): Sept, 1996 ($3.50, one-shot)

1 3.50

EXTREME SACRIFICE
Image Comics (Extreme Studios): Jan, 1995 ($2.50, limited series)

Prelude (#1)-Liefeld wraparound-c; polybagged w/ trading card 2.50
Epilogue (#2)-Liefeld wraparound-c; polybagged w/trading card 2.50
Trade paperback (6/95, $16.95)-Platt-a 17.00

Fables #2 © Bill Willingham & DC

Fallen Angel #1 © Second Age

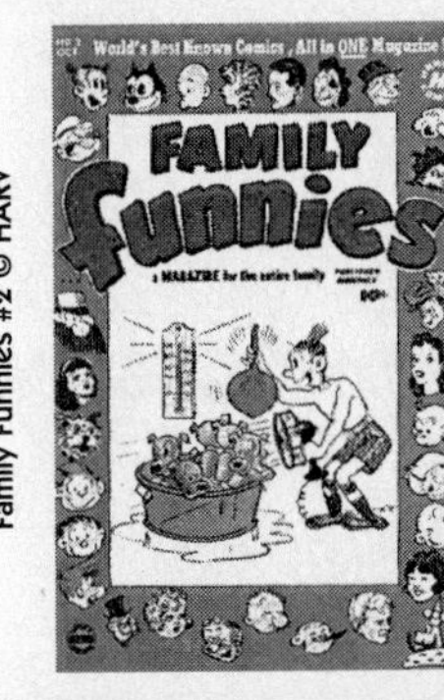

Family Funnies #2 © HARV

	GD	VG	FN	VF	VF/NM	NM-
	2.0	4.0	6.0	8.0	9.0	9.2

GD VG FN VF VF/NM NM- 2.0 4.0 6.0 8.0 9.0 9.2

EXTREME SUPER CHRISTMAS SPECIAL
Image Comics (Extreme Studios): Dec, 1994 ($2.95, one-shot)

1 — 3.00

EXTREMIST, THE
DC Comics (Vertigo): Sept, 1993 - No. 4, Dec, 1993 ($1.95, limited series)

1-4-Peter Milligan scripts; McKeever-c/a — 2.25
1-Platinum Edition — 5.00

EYE OF THE STORM
Rival Productions: Dec, 1994 - No. 7, June, 1995? ($2.95)

1-7: Computer generated comic — 3.00

EYE OF THE STORM
DC Comics (WildStorm): Sept, 2003 ($4.95)

Annual 1-Short stories by various incl. Portacio, Johns, Coker, Pearson, Arcudi — 5.00

FABLES
DC Comics (Vertigo): July, 2002 - Present ($2.50)

1-Willingham-s/Medina-a; two covers by Maleev & Jean — 8.00
2-Medina-a — 5.00
3-5 — 4.00
6-32: 6-10-Buckingham-a. 11-Talbot-a. 18-Medley-a. 26-Preview of The Witching — 2.50
6-RRP Edition wraparound variant-c; promotional giveaway for retailers (200 printed) — 50.00
Animal Farm (2003, $12.95, TPB) r/#6-10; sketch pages by Buckingham & Jean — 13.00
Legends in Exile (2002, $9.95, TPB) r/#1-5; new short story Willingham-s/a — 10.00
...: March of the Wooden Soldiers (2004, $17.95, TPB) r/#19-21 & ...: The Last Castle — 18.00
...: Storybook Love (2004, $14.95, TPB) r/#11-18 — 15.00
...: The Last Castle (2003, $5.95) Hamilton-a/Willingham-s; prequel to title — 6.00

FACE
DC Comics (Vertigo): Jan, 1995 ($4.95, one-shot)

1 — 5.00

FACE, THE (Tony Trent, the Face No. 3 on) (See Big Shot Comics)
Columbia Comics Group: 1941 - No. 2, 1943

	GD	VG	FN	VF	VF/NM	NM-
1-The Face; Mart Bailey-c	89	178	267	556	853	1150
2-Bailey-c	52	104	156	317	484	650

FACTION PARADOX
Image Comics: Aug, 2003 - Present ($2.95)

1,2-Calafiore-a — 3.00

FACTOR X
Marvel Comics: Mar, 1995 - No. 4, July, 1995 ($1.95, limited series)

1-Age of Apocalypse — 3.00
2-4 — 2.50

FACULTY FUNNIES
Archie Comics: June, 1989 - No. 5, May, 1990 (75¢/95¢ #2 on)

1-5: 1,2-The Awesome Four app. — 3.00

FADE FROM GRACE
Beckett Comics: Aug, 2004 - Present (99¢/$1.99)

1-(99¢) Jeff Amano-a/c; Gabriel Benson-s; origin of Fade — 1.00
2,3-($1.99) — 2.00

FAFHRD AND THE GREY MOUSER (Also see Sword of Sorcery & Wonder Woman #202)
Marvel Comics: Oct, 1990 - No. 4, 1991 ($4.50, 52 pgs., squarebound)

1-4: Mignola/Williamson-a; Chaykin scripts — 4.50

FAGIN THE JAW
Doubleday: Oct, 2003 ($15.95, softcover graphic novel)

nn-Will Eisner-s/a; story of Fagin from Dickens' Oliver Twist — 16.00

FAIRY TALE PARADE (See Famous Fairy Tales)
Dell Publishing Co.: June-July, 1942 - No. 121, Oct, 1946 (Most by Walt Kelly)

	GD	VG	FN	VF	VF/NM	NM-
1-Kelly-a begins	123	246	369	876	1376	1875
2(8-9/42)	50	100	150	376	568	760
3-5 (10-11/42 - 2-4/43)	35	70	105	263	407	550
6-9 (5-7/43 - 11-1/43-44)	28	56	84	203	312	420
Four Color 50('44),69('45), 87('45)	26	52	78	187	286	385
Four Color 104,114('46)-Last Kelly issue	20	40	60	141	216	290
Four Color 121('46)-Not by Kelly	12	24	36	87	134	180

NOTE: *#1-9, 4-Color #50, 69 have* ***Kelly*** *c/a; 4-Color #87, 104, 114-****Kelly*** *art only. #9 has a redrawn version of The Reluctant Dragon. This series contains all the classic fairy tales from Jack In The Beanstalk to Cinderella.*

FAIRY TALES
Ziff-Davis Publ. Co. (Approved Comics): No. 10, Apr-May, 1951 - No. 11, June-July, 1951

	GD	VG	FN	VF	VF/NM	NM-
10,11-Painted-c	20	40	60	112	161	210

FAITH
DC Comics (Vertigo): Nov, 1999 - No. 5, Mar, 2000 ($2.50, limited series)

1-5-Ted McKeever-s/c/a — 2.50

FAITHFUL
Marvel Comics/Lovers' Magazine: Nov, 1949 - No. 2, Feb, 1950 (52 pgs.)

	GD	VG	FN	VF	VF/NM	NM-
1,2-Photo-c	10	20	30	58	77	95

FALCON (See Marvel Premiere #49, Avengers #181 & Captain America #117 & 133)
Marvel Comics Group: Nov, 1983 - No. 4, Feb, 1984 (Mini-series)

1-4: 1-Paul Smith-c/a(p). 2-Paul Smith-c/Mark Bright-a. 3-Kupperberg-c — 3.00

FALLEN ANGEL
DC Comics: Sept, 2003 - Present ($2.50/$2.95)

1-9-Peter David-s/David Lopez-a/Stelfreeze-c; intro. Lee — 2.50
10-18: 10-Begin $2.95-c. 13,17-Kaluta-c — 3.00
TPB (2004, $12.95) r/#1-6; intro. by Harlan Ellison — 13.00

FALLEN ANGEL ON THE WORLD OF MAGIC: THE GATHERING
Acclaim (Armada): May, 1996 ($5.95, one-shot)

1-Nancy Collins story — 6.00

FALLEN ANGELS
Marvel Comics Group: April, 1987 - No. 8, Nov, 1987 (Limited series)

1-8 — 2.50

FALLING IN LOVE
Arleigh Pub. Co./National Per. Pub.: Sept-Oct, 1955 - No. 143, Oct-Nov, 1973

	GD	VG	FN	VF	VF/NM	NM-
1	40	80	120	230	335	440
2	21	42	63	118	169	220
3-10	12	24	36	71	98	125
11-20	10	20	30	60	80	100
21-40	8	16	24	46	58	70
41-47: 47-Last 10¢ issue?	7	14	21	37	46	55
48-70	4	8	12	22	30	38
71-99,108: 108-Wood-a (4 pgs., 7/69)	3	6	9	18	23	28
100	4	8	12	25	33	42
101-107,109-124	2	4	6	14	18	22
134-143	2	4	6	11	14	18
125-133: 52 pgs.	3	7	10	21	28	35

NOTE: ***Colan*** *c/a-75, 81. 52 pgs.-#125-133.*

FALLING MAN, THE
Image Comics: Feb, 1998 ($2.95)

1-McCorkindale-s/Hester-a — 3.00

FALL OF THE HOUSE OF USHER, THE (See A Corben Special & Spirit section 8/22/48)

FALL OF THE ROMAN EMPIRE (See Movie Comics)

FAMILY AFFAIR (TV)
Gold Key: Feb, 1970 - No. 4, Oct, 1970 (25¢)

	GD	VG	FN	VF	VF/NM	NM-
1-With pull-out poster; photo-c	7	14	21	50	68	85
1-With poster missing	3	7	10	21	28	35
2-4: 3,4-Photo-c	4	8	12	25	33	42

FAMILY FUNNIES
Parents' Magazine Institute: No. 9, Aug-Sept, 1946

	GD	VG	FN	VF	VF/NM	NM-
9	5	10	15	24	30	35

FAMILY FUNNIES (Tiny Tot Funnies No. 9)
Harvey Publications: Sept, 1950 - No. 8, Apr, 1951

	GD	VG	FN	VF	VF/NM	NM-
1-Mandrake (has over 30 King Feature strips)	10	20	30	60	80	100
2-Flash Gordon, 1 pg.	8	16	24	40	50	60
3-8: 4,5,7-Flash Gordon, 1 pg.	6	12	18	31	38	45

FAMILY MAN
DC Comics (Paradox Press): 1995 - No. 3, 1995 ($4.95, B&W, digest-size, limited series)

1-3 — 5.00

FAMILY MATTER
Kitchen Sink Press: 1998 ($24.95/$15.95, graphic novel)

Hardcover ($24.95) Will Eisner-s/a — 25.00
Softcover ($15.95) — 16.00

FAMOUS AUTHORS ILLUSTRATED (See Stories by...)

FAMOUS CRIMES
Fox Features Syndicate/M.S. Dist. No. 51,52: June, 1948 - No. 19, Sept, 1950; No. 20, Aug,

Famous Crimes #6 © FOX

Famous First Edition F-6 Wonder Woman #1 © DC

Famous Funnies #54 © EAS

GD VG FN VF VF/NM NM-
2.0 4.0 6.0 8.0 9.0 9.2

1951; No. 51, 52, 1953
1-Blue Beetle app. & crime story-r/Phantom Lady #16
50 100 150 305 465 625
2-Has woman dissolved in acid; lingerie-c/panels 40 80 120 233 342 450
3-Injury-to-eye story used in **SOTI**, pg. 112; has two electrocution stories
48 96 144 293 447 600
4-6 24 48 72 135 195 255
7- "Tarzan, the Wyoming Killer" used in **SOTI**, pg. 44; drug trial/ possession story 40 80 120 233 342 450
8-20: 17-Morisi-a. 20-Same cover as #15 18 36 54 100 143 185
51 (nd, 1953) 16 32 48 92 131 170
52 (Exist?) 11 22 33 64 87 110

FAMOUS FEATURE STORIES
Dell Publishing Co.: 1938 (7-1/2x11", 68 pgs.)
1-Tarzan, Terry & the Pirates, King of the Royal Mtd., Buck Jones, Dick Tracy, Smilin' Jack, Dan Dunn, Don Winslow, G-Man, Tailspin Tommy, Mutt & Jeff, Little Orphan Annie reprints - all illustrated text 75 140 210 455 678 900

FAMOUS FIRST EDITION (See Limited Collectors' Edition)
National Periodical Publications/DC Comics: ($1.00, 10x13-1/2", 72 pgs.) (No.6-8, 68 pgs.) 1974 - No. 8, Aug-Sept, 1975; C-61, 1979
(Hardbound editions with dust jackets are from Lyle Stuart, Inc.)
C-26-Action Comics #1; gold ink outer-c 5 10 15 33 44 55
C-26-Hardbound edition w/dust jacket 17 34 51 121 186 250
C-28-Detective #27; silver ink outer-c 7 14 21 46 63 80
C-28-Hardbound edition w/dust jacket 22 44 66 155 238 320
C-30-Sensation #1(1974); bronze ink outer-c 5 10 15 33 44 55
C-30-Hardbound edition w/dust jacket 17 34 51 121 186 250
F-4-Whiz Comics #2(#1)(10-11/74)-Cover not identical to original (dropped "Gangway for Captain Marvel" from cover); gold ink on outer-c 5 10 15 33 44 55
F-4-Hardbound edition w/dust jacket 17 34 51 121 186 250
F-5-Batman #1(F-6 inside); silver ink on outer-c 6 12 18 38 52 65
F-5-Hardbound edition w/dust jacket 17 34 51 121 186 250
V2#F-6-Wonder Woman #1 5 10 15 33 44 55
F-6-Wonder Woman #1 Hardbound w/dust jacket 17 34 51 121 186 250
F-7-All-Star Comics #3 5 10 15 33 44 55
F-8-Flash Comics #1(8-9/75) 5 10 15 33 44 55
V8#C-61-Superman #1(1979, $2.00) 4 8 12 25 33 42
V8#C-61 (Whitman variant) 4 8 12 29 40 50
Warning: The above books are almost **exact** reprints of the originals that they represent except for the Giant-Size format. None of the originals are Giant-Size. The first five issues and C-61 were printed with two covers. Reprint information can be found on the outside cover, but not on the inside cover which was reprinted exactly like the original (inside and out).

FAMOUS FUNNIES
Eastern Color: 1934; July, 1934 - No. 218, July, 1955
A Carnival of Comics (See Promotional Comics section)
Series 1-(Very rare)(nd-early 1934)(68 pgs.) No publisher given (Eastern Color PrintingCo.); sold in chain stores for 10¢. 35,000 print run. Contains Sunday strip reprints of Mutt & Jeff, Reg'lar Fellers, Nipper, Hairbreadth Harry, Strange As It Seems, Joe Palooka, Dixie Dugan, The Nebbs, Keeping Up With the Jones, and others. Inside front and back covers and pages 1-16 of Famous Funnies Series 1, #s 49-64 reprinted from **Famous Funnies**, **A Carnival of Comics**, and most of pages 17-48 reprinted from **Funnies on Parade**.
4058 8116 12,174 28,000 - -
No. 1 (Rare)(7/34-on stands 5/34) - Eastern Color Printing Co. First monthly newsstand comic book. Contains Sunday strip reprints of Toonerville Folks, Mutt & Jeff, Hairbreadth Harry, S'Matter Pop, Nipper, Dixie Dugan, The Bungle Family, Connie, Ben Webster, Tailspin Tommy, The Nebbs, Joe Palooka, & others.
3043 6086 9129 21,000 - -
2 (Rare, 9/34) 560 1120 1680 4200 - -
3-Buck Rogers Sunday strip-r by Rick Yager begins, ends #218; not in #191-208; 1st comic book app. of Buck Rogers; the number of the 1st strip reprinted is pg. 190, Series No. 1
733 1467 2200 5500 - -
4 233 467 700 1750 - -
5-1st Christmas-c on a newsstand comic 220 440 660 1650 - -
6-10 150 300 450 1125 - -
11,12,18-Four pgs. of Buck Rogers in each issue, completes stories in Buck Rogers #1 which lacks these pages. 18-Two pgs. of Buck Rogers reprinted in Daisy Comics #1
102 204 306 612 869 1125
13-17,19,20: 14-Has two Buck Rogers panels missing. 17-2nd Christmas-c on a newsstand comic (12/35) 79 158 237 474 675 875
21,23-30: 27-(10/36)-War on Crime begins (4 pgs.); 1st true crime in comics (reprints); part photo-c. 29-X-Mas-c (12/36) 59 118 177 354 502 650
22-Four pgs. of Buck Rogers needed to complete stories in Buck Rogers #1
62 124 186 372 526 680
31,33,34,36,37,39,40: 33-Careers of Baby Face Nelson & John Dillinger traced
41 82 123 246 348 450

GD VG FN VF VF/NM NM-
2.0 4.0 6.0 8.0 9.0 9.2

32-(3/37) 1st app. the Phantom Magician (costume hero) in Advs. of Patsy
45 90 135 270 385 500
35-Two pgs. Buck Rogers omitted in Buck Rogers #2
45 90 135 270 385 500
38-Full color portrait of Buck Rogers 43 86 129 258 367 475
41-60: 41,53-X-Mas-c. 55-Last bottom panel, pg. 4 in Buck Rogers redrawn in Buck Rogers #3
30 60 90 170 245 320
61,63,64,66,67,69,70 24 48 72 138 199 260
62,65,68,73-78-Two pgs. Kirby-a "Lightnin' & the Lone Rider". 65,77-X-Mas-c
27 54 81 152 219 285
71,79,80: 80-(3/41)-Buck Rogers story continues from Buck Rogers #5
18 36 54 102 146 190
72-Speed Spaulding begins by Marvin Bradley (artist), ends #88. This series was written by Edwin Balmer & Philip Wylie (later appeared as film & book "When Worlds Collide")
21 42 63 118 169 220
81-Origin & 1st app. Invisible Scarlet O'Neil (4/41); strip begins #82, ends #167; 1st non-funny-c (Scarlet O'Neil) 21 42 63 118 169 220
82-Buck Rogers-c 21 42 63 118 169 220
83-87,90: 86-Connie vs. Monsters on the Moon-c (sci/fi). 87 has last Buck Rogers full page-r. 90-Bondage-c 16 32 48 89 127 165
88,89: 88-Buck Rogers in "Moon's End" by Calkins, 2 pgs.(not reprints). Beginning with #88, all Buck Rogers pgs. have rearranged panels. 89-Origin & 1st app. Fearless Flint, the Flint Man 17 34 51 95 135 175
91-93,95,96,98-99,101,103-110: 105-Series 2 begins (Strip Page #1)
14 28 42 81 113 145
94-Buck Rogers in "Solar Holocaust" by Calkins, 3 pgs.(not reprints)
15 30 45 86 123 160
97-War Bond promotion, Buck Rogers by Calkins, 2 pgs.(not reprints)
15 30 45 86 123 160
100-1st comic to reach #100; 100th Anniversary cover features 11 major Famous Funnies characters, including Buck Rogers 17 34 51 95 135 175
102-Chief Wahoo vs. Hitler,Tojo & Mussolini-c (1/43) 52 104 156 317 484 650
111-130 (5/45): 113-X-Mas-c 11 22 33 62 84 105
131-150 (1/47): 137-Strip page No. 110 omitted 10 20 30 56 73 90
151-162,164-168 9 18 27 52 66 80
163-St. Valentine's Day-c 9 18 27 54 70 85
169,170-Two text illos. by Williamson, his 1st comic book work
11 22 33 66 91 115
171-190: 171-Strip pgs. 227,229,230, Series 2 omitted. 172-Strip Pg. 232 omitted. 190-Buck Rogers ends with start of strip pg. 302, Series 2; Oaky Doaks-c/story
8 16 24 46 58 70
191-197,199,201,203,206-208: No Buck Rogers. 191-Barney Carr, Space detective begins, ends #192. 8 16 24 43 54 65
198,200,202,205-One pg. Frazetta ads; no B. Rogers 8 16 24 46 58 70
204-Used in **POP**, pg. 79,99; war-c begin, end #208 9 18 27 51 62 75
209-216: Frazetta-c. 209-Buck Rogers begins (12/53) with strip pg. 480, Series 2; 211-Buck Rogers ads by Anderson begins, ends #217. #215-Contains B. Rogers strip pg. 515-518, series 2 followed by pgs.179-181, Series 3 123 246 369 769 1185 1600
217,218-B. Rogers ends with pg. 199, Series 3. 218-Wee Three-c/story
9 18 27 51 62 75

NOTE: ***Rick Yager** did the Buck Rogers Sunday strips reprinted in Famous Funnies. The Sundays were formerly done by Russ Keaton and Lt. Dick Calkins did the dailies, but would sometimes assist Yager on a panel or two from time to time. Strip No. 169 is Yager's first full Buck Rogers page. Yager did the strip until 1958 when **Murphy Anderson** took over. **Tuska** art from 4/26/59 - 1965. Virtually every panel was rewritten for Famous Funnies. Not identical to the original Sunday page. The Buck Rogers reprints run continuously through Famous Funnies issue No. 190 (Strip No. 302) with no break in story line. The story line has no continuity after No. 190. The Buck Rogers newspaper strips came out in four series: Series 1, 3/30/30 - 9/21/41 (No. 1 - 600); Series 2, 9/28/41 -10/21/51 (No. 1 -525)(Strip No. 110-1/2 (1/2 pg.) published in only a few newspapers); Series 3, 10/28/51 -2/9/58 (No. 100-428)(No No.1-99); Series 4, 2/16/58 - 6/13/65 (No numbers, dates only). **Everett** c-85, 86. **Moulton** a-100. Chief Wahoo c-93, 97, 102, 116, 136, 139, 151. Dickie Dare c-83, 88. Fearless Flint c-89. Invisible Scarlet O'Neil c-81, 87, 95, 121(part), 132. Scorchy Smith c-84, 90.*

FAMOUS FUNNIES
Super Comics: 1964
Super Reprint Nos. 15-18:17-r/Double Trouble #1. 18-Space Comics #?
2 4 6 12 16 20

FAMOUS GANGSTERS (Crime on the Waterfront No. 4)
Avon Periodicals/Realistic No. 3: Apr, 1951 - No. 3, Feb, 1952
1-3: 1-Capone, Dillinger; c-/Avon paperback #329. 2-Dillinger Machine Gun Killer; Wood-c/a (1 pg.); r/Saint #7 & retitled "Mike Strong". 3-Lucky Luciano & Murder, Inc; c-/Avon paperback #66 39 78 117 222 324 425

FAMOUS INDIAN TRIBES
Dell Publishing Co.: July-Sept, 1962; No. 2, July, 1972
12-264-209(#1) (The Sioux) 3 6 9 16 21 26
2(7/72)-Reprints above 1 3 4 6 8 10

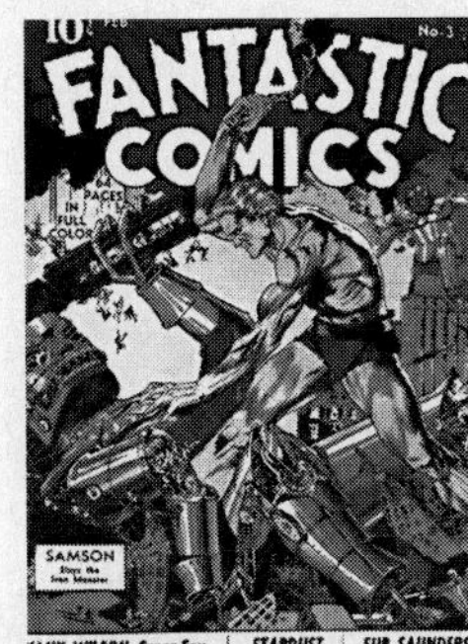

Fantastic Comics #3 © FOX

Fantastic Fears #8 © AJAX

Fantastic Four #15 © MAR

GD VG FN VF VF/NM NM-
2.0 4.0 6.0 8.0 9.0 9.2

FAMOUS STARS
Ziff-Davis Publ. Co.: Nov-Dec, 1950 - No. 6, Spring, 1952 (All have photo-c)

1-Shelley Winters, Susan Peters, Ava Gardner, Shirley Temple; Jimmy Stewart & Shelley Winters photo-c; Whitney-a 37 74 111 209 305 400
2-Betty Hutton, Bing Crosby, Colleen Townsend, Gloria Swanson; Betty Hutton photo-c; Everett-a(2) 24 48 72 138 199 260
3-Farley Granger, Judy Garland's ordeal (life story; she died 6/22/69 at the age of 47), Alan Ladd; Farley Granger photo-c; Whitney-a 28 56 84 158 229 300
4-Al Jolson, Bob Mitchum, Ella Raines, Richard Conte, Vic Damone; Bob Mitchum photo-c; Crandall-a, 6pgs. 21 42 63 118 169 220
5-Liz Taylor, Betty Grable, Esther Williams, George Brent, Mario Lanza; Liz Taylor photo-c; Krigstein-a 40 80 120 233 342 450
6-Gene Kelly, Hedy Lamarr, June Allyson, William Boyd, Janet Leigh, Gary Cooper; Gene Kelly photo-c 18 36 54 102 146 190

FAMOUS STORIES (...Book No. 2)
Dell Publishing Co.: 1942 - No. 2, 1942

1,2: 1-Treasure Island. 2-Tom Sawyer 32 64 96 184 267 350

FAMOUS TV FUNDAY FUNNIES
Harvey Publications: Sept, 1961 (25¢ Giant)

1-Casper the Ghost, Baby Huey, Little Audrey 6 12 18 43 59 75

FAMOUS WESTERN BADMEN (Formerly Redskin)
Youthful Magazines: No. 13, Dec, 1952 - No. 15, Apr, 1953

13-Redskin story 13 26 39 76 106 135
14,15: 15-The Dalton Boys story 10 20 30 58 77 95

FAN BOY
DC Comics: Mar, 1999 - No. 6, Aug, 1999 ($2.50, limited series)

1-6: 1-Art by Aragonés and various in all. 2-Green Lantern-c/a by Gil Kane. 3-JLA. 4-Sgt. Rock art by Heath, Marie Severin. 5-Batman art by Sprang, Adams, Miller, Timm. 6-Wonder Woman; art by Rude, Grell 2.50
TPB (2001, $12.95) r/#1-6 13.00

FANTASTIC (Formerly Captain Science; Beware No. 10 on)
Youthful Magazines: No. 8, Feb, 1952 - No. 9, Apr, 1952

8-Capt. Science by Harrison; decapitation, shrunken head panels 40 80 120 244 372 500
9-Harrison-a 35 70 105 198 287 375

FANTASTIC ADVENTURES
Super Comics: 1963 - 1964 (Reprints)

9,10,12,15,16,18: 9-r/? 10-r/He-Man #2(Toby). 11-Disbrow-a. 12-Unpublished Chesler material? 15-r/Spook #23. 16-r/Dark Shadows #2(Steinway); Briefer-a.18-r/Superior Stories #1 3 7 10 21 28 35
11-Wood-a; r/Blue Bolt #118 4 8 12 29 40 50
17-Baker-a(2) r/Seven Seas #6 4 8 12 29 40 50

FANTASTIC COMICS
Fox Features Syndicate: Dec, 1939 - No. 23, Nov, 1941

1-Intro/origin Samson; Stardust, The Super Wizard, Sub Saunders (by Kiefer), Space Smith, Capt. Kidd begin 465 930 1395 3255 5228 7200
2-Powell text illos 246 492 738 1538 2369 3200
3-Classic Lou Fine Robot-c; Powell text illos 1015 2030 3045 5200 7000 8800
4,5: Last Lou Fine-c 185 370 555 1156 1778 2400
6,7-Simon-c 138 276 414 863 1332 1800
8-10: 10-Intro/origin David, Samson's aide 96 192 288 600 925 1250
11-17,19,20: 16-Stardust ends 77 154 231 481 741 1000
18,23: 18-1st app. Black Fury & sidekick Chuck; ends #23. 23-Origin The Gladiator 79 158 237 494 760 1025
21-The Banshee begins(origin); ends #23; Hitler-c 85 170 255 531 816 1100
22-Hitler-c (likeness of Hitler as furnace on cover) 92 184 276 575 888 1200

NOTE: *Lou Fine c-1-5.* ***Tuska*** *a-3-5, 8. Bondage c-6, 8, 9. Issue #11 has indicia to Mystery Men Comics #15. All issues feature Samson covers.*

FANTASTIC COMICS (Fantastic Fears #1-9; Becomes Samson #12)
Ajax/Farrell Publ.: No. 10, Nov-Dec, 1954 - No. 11, Jan-Feb, 1955

10 (#1) 21 42 63 121 173 225
11-Robot-c 25 50 75 141 203 265

FANTASTIC FABLES
Silverwolf Comics: Feb, 1987 - No. 2, 1987 ($1.50, 28 pgs., B&W)

1,2: 1-Tim Vigil-a (6 pgs.). 2-Tim Vigil-a (7 pgs.) 4.00

FANTASTIC FEARS (Formerly Captain Jet) (Fantastic Comics #10 on)
Ajax/Farrell Publ.: No. 7, May, 1953 - No. 9, Sept-Oct, 1954

7(#1, 5/53)-Tales of Stalking Terror 48 96 114 293 447 600
8(#2, 7/53) 35 70 105 201 293 385
3,4 28 56 84 158 229 300
5-(1-2/54)-Ditko story (1st drawn) is written by Bruce Hamilton; r-in Weird V2#8 (1st pro work for Ditko but Daring Love #1 was published 1st) 83 166 249 519 797 1075
6-Decapitation-girl's head w/paper cutter (classic) 55 110 165 340 520 700
7(5-6/54), 9(9-10/54) 28 56 84 158 229 300
8(7-8/54)-Contains story intended for Jo-Jo; name changed to Kaza; decapitation story 31 62 93 177 256 335

FANTASTIC FIVE
Marvel Comics: Oct, 1999 - No. 5, Feb, 2000 ($1.99)

1-5: 1-M2 Universe; recaps origin; Ryan-a. 2-Two covers 2.25

FANTASTIC FORCE
Marvel Comics: Nov, 1994 - No. 18, Apr, 1996 ($1.75)

1-($2.50)-Foil wraparound-c; intro Fantastic Force w/Huntara, Delvor, Psi-Lord & Vibraxas 3.00
2-18: 13-She-Hulk app. 2.25

FANTASTIC FOUR (See America's Best TV..., Fireside Book Series, Giant-Size..., Giant Size Super-Stars, Marvel Age..., Marvel Collectors Item Classics, Marvel Knights 4, Marvel Milestone Edition, Marvel's Greatest, Marvel Treasury Edition, Marvel Triple Action, Official Marvel Index to..., Power Record Comics & Ultimate...)

FANTASTIC FOUR
Marvel Comics Group: Nov, 1961 - No. 416, Sept, 1996 (Created by Stan Lee & Jack Kirby)

1-Origin & 1st app. The Fantastic Four (Reed Richards: Mr. Fantastic, Johnny Storm: The Human Torch, Sue Storm: The Invisible Girl, & Ben Grimm: The Thing–Marvel's 1st super-hero group since the G.A.; 1st app. S.A. Human Torch); origin/1st app. The Mole Man. 875 1750 2625 9200 22,100 35,000
1-Golden Record Comic Set Reprint (1966)-cover not identical to original 16 32 48 116 178 240
with Golden Record 24 48 72 174 267 360
2-Vs. The Skrulls (last 10¢ issue) 318 636 954 2910 4955 7000
3-Fantastic Four don costumes & establish Headquarters; brief 1pg. origin; intro. The Fantasti-Car; Human Torch drawn w/two left hands on-c 229 458 687 2004 3402 4800
4-1st S. A. Sub-Mariner app. (5/62) 252 504 756 2205 3753 5300
5-Origin & 1st app. Doctor Doom 327 654 981 2992 5096 7200
6-Sub-Mariner, Dr. Doom team up; 1st Marvel villain team-up (2nd S.A. Sub-Mariner app. 147 294 441 1250 2025 2800
7-10: 7-1st app. Kurrgo. 8-1st app. Puppet-Master & Alicia Masters. 9-3rd Sub-Mariner app. 10-Stan Lee & Jack Kirby app. in story 103 206 309 876 1413 1950
11-Origin/1st app. The Impossible Man (2/63) 84 168 252 714 1157 1600
12-Fantastic Four vs. The Hulk (1st meeting); 1st Hulk x-over & ties w/Amazing Spider-Man #1 as 1st Marvel x-over; (3/63) 200 400 600 1750 2875 4000
13-Intro. The Watcher; 1st app. The Red Ghost 50 100 150 425 688 950
14-19: 14-Sub-Mariner x-over. 15-1st app. Mad Thinker. 16-1st Ant-Man x-over (7/63); Wasp cameo. 18-Origin/1st app. The Super Skrull. 19-Intro. Rama-Tut; Stan Lee & Jack Kirby cameo 43 86 129 344 535 725
20-Origin/1st app. The Molecule Man 44 88 132 352 551 750
21-Intro. The Hate Monger; 1st Sgt. Fury x-over (12/63) 41 82 123 305 478 650
22-24: 22-Sue Storm gains more powers 26 52 78 189 290 390
25,26-The Hulk vs. The Thing (their 1st battle). 25-3rd Avengers x-over (1st time w/Captain America)(cameo, 4/64); 2nd S.A. app. Cap (takes place between Avengers #4 & 5. 26-4th Avengers x-over 51 102 153 434 705 975
27-1st Doctor Strange x-over (6/64) 32 64 96 240 370 500
28-Early X-Men x-over (7/64); same date as X-Men #6 44 88 132 352 551 750
29,30: 30-Intro. Diablo 24 48 72 174 267 360
31-40: 31-Early Avengers x-over (10/64). 33-1st app. Attuma; part photo-c. 35-Intro/1st app. Dragon Man. 36-Intro/1st app. Madam Medusa & the Frightful Four (Sandman, Wizard, Paste Pot Pete). 39-Wood inks on Daredevil (early x-over) 19 38 57 138 212 285
41-44,47: 41-43-Frightful Four app. 44-Intro. Gorgon 11 22 33 77 114 150
45-Intro/1st app. The Inhumans (c/story, 12/65); also see Incredible Hulk Special #1 & Thor #146, & 147 19 38 57 138 212 285
46-1st Black Bolt-c (Kirby) & 1st full app. 12 24 36 87 134 180
48-Partial origin/1st app. The Silver Surfer & Galactus (3/66) by Lee & Kirby; Galactus brief app. in last panel; 1st of 3 part story 53 106 159 451 726 1000
49-2nd app./1st cover Silver Surfer & Galactus 36 72 108 270 423 575
50-Silver Surfer battles Galactus; full S.S.-c 41 82 123 305 478 650
51-Classic "This Man...This Monster" story 16 32 48 116 178 240
52-1st app. The Black Panther (7/66) 29 58 87 206 316 425
53-Origin & 2nd app. The Black Panther 14 28 42 97 149 200
54-Inhumans cameo 10 20 30 70 100 130

Fantastic Four #221 © MAR

Fantastic Four #257 © MAR

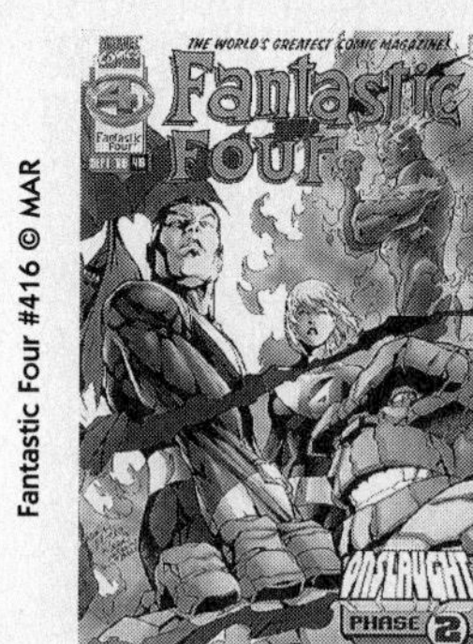

Fantastic Four #416 © MAR

	GD	VG	FN	VF	VF/NM	NM-
	2.0	4.0	6.0	8.0	9.0	9.2

55-Thing battles Silver Surfer; 4th app. Silver Surfer 16 32 48 116 178 240
56-Silver Surfer cameo 10 20 30 72 104 135
57-60: Dr. Doom steals Silver Surfer's powers (also see Silver Surfer: Loftier Than Mortals).
59,60-Inhumans cameo 9 18 27 60 85 110
61-65,68-71: 61-Silver Surfer cameo; Sandman-c/s 7 14 21 46 63 80
66-Begin 2 part origin of Him (Warlock); does not app. (9/67)
13 26 39 90 138 185
66,67-2nd printings (1994) 2 4 6 8 10 12
67-Origin/1st brief app. Him (Warlock); 1 page; see Thor #165,166 for 1st full app.
13 26 39 90 138 185
72-Silver Surfer-c/story (pre-dates Silver Surfer #1) 10 20 30 73 107 140
73-Spider-Man, D.D., Thor x-over; cont'd from Daredevil #38
10 20 30 67 96 125
74-77: Silver Surfer app.(#77 is same date/S.S. #1) 8 16 24 55 78 100
78-80 6 12 18 38 52 65
81-88: 81-Crystal joins & dons costume. 82,83-Inhumans app. 84-87-Dr. Doom app.
88-Last 12¢ issue 5 10 15 36 48 60
89-99,101: 94-Intro. Agatha Harkness. 4 8 12 27 36 45
100 (7/70) F.F. vs Thinker and Puppet-Master 10 20 30 70 100 130
102-104: F.F. vs. Sub-Mariner. 104-Magneto-c/story 4 8 12 27 36 45
105-109,111: 108-Last Kirby issue (not in #103-107) 4 8 12 28 38 48
110-Initial version w/green Thing and blue faces and pink uniforms on-c
5 10 15 33 44 55
110-Corrected-c w/accurately colored faces and uniforms and orange Thing
4 8 12 29 40 50
112-Hulk Vs. Thing (7/71) 11 22 33 80 120 160
113-115: 115-Last 15¢ issue 3 7 10 21 28 35
116 (52 pgs.) 5 10 15 33 44 55
117-120 3 6 9 19 25 32
121-123-Silver Surfer-c/stories. 122,123-Galactus 4 8 12 22 30 38
124,125,127,129-149: 129-Intro. Thundra. 130-Sue leaves F.F. 131-Quicksilver app.
132-Medusa joins. 133-Thundra Vs. Thing. 142-Kirbyish-a by Buckler begins.
143-Dr. Doom-c/story. 147-Sub-Mariner 3 6 9 16 20 24
126-Origin F.F. retold; cover swipe of F.F. #1 3 6 9 18 23 28
128-Four pg. insert of F.F. Friends & Foes 3 6 9 18 23 28
150-Crystal & Quicksilver's wedding 3 6 9 18 24 30
151-154,158-160: 151-Origin Thundra. 159-Medusa leaves; Sue rejoins
2 4 6 9 11 14
155-157: Silver Surfer in all 2 4 6 12 16 20
161-165,168,174-180: 164-The Crusader (old Marvel Boy) revived (origin #165); 1st app.
Frankie Raye. 168-170-Cage app. 176-Re-intro Impossible Man; Marvel artists app.
180-r/#101 by Kirby 1 2 3 5 7 9
166,167-vs. Hulk 2 4 6 11 14 18
169-173-(Regular 25¢ edition)(4-8/75) 1 2 3 5 7 9
169-173-(30¢-c, limited distribution) 2 4 6 9 11 14
181-199: 189-G.A. Human Torch app. & origin retold. 190,191-Fantastic Four break up
1 2 3 5 6 8
183-187-(35¢-c variants, limited dist.)(6-10/77) 2 4 6 8 10 12
200-(11/78, 52 pgs.)-F.F. re-united vs. Dr. Doom 2 4 6 9 11 14
201-208,219,222-231: 207-Human Torch vs. Spider-Man-c/story. 211-1st app. Terrax.
224-Contains unused alternate-c for FF #3 and pin-ups 5.00
209-216,218,220,221-Byrne-a. 209-1st Herbie the Robot. 220-Brief origin 6.00
217-Early app. Dazzler (4/80); by Byrne 6.00
232-Byrne-a begins 6.00
233-235,237-249,251-260: All Byrne-a. 238-Origin Frankie Raye. 244-Frankie Raye becomes
Nova, Herald of Galactus. 252-Reads sideways; Annihilus app.; contains skin "Tattooz"
decals 5.00
236-20th Anniversary issue(11/81, 68 pgs., $1.00)-Brief origin F.F.; Byrne-c/a(p); new Kirby-a(p)
6.00
250-(52 pgs)-Spider-Man x-over; Byrne-a; Skrulls impersonate New X-Men 6.00
261-285: 261-Silver Surfer. 262-Origin Galactus; Byrne writes & draws himself into story.
264-Swipes-c of F.F. #1. 274-Spider-Man's alien costume app. (4th app., 1/85, 2 pgs.) 4.00
286-2nd app. X-Factor continued from Avengers #263; story continues in X-Factor #1 5.00
287-295: 291-Action Comcis #1 cover swipe. 292-Nick Fury app. 293-Last Byrne-a 3.00
296-($1.50)-Barry Smith-c/a; Thing rejoins 4.00
297-318,321-330: 300-Johnny Storm & Alicia Masters wed. 306-New team begins (9/87).
311-Re-intro The Black Panther. 327-Mr. Fantastic & Invisible Girl return 3.00
319,320: 319-Double size. 320-Thing vs. Hulk 4.00
331-346,351-357,359,360: 334-Simonson-c/scripts begin. 337-Simonson-a begins.
342-Spider-Man cameo. 356-F.F. vs. The New Warriors; Paul Ryan-c/a begins.
360-Last $1.00-c 2.50
347-Ghost Rider, Wolverine, Spider-Man, Hulk-c/stories thru #349; Arthur Adams-c/a(p)
in each 4.00
347,348-Gold 2nd printing 2.50
348-350: 350-($1.50, 52 pgs.)-Dr. Doom app. 3.00
358-(11/91, $2.25, 88 pgs.)-30th anniversary issue; gives history of F.F.; die cut-c; Art Adams
back-up story-a 3.00
361-368,370,372-374,376-380,382-386: 362-Spider-Man app. 367-Wolverine app. (brief).
370-Infinity War x-over; Thanos & Magus app. 374-Secret Defenders (Ghost Rider,
Hulk, Wolverine) x-over 2.25
369-Infinity War x-over; Thanos app. 2.50
371-All white embossed-c ($2.00) 4.00
371-All red 2nd printing ($2.00) 2.50
375-($2.95, 52 pgs.)-Holo-grafx foil-c; ann. issue 3.00
376-($2.95)-Variant polybagged w/Dirt Magazine #4 and music tape 5.00
381-Death of Reed Richards (Mister Fantastic) & Dr. Doom 4.00
387-Newsstand ed. ($1.25) 2.25
387-($2.95)-Collector's Ed. w/Die-cut foil-c 3.00
388-393,395-397: 388-bound-in trading card sheet. 394-($1.50-c) 2.25
394,398,399: 394 ($2.95)-Collector's Edition-polybagged w/16 pg. Marvel Action Hour book
and acetate print; pink logo. 398,399-Rainbow Foil-c 3.00
400-Rainbow-Foil-c 4.00
401-415: 401,402-Atlantis Rising. 407,408-Return of Reed Richards. 411-Inhumans app.
414-Galactus vs. Hyperstorm. 415-Onslaught tie-in; X-Men app. 2.25
416-($2.50)-Onslaught tie-in; Dr. Doom app.; wraparound-c 3.00
#500-up (See Fantastic Four Vol. 3; series resumed original numbering after Vol. 3 #70)
Annual 1('63)-Origin F.F.; Ditko-i; early Spidey app. 68 136 204 578 939 1300
Annual 2('64)-Dr. Doom origin & c/story 38 76 114 285 443 600
Annual 3('65)-Reed & Sue wed; r/#6,11 17 34 51 121 186 250
Special 4(11/66)-G.A. Torch x-over (1st S.A. app.) & origin retold; r/#25,26 (Hulk vs. Thing);
Torch vs. Torch battle 12 24 36 82 124 165
Special 5(11/67)-New art; Intro. Psycho-Man; early Black Panther, Inhumans & Silver Surfer
(1st solo story) app. 12 24 36 84 127 170
Special 6(11/68)-Intro. Annihilus; birth of Franklin Richards; new 48 pg. movie length epic;
last non-reprint annual 8 16 24 55 78 100
Special 7(11/69)-r/F.F. #1,2; Marvel staff photos 4 8 12 25 33 42
Special 8-10: All reprints. 8(12/70)-F.F. vs. Sub-Mariner plus gallery of F.F. foes. 9(12/71).
10('73) 3 6 9 18 23 28
Annual 11-14: 11(1976)-New art begins again. 12(1978). 13(1978). 14(1979)
1 2 3 5 7 9
Annual 15-17: 15('80-'94, 68 pgs.).17(1983)-Byrne-c/a 5.00
Annual 18-27: 21(1988)-Evolutionary War x-over. 22-Atlantis Attacks x-over; Sub-Mariner &
The Avengers app.; Buckler-a. 23-Byrne-c; Guice-p. 24-2 pg. origin recap of Fantastic Four;
Guardians of the Galaxy x-over. 25-Moondragon story. 26-Bagged w/card 3.00
Special Edition 1(5/84)-r/Annual #1; Byrne-c/a 3.00
....: Monsters Unleashed nn (1992, $5.95)-r/F.F. #347-349 w/new Arthur Adams-c 6.00
....: Nobody Gets Out Alive (1994, $15.95) TPB r/ #387-392 16.00
... Visionaries (11/01, $19.95) r/#232-240 by John Byrne 20.00
... Visionaries Vol. 2 (2004, $24.99) r/#241-250 by John Byrne 25.00

NOTE: ***Arthur Adams*** *c/a-347-349p.* ***Austin*** *c(i)-232-236, 238, 240-242, 250i, 286i.* ***Buckler*** *c-151, 168.* ***John Buscema*** *a(p)-107, 108(w/**Kirby, Sinnott & Romita**),109-130, 132, 134-141, 160, 173-175, 202, 296-309p, Annual 11, 13; c(p)-107-122, 124-129, 133-139, 202, Annual 12p, Special 10.* ***Byrne*** *a-209-218p, 220p, 221p, 232-265, 266i, 267-273, 274-293p, Annual 17, 19; c-211-214p, 220p, 232-236p, 237, 238p, 239, 240-242p, 243-249, 250p, 251-267, 269-277, 278-281p, 283p, 284, 285, 286p, 288-293, Annual 17, 18.* ***Ditko*** *a-13i, 14i(w/**Kirby**-p), Annual 16.* ***G. Kane*** *c-145p, 146p, 150p, 160p.* ***Kirby*** *a-1-102p, 108p, 180r, 189r, 236p, Special 1-10; c-1-101, 164, 167, 171-177, 180, 181, 190, 200, Annual 11, Special 1-7, 9.* ***Marcos*** *a-Annual 14i.* ***Mooney*** *a-118i, 152i.* ***Perez*** *a(p)-164-167, 170-172, 176-178, 184-188, 191p, 192p. Annual 14p, 15p; c(p)-183-188, 191, 192, 194-197.* ***Simonson*** *a-337-341, 343, 344p, 345p, 346, 350p, 352-354; c-212, 334-341, 342p, 343-346, 350, 353, 354.* ***Steranko*** *c-130-132p.* ***Williamson*** *c-357i.*

FANTASTIC FOUR (Volume Two)
Marvel Comics: V2#1, Nov, 1996 - No. 13, Nov, 1997 ($2.95/$1.95/$1.99) (Produced by WildStorm Productions)

1-($2.95)-Reintro Fantastic Four; Jim Lee-c/a; Brandon Choi scripts; Mole Man app. 5.00
1-($2.95)-Variant-c 1 2 3 4 5 7
2-9: 2-Namor-c/app. 3-Avengers-c/app. 4-Two covers; Dr. Doom cameo 3.00
10,11,13: All $1.99-c. 13-"World War 3"-pt. 1, x-over w/Image 3.00
12-($2.99) "Heroes Reunited"-pt. 1 4.00
...: Heroes Reborn (7/00, $17.95, TPB) r/#1-6 18.00

FANTASTIC FOUR (Volume Three)
Marvel Comics: V3#1, Jan, 1998 - Present ($2.99/$1.99/$2.25)

1-($2.99)-Heroes Return; Lobdell-s/Davis & Farmer-a 5.00
1-Alternate Heroes Return-c 1 2 3 4 5 7
2-4,12: 2-2-covers. 4-Claremont-s/Larroca-a begin; Silver Surfer c/app.
12-($2.99) Wraparound-c by Larroca 4.00
5-11: 6-Heroes For Hire app. 9-Spider-Man-c/app. 3.00
13-24: 13,14-Ronan-c/app. 2.50
25-($2.99) Dr. Doom returns 3.00
26-49: 27-Dr. Doom marries Sue. 30-Begin $2.25-c. 32,42-Namor-c/app. 35-Regular cover;
Pacheco-s/a begins. 37-Super-Skrull-c/app. 38-New Baxter Building 2.25

Fantastic Four V3#500 © MAR

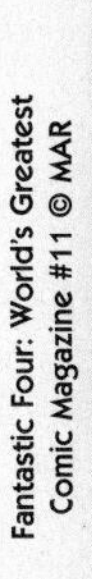

Fantastic Four: World's Greatest Comic Magazine #11 © MAR

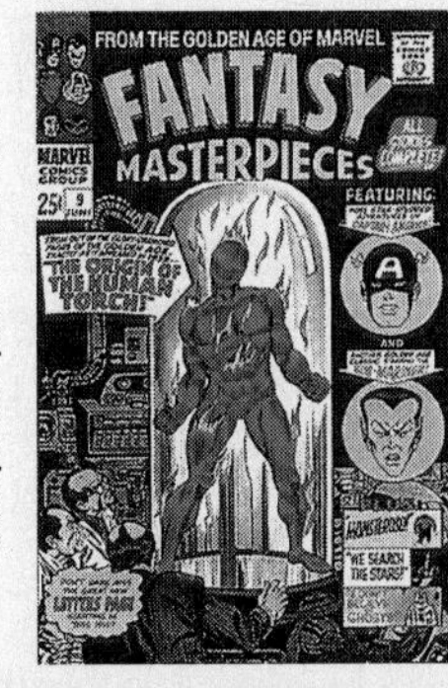

Fantasy Masterpieces #9 © MAR

GD 2.0 | VG 4.0 | FN 6.0 | VF 8.0 | VF/NM 9.0 | NM- 9.2

35-($3.25) Variant foil enhanced-c; Pacheco-s/a begins 3.25
50-($3.99, 64 pgs.) BWS-c; Grummett, Pacheco, Rude, Udon-a 4.00
51-53,55-59: 51-53-Bagley-a(p)/Wieringo-c; Inhumans app. 55,56-Immonen-a 57-59-Warren-s/Grant-a 2.25
54-($3.50, 100 pgs.) Birth of Valeria; r/Annual #6 birth of Franklin 3.50
60-(9¢-c) Waid-s/Wieringo-a begin 2.25
60-($2.25 newsstand edition)(also see Promotional Comics section) 2.25
61-70: 62-64-FF vs. Modulus. 65,66-Buckingham-a. 68-70-Dr. Doom app. 2.25

(After #70 [Aug, 2003] numbering reverted back to original Vol. 1 with #500, Sept, 2003)

500-($3.50) Regular edition; concludes Dr. Doom app.; Dr. Strange app.; Rivera painted-c 3.50
500-($4.99) Director's Cut Edition; chromium-c by Wieringo; sketch and script pages 8.00
501-516: 501,502-Casey Jones-a. 503-508-Porter-a. 509-Wieringo-c/a resumes. 512,513-Spider-Man app. 514-516-Ha-c/Medina-a 2.25
517-520: 517-Begin $2.99-c. 519,520-Galactus app. 3.00
...'98 Annual ($3.50) Immonen-a 3.50
...'99 Annual ($3.50) Ladronn-a 3.50
...'00 Annual ($3.50) Larocca-a; Marvel Girl back-up story 3.50
...'01 Annual ($2.99) Maguire-a; Thing back-up w/Yu-a 3.00
Fantastic 4th Voyage of Sinbad (9/01, $5.95) Claremont-s/Ferry-a 6.00
Flesh and Stone (8/01, $12.95, TPB) r/#35-39 13.00
... Vol. 1 HC (2004, $29.99, TPB) oversized reprint /#60-70, 500-502; Mark Waid intro and series proposal; cover gallery 30.00
... Vol. 1: Imaginauts (2003, $17.99, TPB) r/#56,60-66; Mark Waid's series proposal 18.00
... Vol. 2: Unthinkable (2003, $17.99, TPB) r/#67-70,500-502; #500 Director's Cut extras 18.00
... Vol. 3: Authoritative Action (2004, $12.99, TPB) r/#503-508 13.00
... Vol. 4: Hereafter (2004, $11.99, TPB) r/#509-513 12.00
Wizard #1/2 -Lim-a 10.00

FANTASTIC FOUR: ATLANTIS RISING
Marvel Comics: June, 1995 - No. 2, July, 1995 ($3.95, limited series)

1,2: Acetate-c 5.00
Collector's Preview (5/95, $2.25, 52 pgs.) 2.50

FANTASTIC FOUR: BIG TOWN
Marvel Comics: Jan, 2001 - No. 4, Apr, 2001 ($2.99, limited series)

1-4:"What If?" story; McKone-a/Englehart-s 3.00

FANTASTIC FOUR: FIREWORKS
Marvel Comics: Jan, 1999 - No. 3, Mar, 1999 ($2.99, limited series)

1-3-Remix; Jeff Johnson-a 3.00

FANTASTIC FOUR INDEX (See Official...)

FANTASTIC FOUR: 1 2 3 4
Marvel Comics: Oct, 2001 - No. 4, Jan, 2002 ($2.99, limited series)

1-4-Morrison-s/Jae Lee-a. 2-4-Namor-c/app. 3.00
TPB (2002, $9.99) r/#1-4 10.00

FANTASTIC FOUR ROAST
Marvel Comics Group: May, 1982 (75¢, one-shot, direct sales)

1-Celebrates 20th anniversary of F.F.#1; X-Men, Ghost Rider & many others cameo; Golden, Miller, Buscema, Rogers, Byrne, Anderson art; Hembeck/Austin-c 4.00

FANTASTIC FOUR: THE LEGEND
Marvel Comics: Oct, 1996 ($3.95, one-shot)

1-Tribute issue 4.00

FANTASTIC FOUR 2099
Marvel Comics: Jan, 1996 - No. 8, Aug, 1996 ($3.95/$1.95)

1-($3.95)-Chromium-c; X-Nation preview 4.00
2-8: 4-Spider-Man 2099-c/app. 5-Doctor Strange app. 7-Thibert-c 2.25
NOTE: *Williamson a-1i; c-1i.*

FANTASTIC FOUR UNLIMITED
Marvel Comics: Mar, 1993 - No. 12, Dec, 1995 ($3.95, 68 pgs.)

1-12: 1-Black Panther app. 4-Thing vs. Hulk. 5-Vs. The Frightful Four. 6-Vs. Namor. 7, 9-12-Wraparound-c 4.00

FANTASTIC FOUR UNPLUGGED
Marvel Comics: Sept, 1995 - No. 6, Aug 1996 (99¢, bi-monthly)

1-6 2.25

FANTASTIC FOUR - UNSTABLE MOLECULES
(Indicia for #1 reads STARTLING STORIES: ... ; #2 reads UNSTABLE MOLECULES)
Marvel Comics: Mar, 2003 - No. 4, June, 2003 ($2.99, limited series)

1-4-Guy Davis-c/a 3.00
Fantastic Four Legends Vol. 1 TPB (2003, $13.99) r/#1-4, origin from FF #1 (1963) 14.00

FANTASTIC FOUR VS. X-MEN
Marvel Comics: Feb, 1987 - No. 4, June, 1987 (Limited series)

1-4: 4-Austin-a(i) 4.00

FANTASTIC FOUR: WORLD'S GREATEST COMICS MAGAZINE
Marvel Comics: Feb, 2001 - No. 12 (Limited series)

1-12: Homage to Lee & Kirby era of F.F.; s/a by Larsen & various. 5-Hulk-c/app. 10-Thor app. 3.00

FANTASTIC GIANTS (Formerly Konga #1-23)
Charlton Comics: V2#24, Sept, 1966 (25¢, 68 pgs.)

V2#24-Special Ditko issue; origin Konga & Gorgo reprinted plus two new Ditko stories 8 16 24 53 74 95

FANTASTIC TALES
I. W. Enterprises: 1958 (no date) (Reprint, one-shot)

1-Reprints Avon's "City of the Living Dead" 4 8 12 24 32 40

FANTASTIC VOYAGE (See Movie Comics)
Gold Key: Aug, 1969 - No. 2, Dec, 1969

1 (TV) 6 12 18 43 59 75
2 4 8 12 29 40 55

FANTASTIC VOYAGES OF SINDBAD, THE
Gold Key: Oct, 1965 - No. 2, June, 1967

1-Painted-c on both 7 14 21 51 71 90
2 6 12 18 40 55 70

FANTASTIC WORLDS
Standard Comics: No. 5, Sept, 1952 - No. 7, Jan, 1953

5-Toth, Anderson-a 37 74 111 209 305 400
6-Toth-c/a 31 62 93 178 259 340
7 20 40 60 112 161 210

FANTASY FEATURES
Americomics: 1987 - No. 2, 1987 ($1.75)

1,2 3.00

FANTASY ILLUSTRATED
New Media Publ.: Spring 1982 ($2.95, B&W magazine)

1-P. Craig Russell-c/a; art by Ditko, Sekowsky, Sutton; Englehart-s 1 2 3 4 5 7

FANTASY MASTERPIECES (Marvel Super Heroes No. 12 on)
Marvel Comics Group: Feb, 1966 - No. 11, Oct, 1967; V2#1, Dec, 1979 - No. 14, Jan, 1981

1-Photo of Stan Lee (12¢-c #1,2) 7 14 21 51 71 90
2-r/1st Fin Fang Foom from Strange Tales #89 4 8 12 29 40 50
3-8: 3-G.A. Capt. America-r begin, end #11; 1st 25¢ Giant; Colan-r. 3-6-Kirby-c(p). 4-Kirby-c(p)(i). 7-Begin G.A. Sub-Mariner, Torch-r/M. Mystery. 8-Torch battles the Sub-Mariner-r/Marvel Mystery #9 5 10 15 36 48 60
9-Origin Human Torch-r/Marvel Comics #1 6 12 18 38 52 65
10,11: 10-r/origin & 1st app. All Winners Squad from All Winners #19. 11-r/origin of Toro (H.T. #1) & Black Knight #1 5 10 15 33 44 55
V2#1(12/79, 75¢, 52 pgs.)-r/origin Silver Surfer from Silver Surfer #1 with editing plus reprints cover; J. Buscema-a 6.00
2-14-Reprints Silver Surfer #2-14 w/covers 4.00
NOTE: *Buscema c-V2#7-9(in part).* ***Ditko*** *r-1-3, 7, 9.* ***Everett*** *r-1,7-9.* ***Matt Fox*** *r-9i.* ***Kirby*** *r-1-11; c(p)-3, 4i, 5, 6.* ***Starlin*** *r-8-13. Some direct sale V2#14's had a 50¢ cover price. #3-11 contain Capt. America-r/Capt. America #3-10. #7-11 contain G.A.Human Torch & Sub-Mariner-r.*

FANTASY QUARTERLY (Also see Elfquest)
Independent Publishers Syndicate: Spring, 1978 (B&W)

1-1st app. Elfquest; Dave Sim-a (6 pgs.) 7 14 21 46 63 80

FANTOMAN (Formerly Amazing Adventure Funnies)
Centaur Publications: No. 2, Aug, 1940 - No. 4, Dec, 1940

2-The Fantom of the Fair, The Arrow, Little Dynamite-r begin; origin The Ermine by Filchock; Fantoman app. in 2-4; Burgos, J. Cole, Ernst, Gustavson-a 121 242 363 756 1166 1575
3,4: Gustavson-r. 4-Red Blaze story 96 192 288 600 925 1250

FAREWELL MOONSHADOW (See Moonshadow)
DC Comics (Vertigo): Jan, 1997 ($7.95, one-shot)

nn-DeMatteis-s/Muth-c/a 8.00

FARGO KID (Formerly Justice Traps the Guilty)(See Feature Comics #47
Prize Publications: V11#3(#1), June-July, 1958 - V11#5, Oct-Nov, 1958

V11#3(#1)-Origin Fargo Kid, Severin-c/a; Williamson-a(2); Heath-a 19 38 57 107 154 200
V11#4,5-Severin-c/a 13 26 39 74 102 130

Fast Fiction #2 © Seaboard

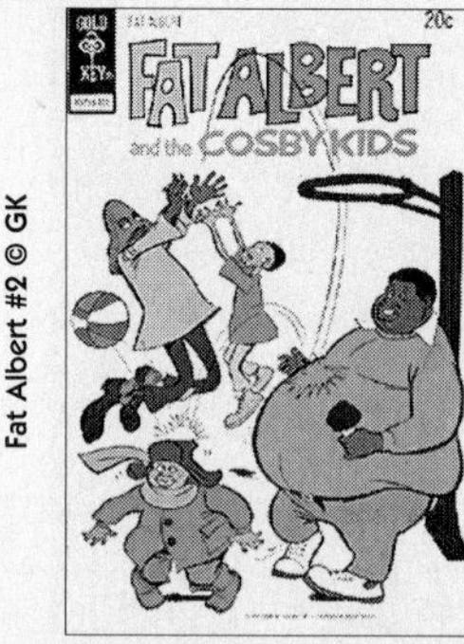

Fat Albert #2 © GK

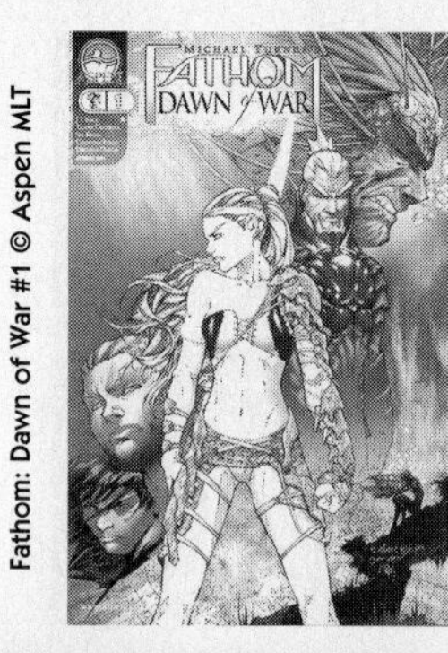

Fathom: Dawn of War #1 © Aspen MLT

GD 2.0 | VG 4.0 | FN 6.0 | VF 8.0 | VF/NM 9.0 | NM- 9.2

GD 2.0 | VG 4.0 | FN 6.0 | VF 8.0 | VF/NM 9.0 | NM- 9.2

FARMER'S DAUGHTER, THE
Stanhall Publ./Trojan Magazines: Feb-Mar, 1954 - No. 3, June-July, 1954; No. 4, Oct, 1954

1-Lingerie, nudity panel 26 52 78 147 211 275
2-4(Stanhall) 15 30 45 86 123 160

FARSCAPE: WAR TORN (Based on TV series)
DC Comics (WildStorm): Apr, 2002 - No. 2, May, 2002 ($4.95, limited series)

1,2-Teranishi-a/Wolfman-s; photo-c 5.00

FASHION IN ACTION
Eclipse Comics: Aug, 1986 - Feb, 1987 (Baxter paper)

Summer Special 1 , Winter Special 1, each Snyder III-c/a 2.25

FASTBALL EXPRESS (Major League Baseball)
Ultimate Sports Force: 2000 ($3.95, one-shot)

1-Polybagged with poster; Johnson, Maddux, Park, Nomo, Clemens app. 4.00

FASTEST GUN ALIVE, THE (Movie)
Dell Publishing Co.: No. 741, Sept, 1956 (one-shot)

Four Color 741-Photo-c 8 16 24 58 82 105

FAST FICTION (...Action) (Stories by Famous Authors Illustrated #6 on)
Seaboard Publ./Famous Authors Ill.: Oct, 1949 - No. 5, Mar, 1950
(All have Kiefer-c)(48 pgs.)

1-Scarlet Pimpernel; Jim Lavery-c/a 38 76 114 219 320 420
2-Captain Blood; H. C. Kiefer-c/a 35 70 105 198 287 375
3-She, by Rider Haggard; Vincent Napoli-a 40 80 120 235 348 460
4-(1/50, 52 pgs.)-The 39 Steps; Lavery-c/a 27 54 81 152 219 285
5-Beau Geste; Kiefer-c/a 27 54 81 152 219 285
NOTE: *Kiefer a-2, 5; c-2, 3,5. Lavery c/a-1, 4. Napoli a-3.*

FAST FORWARD
DC Comics (Piranha Press): 1992 - No. 3, 1993 ($4.95, 68 pgs.)

1-3: 1-Morrison scripts; McKean-c/a. 3-Sam Kieth-a 5.00

FAST WILLIE JACKSON
Fitzgerald Periodicals, Inc.: Oct, 1976 - No. 7, 1977

1 2 4 6 11 14 18
2-7 1 3 4 6 8 10

FAT ALBERT (...& the Cosby Kids) (TV)
Gold Key: Mar, 1974 - No. 29, Feb, 1979

1 4 8 12 25 33 42
2-10 2 4 6 14 18 22
11-29 2 4 6 10 13 16

FATALE (Also see Powers That Be #1 & Shadow State #1,2)
Broadway Comics: Jan, 1996 - No. 6, Aug, 1996 ($2.50)

1-6: J.G. Jones-c/a in all, Preview Edition 1 (11/95, B&W) 2.50

FAT AND SLAT (Ed Wheelan) (Becomes Gunfighter No. 5 on)
E. C. Comics: Summer, 1947 - No. 4, Spring, 1948

1-Intro/origin Voltage, Man of Lightning; "Comics" McCormick, the World's No. 1 Comic Book Fan begins, ends #4 36 72 108 204 297 390
2-4: 4-Comics McCormick-c feature 24 48 72 138 199 260

FAT AND SLAT JOKE BOOK
All-American Comics (William H. Wise): Summer, 1944 (52 pgs., one-shot)

nn-by Ed Wheelan 28 56 84 158 229 300

FATE (See Hand of Fate & Thrill-O-Rama)

FATE
DC Comics: Oct, 1994 - No. 22, Sept, 1996 ($1.95/$2.25)

0,1-22: 8-Begin $2.25-c. 11-14-Alan Scott (Sentinel) app. 10,14-Zatanna app. 21-Phantom Stranger app. 22-Spectre app. 2.25

FATE OF THE BLADE
Dreamwave Productions: Aug, 2002 - Present ($2.95)

1-5: 1-Sarracini-s/Yamen-a; gatefold wraparound--c 3.00

FATHOM
Comico: May, 1987 - No. 3, July, 1987 ($1.50, limited series)

1-3 2.25

FATHOM
Image Comics (Top Cow Prod.): Aug, 1998 - No. 14, May, 2002 ($2.50)

Preview 12.00
0-Wizard supplement 7.00
0-($6.95) DF Alternate 7.00
1/2 (Wizard) origin of Cannon; Turner-a 6.00
1/2 (3/03, $2.99) origin of Cannon 3.00
1-Turner-s/a; three covers; alternate story pages 6.00
1-Wizard World Ed. 9.00
2-14: 12-14-Witchblade app. 13,14-Tomb Raider app. 3.00
9-Green foil-c edition 15.00
9,12-Holofoil editions 18.00
12,13-DFE alternate-c 6.00
13,14-DFE Gold edition 8.00
14-DFE Blue 15.00
... Collected Edition 1 (3/99, $5.95) r/Preview & all three #1's 6.00
... Collected Edition 2-4 (3-12/99, $5.95) 2-r/#2,3. 3-r/#4,5. 4-r/#6,7 6.00
... Collected Edition 5 (4/00, $5.95) 5-r/#8,9 6.00
... Swimsuit Special (5/99, $2.95) Pin-ups by various 3.00
... Swimsuit Special 2000 (12/00, $2.95) Pin-ups by various; Turner-c 3.00
Michael Turner's Fathom HC ('01, $39.95) r/#1-9, black-c w/silver foil 40.00
Michael Turner's Fathom SC ('01, $24.95) r/#1-9, new Turner-c 25.00

FATHOM (MICHAEL TURNER'S...) (Also see Cannon)
Aspen MLT, Inc.: 2004 ($2.50)

0-Caldwell-a 2.50
...: Cannon Hawke #0 ('04, $2.50) Turner-c 2.50

FATHOM: DAWN OF WAR (MICHAEL TURNER'S...)
Aspen MLT, Inc.: Oct, 2004 - Present ($2.99)

1,2-Caldwell-a 3.00

FATHOM: KILLIAN'S TIDE
Image Comics (Top Cow Prod.): Apr, 2001 - No. 4, Nov, 2001 ($2.95)

1-4-Caldwell-a(p); two covers by Caldwell and Turner. 2-Flip-book preview of Universe 3.00
1-DFE Blue, 1-Holographic logo 12.00
4-Foil-c 12.00

FATIMA...CHALLENGE TO THE WORLD
Catechetical Guild: 1951, 36 pgs. (15¢)

nn (not same as 'Challenge to the World') 5 10 14 20 24 28

FATMAN, THE HUMAN FLYING SAUCER
Lightning Comics(Milson Publ. Co.): April, 1967 - No. 3, Aug-Sept, 1967 (68 pgs.)
(Written by Otto Binder)

1-Origin/1st app. Fatman & Tinman by Beck 7 14 21 46 63 80
2-C. C. Beck-a 4 8 12 29 40 50
3-(Scarce)-Beck-a 7 14 21 51 71 90

FAULTLINES
DC Comics (Vertigo): May, 1997 - No. 6, Oct, 1997 ($2.50, limited series)

1-6-Lee Marrs-s/Bill Koeb-a in all 2.50

FAUNTLEROY COMICS (Super Duck Presents...)
Close-Up/Archie Publications: 1950; No. 2, 1951; No. 3, 1952

1-Super Duck-c/stories by Al Fagaly in all 9 18 27 52 66 80
2,3 6 12 18 31 38 45

FAUST
Northstar Publishing/Rebel Studios #7 on: 1989 - No 11, 1997 ($2.00/$2.25, B&W, mature themes)

1-Decapitation-c; Tim Vigil-c/a in all 3 6 9 16 20 24
1-2nd - 4th printings 3.00
2 2 4 6 8 10 12
2-2nd & 3rd printings, 3,5-2nd printing 3.00
3 1 3 4 6 8 10
4-10: 7-Begin Rebel Studios series 5.00
11-($2.25) 3.00

FAWCETT MOTION PICTURE COMICS (See Motion Picture Comics)

FAWCETT MOVIE COMIC
Fawcett Publications: 1949 - No. 20, Dec, 1952 (All photo-c)

nn- "Dakota Lil"; George Montgomery & Rod Cameron (1949) 32 64 96 184 267 350
nn- "Copper Canyon"; Ray Milland & Hedy Lamarr (1950) 25 50 75 141 203 265
nn- "Destination Moon" (1950) 79 158 237 494 760 1025
nn- "Montana"; Errol Flynn & Alexis Smith (1950) 25 50 75 141 203 265
nn- "Pioneer Marshal"; Monte Hale (1950) 25 50 75 141 203 265
nn- "Powder River Rustlers"; Rocky Lane (1950) 36 72 108 204 297 390
nn- "Singing Guns"; Vaughn Monroe, Ella Raines & Walter Brennan (1950) 22 44 66 123 177 230

Fawcett Funny Animals #5 © FAW

Fear #3 © MAR

Feature Books #11 © KING

GD 2.0 | VG 4.0 | FN 6.0 | VF 8.0 | VF/NM 9.0 | NM- 9.2

7- "Gunmen of Abilene"; Rocky Lane; Bob Powell-a (1950) 27 54 81 152 219 285
8- "King of the Bullwhip"; Lash LaRue; Bob Powell-a (1950) 39 78 117 222 324 425
9- "The Old Frontier"; Monte Hale; Bob Powell-a (2/51; mis-dated 2/50) 26 52 78 147 211 275
10- "The Missourians"; Monte Hale (4/51) 26 52 78 147 211 275
11- "The Thundering Trail"; Lash LaRue (6/51) 32 64 96 184 267 350
12- "Rustlers on Horseback"; Rocky Lane (8/51) 27 54 81 152 219 285
13- "Warpath"; Edmond O'Brien & Forrest Tucker (10/51) 19 38 57 107 154 200
14- "Last Outpost"; Ronald Reagan (12/51) 40 80 120 240 360 480
15-(Scarce)- "The Man From Planet X"; Robert Clark; Schaffenberger-a (2/52) 231 462 693 1444 2222 3000
16- "10 Tall Men"; Burt Lancaster 15 30 45 85 120 155
17- "Rose of Cimarron"; Jack Buetel & Mala Powers 12 24 36 69 95 120
18- "The Brigand"; Anthony Dexter & Anthony Quinn; Schaffenberger-a 12 24 36 69 95 120
19- "Carbine Williams"; James Stewart; Costanza-a; James Stewart photo-c 13 26 39 76 106 135
20- "Ivanhoe"; Robert Taylor & Liz Taylor photo-c 23 46 69 132 191 250

FAWCETT'S FUNNY ANIMALS (No. 1-26, 80-on titled "Funny Animals"; becomes Li'l Tomboy No. 92 on?)
Fawcett Publications/Charlton Comics No. 84 on: 12/42 - #79, 4/53; #80, 6/53 - #83, 12?/53; #84, 4/54 - #91, 2/56

1-Capt. Marvel on cover; intro. Hoppy The Captain Marvel Bunny, cloned from Capt. Marvel; Billy the Kid & Willie the Worm begin 56 112 168 350 538 725
2-Xmas-c 35 70 105 198 287 375
3-5: 3(2/43)-Spirit of '43-c 23 46 69 132 191 250
6,7,9,10 15 30 45 83 117 150
8-Flag-c 15 30 45 86 123 160
11-20: 14-Cover is a 1944 calendar 11 22 33 64 87 110
21-40: 25-Xmas-c. 26-St. Valentine's Day-c 9 18 27 51 62 75
41-86,90,91 8 16 24 40 50 60
87-89(10-54-2/55)-Merry Mailman ish (TV/Radio)-part photo-c 9 18 27 51 62 75

NOTE: *Marvel Bunny in all issues to at least No. 68 (not in 49-54).*

FAZE ONE FAZERS
AC Comics: 1986 - No. 4, Sept, 1986 (Limited series)

1-4 2.25

F.B.I., THE
Dell Publishing Co.: Apr-June, 1965

1-Sinnott-a 3 7 10 21 28 35

F.B.I. STORY, THE (Movie)
Dell Publishing Co.: No. 1069, Jan-Mar, 1960

Four Color 1069-Toth-a; James Stewart photo-c 11 22 33 75 100 145

FEAR (Adventure into...)
Marvel Comics Group: Nov, 1970 - No. 31, Dec, 1975

1-Fantasy & Sci-Fi-r in early issues; 68 pg. Giant size; Kirby-a(r) 5 10 15 33 44 55
2-6: 2-4-(68 pgs.). 5,6-(52 pgs.) Kirby-a(r) 3 6 9 19 25 32
7-9-Kirby-a(r) 2 4 6 11 14 18
10-Man-Thing begins (10/72, 4th app.), ends #19; see Savage Tales #1 for 1st app.; 1st solo series; Chaykin/Morrow-c/a; 4 8 12 27 36 45
11,12: 11-N. Adams-c. 12-Starlin/Buckler-a 2 4 6 12 16 20
13,14,16-18: 17-Origin/1st app. Wundarr 2 4 6 10 13 16
15-1st full-length Man-Thing story (8/73) 2 4 6 12 16 20
19-Intro. Howard the Duck; Val Mayerik-a (12/73) 4 8 12 27 36 45
20-Morbius, the Living Vampire begins, ends #31; has history recap of Morbius with X-Men & Spider-Man 4 8 12 27 36 45
21-23,25 2 4 6 10 13 16
24-Blade-c/sty 3 6 9 18 24 30
26-31 2 4 6 8 10 12

NOTE: ***Bolle** a-13i. **Brunner** c-15-17. **Buckler** a-11p, 12i. **Chaykin** a-10i. **Colan** a-23r. **Craig** a-10p. **Ditko** a-6-8r. **Evans** a-30. **Everett** a-9, 10i, 21r. **Gulacy** a-20p. **Heath** a-12r. **Heck** a-8r, 13r. **Gil Kane** a-21p; c(p)-20, 21, 23-28, 31. **Kirby** a-1-9r. **Maneely** a-24r. **Mooney** a-11i, 26r. **Morrow** a-11i. **Paul Reinman** a-14r. **Robbins** a(p)-25-27, 31. **Russell** a-23p, 24p. **Severin** c-8. **Starlin** c-12p.*

FEARBOOK
Eclipse Comics: April, 1986 ($1.75, one-shot, mature)

1-Scholastic Mag- r; Bissette-a 2.25

FEAR EFFECT (Based on the video game)
Image Comics (Top Cow): May, 2000; March, 2001 ($2.95)

Retro Helix 1 (3/01), Special 1 (5/00) 3.00

FEAR IN THE NIGHT (See Complete Mystery No. 3)

FEARLESS FAGAN
Dell Publishing Co.: No. 441, Dec, 1952 (one-shot)

Four Color 441 4 8 12 29 40 50

FEATHER
Image Comics: Aug, 2003 - No. 5, May, 2004 ($2.95)

1-4-Steve Uy-s/a 3.00
5-($5.95) 6.00

FEATURE BOOK (Dell) (See Large Feature Comic)

FEATURE BOOKS (Newspaper-r, early issues)
David McKay Publications: May, 1937 - No. 57, 1948 (B&W)
(Full color, 68 pgs. begin #26 on)

Note: See individual alphabetical listings for prices

nn-Popeye & the Jeep (#1, 100 pgs.); reprinted as Feature Books #3(Very Rare; only 3 known copies, 1-VF, 2-in low grade)
nn-Dick Tracy (#1)-Reprinted as Feature Book #4 (100 pgs.) & in part as 4-Color #1 (Rare, less than 10 known copies)

NOTE: *Above books were advertised together with different covers from Feat. Books #3 & 4.*

1-King of the Royal Mtd. (#1)
3-Popeye (7/37) by Segar;
4-Dick Tracy (8/37)-Same as nn issue but a new cover added
6-Dick Tracy (10/37)
8-Secret Agent X-9 (12/37) -Not by Raymond
9-Dick Tracy (1/38)
11-Little Annie Rooney (#1, 3/38)
13-Inspector Wade (5/38)
15-Barney Baxter (#1) (7/38)
17-Gangbusters (#1, 9/38) (1st app.)
20-Phantom (#1, 12/38)
22-Phantom
24-Lone Ranger (1941)
26-Prince Valiant (1941)-Hal Foster -c/a; newspaper strips reprinted, pgs. 1-28,30-63; color & 68 pg. issues begin; Foster cover is only original comic book artwork by him
36('43),38,40('44),42,43, 45,47-Blondie
39-Phantom
46-Mandrake in the Fire World-(58 pgs.)
48-Maltese Falcon by Dashiell Hammett('46)
51,54-Rip Kirby; Raymond-c/s; origin-#51
53,56,57-Phantom
2-Popeye (6/37) by Segar same as nn issue but a new cover added
5-Popeye (9/37) by Segar
7-Little Orphan Annie (#1, 11/37) (Rare)-Reprints strips from 12/31/34 to 7/17/35
10-Popeye (2/38)
12-Blondie (#1) (4/38) (Rare)
14-Popeye (6/38) by Segar
16-Red Eagle (8/38)
18,19-Mandrake
21-Lone Ranger
23-Mandrake
25-Flash Gordon (#1)-Reprints not by Raymond
27-29,31,34-Blondie
30-Katzenjammer Kids (#1, 1942)
32,35,41,44-Katzenjammer Kids
33(nn)-Romance of Flying; World War II photos
37-Katzenjammer Kids; has photo & biog. of Harold H.Knerr(1883-1949) who took over strip from Rudolph Dirks in 1914
49,50-Perry Mason; based on Gardner novels
52,55-Mandrake

NOTE: *All Feature Books through #25 are over-sized 8-1/2x11-3/8" comics with color covers and black and white interiors. The covers are rough, heavy stock. The page counts, including covers, are as follows: nn, #3, 4-100 pgs.; #1, 2-52 pgs.; #5-25 are all 76 pgs. #33 was found in bound set from publisher.*

FEATURE COMICS (Formerly Feature Funnies)
Quality Comics Group: No. 21, June, 1939 - No. 144, May, 1950

21-The Clock, Jane Arden & Mickey Finn continue from Feature Funnies 69 138 207 397 561 725
22-26: 23-Charlie Chan begins (8/39, 1st app.) 48 96 144 276 388 500
26-(nn, nd)-Cover in one color, (10¢, 36 pgs.; issue No. blanked out. Two variations exist, each contain half of the regular #26) 48 96 144 276 388 500
27-(Rare)-Origin/1st app. Doll Man by Eisner (scripts) & Lou Fine (art); Doll Man begins, ends #139 423 846 1269 2936 4718 6500
28-2nd app. Doll Man by Lou Fine 169 338 507 1056 1628 2200
29 96 192 288 600 925 1250
30-1st Doll Man-c 127 254 381 794 1222 1650
31-Last Clock & Charlie Chan issue (4/40); Charlie Chan moves to Big Shot #1 following month (5/40) 75 150 225 469 722 975
32,34,36: Dollman covers. 32-Rusty Ryan & Samar begin. 34-Captain Fortune app. 62 124 186 388 594 800
33,35,37: 37-Last Fine Doll Man 53 106 159 323 494 665

Note: *A 15¢ Canadian version of Feature Comics #37, made in the US, exists.*

38,40-Dollman covers. 38-Origin the Ace of Space. 40-Bruce Blackburn in costume

Feature Comics #70 © QUA

Felicia Hardy #2 © MAR

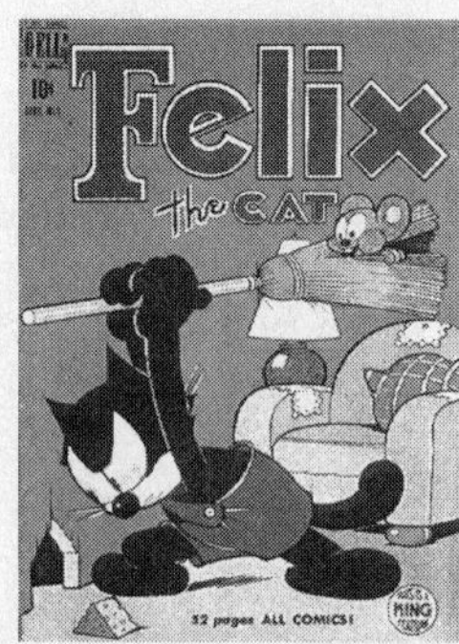
Felix the Cat #14 © KING

GD VG FN VF VF/NM NM-
2.0 4.0 6.0 8.0 9.0 9.2

50 100 150 305 465 625
39,41: 39-Origin The Destroying Demon, ends #40; X-Mas-c.
42 84 126 256 391 525
42,46,48,50-Dollman covers. 42-USA, the Spirit of Old Glory begins. 46-Intro. Boyville Brigadiers in Rusty Ryan. 48-USA ends 40 80 120 233 342 450
43,45,47,49: 47-Fargo Kid begins 33 66 99 190 275 360
44-Doll Man by Crandall begins, ends #63; Crandall-a(2)
50 100 150 305 465 625
51,53,55,57,59: 57-Spider Widow begins 26 52 78 147 211 275
52,54,56,58,60-Dollman covers. 56-Marijuana story in Swing Sisson strip. 60-Raven begins, ends #71 31 62 93 177 256 335
61,63,65,67 23 46 69 132 191 250
62,64,66,68-Dollman covers. 68-(5/43) 27 54 81 154 222 290
69,71-Phantom Lady x-over in Spider Widow 26 52 78 147 211 275
70-Dollman-c; Phantom Lady x-over 30 60 90 170 245 320
72,74,77-80,100-Dollman covers. 72-Spider Widow ends
22 44 66 125 180 235
73,75,76 19 38 57 107 154 200
81-99-All Dollman covers 17 34 51 95 135 175
101-144: 139-Last Doll Man & last Doll Man cover. 140-Intro. Stuntman Stetson (Stuntman Stetson c-140-144) 13 26 39 76 106 135

NOTE: ***Celardo** a-37-43. **Crandall** a-44-60, 62, 63-on(most). **Gustavson** a-(Rusty Ryan)- 32-134. **Powell** a-34, 64-73. The Clock c-25, 28, 29. Doll Man c-30, 32, 34, 36, 38, 40, 42, 44, 46, 48, 50, 52, 54, 56, 58, 60, 62, 64, 66, 68, 70, 72, 74, 77-139. Joe Palooka c-21, 24, 27.*

FEATURE FILMS
National Periodical Publ.: Mar-Apr, 1950 - No. 4, Sept-Oct, 1950 (All photo-c)
1- "Captain China" with John Payne, Gail Russell, Lon Chaney & Edgar Bergen
67 134 201 419 647 875
2- "Riding High" with Bing Crosby 71 142 213 444 685 925
3- "The Eagle & the Hawk" with John Payne, Rhonda Fleming & D. O'Keefe
67 134 201 419 647 875
4- "Fancy Pants"; Bob Hope & Lucille Ball 75 150 225 469 722 975

FEATURE FUNNIES (Feature Comics No. 21 on)
Harry 'A' Chesler: Oct, 1937 - No. 20, May, 1939
1(V9#1-indicia)-Joe Palooka, Mickey Finn (1st app.), The Bungles, Jane Arden, Dixie Dugan (1st app.), Big Top, Ned Brant, Strange As It Seems, & Off the Record strip reprints begin
322 644 966 1770 2369 3200
2-The Hawk app. (11/37); Goldberg-c 150 300 450 825 1110 1500
3-Hawks of Seas begins by Eisner, ends #12; The Clock begins; Christmas-c
117 234 351 644 869 1175
4,5 86 172 258 473 647 875
6-12: 11-Archie O'Toole by Bud Thomas begins, ends #22
67 134 201 369 502 675
13-Espionage, Starring Black X begins by Eisner, ends #20
71 142 213 391 532 720
14-20 50 100 150 275 372 500
NOTE: *Joe Palooka covers 1, 6, 9, 12, 15, 18.*

FEATURE PRESENTATION, A (Feature Presentations Magazine #6) (Formerly Women in Love) (Also see Startling Terror Tales #11)
Fox Features Syndicate: No. 5, April, 1950
5(#1)-Black Tarantula 40 80 120 233 342 450

FEATURE PRESENTATIONS MAGAZINE (Formerly A Feature Presentation #5; becomes Feature Stories Magazine #3 on)
Fox Features Syndicate: No. 6, July, 1950
6(#2)-Moby Dick; Wood-c 33 66 99 190 275 360

FEATURE STORIES MAGAZINE (Formerly Feature Presentations Mag. #6)
Fox Features Syndicate: No. 3, Aug, 1950
3-Jungle Lil, Zegra stories; bondage-c 35 70 105 200 290 380

FEDERAL MEN COMICS (See Adventure Comics #32, The Comics Magazine, New Adventure Comics, New Book of Comics, New Comics & Star Spangled Comics #91)
Gerard Publ. Co.: No. 2, 1945 (DC reprints from 1930's)
2-Siegel/Shuster-a; cover redrawn from Det. #9 40 80 120 233 342 450

FEEDERS
Dark Horse Comics: Oct, 1999 ($2.95, one-shot)
1-Mike Allred-c/a/Shane Hawks-s 3.00

FELICIA HARDY: THE BLACK CAT
Marvel Comics: July, 1994 - No. 4, Oct, 1994 ($1.50, limited series)
1-4: 1,4-Spider-Man app. 2.25

FELIX'S NEPHEWS INKY & DINKY
Harvey Publications: Sept, 1957 - No. 7, Oct, 1958
1-Cover shows Inky's left eye with 2 pupils 10 20 30 56 73 90
2-7 6 12 18 31 38 45
NOTE: ***Messmer** art in 1-6. **Oriolo** a-1-7.*

FELIX THE CAT (See Cat Tales 3-D, The Funnies, March of Comics #24,36,51, New Funnies & Popular Comics)
Dell Publ. No. 1-19/Toby No. 20-61/Harvey No. 62-118/Dell No. 1-12:
1943 - No. 118, Nov, 1961; Sept-Nov, 1962 - No. 12, July-Sept, 1965
Four Color 15 70 140 210 536 868 1200
Four Color 46('44) 39 78 117 293 459 625
Four Color 77('45) 37 74 111 278 432 585
Four Color 119('46)-All new stories begin 34 68 102 255 398 540
Four Color 135('46) 26 52 78 184 282 380
Four Color 162(9/47) 20 40 60 145 223 300
1(2-3/48)(Dell) 28 56 84 199 305 410
2 15 30 45 107 164 220
3-5 12 24 36 86 131 175
6-19(2-3/51-Dell) 10 20 30 70 100 130
20-30,32,33,36,38-61(6/55)-All Messmer issues.(Toby): 28-(2/52)-Some copies have #29 on cover, #28 on inside (Rare in high grade) 22 44 66 158 242 325
31,34,35-No Messmer-a; Messmer-c only 31,34 10 20 30 73 107 140
37-(100 pgs., 25 ¢, 1/15/53, X-Mas-c, Toby; daily & Sunday-r (rare)
41 82 123 318 497 675
62(8/55)-80,100 (Harvey) 6 12 18 40 55 70
81-99 5 10 15 36 48 60
101-118(11/61): 101-117-Reprints. 118-All new-a 4 8 12 25 33 42
12-269-211(#1, 9-11/62)(Dell)-No Messmer 6 12 18 38 52 65
2-12(7-9/65)(Dell, TV)-No Messmer 4 8 12 29 40 50
3-D Comic Book 1(1953-One Shot, 25¢)-w/glasses 30 60 90 213 327 440
Summer Annual nn ('53, 25¢, 100 pgs., Toby)-Daily & Sunday-r
36 72 108 270 423 575
Winter Annual 2 ('54, 25¢, 100 pgs., Toby)-Daily & Sunday-r
34 68 102 255 398 540
(Special note: Despite the covers on Toby 37 and the Summer Annual above proclaiming "all new stories," they were actually reformatted newspaper strips)

NOTE: ***Otto Messmer** went to work for Universal Film as an animator in 1915 and then worked for the Pat Sullivan animation studio in 1916. He created a black cat in the cartoon short, Feline Follies in 1919 that became known as Felix in the early 1920s. The Felix Sunday strip began Aug. 14, 1923 and continued until Sept. 19, 1943 whjen **Messmer** took the character to Dell (Western Publishing) and began doing Felix comic books, first adapting strips to the comic format. The first all new Felix comic was Four Color #119 in 1946 (#4 in the Dell run). The daily Felix was begun on May 9, 1927 by another artist, but by the following year, **Messmer** did it too. King Features took the daily away from **Messmer** in 1954 and he began to do some of his most dynamic art for Toby Press. The daily was continued by **Joe Oriolo** who drew it until it was discontinued Jan. 9, 1967. **Oriolo** was **Messmer's** assistant for many years and inked some of **Messmer's** pencils through the Toby run, as well as doing some of the stories by himself. Though **Messmer** continued to work for Harvey, his contirubitons were limited, and no all **Messmer** stories appeared after the Toby run until some early Toby reprints were published in the 1990s Harvey revival of the title. 4-Color No. 15, 46, 77 and the Toby Annuals are all daily or Sunday newspaper reprints from the 1930's-1940's drawn by **Otto Messmer**. #101-r/#64; 102-r/#65; 103-r/#67; 104-117-r/#68-81. **Messmer**-a in all Dell/Toby/Harvey issues except #31, 34, 35, 97, 98, 100, 118. **Oriolo** a-20, 31-on.*

FELIX THE CAT (Also see The Nine Lives of...)
Harvey Comics/Gladstone: Sept, 1991 - No. 7, Jan, 1993 ($1.25/$1.50, bi-monthly)
1: 1950s-r/Toby issues by Messmer begins. 1-Inky and Dinky back-up story (produced by Gladstone) 4.00
2-7, Big Book , V2#1 (9/92, $1.95, 52 pgs.) 3.00

FELIX THE CAT AND FRIENDS
Felix Comics: 1992 - No. 5, 1993 ($1.95)
1-5: 1-Contains Felix trading cards 3.00

FELIX THE CAT & HIS FRIENDS (Pat Sullivan's...)
Toby Press: Dec, 1953 - No. 3, 1954 (Indicia title for #2&3 as listed)
1 (Indicia title, "Felix and His Friends," #1 only) 31 62 93 175 253 330
2-3 19 38 57 107 154 200

FELIX THE CAT DIGEST MAGAZINE
Harvey Comics: July, 1992 ($1.75, digest-size, 98 pgs.)
1-Felix, Richie Rich stories 6.00

FELIX THE CAT KEEPS ON WALKIN'
Hamilton Comics: 1991 ($15.95, 8-1/2"x11", 132 pgs.)
nn-Reprints 15 Toby Press Felix the Cat and Felix and His Friends stories in new color 16.00

FELON
Image Comics (Minotaur Press): Nov, 2001 - No. 4, Apr, 2002 ($2.95, B&W)
1-4-Rucka-s/Clark-a/c 3.00

FEM FANTASTIQUE
AC Comics: Aug, 1988 ($1.95, B&W)

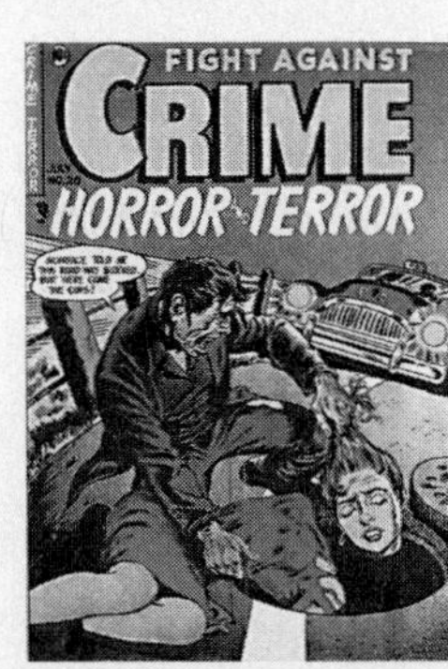

Fight Against Crime #20 © Story

Fight Comics #7 © FH

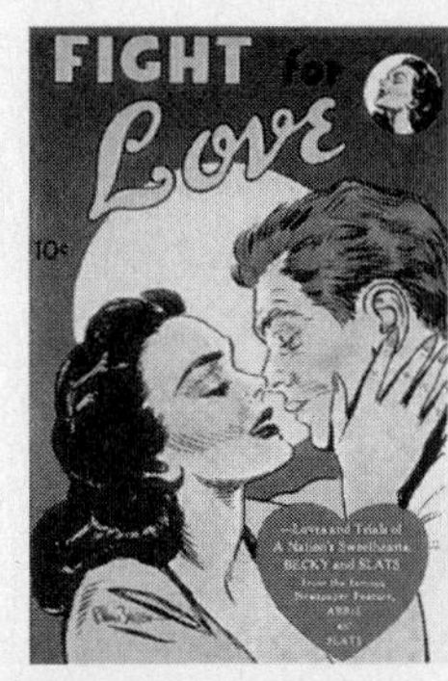

Fight For Love nn © UFS

	GD 2.0	VG 4.0	FN 6.0	VF 8.0	VF/NM 9.0	NM- 9.2
V2#1-By Bill Black; Betty Page pin-up						4.00

FEMFORCE (Also see Untold Origin of the Femforce)
Americomics: Apr, 1985 - No. 109 (1.75-/2.95, B&W #16-56)

	GD	VG	FN	VF	VF/NM	NM-
1-Black-a in most; Nightveil, Ms. Victory begin	1	3	4	6	8	10
2-10						4.00
11-43: 25-Origin/1st app. new Ms. Victory. 28-Colt leaves. 29,30-Camilla-r by Mayo from Jungle Comics. 36-(2.95, 52 pgs.)						4.00
44,64: 44-W/mini-comic, Catman & Kitten #0. 64-Re-intro Black Phantom						5.00
45-63,65-99: 50 (2.95, 52 pgs.)-Contains flexi-disc; origin retold; most AC characters app. 51-Photo-c from movie. 57-Begin color issues. 95-Photo-c						3.00
100-($3.95)						5.00
100-($6.90)-Polybagged	1	2	3	5	6	8
101-109-($4.95)						5.00
Special 1 (Fall, '84)(B&W, 52pgs.)-1st app. Ms. Victory, She-Cat, Blue Bulleteer, Rio Rita & Lady Luger						4.00
Bad Girl Backlash-(12/95, $5.00)						5.00
Frightbook 1 ('92, $2.95, B&W)-Halloween special, In the House of Horror 1 ('89, 2.50, B&W), Night of the Demon 1 ('90, 2.75, B&W), Out of the Asylum Special 1 ('87, B&W, $1.95), Pin-Up Portfolio						3.50
Pin-Up Portfolio (5 issues)						4.00

FEMFORCE UP CLOSE
AC Comics: Apr, 1992 - No. 11, 1995 ($2.75, quarterly)

	GD	VG	FN	VF	VF/NM	NM-
1-11: 1-Stars Nightveil; inside f/c photo from Femforce movie. 2-Stars Stardust. 3-Stars Dragonfly. 4-Stars She-Cat						3.50

FERDINAND THE BULL (See Mickey Mouse Magazine V4#3)
Dell Publishing Co.: 1938 (10¢, large size, some color w/rest B&W)

	GD	VG	FN	VF	VF/NM	NM-
nn	20	40	60	112	161	210

FERRET
Malibu Comics: Sept, 1992; May, 1993 - No. 10, Feb, 1994 ($1.95)

	GD	VG	FN	VF	VF/NM	NM-
1-(1992, one-shot)						3.00
1-10: 1-Die-cut-c. 2-4-Collector's Ed. w/poster. 5-Polybagged w/Skycap						2.50
2-4-($1.95)-Newsstand Edition w/different-c						2.25

FEUD
Marvel Comics (Epic Comics/Heavy Hitters): July, 1993 - No. 4, Oct, 1993 ($1.95, limited series)

	GD	VG	FN	VF	VF/NM	NM-
1-($2.50)-Embossed-c						3.00
2-4						2.25

F5
Image Comics/Dark Horse: Jan, 2000 - No. 4, Oct, 2000 ($2.50/$2.95)

	GD	VG	FN	VF	VF/NM	NM-
Preview (1/00, $2.50) Character bios and b&w pages; Daniel-s/a						2.50
1-($2.95, 48 pages) Tony Daniel-s/a						3.00
1-($20.00) Variant bikini-c						20.00
2-4-($2.50)						2.50
F5 Origin (Dark Horse Comics, 11/01, $2.99) w/cove gallery & sketches						3.00

FIBBER McGEE & MOLLY (Radio)(Also see A-1 Comics)
Magazine Enterprises: No. 25, 1949 (one-shot)

	GD	VG	FN	VF	VF/NM	NM-
A-1 25	11	22	33	62	84	105

55 DAYS AT PEKING (See Movie Comics)

FICTION ILLUSTRATED
Byron Preiss Visual Publ./Pyramid: No. 1, Jan, 1975 - No. 4, Jan, 1977 ($1.00, #1,2 are digest size, 132 pgs.; #3,4 are graphic novels for mail order and specialty bookstores only)

	GD	VG	FN	VF	VF/NM	NM-
1,2: 1-Schlomo Raven; Sutton-a. 2-Starfawn; Stephen Fabian-a.	2	4	6	12	16	20
3-($1.00-c, 4 3/4 x 6 1/2" digest size) Chandler; new Steranko-a	3	6	9	16	20	24
3-($4.95-c, 8 1/2 x 11" graphic novel; low print) same contents and indicia, but "Chandler" is the cover feature title	6	12	18	40	55	70
4-($4.95-c, 8 1/2 x 11" graphic novel; low print) Son of Sherlock Holmes; Reese-a	5	10	15	33	44	55

FIERCE
Dark Horse Comics (Rocket Comics): July, 2004 - No. 4 ($2.99, limited series)

	GD	VG	FN	VF	VF/NM	NM-
1,2-Jeremy Love-s/Robert Love-a						3.00

FIGHT AGAINST CRIME (Fight Against the Guilty #22, 23)
Story Comics: May, 1951 - No. 21, Sept, 1954

	GD	VG	FN	VF	VF/NM	NM-
1-True crime stories #1-4	40	80	120	232	342	450
2	21	42	63	118	169	220
3,5: 5-Frazetta-a, 1 pg.; content change to horror & suspense	18	36	54	102	146	190
4-Drug story "Hopped Up Killers"	19	38	57	107	154	200
6,7: 6-Used in **POP**, pgs. 83,84	16	32	48	89	127	165
8-Last crime format issue	15	30	45	83	117	150

NOTE: *No. 9-21 contain violent, gruesome stories with blood, dismemberment, decapitation, E.C. style plot twists and several E.C. swipes. Bondage c-4, 6, 18, 19.*

	GD	VG	FN	VF	VF/NM	NM-
9-11,13	39	78	117	222	324	425
12-Morphine drug story "The Big Dope"	40	80	120	236	351	465
14-Tothish art by Ross Andru; electrocution-c	40	80	120	233	342	450
15-B&W & color illos in **POP**	39	78	117	222	324	425
16-E.C. story swipe/Haunt of Fear #19; Tothish-a by Ross Andru; bondage-c	40	80	120	236	351	465
17-Wildey E.C. swipe/Shock SuspenStories #9; knife through neck-c (1/54)	40	80	120	235	348	460
18,19: 19-Bondage/torture-c	37	74	111	209	305	400
20-Decapitation cover; contains hanging, ax murder, blood & violence	60	120	180	375	575	775
21-E.C. swipe	31	62	93	178	259	340

NOTE: ***Cameron** a-4, 5, 8. **Hollingsworth** a-3-7, 9, 10, 13. **Wildey** a-6, 15, 16.*

FIGHT AGAINST THE GUILTY (Formerly Fight Against Crime)
Story Comics: No. 22, Dec, 1954 - No. 23, Mar, 1955

	GD	VG	FN	VF	VF/NM	NM-
22-Tothish-a by Ross Andru; Ditko-a; E.C. story swipe; electrocution-c (Last pre-code)	31	62	93	175	253	330
23-Hollingsworth-a	21	42	63	118	169	220

FIGHT COMICS
Fiction House Magazines: Jan, 1940 - No. 83, 11/52; No. 84, Wint, 1952-53; No. 85, Spring, 1953; No. 86, Summer, 1954

	GD	VG	FN	VF	VF/NM	NM-
1-Origin Spy Fighter, Starring Saber; Jack Dempsey life story; Shark Brodie & Chip Collins begin; Fine-c; Eisner-a	334	668	1002	2171	3511	4850
2-Joe Louis life story; Fine/Eisner-c	119	238	357	744	1147	1550
3-Rip Regan, the Power Man begins (3/40)	92	184	276	575	888	1200
4,5: 4-Fine-c	66	132	198	413	637	860
6-10: 6,7-Powell-c	50	100	150	305	465	625
11-14: Rip Regan ends	46	92	138	281	428	575
15-1st app. Super American plus-c (10/41)	60	120	180	375	580	785
16-Captain Fight begins (12/41); Spy Fighter ends	60	120	180	375	580	785
17,18: Super American ends	46	92	138	281	428	575
19-Captain Fight ends; Senorita Rio begins (6/42, origin & 1st app.); Rip Carson, Chute Trooper begins	48	96	144	293	447	600
20	40	80	120	240	360	480
21-30	33	66	99	190	275	360
31-Decapitation-c	37	74	111	209	305	400
32-Tiger Girl begins (6/44, 1st app.?)	40	80	120	233	342	450
33-50: 44-Capt. Fight returns. 48-Used in Love and Death by Legman. 49-Jungle-c begin, end #81	25	50	75	141	203	265
51-Origin Tiger Girl; Patsy Pin-Up app.	39	78	117	222	324	425
52-60,62-64-Last Baker issue	22	44	66	123	177	230
61-Origin Tiger Girl retold	24	48	72	135	195	255
65-78: 78-Used in **POP**, pg. 99	19	38	57	107	154	200
79-The Space Rangers app.	20	40	60	112	161	210
80-85: 81-Last jungle-c. 82-85-War-c/stories	16	32	48	92	131	170
86-Two Tigerman stories by Evans-r/Rangers Comics #40,41; Moreira-r/Rangers Comics #45	16	32	48	92	131	170

NOTE: *Bondage covers, Lingerie, headlights panels are common. Captain Fight by **Kamen**-51-66. Kayo Kirby by **Baker**-#43-64, 67(not by Baker). Senorita Rio by **Kamen**-#57-64; by **Grandenetti**-#65, 66. Tiger Girl by **Baker**-#36-60, 62-64; **Eisner** c-1-3, 5, 10, 11. **Kamen** a-54?, 57? **Tuska** a-1, 5, 8, 10, 21, 29, 34. **Whitman** c-73-84. **Zolnerwich** c-16, 17, 22. Power Man c-5, 6, 9. Super American c-15-17. Tiger Girl c-49-81.*

FIGHT FOR LOVE
United Features Syndicate: 1952 (no month)

	GD	VG	FN	VF	VF/NM	NM-
nn-Abbie & Slats newspaper-r	9	18	27	54	70	85

FIGHT FOR TOMORROW
DC Comics (Vertigo): Nov, 2002 - No. 6, Apr, 2003 ($2.50, limited series)

	GD	VG	FN	VF	VF/NM	NM-
1-6-Denys Cowan-a/Brian Wood-s. 1-Jim Lee-c						2.50

FIGHTING AIR FORCE (See United States Fighting Air Force)

FIGHTIN' AIR FORCE (Formerly Sherlock Holmes?; Never Again? War and Attack #54 on)
Charlton Comics: No. 3, Feb, 1956 - No. 53, Feb-Mar, 1966

	GD	VG	FN	VF	VF/NM	NM-
V1#3	9	18	27	51	62	75
4-10	6	12	18	31	38	45
11(3/58, 68 pgs.)	8	16	24	43	54	65
12 (100 pgs.)-U.S. Nukes Russia	11	22	33	66	91	115
13-30: 13,24-Glanzman-a. 24-Glanzman-c	3	7	10	21	28	35
31-50: 50-American Eagle begins	3	6	9	16	20	24

Fightin' American #2 © S&K

Fightin' Army #17 © CC

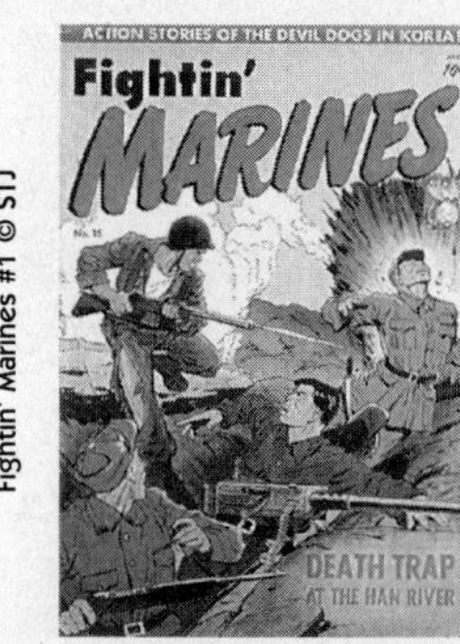

Fightin' Marines #1 © STJ

	GD 2.0	VG 4.0	FN 6.0	VF 8.0	VF/NM 9.0	NM- 9.2
51-53	2	4	6	12	16	20

FIGHTING AMERICAN
Headline Publ./Prize (Crestwood): Apr-May, 1954 - No. 7, Apr-May, 1955

	GD 2.0	VG 4.0	FN 6.0	VF 8.0	VF/NM 9.0	NM- 9.2
1-Origin & 1st app. Fighting American & Speedboy (Capt. America & Bucky clones); S&K-c/a(3); 1st super hero satire series	169	338	507	1056	1628	2200
2-S&K-a(3)	79	158	237	494	760	1025
3-5: 3,4-S&K-a(3). 5-S&K-a(2); Kirby/?-a	63	126	189	394	610	825
6-Origin-r (4 pgs.) plus 2 pgs. by S&K	60	120	180	375	575	775
7-Kirby-a	54	108	162	329	502	675

NOTE: ***Simon** & **Kirby** covers on all. 6 is last pre-code issue.*

FIGHTING AMERICAN
Harvey Publications: Oct, 1966 (25¢)

	GD 2.0	VG 4.0	FN 6.0	VF 8.0	VF/NM 9.0	NM- 9.2
1-Origin Fighting American & Speedboy by S&K-r; S&K-c/a(3); 1 pg. Neal Adams ad	6	12	18	43	59	75

FIGHTING AMERICAN
DC Comics: Feb, 1994 - No. 6, 1994 ($1.50, limited series)

	GD 2.0	VG 4.0	FN 6.0	VF 8.0	VF/NM 9.0	NM- 9.2
1-6						2.50

FIGHTING AMERICAN (Vol. 3)
Awesome Entertainment: Aug, 1997 - No. 2, Oct, 1997 ($2.50)

	GD 2.0	VG 4.0	FN 6.0	VF 8.0	VF/NM 9.0	NM- 9.2
Preview-Agent America (pre-lawsuit)	1	2	3	5	6	7
1-Four covers by Liefeld, Churchill, Platt, McGuinness						2.50
1-Platinum Edition, 1-Gold foil Edition						10.00
1-Comic Cavalcade Edition, 2-American Ent. Spice Ed.						4.00
2-Platt-c, 2-Liefeld variant-c						2.50

FIGHTING AMERICAN: DOGS OF WAR
Awesome-Hyperwerks: Sept, 1998 - No. 3, May, 1999 ($2.50)

	GD 2.0	VG 4.0	FN 6.0	VF 8.0	VF/NM 9.0	NM- 9.2
Limited Convention Special (7/98, B&W) Platt-a						2.50
1-3-Starlin-s/Platt-a/c						2.50

FIGHTING AMERICAN: RULES OF THE GAME
Awesome Entertainment: Nov, 1997 - No. 3, Mar, 1998 ($2.50, lim. series)

	GD 2.0	VG 4.0	FN 6.0	VF 8.0	VF/NM 9.0	NM- 9.2
1-3: 1-Loeb-s/McGuinness-a/c. 2-Flip book with Swat! preview						2.50
1-Liefeld SPICE variant-c, 1-Dynamic Forces Ed.; McGuinness-c						2.50
1-Liefeld Fighting American & cast variant-c						2.50

FIGHTIN' ARMY (Formerly Soldier and Marine Comics) (See Captain Willy Schultz)
Charlton Comics: No. 16, 1/56 - No. 127, 12/76; No. 128, 9/77 - No. 172, 11/84

	GD 2.0	VG 4.0	FN 6.0	VF 8.0	VF/NM 9.0	NM- 9.2
16	9	18	27	51	62	75
17-19,21-23,25-30	6	12	18	31	38	45
20-Ditko-a	9	18	27	51	62	75
24 (3/58, 68 pgs.)	8	16	24	40	50	60
31-45	3	6	9	19	25	32
46-60	3	6	9	16	21	26
61-74	2	4	6	12	16	20
75-1st The Lonely War of Willy Schultz	3	6	9	18	24	30
76-80: 76-92-The Lonely War of Willy Schultz. 79-Devil Brigade	2	4	6	12	16	20
81-88,91,93-99: 82,83-Devil Brigade	2	4	6	10	12	15
89,90,92-Ditko-a	2	4	6	14	18	22
100	2	4	6	11	14	18
101-127	2	4	6	8	10	12
128-140	1	2	3	5	6	8
141-165						6.00
166-172-Low print run	1	2	3	5	6	8
108(Modern Comics-1977)-Reprint						4.00

NOTE: ***Aparo** c-154. **Glanzman** a-77-88. **Montes/Bache** a-48, 49, 51, 69, 75, 76, 170r.*

FIGHTING CARAVANS (See Zane Grey 4-Color 632)

FIGHTING DANIEL BOONE
Avon Periodicals: 1953

	GD 2.0	VG 4.0	FN 6.0	VF 8.0	VF/NM 9.0	NM- 9.2
nn-Kinstler-c/a, 22 pgs.	20	40	60	112	161	210
I.W. Reprint #1-Reprints #1 above; Kinstler-c/a; Lawrence/Alascia-a	3	6	9	16	20	24

FIGHTING DAVY CROCKETT (Formerly Kit Carson)
Avon Periodicals: No. 9, Oct-Nov, 1955

	GD 2.0	VG 4.0	FN 6.0	VF 8.0	VF/NM 9.0	NM- 9.2
9-Kinstler-c	10	20	30	56	73	90

FIGHTIN' FIVE, THE (Formerly Space War) (Also see The Peacemaker)
Charlton Comics: July, 1964 - No. 41, Jan, 1967; No. 42, Oct, 1981 - No. 49, Dec, 1982

	GD 2.0	VG 4.0	FN 6.0	VF 8.0	VF/NM 9.0	NM- 9.2
V2#28-Origin/1st app. Fightin' Five; Montes/Bache-a	6	12	18	43	59	75
29-39,41-Montes/Bache-a in all	4	8	12	22	30	38
40-Peacemaker begins (1st app.)	7	14	21	46	63	80
41-Peacemaker (2nd app.)	5	10	15	33	44	55
42-49: Reprints						5.00

FIGHTING FRONTS!
Harvey Publications: Aug, 1952 - No. 5, Jan, 1953

	GD 2.0	VG 4.0	FN 6.0	VF 8.0	VF/NM 9.0	NM- 9.2
1	10	20	30	56	73	90
2-Extreme violence; Nostrand/Powell-a	11	22	33	62	84	105
3-5: 3-Powell-a	7	14	21	37	46	55

FIGHTING INDIAN STORIES (See Midget Comics)

FIGHTING INDIANS OF THE WILD WEST!
Avon Periodicals: Mar, 1952 - No. 2, Nov, 1952

	GD 2.0	VG 4.0	FN 6.0	VF 8.0	VF/NM 9.0	NM- 9.2
1-Geronimo, Chief Crazy Horse, Chief Victorio, Black Hawk begin; Larsen-a; McCann-a(2)	17	34	51	95	135	175
2-Kinstler-c & inside-c only; Larsen, McCann-a	11	22	33	63	84	105
100 Pg. Annual (1952, 25¢)-Contains three comics rebound; Geronimo, Chief Crazy Horse, Chief Victorio; Kinstler-c	33	66	99	190	275	360

FIGHTING LEATHERNECKS
Toby Press: Feb, 1952 - No. 6, Dec, 1952

	GD 2.0	VG 4.0	FN 6.0	VF 8.0	VF/NM 9.0	NM- 9.2
1- "Duke's Diary"; full pg. pin-ups by Sparling	14	28	42	79	110	140
2-5: 2- "Duke's Diary". 3-5- "Gil's Gals"; full pg. pin-ups	10	20	30	56	73	90
6-(Same as No. 3-5?)	10	20	30	56	73	90

FIGHTING MAN, THE (War)
Ajax/Farrell Publications(Excellent Publ.): May, 1952 - No. 8, July, 1953

	GD 2.0	VG 4.0	FN 6.0	VF 8.0	VF/NM 9.0	NM- 9.2
1	14	28	42	79	110	140
2	8	16	24	43	54	65
3-8	7	14	21	37	46	55
Annual 1 (1952, 25¢, 100 pgs.)	24	48	72	138	199	260

FIGHTIN' MARINES (Formerly The Texan; also see Approved Comics)
St. John(Approved Comics)/Charlton Comics No. 14 on:
No. 15, 8/51 - No. 12, 3/53; No. 14, 5/55 - No. 132, 11/76; No. 133, 10/77 - No. 176, 9/84 (No #13?) (Korean War #1-3)

	GD 2.0	VG 4.0	FN 6.0	VF 8.0	VF/NM 9.0	NM- 9.2
15(#1)-Matt Baker c/a "Leatherneck Jack"; slightly large size; Fightin' Texan No. 16 & 17?	40	80	120	239	357	475
2-1st Canteen Kate by Baker; slightly large size; partial Baker-c	45	90	135	275	418	560
3-9,11-Canteen Kate by Baker; Baker c-#2,3,5-11; 4-Partial Baker-c	26	52	78	147	211	275
10-Matt Baker-c	11	22	33	62	84	105
12-No Baker-a; Last St. John issue?	7	14	21	35	43	50
14 (5/55; 1st Charlton issue; formerly?)-Canteen Kate by Baker; all stories reprinted from #2	19	38	57	107	154	200
15-Baker-c	9	18	27	54	70	85
16,18-20-Not Baker-c	6	12	18	29	36	42
17-Canteen Kate by Baker	14	28	42	79	110	140
21-24	6	12	18	27	33	38
25-(68 pgs.)(3/58)-Check-a?	9	18	27	52	66	80
26-(100 pgs.)(8/58)-Check-a(5)	13	26	39	76	106	135
27-50	3	6	9	19	25	32
51-81: 78-Shotgun Harker & the Chicken series begin	3	6	9	16	20	24
82-(100 pgs.)	5	10	15	33	44	55
83-85: 85-Last 12¢ issue	2	4	6	14	18	22
86-94: 94-Last 15¢ issue	2	4	6	10	13	16
95-100,122: 122-(1975) Pilot issue for "War" title (Fightin' Marines Presents War)	2	4	6	9	11	14
101-121	1	3	4	6	8	10
123-140	1	2	3	5	6	8
141-170						6.00
171-176-Low print run	1	2	3	5	6	8
120(Modern Comics reprint, 1977)						4.00

NOTE: *No. 14 & 16 (CC) reprint St. John issues; No. 16 reprints St. John insignia on cover. **Colan** a-3, 7. **Glanzman** c/a-92, 94. **Montes/Bache** a-48, 53, 55, 64, 65, 72-74, 77-83, 176r.*

FIGHTING MARSHAL OF THE WILD WEST (See The Hawk)

FIGHTIN' NAVY (Formerly Don Winslow)
Charlton Comics: No. 74, 1/56 - No. 125, 4-5/66; No. 126, 8/83 - No. 133, 10/84

	GD 2.0	VG 4.0	FN 6.0	VF 8.0	VF/NM 9.0	NM- 9.2
74	6	12	18	43	59	75
75-81	4	8	12	25	33	42
82-Sam Glanzman-a	4	8	12	27	36	45
83-(100 pgs.)	7	14	21	50	68	85
84-99,101: 101-UFO story	3	6	9	18	24	30

Fighting Yank #1 © Nedor

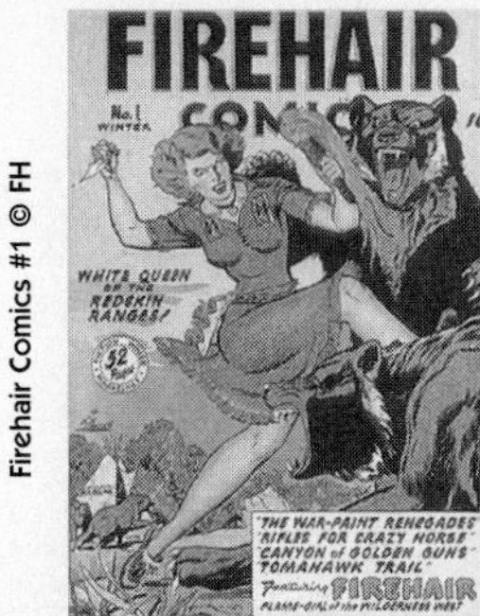

Firehair Comics #1 © FH

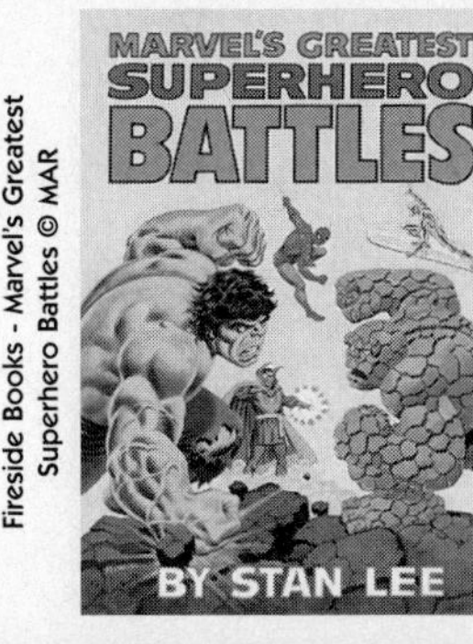

Fireside Books - Marvel's Greatest Superhero Battles © MAR

	GD 2.0	VG 4.0	FN 6.0	VF 8.0	VF/NM 9.0	NM- 9.2
100	3	6	9	19	25	32
102-105,106-125('66)	2	4	6	14	18	22
126-133 (1984)-Low print run	1	2	3	5	6	8

NOTE: ***Montes/Bache** a-109. **Glanzman** a-82, 92, 96, 98, 100, 131r.*

FIGHTING PRINCE OF DONEGAL, THE (See Movie Comics)

FIGHTIN' TEXAN (Formerly The Texan & Fightin' Marines?)
St. John Publishing Co.: No. 16, Sept, 1952 - No. 17, Dec, 1952

	GD	VG	FN	VF	VF/NM	NM-
16,17: Tuska-a each. 17-Cameron-c/a	8	16	24	43	54	65

FIGHTING UNDERSEA COMMANDOS (See Undersea Fighting...)
Avon Periodicals: May, 1952 - No. 5, April, 1953 (U.S. Navy frogmen)

	GD	VG	FN	VF	VF/NM	NM-
1-Cover title is Undersea Fighting... #1 only	15	30	45	86	123	160
2	10	20	30	58	77	95
3-5: 1,3-Ravielli-c. 4-Kinstler-c	9	18	27	52	66	80

FIGHTING WAR STORIES
Men's Publications/Story Comics: Aug, 1952 - No. 5, 1953

	GD	VG	FN	VF	VF/NM	NM-
1	10	20	30	56	73	90
2-5	6	12	18	31	38	45

FIGHTING YANK (See America's Best Comics & Startling Comics)
Nedor/Better Publ./Standard: Sept, 1942 - No. 29, Aug, 1949

	GD	VG	FN	VF	VF/NM	NM-
1-The Fighting Yank begins; Mystico, the Wonder Man app; bondage-c	277	554	831	1731	2666	3600
2	112	224	336	700	1075	1450
3,4: 4-Schomburg-c begin	81	162	243	506	778	1050
5-10: 7-Grim Reaper app. 8,10-Bondage/torture-c	63	126	189	394	610	825
11,13-20: 11-The Oracle app. 15-Bondage/torture-c. 18-The American Eagle app.	52	104	156	317	484	650
12-Hirohito bondage-c	62	124	186	388	594	800
21,24: 21-Kara, Jungle Princess app.; lingerie-c. 24-Miss Masque app.	46	92	138	281	428	575
22-Miss Masque-c/story	53	106	159	323	494	665
23-Classic Schomburg hooded vigilante-c	65	130	195	406	628	850
25-Robinson/Meskin-a; strangulation, lingerie panel; The Cavalier app.	53	106	159	323	494	665
26-29: All-Robinson/Meskin-a. 28-One pg. Williamson-a	44	88	132	268	409	550

NOTE: ***Schomburg (Xela)** c-4-29; airbrush-c 28, 29. Bondage c-1, 4, 8, 10, 11, 12, 15, 17.*

FIGHTMAN
Marvel Comics: June, 1993 ($2.00, one-shot, 52 pgs.)

	GD	VG	FN	VF	VF/NM	NM-
1						2.25

FIGHT THE ENEMY
Tower Comics: Aug, 1966 - No. 3, Mar, 1967 (25¢, 68 pgs.)

	GD	VG	FN	VF	VF/NM	NM-
1-Lucky 7 & Mike Manly begin	4	8	12	29	40	50
2-Boris Vallejo, McWilliams-a	4	8	12	22	30	38
3-Wood-a (1/2 pg.); McWilliams, Bolle-a	4	8	12	22	30	38

FILM FUNNIES
Marvel Comics (CPC): Nov, 1949 - No. 2, Feb, 1950 (52 pgs.)

	GD	VG	FN	VF	VF/NM	NM-
1-Krazy Krow, Wacky Duck	19	38	57	107	154	200
2-Wacky Duck	14	28	42	79	110	140

FILM STARS ROMANCES
Star Publications: Jan-Feb, 1950 - No. 3, May-June, 1950 (True life stories of movie stars)

	GD	VG	FN	VF	VF/NM	NM-
1-Rudy Valentino & Gregory Peck stories; L. B. Cole-c; lingerie panels	44	88	132	268	409	550
2-Liz Taylor/Robert Taylor photo-c & true life story	50	100	150	305	465	625
3-Douglas Fairbanks story; photo-c	27	54	81	152	219	285

FILTH, THE
DC Comics (Vertigo): Aug, 2002 - No. 13, Oct, 2003 ($2.95, limited series)

	GD	VG	FN	VF	VF/NM	NM-
1-13-Morrison-s/Weston & Erskine-a						3.00
TPB (2004, $19.95) r/#1-13						20.00

FINAL CYCLE, THE
Dragon's Teeth Productions: July, 1987 - No. 4, 1988 (Limited series)

	GD	VG	FN	VF	VF/NM	NM-
1-4						2.25

FINAL NIGHT, THE (See DC related titles and Parallax: Emerald Night)
DC Comics: Nov, 1996 - No. 4, Nov, 1996 ($1.95, weekly limited series)

	GD	VG	FN	VF	VF/NM	NM-
1-4: Kesel-s/Immonen-a(p) in all. 4-Parallax's final acts						3.50
Preview						2.25
TPB-(1998, $12.95) r/#1-4, Parallax: Emerald Night #1, and preview						13.00

FINALS
DC Comics (Vertigo): Sept, 1999 - No. 4, Dec, 1999 ($2.95, limited series)

	GD	VG	FN	VF	VF/NM	NM-
1-4-Will Pfeifer-s/Jill Thompson-a						3.00

FIRE
Caliber Press: 1993 - No. 2, 1993 ($2.95, B&W, limited series, 52 pgs.)

	GD	VG	FN	VF	VF/NM	NM-
1,2-Brian Michael Bendis-s/a						3.00
TPB (1999, 2001, $9.95) Restored reprints of series						10.00

FIREARM (Also see Codename: Firearm, Freex #15, Night Man #4 & Prime #10)
Malibu Comics (Ultraverse): Sept, 1993 - No. 18, Mar, 1995 ($1.95/$2.50)

	GD	VG	FN	VF	VF/NM	NM-
0 ($14.95)-Came w/ video containing 1st half of story (comic contains 2nd half); 1st app. Duet						15.00
1,3-6: 1-James Robinson scripts begin; Cully Hamner-a; Chaykin-c; 1st app. Alec Swan. 3-Intro The Sportsmen; Chaykin-c. 4-Break-Thru x-over; Chaykin-c. 5-1st app. Ellen (Swan's girlfriend);2 pg. origin of Prime. 6-Prime app. (story cont'd in Prime #10); Brereton-c						2.50
1-($2.50)-Newsstand edition polybagged w/card						3.00
1-Ultra Limited silver foil-c						5.00
2 ($2.50, 44 pgs.)-Hardcase app.;Chaykin-c; Rune flip-c/story by B. Smith (3 pgs.)						3.00
7-10,12-17: 12-The Rafferty Saga begins, ends #18; 1st app. Rafferty. 15-Night Man & Freex app. 17-Swan marries Ellen						2.50
11-($3.50, 68 pgs.)-Flip book w/Ultraverse Premiere #5						3.50
18-Death of Rafferty; Chaykin-c						3.00

NOTE: ***Brereton** c-6. **Chaykin** c-1-4, 14, 16, 18. **Hamner** a-1-4. **Herrera** a-12. **James Robinson** scripts-0-18.*

FIRE BALL XL5 (See Steve Zodiac & The ...)

FIREBIRDS (See Noble Causes)
Image Comics: Nov, 2004 ($5.95)

	GD	VG	FN	VF	VF/NM	NM-
1-Faerber-s/Ponce-a/c; intro. Firebird						6.00

FIREBRAND (Also see Showcase '96 #4)
DC Comics: Feb, 1996 - No. 9, Oct, 1996 ($1.75)

	GD	VG	FN	VF	VF/NM	NM-
1-9: Brian Augustyn scripts; Velluto-c/a in all. 9-Daredevil #319-c/swipe						2.25

FIREBREATHER
Image Comics: Jan, 2003 - No. 4, Apr, 2003 ($2.95)

	GD	VG	FN	VF	VF/NM	NM-
1-4-Hester-s/Kuhn-a						3.00
TPB (7/04, $13.95) r/#1-4; foreword by Brad Meltzer; gallery and sketch pages						14.00

FIRE FROM HEAVEN
Image Comics (WildStorm Productions): Mar, 1996 ($2.50)

	GD	VG	FN	VF	VF/NM	NM-
1,2-Moore-s						2.50

FIREHAIR COMICS (Formerly Pioneer West Romances #3-6; also see Rangers Comics)
Fiction House Magazines (Flying Stories): Winter/48-49; No. 2, Wint/49-50; No. 7, Spr/51 - No. 11, Spr/52

	GD	VG	FN	VF	VF/NM	NM-
1-Origin Firehair	54	108	162	329	502	675
2-Continues as Pioneer West Romances for #3-6	28	56	84	158	229	300
7-11	19	38	57	107	154	200
I.W. Reprint 8-(nd)-Kinstler-c; reprints Rangers #57; Dr. Drew story by Grandenetti	3	6	9	18	24	30

FIRESIDE BOOK SERIES (Hard and soft cover editions)
Simon and Schuster: 1974 - 1980 (130-260 pgs.), Square bound, color

		GD	VG	FN	VF	VF/NM	NM-
Amazing Spider-Man, The, 1979,	HC	10	20	30	67	96	125
130 pgs., $3.95, Bob Larkin-c	SC	6	12	18	43	59	75
America At War–The Best of DC War	HC	13	26	39	90	138	185
Comics, 1979, $6.95, 260 pgs, Kubert-c	SC	9	18	27	60	85	110
Best of Spidey Super Stories (Electric Company) 1978, $3.95,	SC	7	14	21	51	71	90
Bring On The Bad Guys (Origins of the	HC	9	18	27	65	93	120
Marvel Comics Villains) 1976, $6.95, 260 pgs.; Romita-c	SC	6	12	18	40	55	70
Captain America, Sentinel of Liberty,1979,	HC	10	20	30	67	96	125
130 pgs., $12.95, Cockrum-c	SC	6	12	18	43	59	75
Doctor Strange Master of the Mystic	HC	10	20	30	67	96	125
Arts, 1980, 130 pgs.	SC	6	12	18	43	59	75
Fantastic Four, The, 1979, 130 pgs.	HC	9	18	27	65	93	120
	SC	6	12	18	40	55	70
Heart Throbs–The Best of DC Romance	HC	18	36	54	126	193	260
Comics, 1979, 260 pgs., $6.,95	SC	11	22	33	77	114	150
Incredible Hulk, The, 1978, 260 pgs.	HC	9	18	27	65	93	120
(8 1/4" x 11")	SC	6	12	18	40	55	70

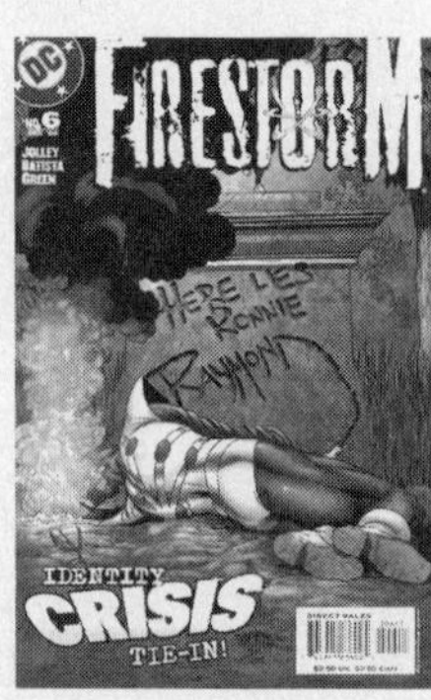

Firestorm ('04) #6 © DC

First Issue Special #13 © DC

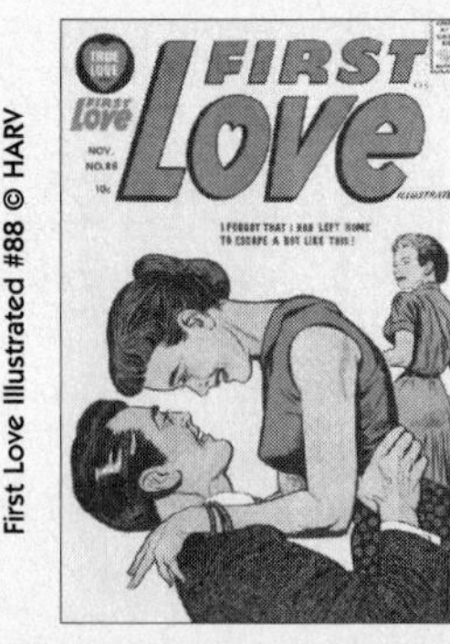

First Love Illustrated #88 © HARV

		GD	VG	FN	VF	VF/NM	NM-
		2.0	4.0	6.0	8.0	9.0	9.2
Marvel's Greatest Superhero Battles,	HC	11	22	33	79	117	155
1978, 260 pgs., $6.95, Romita-c	SC	7	14	21	51	71	90
Mysteries in Space, 1980, $7,95,	HC	10	20	30	73	107	140
Anderson-c. r-DC sci/fi stories	SC	7	14	21	46	63	80
Origins of Marvel Comics, 1974, 260 pgs., $5.95. r-covers & origins of Fantastic							
Four, Hulk, Spider-Man, Thor,	HC	9	18	27	65	93	120
& Doctor Strange	SC	6	12	18	40	55	70
Silver Surfer, The, 1978, 130 pgs.,	HC	10	20	30	67	96	125
$4.95, Norem-c	SC	7	14	21	46	63	80
Son of Origins of Marvel Comics, 1975, 260 pgs., $6.95, Romita-c. Reprints							
covers & origins of X-Men, Iron Man,	HC	9	18	27	65	93	120
Avengers, Daredevil, Silver Surfer	SC	6	12	18	40	55	70
Superhero Women, The–Featuring the	HC	11	22	33	79	117	155
Fabulous Females of Marvel Comics,	SC	7	14	21	51	71	90
1977, 260 pgs., $6.95, Romita-c							

Note: Prices listed are for 1st printings. Later printings have lesser value.

FIRESTAR
Marvel Comics Group: Mar, 1986 - No. 4, June, 1986 (75¢)(From Spider-Man TV series)

1,2: 1-X-Men & New Mutants app. 2-Wolverine-c (not real Wolverine?); Art Adams-a(p) 5.00
3,4: 3-Art Adams/Sienkiewicz-c. 4-B. Smith-c 3.00

FIRESTONE (See Donald And Mickey Merry Christmas)

FIRESTORM (See Cancelled Comic Cavalcade, DC Comics Presents, Flash #289, The Fury of... & Justice League of America #179)
DC Comics: March, 1978 - No. 5, Oct-Nov, 1978

1,5: 1-Origin & 1st app. 1 3 4 6 8 10
2-4: 2-Origin Multiplex. 3-Origin & 1st app. Killer Frost. 4-1st app. Hyena 6.00

FIRESTORM
DC Comics: July, 2004 - Present ($2.50)

1-6: 1-Intro. Jason Rusch; Jolley-s/ChrisCross-a. 6-Identity Crisis tie-in. 7-Bloodhound x-over 8-Killer Frost returns 2.50

FIRESTORM, THE NUCLEAR MAN (Formerly Fury of Firestorm)
DC Comics: No. 65, Nov, 1987 - No. 100, Aug, 1990

65-99: 66-1st app. Zuggernaut; Firestorm vs. Green Lantern. 71-Death of Capt. X. 67,68-Millennium tie-ins. 83-1st new look 2.50
100-($2.95, 68 pgs.) 4.00
Annual 5 (10/87)-1st app. new Firestorm 3.00

FIRST, THE
CrossGeneration Comics: Jan, 2001 - No. 37, Jan, 2004 ($2.95)

1-3: 1-Barbara Kesel-s/Bart Sears & Andy Smith-a 5.00
4-10 4.00
11-37 3.00
Preview (11/00, free) 8 pg. intro 2.25
Two Houses Divided Vol. 1 TPB (11/01, $19.95) r/#1-7; new Moeller-c 20.00
Magnificent Tension Vol. 2 TPB (2002, $19.95) r/#8-13 20.00
Sinister Motives Vol. 3 TPB (2003, $15.95) r/#14-19 16.00
Vol. 4 Futile Endeavors (2003, $15.95) r/#20-25 16.00
Vol. 5 Liquid Alliances (2003, $15.95) r/#26-31 16.00
Vol. 6 Ragnarok (2004, $15.95) r/#32-37 16.00

FIRST ADVENTURES
First Comics: Dec, 1985 - No. 5, Apr, 1986 ($1.25)

1-5: Blaze Barlow, Whisper & Dynamo Joe in all 2.25

FIRST AMERICANS, THE
Dell Publishing Co.: No. 843, Sept, 1957

Four Color 843-Marsh-a 10 20 30 70 100 130

FIRST CHRISTMAS, THE (3-D)
Fiction House Magazines (Real Adv. Publ. Co.): 1953 (25¢, 8-1/4x10-1/4", oversize)(Came w/glasses)

nn-(Scarce)-Kelly Freas painted-c; Biblical theme, birth of Christ; Nativity-c
33 66 99 190 275 360

FIRST COMICS GRAPHIC NOVEL
First Comics: Jan, 1984 - No. 21? (52 pgs./176 pgs., high quality paper)

1,2: 1-Beowulf ($5.95)(both printings). 2-Time Beavers 9.00
3($11.95, 100 pgs.)-American Flagg! Hard Times (2nd printing exists) 15.00
4-Nexus ($6.95)-r/B&W 1-3 12.00
5,7: 5-The Enchanted Apples of Oz ($7.95, 52 pgs.)-Intro by Harlan Ellison (1986). 7-The Secret Island Of Oz ($7.95) 10.00
6-Elric of Melnibone ($14.95, 176 pgs.)-Reprints with new color 18.00
8,10,14,18: Teenage Mutant Ninja Turtles Book I -IV ($9.95, 132 pgs.)-8-r/TMNT #1-3 in color w/12 pgs. new-a; origin. 10-r/TMNT #4-6 in color. 14-r/TMNT #7,8 in color plus new 12 pg. story. 18-r/TMNT #10,11 plus 3 pg. fold-out 11.00
9-Time 2: The Epiphany by Chaykin (11/86, $7.95, 52pgs. - indicia says #8) 10.00
11-Sailor On The Sea of Fate ($14.95) 16.00
nn-Time 2: The Satisfaction of Black Mariah (9/87) 10.00
12-American Flagg! Southern Comfort (10/87, $11.95) 14.00
13,16,17,21: 13-The Ice King Of Oz. 16-The Forgotten Forest of Oz ($8.95). 17-Mazinger (68 pgs., $8.95). 21-Elric, The Weird of the White Wolf; r/#1-5 10.00
15,19: 15-Hex Breaker: Badger ($7.95). 19-The Original Nexus Graphic Novel ($7.95, 104 pgs.)-Reprints First Comics Graphic Novel #4 12.00
20-American Flagg!: State of the Union ($11.95, 96 pgs.); r/A.F. #7-9 15.00
NOTE: *Most or all issues have been reprinted.*

1ST FOLIO (The Joe Kubert School Presents...)
Pacific Comics: Mar, 1984 ($1.50, one-shot)

1-Joe Kubert-c/a(2 pgs.); Adam & Andy Kubert-a 3.00

1ST ISSUE SPECIAL
National Periodical Publications: Apr, 1975 - No. 13, Apr, 1976 (Tryout series)

1,6: 1-Intro. Atlas; Kirby-c/a/script. 6-Dingbats 2 4 6 10 12 15
2,12: 2-Green Team (see Cancelled Comic Cavalcade). 12-Origin/1st app. "Blue" Starman (2nd app. in Starman, 2nd Series #3); Kubert-c 1 3 4 6 8 10
3-Metamorpho by Ramona Fradon 1 3 4 6 8 10
4,10,11: 4-Lady Cop. 10-The Outsiders. 11-Code Name: Assassin; Grell-c
1 2 3 5 7 9
5-Manhunter; Kirby-c/a/script 2 4 6 11 14 18
7,9: 7-The Creeper by Ditko (c/a). 9-Dr. Fate; Kubert-c/Simonson-a.
2 4 6 10 12 15
8,13: 8-Origin/1st app. The Warlord; Grell-c/a (11/75). 13-Return of the New Gods; Darkseid app.; 1st new costume Orion; predates New Gods #12 by more than a year
3 6 9 16 21 26

FIRST KISS
Charlton Comics: Dec, 1957 - No. 40, Jan, 1965

V1#1 5 10 15 36 48 60
V1#2-10 3 7 10 21 28 35
11-40 2 4 6 14 18 22

FIRST LOVE ILLUSTRATED
Harvey Publications(Home Comics)(True Love): 2/49 - No. 9, 6/50; No. 10, 1/51 - No. 86, 3/58; No. 87, 9/58 - No. 88, 11/58; No. 89, 11/62, No. 90, 2/63

1-Powell-a(2) 19 38 57 107 154 200
2-Powell-a 10 20 30 60 80 100
3-"Was I Too Fat To Be Loved" story 10 20 30 60 80 100
4-10 8 16 24 43 54 65
11-30: 13-"I Joined a Teen-age Sex Club" story. 30-Lingerie panel
6 12 18 33 41 48
31-34,37,39-49: 49-Last pre-code (2/55) 6 12 18 29 36 42
35-Used in **SOTI**, illo "The title of this comic book is First Love"
20 40 60 112 161 210
36-Communism story, "Love Slaves" 9 18 27 52 66 80
38-Nostrand-a 8 16 24 43 54 65
50-66,71-90 5 10 15 23 28 32
67-70-Kirby-c 6 12 18 33 41 48
NOTE: ***Disbrow** a-13. **Orlando** c-87. **Powell** a-1, 3-5, 7, 10, 11, 13-17, 19-24, 26-29, 33,35-41, 43, 45, 46, 50, 54, 55, 57, 58, 61-63, 65, 71-73, 76, 79r, 82, 84, 88.*

FIRST MEN IN THE MOON (See Movie Comics)

FIRST ROMANCE MAGAZINE
Home Comics(Harvey Publ.)/True Love: 8/49 - #6, 6/50; #7, 6/51 - #50, 2/58; #51, 9/58 - #52, 11/58

1 16 32 48 92 131 170
2 9 18 27 54 70 85
3-5 8 16 24 46 58 70
6-10,28: 28-Nostrand-a(Powell swipe) 8 16 24 40 50 60
11-20 6 12 18 33 41 48
21-27,29-32: 32-Last pre-code issue (2/55) 6 12 18 29 36 42
33-40,44-52 6 12 18 27 33 38
41-43-Kirby-c 6 12 18 33 41 48
NOTE: ***Powell** a-1-5, 8-10, 14, 18, 20-22, 24, 25, 28, 36, 46, 48, 51.*

FIRST TRIP TO THE MOON (See Space Adventures No. 20)

FIRST WAVE (Based on Sci-Fi Channel TV series)
Andromeda Entertainment: Dec, 2000 - No. 4, Jun, 2001 ($2.99)

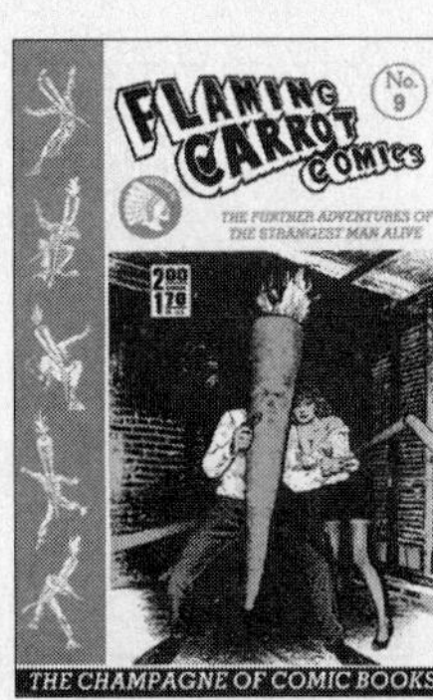

Flaming Carrot Comics #9 © Bob Burden

Flash #107 © DC

Flash #165 © DC

GD 2.0 | VG 4.0 | FN 6.0 | VF 8.0 | VF/NM 9.0 | NM- 9.2

1-4-Kuhoric-s/Parsons-a/Busch-c 3.00

FISH POLICE (Inspector Gill of the...#2, 3)
Fishwrap Productions/Comico V2#5-17/Apple Comics #18 on: Dec, 1985 - No. 11, Nov, 1987 ($1.50, B&W); V2#5, April, 1988 - V2#17, May, 1989 ($1.75, color) No. 18, Aug, 1989 - No. 26, Dec, 1990 ($2.25, B&W)
1-11, 1(5/86),2-2nd print, V2#5-17-(Color): V2#5-11. 12-17, new-a, 18-26 ($2.25-c, B&W). 18-Origin Inspector Gill 2.50
Special 1($2.50, 7/87, Comico) 2.50
Graphic Novel: Hairballs (1987, $9.95, TPB) r/#1-4 in color 10.00

FISH POLICE
Marvel Comics: V2#1, Oct, 1992 - No. 6, Mar, 1993 ($1.25)
V2#1-6: 1-Hairballs Saga begins; r/#1 (1985) 2.50

5 CENT COMICS (Also see Whiz Comics)
Fawcett Publ.: Feb, 1940 (8 pgs., reg. size, B&W)
1-(nn-on c) 1st app. Dan Dare 552 1104 1656 3864 6032 8200
NOTE: Only 2 known copies, in GD and NM condition. A promo comic, same as ***Flash*** & ***Thrill Comics***.

5-STAR SUPER-HERO SPECTACULAR (See DC Special Series No. 1)

FLAME, THE (See Big 3 & Wonderworld Comics)
Fox Features Synd.: Sum, 1940 - No. 8, Jan, 1942 (#1,2: 68 pgs; #3-8: 44 pgs.)
1-Flame stories reprinted from Wonderworld #5-9; origin The Flame; Lou Fine-a (36 pgs.), 317 634 951 2061 3331 4600
2-Fine-a(2); Wing Turner by Tuska; r/Wonderworld #3,10 137 274 411 856 1316 1775
3-8: 3-Powell-a 90 180 270 563 869 1175

FLAME, THE (Formerly Lone Eagle)
Ajax/Farrell Publications (Excellent Publ.): No. 5, Dec-Jan, 1954-55 - No. 3, April-May, 1955
5(#1)-1st app. new Flame 46 92 138 281 428 575
2,3 31 62 93 175 253 330

FLAMING CARROT (...Comics #6? on; see Anything Goes, Cerebus, Teenage Mutant Ninja Turtles/Flaming Carrot Crossover & Visions)
Aardvark-Vanaheim/Renegade Press #6-17/Dark Horse #18 on: 5/84 - No. 5, 1/85; No. 6, 3/85 - Present? ($1.70/$2.00, B&W)
1-Bob Burden story/art 4 8 12 29 40 50
2 3 6 9 16 20 25
3 2 4 6 10 13 16
4-6 2 4 6 8 10 12
7-9 1 2 3 5 7 9
10-12 6.00
13-15 4.00
15-Variant without cover price 6.00
16-(6/87) 1st app. Mystery Men 1 2 3 5 6 8
17-20: 18-1st Dark Horse issue 4.00
21-23,25: 25-Contains trading cards; TMNT app. 3.00
24-(2.50, 52 pgs.)-10th anniversary issue 4.00
26-28: 26-Begin $2.25-c. 26,27-Teenage Mutant Ninja Turtles x-over. 27-McFarlane-c 3.00
29-31-(2.50-c) 3.00
Annual 1(1/97, $5.00) 5.00
... & Reid Fleming, World's Toughest Milkman (12/02, $3.99) listed as #32 in indicia 4.00
... :Fortune Favors the Bold (1998, $16.95, TPB) r/#19-24 17.00
... :Men of Mystery (7/97, $12.95, TPB) r/#1-3, + new material 13.00
... 's Greatest Hits (4/98, $17.95, TPB) r/#12-18, + new material 18.00
... :The Wild Shall Wild Remain (1997, $17.95, TPB) r/#4-11, + new s/a 18.00

FLAMING CARROT COMICS (Also see Junior Carrot Patrol)
Killian Barracks Press: Summer-Fall, 1981 ($1.95, one shot) (Lg size, 8-1/2x11")
1-Bob Burden-c/a/scripts; serially #'ed to 6500 6 12 18 40 55 70

FLAMING LOVE
Quality Comics Group (Comic Magazines): Dec, 1949 - No. 6, Oct, 1950 (Photo covers #2-6) (52 pgs.)
1-Ward-c/a (9 pgs.) 40 80 120 230 335 440
2 18 36 54 100 143 185
3-Ward-a (9 pgs.); Crandall-a 27 54 81 152 219 285
4-6: 4-Gustavson-a 15 30 45 86 123 160

FLAMING WESTERN ROMANCES (Formerly Target Western Romances)
Star Publications: No. 3, Mar-Apr, 1950
3-Robert Taylor, Arlene Dahl photo on-c with biographies inside; L. B. Cole-c 40 80 120 233 342 450

FLARE (Also see Champions for 1st app. & League of Champions)
Hero Comics/Hero Graphics Vol. 2 on: Nov, 1988 - No. 3, Jan, 1989 ($2.75, color, 52 pgs); V2#1, Nov, 1990 - No. 7, Nov, 1991 ($2.95/$3.50, color, mature, 52 pgs.);V2#8, Oct, 1992 - No. 16, Feb, 1994 ($3.50/$3.95, B&W, 36 pgs.)
V1#1-3, V2#1-16: 5-Eternity Smith returns. 6-Intro The Tigress 4.00
Annual 1(1992, $4.50, B&W, 52 pgs.)-Champions-r 4.50

FLARE ADVENTURES
Hero Graphics: Feb, 1992 - No. 12, 1993? ($3.50/$3.95)
1 (90¢, color, 20 pgs.) 2.50
2-12-Flip books w/Champions Classics 4.00

FLASH, THE (See Adventure Comics, The Brave and the Bold, Crisis On Infinite Earths, DC Comics Presents, DC Special, DC Special Series, DC Super-Stars, The Greatest Flash Stories Ever Told, Green Lantern, Impulse, JLA, Justice League of America, Showcase, Speed Force, Super Team Family, Titans & World's Finest)

FLASH, THE (1st Series)(Formerly Flash Comics)(See Showcase #4,8,13,14)
National Periodical Publ./DC: No. 105, Feb-Mar, 1959 - No. 350, Oct, 1985
105-(2-3/59)-Origin Flash(retold), & Mirror Master (1st app.) 423 846 1269 3871 6586 9300
106-Origin Grodd & Pied Piper; Flash's 1st visit to Gorilla City; begin Grodd the Super Gorilla trilogy (Scarce) 145 290 435 1233 1992 2750
107-Grodd trilogy, part 2 75 150 225 638 1032 1425
108-Grodd trilogy ends 63 126 189 536 868 1200
109-2nd app. Mirror Master 50 100 150 407 641 875
110-Intro/origin Kid Flash who later becomes Flash in Crisis On Infinite Earths #12; begin Kid Flash trilogy, ends #112 (also in #114,116,118); 1st app. & origin of The Weather Wizard 121 242 363 1029 1665 2300
111-2nd Kid Flash tryout; Cloud Creatures 41 82 123 305 478 650
112-Origin & 1st app. Elongated Man (4-5/60); also apps. in #115,119,130 46 92 138 368 572 775
113-Origin & 1st app. Trickster 41 82 123 305 478 650
114-Captain Cold app. (see Showcase #8) 32 64 96 240 370 500
115,116,118-120: 119-Elongated Man marries Sue Dearborn. 120-Flash & Kid Flash team-up for 1st time 25 50 75 181 278 375
117-Origin & 1st app. Capt. Boomerang; 1st & only S.A. app. Winky Blinky & Noddy 31 62 93 223 342 460
121,122: 122-Origin & 1st app. The Top 19 38 57 138 212 285
123-(9/61)-Re-intro. Golden Age Flash; origins of both Flashes; 1st mention of an Earth II where DC G. A. heroes live 116 232 348 986 1593 2200
124-Last 10¢ issue 16 32 48 112 171 230
125-128,130: 127-Return of Grodd-c/story. 128-Origin & 1st app. Abra Kadabra. 130-(7/62)-1st Gauntlet of Super-Villains (Mirror Master, Capt. Cold, The Top, Capt. Boomerang & Trickster) 15 30 45 107 164 220
129-2nd G.A. Flash x-over; J.S.A. cameo in flashback (1st S.A. app. G.A. Green Lantern, Hawkman, Atom, Black Canary & Dr. Mid-Nite. Wonder Woman (1st S.A. app.?) appears) 29 58 87 210 323 435
131-136,138,140: 131-Early Green Lantern x-over (9/62). 135-1st app. of Kid Flash's yellow costume (3/63). 136-1st Dexter Miles. 140-Origin & 1st app. Heat Wave 13 26 39 92 141 190
137-G.A. Flash x-over; J.S.A. cameo (1st S.A. app.)(1st real app. since 2-3/51); 1st S.A. app. Vandal Savage & Johnny Thunder; JSA team decides to re-form 41 82 123 318 497 675
139-Origin & 1st app. Prof. Zoom 14 28 42 97 149 200
141-150: 142-Trickster app. 10 20 30 73 107 140
151-Engagement of Barry Allen & Iris West; G.A. Flash vs. The Shade. 13 26 39 90 138 185
152-159 9 18 27 65 93 120
160-(80-Pg. Giant G-21); G.A. Flash & Johnny Quick-r 13 26 39 90 138 185
161-164,166,167: 167-New facts about Flash's origin 8 16 24 55 78 100
165-Barry Allen weds Iris West 9 18 27 60 85 110
168,170: 168-Green Lantern-c/app. 170-Dr. Mid-Nite, Dr. Fate, G.A. Flash x-over 8 16 24 55 78 100
169-(80-Pg. Giant G-34)-New facts about origin 10 20 30 70 100 130
171,172,174,176,177,179,180: 171-JLA, Green Lantern, Atom flashbacks. 174-Barry Allen reveals I.D. to wife. 179-(5/68)-Flash travels to Earth-Prime and meets DC editor Julie Schwartz; 1st unnamed app. Earth-Prime (See Justice League of America #123 for 1st named app. & 3rd app. overall) 7 14 21 51 71 90
173-G.A. Flash x-over 8 16 24 55 78 100
175-2nd Superman/Flash race (12/67) (See Superman #199 & World's Finest #198,199); JLA cameo; gold kryptonite used (on J'onn J'onzz impersonating Superman) 16 32 48 116 178 240
178-(80-Pg. Giant G-46) 9 18 27 65 93 120
181-186,188,189: 186-Re-intro. Sargon. 189-Last 12¢-c 6 12 18 43 59 75
187,196: (68-Pg. Giants G-58, G-70) 7 14 21 51 71 90
190-195,197-199 5 10 15 33 44 55

Flash #225 © DC

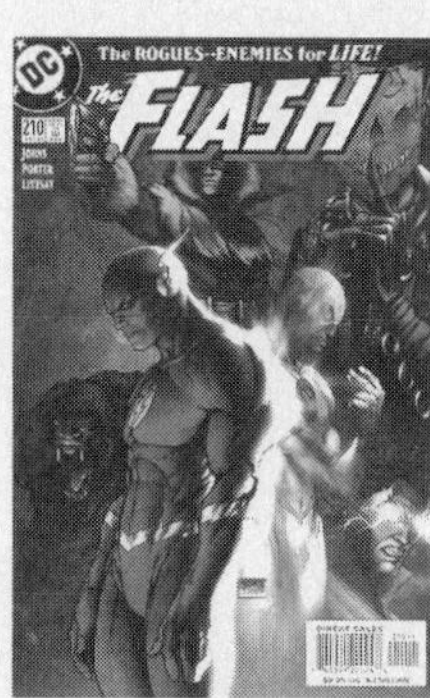
Flash (2nd series) #210 © DC

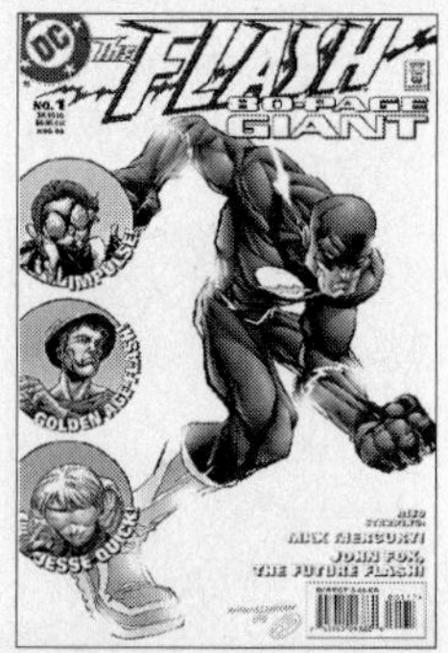
Flash 80-Page Giant #1 © DC

	GD 2.0	VG 4.0	FN 6.0	VF 8.0	VF/NM 9.0	NM- 9.2

200 6 12 18 38 52 65
201-204,206,207: 201-New G.A. Flash story. 206-Elongated Man begins
207-Last 15¢ issue 4 8 12 24 32 40
205-(68-Pg. Giant G-82) 6 12 18 40 55 70
208-213-(52 pg.): 211-G.A. Flash origin-r/#104. 213-Reprints #137
4 8 12 27 36 45
214-DC 100 Page Super Spectacular DC-11; origin Metal Men-r/Showcase #37; never before published G.A. Flash story.
(see DC 100 pg. Super Spec. #11 for price)
215 (52 pgs.)-Flash-r/Showcase #4; G.A. Flash x-over, continued in #216
4 8 12 29 40 50
216,220: 220-1st app. Turtle since Showcase #4 3 6 9 18 24 30
217-219: Neal Adams-a in all. 217-Green Lantern/Green Arrow series begins (9/72); 2nd G.L. & G.A. team-up series (see Green Lantern #76). 219-Last Green Arrow
4 8 12 29 40 50
221-225,227,228,230,231,233: 222-G. Lantern x-over. 228-(7-8/74)-Flash writer Cary Bates travels to Earth-One & meets Flash, Iris Allen & Trickster; 2nd unnamed app. Earth-Prime (See Justice League of America #123 for 1st named app. & 3rd app. overall)
2 4 6 12 16 20
226-Neal Adams-p 3 6 9 18 23 28
229,232-(100 pg. issues)-G.A. Flash-r & new-a 5 10 15 33 44 55
234-250: 235-Green Lantern x-over. 243-Death of The Top. 245-Origin The Floronic Man in Green Lantern back-up, ends #246. 246-Last Green Lantern. 247-Jay Garrick app.
250-Intro Golden Glider 2 4 6 10 12 15
251-274: 256-Death of The Top retold. 265-267-(44 pgs.). 267-Origin of Flash's uniform.
270-Intro The Clown 1 3 4 6 8 10
268,273-276,278,283,286-(Whitman variants; low print run; no issue #s shown on covers
2 4 6 8 10 12
275,276-Iris Allen dies 2 4 6 8 10 12
277-288,290: 286-Intro/origin Rainbow Raider 1 2 3 4 5 7
289-1st Perez DC art (Firestorm); new Firestorm back-up series begins (9/80), ends #304
1 2 3 5 7 9
291-299,301-305: 291-1st app. Saber-Tooth (villain). 295-Gorilla Grodd-c/story. 298-Intro/origin new Shade. 301-Atomic bomb-c. 303-The Top returns. 304-Intro/origin Colonel Computron;
305-G.A. Flash x-over 5.00
300-(52 pgs.)-Origin Flash retold; 25th ann. issue 1 2 3 4 5 7
306-313-Dr. Fate by Giffen. 309-Origin Flash retold 5.00
314-340: 318-323-Creeper back-ups. 323,324-Two part Flash vs. Flash story. 324-Death of Reverse Flash (Professor Zoom). 328-Iris West Allen's death retold. 329-JLA app.
340-Trial of the Flash begins 4.00
341-349: 344-Origin Kid Flash 5.00
350-Double size ($1.25) Final issue 6.00
Annual 1 (10-12/63, 84 pgs.)-Origin Elongated Man & Kid Flash-r; origin Grodd; G.A. Flash-r
39 78 117 293 459 625
Annual 1 Replica Edition (2001, $6.95)-Reprints the entire 1963 Annual 7.00
The Flash Spectacular (See DC Special Series No. 11)
The Life Story of the Flash (1997, $19.95, Hardcover) "Iris Allen's" chronicle of Barry Allen's life; comic panels w/additional text; Waid & Augustyn-s/ Kane & Staton-a/Orbik painted-c
20.00
The Life Story of the Flash (1998, $12.95, Softcover) New Orbik-c 13.00

NOTE: ***N. Adams*** *c-194, 195, 203, 204, 206-208, 211, 213, 215, 226p, 246.* ***M. Anderson*** *c-165, a(i)-195, 200-204, 206-208.* ***Austin*** *a-233i, 234i, 246i.* ***Buckler*** *a-271p, 272p; c(p)-247-250, 252, 253p, 255, 256p, 258, 262, 265-267, 269-271.* ***Giffen*** *a-306-313p; c-310p, 315.* ***Giordano*** *a-226i.* ***Sid Greene*** *a-167-174i, 229i(r).* ***Grell*** *a-237p, 238p, 240-243p; c-236.* ***Heck*** *a-198p.* ***Infantino/Anderson*** *a-135. c-135, 170-174, 192, 200, 201, 328-330.* ***Infantino/Giella*** *c-105-112, 163, 164, 166-168.* ***G. Kane*** *a-195p, 197-199p, 229r, 232r; c-197-199, 312p.* ***Kubert*** *a-108p, 215i(r); c-189-191.* ***Lopez*** *c-272.* ***Meskin*** *a-229r, 232r.* ***Perez*** *a-289-293p; c-293.* ***Starlin*** *a-294-296p.* ***Staton*** *c-263p, 264p. Green Lantern x-over-131, 143, 168, 171, 191.*

FLASH (2nd Series)(See Crisis on Infinite Earths #12 and Justice League Europe)
DC Comics: June, 1987 - Present (75¢-$2.25)

1-Guice-c/a begins; New Teen Titans app. 1 3 4 6 8 10
2-10: 3-Intro. Kilgore. 5-Intro. Speed McGee. 7-1st app. Blue Trinity. 8,9-Millennium tie-ins.
9-1st app. The Chunk 4.00
11-61: 12-Free extra 16 pg. Dr. Light story. 19-Free extra 16 pg. Flash story. 28-Capt. Cold app. 29-New Phantom Lady app. 40-Dr. Alchemy app. 50-($1.75, 52 pgs.) 3.00
62-78,80: 62-Flash: Year One begins, ends #65. 65-Last $1.00-c. 66-Aquaman app. 69,70-Green Lantern app. 70-Gorilla Grodd story ends. 73-Re-intro Barry Allen & begin saga ("Barry Allen's" true ID revealed in #78). 76-Re-intro of Max Mercury (Quality Comics' Quicksilver), not in uniform until #77. 80-($1.25-c) Regular Edition 4.00
79,80 ($2.50): 79-(68 pgs.) Barry Allen saga ends. 80-Foil-c 5.00
81-91,93,94,0,95-99,101: 81,82-Nightwing & Starfire app. 84-Razer app. 94-Zero Hour. 0-(10/94). 95-"Terminal Velocity" begins, ends #100. 96,98,99-Kobra app. 97-Origin Max Mercury; Chillblaine app. 4.00
92-1st Impulse 1 3 4 6 8 10
100 ($2.50)-Newstand edition; Kobra & JLA app. 4.00
100 ($3.50)-Foil-c edition; Kobra & JLA app. 5.00
102-131: 102-Mongul app.; begin-$1.75-c. 105-Mirror Master app. 107-Shazam app. 108-"Dead Heat" begins; 1st app. Savitar. 109-"Dead Heat" Pt. 2 (cont'd in Impulse #10). 110-"Dead Heat" Pt. 4 (cont'd in Impulse #11). 111-"Dead Heat" finale; Savitar disappears into the Speed Force; John Fox cameo (2nd app.). 112-"Race Against Time" begins, ends #118; re-intro John Fox. 113-Tornado Twins app. 119-Final Night x-over. 127-129-Rogue's Gallery & Neron. 128,129-JLA-app.130-Morrison & Millar-s begin 3.00
132-150: 135-GL & GA app. 142-Wally almost marries Linda; Waid-s return. 144-Cobalt Blue origin. 145-Chain Lightning begins.147-Professor Zoom app. 149-Barry Allen app. 150-($2.95) Final showdown with Cobalt Blue 3.00
151-162: 151-Casey-s. 152-New Flash-c. 154-New Flash ID revealed. 159-Wally marries Linda. 162-Last Waid-s. 2.50
163-187,189-196,198,199,201-206: 163-Begin $2.25-c. 164-186-Bolland-c. 183-New Trickster. 196-Winslade-a. 201-Dose-a begins. 205-Batman-c/app. 2.25
188-($2.95) Mirror Master, Weather Wizard, Trickster app. 3.00
197-Origin of Zoom (6/03) 6.00
200-($3.50) Flash vs. Zoom; Barry Allen & Hal Jordan app.; wraparound-c 3.50
207-216: 207-211-Turner-c/Porter-a. 209-JLA app. 210-Nightwing app. 212-Origin Mirror Master. 214-216-Identity Crisis x-over 2.25
#1,000,000 (11/98) 853rd Century x-over 2.50
Annual 1-7,9: 2-('87-'94,'96, 68 pgs), 3-Gives history of G.A.,S.A., & Modern Age Flash in text. 4-Armaggedon 2001. 5-Eclipso-c/story. 7-Elseworlds story. 9-Legends of the Dead Earth story; J.H. Williams-a(p); Mick Gray-a(i) 3.00
Annual 8 (1995, $3.50)-Year One story 3.50
Annual 10 (1997, $3.95)-Pulp Heroes stories 4.00
Annual 11,12 ('98, '99)-11-Ghosts; Wrightson-c. 12-JLApe; Art Adams-c 3.00
Annual 13 ('00, $3.50) Planet DC; Alcatena-c/a 3.50
...: Blitz (2004, $19.95, TPB)-r/#192-200; Kolins-c 20.00
...: Blood Will Run (2002, $17.95, TPB)-r/#170-176, Secret Files #3 18.00
...: Crossfire (2004, $17.95, TPB)-r/#183-191 & parts of Flash Secret Files #3 18.00
Dead Heat (2000, $14.95, TPB)-r/#108-111, Impulse #10,11 15.00
...80-Page Giant (8/98, $4.95) Flash family stories by Waid, Millar and others; Mhan-c 5.00
...80-Page Giant 2 (4/99, $4.95) Stories of Flash family, future Kid Flash, original Teen Titans and XS 5.00
...: Iron Heights (2001, $5.95)-Van Sciver-c/a; intro. Murmur 6.00
...: Our Worlds at War 1 (10/01, $2.95)-Jae Lee-c; Black Racer app. 3.00
...Plus 1 (1/1997, $2.95)-Nightwing-c/app. 3.00
Race Against Time (2001, $14.95, TPB)-r/#112-118 15.00
...: Rogues (2003, $14.95, TPB)-r/#177-182 15.00
...Secret Files 1 (11/97, $4.95) Origin-s & pin-ups 5.00
...Secret Files 2 (11/99, $4.95) Origin of Replicant 5.00
...Secret Files 3 (11/01; $4.95) Intro. Hunter Zolomon (who later becomes Zoom) 5.00
Special 1 (1990, $2.95, 84 pgs.)-50th anniversary issue; Kubert-c; 1st Flash story by Mark Waid; 1st app. John Fox (27th Century Flash) 3.00
Terminal Velocity (1996, $12.95, TPB)-r/#95-100. 13.00
The Return of Barry Allen (1996, $12.95, TPB)-r/#74-79. 13.00
...: Time Flies (2002, $5.95)-Seth Fisher-c/a; Rozum-s 6.00
TV Special 1 (1991, $3.95, 76 pgs.)-Photo-c plus behind the scenes photos of TV show; Saltares-a, Byrne scripts 4.00

NOTE: ***Guice*** *a-1-9p, 11p, Annual 1p; c-1-9p, Annual 1p.* ***Perez*** *c-15-17, Annual 2i.* ***Charest*** *c/a-Annual 5p.*

FLASH, THE (See Tangent Comics/ The Flash)

FLASH AND GREEN LANTERN: THE BRAVE AND THE BOLD
DC Comics: Oct, 1999 - No. 6, Mar, 2000 ($2.50, limited series)

1-6-Waid & Peyer-s/Kitson-a. 4-Green Arrow app.; Grindberg-a(p) 2.50
TPB (2001, $12.95) r/#1-6 13.00

FLASH/ GREEN LANTERN: FASTER FRIENDS (See Green Lantern/Flash...)
DC Comics: No. 2, 1997 ($4.95, continuation of Green Lantern/Flash: Faster Friends #1)

2-Waid/Augustyn-s 5.00

FLASH COMICS (Whiz Comics No. 2 on)
Fawcett Publications: Jan, 1940 (12 pgs., B&W, regular size)
(Not distributed to newsstands; printed for in-house use)

NOTE: *Whiz Comics #2 was preceded by two books, **Flash Comics** and **Thrill Comics**, both dated Jan, 1940, (12 pgs, B&W, regular size) and were not distributed. These two books are identical except for the title, and were sent out to major distributors as ad copies to promote sales. It is believed that the complete 68 page issue of Fawcett's **Flash** and **Thrill Comics** #1 was finished and ready for publication with the January date. Since DC Comics was also about to publish a book with the same date and title, Fawcett hurriedly printed up the black and white version of **Flash Comics** to secure copyright before DC. The inside covers are blank, with the covers and inside pages printed on a high quality uncoated paper stock.The eight page origin story of Captain Thunder is composed of pages 1-7 and 13 of the Captain Marvel story essentially as they appeared in the first issue of **Whiz Comics**. The balloon dialogue on page thirteen was relettered to tie the story into the end of page seven in **Flash** and **Thrill Comics** to produce a shorter version of the origin story for copyright purposes. Obviously, DC acquired the copyright and Fawcett dropped **Flash** as well as **Thrill** and came out with **Whiz Comics** a month later. Fawcett never used the cover to **Flash** and **Thrill** #1, designing a new cover for **Whiz Comics**. Fawcett also must have discovered that Captain Thunder had already been used by another publisher (Captain Terry Thunder by Fiction House). All references to Captain Thunder were relettered to Captain Marvel before appearing in **Whiz**.*

Flash Comics #37 © DC

Flash Gordon #1 © HARV

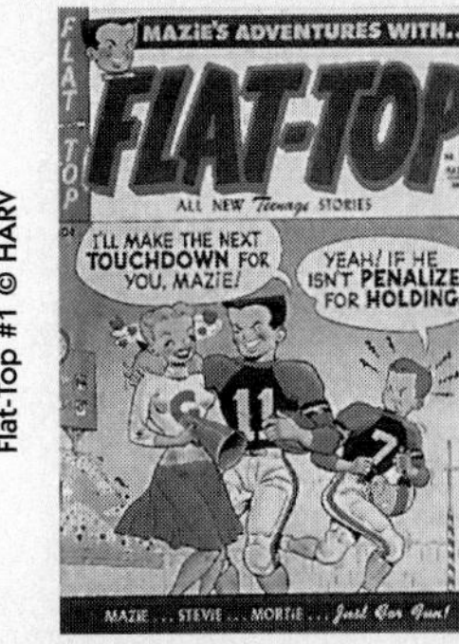

Flat-Top #1 © HARV

	GD 2.0	VG 4.0	FN 6.0	VF 8.0	VF/NM 9.0	NM- 9.2

1 (nn on-c, #1 on inside)-Origin & 1st app. Captain Thunder. Cover by C.C. Beck. Eight copies of Flash and three copies of Thrill exist. All 3 copies of Thrill sold in 1986 for between $4,000-$10,000 each. A NM copy of Thrill sold in 1987 for $12,000. A VG copy of Thrill sold in 1987 for $9000 cash. A VF(8.0) copy of Thrill sold in 2003 for $11,400.

FLASH COMICS (The Flash No. 105 on) (Also see All-Flash)
National Periodical Publ./All-American: Jan, 1940 - No. 104, Feb, 1949

1-The Flash (origin/1st app.) by Harry Lampert, Hawkman (origin/1st app.) by Gardner Fox, The Whip, & Johnny Thunder (origin/1st app.) by Stan Asch; Cliff Cornwall by Moldoff, Flash Picture Novelets (later Minute Movies w/#12) begin; Moldoff (Shelly) cover; 1st app. Shiera Sanders who later becomes Hawkgirl, #24; reprinted in Famous First Edition (on sale 11/10/39); The Flash-c 6467 12,934 19,400 48,500 79,250 110,000

1-Reprint, Oversize 13-1/2x10". **WARNING:** This comic is an exact reprint of the original except for its size. DC published it in 1974 with a second cover titling it as a Famous First Edition. There have been many reported cases of the outer cover being removed and the interior sold as the original edition. The reprint with the new outer cover removed is practically worthless. See Famous First Edition for value.

2-Rod Rian begins, ends #11; Hawkman-c 742 1484 2226 5194 8347 11,500
3-King Standish begins (1st app.), ends #41 (called The King #16-37,39-41); E.E. Hibbard-a begins on Flash 516 1032 1548 3612 5806 8000
4-Moldoff (Shelly) Hawkman begins; The Whip-c 423 846 1269 2790 4495 6200
5-The King-c 345 690 1035 2243 3622 5000
6-2nd Flash-c (alternates w/Hawkman #6 on) 471 942 1413 3297 5299 7300
7-2nd Hawkman-c; 1st Moldoff Hawkman-c 439 878 1317 3073 4937 6800
8-New logo begins; classic Moldoff Flash-c 300 600 900 1925 3063 4200
9,10: 9-Moldoff Hawkman-c; 10-Classic Moldoff Flash-c 317 634 951 2061 3331 4600
11-13,15-20: 12-Les Watts begins; "Sparks" #16 on. 17-Last Cliff Cornwall 208 416 624 1300 2000 2700
14-World War II cover 246 492 738 1538 2369 3200
21-Classic Hawkman-c 204 408 612 1275 1963 2650
22,23 185 370 555 1156 1778 2400
24-Shiera becomes Hawkgirl (12/41); see All-Star Comics #5 for 1st app. 221 442 663 1381 2128 2875
25-28,30: 28-Last Les Sparks. 119 238 357 744 1147 1550
29-Ghost Patrol begins (origin/1st app.), ends #104 131 262 393 819 1260 1700
31,33-Classic Hawkman-c. 33-Origin Shade 119 238 357 744 1147 1550
32,34-40: 36-1st app. Rag Doll 110 220 330 688 1057 1425
41-50 96 192 288 600 925 1250
51-61: 52-1st computer in comics, c/s (4/44). 59-Last Minute Movies. 61-Last Moldoff Hawkman 87 174 261 544 835 1125
62-Hawkman by Kubert begins 113 226 339 706 1091 1475
63-85: 66-68-Hop Harrigan in all. 70-Mutt & Jeff app. 80-Atom begins, ends #104 77 154 231 481 741 1000
86-Intro. The Black Canary in Johnny Thunder (8/47); see All-Star #38. 285 570 855 1781 2741 3700
87,88,90: 87-Intro. The Foil. 88-Origin Ghost. 123 246 369 769 1185 1600
89-Intro villain The Thorn 177 354 531 1106 1703 2300
91,93-99: 98-Atom & Hawkman don new costumes 131 262 393 819 1260 1700
92-1st solo Black Canary plus-c; rare in Mint due to black ink smearing on white-c 345 690 1035 2243 3622 5000
100 (10/48),103(Scarce)-52 pgs. each 300 600 900 1892 2946 4000
101,102(Scarce) 254 508 762 1588 2444 3300
104-Origin The Flash retold (Scarce) 645 1290 1935 4515 7258 10,000

NOTE: ***Irwin Hasen*** *a-Wheaties Giveaway. c-97, Wheaties Giveaway.* ***E.E. Hibbard*** *c-6, 12, 20, 24, 26, 28, 30, 44, 46, 48, 50, 62, 66, 68, 69, 72, 74, 76, 78, 80, 82.* ***Infantino*** *a-86p, 90, 93-95, 99-104; c-90, 92, 93, 97, 99, 101, 103.* ***Kinstler*** *a-87, 89(Hawkman); c-87.* ***Chet Kozlak*** *c-77, 79, 81.* ***Krigstein*** *a-94.* ***Kubert*** *a-62-76, 83, 85, 86, 88-104; c-63, 65, 67, 70, 71, 73, 75, 83, 85, 86, 88, 89, 91, 94, 96, 98, 100, 104.* ***Moldoff*** *a-3; c-3, 7-11, 13-17, plus odd #'s 19-61.* ***Martin Naydell*** *c-52, 54, 56, 58, 60, 64, 84.*

FLASH DIGEST, THE (See DC Special Series #24)

FLASH GORDON (See Defenders Of The Earth, Eat Right to Work..., Giant Comic Album, King Classics, King Comics, March of Comics #118, 133, 142, The Phantom #18, Street Comix & Wow Comics, 1st series)

FLASH GORDON
Dell Publishing Co.: No. 25, 1941; No. 10, 1943 - No. 512, Nov, 1953

Feature Books 25 (#1)(1941))-r-not by Raymond 112 224 336 700 1075 1450
Four Color 10(1943)-by Alex Raymond; reprints "The Ice Kingdom" 90 180 270 680 1103 1525
Four Color 84(1945)-by Alex Raymond; reprints "The Fiery Desert" 41 82 123 330 515 700
Four Color 173 19 38 57 134 205 275
Four Color 190-Bondage-c; "The Adventures of the Flying Saucers"; 5th Flying Saucer story (6/48)- see The Spirit 9/28/47(1st), Shadow Comics V7#10 (2nd, 1/48), Captain Midnight #60 (3rd, 2/48) & Boy Commandos #26 (4th, 3-4/48) 21 42 63 150 230 310
Four Color 204,247 15 30 45 109 167 225
Four Color 424-Painted-c 12 24 36 82 124 165
2(5-7/53-Dell)-Painted-c; Evans-a? 9 18 27 60 85 110
Four Color 512-Painted-c 9 18 27 60 85 110

FLASH GORDON (See Tiny Tot Funnies)
Harvey Publications: Oct, 1950 - No. 4, April, 1951

1-Alex Raymond-a; bondage-c; reprints strips from 7/14/40 to 12/8/40 37 74 111 209 305 400
2-Alex Raymond-a; r/strips 12/15/40-4/27/41 24 48 72 138 199 260
3,4-Alex Raymond-a; 3-bondage-c; r/strips 5/4/41-9/21/41. 4-r/strips 10/24/37-3/27/38 22 44 66 125 180 235
5-(Rare)-Small size-5-1/2x8-1/2"; B&W; 32 pgs.; Distributed to some mail subscribers only 56 112 168 350 538 725
(Also see All-New No. 15, Boy Explorers No. 2, and Stuntman No. 3)

FLASH GORDON
Gold Key: June, 1965

1 (1947 reprint)-Painted-c 6 12 18 43 59 75

FLASH GORDON (Also see Comics Reading Libraries in the Promotional Comics section)
King #1-11/Charlton #12-18/Gold Key #19-23/Whitman #28 on:
9/66 - #11, 12/67; #12, 2/69 - #18, 1/70; #19, 9/78 - #37, 3/82 (Painted covers No. 19-30, 34)

1-1st S.A. app Flash Gordon; Williamson c/a(2); E.C. swipe/Incredible S.F. #32; Mandrake story 7 14 21 51 70 90
1-Army giveaway(1968)("Complimentary" on cover)(Same as regular #1 minus Mandrake story & back-c) 4 8 12 29 40 50
2-8: 2-Bolle, Gil Kane-c; Mandrake story. 3-Williamson-c. 4-Secret Agent X-9 begins, Williamson-c/a(3). 5-Williamson-c/a(2). 6,8-Crandall-a. 7-Raboy-a (last in comics?). 8-Secret Agent X-9-r 4 8 12 27 36 45
9-13: 9,10-Raymond-r. 10-Buckler's 1st pro work (11/67). 11-Crandall-a. 12-Crandall-c/a. 13-Jeff Jones-a (15 pgs.) 4 8 12 24 32 40
14,15: 15-Last 12¢ issue 3 6 9 18 24 30
16,17: 17-Brick Bradford story 3 6 9 16 20 24
18-Kaluta-a (3rd pro work?)(see Teen Confessions) 3 6 9 19 25 32
19(9/78, G.K.), 20-26 1 3 4 6 8 10
27-29.34-37: 34-37-Movie adaptation 2 4 6 8 10 12
30 (10/80) (scarce) 3 6 9 18 24 30
30 (7/81; re-issue), 31-33-single issues 2 4 6 8 10 12
31-33 (Bagged 3-pack): Movie adaptation; Williamson-a. 36.00

NOTE: ***Aparo*** *a-8.* ***Bolle*** *a-21, 22.* ***Boyette*** *a-14-18.* ***Briggs*** *c-10.* ***Buckler*** *a-10.* ***Crandall*** *c-6.* ***Estrada*** *a-3.* ***Gene Fawcette*** *a-29, 30, 34, 37.* ***McWilliams*** *a-31-33, 36.*

FLASH GORDON
DC Comics: June, 1988 - No. 9, Holiday, 1988-'89 ($1.25, mini-series)

1-9: 1,5-Painted-c 3.00

FLASH GORDON
Marvel Comics: June, 1995 - No. 2, July, 1995 ($2.95, limited series)

1,2: Schultz scripts; Williamson-a 3.00

FLASH GORDON THE MOVIE
Western Publishing Co.: 1980 (8-1/4 x 11", $1.95, 68 pgs.)

11294-Williamson-c/a; adapts movie 2 4 6 10 13 16
13743-Hardback edition 3 6 9 16 20 24

FLASHPOINT (Elseworlds Flash)
DC Comics: Dec, 1999 - No. 3, Feb, 2000 ($2.95, limited series)

1-3-Paralyzed Barry Allen; Breyfogle-a/McGreal-s 3.00

FLAT-TOP
Mazie Comics/Harvey Publ.(Magazine Publ.) No. 4 on: 11/53 - No. 3, 5/54; No. 4, 3/55 - No. 7, 9/55

1-Teenage; Flat-Top, Mazie, Mortie & Stevie begin 8 16 24 46 58 70
2,3 5 10 15 24 30 35
4-7 5 10 15 22 26 30

FLESH & BLOOD
Brainstorm Comics: Dec, 1995 ($2.95, B&W, mature)

1-Balent-c; foil-c. 3.00

FLESH AND BONES
Upshot Graphics (Fantagraphics Books): June, 1986 - No. 4, Dec, 1986 (Limited series)

1-4: Alan Moore scripts (r) & Dalgoda by Fujitake 3.00

FLESH CRAWLERS
Kitchen Sink Press: Aug, 1993 - No. 3, 1995 ($2.50, B&W, limited series, mature)

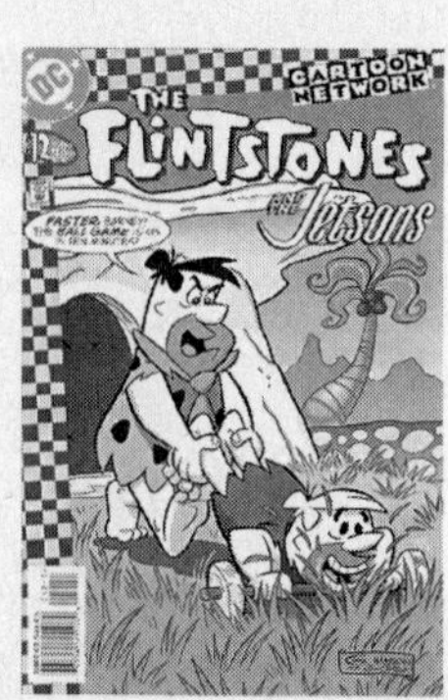

Flintstones & the Jetsons #12 © H-B

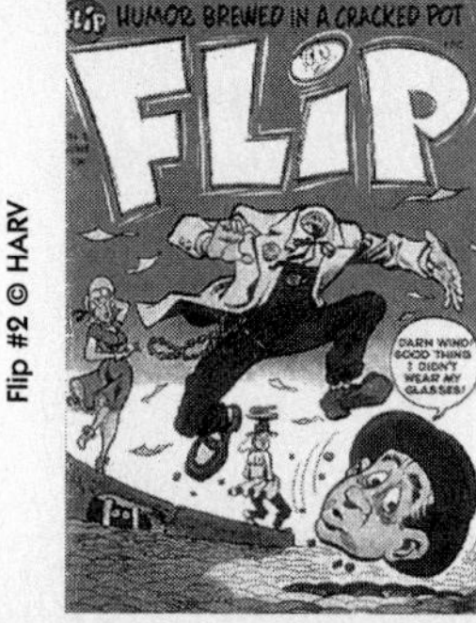

Flip #2 © HARV

Flying Cadet #6 © FCPC

	GD 2.0	VG 4.0	FN 6.0	VF 8.0	VF/NM 9.0	NM- 9.2
1-3						2.50

FLEX MENTALLO (Man of Muscle Mystery) (See Doom Patrol, 2nd Series)
DC Comics (Vertigo): Jun, 1996 - No. 4, Sept, 1996 ($2.50, lim. series, mature)

	GD 2.0	VG 4.0	FN 6.0	VF 8.0	VF/NM 9.0	NM- 9.2
1-4: Grant Morrison scripts & Frank Quitely-c/a in all; banned from reprints due to Charles Atlas legal action	1	3	4	6	8	10

FLINCH (Horror anthology)
DC Comics (Vertigo): Jun, 1999 - No. 16, Jan, 2001 ($2.50)

	GD 2.0	VG 4.0	FN 6.0	VF 8.0	VF/NM 9.0	NM- 9.2
1-16: 1-Art by Jim Lee, Quitely, and Corben. 5-Sale-c. 11-Timm-a						2.50

FLINTSTONE KIDS, THE (TV) (See Star Comics Digest)
Star Comics/Marvel Comics #5 on: Aug, 1987 - No. 11, Apr, 1989

	GD 2.0	VG 4.0	FN 6.0	VF 8.0	VF/NM 9.0	NM- 9.2
1-11						4.50

FLINTSTONES, THE (TV)(See Dell Giant #48 for No. 1)
Dell Publ. Co./Gold Key No. 7 (10/62) on: No. 2, Nov-Dec, 1961 - No. 60, Sept, 1970 (Hanna-Barbera)

	GD 2.0	VG 4.0	FN 6.0	VF 8.0	VF/NM 9.0	NM- 9.2
2-2nd app. (TV show debuted on 9/30/60); 1st app. of Cave Kids; 15¢-c thru #5	12	24	36	84	127	170
3-6(7-8/62): 3-Perry Gunnite begins. 6-1st 12¢-c	8	16	24	55	78	100
7 (10/62; 1st GK)	8	16	24	55	78	100
8-10	7	14	21	46	63	80
11-1st app. Pebbles (6/63)	10	20	30	70	100	130
12-15,17-20	6	12	18	38	52	65
16-1st app. Bamm-Bamm (1/64)	9	18	27	65	93	120
21-23,25-30,33: 26,27-2nd & 3rd app. The Grusomes. 30-1st app. Martian Mopheads (10/65). 33-Meet Frankenstein & Dracula	5	10	15	36	48	60
24-1st app. The Grusomes	7	14	21	50	68	85
31,32,35-40: 31-Xmas-c. 36-Adaptation of "the Man Called Flintstone" movie. 39-Reprints	4	8	12	29	40	50
34-1st app. The Great Gazoo	7	14	21	50	68	85
41-60: 45-Last 12¢ issue	4	8	12	25	33	42
At N. Y. World's Fair ('64)-J.W. Books (25¢)-1st printing; no date on-c (29¢ version exists, 2nd print?) Most H-B characters app.; including Yogi Bear, Top Cat, Snagglepuss and the Jetsons	6	12	18	43	59	75
At N. Y. World's Fair (1965 on-c; re-issue; Warren Pub.) NOTE: Warehouse find in 1984	2	4	6	11	14	18
Bigger & Boulder 1(#30013-211) (Gold Key Giant, 11/62, 25¢, 84 pgs.)	10	20	30	67	96	125
Bigger & Boulder 2-(1966, 25¢)-Reprints B&B No. 1	6	12	18	40	55	70
...On the Rocks (9/61, $1.00, 6-1/4x9", cardboard-c, high quality paper,116 pgs.) B&W new material	10	20	30	73	107	140
...With Pebbles & Bamm Bamm (100 pgs., G.K.)-30028-511 (paper-c, 25¢) (11/65)	10	20	30	67	96	125

NOTE: *(See Comic Album #16, Bamm-Bamm & Pebbles Flintstone, Dell Giant 48, Golden Comics Digest, March of Comics #229, 243, 271, 289, 299, 317, 327, 341, Pebbles Flintstone, Top Comics #2-4, and Whitman Comic Book.)*

FLINTSTONES, THE (TV)(...& Pebbles)
Charlton Comics: Nov, 1970 - No. 50, Feb, 1977 (Hanna-Barbera)

	GD 2.0	VG 4.0	FN 6.0	VF 8.0	VF/NM 9.0	NM- 9.2
1	9	18	27	65	93	120
2	5	10	15	36	48	60
3-7,9,10	4	8	12	24	32	40
8- "Flintstones Summer Vacation" (Summer, 1971, 52 pgs.)	6	12	18	43	59	75
11-20,36: 36-Mike Zeck illos (early work)	3	6	9	18	24	30
21-35,38-41,43-45	3	6	9	16	20	24
37-Byrne text illos (early work; see Nightmare #20)	3	6	9	18	24	30
42-Byrne-a (2 pgs.)	3	6	9	18	24	30
46-50	2	4	6	14	18	22
Digest nn (1972, B&W, 100 pgs.) (low print run)	4	8	12	24	32	40

(Also see Barney & Betty Rubble, Dino, The Great Gazoo, & Pebbles & Bamm-Bamm)

FLINTSTONES, THE (TV)(See Yogi Bear, 3rd series) (Newsstand sales only)
Marvel Comics Group: October, 1977 - No. 9, Feb, 1979 (Hanna-Barbera)

	GD 2.0	VG 4.0	FN 6.0	VF 8.0	VF/NM 9.0	NM- 9.2
1,7-9: 1-(30¢-c). 7-9-Yogi Bear app.	4	8	12	24	32	40
1-(35¢-c variant, limited distribution)	4	8	12	29	40	50
2,3,5,6: Yogi Bear app.	3	6	9	18	23	28
4-The Jetsons app.	3	6	9	19	25	32

FLINTSTONES, THE (TV)
Harvey Comics: Sept, 1992 - No. 13, Jun, 1994 ($1.25/$1.50) (Hanna-Barbera)

	GD 2.0	VG 4.0	FN 6.0	VF 8.0	VF/NM 9.0	NM- 9.2
V2#1-13						3.00
...Big Book 1,2 (11/92, 3/93; both $1.95, 52 pgs.)						3.50
...Giant Size 1-3 (10/92, 4/93, 11/93; $2.25, 68 pgs.)						3.50

FLINTSTONES, THE (TV)
Archie Publications: Sept, 1995 - No. 22, June, 1997 ($1.50)

	GD 2.0	VG 4.0	FN 6.0	VF 8.0	VF/NM 9.0	NM- 9.2
1-22						3.00

FLINTSTONES AND THE JETSONS, THE (TV)
DC Comics: Aug, 1997 - No. 21, May, 1999 ($1.75/$1.95/$1.99)

	GD 2.0	VG 4.0	FN 6.0	VF 8.0	VF/NM 9.0	NM- 9.2
1						6.00
2-21: 19-Bizarro Elroy-c						3.00

FLINTSTONES CHRISTMAS PARTY, THE (See The Funtastic World of Hanna-Barbera No. 1)

FLIP
Harvey Publications: April, 1954 - No. 2, June, 1954 (Satire)

	GD 2.0	VG 4.0	FN 6.0	VF 8.0	VF/NM 9.0	NM- 9.2
1,2-Nostrand-a each. 2-Powell-a	23	46	69	130	188	245

FLIPPER (TV)
Gold Key: Apr, 1966 - No. 3, Nov, 1967 (All have photo-c)

	GD 2.0	VG 4.0	FN 6.0	VF 8.0	VF/NM 9.0	NM- 9.2
1	8	16	24	55	78	100
2,3	6	12	18	38	52	65

FLIPPITY & FLOP
National Per. Publ. (Signal Publ. Co.): 12-1/51-52 - No. 46, 8-10/59; No. 47, 9-11/60

	GD 2.0	VG 4.0	FN 6.0	VF 8.0	VF/NM 9.0	NM- 9.2
1-Sam dog & his pets Flippity The Bird and Flop The Cat begin; Twiddle and Twaddle begin	28	56	84	158	229	300
2	15	30	45	83	117	150
3-5	13	26	39	74	102	130
6-10	11	22	33	64	87	110
11-20: 20-Last precode (3/55)	10	20	30	58	77	95
21-47	9	18	27	52	66	80

FLOATERS
Dark Horse Comics: Sept, 1993 - No. 5, Jan, 1994 ($2.50, B&W, lim. series)

	GD 2.0	VG 4.0	FN 6.0	VF 8.0	VF/NM 9.0	NM- 9.2
1-5						2.50

FLOYD FARLAND (See Eclipse Graphic Album Series #11)

FLY, THE (Also see Adventures of..., Blue Ribbon Comics & Flyman)
Archie Enterprises, Inc.: May, 1983 - No. 9, Oct, 1984

	GD 2.0	VG 4.0	FN 6.0	VF 8.0	VF/NM 9.0	NM- 9.2
1,2: 1-Mr. Justice app; origin Shield; Kirby-a; Steranko-c. 2-Ditko-a; Flygirl app.						5.00
3-5: Ditko-a in all. 4,5-Ditko-c(p)						4.00
6-9: Ditko-a in all. 6-8-Ditko-c(p)						5.00

NOTE: *Ayers c-9.* ***Buckler*** *a-1, 2.* ***Kirby*** *a-1.* ***Nebres*** *c-3, 4, 5i, 6, 7i.* ***Steranko*** *c-1, 2.*

FLY, THE
Impact Comics (DC): Aug, 1991 - No. 17, Dec, 1992 ($1.00)

	GD 2.0	VG 4.0	FN 6.0	VF 8.0	VF/NM 9.0	NM- 9.2
1						3.00
2-17: 4-Vs. The Black Hood. 9-Trading card inside						2.50
Annual 1 ('92, $2.50, 68 pgs.)-Impact trading card						3.00

FLYBOY (Flying Cadets)(Also see Approved Comics #5)
Ziff-Davis Publ. Co. (Approved): Spring, 1952 - No. 2, Oct-Nov, 1952

	GD 2.0	VG 4.0	FN 6.0	VF 8.0	VF/NM 9.0	NM- 9.2
1-Saunders painted-c	20	40	60	112	161	210
2-(10-11/52)-Saunders painted-c	14	28	42	79	110	140

FLYING ACES (Aviation stories)
Key Publications: July, 1955 - No. 5, Mar, 1956

	GD 2.0	VG 4.0	FN 6.0	VF 8.0	VF/NM 9.0	NM- 9.2
1	8	16	24	40	50	60
2-5: 2-Trapani-a	5	10	15	22	26	30

FLYING A'S RANGE RIDER, THE (TV)(See Western Roundup under Dell Giants)
Dell Publishing Co.: #404, 6-7/52; #2, June-Aug, 1953 - #24, Aug, 1959 (All photo-c)

	GD 2.0	VG 4.0	FN 6.0	VF 8.0	VF/NM 9.0	NM- 9.2
Four Color 404(#1)-Titled "The Range Rider"	12	24	36	84	127	170
2	8	16	24	55	78	100
3-10	7	14	21	46	63	80
11-16,18-24	6	12	18	40	55	70
17-Toth-a	7	14	21	50	68	85

FLYING CADET (WW II Plane Photos)
Flying Cadet Publ. Co.; Jan, 1943 - V2#8, 1947 (Half photos, half comics)

	GD 2.0	VG 4.0	FN 6.0	VF 8.0	VF/NM 9.0	NM- 9.2
V1#1-Painted-c	15	30	45	86	123	160
2	9	18	27	52	66	80
3-9 (Two #6's, Sept. & Oct.): 5,6a,6b-Photo-c	8	16	24	46	58	70
V2#1-7(#10-16)	8	16	24	40	50	60
8(#17)-Bare-breasted woman-c	19	38	57	107	154	200

FLYING COLORS 10th ANNIVERSARY SPECIAL
Flying Colors Comics: Fall 1998 ($2.95, one-shot)

	GD 2.0	VG 4.0	FN 6.0	VF 8.0	VF/NM 9.0	NM- 9.2
1-Dan Brereton-c; pin-ups by Jim Lee and Jeff Johnson						3.00

FLYIN' JENNY
Pentagon Publ. Co./Leader Enterprises #2: 1946 - No. 2, 1947 (1945 strip-r)

	GD 2.0	VG 4.0	FN 6.0	VF 8.0	VF/NM 9.0	NM- 9.2
nn-Marcus Swayze strip-r (entire insides)	14	28	42	81	113	145

Foolkiller #1 © MAR

Football Thrills #2 © Z-D

Forbidden Worlds #86 © ACG

	GD 2.0	VG 4.0	FN 6.0	VF 8.0	VF/NM 9.0	NM- 9.2
2-Baker-c; Swayze strip reprints	16	32	48	89	127	165

FLYING MODELS
H-K Publ. (Health-Knowledge Publs.): V61#3, May, 1954 (5¢, 16 pgs.)

	GD	VG	FN	VF	VF/NM	NM-
V61#3 (Rare)	9	18	27	52	66	80

FLYING NUN (TV)
Dell Publishing Co.: Feb, 1968 - No. 4, Nov, 1968

	GD	VG	FN	VF	VF/NM	NM-
1-Sally Field photo-c	7	14	21	46	63	80
2-4: 2-Sally Field photo-c	4	8	12	28	38	48

FLYING NURSES (See Sue & Sally Smith...)

FLYING SAUCERS (See The Spirit 9/28/47(1st app.), Shadow Comics V7#10 (2nd, 1/48), Captain Midnight #60 (3rd, 2/48), Boy Commandos #26 (4th, 3-4/48) & Flash Gordon Four Color 190 (5th, 6/48))

FLYING SAUCERS
Avon Periodicals/Realistic: 1950; 1952; 1953

	GD	VG	FN	VF	VF/NM	NM-
1(1950)-Wood-a, 21 pgs.; Fawcette-c	79	158	237	494	760	1025
nn(1952)-Cover altered plus 2 pgs. of Wood-a not in original	46	92	138	281	428	575
nn(1953)-Reprints above	36	72	108	204	297	390

FLYING SAUCERS (Comics)
Dell Publishing Co.: April, 1967 - No. 4, Nov, 1967; No. 5, Oct, 1969

	GD	VG	FN	VF	VF/NM	NM-
1	4	8	12	29	40	50
2-5	3	7	10	21	28	35

FLY MAN (Formerly Adventures of The Fly; Mighty Comics #40 on)
Mighty Comics Group (Radio Comics) (Archie): No. 32, July, 1965 - No. 39, Sept, 1966 (Also see Mighty Crusaders)

	GD	VG	FN	VF	VF/NM	NM-
32,33-Comet, Shield, Black Hood, The Fly & Flygirl x-over. 33-Re-intro Wizard, Hangman (1st S.A. appearances)	5	10	15	36	48	60
34-39: 34-Shield begins. 35-Origin Black Hood. 36-Hangman x-over in Shield; re-intro. & origin of Web (1st S.A. app.). 37-Hangman, Wizard x-over in Flyman; last Shield issue. 38-Web story. 39-Steel Sterling (1st S.A. app.)	4	8	12	24	32	40

FOES
Ram Comics: 1989 - No. 3, 1989 ($1.95, limited series)

	GD	VG	FN	VF	VF/NM	NM-
1-3						2.25

FOLLOW THE SUN (TV)
Dell Publishing Co.: May-July, 1962 - No. 2, Sept-Nov, 1962 (Photo-c)

	GD	VG	FN	VF	VF/NM	NM-
01-280-207(No.1)	6	12	18	38	52	65
12-280-211(No.2)	5	10	15	33	44	55

FOODANG
Continum Comics: July, 1994 ($1.95, B&W, bi-monthly)

	GD	VG	FN	VF	VF/NM	NM-
1						2.25

FOODINI (TV)(The Great...; see Jingle Dingle & Pinhead &...)
Continental Publ. (Holyoke): March, 1950 - No. 4, Aug, 1950 (All have 52 pgs.)

	GD	VG	FN	VF	VF/NM	NM-
1-Based on TV puppet show (very early TV comic)	23	46	69	132	191	250
2-Jingle Dingle begins	12	24	36	71	98	125
3,4	10	20	30	58	77	95

FOOEY (Magazine) (Satire)
Scoff Publishing Co.: Feb, 1961 - No. 4, May, 1961

	GD	VG	FN	VF	VF/NM	NM-
1	5	10	15	36	48	60
2-4	4	8	12	22	30	38

FOOFUR (TV)
Marvel Comics (Star Comics)/Marvel No. 5 on: Aug, 1987 - No. 6, Jun, 1988

	GD	VG	FN	VF	VF/NM	NM-
1-6						3.00

FOOLKILLER (Also see The Amazing Spider-Man #225, The Defenders #73, Man-Thing #3 & Omega the Unknown #8)
Marvel Comics: Oct, 1990 - No. 10, Oct, 1991 ($1.75, limited series)

	GD	VG	FN	VF	VF/NM	NM-
1-10: 1-Origin 3rd Foolkiller; Greg Salinger app; DeZuniga-a(i) in 1-4. 8-Spider-Man x-over						2.25

FOOM (Friends Of Ol' Marvel)
Marvel Comics: 1973 - No. 22, 1979 (Marvel fan magazine)

	GD	VG	FN	VF	VF/NM	NM-
1	6	12	18	38	52	65
2-Hulk-c by Steranko	4	8	12	25	33	42
3,4	4	8	12	22	30	38
5-11: 11-Kirby-a and interview	3	6	9	19	25	32
12-15: 12-Vision-c. 13-Daredevil-c. 14-Conan. 15-Howard the Duck	3	6	9	18	23	28
16-20: 16-Marvel bullpen. 17-Stan Lee issue. 19-Defenders	3	6	9	16	20	24
21-Star Wars	3	6	9	18	23	28
22-Spider-Man-c; low print run final issue	5	10	15	33	44	55

FOOTBALL THRILLS (See Tops In Adventure)
Ziff-Davis Publ. Co.: Fall-Winter, 1951-52 - No. 2, Fall, 1952 (Edited by "Red" Grange)

	GD	VG	FN	VF	VF/NM	NM-
1-Powell a(2); Saunders painted-c; Red Grange, Jim Thorpe stories	30	60	90	173	249	325
2-Saunders painted-c	20	40	60	112	161	210

FOOT SOLDIERS, THE
Dark Horse Comics: Jan, 1996 - No. 4, Apr, 1996 ($2.95, limited series)

	GD	VG	FN	VF	VF/NM	NM-
1-4: Krueger story & Avon Oeming-a. in all. 1-Alex Ross-c. 4-John K. Snyder, III-c						3.00

FOOT SOLDIERS, THE (Volume Two)
Image Comics: Sept, 1997 - No. 5, May, 1998 ($2.95, limited series)

	GD	VG	FN	VF	VF/NM	NM-
1-5: 1-Yeowell-a. 2-McDaniel, Hester, Sienkiewicz, Giffen-a						3.00

FOR A NIGHT OF LOVE
Avon Periodicals: 1951

	GD	VG	FN	VF	VF/NM	NM-
nn-Two stories adapted from the works of Emile Zola; Astarita, Ravielli-a; Kinstler-c	31	62	93	175	253	330

FORBIDDEN KNOWLEDGE: ADVENTURE BEYOND THE DOORWAY TO SOULS WITH RADICAL DREAMER (Also see Radical Dreamer)
Mark's Giant Economy Size Comics: 1996 ($3.50, B&W, one-shot, 48 pgs.)

	GD	VG	FN	VF	VF/NM	NM-
nn-Max Wrighter app.; Wheatley-c/a/script; painted infinity-c						3.50

FORBIDDEN LOVE
Quality Comics Group: Mar, 1950 - No. 4, Sept, 1950 (52 pgs.)

	GD	VG	FN	VF	VF/NM	NM-
1-(Scarce)-Classic photo-c; Crandall-a	75	150	225	469	722	975
2-(Scarce)-Classic photo-c	63	126	189	394	610	825
3-(Scarce)-Photo-c	40	80	120	236	351	465
4-(Scarce)-Ward/Cuidera-a; photo-c	40	80	120	241	363	485

FORBIDDEN LOVE (See Dark Mansion of...)

FORBIDDEN PLANET
Innovation Publishing: May, 1992 - No. 4, 1992 ($2.50, limited series)

	GD	VG	FN	VF	VF/NM	NM-
1-4: Adapts movie; painted-c						2.50

FORBIDDEN TALES OF DARK MANSION (Formerly Dark Mansion of Forbidden Love #1-4)
National Periodical Publ.: No. 5, May-June, 1972 - No. 15, Feb-Mar, 1974

	GD	VG	FN	VF	VF/NM	NM-
5-(52 pgs.)	5	10	15	36	48	60
6-15: 13-Kane/Howard-a	3	6	9	16	20	24

NOTE: ***N. Adams** c-9. **Alcala** a-9-11, 13. **Chaykin** a-7,15. **Evans** a-14. **Heck** a-5. **Kaluta** a-7i, 8-12; c-7, 8, 13. **G. Kane** a-13. **Kirby** a-6. **Nino** a-8, 12, 15. **Redondo** a-14.*

FORBIDDEN WORLDS
American Comics Group: 7-8/51 - No. 34, 10-11/54; No. 35, 8/55 - No. 145, 8/67 (No. 1-5: 52 pgs.; No. 6-8: 44 pgs.)

	GD	VG	FN	VF	VF/NM	NM-
1-Williamson/Frazetta-a (10 pgs.)	154	308	462	963	1482	2000
2	66	132	198	413	637	860
3-Williamson/Orlando-a (7 pgs.); Wood (2 panels); Frazetta (1 panel)	68	136	204	425	655	885
4	42	84	126	256	391	525
5-Krenkel/Williamson-a (8 pgs.)	55	110	165	336	511	685
6-Harrison/Williamson-a (8 pgs.)	48	96	144	293	447	600
7,8,10: 7-1st monthly issue	31	62	93	178	259	340
9-A-Bomb explosion story	35	70	105	198	287	375
11-20	22	44	66	127	184	240
21-33: 24-E.C. swipe by Landau	17	34	51	95	135	175
34(10-11/54)(Scarce)(becomes Young Heroes #35 on)-Last pre-code issue; A-Bomb explosion story	19	38	57	107	154	200
35(8/55)-Scarce	18	36	54	100	143	185
36-62	12	24	36	69	95	120
63,69,76,78-Williamson-a in all; w/Krenkel #69	12	24	36	71	98	125
64,66-68,70-72,74,75,77,79-85,87-90	10	20	30	56	73	90
65- "There's a New Moon Tonight" listed in #114 as holding 1st record fan mail response	12	24	36	71	98	125
73-1st app. Herbie by Ogden Whitney	40	80	120	233	342	450
86-Flying saucer-c by Schaffenberger	11	22	33	62	84	105
91-93,95-100	6	12	18	40	55	70
94-Herbie (2nd app.)	10	20	30	70	100	130
101-109,111-113,115,117-120	5	10	15	33	44	55
110,116-Herbie app. 116-Herbie goes to Hell	7	14	21	51	71	90
114-1st Herbie-c; contains list of editor's top 20 ACG stories	9	18	27	60	85	110
121-123	4	8	12	27	36	45

Force Works #21 © MAR

Forever People (2nd series) #6 © DC

Four Color Comics #9 © NYNS

GD 2.0 | VG 4.0 | FN 6.0 | VF 8.0 | VF/NM 9.0 | NM- 9.2

124,126-130: 124-Magic Agent app. 4 8 12 29 40 50
125-Magic Agent app.; intro. & origin Magicman series, ends #141
6 12 18 43 59 75
131-139: 133-Origin/1st app. Dragonia in Magicman (1-2/66); returns in #138.
136-Nemesis x-over in Magicman 4 8 12 27 36 45
140-Mark Midnight app. by Ditko 4 8 12 29 40 50
141-145 4 8 12 24 32 40
NOTE: ***Buscema** a-75, 79, 81, 82, 140r. **Cameron** a-5. **Disbrow** a-10. **Ditko** a-137p, 138, 140. **Landau** a-24, 27-29, 31-34, 48, 86r, 96, 143-45. **Lazarus** a-18, 23, 24, 57. **Moldoff** a-27, 31, 139r. **Reinman** a-93. **Whitney** a-115, 116, 137; c-40, 46, 57, 60, 68, 78, 79, 90, 93, 94, 100, 102, 103, 106-108, 114, 129.*

FORCE, THE (See The Crusaders)

FORCE MAJEURE: PRAIRIE BAY (Also see Wild Stars)
Little Rocket Publications: May, 2002 ($2.95, B&W)
1-Tierney-s/Gil-c/a 3.00

FORCE OF BUDDHA'S PALM THE
Jademan Comics: Aug, 1988 - No. 55, Feb, 1993 ($1.50/$1.95, 68 pgs.)
1,55-Kung Fu stories in all 3.00
2-54 2.50

FORCE WORKS
Marvel Comics: July, 1994 - No. 22, Apr, 1996 ($1.50)
1-($3.95)-Fold-out pop-up-c; Iron Man, Wonder Man, Spider-Woman, U.S. Agent & Scarlet Witch (new costume) 4.00
2-11, 13-22: 5-Blue logo & pink logo versions. 9-Intro Dreamguard. 13-Avengers app. 2.25
5-Pink logo ($2.95)-polybagged w/ 16pg. Marvel Action Hour Preview & acetate print 3.00
12 ($2.50)-Flip book w/War Machine. 2.50

FORD ROTUNDA CHRISTMAS BOOK (See Christmas at the Rotunda)

FOREIGN INTRIGUES (Formerly Johnny Dynamite; becomes Battlefield Action #16 on)
Charlton Comics: No. 14, 1956 - No. 15, Aug, 1956
14,15-Johnny Dynamite continues 8 16 24 40 50 60

FOREMOST BOYS (See 4Most)

FOREVER AMBER
Image Comics: July, 1999 - Oct, 1999 ($2.95, B&W)
1-4-Don Hudson-s/a 3.00

FOREVER DARLING (Movie)
Dell Publishing Co.: No. 681, Feb, 1956
Four Color 681-w/Lucille Ball & Desi Arnaz; photo-c 12 24 36 86 131 175

FOREVER MAELSTROM
DC Comics: Jan, 2003 - No. 6, Jun, 2003 ($2.95, limited series)
1-6-Chaykin & Tischman-s/Lucas & Barreto-a 3.00

FOREVER PEOPLE, THE
National Periodical Publications: Feb-Mar, 1971 - No. 11, Oct-Nov, 1972 (Fourth World) (#1-3, 10-11 are 36 pgs; #4-9 are 52 pgs.)
1-1st app. Forever People; Superman x-over; Kirby-c/a begins; 1st full app. Darkseid (3rd anywhere, 3 weeks before New Gods #1); Darkseid storyline begins, ends #8 (app. in 1-4,6,8; cameos in 5,11) 8 16 24 55 78 100
2-9: 4-G.A. reprints thru #9. 9,10-Deadman app. 4 8 12 29 40 50
10,11 3 6 9 19 25 32
Jack Kirby's Forever People TPB ('99, $14.95, B&W&Grey) r/#1-11 plus cover gallery 15.00
NOTE: ***Kirby** c/a(p)-1-11; #4-9 contain Sandman reprints from Adventure #85, 84, 75, 80, 77, 74 in that order.*

FOREVER PEOPLE
DC Comics: Feb, 1988 - No. 6, July, 1988 ($1.25, limited series)
1-6 3.00

FORGE
CrossGeneration Comics: Feb, 2002 - No. 13, May, 2003 ($9.95/$11.95/$7.95, TPB)
1-3: Reprints from various CrossGen titles 10.00
4-8-($11.95) 12.00
9-13-($7.95, 8-1/4" x 5-1/2") digest-sized reprints 8.00

FOR GIRLS ONLY
Bernard Baily Enterprises: 11/53 - No. 2, 6/54 (100 pgs., digest size, 25¢)
1-25% comic book, 75% articles, illos, games 14 28 42 79 110 140
2-Eddie Fisher photo & story. 10 20 30 56 73 90

FORGOTTEN FOREST OF OZ, THE (See First Comics Graphic Novel #16)

FORGOTTEN REALMS (Also see Avatar & TSR Worlds)
DC Comics: Sept, 1989 - No. 25, Sept, 1991 ($1.50/$1.75)
1, Annual 1 (1990, $2.95, 68 pgs.) 3.00

GD 2.0 | VG 4.0 | FN 6.0 | VF 8.0 | VF/NM 9.0 | NM- 9.2

2-25: Based on TSR role-playing game. 18-Avatar story 2.25

FORLORN RIVER (See Zane Grey Four Color 395)

FOR LOVERS ONLY (Formerly Hollywood Romances)
Charlton Comics: No. 60, Aug, 1971 - No. 87, Nov, 1976
60 4 8 12 24 32 40
61-87 2 4 6 12 16 20

FORMERLY KNOWN AS THE JUSTICE LEAGUE
DC Comics: Sept, 2003 - No. 6, Feb, 2004 ($2.50, limited series)
1-Giffen & DeMatteis-s/Maguire-a; Booster Gold, Blue Beetle, Captain Atom, Mary Marvel, Fire, and Elongated Man app. 3.00
2-6: 3,4-Roulette app. 6-JLA app. 2.50
TPB (2004, $12.95) r/#1-6 13.00

FORSAKEN
Image Comics: Aug, 2004 - Present ($2.95)
1-3-Treffiletti-s/Donaldson-a 3.00

FORT: PROPHET OF THE UNEXPLAINED
Dark Horse Comics: June, 2002 - No. 4, Sept, 2002 ($2.99, B&W, limited series)
1-4-Peter Lenkov-s/Frazer Irving-c/a 3.00
TPB (2003, $9.95) r/#1-4 10.00

FORTUNE AND GLORY
Oni Press: Dec, 1999 - No. 3, Apr, 2000 ($4.95, B&W, limited series)
1-3-Brian Michael Bendis in Hollywood 5.00
TPB ($14.95) 15.00

40 BIG PAGES OF MICKEY MOUSE
Whitman Publ. Co.: No. 945, Jan, 1936 (10-1/4x12-1/2", 44 pgs., cardboard-c)
945-Reprints Mickey Mouse Magazine #1, but with a different cover; ads were eliminated and some illustrated stories had expanded text. The book is 3/4" shorter than Mickey Mouse Mag. #1, but the reprints are same size (Rare) 162 324 486 1013 1557 2100

40 oz. COLLECTED
Image Comics: Nov, 2003 ($9.95, digest-size, B&W)
Vol. 1-Reprints Jim Mahfood's mini-comics plus 20 pgs. new material; Grrl Scouts app. 10.00

FOR YOUR EYES ONLY (See James Bond...)

FOUR COLOR
Dell Publishing Co.: Sept?, 1939 - No. 1354, Apr-June, 1962
(Series I are all 68 pgs.)
NOTE: *Four Color only appears on issues #19-25, 1-99,101. Dell Publishing Co. filed these as Series I, #1-25, and Series II, #1-1354. Issues beginning with #710? were printed with and without ads on back cover. Issues without ads are worth more.*

SERIES I:
1(nn)-Dick Tracy 718 1436 2154 5026 8263 11,500
2(nn)-Don Winslow of the Navy (#1) (Rare) (11/39?)
138 276 414 1035 1618 2200
3(nn)-Myra North (1/40) 70 140 210 536 856 1175
4-Donald Duck by Al Taliaferro (1940)(Disney)(3/40?)
875 1750 2625 6800 11,900 17,000
(Prices vary widely on this book)
5-Smilin' Jack (#1) (5/40?) 55 110 165 432 679 925
6-Dick Tracy (Scarce) 135 270 405 1071 1736 2400
7-Gang Busters 36 72 108 270 423 575
8-Dick Tracy 68 136 204 536 868 1200
9-Terry and the Pirates-r/Super #9-29 50 100 150 407 641 875
10-Smilin' Jack 46 92 138 370 578 785
11-Smitty (#1) 34 68 102 255 403 550
12-Little Orphan Annie; reprints strips from 12/19/37 to 6/4/38
43 86 129 344 535 725
13-Walt Disney's Reluctant Dragon('41)-Contains 2 pgs. of photos from film; 2 pg. foreword to Fantasia by Leopold Stokowski; Donald Duck, Goofy, Baby Weems & Mickey Mouse (as the Sorcerer's Apprentice) app. (Disney) 150 300 450 1140 1820 2500
14-Moon Mullins (#1) 34 68 102 255 403 550
15-Tillie the Toiler (#1) 34 68 102 255 398 540
16-Mickey Mouse (#1) (Disney) by Gottfredson 1400 2800 4200 13,500 - -
17-Walt Disney's Dumbo, the Flying Elephant (#1)(1941)-Mickey Mouse, Donald Duck, & Pluto app. (Disney) 185 370 555 1388 2194 3000
18-Jiggs and Maggie (#1)(1936-38-r) 36 72 108 270 423 575
19-Barney Google and Snuffy Smith (#1)-(1st issue with Four Color on the cover)
38 76 115 285 430 575
20-Tiny Tim 29 58 87 206 316 425
21-Dick Tracy 55 110 165 425 688 950

Four Color Comics #19 © DELL

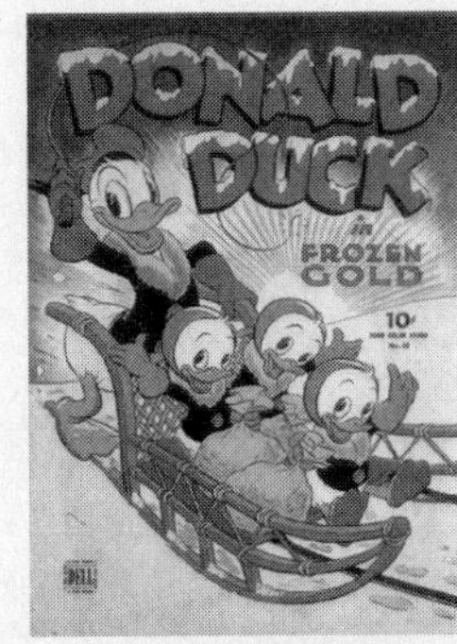

Four Color Comics #62 © WDC

Four Color Comics #64 © NYNS

	GD 2.0	VG 4.0	FN 6.0	VF 8.0	VF/NM 9.0	NM- 9.2
22-Don Winslow	32	64	96	240	370	500
23-Gang Busters	30	60	90	213	327	440
24-Captain Easy	40	80	120	300	468	635
25-Popeye (1942)	60	120	180	475	763	1050
SERIES II:						
1-Little Joe (1942)	50	100	150	400	625	850
2-Harold Teen	30	60	90	218	334	450
3-Alley Oop (#1)	46	92	138	368	572	775
4-Smilin' Jack	41	82	123	305	478	650
5-Raggedy Ann and Andy (#1)	47	94	141	376	588	800
6-Smitty	23	46	69	165	253	340
7-Smokey Stover (#1)	31	62	93	225	355	485
8-Tillie the Toiler	33	66	99	190	275	360
9-Donald Duck Finds Pirate Gold, by Carl Barks & Jack Hannah (Disney) (© 8/17/42)	750	1500	2250	5800	9813	14,000
10-Flash Gordon by Alex Raymond; reprinted from "The Ice Kingdom"	90	180	270	680	1103	1525
11-Wash Tubbs	31	62	93	228	352	475
12-Walt Disney's Bambi (#1)	59	158	177	417	659	900
13-Mr. District Attorney (#1)-See The Funnies #35 for 1st app.	30	60	90	213	327	440
14-Smilin' Jack	33	66	99	248	387	525
15-Felix the Cat (#1)	70	140	210	536	868	1200
16-Porky Pig (#1)(1942)- "Secret of the Haunted House"	74	148	222	629	1015	1400
17-Popeye	44	88	132	352	551	750
18-Little Orphan Annie's Junior Commandos; Flag-c; reprints strips from 6/14/42 to 11/21/42	37	74	111	278	432	585
19-Walt Disney's Thumper Meets the Seven Dwarfs (Disney); reprinted in Silly Symphonies	49	98	147	392	614	835
20-Barney Baxter	29	58	87	209	310	410
21-Oswald the Rabbit (#1)(1943)	45	90	135	360	560	760
22-Tillie the Toiler	18	36	54	131	201	270
23-Raggedy Ann and Andy	37	74	111	278	432	585
24-Gang Busters	30	60	90	213	327	440
25-Andy Panda (#1) (Walter Lantz)	54	108	162	405	628	850
26-Popeye	44	88	132	352	551	750
27-Walt Disney's Mickey Mouse and the Seven Colored Terror	80	160	240	629	1015	1400
28-Wash Tubbs	22	44	66	158	242	325
29-Donald Duck and the Mummy's Ring, by Carl Barks (Disney) (9/43)	513	1026	1539	4000	6750	9500
30-Bambi's Children (1943)-Disney	56	112	168	400	620	840
31-Moon Mullins	20	40	60	141	216	290
32-Smitty	17	34	51	121	186	250
33-Bugs Bunny "Public Nuisance #1"	115	230	345	805	1278	1750
34-Dick Tracy	41	82	123	318	497	675
35-Smokey Stover	18	36	54	129	197	265
36-Smilin' Jack	25	50	75	177	271	365
37-Bringing Up Father	20	40	60	145	273	300
38-Roy Rogers (#1, © 4/44)-1st western comic with photo-c (see Movie Comics #3)	200	400	600	1654	2677	3700
39-Oswald the Rabbit (1944)	33	66	99	248	387	525
40-Barney Google and Snuffy Smith	24	48	72	170	260	350
41-Mother Goose and Nursery Rhyme Comics (#1)-All by Walt Kelly	25	50	75	177	271	365
42-Tiny Tim (1934-r)	18	36	54	126	193	260
43-Popeye (1938-'42-r)	32	64	96	240	370	500
44-Terry and the Pirates (1938-r)	37	74	111	278	432	585
45-Raggedy Ann	31	62	93	225	355	485
46-Felix the Cat and the Haunted Castle	39	78	117	293	459	625
47-Gene Autry (copyright 6/16/44)	41	82	123	330	515	700
48-Porky Pig of the Mounties by Carl Barks (7/44)	86	172	258	706	1128	1550
49-Snow White and the Seven Dwarfs (Disney)	55	110	165	425	675	925
50-Fairy Tale Parade-Walt Kelly art (1944)	26	52	78	187	286	385
51-Bugs Bunny Finds the Lost Treasure	35	70	105	263	412	560
52-Little Orphan Annie; reprints strips from 6/18/38 to 11/19/38	30	60	90	213	327	440
53-Wash Tubbs	16	32	48	114	175	235
54-Andy Panda	31	62	93	228	352	475
55-Tillie the Toiler	14	28	42	102	156	210
56-Dick Tracy	36	72	108	270	423	575
57-Gene Autry	40	80	120	300	468	635
58-Smilin' Jack	25	50	75	177	271	365

	GD 2.0	VG 4.0	FN 6.0	VF 8.0	VF/NM 9.0	NM- 9.2
59-Mother Goose and Nursery Rhyme Comics-Kelly-c/a	21	42	63	148	227	305
60-Tiny Folks Funnies	17	34	51	119	182	245
61-Santa Claus Funnies(11/44)-Kelly art	25	50	75	177	271	365
62-Donald Duck in Frozen Gold, by Carl Barks (Disney) (1/45)	162	332	498	1365	2233	3100
63-Roy Rogers; color photo-all 4 covers	47	94	141	376	588	800
64-Smokey Stover	14	28	42	102	156	210
65-Smitty	14	28	42	97	149	200
66-Gene Autry	40	80	120	300	468	635
67-Oswald the Rabbit	19	38	57	134	205	275
68-Mother Goose and Nursery Rhyme Comics, by Walt Kelly	21	42	63	148	227	305
69-Fairy Tale Parade, by Walt Kelly	26	52	78	187	286	385
70-Popeye and Wimpy	26	52	78	187	296	385
71-Walt Disney's Three Caballeros, by Walt Kelly (© 4/45)-(Disney)	70	140	210	550	875	1200
72-Raggedy Ann	27	54	81	194	297	400
73-The Gumps (#1)	13	26	39	92	141	190
74-Marge's Little Lulu (#1)	115	230	345	850	1325	1800
75-Gene Autry and the Wildcat	31	62	93	230	358	485
76-Little Orphan Annie; reprints strips from 2/28/40 to 6/24/40	25	50	75	181	278	375
77-Felix the Cat	37	74	111	278	432	585
78-Porky Pig and the Bandit Twins	27	54	81	194	297	400
79-Walt Disney's Mickey Mouse in The Riddle of the Red Hat by Carl Barks (8/45)	100	200	300	757	1229	1725
80-Smilin' Jack	16	32	48	116	178	240
81-Moon Mullins	12	24	36	84	127	170
82-Lone Ranger	40	80	120	300	468	635
83-Gene Autry in Outlaw Trail	31	62	93	230	358	485
84-Flash Gordon by Alex Raymond-Reprints from "The Fiery Desert"	41	82	123	330	515	700
85-Andy Panda and the Mad Dog Mystery	18	36	54	126	193	260
86-Roy Rogers; photo-c	35	70	105	263	412	560
87-Fairy Tale Parade by Walt Kelly; Dan Noonan-c	26	52	78	187	286	385
88-Bugs Bunny's Great Adventure (Sci/fi)	24	48	72	170	260	350
89-Tillie the Toiler	14	28	42	102	156	210
90-Christmas with Mother Goose by Walt Kelly (11/45)	19	38	57	134	205	275
91-Santa Claus Funnies by Walt Kelly (11/45)	19	38	57	134	205	275
92-Walt Disney's The Wonderful Adventures Of Pinocchio (1945); Donald Duck by Kelly, 16 pgs. (Disney)	53	106	159	420	660	900
93-Gene Autry in The Bandit of Black Rock	30	60	90	213	327	440
94-Winnie Winkle (1945)	13	26	39	90	138	185
95-Roy Rogers Comics; photo-c	35	70	105	263	412	560
96-Dick Tracy	28	56	84	199	305	410
97-Marge's Little Lulu (1946)	50	100	150	376	576	775
98-Lone Ranger, The	31	62	93	225	355	485
99-Smitty	12	24	36	84	127	170
100-Gene Autry Comics; 1st Gene Autry photo-c	31	62	93	230	358	485
101-Terry and the Pirates	26	52	78	189	290	390

NOTE: No. 101 is last issue to carry "Four Color" logo on cover; all issues beginning with No. 100 are marked "...O. S." (One Shot) which can be found in the bottom left-hand panel on the first page; the numbers following "O. S." relate to the year/month issued.

	GD 2.0	VG 4.0	FN 6.0	VF 8.0	VF/NM 9.0	NM- 9.2
102-Oswald the Rabbit-Walt Kelly art, 1 pg.	16	32	48	112	171	230
103-Easter with Mother Goose by Walt Kelly	19	38	57	134	205	275
104-Fairy Tale Parade by Walt Kelly	20	40	60	141	216	290
105-Albert the Alligator and Pogo Possum (#1) by Kelly (4/46)	60	120	180	502	789	1075
106-Tillie the Toiler (5/46)	11	22	33	77	114	150
107-Little Orphan Annie; reprints strips from 11/16/42 to 3/24/43	22	44	66	155	238	320
108-Donald Duck in The Terror of the River, by Carl Barks (Disney) (© 4/16/46)	125	250	375	1063	1719	2375
109-Roy Rogers Comics; photo-c	29	58	87	206	316	425
110-Marge's Little Lulu	35	70	105	260	398	535
111-Captain Easy	15	30	45	107	164	220
112-Porky Pig's Adventure in Gopher Gulch	17	34	51	121	186	250
113-Popeye; all new Popeye stories begin	15	30	45	105	160	215
114-Fairy Tale Parade by Walt Kelly	20	40	60	141	216	290
115-Marge's Little Lulu	35	70	105	255	390	525
116-Mickey Mouse and the House of Many Mysteries (Disney)	26	52	78	187	286	385

Four Color Comics #125 © Lone Ranger Inc.

Four Color Comics #126 © DELL

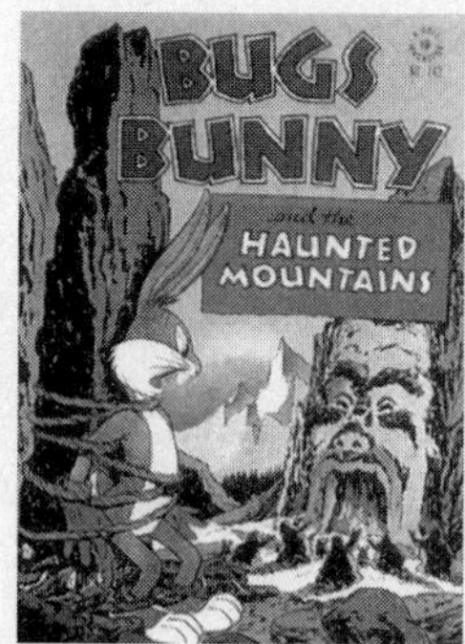

Four Color Comics #142 © WB

	GD 2.0	VG 4.0	FN 6.0	VF 8.0	VF/NM 9.0	NM- 9.2
117-Roy Rogers Comics; photo-c	23	46	69	163	249	335
118-Lone Ranger, The	31	62	93	225	355	485
119-Felix the Cat; all new Felix stories begin	34	68	102	255	398	540
120-Marge's Little Lulu	31	62	93	228	352	475
121-Fairy Tale Parade-(not Kelly)	12	24	36	87	134	180
122-Henry (#1) (10/46)	15	30	45	105	160	215
123-Bugs Bunny's Dangerous Venture	17	34	51	121	186	250
124-Roy Rogers Comics; photo-c	23	46	69	163	249	335
125-Lone Ranger, The	23	46	69	163	249	335
126-Christmas with Mother Goose by Walt Kelly (1946)	14	28	42	102	156	210
127-Popeye	15	30	45	105	160	215
128-Santa Claus Funnies- "Santa & the Angel" by Gollub; "A Mouse in the House" by Kelly	15	30	45	107	164	220
129-Walt Disney's Uncle Remus and His Tales of Brer Rabbit (#1) (1946)-Adapted from Disney movie "Song of the South"	29	58	87	210	323	435
130-Andy Panda (Walter Lantz)	12	24	36	84	127	170
131-Marge's Little Lulu	31	62	93	228	352	475
132-Tillie the Toiler (1947)	11	22	33	77	114	150
133-Dick Tracy	23	46	69	163	249	335
134-Tarzan and the Devil Ogre; Marsh-c/a	55	110	165	460	743	1025
135-Felix the Cat	26	52	78	184	282	380
136-Lone Ranger, The	23	46	69	163	249	335
137-Roy Rogers Comics; photo-c	23	46	69	163	249	335
138-Smitty	10	20	30	73	107	140
139-Marge's Little Lulu (1947)	30	60	90	213	327	440
140-Easter with Mother Goose by Walt Kelly	15	30	45	109	167	225
141-Mickey Mouse and the Submarine Pirates (Disney)	22	44	66	158	242	325
142-Bugs Bunny and the Haunted Mountain	17	34	51	121	186	250
143-Oswald the Rabbit & the Prehistoric Egg	11	22	33	75	110	145
144-Roy Rogers Comics (1947)-Photo-c	23	46	69	163	249	335
145-Popeye	15	30	45	105	160	215
146-Marge's Little Lulu	30	60	90	213	327	440
147-Donald Duck in Volcano Valley, by Carl Barks (Disney) (5/47)	84	168	252	714	1155	1515
148-Albert the Alligator and Pogo Possum by Walt Kelly (5/47)	50	100	150	407	641	875
149-Smilin' Jack	11	22	33	80	120	160
150-Tillie the Toiler (6/47)	10	20	30	72	104	135
151-Lone Ranger, The	20	40	60	141	216	290
152-Little Orphan Annie; reprints strips from 1/2/44 to 5/6/44	14	28	42	102	156	210
153-Roy Rogers Comics; photo-c	20	40	60	145	223	300
154-Walter Lantz Andy Panda	12	24	36	84	127	170
155-Henry (7/47)	10	20	30	73	107	140
156-Porky Pig and the Phantom	12	24	36	86	131	175
157-Mickey Mouse & the Beanstalk (Disney)	22	44	66	158	242	325
158-Marge's Little Lulu	30	60	90	213	327	440
159-Donald Duck in the Ghost of the Grotto, by Carl Barks (Disney) (8/47)	72	144	216	612	994	1375
160-Roy Rogers Comics; photo-c	20	40	60	145	223	300
161-Tarzan and the Fires Of Tohr; Marsh-c/a	51	102	153	408	634	860
162-Felix the Cat (9/47)	20	40	60	145	223	300
163-Dick Tracy	19	38	57	136	208	280
164-Bugs Bunny Finds the Frozen Kingdom	17	34	51	121	186	250
165-Marge's Little Lulu	30	60	90	213	327	440
166-Roy Rogers Comics (52 pgs.)-Photo-c	20	40	60	145	223	300
167-Lone Ranger, The	20	40	60	141	216	290
168-Popeye (10/47)	15	30	45	105	160	215
169-Woody Woodpecker (#1)- "Manhunter in the North"; drug use story	18	36	54	131	201	270
170-Mickey Mouse on Spook's Island (11/47)(Disney)-reprinted in Mickey Mouse #103	19	38	57	136	208	280
171-Charlie McCarthy (#1) and the Twenty Thieves	28	56	84	199	305	410
172-Christmas with Mother Goose by Walt Kelly (11/47)	14	28	42	102	156	210
173-Flash Gordon	19	38	57	134	205	275
174-Winnie Winkle	9	18	27	60	85	110
175-Santa Claus Funnies by Walt Kelly (1947)	15	30	45	107	164	220
176-Tillie the Toiler (12/47)	10	20	30	72	104	135
177-Roy Rogers Comics-(36 pgs.); Photo-c	20	40	60	141	216	290
178-Donald Duck "Christmas on Bear Mountain" by Carl Barks; 1st app. Uncle Scrooge (Disney)(12/47)	100	200	300	850	1375	1900
179-Uncle Wiggily (#1)-Walt Kelly-c	17	34	51	119	182	245
180-Ozark Ike (#1)	11	22	33	80	120	160
181-Walt Disney's Mickey Mouse in Jungle Magic	19	38	57	136	208	280
182-Porky Pig in Never-Never Land (2/48)	12	24	36	86	131	175
183-Oswald the Rabbit (Lantz)	11	22	33	75	110	145
184-Tillie the Toiler	10	20	30	72	104	135
185-Easter with Mother Goose by Walt Kelly (1948)	14	28	42	97	149	200
186-Walt Disney's Bambi (4/48)-Reprinted as Movie Classic Bambi #3 (1956)	18	36	54	126	193	260
187-Bugs Bunny and the Dreadful Dragon	12	24	36	87	134	180
188-Woody Woodpecker (Lantz, 5/48)	12	24	36	86	131	175
189-Donald Duck in The Old Castle's Secret, by Carl Barks (Disney) (6/48)	61	122	183	519	835	1150
190-Flash Gordon (6/48); bondage-c; "The Adventures of the Flying Saucers"; 5th Flying Saucer story- see The Spirit 9/28/47(1st), Shadow Comics V7#10 (2nd, 1/48),Captain Midnight #60 (3rd, 2/48) & Boy Commandos #26 (4th, 3-4/48)	21	42	63	150	230	310
191-Porky Pig to the Rescue	12	24	36	86	131	175
192-The Brownies (#1)-by Walt Kelly (7/48)	15	30	45	107	164	220
193-M.G.M. Presents Tom and Jerry (#1)(1948)	22	44	66	160	245	330
194-Mickey Mouse in The World Under the Sea (Disney)-Reprinted in Mickey Mouse #101	19	38	57	136	208	280
195-Tillie the Toiler	8	16	24	55	78	100
196-Charlie McCarthy in The Haunted Hide-Out; part photo-c	18	36	54	129	197	265
197-Spirit of the Border (#1) (Zane Grey) (1948)	13	26	39	90	138	185
198-Andy Panda	12	24	36	84	127	170
199-Donald Duck in Sheriff of Bullet Valley, by Carl Barks; Barks draws himself on wanted poster, last page; used in Love & Death (Disney) (10/48)	67	134	201	570	920	1270
200-Bugs Bunny, Super Sleuth (10/48)	12	24	36	87	134	180
201-Christmas with Mother Goose by W. Kelly	13	26	39	90	138	185
202-Woody Woodpecker	9	18	27	65	93	120
203-Donald Duck in the Golden Christmas Tree, by Carl Barks (Disney) (12/48)	50	100	150	407	641	875
204-Flash Gordon (12/48)	15	30	45	109	167	225
205-Santa Claus Funnies by Walt Kelly	14	28	42	97	149	200
206-Little Orphan Annie; reprints strips from 11/10/40 to 1/11/41	9	18	27	60	85	110
207-King of the Royal Mounted (#1) (12/48)	15	30	45	109	167	225
208-Brer Rabbit Does It Again (Disney) (1/49)	12	24	36	86	131	175
209-Harold Teen	6	12	18	43	59	75
210-Tippie and Cap Stubbs	6	12	18	38	52	65
211-Little Beaver (#1)	10	20	30	67	96	125
212-Dr. Bobbs	6	12	18	38	52	65
213-Tillie the Toiler	8	16	24	55	78	100
214-Mickey Mouse and His Sky Adventure (2/49)(Disney)-Reprinted in Mickey Mouse #105	14	28	42	102	156	210
215-Sparkle Plenty (Dick Tracy-r by Gould)	12	24	36	86	131	175
216-Andy Panda and the Police Pup (Lantz)	9	18	27	63	89	115
217-Bugs Bunny in Court Jester	12	24	36	87	134	180
218-Three Little Pigs and the Wonderful Magic Lamp (Disney) (3/49)(#1)	12	24	36	87	134	180
219-Swee'pe	10	20	30	70	100	130
220-Easter with Mother Goose by Walt Kelly	14	28	42	97	149	200
221-Uncle Wiggily-Walt Kelly cover in part	10	20	30	73	107	140
222-West of the Pecos (Zane Grey)	8	16	24	58	82	105
223-Donald Duck "Lost in the Andes" by Carl Barks (Disney-4/49) (square egg story)	64	128	192	544	868	1215
224-Little Iodine (#1), by Hatlo (4/49)	12	24	36	84	127	170
225-Oswald the Rabbit (Lantz)	7	14	21	51	71	90
226-Porky Pig and Spoofy, the Spook	10	20	30	73	107	140
227-Seven Dwarfs (Disney)	11	22	33	80	120	160
228-Mark of Zorro, The (#1) (1949)	23	46	69	165	253	340
229-Smokey Stover	7	14	21	51	71	90
230-Sunset Pass (Zane Grey)	8	16	24	58	82	105
231-Mickey Mouse and the Rajah's Treasure (Disney)	14	28	42	102	156	210
232-Woody Woodpecker (Lantz, 6/49)	9	18	27	65	93	120
233-Bugs Bunny, Sleepwalking Sleuth	12	24	36	87	134	180
234-Dumbo in Sky Voyage (Disney)	13	26	39	92	141	190
235-Tiny Tim	6	12	18	40	55	70
236-Heritage of the Desert (Zane Grey) (1949)	8	16	24	58	82	105
237-Tillie the Toiler	8	16	24	55	78	100

Four Color Comics #283 © KING

Four Color Comics #293 © Oskar Lebeck

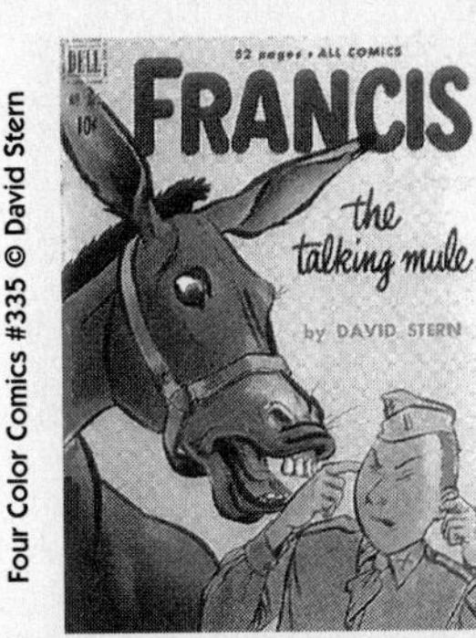
Four Color Comics #335 © David Stern

	GD 2.0	VG 4.0	FN 6.0	VF 8.0	VF/NM 9.0	NM- 9.2
238-Donald Duck in Voodoo Hoodoo, by Carl Barks (Disney) (8/49)	50	100	150	407	641	875
239-Adventure Bound (8/49)	6	12	18	43	59	75
240-Andy Panda (Lantz)	9	18	27	63	89	115
241-Porky Pig, Mighty Hunter	10	20	30	73	107	140
242-Tippie and Cap Stubbs	4	8	12	29	40	50
243-Thumper Follows His Nose (Disney)	12	24	36	84	127	170
244-The Brownies by Walt Kelly	11	22	33	79	117	155
245-Dick's Adventures (9/49)	7	14	21	46	63	80
246-Thunder Mountain (Zane Grey)	6	12	18	40	55	70
247-Flash Gordon	15	30	45	109	167	225
248-Mickey Mouse and the Black Sorcerer (Disney)	14	28	42	102	156	210
249-Woody Woodpecker in the "Globetrotter" (10/49)	9	18	27	65	93	120
250-Bugs Bunny in Diamond Daze; used in **SOTI**, pg. 309	13	26	39	92	141	190
251-Hubert at Camp Moonbeam	6	12	18	43	59	75
252-Pinocchio (Disney)-not by Kelly; origin	12	24	36	84	127	170
253-Christmas with Mother Goose by W. Kelly	13	26	39	90	138	185
254-Santa Claus Funnies by Walt Kelly; Pogo & Albert story by Kelly (11/49)	14	28	42	97	149	200
255-The Ranger (Zane Grey) (1949)	6	12	18	40	55	70
256-Donald Duck in "Luck of the North" by Carl Barks (Disney) (12/49)-Shows #257 on inside	41	82	123	318	497	675
257-Little Iodine	9	18	27	63	89	115
258-Andy Panda and the Balloon Race (Lantz)	9	18	27	63	89	115
259-Santa and the Angel (Gollub art-condensed from #128) & Santa at the Zoo (12/49) -two books in one	6	12	18	38	52	65
260-Porky Pig, Hero of the Wild West (12/49)	10	20	30	73	107	140
261-Mickey Mouse and the Missing Key (Disney)	14	28	42	102	156	210
262-Raggedy Ann and Andy	11	22	33	75	110	145
263-Donald Duck in "Land of the Totem Poles" by Carl Barks (Disney) (2/50)-Has two Barks stories	41	82	123	305	478	650
264-Woody Woodpecker in the Magic Lantern (Lantz)	9	18	27	65	93	120
265-King of the Royal Mounted (Zane Grey)	10	20	30	67	96	125
266-Bugs Bunny on the "Isle of Hercules" (2/50)-Reprinted in Best of Bugs Bunny #1	10	20	30	73	107	140
267-Little Beaver; Harmon-c/a	6	12	18	38	52	65
268-Mickey Mouse's Surprise Visitor (1950)(Disney)	14	28	42	97	149	200
269-Johnny Mack Brown (#1)-Photo-c	25	50	75	177	271	365
270-Drift Fence (Zane Grey) (3/50)	6	12	18	40	55	70
271-Porky Pig in Phantom of the Plains	10	20	30	73	107	140
272-Cinderella (Disney) (4/50)	13	26	39	90	138	185
273-Oswald the Rabbit (Lantz)	7	14	21	51	71	90
274-Bugs Bunny, Hare-brained Reporter	10	20	30	73	107	140
275-Donald Duck in "Ancient Persia" by Carl Barks (Disney) (5/50)	39	78	117	293	459	625
276-Uncle Wiggily	9	18	27	63	89	115
277-Porky Pig in Desert Adventure (5/50)	10	20	30	73	107	140
278-(Wild) Bill Elliott Comics (#1)-Photo-c	14	28	42	102	156	210
279-Mickey Mouse and Pluto Battle the Giant Ants (Disney); reprinted in Mickey Mouse #102 & 245	11	22	33	79	117	155
280-Andy Panda in The Isle Of Mechanical Men (Lantz)	9	18	27	63	89	115
281-Bugs Bunny in The Great Circus Mystery	10	20	30	73	107	140
282-Donald Duck and the Pixilated Parrot by Carl Barks (Disney) (© 5/23/50)	39	78	117	293	459	625
283-King of the Royal Mounted (7/50)	10	20	30	67	96	125
284-Porky Pig in The Kingdom of Nowhere	10	20	30	73	107	140
285-Bozo the Clown & His Minikin Circus (#1) (TV)	21	42	63	150	230	310
286-Mickey Mouse in The Uninvited Guest (Disney	11	22	33	79	117	155
287-Gene Autry's Champion in The Ghost Of Black Mountain; photo-c	12	24	36	86	131	175
288-Woody Woodpecker in Klondike Gold (Lantz)	9	18	27	65	93	120
289-Bugs Bunny in "Indian Trouble"	10	20	30	73	107	140
290-The Chief (#1) (8/50)	7	14	21	51	71	90
291-Donald Duck in "The Magic Hourglass" by Carl Barks (Disney) (9/50)	39	78	117	293	459	625
292-The Cisco Kid Comics (#1)	26	52	78	189	290	390
293-The Brownies-Kelly-c/a	11	22	33	79	117	155
294-Little Beaver	6	12	18	38	52	65
295-Porky Pig in President Porky (9/50)	10	20	30	73	107	140
296-Mickey Mouse in Private Eye for Hire (Disney)	11	22	33	79	117	155
297-Andy Panda in The Haunted Inn (Lantz, 10/50)	9	18	27	63	89	115

	GD 2.0	VG 4.0	FN 6.0	VF 8.0	VF/NM 9.0	NM- 9.2
298-Bugs Bunny in Sheik for a Day	10	20	30	73	107	140
299-Buck Jones & the Iron Horse Trail (#1)	14	28	42	97	149	200
300-Donald Duck in "Big-Top Bedlam" by Carl Barks (Disney) (11/50)	39	78	117	293	459	625
301-The Mysterious Rider (Zane Grey)	6	12	18	40	55	70
302-Santa Claus Funnies (11/50)	7	14	21	46	63	80
303-Porky Pig in The Land of the Monstrous Flies	8	16	24	53	74	95
304-Mickey Mouse in Tom-Tom Island (Disney) (12/50)	10	20	30	70	100	130
305-Woody Woodpecker (Lantz)	7	14	21	46	63	80
306-Raggedy Ann	9	18	27	60	85	110
307-Bugs Bunny in Lumber Jack Rabbit	10	20	30	67	96	125
308-Donald Duck in "Dangerous Disguise" by Carl Barks (Disney) (1/51)	36	72	108	270	423	575
309-Betty Betz' Dollface and Her Gang (1951)	6	12	18	43	59	75
310-King of the Royal Mounted (1/51)	8	16	24	53	74	95
311-Porky Pig in Midget Horses of Hidden Valley	8	16	24	53	74	95
312-Tonto (#1)	11	22	33	80	120	160
313-Mickey Mouse in The Mystery of the Double-Cross Ranch (#1) (Disney) (2/51)	10	20	30	70	100	130

Note: Beginning with the above comic in 1951 Dell/Western began adding #1 in small print on the covers of several long running titles with the evident intention of switching these titles to their own monthly numbers, but when the conversions were made, there was no connection. It is thought that the post office may have stepped in and decreed the sequences should commence as though the first four colors printed had each begun with number one, or the first issues sold by subscription. Since the regular series' numbers don't correctly match to the numbers of earlier issues published, it's not known whether or not the numbering was in error.

	GD 2.0	VG 4.0	FN 6.0	VF 8.0	VF/NM 9.0	NM- 9.2
314-Ambush (Zane Grey)	6	12	18	40	55	70
315-Oswald the Rabbit (Lantz)	7	14	21	46	63	80
316-Rex Allen (#1)-Photo-c; Marsh-a	16	32	48	112	171	230
317-Bugs Bunny in Hair Today Gone Tomorrow (#1)	10	20	30	67	96	125
318-Donald Duck in "No Such Varmint" by Carl Barks (#1)-Indicia shows #317 (Disney, © 1/23/51)	36	72	108	270	423	575
319-Gene Autry's Champion; painted-c	7	14	21	46	63	80
320-Uncle Wiggily (#1)	9	18	27	63	89	115
321-Little Scouts (#1) (3/51)	4	8	12	29	40	50
322-Porky Pig in Roaring Rockets (#1 on-c)	8	16	24	53	74	95
323-Susie Q. Smith (#1) (3/51)	5	10	15	36	48	60
324-I Met a Handsome Cowboy (3/51)	10	20	30	70	100	130
325-Mickey Mouse in The Haunted Castle (#2) (Disney) (4/51)	10	20	30	70	100	130
326-Andy Panda (#1) (Lantz)	7	14	21	46	63	80
327-Bugs Bunny and the Rajah's Treasure (#2)	10	20	30	67	96	125
328-Donald Duck in Old California (#2) by Carl Barks-Peyote drug use issue (Disney) (5/51)	37	56	84	210	398	585
329-Roy Roger's Trigger (#1)(5/51)-Painted-c	16	32	48	116	178	240
330-Porky Pig Meets the Bristled Bruiser (#2)	8	16	24	53	74	95
331-Alice in Wonderland (Disney) (1951)	16	32	48	112	171	230
332-Little Beaver	6	12	18	38	52	65
333-Wilderness Trek (Zane Grey) (5/51)	6	12	18	40	55	70
334-Mickey Mouse and Yukon Gold (Disney) (6/51)	10	20	30	70	100	130
335-Francis the Famous Talking Mule (#1, 6/51)-1st Dell non animated movie comic (all issues based on movie)	11	22	33	80	120	160
336-Woody Woodpecker (Lantz)	7	14	21	46	63	80
337-The Brownies-not by Walt Kelly	6	12	18	38	52	65
338-Bugs Bunny and the Rocking Horse Thieves	10	20	30	67	96	125
339-Donald Duck and the Magic Fountain-not by Carl Barks (Disney) (7-8/51)	10	20	30	73	107	140
340-King of the Royal Mounted (7/51)	8	16	24	53	74	95
341-Unbirthday Party with Alice in Wonderland (Disney) (7/51)	16	32	48	112	171	230
342-Porky Pig the Lucky Peppermint Mine; r/in Porky Pig #3	6	12	18	40	55	70
343-Mickey Mouse in The Ruby Eye of Homar-Guy-Am (Disney)-Reprinted in Mickey Mouse #104	9	18	27	60	85	110
344-Sergeant Preston from Challenge of The Yukon (#1) (TV)	13	26	39	90	138	185
345-Andy Panda in Scotland Yard (8-10/51) (Lantz)	7	14	21	46	63	80
346-Hideout (Zane Grey)	6	12	18	40	55	70
347-Bugs Bunny the Frigid Hare (8-9/51)	10	20	30	67	96	125
348-Donald Duck "The Crocodile Collector"; Barks-c only (Disney) (9-10/51)	19	38	57	134	205	275
349-Uncle Wiggily	8	16	24	53	74	95
350-Woody Woodpecker (Lantz)	7	14	21	46	63	80

Four Color Comics #359 © HILL

Four Color Comics #409 © Walter Lantz

Four Color Comics #470 © WB

	GD 2.0	VG 4.0	FN 6.0	VF 8.0	VF/NM 9.0	NM- 9.2
351-Porky Pig & the Grand Canyon Giant (9-10/51)	6	12	18	40	55	70
352-Mickey Mouse in The Mystery of Painted Valley (Disney)	9	18	27	60	85	110
353-Duck Album (#1)-Barks-c (Disney)	10	20	30	72	104	135
354-Raggedy Ann & Andy	9	18	27	60	85	110
355-Bugs Bunny Hot-Rod Hare	10	20	30	67	96	125
356-Donald Duck in "Rags to Riches"; Barks-c only	19	38	57	134	205	275
357-Comeback (Zane Grey)	5	10	15	36	48	60
358-Andy Panda (Lantz) (11-1/52)	7	14	21	46	63	80
359-Frosty the Snowman (#1)	10	20	30	73	107	140
360-Porky Pig in Tree of Fortune (11-12/51)	6	12	18	40	55	70
361-Santa Claus Funnies	7	14	21	46	63	80
362-Mickey Mouse and the Smuggled Diamonds (Disney)	9	18	27	60	85	110
363-King of the Royal Mounted	7	14	21	46	63	80
364-Woody Woodpecker (Lantz)	6	12	18	38	52	65
365-The Brownies-not by Kelly	6	12	18	38	52	65
366-Bugs Bunny Uncle Buckskin Comes to Town (12-1/52)	10	20	30	67	96	125
367-Donald Duck in "A Christmas for Shacktown" by Carl Barks (Disney) (1-2/52)	31	62	93	230	358	485
368-Bob Clampett's Beany and Cecil (#1)	29	58	87	206	316	425
369-The Lone Ranger's Famous Horse Hi-Yo Silver (#1); Silver's origin	11	22	33	77	114	150
370-Porky Pig in Trouble in the Big Trees	6	12	18	40	55	70
371-Mickey Mouse in The Inca Idol Case (1952) (Disney)	9	18	27	60	85	110
372-Riders of the Purple Sage (Zane Grey)	5	10	15	36	48	60
373-Sergeant Preston (TV)	9	18	27	60	85	110
374-Woody Woodpecker (Lantz)	6	12	18	38	52	65
375-John Carter of Mars (E. R. Burroughs)-Jesse Marsh-a; origin	27	54	81	194	297	400
376-Bugs Bunny, "The Magic Sneeze"	10	20	30	67	96	125
377-Susie Q. Smith	4	8	12	27	36	45
378-Tom Corbett, Space Cadet (#1) (TV)-McWilliams-a	19	38	57	134	205	275
379-Donald Duck in "Southern Hospitality"; Not by Barks (Disney)	10	20	30	73	107	140
380-Raggedy Ann & Andy	9	18	27	60	85	110
381-Marge's Tubby (#1)	22	44	66	158	242	325
382-Snow White and the Seven Dwarfs (Disney)-origin; partial reprint of Four Color #49 (Movie)	11	22	33	80	120	160
383-Andy Panda (Lantz)	5	10	15	36	48	60
384-King of the Royal Mounted (3/52)(Zane Grey)	7	14	21	46	63	80
385-Porky Pig in The Isle of Missing Ships (3-4/52)	6	12	18	40	55	70
386-Uncle Scrooge (#1)-by Carl Barks (Disney) in "Only a Poor Old Man" (3/52)	95	190	285	808	1304	1800
387-Mickey Mouse in High Tibet (Disney) (4-5/52)	9	18	27	60	85	110
388-Oswald the Rabbit (Lantz)	7	14	21	46	63	80
389-Andy Hardy Comics (#1)	5	10	15	36	48	60
390-Woody Woodpecker (Lantz)	6	12	18	38	52	65
391-Uncle Wiggily	8	16	24	53	74	95
392-Hi-Yo Silver	6	12	18	43	59	75
393-Bugs Bunny	10	20	30	67	96	125
394-Donald Duck in Malayalaya-Barks-c only (Disney)	19	38	57	134	205	275
395-Forlorn River(Zane Grey)-First Nevada (5/52)	5	10	15	36	48	60
396-Tales of the Texas Rangers(#1)(TV)-Photo-c	12	24	36	84	127	170
397-Sergeant Preston of the Yukon (TV) (5/52)	9	18	27	60	85	110
398-The Brownies-not by Kelly	6	12	18	38	52	65
399-Porky Pig in The Lost Gold Mine	6	12	18	40	55	70
400-Tom Corbett, Space Cadet (TV)-McWilliams-c/a	11	22	33	80	120	160
401-Mickey Mouse and Goofy's Mechanical Wizard (Disney) (6-7/52)	7	14	21	50	68	85
402-Mary Jane and Sniffles	9	18	27	63	89	115
403-Li'l Bad Wolf (Disney) (6/52)(#1)	8	16	24	58	82	105
404-The Range Rider (#1) (Flying A's...)(TV)-Photo-c	12	24	36	84	127	170
405-Woody Woodpecker (Lantz) (6-7/52)	6	12	18	38	52	65
406-Tweety and Sylvester (#1)	11	22	33	77	114	150
407-Bugs Bunny, Foreign-Legion Hare	8	16	24	58	82	105
408-Donald Duck and the Golden Helmet by Carl Barks (Disney) (7-8/52)	31	63	93	230	358	485
409-Andy Panda (7-9/52)	5	10	15	36	48	60
410-Porky Pig in The Water Wizard (7/52)	6	12	18	40	55	70

	GD 2.0	VG 4.0	FN 6.0	VF 8.0	VF/NM 9.0	NM- 9.2
411-Mickey Mouse and the Old Sea Dog (Disney) (8-9/52)	7	14	21	50	68	85
412-Nevada (Zane Grey)	5	10	15	36	48	60
413-Robin Hood (Disney-Movie) (8/52)-Photo-c (1st Disney movie Four Color book)	11	22	33	80	120	160
414-Bob Clampett's Beany and Cecil (TV)	17	34	51	121	186	250
415-Rootie Kazootie (#1) (TV)	11	22	33	80	120	160
416-Woody Woodpecker (Lantz)	6	12	18	38	52	65
417-Double Trouble with Goober (#1) (8/52)	4	8	12	29	40	50
418-Rusty Riley, a Boy, a Horse, and a Dog (#1)-Frank Godwin-a (strip reprints) (8/52)	6	12	18	38	52	65
419-Sergeant Preston (TV)	9	18	27	60	85	110
420-Bugs Bunny in The Mysterious Buckaroo (8-9/52)	8	16	24	58	82	105
421-Tom Corbett, Space Cadet(TV)-McWilliams-a	11	22	33	80	120	160
422-Donald Duck and the Gilded Man, by Carl Barks (Disney) (9-10/52) (#423 on inside)	31	63	93	230	358	485
423-Rhubarb, Owner of the Brooklyn Ball Club (The Millionaire Cat) (#1)-Painted cover	6	12	18	43	59	75
424-Flash Gordon-Test Flight in Space (9/52)	12	24	36	82	124	165
425-Zorro, the Return of	13	26	39	92	141	190
426-Porky Pig in The Scalawag Leprechaun	6	12	18	40	55	70
427-Mickey Mouse and the Wonderful Whizzix (Disney) (10-11/52)-Reprinted in Mickey Mouse #100	7	14	21	50	68	85
428-Uncle Wiggily	6	12	18	40	55	70
429-Pluto in "Why Dogs Leave Home" (Disney) (10/52)(#1)	10	20	30	73	107	140
430-Marge's Tubby, the Shadow of a Man-Eater	12	24	36	87	134	180
431-Woody Woodpecker (10/52) (Lantz)	6	12	18	38	52	65
432-Bugs Bunny and the Rabbit Olympics	8	16	24	58	82	105
433-Wildfire (Zane Grey) (11-1/52-53)	5	10	15	36	48	60
434-Rin Tin Tin "In Dark Danger" (#1) (TV) (11/52)-Photo-c	16	32	48	112	171	230
435-Frosty the Snowman (11/52)	6	12	18	40	55	70
436-The Brownies-not by Kelly (11/52)	5	10	15	36	48	60
437-John Carter of Mars (E.R. Burroughs)-Marsh-a	17	34	51	119	182	245
438-Annie Oakley (#1) (TV)	16	32	48	116	178	240
439-Little Hiawatha (Disney) (12/52)j(#1)	7	14	21	46	63	80
440-Black Beauty (12/52)	4	8	12	29	40	50
441-Fearless Fagan	4	8	12	29	40	50
442-Peter Pan (Disney) (Movie)	12	24	36	82	124	165
443-Ben Bowie and His Mountain Men (#1)	9	18	27	60	85	110
444-Marge's Tubby	12	24	36	87	134	180
445-Charlie McCarthy	6	12	18	43	59	75
446-Captain Hook and Peter Pan (Disney)(Movie)(1/53)	10	20	30	73	107	140
447-Andy Hardy Comics	4	8	12	24	32	40
448-Bob Clampett's Beany and Cecil (TV)	17	34	51	121	186	250
449-Tappan's Burro (Zane Grey) (2-4/53)	5	10	15	36	48	60
450-Duck Album; Barks-c (Disney)	8	16	24	55	78	100
451-Rusty Riley-Frank Godwin-a (strip-r) (2/53)	4	8	12	29	40	50
452-Raggedy Ann & Andy (1953)	9	18	27	60	85	110
453-Susie Q. Smith (2/53)	4	8	12	27	36	45
454-Krazy Kat Comics; not by Herriman	5	10	15	36	48	60
455-Johnny Mack Brown Comics(3/53)-Photo-c	8	16	24	53	74	95
456-Uncle Scrooge Back to the Klondike (#2) by Barks (3/53) (Disney)	53	106	159	451	726	1000
457-Daffy (#1)	10	20	30	73	107	140
458-Oswald the Rabbit (Lantz)	5	10	15	36	48	60
459-Rootie Kazootie (TV)	8	16	24	58	82	105
460-Buck Jones (4/53)	6	12	18	43	59	75
461-Marge's Tubby	11	22	33	80	120	160
462-Little Scouts	3	7	10	21	28	35
463-Petunia (4/53)	4	8	12	29	40	50
464-Bozo (4/53)	10	20	30	73	107	140
465-Francis the Famous Talking Mule	7	14	21	46	63	80
466-Rhubarb, the Millionaire Cat; painted-c	6	12	18	38	52	65
467-Desert Gold (Zane Grey) (5-7/53)	5	10	15	36	48	60
468-Goofy (#1) (Disney)	13	26	39	92	141	190
469-Beetle Bailey (#1) (5/53	11	22	33	80	120	160
470-Elmer Fudd	7	14	21	51	71	90
471-Double Trouble with Goober	3	6	9	18	24	30
472-Wild Bill Elliott (6/53)-Photo-c	6	12	18	38	52	65
473-Li'l Bad Wolf (Disney) (6/53)(#2)	6	12	18	38	52	65
474-Mary Jane and Sniffles	8	16	24	58	82	105

Four Color Comics #529 © DELL

Four Color Comics #567 © KING

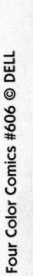

Four Color Comics #606 © DELL

	GD 2.0	VG 4.0	FN 6.0	VF 8.0	VF/NM 9.0	NM- 9.2
475-M.G.M.'s The Two Mouseketeers (#1)	9	18	27	60	85	110
476-Rin Tin Tin (TV)-Photo-c	9	18	27	63	89	115
477-Bob Clampett's Beany and Cecil (TV)	17	34	51	121	186	250
478-Charlie McCarthy	6	12	18	43	59	75
479-Queen of the West Dale Evans (#1)-Photo-c	24	48	72	170	260	350
480-Andy Hardy Comics	4	8	12	24	32	40
481-Annie Oakley And Tagg (TV)	10	20	30	73	107	140
482-Brownies-not by Kelly	5	10	15	36	48	60
483-Little Beaver (7/53)	5	10	15	33	44	55
484-River Feud (Zane Grey) (8-10/53)	5	10	15	36	48	60
485-The Little People-Walt Scott (#1)	9	18	27	60	85	110
486-Rusty Riley-Frank Godwin strip-r	4	8	12	29	40	50
487-Mowgli, the Jungle Book (Rudyard Kipling's)	7	14	21	46	63	80
488-John Carter of Mars (Burroughs)-Marsh-a; painted-c	17	34	51	119	182	245
489-Tweety and Sylvester	6	12	18	43	59	75
490-Jungle Jim (#1)	8	16	24	58	82	105
491-Silvertip (#1) (Max Brand)-Kinstler-a (8/53)	9	18	27	65	93	120
492-Duck Album (Disney)	6	12	18	43	59	75
493-Johnny Mack Brown; photo-c	8	16	24	53	74	95
494-The Little King (#1)	10	20	30	73	107	140
495-Uncle Scrooge (#3) (Disney)-by Carl Barks (9/53)	43	86	129	344	535	725
496-The Green Hornet; painted-c	26	52	81	192	294	385
497-Zorro (Sword of…)-Kinstler-a	14	18	42	97	149	200
498-Bugs Bunny's Album (9/53)	6	12	18	43	59	75
499-M.G.M.'s Spike and Tyke (#1) (9/53)	6	12	18	43	59	75
500-Buck Jones	6	12	18	43	59	75
501-Francis the Famous Talking Mule	6	12	18	38	52	65
502-Rootie Kazootie (TV)	8	16	24	58	82	105
503-Uncle Wiggily (10/53)	6	12	18	40	55	70
504-Krazy Kat; not by Herriman	5	10	15	36	48	60
505-The Sword and the Rose (Disney) (10/53)(Movie)-Photo-c	10	20	30	70	100	130
506-The Little Scouts	3	7	10	21	28	35
507-Oswald the Rabbit (Lantz)	5	10	15	36	48	60
508-Bozo (10/53)	10	20	30	73	107	140
509-Pluto (Disney) (10/53)	7	14	21	50	68	85
510-Son of Black Beauty	4	8	12	27	36	45
511-Outlaw Trail (Zane Grey)-Kinstler-a	6	12	18	40	55	70
512-Flash Gordon (11/53)	9	18	27	60	85	110
513-Ben Bowie and His Mountain Men	5	10	15	33	44	55
514-Frosty the Snowman (11/53)	6	12	18	40	55	70
515-Andy Hardy	4	8	12	24	32	40
516-Double Trouble With Goober	3	6	9	18	24	30
517-Chip 'N' Dale (#1) (Disney)	11	22	33	80	120	160
518-Rivets (11/53)	4	8	12	24	32	40
519-Steve Canyon (#1)-Not by Milton Caniff	10	20	30.	70	100	130
520-Wild Bill Elliott-Photo-c	6	12	18	38	52	65
521-Beetle Bailey (12/53)	7	14	21	46	63	80
522-The Brownies	5	10	15	36	48	60
523-Rin Tin Tin (TV)-Photo-c (12/53)	9	18	27	63	89	115
524-Tweety and Sylvester	6	12	18	43	59	75
525-Santa Claus Funnies	7	14	21	46	63	80
526-Napoleon	3	7	10	21	28	35
527-Charlie McCarthy	6	12	18	43	59	75
528-Queen of the West Dale Evans; photo-c	12	24	36	86	131	175
529-Little Beaver	5	10	15	33	44	55
530-Bob Clampett's Beany and Cecil (TV) (1/54)	17	34	51	121	186	250
531-Duck Album (Disney)	6	12	18	43	59	75
532-The Rustlers (Zane Grey) (2-4/54)	5	10	15	36	48	60
533-Raggedy Ann and Andy	9	18	27	60	85	110
534-Western Marshal(Ernest Haycox's)-Kinstler-a	7	14	21	50	68	85
535-I Love Lucy (#1) (TV) (2/54)-Photo-c	50	100	150	400	625	850
536-Daffy (3/54)	6	12	18	40	55	70
537-Stormy, the Thoroughbred… (Disney-Movie) on top 2/3 of each page; Pluto story on bottom 1/3 of each page (2/54)	5	10	15	36	48	60
538-The Mask of Zorro; Kinstler-a	14	18	42	97	149	200
539-Ben and Me (Disney) (3/54)	4	8	12	29	40	50
540-Knights of the Round Table (3/54) (Movie)-Photo-c	8	16	24	58	82	105
541-Johnny Mack Brown; photo-c	8	16	24	53	74	95
542-Super Circus Featuring Mary Hartline (TV) (3/54)	8	16	24	58	82	105
543-Uncle Wiggily (3/54)	6	12	18	40	55	70
544-Rob Roy (Disney-Movie)-Manning-a; photo-c	9	18	27	63	89	115
545-The Wonderful Adventures of Pinocchio-Partial reprint of Four Color #92 (Disney-Movie)	8	16	24	58	82	105
546-Buck Jones	6	12	18	43	59	75
547-Francis the Famous Talking Mule	6	12	18	38	52	65
548-Krazy Kat; not by Herriman (4/54)	5	10	15	33	44	55
549-Oswald the Rabbit (Lantz)	5	10	15	36	48	60
550-The Little Scouts	3	7	10	21	28	35
551-Bozo (4/54)	10	20	30	73	107	140
552-Beetle Bailey	7	14	21	46	63	80
553-Susie Q. Smith	4	8	12	27	36	45
554-Rusty Riley (Frank Godwin strip-r)	4	8	12	29	40	50
555-Range War (Zane Grey)	5	10	15	36	48	60
556-Double Trouble With Goober (5/54)	3	6	9	18	24	30
557-Ben Bowie and His Mountain Men	5	10	15	33	44	55
558-Elmer Fudd (5/54)	5	10	15	33	44	55
559-I Love Lucy (#2) (TV)-Photo-c	32	64	96	240	370	500
560-Duck Album (Disney) (5/54)	6	12	18	43	59	75
561-Mr. Magoo (5/54)	12	24	36	82	124	165
562-Goofy (Disney)(#2)	8	16	24	58	82	105
563-Rhubarb, the Millionaire Cat (6/54)	6	12	18	38	52	65
564-Li'l Bad Wolf (Disney)(#3)	6	12	18	38	52	65
565-Jungle Jim	5	10	15	36	48	60
566-Son of Black Beauty	4	8	12	27	36	45
567-Prince Valiant (#1)-By Bob Fuje (Movie)-Photo-c	12	24	36	87	134	180
568-Gypsy Colt (Movie) (6/54)	6	12	18	38	52	65
569-Priscilla's Pop	4	8	12	28	38	48
570-Bob Clampett's Beany and Cecil (TV)	17	34	51	121	186	250
571-Charlie McCarthy	6	12	18	43	59	75
572-Silvertip (Max Brand) (7/54); Kinstler-a	6	12	18	38	52	65
573-The Little People by Walt Scott	5	10	15	36	48	60
574-The Hand of Zorro; Kinstler-a	14	18	42	97	149	200
575-Annie Oakley and Tagg (TV)-Photo-c	10	20	30	73	107	140
576-Angel (#1) (8/54)	4	8	12	24	32	40
577-M.G.M.'s Spike and Tyke	4	8	12	27	36	45
578-Steve Canyon (8/54)	6	12	18	43	59	75
579-Francis the Famous Talking Mule	6	12	18	38	52	65
580-Six Gun Ranch (Luke Short-8/54)	4	8	12	29	40	50
581-Chip 'N' Dale (#2) (Disney)	7	14	21	46	63	80
582-Mowgli Jungle Book (Kipling) (8/54)	6	12	18	38	52	65
583-The Lost Wagon Train (Zane Grey)	5	10	15	36	48	60
584-Johnny Mack Brown-Photo-c	8	16	24	53	74	95
585-Bugs Bunny's Album	6	12	18	43	59	75
586-Duck Album (Disney)	6	12	18	43	59	75
587-The Little Scouts	3	7	10	21	28	35
588-King Richard and the Crusaders (Movie) (10/54) Matt Baker-a; photo-c	11	22	33	75	110	145
589-Buck Jones	6	12	18	43	59	75
590-Hansel and Gretel; partial photo-c	8	16	24	53	74	95
591-Western Marshal(Ernest Haycox's)-Kinstler-a	6	12	18	43	59	75
592-Super Circus (TV)	8	16	24	53	74	95
593-Oswald the Rabbit (Lantz)	5	10	15	36	48	60
594-Bozo (10/54)	10	20	30	73	107	140
595-Pluto (Disney)	5	10	15	36	48	60
596-Turok, Son of Stone (#1)	50	100	150	419	672	925
597-The Little King	6	12	18	43	59	75
598-Captain Davy Jones	6	12	18	38	52	65
599-Ben Bowie and His Mountain Men	5	10	15	33	44	55
600-Daisy Duck's Diary (#1) (Disney) (11/54)	8	16	24	55	78	100
601-Frosty the Snowman	6	12	18	40	55	70
602-Mr. Magoo and Gerald McBoing-Boing	12	24	36	82	124	165
603-M.G.M.'s The Two Mouseketeers	6	12	18	40	55	70
604-Shadow on the Trail (Zane Grey)	5	10	15	36	48	60
605-The Brownies-not by Kelly (12/54)	5	10	15	36	48	60
606-Sir Lancelot (not TV)	8	16	24	58	82	105
607-Santa Claus Funnies	7	14	21	46	63	80
608-Silvertip- "Valley of Vanishing Men" (Max Brand)-Kinstler-a	6	12	18	38	52	65
609-The Littlest Outlaw (Disney-Movie) (1/55)-Photo-c	8	16	24	53	74	95
610-Drum Beat (Movie); Alan Ladd photo-c	10	20	30	70	100	130
611-Duck Album (Disney)	6	12	18	43	59	75

Four Color Comics #631 © WDC

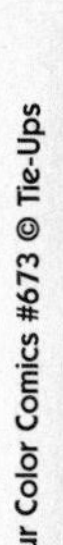
Four Color Comics #673 © Tie-Ups

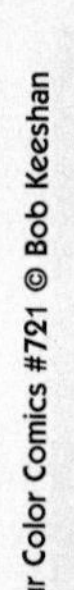
Four Color Comics #721 © Bob Keeshan

	GD 2.0	VG 4.0	FN 6.0	VF 8.0	VF/NM 9.0	NM- 9.2
612-Little Beaver (1/55)	5	10	15	33	44	55
613-Western Marshal (Ernest Haycox's) (2/55)-Kinstler-a	6	12	18	43	59	75
614-20,000 Leagues Under the Sea (Disney) (Movie) (2/55)-Painted-c	10	20	30	72	104	135
615-Daffy	6	12	18	40	55	70
616-To the Last Man (Zane Grey)	5	10	15	36	48	60
617-The Quest of Zorro	13	26	39	92	141	190
618-Johnny Mack Brown; photo-c	8	16	24	53	74	95
619-Krazy Kat; not by Herriman	5	10	15	33	44	55
620-Mowgli Jungle Book (Kipling)	6	12	18	38	52	65
621-Francis the Famous Talking Mule (4/55)	5	10	15	33	44	55
622-Beetle Bailey	7	14	21	46	63	80
623-Oswald the Rabbit (Lantz)	4	8	12	29	40	50
624-Treasure Island(Disney-Movie)(4/55)-Photo-c	10	20	30	67	96	125
625-Beaver Valley (Disney-Movie)	7	14	21	51	71	90
626-Ben Bowie and His Mountain Men	5	10	15	33	44	55
627-Goofy (Disney) (5/55)	8	16	24	58	82	105
628-Elmer Fudd	5	10	15	33	44	55
629-Lady and the Tramp with Jock (Disney)	8	16	24	58	82	105
630-Priscilla's Pop	4	8	12	28	38	48
631-Davy Crockett, Indian Fighter (#1) (Disney) (5/55) (TV)-Fess Parker photo-c	21	42	63	148	227	305
632-Fighting Caravans (Zane Grey)	5	10	15	36	48	60
633-The Little People by Walt Scott (6/55)	5	10	15	36	48	60
634-Lady and the Tramp Album (Disney) (6/55)	6	12	18	40	55	70
635-Bob Clampett's Beany and Cecil (TV)	17	34	51	121	186	250
636-Chip 'N' Dale (Disney)	7	14	21	46	63	80
637-Silvertip (Max Brand)-Kinstler-a	6	12	18	38	52	65
638-M.G.M.'s Spike and Tyke (8/55)	4	8	12	27	36	45
639-Davy Crockett at the Alamo (Disney) (7/55) (TV)-Fess Parker photo-c	17	34	51	119	182	245
640-Western Marshal(Ernest Haycox's)-Kinstler-a	6	12	18	43	59	75
641-Steve Canyon (1955)-by Caniff	6	12	18	43	59	75
642-M.G.M.'s The Two Mouseketeers	6	12	18	40	55	70
643-Wild Bill Elliott; photo-c	5	10	15	33	44	55
644-Sir Walter Raleigh (5/55)-Based on movie "The Virgin Queen"; photo-c	8	16	24	55	78	100
645-Johnny Mack Brown; photo-c	8	16	24	53	74	95
646-Dotty Dripple and Taffy (#1)	5	10	15	33	44	55
647-Bugs Bunny's Album (9/55)	6	12	18	43	59	75
648-Jace Pearson of the Texas Rangers (TV)-Photo-c	6	12	18	43	59	75
649-Duck Album (Disney)	6	12	18	43	59	75
650-Prince Valiant; by Bob Fuje	8	16	24	58	82	105
651-King Colt (Luke Short) (9/55)-Kinstler-a	4	8	12	29	40	50
652-Buck Jones	5	10	15	33	44	55
653-Smokey the Bear (#1) (10/55)	12	24	36	86	131	175
654-Pluto (Disney)	5	10	15	36	48	60
655-Francis the Famous Talking Mule	5	10	15	33	44	55
656-Turok, Son of Stone (#2) (10/55)	32	64	96	240	375	510
657-Ben Bowie and His Mountain Men	5	10	15	33	44	55
658-Goofy (Disney)	8	16	24	58	82	105
659-Daisy Duck's Diary (Disney)(#2)	7	14	21	46	63	80
660-Little Beaver	5	10	15	33	44	55
661-Frosty the Snowman	6	12	18	40	55	70
662-Zoo Parade (TV)-Marlin Perkins (11/55)	6	12	18	40	55	70
663-Winky Dink (TV)	9	18	27	65	93	120
664-Davy Crockett in the Great Keelboat Race (TV) (Disney) (11/55)-Fess Parker photo-c	16	32	48	112	171	230
665-The African Lion (Disney-Movie) (11/55)	7	14	21	46	63	80
666-Santa Claus Funnies	7	14	21	46	63	80
667-Silvertip and the Stolen Stallion (Max Brand) (12/55)-Kinstler-a	6	12	18	38	52	65
668-Dumbo (Disney) (12/55)-First of two printings. Dumbo on cover with starry sky. Reprints 4-Color #234?; same-c as #234	11	22	33	77	114	150
668-Dumbo (Disney) (1/58)-Second printing. Same cover altered, with Timothy Mouse added. Same contents as above	8	16	24	55	78	100
669-Robin Hood (Disney-Movie) (12/55)-Reprints #413 plus-c; photo-c	7	14	21	46	63	80
670-M.G.M's Mouse Musketeers (#1) (1/56)-Formerly the Two Mouseketeers	5	10	15	36	48	60
671-Davy Crockett and the River Pirates (TV) (Disney) (12/55)-Jesse Marsh-a; Fess Parker photo-c	16	32	48	112	171	230
672-Quentin Durward (1/56) (Movie)-Photo-c	8	16	24	55	78	100
673-Buffalo Bill, Jr. (#1) (TV)-James Arness photo-c	9	18	27	63	89	115
674-The Little Rascals (#1) (TV)	10	20	30	70	100	130
675-Steve Donovan, Western Marshal (#1) (TV)-Kinstler-a; photo-c	9	18	27	65	93	120
676-Will-Yum!	4	8	12	27	36	45
677-Little King	6	12	18	43	59	75
678-The Last Hunt (Movie)-Photo-c	9	18	27	63	89	115
679-Gunsmoke (#1) (TV)-Photo-c	19	38	57	134	205	275
680-Out Our Way with the Worry Wart (2/56)	4	8	12	24	32	40
681-Forever Darling (Movie) with Lucille Ball & Desi Arnaz (2/56)-; photo-c	12	24	36	86	131	175
682-The Sword & the Rose (Disney-Movie)-Reprint of #505; Renamed When Knighthood Was in Flower for the novel; photo-c	8	16	24	58	82	105
683-Hi and Lois (3/56)	4	8	12	29	40	50
684-Helen of Troy (Movie)-Buscema-a; photo-c	11	22	33	80	120	160
685-Johnny Mack Brown; photo-c	8	16	24	53	74	95
686-Duck Album (Disney)	6	12	18	43	59	75
687-The Indian Fighter (Movie)-Kirk Douglas photo-c	9	18	27	63	89	115
688-Alexander the Great (Movie) (5/56)-Buscema-a; photo-c	9	18	27	60	85	110
689-Elmer Fudd (3/56)	5	10	15	33	44	55
690-The Conqueror (Movie) - John Wayne photo-c	18	36	54	129	197	265
691-Dotty Dripple and Taffy	4	8	12	22	30	38
692-The Little People-Walt Scott	5	10	15	36	48	60
693-Song of the South (Disney) (1956)-Partial reprint of #129	10	20	30	70	100	130
694-Super Circus (TV)-Photo-c	8	16	24	53	74	95
695-Little Beaver	5	10	15	33	44	55
696-Krazy Kat; not by Herriman (4/56)	5	10	15	33	44	55
697-Oswald the Rabbit (Lantz)	4	8	12	29	40	50
698-Francis the Famous Talking Mule (4/56)	5	10	15	33	44	55
699-Prince Valiant-by Bob Fuje	8	16	24	58	82	105
700-Water Birds and the Olympic Elk (Disney-Movie) (4/56)	6	12	18	43	59	75
701-Jiminy Cricket (#1) (Disney) (5/56)	10	20	30	70	100	130
702-The Goofy Success Story (Disney)	8	16	24	58	82	105
703-Scamp (#1) (Disney)	10	20	30	72	104	135
704-Priscilla's Pop (5/56)	4	8	12	28	38	48
705-Brave Eagle (#1) (TV)-Photo-c	8	16	24	53	74	95
706-Bongo and Lumpjaw (Disney) (6/56)	7	14	21	46	63	80
707-Corky and White Shadow (Disney) (5/56)-Mickey Mouse Club (TV); photo-c	8	16	24	58	82	105
708-Smokey the Bear	7	14	21	51	71	90
709-The Searchers (Movie) - John Wayne photo-c	28	56	84	199	305	410
710-Francis the Famous Talking Mule	5	10	15	33	44	55
711-M.G.M's Mouse Musketeers	4	8	12	27	36	45
712-The Great Locomotive Chase (Disney-Movie) (9/56)-Photo-c	8	16	24	58	82	105
713-The Animal World (Movie) (8/56)	4	8	12	27	36	45
714-Spin and Marty (#1) (TV) (Disney)-Mickey Mouse Club (6/56); photo-c	14	28	42	97	149	200
715-Timmy (8/56)	5	10	15	36	48	60
716-Man in Space (Disney)(A science feature from Tomorrowland)	10	20	30	70	100	130
717-Moby Dick (Movie)-Gregory Peck photo-c	10	20	30	70	100	130
718-Dotty Dripple and Taffy	4	8	12	22	30	38
719-Prince Valiant; by Bob Fuje (8/56)	8	16	24	58	82	105
720-Gunsmoke (TV)-James Arness photo-c	10	20	30	72	104	135
721-Captain Kangaroo (TV)-Photo-c	18	36	54	131	201	270
722-Johnny Mack Brown-Photo-c	8	16	24	53	74	95
723-Santiago (Movie)-Kinstler-a (9/56); Alan Ladd photo-c	11	22	33	75	110	145
724-Bugs Bunny's Album	6	12	18	38	52	65
725-Elmer Fudd (9/56)	4	8	12	27	36	45
726-Duck Album (Disney) (9/56)	6	12	18	43	59	75
727-The Nature of Things (TV) (Disney)-Jesse Marsh-a	6	12	18	43	59	75
728-M.G.M's Mouse Musketeers	4	8	12	27	36	45
729-Bob Son of Battle (11/56)	4	8	12	29	40	50
730-Smokey Stover	6	12	18	40	55	70
731-Silvertip and The Fighting Four (Max Brand)-Kinstler-a	6	12	18	38	52	65
732-Zorro, the Challenge of (10/56)	13	26	39	92	141	190

Four Color Comics #800 © DELL

Four Color Comics #815 © DELL

Four Color Comics #845 © Universal

	GD 2.0	VG 4.0	FN 6.0	VF 8.0	VF/NM 9.0	NM- 9.2
733-Buck Jones	5	10	15	33	44	55
734-Cheyenne (#1) (TV) (10/56)-Clint Walker photo-c	18	36	54	126	193	260
735-Crusader Rabbit (#1) (TV)	32	64	96	232	361	490
736-Pluto (Disney)	5	10	15	36	48	60
737-Steve Canyon-Caniff-a	6	12	18	43	59	75
738-Westward Ho, the Wagons (Disney-Movie)-Fess Parker photo-c	11	22	33	75	110	145
739-Bounty Guns (Luke Short)-Drucker-a	4	8	12	28	38	48
740-Chilly Willy (#1) (Walter Lantz)	7	14	21	50	68	85
741-The Fastest Gun Alive (Movie)(9/56)-Photo-c	8	16	24	58	82	105
742-Buffalo Bill, Jr. (TV)-Photo-c	6	12	18	40	55	70
743-Daisy Duck's Diary (Disney) (11/56)	7	14	21	46	63	80
744-Little Beaver	5	10	15	33	44	55
745-Francis the Famous Talking Mule	5	10	15	33	44	55
746-Dotty Dripple and Taffy	4	8	12	22	30	38
747-Goofy (Disney)	8	16	24	58	82	105
748-Frosty the Snowman (11/56)	6	12	18	38	52	65
749-Secrets of Life (Disney-Movie)-Photo-c	6	12	18	40	55	70
750-The Great Cat Family (Disney-TV/Movie)-Pinocchio & Alice app.	8	16	24	53	74	95
751-Our Miss Brooks (TV)-Photo-c	9	18	27	63	89	115
752-Mandrake, the Magician	12	24	36	82	124	165
753-Walt Scott's Little People (11/56)	5	10	15	36	48	60
754-Smokey the Bear	7	14	21	51	71	90
755-The Littlest Snowman (12/56)	6	12	18	40	55	70
756-Santa Claus Funnies	7	14	21	46	63	80
757-The True Story of Jesse James (Movie)-Photo-c	10	20	30	72	104	135
758-Bear Country (Disney-Movie)	6	12	18	43	59	75
759-Circus Boy (TV)-The Monkees' Mickey Dolenz photo-c (12/56)	14	28	42	102	156	210
760-The Hardy Boys (#1) (TV) (Disney)-Mickey Mouse Club; photo-c	12	24	36	84	127	170
761-Howdy Doody (TV) (1/57)	12	24	36	82	124	165
762-The Sharkfighters (Movie) (1/57); Buscema-a; photo-c	9	18	27	63	89	115
763-Grandma Duck's Farm Friends (#1) (Disney)	9	18	27	60	85	110
764-M.G.M's Mouse Musketeers	4	8	12	27	36	45
765-Will-Yum!	4	8	12	27	36	45
766-Buffalo Bill, Jr. (TV)-Photo-c	6	12	18	40	55	70
767-Spin and Marty (TV) (Disney)-Mickey Mouse Club (2/57)	10	20	30	72	104	135
768-Steve Donovan, Western Marshal (TV)-Kinstler-a; photo-c	8	16	24	53	74	95
769-Gunsmoke (TV)-James Arness photo-c	10	20	30	72	104	135
770-Brave Eagle (TV)-Photo-c	4	8	12	29	40	50
771-Brand of Empire (Luke Short)(3/57)-Drucker-a	4	8	12	28	38	48
772-Cheyenne (TV)-Clint Walker photo-c	10	20	30	67	96	125
773-The Brave One (Movie)-Photo-c	6	12	18	43	59	75
774-Hi and Lois (3/57)	3	7	10	21	28	35
775-Sir Lancelot and Brian (TV)-Buscema-a; photo-c	11	22	33	77	114	150
776-Johnny Mack Brown; photo-c	8	16	24	53	74	95
777-Scamp (Disney) (3/57)	8	16	24	53	74	95
778-The Little Rascals (TV)	7	14	21	46	63	80
779-Lee Hunter, Indian Fighter (3/57)	6	12	18	38	52	65
780-Captain Kangaroo (TV)-Photo-c	15	30	45	105	160	215
781-Fury (#1) (TV) (3/57)-Photo-c	9	18	27	65	93	120
782-Duck Album (Disney)	6	12	18	43	59	75
783-Elmer Fudd	4	8	12	27	36	45
784-Around the World in 80 Days (Movie) (2/57)-Photo-c	8	16	24	55	78	100
785-Circus Boy (TV) (4/57)-The Monkees' Mickey Dolenz photo-c	12	24	36	84	127	170
786-Cinderella (Disney) (3/57)-Partial-r of #272	8	16	24	55	78	100
787-Little Hiawatha (Disney) (4/57)(#2)	6	12	18	38	52	65
788-Prince Valiant; by Bob Fuje	8	16	24	55	78	100
789-Silvertip-Valley Thieves (Max Brand) (4/57)-Kinstler-a	6	12	18	38	52	65
790-The Wings of Eagles (Movie) (John Wayne)-Toth-a; John Wayne photo-c; 10¢ & 15¢ editions exist	16	32	48	112	171	230
791-The 77th Bengal Lancers (TV)-Photo-c	8	16	24	58	82	105
792-Oswald the Rabbit (Lantz)	4	8	12	29	40	50
793-Morty Meekle	3	7	10	21	28	35
794-The Count of Monte Cristo (5/57) (Movie)-Buscema-a	10	20	30	70	100	130
795-Jiminy Cricket (Disney)(#2)	8	16	24	53	74	95
796-Ludwig Bemelman's Madeleine and Genevieve	4	8	12	27	36	45
797-Gunsmoke (TV)-Photo-c	10	20	30	72	104	135
798-Buffalo Bill, Jr. (TV)-Photo-c	6	12	18	40	55	70
799-Priscilla's Pop	4	8	12	28	38	48
800-The Buccaneers (TV)-Photo-c	8	16	24	58	82	105
801-Dotty Dripple and Taffy	4	8	12	22	30	38
802-Goofy (Disney) (5/57)	8	16	24	58	82	105
803-Cheyenne (TV)-Clint Walker photo-c	10	20	30	67	96	125
804-Steve Canyon-Caniff-a (1957)	6	12	18	43	59	75
805-Crusader Rabbit (TV)	26	52	78	184	282	380
806-Scamp (Disney) (6/57)	8	16	24	53	74	95
807-Savage Range (Luke Short)-Drucker-a	4	8	12	28	38	48
808-Spin and Marty (TV)(Disney)-Mickey Mouse Club; photo-c	10	20	30	72	104	135
809-The Little People (Walt Scott)	5	10	15	36	48	60
810-Francis the Famous Talking Mule	4	8	12	29	40	50
811-Howdy Doody (TV) (7/57)	12	24	36	82	124	165
812-The Big Land (Movie); Alan Ladd photo-c	10	20	30	73	107	140
813-Circus Boy (TV)-The Monkees' Mickey Dolenz photo-c	12	24	36	84	127	170
814-Covered Wagons, Ho! (Disney)-Donald Duck (TV) (6/57); Mickey Mouse app.	6	12	18	43	59	75
815-Dragoon Wells Massacre (Movie)-photo-c	9	18	27	63	89	115
816-Brave Eagle (TV)-photo-c	4	8	12	29	40	50
817-Little Beaver	5	10	15	33	44	55
818-Smokey the Bear (6/57)	7	14	21	51	71	90
819-Mickey Mouse in Magicland (Disney) (7/57)	6	12	18	38	52	65
820-The Oklahoman (Movie)-Photo-c	10	20	30	72	104	135
821-Wringle Wrangle (Disney)-Based on movie "Westward Ho, the Wagons"; Marsh-a; Fess Parker photo-c	9	18	27	65	93	120
822-Paul Revere's Ride with Johnny Tremain (TV) (Disney)-Toth-a	10	20	30	72	104	135
823-Timmy	4	8	12	25	33	42
824-The Pride and the Passion (Movie) (8/57)-Frank Sinatra & Cary Grant photo-c	10	20	30	73	107	140
825-The Little Rascals (TV)	7	14	21	46	63	80
826-Spin and Marty and Annette (TV) (Disney)-Mickey Mouse Club; Annette Funicello photo-c	25	50	75	177	271	365
827-Smokey Stover (8/57)	6	12	18	40	55	70
828-Buffalo Bill, Jr. (TV)-Photo-c	6	12	18	40	55	70
829-Tales of the Pony Express (TV) (8/57)-Painted-c	6	12	18	38	52	65
830-The Hardy Boys (TV) (Disney)-Mickey Mouse Club (8/57); photo-c	10	20	30	72	104	135
831-No Sleep 'Til Dawn (Movie)-Karl Malden photo-c	8	16	24	53	74	95
832-Lolly and Pepper (#1)	4	8	12	29	40	50
833-Scamp (Disney) (9/57)	8	16	24	53	74	95
834-Johnny Mack Brown; photo-c	8	16	24	53	74	95
835-Silvertip-The False Rider (Max Brand)	6	12	18	38	52	65
836-Man in Flight (Disney) (TV) (9/57)	8	16	24	58	82	105
837-All-American Athlete Cotton Woods	4	8	12	27	36	45
838-Bugs Bunny's Life Story Album (9/57)	6	12	18	38	52	65
839-The Vigilantes (Movie)	8	16	24	58	82	105
840-Duck Album (Disney) (9/57)	6	12	18	43	59	75
841-Elmer Fudd	4	8	12	27	36	45
842-The Nature of Things (Disney-Movie) ('57)-Jesse Marsh-a (TV series)	6	12	18	43	59	75
843-The First Americans (Disney) (TV)-Marsh-a	10	20	30	70	100	130
844-Gunsmoke (TV)-Photo-c	10	20	30	72	104	135
845-The Land Unknown (Movie)-Alex Toth-a	13	26	39	90	138	185
846-Gun Glory (Movie)-by Alex Toth; photo-c	10	20	30	72	104	135
847-Perri (squirrels) (Disney-Movie)-Two different covers published	6	12	18	43	59	75
848-Marauder's Moon (Luke Short)	4	8	12	28	38	48
849-Prince Valiant; by Bob Fuje	8	16	24	55	78	100
850-Buck Jones	5	10	15	33	44	55
851-The Story of Mankind (Movie) (1/58)-Hedy Lamarr & Vincent Price photo-c	8	16	24	58	82	105
852-Chilly Willy (2/58) (Lantz)	5	10	15	33	44	55
853-Pluto (Disney) (10/57)	5	10	15	36	48	60
854-The Hunchback of Notre Dame (Movie)-Photo-c	14	28	42	97	149	200
855-Broken Arrow (TV)-Photo-c	7	14	21	46	63	80

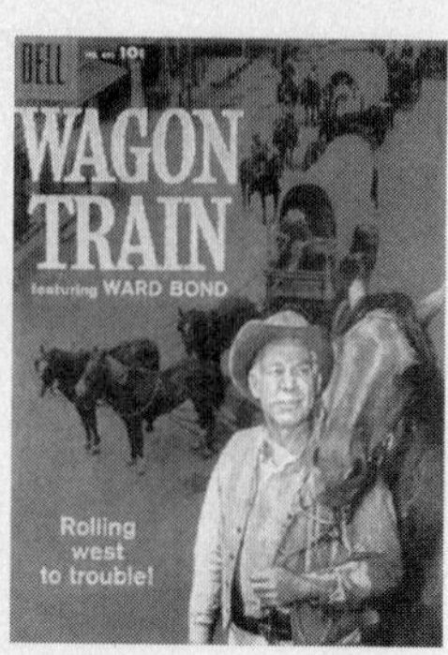

Four Color Comics #895 © Revere

Four Color Comics #920 © WDC

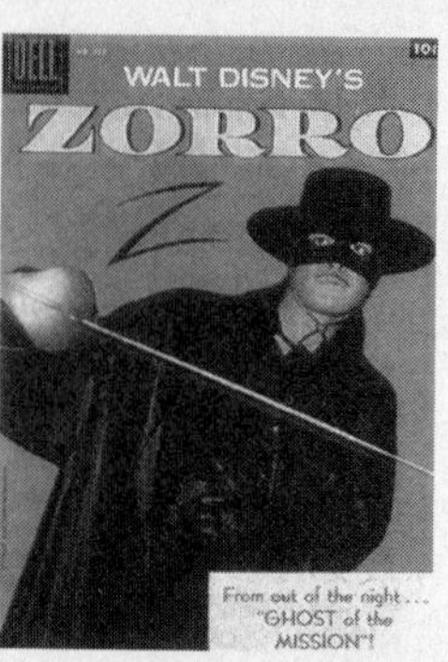

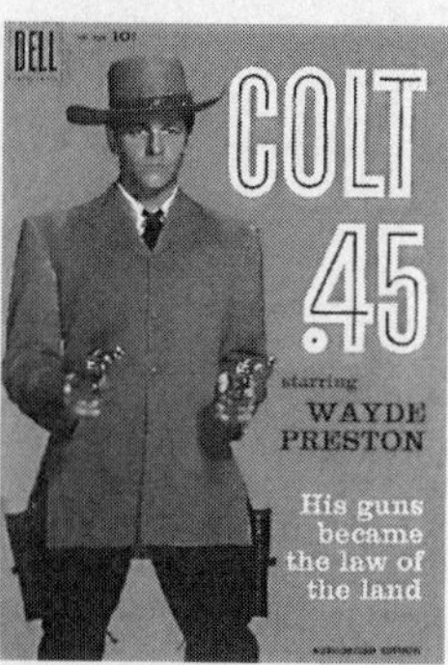

Four Color Comics #924 © WB

	GD 2.0	VG 4.0	FN 6.0	VF 8.0	VF/NM 9.0	NM- 9.2
856-Buffalo Bill, Jr. (TV)-Photo-c	6	12	18	40	55	70
857-The Goofy Adventure Story (Disney) (11/57)	8	16	24	58	82	105
858-Daisy Duck's Diary (Disney) (11/57)	6	12	18	40	55	70
859-Topper and Neil (TV) (11/57)	6	12	18	38	52	65
860-Wyatt Earp (#1) (TV)-Manning-a; photo-c	11	22	33	80	120	160
861-Frosty the Snowman	6	12	18	38	52	65
862-The Truth About Mother Goose (Disney-Movie) (11/57)	9	18	27	60	85	110
863-Francis the Famous Talking Mule	4	8	12	29	40	50
864-The Littlest Snowman	6	12	18	40	55	70
865-Andy Burnett (TV) (Disney) (12/57)-Photo-c	10	20	30	72	104	135
866-Mars and Beyond (Disney-TV)(A science feature from Tomorrowland)	10	20	30	70	100	130
867-Santa Claus Funnies	7	14	21	46	63	80
868-The Little People (12/57)	5	10	15	36	48	60
869-Old Yeller (Disney-Movie)-Photo-c	6	12	18	43	59	75
870-Little Beaver (1/58)	5	10	15	33	44	55
871-Curly Kayoe	4	8	12	27	36	45
872-Captain Kangaroo (TV)-Photo-c	15	30	45	105	160	215
873-Grandma Duck's Farm Friends (Disney)	6	12	18	43	59	75
874-Old Ironsides (Disney-Movie with Johnny Tremain) (1/58)	8	16	24	53	74	95
875-Trumpets West (Luke Short) (2/58)	4	8	12	28	38	48
876-Tales of Wells Fargo (#1)(TV)(2/58)-Photo-c	10	20	30	73	107	140
877-Frontier Doctor with Rex Allen (TV)-Alex Toth-a; Rex Allen photo-c	11	22	33	77	114	150
878-Peanuts (#1)-Schulz-c only (2/58)	18	36	54	126	193	260
879-Brave Eagle (TV) (2/58)-Photo-c	4	8	12	29	40	50
880-Steve Donovan, Western Marshal-Drucker-a (TV)-Photo-c	6	12	18	38	52	65
881-The Captain and the Kids (2/58)	4	8	12	29	40	50
882-Zorro (Disney)-1st Disney issue; by Alex Toth (TV) (2/58); photo-c	17	34	51	123	189	255
883-The Little Rascals (TV)	7	14	21	46	63	80
884-Hawkeye and the Last of the Mohicans (TV) (3/58); photo-c	8	16	24	58	82	105
885-Fury (TV) (3/58)-Photo-c	8	16	24	55	78	100
886-Bongo and Lumpjaw (Disney) (3/58)	6	12	18	38	52	65
887-The Hardy Boys (Disney) (TV)-Mickey Mouse Club (1/58)-Photo-c	10	20	30	72	104	135
888-Elmer Fudd (3/58)	4	8	12	27	36	45
889-Clint and Mac (Disney) (TV) (3/58)-Alex Toth-a; photo-c	14	28	42	97	149	200
890-Wyatt Earp (TV)-by Russ Manning; photo-c	9	18	27	60	85	110
891-Light in the Forest (Disney-Movie) (3/58)-Fess Parker photo-c	9	18	27	63	89	115
892-Maverick (#1) (TV) (4/58)-James Garner photo-c	26	52	78	184	282	380
893-Jim Bowie (TV)-Photo-c	7	14	21	46	63	80
894-Oswald the Rabbit (Lantz)	4	8	12	29	40	50
895-Wagon Train (#1) (TV) (3/58)-Photo-c	12	24	36	87	134	180
896-The Adventures of Tinker Bell (Disney)	10	20	30	70	100	130
897-Jiminy Cricket (Disney)	8	16	24	53	74	95
898-Silvertip (Max Brand)-Kinstler-a (5/58)	6	12	18	38	52	65
899-Goofy (Disney) (5/58)	6	12	18	40	55	70
900-Prince Valiant; by Bob Fuje	8	16	24	55	78	100
901-Little Hiawatha (Disney)	6	12	18	38	52	65
902-Will-Yum!	4	8	12	27	36	45
903-Dotty Dripple and Taffy	4	8	12	22	30	38
904-Lee Hunter, Indian Fighter	4	8	12	27	36	45
905-Annette (Disney) (TV) (5/58)-Mickey Mouse Club; Annette Funicello photo-c	31	62	93	223	342	460
906-Francis the Famous Talking Mule	4	8	12	29	40	50
907-Sugarfoot (#1) (TV)Toth-a; photo-c	14	28	42	97	149	200
908-The Little People and the Giant-Walt Scott (5/58)	5	10	15	36	48	60
909-Smitty	4	8	12	29	40	50
910-The Vikings (Movie)-Buscema-a; Kirk Douglas photo-c	10	20	30	67	96	125
911-The Gray Ghost (TV)-Photo-c	10	20	30	70	100	130
912-Leave It to Beaver (#1) (TV)-Photo-c	18	36	54	129	197	265
913-The Left-Handed Gun (Movie) (7/58); Paul Newman photo-c	11	22	33	75	110	145
914-No Time for Sergeants (Movie)-Andy Griffith photo-c; Toth-a	11	22	33	80	120	160
915-Casey Jones (TV)-Alan Hale photo-c	6	12	18	43	59	75
916-Red Ryder Ranch Comics (7/58)	6	12	18	38	52	65
917-The Life of Riley (TV)-Photo-c	12	24	36	86	131	175
918-Beep Beep, the Roadrunner (#1) (7/58)-Published with two different back covers	11	22	33	80	120	160
919-Boots and Saddles (#1) (TV)-Photo-c	9	18	27	63	89	115
920-Zorro (Disney) (TV) (6/58)Toth-a; photo-c	13	26	39	92	141	190
921-Wyatt Earp (TV)-Manning-a; photo-c	9	18	27	60	85	110
922-Johnny Mack Brown by Russ Manning; photo-c	8	16	24	55	78	100
923-Timmy	4	8	12	25	33	42
924-Colt .45 (#1) (TV) (8/58)-W. Preston photo-c	11	22	33	80	120	160
925-Last of the Fast Guns (Movie) (8/58)-Photo-c	8	16	24	58	82	105
926-Peter Pan (Disney)-Reprint of #442	5	10	15	36	48	60
927-Top Gun (Luke Short) Buscema-a	4	8	12	28	38	48
928-Sea Hunt (#1) (9/58) (TV)-Lloyd Bridges photo-c	13	26	39	92	141	190
929-Brave Eagle (TV)-Photo-c	4	8	12	29	40	50
930-Maverick (TV) (7/58)-James Garner photo-c	12	24	36	84	127	170
931-Have Gun, Will Travel (#1) (TV)-Photo-c	15	30	45	105	160	215
932-Smokey the Bear (His Life Story)	7	14	21	51	71	90
933-Zorro (Disney, 9/58) (TV)-Alex Toth-a; photo-c	13	26	39	92	141	190
934-Restless Gun (#1) (TV)-Photo-c	12	24	36	87	134	180
935-King of the Royal Mounted	5	10	15	33	44	55
936-The Little Rascals (TV)	7	14	21	46	63	80
937-Ruff and Reddy (#1) (9/58) (TV) (1st Hanna-Barbera comic book)	14	28	42	97	149	200
938-Elmer Fudd (9/58)	4	8	12	27	36	45
939-Steve Canyon - not by Caniff	6	12	18	43	59	75
940-Lolly and Pepper (10/58)	3	7	10	21	28	35
941-Pluto (Disney) (10/58)	5	10	15	33	44	55
942-Pony Express (TV)	6	12	18	38	52	65
943-White Wilderness (Disney-Movie) (10/58)	8	16	24	53	74	95
944-The 7th Voyage of Sinbad (Movie) (9/58)-Buscema-a; photo-c	14	28	42	97	149	200
945-Maverick (TV)-James Garner/Jack Kelly photo-c	12	24	36	84	127	170
946-The Big Country (Movie)-Photo-c	8	16	24	58	82	105
947-Broken Arrow (TV)-Photo-c (11/58)	6	12	18	40	55	70
948-Daisy Duck's Diary (Disney) (11/58)	6	12	18	40	55	70
949-High Adventure(Lowell Thomas')(TV)-Photo-c	7	14	21	46	63	80
950-Frosty the Snowman	6	12	18	38	52	65
951-The Lennon Sisters Life Story (TV)-Toth-a, 32 pgs.; photo-c	15	30	45	107	164	220
952-Goofy (Disney) (11/58)	6	12	18	40	55	70
953-Francis the Famous Talking Mule	4	8	12	29	40	50
954-Man in Space-Satellites (TV)	8	16	24	58	82	105
955-Hi and Lois (11/58)	3	7	10	21	28	35
956-Ricky Nelson (#1) (TV)-Photo-c	20	40	60	141	216	290
957-Buffalo Bee (#1) (TV)	10	20	30	72	104	135
958-Santa Claus Funnies	6	12	18	43	59	75
959-Christmas Stories-(Walt Scott's Little People) (1951-56 strip reprints)	5	10	15	36	48	60
960-Zorro (Disney) (TV) (12/58)-Toth art; photo-c	13	26	39	92	141	190
961-Jace Pearson's Tales of the Texas Rangers (TV)-Spiegle-a; photo-c	6	12	18	40	55	70
962-Maverick (TV) (1/59)-James Garner/Jack Kelly photo-c	12	24	36	84	127	170
963-Johnny Mack Brown; photo-c	8	16	24	53	74	95
964-The Hardy Boys (TV) (Disney) (1/59)-Mickey Mouse Club; photo-c	10	20	30	72	104	135
965-Grandma Duck's Farm Friends (Disney)(1/59)	6	12	18	38	52	65
966-Tonka (starring Sal Mineo; Disney-Movie)-Photo-c	10	20	30	67	96	125
967-Chilly Willy (2/59) (Lantz)	5	10	15	33	44	55
968-Tales of Wells Fargo (TV)-Photo-c	10	20	30	70	100	130
969-Peanuts (2/59)	12	24	36	84	127	170
970-Lawman (#1) (TV)-Photo-c	14	28	42	97	149	200
971-Wagon Train (TV)-Photo-c	8	16	24	55	78	100
972-Tom Thumb (Movie)-George Pal (1/59)	10	20	30	72	104	135
973-Sleeping Beauty and the Prince(Disney)(5/59)	12	24	36	87	134	180
974-The Little Rascals (TV) (3/59)	7	14	21	46	63	80
975-Fury (TV)-Photo-c	8	16	24	55	78	100
976-Zorro (Disney) (TV)-Toth-a; photo-c	13	26	39	92	141	190
977-Elmer Fudd (3/59)	4	8	12	27	36	45
978-Lolly and Pepper	3	7	10	21	28	35

Four Color Comics #1006 © Oscar Film

Four Color Comics #1052 © Loew's

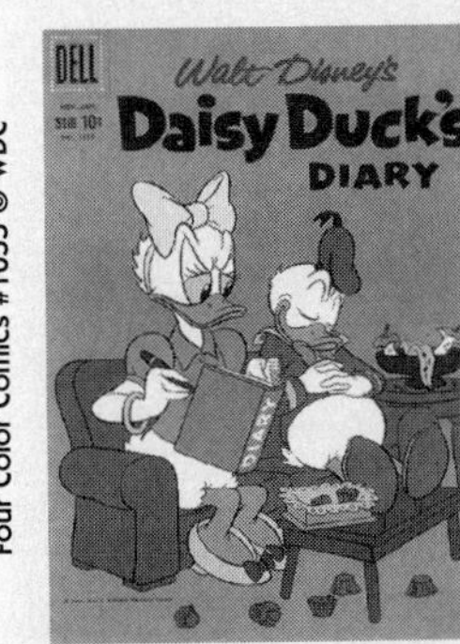

Four Color Comics #1055 © WDC

	GD 2.0	VG 4.0	FN 6.0	VF 8.0	VF/NM 9.0	NM- 9.2
979-Oswald the Rabbit (Lantz)	4	8	12	29	40	50
980-Maverick (TV) (4-6/59)-James Garner/Jack Kelly photo-c	12	24	36	84	127	170
981-Ruff and Reddy (TV) (Hanna-Barbera)	9	18	27	65	93	120
982-The New Adventures of Tinker Bell (TV) (Disney)	9	18	27	65	93	120
983-Have Gun, Will Travel (TV) (4-6/59)-Photo-c	10	20	30	70	100	130
984-Sleeping Beauty's Fairy Godmothers (Disney)	10	20	30	70	100	130
985-Shaggy Dog (Disney-Movie)-Photo-all four covers; Annette on back-c(5/59)	9	18	27	63	89	115
986-Restless Gun (TV)-Photo-c	9	18	27	65	93	120
987-Goofy (Disney) (7/59)	6	12	18	40	55	70
988-Little Hiawatha (Disney)	6	12	18	38	52	65
989-Jiminy Cricket (Disney) (5-7/59)	8	16	24	53	74	95
990-Huckleberry Hound (#1)(TV)(Hanna-Barbera); 1st app. Huck, Yogi Bear, & Pixie & Dixie & Mr. Jinks	13	26	39	92	141	190
991-Francis the Famous Talking Mule	4	8	12	29	40	50
992-Sugarfoot (TV)-Toth-a; photo-c	13	26	39	90	138	185
993-Jim Bowie (TV)-Photo-c	6	12	18	43	59	75
994-Sea Hunt (TV)-Lloyd Bridges photo-c	9	18	27	65	93	120
995-Donald Duck Album (Disney) (5-7/59)(#1)	7	14	21	50	68	85
996-Nevada (Zane Grey)	5	10	15	36	48	60
997-Walt Disney Presents-Tales of Texas John Slaughter (#1) (TV) (Disney)-Photo-c; photo of W. Disney inside-c	9	18	27	60	85	110
998-Ricky Nelson (TV)-Photo-c	20	40	60	141	216	290
999-Leave It to Beaver (TV)-Photo-c	15	30	45	107	164	220
1000-The Gray Ghost (TV) (6-8/59)-Photo-c	10	20	30	70	100	130
1001-Lowell Thomas' High Adventure (TV) (8-10/59)-Photo-c	6	12	18	43	59	75
1002-Buffalo Bee (TV)	8	16	24	55	78	100
1003-Zorro (TV) (Disney)-Toth-a; photo-c	13	26	39	92	141	190
1004-Colt .45 (TV) (6-8/59)-Photo-c	9	18	27	65	93	120
1005-Maverick (TV)-James Garner/Jack Kelly photo-c	12	24	36	84	127	170
1006-Hercules (Movie)-Buscema-a; photo-c	10	20	30	73	107	140
1007-John Paul Jones (Movie)-Robert Stack photo-c	6	12	18	43	59	75
1008-Beep Beep, the Road Runner (7-9/59)	7	14	21	46	63	80
1009-The Rifleman (#1) (TV)-Photo-c	27	54	81	194	297	400
1010-Grandma Duck's Farm Friends (Disney)-by Carl Barks	14	28	42	97	149	200
1011-Buckskin (#1) (TV)-Photo-c	8	16	24	58	82	105
1012-Last Train from Gun Hill (Movie) (7/59)-Photo-c	10	20	30	70	100	130
1013-Bat Masterson (#1) (TV) (8/59)-Gene Barry photo-c	13	26	39	92	141	190
1014-The Lennon Sisters (TV)-Toth-a; photo-c	14	28	42	102	156	210
1015-Peanuts-Schulz-c	12	24	36	84	127	170
1016-Smokey the Bear Nature Stories	5	10	15	36	48	60
1017-Chilly Willy (Lantz)	5	10	15	33	44	55
1018-Rio Bravo (Movie)(6/59)-John Wayne; Toth-a; John Wayne, Dean Martin & Ricky Nelson photo-c	25	50	75	177	271	365
1019-Wagon Train (TV)-Photo-c	8	16	24	55	78	100
1020-Jungle Jim-McWilliams-a	4	8	12	29	40	50
1021-Jace Pearson's Tales of the Texas Rangers (TV)-Photo-c	6	12	18	40	55	70
1022-Timmy	4	8	12	25	33	42
1023-Tales of Wells Fargo (TV)-Photo-c	10	20	30	70	100	130
1024-Darby O'Gill and the Little People (Disney-Movie)-Toth-a; photo-c	11	22	33	80	120	160
1025-Vacation in Disneyland (8-10/59)-Carl Barks-a(24pgs.) (Disney)	19	38	57	134	205	275
1026-Spin and Marty (TV) (Disney) (9-11/59)-Mickey Mouse Club; photo-c	9	18	27	63	89	115
1027-The Texan (#1)(TV)-Photo-c	10	20	30	70	100	130
1028-Rawhide (#1) (TV) (9-11/59)-Clint Eastwood photo-c; Tufts-a	25	50	75	179	275	370
1029-Boots and Saddles (TV) (9/59)-Photo-c	6	12	18	43	59	75
1030-Spanky and Alfalfa, the Little Rascals (TV)	7	14	21	46	63	80
1031-Fury (TV)-Photo-c	8	16	24	55	78	100
1032-Elmer Fudd	4	8	12	27	36	45
1033-Steve Canyon-not by Caniff; photo-c	6	12	18	43	59	75
1034-Nancy and Sluggo Summer Camp (9-11/59)	5	10	15	36	48	60
1035-Lawman (TV)-Photo-c	9	18	27	60	85	110
1036-The Big Circus (Movie)-Photo-c	8	16	24	53	74	95
1037-Zorro (Disney) (TV)-Tufts-a; Annette Funicello photo-c	16	32	48	114	175	235
1038-Ruff and Reddy (TV)(Hanna-Barbera)(1959)	9	18	27	65	93	120
1039-Pluto (Disney) (11-1/60)	5	10	15	33	44	55
1040-Quick Draw McGraw (#1) (TV) (Hanna-Barbera) (12-2/60)	15	30	45	102	156	215
1041-Sea Hunt (TV) (10-12/59)-Toth-a; Lloyd Bridges photo-c	10	20	30	67	96	125
1042-The Three Chipmunks (Alvin, Simon & Theodore) (#1) (TV) (10-12/59)	7	14	21	51	70	90
1043-The Three Stooges (#1)-Photo-c	27	54	81	194	297	400
1044-Have Gun, Will Travel (TV)-Photo-c	10	20	30	70	100	130
1045-Restless Gun (TV)-Photo-c	9	18	27	65	93	120
1046-Beep Beep, the Road Runner (11-1/60)	7	14	21	46	63	80
1047-Gyro Gearloose (#1) (Disney)-All Barks-c/a	19	38	57	134	205	275
1048-The Horse Soldiers (Movie) (John Wayne)-Sekowsky-a; painted cover featuring John Wayne	15	30	45	105	160	215
1049-Don't Give Up the Ship (Movie) (8/59)-Jerry Lewis photo-c	10	20	30	70	100	130
1050-Huckleberry Hound (TV) (Hanna-Barbera) (10-12/59)	9	18	27	65	93	120
1051-Donald in Mathmagic Land (Disney-Movie)	10	20	30	70	100	130
1052-Ben-Hur (Movie) (11/59)-Manning-a	11	22	33	77	114	150
1053-Goofy (Disney) (11-1/60)	6	12	18	40	55	70
1054-Huckleberry Hound Winter Fun (TV) (Hanna-Barbera) (12/59)	9	18	27	65	93	120
1055-Daisy Duck's Diary (Disney)-by Carl Barks (11-1/60)	10	20	30	72	104	135
1056-Yellowstone Kelly (Movie)-Clint Walker photo-c	7	14	21	46	63	80
1057-Mickey Mouse Album (Disney)	5	10	15	33	44	55
1058-Colt .45 (TV)-Photo-c	9	18	27	65	93	120
1059-Sugarfoot (TV)-Photo-c	10	20	30	70	100	130
1060-Journey to the Center of the Earth (Movie)-Pat Boone & James Mason photo-c	12	24	36	87	134	180
1061-Buffalo Bee (TV)	8	16	24	55	78	100
1062-Christmas Stories (Walt Scott's Little People strip-r)	5	10	15	36	48	60
1063-Santa Claus Funnies	6	12	18	43	59	75
1064-Bugs Bunny's Merry Christmas (12/59)	6	12	18	38	52	65
1065-Frosty the Snowman	6	12	18	38	52	65
1066-77 Sunset Strip (#1) (TV)-Toth-a (1-3/60)-Efrem Zimbalist, Jr. & Edd "Kookie" Byrnes photo-c	12	24	36	87	134	180
1067-Yogi Bear (#1) (TV) (Hanna-Barbera)	12	24	36	87	134	180
1068-Francis the Famous Talking Mule	4	8	12	29	40	50
1069-The FBI Story (Movie)-Toth-a; James Stewart photo on-c	11	22	33	75	100	145
1070-Solomon and Sheba (Movie)-Sekowsky-a; photo-c	10	20	30	72	104	135
1071-The Real McCoys (#1) (TV) (1-3/60)-Toth-a; Walter Brennan photo-c	10	20	30	73	107	140
1072-Blythe (Marge's)	6	12	18	43	59	75
1073-Grandma Duck's Farm Friends-Barks-c/a (Disney)	14	28	42	97	149	200
1074-Chilly Willy (Lantz)	5	10	15	33	44	55
1075-Tales of Wells Fargo (TV)-Photo-c	10	20	30	70	100	130
1076-The Rebel (#1) (TV)-Sekowsky-a; photo-c	11	22	33	80	120	160
1077-The Deputy (#1) (TV)-Buscema-a; Henry Fonda photo-c	14	28	42	97	149	200
1078-The Three Stooges (2-4/60)-Photo-c	14	28	42	97	149	200
1079-The Little Rascals (TV) (Spanky & Alfalfa)	7	14	21	46	63	80
1080-Fury (TV) (2-4/60)-Photo-c	8	16	24	55	78	100
1081-Elmer Fudd	4	8	12	27	36	45
1082-Spin and Marty (Disney) (TV)-Photo-c	9	18	27	63	89	115
1083-Men into Space (TV)-Anderson-a; photo-c	6	12	18	43	59	75
1084-Speedy Gonzales	6	12	18	43	59	75
1085-The Time Machine (H.G. Wells) (Movie) (3/60)-Alex Toth-a; Rod Taylor photo-c	16	32	48	112	171	230
1086-Lolly and Pepper	3	7	10	21	28	35
1087-Peter Gunn (TV)-Photo-c	10	20	30	72	104	135
1088-A Dog of Flanders (Movie)-Photo-c	6	12	18	38	52	65
1089-Restless Gun (TV)-Photo-c	9	18	27	65	93	120
1090-Francis the Famous Talking Mule	4	8	12	29	40	50
1091-Jacky's Diary (4-6/60)	6	12	18	38	52	65
1092-Toby Tyler (Disney-Movie)-Photo-c	8	16	24	53	74	95
1093-MacKenzie's Raiders (Movie/TV)-Richard Carlson photo-c from TV show						

Four Color Comics #1099 © WDC

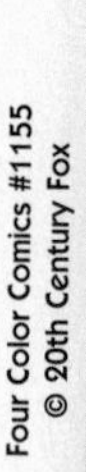

Four Color Comics #1155 © 20th Century Fox

Four Color Comics #1180 © Danny Thomas

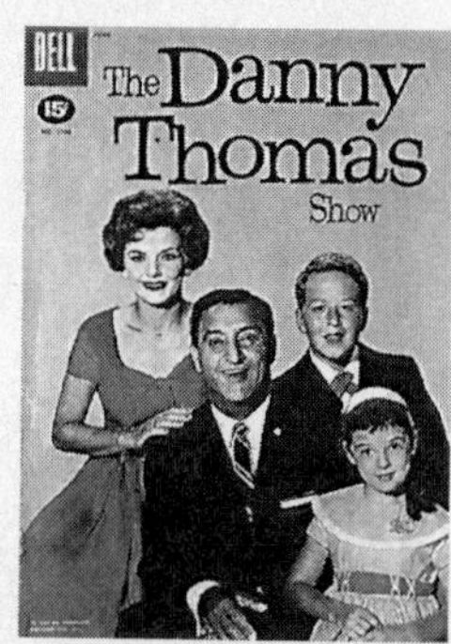

	GD 2.0	VG 4.0	FN 6.0	VF 8.0	VF/NM 9.0	NM- 9.2
	8	16	24	53	74	95
1094-Goofy (Disney)	6	12	18	40	55	70
1095-Gyro Gearloose (Disney)-All Barks-c/a	11	22	33	75	110	145
1096-The Texan (TV)-Rory Calhoun photo-c	9	18	27	65	93	120
1097-Rawhide (TV)-Manning-a; Clint Eastwood photo-c	16	32	48	112	171	230
1098-Sugarfoot (TV)-Photo-c	10	20	30	70	100	130
1099-Donald Duck Album (Disney) (5-7/60)-Barks-c	8	16	24	53	74	95
1100-Annette's Life Story (Disney-Movie) (5/60)-Annette Funicello photo-c	25	50	75	181	278	375
1101-Robert Louis Stevenson's Kidnapped (Disney-Movie) (5/60); photo-c	8	16	24	53	74	95
1102-Wanted: Dead or Alive (#1) (TV) (5-7/60); Steve McQueen photo-c	14	28	42	97	149	200
1103-Leave It to Beaver (TV)-Photo-c	15	30	45	107	164	220
1104-Yogi Bear Goes to College (TV) (Hanna-Barbera) (6-8/60)	9	18	27	60	85	110
1105-Gale Storm (Oh! Susanna) (TV)-Toth-a; photo-c	14	28	42	97	149	200
1106-77 Sunset Strip(TV)(6-8/60)-Toth-a; photo-c	10	20	30	72	104	135
1107-Buckskin (TV)-Photo-c	8	16	24	53	74	95
1108-The Troubleshooters (TV)-Keenan Wynn photo-c	6	12	18	43	59	75
1109-This Is Your Life, Donald Duck (Disney) (TV) (8-10/60)-Gyro flashback to WDC&S #141; origin Donald Duck (1st told)	15	30	45	105	160	215
1110-Bonanza (#1) (TV) (6-8/60)-Photo-c	36	72	108	270	423	575
1111-Shotgun Slade (TV)-Photo-c	7	14	21	51	71	90
1112-Pixie and Dixie and Mr. Jinks (#1) (TV) (Hanna-Barbera) (7-9/60)	9	18	27	63	89	115
1113-Tales of Wells Fargo (TV)-Photo-c	10	20	30	70	100	130
1114-Huckleberry Finn (Movie) (7/60)-Photo-c	6	12	18	43	59	75
1115-Ricky Nelson (TV)-Manning-a; photo-c	16	32	48	112	171	230
1116-Boots and Saddles (TV) (8/60)-Photo-c	6	12	18	43	59	75
1117-Boy and the Pirates (Movie)-Photo-c	8	16	24	53	74	95
1118-The Sword and the Dragon (Movie) (6/60)-Photo-c	9	18	27	63	89	115
1119-Smokey the Bear Nature Stories	5	10	15	36	48	60
1120-Dinosaurus (Movie)-Painted-c	9	18	27	63	89	115
1121-Hercules Unchained (Movie) (8/60)-Crandall/Evans-a	10	20	30	73	107	140
1122-Chilly Willy (Lantz)	5	10	15	33	44	55
1123-Tombstone Territory (TV)-Photo-c	10	20	30	70	100	130
1124-Whirlybirds (#1) (TV)-Photo-c	10	20	30	70	100	130
1125-Laramie (#1) (TV)-Photo-c; G. Kane/Heath-a	10	20	30	72	104	135
1126-Hotel Deparee - Sundance (TV) (8-10/60)-Earl Holliman photo-c	8	16	24	53	74	95
1127-The Three Stooges-Photo-c (8-10/60)	14	28	42	97	149	200
1128-Rocky and His Friends (#1) (TV) (Jay Ward) (8-10/60)	34	68	102	255	398	540
1129-Pollyanna (Disney-Movie)-Hayley Mills photo-c	9	18	27	63	89	115
1130-The Deputy (TV)-Buscema-a; Henry Fonda photo-c	11	22	33	75	110	145
1131-Elmer Fudd (9-11/60)	4	8	12	27	36	45
1132-Space Mouse (Lantz) (8-10/60)	5	10	15	36	48	60
1133-Fury (TV)-Photo-c	8	16	24	55	78	100
1134-Real McCoys (TV)-Toth-a; photo-c	10	20	30	73	107	140
1135-M.G.M.'s Mouse Musketeers (9-11/60)	4	8	12	24	32	40
1136-Jungle Cat (Disney-Movie)-Photo-c	8	16	24	53	74	95
1137-The Little Rascals (TV)	7	14	21	46	63	80
1138-The Rebel (TV)-Photo-c	10	20	30	70	100	130
1139-Spartacus (Movie) (11/60)-Buscema-a; Kirk Douglas photo-c	14	28	42	97	149	200
1140-Donald Duck Album (Disney)-Barks-c	8	16	24	53	74	95
1141-Huckleberry Hound for President (TV) (Hanna-Barbera) (10/60)	9	18	27	63	89	115
1142-Johnny Ringo (TV)-Photo-c	8	16	24	58	82	105
1143-Pluto (Disney) (11-1/61)	5	10	15	33	44	55
1144-The Story of Ruth (Movie)-Photo-c	10	20	30	72	104	135
1145-The Lost World (Movie)-Gil Kane-a; photo-c; 1 pg. Conan Doyle biography by Torres	11	22	33	75	110	145
1146-Restless Gun (TV)-Photo-c; Wildey-a	9	18	27	65	93	120
1147-Sugarfoot (TV)-Photo-c	10	20	30	70	100	130
1148-I Aim at the Stars-the Wernher Von Braun Story (Movie) (11-1/61)-Photo-c	8	16	24	58	82	105
1149-Goofy (Disney) (11-1/61)	6	12	18	40	55	70
1150-Daisy Duck's Diary (Disney) (12-1/61) by Carl Barks	10	20	30	72	104	135
1151-Mickey Mouse Album (Disney) (11-1/61)	5	10	15	33	44	55
1152-Rocky and His Friends (TV) (Jay Ward) (12-2/61)	24	48	72	170	260	350
1153-Frosty the Snowman	6	12	18	38	52	65
1154-Santa Claus Funnies	6	12	18	43	59	75
1155-North to Alaska (Movie)-John Wayne photo-c	18	36	54	131	201	270
1156-Walt Disney Swiss Family Robinson (Movie) (12/60)-Photo-c	9	18	27	60	85	110
1157-Master of the World (Movie) (7/61)	7	14	21	46	63	80
1158-Three Worlds of Gulliver (2 issues exist with different covers) (Movie)-Photo-c	8	16	24	55	78	100
1159-77 Sunset Strip (TV)-Toth-a; photo-c	10	20	30	72	104	135
1160-Rawhide (TV)-Clint Eastwood photo-c	16	32	48	112	171	230
1161-Grandma Duck's Farm Friends (Disney) by Carl Barks (2-4/61)	14	28	42	97	149	200
1162-Yogi Bear Joins the Marines (TV) (Hanna-Barbera) (5-7/61)	9	18	27	60	85	110
1163-Daniel Boone (3-5/61); Marsh-a	6	12	18	43	59	75
1164-Wanted: Dead or Alive (TV)-Steve McQueen photo-c	11	22	33	75	110	145
1165-Ellery Queen (#1) (3-5/61)	12	24	36	86	131	175
1166-Rocky and His Friends (TV) (Jay Ward)	24	48	72	170	260	350
1167-Tales of Wells Fargo (TV)-Photo-c	9	18	27	65	93	120
1168-The Detectives (TV)-Robert Taylor photo-c	11	22	33	80	120	160
1169-New Adventures of Sherlock Holmes	17	34	51	119	182	245
1170-The Three Stooges (3-5/61)-Photo-c	14	28	42	97	149	200
1171-Elmer Fudd	4	8	12	27	36	45
1172-Fury (TV)-Photo-c	8	16	24	55	78	100
1173-The Twilight Zone (#1) (TV) (5/61)-Crandall/Evans-c/a; Crandall tribute to Ingles	23	46	69	165	253	340
1174-The Little Rascals (TV)	6	12	18	38	52	65
1175-M.G.M.'s Mouse Musketeers (3-5/61)	4	8	12	24	32	40
1176-Dondi (Movie)-Origin; photo-c	6	12	18	38	52	65
1177-Chilly Willy (Lantz) (4-6/61)	5	10	15	33	44	55
1178-Ten Who Dared (Disney-Movie) (12/60)-Painted-c; cast member photo on back-c	9	18	27	60	85	110
1179-The Swamp Fox (TV) (Disney)-Leslie Nielsen photo-c	10	20	30	70	100	130
1180-The Danny Thomas Show (TV)-Toth-a; photo-c	18	36	54	129	197	265
1181-Texas John Slaughter (TV) (Walt Disney Presents...) (4-6/61)-Photo-c	8	16	24	58	82	105
1182-Donald Duck Album (Disney) (5-7/61)	6	12	18	38	52	65
1183-101 Dalmatians (Disney-Movie) (3/61)	11	22	33	80	120	160
1184-Gyro Gearloose; All Barks-c/a (Disney) (5-7/61) Two variations exist	11	22	33	75	110	145
1185-Sweetie Pie	5	10	15	36	48	60
1186-Yak Yak (#1) by Jack Davis (2 versions - one minus 3-pg. Davis-c/a)	10	20	30	70	100	130
1187-The Three Stooges (6-8/61)-Photo-c	14	28	42	97	149	200
1188-Atlantis, the Lost Continent (Movie) (5/61)-Photo-c	12	24	36	82	124	165
1189-Greyfriars Bobby (Disney-Movie) (11/61)-Photo-c (scarce)	8	16	24	58	82	105
1190-Donald and the Wheel (Disney-Movie) (11/61); Barks-c	9	18	27	60	85	110
1191-Leave It to Beaver (TV)-Photo-c	15	30	45	107	164	220
1192-Ricky Nelson (TV)-Manning-a; photo-c	16	32	48	112	171	230
1193-The Real McCoys (TV) (6-8/61)-Photo-c	10	20	30	70	100	130
1194-Pepe (Movie) (4/61)-Photo-c	3	6	9	19	25	32
1195-National Velvet (#1) (TV)-Photo-c	8	16	24	58	82	105
1196-Pixie and Dixie and Mr. Jinks (TV) (Hanna-Barbera) (7-9/61)	7	14	21	46	63	80
1197-The Aquanauts (TV) (5-7/61)-Photo-c	8	16	24	58	82	105
1198-Donald in Mathmagic Land (Disney-Movie)-Reprint of #1051	8	16	24	53	74	95
1199-The Absent-Minded Professor (Disney-Movie) (4/61)-Photo-c	9	18	27	63	89	115
1200-Hennessey (TV) (8-10/61)-Gil Kane-a; photo-c	8	16	24	58	82	105
1201-Goofy (Disney) (8-10/61)	6	12	18	40	55	70
1202-Rawhide (TV)-Clint Eastwood photo-c	16	32	48	112	171	230

Four Color Comics #1268 © Walter Lantz

Four Color Comics #1300 © 20th Century Fox

Four Color Comics #1308 © Videocraft

	GD 2.0	VG 4.0	FN 6.0	VF 8.0	VF/NM 9.0	NM- 9.2
1203-Pinocchio (Disney) (3/62)	6	12	18	43	59	75
1204-Scamp (Disney)	5	10	15	36	48	60
1205-David and Goliath (Movie) (7/61)-Photo-c	8	16	24	53	74	95
1206-Lolly and Pepper (9-11/61)	3	7	10	21	28	35
1207-The Rebel (TV)-Sekowsky-a; photo-c	10	20	30	70	100	130
1208-Rocky and His Friends (Jay Ward) (TV)	24	48	72	170	260	350
1209-Sugarfoot (TV)-Photo-c (10-12/61)	10	20	30	70	100	130
1210-The Parent Trap (Disney-Movie) (8/61)-Hayley Mills photo-c	10	20	30	73	107	140
1211-77 Sunset Strip (TV)-Manning-a; photo-c	10	20	30	67	96	125
1212-Chilly Willy (Lantz) (7-9/61)	5	10	15	33	44	55
1213-Mysterious Island (Movie)-Photo-c	10	20	30	70	100	130
1214-Smokey the Bear	5	10	15	36	48	60
1215-Tales of Wells Fargo (TV) (10-12/61)-Photo-c	9	18	27	65	93	120
1216-Whirlybirds (TV)-Photo-c	9	18	27	65	93	120
1218-Fury (TV)-Photo-c	8	16	24	55	78	100
1219-The Detectives (TV)-Robert Taylor & Adam West photo-c	10	20	30	70	100	130
1220-Gunslinger (TV)-Photo-c	10	20	30	70	100	130
1221-Bonanza (TV) (9-11/61)-Photo-c	20	40	60	141	216	290
1222-Elmer Fudd (9-11/61)	4	8	12	27	36	45
1223-Laramie (TV)-Gil Kane-a; photo-c	8	16	24	53	74	95
1224-The Little Rascals (TV) (10-12/61)	6	12	18	38	52	65
1225-The Deputy (TV)-Henry Fonda photo-c	11	22	33	75	110	145
1226-Nikki, Wild Dog of the North (Disney-Movie) (9/61)-Photo-c	6	12	18	43	59	75
1227-Morgan the Pirate (Movie)-Photo-c	9	18	27	63	89	115
1229-Thief of Baghdad (Movie)-Crandall/Evans-a; photo-c	8	16	24	55	78	100
1230-Voyage to the Bottom of the Sea (#1) (Movie)-Photo insert on-c	12	24	36	84	127	170
1231-Danger Man (TV) (9-11/61)-Patrick McGoohan photo-c	12	24	36	86	131	175
1232-On the Double (Movie)	6	12	18	38	52	65
1233-Tammy Tell Me True (Movie) (1961)	8	16	24	53	74	95
1234-The Phantom Planet (Movie) (1961)	8	16	24	58	82	105
1235-Mister Magoo (#1) (12-2/62)	10	20	30	70	100	130
1235-Mister Magoo (3-5/65) 2nd printing; reprint of 12-2/62 issue	7	14	21	51	71	90
1236-King of Kings (Movie)-Photo-c	9	18	27	63	89	115
1237-The Untouchables (#1) (TV)-Not by Toth; photo-c	24	48	72	170	260	350
1238-Deputy Dawg (TV)	12	24	36	87	134	180
1239-Donald Duck Album (Disney) (10-12/61)-Barks-c	8	16	24	53	74	95
1240-The Detectives (TV)-Tufts-a; Robert Taylor photo-c	10	20	30	70	100	130
1241-Sweetie Pie	4	8	12	27	36	45
1242-King Leonardo and His Short Subjects (#1) (TV) (11-1/62)	14	28	42	102	156	210
1243-Ellery Queen	10	20	30	70	100	130
1244-Space Mouse (Lantz) (11-1/62)	5	10	15	36	48	60
1245-New Adventures of Sherlock Holmes	15	30	45	107	164	220
1246-Mickey Mouse Album (Disney)	5	10	15	33	44	55
1247-Daisy Duck's Diary (Disney) (12-2/62)	6	12	18	40	55	70
1248-Pluto (Disney)	5	10	15	33	44	55
1249-The Danny Thomas Show (TV)-Manning-a; photo-c	17	34	51	121	186	250
1250-The Four Horsemen of the Apocalypse (Movie)-Photo-c	8	16	24	53	74	95
1251-Everything's Ducky (Movie) (1961)	6	12	18	38	52	65
1252-The Andy Griffith Show (TV)-Photo-c; 1st show aired 10/3/60	38	76	114	285	443	600
1253-Space Man (#1) (1-3/62)	9	18	27	60	85	110
1254- "Diver Dan" (#1) (TV) (2-4/62)-Photo-c	6	12	18	40	55	75
1255-The Wonders of Aladdin (Movie) (1961)	8	16	24	53	74	95
1256-Kona, Monarch of Monster Isle (#1) (2-4/62)-Glanzman-a	9	18	27	65	93	120
1257-Car 54, Where Are You? (#1) (TV) (3-5/62)-Photo-c	10	20	30	70	100	130
1258-The Frogmen (#1)-Evans-a	9	18	27	65	93	120
1259-El Cid (Movie) (1961)-Photo-c	8	16	24	58	82	105
1260-The Horsemasters (TV, Movie) (Disney) (12-2/62)-Annette Funicello photo-c	14	28	42	97	149	200

	GD 2.0	VG 4.0	FN 6.0	VF 8.0	VF/NM 9.0	NM- 9.2
1261-Rawhide (TV)-Clint Eastwood photo-c	16	32	48	112	171	230
1262-The Rebel (TV)-Photo-c	10	20	30	70	100	130
1263-77 Sunset Strip (TV) (12-2/62)-Manning-a; photo-c	10	20	30	67	96	125
1264-Pixie and Dixie and Mr. Jinks (TV) (Hanna-Barbera)	7	14	21	46	63	80
1265-The Real McCoys (TV)-Photo-c	10	20	30	70	100	130
1266-M.G.M.'s Spike and Tyke (12-2/62)	3	7	10	21	28	35
1267-Gyro Gearloose; Barks-c/a, 4 pgs. (Disney) (12-2/62)	9	18	27	60	85	110
1268-Oswald the Rabbit (Lantz)	4	8	12	29	40	50
1269-Rawhide (TV)-Clint Eastwood photo-c	16	32	48	112	171	230
1270-Bullwinkle and Rocky (#1) (TV) (Jay Ward) (3-5/62)	21	42	63	150	230	310
1271-Yogi Bear Birthday Party (TV) (Hanna-Barbera) (11/61) (Given away for 1 box top from Kellogg's Corn Flakes)	7	14	21	46	63	80
1272-Frosty the Snowman	6	12	18	38	52	65
1273-Hans Brinker (Disney-Movie)-Photo-c (2/62)	8	16	24	53	74	95
1274-Santa Claus Funnies (12/61)	6	12	18	43	59	75
1275-Rocky and His Friends (TV) (Jay Ward)	24	48	72	170	260	350
1276-Dondi	4	8	12	22	30	38
1278-King Leonardo and His Short Subjects (TV)	14	28	42	102	156	210
1279-Grandma Duck's Farm Friends (Disney)	6	12	18	38	52	65
1280-Hennesey (TV)-Photo-c	8	16	24	53	74	95
1281-Chilly Willy (Lantz) (4-6/62)	5	10	15	33	44	55
1282-Babes in Toyland (Disney-Movie) (1/62); Annette Funicello photo-c	15	30	45	105	160	215
1283-Bonanza (TV) (2-4/62)-Photo-c	20	40	60	141	216	290
1284-Laramie (TV)-Heath-a; photo-c	8	16	24	53	74	95
1285-Leave It to Beaver (TV)-Photo-c	15	30	45	107	164	220
1286-The Untouchables (TV)-Photo-c	17	34	51	119	182	245
1287-Man from Wells Fargo (TV)-Photo-c	7	14	21	46	63	80
1288-Twilight Zone (TV) (4/62)-Crandall/Evans-c/a	13	26	39	90	138	185
1289-Ellery Queen	10	20	30	70	100	130
1290-M.G.M.'s Mouse Musketeers	4	8	12	24	32	40
1291-77 Sunset Strip (TV)-Manning-a; photo-c	10	20	30	67	96	125
1293-Elmer Fudd (3-5/62)	4	8	12	27	36	45
1294-Ripcord (TV)	8	16	24	58	82	105
1295-Mister Ed, the Talking Horse (#1) (TV) (3-5/62)-Photo-c	14	28	42	102	156	210
1296-Fury (TV) (3-5/62)-Photo-c	8	16	24	55	78	100
1297-Spanky, Alfalfa and the Little Rascals (TV)	6	12	18	38	52	65
1298-The Hathaways (TV)-Photo-c	6	12	18	38	52	65
1299-Deputy Dawg (TV)	12	24	36	87	134	180
1300-The Comancheros (Movie) (1961)-John Wayne photo-c	17	34	51	121	186	250
1301-Adventures in Paradise (TV) (2-4/62)	7	14	21	46	63	80
1302-Johnny Jason, Teen Reporter (2-4/62)	4	8	12	27	36	45
1303-Lad: A Dog (Movie)-Photo-c	5	10	15	36	48	60
1304-Nellie the Nurse (3-5/62)-Stanley-a	8	16	24	58	82	105
1305-Mister Magoo (3-5/62)	10	20	30	70	100	130
1306-Target: The Corruptors (#1) (TV) (3-5/62)-Photo-c	7	14	21	46	63	80
1307-Margie (TV) (3-5/62)	7	14	21	46	63	80
1308-Tales of the Wizard of Oz (TV) (3-5/62)	13	26	39	90	138	185
1309-87th Precinct (#1) (TV) (4-6/62)-Krigstein-a; photo-c	11	22	33	80	120	160
1310-Huck and Yogi Winter Sports (TV) (Hanna-Barbera) (3/62)	10	20	30	70	100	130
1311-Rocky and His Friends (TV) (Jay Ward)	24	48	72	170	260	350
1312-National Velvet (TV)-Photo-c	5	10	15	33	44	55
1313-Moon Pilot (Disney-Movie)-Photo-c	8	16	24	58	82	105
1328-The Underwater City (Movie) (1961)-Evans-a; photo-c	8	16	24	58	82	105
1329-See Gyro Gearloose #01329-207						
1330-Brain Boy (#1)-Gil Kane-a	14	28	42	97	149	200
1332-Bachelor Father (TV)	9	18	27	63	89	115
1333-Short Ribs (4-6/62)	6	12	18	43	59	75
1335-Aggie Mack (4-6/62)	4	8	12	29	40	50
1336-On Stage; not by Leonard Starr	6	12	18	38	52	65
1337-Dr. Kildare (#1) (TV) (4-6/62)-Photo-c	10	20	30	72	104	135
1341-The Andy Griffith Show (TV) (4-6/62)-Photo-c	35	70	105	263	412	560
1348-Yak Yak (#2)-Jack Davis-c/a	9	18	27	65	93	120
1349-Yogi Bear Visits the U.N. (TV) (Hanna-Barbera) (1/62)-Photo-c						

Four Favorites #4 © ACE

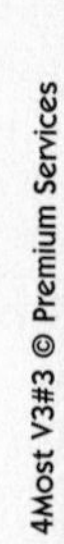
4Most V3#3 © Premium Services

Fox and the Crow #2 © DC

GD 2.0 | VG 4.0 | FN 6.0 | VF 8.0 | VF/NM 9.0 | NM- 9.2

1350-Comanche (Disney-Movie)(1962)-Reprints 4-Color #966 (title change from "Tonka" to "Comanche") (4-6/62)-Sal Mineo photo-c 10 20 30 72 104 135
1354-Calvin & the Colonel (#1) (TV) (4-6/62) 10 20 30 70 100 130
6 12 18 43 59 75
NOTE: *Missing numbers probably do not exist.*

4-D MONKEY, THE (Adventures of... #? on)
Leung's Publications: 1988 - No. 11, 1990 ($1.80/$2.00, 52 pgs.)

1-11: 1-Karate Pig, Ninja Flounder & 4-D Monkey (48 pgs., centerfold is a Christmas card). 2-4 (52 pgs.) 2.50

FOUR FAVORITES (Crime Must Pay the Penalty No. 33 on)
Ace Magazines: Sept, 1941 - No. 32, Dec, 1947

1-Vulcan, Lash Lightning (formerly Flash Lightning in Sure-Fire), Magno the Magnetic Man & The Raven begin; flag/Hitler-c 169 338 507 1056 1628 2200
2-The Black Ace only app. 60 120 180 375 575 775
3-Last Vulcan 50 100 150 305 463 620
4,5: 4-The Raven & Vulcan end; Unknown Soldier begins (see Our Flag), ends #28. 5-Captain Courageous begins (5/42), ends #28 (moves over from Captain Courageous #6); not in #6 45 90 135 275 418 560
6-8: 6-The Flag app.; Mr. Risk begins (7/42) 40 80 120 244 372 500
9-Kurtzman-a (Lash Lightning); robot-c 45 90 135 275 418 560
10-Classic Kurtzman-c/a (Magno & Davey) 51 102 153 311 476 640
11-Kurtzman-a; Hitler, Mussolini, Hirohito-c; L.B. Cole-a; Unknown Soldier by Kurtzman 60 120 180 375 575 775
12-L.B. Cole-a 38 76 114 219 320 420
13-20: 18,20-Palais-c/a 33 66 99 190 275 360
21-No Unknown Soldier; The Unknown app. 24 48 72 138 199 260
22-26: 22-Captain Courageous drops costume. 23-Unknown Soldier drops costume. 25-29-Hap Hazard app. 26-Last Magno 24 48 72 138 199 260
27-29: Hap Hazard app. in all 22 44 66 125 180 235
30-32: 30-Funny-c begin (teen humor), end #32 15 30 45 83 117 150
NOTE: ***Dave Berg** c-5. **Jim Mooney** a-6; c-1-3. **Palais** a-18-20; c-18-25. Torture chamber c-5.*

FOUR HORSEMEN, THE (See The Crusaders)

FOUR HORSEMEN
DC Comics (Vertigo): Feb, 2000 - No. 4, May, 2000 ($2.50, limited series)

1-4-Essad Ribic-c/a; Robert Rodi-s 2.50

FOUR HORSEMEN OF THE APOCALYPSE, THE (Movie)
Dell Publishing Co.: No. 1250, Jan-Mar, 1962 (one-shot)

Four Color 1250-Photo-c 8 16 24 53 74 95

4MOST (Foremost Boys No. 32-40; becomes Thrilling Crime Cases #41 on)
Novelty Publications/Star Publications No. 37-on:
Winter, 1941-42 - V8#5(#36), 9-10/49; #37, 11-12/49 - #40, 4-5/50

V1#1-The Target by Sid Greene, The Cadet & Dick Cole begin with origins retold; produced by Funnies Inc.; quarterly issues begin, end V6#3 146 292 438 913 1407 1900
2-Last Target (Spr/42); WWII cover 62 124 186 388 594 800
3-Dan'l Flannel begins; flag-c 46 92 138 281 428 575
4-1pg. Dr. Seuss (signed) (Aut/42); fish in the face-c 48 96 144 293 447 600
V2#1-3 19 38 57 107 154 200
4-Hitler, Tojo & Mussolini app. as pumpkins on-c 35 70 105 198 287 375
V3#1-4 15 30 45 86 123 160
V4#1-4: 2-Walter Johnson-c 12 24 36 69 95 120
V5#1-4: 1-The Target & Targeteers app. 10 20 30 60 80 100
V6#1-4 9 18 27 54 70 85
5-L. B. Cole-c 21 42 63 121 173 225
V7#1,3,5, V8#1, 37 9 18 27 54 70 85
2,4,6-L. B. Cole-c. 6-Last Dick Cole 21 42 63 121 173 225
V8#2,3,5-L. B. Cole-c/a 25 50 75 141 203 265
4-L. B. Cole-a 15 30 45 83 117 150
38-40: 38-Johnny Weismuller (Tarzan) life story & Jim Braddock (boxer) life story. 38-40-L.B. Cole-c. 40-Last White Rider 18 36 54 102 146 190
Accepted Reprint 38-40 (nd): 40-r/Johnny Weismuller life story; all have L.B. Cole-c 10 20 30 58 77 95

411
Marvel Comics: June, 2003 - No. 3 ($3.50, limited series)

1,2-Tributes to peacemakers; s/a by various. 1-Millar, Quitely, Mack, Winslade & others-s/a. 2-Harris, Phillips, Manco, Bruce Jones. 3.50

FOUR-STAR BATTLE TALES
National Periodical Publications: Feb-Mar, 1973 - No. 5, Nov-Dec, 1973

1-Reprints begin 3 6 9 18 24 30
2-5 2 4 6 11 14 18
NOTE: ***Drucker** r-1, 3-5. **Heath** r-2, 5; c-1. **Krigstein** r-5. **Kubert** r-4; c-2.*

FOUR STAR SPECTACULAR
National Periodical Publications: Mar-Apr, 1976 - No. 6, Jan-Feb, 1977

1 2 4 6 11 14 18
2-6: Reprints in all. 2-Infinity cover 1 3 4 6 8 10
NOTE: *All contain DC Superhero reprints. #1 has 68 pgs.; #2-6, 52 pgs.. #1, 4-Hawkman app.; #2-Kid Flash app.; #3-Green Lantern app; #2, 4, 5-Wonder Woman, Superboy app; #5-Green Arrow, Vigilante app; #6-Blackhawk G.A.-r.*

FOUR TEENERS (Formerly Crime Must Pay The Penalty; Dotty No. 35 on)
A. A. Wyn: No. 34, April, 1948 (52 pgs.)

34-Teen-age comic; Dotty app.; Curly & Jerry continue from Four Favorites 7 14 21 37 46 55

FOURTH WORLD GALLERY, THE (Jack Kirby's...)
DC Comics: 1996 (9/96) ($3.50, one-shot)

nn-Pin-ups of Jack Kirby's Fourth World characters (New Gods, Forever People & Mister Miracle) by John Byrne, Rick Burchett, Dan Jurgens, Walt Simonson & others 3.50

FOUR WOMEN
DC Comics (Homage): Dec, 2001 - No. 5, Apr, 2002 ($2.95, limited series)

1-5-Sam Kieth-s/a 3.00
TPB (2002, $17.95) r/series; foreward by Kieth 18.00

FOX AND THE CROW (Stanley & His Monster No. 109 on) (See Comic Cavalcade & Real Screen Comics)
National Periodical Publications: Dec-Jan, 1951-52 - No. 108, Feb-Mar, 1968

1 112 224 336 700 1075 1450
2(Scarce) 53 106 159 323 492 660
3-5 37 74 111 209 305 400
6-10 27 54 81 152 219 285
11-20 20 40 60 112 161 210
21-30: 22-Last precode issue (2/55) 14 28 42 81 113 145
31-40 11 22 33 66 91 115
41-60 7 14 21 51 71 90
61-80 6 12 18 40 55 70
81-94: 94-(11/65)-The Brat Finks begin 4 8 12 29 40 50
95-Stanley & His Monster begins (origin & 1st app) 6 12 18 40 55 70
96-99,101-108 4 8 12 22 30 38
100 (10-11/66) 4 8 12 25 33 42
NOTE: *Many later covers by **Mort Drucker**.*

FOX AND THE HOUND, THE (Disney)(Movie)
Whitman Publishing Co.: Aug, 1981 - No. 3, Oct, 1981

11292(#1),2,3-Based on animated movie 1 2 3 5 7 9

FOXFIRE (See The Phoenix Resurrection)
Malibu Comics (Ultraverse): Feb, 1996 - No. 4, May, 1996 ($1.50)

1-4: Sludge, Ultraforce app. 4-Punisher app. 2.25

FOX GIANTS (Also see Giant Comics Edition)
Fox Features Syndicate: 1944 - 1950 (25¢, 132 - 196 pgs.)

Album of Crime nn(1949, 132p) 46 92 138 281 428 575
Album of Love nn(1949, 132p) 40 80 120 240 360 480
All Famous Crime Stories nn('49, 132p) 46 92 138 281 428 575
All Good Comics 1(1944, 132p)(R.W. Voigt)-The Bouncer, Purple Tigress,Rick Evans, Puppeteer, Green Mask; Infinity-c 40 80 120 241 363 485
All Great nn(1944, 132p)-Capt. Jack Terry, Rick Evans, Jaguar Man 40 80 120 241 363 485
All Great nn(Chicago Nite Life News)(1945, 132p)-Green Mask, Bouncer, Puppeteer, Rick Evans, Rocket Kelly 40 80 120 241 363 485
All-Great Confessions nn(1949, 132p) 40 80 120 239 357 475
All Great Crime Stories nn('49, 132p) 46 92 138 281 428 575
All Great Jungle Adventures nn('49, 132p) 55 110 165 340 520 700
All Real Confession Magazine 3 (3/49, 132p) 40 80 120 239 357 475
All Real Confession Magazine 4 (4/49, 132p) 40 80 120 239 357 475
All Your Comics 1(1944, 132p)-The Puppeteer, Red Robbins, & Merciless the Sorcerer 40 80 120 240 360 480
Almanac Of Crime nn(1948, 148p)-Phantom Lady 52 104 156 317 484 650
Almanac Of Crime 1(1950, 132p) 44 88 132 268 409 550
Book Of Love nn(1950, 132p) 40 80 120 230 335 440
Burning Romances 1(1949, 132p) 44 88 132 268 409 550
Crimes Incorporated nn(1950, 132p) 42 84 126 256 391 525
Daring Love Stories nn(1950, 132p) 40 80 120 230 335 440
Everybody's Comics 1(1944, 50¢, 196p)-The Green Mask, The Puppeteer, The Bouncer,

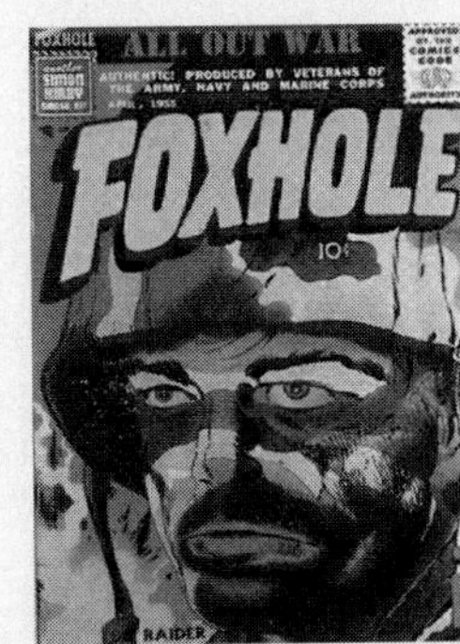

Foxhole #4 © Mainline

Fraction #1 © David Tischman & DC

Frankenstein Mobster #1 © Mark Wheatley

	GD 2.0	VG 4.0	FN 6.0	VF 8.0	VF/NM 9.0	NM- 9.2
Rocket Kelly, Rick Evans	46	92	138	281	428	575
Everybody's Comics 1(1946, 196p)-Green Lama, The Puppeteer	40	80	120	230	335	440
Everybody's Comics 1(1946, 196p)-Same as 1945 Ribtickler	32	64	96	184	267	350
Everybody's Comics nn(1947, 132p)-Jo-Jo, Purple Tigress, Cosmo Cat, Bronze Man	40	80	120	233	342	450
Exciting Romance Stories nn(1949, 132p)	40	80	120	233	342	450
Famous Love nn(1950, 132p)	40	80	120	230	335	440
Intimate Confessions nn(1950, 132p)	40	80	120	230	335	440
Journal Of Crime nn(1949, 132p)	46	92	138	281	428	575
Love Problems nn(1949, 132p)	40	80	120	239	357	475
Love Thrills nn(1950, 132p)	40	80	120	235	348	460
March of Crime nn('48, 132p)-Female w/rifle-c	44	88	132	268	409	550
March of Crime nn('49, 132p)-Cop w/pistol-c	42	84	126	256	391	525
March of Crime nn(1949, 132p)-Coffin & man w/machine-gun-c	42	84	126	256	391	525
Revealing Love Stories nn(1950, 132p)	40	80	120	230	335	440
Ribtickler nn(1945, 50¢, 196p)-Chicago Nite Life News; Marvel Mutt, Cosmo Cat, Flash Rabbit, The Nebbs app.	40	80	120	230	335	440
Romantic Thrills nn(1950, 132p)	40	80	120	230	335	440
Secret Love Stories nn(1949, 132p)	40	80	120	233	342	450
Strange Love nn(1950, 132p)-Photo-c	42	84	126	256	388	520
Sweetheart Scandals nn(1950, 132p)	40	80	120	230	335	440
Teen-Age Love nn(1950, 132p)	40	80	120	230	335	440
Throbbing Love nn(1950, 132p)-Photo-c; used in **POP**, pg. 107	42	84	126	256	388	520
Truth About Crime nn(1949, 132p)	46	92	138	281	428	575
Variety Comics 1(1946, 132p)-Blue Beetle, Jungle Jo	40	80	120	241	363	485
Variety Comics nn(1950, 132p)-Jungle Jo, My Secret Affair(w/Harrison/Wood-a), Crimes by Women & My Story	40	80	120	236	351	465
Western Roundup nn('50, 132p)-Hoot Gibson; Cody of the Pony Express app.	40	80	120	241	363	485

NOTE: Each of the above usually contain four remaindered Fox books minus covers. Since these missing covers often had the first page of the first story, most Giants therefore are incomplete. Approximate values are listed. Books with appearances of Phantom Lady, Rulah, Jo-Jo, etc. could bring more.

FOXHOLE (Becomes Never Again #8?)
Mainline/Charlton No. 5 on: 9-10/54 - No. 4, 3-4/55; No. 5, 7/55 - No. 7, 3/56

	GD	VG	FN	VF	VF/NM	NM-
1-Classic Kirby-c	45	90	135	275	418	560
2-Kirby-c/a(2); Kirby scripts based on his war time experiences	34	68	102	196	283	370
3-5-Kirby-c only	20	40	60	112	161	210
6-Kirby-c/a(2)	29	58	87	164	237	310
7	10	20	30	56	73	90
Super Reprints #10,15-17: 10-r/? 15,16-r/United States Marines #5,8. 17-r/Monty Hall #?	2	4	6	12	16	20
11,12,18-r/Foxhole #1,2,3; Kirby-c	3	6	9	19	25	32

*NOTE: **Kirby** a(r)-Super #11, 12. **Powell** a(r)-Super #15, 16. Stories by actual veterans.*

FOX KIDS FUNHOUSE (TV)
Acclaim Books: 1997 ($4.50, digest size)

1-The Tick 4.50

FOXY FAGAN COMICS (Funny Animal)
Dearfield Publishing Co.: Dec, 1946 - No. 7, Summer, 1948

	GD	VG	FN	VF	VF/NM	NM-
1-Foxy Fagan & Little Buck begin	13	26	39	74	102	130
2	8	16	24	43	54	65
3-7: 6-Rocket ship-c	7	14	21	37	46	55

FRACTION
DC Comics (Focus): June, 2004 - No. 6, Nov, 2004 ($2.50, limited series)

1-6-David Tischman-s/Timothy Green II-a 2.50

FRACTURED FAIRY TALES (TV)
Gold Key: Oct, 1962 (Jay Ward)

	GD	VG	FN	VF	VF/NM	NM-
1 (10022-210)-From Bullwinkle TV show	12	24	36	87	134	180

FRAGGLE ROCK (TV)
Marvel Comics (Star Comics)/Marvel V2#1 on: Apr, 1985 - No. 8, Sept, 1986; V2#1, Apr, 1988 - No. 6, Sept, 1988

1-6 (75¢-c) 5.00
7,8 6.00
V2#1-6-($1.00): Reprints 1st series 2.25

FRANCIS, BROTHER OF THE UNIVERSE
Marvel Comics Group: 1980 (75¢, 52 pgs., one-shot)

nn-John Buscema/Marie Severin-a; story of Francis Bernadone celebrating his 800th birthday in 1982 4.00

FRANCIS THE FAMOUS TALKING MULE (All based on movie)
Dell Publishing Co.: No. 335 (#1), June, 1951 - No. 1090, March, 1960

	GD	VG	FN	VF	VF/NM	NM-
Four Color 335 (#1)	11	22	33	80	120	160
Four Color 465	7	14	21	46	63	80
Four Color 501,547,579	6	12	18	38	52	65
Four Color 621,655,698,710,745	5	10	15	33	44	55
Four Color 810,863,906,953,991,1068,1090	4	8	12	29	40	50

FRANK
Nemesis Comics (Harvey): Apr (Mar inside), 1994 - No. 4, 1994 ($1.75/$2.50, limited series)

1-4-($2.50, direct sale): 1-Foil-c Edition 3.00
1-4-($1.75)-Newsstand Editions; Cowan-a in all 2.25

FRANK
Fantagraphics Books: Sept, 1996 ($2.95, B&W)

1-Woodring-c/a/scripts 3.00

FRANK BUCK (Formerly My True Love)
Fox Features Syndicate: No. 70, May, 1950 - No. 3, Sept, 1950

	GD	VG	FN	VF	VF/NM	NM-
70-Wood a(p)(3 stories)-Photo-c	34	68	102	196	283	370
71-Wood-a (9 pgs.); photo/painted-c	18	36	54	100	143	185
3: 3-Photo/painted-c	14	28	42	79	110	140

NOTE: Based on "Bring 'Em Back Alive" TV show.

FRANKENSTEIN (See Dracula, Movie Classics & Werewolf)
Dell Publishing Co.: Aug-Oct, 1964; No. 2, Sept, 1966 - No. 4, Mar, 1967

	GD	VG	FN	VF	VF/NM	NM-
1(12-283-410)(1964)(2nd printing; see Movie Classics for 1st printing)	7	14	21	46	63	80
2-Intro. & origin super-hero character (9/66)	4	8	12	29	40	50
3,4	3	6	9	19	25	32

FRANKENSTEIN (The Monster of...; also see Monsters Unleashed #2, Power Record Comics, Psycho & Silver Surfer #7)
Marvel Comics Group: Jan, 1973 - No. 18, Sept, 1975

	GD	VG	FN	VF	VF/NM	NM-
1-Ploog-c/a begins, ends #6	6	12	18	43	59	75
2	4	8	12	25	33	42
3-5	3	6	9	18	24	30
6,7,10: 7-Dracula cameo	3	6	9	16	20	24
8,9-Dracula c/sty. 9-Death of Dracula	4	8	12	28	38	48
11-17	2	4	6	11	14	18
18-Wrightson-c(i)	2	4	6	14	18	22

*NOTE: **Adkins** c-17i. **Buscema** a-7-10p. **Ditko** a-12r. **G. Kane** c-15p. **Orlando** a-8r. **Ploog** a-1-3, 4p, 5p, 6; c-1-6. **Wrightson** c-18i.*

FRANKENSTEIN (Mary Wollstonecraft Shelley's...; A Marvel Illustrated Novel)
Marvel Pub.: 1983 ($8.95, B&W, 196 pgs., 8x11" TPB)

	GD	VG	FN	VF	VF/NM	NM-
nn-Wrightson-a; 4 pg. intro. by Stephen King	4	8	12	27	36	45

FRANKENSTEIN COMICS (Also See Prize Comics)
Prize Publ. (Crestwood/Feature): Sum, 1945 - V5#5(#33), Oct-Nov, 1954

	GD	VG	FN	VF	VF/NM	NM-
1-Frankenstein begins by Dick Briefer (origin); Frank Sinatra parody	112	224	336	700	1075	1450
2	54	108	162	329	502	675
3-5	40	80	120	244	372	500
6-10: 7-S&K a(r)/Headline Comics. 8(7-8/47)-Superman satire	37	74	111	209	305	400
11-17(1-2/49)-11-Boris Karloff parody-c/story. 17-Last humor issue	32	64	96	184	267	350
18(3/52)-New origin, horror series begins	40	80	120	244	372	500
19,20(V3#4, 8-9/52)	28	56	84	158	229	300
21(V3#5), 22(V3#6), 23(V4#1) - #28(V4#6)	26	52	78	147	211	275
29(V5#1) - #33(V5#5)	25	50	75	141	203	265

*NOTE: **Briefer** c/a-all. **Meskin** a-21, 29.*

FRANKENSTEIN/DRACULA WAR, THE
Topps Comics: Feb, 1995 - No. 3, May, 1995 ($2.50, limited series)

1-3 3.00

FRANKENSTEIN, JR. (...& the Impossibles) (TV)
Gold Key: Jan, 1966 (Hanna-Barbera)

	GD	VG	FN	VF	VF/NM	NM-
1-Super hero (scarce)	12	24	36	84	127	170

FRANKENSTEIN MOBSTER
Image Comics: No. 0, Oct, 2003 - Present ($2.95)

0-6: 0-Two covers by Wheatley and Hughes; Wheatley-s/a. 1-Variant-c by Wieringo 3.00

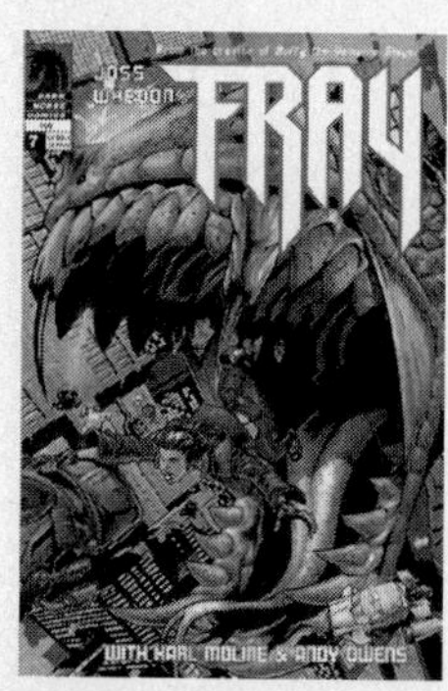

Fray #7 © Joss Whedon

Freaks of the Heartland #1 © Niles & Ruth

Freedom Fighters #3 © DC

	GD 2.0	VG 4.0	FN 6.0	VF 8.0	VF/NM 9.0	NM- 9.2

FRANKENSTEIN: OR THE MODERN PROMETHEUS
Caliber Press: 1994 ($2.95, one-shot)

	GD	VG	FN	VF	VF/NM	NM-
1						3.00

FRANK FRAZETTA FANTASY ILLUSTRATED (Magazine)
Quantum Cat Entertainment: Spring 1998 - No. 8 ($5.95, quarterly)

	GD	VG	FN	VF	VF/NM	NM-
1-Anthology; art by Corben, Horley, Jusko	1	2	3	4	5	7
1-Linsner variant-c						10.00
2-Battle Chasers by Madureira; Harris-a						8.00
2-Madureira Battle Chasers variant-c						12.00
3-8-Frazetta-c						6.00
3-Tony Daniel variant-c						15.00
5,6-Portacio variant-c, 7,8-Alex Nino variant-c						10.00
8-Alex Ross Chicago Comicon variant-c						10.00

FRANK FRAZETTA'S THUN'DA TALES
Fantagraphics Books: 1987 ($2.00, one-shot)

	GD	VG	FN	VF	VF/NM	NM-
1-Frazetta-r						6.00

FRANK FRAZETTA'S UNTAMED LOVE (Also see Untamed Love)
Fantagraphics Books: Nov, 1987 ($2.00, one-shot)

	GD	VG	FN	VF	VF/NM	NM-
1-Frazetta-r from 1950's romance comics						6.00

FRANKIE COMICS (...& Lana No. 13-15) (Formerly Movie Tunes; becomes Frankie Fuddle No. 16 on)
Marvel Comics (MgPC): No. 4, Wint, 1946-47 - No. 15, June, 1949

	GD	VG	FN	VF	VF/NM	NM-
4-Mitzi, Margie, Daisy app.	14	28	42	79	110	140
5-9	9	18	27	51	62	75
10-15: 13-Anti-Wertham editorial	8	16	24	43	54	65

FRANKIE DOODLE (See Sparkler, both series)
United Features Syndicate: No. 7, 1939

	GD	VG	FN	VF	VF/NM	NM-
Single Series 7	33	66	99	190	275	360

FRANKIE FUDDLE (Formerly Frankie & Lana)
Marvel Comics: No. 16, Aug, 1949 - No. 17, Nov, 1949

	GD	VG	FN	VF	VF/NM	NM-
16,17	8	16	24	43	54	65

FRANK LUTHER'S SILLY PILLY COMICS (See Jingle Dingle...)
Children's Comics (Maltex Cereal): 1950 (10¢)

	GD	VG	FN	VF	VF/NM	NM-
1-Characters from radio, records, & TV	8	16	24	43	54	65

FRANK MERRIWELL AT YALE (Speed Demons No. 5 on?)
Charlton Comics: June, 1955 - No. 4, Jan, 1956 (Also see Shadow Comics)

	GD	VG	FN	VF	VF/NM	NM-
1	7	14	21	37	46	55
2-4	5	10	15	24	30	35

FRANTIC (Magazine) (See Ratfink & Zany)
Pierce Publishing Co.: Oct, 1958 - V2#2, Apr, 1959 (Satire)

	GD	VG	FN	VF	VF/NM	NM-
V1#1	11	22	33	64	87	110
2	9	18	27	51	62	75
V2#1,2: 1-Burgos-a, Severin-c/a; Powell-a?	7	14	21	37	46	55

FRAY
Dark Horse Comics: June, 2001 - No. 8, July, 2003 ($2.99, limited series)

	GD	VG	FN	VF	VF/NM	NM-
1-Joss Whedon-s/Moline & Owens-a	1	2	3	5	6	8
1-DF Gold edition	2	4	6	10	12	15
2-8: 6-(3/02). 7-(4/03)						4.00

FREAK FORCE (Also see Savage Dragon)
Image Comics (Highbrow Ent.): Dec, 1993 - No. 18, July, 1995 ($1.95/$2.50)

	GD	VG	FN	VF	VF/NM	NM-
1-18-Superpatriot & Mighty Man in all; Erik Larsen scripts in all. 4-Vanguard app. 8-Begin $2.50-c. 9-Cyberforce-c & app. 13-Variant-c						3.00

FREAK FORCE (Also see Savage Dragon)
Image Comics: Apr, 1997 - No. 3, July, 1997 ($2.95)

	GD	VG	FN	VF	VF/NM	NM-
1-3-Larsen-s						3.00

FREAKS OF THE HEARTLAND
Dark Horse Comics: Jan, 2004 - No. 4, July, 2004 ($2.99)

	GD	VG	FN	VF	VF/NM	NM-
1-4-Steve Niles-s/Greg Ruth-a						3.00

FRECKLES AND HIS FRIENDS (See Crackajack Funnies, Famous Comics Cartoon Book, Honeybee Birdwhistle... & Red Ryder)

FRECKLES AND HIS FRIENDS
Standard Comics/Argo: No. 5, 11/47 - No. 12, 8/49; 11/55 - No. 4, 6/56

	GD	VG	FN	VF	VF/NM	NM-
5-Reprints	9	18	27	51	62	75
6-12-Reprints. 7-9-Airbrush-c (by Schomburg?). 11-Lingerie panels	6	12	18	31	38	45

NOTE: *Some copies of No. 8 & 9 contain a printing oddity. The negatives were elongated in the engraving process, probably to conform to page dimensions on the filler pages. Those pages only look normal when viewed at a 45 degree angle.*

	GD	VG	FN	VF	VF/NM	NM-
1(Argo,'55)-Reprints (NEA Service)	6	12	18	28	34	40
2-4	4	8	12	18	22	25

FREDDY (Formerly My Little Margie's Boy Friends) (Also see Blue Bird)
Charlton Comics: V2#12, June, 1958 - No. 47, Feb, 1965

	GD	VG	FN	VF	VF/NM	NM-
V2#12	4	8	12	24	32	40
13-15	3	6	9	16	20	25
16-47	2	4	6	11	14	18

FREDDY
Dell Publishing Co.: May-July, 1963 - No. 3, Oct-Dec, 1964

	GD	VG	FN	VF	VF/NM	NM-
1	3	7	10	21	28	35
2,3	3	6	9	16	20	24

FREDDY KRUEGER'S A NIGHTMARE ON ELM STREET
Marvel Comics: Oct, 1989 - No. 2, Dec, 1989 ($2.25, B&W, movie adaptation)

	GD	VG	FN	VF	VF/NM	NM-
1,2: Origin Freddy Krueger; Buckler/Alcala-a						3.00

FREDDY'S DEAD: THE FINAL NIGHTMARE
Innovation Publishing: Oct, 1991 - No. 3, Dec 1991 ($2.50, color mini-series, adapts movie)

	GD	VG	FN	VF	VF/NM	NM-
1-3: Dismukes (film poster artist) painted-c						3.00

FRED HEMBECK DESTROYS THE MARVEL UNIVERSE
Marvel Comics: July, 1989 ($1.50, one-shot)

	GD	VG	FN	VF	VF/NM	NM-
1-Punisher app.; Staton-i (5 pgs.)						3.00

FRED HEMBECK SELLS THE MARVEL UNIVERSE
Marvel Comics: Oct, 1990 ($1.25, one-shot)

	GD	VG	FN	VF	VF/NM	NM-
1-Punisher, Wolverine parodies; Hembeck/Austin-c						3.00

FREEDOM AGENT (Also see John Steele)
Gold Key: Apr, 1963 (12¢)

	GD	VG	FN	VF	VF/NM	NM-
1 (10054-304)-Painted-c	5	10	15	33	44	55

FREEDOM FIGHTERS (See Justice League of America #107,108)
National Periodical Publ./DC Comics: Mar-Apr, 1976 - No. 15, July-Aug, 1978

	GD	VG	FN	VF	VF/NM	NM-
1-Uncle Sam, The Ray, Black Condor, Doll Man, Human Bomb, & Phantom Lady begin (all former Quality characters)	2	4	6	12	16	20
2-9: 4,5-Wonder Woman x-over. 7-1st app. Crusaders	2	4	6	8	10	12
10-15: 10-Origin Doll Man; Cat-Man-c/story (4th app; 1st revival since Detective #325). 11-Origin The Ray. 12-Origin Firebrand. 13-Origin Black Condor. 14-Batgirl & Batwoman app. 15-Batgirl & Batwoman app.; origin Phantom Lady	2	4	6	9	11	14

NOTE: ***Buckler** c-5-11p, 13p, 14p.*

FREEMIND
Future Comics: No. 0, Aug, 2002; Nov, 2002 - No. 7, June, 2003 ($3.50)

	GD	VG	FN	VF	VF/NM	NM-
0-($2.25) Giordano-c						2.25
0-($2.25) Variant-c by Layton						2.25
1-7 ($3.50) 1-Two covers by Giordano & Layton; Giordano-a thru #3. 4,5-Leeke-a						3.50

FREE SPEECHES
Oni Press: Aug, 1998 ($2.95, one-shot)

	GD	VG	FN	VF	VF/NM	NM-
1-Speeches against comic censorship; Frank Miller-c						3.00

FREEX
Malibu Comics (Ultraverse): July, 1993 - No. 18, Mar, 1995 ($1.95)

	GD	VG	FN	VF	VF/NM	NM-
1-3,5-14,16-18: 1-Polybagged w/trading card. 2-Some were polybagged w/card. 6-Nightman-c/story. 7-2 pg. origin Hardcase by Zeck. 17-Rune app.						2.25
1-Holographic-c edition						6.00
1-Ultra 5,000 limited silver ink-c						3.00
4-($2.50, 48 pgs.)-Rune flip-c/story by B. Smith (3 pgs.); 3 pg. Night Man preview						2.50
15 ($3.50)-w/Ultraverse Premiere #9 flip book; Alec Swan & Rafferty app.						3.50
Giant Size 1 (1994, $2.50)-Prime app.						2.50

NOTE: ***Simonson** c-1.*

FRENZY (Magazine) (Satire)
Picture Magazine: Apr, 1958 - No. 6, Mar, 1959

	GD	VG	FN	VF	VF/NM	NM-
1	11	22	33	64	87	110
2-6	8	16	24	40	50	60

FRIDAY FOSTER
Dell Publishing Co.: October, 1972

	GD	VG	FN	VF	VF/NM	NM-
1	4	8	12	24	32	40

FRIENDLY GHOST, CASPER, THE (Becomes Casper... #254 on)

Frisky Animals #57 © STAR

From Beyond the Unknown #17 © DC

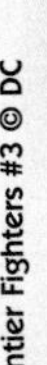
Frontier Fighters #3 © DC

Harvey Publications: Aug, 1958 - No. 224, Oct, 1982; No. 225, Oct, 1986 - No. 253, June, 1990

	GD 2.0	VG 4.0	FN 6.0	VF 8.0	VF/NM 9.0	NM- 9.2
1-Infinity-c	32	64	96	240	370	500
2	15	30	45	107	164	220
3-10: 6-X-Mas-c	9	18	27	60	85	110
11-20: 18-X-Mas-c	6	12	18	43	59	75
21-30	4	8	12	29	40	50
31-50	4	8	12	24	32	40
51-70,100: 54-X-Mas-c	3	6	9	19	25	32
71-99	3	6	9	16	21	26
101-131: 131-Last 12¢ issue	2	4	6	14	18	22
132-159	2	4	6	11	14	18
160-163: All 52 pg. Giants	3	6	9	16	20	24
164-199: 173,179,185-Cub Scout Specials	1	3	4	6	8	10
200	2	4	6	8	10	12
201-224	1	2	3	5	6	8
225-237: 230-X-mas-c. 232-Valentine's-c						5.00
238-253: 238-Begin $1.00-c. 238,244-Halloween-c. 243-Last new material						4.00

FRIENDS OF MAXX (Also see Maxx)
Image Comics (I Before E): Apr, 1996 - No. 3, Mar, 1997 ($2.95)

	GD 2.0	VG 4.0	FN 6.0	VF 8.0	VF/NM 9.0	NM- 9.2
1-3: Sam Kieth-c/a/scripts. 1-Featuring Dude Japan						3.00

FRIGHT
Atlas/Seaboard Periodicals: June, 1975 (Aug on inside)

	GD 2.0	VG 4.0	FN 6.0	VF 8.0	VF/NM 9.0	NM- 9.2
1-Origin/1st app. The Son of Dracula; Frank Thorne-c/a	1	3	4	6	8	10

FRIGHT NIGHT
Now Comics: Oct, 1988 - No. 22, 1990 ($1.75)

	GD 2.0	VG 4.0	FN 6.0	VF 8.0	VF/NM 9.0	NM- 9.2
1-22: 1,2 Adapts movie. 8, 9-Evil Ed horror photo-c from movie						2.25

FRIGHT NIGHT II
Now Comics: 1989 ($3.95, 52 pgs.)

	GD 2.0	VG 4.0	FN 6.0	VF 8.0	VF/NM 9.0	NM- 9.2
1-Adapts movie sequel						4.00

FRISKY ANIMALS (Formerly Frisky Fables; Super Cat #56 on)
Star Publications: No. 44, Jan, 1951 - No. 55, Sept, 1953

	GD 2.0	VG 4.0	FN 6.0	VF 8.0	VF/NM 9.0	NM- 9.2
44-Super Cat; L.B. Cole	24	48	72	135	195	255
45-Classic L. B. Cole-c	34	68	102	196	283	370
46-51,53-55: Super Cat. 54-Super Cat-c begin	22	44	66	125	180	235
52-L. B. Cole-c/a, 3 1/2 pgs.; X-Mas-c	24	48	72	135	195	255

NOTE: *All have* ***L. B. Cole****-c. No. 47-No Super Cat.* ***Disbrow*** *a-49, 52.* ***Fago*** *a-51.*

FRISKY ANIMALS ON PARADE (Formerly Parade Comics; becomes Superspook)
Ajax-Farrell Publ. (Four Star Comic Corp.): Sept, 1957 - No. 3, Dec-Jan, 1957-1958

	GD 2.0	VG 4.0	FN 6.0	VF 8.0	VF/NM 9.0	NM- 9.2
1-L. B. Cole-c	20	40	60	112	161	210
2-No L. B. Cole-c	9	18	27	54	70	85
3-L. B. Cole-c	17	34	51	95	135	175

FRISKY FABLES (Frisky Animals No. 44 on)
Premium Group/Novelty Publ./Star Publ. V5#4 on: Spring, 1945 - No. 43, Oct, 1950

	GD 2.0	VG 4.0	FN 6.0	VF 8.0	VF/NM 9.0	NM- 9.2
V1#1-Funny animal; Al Fago-c/a #1-38	22	44	66	123	177	230
2,3(Fall & Winter, 1945)	11	22	33	64	87	110
V2#1(#4, 4/46) - 9,11,12(#15, 3/47): 4-Flag-c	9	18	27	54	70	85
10-Christmas-c. 12-Valentine's-c	10	20	30	56	73	90
V3#1(#16, 4/47) - 12(#27, 3/48): 4-Flag-c. 7,9-Infinity-c. 10-X-Mas-c. 12-Washington crossing the Delaware parody-c	8	16	24	46	58	70
V4#1(#28, 4/48) - 7(#34, 2-3/49)	8	16	24	43	54	65
V5#1(#35, 4-5/49) - 4(#38, 10-11/49)	8	16	24	43	54	65
39-43-L. B. Cole-c; 40-Xmas-c	24	48	72	135	195	255
Accepted Reprint No. 43 (nd); L.B. Cole-c	9	18	27	54	70	85

FRITZI RITZ (See Comics On Parade, Single Series #5, 1(reprint), Tip Top & United Comics)

FRITZI RITZ (United Comics No. 8-26) (Also see Tip Topper for early Peanuts by Schulz)
United Features Synd./St. John No. 37-55/Dell No. 56 on:
Fall, 1948; No. 3, 1949 - No. 7, 1949; No. 27, 3-4/53 - No. 36, 9-10/54; No. 37 - No. 55, 9-11/57; No. 56, 12-2/57-58 - No. 59, 9-11/58

	GD 2.0	VG 4.0	FN 6.0	VF 8.0	VF/NM 9.0	NM- 9.2
nn(1948)-Special Fall issue; by Ernie Bushmiller	17	34	51	95	135	175
3(#1)	11	22	33	62	84	105
4-7(1949): 6-Abbie & Slats app.	9	18	27	51	62	75
27(1953)-33,37-50,57-59-Early Peanuts (1-4 pgs.) by Schulz. 29-Five pg. Abbie & Slats; 1 pg. Mamie by Russell Patterson. 38(9/55)-41(4/56)-Low print run	8	16	24	46	58	70
34-36,51-56: 36-1 pg. Mamie by Patterson	7	14	21	37	46	55

NOTE: *Abbie & Slats in #6,7, 27-31. Li'l Abner in #32-36.*

FROGMAN COMICS
Hillman Periodicals: Jan-Feb, 1952 - No. 11, May, 1953

	GD 2.0	VG 4.0	FN 6.0	VF 8.0	VF/NM 9.0	NM- 9.2
1	15	30	45	83	117	150
2	9	18	27	49	62	75
3,4,6-11: 4-Meskin-a	8	16	24	40	50	60
5-Krigstein-a	8	16	24	46	58	70

FROGMEN, THE
Dell Publishing Co.: No. 1258, Feb-Apr, 1962 - No. 11, Nov-Jan, 1964-65 (Painted-c)

	GD 2.0	VG 4.0	FN 6.0	VF 8.0	VF/NM 9.0	NM- 9.2
Four Color 1258(#1)-Evans-a	9	18	27	65	93	120
2,3-Evans-a; part Frazetta inks in #2,3	7	14	21	46	63	80
4,6-11	4	8	12	29	40	50
5-Toth-a	5	10	15	36	48	60

FROM BEYOND THE UNKNOWN
National Periodical Publications: 10-11/69 - No. 25, 11-12/73

	GD 2.0	VG 4.0	FN 6.0	VF 8.0	VF/NM 9.0	NM- 9.2
1	6	12	18	38	52	65
2-6	3	6	9	19	25	32
7-11: (64 pgs.) 7-Intro Col. Glenn Merrit	4	8	12	22	30	38
12-17: (52 pgs.) 13-Wood-a(i)(r). 17-Pres. Nixon-c	3	6	9	18	24	30
18-25: Star Rovers-r begin #18,19. Space Museum in #23-25	2	4	6	11	14	18

NOTE: ***N. Adams*** *c-3, 6, 8, 9.* ***Anderson*** *c-2, 4, 5, 10, 11i, 15-17, 22; reprints-3, 4, 6-8, 10, 11, 13-16, 24, 25.* ***Infantino*** *r-1-5, 7-19, 23-25; c-11p.* ***Kaluta*** *c-18, 19.* ***Gil Kane*** *a-9r.* ***Kubert*** *c-1, 7, 12-14.* ***Toth*** *a-2r.* ***Wood*** *a-13i. Photo c-22.*

FROM DUSK TILL DAWN (Movie)
Big Entertainment: 1996 ($4.95, one-shot)

	GD 2.0	VG 4.0	FN 6.0	VF 8.0	VF/NM 9.0	NM- 9.2
nn-Adaptation of the film; Brereton-c						5.00
nn-($9.95)Deluxe Ed. w/ new material						10.00

FROM HELL
Mad Love/Tundra Publishing/Kitchen Sink: 1991 - No. 11, Sept, 1998 (B&W)

	GD 2.0	VG 4.0	FN 6.0	VF 8.0	VF/NM 9.0	NM- 9.2
1-Alan Moore and Eddie Campbell's Jack The Ripper story collected from the Taboo anthology series	2	4	6	12	16	20
1-(2nd printing)	2	4	6	8	10	12
1-(3rd printing)	1	2	3	4	5	7
2	1	2	3	5	6	8
2-(2nd printing)						6.00
2-(3rd printing)						4.00
3-1st Kitchen Sink Press issue	1	2	3	5	6	8
3-(2nd printing)						5.00
4-10: 10-(8/96)	1	2	3	4	5	7
11-Dance of the Gull Catchers (9/98, $4.95) Epilogue	2	4	6	10	12	15
Tundra Publishing reprintings 1-5 ('92)	1	2	3	4	5	7
HC						125.00
HC Ltd. Edition of 1,000 (signed and numbered)						225.00
TPB-1st printing (11/99)						60.00
TPB-2nd printing (3/00)						50.00
TPB-3rd printing (11/00)						40.00
TPB-4th printing (7/01) Regular and movie covers						35.00
TPB-5th printing - Regular and movie covers						35.00

FROM HERE TO INSANITY (Satire) (Formerly Eh! #1-7) (See Frantic & Frenzy)
Charlton Comics: No. 8, Feb, 1955 - V3#1, 1956

	GD 2.0	VG 4.0	FN 6.0	VF 8.0	VF/NM 9.0	NM- 9.2
8	17	34	51	98	139	180
9	15	30	45	86	123	160
10-Ditko-c/a (3 pgs.)	24	48	72	138	199	260
11,12-All Kirby except 4 pgs.	34	68	102	193	279	365
V3#1(1956)-Ward-c/a(2) (signed McCartney); 5 pgs. Wolverton-a; 3 pgs. Ditko-a; magazine format (cover says "Crazy, Man, Crazy" and becomes Crazy, Man, Crazy with V2#2)	40	80	120	235	348	460

FROM THE PIT
Fantagor Press: 1994 ($4.95, one-shot, mature)

	GD 2.0	VG 4.0	FN 6.0	VF 8.0	VF/NM 9.0	NM- 9.2
1-R. Corben-a; HP Lovecraft back-up story	1	2	3	5	6	8

FRONTIER DOCTOR (TV)
Dell Publishing Co.: No. 877, Feb, 1958 (one-shot)

	GD 2.0	VG 4.0	FN 6.0	VF 8.0	VF/NM 9.0	NM- 9.2
Four Color 877-Toth-a, Rex Allen photo-c	11	22	33	77	114	150

FRONTIER FIGHTERS
National Periodical Publications: Sept-Oct, 1955 - No. 8, Nov-Dec, 1956

	GD 2.0	VG 4.0	FN 6.0	VF 8.0	VF/NM 9.0	NM- 9.2
1-Davy Crockett, Buffalo Bill (by Kubert), Kit Carson begin (Scarce)	57	114	171	356	546	735
2	40	80	120	235	348	460
3-8	39	78	117	222	324	425

Frontline Combat #4 © WMG

Fun Comics #10 © STAR

The Funnies #4 © DELL

NOTE: *Buffalo Bill by* ***Kubert*** *in all.*

FRONTIER ROMANCES
Avon Periodicals/I. W.: Nov-Dec, 1949 - No. 2, Feb-Mar, 1950 (Painted-c)

	GD 2.0	VG 4.0	FN 6.0	VF 8.0	VF/NM 9.0	NM- 9.2
1-Used in **SOTI**, pg. 180 (General reference) & illo. "Erotic spanking in a western comic book"	48	96	144	293	447	600
2 (Scarce)-Woodish-a by Stallman	39	78	117	222	324	425
I.W. Reprint #1-Reprints Avon's #1	4	8	12	27	36	45
I.W. Reprint #9-Reprints ?	3	6	9	18	23	28

FRONTIER SCOUT: DAN'L BOONE (Formerly Death Valley; The Masked Raider No. 14 on)
Charlton Comics: No. 10, Jan, 1956 - No. 13, Aug, 1956; V2#14, Mar, 1965

	GD 2.0	VG 4.0	FN 6.0	VF 8.0	VF/NM 9.0	NM- 9.2
10	10	20	30	56	73	90
11-13(1956)	6	12	18	31	38	45
V2#14(3/65)	5	10	14	20	24	28

FRONTIER TRAIL (The Rider No. 1-5)
Ajax/Farrell Publ.: No. 6, May, 1958

	GD 2.0	VG 4.0	FN 6.0	VF 8.0	VF/NM 9.0	NM- 9.2
6	6	12	18	28	34	40

FRONTIER WESTERN
Atlas Comics (PrPI): Feb, 1956 - No. 10, Aug, 1957

	GD 2.0	VG 4.0	FN 6.0	VF 8.0	VF/NM 9.0	NM- 9.2
1	20	40	60	112	161	210
2,3,6-Williamson-a, 4 pgs. each	14	28	42	79	110	140
4,7,9,10: 10-Check-a	9	18	27	54	70	85
5-Crandall, Baker, Davis-a; Williamson text illos	13	26	39	74	102	130
8-Crandall, Morrow, & Wildey-a	10	20	30	56	73	90

NOTE: ***Baker*** *a-9.* ***Colan*** *a-2, 6.* ***Drucker*** *a-3, 4.* ***Heath*** *c-5.* ***Maneely*** *c/a-2, 7, 9.* ***Maurera*** *a-2.* ***Romita*** *a-7.* ***Severin*** *c-6, 8, 10.* ***Tuska*** *a-2.* ***Wildey*** *a-5, 8. Ringo Kid in No. 4.*

FRONTLINE COMBAT
E. C. Comics: July-Aug, 1951 - No. 15, Jan, 1954

	GD 2.0	VG 4.0	FN 6.0	VF 8.0	VF/NM 9.0	NM- 9.2
1-Severin/Kurtzman-a	66	132	198	495	723	950
2	36	72	108	270	398	525
3	28	56	84	210	310	410
4-Used in **SOTI**, pg. 257; contains "Airburst" by Kurtzman which is his personal all-time favorite story	26	52	78	195	285	375
5	22	44	66	165	245	325
6-10	19	38	57	143	212	280
11-15	14	28	42	105	158	210

NOTE: ***Davis*** *a-in all; c-11, 12.* ***Evans*** *a-10-15.* ***Heath*** *a-1.* ***Kubert*** *a-14.* ***Kurtzman*** *a-1-5; c-1-9.* ***Severin*** *a-5-7, 9, 13, 15.* ***Severin/Elder*** *a-2-11; c-10.* ***Toth*** *a-8, 12.* ***Wood*** *a-1-4, 6-10, 12-15; c-13-15. Special issues: No. 7 (Iwo Jima), No. 9 (Civil War), No. 12 (Air Force).*
(Canadian reprints known; see Table of Contents.)

FRONTLINE COMBAT
Russ Cochran/Gemstone Publishing: Aug, 1995 - No. 14 ($2.00/$2.50)

	GD 2.0	VG 4.0	FN 6.0	VF 8.0	VF/NM 9.0	NM- 9.2
1-14-E.C. reprints in all						3.00

FRONT PAGE COMIC BOOK
Front Page Comics (Harvey): 1945

	GD 2.0	VG 4.0	FN 6.0	VF 8.0	VF/NM 9.0	NM- 9.2
1-Kubert-a; intro. & 1st app. Man in Black by Powell; Fuje-c	40	80	120	236	351	465

FROST AND FIRE (See DC Science Fiction Graphic Novel)

FROSTY THE SNOWMAN
Dell Publishing Co.: No. 359, Nov, 1951 - No. 1272, Dec-Feb?/1961-62

	GD 2.0	VG 4.0	FN 6.0	VF 8.0	VF/NM 9.0	NM- 9.2
Four Color 359 (#1)	10	20	30	73	107	140
Four Color 435,514,601,661	6	12	18	40	55	70
Four Color 748,861,950,1065,1153,1272	6	12	18	38	52	65

FRUITMAN SPECIAL
Harvey Publications: Dec, 1969 (68 pgs.)

	GD 2.0	VG 4.0	FN 6.0	VF 8.0	VF/NM 9.0	NM- 9.2
1-Funny super hero	4	8	12	24	32	40

F-TROOP (TV)
Dell Publishing Co.: Aug, 1966 - No. 7, Aug, 1967 (All have photo-c)

	GD 2.0	VG 4.0	FN 6.0	VF 8.0	VF/NM 9.0	NM- 9.2
1	11	22	33	77	114	150
2-7	7	14	21	46	63	80

FUGITIVES FROM JUSTICE
St. John Publishing Co.: Feb, 1952 - No. 5, Oct, 1952

	GD 2.0	VG 4.0	FN 6.0	VF 8.0	VF/NM 9.0	NM- 9.2
1	22	44	66	123	177	230
2-Matt Baker-r/Northwest Mounties #2; Vic Flint strip reprints begin	22	44	66	123	177	230
3-Reprints panel from Authentic Police Cases that was used in **SOTI** with changes; Tuska-a	21	42	63	118	169	220
4	10	20	30	60	80	100
5-Last Vic Flint-r; bondage-c	12	24	36	69	95	120

FUGITOID
Mirage Studios: 1985 (B&W, magazine size, one-shot)

	GD 2.0	VG 4.0	FN 6.0	VF 8.0	VF/NM 9.0	NM- 9.2
1-Ties into Teenage Mutant Ninja Turtles #5	1	2	3	4	5	7

FULL OF FUN
Red Top (Decker Publ.)(Farrell)/I. W. Enterprises: Aug, 1957 - No. 2, Nov, 1957; 1964

	GD 2.0	VG 4.0	FN 6.0	VF 8.0	VF/NM 9.0	NM- 9.2
1(1957)-Funny animal; Dave Berg-a	7	14	21	37	46	55
2-Reprints Bingo, the Monkey Doodle Boy	5	10	15	22	26	30
8-I.W. Reprint('64)	2	4	6	10	12	15

FUN AT CHRISTMAS (See March of Comics No. 138)

FUN CLUB COMICS (See Interstate Theatres...)

FUN COMICS (Formerly Holiday Comics #1-8; Mighty Bear #13 on)
Star Publications: No. 9, Jan, 1953 - No. 12, Oct, 1953

	GD 2.0	VG 4.0	FN 6.0	VF 8.0	VF/NM 9.0	NM- 9.2
9-(25¢ Giant)-L. B. Cole X-Mas-c; X-Mas issue	24	48	72	138	199	260
10-12-L. B. Cole-c. 12-Mighty Bear-c/story	20	40	60	112	161	210

FUNDAY FUNNIES (See Famous TV..., and Harvey Hits No. 35,40)

FUN-IN (TV)(Hanna-Barbera)
Gold Key: Feb, 1970 - No. 10, Jan, 1972; No. 11, 4/74 - No. 15, 12/74

	GD 2.0	VG 4.0	FN 6.0	VF 8.0	VF/NM 9.0	NM- 9.2
1-Dastardly & Muttley in Their Flying Machines; Perils of Penelope Pitstop in #1-4; It's the Wolf in all	7	14	21	51	71	90
2-4,6-Cattanooga Cats in 2-4	4	8	12	25	33	42
5,7-Motormouse & Autocat, Dastardly & Muttley in both; It's the Wolf in #7	4	8	12	28	38	48
8,10-The Harlem Globetrotters, Dastardly & Muttley in #10	4	8	12	28	38	48
9-Where's Huddles?, Dastardly & Muttley, Motormouse & Autocat app.	4	8	12	28	38	48
11-Butch Cassidy	4	8	12	22	30	38
12-15: 12,15-Speed Buggy. 13-Hair Bear Bunch. 14-Inch High Private Eye	4	8	12	22	30	38

FUNKY PHANTOM, THE (TV)
Gold Key: Mar, 1972 - No. 13, Mar, 1975 (Hanna-Barbera)

	GD 2.0	VG 4.0	FN 6.0	VF 8.0	VF/NM 9.0	NM- 9.2
1	6	12	18	40	55	70
2-5	3	7	10	21	28	35
6-13	3	6	9	16	21	26

FUNLAND
Ziff-Davis (Approved Comics): No date (1940s) (25¢)

	GD 2.0	VG 4.0	FN 6.0	VF 8.0	VF/NM 9.0	NM- 9.2
nn-Contains games, puzzles, cut-outs, etc.	19	38	57	107	154	200

FUNLAND COMICS
Croyden Publishers: 1945

	GD 2.0	VG 4.0	FN 6.0	VF 8.0	VF/NM 9.0	NM- 9.2
1-Funny animal	16	32	48	89	127	165

FUNNIES, THE (New Funnies No. 65 on)
Dell Publishing Co.: Oct, 1936 - No. 64, May, 1942

	GD 2.0	VG 4.0	FN 6.0	VF 8.0	VF/NM 9.0	NM- 9.2
1-Tailspin Tommy, Mutt & Jeff, Alley Oop (1st app?), Capt. Easy (1st app.), Don Dixon begin	381	762	1143	2096	3048	4000
2 (11/36)-Scribbly by Mayer begins (see Popular Comics #6 for 1st app.)	171	342	513	941	1371	1800
3	119	238	357	655	953	1250
4,5: 4(1/37)-Christmas-c	90	180	270	495	723	950
6-10	69	138	207	380	553	725
11-20: 16-Christmas-c	64	128	192	352	514	675
21-29: 25-Crime Busters by McWilliams(4pgs.)	51	102	153	281	411	540
30-John Carter of Mars (origin/1st app.) begins by Edgar Rice Burroughs; Warner Bros.' Bosko-c (4/39)	138	276	414	863	1332	1800
31-44: 33-John Coleman Burroughs art begins on John Carter. 34-Last funny-c. 35-(9/39)-Mr. District Attorney begins; based on radio show; 1st cover app. John Carter of Mars	77	154	231	481	741	1000
45-Origin/1st app. Phantasmo, the Master of the World (Dell's 1st super-hero, 7/40) & his sidekick Whizzer McGee	92	184	276	575	888	1200
46-50: 46-The Black Knight begins, ends #62	55	110	165	340	520	700
51-56-Last ERB John Carter of Mars	48	96	144	293	447	600
57-Intro. & origin Captain Midnight (7/41)	345	690	1035	2243	3622	5000
58-60: 58-Captain Midnight-c begin, end #63	98	196	294	613	944	1275
61-Andy Panda begins by Walter Lantz	89	178	267	556	853	1150
62,63: 63-Last Captain Midnight-c; bondage-c	67	134	201	419	647	875
64-Format change; Oswald the Rabbit, Felix the Cat, Li'l Eight Ball app.; origin & 1st app. Woody Woodpecker in Oswald; last Capt. Midnight; Oswald, Andy Panda, Li'l Eight Ball-c	123	246	369	769	1185	1600

NOTE: ***Mayer*** *c-26, 48.* ***McWilliams*** *art in many issues on "Rex King of the Deep". Alley Oop c-17, 20. Captain Midnight c-57(i/2), 58-63. John Carter c-35-37, 40. Phantasmo c-45-56, 57(1/2), 58-61(part). Rex King c-38, 39,*

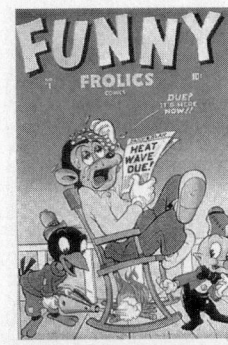

Funny Frolics #1 © MAR

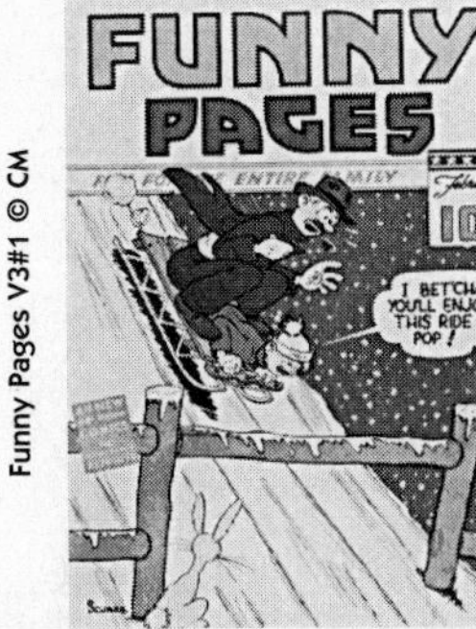

Funny Pages V3#1 © CM

Funny Stuff #26 © DC

GD 2.0 VG 4.0 FN 6.0 VF 8.0 VF/NM 9.0 NM- 9.2

GD 2.0 VG 4.0 FN 6.0 VF 8.0 VF/NM 9.0 NM- 9.2

42. Tailspin Tommy c-41.

FUNNIES ANNUAL, THE
Avon Periodicals: 1959 ($1.00, approx. 7x10", B&W; tabloid-size)

1-(Rare)-Features the best newspaper comic strips of the year: Archie, Snuffy Smith, Beetle Bailey, Henry, Blondie, Steve Canyon, Buz Sawyer, The Little King, Hi & Lois, Popeye, & others. Also has a chronological history of the comics from 2000 B.C. to 1959. 44 88 132 268 409 550

FUNNIES ON PARADE (See Promotional Comics section)

FUNNY ANIMALS (See Fawcett's Funny Animals)
Charlton Comics: Sept, 1984 - No. 2, Nov, 1984

1,2-Atomic Mouse-r; low print 6.00

FUNNYBONE (... The Laugh-Book of Comical Comics)
La Salle Publishing Co.: 1944 (25¢, 132 pgs.)

nn 30 60 90 170 245 320

FUNNY BOOK (...Magazine for Young Folks) (Hocus Pocus No. 9)
Parents' Magazine Press (Funny Book Publishing Corp.):
Dec, 1942 - No. 9, Aug-Sept, 1946 (Comics, stories, puzzles, games)

1-Funny animal; Alice In Wonderland app. 15 30 45 86 123 160
2-Gulliver in Giant-Land 9 18 27 54 70 85
3-9: 4-Advs. of Robin Hood. 9-Hocus-Pocus strip 8 16 24 43 54 65

FUNNY COMICS
Modern Store Publ.: 1955 (7¢, 5x7", 36 pgs.)

1-Funny animal 4 8 12 27 36 45

FUNNY COMIC TUNES (See Funny Tunes)

FUNNY FABLES
Decker Publications (Red Top Comics): Aug, 1957 - V2#2, Nov, 1957

V1#1 6 12 18 31 38 45
V1#2,V2#1,2: V1#2 (11/57)-Reissue of V1#1 5 10 14 20 24 28

FUNNY FILMS (Features funny animal characters from films)
American Comics Group(Michel Publ./Titan Publ.): Sept-Oct, 1949 - No. 29, May-June, 1954 (No. 1-4: 52 pgs.)

1-Puss An' Boots, Blunderbunny begin 20 40 60 112 161 210
2 11 22 33 64 87 110
3-10: 3-X-Mas-c 9 18 27 51 62 75
11-20 7 14 21 35 43 50
21-29 6 12 18 27 33 38

FUNNY FOLKS (Hollywood... on cover only No. 16-26; becomes Hollywood Funny Folks No. 27 on)
National Periodical Publ.: April-May, 1946 - No. 26, June-July, 1950 (52 pgs., #16 on)

1-Nutsy Squirrel begins (1st app.) by Rube Grossman; Grossman-a in most issues 40 80 120 235 348 460
2 20 40 60 112 161 210
3-5: 4-1st Nutsy Squirrel-c 15 30 45 83 117 150
6-10: 6,9-Nutsy Squirrel-c begin 11 22 33 64 87 110
11-26: 16-Begin 52 pg. issues (10-11/48) 10 20 30 56 73 90

NOTE: ***Sheldon Mayer** a-in some issues. **Post** a-18. Christmas c-12.*

FUNNY FROLICS
Timely/Marvel Comics (SPI): Summer, 1945 - No. 5, Dec, 1946

1-Sharpy Fox, Puffy Pig, Krazy Krow 24 48 72 138 199 260
2 13 26 39 74 102 130
3,4 10 20 30 58 77 95
5-Kurtzman-a 11 22 33 64 87 110

FUNNY FUNNIES
Nedor Publishing Co.: April, 1943 (68 pgs.)

1-Funny animals; Peter Porker app. 20 40 60 112 161 210

FUNNYMAN (Also see Cisco Kid Comics & Extra Comics)
Magazine Enterprises: Dec, 1947; No. 1, Jan, 1948 - No. 6, Aug, 1948

nn(12/47)-Prepublication B&W undistributed copy by Siegel & Shuster-(5-3/4x8"), 16 pgs.; Sold at auction in 1997 for $575.00
1-Siegel & Shuster-a in all; Dick Ayers 1st pro work (as assistant) on 1st few issues 46 92 138 281 428 575
2 29 58 87 164 237 310
3-6 24 48 72 135 195 255

FUNNY MOVIES (See 3-D Funny Movies)

FUNNY PAGES (Formerly The Comics Magazine)
Comics Magazine Co./Ultem Publ.(Chesler)/Centaur Publications:
No. 6, Nov, 1936 - No. 42, Oct, 1940

V1#6 (nn, nd)-The Clock begins (2 pgs., 1st app.), ends #11; The Clock is the 1st masked comic book hero 238 476 714 1488 2294 3100
7-11 92 184 276 575 888 1200
V2#1-V2#3: V2#1 (9/37)(V2#2 on-c; V2#1 in indicia). V2#2 (10/37)(V2#3 on-c; V2#2 in indicia). V2#3(11/37)-5 65 130 195 406 628 850
6(1st Centaur, 3/38) 90 180 270 563 869 1175
7-9 65 130 195 406 628 850
10(Scarce, 9/38)-1st app. of The Arrow by Gustavson (Blue costume) 303 606 909 1970 3185 4400
11,12 119 238 357 744 1147 1550
V3#1-Bruce Wayne prototype in "Case of the Missing Heir," by Bob Kane, 3 months before app. Batman (See Det. Pic. Stories #5) 123 246 369 769 1185 1600
2-6,8: 6,8-Last funny covers 108 216 324 675 1038 1400
7-1st Arrow-c (9/39) 246 492 738 1538 2369 3200
9-Tarpe Mills jungle-c 113 226 339 706 1091 1475
10-2nd Arrow-c 192 384 576 1200 1850 2500
V4#1(1/40, Arrow-c)-(Rare)-The Owl & The Phantom Rider app.; origin Mantoka, Maker of Magic by Jack Cole. Mad Ming begins, ends #42; Tarpe Mills-a 246 492 738 1538 2369 3200
35-Classic Arrow-c 246 492 738 1538 2369 3200
36-38-Mad Ming-c 110 220 330 688 1057 1425
39-41-Arrow-c 181 362 543 1131 1741 2350
42 (Scarce,10/40)-Last Arrow; Arrow-c 189 378 567 1181 1816 2450

NOTE: ***Biro** c-V2#9. **Burgos** c-V3#10. **Jack Cole** a-V2#3, 7, 8, 10, 11, V3#2, 6, 9, 10, V4#1, 37; c-V3#2, 4. **Eisner** a-V1#7, 8?, 10. **Ken Ernst** a-V1#7, 8. **Everett** a-V2#11 (illos). **Filchock** c-V2#10, V3#6. **Gill Fox** a-V2#11. **Sid Greene** a-39. **Guardineer** a-V2#2, 3, 5. **Gustavson** a-V2#5, 11, 12, V3#1-10, 35, 38-42; c-V3#7, 35, 39-42. **Bob Kane** a-V3#1. **McWilliams** a-V2#12, V3#1, 3-6. **Tarpe Mills** a-V3#8-10, V4#1; c-V3#9. **Ed Moore Jr.** a-V2#12. **Schwab** c-V3#1. **Bob Wood** a-V2#2, 3, 8, 11, V3#6, 9, 10; c-V2#6, 7. Arrow c-V3#7, 10, V4#1, 35, 40-42.*

FUNNY PICTURE STORIES (Comic Pages V3#4 on)
Comics Magazine Co./Centaur Publications: Nov, 1936 - V3#3, May, 1939

V1#1-The Clock begins (c-feature)(see Funny Pages for 1st app.) 324 648 972 2106 3403 4700
2 119 238 357 744 1147 1550
3-7(6/37): 4-Eisner-a; X-Mas-c. 7-Racial humor-c 81 162 243 506 778 1050
V2#1 (9/37; V1#10 on-c; V2#1 in indicia)-Jack Strand begins 55 110 165 340 520 700
2 (10/37; V1#11 on-c; V2#2 in indicia) 55 110 165 340 520 700
3-5,7-11(11/38): 4-Xmas-c 48 96 144 293 447 600
6-(1st Centaur, 3/38) 81 162 243 506 778 1050
V3#1(1/39)-3 46 92 138 281 428 575

NOTE: ***Biro** c-V2#1, 8, 9, 11. **Guardineer** a-V1#11; c-V2#6, V3#5. **Bob Wood** c/a-V1#11, V2#2; c-V2#3, 5.*

FUNNY STUFF (Becomes The Dodo & the Frog No. 80)
All-American/National Periodical Publications No. 7 on: Summer, 1944 - No. 79, July-Aug, 1954 (#1-7 are quarterly)

1-The Three Mouseketeers (ends #28) & The "Terrific Whatzit" begin; Sheldon Mayer-a; Grossman-a in most issues 89 178 267 556 853 1150
2-Sheldon Mayer-a 42 84 126 256 391 525
3-5: 3-Flash parody. 5-All Mayer-a/scripts issue 31 62 93 175 253 330
6-10 10-(6/46) 21 42 63 118 169 220
11-17,19 16 32 48 89 127 165
18-The Dodo & the Frog (2/47, 1st app?) begin?; X-Mas-c 28 56 84 158 229 300
19-1st Dodo & the Frog-c (3/47) 19 38 57 107 154 200
20-2nd Dodo & the Frog-c (4/47) 14 28 42 79 110 140
21,23-30: 24-Infinity-c. 30-Christmas-c 11 22 33 62 84 105
22-Superman cameo 40 80 120 233 342 450
31-79: 70-1st Bo Bunny by Mayer & begins 10 20 30 56 73 90

NOTE: ***Mayer** a-1-8, 55, ,57, 58, 61, 62, 64, 65, 68, 70, 72, 74-79; c-2, 5, 6, 8.*

FUNNY STUFF STOCKING STUFFER
DC Comics: Mar, 1985 ($1.25, 52 pgs.)

1-Almost every DC funny animal featured 4.00

FUNNY 3-D
Harvey Publications: December, 1953 (25¢, came with 2 pair of glasses)

1-Shows cover in 3-D on inside 12 24 36 69 95 120

FUNNY TUNES (Animated Funny Comic Tunes No. 16-22; Funny Comic Tunes No. 23, on covers only; formerly Krazy Komics #15; Oscar No. 24 on)
U.S.A. Comics Magazine Corp. (Timely): No. 16, Summer, 1944 - No. 23, Fall, 1946

16-Silly Seal, Ziggy Pig, Krazy Krow begin 15 30 45 86 123 160
17 (Fall/44)-Becomes Gay Comics #18 on? 12 24 36 69 95 120
18-22: 21-Super Rabbit app. 10 20 30 58 77 95

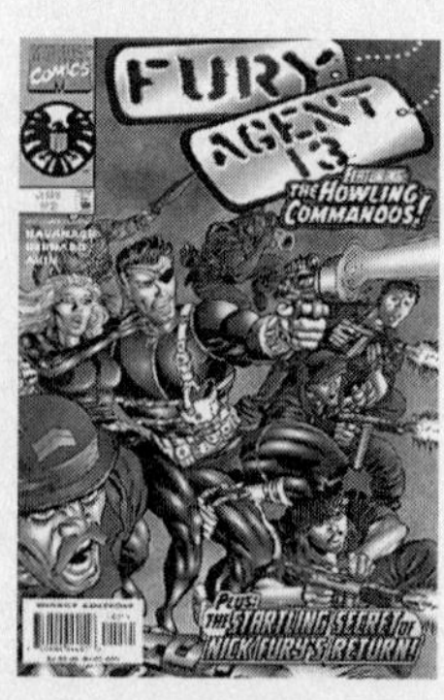

Fury/Agent 13 #2 © MAR

Fused #2 © Steve Niles

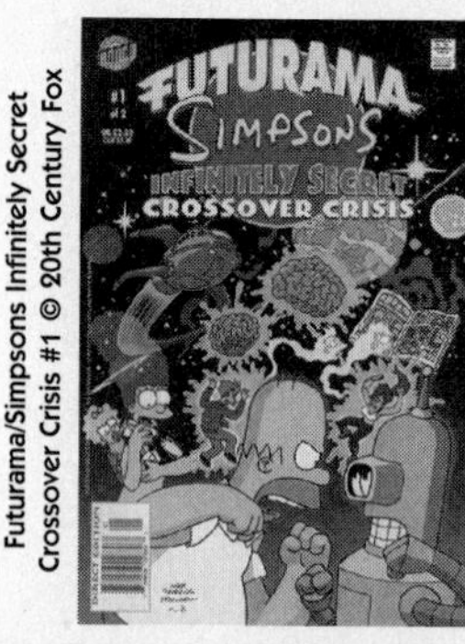

Futurama/Simpsons Infinitely Secret Crossover Crisis #1 © 20th Century Fox

GD VG FN VF VF/NM NM-
2.0 4.0 6.0 8.0 9.0 9.2

23-Kurtzman-a 11 22 33 64 87 110

FUNNY TUNES (Becomes Space Comics #4 on)
Avon Periodicals: July, 1953 - No. 3, Dec-Jan, 1953-54
1-Space Mouse, Peter Rabbit, Merry Mouse, Spotty the Pup, Cicero the Cat begin; all continue in Space Comics 11 22 33 63 84 105
2,3 8 16 24 46 58 70

FUNNY WORLD
Marbak Press: 1947 - No. 3, 1948
1-The Berrys, The Toodles & other strip-r begin 9 18 27 51 62 75
2,3 6 12 18 31 38 45

FUNTASTIC WORLD OF HANNA-BARBERA, THE (TV)
Marvel Comics Group: Dec, 1977 - No. 3, June, 1978 ($1.25, oversized)
1-3: 1-The Flintstones Christmas Party(12/77). 2-Yogi Bear's Easter Parade(3/78). 3-Laff-a-lympics(6/78) 4 8 12 29 40 50

FUN TIME
Ace Periodicals: Spring, 1953; No. 2, Sum, 1953; No. 3(nn), Fall, 1953; No. 4, Wint, 1953-54
1-(25¢, 100 pgs.)-Funny animal 18 36 54 102 146 190
2-4 (All 25¢, 100 pgs.) 15 30 45 83 117 150

FUN WITH SANTA CLAUS (See March of Comics No. 11, 108, 325)

FURTHER ADVENTURES OF CYCLOPS AND PHOENIX (Also see Adventures of Cyclops and Phoenix, Uncanny X-Men & X-Men)
Marvel Comics: June, 1996 - No. 4, Sept, 1996 ($1.95, limited series)
1-4: Origin of Mr. Sinister; Milligan scripts; John Paul Leon-c/a(p). 2-4-Apocalypse app. 3.00
Trade Paperback (1997, $14.99) r/1-4 15.00

FURTHER ADVENTURES OF INDIANA JONES, THE (Movie) (Also see Indiana Jones and the Last Crusade & Indiana Jones and the Temple of Doom)
Marvel Comics Group: Jan, 1983 - No. 34, Mar, 1986
1-Byrne/Austin-a; Austin-c 4.00
2-34: 2-Byrne/Austin-c/a 2.50
NOTE: ***Austin*** *a-1i, 2i, 6i, 9i; c-1, 2i, 6i, 9i.* ***Byrne*** *a-1p, 2p; c-2p.* ***Chaykin*** *a-6p; c-6p, 8p-10p.* ***Ditko*** *a-21p, 25-28, 34.* ***Golden*** *c-24, 25.* ***Simonson*** *c-9. Painted c-14.*

FURTHER ADVENTURES OF NYOKA, THE JUNGLE GIRL, THE (See Nyoka)
AC Comics: 1988 - No. 5, 1989 ($1.95, color; $2.25/$2.50, B&W)
1-5 : 1,2-Bill Black-a plus reprints. 3-Photo-c. 5-(B&W)-Reprints plus movie photos 2.50

FURY (Straight Arrow's Horse...) (See A-1 No. 119)

FURY (TV) (See March Of Comics #200)
Dell Publishing Co./Gold Key: No. 781, Mar, 1957 - Nov, 1962 (All photo-c)
Four Color 781 9 18 27 65 93 120
Four Color 885,975,1031,1080,1133,1172,1218,1296 8 16 24 55 78 100
01292-208(#1-'62), 10020-211(11/62-G.K.) 8 16 24 53 74 95

FURY
Marvel Comics: May, 1994 ($2.95, one-shot)
1-Iron Man, Red Skull, FF, Hatemonger, Logan app.; Origin Nick Fury 3.00

FURY (Volume 3)
Marvel Comics (MAX): Nov, 2001 - No. 6, Apr, 2002 ($2.99, mature content)
1-6-Ennis-s/Robertson-a 3.00

FURY/ AGENT 13
Marvel Comics: June, 1998 - No. 2, July, 1998 ($2.99, limited series)
1,2-Nick Fury returns 3.00

FURY OF FIRESTORM, THE (Becomes Firestorm The Nuclear Man on cover with #50, in indicia with #65) (Also see Firestorm)
DC Comics: June, 1982 - No. 64, Oct, 1987 (75¢ on)
1-Intro The Black Bison; brief origin 6.00
2-40,43-64: 4-JLA x-over. 17-1st app. Firehawk. 21-Death of Killer Frost. 22-Origin. 23-Intro. Byte. 24-(6/84)-1st app. Blue Devil & Bug (origin); origin Byte. 34-1st app./origin Killer Frost II. 39-Weasel's ID revealed. 48-Intro. Moonbow. 53-Origin/1st app. Silver Shade. 55,56-Legends x-over. 58-1st app./origin new Parasite 2.50
41,42-Crisis x-over 3.00
61-Test cover variant; Superman logo 4 8 12 24 32 40
Annual 1-4: 1(1983), 2(1984), 3(1985), 4(1986) 3.00
NOTE: ***Colan*** *a-19p, Annual 4p.* ***Giffen*** *a-Annual 4p.* ***Gil Kane*** *c-30.* ***Nino*** *a-37.* ***Tuska*** *a-(p)-17, 18, 32, 45.*

FURY OF SHIELD
Marvel Comics: Apr, 1995 - No. 4, July, 1995 ($2.50/$1.95, limited series)
1 ($2.50)-Foil-c 3.00
2-4: 4-Bagged w/ decoder 2.50

FUSED
Image Comics: Mar, 2002 - No. 4, Jan, 2003 ($2.95)
1-4-Steve Niles-s. 1,2-Paul Lee-a. 3-Brad Rader-a. 4-Templesmith-a 3.00
Canned Heat TPB (Dark Horse, 6/04, $12.95) r/series; Dan Wickline intro. 13.00

FUSED
Dark Horse Comics: Dec, 2003 - No. 4, Mar, 2004 ($2.95)
1-4-Steve Niles-s/Josh Medors-a. 1-Powell-c 3.00

FUSION
Eclipse Comics: Jan, 1987 - No. 17, Oct, 1989 ($2.00, B&W, Baxter paper)
1-17: 11-The Weasel Patrol begins (1st app.?) 2.25

FUTURAMA (TV)
Bongo Comics: 2000 - Present ($2.50, bi-monthly)
1-Based on the FOX-TV animated series; Groening/Morrison-c 3.50
1-San Diego Comic-Con Premiere Edition 5.00
2-19: 8-CGC cover spoof; X-Men parody 3.00
Futurama Adventures TPB (2004, $14.95) r/#5-9 15.00
Futurama-O-Rama TPB (2002, $12.95) r/#1-4; sketch pages of Fry's development 13.00

FUTURAMA/SIMPSONS INFINITELY SECRET CROSSOVER CRISIS (TV)
Bongo Comics: 2002 - No. 2, 2002 ($2.50, limited series)
1,2-Evil Brain Spawns put Futurama crew into the Simpsons' Springfield 2.50

FUTURE COMICS
David McKay Publications: June, 1940 - No. 4, Sept, 1940
1-(6/40, 64 pgs.)-Origin The Phantom (1st in comics) (4 pgs.); The Lone Ranger (8 pgs.) & Saturn Against the Earth (4 pgs.) begin 277 554 831 1731 2666 3600
2 131 262 393 819 1260 1700
3,4 100 200 300 625 963 1300

FUTURE COP L.A.P.D. (Electronic Arts video game) (Also see PromotionalComics section)
DC Comics (WildStorm): Jan, 1999 ($4.95, magazine sized)
1-Stories & art by various 5.00

FUTURE WORLD COMICS
George W. Dougherty: Summer, 1946 - No. 2, Fall, 1946
1,2: H. C. Kiefer-c; preview of the World of Tomorrow 33 66 99 190 275 360

FUTURE WORLD COMIX (Warren Presents...)
Warren Publications: Sept, 1978 (B&W magazine, 84 pgs.)
1-Corben, Maroto, Morrow, Nino, Sutton-a; Todd-c/a; contains nudity panels 2 4 6 8 10 12

FUTURIANS, THE (See Marvel Graphic Novel #9)
Lodestone Publishing/Eternity Comics: Sept, 1985 - No. 3, 1985 ($1.50)
1-3: Indicia title "Dave Cockrum's..." 2.25
Graphic Novel 1 ($9.95, Eternity)-r/#1-3, plus never published #4 issue 10.00

G-8 (Listed at G-Eight)

GABBY (Formerly Ken Shannon) (Teen humor)
Quality Comics Group: No. 11, Jul, 1953; No. 2, Sep, 1953 - No. 9, Sep, 1954
11(#1)(7/53) 8 16 24 46 58 70
2 6 12 18 28 34 40
3-9 5 10 15 23 28 32

GABBY GOB (See Harvey Hits No. 85, 90, 94, 97, 100, 103, 106, 109)

GABBY HAYES ADVENTURE COMICS
Toby Press: Dec, 1953
1-Photo-c 16 32 48 89 127 165

GABBY HAYES WESTERN (Movie star)(See Monte Hale, Real Western Hero & Western Hero)
Fawcett Publications/Charlton Comics No. 51 on: Nov, 1948 - No. 50, Jan, 1953; No. 51, Dec, 1954 - No. 59, Jan, 1957
1-Gabby & his horse Corker begin; photo front/back-c begin 51 102 153 311 476 640
2 27 54 81 152 219 285
3-5 19 38 57 107 154 200
6-10: 9-Young Falcon begins 15 30 45 86 123 160
11-20: 19-Last photo back-c 12 24 36 71 98 125
21-49: 20,22,24,26,28,29-(52 pgs.) 10 20 30 58 77 95
50-(1/53)-Last Fawcett issue; last photo-c? 11 22 33 64 87 110
51-(12/54)-1st Charlton issue; photo-c 11 22 33 66 91 115
52-59(1955-57): 53,55-Photo-c. 58-Swayze-a 8 16 24 46 58 70

GAGS

Gabby Hayes Western #4 © FAW

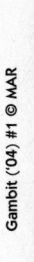

Gambit ('04) #1 © MAR

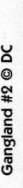

Gangland #2 © DC

GD 2.0 | VG 4.0 | FN 6.0 | VF 8.0 | VF/NM 9.0 | NM- 9.2

United Features Synd./Triangle Publ. No. 9 on: Jul, 1937 - V3#10, Oct, 1944 (13-3/4x10-3/4")
1(7/37)-52 pgs.; 20 pgs. Grin & Bear It, Fellow Citizen 10 20 30 56 73 90
V1#9 (36 pgs.) (7/42) 6 12 18 28 34 40
V3#10 5 10 15 24 30 35

GALACTIC
Dark Horse Comics: Aug, 2003 - Present ($2.99)
1-3-Krueger-s/Greene-a/Pearson-c 3.00

GALACTICA: THE NEW MILLENNIUM
Realm Press: Sept, 1999 ($2.99)
1-Stories by Shooter, Braden, Kuhoric 3.00

GALACTIC GUARDIANS
Marvel Comics: July, 1994 - No. 4, Oct, 1994 ($1.50, limited series)
1-4 2.25

GALACTIC WARS COMIX (Warren Presents... on cover)
Warren Publications: Dec, 1978 (B&W magazine, 84 pgs.)
nn-Wood, Williamson-r; Battlestar Galactica/Flash Gordon photo/text stories 2 4 6 8 10 12

GALACTUS THE DEVOURER
Marvel Comics: Sept, 1999 - No. 6, Mar, 2000 ($3.50/$2.50, limited series)
1-($3.50) L. Simonson-s/Muth & Sienkiewicz-a 3.50
2-5-($2.50) Buscema & Sienkiewicz-a 2.50
6-($3.50) Death of Galactus; Buscema & Sienkiewicz-a 3.50

GALAXIA (Magazine)
Astral Publ.: 1981 ($2.50, B&W, 52 pgs.)
1-Buckler/Giordano-c; Texeira/Guice-a; 1st app. Astron, Sojourner, Bloodwing, Warlords; Buckler-s/a 2 4 6 8 10 12

GALLANT MEN, THE (TV)
Gold Key: Oct, 1963 (Photo-c)
1(1008-310)-Manning-a 4 8 12 22 30 38

GALLEGHER, BOY REPORTER (Disney, TV)
Gold Key: May, 1965
1(10149-505)-Photo-c 3 6 9 18 24 30

GAMBIT (See X-Men #266 & X-Men Annual #14)
Marvel Comics: Dec, 1993 - No. 4, Mar, 1994 ($2.00, limited series)
1-($2.50)-Lee Weeks-c/a in all; gold foil stamped-c. 5.00
1 (Gold) 2 4 6 10 12 15
2-4 3.00

GAMBIT
Marvel Comics: Sept, 1997 - No. 4, Dec, 1997 ($2.50, limited series)
1-4-Janson-a/ Mackie & Kavanagh-s 3.00

GAMBIT
Marvel Comics: Feb, 1999 - No. 25, Feb, 2001 ($2.99/$1.99)
1-($2.99) Five covers; Nicieza-a/Skroce-a 4.00
2-11,13-16-($1.99): 2-Two covers (Skroce & Adam Kubert) 2.50
12-($2.99) 3.50
17-24: 17-Begin $2.25-c. 21-Mystique-c/app. 2.25
25-($2.99) Leads into "Gambit & Bishop" 3.00
...1999 Annual ($3.50) Nicieza-s/McDaniel-a 3.50
...2000 Annual ($3.50) Nicieza-s/Derenick & Smith-a 3.50

GAMBIT
Marvel Comics: Nov, 2004 - Present ($2.99/)
1-4-Jeanty-a/Land-c/Layman-s 3.00

GAMBIT & BISHOP (... : Sons of the Atom on cover)
Marvel Comics: Feb, 2001 - No. 6, May, 2001 ($2.25, bi-weekly limited series)
Alpha (2/01) Prelude to series; Nord-a 2.25
1-6-Jeanty-a/Williams-c 2.25
Genesis (3/01, $3.50) reprints their first apps. and first meeting 3.50

GAMBIT AND THE X-TERNALS
Marvel Comics: Mar, 1995 - No. 4, July, 1995 ($1.95, limited series)
1-4-Age of Apocalypse 2.50

GAMEBOY (Super Mario covers on all)
Valiant: 1990 - No. 5 ($1.95, coated-c)
1-5: 3,4-Layton-c. 4-Morrow-a. 5-Layton-c(i) 4.00

GAMERA
Dark Horse Comics: Aug, 1996 - No. 4, Nov, 1996 ($2.95, limited series)
1-4 3.00

GAMMARAUDERS
DC Comics: Jan, 1989 - No. 10, Dec, 1989 ($1.25/$1.50/$2.00)
1-10-Based on TSR game 2.25

GAMORRA SWIMSUIT SPECIAL
Image Comics (WildStorm Productions): June, 1996 ($2.50, one-shot)
1-Campbell wraparound-c; pinups 2.50

GANDY GOOSE (Movies/TV)(See All Surprise, Giant Comics Edition #5A &10, Paul Terry's Comics & Terry-Toons)
St. John Publ. Co./Pines No. 5,6: Mar, 1953 - No. 5, Nov, 1953; No. 5, Fall, 1956 - No. 6, Sum/58
1-All St. John issues are pre-code 10 20 30 56 73 90
2 6 12 18 31 38 45
3-5(1953)(St. John) 6 12 18 28 34 40
5,6(1956-58)(Pines)-CBS Television Presents... 5 10 15 22 26 30

GANG BUSTERS (See Popular Comics #38)
David McKay/Dell Publishing Co.: 1938 - 1943
Feature Books 17(McKay)('38)-1st app. 63 126 189 394 610 825
Large Feature Comic 10('39)-(Scarce) 63 126 189 394 610 825
Large Feature Comic 17('41) 43 86 129 262 399 535
Four Color 7(1940) 36 72 108 270 423 575
Four Color 23,24('42-43) 30 60 90 213 327 440

GANG BUSTERS (Radio/TV)(Gangbusters #14 on)
National Periodical Publ.: Dec-Jan, 1947-48 - No. 67, Dec-Jan, 1958-59 (No. 1-23: 52 pgs.)
1 89 178 267 556 853 1150
2 40 80 120 244 372 500
3-5 34 68 102 193 279 365
6-10: 9-Dan Barry-a. 9,10-Photo-c 26 52 78 147 211 275
11-13-Photo-c 21 42 63 121 173 225
14,17-Frazetta-a, 8 pgs. each. 14-Photo-c 40 80 120 236 351 465
15,16,18-20,26: 26-Kirby-a 16 32 48 92 131 170
21-25,27-30 14 28 42 79 110 140
31-44: 44-Last Pre-code (2-3/55) 12 24 36 69 95 120
45-67 10 20 30 58 77 95
NOTE: ***Barry** a-6, 8, 10. **Drucker** a-51. **Moreira** a-48, 50, 59. **Roussos** a-8.*

GANGLAND
DC Comics (Vertigo): Jun, 1998 - No. 4, Sept, 1998 ($2.95, limited series)
1-4:Crime anthology by various. 2-Corben-a 3.00
TPB-(2000, $12.95) r/#1-4; Bradstreet-c 13.00

GANGSTERS AND GUN MOLLS
Avon Per./Realistic Comics: Sept, 1951 - No. 4, June, 1952 (Painted c-1-3)
1-Wood-a, 1 pg; c-/Avon paperback #292 48 96 144 293 447 600
2-Check-a, 8 pgs.; Kamen-a; Bonnie Parker story 40 80 120 233 342 450
3-Marijuana mentioned; used in **POP**, pg. 84,85 37 74 111 209 305 400
4-Syd Shores-c 29 58 87 164 237 310

GANGSTERS CAN'T WIN
D. S. Publishing Co.: Feb-Mar, 1948 - No. 9, June-July, 1949 (All 52 pgs?)
1-True crime stories 35 70 105 200 290 380
2 18 36 54 100 143 185
3,5,6 16 32 48 89 127 165
4-Acid in face story 20 40 60 112 161 210
7-9 12 24 36 71 98 125
NOTE: ***Ingles** a-5, 6. **McWilliams** a-5, 7. **Reinman** c-6.*

GANG WORLD
Standard Comics: No. 5, Nov, 1952 - No. 6, Jan, 1953
5-Bondage-c 20 40 60 112 161 210
6 15 30 45 83 117 150

GARGOYLE (See The Defenders #94)
Marvel Comics Group: June, 1985 - No. 4, Sept, 1985 (75¢, limited series)
1-Wrightson-c; character from Defenders 3.50
2-4 2.50

GARGOYLES (TV cartoon)
Marvel Comics: Feb, 1995 - No. 17, June, 1996 ($2.50)
1-17: Based on animated series 3.00

GARRISON'S GORILLAS (TV)

Gay Comics #32 © MAR

Geisha #2 © Andi Watson

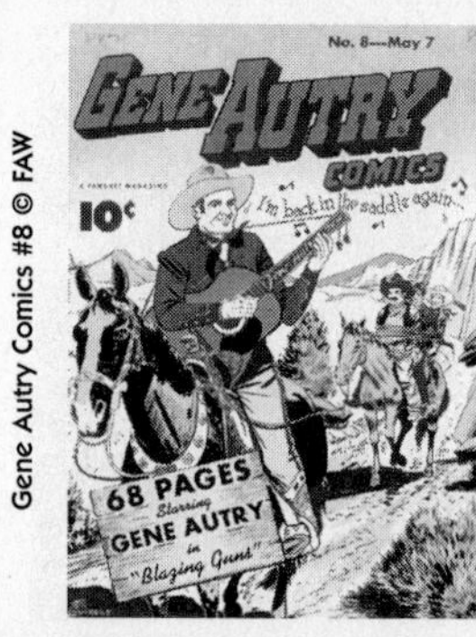

Gene Autry Comics #8 © FAW

	GD 2.0	VG 4.0	FN 6.0	VF 8.0	VF/NM 9.0	NM- 9.2

Dell Publishing Co.: Jan, 1968 - No. 4, Oct, 1968; No. 5, Oct, 1969 (Photo-c)

1	6	12	18	38	52	65
2-5: 5-Reprints #1	4	8	12	24	32	40

GARY GIANNI'S THE MONSTERMEN
Dark Horse Comics: Aug, 1999 ($2.95, one-shot)

1-Gianni-s/c/a; back-up Hellboy story by Mignola 3.00

GASM
Stories, Layouts & Press, Inc.: Nov, 1977 - nn(No. 4), Jun, 1978 (B&W/color)

1-Mark Wheatley-s/a; Gene Day-s/a; Workman-a	2	4	6	12	16	20
nn(#2, 2/78) Day-s/a; Wheatley-a; Workman-a	2	4	6	9	11	14
nn(#3, 4/78) Day-s/a; Wheatley-a; Corben-a	2	4	6	14	18	22
nn(#4, 6/78) Hempel-a; Howarth-a; Corben-a	3	6	9	16	20	24

GASOLINE ALLEY (Top Love Stories No. 3 on?)
Star Publications: Sept-Oct, 1950 - No. 2, Dec, 1950 (Newspaper-r)

1-Contains 1 pg. intro. history of the strip (The Life of Skeezix); reprints 15 scenes of highlights from 1921-1935, plus an adventure from 1935 and 1936 strips; a 2-pg. filler is included on the life of the creator Frank King, with photo of the cartoonist.	22	44	66	125	180	235
2-(1936-37 reprints)-L. B. Cole-c	26	52	78	147	211	275

(See Super Book No. 21)

GASP!
American Comics Group: Mar, 1967 - No. 4, Aug, 1967 (12¢)

1	5	10	15	33	44	55
2-4	3	6	9	19	25	32

GATECRASHER
Black Bull Entertainment: Mar, 2000 - No. 4, Jun, 2000 ($2.50, limited series)

1,2-Waid-s/Conner & Palmiotti-c/a; 1,2-variant-c by J.G. Jones 2.50
3,4: 3-Jusko var-c. 4-Linsner-c 2.50
... Ring of Fire TPB (11/00, $12.95) r/#1-4; Hughes-c; Ennis intro. 13.00

GATECRASHER (Regular series)
Black Bull Entertainment: Aug, 2000 - No. 6, Jan, 2001 ($2.50, limited series)

1-6-Waid-s/Conner & Palmiotti-c/a; 1-3-Variant-c by Fabry. 4-Hildebrandts variant-c. 5-Art Adams var-c. 6-Texeira var-c 2.50

GAY COMICS (Honeymoon No. 41)
Timely Comics/USA Comic Mag. Co. No. 18-24: Mar, 1944 (no month); No. 18, Fall, 1944 - No. 40, Oct, 1949

1-Wolverton's Powerhouse Pepper; Tessie the Typist begins; 1st app. Willie (one shot)	50	100	150	305	465	625
18-(Formerly Funny Tunes #17?)-Wolverton-a	33	66	99	190	275	360
19-29: Wolverton-a in all. 21,24-6 pg., 7 pg. Powerhouse Pepper; additional 2 pg. story in 24). 23-7 pg Wolverton story & 2 two pg stories(total of 11pgs.). 24,29-Kurtzman-a (24-"Hey Look"(2))	28	56	84	158	229	300
30,33,36,37-Kurtzman's "Hey Look"	11	22	33	62	84	105
31-Kurtzman's "Hey Look" (1), Giggles 'N' Grins (1-1/2)	11	22	33	62	84	105
32,35,38-40: 35-Nellie The Nurse begins?	10	20	30	56	73	90
34-Three Kurtzman's "Hey Look"	11	22	33	66	91	115

GAY COMICS (Also see Smile, Tickle, & Whee Comics)
Modern Store Publ.: 1955 (7¢, 5x7-1/4", 52 pgs.)

1	4	8	12	27	36	45

GAY PURR-EE (See Movie Comics)

GAZILLION
Image Comics: Nov, 1998 ($2.50, one-shot)

1-Howard Shum-s/ Keron Grant-a 2.50

GEAR STATION, THE
Image Comics: Mar, 2000 - No. 5, Nov, 2000 ($2.50)

1-Four covers by Ross, Turner, Pat Lee, Fraga 2.50
1-($6.95) DF Cover 7.00
2-5: 2-Two covers by Fraga and Art Adams 2.50

GEEK, THE (See Brother Power... & Vertigo Visions)

GEEKSVILLE (Also see 3 Geeks, The)
3 Finger Prints/ Image: Aug, 1999 - No. 6, Mar, 2001 ($2.75/$2.95, B&W)

1,2,4-6-The 3 Geeks by Koslowski; Innocent Bystander by Sassaman 3.00
3-Includes "Babes & Blades" mini-comic 5.00
0-(3/00) First Image issue 3.00
(Vol. 2) 1-4-($2.95) 3-Mini-comic insert by the Geeks. 4-Steve Borock app. 3.00

G-8 AND HIS BATTLE ACES (Based on pulps)
Gold Key: Oct, 1966

1 (10184-610)-Painted-c	4	8	12	28	38	48

G-8 AND HIS BATTLE ACES
Blazing Comics: 1991 ($1.50, one-shot)

1-Glanzman-a; Truman-c 2.50
NOTE: *Flip book format with "The Spider's Web" #1 on other side w/**Glanzman**-a, **Truman**-c.*

GEISHA (Also see Oni Press Summer Vacation Supercolor Fun Special)
Oni Press: Sept, 1998 - No. 4, Dec, 1998 ($2.95, limited series)

1-4-Andi Watson-s/a. 2-Adam Warren-c 3.00
...One Shot (5/00, $4.50) 4.50
The Complete Geisha TPB (5/03, $15.95, digest size) r/#1-4, One Shot & story from Oni Press Summer Vacation Supercolor Fun Special 16.00

GEM COMICS
Spotlight Publishers: Apr, 1945 (52 pgs)

1-Little Mohee, Steve Strong app.; Jungle bondage-c	44	88	132	268	409	550

GEMINAR
Image Comics: July, 2000 ($4.95, B&W)

1-(72-Page Special) Terry Collins-s/Al Bigley-a 5.00

GEMINI BLOOD
DC Comics (Helix): Sept, 1996 - No. 9, May, 1997 ($2.25, limited series)

1-9: 5-Simonson-c 2.25

GEN ACTIVE
DC Comics (WildStorm): May, 2000 - No. 6, Aug, 2001 ($3.95)

1-6: 1-Covers by Campbell and Madureira; Gen 13 & DV8 app. 5-Mahfood-a; Quitely and Stelfreeze-c. 6-Portacio-a/c 4.00

GENE AUTRY (See March of Comics No. 25, 28, 39, 54, 78, 90, 104, 120, 135, 150 in the Promotional Comics section & Western Roundup under Dell Giants)

GENE AUTRY COMICS (Movie, Radio star; singing cowboy)
Fawcett Publications: 1941 (On sale 12/31/41) - No. 10, 1943 (68 pgs.)
(Dell takes over with No. 11)

1 (Rare)-Gene Autry & his horse Champion begin	774	1548	2322	5418	8709	12,000
2-(1942)	162	324	486	1013	1557	2100
3-5: 3-(11/1/42)	104	208	312	650	1000	1350
6-10	85	170	255	531	816	1100

GENE AUTRY COMICS (...& Champion No. 102 on)
Dell Publishing Co.: No. 11, 1943 - No. 121, Jan-Mar, 1959 (TV - later issues)

11 (1943, 60 pgs.)-Continuation of Fawcett series; photo back-c; first Dell issue	50	100	150	419	672	925
12 (2/44, 60 pgs.)	49	98	147	392	609	825
Four Color 47 (1944, 60 pgs.)	41	82	123	330	515	700
Four Color 57 (11/44),66('45)(52 pgs. each)	40	80	120	300	468	635
Four Color 75,83 ('45, 36 pgs. each)	31	62	93	230	358	485
Four Color 93 ('45, 36 pgs.)	30	60	90	213	327	440
Four Color 100 ('46, 36 pgs.) First Gene Autry photo-c	31	62	93	230	358	485
1 (5-6/46, 52 pgs.)	41	82	123	330	515	700
2 (7-8/46)-Photo-c begin, end #111	25	50	75	181	278	375
3-5: 4-Intro Flapjack Hobbs	19	38	57	138	212	285
6-10	16	32	48	116	178	240
11-20: 20-Panhandle Pete begins	14	28	42	97	149	200
21-29 (36pgs.)	12	24	36	82	124	165
30-40 (52pgs.)	10	20	30	73	107	140
41-56 (52pgs.)	9	18	27	63	89	115
57-66 (36pgs.): 58-X-mas-c	8	16	24	53	74	95
67-80 (52pgs.): 70-X-mas-c	7	14	21	50	68	85
81-90 (52pgs.): 82-X-mas-c. 87-Blank inside-c	6	12	18	43	59	75
91-99 (36pgs. No. 91-on). 94-X-mas-c	6	12	18	38	52	65
100	6	12	18	40	55	70
101-111-Last Gene Autry photo-c	5	10	15	36	48	60
112-121-All Champion painted-c, most by Savitt	5	10	15	33	44	55

NOTE: *Photo back covers 4-18, 20-45, 48-65.* **Manning** *a-118.* **Jesse Marsh** *art: 4-Color No. 66, 75, 93, 100, No. 1-25, 27-37, 39, 40.*

GENE AUTRY'S CHAMPION (TV)
Dell Publ. Co.: No. 287, 8/50; No. 319, 2/51; No. 3, 8-10/51 - No. 19, 8-10/55

Four Color 287(#1)('50, 52pgs.)-Photo-c	12	24	36	86	131	175

Gene Pool nn © Joshua Films

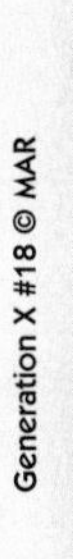

Generation X #18 © MAR

Gen 13 #9 © WSP

	GD 2.0	VG 4.0	FN 6.0	VF 8.0	VF/NM 9.0	NM- 9.2

Four Color 319(#2, '51), 3: 2-Painted-c begin, most by Sam Savitt 7 14 21 46 63 80
4-19: 19-Last painted-c 5 10 15 36 48 60

GENE DOGS
Marvel Comics UK: Oct, 1993 - No. 4, Jan, 1994 ($1.75, limited series)
1-($2.75)-Polybagged w/4 trading cards 3.00
2-4: 2-Vs. Genetix 2.25

GENE POOL
IDW Publishing: Oct, 2003 ($6.99, squarebound)
nn-Wein & Wolfman-s/Cummings-a 7.00

GENERAL DOUGLAS MACARTHUR
Fox Features Syndicate: 1951
nn-True life story 21 42 63 118 169 220

GENERIC COMIC, THE
Marvel Comics Group: Apr, 1984 (one-shot)
1 3.00

GENERATION HEX
DC Comics (Amalgam): June, 1997 ($1.95, one-shot)
1-Milligan-s/ Pollina & Morales-a 2.50

GENERATION NEXT
Marvel Comics: Mar, 1995 - No. 4, June, 1995 ($1.95, limited series)
1-4-Age of Apocalypse; Scott Lobdell scripts & Chris Bachalo-c/a 2.50

GENERATION X (See Gen 13/ Generation X)
Marvel Comics: Oct, 1994 - No. 75, June, 2001 ($1.50/$1.95/$1.99/$2.25)
Collectors Preview ($1.75), "Ashcan" Edition 2.25
-1(7/97) Flashback story 3.00
1/2 (San Diego giveaway) 2 4 6 8 10 12
1-($3.95)-Wraparound chromium-c; Scott Lobdell scripts & Chris Bachalo-a begins 6.00
2-($1.95)-Deluxe edition, Bachalo-a 4.00
3,4-($1.95)-Deluxe Edition; Bachalo-a 3.00
2-10: 2-4-Standard Edition. 5-Returns from "Age of Apocalypse," begin $1.95-c. 6-Bachalo-a(p) ends, returns #17. 7-Roger Cruz-a(p). 10-Omega Red-c/app. 3.00
11-24, 26-28: 13,14-Bishop-app. 17-Stan Lee app. (Stan Lee scripts own dialogue); Bachalo/Buckingham-a; Onslaught update. 18-Toad cameo. 20-Franklin Richards app; Howard the Duck cameo. 21-Howard the Duck app. 22-Nightmare app. 2.50
25-($2.99)-Wraparound-c. Black Tom, Howard the Duck app. 3.50
29-37: 29-Begin $1.99-c, "Operation Zero Tolerance". 33-Hama-s 2.50
38-49: 38-Dodson-a begins. 40-Penance ID revealed. 49-Maggott app. 2.50
50,57-($2.99): 50-Crossover w/X-Man #50 3.50
51-56, 58-62: 59-Avengers & Spider-Man app. 2.25
63-74: 63-Ellis-s begin. 64-Begin $2.25-c. 69-71-Art Adams-c 2.25
75-($2.99) Final issue; Chamber joins the X-Men; Lim-a 3.00
'95 Special-($3.95) 4.00
'96 Special-($2.95)-Wraparound-c; Jeff Johnson-c/a 3.50
'97 Special-($2.99)-Wraparound-c; 3.50
'98 Annual-($3.50)-vs. Dracula 3.50
'99 Annual-($3.50)-Monet leaves 3.50
75¢ Ashcan Edition 3.00
...Holiday Special 1 (2/99, $3.50) Pollina-a 3.50
...Underground Special 1 (5/98, $2.50, B&W) Mahfood-a 2.50

GENERATION X/ GEN 13 (Also see Gen 13/ Generation X)
Marvel Comics: 1997 ($3.99, one-shot)
1-Robinson-s/Larroca-a(p) 4.00

GENE RODDENBERRY'S LOST UNIVERSE
Tekno Comix: Apr, 1995 - No. 7, Oct, 1995 ($1.95)
1-7: 1-3-w/ bound-in game piece & trading card. 4-w/bound-in trading card 2.25

GENE RODDENBERRY'S XANDER IN LOST UNIVERSE
Tekno Comix: No. 0, Nov, 1995; No. 1, Dec, 1995 - No. 8, July, 1996 ($2.25)
0,1-8: 1-5-Jae Lee-c. 4-Polybagged. 8-Pt. 5 of The Big Bang x-over 2.25

GENESIS (See DC related titles)
DC Comics: Oct, 1997 - No. 4, Oct, 1997 ($1.95, weekly limited series)
1-4: Byrne-s/Wagner-a(p) in all. 3.00

GENESIS: THE #1 COLLECTION (WildStorm Archives)
WildStorm Productions: 1998 ($9.99, TPB, B&W)
nn-Reprints #1 issues of WildStorm titles and pin-ups 10.00

GENETIX
Marvel Comics UK: Oct, 1993 - No. 6, Mar, 1994 ($1.75, limited series)
1-($2.75)-Polybagged w/4 cards; Dark Guard app. 3.00
2-6: 2-Intro Tektos. 4-Vs. Gene Dogs 2.25

GEN 12 (Also see Gen13 and Team 7)
Image Comics (WildStorm Productions): Feb, 1998 - No. 5, June, 1998 ($2.50, lim. series)
1-5: 1-Team 7 & Gen13 app.; wraparound-c 3.00

GEN 13 (Also see Wild C.A.T.S. #1 & Deathmate Black #2)
Image Comics (WildStorm Productions): Feb, 1994 - No. 5, July 1994 ($1.95, limited series)
0 (8/95, $2.50)-Ch. 1 w/Jim Lee-p; Ch.4 w/Charest-p 3.00
1/2 1 2 3 4 5 7
1-($2.50)-Created by Jim Lee 1 3 4 6 8 10
1-2nd printing 2.50
1-"3-D" Edition (9/97, $4.95)-w/glasses 5.00
2-($2.50) 1 2 3 4 5 7
3-Pitt-c & story 4.00
4-Pitt-c & story; wraparound-c 3.00
5 4.00
5-Alternate Portacio-c; see Deathblow #5 6.00
...Collected Edition ('94, $12.95)-r/#1-5 13.00
...Rave ($1.50, 3/95)-wraparound-c 3.00
NOTE: *Issues 1-4 contain coupons redeemable for the ashcan edition of Gen 13 #0. Price listed is for a complete book.*

GEN 13
Image Comics (WildStorm Productions): Mar, 1995 - No. 36, Dec, 1998;
DC Comics (WildStorm): No. 37, Mar, 1999 - No. 77, Jul, 2002 ($2.95/$2.50)
1-A (Charge)-Campbell/Garner-c 4.50
1-B (Thumbs Up)-Campbell/Garner-c 4.50
1-C-1-F,1-I-1-M: 1-C (Lil' GEN 13)-Art Adams-c. 1-D (Barbari-GEN)-Simon Bisley-c. 1-E (Your Friendly Neighborhood Grunge)-Cleary-c. 1-F (GEN 13 Goes Madison Ave.)-Golden-c. 1-I (That's the way we became GEN 13)-Campbell/Gibson-c. 1-J (All Dolled Up)-Campbell/McWeeney-c. 1-K (Verti-GEN)-Dunn-c. 1-L (Picto-Fiction). 1-M (Do it Yourself Cover) 1 2 3 4 5 7
1-G (Lin-GEN-re)-Michael Lopez-c 2 4 6 8 10 12
1-H (GEN-et Jackson)-Jason Pearson-c 2 4 6 8 10 12
1-Chromium-c by Campbell 60.00
1-Chromium-c by Jim Lee 80.00
1-"3-D" Edition (2/98, $4.95)-w/glasses 5.00
2 ($1.95, Newsstand)-WildStorm Rising Pt. 4; bound-in card 2.50
2-12: 2-($2.50, Direct Market)-WildStorm Rising Pt. 4, bound-in card. 6,7-Jim Lee-c/a(p). 9-Ramos-a. 10,11-Fire From Heaven Pt. 3. & Pt.9 3.00
11-($4.95)-Special European Tour Edition; chromium-c 2 4 6 11 14 18
13A,13B,13C-($1.30, 13 pgs.): 13A-Archie & Friends app. 13B-Bone-c/app.; Teenage Mutant Ninja Turtles, Madman, Spawn & Jim Lee app. 3.00
14-24: 20-Last Campbell-a 2.50
25-($3.50)-Two covers by Campbell and Charest 3.50
25-($3.50)-Voyager Pack w/Danger Girl preview 4.50
25-Foil-c 10.00
26-32,34: 26-Arcudi-s/Frank-a begins. 34-Back-up story by Art Adams 2.50
33-Flip book w/Planetary preview 4.00
35-49: 36,38,40-Two covers. 37-First DC issue. 41-Last Frank-a 2.50
50-($3.95) Two covers by Lee and Benes; art by various 4.00
51-76: 51-Moy-a; Fairchild loses her powers. 60-Warren-s/a. 66-Art by various incl. Campbell (3 pgs.). 70,75,76-Mays-a. 76-Original team dies 2.50
77-($3.50) Mays, Andrews, Warren-a 3.50
Annual 1 (1997, $2.95) Ellis-s/ Dillon-c/a. 3.50
Annual 1999 ($3.50, DC) Slipstream x-over w/ DV8 3.50
Annual 2000 ($3.50) Devil's Night x-over w/WildStorm titles; Bermejo-c 3.50
...: A Christmas Caper (1/00, $5.95, one-shot) McWeeney-s/a 6.00
... Archives (4/98, $12.99) B&W reprints of mini-series, #0,1/2,1-13ABC; includes cover gallery and sourcebook 13.00
...: Carny Folk (2/00, $3.50) Collect back-up stories 3.50
... European Vacation TPB ($6.95) r/#6,7 7.00
.../ Fantastic Four (2001, $5.95) Maguire-s/c/a(p) 6.00
...: Going West (6/99, $2.50, one-shot) Pruett-s 2.50
...: Grunge Saves the World (5/99, $5.95, one-shot) Altieri-c/a 6.00
... I Love New York TPB ($9.95) r/part #25, 26-29; Frank-c 10.00
... London, New York, Hell TPB ($6.95) r/Annual #1 & Bootleg Ann. #1 7.00
... Lost in Paradise TPB ($6.95) r/#3-5 7.00
.../ Maxx (12/95, $3.50, one-shot) Messner-Loebs-s, 1st Coker-c/a. 3.50
...: Meanwhile (2003, $17.95) r/#43,44,66-70; all Warren-s; art by various 18.00
...: Medicine Song (2001, $5.95) Brent Anderson-c/a(p)/Raab-s 6.00

Gen 13: Magical Drama Queen Roxy #2 © WSP

Georgie Comics #3 © MAR

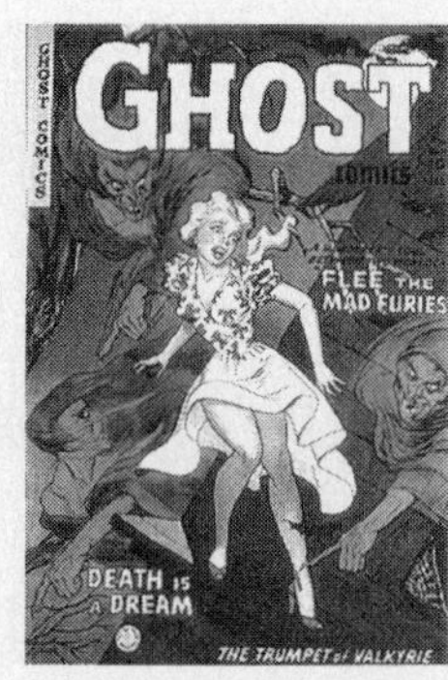

Ghost #4 © FH

	GD 2.0	VG 4.0	FN 6.0	VF 8.0	VF/NM 9.0	NM- 9.2
... Science Friction (2001, $5.95) Haley & Lopresti-a						6.00
... Starting Over TPB ($14.95) r/#1-7						15.00
... Superhuman Like You TPB ($12.95) r/#60-65; Warren-c						13.00
... #13 A,B&C Collected Edition ($6.95, TPB) r/#13A,B&C						7.00
... 3-D Special (1997, $4.95, one-shot) Art Adams-s/a(p)						5.00
...: The Unreal World (7/96, $2.95, one-shot) Humberto Ramos-c/a						3.00
... We'll Take Manhattan TPB ($14.95) r/#45-50; new Benes-c						15.00
...: Wired (4/99, $2.50, one-shot) Richard Bennett-c/a						2.50
... Yearbook 1997 (6/97, $2.50) College-themed stories and pin-ups by various						2.50
...: 'Zine (12/96, $1.95, B&W, digest size) Campbell/Garner-c						2.25
Variant Collection-Four editions (all 13 variants w/Chromium variant-limited, signed)						100.00
GEN 13						
DC Comics (WildStorm): No. 0, Sept, 2002 - No. 16, Feb, 2004 ($2.95)						
0-(13¢-c) Intro. new team; includes previews of 21 Down & The Resistance						2.50
1-Claremont-s/Garza-c/a; Fairchild app.						3.00
2-16: 8-13-Bachs-a. 16-Original team returns						3.00
...: September Song TPB (2003, $19.95) r/#0-6; Garza sketch pages						20.00
GEN 13 BOOTLEG						
Image Comics (WildStorm): Nov, 1996 - No. 20, Jul, 1998 ($2.50)						
1-Alan Davis-a; alternate costumes-c						2.50
1-Team falling variant-c						3.00
2-7: 2-Alan Davis-a. 5,6-Terry Moore-s. 7-Robinson-s/Scott Hampton-a						2.50
8-10-Adam Warren-s/a						4.00
11-20: 11,12-Lopresti-s/a & Simonson-s. 13-Wieringo-s/a. 14-Mariotte-s/Phillips-a. 15,16-Strnad-s/Shaw-a. 18-Altieri-s/a(p)/c, 18-Variant-c by Bruce Timm						2.50
Annual 1 (2/98, $2.95) Ellis-s/Dillon-c/a						3.00
... Grunge: The Movie (12/97, $9.95) r/#8-10, Warren-c						10.00
...Vol. 1 TPB (10/98, $11.95) r/#1-4						12.00
GEN 13/ GENERATION X (Also see Generation X / Gen 13)						
Image Comics (WildStorm Publications): July, 1997 ($2.95, one-shot)						
1-Choi-s/ Art Adams-p/Garner-i. Variant covers by Adams/Garner and Campbell/McWeeney						3.00
1-($4.95) 3-D Edition w/glasses; Campbell-c						5.00
GEN 13 INTERACTIVE						
Image Comics (WildStorm): Oct, 1997 - No. 3, Dec, 1997 ($2.50, lim. series)						
1-3-Internet voting used to determine storyline						2.50
... Plus! (7/98, $11.95) r/series & 3-D Special (in 2-D)						12.00
GEN 13 : MAGICAL DRAMA QUEEN ROXY						
Image Comics (WildStorm): Oct, 1998 - No. 3, Dec, 1998 ($3.50, lim. series)						
1-3-Adam Warren-s/c/a; manga style, 2-Variant-c by Hiroyuki Utatane						3.50
1-($6.95) Dynamic Forces Ed. w/Variant Warren-c						7.00
GEN 13 /MONKEYMAN & O'BRIEN						
Image Comics (WildStorm): Jun, 1998 - No. 2, July, 1998 ($2.50, lim. series)						
1,2-Art Adams-s/a(p); 1-Two covers						2.50
1-($4.95) Chromium-c						5.00
1-($6.95) Dynamic Forces Ed.						7.00
GEN 13: ORDINARY HEROES						
Image Comics (WildStorm Publications): Feb, 1996 - No. 2, July, 1996 ($2.50, limited series)						
1,2-Adam Hughes-c/a/scripts						3.00
TPB (2004, $14.95) r/series, Gen13 Bootleg #1&2 and Wildstorm Thunderbook; new Hughes-c and art pages						15.00
GENTLE BEN (TV)						
Dell Publishing Co.: Feb, 1968 - No. 5, Oct, 1969 (All photo-c)						
1	5	10	15	33	44	55
2-5: 5-Reprints #1	3	6	9	18	24	30
GEOMANCER (Also see Eternal Warrior: Fist & Steel)						
Valiant: Nov, 1994 - No. 8, June, 1995 ($3.75/$2.25)						
1 ($3.75)-Chromium wraparound-c; Eternal Warrior app.						3.75
2-8						2.25
GEORGE OF THE JUNGLE (TV)(See America's Best TV Comics)						
Gold Key: Feb, 1969 - No. 2, Oct, 1969 (Jay Ward)						
1	14	28	42	97	149	200
2	10	20	30	67	96	125
GEORGE PAL'S PUPPETOONS (Funny animal puppets)						
Fawcett Publications: Dec, 1945 - No. 18, Dec, 1947; No. 19, 1950						
1-Captain Marvel-c	42	84	126	256	391	525
2	24	48	72	138	199	260

	GD 2.0	VG 4.0	FN 6.0	VF 8.0	VF/NM 9.0	NM- 9.2
3-10	15	30	45	86	123	160
11-19	12	24	36	71	98	125
GEORGIE COMICS (...& Judy Comics #20-35?; see All Teen & Teen Comics)						
Timely Comics/GPI No. 1-34: Spr, 1945 - No. 39, Oct, 1952 (#1-3 are quarterly)						
1-Dave Berg-a	26	52	78	150	215	280
2	14	28	42	79	110	140
3-5,7,8	11	22	33	64	87	110
6-Georgie visits Timely Comics	14	28	42	79	110	140
9,10-Kurtzman's "Hey Look" (1 & ?); Margie app.	11	22	33	66	91	115
11,12: 11-Margie, Millie app.	9	18	27	52	66	80
13-Kurtzman's "Hey Look", 3 pgs.	10	20	30	56	73	90
14-Wolverton-a(1 pg.); Kurtzman's "Hey Look"	10	20	30	60	80	100
15,16,18-20	8	16	24	46	58	70
17,29-Kurtzman's "Hey Look", 1 pg.	9	18	27	52	66	80
21-24,27,28,30-39: 21-Anti-Wertham editorial	8	16	24	40	50	60
25-Painted-c by classic pin-up artist Peter Driben	10	20	30	60	80	100
26-Logo design swipe from Archie Comics	8	16	24	43	54	65
GERALD McBOING-BOING AND THE NEARSIGHTED MR. MAGOO (TV)						
(Mr. Magoo No. 6 on)						
Dell Publishing Co.: Aug-Oct, 1952 - No. 5, Aug-Oct, 1953						
1	14	28	42	102	156	210
2-5	12	24	36	82	124	165
GERONIMO (See Fighting Indians of the Wild West!)						
Avon Periodicals: 1950 - No. 4, Feb, 1952						
1-Indian Fighter; Maneely-a; Texas Rangers-r/Cowpuncher #1; Fawcette-c	19	38	57	107	154	200
2-On the Warpath; Kit West app.; Kinstler-c/a	12	24	36	69	95	120
3-And His Apache Murderers; Kinstler-c/a(2); Kit West-r/Cowpuncher #6	12	24	36	69	95	120
4-Savage Raids of; Kinstler-c & inside front-c; Kinstlerish-a by McCann(3)	11	22	33	64	87	110
GERONIMO JONES						
Charlton Comics: Sept, 1971 - No. 9, Jan, 1973						
1	2	4	6	12	16	20
2-9	1	3	4	6	8	10
Modern Comics Reprint #7('78)						4.00
GETALONG GANG, THE (TV)						
Marvel Comics (Star Comics): May, 1985 - No. 6, Mar, 1986						
1-6: Saturday morning TV stars						3.00
GET LOST						
Mikeross Publications/New Comics: Feb-Mar, 1954 - No. 3, June-July, 1954 (Satire)						
1-Andru/Esposito-a in all?	31	62	93	175	253	330
2-Andru/Esposito-c; has 4 pg. E.C. parody featuring "The Sewer Keeper"	21	42	63	118	169	220
3-John Wayne 'Hondo' parody	17	34	51	95	135	175
1,2 (10,12/87-New Comics)-B&W r-original						2.25
GET SMART (TV)						
Dell Publ. Co.: June, 1966 - No. 8, Sept, 1967 (All have Don Adams photo-c)						
1	11	22	33	80	120	160
2,3-Ditko-a	8	16	24	58	82	105
4-8: 8-Reprints #1 (cover and insides)	7	14	21	46	63	80
GHOST (...Comics #9)						
Fiction House Magazines: 1951(Winter) - No. 11, Summer, 1954						
1-Most covers by Whitman	71	142	213	444	685	925
2-Ghost Gallery & Werewolf Hunter stories	40	80	120	230	335	440
3-9: 3,6,7,9-Bondage-c. 9-Abel, Discount-a	34	68	102	196	283	370
10,11-Dr. Drew by Grandenetti in each, reprinted from Rangers; 11-Evans-r/Rangers #39; Grandenetti-r/Rangers #49	30	60	90	170	245	320
GHOST (See Comic's Greatest World)						
Dark Horse Comics: Apr, 1995 - No. 36, Apr, 1998 ($2.50/$2.95)						
1-Adam Hughes-a	1	2	3	5	6	8
2,3-Hughes-a						4.00
4-24: 4-Barb Wire app. 5,6-Hughes-c. 12-Ghost/Hellboy preview. 15,21-X app. 18,19-Barb Wire app.						3.00
25-($3.50)-48 pgs. special						3.50
26-36: 26-Begin $2.95-c. 29-Flip book w/Timecop. 33-36-Jade Cathedral; Harris painted-c						3.00
Special 1 (7/94, $3.95, 48 pgs.)	1	2	3	4	5	7
Special 2 (6/98, $3.95) Barb Wire app.						4.00

Ghostbusters: Legion #1 © Columbia Pict.

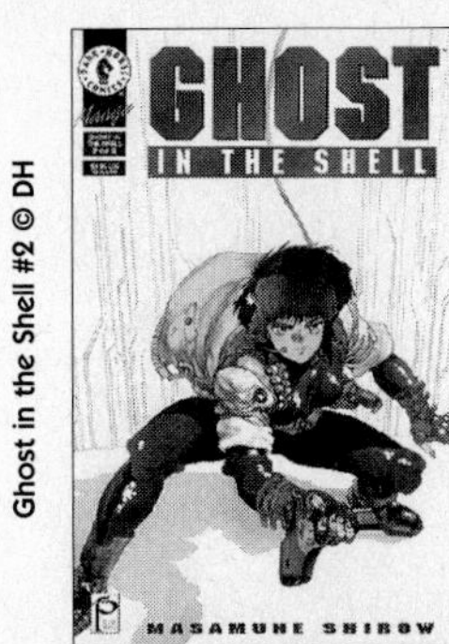

Ghost in the Shell #2 © DH

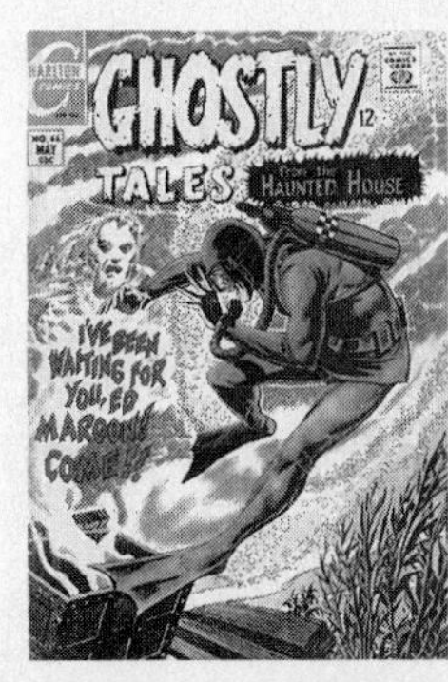

Ghostly Tales #66 © CC

	GD 2.0	VG 4.0	FN 6.0	VF 8.0	VF/NM 9.0	NM- 9.2

...Black October (1/99, $14.95, trade paperback)-r/#6-9,26,27 15.00
...Nocturnes (1996, $9.95, trade paperback)-r/#1-3 & 5 10.00
...Stories (1995, $9.95, trade paperback)-r/Early Ghost app. 10.00

GHOST (Volume 2)
Dark Horse Comics: Sept, 1998 - No. 22, Aug, 2000 ($2.95)

1-22: 1-4-Ryan Benjamin-c/Zanier-a 3.00
Handbook (8/99, $2.95) guide to issues and characters 3.00
Special 3 (12/98, $3.95) 4.00

GHOST AND THE SHADOW
Dark Horse Comics: Dec, 1995 ($2.95, one-shot)

1-Moench scripts 3.00

GHOST/BATGIRL
Dark Horse Comics: Aug, 2000 - No. 4, Dec, 2000 ($2.95, limited series)

1-4-New Batgirl; Oracle & Bruce Wayne app.; Benjamin-c/a 3.00

GHOST/HELLBOY
Dark Horse Comics: May, 1996 - No. 2, June, 1996 ($2.50, limited series)

1,2: Mike Mignola-c/scripts & breakdowns; Scott Benefiel finished-a 3.00

GHOST BREAKERS (Also see Racket Squad in Action, Red Dragon & (CC) Sherlock Holmes Comics)
Street & Smith Publications: Sept, 1948 - No. 2, Dec, 1948 (52 pgs.)

1-Powell-c/a(3); Dr. Neff (magician) app. 40 80 120 244 372 500
2-Powell-c/a(2); Maneely-a 35 70 105 198 287 375

GHOSTBUSTERS (TV) (Also, see Real...and Slimer)
First Comics: Feb, 1987 - No. 6, Aug, 1987 ($1.25)

1-6: Based on new animated TV series 3.00

GHOSTBUSTERS: LEGION (Movie)
88 MPH Studios: Feb, 2004 - No. 4 ($2.95/$3.50)

1-3-Steve Kurth-a/Andrew Dabb-s 3.00
1-3-($3.50) Brereton variant-c 3.50

GHOSTBUSTERS II
Now Comics: Oct, 1989 - No. 3, Dec, 1989 ($1.95, mini-series)

1-3: Movie Adaptation 3.00

GHOST CASTLE (See Tales of...)

GHOSTDANCING
DC Comics (Vertigo): Mar, 1995 - No. 6, Sept, 1995 ($1.95, limited series)

1-6: Case-c/a 2.25

GHOST IN THE SHELL (Manga)
Dark Horse: Mar, 1995 - No. 8, Oct, 1995 ($3.95, B&W/color, lim. series)

1,2 2 4 6 15 19 22
3 2 4 6 8 10 12
4-8 1 2 3 5 6 8

GHOST IN THE SHELL 2: MAN-MADE INTERFACE (Manga)
Dark Horse Comics: Jan, 2003 - No. 11, Dec, 2003 ($3.50, color/B&W, lim. series)

1-11-Masamune Shirow-s/a. 5-B&W 3.50

GHOSTLY HAUNTS (Formerly Ghost Manor)
Charlton Comics: #20, 9/71 - #53, 12/76; #54, 9/77 - #55, 10/77; #56, 1/78 - #58, 4/78

20 3 6 9 18 23 28
21 2 4 6 10 13 16
22-25,27,31-34,36,37-Ditko-c/a. 27-Dr. Graves x-over. 32-New logo. 33-Back to old logo 2 4 6 14 18 22
26,29,30,35-Ditko-c 2 4 6 10 13 16
28,38-40-Ditko-a. 39-Origin & 1st app. Destiny Fox 2 4 6 10 13 16
41,42: 41-Sutton-c; Ditko-a. 42-Newton-c/a 2 4 6 11 14 18
43-46,48,50,52-Ditko-a 2 4 6 10 12 15
47,54,56-Ditko-c/a. 56-Ditko-a(r). 2 4 6 11 14 18
49,51,53,55,57 1 3 4 6 8 10
58 (4/78) Last issue 2 4 6 11 14 18
40,41(Modern Comics-r, 1977, 1978) 4.00

NOTE: ***Ditko** a-22-25, 27, 28, 31-34, 36-41, 43-48, 50, 52, 54, 56r; c-22-27, 29, 30, 33-37, 47, 54, 56. **Glanzman** a-20. **Howard** a-27, 30, 35, 40-43, 48, 54, 57. **Kim** a-38, 41, 57. **Larson** a-48, 50. **Newton** c/a-42. **Staton** a-32, 35; c-28, 46. **Sutton** c-33, 37, 39, 41.*

GHOSTLY TALES (Formerly Blue Beetle No. 50-54)
Charlton Comics: No. 55, 4-5/66 - No. 124, 12/76; No. 125, 9/77 - No. 169, 10/84

55-Intro. & origin Dr. Graves; Ditko-a 7 14 21 46 63 80
56-58,60,61,70,71-Ditko-a. 70-Dr. Graves ends. 71-Last 12¢ issue 4 8 12 22 30 38
59,62-66,68 3 6 9 16 20 25
67,69-Ditko-c/a 4 8 12 27 36 45
72,75,76,79-82,85-Ditko-a 2 4 6 14 18 22
73,77,78,83,84,86-90,92-95,97,99-Ditko-c/a 3 6 9 18 23 28
74,91,98,119,123,124,127-130: 127,130-Sutton-a 2 4 6 9 11 14
96-Ditko-c 2 4 6 12 16 20
100-Ditko-c; Sutton-a 2 4 6 12 16 20
101,103-105-Ditko-a 2 4 6 11 14 18
102,109-Ditko-c/a 2 4 6 14 18 22
110,113-Sutton-c; Ditko-a 2 4 6 11 14 18
106-Ditko & Sutton-a; Sutton-c 2 4 6 11 14 18
107-Ditko, Wood, Sutton-a 2 4 6 12 16 20
108,116,117,126-Ditko-a 2 4 6 11 14 18
111,118,120-122,125-Ditko-c/a 2 4 6 14 18 22
112,114,115: 112,114-Ditko, Sutton-a. 114-Newton-a. 115-Newton, Ditko-a. 2 4 6 11 14 18
131-134,163-Ditko-c/a 2 4 6 10 13 16
135,142,145-151,153,154,156-160 1 2 3 5 6 8
136-141,143,144,152,155-Ditko-a 1 3 4 6 8 10
161,162,164-168-Lower print run. 162-Nudity panel 2 4 6 9 11 14
169 (10/84) Last issue; lower print run 2 4 6 11 14 18

NOTE: ***Aparo** a-65, 66, 68, 72, 137, 141r, 142r; c-71, 72, 74-76, 81, 146r, 149. **Ditko** a-55-58, 60, 61, 67, 69-73, 75-90, 92-95, 97, 99-118, 120-122, 125r, 126r, 131-141r, 143r, 144r, 146, 147, 149-152, 154-157, 159-161, 163; c-67, 69, 73, 77, 78, 83, 84, 86-90, 92-97, 99, 102, 109, 111, 118, 120-122, 125, 131-133, 147, 148, 151, 157-160, 163. **Glanzman** a-167. **Howard** a-95, 98, 99, 108, 117, 129, 131; c-98, 107, 120, 121, 161. **Larson** a-117, 119, 136, 159; c-136. **Morisi** a-83, 84, 86. **Newton** a-114; c-115(painted). **Palais** a-61. **Staton** a-161; c-117. **Sutton** a-106, 107, 111-114, 127, 130, 162; c-100, 106, 110, 113(painted). **Wood** a-107.*

GHOSTLY WEIRD STORIES (Formerly Blue Bolt Weird)
Star Publications: No. 120, Sept, 1953 - No. 124, Sept, 1954

120-Jo-Jo-r 40 80 120 236 351 465
121-124: 121-Jo-Jo-r. 122-The Mask-r/Capt. Flight #5; Rulah-r; has 1pg. story 'Death and the Devil Pills'-r/Western Outlaws #17. 123-Jo-Jo; Disbrow-a(2). 124-Torpedo Man 37 74 111 209 305 400

NOTE: ***Disbrow** a-120-124. **L. B. Cole** covers-all issues (#122 is a sci-fi cover).*

GHOST MANOR (Ghostly Haunts No. 20 on)
Charlton Comics: July, 1968 - No. 19, July, 1971

1 6 12 18 38 52 65
2-6: 6-Last 12¢ issue 3 6 9 19 25 32
7-12,17: 17-Morisi-a 3 6 9 16 21 26
13,14,16-Ditko-a 3 6 9 19 25 32
15,18,19-Ditko-c/a 4 8 12 24 32 40

GHOST MANOR (2nd Series)
Charlton Comics: Oct, 1971-No. 32, Dec, 1976; No. 33, Sept, 1977-No. 77, 11/84

1 4 8 12 29 40 50
2,3,5-7,9-Ditko-c 3 6 9 16 20 24
4,10-Ditko-c/a 3 6 9 18 24 30
8-Wood, Ditko-a; Sutton-c 3 6 9 18 24 30
11,14-Ditko-c/a 3 6 9 16 20 24
12,17,27,30 2 4 6 9 11 14
13,15,16,23-26,29: 13-Ditko-a. 15,16-Ditko-c. 23-Sutton-a. 24-26,29-Ditko-a. 25-Sutton-a. 26-Early Zeck-a; Boyette-c 2 4 6 11 14 18
18-(3/74) Newton 1st pro art; Ditko-a; Sutton-c 3 6 9 16 20 25
19-21: 19-Newton, Sutton-a; nudity panels. 20-Ditko-a. 21-E-Man, Blue Beetle, Capt. Atom cameos; Ditko-a. 2 4 6 11 14 18
22-Newton-c/a; Ditko-a 2 4 6 12 16 20
28,31,37,38-Ditko-c/a: 28-Nudity panels 2 4 6 12 16 20
32-36,39,41,45,48-50,53: 34-Black Cat by Kim 1 2 3 5 7 9
40-Ditko-a; torture & drug use 2 4 6 11 14 18
42,43,46,47,51,52,60,62-Ditko-c/a 2 4 6 10 13 16
44,54,71-Ditko-a 2 4 6 8 10 12
55,56,58,59,61,63,65-70 1 2 3 4 5 7
57-Wood, Ditko, Howard-a 2 4 6 9 11 14
64-Ditko & Newton-a 2 4 6 8 10 12
71-76 (low print) 1 2 3 5 6 8
77-(11/84) Last issue Aparo-r/Space Adventures V3#60 (Paul Mann) 2 4 6 10 13 16
19 (Modern Comics reprint, 1977) 4.00

NOTE: ***Ditko** a-4, 8, 10, 11(2), 13, 14, 18, 20-22, 24-26, 28, 29, 31, 37r, 38r, 40r, 42-44r, 46r, 47, 51r, 52r, 54r, 57, 60, 62(4), 64r, 71; c-2-7, 9-11, 14-16, 28, 31, 37, 38, 42, 43, 46, 47, 51, 52, 60, 62, 64. **Howard** a-4, 8, 12, 17, 19-21, 31, 41, 45, 57. **Newton** a-18-20, 22, 64; c-22. **Staton** a-13, 38, 44, 45. **Sutton** a-19, 23, 25, 45;c-8, 18.*

GHOST RIDER (See A-1 Comics, Best of the West, Black Phantom, Bobby Benson, Great Western, Red Mask & Tim Holt)
Magazine Enterprises: 1950 - No. 14, 1954

Ghost Rider #2 © MAR

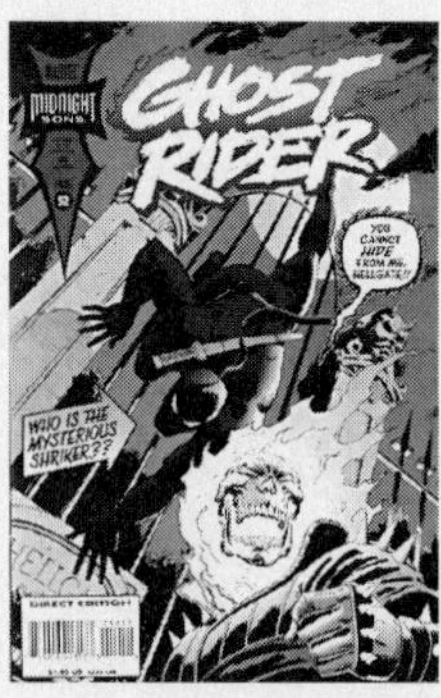

Ghost Rider V2#52 © MAR

Ghosts #90 © DC

NOTE: *The character was inspired by Vaughn Monroe's "Ghost Riders in the Sky", and Disney's movie "The Headless Horseman".*

	GD 2.0	VG 4.0	FN 6.0	VF 8.0	VF/NM 9.0	NM- 9.2
1(A-1 #27)-Origin Ghost Rider	108	216	324	675	1038	1400
2-5: 2(A-1 #29), 3(A-1 #31), 4(A-1 #34), 5(A-1 #37)-All Frazetta-c only	73	146	219	456	703	950
6,7: 6(A-1 #44)-Loco weed story, 7(A-1 #51)	32	64	96	184	267	350
8,9: 8(A-1 #57)-Drug use story, 9(A-1 #69)	27	54	81	154	222	290
10(A-1 #71)-Vs. Frankenstein	29	58	87	164	237	310
11-14: 11(A-1 #75). 12(A-1 #80)-Bondage-c; one-eyed Devil-c. 13(A-1 #84). 14(A-1 #112)	24	48	72	135	195	255

NOTE: ***Dick Ayers** art in all; c-1, 6-14.*

GHOST RIDER, THE (See Night Rider & Western Gunfighters)
Marvel Comics Group: Feb, 1967 - No. 7, Nov, 1967 (Western hero)(12¢)

	GD 2.0	VG 4.0	FN 6.0	VF 8.0	VF/NM 9.0	NM- 9.2
1-Origin & 1st app. Ghost Rider; Kid Colt-reprints begin	9	18	27	65	93	120
2	5	10	15	36	48	60
3-7: 6-Last Kid Colt-r; All Ayers-c/a(p)	4	8	12	29	40	50

GHOST RIDER (See The Champions, Marvel Spotlight #5, Marvel Team-Up #15, 58, Marvel Treasury Edition #18, Marvel Two-In-One #8, The Original Ghost Rider & The Original Ghost Rider Rides Again)
Marvel Comics Group: Sept, 1973 - No. 81, June, 1983 (Super-hero)

	GD 2.0	VG 4.0	FN 6.0	VF 8.0	VF/NM 9.0	NM- 9.2
1-Johnny Blaze, the Ghost Rider begins; 1st brief app. Daimon Hellstrom (Son of Satan)	9	18	27	60	85	110
2-1st full app. Daimon Hellstrom; gives glimpse of costume (1 panel); story continues in Marvel Spotlight #12	4	8	12	27	36	45
3-5: 3-Ghost Rider gets new cycle; Son of Satan app.	3	7	10	21	28	35
6-10: 10-Reprints origin/1st app. from Marvel Spotlight #5; Ploog-a	2	4	6	14	18	22
11-16	2	4	6	9	11	14
17,19-(Reg. 25¢ editions)(4,8/76)	2	4	6	9	11	14
17,19-(30¢-c variants, limited distribution)	2	4	6	12	16	20
18-(Reg. 25¢ edition)(6/76). Spider-Man-c & app.	2	4	6	10	13	16
18-(30¢-c variant, limited distribution)	3	6	9	16	20	24
20-Daredevil x-over; ties into D.D. #138; Byrne-a	2	4	6	14	18	22
21-30: 22-1st app. Enforcer. 29,30-Vs. Dr. Strange	1	2	3	5	7	9
24-26-(35¢-c variants, limited distribution)	2	4	6	9	11	14
31-34,36-49	1	2	3	4	5	7
35-Death Race classic; Starlin-c/a/sty	2	4	6	8	10	12
50-Double size	1	2	3	5	7	9
51-76,78-80: 80-Brief origin recap. 68,77-Origin retold						5.00
81-Death of Ghost Rider (Demon leaves Blaze)	2	4	6	10	13	16

NOTE: **Anderson** *c-64p.* **Infantino** *a(p)-43, 44, 51.* **G. Kane** *a-21p; c(p)-1, 2, 4, 5, 8, 9, 11-13, 19, 20, 24, 25.* **Kirby** *c-21-23.* **Mooney** *a-2-9p, 30i.* **Nebres** *c-26i.* **Newton** *a-23i.* **Perez** *c-26p.* **Shores** *a-2i. J.* **Sparling** *a-62p, 64p, 65p.* **Starlin** *a(p)-35.* **Sutton** *a-1p, 44i, 64i, 65i, 66, 67i.* **Tuska** *a-13p, 14p, 16p.*

GHOST RIDER (Volume 2) (Also see Doctor Strange/Ghost Rider Special, Marvel Comics Presents & Midnight Sons Unlimited)
Marvel Comics (Midnight Sons imprint #44 on): V2#1, May, 1990 - No. 93, Feb, 1998 ($1.50/$1.75/$1.95)

	NM- 9.2
1-($1.95, 52 pgs.)-Origin/1st app. new Ghost Rider; Kingpin app.	6.00
1-2nd printing (not gold)	2.50
2-5: 3-Kingpin app. 5-Punisher app.; Jim Lee-c	3.00
5-Gold background 2nd printing	2.50
6-14,16-24,29,30,32-39: 6-Punisher app. 6,17-Spider-Man/Hobgoblin-c/story. 9-X-Factor app. 10-Reintro Johnny Blaze on the last pg. 11-Stroman-c/a(p). 12,13-Dr. Strange x-over cont'd in D.S. #28. 13-Painted-c. 14-Johnny Blaze vs. Ghost Rider; origin recap 1st Ghost Rider (Blaze). 18-Painted-c by Nelson. 29-Wolverine-c/story. 32-Dr. Strange x-over; Johnny Blaze app. 34-Williamson-a(i). 36-Daredevil app. 37-Archangel app.	2.50
15-Glow in the dark-c	3.00
25-27: 25-($2.75)-Contains pop-up scene insert. 26,27-X-Men x-over; Lee/Williams-c on both	3.00
28,31-($2.50, 52 pgs.)-Polybagged w/poster; part 1 & part 6 of Rise of the Midnight Sons storyline (see Ghost Rider/Blaze #1)	3.00
40-Outer-c is Darkhold envelope made of black parchment w/gold ink; Midnight Massacre; Demogoblin app.	3.00
41-48: 41-Lilith & Centurious app.; begin $1.75-c. 41-43-Neon ink-c. 43-Has free extra 16 pg. insert on Siege of Darkness. 44,45-Siege of Darkness parts 2 & 10. 44-Spot varnish-c. 46-Intro new Ghost Rider. 48-Spider-Man app.	2.25
49,51-60,62-74: 49-Begin $1.95-c; bound-in trading card sheet; Hulk app. 55-Werewolf by Night app. 65-Punisher app. 67,68-Gambit app. 68-Wolverine app. 73,74-Blaze, Vengeance app.	2.25
50,61: 50-($2.50, 52 pgs.)-Regular edition	2.50
50-($2.95, 52 pgs.)-Collectors Ed. die cut foil-c	3.00
75-92: 76-Vs. Vengeance. 77,78-Dr. Strange-app. 78-New costume	2.25
93-($2.99)-Saltares & Texeira-a	3.00
#(-1) Flashback (7/97) Saltares-a	2.25
Annual 1,2 ('93, '94, $2.95, 68 pgs.) 1-Bagged w/card	3.00
...And Cable 1 (9/92, $3.95, stiff-c, 68 pgs.)-Reprints Marvel Comics Presents #90-98 w/new Kieth-c	4.00
...:Crossroads (11/95, $3.95) Die cut cover; Nord-a	5.00
Highway to Hell (2001, $3.50) Reprints origin from Marvel Spotlight #5	3.50
...: Resurrected TPB (2001, $12.95) r/#1-7	13.00

NOTE: **Andy & Joe Kubert** *c/a-28-31.* **Quesada** *c-21.* **Williamson** *a(i)-33-35; c-33i.*

GHOST RIDER (Volume 3)
Marvel Comics: Aug, 2001 - No. 6, Jan, 2002 ($2.99, limited series)

	NM- 9.2
1-6-Grayson-s/Kaniuga-a/c	3.00
...: The Hammer Lane TPB (6/02, $15.95) r/#1-6	16.00

GHOST RIDER/BALLISTIC
Marvel Comics: Feb, 1997 ($2.95, one-shot)

	NM- 9.2
1-Devil's Reign pt. 3	3.00

GHOST RIDER/BLAZE: SPIRITS OF VENGEANCE (Also see Blaze)
Marvel Comics (Midnight Sons imprint #17 on): Aug, 1992 - No. 23, June, 1994 ($1.75)

	NM- 9.2
1-($2.75, 52 pgs.)-Polybagged w/poster; part 2 of Rise of the Midnight Sons storyline; Adam Kubert-c/a begins	3.00
2-11,14-21: 4-Art Adams & Joe Kubert-p. 5,6-Spirits of Venom parts 2 & 4 cont'd from Web of Spider-Man #95,96 w/Demogoblin. 14-17-Neon ink-c. 15-Intro Blaze's new costume & power. 17,18-Siege of Darkness parts 8 & 13. 17-Spot varnish-c	2.25
12-($2.95)-Glow-in-the-dark-c	3.00
13-($2.25)-Outer-c is Darkhold envelope made of black parchment w/gold ink; Midnight Massacre x-over	2.50
22,23: 22-Begin $1.95-c; bound-in trading card sheet	2.25

NOTE: **Adam & Joe Kubert** *c-7, 8.* **Adam Kubert/Steacy** *c-6.* **J. Kubert** *a-13p(6 pgs.)*

GHOST RIDER/CAPTAIN AMERICA: FEAR
Marvel Comics: Oct, 1992 ($5.95, 52 pgs.)

	NM- 9.2
nn-Wraparound gatefold-c; Williamson inks	6.00

GHOST RIDER 2099
Marvel Comics: May, 1994 - No. 25, May, 1996 ($1.50/$1.95)

	NM- 9.2
1 ($2.25)-Collector's Edition w/prismatic foil-c	3.00
1 ($1.50)-Regular Edition; bound-in trading card sheet	2.25
2-24: 7-Spider-Man 2099 app.	2.25
2-(Variant; polybagged with Sega Sub-Terrania poster)	5.00
25 ($2.95)	3.00

GHOST RIDER, WOLVERINE, PUNISHER: THE DARK DESIGN
Marvel Comics: Dec, 1994 ($5.95, one-shot)

	NM- 9.2
nn-Gatefold-c	6.00

GHOST RIDER; WOLVERINE; PUNISHER: HEARTS OF DARKNESS
Marvel Comics: Dec, 1991 ($4.95, one-shot, 52 pgs.)

	NM- 9.2
1-Double gatefold-c; John Romita, Jr.-c/a(p)	5.00

GHOSTS (Ghost No. 1)
National Periodical Publications/DC Comics: Sept-Oct, 1971 - No. 112, May, 1982 (No. 1-5: 52 pgs.)

	GD 2.0	VG 4.0	FN 6.0	VF 8.0	VF/NM 9.0	NM- 9.2
1-Aparo-a	13	26	39	92	141	190
2-Wood-a(i)	7	14	21	51	71	90
3-5-(52 pgs.)	6	12	18	40	55	70
6-10	3	6	9	19	25	32
11-20	2	4	6	14	18	22
21-39	2	4	6	9	11	14
40-(68 pgs.)	3	6	9	16	21	26
41-60	1	2	3	5	7	9
61-96	1	2	3	4	5	7
97-99-The Spectre vs. Dr. 13 by Aparo. 97,98-Spectre-c by Aparo.	2	4	6	9	11	14
100-Infinity-c	1	2	3	5	6	8
101-112						6.00

NOTE: **B. Baily** *a-77.* **Buckler** *c-99, 100.* **J. Craig** *a-108.* **Ditko** *a-77, 111.* **Giffen** *a-104p, 106p, 111p.* **Glanzman** *a-2.* **Golden** *a-88.* **Infantino** *a-8.* **Kaluta** *c-7, 93, 101.* **Kubert** *a-8; c-89, 105-108, 111.* **Mayer** *a-111.* **McWilliams** *a-99.* **Win Mortimer** *a-89, 91, 94.* **Nasser/Netzer** *a-97.* **Newton** *a-92p, 94p.* **Nino** *a-35, 37, 57.* **Orlando** *a-74i; c-80.* **Redondo** *a-8, 13, 45.* **Sparling** *a(p)-90, 93, 94.* **Spiegle** *a-103, 105.* **Tuska** *a-2i. Dr. 13, the Ghostbreaker back-ups in 95-99, 101.*

GHOSTS SPECIAL (See DC Special Series No. 7)

GHOST SPY
Image Comics: May, 2004 - No. 6 ($2.95, limited series)

Giant Comics Edition #15 © STJ

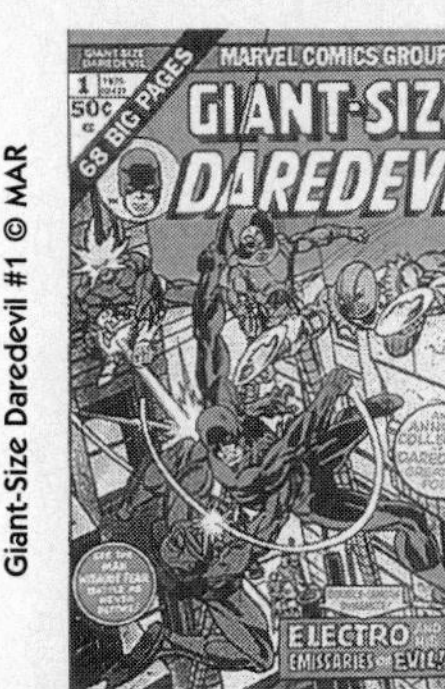

Giant-Size Daredevil #1 © MAR

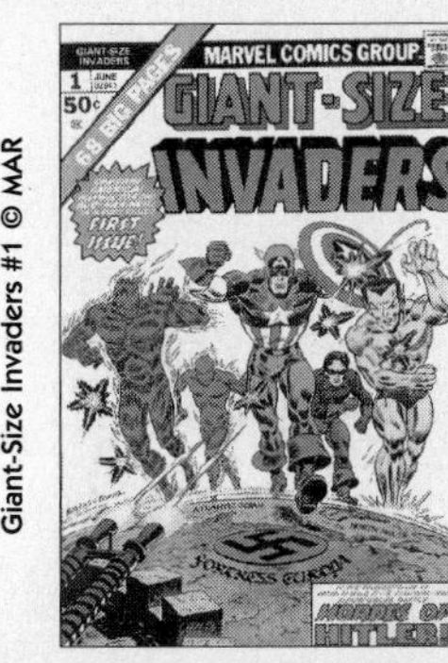

Giant-Size Invaders #1 © MAR

GD VG FN VF VF/NM NM-
2.0 4.0 6.0 8.0 9.0 9.2

GD VG FN VF VF/NM NM-
2.0 4.0 6.0 8.0 9.0 9.2

1-5-Jacob Elijah-s/Steve Albertson-a 3.00

GHOST STORIES (See Amazing Ghost Stories)

GHOST STORIES
Dell Publ. Co.: Sept-Nov, 1962; No. 2, Apr-June, 1963 - No. 37, Oct, 1973

12-295-211(#1)-Written by John Stanley 7 14 21 46 63 80
2 4 8 12 24 32 40
3-10: Two No. 6's exist with different c/a(12-295-406 & 12-295-503)
#12-295-503 is actually #9 with indicia to #6 3 7 10 21 28 35
11-21: 21-Last 12¢ issue 3 6 9 18 23 28
22-37 2 4 6 12 16 20
NOTE: *#21-34, 36, 37 all reprint earlier issues.*

GHOUL TALES (Magazine)
Stanley Publications: Nov, 1970 - No. 5, July, 1971 (52 pgs.) (B&W)

1-Aragon pre-code reprints; Mr. Mystery as host; bondage-c
7 14 21 51 71 90
2,3: 2-(1/71)Reprint/Climax #1. 3-(3/71) 4 8 12 27 36 45
4-(5/71)Reprints story "The Way to a Man's Heart" used in **SOTI**
5 10 15 33 44 55
5-ACG reprints 4 8 12 22 30 38
NOTE: *No. 1-4 contain pre-code Aragon reprints.*

GIANT BOY BOOK OF COMICS (Also see Boy Comics)
Newsbook Publications (Gleason): 1945 (240 pgs., hard-c)

1-Crimebuster & Young Robin Hood; Biro-c 92 184 276 575 888 1200

GIANT COMIC ALBUM
King Features Syndicate: 1972 (59¢, 11x14", 52 pgs., B&W, cardboard-c)

Newspaper reprints: Barney Google, Little Iodine, Katzenjammer Kids, Henry, Beetle Bailey, Blondie, & Snuffy Smith each... 3 6 9 18 24 32
Flash Gordon ('68-69 Dan Barry) 4 8 12 27 36 45
Mandrake the Magician ('59 Falk), Popeye 4 8 12 22 30 38

GIANT COMICS
Charlton Comics: Summer, 1957 - No. 3, Winter, 1957 (25¢, 100 pgs.)

1-Atomic Mouse, Hoppy app. 22 44 66 123 177 230
2,3: 2-Romance. 3-Christmas Book; Atomic Mouse, Atomic Rabbit, Li'l Genius, Li'l Tomboy & Atom the Cat stories 16 32 48 89 127 165
NOTE: *The above may be rebound comics; contents could vary.*

GIANT COMICS (See Wham-O Giant Comics)

GIANT COMICS EDITION (See Terry-Toons) (Also see Fox Giants)
St. John Publishing Co.: 1947 - No. 17, 1950 (25¢, 100-164 pgs.)

1-Mighty Mouse 50 100 150 305 465 625
2-Abbie & Slats 28 56 84 158 229 300
3-Terry-Toons Album; 100 pgs. 40 80 120 239 357 475
4-Crime comics; contains Red Seal No. 16, used & illo. in **SOTI**
55 110 165 336 511 685
5-Police Case Book (4/49, 132 pgs.)-Contents varies; contains remaindered St. John books - some volumes contain 5 copies rather than 4, with 160 pages; Matt Baker-c
53 106 159 323 492 660
5A-Terry-Toons Album (132 pgs.)-Mighty Mouse, Heckle & Jeckle, Gandy Goose & Dinky stories 38 76 114 219 320 420
6-Western Picture Stories; Baker-c/a(3); Tuska-a; The Sky Chief, Blue Monk, Ventrilo app., 132 pgs. 51 102 153 311 473 635
7-Contains a teen-age romance plus 3 Mopsy comics
35 70 105 200 290 380
8-The Adventures of Mighty Mouse (10/49) 38 76 114 219 320 420
9-Romance and Confession Stories; Kubert-a(4); Baker-a; photo-c (132 pgs.)
55 110 165 336 511 685
10-Terry-Toons Album (132 pgs.)-Mighty Mouse, Heckle & Jeckle, Gandy Goose stories
38 76 114 219 320 420
11-Western Picture Stories-Baker-c/a(4); The Sky Chief, Desperado, & Blue Monk app.; another version with Son of Sinbad by Kubert (132 pgs.)
49 98 147 299 455 610
12-Diary Secrets; Baker prostitute-c; 4 St. John romance comics; Baker-a
112 224 336 700 1075 1450
13-Romances; Baker, Kubert-a 49 98 147 299 455 610
14-Mighty Mouse Album (132 pgs.) 38 76 114 219 320 420
15-Romances (4 love comics)-Baker-c 55 110 165 336 511 685
16-Little Audrey; Abbott & Costello, Casper 40 80 120 233 342 450
17(nn)-Mighty Mouse Album (nn, no date, but did follow No. 16); 100 pgs. on cover but has 148 pgs. 38 76 114 219 320 420
NOTE: *The above books contain remaindered comics and contents could vary with each issue. No. 11, 12 have part photo magazine insides.*

GIANT COMICS EDITIONS
United Features Syndicate: 1940's (132 pgs.)

1-Abbie & Slats, Abbott & Costello, Jim Hardy, Ella Cinders, Iron Vic, Gordo, & Bill Bumlin 40 80 120 236 351 465
2-Jim Hardy, Ella Cinders, Elmo & Gordo 30 60 90 170 245 320
NOTE: *Above books contain rebound copies; contents can vary.*

GIANT GRAB BAG OF COMICS (See Archie All-Star Specials under Archie Comics)

GIANTKILLER
DC Comics: Aug, 1999 - No. 6, Jan, 2000 ($2.50, limited series)

1-6-Story and painted art by Dan Brereton 2.50
...A to Z: A Field Guide to Big Monsters (8/99) 2.50

GIANTS (See Thrilling True Story of the Baseball...)

GIANT-SIZE...
Marvel Comics Group: May, 1974 - Dec, 1975 (35/50¢, 52/68 pgs.)
(Some titles quarterly) (Scarce in strict NM or better due to defective cutting, gluing and binding; warping, splitting and off-center pages are common)

Avengers 1(8/74)-New-a plus G.A. H. Torch-r; 1st modern app. The Whizzer; 1st & only modern app. Miss America; 2nd app. Invaders; Kang, Rama-Tut, Mantis app.
4 8 12 29 40 50
Avengers 2,3,5: 2(11/74)-Death of the Swordsman; origin of Rama-Tut. 3(2/75). 5(12/75)-Reprints Avengers Special #1 3 6 9 18 24 30
Avengers 4 (6/75)-Vision marries Scarlet Witch. 4 8 12 24 32 40
Captain America 1(12/75)-r/stories T.O.S. 59-63 by Kirby (#63 reprints origin)
4 8 12 24 32 40
Captain Marvel 1(12/75)-r/Capt. Marvel #17, 20, 21 by Gil Kane (p)
3 6 9 18 23 28
Chillers 1(6/74, 52 pgs)-Curse of Dracula; origin/1st app. Lilith, Dracula's daughter; Heath-r, Colan-c/a(p); becomes Giant-Size Dracula #2 on 5 10 15 36 48 60
Chillers 1(2/75, 50¢, 68 pgs.)-Alcala-a 3 6 9 18 24 30
Chillers 2(5/75)-All-r; Everett-r from Advs. into Weird Worlds
3 6 9 16 20 24
Chillers 3(8/75)-Wrightson-c(new)/a(r); Colan, Kirby, Smith-r
3 6 9 18 24 30
Conan 1(9/74)-B. Smith-r/#3; start adaptation of Howard's "Hour of the Dragon" (ends #4); 1st app. Belit; new-a begins 3 6 9 19 25 32
Conan 2(12/74)-B. Smith-r/#5; Sutton-a(i)(#1 also); Buscema-c
3 6 9 16 20 24
Conan 3-5: 3(4/75)-B. Smith-r/#6; Sutton-a(i). 4(6/75)-B. Smith-r/#7. 5(1975)-B. Smith-r/#14,15; Kirby-c 2 4 6 12 16 20
Creatures 1(5/74, 52 pgs.)-Werewolf app; 1st app. Tigra (formerly Cat); Crandall-r; becomes Giant-Size Werewolf w/#2 4 8 12 27 36 45
Daredevil 1(1975)-Reprints Daredevil Annual #1 3 6 9 16 21 26
Defenders 1(7/74)-Silver Surfer app.; Starlin-a; Ditko, Everett & Kirby reprints
4 8 12 24 32 40
Defenders 2(10/74, 68 pgs.)-New G. Kane-c/a(p); Son of Satan app.; Sub-Mariner-r by Everett; Ditko-r/Strange Tales #119 (Dr. Strange); Maneely-r
3 6 9 18 23 28
Defenders 3-5: 3(1/75)-1st app. Korvac.; Newton, Starlin-a; Ditko, Everett-r. 4(4/75)-Ditko, Everett-r; G. Kane-c. 5-(7/75)-Guardians app. 3 6 9 16 20 24
Doc Savage 1(1975, 68 pgs.)-r/#1,2; Mooney-r 2 4 6 12 16 20
Doctor Strange 1(11/75)-Reprints stories from Strange Tales #164-168; Lawrence, Tuska-r 3 6 9 16 20 24
Dracula 2(9/74, 50¢)-Formerly Giant-Size Chillers 3 6 9 18 23 28
Dracula 3(12/74)-Fox-r/Uncanny Tales #6 3 6 9 16 21 26
Dracula 4(3/75)-Ditko-r(2) 3 6 9 16 21 26
Dracula 5(6/75)-1st Byrne art at Marvel 4 8 12 29 40 50
Fantastic Four 2-4: 2(8/74)-Formerly Giant-Size Super-Stars; Ditko-r. 3(11/74). 4(2/75)-1st Madrox; 2-4-All have Buscema-a 3 6 9 18 24 30
Fantastic Four 5,6: 5(5/75)-All-r; Kirby, G. Kane-r. 6(10/75)-All-r; Kirby-r
2 4 6 14 18 22
Hulk 1(1975) r/Hulk Special #1 3 6 9 18 24 30
Invaders 1(6/75, 50¢, 68 pgs.)-Origin; G.A. Sub-Mariner-r/Sub-Mariner #1; intro Master Man
3 7 10 21 28 35
Iron Man 1(1975)-Ditko reprint 3 6 9 18 23 28
Kid Colt 1-3: 1(1/75). 2(4/75). 3(7/75)-new Ayers-a 6 12 18 40 55 70
Man-Thing 1(8/74)-New Ploog-c/a (25 pgs.); Ditko-r/Amazing Adv. #11; Kirby-r/Strange Tales Ann. #2 & T.O.S. #15; (#1-5 all have new Man-Thing stories, pre-hero-r & are 68 pgs.) 3 7 10 21 28 35
Man-Thing 2,3: 2(11/74)-Buscema-c/a(p); Kirby, Powell-r. 3(2/75)-Alcala-a; Ditko, Kirby, Sutton-r; Gil Kane-c 3 6 9 16 20 24
Man-Thing 4,5: 4(5/75)-Howard the Duck by Brunner-c/a; Ditko-r. 5(8/75)-Howard the Duck by Brunner (p); Dracula cameo in Howard the Duck; Buscema-a(p); Sutton-a(i); G. Kane-c

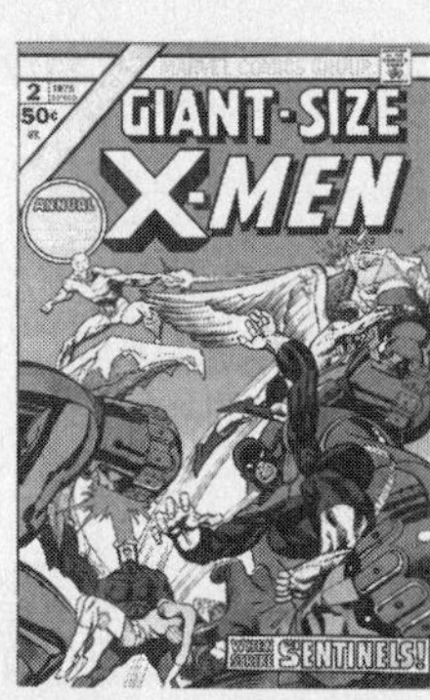

Giant-Size X-Men #2 © MAR

G.I. Combat #12 © QUA

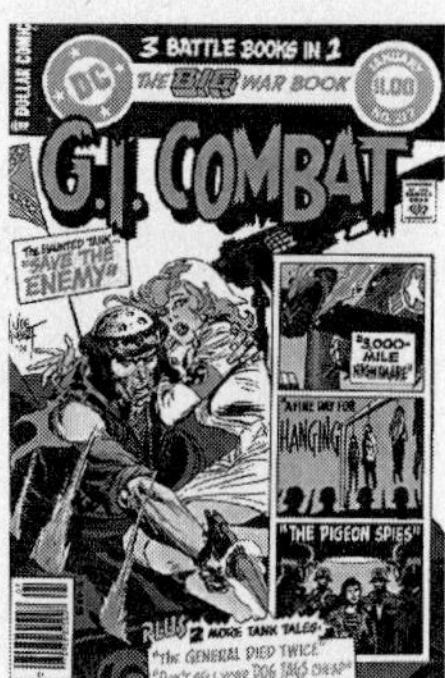

G.I. Combat #217 © DC

GD VG FN VF VF/NM NM-
2.0 4.0 6.0 8.0 9.0 9.2

3 6 9 19 25 32
Marvel Triple Action 1,2: 1(5/75). 2(7/75) 2 4 6 14 18 22
Master of Kung Fu 1(9/74)-Russell-a; Yellow Claw-r in #1-4; Gulacy-a in #1,2
3 6 9 19 25 32
Master of Kung Fu 2-4: 2-(12/74)-r/Yellow Claw #1. 3(3/75)-Gulacy-a; Kirby-a. 4(6/75)-Kirby-a
3 6 9 16 20 24
Power Man 1(1975) 2 4 6 14 18 22
Spider-Man 1(7/74)-Spider-Man /Human Torch-r by Kirby/Ditko; Byrne-r plus new-a (Dracula-c/story) 6 12 18 43 59 75
Spider-Man 2,3: 2(10/74)-Shang-Chi-c/app. 3(1/75)-Doc Savage-c/app.; Daredevil/ Spider-Man-r w/Ditko-a 4 8 12 25 33 42
Spider-Man 4(4/75)-3rd Punisher app.; Byrne, Ditko-r
10 20 30 73 107 140
Spider-Man 5,6: 5(7/75)-Man-Thing/Lizard-c. 6(9/75) 3 7 10 21 28 35
Super-Heroes Featuring Spider-Man 1(6/74, 35¢, 52 pgs.)-Spider-Man vs. Man-Wolf; Morbius, the Living Vampire app.; Ditko-r; G. Kane-a(p); Spidey villains app.
6 12 18 43 59 75
Super-Stars 1(5/74, 35¢, 52 pgs.)-Fantastic Four; Thing vs. Hulk; Kirbyish-c/a by Buckler/Sinnott; F.F. villains profiled; becomes Giant-Size Fantastic Four #2 on
5 10 15 33 44 55
Super-Villain Team-Up 1(3/75, 68 pgs.)-Craig-r(i) (Also see Fantastic Four #6 for 1st super-villain team-up) 3 6 9 18 23 28
Super-Villain Team-Up 2(6/75, 68 pgs.)-Dr. Doom, Sub-Mariner app.; Spider-Man-r from Amazing Spider-Man #8 by Ditko; Sekowsky-a(p) 2 4 6 14 18 22
Thor 1(7/75) 3 7 10 21 28 35
Werewolf 2(10/74, 68 pgs.)-Formerly Giant-Size Creatures; Ditko-r; Frankenstein app.
3 6 9 16 21 26
Werewolf 3,5: 3(1/75, 68 pgs.). 5(7/75, 68 pgs.) 3 6 9 16 21 26
Werewolf 4(4/75, 68 pgs.)-Morbius the Living Vampire app.
3 6 9 19 25 32
X-Men 1(Summer, 1975, 50¢, 68 pgs.)-1st app. new X-Men; intro. Nightcrawler, Storm, Colossus & Thunderbird; 2nd full app. Wolverine after Incredible Hulk #181
58 116 174 493 797 1100
X-Men 2 (11/75)-N. Adams-r (51 pgs) 8 16 24 58 82 105

GIANT SPECTACULAR COMICS (See Archie All-Star Special under Archie Comics)

GIANT SUMMER FUN BOOK (See Terry-Toons…)

G. I. COMBAT
Quality Comics Group: Oct, 1952 - No. 43, Dec, 1956

1-Crandall-c; Cuidera a-1-43i 69 138 207 431 666 900
2 37 74 111 209 305 400
3-5,10-Crandall-c/a 32 64 96 184 267 350
6-Crandall-a 28 56 84 158 229 300
7-9 23 46 69 132 191 250
11-20 18 36 54 102 146 190
21-31,33,35-43: 41-1st S.A. issue 16 32 48 89 127 165
32-Nuclear attack-c/story "Atomic Rocket Assault" 19 38 57 107 154 200
34-Crandall-a 17 34 51 98 139 180

G. I. COMBAT (See DC Special Series #22)
National Periodical Publ./DC Comics: No. 44, Jan, 1957 - No. 288, Mar, 1987

44-Grey tone-c 50 100 150 407 641 875
45 27 54 81 194 297 400
46-50 22 44 66 155 238 320
51-Grey tone-c 23 46 69 163 249 335
52-54,59,60 18 36 54 126 193 268
55-Minor Sgt. Rock prototype by Finger 20 40 60 145 223 300
56-Sgt. Rock prototype by Kanigher/Kubert 24 48 72 174 267 360
57,58-Pre-Sgt. Rock Easy Co. stories 22 44 66 155 238 320
61-65,69-74: 74-American flag-c 14 28 42 97 149 200
66-Pre-Sgt. Rock Easy Co. story 20 40 60 141 216 290
67-1st Tank Killer 23 46 69 165 253 340
68-(1/59) Introduces "The Rock", Sgt. Rock prototype by Kanigher/Kubert; once considered his actual 1st app. (see Our Army at War #82,83) 55 110 165 468 759 1050
75-80: 75-Greytone-c begin, end #109 16 32 48 114 175 235
81,82,84-86 13 26 39 90 138 185
83-1st Big Al, Little Al, & Charlie Cigar 15 30 45 109 167 225
87-1st Haunted Tank; series begins; classic-c 53 106 159 451 726 1000
88-2nd Haunted Tank 22 44 66 155 238 320
89,90: 90-Last 10¢ issue 13 26 39 90 138 185
91-1st Haunted Tank-c 17 34 51 121 186 250
92-99: 92-95,99-Grey tone-c 11 22 33 77 114 150
100,108: 108-1st Sgt. Rock x-over 12 24 36 82 124 165
101-107,109: 104,109-Grey tone-c 9 18 27 65 93 120
110-112,115-120: 119-Grey tone-c 7 14 21 51 71 90
113-Grey tone-c 9 18 27 60 85 110
114-Origin Haunted Tank 14 28 42 102 156 210
121-136: 121-1st app. Sgt. Rock's father. 125-Sgt. Rock app. 136-Last 12¢ issue
6 12 18 38 52 65
137,139,140 4 8 12 29 40 50
138-Intro. The Losers (Capt. Storm, Gunner/Sarge, Johnny Cloud) in Haunted Tank (10-11/69)
10 20 30 67 96 125
141-143 3 6 9 18 24 30
144-148 (68 pgs.) 4 8 12 24 32 40
149,151-154 (52 pgs.): 151-Capt. Storm story. 151,153-Medal of Honor series by Maurer
3 6 9 18 24 30
150- (52 pgs.) Ice Cream Soldier story (tells how he got his name); Death of Haunted Tank-c/s
4 8 12 24 32 40
155-167,169,170,200 2 4 6 10 12 15
168-Neal Adams-c 3 6 9 16 20 24
171-199 2 4 6 8 10 12
201,202 ($1.00 size) Neal Adams-c 2 4 6 12 16 20
203-210 ($1.00 size) 2 4 6 10 12 15
211-230 ($1.00 size) 2 4 6 8 10 12
231-259 ($1.00 size).232-Origin Kana the Ninja. 244-Death of Slim Stryker; 1st app. The Mercenaries. 246-(76 pgs., $1.50)-30th Anniversary issue. 257-Intro. Stuart's Raiders
1 2 3 5 7 9
260-281: 260-Begin $1.25, 52 pg. issues, end #281. 264-Intro Sgt. Bullet; origin Kana. 269-Intro. The Bravos of Vietnam. 274-Cameo of Monitor from Crisis on Infinite Earths 6.00
282-288 (75¢): 282-New advs. begin 6.00
NOTE: ***N. Adams*** *c-168, 201, 202.* ***Check*** *a-168, 173.* ***Drucker*** *a-48, 61, 63, 66, 71, 72, 76, 134, 140, 141, 144, 147, 148, 153.* ***Evans*** *a-135, 138, 158, 164, 166, 201, 202, 204, 205, 215, 256. Giffen a-267.* ***Glanzman*** *a-most issues.* ***Kubert/Heath*** *a-most issues;* ***Kubert*** *covers most issues.* ***Morrow*** *a-159-161(2 pgs.).* ***Redondo*** *a-189, 240i, 243i.* ***Sekowsky*** *a-162p.* ***Severin*** *a-147, 152, 154.* ***Simonson*** *c-169.* ***Thorne*** *a-152, 156.* ***Wildey*** *a-153. Johnny Cloud app.-112, 115, 120. Mlle. Marie app.-123, 132, 200. Sgt. Rock app.-111-113, 115, 120, 125, 141, 146, 147, 149, 200. USS Stevens by* ***Glanzman****-145, 150-153, 157.* ***Grandenetti*** *c-44-48.*

GIDGET (TV)
Dell Publishing Co.: Apr, 1966 - No. 2, Dec, 1966

1-Sally Field photo-c 10 20 30 73 107 140
2 8 16 24 53 74 95

GIFT COMICS
Fawcett Publications: 1942 - No. 4, 1949 (50¢/25¢, 324 pgs./152 pgs.)

1-Captain Marvel, Bulletman, Golden Arrow, Ibis the Invincible, Mr. Scarlet, & Spy Smasher begin; not rebound, remaindered comics, printed at same time as originals; 50¢-c & 324 pgs. begin, end #3. 269 538 807 1681 2591 3500
2-Commando Yank, Phantom Eagle, others app. 162 324 486 1013 1557 2100
3 110 220 330 688 1057 1425
4-(25¢, 152 pgs.)-The Marvel Family, Captain Marvel, etc.; each issue can vary in contents
69 138 207 431 666 900

GIFTS FROM SANTA (See March of Comics No. 137)

GIFTS OF THE NIGHT
DC Comics (Vertigo): Feb, 1999 - No. 4, May, 1999 ($2.95, limited series)

1-4-Bolton-c/a; Chadwick-s 3.00

GIGGLE COMICS (Spencer Spook No. 100) (Also see Ha Ha Comics)
Creston No.1-63/American Comics Group No. 64 on; Oct, 1943 - No. 99, Jan-Feb, 1955

1-Funny animal 35 70 105 198 287 375
2 17 34 51 95 135 175
3-5: Ken Hultgren-a begins? 12 24 36 71 98 125
6-10: 9-1st Superkatt (6/44) 10 20 30 58 77 95
11-20 9 18 27 51 62 75
21-40: 32-Patriotic-c. 37,61-X-Mas-c 8 16 24 43 54 65
41-54,56-59,61-99: Spencer Spook app. in many 7 14 21 37 46 55
55,60-Milt Gross-a 8 16 24 46 58 70

G-I IN BATTLE (G-I No. 1 only)
Ajax-Farrell Publ./Four Star: Aug, 1952 - No. 9, July, 1953; Mar, 1957 - No. 6, May, 1958

1 12 24 36 69 95 120
2 8 16 24 40 50 60
3-9 7 14 21 37 46 55
Annual 1(1952, 25¢, 100 pgs.) 26 52 78 150 215 280
1(1957-Ajax) 8 16 24 43 54 65
2-6 6 12 18 28 34 40

G. I. JANE
Stanhall/Merit No. 11: May, 1953 - No. 11, Mar, 1955 (Misdated 3/54)

1-PX Pete begins; Bill Williams-c/a 14 28 42 79 110 140
2-7(5/54) 8 16 24 46 58 70

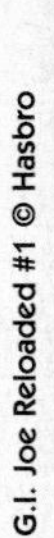
G.I. Joe #21 © Hasbro

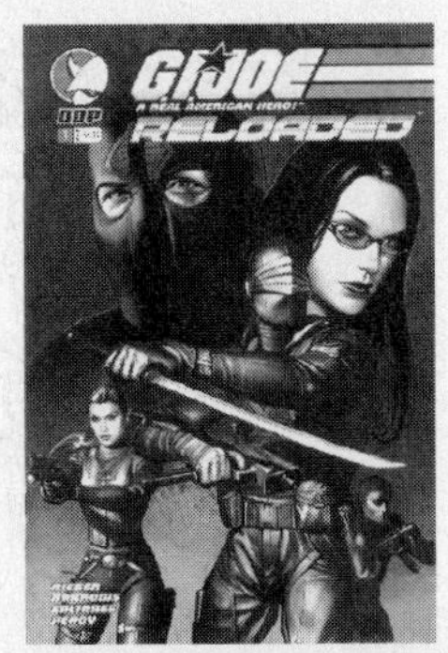
G.I. Joe Reloaded #1 © Hasbro

G.I. Joe Vs. the Transformers #2 © Hasbro

	GD 2.0	VG 4.0	FN 6.0	VF 8.0	VF/NM 9.0	NM- 9.2
8-10(12/54, Stanhall)	8	16	24	40	50	60
11 (3/55, Merit)	7	14	21	37	46	55

G. I. JOE (Also see Advs. of..., Showcase #53, 54 & The Yardbirds)
Ziff-Davis Publ. Co. (Korean War): No. 10, 1950; No. 11, 4-5/51 - No. 51, 6/57(52pgs.: 10-14,6-17?)

	GD	VG	FN	VF	VF/NM	NM-
10(#1, 1950)-Saunders painted-c begin	17	34	51	95	135	175
11-14(#2-5, 10/51): 11-New logo. 12-New logo	11	22	33	62	84	105
V2#6(12/51)-17-(11/52; Last 52 pgs.?)	10	20	30	58	77	95
18-(25¢, 100 pg. Giant, 12-1/52-53)	24	48	72	138	199	260
19-30: 20-22,24,28-31-The Yardbirds app.	9	18	27	52	66	80
31-47,49-51	9	18	27	51	62	75
48-Atom bomb story	9	18	27	52	66	80

NOTE: ***Powell** a-V2#7, 8, 11. **Norman Saunders** painted c-10-14, V2#6-14, 26, 30, 31, 35, 38, 39. **Tuska** a-7. Bondage c-29, 35, 38.*

G. I. JOE (America's Movable Fighting Man)
Custom Comics: 1967 (5-1/8x8-3/8", 36 pgs.)

	GD	VG	FN	VF	VF/NM	NM-
nn-Schaffenberger-a; based on Hasbro toy	4	8	12	24	32	40

G.I. JOE
Dark Horse Comics: Dec, 1995 - No. 4, Apr, 1996 ($1.95, limited series)

1-4: Mike W. Barr scripts. 1-Three Frank Miller covers with title logos in red, white and blue. 2-Breyfogle-c. 3-Simonson-c — 3.00

G.I. JOE
Dark Horse Comics: V2#1, June, 1996 - V2#4, Sept, 1996 ($2.50)

V2#1-4: Mike W. Barr scripts. 4-Painted-c — 3.00

G.I. JOE
Image Comics/Devil's Due Publishing: 2001 - Present ($2.95)

	GD	VG	FN	VF	VF/NM	NM-
1-Campbell-c; back-c painted by Beck; Blaylock-s	2	4	6	8	10	12
1-2nd printing with front & back covers switched						6.00
2,3						5.00
4-($3.50)						4.00
5-20,22-37: 6-SuperPatriot preview. 18-Brereton-c. 31-33-Wraith back-up; Caldwell-a						3.00
21-Silent issue; Zeck-a; two covers by Campbell and Zeck						3.00
...:Cobra Reborn (1/04, $4.95) Bradstreet-c/Jenkins-s						5.00
...:G.I. Joe Reborn (2/04, $4.95) Bradstreet-c/Bennett & Saltares-a						5.00
...: Malfunction (2003, $15.95) r/#11-15						16.00
... M. I. A. (2002, $4.95) r/#1&2; Beck back-c from #1 on cover						5.00
...: Reborn (2004, $9.95) r/Cobra Reborn & G.I. Joe Reborn						10.00
...: Reckonings (2002, $12.95) r/#6-9; Zeck-c						13.00
...: Reinstated (2002, $14.95) r/#1-4						15.00

G. I. JOE AND THE TRANSFORMERS
Marvel Comics Group: Jan, 1987 - No. 4, Apr, 1987 (Limited series)

1-4 — 6.00

G. I. JOE, A REAL AMERICAN HERO (...Starring Snake-Eyes on-c #135 on)
Marvel Comics Group: June, 1982 - No. 155, Dec, 1994

	GD	VG	FN	VF	VF/NM	NM-
1-Printed on Baxter paper; based on Hasbro toy	3	6	9	16	23	28
2-Printed on reg. paper	3	6	9	16	20	25
3-10	2	4	6	11	14	18
11-20: 11-Intro Airborne	2	4	6	9	11	14
21-1st Storm Shadow; silent issue	3	6	9	16	23	28
22	2	4	6	8	10	12
23-25,28-30,60: 60-Todd McFarlane-a	1	2	3	5	6	8
26,27-Origin Snake-Eyes parts 1 & 2	2	4	6	10	13	16
31-50: 33-New headquarters						5.00
51-59,61-90						4.00
91,92,94-99						5.00
93-Snake-Eyes' face first revealed	2	4	6	10	13	16
100,135-138: 135-138-($1.75)-Bagged w/trading card	1	3	4	6	8	10
101-134: 110-1st Ron Garney-a	1	2	3	4	5	7
139-142-New Transformers app.	2	4	6	8	10	12
143,145-149	1	2	3	5	7	9
144-Origin Snake-Eyes	2	4	6	9	11	14
150-Low print thru #155	3	6	9	16	20	24
151-154	2	4	6	14	18	22
155-Last issue	4	8	12	22	30	38
All 2nd printings						2.25
Special #1 (2/95, $1.50) r/#60 w/McFarlane-a	4	8	12	24	32	40
Special Treasury Edition (1982)-r/#1	3	6	9	18	23	28
Volume 1 TPB (4/02, $24.95) r/#1-10; new cover by Michael Golden						25.00
Volume 2 TPB (6/02, $24.95) r/#11-20; new cover by J. Scott Campbell						25.00
Volume 3 TPB (2002, $24.99) r/#21-30; new cover by J. Scott Campbell						25.00
Volume 4 TPB (2002, $25.99) r/#31-40; new cover by J. Scott Campbell						26.00
Volume 5 TPB (2002, $24.99) r/#42-50; new cover by J. Scott Campbell						25.00
Yearbook 1-4: (3/85-3/88)-r/#1; Golden-c. 2-Golden-c/a						5.00

NOTE: ***Garney** a(p)-110. **Golden** c-23, 29, 34, 36. **Heath** a-24. **Rogers** a(p)-75, 77-82, 84, 86; c-77.*

G.I. JOE: BATTLE FILES
Image Comics: 2002 - No. 3, 2002 ($5.95)

1-3-Profile pages of characters and history; Beck-c — 6.00

G. I. JOE COMICS MAGAZINE
Marvel Comics Group: Dec, 1986 - No. 13, 1988 ($1.50, digest-size)

	GD	VG	FN	VF	VF/NM	NM-
1-13: G.I. Joe-r	1	3	4	6	8	10

G.I. JOE EUROPEAN MISSIONS (Action Force in indicia)
Marvel Comics Ltd. (British): Jun, 1988 - No. 15, Dec, 1989 ($1.50/$1.75)
(Series reprints Action Force)

	GD	VG	FN	VF	VF/NM	NM-
1,3-Snake Eyes & Storm Shadow-c/s	1	2	3	5	7	9
2,4-15						6.00

G.I. JOE: FRONT LINE
Image Comics: 2002 - No. 18, Dec, 2003 ($2.95)

	NM-
1-18: 1-Jurgens-a/Hama-s. 1-Two covers by Dorman & Sharpe. 7,8-Harris-c	3.00
...Vol. 1 - The Mission That Never Was TPB (2003, $14.95) r/ #1-4; script pages	15.00
...Vol. 2 - Icebound TPB (3/04, $12.95) r/ #5-8	13.00
...Vol. 3 - History Repeating TPB (4/04, $9.95) r/#11-14	10.00
...Vol. 4 - One-Shots TPB (5/04, $15.95) r/#9,10,15-18	16.00

G.I. JOE: MASTER & APPRENTICE
Image Comics: May, 2004 - Present ($2.95)

1-8: 1-4-Caselli-a/Jerwa-s. 5,6-Rieber-s/Saltares-a. 8-Origin of the Baroness — 3.00

G. I. JOE ORDER OF BATTLE, THE
Marvel Comics Group: Dec, 1986 - No. 4, Mar, 1987 (limited series)

1-4 — 6.00

G.I. JOE: RELOADED
Image Comics: Mar, 2004 - Present ($2.95)

1-9: 1-3-Granov-c/Ney Rieber-s — 3.00

G. I. JOE SPECIAL MISSIONS (Indicia title: Special Missions)
Marvel Comics Group: Oct, 1986 - No. 28, Dec, 1989 ($1.00)

	NM-
1-20	4.00
21-28	5.00

G.I. JOE VS. THE TRANSFORMERS
Image Comics: Jun, 2003 - No. 6, Nov, 2003 ($2.95, limited series)

	NM-
1-Blaylock-s/Mike Miller-a; three covers by Miller, Campbell & Andrews	3.00
1-2nd printing; black cover with logo; back-c by Campbell	3.00
2-6: 2-Two covers by Miller & Brooks	3.00
TPB (3/04, $15.95) r/series; sketch pages	16.00

G.I. JOE VS. THE TRANSFORMERS (Volume 2)
Devil's Due Publ.: Sept, 2004 - No. 4, Dec, 2004 ($4.95/$2.95, limited series)

	NM-
1-($4.95) Three covers; Jolley-s/Su & Seeley-a	5.00
2-4-($2.95) Two covers by Su & Pollina	3.00

G. I. JUNIORS (See Harvey Hits No. 86,91,95,98,101,104,107,110,112,114,116,118,120,122)

GILGAMESH II
DC Comics: 1989 - No. 4, 1989 ($3.95, limited series, prestige format, mature)

1-4: Starlin-c/a/scripts — 4.00

GIL THORP
Dell Publishing Co.: May-July, 1963

	GD	VG	FN	VF	VF/NM	NM-
1-Caniffish-a	4	8	12	27	36	45

GINGER
Archie Publications: 1951 - No. 10, Summer, 1954

	GD	VG	FN	VF	VF/NM	NM-
1-Teenage humor	15	30	45	83	117	150
2-(1952)	9	18	27	52	66	80
3-6: 6-(Sum/53)	8	16	24	43	54	65
7-10-Katy Keene app.	10	20	30	56	73	90

GINGER FOX (Also see The World of Ginger Fox)
Comico: Sept, 1988 - No. 4, Dec, 1988 ($1.75, limited series)

1-4: Part photo-c on all — 2.25

G.I. R.A.M.B.O.T.
Wonder Color Comics/Pied Piper #2: Apr, 1987 - No. 2? ($1.95)

1,2: 2-Exist? — 2.25

Girls' Life #2 © MAR

Girls' Love Stories #3 © DC

The Girl Who Would Be Death #1 © DC

GIRL
DC Comics (Vertigo Verite): Jul, 1996 - No. 3, 1996 ($2.50, lim. series, mature)

	GD 2.0	VG 4.0	FN 6.0	VF 8.0	VF/NM 9.0	NM- 9.2
1-3: Peter Milligan scripts; Fegredo-c/a						2.50

GIRL COMICS (Becomes Girl Confessions No. 13 on)
Marvel/Atlas Comics(CnPC): Oct, 1949 - No. 12, Jan, 1952 (#1-4: 52 pgs.)

	GD 2.0	VG 4.0	FN 6.0	VF 8.0	VF/NM 9.0	NM- 9.2
1-Photo-c	23	46	69	132	191	250
2-Kubert-a; photo-c	13	26	39	74	100	130
3-Everett-a; Liz Taylor photo-c	26	52	78	147	211	275
4-11: 4-Photo-c. 10-12-Sol Brodsky-c	10	20	30	60	80	100
12-Krigstein-a; Al Hartley-c	11	22	33	64	87	110

GIRL CONFESSIONS (Formerly Girl Comics)
Atlas Comics (CnPC/ZPC): No. 13, Mar, 1952 - No. 35, Aug, 1954

	GD 2.0	VG 4.0	FN 6.0	VF 8.0	VF/NM 9.0	NM- 9.2
13-Everett-a	12	24	36	71	98	125
14,15,19,20	9	18	27	52	66	80
16-18-Everett-a	10	20	30	60	80	100
21-35: Robinson-a	8	16	24	40	50	60

GIRL CRAZY
Dark Horse Comics: May, 1996 - No. 3, July, 1996 ($2.95, B&W, limited series)

	GD 2.0	VG 4.0	FN 6.0	VF 8.0	VF/NM 9.0	NM- 9.2
1-3: Gilbert Hernandez-a/scripts.						3.00

GIRL FROM U.N.C.L.E., THE (TV) (Also see The Man From...)
Gold Key: Jan, 1967 - No. 5, Oct, 1967

	GD 2.0	VG 4.0	FN 6.0	VF 8.0	VF/NM 9.0	NM- 9.2
1-McWilliams-a; Stephanie Powers photo front/back-c & pin-ups (no ads, 12¢)	10	20	30	73	107	140
2-5-Leonard Swift-Courier No. 5	8	16	24	53	74	95

GIRLS' FUN & FASHION MAGAZINE (Formerly Polly Pigtails)
Parents' Magazine Institute: V5#44, Jan, 1950 - V5#48, Sept., 1950

	GD 2.0	VG 4.0	FN 6.0	VF 8.0	VF/NM 9.0	NM- 9.2
V5#44	6	12	18	31	38	45
45-48	5	10	15	22	26	30

GIRLS IN LOVE
Fawcett Publications: May, 1950 - No. 2, July, 1950

	GD 2.0	VG 4.0	FN 6.0	VF 8.0	VF/NM 9.0	NM- 9.2
1-Photo-c	12	24	36	71	98	125
2-Photo-c	10	20	30	56	73	90

GIRLS IN LOVE (Formerly G. I. Sweethearts No. 45)
Quality Comics Group: No. 46, Sept, 1955 - No. 57, Dec, 1956

	GD 2.0	VG 4.0	FN 6.0	VF 8.0	VF/NM 9.0	NM- 9.2
46	9	18	27	51	62	75
47-53,55,56	7	14	21	35	43	50
54- 'Commie' story	8	16	24	40	50	60
57-Matt Baker-c/a	9	18	27	54	70	85

GIRLS IN WHITE (See Harvey Comics Hits No. 58)

GIRLS' LIFE (Patsy Walker's Own Magazine For Girls!)
Atlas Comics (BFP): Jan, 1954 - No. 6, Nov, 1954

	GD 2.0	VG 4.0	FN 6.0	VF 8.0	VF/NM 9.0	NM- 9.2
1	12	24	36	69	95	120
2-Al Hartley-c	8	16	24	43	54	65
3-6	7	14	21	37	46	55

GIRLS' LOVE STORIES
National Comics(Signal Publ. No. 9-65/Arleigh No. 83-117): Aug-Sept, 1949 - No. 180, Nov-Dec, 1973 (No. 1-13: 52 pgs.)

	GD 2.0	VG 4.0	FN 6.0	VF 8.0	VF/NM 9.0	NM- 9.2
1-Toth, Kinstler-a, 8 pgs. each; photo-c	55	110	165	340	520	700
2-Kinstler-a?	32	64	96	184	267	350
3-10: 1-9-Photo-c. 7-Infantino-c(p)	22	44	66	123	177	230
11-20	17	34	51	95	135	175
21-33: 21-Kinstler-a. 33-Last pre-code (1-2/55)	11	22	33	64	87	110
34-50	9	18	27	54	70	85
51-70	6	12	18	43	59	75
71-99: 83-Last 10¢ issue	5	10	15	33	44	55
100	5	10	15	36	48	60
101-146: 113-117-April O'Day app.	3	7	10	21	28	35
147-151- "Confessions" serial. 150-Wood-a	3	7	10	21	28	35
152-160,171-179	3	6	9	16	20	24
161-170 (52 pgs.)	4	8	12	24	32	40
180 Last issue	3	7	10	21	28	35

GIRLS' ROMANCES
National Periodical Publ.(Signal Publ. No. 7-79/Arleigh No. 84): Feb-Mar, 1950 - No. 160, Oct, 1971 (No. 1-11: 52 pgs.)

	GD 2.0	VG 4.0	FN 6.0	VF 8.0	VF/NM 9.0	NM- 9.2
1-Photo-c	54	108	162	329	502	675
2-Photo-c; Toth-a	31	62	93	178	259	340
3-10: 3-6-Photo-c	22	44	66	123	177	230
11,12,14-20	15	30	45	85	120	155
13-Toth-c	16	32	48	89	127	165
21-31: 31-Last pre-code (2-3/55)	11	22	33	62	84	105
32-50	7	14	21	46	63	80
51-99: 80-Last 10¢ issue	5	10	15	33	44	55
100	5	10	15	36	48	60
101-108,110-120	3	7	10	21	28	35
109-Beatles-c/story	12	24	36	87	134	180
121-133,135-140	3	6	9	18	24	30
134-Neal Adams-c (splash pg. is same as-c)	5	10	15	36	48	60
141-158	3	6	9	16	20	24
159,160-52 pgs.	4	8	12	24	32	40

GIRL WHO WOULD BE DEATH, THE
DC Comics (Vertigo): Dec, 1998 - No. 4, March, 1999 ($2.50, lim. series)

	GD 2.0	VG 4.0	FN 6.0	VF 8.0	VF/NM 9.0	NM- 9.2
1-4-Kiernan-s/Ormston-a						2.50

G. I. SWEETHEARTS (Formerly Diary Loves; Girls In Love #46 on)
Quality Comics Group: No. 32, June, 1953 - No. 45, May, 1955

	GD 2.0	VG 4.0	FN 6.0	VF 8.0	VF/NM 9.0	NM- 9.2
32	9	18	27	52	66	80
33-45: 44-Last pre-code (3/55)	7	14	21	37	46	55

G.I. TALES (Formerly Sgt. Barney Barker No. 1-3)
Atlas Comics (MCI): No. 4, Feb, 1957 - No. 6, July, 1957

	GD 2.0	VG 4.0	FN 6.0	VF 8.0	VF/NM 9.0	NM- 9.2
4-Severin-a(4)	9	18	27	52	66	80
5	7	14	21	37	46	55
6-Orlando, Powell, & Woodbridge-a	8	16	24	40	50	60

GIVE ME LIBERTY (Also see Dark Horse Presents Fifth Anniversary Special, Dark Horse Presents #100-4, Happy Birthday Martha Washington, Martha Washington Goes to War, Martha Washington Stranded In Space & San Diego Comicon Comics #2)
Dark Horse Comics: June, 1990 - No. 4, 1991 ($4.95, limited series, 52 pgs.)

	GD 2.0	VG 4.0	FN 6.0	VF 8.0	VF/NM 9.0	NM- 9.2
1-4: 1st app. Martha Washington; Frank Miller scripts, Dave Gibbons-c/a in all						5.00

G. I. WAR BRIDES
Superior Publishers Ltd.: Apr, 1954 - No. 8, June, 1955

	GD 2.0	VG 4.0	FN 6.0	VF 8.0	VF/NM 9.0	NM- 9.2
1	9	18	27	52	66	80
2	6	12	18	29	36	42
3-8: 4-Kamen*esque*-a; lingerie panels	6	12	18	27	33	38

G. I. WAR TALES
National Periodical Publications: Mar-Apr, 1973 - No. 4, Oct-Nov, 1973

	GD 2.0	VG 4.0	FN 6.0	VF 8.0	VF/NM 9.0	NM- 9.2
1-Reprints in all; dinosaur-c/s	3	6	9	18	24	30
2-N. Adams-a(r)	2	4	6	11	14	18
3,4: 4-Krigstein-a(r)	2	4	6	10	13	16

NOTE: ***Drucker*** *a-3r, 4r.* ***Heath*** *a-4r.* ***Kubert*** *a-2, 3; c-4r.*

GIZMO (Also see Domino Chance)
Chance Ent.: May-June, 1985 (B&W, one-shot)

	GD 2.0	VG 4.0	FN 6.0	VF 8.0	VF/NM 9.0	NM- 9.2
1						6.00

GIZMO
Mirage Studios: 1986 - No. 6, July, 1987 ($1.50, B&W)

	GD 2.0	VG 4.0	FN 6.0	VF 8.0	VF/NM 9.0	NM- 9.2
1-6						2.50

GLADSTONE COMIC ALBUM
Gladstone: 1987 - No. 28, 1990 ($5.95/$9.95, 8-1/2x11")(All Mickey Mouse albums are by Gottfredson)

	GD 2.0	VG 4.0	FN 6.0	VF 8.0	VF/NM 9.0	NM- 9.2
1-10: 1-Uncle Scrooge; Barks-r; Beck-c. 2-Donald Duck; r/F.C. #108 by Barks. 3-Mickey Mouse-r by Gottfredson. 4-Uncle Scrooge; r/F.C. #456 by Barks w/unedited story. 5-Donald Duck Advs.; r/F.C. #199. 6-Uncle Scrooge-r by Barks. 7-Donald Duck-r by Barks. 8-Mickey Mouse-r. 9-Bambi; r/F.C. #186? 10-Donald Duck Advs.; r/F.C. #275	1	3	4	6	8	10
11-20: 11-Uncle Scrooge; r/U.S. #4. 12-Donald And Daisy; r/F.C. #1055, WDC&S. 13-Donald Duck Advs.; r/F.C. #408. 14-Uncle Scrooge; Barks-r/U.S #21. 15-Donald And Gladstone; Barks-r. 16-Donald Duck Advs.; r/F.C. #238. 17-Mickey Mouse strip-r (The World of Tomorrow, The Pirate Ghost Ship). 18-Donald Duck and the Junior Woodchucks; Barks-r. 19-Uncle Scrooge; r/U.S. #12; Rosa-c. 20-Uncle Scrooge; r/F.C. #386; Barks-c/a(r)	1	3	4	6	8	10
21-25: 21-Donald Duck Family; Barks-c/a(r). 22-Mickey Mouse strip-r. 23-Donald Duck; Barks-r/D.D. #26 w/unedited story. 24-Uncle Scrooge; Barks-r; Rosa-c. 25-D. Duck; Barks-c/a-r/F.C. #367	1	3	4	6	8	10
26-28: All have $9.95-c. 26-Mickey and Donald; Gottfredson-c/a(r). 27-Donald Duck; r/-WDC&S by Barks; Barks painted-c. 28-Uncle Scrooge & Donald Duck; Rosa-c/a (4 stories)	1	3	4	6	8	10

Special 1-7: 1 ('89-'90, $9.95/13.95)-1-Donald Duck Finds Pirate Gold; r/F.C. #9. 2 ('89, $8.95)-

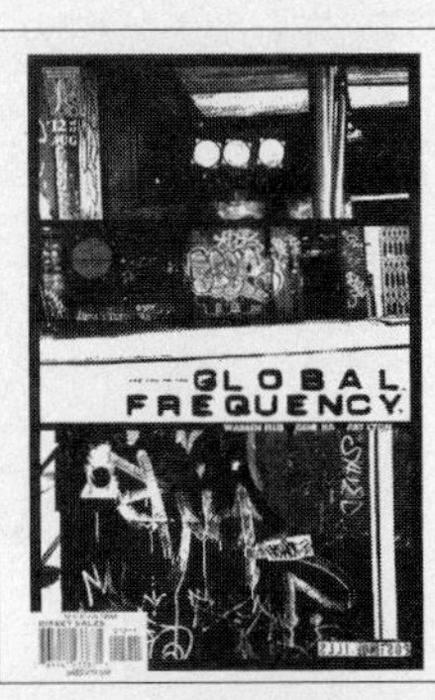

Global Frequency #12 © Warren Ellis & DC

Goddess #1 © Ennis & Winslade

Godzilla #16 © MAR

	GD 2.0	VG 4.0	FN 6.0	VF 8.0	VF/NM 9.0	NM- 9.2

Uncle Scrooge and Donald Duck; Barks-r/Uncle Scrooge #5; Rosa-c. 3 ('89, $8.95)-Mickey Mouse strip-r. 4 ('89, $11.95)-Uncle Scrooge; Rosa-c/a-r/Son of the Sun from U.S. #219 plus Barks-r/U.S. 5 ('90, $11.95)-Donald Duck Advs.; Barks-r/F.C. #282 & 422 plus Barks painted-c. 6 ('90, $12.95)-Uncle Scrooge; Barks-c/a-r/Uncle Scrooge. 7 ('90, $13.95)-Mickey Mouse; Gottfredson strip-r 2 4 6 9 11 14

GLADSTONE COMIC ALBUM (2nd Series)(Also see The Original Dick Tracy)
Gladstone Publishing: 1990 ($5.95, 8-1/2 x 11," stiff-c, 52 pgs.)

1,2-The Original Dick Tracy. 2-Origin of the 2-way wrist radio 6.00
3-D Tracy Meets the Mole-r by Gould ($6.95). 1 2 3 5 6 8

GLAMOROUS ROMANCES (Formerly Dotty)
Ace Magazines (A. A. Wyn): No. 41, July, 1949 - No. 90, Oct, 1956 (Photo-c 68-90)

41-Dotty app. 9 18 27 52 66 80
42-72,74-80: 44-Begin 52 pg. issues. 45,50-61-Painted-c. 80-Last pre-code (2/55) 7 14 21 37 46 55
73-L.B. Cole-r/All Love #27 8 16 24 40 50 60
81-90 7 14 21 35 43 50

GLOBAL FREQUENCY
DC Comics (WildStorm): Dec, 2002 - No. 12, Aug, 2004 ($2.95, limited series)

1-12-Warren Ellis-s. 1-Leach-a. 2-Fabry-a. 3-Dillon-a. 5-Muth-a. 7-Bisley-a. 12-Ha-a 3.00
1-RRP Edition variant-c; promotional giveaway for retailers (200 printed) 10.00
...: Detonation Radio TPB (2005, $14.95) r/#7-12 15.00
...: Planet Ablaze TPB (2003, $14.95) r/#1-6 15.00

GLOOMCOOKIE
SLG Publishing: June, 1999 - Present ($2.95, B&W)

1-21-Serena Valentino-s. 1-6-Ted Naifeh-a. 7-12-Gebbia-a 3.00
...Presents: A Monster's Christmas (12/02, $3.95, color) 4.00

GLORY
Image Comics (Extreme Studios)/Maximum Press: Mar, 1995 - No. 22, Apr, 1997 ($2.50)

0-Deodato-c/a, 1-(3/95)-Deodato-a 2.50
1A-Variant-c 4.00
2-11,13-22: 4-Variant-c by Quesada & Palmiotti. 5-Bagged w/Youngblood gaming card. 7,8-Deodato-c/a(p). 8-Babewatch x-over. 9-Cruz-c; Extreme Destroyer Pt. 5; polybagged w/card. 10-Angela-c/app. 11-Deodato-c. 2.50
12-($3.50)-Photo-c 3.50
Trade Paperback (1995, $9.95)-r/#1-4 10.00

GLORY
Awesome Comics: Mar, 1999 ($2.50)

0-Liefeld-c; story and sketch pages 2.50

GLORY (ALAN MOORE'S...)
Avatar Press: Dec, 2001 - No. 2 ($3.50)

Preview-(9/01, $1.99) B&W pages and cover art; Alan Moore-s 2.25
0-Four regular covers 3.50
1,2: 1-Alan Moore-s/Mychaels & Gebbie-a; nine covers by various. 2-Five covers 3.50

GLORY & FRIENDS BIKINI FEST
Image Comics (Extreme): Sept, 1995 - No. 2, Oct, 1995 ($2.50, limited series)

1,2: 1-Photo-c; centerfold photo; pin-ups 2.50

GLORY & FRIENDS CHRISTMAS SPECIAL
Image Comics (Extreme Studios): Dec, 1995 ($2.50, one-shot)

1-Deodato-c 2.50

GLORY & FRIENDS LINGERIE SPECIAL
Image Comics (Extreme Studios): Sept, 1995 ($2.95, one-shot)

1-Pin-ups w/photos; photo-c; varant-c exists 3.00

GLORY/ANGELA: ANGELS IN HELL (See Angela/Glory: Rage of Angels)
Image Comics (Extreme Studios): Apr, 1996 ($2.50, one-shot)

1-Flip book w/Darkchylde #1 2.50

GLORY/AVENGELYNE
Image Comics (Extreme Studios): Oct, 1995 ($3.95, one-shot)

1-Chromium-c, 1-Regular-c 4.00

GLORY/CELESTINE: DARK ANGEL
Image Comics/Maximum Press (Extreme Studios): Sept, 1996 - No. 3, Nov, 1996 ($2.50, limited series)

1-3 2.50

GNOME MOBILE, THE (See Movie Comics)

GOBBLEDYGOOK
Mirage Studios: 1984 - No. 2, 1984 (B&W)(1st Mirage comics, published at same time)

1-(24 pgs.)-(distribution of approx. 50) Teenage Mutant Ninja Turtles app. on full page back-c ad; Teenage Mutant Ninja Turtles do not appear inside. 1st app of Fugitoid 47 94 141 376 588 800
2-(24 pgs.)-Teenage Mutant Ninja Turtles on full page back-c ad 32 64 96 240 370 500

NOTE: Counterfeit copies exist. Originals feature both black & white covers and interiors. Signed and numbered copies do not exist.

GOBBLEDYGOOK
Mirage Studios: Dec, 1986 ($3.50, B&W, one-shot, 100 pgs.)

1-New 8 pg. TMNT story plus a Donatello/Michaelangelo 7 pg. story & a Gizmo story; Corben-i(r)/TMNT #7 6.00

GOBLIN, THE
Warren Publishing Co.: June, 1982 - No. 3, Dec, 1982 ($2.25, B&W magazine with 8 pg. color insert comic in all)

1-The Gremlin app. Philo Photon & the Troll Patrol, Micro-Buccaneers & Wizard Wormglow begin & app. in all. Tin Man app. Golden-a(p). Nebres-c/a in all 2 4 6 14 18 22
2,3: 2-1st Hobgoblin. 3-Tin Man app. 2 4 6 10 12 15

NOTE: *Bermejo* a-1-3. *Elias* a-1-3. *Laxamana* a-1-3. *Nino* a-3.

GO BOY 7
Dark Horse Comics: July, 2003 - Present ($2.99)

1-5-Peyer-s/Sommariva-a 3.00

GODDESS
DC Comics (Vertigo): June, 1995 - No. 8, Jan, 1996 ($2.95, limited series)

1-Garth Ennis scripts; Phil Winslade-c/a in all 5.00
2-8 4.00
TPB (2002, $19.95) r/#1-8; foreword and sketch pages by Winslade 20.00

GODFATHERS, THE (See The Crusaders)

GOD IS
Spire Christian Comics (Fleming H. Revell Co.): 1973, 1975 (35-49¢)

nn-By Al Hartley 1 3 4 6 8 11

GODS AND TULIPS
Westhampton House: Aug, 1999 ($3.00, B&W, one-shot for the CBLDF)

nn-Neil Gaiman speeches; Kaluta-c 3.00

GOD'S COUNTRY (Also see Marvel Comics Presents)
Marvel Comics: 1994 ($6.95)

nn-P. Craig Russell-a; Colossus story; r/Marvel Comics Presents #10-17 7.00

GOD'S HEROES IN AMERICA
Catechetical Guild Educational Society: 1956 (nn) (25¢/35¢, 68 pgs.)

307 3 6 9 16 21 26

GOD'S SMUGGLER (Religious)
Spire Christian Comics/Fleming H. Revell Co.: 1972 (39¢/40¢)

1-Two variations exist 1 3 4 6 8 11

GODWHEEL
Malibu Comics (Ultraverse): No. 0, Jan, 1995 - No. 3, Feb, 1995 ($2.50, limited series)

0-3: 0-Flip-c. 1-1st app. of Primevil; Thor cameo (1 panel). 3-Perez-a in Chapter 3, Thor app. 2.50

GODZILLA (Movie)
Marvel Comics : August, 1977 - No. 24, July, 1979 (Based on movie series)

1-(Regular 30¢ edition)-Mooney-i 3 6 9 16 20 25
1-(35¢-c variant, limited distribution) 4 8 12 22 30 38
2-(Regular 30¢ edition)-Tuska-i. 2 4 6 8 10 12
2,3-(35¢-c variant, limited distribution) 2 4 6 12 16 20
3-(30¢-c) Champions app.(w/o Ghost Rider) 2 4 6 9 11 14
4-10: 4,5-Sutton-a 1 3 4 6 8 10
11-23: 14-Shield app. 20-F.F. app. 21,22-Devil Dinosaur app. 1 2 3 5 7 9
24-Last issue 2 4 6 8 10 12

GODZILLA (Movie)
Dark Horse Comics: May, 1988 - No. 6, 1988 ($1.95, B&W, limited series) (Based on movie series)

1 6.00
2-6 4.00
...Collection (1990, $10.95)-r/1-6 with new-c 11.00
...Color Special 1 (Sum, 1992, $3.50, color, 44 pgs.)-Arthur Adams wraparound-c/a & part scripts 5.00

Go-Go #6 © CC

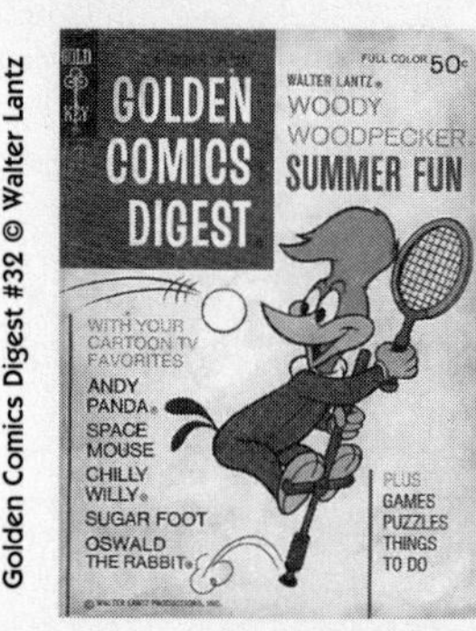

Golden Comics Digest #32 © Walter Lantz

Golden Arrow Western #6 © FAW

GD VG FN VF VF/NM NM-
2.0 4.0 6.0 8.0 9.0 9.2

GD VG FN VF VF/NM NM-
2.0 4.0 6.0 8.0 9.0 9.2

...King Of The Monsters Special (8/87, $1.50)-Origin; Bissette-c/a 4.00
...Vs. Barkley nn (12/93, $2.95, color)-Dorman painted-c 4.00

GODZILLA (King of the Monsters) (Movie)
Dark Horse Comics: May, 1995 - No. 16, Sept, 1996 ($2.50) (Based on movies)

0-16: 0-r/Dark Horse Comics #10,11. 1-3-Kevin Maguire scripts. 3-8-Art Adams-c 4.00
...Vs. Hero Zero ($2.50) 3.00

GOG (VILLAINS) (See Kingdom Come)
DC Comics: Feb, 1998 ($1.95, one-shot)

1-Waid-s/Ordway-a(p)/Pearson-c 3.00

GO GIRL!
Image Comics: Aug, 2000 - Present ($3.50, B&W, quarterly)

1-5-Trina Robbins-s/Anne Timmons-a; pin-up gallery 3.50

GO-GO
Charlton Comics: June, 1966 - No. 9, Oct, 1967

1-Miss Bikini Luv begins w/Jim Aparo's 1st published work; Rolling Stones, Beatles, Elvis, Sonny & Cher, Bob Dylan, Sinatra, parody; Herman's Hermits pin-ups; D'Agostino-c/a in #1-8 9 18 27 60 85 110
2-Ringo Starr, David McCallum & Beatles photos on cover; Beatles story and photos 9 18 27 60 85 110
3,4: 3-Blooperman begins, ends #6; 1 pg. Batman & Robin satire; full pg. photo pin-ups Lovin' Spoonful & The Byrds 5 10 15 36 48 60
5,7,9: 5 (2/67)-Super Hero & TV satire by Jim Aparo & Grass Green begins. 6-8-Aparo-a. 7-Photo of Brian Wilson of Beach Boys on-c & Beach Boys photo inside f/b-c. 9-Aparo-c/a 5 10 15 36 48 60
6-Parody of JLA & DC heroes vs. Marvel heroes; Aparo-a; Elvis parody; Petula Clark photo-c 6 12 18 40 55 70
8-Monkees photo on-c & photo inside f/b-c 7 14 21 46 63 80

GO-GO AND ANIMAL (See Tippy's Friends...)

GOING STEADY (Formerly Teen-Age Temptations)
St. John Publ. Co.: No. 10, Dec, 1954 - No. 13, June, 1955; No. 14, Oct, 1955

10(1954)-Matt Baker-c/a 21 42 63 118 169 220
11(2/55, last precode), 12(4/55)-Baker-c 12 24 36 69 95 120
13(6/55)-Baker-c/a 15 30 45 83 117 150
14(10/55)-Matt Baker-c/a, 25 pgs. 17 34 51 95 135 175

GOING STEADY (Formerly Personal Love)
Prize Publications/Headline: V3#3, Feb, 1960 - V3#6, Aug, 1960; V4#1, Sept-Oct, 1960

V3#3-6, V4#1 3 6 9 17 21 26

GOING STEADY WITH BETTY (Becomes Betty & Her Steady No. 2)
Avon Periodicals: Nov-Dec, 1949

1 15 30 45 83 117 150

GOLDEN AGE, THE
DC Comics (Elseworlds): 1993 - No. 4, 1994 ($4.95, limited series)

1-4: James Robinson scripts; Paul Smith-c/a; gold foil embossed-c 6.00
Trade Paperback (1995, $19.95) 20.00

GOLDEN AGE SECRET FILES
DC Comics: Feb, 2001 ($4.95, one-shot)

1-Origins and profiles of JSA members and other G.A. heroes; Lark-c 5.00

GOLDEN ARROW (See Fawcett Miniatures, Mighty Midget & Whiz Comics)

GOLDEN ARROW (...Western No. 6)
Fawcett Publications: Spring, 1942 - No. 6, Spring, 1947 (68 pgs.)

1-Golden Arrow begins 87 174 261 544 835 1125
2-(1943) 42 84 126 256 391 525
3-5: 3-(Win/45-46). 4-(Spr/46). 5-(Fall/46) 35 70 105 198 287 375
6-Krigstein-a 36 72 108 204 297 390

GOLDEN COMICS DIGEST
Gold Key: May, 1969 - No. 48, Jan, 1976

NOTE: *Whitman editions exist of many titles and are generally valued the same.*

1-Tom & Jerry, Woody Woodpecker, Bugs Bunny 6 12 18 38 52 65
2-Hanna-Barbera TV Fun Favorites; Space Ghost, Flintstones, Atom Ant, Jetsons, Yogi Bear, Banana Splits, others app. 7 14 21 51 71 90
3-Tom & Jerry, Woody Woodpecker 3 6 9 16 21 26
4-Tarzan; Manning & Marsh-a 5 10 15 33 44 55
5,8-Tom & Jerry, W. Woodpecker, Bugs Bunny 3 6 9 16 20 24
6-Bugs Bunny 3 6 9 16 20 24
7-Hanna-Barbera TV Fun Favorites 6 12 18 38 52 65
9-Tarzan 5 10 15 33 44 55
10,12-17: 10-Bugs Bunny. 12-Tom & Jerry, Bugs Bunny, W. Woodpecker Journey to the Sun. 13-Tom & Jerry. 14-Bugs Bunny Fun Packed Funnies. 15-Tom & Jerry, Woody Woodpecker, Bugs Bunny. 16-Woody Woodpecker Cartoon Special. 17-Bugs Bunny 3 6 9 16 20 24
11-Hanna-Barbera TV Fun Favorites 6 12 18 40 55 70
18-Tom & Jerry; Barney Bear-r by Barks 3 6 9 16 21 26
19-Little Lulu 4 8 12 27 36 45
20-22: 20-Woody Woodpecker Falltime Funtime. 21-Bugs Bunny Showtime. 22-Tom & Jerry Winter Wingding 3 6 9 16 20 24
23-Little Lulu & Tubby Fun Fling 4 8 12 27 36 45
24-26,28: 24-Woody Woodpecker Fun Festival. 25-Tom & Jerry. 26-Bugs Bunny Halloween Hulla-Boo-Loo; Dr. Spektor article, also #25. 28-Tom & Jerry 2 4 6 14 18 22
27-Little Lulu & Tubby in Hawaii 4 8 12 25 33 42
29-Little Lulu & Tubby 4 8 12 25 33 42
30-Bugs Bunny Vacation Funnies 2 4 6 14 18 22
31-Turok, Son of Stone; r/4-Color #596,656; c-r/#9 4 8 12 28 38 48
32-Woody Woodpecker Summer Fun 2 4 6 14 18 22
33,36: 33-Little Lulu & Tubby Halloween Fun; Dr. Spektor app. 36-Little Lulu & Her Friends 4 8 12 25 33 42
34,35,37-39: 34-Bugs Bunny Winter Funnies. 35-Tom & Jerry Snowtime Funtime. 37-Woody Woodpecker County Fair. 39-Bugs Bunny Summer Fun 2 4 6 14 18 22
38-The Pink Panther 3 6 9 16 21 26
40,43: 40-Little Lulu & Tubby Trick or Treat; all by Stanley. 43-Little Lulu in Paris 4 8 12 25 33 42
41,42,44,47: 41-Tom & Jerry Winter Carnival. 42-Bugs Bunny. 44-Woody Woodpecker Family Fun Festival. 47-Bugs Bunny 2 4 6 12 16 20
45-The Pink Panther 3 6 9 16 21 26
46-Little Lulu & Tubby 4 8 12 22 30 38
48-The Lone Ranger 3 6 9 18 24 30

NOTE: *#1-30, 164 pgs.; #31 on, 132 pgs..*

GOLDEN LAD
Spark/Fact & Fiction Publ.: July, 1945 - No. 5, June, 1946 (#4, 5: 52 pgs.)

1-Origin & 1st app. Golden Lad & Swift Arrow; Sandusky and the Senator begins 75 150 225 469 722 975
2-Mort Meskin-c/a 39 78 117 222 324 425
3,4-Mort Meskin-c/a 35 70 105 198 287 375
5-Origin & 1st app. Golden Girl; Shaman & Flame app. 39 78 117 222 324 425

NOTE: *All have* ***Robinson,*** *and* ***Roussos*** *art plus* ***Meskin*** *covers and art.*

GOLDEN LEGACY
Fitzgerald Publishing Co.: 1966 - 1972 (Black History) (25¢)

1-12,14-16: 1-Toussaint L'Ouverture (1966), 2-Harriet Tubman (1967), 3-Crispus Attucks & the Minutemen (1967), 4-Benjamin Banneker (1968), 5-Matthew Henson (1969), 6-Alexander Dumas & Family (1969), 7-Frederick Douglass, Part 1 (1969), 8-Frederick Douglass, Part 2 (1970), 9-Robert Smalls (1970), 10-J. Cinque & the Amistad Mutiny (1970), 11-Men in Action: White, Marshall J. Wilkins (1970), 12-Black Cowboys (1972), 14-The Life of Alexander Pushkin (1971), 15-Ancient African Kingdoms (1972), 16-Black Inventors (1972) each.... 3 6 9 16 20 25
13-The Life of Martin Luther King, Jr. (1972) 3 7 10 21 28 35
1-10,12,13,15,16(1976)-Reprints 1 2 3 5 7 9

GOLDEN LOVE STORIES (Formerly Golden West Love)
Kirby Publishing Co.: No. 4, April, 1950

4-Powell-a; Glenn Ford/Janet Leigh photo-c 16 32 48 89 127 165

GOLDEN PICTURE CLASSIC, A
Western Printing Co. (Simon & Shuster): 1956-1957 (Text stories w/illustrations in color; 100 pgs. each)

CL-401: Treasure Island 10 20 30 60 80 100
CL-402,403: 402: Tom Sawyer. 403: Black Beauty 9 18 27 52 66 80
CL-404, 405: CL-404: Little Women. CL-405: Heidi 9 18 27 52 66 80
CL-406: Ben Hur 8 16 24 40 50 60
CL-407: Around the World in 80 Days 8 16 24 40 50 60
CL-408: Sherlock Holmes 8 16 24 46 58 70
CL-409: The Three Musketeers 8 16 24 40 50 60
CL-410: The Merry Advs. of Robin Hood 8 16 24 40 50 60
CL-411,412: 411: Hans Brinker. 412: The Count of Monte Cristo 8 16 24 46 58 70

(Both soft & hardcover editions are valued the same)

NOTE: *Recent research has uncovered new information. Apparently #s 1-6 were issued in 1956 and #7-12 in 1957. But they can be found in five different series listings: CL-1 to CL-12 (softbound); CL-401 to CL-412 (also softbound); CL-101 to CL-112 (hardbound); plus two new series discoveries: A Golden Reading Adventure, publ. by Golden Press; edited down to 60 pages and reduced in size to 6x9"; only #s discovered so far are #381 (CL-4), #382 (CL-*

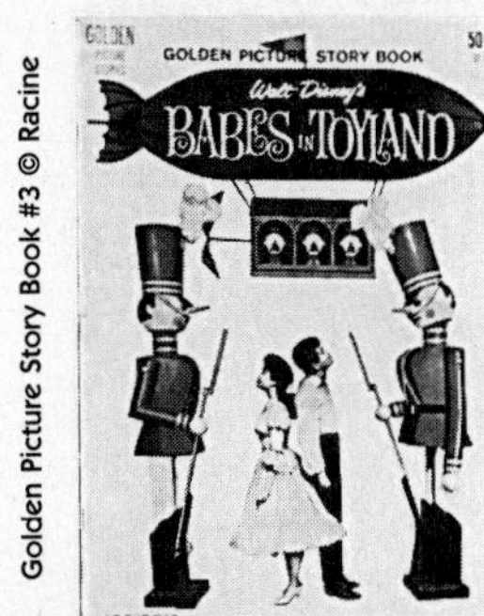

Golden Picture Story Book #3 © Racine

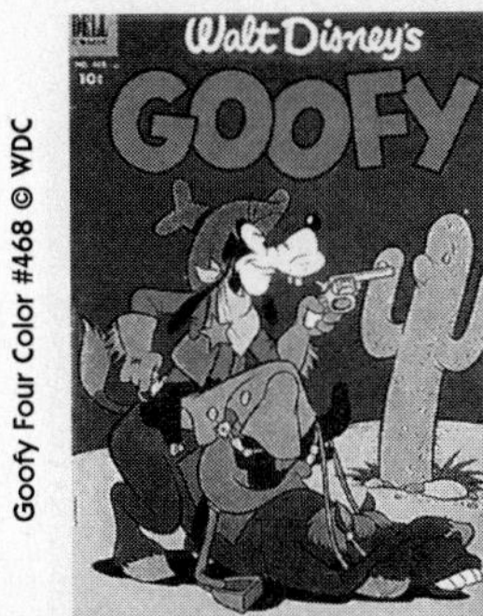

Goofy Four Color #468 © WDC

Goofy Comics #9 © STD

GD 2.0 | VG 4.0 | FN 6.0 | VF 8.0 | VF/NM 9.0 | NM- 9.2

GD 2.0 | VG 4.0 | FN 6.0 | VF 8.0 | VF/NM 9.0 | NM- 9.2

6) & #387 (CL-3). They have no reorder list and some have covers different from GPC. There have also been found British hardbound editions of GPC with dust jackets. Copies of all five listed series vary from scarce to very rare. Some editions of some series have not yet been found at all.

GOLDEN PICTURE STORY BOOK
Racine Press (Western): Dec, 1961 (50¢, Treasury size, 52 pgs.) (All are scarce)

ST-1-Huckleberry Hound (TV); Hokey Wolf, Pixie & Dixie, Quick Draw McGraw, Snooper and Blabber, Augie Doggie app. 20 40 60 141 216 290
ST-2-Yogi Bear (TV); Snagglepuss, Yakky Doodle, Quick Draw McGraw, Snooper and Blabber, Augie Doggie app. 20 40 60 141 216 290
ST-3-Babes in Toyland (Walt Disney's...)-Annette Funicello photo-c 25 50 75 177 271 365
ST-4-(...of Disney Ducks)-Walt Disney's Wonderful World of Ducks (Donald Duck, Uncle Scrooge, Donald's Nephews, Grandma Duck, Ludwig Von Drake, & Gyro Gearloose stories) 25 50 75 177 271 365

GOLDEN RECORD COMIC (See Amazing Spider-Man #1, Avengers #4, Fantastic Four #1, Journey Into Mystery #83)

GOLDEN STORY BOOKS
Western Printing Co. (Simon & Shuster): 1949 (Heavy covers, digest size, 128 pgs.) (Illustrated text in color)

7-Walt Disney's Mystery in Disneyville, a book-length adventure starring Donald and Nephews, Mickey and Nephews, and with Minnie, Daisy and Goofy. Art by Dick Moores & Manuel Gonzales (scarce) 30 60 90 173 249 325
10-Bugs Bunny's Treasure Hunt, a book-length adventure starring Bugs & Porky Pig, with Petunia Pig & Nephew, Cicero. Art by Tom McKimson (scarce) 21 42 63 121 173 225

GOLDEN WEST LOVE (Golden Love Stories No. 4)
Kirby Publishing Co.: Sept-Oct, 1949 - No. 3, Feb, 1950 (All 52 pgs.)

1-Powell-a in all; Roussos-a; painted-c 22 44 66 127 184 240
2,3: Photo-c 16 32 48 89 127 165

GOLDEN WEST RODEO TREASURY (See Dell Giants)

GOLDFISH (See A.K.A. Goldfish)

GOLDILOCKS (See March of Comics No. 1)

GOLD KEY CHAMPION
Gold Key: Mar, 1978 - No. 2, May, 1978 (50¢, 52pgs.)

1,2: 1-Space Family Robinson; half-r. 2-Mighty Samson; half-r 1 3 4 6 8 11

GOLD KEY SPOTLIGHT
Gold Key: May, 1976 - No. 11, Feb, 1978

1-Tom, Dick & Harriet 2 4 6 9 11 14
2-11: 2-Wacky Advs. of Cracky. 3-Wacky Witch. 4-Tom, Dick & Harriet. 5-Wacky Advs. of Cracky. 6-Dagar the Invincible; Santos-a; origin Demonomicon. 7-Wacky Witch & Greta Ghost 10-O. G. Whiz.11-Tom, Dick & Harriet. 8-The Occult Files of Dr. Spektor, Simbar, Lu-sai; Santos-a. 9-Tragg 1 3 4 6 8 10

GOLD MEDAL COMICS
Cambridge House: 1945 (25¢, one-shot, 132 pgs.)

nn-Captain Truth by Fugitani, Crime Detector, The Witch of Salem, Luckyman, others app. 30 60 90 170 245 320

GOMER PYLE (TV)
Gold Key: July, 1966 - No. 3, Jan, 1967

1-Photo front/back-c 10 20 30 67 96 125
2,3 7 14 21 50 68 85

GON
DC Comics (Paradox Press): July, 1996 - No. 4, Oct, 1996; No. 5, 1997 ($5.95, B&W, digest-size, limited series)

1-5: Misadventures of baby dinosaur; 1-Gon. 2-Gon Again. 3-Gon: Here Today, Gone Tomorrow. 4-Gon: Going, Going...Gon. 5-Gon Swimmin'. Tanaka-c/a/scripts in all 1 2 3 5 6 8

GON COLOR SPECTACULAR
DC Comics (Paradox Press): 1998 ($5.95, square-bound)

nn-Tanaka-c/a/scripts 1 2 3 5 6 8

GON ON SAFARI
DC Comics (Paradox Press): 2000 ($7.95, B&W, digest-size)

nn-Tanaka-c/a/scripts 1 2 3 5 6 8

GON UNDERGROUND
DC Comics (Paradox Press): 1999 ($7.95, B&W, digest-size)

nn-Tanaka-c/a/scripts 1 2 3 5 6 8

GON WILD
DC Comics (Paradox Press): 1997 ($9.95, B&W, digest-size)

nn-Tanaka-c/a/scripts in all. (Rep. Gon #3,4) 1 3 4 6 8 10

GOODBYE, MR. CHIPS (See Movie Comics)

GOOD GIRL ART QUARTERLY
AC Comics: Summer, 1990 - No. 15, Spring, 1994 (B&W/color, 52 pgs.)

1,3-15 ($3.50)-All have one new story (often FemForce) & rest reprints by Baker, Ward & other "good girl" artists 4.00
2 ($3.95) 4.00

GOOD GIRL COMICS (Formerly Good Girl Art Quarterly)
AC Comics: No. 16, Summer, 1994 - No. 18, 1995 (B&W)

16-18 4.00

GOOD GUYS, THE
Defiant: Nov, 1993 - No. 9, July, 1994 ($2.50/$3.25/$3.50)

1-($3.50, 52 pgs.)-Glory x-over from Plasm 3.50
2,3,5-9: 9-Pre-Schism issue 2.50
4-($3.25, 52 pgs.) 3.25

GOOD TRIUMPHS OVER EVIL! (Also see Narrative Illustration)
M.C. Gaines: 1943 (12 pgs., 7-1/4"x10", B&W) (not a comic book) (Rare)

nn-A pamphlet, sequel to Narrative Illustration 96 192 288 600 925 1250

GOOFY (Disney)(See Dynabrite Comics, Mickey Mouse Magazine V4#7, Walt Disney Showcase #35 & Wheaties)
Dell Publishing Co.: No. 468, May, 1953 - Sept-Nov, 1962

Four Color 468 (#1) 13 26 39 92 141 190
Four Color 562,627,658,702,747,802,857 8 16 24 58 82 105
Four Color 899,952,987,1053,1094,1149,1201 6 12 18 40 55 70
12-308-211(Dell, 9-11/62) 6 12 18 40 55 70

GOOFY ADVENTURES
Disney Comics: June, 1990 - No. 17, 1991 ($1.50)

1-17: Most new stories. 2-Joshua Quagmire-a w/free poster. 7-WDC&S-r plus new-a. 9-Gottfredson-r. 14-Super Goof story. 15-All Super Goof issue. 17-Gene Colan-a(p) 3.00

GOOFY ADVENTURE STORY (See Goofy No. 857)

GOOFY COMICS (Companion to Happy Comics)(Not Disney)
Nedor Publ. Co. No. 1-14/Standard No. 14-48: June, 1943 - No. 48, 1953 (Animated Cartoons)

1-Funny animal; Oriolo-c 30 60 90 170 245 320
2 15 30 45 86 123 160
3-10 12 24 36 69 95 120
11-19 10 20 30 58 77 95
20-35-Frazetta text illos in all 11 22 33 64 87 110
36-48 9 18 27 51 62 75

GOOFY SUCCESS STORY (See Goofy No. 702)

GOON, THE
Avatar Press: Mar, 1999 - No. 3, July, 1999 ($3.00, B&W)

1- Eric Powell-s/a 20.00
2 12.00
3 8.00
...: Rough Stuff (Albatross, 1/03, $15.95) r/Avatar Press series #1-3 16.00
...: Rough Stuff (Dark Horse, 2/04, $12.95) r/Avatar Press series #1-3 newly colored 13.00

GOON, THE
Albatross Exploding Funny Books: Oct, 2002 - No. 4, Feb, 2003 ($2.95)

1- Eric Powell-s/a 10.00
2-4 6.00
...Color Special 1 (8/02) 10.00
...: Nothin' But Misery Vol. 1 (Dark Horse, 7/03, $15.95, TPB) - Reprints The Goon #1-4 (Albatross series), Color Special, and story from DHP #157 16.00

GOON, THE
Dark Horse Comics: June, 2003 - Present ($2.99)

1-8-Eric Powell-s/a. 7-Hellboy-c/app; framing seq. by Mignola 3.00
...: My Murderous Childhood (And Other Grievous Yarns) (5/04, $13.95, TPB) r/#1-4 and short story from Drawing on Your Nightmares one-shot; intro. by Frank Cho 14.00

GOOSE (Humor magazine)
Cousins Publ. (Fawcett): Sept, 1976 - No. 3, 1976 (75¢, 52 pgs., B&W)

1-Nudity in all 2 4 6 14 18 22
2,3: 2-(10/76) Fonz-c/s; Lone Ranger story. 3-Wonder Woman, King Kong, Six Million

Gorgo #6 © CC

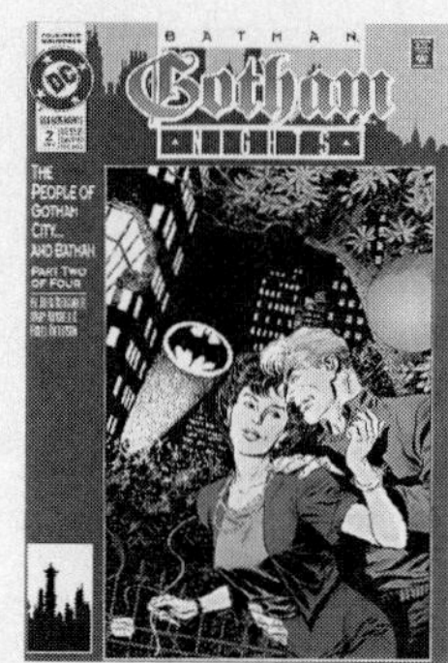

Gotham Nights #2 © DC

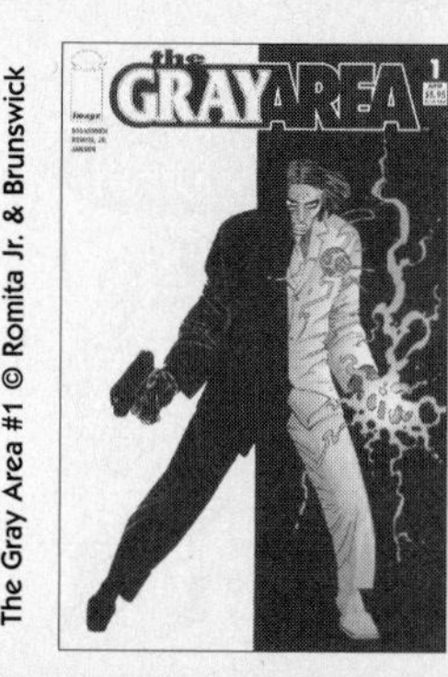

The Gray Area #1 © Romita Jr. & Brunswick

	GD 2.0	VG 4.0	FN 6.0	VF 8.0	VF/NM 9.0	NM- 9.2
Dollar Man stories	2	4	6	10	12	15

GORDO (See Comics Revue No. 5 & Giant Comics Edition)

GORGO (Based on M.G.M. movie) (See Return of...)
Charlton Comics: May, 1961 - No. 23, Sept, 1965

	GD	VG	FN	VF	VF/NM	NM-
1-Ditko-a, 22 pgs.	24	48	72	170	260	350
2,3-Ditko-c/a	12	24	36	86	131	175
4-Ditko-c	8	16	24	58	82	105
5-11,13-16: 11,13-16-Ditko-a	8	16	24	53	74	95
12,17-23: 12-Reptisaurus x-over; Montes/Bache-a-No. 17-23. 20-Giordano-c	5	10	15	33	44	55
Gorgo's Revenge('62)-Becomes Return of...	6	12	18	40	55	70

GOSPEL BLIMP, THE
Spire Christian Comics (Fleming H. Revell Co.): 1973,1974 (35¢/39¢, 36 pgs.)

	GD	VG	FN	VF	VF/NM	NM-
nn	1	3	4	6	8	11

G.O.T.H.
Verotik: Dec, 1995 - No. 3, June, 1996 ($2.95, limited series, mature)

1-3: Danzig scripts; Liam Sharpe-a. 3.00

GOTHAM BY GASLIGHT (A Tale of the Batman)(See Batman: Master of...)
DC Comics: 1989 ($3.95, one-shot, squarebound, 52 pgs.)

nn-Mignola/Russell-a; intro by Robert Bloch 4.00

GOTHAM CENTRAL
DC Comics: Early Feb, 2003 - Present ($2.50)

1-26-Stories of Gotham City Police. 1-Brubaker & Rucka-s/Lark-c/a. 10-Two-Face app. 13,15-Joker-c. 18-Huntress app. 2.50
...: In The Line of Duty (2004, $9.95, TPB) r/#1-5, cover gallery & sketch pages 10.00

GOTHAM GIRLS
DC Comics: Oct, 2002 - No. 5, Feb, 2003 ($2.25, limited series)

1-5-Catwoman, Batgirl, Poison Ivy, Harley Quinn from animated series 2.25

GOTHAM NIGHTS (See Batman: Gotham Nights II)
DC Comics: Mar, 1992 - No. 4, June, 1992 ($1.25, limited series)

1-4: Featuring Batman 2.25

GOTHIC ROMANCES
Atlas/Seaboard Publ.: Dec, 1974 (75¢, B&W, magazine, 76 pgs.)

	GD	VG	FN	VF	VF/NM	NM-
1-Text w/ illos by N. Adams, Chaykin, Heath (2 pgs. ea.); painted cover (scarce)	12	24	36	82	124	165

GOTHIC TALES OF LOVE (Magazine)
Marvel Comics: Apr, 1975 - No. 3, 1975 (B&W, 76 pgs.)

	GD	VG	FN	VF	VF/NM	NM-
1-3-Painted-c/a (scarce)	12	24	36	82	124	165

GOVERNOR & J. J., THE (TV)
Gold Key: Feb, 1970 - No. 3, Aug, 1970 (Photo-c)

	GD	VG	FN	VF	VF/NM	NM-
1	5	10	15	33	44	55
2,3	4	8	12	22	30	38

GRACKLE, THE
Acclaim Comics: Jan, 1997 - No. 4, Apr, 1997 ($2.95, B&W)

1-4: Mike Baron scripts & Paul Gulacy-c/a. 1-4-Doublecross 3.00

GRAFIK MUSIK
Caliber Press: Nov, 1990 - No. 4, Aug, 1991 ($3.50/$2.50)

	GD	VG	FN	VF	VF/NM	NM-
1-($3.50, 48 pgs., color) Mike Allred-c/a/scripts-1st app. in color of Frank Einstein (Madman)	3	6	9	16	20	25
2-($2.50, 24 pgs., color)	2	4	6	10	12	15
3,4-($2.50, 24 pgs., B&W)	2	4	6	8	10	12

GRANDMA DUCK'S FARM FRIENDS(See Walt Disney's C&S 293 & Wheaties)
Dell Publishing Co.: No. 763, Jan, 1957 - No. 1279, Feb, 1962 (Disney)

	GD	VG	FN	VF	VF/NM	NM-
Four Color 763 (#1)	9	18	27	60	85	110
Four Color 873	6	12	18	43	59	75
Four Color 965,1279	6	12	18	38	52	65
Four Color 1010,1073,1161-Barks-a; 1073,1161-Barks c/a	14	28	42	97	149	200

GRAND PRIX (Formerly Hot Rod Racers)
Charlton Comics: No. 16, Sept, 1967 - No. 31, May, 1970

	GD	VG	FN	VF	VF/NM	NM-
16-Features Rick Roberts	4	8	12	24	32	42
17-20	3	6	9	19	25	32
21-31	3	6	9	18	23	28

GRAPHIQUE MUSIQUE
Slave Labor Graphics: Dec, 1989 - No. 3, May, 1990 ($2.95, 52 pgs.)

	GD	VG	FN	VF	VF/NM	NM-
1-Mike Allred-c/a/scripts	4	8	12	24	32	40
2,3	3	6	9	18	24	30

GRAVEDIGGERS
Acclaim Comics: Nov, 1996 - No. 4, Feb, 1997 ($2.95, B&W)

1-4: Moretti scripts 3.00

GRAVESTONE
Malibu Comics: July, 1993 - No. 7, Feb, 1994 ($2.25)

1-6: 3-Polybagged w/Skycap 2.25
7-($2.50) 2.50

GRAVE TALES
Hamilton Comics: Oct, 1991 - No. 3, Feb, 1992 ($3.95, B&W, mag., 52 pgs.)

	GD	VG	FN	VF	VF/NM	NM-
1-Staton-c/a	1	2	3	5	6	8
2,3: 2-Staton-a; Morrow-c						6.00

GRAY AREA, THE
Image Comics: Jun, 2004 - No. 3, Oct, 2004 ($5.95/$3.95, limited series)

1,3-($5.95) Romita, Jr.-a/Brunswick-s; sketch pages and script pages. 3-Pin-up pages 6.00
2-($3.95) 4.00

GRAY GHOST, THE
Dell Publishing Co.: No. 911, July, 1958; No. 1000, June-Aug, 1959

	GD	VG	FN	VF	VF/NM	NM-
Four Color 911 (#1), 1000-Photo-c each	10	20	30	70	100	130

GREAT ACTION COMICS
I. W. Enterprises: 1958 (Reprints with new covers)

	GD	VG	FN	VF	VF/NM	NM-
1-Captain Truth reprinted from Gold Medal #1	3	6	9	18	24	30
8,9-Reprints Phantom Lady #15 & 23	9	18	27	60	85	110

GREAT AMERICAN COMICS PRESENTS - THE SECRET VOICE
Peter George 4-Star Publ./American Features Syndicate: 1945 (10¢)

	GD	VG	FN	VF	VF/NM	NM-
1-Anti-Nazi; "What Really Happened to Hitler"	35	70	105	201	293	385

GREAT AMERICAN WESTERN, THE
AC Comics: 1987 - No. 4, 1990? ($1.75/$2.95/$3.50, B&W with some color)

1-4: 1-Western-r plus Bill Black-a. 2-Tribute to ME comics; Durango Kid photo-c 3-Tribute to Tom Mix plus Roy Rogers, Durango Kid; Billy the Kid-r by Severin; photo-c. 4- ($3.50, 52 pgs., 16 pgs. color)-Tribute to Lash LaRue; photo-c & interior photos; Fawcett-r 4.00
...Presents 1 (1991, $5.00) New Sunset Carson; film history 5.00

GREAT CAT FAMILY, THE (Disney-TV/Movie)
Dell Publishing Co.: No. 750, Nov, 1956 (one-shot)

	GD	VG	FN	VF	VF/NM	NM-
Four Color 750-Pinocchio & Alice app.	8	16	24	53	74	95

GREAT COMICS
Great Comics Publications: Nov, 1941 - No. 3, Jan, 1942

	GD	VG	FN	VF	VF/NM	NM-
1-Origin/1st app. The Great Zarro; Madame Strange & Guy Gorham, Wizard of Science & The Great Zarro begin	138	276	414	863	1332	1800
2-Buck Johnson, Jungle Explorer app.; X-Mas-c	65	130	195	406	628	850
3-Futuro Takes Hitler to Hell-c/s; "The Lost City" movie story (starring William Boyd); continues in Choice Comics #3	269	538	807	1681	2591	3500

GREAT COMICS
Novack Publishing Co./Jubilee Comics/Knockout/Barrel O' Fun: 1945

	GD	VG	FN	VF	VF/NM	NM-
1-(Four publ. variations: Barrel O-Fun, Jubilee, Knockout & Novack)-The Defenders, Capt. Power app.; L. B. Cole-c	40	80	120	233	342	450
1-(Jubilee)-Same cover; Boogey Man, Satanas, & The Sorcerer & His Apprentice	30	60	90	170	245	320
1-(Barrel O' Fun)-L. B. Cole-c; Barrel O' Fun overprinted in indicia; Li'l Cactus, Cuckoo Sheriff (humorous)	20	40	60	112	161	210

GREAT DOGPATCH MYSTERY (See Mammy Yokum & the...)

GREATEST BATMAN STORIES EVER TOLD, THE
DC Comics

Hardcover ($24.95) 50.00
Softcover ($15.95) "Greatest DC Stories Vol. 2" on spine 20.00
Vol. 2 softcover (1992, $16.95)"Greatest DC Stories Vol. 7" on spine 20.00

GREATEST FLASH STORIES EVER TOLD, THE
DC Comics: 1991

nn-Hardcover ($29.95); Infantino-c 45.00
nn-Softcover ($14.95) 18.00

GREATEST GOLDEN AGE STORIES EVER TOLD, THE
DC Comics: 1990 ($24.95, hardcover)

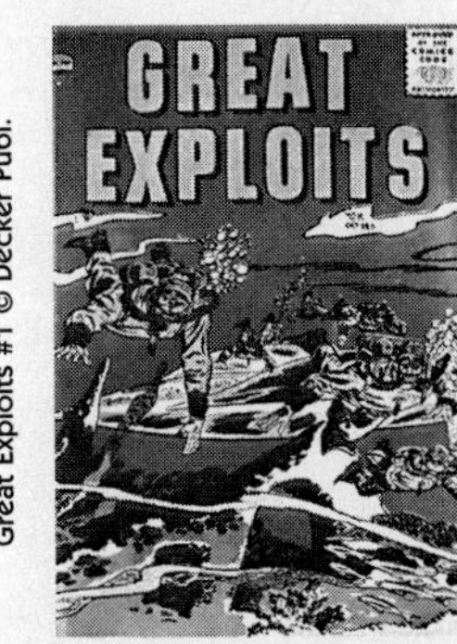

Great Exploits #1 © Decker Publ.

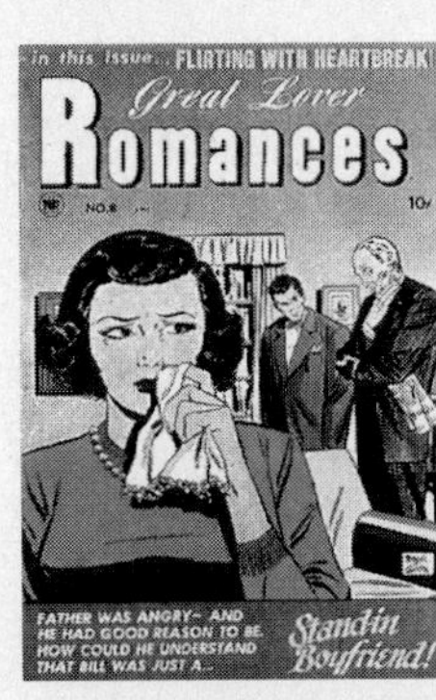

Great Lover Romances #8 © TOBY

Green Arrow ('03) #30 © DC

	GD	VG	FN	VF	VF/NM	NM-
	2.0	4.0	6.0	8.0	9.0	9.2

nn-Ordway-c 60.00

GREATEST JOKER STORIES EVER TOLD, THE (See Batman)
DC Comics: 1983

Hardcover ($19.95)-Kyle Baker painted-c 45.00
Softcover ($14.95) 20.00
Stacked Deck...Expanded Edition (1992, $29.95)-Longmeadow Press Publ. 32.00

GREATEST 1950s STORIES EVER TOLD, THE
DC Comics: 1990

Hardcover ($29.95)-Kubert-c 55.00
Softcover ($14.95) "Greatest DC Stories Vol. 5" on spine 22.00

GREATEST TEAM-UP STORIES EVER TOLD, THE
DC Comics: 1989

Hardcover ($24.95)-DeVries and Infantino painted-c 55.00
Softcover ($14.95) "Greatest DC Stories Vol. 4" on spine; Adams-c 22.00

GREATEST SUPERMAN STORIES EVER TOLD, THE
DC Comics: 1987

Hardcover ($24.95) 50.00
Softcover ($15.95) 22.00

GREAT EXPLOITS
Decker Publ./Red Top: Oct, 1957

1-Krigstein-a(2) (re-issue on cover); reprints Daring Advs. #6 by Approved Comics
8 16 24 40 50 60

GREAT FOODINI, THE (See Foodini)

GREAT GAZOO, THE (The Flintstones)(TV)
Charlton Comics: Aug, 1973 - No. 20, Jan, 1977 (Hanna-Barbera)

1 4 8 12 27 36 45
2-10 2 4 6 14 18 22
11-20 2 4 6 10 13 16

GREAT GRAPE APE, THE (TV)(See TV Stars #1)
Charlton Comics: Sept, 1976 - No. 2, Nov, 1976 (Hanna-Barbera)

1 3 6 9 19 25 32
2 2 4 6 11 14 18

GREAT LOCOMOTIVE CHASE, THE (Disney)
Dell Publishing Co.: No. 712, Sept, 1956 (one-shot)

Four Color 712-Movie, photo-c 8 16 24 58 82 105

GREAT LOVER ROMANCES (Young Lover Romances #4,5)
Toby Press: 3/51; #2, 1951(nd); #3, 1952 (nd); #6, Oct?, 1952 - No. 22, May, 1955 (Photo-c #1-5, 10 ,13, 15, 17) (no #4, 5)

1-Jon Juan story-r/Jon Juan #1 by Schomburg; Dr. Anthony King app.
17 34 51 95 135 175
2-Jon Juan, Dr. Anthony King app. 10 20 30 58 77 95
3,7,9-14,16-22: 10-Rita Hayworth photo-c. 17-Rita Hayworth & Aldo Ray photo-c
8 16 24 40 50 60
6-Kurtzman-a (10/52) 10 20 30 58 77 95
8-Five pgs. of "Pin-Up Pete" by Sparling 10 20 30 58 77 95
15-Liz Taylor photo-c 21 42 63 121 173 225

GREAT RACE, THE (See Movie Classics)

GREAT SCOTT SHOE STORE (See Bulls-Eye)

GREAT SOCIETY COMIC BOOK, THE (Political parody)
Pocket Books Inc./Parallax Pub.: 1966 ($1.00, 36 pgs., 7"x10", one-shot)

nn-Super-LBJ-c/story; 60s politicians app. as super-heroes; Tallarico-a
3 6 9 18 24 30

GREAT WEST (Magazine)
M. F. Enterprises: 1969 (B&W, 52 pgs.)

V1#1 2 4 6 11 14 18

GREAT WESTERN
Magazine Enterprises: No. 8, Jan-Mar, 1954 - No. 11, Oct-Dec, 1954

8(A-1 93)-Trail Colt by Guardineer; Powell Red Hawk-r/Straight Arrow begins, ends #11; Durango Kid story 22 44 66 123 177 230
9(A-1 105), 11(A-1 127)-Ghost Rider, Durango Kid app. in each. 9-Red Mask-c, but no app.
15 30 45 83 117 150
10(A-1 113)-The Calico Kid by Guardineer-r/Tim Holt #8; Straight Arrow, Durango Kid app.
14 28 42 79 110 140
I.W. Reprint #1,2 9: 1,2-r/Straight Arrow #36,42. 9-r/Straight Arrow #?
3 6 9 18 23 28
I.W. Reprint #8-Origin Ghost Rider(r/Tim Holt #11); Tim Holt app.; Bolle-a
3 6 9 19 25 32

NOTE: *Guardineer c-8.* ***Powell*** *a(r)-8-11 (from Straight Arrow).*

GREEN ARROW (See Action #440, Adventure, Brave & the Bold, DC Super Stars #17, Detective #521, Flash #217, Green Lantern #76, Justice League of America #4, Leading Comics, More Fun #73 (1st app.), Showcase '95 #9 & World's Finest Comics)

GREEN ARROW
DC Comics: May, 1983 - No. 4, Aug, 1983 (limited series)

1-Origin; Speedy cameo; Mike W. Barr scripts, Trevor Von Eeden-c/a 5.00
2-4 4.00

GREEN ARROW
DC Comics: Feb, 1988 - No. 137, Oct, 1998 ($1.00-$2.50) (Painted-c #1-3)

1-Mike Grell scripts begin, ends #80 5.00
2-49,51-74,76-86: 27,28-Warlord app. 35-38-Co-stars Black Canary; Bill Wray-i. 40-Grell-a. 47-Begin $1.50-c. 63-No longer has mature readers on-c. 63-66-Shado app. 81-Aparo-a begins, ends #100; Nuklon app. 82-Intro & death of Rival. 83-Huntress-c/story. 84-Deathstroke cameo. 85-Deathstroke-c/app. 86-Catwoman-c/story w/Jim Balent layouts 2.50
50,75-($2.50, 52 pgs.): Anniversary issues. 75-Arsenal (Roy Harper) & Shado app. 3.00
0,87-96: 87-$1.95-c begins. 88-Guy Gardner, Martian Manhunter, & Wonder Woman-c/app.; Flash-c. 89-Anarky app. 90-(9/94)-Zero Hour tie-in. 0-(10/94)-1st app. Connor Hawke; Aparo-a(p). 91-(11/94). 93-1st app. Camorouge. 95-Hal Jordan cameo. 96-Intro new Force of July; Hal Jordan (Parallax) app; Oliver Queen learns that Connor Hawke is his son 2.50
97-99,102-109: 97-Begin $2.25-c; no Aparo-a. 97-99-Arsenal app. 102,103-Underworld Unleashed x-over. 104-GL(Kyle Rayner)-c/app. 105-Robin-c/app. 107-109-Thorn app. 109-Lois Lane cameo; Weeks-c. 2.50
100-($3.95)-Foil-c; Superman app. 1 3 4 6 8 10
101-Death of Oliver Queen; Superman app. 3 6 9 18 24 30
110,111-124: 110,111-GL x-over. 110-Intro Hatchet. 114-Final Night. 115-117-Black Canary & Oracle app. 2.50
125-($3.50, 48 pgs)-GL x-over cont. in GL #92 3.50
126-136: 126-Begin $2.50-c. 130-GL & Flash x-over. 132,133-JLA app. 134,135-Brotherhood of the Fist pts. 1,5. 136-Hal Jordan-c/app. 2.50
137-Last issue; Superman app.; last panel cameo of Oliver Queen
2 4 6 10 12 15
#1,000,000 (11/98) 853rd Century x-over 2.50
Annual 1-6 ('88-'94, 68 pgs.)-1-No Grell scripts. 2-No Grell scripts; recaps origin Green Arrow, Speedy, Black Canary & others. 3-Bill Wray-a. 4-50th anniversary issue. 5-Batman, Eclipso app. 6-Bloodlines; Hook app. 3.50
Annual 7-('95, $3.95)-Year One story 4.00

NOTE: ***Aparo*** *a-0, 81-85, 86 (partial),87p, 88p, 91-95, 96i, 98-100p, 109p; c-81,98-100p.* ***Austin*** *c-96i.* ***Balent*** *layouts-86.* ***Burchett*** *c-91-95.* ***Campanella*** *a-100-108i, 110-113i; c-99i, 101-108i,110-113i.* ***Denys Cowan*** *a-39p, 41-43p, 47p, 48p, 60p; c-41-43.* ***Damaggio*** *a(p)-97p, 100-108p, 110-112p; c-97-99p, 101-108p, 110-113p.* ***Mike Grell*** *c-1-4, 10p, 11, 39, 40, 44, 45, 47-80, Annual 4, 5.* ***Nasser/Netzer*** *a-89, 96.* ***Sienkiewicz*** *a-109i.* ***Springer*** *a-67, 68.* ***Weeks*** *c-109.*

GREEN ARROW
DC Comics: Apr, 2001 - Present ($2.50)

1-Oliver Queen returns; Kevin Smith-s/Hester-a/Wagner-painted-c
2 4 6 10 13 16
1-2nd-4th printings 3.00
2-Batman cameo 1 2 3 4 5 7
2-2nd printing 2.50
3-5: 4-JLA app. 5.00
6-15: 7-Barry Allen & Hal Jordan app. 9,10-Stanley & his Monster app. 10-Oliver regains his soul. 12-Hawkman-c/app. 3.00
16-25: 16-Brad Meltzer-s begin; The Shade app. 18-Solomon Grundy-c/app. 19-JLA app. 22-Beatty-s; Count Vertigo app. 23-25-Green Lantern app.; Raab-s/Adlard-a 2.50
26-44: 26-Winick-s begin. 35-37-Riddler app. 43-Mia learns she's HIV+ 2.50
...: Quiver HC (2002, $24.95) r/#1-10; Smith intro. 25.00
...: Quiver SC (2003, $17.95) r/#1-10; Smith intro. 18.00
...Secret Files & Origins 1-(12/02, $4.95) Origin stories & profiles; Wagner-c 5.00
...: Sounds of Violence HC (2003, $19.95) r/#11-15; Hester intro. & sketch pages 20.00
...: Sounds of Violence SC (2003, $12.95) r/#11-15; Hester intro. & sketch pages 13.00
...: Straight Shooter SC (2004, $12.95) r/#26-31 13.00
...: The Archer's Quest HC (2003, $19.95) r/#16-21; pitch, script and sketch pages 20.00
...: The Archer's Quest SC (2004, $14.95) r/#16-21; pitch, script and sketch pages 15.00

GREEN ARROW: THE LONG BOW HUNTERS
DC Comics: Aug, 1987 - No. 3, Oct, 1987 ($2.95, limited series, mature)

1-Grell-c/a in all 6.00
1,2-2nd printings 3.00
2,3 4.00
Trade paperback (1989, $12.95)-r/#1-3 13.00

Green Giant Comics #1 © Pelican Press

Green Hornet Comics #32 © HARV

Green Lantern #1 © DC

GD VG FN VF VF/NM NM-
2.0 4.0 6.0 8.0 9.0 9.2

GREEN ARROW: THE WONDER YEAR
DC Comics: Feb, 1993 - No. 4, May, 1993 ($1.75, limited series)

1-4: Mike Grell-a(p)/scripts & Gray Morrow-a(i) 2.50

GREEN BERET, THE (See Tales of...)

GREEN CANDLES
DC Comics (Paradox Press): Sept, 1995 - No. 3, Dec, 1995 ($5.95, B&W, limited series, digest size)

1-3 6.00
Paperback ($9.95) 10.00

GREEN GIANT COMICS (Also see Colossus Comics)
Pelican Publ. (Funnies, Inc.): 1940 (No price on cover; distributed in New York City only)

1-Dr. Nerod, Green Giant, Black Arrow, Mundoo & Master Mystic app.; origin Colossus (Rare)
1000 2000 3000 7500 12,250 17,000

NOTE: *The idea for this book came from George Kapitan. Printed by Moreau Publ. of Orange, N.J. as an experiment to see if they could profitably use the idle time of their 40-page Hoe color press. The experiment failed due to the difficulty of obtaining good quality color registration and Mr. Moreau believes the book never reached the stands. The book has no price or date which lends credence to this. Contains five pages reprinted from Motion Picture Funnies Weekly.*

GREEN GOBLIN
Marvel Comics: Oct, 1995 - No. 13, Oct, 1996 ($2.95/$1.95)

1-($2.95)-Scott McDaniel-c/a begins, ends #7; foil-c 3.50
2-13: 2-Begin $1.95-c. 4-Hobgoblin-c/app; Thing app. 6-Daredevil-c/app. 8-Robertson-a; McDaniel-c. 12,13-Onslaught x-over. 13-Green Goblin quits; Spider-Man app. 2.25

GREENHAVEN
Aircel Publishing: 1988 - No. 3, 1988 ($2.00, limited series, 28 pgs.)

1-3 2.25

GREEN HORNET, THE (TV)
Dell Publishing Co./Gold Key: Sept, 1953; Feb, 1967 - No. 3, Aug, 1967

Four Color 496-Painted-c. 26 52 81 192 294 385
1-All have Bruce Lee photo-c 22 44 66 160 245 330
2,3 15 30 45 107 164 220

GREEN HORNET, THE (Also see Kato of the... & Tales of the...)
Now Comics: Nov, 1989 - No. 14, Feb, 1991 ($1.75)
V2#1, Sept, 1991 - V2#40, Jan, 1995 ($1.95)

1 ($2.95, double-size)-Steranko painted-c; G.A. Green Hornet 5.00
1,2: 1-2nd printing ('90, $3.95)-New Butler-c 4.00
3-14: 5-Death of original ('30s) Green Hornet. 6-Dave Dorman painted-c. 11-Snyder-c 3.00
V2#1-11,13-21,24-26,28-30,32-37: 1-Butler painted-c. 9-Mayerik-c 2.50
12-($2.50)-Color Green Hornet button polybagged inside 4.00
22,23-($2.95)-Bagged w/color hologravure card 4.00
27-($2.95)-Newsstand ed. polybagged w/multi-dimensional card (1993 Anniversary Special on cover), 27-($2.95)-Direct Sale ed. polybagged w/multi-dimensional card; cover variations 3.00
31,38: 31-($2.50)-Polybagged w/trading card 2.50
39,40-Low print run 6.00
1-($2.50)-Polybagged w/button (same as #12) 2.50
2,3-($1.95)-Same as #13 & 14 2.25
Annual 1 (12/92, $2.50), Annual 1994 (10/94, $2.95) 3.50

GREEN HORNET: DARK TOMORROW
Now Comics: Jun, 1993 - No. 3, Aug, 1993 ($2.50, limited series)

1-3: Future Green Hornet 3.00

GREEN HORNET: SOLITARY SENTINEL, THE
Now Comics: Dec, 1992 - No. 3, 1993 ($2.50, limited series)

1-3 3.00

GREEN HORNET COMICS (...Racket Buster #44) (Radio, movies)
Helnit Publ. Co.(Holyoke) No. 1-6/Family Comics(Harvey) No. 7-on:
Dec, 1940 - No. 47, Sept, 1949 (See All New #13,14)(Early issues: 68 pgs.)

1-1st app. Green Hornet & Kato; origin of Green Hornet on inside front-c; intro the Black Beauty (Green Hornet's car); painted-c
484 968 1452 3388 5444 7500
2-Early issues based on radio adventures 200 400 600 1250 1925 2600
3 142 284 426 888 1369 1850
4-6: 6-(8/41) 115 230 345 719 1110 1500
7 (6/42)-Origin The Zebra & begins; Robin Hood, Spirit of '76, Blonde Bomber & Mighty Midgets begin; new logo 96 192 288 600 925 1250
8,10 81 162 243 506 778 1050
9-Kirby-c 100 200 300 625 963 1300
11,12-Mr. Q in both 79 158 237 494 760 1025
13-1st Nazi-c; shows Hitler poster on-c 87 174 261 544 835 1125
14-19 60 120 180 375 580 785
20-Classic-c 66 132 198 413 637 860
21-23,25-30 48 96 144 293 447 600
24-Sci-Fi-c 52 104 156 317 484 650
31-The Man in Black Called Fate begins (11-12/45, early app.)
50 100 150 305 465 625
32-36 40 80 120 241 363 485
37,38: Shock Gibson app. by Powell. 37-S&K Kid Adonis reprinted from Stuntman #3. 38-Kid Adonis app. 40 80 120 241 363 485
39-Stuntman story by S&K 50 100 150 305 465 625
40-47: 42-47-Kerry Drake in all. 45-Boy Explorers on-c only. 46- "Case of the Marijuana Racket" cover/story; Kerry Drake app. 35 70 105 201 293 385

NOTE: ***Fuje** a-23, 24, 26. **Henkle** c-7-9. **Kubert** a-20, 30. **Powell** a-7-10, 12, 14, 16-21, 30, 31(2), 32(3), 33, 34(3), 35, 36, 37(2), 38. **Robinson** a-27. **Schomburg** c-15, 17-23. Kirbyish c-7, 15. Bondage c-8, 14, 18, 26, 36.*

GREEN JET COMICS, THE (See Comic Books, Series 1)

GREEN LAMA (Also see Comic Books, Series 1, Daring Adventures #17 & Prize Comics #7)
Spark Publications/Prize No. 7 on: Dec, 1944 - No. 8, Mar, 1946

1-Intro. Lt. Hercules & The Boy Champions; Mac Raboy-c/a #1-8
131 262 393 819 1260 1700
2-Lt. Hercules borrows the Human Torch's powers for one panel
77 154 231 481 741 1000
3-6,8: 4-Dick Tracy take-off in Lt. Hercules story by H. L. Gold (science fiction writer). 5-Lt. Hercules story; Little Orphan Annie, Smilin' Jack & Snuffy Smith take-off (5/45) 62 124 186 388 594 800
7-X-mas-c; Raboy craft tint-c/a (note: a small quantity of NM copies surfaced)
39 78 117 222 324 425

NOTE: ***Robinson** a-3-5, 8. Roussos a-8. Formerly a pulp hero who began in 1940.*

GREEN LANTERN (1st Series) (See All-American, All Flash Quarterly, All Star Comics, The Big All-American & Comic Cavalcade)
National Periodical Publications/All-American: Fall, 1941 - No. 38, May-June, 1949 (#1-18 are quarterly)

1-Origin retold; classic Purcell-c 2975 5950 8925 23,800 39,400 55,000
2-1st book-length story 677 1354 2031 4739 7620 10,500
3-Classic German war-c by Mart Nodell 484 968 1452 3388 5444 7500
4-Green Lantern & Doiby Dickles join the Army 400 800 1200 2600 4200 5800
5 292 584 876 1825 2813 3800
6,8: 8-Hop Harrigan begins; classic-c 231 462 693 1444 2222 3000
7-Robot-c. 246 492 738 1538 2369 3200
9,10: 10-Origin/1st app. Vandal Savage 200 400 600 1250 1925 2600
11-15: 12-Origin/1st app. Gambler 150 300 450 938 1444 1950
16-Classic jungle-c (scarce in high grade) 154 308 462 963 1482 2000
17,19,20 135 270 405 844 1297 1750
18-Christmas-c 169 338 507 1056 1628 2200
21-26,28 119 238 357 744 1147 1550
27-Origin/1st app. Sky Pirate 125 250 375 781 1203 1625
29-All Harlequin issue; classic Harlequin-c 129 258 387 806 1241 1675
30-Origin/1st app. Streak the Wonder Dog by Toth (2-3/48) (scarce)
169 338 507 1056 1628 2200
31-35: 35-Kubert-c. 35-38-New logo 102 204 306 638 982 1325
36-38: 37-Sargon the Sorcerer app. 125 250 375 781 1203 1625

NOTE: *Book-length stories #2-7. **Mayer/Moldoff** c-9. **Mayer/Purcell** c-8. **Purcell** c-1. **Mart Nodell** c-2, 3, 7. **Paul Reinman** c-11, 12, 15-22. **Toth** a-28, 30, 31, 34-38; c-28, 30, 34p, 36-38p. Cover to #8 says Fall while the indicia says Summer Issue. Streak the Wonder Dog c-30 (w/Green Lantern), 34, 36, 38.*

GREEN LANTERN (See Action Comics Weekly, Adventure Comics, Brave & the Bold, Day of Judgment, DC Special, DC Special Series, Flash, Guy Gardner, Guy Gardner Reborn, JLA, JSA, Justice League of America, Parallax: Emerald Night, Showcase, Showcase '93 #12 & Tales of The...Corps)

GREEN LANTERN (2nd Series)(Green Lantern Corps #206 on) (See Showcase #22-24)
National Periodical Publ./DC Comics: Jul/Aug. 1960 - No. 89, Apr/May 1972; No. 90, Aug/Sept. 1976 - No. 205, Oct, 1986

1-(7-8/60)-Origin retold; Gil Kane-c/a continues; 1st app. Guardians of the Universe
327 654 981 2992 5096 7200
2-1st Pieface 74 148 222 629 1015 1400
3-Contains readers poll 47 94 141 376 588 800
4,5: 5-Origin/1st app. Hector Hammond 38 76 114 285 443 600
6-Intro Tomar-Re the alien G.L. 33 66 99 248 384 520
7-Origin/1st app. Sinestro (7-8/61) 32 64 96 240 370 500
8-10: 8-1st 5700 A.D. story; grey tone-c. 9-1st Jordan Brothers; last 10¢ issue
27 54 81 194 297 400
11,12 19 38 57 134 205 275
13-Flash x-over 30 60 90 218 334 450
14-20: 14-Origin/1st app. Sonar. 16-Origin & 1st app. Star Sapphire. 20-Flash x-over
16 32 48 116 178 240
21-30: 21-Origin & 1st app. Dr. Polaris. 23-1st Tattooed Man. 24-Origin & 1st app. Shark.

Green Lantern (2nd) #42 © DC

Green Lantern (3rd) #16 © DC

Green Lantern (3rd) #179 © DC

	GD 2.0	VG 4.0	FN 6.0	VF 8.0	VF/NM 9.0	NM- 9.2
29-JLA cameo; 1st Blackhand	13	26	39	92	141	190
31-39: 37-1st app. Evil Star (villain)	11	22	33	80	120	160
40-1st app. Crisis (10/65); 2nd solo G.A. Green Lantern in Silver Age (see Showcase #55); origin The Guardians; Doiby Dickles app.	46	92	138	368	572	775
41-44,46-50: 42-Zatanna x-over. 43-Flash x-over	10	20	30	70	100	130
45-2nd S.A. app. G.A. Green Lantern in title (6/66)	15	30	45	105	160	215
51,53-58	8	16	24	55	78	100
52-G.A. Green Lantern x-over	10	20	30	72	104	135
59-1st app. Guy Gardner (3/68)	17	34	51	123	189	255
60,62-69: 69-Wood inks; last 12¢ issue	6	12	18	43	59	75
61-G.A. Green Lantern x-over	8	16	24	53	74	95
70-75	5	10	15	36	48	60
76-(4/70)-Begin Green Lantern/Green Arrow series (by Neal Adams #76-89) ends #122 (see Flash #217 for 2nd series)	32	64	96	240	370	500
77	9	18	27	60	85	110
78-80	7	14	21	51	71	90
81-84: 82-Wrightson-i(1 pg.). 83-G.L. reveals i.d. to Carol Ferris. 84-N. Adams/Wrightson-a (22 pgs.); last 15¢-c; partial photo-c	7	14	21	46	63	80
85,86-(52 pgs.)-Anti-drug issues. 86-G.A. Green Lantern-r; Toth-a	9	18	27	60	85	110
87-(52 pgs.): 2nd app. Guy Gardner (cameo); 1st app. John Stewart (12-1/71-72) (becomes 3rd Green Lantern in #182)	6	12	18	40	55	70
88-(2-3/72, 52 pgs.)-Unpubbed G.A. Green Lantern story; Green Lantern-r/Showcase #23. N. Adams-c/a (1 pg.)	4	8	12	27	36	45
89-(4-5/72, 52 pgs.)-G.A. Green Lantern-r; Green Lantern & Green Arrow move to Flash #217 (2nd team-up series)	6	12	18	40	55	70
90 (8-9/76)-Begin 3rd Green Lantern/Green Arrow team-up series; Mike Grell-c/a begins, ends #111	2	4	6	14	18	22
91-99	2	4	6	8	10	12
100-(1/78, Giant)-1st app. Air Wave II	2	4	6	12	16	20
101-107,111,113-115,117-119: 107-1st Tales of the G.L. Corps story	1	2	3	5	7	9
108-110-(44 pgs)-G.A. Green Lantern back-ups in each. 111-Origin retold; G.A. Green Lantern app.	1	3	4	6	8	10
112-G.A. Green Lantern origin retold	2	4	6	10	13	16
116-1st app. Guy Gardner as a G.L. (5/79)	4	8	12	27	36	45
117-119,121-(Whitman variants; low print run; none have issue # on cover)	2	4	6	8	10	12
120-122,124-150: 22-Last Green Lantern/Green Arrow team-up. 130-132-Tales of the G.L. Corps. 132-Adam Strange series begins, ends147. 136,137-1st app. Citadel; Space Ranger app. 141-1st app. Omega Men (6/81). 142,143-Omega Men app.;Perez-c. 144-Omega Men cameo. 148-Tales of the G.L. Corps begins, ends #173. 150-Anniversary issue, 52 pgs.; no G.L. Corps						6.00
123-Green Lantern back to solo action; 2nd app. Guy Gardner as Green Lantern	1	3	4	6	8	10
151-180,183,184,186,187: 159-Origin Evil Star. 160,161-Omega Men app.						4.00
181,182,185,188: 181-Hal Jordan resigns as G.L. 182-John Stewart becomes new G.L.; origin recap of Hal Jordan as G.L. 185-Origin new G.L. (John Stewart).188-I.D. revealed; Alan Moore back-up scripts.						5.00
189-193,196-199,201-205: 191-Re-intro Star Sapphire (cameo). 192-Re-intro & origin of Star Sapphire (1st full app.). 194,198-Crisis x-over. 199-Hal Jordan returns as a member of G.L. Corps (3 G.L.s now). 201-Green Lantern Corps begins (is cover title, says premiere issue); intro. Kilowog						3.50
194-Hal Jordan/Guy Gardner battle; Guardians choose Guy Gardner to become new Green Lantern						6.00
195-Guy Gardner becomes Green Lantern; Crisis on Infinite Earths x-over	2	4	6	8	10	12
200-Double-size						4.00
Annual 1 (Listed as Tales Of The Green Lantern Corps Annual 1)						
Annual 2,3 (See Green Lantern Corps Annual #2,3)						3.50
Special 1 (1988), 2 (1989)-(Both $1.50, 52 pgs.)						3.50

NOTE: ***N. Adams** a-76, 77-87p, 89; c-63, 76-89. **M. Anderson** a-137i. **Austin** a-93i, 94i, 171i. **Chaykin** c-196. **Greene** a-39-49i, 58-63i; c-54-58i. **Grell** a-90-106, 108-111; c-90-106, 108-112. **Heck** a-120-122p. **Infantino** a-137p, 145-147p, 151, 152p. **Gil Kane** a-1-49p, 50-57, 58-61p, 68-75p, 85p(r), 87p(r), 88p(r), 156, 177, 184p; c-1-52, 54-61p, 67-75, 123, 154, 156, 165-171, 177, 184. **Newton** a-148p, 149p, 181. **Perez** c-132p, 141-144. **Sekowsky** a-65p, 170p. **Simonson** c-200. **Sparling** a-63p. **Starlin** c-129, 133. **Staton** a-117p, 123-127p, 128, 129-131p, 132-139, 140p, 141-146, 147p, 148-150, 151-155p; c-107p, 117p, 135(i), 136p, 145p, 146, 147, 148-152p, 155p. **Toth** a-86r, 171p. **Tuska** a-166-168p, 170p.*

GREEN LANTERN (3rd Series)
DC Comics: June, 1990 - No. 181, Nov, 2004 ($1.00/$1.25/$1.50/$1.75/$1.95/$1.99/$2.25)

	NM- 9.2
1-Hal Jordan, John Stewart & Guy Gardner return; Batman & JLA app.	5.00
2-26: 9-12-Guy Gardner solo story. 13-(52 pgs.). 18-Guy Gardner solo story. 19-($1.75, 52 pgs.)-50th anniversary issue; Mart Nodell (original G.A. artist) part-p on G.A. Gr.Lantern; G. Kane-c. 25-($1.75, 52 pgs.)-Hal Jordan/Guy Gardner battle	4.00
27-45,47: 30,31-Gorilla Grodd-c/story(see Flash #69). 38,39-Adam Strange-c/story. 42-Deathstroke-c/s. 47-Green Arrow x-over	3.00
46,48,49,50: 46-Superman app. cont'd in Superman #82. 48-Emerald Twilight part 1. 50-($2.95, 52 pgs.)-Glow-in-the-dark-c	6.00
0, 51-62: 51-1st app. New Green Lantern (Kyle Rayner) with new costume. 53-Superman-c/story. 55-(9/94)-Zero Hour. 0-(10/94). 56-(11/94)	4.00
63,64-Kyle Rayner vs. Hal Jordan.	4.00
65-80,82-92: 63-Begin $1.75-c. 65-New Titans app. 66,67-Flash app. 71-Batman & Robin app. 72-Shazam!-c/app. 73-Wonder Woman-c/app. 73-75-Adam Strange app. 76,77-Green Arrow x-over. 80-Final Night x-over. 87-JLA app. 91-Genesis x-over. 92-Green Arrow x-over	3.00
81-(Regular Ed.)-Memorial for Hal Jordan (Parallax); most DC heroes app.	5.00
81-($3.95, Deluxe Edition)-Embossed prism-c	6.00
93-99: 93-Begin $1.95-c; Deadman app. 94-Superboy app. 95-Starlin-a(p). 98,99-Legion of Super-Heroes-c/app.	2.50
100-($2.95) Two covers (Jordan & Rayner); vs. Sinestro	5.00
101-106: 101-106-Hal Jordan-c/app. 103-JLA-c/app. 104-Green Arrow app. 105,106-Parallax app.	3.00
107-126: 107-Jade becomes a Green Lantern. 119-Hal Jordan/Spectre app. 125-JLA app.	2.25
127-149: 127-Begin $2.25-c. 129-Winick-s begin. 134-136-JLA-c/app. 143-Joker: Last Laugh; Lee-c. 145-Kyle becomes The Ion. 149-Superman-c/app.	2.25
150-($3.50) Jim Lee-c; Kyle becomes Green Lantern again; new costume	3.50
151-181: 151-155-Jim Lee-c: 154-Terry attacked. 155-Spectre-c/app. 162-164-Crossover with Green Arrow #23-25. 165-Raab-s begin. 169-Kilowog returns	2.25
#1,000,000 (11/98) 853rd Century x-over; Hitch & Neary-a/c	3.00
Annual 1-3: ('92-'94, 68 pgs.)-1-Eclipso app. 2 -Intro Nightblade. 3-Elseworlds story	3.50
Annual 4 (1995, $3.50)-Year One story	4.00
Annual 5,7,8 ('96, '98, '99, $2.95): 5-Legends of the Dead Earth. 7-Ghosts; Wrightson-c. 8-JLApe; Art Adams-c	3.00
Annual 6 (1997, $3.95)-Pulp Heroes story	5.00
Annual 9 (2000, $3.50) Planet DC	3.50
...80 Page Giant (12/98, $4.95) Stories by various	5.00
...80 Page Giant 2 (6/99, $4.95) Team-ups	5.00
...80 Page Giant 3 (8/00, $5.95) Darkseid vs. the GL Corps	6.00
...: 1001 Emerald Nights (2001, $6.95) Elseworlds; Guay-a/c; LaBan-s	7.00
...3-D #1 (12/98, $3.95) Jeanty-a	4.00
...: A New Dawn TPB (1998, $9.95)-r/#50-55	10.00
...: Baptism of Fire TPB (1999, $12.95)-r/#59,66,67,70-75	13.00
...: Brother's Keeper (2003, $12.95)-r/#151-155; Green Lantern Secret Files #3	13.00
...: Emerald Allies TPB (2000, $14.95)-r/GL/GA team-ups	15.00
...: Emerald Knights TPB (1998, $12.95)-r/Hal Jordan's return	13.00
...: Emerald Twilight nn (1994, $5.95)-r/#48-50	6.00
...: Emerald Twilight/New Dawn TPB (2003, $19.95)-r/#48-55	20.00
...: Ganthet's Tale nn (1992, $5.95, 68 pgs.)-Silver foil logo; Niven scripts; Byrne-c/a	6.00
.../Green Arrow Vol. 1 (2004, $12.95) -r/GL #76-82; intro. by O'Neil	13.00
.../Green Arrow Vol. 2 (2004, $12.95) -r/GL #83-87,89 & Flash #217-219, 226; cover gallery with 1983-84 GL/GA covers #1-7; intro. by Giordano	13.00
.../Green Arrow Collection, Vol. 2-r/GL #84-87,89 & Flash #217-219 & GL/GA #5-7 by O'Neil/Adams/Wrightson	13.00
...: New Journey, Old Path TPB (2001, $12.95)-r/#129-136	13.00
... : Our Worlds at War (8/01, $2.95) Jae Lee-c; prelude to x-over	3.00
...: Passing The Torch (2004, $12.95, TPB) r/#156,158-161 & GL Secret Files #2	13.00
...Plus 1 (12/1996, $2.95)-The Ray & Polaris-c/app.	3.00
...Secret Files 1-3- (7/98-7/02, $4.95)1- Origin stories & profiles. 2-Grell-c	5.00
.../Superman: Legend of the Green Flame (2000, $5.95) 1988 unpub. Neil Gaiman story of Hal Jordan with new art by various; Frank Miller-c	6.00
...: The Power of Ion (2003, $14.95, TPB) r/#142-150	15.00
...The Road Back nn (1992, $8.95)-r/1-8 w/covers	9.00
...: Traitor TPB (2001, $12.95) r/Legends of the DCU #20,21,28,29,37,38	13.00
...: Willworld (2001, $24.95, HC) Seth Fisher-a/J.M. DeMatteis-s; Hal Jordan	25.00
...: Willworld (2003, $17.95, SC) Seth Fisher-a/J.M. DeMatteis-s; Hal Jordan	18.00

NOTE: ***Staton** a(p)-9-12; c-9-12.*

GREEN LANTERN (See Tangent Comics/ Green Lantern)

GREEN LANTERN ANNUAL NO. 1, 1963
DC Comics: 1998 ($4.95, one-shot)

	NM- 9.2
1-Reprints Golden Age & Silver Age stories in 1963-style 80 pg. Giant format; new Gil Kane sketch art	5.00

GREEN LANTERN: BRIGHTEST DAY; BLACKEST NIGHT
DC Comics: 2002 ($5.95, squarebound, one-shot)

	NM- 9.2
nn-Alan Scott vs. Solomon Grundy in 1944; Snyder III-c/a; Seagle-s	6.00

GREEN LANTERN: CIRCLE OF FIRE
DC Comics: Early Oct, 2000 - No. 2, Late Oct, 2000 (limited series)

	NM- 9.2
1-($4.95) Intro. other Green Lanterns	5.00
2-($3.75)	4.00

Green Lantern: Rebirth #1 © DC

Green Lantern/Sentinel Heart of Darkness #2 © DC

Grendel: Red White and Black #1 © Matt Wagner

GD 2.0 | VG 4.0 | FN 6.0 | VF 8.0 | VF/NM 9.0 | NM- 9.2

Green Lantern (x-overs)- .../Adam Strange; .../Atom; .../Firestorm; ... /Green Lantern, Winick-s; .../Power Girl (all $2.50-c) 2.50
TPB (2002, $17.95) r/#1,2 & x-overs 18.00

GREEN LANTERN CORPS, THE (Formerly Green Lantern; see Tales of...)
DC Comics: No. 206, Nov, 1986 - No. 224, May, 1988

206-223: 212-John Stewart marries Katma Tui. 220,221-Millennium tie-ins 3.00
224-Double-size last issue 4.00
...Corps Annual 2,3- (12/86,8/87) 1-Formerly Tales of ...Annual #1; Alan Moore scripts. 3-Indicia says Green Lantern Annual #3; Moore scripts; Byrne-a 3.00
NOTE: ***Austin** a-Annual 3i. **Gil Kane** a-223, 224p; c-223, 224, Annual 2. **Russell** a-Annual 3i. **Staton** a-207-213p, 217p, 221p, 222p, Annual 3; c-207-213p, 217p, 221p, 222p. **Willingham** a-213p, 219p, 220p, 218p, 219p, Annual 2, 3p; c-218p, 219p.*

GREEN LANTERN CORPS QUARTERLY
DC Comics: Summer, 1992 - No. 8, Spring, 1994 ($2.50/$2.95, 68 pgs.)

1,7,8: 1-G.A. Green Lantern story; Staton-a(p). 7-Painted-c; Tim Vigil-a. 8-Lobo-c/s 3.50
2-6: 2-G.A. G.L.-c/story; Austin-c(i); Gulacy-a(p). 3-G.A. G.L. story. 4-Austin-i 3.00

GREEN LANTERN: DRAGON LORD
DC Comics: 2001 - No. 3, 2001 ($4.95, squarebound, limited series)

1-3: A G.L. in ancient China; Moench-s/Gulacy-c/a 5.00

GREEN LANTERN: EMERALD DAWN (Also see Emerald Dawn)
DC Comics: Dec, 1989 - No. 6, May, 1990 ($1.00, limited series)

1-Origin retold; Giffen plots in all 5.00
2-6: 4-Re-intro. Tomar-Re 4.00

GREEN LANTERN: EMERALD DAWN II (Emerald Dawn II #1 & 2)
DC Comics: Apr, 1991 - No. 6, Sept, 1991 ($1.00, limited series)

1-6 2.50
TPB (2003, $12.95) r/#1-6; Alan Davis-c 13.00

GREEN LANTERN: EVIL'S MIGHT (Elseworlds)
DC Comics: 2002 - No. 3 ($5.95, squarebound, limited series)

1-3-Kyle Rayner in 19th century NYC; Rogers-a; Chaykin & Tischman-s 6.00

GREEN LANTERN: FEAR ITSELF
DC Comics: 1999 (Graphic novel)

Hardcover ($24.95) Ron Marz-s/Brad Parker painted-a 25.00
Softcover ($14.95) 15.00

GREEN LANTERN/FLASH: FASTER FRIENDS (See Flash/Green Lantern...)
DC Comics: 1997 ($4.95, limited series)

1-Marz-s 5.00

GREEN LANTERN GALLERY
DC Comics: Dec, 1996 ($3.50, one-shot)

1-Wraparound-c; pin-ups by various 3.50

GREEN LANTERN/GREEN ARROW (Also see The Flash #217)
DC Comics: Oct, 1983 - No. 7, April, 1984 (52-60 pgs.)

1-7- r-Green Lantern #76-89 4.00
NOTE: ***Neal Adams** r-1-7; c-1-4. **Wrightson** r-4, 5.*

GREEN LANTERN • LEGACY: THE LAST WILL & TESTAMENT OF HAL JORDAN
DC Comics: 2002 ($24.95, hardcover graphic novel)

Hardcover-Anderson & Sienkiewicz-a/c; Kelly-s; Return of Oa 25.00
Softcover (2004, $17.95) 18.00

GREEN LANTERN: MOSAIC (Also see Cosmic Odyssey #2)
DC Comics: June, 1992 - No. 18, Nov, 1993 ($1.25)

1-18: Featuring John Stewart. 1-Painted-c by Cully Hamner 2.25

GREEN LANTERN: REBIRTH
DC Comics: Dec, 2004 - No. 6 ($2.95, limited series)

1-Johns-s/Van Sciver-a; Hal Jordan as The Spectre on-c 5.00
1-2nd printing; Hal Jordan as Green Lantern on-c 3.00
1-3rd printing; B&W-c version of 1st printing 3.00
2-Guy Gardner becomes a Green Lantern again; JLA app. 3.00

GREEN LANTERN/SENTINEL: HEART OF DARKNESS
DC Comics: Mar, 1998 - No. 3, May, 1998 ($1.95, limited series)

1-3-Marz-s/Pelletier-a 3.00

GREEN LANTERN/SILVER SURFER: UNHOLY ALLIANCES
DC Comics: 1995 ($4.95, one-shot)(Prelude to DC Versus Marvel)

nn-Hal Jordan app. 5.00

GREEN LANTERN: THE NEW CORPS
DC Comics:1999 - No. 2, 1999 ($4.95, limited series)

GD 2.0 | VG 4.0 | FN 6.0 | VF 8.0 | VF/NM 9.0 | NM- 9.2

1,2-Kyle recruits new GLs; Eaton-a 5.00

GREEN LANTERN VS. ALIENS
Dark Horse Comics: Sept, 2000 - No. 4, Dec, 2000 ($2.95, limited series)

1-4: 1-Hal Jordan and GL Corps vs. Aliens; Leonardi-p. 2-4-Kyle Rayner 3.00

GREEN MASK, THE (See Mystery Men)
Summer, 1940 - No. 9, 2/42; No. 10, 8/44 - No. 11, 11/44;
Fox Features Syndicate: V2#1, Spring, 1945 - No. 6, 10-11/46

	GD	VG	FN	VF	VF/NM	NM-
V1#1-Origin The Green Mask & Domino; reprints/Mystery Men #1-3,5-7; Lou Fine-c	372	744	1116	2418	3909	5400
2-Zanzibar The Magician by Tuska	135	270	405	844	1297	1750
3-Powell-a; Marijuana story	85	170	255	531	816	1100
4-Navy Jones begins, ends #6	67	134	201	419	647	875
5	55	110	165	340	520	700
6-The Nightbird begins, ends #9; bondage/torture-c	45	90	135	275	418	560
7-9: 9(2/42)-Becomes The Bouncer #10(nn) on? & Green Mask #10 on	40	80	120	230	335	440
10,11: 10-Origin One Round Hogan & Rocket Kelly	32	64	96	184	267	350
V2#1	24	48	72	138	199	260
2-6	21	42	63	118	169	220

GREEN PLANET, THE
Charlton Comics: 1962 (one-shot) (12¢)

	GD	VG	FN	VF	VF/NM	NM-
nn-Giordano-c; sci-fi	8	16	24	53	74	95

GREEN TEAM (See Cancelled Comic Cavalcade & 1st Issue Special)

GREETINGS FROM SANTA (See March of Comics No. 48)

GRENDEL (Also see Primer #2, Mage and Comico Collection)
Comico: Mar, 1983 - No. 3, Feb, 1984 ($1.50, B&W)(#1 has indicia to Skrog #1)

	GD	VG	FN	VF	VF/NM	NM-
1-Origin Hunter Rose	12	24	36	82	124	165
2,3: 2-Origin Argent	9	18	27	60	85	110

GRENDEL
Comico: Oct, 1986 - No. 40, Feb, 1990 ($1.50/$1.95/$2.50, mature)

	GD	VG	FN	VF	VF/NM	NM-
1	1	2	3	5	7	9
1,2: 2nd printings						3.00
2,3,5-15: 13-15-Ken Steacy-c.						4.00
4,16: 4-Dave Stevens-c(i). 16-Re-intro Mage (series begins, ends #19)						6.00
17-40: 24-25,27-28,30-31-Snyder-c/a						3.00
Devil by the Deed (Graphic Novel, 10/86, $5.95, 52 pgs.)-r/Grendel back-ups/ Mage 6-14; Alan Moore intro.	1	2	3	4	5	7
Devil's Legacy ($14.95, 1988, Graphic Novel)	2	4	6	10	12	15
Devil's Vagary (10/87, B&W & red)-No price; included in Comico Collection	2	4	6	8	10	12

GRENDEL (Title series): **Dark Horse Comics**

--BLACK, WHITE, AND RED, 11/98 - No. 4, 2/99 ($3.95, anthology)
1-Wagner-s in all. Art by Sale, Leon and others 5.00
2-4: 2-Mack, Chadwick-a. 3-Allred, Kristensen-a. 4-Pearson, Sprouse-a 4.00

--CLASSICS, 7/95 - 8/95 ($3.95, mature) 1,2-reprints; new Wagner-c 4.00

--CYCLE, 10/95 ($5.95) 1-nn-history of Grendel by M. Wagner & others 6.00

--DEVIL BY THE DEED, 7/93 ($3.95, varnish-c) 1-nn-M. Wagner-c/a/scripts; r/Grendel back-ups from Mage #6-14 4.00
Reprint (12/97, $3.95) w/pin-ups by various 4.00

--DEVIL CHILD, 6/99 - No. 2, 7/99 ($2.95, mature) 1,2-Sale & Kristiansen-a/Schutz-s 3.00

--DEVIL QUEST, 11/95 ($4.95) 1-nn-Prequel to Batman/Grendel II; M. Wagner story & art; r/back-up story from Grendel Tales series. 5.00

--DEVILS AND DEATHS, 10/94 - 11/94 ($2.95, mature) 1,2 3.00

: DEVIL'S LEGACY, 3/00 - No. 12, 2/01 ($2.95, reprints 1986 series, recolored)
1-12-Wagner-s/c; Pander Bros.-a 3.00

: DEVIL'S REIGN, 5/04 - No. 7 ($3.50, repr. 1989 series #34-40, recolored)
1-4-Sale-c/a. 3.50

: GOD AND THE DEVIL, No. 0, 1/03 - No. 10, 12/03 ($3.50/$4.99, repr. 1986 series, recolored)
0-9: 0-Sale-c/a; r/#23. 1-9-Snyder-c 3.50
10-($4.99) Double-sized; Snyder-c 5.00

--RED, WHITE & BLACK, 9/02 - No. 4, 12/02 ($4.99, anthology)
1-4-Wagner-s in all. 1-Art by Thompson, Sakai, Mahfood and others. 2-Kelley Jones, Watson, Brereton, Hester & Parks-a. 3-Oeming, Noto, Cannon, Ashley Wood, Huddleston-a 4-Chiang, Dalrymple, Robertson, Snyder III and Zulli-a 5.00

Grifter & the Mask #1 © WSP/DH

Grimjack #2 © FC

Groo #117 © Sergio Aragonés

GD VG FN VF VF/NM NM-
2.0 4.0 6.0 8.0 9.0 9.2

--TALES: DEVIL'S CHOICES, 3/95 - 6/95 ($2.95, mature) 1-4 3.00

--TALES: FOUR DEVILS, ONE HELL, 8/93 - 1/94 ($2.95, mature)
1-6-Wagner painted-c 3.00
TPB (12/94, $17.95) r/#1-6 18.00

--TALES: HOMECOMING, 12/94 - 2/95 ($2.95, mature) 1-3 3.00

--TALES: THE DEVIL IN OUR MIDST, 5/94 - 9/95 ($2.95, mature) 1-5-Wagner painted-c 3.00

--TALES: THE DEVIL MAY CARE, 12/95 - No. 6, 5/96 ($2.95, mature)
1-6-Terry LaBan scripts. 5-Batman/Grendel II preview 3.00

--TALES: THE DEVIL'S APPRENTICE, 9/97 - No. 3, 11/97 ($2.95, mature)
1-3 3.00

: THE DEVIL INSIDE, 9/01 - No. 3, 11/01 ($2.99)
1-3-r/#13-15 with new Wagner-c 3.00

GRENDEL: WAR CHILD
Dark Horse Comics: Aug, 1992 - No. 10, Jun, 1993 ($2.50, lim. series, mature)
1-9: 1-4-Bisley painted-c; Wagner-i & scripts in all 3.00
10-($3.50, 52 pgs.) Wagner-c 4.00
Limited Edition Hardcover ($99.95) 100.00

GREYFRIARS BOBBY (Disney)(Movie)
Dell Publishing Co.: No. 1189, Nov, 1961 (one-shot)
Four Color 1189-Photo-c (scarce) 8 16 24 58 82 105

GREYLORE
Sirius: 12/85 - No. 5, Sept, 1986 ($1.50/$1.75, high quality paper)
1-5: Bo Hampton-a in all 2.25

GREYSHIRT: INDIGO SUNSET (Also see Tomorrow Stories)
America's Best Comics: Dec, 2001 - No. 6, Aug, 2002 ($3.50, limited series)
1-6-Veitch-s/a. 4-Back-up w/John Severin-a. 6-Cho-a 3.50
TPB (2002, $19.95) r/#1-6; preface by Alan Moore 20.00

GRIDIRON GIANTS
Ultimate Sports Ent.: 2000 - No. 2 ($3.95, cardstock covers)
1,2-NFL players Sanders, Marino, Plummer, T. Davis battle evil 4.00

GRIFFIN, THE
DC Comics: 1991 - No. 6, 1991 ($4.95, limited series, 52 pgs.)
Book 1-6: Matt Wagner painted-c 5.00

GRIFTER (Also see Team 7 & WildC.A.T.S)
Image Comics (WildStorm Prod.): May, 1995 - No. 10, Mar, 1996 ($1.95)
1 ($1.95, Newsstand)-WildStorm Rising Pt. 5 2.50
1-10:1 ($2.50, Direct)-WildStorm Rising Pt. 5, bound-in trading card 3.00

GRIFTER
Image Comics (WildStorm Prod.): V2#1, July, 1996 - No. 14, Aug, 1997 ($2.50)
V2#1-14: Steven Grant scripts 3.00

GRIFTER AND THE MASK
Dark Horse Comics: Sept, 1996 - No. 2, Oct, 1996 ($2.50, limited series)
(1st Dark Horse Comics/Image x-over)
1,2: Steve Seagle scripts 3.00

GRIFTER/BADROCK (Also see WildC.A.T.S & Youngblood)
Image Comics (Extreme Studios): Oct, 1995 - No.2, Nov, 1995 ($2.50, unfinished lim. series)
1,2: 2-Flip book w/Badrock #2 2.50

GRIFTER: ONE SHOT
Image Comics (WildStorm Productions): Jan, 1995 ($4.95, one-shot)
1-Flip-c 5.00

GRIFTER/SHI
Image Comics (WildStorm Productions): Apr, 1996 - No. 2, May, 1996 ($2.95, limited series)
1,2: 1-Jim Lee-c/a(p); Travis Charest-a(p). 2-Billy Tucci-c/a(p); Travis Charest-a(p) 3.00

GRIM GHOST, THE
Atlas/Seaboard Publ.: Jan, 1975 - No. 3, July, 1975
1-3: Fleisher-s in all. 1-Origin. 2-Son of Satan; Colan-a. 3-Heath-c
1 2 3 5 6 8

GRIMJACK (Also see Demon Knight & Starslayer)
First Comics: Aug, 1984 - No. 81, Apr, 1991 ($1.00/$1.95/$2.25)
1-John Ostrander scripts & Tim Truman-c/a begins. 3.00
2-25: 20-Sutton-c/a begins. 22-Bolland-a. 2.25
26-2nd color Teenage Mutant Ninja Turtles 4.00
27-74,76-81 (Later issues $1.95, $2.25): 30-Dynamo Joe x-over; 31-Mandrake-c/a begins. 73,74-Kelley Jones-a 2.50
75-($5.95, 52 pgs.)-Fold-out map; coated stock 6.00
NOTE: *Truman c/a-1-17.*

GRIMJACK CASEFILES
First Comics: Nov, 1990 - No. 5, Mar, 1991 ($1.95, limited series)
1-5 Reprints 1st stories from Starslayer #10 on 2.25

GRIMM'S GHOST STORIES (See Dan Curtis)
Gold Key/Whitman No. 55 on: Jan, 1972 - No. 60, June, 1982 (Painted-c #1-42,44,46-56)
1 4 8 12 24 32 40
2-5,8: 5,8-Williamson-a 2 4 6 12 16 20
6,7,9,10 2 4 6 10 13 16
11-20 2 4 6 8 10 12
21-42,45-54: 32,34-Reprints. 45-Photo-c 1 2 3 5 7 9
43,44,55-60: 43,44-(52 pgs.). 43-Photo-c. 58(2/82). 59(4/82)-Williamson-a(r/#8). 60(6/82)
2 4 6 8 10 12
Mini-Comic No. 1 (3-1/4x6-1/2", 1976) 1 3 4 6 8 10
NOTE: *Reprints-#32?, 34?, 39, 43, 44, 47?, 53; 56-60(1/3).* **Bolle** *a-8, 17, 22-25, 27, 29(2), 33, 35, 41, 43r, 45(2), 48(2), 50, 52.* **Celardo** *a-17, 26, 28p, 30, 31, 43(2), 45.* **Lopez** *a-24, 25.* **McWilliams** *a-33, 44r, 48, 54(2), 57, 58.* **Win Mortimer** *a-31, 33, 49, 51, 55, 56, 58(2), 59, 60.* **Roussos** *a-25, 30.* **Sparling** *a-23, 24, 28, 30, 31, 33, 43r, 44, 45, 51(2), 52, 56, 58, 59(2), 60.* **Spiegle** *a-44.*

GRIN (The American Funny Book) (Satire)
APAG House Pubs: Nov, 1972 - No. 3, April, 1973 (Magazine, 52 pgs.)
1-Parodies-Godfather, All in the Family 3 6 9 18 23 28
2,3 2 4 6 10 13 16

GRIN & BEAR IT (See Gags)
Dell Publishing Co.: No. 28, 1941
Large Feature Comic 28 17 34 51 95 135 175

GRIPS (Extreme violence)
Silverwolf Comics: Sept, 1986 - No. 4, Dec, 1986 ($1.50, B&W, mature)
1-Tim Vigil-c/a in all 6.00
2-4 4.00

GRIP: THE STRANGE WORLD OF MEN
DC Comics (Vertigo): Jan, 2002 - No. 5, May, 2002 ($2.50, limited series)
1-4-Gilbert Hernandez-s/a 2.50

GRIT GRADY (See Holyoke One-Shot No. 1)

GROO (Sergio Aragonés'...)
Image Comics: Dec, 1994 - No. 12, Dec, 1995 ($1.95)
1-12: 2-Indicia reads #1, Jan, 1995; Aragonés-c/a in all 3.50

GROO (Sergio Aragonés'...)
Dark Horse Comics: Jan, 1998 - No. 4, Apr, 1998 ($2.95)
1-4: Aragonés-c/a in all 4.00

GROO CHRONICLES, THE (Sergio Aragonés)
Marvel Comics (Epic Comics): June, 1989 - No. 6, Feb, 1990 ($3.50)
Book 1-6: Reprints early Pacific issues 3.50

GROO SPECIAL
Eclipse Comics: Oct, 1984 ($2.00, 52 pgs., Baxter paper)
1-Aragonés-c/a 3 6 9 16 20 24

GROO THE WANDERER (See Destroyer Duck #1 & Starslayer #5)
Pacific Comics: Dec, 1982 - No. 8, Apr, 1984
1-Aragonés-c/a(p) in all; Aragonés bio., photo 2 4 6 12 16 20
2-5: 5-Deluxe paper (1.00-c) 2 4 6 9 11 14
6-8 2 4 6 10 13 16

GROO THE WANDERER (Sergio Aragonés'...) (See Marvel Graphic Novel #32)
Marvel Comics (Epic Comics): March, 1985 - No. 120, Jan, 1995
1-Aragonés-c/a in all 2 4 6 9 11 14
2-10 1 2 3 4 5 7
11-20,50-($1.50, double size) 5.00
21-49,51-99: 87-direct sale only, high quality paper 3.00
100-($2.95, 52 pgs.) 5.00
101-120 4.00
Groo Carnival, The (12/91, $8.95)-r/#9-12 11.00
Groo Garden, The (4/94, $10.95)-r/#25-28 11.00

GROOVY (Cartoon Comics - not CCA approved)
Marvel Comics Group: March, 1968 - No. 3, July, 1968
1-Monkees, Ringo Starr, Sonny & Cher, Mamas & Papas photos
9 18 27 65 93 120

Guardians of the Galaxy #55 © MAR

Gunfighter #8 © WMG

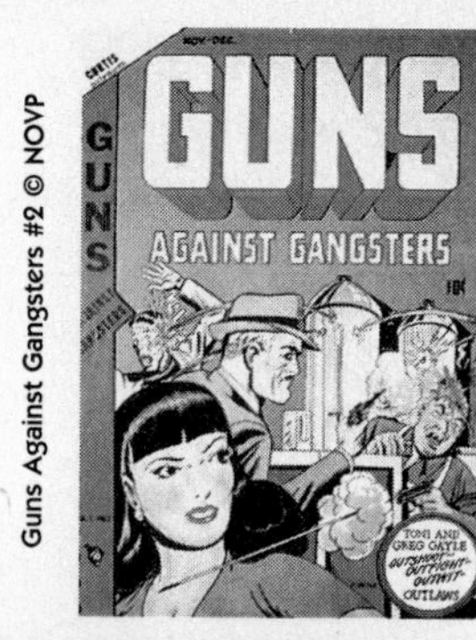

Guns Against Gangsters #2 © NOVP

	GD 2.0	VG 4.0	FN 6.0	VF 8.0	VF/NM 9.0	NM- 9.2

2,3 — 6 12 18 43 59 75

GROSS POINT
DC Comics: Aug, 1997 - No. 14, Aug, 1998 ($2.50)
1-14: 1-Waid/Augustyn-s — 2.50

GROUP LARUE, THE
Innovation Publishing: 1989 - No. 4, 1990 ($1.95, mini-series)
1-4-By Mike Baron — 2.25

GRRL SCOUTS (Jim Mahfood's...) (Also see 40 oz. Collected)
Oni Press: Mar,1999 - No. 4, Dec, 1999 ($2.95, B&W, limited series)
1-4-Mahfood-s/c/a — 3.00
TPB (2003, $12.95) r/#1-4; pin-ups by Warren, Winick, Allred, Fegredo and others — 13.00

GRRL SCOUTS: WORK SUCKS
Image Comics: Feb, 2003 - No. 4, May, 2003 ($2.95, B&W, limited series)
1-4-Mahfood-s/c/a — 3.00
TPB (2004, $12.95) r/#1-4; pin-ups by Oeming, Dwyer, Tennapel and others — 13.00

GUADALCANAL DIARY (See American Library)

GUARDIAN ANGEL
Image Comics: May, 2002 - No. 2, July, 2002 ($2.95)
1,2-Peterson-s/Wiesenfeld-a — 3.00

GUARDIANS
Marvel Comics: Sept, 2004 - No. 5, Dec, 2004 ($2.99, limited series)
1-5-Sumerak-s/Casey Jones-a — 3.00

GUARDIANS OF JUSTICE & THE O-FORCE
Shadow Comics: 1990 (no date) ($1.50, 7-1/2 x10-1/4)
1-Super-hero group — 2.25

GUARDIANS OF METROPOLIS
DC Comics: Nov, 1995 - Feb, 1995 ($1.50, limited series)
1-4: 1-Superman & Granny Goodness app. — 2.25

GUARDIANS OF THE GALAXY (Also see The Defenders #26, Marvel Presents #3, Marvel Super-Heroes #18, Marvel Two-In-One #5)
Marvel Comics: June, 1990 - No. 62, July, 1995 ($1.00/$1.25)
1-Valentino-c/a(p) begin. — 3.00
2-16: 2-Zeck-c(i). 5-McFarlane-c(i). 7-Intro Malevolence (Mephisto's daughter); Perez-c(i). 8-Intro Rancor (descendant of Wolverine) in cameo. 9-1st full app. Rancor; Rob Liefeld-c(i). 10-Jim Lee-c(i). 13,14-1st app. Spirit of Vengeance (futuristic Ghost Rider). 14-Spirit of Vengeance vs. The Guardians. 15-Starlin-c(i). 16-($1.50, 52 pgs.)-Starlin-c(i) — 2.50
17-24,26-38,40-47: 17-20-31st century Punishers storyline. 20-Last $1.00-c. 21-Rancor app. 22-Reintro Starhawk. 24-Silver Surfer-c/story; Ron Lim-c. 26-Origin retold. 27-28-Infinity War x-over; 27-Inhumans app. 43-Intro Wooden (son of Thor) — 2.25
25-($2.50)-Prism foil-c; Silver Surfer/Galactus-c/s — 3.00
25-($2.50)-Without foil-c; newsstand edition — 2.50
39-($2.95, 52 pgs.)-Embossed & holo-grafx foil-c; Dr. Doom vs. Rancor — 3.00
48,49,51-62: 48-bound-in trading card sheet — 2.25
50-($2.00, 52 pgs.)-Newsstand edition — 2.25
50-($2.95, 52 pgs.)-Collectors ed. w/foil embossed-c — 3.00
Annual 1-4: ('91-'94, 68 pgs.)-1-Origin. 2-Spirit of Vengeance-c/story. 3,4-Bagged w/card — 3.00

GUERRILLA WAR (Formerly Jungle War Stories)
Dell Publishing Co.: No. 12, July-Sept, 1965 - No. 14, Mar, 1966
12-14 — 3 6 9 16 21 26

GUFF
Dark Horse Comics: Apr, 1998 ($1.95, B&W)
1-Flip book; Aragonés-c — 2.25

GUILTY (See Justice Traps the Guilty)

GULLIVER'S TRAVELS (See Dell Jr. Treasury No. 3)
Dell Publishing Co.: Sept-Nov, 1965 - No. 3, May, 1966
1 — 6 12 18 43 59 75
2,3 — 4 8 12 29 40 50

GUMBY'S SUMMER FUN SPECIAL
Comico: July, 1987 ($2.50)
1-Art Adams-c/a; B. Burden scripts — 3.00

GUMBY'S WINTER FUN SPECIAL
Comico: Dec, 1988 ($2.50, 44 pgs.)
1-Art Adams-c/a — 3.00

GUMPS, THE (See Merry Christmas..., Popular & Super Comics)
Dell Publ. Co./Bridgeport Herald Corp.: No. 73, 1945; Mar-Apr, 1947 - No. 5, Nov-Dec, 1947
Four Color 73 (Dell)(1945) — 13 26 39 92 141 190
1 (3-4/47) — 16 32 48 92 131 170
2-5 — 10 20 30 60 80 100

GUNFIGHTER (Fat & Slat #1-4) (Becomes Haunt of Fear #15 on)
E. C. Comics (Fables Publ. Co.): No. 5, Sum, 1948 - No. 14, Mar-Apr, 1950
5,6-Moon Girl in each — 55 110 165 340 520 700
7-14: 14-Bondage-c — 40 80 120 240 360 480
NOTE: *Craig & H. C. Kiefer art in most issues.* ***Craig*** *c-5, 6, 13, 14.* ***Feldstein/Craig*** *a-10.* ***Feldstein*** *a-7-11.* ***Harrison/Wood*** *a-13, 14.* ***Ingels*** *a-5-14; c-7-12.*

GUNFIGHTERS, THE
Super Comics (Reprints): 1963 - 1964
10-12,15,16,18: 10,11-r/Billy the Kid #s? 12-r/The Rider #5(Swift Arrow). 15-r/Straight Arrow #42; Powell-r. 16-r/Billy the Kid #?(Toby). 18-r/The Rider #3; Severin-c — 2 4 6 11 14 18

GUNFIGHTERS, THE (Formerly Kid Montana)
Charlton Comics: No. 51, 10/66 - No. 52, 10/67; No. 53, 6/79 - No. 85, 7/84
51,52 — 2 4 6 12 16 20
53,54,56:53,54-Williamson/Torres-r/Six Gun Heroes #47,49. 56-Williamson/Severin-c; Severin-r/Sheriff of Tombstone #1 — 1 3 4 6 8 10
55,57-80 — 6.00
81-84-Lower print run — 1 2 3 5 6 8
85-S&K-r/1955 Bullseye — 1 3 4 6 8 10

GUNFIRE (See Deathstroke Annual #2 & Showcase 94 #1,2)
DC Comics: May, 1994 - No. 13, June, 1995 ($1.75/$2.25)
1-5,0,6-13: 2-Ricochet-c/story. 5-(9/94). 0-(10/94). 6-(11/94) — 2.25

GUN GLORY (Movie)
Dell Publishing Co.: No. 846, Oct, 1957 (one-shot)
Four Color 846-Toth-a, photo-c. — 10 20 30 72 104 135

GUNHAWK, THE (Formerly Whip Wilson)(See Wild Western)
Marvel Comics/Atlas (MCI): No. 12, Nov, 1950 - No. 18, Dec, 1951
(Also see Two-Gun Western #5)
12 — 20 40 60 112 161 210
13-18: 13-Tuska-a. 16-Colan-a. 18-Maneely-c — 14 28 42 79 110 140

GUNHAWKS (Gunhawk No. 7)
Marvel Comics Group: Oct, 1972 - No. 7, October, 1973
1,6: 1-Reno Jones, Kid Cassidy; Shores-c/a(p). 6-Kid Cassidy dies — 3 6 9 16 21 26
2-5,7: 7-Reno Jones solo — 2 4 6 11 14 18

GUNHED
Vix Comics: 1990 - No. 3, 1991? ($4.95, 7-1/8 x 9-1/8, 52 pgs., bi-monthly)
1-3: Japanese sci-fi based on 1991 movie — 5.00

GUNMASTER (Becomes Judo Master #89 on)
Charlton Comics: 9/64 - No. 4, 1965; No. 84, 7/65 - No. 88, 3-4/66; No. 89, 10/67
V1#1 — 4 8 12 27 36 45
2,4, V5#84-86: 84-Formerly Six-Gun Heroes — 3 6 9 18 23 28
V5#87-89 — 2 4 6 12 16 20
NOTE: *Vol. 5 was originally cancelled with #88 (3-4/66). #89 on, became Judo Master, then later in 1967, Charlton issued #89 as a Gunmaster one-shot.*

GUN RUNNER
Marvel Comics UK: Oct, 1993 - No. 6, Mar, 1994 ($1.75, limited series)
1-($2.75)-Polybagged w/4 trading cards; Spirits of Vengeance app. — 3.00
2-6: 2-Ghost Rider & Blaze app. — 2.25

GUNS AGAINST GANGSTERS (True-To-Life Romances #8 on)
Curtis Publications/Novelty Press: Sept-Oct, 1948 - No. 6, July-Aug, 1949; V2#1, Sept-Oct, 1949
1-Toni & Greg Gayle begins by Schomburg; L.B. Cole-c — 40 80 120 230 335 440
2-L.B. Cole-c — 30 60 90 170 245 320
3-6, V2#1: 6-Toni Gayle-c — 25 50 75 144 207 270
NOTE: ***L. B. Cole*** *c-1-6, V2#1, 2; a-1, 2, 3(2), 4-6.*

GUNSLINGER
Dell Publishing Co.: No. 1220, Oct-Dec, 1961 (one-shot)
Four Color 1220-Photo-c — 10 20 30 70 100 130

GUNSLINGER (Formerly Tex Dawson...)
Marvel Comics Group: No. 2, Apr, 1973 - No. 3, June, 1973

Gunsmith Cats: Kidnapped #5 © DH

Gunsmoke #14 © WEST

Guy Gardner Warrior #40 © DC

	GD 2.0	VG 4.0	FN 6.0	VF 8.0	VF/NM 9.0	NM- 9.2
2,3	2	4	6	12	16	20

GUNSLINGERS
Marvel Comics: Feb, 2000 ($2.99)

	GD 2.0	VG 4.0	FN 6.0	VF 8.0	VF/NM 9.0	NM- 9.2
1-Reprints stories of Two-Gun Kid, Rawhide Kid and Caleb Hammer						3.00

GUNSMITH CATS: (Title series), **Dark Horse Comics**

	GD 2.0	VG 4.0	FN 6.0	VF 8.0	VF/NM 9.0	NM- 9.2
--BAD TRIP (Manga), 6/98 - No. 6, 11/98 ($2.95, B&W) 1-6						3.00
--BEAN BANDIT (Manga), 1/99 - No. 9 ($2.95, B&W, limited series) 1-9						3.00
--GOLDIE VS. MISTY (Manga), 11/97 - No. 7, 5/98 ($2.95, B&W) 1-7						3.00
--KIDNAPPED (Manga), 11/99 - No. 10, 8/00 ($2.95, B&W) 1-10						3.00
--MISTER V (Manga), 10/00 - No. 11, 8/01 ($3.50/$2.99), B&W) 1-7,9-11						3.50
8-($2.99)						3.00
--THE RETURN OF GRAY (Manga), 8/96 - No. 7, 2/97 ($2.95, B&W) 1-7						3.00
--SHADES OF GRAY (Manga), 5/97 - No. 5, 9/97 ($2.95, B&W) 1-5						3.00
--SPECIAL (Manga) Nov, 2001 ($2.99, B&W, one-shot)						3.00

GUNSMOKE (Blazing Stories of the West)
Western Comics (Youthful Magazines): Apr-May, 1949 - No. 16, Jan, 1952

	GD 2.0	VG 4.0	FN 6.0	VF 8.0	VF/NM 9.0	NM- 9.2
1-Gunsmoke & Masked Marvel begin by Ingels; Ingels bondage-c	42	84	126	256	391	525
2-Ingels-c/a(2)	30	60	90	170	245	320
3-Ingels bondage-c/a	25	50	75	141	203	265
4-6: Ingels-c	20	40	60	112	161	210
7-10	11	22	33	66	91	115
11-16: 15,16-Western/horror stories	11	22	33	62	84	105

NOTE: ***Stallman** a-11, 14. **Wildey** a-15, 16.*

GUNSMOKE (TV)
Dell Publishing Co./Gold Key (All have James Arness photo-c): No. 679, Feb, 1956 - No. 27, Feb, 1969 - No. 6, Feb, 1970

	GD 2.0	VG 4.0	FN 6.0	VF 8.0	VF/NM 9.0	NM- 9.2
Four Color 679(#1)	19	38	57	134	205	275
Four Color 720,769,797,844 (#2-5),6(11-1/57-58)	10	20	30	72	104	135
7,8,9,11,12-Williamson-a in all, 4 pgs. each	10	20	30	73	107	140
10-Williamson/Crandall-a, 4 pgs.	10	20	30	73	107	140
13-27	9	18	27	60	85	110
1 (Gold Key)	7	14	21	50	68	85
2-6('69-70)	4	8	12	27	36	45

GUNSMOKE TRAIL
Ajax-Farrell Publ./Four Star Comic Corp.: June, 1957 - No. 4, Dec, 1957

	GD 2.0	VG 4.0	FN 6.0	VF 8.0	VF/NM 9.0	NM- 9.2
1	11	22	33	63	84	105
2-4	7	14	21	35	43	50

GUNSMOKE WESTERN (Formerly Western Tales of Black Rider)
Atlas Comics No. 32-35(CPS/NPI); Marvel No. 36 on: No. 32, Dec, 1955 - No. 77, July, 1963

	GD 2.0	VG 4.0	FN 6.0	VF 8.0	VF/NM 9.0	NM- 9.2
32-Baker & Drucker-a	17	34	51	95	135	175
33,35,36-Williamson-a in each: 5,6 & 4 pgs. plus Drucker-a #33. 33-Kinstler-a?	14	28	42	79	110	140
34-Baker-a, 4 pgs.; Kirby-c	12	24	36	69	95	120
37-Davis-a(2); Williamson text illo	11	22	33	64	87	110
38,39: 39-Williamson text illo (unsigned)	9	18	27	54	70	85
40-Williamson/Mayo-a (4 pgs.)	10	20	30	58	77	95
41,42,45,46,48,49,52-54,57,58,60: 49,52-Kid from Texas story. 57-1st Two Gun Kid by Severin. 60-Sam Hawk app. in Kid Colt	8	16	24	43	54	65
43,44-Torres-a	8	16	24	43	54	65
47,51,59,61: 47,51,59-Kirby-a. 61-Crandall-a	9	18	27	52	66	80
50-Kirby, Crandall-a	10	20	30	58	77	95
55,56-Matt Baker-a	9	18	27	54	70	85
62-67,69,71-73,77-Kirby-a. 72-Origin Kid Colt	6	12	18	40	55	70
68,70,74-76: 68-(10¢-c)	5	10	15	33	44	55
68-(10¢ cover price blacked out, 12¢ printed on)	9	18	27	60	85	110

NOTE: ***Colan** a-35-37, 39, 72, 76. **Davis** a-37, 52, 54, 55; c-50, 54. **Ditko** a-66; c-56p. **Drucker** a-32-34. **Heath** c-33. **Jack Keller** a-35, 40, 60, 72; c-72. **Kirby** a-47, 50, 51, 59, 62(3), 63-67, 69, 71, 73, 77; c-56(w/Ditko),57, 58, 60, 61(w/Ayers), 62, 63, 66, 68, 69, 71-77. **Robinson** a-35. **Severin** a-35, 59-61; c-34, 35, 39, 42, 43. **Tuska** a-34. **Wildey** a-10, 37, 42, 56, 57. Kid Colt in all. Two-Gun Kid in No. 57, 59, 60-63. Wyatt Earp in No. 45, 48, 49, 52, 54, 55, 58.*

GUNS OF FACT & FICTION (Also see A-1 Comics)
Magazine Enterprises: No. 13, 1948 (one-shot)

	GD 2.0	VG 4.0	FN 6.0	VF 8.0	VF/NM 9.0	NM- 9.2
A-1 13-Used in **SOTI**, pg. 19; Ingels & J. Craig-a	30	60	90	170	245	320

GUNS OF THE DRAGON
DC Comics: Oct, 1998 - No. 4, Jan, 1999 ($2.50, limited series)

	GD 2.0	VG 4.0	FN 6.0	VF 8.0	VF/NM 9.0	NM- 9.2
1-4-DCU in the 1920's; Enemy Ace & Bat Lash app.						2.50

GUN THEORY
Marvel Comics (Epic): Oct, 2003 - No. 4 ($2.50, limited series)

	GD 2.0	VG 4.0	FN 6.0	VF 8.0	VF/NM 9.0	NM- 9.2
1,2-Daniel Way-s/Jon Proctor-a						2.50

GUNWITCH, THE : OUTSKIRTS OF DOOM (See The Nocturnals)
Oni Press: June, 2001 - No. 3, Oct, 2001 ($2.95, B&W, limited series)

	GD 2.0	VG 4.0	FN 6.0	VF 8.0	VF/NM 9.0	NM- 9.2
1-3-Brereton-s/painted-c/Naifeh-s						3.00

GUY GARDNER (Guy Gardner: Warrior #17 on)(Also see Green Lantern #59)
DC Comics: Oct, 1992 - No. 44, July, 1996 ($1.25/$1.50/$1.75)

	GD 2.0	VG 4.0	FN 6.0	VF 8.0	VF/NM 9.0	NM- 9.2
1-24,0,26-30: 1-Staton-c/a(p) begins. 6-Guy vs. Hal Jordan. 8-Vs. Lobo-c/story. 5-JLA x-over, begin $1.50-c. 18-Begin 4-part Emerald Fallout story; splash page x-over GL #50. 18-21-Vs. Hal Jordan. 24-(9/94)-Zero Hour. 0-(10/94)						2.50
25 (11/94, $2.50, 52 pgs.)						3.00
29 ($2.95)-Gatefold-c						3.50
29-Variant-c (Edward Hopper's Nighthawks)						2.50
31-44: 31-$1.75-c begins. 40-Gorilla Grodd-c/app. 44-Parallax-app. (1 pg.)						2.50
Annual 1 (1995, $3.50)-Year One story						4.00
Annual 2 (1996, $2.95)-Legends of the Dead Earth story						3.00

GUY GARDNER REBORN
DC Comics: 1992 - Book 3, 1992 ($4.95, limited series)

	GD 2.0	VG 4.0	FN 6.0	VF 8.0	VF/NM 9.0	NM- 9.2
1-3: Staton-c/a(p). 1-Lobo-c/cameo. 2,3-Lobo-c/s						5.00

GYPSY COLT
Dell Publishing Co.: No. 568, June, 1954 (one-shot)

	GD 2.0	VG 4.0	FN 6.0	VF 8.0	VF/NM 9.0	NM- 9.2
Four Color 568--Movie	6	12	18	38	52	65

GYRO GEARLOOSE (See Dynabrite Comics, Walt Disney's C&S #140 &Walt Disney Showcase #18)
Dell Publishing Co.: No. 1047, Nov-Jan/1959-60 - May-July, 1962 (Disney)

	GD 2.0	VG 4.0	FN 6.0	VF 8.0	VF/NM 9.0	NM- 9.2
Four Color 1047 (No. 1)-All Barks-c/a	19	38	57	134	205	275
Four Color 1095,1184-All by Carl Barks	11	22	33	75	110	145
Four Color 1267-Barks c/a, 4 pgs.	9	18	27	60	85	110
01329-207 (#1, 5-7/62)-Barks-c only (intended as 4-Color 1329?)	7	14	21	46	63	80

HACKER FILES, THE
DC Comics: Aug, 1992 - No. 12, July, 1993 ($1.95)

	GD 2.0	VG 4.0	FN 6.0	VF 8.0	VF/NM 9.0	NM- 9.2
1-12: 1-Sutton-a(p) begins; computer generated-c						2.25

HACK/SLASH
Devil's Due Publishing: Apr. 2004 ($4.95, one-shots)

	GD 2.0	VG 4.0	FN 6.0	VF 8.0	VF/NM 9.0	NM- 9.2
1-Seeley-s/Caselli-a/c						5.00
...: Girls Gone Dead (10/04) Manfredi-a/Seeley-s						5.00

HAGAR THE HORRIBLE (See Comics Reading Libraries in the Promotional Comics section)

HA HA COMICS (Teepee Tim No. 100 on; also see Giggle Comics)
Scope Mag.(Creston Publ.) No. 1-80/American Comics Group: Oct, 1943 - No. 99, Jan, 1955

	GD 2.0	VG 4.0	FN 6.0	VF 8.0	VF/NM 9.0	NM- 9.2
1-Funny animal	35	70	105	198	287	375
2	17	34	51	95	135	175
3-5: Ken Hultgren-a begins?	12	24	36	71	98	125
6-10	10	20	30	58	77	95
11-20: 14-Infinity-c	9	18	27	51	62	75
21-40	8	16	24	43	54	65
41-94,96-99: 49,61-X-Mas-c	7	14	21	37	46	55
95-3-D effect-c	15	30	45	85	120	155

HAIR BEAR BUNCH, THE (TV) (See Fun-In No. 13)
Gold Key: Feb, 1972 - No. 9, Feb, 1974 (Hanna-Barbera)

	GD 2.0	VG 4.0	FN 6.0	VF 8.0	VF/NM 9.0	NM- 9.2
1	4	8	12	28	38	48
2-9	3	6	9	18	24	30

HALLELUJAH TRAIL, THE (See Movie Classics)

HALL OF FAME FEATURING THE T.H.U.N.D.E.R. AGENTS
JC Productions(Archie Comics Group): May, 1983 - No. 3, Dec, 1983

	GD 2.0	VG 4.0	FN 6.0	VF 8.0	VF/NM 9.0	NM- 9.2
1-3: Thunder Agents-r(Crandall, Kane, Tuska, Wood-a). 2-New Ditko-c						3.00

HALLOWEEN (Movie)
Chaos! Comics: Nov, 2000; Apr, 2001 ($2.95/$2.99, one-shots)

	GD 2.0	VG 4.0	FN 6.0	VF 8.0	VF/NM 9.0	NM- 9.2
1-Brewer-a; Michael Myers childhood at the Sanitarium						3.00
...II: The Blackest Eyes (4/01, $2.99) Beck-a						3.00
...III: The Devil's Eyes (11/01, $2.99) Justiniano-a						3.00

HALLOWEEN HORROR
Eclipse Comics: Oct, 1987 (Seduction of the Innocent #7)($1.75)

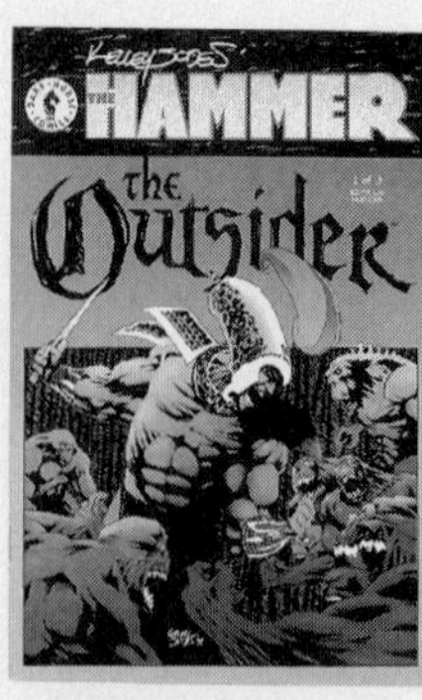

The Hammer: The Outsider #1 © Kelley Jones

Hammer of the Gods: Hammer Hits China #2 © Oeming

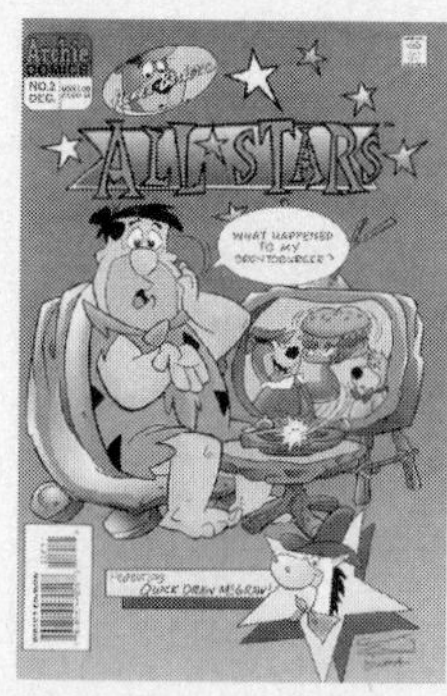

Hanna-Barbera All-Stars #2 © H-B

	GD 2.0	VG 4.0	FN 6.0	VF 8.0	VF/NM 9.0	NM- 9.2

1-Pre-code horror-r 3.00

HALLOWEEN MEGAZINE
Marvel Comics: Dec, 1996 ($3.95, one-shot, 96 pgs.)
1-Reprints Tomb of Dracula 4.00

HALO JONES (See The Ballad of...)

HAMMER, THE
Dark Horse Comics: Oct, 1997 - No. 4, Jan, 1998 ($2.95, limited series)
1-4-Kelley Jones-s/c/a, ...: Uncle Alex (8/98, $2.95) 3.00

HAMMER, THE: THE OUTSIDER
Dark Horse Comics: Feb, 1999 - No. 3, Apr, 1999 ($2.95, limited series)
1-3-Kelley Jones-s/c/a 3.00

HAMMERLOCKE
DC Comics: Sept, 1992 - No. 9, May, 1993 ($1.75, limited series)
1-($2.50, 52 pgs.)-Chris Sprouse-c/a in all 3.00
2-9 2.25

HAMMER OF GOD (Also see Nexus)
First Comics: Feb, 1990 - No. 4, May, 1990 ($1.95, limited series)
1-4 2.50

HAMMER OF GOD: BUTCH
Dark Horse Comics: May, 1994 - No. 4, Aug, 1994 ($2.50, limited series)
1-3 2.50

HAMMER OF GOD: PENTATHLON
Dark Horse Comics: Jan, 1994 ($2.50, one shot)
1-Character from Nexus 2.50

HAMMER OF GOD: SWORD OF JUSTICE
First Comics: Feb 1991 - Mar 1991 ($4.95, lim. series, squarebound, 52 pgs.)
V2#1,2 5.00

HAMMER OF THE GODS
Insight Studio Groups: 2001 - No. 5, 2001 ($2.95, limited series)
1-Michael Oeming & Mark Wheatley-s/a; Frank Cho-c 6.00
2-5: 3-Hughes-c. 5-Dave Johnson-c 3.00
The ColorSaga (2002, $4.95) r/"Enemy of the Gods" internet strip 5.00
Mortal Enemy TPB (2002, $18.95) r/#1-5; intro. by Peter David; afterword by Raven 19.00

HAMMER OF THE GODS: HAMMER HITS CHINA
Image Comics: Feb, 2003 - No. 3, Sept, 2003 ($2.95, limited series)
1-3-Oeming & Wheatley-s/a; Oeming-c. 2-Frankenstein Mobster by Wheatley 3.00

HANDBOOK OF THE CONAN UNIVERSE, THE
Marvel Comics: June, 1985 ($1.25, one-shot)
1-Kaluta-c. 4.00

HAND OF FATE (Formerly Men Against Crime)
Ace Magazines: No. 8, Dec, 1951 - No. 25, Dec, 1954 (Weird/horror stories) (Two #25's)
8-Surrealistic text story 40 80 120 244 372 500
9,10,21-Necronomicon sty; drug belladonna used 25 50 75 144 207 270
11-18,20,22,23 21 42 63 118 169 220
19-Bondage, hypo needle scenes 22 44 66 127 184 240
24-Electric chair-c 32 64 96 184 267 350
25a(11/54), 25b(12/54)-Both have Cameron-a 17 34 51 95 135 175
NOTE: *Cameron a-9, 10, 19-25a, 25b; c-13. Sekowsky a-8, 9, 13, 14.*

HAND OF FATE
Eclipse Comics: Feb, 1988 - No. 3, Apr, 1988 ($1.75/$2.00, Baxter paper)
1-3; 3-B&W 2.25

HANDS OF THE DRAGON
Seaboard Periodicals (Atlas): June, 1975
1-Origin/1st app.; Craig-a(p)/Mooney inks 1 3 4 6 8 10

HANGMAN COMICS (Special Comics No. 1; Black Hood No. 9 on)
(Also see Flyman, Mighty Comics, Mighty Crusaders & Pep Comics)
MLJ Magazines: No. 2, Spring, 1942 - No. 8, Fall, 1943
2-The Hangman, Boy Buddies begin 192 384 576 1200 1850 2500
3-Beheading splash pg.; 1st Nazi war-c 125 250 375 781 1203 1625
4-8: 5-1st Jap war-c. 8-2nd app. Super Duck (ties w/Jolly Jingles #11) 110 220 330 688 1057 1425
NOTE: *Fuje a-7(3), 8(3); c-3. Reinman c/a-3. Bondage c-3. Sahle c-6.*

HANK
Pentagon Publishing Co.: 1946
nn-Coulton Waugh's newspaper reprint 8 16 24 46 58 70

HANNA-BARBERA (See Golden Comics Digest No. 2, 7, 11)

HANNA-BARBERA ALL-STARS
Archie Publications: Oct, 1995 - No. 6, Sept, 1996 ($1.50, bi-monthly)
1-6 3.00

HANNA-BARBERA BANDWAGON (TV)
Gold Key: Oct, 1962 - No. 3, Apr, 1963
1-Giant, 84 pgs. 1-Augie Doggie app.; 1st app. Lippy the Lion, Touché Turtle & Dum Dum, Wally Gator, Loopy de Loop, 14 28 42 97 149 200
2-Giant, 84 pgs.; Mr. & Mrs. J. Evil Scientist (1st app.) in Snagglepuss story; Yakky Doodle, Ruff and Reddy and others app. 10 20 30 73 107 140
3-Regular size; Mr. & Mrs. J. Evil Scientist app. (pre-#1), Snagglepuss, Wally Gator and others app. 8 16 24 58 82 105

HANNA-BARBERA GIANT SIZE
Harvey Comics: Oct, 1992 - No. 3 ($2.25, 68 pgs.)
V2#1-3:Flintstones, Yogi Bear, Magilla Gorilla, Huckleberry Hound, Quick Draw McGraw, Yakky Doodle & Chopper, Jetsons & others 5.00

HANNA-BARBERA HI-ADVENTURE HEROES (See Hi-Adventure...)

HANNA-BARBERA PARADE (TV)
Charlton Comics: Sept, 1971 - No. 10, Dec, 1972
1 9 18 27 60 85 110
2,4-10 5 10 15 33 44 55
3-(52 pgs.)- "Summer Picnic" 7 14 21 46 63 80
NOTE: *No. 4 (1/72) went on sale late in 1972 with the January 1973 issues.*

HANNA-BARBERA PRESENTS
Archie Publications: Nov, 1995 - No. 6 ($1.50, bi-monthly)
1-8: 1-Atom Ant & Secret Squirrel. 2-Wacky Races. 3-Yogi Bear. 4-Quick Draw McGraw & Magilla Gorilla. 5-A Pup Named Scooby-Doo. 6-Superstar Olympics. 7-Wacky Races. 8-Frankenstein Jr. & the Impossibles 3.00

HANNA-BARBERA SPOTLIGHT (See Spotlight)

HANNA-BARBERA SUPER TV HEROES (TV)
Gold Key: Apr, 1968 - No. 7, Oct, 1969 (Hanna-Barbera)
1-The Birdman, The Herculoids(ends #6; not in #3), Moby Dick, Young Samson & Goliath (ends #2,4), and The Mighty Mightor begin; Spiegle-a in all 19 38 57 134 205 275
2-The Galaxy Trio app.; Shazzan begins; 12¢ & 15¢ versions exist 13 26 39 90 138 185
3,6,7-The Space Ghost app. 12 24 36 86 131 175
4,5 11 22 33 77 114 150
NOTE: *Birdman in #1,2,4,5. Herculoids in #2,4-7. Mighty Mightor in #1,2,4-7. Moby Dick in all. Shazzan in #2-5. Young Samson & Goliath in #1,3.*

HANNA-BARBERA TV FUN FAVORITES (See Golden Comics Digest #2,7,11)

HANNA-BARBERA (TV STARS) (See TV Stars)

HANS BRINKER (Disney)
Dell Publishing Co.: No. 1273, Feb, 1962 (one-shot)
Four Color 1273-Movie, photo-c 8 16 24 53 74 95

HANS CHRISTIAN ANDERSEN
Ziff-Davis Publ. Co.: 1953 (100 pgs., Special Issue)
nn-Danny Kaye (movie)-Photo-c; fairy tales 17 34 51 95 135 175

HANSEL & GRETEL
Dell Publishing Co.: No. 590, Oct, 1954 (one-shot)
Four Color 590-Partial photo-c 8 16 24 53 74 95

HANSI, THE GIRL WHO LOVED THE SWASTIKA
Spire Christian Comics (Fleming H. Revell Co.): 1973, 1976 (39¢/49¢)
1973 edition with 39¢-c 4 8 12 27 36 45
1976 edition with 49¢-c 3 6 9 19 25 32

HAP HAZARD COMICS (Real Love No. 25 on)
Ace Magazines (Readers' Research): Summer, 1944 - No. 24, Feb, 1949
(#1-6 are quarterly issues)
1 15 30 45 86 123 160
2 9 18 27 52 66 80
3-10 8 16 24 43 54 65
11-13,15-24 7 14 21 37 46 55
14-Feldstein-c (4/47) 10 20 30 56 73 90

HAP HOPPER (See Comics Revue No. 2)

Harbinger #14 © VAL

Hardcore Station #3 © Jim Starlin

Harlem Globetrotters #10 © GK

GD VG FN VF VF/NM NM-
2.0 4.0 6.0 8.0 9.0 9.2

HAPPIEST MILLIONAIRE, THE (See Movie Comics)

HAPPI TIM (See March of Comics No. 182)

HAPPY BIRTHDAY MARTHA WASHINGTON (Also see Give Me Liberty, Martha Washington Goes To War, & Martha Washington Stranded In Space)
Dark Horse Comics: Mar, 1995 ($2.95, one-shot)

1-Miller script; Gibbons-c/a 3.00

HAPPY COMICS (Happy Rabbit No. 41 on)
Nedor Publ./Standard Comics (Animated Cartoons): Aug, 1943 - No. 40, Dec, 1950 (Companion to Goofy Comics)

	GD	VG	FN	VF	VF/NM	NM-
1-Funny animal	27	54	81	152	219	285
2	14	28	42	79	110	140
3-10	10	20	30	58	77	95
11-19	9	18	27	51	62	75
20-31,34-37-Frazetta text illos in all (2 in #34&35, 3 in #27,28,30). 27-Al Fago-a	10	20	30	58	77	95
32-Frazetta-a, 7 pgs. plus 2 text illos; Roussos-a	21	42	63	118	169	220
33-Frazetta-a(2), 6 pgs. each (Scarce)	29	58	87	164	237	310
38-40	8	16	24	40	50	60

HAPPYDALE: DEVILS IN THE DESERT
DC Comics (Vertigo): 1999 - No. 2, 1999 ($6.95, limited series)

1,2-Andrew Dabb-s/Seth Fisher-a 7.00

HAPPY DAYS (TV)(See Kite Fun Book)
Gold Key: Mar, 1979 - No. 6, Feb, 1980

	GD	VG	FN	VF	VF/NM	NM-
1-Photo-c of TV cast; 35¢-c	3	6	9	18	23	28
2-6-(40¢-c)	2	4	6	9	11	14

HAPPY HOLIDAY (See March of Comics No. 181)

HAPPY HOULIHANS (Saddle Justice No. 3 on; see Blackstone, The Magician Detective)
E. C. Comics: Fall, 1947 - No. 2, Winter, 1947-48

	GD	VG	FN	VF	VF/NM	NM-
1-Origin Moon Girl (same date as Moon Girl #1)	52	104	156	317	484	650
2	31	62	93	175	253	330

HAPPY JACK
Red Top (Decker): Aug, 1957 - No. 2, Nov, 1957

	GD	VG	FN	VF	VF/NM	NM-
V1#1,2	5	10	15	22	26	30

HAPPY JACK HOWARD
Red Top (Farrell)/Decker: 1957

	GD	VG	FN	VF	VF/NM	NM-
nn-Reprints Handy Andy story from E. C. Dandy Comics #5, renamed "Happy Jack"	5	10	15	22	26	30

HAPPY RABBIT (Formerly Happy Comics)
Standard Comics (Animated Cartoons): No. 41, Feb, 1951 - No. 48, Apr, 1952

	GD	VG	FN	VF	VF/NM	NM-
41-Funny animal	7	14	21	37	46	55
42-48	6	12	18	27	33	38

HARBINGER (Also see Unity)
Valiant: Jan, 1992 - No. 41, June, 1995 ($1.95/$2.50)

	GD	VG	FN	VF	VF/NM	NM-
0-Prequel to the series; available by redeeming coupons in #1-6; cover image has pink sky; title logo is blue	3	6	9	19	25	32
0-(2nd printing) cover has blue sky & red logo						4.00
1-1st app.	1	3	4	6	8	10
2-4: 4-Low print run	1	2	3	4	5	7
5,6: 5-Solar app. 6-Torque dies						6.00
7-10: 8,9-Unity x-overs. 8-Miller-c. 9-Simonson-c. 10-1st app. H.A.R.D Corps (10/92)						4.00
11-24,26-41: 14-1st app. Stronghold. 18-Intro Screen. 19-1st app. Stunner. 22-Archer & Armstrong app. 24-Cover similar to #1. 26-Intro New Harbingers. 29-Bound-in trading card. 30-H.A.R.D. Corps app. 32-Eternal Warrior app. 33-Dr. Eclipse app.						2.50
25-($3.50, 52 pgs.)-Harada vs. Sting						3.50
...Files 1,2 (8/94,2/95 $2.50)						2.50
Trade paperback nn (11/92, $9.95)-Reprints #1-4 & comes polybagged with a copy of Harbinger #0 w/new-c. Price for TPB only						10.00

NOTE: *Issues 1-6 have coupons with origin of Harada and are redeemable for Harbinger #0.*

HARD BOILED
Dark Horse Comics: Sept, 1990 - No. 3, Mar, 1992 ($4.95/$5.95, 8 1/2x11", lim. series)

	GD	VG	FN	VF	VF/NM	NM-
1-3-Miller-s; Darrow-c/a; sexually explicit & violent	1	2	3	4	5	7
TPB (5/93, $15.95)						16.00
Big Damn Hard Boiled (12/97, $29.95, B&W) r/#1-3						30.00

HARDCASE (See Break Thru, Flood Relief & Ultraforce, 1st Series)
Malibu Comics (Ultraverse): June, 1993 - No. 26, Aug, 1995 ($1.95/$2.50)

	NM-
1-Intro Hardcase; Dave Gibbons-c; has coupon for Ultraverse Premiere #0; Jim Callahan-a(p) begin, ends #3	3.00
1-With coupon missing	2.25
1-Platinum Edition	4.00
1-Holographic Cover Edition; 1st full-c holograph tied w/Prime 1 & Strangers 1	7.00
1-Ultra Limited silver foil-c	4.00
2,3-Callahan-a, 2-($2.50)-Newsstand edition bagged w/trading card	2.50
4,6-15, 17-19: 4-Strangers app. 7-Break-Thru x-over. 8-Solution app. 9-Vs. Turf. 12-Silver foil logo, wraparound-c. 17-Prime app.	2.50
5-($2.50, 48 pgs.)-Rune flip-c/story by B. Smith (3 pgs.)	2.50
16 ($3.50, 68 pgs.)-Rune pin-up	3.50
20-26: 23-Loki app.	2.50

NOTE: *Perez a-8(2); c-20i.*

HARDCORE STATION
DC Comics: July, 1998 - No. 6, Dec, 1998 ($2.50, limited series)

1-6-Starlin-s/a(p). 3-Green Lantern-c/app. 5,6-JLA-c/app. 3.00

H.A.R.D. CORPS, THE (See Harbinger #10)
Valiant: Dec, 1992 - No. 30, Feb, 1995 ($2.25) (Harbinger spin-off)

	NM-
1-($2.50)-Gatefold-c by Jim Lee & Bob Layton	3.00
1-Gold variant	5.00
2-30: 5-Bloodshot-c/story cont'd from Bloodshot #3. 5-Variant edition; came w/Comic Defense System. 10-Turok app. 17-vs. Armorines. 18-Bound-in trading card. 20-Harbinger app.	2.25

HARD TIME
DC Comics (Focus): Apr, 2004 - Present ($2.50)

	NM-
1-11-Gerber-s/Hurtt-a; 1-Includes previews of other DC Focus series	2.50
...: 50 to Life (2004, $9.95, TPB) r/#1-6; cover gallery with sketches	10.00

HARDWARE
DC Comics (Milestone): Apr, 1993 - No. 50, Apr, 1997 ($1.50/$1.75/$2.50)

	NM-
1-($2.95)-Collector's Edition polybagged w/poster & trading card (direct sale only)	4.00
1-Platinum Edition	6.00
1-15,17-19: 11-Shadow War x-over. 11,14-Simonson-c. 12-Buckler-a(p). 17-Worlds Collide Pt. 2. 18-Simonson-c; Worlds Collide Pt. 9. 15-1st Humberto Ramos DC work	2.50
16,50-($3.95, 52 pgs.)-16-Collector's Edition w/gatefold 2nd cover by Byrne; new armor; Icon app.	4.00
16,20-24,26-49: 16-($2.50, 52 pgs.)-Newsstand Ed. 49-Moebius-c	2.50
25-($2.95, 52 pgs.)	3.00

HARDY BOYS, THE (Disney
Dell Publ. Co.: No. 760, Dec, 1956 - No. 964, Jan, 1959 (Mickey Mouse Club)

	GD	VG	FN	VF	VF/NM	NM-
Four Color 760 (#1)-Photo-c	12	24	36	84	127	170
Four Color 830(8/57), 887(1/58), 964-Photo-c	10	20	30	72	104	135

HARDY BOYS, THE (TV)
Gold Key: Apr, 1970 - No. 4, Jan, 1971

	GD	VG	FN	VF	VF/NM	NM-
1	5	10	15	36	48	60
2-4	3	7	10	21	28	35

HARLAN ELLISON'S DREAM CORRIDOR
Dark Horse Comics: Mar, 1995 - No. 5, July, 1995 ($2.95, anthology)

	NM-
1-5: Adaptation of Ellison stories. 1-4-Byrne-a.	3.00
Special (1/95, $4.95)	5.00
Trade paperback-(1996, $18.95, 192 pgs)-r/#1-5 & Special #1	19.00

HARLAN ELLISON'S DREAM CORRIDOR QUARTERLY
Dark Horse Comics: V2#1, Aug, 1996 ($5.95, anthology, squarebound)

V2#1-Adaptations of Ellison's stories w/new material; Neal Adams-a 6.00

HARLEM GLOBETROTTERS (TV) (See Fun-In No. 8, 10)
Gold Key: Apr, 1972 - No. 12, Jan, 1975 (Hanna-Barbera)

	GD	VG	FN	VF	VF/NM	NM-
1	4	8	12	29	40	50
2-5	3	6	9	16	20	25
6-12	2	4	6	12	16	20

NOTE: *#4, 8, and 12 contain 16 extra pages of advertising.*

HARLEQUIN ROMANCE
Dark Horse Comics: Nov, 2001 ($10.95, hardcover, one-shot)

nn-Neil Gaiman-s; painted-a/c by John Bolton 11.00

HARLEY QUINN
DC Comics: Dec, 2000 - No. 38, Jan, 2004 ($2.95/$2.25/$2.50)

	NM-
1-Joker and Poison Ivy app.; Terry & Rachel Dodson-a/c	4.00
2-11-($2.25). 2-Two-Face-c/app. 3-Slumber party. 6,7-Riddler app.	2.50
12-($2.95) Batman app.	3.00
13-38: 13-Joker: Last Laugh. 17,18-Bizarro-c/app. 23-Begin $2.50-c. 23,24-Martian Manhunter app. 25,32-Joker-c/app.	2.50

Harley & Ivy: Love on the Lam © DC

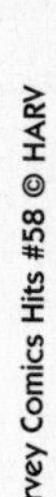

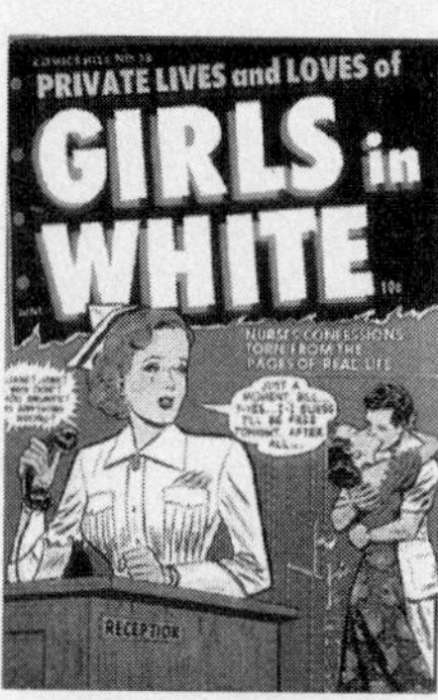

Harvey Comics Hits #58 © HARV

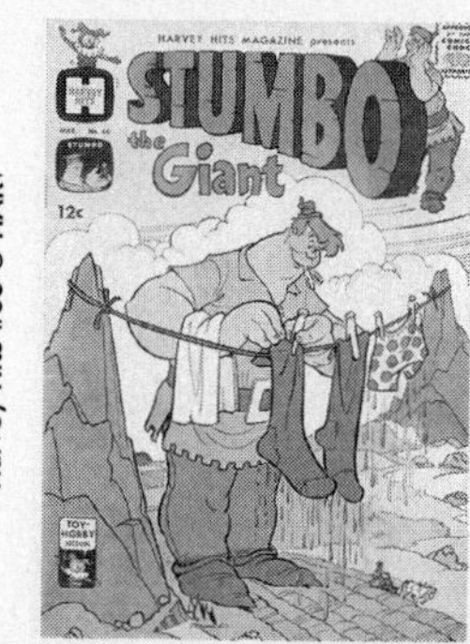

Harvey Hits #66 © HARV

	GD 2.0	VG 4.0	FN 6.0	VF 8.0	VF/NM 9.0	NM- 9.2
Harley & Ivy: Love on the Lam (2001, $5.95) Winick-s/Chiodo-c/a						6.00
...: Our Worlds at War (10/01, $2.95) Jae Lee-c; art by various						3.00
HAROLD TEEN (See Popular Comics, & Super Comics) **Dell Publishing Co.:** No. 2, 1942 - No. 209, Jan, 1949						
Four Color 2	30	60	90	218	334	450
Four Color 209	6	12	18	43	59	75
HARRIERS **Entity Comics:** June, 1995 - No. 3, 1995 ($2.50)						
1-Foil-c; polybagged w/PC game, 1-3 ($2.50)						3.00
HARROWERS, THE (See Clive Barker's...)						
HARRY JOHNSON **Fulp Fiction:** 2004 - No. 2, 2004 ($2.95, limited series)						
1,2-Charles Fulp-s/Craig Rousseau-a/c						3.00
HARSH REALM (Inspired 1999 TV series) **Harris Comics:** 1993- No. 6, 1994 ($2.95, limited series)						
1-6: Painted-c. Hudnall-s/Paquette & Ridgway-a						3.50
TPB (2000, $14.95) r/series						15.00
HARVEY **Marvel Comics:** Oct, 1970; No. 2, 12/70; No. 3, 6/72 - No. 6, 12/72						
1	10	20	30	67	96	125
2-6	6	12	18	43	59	75
HARVEY COLLECTORS COMICS (Titled Richie Rich Collectors Comics on cover of #6-on) **Harvey Publ.:** Sept, 1975 - No. 15, Jan, 1978; No. 16, Oct, 1979 (52 pgs.)						
1-Reprints Richie Rich #1,2	2	4	6	12	16	20
2-10: 7-Splash pg. shows cover to Friendly Ghost Casper #1	2	4	6	8	10	12
11-16: 16-Sad Sack-r	1	2	3	5	6	8
NOTE: *All reprints: Casper-#2, 7, Richie Rich-#1, 3, 5, 6, 8-15, Sad Sack-#16. Wendy-#4.*						
HARVEY COMICS HITS (Formerly Joe Palooka #50) **Harvey Publications:** No. 51, Oct, 1951 - No. 62, Apr, 1953						
51-The Phantom	32	64	96	184	267	350
52-Steve Canyon's Air Power(Air Force sponsored)	14	28	42	79	110	140
53-Mandrake the Magician	24	48	72	138	199	260
54-Tim Tyler's Tales of Jungle Terror	14	28	42	79	110	140
55-Love Stories of Mary Worth	9	18	27	52	66	80
56-The Phantom; bondage-c	27	54	81	154	222	290
57-Rip Kirby Exposes the Kidnap Racket; entire book by Alex Raymond	17	34	51	98	139	180
58-Girls in White (nurses stories)	9	18	27	52	66	80
59-Tales of the Invisible featuring Scarlet O'Neil	13	26	39	74	102	130
60-Paramount Animated Comics #1 (9/52) (3rd app. Baby Huey); 2nd Harvey app. Baby Huey & Casper the Friendly Ghost (1st in Little Audrey #25 (8/52)); 1st app. Herman & Catnip (c/story) & Buzzy the Crow	40	80	120	239	357	475
61-Casper the Friendly Ghost #6 (3rd Harvey Casper, 10/52)-Casper-c	42	84	126	256	357	525
62-Paramount Animated Comics #2; Herman & Catnip, Baby Huey & Buzzy the Crow	17	34	51	95	135	175
HARVEY COMICS LIBRARY **Harvey Publications:** Apr, 1952 - No. 2, 1952						
1-Teen-Age Dope Slaves as exposed by Rex Morgan, M.D.; drug propaganda story; used in **SOTI,** pg. 27	115	230	345	719	1110	1500
2-Dick Tracy Presents Sparkle Plenty in "Blackmail Terror"	24	48	72	138	199	260
HARVEY COMICS SPOTLIGHT **Harvey Comics:** Sept, 1987 - No. 4, Mar, 1988 (75¢/$1.00)						
1-New material; begin 75ç, ends #3; Sand Sack						5.00
2-4: 2,4-All new material. 2-Baby Huey. 3-Little Dot; contains reprints w/5 pg. new story. 4-$1.00-c; Little Audrey						4.00
NOTE: No. 5 was advertised but not published.						
HARVEY HITS **Harvey Publications:** Sept, 1957 - No. 122, Nov, 1967						
1-The Phantom	28	56	84	199	305	410
2-Rags Rabbit (10/57)	5	10	15	36	48	60
3-Richie Rich (11/57)-r/Little Dot; 1st book devoted to Richie Rich; see Little Dot for 1st app.	105	210	315	893	1447	2000
4-Little Dot's Uncles (12/57)	17	34	51	123	189	255
5-Stevie Mazie's Boy Friend (1/58)	4	8	12	29	40	50
6-The Phantom (2/58); Kirby-c; 2pg. Powell-a	19	38	57	136	208	280
7-Wendy the Good Little Witch (3/58, pre-dates Wendy #1; 1st book devoted to Wendy)	25	50	75	181	278	375
8-Sad Sack's Army Life; George Baker-c	8	16	24	53	74	95
9-Richie Rich's Golden Deeds; reprints (2nd book devoted to Richie Rich)	41	82	123	330	515	700
10-Little Lotta's Lunch Box	12	24	36	84	127	170
11-Little Audrey Summer Fun (7/58)	10	20	30	67	96	125
12-The Phantom; Kirby-c; 2pg. Powell-a (8/58)	15	30	45	109	167	225
13-Little Dot's Uncles (9/58); Richie Rich 1pg.	11	22	33	80	120	160
14-Herman & Katnip (10/58, TV/movies)	4	8	12	27	36	45
15-The Phantom (12/58)-1 pg. origin	15	30	45	109	167	225
16-Wendy the Good Little Witch (1/59); Casper app.	12	24	36	84	127	170
17-Sad Sack's Army Life (2/59)	7	14	21	46	63	80
18-Buzzy & the Crow	4	8	12	29	40	50
19-Little Audrey (4/59)	6	12	18	43	59	75
20-Casper & Spooky	9	18	27	60	85	110
21-Wendy the Witch	9	18	27	60	85	110
22-Sad Sack's Army Life	6	12	18	38	52	65
23-Wendy the Witch (8/59)	9	18	27	60	85	110
24-Little Dot's Uncles (9/59); Richie Rich 1pg.	10	20	30	67	96	125
25-Herman & Katnip (10/59)	4	8	12	24	32	40
26-The Phantom (11/59)	12	24	36	86	131	175
27-Wendy the Good Little Witch (12/59)	9	18	27	60	85	110
28-Sad Sack's Army Life (1/60)	4	8	12	29	40	50
29-Harvey-Toon (No.1)('60); Casper, Buzzy	6	12	18	40	55	70
30-Wendy the Witch (3/60)	9	18	27	60	85	110
31-Herman & Katnip (4/60)	4	8	12	24	32	40
32-Sad Sack's Army Life (5/60)	4	8	12	27	36	45
33-Wendy the Witch (6/60)	8	16	24	55	78	100
34-Harvey-Toon (7/60)	4	8	12	29	40	50
35-Funday Funnies (8/60)	4	8	12	24	32	40
36-The Phantom (1960)	11	22	33	80	120	160
37-Casper & Nightmare	7	14	21	46	63	80
38-Harvey-Toon	4	8	12	29	40	50
39-Sad Sack's Army Life (12/60)	4	8	12	25	33	42
40-Funday Funnies (1/61)	3	6	9	19	25	32
41-Herman & Katnip	3	6	9	19	25	32
42-Harvey-Toon (3/61)	4	8	12	22	30	38
43-Sad Sack's Army Life (4/61)	4	8	12	22	30	38
44-The Phantom (5/61)	11	22	33	77	114	150
45-Casper & Nightmare	6	12	18	38	52	65
46-Harvey-Toon (7/61)	3	6	9	19	25	32
47-Sad Sack's Army Life (8/61)	3	6	9	19	25	32
48-The Phantom (9/61)	11	22	33	77	114	150
49-Stumbo the Giant (1st app. in Hot Stuff)	11	22	33	75	110	145
50-Harvey-Toon (11/61)	3	6	9	18	24	30
51-Sad Sack's Army Life (12/61)	3	6	9	18	24	30
52-Casper & Nightmare	5	10	15	36	48	60
53-Harvey-Toons (2/62)	3	6	9	18	23	28
54-Stumbo the Giant	6	12	18	43	59	75
55-Sad Sack's Army Life (4/62)	3	6	9	18	24	30
56-Casper & Nightmare	5	10	15	33	44	55
57-Stumbo the Giant	6	12	18	43	59	75
58-Sad Sack's Army Life	3	6	9	18	24	30
59-Casper & Nightmare (7/62)	5	10	15	33	44	55
60-Stumbo the Giant (9/62)	6	12	18	43	59	75
61-Sad Sack's Army Life	3	6	9	18	23	28
62-Casper & Nightmare	4	8	12	28	38	48
63-Stumbo the Giant	5	10	15	36	48	60
64-Sad Sack's Army Life (1/63)	3	6	9	18	23	28
65-Casper & Nightmare	4	8	12	28	38	48
66-Stumbo The Giant (3/63)	5	10	15	36	48	60
67-Sad Sack's Army Life (4/63)	3	6	9	18	23	28
68-Casper & Nightmare	4	8	12	28	38	48
69-Stumbo the Giant (6/63)	5	10	15	36	48	60
70-Sad Sack's Army Life (7/63)	3	6	9	18	23	28
71-Casper & Nightmare (8/63)	4	8	12	25	33	42
72-Stumbo the Giant	5	10	15	36	48	60
73-Little Sad Sack (10/63)	3	6	9	18	23	28
74-Sad Sack's Muttsy... (11/63)	3	6	9	18	23	28
75-Casper & Nightmare	4	8	12	22	30	38
76-Little Sad Sack	3	6	9	18	23	28
77-Sad Sack's Muttsy...	3	6	9	18	23	28
78-Stumbo the Giant (3/64); JFK caricature	5	10	15	36	48	60

Hate #24 © Peter Bagge

Haunted #21 © CC

The Haunt of Fear #8 © WMG

GD VG FN VF VF/NM NM-
2.0 4.0 6.0 8.0 9.0 9.2

GD VG FN VF VF/NM NM-
2.0 4.0 6.0 8.0 9.0 9.2

79-87: 79-Little Sad Sack (4/64). 80-Sad Sack's Muttsy... (5/64). 81-Little Sad Sack. 82-Sad Sack's Muttsy... 83-Little Sad Sack(8/64). 84-Sad Sack's Muttsy... 85-Gabby Gob (#1) (10/64). 86-G. I. Juniors (#1)(11/64). 87-Sad Sack's Muttsy... (12/64)
3 6 9 18 23 28
88-Stumbo the Giant (1/65) 5 10 15 36 48 60
89-122: 89-Sad Sack's Muttsy... 90-Gabby Gob. 91-G. I. Juniors. 92-Sad Sack's Muttsy... (5/65). 93-Sadie Sack (6/65). 94-Gabby Gob. 95-G. I. Juniors (8/65). 96-Sad Sack's Muttsy... (9/65). 97-Gabby Gob (10/65). 98-G. I. Juniors (11/65). 99-Sad Sack's Muttsy... (12/65). 100-Gabby Gob(1/66). 101-G. I. Juniors (2/66). 102-Sad Sack's Muttsy... (3/66). 103-Gabby Gob. 104- G. I. Juniors. 105-Sad Sack's Muttsy... 106-Gabby Gob (7/66). 107-G. I. Juniors (8/66). 108-Sad Sack's Muttsy...109-Gabby Gob. 110-G. I. Juniors (11/66). 111-Sad Sack's Muttsy... (12/66). 112-G. I. Juniors. 113-Sad Sack's Muttsy... 114-G. I. Juniors. 115-Sad Sack's Muttsy... 116-G. I. Juniors (5/67). 117-Sad Sack's Muttsy... 118-G. I. Juniors. 119-Sad Sack's Muttsy... (8/67). 120-G. I. Juniors (9/67). 121-Sad Sack's Muttsy... (10/67). 122-G. I. Juniors (11/67) 2 4 6 11 14 18

HARVEY HITS COMICS
Harvey Publications: Nov, 1986 - No. 6, Oct, 1987

1-Little Lotta, Little Dot, Wendy & Baby Huey 1 2 3 4 5 7
2-6: 3-Xmas-c 4.50

HARVEY POP COMICS (Rock Happening) (Teen Humor)
Harvey Publications: Oct, 1968 - No. 2, Nov, 1969 (Both are 68 pg. Giants)

1-The Cowsills 6 12 18 43 59 75
2-Bunny 6 12 18 38 52 65

HARVEY 3-D HITS (See Sad Sack)

HARVEY-TOON (...S) (See Harvey Hits No. 29, 34, 38, 42, 46, 50, 53)

HARVEY WISEGUYS (...Digest #? on)
Harvey Comics: Nov, 1987; #2, Nov, 1988; #3, Apr, 1989 - No. 4, Nov, 1989 (98 pgs., digest-size, $1.25/$1.75)

1-Hot Stuff, Spooky, etc. 1 2 3 4 5 7
2-4: 2 (68 pgs.) 4.50

HATARI (See Movie Classics)

HATE
Fantagraphics Books: Spr, 1990 - No. 30, 1998 ($2.50/$2.95, B&W/color)

1 2 4 6 10 12 15
2-3 1 2 3 5 6 8
4-10 5.00
11-20: 16- color begins 4.00
21-29 3.00
30-($3.95) Last issue 4.00
Annual 1 (2/01, $3.95) Peter Bagge-s/a 4.00
Annual 2-4 (12/01, 12/02, 12/03; $4.95) Peter Bagge-s/a 5.00
Buddy Bites the Bullet! (2001, $16.95) r/Buddy stories in color 17.00
Buddy Go Home! (1997, $16.95) r/Buddy stories in color 17.00
Hate-Ball Special Edition ($3.95, giveaway)-reprints 4.00
Hate Jamboree (10/98, $4.50) old & new cartoons 4.50

HATHAWAYS, THE (TV)
Dell Publishing Co.: No. 1298, Feb-Apr, 1962 (one-shot)

Four Color 1298-Photo-c 6 12 18 38 52 65

HAUNTED (See This Magazine Is Haunted)

HAUNTED (Baron Weirwulf's Haunted Library on-c #21 on)
Charlton Comics: 9/71 - No. 30, 11/76; No. 31, 9/77 - No. 75, 9/84

1-All Ditko issue 5 10 15 33 44 55
2-7-Ditko-c/a 3 6 9 18 23 28
8,12,28-Ditko-a 2 4 6 11 14 18
9,19 2 4 6 9 11 14
10,20,15,18: 10,20-Sutton-a. 15-Sutton-c 2 4 6 9 11 14
11,13,14,16-Ditko-c/a 2 4 6 12 16 20
17-Sutton-c/a; Newton-a 2 4 6 10 12 15
21-Newton-c/a; Sutton-a; 1st Baron Weirwulf 3 6 9 18 23 28
22-Newton-c/a; Sutton-a 2 4 6 10 13 16
23,24-Sutton-c; Ditko-a 2 4 6 10 13 16
25-27,29,32,33 1 3 4 6 8 10
30,41,47,49-52,74-Ditko-c/a: 51-Reprints #1 2 4 6 10 13 16
31,35,37,38-Sutton-a 1 3 4 6 8 10
34,36,39,40,42,57,60-Ditko-a 2 4 6 8 10 12
43-46,48,53-56,58,59,61-73: 59-Newton-a. 64-Sutton-c. 71-73-Low print
1 2 3 5 6 8
75-(9/84) Last issue; low print 2 4 6 10 13 16

NOTE: *Aparo c-45.* ***Ditko*** *a-1-8, 11-16, 18, 23, 24, 28, 30, 34r, 36r, 39-42r, 47r, 49-52r, 57, 60, 74. c-1-7, 11, 13, 14, 16, 30, 41, 47, 49-52, 74.* ***Howard*** *a-6, 9, 18, 22, 25, 32.* ***Kim*** *a-9, 19.* ***Morisi*** *a-13.* ***Newton*** *a-17, 21, 59r; c-21, 22(painted).* ***Staton*** *a-11, 12, 18, 21, 22, 30, 33, 35, 38; c-18, 33, 38.* ***Sutton*** *a-10, 17, 20-22, 31, 35, 37, 38; c-15, 17, 18, 23(painted), 24(painted), 27, 64r. #49 reprints Tales of the Mysterious Traveler #4.*

HAUNTED, THE
Chaos! Comics: Jan, 2002 - No. 4, Apr, 2002 ($2.99, limited series)

1-4-Peter David-s/Nat Jones-a 3.00
...: Gray Matters (7/02, $2.99) David-s/Jones-a 3.00

HAUNTED LOVE
Charlton Comics: Apr, 1973 - No. 11, Sept, 1975

1-Tom Sutton-a (16 pgs.) 5 10 15 36 48 60
2,3,6,7,10,11 3 6 9 16 20 25
4,5-Ditko-a 3 6 9 19 25 32
8,9-Newton-c 3 6 9 18 23 28
Modern Comics #1(1978) 2 4 6 9 11 14

NOTE: ***Howard*** *a-8i.* ***Kim*** *a-7-9.* ***Newton*** *c-8, 9.* ***Staton*** *a-1-6.* ***Sutton*** *a-1, 3-5, 10, 11.*

HAUNTED MAN, THE
Dark Horse Comics: Mar, 2000 ($2.95, unfinished limited series)

1-Gerald Jones-s/Mark Badger-a 3.00

HAUNTED THRILLS (Tales of Horror and Terror)
Ajax/Farrell Publications: June, 1952 - No. 18, Nov-Dec, 1954

1-r/Ellery Queen #1 50 100 150 305 465 625
2-L. B. Cole-a r-/Ellery Queen #1 35 70 105 200 290 380
3-5: 3-Drug use story 31 62 93 177 256 335
6-10,12: 7-Hitler story. 26 52 78 150 215 280
11-Nazi death camp story 28 56 84 158 229 300
13-18: 18-Lingerie panels. 14-Jesus Christ apps. in story by Webb. 15-Jo-Jo-r
21 42 63 121 173 225

NOTE: ***Kamenish*** *art in most issues.* ***Webb*** *a-12.*

HAUNT OF FEAR (Formerly Gunfighter)
E. C. Comics: No. 15, May-June, 1950 - No. 28, Nov-Dec, 1954

15(#1, 1950)(Scarce) 276 552 828 2070 3035 4000
16-1st app. "The Witches Cauldron" & the Old Witch (by Kamen); begin series as hostess of Haunt of Fear 117 234 351 878 1289 1700
17-Origin of Crypt of Terror, Vault of Horror, & Haunt of Fear; used in **SOTI**, pg. 43; last pg. Ingels-a used by N.Y. Legis. Comm.; story "Monster Maker" based on Frankenstein. Old Witch by Feldstein 117 234 351 878 1289 1700
4-Ingles becomes regular artist for Old Witch. 1st Vault Keeper & Crypt Keeper app. in HOF; begin series 72 144 216 540 795 1050
5-Injury-to-eye panel, pg. 4 of Wood story 56 112 168 420 618 815
6,7,9,10: 6-Crypt Keeper by Feldstein begins. 9-Crypt Keeper by Davis begins. 10-Ingels biog.
42 84 126 315 463 610
8-Classic Feldstein Shrunken Head-c 45 90 135 338 497 655
11,12: Classic Ingels-c; 11-Kamen biog. 12-Feldstein biog.
34 68 102 255 373 490
13,15,16,18,20: 16,18-Ray Bradbury adaptations. 18-Ray Bradbury biography. 20-Feldstein-r/Vault of Horror #12 32 64 96 240 350 460
14-Origin Old Witch by Ingels; classic-ingels-c 47 94 141 353 514 675
17-Classic Ingels-c 33 66 99 248 362 475
19-Used in **SOTI**, ill. "A comic book baseball game" & Senate investigation on juvenile delinq. bondage/decapitation-c 42 84 126 315 460 605
21-27: 23-Used in **SOTI**, pg. 241. 24-Used in Senate Investigative Report, pg.8. 26-Contains anti-censorship editorial, 'Are you a Red Dupe?' 27-Cannibalism story; Wertham cameo
22 44 66 165 243 320
28-Low distribution 30 60 90 225 330 435

NOTE: *(Canadian reprints known; see Table of Contents).* ***Craig*** *a-15-17, 5, 7, 10, 12, 13; c-15-17, 5-7.* ***Crandall*** *a-20, 21, 26, 27.* ***Davis*** *a-4-26, 28.* ***Evans*** *a-15-19, 22-25, 27.* ***Feldstein*** *a-15-17, 20; c-4, 8-10.* ***Ingels*** *a-16, 17, 4-28; c-11-28.* ***Kamen*** *a-16, 4, 6, 7, 9-11, 13-19, 21-28.* ***Krigstein*** *a-28.* ***Kurtzman*** *a-15(#1), 17(#3).* ***Orlando*** *a-9, 12.* ***Wood*** *a-15, 16, 4-6.*

HAUNT OF FEAR, THE
Gladstone Publishing: May, 1991 - No. 2, July, 1991 ($2.00, 68 pgs.)

1,2: 1-Ghastly Ingels-c(r); 2-Craig-c(r) 3.00

HAUNT OF FEAR
Russ Cochran/Gemstone Publ.: Sept, 1991 - No. 5, 1992 ($2.00, 68 pgs.); Nov, 1992 - Present ($1.50/$2.00/$2.50)

1-25: 1-Ingels-c(r). 1-3-r/HOF #15-17 with original-c. 4,5-r/HOF #4,5 with original-c 2.50
Annual 1-5: 1- r/#1-5. 2- r/#6-10. 3- r/#11-15. 4- r/#16-20. 5- r/#21-25 14.00
Annual 6-r/#26-28 9.00

HAUNT OF HORROR, THE (Digest)
Marvel Comics: Jun, 1973 - No. 2, Aug, 1973 (164 pgs.; text and art)

1-Morrow painted skull-c; stories by Ellison, Howard, and Leiber; Brunner-a

The Hawk #3 © Z-D

Hawkeye ('03) #1 © MAR

Hawkman #25 © DC

	GD	VG	FN	VF	VF/NM	NM-
	2.0	4.0	6.0	8.0	9.0	9.2

	4	8	12	24	32	40
2-Kelly Freas painted bondage-c; stories by McCaffrey, Goulart, Leiber, Ellison; art by Simonson, Brunner, and Buscema	3	6	9	18	23	28

HAUNT OF HORROR, THE (Magazine)
Cadence Comics Publ. (Marvel): May, 1974 - No. 5, Jan, 1975 (75¢) (B&W)

1,2: 2-Origin & 1st app. Gabriel the Devil Hunter; Satana begins	2	4	6	12	16	20
3-5: 4-Neal Adams-a. 5-Evans-a(2)	3	6	9	16	20	25

NOTE: *Alcala a-2. Colan a-2p. Heath r-1. Krigstein r-3. Reese a-1. Simonson a-1.*

HAVE GUN, WILL TRAVEL (TV)
Dell Publishing Co.: No. 931, 8/58 - No. 14, 7-9/62 (All Richard Boone photo-c)

Four Color 931 (#1)	15	30	45	105	160	215
Four Color 983,1044 (#2,3)	10	20	30	70	100	130
4 (1-3/60) - 10	9	18	27	63	89	115
11-14	9	18	27	60	85	110

HAVEN: THE BROKEN CITY (See JLA/Haven: Arrival and JLA/Haven: Anathema)
DC Comics: Feb, 2002 - No. 9, Oct, 2002 ($2.50, limited series)

1-9-Olivetti-c/a: 1- JLA app. Series concludes in JLA/Haven: Anathema 2.50

HAVOK & WOLVERINE - MELTDOWN (See Marvel Comics Presents #24)
Marvel Comics (Epic Comics): Mar, 1989 - No. 4, Oct, 1989 ($3.50, mini-series, square-bound, mature)

1-4: Art by Kent Williams & Jon J. Muth; story by Walt & Louise Simonson 4.00

HAWAIIAN DICK
Image Comics: Dec, 2002 - No. 3, Feb, 2003 ($2.95, limited series)

1-3-B. Clay Moore-s/Steven Griffin-a 3.00
...: Byrd of Paradise TPB (8/03, $14.95) r/#1-3, script & sketch pages 15.00

HAWAIIAN DICK: THE LAST RESORT
Image Comics: Aug, 2004 - No. 4 ($2.95, limited series)

1,2-B. Clay Moore-s/Steven Griffin-a 3.00

HAWAIIAN EYE (TV)
Gold Key: July, 1963 (Troy Donahue, Connie Stevens photo-c)

1 (10073-307)	6	12	18	40	55	70

HAWAIIAN ILLUSTRATED LEGENDS SERIES
Hogarth Press: 1975 (B&W)(Cover printed w/blue, yellow, and green)

1-Kalelealuaka, the Mysterious Warrior 5.00

HAWK, THE (Also see Approved Comics #1, 7 & Tops In Adventure)
Ziff-Davis/St. John Publ. Co. No. 4 on: Wint/51 - No. 3, 11-12/52; No. 4, 1-2/53; No. 8, 9/54 - No. 12, 5/55 (Painted c-1-4)(#5-7 don't exist)

1-Anderson-a	21	42	63	118	169	220
2 (Sum, '52)-Kubert, Infantino-a	12	24	36	69	95	120
3-4,11: 11-Buckskin Belle & The Texan app.	10	20	30	56	73	90
8-10,12: 8(9/54)-Reprints #3 w/different-c by Baker. 9-Baker-c/a; Kubert-a(r)/#2. 10-Baker-c/a; r/one story from #2. 12-Baker-c/a; Buckskin Belle app.	13	26	39	74	102	130
3-D 1(11/53, 25¢)-Came w/glasses; Baker-c	35	70	105	198	287	375

NOTE: *Baker c-8-12. Larsen a-10. Tuska a-1, 9, 12. Painted c-1, 4, 7.*

HAWK AND THE DOVE, THE (See Showcase #75 & Teen Titans) (1st series)
National Periodical Publications: Aug-Sept, 1968 - No. 6, June-July, 1969

1-Ditko-c/a	9	18	27	65	93	120
2-6: 5-Teen Titans cameo	6	12	18	40	55	70

NOTE: *Ditko c/a-1, 2. Gil Kane a-3p, 4p, 5, 6p; c-3-6.*

HAWK AND DOVE (2nd Series)
DC Comics: Oct, 1988 - No. 5, Feb, 1989 ($1.00, limited series)

1-Rob Liefeld-c/a(p) in all 4.00
2-5 3.00
Trade paperback ('93, $9.95)-Reprints #1-5 10.00

HAWK AND DOVE
DC Comics: June, 1989 - No. 28, Oct, 1991 ($1.00)

1-28 2.50
Annual 1,2 ('90, '91; $2.00) 1-Liefeld pin-up. 2-Armageddon 2001 x-over 3.00

HAWK AND DOVE
DC Comics: Nov, 1997 - No. 5, Mar, 1998 ($2.50, limited series)

1-5-Baron-s/Zachary & Giordano-a 2.50

HAWK AND WINDBLADE (See Elflord)
Warp Graphics: Aug, 1997 - No.2, Sept, 1997 ($2.95, limited series)

1,2-Blair-s/Chan-c/a 3.00

HAWKEYE (See The Avengers #16 & Tales Of Suspense #57)
Marvel Comics Group: Sept, 1983 - No. 4, Dec, 1983 (limited series)

1-4: Mark Gruenwald-a/scripts. 1-Origin Hawkeye. 3-Origin Mockingbird. 4-Hawkeye & Mockingbird elope 3.00

HAWKEYE
Marvel Comics: Jan, 1994 - No. 4, Apr, 1994 ($1.75, limited series)

1-4 2.25

HAWKEYE (Volume 2)
Marvel Comics: Dec, 2003 - No. 8, Aug, 2004 ($2.99)

1-8: 1-6-Nicieza-s/Raffaele-a. 7,8-Bennett-a; Black Widow app. 3.00

HAWKEYE & THE LAST OF THE MOHICANS (TV)
Dell Publishing Co.: No. 884, Mar, 1958 (one-shot)

Four Color 884-Photo-c	8	16	24	58	82	105

HAWKEYE: EARTH'S MIGHTIEST MARKSMAN
Marvel Comics: Oct, 1998 ($2.99, one-shot)

1-Justice and Firestar app.; DeFalco-s 3.00

HAWKMAN (See Atom & Hawkman, The Brave & the Bold, DC Comics Presents, Detective Comics, Flash Comics, Hawkworld, JSA, Justice League of America #31, Legend of the Hawkman, Mystery in Space, Shadow War Of..., Showcase, & World's Finest #256)

HAWKMAN (1st Series) (Also see The Atom #7 & Brave & the Bold #34-36, 42-44, 51)
National Periodical Publications: Apr-May, 1964 - No. 27, Aug-Sept, 1968

1-(4-5/64)-Anderson-c/a begins, ends #21	51	102	153	434	705	975
2	24	48	72	174	267	360
3,5: 5-2nd app. Shadow Thief	15	30	45	109	167	225
4-Origin & 1st app. Zatanna (10-11/64)	19	38	57	138	212	285
6	12	24	36	86	131	175
7	10	20	30	72	104	135
8-10: 9-Atom cameo; Hawkman & Atom learn each other's I.D.; 3rd app. Shadow Thief	9	18	27	63	89	115
11-15	7	14	21	50	68	85
16,17-27: 18-Adam Strange x-over (cameo #19). 25-G.A. Hawkman-r by Moldoff. 26-Kirby-a(r). 27-Kubert-c	6	12	18	38	52	65

HAWKMAN (2nd Series)
DC Comics: Aug, 1986 - No. 17, Dec, 1987

1-17: 10-Byrne-c, Special #1 (1986, $1.25) 2.50
Trade paperback (1989, $19.95)-r/Brave and the Bold #34-36,42-44 by Kubert; Kubert-c 20.00

HAWKMAN (4th Series)(See both Hawkworld limited & ongoing series)
DC Comics: Sept, 1993 - No. 33, July, 1996 ($1.75/$1.95/$2.25)

1-($2.50)-Gold foil embossed-c; storyline cont'd from Hawkworld ongoing series; new costume & powers. 3.00
2-13,0,14-33: 2-Green Lantern x-over. 3-Airstryke app. 4,6-Wonder Woman app. 13-(9/94)-Zero Hour. 0-(10/94). 14-(11/94). 15-Aquaman-c & app. 23-Wonder Woman app. 25-Kent Williams-c. 29,30-Chaykin-c. 32-Breyfogle-c 2.50
Annual 1 (1993, $2.50, 68 pgs.)-Bloodlines Earthplague 3.00
Annual 2 (1995, $3.95)-Year One story 4.00

HAWKMAN (See JSA #23 for return)
DC Comics: May, 2002 - Present ($2.50)

1-Johns & Robinson-s/Morales-a 5.00
1-2nd printing 2.50
2-35: 2-4-Shadow Thief app. 5,6-Green Arrow-c/app. 8-Atom-c/app. 13-Van Sciver-a. 14-Gentleman Ghost app. 15-Hawkwoman app. 16-Byth returns. 23-25-Black Reign x-over with JSA #56-58. 26-Byrne-c/a. 27-Phillips-a. 28-Sook-a begins. 29,30-Land-c 2.50
...: Allies & Enemies TPB (2004, $14.95) r/#7-14 & pages fromSecret Files and Origins 15.00
...: Endless Flight TPB (2003, $12.95) r/#1-6 & Secret Files and Origins 13.00
... Secret Files and Origins (10/02, $4.95) profiles and pin-ups by various 5.00

HAWKMOON: THE JEWEL IN THE SKULL
First Comics: May, 1986 - No. 4, Nov, 1986 ($1.75, limited series, Baxter paper)

1-4: Adapts novel by Michael Moorcock 2.50

HAWKMOON: THE MAD GOD'S AMULET
First Comics: Jan, 1987 - No. 4, July, 1987 ($1.75, limited series, Baxter paper)

1-4: Adapts novel by Michael Moorcock 2.50

HAWKMOON: THE RUNESTAFF
First Comics: Jun, 1988 -No. 4, Dec, 1988 ($1.75-$1.95, lim. series, Baxter paper)

1-4: ($1.75) Adapts novel by Michael Moorcock. 3,4 ($1.95) 2.50

HAWKMOON: THE SWORD OF DAWN

Headline Comics #8 © PRIZE

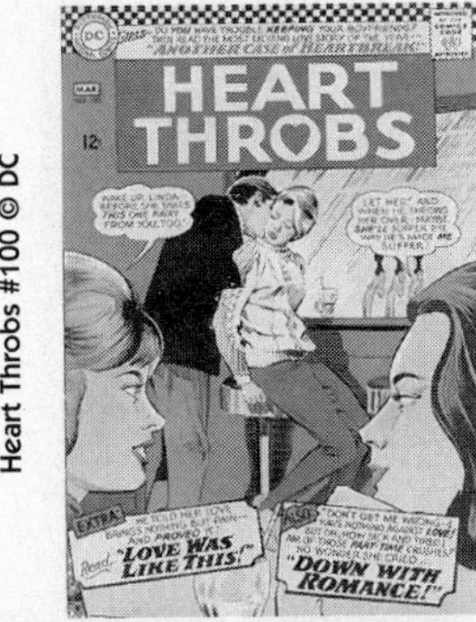

Heart Throbs #100 © DC

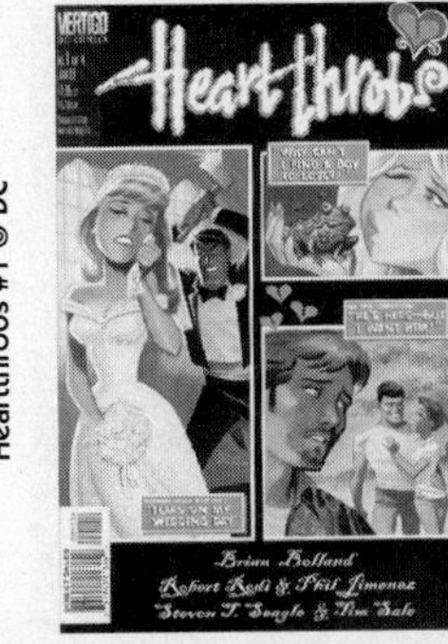

Heartthrobs #1 © DC

	GD 2.0	VG 4.0	FN 6.0	VF 8.0	VF/NM 9.0	NM- 9.2

First Comics: Sept, 1987 - No. 4, Mar, 1988 ($1.75, lim. series, Baxter paper)

1-4: Dorman painted-c; adapts Moorcock novel — 2.50

HAWKS OF THE SEAS (WILL EISNER'S...)
Dark Horse Comics: July, 2003 ($19.95, B&W, hardcover)

nn-Reprints 1937-1939 weekly Pirate serial by Will Eisner; Williamson intro. — 20.00

HAWKWORLD
DC Comics: 1989 - No. 3, 1989 ($3.95, prestige format, limited series)

Book 1-3: 1-Tim Truman story & art in all; Hawkman dons new costume; reintro Byth — 4.00
TPB (1991, $16.95) r/#1-3 — 17.00

HAWKWORLD (3rd Series)
DC Comics: June, 1990 - No. 32, Mar, 1993 ($1.50/$1.75)

1-Hawkman spin-off; story cont'd from limited series. — 3.00
2-32: 15,16-War of the Gods x-over. 22-J'onn J'onzz app. — 2.25
Annual 1-3 ('90-'92, $2.95, 68 pgs.), 2-2nd printing with silver ink-c — 3.00
NOTE: *Truman a-30-32; c-27-32, Annual 1.*

HAYWIRE
DC Comics: Oct, 1988 - No. 13, Sept, 1989 ($1.25, mature)

1-13 — 2.25

HAZARD
Image Comics (WildStorm Prod.): June, 1996 - No. 7, Nov, 1996 ($1.75)

1-7: 1-Intro Hazard; Jeff Mariotte scripts begin; Jim Lee-c(p) — 3.00

HEADHUNTERS
Image Comics: Apr, 1997 - No. 3, June, 1997 ($2.95, B&W)

1-3: Chris Marrinan-s/a — 3.00

HEADLINE COMICS (...For the American Boy) (...Crime No. 32-39)
Prize Publ./American Boys' Comics: Feb, 1943 - No. 22, Nov-Dec, 1946; No. 23, 1947 - No. 77, Oct, 1956

	GD 2.0	VG 4.0	FN 6.0	VF 8.0	VF/NM 9.0	NM- 9.2
1-Junior Rangers-c/stories begin; Yank & Doodle x-over in Junior Rangers (Junior Rangers are Uncle Sam's nephews)	54	108	162	329	502	675
2	31	62	93	177	256	335
3-Used in **POP**, pg. 84	22	44	66	125	180	235
4-7,9,10: 4,9,10-Hitler stories in each	19	38	57	107	154	200
8-Classic Hitler-c	58	116	174	363	557	750
11,12	17	34	51	95	135	175
13-15-Blue Streak in all	18	36	54	102	146	190
16-Origin & 1st app. Atomic Man (11-12/45)	28	56	84	158	229	300
17,18,20,21: 21-Atomic Man ends (9-10/46)	15	30	45	83	117	150
19-S&K-a	31	62	93	178	259	340
22-Last Junior Rangers; Kiefer-c	12	24	36	69	95	120
23,24: (All S&K-a). 23-Valentine's Day Massacre story; content changes to true crime. 24-Dope-crazy killer story	30	60	90	170	245	320
25-35-S&K-c/a. 25-Powell-a	28	56	84	158	229	300
36-S&K-a; photo-c begin	21	42	63	121	173	225
37-1 pg. S&K, Severin-a; rare Kirby photo-c app.	21	42	63	121	173	225
38,40-Meskin-a	9	18	27	52	66	80
39,41-43,46-50,52-55: 41-J. Edgar Hoover 26th Anniversary Issue with photo on-c. 43,49-Meskin-a	8	16	24	43	54	65
44-S&K-c; Severin/Elder, Meskin-a	13	26	39	76	106	135
45-Kirby-a	11	22	33	64	87	110
51-Kirby-c	9	18	27	52	66	80
56-S&K-a	13	26	39	74	102	130
57-77: 72-Meskin-c/a(i)	7	14	21	35	43	50

NOTE: ***Hollingsworth** a-30. Photo c-36-43. **H. C. Kiefer** c-12-16, 22. Atomic Man c-17-19.*

HEADMAN
Innovation Publishing: 1990 ($2.50, mature)

1-Sci/fi — 2.50

HEAP, THE
Skywald Publications: Sept, 1971 (52 pgs.)

	GD 2.0	VG 4.0	FN 6.0	VF 8.0	VF/NM 9.0	NM- 9.2
1-Kinstler-r/Strange Worlds #8; new-s w/Sutton-a	3	6	9	19	25	32

HEART AND SOUL
Mikeross Publications: April-May, 1954 - No. 2, June-July, 1954

	GD 2.0	VG 4.0	FN 6.0	VF 8.0	VF/NM 9.0	NM- 9.2
1,2	8	16	24	40	50	60

HEARTBREAKERS (Also see Dark Horse Presents)
Dark Horse Comics: Apr, 1996 - No. 4, July, 1996 ($2.95, limited series)

1-4: 1-W/paper doll & pin-up. 2-Alex Ross pin-up. 3-Evan Dorkin pin-ups. 4-Brereton-c; Matt Wagner pin-up — 3.00
...Superdigest (7/98, $9.95, digest-size) new stories — 10.00

HEARTLAND (See Hellblazer)
DC Comics (Vertigo): Mar, 1997 ($4.95, one-shot, mature)

1-Garth Ennis-s/Steve Dillon-c/a — 5.00

HEART OF DARKNESS
Hardline Studios: 1994 ($2.95)

1-Brereton-c — 3.00

HEART OF EMPIRE
Dark Horse Comics: Apr, 1999 - No. 9, Dec, 1999 ($2.95, limited series)

1-9-Bryan Talbot-s/a — 3.00

HEART OF THE BEAST, THE
DC Comics (Vertigo): 1994 ($19.95, hardcover, mature)

1-Dean Motter scripts — 20.00

HEARTS OF DARKNESS (See Ghost Rider; Wolverine; Punisher: Hearts of...)

HEART THROBS (Love Stories No. 147 on)
Quality Comics/National Periodical #47(4-5/57) on (Arleigh #48-101): 8/49 - No. 8, 10/50; No. 9, 3/52 - No. 146, Oct, 1972

	GD 2.0	VG 4.0	FN 6.0	VF 8.0	VF/NM 9.0	NM- 9.2
1-Classic Ward-c, Gustavson-a, 9 pgs.	40	80	120	244	372	500
2-Ward-c/a (9 pgs); Gustavson-a	26	52	78	150	215	280
3-Gustavson-a	11	22	33	62	84	105
4,6,8-Ward-a, 8-9 pgs.	15	30	45	83	117	150
5,7	9	18	27	51	62	75
9-Robert Mitchum, Jane Russell photo-c	11	22	33	66	91	115
10,15-Ward-a	11	22	33	66	91	115
11-14,16-20: 12 (7/52)	8	16	24	40	50	60
21-Ward-c	10	20	30	60	80	100
22,23-Ward-a(p)	8	16	24	46	58	70
24-33: 33-Last pre-code (3/55)	7	14	21	37	46	55
34-39,41-46 (12/56; last Quality issue): 45-Baker-a	7	14	21	35	43	50
40-Ward-a; r-7 pgs./#21	8	16	24	40	50	60
47-(4-5/57); 1st DC issue)	23	46	69	163	249	335
48-60, 100	10	20	30	67	96	125
61-70	7	14	21	50	68	85
71-99: 74-Last 10 cent issue	6	12	18	40	55	70
101-The Beatles app. on-c	14	28	42	97	149	200
102-120: 102-123-(Serial)-Three Girls, Their Lives, Their Loves	3	7	10	21	28	35
121-132,143-146	3	6	9	18	23	28
133-142-(52 pgs.)	4	8	12	24	32	40

NOTE: ***Gustavson** a-8. **Tuska** a-128. Photo c-4, 5, 8-10, 15, 17.*

HEART THROBS - THE BEST OF DC ROMANCE COMICS (See Fireside Book Series)

HEART THROBS
DC Comics (Vertigo): Jan, 1999 - No. 4, Apr, 1999 ($2.95, lim. series)

1-4-Romance anthology. 1-Timm-c. 3-Corben-a — 3.00

HEATHCLIFF (See Star Comics Magazine)
Marvel Comics (Star Comics)/Marvel Comics No. 23 on: Apr, 1985 - No. 56, Feb, 1991 (#16-on, $1.00)

1-Post-a most issues — 6.00
2-10,47: 47-Batman parody (Catman vs. the Soaker) — 4.00
11-46,48-56: 43-X-Mas issue — 3.00
Annual 1 ('87) — 3.00

HEATHCLIFF'S FUNHOUSE
Marvel Comics (Star Comics)/Marvel No. 6 on: May, 1987 - No. 10, 1988

1 — 4.00
2-10 — 3.00

HEAVEN'S DEVILS
Image Comics: Sept, 2003 - No. 4, July, 2004 ($2.95/$3.50, B&W, limited series)

1-3-($2.95) Jai Nitz-s/Zach Howard-a — 3.00
4-($3.50) Kevin Sharpe-a — 3.50

HEAVY HITTERS
Marvel Comics (Epic Comics): 1993 ($3.75, 68 pgs.)

1-Bound w/trading card; Lawdog, Feud, Alien Legion, Trouble With Girls, & Spyke — 3.75

HEAVY LIQUID
DC Comics (Vertigo): Oct, 1999 - No. 5, Feb, 2000 ($5.95, limited series)

1-5-Paul Pope-s/a; flip covers — 6.00
TPB (2001, $29.95) r/#1-5 — 30.00

HECKLE AND JECKLE (Paul Terry's...)(See Blue Ribbon, Giant Comics Edition #5A & 10,

Hellblazer #128 © DC

Hellblazer Special: Lady Constantine#4 © DC

Hellboy Premiere Edition © Mike Mignola

GD 2.0 | VG 4.0 | FN 6.0 | VF 8.0 | VF/NM 9.0 | NM- 9.2

Paul Terry's, Terry-Toons Comics)
St. John Publ. Co. No. 1-24/Pines No. 25 on: No. 3, 2/52 - No. 24, 10/55; No. 25, Fall/56 - No. 34, 6/59

3(#1)-Funny animal 26 52 78 150 215 280
4(6/52), 5 12 24 36 71 98 125
6-10(4/53) 9 18 27 51 62 75
11-20 8 16 24 40 50 60
21-34: 25-Begin CBS Television Presents on-c 6 12 18 31 38 45

HECKLE AND JECKLE (TV) (See New Terrytoons)
Gold Key/Dell Publ. Co.: 11/62 - No. 4, 8/63; 5/66; No. 2, 10/66; No. 3, 8/67

1 (11/62; Gold Key) 8 16 24 53 74 95
2-4 4 8 12 27 36 45
1 (5/66; Dell) 5 10 15 33 44 55
2,3 4 8 12 22 30 38
(See March of Comics No. 379, 472, 484)

HECKLE AND JECKLE 3-D
Spotlight Comics: 1987 - No. 2?, 1987 ($2.50)

1,2 5.00

HECKLER, THE
DC Comics: Sept, 1992 - No. 6, Feb, 1993 ($1.25)

1-6-T&M Bierbaum-s/Keith Giffen-c/a 2.25

HECTIC PLANET
Slave Labor Graphics 1998 ($12.95/$14.95)

Book 1,2-r-Dorkin-s/a from Pirate Corp$ Vol. 1 & 2 15.00

HECTOR COMICS (The Keenest Teen in Town)
Key Publications: Nov, 1953 - No. 3, 1954

1-Teen humor 6 12 18 29 36 42
2,3 4 8 12 18 22 25

HECTOR HEATHCOTE (TV)
Gold Key: Mar, 1964

1 (10111-403) 8 16 24 58 82 105

HECTOR THE INSPECTOR (See Top Flight Comics)

HEDGE KNIGHT, THE
Image Comics: Aug, 2003 - No. 6, Apr, 2004 ($2.95, limited series)

1-6-George R.R. Martin-s/Mark Miller-a. 1-Two covers by Kaluta and Miller 3.00
TPB (2004, $14.95) r/series plus new short story 15.00

HEDY DEVINE COMICS (Formerly All Winners #21? or Teen #22?(6/47); Hedy of Hollywood #36 on; also see Annie Oakley, Comedy & Venus)
Marvel Comics (RCM)/Atlas #50: No. 22, Aug, 1947 - No. 50, Sept, 1952

22-1st app. Hedy Devine (also see Joker #32) 26 52 78 150 215 280
23,24,27-30: 23-Wolverton-a, 1 pg; Kurtzman's "Hey Look", 2 pgs. 24,27-30- "Hey Look" by Kurtzman, 1-3 pgs. 18 36 54 102 146 190
25-Classic "Hey Look" by Kurtzman, "Optical Illusion" 20 40 60 112 161 210
26- "Giggles 'n' Grins" by Kurtzman 15 30 45 85 120 155
31-34,36-50: 32-Anti-Wertham editorial 10 20 30 60 80 100
35-Four pgs. "Rusty" by Kurtzman 15 30 45 86 123 160

HEDY-MILLIE-TESSIE COMEDY (See Comedy Comics)

HEDY WOLFE (Also see Patsy & Hedy & Miss America Magazine V1#2)
Atlas Publishing Co. (Emgee): Aug, 1957

1-Patsy Walker's rival; Al Hartley-c 11 22 33 64 87 110

HEE HAW (TV)
Charlton Press: July, 1970 - No. 7, Aug, 1971

1 5 10 15 33 44 55
2-7 3 7 10 21 28 35

HEIDI (See Dell Jr. Treasury No. 6)

HEIRS OF ETERNITY
Image Comics: Apr, 2003 - Present ($2.95)

1-5-Jae Tsai-a/José Torres-s. 4,5-B&W 3.00

HELEN OF TROY (Movie)
Dell Publishing Co.: No. 684, Mar, 1956 (one-shot)

Four Color 684-Buscema-a, photo-c 11 22 33 80 120 160

HELL
Dark Horse Comics: July, 2003 - No. 4, Mar, 2004 ($2.99, limited series)

GD 2.0 | VG 4.0 | FN 6.0 | VF 8.0 | VF/NM 9.0 | NM- 9.2

1-4-Augustyn-s/Demong-a/Meglia-c 3.00

HELLBLAZER (John Constantine) (See Saga of Swamp Thing #37)
(Also see Books of Magic limited series)
DC Comics (Vertigo #63 on): Jan, 1988 - Present ($1.25/$1.50/$1.95/$2.25/$2.50/$2.75)

1-(44 pgs.)-John Constantine; McKean-c thru #21 2 4 6 8 10 12
2-5 1 2 3 4 5 7
6-8,10: 10-Swamp Thing cameo 5.00
9,19: 9-X-over w/Swamp Thing #76. 19-Sandman app. 6.00
11-18,20 5.00
21-26,28-30: 22-Williams-c. 24-Contains bound-in Shocker movie poster. 25,26-Grant Morrison scripts. 5.00
27-Gaiman scripts; Dave McKean-a; low print run 2 4 6 10 12 15
31-39: 36-Preview of World Without End. 4.00
40-($2.25, 52 pgs.)-Dave McKean-a & colors; preview of Kid Eternity 4.00
41-Ennis scripts begin; ends #83 5.00
42-120: 44,45-Sutton-a(i). 50-($3.00, 52 pgs.). 52-Glenn Fabry painted-c begin. 62-Special Death insert by McKean. 63-Silver metallic ink on-c. 77-Totleben-c. 84-Sean Phillips-c/a begins; Delano story. 85-88-Eddie Campbell story. 75-($2.95, 52 pgs.). 89-Paul Jenkins scripts begin; 108-Adlard-a. 100,120($3.50,48 pgs.) 3.50
121-199, 201,202: 129-Ennis-s. 141-Bradstreet-a. 146-150-Corben-a 151-Azzarello-s begin. 175-Carey-s begin; Dillon-a. 176-Begin $2.75-c. 182,183-Bermejo-a 2.75
200-($4.50) Carey-s/Dillon, Frusin, Manco-a 4.50
Annual 1 (1989, $2.95, 68 pgs.)-Bryan Talbot's 1st work in American comics 5.00
Special 1 (1993, $3.95, 68 pgs.)-Ennis story; w/pin-ups. 4.00
...Damnation's Flame (1999, $16.95, TPB) r/#72-77 17.00
...Dangerous Habits (1997, $14.95, TPB) r/#41-46 15.00
...Fear and Loathing (1997, $14.95, TPB) r/#62-67 18.00
...Fear and Loathing (2nd printing, $17.95) 18.00
...: Freezes Over (2003, $14.95, TPB) r/#157-163 15.00
...Good Intentions (2002, $12.95, TPB) r/#151-156 13.00
...Hard Time (2001, $9.95, TPB) r/#146-150 10.00
...Haunting (2003, $12.95, TPB) r/#134-139 13.00
...Highwater (2004, $19.95, TPB) r/#164-174 20.00
...Original Sins (1993, $19.95, TPB) r/#1-9 20.00
...Rake at the Gates of Hell (2003, $19.95, TPB) r/#78-83; Heartland #1 20.00
...: Setting Sun (2004, $12.95, TPB) r/#140-143 13.00
...: Son of Man (2004, $12.95, TPB) r/#129-133 13.00
...Tainted Love (1998, $16.95, TPB) r/#68-71, Vertigo Jam #1 and Hellblazer Special #1 17.00
NOTE: ***Alcala** a-8i, 9i, 18-22i. **Gaiman** scripts-27. **McKean** a-27,40; c-1-21. **Sutton** a-44i, 45i. **Talbot** a-Annual 1.*

HELLBLAZER SPECIAL: BAD BLOOD
DC Comics (Vertigo): Sept, 2000 - No. 4, Dec, 2000 ($2.95, mini-series)

1-4-Delano-s/Bond-a; Constantine in 2025 London 3.00

HELLBLAZER SPECIAL: LADY CONSTANTINE
DC Comics (Vertigo): Feb, 2003 - No. 4, May, 2003 ($2.95, mini-series)

1-4-Story of Johanna Constantine in 1785; Diggle-s/Sudzuka-a/Noto-c 3.00

HELLBLAZER/THE BOOKS OF MAGIC
DC Comics (Vertigo): Dec, 1997 - No. 2, Jan, 1998 ($2.50, mini-series)

1,2-John Constantine and Tim Hunter 2.50

HELLBOY (Also see Danger Unlimited #4, Dark Horse Presents, Gen13 #13B, Ghost/Hellboy, John Byrne's Next Men, San Diego Comic Con #2, & Savage Dragon)

HELLBOY: ALMOST COLOSSUS
Dark Horse Comics (Legend): Jun, 1997 - No. 2, Jul, 1997 ($2.95, lim. series)

1,2-Mignola-s/a 3.00

HELLBOY: BOX FULL OF EVIL
Dark Horse Comics: Aug, 1999 - No. 2, Sept, 1999 ($2.95, lim. series)

1,2-Mignola-s/a; back-up story w/ Matt Smith-a 3.00

HELLBOY CHRISTMAS SPECIAL
Dark Horse Comics: Dec, 1997 ($3.95, one-shot)

nn-Christmas stories by Mignola, Gianni, Darrow, Purcell 4.00

HELLBOY: CONQUEROR WORM
Dark Horse Comics: May, 2001 - No. 4, Aug, 2001 ($2.99, lim. series)

1-4-Mignola-s/a/c 3.00

HELLBOY, JR.
Dark Horse Comics: Oct, 1999 - No. 2, Nov, 1999 ($2.95, limited series)

1,2-Stories and art by various 3.00
TPB (1/04, $14.95) r/#1&2, Halloween; sketch pages; intro. by Steve Niles; Bill Wray-c 15.00

HELLBOY, JR., HALLOWEEN SPECIAL
Dark Horse Comics: Oct, 1997 ($3.95, one-shot)

Hellboy: Weird Tales #6 © Mike Mignola

Hello Pal Comics #1 © HARV

Hellshock #4 © Jae Lee

	GD 2.0	VG 4.0	FN 6.0	VF 8.0	VF/NM 9.0	NM- 9.2

nn-"Harvey" style renditions of Hellboy characters; Bill Wray, Mike Mignola & various-s/a; wraparound-c by Wray 4.00

HELLBOY PREMIERE EDITION
Dark Horse Comics (Wizard): 2004 (no price, one-shot)

nn-2 covers by Mignola & Davis; Mignola-s/a; BPRD story w/Arcudi-s/Davis-a 5.00
Wzard World Los Angeles-Movie photo-c; Mignola-s/a; BPRD story w/Arcudi-s/Davis-a 10.00

HELLBOY: SEED OF DESTRUCTION
Dark Horse Comics (Legend): Mar, 1994 - No. 4, Jun, 1994 ($2.50, lim. series)

1-4-Mignola-c/a w/Byrne scripts; Monkeyman & O'Brien back-up story (origin) by Art Adams. 4.00
Trade paperback (1994, $17.95)-collects all four issues plus r/Hellboy's 1st app. in San Diego Comic Con #2 & pin-ups 18.00
Limited edition hardcover (1995, $99.95)-includes everything in trade paperback plus additional material. 100.00

HELLBOY: THE CHAINED COFFIN AND OTHERS
Dark Horse Comics (Legend): Aug, 1998 ($17.95, TPB)

nn-Mignola-c/a/s; reprints out-of-print one shots; pin-up gallery 18.00

HELLBOY: THE CORPSE
Dark Horse Comics: Mar, 2004 (25¢, one-shot)

nn-Mignola-c/a/scripts; reprints "The Corpse" serial from Capitol City's Advance Comics catalog; development sketches and photos of the Corpse from the Hellboy movie 2.25

HELLBOY: THE CORPSE AND THE IRON SHOES
Dark Horse Comics (Legend): Jan, 1996 ($2.95, one-shot)

nn-Mignola-c/a/scripts; reprints "The Corpse" serial w/new story 3.00

HELLBOY: THE RIGHT HAND OF DOOM
Dark Horse Comics (Legend): Apr, 2000 ($17.95, TPB)

nn-Mignola-c/a/s; reprints 18.00

HELLBOY: THE THIRD WISH
Dark Horse Comics (Maverick): July, 2002 - No. 2, Aug, 2002 ($2.99, limited series)

1,2-Mignola-c/a/s 3.00

HELLBOY: THE WOLVES OF ST. AUGUST
Dark Horse Comics (Legend): 1995 ($4.95, squarebound, one-shot)

nn-Mignola--c/a/scripts; r/Dark Horse Presents #88-91 with additional story 5.00

HELLBOY: WAKE THE DEVIL (Sequel to Seed of Destruction)
Dark Horse Comics (Legend): Jun, 1996 - No. 5, Oct, 1996 ($2.95, lim. series)

1-5: Mignola-c/a & scripts; The Monstermen back-up story by Gary Gianni 3.00
TPB (1997, $17.95) r/#1-5 18.00

HELLBOY: WEIRD TALES
Dark Horse Comics: Feb, 2003 - No. 8, Apr, 2004 ($2.99, limited series, anthology)

1-8-Hellboy stories from other creators. 1-Cassaday-c/s/a; Watson-s/a. 6-Cho-c 3.00
... Vol. 1 (2004, 17.95) r/#1-4 18.00
... Vol. 2 (2004, 17.95) r/#5-8 and Lobster Johnson serial from #1-8 18.00

HELLCAT
Marvel Comics: Sept, 2000 - No. 3, Nov, 2000 ($2.99)

1-3-Englehart-s/Breyfogle-a; Hedy Wolfe app. 3.00

HELLCOP
Image Comics (Avalon Studios): Aug, 1998 - No. 4, Mar, 1999 ($2.50)

1-4: 1-(Oct. on-c) Casey-s 2.50

HELL ETERNAL
DC Comics (Vertigo Verité): 1998 ($6.95, squarebound, one-shot)

1-Delano-s/Phillips-a 7.00

HELLHOLE
Image Comics: July, 1999 - No. 3, Oct, 1999 ($2.50)

1-3-Lobdell-s/Polina-a 2.50

HELLHOUNDS (...: Panzer Cops #3-6)
Dark Horse Comics: 1994 - No. 6, July, 1994 ($2.50, B&W, limited series)

1-6: 1-Hamner-c. 3-(4/94). 2-Joe Phillips-c 3.00

HELLHOUNDS
Image Comics: Aug, 2003 - No. 4 ($2.95)

1-4: 1-Five covers; Singley-s/Abraham-a 3.00

HELLHOUND, THE REDEMPTION QUEST
Marvel Comics (Epic Comics): Dec, 1993 - No. 4, Mar, 1994 ($2.25, lim. series, coated stock)

1-4 2.25

HELLO, I'M JOHNNY CASH
Spire Christian Comics (Fleming H. Revell Co.): 1976 (39¢/49¢)

	GD 2.0	VG 4.0	FN 6.0	VF 8.0	VF/NM 9.0	NM- 9.2
nn-(39¢-c)	2	4	6	10	13	16
nn-(49¢-c)	1	3	4	6	8	11

HELL ON EARTH (See DC Science Fiction Graphic Novel)

HELLO PAL COMICS (Short Story Comics)
Harvey Publications: Jan, 1943 - No. 3, May, 1943 (Photo-c)

	GD 2.0	VG 4.0	FN 6.0	VF 8.0	VF/NM 9.0	NM- 9.2
1-Rocketman & Rocketgirl begin; Yankee Doodle Jones app.; Mickey Rooney photo-c	69	138	207	431	666	900
2-Charlie McCarthy photo-c (scarce)	56	112	168	350	538	725
3-Bob Hope photo-c (scarce)	62	124	186	388	594	800

HELLRAISER/NIGHTBREED – JIHAD (Also see Clive Barker's...)
Epic Comics (Marvel Comics): 1991 - Book 2, 1991 ($4.50, 52 pgs.)

Book 1,2 4.50

HELL-RIDER (Motorcycle themed magazine)
Skywald Publications: Aug, 1971 - No. 2, Oct, 1971 (B&W, 68 pgs.)

	GD 2.0	VG 4.0	FN 6.0	VF 8.0	VF/NM 9.0	NM- 9.2
1-Origin & 1st app.; Butterfly & the Wild Bunch begin; 1st Hell-Rider by Andru, Esposito and Friedrich	6	12	18	38	52	65
2-Andru, Ayers, Buckler, Shores-a	4	8	12	25	33	42

NOTE: *#3 advertised in Psycho #5 but did not come out.* ***Buckler*** *a-1, 2.* ***Rosenbaum*** *c-1,2.*

HELL'S ANGEL (Becomes Dark Angel #6 on)
Marvel Comics UK: July, 1992 - No. 5, Nov, 1993 ($1.75)

1-5: X-Men (Wolverine, Cyclops)-c/stories. 1-Origin. 3-Jim Lee cover swipe 2.25

HELLSHOCK
Image Comics: July, 1994 - No. 4, Nov, 1994 ($1.95, limited series)

1-4-Jae Lee-c/a & scripts. 4-Variant-c. 2.50

HELLSHOCK
Image Comics: Jan, 1997 - No. 3, Jan, 1998 ($2.95/$2.50, limited series)

1-($2.95)-Jae Lee-c/s/a, Villarrubia-painted-a 4.00
2-($2.50) 2.50
Book 3: The Science of Faith (1/98, $2.50) Jae Lee-c/s/a, Villarrubia-painted-a 2.50

HELLSPAWN
Image Comics: Aug, 2000 - Present ($2.50)

1-Bendis-s/Ashley Wood-c/a; Spawn and Clown app. 2.50
2-9: 6-Last Bendis-s; Mike Moran (Miracleman app.). 7-Niles-s 2.50
10-16-Templesmith-a 2.50

HELLSTORM: PRINCE OF LIES (See Ghost Rider #1 & Marvel Spotlight #12)
Marvel Comics: Apr, 1993 - No. 21, Dec, 1994 ($2.00)

1-($2.95)-Parchment-c w/red thermographic ink 3.00
2-21: 14-Bound-in trading card sheet. 18-P. Craig Russell-c 2.50

HE-MAN (See Masters Of The Universe)

HE-MAN (Also see Tops In Adventure)
Ziff-Davis Publ. Co. (Approved Comics): Fall, 1952

	GD 2.0	VG 4.0	FN 6.0	VF 8.0	VF/NM 9.0	NM- 9.2
1-Kinstler painted-c; Powell-a	17	34	51	95	135	175

HE-MAN
Toby Press: May, 1954 - No. 2, July, 1954 (Painted-c by B. Safran)

	GD 2.0	VG 4.0	FN 6.0	VF 8.0	VF/NM 9.0	NM- 9.2
1	16	32	48	92	131	170
2-Shark-c	15	30	45	86	123	160

HENNESSEY (TV)
Dell Publishing Co.: No. 1200, Aug-Oct, 1961 - No. 1280, Mar-May, 1962

	GD 2.0	VG 4.0	FN 6.0	VF 8.0	VF/NM 9.0	NM- 9.2
Four Color 1200-Gil Kane-a, photo-c	8	16	24	58	82	105
Four Color 1280-Photo-c	8	16	24	53	74	95

HENRY (Also see Little Annie Rooney)
David McKay Publications: 1935 (52 pgs.) (Daily B&W strip reprints)(10"x10" cardboard-c)

	GD 2.0	VG 4.0	FN 6.0	VF 8.0	VF/NM 9.0	NM- 9.2
1-By Carl Anderson	40	80	120	236	351	465

HENRY (See King Comics & Magic Comics)
Dell Publishing Co.: No. 122, Oct, 1946 - No. 65, Apr-June, 1961

	GD 2.0	VG 4.0	FN 6.0	VF 8.0	VF/NM 9.0	NM- 9.2
Four Color 122-All new stories begin	15	30	45	105	160	215
Four Color 155 (7/47), 1 (1-3/48)-All new stories	10	20	30	73	107	140
2	6	12	18	40	55	70
3-10	5	10	15	33	44	55
11-20: 20-Infinity-c	4	8	12	24	32	40
21-30	3	6	9	19	25	32
31-40	3	6	9	16	20	25
41-65	2	4	6	12	16	20

Henry Aldrich Comics #3 © DELL

Herbie #21 © ACG

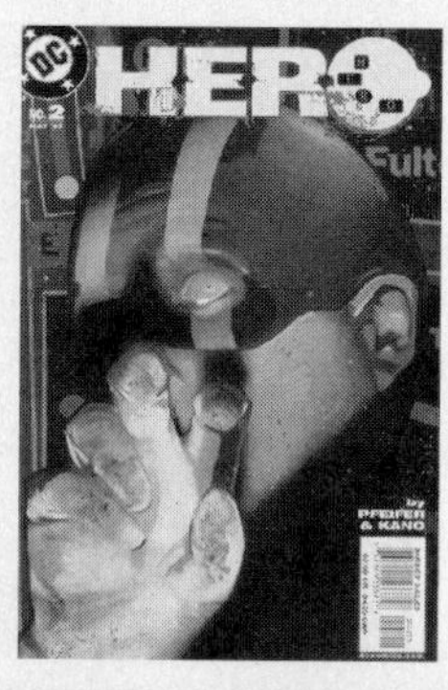

H-E-R-O #2 © DC

	GD 2.0	VG 4.0	FN 6.0	VF 8.0	VF/NM 9.0	NM- 9.2

HENRY (See Giant Comic Album and March of Comics No. 43, 58, 84, 101, 112, 129, 147, 162, 178, 189)

HENRY ALDRICH COMICS (TV)
Dell Publishing Co.: Aug-Sept, 1950 - No. 22, Sept-Nov, 1954

Issue	GD	VG	FN	VF	VF/NM	NM-
1-Part series written by John Stanley; Bill Williams-a	10	20	30	73	107	140
2	6	12	18	40	55	70
3-5	5	10	15	36	48	60
6-10	4	8	12	28	38	48
11-22	4	8	12	22	30	38

HENRY BREWSTER
Country Wide (M.F. Ent.): Feb, 1966 - V2#7, Sept, 1967 (All 25¢ Giants)

Issue	GD	VG	FN	VF	VF/NM	NM-
1	3	6	9	19	25	32
2-6(12/66), V2#7-Powell-a in most	2	4	6	11	14	18

HEPCATS
Antarctic Press: Nov, 1996 - No. 12 ($2.95, B&W)

Issue	GD	VG	FN	VF	VF/NM	NM-
0-12-Martin Wagner-c/s/a: 0-color						3.00
0-($9.95) CD Edition						10.00

HERBIE (See Forbidden Worlds & Unknown Worlds)
American Comics Group: April-May, 1964 - No. 23, Feb, 1967 (All 12¢)

Issue	GD	VG	FN	VF	VF/NM	NM-
1-Whitney-c/a in most issues	17	34	51	121	186	250
2-4	10	20	30	67	96	125
5-Beatles parody (10 pgs.), Dean Martin, Frank Sinatra app.	11	22	33	77	114	150
6,7,9,10	8	16	24	55	78	100
8-Origin & 1st app. The Fat Fury	10	20	30	67	96	125
11-23: 14-Nemesis & Magicman app. 17-r/2nd Herbie from Forbidden Worlds #94. 23-r/1st Herbie from F.W. #73	6	12	18	43	59	75

HERBIE
Dark Horse Comics: Oct, 1992 - No. 12, 1993 ($2.50, limited series)

Issue	GD	VG	FN	VF	VF/NM	NM-
1-Whitney-r plus new-c/a in all; Byrne-c/a & scripts						3.00
2-6: 3-Bob Burden-c/a. 4-Art Adams-c						2.50

HERBIE GOES TO MONTE CARLO, HERBIE RIDES AGAIN (See Walt Disney Showcase No. 24, 41)

HERCULES (See Hit Comics #1-21, Journey Into Mystery Annual, Marvel Graphic Novel #37, Marvel Premiere #26 & The Mighty...)

HERCULES (See Charlton Classics)
Charlton Comics: Oct, 1967 - No. 13, Sept, 1969; Dec, 1968

Issue	GD	VG	FN	VF	VF/NM	NM-
1-Thane of Bagarth begins; Glanzman-a in all	4	8	12	27	36	45
2-13: 1-5,7-10-Aparo-a. 8-(12¢-c)	3	6	9	16	20	25
8-(Low distribution)(12/68, 35¢, B&W); magazine format; new Hercules story plus-r story/#1; Thane-r/#1-3	6	12	18	40	55	70
Modern Comics reprint 10('77), 11('78)						6.00

HERCULES (Prince of Power) (Also see The Champions)
Marvel Comics Group: V1#1, Sept, 1982 - V1#4, Dec, 1982; V2#1, Mar, 1984 - V2#4, Jun, 1984 (color, both limited series)

Issue	GD	VG	FN	VF	VF/NM	NM-
1-4, V2#1-4: Layton-c/a. 4-Death of Zeus.						3.00

NOTE: *Layton a-1, 2, 3p, 4p, V2#1-4; c-1-4, V2#1-4.*

HERCULES: HEART OF CHAOS
Marvel Comics: Aug, 1997 - No. 3, Oct, 1997 ($2.50, limited series)

Issue	GD	VG	FN	VF	VF/NM	NM-
1-3-DeFalco-s, Frenz-a						2.50

HERCULES: OFFICIAL COMICS MOVIE ADAPTION
Acclaim Books: 1997 ($4.50, digest size)

Issue	GD	VG	FN	VF	VF/NM	NM-
nn-Adaption of the Disney animated movie						4.50

HERCULES: THE LEGENDARY JOURNEYS (TV)
Topps Comics: June, 1996 - No. 5, Oct, 1996 ($2.95)

Issue	GD	VG	FN	VF	VF/NM	NM-
1-2: 1-Golden-c.						3.00
3-Xena-c/app.	1	2	3	4	5	7
3-Variant-c	2	4	6	10	12	15
4,5: Xena-c/app.						5.00

HERCULES UNBOUND
National Periodical Publications: Oct-Nov, 1975 - No. 12, Aug-Sept, 1977

Issue	GD	VG	FN	VF	VF/NM	NM-
1-Wood-i begins	2	4	6	9	11	14
2-12: 7-Adams ad. 10-Atomic Knights x-over	1	2	3	5	6	8

NOTE: ***Buckler** c-7p. **Layton** inks-No. 9, 10. **Simonson** a-7-10p, 11, 12; c- 8p, 9-12. **Wood** a-1-8i; c-7i, 8i.*

HERCULES (...Unchained #1121) (Movie)
Dell Publishing Co.: No. 1006, June-Aug, 1959 - No.1121, Aug, 1960

Issue	GD	VG	FN	VF	VF/NM	NM-
Four Color 1006-Buscema-a, photo-c	10	20	30	73	107	140
Four Color 1121-Crandall/Evans-a	10	20	30	73	107	140

HERE COMES SANTA (See March of Comics No. 30, 213, 340)

HERE'S HOWIE COMICS
National Periodical Publications: Jan-Feb, 1952 - No. 18, Nov-Dec, 1954

Issue	GD	VG	FN	VF	VF/NM	NM-
1	26	52	78	150	215	280
2	14	28	42	79	110	140
3-5: 5-Howie in the Army issues begin (9-10/52)	11	22	33	62	84	105
6-10	9	18	27	54	70	85
11-18	9	18	27	51	62	75

HERETIC, THE
Dark Horse (Blanc Noir): Nov, 1996 - No. 4, Mar, 1997 ($2.95, lim. series)

Issue	GD	VG	FN	VF	VF/NM	NM-
1-4:-w/back-up story						3.00

HERITAGE OF THE DESERT (See Zane Grey, 4-Color 236)

HERMAN & KATNIP (See Harvey Comics Hits #60 & 62, Harvey Hits #14,25,31,41 & Paramount Animated Comics #1)

HERMES VS. THE EYEBALL KID
Dark Horse Comics: Dec, 1994 - No. 3,Feb, 1995 ($2.95, B&W, limited series)

Issue	GD	VG	FN	VF	VF/NM	NM-
1-3: Eddie Campbell-c/a/scripts						3.00

H-E-R-O (Dial H For HERO)
DC Comics: Apr, 2003 - No. 22, Jan, 2005 ($2.50)

Issue	GD	VG	FN	VF	VF/NM	NM-
1-Will Pfeiffer-s/Kano-a/Van Fleet-c						3.00
2-22: 2-6-Kano-a. 7,8-Gleason-a. 12-14-Kirk-a. 15-22-Robby Reed app.						2.50
...: Double Feature (6/03, $4.95) r/#1&2						5.00
...: Powers and Abilities (2003, $9.95) r/#1-6; intro. by Geoff Johns						10.00

HERO (Warrior of the Mystic Realms)
Marvel Comics: May, 1990 - No. 6, Oct, 1990 ($1.50, limited series)

Issue	GD	VG	FN	VF	VF/NM	NM-
1-6: 1-Portacio-i						2.25

HERO ALLIANCE, THE
Sirius Comics: Dec, 1985 - No. 2, Sept, 1986 (B&W)

Issue	GD	VG	FN	VF	VF/NM	NM-
1,2: 2-($1.50), Special Edition 1 (7/86, color)						2.25

HERO ALLIANCE
Wonder Color Comics: May, 1987 ($1.95)

Issue	GD	VG	FN	VF	VF/NM	NM-
1-Ron Lim-a						2.25

HERO ALLIANCE
Innovation Publishing: V2#1, Sept, 1989 - V2#17, Nov, 1991 ($1.95, 28 pgs.)

Issue	GD	VG	FN	VF	VF/NM	NM-
V2#1-17: 1,2-Ron Lim-a						2.25
Annual 1 (1990, $2.75, 36 pgs.)-Paul Smith-c/a						2.75
Special 1 (1992, $2.50, 32 pgs.)-Stuart Immonen-a (10 pgs.)						2.50

HERO ALLIANCE: END OF THE GOLDEN AGE
Innovation Publ.: July, 1989 - No. 3, Aug, 1989 ($1.75, bi-weekly lim. series)

Issue	GD	VG	FN	VF	VF/NM	NM-
1-3: Bart Sears & Ron Lim-c/a; reprints & new-a						2.25

HEROES
Marvel Comics: Dec, 2001 ($3.50, magazine-size, one-shot)

Issue	GD	VG	FN	VF	VF/NM	NM-
1-Pin-up tributes to the rescue workers of the Sept. 11 tragedy; art and text by various; cover by Alex Ross						3.50
1-2nd and 3rd printings						3.50

HEROES (Also see Shadow Cabinet & Static)
DC Comics (Milestone): May, 1996 - No. 6, Nov, 1996 ($2.50, limited series)

Issue	GD	VG	FN	VF	VF/NM	NM-
1-6: 1-Intro Heroes (Iota, Donner, Blitzen, Starlight, Payback & Static)						2.50

HEROES AGAINST HUNGER
DC Comics: 1986 ($1.50; one-shot for famine relief)

Issue	GD	VG	FN	VF	VF/NM	NM-
1-Superman, Batman app.; Neal Adams-c(p); includes many artists work; Jeff Jones assist (2 pg.) on B. Smith-a; Kirby-a						4.00

HEROES ALL CATHOLIC ACTION ILLUSTRATED
Heroes All Co.: 1943 - V6#5, Mar 10, 1948 (paper covers)

Issue	GD	VG	FN	VF	VF/NM	NM-
V1#1-(16 pgs., 8x11")	24	48	72	138	199	260
V1#2-(16 pgs., 8x11")	20	40	60	112	161	210
V2#1(1/44)-3(3/44)-(16 pgs., 8x11")	17	34	51	98	139	180
V3#1(1/45)-10(12/45)-(16 pgs., 8x11")	15	30	45	86	123	160
V4#1-35 (12/20/46)-(16 pgs.)	14	28	42	79	110	140
V5#1(1/10/47)-8(2/28/47)-(16 pgs.), V5#9(3/7/47)-20(11/25/47)-(32 pgs.), V6#1(1/10/48)-5(3/10/48)-(32 pgs.)	11	22	33	64	87	110

HEROES ANONYMOUS
Bongo Comics: 2003 - No. 6 ($2.99, limited series)

Hero For Hire #1 © MAR

Heroic Comics #16 © EAS

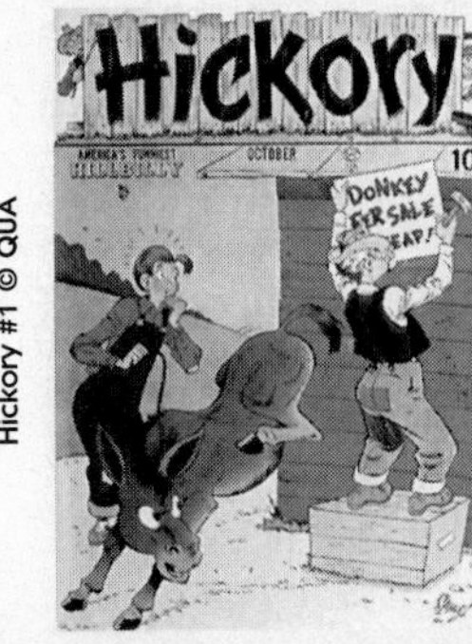

Hickory #1 © QUA

	GD 2.0	VG 4.0	FN 6.0	VF 8.0	VF/NM 9.0	NM- 9.2
1-5-($2.99)-Bill Morrison-c. 2-Guerra-a. 3-Pepoy-a						3.00

HEROES FOR HIRE
Marvel Comics: July, 1997 - No. 19, Jan, 1999 ($2.99/$1.99)

	GD 2.0	VG 4.0	FN 6.0	VF 8.0	VF/NM 9.0	NM- 9.2
1-($2.99)-Wraparound cover						5.00
2-19: 2-Variant cover. 7-Thunderbolts app. 9-Punisher-c/app. 10,11-Deadpool-c/app. 18,19-Wolverine-c/app.						3.00
.../Quicksilver '98 Annual ($2.99) Siege of Wundagore pt.5						3.00

HEROES FOR HOPE STARRING THE X-MEN
Marvel Comics Group: Dec, 1985 ($1.50, one-shot, 52 pgs., proceeds donated to famine relief)

	GD 2.0	VG 4.0	FN 6.0	VF 8.0	VF/NM 9.0	NM- 9.2
1-Stephen King scripts; Byrne, Miller, Corben-a; Wrightson/J. Jones-a (3 pgs.); Art Adams-c; Starlin back-c						5.00

HEROES, INC. PRESENTS CANNON
Wally Wood/CPL/Gang Publ.: 1969 - No. 2, 1976 (Sold at Army PX's)

	GD 2.0	VG 4.0	FN 6.0	VF 8.0	VF/NM 9.0	NM- 9.2
nn-Ditko, Wood-a; Wood-c; Reese-a(p)	2	4	6	10	12	15
2-Wood-c; Ditko, Byrne, Wood-a; 8-1/2x10-1/2"; B&W; $2.00	2	4	6	14	18	22

NOTE: *First issue not distributed by publisher; 1,800 copies were stored and 900 copies were stolen from warehouse. Many copies have surfaced in recent years.*

HEROES OF THE WILD FRONTIER (Formerly Baffling Mysteries)
Ace Periodicals: No. 27, Jan, 1956 - No. 2, Apr, 1956

	GD 2.0	VG 4.0	FN 6.0	VF 8.0	VF/NM 9.0	NM- 9.2
27(#1),2-Davy Crockett, Daniel Boone, Buffalo Bill	6	12	18	29	36	42

HEROES REBORN (one-shots)
Marvel Comics: Jan, 2000 ($1.99)

	GD 2.0	VG 4.0	FN 6.0	VF 8.0	VF/NM 9.0	NM- 9.2
...:Ashema; ...:Doom; ...:Doomsday; ...:Masters of Evil; ...:Rebel; ...:Remnants; ...:Young Allies						2.25

HEROES REBORN: THE RETURN
Marvel Comics: Dec, 1997 - No. 4 ($2.50, weekly mini-series)

	GD 2.0	VG 4.0	FN 6.0	VF 8.0	VF/NM 9.0	NM- 9.2
1-4-Avengers, Fantastic Four, Iron Man & Captain America rejoin regular Marvel Universe; Peter David-s/Larocca-c/a						4.00
1-4-Variant-c for each						6.00
Wizard 1/2	1	2	3	5	7	9
Return of the Heroes TPB ('98, $14.95) r/#1-4						15.00

HERO FOR HIRE (Power Man No. 17 on; also see Cage)
Marvel Comics Group: June, 1972 - No. 16, Dec, 1973

	GD 2.0	VG 4.0	FN 6.0	VF 8.0	VF/NM 9.0	NM- 9.2
1-Origin & 1st app. Luke Cage; Tuska-a(p)	8	16	24	53	75	95
2-Tuska-a(p)	4	8	12	24	32	40
3-5: 3-1st app. Mace. 4-1st app. Phil Fox of the Bugle	3	6	9	18	23	28
6-10: 8,9-Dr. Doom app. 9-F.F. app.	2	4	6	11	14	18
11-16: 14-Origin retold. 15-Everett Sub-Mariner-r('53). 16-Origin Stilletto; death of Rackham	2	4	6	8	10	12

HERO HOTLINE (1st app. in Action Comics Weekly #637)
DC Comics: April, 1989 - No. 6, Sept, 1989 ($1.75, limited series)

	GD 2.0	VG 4.0	FN 6.0	VF 8.0	VF/NM 9.0	NM- 9.2
1-6: Super-hero humor; Schaffenberger-i						2.25

HEROIC ADVENTURES (See Adventures)

HEROIC COMICS (Reg'lar Fellers...#1-15; New Heroic #41 on)
Eastern Color Printing Co./Famous Funnies(Funnies, Inc. No. 1): Aug, 1940 - No. 97, June, 1955

	GD 2.0	VG 4.0	FN 6.0	VF 8.0	VF/NM 9.0	NM- 9.2
1-Hydroman (origin) by Bill Everett, The Purple Zombie (origin) & Mann of India by Tarpe Mills begins (all 1st apps.)	185	370	555	1156	1778	2400
2	77	154	231	481	741	1000
3,4	52	104	156	317	484	650
5,6	42	84	126	256	391	525
7-Origin & 1st app. Man O'Metal (1 pg.)	45	90	135	275	418	560
8-10: 10-Lingerie panels	35	70	105	198	287	375
11,13: 13-Crandall/Fine-a	32	64	96	184	267	350
12-Music Master (origin/1st app.) begins by Everett, ends No. 31; last Purple Zombie & Mann of India	36	72	108	204	297	390
14,15-Hydroman x-over in Rainbow Boy. 14-Origin & 1st app. Rainbow Boy (super hero). 15-1st app. Downbeat	35	70	105	198	287	375
16-20: 16-New logo. 17-Rainbow Boy x-over in Hydroman. 19-Rainbow Boy x-over in Hydroman & vice versa	24	48	72	138	199	260
21-30:25-Rainbow Boy x-over in Hydroman. 28-Last Man O'Metal. 29-Last Hydroman	17	34	51	98	139	180
31,34,38	8	16	24	43	54	65
32,36,37-Toth-a (3-4 pgs. each)	9	18	27	52	66	80
33,35-Toth-a (8 & 9 pgs.)	9	18	27	54	70	85
39-42-Toth, Ingels-a	9	18	27	54	70	85
43,46,47,49-Toth-a (2-4 pgs.). 47-Ingels-a	9	18	27	51	62	75
44,45,50-Toth-a (6-9 pgs.)	9	18	27	52	66	80
48,53,54	8	16	24	40	50	60
51-Williamson-a	9	18	27	52	66	80
52-Williamson-a (3 pg. story)	8	16	24	43	54	65
55-Toth-a	9	18	27	51	62	75
56-60: 60-Everett-a	8	16	24	43	54	65
61-Everett-a	8	16	24	40	50	60
62,64-Everett-c/a	8	16	24	43	54	65
63-Everett-c	8	16	24	40	50	60
65-Williamson/Frazetta-a; Evans-a (2 pgs.)	11	22	33	62	84	105
66,75,94-Frazetta-a (2 pgs. each)	8	16	24	43	54	65
67,73-Frazetta-a (4 pgs. each)	9	18	27	52	66	80
68,74,76-80,84,85,88-93,95-97: 95-Last pre-code	7	14	21	37	46	55
69,72-Frazetta-a (6 & 8 pgs. each); 1st (?) app. Frazetta Red Cross ad	11	22	33	62	84	105
70,71,86,87-Frazetta, 3-4 pgs. each; 1 pg. ad by Frazetta in #70	8	16	24	46	58	70
81,82-Frazetta art (1 pg. each): 81-1st (?) app. Frazetta Boy Scout ad (tied w/ Buster Crabbe #9	8	16	24	40	50	60
83-Frazetta-a (1/2 pg.)	8	16	24	40	50	60

NOTE: ***Evans** a-64, 65. **Everett** a-(Hydroman-c/a-No. 1-9), 44, 60-64; c-1-9, 62-64. **Harvey Fuller** c-28-35. **Sid Greene** a-38-43, 46. **Guardineer** a-42(3), 43, 44, 45(2), 49(3), 50, 60, 61(2), 65, 67(2) 70-72. **Ingels** c-41. **Kiefer** a-46, 48; c-19-22, 24, 44, 46, 48, 51-53, 65, 67-69, 71-74, 76, 77, 79, 80, 82, 85, 86, 88, 89, 94, 95. **Mort Lawrence** a-45. **Tarpe Mills** a-2(2), 3(2), 10. **Ed Moore** a-49, 52-54, 56-63, 65-69, 72-74, 76, 77. **H.G. Peter** a-58-74, 76, 77, 87. **Paul Reinman** a-49. **Rico** a-31. Captain Tootsie by **Beck**-31, 32. Painted-c #16 on. Hydroman c-1-11. Music Master c-12, 13, 15. Rainbow Boy c-14.*

HERO ZERO (Also see Comics' Greatest World & Godzilla Versus Hero Zero)
Dark Horse Comics: Sept, 1994 ($2.50)

	GD 2.0	VG 4.0	FN 6.0	VF 8.0	VF/NM 9.0	NM- 9.2
0						2.50

HEX (Replaces Jonah Hex)
DC Comics: Sept, 1985 - No. 18, Feb, 1987 (Story cont'd from Jonah Hex # 92)

	GD 2.0	VG 4.0	FN 6.0	VF 8.0	VF/NM 9.0	NM- 9.2
1-Hex in post-atomic war world; origin	1	2	3	5	6	8
2-18: 6-Origin Stiletta. 11-13: All contain future Batman storyline. 13-Intro The Dogs of War (origin #15)						5.00

NOTE: ***Giffen** a(p)-15-18; c(p)-15,17,18. **Texeira** a-1, 2p, 3p, 5-7p, 9p, 11-14p; c(p)-1, 2, 4-7, 12.*

HEXBREAKER (See First Comics Graphic Novel #15)

HEY THERE, IT'S YOGI BEAR (See Movie Comics)

HI-ADVENTURE HEROES (TV)
Gold Key: May, 1969 - No. 2, Aug, 1969 (Hanna-Barbera)

	GD 2.0	VG 4.0	FN 6.0	VF 8.0	VF/NM 9.0	NM- 9.2
1-Three Musketeers, Gulliver, Arabian Knights	6	12	18	40	55	70
2-Three Musketeers, Micro-Venture, Arabian Knights	5	10	15	36	48	60

HI AND LOIS
Dell Publishing Co.: No. 683, Mar, 1956 - No. 955, Nov, 1958

	GD 2.0	VG 4.0	FN 6.0	VF 8.0	VF/NM 9.0	NM- 9.2
Four Color 683 (#1)	4	8	12	29	40	50
Four Color 774(3/57),955	3	7	10	21	28	35

HI AND LOIS
Charlton Comics: Nov, 1969 - No. 11, July, 1971

	GD 2.0	VG 4.0	FN 6.0	VF 8.0	VF/NM 9.0	NM- 9.2
1	3	6	9	16	20	25
2-11	2	4	6	10	12	15

HICKORY (See All Humor Comics)
Quality Comics Group: Oct, 1949 - No. 6, Aug, 1950

	GD 2.0	VG 4.0	FN 6.0	VF 8.0	VF/NM 9.0	NM- 9.2
1-Sahl-c/a in all; Feldstein?-a	17	34	51	95	135	175
2	10	20	30	56	73	90
3-6	9	18	27	52	66	80

HIDDEN CREW, THE (See The United States Air Force Presents:...)

HIDE-OUT (See Zane Grey, Four Color No. 346)

HIDING PLACE, THE
Spire Christian Comics (Fleming H. Revell Co.): 1973 (39¢/49¢)

	GD 2.0	VG 4.0	FN 6.0	VF 8.0	VF/NM 9.0	NM- 9.2
nn	1	3	4	6	8	11

HIEROGLYPH
Dark Horse Comics: Nov, 1999 - No. 4, Feb, 2000 ($2.95, limited series)

	GD 2.0	VG 4.0	FN 6.0	VF 8.0	VF/NM 9.0	NM- 9.2
1-4-Ricardo Delgado-s/a						3.00

HIGH ADVENTURE
Red Top(Decker) Comics (Farrell): Oct, 1957

	GD 2.0	VG 4.0	FN 6.0	VF 8.0	VF/NM 9.0	NM- 9.2
1-Krigstein-r from Explorer Joe (re-issue on-c)	5	10	15	23	28	32

HIGH ADVENTURE (TV)

High Roads #2 © Leinil Yu

Hi-School Romance #3 © HARV

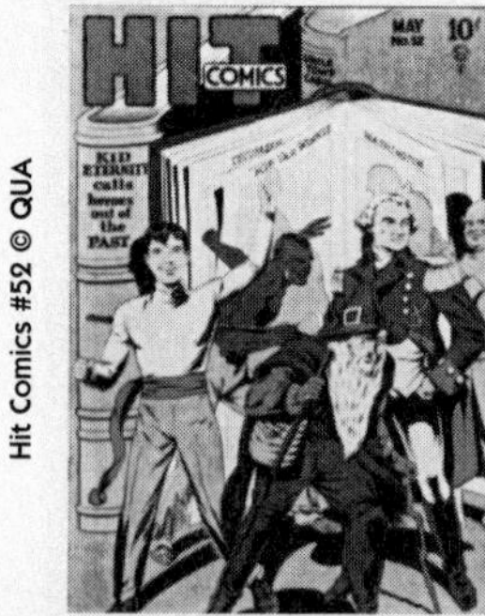

Hit Comics #52 © QUA

GD 2.0 | VG 4.0 | FN 6.0 | VF 8.0 | VF/NM 9.0 | NM- 9.2

Dell Publishing Co.: No. 949, Nov, 1958 - No. 1001, Aug-Oct, 1959 (Lowell Thomas)
Four Color 949 (#1)-Photo-c 7 14 21 46 63 80
Four Color 1001-Lowell Thomas'...(#2) 6 12 18 43 59 75

HIGH CHAPPARAL (TV)
Gold Key: Aug, 1968 (Photo-c)
1 (10226-808)-Tufts-a 6 12 18 40 55 70

HIGH ROADS
DC Comics (Cliffhanger): June, 2002 - No. 6, Nov, 2002 ($2.95, limited series)
1-6-Leinil Yu-c/a; Lobdell-s 3.00
TPB (2003, $14.95) r/#1-6; sketch pages 15.00

HIGH SCHOOL CONFIDENTIAL DIARY (Confidential Diary #12 on)
Charlton Comics: June, 1960 - No. 11, Mar, 1962
1 5 10 15 33 44 55
2-11 3 6 9 19 25 32

HI-HO COMICS
Four Star Publications: nd (2/46?) - No. 3, 1946
1-Funny Animal; L. B. Cole-c 39 78 117 222 324 425
2,3: 2-L. B. Cole-c 22 44 66 123 177 230

HI-JINX (Teen-age Animal Funnies)
La Salle Publ. Co./B&I Publ. Co. (American Comics Group)/Creston: 1945; July-Aug, 1947 - No. 7, July-Aug, 1948
nn-(© 1945, 25 cents, 132 Pgs.)(La Salle) 25 50 75 144 207 270
1-Teen-age, funny animal 17 34 51 98 139 180
2,3 10 20 30 60 80 100
4-7-Milt Gross. 4-X-Mas-c 15 30 45 86 123 160

HI-LITE COMICS
E. R. Ross Publishing Co.: Fall, 1945
1-Miss Shady 20 40 60 112 161 210

HILLBILLY COMICS
Charlton Comics: Aug, 1955 - No. 4, July, 1956 (Satire)
1-By Art Gates 9 18 27 52 66 80
2-4 6 12 18 31 38 45

HILLY ROSE'S SPACE ADVENTURES
Astro Comics: May, 1995 - No. 9 ($2.95, B&W)
1 1 2 3 5 7 9
2-5 5.00
6-9 3.00
Trade Paperback (1996, $12.95)-r/#1-5 13.00

HIP FLASK UNNATURAL SELECTION
Active Images: Sept, 2002 ($2.99)
1-Casey & Starkings-s/Ladronn-a; var.-c by Madureira, Campbell, Churchill 3.00

HIP-IT-TY HOP (See March of Comics No. 15)

HIRE, THE (BMWfilms.com's...)
Dark Horse Comics: July, 2004 - No. 6 ($2.99)
1-Matt Wagner-s/Wagner & Velasco-a 3.00

HI-SCHOOL ROMANCE (...Romances No. 41 on)
Harvey Publ./True Love(Home Comics): Oct, 1949 - No. 5, June, 1950; No. 6, Dec, 1950 - No. 73, Mar, 1958; No. 74, Sept, 1958 - No. 75, Nov, 1958
1-Photo-c 16 32 48 92 131 170
2-Photo-c 9 18 27 54 70 85
3-9: 3,5-Photo-c 8 16 24 43 54 65
10-Rape story 9 18 27 54 70 85
11-20 7 14 21 35 43 50
21-31 6 12 18 27 33 38
32- "Unholy passion" story 8 16 24 43 54 65
33-36: 36-Last pre-code (2/55) 5 10 15 24 30 35
37-53,59-72,74,75 5 10 14 20 24 28
54-58,73-Kirby-c 5 10 15 23 28 32
NOTE: ***Powell** a-1-3, 5, 8, 12-16, 18, 21-23, 25-27, 30-34, 36, 37, 39, 45-48, 50-52, 57, 58, 60, 64, 65, 67, 69.*

HI-SCHOOL ROMANCE DATE BOOK
Harvey Publications: Nov, 1962 - No. 3, Mar, 1963 (25¢ Giants)
1-Powell, Baker-a 6 12 18 38 52 65
2,3 3 7 10 21 28 35

HIS NAME IS SAVAGE (Magazine format)
Adventure House Press: June, 1968 (35¢, 52 pgs.)
1-Gil Kane-a 5 10 15 33 44 55

HI-SPOT COMICS (Red Ryder No. 1 & No. 3 on)
Hawley Publications: No. 2, Nov, 1940
2-David Innes of Pellucidar; art by J. C. Burroughs; written by Edgar Rice Burroughs
123 246 369 769 1185 1600

HISTORY OF THE DC UNIVERSE (Also see Crisis on Infinite Earths)
DC Comics: Sept, 1986 - No. 2, Nov, 1986 ($2.95, limited series)
1,2: 1-Perez-c/a 3.00
Limited Edition hardcover 5 10 15 33 44 55
Softcover (2002, $9.95) new Alex Ross wraparound-c 10.00

HISTORY OF VIOLENCE, A
DC Comics (Paradox Press) 1998?
nn-Paperback ($9.95) 10.00

HITCHHIKERS GUIDE TO THE GALAXY (See Life, the Universe and Everything & Restaraunt at the End of the Universe)
DC Comics: 1993 - No. 3, 1993 ($4.95, limited series)
1-3: Adaptation of Douglas Adams book 5.00
TPB (1997, $14.95) r/#1-3 15.00

HIT COMICS
Quality Comics Group: July, 1940 - No. 65, July, 1950
1-Origin/1st app. Neon, the Unknown & Hercules; intro. The Red Bee; Bob & Swab, Blaze Barton, the Strange Twins, X-5 Super Agent, Casey Jones & Jack & Jill (ends #7) begin
635 1290 1935 4515 7258 10,000
2-The Old Witch begins, ends #14 269 538 807 1681 2591 3500
3-Casey Jones ends; transvestism story "Jack & Jill"
250 500 750 1563 2407 3250
4-Super Agent (ends #17), & Betty Bates (ends #65) begin; X-5 ends
223 446 669 1394 2147 2900
5-Classic Lou Fine cover 542 1084 1626 3794 6097 8400
6-10: 10-Old Witch by Crandall (4 pgs.); 1st work in comics (4/41)
192 384 576 1200 1850 2500
11-Classic cover 173 346 519 1081 1666 2250
12-17: 13-Blaze Barton ends. 17-Last Neon; Crandall Hercules in all; Last Lou Fine-c
119 238 357 744 1147 1550
18-Origin & 1st app. Stormy Foster, the Great Defender (12/41); The Ghost of Flanders begins; Crandall-c 127 254 381 794 1222 1650
19,20 100 200 300 625 963 1300
21-24: 21-Last Hercules. 24-Last Red Bee & Strange Twins
96 192 288 600 925 1250
25-Origin & 1st app. Kid Eternity and begins by Moldoff (12/42); 1st app. The Keeper (Kid Eternity's aide) 185 370 555 1156 1778 2400
26-Blackhawk x-over in Kid Eternity 100 200 300 625 963 1300
27-29 50 100 150 305 465 625
30,31- "Bill the Magnificent" by Kurtzman, 11 pgs. in each
46 92 138 281 428 575
32-40: 32-Plastic Man x-over. 34-Last Stormy Foster
30 60 90 170 245 320
41-50 21 42 63 121 173 225
51-60-Last Kid Eternity 20 40 60 112 161 210
61-63-Crandall-c/a; 61-Jeb Rivers begins 21 42 63 118 169 220
64,65-Crandall-a 20 40 60 112 161 210
NOTE: ***Crandall** a-11-17(Hercules), 23, 24(Stormy Foster); c-18-20, 23, 24. **Fine** c-1-14, 16, 17(most). **Ward** c-33. Bondage c-7, 64. Hercules c-3, 10-17. Jeb Rivers c-61-65. Kid Eternity c-25-60 (w/Keeper-28-34, 36, 39-43, 45-55). Neon the Unknown c-2, 4, 8, 9. Red Bee c-1, 5-7. Stormy Foster c-18-24.*

HITLER'S ASTROLOGER (See Marvel Graphic Novel #35)

HITMAN (Also see Bloodbath #2, Batman Chronicles #4, Demon #43-45 & Demon Annual #2)
DC Comics: May, 1996 - No. 60, Apr, 2001 ($2.25/$2.50)
1-Garth Ennis-s & John McCrea-c/a begin; Batman app.
1 2 3 5 7 9
2-Joker-c;Two Face, Mad Hatter, Batman app. 6.00
3-5: 3-Batman-c/app.; Joker app. 4-1st app. Nightfist 4.00
6-20: 8-Final Night x-over. 10-GL cameo. 11-20: 11,12-GL-c/app. 15-20-"Ace of Killers". 16-18-Catwoman app. 17-19-Demon-app. 3.00
21-59: 34-Superman-c/app. 2.50
60-($3.95) Final issue; includes pin-ups by various 4.00
#1,000,000 (11/98) Hitman goes to the 853rd Century 2.50
Annual 1 (1997, $3.95) Pulp Heroes 4.00
.../Lobo: That Stupid Bastich (7/00, $3.95) Ennis-s/Mahnke-a 4.00
TPB-(1997, $9.95) r/#1-3, Demon Ann. #2, Batman Chronicles #4 10.00
Ace of Killers TPB ('00, $17.95) r/#15-22 18.00

Hollywood Confessions #1 © STJ

Hollywood Secrets #1 © QUA

Holyoke One-Shot #2 © HOKE

GD VG FN VF VF/NM NM-
2.0 4.0 6.0 8.0 9.0 9.2

Local Heroes TPB ('99, $17.95) r/#9-14 & Annual #1 18.00
10,000 Bullets TPB ('98, $9.95) r/#4-8 10.00
Who Dares Wins TPB ('01, $12.95) r/#23-28 13.00

HI-YO SILVER (See Lone Ranger's Famous Horse... and The Lone Ranger; and March of Comics No. 215 in the Promotional Comics section)

HOBBIT, THE
Eclipse Comics: 1989 - No. 3, 1990 ($4.95, squarebound, 52 pgs.)

Book 1-3: Adapts novel; Wenzel-a 7.00
Book 1-Second printing 5.00
Graphic Novel (1990, Ballantine)-r/#1-3 20.00

HOCUS POCUS (See Funny Book #9)

HOGAN'S HEROES (TV)
Dell Publishing Co.: June, 1966 - No. 8, Sept, 1967; No. 9, Oct, 1969

1: #1-7 photo-c 10 20 30 67 96 125
2,3-Ditko-a(p) 6 12 18 43 59 75
4-9: 9-Reprints #1 5 10 15 36 48 60

HOKUM & HEX (See Razorline)
Marvel Comics (Razorline): Sept, 1993 - No. 9, May, 1994 ($1.75/$1.95)

1-($2.50)-Foil embossed-c; by Clive Barker 3.00
2-9: 5-Hyperkind x-over 2.25

HOLIDAY COMICS
Fawcett Publications: 1942 (25¢, 196 pgs.)

1-Contains three Fawcett comics plus two page portrait of Captain Marvel; Capt. Marvel, Nyoka #1, & Whiz. Not rebound, remaindered comics; printed at the same time as originals 162 324 486 1013 1557 2100

HOLIDAY COMICS (Becomes Fun Comics #9-12)
Star Publications: Jan, 1951 - No. 8, Oct, 1952

1-Funny animal contents (Frisky Fables) in all; L. B. Cole X-Mas-c 38 76 114 219 320 420
2-Classic L. B. Cole-c 40 80 120 230 335 440
3-8: 5,8-X-Mas-c; all L.B. Cole-c 25 50 75 144 207 270
Accepted Reprint 4 (nd)-L.B. Cole-c 11 22 33 66 87 110

HOLIDAY DIGEST
Harvey Comics: 1988 ($1.25, digest-size)

1 1 2 3 5 7 9

HOLIDAY PARADE (Walt Disney's...)
W. D. Publications (Disney): Winter, 1990-91(no year given) - No. 2, Winter, 1990-91 ($2.95, 68 pgs.)

1-Reprints 1947 Firestone by Barks plus new-a 4.00
2-Barks-r plus other stories 4.00

HOLI-DAY SURPRISE (Formerly Summer Fun)
Charlton Comics: V2#55, Mar, 1967 (25¢ Giant)

V2#55 4 8 12 25 33 42

HOLLYWOOD COMICS
New Age Publishers: Winter, 1944 (52 pgs.)

1-Funny animal 19 38 57 107 154 200

HOLLYWOOD CONFESSIONS
St. John Publishing Co.: Oct, 1949 - No. 2, Dec, 1949

1-Kubert-c/a (entire book) 32 64 96 184 267 350
2-Kubert-c/a (entire book) (Scarce) 35 70 105 201 293 385
370

HOLLYWOOD DIARY
Quality Comics Group: Dec, 1949 - No. 5, July-Aug, 1950

1-No photo-c 21 42 63 118 169 220
2-Photo-c 13 26 39 76 106 135
3-5-Photo-c. 5-June Allyson/Peter Lawford photo-c 11 22 33 66 91 115

HOLLYWOOD FILM STORIES
Feature Publications/Prize: April, 1950 - No. 4, Oct, 1950 (All photo-c; "Fumetti" type movie comic)

1-June Allyson photo-c 21 42 63 121 173 225
2-4: 2-Lizabeth Scott photo-c. 3-Barbara Stanwick photo-c. 4-Betty Hutton photo-c 15 30 45 86 123 160

HOLLYWOOD FUNNY FOLKS (Formerly Funny Folks; Becomes Nutsy Squirrel #61 on)
National Periodical Publ.: No. 27, Aug-Sept, 1950 - No. 60, July-Aug, 1954

27 14 28 42 79 110 140
28-40 10 20 30 56 73 90
41-60 9 18 27 49 62 75

NOTE: ***Rube Grossman** a-most issues. **Sheldon Mayer** a-27-35, 37-40, 43-46, 48-51, 53, 56, 57, 60.*

HOLLYWOOD LOVE DOCTOR (See Doctor Anthony King...)

HOLLYWOOD PICTORIAL (...Romances on cover)
St. John Publishing Co.: No. 3, Jan, 1950

3-Matt Baker-a; photo-c 24 48 72 138 199 260
(Becomes a movie magazine - Hollywood Pictorial Western with No. 4.)

HOLLYWOOD ROMANCES (Formerly Brides In Love; becomes For Lovers Only #60 on)
Charlton Comics: V2#46, 11/66; #47, 10/67; #48, 11/68;V3#49,11/69-V3#59, 6/71

V2#46-Rolling Stones-c/story 10 20 30 67 96 125
V2#47-V3#59: 56- "Born to Heart Break" begins 2 4 6 14 18 22

HOLLYWOOD SECRETS
Quality Comics Group: Nov, 1949 - No. 6, Sept, 1950

1-Ward-c/a (9 pgs.) 35 70 105 198 287 375
2-Crandall-a, Ward-c/a (9 pgs.) 23 46 69 132 191 250
3-6: All photo-c. 5-Lex Barker (Tarzan)-c 12 24 36 71 98 125
...of Romance, I.W. Reprint #9; r/#2 above w/Kinstler-c 2 4 6 11 14 18

HOLLYWOOD SUPERSTARS
Marvel Comics (Epic Comics): Nov, 1990 - No. 5, Apr, 1991 ($2.25)

1-($2.95, 52 pgs.)-Spiegle-c/a in all; Aragones-a, inside front-c plus 2-4 pgs. 3.00
2-5 ($2.25) 2.25

HOLO-MAN (See Power Record Comics)

HOLYOKE ONE-SHOT
Holyoke Publishing Co. (Tem Publ.): 1944 - No. 10, 1945 (All reprints)

1,2: 1-Grit Grady (on cover only), Miss Victory, Alias X (origin)-All reprints from Captain Fearless. 2-Rusty Dugan (Corporal); Capt. Fearless (origin), Mr. Miracle (origin) app. 17 34 51 95 135 175
3-Miss Victory; r/Crash #4; Cat Man (origin), Solar Legion by Kirby app.; Miss Victory on cover only (1945) 30 60 90 170 245 320
4,6,8: 4-Mr. Miracle; The Blue Streak app. 6-Capt. Fearless, Alias X, Capt. Stone (splash used as-c to #10); Diamond Jim & Rusty Dugan (splash from cover of #2). 8-Blue Streak, Strong Man (story matches cover to #7)-Crash reprints 15 30 45 83 117 150
5,7: 5-U.S. Border Patrol Comics (Sgt. Dick Carter of the...), Miss Victory (story matches cover to #3), Citizen Smith, & Mr. Miracle app. 7-Secret Agent Z-2, Strong Man, Blue Streak (story matches cover to #8); Reprints from Crash #2 17 34 51 95 135 175
9-Citizen Smith, The Blue Streak, Solar Legion by Kirby & Strongman, the Perfect Human app.; reprints from Crash #4 & 5; Citizen Smith on cover only-from story in #5 (1944-before #3) 20 40 60 112 161 210
10-Captain Stone; r/Crash; Solar Legion by S&K 20 40 60 112 161 210

HOLY TERROR
Image Comics: Aug, 2002 - Present ($2.95)

1,2-Phil Hester-a/c; Jason Caskey-s 3.00

HOMER COBB (See Adventures of...)

HOMER HOOPER
Atlas Comics: July, 1953 - No. 4, Dec, 1953

1-Teenage humor 10 20 30 58 77 95
2-4 8 16 24 40 50 60

HOMER, THE HAPPY GHOST (See Adventures of...)
Atlas(ACI/PPI/WPI)/Marvel: 3/55 - No. 22, 11/58; V2#1, 11/69 - V2#4, 5/70

V1#1-Dan DeCarlo-c/a begins, ends #22 22 44 66 127 184 240
2-1st code approved issue 12 24 36 69 95 120
3-10 10 20 30 60 80 100
11-22 9 18 27 52 66 80
V2#1 (11/69) 11 22 33 77 114 150
2-4 6 12 18 43 59 75

HOME RUN (Also see A-1 Comics)
Magazine Enterprises: No. 89, 1953 (one-shot)

A-1 89 (#3)-Powell-a; Stan Musial photo-c 14 28 42 79 110 140

HOMICIDE (Also see Dark Horse Presents)
Dark Horse Comics: Apr, 1990 ($1.95, B&W, one-shot)

1-Detective story 2.25

HONEYMOON (Formerly Gay Comics)
A Lover's Magazine(USA) (Marvel): No. 41, Jan, 1950

Hopalong Cassidy #84 © FAW

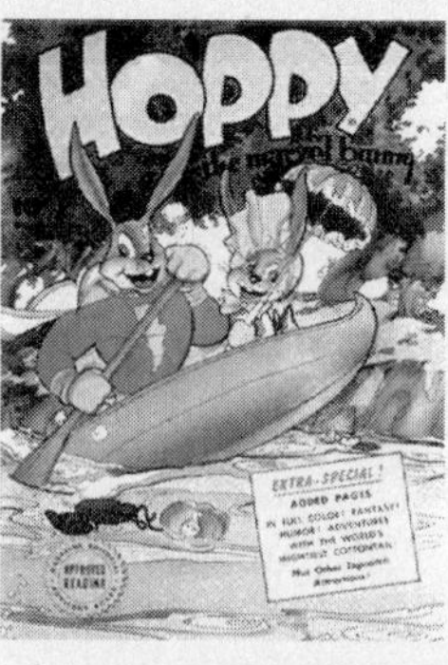

Hoppy the Marvel Bunny #4 © FAW

Horrific #12 © Comic Media

	GD 2.0	VG 4.0	FN 6.0	VF 8.0	VF/NM 9.0	NM- 9.2
41-Photo-c; article by Betty Grable	10	20	30	58	77	95

HONEYMOONERS, THE (TV)
Lodestone: Oct, 1986 ($1.50)

	GD	VG	FN	VF	VF/NM	NM-
1-Photo-c						4.00

HONEYMOONERS, THE (TV)
Triad Publications: Sept, 1987 - No. 13? ($2.00)

	GD	VG	FN	VF	VF/NM	NM-
1-13						4.00

HONEYMOON ROMANCE
Artful Publications (Canadian): Apr, 1950 - No. 2, July, 1950 (25¢, digest size)

	GD	VG	FN	VF	VF/NM	NM-
1,2-(Rare)	38	76	114	219	320	420

HONEY WEST (TV)
Gold Key: Sept, 1966 (Photo-c)

	GD	VG	FN	VF	VF/NM	NM-
1 (10186-609)	11	22	33	80	120	160

HONG KONG PHOOEY (TV)
Charlton Comics: June, 1975 - No. 9, Nov, 1976 (Hanna-Barbera)

	GD	VG	FN	VF	VF/NM	NM-
1	6	12	18	40	55	70
2	3	7	10	21	28	35
3-9	3	6	9	16	21	26

HONG ON THE RANGE
Image/Flypaper Press: Dec, 1997 - No. 3, Feb, 1998 ($2.50, lim. series)

	GD	VG	FN	VF	VF/NM	NM-
1-3: Wu-s/Lafferty-a						2.50

HOOD, THE
Marvel Comics (MAX): Jul, 2002 - No. 6, Dec, 2002 ($2.99, limited series)

	GD	VG	FN	VF	VF/NM	NM-
1-6-Vaughan-s/Hotz-c/a						3.00
Vol. 1 Blood From Stones TPB (2003, $14.99) r/#1-6						15.00

HOODED HORSEMAN, THE (Formerly Blazing West)
American Comics Group (Michel Publ.): No. 21, 1-2/52 - No. 27, 1-2/54; No. 18, 12-1/54-55 - No. 22, 8-9/55

	GD	VG	FN	VF	VF/NM	NM-
21(1-2/52)-Hooded Horseman, Injun Jones cont.	15	30	45	86	123	160
22	10	20	30	58	77	95
23,24,27(1-2/54)	9	18	27	52	66	80
25 (9-10/53)-Cowboy Sahib on cover only; Hooded Horseman i.d. revealed	9	18	27	54	70	85
26-Origin/1st app. Cowboy Sahib by L. Starr	11	22	33	64	87	110
18(12-1/54-55)(Formerly Out of the Night)	10	20	30	56	73	90
19,21,22: 19-Last precode (1-2/55)	8	16	24	46	58	70
20-Origin Johnny Injun	9	18	27	52	66	80

NOTE: ***Whitney** c/a-21('52), 20-22.*

HOODED MENACE, THE (Also see Daring Adventures)
Realistic/Avon Periodicals: 1951 (one-shot)

	GD	VG	FN	VF	VF/NM	NM-
nn-Based on a band of hooded outlaws in the Pacific Northwest, 1900-1906; reprinted in Daring Advs. #15	48	96	144	293	447	600

HOODS UP
Fram Corp.: 1953 (15¢, distributed to service station owners, 16 pgs.)

	GD	VG	FN	VF	VF/NM	NM-
1-(Very Rare; only 2 known); Eisner-c/a in all.	48	96	144	293	447	600
2-6-(Very Rare; only 1 known of #3, 4, 2 known of #2)	48	96	144	288	432	575

NOTE: *Convertible Connie gives tips for service stations, selling Fram oil filters.*

HOOK (Movie)
Marvel Comics: Early Feb, 1992 - No. 4, Late Mar, 1992 ($1.00, limited series)

	GD	VG	FN	VF	VF/NM	NM-
1-4: Adapts movie; Vess-c; 1-Morrow-a(p)						2.25
nn (1991, $5.95, 84 pgs.)-Contains #1-4; Vess-c						6.00
1 (1991, $2.95, magazine, 84 pgs.)-Contains #1-4; Vess-c (same cover as nn issue)						3.00

HOOT GIBSON'S WESTERN ROUNDUP (See Western Roundup under Fox Giants)

HOOT GIBSON WESTERN (Formerly My Love Story)
Fox Features Syndicate: No. 5, May, 1950 - No. 3, Sept, 1950

	GD	VG	FN	VF	VF/NM	NM-
5,6(#1,2): 5-Photo-c. 6-Photo/painted-c	29	58	87	164	237	310
3-Wood-a; painted-c	31	62	93	175	253	330

HOPALONG CASSIDY (Also see Bill Boyd Western, Master Comics, Real Western Hero, Six Gun Heroes & Western Hero; Bill Boyd starred as Hopalong Cassidy in movies, radio & TV)
Fawcett Publications: Feb, 1943; No. 2, Summer, 1946 - No. 85, Nov, 1953

	GD	VG	FN	VF	VF/NM	NM-
1 (1943, 68 pgs.)-H. Cassidy & his horse Topper begin (on sale 1/8/43)-Captain Marvel app. on-c	471	942	1413	3297	5300	7300
2-(Sum, '46)	81	162	243	506	778	1050
3,4: 3-(Fall, '46, 52 pgs. begin)	40	80	120	241	363	485
5- "Mad Barber" story mentioned in **SOTI**, pgs. 308,309; photo-c	37	74	111	209	305	400
6-10: 8-Photo-c	29	58	87	164	237	310
11-19: 11,13-19-Photo-c	21	42	63	121	173	225
20-29 (52 pgs.)-Painted/photo-c	17	34	51	98	139	180
30,31,33,34,37-39,41 (52 pgs.)-Painted-c	12	24	36	69	95	120
32,40 (36pgs.)-Painted-c	11	22	33	62	84	105
35,42,43,45-47,49-51,53,54,56 (52 pgs.)-Photo-c	11	22	33	64	87	110
36,44,48 (36 pgs.)-Photo-c	10	20	30	60	80	100
52,55,57-70 (36 pgs.)-Photo-c	10	20	30	56	73	90
71-84-Photo-c	9	18	27	51	62	75
85-Last Fawcett issue; photo-c	10	20	30	56	73	90

NOTE: *Line-drawn c-1-4, 6, 7, 9, 10, 12.*

	GD	VG	FN	VF	VF/NM	NM-
... & The 5 Men of Evil (AC Comics, 1991, $12.95) r/newspaper strips and Fawcett story "Signature of Death"						13.00

HOPALONG CASSIDY
National Periodical Publications: No. 86, Feb, 1954 - No. 135, May-June, 1959 (All-36 pgs.)

	GD	VG	FN	VF	VF/NM	NM-
86-Gene Colan-a begins, ends #117; photo covers continue	40	80	120	236	351	465
87	23	46	69	130	188	245
88-91: 91-1 pg. Superboy-sty (7/54)	15	30	45	86	123	160
92-99 (98 has #93 on-c; last precode issue, 2/55). 95-Reversed photo-c to #52. 98-Reversed photo-c to #61. 99-Reversed photo-c to #60	14	28	42	79	110	140
100-Same cover as #50	15	30	45	86	123	160
101-108: 105-Same photo-c as #54. 107-Same photo-c as #51. 108-Last photo-c	8	16	24	55	78	100
109-130: 118-Gil Kane-a begins. 123-Kubert-a (2 pgs.). 124-Painted-c	7	14	21	51	71	90
131-135	8	16	24	53	74	95

HOPELESS SAVAGES (Also see Too Much Hopeless Savages; and the Promotional Comics section for Free Comic Book Day edition)
Oni Press: Aug, 2001 - No. 4, Nov, 2001 ($2.95, B&W, limited series)

	GD	VG	FN	VF	VF/NM	NM-
1-4-Van Meter-s/Norrie-a/Clugston-Major-a/Watson-c						3.00
TPB (2002, $13.95, 8" x 5.75") r/#1-4; plus color stories; Watson-c						14.00

HOPELESS SAVAGES: GROUND ZERO
Oni Press: June, 2002 - No. 4, Oct, 2002 ($2.95, B&W, limited series)

	GD	VG	FN	VF	VF/NM	NM-
1-4-Van Meter-s/O'Malley-a/Dodson-c. 1-Watson-a						3.00
TPB (2003, $11.95, 8" x 5.75") r/#1-4; Dodson-c						12.00

HOPE SHIP
Dell Publishing Co.: June-Aug, 1963

	GD	VG	FN	VF	VF/NM	NM-
1	3	6	9	18	23	28

HOPPY THE MARVEL BUNNY (See Fawcett's Funny Animals)
Fawcett Publications: Dec, 1945 - No. 15, Sept, 1947

	GD	VG	FN	VF	VF/NM	NM-
1	30	60	90	173	249	325
2	15	30	45	86	123	160
3-15: 7-Xmas-c	13	26	39	74	102	130

HORACE & DOTTY DRIPPLE (Dotty Dripple No. 1-24)
Harvey Publications: No. 25, Aug, 1952 - No. 43, Oct, 1955

	GD	VG	FN	VF	VF/NM	NM-
25-43	4	8	12	16	19	22

HORIZONTAL LIEUTENANT, THE (See Movie Classics)

HOROBI
Viz Premiere Comics: 1990 - No. 8, 1990 ($3.75, B&W, mature readers, 84 pgs.) V2#1, 1990 - No. 7, 1991 ($4.25, B&W, 68 pgs.)

	GD	VG	FN	VF	VF/NM	NM-
1-8: Japanese manga, Part Two, #1-7						4.50

HORRIFIC (Terrific No. 14 on)
Artful/Comic Media/Harwell/Mystery: Sept, 1952 - No. 13, Sept, 1954

	GD	VG	FN	VF	VF/NM	NM-
1	52	104	156	317	484	650
2	31	62	93	178	259	340
3-Bullet in head-c	55	110	165	340	520	700
4,5,7,9,10: 4-Shrunken head-c. 7-Guillotine-c	28	56	84	158	229	300
6-Jack The Ripper story	29	58	87	164	237	310
8-Origin & 1st app. The Teller (E.C. parody)	32	64	96	184	267	350
11-13: 11-Swipe/Witches Tales #6,27; Devil-c	22	44	66	127	184	240

NOTE: ***Don Heck** a-8; c-3-13. **Hollingsworth** a-4. **Morisi** a-8. **Palais** a-5, 7-12.*

HORRORCIDE
IDW Publishing: Sept, 2004 ($6.99)

	GD	VG	FN	VF	VF/NM	NM-
1-Steve Niles short stories; art by Templesmith, Medors and Chee						7.00

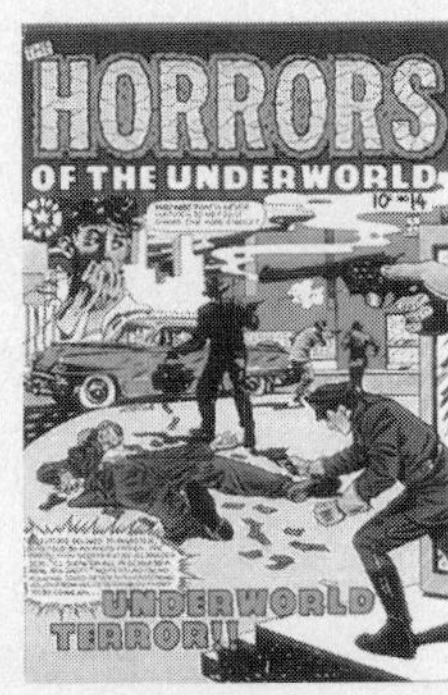

The Horrors #14 © STAR

Hot Rods and Racing Cars #8 © CC

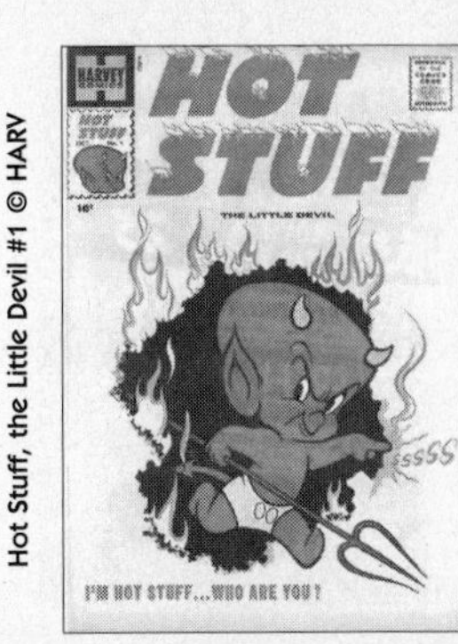

Hot Stuff, the Little Devil #1 © HARV

HORROR FROM THE TOMB (Mysterious Stories No. 2 on)
Premier Magazine Co.: Sept, 1954

	GD 2.0	VG 4.0	FN 6.0	VF 8.0	VF/NM 9.0	NM- 9.2
1-Woodbridge/Torres, Check-a; The Keeper of the Graveyard is host	40	80	120	241	363	485

HORRORIST, THE (Also see Hellblazer)
DC Comics (Vertigo): Dec, 1995 - No. 2, Jan, 1996 ($5.95, lim. series, mature)

	GD 2.0	VG 4.0	FN 6.0	VF 8.0	VF/NM 9.0	NM- 9.2
1,2: Jamie Delano scripts, David Lloyd-c/a; John Constantine (Hellblazer) app.						6.00

HORROR OF COLLIER COUNTY
Dark Horse Comics: Oct, 1999 - No. 5, Feb, 2000 ($2.95, B&W, limited series)

	GD 2.0	VG 4.0	FN 6.0	VF 8.0	VF/NM 9.0	NM- 9.2
1-5-Rich Tommaso-s/a						3.00

HORRORS, THE (Formerly Startling Terror Tales #10)
Star Publications: No. 11, Jan, 1953 - No. 15, Apr, 1954

	GD 2.0	VG 4.0	FN 6.0	VF 8.0	VF/NM 9.0	NM- 9.2
11-Horrors of War; Disbrow-a(2)	31	62	93	175	253	330
12-Horrors of War; color illo in **POP**	29	58	87	164	237	310
13-Horrors of Mystery; crime stories	27	54	81	152	219	285
14,15-Horrors of the Underworld; crime stories	29	58	87	164	237	310

NOTE: *All have **L. B. Cole** covers; a-12. **Hollingsworth** a-13. **Palais** a-13r.*

HORROR TALES (Magazine)
Eerie Publications: V1#7, 6/69 - V6#6, 12/74; V7#1, 2/75; V7#2, 5/76 - V8#5, 1977; V9#1-3, 8/78; V10#1(2/79) (V1-V6: 52 pgs.; V7, V8#2: 112 pgs.; V8#4 on: 68 pgs.) (No V5#3, V8#1,3)

	GD 2.0	VG 4.0	FN 6.0	VF 8.0	VF/NM 9.0	NM- 9.2
V1#7	5	10	15	33	44	55
V1#8,9	4	8	12	22	30	38
V2#1-6('70), V3#1-6('71), V4#1-3,5-7('72)	3	6	9	19	25	32
V4#4-LSD story reprint/Weird V3#5	4	8	12	27	36	45
V5#1,2,4,5(6/73),5(10/73),6(12/73),V6#1-6('74),V7#1,2,4('76),V7#3('76)-Giant issue, V8#2,4,5('77)	3	6	9	19	25	32
V9#1-3(11/78, $1.50), V10#1(2/79)	4	8	12	24	32	40

NOTE: *Bondage-c-V6#1, 3, V7#2.*

HORSE FEATHERS COMICS
Lev Gleason Publ.: Nov, 1945 - No. 4, July(Summer on-c), 1948 (52 pgs.)

	GD 2.0	VG 4.0	FN 6.0	VF 8.0	VF/NM 9.0	NM- 9.2
1-Wolverton's Scoop Scuttle, 2 pgs.	20	40	60	112	161	210
2	10	20	30	60	80	100
3,4: 3-(5/48)	9	18	27	51	62	75

HORSEMAN
Crusade Comics/Kevlar Studios: Mar, 1996 - No. 3, Nov, 1997 ($2.95)

	GD 2.0	VG 4.0	FN 6.0	VF 8.0	VF/NM 9.0	NM- 9.2
0-1st Kevlar Studios issue, 1-(3/96)-Crusade issue; Shi-c/app., 1-(11/96)-3-(11/97)-Kevlar Studios						3.00

HORSEMASTERS, THE (Disney)(TV, Movie)
Dell Publishing Co.: No. 1260, Dec-Feb, 1961/62

	GD 2.0	VG 4.0	FN 6.0	VF 8.0	VF/NM 9.0	NM- 9.2
Four Color 1260-Annette Funicello photo-c	14	28	42	97	149	200

HORSE SOLDIERS, THE
Dell Publishing Co.: No. 1048, Nov-Jan, 1959/60 (John Wayne movie)

	GD 2.0	VG 4.0	FN 6.0	VF 8.0	VF/NM 9.0	NM- 9.2
Four Color 1048-Painted-c, Sekowsky-a	15	30	45	105	160	215

HORSE WITHOUT A HEAD, THE (See Movie Comics)

HOT DOG
Magazine Enterprises: June-July, 1954 - No. 4, Dec-Jan, 1954-55

	GD 2.0	VG 4.0	FN 6.0	VF 8.0	VF/NM 9.0	NM- 9.2
1(A-1 #107)	9	18	27	51	62	75
2,3(A-1 #115),4(A-1 #136)	6	12	18	31	38	45

HOT DOG (See Jughead's Pal, Hotdog)

HOTEL DEPAREE - SUNDANCE (TV)
Dell Publishing Co.: No. 1126, Aug-Oct, 1960 (one-shot)

	GD 2.0	VG 4.0	FN 6.0	VF 8.0	VF/NM 9.0	NM- 9.2
Four Color 1126-Earl Holliman photo-c	8	16	24	53	74	95

HOT ROD AND SPEEDWAY COMICS
Hillman Periodicals: Feb-Mar, 1952 - No. 5, Apr-May, 1953

	GD 2.0	VG 4.0	FN 6.0	VF 8.0	VF/NM 9.0	NM- 9.2
1	30	60	90	170	245	320
2-Krigstein-a	20	40	60	112	161	210
3-5	12	24	36	69	95	120

HOT ROD COMICS (...Featuring Clint Curtis) (See XMas Comics)
Fawcett Publications: Nov, 1951 (no month given) - V2#7, Feb, 1953

	GD 2.0	VG 4.0	FN 6.0	VF 8.0	VF/NM 9.0	NM- 9.2
nn (V1#1)-Powell-c/a in all	35	70	105	201	293	385
2 (4/52)	19	38	57	107	154	200
3-6, V2#7	14	28	42	79	110	140

HOT ROD KING (Also see Speed Smith the Hot Rod King)
Ziff-Davis Publ. Co.: Fall, 1952

	GD 2.0	VG 4.0	FN 6.0	VF 8.0	VF/NM 9.0	NM- 9.2
1-Giacoia-a; Saunders painted-c	28	56	84	158	229	300

HOT ROD RACERS (Grand Prix No. 16 on)
Charlton Comics: Dec, 1964 - No. 15, July, 1967

	GD 2.0	VG 4.0	FN 6.0	VF 8.0	VF/NM 9.0	NM- 9.2
1	9	18	27	63	89	115
2-5	6	12	18	38	52	65
6-15	4	8	12	28	38	48

HOT RODS AND RACING CARS
Charlton Comics (Motor Mag. No. 1): Nov, 1951 - No. 120, June, 1973

	GD 2.0	VG 4.0	FN 6.0	VF 8.0	VF/NM 9.0	NM- 9.2
1-Speed Davis begins; Indianapolis 500 story	30	60	90	170	245	320
2	15	30	45	86	123	160
3-10	11	22	33	64	87	110
11-20	10	20	30	56	73	90
21-33,36-40	8	16	24	46	58	70
34, 35 (? & 6/58, 68 pgs.)	11	22	33	62	84	105
41-60	7	14	21	37	46	55
61-80	4	8	12	22	30	38
81-100	3	6	9	18	23	28
101-120	2	4	6	14	18	22

HOT SHOT CHARLIE
Hillman Periodicals: 1947 (Lee Elias)

	GD 2.0	VG 4.0	FN 6.0	VF 8.0	VF/NM 9.0	NM- 9.2
1	10	20	30	60	80	100

HOT SHOTS: AVENGERS
Marvel Comics: Oct, 1995 ($2.95, one-shot)

	GD 2.0	VG 4.0	FN 6.0	VF 8.0	VF/NM 9.0	NM- 9.2
nn-pin-ups						3.00

HOTSPUR
Eclipse Comics: Jun, 1987 - No. 3, Sep, 1987 ($1.75, lim. series, Baxter paper)

	GD 2.0	VG 4.0	FN 6.0	VF 8.0	VF/NM 9.0	NM- 9.2
1-3						3.00

HOT STUFF (See Stumbo Tinytown)
Harvey Comics: V2#1, Sept, 1991 - No. 12, June, 1994 ($1.00)

	GD 2.0	VG 4.0	FN 6.0	VF 8.0	VF/NM 9.0	NM- 9.2
V2#1-Stumbo back-up story						4.00
2-12 ($1.50)						3.00
...Big Book 1 (11/92), 2 (6/93) (Both $1.95, 52 pgs.)						4.00

HOT STUFF CREEPY CAVES
Harvey Publications: Nov, 1974 - No. 7, Nov, 1975

	GD 2.0	VG 4.0	FN 6.0	VF 8.0	VF/NM 9.0	NM- 9.2
1	4	8	12	27	36	45
2-7	3	6	9	16	21	26

HOT STUFF DIGEST
Harvey Comics: July, 1992 - No. 5, Nov, 1993 ($1.75, digest-size)

	GD 2.0	VG 4.0	FN 6.0	VF 8.0	VF/NM 9.0	NM- 9.2
V2#1-Hot Stuff, Stumbo, Richie Rich stories						6.00
2-5						4.00

HOT STUFF GIANT SIZE
Harvey Comics: Oct, 1992 - No. 3, Oct, 1993 ($2.25, 68 pgs.)

	GD 2.0	VG 4.0	FN 6.0	VF 8.0	VF/NM 9.0	NM- 9.2
V2#1-Hot Stuff & Stumbo stories						4.50
2,3						3.50

HOT STUFF SIZZLERS
Harvey Publications: July, 1960 - No. 59, Mar, 1974; V2#1, Aug, 1992

	GD 2.0	VG 4.0	FN 6.0	VF 8.0	VF/NM 9.0	NM- 9.2
1- 84 pgs. begin, ends #5; Hot Stuff, Stumbo begin	15	30	45	107	164	220
2-5	8	16	24	53	74	95
6-10: 6-68 pgs. begin, ends #45	6	12	18	38	52	65
11-20	4	8	12	28	38	48
21-45	3	6	9	19	25	32
46-52: 52 pgs. begin	3	6	9	16	20	24
53-59	2	4	6	10	13	16
V2#1-(8/92, $1.25)-Stumbo back-up						5.00

HOT STUFF, THE LITTLE DEVIL (Also see Devil Kids & Harvey Hits)
Harvey Publications (Illustrated Humor): 10/57 - No. 141, 7/77; No. 142, 2/78 - No. 164, 8/82; No. 165, 10/86 - No. 171, 11/87; No. 172, 11/88; No. 173, Sept, 1990 - No. 177, 1/91

	GD 2.0	VG 4.0	FN 6.0	VF 8.0	VF/NM 9.0	NM- 9.2
1	41	82	123	305	478	650
2-1st app. Stumbo the Giant (12/57)	21	42	63	150	230	310
3-5	15	30	45	107	164	220
6-10	10	20	30	70	100	130
11-20	7	14	21	51	71	90
21-40	5	10	15	36	48	60
41-60	4	8	12	22	30	38
61-80	3	6	9	18	24	30
81-105	2	4	6	14	18	22
106-112: All 52 pg. Giants	3	6	9	18	24	30

House of Mystery #6 © DC

House of Mystery #174 © DC

House of Secrets #106 © DC

	GD 2.0	VG 4.0	FN 6.0	VF 8.0	VF/NM 9.0	NM- 9.2
113-125	2	4	6	8	10	12
126-141	1	2	3	5	7	9
142-177: 172-177-($1.00)						6.00

HOT WHEELS (TV)
National Periodical Publications: Mar-Apr, 1970 - No. 6, Jan-Feb, 1971

	GD 2.0	VG 4.0	FN 6.0	VF 8.0	VF/NM 9.0	NM- 9.2
1	10	20	30	73	107	140
2,4,5	6	12	18	40	55	70
3-Neal Adams-c	7	14	21	46	63	80
6-Neal Adams-c/a	8	16	24	55	78	100

NOTE: *Toth a-1p, 2-5; c-1p, 5.*

HOURMAN (Justice Society member, see Adventure Comics #48)

HOURMAN (See JLA and DC One Million)
DC Comics: Apr, 1999 - No. 25, Apr, 2001 ($2.50)

	GD 2.0	VG 4.0	FN 6.0	VF 8.0	VF/NM 9.0	NM- 9.2
1-25: 1-JLA app.; McDaniel-c. 2-Tomorrow Woman-c/app. 6,7-Amazo app. 11-13-Justice Legion A app. 16-Silver Age flashback. 18,19-JSA-c/app. 22-Harris-c/a. 24-Hourman Vs. Rex Tyler						2.50

HOUSE OF MYSTERY (See Brave and the Bold #93, Elvira's House of Mystery, Limited Collectors' Edition & Super DC Giant)

HOUSE OF MYSTERY, THE
National Periodical Publications/DC Comics: Dec-Jan, 1951-52 - No. 321, Oct, 1983 (No. 194-203: 52 pgs.)

	GD 2.0	VG 4.0	FN 6.0	VF 8.0	VF/NM 9.0	NM- 9.2
1-DC's first horror comic	238	476	714	1488	2294	3100
2	92	184	276	575	888	1200
3	65	130	195	406	628	850
4,5	52	104	156	317	484	650
6-10	45	90	135	275	418	560
11-15	40	80	120	233	342	450
16(7/53)-25	31	62	93	177	256	335
26-35(2/55)-Last pre-code issue; 30-Woodish-a	24	48	72	138	199	260
36-50: 50-Text story of Orson Welles' War of the Worlds broadcast	14	28	42	97	149	200
51-60: 55-1st S.A. issue	11	22	33	80	120	160
61,63,65,66,69,70,72,76,85-Kirby-a	13	26	39	90	138	185
62,64,67,68,71,73-75,77-83,86-99	10	20	30	72	104	135
84-Prototype of Negative Man (Doom Patrol)	13	26	39	90	138	185
100 (7/60)	11	22	33	77	114	150
101-116: 109-Toth, Kubert-a. 116-Last 10¢ issue	10	20	30	67	96	125
117-130: 117-Swipes-c to HOS #20. 120-Toth-a	9	18	27	60	85	110
131-142	8	16	24	53	74	95
143-J'onn J'onzz, Manhunter begins (6/64), ends #173; story continues from Detective #326; intro. Idol-Head of Diabolu	22	44	66	155	238	320
144	10	20	30	70	100	130
145-155,157-159: 149-Toth-a. 155-The Human Hurricane app. (12/65), Red Tornado prototype. 158-Origin Diabolu Idol-Head	7	14	21	50	68	85
156-Robby Reed begins (origin/1st app.), ends #173	9	18	27	63	89	115
160-(7/66)-Robby Reed becomes Plastic Man in this issue only; 1st S.A. app. Plastic Man; intro Marco Xavier (Martian Manhunter) & Vulture Crime Organization; ends #173	11	22	33	75	110	145
161-173: 169-Origin/1st app. Gem Girl	5	10	15	36	48	60
174-Mystery format begins.	9	18	27	63	89	115
175-1st app. Cain (House of Mystery host)	7	14	21	46	63	80
176,177	6	12	18	40	55	70
178-Neal Adams-a (2/69)	7	14	21	50	68	85
179-N. Adams/Orlando, Wrightson-a (1st pro work, 3 pgs.)	9	18	27	63	89	115
180,181,183: Wrightson-a (3,10, & 3 pgs.). 180-Last 12¢ issue; Kane/Wood-a(2). 183-Wood-a	6	12	18	40	55	70
182,184: 182-Toth-a. 184-Kane/Wood, Toth-a	4	8	12	27	36	45
185-Williamson/Kaluta-a; Howard-a (3 pgs.)	4	8	12	29	40	50
186-N. Adams-c/a; Wrightson-a (10 pgs.)	6	12	18	40	55	70
187,190: Adams-c. 187-Toth-a. 190-Toth-a(r)	4	8	12	24	32	40
188-Wrightson-a (8 & 3pgs.); Adams-c	5	10	15	33	44	55
189,192,197: Adams-c on all. 189-Wood-a(i). 192-Last 15¢-c	4	8	12	24	32	40
191-Wrightson-a (8 & 3pgs.); Adams-c	5	10	15	33	44	55
193-Wrightson-c	4	8	12	25	33	42
194-Wrightson-c; 52 pgs begin, end #203; Toth,Kirby-a	5	10	15	33	44	55
195: Wrightson-c. Swamp creature story by Wrightson similar to Swamp Thing (10 pgs.)(10/71)	7	14	21	46	63	80
196,198	4	8	12	25	33	42
199-Adams-c; Wood-a(8pgs.); Kirby-a	4	8	12	29	40	50
200-(25¢, 52 pgs.)-One third-r (3/72)	5	10	15	33	44	55
201-203-(25¢, 52 pgs.)-One third-r	4	8	12	25	33	42
204-Wrightson-c/a, 9 pgs.	4	8	12	22	30	38
205,206,208,210,212,215,216,218	3	6	9	16	20	24
207-Wrightson c/a; Starlin, Redondo-a	3	7	10	21	28	35
209,211,213,214,217,219-Wrightson-c	3	6	9	18	23	28
220,222,223	2	4	6	12	16	20
221-Wrightson/Kaluta-a(8 pgs.)	3	7	10	21	28	35
224-229: 224-Wrightson-r from Spectre #9; Dillin/Adams-r from House of Secrets #82; begin 100 pg. issues; Phantom Stranger-r. 225,227-(100 pgs.): 225-Spectre app. 226-Wrightson/Redondo-a Phantom Stranger-r. 228-N. Adams inks; Wrightson-r. 229-Wrightson-a(r); Toth-r; last 100 pg. issue	5	10	15	36	48	60
230,232-235,237-250	2	4	6	10	12	15
231-Classic Wrightson-c	3	6	9	18	24	30
236-Wrightson-c; Ditko-a(p); N. Adams-i	2	4	6	12	16	20
251-254-(84 pgs.)-Adams-c. 251-Wood-a	3	6	9	16	20	24
255,256-(84 pgs.)-Wrightson-c	3	6	9	16	20	24
257-259-(84 pgs.)	2	4	6	14	18	22
260-289: 282-(68 pgs.)-Has extra story "The Computers That Saved Metropolis" Radio Shack giveaway by Jim Starlin	1	2	3	5	7	9
290-1st "I, Vampire"	3	6	9	16	20	24
291-299: 291,293,295-299- "I, Vampire"	2	4	6	9	11	14
300,319,321: Death of "I, Vampire"	2	4	6	10	13	16
301-318,320: 301-318-"I, Vampire"	2	4	6	9	11	14
Welcome to the House of Mystery (7/98, $5.95) reprints stories with new framing story by Gaiman and Aragonés						6.00

NOTE: ***Neal Adams** a-236i; c-175-192, 197, 199, 251-254. **Alcala** a-209, 217, 219, 224, 227. **M. Anderson** a-212; c/a-37. **Aparo** a-209. **Aragones** a-185, 186, 194, 196, 200, 202, 229, 251. **Baily** a-279p. **Cameron** a-76, 79. **Colan** a-202r. **Craig** a-263, 275, 295, 300. **Dillin/Adams** r-224. **Ditko** a-236p, 247, 254, 258, 276; c-277. **Drucker** a-37. **Evans** c-218. **Fradon** a-251. **Giffen** a-284. **Giunta** a-199, 227r. **Golden** a-257, 259. **Heath** a-194r; c-203. **Howard** a-182, 185, 187, 196, 229r, 247i, 254, 279i. **Kaluta** a-195, 200, 250r; c-200-202, 210, 212, 233, 260, 261, 263, 265, 267, 268, 273, 276, 284, 287, 288, 293-295, 300, 302, 304, 305, 309-319, 321. **Bob Kane** a-84. **Gil Kane** a-196p, 253p, 300p. **Kirby** a-194r, 199r; c-65, 76, 78, 79, 85. **Kubert** c-282, 283, 285, 286, 289-292, 297-299, 301, 303, 306-308. **Maneely** a-68, 227r. **Mayer** a-317p. **Meskin** a-52-144 (most), 195r, 224r, 229r; c-63, 66, 124, 127. **Mooney** a-24, 159, 160. **Moreira** a-3, 4, 20-50, 58, 59, 62, 68, 77, 79, 90, 108, 113, 123, 201r, 228; c-4-28, 44, 47, 50, 54, 59, 62, 64, 68, 70, 73. **Morrow** a-192, 196, 255, 320i. **Mortimer** a-204(3 pgs.). **Nasser** a-276. **Newton** a-259, 272. **Nino** a-204, 212, 213, 220, 224, 225, 245, 250, 252-256, 283. **Orlando** a-175(2 pgs.), 178, 240i; c-240, 258p, 262, 264p, 270p, 271, 272, 274, 275, 278, 296i. **Redondo** a-194, 195, 197, 202, 203, 207, 211, 214, 217, 219, 226, 227, 229, 235, 241, 287(layout), 302p, 303i, 308; c-229. **Reese** a-195, 200, 205i. **Rogers** a-254, 274, 277. **Roussos** a-65, 84, 224i. **Sekowsky** a-282p. **Sparling** a-203. **Starlin** a-207(2 pgs.), 282p; c-281. **Leonard Starr** a-9. **Staton** a-300p. **Sutton** a-189, 271, 290, 291, 293, 295, 297-299, 302, 303, 306-309, 310-313i, 314. **Tuska** a-293p, 294p, 316p. **Wrightson** c-193-195, 204, 207, 209, 211, 213, 214, 217, 219, 221, 231, 236, 255, 256; r-224.*

HOUSE OF SECRETS (Combined with The Unexpected after #154)
National Periodical Publications/DC Comics: 11-12/56 - No. 80, 9-10/66; No. 81, 8-9/69 - No. 140, 2-3/76; No. 141, 8-9/76 - No. 154, 10-11/78

	GD 2.0	VG 4.0	FN 6.0	VF 8.0	VF/NM 9.0	NM- 9.2
1-Drucker-a; Moreira-c	113	226	339	961	1556	2150
2-Moreira-a	43	86	129	344	535	725
3-Kirby-c/a	38	76	114	285	443	600
4-Kirby-a	29	58	87	206	316	425
5-7	20	40	60	141	216	290
8-Kirby-a	23	46	69	165	253	340
9-11: 11-Lou Cameron-a (unsigned)	17	34	51	123	189	255
12-Kirby-c/a; Lou Cameron-a	19	38	57	136	208	280
13-15: 14-Flying saucer-c	13	26	39	92	141	190
16-20	12	24	36	84	127	170
21,22,24-30	11	22	33	75	110	145
23-1st app. Mark Merlin & begin series (8/59)	12	24	36	84	127	170
31-50: 48-Toth-a. 50-Last 10¢ issue	10	20	30	67	96	125
51-60: 58-Origin Mark Merlin	8	16	24	58	82	105
61-First Eclipso (7-8/63) and begin series	17	34	51	121	186	250
62	10	20	30	67	96	125
63-65-Toth-a on Eclipso (see Brave and the Bold #64)	8	16	24	53	74	95
66-1st Eclipso-c (also #67,70,78,79); Toth-a	10	20	30	67	96	125
67,73: 67-Toth-a on Eclipso. 73-Mark Merlin becomes Prince Ra-Man (1st app.)	8	16	24	53	74	95
68-72,74-80: 76-Prince Ra-Man vs. Eclipso. 80-Eclipso, Prince Ra-Man end	7	14	21	50	68	85
81-Mystery format begins; 1st app. Abel (House Of Secrets host); (cameo in DC Special #4)	9	18	27	63	89	115
82-84: 82-Neal Adams-c(i)	5	10	15	33	44	55
85,90: 85-N. Adams-a(i). 90-Buckler (early work)/N. Adams-a(i)	5	10	15	36	48	60
86,88,89,91	4	8	12	27	36	45
87-Wrightson & Kaluta-a	6	12	18	38	52	65

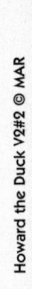

House of Secrets #5 © Seagle & Kristiansen

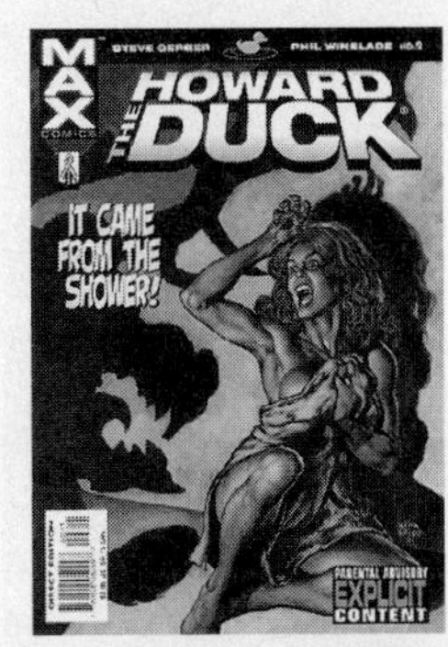

Howard the Duck V2#2 © MAR

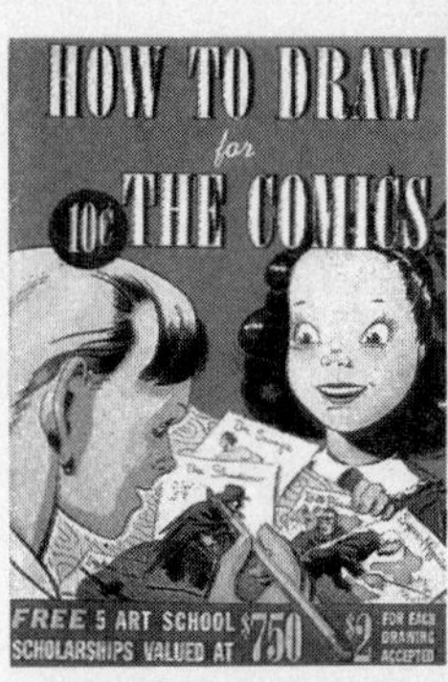

How to Draw For the Comics © CN

GD VG FN VF VF/NM NM-
2.0 4.0 6.0 8.0 9.0 9.2

92-1st app. Swamp Thing-c/story (8 pgs.)(6-7/71) by Berni Wrightson(p)
w/JeffJones/Kaluta/Weiss ink assists; classic-c. 50 100 150 400 625 850
93,94,96-(52 pgs.)-Wrightson-c. 94-Wrightson-a(i); 96-Wood-a
4 8 12 29 40 50
95,97,98-(52 pgs.) 4 8 12 29 40 50
99-Wrightson splash pg. 4 8 12 22 30 38
100-Classic Wrightson-c 5 10 15 33 44 55
101,102,104,105,108-120: 112-Grey tone-c 2 4 6 12 16 20
103,106,107-Wrightson-c 3 6 9 18 23 28
121-133 2 4 6 9 11 14
134-136,139-Wrightson-a 2 4 6 11 14 18
137,138,141-154 1 3 4 6 8 10
140-1st solo origin of the Patchworkman (see Swamp Thing #3)
3 6 9 16 21 26

NOTE: ***Neal Adams** c-81, 82, 84-88, 90, 91. **Alcala** a-104-107. **Anderson** a-91. Aparo a-93, 97, 105. **B. Bailey** a-107. **Cameron** a-13, 15. **Colan** a-63. **Ditko** a-139p, 148. **Elias** a-58. **Evans** a-118. **Finlay** a-7r(Real Fact?). **Glanzman** a-91. **Golden** a-151. **Heath** a-31. **Heck** a-85. **Kaluta** a-87, 98, 99; c-98, 99, 101, 102, 105, 149, 151, 154. **Bob Kane** a-18, 21. **G. Kane** a-85p. **Kirby** c-3, 11, 12. **Kubert** a-39. **Meskin** a-2-68 (most), 94r; c-55-60. **Moreira** a-7, 8, 51, 54, 102-104, 106, 108, 113, 116, 118, 121, 123, 127; c-1, 2, 4-10, 13-20. **Morrow** a-86, 89, 90; c-89, 146-148. **Nino** a-101, 103, 106, 109, 115, 117, 126, 128, 131, 147, 153. **Redondo** a-95, 99, 102, 104p, 113, 116, 134, 136, 139, 140. **Reese** a-85. **Severin** a-91. **Starlin** c-150. **Sutton** a-154. **Toth** a-63-67, 83, 93r, 94r, 96r-98r, 123. **Tuska** a-90, 104. **Wrightson** a-134; c-92-94, 96, 100, 103, 106, 107, 135, 136, 139.*

HOUSE OF SECRETS
DC Comics (Vertigo): Oct, 1996 - No. 25, Dec, 1998 ($2.50) (Creator-owned series)

1-Steven Seagle-s/Kristiansen-c/a. 3.50
2-25: 5,7-Kristiansen-c/a. 6-Fegrado-a 3.00
TPB-(1997, $14.95) r/1-5 15.00

HOUSE OF SECRETS: FACADE
DC Comics (Vertigo): 2001 - No. 2, 2001 ($5.95, limited series)

1,2-Steven Seagle-s/Teddy Kristiansen-c/a. 6.00

HOUSE OF TERROR (3-D)
St. John Publishing Co.: Oct, 1953 (25¢, came w/glasses)

1-Kubert, Baker-a 33 66 99 190 275 360

HOUSE OF YANG, THE (See Yang)
Charlton Comics: July, 1975 - No. 6, June, 1976; 1978

1-Sanho Kim-a in all 2 4 6 11 14 18
2-6 1 2 3 5 7 9
Modern Comics #1,2(1978) 4.00

HOUSE ON THE BORDERLAND
DC Comics (Vertigo): 2000 ($29.95, hardcover, one-shot)

HC-Adaptation of William Hope Hodgson book; Corben-a 30.00
SC (2003, $19.95) 20.00

HOUSE II: THE SECOND STORY
Marvel Comics: Oct, 1987 (One-shot)

1-Adapts movie 2.50

HOWARD CHAYKIN'S AMERICAN FLAGG (See American Flagg!)
First Comics: V2#1, May, 1988 - V2#12, Apr, 1989 ($1.75/$1.95, Baxter paper)

V2#1-9,11,12-Chaykin-c(p) in all 2.25
10-Elvis Presley photo-c 3.00

HOWARD THE DUCK (See Bizarre Adventures #34, Crazy Magazine, Fear, Man-Thing, Marvel Treasury Edition & Sensational She-Hulk #14-17)
Marvel Comics Group: Jan, 1976 - No. 31, May, 1979; No. 32, Jan, 1986; No. 33, Sept, 1986

1-Brunner-c/a; Spider-Man x-over (low distr.) 3 7 10 21 28 35
2-Brunner-c/a 2 4 6 10 12 15
3,4-(Regular 25¢ edition). 3-Buscema-a(p), (7/76) 1 3 4 6 8 10
3,4-(30¢-c, limited distribution) 2 4 6 10 12 15
5 1 3 4 6 8 10
6-11: 8-Howard The Duck for president. 9-1st Sgt. Preston Dudley of RCMP.
10-Spider-Man-c/sty 1 2 3 4 5 7
12-1st brief app. Kiss (3/77) 3 7 10 21 28 35
13-(30¢-c) 1st full app. Kiss (6/77); Daimon Hellstrom app. plus cameo of
Howard as Son of Satan 4 8 12 24 32 40
13-(35¢-c, limited distribution) 5 10 15 36 48 60
14-32: 14-17-(Regular 30¢-c). 14-Howard as Son of Satan-c/story; Son of Satan app.
16-Album issue; 3 pgs. comics. 22,23-Man-Thing-c/stories; Star Wars parody.
30,32-P. Smith-a 4.00
14-17-(35¢-c, limited distribution) 6.00
33-Last issue; low print run 1 2 3 4 5 7
Annual 1(1977, 52 pgs.)-Mayerik-a 1 2 3 4 5 7

NOTE: ***Austin** c-29i. **Bolland** c-33. **Brunner** a-1p, 2p; c-1, 2. **Buckler** c-3p. **Buscema** a-3p. **Colan** a(p)-4-15, 17-20, 24-27, 30, 31; c(p)-4-31, Annual 1p. **Leialoha** a-1-13i; c(i)-3-5, 8-11. **Mayerik** a-22, 23, 33. **Paul Smith** a-30p, 32. Man-Thing app. in #22, 23.*

HOWARD THE DUCK (Magazine)
Marvel Comics Group: Oct, 1979 - No. 9, Mar, 1981 (B&W, 68 pgs.)

1-Art by Colan, Janson, Golden. Kidney Lady app. 1 3 4 6 8 10
2,3,5-9 (nudity in most): 2-Mayerick-c. 3-Xmas issue; Jack Davis-c; Duck World flashback.
5-Dracula app. 6-1st Street People back-up story. 7-Has poster by Byrne; Man-Thing-c/s (46 pgs.). 8-Batman parody w/Marshall Rogers-a; Dave Sim-a (1 pg.). 9-Marie Severin-a; John Pound painted-c 5.00
4-Beatles, John Lennon, Elvis, Kiss & Devo cameos; Hitler app.
2 4 6 8 10 12

NOTE: ***Buscema** a-4p. **Colan** a-1-5p, 7-9p. **Jack Davis** c-3. **Golden** a(p)-1, 5, 6(51pgs.). **Rogers** a-7, 8. **Simonson** a-7.*

HOWARD THE DUCK (Volume 2)
Marvel Comics: Mar, 2002 - No. 6, Aug, 2002 ($2.99)

1-Gerber-s/Winslade-a/Fabry-c 4.00
2-6: 2,4-6-Gerber-s/Winslade-a/Fabry-c. 3-Fabry-a/c 3.00
TPB (9/02, $14.99) r/#1-6 15.00

HOWARD THE DUCK HOLIDAY SPECIAL
Marvel Comics: Feb, 1997 ($2.50, one-shot)

1-Wraparound-c; Hama-s 2.50

HOWARD THE DUCK: THE MOVIE
Marvel Comics Group: Dec, 1986 - No. 3, Feb, 1987 (Limited series)

1-3: Movie adaptation; r/Marvel Super Special 2.50

HOW BOYS AND GIRLS CAN HELP WIN THE WAR
The Parents' Magazine Institute: 1942 (10¢, one-shot)

1-All proceeds used to buy war bonds 26 52 78 150 215 280

HOWDY DOODY (TV)(See Jackpot of Fun-- & Poll Parrot)
Dell Publishing Co.: 1/50 - No. 38, 7-9/56; No. 761, 1/57; No. 811, 7/57

1-(Scarce)-Photo-c; 1st TV comic 90 180 270 714 1157 1600
2-Photo-c 41 82 123 305 478 650
3-5: All photo-c 25 50 75 177 271 365
6-Used in **SOTI**, pg. 309; classic-c; painted covers begin
26 52 78 187 286 385
7-10 17 34 51 121 186 250
11-20: 13-X-Mas-c 14 28 42 97 149 200
21-38, Four Color 761,811 12 24 36 82 124 165

HOW IT BEGAN
United Features Syndicate: No. 15, 1939 (one-shot)

Single Series 15 35 70 105 198 287 375

HOW SANTA GOT HIS RED SUIT (See March of Comics No. 2)

HOW THE WEST WAS WON (See Movie Comics)

HOW TO DRAW FOR THE COMICS
Street and Smith: No date (1942?) (10¢, 64 pgs., B&W & color, no ads)

nn-Art by Robert Winsor McCay (recreating his father's art), George Marcoux (Supersnipe artist), Vernon Greene (The Shadow artist), Jack Binder (with biog.), Thorton Fisher, Jon Small, & Jack Farr; has biographies of each artist
29 58 87 164 237 310

H. P. LOVECRAFT'S CTHULHU
Millennium Publications: Dec, 1991 - No. 3, May, 1992 ($2.50, limited series)

1-3: 1-Contains trading cards on thin stock 3.00

H. R. PUFNSTUF (TV) (See March of Comics #360)
Gold Key: Oct, 1970 - No. 8, July, 1972

1-Photo-c 21 42 63 150 230 310
2-8-Photo-c on all. 6-8-Both Gold Key and Whitman editions exist
11 22 33 79 117 155

HUBERT AT CAMP MOONBEAM
Dell Publishing Co.: No. 251, Oct, 1949 (one shot)

Four Color 251 6 12 18 43 59 75

HUCK & YOGI JAMBOREE (TV)
Dell Publishing Co.: Mar, 1961 ($1.00, 6-1/4x9", 116 pgs., cardboard-c, high quality paper) (B&W original material)

nn (scarce) 11 22 33 75 110 145

HUCK & YOGI WINTER SPORTS (TV)
Dell Publishing Co.: No. 1310, Mar, 1962 (Hanna-Barbara) (one-shot)

Four Color 1310 10 20 30 70 100 130

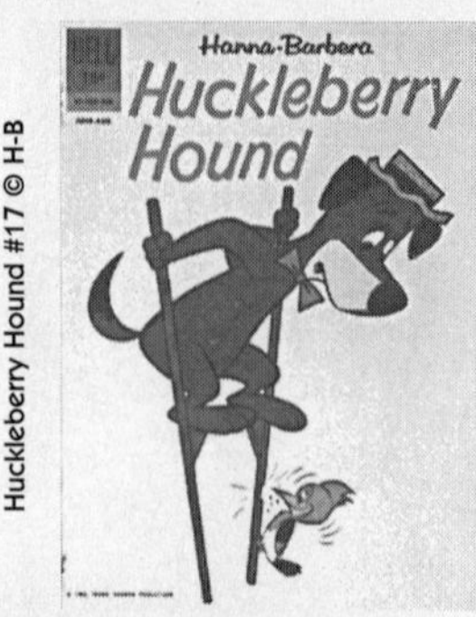

Huckleberry Hound #17 © H-B

Hulk: Nightmerica #1 © MAR

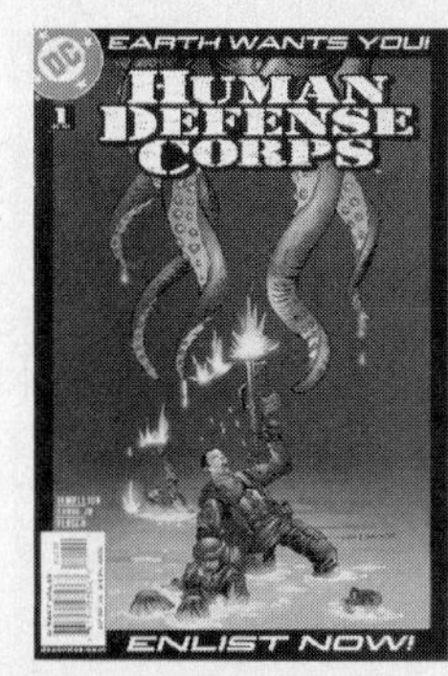

Human Defense Corps #1 © DC

GD VG FN VF VF/NM NM-
2.0 4.0 6.0 8.0 9.0 9.2

GD VG FN VF VF/NM NM-
2.0 4.0 6.0 8.0 9.0 9.2

HUCK FINN (See The New Adventures of... & Power Record Comics)

HUCKLEBERRY FINN (Movie)
Dell Publishing Co.: No. 1114, July, 1960

Four Color 1114-Photo-c 6 12 18 43 59 75

HUCKLEBERRY HOUND (See Dell Giant #31,44, Golden Picture Story Book, Kite Fun Book, March of Comics #199, 214, 235, Spotlight #1 & Whitman Comic Books)

HUCKLEBERRY HOUND (TV)
Dell/Gold Key No. 18 (10/62) on: No. 990, 5-7/59 - No. 43, 10/70 (Hanna-Barbera)

Four Color 990(#1)-1st app. Huckleberry Hound, Yogi Bear, & Pixie & Dixie & Mr. Jinks
13 26 39 92 141 190
Four Color 1050,1054 (12/59) 9 18 27 65 93 120
3(1-2/60) - 7 (9-10/60), Four Color 1141 (10/60) 9 18 27 63 89 115
8-10 7 14 21 51 71 90
11,13-17 (6-8/62) 6 12 18 38 52 65
12-1st Hokey Wolf & Ding-a-Ling 6 12 18 43 59 75
18,19 (84pgs.; 18-20 titled ...Chuckleberry Tales) 9 18 27 63 89 115
20-Titled Chuckleberry Tales 5 10 15 36 48 60
21-30: 28-30-Reprints 4 8 12 28 38 48
31-43: 31,32,35,37-43-Reprints 4 8 12 22 30 38

HUCKLEBERRY HOUND (TV)
Charlton Comics: Nov, 1970 - No. 8, Jan, 1972 (Hanna-Barbera)

1 6 12 18 40 55 70
2-8 3 7 10 21 28 35

HUEY, DEWEY, & LOUIE (See Donald Duck, 1938 for 1st app. Also see Mickey Mouse Magazine V4#2, V5#7 & Walt Disney's Junior Woodchucks Limited Series)

HUEY, DEWEY, & LOUIE BACK TO SCHOOL (See Dell Giant #22, 35, 49 & Dell Giants)

HUEY, DEWEY, AND LOUIE JUNIOR WOODCHUCKS (Disney)
Gold Key No. 1-61/Whitman No. 62 on: Aug, 1966 - No. 81, July, 1984
(See Walt Disney's Comics & Stories #125)

1 7 14 21 46 63 80
2,3(12/68) 4 8 12 27 36 45
4,5(4/70)-r/two WDC&S D.Duck stories by Barks 4 8 12 24 32 40
6-17 3 7 10 21 28 35
18,27-30 3 6 9 16 21 26
19-23,25-New storyboarded scripts by Barks, 13-25 pgs. per issue
4 8 12 22 30 38
24,26: 26-r/Barks Donald Duck WDC&S stories 3 6 9 18 24 30
31-57,60,61: 35,41-r/Barks J.W. scripts 2 4 6 9 11 14
58,59: 58-r/Barks Donald Duck WDC&S stories 2 4 6 10 13 16
62-64 (Whitman) 2 4 6 10 13 16
65-(9/80), 66 (Pre-pack? scarce) 3 6 9 19 25 32
67 (1/81),68 2 4 6 12 16 20
69-74: 72(2/82), 73(2-3/82), 74(3/82) 2 4 6 11 14 18
75-81 (all #90183; pre-pack; nd, nd code; scarce): 75(4/83), 76(5/83), 77(7/83), 78(8/83), 79(4/84), 80(5/84), 81(7/84) 2 4 6 14 18 22

HUGGA BUNCH (TV)
Marvel Comics (Star Comics): Oct, 1986 - No. 6, Aug, 1987

1-6 4.00

HULK (Magazine)(Formerly The Rampaging Hulk)(Also see The Incredible Hulk)
Marvel Comics: No. 10, Aug., 1978 - No. 27, June, 1981 ($1.50)

10-18: 10-Bill Bixby interview. 11-Moon Knight begins. 12-15,17,18-Moon Knight stories. 12-Lou Ferrigno interview. 2 4 6 8 10 12
19-27: 20-Moon Knight story. 23-Last full color issue; Banner is attacked. 24-Part color, Lou Ferrigno interview. 25-Part color. 26,27-are B&W
1 2 3 5 6 8

NOTE: #10-20 have fragile spines which split easily. ***Alcala*** *a(i)-15, 17-20, 22, 24-27.* ***Buscema*** *a-23; c-26.* ***Chaykin*** *a-21-25.* ***Colan*** *a(p)-11, 19, 24-27.* ***Jusko*** *painted c-12.* ***Nebres*** *a-16.* ***Severin*** *a-19i. Moon Knight by* ***Sienkiewicz*** *in 13-15, 17, 18, 20.* ***Simonson*** *a-27; c-23. Dominic Fortune appears in #21-24.*

HULK (Becomes Incredible Hulk Vol. 2 with issue #12)
Marvel Comics: Apr, 1999 - No. 11, Feb, 2000 ($2.99/$1.99)

1-($2.99) Byrne-s/Garney-a 5.00
1-Variant-c 9.00
1-DFE Remarked-c 50.00
1-Gold foil variant 10.00
2-7-($1.99): 2-Two covers. 5-Art by Jurgens, Buscema & Texeira. 7-Avengers app. 4.00
8-Hulk battles Wolverine 7.00
9-11: 11-She-Hulk app. 3.00
1999 Annual ($3.50) Chapter One story; Byrne-s/Weeks-a 3.50
Hulk Vs. The Thing (12/99, $3.99, TPB) reprints their notable battles 4.00

HULK & THING: HARD KNOCKS
Marvel Comics: Nov, 2004 - No. 4, Feb, 2005 ($3.50, limited series)

1-3-Bruce Jones-s/Jae Lee-a/c 3.50

HULK: FUTURE IMPERFECT
Marvel Comics: Jan, 1993 - No. 2, Dec, 1992 (In error) ($5.95, 52 pgs., squarebound, limited series)

1,2: Embossed-c; Peter David story & George Perez-c/a. 1-1st app. Maestro.
1 2 3 5 6 8

HULK: GRAY
Marvel Comics: Dec, 2003 - No. 6, Apr, 2004 ($3.50, limited series)

1-6-Hulk's origin & early days; Loeb-s/Sale-a/c 3.50
HC (2004, $21.99, with dust jacket) oversized r/#1-6 22.00

HULK: NIGHTMERICA
Marvel Comics: Aug, 2003 - No. 6, May, 2004 ($2.99, limited series)

1-6-Brian Ashmore painted-a/c 3.00

HULK/ PITT
Marvel Comics: 1997 ($5.99, one-shot)

1-David-s/Keown-c/a 6.00

HULK SMASH
Marvel Comics: Mar, 2001 - No. 2, Apr, 2001 ($2.99, limited series)

1,2-Ennis-s/McCrea & Janson-a/Nowlan painted-c 3.00

HULK: THE MOVIE
Marvel Comics

...Adaptation (8/03, $3.50) Bruce Jones-s/Bagley-a/Keown-c 3.50
TPB (2003, $12.99) r/Adaptation, Ultimates #5, Inc. Hulk #34, Ult. Marvel Team-Up #2&3 13.00

HULK 2099
Marvel Comics: Dec, 1994 - No. 10, Sept, 1995 ($1.50/$1.95)

1-($2.50)-Green foil-c 3.00
2-10: 2-A. Kubert-c 2.25

HULK/WOLVERINE: 6 HOURS
Marvel Comics: Mar, 2003 - No. 4, May, 2003 ($2.99, limited series)

1-4-Bruce Jones-s/Scott Kolins-a; Bisley-c 3.00
Hulk Legends Vol. 1: Hulk/Wolverine: 6 Hours (2003, $13.99, TPB) r/#1-4 & 1st Wolverine app. from Incredible Hulk #181 14.00

HUMAN DEFENSE CORPS
DC Comics: Jul, 2003 - No. 6, Dec, 2003 ($2.50, limited series)

1-6-Ty Templeton-s/Sauve, Jr & Vlasco-a. 1-Lois Lane app. 2.50

HUMAN FLY
I.W. Enterprises/Super: 1963 - 1964 (Reprints)

I.W. Reprint #1-Reprints Blue Beetle #44('46) 2 4 6 14 18 22
Super Reprint #10-R/Blue Beetle #46('47) 2 4 6 14 18 22

HUMAN FLY, THE
Marvel Comics Group: Sept, 1977 - No. 19, Mar, 1979

1,2,9,19: 1,2-(Regular 30¢-c). 1-Origin; Spider-Man x-over. 2-Ghost Rider app. 9-Daredevil x-over; Byrne-c(p). 19-Last issue 1 2 3 5 6 8
1,2-(35¢-c, limited distribution) 2 4 6 8 10 12
3-8,10-18 4.00

NOTE: ***Austin*** *c-4i, 9i.* ***Elias*** *a-1, 3p, 4p, 7p, 10-12p, 15p, 18p, 19p.* ***Layton*** *c-19.*

HUMANKIND
Image Comics (Top Cow): Sept, 2004 - No. 5 ($2.99, limited series)

1-3-Tony Daniel-a. 1-Three covers by Baniel, Silvestri, and Land 3.00

HUMAN TARGET
DC Comics (Vertigo): Apr, 1999 - No. 4, July, 1999 ($2.95, limited series)

1-4-Milligan-s/Bradstreet-c/Biuković-a 3.00
TPB (2000, $12.95) new Bradstreet-c 13.00

HUMAN TARGET
DC Comics (Vertigo): Oct, 2003 - Present ($2.95)

1-17: 1-5-Milligan-s/Pulido-a/c. 6-Chiang-a 3.00
...: Living in Amerika TPB (2004, $14.95) r/#6-10; Chiang sketch pages 15.00
...: Strike Zones TPB (2004, $9.95) r/#1-5 10.00

HUMAN TARGET: FINAL CUT
DC Comics (Vertigo): 2002 ($29.95/$19.95, graphic novel)

Hardcover (2002, $29.95) Milligan-s/Pulido-a/c 30.00
Softcover (2003, $19.95) 20.00

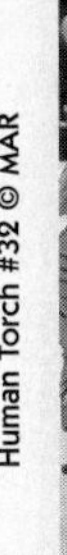
Human Torch #32 © MAR

Humphrey #18 © HARV

Huntress #17 © DC

	GD 2.0	VG 4.0	FN 6.0	VF 8.0	VF/NM 9.0	NM- 9.2

HUMAN TARGET SPECIAL (TV)
DC Comics: Nov, 1991 ($2.00, 52 pgs., one-shot)

1 — 3.00

HUMAN TORCH, THE (Red Raven #1)(See All-Select, All Winners, Marvel Mystery, Men's Adventures, Mystic Comics (2nd series), Sub-Mariner, USA & Young Men)
Timely/Marvel Comics (TP 2,3/TCI 4-9/SePI 10/SnPC 11-25/CnPC 26-35/Atlas Comics (CPC 36-38)): No. 2, Fall, 1940 - No. 15, Spring, 1944; No. 16, Fall, 1944 - No. 35, Mar, 1949 (Becomes Love Tales #36 on); No. 36, April, 1954 - No. 38, Aug, 1954

	GD	VG	FN	VF	VF/NM	NM-
2(#1)-Intro & Origin Toro; The Falcon, The Fiery Mask, Mantor the Magician, & Microman only app.; Human Torch by Burgos, Sub-Mariner by Everett begin (origin of each in text)	2875	5750	8625	21,600	35,800	50,000
3(#2)-40 pg. H.T. story; H.T. & S.M. battle over who is best artist in text-Everett or Burgos	516	1032	1548	3612	5806	8000
4(#3)-Origin The Patriot in text; last Everett Sub-Mariner; Sid Greene-a	423	846	1269	2837	4569	6300
5(#4)-The Patriot app; Angel x-over in Sub-Mariner (Summer, 1941); 1st Nazi war-c this title	345	690	1035	2243	3622	5000
5-Human Torch battles Sub-Mariner (Fall, '41); 60 pg. story	516	1032	1548	3612	5806	8000
6,9	238	476	714	1488	2294	3100
7-1st Japanese war-c	246	492	738	1538	2369	3200
8-Human Torch battles Sub-Mariner; 52 pg. story; Wolverton-a, 1 pg.	345	690	1035	2243	3622	5000
10-Human Torch battles Sub-Mariner, 45 pg. story; Wolverton-a, 1 pg.	300	600	900	1892	2946	4000
11,13-15: 14-1st Atlas Globe logo (Winter, 1943-44; see All Winners #11 also)	185	370	555	1156	1778	2400
12-Classic-c	300	600	900	1934	3117	4300
16-20: 20-Last War issue	131	262	393	819	1260	1700
21,22,24-30: 27-2nd app. (1st-c) Asbestos Lady (see Capt. America Comics #63 for 1st app.)	119	238	357	744	1147	1550
23 (Sum/46)-Becomes Junior Miss 24? Classic Schomburg Robot-c	138	276	414	863	1332	1800
31,32: 31-Namora x-over in Sub-Mariner (also #30); last Toro. 32-Sungirl, Namora app.; Sungirl-c	100	200	300	625	963	1300
33-Capt. America x-over	106	212	318	663	1019	1375
34-Sungirl solo	92	184	276	575	888	1200
35-Captain America & Sungirl app. (1949)	100	200	300	625	963	1300
36-38(1954)-Sub-Mariner in all	89	178	267	556	853	1150

NOTE: ***Ayers*** *Human Torch in 36(3).* ***Brodsky*** *c-25, 31-33?, 37, 38.* ***Burgos*** *c-36.* ***Everett*** *a-1-3, 27, 28, 30, 37, 38.* ***Powell*** *a-36(Sub-Mariner).* ***Schomburg*** *c-1-3, 5-8, 10-23.* ***Sekowsky*** *c-28, 34?, 35?* ***Shores*** *c-24, 26, 27, 29, 30.* ***Mickey Spillane*** *text 4-6. Bondage c-2, 12, 19.*

HUMAN TORCH, THE (Also see Avengers West Coast, Fantastic Four, The Invaders, Saga of the Original... & Strange Tales #101)
Marvel Comics Group: Sept, 1974 - No. 8, Nov, 1975

	GD	VG	FN	VF	VF/NM	NM-
1: 1-8-r/stories from Strange Tales #101-108	2	4	6	12	16	20
2-8: 1st H.T. title since G.A. 7-vs. Sub-Mariner	2	4	6	8	10	12

NOTE: *Golden Age & Silver Age Human Torch-r #1-8.* ***Ayers*** *r-6, 7.* ***Kirby/Ayers*** *r-1-5, 8.*

HUMAN TORCH (From the Fantastic Four)
Marvel Comics: June, 2003 - No. 12, Jun, 2004 ($2.50/$2.99)

1-7-Skottie Young-c/a; Karl Kesel-s — 2.50
8-12-($2.99) 8,10-Dodd-a. 9-Young-a. 11-Porter-a. 12-Medina-a — 3.00

HUMBUG (Satire by Harvey Kurtzman)
Humbug Publications: Aug, 1957 - No. 9, May, 1958; No. 10, June, 1958; No. 11, Oct, 1958

	GD	VG	FN	VF	VF/NM	NM-
1-Wood-a (intro pgs. only)	30	60	90	170	245	320
2	15	30	45	83	117	150
3-9: 8-Elvis in Jailbreak Rock	12	24	36	71	98	125
10,11-Magazine format. 10-Photo-c	16	32	48	92	131	170
Bound Volume(#1-9)(extremely rare)	67	134	201	419	647	875

NOTE: ***Davis*** *a-1-11.* ***Elder*** *a-2-4, 6-9, 11.* ***Heath*** *a-2, 4-8, 10.* ***Jaffee*** *a-2, 4-9.* ***Kurtzman*** *a-11.*

HUMDINGER (Becomes White Rider and Super Horse #3 on?)
Novelty Press/Premium Group: May-June, 1946 - V2#2, July-Aug, 1947

	GD	VG	FN	VF	VF/NM	NM-
1-Jerkwater Line, Mickey Starlight by Don Rico, Dink begin	36	72	108	204	297	390
2	16	32	48	89	127	165
3-6, V2#1,2	11	22	33	64	87	110

HUMONGOUS MAN
Alternative Press (Ikon Press): Sept, 1997 -No. 3 ($2.25, B&W)

1-3-Stepp & Harrison-c/s/a. — 2.25

HUMOR (See All Humor Comics)

HUMPHREY COMICS (Joe Palooka Presents...; also see Joe Palooka)
Harvey Publications: Oct, 1948 - No. 22, Apr, 1952

	GD	VG	FN	VF	VF/NM	NM-
1-Joe Palooka's pal (r); (52 pgs.)-Powell-a	14	28	42	79	110	140
2,3: Powell-a	8	16	24	48	58	70
4-Boy Heroes app.; Powell-a	9	18	27	51	62	75
5-8,10: 5,6-Powell-a. 7-Little Dot app.	7	14	21	37	46	55
9-Origin Humphrey	8	16	24	46	58	70
11-22	7	14	21	35	43	50

HUNCHBACK OF NOTRE DAME, THE
Dell Publishing Co.: No. 854, Oct, 1957 (one shot)

	GD	VG	FN	VF	VF/NM	NM-
Four Color 854-Movie, photo-c	14	28	42	97	149	200

HUNGER DOGS, THE (See DC Graphic Novel #4)

HUNK
Charlton Comics: Aug, 1961 - No. 11, 1963

	GD	VG	FN	VF	VF/NM	NM-
1	4	8	12	29	40	50
2-11	3	6	9	16	20	25

HUNTED (Formerly My Love Memoirs)
Fox Features Syndicate: No. 13, July, 1950; No. 2, Sept, 1950

	GD	VG	FN	VF	VF/NM	NM-
13(#1)-Used in **SOTI**, pg. 42 & illo. "Treating police contemptuously" (lower left); Hollingsworth bondage-c	36	72	108	204	297	390
2	16	32	48	89	127	165

HUNTER-KILLER
Image Comics (Top Cow): Nov, 2004 - Present

0-(11/04, 25¢) Prelude with Silvestri sketch page and Waid afterword — 2.25

HUNTER'S HEART
DC Comics: June, 1995 - No. 3, Aug, 1995 ($5.95, B&W, limited series)

1-3 — 6.00

HUNTER: THE AGE OF MAGIC (See Books of Magic)
DC Comics (Vertigo): Sept, 2001 - No. 25, Sept, 2003 ($2.50/$2.75)

1-25: Horrocks-s/Case-a. 1-8-Bolton-c. 14-Begin $2.75-c. 19-Bachalo-c — 2.75

HUNTRESS, THE (See All-Star Comics #69, Batman Family, Brave & the Bold #62, DC Super Stars #17, Detective #652, Infinity, Inc. #1, Sensation Comics #68 & Wonder Woman #271)
DC Comics: Apr, 1989 - No. 19, Oct, 1990 ($1.00, mature)

1-16: Staton-c/a(p) in all — 2.50
17-19-Batman-c/stories — 3.00

HUNTRESS, THE
DC Comics: June, 1994 - No. 4, Sept, 1994 ($1.50, limited series)

1-4-Netzer-c/a: 2-Batman app. — 2.25

HURRICANE COMICS
Cambridge House: 1945 (52 pgs.)

	GD	VG	FN	VF	VF/NM	NM-
1-(Humor, funny animal)	24	48	72	138	199	260

HYBRIDS
Continunity Comics: Jan, 1994 ($2.50, one-shot)

1-Neal Adams-c(p) & part-a(i); embossed-c. — 3.50

HYBRIDS DEATHWATCH 2000
Continuity Comics: Apr, 1993 - No. 3, Aug, 1993 ($2.50)

0-(Giveaway)-Foil-c; Neal Adams-c(i) & plots (also #1,2) — 3.50
1-3: 1-Polybagged w/card; die-cut-c. 2-Thermal-c. 3-Polybagged w/card; indestructible-c; Adams plot — 3.00

HYBRIDS ORIGIN
Continunity Comics: 1993 - No. 5, Jan, 1994 ($2.50)

1-5: 2,3-Neal Adams-c. 4,5-Valeria the She-Bat app. Adams-c(i) — 3.25

HYDE
IDW Publ.: Oct, 2004 ($7.49, one-shot)

1-Steve Niles-s/Nick Stakal — 7.50

HYDE-25
Harris Publications: Apr, 1995 ($2.95, one-shot)

0-coupon for poster; r/Vampirella's 1st app. — 3.00

HYDROMAN (See Heroic Comics)

HYPERKIND (See Razorline)
Marvel Comics: Sept, 1993 - No. 9, May, 1994 ($1.75/$1.95)

1-($2.50)-Foil embossed-c; by Clive Barker — 3.00
2-9 — 2.25

iCandy #2 © DC

Identity Crisis #1 © DC

I Feel Sick #1 © Jhonen Vasquez

	GD 2.0	VG 4.0	FN 6.0	VF 8.0	VF/NM 9.0	NM- 9.2

HYPERKIND UNLEASED
Marvel Comics: Aug, 1994 ($2.95, 52 pgs., one-shot)

	GD	VG	FN	VF	VF/NM	NM-
1						3.00

HYPER MYSTERY COMICS
Hyper Publications: May, 1940 - No. 2, June, 1940 (68 pgs.)

	GD	VG	FN	VF	VF/NM	NM-
1-Hyper, the Phenomenal begins; Calkins-a	208	416	624	1300	2000	2700
2	106	212	318	663	1019	1375

HYPERSONIC
Dark Horse Comics: Nov, 1997 - No. 4, Feb, 1998 ($2.95, limited series)

	GD	VG	FN	VF	VF/NM	NM-
1-4: Abnett & White/Erskine-a						3.00

I AIM AT THE STARS (Movie)
Dell Publishing Co.: No. 1148, Nov-Jan/1960-61 (one-shot)

	GD	VG	FN	VF	VF/NM	NM-
Four Color 1148-The Werner Von Braun Sty-photo-c	8	16	24	58	82	105

I AM COYOTE (See Eclipse Graphic Album Series & Eclipse Magazine #2)

I AM LEGEND
Eclipse Books: 1991 - No. 4, 1991 ($5.95, B&W, squarebound, 68 pgs.)

	GD	VG	FN	VF	VF/NM	NM-
1-4: Based on 1954 novel by Richard Matheson						6.00

IBIS, THE INVINCIBLE (See Fawcett Miniatures, Mighty Midget & Whiz)
Fawcett Publications: 1942 (Fall?); #2, Mar.,1943; #3, Wint, 1945 - #5, Fall, 1946; #6, Spring, 1948

	GD	VG	FN	VF	VF/NM	NM-
1-Origin Ibis; Raboy-c; on sale 1/2/43	215	430	645	1344	2072	2800
2-Bondage-c (on sale 2/5/43)	98	196	294	613	944	1275
3-Wolverton-a #3-6 (4 pgs. each)	75	150	225	469	722	975
4-6: 5-Bondage-c	50	100	150	305	465	625

NOTE: ***Mac Raboy** c(p)-3-5. **Schaffenberger** c-6.*

I–BOTS (See Isaac Asimov's I-BOTS)

iCANDY
DC Comics: Nov, 2003 - Present ($2.50, limited series)

	GD	VG	FN	VF	VF/NM	NM-
1-6: 1-3-Abnett & Lanning-s/Andrasofszky-a. 4-Udon-a						2.50

ICE AGE ON THE WORLD OF MAGIC: THE GATHERING (See Magic The Gathering)

ICE KING OF OZ, THE (See First Comics Graphic Novel #13)

ICEMAN (Also see The Champions & X-Men #94)
Marvel Comics Group: Dec, 1984 - No. 4, June, 1985 (Limited series)

	GD	VG	FN	VF	VF/NM	NM-
1,2,4: Zeck covers on all						3.50
3-The Defenders, Champions (Ghost Rider) & the original X-Men x-over						4.00

ICEMAN (X-Men)
Marvel Comics: Dec, 2001 - No. 4, Mar, 2002 ($2.50, limited series)

	GD	VG	FN	VF	VF/NM	NM-
1-4-Abnett & Lanning-s/Kerschl-a						3.00

ICON
DC Comics (Milestone): May, 1993 - No. 42, Feb, 1997($1.50/$1.75/$2.50)

	GD	VG	FN	VF	VF/NM	NM-
1-($2.95)-Collector's Edition polybagged w/poster & trading card (direct sale only)						3.00
1-24,30-42: 9-Simonson-c. 15,16-Worlds Collide Pt. 4 & 11. 15-Superboy app. 16-Superman-c/story. 40-Vs. Blood Syndicate						2.50
25-($2.95, 52 pgs.)						3.00

IDAHO
Dell Publishing Co.: June-Aug, 1963 - No. 8, July-Sept, 1965

	GD	VG	FN	VF	VF/NM	NM-
1	3	6	9	19	25	32
2-8: 5-7-Painted-c	2	4	6	10	13	16

IDEAL (... a Classical Comic) (2nd Series) (Love Romances No. 6 on)
Timely Comics: July, 1948 - No. 5, March, 1949 (Feature length stories)

	GD	VG	FN	VF	VF/NM	NM-
1-Antony & Cleopatra	37	74	111	209	305	400
2-The Corpses of Dr. Sacotti	31	62	93	175	253	330
3-Joan of Arc; used in **SOTI**, pg. 308 'Boer War'	29	58	87	164	237	310
4-Richard the Lion-hearted; titled "...the World's Greatest Comics"; The Witness app.	40	80	120	236	351	465
5-Ideal Love & Romance; change to love; photo-c	19	38	57	107	154	200

IDEAL COMICS (1st Series) (Willie Comics No. 5 on)
Timely Comics (MgPC): Fall, 1944 - No. 4, Spring, 1946

	GD	VG	FN	VF	VF/NM	NM-
1-Funny animal; Super Rabbit in all	24	48	72	138	199	260
2	14	28	42	79	110	140
3,4	13	26	39	74	102	130

IDEAL LOVE & ROMANCE (See Ideal, A Classical Comic)

IDEAL ROMANCE (Formerly Tender Romance)
Key Publ.: No. 3, April, 1954 - No. 8, Feb, 1955 (Diary Confessions No. 9 on)

	GD	VG	FN	VF	VF/NM	NM-
3-Bernard Baily-c	9	18	27	52	66	80
4-8: 4-6-B. Baily-c	6	12	18	33	41	48

IDEALS (Secret Stories)
Ideals Publ., USA: 1981 (68 pgs, graphic novels, 7x10", stiff-c)

	GD	VG	FN	VF	VF/NM	NM-
Captain America - Star Spangled Super Hero	3	7	10	21	28	35
Fantastic Four - Cosmic Quartet	3	7	10	21	28	35
Incredible Hulk - Gamma Powered Goliath	3	7	10	21	28	35
Spider-Man - World Famous Wall Crawler	4	8	12	27	36	45

IDENTITY CRISIS
DC Comics: Aug, 2004 - No. 7 ($3.95, limited series)

	GD	VG	FN	VF	VF/NM	NM-
1-Meltzer-s/Morales-a/Turner-c in all; Sue Dibny murdered						6.00
1-(Second printing) black-c with white sketch lines						4.00
1-Diamond Retailer Summit Edition						100.00
2-7: 2-4-Deathstroke app. 5-Firestorm, Jack Drake, Capt. Boomerang killed						4.00

IDENTITY DISC
Marvel Comics: Aug, 2004 - No. 5, Dec, 2004 ($2.99, limited series)

	GD	VG	FN	VF	VF/NM	NM-
1-5-Sabretooth, Bullseye, Sandman, Vulture, Deadpool, Juggernaut app.; Higgins-a						4.00

I DIE AT MIDNIGHT (Vertigo V2K)
DC Comics (Vertigo): 2000 ($6.95, prestige format, one-shot)

	GD	VG	FN	VF	VF/NM	NM-
1-Kyle Baker-s/a						7.00

IDOL
Marvel Comics (Epic Comics): 1992 - No. 3, 1992 ($2.95, mini-series, 52 pgs.)

	GD	VG	FN	VF	VF/NM	NM-
Book 1-3						3.00

I DREAM OF JEANNIE (TV)
Dell Publishing Co.: Apr, 1965 - No. 2, Dec, 1966 (Photo-c)

	GD	VG	FN	VF	VF/NM	NM-
1-Barbara Eden photo-c, each	17	34	51	121	186	250
2	13	26	39	90	138	185

I FEEL SICK
Slave Labor Graphics: Aug, 1999 - No. 2, May, 2000 ($3.95, limited series)

	GD	VG	FN	VF	VF/NM	NM-
1,2-Jhonen Vasquez-s/a						4.00

ILLUMINATOR
Marvel Comics/Nelson Publ.: 1993 - No. 4, 1993 ($4.99/$2.95, 52 pgs.)

	GD	VG	FN	VF	VF/NM	NM-
1,2-($4.99) Religious themed						5.00
3,4						3.00

ILLUSTRATED GAGS
United Features Syndicate: No. 16, 1940

	GD	VG	FN	VF	VF/NM	NM-
Single Series 16	17	34	51	95	135	175

ILLUSTRATED LIBRARY OF..., AN (See Classics Illustrated Giants)

ILLUSTRATED STORIES OF THE OPERAS
Baily (Bernard) Publ. Co.: 1943 (16 pgs.; B&W) (25 cents) (cover-B&W & red)

	GD	VG	FN	VF	VF/NM	NM-
nn-(Rare)(4 diff. issues)-Faust (part-r in Cisco Kid #1), nn-Aida, nn-Carmen; Baily-a, nn-Rigoleito	55	110	165	340	520	700

ILLUSTRATED STORY OF ROBIN HOOD & HIS MERRY MEN, THE (See Classics Giveaways, 12/44)

ILLUSTRATED TARZAN BOOK, THE (See Tarzan Book)

I LOVED (Formerly Rulah; Colossal Features Magazine No. 33 on)
Fox Features Syndicate: No. 28, July, 1949 - No. 32, Mar, 1950

	GD	VG	FN	VF	VF/NM	NM-
28	11	22	33	64	87	110
29-32	8	16	24	46	58	70

I LOVE LUCY
Eternity Comics : 6/90 - No. 6, 1990;V2#1, 11/90 - No. 6, 1991 ($2.95, B&W, mini-series)

	GD	VG	FN	VF	VF/NM	NM-
1-6: Reprints 1950s comic strip; photo-c						4.00
Book II #1-6: Reprints comic strip; photo-c						4.00
...In Full Color 1 (1991, $5.95, 52 pgs.)-Reprints I Love Lucy Comics #4,5,8,16; photo-c with embossed logo (2 versions exist, one with pgs. 18 & 19 reversed, the other corrected)	1	2	3	5	6	8
...In 3-D 1 (1991, $3.95, w/glasses)-Reprints I Love Lucy Comics; photo-c; bagged						6.00

I LOVE LUCY COMICS (TV) (Also see The Lucy Show)
Dell Publishing Co.: No. 535, Feb, 1954 - No. 35, Apr-June, 1962 (Lucille Ball photo-c on all)

	GD	VG	FN	VF	VF/NM	NM-
Four Color 535(#1)	50	100	150	400	625	850
Four Color 559(#2, 5/54)	32	64	96	240	370	500
3 (8-10/54) - 5	20	40	60	145	223	300
6-10	16	32	48	116	178	240
11-20	12	24	36	84	127	170
21-35	10	20	30	73	107	140

I Love You #1 © FAW

Impact #1 © WMG

Impulse/Atom Double Shot #1 © DC

GD 2.0 | VG 4.0 | FN 6.0 | VF 8.0 | VF/NM 9.0 | NM- 9.2

I LOVE NEW YORK
Linsner.com: 2002 ($2.95, B&W, one-shot)
1-Linsner-s/a; benefit book for the Sept. 11 charities 3.00

I LOVE YOU
Fawcett Publications: June, 1950 (one-shot)
1-Photo-c 15 30 45 83 117 150

I LOVE YOU (Formerly In Love)
Charlton Comics: No. 7, 9/55 - No. 121, 12/76; No. 122, 3/79 - No. 130, 5/80
7-Kirby-c; Powell-a 10 20 30 67 96 125
8-10 5 10 15 33 44 55
11-16,18-20 4 8 12 28 38 48
17-(68 pg. Giant) 8 16 24 53 74 95
21-50: 26-No Torres-a 3 7 10 21 28 35
51-59 3 6 9 16 20 24
60-(1/66)-Elvis Presley line drawn c/story 16 32 48 112 171 230
61-85 2 4 6 10 13 16
86-110 1 2 3 5 7 9
111-130 6.00

I, LUSIPHUR (Becomes Poison Elves, 1st series #8 on)
Mulehide Graphics: 1991 - No. 7, 1992 (B&W, magazine size)
1-Drew Hayes-c/a/scripts 4 8 12 27 36 45
2,4,5 2 4 6 12 16 20
3-Low print run 4 8 12 29 40 50
6,7 2 4 6 8 10 12
Poison Elves: Requiem For An Elf (Sirius Ent., 6/96, $14.95, trade paperback) -Reprints I, Lusiphur #1,2 as text, and 3-6 15.00

I'M A COP
Magazine Enterprises: 1954 - No. 3, 1954
1(A-1 #111)-Powell-c/a in all 16 32 48 89 127 165
2(A-1 #126), 3(A-1 #128) 10 20 30 56 73 90

IMAGE GRAPHIC NOVEL
Image Int.: 1984 ($6.95)(Advertised as Pacific Comics Graphic Novel #1)
1-The Seven Samuroid; Brunner-c/a 7.00

IMAGE INTRODUCES...
Image Comics: Oct, 2001 - Present ($2.95, anthology)
Believer #1-Schamberger-s/Thurman & Molder-a; Legend of Isis preview 3.00
Cryptopia #1-Raab-s/Quinn-a 3.00
Dog Soldiers #1-Hunter-s/Pachoumis-a 3.00
Legend of Isis #1-Valdez-a 3.00
Primate #1-Two covers; Beau Smith & Bernhardt-s/Byrd-a 3.00

IMAGES OF A DISTANT SOIL
Image Comics: Feb, 1997 ($2.95, B&W, one-shot)
1-Sketches by various 3.00

IMAGES OF SHADOWHAWK (Also see Shadowhawk)
Image Comics: Sept, 1993 - No. 3, 1994 ($1.95, limited series)
1-3: Keith Giffen-c/a; Trencher app. 2.25

IMAGE TWO-IN-ONE
Image Comics: Mar, 2001 ($2.95, 48 pgs., B&W, one-shot)
1-Two stories; 24 pages produced in 24 hrs. by Larsen and Eliopoulos 3.00

IMAGE ZERO
Image Comics: 1993 (Received through mail w/coupons from Image books)
0-Savage Dragon, StormWatch, Shadowhawk, Strykeforce; 1st app. Troll; 1st app. McFarlane's Freak, Blotch, Sweat and Bludd 5.00

I'M DICKENS - HE'S FENSTER (TV)
Dell Publishing Co.: May-July, 1963 - No. 2, Aug-Oct, 1963 (Photo-c)
1 7 14 21 46 63 80
2 6 12 18 40 55 70

I MET A HANDSOME COWBOY
Dell Publishing Co.: No. 324, Mar, 1951
Four Color 324 10 20 30 70 100 130

IMMORTAL DOCTOR FATE, THE
DC Comics: Jan, 1985 - No. 3, Mar, 1985 ($1.25, limited series)
1-3: 1-Simonson-c/a. 2-Giffen-c/a(p) 4.00

IMMORTALIS (See Mortigan Goth: Immortalis)

IMMORTAL II
Image Comics: Apr, 1997 - No. 5, Feb, 1998 ($2.50, B&W&Grey, limited series)
1-5: 1-B&W w/ color pull-out poster 2.50

IMPACT
E. C. Comics: Mar-Apr, 1955 - No. 5, Nov-Dec, 1955
1-Not code approved 17 34 51 128 184 240
2 10 20 30 75 113 150
3-5: 4-Crandall-a 8 16 24 60 93 125
NOTE: ***Crandall*** *a-1-4.* ***Davis*** *a-2-4; c-1-5.* ***Evans*** *a-1, 4, 5.* ***Ingels*** *a-in all.* ***Kamen*** *a-3.* ***Krigstein*** *a-1, 5.* ***Orlando*** *a-2, 5.*

IMPACT
Gemstone Publishing: Apr, 1999 - No. 5, Aug, 1999 ($2.50)
1-5-Reprints E.C. series 2.50

IMPACT CHRISTMAS SPECIAL
DC Comics (Impact Comics): 1991 ($2.50, 68 pgs.)
1-Gift of the Magi by Infantino/Rogers; The Black Hood, The Fly, The Jaguar, & The Shield stories 2.50

IMPOSSIBLE MAN SUMMER VACATION SPECTACULAR, THE
Marvel Comics: Aug, 1990; No. 2, Sept, 1991 ($2.00, 68 pgs.) (See Fantastic Four#11)
1-Spider Man, Quasar, Dr. Strange, She-Hulk, Punisher & Dr. Doom stories; Barry Crain, Guice-a; Art Adams-c(i) 2.50
2-Ka Zar & Thor app.; Cable Wolverine-c app. 2.50

IMPERIAL GUARD
Marvel Comics: Jan, 1997 - No. 3, Mar, 1997 ($1.95, limited series)
1-3: Augustyn-s in all; 1-Wraparound-c 2.25

IMPULSE (See Flash #92, 2nd Series for 1st app.) (Also see Young Justice)
DC Comics: Apr, 1995 - No. 89, Oct, 2002 ($1.50/$1.75/$1.95/$2.25/$2.50)
1-Mark Waid scripts & Humberto Ramos-c/a(p) begin; brief retelling of origin 6.00
2-12: 9-XS from Legion (Impulse's cousin) comes to the 20th Century, returns to the 30th Century in #12. 10-Dead Heat Pt. 3 (cont'd in Flash #110). 11-Dead Heat Pt. 4 (cont'd in Flash #111); Johnny Quick dies. 3.00
13-25: 14-Trickster app. 17-Zatanna-c/app. 21-Legion-c/app. 22-Jesse Quick-c/app. 24-Origin; Flash app. 25-Last Ramos-a. 2.50
26-55: 26-Rousseau-a begins. 28-1st new Arrowette (see World's Finest #113). 30-Genesis x-over. 47-Superman-c/app. 50-Batman & Joker-c/app. Van Sciver-a begins 2.50
56-62: 56-Young Justice app. 2.50
63-89: 63-Begin $2.50-c. 66-JLA,JSA-c/app. 68,69-Adam Strange, GL app. 77-Our Worlds at War x-over; Young Justice-c/app. 85-World Without Young Justice x-over pt. 2. 2.50
#1,000,000 (11/98) John Fox app. 2.50
Annual 1 (1996, $2.95)-Legends of the Dead Earth; Parobeck-a 4.00
Annual 2 (1997, $3.95)-Pulp Heroes stories; Orbik painted-c 4.00
.../Atom Double-Shot 1(2/98, $1.95) Jurgens-s/Mhan-a 3.00
...: Bart Saves the Universe (4/99, $5.95) JSA app. 6.00
...Plus(9/97, $2.95) w/Gross Out (Scare Tactics)-c/app. 3.00
...Reckless Youth (1997, $14.95, TPB) r/Flash #92-94, Impulse #1-6 15.00

INCAL, THE
Marvel Comics (Epic): Nov, 1988 - No. 3, Jan, 1989 ($10.95/$12.95, mature)
1-3: Moebius-c/a in all; sexual content 14.00

INCOMPLETE DEATH'S HEAD (Also see Death's Head)
Marvel Comics UK: Jan, 1993 - No. 12, Dec, 1993 ($1.75, limited series)
1-($2.95, 56 pgs.)-Die-cut cover 3.00
2-11: 2-Re-intro original Death's Head. 3-Original Death's Head vs. Dragon's Claws 2.25
12-($2.50, 52 pgs.)-She Hulk app. 2.50

INCREDIBLE HULK, THE (See Aurora, The Avengers #1, The Defenders #1, Giant-Size..., Hulk, Marvel Collectors Item Classics, Marvel Comics Presents #26, Marvel Fanfare, Marvel Treasury Edition, Power Record Comics, Rampaging Hulk, She-Hulk & 2099 Unlimited)

INCREDIBLE HULK, THE
Marvel Comics: May, 1962 - No. 6, Mar, 1963; No. 102, Apr, 1968 - No. 474, Mar, 1999
1-Origin & 1st app. (skin is grey colored); Kirby pencils begin, end #5 700 1400 2100 7700 16,350 25,000
2-1st green skinned Hulk; Kirby/Ditko-a 229 458 687 2004 3402 4800
3-Origin retold; 1st app. Ringmaster & Hercules (9/62) 147 294 441 1250 2025 2800
4,5: 4-Brief origin retold 137 274 411 1165 1883 2600
6-(3/63) Intro. Teen Brigade; all Ditko-a 170 340 510 1488 2444 3400
102-(4/68) (Formerly Tales to Astonish)-Origin retold; story continued from Tales to Astonish #101 24 48 72 170 260 350
103 10 20 30 73 107 140
104-Rhino app. 10 20 30 73 107 140

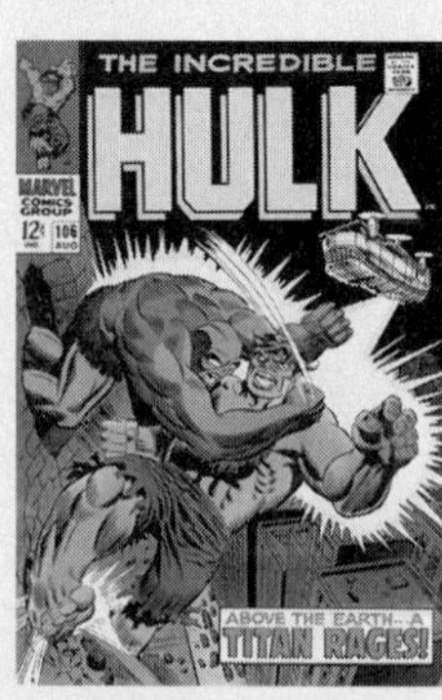

Incredible Hulk #106 © MAR

Incredible Hulk #158 © MAR

Incredible Hulk #474 © MAR

GD 2.0 VG 4.0 FN 6.0 VF 8.0 VF/NM 9.0 NM- 9.2

105-108: 105-1st Missing Link. 107-Mandarin app.(9/68). 108-Mandarin & Nick Fury app.
(10/68) 8 16 24 53 74 95
109,110: 109-Ka-Zar app. 6 12 18 43 59 75
111-117: 117-Last 12¢ issue 5 10 15 36 48 60
118-Hulk vs. Sub-Mariner 6 12 18 43 59 75
119-121,123-125 4 8 12 27 36 45
122-Hulk battles Thing (12/69) 7 14 21 51 71 90
126-1st Barbara Norriss (Valkyrie) 4 8 12 27 36 45
127-139: 131-Hulk vs. Iron Man; 1st Jim Wilson, Hulk's new sidekick. 136-1st Xeron,
The Star-Slayer 3 6 9 19 25 32
140-Written by Harlan Ellison; 1st Jarella, Hulk's love 3 7 10 21 28 35
140-2nd printing (1994) 2 4 6 8 10 12
141-1st app. Doc Samson (7/71) 10 20 30 67 96 125
142-144: 144-Last 15¢ issue 3 6 9 18 24 30
145-(52 pgs.)-Origin retold 4 8 12 29 40 50
146-160: 149-1st app. The Inheritor. 155-1st app. Shaper. 158-Warlock cameo(12/72)
3 6 9 16 20 25
161-The Mimic dies; Beast app. 3 7 10 21 28 35
162-1st app. The Wendigo (4/73); Beast app. 7 14 21 46 63 80
163-171,173-176: 163-1st app. The Gremlin. 164-1st Capt. Omen & Colonel John D. Armbruster. 166-1st Zzzax. 168-1st The Harpy; nudity panels of Betty Brant. 169-1st app. Bi-Beast.176-Warlock cameo (2 panels only); same date as Strange Tales #178 (6/74)
2 4 6 12 16 20
172-X-Men cameo; origin Juggernaut retold 4 8 12 27 36 45
177-1st actual death of Warlock (last panel only) 2 4 6 12 16 20
178-Rebirth of Warlock 2 4 6 12 16 20
179 2 4 6 10 12 15
180-(10/74)-1st brief app. Wolverine (last pg.) 17 34 51 121 186 250
181-(11/74)-1st full Wolverine story; Trimpe-a 80 160 240 640 970 1300
182-Wolverine cameo; see Giant-Size X-Men #1 for next app.; 1st Crackajack Jackson
11 22 33 77 114 150
183-199: 185-Death of Col. Armbruster. 195,196-Abomination app. 197,198-Man-Thing-c/s
2 4 6 8 10 12
198,199, 201,202-(30¢-c variants, lim. distribution) 2 4 6 11 14 18
200-(25¢-c) Silver Surfer app.; anniversary issue 3 6 9 19 25 32
200-(30¢-c variant, limited distribution)(6/76) 4 8 12 28 38 48
201-220: 201-Conan swipe-c/sty. 212-1st app. The Constrictor 6.00
212-216-(35¢-c variant, limited distribution) 1 2 3 5 7 9
221-249: 227-Original Avengers app. 232-Capt. America x-over from C.A. #230. 233-Marvel Man app. 234-(4/79)-1st app. Quasar (formerly called Marvel Man. 243-Cage app. 5.00
250-Giant size; Silver Surfer app. 2 4 6 8 10 12
251-277,280-299: 271-Rocket Raccoon app. 272-Sasquatch & Wendigo app.; Wolverine & Alpha Flight cameo in flashback. 282-284-She-Hulk app. 293-F.F. app. 4.00
278,279-Most Marvel characters app. (Wolverine in both). 279-X-Men & Alpha Flight cameos 5.00
300-(11/84, 52 pgs.)-Spider-Man app in new black costume on-c & 2 pg. cameo 6.00
301-313: 312-Origin Hulk retold 3.00
314-Byrne-c/a begins, ends #319 5.00
315-319: 319-Bruce Banner & Betty Talbot wed 4.00
320-323,325,327-329 3.00
324-1st app. Grey Hulk since #1 (c-swipe of #1) 2 4 6 8 10 12
326-Grey vs. Green Hulk 5.00
330,331: 330-1st McFarlane ish (4/87); Thunderbolt Ross dies. 331-Grey Hulk series begins
3 6 9 16 20 25
332-334,336-339: 336,337-X-Factor app. 2 4 6 9 11 14
335-No McFarlane-a 5.00
340-Hulk battles Wolverine by McFarlane 4 8 12 27 36 45
341-346: 345-($1.50, 52 pgs.). 346-Last McFarlane issue
1 2 3 5 6 8
347-349,351-358,360-366: 347-1st app. Marlo 3.00
350-Hulk/Thing battle 6.00
359-Wolverine app. (illusion only) 3.00
367,372,377: 367-1st Dale Keown-a on Hulk (3/90). 372-Green Hulk app.;Keown-c/a. 377-1st all new Hulk; fluorescent-c; Keown-c/a 1 2 3 5 6 8
368-371,373-376: 368-Sam Kieth-c/a, 1st app. Pantheon. 369,370-Dale Keown-c/a. 370,371-Original Defenders app. 371,373-376: Keown-c/a. 376-Green vs. Grey Hulk 5.00
377-Fluorescent green logo 2nd printing 3.00
378,380,389: No Keown-a. 380-Doc Samson app. 3.00
379,381-388,390-392-Keown-a. 385-Infinity Gauntlet x-over. 389-Last $1.00-c. 392-X-Factor app. 4.00
393-($2.50, 72 pgs.)-30th anniversary issue; green foil stamped-c; swipes-c to #1; has pin-ups of classic battles; Keown-c/a 5.00
393-2nd printing 2.50
394-399: 394-No Keown-c/a; intro Trauma. 395,396-Punisher-c/stories; Keown-c/a. 397-Begin "Ghost of the Past" 4-part sty; Keown c/a. 398-Last Keown-c/a 2.50
400-($2.50, 68 pgs.)-Holo-grafx foil-c & r/TTA #63 3.00
400-416: 400-2nd print-Diff. color foil-c. 402-Return of Doc Samson 2.50
417-424: 417-Begin $1.50-c; Rick Jones' bachelor party; Hulk returns from "Future Imperfect"; bound-in trading card sheet. 418-(Regular edition)-Rick Jones marries Marlo; includes cameo apps of various Marvel characters as well as DC's Death & Peter David. 420-Death of Jim Wilson 2.50
418-($2.50)-Collector's Edition w/gatefold die-cut-c 3.00
425 ($2.25, 52 pgs.) 2.50
425 ($3.50, 52 pgs.)-Holographic-c 4.00
426-434, 436-442: 426-Begin $1.95-c. 427, 428-Man-Thing app. 431,432-Abomination app. 434-Funeral for Nick Fury. 436-Ghosts of the Future begins, ends #440. 439-Hulk becomes Maestro, Avengers app. 440-Thor-c/app. 441,442-She-Hulk-c/app. 2.50
435 ($2.50)-Rhino-app; excerpt from "What Savage Beast" 3.00
443,446-448: 443-Begin $1.50-c; re-app. of Hulk. 446-w/card insert. 447-Begin Deodato-c/a(p) 2.50
444,445: 444-Cable-c/app.; "Onslaught". 445-"Onslaught" 4.00
447-Variant cover 4.00
449-1st app. Thunderbolts 6.00
450-($2.95)-Thunderbolts app.; 2 stories; Heroes Reborn-c/app. 5.00
451-470: 455-X-Men-c/app. 460-Bruce Banner returns. 464-Silver Surfer-c/app. 466,467: Betty dies. 467-Last Peter David-s/Kubert-a. 468-Casey-s/Pulido-a begin 2.50
471-473 3.00
474-($2.99) Last issue; Abomination app. 4.00
#(-1) Flashback (7/97) Kubert-a 2.50
Special 1 (10/68, 25¢, 68 pg.)-New 51 pg. story, Hulk battles The Inhumans (early app.); Steranko-c. 10 20 30 73 107 140
Special 2 (10/69, 25¢, 68 pg.)-Origin retold 6 12 18 40 55 70
Special 3,4: 3-(1/71, 25¢, 68 pg.). 4-(1/72, 52pgs.) 3 6 9 18 24 30
Annual 5 (1976) 2 4 6 10 13 16
Annual 6-8 ('77-79)-7-Byrne/Layton-c/a; Iceman & Angel app. in book-length story. 8-Book-length Sasquatch-c/sty 2 4 6 8 10 12
Annual 9,10: 9('80). 10 ('81) 6.00
Annual 11('82)-Doc Samson back-up by Miller(p)(5 pgs.); Spider-Man & Avengers app. Buckler-a(p) 6.00
Annual 12-17: 12 ('83). 13('84). 14('85). 15('86). 16('90, $2.00, 68 pgs.)-She-Hulk app. 17(1991, $2.00)-Origin retold 3.50
Annual 18-20 ('92-'94 68 pgs.)-18-Return of the Defenders, Pt. I; no Keown-c/a 19-Bagged w/card 3.00
...'97 ($2.99) Pollina-c 3.00
...And Wolverine 1 (10/86, $2.50)-r/1st app. (#180-181) 1 3 4 6 8 10
...: Beauty and the Behemoth ('98, $19.95, TPB) r/Bruce & Betty stories 20.00
...Ground Zero ('95, $12.95) r/#340-346 13.00
...Hercules Unleashed (10/96, $2.50) David-s/Deodato-c/a 2.50
.../Sub-Mariner '98 Annual ($2.99) 3.00
...Versus Quasimodo 1 (3/83, one-shot)-Based on Saturday morning cartoon 4.00
...Vs. Superman 1 (7/99, $5.95, one-shot)-painted-c by Rude 6.00
...Versus Venom 1 (4/94, $2.50, one-shot)-Embossed-c; red foil logo 3.00
Wizard #1 Ace Edition - Reprints #1 with new Andy Kubert-c 14.00
Wizard #181 Ace Edition - Reprints #181 with new Chen-c 14.00
(Also see titles listed under **Hulk**)

NOTE: ***Adkins*** *a-111-116i.* ***Austin*** *a(i)-350, 351, 353, 354; c-302i, 350i.* ***Ayers*** *a-3-5i.* ***Buckler*** *a-Annual 5; c-252.* ***John Buscema*** *c-202p.* ***Byrne*** *a-314-319p; c-314-316, 318, 319, 359, Annual 14i.* ***Colan*** *c-363.* ***Ditko*** *a-2i, 6, 249, Annual 2r(5), 3r, 9p; c-2i, 6, 235, 249.* ***Everett*** *c-133i.* ***Golden*** *c-248, 251.* ***Kane*** *c(p)-193, 194, 196, 198.* ***Dale Keown*** *a(p)-367, 369-377, 381-388, 390-393, 395-398; c-369-377p, 381, 382p, 384, 385, 386, 387p, 388, 390p, 391-393, 395p, 396, 397p, 398.* ***Kirby*** *a-1-5p, Special 2, 3p, Annual 5p; c-1-5, Annual 5.* ***McFarlane*** *a-330-334p, 336-339p, 340-343, 344-346p; c-330p, 340p, 341-343, 344p, 345, 346p.* ***Mignola*** *c-302, 305, 313.* ***Miller*** *c-258p, 261, 264, 268.* ***Mooney*** *a-230p, 287i, 288i.* ***Powell*** *a-Special 3r(2).* ***Romita*** *a-Annual 17p.* ***Severin*** *a(i)-108-110, 131-133, 141-151, 153-155; c(i)-109, 110, 132, 142, 144-155.* ***Simonson*** *c-283, 364-367.* ***Starlin*** *a-222p; c-217.* ***Staton*** *a(i)-187-189, 191-209.* ***Tuska*** *a-102i, 105i, 106i, 218p.* ***Williamson*** *a-310i; c-310i, 311i.* ***Wrightson*** *c-197.*

INCREDIBLE HULK (Vol. 2) (Formerly Hulk #1-11)
Marvel Comics: No. 12, Mar, 2000 - Present ($1.99-$3.50)

12-Jenkins-s/Garney & McKone-a 3.00
13,14-($1.99) Garney & Buscema-a 2.50
15-24,26-32: 15-Begin $2.25-c. 21-Maximum Security x-over. 24-($1.99-c) 2.25
25-($2.99) Hulk vs. The Abomination; Romita Jr.-a 3.00
33-($3.50, 100 pgs.) new Bogdanove-a/Priest-s; reprints 3.50
34-Bruce Jones-s begin; Romita Jr.-a 5.00
35-49,51-54: 35-39-Jones-s/Romita Jr.-a. 40-43-Weeks-a. 44-49-Immonen-a 3.00
50-($3.50) Deodato-a begins; Abomination app. thru #54 3.50
55-74: 55(25¢-c) Absorbing Man returns; Fernandez-a. 60-65-Deodato-a. 66-69-Braithwaite-a. 70-72-Deodato-a. 71-74-Iron Man app. 2.25
75,76-($3.50) The Leader app. 75-Robertson-a/Frank-c. 76-Braithwaite-a 3.50
Annual 2000 ($3.50) Texeira-a/Jenkins-s; Avengers app. 3.50

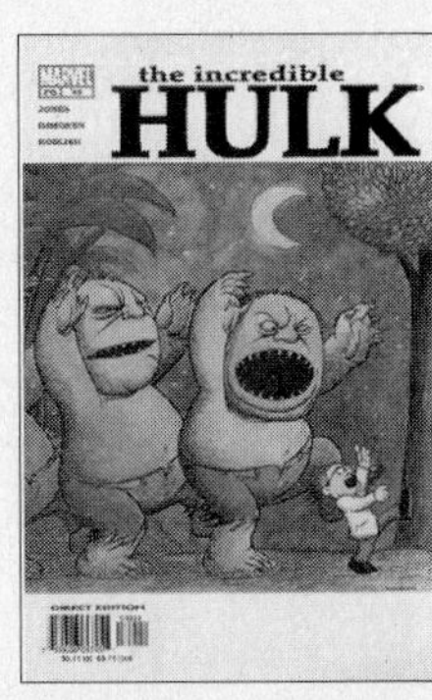
Incredible Hulk V2#49 © MAR

Indian Chief #23 © DELL

Indians #8 © FH

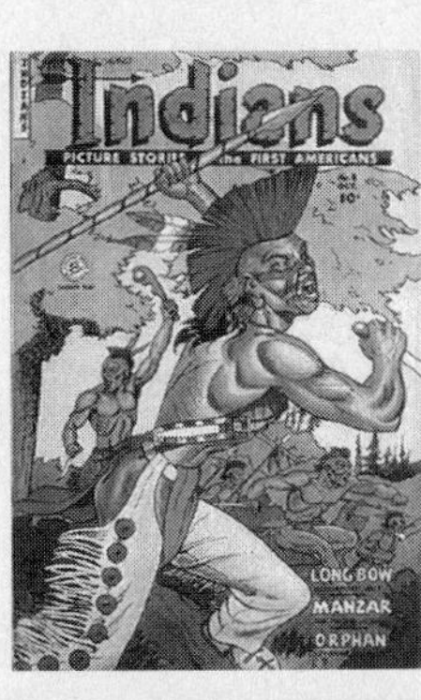

	GD	VG	FN	VF	VF/NM	NM-
	2.0	4.0	6.0	8.0	9.0	9.2

Annual 2001 ($2.99) Thor-c/app.; Larsen-s/Williams III-c 3.00
... : Boiling Point (Volume 2, 2002, $8.99, TPB) r/#40-43; Andrews-c 9.00
Dogs of War (6/01, $19.95, TPB) r/#12-20 20.00
... : Return of the Monster (7/02, $12.99, TPB) r/#34-39 13.00
...: The End (8/02, $5.95) David-s/Keown-a; Hulk in the far future 6.00
...Volume 1 HC (2002, $29.99, oversized) r/#34-43 & Startling Stories: Banner #1-4 30.00
...Volume 2 HC (2003, $29.99, oversized) r/#44-54; sketch pages and cover gallery 30.00
Volume 3: Transfer of Power (2003, $12.99, TPB) r/#44-49 13.00
Volume 4: Abominable (2003, $11.99, TPB) r/#50-54; Abomination app.; Deodato-a 12.00
Volume 5: Hide in Plain Sight (2003, $11.99, TPB) r/#55-59; Fernandez-a 12.00
Volume 6: Split Decisions (2004, $12.99, TPB) r/#60-65; Deodato-a 13.00
Volume 7: Dead Like Me (2004, $12.99, TPB) r/#66-69 & Hulk Smash #1&2 13.00
Volume 8: Big Things (2004, $17.99, TPB) r/#70-76; Iron Man app. 18.00

INCREDIBLE MR. LIMPET, THE (See Movie Classics)

INCREDIBLE SCIENCE FICTION (Formerly Weird Science-Fantasy)
E. C. Comics: No. 30, July-Aug, 1955 - No. 33, Jan-Feb, 1956

30,33: 33-Story-r/Weird Fantasy #18 38 76 114 285 418 550
31-Williamson/Krenkel-a, Wood-a(2) 39 78 117 293 429 565
32-Williamson/Krenkel-a 39 78 117 293 429 565
NOTE: *Davis a-30, 32, 33; c-30-32.* ***Krigstein*** *a-in all.* ***Orlando*** *a-30, 32, 33("Judgement Day" reprint).* ***Wood*** *a-30, 31, 33; c-33.*

INCREDIBLE SCIENCE FICTION (Formerly Weird Science-Fantasy)
Russ Cochran/Gemstone Publ.: No. 8, Aug, 1994 - No. 11, May, 1995 ($2.00)

8-11: Reprints #30-33 of E.C. series 2.50

INDEPENDENCE DAY (Movie)
Marvel Comics: No. 0, June, 1996 - No. 2, Aug, 1996 ($1.95, limited series)

0-Special Edition; photo-c 5.00
0-2 2.50

INDEPENDENT VOICES
Peregrine Entertainment: Sept, 1998; Sept, 1999 ($1.95/$2.95, B&W)

1-Sampler of Indy titles for CBLDF 2.25
2-(9/99, $2.95); 2nd printing-(5/00) 3.00

INDIANA JONES (Title series), **Dark Horse Comics**

--AND THE ARMS OF GOLD, 2/94 - 5/94 ($2.50) 1-4 2.50

--AND THE FATE OF ATLANTIS, 3/91 - 9/91 ($2.50) 1-4-Dorman painted-c on all; contain trading cards (#1 has a 2nd printing, 10/91) 2.50

--AND THE GOLDEN FLEECE, 6/94 - 7/94 ($2.50) 1,2 2.50

--AND THE IRON PHOENIX, 12/94 - 3/95 ($2.50) 1-4 2.50

INDIANA JONES AND THE LAST CRUSADE
Marvel Comics: 1989 - No. 4, 1989 ($1.00, limited series, movie adaptation)

1-4: Williamson-i assist 3.00
1-(1989, $2.95, B&W mag., 80 pgs.) 4.00

--AND THE SHRINE OF THE SEA DEVIL: Dark Horse, 9/94 ($2.50, one shot)
1-Gary Gianni-a 2.50

--AND THE SPEAR OF DESTINY: Dark Horse, 4/95 - 8/95 ($2.50) 1-4 2.50

--THUNDER IN THE ORIENT: Dark Horse, 9/93 - '94 ($2.50)
1-6: Dan Barry story & art in all; 1-Dorman painted-c 2.50

INDIANA JONES AND THE TEMPLE OF DOOM
Marvel Comics Group: Sept, 1984 - No. 3, Nov, 1984 (Movie adaptation)

1-3-r/Marvel Super Special; Guice-a 3.00

INDIAN BRAVES (Baffling Mysteries No. 5 on)
Ace Magazines: March, 1951 - No. 4, Sept, 1951

1-Green Arrowhead begins, ends #3 14 28 42 79 110 140
2 8 16 24 46 58 70
3,4 8 16 24 40 50 60
I.W. Reprint #1 (nd)-r/Indian Braves #4 2 4 6 10 13 16

INDIAN CHIEF (White Eagle...) (Formerly The Chief, Four Color 290)
Dell Publ. Co.: No. 3, July-Sept, 1951 - No. 33, Jan-Mar, 1959 (All painted-c)

3 5 10 15 36 48 60
4-11: 6-White Eagle app. 4 8 12 28 38 48
12-1st White Eagle(10-12/53)-Not same as earlier character
5 10 15 36 48 60
13-29 4 8 12 22 30 38
30-33-Buscema-a 4 8 12 24 32 40

INDIAN CHIEF (See March of Comics No. 94, 110, 127, 140, 159, 170, 187)

INDIAN FIGHTER, THE (Movie)
Dell Publishing Co.: No. 687, May, 1956 (one-shot)

Four Color 687-Kirk Douglas photo-c 9 18 27 63 89 115

INDIAN FIGHTER
Youthful Magazines: May, 1950 - No. 11, Jan, 1952

1 14 28 42 79 110 140
2-Wildey-a/c(bondage) 9 18 27 54 70 85
3-11: 3,4-Wildey-a 8 16 24 40 50 60
NOTE: ***Walter Johnson*** *c-1, 3, 4, 6.* ***Palais*** *a-10.* ***Stallman*** *a-7.* ***Wildey*** *a-2-4; c-2, 5.*

INDIAN LEGENDS OF THE NIAGARA (See American Graphics)

INDIANS
Fiction House Magazines (Wings Publ. Co.): Spring, 1950 - No. 17, Spr, 1953 (1-8: 52 pgs.)

1-Manzar The White Indian, Long Bow & Orphan of the Storm begin
30 60 90 170 245 320
2-Starlight begins 15 30 45 86 123 160
3-5: 5-17-Most-c by Whitman 13 26 39 74 102 130
6-10 11 22 33 64 87 110
11-17 10 20 30 58 77 95

INDIANS OF THE WILD WEST
I. W. Enterprises: Circa 1958? (no date) (Reprints)

9-Kinstler-c; Whitman-a; r/Indians #? 2 4 6 11 14 18

INDIANS ON THE WARPATH
St. John Publishing Co.: No date (Late 40s, early 50s) (132 pgs.)

nn-Matt Baker-c; contains St. John comics rebound. Many combinations possible
35 70 105 198 287 375

INDIAN TRIBES (See Famous Indian Tribes)

INDIAN WARRIORS (Formerly White Rider and Super Horse; becomes Western Crime Cases #9)
Star Publications: No. 7, June, 1951 - No. 8, Sept, 1951

7-White Rider & Superhorse continue; "Last of the Mohicans" serial begins;
L.B. Cole-c 19 38 57 107 154 200
8-L. B. Cole-c 18 36 54 100 143 185
3-D 1(12/53, 25¢)-Came w/glasses; L. B. Cole-c 39 78 117 222 324 425
Accepted Reprint(nn)(inside cover shows White Rider & Superhorse #11)-r/cover to #7;
origin White Rider &...; L. B. Cole-c 7 14 21 37 46 55
Accepted Reprint #8 (nd); L.B. Cole-c (r-cover to #8) 7 14 21 37 46 55

INDOORS-OUTDOORS (See Wisco)

INDOOR SPORTS
National Specials Co.: nd (6x9", 64 pgs., B&W-r, hard-c)

nn-By Tad 5 10 15 24 30 35

INDUSTRIAL GOTHIC
DC Comics (Vertigo): Dec, 1995 - No. 5, Apr, 1996 ($2.50, limited series)

1-5: Ted McKeever-c/a/scripts 2.50

INFANTRY
Devil's Due Publ.: Dec, 2004 - Present ($2.95)

1-Casey-s/Sauve-a; two covers 3.00

INFERIOR FIVE, THE (Inferior 5 #11, 12) (See Showcase #62, 63, 65)
National Periodical Publications (#1-10: 12¢): 3-4/67 - No. 10, 9-10/68; No. 11, 8-9/72 - No. 12, 10-11/72

1-(3-4/67)-Sekowsky-a(p); 4th app. 6 12 18 40 55 70
2-5: 2-Plastic Man, F.F. app. 4-Thor app. 3 7 10 21 28 35
6-9: 6-Stars DC staff 3 6 9 16 21 26
10-Superman x-over; F.F., Spider-Man & Sub-Mariner app.
3 6 9 19 25 32
11,12: Orlando-c/a; both r/Showcase #62,63 2 4 6 12 16 20

INFERNO
Caliber Comics: 1995 - No. 5 ($2.95, B&W)

1-5 3.00

INFERNO (See Legion of Super-Heroes)
DC Comics: Oct, 1997 - No. 4, Feb, 1998 ($2.50, limited series)

1-Immonen-s/c/a in all 4.00
2-4 3.00

INFERNO: HELLBOUND
Image Comics (Top Cow): Jan, 2002 - Present ($2.50/$2.99)

1,2: 1-Seven covers; Silvestri-a/Silvestri and Wohl-s 2.50
3-($2.99) Tan-a 3.00
#0 (7/02, $3.00) Tan-a 3.00

Infinity Gauntlet #3 © MAR

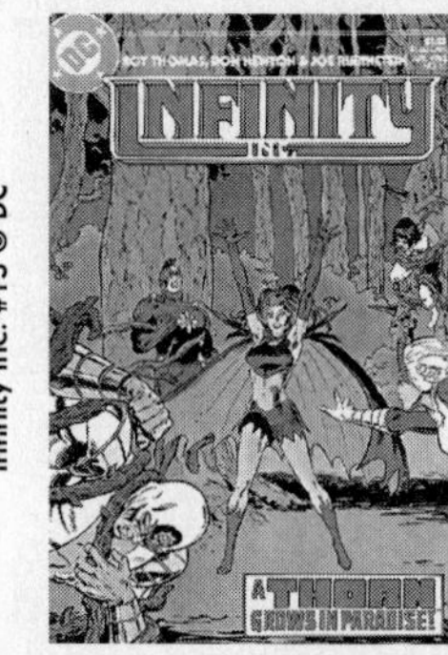

Infinity Inc. #13 © DC

Inhumans V6#1 © MAR

GD 2.0 VG 4.0 FN 6.0 VF 8.0 VF/NM 9.0 NM- 9.2

Wizard #0- Previews series; bagged with Wizard Top Cow Special mag 2.25

INFINITY ABYSS (Also see Marvel Universe: The End)
Marvel Comics: Aug, 2002 - No. 6 ($2.99, limited series)

1-5-Starlin-s/a; Thanos, Captain Marvel, Spider-Man, Dr. Strange app. 3.00
6-($3.50) 3.50
Thanos Vol. 2: Infinity Abyss TPB (2003, $17.99) r/ #1-6 18.00

INFINITY CRUSADE
Marvel Comics: June, 1993 - No. 6, Nov, 1993 ($2.50, limited series, 52 pgs.)

1-6: By Jim Starlin & Ron Lim 2.50

INFINITY GAUNTLET (The... #2 on; see Infinity Crusade, The Infinity War & Warlock & the Infinity Watch)
Marvel Comics: July, 1991 - No. 6, Dec, 1991 ($2.50, limited series)

1-6:Thanos-c/stories in all; Starlin scripts in all; 5,6-Ron Lim-c/a 3.00
TPB (4/99, $24.95) r/#1-6 25.00
NOTE: ***Lim*** *a-3p(part), 5p, 6p; c-5i, 6i.* ***Perez*** *a-1-3p, 4p(part); c-1(painted), 2-4, 5i, 6i.*

INFINITY, INC. (See All-Star Squadron #25)
DC Comics: Mar, 1984 - No. 53, Aug, 1988 ($1.25, Baxter paper, 36 pgs.)

1-Brainwave, Jr., Fury, The Huntress, Jade, Northwind, Nuklon, Obsidian, Power Girl, Silver Scarab & Star Spangled Kid begin 4.00
2-13,38-49,51-53: 2-Dr. Midnite, G.A. Flash, W. Woman, Dr. Fate, Hourman, Green Lantern, Wildcat app. 5-Nudity panels. 46,47-Millennium tie-ins 3.00
14-Todd McFarlane-a (5/85, 2nd full story) 1 2 3 6 8 9
15-37-McFarlane-a (20,23,24: 5 pgs. only; 33: 2 pgs.); 18-24-Crisis x-over. 21-Intro new Hourman & Dr. Midnight. 26-New Wildcat app. 31-Star Spangled Kid becomes Skyman. 32-Green Fury becomes Green Flame. 33-Origin Obsidian. 35-1st modern app. G.A. Fury 4.00
50 ($2.50, 52 pgs.) 3.00
Annual 1,2: 1(12/85)-Crisis x-over. 2('88, $2.00), Special 1 ('87, $1.50) 3.00
NOTE: ***Kubert*** *r-4.* ***McFarlane*** *a-14-37p, Annual 1p; c(p)-14-19, 22, 25, 26, 31-33, 37, Annual 1.* ***Newton*** *a-12p, 13p(last work 4/85).* ***Tuska*** *a-11p. JSA app. 3-10.*

INFINITY WAR, THE (Also see Infinity Gauntlet & Warlock and the Infinity...)
Marvel Comics: June, 1992 - No. 6, Nov, 1992 ($2.50, mini-series)

1-Starlin scripts, Lim-c/a(p), Thanos app. in all 2.50
2-6: All have wraparound gatefold covers 2.50

INFORMER, THE
Feature Television Productions: April, 1954 - No. 5, Dec, 1954

1-Sekowsky-a begins 12 24 36 71 98 125
2 9 18 27 51 62 75
3-5 8 16 24 43 54 65

IN HIS STEPS
Spire Christian Comics (Fleming H. Revell Co.): 1973, 1977 (39/49¢)

nn 1 3 4 6 8 11

INHUMANOIDS, THE (TV)
Marvel Comics (Star Comics): Jan, 1987 - No. 4, July 1987

1-4: Based on Hasbro toys 3.00

INHUMANS, THE (See Amazing Adventures, Fantastic Four #54 & Special #5, Incredible Hulk Special #1, Marvel Graphic Novel & Thor #146)
Marvel Comics Group: Oct, 1975 - No. 12, Aug, 1977

1: #1-4,6 are 25¢ issues 2 4 6 14 18 22
2-4-Peréz-a 1 3 4 6 8 10
5-12: 9-Reprints Amazing Adventures #1,2('70). 12-Hulk app. 1 2 3 5 7 9
4-(30¢-c variant, limited distribution)(4/76) Peréz-a 2 4 6 11 14 18
6-(30¢-c variant, limited distribution)(8/76) 2 4 6 11 14 18
11,12-(35¢-c variants, limited distribution) 2 4 6 11 14 18
Special 1(4/90, $1.50, 52 pgs.)-F.F. cameo 3.00
...: The Great Refuge (5/95, $2.95) 3.00
NOTE: ***Buckler*** *c-2-4p, 5.* ***Gil Kane*** *a-5-7p; c-1p, 7p, 8p.* ***Kirby*** *a-9r.* ***Mooney*** *a-11i.* ***Perez*** *a-1-4p, 8p.*

INHUMANS (Marvel Knights)
Marvel Comics: Nov, 1998 - No. 12, Oct, 1999 ($2.99, limited series)

1-Jae Lee-c/a; Paul Jenkins-s 10.00
1-($6.95) DF Edition; Jae Lee variant-c 7.00
2-Two covers by Lee and Darrow 4.00
3-12 3.00
TPB (10/00, $24.95) r/#1-12 25.00

INHUMANS (Volume 3)
Marvel Comics: Jun, 2000 - No. 4, Oct, 2000 ($2.99, limited series)

1-4-Ladronn-c/Pacheco & Marin-s. 1-3-Ladronn-a. 4-Lucas-a 3.00

INHUMANS (Volume 6)
Marvel Comics: Jun, 2003 - No. 12, Jun, 2004 ($2.50/$2.99)

1-12: 1-6-McKeever-s/Clark-a/JH Williams III-c. 7-Begin $2.99-c. 7,8-Teranishi-a 3.00

INHUMANS 2099
Marvel Comics: Nov, 2004 ($2.99, one-shot)

1-Kirkman-s/Rathburn-a/Pat Lee-c 3.00

INKY & DINKY (See Felix's Nephews...)

IN LOVE (...Magazine on-c; I Love You No. 7 on)
Mainline/Charlton No. 5 (5/55)-on: Aug-Sept, 1954 - No. 6, July, 1955 ('Adult Reading' on-c)

1-Simon & Kirby-a; book-length novel in all issues 40 80 120 230 335 440
2,3-S&K-a. 3-Last pre-code (12-1/54-55) 24 48 72 135 195 255
4-S&K-a.(Rare) 25 50 75 141 203 265
5-S&K-c only 11 22 33 64 87 110
6-No S&K-a 8 16 24 43 54 65

INNOVATION SPECTACULAR
Innovation Publishing: 1991 - No. 2, 1991 ($2.95, squarebound, 100 pgs.)

1,2: Contains rebound comics w/o covers 3.00

INNOVATION SUMMER FUN SPECIAL
Innovation Publishing: 1991 ($3.50, B&W/color, squarebound)

1-Contains rebound comics (Power Factory) 3.50

INSANE
Dark Horse Comics: Feb, 1988 - No. 2 ($1.75, B&W)

1,2: 1-X-Men, Godzilla parodies. 2-Concrete 2.25

INSANE CLOWN POSSE
Chaos Comics: June, 1999 - No. 3, Nov, 1999 ($2.95)

1-3-McCann-s 4.00
TPB ('00, $8.95) r/#1-3 9.00

INSANE CLOWN POSSE: THE PENDULUM
Chaos Comics: Jan, 2000 - No. 12, Dec, 2001 ($2.95)

1-12-($5.95) polybagged w/CD 6.00
...: Hallowicked 1 (11/01, $2.99) 3.00
...: Halls of Illusion 1 (6/02, $2.99) 3.00

IN SEARCH OF THE CASTAWAYS (See Movie Comics)

INSIDE CRIME (Formerly My Intimate Affair)
Fox Features Syndicate (Hero Books): No. 3, July, 1950 - No. 2, Sept, 1950

3-Wood-a (10 pgs.); L. B. Cole-c 30 60 90 170 245 320
2-Used in **SOTI**, pg. 182,183; r/Spook #24 23 46 69 130 188 245
nn(no publ. listed, nd) 10 20 30 58 77 95

INSPECTOR, THE (TV) (Also see The Pink Panther)
Gold Key: July, 1974 - No. 19, Feb, 1978

1 4 8 12 22 30 38
2-5 2 4 6 14 18 22
6-9 2 4 6 11 14 18
10-19: 11-Reprints 2 4 6 8 10 12

INSPECTOR GILL OF THE FISH POLICE (See Fish Police)

INSPECTOR WADE
David McKay Publications: No. 13, May, 1938

Feature Books 13 28 56 84 158 229 300

INSTANT PIANO
Dark Horse Comics: Aug, 1994 - No. 4, Feb, 1995 ($3.95, B&W, bimonthly, mature)

1-4 4.00

INTERFACE
Marvel Comics (Epic Comics): Dec, 1989 - No. 8, Dec, 1990 ($1.95, mature, coated paper)

1-8: Cont. from 1st ESPers series; painted-c/a 2.25
Espers: Interface TPB ('98, $16.95) r/#1-6 17.00

INTERNATIONAL COMICS (...Crime Patrol No. 6)
E. C. Comics: Spring, 1947 - No. 5, Nov-Dec, 1947

1-Schaffenberger-a begins, ends #4 60 120 180 375 575 775
2 43 86 129 262 401 540
3-5 40 80 120 236 351 465

INTERNATIONAL CRIME PATROL (Formerly International Comics #1-5; becomes Crime Patrol No. 7 on)
E. C. Comics: No. 6, Spring, 1948

6-Moon Girl app. 60 120 180 375 575 775

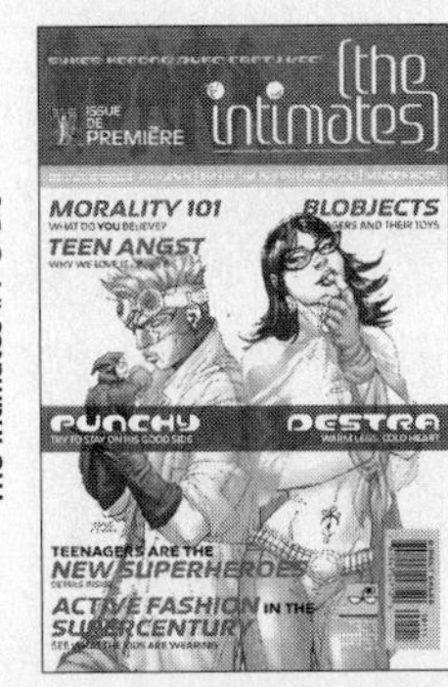

The Intimates #1 © DC

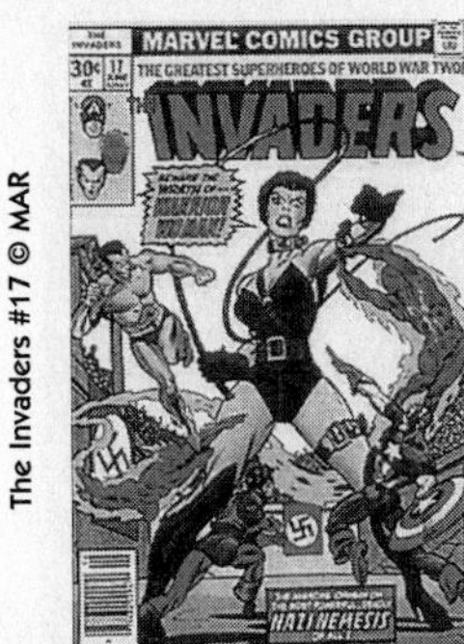

The Invaders #17 © MAR

The Invisibles (2nd) #12 © Grant Morrison

IN THE DAYS OF THE MOB (Magazine)
Hampshire Dist. Ltd. (National): Fall, 1971 (B&W)

	GD 2.0	VG 4.0	FN 6.0	VF 8.0	VF/NM 9.0	NM- 9.2
1-Kirby-a; John Dillinger wanted poster inside (1/2 value if poster is missing)	8	16	24	58	82	105

IN THE PRESENCE OF MINE ENEMIES
Spire Christian Comics/Fleming H. Revell Co.: 1973 (35/49¢)

	GD 2.0	VG 4.0	FN 6.0	VF 8.0	VF/NM 9.0	NM- 9.2
nn	1	3	4	6	8	11

IN THE SHADOW OF EDGAR ALLAN POE
DC Comics (Vertigo): 2002 (Graphic novel)

	GD 2.0	VG 4.0	FN 6.0	VF 8.0	VF/NM 9.0	NM- 9.2
Hardcover (2002, $24.95) Fuqua-s/Phillips and Parke photo-a						25.00
Softcover (2003, $17.95)						18.00

INTIMATE
Charlton Comics: Dec, 1957 - No. 3, May, 1958

	GD 2.0	VG 4.0	FN 6.0	VF 8.0	VF/NM 9.0	NM- 9.2
1	5	10	15	24	30	35
2,3	4	8	11	16	19	22

INTIMATE CONFESSIONS (See Fox Giants)

INTIMATE CONFESSIONS
Realistic Comics: July-Aug, 1951 - No. 7, Aug, 1952; No. 8, Mar, 1953 (All painted-c)

	GD 2.0	VG 4.0	FN 6.0	VF 8.0	VF/NM 9.0	NM- 9.2
1-Kinstler-c/a; c/Avon paperback #222	77	154	231	481	741	1000
2	22	44	66	123	177	230
3-c/Avon paperback #250; Kinstler-c/a	25	50	75	144	207	270
4-8: 4-c/Avon paperback #304; Kinstler-c. 6-c/Avon paperback #120. 8-c/Avon paperback #375; Kinstler-a	22	44	66	123	177	230

INTIMATE CONFESSIONS
I. W. Enterprises/Super Comics: 1964

	GD 2.0	VG 4.0	FN 6.0	VF 8.0	VF/NM 9.0	NM- 9.2
I.W. Reprint #9,10, Super Reprint #10,12,18	2	4	6	11	14	18

INTIMATE LOVE
Standard Comics: No. 5, 1950 - No. 28, Aug, 1954

	GD 2.0	VG 4.0	FN 6.0	VF 8.0	VF/NM 9.0	NM- 9.2
5-8: 6-8-Severin/Elder-a	9	18	27	52	66	80
9	7	14	21	35	43	50
10-Jane Russell, Robert Mitchum photo-c	11	22	33	64	87	110
11-18,20,23,25,27,28	6	12	18	31	38	45
19,21,22,24,26-Toth-a	8	16	24	40	50	60

NOTE: ***Celardo*** *a-8, 10.* ***Colletta*** *a-23.* ***Moreira*** *a-13(2). Photo-c-6, 7, 10, 12, 14, 15, 18-20, 24, 26, 27.*

INTIMATES, THE
DC Comics (WildStorm): Jan, 2005 - Present ($2.95)

	GD 2.0	VG 4.0	FN 6.0	VF 8.0	VF/NM 9.0	NM- 9.2
1,2-Joe Casey-s/Jim Lee-c/Lee and Giuseppe Camuncoli-a						3.00

INTIMATE SECRETS OF ROMANCE
Star Publications: Sept, 1953 - No. 2, Apr, 1954

	GD 2.0	VG 4.0	FN 6.0	VF 8.0	VF/NM 9.0	NM- 9.2
1,2-L. B. Cole-c	20	40	60	112	161	210

INTRIGUE
Quality Comics Group: Jan, 1955

	GD 2.0	VG 4.0	FN 6.0	VF 8.0	VF/NM 9.0	NM- 9.2
1-Horror; Jack Cole reprint/Web of Evil	33	66	99	190	275	360

INTRIGUE
Image Comics: Aug, 1999 - No. 3, Feb, 2000 ($2.50/$2.95)

	GD 2.0	VG 4.0	FN 6.0	VF 8.0	VF/NM 9.0	NM- 9.2
1,2: 1-Two covers (Andrews, Wieringo); Shum-s/Andrews-a						2.50
3-($2.95)						3.00

INTRUDER
TSR, Inc.: 1990 - No. 10, 1991 ($2.95, 44 pgs.)

	GD 2.0	VG 4.0	FN 6.0	VF 8.0	VF/NM 9.0	NM- 9.2
1-10						3.00

INVADERS, THE (TV)
Gold Key: Oct, 1967 - No. 4, Oct, 1968 (All have photo-c)

	GD 2.0	VG 4.0	FN 6.0	VF 8.0	VF/NM 9.0	NM- 9.2
1-Spiegle-a in all	11	22	33	80	120	160
2-4	8	16	24	58	82	105

INVADERS, THE (Also see The Avengers #71 & Giant-Size Invaders)
Marvel Comics Group: August, 1975 - No. 40, May, 1979; No. 41, Sept, 1979

	GD 2.0	VG 4.0	FN 6.0	VF 8.0	VF/NM 9.0	NM- 9.2
1-Captain America & Bucky, Human Torch & Toro, & Sub-Mariner begin; cont'd. from Giant Size Invaders #1; #1-7 are 25¢ issues	5	10	15	33	44	55
2-5: 2-1st app. Brain-Drain. 3-Battle issue; Cap vs. Namor vs. Torch; intro U-Man	2	4	6	14	18	22
6-10: 6,7-(Regular 25¢ edition). 6-(7/76) Liberty Legion app. 7-Intro Baron Blood & intro/1st app. Union Jack; Human Torch origin retold. 8-Union Jack-c/story. 9-Origin Baron Blood. 10-G.A. Capt. America-r/C.A #22	2	4	6	9	11	14
6,7-(30¢-c variants, limited distribution)	2	4	6	14	18	22
11-19: 11-Origin Spitfire; intro The Blue Bullet. 14-1st app. The Crusaders. 16-Re-intro The Destroyer. 17-Intro Warrior Woman. 18-Re-intro The Destroyer w/new origin. 19-Hitler-c/story	1	3	4	6	8	10
17-19,21-(35¢-c variants, limited distribution)	2	4	6	10	12	15
20-(Regular 30¢-c) Reprints origin/1st app. Sub-Mariner from Motion Picture Funnies Weekly with color added & brief write-up about MPFW; 1st app. new Union Jack II	2	4	6	9	11	14
20-(35¢-c variant, limited distribution)	2	4	6	14	18	22
21-(Regular 30¢ edition)-r/Marvel Mystery #10 (battle issue)	1	3	4	6	8	10
22-30,34-40: 22-New origin Toro. 24-r/Marvel Mystery #17 (team-up issue; all-r). 25-All new-a begins. 28-Intro new Human Top & Golden Girl. 29-Intro Teutonic Knight. 34-Mighty Destroyer joins. 35-The Whizzer app.	1	2	3	4	5	7
31-33: 31-Frankenstein-c/sty. 32,33-Thor app.	1	3	4	6	8	10
41-Double size last issue	2	4	6	10	13	16
Annual 1 (9/77)-Schomburg, Rico stories (new); Schomburg-c/a (1st for Marvel in 30 years); Avengers app.; re-intro The Shark & The Hyena	4	8	12	24	32	40

NOTE: ***Buckler*** *a-5.* ***Everett*** *r-20('39), 21(1940), 24, Annual 1.* ***Gil Kane*** *c(p)-13, 17, 18, 20-27.* ***Kirby*** *c(p)-3-12, 14-16, 32, 33.* ***Mooney*** *a-5i, 16, 22.* ***Robbins*** *a-1-4, 6-9, 10(3 pg.), 11-15, 17-21, 23, 25-28; c-28.*

INVADERS (See Namor, the Sub-Mariner #12)
Marvel Comics Group: May, 1993 - No. 4, Aug, 1993 ($1.75, limited series)

	GD 2.0	VG 4.0	FN 6.0	VF 8.0	VF/NM 9.0	NM- 9.2
1-4						2.50

INVADERS (2004 title - see New Invaders)

INVADERS FROM HOME
DC Comics (Piranha Press): 1990 - No. 6, 1990 ($2.50, mature)

	GD 2.0	VG 4.0	FN 6.0	VF 8.0	VF/NM 9.0	NM- 9.2
1-6						2.50

INVASION
DC Comics: Holiday, 1988-'89 - No. 3, Jan, 1989 ($2.95, lim. series, 84 pgs.)

	GD 2.0	VG 4.0	FN 6.0	VF 8.0	VF/NM 9.0	NM- 9.2
1-3:1-McFarlane/Russell-a. 2-McFarlane/Russell & Giffen/Gordon-a						3.00

INVINCIBLE
Image Comics: Jan, 2003 - Present ($2.95)

	GD 2.0	VG 4.0	FN 6.0	VF 8.0	VF/NM 9.0	NM- 9.2
1-17: 1-7-Kirkman-s/Walker-a. 4-Preview of The Moth. 11-Origin of Omni-Man. 14-Cho-c						3.00
Vol. 1: Family Matters TPB (8/03, $12.95) r/#1-4; intro. by Busiek; sketch pages						13.00
Vol. 2: Eight in Enough TPB (3/04, $12.95) r/#5-8; intro. by Larsen; sketch pages						13.00

INVINCIBLE FOUR OF KUNG FU & NINJA
Leung Publications: April, 1988 - No. 6, 1989 ($2.00)

	GD 2.0	VG 4.0	FN 6.0	VF 8.0	VF/NM 9.0	NM- 9.2
1-($2.75)						3.00
2-6: 2-Begin $2.00-c						2.25

INVISIBLE BOY (See Approved Comics)

INVISIBLE MAN, THE (See Superior Stories #1 & Supernatural Thrillers #2)

INVISIBLE PEOPLE
Kitchen Sink Press: 1992 (B&W, lim. series)

	GD 2.0	VG 4.0	FN 6.0	VF 8.0	VF/NM 9.0	NM- 9.2
Book One: Sanctum; Book Two: "The Power": Will Eisner-s/a in all						2.25
Book Three: "Mortal Combat"						4.00
Hardcover ($34.95)						35.00
TPB (DC Comics, 9/00, $12.95) reprints series						13.00

INVISIBLES, THE (1st Series)
DC Comics (Vertigo): Sept, 1994 - No. 25, Oct, 1996 ($1.95/$2.50, mature)

	GD 2.0	VG 4.0	FN 6.0	VF 8.0	VF/NM 9.0	NM- 9.2
1-($2.95, 52 pgs.)-Intro King Mob, Ragged Robin, Boy, Lord Fanny & Dane (Jack Frost); Grant Morrison scripts in all						6.00
2-8: 4-Includes bound-in trading cards. 5-1st app. Orlando; brown paper-c						4.00
9-25: 10-Intro Jim Crow. 13-15-Origin Lord Fanny. 19-Origin King Mob; polybagged. 20-Origin Boy. 21-Mister Six revealed. 25-Intro Division X						2.50
Apocalipstick (2001, $19.95, TPB)-r/#9-16; Bolland-c						20.00
Entropy in the U.K. (2001, $19.95, TPB)-r/#17-25; Bolland-c						20.00
Say You Want A Revolution (1996, $17.50, TPB)-r/#1-8						18.00

NOTE: ***Buckingham*** *a-25p.* ***Rian Hughes*** *c-1, 5.* ***Phil Jimenez*** *a-17p-19p.* ***Paul Johnson*** *a-16, 21.* ***Sean Phillips*** *c-2-4, 6-25.* ***Weston*** *a-10p.* ***Yeowell*** *a-1p-4p, 22p-24p.*

INVISIBLES, THE (2nd Series)
DC Comics (Vertigo): V2#1, Feb, 1997 - No. 22, Feb, 1999 ($2.50, mature)

	GD 2.0	VG 4.0	FN 6.0	VF 8.0	VF/NM 9.0	NM- 9.2
1-Intro Jolly Roger; Grant Morrison scripts, Phil Jimenez-a, & Brian Bolland-c begins						4.00
2-22: 9,14-Weston-a						2.50
Bloody Hell in America TPB ('98, $12.95) r/#1-4						13.00
Counting to None TPB ('99, $19.95) r/#5-13						20.00
Kissing Mr. Quimper TPB ('00, $19.95) r/#14-22						20.00

INVISIBLES, THE (3rd Series) (Issue #'s go in reverse from #12 to #1)
DC Comics (Vertigo): V3#12, Apr, 1999 - No. 1, June, 2000 ($2.95, mature)

	GD 2.0	VG 4.0	FN 6.0	VF 8.0	VF/NM 9.0	NM- 9.2
1-12-Bolland-c; Morrison-s on all. 1-Quitely-a. 2-4-Art by various. 5-8-Phillips-a. 9-12-Phillip Bond-a.						3.00

Iron Fist ('04) #1 © MAR

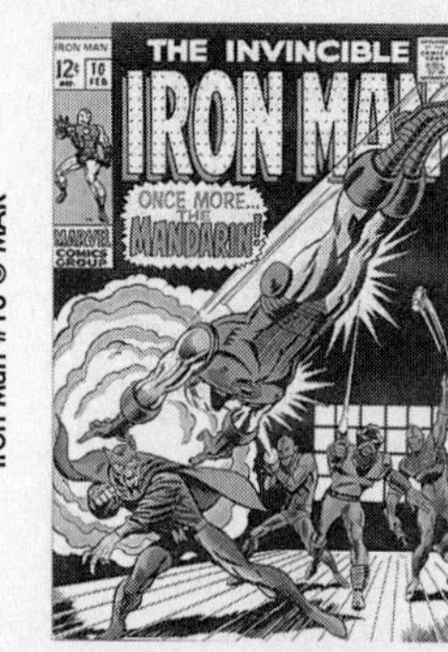

Iron Man #10 © MAR

Iron Man #100 © MAR

	GD	VG	FN	VF	VF/NM	NM-
	2.0	4.0	6.0	8.0	9.0	9.2

The Invisible Kingdom TPB ('02, $19.95) r/#12-1; new Bolland-c 20.00

INVISIBLE SCARLET O'NEIL (Also see Famous Funnies #81 & Harvey Comics Hits #59)
Famous Funnies (Harvey): Dec, 1950 - No. 3, Apr, 1951 (2-3 pgs. of Powell-a in each issue.)

1 15 30 45 83 117 150
2,3 11 22 33 62 84 105

I, PAPARAZZI
DC Comics (Vertigo): 2001 ($29.95, HC, digitally manipulated photographic art)

nn-Pat McGreal-s/Steven Parke-digital-a/Stephen John Phillips-photos 30.00

IRON CORPORAL, THE (See Army War Heroes #22)
Charlton Comics: No. 23, Oct, 1985 - No. 25, Feb, 1986

23-25: Glanzman-a(r); low print 5.00

IRON FIST (See Deadly Hands of Kung Fu, Marvel Premiere & Power Man)
Marvel Comics: Nov, 1975 - No. 15, Sept, 1977

1-Iron Fist battles Iron Man (#1-6: 25¢) 6 12 18 38 52 65
2 3 6 9 19 25 32
3-10: 4-6-(Regular 25¢ edition)(4-6/76). 8-Origin retold
3 6 9 16 20 24
4-6-(30¢-c variant, limited distribution) 3 7 10 21 28 36
11,13: 13-(30¢-c) 2 4 6 11 14 18
12-Capt. America app. 2 4 6 14 18 22
13-(35¢-c variant, limited distribution) 3 6 9 18 23 28
14-1st app. Sabretooth (8/77)(see Power Man) 11 22 33 80 120 160
14-(35¢-c variant, limited distribution) 27 54 81 194 297 400
15-(Regular 30¢ ed.) X-Men app., Byrne-a 6 12 18 40 55 70
15-(35¢-c variant, limited distribution) 10 20 30 73 107 140
NOTE: ***Adkins*** *a-8p, 10i, 13i; c-8i.* ***Byrne*** *a-1-15p; c-8p, 15p.* ***G. Kane*** *c-4-6p.* ***McWilliams*** *a-1i.*

IRON FIST
Marvel Comics: Sept, 1996 - No. 2, Oct, 1996 ($1.50, limited series)

1,2 3.00

IRON FIST
Marvel Comics: Jul, 1998 - No. 3, Sept, 1998 ($2.50, limited series)

1-3: Jurgens-s/Guice-a 2.50

IRON FIST
Marvel Comics: May, 2004 - Present ($2.99)

1-6: 1-4,6-Kevin Lau-c/a. 5-Mays-c/a 3.00

IRON FIST: WOLVERINE
Marvel Comics: Nov, 2000 - No. 4, Feb, 2001 ($2.99, limited series)

1-4-Igle-c/a; Kingpin app. 2-Iron Man app. 3,4-Capt. America app. 3.00

IRONHAND OF ALMURIC (Robert E. Howard's...)
Dark Horse Comics: Aug, 1991 - No. 4, 1991 ($2.00, B&W, mini-series)

1-4: 1-Conrad painted-c 2.25

IRON HORSE (TV)
Dell Publishing Co.: March, 1967 - No. 2, June, 1967

1-Dale Robertson photo covers on both 3 7 10 21 28 35
2 3 6 9 16 21 26

IRONJAW (Also see The Barbarians)
Atlas/Seaboard Publ.: Jan, 1975 - No. 4, July, 1975

1,2-Neal Adams-c. 1-1st app. Iron Jaw; Sekowsky-a(p); Fleisher-s
2 4 6 8 10 12
3,4-Marcos. 4-Origin 1 2 3 4 5 7

IRON LANTERN
Marvel Comics (Amalgam): June, 1997 ($1.95, one-shot)

1-Kurt Busiek-s/Paul Smith & Al Williamson-a 2.50

IRON MAN (Also see The Avengers #1, Giant-Size..., Marvel Collectors Item Classics, Marvel Double Feature, Marvel Fanfare & Tales of Suspense #39)
Marvel Comics: May, 1968 - No. 332, Sept, 1996

1-Origin; Colan-c/a(p); story continued from Iron Man & Sub-Mariner #1
36 72 108 270 423 575
2 12 24 36 87 134 180
3 9 18 27 60 85 110
4,5 7 14 21 51 71 90
6-10: 9-Iron Man battles green Hulk-like android 6 12 18 40 55 70
11-15: 15-Last 12¢ issue 5 10 15 33 44 55
16-20 4 8 12 24 32 40
21-24,26-30: 22-Death of Janice Cord. 27-Intro Firebrand
3 6 9 18 24 30
25-Iron Man battles Sub-Mariner 3 7 10 21 28 35
31-42: 33-1st app. Spymaster. 35-Nick Fury & Daredevil x-over. 42-Last 15¢ issue
3 6 9 16 20 24
43-Intro The Guardsman; 25¢ giant (52 pgs.) 4 8 12 24 32 40
44-46,48-50: 43-Giant-Man back-up by Ayers. 44-Ant-Man by Tuska. 46-The Guardsman dies. 50-Princess Python app. 2 4 6 11 14 18
47-Origin retold; Barry Smith-a(p) 3 6 9 18 23 28
51-53: 53-Starlin part pencils 2 4 6 10 12 15
54-Iron Man battles Sub-Mariner; 1st app. Moondragon (1/73) as Madame MacEvil; Everett part-c 3 6 10 21 28 35
55-1st app. Thanos (brief), Drax the Destroyer, Mentor, Starfox & Kronos (2/73); Starlin-c/a
12 24 36 87 134 180
56-Starlin-a 3 6 9 19 25 32
57-65,67-70: 59-Firebrand returns. 65-Origin Dr. Spectrum. 67-Last 20¢ issue. 68-Sunfire & Unicorn app.; origin retold; Starlin-c 2 4 6 9 11 14
66-Iron Man vs. Thor. 3 6 9 16 21 26
71-84: 72-Cameo portraits of N. Adams. 73-Rename Stark Industries to Stark International; Brunner. 76-r/#9. 2 4 6 8 10 12
85-89-(Regular 25¢ editions): 86-1st app. Blizzard. 87-Origin Blizzard. 88-Thanos app. 89-Daredevil app.; last 25¢-c 2 4 6 8 10 12
85-89-(30¢-c variants, limited distribution)(4-8/76) 2 4 6 11 14 18
90-99: 96-1st app. new Guardsman 1 3 4 6 8 10
99,101-103-(35¢-c variants, limited dist.) 2 4 6 8 10 12
100-(7/77)-Starlin-c 3 6 9 18 23 28
100-(35¢-c variant, limited dist.) 4 8 12 25 33 42
101-117: 101-Intro DreadKnight. 109-1st app. new Crimson Dynamo; 1st app. Vanguard. 110-Origin Jack of Hearts retold; death of Count Nefaria. 114-Avengers app.
1 2 3 5 6 8
118-Byrne-a(p); 1st app. Jim Rhodes 1 3 4 6 8 10
119-127: 120,121-Sub-Mariner x-over. 122-Origin. 123-128-Tony Stark treated for alcohol problem. 125-Ant-Man app. 1 2 3 5 6 8
128-Classic Tony Stark alcoholism cover 2 4 6 10 12 15
129,130,133-149 6.00
131,132-Hulk x-over 1 2 3 5 6 8
150-Double size 1 2 3 5 7 9
151-168: 152-New armor. 161-Moon Knight app. 167-Tony Stark alcohol problem resurfaces
4.00
169-New Iron Man (Jim Rhodes replaces Tony Stark) 6.00
170,171 4.00
172-199: 172-Captain America x-over. 186-Intro Vibro. 190-Scarlet Witch app. 191-198-Tony Stark returns as original Iron Man. 192-Both Iron Men battle 3.00
200-(11/85, $1.25, 52 pgs.)-Tony Stark returns as new Iron Man (red & white armor) thru #230 5.00
201-213,215-224: 213-Intro new Dominic Fortune 3.00
214,225,228,231,234,247: 214-Spider-Woman app. in new black costume (1/87). 225-Double size ($1.25). 228-vs. Capt. America. 231-Intro new Iron Man. 234-Spider-Man x-over. 247-Hulk x-over 4.00
226,227,229,230,232,233,235-243,245,246,248,249: 233-Ant-Man app. 243-Tony Stark loses use of legs 2.50
244-($1.50, 52 pgs.)-New Armor makes him walk 3.00
250-($1.50, 52 pgs.)-Dr. Doom-c/story 3.00
251-274,276-281,283,285-287,289,291-299: 258-277-Byrne scripts. 271-Fin Fang Foom app. 276-Black Widow-c/story; last $1.00-c. 281-1st brief app. War Machine. 283-2nd full app. War Machine 2.50
275-($1.50, 52 pgs.) 3.00
282-1st full app. War Machine (7/92) 4.00
284-Death of Iron Man (Tony Stark) 4.00
288-($2.50, 52pg.)-Silver foil stamped-c; Iron Man's 350th app. in comics 3.00
290-($2.95, 52pg.)-Gold foil stamped-c; 30th ann. 3.00
300-($3.95, 68 pgs.)-Collector's Edition w/embossed foil-c; anniversary issue; War Machine-c/story 4.00
300-($2.50, 68 pgs.)-Newsstand Edition 2.50
301-303: 302-Venom-c/story (cameo #301) 2.50
304-316,318-324,326-331: 304-Begin $1.50-c; bound-in trading card sheet; Thunderstrike-c/story. 310-Orange logo. 312-w/bound-in Power Ranger Card. 319-Prologue to "The Crossing." 326-New Tony Stark; Pratt-c. 330-War Machine & Stockpile app; return of Morgan Stark 2.50
310,325: 310 ($2.95)-Polybagged w/ 16 pg. Marvel Action Hour preview & acetate print; white logo. 325-($2.95)-Wraparound-c 3.00
317 ($2.50)-Flip book 2.50
332-Onslaught x-over 4.00
Special 1 (8/70)-Sub-Mariner x-over; Everett-c 4 8 12 25 33 42
Special 2 (11/71, 52 pgs.)-r/TOS #81,82,91 (all-r) 3 6 9 16 20 24
Annual 3 (1976)-Man-Thing app. 2 4 6 10 12 15

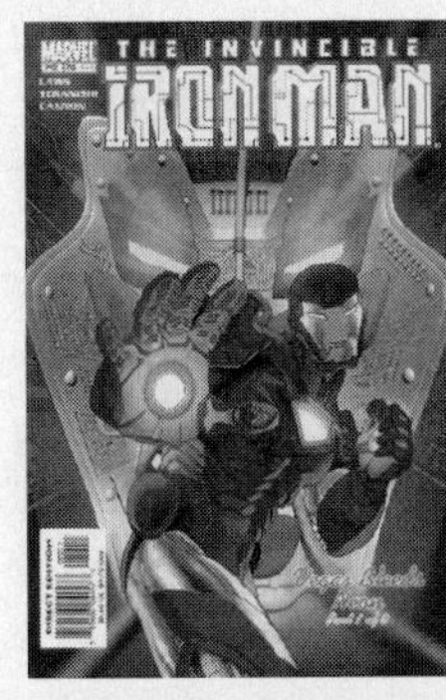

Iron Man V3#70 © MAR

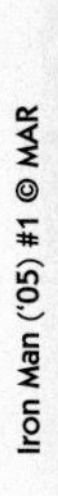
Iron Man ('05) #1 © MAR

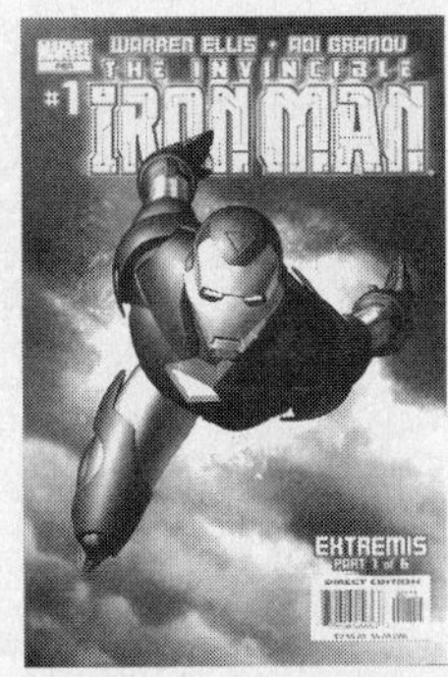

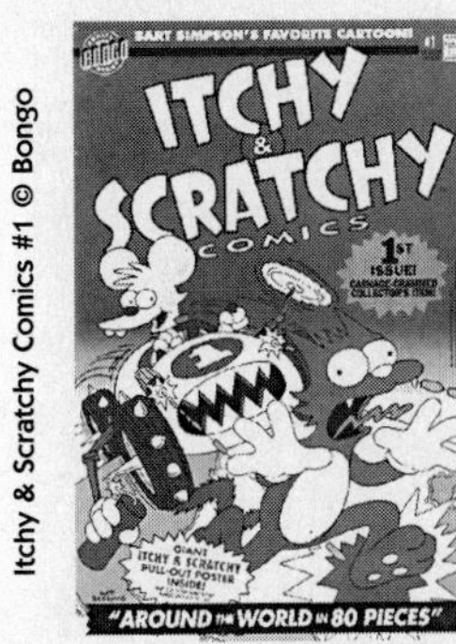

Itchy & Scratchy Comics #1 © Bongo

GD VG FN VF VF/NM NM-
2.0 4.0 6.0 8.0 9.0 9.2

King Size 4 (8/77)-The Champions (w/Ghost Rider) app.; Newton-a(i)
1 3 4 6 8 10
Annual 5 ('82) New-a 6.00
Annual 6-8: ('83-'85) 6-New Iron Man (J. Rhodes) app. 8-X-Factor app. 5.00
Annual 9-15: ('86-'94) 10-Atlantis Attacks x-over; P. Smith-a; Layton/Guice-a; Sub-Mariner app. 11-(1990)-Origin of Mrs. Arbogast by Ditko (p&i). 12-1 pg. origin recap; Ant-Man back-up-s. 13-Darkhawk & Avengers West Coast app.; Colan/Williamson-a. 14-Bagged w/card 3.00
Manual 1 (1993, $1.75)-Operations handbook 2.50
Graphic Novel: Crash (1988, $12.95, Adults, 72 pgs.)-Computer generated art & color; violence & nudity 13.00
...Collector's Preview 1(11/94, $1.95)-wraparound-c; text & illos-no comics 2.50
...Vs. Dr. Doom (12/94, $12.95)-r/#149-150, 249,250. Julie Bell-c 13.00
NOTE: ***Austin*** *c-105i, 109-111i, 151i.* ***Byrne*** *a-118p; c-109p, 197, 253.* ***Colan*** *a-1p, 253, Special 1p(3); c-1p.* ***Craig*** *a-1i, 2-4, 5-13i, 14, 15-19i, 24p, 25p, 26-28i; c-2-4.* ***Ditko*** *a-160p.* ***Everett*** *c-29.* ***Guice*** *a-233-241p.* ***G. Kane*** *c(p)-52-54, 63, 67, 72-75, 77-79, 88, 98.* ***Kirby*** *a-Special 1p; c-13, 80p, 90, 92-95.* ***Mooney*** *a-40i, 43i, 47i.* ***Perez*** *c-103p.* ***Simonson*** *c-Annual 8.* ***B. Smith*** *a-232p, 243i; c-232.* ***P. Smith*** *a-159p, 245p, Annual 10p; c-159.* ***Starlin*** *a-53p(part), 55p, 56p; c-55p, 160, 163.* ***Tuska*** *a-5-13p, 15-23p, 24i, 32p, 38-46p, 48-54p, 57-61p, 63-69p, 70-72p, 78p, 86-92p, 95-106p, Annual 4p.* ***Wood*** *a-Special 1i.*

IRON MAN (The Invincible...) (Volume Two)
Marvel Comics: Nov, 1996 - No. 13, Nov, 1997 ($2.95/$1.95/$1.99)
(Produced by WildStorm Productions)

V2#1-3-Heroes Reborn begins; Scott Lobdell scripts & Whilce Portacio-c/a begin; new origin Iron Man & Hulk. 2-Hulk app. 3-Fantastic Four app. 4.00
1-Variant-c 5.00
4-11: 4-Two covers. 6-Fantastic Four app.; Industrial Revolution; Hulk app. 7-Return of Rebel. 11-($1.99) Dr. Doom-c/app. 3.00
12-($2.99) "Heroes Reunited"-pt. 3; Hulk-c/app. 3.50
13-($1.99) "World War 3"-pt. 3, x-over w/Image 3.00

IRON MAN (The Invincible...) (Volume Three)
Marvel Comics: Feb, 1998 - No. 89, Dec, 2004 ($2.99/$1.99/$2.25)

V3#1-($2.99)-Follows Heroes Return; Busiek scripts & Chen-c/a begin; Deathsquad app. 5.00
1-Alternate Ed. 1 2 3 5 6 8
2-12: 2-Two covers. 6-Black Widow-c/app. 7-Warbird-c/app. 8-Black Widow app. 9-Mandarin returns 3.00
13-($2.99) battles the Controller 3.50
14-24: 14-Fantastic Four-c/app. 3.00
25-($2.99) Iron Man and Warbird battle Ultimo; Avengers app. 3.00
26-30-Quesada-s. 28-Whiplash killed. 29-Begin $2.25-c. 2.50
31-45,47-49,51-54: 35-Maximum Security x-over; FF-c/app. 41-Grant-a begins. 44-New armor debut. 48-Ultron-c/app. 2.25
46-($3.50, 100 pgs.) Sentient armor returns; r/V1#78,140,141 3.50
50-($3.50) Grell-s begin; Black Widow app. 3.50
55-($3.50) 400th issue; Asamiya-c; back-up story Stark reveals ID; Grell-a 3.50
56-66: 56-Reis-a. 57,58-Ryan-a. 59-61-Grell-c/a. 62,63-Ryan-a. 64-Davis-a; Thor-c/app. 2.25
67-89: 67-Begin $2.99-c; Gene Ha-c. 75-83-Granov-c. 84-Avengers Disassembled prologue 85-89-Avengers Disassembled. 85-88-Harris-a. 86-89-Pat Lee-c. 87-Rumiko killed 3.00
.../Captain America '98 Annual ($3.50) vs. Modok 3.50
1999, 2000 Annual ($3.50) 3.50
2001 Annual ($2.99) Claremont-s/Ryan-a 3.00
Mask in the Iron Man (5/01, $14.95, TPB) r/#26-30, #1/2 15.00

IRON MAN (The Invincible...)
Marvel Comics: Jan, 2005 - Present ($3.50)

1-Warren Ellis-s/Adi Granov-c/a 3.50

IRON MAN & SUB-MARINER
Marvel Comics Group: Apr, 1968 (12¢, one-shot) (Pre-dates Iron Man #1 & Sub-Mariner #1)

1-Iron Man story by Colan/Craig continued from Tales of Suspense #99 & continued in Iron Man #1; Sub-Mariner story by Colan continued from Tales to Astonish #101 & continued in Sub-Mariner #1; Colan/Everett-c 15 30 45 107 164 220

IRON MAN: BAD BLOOD
Marvel Comics: Sept, 2000 - No. 4, Dec, 2000 ($2.99, limited series)

1-4-Micheline-s/Layton-a 3.00

IRON MAN: THE IRON AGE
Marvel Comics: Aug, 1998 - No. 2, Sept, 1998 ($5.99, limited series)

1,2-Busiek-s; flashback story from gold armor days 6.00

IRON MAN: THE LEGEND
Marvel Comics: Sept, 1996 ($3.95, one-shot)

1-Tribute issue 4.50

IRON MAN 2020 (Also see Machine Man limited series)
Marvel Comics: June, 1994 ($5.95, one-shot)

nn 6.00

GD VG FN VF VF/NM NM-
2.0 4.0 6.0 8.0 9.0 9.2

IRON MAN/X-O MANOWAR: HEAVY METAL (See X-O Manowar/Iron Man: In Heavy Metal)
Marvel Comics: Sept, 1996 ($2.50, one-shot) (1st Marvel/Valiant x-over)

1-Pt. II of Iron Man/X-O Manowar x-over; Fabian Nicieza scripts; 1st app. Rand Banion 2.50

IRON MARSHALL
Jademan Comics: July, 1990 - No. 32, Feb, 1993 ($1.75, plastic coated-c)

1,32: Kung Fu stories. 1-Poster centerfold 2.25
2-31-Kung Fu stories in all 2.25

IRON VIC (See Comics Revue No. 3 & Giant Comics Editions)
United Features Syndicate/St. John Publ. Co.: 1940

Single Series 22 34 68 102 196 283 370

IRON WINGS
Image Comics: Apr, 2000 - No. 2, May, 2000 ($2.50)

1,2: 1-Two covers 2.50

IRONWOLF
DC Comics: 1986 ($2.00, one shot)

1-r/Weird Worlds 8-10; Chaykin story & art 2.25

IRONWOLF: FIRES OF THE REVOLUTION (See Weird Worlds #8-10)
DC Comics: 1992 ($29.95, hardcover)

nn-Chaykin/Moore story, Mignola-a w/Russell inks. 30.00

ISAAC ASIMOV'S I-BOTS
Tekno Comix: Dec, 1995 - No. 7, May, 1996 ($1.95)

1-7: 1-6-Perez-c/a. 2-Chaykin variant-c exists. 3-Polybagged. 7-Lady Justice-c/app. 2.25

ISAAC ASIMOV'S I-BOTS
BIG Entertainment: V2#1, June, 1996 - No. 9, Feb, 1997 ($2.25)

V2#1-9: 1-Lady Justice-c/app. 6-Gil Kane-c 2.25

ISIS (TV) (Also see Shazam)
National Per.l Publ./DC Comics: Oct-Nov, 1976 - No. 8, Dec-Jan, 1977-78

1-Wood inks 2 4 6 10 13 16
2-8: 5-Isis new look. 7-Origin 1 2 3 5 7 9

ISLAND AT THE TOP OF THE WORLD (See Walt Disney Showcase #27)

ISLAND OF DR. MOREAU, THE (Movie)
Marvel Comics Group: Oct, 1977 (52 pgs.)

1-Gil Kane-c 1 2 3 5 6 8

I SPY (TV)
Gold Key: Aug, 1966 - No. 6, Sept, 1968 (All have photo-c)

1-Bill Cosby, Robert Culp photo covers 23 46 69 165 253 340
2-6: 3,4-McWilliams-a. 5-Last 12¢-c 14 28 42 97 149 200

IT! (See Astonishing Tales No. 21-24 & Supernatural Thrillers No. 1)

ITCHY & SCRATCHY COMICS (The Simpsons TV show)
Bongo Comics: 1993 - No. 3, 1993 ($1.95)

1-3: 1-Bound-in jumbo poster. 3-w/decoder screen trading card 4.00
Holiday Special ('94, $1.95) 4.00

IT GIRL (Also see Atomics, and Madman Comics)
Oni Press: May, 2002 ($2.95, one-shot)

1-Allred-s/Clugston-Major-c/a; Atomics and Madman app. 3.00

IT REALLY HAPPENED
William H. Wise No. 1,2/Standard (Visual Editions): 1944 - No. 11, Oct, 1947

1-Kit Carson & Ben Franklin stories 22 44 66 123 177 230
2 11 22 33 66 91 115
3,4,6,9,11: 6-Joan of Arc story. 9-Captain Kidd & Frank Buck stories
10 20 30 58 77 95
5-Lou Gehrig & Lewis Carroll stories 16 32 48 89 127 165
7-Teddy Roosevelt story 11 22 33 66 91 115
8-Story of Roy Rogers 17 34 51 95 135 175
10-Honus Wagner & Mark Twain stories 13 26 39 76 103 135
NOTE: ***Guardineer*** *a-7(2), 8(2), 11.* ***Schomburg*** *c-1-7, 9-11.*

IT RHYMES WITH LUST (Also see Bold Stories & Candid Tales)
St. John Publishing Co.: 1950 (Digest size, 128 pgs.)

nn (Rare)-Matt Baker & Ray Osrin-a 62 124 186 388 594 800

IT'S A BIRD...
DC Comics: 2004 ($24.95, hardcover with dust jacket)

HC-Semi-autobiographical story of Steven Seagle writing Superman; Kristiansen-a 25.00

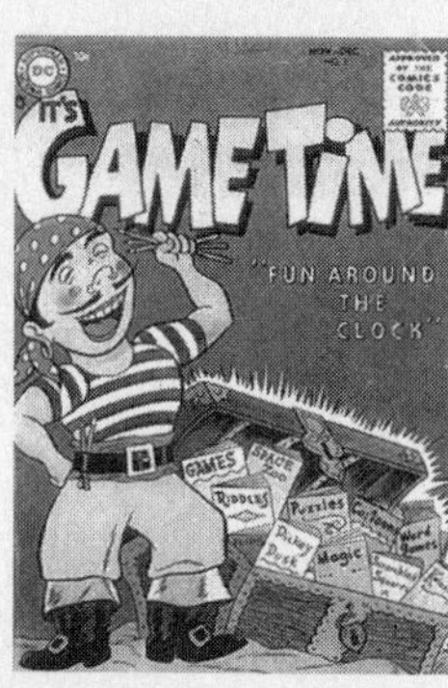

It's Game Time #2 © DC

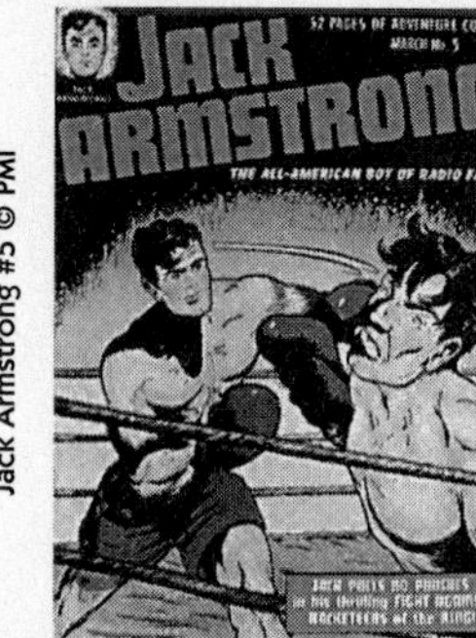

Jack Armstrong #5 © PMI

Jack Kirby's Secret City Saga #0 © Jack Kirby

IT'S ABOUT TIME (TV)
Gold Key: Jan, 1967

	GD 2.0	VG 4.0	FN 6.0	VF 8.0	VF/NM 9.0	NM- 9.2
1 (10195-701)-Photo-c	5	10	15	36	48	60

IT'S A DUCK'S LIFE
Marvel Comics/Atlas(MMC): Feb, 1950 - No. 11, Feb, 1952

	GD 2.0	VG 4.0	FN 6.0	VF 8.0	VF/NM 9.0	NM- 9.2
1-Buck Duck, Super Rabbit begin	15	30	45	86	123	160
2	9	18	27	52	66	80
3-11	8	16	24	46	58	70

IT'S GAMETIME
National Periodical Publications: Sept-Oct, 1955 - No. 4, Mar-Apr, 1956

	GD 2.0	VG 4.0	FN 6.0	VF 8.0	VF/NM 9.0	NM- 9.2
1-(Scarce)-Infinity-c; Davy Crockett app. in puzzle	77	154	231	481	741	1000
2,3 (Scarce): 2-Dodo & The Frog	60	120	180	375	580	785
4 (Rare)	63	126	189	394	610	825

IT'S LOVE, LOVE, LOVE
St. John Publishing Co.: Nov, 1957 - No. 2, Jan, 1958 (10¢)

	GD 2.0	VG 4.0	FN 6.0	VF 8.0	VF/NM 9.0	NM- 9.2
1,2	6	12	18	28	34	40

IVANHOE (See Fawcett Movie Comics No. 20)

IVANHOE
Dell Publishing Co.: July-Sept, 1963

	GD 2.0	VG 4.0	FN 6.0	VF 8.0	VF/NM 9.0	NM- 9.2
1 (12-373-309)	4	8	12	25	33	42

IWO JIMA (See Spectacular Features Magazine)

JACE PEARSON OF THE TEXAS RANGERS (Radio/TV)(4-Color #396 is titled Tales of the Texas Rangers; ...'s Tales of ... #11-on)(See Western Roundup under Dell Giants)
Dell Publishing Co.: No. 396, 5/52 - No. 1021, 8-10/59 (No #10) (All-Photo-c)

	GD 2.0	VG 4.0	FN 6.0	VF 8.0	VF/NM 9.0	NM- 9.2
Four Color 396 (#1)	12	24	36	84	127	170
2(5-7/53) - 9(2-4/55)	8	16	24	53	74	95
Four Color 648(#10, 9/55)	6	12	18	43	59	75
11(11-2/55-56) - 14,17-20(6-8/58)	6	12	18	40	55	70
15,16-Toth-a	6	12	18	43	59	75
Four Color 961,1021: 961-Spiegle-a	6	12	18	40	55	70

NOTE: *Joel McCrea photo c-1-9, F.C. 648 (starred on radio show only); Willard Parker photo c-11-on (starred on TV series).*

JACK ARMSTRONG (Radio)(See True Comics)
Parents' Institute: Nov, 1947 - No. 9, Sept, 1948; No. 10, Mar, 1949 - No. 13, Sept, 1949

	GD 2.0	VG 4.0	FN 6.0	VF 8.0	VF/NM 9.0	NM- 9.2
1-(Scarce) (odd size) Cast intro. inside front-c	44	88	132	268	409	550
2	21	42	63	118	169	220
3-5	15	30	45	86	123	160
6-13: 7-Vic Hardy's Crime Lab begins?	12	24	36	71	98	125

JACK HUNTER
Blackthorne Publishing: July, 1987 - No. 3 ($1.25)

	GD 2.0	VG 4.0	FN 6.0	VF 8.0	VF/NM 9.0	NM- 9.2
1-3						2.25

JACKIE CHAN'S SPARTAN X
Topps Comics: May, 1997 - No. 3 ($2.95, limited series)

	GD 2.0	VG 4.0	FN 6.0	VF 8.0	VF/NM 9.0	NM- 9.2
1-3-Michael Golden-s/a; variant photo-c						3.00

JACKIE CHAN'S SPARTAN X: HELL BENT HERO FOR HIRE
Image Comics (Little Eva Ink): Mar, 1998 - No. 3 ($2.95, B&W)

	GD 2.0	VG 4.0	FN 6.0	VF 8.0	VF/NM 9.0	NM- 9.2
1-3-Michael Golden-s/a: 1-variant photo-c						3.00

JACKIE GLEASON (TV) (Also see The Honeymooners)
St. John Publishing Co.: Sept, 1955 - No. 4, Dec, 1955?

	GD 2.0	VG 4.0	FN 6.0	VF 8.0	VF/NM 9.0	NM- 9.2
1(1955)(TV)-Photo-c	60	120	180	375	580	785
2-4	40	80	120	244	372	500

JACKIE GLEASON AND THE HONEYMOONERS (TV)
National Periodical Publications: June-July, 1956 - No. 12, Apr-May, 1958

	GD 2.0	VG 4.0	FN 6.0	VF 8.0	VF/NM 9.0	NM- 9.2
1-1st app. Ralph Kramden	89	178	267	556	853	1150
2	54	108	162	329	502	675
3-11	40	80	120	244	372	500
12 (Scarce)	60	120	180	375	580	785

JACKIE JOKERS (Became Richie Rich &...)
Harvey Publications: March, 1973 - No. 4, Sept, 1973 (#5 was advertised, but not published)

	GD 2.0	VG 4.0	FN 6.0	VF 8.0	VF/NM 9.0	NM- 9.2
1-1st app.	3	6	9	18	23	28
2-4: 2-President Nixon app.	2	4	6	9	11	14

JACKIE ROBINSON (Famous Plays of...) (Also see Negro Heroes #2 & Picture News #4)
Fawcett Publications: May, 1950 - No. 6, 1952 (Baseball hero) (All photo-c)

	GD 2.0	VG 4.0	FN 6.0	VF 8.0	VF/NM 9.0	NM- 9.2
nn	92	184	276	575	888	1200
2	55	110	165	340	520	700
3-6	46	92	138	281	428	575

JACK IN THE BOX (Formerly Yellowjacket Comics #1-10; becomes Cowboy Western Comics #17 on)
Frank Comunale/Charlton Comics No. 11 on: Feb, 1946; No. 11, Oct, 1946 - No. 16, Nov-Dec, 1947

	GD 2.0	VG 4.0	FN 6.0	VF 8.0	VF/NM 9.0	NM- 9.2
1-Stitches, Marty Mouse & Nutsy McKrow	15	30	45	86	123	160
11-Yellowjacket (early Charlton comic)	20	40	60	112	161	210
12,14,15	10	20	30	56	73	90
13-Wolverton-a	21	42	63	118	169	220
16-12 pg. adapt. of Silas Marner; Kiefer-a	11	22	33	64	87	110

JACK KIRBY'S FOURTH WORLD (See Mister Miracle & New Gods, 3rd Series)
DC Comics: Mar, 1997 - No. 20, Oct, 1998 ($1.95/$2.25)

	GD 2.0	VG 4.0	FN 6.0	VF 8.0	VF/NM 9.0	NM- 9.2
1-20: 1-Byrne-a/scripts & Simonson-c begin; story cont'd from New Gods, 3rd Series #15; retells "The Pact" (New Gods, 1st Series #7); 1st brief DC app. Thor. 2-Thor vs. Big Barda; "Apokolips Then" back-up begins; Kirby-c/swipe (Thor #126) 8-Genesis x-over. 10-Simonson-s/a 13-Simonson back-up story. 20-Superman-c/app.						2.25

JACK KIRBY'S SECRET CITY SAGA
Topps Comics (Kirbyverse): No. 0, Apr, 1993; No. 1, May, 1993 - No. 4, Aug, 1993 ($2.95, limited series)

	GD 2.0	VG 4.0	FN 6.0	VF 8.0	VF/NM 9.0	NM- 9.2
0-(No cover price, 20 pgs.)-Simonson-c/a						3.00
0-Red embossed-c (limited ed.)						5.00
1-4-Bagged w/3 trading cards; Ditko-c/a: 1-Ditko/Art Adams-c. 2-Ditko/Byrne-c; has coupon for Pres. Clinton holo-foil trading card. 3-Dorman poster; has coupon for Gore holo-foil trading card. 4-Ditko/Perez-c						3.00

NOTE: *Issues #1-4 contain coupons redeemable for Kirbychrome version of #1*

JACK KIRBY'S SILVER STAR (Also see Silver Star)
Topps Comics (Kirbyverse): Oct, 1993 ($2.95)(Intended as a 4-issue limited series)

	GD 2.0	VG 4.0	FN 6.0	VF 8.0	VF/NM 9.0	NM- 9.2
1-Silver ink-c; Austin-c/a(i); polybagged w/3 cards						3.00

JACK KIRBY'S TEENAGENTS (See Satan's Six)
Topps Comics (Kirbyverse): Aug, 1993 - No. 4, Nov, 1993 ($2.95, limited series)

	GD 2.0	VG 4.0	FN 6.0	VF 8.0	VF/NM 9.0	NM- 9.2
1-4: Bagged with/3 trading cards; Busiek-s/Austin-c(i): 3-Liberty Project app.						3.00

JACK OF HEARTS (Also see The Deadly Hands of Kung Fu #22 & Marvel Premiere #44)
Marvel Comics Group: Jan, 1984 - No. 4, Apr, 1984 (60¢, limited series)

	GD 2.0	VG 4.0	FN 6.0	VF 8.0	VF/NM 9.0	NM- 9.2
1-4						2.50

JACKPOT COMICS (Jolly Jingles #10 on)
MLJ Magazines: Spring, 1941 - No. 9, Spring, 1943

	GD 2.0	VG 4.0	FN 6.0	VF 8.0	VF/NM 9.0	NM- 9.2
1-The Black Hood, Mr. Justice, Steel Sterling & Sgt. Boyle begin; Biro-c	310	620	930	2015	3258	4500
2-S. Cooper-c	142	284	426	888	1369	1850
3-Hubbell-c	108	216	324	675	1038	1400
4-Archie begins (Win/41; on sale 12/41)-(also see Pep Comics #22); 1st app. Mrs. Grundy, the principal; Novick-c	379	758	1137	2464	3982	5500
5-Hitler, Tojo, Mussolini-c by Montana; 1st definitive Mr. Weatherbee; 1st brief app. Reggie in 1 panel	154	308	462	963	1482	2000
6-9: 6,7-Bondage-c by Novick. 8,9-Sahle-c	110	220	330	688	1057	1425

JACK Q FROST (See Unearthly Spectaculars)

JACK STAFF (Vol. 2; previously published in Britain)
Image Comics: Feb, 2003 - Present ($2.95/$3.50)

	GD 2.0	VG 4.0	FN 6.0	VF 8.0	VF/NM 9.0	NM- 9.2
1-5-Paul Grist-s/a						3.00
6-($3.50) Flashback to the WW2 Freedom Fighters						3.50
Vol. 1: Everything Used to Be Black and White TPB (12/03, $19.95) r/British issues						20.00

JACK THE GIANT KILLER (See Movie Classics)

JACK THE GIANT KILLER (New Adventures of...)
Bimfort & Co.: Aug-Sept, 1953

	GD 2.0	VG 4.0	FN 6.0	VF 8.0	VF/NM 9.0	NM- 9.2
V1#1-H. C. Kiefer-c/a	24	48	72	138	199	260

JACKY'S DIARY
Dell Publishing Co.: No. 1091, Apr-June, 1960 (one-shot)

	GD 2.0	VG 4.0	FN 6.0	VF 8.0	VF/NM 9.0	NM- 9.2
Four Color 1091	6	12	18	38	52	65

JADE (Chaos! Presents: ...)
Chaos! Comics: May, 2001 - No. 4, Aug, 2001 ($2.99, limited series)

	GD 2.0	VG 4.0	FN 6.0	VF 8.0	VF/NM 9.0	NM- 9.2
1-4-Lashley-a/Golden & Sniegoski-a						3.00
...Redemption 1-4 (12/01 - No. 4, 3/02) Tortosa-a						3.00

JADEMAN COLLECTION
Jademan Comics: Dec, 1989 - No. 3, 1990 ($2.50, plastic coated-c, 68 pgs.)

	GD 2.0	VG 4.0	FN 6.0	VF 8.0	VF/NM 9.0	NM- 9.2
1-3: 1-Wraparound-c w/fold-out poster						2.50

Jane Arden #1 © UFS

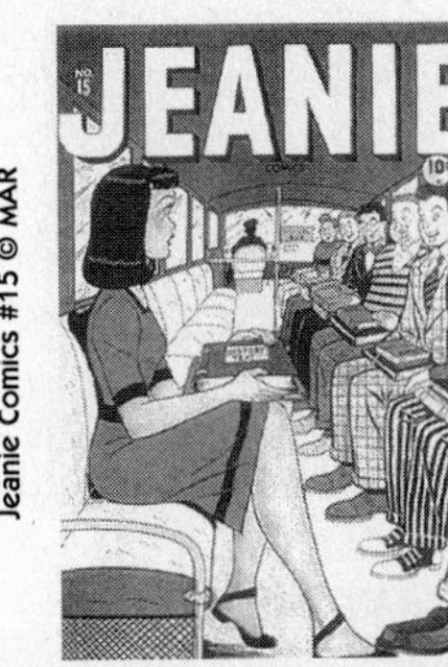

Jeanie Comics #15 © MAR

Jeep Comics #1 © RFL

	GD 2.0	VG 4.0	FN 6.0	VF 8.0	VF/NM 9.0	NM- 9.2

JADEMAN KUNG FU SPECIAL
Jademan Comics: 1988 ($1.50, 64 pgs.)

1 — 2.50

JADE WARRIORS (Mike Deodato's...)
Image Comics (Glass House Graphics): Nov, 1999 - No. 3, 2000 ($2.50)

1-3-Deodato-a — 2.50
1-Variant-c — 2.50

JAGUAR, THE (Also see The Adventures of...)
Impact Comics (DC): Aug, 1991 - No. 14, Oct, 1992 ($1.00)

1-14: 4-The Black Hood x-over. 7-Sienkiewicz-c. 9-Contains Crusaders trading card — 2.25
Annual 1 (1992, $2.50, 68 pgs.)-With trading card — 2.50

JAGUAR GOD
Verotik: Mar, 1995 - No. 7, June, 1997 ($2.95, mature)

0 (2/96, $3.50)-Embossed Frazetta-c; Bisley-a; w/pin-ups. — 4.00
1-Frazetta-c. — 4.00
2-7: 2-Frazetta-c. 3-Bisley-c. 4-Emond-c. 7-($2.95)-Frazetta-c — 3.00

JAKE THRASH
Aircel Publishing: 1988 - No. 3, 1988 ($2.00)

1-3 — 2.25

JAM, THE (...Urban Adventure)
Slave Labor Nos. 1-5/Dark Horse Comics Nos. 6-8/Caliber Comics No. 9 on: Nov, 1989 - No. 14, 1997 ($1.95/$2.50/$2.95, B&W)

1-14: Bernie Mireault-c/a/scripts. 6-1st Dark Horse issue. 9-1st Caliber issue — 3.00

JAMBOREE
Round Publishing Co.: Feb, 1946(no month given) - No. 3, Apr, 1946

	GD	VG	FN	VF	VF/NM	NM-
1-Funny animal	27	54	81	152	219	285
2,3	16	32	48	92	131	170

JAMES BOND 007: A SILENT ARMAGEDDON
Dark Horse Comics/Acme Press: Mar, 1993 - Apr 1993 (limited series)

1,2 — 3.50

JAMES BOND 007: GOLDENEYE (Movie)
Topps Comics: Jan, 1996 ($2.95, unfinished limited series of 3)

1-Movie adaptation; Stelfreeze-c — 3.00

JAMES BOND 007: SERPENT'S TOOTH
Dark Horse Comics/Acme Press: July 1992 - Aug 1992 ($4.95, limited series)

1-3-Paul Gulacy-c/a — 5.00

JAMES BOND 007: SHATTERED HELIX
Dark Horse Comics: Jun 1994 - July 1994 ($2.50, limited series)

1,2 — 3.00

JAMES BOND 007: THE QUASIMODO GAMBIT
Dark Horse Comics: Jan 1995 - May 1995 ($3.95, limited series)

1-3 — 4.50

JAMES BOND FOR YOUR EYES ONLY
Marvel Comics Group: Oct, 1981 - No. 2, Nov, 1981

1,2-Movie adapt.; r/Marvel Super Special #19 — 3.00

JAMES BOND JR. (TV)
Marvel Comics: Jan, 1992 - No. 12, Dec, 1992 (#1: $1.00, #2-on: $1.25)

1-12: Based on animated TV show — 2.25

JAMES BOND: LICENCE TO KILL (See Licence To Kill)

JAMES BOND: PERMISSION TO DIE
Eclipse Comics/ACME Press: 1989 - No. 3, 1991 ($3.95, lim. series, squarebound, 52 pgs.)

1-3: Mike Grell-c/a/scripts in all. 3-($4.95) — 5.00

JAM, THE: SUPER COOL COLOR INJECTED TURBO ADVENTURE #1 FROM HELL!
Comico: May, 1988 ($2.50, 44 pgs., one-shot)

1 — 2.50

JANE ARDEN (See Feature Funnies & Pageant of Comics)
St. John (United Features Syndicate): Mar, 1948 - No. 2, June, 1948

	GD	VG	FN	VF	VF/NM	NM-
1-Newspaper reprints	16	32	48	89	127	165
2	12	24	36	69	95	120

JANN OF THE JUNGLE (Jungle Tales No. 1-7)
Atlas Comics (CSI): No. 8, Nov, 1955 - No. 17, June, 1957

	GD	VG	FN	VF	VF/NM	NM-
8(#1)	35	70	105	198	287	375
9,11-15	20	40	60	112	161	210
10-Williamson/Colletta-c	20	40	60	115	165	215
16,17-Williamson/Mayo-a(3), 5 pgs. each	21	42	63	121	173	225

NOTE: *Everett c-15-17. Heck a-8, 15, 17. Maneely c-11. Shores a-8.*

JAR OF FOOLS
Penny Dreadful Press: 1994 ($5.95, B&W)

1-Jason Lutes-c/a/scripts — 6.00

JAR OF FOOLS
Black Eye Productions: 1994 - No. 2, 1994 ($6.95, B&W)

1,2: 1-Reprints of earlier ed. Jason Lutes-c/a/scripts — 7.00

JASON & THE ARGOBOTS
Oni Press: Aug, 2002 - No. 4, Dec, 2002 ($2.95, B&W, limited series)

1-4-Torres-s/Norton-c/a — 3.00
Vol. 1 Birthquake TPB (6/03, $11.95, digest size) r/#1-4, Sunday comic strips — 12.00
Vol. 2 Machina Ex Deus TPB (9/03, $11.95, digest size) new story — 12.00

JASON & THE ARGONAUTS (See Movie Classics)

JASON GOES TO HELL: THE FINAL FRIDAY (Movie)
Topps Comics: July, 1993 - No. 3, Sept, 1993 ($2.95, limited series)

1-3: Adaptation of film. 1-Glow-in-the-dark-c — 3.00

JASON'S QUEST (See Showcase #88-90)

JASON VS. LEATHERFACE
Topps Comics: Oct, 1995 - No. 3, Jan, 1996 ($2.95, limited series)

1-3: Collins scripts; Bisley-c — 3.00

JAWS 2 (See Marvel Comics Super Special, A)

JAY & SILENT BOB (See Clerks & Oni Double Feature)
Oni Press: July, 1998 - No. 4, Oct, 1999 ($2.95, B&W, limited series)

1-Kevin Smith-s/Fegredo-a; photo-c & Quesada/Palmiotti-c — 8.00
1-San Diego Comic Con variant covers (2 different covers, came packaged with action figures) — 10.00
1-2nd & 3rd printings, 2-4: 2-Allred-c. 3-Flip-c by Jaime Hernandez — 3.00
Chasing Dogma TPB (1999, $11.95) r/#1-4; Alanis Morissette intro. — 12.00
Chasing Dogma TPB (2001, $12.95) r/#1-4 in color; Morissette intro. — 13.00
Chasing Dogma HC (1999, $69.95, S&N) r/#1-4 in color; Morissette intro. — 70.00

JCP FEATURES
J.C. Productions (Archie): Feb, 1982-c; Dec, 1981-indicia ($2.00, one-shot, B&W magazine)

	GD	VG	FN	VF	VF/NM	NM-
1-T.H.U.N.D.E.R. Agents; Black Hood by Morrow & Neal Adams; Texeira-a; 2 pgs. S&K-a from Fly #1	1	3	4	6	8	10

JEANIE COMICS (Formerly All Surprise; Cowgirl Romances #28)
Marvel Comics/Atlas(CPC): No. 13, April, 1947 - No. 27, Oct, 1949

	GD	VG	FN	VF	VF/NM	NM-
13-Mitzi, Willie begin	20	40	60	112	161	210
14,15	14	28	42	79	110	140
16-Used in Love and Death by Legman; Kurtzman's "Hey Look"	16	32	48	89	127	165
17-19,22-Kurtzman's "Hey Look", (1-3 pgs. each)	11	22	33	66	91	115
20,21,23-27	10	20	30	60	80	100

JEEP COMICS (Also see G.I. Comics and Overseas Comics)
R. B. Leffingwell & Co.: Winter, 1944 - No. 3, Mar-Apr, 1948

	GD	VG	FN	VF	VF/NM	NM-
1-Capt. Power, Criss Cross & Jeep & Peep (costumed) begin	58	116	174	363	557	750
2	39	78	117	222	324	425
3-L. B. Cole dinosaur-c	47	94	141	287	436	585

JEFF JORDAN, U.S. AGENT
D. S. Publishing Co.: Dec, 1947 - Jan, 1948

	GD	VG	FN	VF	VF/NM	NM-
1	15	30	45	85	120	155

JEMM, SON OF SATURN
DC Comics: Sept, 1984 - No. 12, Aug, 1985 (Maxi-series, mando paper)

1-12: 3-Origin — 2.50

NOTE: *Colan a-1-12p; c-1-5, 7-12p.*

JENNY FINN
Oni Press: June, 1999 - No. 2, Sept, 1999 ($2.95, B&W, unfinished lim. series)

1,2-Mignola & Nixey-s/Nixey-a/Mignola-c — 3.00

JENNY SPARKS: THE SECRET HISTORY OF THE AUTHORITY
DC Comics (WildStorm): Aug, 2000 - No. 5, Mar, 2001 ($2.50, limited series)

1-Millar-s/McCrea & Hodgkins-a/Hitch & Neary-c — 3.50

Jesse James #2 © AVON

Jet Fighters #5 © STD

The Jetsons #8 © H-B

	GD 2.0	VG 4.0	FN 6.0	VF 8.0	VF/NM 9.0	NM- 9.2
1-Variant-c by McCrea	1	3	4	6	8	10
2-5: 2-Apollo & Midnighter. 3-Jack Hawksmoor. 4-Shen. 5-Engineer						3.00
TPB (2001, $14.95) r/#1-5; Ellis intro.						15.00

JERRY DRUMMER (Formerly Soldier & Marine V2#9)
Charlton Comics: V2#10, Apr, 1957 - V3#12, Oct, 1957

	GD 2.0	VG 4.0	FN 6.0	VF 8.0	VF/NM 9.0	NM- 9.2
V2#10, V3#11,12: 11-Whitman-c/a	6	12	18	29	36	42

JERRY IGER'S... (All titles, Blackthorne/First)(Value: cover or less)

JERRY LEWIS (See The Adventures of...)

JESSE JAMES (The True Story Of..., also seeThe Legend of...)
Dell Publishing Co.: No. 757, Dec, 1956 (one shot)

	GD 2.0	VG 4.0	FN 6.0	VF 8.0	VF/NM 9.0	NM- 9.2
Four Color 757-Movie, photo-c	10	20	30	72	104	135

JESSE JAMES (See Badmen of the West & Blazing Sixguns)
Avon Periodicals: 8/50 - No. 9, 11/52; No. 15, 10/53 - No. 29, 8-9/56

	GD 2.0	VG 4.0	FN 6.0	VF 8.0	VF/NM 9.0	NM- 9.2
1-Kubert Alabam-r/Cowpuncher #1	17	34	51	95	135	175
2-Kubert-a(3)	14	28	42	79	110	140
3-Kubert Alabam-r/Cowpuncher #2	13	26	39	76	106	135
4,9-No Kubert	8	16	24	43	54	65
5,6-Kubert Jesse James-a(3); 5-Wood-a(1pg.)	13	26	39	76	106	135
7-Kubert Jesse James-a(2)	11	22	33	66	91	115
8-Kinstler-a(3)	9	18	27	51	62	75
15-Kinstler-r/#3	7	14	21	37	46	55
16-Kinstler-r/#3 & story-r/Butch Cassidy #1	8	16	24	40	50	60
17-19,21: 17-Jesse James-r/#4; Kinstler-c idea from Kubert splash in #6. 18-Kubert Jesse James-r/#5. 19-Kubert Jesse James-r/#6. 21-Two Jesse James-r/#4, Kinstler-r/#4	7	14	21	35	43	50
20-Williamson/Frazetta-a; r/Chief Vic. Apache Massacre; Kubert Jesse James-r/#6; Kit West story by Larsen	14	28	42	79	110	140
22-29: 22,23-No Kubert. 24-New McCarty strip by Kinstler; Kinstler-r. 25-New McCarty Jesse James strip by Kinstler; Jesse James-r/#7,9. 26,27-New McCarty Jesse James strip plus a Kinstler/McCann Jesse James-r. 28-Reprints most of Red Mountain, Featuring Quantrells Raiders	7	14	21	35	43	50
Annual nn (1952; 25¢, 100 pgs.)- "...Brings Six-Gun Justice to the West"- 3 earlier issues rebound; Kubert, Kinstler-a(3)	29	58	87	164	237	310

NOTE: *Mostly reprints #10 on.* ***Fawcette*** *c-1, 2.* ***Kida*** *a-5.* ***Kinstler*** *a-3, 4, 7-9, 15r, 16r(2), 21-27; c-3, 4, 9, 17-27. Painted c-5-8. 22 has 2 stories r/Sheriff Bob Dixon's Chuck Wagon #1 with name changed to Sheriff Bob Trent.*

JESSE JAMES
Realistic Publications: July, 1953

	GD 2.0	VG 4.0	FN 6.0	VF 8.0	VF/NM 9.0	NM- 9.2
nn-Reprints Avon's #1; same-c, colors different	9	18	27	54	70	85

JEST (Formerly Snap; becomes Kayo #12)
Harry 'A' Chesler: No. 10, 1944; No. 11, 1944

	GD 2.0	VG 4.0	FN 6.0	VF 8.0	VF/NM 9.0	NM- 9.2
10-Johnny Rebel & Yankee Boy app. in text	17	34	51	95	135	175
11-Little Nemo in Adventure Land	17	34	51	95	135	175

JESTER
Harry 'A' Chesler: No. 10, 1945

	GD 2.0	VG 4.0	FN 6.0	VF 8.0	VF/NM 9.0	NM- 9.2
10	15	30	45	85	120	155

JESUS
Spire Christian Comics (Fleming H. Revell Co.): 1979 (49¢)

	GD 2.0	VG 4.0	FN 6.0	VF 8.0	VF/NM 9.0	NM- 9.2
nn	2	4	6	9	11	14

JET (See Jet Powers)

JET (Crimson from Wildcore & Backlash)
DC Comics (WildStorm): Nov, 2000 - No. 4, Feb, 2001 ($2.50, limited series)

	GD 2.0	VG 4.0	FN 6.0	VF 8.0	VF/NM 9.0	NM- 9.2
1-4-Nguyen-a/Abnett & Lanning-s						2.50

JET ACES
Fiction House Magazines: 1952 - No. 4, 1953

	GD 2.0	VG 4.0	FN 6.0	VF 8.0	VF/NM 9.0	NM- 9.2
1	16	32	48	92	131	170
2-4	10	20	30	56	73	90

JETCAT CLUBHOUSE (Also see Land of Nod, The)
Oni Press: Apr, 2001 - No. 3, Aug, 2001 ($3.25)

	GD 2.0	VG 4.0	FN 6.0	VF 8.0	VF/NM 9.0	NM- 9.2
1-3-Jay Stephens-s/a. 1-Wraparound-c						3.25
TPB (8/02, $10.95, 8 3/4" x 5 3/4") r/#1-3 & stories from Nickelodeon mag. & other						11.00

JET DREAM (...and Her Stunt-Girl Counterspies)(See The Man from Uncle #7)
Gold Key: June, 1968 (12¢)

	GD 2.0	VG 4.0	FN 6.0	VF 8.0	VF/NM 9.0	NM- 9.2
1-Painted-c	4	8	12	27	36	45

JET FIGHTERS (Korean War)
Standard Magazines: No. 5, Nov, 1952 - No. 7, Mar, 1953

	GD 2.0	VG 4.0	FN 6.0	VF 8.0	VF/NM 9.0	NM- 9.2
5,7-Toth-a. 5-Toth-c	12	24	36	69	95	120
6-Celardo-a	7	14	21	37	46	55

JET POWER
I.W. Enterprises: 1963

	GD 2.0	VG 4.0	FN 6.0	VF 8.0	VF/NM 9.0	NM- 9.2
I.W. Reprint 1,2-r/Jet Powers #1,2	3	6	9	19	25	32

JET POWERS (American Air Forces No. 5 on)
Magazine Enterprises: 1950 - No. 4, 1951

	GD 2.0	VG 4.0	FN 6.0	VF 8.0	VF/NM 9.0	NM- 9.2
1(A-1 #30)-Powell-c/a begins	37	74	112	213	312	410
2(A-1 #32) Powell dinosaur-c/a; classic-c	37	74	111	209	305	400
3(A-1 #35)-Williamson/Evans-a	40	80	120	239	357	475
4(A-1 #38)-Williamson/Wood-a; "The Rain of Sleep" drug story	40	80	120	239	357	475

JET PUP (See 3-D Features)

JETSONS, THE (TV) (See March of Comics #276, 330, 348 & Spotlight #3)
Gold Key: Jan, 1963 - No. 36, Oct, 1970 (Hanna-Barbera)

	GD 2.0	VG 4.0	FN 6.0	VF 8.0	VF/NM 9.0	NM- 9.2
1-1st comic book app.	27	54	81	192	294	395
2	13	26	39	90	138	185
3-10	10	20	30	73	107	140
11-22	8	16	24	58	82	105
23-36-Reprints	7	14	21	46	63	80

JETSONS, THE (TV) (Also see Golden Comics Digest)
Charlton Comics: Nov, 1970 - No. 20, Dec, 1973 (Hanna-Barbera)

	GD 2.0	VG 4.0	FN 6.0	VF 8.0	VF/NM 9.0	NM- 9.2
1	10	20	30	70	100	130
2	6	12	18	38	52	65
3-10	4	8	12	25	33	42
11-20	3	6	9	19	25	32
nn (1973, 60¢, 100 pgs.) B&W one page gags	4	8	12	27	36	45

JETSONS, THE (TV)
Harvey Comics: V2#1, Sept, 1992 - No. 5, Nov, 1993 ($1.25/$1.50) (Hanna-Barbera)

	GD 2.0	VG 4.0	FN 6.0	VF 8.0	VF/NM 9.0	NM- 9.2
V2#1-5						4.00
...Big Book V2#1,2,3 ($1.95, 52 pgs.): 1-(11/92). 2-(4/93). 3-(7/93)						4.00
...Giant Size 1,2,3 ($2.25, 68 pgs): 1-(10/92). 2-(4/93). 3-(10/93)						4.00

JETSONS, THE (TV)
Archie Comics: Sept, 1995 - No. 17, Aug, 1996 ($1.50)

	GD 2.0	VG 4.0	FN 6.0	VF 8.0	VF/NM 9.0	NM- 9.2
1-17						3.00

JETTA OF THE 21ST CENTURY
Standard Comics: No. 5, Dec, 1952 - No. 7, Apr, 1953 (Teen-age Archie type)

	GD 2.0	VG 4.0	FN 6.0	VF 8.0	VF/NM 9.0	NM- 9.2
5	24	48	72	135	195	255
6,7: 6-Robot-c	14	28	42	79	110	140

JEZEBEL JADE (Hanna-Barbara)
Comico: Oct, 1988 - No. 3, Dec, 1988 ($2.00, mini-series)

	GD 2.0	VG 4.0	FN 6.0	VF 8.0	VF/NM 9.0	NM- 9.2
1-3: Johnny Quest spin-off						3.00

JEZEBELLE (See Wildstorm 2000 Annuals)
DC Comics (WildStorm): Mar, 2001 - No. 6, Aug, 2001 ($2.50, limited series)

	GD 2.0	VG 4.0	FN 6.0	VF 8.0	VF/NM 9.0	NM- 9.2
1-6-Ben Raab-s/Steve Ellis-a						2.50

JIGGS & MAGGIE
Dell Publishing Co.: No. 18, 1941 (one shot)

	GD 2.0	VG 4.0	FN 6.0	VF 8.0	VF/NM 9.0	NM- 9.2
Four Color 18 (#1)-(1936-38-r)	36	72	108	270	423	575

JIGGS & MAGGIE
Standard Comics/Harvey Publications No. 22 on: No. 11, 1949(June) - No. 21, 2/53; No. 22, 4/53 - No. 27, 2-3/54

	GD 2.0	VG 4.0	FN 6.0	VF 8.0	VF/NM 9.0	NM- 9.2
11	13	26	39	74	102	130
12-15,17-21	8	16	24	46	58	70
16-Wood text illos.	8	16	24	52	66	80
22-24-Little Dot app.	9	18	27	51	62	75
25,27	7	14	21	37	46	55
26-Four pgs. partially in 3-D	14	28	42	79	110	140

NOTE: *Sunday page reprints by McManus loosely blended into story continuity. Based on Bringing Up Father strip. Advertised on covers as "All New."*

JIGSAW (Big Hero Adventures)
Harvey Publ. (Funday Funnies): Sept, 1966 - No. 2, Dec, 1966 (36 pgs.)

	GD 2.0	VG 4.0	FN 6.0	VF 8.0	VF/NM 9.0	NM- 9.2
1-Origin & 1st app.; Crandall-a (5 pgs.)	4	8	12	22	30	38
2-Man From S.R.A.M.	3	6	9	16	20	24

JIGSAW OF DOOM (See Complete Mystery No. 2)

JIM BOWIE (Formerly Danger?; Black Jack No. 20 on)
Charlton Comics: No. 16, 1955? - No. 19, Apr, 1957

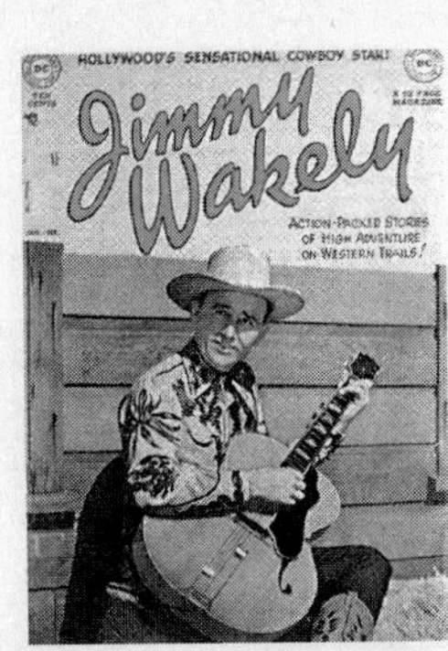

Jimmy Wakely #3 © DC

Jingle Jangle Comics #4 © EAS

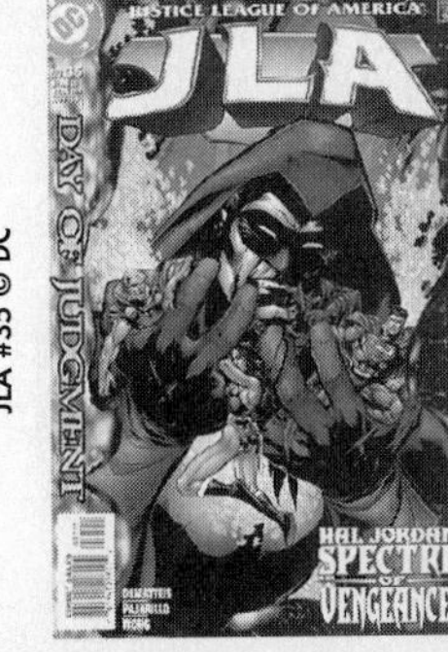

JLA #35 © DC

	GD 2.0	VG 4.0	FN 6.0	VF 8.0	VF/NM 9.0	NM- 9.2
16	8	16	24	43	54	65
17-19	6	12	18	29	36	42

JIM BOWIE (TV, see Western Tales)
Dell Publishing Co.: No. 893, Mar, 1958 - No. 993, May-July, 1959

Four Color 893 (#1)	7	14	21	46	63	80
Four Color 993-Photo-c	6	12	18	43	59	75

JIM DANDY
Dandy Magazine (Lev Gleason): May, 1956 - No. 3, Sept, 1956 (Charles Biro)

1-Biro-c	9	18	27	51	62	75
2,3	6	12	18	29	36	42

JIM HARDY (See Giant Comics Eds., Sparkler & Treasury of Comics #2 & 5)
United Features Syndicate/Spotlight Publ.: 1939; 1942; 1947 - No. 2, 1947

Single Series 6 ('39)	40	80	120	241	363	485
Single Series 27('42)	37	74	111	209	305	400
1('47)-Spotlight Publ.	15	30	45	86	123	160
2	9	18	27	54	70	85

JIM HARDY
Spotlight/United Features Synd.: 1944 (25¢, 132 pgs.) (Tip Top, Sparkler-r)

nn-Origin Mirror Man; Triple Terror app.	40	80	120	236	351	465

JIMINY CRICKET (Disney,, see Mickey Mouse Mag. V5#3 & Walt Disney Showcase #37)
Dell Publishing Co.: No. 701, May, 1956 - No. 989, May-July, 1959

Four Color 701	10	20	30	70	100	130
Four Color 795, 897, 989	8	16	24	53	74	95

JIM LEE SKETCHBOOK
DC Comics (WildStorm): 2002 (no price, 16 pgs.)

nn-Various DC and WildStorm character sketches by Lee 2.50

JIMMY CORRIGAN (See Acme Novelty Library)

JIMMY DURANTE (Also see A-1 Comics)
Magazine Enterprises: No. 18, 1949 - No. 20, 1949

A-1 18,20-Photo-c	43	86	129	262	401	540

JIMMY OLSEN (See Superman's Pal...)

JIMMY OLSEN: ADVENTURES BY JACK KIRBY
DC Comics: 2003, 2004 ($19.95, TPB)

nn-(2003) Reprints Jack Kirby's early issues of Superman's Pal Jimmy Olsen #133-139,141; Mark Evanier intro.; cover by Kirby and Steve Rude 20.00
Vol. 2 (2004) Reprints #142-148; Evanier intro.; cover gallery and sketch pages 20.00

JIMMY WAKELY (Cowboy movie star)
National Per. Publ.: Sept-Oct, 1949 - No. 18, July-Aug, 1952 (1-13: 52pgs.)

1-Photo-c, 52 pgs. begin; Alex Toth-a; Kit Colby Girl Sheriff begins	112	224	336	700	1075	1450
2-Toth-a	46	92	138	281	428	575
3,4,6,7-Frazetta-a in all, 3 pgs. each; Toth-a in all. 7-Last photo-c. 4-Kurtzman "Pot-Shot Pete", 1 pg; Toth-a	48	96	144	293	447	600
5,8-15-Toth-a; 12,14-Kubert-a (3 & 2 pgs.)	39	78	117	222	324	425
16-18	33	66	99	190	275	360

NOTE: *Gil Kane c-10-19p.*

JIM RAY'S AVIATION SKETCH BOOK
Vital Publishers: Mar-Apr, 1946 - No. 2, May-June, 1946

1-Picture stories about planes and pilots	40	80	120	230	335	440
2	27	54	81	152	219	285

JIM SOLAR (See Wisco/Klarer in the Promotional Comics section)

JINGLE BELLE (Paul Dini's...)
Oni Press: Nov, 1999 - No. 2, Dec, 1999 ($2.95, B&W, limited series)

1,2-Paul Dini-s. 2-Alex Ross flip-c 3.00
Jingle Belle: Dash Away All (12/03, $11.95, digest-size) Dini-s/Garibaldi-a 12.00
Jingle Belle's Cool Yule (11/02, $13.95,TPB) r/All-Star Holiday Hullabaloo, The Mighty Elves, and Jubilee; internet strips and a color section w/DeStefano-a 14.00
Paul Dini's Jingle Belle Jubilee (11/01, $2.95) Dini-s; art by Rolston, DeCarlo, Morrison and Bone; pin-ups by Thompson and Aragonés 3.00
Paul Dini's Jingle Belle's All-Star Holiday Hullabaloo (11/00, $4.95) stories by various including Dini, Aragonés, Jeff Smith, Bill Morrison; Frank Cho-c 5.00
Paul Dini's Jingle Belle: The Mighty Elves (7/01, $2.95) Dini-s/Bone-a 3.00
Paul Dini's Jingle Belle Winter Wingding (11/02, $2.95) Dini-s/Clugston-Major-c 3.00
TPB (10/00, $8.95) r/#1&2, and app. from Oni Double Feature #13 9.00

JINGLE BELLS (See March of Comics No. 65)

JINGLE DINGLE CHRISTMAS STOCKING COMICS (See Foodini #2)
Stanhall Publications: V2#1, 1951 (no date listed) (25¢, 100 pgs.; giant-size) (Publ. annually)

V2#1-Foodini & Pinhead, Silly Pilly plus games & puzzles	19	38	57	107	154	200

JINGLE JANGLE COMICS (Also see Puzzle Fun Comics)
Eastern Color Printing Co.: Feb, 1942 - No. 42, Dec, 1949

1-Pie-Face Prince of Old Pretzleburg, Jingle Jangle Tales by George Carlson, Hortense, & Benny Bear begin	46	92	138	281	428	575
2-4: 2,3-No Pie-Face Prince. 4-Pie-Face Prince-c	22	44	66	123	177	230
5	20	40	60	112	161	210
6-10: 8-No Pie-Face Prince	15	30	45	86	123	160
11-15	12	24	36	69	95	120
16-30: 17,18-No Pie-Face Prince. 24,30-XMas-c	10	20	30	58	77	95
31-42: 36,42-Xmas-c	9	18	27	54	70	85

NOTE: ***George Carlson** a-(2) in all except No. 2, 3, 8; c-1-6. **Carlson** 1 pg. puzzles in 9, 10, 12-15, 18, 20. **Carlson** illustrated a series of Uncle Wiggily books in 1930's.*

JING PALS
Victory Publishing Corp.: Feb, 1946 - No. 4, Aug?, 1946 (Funny animal)

1-Wishing Willie, Puggy Panda & Johnny Rabbit begin	15	30	45	86	123	160
2-4	9	18	27	52	66	80

JINKS, PIXIE, AND DIXIE (See Kite Fun Book & Whitman Comic Books)

JINN
Image Comics (Avalon Studios): Mar, 2000 - No. 3, Oct, 2000 ($2.50)

1-3-Rearte-c/a 3.00

JINX
Caliber Press: 1996 - No. 7, 1996 ($2.95, B&W, 32 pgs.)

1-7: Brian Michael Bendis-c/a/scripts. 2-Photo-c 3.00

JINX (Volume 2)
Image Comics: 1997 - No. 5, 1998 ($2.95, B&W, bi-monthly)

1-4: Brian Michael Bendis-c/a/scripts. 3.00
5-($3.95) Brereton-c 4.00
...Buried Treasures ('98, $3.95) short stories, ...Confessions ('98, $3.95) short stories, ...Pop Culture Hoo-Hah ('98, $3.95) humor shorts 4.00
TPB (1997, $10.95) r/Vol 1,#1-4 11.00
...: The Definitive Collection ('01, $24.95) remastered #1-5, sketch pages, art gallery, script excerpts, Mack intro. 25.00

JINX: TORSO
Image Comics: 1998 - No. 6, 1999 ($3.95/$4.95, B&W)

1-6-Based on Eliot Ness' pursuit of America's first serial killer; Brian Michael Bendis & Marc Andreyko-s/Bendis-a. 3-6-($4.95) 5.00
Softcover (2000, $24.95) r/#1-6; intro. by Greg Rucka; photo essay of the actual murders and police documents 25.00
Hardcover (2000, $49.95) signed & numbered 50.00

JLA (See Justice League of America and Justice Leagues)
DC Comics: Jan, 1997 - Present ($1.95/$1.99/$2.25)

1-Morrison-s/Porter & Dell-a. The Hyperclan app.	2	4	6	10	12	15
2	1	3	4	6	8	10
3,4	1	2	3	5	7	9

5-Membership drive; Tomorrow Woman app. 6.00
6-9: 8-Green Arrow joins. 6.00
10-21: 10-Rock of Ages begins. 11-Joker and Luthor-c/app. 15-($2.95) Rock of Ages concludes. 16-New members join; Prometheus app. 17,20-Jorgensen-a. 18-21-Waid-s. 20,21-Adam Strange c/app. 5.00
22-40: 22-Begin $1.99-c; Sandman (Daniel) app. 27-Amazo app. 28-31-JSA app. 35-Hal Jordan/Spectre app. 36-40-World War 3 2.50
41-($2.99) Conclusion of World War 3; last Morrison-s 3.00
42-46: 43-Waid-s; Ra's al Ghul app. 44-Begin $2.25-c. 46-Batman leaves 2.25
47-49: 47-Hitch & Neary-a begins; JLA battles Queen of Fables 2.25
50-($3.75) JLA vs. Dr. Destiny; art by Hitch & various 3.75
51-74: 52-55-Hitch-a. 59-Joker: Last Laugh. 61-68-Kelly-s/Mahnke-a. 69-73-Hunt for Aquaman; bi-monthly with alternating art by Mahnke and Guichet 2.25
75-(1/03, $3.95) leads into Aquaman (4th series) #1 4.00
76-93: 76-Firestorm app. 77-Banks-a. 79-Kanjar Ro app. 91-93-O'Neil-s/Huat-a 2.25
94-99-Byrne & Ordway-a/Claremont-s; Doom Patrol app. 2.25
100-($3.50) Intro. Vera Black; leads into Justice League Elite #1 3.50
101-109: 101-106-Austen-s/Garney-a/c. 107-109-Crime Syndicate app.; Busiek-s 2.25
#1,000,000 (11/98) 853rd Century x-over 2.50
Annual 1 (1997, $3.95) Pulp Heroes; Augustyn-s/Olivetti & Ha-a 4.00

JLA in Crisis Secret Files #1 © DC

JLA/Avengers #3 © DC & MAR

JLA: World Without Grown-Ups #1 © DC

GD 2.0 | VG 4.0 | FN 6.0 | VF 8.0 | VF/NM 9.0 | NM- 9.2

Annual 2 (1998, $2.95) Ghosts; Wrightson-c 4.00
Annual 3 (1999, $2.95) JLApe; Art Adams-c 3.00
Annual 4 (2000, $3.50) Planet DC x-over; Steve Scott-c/a 3.50
...80-Page Giant 1 (7/98, $4.95) stories & art by various 6.00
...80-Page Giant 2 (11/99, $4.95) Green Arrow & Hawkman app. Hitch-c 6.00
...80-Page Giant 3 (10/00, $5.95) Pariah & Harbinger; intro. Moon Maiden 6.00
...Foreign Bodies (1999, $5.95, one-shot) Kobra app.; Semeiks-a 6.00
...Gallery (1997, $2.95) pin-ups by various; Quitely-c 3.00
...God & Monsters (2001, $6.95, one-shot) Benefiel-a/c 7.00
.../ Haven: Anathema (2002, $6.95) Concludes the Haven: The Broken City series 7.00
.../ Haven: Arrival (2001, $6.95) Leads into the Haven: The Broken City series 7.00
...In Crisis Secret Files 1 (11/98, $4.95) recap of JLA in DC x-overs 5.00
...: Island of Dr. Moreau, The (2002, $6.95, one-shot) Elseworlds; Pugh-c/a; Thomas-s 7.00
.../ JSA Secret Files & Origins (1/03, $4.95) prelude to JLA/JSA: Virtue & Vice; short stories and pin-ups by various; Pacheco-c 5.00
.../ JSA: Virtue and Vice HC (2002, $24.95) Teams battle Despero & Johnny Sorrow; Goyer & Johns-s/Pacheco-a/c 25.00
.../ JSA: Virtue and Vice SC (2003, $17.95) 18.00
...: Obsidian Age Book One, The (2003, $12.95) r/#66-71 13.00
...: Obsidian Age Book Two, The (2003, $12.95) r/#72-76 13.00
...: Our Worlds at War (9/01, $2.95) Jae Lee-c; Aquaman presumed dead 3.00
...Primeval (1999, $5.95, one-shot) Abnett & Lanning-s/Olivetti-a 6.00
...: Riddle of the Beast HC (2001, $24.95) Grant-s/painted-a by various; Sweet-c 25.00
...: Riddle of the Beast SC (2003, $14.95) Grant-s/painted-a by various; Kaluta-c 15.00
...: Seven Caskets (2000, $5.95, one-shot) Brereton-s/painted-c/a 6.00
...Showcase 80-Page Giant (2/00, $4.95) Hitch-c 5.00
...Superpower (1999, $5.95, one-shot) Arcudi-s/Eaton-a; Mark Antaeus joins 6.00
...: Shogun of Steel (2002, $6.95, one-shot) Elseworlds; Justiniano-c/a 7.00
...Vs. Predator (DC/Dark Horse, 2000, $5.95, one-shot) Nolan-c/a 6.00
...: Welcome to the Working Week (2003, $6.95, one-shot) Patton Oswalt-s 7.00
...: Zatanna's Search (2003, $12.95, TPB) rep. Zatanna's early app. & origin; Bolland-c 13.00
American Dreams (1998, $7.95, TPB) r/#5-9 8.00
Divided We Fall (2001, $17.95, TPB) r/#47-54 18.00
Golden Perfect (2003, $12.95, TPB) r/#61-65 13.00
Justice For All (1999, $14.95, TPB) r/#24-33 15.00
New World Order (1997, $5.95, TPB) r/#1-4 6.00
One Million (2004, $19.95, TPB) r/#DC One Million #1-4 and other #1,000,000 x-overs 20.00
Rock of Ages (1998, $9.95, TPB) r/#10-15 10.00
Rules of Engagement (2004, $12.95, TPB) r/#77-82 13.00
Strength in Numbers (1998, $12.95, TPB) r/#16-23, Secret Files #2 and Prometheus #1 13.00
Terror Incognita (2002, $12.95, TPB) r/#55-60 13.00
The Tenth Circle (2004, $12.95, TPB) r/#94-99 13.00
Tower of Babel (2001, $12.95, TPB) r/#42-46, Secret Files #3, 80-Page Giant #1 13.00
Trial By Fire (2004, $12.95, TPB) r/#84-89 13.00
World War III (2000, $12.95, TPB) r/#34-41 13.00

JLA: ACT OF GOD
DC Comics: 2000 - No. 3, 2001 ($4.95, limited series)
1-3-Elseworlds; metahumans lose their powers; Moench-s/Dave Ross-a 5.00

JLA: AGE OF WONDER
DC Comics: 2003 - No. 2, 2003 ($5.95, limited series)
1,2-Elseworlds; Superman and the League of Science during the Industrial Revolution 6.00

JLA: A LEAGUE OF ONE
DC Comics: 2000 (Graphic novel)
Hardcover ($24.95) Christopher Moeller-s/painted-a 25.00
Softcover (2002, $14.95) 15.00

JLA/AVENGERS (See Avengers/JLA for #2 & #4)
Marvel Comics: Sept, 2003; No. 3, Dec, 2003 ($5.95, limited series)
1-Busiek-s/Pérez-a; wraparound-c; Krona, Starro, Grandmaster, Terminus app. 6.00
3-Busiek-s/Pérez-a; wraparound-c; Phantom Stranger app. 6.00

JLA: BLACK BAPTISM
DC Comics: May, 2001 - No. 4, Aug, 2001 ($2.50, limited series)
1-4-Saiz-a(p)/Bradstreet-c; Zatanna app. 2.50

JLA: CLASSIFIED
DC Comics: Jan, 2005 - Present ($2.95)
1-Morrison-s/McGuinness-a/c; Ultramarines app. 3.00

JLA: CREATED EQUAL
DC Comics: 2000 - No. 2, 2000 ($5.95, limited series, prestige format)
1,2-Nicieza-s/Maguire-a; Elseworlds-Superman as the last man on Earth 6.00

JLA: DESTINY
DC Comics: 2002 - No. 4, 2002 ($5.95, prestige format, limited series)
1-4-Elseworlds; Arcudi-s/Mandrake-a 6.00

JLA: EARTH 2
DC Comics: 2000 (Graphic novel)
Hardcover ($24.95) Morrison-s/Quitely-a; Crime Syndicate app. 25.00
Softcover ($14.95) 15.00

JLA: GATEKEEPER
DC Comics: 2001 - No. 3, 2001 ($4.95, prestige format, limited series)
1-3-Truman-s/a 5.00

JLA: HEAVEN'S LADDER
DC Comics: 2000 ($9.95, Treasury-size one-shot)
nn-Bryan Hitch & Paul Neary-c/a; Mark Waid-s 10.00

JLA: INCARNATIONS
DC Comics: Jul, 2001 - No. 7, Feb, 2002 ($3.50, limited series)
1-7-Ostrander-s/Semeiks-a; different eras of the Justice League 3.50

JLA: LIBERTY AND JUSTICE
DC Comics: Nov, 2003 ($9.95, Treasury-size one-shot)
nn-Alex Ross-c/a; Paul Dini-s; story of the classic Justice League 10.00

JLA PARADISE LOST
DC Comics: Jan, 1998 - No. 3, Mar, 1998 ($1.95, limited series)
1-3-Millar-s/Olivetti-a 2.50

JLA: SCARY MONSTERS
DC Comics: May, 2003 - No. 6, Oct, 2003 ($2.50, limited series)
1-6-Claremont-s/Art Adams-c 2.50

JLA SECRET FILES
DC Comics: Sept, 1997 - Present ($4.95)
1-Standard Ed. w/origin-s & pin-ups 5.00
1-Collector's Ed. w/origin-s & pin-ups; cardstock-c 6.00
2,3: 2-(8/98) origin-s of JLA #16's newer members. 3-(12/00) 5.00
... 2004 (11/04) Justice League Elite app.; Mahnke & Byrne-a; Crime Syndicate app. 5.00

JLA: SECRET ORIGINS
DC Comics: Nov, 2002 ($7.95, Treasury-size one-shot)
nn-Alex Ross 2-page origins of Justice League members; text by Paul Dini 8.00

JLA: SECRET SOCIETY OF SUPER-HEROES
DC Comics: 2000 - No. 2, 2000 ($5.95, limited series, prestige format)
1,2-Elseworlds JLA; Chaykin and Tischman-s/McKone-a 6.00

JLA /SPECTRE: SOUL WAR
DC Comics: 2003 - No. 2, 2003 ($5.95, limited series, prestige format)
1,2-DeMatteis-s/Banks & Neary-a 6.00

JLA: THE NAIL (Elseworlds) (Also see Justice League of America: Another Nail)
DC Comics: Aug, 1998 - No. 3, Oct, 1998 ($4.95, prestige format)
1-3-JLA in a world without Superman; Alan Davis-s/a(p) 5.00
TPB ('98, $12.95) r/series w/new Davis-c 13.00

JLA / TITANS
DC Comics: Dec, 1998 - No. 3, Feb, 1999 ($2.95, limited series)
1-3-Grayson-s; P. Jimenez-c/a 3.00
...:The Technis Imperative ('99, $12.95, TPB) r/#1-3; Titans Secret Files 13.00

JLA: TOMORROW WOMAN (Girlfrenzy)
DC Comics: June, 1998 ($1.95, one-shot)
1-Peyer-s; story takes place during JLA #5 2.50

JLA / WILDC.A.T.S
DC Comics: 1997 ($5.95, one-shot, prestige format)
1-Morrison-s/Semeiks & Conrad-a 6.00

JLA /WITCHBLADE
DC Comics/Top Cow: 2000 ($5.95, prestige format, one-shot)
1-Pararillo-c/a 6.00

JLA / WORLD WITHOUT GROWN-UPS (See Young Justice)
DC Comics: Aug, 1998 - No. 2, Sept, 1998 ($4.95, prestige format)
1,2-JLA, Robin, Impulse & Superboy app.; Ramos & McKone-a 6.00
TPB ('98, $9.95) r/series & Young Justice: The Secret #1 10.00

JLA: YEAR ONE
DC Comics: Jan, 1998 - No. 12, Dec, 1998 ($2.95/$1.95, limited series)

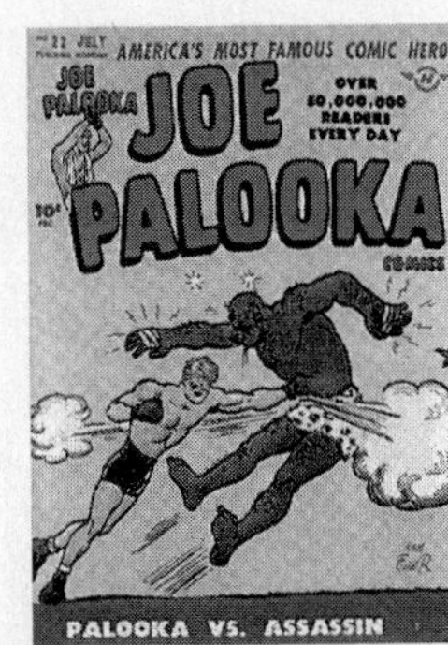

Joe Palooka #22 © CCG

John Byrne's Next Men #18 © DH

John Carter, Warlord of Mars #4 © MAR

GD 2.0 | VG 4.0 | FN 6.0 | VF 8.0 | VF/NM 9.0 | NM- 9.2

GD 2.0 | VG 4.0 | FN 6.0 | VF 8.0 | VF/NM 9.0 | NM- 9.2

1-($2.95)-Waid & Augustyn-s/Kitson-a 5.00
1-Platinum Edition 10.00
2-8-($1.95): 5-Doom Patrol-c/app. 7-Superman app. 4.00
9-12 3.00
TPB ('99, $19.95) r/#1-12; Busiek intro. 20.00

JLA-Z
DC Comics: Nov, 2003 - No. 3, Jan, 2004 ($2.50, limited series)
1-3-Pin-ups and info on current and former JLA members and villains; art by various 2.50

JLX
DC Comics (Amalgam): Apr, 1996 ($1.95, one-shot)
1-Mark Waid scripts 2.50

JLX UNLEASHED
DC Comics (Amalgam): June, 1997 ($1.95, one-shot)
1-Priest-s/ Oscar Jimenez & Rodriquez/a 2.50

JOAN OF ARC (Also see A-1 Comics & Ideal a Classical Comic)
Magazine Enterprises: No. 21, 1949 (one shot)
A-1 21-Movie adaptation; Ingrid Bergman photo-covers & interior photos; Whitney-a 29 58 87 164 237 310

JOE COLLEGE
Hillman Periodicals: Fall, 1949 - No. 2, Wint, 1950 (Teen-age humor, 52 pgs.)
1-Powell-a; Briefer-a 12 24 36 69 95 120
2-Powell-a 10 20 30 56 73 90

JOE JINKS
United Features Syndicate: No. 12, 1939
Single Series 12 31 62 93 178 259 340

JOE LOUIS (See Fight Comics #2, Picture News #6 & True Comics #5)
Fawcett Publications: Sept, 1950 - No. 2, Nov, 1950 (Photo-c) (Boxing champ) (See Dick Cole #10)
1-Photo-c; life story 56 112 168 350 538 725
2-Photo-c 40 80 120 235 348 460

JOE PALOOKA (1st Series)(Also see Big Shot Comics, Columbia Comics & Feature Funnies)
Columbia Comic Corp. (Publication Enterprises): 1942 - No. 4, 1944
1-1st to portray American president; gov't permission required 96 192 288 600 925 1250
2 (1943)-Hitler-c 56 112 168 350 538 725
3-Nazi Sub-c 40 80 120 233 342 450
4 35 70 105 201 293 385

JOE PALOOKA (2nd Series) (Battle Adv. #68-74; ...Advs. #75, 77-81, 83-85, 87; Champ of the Comics #76, 82, 86, 89-93) (See All-New)
Harvey Publications: Nov, 1945 - No. 118, Mar, 1961
1 48 96 144 293 447 600
2 26 52 78 147 211 275
3,4,6,7-1st Flyin' Fool, ends #25 16 32 48 92 131 170
5-Boy Explorers by S&K (7-8/46) 22 44 66 123 177 230
8-10 13 26 39 76 106 135
11-14,16,18-20: 14-Black Cat text-s(2). 18-Powell-a.; Little Max app. 19-Freedom Train-c 10 20 30 60 80 100
15-Origin & 1st app. Humphrey (12/47); Super-heroine Atoma app. by Powell 16 32 48 92 131 170
17-Humphrey vs. Palooka-c/s; 1st app. Little Max 16 32 48 92 131 170
21-26,29,30: 22-Powell-a. 30-Nude female painting 9 18 27 54 70 85
27-Little Max app.; Howie Morenz-s 10 20 30 56 73 90
28-Babe Ruth 4 pg. sty. 10 20 30 56 73 90
31,39,51: 31-Dizzy Dean 4 pg. sty. 39-(12/49) Humphrey & Little Max begin; Sonny Baugh football-s; Sherlock Max-s. 51-Babe Ruth 2 pg. sty; Jake Lamotta 1/2 pg. sty 9 18 217 51 62 75
32-38,40-50,52-61: 35-Little Max-c/story(4 pgs.); Joe Louis 1 pg. sty. 36-Humphrey story. 41-Bing Crosby photo on-c. 44-Palooka marries Ann Howe. 50-(11/51)-Becomes Harvey Comics Hits #51 8 16 24 43 54 65
62-S&K Boy Explorers-r 9 18 27 51 62 75
63-65,73-80,100: 79-Story of 1st meeting with Ann 7 14 21 37 46 55
66,67-'Commie' torture story "Drug-Diet Horror" 9 18 27 51 62 75
68,70-72: 68,70-Joe vs. "Gooks"-c. 71-Bloody bayonets-c. 72-Tank-c 8 16 24 46 58 70
69-1st "Battle Adventures" issue; torture & bondage 9 18 27 51 62 75
81-99,101-115: 104,107-Humphrey & Little Max-s 7 14 21 35 43 50
116-S&K Boy Explorers-r (Giant, '60) 8 16 24 46 58 70
117-(84 pg. Giant) r/Commie issues #66,67; Powell-a 9 18 27 51 62 75
118-(84 pg. Giant) Jack Dempsey 2 pg. sty, Powell-a 8 16 24 46 58 70
...**Visits the Lost City** nn (1945)(One Shot)(50¢)-164 page continuous story strip reprint. Has biography & photo of Ham Fisher; possibly the single longest comic book story published in that era (159 pgs.?) 165 330 495 1031 1591 2150

NOTE: ***Nostrand/Powell** a-73. **Powell** a-7, 8, 10, 12, 14, 17, 19, 26-45, 47-53, 70, 73 at least. Black Cat text stories #8, 12, 13, 19.*

JOE PSYCHO & MOO FROG
Goblin Studios: 1996 - No. 5, 1997 ($2.50, B&W)
1-5: 4-Two covers 2.50
...Full Color Extravagarbonzo ($2.95, color) 3.00

JOE YANK (Korean War)
Standard Comics (Visual Editions): No. 5, Mar, 1952 - No. 16, 1954
5-Toth, Celardo, Tuska-a 10 20 30 56 73 90
6-Toth, Severin/Elder-a 9 18 27 54 70 85
7 7 14 21 35 43 50
8-Toth-c 8 16 24 43 54 65
9-16: 9-Andru-c. 12-Andru-a 6 12 18 31 38 45

JOHN BOLTON'S HALLS OF HORROR
Eclipse Comics: June, 1985 - No. 2, June, 1985 ($1.75, limited series)
1,2-British-r; Bolton-c/a 3.00

JOHN BOLTON'S STRANGE WINK
Dark Horse Comics: Mar, 1998 - No. 3, May, 1998 ($2.95, B&W, limited series)
1-3-Anthology; Bolton-s/c/a 3.00

JOHN BYRNE'S NEXT MEN (See Dark Horse Presents #54)
Dark Horse Comics (Legend imprint #19 on): Jan, 1992 - No. 30, Dec, 1994 ($2.50, mature)
1-Silver foil embossed-c; Byrne-c/a/scripts in all 4.00
1-4: 1-2nd printing with gold ink logo 2.50
0-(2/92)-r/chapters 1-4 from DHP w/new Byrne-c 2.50
5-20,22-30: 7-10-MA #1-4 mini-series on flip side. 16-Origin of Mark IV. 17-Miller-c. 19-22-Faith storyline. 23-26-Power storyline. 27-30-Lies storyline Pt. 1-4 2.50
21-(12/93) 1st Hellboy; cover and Hellboy pages by Mike Mignola; Byrne other pages 3 6 9 18 23 28
...Parallel, Book 2 ($16.95)-TPB; r/#7-12 17.00
...Fame, Book 3($16.95)-TPB r/#13-18 17.00
...Faith, Book 4($14.95)-TPB r/#19-22 15.00

NOTE: *Issues 1 through 6 contain certificates redeemable for an exclusive Next Men trading card set by Byrne. Prices are for complete books. **Cody** painted c-23-26. **Mignola** a-21(part); c-21.*

JOHN BYRNE'S 2112
Dark Horse Comics (Legend): Oct, 1994 ($9.95, TPB)
1-Byrne-c/a/s 10.00

JOHN CARTER OF MARS (See The Funnies & Tarzan #207)
Dell Publishing Co.: No. 375, Mar-May, 1952 - No. 488, Aug-Oct, 1953 (Edgar Rice Burroughs)
Four Color 375 (#1)-Origin; Jesse Marsh-a 27 54 81 194 297 400
Four Color 437, 488-Painted-c 17 34 51 119 182 245

JOHN CARTER OF MARS
Gold Key: Apr, 1964 - No. 3, Oct, 1964
1(10104-404)-r/4-Color #375; Jesse Marsh-a 7 14 21 50 68 85
2(407), 3(410)-r/4-Color #437 & 488; Marsh-a 5 10 15 36 48 60

JOHN CARTER OF MARS
House of Greystroke: 1970 (10-1/2x16-1/2", 72 pgs., B&W, paper-c)
1941-42 Sunday strip-r; John Coleman Burroughs-a 4 8 12 24 32 40

JOHN CARTER, WARLORD OF MARS (Also see Weird Worlds)
Marvel Comics: June, 1977 - No. 28, Oct, 1979
1,18: 1-Origin. 18-Frank Miller-a(p)(1st publ. Marvel work) 1 2 3 5 7 9
1-(35¢-c variant, limited dist.) 2 4 6 11 14 18
2-5-(35¢-c variants, limited dist.) 6.00
2-17,19-28: 11-Origin Dejah Thoris 4.00
Annuals 1-3: 1(1977). 2(1978). 3(1979)-All 52 pgs. with new book-length stories 5.00

NOTE: ***Austin** c-24i. **Gil Kane** a-1-10p; c-1p, 2p, 3, 4-9p, 10, 15p, Annual 1p. **Layton** a-17i. **Miller** c-25, 26p. **Nebres** a-2-4i, 8-16i; c(i)-6-9, 11-22, 25, Annual 1. **Perez** c-24p. **Simonson** a-15p. **Sutton** a-7i.*

JOHN F. KENNEDY, CHAMPION OF FREEDOM
Worden & Childs: 1964 (no month) (25¢)
nn-Photo-c 9 18 27 60 85 110

JOHN F. KENNEDY LIFE STORY
Dell Publishing Co.: Aug-Oct, 1964; Nov, 1965; June, 1966 (12¢)

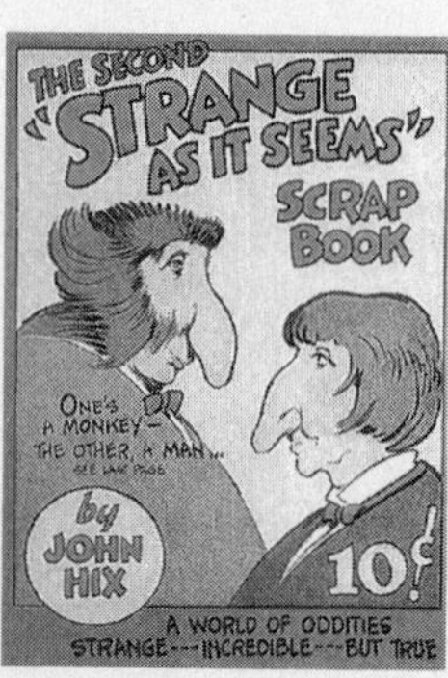

John Hix Scrap Book #2 © EAS

Johnny Hazard #6 © STD

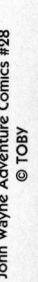

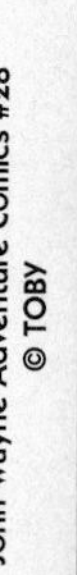
John Wayne Adventure Comics #28 © TOBY

	GD 2.0	VG 4.0	FN 6.0	VF 8.0	VF/NM 9.0	NM- 9.2
12-378-410-Photo-c	7	14	21	51	71	90
12-378-511 (reprint, 11/65)	4	8	12	25	33	42
12-378-606 (reprint, 6/66)	4	8	12	22	30	38

JOHN FORCE (See Magic Agent)

JOHN HIX SCRAP BOOK, THE
Eastern Color Printing Co. (McNaught Synd.): Late 1930's (no date) (10¢, 68 pgs., regular size)

	GD	VG	FN	VF	VF/NM	NM-
1-Strange As It Seems (resembles Single Series books)	40	80	120	230	335	440
2-Strange As It Seems	27	54	81	152	219	285

JOHN JAKES' MULLKON EMPIRE
Tekno Comix: Sept, 1995 - No. 6, Feb, 1996 ($1.95)

	GD	VG	FN	VF	VF/NM	NM-
1-6						2.25

JOHN LAW DETECTIVE (See Smash Comics #3)
Eclipse Comics: April, 1983 ($1.50, Baxter paper)

	GD	VG	FN	VF	VF/NM	NM-
1-Three Eisner stories originally drawn in 1948 for the never published John Law #1; original cover pencilled in 1948 & inked in 1982 by Eisner						3.00

JOHNNY APPLESEED (See Story Hour Series)

JOHNNY CASH (See Hello, I'm...)

JOHNNY DANGER (See Movie Comics, 1946)
Toby Press: 1950 (Based on movie serial)

	GD	VG	FN	VF	VF/NM	NM-
1-Photo-c; Sparling-a	18	36	54	100	143	185

JOHNNY DANGER PRIVATE DETECTIVE
Toby Press: Aug, 1954 (Reprinted in Danger #11 by Super)

	GD	VG	FN	VF	VF/NM	NM-
1-Photo-c; Opium den story	14	28	42	79	110	140

JOHNNY DYNAMITE (Formerly Dynamite #1-9; Foreign Intrigues #14 on)
Charlton Comics: No. 10, June, 1955 - No. 12, Oct, 1955

	GD	VG	FN	VF	VF/NM	NM-
10-12	10	20	30	58	77	95

JOHNNY DYNAMITE
Dark Horse Comics: Sept, 1994 - Dec, 1994 ($2.95, B&W & red, limited series)

	GD	VG	FN	VF	VF/NM	NM-
1-4: Max Allan Collins scripts in all; Terry Beatty-a						3.00
...: Underworld GN (AiT/Planet Lar, 3/03, $12.95, B&W) r/#1-4 in B&W without red						13.00

JOHNNY HAZARD
Best Books (Standard Comics) (King Features): No. 5, Aug, 1948 - No. 8, May, 1949; No. 35, date?

	GD	VG	FN	VF	VF/NM	NM-
5-Strip reprints by Frank Robbins (c/a)	20	40	60	112	161	210
6,8-Strip reprints by Frank Robbins	17	34	51	95	135	175
7,35: 7-New art, not Robbins	11	22	33	64	87	110

JOHNNY JASON (...Teen Reporter)
Dell Publishing Co.: Feb-Apr, 1962 - No. 2, June-Aug, 1962

	GD	VG	FN	VF	VF/NM	NM-
Four Color 1302, 2(01380-208)	4	8	12	27	36	45

JOHNNY LAW, SKY RANGER
Good Comics (Lev Gleason): Apr, 1955 - No. 3, Aug, 1955; No. 4, Nov, 1955

	GD	VG	FN	VF	VF/NM	NM-
1-Edmond Good-c/a	10	20	30	58	77	95
2-4	7	14	21	35	43	50

JOHNNY MACK BROWN (Western star; see Western Roundup under Dell Giants)
Dell Publishing Co.: No. 269, Mar, 1950 - No. 963, Feb, 1959 (All Photo-c)

	GD	VG	FN	VF	VF/NM	NM-
Four Color 269(#1)(3/50, 52pgs.)-Johnny Mack Brown & his horse Rebel begin; photo front/back-c begin; Marsh-a in #1-9	25	50	75	177	271	365
2(10-12/50, 52pgs.)	12	24	36	87	134	180
3(1-3/51, 52pgs.)	10	20	30	72	104	135
4-10 (9-11/52)(36pgs.), Four Color 455,493,541,584,618,645,685,722,776,834,963	8	16	24	53	74	95
Four Color 922-Manning-a	8	16	24	55	78	100

JOHNNY NEMO
Eclipse Comics: Sept, 1985 - No. 3, Feb, 1986 (Mini-series)

	GD	VG	FN	VF	VF/NM	NM-
1-3						2.50

JOHNNY PERIL (See Comic Cavalcade #15, Danger Trail #5, Sensation Comics #107 & Sensation Mystery)

JOHNNY RINGO (TV)
Dell Publishing Co.: No. 1142, Nov-Jan, 1960/61 (one shot)

	GD	VG	FN	VF	VF/NM	NM-
Four Color 1142-Photo-c	8	16	24	58	82	105

JOHNNY STARBOARD (See Wisco)

JOHNNY THE HOMICIDAL MANIAC
Slave Labor Graphics: Aug, 1995 - No. 7, Jan, 1997 ($2.95, B&W, lim. series)

	GD 2.0	VG 4.0	FN 6.0	VF 8.0	VF/NM 9.0	NM- 9.2
1-Jhonen Vasquez-c/s/a	1	3	4	6	8	10
1-Signed & numbered edition	2	4	6	10	12	15
2,3: 2-(11/95). 3-(2/96)						6.00
4-7: 4-(5-96). 5-(8/96)						4.00
Hardcover-($29.95) r/#1-7						30.00
TPB-($19.95)						20.00

JOHNNY THUNDER
National Periodical Publications: Feb-Mar, 1973 - No. 3, July-Aug, 1973

	GD	VG	FN	VF	VF/NM	NM-
1-Johnny Thunder & Nighthawk-r. in all	2	4	6	12	16	20
2,3: 2-Trigger Twins app.	2	4	6	8	10	12

NOTE: *All contain 1950s DC reprints from All-American Western.* ***Drucker*** *r-2, 3.* ***G. Kane*** *r-2, 3.* ***Moriera*** *r-1.* ***Toth*** *r-1, 3; c-1r, 3r. Also see All-American, All-Star Western, Flash Comics, Western Comics, World's Best & World's Finest.*

JOHN PAUL JONES
Dell Publishing Co.: No. 1007, July-Sept, 1959 (one-shot)

	GD	VG	FN	VF	VF/NM	NM-
Four Color 1007-Movie, Robert Stack photo-c	6	12	18	43	59	75

JOHN STEED & EMMA PEEL (See The Avengers, Gold Key series)

JOHN STEELE SECRET AGENT (Also see Freedom Agent)
Gold Key: Dec, 1964

	GD	VG	FN	VF	VF/NM	NM-
1-Freedom Agent	9	18	27	65	93	120

JOHN WAYNE ADVENTURE COMICS (Movie star; See Big Tex, Oxydol-Dreft, Tim McCoy, & With The Marines...#1)
Toby Press: Winter, 1949-50 - No. 31, May, 1955 (Photo-c: 1-12,17,25-on)

	GD	VG	FN	VF	VF/NM	NM-
1 (36pgs.)-Photo-c begin (1st time in comics on-c)	162	324	486	1013	1557	2100
2-4: 2-(4/50, 36pgs.)-Williamson/Frazetta-a(2) 6 & 2 pgs. (one story-r/Billy the Kid #1); photo back-c. 3-(36pgs.)-Williamson/Frazetta-a(2), 16 pgs. total; photo back-c. 4-(52pgs.)-Williamson/Frazetta-a(2), 16 pgs. total	71	142	213	444	685	925
5 (52pgs.)-Kurtzman-a-(Alfred "L" Newman in Potshot Pete)	51	102	153	311	476	640
6 (52pgs.)-Williamson/Frazetta-a (10 pgs.); Kurtzman-a "Pot-Shot Pete", (5 pgs.); & "Genius Jones", (1 pg.)	62	124	186	388	594	800
7 (52pgs.)-Williamson/Frazetta-a (10 pgs.)	55	110	165	340	520	700
8 (36pgs.)-Williamson/Frazetta-a(2) (12 & 9 pgs.)	67	134	201	419	647	875
9-11: Photo western-c	40	80	120	230	335	440
12,14-Photo war-c. 12-Kurtzman-a(2 pg.) "Genius"	40	80	120	230	335	440
13,15: 13,15-Line-drawn-c begin, end #24	35	70	105	201	293	385
16-Williamson/Frazetta-r/Billy the Kid #1	38	76	114	219	320	420
17-Photo-c	38	76	114	219	320	420
18-Williamson/Frazetta-a (r/#4 & 8, 19 pgs.)	40	80	120	236	351	465
19-24: 23-Evans-a?	32	64	96	184	267	350
25-Photo-c resume; end #31; Williamson/Frazetta-r/Billy the Kid #3	40	80	120	236	351	465
26-28,30-Photo-c	36	72	108	204	297	390
29,31-Williamson/Frazetta-a in each (r/#4, 2)	40	80	120	230	335	440

NOTE: *Williamsonish art in later issues by* ***Gerald McCann.***

JO-JO COMICS (...Congo King #7-29; My Desire #30 on)(Also see Fantastic Fears and Jungle Jo)
Fox Feature Syndicate: 1945 - No. 29, July, 1949 (Two No.7's; no #13)

	GD	VG	FN	VF	VF/NM	NM-
nn(1945)-Funny animal, humor	17	34	51	98	139	180
2(Sum,'46)-6(4-5/47): Funny animal. 2-Ten pg. Electro story (Fall/46)	10	20	30	58	77	95
7(7/47)-Jo-Jo, Congo King begins (1st app.); Bronze Man & Purple Tigress app.	90	180	270	563	869	1175
7(#8) (9/47)	65	130	195	406	623	840
8-10(#9-11): 8-Tanee begins	55	110	165	340	520	700
11,12(#12,13),14,16: 11,16-Kamen bondage-c	48	96	144	293	447	600
15,17: 15-Cited by Dr. Wertham in 5/47 Saturday Review of Literature. 17-Kamen bondage-c	50	100	150	305	465	625
18-20	48	96	144	293	447	600
21-29: 21-Hollingsworth-a(4 pgs.; 23-1 pg.)	40	80	120	240	360	480

NOTE: *Many bondage-c/a by* ***Baker/Kamen/Feldstein/Good.*** *No. 7's have Princesses Gwenna, Geesa, Yolda, & Safra before settling down on Tanee.*

JOKEBOOK COMICS DIGEST ANNUAL (...Magazine No. 5 on)
Archie Publications: Oct, 1977 - No. 13, Oct, 1983 (Digest Size)

	GD	VG	FN	VF	VF/NM	NM-
1(10/77)-Reprints; Neal Adams-a	2	4	6	14	18	22
2(4/78)-5	2	4	6	10	12	15
6-13	1	3	4	6	8	10

JOKER, THE (See Batman #1, Batman: The Killing Joke, Brave & the Bold, Detective, Greatest Joker Stories & Justice League Annual #2)
National Periodical Publications: May, 1975 - No. 9, Sept-Oct, 1976

The Joker #9 © DC

Jolly Jingles #12 © MLJ

Jon Sable, Freelance #23 © FC

GD 2.0 | VG 4.0 | FN 6.0 | VF 8.0 | VF/NM 9.0 | NM- 9.2

1-Two-Face app. 4 8 12 29 40 60
2,3: 3-The Creeper app. 3 6 9 16 20 30
4-9: 4-Green Arrow-c/sty. 6-Sherlock Holmes-c/sty. 7-Lex Luthor-c/story. 8-Scarecrow-c/story. 9-Catwoman-c/story 2 4 6 11 14 22

JOKER, THE (See Tangent Comics/ The Joker)

JOKER COMICS (Adventures Into Terror No. 43 on)
Timely/Marvel Comics No. 36 on (TCI/CDS): Apr, 1942 - No. 42, Aug, 1950

1-(Rare)-Powerhouse Pepper (1st app.) begins by Wolverton; Stuporman app. from Daring Comics 277 554 831 1731 2666 3600
2-Wolverton-a; 1st app. Tessie the Typist & begin series 90 180 270 563 869 1175
3-5-Wolverton-a 55 110 165 340 520 700
6-10-Wolverton-a. 6-Tessie-c begin 40 80 120 244 372 500
11-20-Wolverton-a 39 78 117 222 324 425
21,22,24-27,29,30-Wolverton cont'd. & Kurtzman's "Hey Look" in #23-27 33 66 99 190 275 360
23-1st "Hey Look" by Kurtzman; Wolverton-a 35 70 105 201 293 385
28,32,34,37-41: 28-Millie the Model begins. 32-Hedy begins. 41-Nellie the Nurse app. 12 24 36 71 98 125
31-Last Powerhouse Pepper; not in #28 26 52 78 147 211 275
33,35,36-Kurtzman's "Hey Look" 13 26 39 76 106 135
42-Only app. 'Patty Pinup,' clone of Millie the Model 13 26 39 74 102 130

JOKER: DEVIL'S ADVOCATE
DC Comics: 1996 ($24.95/$12.95, one-shot)

nn-(Hardcover)-Dixon scripts/Nolan & Hanna-a 25.00
nn-(Softcover) 13.00

JOKER: LAST LAUGH
DC Comics: Dec, 2001 - No. 6, Jan, 2002 ($2.95, weekly limited series)

1-6: 1,6-Bolland-c 3.00
...Secret Files (12/01, $5.95) Short stories by various; Simonson-c 6.00

JOKER / MASK
Dark Horse Comics: May, 2000 - No. 4, Aug, 2000 ($2.95, limited series)

1-4-Batman, Harley Quinn, Poison Ivy app. 3.00

JOLLY CHRISTMAS, A (See March of Comics No. 269)

JOLLY COMICS: **Four Star Publishing Co.:** 1947 (Advertised, not published)

JOLLY JINGLES (Formerly Jackpot Comics)
MLJ Magazines: No. 10, Sum, 1943 - No. 16, Wint, 1944/45

10-Super Duck begins (origin & 1st app.); Woody The Woodpecker begins (not same as Lantz character) 40 80 120 230 335 440
11 (Fall, '43)-2nd Super Duck(see Hangman #8) 20 40 60 112 161 210
12-Hitler-c 25 50 75 141 203 265
13-16: 13-Sahle-c. 15-Vigoda-c 13 26 39 74 102 130

JONAH HEX (See All-Star Western, Hex and Weird Western Tales)
National Periodical Pub./DC Comics: Mar-Apr, 1977 - No. 92, Aug, 1985

1 11 22 33 77 114 150
2 6 12 18 40 55 70
3,4,9: 9-Wrightson-c. 4 8 12 29 40 50
5,6,10: 5-Rep 1st app. from All-Star Western #10 4 8 12 24 32 40
7,8-Explains Hex's face disfigurement (origin) 5 10 15 33 44 55
11-20: 12-Starlin-c 3 6 9 16 20 25
21-32: 31,32-Origin retold 2 4 6 10 13 16
33-50 1 3 4 6 8 10
51-80 6.00
81-91: 89-Mark Texeira-a. 91-Cover swipe from Superman #243 (hugging a mystery woman) 1 2 3 4 5 7
92-Story cont'd in Hex #1 3 6 9 16 20 24

NOTE: ***Ayers** a(p)-35-37, 40, 41, 44-53, 56, 58-82. **Buckler** a-11; c-11, 13-16. **Kubert** c-43-46. **Morrow** a-90-92; c-10. **Spiegle(Tothish)** a-34, 38, 40, 49, 52. **Texeira** a-89p. Batlash back-ups in 49, 52. El Diablo back-ups in 48, 56-60, 73-75. Scalphunter back-ups in 40, 41, 45-47.*

JONAH HEX AND OTHER WESTERN TALES (Blue Ribbon Digest)
DC Comics: Sept-Oct, 1979 - No. 3, Jan-Feb, 1980 (100 pgs.)

1-3: 1-Origin Scalphunter-r, Ayers/Evans, Neal Adams-a.; painted-c. 2-Weird Western Tales-r; Neal Adams, Toth, Aragones-a. 3-Outlaw-r, Scalphunter-r; Gil Kane, Wildey-a 2 4 6 10 13 16

JONAH HEX: RIDERS OF THE WORM AND SUCH
DC Comics (Vertigo): Mar, 1995 - No. 5, July, 1995 ($2.95, limited series)

1-5-Lansdale story, Truman -a 4.00

JONAH HEX: SHADOWS WEST
DC Comics (Vertigo): Feb, 1999 - No. 3, Apr, 1999 ($2.95, limited series)

1-3-Lansdale-s/Truman -a 4.00

JONAH HEX SPECTACULAR (See DC Special Series No. 16)

JONAH HEX: TWO-GUN MOJO
DC Comics (Vertigo): Aug, 1993 - No. 5, Dec, 1993 ($2.95, limited series)

1-Lansdale scripts in all; Truman/Glanzman-a in all w/Truman-c 6.00
1-Platinum edition with no price on cover 20.00
2-5 4.00
TPB-(1994, $12.95) r/#1-5 13.00

JONESY (Formerly Crack Western)
Comic Favorite/Quality Comics Group: No. 85, Aug, 1953; No. 2, Oct, 1953 - No. 8, Oct, 1954

85(#1)-Teen-age humor 8 16 24 43 54 65
2 5 10 15 24 30 35
3-8 5 10 15 22 26 30

JON JUAN (Also see Great Lover Romances)
Toby Press: Spring, 1950

1-All Schomburg-a (signed Al Reid on-c); written by Siegel; used in **SOTI**, pg. 38 (Scarce) 63 126 189 394 610 825

JONNI THUNDER (...A.K.A. Thunderbolt)
DC Comics: Feb, 1985 - No. 4, Aug, 1985 (75¢, limited series)

1-4: 1-Origin & 1st app. 2.25

JONNY DEMON
Dark Horse Comics: May, 1994 - No. 3, July, 1994 ($2.50, limited series)

1-3 2.50

JONNY DOUBLE
DC Comics (Vertigo): Sept, 1998 - No. 4, Dec, 1998 ($2.95, limited series)

1-4-Azzarello-s 3.00
TPB (2002, $12.95) r/#1-4; Chiarello-c 13.00

JONNY QUEST (TV)
Gold Key: Dec, 1964 (Hanna-Barbera)

1 (10139-412) 35 70 105 263 412 560

JONNY QUEST (TV)
Comico: June 1986 - No. 31, Dec, 1988 ($1.50/$1.75)(Hanna-Barbera)

1 5.00
2,3,5: 3,5-Dave Stevens-c 4.00
4,6-31: 30-Adapts TV episode 3.00
Special 1(9/88, $1.75), 2(10/88, $1.75) 4.00

NOTE: ***M. Anderson** a-9. **Mooney** a-Special 1. **Pini** a-2. **Quagmire** a-31p. **Rude** a-1; c-2i. **Sienkiewicz** c-11. **Spiegle** a-7, 12, 21; c-21 **Staton** a-2i, 11p. **Steacy** c-8. **Stevens** a-4i; c-3,5. **Wildey** a-1, c-1, 7, 12. **Williamson** a-4i; c-4i.*

JONNY QUEST CLASSICS (TV)
Comico: May, 1987 - No. 3, July, 1987 ($2.00) (Hanna-Barbera)

1-3: Wildey-c/a; 3-Based on TV episode 3.00

JON SABLE, FREELANCE (Also see Mike Grell's Sable & Sable)
First Comics: 6/83 - No. 56, 2/88 (#1-17, $1; #18-33, $1.25, #34-on, $1.75)

1-Mike Grell-c/a/scripts 3.00
2-56: 3-5-Origin, parts 1-3. 6-Origin, part 4. 11-1st app. of Maggie the Cat. 14-Mando paper begins. 16-Maggie the Cat. app. 25-30-Shatter app. 34-Deluxe format begins ($1.75) 2.25

NOTE: ***Aragones** a-33; c-33(part). **Grell** a-1-43;c-1-52, 53p, 54-56.*

JOSEPH & HIS BRETHREN (See The Living Bible)

JOSIE (She's... #1-16) (...& the Pussycats #45 on) (See Archie's Pals 'n' Gals #23 for 1st app.) (Also see Archie Giant Series Magazine #528, 540, 551, 562, 571, 584, 597, 610, 622)
Archie Publ./Radio Comics: Feb, 1963; No. 2, Aug, 1963 - No. 106, Oct, 1982

1 17 34 51 121 186 250
2 10 20 30 67 96 125
3-5 7 14 21 50 68 85
6-10 5 10 15 36 48 60
11-20 4 8 12 25 33 42
21, 23-30 3 6 9 19 25 32
22 (9/66)-Mighty Man & Mighty (Josie Girl) app. 4 8 12 28 38 48
31-44 3 6 9 16 21 26
45 (12/69)-Josie and the Pussycats begins (Hanna Barbera TV cartoon); 1st app. of the Pussycats 11 22 33 77 114 150
46-2nd app./1st cover Pussycats 8 16 24 53 74 95
47-3rd app. of the Pussycats 5 10 15 36 48 60
48,49-Pussycats band-c/s 6 12 18 40 55 70

Journey Into Fear #20 © SUPR

Journey Into Mystery #95 © MAR

Journey Into Mystery #515 © MAR

	GD 2.0	VG 4.0	FN 6.0	VF 8.0	VF/NM 9.0	NM- 9.2
50-J&P-c; go to Hollywood, meet Hanna & Barbera	7	14	21	50	68	85
51-54	3	6	9	19	25	32
55-74 (2/74)(52 pg. issues)	3	6	9	18	24	30
75-90(8/76)	2	4	6	11	14	18
91-99	2	4	6	10	12	15
100 (10/79)	2	4	6	12	16	20
101-106	2	4	6	11	14	18

JOSIE & THE PUSSYCATS (TV)
Archie Comics: 1993 - No. 2, 1994 ($2.00, 52 pgs.)(Published annually)

	GD 2.0	VG 4.0	FN 6.0	VF 8.0	VF/NM 9.0	NM- 9.2
1,2-Bound-in pull-out poster in each. 2-(Spr/94)						5.00

JOURNAL OF CRIME (See Fox Giants)

JOURNEY
Aardvark-Vanaheim #1-14/Fantagraphics Books #15-on: 1983 - No. 14, Sept, 1984; No. 15, Apr, 1985 - No. 27, July, 1986 (B&W)

	GD 2.0	VG 4.0	FN 6.0	VF 8.0	VF/NM 9.0	NM- 9.2
1						3.00
2-27: 20-Sam Kieth-a						2.25

JOURNEY INTO FEAR
Superior-Dynamic Publications: May, 1951 - No. 21, Sept, 1954

	GD 2.0	VG 4.0	FN 6.0	VF 8.0	VF/NM 9.0	NM- 9.2
1-Baker-r(2)	67	134	201	419	647	875
2	46	92	138	281	428	575
3,4	40	80	120	239	357	475
5-10,15: 15-Used in **SOTI**, pg. 389	30	60	90	170	245	320
11-14,16-21	27	54	81	154	222	290

NOTE: *Kamenish 'headlight'-a most issues.* ***Robinson** a-10.*

JOURNEY INTO MYSTERY (1st Series) (Thor Nos. 126-502)
Atlas(CPS No. 1-48/AMI No. 49-68/Marvel No. 69 (6/61) on): 6/52 - No. 48, 8/57; No. 49, 11/58 - No. 125, 2/66; 503, 11/96 - No. 521, June, 1998

	GD 2.0	VG 4.0	FN 6.0	VF 8.0	VF/NM 9.0	NM- 9.2
1-Weird/horror stories begin	300	600	900	1948	3124	4300
2	108	216	324	675	1038	1400
3,4	81	162	243	506	778	1050
5-11	55	110	165	340	520	700
12-20,22: 15-Atomic explosion panel. 22-Davis*esque*-a; last pre-code issue (2/55)	43	86	129	262	401	540
21-Kubert-a; Tothish-a by Andru	44	88	132	268	409	550
23-32,35-38,40: 24-Torres?-a. 38-Ditko-a	32	64	96	184	267	350
33-Williamson-a; Ditko-a (his 1st for Atlas?)	35	70	105	201	293	385
34,39: 34-Krigstein-a. 39-1st S.A. issue; Wood-a	33	66	99	190	275	368
41-Crandall-a; Frazetta*esque*-a by Morrow	20	40	60	145	223	300
42,46,48: 42,48-Torres-a. 46-Torres & Krigstein-a	20	40	60	141	216	290
43,44-Williamson/Mayo-a in both	21	42	63	150	230	310
45,47,50,52-54: 50-Davis-a. 54-Williamson-a	19	38	57	136	208	280
49-Matt Fox, Check-a	20	40	60	141	216	290
51-Kirby/Wood-a	21	42	63	152	234	315
55-61,63-65,67-69,71,72,74,75: 74-Contents change to Fantasy. 75-Last 10¢ issue	19	38	57	136	208	280
62-Prototype ish. (The Hulk); 1st app. Xemnu (Titan) called "The Hulk"	29	58	87	210	323	435
66-Prototype ish. (The Hulk)-Return of Xemnu "The Hulk"	26	52	78	184	282	380
70-Prototype ish. (The Sandman)(7/61); similar to Spidey villain	25	50	75	177	271	365
73-Story titled "The Spider" where a spider is exposed to radiation & gets powers of a human and shoots webbing; a reverse prototype of Spider-Man's origin	37	74	111	278	432	585
76,77,80-82: 80-Anti-communist propaganda story	15	30	45	109	167	225
76-(10¢ cover price blacked out, 12¢ printed on)	37	74	111	278	432	585
78-The Sorceror (Dr. Strange prototype) app. (3/62)	25	50	75	177	271	365
79-Prototype issue. (Mr. Hyde)	21	42	63	150	230	310
83-Origin & 1st app. The Mighty Thor by Kirby (8/62) and begin series; Thor-c also begin	455	910	1365	4163	7082	10,000
83-Reprint from the Golden Record Comic Set	14	28	42	97	149	200
With the record (1966)	20	40	60	145	223	300
84-2nd app. Thor	142	284	426	1207	1954	2700
85-1st app. Loki & Heimdall; 1st brief app. Odin (1 panel)	89	178	267	757	1229	1700
86-1st full app. Odin	55	110	165	468	759	1050
87-89: 89-Origin Thor retold	44	88	132	352	551	750
90-No Kirby-a	38	76	114	285	443	600
91,92,94,96-Sinnott-a	32	64	96	232	361	490
93,97-Kirby-a; Tales of Asgard series begins #97 (origin which concludes in #99); origin/1st app. Lava Man	38	76	114	285	443	600
95-Sinnott-a	32	64	96	232	361	490
98,99-Kirby/Heck-a. 98-Origin/1st app. The Human Cobra. 99-1st app. Surtur & Mr. Hyde	27	54	81	194	297	400
100-Kirby/Heck-a; Thor battles Mr. Hyde	27	54	81	194	297	400
101,108: 101-(2/64)-2nd Avengers x-over (w/o Capt. America); see Tales Of Suspense #49 for 1st x-over. 108-(9/64)-Early Dr. Strange & Avengers x-over; ten extra pgs. Kirby-a	20	40	60	145	223	300
102,104-107,110: 102-Intro Sif. 105-109-Ten extra pgs. Kirby-a in each. 107-1st app. Grey Gargoyle	19	38	57	136	208	280
103-1st app. Enchantress	22	44	66	158	242	325
109-Magneto-c & app. (1st x-over, 10/64)	41	82	123	305	478	650
111,113: 113-Origin Loki	15	30	45	107	164	220
112-Thor Vs. Hulk (1/65); Origin Loki	41	82	123	330	515	700
114-Origin/1st app. Absorbing Man	22	44	66	158	242	325
115-Detailed origin of Loki	19	38	57	138	212	285
116-123,125: 118-1st app. Destroyer. 119-Intro Hogun, Fandral, Volstagg	13	26	39	92	141	190
124-Hercules-c/story	14	28	42	97	149	200
503-521: 503-(11/96, $1.50)-The Lost Gods begin; Tom DeFalco scripts & Deodato Studios-c/a. 505-Spider-Man-c/app. 509-Loki-c/app. 514-516-Shang-Chi						2.50
#(-1) Flashback (7/97) Tales of Asgard Donald Blake app.						2.50
Annual 1(1965, 25¢, 72 pgs.)-New Thor vs. Hercules(1st app.)-c/story (see Incredible Hulk #3); Kirby-c/a; r/#85,93,95,97	22	44	66	155	238	320

NOTE: ***Ayers** a-14, 39, 64i, 71i, 74i, 80i. **Bailey** a-43. **Briefer** a-5, 12. **Cameron** a-35. **Check** a-17. **Colan** a-23, 81; c-14. **Ditko** a-33, 38, 50-96; c-58, 67, 71, 88i. **Kirby/Ditko** a-50-83. **Everett** a-20, 48; c-4-7, 9, 36, 37, 39-42, 44, 45, 47. **Forte** a-19, 35, 40, 53. **Heath** a-4-6, 11, 14; c-1, 8, 11, 15, 51. **Heck** a-53, 73. **Kirby** a(p)-51, 52, 56, 57-60, 62-64, 66, 67, 69-89, 93, 97, 98, 100(w/**Heck**), 101-125; c-50-57, 59-66, 68-70, 72-82, 88(w/**Ditko**), 83 & 84(w/**Sinnott**), 85-96(w/**Ayers**), 97-125p. **Leiber/Fox** a-93, 98-102. **Maneely** c-20-22. **Morisi** a-42. **Morrow** a-41, 42. **Orlando** a-30, 45, 57. **Mac Pakula** (Tothish) a-9, 35, 41. **Powell** a-20, 27, 34. **Reinman** a-39, 87, 92, 96i. **Robinson** a-9. **Roussos** a-39. **Robert Sale** a-14. **Severin** a-27; c-30. **Sinnott** a-41; c-50. **Tuska** a-11. **Wildey** a-16.*

JOURNEY INTO MYSTERY (2nd Series)
Marvel Comics: Oct, 1972 - No. 19, Oct, 1975

	GD 2.0	VG 4.0	FN 6.0	VF 8.0	VF/NM 9.0	NM- 9.2
1-Robert Howard adaptation; Starlin/Ploog-a	3	6	9	18	24	32
2-5: 2,3,5-Bloch adapt. 4-H. P. Lovecraft adapt.	2	4	6	14	18	22
6-19: Reprints	2	4	6	10	13	16

NOTE: ***N. Adams** a-2i. **Ditko** r-7, 10, 12, 14, 15, 19; c-10. **Everett** r-9, 14. **G. Kane** a-1p, 2p; c-1-3p. **Kirby** r-7, 13, 15, 18, 19; c-7. **Mort Lawrence** r-2. **Maneely** r-3. **Orlando** r-16. **Reese** a-1, 2i. **Starlin** a-1p, 3p. **Torres** r-16. **Wildey** r-9, 14.*

JOURNEY INTO UNKNOWN WORLDS (Formerly Teen)
Atlas Comics (WFP): No. 36, Sept, 1950 - No. 38, Feb, 1951; No. 4, Apr, 1951 - No. 59, Aug, 1957

	GD 2.0	VG 4.0	FN 6.0	VF 8.0	VF/NM 9.0	NM- 9.2
36(#1)-Science fiction/weird; "End Of The Earth" c/story	238	476	714	1488	2294	3100
37(#2)-Science fiction; "When Worlds Collide" c/story; Everett-c/a; Hitler story	102	204	306	638	982	1325
38(#3)-Science fiction	87	174	261	544	835	1125
4-6,8,10-Science fiction/weird	55	110	165	340	520	700
7-Wolverton-a "Planet of Terror", 6 pgs; electric chair c-inset/story	90	180	270	563	869	1175
9-Giant eyeball story	67	134	201	419	647	875
11,12-Krigstein-a	40	80	120	239	357	475
13,16,17,20	37	74	111	209	305	400
14-Wolverton-a "One of Our Graveyards Is Missing", 4 pgs; Tuska-a	67	134	201	419	647	875
15-Wolverton-a "They Crawl by Night", 5 pgs.; 2 pg. Maneely s/f story	67	134	201	419	647	875
18,19-Matt Fox-a	40	80	120	239	357	475
21-33: 21-Decapitation-c. 24-Sci/fic story. 26-Atom bomb panel. 27-Sid Check-a. 33-Last pre-code (2/55)	27	54	81	154	222	290
34-Kubert, Torres-a	21	42	63	121	173	225
35-Torres-a	19	38	57	107	154	200
36-45,48,50,53,55,59: 43-Krigstein-a. 44-Davis-a. 45,55,59-Williamson-a in all; with Mayo #55,59. 55-Crandall-a. 48,53-Crandall-a (4 pgs. #48). 48-Check-a. 50-Davis, Crandall-a	18	36	54	100	143	185
46,47,49,52,54,56-58: 54-Torres-a	16	32	48	92	131	170
51-Ditko, Wood-a	20	40	60	112	161	210

NOTE: ***Ayers** a-24, 43, **Berg** a-38(#3), 43. **Lou Cameron** a-33. **Colan** a-37(#2), 6, 17, 19, 20, 23, 39. **Ditko** a-45, 51. **Drucker** a-35, 58. **Everett** a-37(#2), 11, 14, 41, 55, 56; c-37(#2), 11, 13, 14, 17, 22, 47, 48, 50, 53-55, 59. **Forte** a-49. **Fox** a-21i. **Heath** a-36(#1), 4, 6-8, 17, 20, 22, 36i; c-18. **Keller** a-15. **Mort Lawrence** a-38, 39. **Maneely** a-7, 8, 15, 16, 22, 49, 58; c-19, 25, 52. **Morrow** a-48. **Orlando** a-44, 57. **Pakula** a-36. **Powell** a-42, 53, 54. **Reinman** a-8. **Rico** a-21. **Robert Sale** a-24, 49. **Sekowsky** a-4, 5, 9. **Severin** a-38, 51; c-38, 48i, 56. **Sinnott** a-9, 21, 24. **Tuska** a-38(#3), 14. **Wildey** a-25, 43, 44.*

JOURNEYMAN
Image Comics: Aug, 1999 - No. 3, Oct, 1999 ($2.95, B&W, limited series)

JSA #67 © DC

Jubilee #1 © MAR

Judo Joe #1 © Jay-Jay Corp.

1-3-Brandon McKinney-s/a 3.00

JOURNEY TO THE CENTER OF THE EARTH (Movie)
Dell Publishing Co.: No. 1060, Nov-Jan, 1959/60 (one-shot)

Four Color 1060-Pat Boone & James Mason photo-c 12 24 36 87 134 180

JSA (Justice Society of America) (Also see All Star Comics)
DC Comics: Aug, 1999 - Present ($2.50)

1-Robinson and Goyer-s; funeral of Wesley Dodds 2 4 6 8 10 12
2-5: 4-Return of Dr. Fate 6.00
6-24: 6-Black Adam-c/app. 11,12-Kobra. 16-20-JSA vs. Johnny Sorrow. 19,20-Spectre app. 22-Hawkgirl origin. 23-Hawkman returns 4.00
25-($3.75) Hawkman rejoins the JSA 1 2 3 5 7 9
26-36, 38-49: 27-Capt. Marvel app. 29-Joker: Last Laugh. 31,32-Snejbjerg-a. 33-Ultra-Humanite. 34-Intro. new Crimson Avenger and Hourman. 42-G.A. Mr. Terrific and the Freedom Fighters app. 46-Eclipso returns 3.00
37-($3.50) Johnny Thunder merges with the Thunderbolt; origin new Crimson Avenger 3.50
50-($3.95) Wraparound-c by Pacheco; Sentinel becomes Green Lantern again 4.00
51-68: 51-Kobra killed. 54-JLA app. 55-Ma Hunkle (Red Tornado) app. 56-58-Black Reign x-over with Hawkman #23-25. 64-Sand returns. 67-Identity Crisis tie-in; Gibbons-a. 68-Ross-c 2.50
Annual 1 (10/00, $3.50) Planet DC; intro. Nemesis 3.50
Darkness Falls TPB (2002, $19.95) r/#6-15 20.00
Fair Play TPB (2003, $14.95) r/#26-31 & Secret Files #2 15.00
Justice Be Done TPB (2000, $14.95) r/Secret Files & #1-5 15.00
...: Our Worlds at War 1 (9/01, $2.95) Jae Lee-c; Saltares-a 3.00
...: Savage Times TPB (2004, $14.95) r/#39-45 15.00
... Secret Files 1 (8/99, $4.95) Origin stories and pin-ups; death of Wesley Dodds (G.A. Sandman); intro new Hawkgirl 5.00
... Secret Files 2 (9/01, $4.95) Short stories and profile pages 5.00
...: Stealing Thunder TPB (2003, $14.95) r/#32-38; JSA vs. The Ultra-Humanite 15.00
...: The Return of Hawkman TPB (2002, $19.95) r/#16-26 & Secret Files #1 20.00

JSA: ALL STARS
DC Comics: July, 2003 - No. 8, Feb, 2004 ($2.50/$3.50, limited series, back-up stories in Golden Age style)

1-6,8-Goyer & Johns-s/Cassaday-c. 1-Velluto-a; intro. Legacy. 2-Hawkman by Loeb/Sale 3-Dr. Fate by Cooke. 4-Starman by Robinson/Harris. 5-Hourman by Chaykin. 6-Dr. Mid-nite by Azzarello/Risso 2.50
7-($3.50) Mr. Terrific back-up story by Chabon; Lark-a 3.50
TPB (2004, $14.95) r/#1-8 15.00

JSA STRANGE ADVENTURES
DC Comics: Oct, 2004 - No. 6 ($3.50, limited series)

1-4-Johnny Thunder as pulp writer; Kitson-a/Watson-c/ Kevin Anderson-s 3.50

JSA: THE LIBERTY FILE (Elseworlds)
DC Comics: Feb, 2000 - No. 2, Mar, 2000 ($6.95, limited series)

1,2-Batman, Dr. Mid-Nite and Hourman vs. WW2 Joker; Tony Harris-c/a 7.00
JSA: The Liberty Files TPB (2004, $19.95) r/The Liberty File and The Unholy Three series 20.00

JSA: THE UNHOLY THREE (Elseworlds)(Sequel to JSA: The Liberty File)
DC Comics: 2003 - No. 2, 2003 ($6.95, limited series)

1,2-Batman, Superman and Hourman; Tony Harris-c/a 7.00

J2 (Also see A-Next and Juggernaut)
Marvel Comics: Oct, 1998 - No. 12, Sept, 1999 ($1.99)

1-12:1-Juggernaut's son; Lim-a. 2-Two covers; X-People app. 3-J2 battles the Hulk 2.25

JUBILEE (X-Men)
Marvel Comics: Nov, 2004 - No. 6 ($2.99)

1-4: 1-Jubilee in a Los Angeles high school; Kirkman-s; Casey Jones-c 3.00

JUDE, THE FORGOTTEN SAINT
Catechetical Guild Education Soc.: 1954 (16 pgs.; 8x11"; full color; paper-c)

nn 5 10 14 20 24 28

J.U.D.G.E.: THE SECRET RAGE
Image Comics: Mar, 2000 - No. 3, May, 2000 ($2.95)

1-3-Greg Horn-s/c/a 3.00

JUDGE COLT
Gold Key: Oct, 1969 - No. 4, Sept, 1970

1 3 6 9 18 24 30
2-4 2 4 6 10 13 16

JUDGE DREDD (...Classics #62 on; also see Batman - Judge Dredd, The Law of Dredd & 2000 A.D. Monthly)
Eagle Comics/IPC Magazines Ltd./Quality Comics #34-35, V2#1-37/ Fleetway #38 on: Nov, 1983 - No. 35, 1986; V2#1, Oct, 1986 - No. 77, 1993

1-Bolland-c/a 6.00
2-35 3.00
V2#1-77: 1-('86)-New look begins. 20-Begin $1.50-c. 21/22, 23/24-Two issue numbers in one. 28-1st app. Megaman (super-hero). 39-Begin $1.75-c. 51-Begin $1.95-c. 53-Bolland-a. 57-Reprints 1st published Judge Dredd story 2.50
Special 1 2.50
NOTE: ***Bolland** a-1-6, 8, 10; c-1-10, 15. **Guice** c-V2#23/24, 26, 27.*

JUDGE DREDD (3rd Series)
DC Comics: Aug, 1994 - No. 18, Jan, 1996 ($1.95)

1-18: 12-Begin $2.25-c 2.50
nn ($5.95)-Movie adaptation, Sienkiewicz-c 6.00

JUDGE DREDD'S CRIME FILE
Eagle Comics: Aug, 1989 - No. 6, Feb, 1986 ($1.25, limited series)

1-6: 1-Byrne-a 2.50

JUDGE DREDD: LEGENDS OF THE LAW
DC Comics: Dec, 1994 - No. 13, Dec, 1995 ($1.95)

1-13: 1-5-Dorman-c 2.50

JUDGE DREDD: THE EARLY CASES
Eagle Comics: Feb, 1986 - No. 6, Jul, 1986 ($1.25, Mega-series, Mando paper)

1-6: 2000 A.D.-r 2.50

JUDGE DREDD: THE JUDGE CHILD QUEST (Judge Child in indicia)
Eagle Comics: Aug, 1984 - No. 5, Oct, 1984 ($1.25, Lim. series, Baxter paper)

1-5: 2000A.D.-r; Bolland-c/a 2.50

JUDGE DREDD: THE MEGAZINE
Fleetway/Quality: 1991 - Present ($4.95, stiff-c, squarebound, 52 pgs.)

1-3 5.00

JUDGE DREDD VS. ALIENS: INCUBUS
Dark Horse Comics: March, 2003 - No. 4, June, 2003 ($2.99, limited series)

1-4-Flint-a/Wagner & Diggle-s 3.00

JUDGE PARKER
Argo: Feb, 1956 - No. 2, 1956

1-Newspaper strip reprints 7 14 21 35 43 50
2 5 10 15 24 30 35

JUDGMENT DAY
Awesome Entertainment: June, 1997 - No. 3, Oct, 1997 ($2.50, limited series)

1-3: 1 Alpha-Moore-s/Liefeld-c/a(p) flashback art by various in all. 2 Omega. 3 Final Judgment. All have a variant cover by Dave Gibbons 2.50
...Aftermath-($3.50) Moore-s/Kane-a; Youngblood, Glory, New Men, Maximage, Allies and Spacehunter short stories. Also has a variant cover by Dave Gibbons 3.50
TPB (Checker Books, 2003, $16.95) r/series 17.00

JUDO JOE
Jay-Jay Corp.: Aug, 1953 - No. 3, Dec, 1953 (Judo lessons in each issue)

1-Drug ring story 9 18 27 54 70 85
2,3: 3-Hypo needle story 7 14 21 35 43 50

JUDOMASTER (Gun Master #84-89) (Also see Crisis on Infinite Earths, Sarge Steel #6 & Special War Series)
Charlton Comics: No. 89, May-June, 1966 - No. 98, Dec, 1967 (Two No. 89's)

89-3rd app. Judomaster 4 8 12 29 40 50
90,92-98: 93-Intro. Tiger 4 8 12 22 32 40
91-Sarge Steel begins 4 8 12 25 33 42
93,94,96,98 (Modern Comics reprint, 1977) 4.00
NOTE: ***Morisi** Thunderbolt #90. #91 has 1 pg. biography on writer/artist Frank McLaughlin.*

JUDY CANOVA (Formerly My Experience) (Stage, screen, radio)
Fox Features Syndicate: No. 23, May, 1950 - No. 3, Sept, 1950

23(#1)-Wood-c,a(p)? 23 46 69 130 188 245
24-Wood-a(p) 22 44 66 125 180 235
3-Wood-c; Wood/Orlando-a 24 48 72 138 199 260

JUDY GARLAND (See Famous Stars)

JUDY JOINS THE WAVES
Toby Press: 1951 (For U.S. Navy)

nn 7 14 21 35 43 50

JUGGERNAUT (See X-Men)
Marvel Comics: Apr, 1997, Nov, 1999 ($2.99, one-shots)

1-(4/97) Kelly-s/ Rouleau-a 3.00

Jughead's Pal Hot Dog #2 © AP

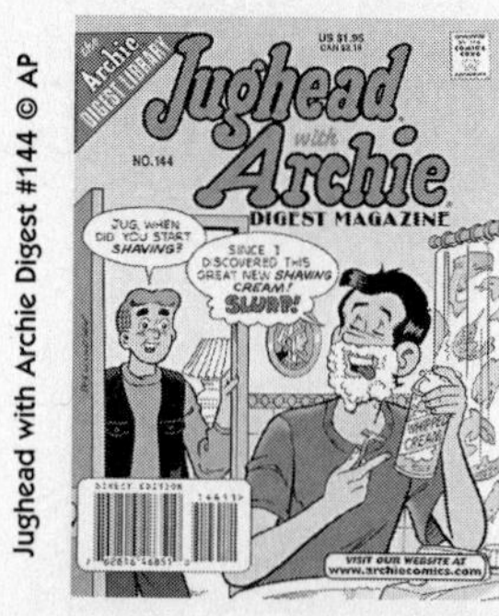

Jughead with Archie Digest #144 © AP

Jumbo Comics #25 © FH

	GD 2.0	VG 4.0	FN 6.0	VF 8.0	VF/NM 9.0	NM- 9.2
1-(11/99) Casey-s; Eighth Day x-over; Thor, Iron Man, Spidey app.						3.00

JUGHEAD (Formerly Archie's Pal...)
Archie Publications: No. 127, Dec, 1965 - No. 352, June, 1987

	GD 2.0	VG 4.0	FN 6.0	VF 8.0	VF/NM 9.0	NM- 9.2
127-130	3	6	9	18	24	30
131,133,135-160(9/68)	3	6	9	16	20	24
132,134: 132-Shield-c; The Fly & Black Hood app.; Shield cameo. 134-Shield-c	4	8	12	22	30	38
161-180	2	4	6	11	14	18
181-199	2	4	6	9	11	14
200(1/'72)	2	4	6	10	13	16
201-240(5/75)	1	3	4	6	8	10
241-270(11/77)	1	2	3	5	6	8
271-299	1	2	3	4	5	7
300(5/80)-Anniversary issue; infinity-c	1	2	3	5	6	8
301-320(1/82)						5.00
321-324,326-352						4.00
325-(10/82) Cheryl Blossom app. (not on cover); same month as intro. (cover & story) in Archie's Girls, Betty & Veronica #320; Jason Blossom app.; DeCarlo-a	3	6	9	18	23	28

JUGHEAD (2nd Series)(Becomes Archie's Pal Jughead Comics #46 on)
Archie Enterprises: Aug, 1987 - No. 45, May, 1993 (.75/$1.00/$1.25)

	GD 2.0	VG 4.0	FN 6.0	VF 8.0	VF/NM 9.0	NM- 9.2
1	1	2	3	4	5	7
2-10						4.00
11-45: 4-X-Mas issue. 17-Colan-c/a						3.00

JUGHEAD AS CAPTAIN HERO (See Archie as Pureheart the Powerful, Archie Giant Series Magazine #142 & Life With Archie)
Archie Publications: Oct, 1966 - No. 7, Nov, 1967

	GD 2.0	VG 4.0	FN 6.0	VF 8.0	VF/NM 9.0	NM- 9.2
1-Super hero parody	7	14	21	46	63	80
2	4	8	12	29	40	50
3-7	4	8	12	24	32	40

JUGHEAD JONES COMICS DIGEST, THE (...Magazine No. 10-64; Jughead Jones Digest Magazine #65)
Archie Publ.: June, 1977 - No. 100, May, 1996 ($1.35/$1.50/$1.75, digest-size, 128 pgs.)

	GD 2.0	VG 4.0	FN 6.0	VF 8.0	VF/NM 9.0	NM- 9.2
1-Neal Adams-a; Capt. Hero-r	4	8	12	24	32	40
2(9/77)-Neal Adams-a	3	6	9	16	21	26
3-6,8-10	2	4	6	11	14	18
7-Origin Jaguar-r; N. Adams-a.	2	4	6	12	16	20
11-20: 13-r/1957 Jughead's Folly	1	3	4	6	8	10
21-50	1	2	3	4	5	7
51-70						5.00
71-100						3.00

JUGHEAD'S BABY TALES
Archie Comics: Spring, 1994 - No. 2, Wint. 1994 ($2.00, 52 pgs.)

	GD 2.0	VG 4.0	FN 6.0	VF 8.0	VF/NM 9.0	NM- 9.2
1,2: 1-Bound-in pull-out poster						4.00

JUGHEAD'S DINER
Archie Comics: Apr, 1990 - No. 7, Apr, 1991 ($1.00)

	GD 2.0	VG 4.0	FN 6.0	VF 8.0	VF/NM 9.0	NM- 9.2
1						4.00
2-7						2.50

JUGHEAD'S DOUBLE DIGEST (...Magazine #5)
Archie Comics: Oct, 1989 - Present ($2.25 - $3.59)

	GD 2.0	VG 4.0	FN 6.0	VF 8.0	VF/NM 9.0	NM- 9.2
1	2	4	6	8	10	12
2-10: 2,5-Capt. Hero stories	1	2	3	5	6	8
11-25						5.00
26-110: 58-Begin $2.99-c. 66-Begin $3.19-c. 75-Begin $3.29-c. 91-Begin $3.59-c						3.60

JUGHEAD'S EAT-OUT COMIC BOOK MAGAZINE (See Archie Giant Series Magazine No. 170)

JUGHEAD'S FANTASY
Archie Publications: Aug, 1960 - No. 3, Dec, 1960

	GD 2.0	VG 4.0	FN 6.0	VF 8.0	VF/NM 9.0	NM- 9.2
1	18	36	54	126	193	260
2	12	24	36	82	124	165
3	10	20	30	70	100	130

JUGHEAD'S FOLLY
Archie Publications (Close-Up): 1957 (36 pgs.)(one-shot)

	GD 2.0	VG 4.0	FN 6.0	VF 8.0	VF/NM 9.0	NM- 9.2
1-Jughead a la Elvis (Rare) (1st reference to Elvis in comics?)	50	100	150	305	465	625

JUGHEAD'S JOKES
Archie Publications: Aug, 1967 - No. 78, Sept, 1982
(No. 1-8, 38 on: reg. size; No. 9-23: 68 pgs.; No. 24-37: 52 pgs.)

	GD 2.0	VG 4.0	FN 6.0	VF 8.0	VF/NM 9.0	NM- 9.2
1	7	14	21	51	71	90
2	4	8	12	27	36	45
3-8	3	6	9	18	24	30
9,10 (68 pgs.)	3	7	10	21	28	35
11-23(4/71) (68 pgs.)	3	6	9	18	23	28
24-37(1/74) (52 pgs.)	2	4	6	11	14	18
38-50(9/76)	1	2	3	5	7	9
51-78						6.00

JUGHEAD'S PAL HOT DOG (See Laugh #14 for 1st app.)
Archie Comics: Jan, 1990 - No. 5, Oct, 1990 ($1.00)

	GD 2.0	VG 4.0	FN 6.0	VF 8.0	VF/NM 9.0	NM- 9.2
1						4.00
2-5						2.50

JUGHEAD'S SOUL FOOD
Spire Christian Comics (Fleming H. Revell Co.): 1979 (49 cents)

	GD 2.0	VG 4.0	FN 6.0	VF 8.0	VF/NM 9.0	NM- 9.2
nn-Low print run	2	4	6	10	13	16

JUGHEAD'S TIME POLICE
Archie Comics: July, 1990 - No. 6, May, 1991 ($1.00, bi-monthly)

	GD 2.0	VG 4.0	FN 6.0	VF 8.0	VF/NM 9.0	NM- 9.2
1						4.00
2-6: Colan a-3-6p; c-3-6						2.50

JUGHEAD WITH ARCHIE DIGEST (...Plus Betty & Veronica & Reggie Too No. 1,2; ...Magazine #33-?, 101-on; ...Comics Digest Mag.)
Archie Pub.: Mar, 1974 - Present ($1.00-$2.39)

	GD 2.0	VG 4.0	FN 6.0	VF 8.0	VF/NM 9.0	NM- 9.2
1	6	12	18	40	55	70
2	4	8	12	27	36	45
3-10	3	6	9	19	25	32
11-13,15-17,19,20: Capt. Hero-r in #14-16; Capt. Pureheart #17,19	2	4	6	10	13	16
14,18,21,22-Pureheart the Powerful in #18,21,22	2	4	6	11	14	18
23-30: 29-The Shield-r. 30-The Fly-r	1	3	4	6	8	10
31-50,100	1	2	3	5	6	8
51-99	1	2	3	4	5	7
101-121						4.00
122-200: 156-Begin $2.19-c. 180-Begin $2.39-c						2.50

JUKE BOX COMICS
Famous Funnies: Mar, 1948 - No. 6, Jan, 1949

	GD 2.0	VG 4.0	FN 6.0	VF 8.0	VF/NM 9.0	NM- 9.2
1-Toth-c/a; Hollingsworth-a	40	80	120	236	351	465
2-Transvestism story	27	54	81	152	219	285
3-6: 3-Peggy Lee story. 4-Jimmy Durante line drawn-c. 6-Features Desi Arnaz plus Arnaz line drawn-c	21	42	63	118	169	220

JUMBO COMICS (Created by S.M. Iger)
Fiction House Magazines (Real Adv. Publ. Co.): Sept, 1938 - No. 167, Mar, 1953 (No. 1-3: 68 pgs.; No. 4-8: 52 pgs.)(No. 1-8 oversized-10-1/2x14-1/2"; black & white)

	GD 2.0	VG 4.0	FN 6.0	VF 8.0	VF/NM 9.0	NM- 9.2
1-(Rare)-Sheena Queen of the Jungle(1st app.) by Meskin, Hawks of the Seas (The Hawk #10 on; see Feature Funnies #3) by Eisner, The Hunchback by Dick Briefer (ends #8), Wilton of the West (ends #24), Inspector Dayton (ends #67) & ZX-5 (ends #140) begin; 1st comic art by Jack Kirby (Count of Monte Cristo & Wilton of the West); Mickey Mouse appears (1 panel) with brief biography of Walt Disney; 1st app. Peter Pupp by Bob Kane. Note: Sheena was created by Iger for publication in England as a newspaper strip. The early issues of Jumbo contain Sheena strip-r; multiple panel-c 1,2,7	2100	4200	6300	21,000	-	-
2-(Rare)-Origin Sheena. Diary of Dr. Hayward by Kirby (also #3) plus 2 other stories; contains strip from Universal Film featuring Edgar Bergen & Charlie McCarthy plus-c (preview of film)	660	1360	2040	6800	-	-
3-Last Kirby issue	480	960	1440	4800	-	-
4-(Scarce)-Origin The Hawk by Eisner; Wilton of the West by Fine (ends #14)(1st comic work); Count of Monte Cristo by Fine (ends #15); The Diary of Dr. Hayward by Fine (cont'd #8,9)	450	900	1350	4500	-	-
5-Christmas-c	385	770	1155	3850	-	-
6-8-Last B&W issue. #8 was a 1939 N. Y. World's Fair Special Edition; Frank Buck's Jungleland story	345	690	1035	3450	-	-
9-Stuart Taylor begins by Fine (ends #140); Fine-c; 1st color issue (8-9/39)-1st Sheena (jungle) cover; 8-1/4x10-1/4" (oversized in width only)	325	650	975	3250	-	-
10-Regular size 68 pg. issues begin; Sheena dons new costume w/origin costume; Stuart Taylor sci/fi-c; classic Lou Fine-c.	188	376	564	1175	1813	2450
11-13: 12-The Hawk-c by Eisner. 13-Eisner-c	127	254	381	794	1222	1650
14-Intro. Lightning (super-hero) on-c only	131	262	393	819	1260	1700
15,17-20: 15-1st Lightning story and begins, ends #41. 17-Lightning part-c	81	162	243	506	778	1050
16-Lightning-c	98	196	294	613	944	1275

Jungle Action #3 © FH

Jungle Comics #5 © FH

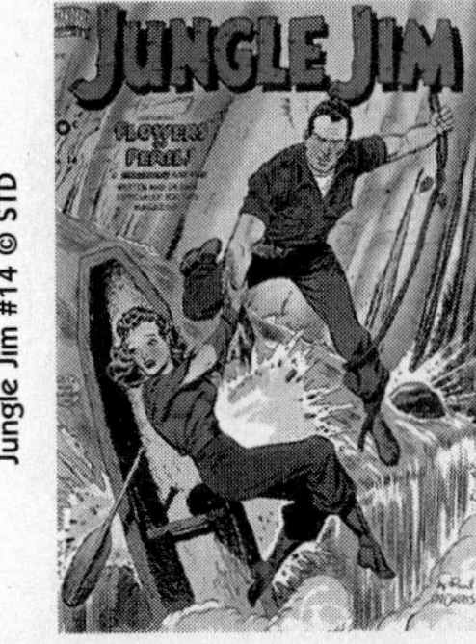

Jungle Jim #14 © STD

GD VG FN VF VF/NM NM-
2.0 4.0 6.0 8.0 9.0 9.2

21-30: 22-1st Tom, Dick & Harry; origin The Hawk retold. 25-Midnight the Black Stallion begins, ends #65 63 126 189 394 610 825
31-40: 31-(9/41)-1st app. Mars God of War in Stuart Taylor story (see Planet Comics #15. 35-Shows V2#11 (correct number does not appear) 52 104 156 317 484 650
41-50: 42-Ghost Gallery begins, ends #167 40 80 120 241 363 485
51-60: 52-Last Tom, Dick & Harry 37 74 111 209 305 400
61-70: 68-Sky Girl begins, ends #130; not in #79 28 56 84 158 229 300
71-93,95-99: 89-ZX5 becomes a private eye. 22 44 66 127 184 240
94-Used in Love and Death by Legman 25 50 75 141 203 265
100 25 50 75 141 203 265
101-121 21 42 63 121 173 225
121-140,150-158: 155-Used in **POP**, pg. 98 18 36 54 102 146 190
141-149-Two Sheena stories. 141-Long Bow, Indian Boy begins, ends #160 17 34 51 98 139 180
159-163: Space Scouts serial in all. 160-Last jungle-c (6/52). 161-Ghost Gallery covers begin, end #167. 163-Suicide Smith app. 16 32 48 92 131 170
164-The Star Pirate begins, ends #165 16 32 48 92 131 170
165-167: 165,167-Space Rangers app. 16 32 48 92 131 170
NOTE: *Bondage covers, negligee panels, torture, etc. are common in this series. Hawks of the Seas, Inspector Dayton, Spies in Action, Sports Shorts, & Uncle Otto by Eisner, #1-7. Hawk by* ***Eisner****-#10-15.* ***Eisner*** *c-1-8, 12-14. 1pg. Patsy pin-ups in 92-97, 99-101. Sheena by* ***Meskin****-#1, 4; by* ***Powell****-#2, 3, 5-28;* ***Powell*** *c-14, 16, 17, 19.* ***Powell/Eisner*** *c-15. Sky Girl by* ***Matt Baker****-#69-78, 80-130. ZX-5 & Ghost Gallery by* ***Kamen****-#90-130.* ***Bailey*** *a-3-8.* ***Briefer*** *a-1-8, 10.* ***Fine*** *a-14; c-9-11.* ***Kamen*** *a-101, 105, 123, 132; c-105, 121-145.* ***Bob Kane*** *a-1-8.* ***Whitman*** *c-146-167(most). Jungle c-9, 13, 15, 17 on.*

JUNGLE ACTION
Atlas Comics (IPC): Oct, 1954 - No. 6, Aug, 1955
1-Leopard Girl begins by Al Hartley (#1,3); Jungle Boy by Forte; Maneely-a in all 39 78 117 222 324 425
2-(3-D effect cover) 39 78 117 222 324 425
3-6: 3-Last precode (2/55) 25 50 75 141 203 265
NOTE: ***Maneely*** *c-1, 2, 5, 6.* ***Romita*** *a-3, 6.* ***Shores*** *a-3, 6; c-3, 4?.*

JUNGLE ACTION (...& Black Panther #18-21?)
Marvel Comics Group: Oct, 1972 - No. 24, Nov, 1976
1-Lorna, Jann-r (All reprints in 1-4) 2 4 6 12 16 20
2-4 2 4 6 8 10 12
5-Black Panther begins (r/Avengers #62) 3 6 9 18 23 28
6-New solo Black Panther stories begin 3 6 9 16 20 24
7,9,10: 9-Contains pull-out centerfold ad by Mark Jewelers 2 4 6 8 10 12
8-Origin Black Panther 2 4 6 11 14 18
11-20,23,24: 19-23-KKK x-over. 23-r/#22. 24-1st Wind Eagle; story contd in Marvel Premiere #51-#53 1 2 3 5 7 9
21,22-(Regular 25¢ edition)(5,7/76) 1 2 3 5 7 9
21,22-(30¢-c variant, limited distribution) 2 4 6 9 11 14
NOTE: ***Buckler*** *a-6-9p, 22; c-8p, 12p.* ***Buscema*** *a-5p; c-22.* ***Byrne*** *c-23.* ***Gil Kane*** *a-8p; c-2, 4, 10p, 11p, 13-17, 19, 24.* ***Kirby*** *c-18.* ***Maneely*** *r-1.* ***Russell*** *a-13i.* ***Starlin*** *c-3p.*

JUNGLE ADVENTURES
Super Comics: 1963 - 1964 (Reprints)
10,12,15,17,18: 10-r/Terrors of the Jungle #4 & #10(Rulah). 12-r/Zoot #14(Rulah).15-r/Kaanga from Jungle #152 & Tiger Girl. 17-All Jo-Jo-r. 18-Reprints/White Princess of the Jungle #1; no Kinstler-a; origin of both White Princess & Cap'n Courage 4 8 12 22 30 38

JUNGLE ADVENTURES
Skywald Comics: Mar, 1971 - No. 3, June, 1971 (25¢, 52 pgs.) (Pre-code reprints & new-s)
1-Zangar origin; reprints of Jo-Jo, Blue Gorilla(origin)/White Princess #3, Kinstler-r/White Princess #2 3 6 9 18 23 28
2,3: 2-Zangar, Sheena-r/Sheena #17 & Jumbo #162, Jo-Jo, origin Slave Girl-r. 3-Zangar, Jo-Jo, White Princess, Rulah-r 2 4 6 11 14 18

JUNGLE BOOK (See King Louie and Mowgli, Movie Comics, Mowgli..., Walt Disney Showcase #45 & Walt Disney's The Jungle Book)

JUNGLE CAT (Disney)
Dell Publishing Co.: No. 1136, Sept-Nov, 1960 (one shot)
Four Color 1136-Movie, photo-c 8 16 24 53 74 95

JUNGLE COMICS
Fiction House Magazines: 1/40 - No. 157, 3/53; No. 158, Spr, 1953 - No. 163, Summer, 1954
1-Origin The White Panther, Kaanga, Lord of the Jungle, Tabu, Wizard of the Jungle; Wambi, the Jungle Boy, Camilla & Capt. Terry Thunder begin (all 1st app.). Lou Fine-c 452 904 1356 3164 5082 7000
2-Fantomah, Mystery Woman of the Jungle begins, ends #51; The Red Panther begins, ends #26 165 330 495 1031 1591 2150
3,4 135 270 405 844 1297 1750
5-Classic Eisner-c 146 292 438 913 1407 1900
6-10: 7,8-Powell-c 77 154 231 481 741 1000
11-20: 13-Tuska-c 55 110 165 340 520 700
21-30: 25-Shows V2#1 (correct number does not appear). #27-New origin Fantomah, Daughter of the Pharoahs; Camilla dons new costume 45 90 135 275 418 560
31-40 37 74 111 209 305 400
41,43-50 31 62 93 178 259 340
42-Kaanga by Crandall, 12 pgs. 34 68 102 196 283 370
51-60 28 56 84 158 229 300
61-70: 67-Cover swipes Crandall splash pg. in #42 25 50 75 144 207 270
71-80: 79-New origin Tabu 21 42 63 118 164 235
81-97,99 21 42 63 118 169 220
98-Used in **SOTI**, pg. 185 & illo "In ordinary comic books, there are pictures within pictures for children who know how to look;" used by N.Y. Legis. Comm. 33 66 99 190 275 360
100 25 50 75 141 203 265
101-110: 104-In Camilla story, villain is Dr. Wertham 20 40 60 112 161 210
111-120: 118-Clyde Beatty app. 20 40 60 112 161 210
121-130 18 36 54 100 143 185
131-163: 135-Desert Panther begins in Terry Thunder (origin), not in #137; ends (dies) #138. 139-Last 52 pg. issue. 141-Last Tabu. 143,145-Used in **POP**, pg. 99. 151-Last Camilla & Terry Thunder. 152-Tiger Girl begins. 158-Last Wambi; Sheena app. 17 34 51 95 135 175
I.W. Reprint #1,9: 1-r/? 9-r/#151 3 6 9 16 25 32
NOTE: *Bondage covers, negligee panels, torture, etc. are common to this series. Camilla by* ***Fran Hopper****-#70-92; by* ***Baker****-#69, 100-113, 115, 116; by* ***Lubbers****-#97-99 by* ***Tuska****-#63, 65. Kaanga by* ***John Celardo****-#80-113; by* ***Larsen****-#71, 75-79; by* ***Moreira****-#58, 60, 61, 63-70, 72-74; by* ***Tuska****-#37, 62; by* ***Whitman****-#114-163. Tabu by* ***Larsen****-#59-75, 82-92; by* ***Whitman****-#93-115. Terry Thunder by* ***Hopper****-#71, 72; by* ***Celardo****-#78, 79; by* ***Lubbers****-#80-85. Tiger Girl-r by* ***Baker****-#152, 153, 155-157, 159. Wambi by* ***Baker****-#62-67, 74.* ***Astarita*** *c-45, 46.* ***Celardo*** *a-78; c-98-113.* ***Crandall*** *c-67 from splash pg.* ***Eisner*** *c-2, 5, 6.* ***Fine*** *c-1.* ***Larsen*** *a-65, 66, 71, 72, 74, 75, 79, 83, 84, 87-90.* ***Moriera*** *c-43, 44.* ***Morisi*** *a-51.* ***Powell*** *c-7, 8.* ***Sultan*** *c-3, 4.* ***Tuska*** *c-13.* ***Whitman*** *c-132-163(most).* ***Zolnerowich*** *c-11, 12, 18-41.*

JUNGLE COMICS
Blackthorne Publishing: May, 1988 - No. 4 ($2.00, B&W/color)
1-Dave Stevens-c; B. Jones scripts in all. 3.00
2-4: 2-B&W-a begins 2.25

JUNGLE GIRL (See Lorna, the...)

JUNGLE GIRL (Nyoka, Jungle Girl No. 2 on)
Fawcett Publications: Fall, 1942 (one-shot)(No month listed)
1-Bondage-c; photo of Kay Aldridge who played Nyoka in movie serial app. on-c. Adaptation of the classic Republic movie serial Perils of Nyoka. 1st comic to devote entire contents to a movie serial adaptation 131 262 393 819 1260 1700

JUNGLE GIRLS
AC Comics: 1989 - No. 16, 1993 (B&W)
1-16: 1-4,10,13-16-New story & "good girl" reprints. 5-9,11,12-All g.g. reprints (Baker, Powell, Lubbers, others) 3.00

JUNGLE JIM (Also see Ace Comics)
Standard Comics (Best Books): No. 11, Jan, 1949 - No. 20, Apr, 1951
11 10 20 30 60 80 100
12-20 7 14 21 37 46 55

JUNGLE JIM
Dell Publishing Co.: No. 490, 8/53 - No. 1020, 8-10/59 (Painted-c)
Four Color 490(#1) 8 16 24 58 82 105
Four Color 565(#2, 6/54) 5 10 15 36 48 60
3(10-12/54)-5 5 10 15 33 44 55
6-19(1-3/59), Four Color 1020(#20) 4 8 12 29 40 50

JUNGLE JIM
King Features Syndicate: No. 5, Dec, 1967
5-Reprints Dell #5; Wood-c 2 4 6 11 14 18

JUNGLE JIM (Continued from Dell series)
Charlton Comics: No. 22, Feb, 1969 - No. 28, Feb, 1970 (#21 was an overseas edition only)
22-Dan Flagg begins; Ditko/Wood-a 4 8 12 25 33 42
23-26: 23-Last Dan Flagg; Howard-c. 24-Jungle People begin 3 6 9 16 21 26
27,28: 27-Ditko/Howard-a. 28-Ditko-a 3 6 9 19 25 32
NOTE: *Ditko cover of #22 reprints story panels*

JUNGLE JO
Fox Feature Syndicate (Hero Books): Mar, 1950 - No. 3, Sept, 1950
nn-Jo-Jo blanked out, leaving Congo King; came out after Jo-Jo #29

Jungle War Stories #8 © DELL

Junior Comics #10 © FOX

Junior Miss #34 © MAR

	GD 2.0	VG 4.0	FN 6.0	VF 8.0	VF/NM 9.0	NM- 9.2
(intended as Jo-Jo #30?)	44	88	132	268	409	550
1-Tangi begins; part Wood-a	46	92	138	281	428	575
2,3	38	76	114	219	320	420

JUNGLE LIL (Dorothy Lamour #2 on; also see Feature Stories Magazine)
Fox Feature Syndicate (Hero Books): April, 1950

	GD	VG	FN	VF	VF/NM	NM-
1	40	80	120	236	351	465

JUNGLE TALES (Jann of the Jungle No. 8 on)
Atlas Comics (CSI): Sept, 1954 - No. 7, Sept, 1955

	GD	VG	FN	VF	VF/NM	NM-
1-Jann of the Jungle	39	78	117	222	324	425
2-7: 3-Last precode (1/55)	27	54	81	152	219	285

NOTE: *Heath c-5.* ***Heck*** *a-6, 7.* ***Maneely*** *a-2; c-1, 3.* ***Shores*** *a-5-7; c-4, 6.* ***Tuska*** *a-2.*

JUNGLE TALES OF CAVEWOMAN
Basement Comics: 1998 ($2.95, B&W)

	GD	VG	FN	VF	VF/NM	NM-
1-Budd Root-s/a						3.00

JUNGLE TALES OF TARZAN
Charlton Comics: Dec, 1964 - No. 4, July, 1965

	GD	VG	FN	VF	VF/NM	NM-
1	6	12	18	43	59	75
2-4	4	8	12	27	36	45

NOTE: ***Giordano*** *c-3p.* ***Glanzman*** *a-1-3.* ***Montes/Bache*** *a-4.*

JUNGLE TERROR (See Harvey Comics Hits No. 54)

JUNGLE THRILLS (Formerly Sports Thrills; Terrors of the Jungle #17 on)
Star Publications: No. 16, Feb, 1952; Dec, 1953; No. 7, 1954

	GD	VG	FN	VF	VF/NM	NM-
16-Phantom Lady & Rulah story-reprint/All Top No. 15; used in **POP**, pg. 98,99; L. B. Cole-c	50	100	150	305	465	625
3-D 1(12/53, 25¢)-Came w/glasses; Jungle Lil & Jungle Jo appear; L. B. Cole-c	50	100	150	305	465	625
7-Titled 'Picture Scope Jungle Adventures;' (1954, 36 pgs, 15¢)-3-D effect c/stories; story & coloring book; Disbrow-a/script; L.B. Cole-c	50	100	150	305	463	620

JUNGLE TWINS, THE (Tono & Kono)
Gold Key/Whitman No. 18: Apr, 1972 - No. 17, Nov, 1975; No. 18, May, 1982

	GD	VG	FN	VF	VF/NM	NM-
1	3	6	9	16	20	24
2-5	2	4	6	8	10	12
6-18: 18(Whitman, 5/82)-Reprints	1	2	3	5	6	8

NOTE: *UFO c/story No. 13. Painted-c No. 1-17.* ***Spiegle*** *c-18.*

JUNGLE WAR STORIES (Guerrilla War No. 12 on)
Dell Publishing Co.: July-Sept, 1962 - No. 11, Apr-June, 1965 (Painted-c)

	GD	VG	FN	VF	VF/NM	NM-
01-384-209 (#1)	4	8	12	27	36	45
2-11	3	6	9	18	24	30

JUNIE PROM (Also see Dexter Comics)
Dearfield Publishing Co.: Winter, 1947-48 - No. 7, Aug, 1949

	GD	VG	FN	VF	VF/NM	NM-
1-Teen-age	13	26	39	74	102	130
2	8	16	24	46	58	70
3-7	7	14	21	37	46	55

JUNIOR
Fantagraphics Books: June, 2000 - No. 5, Jan, 2001 ($2.95, B&W)

	GD	VG	FN	VF	VF/NM	NM-
1-5-Peter Bagge-s/a						3.00

JUNIOR CARROT PATROL (Jr. Carrot Patrol #2)
Dark Horse Comics: May, 1989; No. 2, Nov, 1990 ($2.00, B&W)

	GD	VG	FN	VF	VF/NM	NM-
1,2-Flaming Carrot spin-off. 1-Bob Burden-c(i)						2.50

JUNIOR COMICS (Formerly Li'l Pan; becomes Western Outlaws with #17)
Fox Feature Syndicate: No. 9, Sept, 1947 - No. 16, July, 1948

	GD	VG	FN	VF	VF/NM	NM-
9-Feldstein-c/a; headlights-c	89	178	267	556	853	1150
10-16-Feldstein-c/a; headlights-c on all	79	158	237	494	760	1025

JUNIOR FUNNIES (Formerly Tiny Tot Funnies No. 9)
Harvey Publ. (King Features Synd.): No. 10, Aug, 1951 - No. 13, Feb, 1952

	GD	VG	FN	VF	VF/NM	NM-
10-Partial reprints in all; Blondie, Dagwood, Daisy, Henry, Popeye, Felix, Katzenjammer Kids	6	12	18	28	34	40
11-13	5	10	15	24	30	35

JUNIOR HOPP COMICS
Stanmor Publ.: Feb, 1952 - No. 3, July, 1952

	GD	VG	FN	VF	VF/NM	NM-
1-Teenage humor	10	20	30	56	73	90
2,3: 3-Dave Berg-a	6	12	18	31	38	45

JUNIOR MEDICS OF AMERICA, THE
E. R. Squire & Sons: No. 1359, 1957 (15¢)

	GD	VG	FN	VF	VF/NM	NM-
1359	4	8	12	17	21	24

JUNIOR MISS
Timely/Marvel (CnPC): Wint, 1944; No. 24, Apr, 1947 - No. 39, Aug, 1950

	GD	VG	FN	VF	VF/NM	NM-
1-Frank Sinatra & June Allyson life story	30	60	90	170	245	320
24-Formerly The Human Torch #23?	14	28	42	81	113	145
25-38: 29,31,34-Cindy-c/stories (others?)	9	18	27	51	62	75
39-Kurtzman-a	10	20	30	58	77	95

NOTE: *Painted-c 35-37. 35, 37-all romance. 36, 38-mostly teen humor.*

JUNIOR PARTNERS (Formerly Oral Roberts' True Stories)
Oral Roberts Evangelistic Assn.: No. 120, Aug, 1959 - V3#12, Dec, 1961

	GD	VG	FN	VF	VF/NM	NM-
120(#1)	4	8	12	29	40	50
2(9/59)	3	6	9	19	25	32
3-12(7/60)	2	4	6	14	18	22
V2#1(8/60)-5(12/60)	2	4	6	10	13	16
V3#1(1/61)-12	2	4	6	8	10	12

JUNIOR TREASURY (See Dell Junior...)

JUNIOR WOODCHUCKS GUIDE (Walt Disney's...)
Danbury Press: 1973 (8-3/4"x5-3/4", 214 pgs., hardcover)

	GD	VG	FN	VF	VF/NM	NM-
nn-Illustrated text based on the long-standing J.W. Guide used by Donald Duck's nephews Huey, Dewey & Louie by Carl Barks. The guidebook was a popular plot device to enable the nephews to solve problems facing their uncle or Scrooge McDuck (scarce)	6	12	18	40	55	70

JUNIOR WOODCHUCKS LIMITED SERIES (Walt Disney's...)
W. D. Publications (Disney): July, 1991 - No. 4, Oct, 1991 ($1.50, limited series; new & reprint-a)

	GD	VG	FN	VF	VF/NM	NM-
1-4: 1-The Beagle Boys app.; Barks-r						2.50

JUNIOR WOODCHUCKS (See Huey, Dewey & Louie...)

JUNK CULTURE
DC Comics (Vertigo): July, 1997 - No. 2, Aug, 1997 ($2.50, limited series)

	GD	VG	FN	VF	VF/NM	NM-
1,2: Ted McKeever-s/a in all						3.00

JURASSIC PARK
Topps Comics: June, 1993 - No. 4, Aug, 1993; No. 5, Oct, 1994 - No. 10, Feb, 1995

	GD	VG	FN	VF	VF/NM	NM-
1-($2.50)-Newsstand Edition; Kane/Perez-a in all; 1-4: movie adaptation						2.50
1-($2.95)-Collector's Ed.; polybagged w/3 cards						4.00
1-Amberchrome Edition w/no price or ads	1	2	3	4	5	7
2-4-($2.50)-Newsstand Edition						2.50
2,3-($2.95)-Collector's Ed.; polybagged w/3 cards						3.00
4-10: 4-($2.95)-Collector's Ed.; polybagged w/1 of 4 different action hologram trading card; Gil Kane/Perez-a. 5-becomes Advs. of						3.00
Annual 1 ($3.95, 5/95)						4.00
Trade paperback (1993, $9.95)-r/#1-4; bagged w/#0						10.00

JURASSIC PARK: RAPTOR
Topps Comics: Nov, 1993 - No. 2, Dec, 1993 ($2.95, limited series)

	GD	VG	FN	VF	VF/NM	NM-
1,2: 1-Bagged w/3 trading cards & Zorro #0; Golden c-1,2						3.00

JURASSIC PARK: RAPTORS ATTACK
Topps Comics: Mar, 1994 - No. 4, June, 1994 ($2.50, limited series)

	GD	VG	FN	VF	VF/NM	NM-
1-4-Michael Golden-c/frontispiece						2.50

JURASSIC PARK: RAPTORS HIJACK
Topps Comics: July, 1994 - No. 4, Oct, 1994 ($2.50, limited series)

	GD	VG	FN	VF	VF/NM	NM-
1-4: Michael Golden-c/front piece						2.50

JUST A PILGRIM
Black Bull Entertainment: May, 2001 - No. 5, Sept, 2001 ($2.99)

	GD	VG	FN	VF	VF/NM	NM-
Limited Preview Edition (12/00, $7.00) Ennis & Ezquerra interviews						7.00
1-Ennis-s/Ezquerra-a; two covers by Texeira & JG Jones						3.00
2-5: 2-Fabry-c. 3-Nowlan-c. 4-Sienkiewicz-c						3.00
TPB (11/01, $12.99) r/#1-5; Waid intro.						13.00

JUST A PILGRIM: GARDEN OF EDEN
Black Bull Entertainment: May, 2002 - No. 4, Aug, 2002 ($2.99, limited series)

	GD	VG	FN	VF	VF/NM	NM-
Limited Preview Ed. (1/02, $7.00) Ennis & Ezquerra interviews; Jones-c						7.00
1-4-Ennis-s/Ezquerra-a						3.00
TPB (11/02, $12.99) r/#1-4; Gareb Shamus intro.						13.00

JUSTICE
Marvel Comics Group (New Universe): Nov, 1986 - No. 32, June, 1989

	GD	VG	FN	VF	VF/NM	NM-
1-32: 26-32-$1.50-c (low print run)						2.25

JUSTICE COMICS (Formerly Wacky Duck; Tales of Justice #53 on)
Marvel/Atlas Comics (NPP 7-9,4-19/CnPC 20-23/MjMC 24-38/Male 39-52:
No. 7, Fall/47 - No. 9, 6/48; No. 4, 8/48 - No. 52, 3/55

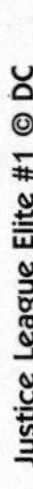

Justice League Elite #1 © DC

Justice League Europe #28 © DC

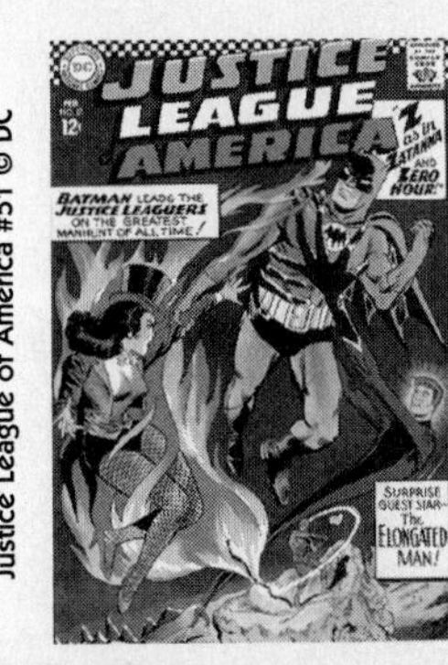
Justice League of America #51 © DC

	GD 2.0	VG 4.0	FN 6.0	VF 8.0	VF/NM 9.0	NM- 9.2
7(#1, 1947)	29	58	87	167	241	315
8(#2)-Kurtzman-a "Giggles 'n' Grins" (3)	20	40	60	112	161	210
9(#3, 6/48)	18	36	54	100	143	185
4	16	32	48	89	127	165
5(9/48)-9: 8-Anti-Wertham editorial	14	28	42	79	110	140
10-15-Photo-c	11	22	33	64	87	110
16-30	10	20	30	58	77	95
31-40,42-52: 35-Gene Colan-a. 48-Last precode; Pakula & Tuska-a.	9	18	27	54	70	85
41-Electrocution-c	17	34	51	95	135	175

NOTE: ***Heath*** *a-24.* ***Maneely*** *c-44, 52.* ***Pakula*** *a-43, 45, 48.* ***Louis Ravielli*** *a-39.* ***Robinson*** *a-22, 25, 41.* ***Shores*** *c-7(#1), 8(#2)?* ***Tuska*** *a-48.* ***Wildey*** *a-52.*

JUSTICE: FOUR BALANCE
Marvel Comics: Sept, 1994 - No. 4, Dec, 1994 ($1.75, limited series)

1-4: 1-Thing & Firestar app. 2.25

JUSTICE, INC. (The Avenger) (Pulp)
National Periodical Publications: May-June, 1975 - No. 4, Nov-Dec, 1975

	GD	VG	FN	VF	VF/NM	NM-
1-McWilliams-a, Kubert-c; origin	2	4	6	9	11	14
2-4: 2-4-Kirby-a(p), c-2,3p. 4-Kubert-c	2	4	6	8	10	12

NOTE: *Adapted from Kenneth Robeson novel, creator of Doc Savage.*

JUSTICE, INC. (Pulp)
DC Comics: 1989 - No. 2, 1989 ($3.95, 52 pgs., squarebound, mature)

1,2: Re-intro The Avenger; Andrew Helfer scripts & Kyle Baker-c/a 4.00

JUSTICE LEAGUE (...International #7-25; ...America #26 on)
DC Comics: May, 1987 - No. 113, Aug, 1996 (Also see Legends #6)

	GD	VG	FN	VF	VF/NM	NM-
1-Batman, Green Lantern (Guy Gardner), Blue Beetle, Mr. Miracle, Capt. Marvel & Martian Manhunter begin	1	2	3	4	5	7
2,3: 3-Regular-c (white background)						5.00
3-Limited-c (yellow background, Superman logo)	4	8	12	29	40	50

4-10: 4-Booster Gold joins. 5-Origin Gray Man; Batman vs. Guy Gardner; Creeper app. 7-($1.25, 52 pgs.)-Capt. Marvel & Dr. Fate resign; Capt. Atom & Rocket Red join. 9,10-Millennium x-over 3.00
11-17,22,23,25-49,51-68,72-82: 16-Bruce Wayne-c/story. 31,32-J. L. Europe x-over. 58-Lobo app. 61-New team begins; swipes-c to J.L. of A. #1('60). 70-Newsstand version w/o outer-c. 71-Direct sales version w/black outer-c. 71-Newsstand version w/o outer-c. 80-Intro new Booster Gold. 82,83-Guy Gardner-c/stories 2.50
18-21,24,50: 18-21-Lobo app. 24-($1.50)-1st app. Justice League Europe. 50-($1.75, 52 pgs.) 3.00
69-Doomsday tie-in; takes place between Superman: The Man of Steel #18 & Superman #74 5.00
69,70-2nd printings 2.25
70-Funeral for a Friend part 1; red 3/4 outer-c 4.00
83-99,101-113: 92-(9/94)-Zero Hour x-over; Triumph app. 113-Green Lantern, Flash & Hawkman app. 2.50
100 ($3.95)-Foil-c; 52 pgs. 4.00
100 ($2.95)-Newstand 3.00
#0-(10/94) Zero Hour (publ between #92 & #93); new team begins (Hawkman, Flash, Wonder Woman, Metamorpho, Nuklon, Crimson Fox, Obsidian & Fire) 2.50
Annual 1-8,10 ('87-'94, '96, 68 pgs.): 2-Joker-c/story; Batman cameo. 5-Armageddon 2001 x-over; Silver ink 2nd print. 7-Bloodlines x-over. 8-Elseworlds story. 10-Legends of the Dead Earth 3.00
Annual 9 (1995, $3.50)-Year One story 3.50
Special 1,2 ('90,'91, 52 pgs.): 1-Giffen plots. 2-Staton-a(p) 3.00
Spectacular 1 (1992, $1.50, 52 pgs.)-Intro new JLI & JLE teams; ties into JLI #61 & JLE #37; two interlocking covers by Jurgens 3.00
A New Beginning Trade Paperback (1989, $12.95)-r/#1-7 13.00

NOTE: ***Anderson*** *c-61i.* ***Austin*** *a-1i, 60i; c-1i.* ***Giffen*** *a-13; c-21p.* ***Guice*** *a-62i.* ***Maguire*** *a-1-12, 16-19, 22, 23.* ***Russell*** *a-Annual 1i; c-54i.* ***Willingham*** *a-30p, Annual 2.*

JUSTICE LEAGUE ADVENTURES (Based on Cartoon Network series)
DC Comics: Jan, 2002 - No. 34, Oct, 2004 ($1.99/$2.25)

1-Timm & Ross-c 3.00
2-32: 3-Nicieza-s. 5-Starro app. 10-Begin $2.25-c. 14-Includes 16 pg. insert for VERB with Haberlin CG-art. 15,29-Amancio-a. 16-McCloud-s. 20-Psycho Pirate app. 25,26-Adam Strange-c/app. 28-Legion of Super-Heroes app. 30-Kamandi app. 2.25
Free Comic Book Day giveaway - (See Promotional Comics section)
TPB (2003, $9.95) r/#1,3,6,10-13; Timm/Ross-c from #1 10.00
...Vol. 1: The Magnificent Seven (2004, $6.95) digest-size reprints #3,6,10-12 7.00
...Vol. 2: Friends and Foes (2004, $6.95) digest-size reprints #13,14,16,19,20 7.00

JUSTICE LEAGUE: A MIDSUMMER'S NIGHTMARE
DC Comics: Sept, 1996 - No. 3, Nov, 1996 ($2.95, limited series, 38 pgs.)

1-3: Re-establishes Superman, Batman, Green Lantern, The Martian Manhunter, Flash, Aquaman & Wonder Woman as the Justice League; Mark Waid & Fabian Nicieza co-scripts; Jeff Johnson & Darick Robertson-a(p); Kevin Maguire-c 5.00
TPB-(1997, $8.95) r/1-3 9.00

JUSTICE LEAGUE ELITE (See JLA #100 and JLA Secret Files 2004)
DC Comics: Sept, 2004 - Present ($2.50)

1-6-Flash, Green Arrow, Vera Black and others; Kelly-s/Mahnke-a. 5,6-JSA app. 2.50

JUSTICE LEAGUE EUROPE (Justice League International #51 on)
DC Comics: Apr, 1989 - No. 68, Sept., 1994 (75¢/$1.00/$1.25/$1.50)

1-Giffen plots in all, breakdowns in #1-8,13-30; Justice League #1-c/swipe 3.00
2-10: 7-9-Batman app. 7,8-JLA x-over. 8,9-Superman app. 2.50
11-49: 12-Metal Men app. 20-22-Rogers-c/a(p). 33,34-Lobo vs. Despero. 37-New team begins; swipes-c to JLA #9; see JLA Spectacular 2.50
50-($2.50, 68 pgs.)-Battles Sonar 3.00
51-68: 68-Zero Hour x-over; Triumph joins Justice League Task Force (See JLTF #17) 2.25
Annual 1-5 ('90-'94, 68 pgs.)-1-Return of the Global Guardians; Giffen plots/breakdowns. 2-Armageddon 2001; Giffen-a(p); Rogers-a(p); Golden-a(i). 3-Eclipso app. 4-Intro Lionheart. 5-Elseworlds story 3.00

NOTE: ***Phil Jimenez*** *a-68p.* ***Rogers*** *c/a-20-22.* ***Sears*** *a-1-12, 14-19, 23-29; c-1-10, 12, 14-19, 23-29.*

JUSTICE LEAGUE INTERNATIONAL (See Justice League Europe)

JUSTICE LEAGUE OF AMERICA (See Brave & the Bold #28-30, Mystery In Space #75 & Official... Index) (See Crisis on Multiple Earths TPBs for reprints of JLA/JSA crossovers)
National Periodical Publ./DC Comics: Oct-Nov, 1960 - No. 261, Apr, 1987 (#91-99,139-157: 52 pgs.)

	GD 2.0	VG 4.0	FN 6.0	VF 8.0	VF/NM 9.0	NM- 9.2
1-(10-11/60)-Origin & 1st app. Despero; Aquaman, Batman, Flash, Green Lantern, J'onn J'onzz, Superman & Wonder Woman continue from Brave and the Bold	364	728	1092	3331	5666	8000
2	92	184	276	782	1266	1750
3-Origin/1st app. Kanjar Ro (see Mystery in Space #75)(scarce in high grade due to black-c)	74	148	222	629	1015	1400
4-Green Arrow joins JLA	50	100	150	407	641	875
5-Origin & 1st app. Dr. Destiny	45	90	135	360	568	775
6-8,10: 6-Origin & 1st app. Prof. Amos Fortune. 7-(10-11/61)-Last 10¢ issue. 10-(3/62)-Origin & 1st app. Felix Faust; 1st app. Lord of Time	34	68	102	255	403	550
9-(2/62)-Origin JLA (1st origin)	42	84	126	336	531	725
11-15: 12-(6/62)-Origin & 1st app. Dr. Light. 13-(8/62)-Speedy app. 14-(9/62)-Atom joins JLA.	22	44	66	158	242	325
16-20: 17-Adam Strange flashback	19	38	57	136	208	280
21-(8/63)-"Crisis on Earth-One"; re-intro. of JSA in this title (see Flash #129) (1st S.A. app. Hourman & Dr. Fate)	34	68	102	255	398	540
22- "Crisis on Earth-Two"; JSA x-over (story continued from #21)	31	62	93	223	342	460
23-28: 24-Adam Strange app. 27-Robin app.	14	28	42	102	156	210
29-JSA x-over; 1st S.A. app. Starman; "Crisis on Earth-Three"	18	36	54	126	193	260
30-JSA x-over	16	32	48	114	175	235
31-Hawkman joins JLA, Hawkgirl cameo (11/64)	12	24	36	86	131	175
32,34: 32-Intro & Origin Brain Storm. 34-Joker-c/sty	10	20	30	73	107	140
33,35,36,40,41: 40-3rd S.A. Penguin app. 41-Intro & origin The Key	10	20	30	67	96	125
37-39: 37,38-JSA x-over. 37-1st S.A. app. Mr. Terrific; Batman cameo. 38-"Crisis on Earth-A". 39-Giant G-16; r/B&B #28,30 & JLA #5	12	24	36	86	131	175
42-45: 42-Metamorpho app. 43-Intro. Royal Flush Gang	8	16	24	55	78	100
46-JSA x-over; 1st S.A. app. Sandman; 3rd S.A. app. of G.A. Spectre (8/66)	13	26	39	90	138	185
47-JSA x-over; 4th S.A. app of G.A. Spectre.	10	20	30	67	96	125
48-Giant G-29; r/JLA #2,3 & B&B #29	9	18	27	65	93	120
49-54,57,59,60	7	14	21	51	71	90
55-Intro. Earth 2 Robin (1st G.A. Robin in S.A.)	10	20	30	67	96	125
56-JLA vs. JSA (1st G.A. Wonder Woman in S.A.)	8	16	24	58	82	105
58-Giant G-41; r/JLA #6,8,1	8	16	24	58	82	105
61-63,66,68-72: 69-Wonder Woman quits. 71-Manhunter leaves. 72-Last 12¢ issue	6	12	18	40	55	70
64,65-JSA story. 64-(8/68)-Origin/1st app. S.A. Red Tornado	7	14	21	46	63	80
67-Giant G-53; r/JLA #4,14,31	8	16	24	55	78	100
73-1st S.A. app. of G.A. Superman	7	14	21	46	63	80
74-Black Canary joins; 1st meeting of G.A. & S.A. Superman; Neal Adams-c	7	14	21	46	63	80
75-2nd app. Green Arrow in new costume (see Brave & the Bold #85)	6	12	18	43	59	75
76-Giant G-65	7	14	21	46	63	80

Justice League of America #92 © DC

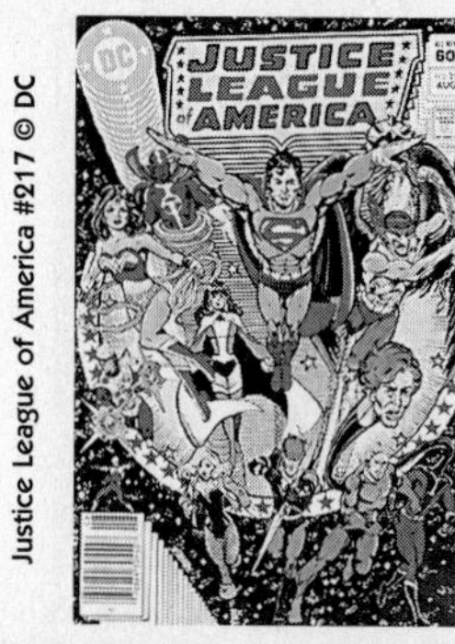
Justice League of America #217 © DC

Justice League Unlimited #1 © DC

GD VG FN VF VF/NM NM-
2.0 4.0 6.0 8.0 9.0 9.2

77-80: 78-Re-intro Vigilante (1st S.A. app?) 4 8 12 27 36 45
81-84,86-90: 82-1st S.A. app. of G.A. Batman (cameo). 83-Apparent death of The Spectre.
90-Last 15¢ issue 4 8 12 24 32 40
85,93-(Giant G-77,G-89; 68 pgs.) 5 10 15 36 48 60
91,92: 91-1st meeting of the G.A. & S.A. Robin; begin 25¢, 52 pgs. issues, ends #99.
92-S.A. Robin tries on costume that is similar to that of G.A. Robin in All Star Comics #58 4 8 12 29 40 50
94-Reprints 1st Sandman story (Adv. #40) & origin/1st app. Starman (Adventure #61);
Deadman x-over; N. Adams-a (4 pgs.) 9 18 27 65 93 120
95,96: 95-Origin Dr. Fate & Dr. Midnight -r/ More Fun #67, All-American #25).
96-Origin Hourman (Adv. #48); Wildcat-r 5 10 15 33 44 55
97-99: 97-Origin JLA retold; Sargon, Starman-r. 98-G.A. Sargon, Starman-r.
99-G.A. Sandman, Atom-r; last 52 pg. issue 4 8 12 27 36 45
100-(8/72)-1st meeting of G.A. & S.A. W. Woman 5 10 15 33 44 55
101,102: JSA x-overs. 102-Red Tornado dies 4 8 12 24 32 40
103-106,109: 103-Rutland Vermont Halloween x-over; Phantom Stranger joins.
105-Elongated Man joins. 106-New Red Tornado joins. 109-Hawkman resigns 3 6 9 16 20 24
107,108-JSA x-over; 1st revival app. of G.A. Uncle Sam, Black Condor, The Ray, Dollman,
Phantom Lady & The Human Bomb 3 6 9 16 21 26
110-116: All 100 pgs. 111-JLA vs. Injustice Gang; Shining Knight, Green Arrow-r. 112-Amazo app; Crimson Avenger, Vigilante-r; origin Starman-r/Adv. #81. 115-Martian Manhunter app. 4 8 12 29 40 50
117-122,125-134: 117-Hawkman rejoins. 120,121-Adam Strange app. 125,126-Two-Face-app.
128-Wonder Woman rejoins. 129-Destruction of Red Tornado 2 4 6 11 14 18
123-(10/75),124: JLA/JSA x-over. DC editor Julie Schwartz & JLA writers Cary Bates & Elliot S! Maggin appear in story as themselves. 1st named app. Earth-Prime (3rd app. after Flash; 1st Series #179 & 228) 2 4 6 12 16 20
135-136: 135-137-G.A. Bulletman, Bulletgirl, Spy Smasher, Mr. Scarlet, Pinky & Ibis x-over, 1st appearances since G.A. 2 4 6 12 16 20
137-Superman battles G.A. Capt. Marvel 3 6 9 16 20 24
138,139-157: 138-Adam Strange app. w/c by Neal Adams; 1st app. Green Lantern of the 73rd Century. 139-157-(52 pgs.): 139-Adam Strange app. 144-Origin retold; origin J'onn J'onzz. 145-Red Tornado resurrected. 147,148-Legion of Super-Heroes x-over 2 4 6 10 12 15
158-160-(44 pgs.) 1 3 4 6 8 10
158,160-162,168,169,171,172,173,176-179,181-(Whitman variants; low print run, none show issue # on cover) 2 4 6 8 10 12
161-182: 161-Zatanna joins & new costume. 171-Mr. Terrific murdered. 178-Cover similar to #1; J'onn J'onzz app. 179-Firestorm joins. 181-Green Arrow leaves JLA 6.00
183-185-JSA/New Gods/Darkseid/Mr.Miracle x-over 1 2 3 4 5 7
186-199: 192,193-Real origin Red Tornado. 193-1st app. All-Star Squadron as free 16 pg. insert 5.00
200 ($1.50, Anniversary issue, 76pgs.)-JLA origin retold; Green Arrow rejoins; Bolland, Aparo, Giordano, Gil Kane, Infantino, Kubert-a; Perez-c/a 6.00
201-206,209-243,246-259: 203-Intro/origin new Royal Flush Gang. 219,220-True origin Black Canary. 228-Re-intro Martian Manhunter. 228-230-War of the Worlds storyline; JLA Satellite destroyed by Martians. 233-Story cont'd from Annual #2. 243-Aquaman leaves.
250-Batman rejoins. 253-Origin Despero. 258-Death of Vibe. 258-261-Legends x-over 3.00
207,208-JSA, JLA, & All-Star Squadron team-up 4.00
244,245-Crisis x-over 4.00
260-Death of Steel 5.00
261-Last issue 1 2 3 4 5 7
Annual 1-3 ('83-'85), 2-Intro new J.L.A. (Aquaman, Martian Manhunter, Steel, Gypsy, Vixen, Vibe, Elongated Man, & Zatanna). 3-Crisis x-over 3.00

NOTE: ***Neal Adams** c-63, 66, 67, 70, 74, 79, 81, 82, 86-89, 91, 92, 94, 96-98, 138, 139. **M. Anderson** c-1-4, 6, 7, 10, 12-14. **Aparo** a-200. **Austin** a-200i. **Baily** a-96r. **Bolland** a-200. **Buckler** c-158, 163, 164. **Burnley** r-94, 98, 99. **Greene** a-46-61i, 64-73i, 110i(r). **Grell** c-117, 122. **Kaluta** c-154p. **Gil Kane** a-200. **Krigstein** a-96(r/Sensation #84). **Kubert** a-200; c-72, 73. **Nino** a-228i, 230i. **Orlando** c-151i. **Perez** a-184-186p, 192-197p, 200p; c-184p, 186, 192-195, 196p, 197p, 199, 200, 201p, 202, 203-205p, 207-209, 212-215, 217, 219, 220. **Reinman** r-97. **Roussos** a-62i. **Sekowsky** a-37, 38, 44-63p, 110-112p(r); c-46-48p, 51p. **Sekowsky/Anderson** c-5, 8, 9, 11, 15. **B. Smith** c-185i. **Starlin** c-178-180, 183, 185p. **Staton** a-244p; c-157p, 244p. **Toth** r-110. **Tuska** a-153, 228p, 241-243p. JSA x-overs-21, 22, 29, 30, 37, 38, 46, 47, 55, 56, 64, 65, 73, 74, 82, 83, 91, 92, 100, 101, 102, 107, 108, 110, 113, 115, 123, 124, 135-137, 147, 148, 159, 160, 171, 172, 183-185, 195-197, 207-209, 219, 220, 231, 232, 244.*

JUSTICE LEAGUE OF AMERICA : ANOTHER NAIL (Elseworlds) (Also see JLA: The Nail)
DC Comics: 2004 - No. 3, 2004 ($5.95, prestige format)

1-3-Sequel to JLA: The Nail; Alan Davis-s/a(p) 6.00
TPB (2004, $12.95) r/series 13.00

JUSTICE LEAGUE OF AMERICA SUPER SPECTACULAR
DC Comics: 1999 ($5.95, mimics format of DC 100 Page Super Spectaculars)

1-Reprints Silver Age JLA and Golden Age JSA 6.00

JUSTICE LEAGUE QUARTERLY (...International Quarterly #6 on)
DC Comics: Winter, 1990-91 - No. 17, Winter, 1994 ($2.95/$3.50, 84 pgs.)

GD VG FN VF VF/NM NM-
2.0 4.0 6.0 8.0 9.0 9.2

1-12,14-17: 1-Intro The Conglomerate (Booster Gold, Praxis, Gypsy, Vapor, Echo, Maxi-Man, & Reverb); Justice League #1-c/swipe. 1,2-Giffen plots/breakdowns. 3-Giffen plot; 72 pg. story. 4-Rogers/Russell-a in back-up. 5,6-Waid scripts. 8,17-Global Guardians app.
12-Waid script 3.50
13-Linsner-c 6.00
NOTE: ***Phil Jimenez** a-17p. **Sprouse** a-1p.*

JUSTICE LEAGUES...
DC Comics: Mar, 2001 ($2.50, limited series)

JL?, Justice League of Amazons, Justice League of Atlantis, Justice League of Arkham, Justice League of Aliens, JLA: JLA split by the Advance Man; Perez-c in all; s&a by various 2.50

JUSTICE LEAGUE TASK FORCE
DC Comics: June, 1993 - No. 37, Aug, 1996 ($1.25/$1.50/$1.75)

1-16,0,17-37: Aquaman, Nightwing, Flash, J'onn J'onzz, & Gypsy form team. 5,6-Knight-quest tie-ins (new Batman cameo #5, 1 pg.). 15-Triumph cameo. 16-(9/94)-Zero Hour x-over; Triumph app. 0-(10/94). 17-(11/94)-Triumph becomes part of Justice League Task Force (See JLE #68). 26-Impulse app. 35-Warlord app. 37-Triumph quits team 2.25

JUSTICE LEAGUE UNLIMITED (Based on Cartoon Network animated series)
DC Comics: Nov, 2004 - Present ($2.25)

1-4: 1-Zatanna app. 2-Royal Flush Gang app. 4-Adam Strange app. 2.25

JUSTICE MACHINE, THE
Noble Comics: June, 1981 - No. 5, Nov, 1983 ($2.00, nos. 1-3 are mag. size)

1-Byrne-c(p) 3 6 9 16 21 26
2-Austin-c(i) 2 4 6 10 12 15
3 1 3 4 6 8 10
4,5, Annual 1: Ann. 1-(1/84, 68 pgs.)(published by Texas Comics); 1st app. The Elementals; Golden-c(p); new Thunder Agents story (43 pgs.) 6.00

JUSTICE MACHINE (Also see The New Justice Machine)
Comico/Innovation Publishing: Jan, 1987 - No. 29, May 1989 ($1.50/$1.75)

1-29 2.25
Annual 1(6/89, $2.50, 36 pgs.)-Last Comico ish. 3.00
Summer Spectacular 1 ('89, $2.75)-Innovation Publ.; Byrne/Gustovich-c 3.00

JUSTICE MACHINE, THE
Innovation Publishing: 1990 - No. 4, 1990 ($1.95/$2.25, deluxe format, mature)

1-4: Gustovich-c/a in all 2.25

JUSTICE MACHINE FEATURING THE ELEMENTALS
Comico: May, 1986 - No. 4, Aug, 1986 ($1.50, limited series)

1-4 2.25

JUSTICE RIDERS
DC Comics: 1997 ($5.95, one-shot, prestige format)

1-Elseworlds; Dixon-s/Williams & Gray-a 6.00

JUSTICE SOCIETY OF AMERICA (See Adventure #461 & All-Star #3)
DC Comics: April, 1991 - No. 8, Nov, 1991 ($1.00, limited series)

1-8: 1-Flash. 2-Black Canary. 3-Green Lantern. 4-Hawkman. 5-Flash/Hawkman.
6-Green Lantern/Black Canary. 7-JSA 2.50

JUSTICE SOCIETY OF AMERICA (Also see Last Days of the... Special)
DC Comics: Aug, 1992 - No. 10, May, 1993 ($1.25)

1-10 2.50

JUSTICE SOCIETY OF AMERICA 100-PAGE SUPER SPECTACULAR
DC Comics: 2000 ($6.95, mimics format of DC 100 Page Super Spectaculars)

1-"1975 Issue" reprints Flash team-up and Golden Age JSA 7.00

JUSTICE SOCIETY RETURNS, THE (See All Star Comics (1999) for related titles)
DC Comics: 2003 ($19.95, TPB)

TPB-Reprints 1999 JSA x-over from All-Star Comics #1,2 and related one-shots 20.00

JUSTICE TRAPS THE GUILTY (Fargo Kid V11#3 on)
Prize/Headline Publications: Oct-Nov, 1947 - V11#2(#92), Apr-May, 1958 (True FBI Cases)

	GD 2.0	VG 4.0	FN 6.0	VF 8.0	VF/NM 9.0	NM- 9.2
V2#1-S&K-c/a; electrocution-c	59	118	177	369	565	760
2-S&K-c/a	37	74	111	209	305	400
3-5-S&K-c/a	35	70	105	198	287	375
6-S&K-c/a; Feldstein-a	36	72	108	204	297	390
7,9-S&K-c/a. 7-9-V2#1-3 in indicia; #7-9 on-c	30	60	90	173	249	325
8-Krigstein-a; S&K-c	29	58	87	164	237	310
10-Krigstein-a; S&K-c/a	30	60	90	173	249	325
11,18,19-S&K-c	15	30	45	86	123	160
12,14-17,20-No S&K. 14-Severin/Elder-a (8pg.)	9	18	27	54	70	85
13-Used in **SOTI**, pg. 110-111	10	20	30	60	80	100

Just Imagine Stan Lee with Chris Bachalo Creating Catwoman © DC

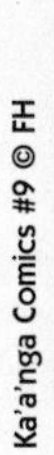

Ka'a'nga Comics #9 © FH

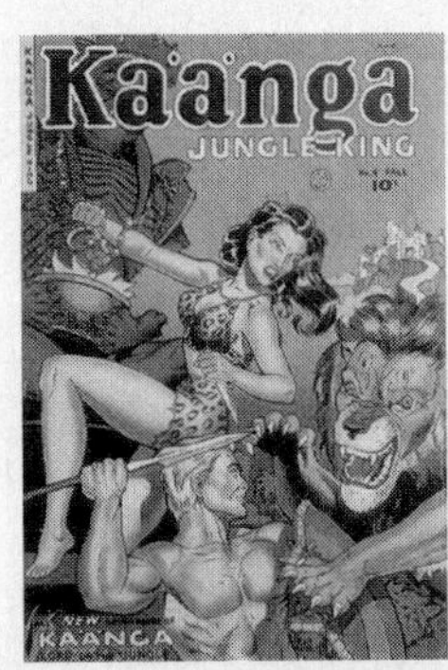

Kabuki V7#1 © David Mack

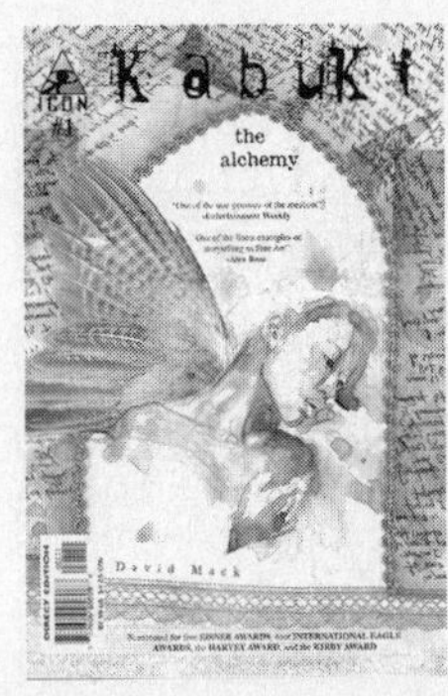

	GD 2.0	VG 4.0	FN 6.0	VF 8.0	VF/NM 9.0	NM- 9.2
21,30-S&K-c/a	15	30	45	86	123	160
22,23,27-S&K-c	11	22	33	62	84	105
24-26,29,31-50: 32-Meskin story	8	16	24	46	58	70
28-Kirby-c	10	20	30	56	73	90
51-55,57,59-70	8	16	24	40	50	60
56-Ben Oda, Joe Simon, Joe Genola, Mort Meskin & Jack Kirby app. in police line-up on classic-c	11	22	33	62	84	105
58-Illo. in **SOTI**, "Treating police contemptuously" (top left); text on heroin	27	54	81	152	219	285
71-92: 76-Orlando-a	7	14	21	35	43	50

NOTE: *Bailey a-12, 13.* ***Elder*** *a-8.* ***Kirby*** *a-19p.* ***Meskin*** *a-22, 27, 63, 64; c-45, 46.* ***Robinson/Meskin*** *a-5, 19.* ***Severin*** *a-8, 11p. Photo c-12, 15-17.*

JUST IMAGINE STAN LEE WITH... (Stan Lee re-invents DC icons)
DC Comics: 2001 - 2002 ($5.95, prestige format, one-shots)
(Adam Hughes back-c on all)(Michael Uslan back-up stories in all, diff. artists)

	NM-
Scott McDaniel Creating **Aquaman**- Back-up w/Fradon-a	6.00
Joe Kubert Creating **Batman**- Back-up w/Kaluta-a	6.00
Chris Bachalo Creating **Catwoman**- Back-up w/Cooke & Allred-a	6.00
John Cassaday Creating **Crisis**- no back-up story	6.00
Kevin Maguire Creating **The Flash**- Back-up w/Aragonés-a	6.00
Dave Gibbons Creating **Green Lantern**- Back-up w/Giordano-a	6.00
Jerry Ordway Creating **JLA**	6.00
John Byrne Creating **Robin**- Back-up w/John Severin-a	6.00
Walter Simonson Creating **Sandman**- Back-up w/Corben-a	6.00
Gary Frank Creating **Shazam!**- Back-up w/Kano-a	6.00
John Buscema Creating **Superman**- Back-up w/Kyle Baker-a	6.00
Jim Lee Creating **Wonder Woman**- Back-up w/Gene Colan-a	6.00
Secret Files and Origins #1 (3/02, $4.95) Crisis prologue; Jurgens-a	5.00
TPB -Just Imagine Stan Lee Creating the DC Universe: Book One (2002, $19.95) r/Batman, Wonder Woman, Superman, Green Lantern	20.00
TPB -Just Imagine Stan Lee Creating the DC Universe: Book Two (2003, $19.95) r/Flash, JLA, Secret Files and Origins, Robin, Shazam; sketch pages	20.00
TPB -Just Imagine Stan Lee Creating the DC Universe: Book Three (2004, $19.95) r/Aquaman, Catwoman, Sandman, Crisis; profile pages	20.00

JUST MARRIED
Charlton Comics: January, 1958 - No. 114, Dec, 1976

	GD	VG	FN	VF	VF/NM	NM-
1	7	14	21	50	68	85
2	4	8	12	25	33	42
3-10	3	6	9	19	25	32
11-30	3	6	9	16	20	24
31-50	2	4	6	11	14	18
51-70	2	4	6	10	12	15
71-90	2	4	6	8	10	12
91-114	1	3	4	6	8	10

JUSTY
Viz Comics: Dec 6, 1988 - No. 9, 1989 ($1.75, B&W, bi-weekly mini-series)

	NM-
1-9: Japanese manga	2.50

KA'A'NGA COMICS (...Jungle King)(See Jungle Comics)
Fiction House Magazines (Glen-Kel Publ. Co.): Spring, 1949 - No. 20, Summer, 1954

	GD	VG	FN	VF	VF/NM	NM-
1-Ka'a'nga, Lord of the Jungle begins	52	104	157	317	484	650
2 (Winter, '49-'50)	30	60	90	173	249	325
3,4	22	44	66	125	180	235
5-Camilla app.	17	34	51	95	135	175
6-10: 7-Tuska-a. 9-Tabu, Wizard of the Jungle app. 10-Used in **POP**, pg. 99	15	30	45	83	117	150
11-15: 15-Camilla-r by Baker/Jungle #106	12	24	36	69	95	120
16-Sheena app.	13	26	39	74	102	130
17-20	11	22	33	64	87	110
I.W. Reprint #1,8: 1-r/#18; Kinstler-c. 8-r/#10	3	6	9	16	20	25

NOTE: *Celardo c-1.* ***Whitman*** *c-8-20(most).*

KABOOM
Awesome Entertainment: Sept, 1997 - No. 3, Nov, 1997 ($2.50)

	NM-
1-3: 1-Matsuda-a/Loeb-s; 4 covers exist (Matsuda, Sale, Pollina and McGuinness), 1-Dynamic Forces Edition, 2-Regular, 2-Alicia Watcher variant-c, 2-Gold logo variant-c, 3-Two covers by Liefeld & Matsuda, 3-Dynamic Forces Ed., Prelude Ed.	2.50
Prelude Gold Edition	4.00

KABOOM (2nd series)
Awesome Entertainment: July, 1999 - No. 3, Dec, 1999 ($2.50)

	NM-
1-3: 1-Grant-a(p); at least 4 variant covers	2.50

KABUKI
Caliber: Nov, 1994 ($3.50, B&W, one-shot)

	GD	VG	FN	VF	VF/NM	NM-
nn-(Fear The Reaper) 1st app.; David Mack-c/a/s	1	2	3	5	6	8
Color Special (1/96, $2.95)-Mack-c/a/scripts; pin-ups by Tucci, Harris & Quesada						4.00
Gallery (8/95, $2.95)- pinups from Mack, Bradstreet, Paul Pope & others						3.00

KABUKI
Image Comics: Oct, 1997 - No. 9, Mar, 2000 ($2.95, color)

	GD	VG	FN	VF	VF/NM	NM-
1-David Mack-c/s/a						5.00
1-($10.00)-Dynamic Forces Edition	1	3	4	6	8	10
2-5						4.00
6-9						3.00
#1/2 (9/01, $2.95) r/Wizard 1/2; Eklipse Mag. article; bio						3.00
...Classics (2/99, $3.95) Reprints Fear the Reaper						4.00
...Classics 2 (3/99, $3.95) Reprints Dance of Dance						4.00
...Classics 3-5 (3-6/99, $4.95) Reprints Circle of Blood-Acts 1-3						5.00
...Classics 6-12 (7/99-3/00, $3.25) Various reprints						3.25
...Images (6/98, $4.95) r/#1 with new pin-ups						5.00
...Images 2 (1/99, $4.95) r/#1 with new pin-ups						5.00
...Metamorphosis TPB (10/00, $24.95) r/#1-9; Sienkiewicz intro.						25.00
...Reflections 1-4 (7/98-5/02; $4.95) new story plus art techniques						5.00
... The Ghost Play (11/02, $2.95) new story plus interview						3.00

KABUKI
Marvel Comics (Icon): July, 2004 - Present ($2.99, color)

	NM-
1,2: 1-David Mack-c/s/a in all; variant-c by Alex Maleev	3.00

KABUKI AGENTS (SCARAB)
Image Comics: Aug, 1999 - No. 8, Aug, 2001 ($2.95, B&W)

	NM-
1-8-David Mack-s/Rick Mays-a	3.00
Lost in Translation HC (3/02, $29.95) r/#1-8; intro. by Paul Pope	30.00
Lost in Translation SC (3/02, $19.95) r/#1-8; intro. by Paul Pope	20.00

KABUKI: CIRCLE OF BLOOD
Caliber Press: Jan, 1995 - No. 6, Nov, 1995 ($2.95, B&W)

	NM-
1-David Mack story/a in all	5.00
2-6: 3-#1 on inside indicia.	3.00
6-Variant-c	3.00
TPB ($16.95) r/#1-6, intro. by Steranko	17.00
TPB (1997, $17.95) Image Edition-r/#1-6, intro. by Steranko	18.00
TPB ($24.95) Deluxe Edition	25.00

KABUKI: DANCE OF DEATH
London Night Studios: Jan, 1995 ($3.00, B&W, one-shot)

	GD	VG	FN	VF	VF/NM	NM-
1-David Mack-c/a/scripts	1	2	3	5	6	8

KABUKI: DREAMS
Image Comics: Jan, 1998 ($4.95, TPB)

	NM-
nn-Reprints Color Special & Dreams of the Dead	5.00

KABUKI: DREAMS OF THE DEAD
Caliber: July, 1996 ($2.95, one-shot)

	NM-
nn-David Mack-c/a/scripts	3.00

KABUKI FAN EDITION
Gemstone Publ./Caliber: Feb, 1997 (mail-in offer, one-shot)

	NM-
nn-David Mack-c/a/scripts	4.00

KABUKI: MASKS OF THE NOH
Caliber: May, 1996 - No. 4, Feb, 1997 ($2.95, limited series)

	NM-
1-4: 1-Three-c (1A-Quesada, 1B-Buzz, &1C-Mack). 3-Terry Moore pin-up	3.00
TPB-(4/98, $10.95) r/#1-4; intro by Terry Moore	11.00

KABUKI: SKIN DEEP
Caliber Comics: Oct, 1996 - No. 3, May, 1997 ($2.95)

	NM-
1-3:David Mack-c/a/scripts. 2-Two-c (1-Mack, 1-Ross)	3.00
TPB-(5/98, $9.95) r/#1-3; intro by Alex Ross	10.00

KAMANDI: AT EARTH'S END
DC Comics: June, 1993 - No. 6, Nov, 1993 ($1.75, limited series)

	NM-
1-6: Elseworlds storyline	2.50

KAMANDI, THE LAST BOY ON EARTH (Also see Alarming Tales #1, Brave and the Bold #120 & 157 & Cancelled Comic Cavalcade)
National Periodical Publ./DC Comics: Oct-Nov, 1972 - No. 59, Sept-Oct, 1978

	GD	VG	FN	VF	VF/NM	NM-
1-Origin & 1st app. Kamandi	7	14	21	50	68	85
2,3	4	8	12	27	36	45
4,5: 4-Intro. Prince Tuftan of the Tigers	3	7	10	18	28	35
6-10	3	6	9	16	21	26

Kamandi, The Last Boy on Earth #28 © DC

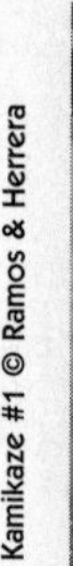
Kamikaze #1 © Ramos & Herrera

Katy Keene Special #5 © AP

	GD 2.0	VG 4.0	FN 6.0	VF 8.0	VF/NM 9.0	NM- 9.2
11-20	2	4	6	11	14	18
21-28,30,31,33-40: 24-Last 20¢ issue. 31-Intro Pyra.	2	4	6	10	13	16
29,32: 29-Superman x-over. 32-(68 pgs.)-r/origin from #1 plus one new story; 4 pg. biog. of Jack Kirby with B&W photos	2	4	6	12	16	20
41-57	2	4	6	8	10	12
58-(44 pgs.)-Karate Kid x-over from LSH	2	4	6	11	14	18
59-(44 pgs.)-Cont'd in B&B #157; The Return of Omac back-up by Starlin-c/a(p)	2	4	6	11	14	18

NOTE: ***Ayers** a(p)-48-59 (most). **Giffen** a-44p, 45p. **Kirby** a-1-40p; c-1-33. **Kubert** c-34-41. **Nasser** a-45p, 46p. **Starlin** a-59p; c-57, 59p.*

KAMIKAZI
DC Comics (Cliffhanger): Dec, 2003 - No. 6, May, 2004 ($2.95, limited series)

	GD 2.0	VG 4.0	FN 6.0	VF 8.0	VF/NM 9.0	NM- 9.2
1-6-Herrera-a						3.00

KAMUI (Legend Of...#2 on)
Eclipse Comics/Viz Comics: May 12, 1987 - No. 37, Nov. 15, 1988 ($1.50, B&W, bi-weekly)

	GD 2.0	VG 4.0	FN 6.0	VF 8.0	VF/NM 9.0	NM- 9.2
1-37: 1-3 have 2nd printings						2.50

KAOS MOON (Also see Negative Burn #34)
Caliber Comics: 1996 - No. 4, 1997 ($2.95, B&W)

	GD 2.0	VG 4.0	FN 6.0	VF 8.0	VF/NM 9.0	NM- 9.2
1-4-David Boller-s/a						3.00
3,4-Limited Alternate-c						4.00
3,4-Gold Alternate-c, Full Circle TPB ($5.95) r/#1,2						6.00

KARATE KID (See Action, Adventure, Legion of Super-Heroes, & Superboy)
National Periodical Publications/DC Comics: Mar-Apr, 1976 - No. 15, July-Aug, 1978
(Legion of Super-Heroes spin-off)

	GD 2.0	VG 4.0	FN 6.0	VF 8.0	VF/NM 9.0	NM- 9.2
1,15: 1-Meets Iris Jacobs; Estrada/Staton-a. 15-Continued into Kamandi #58	2	4	6	9	11	14
2-14: 2-Major Disaster app. 14-Robin x-over	1	2	3	5	6	8

NOTE: ***Grell** c-1-4, 5p, 6p, 7, 8. **Staton** a-1-9i. Legion x-over-No. 1, 2, 4, 6, 10, 12, 13. Princess Projectra x-over-#8, 9.*

KATHY
Standard Comics: Sept, 1949 - No. 17, Sept, 1955

	GD 2.0	VG 4.0	FN 6.0	VF 8.0	VF/NM 9.0	NM- 9.2
1-Teen-age	12	24	36	69	95	120
2-Schomburg-c	9	18	27	52	66	80
3-5	7	14	21	35	43	50
6-17: 17-Code approved	6	12	18	28	34	40

KATHY (The Teenage Tornado)
Atlas Comics/Marvel (ZPC): Oct, 1959 - No. 27, Feb, 1964

	GD 2.0	VG 4.0	FN 6.0	VF 8.0	VF/NM 9.0	NM- 9.2
1-Teen-age	7	14	21	51	70	90
2	4	8	12	27	36	45
3-15	3	6	9	19	25	32
16-27	2	4	6	14	18	22

KAT KARSON
I. W. Enterprises: No date (Reprint)

	GD 2.0	VG 4.0	FN 6.0	VF 8.0	VF/NM 9.0	NM- 9.2
1-Funny animals	2	4	6	10	12	15

KATO OF THE GREEN HORNET (Also see The Green Hornet)
Now Comics: Nov, 1991 - No. 4, Feb, 1992 ($2.50, mini-series)

	GD 2.0	VG 4.0	FN 6.0	VF 8.0	VF/NM 9.0	NM- 9.2
1-4: Brent Anderson-c/a						2.50

KATO OF THE GREEN HORNET II (Also see The Green Hornet)
Now Comics: Nov, 1992 - No. 2, Dec, 1993 ($2.50, mini-series)

	GD 2.0	VG 4.0	FN 6.0	VF 8.0	VF/NM 9.0	NM- 9.2
1,2-Baron-s/Mayerik & Sherman-a						2.50

KATY KEENE (Also see Kasco Komics, Laugh, Pep, Suzie, & Wilbur)
Archie Publ./Close-Up/Radio Comics: 1949 - No. 4, 1951; No. 5, 3/52 - No. 62, Oct, 1961
(50-53-Adventures of...on-c) (Cut and missing pages are common)

	GD 2.0	VG 4.0	FN 6.0	VF 8.0	VF/NM 9.0	NM- 9.2
1-Bill Woggon-c/a begins; swipes-c to Mopsy #1	108	216	324	675	1038	1400
2-(1950)	52	104	156	317	484	650
3-5: 3-(1951). 4-(1951)	40	80	120	239	357	475
6-10	35	70	105	201	293	385
11,13-21: 21-Last pre-code issue (3/55)	30	60	90	170	245	320
12-(Scarce)	35	70	105	201	293	385
22-40	21	42	63	121	173	225
41-60: 54-Wedding Album plus wedding pin-up	17	34	51	95	135	175
61,62: 62-Robot-c	19	38	57	107	154	200
Annual 1('54, 25¢)-All new stories; last pre-code	48	96	144	293	447	600
Annual 2-6('55-59, 25¢)-All new stories	30	60	90	173	249	325
3-D 1(1953, 25¢, large size)-Came w/glasses	40	80	120	236	351	465
Charm 1(9/58)-Woggon-c/a; new stories, and cut-outs	30	60	90	173	249	325
Glamour 1(1957)-Puzzles, games, cut-outs	30	60	90	173	249	325
Spectacular 1('56)	30	60	90	173	249	325

NOTE: *Debby's Diary in #45, 47-49, 52, 57.*

KATY KEENE COMICS DIGEST MAGAZINE
Close-Up, Inc. (Archie Ent.): 1987 - No. 10, July, 1990 ($1.25/$1.35/$1.50, digest size)

	GD 2.0	VG 4.0	FN 6.0	VF 8.0	VF/NM 9.0	NM- 9.2
1	2	4	6	10	13	16
2-10	1	2	3	5	7	9

KATY KEENE FASHION BOOK MAGAZINE
Radio Comics/Archie Publications: 1955 - No. 13, Sum, '56 - N. 23, Wint, '58-59 (nn 3-10)

	GD 2.0	VG 4.0	FN 6.0	VF 8.0	VF/NM 9.0	NM- 9.2
1-Bill Woggon-c/a	48	96	144	293	447	600
2	30	60	90	173	249	325
11-18: 18-Photo Bill Woggon	22	44	66	127	184	240
19-23	18	36	54	102	146	190

KATY KEENE HOLIDAY FUN (See Archie Giant Series Magazine No. 7, 12)

KATY KEENE PINUP PARADE
Radio Comics/Archie Publications: 1955 - No. 15, Summer, 1961 (25¢)
(Cut-out & missing pages are common)

	GD 2.0	VG 4.0	FN 6.0	VF 8.0	VF/NM 9.0	NM- 9.2
1-Cut-outs in all?; last pre-code issue	48	96	144	293	447	600
2-(1956)	30	60	90	173	249	325
3-5: 3-(1957)	25	50	75	141	203	265
6-10,12-14: 8-Mad parody. 10-Bill Woggon photo	21	42	63	118	169	220
11-Story of how comics get CCA approved, narrated by Katy	26	52	78	147	211	275
15(Rare)-Photo artist & family	40	80	120	239	357	475

KATY KEENE SPECIAL (Katy Keene #7 on; see Laugh Comics Digest)
Archie Ent.: Sept, 1983 - No. 33, 1990 (Later issues published quarterly)

	GD 2.0	VG 4.0	FN 6.0	VF 8.0	VF/NM 9.0	NM- 9.2
1-10: 1-Woggon-r; new Woggon-c. 3-Woggon-r						5.00
11-25: 12-Spider-Man parody						6.00
26-32-(Low print run)	1	2	3	5	7	9
33	2	4	6	8	10	12

KATZENJAMMER KIDS, THE (See Captain & the Kids & Giant Comic Album)
David McKay Publ./Standard No. 12-21(Spring/'50 - 53)/Harvey No. 22, 4/53 on: 1945-1946; Summer, 1947 - No. 27, Feb-Mar, 1954

	GD 2.0	VG 4.0	FN 6.0	VF 8.0	VF/NM 9.0	NM- 9.2
Feature Books 30	20	40	60	112	161	210
Feature Books 32,35('45),41,44('46)	18	36	54	100	143	185
Feature Book 37-Has photos & biography of Harold Knerr	19	38	57	107	154	200
1(1947)-All new stories begin	19	38	57	107	154	200
2	10	20	30	60	80	100
3-11	8	16	24	46	58	70
12-14(Standard)	7	14	21	35	43	50
15-21(Standard)	6	12	18	31	38	45
22-25,27(Harvey): 22-24-Henry app.	6	12	18	31	38	45
26-Half in 3-D	17	34	51	95	135	175

KAYO (Formerly Bullseye & Jest; becomes Carnival Comics)
Harry 'A' Chesler: No. 12, Mar, 1945

	GD 2.0	VG 4.0	FN 6.0	VF 8.0	VF/NM 9.0	NM- 9.2
12-Green Knight, Capt. Glory, Little Nemo (not by McCay)	17	34	51	95	135	175

KA-ZAR (Also see Marvel Comics #1, Savage Tales #6 & X-Men #10)
Marvel Comics Group: Aug, 1970 - No. 3, Mar, 1971 (Giant-Size, 68 pgs.)

	GD 2.0	VG 4.0	FN 6.0	VF 8.0	VF/NM 9.0	NM- 9.2
1-Reprints earlier Ka-Zar stories; Avengers x-over in Hercules; Daredevil, X-Men app.; hidden profanity-c	4	8	12	22	30	38
2,3-Daredevil-r. 2-r/Daredevil #13 w/Kirby layouts; Ka-Zar origin, Angel-r from X-Men by Tuska. 3-Romita & Heck-a (no Kirby)	3	6	9	16	21	26

NOTE: ***Buscema** r-2. **Colan** a-1p(r). **Kirby** c/a-1, 2. #1-Reprints X-Men #10 & Daredevil #24*

KA-ZAR
Marvel Comics Group: Jan, 1974 - No. 20, Feb, 1977 (Regular Size)

	GD 2.0	VG 4.0	FN 6.0	VF 8.0	VF/NM 9.0	NM- 9.2
1	2	4	6	11	14	18
2-10	1	2	3	5	7	9
11-14,16,18-20						6.00
15,17-(Regular 25¢ edition)(8/76)						6.00
15,17-(30¢-c variants, limited distribution)	1	2	3	5	6	8

NOTE: ***Alcala** a-6i, 8i. **Brunner** c-4. **J. Buscema** a-6-10p; c-1, 5, 7. **Heath** a-12. **G. Kane** c(p)-3, 5, 8-11, 15, 20. **Kirby** c-12p. **Reinman** a-1p.*

KA-ZAR (Volume 2)
Marvel Comics: May, 1997 - No. 20, Dec, 1998 ($1.95/$1.99)

	GD 2.0	VG 4.0	FN 6.0	VF 8.0	VF/NM 9.0	NM- 9.2
1-Waid-s/Andy Kubert-c/a. thru #4						3.00
1-2nd printing; new cover						2.25
2,4: 2-Two-c						2.50
3-Alpha Flight #1 preview						3.00

Keen Detective Funnies V2#5 © CEN

Ken Shannon #5 © QUA

The Kents #12 © DC

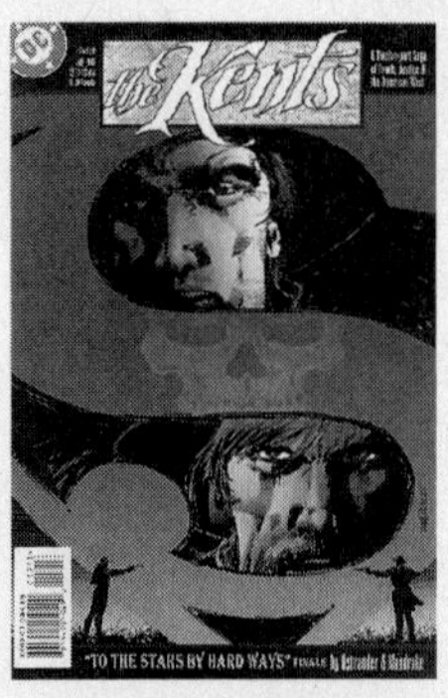

	GD 2.0	VG 4.0	FN 6.0	VF 8.0	VF/NM 9.0	NM- 9.2

5-13,15-20: 8-Includes Spider-Man Cybercomic CD-ROM. 9-11-Thanos app. 15-Priest-s/Martinez & Rodriguez-a begin; Punisher app. 2.25
14-($2.99) Last Waid/Kubert issue; flip book with 2nd story previewing new creative team of Priest-s/Martinez & Rodriguez-a 3.00
'97 Annual ($2.99)-Wraparound-c 3.00

KA-ZAR OF THE SAVAGE LAND
Marvel Comics: Feb, 1997 ($2.50, one-shot)

1-Wraparound-c 2.50

KA-ZAR: SIBLING RIVALRY
Marvel Comics: July, 1997 ($1.95, one-shot)

(# -1) Flashback story w/Alpha Flight #1 preview 2.25

KA-ZAR THE SAVAGE (See Marvel Fanfare)
Marvel Comics Group: Apr, 1981 - No. 34, Oct, 1984 (Regular size)(Mando paper #10 on)

1 4.00
2-20,24,27,28,30-34: 11-Origin Zabu. 12-One of two versions with panel missing on pg. 10. 20-Kraven the Hunter-c/story (also apps. in #21) 2.50
12-Version with panel on pg. 10 (1600 printed) 6.00
21-23, 25,26-Spider-Man app. 26-Photo-c. 3.00
29-Double size; Ka-Zar & Shanna wed 3.00

NOTE: ***B. Anderson** a-1-15p, 18, 19; c-1-17, 18p, 20(back). **G. Kane** a(back-up)-11, 12, 14.*

KEEN DETECTIVE FUNNIES (Formerly Detective Picture Stories?)
Centaur Publications: No. 8, July, 1938 - No. 24, Sept, 1940

V1#8-The Clock continues-r/Funny Picture Stories #1; Roy Crane-a (1st?) 231 462 693 1444 2222 3000
9-Tex Martin by Eisner; The Gang Buster app. 87 174 261 544 835 1125
10,11: 11-Dean Denton story (begins?) 77 154 231 481 741 1000
V2#1,2-The Eye Sees by Frank Thomas begins; ends #23(Not in V2#3&5). 2-Jack Cole-a 71 142 213 444 685 925
3-6: 3-TNT Todd begins. 4-Gabby Flynn begins. 5,6-Dean Denton story 67 134 201 419 647 875
7-The Masked Marvel by Ben Thompson begins (7/39, 1st app.)(scarce) 242 484 726 1513 2332 3150
8-Nudist ranch panel w/four girls 87 174 261 544 835 1125
9-11 75 150 225 469 722 975
12(12/39)-Origin The Eye Sees by Frank Thomas; death of Masked Marvel's sidekick ZL 92 184 276 575 888 1200
V3#1,2 69 138 207 431 666 900
18,19,21,22: 18-Bondage/torture-c 69 138 207 431 666 900
20-Classic Eye Sees-c by Thomas 98 196 294 613 944 1275
23-Air Man begins (intro); Air Man-c 92 184 276 575 888 1200
24-(scarce) Air Man-c 96 192 288 600 925 1250

NOTE: ***Burgos** a-V2#2. **Jack Cole** a-V2#2. **Eisner** a-10, V2#6r. **Ken Ernst** a-V2#4-7, 9, 10, 19, 21; c-V2#4. **Everett** a-V2#6, 7, 9, 11, 12, 20. **Guardineer** a-V2#5, 66. **Gustavson** a-V2#4-6. **Simon** c-V3#1. **Thompson** c-V2#7, 9, 10, 22.*

KEEN KOMICS
Centaur Publications: V2#1, May, 1939 - V2#3, Nov, 1939

V2#1(Large size)-Dan Hastings (s/f), The Big Top, Bob Phantom the Magician, The Mad Goddess app. 96 192 288 600 925 1250
V2#2(Reg. size)-The Forbidden Idol of Machu Picchu; Cut Carson by Burgos begins 62 124 186 388 594 800
V2#3-Saddle Sniffl by Jack Cole, Circus Pays, Kings Revenge app. 62 124 186 388 594 800

NOTE: ***Binder** a-V2#2. **Burgos** a-V2#2, 3. **Ken Ernst** a-V2#3. **Gustavson** a-V2#2. **Jack Cole** a-V2#3.*

KEEN TEENS (Girls magazine)
Life's Romances Publ./Leader/Magazine Ent.: 1945 - No. 6, Aug-Sept, 1947

nn (#1)-14 pgs. Claire Voyant (cont'd. in other nn issue) movie photos, Dotty Dripple, Gertie O'Grady & Sissy; Van Johnson, Frank Sinatra photo-c 39 78 117 222 324 425
nn (#2, 1946)-16 pgs. Claire Voyant & 16 pgs. movie photos 28 56 84 158 229 300
3-6: 4-Glenn Ford photo-c. 5-Perry Como-c 12 24 36 71 98 125

KEIF LLAMA
Oni Press: Mar, 1999 ($2.95, B&W, one-shot)

1-Matt Howarth-s/a 3.00

KELLYS, THE (Formerly Rusty Comics; Spy Cases No. 26 on)
Marvel Comics (HPC): No. 23, Jan, 1950 - No. 25, June, 1950 (52 pgs.)

23-Teenage 12 24 36 71 98 125
24,25: 24-Margie app. 9 18 27 51 62 75

KELVIN MACE
Vortex Publications: 1986 - No. 2, 1986 ($2.00, B&W)

1,2: 1-(B&W). 1-2nd print (1/87, $1.75). 2-(Color) 2.25

KEN MAYNARD WESTERN (Movie star)(See Wow Comics, 1936)
Fawcett Publ.: Sept, 1950 - No. 8, Feb, 1952 (All 36 pgs; photo front/back-c)

1-Ken Maynard & his horse Tarzan begin 60 120 180 375 580 785
2 39 78 117 222 324 425
3-8: 6-Atomic bomb explosion panel 30 60 90 170 245 320

KEN SHANNON (Becomes Gabby #11 on) (Also see Police Comics #103)
Quality Comics Group: Oct, 1951 - No. 10, Apr, 1953 (A private eye)

1-Crandall-a 40 80 120 230 335 440
2-Crandall c/a(2) 31 62 93 175 253 330
3-5-Crandall-a. 3-Horror-c 22 44 66 123 177 230
6-Crandall-c/a; "The Weird Vampire Mob"-c/s 25 50 75 141 203 265
7,10: 7-Crandall-a. 10-Crandall-c 18 36 54 100 143 185
8,9: 8-Opium den drug use story 17 34 51 98 139 180

NOTE: ***Crandall/Cuidera** c-1-10. **Jack Cole** a-1-9. #1-15 published after title change to Gabby.*

KEN STUART
Publication Enterprises: Jan, 1949 (Sea Adventures)

1-Frank Borth-c/a 10 20 30 56 73 90

KENT BLAKE OF THE SECRET SERVICE (Spy)
Marvel/Atlas Comics(20CC): May, 1951 - No. 14, July, 1953

1-Injury to eye, bondage, torture; Brodsky-c 21 42 63 118 169 220
2-Drug use w/hypo scenes; Brodsky-c 15 30 45 83 117 150
3-14: 8-R.Q. Sale-a (2 pgs.) 9 18 27 54 70 85

NOTE: ***Heath** c-5, 7, 8. **Infantino** c-12. **Maneely** c-3. **Sinnott** a-2(3). **Tuska** a-8(3pg.).*

KENTS, THE
DC Comics: Aug, 1997 - No. 12, July, 1998 ($2.50, limited series)

1-12-Ostrander-s/art by Truman and Bair (#1-8), Mandrake (#9-12) 3.00
TPB ($19.95) r/#1-12 20.00

KERRY DRAKE (Also see A-1 Comics)
Argo: Jan, 1956 - No. 2, March, 1956

1,2-Newspaper-r 8 16 24 46 58 70

KERRY DRAKE DETECTIVE CASES (...Racket Buster No. 32,33)
(Also see Chamber of Clues & Green Hornet Comics #42-47)
Life's Romances/Com/Magazine Ent. No.1-5/Harvey No.6 on: 1944 - No. 5, 1944; No. 6, Jan, 1948 - No. 33, Aug, 1952

nn(1944)(A-1 Comics)(slightly over-size) 31 62 93 178 259 340
2 19 38 57 107 154 200
3-5(1944) 16 32 48 92 131 170
6,8(1948): Lady Crime by Powell. 8-Bondage-c 11 22 33 64 87 110
7-Kubert-a; biog of Andriola (artist) 12 24 36 71 98 125
9,10-Two-part marijuana story; Kerry smokes marijuana in #10 16 32 48 89 127 165
11-15 10 20 30 58 77 95
16-33 9 18 27 51 62 75

NOTE: ***Andiola** c-6-9. **Berg** a-5. **Powell** a-10-23, 28, 29.*

KEWPIES
Will Eisner Publications: Spring, 1949

1-Feiffer-a; Kewpie Doll ad on back cover 46 92 138 281 428 575

KEY COMICS
Consolidated Magazines: Jan, 1944 - No. 5, Aug, 1946

1-The Key, Will-O-The-Wisp begin 40 80 120 244 372 500
2 (3/44) 23 46 69 132 191 250
3,4: 4-(5/46)-Origin John Quincy The Atom (begins); Walter Johnson c-3-5 20 40 60 112 161 210
5-4pg. Faust Opera adaptation; Kiefer-a; back-c advertises "Masterpieces Illustrated" by Lloyd Jacquet after he left Classic Comics (no copies of Masterpieces Illustrated known) 25 50 75 144 207 270

KEY RING COMICS
Dell Publishing Co.: 1941 (16 pgs.; two colors) (sold 5 for 10¢)

1-Sky Hawk, 1-Viking Carter, 1-Features Sleepy Samson, 1-Origin Greg Gilday-r/War Comics #2 8 16 24 46 58 70
1-Radior (Super hero) 9 18 27 54 70 85

NOTE: *Each book has two holes in spine to put in binder.*

KICKERS, INC.
Marvel Comics Group: Nov, 1986 - No. 12, Oct, 1987

1-12 2.25

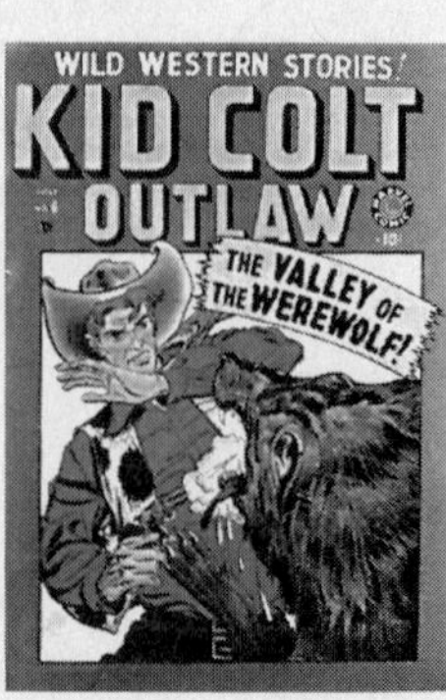

Kid Colt Outlaw #6 © Z-D

Kid Eternity #11 © QUA

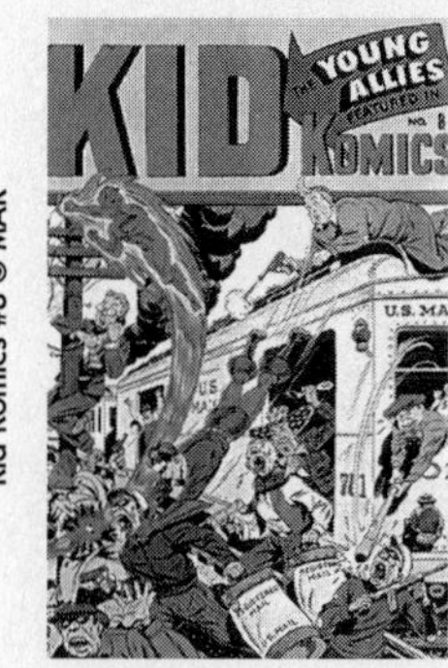

Kid Komics #8 © MAR

GD 2.0 | VG 4.0 | FN 6.0 | VF 8.0 | VF/NM 9.0 | NM- 9.2

KID CARROTS
St. John Publishing Co.: September, 1953
1-Funny animal 8 16 24 40 50 60

KID COLT OUTLAW (Kid Colt #1-4; ...Outlaw #5-on)(Also see All Western Winners, Best Western, Black Rider, Giant-Size..., Two-Gun Kid, Two-Gun Western, Western Winners, Wild Western, Wisco)
Marvel Comics(LCC) 1-16; Atlas(LMC) 17-102; Marvel 103-on: 8/48 - No. 139, 3/68; No. 140, 11/69 - No. 229, 4/79
1-Kid Colt & his horse Steel begin. 100 200 300 625 963 1300
2 50 100 150 305 465 625
3-5: 4-Anti-Wertham editorial; Tex Taylor app. 5-Blaze Carson app.
40 80 120 244 372 500
6-8: 6-Tex Taylor app; 7-Nimo the Lion begins, ends #10
30 60 90 170 245 320
9,10 (52 pgs.) 30 60 90 170 245 320
11-Origin 34 68 102 196 283 370
12-20 21 42 63 118 169 220
21-32 17 34 51 98 139 180
33-45: Black Rider in all 13 26 39 76 106 135
46,47,49,50 11 22 33 64 87 110
48-Kubert-a 11 22 33 66 91 115
51-53,55,56 9 18 27 54 70 85
54-Williamson/Maneely-c 10 20 30 58 77 95
57-60,66: 4-pg. Williamson-a in all 8 16 24 55 78 100
61-63,67-78,80-86: 70-Severin-c. 73-Maneely-c. 86-Kirby-a(r).
6 12 18 40 55 70
64,65-Crandall-a 6 12 18 43 59 75
79,87: 79-Origin retold. 87-Davis-a(r) 6 12 18 43 59 75
88,89-Williamson-a in both (4 pgs.). 89-Redrawn Matt Slade #2
7 14 21 46 63 80
90-99,101-106,108,109: 91-Kirby/Ayers-c. 95-Kirby/Ayers-c/story. 102-Last 10¢ issue
5 10 15 36 48 60
100 6 12 18 38 52 65
107-Only Kirby sci-fi cover of title; Kirby -a. 6 12 18 43 59 75
110-(5/63)-1st app. Iron Mask (Iron Man type villain) 6 12 18 43 59 75
111-120: 114-(1/64)-2nd app. Iron Mask 4 8 12 27 36 45
121-129,133-139: 121-Rawhide Kid x-over. 125-Two-Gun Kid x-over. 139-Last 12¢ issue
3 7 10 21 28 35
130-132 (68 pgs.)-one new story each. 130-Origin 4 8 12 27 36 45
140-155: 140-Reprints begin (later issues mostly-r). 155-Last 15¢ issue
2 4 6 12 16 20
156-Giant; reprints (52 pgs.) 3 6 9 18 24 30
157-180,200: 170-Origin retold. 2 4 6 10 13 16
181-199 2 4 6 8 10 12
201-229: 201-New material w/Rawhide Kid app; Kane-c. 229-Rawhide Kid-r
1 3 4 6 8 10
205-209-(30¢-c variants, limited dist.) 4 8 12 29 40 50
218-220-(35¢-c variants, limited dist.) 6 12 18 43 59 75
...Album (no date; 1950's; Atlas Comics)-132 pgs.; random binding, cardboard cover,
B&W stories; contents can vary (Rare) 81 162 243 506 778 1050

NOTE: ***Ayers*** *a-many.* ***Colan*** *a-52, 53; c(p)-223, 228, 229.* ***Crandall*** *a-140r, 167r.* ***Everett*** *a-90, 137i, 225i(r).* ***Heath*** *a-8(2); c-34, 35, 39, 44, 46, 48, 49, 57, 64.* ***Heck*** *a-135, 139.* ***Jack Keller*** *a-25(2), 26-68(3-4), 78, 94p, 98, 99, 108, 110, 130, 132, 140-150r.* ***Kirby*** *a-86r, 93, 96, 107, 119, 176(part); c-87, 92-95, 97, 99-112, 114-117, 121-123, 197r; w/****Ditko*** *c-89.* ***Maneely*** *a-12, 68, 81; c-17, 19, 40-43, 47, 52, 53, 62, 65, 68, 78, 81, 142r, 150r.* ***Morrow*** *a-173r, 216r.* ***Rico*** *a-13, 18.* ***Severin*** *c-58, 59, 143, 148, 149i.* ***Shores*** *a-39, 41-43, 143r; c-1-10(most), 24.* ***Sutton*** *a-136, 137p, 225p(r).* ***Wildey*** *a-47, 54, 82, 144r.* ***Williamson*** *r-147, 170, 172, 216.* ***Woodbridge*** *a-64, 81. Black Rider in #33-45, 74, 86. Iron Mask in #110, 114, 121, 127. Sam Hawk in #80, 84, 101, 111, 121, 146, 174, 181, 188.*

KID COWBOY (Also see Approved Comics #4 & Boy Cowboy)
Ziff-Davis Publ./St. John (Approved Comics) #11,14: 1950 - No. 11, Wint, '52-'53; No. 14, June, 1954 (No #12,13) (Painted covers #1-10, 14)
1-Lucy Belle & Red Feather begin 16 32 48 92 131 170
2-Maneely-c 10 20 30 60 80 100
3-11,14: (#3, spr. '51). 5-Berg-a. 14-Code approved 9 18 27 54 70 85

KID DEATH & FLUFFY HALLOWEEN SPECIAL
Event Comics: Oct, 1997 ($2.95, B&W, one-shot)
1-Variant-c by Cebollero & Quesada/Palmiotti 3.00

KID DEATH & FLUFFY SPRING BREAK SPECIAL
Event Comics: July, 1996 ($2.50, B&W, one-shot)
1-Quesada & Palmiotti-c/scripts 2.50

KIDDIE KAPERS
Kiddie Kapers Co., 1945/Decker Publ. (Red Top-Farrell): 1945?(nd); Oct, 1957; 1963 - 1964
1(nd, 1945-46?, 36 pgs.)-Infinity-c; funny animal 9 18 27 52 66 80
1(10/57)(Decker)-Little Bit-r from Kiddie Karnival 5 10 15 22 26 30
Super Reprint #7, 10('63), 12, 14('63), 15,17('64), 18('64): 10, 14-r/Animal Adventures #1. 15-Animal Adventures #? 17-Cowboys 'N' Injuns #?
2 4 6 9 11 14

KIDDIE KARNIVAL
Ziff-Davis Publ. Co. (Approved Comics): 1952 (25¢, 100 pgs.) (One Shot)
nn-Rebound Little Bit #1,2; painted-c 38 76 114 219 320 420

KID ETERNITY (Becomes Buccaneers) (See Hit Comics)
Quality Comics Group: Spring, 1946 - No. 18, Nov, 1949
1 100 200 300 625 963 1300
2 40 80 120 241 363 485
3-Mac Raboy-a 40 80 120 244 372 500
4-10 26 52 78 147 211 275
11-18 20 40 60 112 161 210

KID ETERNITY
DC Comics: 1991 - No. 3, Nov, 1991 ($4.95, limited series)
1-3: Grant Morrison scripts 6.00

KID ETERNITY
DC Comics (Vertigo): May, 1993 - No. 16, Sept, 1994 ($1.95, mature)
1-16: 1-Gold ink-c. 6-Photo-c. All Sean Phillips-c/a except #15 (Phillips-c/i only) 2.25

KID FROM DODGE CITY, THE
Atlas Comics (MMC): July, 1957 - No. 2, Sept, 1957
1-Don Heck-c 10 20 30 56 73 90
2-Everett-c 7 14 21 35 43 50

KID FROM TEXAS, THE (A Texas Ranger)
Atlas Comics (CSI): June, 1957 - No. 2, Aug, 1957
1-Powell-a; Severin-c 10 20 30 56 73 90
2 7 14 21 35 43 50

KID KOKO
I. W. Enterprises: 1958
Reprint #1,2-(r/M.E.'s Koko & Kola #4, 1947) 2 4 6 9 11 14

KID KOMICS (Kid Movie Komics No. 11)
Timely Comics (USA 1,2/FCI 3-10): Feb, 1943 - No. 10, Spring, 1946
1-Origin Captain Wonder & sidekick Tim Mullrooney, & Subbie; intro the Sea-Going Lad, Pinto Pete, & Trixie Trouble; Knuckles & Whitewash Jones (from Young Allies) app.; Wolverton-a (7 pgs.) 423 846 1269 2837 4569 6300
2-The Young Allies, Red Hawk, & Tommy Tyme begin; last Captain Wonder & Subbie
196 392 588 1225 1888 2550
3-The Vision, Daredevils & Red Hawk app. 150 300 450 938 1444 1950
4-The Destroyer begins; Sub-Mariner app.; Red Hawk & Tommy Tyme end
125 250 375 781 1203 1625
5,6: 5-Tommy Tyme begins, ends #10 96 192 288 600 925 1250
7-10: 7,10-The Whizzer app. Destroyer not in #7,8. 10-Last Destroyer, Young Allies & Whizzer 85 170 255 531 816 1100

NOTE: ***Brodsky*** *c-5.* ***Schomburg*** *c-2-4, 6-10.* ***Shores*** *c-1. Captain Wonder c-1, 2. The Young Allies c-3-10.*

KID MONTANA (Formerly Davy Crockett Frontier Fighter; The Gunfighters No. 51 on)
Charlton Comics: V2#9, Nov, 1957 - No. 50, Mar, 1965
V2#9 (#1) 5 10 15 36 48 60
10 4 8 12 24 32 40
11,12,14-20 3 6 9 18 23 28
13-Williamson-a 4 8 12 24 32 40
21-35: 25,31-Giordano-c. 32-Origin Kid Montana. 34-Geronimo-c/s. 35-Snow Monster-c/s
2 4 6 12 16 20
36-50: 36-Dinosaur-c/s. 37,48-Giordano-c 2 4 6 10 12 15

NOTE: *Title change to Montana Kid on cover only #44 & 45; remained Kid Montana on inside.* ***Chasal*** *a-29,30.* ***Giordano*** *c-25,31,37,48.* ***Giordano/Alascia*** *c-12.* ***Mastroserio*** *a-9,11,13,14,22; c-11,14.* ***Masulli/Mastroserio*** *c-13.* ***Montes/Bache*** *c-42.* ***Morisi*** *c-16,32-34,36?,40,41,44,46; a-13,15;16,31-50.* ***Nicholas/Alascia*** *a-44,48.*

KID MOVIE KOMICS (Formerly Kid Komics; Rusty Comics #12 on)
Timely Comics: No. 11, Summer, 1946
11-Silly Seal & Ziggy Pig; 2 pgs. Kurtzman "Hey Look" plus 6 pg. "Pigtales" story 27 54 81 152 219 285

KIDNAPPED (Robert Louis Stevenson's...also see Movie Comics)(Disney)
Dell Publishing Co.: No. 1101, May, 1960
Four Color 1101-Movie, photo-c 8 16 24 53 74 95

KIDNAP RACKET (See Harvey Comics Hits No. 57)

Killraven #1 © MAR

Kinetic #8 © Plunkett & Purepop

King Comics #39 © KING

	GD 2.0	VG 4.0	FN 6.0	VF 8.0	VF/NM 9.0	NM- 9.2

KID SLADE GUNFIGHTER (Formerly Matt Slade...)
Atlas Comics (SPI): No. 5, Jan, 1957 - No. 8, July, 1957

	GD	VG	FN	VF	VF/NM	NM-
5-Maneely, Roth, Severin-a in all; Maneely-c	13	26	39	74	102	130
6,8-Severin-c	8	16	24	46	58	70
7-Williamson/Mayo-a, 4 pgs.	10	20	30	58	77	95

KID SUPREME (See Supreme)
Image Comics (Extreme Studios): Mar, 1996 - No. 3, July, 1996 ($2.50)

1-3: Fraga-a/scripts. 3-Glory-c/app. 2.50

KID TERRIFIC
Image Comics: Nov, 1998 ($2.95, B&W)

1-Snyder & Diliberto-s/a 3.00

KID ZOO COMICS
Street & Smith Publications: July, 1948 (52 pgs.)

	GD	VG	FN	VF	VF/NM	NM-
1-Funny Animal	29	58	87	164	237	310

KILLER (...Tales By Timothy Truman)
Eclipse Comics: March, 1985 ($1.75, one-shot, Baxter paper)

1-Timothy Truman-c/a 2.50

KILLER INSTINCT (Video game)
Acclaim Comics: June, 1996 - No. 6 ($2.50, limited series)

1-6: 1-Bart Sears-a(p). 4-Special #1. 5-Special #2. 6-Special #3 3.00

KILLER PRINCESSES
Oni Press: Dec, 2001 - No. 3, Apr, 2003 ($2.95, limited series)

1-3-Gail Simone-s/Lea Hernandez-a 3.00

KILLERS, THE
Magazine Enterprises: 1947 - No. 2, 1948 (No month)

	GD	VG	FN	VF	VF/NM	NM-
1-Mr. Zin, the Hatchet Killer; mentioned in **SOTI**, pgs. 179,180; used by N.Y. Legis. Comm.; L. B. Cole-c	108	216	324	675	1038	1400
2-(Scarce)-Hashish smoking story; "Dying, Dying, Dead" drug story; Whitney, Ingels-a; Whitney hanging-c	89	178	267	556	853	1150

KILLING JOKE, THE (See Batman: The Killing Joke under Batman one-shots)

KILLPOWER: THE EARLY YEARS
Marvel Comics UK: Sept, 1993 - No. 4, Dec, 1993 ($1.75, mini-series)

1-($2.95)-Foil embossed-c 3.00
2-4: 2-Genetix app. 3-Punisher app. 2.25

KILLRAVEN (See Amazing Adventures #18 (5/73))
Marvel Comics: Feb, 2001 ($2.99, one-shot)

1-Linsner-s/a/c 3.00

KILLRAVEN
Marvel Comics: Dec, 2002 - No. 6, May, 2003 ($2.99, limited series)

1-6-Alan Davis-s/a(p)/Mark Farmer-i 3.00

KILLRAZOR
Image Comics (Top Cow Productions): Aug, 1995 ($2.50, one-shot)

1 2.50

KILL YOUR BOYFRIEND
DC Comics (Vertigo): June, 1995 ($4.95, one-shot)

1-Grant Morrison story 6.00
1($5.95, 1998) 2nd printing 6.00

KILROY (Volume 2)
Caliber Press: 1998 ($2.95, B&W)

1-Pruett-s 3.00

KILROY IS HERE
Caliber Press: 1995 ($2.95, B&W)

1-10 3.00

KILROYS, THE
B&I Publ. Co. No. 1-19/American Comics Group: June-July, 1947 - No. 54, June-July, 1955

	GD	VG	FN	VF	VF/NM	NM-
1	23	46	69	132	191	250
2	12	24	36	71	98	125
3-5: 5-Gross-a	10	20	30	58	77	95
6-10: 8-Milt Gross's Moronica	9	18	27	51	62	75
11-20: 14-Gross-a	8	16	24	43	54	65
21-30	7	14	21	37	46	55
31-47,50-54	7	14	21	35	43	50
48,49-(3-D effect-c/stories)	18	36	54	100	143	185

KILROY: THE SHORT STORIES
Caliber Press: 1995 ($2.95, B&W)

1 3.00

KIN
Image Comics (Top Cow): Mar, 2000 - No. 6, Sept, 2000 ($2.95)

1-5-Gary Frank-s/c/a 3.00
1-($6.95) DF Alternate footprint cover 7.00
6-($3.95) 4.00
... Descent of Man TPB (2002, $19.95) r/ #1-6 20.00

KINDRED, THE
Image Comics (WildStorm Productions): Mar, 1994 - No. 4, July, 1995 ($1.95, limited series)

1-($2.50)-Grifter & Backlash app. in all; bound-in trading card 2.50
2-4 2.50
2,3: 2-Variant-c. 3-Alternate-c by Portacio, see Deathblow #5 4.00
Trade paperback (2/95, $9.95) 10.00
NOTE: *Booth c/a-1-4. The first four issues contain coupons redeemable for a Jim Lee Grifter/Backlash print.*

KINDRED II, THE
DC Comics (WildStorm): Mar, 2002 - No. 4, June, 2002 ($2.50, limited series)

1-4-Booth-s/Booth & Regla-a 2.50

KINETIC
DC Comics (Focus): May, 2004 - No. 8, Dec, 2004 ($2.50)

1-8-Puckett-s/Pleece-a/c 2.50

KING ARTHUR AND THE KNIGHTS OF JUSTICE
Marvel Comics UK: Dec, 1993 - No. 3, Feb, 1994 ($1.25, limited series)

1-3: TV adaptation 2.25

KING CLASSICS
King Features : 1977 (36 pgs., cardboard-c) (Printed in Spain for U.S. distr.)

	GD	VG	FN	VF	VF/NM	NM-
1-Connecticut Yankee, 2-Last of the Mohicans, 3-Moby Dick, 4-Robin Hood, 5-Swiss Family Robinson, 6-Robinson Crusoe, 7-Treasure Island, 8-20,000 Leagues, 9-Christmas Carol, 10-Huck Finn, 11-Around the World in 80 Days, 12-Davy Crockett, 13-Don Quixote, 14-Gold Bug, 15-Ivanhoe, 16-Three Musketeers, 17-Baron Munchausen, 18-Alice in Wonderland, 19-Black Arrow, 20-Five Weeks in a Balloon, 21-Great Expectations, 22-Gulliver's Travels, 23-Prince & Pauper, 24-Lawrence of Arabia (Originals, 1977-78) each....	2	4	6	10	12	15
Reprints (1979; HRN-24)	1	2	3	5	7	9

NOTE: *The first eight issues were not numbered. Issues No. 25-32 were advertised but not published. The 1977 originals have HRN 32a; the 1978 originals have HRN 32b.*

KING COLT (See Luke Short's Western Stories)

KING COMICS (Strip reprints)
David McKay Publications/Standard #156-on: 4/36 - No. 155, 11-12/49; No. 156, Spr/50 - No. 159, 2/52 (Winter on-c)

	GD	VG	FN	VF	VF/NM	NM-
1-1st app. Flash Gordon by Alex Raymond; Brick Bradford (1st app.), Popeye, Henry (1st app.) & Mandrake the Magician (1st app.) begin; Popeye-c begin	1233	2466	3700	9700	-	-
2	345	690	1035	1898	2674	3450
3	235	470	705	1293	1822	2350
4	180	360	540	990	1395	1800
5	130	260	390	715	1008	1300
6-10: 9-X-Mas-c	90	180	270	495	698	900
11-20	70	140	210	385	543	700
21-30: 21-X-Mas-c	52	104	156	286	403	520
31-40: 33-Last Segar Popeye	42	84	126	231	326	420
41-50: 46-Text illos by Marge Buell contain characters similar to Lulu, Alvin & Tubby. 50-The Lone Ranger begins	34	68	102	196	283	370
51-60: 52-Barney Baxter begins?	24	48	72	138	199	260
61-The Phantom begins	26	52	78	147	211	275
62-80: 76-Flag-c. 79-Blondie begins	18	36	54	100	143	185
81-99	14	28	42	79	110	140
100	17	34	51	95	135	175
101-114: 114-Last Raymond issue (1 pg.); Flash Gordon by Austin Briggs begins, ends #155	13	26	39	74	102	130
115-145: 117-Phantom origin retold	10	20	30	56	73	90
146,147-Prince Valiant in both	9	18	27	49	62	75
148-155: 155-Flash Gordon ends (11-12/49)	9	18	27	49	62	75
156-159: 156-New logo begins (Standard)	8	16	24	46	58	70

NOTE: *Marge Buell text illos in No. 24-46 at least.*

KING CONAN (Conan The King No. 20 on)
Marvel Comics Group: Mar, 1980 - No. 19, Nov, 1983 (52 pgs.)

1 6.00
2-19: 4-Death of Thoth Amon. 7-1st Paul Smith-a, 1 pg. pin-up (9/81) 4.00
NOTE: ***J. Buscema** a-1-9p, 17p; c(p)-1-5, 7-9, 14, 17. **Kaluta** c-19. **Nebres** a-17i, 18, 19i. **Severin** c-18.*

The Kingdom #2 © DC

KISS #3 © KISS Catalogue Inc.

Kiss Kiss Bang Bang #1 © CRO

	GD 2.0	VG 4.0	FN 6.0	VF 8.0	VF/NM 9.0	NM- 9.2
Simonson c-6.						

KING DAVID
DC Comics (Vertigo): 2002 ($19.95, 8 1/2" x 11")

	GD	VG	FN	VF	VF/NM	NM-
nn-Story of King David; Kyle Baker-s/a						20.00

KINGDOM, THE
DC Comics: Feb, 1999 - No. 2, Feb, 1999 ($2.95/$1.99, limited series)

	GD	VG	FN	VF	VF/NM	NM-
1,2-Waid-s; sequel to Kingdom Come; introduces Hypertime						4.00
...: Kid Flash 1 (2/99, $1.99) Waid-s/Pararillo-a, ...: Nightstar 1 (2/99, $1.99) Waid-s/Haley-a, ...: Offspring 1 (2/99, $1.99) Waid-s/Quitely-a, ...: Planet Krypton 1 (2/99, $1.99) Waid-s/Kitson-a, ...: Son of the Bat 1 (2/99, $1.99) Waid-s/Apthorp-a						2.25

KINGDOM COME
DC Comics: 1996 - No. 4, 1996 ($4.95, painted limited series)

	GD	VG	FN	VF	VF/NM	NM-
1-Mark Waid scripts & Alex Ross-painted c/a in all; tells the last days of the DC Universe; 1st app. Magog	1	2	3	5	6	8
2-Superman forms new Justice League	1	2	3	4	5	7
3-Return of Captain Marvel						5.00
4-Final battle of Superman and Captain Marvel	1	2	3	4	5	7
Deluxe Slipcase Edition-($89.95) w/Revelations companion book, 12 new story pages, foil stamped covers, signed and numbered						120.00
Hardcover Edition-($29.95)-Includes 12 new story pages and artwork from Revelations, new cover artwork with gold foil inlay						35.00
Hardcover 2nd printing						30.00
Softcover Ed.-($14.95)-Includes 12 new story pgs. & artwork from Revelations, new c-artwork						15.00

KING KONG (See Movie Comics)

KING LEONARDO & HIS SHORT SUBJECTS (TV)
Dell Publishing Co./Gold Key: Nov-Jan, 1961-62 - No. 4, Sept, 1963

	GD	VG	FN	VF	VF/NM	NM-
Four Color 1242,1278	14	28	42	102	156	210
01390-207(5-7/62)(Dell)	11	22	33	75	110	145
1 (10/62)	12	24	36	87	134	180
2-4	10	20	30	70	100	130

KING LOUIE & MOWGLI (See Jungle Book under Movie Comics)
Gold Key: May, 1968 (Disney)

	GD	VG	FN	VF	VF/NM	NM-
1 (#10223-805)-Characters from Jungle Book	3	7	10	21	28	35

KING OF DIAMONDS (TV)
Dell Publishing Co.: July-Sept, 1962

	GD	VG	FN	VF	VF/NM	NM-
01-391-209-Photo-c	4	8	12	29	40	50

KING OF KINGS (Movie)
Dell Publishing Co.: No. 1236, Oct-Nov, 1961

	GD	VG	FN	VF	VF/NM	NM-
Four Color 1236-Photo-c	9	18	27	63	89	115

KING OF THE BAD MEN OF DEADWOOD
Avon Periodicals: 1950 (See Wild Bill Hickok #16)

	GD	VG	FN	VF	VF/NM	NM-
nn-Kinstler-c; Kamen/Feldstein-r/Cowpuncher #2	16	32	48	89	127	165

KING OF THE ROYAL MOUNTED (See Famous Feature Stories, King Comics, Red Ryder #3 & Super Book #2, 6)

KING OF THE ROYAL MOUNTED (Zane Grey's...)
David McKay/Dell Publishing Co.: No. 1, May, 1937; No. 9, 1940; No. 207, Dec, 1948 - No. 935, Sept-Nov, 1958

	GD	VG	FN	VF	VF/NM	NM-
Feature Books 1 (5/37)(McKay)	85	170	255	531	816	1100
Large Feature Comic 9 (1940)	48	96	144	293	447	600
Four Color 207(#1, 12/48)	15	30	45	109	167	225
Four Color 265,283	10	20	30	67	96	125
Four Color 310,340	8	16	24	53	74	95
Four Color 363,384, 8(6-8/52)-10	7	14	21	46	63	80
11-20	6	12	18	40	55	70
21-28(3-5/58), Four Color 935(9-11/58)	5	10	15	33	44	55

NOTE: *4-Color No. 207, 265, 283, 310, 340, 363, 384 are all newspaper reprints with* ***Jim Gary*** *art. No. 8 on are all Dell originals. Painted c-No. 9-on.*

KINGPIN
Marvel Comics: Nov, 1997 ($5.99, squarebound, one-shot)

	GD	VG	FN	VF	VF/NM	NM-
nn-Spider-Man & Daredevil vs. Kingpin; Stan Lee-s/ John Romita Sr.-a						6.00

KINGPIN
Marvel Comics: Aug, 2003 - No. 7, Jan, 2004 ($2.50/$2.99, limited series)

	GD	VG	FN	VF	VF/NM	NM-
1-6-Bruce Jones-s/Sean Phillips & Klaus Janson-a						2.50
7-($2.99)						3.00

KING RICHARD & THE CRUSADERS
Dell Publishing Co.: No. 588, Oct, 1954

	GD	VG	FN	VF	VF/NM	NM-
Four Color 588-Movie, Matt Baker-a, photo-c	11	22	33	75	110	145

KINGS OF THE NIGHT
Dark Horse Comics: 1990 - No. 2, 1990 ($2.25, limited series)

	GD	VG	FN	VF	VF/NM	NM-
1,2-Robert E. Howard adaptation; Bolton-c						2.25

KING SOLOMON'S MINES (Movie)
Avon Periodicals: 1951

	GD	VG	FN	VF	VF/NM	NM-
nn (#1 on 1st page)	40	80	120	235	348	460

KING TIGER & MOTORHEAD
Dark Horse Comics: Aug, 1996 - No. 2, Sept, 1996 ($2.95, limited series)

	GD	VG	FN	VF	VF/NM	NM-
1,2: Chichester scripts						3.00

KIPLING, RUDYARD (See Mowgli, The Jungle Book)

KISS (See Crazy Magazine, Howard the Duck #12, 13, Marvel Comics Super Special #1, 5, Rock Fantasy Comics #10 & Rock N' Roll Comics #9)

KISS
Dark Horse Comics: June, 2002 - No. 13, Sept, 2003 ($2.99, limited series)

	GD	VG	FN	VF	VF/NM	NM-
1-Photo-c and J. Scott Campbell-c; Casey-s						4.00
2-13: 2-Photo-c and J. Scott Campbell-c. 3-Photo-c and Leinil Yu-c						3.00
...: Men and Monsters TPB (9/03, $12.95) r/#7-10						13.00
...: Rediscovery TPB (2003, $9.95) r/#1-3						10.00
...: Return of the Phantom TPB (2003, $9.95) r/#4-6						10.00
...: Unholy War TPB (2004, $9.95) r/#11-13						10.00

KISS: THE PSYCHO CIRCUS
Image Comics: Aug, 1997 - No. 31, June, 2000 ($1.95/$2.25/$2.50)

	GD	VG	FN	VF	VF/NM	NM-
1-Holguin-s/Medina-a(p)	1	2	3	5	6	8
1-2nd & 3rd printings						2.50
2						5.00
3,4: 4-Photo-c						4.00
5-8: 5-Begin $2.25-c						3.00
9-29						2.50
30,31: 30-Begin $2.50-c						2.50
Book 1 TPB ('98, $12.95) r/#1-6						13.00
Book 2 Destroyer TPB (8/99, $9.95) r/#10-13						10.00
Book 3 Whispered Scream TPB ('00, $9.95) r/#7-9,18						10.00
...Magazine 1 ($6.95) r/#1-3 plus interviews						7.00
...Magazine 2-5 ($4.95) 2-r/#4,5 plus interviews. 3-r/#6,7. 4-r/#8,9						5.00
Wizard Edition ('98, supplement) Bios, tour preview and interviews						2.25

KISSING CHAOS
Oni Press: Sept, 2001 - No. 8, Mar, 2002 ($2.25, B&W, 6" x 9", limited series)

	GD	VG	FN	VF	VF/NM	NM-
1-8-Arthur Dela Cruz-s/a						2.25
...: Nine Lives (12/03, $2.99, regular comic-sized)						3.00
...: 1000 Words (7/03, $2.99, regular comic-sized)						3.00
TPB (9/02, $17.95) r/#1-8						18.00

KISSING CHAOS: NONSTOP BEAUTY
Oni Press: Oct, 2002 - No. 4, March, 2003 ($2.95, B&W, 6" x 9", limited series)

	GD	VG	FN	VF	VF/NM	NM-
1-4-Arthur Dela Cruz-s/a						3.00
TPB (9/03, $11.95) r/#1-4						12.00

KISS KISS BANG BANG
CrossGen Comics: Feb, 2004 - No. 5, Jun, 2004 ($2.95)

	GD	VG	FN	VF	VF/NM	NM-
1-5-Bedard-s/Perkins-a						3.00

KISSYFUR (TV)
DC Comics: 1989 (Sept.) ($2.00, 52 pgs., one-shot)

	GD	VG	FN	VF	VF/NM	NM-
1-Based on Saturday morning cartoon						4.00

KIT CARSON (Formerly All True Detective Cases No. 4; Fighting Davy Crockett No. 9; see Blazing Sixguns & Frontier Fighters)
Avon Periodicals: 1950; No. 2, 8/51 - No. 3, 12/51; No. 5, 11-12/54 - No. 8, 9/55 (No #4)

	GD	VG	FN	VF	VF/NM	NM-
nn(#1) (1950)- "...Indian Scout" ; r-Cowboys 'N' Injuns #?	14	28	42	79	110	140
2(8/51)	10	20	30	56	73	90
3(12/51)- "...Fights the Comanche Raiders"	9	18	27	49	62	75
5-6,8(11-12/54-9/55): 5-Formerly All True Detective Cases (last pre-code); titled "...and the Trail of Doom"	8	16	24	46	58	70
7-McCann-a?	8	16	24	46	58	70
I.W. Reprint #10('63)-r/Kit Carson #1; Severin-c	2	4	6	12	16	20

NOTE: ***Kinstler*** *c-1-3, 5-8.*

KIT CARSON & THE BLACKFEET WARRIORS
Realistic: 1953

	GD	VG	FN	VF	VF/NM	NM-
nn-Reprint; Kinstler-c	9	18	27	54	70	85

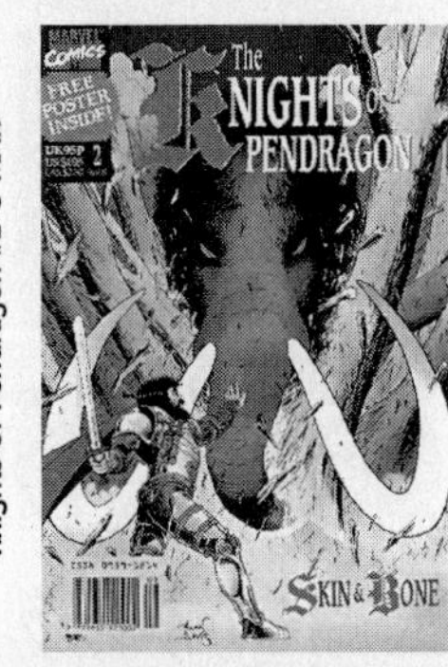

Knights of Pendragon #2 © MAR

Knight Watchman #1 © Carlson & Ecker

Konga #1 © CC

	GD	VG	FN	VF	VF/NM	NM-
	2.0	4.0	6.0	8.0	9.0	9.2

KIT KARTER
Dell Publishing Co.: May-July, 1962
1 — 4 8 12 22 30 38

KITTY
St. John Publishing Co.: Oct, 1948
1-Teenage; Lily Renee-c/a — 8 16 24 43 54 65

KITTY PRYDE, AGENT OF S.H.I.E.L.D. (Also see Excalibur and Mekanix)
Marvel Comics: Dec, 1997 - No. 3, Feb, 1998 ($2.50, limited series)
1-3-Hama-s — 2.50

KITTY PRYDE AND WOLVERINE (Also see Uncanny X-Men & X-Men)
Marvel Comics Group: Nov, 1984 - No. 6, Apr, 1985 (Limited series)
1-6: Characters from X-Men — 4.50

KLARER GIVEAWAYS (See Wisco in the Promotional Comics section)

KNIGHTHAWK
Acclaim Comics (Windjammer): Sept, 1995 - No. 6, Nov, 1995 ($2.50, lim. series)
1-6: 6-origin — 2.50

KNIGHTMARE
Antarctic Press: July, 1994 - May, 1995 ($2.75, B&W, mature readers)
1-6 — 2.75

KNIGHTMARE
Image Comics (Extreme Studios): Feb, 1995 - No. 5, June, 1995 ($2.50)
0 ($3.50) — 3.50
1-5: 4-Quesada & Palmiotti variant-c, 5-Flip book w/Warcry — 2.50

KNIGHTS 4 (See Marvel Knights 4)

KNIGHTS OF PENDRAGON, THE (Also see Pendragon)
Marvel Comics Ltd.: July, 1990 - No. 18, Dec, 1991 ($1.95)
1-18: 1-Capt. Britain app. 2,8-Free poster inside. 9,10-Bolton-c. 11,18-Iron Man app. — 2.25

KNIGHTS OF THE ROUND TABLE
Dell Publishing Co.: No. 540, Mar, 1954
Four Color 540-Movie, photo-c — 8 16 24 58 82 105

KNIGHTS OF THE ROUND TABLE
Pines Comics: No. 10, April, 1957
10 — 5 10 15 24 30 35

KNIGHTS OF THE ROUND TABLE
Dell Publishing Co.: Nov-Jan, 1963-64
1 (12-397-401)-Painted-c — 4 8 12 25 33 42

KNIGHTSTRIKE (Also see Operation: Knightstrike)
Image Comics (Extreme Studios): Jan, 1996 ($2.50)
1-Rob Liefeld & Eric Stephenson story; Extreme Destroyer Part 6. — 2.50

KNIGHT WATCHMAN (See Big Bang Comics & Dr. Weird)
Image Comics: June, 1998 - No. 4, Oct, 1998 ($2.95/$3.50, B&W, lim. series)
1-3-Ben Torres-c/a in all — 3.00
4-($3.50) — 3.50

KNIGHT WATCHMAN: GRAVEYARD SHIFT
Caliber Press: 1994 ($2.95, B&W)
1,2-Ben Torres-a — 3.00

KNOCK KNOCK (...Who's There?)
Whitman Publ./Gerona Publications: No. 801, 1936 (52 pgs.) (8x9", B&W)
801-Joke book; Bob Dunn-a — 9 18 27 51 62 75

KNOCKOUT ADVENTURES
Fiction House Magazines: Winter, 1953-54
1-Reprints Fight Comics #53 w/Rip Carson-c/s — 14 28 42 79 110 140

KNUCKLES (Spin-off of Sonic the Hedgehog)
Archie Publications: Apr, 1997 - Present ($1.50/$1.75/$1.79)
1-29 — 2.25

KNUCKLES' CHAOTIX
Archie Publications: Jan, 1996 ($2.00, annual)
1 — 3.00

KOBALT
DC Comics (Milestone): June, 1994 - No. 16, Sept, 1995 ($1.75/$2.50)
1-16: 1-Byrne-c. 4-Intro Page. 16-Kent Williams-c — 2.50

KOBRA (Unpublished #8 appears in DC Special Series No. 1)
National Periodical Publications: Feb-Mar, 1976 - No. 7, Mar-Apr, 1977
1-1st app.; Kirby-a redrawn by Marcos; only 25¢-c — 1 3 4 6 8 10
2-7: (All 30¢ issues) 3-Giffen-a — 6.00
NOTE: *Austin a-3i. **Buckler** a-5p; c-5p. **Kubert** c-4. **Nasser** a-6p, 7; c-7.*

KOKEY KOALA (...and the Magic Button)
Toby Press: May, 1952
1 — 11 22 33 64 87 110

KOKO AND KOLA (Also see A-1 Comics #16 & Tick Tock Tales)
Com/Magazine Enterprises: Fall, 1946 - No. 5, May, 1947; No. 6, 1950
1-Funny animal — 11 22 33 64 87 110
2-X-Mas-c — 8 16 24 43 54 65
3-6: 6(A-1 28) — 7 14 21 37 46 55

KO KOMICS
Gerona Publications: Oct, 1945 (scarce)
1-The Duke of Darkness & The Menace (hero) — 71 142 213 444 685 925

KOLCHAK: THE NIGHT STALKER (TV)
Moonstone: 2002 - Present ($6.50/$6.95)
1-($6.50) Jeff Rice-s/Gordon Purcell-a — 6.50
... Devil in the Details (2003, $6.95) Trevor Von Eeden-a — 7.00
... Fever Pitch (2002, $6.95) Christopher Jones-a — 7.00
... Get of Belial (2002, $6.95) Art Nichols-a — 7.00
... Lambs to the Slaughter (2003, $6.95) Trevor Von Eeden-a — 7.00
... Pain Most Human (2004, $6.95) Greg Scott-a — 7.00
... Tales of the Night Stalker 1-4 (2003-Present, $3.50) two covers by Moore & Ulanski — 3.50
TPB (2004, $17.95) r/#1, Get of Belial & Fever Pitch — 18.00

KOMIC KARTOONS
Timely Comics (EPC): Fall, 1945 - No. 2, Winter, 1945
1,2-Andy Wolf, Bertie Mouse — 20 40 60 112 161 210

KOMIK PAGES (Formerly Snap; becomes Bullseye #11)
Harry 'A' Chesler, Jr. (Our Army, Inc.): Apr, 1945 (All reprints)
10(#1 on inside)-Land O' Nod by Rick Yager (2 pgs.), Animal Crackers, Foxy GrandPa, Tom, Dick & Mary, Cheerio Minstrels, Red Starr plus other 1-2 pg. strips; Cole-a — 24 48 72 135 195 255

KONA (...Monarch of Monster Isle)
Dell Publishing Co.: Feb-Apr, 1962 - No. 21, Jan-Mar, 1967 (Painted-c)
Four Color 1256 (#1) — 9 18 27 65 93 120
2-10: 4-Anak begins. 6-Gil Kane-c — 5 10 15 36 48 60
11-21 — 4 8 12 27 36 45
NOTE: ***Glanzman** a-all issues.*

KONGA (Fantastic Giants No. 24) (See Return of...)
Charlton Comics: 1960; No. 2, Aug, 1961 - No. 23, Nov, 1965
1(1960)-Based on movie; Giordano-c — 25 50 75 177 271 365
2-5: 2-Giordano-c; no Ditko-a — 11 22 33 80 120 160
6-15 — 10 20 30 67 96 125
16-23 — 6 12 18 40 55 70
NOTE: ***Ditko** a-1, 3-15; c-4, 6-9. **Glanzman** a-12. **Montes** & **Bache** a-16-23.*

KONGA'S REVENGE (Formerly Return of...)
Charlton Comics: No. 2, Summer, 1963 - No. 3, Fall, 1964; Dec, 1968
2,3: 2-Ditko-c/a — 7 14 21 50 68 85
1(12/68)-Reprints Konga's Revenge #3 — 3 6 9 19 25 32

KONG THE UNTAMED
National Periodical Publications: June-July, 1975 - V2#5, Feb-Mar, 1976
1-1st app. Kong; Wrightson-c; Alcala-a — 2 4 6 8 10 12
2-Wrightson-c; Alcala-a — 1 2 3 5 7 9
3-5: 3-Alcala-a — 6.00

KOOKIE
Dell Publishing Co.: Feb-Apr, 1962 - No. 2, May-July, 1962 (15 cents)
1-Written by John Stanley; Bill Williams-a — 10 20 30 67 96 125
2 — 9 18 27 60 85 110

KOOSH KINS
Archie Comics: Oct, 1991 - No. 3, Feb, 1992 ($1.00, bi-monthly, limited series)
1-3 — 2.25
NOTE: *No. 4 was planned, but cancelled.*

KORAK, SON OF TARZAN (Edgar Rice Burroughs)(See Tarzan #139)
Gold Key: Jan, 1964 - No. 45, Jan, 1972 (Painted-c No. 1-?)

Krazy Comics #9 © MAR

Krusty Comics #1 © Bongo

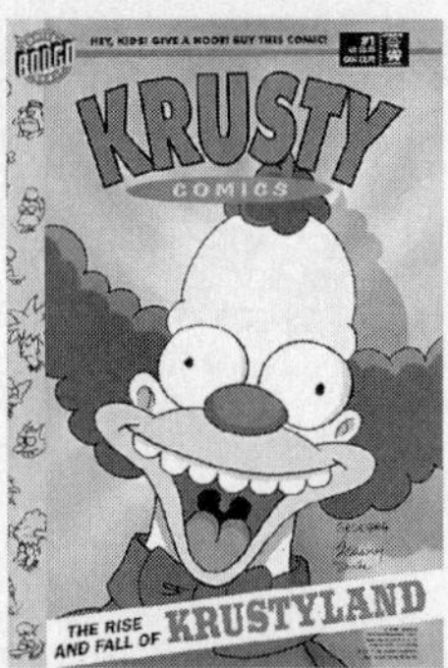

Kull the Conqueror #1 © MAR

	GD 2.0	VG 4.0	FN 6.0	VF 8.0	VF/NM 9.0	NM- 9.2
1-Russ Manning-a	9	18	27	60	85	110
2-5-Russ Manning-a	5	10	15	33	44	55
6-11-Russ Manning-a	4	8	12	29	40	50
12-23: 12,13-Warren Tufts-a. 14-Jon of the Kalahari ends. 15-Mabu, Jungle Boy begins. 21-Manning-a. 23-Last 12¢ issue	4	8	12	27	36	45
24-30	3	6	9	19	25	32
31-45	3	6	9	16	20	24

KORAK, SON OF TARZAN (Tarzan Family #60 on; see Tarzan #230)
National Periodical Publications: V9#46, May-June, 1972 - V12#56, Feb-Mar, 1974; No. 57, May-June, 1975 - No. 59, Sept-Oct, 1975 (Edgar Rice Burroughs)

	GD	VG	FN	VF	VF/NM	NM-
46-(52 pgs.)-Carson of Venus begins (origin), ends #56; Pellucidar feature; Weiss-a	2	4	6	14	18	22
47-59: 49-Origin Korak retold	1	3	4	6	8	10

NOTE: *All have covers by* ***Joe Kubert. Manning*** *strip reprints-No. 57-59.* ***Murphy Anderson*** *a-52.* ***Michael Kaluta*** *a-46-56.* ***Frank Thorne*** *a-46-51.*

KORE
Image Comics: Apr, 2003 - No. 5, Sept, 2003 ($2.95)

	GD	VG	FN	VF	VF/NM	NM-
1-5: 1-Two covers by Capullo and Seeley; Seeley-a (p)						3.00

KORG: 70,000 B. C. (TV)
Charlton Publications: May, 1975 - No. 9, Nov, 1976 (Hanna-Barbera)

	GD	VG	FN	VF	VF/NM	NM-
1,2: 1-Boyette-c/a. 2-Painted-c; Byrne text illos	2	4	6	11	14	18
3-9	2	4	6	8	10	12

KORNER KID COMICS: Four Star Publications: 1947 (Advertised, not pub.)

KOSMIC KAT ACTIVITY BOOK (See Deity)
Image Comics: Aug, 1999 ($2.95, one-shot)

	GD	VG	FN	VF	VF/NM	NM-
1-Stories and games by various						3.00

KRAZY KAT
Holt: 1946 (Hardcover)

	GD	VG	FN	VF	VF/NM	NM-
Reprints daily & Sunday strips by Herriman	60	120	180	375	580	785
dust jacket only	46	92	138	281	428	575

KRAZY KAT (See Ace Comics & March of Comics No. 72, 87)

KRAZY KAT COMICS (...& Ignatz the Mouse early issues)
Dell Publ. Co./Gold Key: May-June, 1951 - F.C. #696, Apr, 1956; Jan, 1964 (None by Herriman)

	GD	VG	FN	VF	VF/NM	NM-
1(1951)	9	18	27	65	93	120
2-5 (#5, 8-10/52)	6	12	18	38	52	65
Four Color 454,504	5	10	15	36	48	60
Four Color 548,619,696 (4/56)	5	10	15	33	44	55
1(10098-401)(1/64-Gold Key)(TV)	5	10	15	33	44	55

KRAZY KOMICS (1st Series) (Cindy Comics No. 27 on) (Also see Ziggy Pig)
Timely Comics (USA No. 1-21/JPC No. 22-26): July, 1942 - No. 26, Spr, 1947

	GD	VG	FN	VF	VF/NM	NM-
1-Toughy Tomcat, Ziggy Pig (by Jaffee) & Silly Seal begin	60	120	180	375	575	775
2	29	58	87	164	237	310
3-8,10	20	40	60	112	161	210
9-Hitler parody	21	42	63	121	173	225
11,13,14	15	30	45	83	117	150
12-Timely's entire art staff drew themselves into a Creeper story	26	52	78	150	215	280
15-(8-9/44)-Becomes Funny Tunes #16; has "Super Soldier" by Pfc. Stan Lee	15	30	45	83	117	150
16-24,26: 16-(10-11/44). 26-Super Rabbit-c/story	12	24	36	71	98	125
25-Wacky Duck-c/story & begin; Kurtzman-a (6pgs.)	15	30	45	83	117	150

KRAZY KOMICS (2nd Series)
Timely/Marvel Comics: Aug, 1948 - No. 2, Nov, 1948

	GD	VG	FN	VF	VF/NM	NM-
1-Wolverton (10 pgs.) & Kurtzman (8 pgs.)-a; Eustice Hayseed begins (Li'l Abner swipe)	42	84	126	256	391	525
2-Wolverton-a (10 pgs.); Powerhouse Pepper cameo	33	66	99	190	275	360

KRAZY KROW (Also see Dopey Duck, Film Funnies, Funny Frolics & Movie Tunes)
Marvel Comics (ZPC): Summer, 1945 - No. 3, Wint, 1945/46

	GD	VG	FN	VF	VF/NM	NM-
1	21	42	63	121	173	225
2,3	13	26	39	74	102	130
I.W. Reprint #1('57), 2('58), 7	2	4	6	12	16	20

KRAZYLIFE (Becomes Nutty Life #2)
Fox Feature Syndicate: 1945 (no month)

	GD	VG	FN	VF	VF/NM	NM-
1-Funny animal	18	36	54	102	146	190

KREE/SKRULL WAR STARRING THE AVENGERS, THE
Marvel Comics: Sept, 1983 - No. 2, Oct, 1983 ($2.50, 68 pgs., Baxter paper)

	GD	VG	FN	VF	VF/NM	NM-
1,2						4.00

NOTE: ***Neal Adams*** *p-1r, 2.* ***Buscema*** *a-1r, 2r.* ***Simonson*** *a-1p; c-1p.*

KROFFT SUPERSHOW (TV)
Gold Key: Apr, 1978 - No. 6, Jan, 1979

	GD	VG	FN	VF	VF/NM	NM-
1-Photo-c	3	6	9	18	26	30
2-6: 6-Photo-c	2	4	6	12	16	20

KRULL
Marvel Comics Group: Nov, 1983 - No. 2, Dec, 1983

	GD	VG	FN	VF	VF/NM	NM-
1,2-Adaptation of film; r/Marvel Super Special. 1-Photo-c from movie						2.50

KRUSTY COMICS (TV)(See Simpsons Comics)
Bongo Comics: 1995 - No. 3, 1995 ($2.25, limited series)

	GD	VG	FN	VF	VF/NM	NM-
1-3						2.50

KRYPTON CHRONICLES
DC Comics: Sept, 1981 - No. 3, Nov, 1981

	GD	VG	FN	VF	VF/NM	NM-
1-3: 1-Buckler-c(p)						4.00

KULL AND THE BARBARIANS
Marvel Comics: May, 1975 - No. 3, Sept, 1975 ($1.00, B&W, magazine)

	GD	VG	FN	VF	VF/NM	NM-
1-(84 pgs.) Andru/Wood-r/Kull #1; 2 pgs. Neal Adams; Gil Kane(p), Marie & John Severin-a(r); Krenkel text illo.	2	4	6	12	16	20
2,3: 2-(84 pgs.) Red Sonja by Chaykin begins; Solomon Kane by Weiss/Adams; Gil Kane-a; Solomon Kane pin-up by Wrightson. 3-(76 pgs.) Origin Red Sonja by Chaykin; Adams-a; Solomon Kane app.	2	4	6	10	13	16

KULL THE CONQUEROR (...the Destroyer #11 on; see Conan #1, Creatures on the Loose #10, Marvel Preview, Monsters on the Prowl)
Marvel Comics Group: June, 1971 - No. 2, Sept, 1971; No. 3, July, 1972 - No. 15, Aug, 1974; No. 16, Aug, 1976 - No. 29, Oct, 1978

	GD	VG	FN	VF	VF/NM	NM-
1-Andru/Wood-a; 2nd app. & origin Kull; 15¢ issue	4	8	12	29	40	50
2-5: 2-3rd Kull app. Last 15¢ iss. 3-13: 20¢ issues	2	4	6	12	16	20
6-10	2	4	6	8	10	12
11-15: 11-15-Ploog-a. 14,15: 25¢ issues	1	2	3	5	7	9
16-(Regular 25¢ edition)(8/76)	1	2	3	4	5	7
16-(30¢-c variant, limited distribution)	1	3	4	6	8	10
17-29: 21-23-(Reg. 30¢ editions)	1	2	3	4	5	7
21-23-(35¢-c variants, limited distribution)	1	3	4	6	8	10

NOTE: *No. 1, 2, 7-9, 11 are based on Robert E. Howard stories.* ***Alcala*** *a-17p, 18-20i; c-24.* ***Ditko*** *a-12r, 15r.* ***Gil Kane*** *c-15p, 21.* ***Nebres*** *a-22i-27i; c-25i, 27i.* ***Ploog*** *c-11, 12p, 13.* ***Severin*** *a-2-9i; c-2-10i, 19.* ***Starlin*** *c-14.*

KULL THE CONQUEROR
Marvel Comics Group: Dec, 1982 - No. 2, Mar, 1983 (52 pgs., Baxter paper)

	GD	VG	FN	VF	VF/NM	NM-
1,2: 1-Buscema-a(p)						4.00

KULL THE CONQUEROR (No. 9,10 titled "Kull")
Marvel Comics Group: 5/83 - No. 10, 6/85 (52 pgs., Baxter paper)

	GD	VG	FN	VF	VF/NM	NM-
V3#1-10: Buscema-a in #1-3,5-10						3.00

NOTE: Bolton a-4. Golden painted c-3-8. Guice a-4p. Sienkiwicz a-4; c-2.

KUNG FU (See Deadly Hands of..., & Master of...)

KUNG FU FIGHTER (See Richard Dragon...)

KURT BUSIEK'S ASTRO CITY (Limited series) (Also see Astro City: Local Heroes)
Image Comics (Juke Box Productions): Aug, 1995 - No. 6, Jan, 1996 ($2.25)

	GD	VG	FN	VF	VF/NM	NM-
1-Kurt Busiek scripts, Brent Anderson-a & Alex Ross front & back-c begins; 1st app. Samaritan & Honor Guard (Cleopatra, MHP, Beautie, The Black Rapier, Quarrel & N-Forcer)	2	4	6	8	10	12
2-6: 2-1st app. The Silver Agent, The Old Soldier, & the "original" Honor Guard (Max O'Millions, Starwoman, the "original" Cleopatra, the "original" N-Forcer, the Bouncing Beatnik, Leopardman & Kitkat). 3-1st app. Jack-in-the-Box & The Deacon. 4-1st app. Winged Victory (cameo), The Hanged Man & The First Family. 5-1st app. Crackerjack, The Astro City Irregulars, Nightingale & Sunbird. 6-Origin Samaritan; 1st full app. Winged Victory	1	3	4	6	8	10
Life In The Big City-(8/96, $19.95, trade paperback)-r/Image Comics limited series w/sketchbook & cover gallery; Ross-c						20.00
Life In The Big City-(8/96, $49.95, hardcover, 1000 print run)-r/Image Comics limited series w/sketchbook & cover gallery; Ross-c						50.00

KURT BUSIEK'S ASTRO CITY (1st Homage Comics series)
Image Comics (Homage Comics): V2#1, Sept, 1996 - No. 15, Dec, 1998;
DC Comics (Homage Comics): No. 16, Mar, 1999 - No. 22, Aug, 2000 ($2.50)

	GD	VG	FN	VF	VF/NM	NM-
1/2-(10/96)-The Hanged Man story; 1st app. The All-American & Slugger, The Lamplighter, The Time-Keeper & Eterneon	1	3	4	6	8	10

La Cosa Nostoid #4 © Rob Schrab

Lady Death: A Medieval Tale #2 © CRO

Lady Death: The Wild Hunt #1 © CRO

	GD 2.0	VG 4.0	FN 6.0	VF 8.0	VF/NM 9.0	NM- 9.2
1/2-(1/98) 2nd printing w/new cover						2.50
1- Kurt Busiek scripts, Alex Ross-c, Brent Anderson-p & Will Blyberg-i begin; intro The Gentleman, Thunderhead & Helia.	1	2	3	5	6	8
1-(12/97, $4.95) "3-D Edition" w/glasses						5.00
2-Origin The First Family; Astra story	1	2	3	4	5	7
3-5: 4-1st app. The Crossbreed, Ironhorse, Glue Gun & The Confessor (cameo)						6.00
6-10						5.00
11-22: 14-20-Steeljack story arc. 16-(3/99) First DC issue						2.50
TPB-($19.95) Ross-c, r/#4-9, #1/2 w/sketchbook						20.00
Family Album TPB ($19.95) r/#1-3,10-13						20.00
The Tarnished Angel HC ($29.95) r/#14-20; new Ross dust jacket; sketch pages by Anderson & Ross; cover gallery with reference photos						30.00
The Tarnished Angel SC ($19.95) r/#14-20; new Ross-c						20.00
LABMAN						
Image Comics: Nov, 1996 ($3.50, one-shot)						
1-Allred-c						4.00
LAB RATS						
DC Comics: June, 2002 - No. 8, Jan, 2003 ($2.50)						
1-8-John Byrne-s/a. 5,6-Superman app.						2.50
LABYRINTH						
Marvel Comics Group: Nov, 1986 - No. 3, Jan, 1987 (Limited series)						
1-3: David Bowie movie adaptation; r/Marvel Super Special #40						4.00
LA COSA NOSTROID (See Scud: The Disposible Assassin)						
Fireman Press: Mar, 1996 - No. 9, 1998 ($2.95, B&W)						
1-9-Dan Harmon-s/Rob Schrab-c/a						3.00
LAD: A DOG (Movie)						
Dell Publishing Co.: 1961 - No. 2, July-Sept, 1962						
Four Color 1303	5	10	15	36	48	60
2	4	8	12	29	40	50
LADY AND THE TRAMP (Disney, See Dell Giants & Movie Comics)						
Dell Publishing Co.: No. 629, May, 1955 - No. 634, June, 1955						
Four Color 629 (#1)-..with Jock	8	16	24	58	82	105
Four Color 634-...Album	6	12	18	40	55	70
LADY COP (See 1st Issue Special)						
LADY DEATH (See Evil Ernie)						
Chaos! Comics: Jan, 1994 - No. 3, Mar, 1994 ($2.75, limited series)						
1/2-S. Hughes-c/a in all, 1/2 Velvet	1	2	3	4	5	7
1/2 Gold	1	3	4	6	8	10
1/2 Signed Limited Edition	2	4	6	8	10	12
1-($3.50)-Chromium-c	2	4	6	11	14	18
1-Commemorative	2	4	6	10	13	16
1-(9/96, $2.95) "Encore Presentation"; r/#1						3.00
2	1	2	3	5	6	8
3						5.00
... And Jade (4/02, $2.99) Augustyn-s/Reis-a						3.00
...And The Women of Chaos! Gallery #1 (11/96, $2.25) pin-ups by various						3.00
.../Bad Kitty (9/01, $2.99) Mota-c/a						3.00
.../Bedlam (6/02, $2.99) Augustyn-s/Reis-c						3.00
...By Steven Hughes (6/00, $2.95) Tribute issue to Steven Hughes						3.00
...By Steven Hughes Deluxe Edition(6/00, $15.95)						16.00
.../Chastity (1/02, $2.99) Mota-c/a; Augustyn-s						3.00
...Death Becomes Her #0 (11/97, $2.95) Hughes-c/a						3.00
...FAN Edition: All Hallow's Eve #1 (1/97, mail-in)						5.00
...In Lingerie #1 (8/95, $2.95) pin-ups, wraparound-c						3.00
...In Lingerie #1-Leather Edition (10,000)						12.00
...In Lingerie #1-Micro Premium Edition; Lady Demon-c (2,000)						35.00
...: Love Bites (3/01, $2.99) Kaminski-s/Luke Ross-a						3.00
.../Medieval Witchblade (8/01, $3.50) covers by Molenaar and Silvestri						3.50
.../Medieval Witchblade Preview Ed. (8/01, $1.99) Molenaar-c						2.25
...: Mischief Night (11/01, $2.99) Ostrander-s/Reis-a						3.00
...: Re-Imagined (7/02, $2.99) Gossett-c						3.00
...: River of Fear (4/01, $2.99) Bennett-a(p)/Cleavenger-c						3.00
...Swimsuit Special #1-($2.50)-Wraparound-c						3.00
...Swimsuit Special #1-Red velvet-c						14.00
...Swimsuit 2001 #1-(2/01, $2.99)-Reis-c; art by various						3.00
...: The Reckoning (7/94, $6.95)-r/#1-3						7.00
...: The Reckoning (8/95, $12.95)- new printing including Lady Death 1/2 & Swimsuit Special #1						13.00
.../Vampirella (3/99, $3.50) Hughes-c/a						3.50

	GD 2.0	VG 4.0	FN 6.0	VF 8.0	VF/NM 9.0	NM- 9.2
.../Vampirella 2 (3/00, $3.50) Deodato-c/a						3.50
... Vs. Purgatori (12/99, $3.50) Deodato-a						3.50
... Vs. Vampirella Preview (2/00, $1.00) Deodato-a/c						2.25
LADY DEATH (Ongoing series)						
Chaos! Comics: Feb, 1998 - No. 16, May, 1999 ($2.95)						
1-16: 1-4: Pulido-s/Hughes-c/a. 5-8,13-16-Deodato-a. 9-11-Hughes-a						3.00
...Retribution (8/98, $2.95) Jadsen-a						3.00
...Retribution Premium Ed.						6.00
LADY DEATH: ALIVE						
Chaos! Comics: May, 2001 - No. 4, Aug, 2001 ($2.99, limited series)						
1-4-Ivan Reis-a; Lady Death becomes mortal						3.00
LADY DEATH: A MEDIEVAL TALE (Brian Pulido's...)						
CG Entertainment: Mar, 2003 - No. 12, Apr, 2004 ($2.95)						
1-12: 1-Brian Pulido-s/Ivan Reis-a; Lady Death in the CrossGen Universe						3.00
Vol.1 TPB (2003, $9.95) digest-sized reprint of #1-6						10.00
LADY DEATH: DARK ALLIANCE						
Chaos! Comics: July, 2002 - No. 5, ($2.99, limited series)						
1-3-Reis-a/Ostrander-s						3.00
LADY DEATH: DARK MILLENNIUM						
Chaos! Comics: Feb, 2000 - No. 3, Apr, 2000 ($2.95, limited series)						
Preview (6/00, $5.00)						5.00
1-3-Ivan Reis-a						3.00
LADY DEATH: GODDESS RETURNS						
Chaos! Comics: Jun, 2002 - No. 2, Aug, 2002 ($2.99, limited series)						
1,2-Mota-a/Ostrander-s						3.00
LADY DEATH: HEARTBREAKER						
Chaos! Comics: Mar, 2002 - No. 4, ($2.99, limited series)						
1-Molenaar-a/Ostrander-s						3.00
LADY DEATH: JUDGEMENT WAR						
Chaos! Comics: Nov, 1999 - No. 3, Jan, 2000 ($2.95, limited series)						
Prelude (10/99) two covers						3.00
1-3-Ivan Reis-a						3.00
LADY DEATH: LAST RITES						
Chaos! Comics: Oct, 2001 - No. 4, Feb, 2001 ($2.99, limited series)						
1-4-Ivan Reis-a/Ostrander-s						3.00
LADY DEATH: THE CRUCIBLE						
Chaos! Comics: Nov, 1996 - No. 6, Oct, 1997 ($3.50/$2.95, limited series)						
1/2						4.00
1/2 Cloth Edition						8.00
1-Wraparound silver foil embossed-c						4.00
2-6-($2.95)						3.00
LADY DEATH: THE GAUNTLET						
Chaos! Comics: Apr, 2002 - No. 2, May, 2002 ($2.99, limited series)						
1,2: 1-J. Scott Campbell-c/redesign of Lady Death's outfit; Mota-a						3.00
LADY DEATH: THE ODYSSEY						
Chaos! Comics: Apr, 1996 - No. 4, Aug, 1996 ($3.50/$2.95)						
1-($1.50)-Sneak Peek Preview						2.25
1-($1.50)-Sneak Peek Preview Micro Premium Edition (2500 print run)	2	4	6	8	10	12
1-($3.50)-Embossed, wraparound goil foil-c						5.00
1-Black Onyx Edition (200 print run)	7	14	21	46	63	80
1-($19.95)-Premium Edition (10,000 print run)						20.00
2-4-($2.95)						3.00
LADY DEATH: THE RAPTURE						
Chaos! Comics: Jun, 1999 - No. 4, Sept, 1999 ($2.95, limited series)						
1-4-Ivan Reis-c/a; Pulido-s						3.00
LADY DEATH: THE WILD HUNT (Brian Pulido's...)						
CG Entertainment: Apr, 2004 - Present ($2.95)						
1-2: 1-Brian Pulido-s/Jim Cheung-a						3.00
LADY DEATH: TRIBULATION						
Chaos! Comics: Dec, 2000 - No. 4, Mar, 2001 ($2.95, limited series)						
1-4-Ivan Reis-a; Kaminski-s						3.00
LADY DEATH II: BETWEEN HEAVEN & HELL						
Chaos! Comics: Mar, 1995 - No. 4, July, 1995 ($3.50, limited series)						

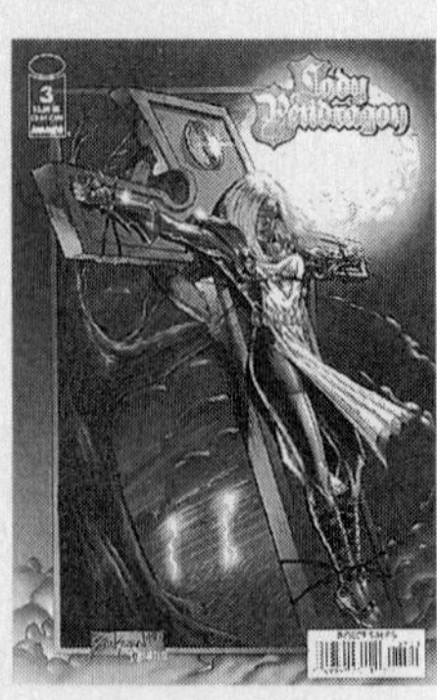
Lady Pendragon #3 © Matt Hawkins

Lana #7 © MAR

Land of the Giants #1 © GK

	GD 2.0	VG 4.0	FN 6.0	VF 8.0	VF/NM 9.0	NM- 9.2
1-Chromium wraparound-c; Evil Ernie cameo						5.00
1-Commemorative (4,000), 1-Black Velvet-c	2	4	6	11	14	18
1-Gold	1	3	4	6	8	10
1-"Refractor" edition (5,000)	2	4	6	12	16	20
2-4						3.50
4-Lady Demon variant-c	1	2	3	5	7	9
Trade paperback-($12.95)-r/#1-4						13.00

LADY DEMON
Chaos! Comics: Mar, 2000 - No. 3, May, 2000 ($2.95, limited series)

	GD	VG	FN	VF	VF/NM	NM-
1-3-Kaminski-s/Brewer-a						3.00
1-Premium Edition						10.00

LADY FOR A NIGHT (See Cinema Comics Herald)

LADY JUSTICE (See Neil Gaiman's...)

LADY LUCK (Formerly Smash #1-85) (Also see Spirit Sections #1)
Quality Comics Group: No. 86, Dec, 1949 - No. 90, Aug, 1950

	GD	VG	FN	VF	VF/NM	NM-
86(#1)	90	180	270	563	869	1175
87-90	65	130	195	406	628	850

LADY PENDRAGON
Maximum Press: Mar, 1996 ($2.50)

	GD	VG	FN	VF	VF/NM	NM-
1-Matt Hawkins script						2.50

LADY PENDRAGON
Image Comics: Nov, 1998 - No. 3, Jan, 1999 ($2.50, mini-series)

	GD	VG	FN	VF	VF/NM	NM-
Preview (6/98) Flip book w/ Deity preview						3.00
1-3: 1-Matt Hawkins-s/Stinsman-a						3.00
1-($6.95) DF Ed. with variant-c by Jusko						7.00
2-($4.95)Variant edition						5.00
0-(3/99) Origin; flip book						2.50

LADY PENDRAGON (Volume 3)
Image Comics: Apr, 1999 - No. 9, Mar, 2000 ($2.50, mini-series)

	GD	VG	FN	VF	VF/NM	NM-
1,2,4-6,8-10: 1-Matt Hawkins-s/Stinsman-a. 2-Peterson-c						2.50
3-Flip book w/Alley Cat preview (1st app.)						3.00
7-($3.95) Flip book; Stinsman-a/Cleavenger painted-a						4.00
Gallery Edition (10/99, $2.95) pin-ups						3.00
...Merlin (1/00, $2.95) Stinsman-a						3.00

LADY PENDRAGON/ MORE THAN MORTAL
Image Comics: May, 1999 ($2.50, one-shot)

	GD	VG	FN	VF	VF/NM	NM-
Preview (2/99) Diamond Dateline suppl.						2.25
1-Scott-s/Norton-a; 2 covers by Norton & Finch						2.50

LADY RAWHIDE
Topps Comics: July, 1995 - No. 5, Mar, 1996 ($2.95, bi-monthly, limited series)

	GD	VG	FN	VF	VF/NM	NM-
1-5: Don McGregor scripts & Mayhew-a. in all. 2-Stelfreeze-c. 3-Hughes-c. 4-Golden-c. 5-Julie Bell-c.						3.00
It Can't Happen Here TPB (8/99, $16.95) r/#1-5						17.00
Mini Comic 1 (7/95) Maroto-a; Zorro app.						2.25
Special Edition 1 (6/95, $3.95)-Reprints						4.00

LADY RAWHIDE (Volume 2)
Topps Comics: Oct, 1996 -No. 5, June, 1997 ($2.95, limited series)

	GD	VG	FN	VF	VF/NM	NM-
1-5: 1-Julie Bell-c.						3.00

LADY RAWHIDE OTHER PEOPLE'S BLOOD (ZORRO'S ...)
Image Comics: Mar, 1999 - No. 5, July, 1999 ($2.95, B&W)

	GD	VG	FN	VF	VF/NM	NM-
1-5-Reprints Lady Rawhide series in B&W						3.00

LADY SUPREME (See Asylum)(Also see Supreme & Kid Supreme)
Image Comics (Extreme): May, 1996 - No. 2, June, 1996 ($2.50, limited series)

	GD	VG	FN	VF	VF/NM	NM-
1,2-Terry Moore -s: 1-Terry Moore-c. 2-Flip book w/Newmen preview						2.50

LAFF-A-LYMPICS (TV)(See The Funtastic World of Hanna-Barbera)
Marvel Comics: Mar, 1978 - No. 13, Mar, 1979 (Newsstand sales only)

	GD	VG	FN	VF	VF/NM	NM-
1-Yogi Bear, Scooby Doo, Pixie & Dixie, etc.	3	6	9	19	25	32
2-8	2	4	6	14	18	22
9-13: 11-Jetsons x-over; 1 pg. illustrated bio of Mighty Mightor, Herculoids, Shazzan, Galaxy Trio & Space Ghost	3	6	9	18	23	28

LAFFY-DAFFY COMICS
Rural Home Publ. Co.: Feb, 1945 - No. 2, Mar, 1945

	GD	VG	FN	VF	VF/NM	NM-
1,2-Funny animal	10	20	30	56	73	90

LANA (Little Lana No. 8 on)
Marvel Comics (MjMC): Aug, 1948 - No. 7, Aug, 1949 (Also see Annie Oakley)

	GD 2.0	VG 4.0	FN 6.0	VF 8.0	VF/NM 9.0	NM- 9.2
1-Rusty, Millie begin	21	42	63	121	173	225
2-Kurtzman's "Hey Look" (1); last Rusty	12	24	36	71	98	125
3-7: 3-Nellie begins	9	18	27	54	70	85

LANCELOT & GUINEVERE (See Movie Classics)

LANCELOT LINK, SECRET CHIMP (TV)
Gold Key: Apr, 1971 - No. 8, Feb, 1973

	GD	VG	FN	VF	VF/NM	NM-
1-Photo-c	7	14	21	51	71	90
2-8: 2-Photo-c	4	8	12	28	38	48

LANCELOT STRONG (See The Shield)

LANCE O'CASEY (See Mighty Midget & Whiz Comics)
Fawcett Publications: Spring, 1946 - No. 3, Fall, 1946; No. 4, Summer, 1948

	GD	VG	FN	VF	VF/NM	NM-
1-Captain Marvel app. on-c	37	74	111	209	305	400
2	24	48	72	135	195	255
3,4	18	36	54	100	143	185

NOTE: *The cover for the 1st issue was done in 1942 but was not published until 1946. The cover shows 68 pages but actually has only 36 pages.*

LANCER (TV)(Western)
Gold Key: Feb, 1969 - No. 3, Sept, 1969 (All photo-c)

	GD	VG	FN	VF	VF/NM	NM-
1	4	8	12	29	40	50
2,3	3	7	10	21	28	35

LAND OF NOD, THE
Dark Horse Comics: July, 1997 - No. 3, Feb, 1998 ($2.95, B&W)

	GD	VG	FN	VF	VF/NM	NM-
1-3-Jetcat; Jay Stephens-s/a						3.00

LAND OF OZ
Arrow Comics: 1998 - No. 9 ($2.95, B&W)

	GD	VG	FN	VF	VF/NM	NM-
1-9-Bishop-s/Bryan-s/a						3.00

LAND OF THE GIANTS (TV)
Gold Key: Nov, 1968 - No. 5, Sept, 1969 (All have photo-c)

	GD	VG	FN	VF	VF/NM	NM-
1	7	14	21	51	71	90
2-5	4	8	12	29	40	50

LAND OF THE LOST COMICS (Radio)
E. C. Comics: July-Aug, 1946 - No. 9, Spring, 1948

	GD	VG	FN	VF	VF/NM	NM-
1	37	74	112	213	312	410
2	24	48	72	138	199	260
3-9	20	40	60	112	161	210

LAND UNKNOWN, THE (Movie)
Dell Publishing Co.: No. 845, Sept, 1957

	GD	VG	FN	VF	VF/NM	NM-
Four Color 845-Alex Toth-a	13	26	39	90	138	185

LA PACIFICA
DC Comics (Paradox Press): 1994/1995 ($4.95, B&W, limited series, digest size, mature readers)

	GD	VG	FN	VF	VF/NM	NM-
1-3						5.00

LARAMIE (TV)
Dell Publishing Co.: Aug, 1960 - July, 1962 (All photo-c)

	GD	VG	FN	VF	VF/NM	NM-
Four Color 1125-Gil Kane/Heath-a	10	20	30	72	104	135
Four Color 1223,1284, 01-418-207 (7/62)	8	16	24	53	74	95

LAREDO (TV)
Gold Key: June, 1966

	GD	VG	FN	VF	VF/NM	NM-
1 (10179-606)-Photo-c	4	8	12	27	36	45

LARGE FEATURE COMIC (Formerly called Black & White in previous guides)
Dell Publishing Co.: 1939 - No. 13, 1943

Note: See individual alphabetical listings for prices

1 (Series I)-Dick Tracy Meets the Blank
2-Terry and the Pirates (#1)
3-Heigh-Yo Silver! The Lone Ranger (text & ill.)(76 pgs.); also exists as a Whitman #710; based on radio
4-Dick Tracy Gets His Man
5-Tarzan of the Apes (#1) by Harold Foster (origin); reprints 1st Tarzan dailies from 1929
6-Terry & the Pirates & The Dragon Lady; reprints dailies from 1936
7-(Scarce, 52 pgs.)-Hi-Yo Silver the Lone Ranger to the Rescue; also exists as a Whitman #715, based on radio program
8-Dick Tracy the Racket Buster
9-King of the Royal Mounted (Zane Grey's...)
10-(Scarce)-Gang Busters (No. appears on inside front cover); first slick cover (based on radio program)
11-Dick Tracy Foils the Mad Doc Hump
12-Smilin' Jack; no number on-c
13-Dick Tracy and Scottie of Scotland Yard
14-Smilin' Jack Helps G-Men Solve a Case!
15-Dick Tracy and the Kidnapped Princes
16-Donald Duck; 1st app. Daisy Duck on

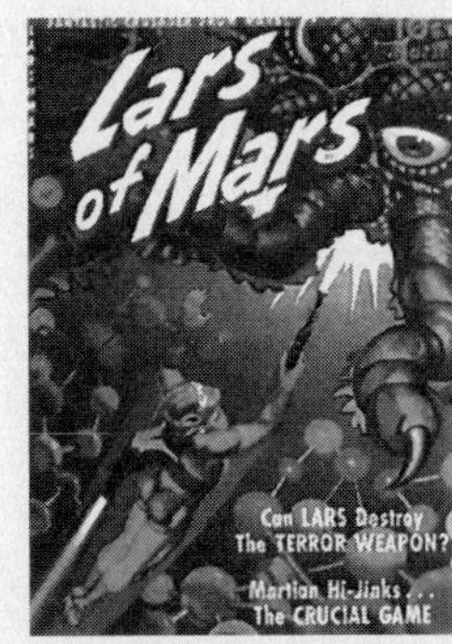

Lars of Mars #11 © Z-D

Lash Larue Western #46 © FAW

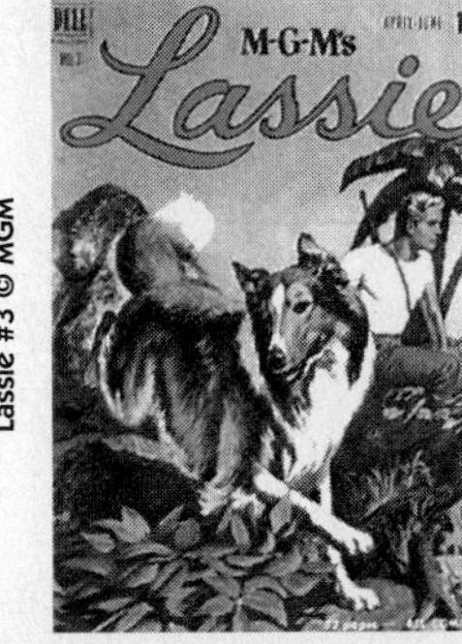

Lassie #3 © MGM

17-Gang Busters (1941)
18-Phantasmo (see The Funnies #45)
20-Donald Duck Comic Paint Book (rarer than #16) (Disney)
21,22: 21-Private Buck. 22-Nuts & Jolts
24-Popeye in "Thimble Theatre" by Segar
26-Smitty
28-Grin and Bear It
30-Tillie the Toiler
2-Winnie Winkle (#1)
3-Dick Tracy
4-Tiny Tim (#1)
6-Terry and the Pirates; Caniff-a
8-Bugs Bunny (#1)('42)
9-Bringing Up Father
10-Popeye (Thimble Theatre)
11-Barney Google and Snuffy Smith
13-(nn)-1001 Hours Of Fun; puzzles & games; by A. W. Nugent. This book was bound as #13 with Large Feature Comics in publisher's files
back cover (6/41-Disney)
19-Dumbo Comic Paint Book (Disney); partial-r from 4-Color #17
23-The Nebbs
25-Smilin' Jack-1st issue to show title on-c
27-Terry and the Pirates; Caniff-c/a
29-Moon Mullins
1 (Series II)-Peter Rabbit by Harrison Cady; arrival date-3/27/42
5-Toots and Casper
7-Pluto Saves the Ship (#1) (Disney)-Written by Carl Barks, Jack Hannah, & Nick George (Barks' 1st comic book work)
12-Private Buck

NOTE: *The Black & White Feature Books are oversized 8-1/2x11-3/8" comics with color covers and black and white interiors. The first nine issues all have rough, heavy stock covers and, except for #7, all have 76 pages, including covers. #7 and #10-on all have 52 pages. Beginning with #10 the covers are slick and thin and, because of their size, are difficult to handle without damaging. For this reason, they are seldom found in fine to mint condition. The paper stock, unlike Wow #1 and Capt. Marvel #1, is itself not unstable ...just thin.*

LARRY DOBY, BASEBALL HERO
Fawcett Publications: 1950 (Cleveland Indians)

	GD 2.0	VG 4.0	FN 6.0	VF 8.0	VF/NM 9.0	NM- 9.2
nn-Bill Ward-a; photo-c	77	154	231	481	741	1000

LARRY HARMON'S LAUREL AND HARDY (...Comics)
National Periodical Publ.: July-Aug, 1972 (Digest advertised, not published)

	GD 2.0	VG 4.0	FN 6.0	VF 8.0	VF/NM 9.0	NM- 9.2
1-Low print run	9	18	27	63	89	115

LARS OF MARS
Ziff-Davis Publishing Co.: No. 10, Apr-May, 1951 - No. 11, July-Aug, 1951 (Painted-c) (Created by Jerry Siegel, editor)

	GD 2.0	VG 4.0	FN 6.0	VF 8.0	VF/NM 9.0	NM- 9.2
10-Origin; Anderson-a(3) in each; classic robot-c	81	162	243	506	778	1050
11-Gene Colan-a; classic-c	65	130	195	406	623	840

LARS OF MARS 3-D
Eclipse Comics: Apr, 1987 ($2.50)

	NM- 9.2
1-r/Lars of Mars #10,11 in 3-D plus new story	4.00
2-D limited edition (B&W, 100 copies)	6.00

LASER ERASER & PRESSBUTTON (See Axel Pressbutton & Miracle Man 9)
Eclipse Comics: Nov, 1985 - No. 6, 1987 (95¢/$2.50, limited series)

	NM- 9.2
1-6: 5,6-(95¢)	2.25
...In 3-D 1 (8/86, $2.50)	4.00
2-D 1 (B&W, limited to 100 copies signed & numbered)	8.00

LASH LARUE WESTERN (Movie star; King of the bullwhip)(See Fawcett Movie Comic, Motion Picture Comics & Six-Gun Heroes)
Fawcett Publications: Sum, 1949 - No. 46, Jan, 1954 (36pgs., 1-7,9,13,16-on)

	GD 2.0	VG 4.0	FN 6.0	VF 8.0	VF/NM 9.0	NM- 9.2
1-Lash & his horse Black Diamond begin; photo front/back-c begin	110	220	330	686	1057	1425
2(11/49)	46	92	138	281	428	575
3-5	40	80	120	236	351	465
6,7,9: 6-Last photo back-c; intro. Frontier Phantom (Lash's twin brother)	35	70	105	198	287	375
8,10 (52pgs.)	36	72	108	204	297	390
11,12,14,15 (52pgs.)	24	48	72	138	199	260
13,16-20 (36pgs.)	21	42	63	121	173	225
21-30: 21-The Frontier Phantom app.	18	36	54	100	143	185
31-45	15	30	45	86	123	160
46-Last Fawcett issue & photo-c	16	32	48	92	131	170

LASH LARUE WESTERN (Continues from Fawcett series)
Charlton Comics: No. 47, Mar-Apr, 1954 - No. 84, June, 1961

	GD 2.0	VG 4.0	FN 6.0	VF 8.0	VF/NM 9.0	NM- 9.2
47-Photo-c	20	40	60	112	161	210
48	15	30	45	86	123	160
49-60, 67,68-(68 pgs.). 68-Check-a	12	24	36	69	95	120
61-66,69,70: 52-r/#8; 53-r/#22	10	20	30	60	80	100
71-83	9	18	27	51	62	75
84-Last issue	10	20	30	58	77	95

LASH LARUE WESTERN
AC Comics: 1990 ($3.50, 44 pgs) (24 pgs. of color, 16 pgs. of B&W)

	NM- 9.2
1-Photo covers; r/Lash #6; r/old movie posters	3.50
Annual 1 (1990, $2.95, B&W, 44 pgs.)-Photo covers	3.00

LASSIE (TV)(M-G-M's... #1-36; see Kite Fun Book)
Dell Publ. Co./Gold Key No. 59 (10/62) on: June, 1950 - No. 70, July, 1969

	GD 2.0	VG 4.0	FN 6.0	VF 8.0	VF/NM 9.0	NM- 9.2
1 (52 pgs.)-Photo-c; inside lists One Shot #282 in error	16	32	48	112	171	230
2-Painted-c begin	8	16	24	58	82	105
3-10	6	12	18	43	59	75
11-19: 12-Rocky Langford (Lassie's master) marries Gerry Lawrence. 15-1st app. Timbu	5	10	15	36	48	60
20-22-Matt Baker-a	6	12	18	38	52	65
23-38,40: 33-Robinson-a.	5	10	15	33	44	55
39-1st app. Timmy as Lassie picks up her TV family	7	14	21	46	63	80
41-50	5	10	15	33	44	55
51-58	4	8	12	29	40	50
59 (10/62)-1st Gold Key	5	10	15	36	48	60
60-70: 63-Last Timmy (10/63). 64-r/#19. 65-Forest Ranger Corey Stuart begins, ends #69. 70-Forest Rangers Bob Ericson & Scott Turner app. (Lassie's new masters)	4	8	12	27	36	45
11193(1978, $1.95, 224 pgs., Golden Press)-Baker-r (92 pgs.)	5	10	15	33	44	55

NOTE: *Photo c-57, 63. (See March of Comics #210, 217, 230, 254, 266, 278, 296, 308, 324, 334, 346, 358, 370, 381, 394, 411, 432)*

LAST AMERICAN, THE
Marvel Comics (Epic): Dec, 1990 - No. 4, March, 1991 ($2.25, mini-series)

	NM- 9.2
1-4: Alan Grant scripts	2.25

LAST AVENGERS STORY, THE (Last Avengers #1)
Marvel Comics: Nov, 1995 - No. 2, Dec, 1995 ($5.95, painted, limited series) (Alterniverse)

	NM- 9.2
1,2: Peter David story; acetate-c in all. 1-New team (Hank Pym, Wasp, Human Torch, Cannonball, She-Hulk, Hotshot, Bombshell, Tommy Maximoff, Hawkeye & Mockingbird) forms to battle Ultron 59, Kang the Conqueror, The Grim Reaper & Oddball	6.00

LAST DAYS OF THE JUSTICE SOCIETY SPECIAL
DC Comics: 1986 ($2.50, one-shot, 68 pgs.)

	GD 2.0	VG 4.0	FN 6.0	VF 8.0	VF/NM 9.0	NM- 9.2
1-62 pg. JSA story plus unpubbed G.A. pg.	1	2	3	5	7	9

LAST GENERATION, THE
Black Tie Studios: 1986 - No. 5, 1989 ($1.95, B&W, high quality paper)

	NM- 9.2
1-5	2.25
Book 1 (1989, $6.95)-By Caliber Press	7.00

LAST HUNT, THE
Dell Publishing Co.: No. 678, Feb, 1956

	GD 2.0	VG 4.0	FN 6.0	VF 8.0	VF/NM 9.0	NM- 9.2
Four Color 678-Movie, photo-c	9	18	27	63	89	115

LAST KISS
ACME Press (Eclipse): 1988 ($3.95, B&W, squarebound, 52 pgs.)

	NM- 9.2
1-One story adapts E.A. Poe's The Black Cat	4.00

LAST OF THE COMANCHES (Movie) (See Wild Bill Hickok #28)
Avon Periodicals: 1953

	GD 2.0	VG 4.0	FN 6.0	VF 8.0	VF/NM 9.0	NM- 9.2
nn-Kinstler-c/a, 21pgs.; Ravielli-a	16	32	48	89	127	165

LAST OF THE ERIES, THE (See American Graphics)

LAST OF THE FAST GUNS, THE
Dell Publishing Co.: No. 925, Aug, 1958

	GD 2.0	VG 4.0	FN 6.0	VF 8.0	VF/NM 9.0	NM- 9.2
Four Color 925-Movie, photo-c	8	16	24	58	82	105

LAST OF THE MOHICANS (See King Classics & White Rider and...)

LAST OF THE VIKING HEROES, THE (Also see Silver Star #1)
Genesis West Comics: Mar, 1987 - No. 12 ($1.50/$1.95)

	NM- 9.2
1-4,5A,5B,6-12: 4-Intro The Phantom Force, 1-Signed edition ($1.50), 5A-Kirby/Stevens-c. 5B,6 ($1.95). 7-Art Adams-c. 8-Kirby back-c.	4.00
Summer Special 1-3: 1-(1988)-Frazetta-c & illos. 2 (1990, $2.50)-A TMNT app. 3 (1991, $2.50)-Teenage Mutant Ninja Turtles	4.00
Summer Special 1-Signed edition (sold for $1.95)	4.00

NOTE: ***Art Adams** c-7. **Byrne** c-3. **Kirby** c-1p, 5p. **Perez** c-2i. **Stevens** c-5Ai.*

LAST ONE, THE
DC Comics (Vertigo): July, 1993 - No. 6, Dec, 1993 ($2.50, lim. series, mature)

	NM- 9.2
1-6	2.50

Laugh Comics #35 © AP

Laurel and Hardy #3 © DELL

Law Against Crime #1 © Essenkay

	GD 2.0	VG 4.0	FN 6.0	VF 8.0	VF/NM 9.0	NM- 9.2

LAST SHOT
Image Comics: Aug, 2001 - No. 4, Mar, 2002 ($2.95, limited series)

	GD	VG	FN	VF	VF/NM	NM-
1-4: 1-Wraparound-c; by Studio XD						3.00
...: First Draw (5/01, $2.95) Introductory one-shot						3.00

LAST STARFIGHTER, THE
Marvel Comics Group: Oct, 1984 - No. 3, Dec, 1984 (75¢, movie adaptation)

	GD	VG	FN	VF	VF/NM	NM-
1-3: r/Marvel Super Special; Guice-c						2.25

LAST TEMPTATION, THE
Marvel Comics: 1994 - No. 3, 1994 ($4.95, limited series)

	GD	VG	FN	VF	VF/NM	NM-
1-3-Alice Cooper story; Neil Gaiman scripts; McKean-c; Zulli-a: 1-Two covers						5.00

LAST TRAIN FROM GUN HILL
Dell Publishing Co.: No. 1012, July, 1959

	GD	VG	FN	VF	VF/NM	NM-
Four Color 1012-Movie, photo-c	10	20	30	70	100	130

LAST TRAIN TO DEADSVILLE: A CAL McDONALD MYSTERY
Dark Horse Comics: May, 2004 - No. 4, Aug, 2004 ($2.99, limited series)

	GD	VG	FN	VF	VF/NM	NM-
1-4-Steve Niles-s/Kelley Jones-a/c						3.00
TPB (2005, $14.95) r/series						15.00

LATEST ADVENTURES OF FOXY GRANDPA (See Foxy Grandpa)

LATEST COMICS (Super Duper No. 3?)
Spotlight Publ./Palace Promotions (Jubilee): Mar, 1945 - No. 2, 1945?

	GD	VG	FN	VF	VF/NM	NM-
1-Super Duper	17	34	51	95	135	170
2-Bee-29 (nd); Jubilee in indicia blacked out	13	26	39	74	102	130

LAUGH
Archie Enterprises: June, 1987 - No. 29, Aug, 1991 (75¢/$1.00)

	GD	VG	FN	VF	VF/NM	NM-
V2#1						5.00
2-10,14,24: 5-X-Mas issue. 14-1st app. Hot Dog. 24-Re-intro Super Duck						4.00
11-13,15-23,25-29: 19-X-Mas issue						3.00

LAUGH COMICS (Teenage) (Formerly Black Hood #9-19) (Laugh #226 on)
Archie Publications (Close-Up): No. 20, Fall, 1946 - No. 400, Apr, 1987

	GD	VG	FN	VF	VF/NM	NM-
20-Archie begins; Katy Keene & Taffy begin by Woggon; Suzie & Wilbur also begin; Archie covers begin	63	126	189	394	610	825
21-23,25	36	72	108	204	297	390
24- "Pipsy" by Kirby (6 pgs.)	37	74	111	209	305	400
26-30	20	40	60	112	161	210
31-40	15	30	45	86	123	160
41-60: 41,54-Debbi by Woggon	11	22	33	66	91	115
61-80: 67-Debbi by Woggon	9	18	27	52	66	80
81-99	6	12	18	38	52	65
100	6	12	18	40	55	70
101-126: 106-109,111,113-Neal Adams-a (1 pg.) in each. 125-Debbi app.	5	10	15	33	44	55
127-144: Super-hero app. in all (see note)	5	10	15	36	48	60
145-(4/63) Josie by DeCarlo begins	6	12	18	43	59	75
146-149-early Josie app. by DeCarlo	4	8	12	29	40	50
150,162,163,165,167,169,170-No Josie	3	6	9	19	25	32
151-161,164,168-Josie app. by DeCarlo	4	8	12	27	36	45
166-Beatles-c (1/65)	6	12	18	38	52	65
171-180, 200 (12/67)	3	6	9	18	24	30
181-199	3	6	9	16	20	24
201-240(3/71)	2	4	6	10	13	16
241-280(7/74)	2	4	6	9	11	14
281-299	1	3	4	6	8	10
300(3/76)	2	4	6	8	10	12
301-340 (7/79)	1	2	3	5	6	8
341-370 (1/82)						6.00
371-380,385-399						5.00
381-384,400: 381-384-Katy Keene app.; by Woggon-381,382						6.00

NOTE: *The Fly app. in 128, 129, 132, 134, 138, 139. Flygirl app. in 136, 137, 143. Flyman app. in 137. The Jaguar app. in 127, 130, 131, 133, 135, 140-142, 144. Josie app. in 145-149, 151-161, 164, 168. Katy Keene app. in 20-125, 129, 130, 133. Horror/Sci-Fi covers on 128-135, 137, 139. Many issues contain paper dolls.* ***Al Fagaly*** *c-20-29.* ***Montana*** *c-33, 36, 37, 42.* ***Bill Vigoda*** *c-30, 50.*

LAUGH COMICS DIGEST (...Magazine #23-89; Laugh Digest Mag. #90 on)
Archie Publ. (Close-Up No. 1, 3 on): 8/74; No. 2, 9/75; No. 3, 3/76 - Present (Digest-size) (Josie and Sabrina app. in most issues)

	GD	VG	FN	VF	VF/NM	NM-
1-Neal Adams-a	5	10	15	36	48	60
2,7,8,19-Neal Adams-a	3	6	9	19	25	32
3-6,9,10	3	6	9	16	20	24
11-18,20	2	4	6	10	13	16
21-40	2	4	6	9	11	14
41-60	1	3	4	6	8	10
61-80	1	2	3	5	6	8
81-99						5.00
100						6.00
101-138						3.00
139-200: 139-Begin $1.95-c. 148-Begin $1.99-c. 156-Begin $2.19-c. 180-Begin $2.39-c						2.50

NOTE: *Katy Keene in 23, 25, 27, 32-38, 40, 45-48, 50. The Fly-r in 19, 20. The Jaguar-r in 25, 27. Mr. Justice-r in 21. The Web-r in 23.*

LAUGH COMIX (Formerly Top Notch Laugh; Suzie Comics No. 49 on)
MLJ Magazines: No. 46, Summer, 1944 - No. 48, Winter, 1944-45

	GD	VG	FN	VF	VF/NM	NM-
46-Wilbur & Suzie in all; Harry Sahle-c	24	48	72	138	199	260
47,48: 47-Sahle-c. 48-Bill Vigoda-c	16	32	48	92	131	170

LAUGH-IN MAGAZINE (TV)(Magazine)
Laufer Publ. Co.: Oct, 1968 - No. 12, Oct, 1969 (50¢) (Satire)

	GD	VG	FN	VF	VF/NM	NM-
V1#1	6	12	18	38	52	65
2-12	4	8	12	25	33	42

LAUREL & HARDY (See Larry Harmon's... & March of Comics No. 302, 314)

LAUREL AND HARDY (...Comics)
St. John Publ. Co.: 3/49 - No. 3, 9/49; No. 26, 11/55 - No. 28, 3/56 (No #4-25)

	GD	VG	FN	VF	VF/NM	NM-
1	71	142	213	444	685	925
2	40	80	120	239	357	475
3	31	62	93	178	259	340
26-28 (Reprints)	17	34	51	95	135	175

LAUREL AND HARDY (TV)
Dell Publishing Co.: Oct, 1962 - No. 4, Sept-Nov, 1963

	GD	VG	FN	VF	VF/NM	NM-
12-423-210 (8-10/62)	7	14	21	50	68	85
2-4 (Dell)	5	10	15	36	48	60

LAUREL AND HARDY (Larry Harmon's...)
Gold Key: Jan, 1967 - No. 2, Oct, 1967

	GD	VG	FN	VF	VF/NM	NM-
1-Photo back-c	6	12	18	40	55	70
2	5	10	15	36	48	60

LAUREL AND HARDY DIGEST: DC Comics. 1972 (Advertised, not published)

L.A.W., THE (LIVING ASSAULT WEAPONS)
DC Comics: Sept, 1999 - No. 6, Feb, 2000 ($2.50, limited series)

	GD	VG	FN	VF	VF/NM	NM-
1-6-Blue Beetle, Question, Judomaster, Capt. Atom app.; Giordano-a 5-JLA app.						2.50

LAW AGAINST CRIME (Law-Crime on cover)
Essenkay Publishing Co.: April, 1948 - No. 3, Aug, 1948 (Real Stories from Police Files)

	GD	VG	FN	VF	VF/NM	NM-
1-(#1-3 are half funny animal, half crime stories)-L. B. Cole-c/a in all; electrocution-c	73	140	219	456	703	950
2-L. B. Cole-c/a	55	110	165	340	520	700
3-Used in **SOTI**, pg. 180,181 & illo "The wish to hurt or kill couples in lovers' lanes;" reprinted in All-Famous Crime #9	69	138	207	431	666	900

LAW AND ORDER
Maximum Press: Sept, 1995 - No. 2, 1995 ($2.50, unfinished limited series)

	GD	VG	FN	VF	VF/NM	NM-
1,2						2.50

LAWBREAKERS (...Suspense Stories No. 10 on)
Law and Order Magazines (Charlton): Mar, 1951 - No. 9, Oct-Nov, 1952

	GD	VG	FN	VF	VF/NM	NM-
1	40	80	120	230	335	440
2	23	46	69	130	188	245
3,5,6,8,9	18	36	54	104	150	190
4- "White Death" junkie story	22	44	66	125	180	235
7- "The Deadly Dopesters" drug story	22	44	66	125	180	235

LAWBREAKERS ALWAYS LOSE!
Marvel Comics (CBS): Spring, 1948 - No. 10, Oct, 1949

	GD	VG	FN	VF	VF/NM	NM-
1-2pg. Kurtzman-a, "Giggles 'n' Grins"	35	70	105	201	293	385
2	19	38	57	107	154	200
3-5: 4-Vampire story	15	30	45	83	117	150
6(2/49)-Has editorial defense against charges of Dr. Wertham	16	32	48	92	131	170
7-Used in **SOTI**, illo "Comic-book philosophy"	31	62	93	175	253	330
8-10: 9,10-Photo-c	13	26	39	74	102	130

NOTE: ***Brodsky*** *c-4, 5.* ***Shores*** *c-1-3, 6-8.*

LAWBREAKERS SUSPENSE STORIES (Formerly Lawbreakers; Strange Suspense Stories No. 16 on)
Capitol Stories/Charlton Comics: No. 10, Jan, 1953 - No. 15, Nov, 1953

	GD	VG	FN	VF	VF/NM	NM-
10	40	80	120	233	342	450
11 (3/53)-Severed tongues-c/story & woman negligee scene						

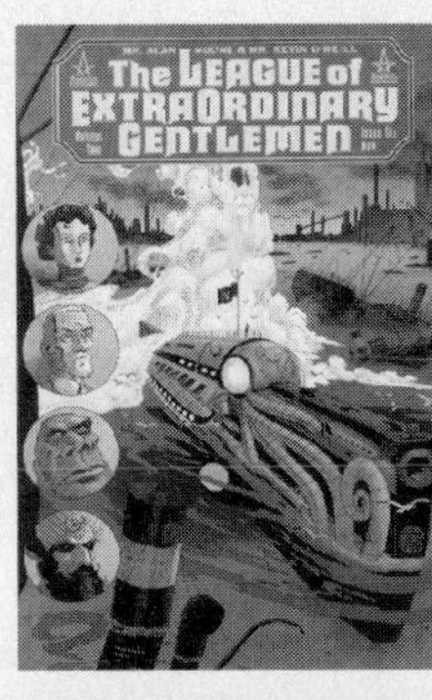

The League of Extraordinary Gentlemen V2#6 © Alan Moore & Kevin O'Neill

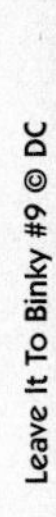

Leave It To Binky #9 © DC

Legacy #1 © Roaring Studios

	GD 2.0	VG 4.0	FN 6.0	VF 8.0	VF/NM 9.0	NM- 9.2
	98	196	294	613	944	1275
12-14: 13-Giordano-c begin, end #15	25	50	75	144	207	270
15-Acid-in-face-c/story; hands dissolved in acid sty	51	102	153	311	476	640

LAW-CRIME (See Law Against Crime)

LAWDOG
Marvel Comics (Epic Comics): May, 1993 - No. 10, Feb, 1993

1-10 2.25

LAWDOG/GRIMROD: TERROR AT THE CROSSROADS
Marvel Comics (Epic Comics): Sept, 1993 ($3.50)

1 3.50

LAWMAN (TV)
Dell Publishing Co.: No. 970, Feb, 1959 - No. 11, Apr-June, 1962 (All photo-c)

	GD	VG	FN	VF	VF/NM	NM-
Four Color 970(#1)	14	28	42	97	149	200
Four Color 1035('60), 3(2-4/60)-Toth-a	9	18	27	60	85	110
4-11	7	14	21	46	63	80

LAW OF DREDD, THE (Also see Judge Dredd)
Quality Comics/Fleetway #8 on: 1989 - No. 33, 1992 ($1.50/$1.75)

1-33: Bolland a-1-6,8,10-12,14(2 pg),15,19 2.50

LAWRENCE (See Movie Classics)

LAZARUS CHURCHYARD
Tundra Publishing: June, 1992 - No. 3, 1992 ($3.95, 44 pgs., coated stock)

1-3 4.00
The Final Cut (Image, 1/01, $14.95, TPB) Reprints Ellis/D'Israeli strips 15.00

LAZARUS FIVE
DC Comics: July, 2000 - No. 5, Nov, 2000 ($2.50, limited series)

1-5-Harris-c/Abell-a(p) 2.50

LAZARUS JACK
Dark Horse Comics: Sept, 2004 ($14.95, 6 x 9", graphic novel)

nn-Mark Ricketts-s/Horacio Domingues-a 15.00

LEADING COMICS (...Screen Comics No. 42 on)
National Periodical Publications: Winter, 1941-42 - No. 41, Feb-Mar, 1950

	GD	VG	FN	VF	VF/NM	NM-
1-Origin The Seven Soldiers of Victory; Crimson Avenger, Green Arrow & Speedy, Shining Knight, The Vigilante, Star Spangled Kid & Stripesy begin; The Dummy (Vigilante villain) 1st app.	465	930	1395	3255	5228	7200
2-Meskin-a; Fred Ray-c	165	330	495	1031	1591	2150
3	127	254	381	794	1222	1650
4,5	90	180	270	563	869	1175
6-10	79	158	237	494	760	1025
11,12,14(Spring, 1945)	55	110	165	34	520	700
13-Classic robot-c	98	196	294	613	944	1275
15-(Sum,'45)-Contents change to funny animal	30	60	90	170	245	320
16-22,24-30: 16-Nero Fox-c begin, end #22	13	26	39	74	102	130
23-1st app. Peter Porkchops by Otto Feuer & begins	30	60	90	170	245	320
31,32,34-41: 34-41-Leading Screen... on-c only	10	20	30	60	80	100
33-(Scarce)	21	42	63	118	169	220

NOTE: *Otto Feuer-a most #15-on; **Rube Grossman**-a most #15-on;c-15-41. **Post** a-23-37, 39, 41.*

LEADING SCREEN COMICS (Formerly Leading Comics)
National Periodical Publ.: No. 42, Apr-May, 1950 - No. 77, Aug-Sept, 1955

	GD	VG	FN	VF	VF/NM	NM-
42-Peter Porkchops-c/stories continue	11	22	33	64	87	110
43-77	10	20	30	58	77	95

NOTE: ***Grossman** a-most. **Mayer** a-45-48, 50, 54-57, 60, 62-74, 75(3), 76, 77.*

LEAGUE OF CHAMPIONS, THE (Also see The Champions)
Hero Graphics: Dec, 1990 - No. 12, 1992 ($2.95, 52 pgs.)

1-12: 1-Flare app. 2-Origin Malice 3.00

LEAGUE OF EXTRAORDINARY GENTLEMEN, THE
America's Best Comics: Mar, 1999 - No. 6, Sept, 2000 ($2.95, limited series)

	GD	VG	FN	VF	VF/NM	NM-
1-Alan Moore-s/Kevin O'Neill-a	1	2	3	5	7	9
1-DF Edition ($10.00) O'Neill-c	2	4	6	8	10	12
2,3						5.00
4-6: 5-Revised printing with "Wonder Co. Syringe" parody ad						3.50
5-Initial printing recalled because of "Marvel Co. Syringe" parody ad						30.00
... Compendium 1,2: 1-r/#1,2. 2-r/#3,4						6.00
Hardcover (2000, $24.95) r/#1-6 plus cover gallery						25.00

LEAGUE OF EXTRAORDINARY GENTLEMEN, THE (Volume 2)
America's Best Comics: Sept, 2002 - No. 6, Nov, 2003 ($3.50, limited series)

1-6-Alan Moore-s/Kevin O'Neill-a 3.50
... Bumper Compendium 1,2: 1-r/#1,2. 2-r/#3,4 6.00

LEAGUE OF JUSTICE
DC Comics (Elseworlds): 1996 - No. 2, 1996 ($5.95, 48 pgs., squarebound)

1,2: Magic-based alternate DC Universe story; Giordano-i 6.00

LEATHERFACE
Arpad Publishing: May (April on-c), 1991 - No. 4, May, 1992 ($2.75, painted-c)

1-4-Based on Texas Chainsaw movie; Dorman-c 3.00

LEATHERNECK THE MARINE (See Mighty Midget Comics)

LEAVE IT TO BEAVER (TV)
Dell Publishing Co.: No. 912, June, 1958; May-July, 1962 (All photo-c)

	GD	VG	FN	VF	VF/NM	NM-
Four Color 912	18	36	54	129	197	265
Four Color 999,1103,1191,1285, 01-428-207	15	30	45	107	164	220

LEAVE IT TO BINKY (Binky No. 72 on) (Super DC Giant) (No. 1-22: 52 pgs.)
National Periodical Publications: 2-3/48 - #60, 10/58; #61, 6-7/68 - #71, 2-3/70 (Teen-age humor)

	GD	VG	FN	VF	VF/NM	NM-
1-Lucy wears Superman costume	37	74	111	209	305	400
2	19	38	57	107	154	200
3,4	12	24	36	69	95	120
5-Superman cameo	18	36	54	100	143	185
6-10	10	20	30	58	77	95
11-14,16-22: Last 52 pg. issue	9	18	27	52	66	80
15-Scribbly story by Mayer	10	20	30	60	80	100
23-28,30-45: 45-Last pre-code (2/55)	8	16	24	40	50	60
29-Used in **POP**, pg. 78	8	16	24	43	54	65
46-60: 60-(10/58)	5	10	15	33	44	55
61 (6-7/68) 1950's reprints with art changes	6	12	18	38	52	65
62-69: 67-Last 12¢ issue	4	8	12	24	32	40
70-7pg. app. Bus Driver who looks like Ralph from Honeymooners	4	8	12	28	38	48
71-Last issue	4	8	12	27	36	45

NOTE: ***Aragones**-a-61, 62, 67. **Drucker** a-28. **Mayer** a-1, 2, 15. Created by **Mayer**.*

LEAVE IT TO CHANCE (Also see Promotional Comics section for FCBD Ed.)
Image Comics (Homage Comics): Sept, 1996 - No. 11, Sept, 1998; No. 13, July, 2002
DC Comics (Homage Comics): No. 12, Jun, 1999 ($2.50/$2.95/$4.95)

1-3: 1-Intro Chance Falconer & St. George; James Robinson scripts & Paul Smith-c/a 5.00
4-12: 12-(6/99) 3.00
13-(7/02, $4.95) includes sketch pages and pin-ups 5.00
Shaman's Rain TPB (1997, $9.95) r/#1-4 10.00
Shaman's Rain HC (2002, $14.95, over-sized 8 1/4" x 12") r/#1-4 15.00
Trick or Threat TPB (1997, $12.95) r/#5-8 13.00
Trick or Threat HC (2002, $14.95, over-sized 8 1/4" x 12") r/#5-8 15.00
Vol. 3: Monster Madness and Other Stories HC (2003, $14.95, 8 1/4" x 12") r/#9-11 15.00

LEE HUNTER, INDIAN FIGHTER
Dell Publishing Co.: No. 779, Mar, 1957; No. 904, May, 1958

	GD	VG	FN	VF	VF/NM	NM-
Four Color 779 (#1)	6	12	18	38	52	65
Four Color 904	4	8	12	27	36	45

LEFT-HANDED GUN, THE (Movie)
Dell Publishing Co.: No. 913, July, 1958

	GD	VG	FN	VF	VF/NM	NM-
Four Color 913-Paul Newman photo-c	11	22	33	75	110	145

LEGACY
Majestic Entertainment: Oct, 1993 - No. 2, Nov, 1993; No. 0, 1994 ($2.25)

1-2,0: 1-Glow-in-the-dark-c. 0-Platinum 2.25

LEGACY
Image Comics: May, 2003 - No. 4, Feb, 2004 ($2.95)

1-4: 1-Francisco-a/Treffiletti-s 3.00

LEGACY OF KAIN (Based on the Eidos video game)
Top Cow Productions: Oct, 1999; Jan, 2004 ($2.99)

...Defiance 1 (1/04, $2.99) Cha-c; Kirkham-a 3.00
...Soul Reaver 1 (10/99, Diamond Dateline supplement) Benitez-c 2.25

LEGEND OF CUSTER, THE (TV)
Dell Publishing Co.: Jan, 1968

	GD	VG	FN	VF	VF/NM	NM-
1-Wayne Maunder photo-c	3	7	10	21	28	35

LEGEND OF JESSE JAMES, THE (TV)
Gold Key: Feb, 1966

	GD	VG	FN	VF	VF/NM	NM-
10172-602-Photo-c	3	7	10	21	28	35

LEGEND OF KAMUI, THE (See Kamui)

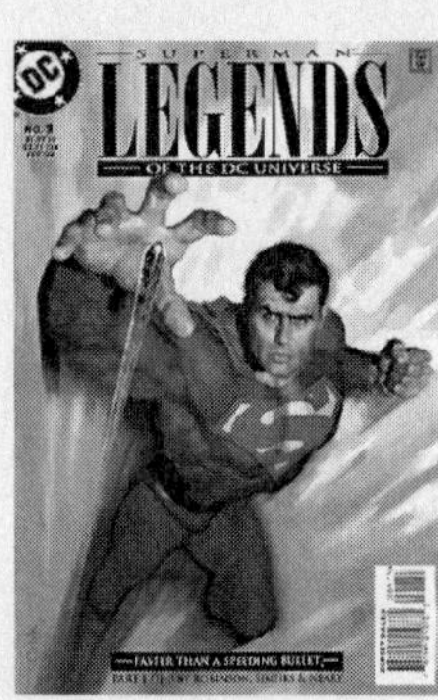

Legends of the DC Universe #1 © DC

Legends of the Legion #1 © DC

The Legion #25 © DC

GD VG FN VF VF/NM NM-
2.0 4.0 6.0 8.0 9.0 9.2

GD VG FN VF VF/NM NM-
2.0 4.0 6.0 8.0 9.0 9.2

LEGEND OF LOBO, THE (See Movie Comics)

LEGEND OF MOTHER SARAH (Manga)
Dark Horse Comics: Apr, 1995 - No. 8, Nov, 1995 ($2.50, limited series)

1-8: Katsuhiro Otomo scripts 4.00

LEGEND OF MOTHER SARAH: CITY OF THE ANGELS (Manga)
Dark Horse Comics: Oct, 1996 - No. 9 ($3.95, B&W, limited series)

1(10/96),.2(12/97),3-9: Otomo scripts 4.00

LEGEND OF MOTHER SARAH: CITY OF THE CHILDREN (Manga)
Dark Horse Comics: Jan, 1996 - No. 7, July, 1996 ($3.95, B&W, limited series)

1-7:Otomo scripts 4.00

LEGEND OF SUPREME
Image Comics (Extreme): Dec, 1994 - No. 3, Feb, 1995 ($2.50, limited series)

1-3 2.50

LEGEND OF THE ELFLORD
DavDez Arts: July, 1998 - No. 2, Sept, 1998 ($2.95)

1,2-Barry Blair & Colin Chin-s/a 3.00

LEGEND OF THE HAWKMAN
DC Comics: 2000 - No. 3, 2000 ($4.95, limited series)

1-3-Raab-s/Lark-c/a 5.00

LEGEND OF THE SAGE
Chaos Comics: Aug, 2001 - No. 4, Dec, 2001 ($2.99, limited series)

Preview Book (6/01, $1.99) 2.50
1-4-($2.99) Augustyn-s/Molenaar-a/c 3.00

LEGEND OF THE SHIELD, THE
DC Comics (Impact Comics): July, 1991 - No. 16, Oct, 1992 ($1.00)

1-16: 6,7-The Fly x-over. 12-Contains trading card 2.50
Annual 1 (1992, $2.50, 68 pgs.)-Snyder-a; w/trading card 2.50

LEGEND OF WONDER WOMAN, THE
DC Comics: May, 1986 - No. 4, Aug, 1986 (75¢, limited series)

1-4 4.00

LEGEND OF YOUNG DICK TURPIN, THE (Disney)(TV)
Gold Key: May, 1966

1 (10176-605)-Photo/painted-c 3 7 10 21 28 35

LEGEND OF ZELDA, THE (Link: The Legend... in indicia)
Valiant Comics: 1990 - No. 4, 1990 ($1.95, coated stiff-c) V2#1, 1990 - No. 5, 1990 ($1.50)

1-4: 4-Layton-c(i) 3.00
V2#1-5 3.00

LEGENDS
DC Comics: Nov, 1986 - No. 6, Apr, 1987 (75¢, limited series)

1-5: 1-Byrne-c/a(p) in all; 1st app. new Capt. Marvel. 3-1st app. new Suicide Squad; death of Blockbuster 4.00
6-1st app. new Justice League 6.00

LEGENDS OF DANIEL BOONE, THE (...Frontier Scout)
National Periodical Publications: Oct-Nov, 1955 - No. 8, Dec-Jan, 1956-57

1 (Scarce)-Nick Cardy c-1-8 60 120 180 375 575 775
2 (Scarce) 43 86 129 262 401 540
3-8 (Scarce) 39 78 117 222 324 425

LEGENDS OF KID DEATH AND FLUFFY
Event Comics: Feb, 1997 ($2.95, B&W, one-shot)

1-Five covers 3.00

LEGENDS OF NASCAR, THE
Vortex Comics: Nov, 1990 - No. 14, 1992? (#1 3rd printing (1/91) says 2nd printing inside)

1-Bill Elliott biog.; Trimpe-a ($1.50) 5.00
1-2nd printing (11/90, $2.00) 2.25
1-3rd print; contains Maxx racecards ($3.00) 3.00
2-14: 2-Richard Petty. 3-Ken Schrader (7/91). 4-Bobby Allison; Spiegle-a(p); Adkins part-i. 5-Sterling Marlin. 6-Bill Elliott. 7-Junior Johnson; Spiegle-c/a. 8-Benny Parsons; Heck-a3.00
1-13-Hologram cover versions. 2-Hologram shows Bill Elliott's car by mistake (all are numbered & limited) 5.00
2-Hologram corrected version 5.00
Christmas Special ($5.95) 6.00

LEGENDS OF THE DARK CLAW
DC Comics (Amalgam): Apr, 1996 ($1.95)

1-Jim Balent-c/a 3.00

LEGENDS OF THE DARK KNIGHT (See Batman: ...)

LEGENDS OF THE DC UNIVERSE
DC Comics: Feb, 1998 - No. 41, June, 2001 ($1.95/$1.99/$2.50)

1-13,15-21: 1-3-Superman; Robinson-s/Semeiks-a/Orbik-painted-c. 4,5-Wonder Woman; Deodato-a/Rude painted-c. 8-GL/GA, O'Neil-s. 10,11-Batgirl; Dodson-a. 12,13-Justice League. 15-17-Flash. 18-Kid Flash; Guice-a. 19-Impulse; prelude to JLApe Annuals. 20,21-Abin Sur 3.00
14-($3.95) Jimmy Olsen; Kirby-esque-c by Rude 4.00
22-27,30: 22,23-Superman; Rude-c/Ladronn-a. 26,27-Aquaman/Joker 2.50
28,29: Green Lantern & the Atom; Gil Kane-a; covers by Kane and Ross 2.50
31,32: 32-Begin $2.50-c; Wonder Woman; Texeira-c 2.50
33-36-Hal Jordan as The Spectre; DeMatteis-s/Zulli-a; Hale painted-c 2.50
37-41: 37,38-Kyle Rayner. 39-Superman. 40,41-Atom; Harris-c 2.50
... Crisis on Infinite Earths 1 (2/99, $4.95) Untold story during and after Crisis on Infinite Earths #4; Wolfman-s/Ryan-a/Orbik-c 5.00
... 80 Page Giant 1 (9/98, $4.95) Stories and art by various incl. Ditko, Perez, Gibbons, Mumy; Joe Kubert-c 5.00
... 80 Page Giant 2 (1/00, $4.95) Stories and art by various incl. Challengers by Art Adams; Sean Phillips-c 5.00
... 3-D Gallery (12/98, $2.95) Pin-ups w/glasses 3.00

LEGENDS OF THE LEGION (See Legion of Super-Heroes)
DC Comics: Feb, 1998 - No. 4, May, 1998 ($2.25, limited series)

1-4:1-Origin-s of Ultra Boy. 2-Spark. 3-Umbra. 4-Star Boy 3.00

LEGENDS OF THE STARGRAZERS (See Vanguard Illustrated #2)
Innovation Publishing: Aug, 1989 - No. 6, 1990 ($1.95, limited series, mature)

1-6: 1-Redondo part inks 2.25

LEGENDS OF THE WORLD'S FINEST (See World's Finest)
DC Comics: 1994 - No. 3, 1994 ($4.95, squarebound, limited series)

1-3: Simonson scripts; Brereton-c/a; embossed foil logos 6.00
TPB-(1995, $14.95) r/#1-3 15.00

L.E.G.I.O.N. (The # to right of title represents year of print)(Also see Lobo & R.E.B.E.L.S.)
DC Comics: Feb, 1989 - No. 70, Sept, 1994 ($1.50/$1.75)

1-Giffen plots/breakdowns in #1-12,28 5.00
2-22,24-47: 3-Lobo app. #3 on. 4-1st Lobo-c this title. 5-Lobo joins L.E.G.I.O.N. 13-Lar Gand app. 16-Lar Gand joins L.E.G.I.O.N., leaves #19. 31-Capt. Marvel app. 35-L.E.G.I.O.N. '92 begins 3.00
23,70-($2.50, 52 pgs.)-L.E.G.I.O.N. '91 begins. 70-Zero Hour 4.00
48,49,51-69: 48-Begin $1.75-c. 63-L.E.G.I.O.N. '94 begins; Superman x-over 3.00
50-($3.50, 68 pgs.) 4.00
Annual 1-5 ('90-94, 68 pgs.): 1-Lobo, Superman app. 2-Alan Grant scripts. 5-Elseworlds story; Lobo app. 4.00
NOTE: *Alan Grant scripts in #1-39, 51, Annual 1, 2.*

LEGION, THE (Continued from Legion Lost & Legion Worlds)
DC Comics: Dec, 2001 - No. 38, Oct, 2004 ($2.50)

1-Abnett & Lanning-s; Coipel & Lanning-c/a 4.00
2-24: 3-8-Ra's al Ghul app. 5-Snejbjerg-a. 9-DeStefano-a. 12-Legion vs. JLA. 16-Fatal Five app.; Walker-a 17,18-Ra's al Ghul app. 20-23-Universo app. 2.50
25-($3.95) Art by Harris, Cockrum, Rivoche; teenage Clark Kent app.; Harris-c 4.00
26-38-Superboy in classic costume. 26-30-Darkseid app. 31-Giffen-a. 35-38-Jurgens-a 2.50
...Secret Files 3003 (1/04, $4.95) Kirk-a, Harris-c/a; Superboy app. 5.00
...Foundations TPB (2004, $19.95) r/#25-30 & Secret Files 3003; Harris-c 20.00

LEGION LOST (Continued from Legion of Super-Heroes [4th series] #125)
DC Comics: May, 2000 - No. 12, Apr, 2001 ($2.50, limited series)

1-Abnett & Lanning-s. Coipel & Lanning-c/a 1 2 3 4 5 7
2-12-Abnett & Lanning-s. Coipel & Lanning-c/a in most. 4,9-Alixe-a 3.00

LEGIONNAIRES (See Legion of Super-Heroes #40, 41 & Showcase 95 #6)
DC Comics: Apr, 1992 - No. 81, Mar, 2000 ($1.25/$1.50/$2.25)

0-(10/94)-Zero Hour restart of Legion; released between #18 & #19 2.50
1-49,51-77: 1-(4/92)-Chris Sprouse-c/a; polybagged w/SkyBox trading card. 11-Kid Quantum joins. 18-(9/94)-Zero Hour. 19(11/94). 37-Valor (Lar Gand) becomes M'onel (5/96). 43-Legion tryouts; reintro Princess Projectra, Shadow Lass & others. 47-Forms one cover image with LSH #91. 60-Karate Kid & Kid Quantum join. 61-Silver Age & 70's Legion app. 76-Return of Wildfire. 79,80-Coipel-c/a; Legion vs. the Blight 2.50
50-($3.95) Pullout poster by Davis/Farmer 4.00
#1,000,000 (11/98) Sean Phillips-a 2.50
Annual 1,3 ('94,'96 $2.95)-1-Elseworlds-s. 3-Legends of the Dead Earth-s 3.00
Annual 2 (1995, $3.95)-Year One-s 4.50

LEGIONNAIRES THREE
DC Comics: Jan, 1986 - No. 4, May, 1986 (75¢, limited series)

Legion of Super-Heroes (3rd) #8 © DC

Legion of Super-Heroes (3rd) #122 © DC

Lenore #11 © Roman Dirge

GD 2.0 | VG 4.0 | FN 6.0 | VF 8.0 | VF/NM 9.0 | NM- 9.2

1-4 3.00

LEGION OF MONSTERS (Also see Marvel Premiere #28 & Marvel Preview #8)
Marvel Comics Group: Sept, 1975 ($1.00, B&W, magazine, 76 pgs.)

1-Origin & 1st app. Legion of Monsters; Neal Adams-c; Morrow-a; origin & only app. The Manphibian; Frankenstein by Mayerik; Bram Stoker's Dracula adaptation; Reese-a; painted-c (#2 was advertised with Morbius & Satana, but was never published) 4 8 12 24 32 40

LEGION OF NIGHT, THE
Marvel Comics: Oct, 1991 - No. 2, Oct, 1991 ($4.95, 52 pgs.)

1,2-Whilce Portacio-c/a(p) 5.00

LEGION OF SUBSTITUTE HEROES SPECIAL (See Adventure Comics #306)
DC Comics: July, 1985 ($1.25, one-shot, 52 pgs.)

1-Giffen-c/a(p) 3.00

LEGION OF SUPER-HEROES (See Action Comics, Adventure, All New Collectors Edition, Legionnaires, Legends of the Legion, Limited Collectors Edition, Secrets of the..., Superboy & Superman)
National Periodical Publications: Feb, 1973 - No. 4, July-Aug, 1973

1-Legion & Tommy Tomorrow reprints begin 3 6 9 19 25 32
2-4: 2-Forte-r. 3-r/Adv. #340. Action #240. 4-r/Adv. #341, Action #233; Mooney-r 2 4 6 10 13 16

LEGION OF SUPER-HEROES, THE (Formerly Superboy and...; Tales of The Legion No. 314 on)
DC Comics: No. 259, Jan, 1980 - No. 313, July, 1984

259(#1)-Superboy leaves Legion 2 4 6 9 11 14
260-270,285-290,294: 265-Contains 28 pg. insert "Superman & the TRS-80 computer"; origin Tyroc; Tyroc leaves Legion. 290-294-Great Darkness saga. 294-Double size (52 pgs.) 1 2 3 5 6 8
261,263,264,266-(Whitman variants; low print run; no cover #'s) 1 3 4 6 8 10
271-284,291-293: 272-Blok joins; origin; 20 pg. insert-Dial 'H' For Hero. 277-Intro. Reflecto. 280-Superboy re-joins Legion. 282-Origin Reflecto. 283-Origin Wildfire 5.00
295-299,301-313: 297-Origin retold. 298-Free 16pg. Amethyst preview. 306-Brief origin Star Boy (Swan art). 311-Colan-a 3.00
300-(68 pgs., Mando paper)-Anniversary issue; has c/a by almost everyone at DC 5.00
Annual 1-3(82-84, 52 pgs.)-1-Giffen-c/a; 1st app./origin new Invisible Kid who joins Legion. 2-Karate Kid & Princess Projectra wed & resign 3.00
...The Great Darkness Saga (1989, $17.95, 196 pgs.)-r/LSH #287,290-294 & Annual #3; Giffen-c/a 2 4 6 11 14 18

NOTE: ***Aparo*** *c-282, 283, 300(part).* ***Austin*** *c-268i.* ***Buckler*** *c-273p, 274p, 276p.* ***Colan*** *a-311p.* ***Ditko*** *a(p)-267, 268, 272, 274, 276, 281.* ***Giffen*** *a-285-313p, Annual 1p; c-287p, 288p, 289, 290p, 291p, 292, 293, 294-299p, 300, 301-313p, Annual 1p, 2p.* ***Perez*** *c-268p, 277-280, 281p.* ***Starlin*** *a-265.* ***Staton*** *a-259p, 260p, 280.* ***Tuska*** *a-308p.*

LEGION OF SUPER-HEROES (3rd Series) (Reprinted in Tales of the Legion)
DC Comics: Aug, 1984 - No. 63, Aug, 1989 ($1.25/$1.75, deluxe format)

1-Silver ink logo 5.00
2-36,39-44,46-49,51-62: 4-Death of Karate Kid. 5-Death of Nemesis Kid. 12-Cosmic Boy, Lightning Lad, & Saturn Girl resign. 14-Intro new members: Tellus, Sensor Girl, Quislet. 15-17-Crisis tie-ins. 18-Crisis x-over. 25-Sensor Girl i.d. revealed as Princess Projectra. 35-Saturn Girl rejoins. 42,43-Millennium tie-ins. 44-Origin Quislet 3.00
37,38-Death of Superboy 2 4 6 9 11 14
45,50: 45 ($2.95, 68 pgs.)-Anniversary ish. 50-Double size ($2.50-c) 4.00
63-Final issue 4.00
Annual 1-4 (10/85-'88, 52 pgs.)-1-Crisis tie-in 3.00

NOTE: ***Byrne*** *c-36p.* ***Giffen*** *a(p)-1, 2, 50-55, 57-63, Annual 1p, 2; c-1-5p, 54p, Annual 1.* ***Orlando*** *a-6p.* ***Steacy*** *c-45-50, Annual 3.*

LEGION OF SUPER-HEROES (4th Series)
DC Comics: Nov, 1989 - No. 125, Mar, 2000 ($1.75/$1.95/$2.25)

0-(10/94)-Zero Hour restart of Legion; released between #61 & #62 2.50
1-Giffen-c/a(p)/scripts begin (4 pg.-a only #18) 4.00
2-20,26-49,51-53,55-58: 4-Mon-El (Lar Gand) destroys Time Trapper, changes reality. 5-Alt. reality story where Mordru rules all; Ferro Lad app. 6-1st app. of Laurel Gand (Lar Gand's cousin). 8-Origin. 13-Free poster by Giffen showing new costumes. 15-(2/91)-1st reference of Lar Gand as Valor. 26-New map of headquarters. 34-Six pg. preview of Timber Wolf mini-series. 40-Minor Legionnaires app. 41-(3/93)-SW6 Legion renamed Legionnaires w/new costumes and some new code-names 3.00
21-25: 21-24-Lobo & Darkseid storyline. 24-Cameo SW6 younger Legion duplicates. 25-SW6 Legion full intro. 3.50
50-($3.50, 68 pgs.) 4.00
54-($2.95)-Die-cut & foil stamped-c 4.00
59-99: 61-(9/94)-Zero Hour. 62-(11/94). 75-XS travels back to the 20th Century (cont'd in Impulse #9). 77-Origin of Brainiac 5. 81-Reintro Sun Boy. 85-Half of the Legion sent to the 20th century, Superman-c/app. 86-Final Night. 87-Deadman-c/app. 88-Impulse-c/app. Adventure Comics #247 cover swipe. 91-Forms one cover image with Legionnaires #47. 96-Wedding of Ultra Boy and Apparition. 99-Robin, Impulse, Superboy app. 2.50
100-($5.95, 96 pgs.)-Legionnaires return to the 30th Century; gatefold-c; 5 stories-art by Simonson, Davis and others 1 2 3 4 5 7
101-121: 101-Armstrong-a(p) begins. 105-Legion past & present vs. Time Trapper. 109-Moder-a. 110-Thunder joins. 114,115-Bizarro Legion. 120,121-Fatal Five. 2.50
122-124: 122,123-Coipel-c/a. 124-Coipel-c 3.00
125-Leads into "Legion Lost" maxi-series; Coipel-c 5.00
#1,000,000 (11/98) Giffen-a 2.50
Annual 1-5 (1990-1994, $3.50, 68 pgs.): 4-Bloodlines. 5-Elseworlds story 3.50
Annual 6 (1995,$3.95)-Year One story 4.00
Annual 7 (1996, $3.50, 48 pgs.)-Legends of the Dead Earth story; intro 75th Century Legion of Super-Heroes; Wildfire app. 3.50
Legion: Secret Files 1 (1/98, $4.95) Retold origin & pin-ups 5.00
Legion: Secret Files 2 (6/99, $4.95) Story and profile pages 5.00
The Beginning of Tomorrow TPB ('99, $17.95) r/post-Zero Hour reboot 18.00

NOTE: ***Giffen*** *a-1-24; breakdowns-26-32, 34-36; c-1-7, 8(part), 9-24.* ***Brandon Peterson*** *a(p)-15(1st for DC), 16, 18, Annual 2(54 pgs.); c-Annual 2p.* ***Swan/Anderson*** *c-8(part).*

LEGION: SCIENCE POLICE (See Legion of Super-Heroes)
DC Comics: Aug, 1998 - No. 4, Nov, 1998 ($2.25, limited series)

1-4-Ryan-a 2.50

LEGION WORLDS (Follows Legion Lost series)
DC Comics: Jun, 2001 - No. 6, Nov, 2001 ($3.95, limited series)

1-6-Abnett & Lanning-s; art by various. 5-Dillon-a. 6-Timber Wolf app. 4.00

LEMONADE KID, THE (See Bobby Benson's B-Bar-B Riders)
AC Comics: 1990 ($2.50, 28 pgs.)

1-Powell-c(r); Red Hawk-r by Powell; Lemonade Kid-r/Bobby Benson by Powell (2 stories) 2.50

LENNON SISTERS LIFE STORY, THE
Dell Publishing Co.: No. 951, Nov, 1958 - No. 1014, Aug, 1959

Four Color 951 (#1)-Toth-a, 32pgs, photo-c 15 30 45 107 164 220
Four Color 1014-Toth-a, photo-c 14 28 42 102 156 210

LENORE
Slave Labor Graphics: Feb, 1998 - Present ($2.95, B&W)

1-11: 1-Roman Dirge-s/a, 1,2-2nd printing 3.00
...: Noogies TPB ($11.95) r/#1-4 12.00
...: Wedgies TPB (2000, $13.95) r/#5-8 14.00

LEONARD NIMOY'S PRIMORTALS
Tekno Comix: Mar, 1995 - No. 15, May, 1996 ($1.95)

1-15: Concept by Leonard Nimoy & Isaac Asimov 1-3-w/bound-in game piece & trading card. 4-w/Teknophage Steel Edition coupon. 13,14-Art Adams-c. 15-Simonson-c 2.25

LEONARD NIMOY'S PRIMORTALS
BIG Entertainment: V2#0, June, 1996 - No. 8, Feb, 1997 ($2.25)

V2#0-8: 0-Includes Pt. 9 of "The Big Bang" x-over. 0,1-Simonson-c. 3-Kelley Jones-c 2.25

LEONARD NIMOY'S PRIMORTALS ORIGINS
Tekno Comix: Nov, 1995 - No. 2, Dec, 1995 ($2.95, limited series)

1,2: Nimoy scripts; Art Adams-c; polybagged 3.00

LEONARDO (Also see Teenage Mutant Ninja Turtles)
Mirage Studios: Dec, 1986 ($1.50, B&W, one-shot)

1 6.00

LEO THE LION
I. W. Enterprises: No date(1960s) (10¢)

1-Reprint 2 4 6 10 13 16

LEROY (Teen-age)
Standard Comics: Nov, 1949 - No. 6, Nov, 1950

1 10 20 30 60 80 100
2-Frazetta text illo. 8 16 24 43 54 65
3-6: 3-Lubbers-a 7 14 21 35 43 50

LETHAL (Also see Brigade)
Image Comics (Extreme Studios): Feb, 1996 ($2.50, unfinished limited series)

1-Marat Mychaels-c/a. 2.50

LETHAL FOES OF SPIDER-MAN (Sequel to Deadly Foes of Spider-Man)
Marvel Comics: Sept, 1993 - No. 4, Dec, 1993 ($1.75, limited series)

1-4 2.50

LETHARGIC LAD

Liberty Comics #12 © Green Pub. Co.

Liberty Meadows #27 © Frank Cho

Life Story #2 © FAW

	GD 2.0	VG 4.0	FN 6.0	VF 8.0	VF/NM 9.0	NM- 9.2

Crusade Ent.: June, 1996 - No. 3, Sept, 1996 ($2.95, B&W, limited series)
1,2 3.00
3-Alex Ross-c/swipe (Kingdom Come) 4.00
...Jumbo Sized Annual #1 (Summer 2002, $3.99) prints comic stories from internet 4.00

LETHARGIC LAD ADVENTURES
Crusade Ent./Destination Ent.#3 on: Oct, 1997 - No. 12, Sept./Oct. 1999 ($2.95, B&W)
1-12-Hyland-s/a. 9-Alex Ross sketch page & back-c 3.00

LET'S PRETEND (CBS radio)
D. S. Publishing Co.: May-June, 1950 - No. 3, Sept-Oct, 1950
1 17 34 51 98 139 180
2,3 13 26 39 74 102 130

LET'S READ THE NEWSPAPER
Charlton Press: 1974
nn-Features Quincy by Ted Sheares 1 3 4 6 8 10

LET'S TAKE A TRIP (TV) (CBS Television Presents)
Pines Comics: Spring, 1958
1-Marv Levy-c/a 5 10 15 23 28 32

LETTERS TO SANTA (See March of Comics No. 228)

LEX LUTHOR: THE UNAUTHORIZED BIOGRAPHY
DC Comics: 1989 ($3.95, 52 pgs., one-shot, squarebound)
1-Painted-c; Clark Kent app. 4.00

LEX TALIONIS: A JUNGLE TALE
Image Comics: Jan, 2004 ($5.95, one-shot, reads sideways)
1-Aneurin Wright-s/a 6.00

LIBERTY COMICS (Miss Liberty No. 1)
Green Publishing Co.: No. 5, May, '46 - No. 15, July, 1946 (MLJ & other-r)
5 (5/46)-The Prankster app; Starr-a 21 42 63 121 173 225
10-Hangman & Boy Buddies app.; reprints 3 Hangman stories, incl. Hangman #8
22 44 66 127 184 240
11(V2#2, 1/46)-Wilbur in women's clothes 18 36 54 102 146 190
12-Black Hood & Suzie app.; classic Skull-c 52 104 156 317 484 650
14,15-Patty of Airliner; Starr-a in both 14 28 42 79 110 140

LIBERTY GUARDS
Chicago Mail Order: No date (1946?)
nn-Reprints Man of War #1 with cover of Liberty Scouts #1; Gustavson-c
37 74 111 209 305 400

LIBERTY MEADOWS
Insight Studios Group/Image Comics #27 on: 1999 - Present ($2.95, B&W)
1-Frank Cho-s/a; reprints newspaper strips 3 6 9 16 20 25
2,3 2 4 6 9 11 14
4-10 1 2 3 4 5 7
11-25,27-36: 20-Adam Hughes-c. 22-Evil Brandy vs. Brandy. 27-1st Image issue, printed sideways 3.00
...: Eden Book 1 SC (Image, 2002, $14.95) r/#1-9; sketch gallery 15.00
...: Eden Book 1 SC 2nd printing (Image, 2004, $19.95) r/#1-9; sketch gallery 20.00
...: Eden Book 1 HC (Image, 2003, $24.95, with dustjacket) r/#1-9; sketch gallery 25.00
...: Creature Comforts Book 2 HC (Image, 2004, $24.95, with d.j.) r/#10-18; sketch gallery 25.00
... Sourcebook (5/04, $4.95) character info and unpublished strips 3.00
... Wedding Album (#26) (2002, $2.95) 3.00

LIBERTY PROJECT, THE
Eclipse Comics: June, 1987 - No. 8, May, 1988 ($1.75, color, Baxter paper)
1-8: 6-Valkyrie app. 2.25

LIBERTY SCOUTS (See Liberty Guards & Man of War)
Centaur Publications: No. 2, June, 1941 - No. 3, Aug, 1941
2(#1)-Origin The Fire-Man, Man of War; Vapo-Man & Liberty Scouts begin; intro Liberty Scouts; Gustavson-c/a in both 129 258 387 806 1241 1675
3(#2)-Origin & 1st app. The Sentinel 94 188 282 588 907 1225

LICENCE TO KILL (James Bond 007) (Movie)
Eclipse Comics: 1989 ($7.95, slick paper, 52 pgs.)
nn-Movie adaptation; Timothy Dalton photo-c 1 2 3 5 6 8
Limited Hardcover ($24.95) 25.00

LIDSVILLE (TV)
Gold Key: Oct, 1972 - No. 5, Oct, 1973
1-Photo-c 6 12 18 40 55 70
2-5 4 8 12 24 32 40

LIEUTENANT, THE (TV)
Dell Publishing Co.: April-June, 1964
1-Photo-c 3 7 10 21 28 35

LIEUTENANT BLUEBERRY (Also see Blueberry)
Marvel Comics (Epic Comics): 1991 - No. 3, 1991 (Graphic novel)
1,2 ($8.95)-Moebius-a in all 9.00
3 ($14.95) 15.00

LT. ROBIN CRUSOE, U.S.N. (See Movie Comics & Walt Disney Showcase #26)

LIFE EATERS, THE
DC Comics (WildStorm): 2003 ($29.95, hardcover with dust jacket)
HC-David Brin-s; Scott Hampton-painted-a/c; Norse Gods team with the Nazis 30.00
SC-(2004, $19.95) 20.00

LIFE OF CAPTAIN MARVEL, THE
Marvel Comics Group: Aug, 1985 - No. 5, Dec, 1985 ($2.00, Baxter paper)
1-5: 1-All reprint Starlin issues of Iron Man #55, Capt. Marvel #25-34 plus Marvel Feature #12 (all with Thanos). 4-New Thanos back-c by Starlin 3.00

LIFE OF CHRIST, THE
Catechetical Guild Educational Society: No. 301, 1949 (35¢, 100 pgs.)
301-Reprints from Topix(1949)-V5#11,12 9 18 27 52 66 80

LIFE OF CHRIST: THE CHRISTMAS STORY, THE
Marvel Comics/Nelson: Feb, 1993 ($2.99, slick stock)
nn 5.00

LIFE OF CHRIST: THE EASTER STORY, THE
Marvel Comics/Nelson: 1993 ($2.99, slick stock)
nn 5.00

LIFE OF CHRIST VISUALIZED
Standard Publishers: 1942 - No. 3, 1943
1-3: All came in cardboard case, each... 8 16 24 43 54 65
Case only..... 10 20 30 56 73 90

LIFE OF CHRIST VISUALIZED
The Standard Publ. Co.: 1946? (48 pgs. in color)
nn 6 12 18 28 34 40

LIFE OF ESTHER VISUALIZED
The Standard Publ. Co.: No. 2062, 1947 (48 pgs. in color)
2062 6 12 18 28 34 40

LIFE OF JOSEPH VISUALIZED
The Standard Publ. Co.: No. 1054, 1946 (48 pgs. in color)
1054 6 12 18 28 34 40

LIFE OF PAUL (See The Living Bible)

LIFE OF POPE JOHN PAUL II, THE
Marvel Comics Group: Jan, 1983 ($1.50/$1.75)
1 6.00

LIFE OF RILEY, THE (TV)
Dell Publishing Co.: No. 917, July, 1958
Four Color 917-Photo-c 12 24 36 86 131 175

LIFE ON ANOTHER PLANET
Kitchen Sink Press: 1978 (B&W, graphic novel, magazine size)
nn-Will Eisner-s/a 13.00
Reprint (DC Comics, 5/00, $12.95) 13.00

LIFE'S LIKE THAT
Croyden Publ. Co.: 1945 (25¢, B&W, 68 pgs.)
nn-Newspaper Sunday strip-r by Neher 7 14 21 35 43 50

LIFE STORIES OF AMERICAN PRESIDENTS (See Dell Giants)

LIFE STORY
Fawcett Publications: Apr, 1949 - V8#46, Jan, 1953; V8#47, Apr, 1953 (All have photo-c?)
V1#1 14 28 42 81 113 145
2 8 16 24 46 58 70
3-6, V2#7-12 8 16 24 40 50 60
V3#13-Wood-a 14 28 42 81 113 145
V3#14-18, V4#19-24, V5#25-30, V6#31-35 7 14 21 35 43 50
V6#36- "I sold drugs" on-c 8 16 24 46 58 70
V7#37,40-42, V8#44,45 6 12 18 31 38 45
V7#38, V8#43-Evans-a 7 14 21 35 43 50

Life With Archie #2 © AP

Lillith #1 © Ben Dunn

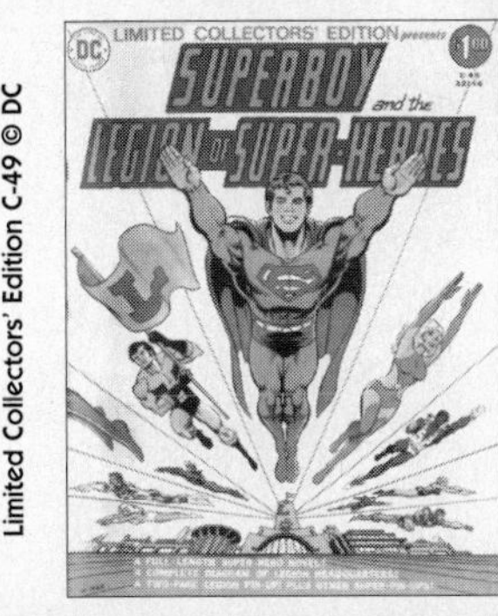

Limited Collectors' Edition C-49 © DC

	GD 2.0	VG 4.0	FN 6.0	VF 8.0	VF/NM 9.0	NM- 9.2
V7#39-Drug Smuggling & Junkie story	8	16	24	40	50	60
V8#46,47 (Scarce)	8	16	24	40	50	60

NOTE: *Powell a-13, 23, 24, 26, 28, 30, 32, 39. **Marcus Swayze** a-1-3, 10-12, 15, 16, 20, 21, 23-25, 31, 35, 37, 40, 44, 46.*

LIFE, THE UNIVERSE AND EVERYTHING (See Hitchhikers Guide to the Galaxy & Restaurant at the End of the Universe)
DC Comics: 1996 - No. 3, 1996 ($6.95, squarebound, limited series)

	GD 2.0	VG 4.0	FN 6.0	VF 8.0	VF/NM 9.0	NM- 9.2
1-3: Adaptation of novel by Douglas Adams.	1	2	3	4	5	7

LIFE WITH ARCHIE
Archie Publications: Sept, 1958 - No. 286, Sept, 1991

	GD 2.0	VG 4.0	FN 6.0	VF 8.0	VF/NM 9.0	NM- 9.2
1	28	56	84	199	305	410
2-(9/59)	14	28	42	97	149	200
3-5: 3-(7/60)	10	20	30	72	104	135
6-10	8	16	24	55	78	100
11-20	6	12	18	43	59	75
21(7/63)-30	5	10	15	33	44	55
31-41: 35,39-Horror/Sci-Fi-c	4	8	12	25	33	42
42-Pureheart begins (1st app.-c/s, 10/65)	8	16	24	53	74	95
43,44	5	10	15	36	48	60
45(1/66) 1st Man From R.I.V.E.R.D.A.L.E.	7	14	21	46	63	80
46-Origin Pureheart	5	10	15	36	48	60
47-49	4	8	12	27	36	45
50-United Three begin: Pureheart (Archie), Superteen (Betty), Captain Hero (Jughead)	5	10	15	36	48	60
51-59: 59-Pureheart ends	4	8	12	27	36	45
60-Archie band begins, ends #66	5	10	15	36	48	60
61-66: 61-Man From R.I.V.E.R.D.A.L.E.-c/s	4	8	12	24	32	40
67-80	3	6	9	16	20	24
81-99	2	4	6	14	18	22
100 (8/70), 113-Sabrina & Salem app.	3	6	9	19	25	32
101-112, 114-130(2/73), 139(11/73)-Archie Band c/s	2	4	6	10	13	16
131,134-138,140-146,148-161,164-170(6/76)	2	4	6	8	10	12
132,133,147,163-all horror-c/s	2	4	6	11	14	18
162-UFO c/s	2	4	6	11	14	18
171,173-175,177-184,186,189,191-194,196	1	2	3	5	6	8
172,185,197 : 172-(9/77)-Bi-Cent. spec. ish, 185-2nd 24th cent.-c/s, 197-Time machine/ SF-c/s	1	2	3	5	7	9
176(12/76)-1st app. Capt. Archie of Starship Rivda, in 24th century c/s; 1st app. Stella the Robot	2	4	6	11	14	18
187,188,195,198,199-all horror-c/s	1	3	4	6	8	10
190-1st Dr. Doom-c/s	1	3	4	6	8	10
200 (12/78) Maltese Pigeon-s	1	2	3	5	7	9
201-203,205-237,239,240(1/84): 208-Reintro Veronica.						6.00
204-Flying saucer-c/s	1	2	3	5	6	8
238-(9/83)-25th anniversary issue; Ol' Betsy (jalopy) replaced	1	2	3	4	5	7
241-278,280-285: 250-Comic book convention-s						5.00
279,286: 279-Intro Mustang Sally ($1.00, 7/90)						6.00

NOTE: *Gene Colan a-272-279, 285, 286. Horror/Sci-Fi-c 9, 11, 35, 39, 162.*

LIFE WITH MILLIE (Formerly A Date With Millie) (Modeling With Millie #21 on)
Atlas/Marvel Comics Group: No. 8, Dec, 1960 - No. 20, Dec, 1962

	GD 2.0	VG 4.0	FN 6.0	VF 8.0	VF/NM 9.0	NM- 9.2
8-Teenage	9	18	27	60	85	110
9-11	6	12	18	40	55	70
12-20	5	10	15	36	48	60

LIFE WITH SNARKY PARKER (TV)
Fox Feature Syndicate: Aug, 1950

	GD 2.0	VG 4.0	FN 6.0	VF 8.0	VF/NM 9.0	NM- 9.2
1-Early TV comic; photo-c from TV puppet show	28	56	84	158	229	300

LIGHT AND DARKNESS WAR, THE
Marvel Comics (Epic Comics): Oct, 1988 - No. 6, Dec, 1989 ($1.95, lim. series)

	GD 2.0	VG 4.0	FN 6.0	VF 8.0	VF/NM 9.0	NM- 9.2
1-6						2.25

LIGHT BRIGADE, THE
DC Comics: 2004 - No. 4, 2004 ($5.95, limited series)

	GD 2.0	VG 4.0	FN 6.0	VF 8.0	VF/NM 9.0	NM- 9.2
1-4-Archangels in World War II; Tomasi-s/Snejbjerg-a						6.00

LIGHT FANTASTIC, THE (Terry Pratchett's)
Innovation Publishing: June, 1992 - No. 4, Sept, 1992 ($2.50, mini-series)

	GD 2.0	VG 4.0	FN 6.0	VF 8.0	VF/NM 9.0	NM- 9.2
1-4: Adapts 2nd novel in Discworld series						2.50

LIGHT IN THE FOREST (Disney)
Dell Publishing Co.: No. 891, Mar, 1958

	GD 2.0	VG 4.0	FN 6.0	VF 8.0	VF/NM 9.0	NM- 9.2
Four Color 891-Movie, Fess Parker photo-c	9	18	27	63	89	115

LIGHTNING COMICS (Formerly Sure-Fire No. 1-3)
Ace Magazines: No. 4, Dec, 1940 - No. 13(V3#1), June, 1942

	GD 2.0	VG 4.0	FN 6.0	VF 8.0	VF/NM 9.0	NM- 9.2
4-Characters continue from Sure-Fire	100	200	300	625	963	1300
5,6: 6-Dr. Nemesis begins	68	136	204	425	655	885
V2#1-6: 2- "Flash Lightning" becomes "Lash..."	55	110	165	336	511	685
V3#1-Intro. Lightning Girl & The Sword	55	110	165	336	511	685

NOTE: ***Anderson** a-V2#6. **Mooney** c-V1#5, 6, V2#1-6, V3#1. Bondage c-V2#6. Lightning-c on all.*

LIGHTNING COMICS PRESENTS
Lightning Comics: May, 1994 ($3.50)

	GD 2.0	VG 4.0	FN 6.0	VF 8.0	VF/NM 9.0	NM- 9.2
1-Red foil-c distr. by Diamond Distr., 1-Black/yellow/blue-c distrib. by Capital Distr., 1-Red/yellow-c distributed by H. World, 1-Platinum						3.50

LI'L ... (See Little ...)

LILI
Image Comics: No. 0, 1999 ($4.95, B&W)

	GD 2.0	VG 4.0	FN 6.0	VF 8.0	VF/NM 9.0	NM- 9.2
0-Bendis & Yanover-s						5.00

LILLITH (See Warrior Nun...)
Antarctic Press: Sept, 1996 - No. 3, Feb, 1997 ($2.95, limited series)

	GD 2.0	VG 4.0	FN 6.0	VF 8.0	VF/NM 9.0	NM- 9.2
1-3: 1-Variant-c						3.00

LIMITED COLLECTORS' EDITION (See Famous First Edition, Marvel Treasury #28, Rudolph The Red-Nosed Reindeer, & Superman Vs. The Amazing Spider-Man; becomes All-New Collectors' Edition)
National Periodical Publications/DC Comics:
(#21-34,51-59: 84 pgs.; #35-41: 68 pgs.; #42-50: 60 pgs.)
C-21, Summer, 1973 - No. C-59, 1978 ($1.00) (10x13-1/2")

	GD 2.0	VG 4.0	FN 6.0	VF 8.0	VF/NM 9.0	NM- 9.2
(Rudolph...C-20 (implied), 12/72)-See Rudolph The Red-Nosed Reindeer						
C-21: Shazam (TV); r/Captain Marvel Jr. #11 by Raboy; C.C. Beck-c, biog. & photo	4	8	12	22	30	38
C-22: Tarzan; complete origin reprinted from #207-210; all Kubert-c/a; Joe Kubert biography & photo inside	3	6	9	18	24	30
C-23: House of Mystery; Wrightson, N. Adams/Orlando, G. Kane/Wood, Toth, Aragones, Sparling reprints	4	8	12	27	36	45
C-24: Rudolph The Red-Nosed Reindeer	8	16	24	53	74	95
C-25: Batman; Neal Adams-c/a(r); G.A. Joker-r; Batman/Enemy Ace-r; Novick-a(r); has photos from TV show	4	8	12	29	40	50
C-26: See Famous First Edition C-26 (same contents)						
C-27,C-29,C-31: C-27: Shazam (TV); G.A. Capt. Marvel & Mary Marvel-r; Beck-r. C-29: Tarzan; reprints "Return of Tarzan" from #219-223 by Kubert; Kubert-c. C-31: Superman; origin-r; Giordano-a; photos of George Reeves from 1950s TV show on inside b/c; Burnley, Boring-r	3	6	9	18	23	28
C-32: Ghosts (new-a)	4	8	12	25	33	42
C-33: Rudolph The Red-Nosed Reindeer(new-a)	7	14	21	50	68	85
C-34: Christmas with the Super-Heroes; unpublished Angel & Ape story by Oksner & Wood; Batman & Teen Titans-r	3	6	9	18	23	28
C-35: Shazam (TV); photo cover features TV's Captain Marvel, Jackson Bostwick; Beck-r; TV photos inside b/c	3	6	9	16	20	25
C-36: The Bible; all new adaptation beginning with Genesis by Kubert, Redondo & Mayer; Kubert-c	3	6	9	16	20	25
C-37: Batman; r-1946 Sundays; inside b/c photos of Batman TV show villains (all villain issue; r/G.A. Joker, Catwoman, Penguin, Two-Face, & Scarecrow stories plus 1946 Sundays-r)	3	6	9	19	25	32
C-38: Superman; 1 pg. N. Adams; part photo-c; photos from TV show on inside back-c	3	6	9	16	20	25
C-39: Secret Origins of Super-Villains; N. Adams-i(r); collection reprints 1950's Joker origin, Luthor origin from Adv. Comics #271, Captain Cold origin from Showcase #8 among others; G.A. Batman-r; Beck-r	3	6	9	16	20	25
C-40: Dick Tracy by Gould featuring Flattop; newspaper-r from 12/21/43 - 5/17/44; biog. of Chester Gould	3	6	9	16	20	25
C-41: Super Friends (TV); JLA-r(1965); Toth-c/a	3	6	9	18	23	28
C-42: Rudolph	5	10	15	33	44	55
C-43-C-47: C-43: Christmas with the Super-Heroes; Wrightson, S&K, Neal Adams-a. C-44: Batman; N. Adams-p(r) & G.A.-r; painted-c. C-45: More Secret Origins of Super-Villains; Flash-r/#105; G.A. Wonder Woman & Batman/Catwoman-r. C-46: Justice League of America(1963-r); 3 pgs. Toth-a C-47: Superman Salutes the Bicentennial (Tomahawk interior); 2 pgs. new-a	3	6	9	16	20	24
C-48,C-49: C-48: Superman Vs. The Flash (Superman/Flash race); swipes-c to Superman #199; r/Superman #199 & Flash #175; 6 pgs. Neal Adams-a. C-49: Superboy & the Legion of Super-Heroes	3	6	9	18	23	28
C-50: Rudolph The Red-Nosed Reindeer; contains poster (1/2 price if poster is missing)	5	10	15	33	44	55
C-51: Batman; Neal Adams-c/a	3	6	9	18	24	30
C-52,C-57: C-52: The Best of DC; Neal Adams-c/a; Toth, Kubert-a. C-57: Welcome Back,						

Li'l Abner Comics #62 © TOBY

Little Ambrose #1 © AP

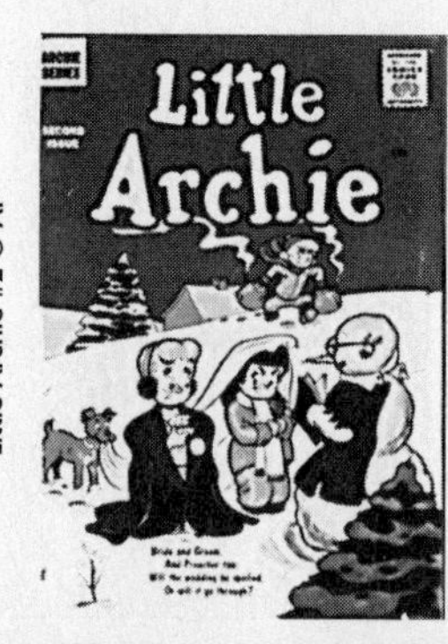

Little Archie #2 © AP

	GD 2.0	VG 4.0	FN 6.0	VF 8.0	VF/NM 9.0	NM- 9.2
Kotter-r(TV)(5/78) includes unpublished #11	3	6	9	16	20	25
C-59: Batman's Strangest Cases; N. Adams-r; Wrightson-r/Swamp Thing #7; N. Adams/Wrightson-c	3	6	9	16	20	25

NOTE: *All-r with exception of some special features and covers.* ***Aparo*** *a-52r; c-37.* ***Grell*** *c-49.* ***Infantino*** *a-25, 39, 44, 45, 52.* ***Bob Kane*** *r-25.* ***Robinson*** *r-25, 44.* ***Sprang*** *r-44. Issues #21-31, 35-39, 45, 48 have back cover cut-outs.*

LINDA (Everybody Loves...) (Phantom Lady No. 5 on)
Ajax-Farrell Publ. Co.: Apr-May, 1954 - No. 4, Oct-Nov, 1954

	GD	VG	FN	VF	VF/NM	NM-
1-Kamenish-a	16	32	48	89	127	165
2-Lingerie panel	13	26	39	74	102	130
3,4	10	20	30	58	77	95

LINDA CARTER, STUDENT NURSE
Atlas Comics (AMI): Sept, 1961 - No. 9, Jan, 1963

	GD	VG	FN	VF	VF/NM	NM-
1-Al Hartley-c	6	12	18	38	52	65
2-9	4	8	12	25	33	42

LINDA LARK
Dell Publishing Co.: Oct-Dec, 1961 - No. 8, Aug-Oct, 1963

	GD	VG	FN	VF	VF/NM	NM-
1	4	8	12	22	30	38
2-8	3	6	9	16	20	24

LINUS, THE LIONHEARTED (TV)
Gold Key: Sept, 1965

	GD	VG	FN	VF	VF/NM	NM-
1 (10155-509)	10	20	30	67	96	125

LION, THE (See Movie Comics)

LIONHEART
Awesome Comics: Sept, 1999 - No. 2 ($2.99/$2.50)

	GD	VG	FN	VF	VF/NM	NM-
1-Ian Churchill-story/a, Jeph Loeb-s; Coven app.						3.00
2-Flip book w/Coven #4						2.50

LION OF SPARTA (See Movie Classics)

LIPPY THE LION AND HARDY HAR HAR (TV)
Gold Key: Mar, 1963 (12¢) (See Hanna-Barbera Band Wagon #1)

	GD	VG	FN	VF	VF/NM	NM-
1 (10049-303)	11	22	33	75	110	145

LISA COMICS (TV)(See Simpsons Comics)
Bongo Comics: 1995 ($2.25)

	GD	VG	FN	VF	VF/NM	NM-
1-Lisa in Wonderland						3.00

LI'L ABNER (See Comics on Parade, Sparkle, Sparkler Comics, Tip Top Comics & Tip Topper)
United Features Syndicate: 1939 - 1940

	GD	VG	FN	VF	VF/NM	NM-
Single Series 4 ('39)	75	150	225	469	722	975
Single Series 18 ('40) (#18 on inside, #2 on-c)	60	120	180	375	580	785

LI'L ABNER (Al Capp's; continued from Comics on Parade #58)
Harvey Publ. No. 61-69 (2/49)/Toby Press No. 70 on: No. 61, Dec, 1947 - No. 97, Jan, 1955 (See Oxydol-Dreft in Promotional Comics section)

	GD	VG	FN	VF	VF/NM	NM-
61(#1)-Wolverton & Powell-a	35	70	105	201	293	385
62-65: 63-The Wolf Girl app. 65-Powell-a	21	42	63	121	173	225
66,67,69,70	19	38	57	107	154	200
68-Full length Fearless Fosdick-c/story	20	40	60	115	165	215
71-74,76,80	15	30	45	86	123	160
75,77-79,86,91-All with Kurtzman art; 86-Sadie Hawkins Day. 91-r/#77	19	38	57	107	154	200
81-85,87-90,92-94,96,97: 83-Evil-Eye Fleegle & Double Whammy app. 88-Cousin Weakeyes goes hunting. 94-Six lessons from Adam Lazonga. 96-Football issue	15	30	45	83	117	150
95-Full length Fearless Fosdick story	16	32	48	92	131	170

LI'L ABNER
Toby Press: 1951

	GD	VG	FN	VF	VF/NM	NM-
1	19	38	57	107	154	200

LI'L ABNER'S DOGPATCH (See Al Capp's...)

LITTLE AL OF THE F.B.I.
Ziff-Davis Publications: No. 10, 1950 (no month) - No. 11, Apr-May, 1951 (Saunders painted-c)

	GD	VG	FN	VF	VF/NM	NM-
10(1950)	17	34	51	95	135	175
11(1951)	14	28	42	79	110	140

LITTLE AL OF THE SECRET SERVICE
Ziff-Davis Publications: No. 10, 7-8/51; No, 2, 9-10/51; No. 3, Winter, 1951 (Saunders painted-c)

	GD	VG	FN	VF	VF/NM	NM-
10(#1)	17	34	51	95	135	175
2,3	14	28	42	79	110	140

LITTLE AMBROSE
Archie Publications: September, 1958

	GD	VG	FN	VF	VF/NM	NM-
1-Bob Bolling-c	15	30	45	83	117	150

LITTLE ANGEL
Standard (Visual Editions)/Pines: No. 5, Sept, 1954; No. 6, Sept, 1955 - No. 16, Sept, 1959

	GD	VG	FN	VF	VF/NM	NM-
5-Last pre-code issue	8	16	24	40	50	60
6-16	5	10	15	24	30	35

LITTLE ANNIE ROONEY (Also see Henry)
David McKay Publ.: 1935 (25¢, B&W dailies, 48 pgs.)(10"x10", cardboard-c)

	GD	VG	FN	VF	VF/NM	NM-
Book 1-Daily strip-r by Darrell McClure	40	80	120	230	335	440

LITTLE ANNIE ROONEY (See King Comics & Treasury of Comics)
David McKay/St. John/Standard: 1938; Aug, 1948 - No. 3, Oct, 1948

	GD	VG	FN	VF	VF/NM	NM-
Feature Books 11 (McKay, 1938)	40	80	120	230	335	440
1 (St. John)	16	32	48	92	131	170
2,3	9	18	27	54	70	85

LITTLE ARCHIE (The Adventures of... #13-on) (See Archie Giant Series Mag. #527, 534, 538, 545, 549, 556, 560, 566, 570, 583, 594, 596, 607, 609, 619)
Archie Publications: 1956 - No. 180, Feb, 1983 (Giants No. 3-84)

	GD	VG	FN	VF	VF/NM	NM-
1-(Scarce)	55	110	165	468	759	1050
2 (1957)	26	52	78	187	286	385
3-5: 3-(1958)-Bob Bolling-c & giant issues begin	15	30	45	107	164	220
6-10	11	22	33	80	120	160
11-22 (84 pgs.): 18,20,22-Horror/Sci-Fi-c	9	18	27	60	85	110
23-39 (68 pgs.)	7	14	21	46	63	80
40 (Fall/66)-Intro. Little Pureheart-c/s (68 pgs.)	7	14	21	51	71	90
41,44-Little Pureheart (68 pgs.)	6	12	18	43	59	75
42-Intro The Little Archies Band, ends #66 (68 pgs.)	7	14	21	50	68	85
43-1st Boy From R.I.V.E.R.D.A.L.E. (68 pgs.)	7	14	21	46	63	80
45-58 (68pgs.)	5	10	15	33	44	55
59 (68pgs.)-Little Sabrina begins	9	18	27	60	85	110
60-66 (68 pgs.)	4	8	12	28	38	48
67(9/71)-84: 84-Last 52pg. Giant-Size (2/74)	3	6	9	18	24	30
85-99	2	4	6	10	12	15
100	2	4	6	11	14	18
101-112,114-116,118-129	1	2	3	5	7	9
113,117,130: 113-Halloween Special issue(12/76). 117-Donny Osmond-c cameo 130-UFO cover (5/78)	2	4	6	8	10	12
131-150(1/80), 180(Last issue, 2/83)	1	2	3	4	5	7
151-179						5.00
...In Animal Land 1 (1957)	13	26	39	90	138	185
...In Animal Land 17 (Winter, 1957-58)-19 (Summer,1958)-Formerly Li'l Jinx	8	16	24	53	74	95
Archie Classics - The Adventures of Little Archie Vol. 1 TPB (2004, $10.95) reprints						11.00

NOTE: *Little Archie Band app. 42-66. Little Sabrina in 59-78,80-180*

LITTLE ARCHIE CHRISTMAS SPECIAL (See Archie Giant Series #581)

LITTLE ARCHIE COMICS DIGEST ANNUAL (...Magazine #5 on)
Archie Publications: 10/77 - No. 48, 5/91 (Digest-size, 128 pgs., later issues $1.35-$1.50)

	GD	VG	FN	VF	VF/NM	NM-
1(10/77)-Reprints	3	6	9	18	23	28
2(4/78,3(11/78)-Neal Adams-a. 3-The Fly-r by S&K	3	6	9	16	20	24
4(4/79) - 10	2	4	6	10	13	16
11-20	1	3	4	6	8	10
21-30: 28-Christmas-c	1	2	3	4	5	7
31-48: 40,46-Christmas-c						5.00

NOTE: *Little Archie, Little Jinx, Little Jughead & Little Sabrina in most issues.*

LITTLE ARCHIE DIGEST MAGAZINE
Archie Comics: July, 1991 - No. 21, Mar, 1998 ($1.50/$1.79/$1.89, digest size, bi-annual)

	GD	VG	FN	VF	VF/NM	NM-
V2#1						6.00
2-10						3.50
11-21						2.50

LITTLE ARCHIE MYSTERY
Archie Publications: Aug, 1963 - No. 2, Oct, 1963 (12¢ issues)

	GD	VG	FN	VF	VF/NM	NM-
1	12	24	36	84	127	170
2	7	14	21	50	68	85

LITTLE ASPIRIN (See Little Lenny & Wisco)
Marvel Comics (CnPC): July, 1949 - No. 3, Dec, 1949 (52 pgs.)

	GD	VG	FN	VF	VF/NM	NM-
1-Oscar app.; Kurtzman-a (4 pgs.)	17	34	51	98	139	180
2-Kurtzman-a (4 pgs.)	10	20	30	58	77	95
3-No Kurtzman-a	8	16	24	43	54	65

Little Audrey TV Funtime #1 © HARV

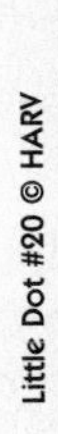

Little Dot #20 © HARV

Little Eva #3 © STJ

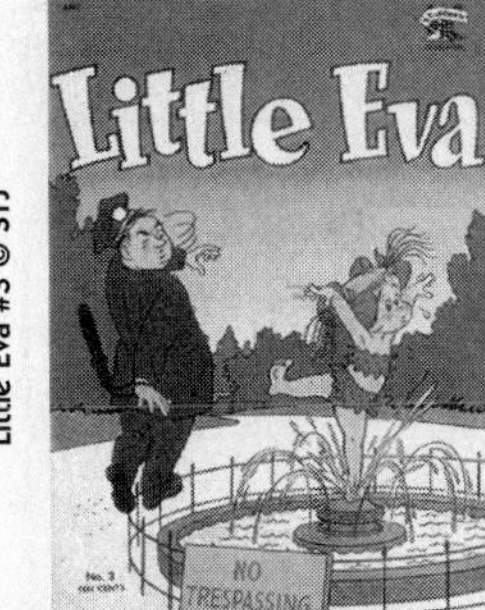

LITTLE AUDREY (Also see Playful...)
St. John Publ.: Apr, 1948 - No. 24, May, 1952

	GD 2.0	VG 4.0	FN 6.0	VF 8.0	VF/NM 9.0	NM- 9.2
1-1st app. Little Audrey	44	88	132	268	409	550
2	25	50	75	144	207	270
3-5	17	34	51	95	135	175
6-10	12	24	36	71	98	125
11-20: 16-X-Mas-c	9	18	27	54	70	85
21-24	8	16	24	46	58	70

LITTLE AUDREY (See Harvey Hits #11, 19)
Harvey Publications: No. 25, Aug, 1952 - No. 53, April, 1957

	GD 2.0	VG 4.0	FN 6.0	VF 8.0	VF/NM 9.0	NM- 9.2
25-(Paramount Pictures Famous Star... on-c); 1st Harvey Casper and Baby Huey (1 month earlier than Harvey Comic Hits #60(9/52))	14	28	42	97	149	200
26-30: 26-28-Casper app.	8	16	24	55	78	100
31-40: 32-35-Casper app.	7	14	21	46	63	80
41-53	5	10	15	33	44	55
...Clubhouse 1 (9/61, 68 pg. Giant)-New stories & reprints	9	18	27	65	93	120

LITTLE AUDREY
Harvey Comics: Aug, 1992 - No. 8, July, 1994 ($1.25/$1.50)

	GD 2.0	VG 4.0	FN 6.0	VF 8.0	VF/NM 9.0	NM- 9.2
V2#1						3.00
2-8						2.25

LITTLE AUDREY (...Yearbook)
St. John Publishing Co.: 1950 (50¢, 260 pgs.)

	GD 2.0	VG 4.0	FN 6.0	VF 8.0	VF/NM 9.0	NM- 9.2
Contains 8 complete 1949 comics rebound; Casper, Alice in Wonderland, Little Audrey, Abbott & Costello, Pinocchio, Moon Mullins, Three Stooges (from Jubilee), Little Annie Rooney app. (Rare)	67	134	201	419	647	875

(Also see All Good & Treasury of Comics)

NOTE: *This book contains remaindered St. John comics; many variations possible.*

LITTLE AUDREY & MELVIN (Audrey & Melvin No. 62)
Harvey Publications: May, 1962 - No. 61, Dec, 1973

	GD 2.0	VG 4.0	FN 6.0	VF 8.0	VF/NM 9.0	NM- 9.2
1	10	20	30	73	107	140
2-5	6	12	18	40	55	70
6-10	5	10	15	33	44	55
11-20	3	6	9	19	25	32
21-40: 22-Richie Rich app.	3	6	9	16	20	24
41-50,55-61	2	4	6	11	14	18
51-54: All 52 pg. Giants	3	6	9	16	20	24

LITTLE AUDREY TV FUNTIME
Harvey Publ.: Sept, 1962 - No. 33, Oct, 1971 (#1-31: 68 pgs.; #32,33: 52 pgs.)

	GD 2.0	VG 4.0	FN 6.0	VF 8.0	VF/NM 9.0	NM- 9.2
1-Richie Rich app.	10	20	30	73	107	140
2,3: Richie Rich app.	6	12	18	43	59	75
4,5: 5-25¢ & 35¢ issues exist	6	12	18	38	52	65
6-10	4	8	12	24	32	40
11-20	3	6	9	16	21	26
21-33	2	4	6	14	18	22

LITTLE BAD WOLF (Disney; seeWalt Disney's C&S #52, Walt Disney Showcase #21 & Wheaties)
Dell Publishing Co.: No. 403, June, 1952 - No. 564, June, 1954

	GD 2.0	VG 4.0	FN 6.0	VF 8.0	VF/NM 9.0	NM- 9.2
Four Color 403 (#1)	8	16	24	58	82	105
Four Color 473 (6/53), 564	6	12	18	38	52	65

LITTLE BEAVER
Dell Publishing Co.: No. 211, Jan, 1949 - No. 870, Jan, 1958 (All painted-c)

	GD 2.0	VG 4.0	FN 6.0	VF 8.0	VF/NM 9.0	NM- 9.2
Four Color 211('49)-All Harman-a	10	20	30	67	96	125
Four Color 267,294,332(5/51)	6	12	18	38	52	65
3(10-12/51)-8(1-3/53)	5	10	15	36	48	60
Four Color 483(8-10/53),529	5	10	15	33	44	55
Four Color 612,660,695,744,817,870	5	10	15	33	44	55

LITTLE BIT
Jubilee/St. John Publishing Co.: Mar, 1949 - No. 2, June, 1949

	GD 2.0	VG 4.0	FN 6.0	VF 8.0	VF/NM 9.0	NM- 9.2
1	9	18	27	54	70	85
2	7	14	21	37	46	55

LITTLE DOT (See Humphrey, Li'l Max, Sad Sack, and Tastee-Freez Comics)
Harvey Publications: Sept, 1953 - No. 164, Apr, 1976

	GD 2.0	VG 4.0	FN 6.0	VF 8.0	VF/NM 9.0	NM- 9.2
1-Intro./1st app. Richie Rich & Little Lotta	177	354	531	1106	1703	2300
2-1st app. Freckles & Pee Wee (Richie Rich's poor friends)	63	126	189	394	610	825
3	44	88	132	268	409	550
4	40	80	120	233	342	450
5-Origin dots on Little Dot's dress	44	88	132	268	409	550
6-Richie Rich, Little Lotta, & Little Dot all on cover; 1st Richie Rich cover featured	44	88	132	268	409	550
7-10: 9-Last pre-code issue (1/55)	26	52	78	147	211	275
11-20	17	34	51	98	139	180
21-30	12	24	36	69	95	120
31-40	10	20	30	56	73	90
41-50	8	16	24	43	54	65
51-60	7	14	21	37	46	55
61-80	4	8	12	25	33	42
81-100	3	6	9	19	25	32
101-141	3	6	9	16	20	24
142-145: All 52 pg. Giants	3	6	9	18	23	28
146-164	2	4	6	10	13	16

NOTE: *Richie Rich & Little Lotta in all.*

LITTLE DOT
Harvey Comics: Sept, 1992 - No. 7, June, 1994 ($1.25/$1.50)

	GD 2.0	VG 4.0	FN 6.0	VF 8.0	VF/NM 9.0	NM- 9.2
V2#1-Little Dot, Little Lotta, Richie Rich in all						3.00
2-7 ($1.50)						2.50

LITTLE DOT DOTLAND (Dot Dotland No. 62, 63)
Harvey Publications: July, 1962 - No. 61, Dec, 1973

	GD 2.0	VG 4.0	FN 6.0	VF 8.0	VF/NM 9.0	NM- 9.2
1-Richie Rich begins	12	24	36	84	127	170
2,3	7	14	21	50	68	85
4,5	6	12	18	43	59	75
6-10	5	10	15	33	44	55
11-20	4	8	12	22	33	38
21-30	3	6	9	18	23	28
31-50	3	6	9	16	20	24
51-54: All 52 pg. Giants	3	6	9	18	23	28
55-61	2	4	6	10	13	16

LITTLE DOT'S UNCLES & AUNTS (See Harvey Hits No. 4, 13, 24)
Harvey Enterprises: Oct, 1961; No. 2, Aug, 1962 - No. 52, Apr, 1974

	GD 2.0	VG 4.0	FN 6.0	VF 8.0	VF/NM 9.0	NM- 9.2
1-Richie Rich begins; 68 pgs. begin	14	28	42	97	149	200
2,3	8	16	24	55	78	100
4,5	6	12	18	43	59	75
6-10	5	10	15	36	48	60
11-20	4	8	12	25	33	42
21-37: Last 68 pg. issue	3	6	9	18	24	30
38-52: All 52 pg. Giants	3	6	9	16	20	24

LITTLE DRACULA
Harvey Comics: Jan, 1992 - No. 3, May, 1992 ($1.25, quarterly, mini-series)

	GD 2.0	VG 4.0	FN 6.0	VF 8.0	VF/NM 9.0	NM- 9.2
1-3						3.00

LITTLE ENDLESS STORYBOOK, THE (See The Sandman titles)
DC Comics: 2001 ($5.95, Prestige format, one-shot)

	GD 2.0	VG 4.0	FN 6.0	VF 8.0	VF/NM 9.0	NM- 9.2
nn-Jill Thompson-s/painted-a/c; puppy Barnabas searches for Delirium						20.00

LITTLE EVA
St. John Publishing Co.: May, 1952 - No. 31, Nov, 1956

	GD 2.0	VG 4.0	FN 6.0	VF 8.0	VF/NM 9.0	NM- 9.2
1	16	32	48	89	127	165
2	9	18	27	52	66	80
3-5	8	16	24	40	50	60
6-10	7	14	21	35	43	50
11-31	6	12	18	31	38	45
3-D 1,2(10/53, 11/53, 25¢)-Both came w/glasses. 1-Infinity-c	23	46	69	130	188	245
I.W. Reprint #1-3,6-8: 1-r/Little Eva #28. 2-r/Little Eva #29. 3-r/Little Eva #24	2	4	6	9	11	14
Super Reprint #10,12('63),14,16,18('64): 18-r/Little Eva #25.	2	4	6	9	11	14

LI'L GENIUS (Formerly Super Brat; Summer Fun No. 54) (See Blue Bird & Giant Comics #3)
Charlton Comics: 1954 - No. 52, 1/65; No. 53, 10/65; No. 54, 10/85 - No. 55, 1/86

	GD 2.0	VG 4.0	FN 6.0	VF 8.0	VF/NM 9.0	NM- 9.2
5(#1?)	11	22	33	66	88	110
6-10	7	14	21	37	46	55
11-15,19,20	6	12	18	29	36	42
16,17-(68 pgs.)	8	16	24	40	50	60
18-(100 pgs., 10/58)	11	22	33	63	84	105
21-35	3	6	9	18	23	28
36-53	2	4	6	11	14	18
54,55 (Low print)						5.00

LI'L GHOST

Little Lizzie #2 © MAR

Little Lotta #3 © HARV

Little Lulu #221 © Marjorie Buell

	GD 2.0	VG 4.0	FN 6.0	VF 8.0	VF/NM 9.0	NM- 9.2

St. John Publ. Co./Fago No. 1 on: 2/58; No. 2,1/59 - No. 3, Mar, 1959

	GD	VG	FN	VF	VF/NM	NM-
1(St. John)	9	18	27	52	66	80
2,3	6	12	18	28	34	40

LITTLE GIANT COMICS
Centaur Publications: 7/38 - No. 3, 10/38; No. 4, 2/39 (132 pgs.) (6-3/4x4-1/2")

	GD	VG	FN	VF	VF/NM	NM-
1-B&W with color-c; stories, puzzles, magic	67	134	201	419	647	875
2,3-B&W with color-c	55	110	165	340	520	700
4 (6-5/8x9-3/8")(68 pgs., B&W inside)	55	110	165	340	520	700

NOTE: *Filchock c-2, 4.* ***Gustavson*** *a-1.* ***Pinajian*** *a-4.* ***Bob Wood*** *a-1.*

LITTLE GIANT DETECTIVE FUNNIES
Centaur Publ.: Oct, 1938; No. 4, Jan, 1939 (6-3/4x4-1/2", 132 pgs., B&W)

	GD	VG	FN	VF	VF/NM	NM-
1-B&W with color-c	77	154	231	481	741	1000
4(1/39, B&W; color-c; 68 pgs., 6-1/2x9-1/2")-Eisner-r	55	110	165	340	520	700

LITTLE GIANT MOVIE FUNNIES
Centaur Publ.: Aug, 1938 - No. 2, Oct, 1938 (6-3/4x4-1/2", 132 pgs., B&W)

	GD	VG	FN	VF	VF/NM	NM-
1-Ed Wheelan's "Minute Movies" reprints	77	154	231	481	741	1000
2-Ed Wheelan's "Minute Movies" reprints	55	110	165	340	520	700

LITTLE GROUCHO (...the Red-Headed Tornado; ...Grouchy No. 2)
Reston Publ. Co.: No. 16; Feb-Mar, 1955 - No. 2, June-July, 1955 (See Tippy Terry)

	GD	VG	FN	VF	VF/NM	NM-
16, 1 (2-3/55)	8	16	24	43	54	65
2(6-7/55)	6	12	18	27	33	38

LITTLE HIAWATHA (Disney; see Walt Disney's C&S #143)
Dell Publishing Co.: No. 439, Dec, 1952 - No. 988, May-July, 1959

	GD	VG	FN	VF	VF/NM	NM-
Four Color 439 (#1)	7	14	21	46	63	80
Four Color 787 (4/57), 901 (5/58), 988	6	12	18	38	52	65

LITTLE IKE
St. John Publishing Co.: April, 1953 - No. 4, Oct, 1953

	GD	VG	FN	VF	VF/NM	NM-
1	10	20	30	56	73	90
2	6	12	18	31	38	45
3,4	5	10	15	24	30	35

LITTLE IODINE (See Giant Comic Album)
Dell Publ. Co.: No. 224, 4/49 - No. 257, 1949: 3-5/50 - No. 56, 4-6/62 (1-4-52pgs.)

	GD	VG	FN	VF	VF/NM	NM-
Four Color 224-By Jimmy Hatlo	12	24	36	84	127	170
Four Color 257	9	18	27	63	89	115
1(3-5/50)	10	20	30	73	107	140
2-5	6	12	18	38	52	65
6-10	4	8	12	28	38	48
11-20	4	8	12	22	30	38
21-30: 27-Xmas-c	3	7	10	21	28	35
31-40	3	6	9	18	24	30
41-56	3	6	9	16	20	24

LITTLE JACK FROST
Avon Periodicals: 1951

	GD	VG	FN	VF	VF/NM	NM-
1	10	20	30	60	80	100

LI'L JINX (Little Archie in Animal Land #17) (Also see Pep Comics #62)
Archie Publications: No. 11, Nov, 1956 - No. 16, Sept, 1957

	GD	VG	FN	VF	VF/NM	NM-
11-By Joe Edwards; "First Issue" on cover	13	26	39	74	102	130
12(1/57)-16	10	20	30	56	73	90

LI'L JINX (See Archie Giant Series Magazine No. 223)

LI'L JINX CHRISTMAS BAG (See Archie Giant Series Mag. No. 195, 206, 219)

LI'L JINX GIANT LAUGH-OUT (See Archie Giant Series Mag. No. 176, 185)
Archie Publications: No. 33, Sept, 1971 - No. 43, Nov, 1973 (52 pgs.)

	GD	VG	FN	VF	VF/NM	NM-
33-43 (52 pgs.)	2	4	6	12	16	20

LITTLE JOE (See Popular Comics & Super Comics)
Dell Publishing Co.: No. 1, 1942

	GD	VG	FN	VF	VF/NM	NM-
Four Color 1	50	100	150	400	625	850

LITTLE JOE
St. John Publishing Co.: Apr, 1953

	GD	VG	FN	VF	VF/NM	NM-
1	5	10	15	24	30	35

LI'L KIDS (Also see Li'l Pals)
Marvel Comics Group: 8/70 - No. 2, 10/70; No. 3, 11/71 - No. 12, 6/73

	GD	VG	FN	VF	VF/NM	NM-
1	7	14	21	50	68	85
2-9	4	8	12	27	36	45
10-12-Calvin app.	4	8	12	29	40	50

LITTLE KING
Dell Publishing Co.: No. 494, Aug, 1953 - No. 677, Feb, 1956

	GD	VG	FN	VF	VF/NM	NM-
Four Color 494 (#1)	10	20	30	73	107	140
Four Color 597, 677	6	12	18	43	59	75

LITTLE LANA (Formerly Lana)
Marvel Comics (MjMC): No. 8, Nov, 1949; No. 9, Mar, 1950

	GD	VG	FN	VF	VF/NM	NM-
8,9	9	18	27	54	70	85

LITTLE LENNY
Marvel Comics (CDS): June, 1949 - No. 3, Nov, 1949

	GD	VG	FN	VF	VF/NM	NM-
1-Little Aspirin app.	12	24	36	69	95	120
2,3	8	16	24	40	50	60

LITTLE LIZZIE
Marvel Comics (PrPI)/Atlas (OMC): 6/49 - No. 5, 4/50; 9/53 - No. 3, Jan, 1954

	GD	VG	FN	VF	VF/NM	NM-
1	13	26	39	74	102	130
2-5	8	16	24	43	54	65
1 (9/53, 2nd series by Atlas)-Howie Post-c	9	18	27	49	62	75
2,3	7	14	21	35	43	50

LITTLE LOTTA (See Harvey Hits No. 10)
Harvey Publications: 11/55 - No. 110, 11/73; No. 111, 9/74 - No. 120, 5/76
V2#1, Oct, 1992 - No. 4, July, 1993 ($1.25)

	GD	VG	FN	VF	VF/NM	NM-
1-Richie Rich (r) & Little Dot begin	34	68	102	255	403	550
2,3	16	32	48	116	178	240
4,5	11	22	33	77	114	150
6-10	8	16	24	58	82	105
11-20	6	12	18	43	59	75
21-40	4	8	12	25	33	42
41-60	3	7	10	21	28	35
61-80: 62-1st app. Nurse Jenny	3	6	9	16	20	25
81-99	2	4	6	11	14	18
100-103: All 52 pg. Giants	2	4	6	14	18	22
104-120	1	3	4	6	8	10
V2#1-4 (1992-93)						3.00

NOTE: *No. 121 was advertised, but never released.*

LITTLE LOTTA FOODLAND
Harvey Publications: 9/63 - No. 14, 10/67; No. 15, 10/68 - No. 29, Oct, 1972

	GD	VG	FN	VF	VF/NM	NM-
1-Little Lotta, Little Dot, Richie Rich, 68 pgs. begin	13	26	39	92	141	190
2,3	9	18	27	63	89	115
4,5	7	14	21	46	63	80
6-10	5	10	15	36	48	60
11-20	3	7	10	21	28	35
21-26: 26-Last 68 pg. issue	3	6	9	16	21	26
27,28: Both 52 pgs.	2	4	6	14	18	22
29-(36 pgs.)	2	4	6	9	11	14

LITTLE LULU (Formerly Marge's Little Lulu)
Gold Key 207-257/Whitman 258 on: No. 207, Sept, 1972 - No. 268, Mar, 1984

	GD	VG	FN	VF	VF/NM	NM-
207,209,220-Stanley-r. 207-1st app. Henrietta	2	4	6	12	16	20
208,210-219: 208-1st app. Snobbly, Wilbur's butler	2	4	6	10	12	15
221-240,242-249, 250(r/#166), 251-254(r/#206)	1	2	3	5	7	9
241,263-Stanley-r	1	3	4	6	8	10
255-257(Gold Key): 256-r/#212	1	2	3	5	6	8
258,259,262,264(2/82),265(3/82) (Whitman)	2	4	6	8	10	12
260-(9/80)(Whitman pre-pack only - low distribution)	15	30	45	109	167	225
261-(11/80)(Whitman pre-pack only)	4	8	12	24	32	40
266-268 (All #90028 on-c; no date, no date code; 3-pack): 266(7/83). 267(8/83). 268(3/84)-Stanley-r	2	4	6	14	18	22

LITTLE MARY MIXUP (See Comics On Parade)
United Features Syndicate: No. 10, 1939, - No. 26, 1940

	GD	VG	FN	VF	VF/NM	NM-
Single Series 10, 26	36	72	108	204	297	390

LITTLE MAX COMICS (Joe Palooka's Pal; see Joe Palooka)
Harvey Publications: Oct, 1949 - No. 73, Nov, 1961

	GD	VG	FN	VF	VF/NM	NM-
1-Infinity-c; Little Dot begins; Joe Palooka on-c	22	44	66	127	184	240
2-Little Dot app.; Joe Palooka on-c	12	24	36	69	95	120
3-Little Dot app.; Joe Palooka on-c	10	20	30	56	73	90
4-10: 5-Little Dot app., 1pg.	8	16	24	43	54	65
11-20	7	14	21	37	46	55
21-40: 23-Little Dot app. 38-r/#20	6	12	18	29	36	42
41-62,66	3	6	9	19	25	32
63-65,67-73-Include new five pg. Richie Rich stories. 70-73-Little Lotta app.	3	6	9	19	25	32

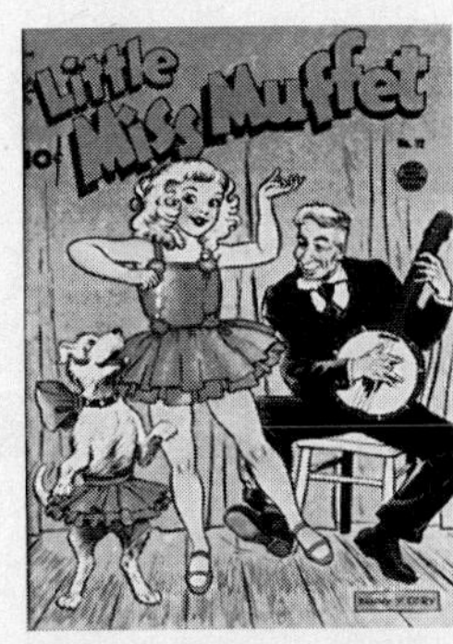

Little Miss Muffet #12 © STD

Little Orphan Annie Four Color #107 © NYNS

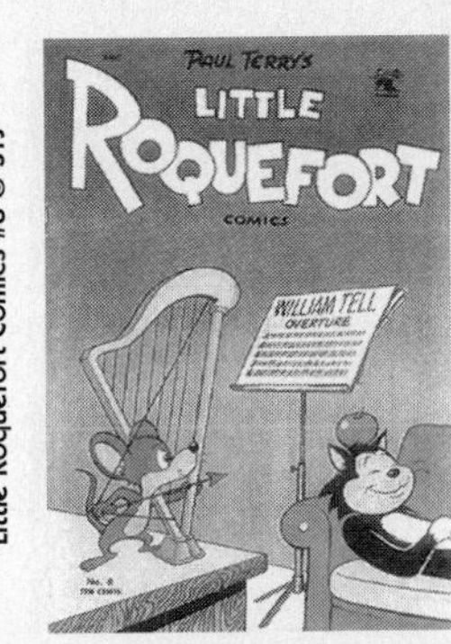

Little Roquefort Comics #8 © STJ

LI'L MENACE
Fago Magazine Co.: Dec, 1958 - No. 3, May, 1959

	GD 2.0	VG 4.0	FN 6.0	VF 8.0	VF/NM 9.0	NM- 9.2
1-Peter Rabbit app.	8	16	24	46	58	70
2-Peter Rabbit (Vincent Fago's)	7	14	21	35	43	50
3	6	12	18	28	34	40

LITTLE MERMAID, THE (Walt Disney's...; also see Disney's...)
W. D. Publications (Disney): 1990 (no date given)($5.95, no ads, 52 pgs.)

	GD 2.0	VG 4.0	FN 6.0	VF 8.0	VF/NM 9.0	NM- 9.2
nn-Adapts animated movie	1	2	3	4	5	7
nn-Comic version ($2.50)						3.00

LITTLE MERMAID, THE
Disney Comics: 1992 - No. 4, 1992 ($1.50, mini-series)

	GD 2.0	VG 4.0	FN 6.0	VF 8.0	VF/NM 9.0	NM- 9.2
1-4: Based on movie						3.00
1-4: 2nd printings sold at Wal-Mart w/different-c						2.25

LITTLE MISS MUFFET
Best Books (Standard Comics)/King Features Synd.: No. 11, Dec, 1948 - No. 13, March, 1949

	GD 2.0	VG 4.0	FN 6.0	VF 8.0	VF/NM 9.0	NM- 9.2
11-Strip reprints; Fanny Cory-c/a	8	16	24	43	54	65
12,13-Strip reprints; Fanny Cory-c/a	6	12	18	28	34	40

LITTLE MISS SUNBEAM COMICS
Magazine Enterprises/Quality Bakers of America: June-July, 1950 - No. 4, Dec-Jan, 1950-51

	GD 2.0	VG 4.0	FN 6.0	VF 8.0	VF/NM 9.0	NM- 9.2
1	17	34	51	95	135	175
2-4	10	20	30	56	73	90
...Advs. In Space ('55)	7	14	21	35	43	50

LITTLE MONSTERS, THE (See March of Comics #423, Three Stooges #17)
Gold Key: Nov, 1964 - No. 44, Feb, 1978

	GD 2.0	VG 4.0	FN 6.0	VF 8.0	VF/NM 9.0	NM- 9.2
1	7	14	21	46	63	80
2	4	8	12	24	32	40
3-10	3	6	9	19	25	32
11-20	3	6	9	16	21	26
21-30	2	4	6	12	16	20
31-44: 20,34-39,43-Reprints	2	4	6	9	11	14

LITTLE MONSTERS (Movie)
Now Comics: 1989 - No. 6, June, 1990 ($1.75)

	GD 2.0	VG 4.0	FN 6.0	VF 8.0	VF/NM 9.0	NM- 9.2
1-6: Photo-c from movie						2.25

LITTLE NEMO (See Cocomalt, Future Comics, Help, Jest, Kayo, Punch, Red Seal, & Superworld; most by Winsor McCay Jr., son of famous artist) (Other McCay books: see Little Sammy Sneeze & Dreams of the Rarebit Fiend)

LITTLE NEMO (...in Slumberland)
McCay Features/Nostalgia Press('69): 1945 (11x7-1/4", 28 pgs., B&W)

	GD 2.0	VG 4.0	FN 6.0	VF 8.0	VF/NM 9.0	NM- 9.2
1905 & 1911 reprints by Winsor McCay	10	20	30	58	77	95
1969-70 (Exact reprint)	2	4	6	10	12	15

LITTLE ORPHAN ANNIE (See Annie, Famous Feature Stories, Marvel Super Special, Merry Christmas..., Popular Comics, Super Book #7, 11, 23 & Super Comics)

LITTLE ORPHAN ANNIE
David McKay Publ./Dell Publishing Co.: No. 7, 1937 - No. 3, Sept-Nov, 1948; No. 206, Dec, 1948

	GD 2.0	VG 4.0	FN 6.0	VF 8.0	VF/NM 9.0	NM- 9.2
Feature Books(McKay) 7-(1937) (Rare)	96	192	288	600	925	1250
Four Color 12(1941)	43	86	129	344	535	725
Four Color 18(1943)-Flag-c	37	74	111	278	432	585
Four Color 52(1944)	30	60	90	213	327	440
Four Color 76(1945)	25	50	75	181	278	375
Four Color 107(1946)	22	44	66	155	238	320
Four Color 152(1947)	14	28	42	102	156	210
1(3-5/48)-r/strips from 5/7/44 to 7/30/44	14	28	42	102	156	210
2-r/strips from 7/21/40 to 9/9/40	10	20	30	73	107	140
3-r/strips from 9/10/40 to 11/9/40	10	20	30	73	107	140
Four Color 206(12/48)	9	18	27	60	85	110

LI'L PALS (Also see Li'l Kids)
Marvel Comics Group: Sept, 1972 - No. 5, May, 1973

	GD 2.0	VG 4.0	FN 6.0	VF 8.0	VF/NM 9.0	NM- 9.2
1	6	12	18	43	59	75
2-5	4	8	12	27	36	45

LI'L PAN (Formerly Rocket Kelly; becomes Junior Comics with #9)
Fox Features Syndicate: No. 6, Dec-Jan, 1946-47 - No. 8, Apr-May, 1947
(Also see Wotalife Comics)

	GD 2.0	VG 4.0	FN 6.0	VF 8.0	VF/NM 9.0	NM- 9.2
6	10	20	30	56	73	90
7,8: 7-Atomic bomb story; robot-c	8	16	24	40	50	60

LITTLE PEOPLE (Also see Darby O'Gill & the...)
Dell Publishing Co.: No. 485, Aug-Oct, 1953 - No. 1062, Dec, 1959
(Walt Scott's)

	GD 2.0	VG 4.0	FN 6.0	VF 8.0	VF/NM 9.0	NM- 9.2
Four Color 485 (#1)	9	18	27	60	85	110
Four Color 573(7/54), 633(6/55)	5	10	15	36	48	60
Four Color 692(3/56),753(11/56),809(7/57),868(12/57),908(5/58), 959(12/58), 1062	5	10	15	36	48	60

LITTLE RASCALS
Dell Publishing Co.: No. 674, Jan, 1956 - No. 1297, Mar-May, 1962

	GD 2.0	VG 4.0	FN 6.0	VF 8.0	VF/NM 9.0	NM- 9.2
Four Color 674 (#1)	10	20	30	70	100	130
Four Color 778(3/57),825(8/57)	7	14	21	46	63	80
Four Color 883(3/58),936(9/58),974(3/59),1030(9/59),1079(2-4/60),1137(9-11/60)	7	14	21	46	63	80
Four Color 1174(3-5/61),1224(10-12/61),1297	6	12	18	38	52	65

LI'L RASCAL TWINS (Formerly Nature Boy)
Charlton Comics: No. 6, 1957 - No. 18, Jan, 1960

	GD 2.0	VG 4.0	FN 6.0	VF 8.0	VF/NM 9.0	NM- 9.2
6-Li'l Genius & Tomboy in all	6	12	18	29	36	42
7-18: 7-Timmy the Timid Ghost app.	4	8	12	18	22	25

LITTLE RED HOT: (CHANE OF FOOLS)
Image Comics: Feb, 1999 - No. 3, Apr, 1999 ($2.95/$3.50, B&W, limited series)

	GD 2.0	VG 4.0	FN 6.0	VF 8.0	VF/NM 9.0	NM- 9.2
1-3-Dawn Brown-s/a. 2,3-($3.50-c)						3.50
The Foolish Collection TPB ($12.95) r/#1-3						13.00

LITTLE RED HOT: BOUND
Image Comics: July, 2001 - No. 3, Nov, 2001 ($2.95, color, limited series)

	GD 2.0	VG 4.0	FN 6.0	VF 8.0	VF/NM 9.0	NM- 9.2
1-3-Dawn Brown-s/a.						3.00

LITTLE ROQUEFORT COMICS (See Paul Terry's Comics #105)
St. John Publishing Co.(all pre-code)/Pines No. 10: June, 1952 - No. 9, Oct, 1953; No. 10, Summer, 1958

	GD 2.0	VG 4.0	FN 6.0	VF 8.0	VF/NM 9.0	NM- 9.2
1-By Paul Terry	10	20	30	56	73	90
2	6	12	18	31	38	45
3-10: 10-CBS Television Presents on-c	5	10	15	24	30	35

LITTLE SAD SACK (See Harvey Hits No. 73, 76, 79, 81, 83)
Harvey Publications: Oct, 1964 - No. 19, Nov, 1967

	GD 2.0	VG 4.0	FN 6.0	VF 8.0	VF/NM 9.0	NM- 9.2
1-Richie Rich app. on cover only	6	12	18	38	52	65
2-10	3	6	9	19	25	32
11-19	3	6	9	16	20	25

LITTLE SCOUTS
Dell Publishing Co.: No. 321, Mar, 1951 - No. 587, Oct, 1954

	GD 2.0	VG 4.0	FN 6.0	VF 8.0	VF/NM 9.0	NM- 9.2
Four Color #321 (#1, 3/51)	4	8	12	29	40	50
2(10-12/51) - 6(10-12/52)	3	7	10	21	28	35
Four Color #462,506,550,587	3	7	10	21	28	35

LITTLE SHOP OF HORRORS SPECIAL (Movie)
DC Comics: Feb, 1987 ($2.00, 68 pgs.)

	GD 2.0	VG 4.0	FN 6.0	VF 8.0	VF/NM 9.0	NM- 9.2
1-Colan-c/a						4.00

LITTLE SPUNKY
I. W. Enterprises: No date (1963?) (10¢)

	GD 2.0	VG 4.0	FN 6.0	VF 8.0	VF/NM 9.0	NM- 9.2
1-r/Frisky Fables #1	2	4	6	9	11	14

LITTLE STOOGES, THE (The Three Stooges' Sons)
Gold Key: Sept, 1972 - No. 7, Mar, 1974

	GD 2.0	VG 4.0	FN 6.0	VF 8.0	VF/NM 9.0	NM- 9.2
1-Norman Maurer cover/stories in all	4	8	12	24	32	40
2-7	3	6	9	16	20	24

LITTLEST OUTLAW (Disney)
Dell Publishing Co.: No. 609, Jan, 1955

	GD 2.0	VG 4.0	FN 6.0	VF 8.0	VF/NM 9.0	NM- 9.2
Four Color 609-Movie, photo-c	8	16	24	53	74	95

LITTLEST SNOWMAN, THE
Dell Publishing Co.: No. 755, 12/56; No. 864, 12/57; 12-2/1963-64

	GD 2.0	VG 4.0	FN 6.0	VF 8.0	VF/NM 9.0	NM- 9.2
Four Color #755,864, 1(1964)	6	12	18	40	55	70

LI'L TOMBOY (Formerly Fawcett's Funny Animals; see Giant Comics #3)
Charlton Comics: V14#92, Oct, 1956; No. 93, Mar, 1957 - No. 107, Feb, 1960

	GD 2.0	VG 4.0	FN 6.0	VF 8.0	VF/NM 9.0	NM- 9.2
V14#92	5	10	15	24	30	35
93-107: 97-Atomic Bunny app.	5	10	14	20	24	28

LI'L WILLIE COMICS (Formerly & becomes Willie Comics #22 on)
Marvel Comics (MgPC): No. 20, July, 1949 - No. 21, Sept, 1949

	GD 2.0	VG 4.0	FN 6.0	VF 8.0	VF/NM 9.0	NM- 9.2
20,21: 20-Little Aspirin app.	11	22	33	62	84	105

LITTLE WOMEN (See Power Record Comics)

Lobo Unbound #1 © DC

Loki #1 © MAR

Lone Ranger #38 © Lone Ranger Inc.

	GD 2.0	VG 4.0	FN 6.0	VF 8.0	VF/NM 9.0	NM- 9.2

LIVE IT UP
Spire Christian Comics (Fleming H. Revell Co.): 1973, 1976 (39-49 cents)
nn 1 3 4 6 8 11

LIVING BIBLE, THE
Living Bible Corp.: Fall, 1945 - No. 3, Spring, 1946
1-The Life of Paul; all have L. B. Cole-c 40 80 120 236 351 465
2-Joseph & His Brethren; Jonah & the Whale 30 60 90 173 249 325
3-Chaplains At War (classic-c) 40 80 120 241 363 485

LOBO
Dell Publishing Co.: Dec, 1965; No. 2, Oct, 1966
1-1st black character to have his own title 4 8 12 24 32 40
2 3 6 9 18 24 30

LOBO (Also see Action #650, Adventures of Superman, Demon (2nd series), Justice League, L.E.G.I.O.N., Mister Miracle, Omega Men #3 & Superman #41)
DC Comics: Nov, 1990 - No. 4, Feb, 1991 ($1.50, color, limited series)
1-(99¢)-Giffen plots/Breakdowns in all 4.00
1-2nd printing 2.50
2-4: 2-Legion '89 spin-off. 1-4 have Bisley painted covers & art 2.50
...: Blazing Chain of Love 1 (9/92, $1.50)-Denys Cowan-c/a; Alan Grant scripts, ...Convention Special 1 (1993, $1.75), ...Paramilitary Christmas Special 1 (1991, $2.39, 52 pgs.) -Bisley-c/a, ...: Portrait of a Victim 1 (1993, $1.75) 2.50

LOBO (Also see Showcase '95 #9)
DC Comics: Dec, 1993 - No. 64, Jul, 1999 ($1.75/$1.95/$2.25/$2.50, mature)
1 ($2.95)-Foil enhanced-c; Alan Grant scripts begin 3.00
2-9,0,10-64: 2-7-Alan Grant scripts. 9-(9/94). 0-(10/94)-Origin retold. 50-Lobo vs. the DCU. 58-Giffen-a 2.50
#1,000,000 (11/98) 853rd Century x-over 2.50
Annual 1 (1993, $3.50, 68 pgs.)-Bloodlines x-over 3.50
Annual 2 (1994, $3.50)-21 artists (20 listed on-c); Alan Grant script; Elseworlds story 3.50
Annual 3 (1995, $3.95)-Year One story 4.00
...Big Babe Spring Break Special (Spr, '95, $1.95)-Balent-a 2.50
...Bounty Hunting for Fun and Profit ('95)-Bisley-c 5.00
... Chained (5/97, $2.50)-Alan Grant story 2.50
.../Deadman: The Brave And The Bald (2/95, $3.50) 3.50
.../Demon: Helloween (12/96, $2.25)-Giarrano-a 2.50
...Fragtastic Voyage 1 ('97, $5.95)-Mejia painted-c/a 6.00
...Gallery (9/95, $3.50)-pin-ups. 3.50
...In the Chair 1 (8/94, $1.95, 36 pgs.), ...I Quit-(12/95, $2.25) 2.50
.../Judge Dredd ('95, $4.95). 5.00
...Lobocop 1 (2/94, $1.95)-Alan Grant scripts; painted-c 2.50

LOBO: (Title Series), DC Comics
--A CONTRACT ON GAWD, 4/94 - 7/94 (mature) 1-4: Alan Grant scripts. 3-Groo cameo 2.50
--DEATH AND TAXES, 10/96 - No. 4, 1/97, 1-4-Giffen/Grant scripts 2.50
--GOES TO HOLLYWOOD, 8/96 ($2.25), 1-Grant scripts 2.50
--INFANTICIDE, 10/92 - 1/93 ($1.50, mature), 1-4-Giffen-c/a; Grant scripts 2.50
--/ MASK, 2/97 - No. 2, 3/97 ($5.95), 1,2 6.00
--'S BACK, 5/92 - No. 4, 11/92 ($1.50, mature), 1-4: 1-Has 3 outer covers. Bisley painted-c 1,2; a-1-3. 3-Sam Kieth-c; all have Giffen plots/breakdown & Grant scripts 2.50
Trade paperback (1993, $9.95)-r/1-4 10.00
--THE DUCK, 6/97 ($1.95), 1-A. Grant-s/V. Semeiks & R. Kryssing-a 2.50
--UNAMERICAN GLADIATORS, 6/93 - No. 4, 9/93 ($1.75, mature), 1-4-Mignola-c; Grant/Wagner scripts 2.50
--UNBOUND, 8/03 - No. 6, 5/04 ($2.95), 1-6-Giffen-s/Horley-c/a. 4-6-Ambush Bug app. 3.00

LOCKE!
Blackthorne Publishing: 1987 - No. 3, ($1.25, limited series)
1-3 2.25

LOCO (Magazine) (Satire)
Satire Publications: Aug, 1958 - V1#3, Jan, 1959
V1#1-Chic Stone-a 9 18 27 51 62 75
V1#2,3-Severin-a, 2 pgs. Davis; 3-Heath-a 7 14 21 35 43 50

LOGAN: PATH OF THE WARLORD
Marvel Comics: Feb, 1996 ($5.95, one-shot)
1-John Paul Leon-a 6.00

LOGAN: SHADOW SOCIETY
Marvel Comics: 1996 ($5.95, one-shot)
1 6.00

LOGAN'S RUN
Marvel Comics Group: Jan, 1977 - No. 7, July, 1977
1: 1-5-Based on novel & movie 1 3 4 6 8 10
2-5,7: 6,7-New stories adapted from novel 6.00
6-1st Thanos (also see Iron Man #55) solo story (back-up) by Zeck (6/77) 3 6 9 16 20 25
6-(35¢-c variant, limited distribution) 4 8 12 22 30 38
7-(35¢-c variant, limited distribution) 1 2 3 5 7 9
NOTE: *Austin a-6i. Gulacy c-6. Kane c-7p. Perez a-1-5p; c-1-5p. Sutton a-6p, 7p.*

LOIS & CLARK, THE NEW ADVENTURES OF SUPERMAN
DC Comics: 1994 ($9.95, one-shot)
1-r/Man of Steel #2, Superman Ann. 1, Superman #9 & 11, Action #600 & 655, Adventures of Superman #445, 462 & 466 1 3 4 6 8 10

LOIS LANE (Also see Daring New Adventures of Supergirl, Showcase #9,10 & Superman's Girlfriend...)
DC Comics: Aug, 1986 - No. 2, Sept, 1986 ($1.50, 52 pgs.)
1,2-Morrow-c/a in each 4.00

LOKI (Thor)
Marvel Comics: Sept, 2004 - No. 4, Nov, 2004 ($3.50)
1-4-Rodi-s/Ribic-a/c 3.50

LOLLY AND PEPPER
Dell Publishing Co.: No. 832, Sept, 1957 - July, 1962
Four Color 832(#1) 4 8 12 29 40 50
Four Color 940,978,1086,1206 3 7 10 21 28 35
01-459-207 (7/62) 3 6 9 19 25 32

LOMAX (See Police Action)

LONDON'S DARK
Escape/Titan: 1989 ($8.95, B&W, graphic novel)
nn-James Robinson script; Paul Johnson-c/a 1 2 3 5 7 9

LONE
Dark Horse Comics: Sept, 2003 - No. 6, Mar, 2004 ($2.99)
1-6-Stuart Moore-s/Jerome Opeña-a/Templesmith-c 3.00

LONE EAGLE (The Flame No. 5 on)
Ajax/Farrell Publications: Apr-May, 1954 - No. 4, Oct-Nov, 1954
1 13 26 39 74 102 130
2-4: 3-Bondage-c 9 18 27 52 66 80

LONE GUNMEN, THE (From the X-Files)
Dark Horse Comics: June, 2001 ($2.99, one-shot)
1-Paul Lee-a; photo-c 3.00

LONELY HEART (Formerly Dear Lonely Hearts; Dear Heart #15 on)
Ajax/Farrell Publ. (Excellent Publ.): No. 9, Mar, 1955 - No. 14, Feb, 1956
9-Kamenesque-a; (Last precode) 10 20 30 56 73 90
10-14 7 14 21 37 46 55

LONE RANGER, THE (See Ace Comics, Aurora, Dell Giants, Future Comics, Golden Comics Digest #48, King Comics, Magic Comics & March of Comics #165, 174, 193, 208, 225, 238, 310, 322, 338, 350)

LONE RANGER, THE
Dell Publishing Co.: No. 3, 1939 - No. 167, Feb, 1947
Large Feature Comic 3(1939)-Heigh-Yo Silver; text with illus. by Robert Weisman; also exists as a Whitman #710 131 262 393 819 1260 1700
Large Feature Comic 7(1939)-Illustr. by Henry Vallely; Hi-Yo Silver the Lone Ranger to the Rescue; also exists as a Whitman #715 125 250 375 781 1203 1625
Feature Book 21(1940), 24(1941) 81 162 243 506 778 1050
Four Color 82(1945) 40 80 120 300 468 635
Four Color 98(1945),118(1946) 31 62 93 225 355 485
Four Color 125(1946),136(1947) 23 46 69 163 249 335
Four Color 151,167(1947) 20 40 60 141 216 290

LONE RANGER, THE (Movie, radio & TV; Clayton Moore starred as Lone Ranger in the movies; No. 1-37: strip reprints)(See Dell Giants)
Dell Publishing Co.: Jan-Feb, 1948 - No. 145, May-July, 1962
1 (36 pgs.)-The Lone Ranger, his horse Silver, companion Tonto & his horse Scout begin 53 106 159 451 726 1000
2 (52 pgs. begin, end #41) 30 60 90 218 334 450
3-5 23 46 69 165 253 340
6,7,9,10 19 38 57 136 208 280
8-Origin retold; Indian back-c begin, end #35 23 46 69 163 249 335

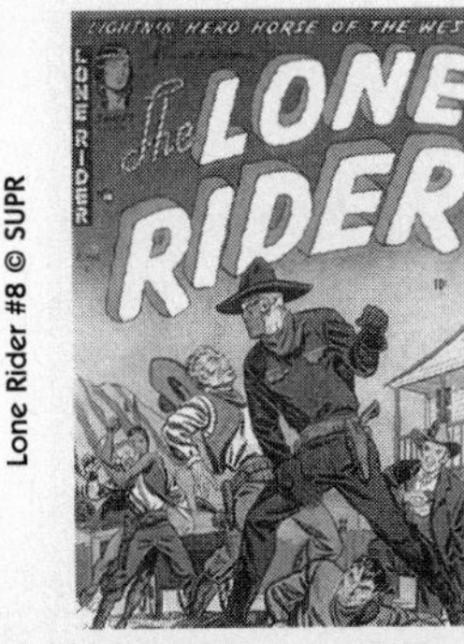

Lone Rider #8 © SUPR

Lone Wolf 2100 #1 © DH

Looney Tunes #100 © WB

GD VG FN VF VF/NM NM-
2.0 4.0 6.0 8.0 9.0 9.2

11-20: 11- "Young Hawk" Indian boy serial begins, ends #145
14 28 42 97 149 200
21,22,24-31: 51-Reprint. 31-1st Mask logo 11 22 33 80 120 160
23-Origin retold 14 28 42 102 156 210
32-37: 32-Painted-c begin. 36-Animal photo back-c begin, end #49. 37-Last newspaper-r issue; new outfit; red shirt becomes blue; most known copies show the blue shirt on-c & inside 10 20 30 70 100 130
37-Variant issue; Long Ranger wears a red shirt on-c and inside. A few copies of the red shirt outfit were printed before catching the mistake and changing the color to blue (rare)
18 36 54 126 193 260
38-41 (All 52 pgs.) 38-Paul S. Newman-s (wrote most of the stories #38-on)
10 20 30 70 100 130
42-50 (36 pgs.) 8 16 24 58 82 105
51-74 (52 pgs.): 56-One pg. origin story of Lone Ranger & Tonto. 71-Blank inside-c
8 16 24 55 78 100
75,77-99: 79-X-mas-c 7 14 21 51 71 90
76-Classic flag-c 8 16 24 55 78 100
100 9 18 27 60 85 110
101-111: Last painted-c 7 14 21 50 68 85
112-Clayton Moore photo-c begin, end #145 20 40 60 141 216 290
113-117: 117-10¢ &15¢-c exist 11 22 33 80 120 160
118-Origin Lone Ranger, Tonto, & Silver retold; Special anniversary issue
25 50 75 177 271 365
119-140: 139-Fran Striker-s 10 20 30 73 107 140
141-145 11 22 33 77 114 150

NOTE: ***Hank Hartman*** *painted c(signed)-65, 66, 70, 75, 82; unsigned-64?, 67-69?, 71, 72, 73?, 74?, 76-78, 80, 81, 83-91, 92?, 93-111.* ***Ernest Nordli*** *painted c(signed)-42, 50, 52, 53, 56, 59, 60; unsigned-39-41, 44-49, 51, 54, 55, 57, 58, 61-63?*

LONE RANGER, THE
Gold Key (Reprints in #13-20): 9/64 - No. 16, 12/69; No. 17, 11/72; No. 18, 9/74 - No. 28, 3/77

1-Retells origin 7 14 21 50 68 85
2 4 8 12 25 33 42
3-10: Small Bear-r in #6-12. 10-Last 12¢ issue 4 8 12 22 30 38
11-17 3 6 9 16 21 26
18-28 2 4 6 12 16 20
Golden West 1(30029-610, 10/66)-Giant; r/most Golden West #3 including Clayton Moore photo front/back-c 8 16 24 55 78 100

LONE RANGER AND TONTO, THE
Topps Comics: Aug, 1994 - No. 4, Nov, 1994 ($2.50, limited series)

1-4: 3-Origin of Lone Ranger; Tonto leaves; Lansdale story, Truman-c/a in all. 2.50
1-4: Silver logo. 1-Signed by Lansdale and Truman 6.00
Trade paperback (1/95, $9.95) 10.00

LONE RANGER'S COMPANION TONTO, THE (TV)
Dell Publishing Co.: No. 312, Jan, 1951 - No. 33, Nov-Jan/58-59 (All painted-c)

Four Color 312(#1, 1/51) 11 22 33 80 120 160
2(8-10/51),3: (#2 titled "Tonto") 7 14 21 46 63 80
4-10 6 12 18 40 55 70
11-20 5 10 15 36 48 60
21-33 4 8 12 29 40 50

NOTE: ***Ernest Nordli*** *painted c(signed)-2, 7; unsigned-3-6, 8-11, 12?, 13, 14, 18?, 22-24? See Aurora Comic Booklets.*

LONE RANGER'S FAMOUS HORSE HI-YO SILVER, THE (TV)
Dell Publishing Co.: No. 369, Jan, 1952 - No. 36, Oct-Dec, 1960 (All painted-c, most by Sam Savitt) (Lone Ranger appears in most issues)

Four Color 369(#1)-Silver's origin as told by The Lone Ranger
11 22 33 77 114 150
Four Color 392(#2, 4/52) 6 12 18 43 59 75
3(7-9/52)-10(4-6/52) 6 12 18 38 52 65
11-36 5 10 15 33 44 55

LONE RIDER (Also see The Rider)
Superior Comics(Farrell Publ.): Apr, 1951 - No. 26, Jul, 1955 (#3-on: 36 pgs.)

1 (52 pgs.)-The Lone Rider & his horse Lightnin' begin; Kamenish-a begins
31 62 93 178 259 340
2 (52 pgs.)-The Golden Arrow begins (origin) 16 32 48 92 131 170
3-6: 6-Last Golden Arrow 15 30 45 86 123 160
7-Golden Arrow becomes Swift Arrow; origin of his shield
16 32 48 92 131 170
8-Origin Swift Arrow 17 34 51 98 139 180
9,10 10 20 30 60 80 100
11-14 9 18 27 51 62 75
15-Golden Arrow origin-r from #2, changing name to Swift Arrow
10 20 30 56 73 90
16-20,22-26: 23-Apache Kid app. 8 16 24 43 54 65
21-3-D effect-c 16 32 48 92 131 170

LONE WOLF AND CUB
First Comics: May, 1987 - No. 45, Apr, 1991 ($1.95-$3.25, B&W, deluxe size)

1-Frank Miller-c & intro.; reprints manga series by Koike & Kojima
1 2 3 6 8 10
1-2nd print, 3rd print, 2-2nd print 3.25
2-12: 6-72 pgs. origin issue 5.50
13-38,40: 40-Ploog-c 4.00
39-($5.95, 120 pgs.)-Ploog-c 6.50
41-44: 41-($3.95, 84 pgs.)-Ploog-c. 42-Ploog-c 6.00
45-Last issue; low print 1 2 3 5 6 8
Deluxe Edition ($19.95, B&W) 20.00

NOTE: ***Sienkiewicz*** *c-13-24.* ***Matt Wagner*** *c-25-30.*

LONE WOLF AND CUB (Trade paperbacks)
Dark Horse Comics: Aug, 2000 - No. 28 ($9.95, B&W, 4" x 6", approx. 300 pgs.)

1-Collects First Comics reprint series; Frank Miller-c 18.00
1-(2nd printing) 12.00
1-(3rd-5th printings) 10.00
2,3-(1st printings) 12.00
2,3-(2nd printings) 10.00
4-28 10.00

LONE WOLF 2100 (Also see Reveal)
Dark Horse Comics: May, 2002 - No. 11, Dec, 2003 ($2.99, color)

1-New homage to Lone Wolf and Cub; Kennedy-s/Velasco-a 4.00
2-11 3.00
...: The Red File (1/03, $2.99) character and story background files 3.00
... Vol. 1 - Shadows on Saplings TPB (2003, $12.95, 6" x 9") r/#1-4 13.00
... Vol. 2 - The Language of Chaos TPB (2003, $12.95, 6" x 9") r/#5-8, Dirty Tricks short story from Reveal 13.00

LONG BOW (...Indian Boy)(See Indians & Jumbo Comics #141)
Fiction House Mag. (Real Adventures Publ.): 1951 - No. 9, Wint, 1952/53

1-Most covers by Maurice Whitman 17 34 51 95 135 175
2 10 20 30 58 77 95
3-9 9 18 27 52 66 80

LONG HOT SUMMER, THE
DC Comics (Milestone): Jul, 1995 - No. 3, Sept, 1995 ($2.95/$2.50, lim. series)

1-3: 1-($2.95-c). 2,3-($2.50-c) 3.00

LONG JOHN SILVER & THE PIRATES (Formerly Terry & the Pirates)
Charlton Comics: No. 30, Aug, 1956 - No. 32, March, 1957 (TV)

30-32: Whitman-c 10 20 30 56 73 90

LONGSHOT (Also see X-Men, 2nd Series #10)
Marvel Comics: Sept, 1985 - No. 6, Feb, 1986 (60¢, limited series)

1-6: 1-Art Adams/Whilce Portacio-c/a in all. 4-Spider-Man app. 6-Double size
1 2 3 4 5 7
Trade Paperback (1989, $16.95)-r/#1-6 17.00

LONGSHOT
Marvel Comics: Feb, 1998 ($3.99, one-shot)

1-DeMatteis-s/Zulli-a 4.00

LOONEY TUNES (2nd Series) (TV)
Gold Key/Whitman: April, 1975 - No. 47, June, 1984

1-Reprints 4 8 12 24 32 40
2-10: 2,4-reprints 2 4 6 12 16 20
11-20: 16-reprints 2 4 6 9 11 14
21-30 1 2 3 5 7 9
31,32,36-42(2/82) 1 2 3 4 5 7
33-(8/80)-35 (Whitman pre-pack only, scarce) 3 6 9 16 20 24
43(4/82),44(6/83) (low distribution) 2 4 6 9 11 14
45-47 (All #90296 on-c; nd, nd code, pre-pack) 45(8/83), 46(3/84), 47(6/84)
2 4 6 14 18 22

LOONEY TUNES (3rd Series) (TV)
DC Comics: Apr, 1994 - Present ($1.50/$1.75/$1.95/$1.99/$2.25)

1-10,120: 1-Marvin Martian-c/sty; Bugs Bunny, Roadrunner, Daffy begin. 120-($2.95-C) 3.00
11-119,121: 23-34-($1.75-c). 35-43-($1.95-c). 44-Begin $1.99-c. 83-Giffen-s. 93-Begin $2.25-c.
100-Art by various incl. Kyle Baker, Marie Severin, Darwyn Cooke, Jill Thompson 2.25
...Back In Action Movie Adaptation (12/03, $3.95) photo-c 4.00

LOONEY TUNES AND MERRIE MELODIES COMICS ("Looney Tunes" #166(8/55) on)

Looney Tunes and Merrie Melodies #10 © WB

Lorna, the Jungle Girl #7 © MAR

Lost in Space #1 © New Line

(Also see Porky's Duck Hunt)
Dell Publishing Co.: 1941 - No. 246, July-Sept, 1962

	GD 2.0	VG 4.0	FN 6.0	VF 8.0	VF/NM 9.0	NM- 9.2
1-Porky Pig, Bugs Bunny, Daffy Duck, Elmer Fudd, Mary Jane & Sniffles, Pat Patsy and Pete begin (1st comic book app. of each). Bugs Bunny story by Win Smith (early Mickey Mouse artist)	1000	2000	3000	7500	12,250	17,000
2 (11/41)	142	284	426	1207	1954	2700
3-Kandi the Cave Kid begins by Walt Kelly; also in #4-6,8,11,15	105	210	315	893	1447	2000
4-Kelly-a	105	210	315	893	1447	2000
5-Bugs Bunny The Super-Duper Rabbit story (1st funny animal super hero, 3/42; also see Coo Coo); Kelly-a	82	164	246	697	1124	1550
6,8-Kelly-a	59	118	177	502	814	1125
7,9,10: 9-Painted-c. 10-Flag-c	50	100	150	407	641	875
11,15-Kelly-a; 15-X-Mas-c	50	100	150	407	641	875
12-14,16-19	40	80	120	300	468	635
20-25: Pat, Patsy & Pete by Walt Kelly in all	33	66	99	248	387	525
26-30	25	50	75	181	278	375
31-40: 33-War bond-c. 39-X-Mas-c	21	42	63	152	234	315
41-50	16	32	48	112	171	230
51-60	12	24	36	87	134	180
61-80	9	18	27	63	89	115
81-99: 87-X-Mas-c	8	16	24	53	74	95
100	8	16	24	58	82	105
101-120	7	14	21	46	63	80
121-150	6	12	18	38	52	65
151-200: 159-X-Mas-c	5	10	15	33	44	55
201-240	4	8	12	29	40	50
241-246	5	10	15	33	44	55

LOONY SPORTS (Magazine)
3-Strikes Publishing Co.: Spring, 1975 (68 pgs.)

	GD 2.0	VG 4.0	FN 6.0	VF 8.0	VF/NM 9.0	NM- 9.2
1-Sports satire	2	4	6	9	11	14

LOOSE CANNON (Also see Action Comics Annual #5 & Showcase '94 #5)
DC Comics: June, 1995 - No. 4, Sept, 1995 ($1.75, limited series)

1-4: Adam Pollina-a. 1-Superman app. 2.50

LOOY DOT DOPE
United Features Syndicate: No. 13, 1939

	GD 2.0	VG 4.0	FN 6.0	VF 8.0	VF/NM 9.0	NM- 9.2
Single Series 13	31	62	93	177	256	335

LORD JIM (See Movie Comics)

LORD PUMPKIN
Malibu Comics (Ultraverse): Oct, 1994 ($2.50, one-shot)

0-Two covers 2.50

LORD PUMPKIN/NECROMANTRA
Malibu Comics (Ultraverse): Apr, 1995 - No. 4, July, 1995 ($2.95, limited series, flip book)

1-4 3.00

LORDS OF MISRULE
Dark Horse Comics: Jan, 1997 - No. 6, Jun, 1997 ($2.95, B&W, limited series)

1-6: 1-Wraparound-c 3.00

LORDS OF THE ULTRA-REALM
DC Comics: June, 1986 - No. 6, Nov, 1986 (Mini-series)

1-6, Special 1(12/87, $2.25) 2.25

LORNA THE JUNGLE GIRL (...Jungle Queen #1-5)
Atlas Comics (NPI 1/OMC 2-11/NPI 12-26): July, 1953 - No. 26, Aug, 1957

	GD 2.0	VG 4.0	FN 6.0	VF 8.0	VF/NM 9.0	NM- 9.2
1-Origin & 1st app.	40	80	120	230	335	440
2-Intro. & 1st app. Greg Knight	20	40	60	112	161	210
3-5	17	34	51	98	139	180
6-11: 11-Last pre-code (1/55)	14	28	42	79	110	140
12-17,19-26: 14-Colletta & Maneely-c	11	22	33	64	87	110
18-Williamson/Colletta-c	12	24	36	69	95	120

NOTE: ***Brodsky** c-1-3, 5, 9. **Everett** c-21, 23-26. **Heath** c-6, 7. **Maneely** c-12, 15. **Romita** a-20, 22, 24, 26. **Shores** a-14-16, 24, 26; c-11, 13, 16. **Tuska** a-6.*

LOSERS
DC Comics (Vertigo): Aug, 2003 - Present ($2.95)

1-Andy Diggle-s/Jock-a 4.00
2-18: 15-Bagged with Sky Captain CD 3.00
...: Ante Up TPB (2004, $9.95) r/#1-6 10.00
...: Double Down TPB (2004, $12.95) r/#7-12 13.00

LOSERS SPECIAL (See Our Fighting Forces #123)(Also see G.I. Combat & Our Fighting Forces)

DC Comics: Sept, 1985 ($1.25, one-shot)

1-Capt. Storm, Gunner & Sarge; Crisis x-over 5.00

LOST, THE
Chaos! Comics: Dec, 1997 - No. 3 ($2.95, B&W, unfinished limited series)

1-3-Andreyko-script: 1-Russell back-c 3.00

LOST CONTINENT
Eclipse Int'l: Sept, 1990 - No. 6, 1991 ($3.50, B&W, squarebound, 60 pgs.)

1-6: Japanese story translated to English 3.50

LOST HEROES
Davdez Arts: Mar, 1998 - No. 4 ($2.95)

0-4-Rob Prior-s/painted-a 3.00

LOST IN SPACE (Movie)
Dark Horse Comics: Apr, 1998 - No. 3, July, 1998 ($2.95, limited series)

1-3-Continuation of 1998 movie; Erskine-c 3.00

LOST IN SPACE (TV)(Also see Space Family Robinson)
Innovation Publishing: Aug, 1991 - No. 12, Jan, 1993 ($2.50, limited series)

1-12: Bill Mumy (Will Robinson) scripts in #1-9. 9-Perez-c 3.00
1,2-Special Ed.; r/#1,2 plus new art & new-c 3.00
Annual 1,2 (1991, 1992, $2.95, 52 pgs.) 3.00
...: Project Robinson (11/93, $2.50) 1st & only part of intended series 3.00

LOST IN SPACE: VOYAGE TO THE BOTTOM OF THE SOUL
Innovation Publishing: No. 13, Aug, 1993 - No. 18, 1994 ($2.50, limited series)

13(V1#1, $2.95)-Embossed silver logo edition; Bill Mumy scripts begin; painted-c 3.00
13(V1#1, $4.95)-Embossed gold logo edition bagged w/poster 5.00
14-18: Painted-c 3.00

NOTE: *Originally intended to be a 12 issue limited series.*

LOST ONES, THE
Image Comics: Mar, 2000 ($2.95)

1-Ken Penders-s/a 3.00

LOST PLANET
Eclipse Comics: 5/87 - No. 5, 2/88; No. 6, 3/89 (Mini-series, Baxter paper)

1-6-Bo Hampton-c/a in all 2.25

LOST WAGON TRAIN, THE (See Zane Grey Four Color 583)

LOST WORLD, THE
Dell Publishing Co.: No. 1145, Nov-Jan, 1960-61

	GD 2.0	VG 4.0	FN 6.0	VF 8.0	VF/NM 9.0	NM- 9.2
Four Color 1145-Movie, Gil Kane-a, photo-c; 1pg. Conan Doyle biography by Torres	11	22	33	75	110	145

LOST WORLD, THE (See Jurassic Park)
Topps Comics: May, 1997 - No. 4, Aug, 1997 ($2.95, limited series)

1-4-Movie adaption 3.00

LOST WORLDS (Weird Tales of the Past and Future)
Standard Comics: No. 5, Oct, 1952 - No. 6, Dec, 1952

	GD 2.0	VG 4.0	FN 6.0	VF 8.0	VF/NM 9.0	NM- 9.2
5- "Alice in Terrorland" by Alex Toth; J. Katz-a	43	86	129	262	401	540
6-Toth-a	38	76	114	219	320	420

LOTS 'O' FUN COMICS
Robert Allen Co.: 1940's? (5¢, heavy stock, blue covers)

nn-Contents can vary; Felix, Planet Comics known; contents would determine value. Similar to Up-To-Date Comics. Remainders - re-packaged.

LOU GEHRIG (See The Pride of the Yankees)

LOVE ADVENTURES (Actual Confessions #13)
Marvel (IPS)/Atlas Comics (MPI): Oct, 1949; No. 2, Jan, 1950; No. 3, Feb, 1951 - No. 12, Aug, 1952

	GD 2.0	VG 4.0	FN 6.0	VF 8.0	VF/NM 9.0	NM- 9.2
1-Photo-c	17	34	51	98	139	180
2-Powell-a; Tyrone Power, Gene Tierney photo-c	15	30	45	86	123	160
3-8,10-12: 8-Robinson-a	9	18	27	52	66	80
9-Everett-a	9	18	27	54	70	85

LOVE AND MARRIAGE
Superior Comics Ltd. (Canada): Mar, 1952 - No. 16, Sept, 1954

	GD 2.0	VG 4.0	FN 6.0	VF 8.0	VF/NM 9.0	NM- 9.2
1	14	28	42	79	110	140
2	8	16	24	43	54	65
3-10	7	14	21	37	46	55
11-16	6	12	18	31	38	45
I.W. Reprint #1,2,8,11,14: 8-r/Love and Marriage #3. 11-r/Love and Marriage #11	2	4	6	10	13	16

Love Confessions #4 © QUA

Love Diary #34 © CC

Love Letters #2 © QUA

	GD 2.0	VG 4.0	FN 6.0	VF 8.0	VF/NM 9.0	NM- 9.2
Super Reprint #10('63),15,17('64):15-Love and Marriage #?	2	4	6	10	13	16

NOTE: *All issues have* ***Kamenish*** *art.*

LOVE AND ROCKETS
Fantagraphics Books: July, 1982 - No. 50, May, 1996 ($2.95/$2.50/$4.95, B&W, mature)

	GD 2.0	VG 4.0	FN 6.0	VF 8.0	VF/NM 9.0	NM- 9.2
1-B&W-c (6/82, $2.95; small size, publ. by Hernandez Bros.)(800 printed)	4	8	12	29	40	50
1 (Fall, '82; color-c)	3	6	9	18	24	30
1-2nd & 3rd printing, 2-11,29-31: 2nd printings						3.00
2	1	3	4	6	8	10
3-10	1	2	3	5	6	8
11-49: 30 ($2.95, 52 pgs.)						5.00
50-($4.95)						6.00

LOVE AND ROCKETS (Volume 2)
Fantagraphics Books: Spring, 2001 - Present ($3.95/$5.95, B&W, mature)

	GD 2.0	VG 4.0	FN 6.0	VF 8.0	VF/NM 9.0	NM- 9.2
1-9-Gilbert, Jaime and Mario Hernandez-s/a						4.00
10-($5.95)						6.00
11-($4.50)						4.50

LOVE AND ROMANCE
Charlton Comics: Sept, 1971 - No. 24, Sept, 1975

	GD 2.0	VG 4.0	FN 6.0	VF 8.0	VF/NM 9.0	NM- 9.2
1	3	6	9	19	25	32
2-10	2	4	6	10	13	16
11-24	1	3	4	6	8	10

LOVE AT FIRST SIGHT
Ace Magazines (RAR Publ. Co./Periodical House): Oct, 1949 - No. 43, Nov, 1956 (Photo-c: 21-42)

	GD 2.0	VG 4.0	FN 6.0	VF 8.0	VF/NM 9.0	NM- 9.2
1-Painted-c	15	30	45	83	117	150
2-Painted-c	9	18	27	51	62	75
3-10: 4-Painted-c	8	16	24	40	50	60
11-20	7	14	21	37	46	55
21-33: 33-Last pre-code	7	14	21	35	43	50
34-43	6	12	18	31	38	45

LOVE BUG, THE (See Movie Comics)

LOVEBUNNY AND MR. HELL
Devil's Due Publ./Image Comics: 2002 - Present ($2.95, B&W, one-shots)

	GD 2.0	VG 4.0	FN 6.0	VF 8.0	VF/NM 9.0	NM- 9.2
1-Tim Seeley-s						3.00
...: A Day in the Lovelife (Image, 2003) Blaylock-a						3.00
...: Savage Love (Image, 2003) Seeley-s/a; Savage Dragon app.; Seeley & Larsen-c						3.00
TPB (4/04, $9.95, digest-sized) reprints						10.00

LOVE CLASSICS
A Lover's Magazine/Marvel: Nov, 1949 - No. 2, Feb, 1950 (Photo-c, 52 pgs.)

	GD 2.0	VG 4.0	FN 6.0	VF 8.0	VF/NM 9.0	NM- 9.2
1,2: 2-Virginia Mayo photo-c; 30 pg. story "I Was a Small Town Flirt"	15	30	45	83	117	150

LOVE CONFESSIONS
Quality Comics: Oct, 1949 - No. 54, Dec, 1956 (Photo-c: 3,4,6,7,9,11-18,21)

	GD 2.0	VG 4.0	FN 6.0	VF 8.0	VF/NM 9.0	NM- 9.2
1-Ward-c/a, 9 pgs; Gustavson-a	32	64	96	184	267	350
2-Gustavson-a; Ward-c	15	30	45	86	123	160
3	10	20	30	56	73	90
4-Crandall-a	11	22	33	62	84	105
5-Ward-a, 7 pgs.	12	24	36	71	98	125
6,7,9,11-13,15,16,18: 7-Van Johnson photo-c. 8-Robert Mitchum & Jane Russell photo-c	8	16	24	43	54	65
8,10-Ward-a (2 stories in #10)	12	24	36	71	98	125
14,17,19,22-Ward-a; 17-Faith Domerque photo-c	11	22	33	66	91	115
20-Ward-a(2)	12	24	36	71	98	125
21,23-28,30-38,40-42: Last precode, 4/55	7	14	21	35	43	50
29-Ward-a	11	22	33	62	84	105
39,53-Matt Baker-a	8	16	24	46	58	70
43,44,46,47,50-52,54: 47-Ward-c?	6	12	18	31	38	45
45,48-Ward-a	8	16	24	43	54	65
49-Baker-c/a	9	18	27	52	66	80

LOVECRAFT
DC Comics: 2003 (graphic novel)

	GD 2.0	VG 4.0	FN 6.0	VF 8.0	VF/NM 9.0	NM- 9.2
Hardcover ($24.95) Rodionoff & Giffen-s/Breccia-a; intro. by John Carpenter						25.00
Softcover ($17.95)						18.00

LOVE DIARY
Our Publishing Co./Toytown/Patches: July, 1949 - No. 48, Oct, 1955 (Photo-c: 1-24,27-29) (52 pgs. #1-11?)

	GD 2.0	VG 4.0	FN 6.0	VF 8.0	VF/NM 9.0	NM- 9.2
1-Krigstein-a	20	40	60	112	161	210
2,3-Krigstein & Mort Leav-a in each	12	24	36	71	98	125
4-8	8	16	24	46	58	70
9,10-Everett-a	9	18	27	51	62	75
11-20: 16- Mort Leav-a, 3 pg. Baker-sty. Leav-a	8	16	24	43	54	65
21-30,32-48: 45-Leav-a. 47-Last precode(12/54)	8	16	24	40	50	60
31-John Buscema headlights-c	8	16	24	46	58	70

LOVE DIARY (Diary Loves #2 on; title change due to previously published title)
Quality Comics Group: Sept, 1949

	GD 2.0	VG 4.0	FN 6.0	VF 8.0	VF/NM 9.0	NM- 9.2
1-Ward-c/a, 9 pgs.	32	64	96	184	267	350

LOVE DIARY
Charlton Comics: July, 1958 - No. 102, Dec, 1976

	GD 2.0	VG 4.0	FN 6.0	VF 8.0	VF/NM 9.0	NM- 9.2
1	9	18	27	54	70	85
2	7	14	21	35	43	50
3-5,7-10: 10-Photo-c	6	12	18	28	34	40
6-Torres-a	6	12	18	31	38	45
11-20: 20-Photo-c	3	6	9	18	24	30
21-40	3	6	9	16	20	24
41-60	2	4	6	11	14	18
61-80,100-102	2	4	6	9	11	14
81-99	1	3	4	6	8	10

LOVE DOCTOR (See Dr. Anthony King...)

LOVE DRAMAS (True Secrets No. 3 on?)
Marvel Comics (IPS): Oct, 1949 - No. 2, Jan, 1950

	GD 2.0	VG 4.0	FN 6.0	VF 8.0	VF/NM 9.0	NM- 9.2
1-Jack Kamen-a; photo-c	19	38	57	107	154	200
2	13	26	39	74	102	130

LOVE EXPERIENCES (Challenge of the Unknown No. 6)
Ace Periodicals (A.A. Wyn/Periodical House): Oct, 1949 - No. 5, June, 1950; No. 6, Apr, 1951 - No. 38, June, 1956

	GD 2.0	VG 4.0	FN 6.0	VF 8.0	VF/NM 9.0	NM- 9.2
1-Painted-c	14	28	42	79	110	140
2	8	16	24	46	58	70
3-5: 5-Painted-c	8	16	24	40	50	60
6-10	7	14	21	37	46	55
11-30: 30-Last pre-code (2/55)	6	12	18	31	38	45
31-38: 38-Indicia date-6/56; c-date-8/56	6	12	18	27	33	38

NOTE: ***Anne Brewster*** *a-15. Photo c-4, 15-35, 38.*

LOVE FIGHTS (Also see Free Comic Book Day Edition in the Promotional Comics section)
Oni Press: June, 2003 - No. 12, Aug, 2004 ($2.99, B&W)

	GD 2.0	VG 4.0	FN 6.0	VF 8.0	VF/NM 9.0	NM- 9.2
1-12-Andi Watson-s/a						3.00
Vol.1 TPB (4/04, $14.95, digest-size) r/#1-6						15.00

LOVE JOURNAL
Our Publishing Co.: No. 10, Oct, 1951 - No. 25, July, 1954

	GD 2.0	VG 4.0	FN 6.0	VF 8.0	VF/NM 9.0	NM- 9.2
10	10	20	30	60	80	100
11-25: 19-Mort Leav-a	8	16	24	40	50	60

LOVELAND
Mutual Mag./Eye Publ. (Marvel): Nov, 1949 - No. 2, Feb, 1950 (52 pgs.)

	GD 2.0	VG 4.0	FN 6.0	VF 8.0	VF/NM 9.0	NM- 9.2
1,2-Photo-c	11	22	33	64	87	110

LOVE LESSONS
Harvey Comics/Key Publ. No. 5: Oct, 1949 - No. 5, June, 1950

	GD 2.0	VG 4.0	FN 6.0	VF 8.0	VF/NM 9.0	NM- 9.2
1-Metallic silver-c printed over the cancelled covers of Love Letters #1; indicia title is "Love Letters"	15	30	45	83	117	150
2-Powell-a; photo-c	9	18	27	51	62	75
3-5: 3-Photo-c	8	16	24	40	50	60

LOVE LETTERS (10/49, Harvey; advertised but never published; covers were printed before cancellation and were used as the cover to Love Lessions #1)

LOVE LETTERS (Love Secrets No. 32 on)
Quality Comics: 11/49 - #6, 9/50; #7, 3/51 - #31, 6/53; #32, 2/54 - #51, 12/56

	GD 2.0	VG 4.0	FN 6.0	VF 8.0	VF/NM 9.0	NM- 9.2
1-Ward-c, Gustavson-a	25	50	75	144	207	270
2-Ward-c, Gustavson-a	20	40	60	112	161	210
3-Gustavson-a	14	28	42	81	113	145
4-Ward-a, 9 pgs.	19	38	57	107	154	200
5-8,10	8	16	24	46	58	70
9-One pg. Ward "Be Popular with the Opposite Sex"; Robert Mitchum photo-c	9	18	27	54	70	85
11-Ward-r/Broadway Romances #2 & retitled	9	18	27	54	70	85
12-15,18-20	8	16	24	40	50	60
16,17-Ward-a; 16-Anthony Quinn photo-c. 17-Jane Russell photo-c	12	24	36	71	98	125

Love Me Tenderloin #1 © DH

Lovers' Lane #4 © LEV

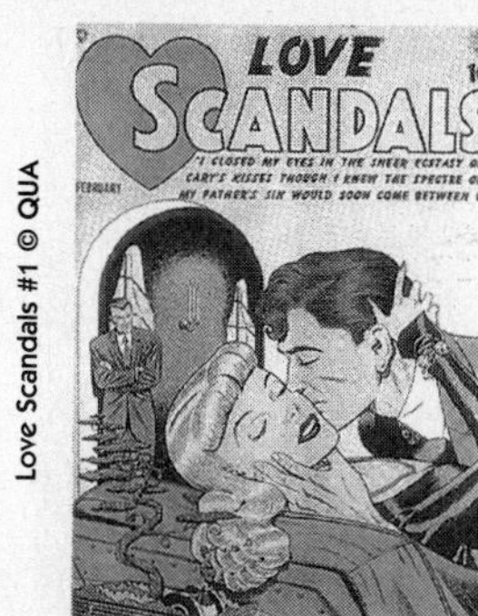

Love Scandals #1 © QUA

	GD 2.0	VG 4.0	FN 6.0	VF 8.0	VF/NM 9.0	NM- 9.2
21-29	7	14	21	37	46	55
30,31(6/53)-Ward-a	9	18	27	51	62	75
32(2/54)-39: 37-Ward-a. 38-Crandall-a. 39-Last precode (4/55)	6	12	18	33	41	48
40-48	6	12	18	29	36	42
49,50-Baker-a	9	18	27	54	70	85
51-Baker-c	8	16	24	46	58	70

NOTE: *Photo-c on most 3-28.*

LOVE LIFE
P. L. Publishing Co.: Nov, 1951

	GD	VG	FN	VF	VF/NM	NM-
1	10	20	30	58	77	95

LOVELORN (Confessions of the Lovelorn #52 on)
American Comics Group (Michel Publ./Regis Publ.): Aug-Sept, 1949 - No. 51, July, 1954 (No. 1-26: 52 pgs.)

	GD	VG	FN	VF	VF/NM	NM-
1	16	32	48	89	127	165
2	9	18	27	54	70	85
3-10	8	16	24	43	54	65
11-20,22-48: 18-Drucker-a(2 pgs.). 46-Lazarus-a	7	14	21	37	46	55
21-Prostitution story	9	18	27	49	62	75
49-51-Has 3-D effect-c/stories	16	32	48	89	127	165

LOVE MEMORIES
Fawcett Publications: 1949 (no month) - No. 4, July, 1950 (All photo-c)

	GD	VG	FN	VF	VF/NM	NM-
1	16	32	48	89	127	165
2-4: 2-(Win/49-50)	9	18	27	54	70	85

LOVE ME TENDERLOIN: A CAL McDONALD MYSTERY
Dark Horse Comics: Jan, 2004 ($2.99, one-shot)

	GD	VG	FN	VF	VF/NM	NM-
1-Niles-s/Templesmith-a/c						3.00

LOVE MYSTERY
Fawcett Publications: June, 1950 - No. 3, Oct, 1950 (All photo-c)

	GD	VG	FN	VF	VF/NM	NM-
1-George Evans-a	23	46	69	132	191	250
2,3-Evans-a. 3-Powell-a	17	34	51	95	135	175

LOVE PROBLEMS (See Fox Giants)

LOVE PROBLEMS AND ADVICE ILLUSTRATED (see True Love...)

LOVE ROMANCES (Formerly Ideal #5)
Timely/Marvel/Atlas(TCI No. 7-71/Male No. 72-106): No. 6, May, 1949 - No. 106, July, 1963

	GD	VG	FN	VF	VF/NM	NM-
6-Photo-c	16	32	48	92	131	170
7-Photo-c; Kamen-a	10	20	30	58	77	95
8-Kubert-a; photo-c	10	20	30	58	77	95
9-20: 9-12-Photo-c	9	18	27	52	66	80
21,24-Krigstein-a	10	20	30	56	73	90
22,23,25-35,37,39,40	9	18	27	51	62	75
36,38-Krigstein-a	9	18	27	52	66	80
41-44,46,47: Last precode (2/55)	8	16	24	46	58	70
45,57-Matt Baker-a	10	20	30	56	73	90
48,50-52,54-56,58-74	5	10	15	36	48	60
49,53-Toth-a, 6 & ? pgs.	6	12	18	40	55	70
75,77,82-Matt Baker-a	7	14	21	46	63	80
76,78-81,86,88-90,92-95: 80-Heath-c. 95-Last 10¢-c?	5	10	15	33	44	55
83,84,87,91-Kirby-c. 83-Severin-a	7	14	21	46	63	80
85,96,97,99-106-Kirby-c/a	8	16	24	55	78	100
98-Kirby-c/a	8	16	24	58	82	105

NOTE: ***Anne Brewster** a-67, 72. **Colletta** a-37, 40, 42, 44, 67(2); c-42, 44, 49, 54, 80. **Everett** c-70. **Heath** a-87. **Kirby** c-80, 85, 88. **Robinson** a-29.*

LOVERS (Formerly Blonde Phantom)
Marvel Comics No. 23,24/Atlas No. 25 on (ANC): No. 23, May, 1949 - No. 86, Aug?, 1957

	GD	VG	FN	VF	VF/NM	NM-
23-Photo-c begin, end #28	16	32	48	92	131	170
24-Toth-*ish* plus Robinson-a	9	18	27	54	70	85
25,30-Kubert-a; 7, 10 pgs.	10	20	30	56	73	90
26-29,31-36,39,40	8	16	24	46	58	70
37,38-Krigstein-a	9	18	27	54	70	85
41-Everett-a(2)	9	18	27	54	70	85
42,44-65: 65-Last pre-code (1/55)	8	16	24	40	50	60
43-Frazetta 1 pg. ad	8	16	24	43	54	65
66,68-86: 81-Baker-a	7	14	21	37	46	55
67-Toth-a	8	16	24	43	54	65

NOTE: ***Anne Brewster** a-86. **Colletta** a-54, 59, 62, 64, 65, 69, 85; c-61, 64, 65, 75. **Heath** a-61. **Maneely** a-57. **Powell** a-27, 30. **Robinson** a-54, 56.*

LOVERS' LANE
Lev Gleason Publications: Oct, 1949 - No. 41, June, 1954 (No. 1-18: 52 pgs.)

	GD	VG	FN	VF	VF/NM	NM-
1-Biro-c	12	24	36	69	95	120
2-Biro-c	8	16	24	43	54	65
3-20: 3,4-Painted-c. 20-Frazetta 1 pg. ad	7	14	21	37	46	55
21-38,40,41	6	12	18	29	36	42
39-Story narrated by Frank Sinatra	8	16	24	43	54	65

NOTE: ***Briefer** a-6, 21. **Fuje** a-4, 16; c-many. **Guardineer** a-1. **Kinstler** c-41. **Tuska** a-6. Painted c-3-18. Photo c-19-22, 26-28.*

LOVE SCANDALS
Quality Comics: Feb, 1950 - No. 5, Oct, 1950 (Photo-c #2-5) (All 52 pgs.)

	GD	VG	FN	VF	VF/NM	NM-
1-Ward-c/a, 9 pgs.	27	54	81	154	222	290
2,3: 2-Gustavson-a	11	22	33	66	91	115
4-Ward-a, 18 pgs; Gil Fox-a	21	42	63	118	169	220
5-C. Cuidera-a; tomboy story "I Hated Being a Woman"	11	22	33	66	91	115

LOVE SECRETS
Marvel Comics(IPC): Oct, 1949 - No. 2, Jan, 1950 (52 pgs., photo-c)

	GD	VG	FN	VF	VF/NM	NM-
1	16	32	48	92	131	170
2	10	20	30	58	77	95

LOVE SECRETS (Formerly Love Letters #31)
Quality Comics Group: No. 32, Aug, 1953 - No. 56, Dec, 1956

	GD	VG	FN	VF	VF/NM	NM-
32	11	22	33	62	84	105
33,35-39	7	14	21	37	46	55
34-Ward-a	11	22	33	62	84	105
40-Matt Baker-c	8	16	24	46	58	70
41-43: 43-Last precode (3/55)	7	14	21	37	46	55
44,47-50,53,54	6	12	18	29	36	42
45,46-Ward-a. 46-Baker-a	9	18	27	52	66	80
51,52-Ward(r). 52-r/Love Confessions #17	7	14	21	37	46	55
55,56: 55-Baker-a. 56-Baker-c	8	16	24	43	54	65

LOVE STORIES (See Top Love Stories)

LOVE STORIES (Formerly Heart Throbs)
National Periodical Publ.: No. 147, Nov, 1972 - No. 152, Oct-Nov, 1973

	GD	VG	FN	VF	VF/NM	NM-
147-152	2	4	6	14	18	22

LOVE STORIES OF MARY WORTH (See Harvey Comics Hits #55 & Mary Worth)
Harvey Publications: Sept, 1949 - No. 5, May, 1950

	GD	VG	FN	VF	VF/NM	NM-
1-1940's newspaper reprints-#1-4	9	18	27	51	62	75
2-5: 3-Kamen/Baker-a?	6	12	18	31	38	45

LOVE TALES (Formerly The Human Torch #35)
Marvel/Atlas Comics (ZPC No. 36-50/MMC No. 67-75): No. 36, 5/49 - No. 58, 8/52; No. 59, date? - No. 75, Sept, 1957

	GD	VG	FN	VF	VF/NM	NM-
36-Photo-c	16	32	48	92	131	170
37	9	18	27	54	70	85
38-44,46-50: 39-41-Photo-c	9	18	27	51	62	75
45,51,52,69: 45-Powell-a. 51,69-Everett-a. 52-Krigstein-a	9	18	27	52	66	80
53-60: 60-Last pre-code (2/55)	7	14	21	37	46	55
61-68,70-75: 75-Brewster, Cameron, Colletta-a	7	14	21	35	43	50

LOVE THRILLS (See Fox Giants)

LOVE TRAILS (Western romance)
A Lover's Magazine (CDS)(Marvel): Dec, 1949 - No. 2, Mar, 1950 (52 pgs.)

	GD	VG	FN	VF	VF/NM	NM-
1,2: 1-Photo-c	15	30	45	86	123	160

LOWELL THOMAS' HIGH ADVENTURE (See High Adventure)

LT. (See Lieutenant)

LUBA
Fantographics Books: Feb, 1998 - Present ($2.95/$3.50, B&W, mature)

	GD	VG	FN	VF	VF/NM	NM-
1-4-Gilbert Hernandez-s/a						3.00
5-9-($3.50)						3.50

LUBA'S COMICS AND STORIES
Fantographics Books: Mar, 2000 - Present ($2.95/$3.50, B&W, mature)

	GD	VG	FN	VF	VF/NM	NM-
1-Gilbert Hernandez-s/a						3.00
2-5-($3.50)						3.50

LUCIFER (See The Sandman #4)
DC Comics (Vertigo): Jun, 2000 - Present ($2.50)

	GD	VG	FN	VF	VF/NM	NM-
1-Carey-s/Weston-a/Fegredo-c						8.00
2,3-Carey-s/Weston-a/Fegredo-c						5.00

Lucifer #47 © DC

Lucy, The Real Gone Gal #1 © STJ

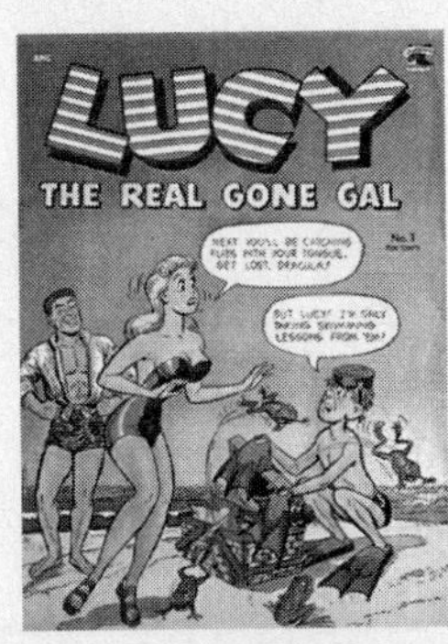

Machine Man #10 © MAR

GD VG FN VF VF/NM NM-
2.0 4.0 6.0 8.0 9.0 9.2

4-10: 4-Pleece-a. 5-Gross-a 4.00
11-49,51-57: 16-Moeller-c begin. 25,26-Death app. 45-Naifeh-a. 53-57-Kaluta-c 2.50
50-($3.50) P. Craig Russell-a; Mazikeen app. 3.50
Preview-16 pg. flip book w/Swamp Thing Preview 3.00
A Dalliance With the Damned TPB ('02, $14.95) r/#14-20 15.00
Children and Monsters TPB ('01, $17.95) r/#5-13 18.00
Devil in the Gateway TPB ('01, $14.95) r/#1-4 & Sandman Presents:..#1-3 15.00
...: Inferno TPB (2003, $14.95) r/#29-35 15.00
...: Mansions of the Silence TPB (2004, $14.95) r/#36-41 15.00
...: Nirvana (2002, $5.95) Carey-s/Muth-painted-c/a; Daniel app. 6.00
...: The Divine Comedy TPB (2003, $17.95) r/#21-28 18.00

LUCIFER'S HAMMER (Larry Niven & Jerry Pournelle's...)
Innovation Publishing: Nov, 1993 - No. 6, 1994 ($2.50, painted, limited series)
1-6: Adaptatin of novel, painted-c & art 2.50

LUCKY COMICS
Consolidated Magazines: Jan, 1944; No. 2, Sum, 1945 - No. 5, Sum, 1946
1-Lucky Starr & Bobbie begin 22 44 66 125 180 235
2-5: 5-Devil-c by Walter Johnson 12 24 36 71 98 125

LUCKY DUCK
Standard Comics (Literary Ent.): No. 5, Jan, 1953 - No. 8, Sept, 1953
5-Funny animal; Irving Spector-a 11 22 33 63 84 105
6-8-Irving Spector-a 10 20 30 56 73 90
NOTE: *Harvey Kurtzman tried to hire Spector for Mad #1.*

LUCKY "7" COMICS
Howard Publishers Ltd.: 1944 (No date listed)
1-Pioneer, Sir Gallagher, Dick Royce, Congo Raider, Punch Powers; bondage-c
39 78 117 222 324 425

LUCKY STAR (Western)
Nation Wide Publ. Co.: 1950 - No. 7, 1951; No. 8, 1953 - No. 14, 1955 (5x7-1/4"; full color, 5¢)
nn (#1)-(5¢, 52 pgs.)-Davis-a 18 36 54 100 143 185
2,3-(5¢, 52 pgs.)-Davis-a 11 22 33 64 87 110
4-7-(5¢, 52 pgs.)-Davis-a 10 20 30 58 77 95
8-14-(36 pgs.)(Exist?) 8 16 24 46 58 70
Given away with Lucky Star Western Wear by the Juvenile Mfg. Co.
6 12 18 31 38 45

LUCY SHOW, THE (TV) (Also see I Love Lucy)
Gold Key: June, 1963 - No. 5, June, 1964 (Photo-c: 1,2)
1 14 28 42 97 149 200
2 8 16 24 58 82 105
3-5: Photo back c-1,2,4,5 8 16 24 53 74 95

LUCY, THE REAL GONE GAL (Meet Miss Pepper #5 on)
St. John Publishing Co.: June, 1953 - No. 4, Dec, 1953
1-Negligee panels 13 26 39 76 106 135
2 8 16 24 46 58 70
3,4: 3-Drucker-a 8 16 24 40 50 60

LUDWIG BEMELMAN'S MADELEINE & GENEVIEVE
Dell Publishing Co.: No. 796, May, 1957
Four Color 796 4 8 12 27 36 45

LUDWIG VON DRAKE (TV)(Disney)(See Walt Disney's C&S #256)
Dell Publishing Co.: Nov-Dec, 1961 - No. 4, June-Aug, 1962
1 8 16 24 55 78 100
2-4 6 12 18 40 55 70

LUFTWAFFE: 1946 (Volume 1)
Antarctic Press: July, 1996 - No. 4, Jan, 1997 ($2.95, B&W, limited series)
1-4-Ben Dunn & Ted Nomura-s/a, ...Special Ed. 3.00

LUFTWAFFE: 1946 (Volume 2)
Antarctic Press: Mar, 1997 - No. 18 ($2.95/$2.99, B&W, limited series)
1-18: 8-Reviews Tigers of Terra series 3.00
Annual 1 (4/98, $2.95)-Reprints early Nomura pages 3.00
...Color Special (4/98) 3.00
...Technical Manual 1,2 (2/98, 4/99) 4.00

LUGER
Eclipse Comics: Oct, 1986 - No. 3, Feb, 1987 ($1.75, miniseries, Baxter paper)
1-3: Bruce Jones scripts; Yeates-c/a 2.25

LUKE CAGE (See Cage & Hero for Hire)

LUKE SHORT'S WESTERN STORIES
Dell Publishing Co.: No. 580, Aug, 1954 - No. 927, Aug, 1958
Four Color 580(8/54), 651(9/55)-Kinstler-a 4 8 12 29 40 50
Four Color 739,771,807,848,875,927 4 8 12 28 38 48

LUNATIC FRINGE, THE
Innovation Publishing: July, 1989 - No. 2, 1989 ($1.75, deluxe format)
1,2 2.25

LUNATICKLE (Magazine) (Satire)
Whitstone Publ.: Feb, 1956 - No. 2, Apr, 1956
1,2-Kubert-a (scarce) 6 12 18 31 38 45

LUNATIK
Marvel Comics: Dec, 1995 - No. 3, Feb, 1996 ($1.95, limited series)
1-3 2.25

LURKERS, THE
IDW Publ.: Oct, 2004 - Present ($3.99)
1,2-Niles-s/Casanova-a 4.00

LUST FOR LIFE
Slave Labor Graphics: Feb, 1997 - No. 4, Jan, 1998 ($2.95, B&W)
1-4: 1-Jeff Levin-s/a 3.00

LYCANTHROPE LEO
Viz Communications: 1994 - No. 7($2.95, B&W, limited series, 44 pgs.)
1-7 3.00

LYNCH (See Gen [13])
Image Comics (WildStorm Productions): May, 1997 ($2.50, one-shot)
1-Helmut-c/app. 2.50

LYNCH MOB
Chaos! Comics: June, 1994 - No. 4, Sept, 1994 ($2.50, limited series)
1-4 2.50
1-Special edition full foil-c 5.00

LYNDON B. JOHNSON
Dell Publishing Co.: Mar, 1965
12-445-503-Photo-c 4 8 12 22 30 38

M
Eclipse Books: 1990 - No. 4, 1991 ($4.95, painted, 52 pgs.)
1-Adapts movie; contains flexi-disc ($5.95) 6.00
2-4 5.00

MACE GRIFFIN BOUNTY HUNTER (Based on video game)
Image Comics (Top Cow): May, 2003 ($2.99, one-shot)
1-Nocon-a 3.00

MACHINE, THE
Dark Horse Comics: Nov, 1994 - No. 4, Feb, 1995 ($2.50, limited series)
1-4 2.50

MACHINE MAN (Also see 2001, A Space Odyssey)
Marvel Comics Group: Apr, 1978 - No. 9, Dec, 1978; No. 10, Aug, 1979 - No. 19, Feb, 1981
1-Jack Kirby-c/a/scripts begin; end #9 2 4 6 10 13 16
2-9-Kirby-c/a/s. 9-(12/78) 1 2 3 5 6 8
10-17: 10-(8/79) Marv Wolfman scripts & Ditko-a begins 5.00
18-Wendigo, Alpha Flight-ties into X-Men #140 2 4 6 12 16 20
19-Intro/1st app. Jack O'Lantern (Macendale), later becomes 2nd Hobgoblin
2 4 6 10 13 16
NOTE: ***Austin** c-7i, 19i. **Buckler** c-17p, 18p. **Byrne** c-14p. **Ditko** a-10-19; c-10-13, 14i, 15, 16. **Kirby** a-1-9p; c-1-5, 7-9p. **Layton** c-7i. **Miller** c-19p. **Simonson** c-6.*

MACHINE MAN (Also see X-51)
Marvel Comics Group: Oct, 1984 - No. 4, Jan, 1985 (Limited-series)
1-4-Barry Smith-c/a(i) & colors in all 4.00
TPB (1988, $6.95) r/ #1-4; Barry Smith-c 7.00
.../Bastion '98 Annual ($2.99) wraparound-c 3.00

MACHINE MAN 2020
Marvel Comics: Aug, 1994 - Nov, 1994 ($2.00, 52 pgs., limited series)
1-4: Reprints Machine Man limited series; Barry Windsor-Smith-c/i(r) 2.25

MACK BOLAN: THE EXECUTIONER (Don Pendleton's...)
Innovation Publishing: July, 1993 ($2.50)
1-3-($2.50) 2.50
1-($3.95)-Indestructible Cover Edition 4.00
1-($2.95)-Collector's Gold Edition; foil stamped 3.00

Mad #8 © E.C. Publ.

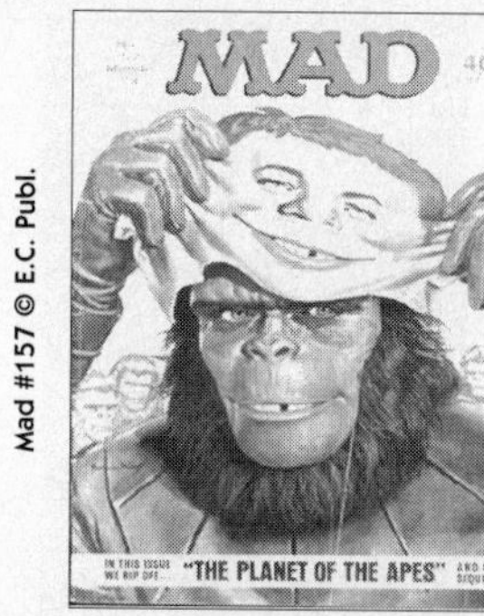

Mad #157 © E.C. Publ.

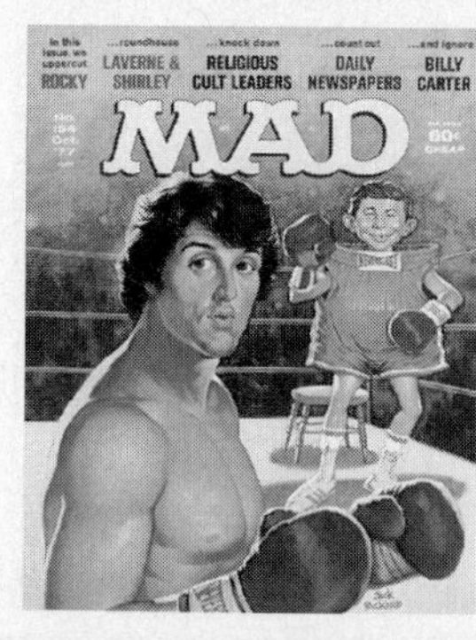

Mad #194 © E.C. Publ.

GD VG FN VF VF/NM NM-
2.0 4.0 6.0 8.0 9.0 9.2

1-($3.50)-Double Cover Edition; red foil outer-c 3.50

MACKENZIE'S RAIDERS (Movie, TV)
Dell Publishing Co.: No. 1093, Apr-June, 1960

Four Color 1093-Richard Carlson photo-c from TV show 8 16 24 53 74 95

MACROSS (Becomes Robotech: The Macross Saga #2 on)
Comico: Dec, 1984 ($1.50)(Low print run)

1-Early manga app. 3 6 9 16 20 25

MACROSS II
Viz Select Comics: 1992 - No. 10, 1993 ($2.75, B&W, limited series)

1-10: Based on video series 2.75

MAD (Tales Calculated to Drive You...)
E. C. Comics (Educational Comics): Oct-Nov, 1952 - Present (No. 24-on are magazine format) (Kurtzman editor No. 1-28, Feldstein No. 29 - No. ?)

1-Wood, Davis, Elder start as regulars 462 924 1386 3465 5083 6700
2-Dick Tracy cameo 121 242 363 908 1329 1750
3,4: 3-Stan Lee mentioned. 4-Reefer mention story "Flob Was a Slob" by Davis; Superman parody 76 152 228 570 835 1100
5-Low distr.; W.M. Gaines biog. 152 304 456 1140 1670 2200
6-11: 6-Popeye cameo. 7,8- "Hey Look" reprints by Kurtzman. 11-Wolverton-a; Davis story was-r/Crime Suspenstories #12 w/new Kurtzman dialogue 59 118 177 443 652 860
12-15: 15,18-Pot Shot Pete-r by Kurtzman 47 94 141 353 514 675
16-23(5/55): 18-Alice in Wonderland by Jack Davis. 21-1st app. Alfred E. Neuman on-c in fake ad. 22-All by Elder plus photo-montages by Kurtzman. 23-Special cancel announcement 40 80 120 300 438 575
24(7/55)-1st magazine issue (25¢); Kurtzman logo & border on-c; 1st "What? Me Worry?" on-c; 2nd printing exists 93 186 279 698 1024 1350
25-Jaffee starts as regular writer 43 86 129 323 474 625
26,27: 27-Jaffee starts as story artist; new logo 39 78 117 244 397 550
28-Last issue edited by Kurtzman; (three cover variations exist with different wording on contents banner on lower right of cover; value of each the same) 34 68 102 213 319 425
29-Kamen-a; Don Martin starts as regular; Feldstein editing begins 34 68 102 213 319 425
30-1st A. E. Neuman cover by Mingo; last Elder-a; Bob Clarke starts as regular; Disneyland & Elvis Presley spoof 52 104 156 325 488 650
31-Freas starts as regular; last Davis-a until #99 30 60 90 188 282 375
32,33: 32-Orlando, Drucker, Woodbridge start as regulars; Wood back-c. 33-Orlando back-c 26 52 78 163 242 320
34-Berg starts as regular 21 42 63 131 201 270
35-Mingo wraparound-c; Crandall-a 21 42 63 131 201 270
36-40 (7/58): 39-Beall-c 16 32 48 100 150 200
41-50: 42-Danny Kaye-s. 44-Xmas-c. 47-49-Sid Caesar-s. 48-Uncle Sam-c. 50 (10/59)-Peter Gunn-s 13 26 39 81 123 165
51-59: 52-Xmas-c; 77 Sunset Strip. 53-Rifleman-s. 54-Jaffee-a begins. 55-Sid Caesar-s. 59-Strips of Superman, Flash Gordon, Donald Duck & others. 59-Halloween/Headless Horseman-c 11 22 33 69 105 140
60 (1/61)-JFK/Nixon flip-c; 1st Spy vs. Spy by Prohias, who starts as regular 13 26 39 81 123 165
61-70: 64-Rickard starts as regular. 65-JFK-s. 66-JFK-c. 68-Xmas-c by Martin. 70-Route 66-s 8 16 24 50 78 105
71-75,77-80 (7/63): 72-10th Anniv. special; 1/3 pg. strips of Superman, Tarzan & others. 73-Bonanza-s. 74-Dr. Kildare-s 6 12 18 40 55 70
76-Aragonés starts as regular 7 14 21 46 63 80
81-85: 81-Superman strip. 82-Castro-c. 85-Lincoln-c 5 10 15 36 48 60
86-1st Fold-in; commonly creased back covers makes these and later issues scarcer in NM 6 12 18 43 59 75
87,88 6 12 18 40 55 70
89,90: 89-One strip by Walt Kelly; Frankenstein-c; Fugitive-s. 90-Ringo back-c by Frazetta; Beatles app. 6 12 18 43 59 75
91,94,96,100: 94-King Kong-c. 96-Man From U.N.C.L.E. 100-(1/66)-Anniversary issue 5 10 15 36 48 60
92,93,95,97-99: 99-Davis-a resumes 5 10 15 33 44 55
101,104,106,108,114,115,119,121: 101-Infinity-c; Voyage to the Bottom of the Sea-s. 104-Lost in Space-s. 106-Tarzan back-c by Frazetta; 2 pg. Batman by Aragonés. 108-Hogan's Heroes by Davis. 114-Rat Patrol-s. 115-Star Trek. 119-Invaders (TV). 121-Beatles-c; Ringo pin-up; flip-c of Sik-Teen; Flying Nun-s 4 8 12 25 33 42
102,103,107,109-113,116-118,120(7/68): 118-Beatles cameo 4 8 12 22 30 38
105-Batman-c/s, TV show parody (9/66) 4 8 12 29 40 50
122,124,126,128,129,131-134,136,137,139,140: 122-Ronald Reagan photo inside; Drucker & Mingo-c. 126-Family Affair-s. 128-Last Orlando. 131-Reagan photo back-c. 132-Xmas-c. 133-John Wayne/True Grit. 136-Room 222 3 6 9 18 23 28

GD VG FN VF VF/NM NM-
2.0 4.0 6.0 8.0 9.0 9.2

123-Three different covers 3 6 9 18 24 30
125,127,130,135,138: 125-2001 Space Odyssey; Hitler back-c. 127-Mod Squad-c/s. 130-Land of the Giants-s; Torres begins as reg. 135-Easy Rider-c by Davis. 138-Snoopy-c; MASH-s 3 6 9 19 25 32
141-149,151-156,158-165,167-170: 141-Hawaii Five-0. 147-All in the Family-s. 153-Dirty Harry-s. 155-Godfather-c/s. 156-Columbo-s. 159-Clockwork Orange-c/s. 161-Tarzan-s. 164-Kung Fu (TV)-s. 165-James Bond-s; Dean Martin-c. 169-Drucker-c; McCloud-s. 170-Exorcist-s 3 6 9 16 20 24
150-(4/72) Partridge Family-s 3 6 9 16 21 26
157-(3/73) Planet of the Apes-c/s 3 6 9 18 24 30
166-(4/74) Classic finger-c 3 6 9 18 24 30
171-185,187,189-192,194,195,198,199: 172-Six Million Dollar Man-s; Hitler back-c. 178-Godfather II-c/s. 180-Jaws-c/s (1/76). 182-Bob Jones starts as regular.185-Starsky & Hutch-s. 187-Fonz/Happy Days-c/s; Harry North starts as regular. 189-Travolta/Kotter-c/s. 190-John Wayne-c/s. 192-King Kong-c/s. 194-Rocky-c/s; Laverne & Shirley-s. 199-James Bond-s 2 4 6 11 14 18
186,188,197,200: 186-Star Trek-c/s. 188-Six Million Dollar Man/ Bionic Woman. 197-Spock-s; Star Wars-s. 200-Close Encounters 2 4 6 14 18 22
193,196: 193-Farrah/Charlie's Angels-c/s. 196-Star Wars-c/s 3 6 9 16 20 24
201,203,205,220: 201-Sat. Night Fever-c/s. 203-Star Wars. 205-Travolta/Grease. 220-Yoda-c, Empire Strikes Back-s 2 4 6 10 13 16
202,204,206,207,209,211-219,221-227,229,230: 204-Hulk TV show. 206-Tarzan. 208-Superman movie. 209-Mork & Mindy. 212-Spider-Man-s; Alien (movie)-s. 213-James Bond, Dracula, Rocky II-s 216-Star Trek. 219-Martin-c. 221-Shining-s. 223-Dallas-c/s. 225-Popeye. 226-Superman II. 229-James Bond. 230-Star Wars 1 3 4 6 8 10
208,228: 208-Superman movie-c/s; Battlestar Galactica-s. 228-Raiders of the Lost Ark-c/s 2 4 6 10 12 15
210-Lord of the Rings 2 4 6 10 13 16
231-235,237-241,243-249,251-260: 233-Pac-Man-c. 234-MASH-c/s. 235-Flip-c with Rocky III & Conan; Boris-a. 239-Mickey Mouse-c. 241-Knight Rider-s. 243-Superman III. 245- Last Rickard-a. 247-Seven Dwarfs-c. 253-Supergirl movie-s; Prince/Purple Rain-s. 254-Rock stars-s. 255-Reagan-c; Cosby-s. 256-Last issue edited by Feldstein; Dynasty, Bev. Hills Cop. 259-Rambo. 260-Back to the Future-c/s; Honeymooners-s 1 2 3 5 6 8
236,242,250: 236-E.T.-c/s;Star Trek II-s. 242-Star Wars/A-Team-c/s. 250-Temple of Doom-c/s; Tarzan-s 1 2 3 5 7 9
261-267,269-276,278-288,290-297: 261-Miami Vice. 262-Rocky IV-c/s, Leave It To Beaver-s. 263-Young Sherlock Holmes-s. 264-Hulk Hogan-c; Rambo-s. 267-Top Gun. 271-Star Trek IV-c/s. 272-ALF-c; Get Smart-s. 273-Pee Wee Herman-c/s. 274-Last Martin-a. 281-California Raisins-c. 282-Star Trek:TNG-s; ALF-s. 283-Rambo III-c/s. 284-Roger Rabbit-c/s. 285-Hulk Hogan-c. 287-3 pgs. Eisner-a. 291-TMNT-c; Indiana Jones-s. 292-Super Mario Bros.-c; Married with Children-s. 295-Back to the Future II. 297-Mike Tyson-c 1 2 3 4 5 7
268,277,289,298-300: 268-Aliens-c/s. 277-Michael Jackson-c/s; Robocop-s. 289-Batman movie parody. 298-Gremlins II-c/s; Robocop II. Batman-s. 299-Simpsons-c/story; Total Recall-s. 300(1/91) Casablanca-s, Dick Tracy-s, Wizard of Oz-s, Gone With The Wind-s 1 2 3 5 6 8
300-303 (1/91-6/91)-Special Hussein Asylum Editions; only distributed to the troops in the Middle East (see Mad Super Spec.) 2 4 6 14 18 22
301-310,312,313,315-320,322,324,326-334,337-349: 303-Home Alone-c/s. 305-Simpsons-s. 306-TMNT II movie. 308-Terminator II. 315-Tribute to William Gaines. 316-Photo-c. 319-Dracula-c/s. 320-Disney's Aladdin-s. 322-Batman Animated series. 327-Seinfeld-s; X-Men-s. 331-Flintstones-c/s. 332-O.J. Simpson-c/s; Simpsons app. in Lion King. 334-Frankenstein-c/s. 338-Judge Dredd-c by Frazetta. 341-Pocahontas-s. 345-Beatles app. (1 pg.) 347-Broken Arrow & Mission Impossible 5.00
311,314,321,323,325,335,336,350,354,358: 311-Addams Family-c/story, Home Improvement-s. 314-Batman Returns-c/story. 321-Star Trek DS9-c/s. 323-Jurassic Park-c/s. 325,336-Beavis & Butthead-c/s. 335-X-Files-s; Pulp Fiction-s; Interview with the Vampire-s. 336-Lois & Clark-s. 350-Polybagged w/CD Rom. 354-Star Wars; Beavis & Butthead-s. 358-X-Files 6.00
351-353,355-357,359-400 4.00
401-452 3.50
Mad About Super Heroes (2002, $9.95) r/super hero app.; Alex Ross-c 10.00

NOTE: ***Aragones** c-210, 293. **Beall** c-39. **Davis** c-2, 27, 135, 139, 173, 178, 212, 213, 219, 246, 260, 296, 308. **Drucker** a-35-62; c-122, 169, 176, 225, 234, 264, 266, 274, 280, 285, 297, 299, 303, 314, 315, 321. **Elder** c-5, 259, 261, 268. **Elder/Kurtzman** a-258-274. **Jules Feiffer** a(r)-42. **Freas** c-40-59, 62-67, 69-70, 72, 74. **Heath** a-14, 27. **Jaffee** c-199, 217, 224, 258. **Kamen** a-29. **Krigstein** a-12, 17, 24, 26. **Kurtzman** c-1, 3, 4, 6-10, 13, 16, 18. **Martin** a-29-62; c-68, 165, 229. **Mingo** c-30-37, 61, 71, 75-80, 82-114, 117-124, 126, 129, 131, 133, 134, 136, 140, 143-148, 150-162, 164, 166-168, 171, 172, 174, 175, 177, 179, 181, 183, 185, 198, 206, 209, 211, 214, 218, 221, 222, 300. **John Severin** a-1-6, 9, 10. **Wolverton** c-11; a-11, 17, 29, 31, 36, 40, 82, 137. **Wood** a-1-21, 23-62; c-26, 28, 29. **Woodbridge** a-35-62. Issues 1-23 are 36 pgs.; 24-28 are 58 pgs.; 29 on are 52 pgs.*

MAD (See Mad Follies, ...Special, More Trash from..., and The Worst from...)

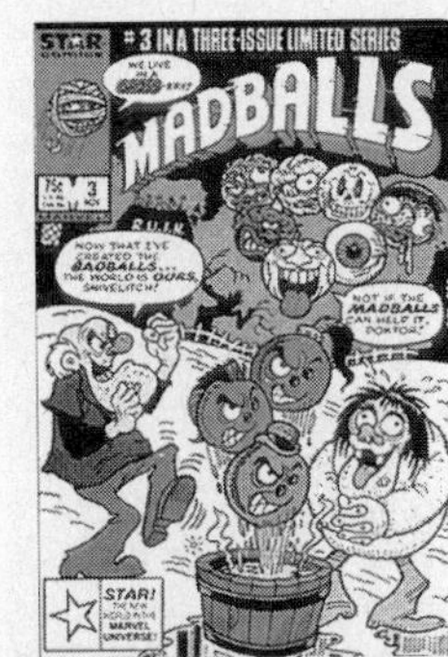

Madballs #3 © MAR

Madhouse #2 © AJAX

Madman Comics #1 © Mike Allred

MAD ABOUT MILLIE (Also see Millie the Model)
Marvel Comics Group: April, 1969 - No. 16, Nov, 1970

	GD 2.0	VG 4.0	FN 6.0	VF 8.0	VF/NM 9.0	NM- 9.2
1-Giant issue	8	16	24	58	82	105
2,3 (Giants)	6	12	18	38	52	65
4-10	4	8	12	22	30	38
11-16: 16-r	3	6	9	19	25	32
Annual 1(11/71, 52 pgs.)	4	8	12	22	30	38

MADAME XANADU
DC Comics: July, 1981 ($1.00, no ads, 36 pgs.)

	GD 2.0	VG 4.0	FN 6.0	VF 8.0	VF/NM 9.0	NM- 9.2
1-Marshall Rogers-a(25 pgs.); Kaluta-c/a(2pgs.); pin-up						5.00

MADBALLS
Star Comics/Marvel Comics #9 on: Sept, 1986 - No. 3, Nov, 1986; No. 4, June, 1987 - No. 10, June, 1988

	GD 2.0	VG 4.0	FN 6.0	VF 8.0	VF/NM 9.0	NM- 9.2
1-10: Based on toys. 9-Post-a						4.00

MAD DISCO
E.C. Comics: 1980 (one-shot, 36 pgs.)

	GD 2.0	VG 4.0	FN 6.0	VF 8.0	VF/NM 9.0	NM- 9.2
1-Includes 30 minute flexi-disc of Mad disco music	2	4	6	12	16	20

MAD-DOG
Marvel Comics: May, 1993 - No. 6, Oct, 1993 ($1.25)

	GD 2.0	VG 4.0	FN 6.0	VF 8.0	VF/NM 9.0	NM- 9.2
1-6-Flip book w/2nd story "created" by Bob Newhart's character from his TV show "Bob" set at a comic book company; actual s/a-Ty Templeton						2.50

MAD DOGS
Eclipse Comics: Feb, 1992 - No. 3, July, 1992 ($2.50, B&W, limited series)

	GD 2.0	VG 4.0	FN 6.0	VF 8.0	VF/NM 9.0	NM- 9.2
1-3						2.50

MAD 84 (Mad Extra)
E.C. Comics: 1984 (84 pgs.)

	GD 2.0	VG 4.0	FN 6.0	VF 8.0	VF/NM 9.0	NM- 9.2
1	1	3	4	6	8	10

MAD FOLLIES (Special)
E. C. Comics: 1963 - No. 7, 1969

	GD 2.0	VG 4.0	FN 6.0	VF 8.0	VF/NM 9.0	NM- 9.2
nn(1963)-Paperback book covers	25	50	75	181	278	375
2(1964)-Calendar	19	38	57	136	208	280
3(1965)-Mischief Stickers	15	30	45	105	160	215
4(1966)-Mobile; Frazetta-r/back-c Mad #90	11	22	33	79	117	155
5,6: 5(1967)-Stencils. 6(1968)-Mischief Stickers	9	18	27	60	85	110
7(1969)-Nasty Cards	9	18	27	60	85	110

(If bonus is missing, issue is half price)
NOTE: *Clarke c-4. Frazetta r-4, 6 (1 pg. ea.). Mingo c-1-3. Orlando a-5.*

MAD HATTER, THE (Costumed Hero)
O. W. Comics Corp.: Jan-Feb, 1946; No. 2, Sept-Oct, 1946

	GD 2.0	VG 4.0	FN 6.0	VF 8.0	VF/NM 9.0	NM- 9.2
1-Freddy the Firefly begins; Giunta-c/a	89	178	267	556	853	1150
2-Has ad for E.C.'s Animal Fables #1	42	84	126	256	391	525

MADHOUSE
Ajax/Farrell Publ. (Excellent Publ./4-Star): 3-4/54 - No. 4, 9-10/54; 6/57 - No. 4, Dec?, 1957

	GD 2.0	VG 4.0	FN 6.0	VF 8.0	VF/NM 9.0	NM- 9.2
1(1954)	32	64	96	184	267	350
2,3	17	34	51	95	135	175
4-Surrealistic-c	26	52	78	147	211	275
1(1957, 2nd series)	14	28	42	79	110	140
2-4 (#4 exist?)	10	20	30	56	73	90

MAD HOUSE (Formerly Madhouse Glads; ...Comics #104? on)
Red Circle Productions/Archie Publications: No. 95, 9/74 - No. 97, 1/75; No. 98, 8/75 - No. 130, 10/82

	GD 2.0	VG 4.0	FN 6.0	VF 8.0	VF/NM 9.0	NM- 9.2
95,96-Horror stories through #97; Morrow-c	2	4	6	10	13	16
97-Intro. Henry Hobson; Morrow-a/c, Thorne-a	2	4	6	8	10	12
98,99,101-120-Satire/humor stories. 110-Sabrina app.,1pg.	1	2	3	5	7	9
100	1	3	4	6	8	10
121-129	1	3	4	6	8	10
130	2	4	6	10	12	15
Annual 8(1970-71)-Formerly Madhouse Ma-ad Annual; Sabrina app. (6 pgs.)	4	8	12	28	38	48
Annual 9- 12(1974-75): 11-Wood-a(r)	2	4	6	12	16	20
...Comics Digest 1('75-76)	2	4	6	11	14	18
2-8(8/82)(...Mag. #5 on)-Sabrina in many	2	4	6	9	11	14

NOTE: *B. Jones a-96. McWilliams a-97. Wildey a-95, 96. See Archie Comics Digest #1, 13.*

MADHOUSE GLADS (Formerly ...Ma-ad; Madhouse #95 on)
Archie Publ.: No. 73, May, 1970 - No. 94, Aug, 1974 (No. 78-92: 52 pgs.)

	GD 2.0	VG 4.0	FN 6.0	VF 8.0	VF/NM 9.0	NM- 9.2
73-77,93,94: 74-1 pg. Sabrina	2	4	6	10	13	16
78-92 (52 pgs.)	2	4	6	12	16	20

MADHOUSE MA-AD (...Jokes #67-70; ...Freak-Out #71-74)
(Formerly Archie's Madhouse) (Becomes Madhouse Glads #73 on)
Archie Publications: No. 67, April, 1969 - No. 72, Jan, 1970

	GD 2.0	VG 4.0	FN 6.0	VF 8.0	VF/NM 9.0	NM- 9.2
67-71: 70-1 pg. Sabrina	2	4	6	14	18	22
72-6 pgs. Sabrina	4	8	12	22	30	38
...Annual 7(1969-70)-Formerly Archie's Madhouse Annual; becomes Madhouse Annual; 6 pgs. Sabrina	4	8	12	28	38	48

MADMAN (See Creatures of the Id #1)
Tundra Publishing: Mar, 1992 - No. 3, 1992 ($3.95, duotone, high quality, lim. series, 52 pgs.)

	GD 2.0	VG 4.0	FN 6.0	VF 8.0	VF/NM 9.0	NM- 9.2
1-Mike Allred-c/a in all	2	4	6	8	10	12
1-2nd printing						4.00
2,3						6.00

MADMAN ADVENTURES
Tundra Publishing: 1992 - No. 3, 1993 ($2.95, limited series)

	GD 2.0	VG 4.0	FN 6.0	VF 8.0	VF/NM 9.0	NM- 9.2
1-Mike Allred-c/a in all	1	2	3	5	7	9
2,3						5.00
TPB (Oni Press, 2002, $14.95) r/#1-3 & first app. of Frank Einstein from Creatures of the Id in color; gallery pages						15.00

MADMAN COMICS (Also see The Atomics)
Dark Horse Comics (Legend No. 2 on): Apr, 1994 - No. 20, Dec, 2000 ($2.95/$2.99)

	GD 2.0	VG 4.0	FN 6.0	VF 8.0	VF/NM 9.0	NM- 9.2
1-Allred-c/a; F. Miller back-c.	1	2	3	5	6	8
2-3: 3-Alex Toth back-c.						5.00
4-11: 4-Dave Stevens back-c. 6,7-Miller/Darrow's Big Guy app. 6-Bruce Timm back-c. 7-Darrow back-c. 8-Origin?; Bagge back-c. 10-Allred/Ross-c; Ross back-c. 11-Frazetta back-c						4.00
12-16: 12-(4/99)						3.00
17-20: 17-The G-Men From Hell #1 on cover; Brereton back-c. 18-(#2). 19,20-($2.99-c). 20-Clowes back-c						3.00
... Boogaloo TPB (6/99, $8.95) r/Nexus Meets Madman & Madman/The Jam						9.00
Ltd. Ed. Slipcover (1997, $99.95, signed and numbered) w/Vol.1 & Vol. 2. Vol.1- reprints #1-5; Vol. 2- reprints #6-10						100.00
The Complete Madman Comics: Vol. 2 (11/96, $17.95, TPB) r/#6-10 plus new material						18.00
Madman King-Size Super Groovy Special (Oni Press, 7/03, $6.95) new short stories by Allred, Derington, Krall and Weissman						7.00
Madman Picture Exhibition No. 1-4 (4-7/02, $3.95) pin-ups by various						4.00
Madman Picture Exhibition Limited Edition (10/02, $29.95) Hardcover collects MPE #1-4						30.00
Yearbook '95 (1996, $17.95, TPB)-r/#1-5, intro by Teller						18.00

MADMAN / THE JAM
Dark Horse Comics: Jul, 1998 - No. 2, Aug, 1998 ($2.95, mini-series)

	GD 2.0	VG 4.0	FN 6.0	VF 8.0	VF/NM 9.0	NM- 9.2
1,2-Allred & Mireault-s/a						3.00

MAD MONSTER PARTY (See Movie Classics)

MADNESS IN MURDERWORLD
Marvel Comics: 1989 (Came with computer game from Paragon Software)

	GD 2.0	VG 4.0	FN 6.0	VF 8.0	VF/NM 9.0	NM- 9.2
V1#1-Starring The X-Men						2.25

MADRAVEN HALLOWEEN SPECIAL
Hamilton Comics: Oct, 1995 ($2.95, one-shot)

	GD 2.0	VG 4.0	FN 6.0	VF 8.0	VF/NM 9.0	NM- 9.2
nn-Morrow-a						3.00

MADROX (from X-Factor)
Marvel Comics (Marvel Knights): Nov, 2004 - Present ($2.99)

	GD 2.0	VG 4.0	FN 6.0	VF 8.0	VF/NM 9.0	NM- 9.2
1-3-Peter David-s/Pablo Raimondi-a; Strong Guy app.						3.00

MAD SPECIAL (...Super Special)
E. C. Publications, Inc.: Fall, 1970 - Present (84 - 116 pgs.)
(If bonus is missing, issue is one half price)

	GD 2.0	VG 4.0	FN 6.0	VF 8.0	VF/NM 9.0	NM- 9.2
Fall 1970(#1)-Bonus-Voodoo Doll; contains 17 pgs. new material	10	20	30	73	107	140
Spring 1971(#2)-Wall Nuts; 17 pgs. new material	6	12	18	40	55	70
3-Protest Stickers	6	12	18	40	55	70
4-8: 4-Mini Posters. 5-Mad Flag. 6-Mad Mischief Stickers. 7-Presidential candidate posters, Wild Shocking Message posters. 8-TV Guise	5	10	15	36	48	60
9(1972)-Contains Nostalgic Mad #1 (28 pgs.)	4	8	12	27	36	45
10-13: 10-Nonsense Stickers (Don Martin). 13-Sickie Stickers; 3 pgs. Wolverton-r/Mad #137. 11-Contains 33-1/3 RPM record. 12-Contains Nostalgic Mad #2 (36 pgs.); Davis, Wolverton-a	4	8	12	22	30	38
14,16-21,24: 4-Vital Message posters & Art Depreciation paintings. 16-Mad-hesive Stickers. 17-Don Martin posters. 20-Martin Stickers. 18-Contains Nostalgic Mad #4 (36 pgs.). 21,24-Contains Nostalgic Mad #5 (28 pgs.) & #6 (28 pgs.)	3	6	9	18	23	28

Mage - The Hero Defined #6 © Matt Wagner

Magic Comics #19 © KING

Magneto Rex #1 © MAR

	GD 2.0	VG 4.0	FN 6.0	VF 8.0	VF/NM 9.0	NM- 9.2
15-Contains Nostalgic Mad #3 (28 pgs.)	3	6	9	18	24	30
22,23,25,27-29,30: 22-Diplomas. 23-Martin Stickers. 25-Martin Posters.27-Mad Shock-Sticks. 28-Contains Nostalgic Mad #7 (36 pgs.). 29-Mad Collectable-Correctables Posters. 30-The Movies	2	4	6	10	13	16
26-Has 33-1/3 RPM record	2	4	6	14	18	22
31,33-35,37-50	2	4	6	9	11	14
32-Contains Nostalgic Mad #8. 36-Has 96 pgs. of comic book & comic strip spoofs: titles "The Comics" on-c	2	4	6	10	13	16
51-70	1	3	4	6	8	10
71-88,90-100: 71-Batman parodies-r by Wood, Drucker. 72-Wolverton-c r-from 1st panel in Mad #11; Wolverton-s r/new dialogue. 83-All Star Trek spoof issue	1	2	3	5	6	8
76-(Fall, 1991)-Special Hussein Asylum Edition; distributed only to the troops in the Middle East (see Mad #300-303)	2	4	6	14	18	22
89-($3.95)-Polybagged w/1st of 3 Spy vs. Spy hologram trading cards (direct sale only issue) (other cards came w/card set)	1	3	4	6	8	10
101-135: 117-Sci-Fi parodies-r.						4.00

NOTE: *#28-30 have no number on cover.* ***Freas*** *c-76.* ***Mingo*** *c-9, 11, 15, 19, 23.*

MAGDALENA, THE (See The Darkness)
Image Comics (Top Cow): Apr, 2000 - No. 3, Jan, 2001 ($2.50)

	GD 2.0	VG 4.0	FN 6.0	VF 8.0	VF/NM 9.0	NM- 9.2
Preview Special ('00, $4.95) Flip book w/Blood Legacy preview						5.00
1-Benitez-c/a; variant covers by Silvestri & Turner						2.50
2,3: 2-Two covers						2.50
.../Angelus #1/2 (11/01, $2.95) Benitez-c/Ching-a						3.00
...Blood Divine (2002, $9.95) r/#1-3 & #1/2; cover gallery						10.00
.../Vampirella (7/03, $2.99) Wohl-s/Benitez-a; two covers						3.00

MAGDALENA, THE (Volume 2)
Image Comics (Top Cow): Aug, 2003 - Present ($2.99)

	GD 2.0	VG 4.0	FN 6.0	VF 8.0	VF/NM 9.0	NM- 9.2
Preview (6/03) B&W preview; Wizard World East logo on cover						2.25
1-4-Holguin-s/Basaldua-a						3.00
1-Variant-c by Jim Silke benefitting ACTOR charity						5.00
.../Vampirella (12/04, $2.99) Kirkman-s/Manapul-a; two covers by Manapul and Bachalo						3.00

MAGE (The Hero Discovered...; also see Grendel #16)
Comico: Feb, 1984 (no month) - No. 15, Dec, 1986 ($1.50, Mando paper)

	GD 2.0	VG 4.0	FN 6.0	VF 8.0	VF/NM 9.0	NM- 9.2
1-Comico's 1st color comic	2	4	6	9	11	14
2-5: 3-Intro Edsel						6.00
6-Grendel begins (1st in color)	3	6	9	16	20	25
7-1st new Grendel story	2	4	6	8	10	12
8-14: 13-Grendel dies. 14-Grendel story ends						6.00
15-($2.95) Double size w/pullout poster	1	2	3	5	6	8
TPB Volume 1-4 (Image, $5.95) 1- r/#1,2. 2- r/#3,4. 3- r/#5,6. 4- r/#7,8						7.00
TPB Volume 5-7 (Image, $6.95) 5- r/#9,10. 6- r/#11,12. 7- r/#13,14						7.00
TPB Volume 8 (Image, 9/99, $7.50) r/#15						7.50

MAGE (The Hero Defined)
Image Comics: July, 1997 - No. 15, Oct, 1999 ($2.50)

	GD 2.0	VG 4.0	FN 6.0	VF 8.0	VF/NM 9.0	NM- 9.2
0-(7/97, $5.00) American Ent. Ed.						5.00
1-14:Matt Wagner-c/s/a in all. 13-Three covers						2.50
1-"3-D Edition" (2/98, $4.95) w/glasses						5.00
15-($5.95) Acetate cover						6.00
Volume 1,2 TPB ('98,'99, $9.95) 1- r/#1-4. 2-r/#5-8						10.00
Volume 3 TPB ('00, $12.95) r/#9-12						13.00
Volume 4 TPB ('01, $14.95) r/#13-15						15.00

MAGE KNIGHT: STOLEN DESTINY (Based on the fantasy game Mage Knight)
Idea + Design Works: Oct, 2002 - No. 5, Feb, 2003 ($3.50, limited series)

	GD 2.0	VG 4.0	FN 6.0	VF 8.0	VF/NM 9.0	NM- 9.2
1-5: 1-J. Scott Campbell-c; Cabrera-a/Dezago-s, 2-Dave Johnson-c						3.50

MAGGIE AND HOPEY COLOR SPECIAL (See Love and Rockets)
Fantagraphics Books: May, 1997 ($3.50, one-shot)

	GD 2.0	VG 4.0	FN 6.0	VF 8.0	VF/NM 9.0	NM- 9.2
1						3.50

MAGGIE THE CAT (Also see Jon Sable, Freelance #11 & Shaman's Tears #12)
Image Comics (Creative Fire Studio): Jan, 1996 - No. 2, Feb, 1996 ($2.50, unfinished limited series)

	GD 2.0	VG 4.0	FN 6.0	VF 8.0	VF/NM 9.0	NM- 9.2
1,2: Mike Grell-c/a/scripts						2.50

MAGICA DE SPELL (See Walt Disney Showcase #30)

MAGIC AGENT (See Forbidden Worlds & Unknown Worlds)
American Comics Group: Jan-Feb, 1962 - No. 3, May-June, 1962

	GD 2.0	VG 4.0	FN 6.0	VF 8.0	VF/NM 9.0	NM- 9.2
1-Origin & 1st app. John Force	4	8	12	29	40	50
2,3	3	7	10	21	28	35

MAGICAL POKÉMON JOURNEY
Viz Comics: 2000 - Present ($4.95, B&W, magazine-size)

	GD 2.0	VG 4.0	FN 6.0	VF 8.0	VF/NM 9.0	NM- 9.2
1-4						5.00
Part 2: 1-3; Part 3: 1-4: 1-Includes color poster; Part 4: 1-4; Part 5: 1-4; Part 6: 1-4						5.00

MAGIC COMICS
David McKay Publications: Aug, 1939 - No. 123, Nov-Dec, 1949

	GD 2.0	VG 4.0	FN 6.0	VF 8.0	VF/NM 9.0	NM- 9.2
1-Mandrake the Magician, Henry, Popeye , Blondie, Barney Baxter, Secret Agent X-9 (not by Raymond), Bunky by Billy DeBeck & Thornton Burgess text stories illustrated by Harrison Cady begin; Henry covers begin	343	686	1029	1887	2744	3600
2	121	242	363	666	971	1275
3	90	180	270	495	723	950
4	70	140	210	385	563	740
5	56	112	168	308	447	585
6-10: 8-11,21-Mandrake/Henry-c	45	90	135	248	362	475
11-16,18,20: 12-Mandrake-c begin.	38	76	114	209	305	400
17-The Lone Ranger begins	42	84	126	231	336	440
19-Robot-c	45	90	135	248	362	475
21-30: 25-Only Blondie-c. 26-Dagwood-c begin	25	50	75	141	203	265
31-40: 36-Flag-c	18	36	54	102	146	190
41-50	15	30	45	83	117	150
51-60	12	24	36	71	98	125
61-70	11	22	33	62	84	105
71-99, 107,108-Flash Gordon app; not by Raymond	9	18	27	54	70	85
100	10	20	30	58	77	95
101-106,109-123: 123-Last Dagwood-c	9	18	27	51	62	75

MAGIC FLUTE, THE (See Night Music #9-11)

MAGIC PICKLE
Oni Press: Sept, 2001 - No. 4, Dec, 2001 ($2.95, limited series)

	GD 2.0	VG 4.0	FN 6.0	VF 8.0	VF/NM 9.0	NM- 9.2
1-4-Scott Morse-s/a; Mahfood-a (2 pgs.)						3.00

MAGIC SWORD, THE (See Movie Classics)

MAGIC THE GATHERING (Title Series), **Acclaim Comics (Armada)**

	GD 2.0	VG 4.0	FN 6.0	VF 8.0	VF/NM 9.0	NM- 9.2
...ANTIQUITIES WAR,11/95 - 2/96 ($2.50), 1-4-Paul Smith-a(p)						2.50
...ARABIAN NIGHTS, 12/95 - 1/96 ($2.50), 1,2						2.50
...COLLECTION ,'95 ($4.95), 1,2-polybagged						5.00
...CONVOCATIONS, '95 ($2.50), 1-nn-pin-ups						2.50
...ELDER DRAGONS ,'95 ($2.50), 1,2-Doug Wheatley-a						2.50
...FALLEN ANGEL ,'95 ($5.95), nn						6.00
...FALLEN EMPIRES ,9/95 - 10/95 ($2.75), 1,2						3.00
...Collection ($4.95)-polybagged						5.00
...HOMELANDS ,'95 ($5.95), nn-polybagged w/card; Hildebrandts-c						6.00
... ICE AGE (On The World of...) ,7/5 -11/95 ($2.50), 1-4: 1,2-bound-in Magic Card. 3,4-bound-in insert						2.50
...LEGEND OF JEDIT OJANEN, '96 ($2.50), 1,2						2.50
...NIGHTMARE, '95 ($2.50, one shot), 1						2.50
...THE SHADOW MAGE, 7/95 - 10/95 ($2.50), 1-4-bagged w/Magic The Gathering card						2.50
...Collection 1,2 (1995, $4.95)-Trade paperback; polybagged						5.00
...SHANDALAR ,'96 ($2.50), 1,2						2.50
...WAYFARER ,11/95 - 2/96 ($2.50), 1-5						2.50

MAGIC: THE GATHERING: GERRARD'S QUEST
Dark Horse Comics: Mar, 1998 - No. 4, June, 1998 ($2.95, limited series)

	GD 2.0	VG 4.0	FN 6.0	VF 8.0	VF/NM 9.0	NM- 9.2
1-4: Grell-s/Mhan-a						3.00

MAGIK (Illyana and Storm Limited Series)
Marvel Comics Group: Dec, 1983 - No. 4, Mar, 1984 (60¢, limited series)

	GD 2.0	VG 4.0	FN 6.0	VF 8.0	VF/NM 9.0	NM- 9.2
1-4: 1-Characters from X-Men; Inferno begins; X-Men cameo (Buscema pencils in #1,2; c-1p. 2-4: 2-Nightcrawler app. & X-Men cameo						3.00

MAGIK (See Black Sun mini-series)
Marvel Comics: Dec, 2000 - No. 4, Mar, 2001 ($2.99, limited series)

	GD 2.0	VG 4.0	FN 6.0	VF 8.0	VF/NM 9.0	NM- 9.2
1-4-Liam Sharp-a/Abnett & Lanning-s; Nightcrawler app.						3.00

MAGILLA GORILLA (TV) (See Kite Fun Book)
Gold Key: May, 1964 - No. 10, Dec, 1968 (Hanna-Barbera)

	GD 2.0	VG 4.0	FN 6.0	VF 8.0	VF/NM 9.0	NM- 9.2
1-1st comic app.	11	22	33	80	120	160
2-4: 3-Vs. Yogi Bear for President. 4-1st Punkin Puss & Mushmouse, Ricochet Rabbit & Droop-a-Long	8	16	24	53	74	95
5-10: 10-Reprints	7	14	21	46	63	80

MAGILLA GORILLA (TV)(See Spotlight #4)

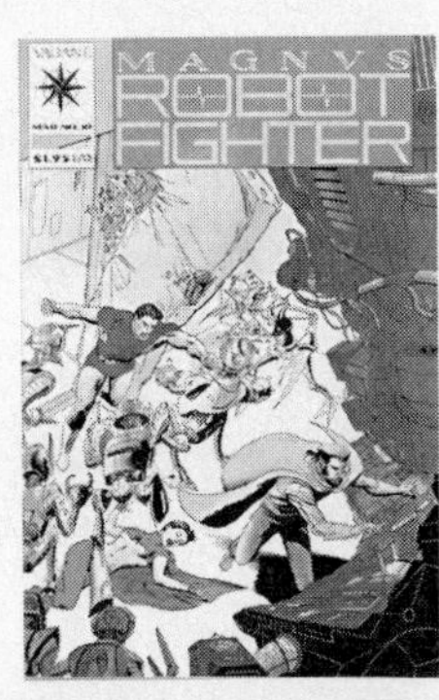

Magnus Robot Fighter #10 © VAL

Majestic #1 © DC

Man Comics #15 © MAR

GD 2.0 | VG 4.0 | FN 6.0 | VF 8.0 | VF/NM 9.0 | NM- 9.2

Charlton Comics: Nov, 1970 - No. 5, July, 1971 (Hanna-Barbera)
1 6 12 18 40 55 70
2-5 4 8 12 24 32 40

MAGNETIC MEN FEATURING MAGNETO
Marvel Comics (Amalgam): June, 1997 ($1.95, one-shot)
1-Tom Peyer-s/Barry Kitson & Dan Panosian-a 2.50

MAGNETO (See X-Men #1)
Marvel Comics: nd (Sept, 1993) (Giveaway) (one-shot)
0-Embossed foil-c by Sienkiewicz; r/Classic X-Men #19 & 12 by Bolton 5.00

MAGNETO
Marvel Comics: Nov, 1996 - No. 4, Feb, 1997 ($1.95, limited series)
1-4: Peter Milligan scripts & Kelley Jones-a(p) 2.50

MAGNETO AND THE MAGNETIC MEN
Marvel Comics (Amalgam): Apr, 1996 ($1.95, one-shot)
1-Jeff Matsuda-a(p) 2.50

MAGNETO ASCENDANT
Marvel Comics: May, 1999 ($3.99, squarebound one-shot)
1-Reprints early Magneto appearances 4.00

MAGNETO: DARK SEDUCTION
Marvel Comics: Jun, 2000 - No. 4, Sept, 2000 ($2.99, limited series)
1-4: Nicieza-s/Cruz-a. 3,4-Avengers-c/app. 3.00

MAGNETO REX
Marvel Comics: Apr, 1999 - No. 3, July, 1999 ($2.50, limited series)
1-3-Rogue, Quicksilver app.; Peterson-a(p) 2.50

MAGNUS, ROBOT FIGHTER (...4000 A.D.)(See Doctor Solar)
Gold Key: Feb, 1963 - No. 46, Jan, 1977 (All painted covers except #5,31)
1-Origin & 1st app. Magnus; Aliens (1st app.) series begins
25 50 75 177 271 365
2,3 11 22 33 80 120 160
4-10: 10-Simonson fan club illo (5/65, 1st-a?) 8 16 24 53 74 95
11-20 6 12 18 38 52 65
21,24-28: 28-Aliens ends 4 8 12 25 33 42
22,23: 22-Origin-r/#1; last 12¢ issue 4 8 12 27 36 45
29-46-Mostly reprints 2 4 6 12 16 20
NOTE: ***Manning** a-1-22, 28-43(r). **Spiegle** a-23, 44r.*

MAGNUS ROBOT FIGHTER (Also see Vintage Magnus)
Valiant/Acclaim Comics: May, 1991 - No. 64, Feb, 1996 ($1.75/$1.95/$2.25/$2.50)
1-Nichols/Layton-c/a; 1-8 have trading cards 1 2 3 5 6 8
2-8: 4-Rai cameo. 5-Origin & 1st full app. Rai (10/91); 5-8 are in flip book format and back-c & half of book are Rai #1-4 mini-series. 6-1st Solar x-over. 7-Magnus vs. Rai-c/story; 1st X-O Armor 6.00
0-Origin issue; Layton-a; ordered through mail w/coupons from 1st 8 issues plus 50¢; B. Smith trading card 1 2 3 5 6 8
0-Sold thru comic shops without trading card 3.00
9-11 3.00
12-(3.25, 44 pgs.)-Turok-c/story (1st app. in Valiant universe, 5/92); has 8 pg. Magnus story insert 1 2 3 5 7 9
13-24,26-48: 14-1st app. Isak. 15,16-Unity x-overs. 15-Miller-c. 16-Birth of Magnus. 21-New direction & new logo. 21-Gold ink variant. 24-Story cont'd in Rai & the Future Force #9. 33-Timewalker app.36-Bound-in trading cards. 37-Rai & Starwatchers app. 44-Bound-in sneak peek card. 2.50
25-($2.95)-Embossed silver foil-c; new costume 3.00
49-63 3.00
64-($2.50): 64-Magnus dies? 4.00
...Invasion (1994, $9.95)-r/Rai #1-4 & Magnus #5-8 10.00
Magnus Steel Nation (1994, $9.95) r/#1-4 10.00
Yearbook (1994, $3.95, 52 pgs.) 4.00
NOTE: ***Ditko/Reese** a-18. **Layton** a(i)-5; c-6-9i, 25; back(i)-5-8. **Reese** a(i)-22, 25, 28; c(i)-22, 24, 28. **Simonson** c-16. Prices for issues 1-8 are for trading cards and coupons intact.*

MAGNUS ROBOT FIGHTER
Acclaim Comics (Valiant Heroes): V2#1, May, 1997 - No. 18, Jun, 1998 ($2.50)
1-18: 1-Reintro Magnus; Donavon Wylie (X-O Manowar) cameo; Tom Peyer scripts & Mike McKone-c/a begin; painted variant-c exists 2.50

MAGNUS ROBOT FIGHTER/NEXUS
Valiant/Dark Horse Comics: Dec, 1993 - No. 2, Apr, 1994 ($2.95, lim. series)
1,2: Steve Rude painted-c & pencils in all 3.00

MAID OF THE MIST (See American Graphics)

MAI, THE PSYCHIC GIRL
Eclipse Comics: May, 1987 - No. 28, July, 1989 ($1.50, B&W, bi-weekly, 44pgs.)
1-28, 1,2-2nd print 2.50

MAJESTIC (Mr. Majestic from WildCATS)
DC Comics: Oct, 2004 - No. 4, Jan, 2005 ($2.95, limited series)
1-4-Kerschl-a/Abnett & Lanning-s. 1-Superman app.; Superman #1 cover swipe 3.00

MAJOR BUMMER
DC Comics: Aug, 1997 - No. 15, Oct, 1998 ($2.50)
1-15: 1-Origin and 1st app. Major Bummer 2.50

MAJOR HOOPLE COMICS (See Crackajack Funnies)
Nedor Publications: nd (Jan, 1943)
1-Mary Worth, Phantom Soldier app. by Moldoff 40 80 120 239 357 475

MAJOR VICTORY COMICS (Also see Dynamic Comics)
H. Clay Glover/Service Publ./Harry 'A' Chesler: 1944 - No. 3, Summer, 1945
1-Origin Major Victory (patriotic hero) by C. Sultan (reprint from Dynamic #1); 1st app. Spider Woman 65 130 195 406 628 850
2-Dynamic Boy app. 40 80 120 236 351 465
3-Rocket Boy app. 39 78 117 222 324 425

MALIBU ASHCAN: RAFFERTY (See Firearm #12)
Malibu Comics (Ultraverse): Nov, 1994 (99¢, B&W w/color-c; one-shot)
1-Previews "The Rafferty Saga" storyline in Firearm; Chaykin-c 2.25

MALTESE FALCON
David McKay Publications: No. 48, 1946
Feature Books 48-by Dashiell Hammett 77 154 231 481 741 1000

MALU IN THE LAND OF ADVENTURE
I. W. Enterprises: 1964 (See White Princess of Jungle #2)
1-r/Avon's Slave Girl Comics #1; Severin-c 6 12 18 38 52 65

MAMMOTH COMICS
Whitman Publishing Co.(K. K. Publ.): 1938 (84 pgs.) (B&W, 8-1/2x11-1/2")
1-Alley Oop, Terry & the Pirates, Dick Tracy, Little Orphan Annie, Wash Tubbs, Moon Mullins, Smilin' Jack, Tailspin Tommy, Don Winslow, Dan Dunn, Smokey Stover & other reprints (scarce) 208 416 624 1300 2000 2700

MAN AGAINST TIME
Image Comics (Motown Machineworks): May, 1996 - No. 4, Aug, 1996 ($2.25, limited series)
1-4: 1-Simonson-c. 2,3-Leon-c. 4-Barreto & Leon-c 2.25

MAN-BAT (See Batman Family, Brave & the Bold, & Detective #400)
National Periodical Publ./DC Comics: Dec-Jan, 1975-76 - No. 2, Feb-Mar, 1976; Dec, 1984
1-Ditko-a(p); Aparo-c; Batman app.; 1st app. She-Bat?
2 4 6 12 16 20
2-Aparo-c 2 4 6 8 10 12
1 (12/84)-N. Adams-r(3)/Det.(Vs. Batman on-c) 4.00

MAN-BAT
DC Comics: Feb, 1996 - No. 3, Apr, 1996 ($2.25, limited series)
1-3: Dixon scripts in all. 2-Killer Croc-c/app. 2.25

MAN CALLED A-X, THE
Malibu Comics (Bravura): Nov, 1994 - No. 4, Jun, 1995 ($2.95, limited series)
0-4: Marv Wolfman scripts & Shawn McManus-c/a. 0-(2/95). 1-"1A" on cover 3.00

MAN CALLED A-X, THE
DC Comics: Oct, 1997 - No. 8, May, 1998 ($2.50)
1-8: Marv Wolfman scripts & Shawn McManus-c/a. 2.50

MAN COMICS
Marvel/Atlas Comics (NPI): Dec, 1949 - No. 28, Sept, 1953 (#1-6: 52 pgs.)
1-Tuska-a 24 48 72 135 195 255
2-Tuska-a 14 28 42 79 110 140
3-6 10 20 30 60 80 100
7,8 10 20 30 58 77 95
9-13,15: 9-Format changes to war 8 16 24 46 58 70
14-Henkel (3 pgs.); Pakula-a 9 18 27 52 66 80
16-21,23-28: 28-Crime issue (Bob Brant) 8 16 24 40 50 60
22-Krigstein-a, 5 pgs. 9 18 27 52 66 80
NOTE: ***Berg** a-14, 15, 19. **Colan** a-9, 21. **Everett** a-8, 22; c-22, 25. **Heath** a-11, 17, 21. Kubertish a-by **Bob Brown**-3. **Maneely** a-11; c-10, 11. **Reinman** a-11. **Robinson** a-7, 10, 14. **Robert Sale** a-9, 11. **Sinnott** a-22, 23. **Tuska** a-14, 23.*

MANDRAKE THE MAGICIAN (See Defenders Of The Earth, 123, 46, 52, 55, Giant Comic Album, King Comics, Magic Comics, The Phantom #21, Tiny Tot Funnies & Wow Comics, '36)

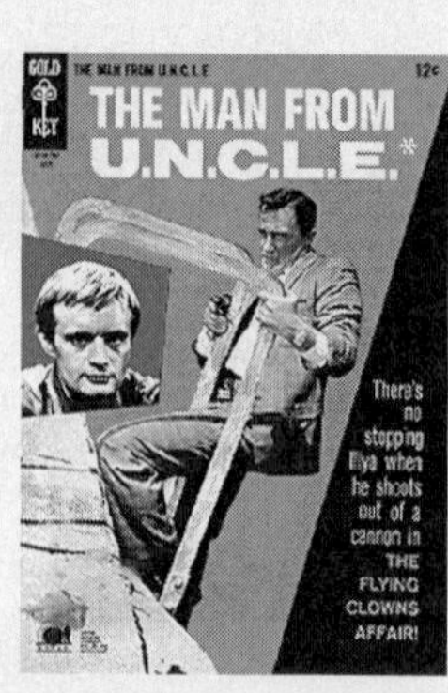

The Man From U.N.C.L.E. #13 © GK

Manhunt! #3 © ME

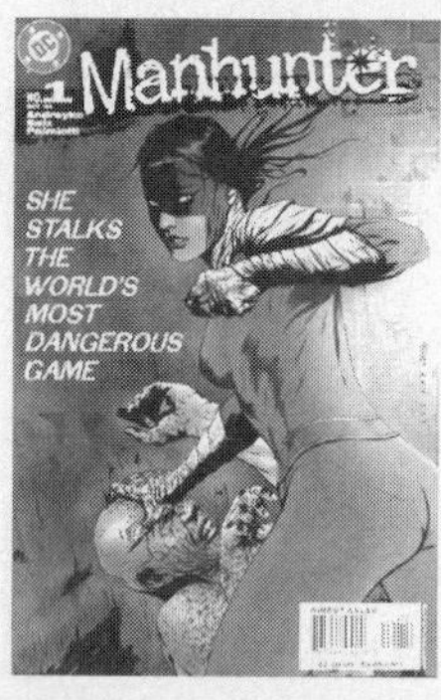

Manhunter ('04) #1 © DC

	GD 2.0	VG 4.0	FN 6.0	VF 8.0	VF/NM 9.0	NM- 9.2

MANDRAKE THE MAGICIAN (See Harvey Comics Hits #53)
David McKay Publ./Dell/King Comics (All 12¢): 1938 - 1948; Sept, 1966 - No. 10, Nov, 1967 (Also see Four Color #752)

	GD	VG	FN	VF	VF/NM	NM-
Feature Books 18,19,23 (1938)	60	120	180	375	575	775
Feature Books 46	44	88	132	268	409	550
Feature Books 52,55	37	74	111	213	312	410
Four Color 752 (11/56)	12	24	36	82	124	165
1-Begin S.O.S. Phantom, ends #3	6	12	18	40	55	70
2-7,9: 4-Girl Phantom app. 5-Flying Saucer-c/story. 5,6-Brick Bradford app. 7-Origin Lothar. 9-Brick Bradford app.	4	8	12	22	30	38
8-Jeff Jones-a (4 pgs.)	4	8	12	25	33	42
10-Rip Kirby app.; Raymond-a (14 pgs.)	4	8	12	29	40	50

MANDRAKE THE MAGICIAN
Marvel Comics: Apr, 1995 - No. 2, May, 1995 ($2.95, unfinished limited series)

1,2: Mike Barr scripts 3.00

MAN-EATING COW (See Tick #7,8)
New England Comics: July, 1992 - No. 10, 1994? ($2.75, B&W, limited series)

1-10 3.00
Man-Eating Cow Bonanza (6/96, $4.95, 128 pgs.)-r/#1-4. 5.00

MAN FROM ATLANTIS (TV)
Marvel Comics: Feb, 1978 - No. 7, Aug, 1978

	GD	VG	FN	VF	VF/NM	NM-
1-(84 pgs.)-Sutton-a(p), Buscema-c; origin & cast photos	1	3	4	6	8	10
2-7						4.00

MAN FROM PLANET X, THE
Planet X Productions: 1987 (no price; probably unlicensed)

1-Reprints Fawcett Movie Comic 2.25

MAN FROM U.N.C.L.E., THE (TV) (Also see The Girl From Uncle)
Gold Key: Feb, 1965 - No. 22, Apr, 1969 (All photo-c)

	GD	VG	FN	VF	VF/NM	NM-
1	16	32	48	112	171	230
2-Photo back c-2-8	9	18	27	65	93	120
3-10: 7-Jet Dream begins (1st app., also see Jet Dream) (all new stories)	7	14	21	51	71	90
11-22: 19-Last 12¢ issue. 21,22-Reprint #10 & 7	7	14	21	46	63	80

MAN FROM U.N.C.L.E., THE (TV)
Entertainment Publishing: 1987 - No. 11 ($1.50/$1.75, B&W)

1-7 ($1.50), 8-11 ($1.75) 3.00

MAN FROM WELLS FARGO (TV)
Dell Publishing Co.: No. 1287, Feb-Apr, 1962 - May-July, 1962 (Photo-c)

	GD	VG	FN	VF	VF/NM	NM-
Four Color 1287, #01-495-207	7	14	21	46	63	80

MANGA SHI (See Tomoe)
Crusade Entertainment: Aug, 1996 ($2.95)

1-Printed backwards (manga-style) 3.00

MANGA SHI 2000
Crusade Entertainment: Feb, 1997 - No. 3, June, 1997 ($2.95, mini-series)

1-3: 1-Two covers 3.00

MANGA ZEN (Also see Zen Intergalactic Ninja)
Zen Comics (Fusion Studios): 1996 - No. 3, 1996 ($2.50, B&W)

1-3 2.50

MANGAZINE
Antarctic Press: Aug, 1985 - No. 4, Sept, 1986 (B&W)

	GD	VG	FN	VF	VF/NM	NM-
1-Soft paper-c	2	4	6	11	14	18
2-4	2	4	6	8	10	12

MANGLE TANGLE TALES
Innovation Publishing: 1990 ($2.95, deluxe format)

1-Intro by Harlan Ellison 3.00

MANHUNT! (Becomes Red Fox #15 on)
Magazine Enterprises: 10/47 - No. 11, 8/48; #13,14, 1953 (no #12)

	GD	VG	FN	VF	VF/NM	NM-
1-Red Fox by L. B. Cole, Undercover Girl by Whitney, Space Ace begin (1st app.); negligee panels	50	100	150	305	465	625
2-Electrocution-c	40	80	120	233	342	450
3-6	34	68	102	193	279	365
7-10: 7-Space Ace ends. 8-Trail Colt begins (intro/1st app., 5/48) by Guardineer; Trail Colt-c. 10-G. Ingels-a	30	60	90	170	245	320
11(8/48)-Frazetta-a, 7 pgs.; The Duke, Scotland Yard begin	40	80	120	238	354	470
13(A-1 #63)-Frazetta, r-/Trail Colt #1, 7 pgs.	40	80	120	230	335	440
14(A-1 #77)-Bondage/hypo-c; last L. B. Cole Red Fox; Ingels-a	33	66	99	190	275	360

NOTE: *Guardineer a-1-5; c-8.* ***Whitney*** *a-2-14; c-1-6, 10. Red Fox by* ***L. B. Cole****-#1-14. #15 was advertised but came out as Red Fox #15. Bondage c-6.*

MANHUNTER (See Adventure #58, 73, Brave & the Bold, Detective Comics, 1st Issue Special, House of Mystery #143 and Justice League of America)
DC Comics: 1984 ($2.50, 76 pgs; high quality paper)

1-Simonson-c/a(r)/Detective; Batman app. 3.50

MANHUNTER
DC Comics: July, 1988 - No. 24, Apr, 1990 ($1.00)

1-24: 8,9-Flash app. 9-Invasion. 17-Batman-c/sty 2.25

MANHUNTER
DC Comics: No. 0, Nov, 1994 - No. 12, Nov, 1995 ($1.95/$2.25)

0-12 2.25

MANHUNTER
DC Comics: Oct, 2004 - Present ($2.50)

1-4: 1-Intro. Kate Spencer; Saiz-a/Jae Lee-c/Andreyko-s. 2,3 Shadow Thief app. 2.50

MANHUNTER: THE SPECIAL EDITION
DC Comics: 1999 ($9.95)

TPB-Reprints Detective Comics stories by Goodwin and Simonson 10.00

MAN IN BLACK (See Thrill-O-Rama) (Also see All New Comics, Front Page, Green Hornet #31, Strange Story & Tally-Ho Comics)
Harvey Publications: Sept, 1957 - No. 4, Mar, 1958

	GD	VG	FN	VF	VF/NM	NM-
1-Bob Powell-c/a	18	36	54	100	143	185
2-4: Powell-c/a	14	28	42	79	110	140

MAN IN BLACK
Lorne-Harvey Publications (Recollections): 1990 - No. 2, July, 1991 (B&W)

1,2 3.00

MAN IN FLIGHT (Disney, TV)
Dell Publishing Co.: No. 836, Sept, 1957

	GD	VG	FN	VF	VF/NM	NM-
Four Color 836	8	16	24	58	82	105

MAN IN SPACE (Disney, TV, see Dell Giant #27)
Dell Publishing Co.: No. 716, Aug, 1956 - No. 954, Nov, 1958

	GD	VG	FN	VF	VF/NM	NM-
Four Color 716-A science feat. from Tomorrowland	10	20	30	70	100	130
Four Color 954-Satellites	8	16	24	58	82	105

MANKIND (WWF Wrestling)
Chaos Comics: Sept, 1999 ($2.95, one-shot)

1-Regular and photo-c 3.00
1-Premium Edition ($10.00) Dwayne Turner & Danny Miki-c 10.00

MANN AND SUPERMAN
DC Comics: 2000 ($5.95, prestige format, one-shot)

nn-Michael T. Gilbert-s/a 6.00

MAN OF STEEL, THE (Also see Superman: The Man of Steel)
DC Comics: 1986 (June release) - No. 6, 1986 (75¢, limited series)

1-6: 1-Silver logo; Byrne-c/a/scripts in all; origin, 1-Alternate-c for newsstand sales,1-Distr. to toy stores by So Much Fun, 2-6: 2-Intro. Lois Lane, Jimmy Olsen. 3-Intro/origin Magpie; Batman-c/story. 4-Intro. new Lex Luthor 4.00
1-6-Silver Editions (1993, $1.95)-r/1-6 3.00
...The Complete Saga nn-Contains #1-6, given away in contest 26.00

	GD	VG	FN	VF	VF/NM	NM-
Limited Edition, softcover	5	10	15	36	48	60

NOTE: *Issues 1-6 were released between Action #583 (9/86) & Action #584 (1/87) plus Superman #423 (9/86) & Advs. of Superman #424 (1/87).*

MAN OF THE ATOM (See Solar, Man of the Atom Vol. 2)

MAN OF WAR (See Liberty Guards & Liberty Scouts)
Centaur Publications: Nov, 1941 - No. 2, Jan, 1942

	GD	VG	FN	VF	VF/NM	NM-
1-The Fire-Man, Man of War, The Sentinel, Liberty Guards, & Vapo-Man begin; Gustavson-c/a; Flag-c	169	338	507	1056	1628	2200
2-Intro The Ferret; Gustavson-c/a	125	250	375	781	1203	1625

MAN OF WAR
Eclipse Comics: Aug, 1987 - No. 3, Feb, 1988 ($1.75, Baxter paper)

1-3: Bruce Jones scripts 2.25

MAN OF WAR (See The Protectors)
Malibu Comics: 1993 - No, 8, Feb, 1994 ($1.95/$2.50/$2.25)

1-5 ($1.95)-Newsstand Editions w/different-c 2.25

Man O' Mars #1 © FH

Man-Thing ('04) #1 © MAR

Marge's Little Lulu #1 © Marjorie Buell

GD 2.0 | VG 4.0 | FN 6.0 | VF 8.0 | VF/NM 9.0 | NM- 9.2

1-8-1-5-Collector's Edi. w/poster. 6-8 ($2.25): 6-Polybagged w/Skycap. 8-Vs. Rocket Rangers 2.50

MAN O' MARS
Fiction House Magazines: 1953; 1964

1-Space Rangers; Whitman-c 42 84 126 256 391 525
I.W. Reprint #1-r/Man O'Mars #1 & Star Pirate; Murphy Anderson-a 6 12 18 40 55 70

MANTECH ROBOT WARRIORS
Archie Enterprises, Inc.: Sept, 1984 - No. 4, Apr, 1985 (75¢)

1-4: Ayers-c/a(p). 1-Buckler-c(i) 3.00

MAN-THING (See Fear, Giant-Size..., Marvel Comics Presents, Marvel Fanfare, Monsters Unleashed, Power Record Comics & Savage Tales)
Marvel Comics Group: Jan, 1974 - No. 22, Oct, 1975; V2#1, Nov, 1979 - V2#11, July, 1981

1-Howard the Duck(2nd app.) cont'd/Fear #19 5 10 15 36 48 60
2 3 6 9 16 20 25
3-1st app. original Foolkiller 2 4 6 12 16 20
4-Origin Foolkiller; last app. 1st Foolkiller 2 4 6 11 14 18
5-11-Ploog-a. 11-Foolkiller cameo (flashback) 2 4 6 11 14 18
12-22: 19-1st app. Scavenger. 20-Spidey cameo. 21-Origin Scavenger, Man-Thing. 22-Howard the Duck cameo 1 3 4 6 8 10
V2#1(1979) 1 2 3 5 6 8
V2#2-11: 4-Dr. Strange-c/app. 11-Mayerik-a 4.00
NOTE: ***Alcala*** *a-14.* ***Brunner*** *c-1. J.* ***Buscema*** *a-12p, 13p, 16p.* ***Gil Kane*** *c-4p, 10p, 12-20p, 21.* ***Mooney*** *a-17, 18, 19p, 20-22, V2#1-3p.* ***Ploog*** *Man-Thing-5p, 6p, 7, 8, 9-11p; c-5, 6, 8, 9, 11.* ***Sutton*** *a-13i. No. 19 says #10 in indicia.*

MAN-THING (Volume Three, continues in Strange Tales #1 (9/98))
Marvel Comics: Dec, 1997 - No. 8, July, 1998 ($2.99)

1-8-DeMatteis-s/Sharp-a. 2-Two covers. 6-Howard the Duck-c/app. 3.00

MAN-THING (Prequel to 2005 movie)
Marvel Comics: Sept, 2004 - No. 3, Nov, 2004 ($2.99, limited series)

1-3-Hans Rodionoff-s/Kyle Hotz-a 3.00

MANTRA
Malibu Comics (Ultraverse): July, 1993 - No. 24, Aug, 1995 ($1.95/$2.50)

1-Polybagged w/trading card & coupon 3.00
1-Newsstand edition w/o trading card or coupon 2.25
1-Full cover holographic edition 1 3 4 6 8 10
1-Ultra-limited silver foil-c 5.00
2-9,11-24: 3-Intro Warstrike & Kismet. 6-Break-Thru x-over. 2-($2.50-Newsstand edition bagged w/card. 4-($2.50, 48 pgs.)-Rune flip-c/story by B. Smith (3 pgs.). 7-Prime app.; origin Prototype by Jurgens/Austin (2 pgs.). 11-New costume. 17-Intro NecroMantra & Pinnacle; prelude to Godwheel 2.50
10-($3.50, 68 pgs.)-Flip-c w/Ultraverse Premiere #2 3.50
Giant Size 1 (7/94, $2.50, 44 pgs.) 2.50
...Spear of Destiny 1,2 (4/95, $2.50, 36pgs.) 2.50

MANTRA (2nd Series) (Also See Black September)
Malibu Comics (Ultraverse): Infinity, Sept, 1995 - No. 7, Apr, 1996 ($1.50)

Infinity (9/95, $1.50)-Black September x-over, Intro new Mantra 2.25
1-7: 1-(10/95). 5-Return of Eden (original Mantra). 6,7-Rush app. 2.25

MAN WITH THE X-RAY EYES, THE (See X,... under Movie Comics)

MANY GHOSTS OF DR. GRAVES, THE (Doctor Graves #73 on)
Charlton Comics: 5/67 - No. 60, 12/76; No. 61, 9/77 - No. 62, 10/77; No. 63, 2/78 - No. 65, 4/78; No. 66, 6/81 - No. 72, 5/82

1-Ditko-a; Palais-a; early issues 12¢-c 6 12 18 38 52 65
2-6,8,10 3 6 9 18 23 28
7,9-Ditko-a 3 6 9 19 25 32
11-13,16-18-Ditko-c/a 3 6 9 16 20 24
14,19,23,25 2 4 6 9 11 14
15,20,21-Ditko-a 2 4 6 10 13 16
22,24,26,27,29-35,38,40-Ditko-c/a 2 4 6 11 14 18
28-Ditko-c 2 4 6 10 13 16
36,46,56,57,59,66-69,71 1 2 3 5 7 9
37,41,43,51,60,61-Ditko-a 2 4 6 8 10 12
39,58-Ditko-c. 39-Sutton-a. 58-Ditko-a 2 4 6 8 10 12
42,44,53-Sutton-c; Ditko-a. 42-Sutton-a 2 4 6 8 10 12
45-(5/74) 2nd Newton comic work (8 pgs.); new logo; Sutton-c 2 4 6 10 13 16
47-Newton, Sutton, Ditko-a 2 4 6 9 11 14
48-Ditko, Sutton-a 2 4 6 8 10 12
49-Newton-c/a; Sutton-a. 1 3 4 6 8 10
50-Sutton-a 1 2 3 5 7 9
52-Newton-c; Ditko-a 2 4 6 8 10 12
54-Early Byrne-c; Ditko-a 2 4 6 8 10 12
55-Ditko-c; Sutton-a 2 4 6 8 10 12
62-65-Ditko-c/a. 65-Sutton-a 2 4 6 10 13 16
70,72-Ditko-a 2 4 6 9 11 14
Modern Comics Reprint 12,25 (1978) 4.00
NOTE: ***Aparo*** *a-4, 5, 7, 8, 66r, 69r; c-8, 14, 19, 66r, 67r.* ***Byrne*** *c-54.* ***Ditko*** *a-1, 7, 9, 11-13, 15-18, 20-22, 24, 26, 27, 29, 30-35, 37, 38, 40-44, 47, 48, 51-54, 58, 60r-65r, 70, 72; c-11-13, 16-18, 22, 24, 26-35, 38, 40, 55, 58, 62-65.* ***Howard*** *a-38, 39, 45i, 65; c-48.* ***Kim*** *a-36, 46, 52.* ***Larson*** *a-58.* ***Morisi*** *a-13, 14, 23, 26.* ***Newton*** *a-45, 47p, 49p; c-49, 52.* ***Staton*** *a-36, 37, 41, 43.* ***Sutton*** *a-39, 42, 47-50, 55, 65; c-42, 44, 45; painted c-53.* ***Zeck*** *a-56, 59.*

MANY LOVES OF DOBIE GILLIS (TV)
National Periodical Publications: May-June, 1960 - No. 26, Oct, 1964

1-Most covers by Bob Oskner 25 50 75 181 278 375
2-5 14 28 42 97 149 200
6-10: 10-Last 10¢-c 10 20 30 67 96 125
11-26: 20-Drucker-a. 24-(3-4/64). 25-(9/64) 9 18 27 60 85 110

MANY WORLDS OF TESLA STRONG, THE (Also see Tom Strong)
America's Best Comics: July, 2003 ($5.95, one-shot)

1-Two covers by Timm & Art Adams; art by various incl. Campbell, Cho, Noto, Hughes 6.00

MARAUDER'S MOON (See Luke Short, Four Color #848)

MARCH OF COMICS (See Promotional Comics section)

MARCH OF CRIME (Formerly My Love Affair #1-6) (See Fox Giants)
Fox Features Synd.: No. 7, July, 1950 - No. 2, Sept, 1950; No. 3, Sept, 1951

7(#1)(7/50)-True crime stories; Wood-a 40 80 120 235 348 460
2(9/50)-Wood-a (exceptional) 40 80 120 230 335 440
3(9/51) 19 38 57 107 154 200

MARCO POLO
Charlton Comics Group: 1962 (Movie classic)

nn (Scarce)-Glanzman-c/a (25 pgs.) 11 22 33 77 114 150

MARC SILVESTRI SKETCHBOOK
Image Comics (Top Cow): Jan, 2004 ($2.99, one-shot)

1-Character sketches, concept artwork, storyboards of Witchblade, Darkness & others 3.00

MARC SPECTOR: MOON KNIGHT (Also see Moon Knight)
Marvel Comics: June, 1989 - No. 60, Mar, 1994 ($1.50/$1.75, direct sales)

1-24,26-49,51-54,58,59: 4-Intro new Midnight. 8,9-Punisher app. 15-Silver Sable app. 19-21-Spider-Man & Punisher app. 25-(52 pgs.)-Ghost Rider app. 32,33-Hobgoblin II (Macendale) & Spider-Man (in black costume) app. 35-38-Punisher story. 42-44-Infinity War x-over. 46-Demogoblin app. 51,53-Gambit app. 55-New look. 57-Spider-Man-c/story. 60-Moon Knight dies 2.50
50-(56 pgs.)-Special die-cut-c 3.00
55-57,60-Platt a 3.50
...: Divided We Fall ($4.95, 52 pgs.) 5.00
Special 1 (1992, $2.50) 2.50
NOTE: *Cowan c(p) 20-23. Guice c-20. Heath c/a-4. Platt -a 55-57,60; c-55-60.*

MARGARET O'BRIEN (See The Adventures of...)

MARGE'S LITTLE LULU (Continues as Little Lulu from #207 on)
Dell Publishing Co./Gold Key #165-206: No. 74, 6/45 - No. 164, 7-9/62; No. 165, 10/62 - No. 206, 8/72
Marjorie Henderson Buell, born in Philadelphia, Pa., in 1904, created Little Lulu, a cartoon character that appeared weekly in the Saturday Evening Post from Feb. 23, 1935 through Dec. 30, 1944. She was not responsible for any of the comic books. **John Stanley** did pencils only on all Little Lulu comics through at least #135 (1959). He did pencils and inks on Four Color #74 & 97. **Irving Tripp** began inking stories from #1 on, and remained the comic's illustrator throughout its entire run. **Stanley** did storyboards (layouts), pencils, and scripts in all cases and inking only on covers. His word balloons were written in cursive. **Tripp** and occasionally other artists at Western Publ. in Poughkeepsie, N.Y. blew up the pencilled pages, inked the blowups, and lettered them. **Arnold Drake** did storyboards, pencils and scripts starting with #197 (1970) on, amidst reprinted issues. **Buell** sold her rights exclusively to Western Publ. in Dec., 1971. The earlier issues had to be approved by **Buell** prior to publication.

Four Color 74('45)-Intro Lulu, Tubby & Alvin 115 230 345 850 1325 1800
Four Color 97(2/46) 50 100 150 376 576 775
(Above two books are all John Stanley - cover, pencils, and inks.)
Four Color 110('46)-1st Alvin Story Telling Time; 1st app. Willy; variant cover exists 35 70 105 260 398 535
Four Color 115-1st app. Boys' Clubhouse 35 70 105 255 390 525
Four Color 120, 131: 120-1st app. Eddie 31 62 93 228 352 475
Four Color 139('47),146,158 30 60 90 213 327 440
Four Color 165 (10/47)-Smokes doll hair & has wild hallucinations. 1st Tubby detective story 30 60 90 213 327 440
1(1-2/48)-Lulu's Diary feature begins 55 110 165 400 675 950
2-1st app. Gloria; 1st Tubby story in a L.L. comic; 1st app. Miss Feeny 30 60 90 213 327 440

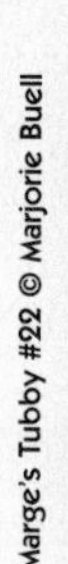
Marge's Little Lulu #44 © Marjorie Buell

Marge's Tubby #22 © Marjorie Buell

Marines in Battle #3 © MAR

	GD 2.0	VG 4.0	FN 6.0	VF 8.0	VF/NM 9.0	NM- 9.2
3-5	28	56	84	199	305	410
6-10: 7-1st app. Annie; Xmas-c	22	44	66	155	238	320
11-20: 18-X-Mas-c. 19-1st app. Wilbur. 20-1st app. Mr. McNabbem	19	38	57	134	205	275
21-30: 26-r/F.C. 110. 30-Xmas-c	15	30	45	109	167	225
31-38,40: 35-1st Mumday story	13	26	39	90	138	185
39-Intro. Witch Hazel in "That Awful Witch Hazel"	14	28	42	97	149	200
41-60: 42-Xmas-c. 45-2nd Witch Hazel app. 49-Gives Stanley & others credit	12	24	36	84	127	170
61-80: 63-1st app. Chubby (Tubby's cousin). 68-1st app. Prof. Cleff. 78-Xmas-c. 80-Intro. Little Itch (2/55)	10	20	30	67	96	125
81-99: 90-Xmas-c	8	16	24	55	78	100
100	8	16	24	58	82	105
101-130: 123-1st app. Fifi	7	14	21	46	63	80
131-164: 135-Last Stanley-p	6	12	18	40	55	70
165-Giant; ...in Paris ('62)	12	24	36	86	131	175
166-Giant; ...Christmas Diary (1962 - '63)	12	24	36	86	131	175
167-169	5	10	15	36	48	60
170,172,175,176,178-196,198-200-Stanley-r. 182-1st app. Little Scarecrow Boy	3	6	9	18	24	30
171,173,174,177,197	3	6	9	16	20	24
201,203,206-Last issue to carry Marge's name	2	4	6	14	18	22
202,204,205-Stanley-r	3	6	9	16	20	24
...& Tubby in Japan (12¢)(5-7/62) 01476-207	8	16	24	55	78	100
...Summer Camp 1(8/67-G.K.-Giant) '57-58-r	6	12	18	43	59	75
...Trick 'N' Treat 1(12¢)(12/62-Gold Key)	7	14	21	50	68	85

NOTE: *See Dell Giant Comics #23, 29, 36, 42, 50, & Dell Giants for annuals. All Giants not by Stanley from L.L. on Vacation (7/54) on. Irving Tripp a-#1-on. Christmas c-7, 18, 30, 42, 78, 90, 126, 166, 250. Summer Camp issues #173, 177, 181, 189, 197, 201, 206.*

MARGE'S LITTLE LULU (See Golden Comics Digest #19, 23, 27, 29, 33, 36, 40, 43, 46, & March of Comics #251, 267, 275, 293, 307, 323, 335, 349, 355, 369, 385, 406, 417, 427, 439, 456, 468, 475, 488)

MARGE'S TUBBY (Little Lulu)(See Dell Giants)
Dell Publishing Co./Gold Key: No. 381, Aug, 1952 - No. 49, Dec-Feb, 1961-62

	GD 2.0	VG 4.0	FN 6.0	VF 8.0	VF/NM 9.0	NM- 9.2
Four Color 381(#1)-Stanley script; Irving Tripp-a	22	44	66	158	242	325
Four Color 430,444-Stanley-a	12	24	36	87	134	180
Four Color 461 (4/53)-1st Tubby & Men From Mars story; Stanley-a	11	22	33	80	120	160
5 (7-9/53)-Stanley-a	10	20	30	67	96	125
6-10	8	16	24	55	78	100
11-20	6	12	18	40	55	70
21-30	5	10	15	33	44	55
31-49	4	8	12	28	38	48
...& the Little Men From Mars No. 30020-410(10/64-G.K.)-25¢, 68 pgs.	9	18	27	63	89	115

NOTE: ***John Stanley** did all storyboards & scripts through at least #35 (1959). **Lloyd White** did all art except F.C. 381, 430, 444, 461 & #5.*

MARGIE (See My Little...)

MARGIE (TV)
Dell Publ. Co.: No. 1307, Mar-May, 1962 - No. 2, July-Sept, 1962 (Photo-c)

	GD 2.0	VG 4.0	FN 6.0	VF 8.0	VF/NM 9.0	NM- 9.2
Four Color 1307(#1)	7	14	21	46	63	80
2	6	12	18	38	52	65

MARGIE COMICS (Formerly Comedy Comics; Reno Browne #50 on)
(Also see Cindy Comics & Teen Comics)
Marvel Comics (ACI): No. 35, Winter, 1946-47 - No. 49, Dec, 1949

	GD 2.0	VG 4.0	FN 6.0	VF 8.0	VF/NM 9.0	NM- 9.2
35	16	32	48	92	131	170
36-38,42,45,47-49	9	18	27	54	70	85
39,41,43(2),44,46-Kurtzman's "Hey Look"	10	20	30	60	80	100
40-Three "Hey Looks", three "Giggles 'n' Grins" by Kurtzman	12	24	36	69	95	120

MARINES (See Tell It to the...)

MARINES ATTACK
Charlton Comics: Aug, 1964 - No. 9, Feb-Mar, 1966

	GD 2.0	VG 4.0	FN 6.0	VF 8.0	VF/NM 9.0	NM- 9.2
1-Glanzman-a begins	4	8	12	27	36	45
2-9	3	6	9	16	20	24

MARINES AT WAR (Formerly Tales of the Marines #4)
Atlas Comics (OPI): No. 5, Apr, 1957 - No. 7, Aug, 1957

	GD 2.0	VG 4.0	FN 6.0	VF 8.0	VF/NM 9.0	NM- 9.2
5-7	9	18	27	51	62	75

NOTE: ***Colan** a-5. **Drucker** a-5. **Everett** a-5. **Maneely** a-5. **Orlando** a-7. **Severin** c-5.*

MARINES IN ACTION
Atlas News Co.: June, 1955 - No. 14, Sept, 1957

	GD 2.0	VG 4.0	FN 6.0	VF 8.0	VF/NM 9.0	NM- 9.2
1-Rock Murdock, Boot Camp Brady begin	11	22	33	64	87	110
2-14	9	18	27	51	62	75

NOTE: ***Berg** a-2, 8, 9, 11, 14. **Heath** c-2, 9. **Maneely** c-1. **Severin** a-4; c-7-11, 14.*

MARINES IN BATTLE
Atlas Comics (ACI No. 1-12/WPI No. 13-25): Aug, 1954 - No. 25, Sept, 1958

	GD 2.0	VG 4.0	FN 6.0	VF 8.0	VF/NM 9.0	NM- 9.2
1-Heath-c; Iron Mike McGraw by Heath; history of U.S. Marine Corps. begins	21	42	63	118	169	220
2-Heath-c	11	22	33	64	87	110
3-6,8-10: 4-Last precode (2/55)	9	18	27	54	70	85
7-Kubert/Moskowitz-a (6 pgs.)	10	20	30	56	73	90
11-16,18-21,24	9	18	27	51	62	75
17-Williamson-a (3 pgs.)	10	20	30	58	77	95
22,25-Torres-a	9	18	27	52	66	80
23-Crandall-a; Mark Murdock app.	9	18	27	54	70	85

NOTE: ***Berg** a-22. **G. Colan** a-22, 23. **Drucker** a-6. **Everett** a-4, 15; c-21. **Heath** c-1, 2, 4. **Maneely** c-23, 24. **Orlando** a-14. **Pakula** a-6, 23. **Powell** a-16. **Severin** a-22; c-12. **Sinnott** a-23. **Tuska** a-15.*

MARINE WAR HEROES (Charlton Premiere #19 on)
Charlton Comics: Jan, 1964 - No. 18, Mar, 1967

	GD 2.0	VG 4.0	FN 6.0	VF 8.0	VF/NM 9.0	NM- 9.2
1-Montes/Bache-c/a	4	8	12	27	36	45
2-18: 14,18-Montes/Bache-a	3	6	9	16	20	24

MARK, THE (Also see Mayhem)
Dark Horse Comics: Dec, 1993 - No. 4, Mar, 1994 ($2.50, limited series)

	GD 2.0	VG 4.0	FN 6.0	VF 8.0	VF/NM 9.0	NM- 9.2
1-4						2.50

MARK HAZZARD: MERC
Marvel Comics Group: Nov, 1986 - No. 12, Oct, 1987 (75¢)

	GD 2.0	VG 4.0	FN 6.0	VF 8.0	VF/NM 9.0	NM- 9.2
1-12: Morrow-a, Annual 1 (11/87, $1.25)						2.25

MARK OF CHARON (See Negation)
CG Entertainment: Apr, 2003 - No. 5, Aug, 2003 ($2.95, limited series)

	GD 2.0	VG 4.0	FN 6.0	VF 8.0	VF/NM 9.0	NM- 9.2
1-5-Bedard-s/Bennett-a						3.00

MARK OF ZORRO (See Zorro, Four Color #228)

MARK 1 COMICS (Also see Shaloman)
Mark 1 Comics: Apr, 1988 - No. 3, Mar, 1989 ($1.50)

	GD 2.0	VG 4.0	FN 6.0	VF 8.0	VF/NM 9.0	NM- 9.2
1-3: Early Shaloman app. 2-Origin						2.25

MARKSMAN, THE (Also see Champions)
Hero Comics: Jan, 1988 - No. 5, 1988 ($1.95)

	GD 2.0	VG 4.0	FN 6.0	VF 8.0	VF/NM 9.0	NM- 9.2
1-5: 1-Rose begins. 1-3-Origin The Marksman						2.25
Annual 1 ('88, $2.75, 52pgs)-Champions app.						2.75

MARK TRAIL
Standard Magazines (Hall Syndicate)/Fawcett Publ. No. 5: Oct, 1955; No. 5, Summer, 1959

	GD 2.0	VG 4.0	FN 6.0	VF 8.0	VF/NM 9.0	NM- 9.2
1(1955)-Sunday strip-r	7	14	21	37	46	55
5(1959)	5	10	15	22	26	30
...Adventure Book of Nature 1 (Summer, 1958, 25¢, Pines)-100 pg. Giant; Special Camp Issue; contains 78 Sunday strip-r	9	18	27	54	70	85

MARMADUKE MONK
I. W. Enterprises/Super Comics: No date; 1963 (10¢)

	GD 2.0	VG 4.0	FN 6.0	VF 8.0	VF/NM 9.0	NM- 9.2
I.W. Reprint 1 (nd)	2	4	6	9	11	14
Super Reprint 14 (1963)-r/Monkeyshines Comics #?	2	4	6	8	10	12

MARMADUKE MOUSE
Quality Comics Group (Arnold Publ.): Spring, 1946 - No. 65, Dec, 1956 (Early issues: 52 pgs.)

	GD 2.0	VG 4.0	FN 6.0	VF 8.0	VF/NM 9.0	NM- 9.2
1-Funny animal	18	36	54	102	146	190
2	10	20	30	58	77	95
3-10	8	16	24	43	54	65
11-30	6	12	18	33	41	48
31-65: Later issues are 36 pgs.	6	12	18	27	33	38
Super Reprint #14(1963)	2	4	6	10	12	15

MARQUIS, THE
Oni Press

	GD 2.0	VG 4.0	FN 6.0	VF 8.0	VF/NM 9.0	NM- 9.2
...: A Sin of One ($2.99, 5/03) Guy Davis-s/a; Michael Gaydos-c						3.00
...: Intermezzo TPB ($11.95, 12/03) r/A Sin of One and Hell's Courtesan #1,2						12.00

MARQUIS, THE: DANSE MACABRE
Oni Press: May, 2000 - No. 5, Feb, 2001 ($2.95, B&W, limited series)

	GD 2.0	VG 4.0	FN 6.0	VF 8.0	VF/NM 9.0	NM- 9.2
1-5-Guy Davis-s/a. 1-Wagner-c. 2-Mignola-c. 3-Vess-c. 5-K. Jones-c						3.00
TPB (8/2001, $18.95) r/1-5 & Les Preludes; Seagle intro.						19.00

MARQUIS, THE: DEVIL'S REIGN: HELL'S COURTESAN
Oni Press: Feb, 2002 - No. 2, Apr, 2002 ($2.95, B&W, limited series)

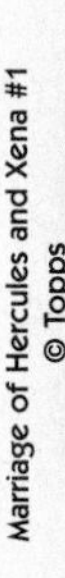

Marriage of Hercules and Xena #1 © Topps

Martian Manhunter #1 © DC

Marvel Age Fantastic Four #1 © MAR

GD 2.0 | VG 4.0 | FN 6.0 | VF 8.0 | VF/NM 9.0 | NM- 9.2

1,2-Guy Davis-s/a 3.00

MARRIAGE OF HERCULES AND XENA, THE
Topps Comics: July, 1998 ($2.95, one-shot)

1-Photo-c; Lopresti-a; Alex Ross pin-up, 1-Alex Ross painted-c 3.00
1-Gold foil logo-c 5.00

MARRIED ... WITH CHILDREN (TV)(Based on Fox TV show)
Now Comics: June, 1990 - No. 7, Feb, 1991(12/90 inside) ($1.75)
V2#1, Sept, 1991 - No. 12, 1992 ($1.95)

1-7: 2-Photo-c, 1,2-2nd printing, V2#1-12: 1,4,5,9-Photo-c 2.25
...Buck's Tale (6/94, $1.95) 2.25
...1994 Annual nn (2/94, $2.50, 52 pgs.)-Flip book format 2.50
Special 1 (7/92, $1.95)-Kelly Bundy photo-c/poster 2.25

MARRIED ... WITH CHILDREN: KELLY BUNDY
Now Comics: Aug, 1992 - No. 3, Oct, 1992 ($1.95, limited series)

1-3: Kelly Bundy photo-c & poster in each 2.25

MARRIED ... WITH CHILDREN: QUANTUM QUARTET
Now Comics: Oct, 1993 - No. 4, 1994, ($1.95, limited series)

1-4: Fantastic Four parody 2.25

MARRIED ... WITH CHILDREN: 2099
Now Comics: June, 1993 - No. 3, Aug, 1993 ($1.95, limited series)

1-3 2.25

MARS
First Comics: Jan, 1984 - No. 12, Jan, 1985 ($1.00, Mando paper)

nn: 1-12: Marc Hempel & Mark Wheatley story & art. 2-The Black Flame begins. 10-Dynamo Joe begins 2.25

MARS & BEYOND (Disney, TV)
Dell Publishing Co.: No. 866, Dec, 1957

Four Color 866-A Science feat. from Tomorrowland 10 20 30 70 100 130

MARS ATTACKS
Topps Comics: May, 1994 - No. 5, Sept, 1994 ($2.95, limited series)

1-5-Giffen story; flip books 4.50
Special Edition 2 4 6 8 10 12
Trade paperback (12/94, $12.95)-r/limited series plus new 8 pg. story 13.00

MARS ATTACKS
Topps Comics: V2#1, 8/95 - V2#3, 10/95; V2#4, 1/96 - No. 7, 5/96($2.95, bi-monthly #6 on)

V2#1-7: 1-Counterstrike storyline begins. 4-(1/96). 5-(1/96). 5,7-Brereton-c. 6-(3/96)-Simonson-c. 7-Story leads into Baseball Special #1 3.00
Baseball Special 1 (6/96, $2.95)-Bisley-c. 3.00

MARS ATTACKS HIGH SCHOOL
Topps Comics: May, 1997 - No. 2, Sept, 1997 ($2.95, B&W, limited series)

1,2-Stelfreeze-c 3.00

MARS ATTACKS IMAGE
Topps Comics: Dec, 1996 - No. 4, Mar, 1997 ($2.50, limited series)

1-4-Giffen-s/Smith/Sienkiewicz-a 3.00

MARS ATTACKS THE SAVAGE DRAGON
Topps Comics: Dec, 1996 - No. 4, Mar, 1997 ($2.95, limited series)

1-4: 1-w/bound-in card 3.00

MARSHAL BLUEBERRY (See Blueberry)
Marvel Comics (Epic Comics): 1991 ($14.95, graphic novel)

1-Moebius-a 15.00

MARSHAL LAW (Also see Crime And Punishment: Marshall Law...)
Marvel Comics (Epic Comics): Oct, 1987 - No. 6, May, 1989 ($1.95, mature)

1-6 2.25

M.A.R.S. PATROL TOTAL WAR (Formerly Total War #1,2)
Gold Key: No. 3, Sept, 1966 - No. 10, Aug, 1969 (All-Painted-c except #7)

3-Wood-a; aliens invade USA 7 14 21 50 68 85
4-10 4 8 12 28 38 48
Wally Wood's M.A.R.S. Patrol Total War TPB (Dark Horse, 9/04, $12.95) r/#3 & Total War #1&2; foreward by Batton Lash; afterword by Dan Adkins 13.00

MARTHA WASHINGTON (Also see Dark Horse Presents Fifth Anniversary Special, Dark Horse Presents #100-4, Give Me Liberty, Happy Birthday Martha Washington & San Diego Comicon Comics #2)

MARTHA WASHINGTON GOES TO WAR
Dark Horse Comics (Legend): May, 1994 - No. 5, Sep, 1994 ($2.95, lim. series)

1-5-Miller scripts; Gibbons-c/a 3.00
TPB ($17.95) r/#1-5 18.00

MARTHA WASHINGTON SAVES THE WORLD
Dark Horse Comics: Dec, 1997 - No. 3, Feb, 1998 ($2.95/$3.95, lim. series)

1,2-Miller scripts; Gibbons-c/a in all 3.00
3-($3.95) 4.00

MARTHA WASHINGTON STRANDED IN SPACE
Dark Horse Comics (Legend): Nov, 1995 ($2.95, one-shot)

nn-Miller-s/Gibbons-a; Big Guy app. 3.00

MARTHA WAYNE (See The Story of...)

MARTIAN MANHUNTER (See Detective Comics & Showcase '95 #9)
DC Comics: May, 1988 - No. 4, Aug,. 1988 ($1.25, limited series)

1-4: 1,4-Batman app. 2-Batman cameo 2.50
Special 1-(1996, $3.50) 3.50

MARTIAN MANHUNTER (See JLA)
DC Comics: No. 0, Oct, 1998 - No. 36, Nov, 2001 ($1.99)

0-(10/98) Origin retold; Ostrander-s/Mandrake-c/a 3.00
1-36: 1-(12/98). 6-9-JLA app. 18,19-JSA app. 24-Mahnke-a 2.50
#1,000,000 (11/98) 853rd Century x-over 2.50
Annual 1,2 (1998,1999; $2.95) 1-Ghosts; Wrightson-c. 2-JLApe 3.00

MARTIAN MANHUNTER: AMERICAN SECRETS
DC Comics: 1992 - Book Three, 1992 ($4.95, limited series, prestige format)

1-3: Barreto-a 5.00

MARTIN KANE (William Gargan as... Private Eye)(Stage/Screen/Radio/TV)
Fox Features Syndicate (Hero Books): No. 4, June, 1950 - No. 2, Aug, 1950 (Formerly My Secret Affair)

4(#1)-True crime stories; Wood-c/a(2); used in **SOTI**, pg. 160; photo back-c 31 62 93 175 253 330
2-Wood/Orlando story, 5 pgs; Wood-a(2) 24 48 72 135 195 255

MARTIN MYSTERY
Dark Horse (Bonelli Comics): Mar, 1999 - No. 6, Aug, 1999 ($4.95, B&W, digest size)

1-6-Reprints Italian series in English; Gibbons-c on #1-3 5.00

MARTY MOUSE
I. W. Enterprises: No date (1958?) (10¢)

1-Reprint 2 4 6 10 12 15

MARVEL ACTION HOUR FEATURING IRON MAN (TV cartoon)
Marvel Comics: Nov, 1994 - No. 8, June, 1995 ($1.50/$2.95)

1-8: Based on cartoon series 2.25
1 ($2.95)-Polybagged w/16 pg Marvel Action Hour Preview & acetate print 3.00

MARVEL ACTION HOUR FEATURING THE FANTASTIC FOUR (TV cartoon)
Marvel Comics: Nov, 1994 - No. 8, June, 1995 ($1.50/$2.95)

1-8: Based on cartoon series 2.25
1-($2.95)-Polybagged w/ 16 pg. Marvel Action Hour Preview & acetate print 3.00

MARVEL ACTION UNIVERSE (TV cartoon)
Marvel Comics: Jan, 1989 ($1.00, one-shot)

1-r/Spider-Man And His Amazing Friends 4.00

MARVEL ADVENTURES
Marvel Comics: Apr, 1997 - No. 18, Sept, 1998 ($1.50)

1-18-"Animated style": 1,4,7-Hulk-c/app. 2,11-Spider-Man. 3,8,15-X-Men. 5-Spider-Man & X-Men. 6-Spider-Man & Human Torch. 9,12-Fantastic Four. 10,16-Silver Surfer. 13-Spider-Man & Silver Surfer. 14-Hulk & Dr. Strange. 18-Capt. America 2.25

MARVEL ADVENTURES STARRING DAREDEVIL (...Adventure #3 on)
Marvel Comics Group: Dec, 1975 - No. 6, Oct, 1976

1 1 3 4 6 8 10
2-6-r/Daredevil #22-27 by Colan. 3-5-(25¢-c) 6.00
3-5-(30¢-c variants, limited distribution)(4,6,8/76) 2 4 6 10 13 16

MARVEL AGE FANTASTIC FOUR
Marvel Comics: Jun, 2004 - Present ($2.25)

1-8-Lee & Kirby stories retold with new art by various 2.25
Vol. 1: All For One TPB (2004, $5.99, digest size) r/#1-4 6.00
Vol. 2: Doom TPB (2004, $5.99, digest size) r/#5-8 6.00
Vol. 3: The Return of Doctor Doom TPB (2005, $5.99, digest size) r/#9-12 6.00

MARVEL AGE HULK
Marvel Comics: Nov, 2004 - Present ($1.75)

Marvel Age Spider-Man #1 © MAR

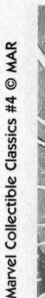

Marvel Collectible Classics #4 © MAR

Marvel Comics Presents #134 © MAR

	GD	VG	FN	VF	VF/NM	NM-
	2.0	4.0	6.0	8.0	9.0	9.2

1-3-Lee & Kirby stories retold with new art by various 2.25

MARVEL AGE SPIDER-MAN (Also see Free Comic Book Day edition in the Promotional Comics section)
Marvel Comics: May, 2004 - Present ($2.25)

1-17-Lee & Ditko stories retold with new art. 4-Doctor Doom app. 5-Lizard app. 2.25
Vol. 1-4 TPB (2004, $5.99, digest size) 1-r/#1-4. 2-r/#5-8. 3-r/#9-12. 4-r/#13-16 6.00
Vol. 2: Everyday Hero TPB (2004, $5.99, digest size) r/#5-8 6.00
Vol. 3: Swingtime TPB (2004, $5.99, digest size) r/#9-12 6.00

MARVEL AGE TEAM-UP
Marvel Comics: Nov, 2004 - Present ($1.75)

1-3-Stories retold with new art by various. 1-Fantastic Four app. 3-Kitty Pryde app. 2.25

MARVEL AND DC PRESENT FEATURING THE UNCANNY X-MEN AND THE NEW TEEN TITANS
Marvel Comics/DC Comics: 1982 ($2.00, 68 pgs., one-shot, Baxter paper)

1-3rd app. Deathstroke the Terminator; Darkseid app.; Simonson/Austin-c/a
2 4 6 12 16 20

MARVEL BOY (Astonishing #3 on; see Marvel Super Action #4)
Marvel Comics (MPC): Dec, 1950 - No. 2, Feb, 1951

1-Origin Marvel Boy by Russ Heath 108 216 324 675 1038 1400
2-Everett-a 77 154 231 481 741 1000

MARVEL BOY (Marvel Knights)
Marvel Comics: Aug, 2000 - No. 6, Mar, 2001 ($2.99, limited series)

1-Intro. Marvel Boy; Morrison-s/J.G. Jones-c/a 3.50
1-DF Variant-c 5.00
2-6 3.00
TPB (6/01, $15.95) 16.00

MARVEL CHILLERS (Also see Giant-Size Chillers)
Marvel Comics Group: Oct, 1975 - No. 7, Oct, 1976 (All 25¢ issues)

1-Intro. Modred the Mystic, ends #2; Kane-c(p) 2 4 6 10 12 15
2,4,5,7: 4-Kraven app. 5,6-Red Wolf app. 7-Kirby-c; Tuska-p
1 2 3 5 7 9
3-Tigra, the Were-Woman begins (origin), ends #7 (see Giant-Size Creatures #1). Chaykin/Wrightson-c. 2 4 6 14 18 22
4-6-(30¢-c variants, limited distribution)(4-8/76) 2 4 6 11 14 18
6-Byrne-a(p); Buckler-c(p) 2 4 6 8 10 12
NOTE: *Bolle a-1. Buckler c-2. Kirby c-7.*

MARVEL CLASSICS COMICS SERIES FEATURING...
(Also see Pendulum Illustrated Classics)
Marvel Comics Group: 1976 - No. 36, Dec, 1978 (52 pgs., no ads)

1-Dr. Jekyll and Mr. Hyde 2 4 6 11 14 18
2-10,28: 28-1st Golden-c/a; Pit and the Pendulum 2 4 6 8 10 12
11-27,29-36 1 2 3 5 7 9
NOTE: ***Adkins** c-1i, 4i, 12i. **Alcala** a-34i; c-34. **Bolle** a-35. **Buscema** c-17p, 19p, 26p. **Golden** c/a-28. **Gil Kane** c-1-16p, 21p, 22p, 24p, 32p. **Nebres** a-5; c-24i. **Nino** a-2, 8, 12. **Redondo** a-1, 9. No. 1-12 were reprinted from Pendulum Illustrated Classics.*

MARVEL COLLECTIBLE CLASSICS: AVENGERS
Marvel Comics: 1998 ($10.00, reprints with chromium wraparound-c)

1-Reprints Avengers Vol.3, #1; Perez-c 10.00

MARVEL COLLECTIBLE CLASSICS: SPIDER-MAN
Marvel Comics: 1998 ($10.00, reprints with chromium wraparound-c)

1-Reprints Amazing Spider-Man #300; McFarlane-c 10.00
2-Reprints Spider-Man #1; McFarlane-c 10.00

MARVEL COLLECTIBLE CLASSICS: X-MEN
Marvel Comics: 1998 ($10.00, reprints with chromium wraparound-c)

1-6: 1-Reprints (Uncanny) X-Men #1 & 2; Adam Kubert-c. 2-Reprints Uncanny X-Men #141 & 142; Byrne-c. 3-Reprints (Uncanny) X-Men #137; Larroca-c. 4-Reprints X-Men #25; Andy Kubert-c. 5-Reprints Giant Size X-Men #1; Gary Frank-c. 6-Reprints X-Men V2#1; Ramos-c 10.00

MARVEL COLLECTOR'S EDITION
Marvel Comics: 1992 (Ordered thru mail with Charleston Chew candy wrapper)

1-Flip-book format; Spider-Man, Silver Surfer, Wolverine (by Sam Kieth), & Ghost Rider stories; Wolverine back-c by Kieth 3.00

MARVEL COLLECTORS' ITEM CLASSICS (Marvel's Greatest #23 on)
Marvel Comics Group(ATF): Feb, 1965 - No. 22, Aug, 1969 (25¢, 68 pgs.)

1-Fantastic Four, Spider-Man, Thor, Hulk, Iron Man-r begin
10 20 30 73 107 140
2 (4/66) 6 12 18 40 55 70

3,4 4 8 12 29 40 50
5-10 4 8 12 24 32 40
11-22: 22-r/The Man in the Ant Hill/TTA #27 3 6 9 18 24 30
NOTE: *All reprints; **Ditko, Kirby** art in all.*

MARVEL COMICS (Marvel Mystery Comics #2 on)
Timely Comics (Funnies, Inc.): Oct, Nov, 1939

NOTE: The first issue was originally dated October 1939. Most copies have a black circle stamped over the date (on cover and inside) with "November" printed over it. However, some copies do not have the November overprint and could have a higher value. Most No. 1's have printing defects, i.e., tilted pages which caused trimming into the panels usually on right side and bottom. Covers exist with and without gloss finish.

1-Origin Sub-Mariner by Bill Everett(1st newsstand app.); 1st 8 pgs. were produced for Motion Picture Funnies Weekly #1 which was probably not distributed outside of advance copies; intro Human Torch by Carl Burgos, Kazar the Great (1st Tarzan clone), & Jungle Terror(only app.); intro. The Angel by Gustavson, The Masked Raider & his horse Lightning (ends #12); cover by sci/fi pulp illustrator Frank R. Paul
20,000 40,000 60,000 144,000 254,500 365,000

MARVEL COMICS PRESENTS
Marvel Comics (Midnight Sons imprint #143 on): Early Sept, 1988 - No. 175, Feb, 1995 ($1.25/$1.50/$1.75, bi-weekly)

1-Wolverine by Buscema in #1-10 6.00
2-5 4.00
6-10: 6-Sub-Mariner app. 10-Colossus begins 3.00
11-47,51-71: 17-Cyclops begins. 19-1st app. Damage Control. 24-Havok begins. 25-Origin/1st app. Nth Man. 26-Hulk begins by Rogers. 29-Quasar app. 31-Excalibur begins by Austin (i). 32-McFarlane-a(p). 37-Devil-Slayer app. 33-Capt. America; Jim Lee-a. 38-Wolverine begins by Buscema; Hulk app. 39-Spider-Man app. 46-Liefeld Wolverine-c. 51-53-Wolverine by Rob Liefeld. 54-61-Wolverine/Hulk story: 54-Werewolf by Night begins; The Shroud by Ditko. 58-Iron Man by Ditko. 59-Punisher. 62-Deathlok & Wolverine stories 63-Wolverine. 64-71-Wolverine/Ghost Rider 8-part story. 70-Liefeld Ghost Rider/ Wolverine-c 2.50
48-50-Wolverine & Spider-Man team-up by Erik Larsen-c/a. 48-Wasp app. 49,50-Savage Dragon prototype app. by Larsen. 50-Silver Surfer. 50-53-Comet Man; Mumy scripts 4.00
72-Begin 13-part Weapon-X story (Wolverine origin) by B. Windsor-Smith (prologue) 5.00
73-Weapon-X part 1; Black Knight, Sub-Mariner 4.00
74-84: 74-Weapon-X part 2; Black Knight, Sub-Mariner. 76-Death's Head story. 77-Mr. Fantastic story. 78-Iron Man by Steacy. 80,81-Capt. America by Ditko/Austin. 81-Daredevil by Rogers/Williamson. 82-Power Man. 83-Human Torch by Ditko(a&scripts); $1.00-c direct, $1.25 newsstand. 84-Last Weapon-X (24 pg. conclusion) 3.00
85-Begin 8-part Wolverine story by Sam Kieth (c/a); 1st Kieth-a on Wolverine; begin 8-part Beast story by Jae Lee(p) with Liefeld part pencils #85,86; 1st Jae Lee-a (assisted w/Liefeld, 1991) 4.00
86-90: 86-89-Wolverine, Beast stories continue. 90-Begin 8-part Ghost Rider & Cable story, ends #97; begin flip book format w/two-c 3.00
91-175: 93-Begin 6-part Wolverine story, ends #98. 98-Begin 2-part Ghost Rider story. 99-Spider-Man story. 101-Begin 6-part Ghost Rider/Dr. Strange story & begin 8-part Wolverine/Nightcrawler story by Colan/Williamson; Punisher story. 107-Begin 6-part Ghost Rider/Werewolf by Night story. 112-Demogoblin story by Colan/Williamson; Pip the Troll story w/Starlin scripts & Gamora cameo. 113-Begin 6-part Giant-Man & begin 6-part Ghost Rider/Iron Fist stories. 100-Full-length Ghost Rider/Wolverine story by Sam Kieth w/Tim Vigil assists; anniversary issue, non flip-book. 108-Begin 4 part Thanos story; Starlin scripts. 109-Begin 8 part Wolverine/Typhoid Mary story. 111-Iron Fist. 117-Preview of Ravage 2099 (1st app.); begin 6 part Wolverine/Venom story w/Kieth-a. 118-Preview of Doom 2099 (1st app.). 119-Begin Ghost Rider/Cloak & Dagger by Colan. 120,136,138-Spider-Man. 123-Begin 8-part Ghost Rider/Typhoid Mary story; begin 4-part She Hulk story; begin 8-part Wolverine/Lynx story. 125-Begin 6-part Iron Fist story. 129-Jae Lee back-c. 130-Begin 6-part Ghost Rider/ Cage story. 131-Begin 6-part Ghost Rider/Cage story. 132-Begin 5-part Wolverine story. 133-136-Iron Fist vs. Sabretooth. 136-Daredevil. 137-Begin 6-part Wolverine story & 6-part Ghost Rider story. 147-Begin 2-part Vengeance-c/story w/new Ghost Rider. 149-Vengeance-c/story w/new Ghost Rider. 150-Silver ink-c; begin 2-part Bloody Mary story w/Typhoid Mary,Wolverine, Daredevil, new Ghost Rider; intro Steel Raven. 152-Begin 4-part Wolverine, 4-part War Machine, 4-part Vengeance, 3-part Moon Knight stories; same date as War Machine #1. 143-146: Siege of Darkness parts 3,6,11,14; all have spot-varnished-c. 143-Ghost Rider/Scarlet Witch; intro new Werewolf. 144-Begin 2-part Morbius story. 145-Begin 2-part Nightstalkers story. 153-155-Bound-in Spider-Man trading card sheet 2.50
...Colossus: God's Country (1994, $6.95) r/#10-17 1 2 3 4 5 7
NOTE: ***Austin** a-31-37i; c(i)-48, 50, 99, 122. **Buscema** a-1-10, 38-47; c-6. **Byrne** a-79; c-71. **Colan** a(p)-36, 37. **Colan/Williamson** a-101-108. **Ditko** a-7p, 10, 56p, 58, 80, 81, 83. **Guice** a-62. **Sam Kieth** a-85-92, 117-122; c-85-98, 99p, 100-108, 117, 118, 120-122; back c-109-113, 117. **Jae Lee** c-129(back). **Liefeld** a-51, 52, 53p(2), 85p; c-46, 70. **McFarlane** c-32. **Mooney** a-73. **Rogers** a-26, 38, 46i, 81p. **Russell** a-10-14,16,17i; c-4,19, 30,31i. **Saltares** a-8p(early), 38-45p. **Simonson** c-1. **B. Smith** a-72-84; c-72-84. **P. Smith** c-34. **Sparling** a-33. **Starlin** a-89i. **Staton** a-74. **Steacy** a-78. **Sutton** a-101-105. **Williamson** c-62i. Two Gun Kid by **Gil Kane** in #116, 122.*

MARVEL COMICS SUPER SPECIAL, A (Marvel Super Special #5 on)
Marvel Comics: Sept, 1977 - No. 41(?), Nov, 1986 (nn 7) ($1.50, magazine)

Marvel Double Feature #20 © MAR

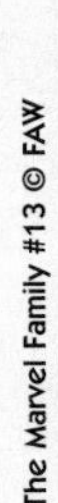
The Marvel Family #13 © FAW

Marvel Fanfare #11 © MAR

GD 2.0 | VG 4.0 | FN 6.0 | VF 8.0 | VF/NM 9.0 | NM- 9.2

GD 2.0 | VG 4.0 | FN 6.0 | VF 8.0 | VF/NM 9.0 | NM- 9.2

1-Kiss, 40 pgs. comics plus photos & features; Simonson-a(p); also see Howard the Duck #12; ink contains real KISS blood; Dr. Doom, Spider-Man, Avengers, Fantastic Four, Mephisto app. 12 24 36 86 131 175
2-Conan (1978) 2 4 6 12 16 20
3-Close Encounters of the Third Kind (1978); Simonson-a 2 4 6 9 11 14
4-The Beatles Story (1978)-Perez/Janson-a; has photos & articles 4 8 12 29 40 50
5-Kiss (1978)-Includes poster 12 24 36 86 131 175
6-Jaws II (1978) 2 4 6 9 11 14
7-Sgt. Pepper; Beatles movie adaptation; withdrawn from U.S. distribution (French ed. exists)
8-Battlestar Galactica; tabloid size ($1.50, 1978); adapts TV show 2 4 6 11 14 18
8-Modern-r of tabloid size 2 4 6 11 14 18
8-Battlestar Galactica; publ. in regular magazine format; low distribution ($1.50, 8-1/2x11") 2 4 6 12 16 20
9-Conan 2 4 6 10 13 16
10-Star-Lord 2 4 6 8 10 12
11-13-Weirdworld begins #11; 25 copy special press run of each with gold seal and signed by artists (Proof quality), Spring-June, 1979 9 18 27 60 85 110
11-15: 11-13-Weirdworld (regular issues): 11-Fold-out centerfold. 14-Miller-c(p); adapts movie "Meteor." 15-Star Trek with photos & pin-ups ($1.50-c) 1 2 3 5 7 9
15-With $2.00 price; the price was changed at tail end of a 200,000 press run 2 4 6 8 10 12
16-Empire Strikes Back adaption; Williamson-a 2 4 6 8 10 12
17-20 (Movie adaptations):17-Xanadu. 18-Raiders of the Lost Ark. 19-For Your Eyes Only (James Bond). 20-Dragonslayer 6.00
21-26,28-30 (Movie adaptations): 21-Conan. 22-Blade Runner; Williamson-a; Steranko-c. 23-Annie. 24-The Dark Crystal. 25-Rock and Rule-w/photos; artwork is from movie. 26-Octopussy (James Bond). 28-Krull; photo-c. 29-Tarzan of the Apes (Greystoke movie). 30-Indiana Jones and the Temple of Doom 1 2 3 4 5 7
27,31-41: 27-Return of the Jedi. 31-The Last Star Fighter. 32-The Muppets Take Manhattan. 33-Buckaroo Banzai. 34-Sheena. 35-Conan The Destroyer. 36-Dune. 37-2010. 38-Red Sonja. 39-Santa Claus:The Movie. 40-Labyrinth. 41-Howard The Duck 1 2 3 5 7 9

NOTE: ***J. Buscema*** *a-1, 2, 9, 11-13, 18p, 21, 35, 40; c-11(part), 12.* ***Chaykin*** *a-9, 19p; c-18, 19.* ***Colan*** *a(p)-6, 10, 14.* ***Morrow*** *a-34; c-1i, 34.* ***Nebres*** *a-11.* ***Spiegle*** *a-29.* ***Stevens*** *a-27.* ***Williamson*** *a-27. #22-28 contain photos from movies.*

MARVEL COMICS: 2001
Marvel Comics: 2001 (no cover price, one-shot)

1-Previews new titles for Fall 2001; Wolverine-c 2.25

MARVEL DOUBLE FEATURE
Marvel Comics Group: Dec, 1973 - No. 21, Mar, 1977

1-Capt. America, Iron Man-r/T.O.S. begin 2 4 6 10 13 16
2-10: 3-Last 20¢ issue 1 3 4 6 8 10
11-17,20,21:17-Story-r/Iron Man & Sub-Mariner #1; last 25¢ issue 6.00
15-17-(30¢-c variants, limited distribution)(4,6,8/76) 1 3 4 6 8 10
18,19-Colan/Craig-r from Iron Man #1 in both 1 2 3 5 6 8

NOTE: ***Colan*** *r-1-19p.* ***Craig*** *r-17-19i.* ***G. Kane*** *r-15p; c-15p.* ***Kirby*** *r-1-16p, 20, 21; c-17-20.*

MARVEL DOUBLE SHOT
Marvel Comics: Jan, 2003 - No. 4, April, 2003 ($2.99, limited series)

1-4: 1-Hulk by Haynes; Thor w/Asamiya-a; Jusko-c. 2-Dr. Doom by Rivera; Simpsons-style Avengers by Bill Morrison 3.00

MARVEL FAMILY (Also see Captain Marvel Adventures No. 18)
Fawcett Publications: Dec, 1945 - No. 89, Jan, 1954

1-Origin Captain Marvel, Captain Marvel Jr., Mary Marvel, & Uncle Marvel retold; origin/1st app. Black Adam 177 354 531 1106 1703 2300
2-The 3 Lt. Marvels & Uncle Marvel app. 77 154 231 481 741 1000
3 55 110 165 340 520 700
4,5 45 90 135 275 418 560
6-10: 7-Shazam app. 40 80 120 230 335 440
11-20 30 60 90 173 249 325
21-30 26 52 78 147 211 275
31-40 21 42 63 121 173 225
41-46,48-50 17 34 51 98 139 180
47-Flying Saucer-c/story (5/50) 24 48 72 135 195 255
51-76 15 30 45 86 123 160
77-Communist Threat-c 25 50 75 141 203 265
78,81-Used in **POP**, pg. 92,93. 18 36 54 100 143 185
79,80,82-89: 79-Horror satire-c 17 34 51 98 139 180

MARVEL FANFARE (1st Series)
Marvel Comics Group: Mar, 1982 - No. 60, Jan, 1992 ($1.25/$2.25, slick paper, direct sales)

1-Spider-Man/Angel team-up; 1st Paul Smith-a (1st full story; see King Conan #7); Daredevil app. (many copies were printed missing the centerfold) 1 2 3 5 6 8
2-Spider-Man, Ka-Zar, The Angel. F.F. origin retold 6.00
3,4-X-Men & Ka-Zar. 4-Deathlok, Spidey app. 5.00
5-14: 5-Dr. Strange, Capt. America. 6-Spider-Man, Scarlet Witch. 7-Incredible Hulk; D.D. back-up(also 15). 8-Dr. Strange; Wolf Boy begins. 9-Man-Thing. 10-13-Black Widow. 14-The Vision 3.00
15,24,33: 15-The Thing by Barry Smith, c/a. 24-Weirdworld; Wolverine back-up. 33-X-Men, Wolverine app.; Punisher pin-up 4.00
16-23,25-32,34-44,46-50: 16,17-Skywolf. 16-Sub-Mariner back-up. 17-Hulk back-up. 18-Capt. America by Miller. 19-Cloak and Dagger. 20-Thing/Dr. Strange. 21-Thing/Dr. Strange /Hulk. 22,23-Iron Man vs. Dr. Octopus. 25,26-Weirdworld. 27-Daredevil/Spider-Man. 28-Alpha Flight. 29-Hulk. 30-Moon Knight. 31,32-Captain America. 34-37-Warriors Three. 38-Moon Knight/Dazzler. 39-Moon Knight/Hawkeye. 40-Angel/Rogue & Storm. 41-Dr. Strange. 42-Spider-Man. 43-Sub-Mariner/Human Torch. 44-Iron Man vs. Dr. Doom by Ken Steacy. 46-Fantastic Four. 47-Hulk. 48-She-Hulk/Vision. 49-Dr. Strange/Nick Fury. 50-X-Factor 2.50
45-All pin-up issue by Steacy, Art Adams & others 4.00
51-($2.95, 52 pgs.)-Silver Surfer; Fantastic Four & Capt. Marvel app.; 51,52-Colan/Williamson back-up (Dr. Strange) 3.00
52,53,56-60: 52,53-Black Knight; 53-Iron Man back up. 56-59-Shanna the She-Devil. 58-Vision & Scarlet Witch back-up. 60-Black Panther/Rogue/Daredevil stories 2.50
54,55-Wolverine back-ups. 54-Black Knight. 55-Power Pack 4.00

NOTE: ***Art Adams*** *c-13.* ***Austin*** *a-1i, 4i, 33i, 38i; c-8i, 33i.* ***Buscema*** *a-51p.* ***Byrne*** *a-1p, 29, 48; c-29.* ***Chiodo*** *painted c-56-59.* ***Colan*** *a-51p.* ***Cowan/Simonson*** *c/a-60.* ***Golden*** *a-1, 2, 4p, 47; c-1, 2, 47.* ***Infantino*** *c/a(p)-8.* ***Gil Kane*** *a-8-11p.* ***Miller*** *a-18; c-1(Back-c), 18.* ***Perez*** *a-10, 11p, 12, 13p; c-10-13p.* ***Rogers*** *a-5p; c-5p.* ***Russell*** *a-5i, 6i, 8-11i, 43i; c-5i, 6.* ***Paul Smith*** *a-1p, 4p, 32, 60; c-4p. Staton c/a-50(p).* ***Williamson*** *a-30i, 51i.*

MARVEL FANFARE (2nd Series)
Marvel Comics: Sept, 1996 - No. 6, Feb, 1997 (99¢)

1-6: 1-Capt. America & The Falcon-c/story; Deathlok app. 2-Wolverine & Hulk-c/app. 3-Ghost Rider & Spider-Man-c/app. 5-Longshot-c/app. 6-Sabretooth, Power Man, & Iron Fist-c/app 2.25

MARVEL FEATURE (See Marvel Two-In-One)
Marvel Comics Group: Dec, 1971 - No. 12, Nov, 1973 (1,2: 25¢, 52 pg. giants) (#1-3: quarterly)

1-Origin/1st app. The Defenders (Sub-Mariner, Hulk & Dr. Strange); see Sub-Mariner #34,35 for prequel; Dr. Strange solo story (predates Dr.Strange #1) plus 1950s Sub-Mariner-r; Neal Adams-c 15 30 45 109 167 225
2-2nd app. Defenders; 1950s Sub-Mariner-r. Rutland, Vermont Halloween x-over 8 16 24 55 78 100
3-Defenders ends 6 12 18 40 55 70
4-Re-intro Antman (1st app. since 1960s), begin series; brief origin; Spider-Man app. 3 6 9 18 24 30
5-7,9,10: 6-Wasp app. & begins team-ups. 9-Iron Man app. 10-Last Antman 2 4 6 9 11 14
8-Origin Antman & Wasp-r/TTA #44; Kirby-a 2 4 6 11 14 18
11-Thing vs. Hulk; 1st Thing solo book (9/73); origin Fantastic Four retold 6 12 18 38 52 65
12-Thing/Iron Man; early Thanos app.; occurs after Capt. Marvel #33; Starlin-a(p) 3 6 9 19 25 32

NOTE: ***Bolle*** *a-9i.* ***Everett*** *a-1i, 3i.* ***Hartley*** *r-10.* ***Kane*** *c-3p, 7p.* ***Russell*** *a-7-10p.* ***Starlin*** *a-8, 11, 12; c-8.*

MARVEL FEATURE (Also see Red Sonja)
Marvel Comics: Nov, 1975 - No. 7, Nov, 1976 (Story cont'd in Conan #68)

1,7: 1-Red Sonja begins (pre-dates Red Sonja #1); adapts Howard short story; Adams-r/Savage Sword of Conan #1. 7-Battles Conan 1 3 4 6 8 10
2-6: Thorne-c/a in #2-7. 4,5-(Regular 25¢ edition)(5,7/76) 6.00
4,5-(30¢-c variants, limited distribution) 2 4 6 11 14 18

MARVEL FRONTIER COMICS UNLIMITED
Marvel Frontier Comics: Jan, 1994 ($2.95, 68 pgs.)

1-Dances with Demons, Immortalis, Children of the Voyager, Evil Eye, The Fallen stories 3.00

MARVEL FUMETTI BOOK
Marvel Comics Group: Apr, 1984 ($1.00, one-shot)

1-All photos; Stan Lee photo-c; Art Adams touch-ups 4.00

MARVEL FUN & GAMES
Marvel Comics Group: 1979/80 (color comic for kids)

1,11: 1-Games, puzzles, etc. 11-X-Men-c 1 2 3 5 7 9
2-10,12,13: (beware marked pages) 6.00

MARVEL GRAPHIC NOVEL

Marvel Knights Double Shot #1 © MAR

Marvel Knights 4 #1 © MAR

Marvel Knights Spider-Man #5 © MAR

	GD 2.0	VG 4.0	FN 6.0	VF 8.0	VF/NM 9.0	NM- 9.2
Marvel Comics Group (Epic Comics): 1982 - No. 38, 1990? ($5.95/$6.95)						
1-Death of Captain Marvel (2nd Marvel graphic novel); Capt. Marvel battles Thanos by Jim Starlin (c/a/scripts)	2	4	6	12	16	20
1 (2nd & 3rd printings)	1	2	3	5	6	8
2-Elric: The Dreaming City	2	4	6	8	10	12
3-Dreadstar; Starlin-c/a, 52 pgs.	2	4	6	9	11	14
4-Origin/1st app. The New Mutants (1982)	2	4	6	9	11	14
4,5-2nd printings	1	2	3	4	5	7
5-X-Men; book-length story (1982)	2	4	6	11	14	18
6-15,20,23,25,30,31: 6-The Star Slammers. 7-Killraven. 8-Super Boxers; Byrne scripts. 9-The Futurians. 10-Heartburst. 11-Void Indigo. 12-Dazzler. 13-Starstruck. 14-The Swords Of The Swashbucklers. 15-The Raven Banner (a Tale of Asgard). 20-Greenberg the Vampire. 23-Dr. Strange. 25-Alien Legion. 30-A Sailor's Story. 31-Wolfpack	1	2	3	5	7	9
16,17,21,29: 16-The Aladdin Effect (Storm, Tigra, Wasp, She-Hulk). 17-Revenge Of The Living Monolith (Spider-Man, Avengers, FF app.). 21-Marada the She-Wolf. 29-The Big Chance (Thing vs. Hulk)	1	2	3	5	7	9
18,19,26-28: 18-She Hulk. 19-Witch Queen of Acheron (Conan). 26-Dracula. 27-Avengers (Emperor Doom). 28-Conan the Reaver	2	4	6	9	11	13
22-Amaz. Spider-Man in Hooky by Wrightson	2	4	6	10	12	15
24-Love and War (Daredevil); Miller scripts	2	4	6	9	11	14
32-Death of Groo	2	4	6	10	12	15
32-2nd printing ($5.95)	1	2	3	5	6	8
33,34,36,37: 33-Thor. 34-Predator & Prey (Cloak & Dagger). 36-Willow (movie adapt.). 37-Hercules	1	3	4	6	8	10
35-Hitler's Astrologer (The Shadow, $12.95, HC)	2	4	6	10	13	16
35-Soft-c reprint (1990, $10.95)	2	4	6	8	10	12
38-Silver Surfer (Judgement Day)($14.95, HC)	2	4	6	11	14	18
38-Soft-c reprint (1990, $10.95)	2	4	6	9	11	14
nn-Abslom Daak: Dalak Killer (1990, $8.95) Dr. Who	1	3	4	6	8	10
nn-Arena by Bruce Jones (1989, $5.95) Dinosaurs	1	2	3	5	6	8
nn- A-Team Storybook Comics Illustrated (1983) r/ A-Team mini-series #1-3	1	3	4	6	8	10
nn-Ax (1988, $5.95) Ernie Colan-s/a	1	3	4	6	8	10
nn-Black Widow Coldest War (4/90, $9.95)	2	4	6	8	10	12
nn-Chronicles of Genghis Grimtoad (1990, $8.95)-Alan Grant-s	1	3	4	6	8	10
nn-Conan the Barbarian in the Horn of Azoth (1990, $8.95)	2	4	6	8	10	12
nn-Conan of Isles ($8.95)	2	4	6	8	10	12
nn-Conan Ravagers of Time (1992, $9.95) Kull & Red Sonja app.	2	4	6	8	10	12
nn-Conan -The Skull of Set	2	4	6	8	10	12
nn-Doctor Strange and Doctor Doom Triumph and Torment (1989, $17.95, HC)	2	4	6	14	18	22
nn-Dreamwalker (1989, $6.95)-Morrow-a	1	2	3	5	7	9
nn-Excalibur Weird War III (1990, $9.95)	2	4	6	8	10	12
nn-G.I. Joe - The Trojan Gambit (1983, 68 pgs.)	2	4	6	8	10	12
nn-Harvey Kurtzman Strange Adventures (Epic, $19.95, HC) Aragonés, Crumb	3	6	9	16	20	25
nn-Hearts and Minds (1990, $8.95) Heath-a	1	3	4	6	8	10
nn-Inhumans (1988, $7.95)-Williamson-i	1	2	3	5	7	9
nn-Jhereg (Epic, 1990, $8.95)	1	3	4	6	8	10
nn-Kazar-Guns of the Savage Land (7/90, $8.95)	1	3	4	6	8	10
nn-Kull-The Vale of Shadow ('89, $6.95)	1	3	4	6	8	10
nn-Last of the Dragons (1988, $6.95) Austin-a(i)	1	2	3	4	5	7
nn-Nightraven: House of Cards (1991, $14.95)	2	4	6	10	12	15
nn-Nightraven: The Collected Stories (1990, $9.95) Bolton-r/British Hulk mag.; David Lloyd-c/a	2	4	6	8	10	12
nn-Original Adventures of Cholly and Flytrap (Epic, 1991, $9.95) Suydam-s/c/a	2	4	6	10	12	15
nn-Rick Mason Agent (1989, $9.95)	1	3	4	6	8	10
nn-Roger Rabbit In The Resurrection Of Doom (1989, $8.95)	1	3	4	6	8	10
nn-A Sailor's Story Book II: Winds, Dreams and Dragons ('86, $6.95, softcover) Glansman-s/c/a	1	3	4	6	8	10
nn-Squadron Supreme: Death of a Universe (1989, $9.95) Gruenwald-s; Ryan & Williamson-a	1	3	4	6	8	10
nn-Who Framed Roger Rabbit (1989, $6.95)	1	3	4	6	8	10

NOTE: ***Aragones** a-27, 32. **Buscema** a-38. **Byrne** c/a-18. **Heath** a-35i. **Kaluta** a-13, 35p; c-13. **Miller** a-24p. **Simonson** a-6; c-6. **Starlin** c/a-1,3. **Williamson** a-34. **Wrightson** c-29i.*

MARVEL-HEROES & LEGENDS
Marvel Comics: Oct, 1996; 1997 ($2.95)

	GD	VG	FN	VF	VF/NM	NM-
nn-Wraparound-c, ...1997 ($2.99) -Original Avengers story						3.00

MARVEL HOLIDAY SPECIAL
Marvel Comics: No. 1, 1991 ($2.25, 84 pgs.) - 1996

	GD 2.0	VG 4.0	FN 6.0	VF 8.0	VF/NM 9.0	NM- 9.2
1-X-Men, Fantastic Four, Punisher, Thor, Capt. America, Ghost Rider, Capt. Ultra, Spidey stories; Art Adams-c/a						3.00
nn (1/93)-Wolverine, Thanos (by Starlin/Lim/Austin)						3.00
nn (1994)-Capt. America, X-Men, Silver Surfer						3.00
...1996-Spider-Man by Waid & Olliffe; X-Men, Silver Surfer						3.00
...2004-Spider-Man by DeFalco & Miyazawa; X-Men, Fantastic Four						3.00

NOTE: ***Art Adams** c-'93. **Golden** a-'93. **Perez** c-'94.*

MARVEL ILLUSTRATED: SWIMSUIT ISSUE (Also see Marvel Swimsuit Special)
Marvel Comics: 1991 ($3.95, magazine, 52 pgs.)

	GD	VG	FN	VF	VF/NM	NM-
V1#1-Parody of Sports Illustrated swimsuit issue; Mary Jane Parker centerfold pin-up by Jusko; 2nd print exists	1	3	4	6	8	10

MARVEL KNIGHTS (See Black Panther, Daredevil, Inhumans, & Punisher)
Marvel Comics: 1998 (Previews for upcoming series)

	GD	VG	FN	VF	VF/NM	NM-
Sketchbook-Wizard suppl.; Quesada & Palmiotti-c						3.00
Tourbook-($2.99) Interviews and art previews						3.00

MARVEL KNIGHTS
Marvel Comics: July, 2000 - No. 15, Sept, 2001 ($2.99)

	GD	VG	FN	VF	VF/NM	NM-
1-Daredevil, Punisher, Black Widow, Shang-Chi, Dagger app.						4.00
2-15: 2-Two covers by Barreto & Quesada						3.00
.../Marvel Boy Genesis Edition (6/00) Sketchbook preview						2.25
...: Millennial Visions (2/02, $3.99) Pin-ups by various; Harris-c						4.00

MARVEL KNIGHTS (Volume 2)
Marvel Comics: May, 2002 - No. 6, Oct, 2002 ($2.99)

	GD	VG	FN	VF	VF/NM	NM-
1-6-Daredevil, Punisher, Black Widow app.; Ponticelli-a						3.00

MARVEL KNIGHTS: DOUBLE SHOT
Marvel Comics: June, 2002 - No. 4 ($2.99, limited series)

	GD	VG	FN	VF	VF/NM	NM-
1-5: 1-Punisher by Ennis & Quesada; Daredevil by Haynes; Fabry-c						3.00

MARVEL KNIGHTS 4 (Fantastic Four) (Issues #1&2 are titled **Knights 4**)
Marvel Comics: Apr, 2004 - Present ($2.99)

	GD	VG	FN	VF	VF/NM	NM-
1-12: 1-7-McNiven-c/a; Aguirre-Sacasa-a. 8,9-Namor app.						3.00

MARVEL KNIGHTS MAGAZINE
Marvel Comics: May, 2001 - No. 6, Oct, 2001 ($3.99, magazine size)

	GD	VG	FN	VF	VF/NM	NM-
1-6-Reprints of recent Daredevil, Punisher, Black Widow, Inhumans						4.00

MARVEL KNIGHTS SPIDER-MAN
Marvel Comics: Jun, 2004 - Present ($2.99)

	GD	VG	FN	VF	VF/NM	NM-
1-Wraparound-c by Dodson; Millar-s/Dodson-a; Green Goblin app.						3.00
2-7: 2-Avengers app. 2,3-Vulture & Electro app. 5,8-Cho-c/a. 6-8-Venom app.						3.00
...Vol. 1: Down Among the Dead Men (2004, $9.99, TPB) r/#1-4						10.00

MARVEL MANGAVERSE:... (one-shots)
Marvel Comics: March 2002 ($2.25, manga-inspired one-shots)

	GD	VG	FN	VF	VF/NM	NM-
Avengers Assemble! - Udon Studio-s/a						2.25
Eternity Twilight ($3.50) - Ben Dunn-s/a/wrap-around-c						3.50
Fantastic Four - Adam Warren-s/Keron Grant-a						2.25
Ghost Riders - Chuck Austen-s/a						2.25
Punisher - Peter David-s/Lea Hernandez-a						2.25
Spider-Man - Kaare Andrews-s/a						2.25
X-Men - C.B. Cebulski-s/Jeff Matsuda-a						2.25

MARVEL MANGAVERSE (Manga series)
Marvel Comics: June, 2002 - No. 6, Nov., 2002 ($2.25)

	GD	VG	FN	VF	VF/NM	NM-
1-6: 1-Ben Dunn-s/a; intro. manga Captain Marvel						2.25
Vol. 1 TPB (2002, $24.95) r/one-shots						25.00
Vol. 2 TPB (2002, $12.99) r/#1-6						13.00
Vol. 3: Spider-Man-Legend of the Spider-Clan (2003, $11.99, TPB) r/series						12.00

MARVEL MASTERPIECES COLLECTION, THE
Marvel Comics: May, 1993 - No. 4, Aug, 1993 ($2.95, coated paper, lim. series)

	GD	VG	FN	VF	VF/NM	NM-
1-4-Reprints Marvel Masterpieces trading cards w/ new Jusko paintings in each; Jusko painted-c/a						3.00

MARVEL MASTERPIECES 2 COLLECTION, THE
Marvel Comics: July, 1994 - No. 3, Sept, 1994 ($2.95, limited series)

	GD	VG	FN	VF	VF/NM	NM-
1-3: 1-Kaluta-c; r/trading cards; new Steranko centerfold						3.00

MARVEL MILESTONE EDITION
Marvel Comics: 1991 - 1999 ($2.95, coated stock)(r/originals with original ads w/silver ink-c)

	GD	VG	FN	VF	VF/NM	NM-
...: X-Men #1-Reprints X-Men #1 (1991)						3.00

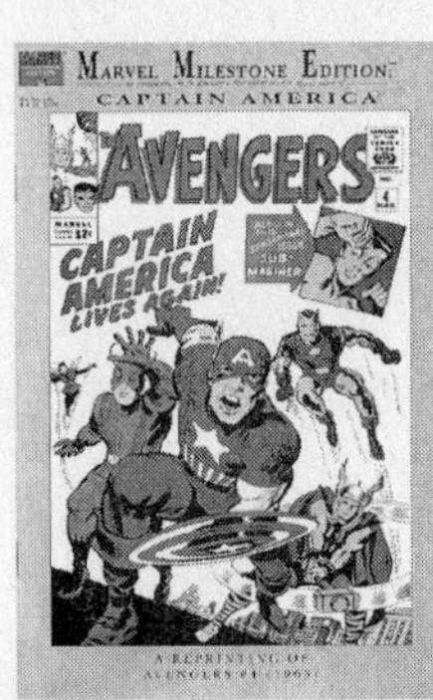

Marvel Milestone Edition Avengers #4 © MAR

Marvel Mystery Comics #3 © MAR

Marvel Mystery Comics #47 © MAR

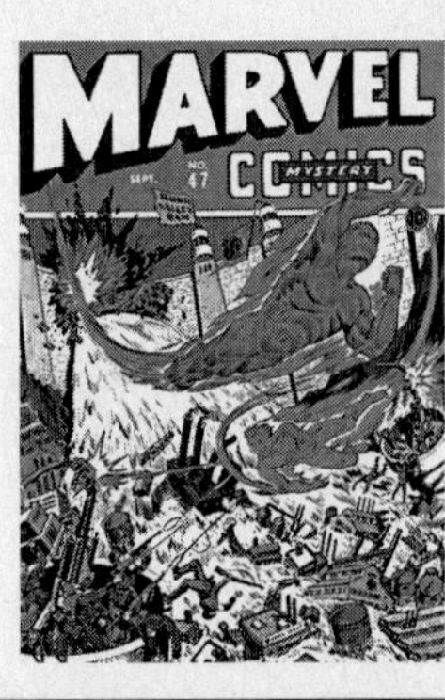

GD 2.0 | VG 4.0 | FN 6.0 | VF 8.0 | VF/NM 9.0 | NM- 9.2

...: Giant Size X-Men #1-(1991, $3.95, 68 pgs.) 4.00
...: Fantastic Four #1 (11/91), ...: Incredible Hulk #1 (3/92, says 3/91 by error), ...: Amazing Fantasy #15 (3/92), ...: Fantastic Four #5 (11/92), ...: Amazing Spider-Man #129 (11/92), ...: Iron Man #55 (11/92), ...: Iron Fist #14 (11/92), ...: Amazing Spider-Man #1 (1/93), ...: Amazing Spider-Man #1 (1/93) variation- no price on-c, ...: Tales of Suspense #39 (3/93), ...: Avengers #1 (9/93), ...: X-Men #9 (10/93), ...: Avengers #16 (10/93), ...:Amazing Spider-Man #149 (11/94, $2.95), ...:X-Men #28 (11/94, $2.95) 3.00
...:Captain America #1 (3/95, $3.95) 4.00
...:Amazing Spider-Man #3 (3/95, $2.95), ...:Avengers #4 (3/95, $2.95), ...:Strange Tales-r/Dr. Strange stories from #110, 111, 114, & 115 3.00
....:Hulk #181 (8/99, $2.99) 3.00

MARVEL MINI-BOOKS (See Promotional Comics section)

MARVEL MOVIE PREMIERE (Magazine)
Marvel Comics Group: Sept, 1975 (B&W, one-shot)

1-Burroughs' "The Land That Time Forgot" adapt. 2 4 6 8 10 12

MARVEL MOVIE SHOWCASE FEATURING STAR WARS
Marvel Comics Group: Nov, 1982 - No. 2, Dec, 1982 ($1.25, 68 pgs.)

1,2-Star Wars movie adaptation; reprints Star Wars #1-6 by Chaykin; 1-Reprints-c to Star Wars #1. 2-Stevens-r 4.00

MARVEL MOVIE SPOTLIGHT FEATURING RAIDERS OF THE LOST ARK
Marvel Comics Group: Nov, 1982 ($1.25, 68 pgs.)

1-Edited-r/Raiders of the Lost Ark #1-3; Buscema-c/a(p); movie adapt. 3.00

MARVEL MUST HAVES (Reprints of recent sold-out issues)
Marvel Comics: Dec, 2001 - Present ($3.99/$2.99)

1,2,4-6: 1-r/Wolverine: Origin #1, Startling Stories: Banner #1, Tangled Web #4 and Cable #97. 2-Amazing Spider-Man #36 and others. 4-Truth #1, Capt. America V4 #1, and The Ultimates #1. 5-r/Ultimate War #1, Ult. X-Men #26, Ult Spider-Man #33. 6-Ult. Spider-Man #33-36 4.00
3-r/Call of Duty: The Brotherhood #1 & Daredevil #32,33 3.00
Amazing Spider-Man #30-32; Incredible Hulk #34-36; The Ultimates #1-3; Ultimate Spider-Man #1-3; Ultimate X-Men #1-3; (New) X-Men #114-116 each.... 4.00

MARVEL MYSTERY COMICS (Formerly Marvel Comics) (Becomes Marvel Tales No. 93 on)
Timely /Marvel Comics (TP #2-17/TCI #18-54/MCI #55-92): No. 2, Dec, 1939 - No. 92, June, 1949 (Some material from #8-10 reprinted in 2004's Marvel 65th Anniversary Special #1)

2-(Rare)-American Ace begins, ends #3; Human Torch (blue costume) by Burgos, Sub-Mariner by Everett continue; 2 pg. origin recap of Human Torch
2460 4920 7380 18,600 30,800 43,000
3-New logo from Marvel pulp begins; 1st app. of television in comics? in Human Torch story (1/40) 1294 2588 3882 9705 15,853 22,000
4-Intro. Electro, the Marvel of the Age (ends #19), The Ferret, Mystery Detective (ends #9); 1st Sub-Mariner-c by Schomburg; 2nd German swastika on-c of a comic (2/40); one month after Top-Notch Comics #2 1088 2176 3264 8160 13,330 18,500
5 Classic Schomburg-c (Scarce) 1950 3900 5850 14,600 24,300 34,000
6,7: 6-Gustavson Angel story 742 1484 2226 5194 8347 11,500
8-1st Human Torch & Sub-Mariner battle(6/40) 1000 2000 3000 7167 11,584 16,000
9-(Scarce)-Human Torch & Sub-Mariner battle (cover/story); classic-c
2300 4600 6900 17,400 28,700 40,000
10-Human Torch & Sub-Mariner battle, conclusion; Terry Vance, the Schoolboy Sleuth begins, ends #57 806 1612 2418 5642 9071 12,500
11 352 704 1056 2288 3694 5100
12-Classic Kirby-c 400 800 1200 2600 4200 5800
13-Intro. & 1st app. The Vision by S&K (11/40); Sub-Mariner dons new costume, ends #15
497 994 1491 3479 5590 7700
14-16: 14-Shows-c to Human Torch #1 on-c (12/40). 15-S&K Vision, Gustavson Angel story
265 530 795 1656 2553 3450
17-Human Torch/Sub-Mariner team-up by Burgos/Everett; pin-up on back-c; shows-c to Human Torch #2 on-c 300 600 900 1875 2888 3900
18 246 492 738 1538 2369 3200
19,20: 19-Origin Toro in text; shows-c to Sub-Mariner #1 on-c. 20-Origin The Angel in text
254 508 762 1588 2444 3300
21-The Patriot begins, (intro. in Human Torch #4 (#3)); not in #46-48; pin-up on back-c (7/41)
246 492 738 1538 2369 3200
22-25: 23-Last Gustavson Angel; origin The Vision in text. 24-Injury-to-eye story
223 446 669 1394 2147 2900
26-30: 27-Ka-Zar ends; last S&K Vision who battles Satan. 28-Jimmy Jupiter in the Land of Nowhere begins, ends #48; Sub-Mariner vs. The Flying Dutchman. 30-1st Japanese war-c
196 392 588 1225 1888 2550
31-33,35,36,38,39: 31-Sub-Mariner by Everett ends, resumes #84. 32-1st app. The Boboes
177 354 531 1106 1703 2300
34-Everett, Burgos, Martin Goodman, Funnies, Inc. office appear in story & battles Hitler; last Burgos Human Torch 204 408 612 1275 1963 2650
37-Classic Hitler-c 204 408 612 1275 1963 2650
40-Classic Zeppelin-c 196 392 588 1225 1888 2550
41-43,45,47,48: 48-Last Vision; flag-c 146 292 438 913 1407 1900
44-Classic Super Plane-c 165 330 495 1031 1591 2150
46-Classic Hitler-c 165 330 495 1031 1591 2150
49-Origin Miss America 188 376 564 1175 1813 2450
50-Mary becomes Miss Patriot (origin) 154 308 462 963 1482 2000
51-60: 54-Bondage-c 131 262 393 819 1260 1700
61,62,64-Last German war-c 127 254 381 794 1222 1650
63-Classic Hitler War-c; The Villainess Cat-Woman only app.
146 292 438 913 1407 1900
65,66-Last Japanese War-c 127 254 381 794 1222 1650
67-78: 74-Last Patriot. 75-Young Allies begin. 76-Ten Chapter Miss America serial begins, ends #85 115 230 345 719 1110 1500
79-New cover format; Super Villains begin on cover; last Angel
119 238 357 744 1147 1550
80-1st app. Capt. America in Marvel Comics 140 280 420 875 1350 1825
81-Captain America app. 112 224 336 700 1075 1450
82-Origin & 1st app. Namora (5/47); 1st Sub-Mariner/Namora team-up; Captain America app.
277 554 831 1731 2666 3600
83,85: 83-Last Young Allies. 85-Last Miss America; Blonde Phantom app.
98 196 294 613 944 1275
84-Blonde Phantom begins (on-c of #84,88,89); Sub-Mariner by Everett begins; Captain America app. 138 276 414 863 1332 1800
86-Blonde Phantom i.d. revealed; Captain America app.; last Bucky app.
106 212 318 663 1019 1375
87-1st Capt. America/Golden Girl team-up; last Toro app. (8/48)
115 230 345 719 1110 1500
88-Golden Girl, Namora, & Sun Girl (1st in Marvel Comics) x-over; Captain America, Blonde Phantom app. 106 212 318 663 1019 1375
89-1st Human Torch/Sun Girl team-up; 1st Captain America solo; Blonde Phantom app.
106 212 318 663 1019 1375
90,91: 90-Blonde Phantom un-masked; Captain America app. 91-Capt. America app.; Blonde Phantom & Sub-Mariner end; early Venus app. (4/49) (scarce)
131 262 393 819 1260 1700
92-Feature story on the birth of the Human Torch and the death of Professor Horton (his creator); 1st app. The Witness in Marvel Comics; Captain America app. (scarce)
300 600 900 1925 3063 4200
132 Pg. issue, B&W, 25¢ (1943-44)-printed in N. Y.; square binding, blank inside covers); has Marvel No. 33-c in color; contains Capt. America #18 & Marvel Mystery Comics #33; same contents as Captain America Annual (Less than 5 copies known to exist)
3400 6800 10,200 24,000 - -
132 Pg. issue (with variant contents), B&W, 25¢ (1942-'43)- square binding, blank inside covers; has same Marvel No. 33-c in color but contains Capt. America #22 & Marvel Mystery Comics #41 instead (possibly scarcer than other version)
(a G+ copy sold in 2002 for $7,500)

NOTE: ***Brodsky** c-49, 72, 86, 88-92. **Crandall** a-26i. **Everett** c-7-9, 27, 84. **Gabrielle** c-30-32. **Schomburg** c-3-11, 13-29, 33-36, 39-48, 50-59, 63-69, 74, 76, 132 pg. issue. **Shores** c-37, 38, 75p, 77, 78p, 79p, 80, 81p, 82-84, 85p, 87p. **Sekowsky** c-73. Bondage covers-3, 4, 7, 12, 28, 29, 49, 50, 52, 56, 57, 58, 59, 65. Angel c-2, 3, 8, 12. Remember Pearl Harbor issues-#30-32.*

MARVEL MYSTERY COMICS
Marvel Comics: Dec, 1999 ($3.95, reprints)

1-Reprints original 1940s stories; Schomburg-c from #74 4.00

MARVEL NO-PRIZE BOOK, THE (The Official... on-c)
Marvel Comics Group: Jan, 1983 (one-shot, direct sales only)

1-Golden-c; Kirby-a 4.00

MARVELOUS ADVENTURES OF GUS BEEZER
Marvel Comics: May, 2003; Feb, 2004 ($2.99, one-shots)

...: Gus Beezer & Spider-Man 1 - (5/03) Gurihiru-a 3.00
...: Hulk 1 - (5/03) Simone-s/Lethcoe-a; She-Hulk app. 3.00
...: Spider-Man 1 - (5/03) Simone-s/Lethcoe-a; The Lizard & Dr. Doom app. 3.00
...: X-Men 1 - (5/03) Simone-s/Lethcoe-a 3.00

MARVEL PREMIERE
Marvel Comics Group: April, 1972 - No. 61, Aug, 1981 (A tryout book for new characters)

1-Origin Warlock (pre-#1) by Gil Kane/Adkins; origin Counter-Earth; Hulk & Thor cameo (#1-14 are 20¢-c) 7 14 21 46 63 80
2-Warlock ends; Kirby Yellow Claw-r 3 7 10 21 28 35
3-Dr. Strange series begins (pre #1, 7/72), B. Smith-c/a(p)
6 12 18 40 55 70
4-Smith/Brunner-a 3 6 9 18 23 28
5-9: 8-Starlin-c/a(p) 2 4 6 11 14 18
10-Death of the Ancient One 3 6 9 16 20 24

Marvel Premiere #50 © MAR

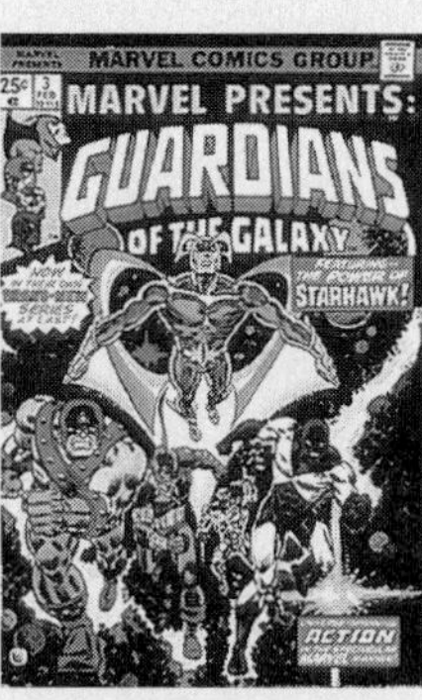

Marvel Presents #3 © MAR

Marvel 1602 #4 © MAR

GD VG FN VF VF/NM NM-
2.0 4.0 6.0 8.0 9.0 9.2

11-14: 11-Dr. Strange origin-r by Ditko. 14-Last Dr. Strange (3/74), gets own title 3 months later 2 4 6 8 10 12
15-Origin/1st app. Iron Fist (5/74), ends #25 8 16 24 55 78 100
16,25: 16-2nd app. Iron Fist; origin cont'd from #15; Hama's 1st Marvel-a. 25-1st Byrne Iron Fist (moves to own title next) 3 7 10 21 28 35
17-24: Iron Fist in all 2 4 6 14 18 22
26-Hercules. 1 2 3 5 6 8
27-Satana 1 3 4 6 8 10
28-Legion of Monsters (Ghost Rider, Man-Thing, Morbius, Werewolf) 2 4 6 12 16 20
29-46,49: 29,30-The Liberty Legion. 29-1st modern app. Patriot. 31-1st app. Woodgod; last 25¢ issue. 32-1st app. Monark Starstalker. 33,34-1st color app. Solomon Kane (Robert E. Howard adaptation "Red Shadows".) 35-Origin/1st app. 3-D Man. 36,37-3-D Man. 38-1st Weirdworld. 39,40-Torpedo. 41-1st Seeker 3000! 42-Tigra. 43-Paladin. 44-Jack of Hearts (1st solo book, 10/78). 45,46-Man-Wolf. 49-The Falcon (1st solo book, 8/79) 4.00
29-31-(30¢-c variants, limited distribution)(4,6,8/76) 2 4 6 10 12 15
36-38-(35¢-c variants, limited distribution)(6,8,10/77) 2 4 6 10 12 15
47,48-Byrne-a: 47-Origin/1st app. new Ant-Man. 48-Ant-Man 1 2 3 5 7 9
50-1st app. Alice Cooper; co-plotted by Alice 2 4 6 10 12 15
51-56,58-61: 51-53-Black Panther. 54-1st Caleb Hammer. 55-Wonder Man. 56-1st color app. Dominic Fortune. 58-60-Dr. Who. 61-Star Lord 4.00
57-Dr. Who (2nd U.S. app.-see Movie Classics) 6.00

NOTE: ***N. Adams*** *(Crusty Bunkers) part inks-10, 12, 13.* ***Austin*** *a-50i, 56i; c-46i, 50i, 56i, 58.* ***Brunner*** *a-4i, 6p, 9-14p; c-9-14.* ***Byrne*** *a-47p, 48p.* ***Chaykin*** *a-32-34; c-32, 33, 56.* ***Giffen*** *a-31p, 44p; c-44.* ***Gil Kane*** *a(p)-1, 2, 15; c(p)-1, 2, 15, 16, 22-24, 27, 36, 37.* ***Kirby*** *c-26, 29-31, 35.* ***Layton*** *a-47i, 48i; c-47.* ***McWilliams*** *a-25i.* ***Miller*** *c-49p, 53p, 58p.* ***Nebres*** *a-44i; c-38i.* ***Nino*** *a-38i.* ***Perez*** *c/a-38p, 45p, 46p.* ***Ploog*** *a-38; c-5-7.* ***Russell*** *a-7p.* ***Simonson*** *a-60(2pgs.); c-57.* ***Starlin*** *a-8p; c-8.* ***Sutton*** *a-41, 43, 50p, 61; c-50p, 61. #57-60 publ'd w/two different prices on-c.*

MARVEL PRESENTS
Marvel Comics: October, 1975 - No. 12, Aug, 1977 (#1-6 are 25¢ issues)

1-Origin & 1st app. Bloodstone 2 4 6 8 10 12
2-Origin Bloodstone continued; Kirby-c 1 2 3 4 5 7
3-Guardians of the Galaxy (1st solo book, 2/76) begins, ends #12 2 4 6 10 13 16
4-7,9-12: 9,10-Origin Starhawk 1 2 3 5 6 8
4-6-(30¢-c variants, limited distribution)(4-8/76) 2 4 6 8 10 12
8-r/story from Silver Surfer #2 plus 4 pgs. new-a 1 2 3 5 6 8
11,12-(35¢-c variants, limited distribution)(6,8/77) 2 4 6 8 10 12

NOTE: ***Austin*** *a-6i.* ***Buscema*** *r-8p.* ***Chaykin*** *a-5p.* ***Kane*** *c-1p.* ***Starlin*** *layouts-10.*

MARVEL PREVIEW (Magazine) (Bizarre Adventures #25 on)
Marvel Comics: Feb (no month), 1975 - No. 24, Winter, 1980 (B&W) ($1.00)

1-Man-Gods From Beyond the Stars; Crusty Bunkers (Neal Adams)-a(i) & cover; Nino-a 2 4 6 11 14 18
2-1st origin The Punisher (see Amaz. Spider-Man #129 & Classic Punisher); 1st app. Dominic Fortune; Morrow-c 9 18 27 65 93 120
3,8,10: 3-Blade the Vampire Slayer. 8-Legion of Monsters; Morbius app. 10-Thor the Mighty; Starlin frontispiece 2 4 6 14 18 22
4,5: 4-Star-Lord & Sword in the Star (origins & 1st app.). 5,6-Sherlock Holmes. 2 4 6 10 13 16
6,9: 6-Sherlock Holmes; N. Adams frontispiece. 9-Man-God; origin Star Hawk, ends #20 2 4 6 8 10 12
7-Satana, Sword in the Star app. 2 4 6 9 11 14
11,12,16,19: 11-Star-Lord; Byrne-a; Starlin frontispiece. 12-Haunt of Horror. 16-Masters of Terror. 19-Kull 1 2 3 5 6 8
13-15,17,18,20-24: 14,15-Star-Lord. 14-Starlin painted-c. 17-Blackmark by G. Kane (see SSOC #1-3). 18-Star-Lord. 20-Bizarre Advs. 21-Moon Knight (Spr/80)-Predates Moon Knight #1; The Shroud by Ditko. 22-King Arthur. 23-Bizarre Advs.; Miller-a. 24-Debut Paradox 5.00

NOTE: ***N. Adams*** *(C. Bunkers) r-20i.* ***Buscema*** *a-22, 23.* ***Byrne*** *a-11.* ***Chaykin*** *a-20r; c-20 (new).* ***Colan*** *a-8, 16p(3), 18p, 23p; c-16p.* ***Elias*** *a-18.* ***Giffen*** *a-7.* ***Infantino*** *a-14p.* ***Kaluta*** *a-12; c-15.* ***Miller*** *a-23.* ***Morrow*** *a-8i; c-2-4.* ***Perez*** *a-20p.* ***Ploog*** *a-8.* ***Starlin*** *c-13, 14. Nudity in some issues*

MARVEL RIOT
Marvel Comics: Dec, 1995 ($1.95, one-shot)

1-"Age of Apocalypse" spoof; Lobdell script 2.25

MARVELS
Marvel Comics: Jan, 1994 - No. 4, Apr, 1994 ($5.95, painted lim. series)
No. 1 (2nd Printing), Apr, 1996 - No. 4 (2nd Printing), July, 1996 ($2.95)

1-4: Kurt Busiek scripts & Alex Ross painted-c/a in all; double-c w/acetate overlay 1 2 3 5 6 8
Marvel Classic Collectors Pack ($11.90)-Issues #1 & 2 boxed (1st printings). 2 4 6 10 13 16
0-(8/94, $2.95)-no acetate overlay. 4.00
1-4-(2nd printing): r/original limited series w/o acetate overlay 3.00
Hardcover (1994, $59.95)-r/#0-4; w/intros by Stan Lee, John Romita, Sr., Kurt Busiek & Scott McCloud. 60.00
...: 10th Anniversary Edition (2004, $49.99, hardcover w/dustjacket) r/#0-4; scripts and commentaries; Ross sketch pages, cover gallery, behind the scenes art 50.00
Trade paperback ($19.95) 20.00

MARVEL SAGA, THE
Marvel Comics Group: Dec, 1985 - No. 25, Dec, 1987

1,21-25 2.25
2-20 2.25

NOTE: ***Williamson*** *a(i)-9, 10; c(i)-7, 10-12, 14, 16.*

MARVELS COMICS: ... (Marvel-type comics read in the Marvel Universe)
Marvel Comics: Jul, 2000 ($2.25, one-shots)

...Captain America #1 -Frenz & Sinnott-a; ...Daredevil #1 -Isabella-s/Newell-a; ...Fantastic Four #1 -Kesel-s/Paul Smith-a; Spider-Man #1 -Oliff-a; ...Thor #1 -Templeton-s/Aucoin-a 2.25
...X-Men #1 -Millar-s/ Sean Phillips & Duncan Fegredo-a 2.25
The History of Marvels Comics (no cover price)-Faux history; previews titles 2.25

MARVEL SELECTS:
Marvel Comics: Jan, 2000 - No. 6, June, 2000 ($2.75/$2.99, reprints)

...Fantastic Four 1-6: Reprints F.F. #107-112; new Davis-c 2.75
...Spider-Man 1,2,4-6: Reprints AS-M #100,101,103,104,93; Wieringo-c 2.75
...Spider-Man 3 ($2.99): Reprints AS-M #102; new Wieringo-c 3.00

MARVEL'S GREATEST COMICS (Marvel Collectors' Item Classics #1-22)
Marvel Comics Group: No. 23, Oct, 1969 - No. 96, Jan, 1981

23-34 (Giants). Begin Fantastic Four-r/#30s?-116 3 6 9 16 20 24
35-37-Silver Surfer-r/Fantastic Four #48-50 2 4 6 8 10 12
38-50: 42-Silver Surfer-r/F.F.(others?) 1 2 3 5 6 8
51-70: 63,64-(25¢ editions) 5.00
63,64-(30¢-c variants, limited distribution)(5,7/76) 1 2 3 4 5 7
71-96: 71-73-(30¢ editions) 4.00
71-73-(35¢-c variants, limited distribution)(7,9-10/77) 6.00

NOTE: *Dr. Strange, Fantastic Four, Iron Man, Watcher-#23, 24. Capt. America, Dr. Strange, Iron Man, Fantastic Four-#25-28. Fantastic Four-#38-96.* ***Buscema*** *r-85-92; c-87-92r.* ***Ditko*** *r-23-28.* ***Kirby*** *r-23-82; c-75, 77p, 80p. #81 reprints Fantastic Four #100.*

MARVEL'S GREATEST SUPERHERO BATTLES (See Fireside Book Series)

MARVEL: SHADOWS AND LIGHT
Marvel Comics: Feb, 1997 ($2.95, B&W, one-shot)

1-Tony Daniel-c 3.00

MARVEL 1602
Marvel Comics: Nov, 2003 - No. 8, June, 2004 ($3.50, limited series)

1-8-Neil Gaiman-s; Andy Kubert & Richard Isanove-a 3.50
HC (2004, $24.99) r/series; script pages for #1, sketch pages and Gaiman afterword 25.00

MARVEL 65TH ANNIVERSARY SPECIAL
Marvel Comics: 2004 ($4.99, one-shot)

1-Reprints Sub-Mariner & Human Torch battle from Marvel Mystery Comics #8-10 5.00

MARVELS OF SCIENCE
Charlton Comics: March, 1946 - No. 4, June, 1946

1-A-Bomb story 24 48 72 138 199 260
2-4 14 28 42 79 110 140

MARVEL SPECIAL EDITION FEATURING... (Also see Special Collectors' Ed.)
Marvel Comics Group: 1975 - 1978 (84 pgs.) (Oversized)

1-The Spectacular Spider-Man ($1.50); r/Amazing Spider-Man #6,35, Annual 1; Ditko-a(r) 3 6 9 18 24 30
1,2-Star Wars ('77,'78; r/Star Wars #1-3 & #4-6; regular edition and Whitman variant exist 2 4 6 11 14 18
3-Star Wars ('78, $2.50, 116 pgs.); r/S. Wars #1-6; regular edition and Whitman variant exist 3 6 9 16 20 24
3-Close Encounters of the Third Kind (1978, $1.50, 56 pgs.)-Movie adaptation; Simonson-a(p) 2 4 6 10 13 16
V2#2(Spring, 1980, $2.00, oversized)- "Star Wars: The Empire Strikes Back"; r/Marvel Comics Super Special #16 3 6 9 18 23 28

NOTE: ***Chaykin*** *c/a(r)-1(1977), 2, 3.* ***Stevens*** *a(r)-2i, 3i.* ***Williamson*** *a(r)-V2#2.*

MARVEL SPECTACULAR
Marvel Comics Group: Aug, 1973 - No. 19, Nov, 1975

1-Thor-r from mid-sixties begin by Kirby 2 4 6 8 10 12
2-19 6.00

MARVELS: PORTRAITS
Marvel Comics: Mar, 1995 - No. 4, June, 1995 ($2.95, limited series)

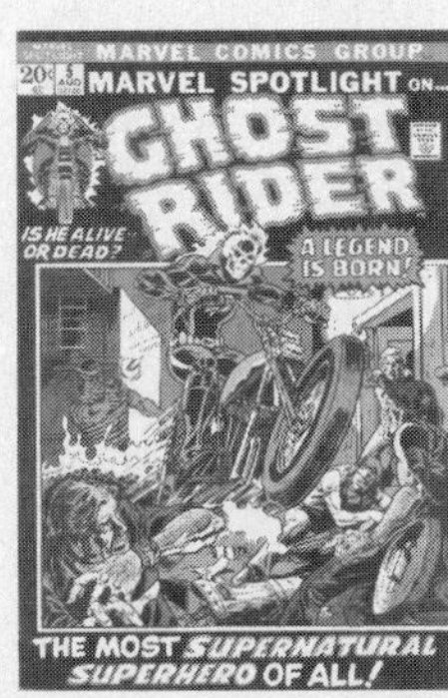

Marvel Spotlight #5 © MAR

Marvel Super-Heroes #77 © MAR

Marvel Tales #96 © MAR

GD 2.0 | VG 4.0 | FN 6.0 | VF 8.0 | VF/NM 9.0 | NM- 9.2

1-4:Different artists renditions of Marvel characters 3.00

MARVEL SPOTLIGHT (...& Son of Satan #19, 20, 23, 24)
Marvel Comics Group: Nov, 1971 - No. 33, Apr, 1977; V2#1, July, 1979 - V2#11, Mar, 1981
(A try-out book for new characters)

1-Origin Red Wolf (western hero)(1st solo book, pre-#1); Wood inks, Neal Adams-c; only 15¢ issue 4 8 12 29 40 50
2-(25¢, 52 pgs.)-Venus-r by Everett; origin/1st app. Werewolf By Night (begins) by Ploog; N. Adams-c 16 32 48 112 171 230
3,4: 4-Werewolf By Night ends (6/72); gets own title 9/72 6 12 18 40 55 70
5-Origin/1st app. Ghost Rider (8/72) & begins 15 30 45 107 164 220
6-8: 6-Origin G.R. retold. 8-Last Ploog issue 5 10 15 33 44 55
9-11-Last Ghost Rider (gets own title next mo.) 4 8 12 25 33 42
12-Origin & 2nd full app. The Son of Satan (10/73); story cont'd from Ghost Rider #2 & into #3; series begins, ends #24 4 8 12 24 32 40
13-24: 13-Partial origin Son of Satan. 14-Last 20¢ issue. 22-Ghost Rider-c & cameo (5 panels). 24-Last Son of Satan (10/75); gets own title 12/75 2 4 6 8 10 12
25,27,30,31: 27-(Regular 25¢-c), Sub-Mariner app. 30-The Warriors Three. 31-Nick Fury 6.00
26-Scarecrow 1 3 4 6 8 10
27-(30¢-c variant, limited distribution) 2 4 6 11 14 18
28-(Regular 25¢-c) 1st solo Moon Knight app. 3 7 10 21 28 35
28-(30¢-c variant, limited distribution) 6 12 18 40 55 70
29,32: 29-(Regular 25¢-c) (8/76) Moon Knight app.; last 25¢ issue. 32-1st app./partial origin Spider-Woman (2/77); Nick Fury app. 3 6 9 16 20 24
29-(30¢-c variant, limited distribution) 4 8 12 29 40 50
33-Deathlok; 1st app. Devil-Slayer 1 2 3 5 6 8
V2#1-7,9-11: 1-4-Capt. Marvel. 5-Dragon Lord. 6,7-StarLord; origin #6. 9-11-Capt. Universe (see Micronauts #8) 3.00
1-Variant copy missing issue #1 on cover 2 4 6 8 10 12
8-Capt. Marvel; Miller-c/a(p) 6.00

NOTE: ***Austin*** *c-V2#2i, 8.* ***J. Buscema*** *c/a-30p.* ***Chaykin*** *a-31; c-26, 31.* ***Colan*** *a-18p, 19p.* ***Ditko*** *a-V2#4, 5, 9-11; c-V2#4, 9-11.* ***Kane*** *c-21p, 32p.* ***Kirby*** *c-29p.* ***McWilliams*** *a-20i.* ***Miller*** *a-V2#8p; c(p)-V2#2, 5, 7, 8.* ***Mooney*** *a-8i, 10i, 14p, 15, 16p, 17p, 24p, 27, 32i.* ***Nasser*** *a-33p.* ***Ploog*** *a-2-5, 6-8p; c-3-9.* ***Romita*** *c-13.* ***Sutton*** *a-9-11p, V2#6, 7. #29-25¢ & 30¢ issues exist.*

MARVEL SUPER ACTION (Magazine)
Marvel Comics Group: Jan, 1976 (B&W, 76 pgs.)

1-Origin/2nd app. Dominic Fortune(see Marvel Preview); early Punisher app.; Weird World & The Huntress; Evans, Ploog-a 6 12 18 43 59 75

MARVEL SUPER ACTION
Marvel Comics Group: May, 1977 - No. 37, Nov, 1981

1-Reprints Capt. America #100 by Kirby 2 4 6 8 10 12
2-13: 2,3,5-13 reprint Capt. America #101,102,103-111. 4-Marvel Boy-r(origin)/M. Boy #1. 11-Origin-r. 12,13-Classic Steranko-c/a(r). 1 2 3 4 5 7
2,3-(35¢-c variants, limited distribution)(6,8/77) 1 2 3 6 8 10
14-20: r/Avengers #55,56, Annual 2, others 4.00
21-37: 30-r/Hulk #6 from U.K. 3.50

NOTE: ***Buscema*** *a(r)-14p, 15p; c-18-20, 22, 35r-37.* ***Everett*** *a-4.* ***Heath*** *a-4r.* ***Kirby*** *r-1-3, 5-11.* ***B. Smith*** *a-27r, 28r.* ***Steranko*** *a(r)-12p, 13p; c-12r, 13r.*

MARVEL SUPER HERO CONTEST OF CHAMPIONS
Marvel Comics Group: June, 1982 - No. 3, Aug, 1982 (Limited series)

1-3: Features nearly all Marvel characters currently appearing in their comics; 1st Marvel limited series 1 2 3 5 6 8

MARVEL SUPER HEROES
Marvel Comics Group: October, 1966 (25¢, 68 pgs.) (1st Marvel one-shot)

1-r/origin Daredevil from D.D. #1; r/Avengers #2; G.A. Sub-Mariner-r/Marvel Mystery #8 (Human Torch app.). Kirby-a 11 22 33 80 120 160

MARVEL SUPER-HEROES (Formerly Fantasy Masterpieces #1-11)
(Also see Giant-Size Super Heroes) (#12-20: 25¢, 68 pgs.)
Marvel Comics: No. 12, 12/67 - No. 31, 11/71; No. 32, 9/72 - No. 105, 1/82

12-Origin & 1st app. Capt. Marvel of the Kree; G.A. Human Torch, Destroyer, Capt. America, Black Knight, Sub-Mariner-r (#12-20 all contain new stories and reprints) 13 26 39 92 144 190
13-2nd app. Capt. Marvel; G.A. Black Knight, Torch, Vision, Capt. America, Sub-Mariner-r 7 14 21 50 68 85
14-Amazing Spider-Man (5/68, new-a by Andru/Everett); G.A. Sub-Mariner, Torch, Mercury (1st Kirby-a at Marvel), Black Knight, Capt. America reprints 9 18 27 65 93 120
15-17: 15-Black Bolt cameo in Medusa (new-a); Black Knight, Sub-Mariner, Black Marvel, Capt. America-r. 16-Origin & 1st app. S. A. Phantom Eagle; G.A. Torch, Capt. America, Black Knight, Patriot, Sub-Mariner-r. 17-Origin Black Knight (new-a); G.A. Torch, Sub-Mariner-r; reprint from All-Winners Squad #21 (cover & story) 4 8 12 27 36 45
18-Origin/1st app. Guardians of the Galaxy (1/69); G.A. Sub-Mariner, All-Winners Squad-r 6 12 18 40 55 70
19-Ka-Zar (new-a); G.A. Torch, Marvel Boy, Black Knight, Sub-Mariner reprints; Smith-c(p); Tuska-a(r) 3 6 9 18 24 30
20-Doctor Doom (5/69); r/Young Men #24 w/-c 4 8 12 24 32 40
21-31: All-r issues. 21-X-Men, Daredevil, Iron Man-r begin, end #31. 31-Last Giant issue 2 4 6 10 13 16
32-50: 32-Hulk/Sub-Mariner-r begin from TTA. 6.00
51-70,100: 56-r/origin Hulk/Inc. Hulk #102; Hulk-r begin 4.00
57,58-(30¢-c variants, limited distribution)(5,7/76) 6.00
65,66-(35¢-c variants, limited distribution)(7,9/77) 6.00
71-99,101-105 3.00

NOTE: ***Austin*** *a-104.* ***Colan*** *a(p)-12, 13, 15, 18; c-12, 13, 15, 18.* ***Everett*** *a-14i(new); r-14, 15i, 18, 19, 33; c-85(r). New* ***Kirby*** *c-22, 27, 54.* ***Maneely*** *r-14, 15, 19.* ***Severin*** *r-83-85i, 100-102; c-100-102r.* ***Starlin*** *c-47.* ***Tuska*** *a-19p. Black Knight-r by* ***Maneely*** *in 12-16, 19. Sub-Mariner-r by* ***Everett*** *in 12-20.*

MARVEL SUPER-HEROES
Marvel Comics: May, 1990 - V2#15, Oct, 1993 ($2.95/$2.50, quart., 68-84 pgs.)

1-Moon Knight, Hercules, Black Panther, Magik, Brother Voodoo, Speedball (by Ditko) & Hellcat; Hembeck-a 3.00
2,4,5,V2#3,6-15: 2-Summer Special(7/90); Rogue, Speedball (by Ditko), Iron Man, Falcon, Tigra & Daredevil. 4-Spider-Man/Nick Fury, Daredevil,Speedball, Wonder Man, Spitfire & Black Knight; Byrne-c. 5-Thor, Dr. Strange, Thing & She-Hulk; Speedball by Ditko(p). V2#3-Retells origin Capt. America w/new facts; Blue Shield, Capt. Marvel,Speedball, Wasp; Hulk by Ditko/Rogers V2#6-9: 6-8-$2.25-c. 6,7-X-Men, Cloak & Dagger, The Shroud (by Ditko) & Marvel Boy in each. 8-X-Men, Namor & Iron Man (by Ditko); Larsen-c. 9-West Coast Avengers, Iron Man app.; Kieth-c(p). V2#10-Ms. Marvel/Sabretooth-c/story (intended for Ms. Marvel #24; shows-c to #24); Namor, Vision, Scarlet Witch stories. V2#11,12 :11-Original Ghost Rider-c/story; Giant-Man, Ms. Marvel stories. 12-Dr. Strange, Falcon, Iron Man. V2#13-15 ($2.75, 84 pgs.): 13-All Iron Man 30th anniversary.
15-Iron Man/Thor/Volstagg/Dr. Druid 2.75

MARVEL SUPER-HEROES MEGAZINE
Marvel Comics: Oct, 1994 - No. 6, Mar, 1995 ($2.95, 100 pgs.)

1-6: 1-r/FF #232, DD #159, Iron Man #115, Incred. Hulk #314 3.00

MARVEL SUPER-HEROES SECRET WARS (See Secret Wars II)
Marvel Comics Group: May, 1984 - No. 12, Apr, 1985 (limited series)

1 1 2 3 5 6 8
1-3-(2nd printings, sold in multi-packs) 2.50
2-6,9-11: 6-The Wasp dies 6.00
7,12: 7-Intro. new Spider-Woman. 12-($1.00, 52 pgs.) 1 2 3 4 5 7
8-Spider-Man's new black costume explained as alien costume (1st app. Venom as alien costume) 3 6 9 18 23 28

NOTE: ***Zeck*** *a-1-12; c-1,3,8-12. Additional artists (John Romita Sr., Art Adams and others) had uncredited art in #12.*

MARVEL SUPER SPECIAL, A (See Marvel Comics Super...)

MARVEL SWIMSUIT SPECIAL (Also see Marvel Illustrated...)
Marvel Comics: 1992 - No. 4, 1995 ($3.95/$4.50, magazine, 52 pgs.)

1-4-Silvestri-c; pin-ups by diff. artists. 2-Jusko-c. 3-Hughes-c 1 2 3 5 6 8

MARVEL TAILS STARRING PETER PORKER THE SPECTACULAR SPIDER-HAM
(Also see Peter Porker...)
Marvel Comics Group: Nov, 1983 (one-shot)

1-Peter Porker, the Spectacular Spider-Ham, Captain Americat, Goose Rider, Hulk Bunny app. 4.00

MARVEL TALES (Formerly Marvel Mystery Comics #1-92)
Marvel/Atlas Comics (MCI): No. 93, Aug, 1949 - No. 159, Aug, 1957

93-Horror/weird stories begin 146 292 438 913 1407 1900
94-Everett-a 94 188 282 588 907 1225
95,96,99,101,103,105: 95-New logo 65 130 195 406 623 840
97-Sun Girl, 2 pgs; Kirbyish-a; one story used in N.Y. State Legislative document 77 154 231 481 741 1000
98,100: 98-Krigstein-a 67 134 201 419 642 865
102-Wolverton-a "The End of the World", (6 pgs.) 92 184 276 575 888 1200
104-Wolverton-a "Gateway to Horror", (6 pgs.) 90 180 270 563 869 1175
106,107-Krigstein-a. 106-Decapitation story 54 108 162 329 502 675
108-120: 118-Hypo-c/panels in End of World story. 120-Jack Katz-a 40 80 120 239 357 475
121,123-131: 128-Flying Saucer-c. 131-Last precode (2/55) 34 68 102 193 279 365
122-Kubert-a 34 68 102 196 283 370

Marvel Tales #130 © MAR

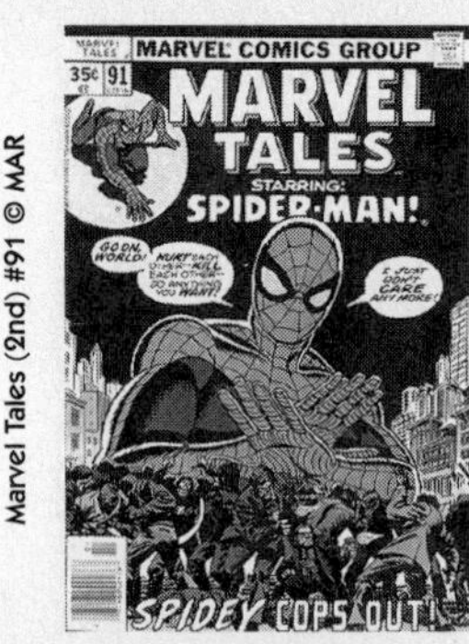

Marvel Tales (2nd) #91 © MAR

Marvel Team-Up #68 © MAR

GD 2.0 | VG 4.0 | FN 6.0 | VF 8.0 | VF/NM 9.0 | NM- 9.2

132,133,135-141,143,145 22 44 66 125 180 235
134-Krigstein, Kubert-a; flying saucer-c 24 48 72 135 195 255
142-Krigstein-a 23 46 69 130 188 245
144-Williamson/Krenkel-a, 3 pgs. 23 46 69 130 188 245
146,148-151,154-156,158: 150-1st S.A. issue. 156-Torres-a
17 34 51 98 139 180
147,152: 147-Ditko-a. 152-Wood, Morrow-a 20 40 60 112 161 210
153-Everett End of World c/story 22 44 66 123 177 230
157,159-Krigstein-a 18 36 54 100 143 185

NOTE: ***Andru** a-103. **Briefer** a-118. **Check** a-147. **Colan** a-105, 107, 118, 120, 121, 127, 131. **Drucker** a-127, 135, 141, 146, 150. **Everett** a-98, 104, 106(2), 108(2), 131, 148, 151, 153, 155; c-107, 109, 111, 112, 114, 117, 127, 143, 147-151, 153, 155, 156. **Forte** a-119, 125, 130. **Heath** a-110, 113, 118, 119; c-104-106, 110, 130. **Gil Kane** a-117. **Lawrence** a-130. **Maneely** a-111, 126, 129; c-108, 116, 120, 129, 152. **Mooney** a-114. **Morisi** a-153. **Morrow** a-150, 152, 156. **Orlando** a-149, 151, 157. **Pakula** a-119, 121, 135, 144, 150, 152, 156. **Powell** a-136, 137, 150, 154. **Ravielli** a-117. **Rico** a-97, 99. **Romita** a-108. **Sekowsky** a-96-98. **Shores** a-110; c-96. **Sinnott** a-105, 116. **Tuska** a-114. **Whitney** a-107. **Wildey** a-126, 138.*

MARVEL TALES (...Annual #1,2; ...Starring Spider-Man #123 on)
Marvel Comics Group (NPP earlier issues): 1964 - No. 291, Nov, 1994 (No. 1-32: 72 pgs.)
(#1-3 have Canadian variants; back & inside-c are blank, same value)

1-Reprints origins of Spider-Man/Amazing Fantasy #15, Hulk/Inc. Hulk#1, Ant-Man/T.T.A. #35, Giant Man/T.T.A. #49, Iron Man/T.O.S. #39,48, Thor/J.I.M. #83 & r/Sgt. Fury #1
30 60 90 218 334 450
2 ('65)-r/X-Men #1(origin), Avengers #1(origin), origin Dr. Strange-r/Strange Tales #115 & origin Hulk(Hulk #3) 11 22 33 80 120 160
3 (7/66)-Spider-Man, Strange Tales (H. Torch), Journey into Mystery (Thor), Tales to Astonish (Ant-Man)-r begin (r/Strange Tales #101) 6 12 18 43 59 75
4,5 4 8 12 29 40 50
6-8,10: 10-Reprints 1st Kraven/Amaz. S-M #15 3 6 9 18 24 30
9-r/Amazing Spider-Man #14 w/cover 3 7 10 21 28 35
11-33: 11-Spider-Man battles Daredevil-r/Amaz. Spider-Man #16. 13-Origin Marvel Boy-r from M. Boy #1. 22-Green Goblin-c/story-r/Amaz. Spider-Man #27. 30-New Angel story (x-over w/Ka-Zar #2,3). 32-Last 72 pg. iss. 33-(52 pgs.) Kraven-r
2 4 6 12 16 20
34-50: 34-Begin regular size issues 1 2 3 4 5 7
51-65 5.00
66-70-(Regular 25¢ editions)(4-8/76) 4.00
66-70-(30¢-c variants, limited distribution) 6.00
71-105: 75-Origin Spider-Man-r. 77-79-Drug issues-r/Amaz. Spider-Man #96-98. 98-Death of Gwen Stacy-r/Amaz. Spider-Man #121 (Green Goblin). 99-Death Green Goblin-r/Amaz. Spider-Man #122. 100-(52 pgs.)-New Hawkeye/Two Gun Kid story.
101-105-All Spider-Man-r 3.00
80-84-(35¢-c variants, limited distribution)(6-10/77) 5.00
106-r/1st Punisher-Amazing Spider-Man #129 1 2 3 5 6 8
107-136: 107-133-All Spider-Man-r. 111,112-r/Spider-Man #134,135 (Punisher). 113,114-r/Spider-Man #136,137(Green Goblin). 126-128-r/clone story from Amazing Spider-Man #149-151. 134-136-Dr. Strange-r begin; SpM stories continue.
134-Dr. Strange-r/Strange Tales #110 3.00
137-Origin-r Dr. Strange; shows original unprinted-c & origin Spider-Man/Amazing Fantasy #15
6.00
137-Nabisco giveaway 1 2 3 4 5 7
138-Reprints all Amazing Spider-Man #1; begin reprints of Spider-Man with covers similar to originals 5.00
139-144: r/Amazing Spider-Man #2-7 3.00
145-149,151-190,193-199: Spider-Man-r continue w/#8 on. 149-Contains skin "Tattooz" decals. 153-r/1st Kraven/Spider-Man #15. 155-r/2nd Green Goblin/Spider-Man #17. 161,164,165-Gr. Goblin-c/stories-r/Spider-Man #23,26,27. 178,179-Green Goblin-c/story-r/ Spider-Man #39,40. 187,189-Kraven-r. 193-Byrne-r/Marvel Team-Up begin w/scripts 2.50
150,191,192,200: 150-($1.00, 52pgs.)-r/Spider-Man Annual #1(Kraven app.). 191-($1.50, 68 pgs.)-r/Spider-Man #96-98. 192-($1.25, 52 pgs.)-r/Spider-Man #121,122. 200-Double size ($1.25)-Miller-c & r/Annual #14 4.00
201-257: 208-Last Byrne-r. 210,211-r/Spidey #134,135. 212,213-r/Giant-Size Spidey #4. 213-r/1st solo Silver Surfer story/F.F. Annual #5. 214,215-r/Spidey #161,162. 222-Reprints origin Punisher/Spectacular Spider-Man #83; last Punisher reprint. 209-Reprints 1st app. The Punisher/Amazing Spider-Man #129; Punisher reprints begin, end #222. 223-McFarlane-c begins, end #239. 233-Spider-Man/X-Men team-ups begin; r/X-Men #35. 234-r/Marvel Team-Up #4. 235,236-r/M. Team-Up Annual #1. 237,238-r/M. Team-Up #150. 239,240-r/M. Team-Up #38,90(Beast). 242-r/M.Team-Up #89. 243-r/M. Team-Up #117 (Wolverine). 250-($1.50, 52pgs.)-r/1st Karma/M. Team-Up #100. 251-r/Spider-Man #100 (Green Goblin-c/story). 252-r/1st app. Morbius/Amaz. Spider-Man #101. 253-($1.50, 52 pgs.) -r/Amaz. S-M #102254-r/M. Team-Up #15(Ghost Rider); new painted-c. 255,256-Spider-Man & Ghost Rider-r/Marvel Team-Up #58,91. 257-Hobgoblin-r begin (r/Amazing Spider-Man #238) 2.25
258-291: 258-261-r/A. Spider-Man #239,249-251(Hobgoblin). 262,263-r/Marv. Team-Up #53,54. 262-New X-Men vs. Sunstroke story. 263-New Woodgod origin story. 264,265-r/Amazing Spider-Man Annual 5. 266-273-Reprints alien costume stories/A. S-M 252-259. 277-r/1st Silver Sable/A. S-M 265. 283-r/A. S-M 275 (Hobgoblin). 284-r/A. S-M 276 (Hobgoblin) 2.25
285-variant w/Wonder-Con logo on c-no price-giveaway 2.25
286-($2.95)-p/bagged w/16 page insert & animation print 3.00

NOTE: *All contain reprints; some have new art. #89-97-r/Amazing Spider-Man #110-118; #98-136-r/#121-159; #137-150-r/Amazing Fantasy #15, #1-12 & Annual 1; #151-167-r/#13-28 & Annual 2; #168-186-r/#29-46. **Austin** a-100i; c-272i, 273i. **Byrne** a(r)-193-198p, 201-208p. **Ditko** a-1-30, 83, 100, 137-155. **G. Kane** a-71, 81, 98-101p, 249r; c-125-127p, 130p, 137-155. **Sam Kieth** c-255, 262, 263. **Ron Lim** c-266p-281p, 283p-285p. **McFarlane** c-223-239. **Mooney** a-63, 95-97i, 103(i). **Nasser** a-100p. **Nebres** a-242i. **Perez** c-259-261. **Rogers** c-240, 241, 243-252.*

MARVEL TEAM-UP (See Marvel Treasury Edition #18 & Official Marvel Index To...)
(Replaced by Web of Spider-Man)
Marvel Comics Group: March, 1972 - No. 150, Feb, 1985
NOTE: *Spider-Man team-ups in all but Nos. 18, 23, 26, 29, 32, 35, 97, 104, 105, 137.*

1-Human Torch 13 26 39 92 141 190
2-Human Torch 5 10 15 36 48 60
3-Spider-Man/Human Torch vs. Morbius (part 1); 3rd app. of Morbius (7/72)
6 12 18 40 55 70
4-Spider-Man/X-Men vs. Morbius (part 2 of story); 4th app. of Morbius
6 12 18 40 55 70
5-10: 5-Vision. 6-Thing. 7-Thor. 8-The Cat (4/73, came out between The Cat #3 & 4). 9-Iron Man. 10-H-T 3 6 9 16 21 26
11,13,14,16-20: 11-Inhumans. 13-Capt. America. 14-Sub-Mariner. 16-Capt. Marvel. 17-Mr. Fantastic. 18-H-T/Hulk. 19-Ka-Zar. 20-Black Panther; last 20¢ issue
2 4 6 10 13 16
12-Werewolf (8/73, 1 month before Werewolf #1). 3 6 9 18 24 30
15-1st Spider-Man/Ghost Rider team-up (11/73) 3 6 9 16 20 24
21-30: 21-Dr. Strange. 22-Hawkeye. 23-H-T/Iceman (X-Men cameo). 24-Brother Voodoo. 25-Daredevil. 26-H-T/Thor. 27-Hulk. 28-Hercules. 29-H-T/Iron Man. 30-Falcon
1 3 4 6 8 10
31-45,47-50: 31-Iron Fist. 32-H-T/Son of Satan. 33-Nighthawk. 34-Valkyrie. 35-H-T/Dr. Strange. 36-Frankenstein. 37-Man-Wolf. 38-Beast. 39-H-T. 40-Sons of the Tiger/H-T. 41-Scarlet Witch. 42-The Vision. 43-Dr. Doom; retells origin. 44-Moondragon. 45-Killraven. 47-Thing. 48-Iron Man; last 25¢ issue. 49-Dr. Strange; Iron Man app. 50-Iron Man; Dr. Strange app.
1 2 3 4 5 7
44-48-(30¢-c variants, limited distribution)(4-8/76) 2 4 6 11 14 18
46-Spider-Man/Deathlok team-up 1 2 3 5 6 8
51,52,56,57: 51-Iron Man; Dr. Strange app. 52-Capt. America. 56-Daredevil. 57-Black Widow
6.00
53-Hulk; Woodgod & X-Men app., 1st Byrne-a on X-Men (1/77)
3 6 9 19 25 32
54,55,58-60: 54,59,60: 54-Hulk; Woodgod app. 59-Yellowjacket/The Wasp. 60-The Wasp (Byrne-a in all). 55-Warlock-c/story; Byrne-a. 58-Ghost Rider
1 2 3 5 6 8
58-62-(35¢-c variants, limited distribution)(6-10/77) 2 4 6 11 14 18
61-70: All Byrne-a; 61-H-T. 62-Ms. Marvel; last 30¢ issue. 63-Iron Fist. 64-Daughters of the Dragon. 65-Capt. Britain (1st U.S. app.). 66-Capt. Britain; 1st app. Arcade. 67-Tigra; Kraven the Hunter app. 68-Man-Thing. 69-Havok (from X-Men). 70-Thor
1 2 3 4 5 7
71-74,76-78,80: 71-Falcon. 72-Iron Man. 73-Daredevil. 74-Not Ready for Prime Time Players (Belushi). 76-Dr. Strange. 77-Ms. Marvel. 78-Wonder Man. 80-Dr. Strange/Clea; last 35¢ issue 4.00
75,79,81: Byrne-a(p). 75-Power Man; Cage app. 79-Mary Jane Watson as Red Sonja; Clark Kent cameo (1 panel, 3/79). 81-Death of Satana 6.00
82-99: 82-Black Widow. 83-Nick Fury. 84-Shang-Chi. 86-Guardians of the Galaxy. 89-Nightcrawler (from X-Men). 91-Ghost Rider. 92-Hawkeye. 93-Werewolf by Night. 94-Spider-Man vs. The Shroud. 95-Mockingbird (intro.); Nick Fury app. 96-Howard the Duck; last 40¢ issue. 97-Spider-Woman/ Hulk. 98-Black Widow. 99-Machine Man. 85-Shang-Chi/ Black Widow/Nick Fury. 87-Black Panther. 88-Invisible Girl. 90-Beast 3.00
100-(Double-size)-Fantastic Four/Storm/Black Panther; origin/1st app. Karma, one of the New Mutants; origin Storm; X-Men x-over; Miller-c/a(p); Byrne-a (on X-Men app. only)
1 2 3 4 5 7
101-116: 101-Nighthawk(Ditko-a). 102-Doc Samson. 103-Ant-Man. 104-Hulk/Ka-Zar. 105-Hulk/Powerman/Iron Fist. 106-Capt. America. 107-She-Hulk. 108-Paladin; Dazzler cameo. 109-Dazzler; Paladin app. 110-Iron Man. 111-Devil-Slayer. 112-King Kull; last 50¢ issue. 113-Quasar. 114-Falcon. 115-Thor. 116-Valkyrie 3.00
117-Wolverine-c/story 1 3 4 6 8 10
118-140,142-149: 118-Professor X; Wolverine app. (4 pgs.); X-Men cameo. 119-Gargoyle. 120-Dominic Fortune. 121-Human Torch. 122-Man-Thing. 123-Daredevil. 124-The Beast. 125-Tigra. 126-Hulk & Powerman/Son of Satan. 127-The Watcher. 128-Capt. America; Spider-Man/Capt. America photo-c. 129-The Vision. 130-Scarlet Witch. 131-Frogman. 132-Mr. Fantastic. 133-Fantastic Four. 134-Jack of Hearts. 135-Kitty Pryde; X-Men cameo. 136-Wonder Man. 137-Aunt May/Franklin Richards. 138-Sandman. 139-Nick Fury. 140-Black Widow. 142-Capt. Marvel. 143-Starfox. 144-Moon Knight. 145-Iron Man. 146-Nomad. 147-Human Torch; Spider-Man back to old costume. 148-Thor. 149-Cannonball
2.50

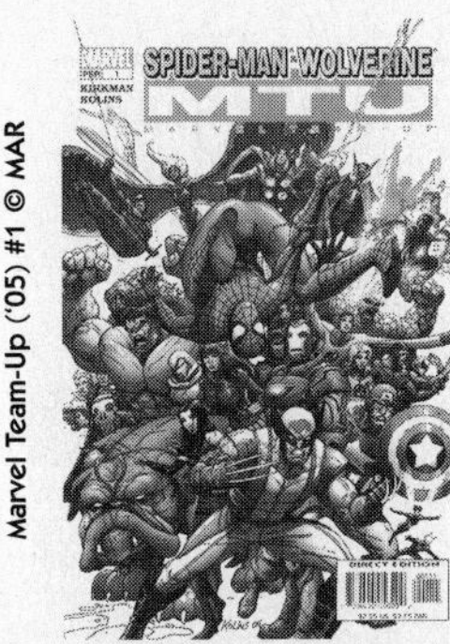

Marvel Team-Up ('05) #1 © MAR

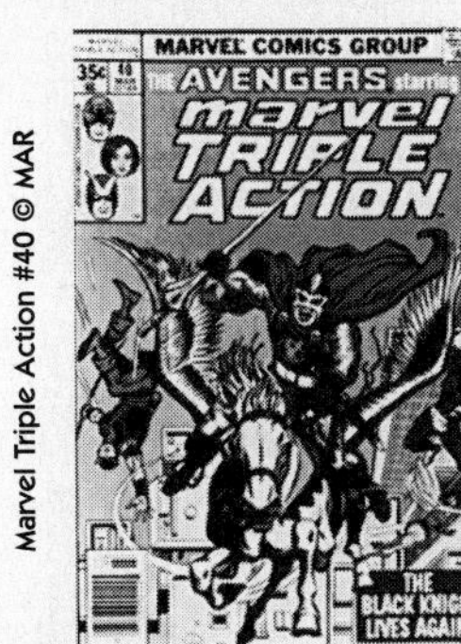

Marvel Triple Action #40 © MAR

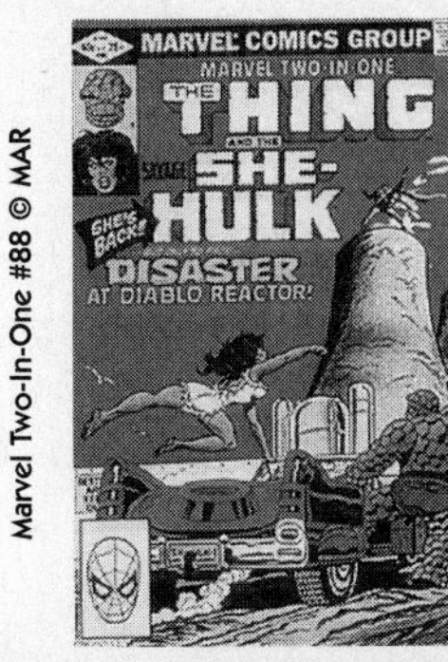

Marvel Two-In-One #88 © MAR

GD VG FN VF VF/NM NM-
2.0 4.0 6.0 8.0 9.0 9.2

141-Daredevil; SpM/Black Widow app. (Spidey in new black costume; ties w/ Amazing Spider-Man #252 for 1st black costume) 1 3 4 6 8 10
150-X-Men ($1.00, double-size); B. Smith-c 5.00
Annual 1 (1976)-Spider-Man/X-Men (early app.) 3 6 9 18 24 30
Annual 2 (1979)-Spider-Man/Hulk 1 2 3 5 7 9
Annuals 3,4: 3 (1980)-Hulk/Power Man/Machine Man/Iron Fist; Miller-c(p). 4 (1981)-Spider-Man /Daredevil/Moon Knight/Power Man/Iron Fist; brief origins of each; Miller-c; Miller scripts on Daredevil 6.00
Annuals 5-7: 5 (1982)-SpM/The Thing/Scarlet Witch/Dr. Strange/Quasar. 6 (1983)-Spider-Man/ New Mutants (early app.), Cloak & Dagger. 7(1984)-Alpha Flight; Byrne-c(i) 5.00

NOTE: ***Art Adams*** *c-141p.* ***Austin*** *a-79i; c-76i, 79i, 96i, 101i, 112i, 130i.* ***Bolle*** *a-9i.* ***Byrne*** *a(p)-53-55, 59-70, 75, 79, 100; c-68p, 70p, 72p, 75, 76p, 79p, 129i, 133i.* ***Colan*** *a-87p.* ***Ditko*** *a-101.* ***Kane*** *a(p)-4-6, 13, 14, 16-19, 23; c(p)-4, 13, 14, 17-19, 23, 25, 26, 32-35, 37, 41, 44, 45, 47, 53, 54.* ***Miller*** *a-100p; c-95p, 99p, 100p, 102p, 106.* ***Mooney*** *a-2i, 7i, 8, 10p, 11p, 16i, 24-31p, 72, 93i, Annual 5i.* ***Nasser*** *a-89p; c-101p.* ***Simonson*** *c-99i, 148.* ***Paul Smith*** *c-131, 132.* ***Starlin*** *c-27.* ***Sutton*** *a-93p. "H-T" means Human Torch; "SpM" means Spider-Man; "S-M" means Sub-Mariner.*

MARVEL TEAM-UP (2nd Series)
Marvel Comics: Sept, 1997 - No. 11, July, 1998 ($1.99)

1-11: 1-Spider-Man team-ups begin, Generation x-app. 2-Hercules-c/app.; two covers. 3-Sandman. 4-Man-Thing. 7-Blade. 8-Namor team-ups begin, Dr. Strange app. 9-Capt. America. 10-Thing. 11-Iron Man 2.25

MARVEL TEAM-UP
Marvel Comics: Jan, 2005 - Present ($2.25)

1,2-Spider-Man & Wolverine; Kirkman-s/Kolins-a 2.25

MARVEL: THE LOST GENERATION
Marvel Comics: No. 12, Mar, 2000 - No. 1, Feb, 2001 ($2.99, issue #s go in reverse)

1-12-Stern-s/Byrne-s/a; untold story of The First Line. 5-Thor app. 3.00

MARVEL TREASURY EDITION
Marvel Comics Group/Whitman #17,18: 1974; #2, Dec, 1974 - #28, 1981 ($1.50/$2.50, 100 pgs., oversized, new-a &-r)(Also see Amazing Spider-Man, The, Marvel Spec. Ed. Feat.--, Savage Fists of Kung Fu, Superman Vs. , & 2001, A Space Odyssey)

1-Spectacular Spider-Man; story-r/Marvel Super-Heroes #14; Romita-c/a(r); G. Kane, Ditko-r; Green Goblin/Hulk-r 6 12 18 38 52 65
1-1,000 numbered copies signed by Stan Lee & John Romita on front-c & sold thru mail for $5.00; these were the1st 1,000 copies off the press 11 22 33 77 114 150
2-10: 2-Fantastic Four-r/F.F. 6,11,48-50(Silver Surfer). 3-The Mighty Thor-r/Thor #125-130. 4-Conan the Barbarian; Barry Smith-c/a(r)/Conan #11. 5-The Hulk (origin-r/Hulk #3). 6-Dr. Strange. 7-Mighty Avengers. 8-Giant Superhero Holiday Grab-Bag; Spider-Man, Hulk, Nick Fury. 9-Giant; Super-hero Team-up. 10-Thor; r/Thor #154-157 3 6 9 16 20 25
11-20: 11-Fantastic Four. 12-Howard the Duck (r/#H. the Duck #1 & G.S. Man-Thing #4,5) plus new Defenders story. 13-Giant Super-Hero Holiday Grab-Bag. 14-The Sensational Spider-Man; r/1st Morbius from Amazing S-M #101,102 plus #100 & r/Not Brand Echh #6. 15-Conan; B. Smith, Neal Adams-i; r/Conan #24. 16-The Defenders (origin) & Valkyrie; r/Defenders #1,4,13,14. 17-The Hulk. 18-The Astonishing Spider-Man; r/Spider-Man's 1st team-ups with Iron Fist, The X-Men, Ghost Rider & Werewolf by Night; inside back-c has photos from 1978 Spider-Man TV show. 19-Conan the Barbarian. 20-Hulk 2 4 6 10 13 16
21-25,27: 21-Fantastic Four. 22-Spider-Man. 23-Conan. 24-Rampaging Hulk. 25-Spider-Man vs. The Hulk. 27-Spider-Man 2 4 6 10 13 16
26-The Hulk; 6 pg. new Wolverine/Hercules-s 2 4 6 12 16 20
28-Spider-Man/Superman; (origin of each) 4 8 12 29 40 50

NOTE: *Reprints-2, 3, 5, 7-9, 13, 14, 16, 17.* ***Neal Adams*** *a(i)-6, 15.* ***Brunner*** *a-6, 12; c-6.* ***Buscema*** *a-15, 19, 28; c-28.* ***Colan*** *a-6r; c-12p.* ***Ditko*** *a-1, 6.* ***Gil Kane*** *c-16p.* ***Kirby*** *a-1-3, 5, 7, 9-11; c-7.* ***Perez*** *a-26.* ***Romita*** *c-1, 5.* ***B. Smith*** *a-4, 15, 19; c-4, 19.*

MARVEL TREASURY OF OZ FEATURING THE MARVELOUS LAND OF OZ
Marvel Comics Group: 1975 ($1.50, oversized) (See MGM's Marvelous…)

1-Buscema-a; Romita-c 3 6 9 16 20 24

MARVEL TREASURY SPECIAL (Also see 2001: A Space Odyssey)
Marvel Comics Group: 1974; 1976 ($1.50, oversized, 84 pgs.)

Vol. 1-Spider-Man, Torch, Sub-Mariner, Avengers "Giant Superhero Holiday Grab-Bag"; Wood, Colan/Everett, plus 2 Kirby-r; reprints Hulk vs. Thing from Fantastic Four #25,26 3 6 9 16 20 24
Vol. 1-... Featuring Captain America's Bicentennial Battles (6/76)-Kirby-a; B. Smith inks, 11 pgs. 3 6 9 16 21 26

MARVEL TRIPLE ACTION (See Giant-Size...)
Marvel Comics Group: Feb, 1972 - No. 24, Mar, 1975; No. 25, Aug, 1975 - No. 47, Apr, 1979

1-(25¢ giant, 52 pgs.)-Dr. Doom, Silver Surfer, The Thing begin, end #4 ('66 reprints from Fantastic Four) 3 6 9 16 20 24
2-5 2 4 6 8 10 12

GD VG FN VF VF/NM NM-
2.0 4.0 6.0 8.0 9.0 9.2

6-10 1 2 3 4 5 7
11-47: 45-r/X-Men #45. 46-r/Avengers #53(X-Men) 4.00
29,30-(30¢-c variants, limited distribution)(5,7/76) 6.00
36,37-(35¢-c variants, limited distribution)(7,9/77) 6.00

NOTE: *#5-44, 46, 47 reprint Avengers #11 thru ?. #40-r/Avengers #48(1st Black Knight).* ***Buscema*** *a(r)-35p, 36p, 38p, 39p, 41, 42, 43p, 44p, 46p, 47p.* ***Ditko*** *a-2r; c-47.* ***Kirby*** *a(r)-1-4p; c-1-4, 9-19, 22, 24, 29.* ***Starlin*** *c-7.* ***Tuska*** *a(r)-40p, 43i, 46i, 47i. #2 through #17 are 20¢-c.*

MARVEL TWO-IN-ONE (...Featuring ... #82 on; also see The Thing)
Marvel Comics Group: January, 1974 - No. 100, June, 1983

1-Thing team-ups begin; Man-Thing 6 12 18 43 59 75
2,3: 2-Sub-Mariner; last 20¢ issue. 3-Daredevil 3 6 9 16 20 25
4-6: 4-Capt. America. 5-Guardians of the Galaxy (9/74, 2nd app.?). 6-Dr. Strange (11/74) 2 4 6 11 14 18
7,9,10 2 4 6 8 10 12
8-Early Ghost Rider app. (3/75) 2 4 6 10 13 16
11-14,19,20: 13-Power Man. 14-Son of Satan (early app.) 1 2 3 5 6 8
15-18-(Regular 25¢ editions)(5-7/76) 17-Spider-Man. 1 2 3 5 6 8
15-18-(30¢-c variants, limited distribution) 2 4 6 11 14 18
21-29: 27-Deathlok. 29-Master of Kung Fu; Spider-Woman cameo 6.00
28,29,31-(35¢-c variants, limited distribution) 2 4 6 11 14 18
30-2nd full app. Spider-Woman (see Marvel Spotlight #32 for 1st app.) 1 3 4 6 8 10
30-(35¢-c variant, limited distribution)(8/77) 2 4 6 12 16 20
31-40: 31-33-Spider-Woman. 39-Vision 6.00
41,42,44,45,47-49: 42-Capt. America. 45-Capt. Marvel 4.00
43,50,53,55-Byrne-a(p). 53-Quasar(7/79, 2nd app.) 6.00
46-Thing battles Hulk-c/story 1 3 4 6 8 10
51-The Beast, Nick Fury, Ms. Marvel; Miller-p 1 2 3 4 5 7
52-Moon Knight app. 3.00
54-Death of Deathlok: Byrne-a 1 3 4 6 8 10
56-60,64-74,76-79,81,82: 60-Intro. Impossible Woman. 68-Angel. 69-Guardians of the Galaxy. 71-1st app. Maelstrom. 76-Iceman 3.00
61-63: 61-Starhawk (from Guardians); "The Coming of Her" storyline begins, ends #63; cover similar to F.F. #67 (Him-c). 62-Moondragon; Thanos & Warlock cameo in flashback; Starhawk app. 63-Warlock revived shortly; Starhawk & Moondragon app. 4.00
75-Avengers (52 pgs.) 4.00
80,90,100: 80-Ghost Rider. 90-Spider-Man. 100-Double size, Byrne-s 4.00
83-89,91-99: 83-Sasquatch. 84-Alpha Flight app. 93-Jocasta dies. 96-X-Men-c & cameo 3.00
Annual 1(1976, 52 pgs.)-Thing/Liberty Legion; Kirby-c 2 4 6 8 10 12
Annual 2(1977, 52 pgs.)-Thing/Spider-Man; 2nd death of Thanos; end of Thanos saga; Warlock app.; Starlin-c/a 4 8 12 24 32 40
Annual 3,4 (1978-79, 52 pgs.): 3-Nova. 4-Black Bolt 6.00
Annual 5-7 (1980-82, 52 pgs.): 5-Hulk. 6-1st app. American Eagle. 7-The Thing/Champion; Sasquatch, Colossus app.; X-Men cameo (1 pg.) 4.00

NOTE: ***Austin*** *c(i)-42, 54, 56, 58, 61, 63, 66.* ***John Buscema*** *a-30p, 45; c-30p.* ***Byrne*** *(p)-43, 50, 53-55; c-43, 53p, 56p, 98i, 99i.* ***Gil Kane*** *a-1p, 2p; c(p)-1-3, 9, 11, 14, 28.* ***Kirby*** *c-10, 12, 19p, 20, 25, 27.* ***Mooney*** *a-18i, 38i, 90i.* ***Nasser*** *a-70p.* ***Perez*** *a(p)-56-58, 60, 64, 65; c(p)-32, 33, 42, 50-52, 54, 55, 57, 58, 61-66, 70.* ***Roussos*** *a-Annual 1i.* ***Simonson*** *c-43i, 97p, Annual 6i.* ***Starlin*** *c-6, Annual 1.* ***Tuska*** *a-6p.*

MARVEL UNIVERSE (See Official Handbook Of The...)

MARVEL UNIVERSE (Title on variant covers for newsstand editions of some 2001 Marvel titles. See indicia for actual titles and issue numbers)

MARVEL UNIVERSE
Marvel Comics: June, 1998 - No. 7, Dec, 1998 ($2.99/$1.99)

1-($2.99)-Invaders stories from WW2; Stern-s 3.00
2-7-($1.99): 2-Two covers. 4-7-Monster Hunters; Manley-a/Stern-s 2.25

MARVEL UNIVERSE: MILLENNIAL VISIONS
Marvel Comics: Feb, 2002 ($3.99, one-shot)

1-Pin-ups by various; wraparound-c by JH Williams & Gray 4.00

MARVEL UNIVERSE: THE END (Also see Infinity Abyss)
Marvel Comics: May, 2003 - No. 6, Aug, 2003 ($3.50/$2.99, limited series)

1-($3.50)-Thanos, X-Men, FF, Avengers, Spider-Man, Daredevil app.; Starlin-s/a(p) 3.50
2-6-($2.99) Akhenaten, Eternity, Living Tribunal app. 3.00
Thanos Vol. 3: Marvel Universe - The End (2003, $16.99) r/#1-6 17.00

MARVEL UNLIMITED (Title on variant covers for newsstand editions of some 2001 Daredevil issues. See indicia for actual titles and issue numbers)

MARVEL VALENTINE SPECIAL
Marvel Comics: Mar, 1997 ($2.99, one-shot)

1-Valentine stories w/Spider-Man, Daredevil, Cyclops, Phoenix 3.00

MARVEL VERSUS DC (See DC Versus Marvel) (Also see Amazon, Assassins, Bruce Wayne: Agent of S.H.I.E.L.D., Bullets & Bracelets, Doctor Strangefate, JLX, Legend of the Dark Claw,

Mary Jane #1 © MAR

Mary Marvel Comics #16 © FAW

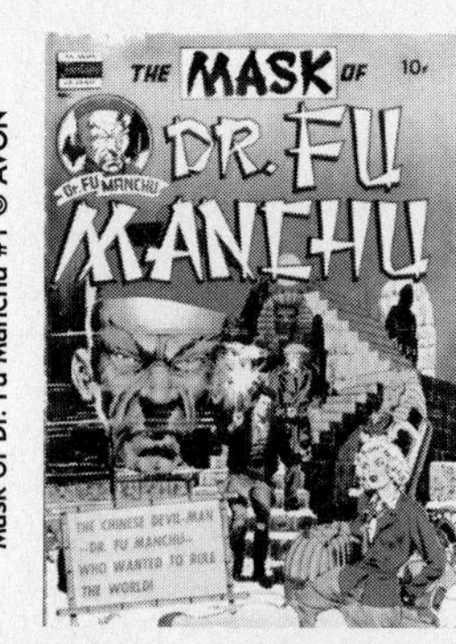

Mask of Dr. Fu Manchu #1 © AVON

GD 2.0 | VG 4.0 | FN 6.0 | VF 8.0 | VF/NM 9.0 | NM- 9.2

Magneto & The Magnetic Men, Speed Demon, Spider-Boy, Super Soldier, & X-Patrol)
Marvel Comics: No. 2, 1996 - No. 3, 1996 ($3.95, limited series)
2,3: 2-Peter David script. 3-Ron Marz script; Dan Jurgens-a(p). 1st app. of Super Soldier, Spider-Boy, Dr. Doomsday, Doctor Strangefate, The Dark Claw, Nightcreeper, Amazon, Wraith & others. Storyline continues in Amalgam books. 4.00

MARVEL VISIONARIES
Marvel Comics: 2002 - Present (various prices, HC and TPB)
...: Gil Kane (8/02, $24.95) r/Amazing Spider-Man #99, Marvel Premiere #1,#15, TOA #76 & others; plus sketch pages and a cover gallery 25.00
...: Jack Kirby HC (2004, $29.99) r/career highlights- Red Raven Comics #1 (1st work), Captain America Comics #1, Avengers #4, Fantastic Four #48-50 and more 30.00
...: Jim Steranko (9/02, $14.95) r/Captain America #110,111,113; X-Men #50,51 and stories from Tower of Shadows #1 and Our Love Story #5; plus a cover gallery 15.00

MARVEL X-MEN COLLECTION, THE
Marvel Comics: Jan, 1994 - No. 3, Mar, 1994 ($2.95, limited series)
1-3-r/X-Men trading cards by Jim Lee 3.00

MARVEL - YEAR IN REVIEW (Magazine)
Marvel Comics: 1989 - No. 3, 1991 (52 pgs.)
1-3: 1-Spider-Man-c by McFarlane. 2-Capt. America-c. 3-X-Men/Wolverine-c 5.00

MARVILLE
Marvel Comics: Nov, 2002 - No. 7, Jul, 2003 ($2.25, limited series)
1-6-Satire on DC/AOL-Time-Warner; Jemas-a/Bright-a/Horn-c 2.25
1-($3.95) Variant foil cover by Udon Studios; bonus sketch pages and Jemas afterword 4.00
7-($2.99) Intro. to Epic Comics line with submission guidelines 3.00

MARVIN MOUSE
Atlas Comics (BPC): September, 1957
1-Everett-c/a; Maneely-a 13 26 39 74 102 130

MARY JANE (Spider-Man)
Marvel Comics: Aug, 2004 - No. 4, Nov, 2004 ($2.25)
1-4-Marvel Age series with teen-age MJ Watson; Miyazawa-c/a; McKeever-s 2.25
... Vol. 1: Circle of Friends (2004, $5.99, digest-size) r/#1-4 6.00

MARY JANE & SNIFFLES (See Looney Tunes)
Dell Publishing Co.: No. 402, June, 1952 - No. 474, June, 1953
Four Color 402 (#1) 9 18 27 63 89 115
Four Color 474 8 16 24 58 82 105

MARY MARVEL COMICS (Monte Hale #29 on) (Also see Captain Marvel #18, Marvel Family, Shazam, & Wow Comics)
Fawcett Publications: Dec, 1945 - No. 28, Sept, 1948
1-Captain Marvel introduces Mary on-c; intro/origin Georgia Sivana
208 416 624 1300 2000 2700
2 77 154 231 481 741 1000
3,4: 3-New logo 54 108 162 329 502 675
5-8: 8-Bulletgirl x-over in Mary Marvel; X-Mas-c 40 80 120 239 357 475
9,10 38 76 114 219 320 420
11-20 26 52 78 147 211 275
21-28: 28-Western-c 21 42 63 121 173 225

MARY POPPINS (See Movie Comics & Walt Disney Showcase No. 17)

MARY SHELLEY'S FRANKENSTEIN
Topps Comics: Oct, 1994 - Jan, 1995 ($2.95, limited series)
1-4-polybagged w/3 trading cards 3.00
1-4 ($2.50)-Newstand ed. 2.50

MARY WORTH (See Harvey Comics Hits #55 & Love Stories of...)
Argo: March, 1956 (Also see Romantic Picture Novelettes)
1 8 16 24 43 54 65

MASK (TV)
DC Comics: Dec, 1985 - No. 4, Mar, 1986; Feb, 1987 - No. 9, Oct, 1987
1-4; 1-9 (2nd series)-Sat. morning TV show. 2.50

MASK, THE (Also see Mayhem)
Dark Horse Comics: Aug, 1991 - No. 4, Oct, 1991; No. 0, Dec, 1991 ($2.50, 36 pgs., limited series)
1-4: 1-1st app. Lt. Kellaway as The Mask (see Dark Horse Presents #10 for 1st app.) 5.00
0-(12/91, B&W, 56 pgs.)-r/Mayhem #1-4 4.00
...: HUNT FOR GREEN OCTOBER July, 1995 - Oct, 1995 ($2.50, lim. series)
1-4-Evan Dorkin scripts 2.50
.../ MARSHALL LAW Feb, 1998 - No. 2, Mar, 1998 ($2.95, lim. series)
1,2-Mills-s/O'Neill-a 3.00
...: OFFICIAL MOVIE ADAPTATION July, 1994 - Aug, 1994 ($2.50, lim. series)
1,2 2.50
... RETURNS Oct, 1992 - No. 4, Mar, 1993 ($2.50, limited series)
1-4 4.00
... SOUTHERN DISCOMFORT Mar, 1996 - No. 4, July, 1996 ($2.50, lim. series)
1-4 2.50
... STRIKES BACK Feb, 1995 - No. 5, Jun, 1995 ($2.50, limited series)
1-5 2.50
... SUMMER VACATION July, 1995 ($10.95, one shot, hard-c)
1-nn-Rick Geary-c/a 11.00
... TOYS IN THE ATTIC Aug, 1998 - No. 4, Nov, 1998 ($2.95, limited series)
1-4-Fingerman-s 3.00
... VIRTUAL SURREALITY July, 1997 ($2.95, one shot)
nn-Mignola, Aragonés, and others-s/a 3.00
... WORLD TOUR Dec, 1995 - No. 4, Mar, 1996 ($2.50, limited series)
1-4: 3-X & Ghost-c/app. 2.50

MASK COMICS
Rural Home Publ.: Feb-Mar, 1945 - No. 2, Apr-May, 1945; No. 2, Fall, 1945
1-Classic L. B. Cole Satan-c/a; Palais-a 292 584 876 1825 2813 3800
2-(Scarce)-Classic L. B. Cole Satan-c; Black Rider, The Boy Magician, & The Collector app.
181 362 543 1131 1741 2350
2-(Fall, 1945)-No publ.-same as regular #2; L. B. Cole-c
142 284 426 888 1369 1850

MASKED BANDIT, THE
Avon Periodicals: 1952
nn-Kinstler-a 17 34 51 95 135 175

MASKED MAN, THE
Eclipse Comics: 12/84 - #10, 4/86; #11, 10/87; #12, 4/88 ($1.75/$2.00, color/B&W #9 on, Baxter paper)
1-12: 1-Origin retold. 3-Origin Aphid-Man; begin $2.00-c 2.25

MASKED MARVEL (See Keen Detective Funnies)
Centaur Publications: Sept, 1940 - No. 3, Dec, 1940
1-The Masked Marvel begins 169 338 507 1056 1628 2200
2,3: 2-Gustavson, Tarpe Mills-a 113 226 339 706 1091 1475

MASKED RAIDER, THE (Billy The Kid #9 on; Frontier Scout, Daniel Boone #10-13) (Also see Blue Bird)
Charlton Comics: June, 1955 - No. 8, July, 1957; No. 14, Aug, 1958 - No. 30, June, 1961
1-Masked Raider & Talon the Golden Eagle begin; painted-c
13 26 39 74 102 130
2 8 16 24 43 54 65
3-8,15: 8-Billy The Kid app. 15-Williamson-a, 7 pgs. 6 12 18 31 38 45
14,16-30: 22-Rocky Lane app. 5 10 15 24 30 35

MASKED RANGER
Premier Magazines: Apr, 1954 - No. 9, Aug, 1955
1-The Masked Ranger, his horse Streak, & The Crimson Avenger (origin) begin, end #9; Woodbridge/Frazetta-a 40 80 120 239 357 475
2,3 15 30 45 83 117 150
4-8-All Woodbridge-a. 5-Jesse James by Woodbridge. 6-Billy The Kid by Woodbridge. 7-Wild Bill Hickok by Woodbridge. 8-Jim Bowie's Life Story
15 30 45 86 123 160
9-Torres-a; Wyatt Earp by Woodbridge; Says Death of Masked Ranger on-c
16 32 48 92 131 170
NOTE: *Check a-1. **Woodbridge** c/a-1, 4-9.*

MASK OF DR. FU MANCHU, THE (See Dr. Fu Manchu)
Avon Periodicals: 1951
1-Sax Rohmer adapt.; Wood-c/a (26 pgs.); Hollingsworth-a
92 184 276 575 888 1200

MASK OF ZORRO, THE
Image Comics: Aug, 1998 - No. 4, Dec, 1998 ($2.95, limited series)
1-4-Movie adapt. Photo variant-c 3.00

MASKS: TOO HOT FOR TV!
DC Comics (WildStorm): Feb, 2004 ($4.95)
1-Short stories by various incl. Thompson, Brubaker, Mahnke, Conner; Fabry-c 5.00

MASQUE OF THE RED DEATH (See Movie Classics)

Master Comics #96 © FAW

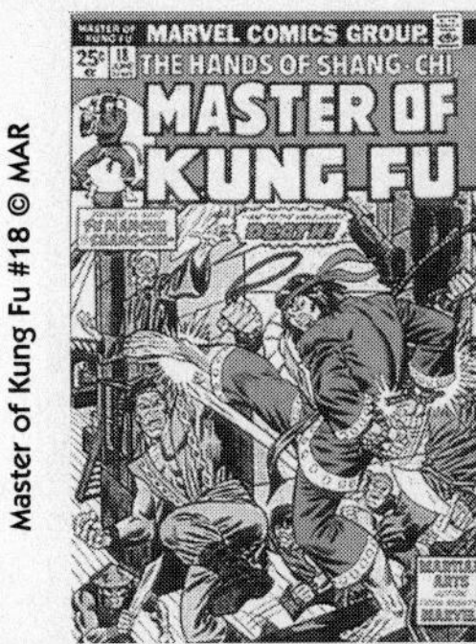

Master of Kung Fu #18 © MAR

Masters of the Universe V3#3 © Mattel

GD VG FN VF VF/NM NM-
2.0 4.0 6.0 8.0 9.0 9.2

GD VG FN VF VF/NM NM-
2.0 4.0 6.0 8.0 9.0 9.2

MASTER COMICS (Combined with Slam Bang Comics #7 on)
Fawcett Publications: Mar, 1940 - No. 133, Apr, 1953 (No. 1-6: oversized issues) (#1-3: 15¢, 52 pgs.; #4-6: 10¢, 36 pgs.; #7-Begin 68 pg. issues)

1-Origin & 1st app. Master Man; The Devil's Dagger, El Carim, Master of Magic, Rick O'Say, Morton Murch, White Rajah, Shipwreck Roberts, Frontier Marshal, Streak Sloan, Mr. Clue begin (all features end #6) 774 1548 2322 5418 8709 12,000
2 238 476 714 1488 2294 3100
3-6: 6-Last Master Man 173 346 519 1081 1666 2250
NOTE: *#1-6 rarely found in near mint or very fine condition due to large-size format.*
7-(10/40)-Bulletman, Zoro, the Mystery Man (ends #22), Lee Granger, Jungle King, & Buck Jones begin; only app. The War Bird & Mark Swift & the Time Retarder; Zoro, Lee Granger, Jungle King & Mark Swift all continue from Slam Bang; Bulletman moves from Nickel 300 600 900 1875 2888 3900
8-The Red Gaucho (ends #13), Captain Venture (ends #22) & The Planet Princess begin 154 308 462 963 1482 2000
9,10: 10-Lee Granger ends 121 242 363 756 1166 1575
11-Origin & 1st app. Minute-Man (2/41) 265 530 795 1656 2553 3450
12 129 258 387 806 1241 1675
13-Origin & 1st app. Bulletgirl; Hitler-c 202 404 606 1263 1944 2625
14-16: 14-Companions Three begins, ends #31 110 220 330 688 1057 1425
17-20: 17-Raboy-a on Bulletman begins. 20-Captain Marvel cameo app. in Bulletman 102 204 306 638 982 1325
21-(12/41; Scarce)-Captain Marvel & Bulletman team up against Capt. Nazi; origin & 1st app. Capt. Marvel Jr's most famous nemesis Captain Nazi who will cause creation of Capt. Marvel Jr. in Whiz #25. Part I of trilogy origin of Capt. Marvel Jr.; 1st Mac Raboy-c for Fawcett; Capt. Nazi-c 506 1012 1518 3542 5696 7850
22-(1/42)-Captain Marvel Jr. moves over from Whiz #25 & teams up with Bulletman against Captain Nazi; part III of trilogy origin of Capt. Marvel Jr. & his 1st cover and adventure 452 904 1356 3164 5082 7000
23-Capt. Marvel Jr. c/stories begin (1st solo story); fights Capt. Nazi by himself. 289 578 867 1806 2778 3750
24,25 98 196 294 613 944 1275
26-28,30-Captain Marvel Jr. vs. Capt. Nazi. 28-Liberty Bell-c. 30-Flag-c 87 174 261 544 835 1125
29-Hitler & Hirohito-c 110 220 330 688 1057 1425
31-33,35: 32-Last El Carim & Buck Jones; intro Balbo, the Boy Magician in El Carim story; classic Eagle-c by Raboy. 33-Balbo, the Boy Magician (ends #47), Hopalong Cassidy (ends #49) begins 65 130 195 406 628 850
34-Capt. Marvel Jr. vs. Capt. Nazi-c/story 74 148 222 463 712 960
36-40: 40-Flag-c 60 120 180 375 580 785
41-(8/43)-Bulletman, Capt. Marvel Jr. & Bulletgirl x-over in Minute-Man; only app. Crime Crusaders Club (Capt. Marvel Jr., Minute-Man, Bulletman & Bulletgirl) 65 130 195 406 623 840
42-47,49: 47-Hitler becomes Corpl. Hitler Jr. 49-Last Minute-Man 40 80 120 239 357 475
48-Intro. Bulletboy; Capt. Marvel cameo in Minute-Man 46 92 138 281 428 575
50-Intro Radar & Nyoka the Jungle Girl & begin series (5/44); Radar also intro in Captain Marvel #35 (same date); Capt. Marvel x-over in Radar; origin Radar; Capt. Marvel & Capt. Marvel, Jr. introduce Radar on-c 40 80 120 244 372 500
51-58 25 50 75 141 203 265
59-62: Nyoka serial "Terrible Tiara" in all; 61-Capt. Marvel Jr. 1st meets Uncle Marvel 27 54 81 154 222 290
63-80 19 38 57 107 154 200
81,83-87,89-91,95-99: 88-Hopalong Cassidy begins (ends #94). 95-Tom Mix begins (cover only in #123, ends #133) 16 32 48 92 131 170
82,88,92-94-Krigstein-a 17 34 51 98 139 180
100 17 34 51 98 139 180
101-106-Last Bulletman (not in #104) 15 30 45 86 123 160
107-120: 118-Mary Marvel 15 30 45 83 117 150
121-131-(lower print run): 123-Tom Mix-c only 15 30 45 86 123 160
132-B&W and color illos in **POP**; last Nyoka 16 32 48 89 127 165
133-Bill Battle app. 21 42 63 121 173 225
NOTE: ***Mac Raboy** a-15-39, 40(part), 42, 58. c-21-49, 51, 52, 54, 56, 58, 68(part), 69(part). Bulletman c-7-11, 13(half), 15, 18(part), 19, 20, 21(w/Capt. Marvel & Capt. Nazi), 22(w/Capt. Marvel, Jr.). Capt. Marvel, Jr. c-23-133. Master Man c-1-6. Minute Man c-12, 13(half), 14, 16, 17, 18(part).*

MASTER DARQUE
Acclaim Comics (Valiant): Feb, 1998 ($3.95)

1-Manco-a/Christina Z.-s 4.00

MASTER DETECTIVE
Super Comics: 1964 (Reprints)

17-r/Criminals on the Loose V4 #2; r/Young King Cole #?; McWilliams-r 2 4 6 9 11 14

MASTER OF KUNG FU (Formerly Special Marvel Edition; see Deadly Hands of Kung Fu & Giant-Size...)
Marvel Comics Group: No. 17, April, 1974 - No. 125, June, 1983

17-Starlin-a; intro Black Jack Tarr; 3rd Shang-Chi (ties w/Deadly Hands #1) 3 6 9 18 24 30
18,20 2 4 6 10 12 15
19-Man-Thing-c/story 2 4 6 11 14 18
21-23,25-30 1 3 4 6 8 10
24-Starlin, Simonson-a 2 4 6 8 10 12
31-50: 33-1st Leiko Wu. 43-Last 25¢ issue 6.00
39-43-(30¢-c variants, limited distribution)(5-7/76) 2 4 6 10 12 15
51-99 4.00
53-57-(35¢-c variants, limited distribution)(6-10/77) 2 4 6 10 12 15
100,118,125-Double size 5.00
101-117,119-124 3.00
Annual 1(4/76)-Iron Fist app. 2 4 6 14 18 22
NOTE: ***Austin** c-63i, 74i. **Buscema** c-44p. **Gulacy** a(p)-18-20, 22, 25, 29-31, 33-35, 38, 39, 40(p&i), 42-50, 53r(#20); c-51, 55, 64, 67. **Gil Kane** c(p)-20, 38, 39, 42, 45, 59, 63. **Nebres** c-73i. **Starlin** a-17p, 24; c-54. **Sutton** a-42i. #53 reprints #20.*

MASTER OF KUNG-FU, SHANG-CHI:... (2002 series, see Shang Chi:...)

MASTER OF KUNG-FU: BLEEDING BLACK
Marvel Comics: Feb, 1991 ($2.95, 84 pgs., one-shot)

1-The Return of Shang-Chi 3.00

MASTER OF THE WORLD
Dell Publishing Co.: No. 1157, July, 1961

Four Color 1157-Movie 7 14 21 46 63 80

MASTERS OF TERROR (Magazine)
Marvel Comics Group: July, 1975 - No. 2, Sept, 1975 (B&W) (All reprints)

1-Brunner, Barry Smith-a; Morrow/Steranko-c; Starlin-a(p); Gil Kane-a 2 4 6 12 16 20
2-Reese, Kane, Mayerik-a; Adkins/Steranko-c 2 4 6 10 12 15

MASTERS OF THE UNIVERSE (See DC Comics Presents #47 for 1st app.)
DC Comics: Dec, 1982 - No. 3, Feb, 1983 (Mini-series)

1 6.00
2,3: 2-Origin He-Man & Ceril 4.00
NOTE: ***Alcala** a-1i,, 2i. **Tuska** a-1-3p; c-1-3p. #2 has 75 & 95 cent cover price.*

MASTERS OF THE UNIVERSE (Comic Album)
Western Publishing Co.: 1984 (8-1/2x11", $2.95, 64 pgs.)

11362-Based on Mattel toy & cartoon 2 4 6 10 13 16

MASTERS OF THE UNIVERSE
Star Comics/Marvel #7 on: May 1986 - No. 13, May, 1988 (75¢/$1.00)

1 6.00
2-11: 8-Begin $1.00-c 4.00
12-Death of He-Man (1st Marvel app.) 1 2 3 5 6 8
13-Return of He-Man & death of Skeletor 1 2 3 5 6 8
The Motion Picture (11/87, $2.00)-Tuska-p 5.00

MASTERS OF THE UNIVERSE
Image Comics: Nov, 2002 - No. 4, March, 2003 ($2.95, limited series)

1-($2.95) Two covers by Santalucia and Campbell; Santalucia-a 3.00
1-($5.95) Variant-c by Norem w/gold foil logo 6.00
2-4($2.95) 2-Two covers by Santalucia and Manapul. 3,4-Two covers 3.00
TPB (CrossGen, 2003, $9.95, 8-1/4" x 5-1/2") digest-sized reprints #1-4 10.00

MASTERS OF THE UNIVERSE (Volume 2)
Image Comics: March, 2003 - No. 6, Aug, 2003 ($2.95)

1-6-($2.95) 1-Santalucia-c. 2-Two covers by Santalucia & JJ Kirby 3.00
1-($5.95) Wraparound variant-c by Struzan w/silver foil logo 6.00
3,4-($5.95) Wraparound variant holofoil-c. 3-By Edwards 4-By Boris Vallejo & Julie Bell 6.00
Volume 2 Dark Reflections TPB (2004, $18.95) r/#1-6 19.00

MASTERS OF THE UNIVERSE (Volume 3)
MVCreations: Apr, 2004 - Present ($2.95)

1-7: 1-Santalucia-c 3.00

MASTERS OF THE UNIVERSE...
CrossGen Comics

...Rise of the Snake-Men (Nov, 2003 - No. 3, $2.95) Meyers-a 3.00
...The Power of Fear (12/03, $2.95, one-shot) Santalucia-a 3.00

MASTERS OF THE UNIVERSE, ICONS OF EVIL
Image Comics/CrossGen Comics: 2003 ($4.95, one-shots)

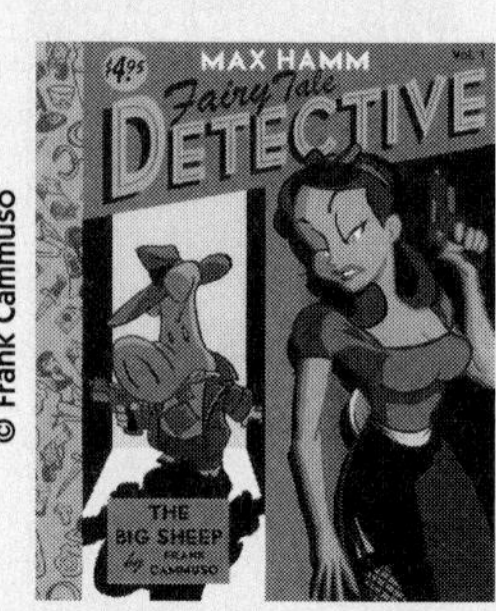

Max Hamm Fairy Tale Detective #1 © Frank Cammuso

McHale's Navy #2 © DELL

MD #3 © WMG

	GD 2.0	VG 4.0	FN 6.0	VF 8.0	VF/NM 9.0	NM- 9.2
...Beastman -(Image) Origin of Beast Man; Tony Moore-a						5.00
...Mer-Man -(CrossGen)						5.00
...Trapjaw -(CrossGen)						5.00
...Tri-Klops -(CrossGen) Walker-c						5.00
TPB (3/04, $18.95, MVCreations) r/one-shots; sketch pages						19.00

MASTERWORKS SERIES OF GREAT COMIC BOOK ARTISTS, THE
Sea Gate Dist./DC Comics: May, 1983 - No. 3, Dec, 1983 (Baxter paper)

	GD 2.0	VG 4.0	FN 6.0	VF 8.0	VF/NM 9.0	NM- 9.2
1-3: 1,2-Shining Knight by Frazetta r-/Adventure. 2-Tomahawk by Frazetta-r. 3-Wrightson-c/a(r)						5.00

MATRIX COMICS, THE (Movie)
Burlyman Entertainment: 2003 ($21.95, trade paperback)

	GD 2.0	VG 4.0	FN 6.0	VF 8.0	VF/NM 9.0	NM- 9.2
nn-Short stories by various incl. Wachowskis, Darrow, Gaiman, Sienkiewicz, Bagge						22.00
...Volume One Preview (7/03, no cover price) bios of creators; Chadwick-s/a						2.25

MATT SLADE GUNFIGHTER (Kid Slade Gunfighter #5 on; See Western Gunfighters)
Atlas Comics (SPI): May, 1956 - No. 4, Nov, 1956

	GD 2.0	VG 4.0	FN 6.0	VF 8.0	VF/NM 9.0	NM- 9.2
1-Intro Matt & horse Eagle; Williamson/Torres-a	21	42	63	118	169	220
2-Williamson-a	13	26	39	74	102	130
3,4	10	20	30	58	77	95

NOTE: ***Maneely*** *a-1, 3, 4; c-1, 2, 4.* ***Roth*** *a-2-4.* ***Severin*** *a-1, 3, 4.* ***Maneely*** *c/a-1. Issue #s stamped on cover after printing.*

MAUS: A SURVIVOR'S TALE (First graphic novel to win a Pulitzer Prize)
Pantheon Books: 1986, 1991 (B&W)

	GD 2.0	VG 4.0	FN 6.0	VF 8.0	VF/NM 9.0	NM- 9.2
Vol. 1-(...: My Father Bleeds History)(1986) Art Spiegelman-s/a; recounts stories of Spiegelman's father in 1930s-40s Nazi-occupied Poland; collects first six stories serialized in Raw Magazine from 1980-1985						20.00
Vol. 2-(...: And Here My Troubles Began)(1991)						20.00
Complete Maus Survivor's Tale -HC Vols. 1& 2 w/slipcase						35.00
Hardcover Vol. 1 (1991)						24.00
Hardcover Vol. 2 (1991)						24.00
TPB (1992, $14.00) Vols. 1& 2						14.00

MAVERICK (TV)
Dell Publishing Co.: No. 892, 4/58 - No. 19, 4-6/62 (All have photo-c)

	GD 2.0	VG 4.0	FN 6.0	VF 8.0	VF/NM 9.0	NM- 9.2
Four Color 892 (#1)-James Garner photo-c begin	26	52	78	184	282	380
Four Color 930,945,962,980,1005 (6-8/59): 945-James Garner/Jack Kelly photo-c begin	12	24	36	84	127	170
7 (10-12/59) - 14: Last Garner/Kelly-c	10	20	30	70	100	130
15-18: Jack Kelly/Roger Moore photo-c	8	16	24	58	82	105
19-Jack Kelly photo-c (last issue)	9	18	27	60	85	110

MAVERICK (See X-Men)
Marvel Comics: Jan, 1997 ($2.95, one-shot)

	GD 2.0	VG 4.0	FN 6.0	VF 8.0	VF/NM 9.0	NM- 9.2
1-Hama-s						3.00

MAVERICK (See X-Men)
Marvel Comics: Sept, 1997 - No. 12, Aug, 1998 ($2.99/$1.99)

	GD 2.0	VG 4.0	FN 6.0	VF 8.0	VF/NM 9.0	NM- 9.2
1,12: 1-($2.99)-Wraparound-c. 12-($2.99) Battles Omega Red						4.00
2-11: 2-Two covers. 4-Wolverine app. 6,7-Sabretooth app.						3.00

MAVERICK MARSHAL
Charlton Comics: Nov, 1958 - No. 7, May, 1960

	GD 2.0	VG 4.0	FN 6.0	VF 8.0	VF/NM 9.0	NM- 9.2
1	6	12	18	31	38	45
2-7	5	10	15	22	26	30

MAVERICKS
Daggar Comics Group: Jan, 1994 - No. 5, 1994 (#1-$2.75, #2-5-$2.50)

	GD 2.0	VG 4.0	FN 6.0	VF 8.0	VF/NM 9.0	NM- 9.2
1-5: 1-Bronze. 1-Gold. 1-Silver						2.75

MAX BRAND (See Silvertip)

MAX HAMM FAIRY TALE DETECTIVE
Nite Owl Comix: 2002 - 2004 ($4.95, B&W, 6 1/2" x 8")

	GD 2.0	VG 4.0	FN 6.0	VF 8.0	VF/NM 9.0	NM- 9.2
1-(2002) Frank Cammuso-s/a						5.00
Vol. 2 #1-3 (2003-2004) Frank Cammuso-s/a						5.00

MAXIMAGE
Image Comics (Extreme Studios): Dec, 1995 - No. 7, June 1996 ($2.50)

	GD 2.0	VG 4.0	FN 6.0	VF 8.0	VF/NM 9.0	NM- 9.2
1-7: 1-Liefeld-c. 2-Extreme Destroyer Pt. 2; polybagged w/card. 4-Angela & Glory-c/app.						2.50

MAXIMO
Dreamwave Prods.: Jan, 2004 ($3.95, one-shot)

	GD 2.0	VG 4.0	FN 6.0	VF 8.0	VF/NM 9.0	NM- 9.2
1-Based on the Capcom video game						4.00

MAXIMUM SECURITY (Crossover)
Marvel Comics: Oct, 2000 - No. 3, Jan, 2001 ($2.99)

	GD 2.0	VG 4.0	FN 6.0	VF 8.0	VF/NM 9.0	NM- 9.2
1-3-Busiek-s/Ordway-a; Ronan the Accuser, Avengers app.						3.00
...Dangerous Planet 1: Busiek-s/Ordway-a; Ego, the Living Planet						3.00
Thor vs. Ego (11/00, $2.99) Reprints Thor #133,160,161; Kirby-a						3.00

MAXX (Also see Darker Image, Primer #5, & Friends of Maxx)
Image Comics (I Before E): Mar, 1993 - No. 35, Feb, 1998 ($1.95)

	GD 2.0	VG 4.0	FN 6.0	VF 8.0	VF/NM 9.0	NM- 9.2
1/2	1	3	4	6	8	10
1/2 (Gold)						20.00
1-Sam Kieth-c/a/scripts						4.00
1-Glow-in-the-dark variant	2	4	6	8	10	12
1-"3-D Edition" (1/98, $4.95) plus new back-up story						5.00
2-12: 6-Savage Dragon cameo(1 pg.). 7,8-Pitt-c & story						2.50
13-16						2.50
17-35: 21-Alan Moore-s						2.50
Volume 1 TPB (DC/WildStorm, 2003, $17.95) r/#1-6						18.00
Volume 2 TPB (DC/WildStorm, 2004, $17.95) r/#7-13						18.00
Volume 3 TPB (DC/WildStorm, 2004, $17.95) r/#14-20						18.00

MAYA (See Movie Classics)
Gold Key: Mar, 1968

	GD 2.0	VG 4.0	FN 6.0	VF 8.0	VF/NM 9.0	NM- 9.2
1 (10218-803)(TV)	3	6	9	19	25	32

MAYHEM
Dark Horse Comics: May, 1989 - No. 4, Sept, 1989 ($2.50, B&W, 52 pgs.)

	GD 2.0	VG 4.0	FN 6.0	VF 8.0	VF/NM 9.0	NM- 9.2
1- Four part Stanley Ipkiss/Mask story begins; Mask-c	1	3	4	6	8	10
2-4: 2-Mask 1/2 back-c. 4-Mask-c	1	2	3	5	7	9

MAZE AGENCY, THE
Comico/Innovation Publ. #8 on: Dec, 1988 - No. 20, 1991 ($1.95-$2.50, color)

	GD 2.0	VG 4.0	FN 6.0	VF 8.0	VF/NM 9.0	NM- 9.2
1-20: 9-Ellery Queen app. 7 ($2.50)-Last Comico issue						2.50
Annual 1 (1990, $2.75)-Ploog-c; Spirit tribute ish						2.75
Special 1 (1989, $2.75)-Staton-p (Innovation)						2.75

MAZE AGENCY, THE (Vol. 2)
Caliber Comics: July, 1997 - Present ($2.95, B&W)

	GD 2.0	VG 4.0	FN 6.0	VF 8.0	VF/NM 9.0	NM- 9.2
1-3: 1-Barr-s/Gonzales-a(p). 3-Hughes-c						3.00

MAZIE (...& Her Friends) (See Flat-Top, Mortie, Stevie & Tastee-Freez)
Mazie Comics(Magazine Publ.)/Harvey Publ. No. 13-on: 1953 - #12, 1954; #13, 12/54 - #22, 9/56; #23, 9/57 - #28, 8/58

	GD 2.0	VG 4.0	FN 6.0	VF 8.0	VF/NM 9.0	NM- 9.2
1-(Teen-age)-Stevie's girlfriend	9	18	27	54	70	85
2	6	12	18	29	36	42
3-10	6	12	18	27	33	38
11-28	5	10	14	20	24	28

MAZIE
Nation Wide Publishers: 1950 - No. 7, 1951 (5¢) (5x7-1/4"-miniature)(52 pgs.)

	GD 2.0	VG 4.0	FN 6.0	VF 8.0	VF/NM 9.0	NM- 9.2
1-Teen-age	16	32	48	92	131	170
2-7	9	18	27	54	70	85

MAZINGER (See First Comics Graphic Novel #17)

'MAZING MAN
DC Comics: Jan, 1986 - No. 12, Dec, 1986

	GD 2.0	VG 4.0	FN 6.0	VF 8.0	VF/NM 9.0	NM- 9.2
1-11: 7,8-Hembeck-a						2.50
12-Dark Knight part-c by Miller						3.00
Special 1 ('87), 2 (4/88), 3 ('90)-All $2.00, 52pgs.						2.50

McCANDLESS & COMPANY
Mandalay Books: 2001 ($7.95)

	GD 2.0	VG 4.0	FN 6.0	VF 8.0	VF/NM 9.0	NM- 9.2
...: Dead Razor - J.C. Vaughn-s/Busch & Sheehan-a; 3 covers						8.00

McHALE'S NAVY (TV) (See Movie Classics)
Dell Publ. Co.: May-July, 1963 - No. 3, Nov-Jan, 1963-64 (All have photo-c)

	GD 2.0	VG 4.0	FN 6.0	VF 8.0	VF/NM 9.0	NM- 9.2
1	8	16	24	55	78	100
2,3	6	12	18	40	55	70

McKEEVER & THE COLONEL (TV)
Dell Publishing Co.: Feb-Apr, 1963 - No. 3, Aug-Oct, 1963

	GD 2.0	VG 4.0	FN 6.0	VF 8.0	VF/NM 9.0	NM- 9.2
1-Photo-c	7	14	21	50	68	85
2,3	6	12	18	38	52	65

McLINTOCK (See Movie Comics)

MD
E. C. Comics: Apr-May, 1955 - No. 5, Dec-Jan, 1955-56

	GD 2.0	VG 4.0	FN 6.0	VF 8.0	VF/NM 9.0	NM- 9.2
1-Not approved by code; Craig-c	13	26	39	98	144	190
2-5	9	18	27	68	99	130

NOTE: ***Crandall, Evans, Ingels, Orlando*** *art in all issues;* ***Craig*** *c-1-5.*

Medal Of Honor #2 © DH

Megalith #8 © Continuity

Megaton #5 © Gary Carlson

GD 2.0 | VG 4.0 | FN 6.0 | VF 8.0 | VF/NM 9.0 | NM- 9.2

GD 2.0 | VG 4.0 | FN 6.0 | VF 8.0 | VF/NM 9.0 | NM- 9.2

MD
Russ Cochran/Gemstone Publishing: Sept, 1999 - No. 5, Jan, 2000 ($2.50)

1-5-Reprints original EC series 2.50
Annual 1 (1999, $13.50) r/#1-5 14.00

M.D. GEIST
CPM Comics: 1995 - No. 3, 1995 (Limited series)

1-3 3.00

M.D. GEIST DATA ALBUM
CPM Comics: June, 1996 ($9.95, trade paperback)

1 10.00

M.D. GEIST: GROUND ZERO
CPM Comics: Mar, 1996 - No. 3, May, 1996 ($2.95, limited series)

1-3 3.00

MEASLES
Fantagraphics Books: Christmas 1998 - Present ($2.95, B&W, quarterly)

1-8-Anthology: 1-Venus-s by Hernandez 3.00

MEAT CAKE
Iconographix: 1992 (B&W)

1 2.50

MEAT CAKE
Fantagraphics Books: No. 1, Oct, 1993 - Present (B&W)

0-8: 3-Sal Buscema-a. 0-(1996)-r/Meat Cake #1 from Iconographix 2.50
9-($3.95) Alan Moore-s 4.00

MECHA (Also see Mayhem)
Dark Horse Comics: June, 1987 - No. 6, 1988 ($1.50/$1.95, color/B&W)

1-6: 1,2 ($1.95, color), 3,4-($1.75, B&W), 5,6-($1.50, B&W) 2.50

MECHANIC, THE
Image Comics: 1998 ($5.95, one-shot, squarebound)

1-Chiodo-painted art; Peterson-s 6.00
1-($10.00) DF Alternate Cover Ed. 10.00

MECHA SPECIAL
Dark Horse Comics: May, 1995 ($2.95, one-shot)

1 3.00

MECH DESTROYER
Image Comics: Apr, 2001 - No. 4, Sept, 2001 ($2.95, limited series)

1-4-Jae Kim-c/a; Robert Chong-s 3.00

MEDAL FOR BOWZER, A
American Visuals: 1966 (8 pgs.)

nn-Eisner-c/script 27 54 81 152 219 285

MEDAL OF HONOR COMICS
A. S. Curtis: Spring, 1946

1-War stories 12 24 36 71 98 125

MEDAL OF HONOR SPECIAL
Dark Horse Comics: 1994 ($2.50, one-shot)

1-Kubert-c/a (first story) 2.50

MEDIA STARR
Innovation Publ.: July, 1989 - No. 3, Sept, 1989 ($1.95, mini-series, 28pgs.)

1-3: Deluxe format 2.25

MEDIEVAL SPAWN/WITCHBLADE
Image Comics (Top Cow Productions): May, 1996 - No. 3, June, 1996 ($2.95, limited series)

1-3-Garth Ennis scripts in all 6.00
1-Platinum foil-c (500 copies from Pittsburgh Con) 35.00
1-Gold 10.00
1-ETM Exclusive Edition; gold foil logo 7.00
TPB ($9.95) r/#1-3 10.00

MEET ANGEL (Formerly Angel & the Ape)
National Periodical Publications: No. 7, Nov-Dec, 1969

7-Wood-a(i) 3 7 10 21 28 35

MEET CORLISS ARCHER (Radio/Movie)(My Life #4 on)
Fox Features Syndicate: Mar, 1948 - No. 3, July, 1948

1-(Teen-age)-Feldstein-c/a; headlight-c 100 200 300 625 963 1300
2 55 110 165 340 520 700
3-Part Feldstein-c only 50 100 150 305 465 625

NOTE: *No. 1-3 used in Seduction of the Innocent, pg. 39.*

MEET HERCULES (See Three Stooges)

MEET MERTON
Toby Press: Dec, 1953 - No. 4, June, 1954

1-(Teen-age)-Dave Berg-c/a 9 18 27 54 70 85
2-Dave Berg-c/a 6 12 18 29 36 42
3,4-Dave Berg-c/a 6 12 18 27 33 38
I.W. Reprint #9, Super Reprint #11('63), 18 2 4 6 9 11 14

MEET MISS BLISS (Becomes Stories Of Romance #5 on)
Atlas Comics (LMC): May, 1955 - No. 4, Nov, 1955

1-Al Hartley-c/a 14 28 42 79 110 140
2-4 9 18 27 52 66 80

MEET MISS PEPPER (Formerly Lucy, The Real Gone Gal)
St. John Publishing Co.: No. 5, April, 1954 - No. 6, June, 1954

5-Kubert/Maurer-a 21 42 63 121 173 225
6-Kubert/Maurer-a; Kubert-c 17 34 51 95 135 175

MEGACITY909
Devil's Due Publ.: Sept, 2004 - Present ($2.95)

1-3-Kano Kang & Zack Suh-a 3.00

MEGA DRAGON & TIGER
Image Comics: Mar, 1999 - No. 5 ($2.95)

1-5-Tony Wong-s/a 3.00

MEGAHURTZ
Image Comics: Aug, 1997 - No. 3, Oct, 1997 ($2.95, B&W)

1-3-St. Pierre-s 3.00

MEGALITH (Megalith Deathwatch 2000 #1,2 of second series)
Continuity: 1989 - No. 9, Mar, 1992; No, 0, Apr, 1993 - No. 7, Jan, 1994

1-9-($2.00-c) 1-Neal Adams & Mark Texiera-c/Texiera & Nebres-a 3.00
2nd series: 0-(4/93)-Foil-c; no c-price, giveaway; Adams plot 3.00
1-7: 1-3-Bagged w/card: 1-Gatefold-c by Nebres; Adams plot. 2-Fold-out-c; Adams plot. 3-Indestructible-c. 4-7-Embossed-c: 4-Adams/Nebres-c; Adams part-i. 5-Sienkiewicz-i. 6-Adams part-i. 7-Adams-c(p); Adams plot 3.00

MEGAMAN
Dreamwave Productions: Sept, 2003 - Present ($2.95)

1-4-Brian Augustyn-s/Mic Fong-a 3.00
1-($5.95) Chromium wraparound variant-c 6.00

MEGATON (A super hero)
Megaton Publ.: Nov, 1983; No. 2, Oct, 1985 - No. 8, Aug, 1987 (B&W)

1-($2.00, 68 pgs.)-Erik Larsen's 1st pro work; Vanguard by Larsen begins (1st app.), ends #4; 1st app. Megaton, Berzerker, & Ethrian; Guice-c/a(p); Gustovich-a(p) in #1,2 2 4 6 10 12 15
2-($2.00, 68 pgs.)-1st brief app. The Dragon (1 pg.) by Larsen (later The Savage Dragon in Image Comics); Guice-c/a(p) 2 4 6 8 10 12
3-(44 pgs.)-1st full app. Savage Dragon-c/story by Larsen; 1st comic book work by Angel Medina (pin-up) 2 4 6 11 14 18
4-(52 pgs.)-2nd full app. Savage Dragon by Larsen; 4,5-Wildman by Grass Green 1 3 4 6 8 10
5-1st Liefeld published-a (inside f/c, 6/86) 1 2 3 4 5 7
6,7: 6-Larsen-c 6.00
8-1st Liefeld story-a (7 pg. super hero story) plus 1 pg. Youngblood ad 1 2 3 5 7 9
...Explosion (6/87, 16 pg. color giveaway)-1st app. Youngblood by Rob Liefeld (2 pg. spread); shows Megaton heroes 2 4 6 14 18 22
...Holiday Special 1 (1994, $2.95, color, 40 pgs., publ. by Entity Comics)-Gold foil logo; bagged w/Kelley Jones card; Vanguard, Megaton plus shows unpublished-c to 1987 Youngblood #1 by Liefeld/Ordway 4.00

NOTE: *Copies of Megaton Explosion were also released in early 1992 all signed by Rob Liefeld and were made available to retailers.*

MEGATON MAN (See Don Simpson's Bizarre Heroes)
Kitchen Sink Enterprises: Nov, 1984 - No. 10, 1986

1-10, 1-2nd printing (1989) 3.00
...Meets The Uncategorizable X-Thems 1 (4/89, $2.00) 3.00

MEGATON MAN: BOMB SHELL
Image Comics: Jul, 1999 - No. 2 ($2.95, B&W, mini-series)

1-Reprints stories from Megaton Man internet site 3.00

MEGATON MAN: HARD COPY
Image Comics: Feb, 1999 - No. 2, Apr, 1999 ($2.95, B&W, mini-series)

Menace #11 © ATLAS

Men in Action #3 © MAR

Men's Adventures #21 © MAR

	GD 2.0	VG 4.0	FN 6.0	VF 8.0	VF/NM 9.0	NM- 9.2
1,2-Reprints stories from Megaton Man internet site						3.00

MEGATON MAN VS. FORBIDDEN FRANKENSTEIN
Fiasco Comics: Apr, 1996 ($2.95, B&W, one-shot)

	GD	VG	FN	VF	VF/NM	NM-
1-Intro The Tomb Team (Forbidden Frankenstein, Drekula, Bride of the Monster, & Moon Wolf).						3.00

MEK (See Reload/Mek flipbook for TPB reprint)
DC Comics (Homage): Jan, 2003 - No. 3, Mar, 2003 ($2.95, limited series)

	GD	VG	FN	VF	VF/NM	NM-
1-3-Warren Ellis-s/Steve Rolston-a						3.00

MEKANIX (See X-Men titles) (See X-Treme X-Men Vol. 4 for TPB)
Marvel Comics: Dec, 2002 - No. 6, May, 2003 ($2.99, limited series)

	GD	VG	FN	VF	VF/NM	NM-
1-6-Kitty Pryde in college; Claremont-s/Bobillo & Sosa-a						3.00

MEL ALLEN SPORTS COMICS (The Voice of the Yankees)
Standard Comics: No. 5, Nov, 1949; No. 6, June, 1950

	GD	VG	FN	VF	VF/NM	NM-
5(#1 on inside)-Tuska-a	24	48	72	138	199	260
6(#2)-Lou Gehrig story	16	32	48	92	131	170

MELTING POT
Kitchen Sink Press: Dec, 1993 - No. 4, Sept, 1994 ($2.95)

	GD	VG	FN	VF	VF/NM	NM-
1-4: Bisley-painted-c						3.00

MELVIN MONSTER
Dell Publishing Co.: Apr-June, 1965 - No. 10, Oct, 1969

	GD	VG	FN	VF	VF/NM	NM-
1-By John Stanley	11	22	33	80	120	160
2-10-All by Stanley. #10-r/#1	9	18	27	60	85	110

MELVIN THE MONSTER (See Peter, the Little Pest & Dexter The Demon #7)
Atlas Comics (HPC): July, 1956 - No. 6, July, 1957

	GD	VG	FN	VF	VF/NM	NM-
1-Maneely-c/a	14	28	42	79	110	140
2-6: 4-Maneely-c/a	10	20	30	56	73	90

MENACE
Atlas Comics (HPC): Mar, 1953 - No. 11, May, 1954

	GD	VG	FN	VF	VF/NM	NM-
1-Horror & sci/fi stories begin; Everett-c/a	67	134	201	419	647	875
2-Post-atom bomb disaster by Everett; anti-Communist propaganda/torture scenes; Sinnott sci/fi story "Rocket to the Moon"	47	94	141	287	436	585
3,4,6-Everett-a. 4-Sci/fi story "Escape to the Moon". 6-Romita sci/fi story "Science Fiction"	40	80	120	233	342	450
5-Origin & 1st app. The Zombie by Everett (reprinted in Tales of the Zombie #1)(7/53); 5-Sci/fi story "Rocket Ship"	55	110	165	340	520	700
7,8,10,11: 7-Frankenstein story. 8-End of world story; Heath 3-D art(3 pgs.). 10-H-Bomb panels	31	62	93	178	259	340
9-Everett-a r-in Vampire Tales #1	36	72	108	204	297	390

NOTE: ***Brodsky*** *c-7, 8, 11.* ***Colan*** *a-6; c-9.* ***Everett*** *a-1-6, 9; c-1-6.* ***Heath*** *a-1-8; c-10.* ***Katz*** *a-11.* ***Maneely*** *a-3, 5, 7-9.* ***Powell*** *a-11.* ***Romita*** *a-3, 6, 8, 11.* ***Shelly*** *a-10.* ***Shores*** *a-7.* ***Sinnott*** *a-2, 7.* ***Tuska*** *a-1, 2, 5.*

MENACE
Awesome-Hyperwerks: Nov, 1998 ($2.50)

	GD	VG	FN	VF	VF/NM	NM-
1-Jada Pinkett Smith-s/Fraga-a						2.50

MEN AGAINST CRIME (Formerly Mr. Risk; Hand of Fate #8 on)
Ace Magazines: No. 3, Feb, 1951 - No. 7, Oct, 1951

	GD	VG	FN	VF	VF/NM	NM-
3-Mr. Risk app.	11	22	33	62	84	105
4-7: 4-Colan-a; entire book-r as Trapped! #4. 5-Meskin-a	8	16	24	46	58	70

MEN, GUNS, & CATTLE (See Classics Illustrated Special Issue)

MEN IN ACTION (Battle Brady #10 on)
Atlas Comics (IPS): April, 1952 - No. 9, Dec, 1952 (War stories)

	GD	VG	FN	VF	VF/NM	NM-
1-Berg, Reinman-a	17	34	51	98	139	180
2,3: 3-Heath-c/a	10	20	30	58	77	95
4-6,8,9	9	18	27	52	66	80
7-Krigstein-a; Heath-c	10	20	30	58	77	95

NOTE: ***Brodsky*** *c-1, 4-6.* ***Maneely*** *c-5.* ***Pakula*** *a-1, 6.* ***Robinson*** *c-8.* ***Shores*** *c-9.*

MEN IN ACTION
Ajax/Farrell Publications: April, 1957 - No. 6, 1958

	GD	VG	FN	VF	VF/NM	NM-
1	9	18	27	52	66	80
2	6	12	18	31	38	45
3-6	6	12	18	27	33	38

MEN IN BLACK, THE (1st series)
Aircel Comics (Malibu): Jan, 1990 - No. 3 Mar, 1990 ($2.25, B&W, lim. series)

	GD	VG	FN	VF	VF/NM	NM-
1-Cunningham-s/a in all	4	8	12	29	40	50
2,3	3	6	9	18	23	28
Graphic Novel (Jan, 1991) r/#1-3	3	6	9	16	20	25

GD VG FN VF VF/NM NM-
2.0 4.0 6.0 8.0 9.0 9.2

MEN IN BLACK (2nd series)
Aircel Comics (Malibu): May, 1991 - No. 3, Jul, 1991 ($2.50, B&W, lim. series)

	GD	VG	FN	VF	VF/NM	NM-
1-Cunningham-s/a in all	3	6	9	16	20	28
2,3	2	4	6	8	10	14

MEN IN BLACK: FAR CRY
Marvel Comics: Aug, 1997 ($3.99, color, one-shot)

	GD	VG	FN	VF	VF/NM	NM-
1-Cunningham-s						4.00

MEN IN BLACK: RETRIBUTION
Marvel Comics: Dec, 1997 ($3.99, color, one-shot)

	GD	VG	FN	VF	VF/NM	NM-
1-Cunningham-s; continuation of the movie						4.00

MEN IN BLACK: THE MOVIE
Marvel Comics: Oct, 1997 ($3.99, one-shot, movie adaption)

	GD	VG	FN	VF	VF/NM	NM-
1-Cunningham-s						4.00

MEN INTO SPACE
Dell Publishing Co.: No. 1083, Feb-Apr, 1960

	GD	VG	FN	VF	VF/NM	NM-
Four Color 1083-Anderson-a, photo-c	6	12	18	43	59	75

MEN OF BATTLE (Also see New Men of Battle)
Catechetical Guild: V1#5, March, 1943 (Hardcover)

	GD	VG	FN	VF	VF/NM	NM-
V1#5-Topix reprints	6	12	18	28	34	40

MEN OF WAR
DC Comics, Inc.: August, 1977 - No. 26, March, 1980 (#9,10: 44 pgs.)

	GD	VG	FN	VF	VF/NM	NM-
1-Enemy Ace, Gravedigger (origin #1,2) begin	2	4	6	12	16	20
2-4,8-10,12-14,19,20: All Enemy Ace stories. 4-1st Dateline Frontline. 9-Unknown Soldier app.	1	3	4	6	8	10
5-7,11,15-18,21-25: 17-1st app. Rosa	1	2	3	5	6	8
26-Sgt. Rock & Easy Co.-c/s	2	4	6	10	12	15

NOTE: ***Chaykin*** *a-9, 10, 12-14, 19, 20.* ***Evans*** *c-25.* ***Kubert*** *c-2-23, 24p, 26.*

MEN'S ADVENTURES (Formerly True Adventures)
Marvel/Atlas Comics (CCC): No. 4, Aug, 1950 - No. 28, July, 1954

	GD	VG	FN	VF	VF/NM	NM-
4(#1)(52 pgs.)	33	66	99	190	275	360
5-Flying Saucer story	21	42	63	118	169	220
6-8: 7-Buried alive story. 8-Sci/fic story	19	38	57	107	154	200
9-20: All war format	12	24	36	69	95	120
21,22,24,26: All horror format	21	42	63	121	173	225
23-Crandall-a; Fox-a(i); horror format	22	44	66	125	180	235
25-Shrunken head-c	34	68	102	196	283	370
27,28-Human Torch & Toro-c/stories; Captain America & Sub-Mariner stories in each (also see Young Men #24-28)	102	204	306	638	982	1325

NOTE: ***Ayers*** *a-27(H. Torch).* ***Berg*** *a-15, 16.* ***Brodsky*** *c-4-9, 11, 12, 16-18, 24.* ***Burgos*** *c-27, 28(Human Torch).* ***Colan*** *a-14, 19.* ***Everett*** *a-10, 14, 22, 25, 28; c-14, 21-23.* ***Heath*** *a-8, 11, 24; c-13, 20, 26.* ***Lawrence*** *a-23; 27(Captain America).* ***Maneely*** *a-24; c-10, 15.* ***Mac Pakula*** *a-15, 25.* ***Post*** *a-23.* ***Powell*** *a-27(Sub-Mariner).* ***Reinman*** *a-11, 12.* ***Robinson*** *c-19.* ***Romita*** *a-22.* ***Shores*** *c-25.* ***Sinnott*** *a-21.* ***Tuska*** *a-24. Adventure-#4-8; War-#9-20; Weird/Horror-#21-26.*

MENZ INSANA
DC Comics (Vertigo): 1997 ($7.95, one-shot)

	GD	VG	FN	VF	VF/NM	NM-
nn-Fowler-s/Bolton painted art	1	2	3	5	6	8

MEPHISTO VS... (See Silver Surfer #3)
Marvel Comics Group: Apr, 1987 - No. 4, July, 1987 ($1.50, mini-series)

	GD	VG	FN	VF	VF/NM	NM-
1-4: 1-Fantastic Four; Austin-i. 2-X-Factor. 3-X-Men. 4-Avengers						3.00

MERC (See Mark Hazzard: Merc)

MERCHANTS OF DEATH
Acme Press (Eclipse): Jul, 1988 - No. 4, Nov, 1988 ($3.50, B&W/16 pgs. color, 44 pg. mag.)

	GD	VG	FN	VF	VF/NM	NM-
1-4: 4-Toth-c						3.50

MERCY
DC Comics (Vertigo): 1993 ($5.95, 68 pgs., mature)

	GD	VG	FN	VF	VF/NM	NM-
nn						6.00

MERIDIAN
CrossGeneration Comics: Jul, 2000 - No. 44, Apr, 2004 ($2.95)

	GD	VG	FN	VF	VF/NM	NM-
1-44: Barbara Kesel-s						3.00
Flying Solo Vol. 1 TPB (2001, $19.95) r/#1-7; cover by Steve Rude						20.00
Going to Ground Vol. 2 TPB (2002, $19.95) r/#8-14						20.00
Taking the Skies Vol. 3 TPB (2002, $15.95) r/#15-20						16.00
Vol. 4: Coming Home (12/02, $15.95) r/#21-26						16.00
Vol. 5: Minister of Cadador (7/03, $15.95) r/#27-32						16.00
Vol. 6: Changing Course (1/04, $15.95) r/#33-38						16.00
Traveler Vol. 1-4 ($9.95): Digest-size reprints of TPBs						10.00

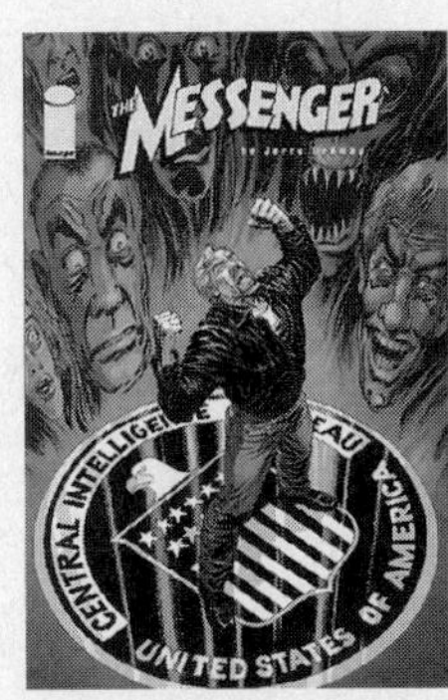

The Messenger #1 © Jerry Ordway

Metallix #1 © Michelinie & Layton

Metal Men #4 © DC

GD 2.0 | VG 4.0 | FN 6.0 | VF 8.0 | VF/NM 9.0 | NM- 9.2

MERLIN JONES AS THE MONKEY'S UNCLE (See Movie Comics and The Misadventures of... under Movie Comics)

MERRILL'S MARAUDERS (See Movie Classics)

MERRY CHRISTMAS (See A Christmas Adventure, Donald Duck..., Dell Giant #39, & March of Comics #153 in the Promotional Comics section)

MERRY COMICS
Carlton Publishing Co.: Dec, 1945 (No cover price)

nn-Boogeyman app. 21 42 63 118 169 220

MERRY COMICS: Four Star Publications: 1947 (Advertised, not published)

MERRY-GO-ROUND COMICS
LaSalle Publ. Co./Croyden Publ./Rotary Litho.: 1944 (25¢, 132 pgs.); 1946; 9-10/47 - No. 2, 1948

nn(1944)(LaSalle)-Funny animal; 29 new features 19 38 57 107 154 200
21 (Publisher?) 9 18 27 51 62 75
1(1946)(Croyden)-Al Fago-c; funny animal 10 20 30 60 80 100
V1#1,2(1947-48; 52 pgs.)(Rotary Litho. Co. Ltd., Canada); Ken Hultgren-a 9 18 27 51 62 75

MERRY MAILMAN (See Fawcett's Funny Animals #87-89)

MERRY MOUSE (Also see Funny Tunes & Space Comics)
Avon Periodicals: June, 1953 - No. 4, Jan-Feb, 1954

1-1st app.; funny animal; Frank Carin-c/a 10 20 30 56 73 90
2-4 7 14 21 35 43 50

MERV PUMPKINHEAD, AGENT OF D.R.E.A.M. (See The Sandman)
DC Comics (Vertigo): 2000 ($5.95, one-shot)

1-Buckingham-a(p); Nowlan painted-c 6.00

MESSENGER, THE
Image Comics: July, 2000 ($5.95, one-shot)

1-Ordway-s/c/a 6.00

META-4
First Comics: Feb, 1991 - No. 4, 1991 ($2.25)

1-($3.95, 52pgs.) 4.00
2-4 2.25

METAL GEAR SOLID (Based in the video game)
IDW Publ.: Sept, 2004 - Present ($3.99)

1-3: 1-Two covers; Ashley Wood-a/Kris Oprisko-s 4.00
1-Retailer edition with foil cover 20.00

METALLIX (Also see Promotional Comics section for FCBD Ed.)
Future Comics: Dec, 2002 - No. 6, June, 2003 ($3.50)

0-6-Ron Lim-a. 0-(6/03) Origin. 1-Layton-c 3.50
1-Collector's Edition with variant cover by Lim 3.50

METAL MEN (See Brave & the Bold, DC Comics Presents, and Showcase #37-40)
National Periodical Publications/DC Comics: 4-5/63 - No. 41, 12-1/69-70; No. 42, 2-3/73 - No. 44, 7-8/73; No. 45, 4-5/76 - No. 56, 2-3/78

1-(4-5/63)-5th app. Metal Men 54 108 162 432 679 925
2 20 40 60 145 223 300
3-5 13 26 39 92 141 190
6-10 9 18 27 65 93 120
11-20: 12-Beatles cameo (2-3/65) 7 14 21 51 71 90
21-Batman, Robin & Flash x-over 6 12 18 40 55 70
22-26,28-30 5 10 15 36 48 60
27-Origin Metal Men retold 7 14 21 51 70 90
31-41(1968-70): 38-Last 12¢ issue. 41-Last 15¢ 4 8 12 29 40 50
42-44(1973)-Reprints 2 4 6 10 12 15
45('76)-49-Simonson-a in all: 48,49-Re-intro Eclipso 1 2 3 6 8 10
50-56: 50-Part-r. 54,55-Green Lantern x-over 1 2 3 6 8 10

NOTE: *Andru/Esposito c-1-30. Aparo c-53-56. Giordano c-45, 46. Kane/Esposito a-30, 31; c-31. Simonson a-45-49; c-47-52. Staton a-50-56.*

METAL MEN
DC Comics: Oct, 1993 - No. 4, Jan, 1994 ($1.25, mini-series)

1-($2.50)-Multi-colored foil-c 4.00
2-4: 2-Origin 2.50

METAL MEN (See Tangent Comics/ Metal Men)

METAMORPHO (See Action Comics #413, Brave & the Bold #57,58, 1st Issue Special, & World's Finest #217)
National Periodical Publications: July-Aug, 1965 - No. 17, Mar-Apr, 1968 (All 12¢ issues)

1-(7-8/65)-3rd app. Metamorpho 12 24 36 87 134 180
2,3 7 14 21 50 68 85
4-6,10:10-Origin & 1st app. Element Girl (1-2/67) 6 12 18 38 52 65
7-9 5 10 15 33 44 55
11-17: 17-Sparling-c/a 4 8 12 27 36 45

NOTE: *Ramona Fradon a-B&B 57, 58, 1-4. Orlando a-5, 6; c-5-9, 11. Trapani a(p)-7-16; i-16.*

METAMORPHO
DC Comics: Aug, 1993 - No. 4, Nov, 1993 ($1.50, mini-series)

1-4 2.50

METAPHYSIQUE
Malibu Comics (Bravura): Apr, 1995 - No. 6, Oct, 1995 ($2.95, limited series)

1-6: Norm Breyfogle-c/a/scripts 3.00

METEOR COMICS
L. L. Baird (Croyden): Nov, 1945

1-Captain Wizard, Impossible Man, Race Wilkins app.; origin Baldy Bean, Capt. Wizard's sidekick; bare-breasted mermaids story 40 80 120 236 351 465

METEOR MAN
Marvel Comics: Aug, 1993 - No. 6, Jan, 1994 ($1.25, limited series)

1-6: 1-Regular unbagged. 4-Night Thrasher-c/story. 6-Terry Austin-c(i) 2.25
1-Polybagged w/button & rap newspaper 4.00
...: The Movie (4/93 [7/93 on cover], $2.25) movie adaptation 2.25

METROPOL (See Ted McKeever's...)

METROPOL A.D. (See Ted McKeever's...)

METROPOLIS S.C.U. (Also see Showcase '96 #1)
DC Comics: Nov, 1995 - No. 4, Feb, 1996 ($1.50, limited series)

1-4:1-Superman-c & app. 2.25

MEZZ: GALACTIC TOUR 2494 (Also See Nexus)
Dark Horse Comics: May, 1994 ($2.50, one-shot)

1 2.50

MGM'S MARVELOUS WIZARD OF OZ (See Marvel Treasury of Oz)
Marvel Comics Group/National Periodical Publications: 1975 ($1.50, 84 pgs.; oversize)

1-Adaptation of MGM's movie; J. Buscema-a 3 6 9 16 20 24

M.G.M'S MOUSE MUSKETEERS (Formerly M.G.M.'s The Two Mouseketeers)
Dell Publishing Co.: No. 670, Jan, 1956 - No. 1290, Mar-May, 1962

Four Color 670 (#4) 5 10 15 36 48 60
Four Color 711,728,764 4 8 12 27 36 45
8 (4-6/57) - 21 (3-5/60) 4 8 12 24 32 40
Four Color 1135,1175,1290 4 8 12 24 32 40

M.G.M.'S SPIKE AND TYKE (also see Tom & Jerry #79)
Dell Publishing Co.: No. 499, Sept, 1953 - No. 1266, Dec-Feb, 1961-62

Four Color 499 (#1) 6 12 18 43 59 75
Four Color 577,638 4 8 12 27 36 45
4(12-2/55-56)-10 4 8 12 22 30 38
11-24(12-2/60-61) 3 6 9 19 25 32
Four Color 1266 3 7 10 21 28 35

M.G.M.'S THE TWO MOUSKETEERS
Dell Publishing Co.: No. 475, June, 1953 - No. 642, July, 1955

Four Color 475 (#1) 9 18 27 60 85 110
Four Color 603 (11/54), 642 6 12 18 40 55 70

MICHAELANGELO CHRISTMAS SPECIAL (See Teenage Mutant Ninja Turtles Christmas Special)

MICHAELANGELO, TEENAGE MUTANT NINJA TURTLE
Mirage Studios: 1986 (One shot) ($1.50, B&W)

1 5.00
1-2nd printing ('89, $1.75)-Reprint plus new-a 2.50

MICHAEL CHABON PRESENTS THE AMAZING ADVENTURES OF THE ESCAPIST
Dark Horse Comics: Feb, 2004 - Present ($8.95, squarebound)

1-4-Short stories by Chabon and various incl. Chaykin, Starlin, Brereton, Kyle Baker 9.00
... Vol. 1 (5/04, $17.95, digest-size) r/#1&2; wraparound-c by Chris Ware 18.00
... Vol. 2 (11/04, $17.95, digest-size) r/#3&4; wraparound-c by Matt Kindt 18.00

MICHAEL MOORCOCK'S ELRIC: THE MAKING OF A SORCEROR
DC Comics: 2004 - No. 4 ($5.95, prestige format, limited series)

1-Moorcock-s/Simonson-a 6.00

MICHAEL MOORCOCK'S MULTIVERSE
DC Comics (Helix): Nov, 1997 - No. 12, Oct, 1998 ($2.50, limited series)

1-12: Simonson, Reeve & Ridgway-a 2.50

Mickey Finn #1 © McNaught Synd.

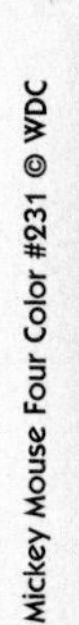
Mickey Mouse Four Color #231 © WDC

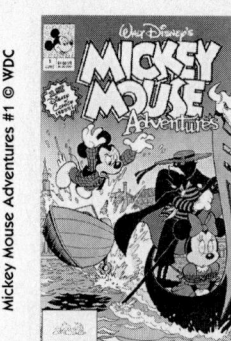

Mickey Mouse Adventures #1 © WDC

GD VG FN VF VF/NM NM-
2.0 4.0 6.0 8.0 9.0 9.2

TPB (1999, $19.95) r/#1-12 20.00

MICHAEL TURNER PRESENTS: ASPEN (See Aspen)

MICKEY AND DONALD (See Walt Disney's...)

MICKEY AND DONALD IN VACATIONLAND (See Dell Giant No. 47)

MICKEY & THE BEANSTALK (See Story Hour Series)

MICKEY & THE SLEUTH (See Walt Disney Showcase #38, 39, 42)

MICKEY FINN (Also see Big Shot Comics #74 & Feature Funnies)
Eastern Color 1-4/McNaught Synd. #5 on (Columbia)/Headline V3#2:
Nov?, 1942 - V3#2, May, 1952

1 31 62 93 175 253 330
2 16 32 48 89 127 165
3-Charlie Chan story 11 22 33 64 87 110
4 9 18 27 52 66 80
5-10 8 16 24 43 54 65
11-15(1949): 12-Sparky Watts app. 7 14 21 35 43 50
V3#1,2(1952) 6 12 18 28 34 40

MICKEY MALONE
Hale Nass Corp.: 1936 (Color, punchout-c) (B&W-a on back)

nn-1pg. of comics 185 370 740 - - -

MICKEY MANTLE (See Baseball's Greatest Heroes #1)

MICKEY MOUSE (See Adventures of Mickey Mouse, The Best of Walt Disney Comics, Cheerios giveaways, Donald and ..., Dynabrite Comics, 40 Big Pages..., Gladstone Comic Album, Merry Christmas From..., Walt Disney's Mickey and Donald, Walt Disney's Comics & Stories, Walt Disney's..., & Wheaties)

MICKEY MOUSE (...Secret Agent #107-109; Walt Disney's... #148-205?)
(See Dell Giants for annuals) (#204 exists from both G.K. & Whitman)
Dell Publ. Co./Gold Key #85-204/Whitman #204-218/Gladstone #219 on:
#16, 1941 - #84, 7-9/62; #85, 11/62 - #218, 6/84; #219, 10/86 - #256, 4/90

Four Color 16(1941)-1st Mickey Mouse comic book; "...vs. the Phantom Blot" by Gottfredson 1400 2800 4200 13,500 - -
Four Color 27(1943)- "7 Colored Terror" 80 160 240 629 1015 1400
Four Color 79(1945)-By Carl Barks (1 story) 100 200 300 757 1229 1725
Four Color 116(1946) 26 52 78 187 286 385
Four Color 141,157(1947) 22 44 66 158 242 325
Four Color 170,181,194('48) 19 38 57 136 208 280
Four Color 214('49),231,248,261 14 28 42 102 156 210
Four Color 268-Reprints/WDC&S #22-24 by Gottfredson ("Surprise Visitor") 14 28 42 97 149 200
Four Color 279,286,296 11 22 33 79 117 155
Four Color 304,313(#1),325(#2),334 10 20 30 70 100 130
Four Color 343,352,362,371,387 9 18 27 60 85 110
Four Color 401,411,427(10-11/52) 7 14 21 50 68 85
Four Color 819-Mickey Mouse in Magicland 6 12 18 38 52 65
Four Color 1057,1151,1246(1959-61)-Album; #1057 has 10¢ & 12¢ editions; back covers are different 5 10 15 33 44 55
28(12-1/52-53)-32,34 6 12 18 38 52 65
33-(Exists with 2 dates, 10-11/53 & 12-1/54) 6 12 18 38 52 65
35-50 5 10 15 33 44 55
51-73,75-80 4 8 12 25 33 42
74-Story swipe "The Rare Stamp Search" from 4-Color #422- "The Gilded Man" 4 8 12 28 34 48
81-105: 93,95-titled "Mickey Mouse Club Album". 100-105: Reprint 4-Color #427,194,279, 170,343,214 in that order 4 8 12 22 30 38
106-120 3 6 9 18 23 28
121-130 2 4 6 14 18 22
131-146 2 4 6 12 16 20
147,148: 147-Reprints "The Phantom Fires" from WDC&S #200-202.148-Reprints "The Mystery of Lonely Valley" from WDC&S #208-210 2 4 6 12 16 20
149-158 2 4 6 9 11 14
159-Reprints "The Sunken City" from WDC&S #205-207 2 4 6 9 11 14
160-178: 162-165,167-170-r 2 4 6 10 13 16
179-(52 pgs.) 1 3 4 6 8 10
180-203: 200-r/Four Color #371 1 2 3 5 7 9
204-(Whitman or G.K.), 205,206 2 4 6 9 11 14
207(8/80), 209(pre-pack?) 3 6 9 19 25 32
208-(8-12/80)-Only distr. in Whitman 3-pack 7 14 21 51 71 90
210(2/81),211-214 2 4 6 9 11 14
215-218: 215(2/82), 216(4/82), 217(3/84), 218(misdated 8/82; actual date 7/84) 2 4 6 10 13 16
219-1st Gladstone issue; The Seven Ghosts serial-r begins by Gottfredson 2 4 6 11 14 18
220,221 1 2 3 5 7 9
222-225: 222-Editor-in Grief strip-r 4.00
226-230 4.00
231-243,246-254: 240-r/March of Comics #27. 245-r/F.C. #279. 250-r/F.C. #248 3.00
244 (1/89, $2.95, 100 pgs.)-Squarebound 60th anniversary issue; gives history of Mickey 4.00
245, 256: 245-r/F.C. #279. 256-$1.95, 68 pgs. 4.00
255 ($1.95, 68 pgs.) 3.00
NOTE: *Reprints #195-197, 198(2/3), 199(1/3), 200-208, 211(1/2), 212, 213, 215(1/3), 216-on.* ***Gottfredson*** *Mickey Mouse serials in #219-239, 241-244, 246-249, 251-253, 255.*
Album 01-518-210(Dell), 1(10082-309)(9/63-Gold Key) 4 8 12 22 30 38
...Club 1(1/64-Gold Key)(TV) 4 8 12 25 33 42
Mini Comic 1(1976)(3-1/4x6-1/2")-Reprints 158 1 2 3 5 6 8
Surprise Party 1(30037-901, G.K.)(1/69)-40th Anniversary (see Walt Disney Showcase #47) 4 8 12 25 33 42
Surprise Party 1(1979)-r/1969 issue 1 2 3 5 6 8

MICKEY MOUSE ADVENTURES
Disney Comics: June, 1990 - No. 18, Nov, 1991 ($1.50)

1,8,9: 1-Bradbury, Murry-r/M.M. #45,73 plus new-a. 8-Byrne-c. 9-Fantasia 50th ann. issue w/new adapt. of movie 3.00
2-7,10-18: 2-Begin all new stories. 10-r/F.C. #214 2.50

MICKEY MOUSE CLUB FUN BOOK
Golden Press: 1977 (1.95, 228 pgs.)(square bound)

11190-1950s-r; 20,000 Leagues, M. Mouse Silly Symphonys, The Reluctant Dragon, etc. 4 8 12 25 33 42

MICKEY MOUSE CLUB MAGAZINE (See Walt Disney...)

MICKEY MOUSE COMICS DIGEST
Gladstone: 1986 - No. 5, 1987 (96 pgs.)

1 ($1.25-c) 1 2 3 5 6 8
2-5: 3-5 ($1.50-c) 5.00

MICKEY MOUSE IN COLOR
Another Rainbow/Pantheon: 1988 (Deluxe, 13"x17", hard-c, $250.00)
(Trade, 9-7/8"x11-1/2", hard-c, $39.95)

Deluxe limited edition of 3,000 copies signed by Floyd Gottfredson and Carl Barks, designated as the "Official Mickey Mouse 60th Anniversary" book. Mickey Sunday and daily reprints, plus Barks "Riddle of the Red Hat" from Four Color #79. Comes with 45 r.p.m. record interview with Gottfredson and Barks. 240 pgs. 20 40 60 142 209 275
Deluxe, limited to 100 copies, as above, but with a unique colored pencil original drawing of Mickey Mouse by Carl Barks. Add value of art to book price. 800.00
Pantheon trade edition, edited down & without Barks, 192 pgs. 4 8 12 24 32 40

MICKEY MOUSE MAGAZINE (Becomes Walt Disney's Comics & Stories)
K. K. Publ./Western Publishing Co.: Summer, 1935 (June-Aug, indicia) - V5#12, Sept, 1940; V1#1-5, V3#11,12, V4#1-3 are 44 pgs; V2#3-100 pgs; V5#12-68 pgs; rest are 36 pgs.(No V3#1, V4#6)

V1#1 (Large size, 13-1/4x10-1/4"; 25¢)-Contains puzzles, games, cels, stories & comics of Disney characters. Promotional magazine for Disney cartoon movies and paraphernalia 1250 2500 3750 8000 16,500 -
Note: *Some copies were autographed by the editors & given away with all early one year subscriptions.*
2 (Size change, 11-1/2x8-1/2"; 10/35; 10¢)-High quality paper begins; Messmer-a 218 436 654 1850 - -
3,4: 3-Messmer-a 112 224 336 950 - -
5-1st Donald Duck solo-c; 2nd cover app. ever; last 44 pg. & high quality paper issue 188 376 564 1600 - -
6-9: 6-36 pg. issues begin; Donald becomes editor. 8-2nd Donald solo-c. 9-1st Mickey/Minnie-c 106 212 318 900 - -
10-12, V2#1,2: 11-1st Pluto/Mickey-c; Donald fires himself and appoints Mickey as editor 100 200 300 850 - -
V2#3-Special 100 pg. Christmas issue (25¢); Messmer-a; Donald becomes editor of Wise Quacks 365 730 1095 3100 - -
4-Mickey Mouse Comics & Roy Ranger (adventure strip) begin; both end V2#9; Messmer-a 85 170 255 725 - -
5-9: 5-Ted True (adventure strip, ends V2#9) & Silly Symphony Comics (ends V3#3) begin. 6-1st solo Minnie-c. 6-9-Mickey Mouse Movies cut-out in each 50 100 150 305 465 625
10-1st full color issue; Mickey Mouse (by Gottfredson; ends V3#12) & Silly Symphony (ends V3#3) full color Sunday-r, Peter The Farm Detective (ends V5#8) & Ole Of The North (ends V3#3) begins 75 150 225 469 722 975
11-13: 12-Hiawatha-c & feature story 48 96 144 293 447 600

Mickey Mouse Magazine V4#7 © WDC

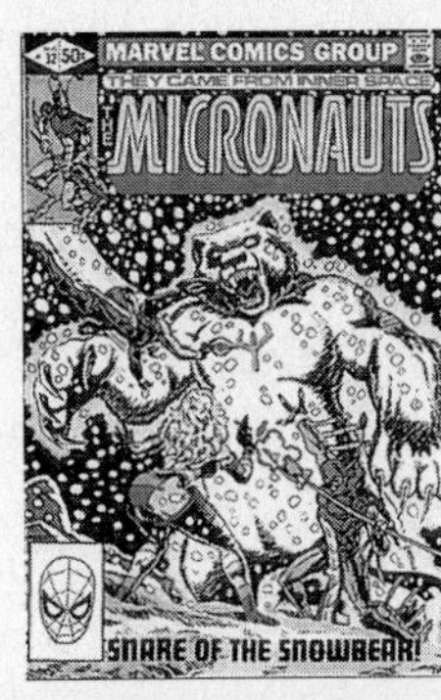

Micronauts #32 © MAR

Midnight Mass #1 © John Rozum & DC

GD 2.0 | VG 4.0 | FN 6.0 | VF 8.0 | VF/NM 9.0 | NM- 9.2

V3#2-Big Bad Wolf Halloween-c 56 112 168 350 538 725
3 (12/37)-1st app. Snow White & The Seven Dwarfs (before release of movie) (possibly 1st in print); Mickey X-Mas-c 102 204 306 638 982 1325
4 (1/38)-Snow White & The Seven Dwarfs serial begins (on stands before release of movie); Ducky Symphony (ends V3#11) begins 85 170 255 531 816 1100
5-1st Snow White & Seven Dwarfs-c (St. Valentine's Day) 104 208 312 650 1000 1350
6-Snow White serial ends; Lonesome Ghosts app. (2 pp.) 56 112 168 350 538 725
7-Seven Dwarfs Easter-c 54 108 162 329 502 675
8-10: 9-Dopey-c. 10-1st solo Goofy-c 44 88 132 268 409 550
11,12 (44 pgs; 8 more pgs. color added). 11-Mickey the Sheriff serial (ends V4#3) & Donald Duck strip-r (ends V3#12) begin. Color feature on Snow White's Forest Friends 48 96 144 293 447 600
V4#1 (10/38; 44 pgs.)-Brave Little Tailor-c/feature story, nominated for Academy Award; Bobby & Chip by Otto Messmer (ends V4#2) & The Practical Pig (ends V4#2) begin 48 96 144 293 447 600
2 (44 pgs.)-1st Huey, Dewey & Louie-c 50 100 150 305 465 625
3 (12/38, 44 pgs.)-Ferdinand The Bull-c/feature story, Academy Award winner; Mickey Mouse & The Whalers serial begins, ends V4#12 48 96 144 293 447 600
4-Spotty, Mother Pluto strip-r begin, end V4#8 44 88 132 268 409 550
5-St. Valentine's day-c. 1st Pluto solo-c 51 102 153 311 476 640
7 (3/39)-The Ugly Duckling-c/feature story, Academy Award winner 48 96 144 293 447 600
7 (4/39)-Goofy & Wilbur The Grasshopper classic-c/feature story from 1st Goofy solo cartoon movie; Timid Elmer begins, ends V5#5 48 96 144 293 447 600
8-Big Bad Wolf-c from Practical Pig movie poster; Practical Pig feature story 48 96 144 293 447 600
9-Donald Duck & Mickey Mouse Sunday-r begin; The Pointer feature story, nominated for Academy Award 48 96 144 293 447 600
10-Classic July 4th drum & fife-c; last Donald Sunday-r 60 120 180 375 575 775
11-1st slick-c; last over-sized issue 44 88 132 268 409 550
12 (9/39; format change, 10-1/4x8-1/4")-1st full color, cover to cover issue; Donald's Penguin-c/feature story 54 108 162 329 502 675
V5#1-Black Pete-c; Officer Duck-c/feature story; Autograph Hound feature story; Robinson Crusoe serial begins 53 106 159 323 492 660
2-Goofy-c; 1st brief app. Pinocchio 69 138 207 431 666 900
3 (12/39)-Pinocchio Christmas-c (Before movie release). 1st app. Jiminy Cricket; Pinocchio serial begins 79 158 237 494 760 1025
4,5: 5-Jiminy Cricket-c; Pinocchio serial ends; Donald's Dog Laundry feature story 53 106 159 323 492 660
6,7: 6-Tugboat Mickey feature story; Rip Van Winkle feature begins, ends V5#8. 7-2nd Huey, Dewey & Louie-c 51 102 153 311 476 640
8-Last magazine size issue; 2nd solo Pluto-c; Figaro & Cleo feature story 53 106 159 323 492 660
9-11: 9 (6/40; change to comic book size)-Jiminy Cricket feature story; Donald-c & Sunday-r begin. 10-Special Independence Day issue. 11-Hawaiian Holiday & Mickey's Trailer feature stories; last 36 pg. issue 56 112 168 350 538 725
12 (Format change)-The transition issue (68 pgs.) becoming a comic book. With only a title change to follow, becomes Walt Disney's Comics & Stories #1 with the next issue 439 878 1317 3073 4937 6800

NOTE: ***Otto Messmer**-a is in many issues of the first two-three years. The following story titles and issues have gags created by **Carl Barks:** V4#3(12/38)-'Donald's Better Self' & 'Donald's Golf Game;' V4#4(1/39)-'Donald's Lucky Day;' V4#7(3/39)-'Hockey Champ;' V4#7(4/39)-'Donald's Cousin Gus;' V4#9(6/39)-'Sea Scouts;' V4#12(9/39)-'Donald's Penguin;' V5#9 (6/40)-'Donald's Vacation;' V5#10(7/40)-'Bone Trouble;' V5#12(9/40)-'Window Cleaners.'*

MICKEY MOUSE MAGAZINE (Russian Version)
May 16, 1991 (1st Russian printing of a modern comic book)
1-Bagged w/gold label commemoration in English 10.00

MICKEY MOUSE MARCH OF COMICS (See March of Comics #8,27,45,60,74)

MICKEY MOUSE'S SUMMER VACATION (See Story Hour Series)

MICKEY MOUSE SUMMER FUN (See Dell Giants)

MICKEY SPILLANE'S MIKE DANGER
Tekno Comix: Sept, 1995 - No. 11, May, 1996 ($1.95)
1-11: 1-Frank Miller-c. 7-polybagged; Simonson-c. 8,9-Simonson-c 2.25

MICKEY SPILLANE'S MIKE DANGER
Big Entertainment: V2#1, June, 1996 - No. 10, Apr, 1997 ($2.25)
V2#1-10: Max Allan Collins scripts 2.25

MICKEY'S TWICE UPON A CHRISTMAS (Disney)
Gemstone Publishing: 2004 ($3.95, square-bound, one-shot)
nn-Christmas short stories with Mickey, Minnie, Donald, Uncle Scrooge, Goofy and others 4.00

MICROBOTS, THE
Gold Key: Dec, 1971 (one-shot)
1 (10271-112) 3 6 9 16 21 26

MICRONAUTS (Toys)
Marvel Comics Group: Jan, 1979 - No. 59, Aug, 1984 (Mando paper #53 on)
1-Intro/1st app. Baron Karza 5.00
2-10,35,37,57: 7-Man-Thing app. 8-1st app. Capt. Universe (8/79). 9-1st app. Cilicia. 35-Double size; origin Microverse; intro Death Squad; Dr. Strange app. 37-Nightcrawler app.; X-Men cameo (2 pgs.). 57-(52 pgs.) 3.00
11-34,36,38-56,58,59: 13-1st app. Jasmine. 15-Death of Microtron. 15-17-Fantastic Four app. 17-Death of Jasmine. 20-Ant-Man app. 21-Microverse series begins. 25-Origin Baron Karza. 25-29-Nick Fury app. 27-Death of Biotron. 34-Dr. Strange app. 38-First direct sale. 40-Fantastic Four app. 48-Early Guice-a begins. 59-Golden painted-c 2.50
nn-Reprints #1-3; blank UPC; diamond on top 2.25
Annual 1,2 (12/79,10/80)-Ditko-c/a 3.00

NOTE: *#38-on distributed only through comic shops. **N. Adams** c-7i. **Chaykin** a-13-18p. **Ditko** a-39p. **Giffen** a-36p, 37p(part). **Golden** a-1-12p; c-2-7p, 8-23, 24p, 38, 39, 59. **Guice** a-48-58p; c-49-58. **Gil Kane** a-38, 40-45p; c-40-45. **Layton** c-33-37. **Miller** c-31.*

MICRONAUTS (Toys)
Marvel Comics Group: Oct, 1984 - No. 20, May, 1986
V2#1-20 2.50

NOTE: ***Kelley Jones** a-1; c-1, 6. **Guice** a-4p; c-2p.*

MICRONAUTS
Image Comics: 2002 - No. 11, Sept, 2003 ($2.95)
2002 Convention Special (no cover price, B&W) previews series 2.25
1-11: 1-3-Hanson-a; Dave Johnson-c. 4-Su-a; 2 covers by Linsner & Hanson 3.00
...Vol. 1: Revolution (2003, $12.95, digest size) r/#1-5 13.00

MICRONAUTS (Volume 2)
Devil's Due Publishing: Mar, 2004 - Present ($2.95)
1-3-Jolley-s/Broderick-a 3.00

MICRONAUTS: KARZA
Image Comics: Feb, 2003 - No. 4, May, 2003 ($2.95)
1-4-Krueger-s/Kurth-a 3.00

MICRONAUTS SPECIAL EDITION
Marvel Comics Group: Dec, 1983 - No. 5, Apr, 1984 ($2.00, limited series, Baxter paper)
1-5: r-/original series 1-12; Guice-c(p)-all 3.00

MIDGET COMICS (Fighting Indian Stories)
St. John Publishng Co.: Feb, 1950 - No. 2, Apr, 1950 (5-3/8x7-3/8", 68 pgs.)
1-Fighting Indian Stories; Matt Baker-c 20 40 60 112 161 210
2-Tex West, Cowboy Marshal (also in #1) 10 20 30 58 77 95

MIDNIGHT (See Smash Comics #18)

MIDNIGHT
Ajax/Farrell Publ. (Four Star Comic Corp.): Apr, 1957 - No. 6, June, 1958
1-Reprints from Voodoo & Strange Fantasy with some changes 15 30 45 86 123 160
2-6 9 18 27 54 70 85

MIDNIGHT EYE
Viz Premiere Comics: 1991 - No. 6, 1992 ($4.95, 44 pgs., mature)
1-6: Japanese stories translated into English 5.00

MIDNIGHT MASS
DC Comics (Vertigo): Jun, 2002 - No. 8, Jan, 2003 ($2.50)
1-8-Rozum-s/Saiz & Palmiotti-a 2.50

MIDNIGHT MASS: HERE THERE BE MONSTERS
DC Comics (Vertigo): March, 2004 - No. 6, Aug, 2004 ($2.95, limited series)
1-6-Rozum-s/Paul Lee-a 3.00

MIDNIGHT MEN
Marvel Comics (Epic Comics/Heavy Hitters): June, 1993 - No. 4, Sept, 1993 ($2.50/$1.95, limited series)
1-($2.50)-Embossed-c; Chaykin-c/a & scripts in all 3.00
2-4 2.25

MIDNIGHT MYSTERY
American Comics Group: Jan-Feb, 1961 - No. 7, Oct, 1961

Midnight Nation #11 © J. Michael Straczynski & TCOW

The Mighty Crusaders #8 © AP

Mighty Love HC © Howard Chaykin

	GD	VG	FN	VF	VF/NM	NM-
	2.0	4.0	6.0	8.0	9.0	9.2

1-Sci/Fi story 9 18 27 65 93 120
2-7: 7-Gustavson-a 5 10 15 36 48 60
NOTE: ***Reinman** a-1, 3. **Whitney** a-1, 4-6; c-1-3, 5, 7.*

MIDNIGHT NATION
Image Comics (Top Cow): Oct, 2000 - No. 12, July, 2002 ($2.50/$2.95)
1-Straczynski-s/Frank-a; 2 covers 3.00
2-11: 9-Twin Towers cover 2.50
12-($2.95)Last issue 3.00
Wizard #1/2 (2001) Michael Zulli-a; two covers by Frank 3.00
Vol. 1 ('03, $29.99, TPB) r/#1-12 & Wizard #1/2; cover gallery; afterword by Straczynski 30.00

MIDNIGHT SONS UNLIMITED
Marvel Comics (Midnight Sons imprint #4 on): Apr, 1993 - No. 9, May, 1995 ($3.95, 68 pgs.)
1-9: Blaze, Darkhold (by Quesada #1), Ghost Rider, Morbius & Nightstalkers in all. 1-Painted-c. 3-Spider-Man app. 4-Siege of Darkness part 17; new Dr. Strange & new Ghost Rider app.; spot varnish-c 4.00
NOTE: ***Sears** a-2.*

MIDNIGHT TALES
Charlton Press: Dec, 1972 - No. 18, May, 1976
V1#1 2 4 6 14 18 22
2-10 2 4 6 9 11 14
11-18: 11-14-Newton-a(p) 1 3 4 6 8 10
12,17(Modern Comics reprint, 1977) 5.00
NOTE: ***Adkins** a-12i, 13i. **Ditko** a-12. **Howard** (Wood imitator) a-1-15, 17, 18; c-1-18. **Don Newton** a-11-14p. **Staton** a-1, 3-11, 13. **Sutton** a-3-10.*

MIGHTY ATOM, THE (...& the Pixies #6) (Formerly The Pixies #1-5)
Magazine Enterprises: No. 6, 1949; Nov, 1957 - No. 6, Aug-Sept, 1958
6(1949-M.E.)-no month (1st Series) 7 14 21 35 43 50
1-6(2nd Series)-Pixies-r 4 8 12 18 22 25
I.W. Reprint #1(nd) 2 4 6 9 11 14

MIGHTY BEAR (Formerly Fun Comics; becomes Unsane #15)
Star Publ. No. 13,14/Ajax-Farrell (Four Star): No. 13, Jan, 1954 - No. 14, Mar, 1954; 9/57 - No. 3, 2/58
13,14-L. B. Cole-c 19 38 57 107 154 200
1-3('57-58)Four Star; becomes Mighty Ghost #4 7 14 21 35 43 50

MIGHTY COMICS (...Presents) (Formerly Flyman)
Radio Comics (Archie): No. 40, Nov, 1966 - No. 50, Oct, 1967 (All 12¢ issues)
40-Web 4 8 12 24 32 40
41-50: 41-Shield, Black Hood. 42-Black Hood. 43-Shield, Web & Black Hood. 44-Black Hood, Steel Sterling & The Shield. 45-Shield & Hangman; origin Web retold. 46-Steel Sterling, Web & Black Hood. 47-Black Hood & Mr. Justice. 48-Shield & Hangman; Wizard x-over in Shield. 49-Steel Sterling & Fox; Black Hood x-over in Steel Sterling. 50-Black Hood & Web; Inferno x-over in Web 3 7 10 21 28 35
NOTE: ***Paul Reinman** a-40-50.*

MIGHTY CRUSADERS, THE (Also see Adventures of the Fly, The Crusaders & Fly Man)
Mighty Comics Group (Radio Comics): Nov, 1965 - No. 7, Oct, 1966 (All 12¢)
1-Origin The Shield 7 14 21 46 63 80
2-Origin Comet 4 8 12 25 33 42
3,5-7: 3-Origin Fly-Man. 5-Intro. Ultra-Men (Fox, Web, Capt. Flag) & Terrific Three (Jaguar, Mr. Justice, Steel Sterling). 7-Steel Sterling feature; origin Fly-Girl
4 8 12 24 32 40
4-1st S.A. app. Fireball, Inferno & Fox; Firefly, Web, Bob Phantom, Blackjack, Hangman, Zambini, Kardak, Steel Sterling, Mr. Justice, Wizard, Capt. Flag, Jaguar x-over
4 8 12 27 36 45
Volume 1: Origin of a Super Team TPB (2003, $12.95) r/#1 & Fly Man #31-33 13.00
NOTE: ***Reinman** a-6.*

MIGHTY CRUSADERS, THE (All New Advs. of...#2)
Red Circle Prod./Archie Ent. No. 6 on: Mar, 1983 - No. 13, Sept, 1985 ($1.00, 36 pgs, Mando paper)
1-Origin Black Hood, The Fly, Fly Girl, The Shield, The Wizard, The Jaguar, Pvt. Strong & The Web. 6.00
2-10: 2-Mister Midnight begins. 4-Darkling replaces Shield. 5-Origin Jaguar, Shield begins. 7-Untold origin Jaguar. 10-Veitch-a 4.00
11-13-Lower print run 5.00
NOTE: ***Buckler** a-1-3, 4i, 5p, 7p, 8i, 9i; c-1-10p.*

MIGHTY GHOST (Formerly Mighty Bear #1-3)
Ajax/Farrell Publ.: No. 4, June, 1958
4 6 12 18 28 34 40

MIGHTY HERCULES, THE (TV)
Gold Key: July, 1963 - No. 2, Nov, 1963
1 (10072-307) 16 32 48 112 171 230
2 (10072-311) 15 30 45 105 160 215

MIGHTY HEROES, THE (TV) (Funny)
Dell Publishing Co.: Mar, 1967 - No. 4, July, 1967
1-Also has a 1957 Heckle & Jeckle-r 15 30 45 105 160 215
2-4: 4-Has two 1958 Mighty Mouse-r 10 20 30 73 107 140

MIGHTY HEROES
Spotlight Comics: 1987 (B&W, one-shot)
1-Heckle & Jeckle backup 5.00

MIGHTY HEROES
Marvel Comics: Jan, 1998 ($2.99, one-shot)
1-Origin of the Mighty Heroes 3.00

MIGHTY LOVE
DC Comics: 2003 ($24.99, graphic novel)
HC-Howard Chaykin-s/a; intro. Skylark and the Iron Angel 25.00

MIGHTY MARVEL TEAM-UP THRILLERS
Marvel Comics: 1983 ($5.95, trade paperback)
1-Reprints team-up stories 38.00

MIGHTY MARVEL WESTERN, THE
Marvel Comics Group (LMC earlier issues): Oct, 1968 - No. 46, Sept, 1976 (#1-14: 68 pgs.; #15,16: 52 pgs.)
1-Begin Kid Colt, Rawhide Kid, Two-Gun Kid-r 6 12 18 40 55 70
2-5: (2-14 are 68 pgs.) 4 8 12 27 36 45
6-16: (15,16 are 52 pgs.) 4 8 12 24 32 40
17-20 2 4 6 12 16 20
21-30,32,37: 24-Kid Colt-r end. 25-Matt Slade-r begin. 32-Origin-r/Rawhide Kid #23; Williamson-r/Kid Slade #7. 37-Williamson, Kirby-r/Two-Gun Kid 51
2 4 6 10 12 15
31,33-36,38-46: 31-Baker-r. 2 4 6 8 10 12
45-(30¢-c variant, limited distribution)(6/76) 2 4 6 11 14 18
NOTE: ***Jack Davis** a(r)-21-24. **Keller** r-1-13, 22. **Kirby** a(r)-1-3, 6, 9, 12-14, 16, 25-29, 32-38, 40, 41, 43-46; c-29. **Maneely** a(r)-22. **Severin** c-3i, 9. No Matt Slade-#43.*

MIGHTY MIDGET COMICS, THE (Miniature)
Samuel E. Lowe & Co.: No date; circa 1942-1943 (Sold 2 for 5¢, B&W and red, 36 pgs, approx. 5x4")
Bulletman #11(1943)-r/cover/Bulletman #3 23 46 69 130 188 245
Captain Marvel Adventures #11 23 46 69 130 188 245
Captain Marvel #11 (Same as above except for full color ad on back cover; this issue was glued to cover of Captain Marvel #20 and is not found in fine-mint condition)
340 680 1020 - - -
Captain Marvel Jr. #11 (Same-c as Master #27 23 46 69 130 188 245
Captain Marvel Jr. #11 (Same as above except for full color ad on back-c; this issue was glued to cover of Captain Marvel #21 and is not found in fine-mint condition)
340 680 1020 - - -
Golden Arrow #11 21 42 63 121 173 225
Golden Arrow #11 (Same as above except for full color ad on back-c; this issue was glued to cover of Captain Marvel #21 and is not found in fine-mint condition)
280 560 840 - - -
Ibis the Invincible #11(1942)-Origin; reprints cover to Ibis #1 (Predates Fawcett's Ibis the Invincible #1). 23 46 69 130 188 245
Spy Smasher #11(1942) 23 46 69 130 188 245
NOTE: *The above books came in a box called "box full of books" and was distributed with other Samuel Lowe puzzles, paper dolls, coloring books, etc. They are not titled Mighty Midget Comics. All have a war bond seal on back cover which is otherwise blank. These books came in a "Mighty Midget" flat cardboard counter display rack.*
Balbo, the Boy Magician #12 (1943)-1st book devoted entirely to character.
12 24 36 71 98 125
Bulletman #12 17 34 51 95 135 175
Commando Yank #12 (1943)-Only comic devoted entirely to character.
14 28 42 79 110 140
Dr. Voltz the Human Generator (1943)-Only comic devoted entirely to character.
12 24 36 71 98 125
Lance O'Casey #12 (1943)-1st comic devoted entirely to character (Predates Fawcett's Lance O'Casey #1). 12 24 36 71 98 125
Leatherneck the Marine (1943)-Only comic devoted entirely to character.
12 24 36 71 98 125
Minute Man #12 17 34 51 95 135 175
Mister "Q" (1943)-Only comic devoted entirely to character.
12 24 36 71 98 125
Mr. Scarlet and Pinky #12 (1943)-Only comic devoted entirely to character.
14 28 42 81 113 145

Mighty Mouse #72 © Viacom

Mike Grell's Sable #8 © First Publ.

Military Comics #42 © QUA

GD 2.0 | VG 4.0 | FN 6.0 | VF 8.0 | VF/NM 9.0 | NM- 9.2

Pat Wilton and His Flying Fortress (1943)-1st comic devoted entirely to character. 12 24 36 71 98 125
The Phantom Eagle #12 (1943)-Only comic devoted entirely to character. 12 24 36 71 98 125
State Trooper Stops Crime (1943)-Only comic devoted entirely to character. 12 24 36 71 98 125
Tornado Tom (1943)-Origin, r/from Cyclone #1-3; only comic devoted entirely to character. 12 24 36 71 98 125

MIGHTY MORPHIN' POWER RANGERS: THE MOVIE (Also see Saban's Mighty Morphin' Power Rangers)
Marvel Comics: Sept, 1995 ($3.95, one-shot)
nn-adaptation of movie 4.00

MIGHTY MOUSE (See Adventures of..., Dell Giant #43, Giant Comics Edition, March of Comics #205, 237, 247, 257, 447, 459, 471, 483, Oxydol-Dreft, Paul Terry's, & Terry-Toons Comics)

MIGHTY MOUSE (1st Series)
Timely/Marvel Comics (20th Century Fox): Fall, 1946 - No. 4, Summer, 1947
1 131 262 393 819 1260 1700
2 56 112 168 350 538 725
3,4 40 80 120 239 357 475

MIGHTY MOUSE (2nd Series) (Paul Terry's... #62-71)
St. John Publishing Co./Pines No. 68 (3/56) on (TV issues #72 on): Aug, 1947 - No. 67, 11/55; No. 68, 3/56 - No. 83, 6/59
5(#1) 40 80 120 233 342 450
6-10: 10-Over-sized issue 20 40 60 112 161 210
11-19 13 26 39 76 106 135
20 (11/50) - 25-(52 pg. editions) 10 20 30 60 80 100
20-25-(36 pg. editions) 9 18 27 54 70 85
26-37: 35-Flying saucer-c 8 16 24 46 58 70
38-45-(100 pgs.) 19 38 57 107 154 200
46-83: 62-64,67-Painted-c. 82-Infinity-c 8 16 24 43 54 65
Album nn (nd, 1952/53?, St. John)(100 pgs.)(Rebound issues w/new cover) 23 46 69 132 191 250
Album 1(10/52, 25¢, 100 pgs., St. John)-Gandy Goose app. 29 58 87 164 237 310
Album 2,3(11/52 & 12/52, St. John) (100 pgs.) 23 46 69 132 191 250
Fun Club Magazine 1(Fall, 1957-Pines, 25¢, 100 pgs.) (CBS TV)-Tom Terrific, Heckle & Jeckle, Dinky Duck, Gandy Goose 16 32 48 92 131 170
Fun Club Magazine 2-6(Winter, 1958-Pines) 10 20 30 60 80 100
3-D 1-(1st printing-9/53, 25¢)(St. John)-Came w/glasses; stiff covers; says World's First! on-c; 1st 3-D comic 31 62 93 175 253 330
3-D 1-(2nd printing-10/53, 25¢)-Came w/glasses; slick, glossy covers, slightly smaller 27 54 81 152 219 285
3-D 2,3(11/53, 12/53, 25¢)-(St. John)-With glasses 26 52 78 147 211 275

MIGHTY MOUSE (TV)(3rd Series)(Formerly Adventures of Mighty Mouse)
Gold Key/Dell Publ. Co. No. 166-on: No. 161, Oct, 1964 - No. 172, Oct, 1968
161(10/64)-165(9/65)-(Becomes Adventures of... No. 166 on) 6 12 18 38 52 65
166(3/66), 167(6/66)-172 4 8 12 25 33 42

MIGHTY MOUSE (TV)
Spotlight Comics: 1987 - No. 2, 1987 ($1.50, color)
1,2-New stories 3.00
...And Friends Holiday Special (11/87, $1.75) 3.00

MIGHTY MOUSE (TV)
Marvel Comics: Oct, 1990 - No. 10, July, 1991 ($1.00)(Based on Sat. cartoon)
1-10: 1-Dark Knight-c parody. 2-10: 3-Intro Bat-Bat; Byrne-c. 4,5-Crisis-c/story parodies w/Perez-c. 6-Spider-Man-c parody. 7-Origin Bat-Bat 2.25

MIGHTY MOUSE ADVENTURE MAGAZINE
Spotlight Comics: 1987 ($2.00, B&W, 52 pgs., magazine size, one-shot)
1-Deputy Dawg, Heckle & Jeckle backup stories 5.00

MIGHTY MOUSE ADVENTURES (Adventures of... #2 on)
St. John Publishing Co.: November, 1951
1 34 68 102 193 279 365

MIGHTY MOUSE ADVENTURE STORIES (Paul Terry's... on-c only)
St. John Publishing Co.: 1953 (50¢, 384 pgs.)
nn-Rebound issues 43 86 129 262 401 540

MIGHTY MUTANIMALS (See Teenage Mutant Ninja Turtles Adventures #19)
May, 1991 - No. 3, July, 1991 ($1.00, limited series)
Archie Comics: Apr, 1992 - No. 8, June, 1993 ($1.25)
1-3: 1-Story cont'd from TMNT Advs. #19. 2.25
1-9 (1992): 7-1st app. Merdude 2.25

MIGHTY SAMSON (Also see Gold Key Champion)
Gold Key/Whitman #32: July, 1964 - No. 20, Nov, 1969; No. 21, Aug, 1972; No. 22, Dec, 1973 - No. 31, Mar, 1976; No. 32, Aug, 1982 (Painted-c #1-31)
1-Origin/1st app.; Thorne-a begins 10 20 30 70 100 130
2-5 6 12 18 38 52 65
6-10: 7-Tom Morrow begins, ends #20 4 8 12 25 33 42
11-20 3 6 9 19 25 32
21-31: 21,22-r 3 6 9 16 20 24
32(Whitman, 8/82)-r 2 4 6 9 11 14

MIGHTY THOR (See Thor)

MIKE BARNETT, MAN AGAINST CRIME (TV)
Fawcett Publications: Dec, 1951 - No. 6, Oct, 1952
1 20 40 60 112 161 210
2 12 24 36 69 95 120
3,4,6 10 20 30 58 77 95
5- "Market for Morphine" cover/story 13 26 39 76 106 135

MIKE DANGER (See Mickey Spillane's...)

MIKE DEODATO'S...
Caliber Comics: 1996, ($2.95, B&W)
...FALLOUT 3000 #1, **...JONAS** (mag. size) #1,**...PRIME CUTS** (mag. size) #1, **...PROTHEUS** #1,2, **...RAMTHAR** #1,**...RAZOR NIGHTS** #1 3.00

MIKE GRELL'S SABLE (Also see Jon Sable & Sable)
First Comics: Mar, 1990 - No. 10, Dec, 1990 ($1.75)
1-10: r/Jon Sable Freelance #1-10 by Grell 2.25

MIKE MIST MINUTE MIST-ERIES (See Ms. Tree/Mike Mist in 3-D)
Eclipse Comics: April, 1981 ($1.25, B&W, one-shot)
1 2.25

MIKE SHAYNE PRIVATE EYE
Dell Publishing Co.: Nov-Jan, 1962 - No. 3, Sept-Nov, 1962
1 4 8 12 27 36 45
2,3 3 6 9 18 24 30

MILITARY COMICS (Becomes Modern Comics #44 on)
Quality Comics Group: Aug, 1941 - No. 43, Oct, 1945
1-Origin/1st app. Blackhawk by C. Cuidera (Eisner scripts); Miss America, The Death Patrol by Jack Cole (also #2-7,27-30), & The Blue Tracer by Guardineer; X of the Underground, The Yankee Eagle, Q-Boat & Shot & Shell, Archie Atkins, Loops & Banks by Bud Ernest (Bob Powell)(ends #13) begin 935 1870 2805 6545 10,523 14,500
2-Secret War News begins (by McWilliams #2-16); Cole-a; new uniform with yellow circle & hawk's head for Blackhawk 269 538 807 1681 2591 3500
3-Origin/1st app. Chop Chop (9/41) 235 470 705 1469 2260 3050
4 188 376 564 1175 1813 2450
5-The Sniper begins; Miss America in costume #4-7 158 316 474 988 1519 2050
6-9: 8-X of the Underground begins (ends #13). 9-The Phantom Clipper begins (ends #16) 113 226 339 706 1091 1475
10-Classic Eisner-c 123 246 369 769 1185 1600
11-Flag-c 92 184 276 575 888 1200
12-Blackhawk by Crandall begins, ends #22 113 226 339 706 1091 1475
13-15: 14-Private Dogtag begins (ends #83) 87 174 261 544 835 1125
16-20: 16-Blue Tracer ends. 17-P.T. Boat begins 75 150 225 469 722 975
21-31: 22-Last Crandall Blackhawk. 23-Shrunken head-c. 27-Death Patrol revived 63 126 189 394 610 825
32-43 55 110 165 336 511 685
NOTE: *Berg a-6.* ***Al Bryant*** *c-31-34, 38, 40-43.* ***J. Cole*** *a-1-3, 27-32.* ***Crandall*** *a-12-22; c-13-20.* ***Cuidera*** *c-2-9.* ***Eisner*** *c-1, 2(part), 9, 10.* ***Kotsky*** *c-21-29, 35, 37, 39.* ***McWilliams*** *a-2-16.* ***Powell*** *a-1-13.* ***Ward*** *Blackhawk-30, 31(15 pgs. each); c-30.*

MILK AND CHEESE (Also see Cerebus Bi-Weekly #20)
Slave Labor: 1991 - Present ($2.50, B&W)
1-Evan Dorkin story & art in all 4 8 12 29 40 50
1-2nd-6th printings 4.00
2-"Other #1" 3 6 9 18 24 30
2-reprint 3.00
3-"Third #1" 2 4 6 12 16 20
4-"Fourth #1", 5-"First Second Issue" 1 3 4 6 8 10
6,7: 6-"#666" 5.00
NOTE: *Multiple printings of all issues exist and are worth cover price unless listed here.*

MILKMAN MURDERS, THE

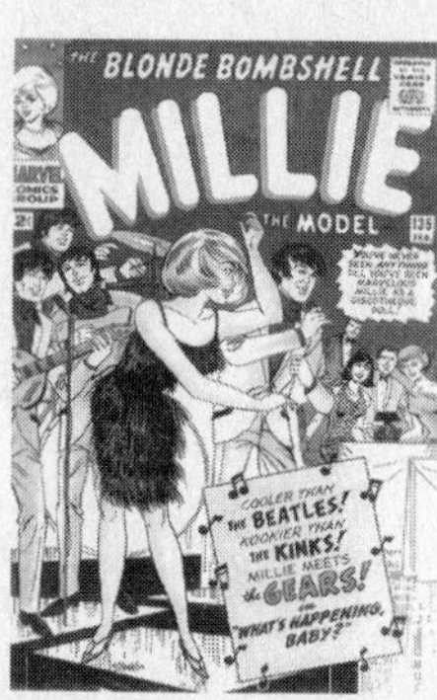

Millie the Model #135 © MAR

Ministry of Space #3 © Ellis & Weston

Miracleman #19 © ECL

	GD 2.0	VG 4.0	FN 6.0	VF 8.0	VF/NM 9.0	NM- 9.2

Dark Horse Comics: Jun, 2004 - No. 3, Aug, 2004 ($2.99, limited series)

	GD	VG	FN	VF	VF/NM	NM-
1-3-Casey-s/Parkhouse-a						3.00

MILLENNIUM
DC Comics: Jan, 1988 - No. 8, Feb, 1988 (Weekly limited series)

	GD	VG	FN	VF	VF/NM	NM-
1-Staton c/a(p) begins						3.00
2-8						2.50

MILLENNIUM EDITION:... (Reprints of classic DC issues)
DC Comics: Feb, 2000 - Feb, 2001 (gold foil cover stamps)

	GD	VG	FN	VF	VF/NM	NM-
Action Comics #1, Adventure Comics #61, All Star Comics #3, All Star Comics #8, Batman #1, Detective Comics #1, Detective Comics #27, Detective Comics #38, Flash Comics #1, Military Comics #1, More Fun Comics #73, Police Comics #1, Sensation Comics #1, Superman #1, Whiz Comics #2, Wonder Woman #1 -($3.95-c)						4.00
Action Comics #252, Adventure Comics #247, Brave and the Bold #28, Brave and the Bold #85, Crisis on Infinite Earths #1, Detective #225, Detective #327, Detective #359, Detective #395, Flash #123, Gen13 #1, Green Lantern #76, House of Mystery #1, House of Secrets #92, JLA #1, Justice League #1, Mad #1, Man of Steel #1, Mysterious Suspense #1, New Gods, #1, New Teen Titans #1, Our Army at War #81, Plop! #1, Saga of the Swamp Thing #21, Shadow #1, Showcase #4, Showcase #9, Showcase #22, Superman #233, Superman (2nd) #75, Superman's Pal Jimmy Olsen #1, Watchmen #1, WildC.A.T.s #1, Wonder Woman (2nd) #1, World's Finest #71 -($2.50-c)						2.50
All-Star Western #10, Hellblazer #1, More Fun Comics #101, Preacher #1, Sandman #1, Spirit #1, Superboy #1, Superman #76, Young Romance #1-($2.95-c)						3.00
Batman: The Dark Knight Returns #1, Kingdom Come #1 -($5.95-c)						6.00
All Star Comics #3, Batman #1, Justice League #1: Chromium cover						10.00
Crisis on Infinite Earths #1 Chromium cover						20.00

MILLENNIUM FEVER
DC Comics (Vertigo): Oct, 1995 - No.4, Jan, 1996 ($2.50, limited series)

	GD	VG	FN	VF	VF/NM	NM-
1-4: Duncan Fegredo-c/a						2.50

MILLENNIUM INDEX
Independent Comics Group: Mar, 1988 - No. 2, Mar, 1988 ($2.00)

	GD	VG	FN	VF	VF/NM	NM-
1,2						2.25

MILLENNIUM 2.5 A.D.
ACG Comics: No. 1, 2000 ($2.95)

	GD	VG	FN	VF	VF/NM	NM-
1-Reprints 1934 Buck Rogers daily strips #1-48						3.00

MILLIE, THE LOVABLE MONSTER
Dell Publishing Co.: Sept-Nov, 1962 - No. 6, Jan, 1973

	GD	VG	FN	VF	VF/NM	NM-
12-523-211	6	12	18	40	55	70
2(8-10/63)-Bill Woggon c/a	5	10	15	36	48	60
3(8-10/64)	4	8	12	29	40	50
4(7/72), 5(10/72), 6(1/73)	2	4	6	14	18	22

NOTE: ***Woggon** a-3-6; c-3-6. 4 reprints 1; 5 reprints 2; 6 reprints 3.*

MILLIE THE MODEL (See Comedy Comics, A Date With..., Joker Comics #28, Life With..., Mad About..., Marvel Mini-Books, Misty & Modeling With...)
Marvel/Atlas/Marvel Comics(CnPC #1)(SPI/Male/VPI):1945 - No. 207, Dec, 1973

	GD	VG	FN	VF	VF/NM	NM-
1-Origin	85	170	255	531	816	1100
2 (10/46)-Millie becomes The Blonde Phantom to sell Blonde Phantom perfume; a pre-Blonde Phantom app. (see All-Select #11, Fall, 1946)	40	80	120	244	372	500
3-8,10: 4-7-Willie app. 7-Willie smokes extra strong tobacco. 8,10-Kurtzman's "Hey Look". 8-Willie & Rusty app.	31	62	93	175	253	330
9-Powerhouse Pepper by Wolverton, 4 pgs.	35	70	105	198	287	375
11-Kurtzman-a, "Giggles 'n' Grins"	21	42	63	118	169	220
12,15,17-20: 12-Rusty & Hedy Devine app.	15	30	45	86	123	160
13,14,16-Kurtzman's "Hey Look". 13-Hedy Devine app.	16	32	48	92	131	170
21-30	11	22	33	64	87	110
31-40	7	14	21	51	71	90
41-60	6	12	18	43	59	75
61-99	5	10	15	33	44	55
100	6	12	18	38	52	65
101-130: 107-Jack Kirby app. in story	4	8	12	28	38	48
131-134,136,138-153: 141-Groovy Gears-c/s	4	8	12	22	30	38
135-(2/66) 1st app. Groovy Gears	4	8	12	28	38	48
137-2nd app. Groovy Gears	4	8	12	25	33	42
154-New Millie begins (10/67)	5	10	15	33	44	55
155-190	3	7	10	21	28	35
191,193-199,201-206	3	6	9	18	23	28
192-(52 pgs.)	4	8	12	24	32	40
200,207(Last issue)	4	8	12	24	32	40

(Beware: cut-up pages are common in all Annuals)

	GD	VG	FN	VF	VF/NM	NM-
Annual 1(1962)-Early Marvel annual (2nd?)	21	42	63	150	230	310
Annual 2(1963)	14	28	42	97	149	200
Annual 3-5 (1964-1966)	9	18	27	65	93	120
Annual 6-10(1967-11/71)	8	16	24	53	74	95
Queen-Size 11(9/74), 12(1975)	7	14	21	46	63	80

NOTE: ***Dan DeCarlo** a-18-93.*

MILLION DOLLAR DIGEST (Richie Rich... #23 on; also see Richie Rich...)
Harvey Publications: 11/86 - No. 7, 11/87; No. 8, 4/88 - No. 34, Nov, 1994 ($1.25/$1.75, digest size)

	GD	VG	FN	VF	VF/NM	NM-
1	1	2	3	4	5	7
2-8: 8-(68 pgs.)						5.00
9-34: 9-Begin $1.75-c. 14-May not exist						3.50

MILT GROSS FUNNIES (Also see Picture News #1)
Milt Gross, Inc. (ACG?): Aug, 1947 - No. 2, Sept, 1947

	GD	VG	FN	VF	VF/NM	NM-
1	21	42	63	121	173	225
2	15	30	45	83	117	150

MILTON THE MONSTER & FEARLESS FLY (TV)
Gold Key: May, 1966

	GD	VG	FN	VF	VF/NM	NM-
1 (10175-605)	11	22	33	75	110	145

MINIMUM WAGE
Fantagraphics Books: V1#1, July, 1995 ($9.95, B&W, graphic novel, mature)
V2#1, 1995 - Present ($2.95, B&W, mature)

	GD	VG	FN	VF	VF/NM	NM-
V1#1-Bob Fingerman story & art	1	3	4	6	8	10
V2#1-9($2.95): Bob Fingerman story & art. 2-Kevin Nowlan back-c. 4-w/pin-ups. 5-Mignola back-c						3.00
Book Two TPB ('97, $12.95) r/V2#1-5						13.00

MINISTRY OF SPACE
Image Comics: Apr, 2001 - No. 3, Apr, 2004 ($2.95, limited series)

	GD	VG	FN	VF	VF/NM	NM-
1-3-Warren Ellis-s/Chris Weston-a						3.00
...Vol. 1 Omnibus (3/04, $4.95) r/1&2						5.00

MINOR MIRACLES
DC Comics: 2000 ($12.95, B&W, squarebound)

	GD	VG	FN	VF	VF/NM	NM-
nn-Will Eisner-s/a						13.00

MINUTE MAN (See Master Comics & Mighty Midget Comics)
Fawcett Publications: Summer, 1941 - No. 3, Spring, 1942 (68 pgs.)

	GD	VG	FN	VF	VF/NM	NM-
1	208	416	624	1300	2000	2700
2,3	127	254	381	794	1222	1650

MINX, THE
DC Comics (Vertigo): Oct, 1998 - No. 8, May, 1999 ($2.50, limited series)

	GD	VG	FN	VF	VF/NM	NM-
1-8-Milligan-s/Phillips-c/a						3.00

MIRACLE COMICS
Hillman Periodicals: Feb, 1940 - No. 4, Mar, 1941

	GD	VG	FN	VF	VF/NM	NM-
1-Sky Wizard Master of Space, Dash Dixon, Man of Might, Pinkie Parker, Dusty Doyle, The Kid Cop, K-7, Secret Agent, The Scorpion, & Blandu, Jungle Queen begin; Masked Angel only app. (all 1st app.)	185	370	555	1156	1778	2400
2	92	184	276	575	888	1200
3,4: 3-Bill Colt, the Ghost Rider begins. 4-The Veiled Prophet & Bullet Bob (by Burnley) app.	79	158	237	494	760	1025

MIRACLEMAN
Eclipse Comics: Aug, 1985 - No. 15, Nov, 1988; No. 16, Dec, 1989 - No. 24, 1994

	GD	VG	FN	VF	VF/NM	NM-
1-r/British Marvelman series; Alan Moore scripts in #1-16	1	2	3	5	7	9
1-Gold variant (edition of 400, signed by Alan Moore, came with signed & #'d certificate of authenticity)						1500.00
1-Blue variant (edition of 600, came with signed certificate of authenticity)						800.00
2-12: 8-Airboy preview. 9,10-Origin Miracleman. 9-Shows graphic scenes of childbirth. 10-Snyder-c	1	2	3	5	6	8
13,14	2	4	6	10	12	15
15-($1.75-c, scarce) end of Kid Miracleman	6	12	18	40	55	70
16-Last Alan Moore-s; 1st $1.95-c (low print)	2	4	6	14	18	22
17,18-($1.95): 17-"The Golden Age" begins, ends #22. Dave McKean-c begins, end #22; Neil Gaiman scripts in #17-24	2	4	6	9	11	14
19-23-($2.50); 23-"The Silver Age" begins; BWS-c	1	2	3	5	7	9
24-Last issue; B. Smith-c	2	4	6	10	12	15
3-D 1 (12/85)	1	2	3	5	6	8
Book One: A Dream of Flying (1988, $9.95, TPB) r/#1-5; Leach-c						22.00
Book One: A Dream of Flying-Hardcover (1988, $29.95) r/#1-5						70.00

Miss America Magazine #3 © MAR

Miss Fury #6 © MAR

Mr. District Attorney #2 © DC

GD 2.0 | VG 4.0 | FN 6.0 | VF 8.0 | VF/NM 9.0 | NM- 9.2

Book Two: The Red King Syndrome (1990, $12.95, TPB) r/#6-10; Bolton-c 22.00
Book Two: The Red King Syndrome-Hardcover (1990, $30.95) r/#6-10 85.00
Book Three: Olympus (1990, $12.95, TPB) r/#11-16 100.00
Book Three: Olympus-Hardcover (1990, $30.95) r/#11-16 200.00
Book Four: The Golden Age (1992, $15.95, TPB) r/#17-22 30.00
Book Four: The Golden Age Hardcover (1992, $33.95) r/#17-22 50.00
Book Four: The Golden Age (1993, $12.99, TPB) new McKean-c 15.00
NOTE: ***Chaykin*** *c-3.* ***Gulacy*** *c-7.* ***McKean*** *c-17-22.* ***B. Smith*** *c-23, 24.* ***Starlin*** *c-4.* ***Totleben*** *a-11-13; c-9, 11-13.* ***Truman*** *c-6.*

MIRACLEMAN: APOCRYPHA
Eclipse Comics: Nov, 1991 - No. 3, Feb, 1992 ($2.50, limited series)
1-3: 1-Stories by Neil Gaiman, Mark Buckingham, Alex Ross & others. 3-Stories by James Robinson, Kelley Jones, Matt Wagner, Neil Gaiman, Mark Buckingham & others 1 2 3 4 5 7
TPB (12/92, $15.95) r/#1-3; Buckingham-c 20.00

MIRACLEMAN FAMILY
Eclipse Comics: May, 1988 - No. 2, Sept, 1988 ($1.95, lim. series, Baxter paper)
1,2: 2-Gulacy-c 5.00

MIRACLE OF THE WHITE STALLIONS, THE (See Movie Comics)

MIRACLE SQUAD, THE
Upshot Graphics (Fantagraphics Books): Aug, 1986 - No. 4, 1987 ($2.00)
1-4 2.25

MIRACLE SQUAD: BLOOD AND DUST, THE
Apple Comics: Jan, 1989 - No. 4, July, 1989 ($1.95, B&W, limited series)
1-4 2.25

MISADVENTURES OF MERLIN JONES, THE (See Movie Comics & Merlin Jones as the Monkey's Uncle under Movie Comics)

MISPLACED
Image Comics: May, 2003 - No. 4, Dec, 2004 ($2.95)
1-4: 1-Three covers by Blaylock, Green and Clugston-Major; Blaylock-s/a 3.00

MISS AMERICA COMICS (Miss America Magazine #2 on; also see Blonde Phantom & Marvel Mystery Comics)
Marvel Comics (20CC): 1944 (one-shot)
1-2 pgs. pin-ups 165 330 495 1031 1591 2150

MISS AMERICA MAGAZINE (Formerly Miss America; Miss America #51 on)
Miss America Publ. Corp./Marvel/Atlas (MAP): V1#2, Nov, 1944 - No. 93, Nov, 1958
V1#2-Photo-c of teenage girl in Miss America costume; Miss America, Patsy Walker (intro.) comic stories plus movie reviews & stories; intro. Buzz Baxter & Hedy Wolfe; 1 pg. origin Miss America 131 262 393 819 1260 1700
3-5-Miss America & Patsy Walker stories 48 96 144 293 447 600
6-Patsy Walker only 15 30 45 86 123 160
V2#1(4/45)-6(9/45)-Patsy Walker continues 10 20 30 58 77 95
V3#1(10/45)-6(4/46) 9 18 27 54 70 85
V4#1(5/46),2,5(9/46) 9 18 27 52 66 80
V4#3(7/46)-Liz Taylor photo-c 21 42 63 121 173 225
V4#4 (8/46; 68 pgs.), V4#6 (10/46; 92 pgs.) 8 16 24 46 58 70
V5#1(11/46)-6(4/47), V6#1(5/47)-3(7/47) 8 16 24 46 58 70
V7#1(8/47)-14,16-23(#56, 6/49) 8 16 24 43 54 65
V7#15-All comics 9 18 27 51 62 75
V7#24(#57, 7/49)-Kamen-a (becomes Best Western #58 on?) 8 16 24 46 58 70
V7#25(8/49), 27-44(3/52), VII,nn(5/52) 8 16 24 40 50 60
V7#26(9/49)-All comics 8 16 24 46 58 70
V1,nn(7/52)-V1,nn(1/53)(#46-49), V7#50(Spring '53), V7#51-V7?#54(7/53), 55-93 7 14 21 37 46 55
NOTE: *Photo-c #1, 4, V2#1, 4, 5, V3#5, V4#3, 4, 6, V7#15, 16, 24, 26, 34, 37, 38. Painted c-3.* ***Powell*** *a-V7#31.*

MISS BEVERLY HILLS OF HOLLYWOOD (See Adventures of Bob Hope)
National Periodical Publ.: Mar-Apr, 1949 - No. 9, July-Aug, 1950 (52 pgs.)
1 (Meets Alan Ladd) 60 120 180 375 580 785
2-William Holden photo on-c 44 88 132 268 409 550
3-5: 2-9-Part photo-c. 5-Bob Hope photo on-c 40 80 120 236 351 465
6,7,9: 6-Lucille Ball photo on-c 37 74 111 209 305 400
8-Reagan photo on-c 40 80 120 239 357 475
NOTE: *Beverly meets Alan Ladd in #1, Eve Arden #2, Betty Hutton #4, Bob Hope #5.*

MISS CAIRO JONES
Croyden Publishers: 1945
1-Bob Oksner daily newspaper-r (1st strip story); lingerie panels 21 42 63 118 169 220

MISS FURY COMICS (Newspaper strip reprints)
Timely Comics (NPI 1/CmPI 2/MPC 3-8): Winter, 1942-43 - No. 8, Winter, 1946 (Published quarterly)
1-Origin Miss Fury by Tarpe' Mills (68 pgs.) in costume w/pin-ups 379 758 1137 2464 3982 5500
2-(60 pgs.)-In costume w/pin-ups 192 384 576 1200 1850 2500
3-(60 pgs.)-In costume w/pin-ups; Hitler-c 154 308 462 963 1482 2000
4-(52 pgs.)-In costume, 2 pgs. w/pin-ups 117 234 351 731 1128 1525
5-(52 pgs.)-In costume w/pin-ups 98 196 294 613 944 1275
6-(52 pgs.)-Not in costume in inside stories, w/pin-ups 94 188 282 588 907 1225
7,8-(36 pgs.)-In costume 1 pg. each; no pin-ups 81 162 243 506 778 1050
NOTE: ***Schomburg*** *c-1, 5, 6.*

MISS FURY
Adventure Comics: 1991 - No. 4, 1991 ($2.50, limited series)
1-4: 1-Origin; granddaughter of original Miss Fury 3.00
1-Limited ed. ($4.95) 5.00

MISSION IMPOSSIBLE (TV)
Dell Publ. Co.: May, 1967 - No. 4, Oct, 1968; No. 5, Oct, 1969 (All have photo-c)
1 10 20 30 72 104 135
2-5: 5-Reprints #1 7 14 21 51 71 90

MISSION IMPOSSIBLE (Movie)
Marvel Comics (Paramount Comics): May, 1996 ($2.95, one-shot) (1st Paramount Comics book)
1-Liefeld-c & back-up story 3.00

MISS LIBERTY (Becomes Liberty Comics)
Burten Publishing Co.: 1945 (MLJ reprints)
1-The Shield & Dusty, The Wizard, & Roy, the Super Boy app.; r/Shield-Wizard #13 30 60 90 170 245 320

MISS MELODY LANE OF BROADWAY (See The Adventures of Bob Hope)
National Periodical Publ.: Feb-Mar, 1950 - No. 3, June-July, 1950 (52 pgs.)
1-Movie stars photos app. on all-c. 60 120 180 375 580 785
2,3: 3-Ed Sullivan photo on-c. 40 80 120 236 351 465

MISS PEACH
Dell Publishing Co.: Oct-Dec, 1963; 1969
1-Jack Mendelsohn-a/script 9 18 27 65 93 120
...Tells You How to Grow (1969; 25¢)-Mel Lazarus-a; also given away (36 pgs.) 6 12 18 38 52 65

MISS PEPPER (See Meet Miss Pepper)

MISS SUNBEAM (See Little Miss...)

MISS VICTORY (See Captain Fearless #1,2, Holyoke One-Shot #3, Veri Best Sure Fire & Veri Best Sure Shot Comics)

MISTER AMERICA
Endeavor Comics: Apr, 1994 - No. 2, May, 1994 ($2.95, limited series)
1,2 3.00

MR. & MRS. BEANS
United Features Syndicate: No. 11, 1939
Single Series 11 36 72 108 204 297 390

MR. & MRS. J. EVIL SCIENTIST (TV)(See The Flintstones & Hanna-Barbera Band Wagon #3)
Gold Key: Nov, 1963 - No. 4, Sept, 1966 (Hanna-Barbera, all 12¢)
1 9 18 27 65 93 120
2-4 6 12 18 43 59 75

MR. ANTHONY'S LOVE CLINIC (Based on radio show)
Hillman Periodicals: Nov, 1949 - No. 5, Apr-May, 1950 (52 pgs.)
1-Photo-c 15 30 45 83 117 150
2 9 18 27 54 70 85
3-5: 5-Photo-c 9 18 27 51 62 75

MISTER BLANK
Amaze Ink: No. 0, Jan, 1996 - No. 14, May, 2000 ($1.75/$2.95, B&W)
0-($1.75, 16 pgs.) Origin of Mr. Blank 2.25
1-14-($2.95) Chris Hicks-s/a 3.00

MR. DISTRICT ATTORNEY (Radio/TV)
National Per. Publ.: Jan-Feb, 1948 - No. 67, Jan-Feb, 1959 (1-23: 52 pgs.)
1-Howard Purcell c-5-23 (most) 100 200 300 625 963 1300
2 46 92 138 281 428 575

Mister Miracle #19 © DC

Mister Mystery #15 © Media Pub.

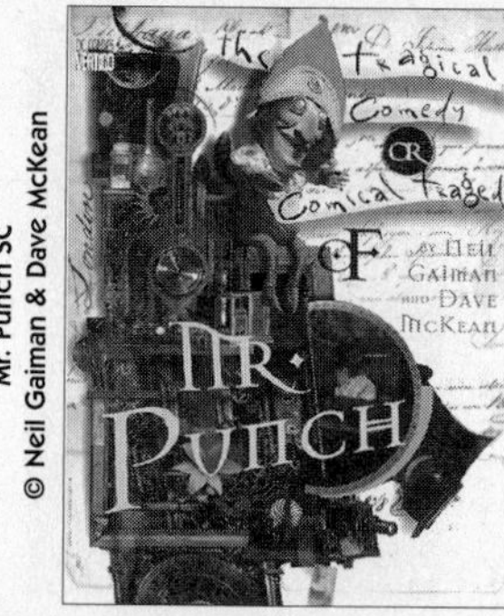

Mr. Punch SC
© Neil Gaiman & Dave McKean

	GD 2.0	VG 4.0	FN 6.0	VF 8.0	VF/NM 9.0	NM- 9.2
3-5	36	72	108	204	297	390
6-10	29	58	87	164	237	310
11-20	22	44	66	123	177	230
21-43: 43-Last pre-code (1-2/55)	15	30	45	83	117	150
44-67	12	24	36	69	95	120

MR. DISTRICT ATTORNEY (SeeThe Funnies #35)
Dell Publishing Co.: No. 13, 1942

	GD	VG	FN	VF	VF/NM	NM-
Four Color 13-See The Funnies #35 for 1st app.	30	60	90	213	327	440

MISTER E (Also see Books of Magic limited series)
DC Comics: Jun, 1991- No. 4, Sept, 1991($1.75, limited series)

	GD	VG	FN	VF	VF/NM	NM-
1-4-Snyder III-c/a; follow-up to Books of Magic limited series						3.00

MISTER ED, THE TALKING HORSE (TV)
Dell Publishing Co./Gold Key: Mar-May, 1962 - No. 6, Feb, 1964 (All photo-c; photo back-c: 1-6)

	GD	VG	FN	VF	VF/NM	NM-
Four Color 1295	14	28	42	102	156	210
1(11/62) (Gold Key)-Photo-c	10	20	30	73	107	140
2-6: Photo-c	7	14	21	46	63	80

(See March of Comics #244, 260, 282, 290)

MR. GUM (From The Atomics)
Oni Press: April, 2003 ($2.99, one-shot)

	GD	VG	FN	VF	VF/NM	NM-
1-Mike Allred-s/J. Bone-a; Madman & The Atomics app.						3.00

MR. HERO, THE NEWMATIC MAN (See Neil Gaiman's...)

MR. MAGOO (TV) (The Nearsighted..., ...& Gerald McBoing Boing 1954 issues; formerly Gerald McBoing-Boing And ...)
Dell Publishing Co.: No. 6, Nov-Jan, 1953-54; 5/54 - 3-5/62; 9-11/63 - 3-5/65

	GD	VG	FN	VF	VF/NM	NM-
6	12	24	36	82	124	165
Four Color 561(5/54),602(11/54)	12	24	36	82	124	165
Four Color 1235(#1, 12-2/62),1305(#2, 3-5/62)	10	20	30	70	100	130
3(9-11/63) - 5	9	18	27	63	89	115
Four Color 1235(12-536-505)(3-5/65)-2nd Printing	7	14	21	51	71	90

MR. MAJESTIC (See WildC.A.T.S.)
DC Comics (WildStorm): Sept, 1999 - No. 9, May, 2000 ($2.50)

	GD	VG	FN	VF	VF/NM	NM-
1-9: 1-McGuinness-a/Casey & Holguin-s. 2-Two covers						2.50
TPB (2002, $14.95) r/#1-6 & Wildstorm Spotlight #1						

MISTER MIRACLE (1st series) (See Cancelled Comic Cavalcade)
National Periodical Publications/DC Comics: 3-4/71 - V4#18, 2-3/74; V5#19, 9/77 - V6#25, 8-9/78; 1987 (Fourth World)

	GD	VG	FN	VF	VF/NM	NM-
1-1st app. Mr. Miracle (#1-3 are 15¢)	8	16	24	53	74	95
2,3: 2-Intro. Granny Goodness. 3-Last 15¢ issue	4	8	12	29	40	50
4-8: 4-Intro. Barda; Boy Commandos-r begin; all 52 pgs.	4	8	12	29	40	50
9-18: 9-Origin Mr. Miracle; Darkseid cameo. 15-Intro/1st app. Shilo Norman. 18-Barda & Scott Free wed; New Gods app. & Darkseid cameo; Last Kirby issue.	3	6	9	16	20	24
19-25 (1977-78)	1	2	3	5	7	9
Special 1(1987, $1.25, 52 pgs.)						3.00
Jack Kirby's Fourth World TPB ('01, $12.95) B&W&Grey-toned reprint of #11-18; Mark Evanier intro.						13.00
Jack Kirby's Mister Miracle TPB ('98, $12.95) B&W&Grey-toned reprint of #1-10; David Copperfield intro.						13.00

NOTE: *Austin a-19i. Ditko a-6r. Golden a-23-25p; c-25p. Heath a-24i, 25i; c-25i. Kirby a(p)/c-1-18. Nasser a-19i. Rogers a-19-22p; c-19, 20p, 21p, 22-24. 4-8 contain Simon & Kirby Boy Commandos reprints from Detective 82,76, Boy Commandos 1, 3 & Detective 64 in that order.*

MISTER MIRACLE (2nd Series) (See Justice League)
DC Comics: Jan, 1989 - No. 28, June, 1991 ($1.00/$1.25)

	GD	VG	FN	VF	VF/NM	NM-
1-28: 13,14-Lobo app. 22-1st new Mr. Miracle w/new costume						2.50

MISTER MIRACLE (3rd Series)
DC Comics: Apr, 1996 - No. 7, Oct, 1996 ($1.95)

	GD	VG	FN	VF	VF/NM	NM-
1-7: 2-Vs. JLA. 6-Simonson-c						2.25

MR. MIRACLE (See Capt. Fearless #1 & Holyoke One-Shot #4)

MR. MONSTER (1st Series)(Doc Stearn... #7 on; See Airboy-Mr. Monster Special, Dark Horse Presents, Super Duper Comics & Vanguard Illustrated #7)
Eclipse Comics: Jan, 1985 - No. 10, June, 1987 ($1.75, Baxter paper)

	GD	VG	FN	VF	VF/NM	NM-
1-3: 1-1st story-r from Vanguard Ill. #7(1st app.). 2-Dave Stevens-c. 3-Alan Moore scripts; Wolverton-r/Weird Mysteries #5.						5.00
4-10: 6-Ditko-r/Fantastic Fears #5 plus new Giffen-a. 10- "6-D" issue						4.00

MR. MONSTER
Dark Horse Comics: Feb, 1988 - No. 8, July, 1991 ($1.75, B&W)

	GD	VG	FN	VF	VF/NM	NM-
1-7						3.00
8-($4.95, 60 pgs.)-Origins conclusion						5.00

MR. MONSTER ATTACKS! (Doc Stearn...)
Tundra Publ.: Aug, 1992 - No. 3, Oct, 1992 ($3.95, limited series, 32 pgs.)

	GD	VG	FN	VF	VF/NM	NM-
1-3: Michael T. Gilbert-a/scripts; Gilbert/Dorman painted-c						4.00

MR. MONSTER PRESENTS (CRACK-A-BOOM!)
Caliber Comics: 1997 - No. 3, 1997 ($2.95, B&W&Red, limited series)

	GD	VG	FN	VF	VF/NM	NM-
1-3: Michael T. Gilbert-a/scripts: 1-Wraparound-c						3.00

MR. MONSTER'S GAL FRIDAY...KELLY!
Image Comics: Jan, 2000 - No. 3, May, 2004 ($3.50, B&W)

	GD	VG	FN	VF	VF/NM	NM-
1-3-Michael T. Gilbert-c; story & art by various. 3-Alan Moore-s						3.50

MR. MONSTER'S SUPER-DUPER SPECIAL
Eclipse Comics: May, 1986 - No. 8, July, 1987

	GD	VG	FN	VF	VF/NM	NM-
1-(5/86)...3-D High Octane Horror #1						5.00
1-(5/86)...2-D version, 100 copies	2	4	6	10	13	16
2-(8/86)...High Octane Horror #1, 3-(9/86)...True Crime #1, 4-(11/86)...True Crime #2, 5-(1/87)...Hi-Voltage Super Science #1, 6-(3/87)...High Shock Schlock #1, 7-(5/87)...High Shock Schlock #2, 8-(7/87)...Weird Tales Of The Future #1						4.00

NOTE: *Jack Cole r-3, 4. Evans a-2r. Kubert a-1r. Powell a-5r. Wolverton a-2r, 7r, 8r.*

MR. MONSTER VS. GORZILLA
Image Comics: July, 1998 ($2.95, one-shot)

	GD	VG	FN	VF	VF/NM	NM-
1-Michael T. Gilbert-a						3.00

MR. MONSTER: WORLDS WAR TWO
Atomeka Press: 2004 ($6.99, one-shot)

	GD	VG	FN	VF	VF/NM	NM-
nn-Michael T. Gilbert-s/George Freeman-a; two covers by Horley & Dorman						7.00

MR. MUSCLES (Formerly Blue Beetle #18-21)
Charlton Comics: No. 22, Mar, 1956; No. 23, Aug, 1956

	GD	VG	FN	VF	VF/NM	NM-
22,23	8	16	24	46	58	70

MR. MXYZPTLK (VILLAINS)
DC Comics: Feb, 1998 ($1.95, one-shot)

	GD	VG	FN	VF	VF/NM	NM-
1-Grant-s/Morgan-a/Pearson-c						2.25

MISTER MYSTERY (Tales of Horror and Suspense)
Mr. Publ. (Media Publ.) No. 1-3/SPM Publ./Stanmore (Aragon): Sept, 1951 - No. 19, Oct, 1954

	GD	VG	FN	VF	VF/NM	NM-
1-Kurtzman*esque* horror story	90	180	270	563	869	1175
2,3-Kurtzman*esque* story. 3-Anti-Wertham edit.	60	120	180	375	575	775
4,6: Bondage-c; 6-Torture	60	120	180	375	575	775
5,8,10	55	110	165	340	520	700
7- "The Brain Bats of Venus" by Wolverton; partially re-used in Weird Tales of the Future #7	121	242	363	756	1166	1575
9-Nostrand-a	55	110	165	340	520	700
11-Wolverton "Robot Woman" story/Weird Mysteries #2, cut up, rewritten & partially redrawn	81	162	243	506	778	1050
12-Classic injury to eye-c	123	246	369	769	1185	1600
13-17,19: 15- "Living Dead" junkie story. 17-Severed heads-c. 19-Reprints	40	80	120	244	372	500
18- "Robot Woman" by Wolverton reprinted from Weird Mysteries #2; decapitation, bondage-c	60	120	180	375	580	785

NOTE: *Andru a-1, 2p, 3p. Andru/Esposito c-1-3. Baily c-10-18(most). Mortellaro c-5-7. Bondage c-7. Some issues have graphic dismemberment scenes.*

MR. PUNCH
DC Comics (Vertigo): 1994 ($24.95, one-shot)

	GD	VG	FN	VF	VF/NM	NM-
nn (Hard-c)-Gaiman scripts; McKean-c/a						40.00
nn (Soft-c)						15.00

MISTER Q (See Mighty Midget Comics & Our Flag Comics #5)

MR. RISK (Formerly All Romances; Men Against Crime #3 on)(Also see Our Flag Comics & Super-Mystery Comics)
Ace Magazines: No. 7, Oct, 1950; No. 2, Dec, 1950

	GD	VG	FN	VF	VF/NM	NM-
7,2	9	18	27	52	66	80

MR. SCARLET & PINKY (See Mighty Midget Comics)

MR. T AND THE T-FORCE
Now Comics: June, 1993 - No. 10, May, 1994 ($1.95, color)

1-10-Newsstand editions: 1-7-polybagged with photo trading card in each.

Mitzi's Romances #8 © MAR

Modeling With Millie #48 © MAR

Mod Wheels #17 © GK

Issue	GD 2.0	VG 4.0	FN 6.0	VF 8.0	VF/NM 9.0	NM- 9.2
1,2-Neal Adams-c/a(p). 3-Dave Dorman painted-c						2.25
1-10-Direct Sale editions polybagged w/line drawn trading cards. 1-Contains gold foil trading card by Neal Adams						2.25

MISTER UNIVERSE (Professional wrestler)
Mr. Publications Media Publ. (Stanmor, Aragon): July, 1951; No. 2, Oct, 1951 - No. 5, April, 1952

Issue	GD 2.0	VG 4.0	FN 6.0	VF 8.0	VF/NM 9.0	NM- 9.2
1	22	44	66	125	180	235
2- "Jungle That Time Forgot", (24 pg. story); Andru/Esposito-c	14	28	42	79	110	140
3-Marijuana story	14	28	42	79	110	140
4,5- "Goes to War" cover/stories	10	20	30	58	77	95

MISTER X (See Vortex)
Mr. Publications/Vortex Comics/Caliber V3#1 on: 6/84 - No. 14, 8/88 ($1.50/$2.25, direct sales, coated paper);V2#1, Apr, 1989 - V2#12, Mar, 1990 ($2.00/$2.50, B&W, newsprint) V3#1, 1996 - Present ($2.95, B&W)

Issue	GD 2.0	VG 4.0	FN 6.0	VF 8.0	VF/NM 9.0	NM- 9.2
1-14: 11-Dave McKean story & art (6 pgs.)						4.00
V2 #1-12: 1-11 (Second Coming, B&W): 1-Four diff.-c. 10-Photo-c						3.00
V3 #1-4						3.00
Return of... ($11.95, graphic novel)-r/V1#1-4						12.00
Return of... ($34.95, hardcover limited edition)-r/1-4						35.00
Special (no date, 1990?)						3.00

MISTY
Marvel Comics (Star Comics): Dec, 1985 - No. 6, May, 1986 (Limited series)

Issue	GD 2.0	VG 4.0	FN 6.0	VF 8.0	VF/NM 9.0	NM- 9.2
1-6: Millie The Model's niece						3.00

MITZI COMICS (Becomes Mitzi's Boy Friend #2-7)(See All Teen)
Timely Comics: Spring, 1948 (one-shot)

Issue	GD 2.0	VG 4.0	FN 6.0	VF 8.0	VF/NM 9.0	NM- 9.2
1-Kurtzman's "Hey Look" plus 3 pgs. "Giggles 'n' Grins"	26	52	78	150	215	280

MITZI'S BOY FRIEND (Formerly Mitzi Comics; becomes Mitzi's Romances)
Marvel Comics (TCI): No. 2, June, 1948 - No. 7, April, 1949

Issue	GD 2.0	VG 4.0	FN 6.0	VF 8.0	VF/NM 9.0	NM- 9.2
2	14	28	42	79	110	140
3-7	11	22	33	62	84	105

MITZI'S ROMANCES (Formerly Mitzi's Boy Friend)
Timely/Marvel Comics (TCI): No. 8, June, 1949 - No. 10, Dec, 1949

Issue	GD 2.0	VG 4.0	FN 6.0	VF 8.0	VF/NM 9.0	NM- 9.2
8-Becomes True Life Tales #8 (10/49) on?	11	22	33	66	91	115
9,10: 10-Painted-c	10	20	30	56	73	90

MOBFIRE
DC Comics (Vertigo): Dec, 1994 - No. 6, May, 1995 ($2.50, limited series)

Issue	GD 2.0	VG 4.0	FN 6.0	VF 8.0	VF/NM 9.0	NM- 9.2
1-6						2.50

MOBY DICK (See Feature Presentations #6, and King Classics)
Dell Publishing Co.: No. 717, Aug, 1956

Issue	GD 2.0	VG 4.0	FN 6.0	VF 8.0	VF/NM 9.0	NM- 9.2
Four Color 717-Movie, Gregory Peck photo-c	10	20	30	70	100	130

MOBY DUCK (See Donald Duck #112 & Walt Disney Showcase #2,11)
Gold Key (Disney): Oct, 1967 - No. 11, Oct, 1970; No. 12, Jan, 1974 - No. 30, Feb, 1978

Issue	GD 2.0	VG 4.0	FN 6.0	VF 8.0	VF/NM 9.0	NM- 9.2
1	4	8	12	25	33	42
2-5	2	4	6	12	16	20
6-11	2	4	6	10	13	16
12-30: 21,30-r	1	3	4	6	8	10

MODEL FUN (With Bobby Benson)
Harle Publications: No. 3, Winter, 1954-55 - No. 5, July, 1955

Issue	GD 2.0	VG 4.0	FN 6.0	VF 8.0	VF/NM 9.0	NM- 9.2
3-Bobby Benson	7	14	21	35	43	50
4,5-Bobby Benson	5	10	15	23	28	32

MODELING WITH MILLIE (Formerly Life With Millie)
Atlas/Marvel Comics (Male Publ.): No. 21, Feb, 1963 - No. 54, June, 1967

Issue	GD 2.0	VG 4.0	FN 6.0	VF 8.0	VF/NM 9.0	NM- 9.2
21	9	18	27	60	85	110
22-30	5	10	15	36	48	60
31-54	4	8	12	27	36	45

MODERN COMICS (Formerly Military Comics #1-43)
Quality Comics Group: No. 44, Nov, 1945 - No. 102, Oct, 1950

Issue	GD 2.0	VG 4.0	FN 6.0	VF 8.0	VF/NM 9.0	NM- 9.2
44-Blackhawk continues	55	110	165	340	520	700
45-52: 49-1st app. Fear, Lady Adventuress	40	80	120	236	351	465
53-Torchy by Ward begins (9/46)	42	84	126	252	391	525
54-60: 55-J. Cole-a	35	70	105	201	293	385
61-77,79,80: 73-J. Cole-a	33	66	99	190	275	360
78-1st app. Madame Butterfly	35	70	105	201	293	385
81-99,101: 82,83-One pg. J. Cole-a. 83-Last 52 pg. issue						
99-Blackhawks on the moon-c/story	31	62	93	177	256	335
100	33	66	99	190	275	360
102-(Scarce)-J. Cole-a; Spirit by Eisner app.	39	78	117	222	324	425

NOTE: ***Al Bryant*** *c-44-51, 54, 55, 66, 69.* ***Jack Cole*** *a-55, 73.* ***Crandall*** *Blackhawk-#46, 47, 50, 51, 54, 56, 58-60, 64, 67-70, 73, 74, 76-78, 80-83; c-60-65, 67, 68, 70-95.* ***Crandall/Cuidera*** *c-56-59, 96-102.* ***Gustavson*** *a-47, 49.* ***Ward*** *Blackhawk-#52, 53, 55 (15 pgs. each). Torchy in #53-102; by* ***Ward*** *only in #53-89(9/49); by* ***Gil Fox*** *#92, 93, 102.*

MODERN LOVE
E. C. Comics: June-July, 1949 - No. 8, Aug-Sept, 1950

Issue	GD 2.0	VG 4.0	FN 6.0	VF 8.0	VF/NM 9.0	NM- 9.2
1-Feldstein, Ingels-a	67	134	201	419	647	875
2-Craig/Feldstein-c/s	43	86	129	262	401	540
3	40	80	120	239	357	475
4-6 (Scarce): 4-Bra/panties panels	51	102	153	311	476	640
7,8	40	80	120	239	357	475

NOTE: ***Craig*** *a-3.* ***Feldstein*** *a-in most issues; c-1, 2i, 3-8.* ***Harrison*** *a-4.* ***Iger*** *a-6-8.* ***Ingels*** *a-1, 2, 4-7.* ***Palais*** *a-5.* ***Wood*** *a-7.* ***Wood/Harrison*** *a-5-7. (Canadian reprints known; see Table of Contents.)*

MOD LOVE
Western Publishing Co.: 1967 (50¢, 36 pgs.)

Issue	GD 2.0	VG 4.0	FN 6.0	VF 8.0	VF/NM 9.0	NM- 9.2
1-(Low print)	6	12	18	38	52	65

MODNIKS, THE
Gold Key: Aug, 1967 - No. 2, Aug, 1970

Issue	GD 2.0	VG 4.0	FN 6.0	VF 8.0	VF/NM 9.0	NM- 9.2
10206-708(#1)	4	8	12	24	32	40
2	3	6	9	16	21	26

MOD SQUAD (TV)
Dell Publishing Co.: Jan, 1969 - No. 3, Oct, 1969 - No. 8, April, 1971

Issue	GD 2.0	VG 4.0	FN 6.0	VF 8.0	VF/NM 9.0	NM- 9.2
1-Photo-c	8	16	24	53	74	95
2-4: 2-4-Photo-c	5	10	15	33	44	55
5-8: 8-Photo-c; Reprints #2	4	8	12	27	36	45

MOD WHEELS
Gold Key: Mar, 1971 - No. 19, Jan, 1976

Issue	GD 2.0	VG 4.0	FN 6.0	VF 8.0	VF/NM 9.0	NM- 9.2
1	4	8	12	29	40	50
2-9	3	6	9	18	23	28
10-19: 11,15-Extra 16 pgs. ads	2	4	6	14	18	22

MOE & SHMOE COMICS
O. S. Publ. Co.: Spring, 1948 - No. 2, Summer, 1948

Issue	GD 2.0	VG 4.0	FN 6.0	VF 8.0	VF/NM 9.0	NM- 9.2
1	9	18	27	49	62	75
2	6	12	18	31	38	45

MOEBIUS (Graphic novel)
Marvel Comics (Epic Comics): Oct, 1987 - No. 6, 1988; No. 7, 1990; No. 8, 1991 ($9.95, 8x11", mature)

Issue	GD 2.0	VG 4.0	FN 6.0	VF 8.0	VF/NM 9.0	NM- 9.2
1,2,4-6,8: (#2, 2nd printing, $9.95)						10.00
3,7,0: 3-(1st & 2nd printings, $12.95). 0 (1990, $12.95)						13.00
Moebius I-Signed & #'d hard-c ($45.95, Graphitti Designs, 1,500 copies printed)-r/#1-3						46.00

MOEBIUS COMICS
Caliber: May, 1996 - No. 6 ($2.95, B&W)

Issue	GD 2.0	VG 4.0	FN 6.0	VF 8.0	VF/NM 9.0	NM- 9.2
1-6: Moebius-c/a. 1-William Stout-a						3.00

MOEBIUS: THE MAN FROM CIGURI
Dark Horse Comics: 1996 ($7.95, digest-size)

Issue	GD 2.0	VG 4.0	FN 6.0	VF 8.0	VF/NM 9.0	NM- 9.2
nn-Moebius-c/a						8.00

MOLLY MANTON'S ROMANCES (Romantic Affairs #3)
Marvel Comics (SePI): Sept, 1949 - No. 2, Dec, 1949 (52 pgs.)

Issue	GD 2.0	VG 4.0	FN 6.0	VF 8.0	VF/NM 9.0	NM- 9.2
1-Photo-c (becomes Blaze the Wonder Collie #2 (10/49) on? & Molly Manton's Romances #2	16	32	48	92	131	170
2-Titled "Romances of..."; photo-c	11	22	33	62	84	105

MOLLY O'DAY (Super Sleuth)
Avon Periodicals: February, 1945 (1st Avon comic)

Issue	GD 2.0	VG 4.0	FN 6.0	VF 8.0	VF/NM 9.0	NM- 9.2
1-Molly O'Day, The Enchanted Dagger by Tuska (r/Yankee #1), Capt'n Courage, Corporal Grant app.	55	110	165	336	511	685

MOMENT OF SILENCE
Marvel Comics: Feb, 2002 ($3.50, one-shot)

Issue	GD 2.0	VG 4.0	FN 6.0	VF 8.0	VF/NM 9.0	NM- 9.2
1-Tributes to the heroes and victims of Sept. 11; s/a by various						3.50

MONA
Kitchen Sink Press: 1999 ($4.95, B&W, one-shot)

Issue	GD 2.0	VG 4.0	FN 6.0	VF 8.0	VF/NM 9.0	NM- 9.2
1-Cartoons by Kurtzman and various; Hernandez-c						5.00

MONARCHY, THE (Also see The Authority and StormWatch)
DC Comics (WildStorm): Apr, 2001 - No. 12, May, 2002 ($2.50)

The Monkees #8 © DELL

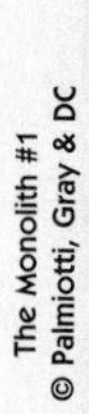

The Monolith #1 © Palmiotti, Gray & DC

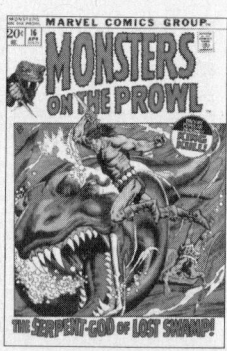

Monsters on the Prowl #16 © MAR

	GD 2.0	VG 4.0	FN 6.0	VF 8.0	VF/NM 9.0	NM- 9.2

1-McCrea & Leach-a/Young-s 2.50
2-12 2.50
Bullets Over Babylon TPB (2001, $12.95) r/#1-4, Authority #21 13.00

MONKEES, THE (TV)(Also see Circus Boy, Groovy, Not Brand Echh #3, Teen-Age Talk, Teen Beam & Teen Beat)
Dell Publishing Co.: March, 1967 - No. 17, Oct, 1969

1-Photo-c 11 22 33 80 120 160
2-17: All photo-c. 17-Reprints #1 7 14 21 51 71 90

MONKEY AND THE BEAR, THE
Atlas Comics (ZPC): Sept, 1953 - No. 3, Jan, 1954

1-Howie Post-c/a in all; funny animal 9 18 27 52 66 80
2,3 6 12 18 33 41 48

MONKEYMAN AND O'BRIEN (Also see Dark Horse Presents #80, 100-5, Gen[13]/..., Hellboy: Seed of Destruction, & San Diego Comic Con #2)
Dark Horse Comics (Legend): Jul, 1996 - No. 3, Sept, 1996 ($2.95, lim. series)

1-3: New stories; Art Adams-c/a/scripts 3.50
nn-(2/96, $2.95)-r/back-up stories from Hellboy: Seed of Destruction; Adams-c/a/scripts 3.50

MONKEYSHINES COMICS
Ace Periodicals/Publishers Specialists/Current Books/Unity Publ.: Summer, 1944 - No. 27, July, 1949

1-Funny animal 14 28 42 79 110 140
2-(Aut/44) 8 16 24 46 58 70
3-10: 3-(Win/44) 8 16 24 40 50 60
11-18,20-27: 23,24-Fago-c/a 7 14 21 37 46 55
19-Frazetta-a 8 16 24 46 58 70

MONKEY'S UNCLE, THE (See Merlin Jones As... under Movie Comics)

MONOLITH, THE
DC Comics: Apr, 2004 - Present ($3.50/$2.95)

1-($3.50) Palmiotti & Gray-s/Winslade-a 3.50
2-10-($2.95): 6-8-Batman app.; Coker-a 3.00

MONROES, THE (TV)
Dell Publishing Co.: Apr, 1967

1-Photo-c 3 7 10 21 28 35

MONSTER
Fiction House Magazines: 1953 - No. 2, 1953

1-Dr. Drew by Grandenetti; reprint from Rangers Comics #48; Whitman-c
50 100 150 305 465 625
2-Whitman-c 40 80 120 233 342 450

MONSTER CRIME COMICS (Also see Crime Must Stop)
Hillman Periodicals: Oct, 1952 (15¢, 52 pgs.)

1 (Scarce) 115 230 345 719 1110 1500

MONSTER FIGHTERS INC.
Image Comics (Bright Anvil Studios): Apr, 1999; Dec, 1999 ($3.50/$3.95)

1-Torres-s/Lubera & Yeung-a 3.50
...: The Black Book 1 (9/00, $3.50) Manapul-a 3.50
...The Ghosts of Christmas 1 (12/99, $3.95) 4.00

MONSTER HOWLS (Magazine)
Humor-Vision: December, 1966 (Satire) (35¢, 68 pgs.)

1 6 12 18 38 52 65

MONSTER HUNTERS
Charlton Comics: Aug, 1975 - No. 9, Jan, 1977; No. 10, Oct, 1977 - No. 18, Feb, 1979

1-Howard-a; Newton-c; 1st Countess Von Bludd and Colonel Whiteshroud
3 6 9 18 24 30
2-Sutton-c/a; Ditko-a 2 4 6 12 16 20
3,4,5,7: 4-Sutton-c/a 2 4 6 8 10 12
6,8,10: 6,8,10-Ditko-a 2 4 6 10 12 15
9,11,12 1 2 3 5 7 9
13,15,18-Ditko-c/a. 18-Sutton-a 2 4 6 10 12 15
14-Special all-Ditko issue 3 6 9 18 23 28
16,17-Sutton-a 1 2 3 5 7 9
1,2 (Modern Comics reprints, 1977) 4.00

NOTE: *Ditko a-2, 6, 8, 10, 13-15r, 18r; c-13-15, 18.* **Howard** *a-1, 3, 17; r-13.* **Morisi** *a-1.* **Staton** *a-1, 13.* **Sutton** *a-2, 4; c-2, 4; r-16-18.* **Zeck** *a-4-9. Reprints in #12-18.*

MONSTER MADNESS (Magazine)
Marvel Comics: 1972 - No. 3, 1973 (60¢, B&W)

1-3: Stories by "Sinister" Stan Lee 4 8 12 24 32 40

MONSTER MAN
Image Comics (Action Planet): Sept, 1997 ($2.95, B&W)

1-Mike Manley-c/s/a 3.00

MONSTER MASTERWORKS
Marvel Comics: 1989 ($12.95, TPB)

nn-Reprints 1960's monster stories; art by Kirby, Ditko, Ayers, Everett 13.00

MONSTER MATINEE
Chaos! Comics: Oct, 1997 - No. 3, Oct, 1997 ($2.50, limited series)

1-3: pin-ups 2.50

MONSTER MENACE
Marvel Comics: Dec, 1993 - No. 4, Mar, 1994 ($1.25, limited series)

1-4: Pre-code Atlas horror reprints. 4.00

NOTE: ***Ditko**-r & **Kirby**-r in all.*

MONSTER OF FRANKENSTEIN (See Frankenstein and Essential Monster of Frankenstein)

MONSTERS ATTACKS (Magazine)
Globe Communications Corpse: Sept, 1989 - No. 3, July, 1990 (B&W)

1-3-Ditko, Morrow, J. Severin-a 5.00

MONSTERS ON THE PROWL (Chamber of Darkness #1-8)
Marvel Comics Group (No. 13,14: 52 pgs.): No. 9, 2/71 - No. 27, 11/73; No. 28, 6/74 - No. 30, 10/74

9-Barry Smith inks 4 8 12 22 30 38
10-12,15: 12-Last 15¢ issue 2 4 6 14 18 22
13,14-(52 pgs.) 3 6 9 18 23 28
16-(4/72)-King Kull 4th app.; Severin-c 3 6 9 16 20 25
17-30 2 4 6 11 14 18

NOTE: ***Ditko** r-9, 14, 16. **Kirby** r-10-17, 21, 23, 25, 27, 28, 30; c-9, 25. **Kirby/Ditko** r-14, 17-20, 22, 24, 26, 29. **Marie/John Severin** a-16(Kull). 9-13, 15 contain one new story. Woodish art by **Reese**-11. King Kull created by Robert E. Howard.*

MONSTERS TO LAUGH WITH (Magazine) (Becomes Monsters Unlimited #4)
Marvel Comics Group: 1964 - No. 3, 1965 (B&W)

1-Humor by Stan Lee 7 14 21 51 70 90
2,3 4 8 12 29 40 50

MONSTERS UNLEASHED (Magazine)
Marvel Comics Group: July, 1973 - No. 11, Apr, 1975; Summer, 1975 (B&W)

1-Soloman Kane sty; Werewolf app. 4 8 12 25 33 42
2-4: 2-The Frankenstein Monster begins, ends #10. 3-Neal Adams-c/a; The Man-Thing begins (origin-r); Son of Satan preview. 4-Werewolf app. 3 7 10 21 28 35
5-7: Werewolf in all. 5-Man-Thing. 7-Williamson-a(r) 3 6 9 16 20 25
8-11: 8-Man-Thing; N. Adams-r. 9-Man-Thing; Wendigo app. 10-Origin Tigra
3 6 9 18 23 28
Annual 1 (Summer,1975, 92 pgs.)-Kane-a 3 6 9 16 20 25

NOTE: ***Boris** c-2, 6. **Brunner** a-2; c-11. **J. Buscema** a-2p, 4p, 5p. **Colan** a-1, 4r. **Davis** a-3r. **Everett** a-2r. **G. Kane** a-3. **Krigstein** r-4. **Morrow** a-3; c-1. **Perez** a-8. **Ploog** a-6. **Reese** a-1, 2. **Tuska** a-3p. **Wildey** a-1r.*

MONSTERS UNLIMITED (Magazine) (Formerly Monsters To Laugh With)
Marvel Comics Group: No. 4, 1965 - No. 7, 1966 (B&W)

4-7 4 8 12 27 36 45

MONSTER WORLD
DC Comics (WildStorm): Jul, 2001 - No. 4, Oct, 2001 ($2.50, limited series)

1-4-Lobdell-s/Meglia-c/a 2.50

MONTANA KID, THE (See Kid Montana)

MONTE HALE WESTERN (Movie star; Formerly Mary Marvel #1-28; also see Fawcett Movie Comic, Motion Picture Comics, Picture News #8, Real Western Hero, Six-Gun Heroes, Western Hero & XMas Comics)
Fawcett Publ./Charlton No. 83 on: No. 29, Oct, 1948 - No. 88, Jan, 1956

29-(#1, 52 pgs.)-Photo-c begin, end #82; Monte Hale & his horse Pardner begin
50 100 150 305 465 625
30-(52 pgs.)-Big Bow and Little Arrow begin, end #34; Captain Tootsie by Beck
27 54 81 152 219 285
31-36,38-40-(52 pgs.): 34-Gabby Hayes begins, ends #80. 39-Captain Tootsie by Beck
20 40 60 112 161 210
37,41,45,49-(36 pgs.) 15 30 45 85 120 155
42-44,46-48,50-(52 pgs.): 47-Big Bow & Little Arrow app.
16 32 48 92 131 170
51,52,54-56,58,59-(52 pgs.) 12 24 36 71 98 125
53,57-(36 pgs.): 53-Slim Pickens app. 10 20 30 60 80 100
60-81: 36 pgs. #60-on. 80-Gabby Hayes ends 10 20 30 58 77 95
82-Last Fawcett issue (6/53) 12 24 36 69 95 120
83-1st Charlton issue (2/55); B&W photo back-c begin. Gabby Hayes returns, ends #86

A Moon, A Girl... Romance #10 © WMG

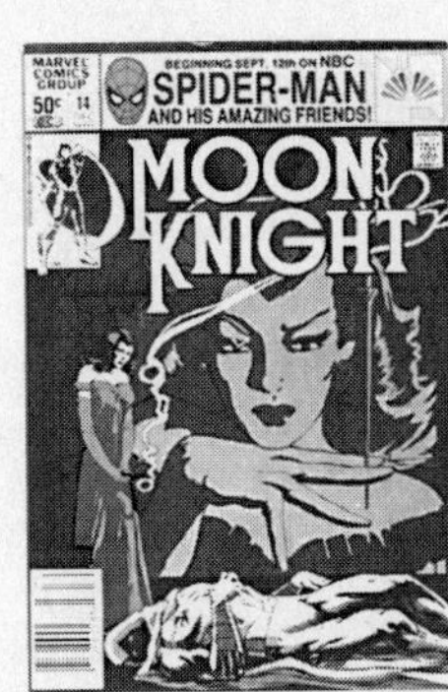

Moon Knight V1#14 © MAR

Moonshadow #7 © Dematteis & Muth

GD 2.0 | VG 4.0 | FN 6.0 | VF 8.0 | VF/NM 9.0 | NM- 9.2

14 28 42 79 110 140
84 (4/55) 10 20 30 60 80 100
85-86 10 20 30 58 77 95
87,88: 87-Wolverton-r, 1/2 pg. 88-Last issue 10 20 30 60 80 100
NOTE: *Gil Kane a-33?, 34? Rocky Lane -1 pg. (Carnation ad)-38, 40, 41, 43, 44, 46, 55.*

MONTY HALL OF THE U.S. MARINES (See With the Marines...)
Toby Press: Aug, 1951 - No. 11, Apr, 1953
1 11 22 33 66 91 115
2 8 16 24 40 50 60
3-5 7 14 21 37 46 55
6-11 7 14 21 35 43 50
NOTE: *Full page pin-ups (Pin-Up Pete) by* ***Jack Sparling*** *in #1-9.*

MOON, A GIRL...ROMANCE, A (Becomes Weird Fantasy #13 on; formerly Moon Girl #1-8)
E. C. Comics: No. 9, Sept-Oct, 1949 - No. 12, Mar-Apr, 1950
9-Moon Girl cameo 71 142 213 444 685 925
10,11 58 116 174 363 557 750
12-(Scarce) 71 142 213 444 685 925
NOTE: ***Feldstein, Ingels*** *art in all.* ***Feldstein*** *c-9-12.* ***Wood/Harrison*** *a-10-12. Canadian reprints known; see Table of Contents.*

MOON GIRL AND THE PRINCE (#1) (Moon Girl #2-6; Moon Girl Fights Crime #7, 8; becomes A Moon, A Girl, Romance #9 on)(Also see Animal Fables #7 and Happy Houlihans)
E. C. Comics: Fall, 1947 - No. 8, Summer, 1949
1-Origin Moon Girl (see Happy Houlihans #1) 96 192 288 600 925 1250
2 55 110 165 336 511 685
3,4: 4-Moon Girl vs. a vampire 48 96 114 293 447 600
5-E.C.'s 1st horror story, "Zombie Terror" 106 212 318 663 1019 1375
6-8 (Scarce): 7-Origin Star (Moongirl's sidekick) 55 110 165 336 511 685
NOTE: ***Craig*** *a-2, 5.; c-1,2.* ***Moldoff*** *a-1-8; c-2-6.* ***Wheelan's*** *Fat and Slat app. in #3, 4, 6. #2 & #3 are 52 pgs., #4 on, 36 pgs. Canadian reprints known; (see Table of Contents.)*

MOON KNIGHT (Also see The Hulk, Marc Spector..., Marvel Preview #21, Marvel Spotlight & Werewolf by Night #32)
Marvel Comics Group: Nov, 1980 - No. 38, Jul, 1984 (Mando paper #33 on)
1-Origin resumed in #4 5.00
2-15,25,35: 4-Intro Midnight Man. 25-Double size. 35-($1.00, 52 pgs.)-X-Men app.; F.F. cameo 3.00
16-24,26-34,36-38: 16-The Thing app. 2.50
NOTE: ***Austin*** *c-27i, 31i.* ***Cowan*** *a-16; c-16, 17.* ***Kaluta*** *c-36-38; back c-35.* ***Miller*** *c-9, 12p, 13p, 15p, 27p.* ***Ploog*** *back c-35.* ***Sienkiewicz*** *a-1-15, 17-20, 22-26, 28-30, 33i, 36(4), 37; c-1-5, 7, 8, 10, 11, 14-16, 18-26, 28-30, 31p, 33, 34.*

MOON KNIGHT
Marvel Comics Group: June, 1985 - V2#6, Dec, 1985
V2#1-6: 1-Double size; new costume. 6-Sienkiewicz painted-c. 2.50

MOON KNIGHT
Marvel Comics: Jan, 1998 - No. 4, Apr, 1998 ($2.50, limited series)
1-4-Moench-s/Edwards-c/a 2.50

MOON KNIGHT (Volume 3)
Marvel Comics: Jan, 1999 - No. 4, Feb, 1999 ($2.99, limited series)
1-4-Moench-s/Texeira-a(p) 3.00

MOON KNIGHT: DIVIDED WE FALL
Marvel Comics: 1992 ($4.95, 52 pgs.)
nn-Denys Cowan-c/a(p) 5.00

MOON KNIGHT SPECIAL
Marvel Comics: Oct, 1992 ($2.50, 52 pgs.)
1-Shang Chi, Master of Kung Fu-c/story 2.50

MOON KNIGHT SPECIAL EDITION
Marvel Comics Group: Nov, 1983 - No. 3, Jan, 1984 ($2.00, limited series, Baxter paper)
1-3: Reprints from Hulk mag. by Sienkiewicz 3.00

MOON MULLINS (See Popular Comics, Super Book #3 & Super Comics)
Dell Publishing Co.: 1941 - 1945
Four Color 14(1941) 34 68 102 255 403 550
Large Feature Comic 29(1941) 36 72 108 204 297 390
Four Color 31(1943) 20 40 60 141 216 290
Four Color 81(1945) 12 24 36 84 127 170

MOON MULLINS
Michel Publ. (American Comics Group)#1-6/St. John #7,8: Dec-Jan, 1947-48 - No. 8, 1949 (52 pgs)
1-Alternating Sunday & daily strip-r 22 44 66 123 177 230
2 11 22 33 66 91 115
3-8: 7,8-St. John Publ. 8-...Featuring Kayo on-c 11 22 33 62 84 105
NOTE: ***Milt Gross*** *a-2-6, 8.* ***Frank Willard*** *r-all.*

MOON PILOT
Dell Publishing Co.: No. 1313, Mar-May, 1962
Four Color 1313-Movie, photo-c 8 16 24 58 82 105

MOONSHADOW (Also see Farewell, Moonshadow)
Marvel Comics (Epic Comics): 5/85 - #12, 2/87 ($1.50/$1.75, mature)
(1st fully painted comic book)
1-Origin; J. M. DeMatteis scripts & Jon J. Muth painted-c/a. 6.00
2-12: 11-Origin 4.00
Trade paperback (1987?)-r/#1-12 14.00
Signed & numbered hard-c ($39.95, 1,200 copies)-r/#1-12 5 10 15 36 48 60

MOONSHADOW
DC Comics (Vertigo): Oct, 1994 - No. 12, Aug, 1995 ($2.25/$2.95)
1-11: Reprints Epic series. 2.50
12 ($2.95)-w/expanded ending 3.00
The Complete Moonshadow TPB ('98, $39.95) r/#1-12 and Farewell Moonshadow; new Muth painted-c 40.00

MOON-SPINNERS, THE (See Movie Comics)

MOONSTONE MONSTERS
Moonstone: 2003, 2004 ($2.95, B&W)
...: Demons ($2.95) - Short stories by various; Frenz-c 3.00
...: Ghosts ($2.95) - Short stories by various; Frenz-c 3.00
...: Sea Creatures ($2.95) - Short stories by various; Frenz-c 3.00
...: Witches ($2.95) - Short stories by various; Frenz-c 3.00

MOONSTONE NOIR
Moonstone: 2003 - Present ($2.95/$4.95/$5.50, B&W)
...: Bulldog Drummond (2004, $4.95) - Messner-Loebs-s/Barkley-a 5.00
...: Johnny Dollar ($4.95) - Gallaher-s/Theriault-a 5.00
...: Mr. Keen, Tracer of Lost Persons 1,2 ($2.95, limited series) - Ferguson-a 3.00
...: Mysterious Traveler (2003, $5.50) - Trevor Von Eeden-a/Joe Gentile-s 5.50
...: Mysterious Traveler Returns (2004, $4.95) - Trevor Von Eeden-a/Joe Gentile-s 5.00
...: The Lone Wolf ($4.95) - Jolley-s/Croall-a 5.00

MOPSY (See Pageant of Comics & TV Teens)
St. John Publ. Co.: Feb, 1948 - No. 19, Sept, 1953
1-Part-r; reprints "Some Punkins" by Neher 19 38 57 107 154 200
2 10 20 30 60 80 100
3-10(1953): 8-Lingerie panels 9 18 27 54 70 85
11-19: 19-Lingerie-c 9 18 27 51 62 75
NOTE: *#1, 3-6, 13, 18, 19 have paper dolls.*

MORBIUS REVISITED
Marvel Comic: Aug, 1993 - No. 5, Dec, 1993 ($1.95, mini-series)
1-5-Reprints Fear #27-31 2.25

MORBIUS: THE LIVING VAMPIRE (Also see Amazing Spider-Man #101,102, Fear #20, Marvel Team-Up #3, 4, Midnight Sons Unl. & Vampire Tales)
Marvel Comics (Midnight Sons imprint #16 on): Sep, 1992 - No. 32, Apr, 1995 ($1.75/$1.95)
1-($2.75, 52 pgs.)-Polybagged w/poster; Ghost Rider & Johnny Blaze x-over (part 3 of Rise of the Midnight Sons) 3.00
2-11,13-24,26-32: 3,4-Vs. Spider-Man-c/s.15-Ghost Rider app. 16-Spot varnish-c. 16,17-Siege of Darkness,parts 5 &13. 18-Deathlok app. 21-Bound-in Spider-Man trading card sheet; Spider-Man app. 2.25
12-($2.25)-Outer-c is a Darkhold envelope made of black parchment w/gold ink; Midnight Massacre x-over 2.50
25-($2.50, 52 pgs.)-Gold foil logo 2.50

MORE FUN COMICS (Formerly New Fun Comics #1-6)
National Periodical Publications: No. 7, Jan, 1936 - No. 127, Nov-Dec, 1947 (No. 7,9-11: paper-c)
7(1/36)-Oversized, paper-c; 1 pg. Kelly-a 780 1560 2340 5600 - -
8(2/36)-Oversized (10x12"), paper-c; 1 pg. Kelly-a; Sullivan-c 780 1560 2340 5600 - -
9(3-4/36)(Very rare, 1st standard-sized comic book with original material)-Last multiple panel-c 935 1870 2805 6700 - -
10,11(7/36): 10-Last Henri Duval by Siegel & Shuster. 11-1st "Calling All Cars" by Siegel & Shuster; new classic logo begins 545 1090 1635 3900 - -
12(8/36)-Slick-c begin 430 860 1290 3100 - -
V2#1(9/36, #13) 395 790 1185 2850 - -
2(10/36, #14)-Dr. Occult in costume (1st in color)(Superman proto-type; 1st DC

More Fun Comics #61 © DC

More Fun Comics #117 © DC

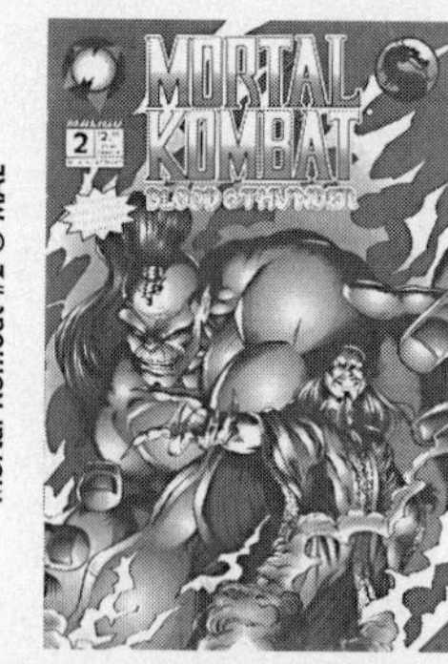

Mortal Kombat #2 © MAL

GD VG FN VF VF/NM NM-
2.0 4.0 6.0 8.0 9.0 9.2

appearance) continues from The Comics Magazine, ends #17
1850 3700 5550 13,200 - -
V2#3(11/36, #15), 16(V2#4), 17(V2#5): 16-Cover numbering begins; Xmas-c; last Superman tryout issue 745 1490 2235 5300 - -
18-20(V2#8, 5/37) 300 600 900 2150 - -
21(V2#9)-24(V2#12, 9/37) 276 552 828 1518 2009 2500
25(V3#1, 10/37)-27(V3#3, 12/37): 27-Xmas-c 276 552 828 1518 2009 2500
28-30: 30-1st non-funny cover 250 500 750 1375 1813 2250
31-Has ad for Action #1 265 530 795 1458 1929 2400
32-35: 32-Last Dr. Occult 250 500 750 1375 1813 2250
36-40: 36-(10/38)-The Masked Ranger & sidekick Pedro begins; Ginger Snap by Bob Kane (2 pgs.; 1st-a?). 39-Xmas-c 250 500 750 1375 1813 2250
41-50: 41-Last Masked Ranger 212 424 636 1166 1583 2000
51-The Spectre app. (in costume) in one panel ad at end of Buccaneer story
741 1482 2223 4076 5538 7000
52-(2/40)-Origin/1st app. The Spectre (in costume splash panel only), part 1 by Bernard Baily (parts 1 & 2 written by Jerry Siegel; Spectre's costume changes color from purple & blue to green & grey; last Wing Brady; Spectre-c 5350 10,700 16,050 40,400 65,200 90,000
53-Origin The Spectre (in costume at end of story), part 2; Capt. Desmo begins; Spectre-c 2575 5150 7725 18,400 32,200 46,000
54-The Spectre in costume; last King Carter; classic-Spectre-c
1118 2236 3354 8385 13,693 19,000
55-(Scarce, 5/40)-Dr. Fate begins (1st app.); last Bulldog Martin; Spectre-c
1235 2470 3705 9263 15,132 21,000
56-1st Dr. Fate-c (classic), origin continues. Congo Bill begins (6/40), 1st app.;
613 1226 1839 4291 6896 9500
57-60-All Spectre-c 366 732 1098 2379 3840 5300
61,65: 61-Classic Dr. Fate-c. 65-Classic Spectre-c 338 676 1014 2197 3549 4900
62-64,66: 63-Last St. Bob Neal. 64-Lance Larkin begins; all Spectre-c
300 600 900 1908 3004 4100
67-(5/41)-Origin (1st) Dr. Fate; last Congo Bill & Biff Bronson (Congo Bill continues in Action Comics #37, 6/41)-Spectre-c 677 1354 2031 4739 7620 10,500
68-70: 68-Clip Carson begins. 70-Last Lance Larkin; all Dr. Fate-c
246 492 738 1538 2369 3200
71-Origin & 1st app. Johnny Quick by Mort Weisinger (9/41); classic sci/fi Dr. Fate-c
516 1032 1548 3612 5806 8000
72-Dr. Fate's new helmet; last Sgt. Carey, Sgt. O'Malley & Captain Desmo; German submarine-c (only German war-c) 242 484 726 1513 2332 3150
73-Origin & 1st app. Aquaman (11/41) by Paul Norris; intro. Green Arrow & Speedy; Dr. Fate-c 1176 2352 3528 8820 14,410 20,000
74-2nd Aquaman; 1st Percival Popp, Supercop; Dr. Fate-c
296 592 888 1850 2850 3850
75,76: 75-New origin Spectre; Nazi spy ring cover w/Hitler's photo. 76-Last Dr. Fate-c; Johnny Quick (by Meskin #76-97) begins, ends #107; last Clip Carson
246 492 738 1538 2369 3200
77-80: 77-Green Arrow-c begin 204 408 612 1275 1963 2650
81-83,85,88,90: 81-Last large logo. 82-1st small logo.
133 266 399 831 1278 1725
84-Green Arrow Japanese war-c 136 272 408 850 1313 1775
86,87-Johnny Quick-c. 87-Last Radio Squad 133 266 399 831 1278 1725
89-Origin Green Arrow & Speedy Team-up 142 284 426 888 1369 1850
91-97,99: 91-1st bi-monthly issue. 93-Dover & Clover begin (1st app., 9-10/43). 97-Kubert-a 87 174 261 544 835 1125
98-Last Dr. Fate (scarce) 104 208 312 650 1000 1350
100 (11-12/44)-Johnny Quick-c 121 242 363 756 1166 1575
101-Origin & 1st app. Superboy (1-2/45)(not by Siegel & Shuster); last Spectre issue; Green Arrow-c 839 1678 2517 5873 9437 13,000
102-2nd Superboy app; 1st Dover & Clover-c 131 262 393 819 1260 1700
103-3rd Superboy app; last Green Arrow-c 98 196 294 613 944 1275
104-1st Superboy-c w/Dover & Clover 85 170 255 531 816 1100
105,106-Superboy-c 79 158 237 494 760 1025
107-Last Johnny Quick & Superboy 79 158 237 494 760 1025
108-120: 108-Genius Jones begins; 1st c-app. (3-4/46; cont'd from Adventure Comics #102)
24 48 72 138 199 260
121-124,126: 121-123,126-Post funny animal (Jimminy & the Magic Book)-c
22 44 66 125 180 235
125-Superman c-app.w/Jimminy 77 154 231 481 741 1000
127-(Scarce)-Post-c/a 37 74 111 209 305 400

NOTE: *All issues are scarce to rare. Cover features: The Spectre-#52-55, 57-60, 62-67. Dr. Fate-#56, 61, 68-76. The Green Arrow & Speedy-#77-85, 88-97, 99, 101 (w/Dover & Clover-#98, 103). Johnny Quick-#86, 87, 100. Dover & Clover-#102, (104, 106 w/Superboy), 107, 108(w/Genius Jones), 110, 112, 114, 117, 119. Genius Jones-#109, 111, 113, 115, 118, 120.* ***Baily*** *a-45, 52-on; c-52-55, 57-60, 62-67.* ***Al Capp*** *a-45(signed Koppy).* ***Ellsworth*** *c-7.* ***Creig Flessel*** *c-30, 31, 35-48(most).* ***Guardineer*** *c-47, 49, 50.* ***Kiefer*** *a-20.* ***Meskin*** *c-86, 87, 100?* ***Moldoff*** *c-51.* ***George Papp*** *c-77-85.* ***Post*** *c-121-127.* ***Vincent Sullivan*** *c-8-28, 32-34.*

MORE FUND COMICS (Benefit book for the Comic Book Legal Defense Fund)
(Also see Even More Fund Comics)
Sky Dog Press: Sept, 2003 ($10.00, B&W, trade paperback)
nn-Anthology of short stories and pin-ups by various; Hulk-c by Pérez 10.00

MORE SEYMOUR (See Seymour My Son)
Archie Publications: Oct, 1963
1-DeCarlo-a? 3 7 10 21 28 35

MORE THAN MORTAL (Also see Lady Pendragon/...)
Liar Comics: June, 1997 - No. 4, Apr, 1998 ($2.95, limited series)
Image Comics: No. 5, Dec, 1999 - Present ($2.95)
1-Blue forest background-c, 1-Variant-c 4.00
1-White-c 6.00
1-2nd printing; purple sky cover 3.00
2-4: 3-Silvestri-c, 4-Two-c, one by Randy Queen 3.00
5,6: 5-1st Image Comics issue 3.00

MORE THAN MORTAL: OTHERWORLDS
Image Comics: July, 1999 - No. 4, Dec, 1999 ($2.95, limited series)
1-4-Firchow-a. 1-Two covers 3.00

MORE THAN MORTAL SAGAS
Liar Comics: Jun, 1998 - No. 3, Dec, 1998 ($2.95, limited series)
1,2-Painted art by Romano. 2-Two-c, one by Firchow 3.00
1-Variant-c by Linsner 5.00

MORE THAN MORTAL TRUTHS AND LEGENDS
Liar Comics: Aug, 1998 - No. 6, Apr, 1999 ($2.95)
1-6-Firchow-a(p) 3.00
1-Variant-c by Dan Norton 4.50

MORE TRASH FROM MAD (Annual)
E. C. Comics: 1958 - No. 12, 1969
(Note: Bonus missing = half price)
nn(1958)-8 pgs. color Mad reprint from #20 21 42 63 150 230 310
2(1959)-Market Product Labels 15 30 45 109 167 225
3(1960)-Text book covers 14 28 42 97 149 200
4(1961)-Sing Along with Mad booklet 14 28 42 97 149 200
5(1962)-Window Stickers; r/from Mad #39 10 20 30 73 107 140
6(1963)-TV Guise booklet 10 20 30 73 107 140
7(1964)-Alfred E. Neuman commemorative stamps 9 18 27 60 85 110
8(1965)-Life size poster-Alfred E. Neuman 7 14 21 46 63 80
9-12: 9,10(1966-67)-Mischief Sticker. 11(1968)-Campaign poster & bumper sticker. 12(1969)-Pocket medals 7 14 21 46 63 80
NOTE: ***Kelly Freas*** *c-1, 2, 4.* ***Mingo*** *c-3, 5-9, 12.*

MORGAN THE PIRATE (Movie)
Dell Publishing Co.: No. 1227, Sept-Nov, 1961
Four Color 1227-Photo-c 9 18 27 63 89 115

MORLOCKS
Marvel Comics: June, 2002 - No. 4, Sept, 2002 ($2.50, limited series)
1-4-Johns-s/Martinbrough-c/a 2.50

MORLOCK 2001
Atlas/Seaboard Publ.: Feb, 1975 - No. 3, July, 1975
1,2: 1-(Super-hero)-Origin & 1st app.; Milgrom-c 1 2 3 5 6 8
3-Ditko/Wrightson-a; origin The Midnight Man & The Mystery Men
1 3 4 6 8 10

MORNINGSTAR SPECIAL
Comico: Apr, 1990 ($2.50)
1-From the Elementals; Willingham-c/a/scripts 3.00

MORRIGAN
Dimension X: Aug, 1993 ($2.75, B&W)
1-Foil stamped-c 3.00

MORRIGAN
Sirius Entertainment: 1997 ($2.95, limited series)
1-Tenuta-c/a 3.00

MORTAL KOMBAT
Malibu Comics: July, 1994 - No. 6, Dec, 1994 ($2.95)
1-6: 1-Two diff. covers exist 3.00
1-Limited edition gold foil embossed-c 4.00
0 (12/94), Special Edition 1 (11/94) 3.00
Tournament Edition I12/94, $3.95), II('95)($3.95) 4.00

The Moth #1 © Steve Rude & Gary Martin

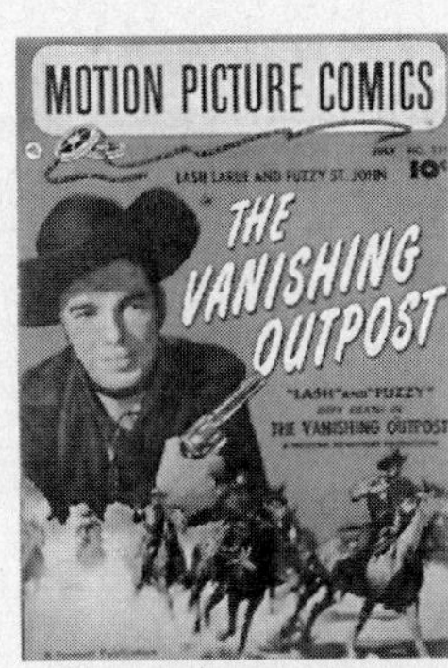

Motion Picture Comics #111 © FAW

Movie Classics - The Incredible Mr. Limpet © DELL

	GD 2.0	VG 4.0	FN 6.0	VF 8.0	VF/NM 9.0	NM- 9.2

...: **BARAKA** ,June, 1995 ($2.95, one-shot) #1; ...**BATTLEWAVE** ,2/95 - No. 6, 7/95 , #1-6; ...**GORO, PRINCE OF PAIN** ,9/94 - No. 3, 11/94, #1-3; ...**KITANA AND MILEENA** ,8/95 , ...**KUNG LAO** ,7/95 , #1; ... **RAYDON & KANO** ,3/95 - No. 3, 5/95, #1-3: ...(all $2.95-c) 3.00

...: **U.S. SPECIAL FORCES** ,1/95 - No. 2, ($3.50), #1,2 3.50

MORTIE (Mazie's Friend; also see Flat-Top)
Magazine Publishers: Dec, 1952 - No. 4, June, 1953?

1 9 18 27 51 62 75
2-4 6 12 18 27 33 38

MORTIGAN GOTH: IMMORTALIS (See Marvel Frontier Comics Unlimited)
Marvel Comics: Sept, 1993 - No. 4, Mar, 1994 ($1.95, mini-series)

1-($2.95)-Foil-c 3.00
2-4 2.25

MORT THE DEAD TEENAGER
Marvel Comics: Nov, 1993 - No. 4, Mar, 1994 ($1.75, mini-series)

1-4 2.25

MORTY MEEKLE
Dell Publishing Co.: No. 793, May, 1957

Four Color 793 3 7 10 21 28 35

MOSES & THE TEN COMMANDMENTS (See Dell Giants)

MOSTLY WANTED
DC Comics (WildStorm): Jul, 2000 - No. 4, Nov, 2000 ($2.50, limited series)

1-4-Lobdell-s/Flores-a 2.50

MOTH, THE
Dark Horse Comics: Apr, 2004 - Present ($2.99)

1-4-Steve Rude-c/a; Gary Martin-s 3.00
... Special (3/04, $4.95) 5.00

MOTHER GOOSE AND NURSERY RHYME COMICS (See Christmas With Mother Goose)
Dell Publishing Co.: No. 41, 1944 - No. 862, Nov, 1957

Four Color 41-Walt Kelly-c/a 25 50 75 177 271 365
Four Color 59, 68-Kelly c/a 21 42 63 148 227 305
Four Color 862-The Truth About..., Movie (Disney) 9 18 27 60 85 110

MOTHER TERESA OF CALCUTTA
Marvel Comics Group: 1984

1-(52 pgs.) No ads 4.00

MOTION PICTURE COMICS (See Fawcett Movie Comics)
Fawcett Publications: No. 101, 1950 - No. 114, Jan, 1953 (All-photo-c)

101- "Vanishing Westerner"; Monte Hale (1950) 31 62 93 175 253 330
102- "Code of the Silver Sage"; Rocky Lane (1/51) 28 56 84 158 229 300
103- "Covered Wagon Raid"; Rocky Lane (3/51) 28 56 84 158 229 300
104- "Vigilante Hideout"; Rocky Lane (5/51)-Book length Powell-a 28 56 84 158 229 300
105- "Red Badge of Courage"; Audie Murphy; Bob Powell-a (7/51) 34 68 102 196 283 370
106- "The Texas Rangers"; George Montgomery (9/51) 29 58 87 164 237 310
107- "Frisco Tornado"; Rocky Lane (11/51) 26 52 78 147 211 275
108- "Mask of the Avenger"; John Derek 20 40 60 112 161 210
109- "Rough Rider of Durango"; Rocky Lane 27 54 81 152 219 285
110- "When Worlds Collide"; George Evans-a (5/52); Williamson & Evans drew themselves in story; (also see Famous Funnies No. 72-88) 96 192 288 600 925 1250
111- "The Vanishing Outpost"; Lash LaRue 32 64 96 184 267 350
112- "Brave Warrior"; Jon Hall & Jay Silverheels 19 38 57 107 154 200
113- "Walk East on Beacon"; George Murphy; Schaffenberger-a 14 28 42 81 113 145
114- "Cripple Creek"; George Montgomery (1/53) 15 30 45 85 120 155

MOTION PICTURE FUNNIES WEEKLY (See Promotional Comics section)

MOTORHEAD (See Comic's Greatest World)
Dark Horse Comics: Aug, 1995 - No. 6, Jan, 1996 ($2.50)

1-6: Bisley-c on all. 1-Predator app. 2.50
Special 1 (3/94, $3.95, 52pgs.)-Jae Lee-c; Barb Wire, The Machine & Wolf Gang app. 4.00

MOTORMOUTH (... & Killpower #7? on)
Marvel Comics UK: June, 1992 - No. 12, May, 1993 ($1.75)

1-13: 1,2-Nick Fury app. 3-Punisher-c/story. 5,6-Nick Fury & Punisher app. 6-Cable cameo. 7-9-Cable app. 2.25

MOUNTAIN MEN (See Ben Bowie)

MOUSE MUSKETEERS (See M.G.M.'s...)

MOUSE ON THE MOON, THE (See Movie Classics)

MOVIE CLASSICS
Dell Publishing Co.: Apr, 1956; May-Jul, 1962 - Dec, 1969

(Before 1963, most movie adaptations were part of the 4-Color series)
(Disney movie adaptations after 1970 are in Walt Disney Showcase)

Around the World Under the Sea 12-030-612 (12/66) 4 8 12 24 32 40
Bambi 3(4/56)-Disney; r/4-Color #186 4 8 12 28 38 48
Battle of the Bulge 12-056-606 (6/66) 4 8 12 25 33 42
Beach Blanket Bingo 12-058-509 8 16 24 55 78 100
Bon Voyage 01-068-212 (12/62)-Disney; photo-c 4 8 12 27 36 45
Castilian, The 12-110-401 4 8 12 24 32 40
Cat, The 12-109-612 (12/66) 4 8 12 22 30 38
Cheyenne Autumn 12-112-506 (4-6/65) 6 12 18 43 59 75
Circus World, Samuel Bronston's 12-115-411; John Wayne app.; John Wayne photo-c 11 22 33 77 114 150
Countdown 12-150-710 (10/67)-James Caan photo-c 4 8 12 25 33 42
Creature, The 1 (12-142-302) (12-2/62-63) 8 16 24 58 82 105
Creature, The 12-142-410 (10/64) 6 12 18 38 52 65
David Ladd's Life Story 12-173-212 (10-12/62)-Photo-c 8 16 24 58 82 105
Die, Monster, Die 12-175-603 (3/66)-Photo-c 6 12 18 40 55 70
Dirty Dozen 12-180-710 (10/67) 5 10 15 36 48 60
Dr. Who & the Daleks 12-190-612 (12/66)-Peter Cushing photo-c; 1st U.S. app. of Dr. Who 11 22 33 77 114 150
Dracula 12-231-212 (10-12/62) 7 14 21 51 71 90
El Dorado 12-240-710 (10/67)-John Wayne; photo-c 13 26 39 92 141 190
Ensign Pulver 12-257-410 (8-10/64) 4 8 12 22 30 38
Frankenstein 12-283-305 (3-5/63)(see Frankenstein 8-10/64 for 2nd printing) 8 16 24 53 74 95
Great Race, The 12-299-603 (3/66)-Natallie Wood, Tony Curtis photo-c 5 10 15 36 48 60
Hallelujah Trail, The 12-307-602 (2/66) (Shows 1/66 inside); Burt Lancaster, Lee Remick photo-c 6 12 18 38 52 65
Hatari 12-340-301 (1/63)-John Wayne 9 18 27 63 89 115
Horizontal Lieutenant, The 01-348-210 (10/62) 4 8 12 22 30 38
Incredible Mr. Limpet, The 12-370-408; Don Knotts photo-c 5 10 15 33 44 55
Jack the Giant Killer 12-374-301 (1/63) 9 18 27 63 89 115
Jason & the Argonauts 12-376-310 (8-10/63)-Photo-c 10 20 30 72 104 135
Lancelot & Guinevere 12-416-310 (10/63) 6 12 18 40 55 70
Lawrence 12-426-308 (8/63)-Story of Lawrence of Arabia; movie ad on back-c; not exactly like movie 6 12 18 40 55 70
Lion of Sparta 12-439-301 (1/63) 4 8 12 27 36 45
Mad Monster Party 12-460-801 (9/67)-Based on Kurtzman's screenplay 9 18 27 60 85 110
Magic Sword, The 01-496-209 (9/62) 6 12 18 43 59 75
Masque of the Red Death 12-490-410 (8-10/64)-Vincent Price photo-c 7 14 21 50 68 85
Maya 12-495-612 (12/66)-Clint Walker & Jay North part photo-c 4 8 12 29 40 50
McHale's Navy 12-500-412 (10-12/64) 5 10 15 36 48 60
Merrill's Marauders 12-510-301 (1/63)-Photo-c 4 8 12 22 30 38
Mouse on the Moon, The 12-530-312 (10/12/63)-Photo-c 4 8 12 27 36 45
Mummy, The 12-537-211 (9-11/62) 2 versions with different back-c 8 16 24 55 78 100
Music Man, The 12-538-301 (1/63) 4 8 12 24 32 40
Naked Prey, The 12-545-612 (12/66)-Photo-c 6 12 18 43 59 75
Night of the Grizzly, The 12-558-612 (12/66)-Photo-c 4 8 12 27 36 45
None But the Brave 12-565-506 (4-6/65) 6 12 18 43 59 75
Operation Bikini 12-597-310 (10/63)-Photo-c 4 8 12 24 32 40
Operation Crossbow 12-590-512 (10-12/65) 4 8 12 24 32 40
Prince & the Pauper, The 01-654-207 (5-7/62)-Disney 4 8 12 27 36 45
Raven, The 12-680-309 (9/63)-Vincent Price photo-c 7 14 21 46 63 80
Ring of Bright Water 01-701-910 (10/69) (inside shows #12-701-909) 4 8 12 27 36 45
Runaway, The 12-707-412 (10-12/64) 4 8 12 22 30 38
Santa Claus Conquers the Martians #? (1964)-Photo-c 10 20 30 72 104 135
Santa Claus Conquers the Martians 12-725-603 (3/66, 12¢)-Reprints 1964 issue;

Movie Comics #3 © FH

Movie Comics - First Men in the Moon © DELL

Movie Comics - The Gnome Mobile © WDC

	GD 2.0	VG 4.0	FN 6.0	VF 8.0	VF/NM 9.0	NM- 9.2
photo-c	8	16	24	58	82	105
Another version given away with a Golden Record, SLP 170, nn, no price (3/66)-Complete with record	14	28	42	102	156	210
Six Black Horses 12-750-301 (1/63)-Photo-c	4	8	12	24	32	40
Ski Party 12-743-511 (9-11/65)-Frankie Avalon photo-c; photo inside-c; Adkins-a	6	12	18	38	52	65
Smoky 12-746-702 (2/67)	4	8	12	22	30	38
Sons of Katie Elder 12-748-511 (9-11/65); John Wayne app.; photo-c	13	26	39	94	145	195
Tales of Terror 12-793-302 (2/63)-Evans-a	6	12	18	43	59	75
Three Stooges Meet Hercules 01-828-208 (8/62)-Photo-c	10	20	30	72	104	135
Tomb of Ligeia 12-830-506 (4-6/65)	6	12	18	43	59	75
Treasure Island 01-845-211 (7-9/62)-Disney; r/4-Color #624	4	8	12	24	32	40
Twice Told Tales (Nathaniel Hawthorne) 12-840-401 (11-1/63-64); Vincent Price photo-c	7	14	21	46	63	80
Two on a Guillotine 12-850-506 (4-6/65)	4	8	12	27	36	45
Valley of Gwangi 01-880-912 (12/69)	10	20	30	72	104	135
War Gods of the Deep 12-900-509 (7-9/65)	4	8	12	24	32	40
War Wagon, The 12-533-709 (9/67); John Wayne app.	10	20	30	67	96	125
Who's Minding the Mint? 12-924-708 (8/67)	4	8	12	22	30	38
Wolfman, The 12-922-308 (6-8/63)	8	16	24	53	74	95
Wolfman, The 1(12-922-410)(8-10/64)-2nd printing; r/#12-922-308	4	8	12	28	38	48
Zulu 12-950-410 (8-10/64)-Photo-c	9	18	27	60	85	110

MOVIE COMICS (See Cinema Comics Herald & Fawcett Movie Comics)

MOVIE COMICS

National Periodical Publications/Picture Comics: April, 1939 - No. 6, Sept-Oct, 1939 (Most all photo-c)

	GD 2.0	VG 4.0	FN 6.0	VF 8.0	VF/NM 9.0	NM- 9.2
1- "Gunga Din", "Son of Frankenstein", "The Great Man Votes", "Fisherman's Wharf", & "Scouts to the Rescue" part 1; Wheelan "Minute Movies" begin	331	662	993	2152	3476	4800
2- "Stagecoach", "The Saint Strikes Back", "King of the Turf","Scouts to the Rescue" part 2, "Arizona Legion", Andy Devine photo-c	231	462	693	1444	2222	3000
3- "East Side of Heaven", "Mystery in the White Room", "Four Feathers", "Mexican Rose" with Gene Autry, "Spirit of Culver", "Many Secrets", "The Mikado" (1st Gene Autry photo cover)	165	330	495	1031	1591	2150
4- "Captain Fury", Gene Autry in "Blue Montana Skies", "Streets of N.Y." with Jackie Cooper, "Oregon Trail" part 1 with Johnny Mack Brown, "Big Town Czar" with Barton MacLane, & "Star Reporter" with Warren Hull	131	262	393	819	1260	1700
5- "The Man in the Iron Mask", "Five Came Back", "Wolf Call", "The Girl & the Gambler", "The House of Fear", "The Family Next Door", "Oregon Trail" part 2	154	308	462	963	1482	2000
6- "The Phantom Creeps", "Chumps at Oxford", & "The Oregon Trail" part 3; 2nd Robot-c	192	384	576	1200	1850	2500

NOTE: *Above books contain many original movie stills with dialogue from movie scripts. All issues are scarce.*

MOVIE COMICS

Fiction House Magazines: Dec, 1946 - No. 4, 1947

	GD 2.0	VG 4.0	FN 6.0	VF 8.0	VF/NM 9.0	NM- 9.2
1-Big Town (by Lubbers), Johnny Danger begin; Celardo-a; Mitzi of the Movies by Fran Hopper	55	110	165	340	520	700
2-(2/47)- "White Tie & Tails" with William Bendix; Mitzi of the Movies begins by Matt Baker, ends #4	40	80	120	241	363	485
3-(6/47)-Andy Hardy starring Mickey Rooney	40	80	120	241	363	485
4-Mitzi In Hollywood by Matt Baker; Merton of the Movies with Red Skelton; Yvonne DeCarlo & George Brent in "Slave Girl"	48	96	144	293	447	600

MOVIE COMICS

Gold Key/Whitman: Oct, 1962 - 1984

	GD 2.0	VG 4.0	FN 6.0	VF 8.0	VF/NM 9.0	NM- 9.2
Alice in Wonderland 10144-503 (3/65)-Disney; partial reprint of 4-Color #331	4	8	12	27	36	45
Alice In Wonderland #1 (Whitman pre-pack, 3/84)	2	4	6	8	10	12
Aristocats, The 1 (30045-103)(3/71)-Disney; with pull-out poster (25¢) (No poster = half price)	8	16	24	58	82	105
Bambi 1 (10087-309)(9/63)-Disney; r/4-C #186	4	8	12	29	40	50
Bambi 2 (10087-607)(7/66)-Disney; r/4-C #186	4	8	12	24	32	40
Beneath the Planet of the Apes 30044-012 (12/70)-with pull-out poster; photo-c (No poster = half price)	10	20	30	72	104	135
Big Red 10026-211 (11/62)-Disney; photo-c	4	8	12	24	32	40
Big Red 10026-503 (3/65)-Disney; reprints 10026-211; photo-c	3	6	9	18	24	30
Blackbeard's Ghost 10222-806 (6/68)-Disney	4	8	12	22	30	38
Bullwhip Griffin 10181-706 (6/67)-Disney; Spiegle-a; photo-c	4	8	12	27	36	45
Captain Sindbad 10077-309 (9/63)-Manning-a; photo-c	7	14	21	50	68	85
Chitty Chitty Bang Bang 1 (30038-902)(2/69)-with pull-out poster; Disney; photo-c (No poster = half price)	8	16	24	53	74	95
Cinderella 10152-508 (8/65)-Disney; r/4-C #786	5	10	15	33	44	55
Darby O'Gill & the Little People 10251-001(1/70)-Disney; reprints 4-Color #1024 (Toth-a); photo-c	6	12	18	38	52	65
Dumbo 1 (10090-310)(10/63)-Disney; r/4-C #668	4	8	12	25	33	42
Emil & the Detectives 10120-502 (11/64)-Disney; photo-c	4	8	12	24	32	40
Escapade in Florence 1 (10043-301)(1/63)-Disney; starring Annette Funicello	9	18	27	63	89	115
Fall of the Roman Empire 10118-407 (7/64); Sophia Loren photo-c	4	8	12	27	36	45
Fantastic Voyage 10178-702 (2/67)-Wood/Adkins-a; photo-c	6	12	18	43	59	75
55 Days at Peking 10081-309 (9/63)-Photo-c	4	8	12	24	32	40
Fighting Prince of Donegal, The 10193-701 (1/67)-Disney	4	8	12	22	30	38
First Men in the Moon 10132-503 (3/65)-Fred Fredericks-a; photo-c	4	8	12	25	33	42
Gay Purr-ee 30017-301(1/63, 84 pgs.)	6	12	18	40	55	70
Gnome Mobile, The 10207-710 (10/67)-Disney	4	8	12	27	36	45
Goodbye, Mr. Chips 10246-006 (6/70)-Peter O'Toole photo-c	4	8	12	24	32	40
Happiest Millionaire, The 10221-804 (4/68)-Disney	4	8	12	27	36	45
Hey There, It's Yogi Bear 10122-409 (9/64)-Hanna-Barbera	8	16	24	53	74	95
Horse Without a Head, The 10109-401 (1/64)-Disney	4	8	12	22	30	38
How the West Was Won 10074-307 (7/63)-Based on the L'Amour novel; Tufts-a	5	10	15	36	48	60
In Search of the Castaways 10048-303 (3/63)-Disney; Hayley Mills photo-c	8	16	24	53	74	95
Jungle Book, The 1 (6022-801)(1/68-Whitman)-Disney; large size (10x13-1/2"); 59¢	8	16	24	53	74	95
Jungle Book, The 1 (30033-803)(3/68, 68 pgs.)-Disney; same contents as Whitman #1	4	8	12	29	40	50
Jungle Book, The 1 (6/78, $1.00 tabloid)	3	6	9	18	24	30
Jungle Book (7/84)-r/Giant; Whitman pre-pack	2	4	6	8	10	12
Kidnapped 10080-306 (6/63)-Disney; reprints 4-Color #1101; photo-c	4	8	12	24	32	40
King Kong 30036-809(9/68-68 pgs.)-painted-c	4	8	12	29	40	50
King Kong nn-Whitman Treasury($1.00, 68 pgs.,1968), same cover as Gold Key issue	6	12	18	40	55	70
King Kong 11299(#1-786, 10x13-1/4", 68 pgs., $1.00, 1978)	3	6	9	18	24	30
Lady and the Tramp 10042-301 (1/63)-Disney; r/4-Color #629	4	8	12	25	33	42
Lady and the Tramp 1 (1967-Giant; 25¢)-Disney; reprints part of Dell #1	6	12	18	43	59	75
Lady and the Tramp 2 (10042-203)(3/72)-Disney; r/4-Color #629	3	6	9	18	24	30
Legend of Lobo, The 1 (10059-303)(3/63)-Disney; photo-c	3	6	9	18	24	30
Lt. Robin Crusoe, U.S.N. 10191-610 (10/66)-Disney; Dick Van Dyke photo-c	3	7	10	21	28	35
Lion, The 10035-301 (1/63)-Photo-c	3	6	9	19	25	32
Lord Jim 10156-509 (9/65)-Photo-c	3	6	9	19	25	32
Love Bug, The 10237-906 (6/69)-Disney; Buddy Hackett photo-c	4	8	12	24	32	40
Mary Poppins 10136-501 (1/65)-Disney; photo-c	5	10	15	36	48	60
Mary Poppins 30023-501 (1/65-68 pgs.)-Disney; photo-c	8	16	24	53	74	95
McLintock 10110-403 (3/64); John Wayne app.; John Wayne & Maureen O'Hara photo-c	13	26	39	90	138	185
Merlin Jones as the Monkey's Uncle 10115-510 (10/65)-Disney; Annette Funicello front/back photo-c	7	14	21	46	63	80
Miracle of the White Stallions, The 10065-306 (6/63)-Disney	4	8	12	22	30	38
Misadventures of Merlin Jones, The 10115-405 (5/64)-Disney; Annette Funicello photo front/back-c	7	14	21	46	63	80
Moon-Spinners, The 10124-410 (10/64)-Disney; Haley Mills photo-c						

Movie Comics - Toby Tyler © WDC

Mowgli Jungle Book Four Color #487 © WDC

Ms. Marvel #7 © MAR

GD VG FN VF VF/NM NM-
2.0 4.0 6.0 8.0 9.0 9.2

8 16 24 53 74 95
Mutiny on the Bounty 1 (10040-302)(2/63)-Marlon Brando photo-c
4 8 12 24 32 40
Nikki, Wild Dog of the North 10141-412 (12/64)-Disney; reprints 4-Color #1226
3 6 9 18 24 30
Old Yeller 10168-601 (1/66)-Disney; reprints 4-Color #869; photo-c
3 6 9 18 24 30
One Hundred & One Dalmations 1 (10247-002) (2/70)-Disney; reprints Four Color #1183
3 7 10 21 28 35
Peter Pan 1 (10086-309)(9/63)-Disney; reprints Four Color #442
4 8 12 25 33 42
Peter Pan 2 (10086-909)(9/69)-Disney; reprints Four Color #442
3 6 9 18 24 30
Peter Pan 1 (3/84)-r/4-Color #442; Whitman pre-pack 2 4 6 8 10 12
P.T. 109 10123-409 (9/64)-John F. Kennedy 6 12 18 38 52 65
Rio Conchos 10143-503(3/65) 4 8 12 27 36 45
Robin Hood 10163-506 (6/65)-Disney; reprints Four Color #413
3 6 9 19 25 32
Shaggy Dog & the Absent-Minded Professor 30032-708 (8/67-Giant, 68 pgs.) Disney; reprints 4-Color #985,1199 6 12 18 40 55 70
Sleeping Beauty 1 (30042-009)(9/70)-Disney; reprints Four Color #973; with pull-out poster (No poster = half price) 8 16 24 53 74 95
Snow White & the Seven Dwarfs 1 (10091-310)(10/63)-Disney; reprints Four Color #382
4 8 12 24 32 40
Snow White & the Seven Dwarfs 10091-709 (9/67)-Disney; reprints Four Color #382
3 6 9 18 24 30
Snow White & the Seven Dwarfs 90091-204 (2/84)-Reprints Four Color #382; Whitman pre-pack 2 4 6 8 10 12
Son of Flubber 1 (10057-304)(4/63)-Disney; sequel to "The Absent-Minded Professor"
4 8 12 27 36 45
Summer Magic 10076-309 (9/63)-Disney; Hayley Mills photo-c; Manning-a
8 16 24 53 74 95
Swiss Family Robinson 10236-904 (4/69)-Disney; reprints Four Color #1156; photo-c
3 7 10 21 28 35
Sword in the Stone, The 30019-402 (2/64-Giant, 68 pgs.)-Disney (see March of Comics #258 & Wart and the Wizard 8 16 24 53 74 95
That Darn Cat 10171-602 (2/66)-Disney; Hayley Mills photo-c
8 16 24 53 74 95
Those Magnificent Men in Their Flying Machines 10162-510 (10/65); photo-c
4 8 12 24 32 40
Three Stooges in Orbit 30016-211 (11/62-Giant, 32 pgs.)-All photos from movie; stiff-photo-c
11 22 33 80 120 160
Tiger Walks, A 10117-406 (6/64)-Disney; Torres?, Tufts-a; photo-c
4 8 12 29 40 50
Toby Tyler 10142-502 (2/65)-Disney; reprints Four Color #1092; photo-c
3 7 10 21 28 35
Treasure Island 1 (10200-703)(3/67)-Disney; reprints Four Color #624; photo-c
3 6 9 18 24 30
20,000 Leagues Under the Sea 1 (10095-312)(12/63)-Disney; reprints Four Color #614
3 7 10 21 28 35
Wonderful Adventures of Pinocchio, The 1 (10089-310)(10/63)-Disney; reprints Four Color #545 (see Wonderful Advs. of...) 4 8 12 25 33 42
Wonderful Adventures of Pinocchio, The 10089-109 (9/71)-Disney; reprints Four Color #545
3 6 9 18 24 30
Wonderful World of the Brothers Grimm 1 (10008-210)(10/62)
5 10 15 36 48 60
X, the Man with the X-Ray Eyes 10083-309 (9/63)-Ray Milland photo on-c
8 16 24 58 82 105
Yellow Submarine 35000-902 (2/69-Giant, 68 pgs.)-With pull-out poster; The Beatles cartoon movie; Paul S. Newman-s 24 48 72 174 267 360
Without poster 10 20 30 67 96 125

MOVIE LOVE (Also see Personal Love)
Famous Funnies: Feb, 1950 - No. 22, Aug, 1953 (All photo-c)

1-Dick Powell, Evelyn Keyes, & Mickey Rooney photo-c
16 32 48 92 131 170
2-Myrna Loy photo-c 9 18 27 54 70 85
3-7,9: 6-Ricardo Montalban photo-c. 9-Gene Tierney, John Lund, Glenn Ford, & Rhonda Fleming photo-c. 9 18 27 51 62 75
8-Williamson/Frazetta-a, 6 pgs. 41 82 123 250 380 510
10-Frazetta-a, 6 pgs. 42 84 126 256 388 520
11,14-16: 14-Janet Leigh photo-c 8 16 24 46 58 70
12-Dean Martin & Jerry Lewis photo-c (12/51, pre-dates Advs. of Dean Martin & Jerry Lewis comic) 17 34 51 95 135 175
13-Ronald Reagan photo-c with 1 pg. biog. 24 48 72 138 199 260
17-Leslie Caron & Ralph Meeker photo-c; 1 pg. Frazetta ad
9 18 27 51 62 75
18-22: 19-John Derek photo-c. 20-Donald O'Connor & Debbie Reynolds photo-c. 21-Paul Henreid & Patricia Medina photo-c. 22-John Payne & Coleen Gray photo-c
8 16 24 43 54 65

NOTE: *Each issue has a full-length movie adaptation with photo covers.*

MOVIE THRILLERS (Movie)
Magazine Enterprises: 1949

1-Adaptation of "Rope of Sand" w/Burt Lancaster; Burt Lancaster photo-c
31 62 93 175 253 330

MOVIE TOWN ANIMAL ANTICS (Formerly Animal Antics; becomes Raccoon Kids #52 on)
National Periodical Publ.: No. 24, Jan-Feb, 1950 - No. 51, July-Aug, 1954

24-Raccoon Kids continue 12 24 36 69 95 120
25-51 10 20 30 56 73 90

NOTE: ***Sheldon Mayer** a-28-33, 35, 37-41, 43, 44, 47, 49-51.*

MOVIE TUNES COMICS (Formerly Animated...; Frankie No. 4 on)
Marvel Comics (MgPC): No. 3, Fall, 1946

3-Super Rabbit, Krazy Krow, Silly Seal & Ziggy Pig 13 26 39 74 102 130

MOWGLI JUNGLE BOOK (Rudyard Kipling's...)
Dell Publ. Co.: No. 487, Aug-Oct, 1953 - No. 620, Apr, 1955

Four Color 487 (#1) 7 14 21 46 63 80
Four Color 582 (8/54), 620 6 12 18 38 52 65

MR. (See Mister)

M. REX
Image Comics: July, 1999 - No. 2, Dec, 1999 ($2.95)

Preview ($5.00) B&W pages and sketchbook; Rouleau-a 5.00
1,2-($2.95) 1-Joe Kelly-s/Rouleau-a/Anacleto-c. 2-Rouleau-c 3.00

MS. CYANIDE & ICE
Blackout Comics: June, 1995 - No. 1, 1995 ($2.95, B&W)

0,1 3.00

MS. FORTUNE
Image Comics: Jan, 1998 ($2.95, B&W, one-shot)

1-Chris Marrinan-s/a 3.00

MS. MARVEL (Also see The Avengers #183)
Marvel Comics Group: Jan, 1977 - No. 23, Apr, 1979

1-1st app. Ms. Marvel; Scorpion app. in #1,2 2 4 6 8 10 12
2-10: 2-Origin. 5-Vision app. 6-10-(Reg. 30¢-c). 10-Last 30¢ issue 6.00
6-10-(35¢-c variants, limited dist.)(6/77) 1 2 3 5 7 9
11-15,19-23: 19-Capt. Marvel app. 20-New costume. 23-Vance Astro (leader of the Guardians) app. 5.00
16,17-1st brief app. Mystique 2 4 6 10 12 15
18-1st full app. Mystique; Avengers x-over 3 6 9 16 20 25

NOTE: ***Austin** c-14i, 16i, 17i, 22i. **Buscema** a-1-3p; c(p)-2, 4, 6, 7, 15. **Infantino** a-14p, 19p. **Gil Kane** c-8. **Mooney** a-4-8p, 13p, 15-18p. **Starlin** c-12.*

MS. MYSTIC
Pacific Comics: Oct, 1982 - No. 2, Feb, 1984 ($1.00/$1.50)

1,2: Neal Adams-c/a/script. 1-Origin; intro Erth, Ayre, Fyre & Watr 4.00

MS. MYSTIC
Continuity Comics: 1988 - No. 9, May, 1992 ($2.00)

1-9: 1,2-Reprint Pacific Comics issues 3.00

MS. MYSTIC
Continunity Comics: V2#1, Oct, 1993 - V2#4, Jan, 1994 ($2.50)

V2#1-4: 1-Adams-c(i)/part-i. 2-4-Embossed-c. 2-Nebres part-i. 3-Adams-c(i)/plot. 4-Adams-c(p)/plot 2.50

MS. MYSTIC DEATHWATCH 2000 (Ms. Mystic #3)
Continuity: May, 1993 - No. 3, Aug, 1993 ($2.50)

1-3-Bagged w/card; Adams plots 2.50

MS. TREE QUARTERLY / SPECIAL
DC Comics: Summer, 1990 -No. 10, 1992 ($3.95/$3.50, 84 pgs, mature)

1-10: 1-Midnight story; Batman text story, Grell-a. 2,3-Midnight stories; The Butcher text stories 4.00

NOTE: ***Cowan** c-2. **Grell** c-1, 6. **Infantino** a-8.*

MS. TREE'S THRILLING DETECTIVE ADVS (Ms. Tree #4 on; also see The Best of Ms. Tree) (Baxter paper #4-9)
Eclipse Comics/Aardvark-Vanaheim 10-18/Renegade Press 19 on:
2/83 - #9, 7/84; #10, 8/84 - #18, 5/85; #19, 6/85 - #50, 6/89

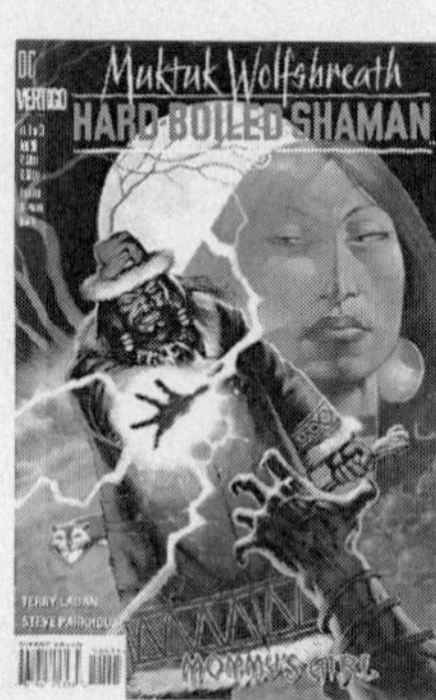

Muktuk Wolfsbreath #1 © Terry Laban

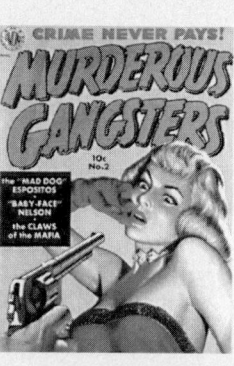

Murderous Gangsters #2 © AVON

Mutant, Texas #1 © Oni Press

	GD 2.0	VG 4.0	FN 6.0	VF 8.0	VF/NM 9.0	NM- 9.2
1						3.00
2-49: 2-Schythe begins. 9-Last Eclipse & last color issue. 10,11-two-tone						2.50
50-Contains flexi-disc ($3.95, 52pgs.)						4.00
Summer Special 1 (8/86)						3.00
1950s 3-D Crime (7/87, no glasses)-Johnny Dynamite in 3-D						3.00
Mike Mist in 3-D (8/85)-With glasses						3.00

NOTE; ***Miller** pin-up 1-4. Johnny Dynamite-r begin #36 by **Morisi**.*

MS. VICTORY SPECIAL(Also see Capt. Paragon & Femforce)
Americomics: Jan, 1985 (nd)

	GD 2.0	VG 4.0	FN 6.0	VF 8.0	VF/NM 9.0	NM- 9.2
1						2.50

MU
Devil's Due Publ.: Nov, 2004 - Present ($2.95)

	GD 2.0	VG 4.0	FN 6.0	VF 8.0	VF/NM 9.0	NM- 9.2
1-Mark Lee-a						3.00

MUCHA LUCHA (Based on Kids WB animated TV show)
DC Comics: Jun, 2003 - No. 3, Aug, 2003 ($2.25, limited series)

	GD 2.0	VG 4.0	FN 6.0	VF 8.0	VF/NM 9.0	NM- 9.2
1-3-Rikochet, Buena Girl and The Flea app.						2.25

MUGGSY MOUSE (Also see Tick Tock Tales)
Magazine Enterprises: 1951 - No. 3, 1951; No. 4, 1954 - No. 5, 1954; 1963

	GD 2.0	VG 4.0	FN 6.0	VF 8.0	VF/NM 9.0	NM- 9.2
1(A-1 #33)	8	16	24	46	58	70
2(A-1 #36)-Racist-c	10	20	30	60	80	100
3(A-1 #39), 4(A-1 #95), 5(A-1 #99)	6	12	18	31	38	45
Super Reprint #14(1963), I.W. Reprint #1,2 (nd)	2	4	6	9	11	14

MUGGY-DOO, BOY CAT
Stanhall Publ.: July, 1953 - No. 4, Jan, 1954

	GD 2.0	VG 4.0	FN 6.0	VF 8.0	VF/NM 9.0	NM- 9.2
1-Funny animal; Irving Spector-a	9	18	27	51	62	75
2-4	6	12	18	27	33	38
Super Reprint #12('63), 16('64)	2	4	6	9	11	14

MUKTUK WOLFSBREATH: HARD-BOILED SHAMAN
DC Comics (Vertigo): Aug, 1998 - No. 3, Oct, 1998 ($2.50)

	GD 2.0	VG 4.0	FN 6.0	VF 8.0	VF/NM 9.0	NM- 9.2
1-3-Terry LaBan-s/Steve Parkhouse-a						2.50

MULLKON EMPIRE (See John Jake's...)

MUMMY, THE (See Universal Presents... under Dell Giants & Movie Classics)

MUMMY, THE: VALLEY OF THE GODS (Movie adaption)
Chaos! Comics: May, 2001 - No. 3 ($2.99, limited series)

	GD 2.0	VG 4.0	FN 6.0	VF 8.0	VF/NM 9.0	NM- 9.2
1-Based on "The Mummy Returns" movie; Broome-a; Broome & photo-c						3.00

MUNDEN'S BAR ANNUAL
First Comics: Apr, 1988; 1989 ($2.95/$5.95)

	GD 2.0	VG 4.0	FN 6.0	VF 8.0	VF/NM 9.0	NM- 9.2
1-($2.95)-r/from Grimjack; Fish Police story; Ordway-c						3.00
2-($5.95)-Teenage Mutant Ninja Turtles app.						6.00

MUNSTERS, THE (TV)
Gold Key: Jan, 1965 - No. 16, Jan, 1968 (All photo-c)

	GD 2.0	VG 4.0	FN 6.0	VF 8.0	VF/NM 9.0	NM- 9.2
1 (10134-501)	20	40	60	141	216	290
2	11	22	33	75	110	145
3-5	9	18	27	65	93	120
6-16	8	16	24	55	78	100

MUNSTERS, THE (TV)
TV Comics!: Aug, 1997 - No. 4 ($2.95, B&W)

	GD 2.0	VG 4.0	FN 6.0	VF 8.0	VF/NM 9.0	NM- 9.2
1-4-All have photo-c						3.00
1,4-($7.95)-Variant-c						8.00
2-Variant-c w/Beverly Owens as Marilyn						3.00
Special Comic Con Ed. (7/97, $9.95)						10.00

MUPPET BABIES, THE (TV)(See Star Comics Magazine)
Marvel Comics (Star Comics)/Marvel #18 on: Aug, 1985 - No. 26, July, 1989 (Children's book)

	GD 2.0	VG 4.0	FN 6.0	VF 8.0	VF/NM 9.0	NM- 9.2
1-26						3.00

MUPPETS TAKE MANHATTAN, THE
Marvel Comics (Star Comics): Nov, 1984 - No. 3, Jan, 1985

	GD 2.0	VG 4.0	FN 6.0	VF 8.0	VF/NM 9.0	NM- 9.2
1-3-Movie adapt. r-/Marvel Super Special						3.00

MURCIELAGA, SHE-BAT
Heroic Publishing: Jan, 1993 - No. 2, 1993 (B&W)

	GD 2.0	VG 4.0	FN 6.0	VF 8.0	VF/NM 9.0	NM- 9.2
1-($1.50, 28 pgs.)						2.50
2-($2.95, 36 pgs.)-Coated-c						3.00

MURDER CAN BE FUN
Slave Labor Graphics: Feb, 1996 - No. 12 ($2.95, B&W)

	GD 2.0	VG 4.0	FN 6.0	VF 8.0	VF/NM 9.0	NM- 9.2
1-12: 1-Dorkin-c. 2-Vasquez-c.						3.00

MURDER INCORPORATED (My Private Life #16 on)
Fox Feature Syndicate: 1/48 - No. 15, 12/49; (2 No.9's); 6/50 - No. 3, 8/51

	GD 2.0	VG 4.0	FN 6.0	VF 8.0	VF/NM 9.0	NM- 9.2
1 (1st Series); 1,2 have 'For Adults Only' on-c	50	100	150	305	465	625
2-Electrocution story	40	80	120	236	351	465
3-7,9(4/49),10(5/49),11-15	24	48	72	135	195	255
8-Used in **SOTI**, pg. 160	26	52	78	150	215	280
9(3/49)-Possible use in **SOTI**, pg. 145; r/Blue Beetle #56('48)	24	48	72	135	195	255
5(#1, 6/50)(2nd Series)-Formerly My Desire #4; bondage-c.	19	38	57	107	154	200
2(8/50)-Morisi-a	16	32	48	92	131	170
3(8/51)-Used in **POP**, pg. 81; Rico-a; lingerie-c/panels	18	36	54	100	143	185

MURDER ME DEAD
El Capitán Books: July, 2000 - No. 9, Oct, 2001 ($2.95/$4.95, B&W)

	GD 2.0	VG 4.0	FN 6.0	VF 8.0	VF/NM 9.0	NM- 9.2
1-8-David Lapham-s/a						3.00
9-($4.95)						5.00

MURDEROUS GANGSTERS
Avon Per./Realistic No. 3 on: Jul, 1951; No. 2, Dec, 1951 - No. 4, Jun, 1952

	GD 2.0	VG 4.0	FN 6.0	VF 8.0	VF/NM 9.0	NM- 9.2
1-Pretty Boy Floyd, Leggs Diamond; 1 pg. Wood-a	44	88	132	268	409	550
2-Baby-Face Nelson; 1 pg. Wood-a; painted-c	30	60	90	170	245	320
3-Painted-c	24	48	72	135	195	255
4- "Murder by Needle" drug story; Mort Lawrence-a; Kinstler-c	30	60	90	170	245	320

MURDER MYSTERIES (Neil Gaiman's...)
Dark Horse Comics: 2002 ($13.95, HC, one-shot)

	GD 2.0	VG 4.0	FN 6.0	VF 8.0	VF/NM 9.0	NM- 9.2
HC-Adapts Gaiman story; P. Craig Russell-script/art						14.00

MURDER TALES (Magazine)
World Famous Publications: V1#10, Nov, 1970 - V1#11, Jan, 1971 (52 pgs.)

	GD 2.0	VG 4.0	FN 6.0	VF 8.0	VF/NM 9.0	NM- 9.2
V1#10-One pg. Frazetta ad	4	8	12	27	36	45
11-Guardineer-r; bondage-c	3	7	10	21	28	35

MUSHMOUSE AND PUNKIN PUSS (TV)
Gold Key: September, 1965 (Hanna-Barbera)

	GD 2.0	VG 4.0	FN 6.0	VF 8.0	VF/NM 9.0	NM- 9.2
1 (10153-509)	10	20	30	72	104	135

MUSIC MAN, THE (See Movie Classics)

MUTANT CHRONICLES (Video game)
Acclaim Comics (Armada): May, 1996 - No. 4, Aug, 1996 ($2.95, lim. series)

	GD 2.0	VG 4.0	FN 6.0	VF 8.0	VF/NM 9.0	NM- 9.2
1-4: Simon Bisley-c on all, Sourcebook (#5)						3.00

MUTANT EARTH (Stan Winston's...)
Image Comics: April, 2002 - No. 4, Jan, 2003 ($2.95)

	GD 2.0	VG 4.0	FN 6.0	VF 8.0	VF/NM 9.0	NM- 9.2
1-4-Flip book w/Realm of the Claw						3.00
Trakk...His Adventures in Mutant Earth TPB (2003, $16.95) r/#1-4; Winston interview						17.00

MUTANT MISADVENTURES OF CLOAK AND DAGGER, THE
(Becomes Cloak and Dagger #14 on)
Marvel Comics: Oct, 1988 - No. 19, Aug, 1991 ($1.25/$1.50)

	GD 2.0	VG 4.0	FN 6.0	VF 8.0	VF/NM 9.0	NM- 9.2
1-8,10-15: 1-X-Factor app. 10-Painted-c. 12-Dr. Doom app. 14-Begin new direction						2.25
9,16-19: 9-(52 pgs.) The Avengers x-over; painted-c. 16-18-Spider-Man x-over. 18-Infinity Gauntlet x-over; Thanos cameo; Ghost Rider app. 19-(52 pgs.) Origin Cloak & Dagger						2.50

NOTE: ***Austin** a-12i; c(i)-4, 12, 13; scripts-all. **Russell** a-2i. **Williamson** a-14i-16i; c-15i.*

MUTANTS & MISFITS
Silverline Comics (Solson): 1987 - No. 3, 1987 ($1.95)

	GD 2.0	VG 4.0	FN 6.0	VF 8.0	VF/NM 9.0	NM- 9.2
1-3						2.25

MUTANTS VS. ULTRAS
Malibu Comics (Ultraverse): Nov, 1995 ($6.95, one-shot)

	GD 2.0	VG 4.0	FN 6.0	VF 8.0	VF/NM 9.0	NM- 9.2
1-r/Exiles vs. X-Men, Night Man vs. Wolverine, Prime vs. Hulk						7.00

MUTANT, TEXAS: TALES OF SHERIFF IDA RED (Also see Jingle Belle)
Oni Press: May, 2002 - No. 4, Nov, 2002 ($2.95, B&W, limited series)

	GD 2.0	VG 4.0	FN 6.0	VF 8.0	VF/NM 9.0	NM- 9.2
1-4-Paul Dini-s/J. Bone-c/a						3.00
TPB (2003, $11.95) r/#1-4; intro. by Joe Lansdale						12.00

MUTANT 2099
Marvel Comics (Marvel Knights): Nov, 2004 ($2.99, one-shot)

	GD 2.0	VG 4.0	FN 6.0	VF 8.0	VF/NM 9.0	NM- 9.2
1-Kirkman-s/Pat Lee-c						3.00

MUTANT X (See X-Factor)
Marvel Comics: Nov, 1998 - No. 32, June, 2001 ($2.99/$1.99/$2.25)

Muties #2 © MAR

My Experience #19(#1) © FOX

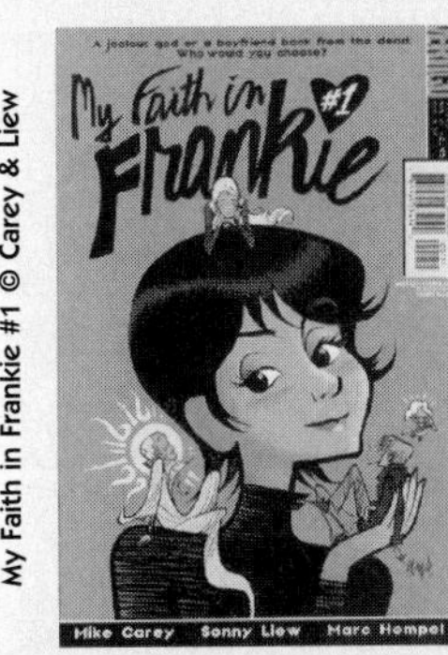
My Faith in Frankie #1 © Carey & Liew

	GD 2.0	VG 4.0	FN 6.0	VF 8.0	VF/NM 9.0	NM- 9.2
1-($2.99) Alex Summers with alternate world's X-Men						3.00
2-11,13-19-($1.99): 2-Two covers. 5-Man-Spider-c/app.						2.25
12,25-($2.99): 12-Pin-up gallery by Kaluta, Romita, Byrne						3.00
20-24,26-32: 20-Begin $2.25-c. 28-31-Logan-c/app. 32-Last issue						2.25
Annual '99, '00 (5/99,'00, $3.50) '00-Doran-a(p)						3.50
Annual 2001 ($2.99) Story oocurs between #31 & #32; Dracula app.						3.00

MUTANT X (Based on TV show)
Marvel Comics: May, 2002 - Present ($3.50)

	GD	VG	FN	VF	VF/NM	NM-
...: Dangerous Decisions (6/02) -Kuder-s/Immonen-a						3.50
...: Origin (5/02) -Tischman & Chaykin-s/Ferguson-a						3.50

MUTATIS
Marvel Comics (Epic Comics): 1992 - No. 3, 1992 ($2.25, mini-series)

	GD	VG	FN	VF	VF/NM	NM-
1-3: Painted-c						2.25

MUTIES
Marvel Comics: Apr, 2002 - No. 6, Sept, 2002 ($2.50)

	GD	VG	FN	VF	VF/NM	NM-
1-6: 1-Bollars-s/Ferguson-a. 2-Spaziante-a. 3-Haspiel-a. 4-Kanuiga-a						2.50

MUTINY (Stormy Tales of the Seven Seas)
Aragon Magazines: Oct, 1954 - No. 3, Feb, 1955

	GD	VG	FN	VF	VF/NM	NM-
1	17	34	51	95	135	175
2,3: 2-Capt. Mutiny. 3-Bondage-c	14	28	42	79	110	140

MUTINY ON THE BOUNTY (See Classics Illustrated #100 & Movie Comics)

MUTT AND JEFF (See All-American, All-Flash #18, Cicero's Cat, Comic Cavalcade, Famous Feature Stories, The Funnies, Popular & Xmas Comics)
All American/National 1-103(6/58)/Dell 104(10/58)-115 (10-12/59)/ Harvey 116(2/60)-148: Summer, 1939 (nd) - No. 148, Nov, 1965

	GD	VG	FN	VF	VF/NM	NM-
1(nn)-Lost Wheels	131	262	393	819	1260	1700
2(nn)-Charging Bull (Summer, 1940, nd; on sale 6/20/40)	67	134	201	419	647	875
3(nn)-Bucking Broncos (Summer, 1941, nd)	48	96	144	293	447	600
4(Winter, '41), 5(Summer, '42)	44	88	132	268	409	550
6-10: 6-Includes Minute Man Answers the Call	26	52	78	147	211	275
11-20: 20-X-Mas-c	18	36	54	102	146	190
21-30	13	26	39	76	106	135
31-50: 32-X-Mas-c	10	20	30	60	80	100
51-75-Last Fisher issue. 53-Last 52 pgs.	9	18	27	51	62	75
76-99,101-103: 76-Last pre-code issue(1/55)	5	10	15	36	48	60
100	6	12	18	38	52	65
104-115,132-148	4	8	12	29	40	50
116-131-Richie Rich app.	5	10	15	33	44	55
...Jokes 1-3(8/60-61, Harvey)-84 pgs.; Richie Rich in all; Little Dot in #2,3; Lotta in #2	4	8	12	29	40	50
...New Jokes 1-4(10/63-11/65, Harvey)-68 pgs.; Richie Rich in #1-3; Stumbo in #1	4	8	12	22	30	38

NOTE: *Most all issues by* ***Al Smith****. Issues from 1963 on have* ***Fisher*** *reprints. Clarification: early issues signed by Fisher are mostly drawn by Smith.*

MY BROTHERS' KEEPER
Spire Christian Comics (Fleming H. Revell Co.): 1973 (35/49¢, 36 pgs.)

	GD	VG	FN	VF	VF/NM	NM-
nn	1	3	4	6	8	11

MY CONFESSIONS (My Confession #7&8; formerly Western True Crime; A Spectacular Feature Magazine #11)
Fox Feature Syndicate: No. 7, Aug, 1949 - No. 10, Jan-Feb, 1950

	GD	VG	FN	VF	VF/NM	NM-
7-Wood-a (10 pgs.)	24	48	72	135	195	255
8,9: 8-Harrison/Wood-a (19 pgs.). 9-Wood-a	22	44	66	123	177	230
10	10	20	30	60	80	100

MY DATE COMICS (Teen-age)
Hillman Periodicals: July, 1947 - V1#4, Jan, 1948 (2nd Romance comic; see Young Romance)

	GD	VG	FN	VF	VF/NM	NM-
1-S&K-c/a	38	76	114	219	320	420
2-4-S&K-c/a; Dan Barry-a	26	52	78	150	215	280

MY DESIRE (Formerly Jo-Jo Comics; becomes Murder, Inc. #5 on)
Fox Feature Syndicate: No. 30, Aug, 1949 - No. 4, April, 1950

	GD	VG	FN	VF	VF/NM	NM-
30(#1)	17	34	51	98	139	180
31 (#2, 10/49),3(2/50),4	11	22	33	66	91	115
31 (Canadian edition)	8	16	24	40	50	60
32(12/49)-Wood-a	21	42	63	118	169	220

MY DIARY (Becomes My Friend Irma #3 on?)
Marvel Comics (A Lovers Mag.): Dec, 1949 - No. 2, Mar, 1950

	GD	VG	FN	VF	VF/NM	NM-
1,2-Photo-c	15	30	45	86	123	160

MY EXPERIENCE (Formerly All Top; becomes Judy Canova #23 on)
Fox Feature Syndicate: No. 19, Sept, 1949 - No. 22, Mar, 1950

	GD	VG	FN	VF	VF/NM	NM-
19,21: 19-Wood-a. 21-Wood-a(2)	26	52	78	150	215	280
20	11	22	33	66	91	115
22-Wood-a (9 pgs.)	21	42	63	118	169	220

MY FAITH IN FRANKIE
DC Comics (Vertigo): March, 2004 - No. 4, June, 2004 ($2.95, limited series)

	GD	VG	FN	VF	VF/NM	NM-
1-4-Mike Carey-s/Sonny Liew & Marc Hempel-a						3.00
TPB (2004, $6.95, digest-size) r/series in B&W; Dead Boy Detectives preview						7.00

MY FAVORITE MARTIAN (TV)
Gold Key: 1/64; No.2, 7/64 - No. 9, 10/66 (No. 1,3-9 have photo-c)

	GD	VG	FN	VF	VF/NM	NM-
1-Russ Manning-a	14	28	42	97	149	200
2	8	16	24	55	78	100
3-9	7	14	21	51	71	90

MY FRIEND IRMA (Radio/TV) (Formerly My Diary? and/or Western Life Romances?)
Marvel/Atlas Comics (BFP): No. 3, June, 1950 - No. 47, Dec, 1954; No. 48, Feb, 1955

	GD	VG	FN	VF	VF/NM	NM-
3-Dan DeCarlo-a in all; 52 pgs. begin, end ?	18	36	54	100	143	185
4-Kurtzman-a (10 pgs.)	19	38	57	107	154	200
5- "Egghead Doodle" by Kurtzman (4 pgs.)	15	30	45	85	120	155
6,8-10: 9-Paper dolls, 1 pg; Millie app. (5 pgs.)	11	22	33	64	87	110
7-One pg. Kurtzman-a	11	22	33	66	91	115
11-23: 23-One pg. Frazetta-a	8	16	24	46	58	70
24-48: 41,48-Stan Lee & Dan DeCarlo app.	7	14	21	37	46	55

MY GIRL PEARL
Atlas Comics: 4/55 - #4, 10/55; #5, 7/57 - #6, 9/57; #7, 8/60 - #11, ?/61

	GD	VG	FN	VF	VF/NM	NM-
1-Dan DeCarlo-c/a in #1-6	15	30	45	84	115	150
2	8	16	24	46	58	75
3-6	7	14	21	35	43	55
7-11	4	8	12	24	32	45

MY GREATEST ADVENTURE (Doom Patrol #86 on)
National Periodical Publications: Jan-Feb, 1955 - No. 85, Feb, 1964

	GD	VG	FN	VF	VF/NM	NM-
1-Before CCA	130	260	390	875	1538	2200
2	50	100	150	400	625	850
3-5	36	72	108	270	423	575
6-10: 6-Science fiction format begins	31	62	93	228	352	475
11-14: 12-1st S.A. issue	23	46	69	165	253	340
15-17: Kirby-a in all	25	50	75	179	275	370
18-Kirby-c/a	29	58	87	206	316	425
19,22-25	19	38	57	136	208	280
20,21,28-Kirby-a	23	46	69	165	253	340
26,27,29,30	14	28	42	97	149	200
31-40	12	24	36	84	127	170
41,42,44-57,59	10	20	30	72	104	135
43-Kirby-a	11	22	33	77	114	150
58,60,61-Toth-a; Last 10¢ issue	10	20	30	73	107	140
62-76,78,79: 79-Promotes "Legion of the Strange" for next issue; renamed Doom Patrol for #80	8	16	24	53	74	95
77-Toth-a; Robotman prototype	8	16	24	55	78	100
80-(6/63)-Intro/origin Doom Patrol and begin series; origin & 1st app. Negative Man, Elasti-Girl & S.A. Robotman	45	90	135	360	568	775
81,85-Toth-a	18	36	54	129	197	265
82-84	16	32	48	116	178	240

NOTE: ***Anderson*** *a-42.* ***Cameron*** *a-24.* ***Colan*** *a-77.* ***Meskin*** *a-25, 26, 32, 39, 45, 50, 56, 57, 61, 64, 70, 73, 74, 76, 79; c-76.* ***Moreira*** *a-11, 12, 15, 17, 20, 23, 25, 27, 37, 40-43, 46, 48, 55-57, 59, 60, 62-65, 67, 69, 70; c-1-4, 7-10.* ***Roussos*** *c/a-71-73.* ***Wildey*** *a-32.*

MY GREAT LOVE (Becomes Will Rogers Western #5)
Fox Feature Syndicate: Oct, 1949 - No. 4, Apr, 1950

	GD	VG	FN	VF	VF/NM	NM-
1	15	30	45	86	123	160
2-4	9	18	27	54	70	85

MY INTIMATE AFFAIR (Inside Crime #3)
Fox Feature Syndicate: Mar, 1950 - No. 2, May, 1950

	GD	VG	FN	VF	VF/NM	NM-
1	15	30	45	86	123	160
2	9	18	27	54	70	85

MY LIFE (Formerly Meet Corliss Archer)
Fox Feature Syndicate: No. 4, Sept, 1948 - No. 15, July, 1950

	GD	VG	FN	VF	VF/NM	NM-
4-Used in **SOTI**, pg. 39; Kamen/Feldstein-a	40	80	120	236	351	465
5-Kamen-a	24	48	72	135	195	255
6-Kamen/Feldstein-a	26	52	78	150	215	280
7-Wood-a; wash cover	21	42	63	118	169	220

My Little Margie #9 © CC

My Love Affair #1 © FOX

My Love Memoirs #11 © FOX

	GD 2.0	VG 4.0	FN 6.0	VF 8.0	VF/NM 9.0	NM- 9.2
8,9,11-15	10	20	30	60	80	100
10-Wood-a	19	38	57	107	154	200
MY LITTLE MARGIE (TV)						
Charlton Comics: July, 1954 - No. 54, Nov, 1964						
1-Photo front/back-c	37	74	111	209	305	400
2-Photo front/back-c	18	36	54	102	146	190
3-7,10	11	22	33	62	84	105
8,9-Infinity-c	11	22	33	64	87	110
11-14: Part-photo-c (#13, 8/56)	10	20	30	56	73	90
15-19	9	18	27	52	66	80
20-(25¢, 100 pg. issue)	15	30	45	86	123	160
21-40: 40-Last 10¢ issue	6	12	18	38	52	65
41-53	5	10	15	33	44	55
54-(11/64) Beatles on cover; lead story spoofs the Beatle haircut craze of the 1960's; Beatles app. (scarce)	18	36	54	126	193	260
NOTE: *Doll cut-outs in 32, 33, 40, 45, 50.*						
MY LITTLE MARGIE'S BOY FRIENDS (TV) (Freddy V2#12 on)						
Charlton Comics: Aug, 1955 - No. 11, Apr?, 1958						
1-Has several Archie swipes	15	30	45	86	123	160
2	9	18	27	54	70	85
3-11	8	16	24	46	58	70
MY LITTLE MARGIE'S FASHIONS (TV)						
Charlton Comics: Feb, 1959 - No. 5, Nov, 1959						
1	14	28	42	79	110	140
2-5	8	16	24	46	58	70
MY LOVE (Becomes Two Gun Western #5 (11/50) on?)						
Marvel Comics (CLDS): July, 1949 - No. 4, Apr, 1950 (All photo-c)						
1	15	30	45	83	117	150
2,3	9	18	27	54	70	85
4-Bettie Page photo-c (see Cupid #2)	35	70	105	201	293	385
MY LOVE						
Marvel Comics Group: Sept, 1969 - No. 39, Mar, 1976						
1	6	12	18	43	59	75
2-9: 4-6-Colan-a	4	8	12	22	30	38
10-Williamson-r/My Own Romance #71; Kirby-a	4	8	12	24	32	40
11-13,15-19	3	6	9	18	24	30
14-(52 pgs.)-Woodstock-c/sty; Morrow-c/a; Kirby/Colletta-r	5	10	15	33	44	55
20-Starlin-a	3	7	10	21	28	35
21,22,24-27,29-38: 38-Reprints	3	6	9	16	21	26
23-Steranko-r/Our Love Story #5	3	7	10	21	28	35
28-Kirby-a	3	6	9	18	24	30
39-Last issue; reprints	3	6	9	18	24	30
Special 1 (12/71)(52 pgs.)	5	10	15	33	44	55
NOTE: ***John Buscema** a-1-7, 10, 18-21, 22r(2), 24r, 25r, 29r, 34r, 36r, 37r, Spec. (r)(4); c-13, 15, 25, 27, Spec. **Colan** a-4, 5, 6, 8, 9, 16, 17, 20, 21, 22, 24r, 27r, 30r, 35r, 39r. **Colan/Everett** a-13, 15, 16, 27(r/#13). **Kirby** a-(r)-10, 14, 26, 28. **Romita** a-1-3, 19, 20, 25, 34, 38; c-1-3, 15.*						
MY LOVE AFFAIR (March of Crime #7 on)						
Fox Feature Syndicate: July, 1949 - No. 6, May, 1950						
1	15	30	45	86	123	160
2	9	18	27	54	70	85
3-6-Wood-a. 5-(3/50)-Becomes Love Stories #6	19	38	57	107	154	200
MY LOVE LIFE (Formerly Zegra)						
Fox Feature Synd.: No. 6, June, 1949 - No. 13, Aug, 1950; No. 13, Sept, 1951						
6-Kamenish-a	16	32	48	92	131	170
7-13	9	18	27	54	70	85
13 (9/51)(Formerly My Story #12)	9	18	27	52	66	80
MY LOVE MEMOIRS (Formerly Women Outlaws; Hunted #13 on)						
Fox Feature Syndicate: No. 9, Nov, 1949 - No. 12, May, 1950						
9,11,12-Wood-a	19	38	57	107	154	200
10	9	18	27	54	70	85
MY LOVE SECRET (Formerly Phantom Lady; Animal Crackers #31)						
Fox Feature Syndicate/M. S. Distr.: No. 24, June, 1949 - No. 30, June, 1950; No. 53, 1954						
24-Kamen/Feldstein-a	19	38	57	107	154	200
25-Possible caricature of Wood on-c?	12	24	36	69	95	120
26,28-Wood-a	19	38	57	107	154	200
27,29,30: 30-Photo-c	10	20	30	58	77	95
53-(Reprint, M.S. Distr.) 1954? nd given; formerly Western Thrillers; becomes Crimes by Women #54; photo-c	7	14	21	35	43	50

	GD 2.0	VG 4.0	FN 6.0	VF 8.0	VF/NM 9.0	NM- 9.2
MY LOVE STORY (Hoot Gibson Western #5 on)						
Fox Feature Syndicate: Sept, 1949 - No. 4, Mar, 1950						
1	15	30	45	86	123	160
2	9	18	27	54	70	85
3,4-Wood-a	19	38	57	107	154	200
MY LOVE STORY						
Atlas Comics (GPS): April, 1956 - No. 9, Aug, 1957						
1	12	24	36	69	95	120
2	8	16	24	40	50	60
3,7: Matt Baker-a. 7-Toth-a	9	18	27	54	70	85
4-6,8,9	7	14	21	37	46	55
NOTE: ***Brewster** a-3. **Colletta** a-1(2), 3, 4(2), 5; c-3.*						
MY NAME IS CHAOS						
DC Comics: 1992 - No. 4, 1992 ($4.95, limited series, 52 pgs.)						
Book 1-4: Tom Veitch scripts; painted-c						5.00
MY NAME IS HOLOCAUST						
DC Comics: May, 1995 - No. 5, Sept, 1995 ($2.50, limited series)						
1-5						2.50
MY ONLY LOVE						
Charlton Comics: July, 1975 - No. 9, Nov, 1976						
1	2	4	6	14	18	22
2,4-9	2	4	6	10	12	15
3-Toth-a	2	4	6	11	14	18
MY OWN ROMANCE (Formerly My Romance; Teen-Age Romance #77 on)						
Marvel/Atlas (MjPC/RCM No. 4-59/ZPC No. 60-76): No. 4, Mar, 1949 - No. 76, July, 1960						
4-Photo-c	16	32	48	92	131	170
5-10: 5,6,8-10-Photo-c	9	18	27	54	70	85
11-20: 14-Powell-a	9	18	27	51	62	75
21-42,55: 42-Last precode (2/55). 55-Toth-a	8	16	24	46	58	70
43-54,56-60	5	10	15	33	44	55
61-70,72,73,75,76	4	8	12	28	38	48
71-Williamson-a	5	10	15	36	48	60
74-Kirby-a	5	10	15	36	48	60
NOTE: ***Brewster** a-59. **Colletta** a-45(2), 48, 50, 55, 57(2), 59; c-58i, 59, 61. **Everett** a-25; c-58p. **Kirby** c-71, 75, 76. **Morisi** a-18. **Orlando** a-61. **Romita** a-36. **Tuska** a-10.*						
MY PAL DIZZY (See Comic Books, Series I)						
MY PAST (...Confessions) (Formerly Western Thrillers)						
Fox Feature Syndicate: No. 7, Aug, 1949 - No. 11, Apr, 1950 (Crimes Inc. #12)						
7	15	30	45	86	123	160
8-10	9	18	27	54	70	85
11-Wood-a	19	38	57	107	154	200
MY PERSONAL PROBLEM						
Ajax/Farrell/Steinway Comic: 11/55; No. 2, 2/56; No. 3, 9/56 - No. 4, 11/56; 10/57 - No. 3, 5/58						
1	9	18	27	52	66	80
2-4	6	12	18	33	41	48
1-3('57-'58)-Steinway	6	12	18	27	33	38
MY PRIVATE LIFE (Formerly Murder, Inc.; becomes Pedro #18)						
Fox Feature Syndicate: No. 16, Feb, 1950 - No. 17, April, 1950						
16,17	13	26	39	74	102	130
MYRA NORTH (See The Comics, Crackajack Funnies & Red Ryder)						
Dell Publishing Co.: No. 3, Jan, 1940						
Four Color 3	70	140	210	536	856	1175
MY REAL LOVE						
Standard Comics: No. 5, June, 1952 (Photo-c)						
5-Toth-a, 3 pgs.; Tuska, Cardy, Vern Greene-a	14	28	42	79	110	140
MY ROMANCE (Becomes My Own Romance #4 on)						
Marvel Comics (RCM): Sept, 1948 - No. 3, Jan, 1949						
1	15	30	45	86	123	160
2,3: 2-Anti-Wertham editorial (11/48)	9	18	27	54	70	85
MY ROMANTIC ADVENTURES (Formerly Romantic Adventures)						
American Comics Group: No. 68, 8/56 - No. 115, 12/60; No. 116, 7/61 - No. 138, 3/64						
68	9	18	27	52	66	80
69-85	6	12	18	28	34	40
86-Three pg. Williamson-a (2/58)	8	16	24	43	54	65
87-100	3	6	9	19	25	32

My Secret Confession #1 © Sterling

Mysterious Adventures #9 © Story

Mystery Comics #2 © WHW

	GD 2.0	VG 4.0	FN 6.0	VF 8.0	VF/NM 9.0	NM- 9.2
101-138	3	6	9	16	20	24

NOTE: *Whitney art in most issues.*

MY SECRET (Becomes Our Secret #4 on)
Superior Comics, Ltd.: Aug, 1949 - No. 3, Oct, 1949

	GD 2.0	VG 4.0	FN 6.0	VF 8.0	VF/NM 9.0	NM- 9.2
1	14	28	42	79	110	140
2,3	9	18	27	52	66	80

MY SECRET AFFAIR (Becomes Martin Kane #4)
Hero Book (Fox Feature Syndicate): Dec, 1949 - No. 3, April, 1950

	GD 2.0	VG 4.0	FN 6.0	VF 8.0	VF/NM 9.0	NM- 9.2
1-Harrison/Wood-a (10 pgs.)	22	44	66	127	184	240
2-Wood-a	18	36	54	102	146	190
3-Wood-a	19	38	57	107	154	200

MY SECRET CONFESSION
Sterling Comics: September, 1955

	GD 2.0	VG 4.0	FN 6.0	VF 8.0	VF/NM 9.0	NM- 9.2
1-Sekowsky-a	9	18	27	52	66	80

MY SECRET LIFE (Formerly Western Outlaws; Romeo Tubbs #26 on)
Fox Feature Syndicate: No. 22, July, 1949 - No. 27, July, 1950; No. 27, 9/51

	GD 2.0	VG 4.0	FN 6.0	VF 8.0	VF/NM 9.0	NM- 9.2
22	11	22	33	64	87	110
23,26-Wood-a, 6 pgs.	18	36	54	100	143	185
24,25,27	10	20	30	56	73	90
27 (9/51)	9	18	27	52	66	80

NOTE: *The title was changed to Romeo Tubbs after #25 even though #26 & 27 did come out.*

MY SECRET LIFE (Formerly Young Lovers; Sue & Sally Smith #48)
Charlton Comics: No. 19, Aug, 1957 - No. 47, Sept, 1962

	GD 2.0	VG 4.0	FN 6.0	VF 8.0	VF/NM 9.0	NM- 9.2
19	4	8	12	25	33	42
20-35	3	6	9	16	20	24
36-47: 44-Last 10¢ issue	2	4	6	12	16	20

MY SECRET MARRIAGE
Superior Comics, Ltd.: May, 1953 - No. 24, July, 1956 (Canadian)

	GD 2.0	VG 4.0	FN 6.0	VF 8.0	VF/NM 9.0	NM- 9.2
1	13	26	39	74	102	130
2	8	16	24	43	54	65
3-24	7	14	21	35	43	50
I.W. Reprint #9	2	4	6	9	11	14

NOTE: *Many issues contain **Kamen-ish** art.*

MY SECRET ROMANCE (Becomes A Star Presentation #3)
Hero Book (Fox Feature Syndicate): Jan, 1950 - No. 2, March, 1950

	GD 2.0	VG 4.0	FN 6.0	VF 8.0	VF/NM 9.0	NM- 9.2
1	15	30	45	83	117	150
2-Wood-a	19	38	57	107	154	200

MY SECRET STORY (Formerly Captain Kidd #25; Sabu #30 on)
Fox Feature Syndicate: No. 26, Oct, 1949 - No. 29, April, 1950

	GD 2.0	VG 4.0	FN 6.0	VF 8.0	VF/NM 9.0	NM- 9.2
26	15	30	45	86	123	160
27-29	9	18	27	54	70	85

MYS-TECH WARS
Marvel Comics UK: Mar, 1993 - No. 4, June, 1993 ($1.75, mini-series)

	GD 2.0	VG 4.0	FN 6.0	VF 8.0	VF/NM 9.0	NM- 9.2
1-4: 1-Gatefold-c						2.25

MYSTERIES (...Weird & Strange)
Superior/Dynamic Publ. (Randall Publ. Ltd.): May, 1953 - No. 11, Jan, 1955

	GD 2.0	VG 4.0	FN 6.0	VF 8.0	VF/NM 9.0	NM- 9.2
1-All horror stories	40	80	120	240	360	480
2-A-Bomb blast story	27	54	81	152	219	285
3-11: 10-Kamenish-c/a reprinted from Strange Mysteries #2; cover is from a panel in Strange Mysteries #2	23	46	69	132	191	250

MYSTERIES IN SPACE (See Fireside Book Series)

MYSTERIES OF SCOTLAND YARD (Also see A-1 Comics)
Magazine Enterprises: No. 121, 1954 (one shot)

	GD 2.0	VG 4.0	FN 6.0	VF 8.0	VF/NM 9.0	NM- 9.2
A-1 121-Reprinted from Manhunt (5 stories)	17	34	51	95	135	175

MYSTERIES OF UNEXPLORED WORLDS (See Blue Bird)(Becomes Son of Vulcan V2#49 on)
Charlton Comics: Aug, 1956; No. 2, Jan, 1957 - No. 48, Sept, 1965

	GD 2.0	VG 4.0	FN 6.0	VF 8.0	VF/NM 9.0	NM- 9.2
1	37	74	112	213	312	410
2-No Ditko	15	30	45	86	123	160
3,4,8,9 Ditko-a. 3-Diko c/a (4). 4-Ditko c/a (2).	30	60	90	170	245	320
5,6,10,11: 5,6-Ditko-c/a (all). 10-Ditko-c/a(4). 11-Ditko-c/a(3); signed J. Kotdi	31	62	93	178	259	340
7-(2/58, 68 pgs.) 4 stories w/Ditko-a	35	70	105	198	287	375
12,19,21-24,26-Ditko-a. 12-Ditko sty (3); Baker story "The Charm Bracelet."	22	44	66	127	184	240
13-18,20	9	18	27	52	66	80
25,27-30	5	10	15	33	44	55
31-45	4	8	12	25	33	42
46(5/65)-Son of Vulcan begins (origin/1st app.)	5	10	15	33	44	55
47,48	4	8	12	25	33	42

NOTE: ***Ditko** c-3-6, 10, 11, 19, 21-24. Covers to #19, 21-24 reprint story panels.*

MYSTERIOUS ADVENTURES
Story Comics: Mar, 1951 - No. 24, Mar, 1955; No. 25, Aug, 1955

	GD 2.0	VG 4.0	FN 6.0	VF 8.0	VF/NM 9.0	NM- 9.2
1-All horror stories	63	126	189	394	610	825
2	37	74	112	213	312	410
3,4,6,10	35	70	105	198	287	375
5-Bondage-c	37	74	112	213	312	410
7-Daggar in eye panel	40	80	120	244	372	500
8-Eyeball story	48	96	144	293	447	600
9-Extreme violence (8/52)	39	78	117	227	331	435
11(12/52)-Used in **SOTI**, pg. 84	39	78	117	227	331	435
12,14: 14-E.C. Old Witch swipe	35	70	105	198	287	375
13-Classic skull-c	40	80	120	230	335	440
15-21: 18-Used in Senate Investigative report, pgs. 5,6; E.C. swipe/TFTC #35; The Coffin-Keeper & Corpse (hosts). 20-Used by Wertham in the Senate hearings. 21-Bondage/beheading-c	40	80	120	236	351	465
22- "Cinderella" parody	35	70	105	198	287	375
23-Disbrow-a (6 pgs.); E.C. swipe "The Mystery Keeper's Tale" (host) and "Mother Ghoul's Nursery Tale"	35	70	105	198	287	375
24,25	25	50	75	144	207	270

NOTE: ***Tothish** art by **Ross Andru**-#22, 23. **Bache** a-8. **Cameron** a-5-7. **Harrison** a-12. **Hollingsworth** a-3-8, 12. **Schaffenberger** a-24, 25. **Wildey** a-15, 17.*

MYSTERIOUS ISLAND
Dell Publishing Co.: No. 1213, July-Sept, 1961

	GD 2.0	VG 4.0	FN 6.0	VF 8.0	VF/NM 9.0	NM- 9.2
Four Color 1213-Movie, photo-c	10	20	30	70	100	130

MYSTERIOUS ISLE
Dell Publishing Co.: Nov-Jan, 1963/64 (Jules Verne)

	GD 2.0	VG 4.0	FN 6.0	VF 8.0	VF/NM 9.0	NM- 9.2
1	4	8	12	24	32	40

MYSTERIOUS RIDER, THE (See Zane Grey, 4-Color 301)

MYSTERIOUS STORIES (Formerly Horror From the Tomb #1)
Premier Magazines: No. 2, Dec-Jan, 1954-1955 - No. 7, Dec, 1955

	GD 2.0	VG 4.0	FN 6.0	VF 8.0	VF/NM 9.0	NM- 9.2
2-Woodbridge-c; last pre-code issue	47	94	141	287	436	585
3-Woodbridge-c/a	33	66	99	190	275	360
4-7: 5-Cinderella parody. 6-Woodbridge-c	31	62	93	175	253	330

NOTE: ***Hollingsworth** a-2, 4.*

MYSTERIOUS SUSPENSE (Also see Blue Beetle #1 (1967))
Charlton Comics: Oct, 1968 (12¢)

	GD 2.0	VG 4.0	FN 6.0	VF 8.0	VF/NM 9.0	NM- 9.2
1-Return of the Question by Ditko (c/a)	7	14	21	51	71	90

MYSTERIOUS TRAVELER (See Tales of the...)

MYSTERIOUS TRAVELER COMICS (Radio)
Trans-World Publications: Nov, 1948

	GD 2.0	VG 4.0	FN 6.0	VF 8.0	VF/NM 9.0	NM- 9.2
1-Powell-c/a(2); Poe adaptation, "Tell Tale Heart"	56	112	168	350	538	725

MYSTERY COMICS
William H. Wise & Co.: 1944 - No. 4, 1944 (No months given)

	GD 2.0	VG 4.0	FN 6.0	VF 8.0	VF/NM 9.0	NM- 9.2
1-The Magnet, The Silver Knight, Brad Spencer, Wonderman, Dick Devins, King of Futuria, & Zudo the Jungle Boy begin (all 1st app.); Schomburg-c on all	113	226	339	706	1091	1475
2-Bondage-c	69	138	207	431	666	900
3,4: 3-Lance Lewis, Space Detective begins (1st app.); Robot-c. 4(V2#1 inside)	62	124	186	388	594	800

MYSTERY COMICS DIGEST
Gold Key/Whitman?: Mar, 1972 - No. 26, Oct, 1975

	GD 2.0	VG 4.0	FN 6.0	VF 8.0	VF/NM 9.0	NM- 9.2
1-Ripley's Believe It or Not; reprint of Ripley's #1 origin Ra-Ka-Tep the Mummy; Wood-a	4	8	12	28	38	48
2-9: 2-Boris Karloff Tales of Mystery; Wood-a; 1st app. Werewolf Count Wulfstein. 3-Twilight Zone (TV); Crandall, Toth & George Evans-a; 1st app. Tragg & Simbar the Lion Lord; (2) Crandall/Frazetta-r/Twilight Zone #1 4-Ripley's Believe It or Not; 1st app. Baron Tibor, the Vampire. 5-Boris Karloff Tales of Mystery; 1st app. Dr. Spektor. 6-Twilight Zone (TV); 1st app. U.S. Marshal Reid & Sir Duane; Evans-r. 7-Ripley's Believe It or Not; origin The Lurker in the Swamp; 1st app. Duroc. 8-Boris Karloff Tales of Mystery; McWilliams-r; Orlando-r. 9-Twilight Zone (TV); Williamson, Crandall, McWilliams-a; 2nd Tragg app.;Torres, Evans, Heck/Tuska-r	3	7	10	21	28	35
10-26: 10,13-Ripley's Believe It or Not: 13-Orlando-r. 11,14-Boris Karloff Tales of Mystery. 14-1st app. Xorkon. 12,15-Twilight Zone (TV). 16,19,22,25-Ripley's Believe It or Not. 17-Boris Karloff Tales of Mystery; Williamson-r; Orlando-r. 18,21,24-Twilight Zone (TV). 20,23,26-Boris Karloff Tales of Mystery	3	6	9	16	21	26

Mystery in Space #24 © DC

Mystery Men Comics #1 © FOX

Mystic #9 © CRO

GD VG FN VF VF/NM NM-
2.0 4.0 6.0 8.0 9.0 9.2

GD VG FN VF VF/NM NM-
2.0 4.0 6.0 8.0 9.0 9.2

NOTE: *Dr. Spektor app.-#5, 10-12, 21. Durak app.-#15. Duroc app.-#14 (later called Durak). King George 1st app.-#8.*

MYSTERY IN SPACE (Also see Fireside Book Series and Pulp Fiction Library: ...)
National Periodical Pub.: 4-5/51 - No. 110, 9/66; No. 111, 9/80 - No. 117, 3/81 (#1-3: 52 pgs.)

1-Frazetta-a, 8 pgs.; Knights of the Galaxy begins, ends #8
229 458 687 2004 3402 4800
2 89 178 267 757 1229 1700
3 71 142 213 604 977 1350
4,5 59 118 177 502 814 1125
6-10: 7-Toth-a 48 96 144 384 605 825
11-15 38 76 114 285 443 600
16-18,20-25: Interplanetary Insurance feature by Infantino in all. 21-1st app. Space Cabbie. 24-Last pre-code issue 33 66 99 248 387 525
19-Virgil Finlay-a 36 72 108 270 428 585
26-40: 26-Space Cabbie feature begins. 34-1st S.A. issue
29 58 87 210 323 435
41-52: 47-Space Cabbie feature ends 22 44 66 158 242 325
53-Adam Strange begins (8/59, 10pg. sty); robot-c 153 306 459 1300 2100 2900
54 45 90 135 360 568 775
55-Grey tone-c 38 76 114 285 443 600
56-60: 59-Kane/Anderson-a 23 46 69 163 249 335
61-71: 61-1st app. Adam Strange foe Ulthoon. 62-1st app. A.S. foe Mortan. 63-Origin Vandor. 66-Star Rovers begin (1st app.). 68-1st app. Dust Devils (6/61). 69-1st Mailbag. 70-2nd app. Dust Devils. 71-Last 10¢ issue 18 36 54 126 193 260
72-74,76-80 12 24 36 87 134 180
75-JLA x-over in Adam Strange (5/62)(sequel to J.L.A. #3)
25 50 75 181 278 375
81-86 11 22 33 75 110 145
87-(11/63)-Adam Strange/Hawkman double feat begins; 3rd Hawkman tryout series
19 38 57 136 208 280
88-Adam Strange & Hawkman stories 17 34 51 121 186 250
89-Adam Strange & Hawkman stories 16 32 48 116 178 240
90-Adam Strange & Hawkman team-up for 1st time (3/64); Hawkman moves to own title next month 19 38 57 134 205 275
91-102: 91-End Infantino art on Adam Strange; double-length Adam Strange story. 92-Space Ranger begins (6/64), ends #103. 92-94,96,98-Space Ranger-c. 94,98-Adam Strange/ Space Ranger team-up. 102-Adam Strange ends (no Space Ranger)
7 14 21 46 63 80
103-Origin Ultra, the Multi-Alien; last Space Ranger 6 12 18 43 59 75
104-110: 110-(9/66)-Last 12¢ issue 5 10 15 33 44 55
V17#111(9/80)-117: 117-Newton-a(3 pgs.) 1 3 4 6 8 10

NOTE: ***Anderson** a-2, 4, 8-10, 12-17, 19, 45-48, 51, 57, 59i, 61-64, 70, 76, 87-91; c-9, 10, 15-25, 87, 89, 105-108, 110. **Aparo** a-111. **Austin** a-112i. **Bolland** a-115. **Craig** a-114, 116. **Ditko** a-111, 114-116. **Drucker** a-13, 14. **Elias** a-98, 102, 103. **Golden** a-113p. **Sid Greene** a-78, 91. **Infantino** a-1-8, 11, 14-25, 27-46, 48, 49, 51, 53-91, 103, 117; c-60-86, 88, 90, 91, 105, 107. **Gil Kane** a-14p, 15p, 18p, 19p, 26p, 29-59p(most), 100-102; c-52, 101. **Kubert** a-113; c-111-115. **Moriera** c-27, 28. **Rogers** a-111. **Sekowsky** a-52. **Simon & Kirby** a-4(2 pgs.). **Spiegle** a-111, 114. **Starlin** c-116. **Sutton** a-112. **Tuska** a-115p, 117p.*

MYSTERY MEN COMICS
Fox Features Syndicate: Aug, 1939 - No. 31, Feb, 1942

1-Intro. & 1st app. The Blue Beetle, The Green Mask, Rex Dexter of Mars by Briefer, Zanzibar by Tuska, Lt. Drake, D-13-Secret Agent by Powell, Chen Chang, Wing Turner, & Captain Denny Scott 1000 2000 3000 7000 11,250 15,500
2-Robot & sci/fi-c (2nd Robot-c w/Movie #6) 331 662 993 2152 3476 4800
3 (10/39)-Classic Lou Fine-c 414 828 1242 2691 4346 6000
4,5: 4-Capt. Savage begins (11/39) 254 508 762 1588 2444 3300
6-Tuska-c 208 416 624 1300 2000 2700
7-1st Blue Beetle-c app. 254 508 762 1588 2444 3300
8-Lou Fine-c 231 462 693 1444 2222 3000
9-The Moth begins; Lou Fine-c 115 230 345 719 1110 1500
10-12: All Joe Simon-c. 10-Wing Turner by Kirby; Simon-c. 11-Intro. Domino
96 192 288 600 925 1250
13-Intro. Lynx & sidekick Blackie (8/40) 65 130 195 406 623 840
14-18 62 124 186 388 594 800
19-Intro. & 1st app. Miss X (ends #21) 65 130 195 406 623 840
20-31: 26-The Wraith begins 60 120 180 375 575 775

NOTE: ***Briefer** a-1-15, 20, 24; c-9. **Cuidera** a-22. **Lou Fine** c-1-5,8,9. **Powell** a-1-15, 24. **Simon** c-10-12. **Tuska** a-1-16, 22, 24, 27; c-6. Bondage-c 1, 3, 7, 8, 25, 27-29, 31. Blue Beetle c-7, 8, 10-31. D-13 Secret Agent c-6. Green Mask c-1, 3-5. Rex Dexter of Mars c-2, 9.*

MYSTERY MEN MOVIE ADAPTION
Dark Horse Comics: July, 1999 - No. 2, Aug, 1999 ($2.95, mini-series)

1,2-Fingerman-s; photo-c 3.00

MYSTERY PLAY, THE
DC Comics (Vertigo): 1994 ($19.95, one-shot)

nn-Hardcover-Morrison-s/Muth-painted art 25.00
Softcover ($9.95)-New Muth cover 10.00

MYSTERY TALES
Atlas Comics (20CC): Mar, 1952 - No. 54, Aug, 1957

1-Horror/weird stories in all 87 174 261 544 835 1125
2-Krigstein-a 46 92 138 281 428 575
3-10: 6-A-Bomb panel. 10-Story similar to "The Assassin" from Shock SuspenStories
40 80 120 236 351 465
11,13-21: 14-Maneely s/f story. 20-Electric chair issue. 21-Matt Fox-a; decapitation story 30 60 90 170 245 320
12,22: 12-Matt Fox-a. 22-Forte/Matt Fox-c; a(i) 33 66 99 190 275 360
23-26 (2/55)-Last precode issue 24 48 72 135 195 255
27,29-35,37,38,41-43,48,49: 43-Morisi story contains Frazetta art swipes from Untamed Love
19 38 57 107 154 200
28,36,39,40,45: 28-Jack Katz-a. 36,39-Krigstein-a. 40,45-Ditko-a (#45 is 3 pgs. only)
20 40 60 112 161 210
44,51-Williamson/Krenkel-a 21 42 63 121 173 225
46-Williamson/Krenkel-a; Crandall text illos 21 42 63 121 173 225
47-Crandall, Ditko, Powell-a 21 42 63 121 173 225
50,52,53: 50-Torres, Morrow-a 19 38 57 107 154 200
54-Crandall, Check-a 20 40 60 112 161 210

NOTE: ***Ayers** a-18, 49, 52. **Berg** a-17, 51. **Colan** a-1, 3, 18, 35, 43. **Colletta** a-18. **Drucker** a-41. **Everett** a-2, 29, 33, 35, 41; c-8-11, 14, 38, 39, 41, 43, 44, 46, 48-51, 53. **Fass** a-16. **Forte** a-21, 22, 45, 46. **Matt Fox** a-12?, 21, 22; c-22. **Heath** a-3; c-3, 15, 17, 26. **Heck** a-25. **Kinstler** a-15. **Mort Lawrence** a-26, 32, 34. **Maneely** a-1, 9, 14, 22; c-12, 23, 24, 27. **Mooney** a-3, 40. **Morisi** a-43, 49, 52. **Morrow** a-50. **Orlando** a-51. **Pakula** a-16. **Powell** a-21, 29, 37, 38, 47. **Reinman** a-1, 14, 17. **Robinson** a-7p, 42. **Romita** a-37. **Roussos** a-4, 44. **R.Q. Sale** a-45, 46, 49. **Severin** c-52. **Shores** a-17, 45. **Tuska** a-10, 12, 14. **Whitney** a-2. **Wildey** a-37.*

MYSTERY TALES
Super Comics: 1964

Super Reprint #16,17('64): 16-r/Tales of Horror #2. 17-r/Eerie #14(Avon), 18-Kubert-r/Strange Terrors #4 3 6 9 16 20 25

MYSTIC (3rd Series)
Marvel/Atlas Comics (CLDS 1/CSI 2-21/OMC 22-35/CSI 35-61): March, 1951 - No. 61, Aug, 1957

1-Atom bomb panels; horror/weird stories in all 92 184 276 575 888 1200
2 50 100 150 305 465 625
3-Eyes torn out 44 88 132 268 409 550
4- "The Devil Birds" by Wolverton (6 pgs.) 79 158 237 494 760 1025
5,7-10 35 70 105 198 287 375
6- "The Eye of Doom" by Wolverton (7 pgs.) 79 158 237 494 760 1025
11-20: 16-Bondage/torture c/story 29 58 87 164 237 310
21-25,27-36-Last precode (3/55). 25-E.C. swipe 24 48 72 135 195 255
26-Atomic War, severed head stories 26 52 78 150 215 280
37-51,53-56,61 20 40 60 112 161 210
52-Wood-a; Crandall-a? 22 44 66 125 180 235
57-Story "Trapped in the Ant-Hill" (1957) is very similar to "The Man in the Ant Hill" in TTA #27
23 46 69 130 188 245
58,59-Krigstein-a 20 40 60 115 165 215
60-Williamson/Mayo-a (4 pgs.) 20 40 60 115 165 215

NOTE: ***Andru** a-23, 25. **Ayers** a-35, 53; c-8. **Berg** a-49. **Cameron** a-49, 51. **Check** a-31, 60. **Colan** a-3, 7, 12, 21, 37, 60. **Colletta** a-29. **Drucker** a-46, 52, 56. **Everett** a-8, 9, 17, 40, 44, 57; c-13, 18, 21, 42, 47, 49, 51-55, 57-59, 61. **Forte** a-35, 52, 58. **Fox** a-24i. **Al Hartley** a-35. **Heath** a-10; c-10, 20, 22, 23, 25, 30. **Infantino** a-12. **Kane** a-8, 24p. **Jack Katz** a-31, 33. **Mort Law.rence** a-19, 37. **Maneely** a-22, 24, 58; c-7, 15, 28, 29, 31. **Moldoff** a-29. **Morisi** a-48, 49, 52. **Morrow** a-51. **Orlando** a-57, 61. **Pakula** a-52, 57, 59. **Powell** a-52, 54-56. **Robinson** a-5. **Romita** a-11, 15. **R.Q. Sale** a-35, 53, 58. **Sekowsky** a-1, 2, 4, 5. **Severin** c-56, 60. **Tuska** a-15. **Whitney** a-33. **Wildey** a-28, 30. **Ed Win** a-17, 20. Canadian reprints known-title 'Startling.'*

MYSTIC (Also see CrossGen Chronicles)
CrossGeneration Comics: Jul, 2000 - No. 43, Jan, 2004 ($2.95)

1-43: 1-Marz-s/Peterson & Dell-a. 15-Cameos by DC & Marvel characters 3.00
...: Rite of Passage Vol. 1 TPB (5/01, $19.95) r/#1-7; Linsner-c 20.00
...: The Demon Queen Vol. 2 TPB (2002, $19.95) r/#8-14 20.00
...: Siege of Scales Vol. 3 TPB (2002, $15.95) r/#15-20 16.00
...: Out All Night Vol.4 TPB (2003, $15.95) r/#21-26 16.00
Vol. 5: Master Class (2003, $15.95) r/#27-32 16.00

MYSTICAL TALES
Atlas Comics (CCC 1/EPI 2-8): June, 1956 - No. 8, Aug, 1957

1-Everett-c/a 48 96 144 293 447 600
2-4: 2-Berg-a. 3,4-Crandall-a. 27 54 81 154 222 290
5-Williamson-a (4 pgs.) 29 58 87 164 237 310
6-Torres, Krigstein-a 25 50 75 144 207 270
7-Bolle, Forte, Torres, Orlando-a 25 50 75 141 203 265
8-Krigstein, Check-a 25 50 75 144 207 270

NOTE: ***Everett** a-1; c-1-4, 6, 7. **Orlando** a-1, 2, 7. **Pakula** a-3. **Powell** a-1, 4.*

Mystic Comics #9 © MAR

Mystique #1 © MAR

Namor V2#1 © MAR

GD VG FN VF VF/NM NM-
2.0 4.0 6.0 8.0 9.0 9.2

MYSTIC COMICS (1st Series)
Timely Comics (TPI 1-5/TCI 8-10): March, 1940 - No. 10, Aug, 1942

1-Origin The Blue Blaze, The Dynamic Man, & Flexo the Rubber Robot; Zephyr Jones, 3X's & Deep Sea Demon app.; The Magician begins (all 1st app.); c-from Spider pulp V18#1, 6/39 1294 2588 3882 9705 15,853 22,000
2-The Invisible Man & Master Mind Excello begin; Space Rangers, Zara of the Jungle, Taxi Taylor app. (scarce) 426 852 1278 2982 4791 6600
3-Origin Hercules, who last appears in #4 317 634 951 2061 3331 4600
4-Origin The Thin Man & The Black Widow; Merzak the Mystic app.; last Flexo, Dynamic Man, Invisible Man & Blue Blaze (some issues have date sticker on cover; others have July w/August overprint in silver color); Roosevelt assassination-c 345 690 1035 2243 3622 5000
5-(3/41)-Origin The Black Marvel, The Blazing Skull, The Sub-Earth Man, Super Slave & The Terror; The Moon Man & Black Widow app.; 5-German war-c begin, end #10 317 634 951 2061 3331 4600
6-(10/41)-Origin The Challenger & The Destroyer (1st app.?; also see All-Winners #2, Fall, 1941) 379 758 1137 2464 3982 5500
7-The Witness begins (12/41, origin & 1st app.); origin Davey & the Demon; last Black Widow; Hitler opens his trunk of terror-c by Simon & Kirby (classic-c) 400 800 1200 2600 4200 5800
8,10: 10-Father Time, World of Wonder, & Red Skeleton app.; last Challenger & Terror 223 446 669 1394 2147 2900
9-Gary Gaunt app.; last Black Marvel, Mystic & Blazing Skull; Hitler-c 238 476 714 1488 2294 3100

NOTE: ***Gabrielle*** *c-8-10.* ***Kirby/Schomburg*** *c-6.* ***Rico*** *a-9(2).* ***Schomburg*** *a-1-4; c-1-5.* ***Sekowsky*** *a-9.* ***Sekowsky/Klein*** *a-8(Challenger). Bondage c-1, 2, 9.*

MYSTIC COMICS (2nd Series)
Timely Comics (ANC): Oct, 1944 - No. 3, Win, 1944-45; No. 4, Mar, 1945

1-The Angel, The Destroyer, The Human Torch, Terry Vance the Schoolboy Sleuth, & Tommy Tyme begin 246 492 738 1538 2369 3200
2-(Fall/44)-Last Human Torch & Terry Vance; bondage/hypo-c 129 258 387 806 1241 1675
3-Last Angel (two stories) & Tommy Tyme 121 242 363 756 1166 1575
4-The Young Allies-c & app.; Schomburg-c 113 226 339 706 1091 1475

MYSTIC EDGE (Manga)
Antarctic Press: Oct, 1998 ($2.95, one-shot)

1-Ryan Kinnaird-s/a/c 3.00

MYSTIQUE (See X-Men titles)
Marvel Comics: June, 2003 - Present ($2.99)

1-21: 1-6-Linsner-c/Vaughan-s/Lucas-a. 7-Ryan-a begins. 8-Horn-c. 9-21-Mayhew-c 3.00
... Vol. 1: Drop Dead Gorgeous TPB (2004, $14.99) r/#1-6 15.00
... Vol. 2: Tinker, Tailor, Mutant, Spy TPB (2004, $17.99) r/#7-13 18.00

MYSTIQUE & SABRETOOTH (Sabretooth and Mystique on-c)
Marvel Comics: Dec, 1996 - No. 4, Mar, 1997 ($1.95, limited series)

1-4: Characters from X-Men 3.00

MY STORY (...True Romances in Pictures #5,6; becomes My Love Life #13) (Formerly Zago)
Hero Books (Fox Features Syndicate): No. 5, May, 1949 - No. 12, Aug, 1950

5-Kamen/Feldstein-a 21 42 63 121 173 225
6-8,11,12: 12-Photo-c 10 20 30 60 80 100
9,10-Wood-a 19 38 57 107 154 200

MYTHOGRAPHY
Bardic Press: Sept, 1996 - No. 8, May, 1998 ($3.95/$4.25, B&W, anthology)

1-3: 1-Drew Hayes-s/a 5.00
4-8 4.25

MYTHOS: THE FINAL TOUR
DC Comics/Vertigo: Dec, 1996 - No. 3, Feb, 1997 ($5.95, limited series)

1-3: 1-Ney Rieber-s/Amaro-a. 2-Snejbjerg-a; Constantine-app. 3-Kristiansen-a; Black Orchid-app. 6.00

MYTHSTALKERS
Image Comics: Mar, 2003 - No. 8, Mar, 2004 ($2.95)

1-8-Jiro-a 3.00

MYTH WARRIORS
Image Comics (Top Cow): Nov, 2004 ($9.95, B&W, digest-size)

1-Manapul-c 10.00

MY TRUE LOVE (Formerly Western Killers #64; Frank Buck #70 on)
Fox Features Syndicate: No. 65, July, 1949 - No. 69, March, 1950

65 16 32 48 92 131 170
66,68,69: 69-Morisi-a 10 20 30 60 80 100
67-Wood-a 19 38 57 107 154 200

NAIL, THE
Dark Horse Comics: June, 2004 - No. 4 ($2.99, limited series)

1-3-Rob Zombie & Steve Niles-s/Nat Jones-a/Simon Bisley-c 3.00
TPB (2005, $12.95) r/series 13.00

NAKED BRAIN (Marc Hempel's...)
Insight Studios Group: 2002 - No. 3, 2002 ($2.95, B&W, limited series)

1-3-Marc Hempel cartoons and sketches; Tug & Buster app. 3.00

NAKED PREY, THE (See Movie Classics)

'NAM, THE (See Savage Tales #1, 2nd series & Punisher Invades...)
Marvel Comics Group: Dec, 1986 - No. 84, Sept, 1993

1-Golden a(p)/c begins, ends #13 3.00
1 (2nd printing) 2.25
2-8,10-66,70-74: 7-Golden-a (2 pgs.). 32-Death R. Kennedy. 52,53-Frank Castle (The Punisher) app. 52,53-Gold 2nd printings. 58-Silver logo. 65-Heath-c/a. 70-Lomax scripts begin 2.25
9-1st app. Fudd Verzyl, Tunnel Rat 3.00
67-69,76-84: 67-69-Punisher 3 part story 3.00
75-($2.25, 52 pgs.) 2.50
Trade Paperback 1,2: 1-r/#1-4. 2-r/#5-8 5.00
TPB ('99, $14.95) r/#1-4; recolored 15.00

'NAM MAGAZINE, THE
Marvel Comics: Aug, 1988 - No. 10, May, 1989 ($2.00, B&W, 52pgs.)

1-10: Each issue reprints 2 issues of the comic 2.25

NAMELESS, THE
Image Comics: May, 1997 - No. 5, Sept, 1997 ($2.95, B&W)

1-5: Pruett/Hester-s/a 3.00

NAMES OF MAGIC, THE (Also see Books of Magic)
DC Comics (Vertigo): Feb, 2001 - No. 5, June, 2001 ($2.50, limited series)

1-5: Bolton painted-c on all; Case-a; leads into Hunter: The Age of Magic 2.50
TPB (2002, $14.95) r/#1-5 15.00

NAME OF THE GAME, THE
DC Comics: 2001 ($29.95, graphic novel)

Hardcover ($29.95) Will Eisner-s/a 30.00

NAMOR (Volume 2)
Marvel Comics: June, 2003 - No. 12, May, 2004 (25¢/$2.25/$2.99)

1-(25¢-c)Young Namor in the 1920s; Larroca-c/a 2.25
2-6-($2.25) Larroca-a 2.25
7-12-($2.99): 7-Olliffe-a begins 3.00

NAMORA (See Marvel Mystery Comics #82 & Sub-Mariner Comics)
Marvel Comics (PrPl): Fall, 1948 - No. 3, Dec, 1948

1-Sub-Mariner x-over in Namora; Namora by Everett(2), Sub-Mariner by Rico (10 pgs.) 262 524 786 1638 2519 3400
2-The Blonde Phantom & Sub-Mariner story; Everett-a 133 266 399 831 1278 1725
3-(Scarce)-Sub-Mariner app.; Everett-a 142 284 426 888 1369 1850

NAMOR, THE SUB-MARINER (See Prince Namor & Sub-Mariner)
Marvel Comics: Apr, 1990 - No. 62, May, 1995 ($1.00/$1.25/$1.50)

1-Byrne-c/a/scripts in 1-25 (scripts only #26-32) 4.00
2-5: 5-Iron Man app. 3.00
6-11,13-23,25,27-49,51-62: 16-Re-intro Iron Fist (8-cameo only). 18-Punisher cameo (1 panel); 21-23,25-Wolverine cameos. 22,23-Iron Fist app. 28-Iron Fist-c/story. 31-Dr. Doom-c/story. 33,34-Iron Fist cameo. 35-New Tiger Shark-c/story. 37-Aqua holografx foil-c. 48-The Thing app. 2.25
12,24: 12-(52pgs.)-Re-intro. The Invaders. 24-Namor vs. Wolverine 2.50
26-Namor w/new costume; 1st Jae Lee-c/a this title (5/92) & begins 3.00
50-($1.75, 52 pgs.)-Newsstand ed.; w/bound-in S-M trading card sheet (both versions) 2.25
50-($2.95, 52 pgs.)-Collector edition w/foil-c 3.00
Annual 1-4 ('91-94, 68 pgs.): 1-3 pg. origin recap. 2-Return/Defenders. 3-Bagged w/card. 4-Painted-c 3.00

NOTE: ***Jae Lee*** *a-26-30p, 31-37, 38p, 39, 40; c-26-40.*

NANCY AND SLUGGO (See Comics On Parade & Sparkle Comics)
United Features Syndicate: No. 16, 1949 - No. 23, 1954

16(#1) 9 18 27 54 70 85
17-23 7 14 21 35 43 50

NANCY & SLUGGO (Nancy #146-173; formerly Sparkler Comics)

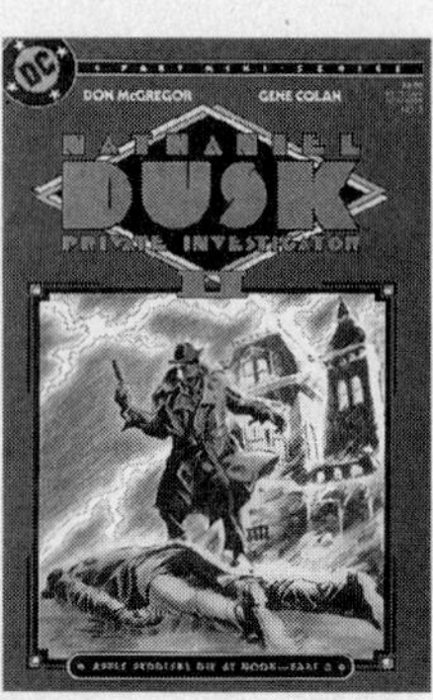

Nathaniel Dusk II #3 © DC

National Comics #27 © QUA

Navy Action #1 © MAR

St. John/Dell #146-187/Gold Key #188 on: No. 121, Apr, 1955-No. 192, Oct, 1963

Issue	GD 2.0	VG 4.0	FN 6.0	VF 8.0	VF/NM 9.0	NM- 9.2
121(4/55)(St. John)	8	16	24	46	58	70
122-145(7/57)(St. John)	7	14	21	37	46	55
146(9/57)-Peanuts begins, ends #192 (Dell)	6	12	18	43	59	75
147-161 (Dell) Peanuts in all	6	12	18	38	52	65
162-165,177-180-John Stanley-a	8	16	24	58	82	105
166-176-Oona & Her Haunted House series; Stanley-a	9	18	27	65	93	120
181-187(3-5/62)(Dell)	5	10	15	36	48	60
188(10/62)-192 (Gold Key)	5	10	15	36	48	60
Four Color 1034(9-11/59)-Summer Camp	5	10	15	36	48	60

(See Dell Giant #34, 45 & Dell Giants)

NANNY AND THE PROFESSOR (TV)
Dell Publishing Co.: Aug, 1970 - No. 2, Oct, 1970 (Photo-c)

Issue	GD 2.0	VG 4.0	FN 6.0	VF 8.0	VF/NM 9.0	NM- 9.2
1-(01-546-008)	6	12	18	40	55	70
2	5	10	15	33	44	55

NAPOLEON
Dell Publishing Co.: No. 526, Dec, 1953

Issue	GD 2.0	VG 4.0	FN 6.0	VF 8.0	VF/NM 9.0	NM- 9.2
Four Color 526	3	7	10	21	28	35

NAPOLEON & SAMANTHA (See Walt Disney Showcase No. 10)

NAPOLEON & UNCLE ELBY (See Clifford McBride's...)
Eastern Color Printing Co.: July, 1942 (68 pgs.) (One Shot)

Issue	GD 2.0	VG 4.0	FN 6.0	VF 8.0	VF/NM 9.0	NM- 9.2
1	44	88	132	268	409	550
1945-American Book-Strafford Press (128 pgs.) (8x10-1/2"; B&W reprints; hardcover)	15	30	45	83	117	150

NARRATIVE ILLUSTRATION, THE STORY OF THE COMICS (Also see Good Triumphs Over Evil!)
M.C. Gaines: Summer, 1942 (32 pgs., 7-1/4"x10", B&W w/color inserts)

nn-16 pgs. text with illustrations of ancient art, strips and comic covers; 4 pg. WWII War Bond promo, "The Minute Man Answers the Call" color comic drawn by Shelly and a special 8-page color comic insert of "The Story of Saul" (from Picture Stories from the Bible #10 or soon to appear in PS #10) or "Noah and His Ark" or "The Story of Ruth". Insert has special title page indicating it was part of a Sunday newspaper supplement insert series that had already run in a New England "Sunday Herald." Another version exists with insert from Picture Stories from the Bible #7. (very rare) Estimated value... 1500.00

NASH (WCW Wrestling)
Image Comics: July, 1999 - No. 2, July, 1999 ($2.95)

Issue	GD 2.0	VG 4.0	FN 6.0	VF 8.0	VF/NM 9.0	NM- 9.2
1,2-Regular and photo-c						3.00
1-($6.95) Photo-split-cover Edition						7.00

NATHANIEL DUSK
DC Comics: Feb, 1984 - No. 4, May, 1984 ($1.25, mini-series, direct sales, Baxter paper)

Issue	GD 2.0	VG 4.0	FN 6.0	VF 8.0	VF/NM 9.0	NM- 9.2
1-4: 1-Intro/origin; Gene Colan-c/a in all						2.25

NATHANIEL DUSK II
DC Comics: Oct, 1985 - No. 4, Jan, 1986 ($2.00, mini-series, Baxter paper)

Issue	GD 2.0	VG 4.0	FN 6.0	VF 8.0	VF/NM 9.0	NM- 9.2
1-4: Gene Colan-c/a in all						2.25

NATHAN NEVER
Dark Horse (Bonelli Comics): Mar, 1999 - No. 6, Aug, 1999 ($4.95, B&W, digest size)

Issue	GD 2.0	VG 4.0	FN 6.0	VF 8.0	VF/NM 9.0	NM- 9.2
1-6-Reprints Italian series in English. 1-4-Art Adams-c						5.00

NATIONAL COMICS
Quality Comics Group: July, 1940 - No. 75, Nov, 1949

Issue	GD 2.0	VG 4.0	FN 6.0	VF 8.0	VF/NM 9.0	NM- 9.2
1-Uncle Sam begins (1st app.); origin sidekick Buddy by Eisner; origin Wonder Boy & Kid Dixon; Merlin the Magician (ends #45); Cyclone, Kid Patrol, Sally O'Neil Policewoman, Pen Miller (by Klaus Nordling; ends #22), Prop Powers (ends #26), & Paul Bunyan (ends #22) begin	517	1034	1551	3619	5810	8000
2	246	492	738	1538	2369	3200
3-Last Eisner Uncle Sam	173	346	519	1081	1666	2250
4-Last Cyclone	135	270	405	844	1297	1750
5-(11/40)-Quicksilver begins (1st app.; 3rd w/lightning speed?; re-intro'd by DC in 1993 as Max Mercury in Flash #76, 2nd series); origin Uncle Sam; bondage-c	154	308	462	963	1482	2000
6,8-11: 8-Jack & Jill begins (ends #22). 9-Flag-c	129	258	387	806	1241	1675
7-Classic Lou Fine-c	231	462	693	1444	2222	3000
12	96	192	288	600	925	1250
13-16-Lou Fine-a	87	174	261	544	835	1125
17,19-22: 22-Last Pen Miller (moves to Crack #23)	67	134	201	419	647	875
18-(12/41)-Shows orientals attacking Pearl Harbor; on stands one month before actual event	121	242	363	756	1166	1575
23-The Unknown & Destroyer 171 begin	69	138	207	431	666	900
24-Japanese War-c	69	138	207	431	666	900
25-30: 26-Wonder Boy ends. 27- G-2 the Unknown begins (ends #46). 29-Origin The Unknown	48	96	144	293	447	600
31-33: 33-Chic Carter begins (ends #47)	44	88	132	268	409	550
34-37,40: 35-Last Kid Patrol	40	80	120	230	335	440
38-Hitler, Tojo, Mussolini-c	44	88	132	268	409	550
39-Hitler-c	46	92	138	281	428	575
41-50: 42-The Barker begins (1st app?, 5/44); The Barker covers begin. 48-Origin The Whistler	24	48	72	138	199	260
51-Sally O'Neil by Ward, 8 pgs. (12/45)	29	58	87	164	237	310
52-60	20	40	60	112	161	210
61-67: 67-Format change; Quicksilver app.	15	30	45	85	120	155
68-75: The Barker ends	12	24	36	71	98	125

NOTE: ***Cole*** *Quicksilver-13; Barker-43; c-43, 46, 47, 49-51.* ***Crandall*** *Uncle Sam-11-13 (with* ***Fine****), 25, 26; c-24-26, 30-33, 43.* ***Crandall*** *Paul Bunyan-10-13.* ***Fine*** *Uncle Sam-13 (w/****Crandall****), 17, 18; c-1-14, 16, 18, 21.* ***Gill Fox*** *c-69-74.* ***Guardineer*** *Quicksilver-27, 35.* ***Gustavson*** *Quicksilver-14-26.* ***McWilliams*** *a-23-28, 55, 57. Uncle Sam c-1-41. Barker c-42-75.*

NATIONAL COMICS (Also see All Star Comics 1999 crossover titles)
DC Comics: May, 1999 ($1.99, one-shot)

Issue	GD 2.0	VG 4.0	FN 6.0	VF 8.0	VF/NM 9.0	NM- 9.2
1-Golden Age Flash and Mr. Terrific; Waid-s/Lopresti-a						2.25

NATIONAL CRUMB, THE (Magazine-Size)
Mayfair Publications: August, 1975 (52 pgs., B&W) (Satire)

Issue	GD 2.0	VG 4.0	FN 6.0	VF 8.0	VF/NM 9.0	NM- 9.2
1-Grandenetti-c/a, Ayers-a	2	4	6	12	16	20

NATIONAL VELVET (TV)
Dell Publishing Co./Gold Key: May-July, 1961 - No. 2, Mar, 1963 (All photo-c)

Issue	GD 2.0	VG 4.0	FN 6.0	VF 8.0	VF/NM 9.0	NM- 9.2
Four Color 1195 (#1)	8	16	24	58	82	105
Four Color 1312, 01-556-207, 12-556-210 (Dell)	5	10	15	33	44	55
1,2: 1(12/62) (Gold Key). 2(3/63)	5	10	15	33	44	55

NATION OF SNITCHES
Piranha Press (DC): 1990 ($4.95, color, 52 pgs.)

Issue	GD 2.0	VG 4.0	FN 6.0	VF 8.0	VF/NM 9.0	NM- 9.2
nn						5.00

NATURE BOY (Formerly Danny Blaze; Li'l Rascal Twins #6 on)
Charlton Comics: No. 3, March, 1956 - No. 5, Feb, 1957

Issue	GD 2.0	VG 4.0	FN 6.0	VF 8.0	VF/NM 9.0	NM- 9.2
3-Origin; Blue Beetle story; Buscema-c/a	24	48	72	135	195	255
4,5	17	34	51	95	135	175

NOTE: ***John Buscema*** *a-3, 4p, 5; c-3.* ***Powell*** *a-4.*

NATURE OF THINGS (Disney, TV/Movie)
Dell Publishing Co.: No. 727, Sept, 1956 - No. 842, Sept, 1957

Issue	GD 2.0	VG 4.0	FN 6.0	VF 8.0	VF/NM 9.0	NM- 9.2
Four Color 727 (#1), 842-Jesse Marsh-a	6	12	18	43	59	75

NAUSICAA OF THE VALLEY OF WIND
Viz Comics: 1988 - No. 7, 1989; 1989 - No. 4, 1990 ($2.50, B&W, 68pgs.)

Issue	GD 2.0	VG 4.0	FN 6.0	VF 8.0	VF/NM 9.0	NM- 9.2
Book 1-7: 1-Contains Moebius poster						3.25
Part II, Book 1-4 ($2.95)						3.25

NAVY ACTION (Sailor Sweeney #12-14)
Atlas Comics (CDS): Aug, 1954 - No. 11, Apr, 1956; No. 15, 1/57 - No. 18, 8/57

Issue	GD 2.0	VG 4.0	FN 6.0	VF 8.0	VF/NM 9.0	NM- 9.2
1-Powell-a	19	38	57	107	154	200
2-Lawrence-a	10	20	30	60	80	100
3-11: 4-Last precode (2/55)	9	18	27	51	62	75
15-18	8	16	24	46	58	70

NOTE: ***Berg*** *a-7, 9.* ***Colan*** *a-8.* ***Drucker*** *a-7, 17.* ***Everett*** *a-3, 7, 16; c-16, 17.* ***Heath*** *c-1, 2, 6.* ***Maneely*** *a-7, 8, 18; c-9, 11.* ***Pakula*** *a-2, 3, 9.* ***Reinman*** *a-17.*

NAVY COMBAT
Atlas Comics (MPI): June, 1955 - No. 20, Oct, 1958

Issue	GD 2.0	VG 4.0	FN 6.0	VF 8.0	VF/NM 9.0	NM- 9.2
1-Torpedo Taylor begins by Don Heck	19	38	57	107	154	200
2	10	20	30	60	80	100
3-10	9	18	27	51	62	75
11,13,15,16,18-20	8	16	24	46	58	70
12-Crandall-a	10	20	30	58	77	95
14-Torres-a	9	18	27	51	62	75
17-Williamson-a, 4 pgs.; Torres-a	9	18	27	52	66	80

NOTE: ***Berg*** *a-10, 11.* ***Colan*** *a-11.* ***Drucker*** *a-7.* ***Everett*** *a-3, 20; c-8 & 9 w/****Tuska****, 10, 13-16.* ***Heck*** *a-11(2).* ***Maneely*** *c-1, 6, 11, 17.* ***Morisi*** *a-8.* ***Pakula*** *a-7.* ***Powell*** *a-20.*

NAVY HEROES
Almanac Publishing Co.: 1945

Issue	GD 2.0	VG 4.0	FN 6.0	VF 8.0	VF/NM 9.0	NM- 9.2
1-Heavy in propaganda	12	24	36	71	98	125

NAVY PATROL
Key Publications: May, 1955 - No. 4, Nov, 1955

Negative Burn #24 © Caliber

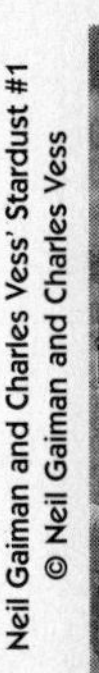

Neil Gaiman and Charles Vess' Stardust #1 © Neil Gaiman and Charles Vess

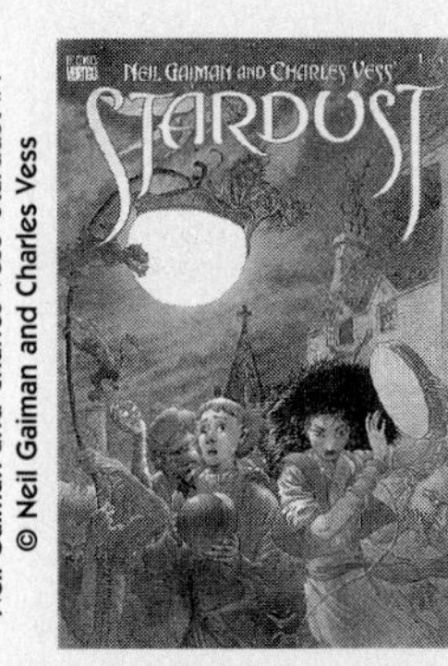

Nellie the Nurse #10 © MAR

	GD 2.0	VG 4.0	FN 6.0	VF 8.0	VF/NM 9.0	NM- 9.2
1	8	16	24	40	50	60
2-4	5	10	15	24	30	35

NAVY TALES
Atlas Comics (CDS): Jan, 1957 - No. 4, July, 1957

	GD 2.0	VG 4.0	FN 6.0	VF 8.0	VF/NM 9.0	NM- 9.2
1-Everett-c; Berg, Powell-a	16	32	48	89	127	165
2-Williamson/Mayo-a(5 pgs); Crandall-a	14	28	42	79	110	140
3,4-Reinman-a; Severin-c. 4-Crandall-a	12	24	36	69	95	120

NOTE: ***Colan** a-4. **Maneely** c-2. **Sinnott** a-4.*

NAVY TASK FORCE
Stanmor Publications/Aragon Mag. No. 4-8: Feb, 1954 - No. 8, April, 1956

	GD 2.0	VG 4.0	FN 6.0	VF 8.0	VF/NM 9.0	NM- 9.2
1	8	16	24	46	58	70
2	5	10	15	24	30	35
3-8: #8-r/Navy Patrol #1	5	10	15	22	26	30

NAVY WAR HEROES
Charlton Comics: Jan, 1964 - No. 7, Mar-Apr, 1965

	GD 2.0	VG 4.0	FN 6.0	VF 8.0	VF/NM 9.0	NM- 9.2
1	4	8	12	22	30	38
2-7	2	4	6	14	18	22

NAZA (Stone Age Warrior)
Dell Publishing Co.: Nov-Jan, 1963-64 - No. 9, March, 1966

	GD 2.0	VG 4.0	FN 6.0	VF 8.0	VF/NM 9.0	NM- 9.2
12-555-401 (#1)-Painted-c	5	10	15	36	48	60
2-9: 2-4-Painted-c	4	8	12	22	30	38

NAZZ, THE
DC Comics: 1990 - No. 4, 1991 ($4.95, 52 pgs., mature)

	NM- 9.2
1-4	5.00

NEBBS, THE (Also see Crackajack Funnies)
Dell Publishing Co./Croydon Publishing Co.: 1941; 1945

	GD 2.0	VG 4.0	FN 6.0	VF 8.0	VF/NM 9.0	NM- 9.2
Large Feature Comic 23(1941)	21	42	63	121	173	225
1(1945, 36 pgs.)-Reprints	13	26	39	76	106	135

NECROMANCER: THE GRAPHIC NOVEL
Marvel Comics (Epic Comics): 1989 ($8.95)

	NM- 9.2
nn	9.00

NECROWAR
Dreamwave Productions: July, 2003 - No. 3, Sept, 2003 ($2.95)

	NM- 9.2
1-3-Furman-s/Granov-digital art	3.00

NEGATION
CrossGeneration Comics: Dec; 2001 - No. 27, Mar, 2004 ($2.95)

	NM- 9.2
Prequel (12/01)	3.00
1-27: 1-(1/02) Pelletier-a/Bedard & Waid-s	3.00
... Lawbringer (11/02, $2.95) Nebres-a	3.00
Vol. 1: Bohica! (10/02, $19.95, TPB) r/ Prequel & #1-6	20.00
Vol. 2: Baptism of Fire (5/03, $15.95, TPB) r/#7-12	16.00
Vol. 3: Hounded (12/03, $15.95, TPB) r/#13-18	16.00

NEGATION WAR
CrossGeneration Comics: Apr, 2004 - No. 6 ($2.95)

	NM- 9.2
1-2-Bedard-s/Pelletier-a	3.00

NEGATIVE BURN
Caliber: 1993 - No. 50, 1997 ($2.95, B&W, anthology)

	GD 2.0	VG 4.0	FN 6.0	VF 8.0	VF/NM 9.0	NM- 9.2
1,2,4-12,14-47: Anthology by various including Bolland, Burden, Doran, Gaiman, Moebius, Moore, & Pope						4.00
3,13: 3-Bone story. 13-Strangers in Paradise story	2	4	6	8	10	12
48,49-($4.95)						5.00
50-($6.95, 96 pgs.)-Gaiman, Robinson, Bolland						7.00

NEGRO (See All-Negro)

NEGRO HEROES (Calling All Girls, Real Heroes, & True Comics reprints)
Parents' Magazine Institute: Spring, 1947 - No. 2, Summer, 1948

	GD 2.0	VG 4.0	FN 6.0	VF 8.0	VF/NM 9.0	NM- 9.2
1	87	174	261	544	835	1125
2-Jackie Robinson-c/story	94	188	282	588	907	1225

NEGRO ROMANCE (Negro Romances #4)
Fawcett Publications: June, 1950 - No. 3, Oct, 1950 (All photo-c)

	GD 2.0	VG 4.0	FN 6.0	VF 8.0	VF/NM 9.0	NM- 9.2
1-Evans-a	115	230	345	719	1110	1500
2,3	87	174	261	544	835	1125

NEGRO ROMANCES (Formerly Negro Romance; Romantic Secrets #5 on)
Charlton Comics: No. 4, May, 1955

	GD 2.0	VG 4.0	FN 6.0	VF 8.0	VF/NM 9.0	NM- 9.2
4-Reprints Fawcett #2	69	138	207	431	666	900

NEIL GAIMAN AND CHARLES VESS' STARDUST
DC Comics (Vertigo): 1997 - No. 4, 1998 ($5.95/$6.95, square-bound, lim. series)

	NM- 9.2
1-4: Gaiman text with Vess paintings in all	7.00
Hardcover (1998, $29.95) r/series with new sketches	35.00
Softcover (1999, $19.95) oversized; new Vess-c	20.00

NEIL GAIMAN'S LADY JUSTICE
Tekno Comix: Sept, 1995 - No. 11, May, 1996 ($1.95/$2.25)

	NM- 9.2
1-11: 1-Sienkiewicz-c; pin-ups. 1-5-Brereton-c. 7-Polybagged. 11-The Big Bang Pt. 7	2.25

NEIL GAIMAN'S LADY JUSTICE
BIG Entertainment: V2#1, June, 1996 - No. 9, Feb, 1997 ($2.25)

	NM- 9.2
V2#1-9: Dan Brereton-c on all. 6-8-Dan Brereton script	2.25

NEIL GAIMAN'S MIDNIGHT DAYS
DC Comics (Vertigo): 1999 ($17.95, trade paperback)

	NM- 9.2
nn-Reprints Gaiman's short stories; new Swamp Thing w/ Bissette-a	18.00

NEIL GAIMAN'S MR. HERO-THE NEWMATIC MAN
Tekno Comix: Mar, 1995 - No. 17, May, 1996 ($1.95/$2.25)

	NM- 9.2
1-17: 1-Intro Mr. Hero & Teknophage; bound-in game piece and trading card. 4-w/Steel edition Neil Gaiman's Teknophage #1 coupon. 13-Polybagged	2.25

NEIL GAIMAN'S MR. HERO-THE NEWMATIC MAN
BIG Entertainment: V2#1, June, 1996 ($2.25)

	NM- 9.2
V2#1-Teknophage destroys Mr. Hero; includes The Big Bang Pt. 10	2.25

NEIL GAIMAN'S PHAGE-SHADOWDEATH
BIG Entertainment: June, 1996 - No. 6, Nov, 1996 ($2.25, limited series)

	NM- 9.2
1-6: Bryan Talbot-c & scripts in all. 1-1st app. Orlando Holmes	2.25

NEIL GAIMAN'S TEKNOPHAGE
Tekno Comix: Aug, 1995 - No. 10, Mar, 1996 ($1.95/$2.25)

	NM- 9.2
1-6-Rick Veitch scripts & Bryan Talbot-c/a.	2.25
1-Steel Edition	4.00
7-10: Paul Jenkins scripts in all. 8-polybagged	2.25

NEIL GAIMAN'S WHEEL OF WORLDS
Tekno Comix: Apr, 1995 - No. 1, May, 1996 ($2.95/$3.25)

	NM- 9.2
0-1st app. Lady Justice; 48 pgs.; bound-in poster	3.25
0-Regular edition	2.25
1 ($3.25, 5/96)-Bruce Jones scripts; Lady Justice & Teknophage app.; CGI photo-c	3.25

NEIL THE HORSE (See Charlton Bullseye #2)
Aardvark-Vanaheim #1-10/Renegade Press #11 on: 2/83 - No. 10, 12/84; No. 11, 4/85 - #15, 1985 (B&W)

	NM- 9.2
1($1.40)	4.00
1-2nd print	2.25
2-13: 13-Double size; 11,13-w/paperdolls	2.25
14,15: Double size ($3.00). 15 is a flip book(2-c)	3.00

NELLIE THE NURSE (Also see Gay Comics & Joker Comics)
Marvel/Atlas Comics (SPI/LMC): 1945 - No. 36, Oct, 1952; 1957

	GD 2.0	VG 4.0	FN 6.0	VF 8.0	VF/NM 9.0	NM- 9.2
1-(1945)	40	80	120	236	351	465
2-(Spring/46)	20	40	60	112	161	210
3,4: 3-New logo (9/46)	15	30	45	86	123	160
5-Kurtzman's "Hey Look" (3); Georgie app.	17	34	51	98	139	180
6-8,10: 7,8-Georgie app. 10-Millie app.	15	30	45	83	117	150
9-Wolverton-a (1 pg.); Mille the Model app.	15	30	45	85	120	155
11,14-16,18-Kurtzman's "Hey Look"	15	30	45	86	123	160
12- "Giggles 'n' Grins" by Kurtzman	15	30	45	83	117	150
13,17,19,20: 17-Annie Oakley app.	11	22	33	62	84	105
21-27,29,30	10	20	30	58	77	95
28-Mr. Nexdoor-r (3 pgs.) by Kurtzman/Rusty #22	10	20	30	58	77	95
31-36: 36-Post-c	9	18	27	52	66	80
1('57)-Leading Mag. (Atlas)-Everett-a, 20 pgs	10	20	30	56	73	90

NELLIE THE NURSE
Dell Publishing Co.: No. 1304, Mar-May, 1962

	GD 2.0	VG 4.0	FN 6.0	VF 8.0	VF/NM 9.0	NM- 9.2
Four Color 1304-Stanley-a	8	16	24	58	82	105

NEMESIS THE WARLOCK (Also see Spellbinders)
Eagle Comics: Sept, 1984 - No. 7, Mar, 1985 (limited series, Baxter paper)

	NM- 9.2
1-7: 2000 A.D. reprints	2.25

NEMESIS THE WARLOCK
Quality Comics/Fleetway Quality #2 on: 1989 - No. 19, 1991 ($1.95, B&W)

	NM- 9.2
1-19	2.25

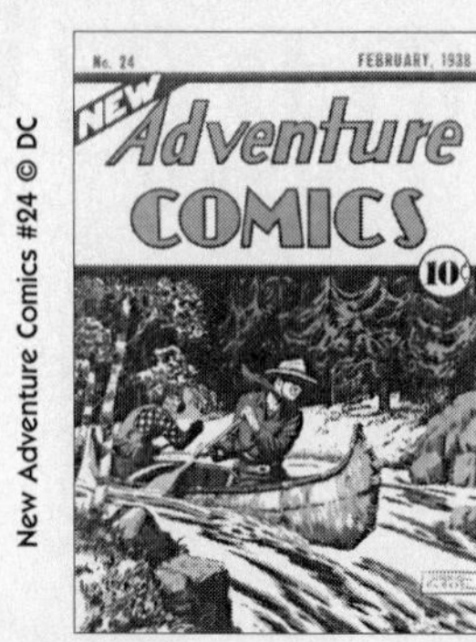

New Adventure Comics #24 © DC

New Adventures of Charlie Chan #2 © DC

The New Avvengers #1 © MAR

GD VG FN VF VF/NM NM-
2.0 4.0 6.0 8.0 9.0 9.2

NEON CYBER
Image Comics (Dreamwave Prod.): Jul, 1999 - No. 8, Jun, 2000 ($2.50)
1-8-Adrian Tsang-s 2.50

NEUTRO
Dell Publishing Co.: Jan, 1967
1-Jack Sparling-c/a (super hero); UFO-s 5 10 15 33 44 55

NEVADA (See Zane Grey's Four Color 412, 996 & Zane Grey's Stories of the West #1)

NEVADA (Also see Vertigo Winter's Edge #1)
DC Comics (Vertigo): May, 1998 - No. 6, Oct, 1998 ($2.50, limited series)
1-6-Gerber-s/Winslade-c/a 2.50
TPB-(1999, $14.95) r/#1-6 & Vertigo Winter's Edge preview 15.00

NEVER AGAIN (War stories; becomes Soldier & Marine V2#9)
Charlton Comics: Aug, 1955; No. 8, July, 1956 (No #2-7)
1 9 18 27 52 66 80
8-(Formerly Foxhole?) 6 12 18 28 34 40

NEVERMEN, THE (See Dark Horse Presents #148-150)
Dark Horse Comics: May, 2000 - No. 4, Aug, 2000 ($2.95, limited series)
1-4-Phil Amara-s/Guy Davis-a 3.00

NEVERMEN, THE: STREETS OF BLOOD
Dark Horse Comics: Jan, 2003 - No. 3, Apr, 2003 ($2.99, limited series)
1-3-Phil Amara-s/Guy Davis-a 3.00
TPB (7/03, $9.95) r/#1-3; Paul Jenkins intro.; Davis sketch pages 10.00

NEW ADVENTURE COMICS (Formerly New Comics; becomes Adventure Comics #32 on; V1#12 indicia says NEW COMICS #12)
National Periodical Publications: V1#12, Jan, 1937 - No. 31, Oct, 1938
V1#12-Federal Men by Siegel & Shuster continues; Jor-L mentioned; Whitney Ellsworth-c begin, end #14 508 1016 1523 3600 – –
V2#1(2/37, #13)-(Rare) 477 954 1431 3400 – –
V2#2 (#14) 415 830 1246 3000 – –
15(V2#3)-20(V2#8): 15-1st Adventure logo; Creig Flessel-c begin, end #31. 16-1st non-funny cover. 17-Nadir, Master of Magic begins, ends #30 356 712 1068 1958 2729 3500
21(V2#9),22(V2#10, 2/37): 22-X-Mas-c 317 634 951 1744 2372 3000
23-31 267 534 800 1469 1985 2500

NEW ADVENTURES OF ABRAHAM LINCOLN, THE
Image Comics (Homage): 1998 ($19.95, one-shot)
1-Scott McCloud-s/computer art 20.00

NEW ADVENTURES OF CHARLIE CHAN, THE (TV)
National Periodical Publications: May-June, 1958 - No. 6, Mar-Apr, 1959
1 (Scarce)-Gil Kane/Sid Greene-a in all 71 142 213 444 685 925
2 (Scarce) 46 92 138 281 428 575
3-6 (Scarce)-Greene/Giella-a 40 80 120 236 351 465

NEW ADVENTURES OF HUCK FINN, THE (TV)
Gold Key: December, 1968 (Hanna-Barbera)
1- "The Curse of Thut"; part photo-c 4 8 12 27 36 45

NEW ADVENTURES OF PINOCCHIO (TV)
Dell Publishing Co.: Oct-Dec, 1962 - No. 3, Sept-Nov, 1963
12-562-212(#1) 10 20 30 70 100 130
2,3 8 16 24 55 78 100

NEW ADVENTURES OF ROBIN HOOD (See Robin Hood)

NEW ADVENTURES OF SHERLOCK HOLMES (Also see Sherlock Holmes)
Dell Publishing Co.: No. 1169, Mar-May, 1961 - No. 1245, Nov-Jan, 1961/62
Four Color 1169(#1) 17 34 51 119 182 245
Four Color 1245 15 30 45 107 164 220

NEW ADVENTURES OF SPEED RACER
Now Comics: Dec, 1993 - No. 7, 1994? ($1.95)
1-7 2.25
0-(Premiere)-3-D cover 3.00

NEW ADVENTURES OF SUPERBOY, THE (Also see Superboy)
DC Comics: Jan, 1980 - No. 54, June, 1984
1 5.00
2-6,8-10 4.00
11-49,51-54: 11-Superboy gets new power. 14-Lex Luthor app. 15-Superboy gets new parents. 28-Dial "H" For Hero begins, ends #49. 45-47-1st app. Sunburst. 48-Begin 75¢-c. 3.00
1,2,5,6,8 (Whitman variants; low print run; no issue # shown on cover) 1 2 3 4 5 7
7,50: 7-Has extra story "The Computers That Saved Metropolis" by Starlin (Radio Shack giveaway w/indicia). 50-Legion app. 5.00
NOTE: ***Buckler** a-9p; c-36p. **Giffen** a-50; c-50. 40i. **Gil Kane** c-32p, 33p, 35, 39, 41-49. **Miller** c-51. **Starlin** a-7. Krypto back-ups in 17, 22. Superbaby in 11, 14, 19, 24.*

NEW ADVENTURES OF THE PHANTOM BLOT, THE (See The Phantom Blot)

NEW AMERICA
Eclipse Comics: Nov, 1987 - No. 4, Feb, 1988 ($1.75, Baxter paper)
1-4: Scout limited series 2.25

NEW ARCHIES, THE (TV)
Archie Comic Publications: Oct, 1987 - No. 22, May, 1990 (75¢)
1 5.00
2-10: 3-Xmas issue 4.00
11-22: 17-22 (95¢-$1.00): 21-Xmas issue 3.00

NEW ARCHIES DIGEST (TV)(...Comics Digest Magazine #4?-10; ...Digest Magazine #11 on)
Archie Comics: May, 1988 - No. 14, July, 1991 ($1.35/$1.50, quarterly)
1 6.00
2-14: 6-Begin $1.50-c 3.50

NEW AVENGERS, THE
Marvel Comics: Jan, 2005 - Present ($2.25)
1-Bendis-s/Finch-a; Spider-Man app.; re-intro The Sentry 2.25

NEW BOOK OF COMICS (Also see Big Book Of Fun)
National Periodical Publ.: 1937; No. 2, Spring, 1938 (100 pgs. each) (Reprints)
1(Rare)-1st regular size comic annual; 2nd DC annual; contains r/New Comics #1-4 & More Fun #9; r/Federal Men (8 pgs.), Henri Duval (1 pg.), & Dr. Occult in costume (1 pg.) by Siegel & Shuster; Moldoff, Sheldon Mayer (15 pgs.)-a 2000 4000 6000 13,000 20,000 27,000
2-Contains-r/More Fun #15 & 16; r/Dr. Occult in costume (a Superman prototype), & Calling All Cars (4 pgs.) by Siegel & Shuster 1000 2000 3000 6500 10,000 13,500

NEW COMICS (New Adventure #12 on)
National Periodical Publ.: 12/35 - No. 11, 12/36 (No. 1-6: paper cover) (No. 1-5: 84 pgs.)
V1#1-Billy the Kid, Sagebrush 'n' Cactus, Jibby Jones, Needles, The Vikings, Sir Loin of Beef, Now-When I Was a Boy, & other 1-2 pg. strips; 2 pgs. Kelly art(1st)-(Gulliver's Travels); Sheldon Mayer-a(1st)(2 2pg. strips); Vincent Sullivan-c(1st) 2900 5800 8700 20,000 – –
2-1st app. Federal Men by Siegel & Shuster & begins (also see The Comics Magazine #2); Mayer, Kelly-a (Rare)(1/36) 1033 2066 3100 7200 – –
3-6: 3,4-Sheldon Mayer-a which continues in The Comics Magazine #1. 3-Vincent Sullivan-c. 4-Dickens' "A Tale of Two Cities" adaptation begins. 5-Junior Federal Men Club; Kiefer-a. 6- "She" adaptation begins 675 1350 2025 5000 – –
7-11: 11-Christmas-c 490 980 1470 3400 – –
NOTE: *#1-6 rarely occur in mint condition. **Whitney Ellsworth** c-4-11.*

NEW DEFENDERS (See Defenders)

NEW DNAGENTS, THE (Formerly DNAgents)
Eclipse Comics: V2#1, Oct, 1985 - V2#17, Mar, 1987 (Whole #s 25-40; Mando paper)
V2#1-17: 1-Origin recap. 7-Begin 95 cent-c. 9,10-Airboy preview 2.25
3-D 1 (1/86, $2.25) 2.25
2-D 1 (1/86)-Limited ed. (100 copies) 10.00

NEW ETERNALS: APOCALYPSE NOW (Also see Eternals, The)
Marvel Comics: Feb, 2000 ($3.99, one-shot)
1-Bennett & Hanna-a; Ladronn-c 4.00

NEWFORCE (Also see Newmen)
Image Comics (Extreme Studios): Jan, 1996-No. 4, Apr, 1996 ($2.50, lim. series)
1-4: 1-"Extreme Destroyer" Pt. 8; polybagged w/gaming card. 4-Newforce disbands 2.50

NEW FUN COMICS (More Fun #7 on; see Big Book of Fun Comics)
National Periodical Publications: Feb, 1935 - No. 6, Oct, 1935 (10x15", No. 1-4,: slick-c) (No. 1-5: 36 pgs; 40 pgs. No. 6)
V1#1 (1st DC comic); 1st app. Oswald The Rabbit; Jack Woods (cowboy) begins 6650 13,300 19,950 46,000 – –
2(3/35)-(Very Rare) 2800 5600 8400 19,000 – –
3-5(8/35): 3-Don Drake on the Planet Soro-c/story (sci/fi, 4/35). 5-Soft-c 1433 2866 4300 9600 – –
6(10/35)-1st Dr. Occult by Siegel & Shuster (Leger & Reuths); last "New Fun" title. "New Comics" #1 begins in Dec. which is reason for title change to More Fun; Henri Duval (ends #10) by Siegel & Shuster begins; paper-c 3150 6300 9450 21,000 – –

New Funnies #76 © DELL

New Gods (2nd) #10 © DC

New Mutants #10 © MAR

GD VG FN VF VF/NM NM-
2.0 4.0 6.0 8.0 9.0 9.2

NEW FUNNIES (The Funnies #1-64; Walter Lantz...#109 on; New TV... #259, 260, 272, 273; TV Funnies #261-271)
Dell Publishing Co.: No. 65, July, 1942 - No. 288, Mar-Apr, 1962

65(#1)-Andy Panda in a world of real people, Raggedy Ann & Andy, Oswald the Rabbit (with Woody Woodpecker x-overs), Li'l Eight Ball & Peter Rabbit begin; Bugs Bunny and Elmer app. 66 132 198 561 906 1250
66-70: 66-Felix the Cat begins. 67-Billy & Bonny Bee by Frank Thomas begins. 69-Kelly-a (2 pgs.); The Brownies begin (not by Kelly) 33 66 99 248 387 525
71-75: 72-Kelly illos. 75-Brownies by Kelly? 23 46 69 163 249 335
76-Andy Panda (Carl Barks & Pabian-a); Woody Woodpecker x-over in Oswald ends 80 160 240 655 1040 1425
77,78: 77-Kelly-c. 78-Andy Panda in a world with real people ends 23 46 69 163 249 335
79-81 15 30 45 109 167 225
82-Brownies by Kelly begins; Homer Pigeon begins 16 32 48 114 175 235
83-85-Brownies by Kelly in ea. 83-X-mas-c; Homer Pigeon begins. 85-Woody Woodpecker, 1 pg. strip begins 16 32 48 114 175 235
86-90: 87-Woody Woodpecker stories begin 12 24 36 82 124 165
91-99 9 18 27 65 93 120
100 (6/45) 10 20 30 67 96 125
101-120: 119-X-Mas-c 7 14 21 51 71 90
121-150: 131,143-X-Mas-c 6 12 18 43 59 75
151-200: 155-X-Mas-c. 167-X-Mas-c. 182-Origin & 1st app. Knothead & Splinter. 191-X-Mas-c 5 10 15 36 48 60
201-240 4 8 12 29 40 50
241-288: 270,271-Walter Lantz c-app. 281-1st story swipes/WDC&S #100 4 8 12 27 36 45

NOTE: *Early issues written by* ***John Stanley.***

NEW GODS, THE (1st Series)(New Gods #12 on)(See Adventure #459, DC Graphic Novel #4, 1st Issue Special #13 & Super-Team Family)
National Periodical Publications/DC Comics: 2-3/71 - V2#11, 10-11/72; V3#12, 7/77 - V3#19, 7-8/78 (Fourth World)

1-Intro/1st app. Orion; 4th app. Darkseid (cameo; 3 weeks after Forever People #1) (#1-3 are 15¢ issues) 10 20 30 70 100 130
2-Darkseid-c/story (2nd full app., 4-5/71) 6 12 18 38 52 65
3-1st app. Black Racer; last 15¢ issue 4 8 12 27 36 45
4-9: (25¢, 52 pg. giants): 4-Darkseid cameo; origin Manhunter-r. 5,7,8-Young Gods feature. 7-Darkseid app. (2-3/72); origin Orion; 1st origin of all New Gods as a group. 9-1st app. Forager 4 8 12 27 36 45
10,11: 11-Last Kirby issue. 3 6 9 18 24 30
12-19: Darkseid storyline w/minor apps. 12-New costume Orion (see 1st Issue Special #13 for 1st new costume). 19-Story continued in Adventure Comics #459,460 1 2 3 5 7 9
Jack Kirby's New Gods TPB ('98, $11.95, B&W&Grey) r/#1-11 plus cover gallery of original series and "84 reprints 12.00

NOTE: *#4-9(25¢, 52 pgs.) contain Manhunter-r by* ***Simon*** *&* ***Kirby*** *from Adventure #73, 74, 75, 76, 77, 78 with covers in that order.* ***Adkins*** *i-12-14, 17-19.* ***Buckler*** *a(p)-15.* ***Kirby*** *c/a-1-11p.* ***Newton*** *a(p)-12-14, 16-19.* ***Starlin*** *c-17.* ***Staton*** *c-19p.*

NEW GODS (Also see DC Graphic Novel #4)
DC Comics: June, 1984 - No. 6, Nov, 1984 ($2.00, Baxter paper)

1-5: New Kirby-c; r/New Gods #1-10. 4.00
6-Reprints New Gods #11 w/48 pgs of new Kirby story & art; leads into DC Graphic Novel #4 2 4 6 8 10 12

NEW GODS (2nd Series)
DC Comics: Feb, 1989 - No. 28, Aug, 1991 ($1.50)

1-28 2.50

NEW GODS (3rd Series) (Becomes Jack Kirby's Fourth World) (Also see Showcase '94 #1 & Showcase '95 #7)
DC Comics: Oct, 1995 - No. 15, Feb, 1997 ($1.95)

1-11,13-15: 9-Giffen-a(p). 10,11-Superman app. 13-Takion, Mr. Miracle & Big Barda app. 13-15-Byrne-a(p)/scripts & Simonson-c. 15-Apokolips merged w/ New Genesis; story cont'd in Jack Kirby's Fourth World 2.50
12-(11/96, 99¢)-Byrne-a(p)/scripts & Simonson-c begin; Takion cameo; indicia reads October 1996 2.50
...Secret Files 1 (9/98, $4.95) Origin-s 5.00

NEW GUARDIANS, THE
DC Comics: Sept, 1988 - No. 12, Sept, 1989 ($1.25)

1-($2.00, 52pgs)-Staton-c/a in #1-9 3.00
2-12 2.25

NEW HEROIC (See Heroic)

NEW INVADERS (Titled Invaders for #0 & #1) (See Avengers V3#83,84)
Marvel Comics: No. 0, Aug, 2004 - Present ($2.99)

0-4-Roster of U.S. Agent, Sub-Mariner, Blazing Skull and others. 0-Avengers app. 3.00

NEW JUSTICE MACHINE, THE (Also see The Justice Machine)
Innovation Publishing: 1989 - No. 3, 1989 ($1.95, limited series)

1-3 2.25

NEW KIDS ON THE BLOCK, THE (Also see Richie Rich and...)
Harvey Comics: Dec, 1990 - No. 8, Dec, 1991 ($1.25)

1-8 2.25
...**Back Stage Pass** 1(12/90) - 7(11/91) **Chillin'** 1(12/90) - 7(12/91): 1-Photo-c ...**Comic Tour** '90/91 1 (12/90) - 7(12/91) **Digest** 1(1/91) - 5(1/92) **Hanging Tough** 1 (2/91) **Magic Summer Tour** 1 (Fall/90) **Magic Summer Tour** nn (Fall/90, sold at concerts) **Step By Step** 1 (Fall/90, one-shot) **Valentine Girl** 1 (Fall/90, one-shot)-Photo-c 2.25

NEW LOVE (See Love & Rockets)
Fantagraphics Books: Aug, 1996 - No. 6, Dec, 1997 ($2.95, B&W, lim. series)

1-6: Gilbert Hernandez-s/a 3.00

NEWMAN
Image Comics (Extreme Studios): Jan, 1996 - No. 4, Apr, 1996 ($2.50, lim. series)

1-4: 1-Extreme Destroyer Pt. 3; polybagged w/card. 4-Shadowhunt tie-in; Eddie Collins becomes new Shadowhawk 2.50

NEWMEN (becomes The Adventures Of The...#22)
Image Comics (Extreme Studios): Apr, 1994 - No. 20, Nov, 1995; No. 21, Nov, 1996 ($1.95/$2.50)

1-21: 1-5: Matsuda-c/a. 1-Liefeld/Matsuda plot. 10-Polybagged w/trading card. 11-Polybagged. 20-Has a variant-c; Babewatch! x-over. 21-(11/96)-Series relaunch; Chris Sprouse-a begins; pin-up. 16-Has a variant-c by Quesada & Palmiotti 2.50
TPB-(1996, $12.95) r/#1-4 w/pin-ups 13.00

NEW MEN OF BATTLE, THE
Catechetical Guild: 1949 (nn) (Carboard-c)

nn(V8#1-3,5,6)-192 pgs.; contains 5 issues of Topix rebound 9 18 27 51 62 75
nn(V8#7-V8#11)-160 pgs.; contains 5 iss. of Topix 9 18 27 51 62 75

NEW MUTANTS, THE (See Marvel Graphic Novel #4 for 1st app.)(Also see X-Force & Uncanny X-Men #167)
Marvel Comics Group: Mar, 1983 - No. 100, Apr, 1991

1 5.00
2-10: 3,4-Ties into X-Men #167. 10-1st app. Magma 3.00
11-17,19,20: 13-Kitty Pryde app. 16-1st app. Warpath (w/out costume); see X-Men #193 2.50
18,21: 18-Intro. new Warlock. 21-Double size; origin new Warlock; newsstand version has cover price written in by Sienkiewicz 3.00
22-24,27-30: 23-25-Cloak & Dagger app. 2.50
25,26: 25-1st brief app. Legion. 26-1st full Legion app. 4.00
31-58: 35-Magneto intro'd as new headmaster. 43-Portacio-i. 50-Double size. 58-Contains pull-out mutant registration form 2.50
59-61: Fall of The Mutants series. 60(52 pgs.) 3.00
62-85: 68-Intro Spyder. 63-X-Men & Wolverine clones app. 73-(52 pgs.). 76-X-Factor & X-Terminator app. 85-Liefeld-c begin 2.50
86-Rob Liefeld-a begins; McFarlane-c(i) swiped from Ditko splash pg.; 1st brief app. Cable (last page teaser) 6.00
87-1st full app. Cable (3/90) 2 4 6 12 16 20
87-2nd printing; gold metallic ink-c ($1.00) 2.50
88-2nd app. Cable 1 2 3 4 5 7
92-No Liefeld-a; Liefeld-c 4.00
89,90,91,93-100: 89-3rd app. Cable. 90-New costumes. 90,91-Sabretooth app. 93,94-Cable vs. Wolverine. 95-97-X-Tinction Agenda x-over. 95-Death of new Warlock. 97-Wolverine & Cable-c, but no app. 98-1st app. Deadpool, Gideon & Domino (2/91); 2nd Shatterstar (cameo). 99-1st app. of Feral (of X-Force); Byrne-c/swipe (X-Men, 1st Series #138). 100-(52 pgs.)-1st brief app. X-Force. 5.00
95,100-Gold 2nd printing. 100-Silver ink 3rd printing 2.50
Annual 1 (1984) 4.00
Annual 2 (1986, $1.25)-1st Psylocke 1 2 3 5 6 8
Annual 3,4,6,7 ('87, '88,'90,'91, 68 pgs.): 4-Evolutionary War x-over. 6-1st new costumes by Liefeld (3 pgs.); 1st brief app. Shatterstar (of X-Force). 7-Liefeld pin-up only; X-Terminators back-up story; 2nd app. X-Force (cont'd in New Warriors Annual #1) 3.00
Annual 5 (1989, $2.00, 68 pgs.)-Atlantis Attacks; 1st Liefeld-a on New Mutants 4.00
Special 1-Special Edition ('85, 68 pgs.)-Ties in w/X-Men Alpha Flight limited series; cont'd in X-Men Annual #9; Art Adams/Austin-a 5.00
Summer Special 1(Sum/90, $2.95, 84 pgs.) 3.00

NOTE: ***Art Adams*** *c-38, 39.* ***Austin*** *c-57i.* ***Byrne*** *c/a-75p.* ***Liefeld*** *a-86-91p, 93-96p, 98-100, Annual 5p, 6(3 pgs.); c-85-91p, 92, 93p, 94, 95, 96p, 97-100, Annual 5, 6p.* ***McFarlane*** *c-85-89i, 93i.* ***Portacio*** *a(i)-43.* ***Russell*** *a-48i.*

New Mutants V2#4 © MAR

New Teen Titans #1 © DC

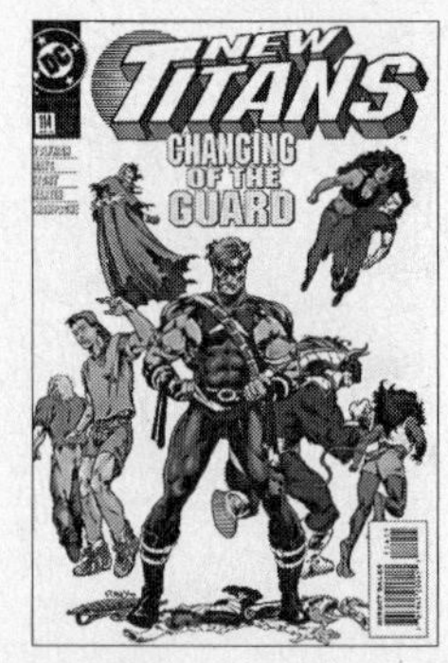

New Titans #114 © DC

GD VG FN VF VF/NM NM-
2.0 4.0 6.0 8.0 9.0 9.2

*Sienkiewicz a-18-31, 35-38i; c-17-31, 35i, 37i, Annual 1. **Simonson** c-11p. **B. Smith** c-36, 40-48. **Williamson** a(i)-69, 71-73, 78-80, 82, 83; c(i)-69, 72, 73, 78i.*

NEW MUTANTS (Continues as New X-Men (Academy X))
Marvel Comics: July, 2003 - No. 13, June, 2004 ($2.50/$2.99)

1-7: 1-6-Josh Middleton-c. 7-Bachalo-c 2.50
8-13 ($2.99) 8-11-Bachalo-c 3.00

NEW MUTANTS, THE: TRUTH OR DEATH
Marvel Comics: Nov, 1997 - No. 3, Jan, 1998 ($2.50, limited series)

1-3-Raab-s/Chang-a(p) 2.50

NEW ORDER, THE
CFD Publishing: Nov, 1994 ($2.95)

1 3.00

NEW PEOPLE, THE (TV)
Dell Publishing Co.: Jan, 1970 - No. 2, May, 1970

	GD	VG	FN	VF	VF/NM	NM-
1	3	6	9	19	25	32
2	3	6	9	16	21	26

NEW ROMANCES
Standard Comics: No. 5, May, 1951 - No. 21, May, 1954

	GD	VG	FN	VF	VF/NM	NM-
5-Photo-c	14	28	42	79	110	140
6-9: 6-Barbara Bel Geddes, Richard Basehart "Fourteen Hours" photo-c. 7-Ray Milland & Joan Fontaine photo-c. 9-Photo-c from '50s movie	9	18	27	51	62	75
10,14,16,17-Toth-a	9	18	27	54	70	85
11-Toth-a; Liz Taylor, Montgomery Cliff photo-c	22	44	66	127	184	240
12,13,15,18-21	8	16	24	43	54	65

NOTE: ***Celardo** a-9. **Moreira** a-6. **Tuska** a-7, 20. Photo c-5-16.*

NEW SHADOWHAWK, THE (Also see Shadowhawk & Shadowhunt)
Image Comics (Shadowline Ink): June, 1995 - No. 7, Mar, 1996 ($2.50)

1-7: Kurt Busiek scripts in all 3.00

NEW STATESMEN, THE
Fleetway Publications (Quality Comics): 1989 - No. 5, 1990 ($3.95, limited series, mature readers, 52pgs.)

1-5: Futuristic; squarebound; 3-Photo-c 4.00

NEWSTRALIA
Innovation Publ.: July, 1989 - No. 5, 1989 ($1.75, color)(#2 on, $2.25, B&W)

1-5: 1,2: Timothy Truman-c/a; Gustovich-i 2.25

NEW TALENT SHOWCASE (Talent Showcase #16 on)
DC Comics: Jan, 1984 - No. 19, Oct, 1985 (Direct sales only)

1-19: Features new strips & artists. 18-Williamson-c(i) 2.25

NEW TEEN TITANS, THE (See DC Comics Presents #26, Marvel and DC Present & Teen Titans; Tales of the Teen Titans #41 on)
DC Comics: Nov, 1980 - No. 40, Mar, 1984

	GD	VG	FN	VF	VF/NM	NM-
1-Robin, Kid Flash, Wonder Girl, The Changeling (1st app.), Starfire, The Raven, Cyborg begin; partial origin	1	3	4	6	8	10

2-1st app. Deathstroke the Terminator 6.00
3-10: 3-Origin Starfire; Intro The Fearsome Five. 4-Origin continues; J.L.A. app. 6-Origin Raven. 7-Cyborg origin. 8-Origin Kid Flash retold. 9-Minor app. Deathstroke on last pg. 10-2nd app. Deathstroke the Terminator (see Marvel & DC Present for 3rd app.); origin Changeling retold 5.00
11-40: 13-Return of Madame Rouge & Capt. Zahl; Robotman revived. 14-Return of Mento; origin Doom Patrol. 15-Death of Madame Rouge & Capt. Zahl; intro. new Brotherhood of Evil. 16-1st app. Captain Carrot (free 16 pg. preview). 18-Return of Starfire. 19-Hawkman teams-up. 21-Intro Night Force in free 16 pg. insert; intro Brother Blood. 23-1st app. Vigilante (not in costume), & Blackfire. 24-Omega Men app. 25-Omega Men cameo; free 16 pg. preview Masters of the Universe. 26-1st app. Terra. 27-Free 16 pg. preview Atari Force. 29-The New Brotherhood of Evil & Speedy app. 30-Terra joins the Titans. 34-4th app. Deathstroke the Terminator.37-Batman & The Outsiders x-over. 38-Origin Wonder Girl. 39-Last Dick Grayson as Robin; Kid Flash quits 3.00
Annual 1(11/82)-Omega Men app. 4.00
Annual V2#2(9/83)-1st app. Vigilante in costume 3.50
Annual 3 (See Tales of the Teen Titans Annual #3)
...: The Judas Contract TPB (2003, $19.95) r/#39,40 plus Tales of the Teen Titans #41-44 & Annual #3 20.00

NOTE: ***Perez** a-1-4p, 6-34p, 37-40p, Annual 1p, 2p; c-1-12, 13-17p, 18-21, 22p, 23p, 24-37, 38, 39(painted), 40, Annual 1, 2.*

NEW TEEN TITANS, THE (Becomes The New Titans #50 on)
DC Comics: Aug, 1984 - No. 49, Nov, 1988 ($1.25/$1.75; deluxe format)

1-New storyline; Perez-c/a begins 5.00
2,3: 2-Re-intro Lilith 4.00
4-10: 5-Death of Trigon. 7-9-Origin Lilith. 8-Intro Kole. 10-Kole joins 3.00
11-49: 13,14-Crisis x-over. 20-Robin (Jason Todd) joins; original Teen Titans return. 38-Infinity, Inc. x-over. 47-Origin of all Titans; Titans (East & West) pin-up by Perez 2.50
Annual 1-4 (9/85-'88): 1-Intro. Vanguard. 2-Byrne c/a(p); origin Brother Blood; intro new Dr. Light. 3-Intro. Danny Chase. 4-Perez-c 3.00
...: The Terror of Trigon TPB (2003, $17.95) r/#1-5; new cover by Phil Jimenez 18.00

NOTE: ***Buckler** c-10. **Kelley Jones** a-47, Annual 4. **Erik Larsen** a-33. **Orlando** c-33p. **Perez** a-1-5; c-1-7, 19-23, 43. **Steacy** c-47.*

NEW TERRYTOONS (TV)
Dell Publishing Co./Gold Key: 6-8/60 - No. 8, 3-5/62; 10/62 - No. 54, 1/79

	GD	VG	FN	VF	VF/NM	NM-
1(1960-Dell)-Deputy Dawg, Dinky Duck & Hashimoto-San begin (1st app. of each)	7	14	21	51	71	90
2-8(1962)	4	8	12	27	36	45
1(30010-210)(10/62-Gold Key, 84 pgs.)-Heckle & Jeckle begins	9	18	27	63	89	115
2(30010-301)-84 pgs.	8	16	24	55	78	100
3-5	4	8	12	25	33	42
6-10	3	7	10	21	28	35
11-20	3	6	9	16	20	24
21-30	2	4	6	10	12	15
31-43	1	3	4	6	8	10
44-54: Mighty Mouse-c/s in all	2	4	6	9	11	14

NOTE: *Reprints: #4-12, 38, 40, 47. (See March of Comics #379, 393, 412, 435)*

NEW TESTAMENT STORIES VISUALIZED
Standard Publishing Co.: 1946 - 1947

	GD	VG	FN	VF	VF/NM	NM-
"New Testament Heroes–Acts of Apostles Visualized, Book I" "New Testament Heroes–Acts of Apostles Visualized, Book II" "Parables Jesus Told" Set....	16	32	48	89	127	165

NOTE: *All three are contained in a cardboard case, illustrated on front and info about the set.*

NEW THUNDERBOLTS
Marvel Comics: Jan, 2005 - Present ($2.99)

1,2-Grummett-a/Nicieza-s. 1-Captain Marvel app. 2-Namor app. 3.00

NEW TITANS, THE (Formerly The New Teen Titans)
DC Comics: No. 50, Dec, 1988 - No. 130, Feb, 1996 ($1.75/$2.25)

50-Perez-c/a begins; new origin Wonder Girl 6.00
51-59: 50-55-Painted-c. 55-Nightwing (Dick Grayson) forces Danny Chase to resign; Batman app. in flashback, Wonder Girl becomes Troia 3.00
60,61: 60-A Lonely Place of Dying Part 2 continues from Batman #440; new Robin tie-in; Timothy Drake app. 61-A Lonely Place of Dying Part 4 3.00
62-99,101-124,126-130: 62-65: Deathstroke the Terminator app. 65-Tim Drake (Robin) app. 70-1st Deathstroke solo cover/sty. 71-(44 pgs.)-10th anniversary issue; Deathstroke cameo. 72-79-Deathstroke in all: 74-Intro. Pantha. 79-Terra brought back to life; 1 panel cameo Team Titans (1st app.). Deathstroke in #80-84,86. 80-2nd full app. Team Titans. 83,84-Deathstroke kills his son, Jericho. 85-Team Titans app. 86-Deathstroke vs. Nightwing-c/story; last Deathstroke app. 87-New costume Nightwing. 90-92-Parts 2,5,8 Total Chaos (Team Titans). 115-(11/94) 2.50
100-($3.50, 52 pgs.)-Holo-grafx foil-c 3.50
125 (3.50)-wraparound-c 3.50
#0-(10/94) Zero Hour, released between #114 & 115 2.50
Annual 5-10 ('89-'94, 68 pgs.. 7-Armaggedon 2001 x-over; 1st full app. Teen (Team) Titans (new group). 8-Deathstroke app.; Eclipso app. (minor). 10-Elseworlds story 3.50
Annual 11 (1995, $3.95)-Year One story 4.00

NOTE: ***Perez** a-50-55p, 57,60p, 58,59,61(layouts); c-50-61, 62-67i, Annual 5i; co-plots-66.*

NEW TV FUNNIES (See New Funnies)

NEW TWO-FISTED TALES, THE
Dark Horse Comics/Byron Preiss: 1993 ($4.95, limited series, 52 pgs.)

1-Kurtzman-r & new-a 5.00

NOTE: ***Eisner** c-1i. **Kurtzman** c-1p, 2.*

NEW WARRIORS, THE (See Thor #411,412)
Marvel Comics: July, 1990 - No. 75, 1996 ($1.00/$1.25/$1.50)

1-Williamson-i; Bagley-c/a(p) in 1-13, Annual 1 5.00
1-Gold 2nd printing (7/91) 2.25
2-5: 1,3-Guice-c(i). 2-Williamson-c/a(i). 3.00
6-24,26-49,51-75: 7-Punisher cameo (last pg.). 8,9-Punisher app. 14-Darkhawk & Namor x-over. 17-Fantastic Four & Silver Surfer x-over. 19-Gideon (of X-Force) app. 28-Intro Turbo & Cardinal. 31-Cannonball & Warpath app. 42-Nova vs. Firelord. 46-Photo-c. 47-Bound-in S-M trading card sheet. 52-12 pg. ad insert. 62-Scarlet Spider-c/app. 70-Spider-Man-c/app. 72-Avengers-c/app. 2.25
25-($2.50, 52 pgs.)-Die-cut cover 2.50
40,60: 40-($2.25)-Gold foil collector's edition 2.50

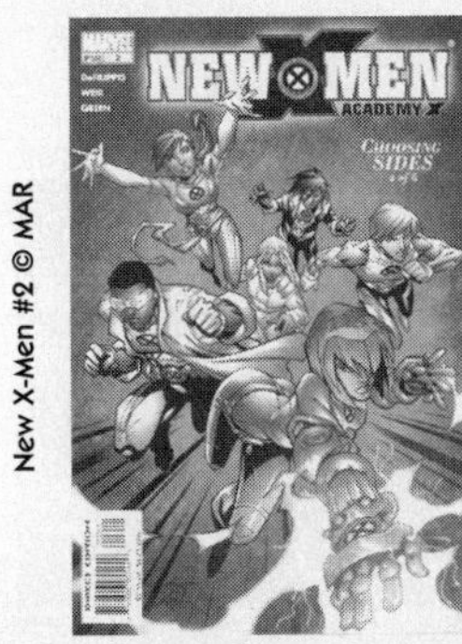

New X-Men #2 © MAR

Nexus #89 © DH

Nickel Comics #2 © FAW

GD 2.0 | VG 4.0 | FN 6.0 | VF 8.0 | VF/NM 9.0 | NM- 9.2

50-($2.95, 52 pgs.)-Glow in the dark-c 3.00

Annual 1-4('91-'94,68 pgs.)-1-Origins all members; 3rd app. X-Force (cont'd from New Mutants Ann. #7 & cont'd in X-Men Ann. #15); x-over before X-Force #1. 3-Bagged w/card 3.00

NEW WARRIORS, THE
Marvel Comics: Oct, 1999 - No. 10, July, 2000 ($2.99/$2.50)

0-Wizard supplement; short story and preview sketchbook 2.25
1-($2.99) 3.00
2-10: 2-Two covers. 5-Generation X app. 9-Iron Man-c 2.50

NEW WAVE, THE
Eclipse Comics: 6/10/86 - No. 13, 3/87 (#1-8: bi-weekly, 20pgs; #9-13: monthly)

1-13:1-Origin, concludes #5. 6-Origin Megabyte. 8,9-The Heap returns. 13-Snyder-c 2.25
...Versus the Volunteers 3-D #1,2(4/87): 1-Snyder-c 2.50

NEW WORLD (See Comic Books, series I)

NEW WORLDS
Caliber: 1996 - No. 6 ($2.95/$3.95, 80 pgs., B&W, anthology)

1-6: 1-Mister X & other stories 4.00

NEW X-MEN (See X-Men *2nd series* #114-156)

NEW X-MEN (Academy X) (Continued from New Mutants)
Marvel Comics: July, 2004 - Present ($2.99)

1-7: 1,2-Green-c/a 3.00

NEW YORK GIANTS (See Thrilling True Story of the Baseball Giants)

NEW YORK STATE JOINT LEGISLATIVE COMMITTEE TO STUDY THE PUBLICATION OF COMICS, THE
N.Y. State Legislative Document: 1951, 1955

This document was referenced by Wertham for **Seduction of the Innocent.** Contains numerous repros from comics showing violence, sadism, torture, and sex. 1955 version (196p, No. 37, 2/23/55) - Sold for $180 in 1986.

NEW YORK, THE BIG CITY
Kitchen Sink Press: 1986 ($10.95, B&W); **DC Comics:** July, 2000 ($12.95, B&W)

nn-Will Eisner-s/a 13.00

NEW YORK WORLD'S FAIR (Also see Big Book of Fun & New Book of Fun)
National Periodical Publ.: 1939, 1940 (100 pgs.; cardboard covers)
(DC's 4th & 5th annuals)

1939-Scoop Scanlon, Superman (blond haired Superman on-c), Sandman, Zatara, Slam Bradley, Ginger Snap by Bob Kane begin; 1st published app. The Sandman (see Adventure #40 for his 1st drawn story); Vincent Sullivan-c; cover background by Guardineer 2100 4200 6300 14,700 30,000 –

1940-Batman, Hourman, Johnny Thunderbolt, Red, White & Blue & Hanko (by Creig Flessel) app.; Superman, Batman & Robin-c (1st time they all appear together); early Robin app.; 1st Burnley-c/a (per Burnley) 1128 2256 3384 7895 16,800 –

NOTE: *The 1939 edition was published 4/29/39 and released 4/30/39, the day the fair opened, at 25¢, and was first sold only at the fair. Since all other comics were 10¢, it didn't sell. Remaining copies were advertised beginning in the August issues of most DC comics for 25¢, but soon the price was dropped to 15¢. Everyone that sent a quarter through the mail for it received a free Superman #1 or a #2 to make up the dime difference. 15¢ stickers were placed over the 25¢ price. Four variations on the 15¢ stickers are known. The 1940 edition was published 5/11/40 and was priced at 15¢. It was a precursor to World's Best #1.*

NEW YORK: YEAR ZERO
Eclipse Comics: July, 1988 - No. 4, Oct, 1988 ($2.00, B&W, limited series)

1-4 2.25

NEXT MAN
Comico: Mar, 1985 - No. 5, Oct, 1985 ($1.50, color, Baxter paper)

1-5 2.25

NEXT MEN (See John Byrne's...)

NEXT NEXUS, THE
First Comics: Jan, 1989 - No. 4, April, 1989 ($1.95, limited series, Baxter paper)

1-4: Mike Baron scripts & Steve Rude-c/a. 2.25
TPB (10/89, $9.95) r/series 10.00

NEXUS (See First Comics Graphic Novel #4, 19 & The Next Nexus)
Capital Comics/First Comics No. 7 on: June, 1981 - No. 6, Mar, 1984; No. 7, Apr, 1985 - No. 80?, May, 1991 (Direct sales only, 36 pgs.; V2#1('83)-printed on Baxter paper)

1-B&W version; mag. size; w/double size poster 3 6 9 16 20 24
1-B&W 1981 limited edition; 500 copies printed and signed; same as above except this version has a 2-pg. poster & a pencil sketch on paperboard by Steve Rude 4 8 12 24 32 40
2-B&W, magazine size 2 4 6 11 14 18
3-B&W, magazine size; Brunner back-c; contains 33-1/3 rpm record ($2.95 price) 2 4 6 9 11 14

V2#1-Color version 4.00
2-49,51-80: 2-Nexus' origin begins. 67-Snyder-c/a 2.25
50-($3.50, 52 pgs.) 3.50

NOTE: ***Bissette*** *c-V2#29.* ***Giffen*** *c/a-V2#23.* ***Gulacy*** *c-1 (B&W), 2(B&W).* ***Mignola*** *c/a-V2#28.* ***Rude*** *c-3(B&W), V2#1-22, 24-27, 33-36, 39-42, 45-48, 50, 58-60, 75; a-1-3, V2#1-7, 8-16p, 18-22p, 24-27p, 33-36p, 39-42p, 45-48p, 50, 58, 59p, 60.* ***Paul Smith*** *a-V2#37, 38, 43, 44, 51-55p; c-V2#37, 38, 43, 44, 51-55.*

NEXUS: ALIEN JUSTICE
Dark Horse Comics: Dec, 1992 - No. 3, Feb, 1993 ($3.95, limited series)

1-3: Mike Baron scripts & Steve Rude-c/a 4.00

NEXUS: EXECUTIONER'S SONG
Dark Horse Comics: June, 1996 - No. 4, Sept, 1996 ($2.95, limited series)

1-4: Mike Baron scripts & Steve Rude-c/a 3.00

NEXUS FILES
First Comics: 1989 ($4.50, color/16pgs. B&W, one-shot, squarebound, 52pgs.)

1-New Rude-a; info on Nexus 4.50

NEXUS: GOD CON
Dark Horse Comics: Apr, 1997 - No. 2, May, 1997 ($2.95, limited series)

1,2-Baron-s/Rude-c/a 3.00

NEXUS LEGENDS
First Comics: May, 1989 - No. 23, Mar, 1991 ($1.50, Baxter paper)\

1-23: R/1-3(Capital) & early First Comics issues w/new Rude covers #1-6,9,10 2.25

NEXUS MEETS MADMAN (...Special)
Dark Horse Comics: May, 1996 ($2.95, one-shot)

nn-Mike Baron & Mike Allred scripts, Steve Rude-c/a. 3.00

NEXUS: NIGHTMARE IN BLUE
Dark Horse Comics: July, 1997 - No. 4, Oct, 1997 ($2.95, limited series)

1-4: 1,2,4-Adam Hughes-c 3.00

NEXUS: THE LIBERATOR
Dark Horse Comics: Aug, 1992 - No. 4, Nov, 1992 ($2.95, limited series)

1-4 3.00

NEXUS: THE ORIGIN
Dark Horse Comics: July, 1996 ($3.95, one-shot)

nn-Mike Baron- scripts, Steve Rude-c/a. 4.00

NEXUS: THE WAGES OF SIN
Dark Horse Comics: Mar, 1995 - No. 4, June, 1995 ($2.95, limited series)

1-4 3.00

NFL SUPERPRO
Marvel Comics: Oct, 1991 - No. 12, Sept, 1992 ($1.00)

1-12: 1-Spider-Man-c/app. 2.25
Special Edition (9/91, $2.00) Jusko painted-c 3.00
Super Bowl Edition (3/91, squarebound) Jusko painted-c 4.00

NICKEL COMICS
Dell Publishing Co.: 1938 (Pocket size - 7-1/2x5-1/2")(68 pgs.)

1- "Bobby & Chip" by Otto Messmer, Felix the Cat artist. Contains some English reprints 79 158 237 494 760 1025

NICKEL COMICS
Fawcett Publications: May, 1940 - No. 8, Aug, 1940 (36 pgs.; Bi-Weekly; 5¢)

	GD	VG	FN	VF	VF/NM	NM-
1-Origin/1st app. Bulletman	400	800	1200	2600	4200	5800
2	131	262	393	819	1260	1700
3	98	196	294	613	944	1275
4-The Red Gaucho begins	81	162	243	506	778	1050
5-7	77	154	231	481	741	1000
8-World's Fair-c; Bulletman moved to Master Comics #7 in October (scarce)	89	178	267	556	853	1150

NOTE: ***Beck*** *c-5-8.* ***Jack Binder*** *c-1-4. Bondage c-5. Bulletman c-1-8.*

NICK FURY, AGENT OF SHIELD (See Fury, Marvel Spotlight #31 & Shield)
Marvel Comics Group: 6/68 - No. 15, 11/69; No. 16, 11/70 - No. 18, 3/71

	GD	VG	FN	VF	VF/NM	NM-
1	10	20	30	73	107	140
2-4: 4-Origin retold	6	12	18	40	55	70
5-Classic-c	7	14	21	46	63	80
6,7: 7-Salvador Dali painting swipe	5	10	15	36	48	60
8-11,13: 9-Hate Monger begins, ends #11. 10-Smith layouts/pencil. 11-Smith-c. 13-1st app. Super-Patriot; last 12¢ issue	3	7	10	21	28	35
12-Smith-c/a	4	8	12	22	30	38
14-Begin 15¢ issues	3	6	9	18	24	30
15-1st app. & death of Bullseye-c/story(11/69); Nick Fury shot & killed; last 15¢ issue	7	14	21	50	68	85

Nightcrawler ('04) #1 © MAR

Night Man #12 © MAL

Nightmare #7 © Skywald

GD VG FN VF VF/NM NM-
2.0 4.0 6.0 8.0 9.0 9.2

16-18-(25¢, 52 pgs.)-r/Str. Tales #135-143 3 6 9 16 21 26
TPB (May 2000, $19.95) r/ Strange Tales #150-168 20.00
...: Who is Scorpio? TPB (11/00, $12.95) r/#1-3,5; Steranko-c 13.00
NOTE: ***Adkins** a-3i. **Craig** a-10i. **Sid Greene** a-12i. **Kirby** a-16-18r. **Springer** a-4, 6, 7, 8p, 9, 10p, 11; c-8, 9. **Steranko** a(p)-1-3, 5; c-1-7.*

NICK FURY AGENT OF SHIELD (Also see Strange Tales #135)
Marvel Comics: Dec, 1983 - No. 2, Jan, 1984 (2.00, 52 pgs., Baxter paper)
1,2-r/Nick Fury #1-4; new Steranko-c 3.50

NICK FURY, AGENT OF S.H.I.E.L.D.
Marvel Comics: Sept, 1989 - No. 47, May, 1993 ($1.50/$1.75)
V2#1-26,30-47: 10-Capt. America app. 13-Return of The Yellow Claw. 15-Fantastic Four app. 30,31-Deathlok app. 36-Cage app. 37-Woodgod c/story. 38-41-Flashes back to pre-Shield days after WWII. 44-Capt. America-c/s. 45-Viper-c/s. 46-Gideon x-over 2.25
27-29-Wolverine-c/stories 2.50
NOTE: ***Alan Grant** scripts-11. **Guice** a(p)-20-23, 25, 26; c-20-28.*

NICK FURY VS. S.H.I.E.L.D.
Marvel Comics: June, 1988 - No. 6, Nov, 1988 ($3.50, 52 pgs, deluxe format)
1,2: 1-Steranko-c. 2-(Low print run) Sienkiewicz-c 5.00
3-6 4.00

NICK HALIDAY (Thrill of the Sea)
Argo: May, 1956
1-Daily & Sunday strip-r by Petree 8 16 24 46 58 70

NIGHT AND THE ENEMY (Graphic Novel)
Comico: 1988 (8-1/2x11") ($11.95, color, 80 pgs.)
1-Harlan Ellison scripts/Ken Steacy-c/a; r/Epic Illustrated & new-a (1st & 2nd printings) 12.00
1-Limited edition ($39.95) 40.00

NIGHT BEFORE CHRISTMAS, THE (See March of Comics No. 152 in the Promotional Comics section)

NIGHT BEFORE CHRISTMASK, THE
Dark Horse Comics: Nov, 1994 ($9.95, one-shot)
nn-Hardcover book; The Mask; Rick Geary-c/a 10.00

NIGHTBREED (See Clive Barker's Nightbreed)

NIGHTCRAWLER
Marvel Comics Group: Nov, 1985 - No. 4, Feb, 1986 (Mini-series from X-Men)
1-4: 1-Cockrum-c/a 3.50

NIGHTCRAWLER (Volume 2)
Marvel Comics: Feb, 2002 - No. 4, May, 2002 ($2.50, limited series)
1-4-Matt Smith-a 2.50

NIGHTCRAWLER
Marvel Comics: Nov, 2004 ($2.99, limited series)
1,2-Robertson-a/Land-c. 2-Magik app. 3.00

NIGHTFALL: THE BLACK CHRONICLES
DC Comics (Homage): Dec, 1999 - No. 3, Feb, 2000 ($2.95, limited series)
1-3-Coker-a/Gilmore-s 3.00

NIGHT FORCE, THE (See New Teen Titans #21)
DC Comics: Aug, 1982 - No. 14, Sept, 1983 (60¢)
1 4.00
2-14: 13-Origin Baron Winter. 14-Nudity panels 3.00
NOTE: ***Colan** c/a-1-14p. **Giordano** c-1i, 2i, 4i, 5i, 7i, 12i.*

NIGHT FORCE
DC Comics: Dec, 1996 - No. 12, Nov, 1997 ($2.25)
1-12: 1-3-Wolfman-s/Anderson-a(p). 8-"Convergence" part 2 2.25

NIGHT GLIDER
Topps Comics (Kirbyverse): April, 1993 ($2.95, one-shot)
1-Kirby c-1, Heck-a; polybagged w/Kirbychrome trading card 3.00

NIGHTHAWK
Marvel Comics: Sept, 1998 - No. 3, Nov, 1998 ($2.99, mini-series)
1-3-Krueger-s; Daredevil app. 3.00

NIGHTINGALE, THE
Henry H. Stansbury Once-Upon-A-Time Press, Inc.: 1948 (10¢, 7-1/4x10-1/4", 14 pgs., 1/2 B&W)
(Very Rare)-Low distribution; distributed to Westchester County & Bronx, N.Y. only; used in **Seduction of the Innocent**, pg. 312,313 as the 1st and only "good" comic book ever published. Ill. by Dong Kingman; 1,500 words of text, printed on high quality paper & no word balloons. Copyright registered 10/22/48, distributed week of 12/5/48. (By Hans Christian Andersen)
Estimated value........ $250

NIGHT MAN, THE (See Sludge #1)
Malibu Comics (Ultraverse): Oct, 1993 - No. 23, Aug, 1995 ($1.95/$2.50)
1-($2.50, 48 pgs.)-Rune flip-c/story by B. Smith (3 pgs.) 2.50
1-Ultra-Limited silver foil-c 6.00
2-15, 17: 3-Break-Thru x-over; Freex app. 4-Origin Firearm (2 pgs.) by Chaykin. 6-TNTNT app. 8-1st app. Teknight 2.50
16 ($3.50)-flip book (Ultraverse Premiere #11) 3.50
...:The Pilgrim Conundrum Saga (1/95, $3.95, 68 pgs.)-Strangers app. 4.00
18-23: 22-Loki-c/a 2.50
Infinity ($1.50) 2.50
...Vs. Wolverine #0-Kelley Jones-c; mail in offer 1 3 4 6 8 10
NOTE: ***Zeck** a-16.*

NIGHT MAN, THE
Malibu Comics (Ultraverse): Sept, 1995 - No.4, Dec, 1995 ($1.50, lim. series)
1-4: Post Black September storyline 2.50

NIGHT MAN, THE /GAMBIT
Malibu Comics (Ultraverse): Mar, 1996 - No. 3, May, 1996 ($1.95, lim. series)
0-Limited Premium Edition 4.00
1-3: David Quinn scripts in all. 3-Rhiannon discovered to be The Night Man's mother 2.50

NIGHTMARE
Ziff-Davis (Approved Comics)/St. John No. 3: Summer, 1952 - No. 3, Winter, 1952, 53 (Painted-c)
1-1 pg. Kinstler-a; Tuska-a(2) 55 110 165 340 520 700
2-Kinstler-a-Poe's "Pit & the Pendulum" 40 80 120 236 351 465
3-Kinstler-a 36 72 108 204 297 390

NIGHTMARE (Weird Horrors #1-9) (Amazing Ghost Stories #14 on)
St. John Publishing Co.: No. 10, Dec, 1953 - No. 13, Aug, 1954
10-Reprints Ziff-Davis Weird Thrillers #2 w/new Kubert-c plus 2 pgs. Kinstler-a; Anderson, Colan & Toth-a 55 110 165 340 520 700
11-Krigstein-a; painted-c; Poe adapt., "Hop Frog" 40 80 120 236 351 465
12-Kubert bondage-c; adaptation of Poe's "The Black Cat"; Cannibalism story 40 80 120 230 335 440
13-Reprints Z-D Weird Thrillers #3 with new cover; Powell-a(2), Tuska-a; Baker-c 29 58 87 164 237 310

NIGHTMARE (Magazine) (Also see Psycho)
Skywald Publishing Corp.: Dec, 1970 - No. 23, Feb, 1975 (B&W, 68 pgs.)
1-Everett-a; Heck-a; Shores-a 8 16 24 55 78 100
2-5,8,9: 2,4-Decapitation story. 5-Nazi-s; Boris Karloff 4 pg. photo/text-s. 8-Features E.C. movie "Tales From the Crypt"; reprints some E.C. comics panels. 9-Wrightson-a; bondage-c; 1st Lovecraft Saggoth Chronicles/Cthulhu 4 8 12 29 40 50
6-Kaluta-a; Jeff Jones-c, photo & interview; 1st Living Gargoyle; Love Witch-s w/nudity; Boris Karloff-s 5 10 15 33 44 55
7 4 8 12 22 30 38
10-Wrightson-a (1 pg.); Princess of Earth-c/s; Edward & Mina Sartyros, the Human Gargoyles series continues from Psycho #8 5 10 15 33 44 55
11-19: 12-Excessive gore, severed heads. 13-Lovecraft-s. 15-Dracula-c/s. 17-Vampires issue; Autobiography of a Vampire series begins 3 6 9 19 25 32
20-John Byrne's 1st artwork (2 pgs.)(8/74); severed head-c; Hitler app. 6 12 18 43 59 75
21-23: 21-(1974 Summer Special)-Kaluta-a. 22-Tomb of Horror issue. 23-(1975 Winter Special) 4 8 12 24 32 40
Annual 1(1972)-Squarebound; B. Jones-a 4 8 12 24 32 40
Winter Special 1(1973)-All new material 3 6 9 19 25 32
Yearbook nn(1974)-B. Jones, Reese, Wildey-a 3 6 9 19 25 32
NOTE: ***Adkins** a-5. **Boris** c-2, 3, 5 (#4 is not by Boris). **Buckler** a-3, 15. **Byrne** a-20p. **Everett** a-1, 2, 4, 5, 12. **Jeff Jones** a-6, 21r(Psycho #6); c-6. **Katz** a-3, 5, 21. **Reese** a-4, 5. **Wildey** a-4, 5, 6, 21, '74 Yearbook. **Wrightson** a-9, 10.*

NIGHTMARE (Alex Nino's)
Innovation Publishing: 1989 ($1.95)
1-Alex Nino-a 2.25

NIGHTMARE
Marvel Comics: Dec, 1994 - No. 4, Mar, 1995 ($1.95, limited series)
1-4 2.25

NIGHTMARE & CASPER (See Harvey Hits #71) (Casper & Nightmare #6 on) (See Casper The Friendly Ghost #19)
Harvey Publications: Aug, 1963 - No. 5, Aug, 1964 (25¢)
1-All reprints? 9 18 27 60 85 110
2-5: All reprints? 5 10 15 36 48 60

NIGHTMARE ON ELM STREET, A (See Freddy Krueger's...)

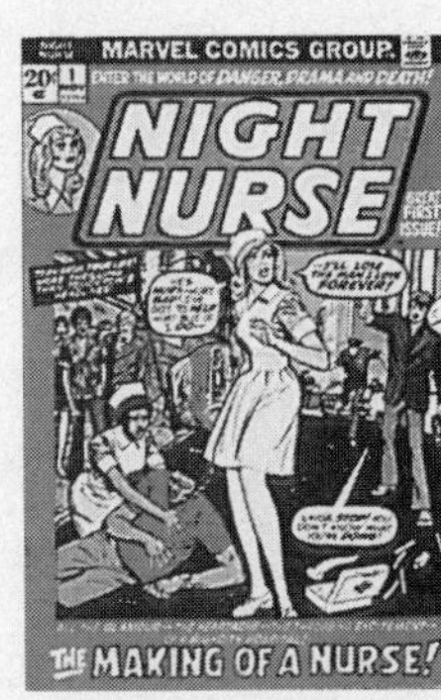

Night Nurse #1 © MAR

Nightwing #10 © DC

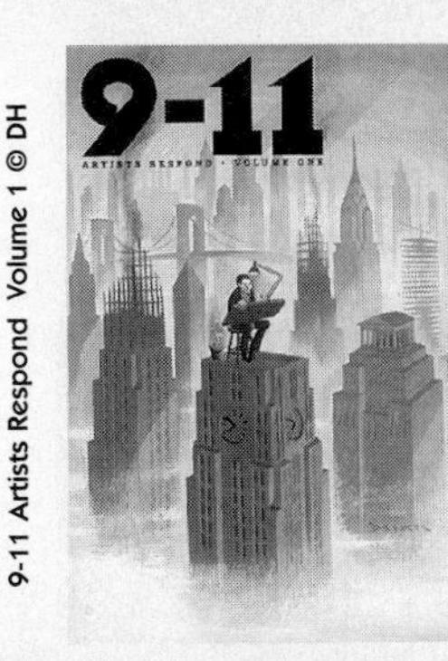

9-11 Artists Respond Volume 1 © DH

	GD 2.0	VG 4.0	FN 6.0	VF 8.0	VF/NM 9.0	NM- 9.2

NIGHTMARES (See Do You Believe in Nightmares)

NIGHTMARES
Eclipse Comics: May, 1985 - No. 2, May, 1985 ($1.75, Baxter paper)
1,2 — 3.00

NIGHTMARE THEATER
Chaos! Comics: Nov, 1997 - No. 4, Nov, 1997 ($2.50, mini-series)
1-4-Horror stories by various; Wrightson-a — 2.50

NIGHTMARK: BLOOD & HONOR
Alpha Productions: 1994 - No. 3, 1994 ($2.50, B&W, mini-series)
1,2 — 2.50

NIGHTMARK MYSTERY SPECIAL
Alpha Productions: Jan, 1994 ($2.50, B&W)
1 — 2.50

NIGHTMASK
Marvel Comics Group: Nov, 1986 - No. 12, Oct, 1987
1-12 — 2.25

NIGHT MASTER
Silverwolf: Feb, 1987 ($1.50, B&W)
1-Tim Vigil-c/a — 3.00

NIGHT MUSIC (See Eclipse Graphic Album Series, The Magic Flute)
Eclipse Comics: Dec, 1984 - No. 11, 1990 ($1.75/$3.95/$4.95, Baxter paper)
1-7: 3-Russell's Jungle Book adapt. 4,5-Pelleas And Melisande (double titled) 6-Salomé (double titled). 7-Red Dog #1 — 2.25
8-($3.95) Ariane and Bluebeard — 4.00
9-11-($4.95) The Magic Flute; Russell adapt. — 5.00

NIGHT NURSE
Marvel Comics Group: Nov, 1972 - No. 4, May, 1973

	GD	VG	FN	VF	VF/NM	NM-
1	11	22	33	80	120	160
2-4	8	16	24	58	82	105

NIGHT OF MYSTERY
Avon Periodicals: 1953 (no month) (one-shot)

	GD	VG	FN	VF	VF/NM	NM-
nn-1 pg. Kinstler-a, Hollingsworth-c	44	88	132	268	409	550

NIGHT OF THE GRIZZLY, THE (See Movie Classics)

NIGHTRAVEN (See Marvel Graphic Novel)

NIGHT RIDER (Western)
Marvel Comics Group: Oct, 1974 - No. 6, Aug, 1975

	GD	VG	FN	VF	VF/NM	NM-
1: 1-6 reprint Ghost Rider #1-6 (#1-origin)	2	4	6	10	13	16
2-6	1	3	4	6	8	10

NIGHT'S CHILDREN: THE VAMPIRE
Millenium: July, 1995 - No. 2, Aug, 1995 ($2.95, B&W)
1,2: Wendy Snow-Lang story & art — 3.00

NIGHTSIDE
Marvel Comics: Dec, 2001 - No. 4, Mar, 2002 ($2.99)
1-4: 1-Weinberg-s/Derenick-a; intro Sydney Taine — 3.00

NIGHTS INTO DREAMS (Based on video game)
Archie Comics: Feb, 1998 -No. 6, Oct, 1998 ($1.75, limited series)
1-6 — 2.25

NIGHTSTALKERS (Also see Midnight Sons Unlimited)
Marvel Comics (Midnight Sons #14 on): Nov, 1992 - No. 18, Apr, 1994 ($1.75)
1-($2.75, 52 pgs.)-Polybagged w/poster; part 5 of Rise of the Midnight Sons storyline; Garney/Palmer-c/a begins; Hannibal King, Blade & Frank Drake begin (see Tomb of Dracula for & Dr. Strange) — 3.00
2-9,11-18: 5-Punisher app. 7-Ghost Rider app. 8,9-Morbius app. 14-Spot varnish-c. 14,15-Siege of Darkness Pts 1 & 9 — 2.25
10-($2.25)-Outer-c is a Darkhold envelope made of black parchment w/gold ink; Midnight Massacre part 1 — 2.50

NIGHT TERRORS,THE
Chanting Monks Studios: 2000 ($2.75, B&W)
1-Bernie Wrightson-c; short stories, one by Wrightson-s/a — 2.75

NIGHT THRASHER (Also see The New Warriors)
Marvel Comics: Aug, 1993 - No. 21, Apr, 1995 ($1.75/$1.95)
1-($2.95, 52 pgs.)-Red holo-grafx foil-c; origin — 3.00
2-21: 2-Intro Tantrum. 3-Gideon (of X-Force) app. 10-Bound-in trading card sheet; Iron Man app. 15-Hulk app. — 2.25

NIGHT THRASHER: FOUR CONTROL
Marvel Comics: Oct, 1992 - No. 4, Jan, 1993 ($2.00, limited series)
1-4: 2-Intro Tantrum. 3-Gideon (of X-Force) app. — 2.25

NIGHT TRIBES
DC Comics (WildStorm): July, 1999 ($4.95, one-shot)
1-Golden & Sniegoski-s/Chin-a — 5.00

NIGHTVEIL (Also see Femforce)
Americomics/AC Comics: Nov, 1984 - No. 7, 1987 ($1.75)
1-7 — 2.25
...'s Cauldron Of Horror 1 (1989, B&W)-Kubert, Powell, Wood-r plus new Nightveil story — 3.00
...'s Cauldron Of Horror 2 (1990, $2.95, B&W)-Pre-code horror-r by Kubert & Powell — 3.00
...'s Cauldron Of Horror 3 (1991) — 3.00
Special 1 ('88, $1.95)-Kaluta-c — 2.25
One Shot ('96, $5.95)-Flip book w/ Colt — 6.00

NIGHTWATCH
Marvel Comics: Apr, 1994 - No. 12, Mar, 1995 ($1.50)
1-($2.95)-Collectors edition; foil-c; Ron Lim-c/a begins; Spider-Man app. — 3.00
1-12-Regular edition. 2-Bound-in S-M trading card sheet; 5,6-Venom-c & app. 7,11-Cardiac app. — 2.25

NIGHTWING (Also see New Teen Titans, New Titans, Showcase '93 #11,12, Tales of the New Teen Titans & Teen Titans Spotlight)
DC Comics: Sept, 1995 - No. 4, Dec, 1995 ($2.25, limited series)
1-Dennis O'Neil story/Greg Land-a in all — 5.00
2-4 — 4.00
...: Alfred's Return (7/95, $3.50) Giordano-a — 4.00
...Ties That Bind (1997, $12.95, TPB) r/mini-series & Alfred's Return — 13.00

NIGHTWING
DC Comics: Oct, 1996 - Present ($1.95/$1.99/$2.25)

	GD	VG	FN	VF	VF/NM	NM-
1-Chuck Dixon scripts & Scott McDaniel-c/a	2	4	6	9	11	12

2,3 — 6.00
4-10: 6-Robin-c/app. — 4.00
11-20: 13-15-Batman app. 19,20-Cataclysm pts. 2,11 — 3.00
21-49,51-64: 23-Green Arrow app. 26-29-Huntress-c/app. 30-Superman-c/app. 35-39-No Man's Land. 41-Land/Geraci-a begins. 46-Begin $2.25-c. 47-Texiera-c. 52-Catwoman-c/app. 54-Shrike app. — 2.50
50-($3.50) Nightwing battles Torque — 3.50
65-74,76-99: 65,66-Bruce Wayne: Murderer x-over pt. 3,9. 68,69: B.W.: Fugitive pt. 6,9. 70-Last Dixon-s. 71-Devin Grayson-s begin. 81-Batgirl vs. Deathstroke. 93-Blockbuster killed. 94-Copperhead app. 96-Bagged w/CD. 96-98-War Games — 2.50
75-(1/03, $2.95) Intro. Tarantula — 3.00
100-(2/05, $2.95) Tarantula app. — 3.00
#1,000,000 (11/98) teams with future Batman — 2.25
Annual 1(1997, $3.95) Pulp Heroes — 4.00
...Eighty Page Giant 1 (12/00, $5.95) Intro. of Hella; Dixon-s/Haley-c — 6.00
...: Big Guns (2004, $14.95, TPB) r/#47-50; Secret Files 1, Eighty Page Giant 1 — 15.00
...: A Darker Shade of Justice (2001, $19.95, TPB) r/#30-39,Secret Files #1 — 20.00
...: A Knight in Blüdhaven (1998, $14.95, TPB) r/#1-8 — 15.00
...: Love and Bullets (2000, $17.95, TPB) r/#1/2, 19,21,22,24-29 — 18.00
...: Our Worlds at War (9/01, $2.95) Jae Lee-c — 3.00
...: Rough Justice (1999, $17.95, TPB) r/#9-18 — 18.00
Secret Files 1 (10/99, $4.95) Origin-s and pin-ups — 5.00
...: The Hunt for Oracle (2003, $14.95, TPB) r/#41-46 & Birds of Prey #20,21 — 15.00
...: The Target (2001, $5.95) McDaniel-c/a — 6.00
Wizard 1/2 (Mail offer) — 5.00

NIGHTWING (See Tangent Comics/ Nightwing)

NIGHTWING AND HUNTRESS
DC Comics: May, 1998 - No. 4, Aug, 1998 ($1.95, limited series)
1-4-Grayson-s/Land & Sienkiewicz-a — 2.50
TPB (2003, $9.95) r/#1/4; cover gallery — 10.00

NIGHTWINGS (See DC Science Fiction Graphic Novel)

NIKKI, WILD DOG OF THE NORTH (Disney, see Movie Comics)
Dell Publishing Co.: No. 1226, Sept, 1961

	GD	VG	FN	VF	VF/NM	NM-
Four Color 1226-Movie, photo-c	6	12	18	43	59	75

9-11 - ARTISTS RESPOND
Dark Horse Comics: 2002 ($9.95, TPB, proceeds donated to charities)
Volume 1-Short stories about the September 11 tragedies by various Dark Horse, Chaos! and Image writers and artists; Eric Drooker-c — 10.00

Ninjak #7 © VAL

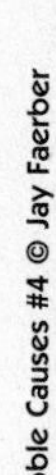

Noble Causes #4 © Jay Faerber

The Nocturnals #1 © Dan Brereton

GD VG FN VF VF/NM NM-
2.0 4.0 6.0 8.0 9.0 9.2

9-11: EMERGENCY RELIEF
Alternative Comics: 2002 ($14.95, TPB, proceeds donated to the Red Cross)

nn-Short stories by various inc. Pekar, Eisner, Hester, Oeming, Noto; Cho-c 15.00

9-11 - THE WORLD'S FINEST COMIC BOOK WRITERS AND ARTISTS TELL STORIES TO REMEMBER
DC Comics: 2002 ($9.95, TPB, proceeds donated to charities)

Volume 2-Short stories about the September 11 tragedies by various DC, MAD, and WildStorm writers and artists ; Alex Ross-c 10.00

NINE RINGS OF WU-TANG
Image Comics: July, 1999 - No. 5, July, 2000 ($2.95)

Preview (7/99, $5.00, B&W) 5.00
1-5: 1-(11/99, $2.95) Clayton Henry-a 3.00
Tower Records Variant-c 5.00
Wizard #0 Prelude 2.25
TPB (1/01, $19.95) r/#1-5, Preview & Prelude; sketchbook & cover gallery 20.00

1963
Image Comics (Shadowline Ink): Apr, 1993 - No. 6, Oct, 1993 ($1.95, lim. series)

1-6: Alan Moore scripts; Veitch, Bissette & Gibbons-a(p) 2.25
1-Gold 3.00

*NOTE: **Bissette** a-2-4; **Gibbons** a-1i, 2i, 6i; c-2.*

1984 (Magazine) (1994 #11 on)
Warren Publishing Co.: June, 1978 - No. 10, Jan, 1980 ($1.50, B&W with color inserts, mature content with nudity; 84 pgs. except #4 has 92 pgs.)

1-Nino-a in all; Mutant World begins by Corben 2 4 6 12 16 20
2-10: 4-Rex Havoc begins. 7-1st Ghita of Alizarr by Thorne. 9-1st Starfire 2 4 6 8 10 12

*NOTE: **Alcala** a-1-3,5,7i. **Corben** a-1-8; c-1,2. **Nebres** a-1-8,10. **Thorne** a-7,8,10. **Wood** a-1,2,5i.*

1994 (Formerly 1984) (Magazine)
Warren Publishing Co.: No. 11, Feb, 1980 - No. 29, Feb, 1983 (B&W with color; mature; #11-(84 pgs.); #12-16,18-21,24-(76 pgs.); #17,22,23,25-29-(68 pgs.)

11,17,18,20,22,23,29: 11,17-8 pgs. color insert. 18-Giger-c. 20-1st Diana Jacklighter Manhuntress by Maroto. 22-1st Sigmund Pavlov by Nino; 1st Ariel Hart by Hsu. 23-All Nino issue 2 4 6 8 10 12
12-16,19,21,24-28: 21-1st app. Angel by Nebres. 27-The Warhawks return 1 2 3 5 6 8

*NOTE: **Corben** c-26. **Maroto** a-20, 21, 24-28. **Nebres** a-11-13, 15, 16, 18, 21, 22, 25, 28. **Nino** a-11-19, 20(2), 21, 25, 26, 28; c-21. **Redondo** c-20. **Thorne** a-11-14, 17-21, 24-26, 28, 29.*

NINE VOLT
Image Comics (Top Cow Productions): July, 1997 - No. 4, Oct, 1997 ($2.50)

1-4 2.50

NINJA BOY
DC Comics (WildStorm): Oct, 2001 - No. 6, Mar, 2002 ($3.50/$2.95)

1-($3.50) Ale Garza-a/c 3.50
2-6-($2.95) 3.00
...: Faded Dreams TPB (2003, $14.95) r/#1-6; sketch pages 15.00

NINJA HIGH SCHOOL (1st series)
Antarctic Press: 1986 - No. 3, Aug, 1987 (B&W)

1-Ben Dunn-s/c/a; early Manga series 2 4 6 10 12 15
2,3 1 3 4 6 8 10

NINJAK (See Bloodshot #6, 7 & Deathmate)
Valiant/Acclaim Comics (Valiant) No. 16 on: Feb, 1994 - No. 26, Nov. 1995 ($2.25/$2.50)

1 ($3.50)-Chromium-c; Quesada-c/a(p) in #1-3 3.50
1-Gold 5.00
2-13: 3-Batman, Spawn & Random (from X-Factor) app. as costumes at party (cameo). 4-w/bound-in trading card. 5,6-X-O app. 2.50
0,00,14-26: 14-(4/95)-Begin $2.50-c. 0-(6/95, $2.50). 00-(6/95, $2.50) 2.50
Yearbook 1 (1994, $3.95) 4.00

NINJAK
Acclaim Comics (Valiant Heroes): V2#1, Mar, 1997 -No. 12, Feb, 1998 ($2.50)

V2#1-12: 1-Intro new Ninjak; 1st app. Brutakon; Kurt Busiek scripts begin; painted variant-c exists. 2-1st app. Karnivor & Zeer. 3-1st app. Gigantik, Shurikai, & Nixie. 4-Origin; 1st app. Yasuiti Motomiya; intro The Dark Dozen; Colin King cameo. 9-Copycat-c 2.50

NINTENDO COMICS SYSTEM (Also see Adv. of Super Mario Brothers)
Valiant Comics: Feb, 1990 - No. 9, Oct, 1991 ($4.95, card stock-c, 68pgs.)

1-9: 1-Featuring Game Boy, Super Mario, Clappwall. 3-Layton-c. 5-8-Super Mario Bros. 9-Dr. Mario 1st app. 5.00

N.I.O.

GD VG FN VF VF/NM NM-
2.0 4.0 6.0 8.0 9.0 9.2

Acclaim Comics: Nov, 1998 - No. 4, Feb, 1999 ($2.50, limited series)

1-4-Bury-s 2.50

NOAH'S ARK
Spire Christian Comics/Fleming H. Revell Co.: 1973 (35/49¢)

nn-By Al Hartley 1 3 4 6 8 11

NOBLE CAUSES
Image Comics: July, 2001; Jan, 2002 - No. 4, May, 2002 ($2.95)

...First Impressions (7/01) Intro. the Noble family; Faerber-s 3.00
1-4: 1-(1/02) Back-up-s with Conner-a. 2-Igle back-up-a. 2-4-Two covers 3.00
...: Extended Family (5/03, $6.95) short stories by various 7.00
...: Extended Family 2 (6/04, $7.95) short stories by various 8.00
Vol. 1: In Sickness and in Health (2003, $12.95) r/#1-4 & ...First Impresssions 13.00

NOBLE CAUSES (Volume 3)
Image Comics: July, 2004 - Present ($3.50)

1-4-Faerber-s; 2 covers on each. 2-Venture app. 3.50

NOBLE CAUSES: DISTANT RELATIVES
Image Comics: Jul, 2003 - No. 4, Oct, 2003 ($2.95, B&W, limited series)

1-4-Faerber-s/Richardson & Ponce-a 3.00

NOBLE CAUSES: FAMILY SECRETS
Image Comics: Oct, 2002 - No. 4, Jan, 2003 ($2.95, limited series)

1-4-Faerber-s/Oeming-c. 1-Variant cover by Walker. 2,3-Valentino var-c. 4-Hester var-c 3.00
Vol. 2 (2004, $12.95) r/#1-4; sketch pages 13.00

NOBODY (Amado, Cho & Adlard's...)
Oni Press: Nov, 1998 - No. 4, Feb, 1999 ($2.95, B&W, mini-series)

1-4 3.00

NOCTURNALS, THE
Malibu Comics (Bravura): Jan, 1995 - No. 6, Aug, 1995 ($2.95, limited series)

1-6: Dan Brereton painted-c/a & scripts 3.00
1-Glow-in-the-Dark premium edition 5.00

NOCTURNALS, THE
Dark Horse Comics/Oni Press: one-shots and trade paperbacks

Black Planet TPB (Oni Press, 1998, $19.95) r/#1-6 (Malibu Comics series) 20.00
Troll Bridge (Oni Press, 2000, $4.95, B&W & orange) Brereton-s/painted-c; art by Brereton, Chin, Art Adams, Sakai, Timm, Warren, Thompson, Purcell, Stephens and others 5.00
Unhallowed Eve TPB (Oni Press, 10/02, $9.95) r/Witching Hour & Troll Bridge one-shots 10.00
Witching Hour (Dark Horse, 5/98, $4.95) Brereton-s/a; reprints DHP stories + 8 new pgs. 5.00

NOCTURNALS: THE DARK FOREVER
Oni Press: Jul, 2001 -No. 3, Feb, 2002 ($2.95, limited series)

1-3-Brereton-s/painted-a/c 3.00
TPB (5/02, $9.95) r/#1-3; afterword & pin-ups by Alex Ross 10.00

NOCTURNE
Marvel Comics: June, 1995 - No. 4, Sept. 1995 ($1.50, limited series)

1-4 2.25

NO ESCAPE (Movie)
Marvel Comics: June, 1994 - No. 3, Aug, 1994 ($1.50)

1-3: Based on movie 2.25

NO HONOR
Image Comics (Top Cow): Feb, 2001 - No. 4, July, 2001 ($2.50)

Preview (12/00, B&W) Silvestri-c 2.25
1-4-Avery-s/Crain-a 2.50
TPB (8/03, $12.99) r/#1-4; intro. by Straczynski 13.00

NOMAD (See Captain America #180)
Marvel Comics: Nov, 1990 - No. 4, Feb, 1991 ($1.50, limited series)

1-4: 1,4-Captain America app. 2.25

NOMAD
Marvel Comics: V2#1, May, 1992 - No. 25, May, 1994 ($1.75)

V2#1-25: 1-Has gatefold-c w/map/wanted poster. 4-Deadpool x-over. 5-Punisher vs. Nomad-c/story. 6-Punisher & Daredevil-c/story cont'd in Punisher War Journal #48. 7-Gambit-c/story. 10-Red Wolf app. 21-Man-Thing-c/story. 25-Bound-in trading card sheet 2.25

NOMAN (See Thunder Agents)
Tower Comics: Nov, 1966 - No. 2, March, 1967 (25¢, 68 pgs.)

1-Wood/Williamson-c; Lightning begins; Dynamo cameo; Kane-a(p) & Whitney-a 9 18 27 65 93 120
2-Wood-c only; Dynamo x-over; Whitney-a 6 12 18 40 55 70

Nova #9 © MAR

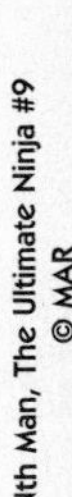

Nth Man, The Ultimate Ninja #9 © MAR

Nuts! #3 © PG

	GD	VG	FN	VF	VF/NM	NM-
	2.0	4.0	6.0	8.0	9.0	9.2

NONE BUT THE BRAVE (See Movie Classics)

NOODNIK COMICS (See Pinky the Egghead)
Comic Media/Mystery/Biltmore: Dec, 1953; No. 2, Feb, 1954 - No. 5, Aug, 1954

3-D(1953, 25¢; Comic Media)(#1)-Came w/glasses	33	66	99	190	275	360
2-5	9	18	27	52	66	80

NORMALMAN (See Cerebus the Aardvark #55, 56)
Aardvark-Vanaheim/Renegade Press #6 on: Jan, 1984 - No. 12, Dec, 1985 ($1.70/$2.00)

1-12: 1-Jim Valentino-c/a in all. 6-12 ($2.00, B&W): 10-Cerebus cameo; Sim-a (2 pgs.) 2.25
...- Megaton Man Special 1 (Image Comics, 8/94, $2.50) 2.50
...3-D 1 (Annual, 1986, $2.25) 2.25
...Twentieth Anniversary Special (7/04, $2.95) 3.00

NORTH AVENUE IRREGULARS (See Walt Disney Showcase #49)

NORTHSTAR
Marvel Comics: Apr, 1994 - No. 4, July, 1994 ($1.75, mini-series)

1-4: Character from Alpha Flight 2.25

NORTH TO ALASKA
Dell Publishing Co.: No. 1155, Dec, 1960

Four Color 1155-Movie, John Wayne photo-c	18	36	54	131	201	270

NORTHWEST MOUNTIES (Also see Approved Comics #12)
Jubilee Publications/St. John: Oct, 1948 - No. 4, July, 1949

1-Rose of the Yukon by Matt Baker; Walter Johnson-a; Lubbers-c	46	92	138	281	428	575
2-Baker-a; Lubbers-c. Ventrilo app.	39	78	117	222	324	425
3-Bondage-c, Baker-a; Sky Chief, K-9 app.	40	80	120	233	342	450
4-Baker-c/a(2 pgs.); Blue Monk & The Desperado app.	40	80	120	233	342	450

NO SLEEP 'TIL DAWN
Dell Publishing Co.: No. 831, Aug, 1957

Four Color 831-Movie, Karl Malden photo-c	8	16	24	53	74	95

NOSTALGIA ILLUSTRATED
Marvel Comics: Nov, 1974 - V2#8, Aug, 1975 (B&W, 76 pgs.)

V1#1	3	6	9	19	25	32
V1#2, V2#1-8	2	4	6	12	16	20

NOT BRAND ECHH (Brand Echh #1-4; See Crazy, 1973)
Marvel Comics Group (LMC): Aug, 1967 - No. 13, May, 1969
(1st Marvel parody book)

1: 1-8 are 12¢ issues	7	14	21	46	63	80
2-8: 3-Origin Thor, Hulk & Capt. America; Monkees, Alfred E. Neuman cameo. 4-X-Men app. 5-Origin/intro. Forbush Man. 7-Origin Fantastical-4 & Stuporman. Beatles cameo; X-Men satire; last 12¢-c	4	8	12	24	32	40
9-13 (25¢, 68 pgs., all Giants) 9-Beatles cameo. 10-All-r; The Old Witch, Crypt Keeper & Vault Keeper cameos. 12,13-Beatles cameo	5	10	15	33	44	55

NOTE: *Colan a(p)-4, 5, 8, 9, 13.* ***Everett*** *a-1i.* ***Kirby*** *a(p)-1, 3, 5-7, 10r; c-1p.* ***J. Severin*** *a-1; c-3, 6-8, 11.* ***M. Severin*** *a-1-13; c-2, 9, 10, 12, 13.* ***Sutton*** *a-3, 4, 5i, 6i, 8, 9, 10r, 11-13; c-5. Archie satire in #9. Avengers satire in #8, 12.*

NOTHING CAN STOP THE JUGGERNAUT
Marvel Comics: 1989 ($3.95)

1-r/Amazing Spider-Man #229 & 230 4.00

NO TIME FOR SERGEANTS (TV)
Dell Publ. Co.: No. 914, July, 1958; Feb-Apr, 1965 - No. 3, Aug-Oct, 1965

Four Color 914 (Movie)-Toth-a; Andy Griffith photo-c	11	22	33	80	120	160
1(2-4/65) (TV): Photo-c	7	14	21	50	68	85
2,3 (TV): Photo-c	6	12	18	38	52	65

NOVA (The Man Called... No. 22-25)(See New Warriors)
Marvel Comics Group: Sept, 1976 - No. 25, May, 1979

1-Origin/1st app. Nova	2	4	6	11	14	18
2-4,12: 4-Thor x-over. 12-Spider-Man x-over	1	2	3	5	7	9
5-11						6.00
10,11-(35¢-c variants, limited distribution)(6,7/77)	2	4	6	10	12	15
12-(35¢-c variant, limited distribution)(8/77)	2	4	6	12	16	20
13,14-(Regular 30¢ editions)(9/77) 13-Intro Crime-Buster.						5.00
13,14-(35¢-c variants, limited distribution)	2	4	6	10	12	15
15-24: 18-Yellow Claw app. 19-Wally West (Kid Flash) cameo						5.00
25-Last issue	1	2	3	5	6	8

NOTE: ***Austin*** *c-21i, 23i.* ***John Buscema*** *a(p)-1-3, 8, 21; c-1p, 2, 15.* ***Infantino*** *a(p)-15-20, 22-25; c-17-20, 21p, 23p, 24p.* ***Kirby*** *c-4p, 5, 7.* ***Nebres*** *c-25i.* ***Simonson*** *a-23i.*

NOVA
Marvel Comics: Jan, 1994 - June, 1995 ($1.75/$1.95)
(Started as 4-part mini-series)

1-($2.95, 52 pgs.)-Collector's Edition w/gold foil-c; new Nova costume 3.00
1-($2.25, 52 pgs.)-Newsstand Edition w/o foil-c 2.25
2-18: 3-Spider-Man-c/story. 5-Stan Lee app. 5-Bound-in card sheet. 13-Firestar & Night Thrasher app.14-Darkhawk 2.25

NOVA
Marvel Comics: May, 1999 - No. 7, Nov, 1999 ($2.99/$1.99)

1-($2.99) Larsen-s/Bennett-a; wraparound-c by Larsen 3.00
2-7-($1.99): 2-Two covers; Capt. America app. 5-Spider-Man. 7-Venom 2.25

NOW AGE ILLUSTRATED (See Pendulum Illustrated Classics)

NOW AGE BOOKS ILLUSTRATED (See Pendulum Illustrated Classics)

NTH MAN THE ULTIMATE NINJA (See Marvel Comics Presents #25)
Marvel Comics: Aug, 1989 - No. 16, Sept, 1990 ($1.00)

1-16-Ninja mercenary. 8-Dale Keown's 1st Marvel work (1/90, pencils) 2.25

NUCLEUS (Also see Cerebus)
Heiro-Graphic Publications: May, 1979 ($1.50, B&W, adult fanzine)

1-Contains "Demonhorn" by Dave Sim; early app. of Cerebus The Aardvark (4 pg. story)	4	8	12	29	40	50

NUKLA
Dell Publishing Co.: Oct-Dec, 1965 - No. 4, Sept, 1966

1-Origin & 1st app. Nukla (super hero)	5	10	15	36	48	60
2,3	4	8	12	22	30	38
4-Ditko-a, c(p)	4	8	12	28	38	48

NURSE BETSY CRANE (Formerly Teen Secret Diary) (Also see Registered Nurse for reprints)
Charlton Comics: V2#12, Aug, 1961 - V2#27, Mar, 1964 (See Soap Opera Romances)

V2#12-27	3	6	9	16	21	26

NURSE HELEN GRANT (See The Romances of...)

NURSE LINDA LARK (See Linda Lark)

NURSERY RHYMES
Ziff-Davis Publ. Co. (Approved Comics): No. 10, July-Aug, 1951 - No. 2, Winter, 1951 (Painted-c)

10 (#1), 2: 10-Howie Post-a	16	32	48	89	127	165

NURSES, THE (TV)
Gold Key: April, 1963 - No. 3, Oct, 1963 (Photo-c: #1,2)

1	4	8	12	28	38	48
2,3	3	6	9	19	25	32

NUTS! (Satire)
Premiere Comics Group: March, 1954 - No. 5, Nov, 1954

1-Hollingsworth-a	31	62	93	175	253	330
2,4,5: 5-Capt. Marvel parody	21	42	63	118	169	220
3-Drug "reefers" mentioned	21	42	63	118	169	220

NUTS (Magazine) (Satire)
Health Knowledge: Feb, 1958 - No. 2, April, 1958

1	9	18	27	54	70	85
2	7	14	21	35	43	50

NUTS & JOLTS
Dell Publishing Co.: No. 22, 1941

Large Feature Comic 22	16	32	48	92	131	170

NUTSY SQUIRREL (Formerly Hollywood Funny Folks)(See Comic Cavalcade)
National Periodical Publications: #61, 9-10/54 - #69, 1-2/56; #70, 8-9/56 - #71, 10-11/56; #72, 11/57

61-Mayer-a; Grossman-a in all	14	28	42	79	110	140
62-72: Mayer a-62,65,67-72	10	20	30	56	73	90

NUTTY COMICS
Fawcett Publications: Winter, 1946 (Funny animal)

1-Capt. Kidd story; 1 pg. Wolverton-a	14	28	42	79	110	140

NUTTY COMICS
Home Comics (Harvey Publications): 1945; No. 4, May-June, 1946 - No. 8, June-July, 1947 (No #2,3)

nn-Helpful Hank, Bozo Bear & others (funny animal)	9	18	27	52	66	80
4	7	14	21	37	46	55
5-Rags Rabbit begins(1st app.); infinity-c	8	16	24	40	50	60
6-8	6	12	18	31	38	45

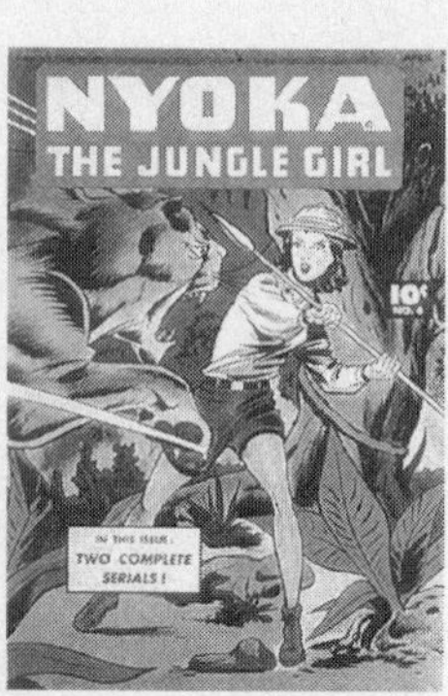

Nyoka the Jungle Girl #6 © FAW

NYX #3 © MAR

Ocean #1 © Ellis & Sprouse

GD VG FN VF VF/NM NM-
2.0 4.0 6.0 8.0 9.0 9.2

NUTTY LIFE (Formerly Krazy Life #1; becomes Wotalife Comics #3 on)
Fox Features Syndicate: No. 2, Summer, 1946

2 — 13 26 39 76 106 135

NYC MECH
Image Comics: Apr, 2004 - No. 6, Sept, 2004 ($2.95)

1-6: 1-MacDonald-a/Brandon & Gunter-s. 1-Dave Johnson-c — 3.00

NYOKA, THE JUNGLE GIRL (Formerly Jungle Girl; see The Further Adventures of..., Master Comics #50 & XMas Comics)
Fawcett Publications: No. 2, Winter, 1945 - No. 77, June, 1953 (Movie serial)

2 — 56 112 168 350 538 725
3 — 35 70 105 201 293 385
4,5 — 30 60 90 170 245 320
6-11,13,14,16-18-Krigstein-a: 17-Sam Spade ad by Lou Fine — 21 42 63 121 173 225
12,15,19,20 — 19 38 57 107 154 200
21-30: 25-Clayton Moore photo-c? — 13 26 39 76 106 135
31-40 — 10 20 30 60 80 100
41-50 — 9 18 27 54 70 85
51-60 — 8 16 24 46 58 70
61-77 — 8 16 24 43 54 65

NOTE: *Photo-c from movies 25, 30-70, 72, 75-77. Bondage c-4, 5, 7, 8, 14, 24.*

NYOKA, THE JUNGLE GIRL (Formerly Zoo Funnies; Space Adventures #23 on)
Charlton Comics: No. 14, Nov, 1955 - No. 22, Nov, 1957

14 — 11 22 33 64 87 110
15-22 — 9 18 27 54 70 85

NYX
Marvel Comics: Nov, 2003 - No. 5, Sept, 2004 ($2.99)

1,2: 1-Quesada-s/Middleton-a/c; intro. Kiden Nixon — 3.00
3-1st app. X-23 — 4.00
4,5: 5-Teranishi-a — 3.00

OAKLAND PRESS FUNNYBOOK, THE
The Oakland Press: 9/17/78 - 4/13/80 (16 pgs.) (Weekly)
Full color in comic book form; changes to tabloid size 4/20/80-on

Contains Tarzan by Manning, Marmaduke, Bugs Bunny, etc. (low distribution); 9/23/79 - 4/13/80 contain Buck Rogers by Gray Morrow & Jim Lawrence — 2.50

OAKY DOAKS (See Famous Funnies #190)
Eastern Color Printing Co.: July, 1942 (One Shot)

1 — 36 72 108 204 297 390

OBERGEIST: RAGNAROK HIGHWAY
Image Comics (Top Cow/Minotaur): May, 2001 - No. 6, Nov, 2001 ($2.95, limited series)

Preview ('01, B&W, 16 pgs.) Harris painted-c — 2.25
1-6-Harris-c/a/Jolley-s. 1-Three covers — 3.00
... :The Directors' Cut (2002, $19.95, TPB) r/#1-6; Bruce Campbell intro. — 20.00
... :The Empty Locket (3/02, $2.95, B&W) Harris & Snyder-a — 3.00

OBIE
Store Comics: 1953 (6¢)

1 — 6 12 18 28 34 40

OBJECTIVE FIVE
Image Comics: July, 2000 - No. 6, Jan, 2001($2.95)

1-6-Lizalde-a — 3.00

OBLIVION
Comico: Aug, 1995 - No. 3, May, 1996 ($2.50)

1-3: 1-Art Adams-c. 2-(1/96)-Bagged w/gaming card. 3-(5/96)-Darrow-c — 2.50

OBNOXIO THE CLOWN (Character from Crazy Magazine)
Marvel Comics Group: April, 1983 (one-shot)

1-Vs. the X-Men — 3.00

OCCULT FILES OF DR. SPEKTOR, THE
Gold Key/Whitman No. 25: Apr, 1973 - No. 24, Feb, 1977; No. 25, May, 1982 (Painted-c #1-24)

1-1st app. Lakota; Baron Tibor begins — 4 8 12 28 38 48
2-5: 3-Mummy-c/s. 5-Jekyll & Hyde-c/s — 2 4 6 14 18 22
6-10: 6,9-Frankenstein. 8,9-Dracula c/s. 9.-Jekyll & Hyde c/s. 9,10-Mummy-c/s — 2 4 6 10 13 16
11-13,15-17,19-22,24: 11-1st app. Spektor as Werewolf. 11-13-Werewolf-c/s. 12,16-Frankenstein c/s. 17-Zombie/Voodoo-c. 19-Sea monster-c/s. 20-Mummy-s. 21-Swamp monster-c/s. 24-Dragon-c/s — 1 3 4 6 8 10
14-Dr. Solar app. — 3 6 9 16 20 24

GD VG FN VF VF/NM NM-
2.0 4.0 6.0 8.0 9.0 9.2

18,23-Dr. Solar cameo — 2 4 6 10 12 15
22-Return of the Owl c/s — 2 4 6 10 12 15
25(Whitman, 5/82)-r/#1 with line drawn-c — 1 3 4 6 8 10

NOTE: *Also see Dan Curtis, Golden Comics Digest 33, Gold Key Spotlight, Mystery Comics Digest 5, & Spine Tingling Tales.*

OCEAN
DC Comics (WildStorm): Dec, 2005 - No. 6 ($2.95, limited series)

1-3-Warren Ellis-s/Chris Sprouse-a — 3.00

ODELL'S ADVENTURES IN 3-D (See Adventures in 3-D)

OFFCASTES
Marvel Comics (Epic Comics/Heavy Hitters): July, 1993 - No. 3, Sept, 1993 ($1.95, limited series)

1-3: Mike Vosburg-c/a/scripts in all — 2.25

OFFICIAL CRISIS ON INFINITE EARTHS INDEX, THE
Independent Comics Group (Eclipse): Mar, 1986 ($1.75)

1 — 5.00

OFFICIAL CRISIS ON INFINITE EARTHS CROSSOVER INDEX, THE
Independent Comics Group (Eclipse): July, 1986 ($1.75)

1-Perez-c. — 5.00

OFFICIAL DOOM PATROL INDEX, THE
Independent Comics Group (Eclipse): Feb, 1986 - No. 2, Mar, 1986 ($1.50, limited series)

1,2: Byrne-c. — 4.00

OFFICIAL HANDBOOK OF THE CONAN UNIVERSE (See Handbook of...)

OFFICIAL HANDBOOK OF THE MARVEL UNIVERSE, THE
Marvel Comics Group: Jan, 1983 - No. 15, May, 1984 (Limited series)

1-Lists Marvel heroes & villains (letter A) — 5.00
2-15: 2 (B-C, 3-(C-D). 4-(D-G). 5-(H-J), 6-(K-L). 7-(M). 8-(N-P); Punisher-c. 9-(Q-S), 10-(S). 11-(S-U). 12-(V-Z); Wolverine-c. 13,14-Book of the Dead. 15-Weaponry catalogue — 4.00

NOTE: ***Bolland** a-8. **Byrne** c/a(p)-1-14; c-15p. **Grell** a-6, 9. **Kirby** a-1, 3. **Layton** a-2, 5, 7. **Mignola** a-3, 4, 5, 6, 8, 12. **Miller** a-4-6, 8, 10. **Nebres** a-3, 4, 8. **Redondo** a-3, 4, 8, 13, 14. **Simonson** a-1, 4, 6-13. **Paul Smith** a-1-12. **Starlin** a-5, 7, 8, 10, 13, 14. **Steranko** a-8p. **Zeck**-2-14.*

OFFICIAL HANDBOOK OF THE MARVEL UNIVERSE, THE
Marvel Comics Group: Dec, 1985 - No. 20, Feb, 1988 ($1.50, maxi-series)

V2#1-Byrne-c — 4.00
2-20: 2,3-Byrne-c — 3.00
Trade paperback Vol. 1-10 ($6.95) — 1 3 4 6 8 10

NOTE: ***Art Adams** a-7, 8, 11, 12, 14. **Bolland** a-8, 10, 13. **Buckler** a-1, 3, 5, 10. **Buscema** a-1, 5, 8, 9, 10, 13, 14. **Byrne** a-1-14; c-1-11. **Ditko** a-1, 2, 4, 6, 7, 11, 13. a-7, 11. **Mignola** a-2, 4, 9, 11, 13. **Miller** a-2, 4, 12. **Simonson** a-1, 2, 4-13, 15. **Paul Smith** a-1-5, 7-12, 14. **Starlin** a-6, 8, 9, 12, 16. **Zeck** a-1-4, 6, 7, 9-14, 16.*

OFFICIAL HANDBOOK OF THE MARVEL UNIVERSE, THE
Marvel Comics: July, 1989 - No. 8, Mid-Dec, 1990 ($1.50, lim. series, 52 pgs.)

V3#1-8: 1-McFarlane-a (2 pgs.) — 3.00

OFFICIAL HANDBOOK OF THE MARVEL UNIVERSE, THE
Marvel Comics: 2004 ($3.99, one-shots)

...: Avengers 2004 - Profile pages; art by various; lists of character origins and 1st apps. — 4.00
...: Book of the Dead 2004 - Profile pages of deceased Marvel characters; art by various; — 4.00
...: Daredevil 2004 - Profile pages; art by various; lists of character origins and 1st apps. — 4.00
...: Hulk 2004 - Profile pages; art by various; lists of character origins and 1st apps. — 4.00
...: Spider-Man 2004 - Profile pages; art by various; lists of character origins and 1st apps. — 4.00
...: Wolverine 2004 - Profile pages; art by various; lists of character origins and 1st apps. — 4.00
...: X-Men 2004 - Profile pages; art by various; lists of character origins and 1st apps. — 4.00

OFFICIAL HAWKMAN INDEX, THE
Independent Comics Group: Nov, 1986 - No. 2, Dec, 1986 ($2.00)

1,2 — 4.00

OFFICIAL JUSTICE LEAGUE OF AMERICA INDEX, THE
Independent Comics Group (Eclipse): April, 1986 - No. 8, Mar, 1987 ($2.00, Baxter paper)

1-8: 1,2-Perez-c. — 6.00

OFFICIAL LEGION OF SUPER-HEROES INDEX, THE
Independent Comics Group (Eclipse): Dec, 1986 - No. 5, 1987 ($2.00, limited series)
(No Official in Title #2 on)

1-5: 4-Mooney-c — 6.00

OFFICIAL MARVEL INDEX TO MARVEL TEAM-UP
Marvel Comics Group: Jan, 1986 - No. 6, 1987 ($1.25, limited series)

1-6 — 4.00

OFFICIAL MARVEL INDEX TO THE AMAZING SPIDER-MAN
Marvel Comics Group: Apr, 1985 - No. 9, Dec, 1985 ($1.25, limited series)

Official Handbook of the Marvel Universe X-Men 2004 © MAR

Oh My Goddess Pt. 6 #3 © DH

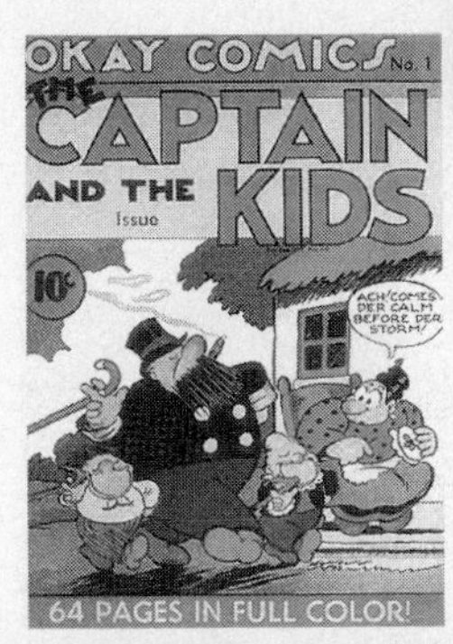

Okay Comics #1 © UFS

	GD 2.0	VG 4.0	FN 6.0	VF 8.0	VF/NM 9.0	NM- 9.2
1 ($1.00)-Byrne-c.						4.00
2-9: 5,6,8,9-Punisher-c.						3.00

OFFICIAL MARVEL INDEX TO THE AVENGERS, THE
Marvel Comics: Jun, 1987 - No. 7, Aug, 1988 ($2.95, limited series)

1-7 — 5.00

OFFICIAL MARVEL INDEX TO THE AVENGERS, THE
Marvel Comics: V2#1, Oct, 1994 - V2#6, 1995 ($1.95, limited series)

V2#1-#6 — 3.00

OFFICIAL MARVEL INDEX TO THE FANTASTIC FOUR
Marvel Comics Group: Dec, 1985 - No. 12, Jan, 1987 ($1.25, limited series)

1-12: 1-Byrne-c. 1,2-Kirby back-c (unpub. art) — 3.00

OFFICIAL MARVEL INDEX TO THE X-MEN, THE
Marvel Comics: May, 1987 - No. 7, July, 1988 ($2.95, limited series)

1-7 — 5.00

OFFICIAL MARVEL INDEX TO THE X-MEN, THE
Marvel Comics: V2#1, Apr, 1994 - V2#5, 1994 ($1.95, limited series)

V2#1-5: 1-Covers X-Men #1-51. 2-Covers #52-122,Special #1,2,Giant-Size #1,2. 3-Byrne-c; covers #123-177, Annuals 3-7, Spec. Ed. #1. 4-Covers Uncanny X-Men #178-234, Annuals 8-12. 5-Covers #235-287, Annuals 13-15 — 3.00

OFFICIAL SOUPY SALES COMIC (See Soupy Sales)

OFFICIAL TEEN TITANS INDEX, THE
Indep. Comics Group (Eclipse): Aug, 1985 - No. 5, 1986 ($1.50, lim. series)

1-5 — 4.00

OFFICIAL TRUE CRIME CASES (Formerly Sub-Mariner #23; All-True Crime Cases #26 on)
Marvel Comics (OCI): No. 24, Fall, 1947 - No. 25, Winter, 1947-48

	GD	VG	FN	VF	VF/NM	NM-
24(#1)-Burgos-a; Syd Shores-c	24	48	72	138	199	260
25-Syd Shores-c; Kurtzman's "Hey Look"	19	38	57	107	154	200

OF SUCH IS THE KINGDOM
George A. Pflaum: 1955 (15¢, 36 pgs.)

	GD	VG	FN	VF	VF/NM	NM-
nn-Reprints from 1951 Treasure Chest	4	7	10	14	17	20

O.G. WHIZ (See Gold Key Spotlight #10)
Gold Key: 2/71 - No. 6, 5/72; No. 7, 5/78 - No. 11, 1/79 (No. 7: 52 pgs.)

	GD	VG	FN	VF	VF/NM	NM-
1,2-John Stanley scripts	7	14	21	46	63	80
3-6(1972)	4	8	12	24	32	40
7-11(1978-79)-Part-r: 9-Tubby issue	2	4	6	11	14	18

OH, BROTHER! (Teen Comedy)
Stanhall Publ.: Jan, 1953 - No. 5, Oct, 1953

	GD	VG	FN	VF	VF/NM	NM-
1-By Bill Williams	8	16	24	40	50	60
2-5	5	10	15	24	30	35

OH MY GODDESS! (Manga)
Dark Horse Comics: Aug, 1994 - Present ($2.50-$3.50, B&W)

1-6-Kosuke Fujishima-s/a in all — 3.00
... **PART II** 2/95 - No. 9, 9/95 ($2.50, B&W, lim.series) #1-9 — 3.00
... **PART III** 11/95 - No. 11, 9/96 ($2.95, B&W, lim. series) #1-11 — 3.00
... **PART IV** 12/96 - No. 8, 7/97 ($2.95, B&W, lim. series) #1-8
3.00
... **PART V** 9/97 - Np. 12, 8/98 ($2.95, B&W, lim. series)
1,2,5,8: 5-Ninja Master pt. 1 — 3.00
3,4,6,7,10-12-($3.95, 48 pgs.) 10-Fallen Angel. 11-Play The Game — 4.00
9-($3.50) "It's Lonely At The Top" — 3.50
... **PART VI** 10/98 - No. 5, 3/99 ($3.50/$2.95, B&W, lim. series)
1-($3.50) — 3.50
2-6-($2.95)-6-Super Urd one-shot — 3.00
... **PART VII** 5/99 - No. 8, 12/99 ($2.95, B&W, lim. series) #1-3 — 3.00
4-8-($3.50) — 3.50
... **PART VIII** 1/00 - No. 6, 6/00 ($3.50, B&W, lim. series) #1-3,5,7 — 3.50
4-($2.95) "Hail To The Chief" begins — 3.00
... **PART IX** 7/00 - No. 7, 1/01 ($3.50/$2.99) #1-4: 3-Queen Sayoko — 3.50
5-7-($2.99) — 3.00
... **PART X** 2/01 - No. 5, 6/01 ($3.50) #1-5 — 3.50
... **PART XI** 10/01 - No. 10, 3/02 ($3.50) #1,2,7,8 — 3.50
3-6,9-($2.99) Mystery Child — 3.00
10-($3.99) — 4.00
(Series adapts new numbering) 88-90-($3.50) Learning tto Love — 3.50
91-94,96-103,105,107-110: 91-94 ($2.99) Traveler. 96-98-The Phantom Racer — 3.00
95,104,106-($3.50) 95-Traveler pt. 5 — 3.50
111,112-($3.99) — 4.00

OH MY GOTH
Sirius Entertainment (Dog Star Press): 1998 - No. 4, 1999 ($2.95, B&W)

1-4-Voltaire-s/a — 3.00
... Humans Suck! (2000 - No. 3) 1,2-Voltaire-s/a — 3.00

OH SUSANNA (TV)
Dell Publishing Co.: No. 1105, June-Aug, 1960 (Gale Storm)

	GD	VG	FN	VF	VF/NM	NM-
Four Color 1105-Toth-a, photo-c	14	28	42	97	149	200

OINK: BLOOD AND CIRCUS
Kitchen Sink: 1998 - No. 4, July, 1998 ($4.95, limited series)

1-4-John Mueller-s/a — 5.00

OJO
Oni Press: Aug, 2004 - No. 5 ($2.99, B&W, limited series)

1-3-Sam Kieth-s/Kieth & Alex Pardee-a — 3.00

OKAY COMICS
United Features Syndicate: July, 1940

	GD	VG	FN	VF	VF/NM	NM-
1-Captain & the Kids & Hawkshaw the Detective reprints	44	88	132	268	409	550

O.K. COMICS
United Features Syndicate/Hit Publications: July, 1940 - No. 2, Oct, 1940

	GD	VG	FN	VF	VF/NM	NM-
1-Little Giant (w/super powers), Phantom Knight, Sunset Smith, & The Teller Twins begin	75	150	225	469	722	975
2 (Rare)-Origin Mister Mist by Chas. Quinlan	77	154	231	481	741	1000

OKLAHOMA KID
Ajax/Farrell Publ.: June, 1957 - No. 4, 1958

	GD	VG	FN	VF	VF/NM	NM-
1	11	22	33	63	84	105
2-4	7	14	21	37	46	55

OKLAHOMAN, THE
Dell Publishing Co.: No. 820, July, 1957

	GD	VG	FN	VF	VF/NM	NM-
Four Color 820-Movie, photo-c	10	20	30	72	104	135

OKTANE
Dark Horse Comics: Aug, 1995 - Nov, 1995 ($2.50, color, limited series)

1-4-Gene Ha-a — 2.50

OKTOBERFEST COMICS
Now & Then Publ.: Fall 1976 (75¢, Canadian, B&W, one-shot)

	GD	VG	FN	VF	VF/NM	NM-
1-Dave Sim-s/a; Gene Day-a; 1st app. Uncle Hans & Natter P. Bombast; The Beavers sty; 1st Cap'n Riverrat, Sim-s/Day-a	2	4	6	14	18	22

OLD IRONSIDES (Disney)
Dell Publishing Co.: No. 874, Jan, 1958

	GD	VG	FN	VF	VF/NM	NM-
Four Color 874-Movie w/Johnny Tremain	8	16	24	53	74	95

OLD YELLER (Disney, see Movie Comics, and Walt Disney Showcase #25)
Dell Publishing Co.: No. 869, Jan, 1958

	GD	VG	FN	VF	VF/NM	NM-
Four Color 869-Movie, photo-c	6	12	18	43	59	75

OLYMPUS HEIGHTS
IDW Publ.: July, 2004 - No. 5 ($3.99, limited series)

1-4-Kevin Munroe-s/a — 4.00

OMAC (One Man Army; ...Corps. #4 on; also see Kamandi #59 & Warlord)
(See Cancelled Comic Cavalcade)
National Periodical Publications: Sept-Oct, 1974 - No. 8, Nov-Dec, 1975

	GD	VG	FN	VF	VF/NM	NM-
1-Origin	4	8	12	29	40	50
2-8: 8-2 pg. Neal Adams ad	2	4	6	14	18	22

NOTE: *Kirby a-1-8p; c-1-7p. Kubert c-8.*

OMAC: ONE MAN ARMY CORPS
DC Comics: 1991 - No. 4, 1991 ($3.95, B&W, mini-series, mature, 52 pgs.)

Book One - Four: John Byrne-c/a & scripts — 4.00

O'MALLEY AND THE ALLEY CATS
Gold Key: April, 1971 - No. 9, Jan, 1974 (Disney)

	GD	VG	FN	VF	VF/NM	NM-
1	3	6	9	18	24	30
2-9	2	4	6	10	13	16

OMEGA ELITE
Blackthorne Publishing: 1987 ($1.25)

1-Starlin-c — 3.00

OMEGA MEN, THE (See Green Lantern #141)
DC Comics: Dec, 1982 - No. 38, May, 1986 ($1.00/$1.25/$1.50; Baxter paper)

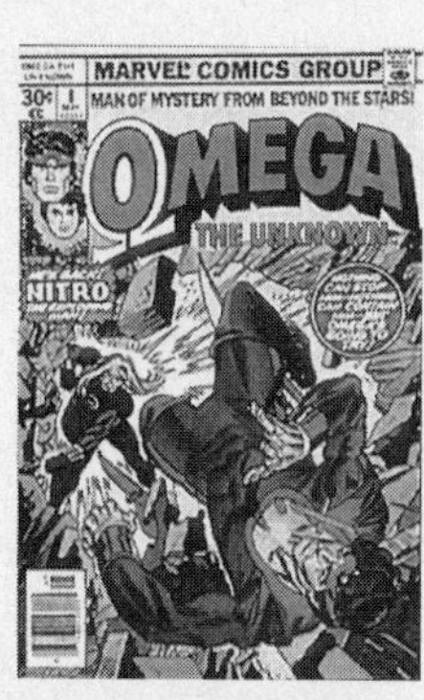

Omega the Unknown #8 © MAR

Omen: Vexed #1 © Chaos!

Oni Press Color Special 2001 © Oni

GD 2.0 | VG 4.0 | FN 6.0 | VF 8.0 | VF/NM 9.0 | NM- 9.2

1,20: 20-2nd full Lobo story 3.00
2,4-9,11-19,21-25,28-30,32,33,36,38: 2-Origin Broot. 5,9-2nd & 3rd app. Lobo (cameo, 2 pgs. each). 7-Origin The Citadel. 19-Lobo cameo. 30-Intro new Primus 2.50
3-1st app. Lobo (5 pgs.)(6/83); Lobo-c 1 2 3 4 5 7
10-1st full Lobo story 5.00
26,27,31,34,35: 26,27-Alan Moore scripts. 31-Crisis x-over. 34,35-Teen Titans x-over 3.00
37-1st solo Lobo story (8 pg. back-up by Giffen) 4.00
Annual 1(11/84, 52 pgs.), 2(11/85) 3.00
NOTE: *Giffen c/a-1-6p. Morrow a-24r. Nino c/a-16, 21; a-Annual 1i.*

OMEGA THE UNKNOWN
Marvel Comics Group: March, 1976 - No. 10, Oct, 1977

1-1st app. Omega 2 4 6 8 10 12
2,3-(Regular 25¢ editions). 2-Hulk-c/story. 3-Electro-c/story. 6.00
2,3-(30¢-c variants, limited distribution) 2 4 6 10 12 15
4-10: 8-1st brief app. 2nd Foolkiller (Greg Salinger), 1 panel only. 9,10-(Reg. 30¢ editions). 9-1st full app. 2nd Foolkiller 6.00
9,10-(35¢-c variants, limited distribution) 2 4 6 10 12 15
NOTE: *Kane c(p)-3, 5, 8, 9. Mooney a-1-3, 4p, 5, 6p, 7, 8i, 9, 10.*

OMEN
Northstar Publishing: 1989 - No. 3, 1989 ($2.00, B&W, mature)

1-Tim Vigil-c/a in all 1 2 3 5 7 9
1, (2nd printing) 3.00
2,3 6.00

OMEN, THE
Chaos! Comics: May, 1998 - No. 5, Sept, 1998 ($2.95, limited series)

1-5: 1-Six covers, ...: Vexed (10/98, $2.95) Chaos! characters appear 3.00

OMNI MEN
Blackthorne Publishing: 1987 - No. 3, 1987 ($1.25)

1-3 2.25
Graphic Novel (1989, $3.50) 3.50

ONE, THE
Marvel Comics (Epic Comics): July, 1985 - No. 6, Feb, 1986 (Limited series, mature)

1-6: Post nuclear holocaust super-hero. 2-Intro The Other 2.25

ONE-ARM SWORDSMAN, THE
Victory Prod./Lueng's Publ. #4 on: 1987 - No. 12, 1990 ($2.75/$1.80, 52 pgs.)

1-3 ($2.75) 2.75
4-12: 4-6-$1.80-c. 7-12-$2.00-c 2.25

ONE HUNDRED AND ONE DALMATIANS (Disney, see Cartoon Tales, Movie Comics, and Walt Disney Showcase #9, 51)
Dell Publishing Co.: No. 1183, Mar, 1961

Four Color 1183-Movie 11 22 33 80 120 160

101 DALMATIONS (Movie)
Disney Comics: 1991 (52 pgs., graphic novel)

nn-($4.95, direct sales)-r/movie adaptation & more 5.00
1-($2.95, newsstand edition) 3.00

101 WAYS TO END THE CLONE SAGA (See Spider-Man)
Marvel Comics: Jan, 1997 ($2.50, one-shot)

1 2.50

100 BULLETS
DC Comics (Vertigo): Aug, 1999 - Present ($2.50)

1-Azzarello-s/Risso-a/Dave Johnson-c 4.00
2-5 3.00
6-49,51-56: 26-Series summary; art by various. 45-Preview of Losers 2.50
50-($3.50) History of the Trust 3.50
...: A Foregone Tomorrow TPB (2002, $17.95) r/#20-30 18.00
...: First Shot, Last Call TPB (2000, $9.95) r/#1-5, Vertigo Winter's Edge #3 10.00
...: Hang Up on the Hang Low TPB (2001, $9.95) r/#15-19; Jim Lee intro. 10.00
...: Samurai TPB (2003, $12.95) r/#43-49 13.00
...: Six Feet Under the Gun TPB (2003, $12.95) r/#37-42 13.00
...: Split Second Chance TPB (2001, $14.95) r/#6-14 15.00
...: The Counterfifth Detective TPB (2003, $12.95) r/#31-36 13.00

100 GREATEST MARVELS OF ALL TIME
Marvel Comics: Dec, 2001 ($7.50/$3.50, limited series)

1-5-Reprints top #6-#25 stories voted by poll for Marvel's 40th ann. 7.50
6-($3.50) (#5 on-c) Reprints X-Men (2nd series) #1 3.50
7-($3.50) (#4 on-c) Reprints Giant-Size X-Men #1 3.50
8-($3.50) (#3 on-c) Reprints (Uncanny) X-Men #137 (Death of Jean Grey) 3.50
9-($3.50) (#2 on-c) Reprints Fantastic Four #1 3.50
10-($3.50) (#1 on-c) Reprints Amazing Fantasy #15 (1st app. Spider-Man) 3.50

100 PAGES OF COMICS
Dell Publishing Co.: 1937 (Stiff covers, square binding)

101(Found on back cover)-Alley Oop, Wash Tubbs, Capt. Easy, Og Son of Fire, Apple Mary, Tom Mix, Dan Dunn, Tailspin Tommy, Doctor Doom
164 328 492 1066 1533 2000

100 PAGE SUPER SPECTACULAR (See DC 100 Page Super Spectacular)

100%
DC Comics (Vertigo): Aug, 2002 - No. 5, July, 2003 ($5.95, B&W, limited series)

1-5-Paul Pope-s/a 6.00

100% TRUE?
DC Comics (Paradox Press): Summer 1996 - No. 2 ($4.95, B&W)

1,2-Reprints stories from various Paradox Press books. 5.00

$1,000,000 DUCK (See Walt Disney Showcase #5)

ONE MILLION YEARS AGO (Tor #2 on)
St. John Publishing Co.: Sept, 1953

1-Origin & 1st app. Tor; Kubert-c/a; Kubert photo inside front cover
21 42 63 121 173 225

ONE PLUS ONE
Oni Press: Sept, 2002 - No. 5, March, 2003 ($2.95, B&W, limited series)

1-5-Shaffer-s/Krall-a 3.00
TPB (9/03, $14.95, digest-size) r/#1-5 & story from Oni Press Color Special 2002 15.00

ONE SHOT (See Four Color...)

1001 HOURS OF FUN
Dell Publishing Co.: No. 13, 1943

Large Feature Comic 13 (nn)-Puzzles & games; by A.W. Nugent. This book was bound as #13 w/Large Feature Comics in publisher's files 29 58 87 164 237 310

ONE TRICK RIP OFF, THE (See Dark Horse Presents)

ONI (Adaption of video game)
Dark Horse Comics: Feb, 2001 - No. 3, Apr, 2001 ($2.99, limited series)

1-3-Sunny Lee-a(p) 3.00

ONI DOUBLE FEATURE (See Clerks: The Comic Book and Jay & Silent Bob)
Oni Press: Jan, 1998 - No. 13, Sept, 1999 ($2.95, B&W)

1-Jay & Silent Bob; Kevin Smith-s/Matt Wagner-a 1 3 4 6 8 10
1-2nd printing 3.00
2-11,13: 2,3-Paul Pope-s/a. 3,4-Nixey-s/a. 4,5-Sienkewicz-s/a. 6,7-Gaiman-s. 9-Bagge-c. 13-All Paul Dini-s; Jingle Belle 3.00
12-Jay & Silent Bob as Bluntman & Chronic; Smith-s/Allred-a 5.00

ONIGAMI (See Warrior Nun Areala: Black & White)
Antarctic Press: Apr, 1998 - No. 3, July, 1998 ($2.95, B&W, limited series)

1-3-Michel Lacombe-s/a 3.00

ONI PRESS COLOR SPECIAL
Oni Press: Jun, 2001; Jul, 2002 ($5.95, annual)

...2001-Oeming "Who Killed Madman?" cover; stories & art by various 6.00
...2002-Allred wraparound-c; stories & art by various 6.00

ONSLAUGHT: EPILOGUE
Marvel Comics: Feb, 1997 ($2.95, one-shot)

1-Hama-s/Green-a; Xavier-c; Bastion-app. 3.00

ONSLAUGHT: MARVEL
Marvel Comics: Oct, 1996 ($3.95, one-shot)

1-Conclusion to Onslaught x-over; wraparound-c 1 2 3 4 5 7

ONSLAUGHT: X-MEN
Marvel Comics: Aug, 1996 ($3.95, one-shot)

1-Waid & Lobdell script; Fantastic Four & Avengers app.; Xavier as Onslaught 5.00
1-Variant-c 2 4 6 8 10 12

ON STAGE
Dell Publishing Co.: No. 1336, Apr-June, 1962

Four Color 1336-Not by Leonard Starr 6 12 18 38 52 65

ON THE DOUBLE (Movie)
Dell Publishing Co.: No. 1232, Sept-Nov, 1961

Four Color 1232 6 12 18 38 52 65

ON THE ROAD TO PERDITION (Movie)

The Order #1 © MAR

Original E-Man and Michael Mauser #4 © CC

Original Ghost Rider #12 © MAR

GD 2.0 | VG 4.0 | FN 6.0 | VF 8.0 | VF/NM 9.0 | NM- 9.2

DC Comics (Paradox Press): 2003 - Book 3, 2004 ($7.95, 8"x5 1/2", B&W, limited series)
...: Oasis, Book 1-Max Allan Collins-s/José Luis García-López-a/David Beck-c 8.00
...: Sanctuary, Book 2-Max Allan Collins-s/Steve Lieber-a/José Luis García-López-c 8.00
...: Detour, Book 3-Max Allan Collins-s/José Luis García-López-a/Steve Lieber-c/a(i) 8.00
Road to Perdition 2: On the Road (2004, $14.95) r/series; Collins intro. 15.00

ON THE ROAD WITH ANDRAE CROUCH
Spire Christian Comics (Fleming H. Revell): 1973, 1977 (39¢)
nn 1 3 4 6 8 11

ON THE SCENE PRESENTS:...
Warren Publishing Co.: Oct, 1966 - No. 2, 1967 (B&W magazine, two #1 issues)
#1 "Super Heroes" (68 pgs.) Batman 1966 movie photo-c/s; has articles/photos/comic art from serials on Superman, Flash Gordon, Capt. America, Capt. Marvel and The Phantom 4 8 12 27 36 45
#1 "Freak Out, USA" (Fall/1966, 60 pgs.) (lower print run) articles on musicians like Zappa, Jefferson Airplane, Supremes 5 10 15 33 44 55
#2 "Freak Out, USA" (2/67, 52 pgs.) Beatles, Country Joe, Doors/Jim Morrison, Bee Gees 4 8 12 27 36 45

ON THE SPOT (Pretty Boy Floyd...)
Fawcett Publications: Fall, 1948
nn-Pretty Boy Floyd photo on-c; bondage-c 35 70 105 198 287 375

ONYX OVERLORD
Marvel Comics (Epic): Oct, 1992 - No. 4, Jan, 1993 ($2.75, mini-series)
1-4: Moebius scripts 2.75

OPEN SPACE
Marvel Comics: Mid-Dec, 1989 - No. 4, Aug, 1990 ($4.95, bi-monthly, 68 pgs.)
1-4: 1-Bill Wray-a; Freas-c 5.00
0-(1999) Wizard supplement; unpubl. early Alex Ross-a; new Ross-c 2.25

OPERATION BIKINI (See Movie Classics)

OPERATION BUCHAREST (See The Crusaders)

OPERATION CROSSBOW (See Movie Classics)

OPERATION: KNIGHTSTRIKE (See Knightstrike)
Image Comics (Extreme Studios): May, 1995 - No.3, July, 1995 ($2.50)
1-3 2.50

OPERATION PERIL
American Comics Group (Michel Publ.): Oct-Nov, 1950 - No. 16, Apr-May, 1953 (#1-5: 52 pgs.)
1-Time Travelers, Danny Danger (by Leonard Starr) & Typhoon Tyler (by Ogden Whitney) begin 40 80 120 230 335 440
2-War-c 24 48 72 135 195 255
3-War-c; horror story 21 42 63 118 169 220
4,5-Sci/fi-c/story 24 48 72 135 195 255
6-10: 6,8,9,10-Sci/fi-c. 6-Dinosaur-c. 7-Sabretooth-c 20 40 60 112 161 210
11,12-War-c; last Time Travelers 14 28 42 79 110 140
13-16: All war format 10 20 30 58 77 95
NOTE: *Starr a-2, 5. Whitney a-1, 2, 5-10, 12; c-1, 3, 5, 8, 9.*

OPERATION: STORMBREAKER
Acclaim Comics (Valiant Heroes): Aug, 1997 ($3.95, one-shot)
1-Waid/Augustyn-s, Braithwaite-a 4.00

OPTIC NERVE
Drawn and Quarterly: Apr, 1995 - Present ($2.95-$3.95, bi-annual)
1-7: Adrian Tomine-c/a/scripts in all 3.00
8,9: 8-($3.50). 9-($3.95) 4.00
32 Stories-($9.95, trade paperback)-r/Optic Nerve mini-comics 10.00
32 Stories-($29.95, hardcover)-r/Optic Nerve mini-comics; signed & numbered 30.00

ORAL ROBERTS' TRUE STORIES (Junior Partners #120 on)
TelePix Publ. (Oral Roberts' Evangelistic Assoc./Healing Waters): 1956 (no month) - No. 119, 7/59 (15¢)(No. 102: 25¢)
V1#1(1956)-(Not code approved)- "The Miracle Touch" 21 42 63 118 169 220
102-(Only issue approved by code, 10/56) "Now I See" 13 26 39 74 102 130
103-119: 115-(114 on inside) 9 18 27 54 70 85
NOTE: *Also see Happiness & Healing For You.*

ORANGE BIRD, THE
Walt Disney Educational Media Co.: No date (1980) (36 pgs.; in color; slick cover)
nn-Included with educational kit on foods, ...in Nutrition Adventures nn (1980) ...and the Nutrition Know-How Revue nn (1983) 3.00

ORB (Magazine)
Orb Publishing: 1974 - No. 6, Mar/Apr 1976 (B&W/color)
1-1st app. Northern Light & Kadaver, both series begin 3 7 10 21 28 35
2,3 (72 pgs.) 2 4 6 12 16 20
4-6 (60 pgs.): 4,5-origin Northern Light 2 4 6 10 12 15
NOTE: *Allison a-1-3. Gene Day a-1-6. P. Hsu a-4-6. Steacy s/a-3,4.*

ORBIT
Eclipse Books: 1990 - No. 3, 1990 ($4.95, 52 pgs., squarebound)
1-3: Reprints from Isaac Asimov's Science Fiction Magazine; 1-Dave Stevens-c, Bolton-a. 3-Bolton-c/a, Yeates-a 5.00

ORBITER
DC Comics (Vertigo): 2003 ($24.95, hardcover with dust jacket)
HC-Warren Ellis-s/Colleen Doran-a 25.00
SC-(2004, $17.95) Warren Ellis-s/Colleen Doran-a 18.00

ORDER, THE (cont'd from Defenders V2#12)
Marvel Comics: Apr, 2002 - No. 6, Sept, 2002 ($2.25, limited series)
1-6: 1-Haley-a/Duffy & Busiek-s. 3-Avengers-c/app. 4-Jurgens-a 2.25

ORIENTAL HEROES
Jademan Comics: Aug, 1988 - No. 55, Feb, 1993 ($1.50/$1.95, 68 pgs.)
1,55 2.25
2-54 2.25

ORIGINAL ASTRO BOY, THE
Now Comics: Sept, 1987 - No. 20, Jun, 1989 ($1.50/$1.75)
1-20-All have Ken Steacy painted-c/a 3.00

ORIGINAL BLACK CAT, THE
Recollections: Oct. 6, 1988 - No. 9, 1992 ($2.00, limited series)
1-9: Elias-r; 1-Bondage-c. 2-Murphy Anderson-c 4.00

ORIGINAL DICK TRACY, THE
Gladstone Publishing: Sept, 1990 - No. 5, 1991 ($1.95, bi-monthly, 68pgs.)
1-5: 1-Vs. Pruneface. 2-& the Evil influence; begin $2.00-c 2.25
NOTE: *#1 reprints strips 7/16/43 - 9/30/43. #2 reprints strips 12/1/46 - 2/2/47. #3 reprints 8/31/46 - 11/14/46. #4 reprints 9/17/45 - 12/23/45. #5 reprints 6/10/46 - 8/28/46.*

ORIGINAL DOCTOR SOLAR, MAN OF THE ATOM, THE
Valiant: Apr, 1995 ($2.95, one-shot)
1-Reprints Doctor Solar, Man of the Atom #1,5; Bob Fugitani-r; Paul Smith-c; afterword by Seaborn Adamson 4.00

ORIGINAL E-MAN AND MICHAEL MAUSER, THE
First Comics: Oct, 1985 - No. 7, April, 1986 ($1.75, Baxter paper)
1-7: 1-Has r-/Charlton's E-Man, Vengeance Squad. 2-Shows #4 in indicia by mistake. 7-($2.00, 44pgs.)-Staton-a 2.25

ORIGINAL GHOST RIDER, THE
Marvel Comics: July, 1992 - No. 20, Feb, 1994 ($1.75)
1-20: 1-7-r/Marvel Spotlight #5-11 by Ploog w/new-c. 3-New Phantom Rider (former Night Rider) back-ups begin by Ayers. 4-Quesada-c(p). 8-Ploog-c. 8,9-r/Ghost Rider #1,2. 10-r/Marvel Spotlight #12. 11-18,20-r/Ghost Rider #3-12. 19-r/Marvel Two-in-One #8 2.25

ORIGINAL GHOST RIDER RIDES AGAIN, THE
Marvel Comics: July, 1991 - No. 7, Jan, 1992, ($1.50, limited series, 52 pgs.)
1-7: 1-r/Ghost Rider #68(origin),69 w/covers. 2-7: R/ G.R. #70-81 w/covers 2.25

ORIGINAL MAGNUS ROBOT FIGHTER, THE
Valiant: Apr, 1995 ($2.95, one-shot)
1-Reprints Magnus, Robot Fighter 4000 #2; Russ Manning-r; Rick Leonardi-c; afterword by Seaborn Adamson 4.00

ORIGINAL NEXUS GRAPHIC NOVEL (See First Comics Graphic Novel #19)

ORIGINAL SHIELD, THE
Archie Enterprises, Inc.: Apr, 1984 - No. 4, Oct, 1984
1-4: 1,2-Origin Shield; Ayers p-1-4, Nebres c-1,2 4.00

ORIGINAL SWAMP THING SAGA, THE (See DC Special Series #2, 14, 17, 20)

ORIGINAL TUROK, SON OF STONE, THE
Valiant: Apr, 1995 - No. 2, May, 1995 ($2.95, limited series)
1,2: 1-Reprints Turok, Son of Stone #24,25,42; Alberto Gioletti-r; Rags Morales-c; afterword by Seaborn Adamson. 2-Reprints Turok, Son of Stone #24,33; Gioletti-r; McKone-c 4.00

ORIGIN OF GALACTUS (See Fantastic Four #48-50)
Marvel Comics: Feb, 1996 ($2.50, one-shot)

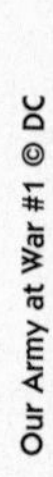
Oswald the Rabbit Four Color #183 © Walter Lantz

Our Army at War #1 © DC

Our Army at War #138 © DC

GD 2.0 | VG 4.0 | FN 6.0 | VF 8.0 | VF/NM 9.0 | NM- 9.2

1-Lee & Kirby reprints w/pin-ups 2.50

ORIGIN OF THE DEFIANT UNIVERSE, THE
Defiant Comics: Feb, 1994 ($1.50, 20 pgs., one-shot)
1-David Lapham, Adam Pollina & Alan Weiss-a; Weiss-c 5.00
NOTE: *The comic was originally published as Defiant Genesis and was distributed at the 1994 Philadelphia ComicCon.*

ORIGINS OF MARVEL COMICS (See Fireside Book Series)

ORION (Manga)
Dark Horse Comics: Sept, 1992 - No. 6, July, 1993 ($2.95/$3.95, B&W, bimonthly, lim. series)
1-6:1,2,6-Squarebound): 1-Masamune Shirow-c/a/s in all 4.00

ORION (See New Gods)
DC Comics: June, 2000 - No. 25, June, 2002 ($2.50)
1-14-Simonson-s/a. 3-Back-up story w/Miller-a. 4-Gibbons-a back-up. 7-Chaykin back-up. 8-Loeb/Liefeld back-up. 10-A. Adams back-up-a 12-Jim Lee back-up-a. 13-JLA-c/app.; Byrne-a 2.50
15-($3.95) Black Racer app.; back-up story w/J.P. Leon-a 4.00
16-24-Simonson-s/a: 19-Joker: Last Laugh x-over 2.50
25-($3.95) Last issue; Mister Miracle-c/app. 4.00
The Gates of Apocalypse (2001, $12.95, TPB) r/#1-5 & various short-s 13.00

OSBORNE JOURNALS (See Spider-Man titles)
Marvel Comics: Feb, 1997 ($2.95, one-shot)
1-Hotz-c/a 3.00

OSCAR COMICS (Formerly Funny Tunes; Awful...#11 & 12) (Also see Cindy Comics)
Marvel Comics: No. 24, Spring, 1947 - No. 10, Apr, 1949; No. 13, Oct, 1949

	GD	VG	FN	VF	VF/NM	NM-
24(#1, Spring, 1947)	18	36	54	102	146	190
25(#2, Sum, 1947)-Wolverton-a plus Kurtzman's "Hey Look"	20	40	60	112	161	210
26(#3)-Same as regular #3 except #26 was printed over in black ink with #3 appearing on-c below the over print	11	22	33	66	91	115
3-9,13: 8-Margie app.	11	22	33	66	91	115
10-Kurtzman's "Hey Look"	13	26	39	76	106	135

OSWALD THE RABBIT (Also see New Fun Comics #1)
Dell Publishing Co.: No. 21, 1943 - No. 1268, 12-2/61-62 (Walter Lantz)

	GD	VG	FN	VF	VF/NM	NM-
Four Color 21(1943)	45	90	135	360	560	760
Four Color 39(1943)	33	66	99	248	387	525
Four Color 67(1944)	19	38	57	134	205	275
Four Color 102(1946)-Kelly-a, 1 pg.	16	32	48	112	171	230
Four Color 143,183	11	22	33	75	110	145
Four Color 225,273	7	14	21	51	71	90
Four Color 315,388	7	14	21	46	63	80
Four Color 458,507,549,593	5	10	15	36	48	60
Four Color 623,697,792,894,979,1268	4	8	12	29	40	50

OSWALD THE RABBIT (See The Funnies, March of Comics #7, 38, 53, 67, 81, 95, 111, 126, 141, 156, 171, 186, New Funnies & Super Book #8, 20)

OTHERS, THE
Image Comics (Shadowline Ink): 1995 - No. 3, 1995 ($2.50)
0 ($1.00)-16 pg. preview 2.25
1-3 2.50

OTIS GOES TO HOLLYWOOD
Dark Horse Comics: Apr, 1997 - No.2, May, 1997 ($2.95, B&W, mini-series)
1,2-Fingerman-c/s/a 3.00

OUR ARMY AT WAR (Becomes Sgt. Rock #302 on; also see Army At War)
National Periodical Publications: Aug, 1952 - No. 301, Feb, 1977

	GD	VG	FN	VF	VF/NM	NM-
1	147	294	441	1250	2025	2800
2	63	126	189	536	868	1200
3,4: 4-Krigstein-a	50	100	150	413	657	900
5-7	41	82	123	330	515	700
8-11,14-Krigstein-a	41	82	123	305	478	650
12,15-20	33	66	99	248	387	525
13-Krigstein-c/a; flag-c	41	82	123	318	497	675
21-31: Last precode (2/55)	24	48	72	174	267	360
32-40	20	40	60	145	223	300
41-60: 51-1st S.A. issue	16	32	48	116	178	240
61-70: 67-Minor Sgt. Rock prototype	14	28	42	102	156	210
71-80	12	24	36	86	131	175
81- (4/59)-Sgt. Rocky of Easy Co. app. by Andru & Esposito-a/ Haney-s; (the last Sgt. Rock prototype)	200	400	600	1750	2875	4000
82-1st Sgt. Rock app., in name only, in Easy Co. story (6 panels) by Kanigher & Drucker	50	100	150	413	657	900
83-(6/59)-1st true Sgt. Rock app. in "The Rock and the Wall" by Kubert & Kanigher; (most similar to prototype in G.I. Combat #68)	160	320	480	1400	2300	3200
84-Kubert-c	30	60	90	213	327	440
85-Origin & 1st app. Ice Cream Soldier	38	76	114	285	443	600
86,87-Early Sgt. Rock; Kubert-a	28	56	84	203	312	420
88-1st Sgt. Rock-c; Kubert-c/a	31	62	93	228	352	475
89	25	50	75	181	278	375
90-Kubert-c/a; How Rock got his stripes	32	64	96	240	370	500
91-All-Sgt. Rock issue; Grandenetti-c/Kubert-a	58	116	174	493	797	1100
92,94,96-99: 97-Regular Kubert-c begin	18	36	54	126	193	260
93-1st Zack Nolan	18	36	54	131	201	270
95,100: 95-1st app. Bulldozer	19	38	57	138	212	285
101,105,108,113,115: 101-1st app. Buster. 105-1st app. Junior. 113-1st app. Wildman & Jackie Johnson. 115-Rock revealed as orphan; 1st x-over Mlle. Marie. 1st Sgt. Rock's battle family	14	28	42	97	149	200
102-104,106,107,109,110,114,116-120: 104-Nurse Jane-c/s. 109-Pre Easy Co. Sgt. Rock-s. 118-Sunny injured	12	24	36	86	131	175
111-1st app. Wee Willie & Sunny	15	30	45	109	167	225
112-Classic Easy Co. roster-c	16	32	48	116	178	240
121-125,130-133,135-139,141-150: 138-1st Sparrow. 141-1st Shaker. 147,148-Rock becomes a General	9	18	27	65	93	120
126,129,134: 126-1st app. Canary; grey tone-c	10	20	30	70	100	130
127-2nd all-Sgt. Rock issue; 1st app. Little Sure	11	22	33	77	114	150
128-Training & origin Sgt. Rock; 1st Sgt. Krupp	25	50	75	181	278	375
140-3rd all-Sgt. Rock issue	10	20	30	70	100	130
151-Intro. Enemy Ace by Kubert (2/65), black-c	38	76	114	285	443	600
152-4th all-Sgt. Rock issue	10	20	30	70	100	130
153-2nd app. Enemy Ace (4/65)	18	36	54	131	201	270
154,156,157,159-161,165-167: 157-2 pg. pin-up: 159-1st Nurse Wendy Winston-c/s. 165-2nd Iron Major	8	16	24	55	78	100
155-3rd app. Enemy Ace (6/65)(see Showcase)	12	24	36	87	134	180
158-Origin & 1st app. Iron Major(9/65), formerly Iron Captain	9	18	27	65	93	120
162,163-Viking Prince x-over in Sgt. Rock	9	18	27	63	89	115
164-Giant G-19	14	28	42	97	149	200
168-1st Unknown Soldier app.; referenced in Star-Spangled War Stories #157; (Sgt. Rock x-over) (6/66)	12	24	36	87	134	180
169,170	7	14	21	51	71	90
171-176,178-181: 171-1st Mad Emperor	7	14	21	46	63	80
177-(80 pg. Giant G-32)	10	20	30	70	100	130
182,183,186-Neal Adams-a. 186-Origin retold	7	14	21	51	71	90
184-Wee Willie dies	8	16	24	55	78	100
185,187,188,193-195,197-199	6	12	18	38	52	65
189,191,192,196: 189-Intro. The Teen-age Underground Fighters of Unit 3. 196-Hitler cameo	6	12	18	40	55	70
190-(80 pg. Giant G-44)	8	16	24	55	78	100
200-12 pg. Rock story told in verse; Evans-a	6	12	18	43	59	75
201,202,204-207: 201-Krigstein-r/#14. 204,205-All reprints; no Sgt. Rock. 207-Last 12¢ cover	4	8	12	27	36	45
203-(80 pg. Giant G-56)-All-r, Sgt. Rock story	7	14	21	50	68	85
208-215	3	7	10	21	28	35
216,229-(80 pg. Giants G-68, G-80): 216-Has G-58 on-c by mistake	6	12	18	43	59	75
217-219: 218-1st U.S.S. Stevens	3	6	9	18	24	30
220-Classic dinosaur/Sgt. Rock-c/s	3	7	10	21	28	35
221-228,230-234: 231-Intro/death Rock's brother. 234-Last 15¢ issue	3	6	9	16	20	24
235-239,241: 52 pg. Giants	3	7	10	21	28	35
240-Neal Adams-a; 52 pg. Giant	4	8	12	27	36	45
242-Also listed as **DC 100 Page Super Spectacular #9**; see for price						
243-246: (All 52 pgs.) 244-No Adams-a	3	6	9	19	25	32
247-250,254-268,270: 247-Joan of Arc	2	4	6	11	14	18
251-253-Return of Iron Major	2	4	6	14	18	22
269,275-(100 pgs.)	4	8	12	29	40	50
271-274,276-279: 273-Crucifixion-c	2	4	6	10	13	16
280-(68 pgs.)-200th app. Sgt. Rock; reprints Our Army at War #81,83	3	6	9	19	25	32
281-299,301: 295-Bicentennial cover	2	4	6	10	12	15
300-Sgt. Rock-s by Kubert (2/77)	2	4	6	11	14	18

NOTE ***Alcala*** *a-251.* ***Drucker*** *a-27, 67, 68, 79, 82, 83, 96, 164, 177, 203, 212, 243r, 244, 269r, 275r, 280r.* ***Evans*** *a-165-175, 200, 266, 269, 270, 274, 276, 278, 280.* ***Glanzman*** *a-218, 220, 222, 223, 225, 227, 230-232, 238-241, 244, 247, 248, 256-259, 261, 265-267, 271, 282, 283, 298.* ***Grandenetti*** *c-91,120.* ***Grell*** *a-287.* ***Heath*** *a-50, 164, & most 176-281.* ***Kubert*** *a-38, 59, 67, 68 & most issues from 83-165, 171, 233, 236, 267, 275, 300; c-84, 280.* ***Maurer*** *a-233, 237, 239, 240, 45, 280, 284, 288, 290, 291, 295.* ***Severin*** *a-236, 252, 265, 267, 269r, 272.* ***Toth*** *a-*

Out For Blood #2 © DH

	GD 2.0	VG 4.0	FN 6.0	VF 8.0	VF/NM 9.0	NM- 9.2

235, 241, 254. ***Wildey*** *a-283-285, 287p.* ***Wood*** *a-249.*

OUR FIGHTING FORCES
National Per. Publ./DC Comics: Oct-Nov, 1954 - No. 181, Sept-Oct, 1978

	GD 2.0	VG 4.0	FN 6.0	VF 8.0	VF/NM 9.0	NM- 9.2
1-Grandenetti-c/a	92	184	276	782	1266	1750
2	41	82	123	330	515	700
3-Kubert-c; last precode issue (3/55)	36	72	108	270	423	575
4,5	30	60	90	218	334	450
6-9: 7-1st S.A. issue	25	50	75	181	278	375
10-Wood-a	26	52	78	187	286	385
11-19	20	40	60	145	223	300
20-Grey tone-c (4/57)	23	46	69	165	253	340
21-30	14	28	42	102	156	210
31-40	13	26	39	90	138	185
41-Unknown Soldier tryout	16	32	48	116	178	240
42-44	12	24	36	82	124	165
45-Gunner & Sarge begins, end #94	38	76	114	285	443	600
46	16	32	48	116	178	240
47	12	24	36	84	127	170
48,50	11	22	33	77	114	150
49-1st Pooch	14	28	42	97	149	200
51-Grey tone-c	10	20	30	72	104	135
52-64: 64-Last 10¢ issue	9	18	27	63	89	115
65-70	7	14	21	50	68	85
71-Grey tone-c	7	14	21	46	63	80
72-80	6	12	18	38	52	65
81-90	5	10	15	36	48	60
91-98: 95-Devil-Dog begins, ends #98.	4	8	12	27	36	45
99-Capt. Hunter begins, ends #106	4	8	12	29	40	50
100	4	8	12	28	38	48
101-105,107-120: 116-Mlle. Marie app. 120-Last 12¢ issue	3	7	10	21	28	35
106-Hunters Hellcats begin	4	8	12	22	30	38
121,122: 121-Intro. Heller	3	6	9	18	24	30
123-The Losers (Capt. Storm, Gunner & Sarge, Johnny Cloud) begin	6	12	18	43	59	75
124-132: 132-Last 15¢ issue	3	6	9	16	20	24
133-137 (Giants). 134-Toth-a	3	6	9	19	25	32
138-145,147-150: 146-Toth-a	2	4	6	10	13	16
146-Classic Toth & Goodwin-a	2	4	6	12	16	20
151-162-Kirby a(p)	2	4	6	14	18	22
163-180	2	4	6	9	11	14
181-Last issue	2	4	6	10	13	16

NOTE: ***N. Adams*** *c-147.* ***Drucker*** *a-28, 37, 39, 42-44, 49, 53, 133r.* ***Evans*** *a-149, 164-174, 177-181.* ***Glanzman*** *a-125-128, 132, 134, 138-141, 143, 144.* ***Heath*** *a-2, 16, 18, 28, 41, 44, 49, 114, 135-138r; c-51.* ***Kirby*** *a-151-162p; c-152-159.* ***Kubert*** *c/a in many issues.* ***Maurer*** *a-135.* ***Redondo*** *a-166.* ***Severin*** *a-123-130, 131i, 132-150.*

OUR FIGHTING MEN IN ACTION (See Men In Action)

OUR FLAG COMICS
Ace Magazines: Aug, 1941 - No. 5, April, 1942

	GD 2.0	VG 4.0	FN 6.0	VF 8.0	VF/NM 9.0	NM- 9.2
1-Captain Victory, The Unknown Soldier (intro.) & The Three Cheers begin	277	554	831	1731	2666	3600
2-Origin The Flag (patriotic hero); 1st app?	119	238	357	744	1147	1550
3-5: 5-Intro & 1st app. Mr. Risk	90	180	270	563	869	1175

NOTE: ***Anderson*** *a-1, 4.* ***Mooney*** *a-1, 2; c-2.*

OUR GANG COMICS (With Tom & Jerry #39-59; becomes Tom & Jerry #60 on; based on film characters)
Dell Publishing Co.: Sept-Oct, 1942 - No. 59, June, 1949

	GD 2.0	VG 4.0	FN 6.0	VF 8.0	VF/NM 9.0	NM- 9.2
1-Our Gang & Barney Bear by Kelly, Tom & Jerry, Pete Smith, Flip & Dip, The Milky Way begin (all 1st app.)	85	170	255	638	1032	1425
2-Benny Burro begins (#2 by Kelly)	41	82	123	330	515	700
3-5	30	60	90	218	334	450
6-Bumbazine & Albert only app. by Kelly	39	78	117	293	459	625
7-No Kelly story	22	44	66	160	245	330
8-Benny Burro begins by Barks	49	98	147	392	609	825
9-Barks-a(2): Benny Burro & Happy Hound; no Kelly story	44	88	132	352	546	740
10-Benny Burro by Barks	33	66	99	248	387	525
11-1st Barney Bear & Benny Burro by Barks (5-6/44); Happy Hound by Barks	44	88	132	352	546	740
12-20	23	46	69	165	253	340
21-30: 30-X-Mas-c	16	32	48	112	171	230
31-36-Last Barks issue	12	24	36	87	134	180
37-40	9	18	27	60	85	110
41-50	7	14	21	51	71	90
51-57	7	14	21	46	63	80
58,59-No Kelly art or Our Gang stories	6	12	18	40	55	70

NOTE: ***Barks*** *art in part only.* ***Barks*** *did not write Barney Bear stories #30-34. (See March of Comics #3, 26). Early issues have photo back-c.*

OUR LADY OF FATIMA
Catechetical Guild Educational Society: 3/11/55 (15¢) (36 pgs.)

	GD 2.0	VG 4.0	FN 6.0	VF 8.0	VF/NM 9.0	NM- 9.2
395	6	12	18	27	33	38

OUR LOVE (True Secrets #3 on? or Romantic Affairs #3 on?)
Marvel Comics (SPC): Sept, 1949 - No. 2, Jan, 1950

	GD 2.0	VG 4.0	FN 6.0	VF 8.0	VF/NM 9.0	NM- 9.2
1-Photo-c	15	30	45	86	123	160
2-Photo-c	10	20	30	58	77	95

OUR LOVE STORY
Marvel Comics Group: Oct, 1969 - No. 38, Feb, 1976

	GD 2.0	VG 4.0	FN 6.0	VF 8.0	VF/NM 9.0	NM- 9.2
1	7	14	21	46	63	80
2-4,6-8,10,11	3	7	10	21	28	35
5-Steranko-a	9	18	27	63	89	115
9,12-Kirby-a	4	8	12	22	30	38
13-(10/71, 52 pgs.)	4	8	12	28	38	48
14-New story by Gary Fredrich & Tarpe' Mills	4	8	12	22	30	38
15-20,27:27-Colan/Everett-a(r?); Kirby/Colletta-r	3	6	9	16	21	26
21-26,28-37	2	4	6	12	16	20
38-Last issue	3	6	9	18	23	28

NOTE: ***J. Buscema*** *a-1-3, 5-7, 9, 13r, 16r, 19r(2), 21r, 22r(2), 23r, 34r, 35r; c-11, 13, 16, 22, 23, 24, 27, 35.* ***Colan*** *a-3-6, 21r(#6), 22r, 23r(#3), 24r(#4), 27; c-19.* ***Katz*** *a-17.* ***Maneely*** *a-13r.* ***Romita*** *a-13r; c-1, 2, 4-6.* ***Weiss*** *a-16, 17, 29r(#17).*

OUR MISS BROOKS
Dell Publishing Co.: No. 751, Nov, 1956

	GD 2.0	VG 4.0	FN 6.0	VF 8.0	VF/NM 9.0	NM- 9.2
Four Color 751-Photo-c	9	18	27	63	89	115

OUR SECRET (Exciting Love Stories)(Formerly My Secret)
Superior Comics Ltd.: No. 4, Nov, 1949 - No. 8, Jun, 1950

	GD 2.0	VG 4.0	FN 6.0	VF 8.0	VF/NM 9.0	NM- 9.2
4-Kamen-a; spanking scene	19	38	57	107	154	200
5,6,8	10	20	30	60	80	100
7-Contains 9 pg. story intended for unpublished Ellery Queen #5; lingerie panels	11	22	33	64	87	110

OUTBREED 999
Blackout Comics: May, 1994 - No. 6, 1994 ($2.95)

	GD 2.0	VG 4.0	FN 6.0	VF 8.0	VF/NM 9.0	NM- 9.2
1-6: 4-1st app. of Extreme Violet in 7 pg. backup story						3.00

OUTCAST, THE
Valiant: Dec, 1995 ($2.50, one-shot)

	GD 2.0	VG 4.0	FN 6.0	VF 8.0	VF/NM 9.0	NM- 9.2
1-Breyfogle-a.						2.50

OUTCASTS
DC Comics: Oct, 1987 - No. 12, Sept, 1988 ($1.75, limited series)

	GD 2.0	VG 4.0	FN 6.0	VF 8.0	VF/NM 9.0	NM- 9.2
1-12: John Wagner & Alan Grant scripts in all						2.25

OUTER LIMITS, THE (TV)
Dell Publishing Co.: Jan-Mar, 1964 - No. 18, Oct, 1969 (Most painted-c)

	GD 2.0	VG 4.0	FN 6.0	VF 8.0	VF/NM 9.0	NM- 9.2
1	13	26	39	92	141	190
2-5	8	16	24	55	78	100
6-10	7	14	21	46	63	80
11-18: 17-Reprints #1. 18-r/#2	6	12	18	38	52	65

OUTER SPACE (Formerly This Magazine Is Haunted, 2nd Series)
Charlton Comics: No. 17, May, 1958 - No. 25, Dec, 1959; Nov, 1968

	GD 2.0	VG 4.0	FN 6.0	VF 8.0	VF/NM 9.0	NM- 9.2
17-Williamson/Wood style art; not by them (Sid Check?)	15	30	45	83	117	150
18-20-Ditko-a	24	48	72	135	195	255
21-25: 21-Ditko-c	15	30	45	83	117	150
V2#1(11/68)-Ditko-a, Boyette-c	6	12	18	40	55	70

OUTER SPACE BABES, THE
Silhouette Studios: Feb, 1994 ($2.95)

	GD 2.0	VG 4.0	FN 6.0	VF 8.0	VF/NM 9.0	NM- 9.2
V3#1						3.00

OUT FOR BLOOD
Dark Horse: Sept, 1999 - No. 4, Dec, 1999 ($2.95, B&W, limited series)

	GD 2.0	VG 4.0	FN 6.0	VF 8.0	VF/NM 9.0	NM- 9.2
1-4-Kelley Jones-c; Erskine-a						3.00

OUTLANDERS (Manga)
Dark Horse Comics: Dec, 1988 - No. 33, Sept,1991 ($2.00-$2.50, B&W, 44 pgs.)

	GD 2.0	VG 4.0	FN 6.0	VF 8.0	VF/NM 9.0	NM- 9.2
1-33: Japanese Sci-fi manga						2.50

OUTLAW (See Return of the...)

Outlaw Kid #8 © MAR

Outlaw Nation #3 © Delano & Sudzuka

Out of the Vortex #8 © DH

OUTLAW FIGHTERS
Atlas Comics (IPC): Aug, 1954 - No. 5, Apr, 1955

	GD 2.0	VG 4.0	FN 6.0	VF 8.0	VF/NM 9.0	NM- 9.2
1-Tuska-a	14	28	42	79	110	140
2-5: 5-Heath-c/a, 7 pgs.	9	18	27	52	66	80

NOTE: ***Heath** c/a-5. **Maneely** c-2. **Pakula** a-2. **Reinman** a-2. **Tuska** a-1, 2.*

OUTLAW KID, THE (1st Series; see Wild Western)
Atlas Comics (CCC No. 1-11/EPI No. 12-29): Sept, 1954 - No. 19, Sept, 1957

	GD 2.0	VG 4.0	FN 6.0	VF 8.0	VF/NM 9.0	NM- 9.2
1-Origin; The Outlaw Kid & his horse Thunder begin; Black Rider app.	29	58	87	164	237	310
2-Black Rider app.	14	28	42	79	110	140
3-7,9: 3-Wildey-a(3)	12	24	36	69	95	120
8-Williamson/Woodbridge-a, 4 pgs.	13	26	39	74	102	130
10-Williamson-a	13	26	39	74	102	130
11-17,19: 13-Baker text illo. 15-Williamson text illo (unsigned)	9	18	27	52	66	80
18-Williamson/Mayo-a	10	20	30	56	73	90

NOTE: ***Berg** a-4, 7, 13. **Maneely** c-1-3, 5-8, 11-13, 15, 16, 18. **Pakula** a-3. **Severin** c-10, 17, 19. **Shores** a-1. **Wildey** a-1(3), 2-8, 10, 11, 12(4), 13(4), 15-19(4 each); c-4.*

OUTLAW KID, THE (2nd Series)
Marvel Comics Group: Aug, 1970 - No. 30, Oct, 1975

	GD 2.0	VG 4.0	FN 6.0	VF 8.0	VF/NM 9.0	NM- 9.2
1-Reprints; 1-Orlando-r, Wildey-r(3)	3	7	10	21	28	35
2,3,9: 2-Reprints. 3,9-Williamson-a(r)	2	4	6	11	14	18
4-7: 7-Last 15¢ issue	2	4	6	10	13	16
8-Double size (52 pgs.); Crandall-r	3	6	9	18	23	28
10-Origin	3	7	10	21	28	35
11-20: new-a in #10-16	2	4	6	11	14	18
21-30: 27-Origin-r/#10	2	4	6	8	10	12

NOTE: ***Ayers** a-10, 27r. **Berg** a-7, 25r. **Everett** a-2(2 pgs.). **Gil Kane** c-10, 11, 15, 27r, 28. **Roussos** a-10i, 27i(r). **Severin** c-1, 9, 20, 25. **Wildey** r-1-4, 6-9, 19-22, 25, 26. **Williamson** a-28r. **Woodbridge/Williamson** a-9r.*

OUTLAW NATION
DC Comics (Vertigo): Nov, 2000 - No. 19, May, 2002 ($2.50)

	GD 2.0	VG 4.0	FN 6.0	VF 8.0	VF/NM 9.0	NM- 9.2
1-19-Fabry painted-c/Delano-s/Sudzuka-a						2.50

OUTLAWS
D. S. Publishing Co.: Feb-Mar, 1948 - No. 9, June-July, 1949

	GD 2.0	VG 4.0	FN 6.0	VF 8.0	VF/NM 9.0	NM- 9.2
1-Violent & suggestive stories	35	70	105	201	293	385
2-Ingels-a; Baker-a	35	70	105	201	293	385
3,5,6: 3-Not Frazetta. 5-Sky Sheriff by Good app. 6-McWilliams-a	16	32	48	92	131	170
4-Orlando-a	18	36	54	100	143	185
7,8-Ingels-a in each	26	52	78	147	211	275
9-(Scarce)-Frazetta-a (7 pgs.)	48	96	144	293	447	600

NOTE: *Another #3 was printed in Canada with **Frazetta** art "Prairie Jinx," 7 pgs.*

OUTLAWS, THE (Formerly Western Crime Cases)
Star Publishing Co.: No. 10, May, 1952 - No. 13, Sep, 1953; No. 14, Apr, 1954

	GD 2.0	VG 4.0	FN 6.0	VF 8.0	VF/NM 9.0	NM- 9.2
10-L. B. Cole-c	22	44	66	123	177	230
11-14-L. B. Cole-c. 14-Reprints Western Thrillers #4 (Fox) w/new L.B. Cole-c; Kamen, Feldstein-r	17	34	51	95	135	175

OUTLAWS
DC Comics: Sept, 1991 - No. 8, Apr, 1992 ($1.95, limited series)

	GD 2.0	VG 4.0	FN 6.0	VF 8.0	VF/NM 9.0	NM- 9.2
1-8: Post-apocalyptic Robin Hood.						2.25

OUTLAW 7
Dark Horse Comics: Aug, 2001 - No. 4 ($2.99, limited series)

	GD 2.0	VG 4.0	FN 6.0	VF 8.0	VF/NM 9.0	NM- 9.2
1-3-Lubera & Feric-s/Lubera & Yeung-a						3.00

OUTLAWS OF THE WEST (Formerly Cody of the Pony Express #10)
Charlton Comics: No. 11, 7/57 - No. 81, 5/70; No. 82, 7/79 - No. 88, 4/80

	GD 2.0	VG 4.0	FN 6.0	VF 8.0	VF/NM 9.0	NM- 9.2
11	8	16	24	43	54	65
12,13,15-17,19,20	5	10	15	24	30	35
14-(68 pgs., 2/58)	9	18	27	49	62	75
18-Ditko-a	10	20	30	56	73	90
21-30	3	6	9	18	23	28
31-50: 34-Gunmaster app.	2	4	6	12	16	20
51-63,65,67-70: 54-Kid Montana app.	2	4	6	10	13	16
64,66: 64-Captain Doom begins (1st app.). 68-Kid Montana series begins	2	4	6	12	16	20
71-79: 73-Origin & 1st app. The Sharp Shooter, last app. #74. 75-Last Capt. Doom	2	4	6	9	11	14
80,81-Ditko-a	2	4	6	12	16	20
82-88						5.00
64,79(Modern Comics-r, 1977, '78)						4.00

OUTLAWS OF THE WILD WEST
Avon Periodicals: 1952 (25¢, 132 pgs.) (4 rebound comics)

	GD 2.0	VG 4.0	FN 6.0	VF 8.0	VF/NM 9.0	NM- 9.2
1-Wood back-c; Kubert-a (3 Jesse James-r)	35	70	105	198	287	375

OUTLAW TRAIL (See Zane Grey 4-Color 511)

OUT OF SANTA'S BAG (See March of Comics #10 in the Promotional Comics section)

OUT OF THE NIGHT (The Hooded Horseman #18 on)
Amer. Comics Group (Creston/Scope): Feb-Mar, 1952 - No. 17, Oct-Nov, 1954

	GD 2.0	VG 4.0	FN 6.0	VF 8.0	VF/NM 9.0	NM- 9.2
1-Williamson/LeDoux-a (9 pgs.)	65	130	195	406	628	850
2-Williamson-a (5 pgs.)	48	96	144	293	447	600
3,5-10: 9-Sci/Fic story	30	60	90	170	245	320
4-Williamson-a (7 pgs.)	40	80	120	241	363	485
11-17: 13-Nostrand-a? 17-E.C. Wood swipe	23	46	69	132	191	250

NOTE: ***Landau** a-14, 16, 17. **Shelly** a-12.*

OUT OF THE SHADOWS
Standard Comics/Visual Editions: No. 5, July, 1952 - No. 14, Aug, 1954

	GD 2.0	VG 4.0	FN 6.0	VF 8.0	VF/NM 9.0	NM- 9.2
5-Toth-p; Moreira, Tuska-a; Roussos-c	55	110	165	340	520	700
6-Toth/Celardo-a; Katz-a(2)	40	80	120	236	351	465
7,9: 7-Jack Katz-c/a(2). 9-Crandall-a(2)	31	62	93	178	259	340
8-Katz shrunken head-c	50	100	150	305	465	625
10-Spider-c; Sekowsky-a	31	62	93	178	259	340
11-Toth-a, 2 pgs.; Katz-a; Andru-c	31	62	93	178	259	340
12-Toth/Peppe-a(2); Katz-a	40	80	120	233	342	450
13-Cannabalism story; Sekowsky-a; Roussos-c	37	74	112	213	312	410
14-Toth-a	31	62	93	178	259	340

OUT OF THE VORTEX (Comics' Greatest World:... #1-4)
Dark Horse Comics: Oct., 1993 - No. 12, Oct, 1994 ($2.00, limited series)

	GD 2.0	VG 4.0	FN 6.0	VF 8.0	VF/NM 9.0	NM- 9.2
1-11: 1-Foil logo. 4-Dorman-c(p). 6-Hero Zero x-over						2.25
12 ($2.50)						2.50

NOTE: ***Art Adams** c-7. **Golden** c-8. **Mignola** c-2. **Simonson** c-3. **Zeck** c-10.*

OUT OF THIS WORLD
Charlton Comics: Aug, 1956 - No. 16, Dec, 1959

	GD 2.0	VG 4.0	FN 6.0	VF 8.0	VF/NM 9.0	NM- 9.2
1	26	52	78	150	215	280
2	13	26	39	76	106	135
3-6-Ditko-c/a (3) each	32	64	96	184	267	350
7-(2/58, 15¢, 68 pgs.)-Ditko-c/a(4)	34	68	102	196	283	370
8-(5/58, 15¢, 68 pgs.)-Ditko-a(2)	30	60	90	170	245	320
9,10,12,16-Ditko-a	22	44	66	127	184	240
11-Ditko c/a (3)	27	54	81	154	222	290
13-15	10	20	30	60	80	100

NOTE: ***Ditko** c-3-12, 16. **Reinman** a-10.*

OUT OF THIS WORLD
Avon Periodicals: June, 1950; Aug, 1950

	GD 2.0	VG 4.0	FN 6.0	VF 8.0	VF/NM 9.0	NM- 9.2
1-Kubert-a(2) (one reprinted/Eerie #1, 1947) plus Crom the Barbarian by Gardner Fox & John Giunta (origin); Fawcette-c	69	138	207	431	666	900
1-(8/50) Reprint; no month on cover	46	92	138	281	428	575

OUT OF THIS WORLD ADVENTURES
Avon Periodicals: July, 1950 - No. 2, Dec, 1950 (25¢ pulp)

	GD 2.0	VG 4.0	FN 6.0	VF 8.0	VF/NM 9.0	NM- 9.2
1-Kubert-a	67	134	201	419	647	875
2-Kubert-a plus The Spider God of Akka by Gardner Fox & John Giunta pulp magazine w/comic insert	46	92	138	281	428	575

NOTE: *Out of This World Adventures is a sci-fi pulp magazine w/32 pgs. of color comics.*

OUT OUR WAY WITH WORRY WART
Dell Publishing Co.: No. 680, Feb, 1956

	GD 2.0	VG 4.0	FN 6.0	VF 8.0	VF/NM 9.0	NM- 9.2
Four Color 680	4	8	12	24	32	40

OUTPOSTS
Blackthorne Publishing: June, 1987 - No. 4, 1987 ($1.25)

	GD 2.0	VG 4.0	FN 6.0	VF 8.0	VF/NM 9.0	NM- 9.2
1-4: 1-Kaluta-c(p)						2.25

OUTSIDERS, THE
DC Comics: Nov, 1985 - No. 28, Feb, 1988

	GD 2.0	VG 4.0	FN 6.0	VF 8.0	VF/NM 9.0	NM- 9.2
1						3.00
2-17						2.25
18-28: 18-26-Batman returns. 21-Intro. Strike Force Kobra; 1st app. Clayface IV 22-E.C. parody; Orlando-a. 21- 25-Atomic Knight app. 27,28-Millennium tie-ins						2.25
Annual 1 (12/86, $2.50), Special 1 (7/87, $1.50)						2.50

NOTE: ***Aparo** a-1-7, 9-14, 17-22, 25, 26; c-1-7, 9-14, 17, 19-26. **Byrne** a-11. **Bolland** a-6, 18; c-16. **Ditko** a-13p. **Erik Larsen** a-24, 27 28; c-27, 28. **Morrow** a-12.*

OUTSIDERS
DC Comics: Nov, 1993 - No. 24, Nov, 1995 ($1.75/$1.95/$2.25)

Outsiders ('03) #2 © DC

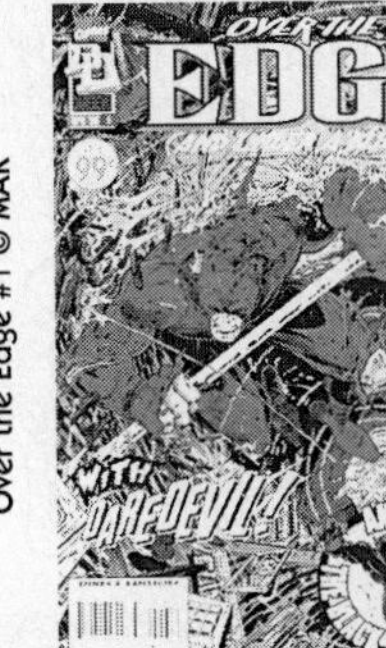

Over the Edge #1 © MAR

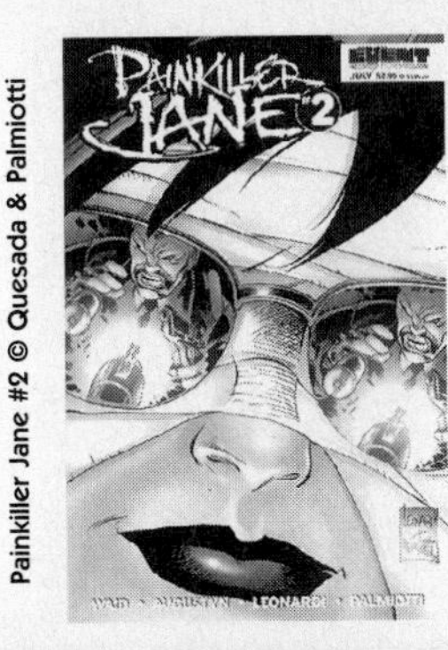

Painkiller Jane #2 © Quesada & Palmiotti

GD 2.0 | VG 4.0 | FN 6.0 | VF 8.0 | VF/NM 9.0 | NM- 9.2

1-11,0,12-24: 1-Alpha; Travis Charest-c. 1-Omega; Travis Charest-c. 5-Atomic Knight app. 8-New Batman-c/story. 11-(9/94)-Zero Hour. 0-(10/94).12-(11/94). 21-Darkseid cameo. 22-New Gods app. 2.25

OUTSIDERS (See Titans/Young Justice: Graduation Day)
DC Comics: Aug, 2003 - Present ($2.50)

1-Nightwing, Arsenal, Metamorpho app.; Winick-s/Raney-a 5.00
2-Joker and Grodd app. 3.00
3-18: 3-Joker-c. 5,6-ChrisCross-a. 8-Huntress app. 9,10-Capt. Marvel Jr. app. 2.50
... Double Feature (10/03, $4.95) r/#1,2 5.00
...: Looking For Trouble TPB (2004, $12.95) r/#1-7 & Teen Titans/Outsiders Secret Files & Origins 2003; intro. by Winick 13.00
...: Sum of All Evil TPB (2004, $14.95) r/#8-15 15.00

OUT THERE
DC Comics(Cliffhanger): July, 2001 - No. 18, Aug, 2003 ($2.50/$2.95)

1-Humberto Ramos-c/a; Brian Augustyn-s 3.00
1-Variant-c by Carlos Meglia 4.00
2-8: 3-Variant-c by Bruce Timm 2.50
9-18: 9-Begin $2.95-c 3.00
...: The Evil Within TPB (2002, $12.95) r/#1-6; Ramos sketch pages 13.00

OVERKILL: WITCHBLADE/ ALIENS/ DARKNESS/ PREDATOR
Image Comics/Dark Horse Comics: Dec, 2000 - No. 2, 2001 ($5.95)

1,2-Jenkins-s/Lansing, Ching & Benitez-a 6.00

OVER THE EDGE
Marvel Comics: Nov, 1995 - No. 10, Aug, 1996 (99¢)

1-10: 1,6,10-Daredevil-c/story. 2,7-Dr. Strange-c/story. 3-Hulk-c/story. 4,9-Ghost Rider-c/story. 5-Punisher-c/story. 8-Elektra-c/story 2.25

OWL, THE (See Crackajack Funnies #25, Popular Comics #72 and Occult Files of Dr. Spektor #22)
Gold Key: April, 1967; No. 2, April, 1968

1-Written by Jerry Siegel; '40s super hero 7 14 21 50 68 85
2 6 12 18 38 52 65

OZ (See First Comics Graphic Novel, Marvel Treaury Of Oz & MGM's Marvelous...)

OZ
Caliber Press: 1994 - 1997 ($2.95, B&W)

0-20: 0-Released between #10 & #11 3.00
1 ($5.95)-Limited Edition; double-c 6.00
...Specials: Freedom Fighters. Lion. Scarecrow. Tin Man 3.00

OZARK IKE
Dell Publishing Co./Standard Comics B11 on: Feb, 1948; Nov, 1948 - No. 24, Dec, 1951; No. 25, Sept, 1952

Four Color 180(1948-Dell) 11 22 33 80 120 160
B11, B12, 13-15 9 18 27 54 70 85
16-25 8 16 24 46 58 70

OZ: DAEMONSTORM
Caliber Press: 1997 ($3.95, B&W, one-shot)

1 4.00

OZ: ROMANCE IN RAGS
Caliber Press: 1996 ($2.95, B&W, limited series)

1-3, ..Special 3.00

OZ SQUAD
Brave New Worlds/Patchwork Press: 1992 - No. 4, 1994 ($2.50/$2.75, B&W)

1-4-Patchwork Press 3.00

OZ SQUAD
Patchwork Press: Dec, 1995 - No. 10, 1996 ($3.95/$2.95, B&W)

1-($3.95) 4.00
2-10 3.00

OZ: STRAW AND SORCERY
Caliber Press: 1997 ($2.95, B&W, limited series)

1-3 3.00

OZ-WONDERLAND WARS, THE
DC Comics: Jan, 1986 - No. 3, March, 1986 (Mini-series)(Giants)

1-3-Capt Carrot app.; funny animals 4.00

OZZIE & BABS (TV Teens #14 on)
Fawcett Publications: Dec, 1947 - No. 13, Fall, 1949

1-Teen-age 9 18 27 54 70 85

GD 2.0 | VG 4.0 | FN 6.0 | VF 8.0 | VF/NM 9.0 | NM- 9.2

2 6 12 18 29 36 42
3-13 5 10 15 24 30 35

OZZIE AND HARRIET (The Adventures of... on cover) (Radio)
National Periodical Publications: Oct-Nov, 1949 - No. 5, June-July, 1950

1-Photo-c 96 192 288 600 925 1250
2 48 96 144 293 447 600
3-5 40 80 120 239 357 475

OZZY OSBOURNE (Todd McFarland Presents)
Image Comics (Todd McFarlane Prod.): June, 1999 ($4.95, magazine-sized)

1-Bio, interview and comic story; Ormston painted-a; Ashley Wood-c 5.00

PACIFIC COMICS GRAPHIC NOVEL (See Image Graphic Novel)

PACIFIC PRESENTS (Also see Starslayer #2, 3)
Pacific Comics: Oct, 1982 - No. 2, Apr, 1983; No. 3, Mar, 1984 - No. 4, Jun, 1984

1-Chapter 3 of The Rocketeer; Stevens-c/a; Bettie Page model 1 2 3 4 5 7
2-Chapter 4 of The Rocketeer (4th app.); nudity; Stevens-c/a 1 2 3 4 5 7
3,4: 3-1st app. Vanity 3.00
NOTE: *Conrad a-3, 4; c-3. Ditko a-1-3; c-1(1/2). Dave Stevens a-1, 2; c-1(1/2), 2.*

PACT, THE
Image Comics: Feb, 1994 - No. 3, June, 1994 ($1.95, limited series)

1-3: Valentino co-scripts & layouts 2.25

PAGEANT OF COMICS (See Jane Arden & Mopsy)
Archer St. John: Sept, 1947 - No. 2, Oct, 1947

1,2: 1-Mopsy strip-r. 2-Jane Arden strip-r 10 20 30 56 73 90

PAINKILLER JANE
Event Comics: June, 1997 - No. 5, Nov, 1997 ($3.95/$2.95)

1-Augustyn/Waid-s/Leonardi/Palmiotti-a, variant-c 4.00
2-5: Two covers (Quesada, Leonardi) 3.00
0-(1/99, $3.95) Retells origin; two covers 4.00

PAINKILLER JANE / DARKCHYLDE
Event Comics: Oct, 1998 ($2.95, one-shot)

Preview-($6.95) DF Edition, 1-($6.95) DF Edition 7.00
1-Three covers; J.G. Jones-a 3.00

PAINKILLER JANE / HELLBOY
Event Comics: Aug, 1998 ($2.95, one-shot)

1-Leonardi & Palmiotti-a 3.00

PAINKILLER JANE VS. THE DARKNESS
Event Comics: Apr, 1997 ($2.95, one-shot)

1-Ennis-s; four variant-c (Conner, Hildebrandts, Quesada, Silvestri) 3.50

PAKKINS' LAND
Caliber Comics (Tapestry): Oct, 1996 - No. 6, July, 1997 ($2.95, B&W)

1-Gary and Rhoda Shipman-s/a 6.00
2,3 4.00
1-3-2nd printing 3.00
4-6 3.00
0-(6/97, $1.95) 3.00

PAKKINS' LAND: FORGOTTEN DREAMS
Caliber Comics/Image Comics #4: Apr, 1998 - No. 4, Mar, 2000 ($2.95, B&W)

1-4-Gary and Rhoda Shipman-s/a 3.00

PAKKINS' LAND: QUEST FOR KINGS
Caliber Comics: Aug, 1997 - No. 6, Mar, 1998 ($2.95, B&W)

1-6: 1-Gary and Rhoda Shipman-s/a; Jeff Smith var-c 3.00

PANCHO VILLA
Avon Periodicals: 1950

nn-Kinstler-c 25 50 75 141 203 265

PANDEMONIUM
Chaos! Comics: Sept, 1998 ($2.95, one-shot)

1-Al Rio-c 3.00

PANHANDLE PETE AND JENNIFER (TV) (See Gene Autry #20)
J. Charles Laue Publishing Co.: July, 1951 - No. 3, Nov, 1951

1 10 20 30 56 73 90
2,3: 2-Interior photo-cvrs 7 14 21 37 46 55

PANIC (Companion to Mad)

Panic #3 © WMG

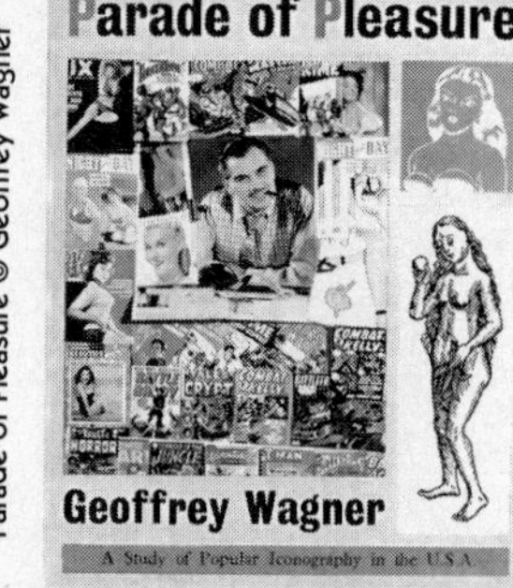

Parade of Pleasure
Geoffrey Wagner
A Study of Popular Iconography in the U.S.A.

Parade of Pleasure © Geoffrey Wagner

Paradise Too #12 © Terry Moore

GD VG FN VF VF/NM NM-
2.0 4.0 6.0 8.0 9.0 9.2

E. C. Comics (Tiny Tot Comics): Feb-Mar, 1954 - No. 12, Dec-Jan, 1955-56

1-Used in Senate Investigation hearings; Elder draws entire E. C. staff; Santa Claus & Mickey Spillane parody 30 60 90 213 327 440
2 14 28 42 102 156 210
3,4: 3-Senate Subcommittee parody; Davis draws Gaines, Feldstein & Kelly, 1 pg.; Old King Cole smokes marijuana. 4-Infinity-c; John Wayne parody
11 22 33 82 124 165
5-11: 8-Last pre-code issue (5/55). 9-Superman, Smilin' Jack & Dick Tracy app. on-c; has photo of Walter Winchell on-c. 11-Wheedies cereal box-c
11 22 33 75 110 145
12 (Low distribution; thousands were destroyed) 13 26 39 94 145 195
NOTE: *Davis a-1-12; c-12. Elder a-1-12. Feldstein c-1-3, 5. Kamen a-1. Orlando a-1-9. Wolverton c-4, panel-3. Wood a-2-9, 11, 12.*

PANIC (Magazine) (Satire)
Panic Publ.: July, 1958 - No. 6, July, 1959; V2#10, Dec, 1965 - V2#12, 1966

1 12 24 36 69 95 120
2-6 8 16 24 43 54 65
V2#10-12: Reprints earlier issues 3 6 9 18 24 30
NOTE: *Davis a-3(2 pgs.), 4, 5, 10; c-10. Elder a-5. Powell a-V2#10, 11. Torres a-1-5. Tuska a-V2#11.*

PANIC
Gemstone Publishing: March, 1997 - No. 11 ($2.50, quarterly)

1-11: E.C. reprints 2.50

PANTHA (See Vampirella-The New Monthly #16,17)

PANTHA: HAUNTED PASSION (Also see Vampirella Monthly #0)
Harris Comics: May, 1997 ($2.95, B&W, one-shot)

1-r/Vampirella #30,31 3.00

PARADE (See Hanna-Barbera...)

PARADE COMICS (Frisky Animals on Parade #2 on)
Ajax/Farrell Publ. (World Famous Publ.): Sept, 1957

1 9 18 27 52 66 80
NOTE: *Cover title: Frisky Animals on Parade.*

PARADE OF PLEASURE
Derric Verschoyle Ltd., London, England: 1954 (192 pgs.) (Hardback book)

By Geoffrey Wagner. Contains section devoted to the censorship of American comic books with illustrations in color and black and white. (Also see **Seduction of the Innocent**). Distributed in USA by Library Publishers, N. Y. 50 100 150 275 375 475
with dust jacket.... 105 210 315 578 777 975

PARADIGM
Image Comics: Sept, 2002 - Present ($3.50/$2.95, B&W)

1-4,9-11-($3.50) Matthew Cashel & Jeremy Haun-s/a. 10-Savage Dragon cameo 3.50
5-8-($2.95) 3.00
12-($3.95) 4.00
Vol. 1: Segue To An Interlude TPB (8/03, $13.95) r/#1-4; sketch pages 14.00

PARADISE TOO!
Abstract Studios: 2000 - No. 14, 2003 ($2.95, B&W)

1-14-Terry Moore's unpublished newspaper strips and sketches 3.00
...: Checking For Weirdos TPB (4/03, $14.95) r/#8-12 15.00
...: Drunk Ducks! TPB (7/02, $15.95) r/#1-7 16.00

PARADISE X (Also see Earth X and Universe X)
Marvel Comics: Apr, 2002 - No. 11, July, 2003 ($4.50/$2.99)

0-Ross-c; Braithwaite-a 4.50
1-11-($2.99) Ross-c; Braithwaite-a. 7-Punisher on-c. 10-Kingpin on-c 3.00
...:A (10/03, $2.99) Braithwaite-a; Ross-c 3.00
...:Devils (11/02, $4.50) Sadowski-a; Ross-c 4.50
...:Ragnarok 1,2 (3/02, 4/03; $2.99) Yeates-a; Ross-c 3.00
...:X (11/03, $2.99) Braithwaite-a; Ross-c; conclusion of story 3.00
...:Xen (7/02, $4.50) Yeowell & Sienkiewicz-a; Ross-c 4.50
Earth X Vol. 4: Paradise X Book 1 (2003, $29.99, TPB) r/#0,1-5, ...: Xen; Heralds #1-3 30.00
Vol. 5: Paradise X Book 2 (2004, $29.99, TPB) r/#6-12, Ragnarok #1&2; Devils, A & X 30.00

PARADISE X: HERALDS (Also see Earth X and Universe X)
Marvel Comics: Dec, 2001 - No. 3, Feb, 2002 ($3.50)

1-3-Prelude to Paradise X series; Ross-c; Pugh-a 3.50
Special Edition (Wizard preview) Ross-c 2.25

PARADOX
Dark Visions Publ: June, 1994 - No. 2, Aug, 1994 ($2.95, B&W, mature)

1,2: 1-Linsner-c. 2-Boris-c. 3.00

PARALLAX: EMERALD NIGHT (See Final Night)

GD VG FN VF VF/NM NM-
2.0 4.0 6.0 8.0 9.0 9.2

DC Comics: Nov, 1996 ($2.95, one-shot, 48 pgs.)

1-Final Night tie-in; Green Lantern (Kyle Rayner) app. 4.00

PARAMOUNT ANIMATED COMICS (See Harvey Comics Hits #60, 62)
Harvey Publications: No. 3, Feb, 1953 - No. 22, July, 1956

3-Baby Huey, Herman & Katnip, Buzzy the Crow begin
23 46 69 132 191 250
4-6 11 22 33 66 91 115
7-Baby Huey becomes permanent cover feature; cover title becomes Baby Huey with #9
22 44 66 127 184 240
8-10: 9-Infinity-c 11 22 33 64 87 110
11-22 9 18 27 52 66 80

PARENT TRAP, THE (Disney)
Dell Publishing Co.: No. 1210, Oct-Dec, 1961

Four Color 1210-Movie, Haley Mills photo-c 10 20 30 73 107 140

PARLIAMENT OF JUSTICE
Image Comics: Mar, 2003 ($5.95, B&W, one-shot, square-bound)

1-Michael Avon Oeming-c/s; Neil Vokes-a 6.00

PARODY
Armour Publishing: Mar, 1977 - No. 3, Aug, 1977 (B&W humor magazine)

1 2 4 6 12 16 20
2,3: 2-King Kong, Happy Days. 3-Charlie's Angels, Rocky
2 4 6 10 12 15

PAROLE BREAKERS
Avon Periodicals/Realistic #2 on: Dec, 1951 - No. 3, July, 1952

1(#2 on inside)-r-c/Avon paperback #283 (painted-c)
44 88 132 268 409 550
2-Kubert-a; r-c/Avon paperback #114 (photo-c) 33 66 99 190 275 360
3-Kinstler-c 30 60 90 170 245 320

PARTRIDGE FAMILY, THE (TV)(Also see David Cassidy)
Charlton Comics: Mar, 1971 - No. 21, Dec, 1973

1 7 14 21 51 70 90
2-4,6-10 4 8 12 27 36 45
5-Partridge Family Summer Special (52 pgs.); The Shadow, Lone Ranger, Charlie McCarthy, Flash Gordon, Hopalong Cassidy, Gene Autry & others app.
8 16 24 58 82 105
11-21 4 8 12 22 30 38

PARTS OF A HOLE
Caliber Press: 1991 ($2.50, B&W)

1-Short stories & cartoons by Brian Michael Bendis 3.00

PARTS UNKNOWN
Eclipse Comics/FX: July, 1992 - No. 4, Oct, 1992 ($2.50, B&W, mature)

1-4: All contain FX gaming cards 2.50

PARTS UNKNOWN
Image Comics: May, 2000 - Present ($2.95, B&W)

...: Killing Attractions 1 (5/00) Beau Smith-s/Brad Gorby-a 3.00
...: Hostile Takeover 1-4 (6-9/00) 3.00

PASSION, THE
Catechetical Guild: No. 394, 1955

394 5 10 15 24 30 35

PASSOVER (See Avengelyne)
Maximum Press: Dec, 1996 ($2.99, one-shot)

1 3.00

PAT BOONE (TV)(Also see Superman's Girlfriend Lois Lane #9)
National Per. Publ.: Sept-Oct, 1959 - No. 5, May-Jun, 1960 (All have photo-c)

1 46 92 138 281 428 575
2-5: 3-Fabian, Connie Francis & Paul Anka photos on-c. 4-Previews "Journey To The Center Of The Earth". 4-Johnny Mathis & Bobby Darin photos on-c. 5-Dick Clark & Frankie Avalon photos on-c 39 78 117 222 324 425

PATCHES
Rural Home/Patches Publ. (Orbit): Mar-Apr, 1945 - No. 11, Nov, 1947

1-L. B. Cole-c 40 80 120 236 351 465
2 15 30 45 86 123 160
3,4,6,8-11: 6-Henry Aldrich story. 8-Smiley Burnette-c/s (6/47); pre-dates Smiley Burnette #1. 9-Mr. District Attorney story (radio). Leav/Keigstein-a (16 pgs.). 9-11-Leav-c. 10-Jack Carson (radio) c/story; Leav-c. 11-Red Skelton story 15 30 45 83 117 150

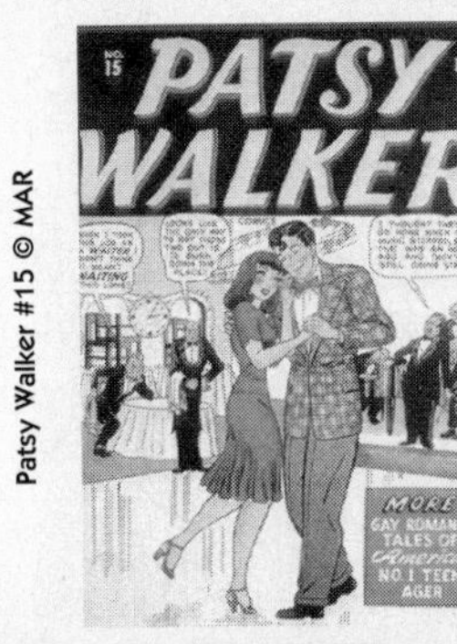

Patsy Walker #15 © MAR

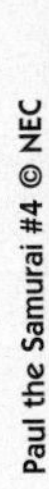

Paul the Samurai #4 © NEC

Peanuts #1 © UFS

	GD 2.0	VG 4.0	FN 6.0	VF 8.0	VF/NM 9.0	NM- 9.2
5-Danny Kaye-c/story; L.B. Cole-c.	21	42	63	121	173	225
7-Hopalong Cassidy-c/story	18	36	54	100	143	185

PATH, THE (Also see Negation War)
CrossGeneration Comics: Apr, 2002 - No. 23, Apr, 2004 ($2.95)

	GD	VG	FN	VF	VF/NM	NM-
1-23: 1-Ron Marz-s/Bart Sears-a. 13-Matthew Smith-a begins						3.00
Vol. 1: Crisis of Faith (2002, $15.95, TPB) r/#1-6						16.00
Vol. 2: Blood on Snow (5/03, $15.95, TPB) r/#7-12						16.00
Vol. 3: Death and Dishonor ('03, $15.95, TPB) r/#13-18						16.00

PATHWAYS TO FANTASY
Pacific Comics: July, 1984

	GD	VG	FN	VF	VF/NM	NM-
1-Barry Smith-c/a; Jeff Jones-a (4 pgs.)						4.00

PATIENT ZERO
Image Comics: Mar, 2004 - No. 4, Jun, 2004 ($2.95, limited series)

	GD	VG	FN	VF	VF/NM	NM-
1-4-Brent White-a/John McLean-Foreman-s						3.00

PATORUZU (See Adventures of...)

PATRIOTS, THE
DC Comics (WildStorm): Jan, 2000 - No. 10, Oct, 2000 ($2.50)

	GD	VG	FN	VF	VF/NM	NM-
1-10-Choi and Peterson-s/Ryan-a						2.50

PATSY & HEDY (Teenage)(Also see Hedy Wolfe)
Atlas Comics/Marvel (GPI/Male): Feb, 1952 - No. 110, Feb, 1967

	GD	VG	FN	VF	VF/NM	NM-
1-Patsy Walker & Hedy Wolfe; Al Jaffee-c	23	46	69	132	191	250
2	13	26	39	76	106	135
3-10: 3,7,8-Al Jaffee-c	10	20	30	60	80	100
11-20: 17-Al Jaffee-c	9	18	27	52	66	80
21-40	8	16	24	40	50	60
41-50	6	12	18	35	45	55
51-60	4	8	12	29	40	50
61-80,100: 88-Lingerie panel	4	8	12	24	32	40
81-87,89-99,101-110	3	7	10	21	28	35
Annual 1(1963)-Early Marvel annual	10	20	30	70	100	130

PATSY & HER PALS (Teenage)
Atlas Comics (PPI): May, 1953 - No. 29, Aug, 1957

	GD	VG	FN	VF	VF/NM	NM-
1-Patsy Walker	19	38	57	107	154	200
2	10	20	30	60	80	100
3-10	9	18	27	54	70	85
11-29: 24-Everett-c	8	16	24	43	54	65

PATSY WALKER (See All Teen, A Date With Patsy, Girls' Life, Miss America Magazine, Patsy & Hedy, Patsy & Her Pals & Teen Comics)
Marvel/Atlas Comics (BPC): 1945 (no month) - No. 124, Dec, 1965

	GD	VG	FN	VF	VF/NM	NM-
1-Teenage	52	104	156	317	484	650
2	28	56	84	158	229	300
3,4,6-10	22	44	66	123	177	230
5-Injury-to-eye-c	25	50	75	141	203	265
11,12,15,16,18	14	28	42	81	113	145
13,14,17,19-22-Kurtzman's "Hey Look"	15	30	45	85	120	155
23,24	11	22	33	64	87	110
25-Rusty by Kurtzman; painted-c	15	30	45	85	120	155
26-29,31: 26-31: 52 pgs.	10	20	30	58	77	95
30(52 pgs.)-Egghead Doodle by Kurtzman (1 pg.)	11	22	33	62	84	105
32-57: Last precode (3/55)	8	16	24	46	58	70
58-80,100	4	8	12	29	40	50
81-99: 92,98-Millie x-over. 99-Linda Carter x-over	4	8	12	24	32	40
101-124	3	7	10	21	28	35
Fashion Parade 1(1966, 68 pgs.) (Beware cut-out & marked pages)	9	18	27	63	89	115

NOTE: *Painted c-25-28. Anti-Wertham editorial in #21. Georgie app. in #8, 11. Millie app. in #10, 92, 98. Mitzi app. in #11. Rusty app. in #12, 25. Willie app. in #12.* ***Al Jaffee*** *c-57, 58.*

PAT THE BRAT (Adventures of Pipsqueak #34 on)
Archie Publications (Radio): June, 1953; Summer, 1955 - No. 4, 5/56; No. 15, 7/56 - No. 33, 7/59

	GD	VG	FN	VF	VF/NM	NM-
nn(6/53)	14	28	42	79	110	140
1(Summer, 1955)	10	20	30	56	73	90
2-4-(5/56) (#5-14 not published)	7	14	21	37	46	55
15-(7/56)-33	4	8	12	27	36	45

PAT THE BRAT COMICS DIGEST MAGAZINE
Archie Publications: October, 1980

	GD	VG	FN	VF	VF/NM	NM-
1-Li'l Jinx & Super Duck app.	2	4	6	10	12	15

PATTY CAKE
Permanent Press: Mar, 1995 - No. 9, Jul, 1996 ($2.95, B&W)

	GD	VG	FN	VF	VF/NM	NM-
1-9: Scott Roberts-s/a						3.00

PATTY CAKE
Caliber Press (Tapestry): Oct, 1996 - No. 3, Apr, 1997 ($2.95, B&W)

	GD	VG	FN	VF	VF/NM	NM-
1-3: Scott Roberts-s/a, ...Christmas (12/96)						3.00

PATTY CAKE & FRIENDS
Slave Labor Graphics: Nov, 1997 - Present ($2.95, B&W)

	GD	VG	FN	VF	VF/NM	NM-
Here There Be Monsters (10/97), 1-14: Scott Roberts-s/a						3.00
Volume 2 #1 (11/00, $4.95)						5.00

PATTY POWERS (Formerly Della Vision #3)
Atlas Comics: No. 4, Oct, 1955 - No. 7, Oct, 1956

	GD	VG	FN	VF	VF/NM	NM-
4	10	20	30	58	77	95
5-7	6	12	18	33	41	48

PAT WILTON (See Mighty Midget Comics)

PAUL
Spire Christian Comics (Fleming H. Revell Co.): 1978 (49¢)

	GD	VG	FN	VF	VF/NM	NM-
nn	1	3	4	6	8	11

PAULINE PERIL (See The Close Shaves of...)

PAUL REVERE'S RIDE (TV, Disney, see Walt Disney Showcase #34)
Dell Publishing Co.: No. 822, July, 1957

	GD	VG	FN	VF	VF/NM	NM-
Four Color 822-w/Johnny Tremain, Toth-a	10	20	30	72	104	135

PAUL TERRY (See Heckle and Jeckle)

PAUL TERRY'S ADVENTURES OF MIGHTY MOUSE (See Adventures of...)

PAUL TERRY'S COMICS (Formerly Terry-Toons Comics; becomes Adventures of Mighty Mouse No. 126 on)
St. John Publishing Co.: No. 85, Mar, 1951 - No. 125, May, 1955

	GD	VG	FN	VF	VF/NM	NM-
85,86-Same as Terry-Toons #85, & 86 with only a title change; published at same time?; Mighty Mouse, Heckle & Jeckle & Gandy Goose continue from Terry-Toons	11	22	33	63	84	105
87-99	8	16	24	46	58	70
100	9	18	27	52	66	80
101-104,107-125: 121,122,125-Painted-c	8	16	24	43	54	65
105,106-Giant Comics Edition (25¢, 100 pgs.) (9/53 & ?). 105-Little Roquefort-c/story	19	38	57	107	154	200

PAUL TERRY'S MIGHTY MOUSE (See Mighty Mouse)

PAUL TERRY'S MIGHTY MOUSE ADVENTURE STORIES (See Mighty Mouse Adventure Stories)

PAUL THE SAMURAI (See The Tick #4)
New England Comics: July, 1992 - No. 6, July, 1993 ($2.75, B&W)

	GD	VG	FN	VF	VF/NM	NM-
1-6						2.75

PAWNEE BILL
Story Comics (Youthful Magazines?): Feb, 1951 - No. 3, July, 1951

	GD	VG	FN	VF	VF/NM	NM-
1-Bat Masterson, Wyatt Earp app.	13	26	39	74	102	130
2,3: 3-Origin Golden Warrior; Cameron-a	8	16	24	43	54	65

PAY-OFF (This Is the..., ...Crime, ...Detective Stories)
D. S. Publishing Co.: July-Aug, 1948 - No. 5, Mar-Apr, 1949 (52 pgs.)

	GD	VG	FN	VF	VF/NM	NM-
1-True Crime Cases #1,2	26	52	78	150	215	280
2	16	32	48	89	127	165
3-5-Thrilling Detective Stories	14	28	42	79	110	140

PEACEMAKER, THE (Also see Fightin' Five)
Charlton Comics: V3#1, Mar, 1967 - No. 5, Nov, 1967 (All 12¢ cover price)

	GD	VG	FN	VF	VF/NM	NM-
1-Fightin' Five begins	6	12	18	40	55	70
2,3,5	4	8	12	24	32	40
4-Origin The Peacemaker	4	8	12	29	40	50
1,2(Modern Comics reprint, 1978)						5.00

PEACEMAKER (Also see Crisis On Infinite Earths & Showcase '93 #7,9,10)
DC Comics: Jan, 1988 - No. 4, Apr, 1988 ($1.25, limited series)

	GD	VG	FN	VF	VF/NM	NM-
1-4						2.50

PEANUTS (Charlie Brown) (See Fritzi Ritz, Nancy & Sluggo, Sparkle & Sparkler, Tip Top, Tip Topper & United Comics)
Dell Publishing Co./Gold Key: 1953-54; No. 878, 2/58 - No. 13, 5-7/62; 5/63 - No. 4, 2/64

	GD	VG	FN	VF	VF/NM	NM-
1(1953-54)-Reprints United Features' Strange As It Seems, Willie, Ferdnand	13	26	39	90	138	185
Four Color 878(#1) Schulz-s/a, with assistance from Dale Hale and Jim Sasseville thru #4	18	36	54	126	193	260

Penny #1 © AVON

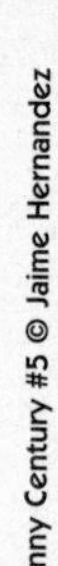
Penny Century #5 © Jaime Hernandez

Pep Comics #48 © AP

	GD 2.0	VG 4.0	FN 6.0	VF 8.0	VF/NM 9.0	NM- 9.2
Four Color 969,1015('59)	12	24	36	84	127	170
4(2-4/60) Schulz-s/a; one story by Anthony Pocrnich, Schulz's assistant cartoonist	10	20	30	72	104	135
5-13-Schulz-c only; s/a by Pocrnich	9	18	27	63	89	115
1(Gold Key, 5/63)	12	24	36	82	124	165
2-4	8	16	24	58	82	105

PEBBLES & BAMM BAMM (TV) (See Cave Kids #7, 12)
Charlton Comics: Jan, 1972 - No. 36, Dec, 1976 (Hanna-Barbera)

	GD	VG	FN	VF	VF/NM	NM-
1-From the Flintstones; "Teen Age..." on cover	6	12	18	38	52	65
2-10	3	6	9	19	25	32
11-20	2	4	6	14	18	22
21-36	2	4	6	10	13	16
nn (1973, 100 pgs.) B&W one page gags	3	6	9	19	25	32

PEBBLES & BAMM BAMM (TV)
Harvey Comics: Nov, 1993 - No. 3, Mar, 1994 ($1.50) (Hanna-Barbera)

	GD	VG	FN	VF	VF/NM	NM-
V2#1-3						3.00
...Giant Size 1 (10/93, $2.25, 68 pgs.)("Summer Special" on-c)						4.00

PEBBLES FLINTSTONE (TV) (See The Flintstones #11)
Gold Key: Sept, 1963 (Hanna-Barbera)

	GD	VG	FN	VF	VF/NM	NM-
1 (10088-309)-Early Pebbles app.	10	20	30	73	107	140

PEDRO (Formerly My Private Life #17; also see Romeo Tubbs)
Fox Features Syndicate: No. 18, June, 1950 - No. 2, Aug, 1950?

	GD	VG	FN	VF	VF/NM	NM-
18(#1)-Wood-c/a(p)	24	48	72	135	195	255
2-Wood-a?	17	34	51	95	135	175

PEE-WEE PIXIES (See The Pixies)

PELLEAS AND MELISANDE (See Night Music #4, 5)

PENALTY (See Crime Must Pay the...)

PENDRAGON (Knights of... #5 on; also see Knights of...)
Marvel Comics UK, Ltd.: July, 1992 - No. 15, Sept, 1993 ($1.75)

	GD	VG	FN	VF	VF/NM	NM-
1-15: 1-4-Iron Man app. 6-8-Spider-Man app.						2.25

PENDULUM ILLUSTRATED BIOGRAPHIES
Pendulum Press: 1979 (B&W)

19-355x-George Washington/Thomas Jefferson, 19-3495-Charles Lindbergh/Amelia Earhart, 19-3509-Harry Houdini/Walt Disney, 19-3517-Davy Crockett/Daniel Boone-Redondo-a, 19-3525-Elvis Presley/Beatles, 19-3533-Benjamin Franklin/Martin Luther King Jr, 19-3541-Abraham Lincoln/Franklin D. Roosevelt, 19-3568-Marie Curie/Albert Einstein-Redondo-a, 19-3576-Thomas Edison/Alexander Graham Bell-Redondo-a, 19-3584-Vince Lombardi/Pele, 19-3592-Babe Ruth/Jackie Robinson, 19-3606-Jim Thorpe/Althea Gibson

	GD	VG	FN	VF	VF/NM	NM-
Softback						3.00
Hardback						5.00

NOTE: *Above books still available from publisher.*

PENDULUM ILLUSTRATED CLASSICS (Now Age Illustrated)
Pendulum Press: 1973 - 1978 (75¢, 62pp, B&W, 5-3/8x8")
(Also see Marvel Classics)

64-100x(1973)-Dracula-Redondo art, 64-131x-The Invisible Man-Nino art, 64-0968-Dr. Jekyll and Mr. Hyde-Redondo art, 64-1005-Black Beauty, 64-1010-Call of the Wild, 64-1020-Frankenstein, 64-1025-Hucklebury Finn, 64-1030-Moby Dick-Nino-a, 64-1040-Red Badge of Courage, 64-1045-The Time Machine-Nino-a, 64-1050-Tom Sawyer, 64-1055-Twenty Thousand Leagues Under the Sea, 64-1069-Treasure Island, 64-1328(1974)-Kidnapped, 64-1336-Three Musketeers-Nino art, 64-1344-A Tale of Two Cities, 64-1352-Journey to the Center of the Earth, 64-1360-The War of the Worlds-Nino-a, 64-1379-The Greatest Advs. of Sherlock Holmes-Redondo art, 64-1387-Mysterious Island, 64-1395-Hunchback of Notre Dame, 64-1409-Helen Keller-story of my life, 64-1417-Scarlet Letter, 64-1425-Gulliver's Travels, 64-2618(1977)-Around the World in Eighty Days, 64-2626-Captains Courageous, 64-2634-Connecticut Yankee, 64-2642-The Hound of the Baskervilles, 64-2650-The House of Seven Gables, 64-2669-Jane Eyre, 64-2677-The Last of the Mohicans, 64-2685-The Best of O'Henry, 64-2693-The Best of Poe-Redondo-a, 64-2707-Two Years Before the Mast, 64-2715-White Fang, 64-2723-Wuthering Heights, 64-3126(1978)-Ben Hur-Redondo art, 64-3134-A Christmas Carol, 64-3142-The Food of the Gods, 64-3150-Ivanhoe, 64-3169-The Man in the Iron Mask, 64-3177-The Prince and the Pauper, 64-3185-The Prisoner of Zenda, 64-3193-The Return of the Native, 64-3207-Robinson Crusoe, 64-3215-The Scarlet Pimpernel, 64-3223-The Sea Wolf, 64-3231-The Swiss Family Robinson, 64-3851-Billy Budd, 64-386x-Crime and Punishment, 64-3878-Don Quixote, 64-3886-Great Expectations, 64-3894-Heidi, 64-3908-The Iliad, 64-3916-Lord Jim, 64-3924-The Mutiny on Board H.M.S. Bounty, 64-3932-The Odyssey, 64-3940-Oliver Twist, 64-3959-Pride and Prejudice, 64-3967-The Turn of the Screw

	GD	VG	FN	VF	VF/NM	NM-
Softback						3.00
Hardback						5.00

NOTE: *All of the above books can be ordered from the publisher; some were reprinted as Marvel Classic Comics #1-12. In 1972 there was another brief series of 12 titles which contained Classics Ill. artwork. They were entitled* ***Now Age Books*** *Illustrated, but can be easily distinguished from later series by the small Classics Illustrated logo at the top of the front cover. The format is the same as the later series. The 48 pg. C.I. art was stretched out to make 62 pgs. After Twin Circle Publ. terminated the Classics Ill. series in 1971, they made a one year contract with Pendulum Press to print these twelve titles of C.I. art. Pendulum was unhappy with the contract, and at the end of 1972 began their own art series, utilizing the talents of the Filipino artist group. One detail which makes this rather confusing is that when they redid the art in 1973, they gave it the same identifying no. as the 1972 series. All 12 of the 1972 C.I. editions have new covers, taken from internal art panels. In spite of their recent age, all of the 1972 C.I. series are very rare. Mint copies would fetch at least $50. Here is a list of the 1972 series, with C.I. title no. counterpart:*

64-1005 (CI#60-A2) 64-1010 (CI#91) 64-1015 (CI-Jr #503) 64-1020 (CI#26)
64-1025 (CI#19-A2) 64-1030 (CI#5-A2) 64-1035 (CI#169) 64-1040 (CI#98)
64-1045 (CI#133) 64-1050 (CI#50-A2) 64-1055 (CI#47) 64-1060 (CI-Jr#535)

PENDULUM ILLUSTRATED ORIGINALS
Pendulum Press: 1979 (In color)

	GD	VG	FN	VF	VF/NM	NM-
94-4254-Solarman: The Beginning (See Solarman)						6.00

PENDULUM'S ILLUSTRATED STORIES
Pendulum Press: 1990 - No. 72, 1990? (No cover price ($4.95), squarebound, 68 pgs.)

	GD	VG	FN	VF	VF/NM	NM-
1-72: Reprints Pendulum Ill. Classics series						5.00

PENNY
Avon Comics: 1947 - No. 6, Sept-Oct, 1949 (Newspaper reprints)

	GD	VG	FN	VF	VF/NM	NM-
1-Photo & biography of creator	12	24	36	69	95	120
2-5	8	16	24	43	54	65
6-Perry Como photo on-c	9	18	27	52	66	80

PENNY CENTURY (See Love and Rockets)
Fantagraphics Books: Dec, 1997 - Present ($2.95, B&W, mini-series)

	GD	VG	FN	VF	VF/NM	NM-
1-7-Jaime Hernandez-s/a						3.00

PENTHOUSE COMIX
General Media Int.: 1994 - No. 33, July, 1998 ($4.95, bimonthly, magazine & comic sized, mature)

	GD	VG	FN	VF	VF/NM	NM-
1	2	4	6	8	10	12
2-5	1	2	3	5	7	9
6-33: 15-Corben-c. 16-Dorman-c. 17-Manara-c. 20-Chiodo-c. 21,23-Boris-c. 24-Scott Hampton-c. 26-33-Comic-sized	1	2	3	4	5	7

PENTHOUSE MAX
General Media International: July, 1996 - No. 3 ($4.95, magazine, mature)

	GD	VG	FN	VF	VF/NM	NM-
1-3: 1-Giffen, Sears, Maguire-a. 2-Political satire. 3-Mr. Monster-c/app.; Dorman-c	1	2	3	4	5	7

PENTHOUSE MEN'S ADVENTURE COMIX
General Media International: 1995 - No. 7, 1996 ($4.95, magazine, mature)

	GD	VG	FN	VF	VF/NM	NM-
1-7 (Magazine Size): 1-Boris-c, 1-5 (Comic Size): 1-Boris-c	1	2	3	4	5	7

PEP COMICS (See Archie Giant Series #576, 589, 601, 614, 624)
MLJ Magazines/Archie Publications No. 56 (3/46) on: Jan, 1940 - No. 411, Mar, 1987

	GD	VG	FN	VF	VF/NM	NM-
1-Intro. The Shield (1st patriotic hero) by Irving Novick; origin & 1st app. The Comet by Jack Cole, The Queen of Diamonds & Kayo Ward; The Rocket, The Press Guardian (The Falcon #1 only), Sergeant Boyle, Fu Chang, & Bentley of of Scotland Yard; Robot-c; Shield-c begin	968	1936	2904	6776	10,888	15,000
2-Origin The Rocket	250	500	750	1563	2407	3250
3	185	370	555	1156	1778	2400
4-Wizard cameo; early robot-s	150	300	450	938	1444	1950
5-Wizard cameo in Shield story	150	300	450	938	1444	1950
6-10: 8-Last Cole Comet; no Cole-a in #6,7	115	230	345	719	1110	1500
11-Dusty, Shield's sidekick begins (1st app.); last Press Guardian, Fu Chang	119	238	357	744	1147	1550
12-Origin & 1st app. Fireball (2/41); last Rocket & Queen of Diamonds; Danny in Wonderland begins	138	276	414	863	1332	1800
13-15	96	192	288	600	925	1250
16-Origin Madam Satan; blood drainage-c	150	300	450	938	1444	1950
17-Origin/1st app. The Hangman (7/41); death of The Comet; Comet is revealed as Hangman's brother	338	676	1014	2197	3549	4900
18-21: 20-Last Fireball. 21-Last Madam Satan	87	174	261	544	835	1125
22-Intro. & 1st app. Archie, Betty, & Jughead(12/41); (also see Jackpot)	1294	2588	3882	9705	15,853	22,000
23	173	346	519	1081	1666	2250
24,25: 24-Coach Kleets app. (unnamed until Archie #94); bondage/torture-c. 25-1st app. Archie's jalopy; 1st skinny Mr. Weatherbee prototype	123	246	369	769	1185	1600
26-1st app. Veronica Lodge (4/42); "Remember Pearl Harbor!" cover caption	177	354	531	1106	1703	2300
27-30: 29-Origin Shield retold; 30-Capt. Commando begins; bondage/torture-c; 1st Miss Grundy (definitive version); see Jackpot #4	94	188	282	588	907	1225
31-35: 31-MLJ offices & artists are visited in Sgt. Boyle story; 1st app. Mr. Lodge. 32-Shield dons new costume. 34-Bondage/Hypo-c. 33-Pre-Moose tryout (see Jughead #1)	75	150	225	469	722	975
36-1st Archie-c (2/43) w/Shield & Hangman	192	384	576	1200	1850	2500
37-40	55	110	165	340	520	700
41-50: 41-Archie-c begin. 47-Last Hangman issue; infinity-c. 48-Black Hood begins (5/44); ends #51,59,60	40	80	120	236	351	465

The Perfect Crime #13 © Cross Publ.

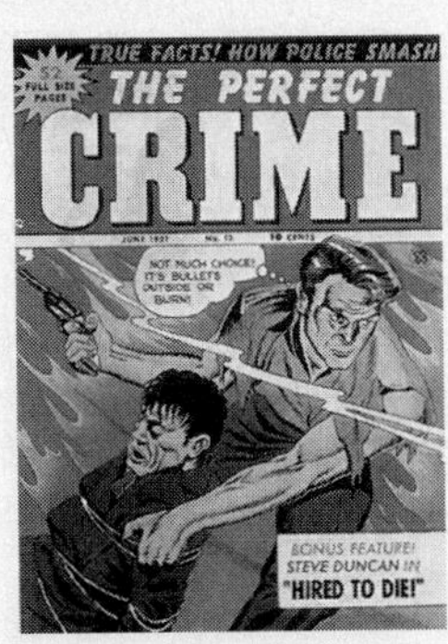

Personal Love #14 © FF

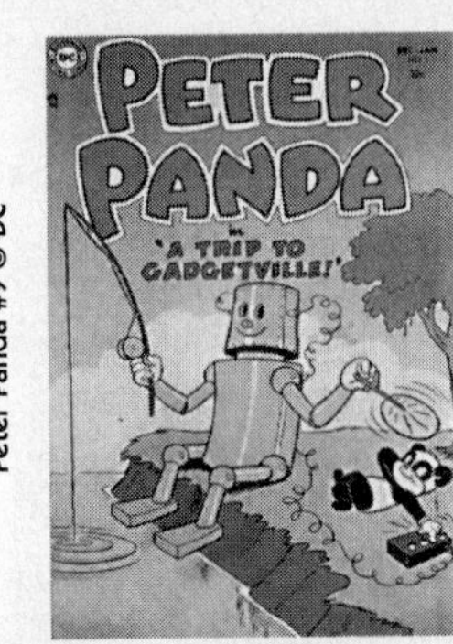

Peter Panda #9 © DC

	GD 2.0	VG 4.0	FN 6.0	VF 8.0	VF/NM 9.0	NM- 9.2
51-60: 52-Suzie begins; 1st Mr Weatherbee-c. 56-Last Capt. Commando. 59-Black Hood not in costume; lingerie panels; Archie dresses as his aunt; Suzie ends. 60-Katy Keene begins(3/47), ends #154	28	56	84	158	229	300
61-65-Last Shield. 62-1st app. Li'l Jinx (7/47)	24	48	72	138	199	260
66-80: 66-G-Man Club becomes Archie Club (2/48); Nevada Jones by Bill Woggon. 78-1st app. Dilton	15	30	45	85	120	155
81-99	11	22	33	66	91	115
100	15	30	45	83	117	150
101-130	8	16	24	46	58	70
131(2/59)-140: 138-140-Neal Adams-a (1 pg.) in each	6	12	18	36	46	55
141-149(9/61)	4	8	12	27	36	45
150-160-Super-heroes app. in each (see note). 150 (10/61?)-2nd or 3rd app. The Jaguar? 151-154,156-158-Horror/Sci/Fi-c. 157-Li'l Jinx	5	10	15	36	48	60
161(3/63)-167,169-180	3	6	9	19	25	32
168,200: 168-(1/64)-Jaguar app. 200-(12/66)	4	8	12	22	30	38
181(5/65)-199: 192-UFO-c. 198-Giantman-c(only)	3	6	9	16	21	26
201-217,219-226,228-240(4/70)	2	4	6	12	16	20
218,227-Archies Band-c only	2	4	6	14	18	22
241-270(10/72)	2	4	6	10	12	15
271-297,299	1	3	4	6	8	10
298-Josie and the Pussycats-c	2	4	6	10	12	15
300(4/75)	2	4	6	10	12	15
301-340(8/78)	1	2	3	5	6	8
341-382						5.00
383(4/82),393(3/84): 383-Marvelous Maureen begins (Sci/fi). 393-Thunderbunny begins						6.00
384-392,394-399,401-410						4.00
400(5/85),411: 400-Story featuring Archie staff (DeCarlo-a)						6.00

NOTE: *Biro a-2, 4, 5.* ***Jack Cole*** *a-1-5, 8.* ***Al Fagaly*** *c-55-72.* ***Fuje*** *a-39, 45, 47; c-34.* ***Meskin*** *a-2, 4, 5, 11(2).* ***Montana*** *c-30, 32, 33, 36, 73-87(most).* ***Novick*** *c-1-28, 29(w/****Schomburg****), 31i.* ***Harry Sahle*** *c-35, 39-50.* ***Schomburg*** *c-38.* ***Bob Wood*** *a-2, 4-6, 11. The Fly app. in 151, 154, 160. Flygirl app. in 153, 155, 156, 158. Jaguar app. in 150, 152, 157, 159, 168. Josie by* ***DeCarlo*** *in 161-166, 168-171, 173, 175-177, 179, 181. Katy Keene by* ***Bill Woggon*** *in 73-126. Bondage c-7, 12, 13, 15, 18, 21, 31, 32. Cover features: Shield #1-16; Shield/Hangman #17-27, 29-41; Hangman #28. Archie #36, 41-on.*

PEPE
Dell Publishing Co.: No. 1194, Apr, 1961

	GD 2.0	VG 4.0	FN 6.0	VF 8.0	VF/NM 9.0	NM- 9.2
Four Color 1194-Movie, photo-c	3	6	9	19	25	32

PERFECT CRIME, THE
Cross Publications: Oct, 1949 - No. 33, May, 1953 (#2-12, 52 pgs.)

	GD 2.0	VG 4.0	FN 6.0	VF 8.0	VF/NM 9.0	NM- 9.2
1-Powell-a(2)	35	70	105	198	287	375
2 (4/50)	19	38	57	107	154	200
3-10: 7-Steve Duncan begins, ends #30. 10-Flag-c	16	32	48	92	131	170
11-Used in **SOTI**, pg. 159	18	36	54	100	143	185
12-14	15	30	45	86	123	160
15- "The Most Terrible Menace" 2 pg. drug editorial	16	32	48	92	131	170
16,17,19-25,27-29,31-33	11	22	33	64	87	110
18-Drug cover, heroin drug propaganda story, plus 2 pg. anti-drug editorial	24	48	72	135	195	255
26-Drug-c with hypodermic needle; drug propaganda story	25	50	75	144	207	270
30-Strangulation cover	25	50	75	144	207	270

NOTE: ***Powell*** *a-No. 1, 2, 4.* ***Wildey*** *a-1, 5. Bondage c-11.*

PERFECT LOVE
Ziff-Davis(Approved Comics)/St. John No. 9 on: #10, 8-9/51 (cover date; 5-6/51 indicia date); #2, 10-11/51 - #10, 12/53

	GD 2.0	VG 4.0	FN 6.0	VF 8.0	VF/NM 9.0	NM- 9.2
10(#1)(8-9/51)-Painted-c	21	42	63	118	169	220
2(10-11/51)	14	28	42	81	113	145
3,5-7: 3-Painted-c. 5-Photo-c	11	22	33	64	87	110
4,8 (Fall, 1952)-Kinstler-a; last Z-D issue	11	22	33	66	91	115
9,10 (10/53, 12/53, St. John): 9-Painted-c. 10-Photo-c	11	22	33	62	84	105

PERRI (Disney)
Dell Publishing Co.: No. 847, Jan, 1958

	GD 2.0	VG 4.0	FN 6.0	VF 8.0	VF/NM 9.0	NM- 9.2
Four Color 847-Movie, w/2 diff-c publ.	6	12	18	43	59	75

PERRY MASON
David McKay Publications: No. 49, 1946 - No. 50, 1946

	GD 2.0	VG 4.0	FN 6.0	VF 8.0	VF/NM 9.0	NM- 9.2
Feature Books 49, 59-Based on Gardner novels	31	62	93	178	259	340

PERRY MASON MYSTERY MAGAZINE (TV)
Dell Publishing Co.: June-Aug, 1964 - No. 2, Oct-Dec, 1964

	GD 2.0	VG 4.0	FN 6.0	VF 8.0	VF/NM 9.0	NM- 9.2
1	6	12	18	40	55	70
2-Raymond Burr photo-c	5	10	15	33	44	55

PERSONAL LOVE (Also see Movie Love)
Famous Funnies: Jan, 1950 - No. 33, June, 1955

	GD 2.0	VG 4.0	FN 6.0	VF 8.0	VF/NM 9.0	NM- 9.2
1-Photo-c	20	40	60	112	161	210
2-Kathryn Grayson & Mario Lanza photo-c	11	22	33	62	84	105
3-7,10: 7-Robert Walker & Joanne Dru photo-c. 10-Loretta Young & Joseph Cotton photo-c	10	20	30	56	73	90
8,9: 8-Esther Williams & Howard Keel photo-c. 9-Debra Paget & Louis Jourdan photo-c	10	20	30	58	77	95
11-Toth-a; Glenn Ford & Gene Tierney photo-c	12	24	36	69	95	120
12,16,17-One pg. Frazetta each. 17-Rock Hudson & Yvonne DeCarlo photo-c	10	20	30	56	73	90
13-15,18-23: 12-Jane Greer & William Lundigan photo-c. 14-Kirk Douglas photo-c. 15-Dale Robertson & Joanne Dru photo-c. 18-Gregory Peck & Susan Hayworth photo-c. 19-Anthony Quinn & Suzan Ball photo-c. 20-Robert Wagner & Kathleen Crowley photo-c. 21-Roberta Peters & Byron Palmer photo-c. 22-Dale Robertson photo-c. 23-Rhonda Fleming-c	9	18	27	52	66	80
24,27,28-Frazetta-a in each (8,8&6 pgs.). 27-Rhonda Fleming & Fernando Lamas photo-c. 28-Mitzi Gaynor photo-c	40	80	120	244	372	500
25-Frazetta-a (tribute to Betty Page, 7 pg. story); Tyrone Power/Terry Moore photo-c from "King of the Khyber Rifles"	50	100	150	305	465	625
26,29,30,33: 26-Constance Smith & Byron Palmer photo-c. 29-Charlton Heston & Nicol Morey photo-c. 30-Johnny Ray & Mitzi Gaynor photo-c. 33-Dana Andrews & Piper Laurie photo-c	9	18	27	52	66	80
31-Marlon Brando & Jean Simmons photo-c; last pre-code (2/55)	11	22	33	62	84	105
32-Classic Frazetta-a (8 pgs.); Kirk Douglas & Bella Darvi photo-c	54	108	162	329	502	675

NOTE: *All have photo-c. Many feature movie stars.* ***Everett*** *a-5, 9, 10, 24.*

PERSONAL LOVE (Going Steady V3#3 on)
Prize Publ. (Headline): V1#1, Sept, 1957 - V3#2, Nov-Dec, 1959

	GD 2.0	VG 4.0	FN 6.0	VF 8.0	VF/NM 9.0	NM- 9.2
V1#1	9	18	27	52	66	80
2	6	12	18	28	34	40
3-6(7-8/58)	6	12	18	27	33	38
V2#1(9-10/58)-V2#6(7-8/59)	5	10	15	23	28	32
V3#1-Wood?/Orlando-a	6	12	18	28	34	40
2	5	10	15	22	26	30

PETER CANNON - THUNDERBOLT (See Crisis on Infinite Earths)(Also see Thunderbolt)
DC Comics: Sept, 1992 - No. 12, Aug, 1993 ($1.25)

	GD 2.0	VG 4.0	FN 6.0	VF 8.0	VF/NM 9.0	NM- 9.2
1-12						2.25

PETER COTTONTAIL
Key Publications: Jan, 1954; Feb, 1954 - No. 2, Mar, 1954 (Says 3/53 in error)

	GD 2.0	VG 4.0	FN 6.0	VF 8.0	VF/NM 9.0	NM- 9.2
1(1/54)-Not 3-D	9	18	27	52	66	80
1(2/54)-(3-D, 25¢)-Came w/glasses; written by Bruce Hamilton	23	46	69	130	188	245
2-Reprints 3-D #1 but not in 3-D	6	12	18	31	38	45

PETER GUNN (TV)
Dell Publishing Co.: No. 1087, Apr-June, 1960

	GD 2.0	VG 4.0	FN 6.0	VF 8.0	VF/NM 9.0	NM- 9.2
Four Color 1087-Photo-c	10	20	30	72	104	135

PETE ROSE: HIS INCREDIBLE BASEBALL CAREER
Masstar Creations Inc.: 1995

	GD 2.0	VG 4.0	FN 6.0	VF 8.0	VF/NM 9.0	NM- 9.2
1-John Tartaglione-a						2.25

PETER PAN (Disney) (See Hook, Movie Classics & Comics, New Adventures of... & Walt Disney Showcase #36)
Dell Publishing Co.: No. 442, Dec, 1952 - No. 926, Aug, 1958

	GD 2.0	VG 4.0	FN 6.0	VF 8.0	VF/NM 9.0	NM- 9.2
Four Color 442 (#1)-Movie	12	24	36	82	124	165
Four Color 926-Reprint of 442	5	10	15	36	48	60

PETER PAN
Disney Comics: 1991 ($5.95, graphic novel, 68 pgs.)(Celebrates video release)

	GD 2.0	VG 4.0	FN 6.0	VF 8.0	VF/NM 9.0	NM- 9.2
nn-r/Peter Pan Treasure Chest from 1953						7.00

PETER PANDA
National Periodical Publications: Aug-Sept, 1953 - No. 31, Aug-Sept, 1958

	GD 2.0	VG 4.0	FN 6.0	VF 8.0	VF/NM 9.0	NM- 9.2
1-Grossman-c/a in all	42	84	126	256	391	525
2	24	48	72	138	199	260
3,4,6-8,10	20	40	60	112	161	210
5-Classic-c (scarce)	40	80	120	233	342	450
9-Robot-c	24	48	72	138	199	260
11-31	13	26	39	74	102	130

PETER PAN TREASURE CHEST (See Dell Giants)

PETER PARKER (See The Spectacular Spider-Man)

Peter Parker: Spider-Man #45 © MAR

Peter Porkchops #6 © DC

The Phantom #1 © KFS

PETER PARKER: SPIDER-MAN
Marvel Comics: Jan, 1999 - No. 57, Aug, 2003 ($2.99/$1.99/$2.25)

	GD 2.0	VG 4.0	FN 6.0	VF 8.0	VF/NM 9.0	NM- 9.2
1-Mackie-s/Romita Jr.-a; wraparound-c						3.00
1-($6.95) DF Edition w/variant cover by the Romitas						7.00
2-11,13-17-($1.99): 2-Two covers; Thor app. 3-Iceman-c/app. 4-Marrow-c/app. 5-Spider-Woman app. 7,8-Blade app. 9,10-Venom app. 11-Iron Man & Thor-c/app.						2.25
12-($2.99) Sinister Six and Venom app.						3.00
18-24,26-43: 18-Begin $2.25-c. 20-Jenkins-s/Buckingham-a start. 23-Intro Typeface. 24-Maximum Security x-over. 29-Rescue of MJ. 30-Ramos-c. 42,43-Mahfood-a						2.25
25-($2.99) Two covers; Spider-Man & Green Goblin						3.00
44-47-Humberto Ramos-c/a; Green Goblin-c/app.						3.00
48,49,51-57: 48,49-Buckingham-c/a. 51,52-Herrera-a. 56,57-Kieth-a; Sandman returns						2.25
50-($3.50) Buckingham-c/a						3.50
...'99 Annual (8/99, $3.50) Man-Thing app.						3.50
...'00 Annual ($3.50) Bounty app.; Joe Bennett-a; Black Cat back-up story						3.50
...'01 Annual ($2.99) Avery-s						3.00
...: A Day in the Life TPB (5/01, $14.95) r/#20-22,26; Webspinners #10-12						15.00
...: One Small Break TPB (2002, $16.95) r/#27,28,30-34; Andrews-c						17.00
Spider-Man: Return of the Goblin TPB (2002, $8.99) r/#44-47; Ramos-c						9.00
...Vol. 4: Trials & Tribulations TPB (2003, $11.99) r/#35,37,48-50; Cho-c						12.00

PETER PAT
United Features Syndicate: No. 8, 1939

	GD	VG	FN	VF	VF/NM	NM-
Single Series 8	37	74	111	209	305	400

PETER PAUL'S 4 IN 1 JUMBO COMIC BOOK
Capitol Stories (Charlton): No date (1953)

	GD	VG	FN	VF	VF/NM	NM-
1-Contains 4 comics bound; Space Adventures, Space Western, Crime & Justice, Racket Squad in Action	40	80	120	233	342	450

PETER PIG
Standard Comics: No. 5, May, 1953 - No. 6, Aug, 1953

	GD	VG	FN	VF	VF/NM	NM-
5,6	7	14	21	35	43	50

PETER PORKCHOPS (See Leading Comics #23)
National Periodical Publications: 11-12/49 - No. 61, 9-11/59; No. 62, 10-12/60 (1-11: 52 pgs.)

	GD	VG	FN	VF	VF/NM	NM-
1	35	70	105	200	290	380
2	17	34	51	95	135	175
3-10: 6- "Peter Rockets to Mars!" c/story	13	26	39	74	102	130
11-30	10	20	30	58	77	95
31-62	9	18	27	49	62	75

NOTE: *Otto Feuer a-all.* ***Rube Grossman****-a most issues.* ***Sheldon Mayer*** *a-30-38, 40-44, 46-52, 61.*

PETER PORKER, THE SPECTACULAR SPIDER-HAM
Star Comics (Marvel): May, 1985 - No. 17, Sept, 1987 (Also see Marvel Tails)

	GD	VG	FN	VF	VF/NM	NM-
1-Michael Golden-c						5.00
2-17: 12-Origin/1st app. Bizarro Phil. 13-Halloween issue						4.00

NOTE: *Back-up features: 2-X-Bugs. 3-Iron Mouse. 4-Croctor Strange. 5-Thrr, Dog of Thunder.*

PETER POTAMUS (TV)
Gold Key: Jan, 1965 (Hanna-Barbera)

	GD	VG	FN	VF	VF/NM	NM-
1-1st app. Peter Potamus & So-So, Breezly & Sneezly	11	22	33	77	114	150

PETER RABBIT (See New Funnies #65 & Space Comics)
Dell Publishing Co.: No. 1, 1942

	GD	VG	FN	VF	VF/NM	NM-
Large Feature Comic 1	56	112	168	350	538	725

PETER RABBIT (Adventures of...; New Advs. of... #9 on)(Also see Funny Tunes & Space Comics)
Avon Periodicals: 1947 - No. 34, Aug-Sept, 1956

	GD	VG	FN	VF	VF/NM	NM-
1(1947)-Reprints 1943-44 Sunday strips; contains a biography & drawing of Cady	36	72	108	204	297	390
2 (4/48)	26	52	78	147	211	275
3 ('48) - 6(7/49)-Last Cady issue	23	46	69	130	188	245
7-10(1950-8/51): 9-New logo	10	20	30	56	73	90
11(11/51)-34('56)-Avon's character	8	16	24	46	58	70
...Easter Parade (1952, 25¢, 132 pgs.)	20	40	60	112	161	210
...Jumbo Book (1954-Giant Size, 25¢)-Jesse James by Kinstler (6 pgs.); space ship-c	25	50	75	141	203	265

PETER RABBIT 3-D
Eternity Comics: April, 1990 ($2.95, with glasses; sealed in plastic bag)

	GD	VG	FN	VF	VF/NM	NM-
1-By Harrison Cady (reprints)						3.00

PETER, THE LITTLE PEST (#4 titled Petey)
Marvel Comics Group: Nov, 1969 - No. 4, May, 1970

	GD	VG	FN	VF	VF/NM	NM-
1	7	14	21	46	63	80
2-4-r-Dexter the Demon & Melvin the Monster	4	8	12	29	40	50

PETE'S DRAGON (See Walt Disney Showcase #43)

PETE THE PANIC
Stanmor Publications: November, 1955

	GD	VG	FN	VF	VF/NM	NM-
nn-Code approved	5	10	15	23	28	32

PETEY (See Peter, the Little Pest)

PETTICOAT JUNCTION (TV, inspired Green Acres)
Dell Publ. Co.: Oct-Dec, 1964 - No. 5, Oct-Dec, 1965 (#1-3, 5 have photo-c)

	GD	VG	FN	VF	VF/NM	NM-
1	8	16	24	58	82	105
2-5	6	12	18	40	55	70

PETUNIA (Also see Looney Tunes and Porky Pig)
Dell Publishing Co.: No. 463, Apr, 1953

	GD	VG	FN	VF	VF/NM	NM-
Four Color 463	4	8	12	29	40	50

PHAGE (See Neil Gaiman's Teknophage & Neil Gaiman's Phage-Shadowdeath)

PHANTACEA
McPherson Publishing Co.: Sept, 1977 - No. 6, Summer, 1980 (B&W)

	GD	VG	FN	VF	VF/NM	NM-
1-Early Dave Sim-a (32 pgs.)	3	7	10	21	28	35
2-Dave Sim-a(10 pgs.)	2	4	6	12	16	20
3,5: 3-Flip-c w/Damnation Bridge	2	4	6	9	11	14
4,6: 4-Gene Day-a	2	4	6	9	11	14

PHANTASMO (See The Funnies #45)
Dell Publishing Co.: No. 18, 1941

	GD	VG	FN	VF	VF/NM	NM-
Large Feature Comic 18	37	74	112	213	312	410

PHANTOM, THE
David McKay Publishing Co.: 1939 - 1949

	GD	VG	FN	VF	VF/NM	NM-
Feature Books 20	87	174	261	544	835	1125
Feature Books 22	65	130	195	406	628	850
Feature Books 39	51	102	153	311	473	635
Feature Books 53,56,57	40	80	120	241	363	485

PHANTOM, THE (See Ace Comics, Defenders Of The Earth, Eat Right to Work and Win, Future Comics, Harvey Comics Hits #51,56, Harvey Hits #1, 6, 12, 15, 26, 36, 44, 48, & King Comics)

PHANTOM, THE (nn (#29)-Published overseas only) (Also see Comics Reading Libraries in the Promotional Comics section)
Gold Key(#1-17)/King(#18-28)/Charlton(#30 on): Nov, 1962 - No. 17, Jul, 1966; No. 18, Sept, 1966 - No. 28, Dec, 1967; No. 30, Feb, 1969 - No. 74, Jan, 1977

	GD	VG	FN	VF	VF/NM	NM-
1-Origin revealed on inside-c & back-c	17	34	51	119	182	245
2-King, Queen & Jack begins, ends #11	9	18	27	65	93	120
3-5	8	16	24	58	82	105
6-10	8	16	24	55	78	100
11-17: 12-Track Hunter begins	7	14	21	46	63	80
18-Flash Gordon begins; Wood-a	6	12	18	38	52	65
19-24: 20-Flash Gordon ends (both by Gil Kane). 21-Mandrake begins. 20,24-Girl Phantom app.	5	10	15	36	48	60
25-28: 25-Jeff Jones-a(4 pgs.); 1 pg. Williamson ad. 26-Brick Bradford app. 28(nn)-Brick Bradford app.	4	8	12	29	40	50
30-33: 33-Last 12¢ issue	4	8	12	22	30	38
34-40: 36,39-Ditko-a	3	7	10	21	28	35
41-66: 46-Intro. The Piranha. 62-Bolle-c	3	6	9	16	20	24
67-Origin retold; Newton-c/a	3	6	9	19	25	32
68-73-Newton-c/a	2	4	6	14	18	22
74-Classic flag-c by Newton; Newton-a;	3	6	9	18	24	30

NOTE: ***Aparo*** *a-31-34, 36-38; c-31-38, 60, 61. Painted c-1-17.*

PHANTOM, THE
DC Comics: May, 1988 - No. 4, Aug, 1988 ($1.25, mini-series)

	GD	VG	FN	VF	VF/NM	NM-
1-4: Orlando-c/a in all						3.00

PHANTOM, THE
DC Comics: Mar, 1989 - No. 13, Mar, 1990 ($1.50)

	GD	VG	FN	VF	VF/NM	NM-
1-13: 1-Brief origin						3.00

PHANTOM, THE
Wolf Publishing: 1992 - No. 8, 1993 ($2.25)

	GD	VG	FN	VF	VF/NM	NM-
1-8						2.25

PHANTOM, THE
Moonstone: 2003 - No. 4, 2004 ($3.50)

	GD	VG	FN	VF	VF/NM	NM-
1-4: 1-Cassaday-c/Raab-s/Quinn-a						3.50

PHANTOM BLOT, THE (#1 titled New Adventures of...)
Gold Key: Oct, 1964 - No. 7, Nov, 1966 (Disney)

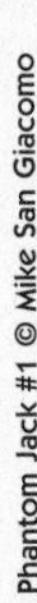
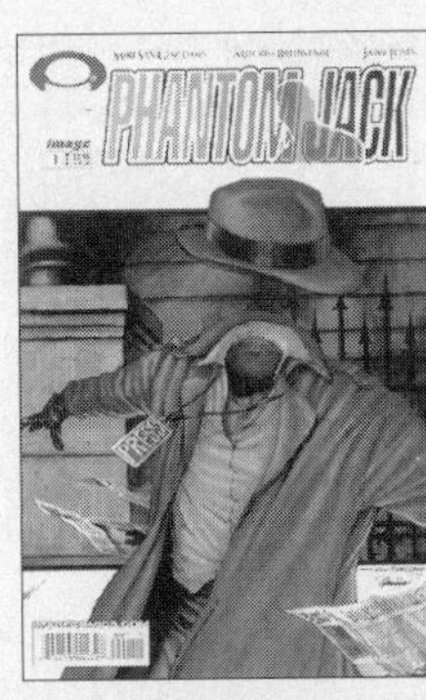

Phantom Jack #1 © Mike San Giacomo

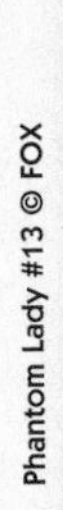

Phantom Lady #13 © FOX

Pictorial Romances #4 © STJ

GD 2.0 | VG 4.0 | FN 6.0 | VF 8.0 | VF/NM 9.0 | NM- 9.2

1 (Meets The Mysterious Mr. X) 7 14 21 46 63 80
2-1st Super Goof 6 12 18 40 55 70
3-7 4 8 12 24 32 40

PHANTOM EAGLE (See Mighty Midget, Marvel Super Heroes #16 & Wow #6)

PHANTOM FORCE
Image Comics/Genesis West #0, 3-7: 12/93 - #2, 1994; #0, 3/94; #3, 5/94 - #8, 10/94 ($2.50/$3.50, limited series)

0 (3/94, $2.50)-Kirby/Jim Lee-c; Kirby-p pgs. 1,5,24-29. 3.00
1 (12/93, $2.50)-Polybagged w/trading card; Kirby Liefeld-c; Kirby plots/pencils w/inks by Liefeld, McFarlane, Jim Lee, Silvestri, Larsen, Williams, Ordway & Miki 3.00
2 ($3.50)-Kirby-a(p); Kirby/Larson-c 3.50
3-8: 3-(5/94, $2.50)-Kirby/McFarlane-c 4-(5/94)-Kirby-c(p). 5-(6/94) 3.00

PHANTOM GUARD
Image Comics (WildStorm Productions): Oct, 1997 - No. 6, Mar, 1998 ($2.50)

1-6: 1-Two covers 3.00
1-($3.50)-Voyager Pack w/Wildcore preview 3.50

PHANTOM JACK
Image Comics: Mar, 2004 - No. 5, July, 2004 ($2.95)

1-5-Mike San Giacomo-s/Mitchell Breitweiser-a. 4-Initial printings with errors exist 3.00

PHANTOM LADY (1st Series) (My Love Secret #24 on) (Also see All Top, Daring Adventures, Freedom Fighters, Jungle Thrills, & Wonder Boy)
Fox Features Syndicate: No. 13, Aug, 1947 - No. 23, Apr, 1949

13(#1)-Phantom Lady by Matt Baker begins (1st app.); Blue Beetle story 414 828 1242 2691 4346 6000
14-16: 14(#2)-Not Baker-c. 15-P.L. injected with experimental drug. 16-Negligee-c, panels; true crime stories begin 254 508 762 1588 2444 3300
17-Classic bondage cover; used in **SOTI**, illo "Sexual stimulation by combining 'headlights' with the sadist's dream of tying up a woman" 548 1096 1644 3836 6168 8500
18,19 177 354 531 1106 1703 2300
20-22 142 284 426 888 1369 1850
23-Bondage-c 154 308 462 963 1482 2000

NOTE: ***Matt Baker** a-in all; c-13, 15-21. **Kamen** a-22, 23.*

PHANTOM LADY (2nd Series) (See Terrific Comics) (Formerly Linda)
Ajax/Farrell Publ.: V1#5, Dec-Jan, 1954/1955 - No. 4, June, 1955

V1#5(#1)-By Matt Baker 115 230 345 719 1110 1500
V1#2-Last pre-code 87 174 261 544 835 1125
3,4-Red Rocket. 3-Heroin story 69 138 207 431 666 900

PHANTOM LADY
Verotik Publications: 1994 ($9.95)

1-Reprints G. A. stories from Phantom Lady and All Top Comics; Adam Hughes-c 10.00

PHANTOM PLANET, THE
Dell Publishing Co.: No. 1234, 1961

Four Color 1234-Movie 8 16 24 58 82 105

PHANTOM STRANGER, THE (1st Series)(See Saga of Swamp Thing)
National Periodical Publications: Aug-Sept, 1952 - No. 6, June-July, 1953

1(Scarce)-1st app. 192 384 576 1200 1850 2500
2 (Scarce) 110 220 330 688 1057 1425
3-6 (Scarce) 94 188 282 588 907 1225

PHANTOM STRANGER, THE (2nd Series) (See Showcase #80)
National Periodical Publications: May-June, 1969 - No. 41, Feb-Mar, 1976

1-2nd S.A. app. P. Stranger; only 12¢ issue 11 22 33 77 114 150
2,3 6 12 18 38 52 65
4-1st new look Phantom Stranger; N. Adams-a 6 12 18 40 55 70
5-7 4 8 12 29 40 50
8-14: 14-Last 15¢ issue 3 6 9 19 25 32
15-19: All 25¢ giants (52 pgs.) 4 8 12 22 30 38
20-Dark Circle begins, ends #24. 2 4 6 14 18 22
21,22 2 4 6 10 13 16
23-Spawn of Frankenstein begins by Kaluta 4 8 12 24 32 40
24,25,27-30-Last Spawn of Frankenstein 3 6 9 18 24 30
26- Book-length story featuring Phantom Stranger, Dr. 13 & Spawn of Frankenstein 3 6 9 19 25 32
31-The Black Orchid begins (6-7/74). 3 6 9 18 24 30
32,34-38: 34-Last 20¢ issue (#35 on are 25¢) 2 4 6 10 13 16
33,39-41: 33-Deadman-c/story. 39-41-Deadman app. 2 4 6 12 16 20

NOTE: ***N. Adams** a-4; c-3-19. **Anderson** a-4, 5i. **Aparo** a-7-17, 19-26; c-20-24, 33-41. **B. Bailey** a-27-30. **DeZuniga** a-12-16, 18, 19, 21, 22, 31, 34. **Grell** a-33. **Kaluta** a-23-25; c-26. **Meskin** r-15, 16, 18, 19. **Redondo** a-32, 35, 36. **Sparling** a-20. **Starr** a-17r. **Toth** a-15r. Black Orchid by **Carrilo**-38-41. Dr. 13 solo in-13, 18, 19, 20, 21, 34. Frankenstein by **Kaluta**-23-25; by **Baily**-27-30. No Black Orchid-33, 34, 37.*

GD 2.0 | VG 4.0 | FN 6.0 | VF 8.0 | VF/NM 9.0 | NM- 9.2

PHANTOM STRANGER (See Justice League of America #103)
DC Comics: Oct, 1987 - No. 4, Jan, 1988 (75¢, limited series)

1-4-Mignola/Russell-c/a & Eclipso app. in all. 3,4-Eclipso-c 3.00

PHANTOM STRANGER (See Vertigo Visions-The Phantom Stranger)

PHANTOM: THE GHOST WHO WALKS
Marvel Comics: Feb, 1995 - No. 3, Apr, 1995 ($2.95, limited series)

1-3 4.00

PHANTOM: THE GHOST WHO WALKS
Moonstone: 2003 ($16.95, TPB)

nn-Three new stories by Raab, Goulart, Collins, Blanco and others; Klauba painted-c 17.00

PHANTOM 2040 (TV cartoon)
Marvel Comics: May, 1995 - No. 4, Aug, 1995 ($1.50)

1-4-Based on animated series; Ditko-a(p) in all 3.00

PHANTOM WITCH DOCTOR (Also see Durango Kid #8 & Eerie #8)
Avon Periodicals: 1952

1-Kinstler-c/a (7 pgs.) 46 92 138 281 428 575

PHANTOM ZONE, THE (See Adventure #283 & Superboy #100, 104)
DC Comics: January, 1982 - No. 4, April, 1982

1-4-Superman app. in all. 2-4: Batman, Green Lantern app. 3.00

NOTE: ***Colan** a-1-4p; c-1-4p. **Giordano** c-1-4i.*

PHAZE
Eclipse Comics: Apr, 1988 - No. 2, Oct, 1988 ($2.25)

1,2: 1-Sienkiewicz-c. 2-Gulacy painted-c 2.25

PHIL RIZZUTO (Baseball Hero)(See Sport Thrills, Accepted reprint)
Fawcett Publications: 1951 (New York Yankees)

nn-Photo-c 71 142 213 444 685 925

PHOENIX
Atlas/Seaboard Publ.: Jan, 1975 - No. 4, Oct, 1975

1-Origin; Rovin-s/Amendola-a 1 3 4 6 8 10
2-4: 3-Origin & only app. The Dark Avenger. 4-New origin/costume The Protector (formerly Phoenix) 1 2 3 5 7 9

NOTE: ***Infantino** appears in #1, 2. **Austin** a-3i. **Thorne** c-3.*

PHOENIX (...The Untold Story)
Marvel Comics Group: April, 1984 ($2.00, one-shot)

1-Byrne/Austin-r/X-Men #137 with original unpublished ending 2 4 6 8 10 12

PHOENIX RESURRECTION, THE
Malibu Comics (Ultraverse): 1995 - 1996 ($3.95)

Genesis #1 (12/95)-X-Men app; wraparound-c, Revelations #1 (12/95)-X-Men app; wraparound-c, Aftermath #1 (1/96)-X-Men app. 4.00
0-($1.95)-r/series 2.25
0-American Entertainment Ed. 4.00

PICNIC PARTY (See Dell Giants)

PICTORIAL CONFESSIONS (Pictorial Romances #4 on)
St. John Publishing Co.: Sept, 1949 - No. 3, Dec, 1949

1-Baker-c/a(3) 31 62 93 178 259 340
2-Baker-a; photo-c 20 40 60 112 161 210
3-Kubert, Baker-a; part Kubert-c 22 44 66 125 180 235

PICTORIAL LOVE STORIES (Formerly Tim McCoy)
Charlton Comics: No. 22, Oct, 1949 - No. 26, July, 1950 (all photo-c)

22-26: All have "Me-Dan Cupid". 25-Fred Astaire-c 21 42 63 118 169 220

PICTORIAL LOVE STORIES
St. John Publishing Co.: October, 1952

1-Baker-c 29 58 87 164 237 310

PICTORIAL ROMANCES (Formerly Pictorial Confessions)
St. John Publ. Co.: No. 4, Jan, 1950; No. 5, Jan, 1951 - No. 24, Mar, 1954

4-Baker-a; photo-c 30 60 90 170 245 320
5,10-All Matt Baker issues. 5-Reprints all stories from #4 w/new Baker-c 23 46 69 130 188 245
6-9,12,13,15,16-Baker-c, 2-3 stories 17 34 51 98 139 180
11-Baker-c/a(3); Kubert-r/Hollywood Confessions #1 19 38 57 107 154 200
14,21-24: Baker-c/a each. 21,24-Each has signed story by Estrada 15 30 45 86 123 160

Picture News #5 © 299 Lafayette

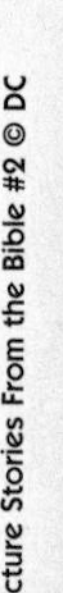

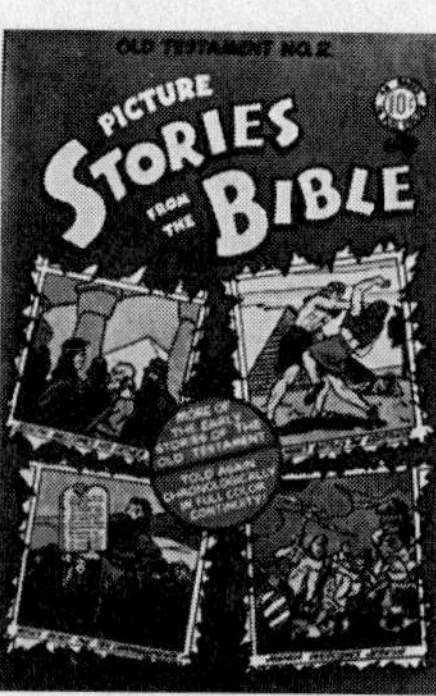

Picture Stories From the Bible #2 © DC

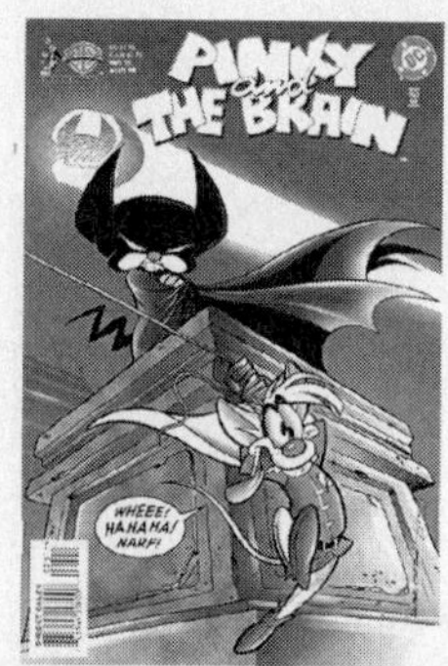

Pinky and the Brain #25 © WB

	GD 2.0	VG 4.0	FN 6.0	VF 8.0	VF/NM 9.0	NM- 9.2
17-20(7/53, 25¢, 100 pgs.): Baker-c/a; each has two signed stories by Estrada	31	62	93	175	253	330

NOTE: ***Matt Baker** art in most issues. **Estrada** a-17-20(2), 21, 24.*

PICTURE NEWS
Lafayette Street Corp.: Jan, 1946 - No. 10, Jan-Feb, 1947

	GD	VG	FN	VF	VF/NM	NM-
1-Milt Gross begins, ends No. 6; 4 pg. Kirby-a; A-Bomb-c/story	40	80	120	240	360	480
2-Atomic explosion panels; Frank Sinatra/Perry Como story	22	44	66	127	184	240
3-Atomic explosion panels; Frank Sinatra, June Allyson, Benny Goodman stories	19	38	57	107	154	200
4-Atomic explosion panels; "Caesar and Cleopatra" movie adapt. w/Claude Raines & Vivian Leigh; Jackie Robinson story	21	42	63	121	173	225
5-7: 5-Hank Greenberg story. 6-Joe Louis-c/story	15	30	45	86	123	160
8,10: 8-Monte Hale story (9-10/46; 1st?). 10-Dick Quick; A-Bomb story; Krigstein, Gross-a	16	32	48	92	131	170
9-A-Bomb story; "Crooked Mile" movie adaptation; Joe DiMaggio story.	19	38	57	107	154	200

PICTURE PARADE (Picture Progress #5 on)
Gilberton Company (Also see A Christmas Adventure): Sept, 1953 - V1#4, Dec, 1953 (28 pgs.)

	GD	VG	FN	VF	VF/NM	NM-
V1#1-Andy's Atomic Adventures; A-bomb blast-c; (Teachers version distributed to schools exists)	21	42	63	118	169	220
2-Around the World with the United Nations	12	24	36	69	95	120
3-Adventures of the Lost One(The American Indian), 4-A Christmas Adventure (r-under same title in 1969)	12	24	36	69	95	120

PICTURE PROGRESS (Formerly Picture Parade)
Gilberton Corp.: V1#5, Jan, 1954 - V3#2, Oct, 1955 (28-36 pgs.)

	GD	VG	FN	VF	VF/NM	NM-
V1#5-9,V2#1-9: 5-News in Review 1953. 6-The Birth of America. 7-The Four Seasons. 8-Paul Revere's Ride. 9-The Hawaiian Islands(5/54). V2#1-The Story of Flight(9/54). 2-Vote for Crazy River (The Meaning of Elections). 3-Louis Pasteur. 4-The Star Spangled Banner. 5-News in Review 1954. 6-Alaska: The Great Land. 7-Life in the Circus. 8-The Time of the Cave Man. 9-Summer Fun(5/55)	8	16	24	43	54	65
V3#1,2: 1-The Man Who Discovered America. 2-The Lewis & Clark Expedition	8	16	24	43	54	65

PICTURE SCOPE JUNGLE ADVENTURES (See Jungle Thrills)

PICTURE STORIES FROM AMERICAN HISTORY
National/All-American/E. C. Comics: 1945 - No. 4, Sum, 1947 (#1,2: 10¢, 56 pgs.; #3,4: 15¢, 52 pgs.)

	GD	VG	FN	VF	VF/NM	NM-
1	31	62	93	178	259	340
2-4	25	50	75	141	203	265

PICTURE STORIES FROM SCIENCE
E.C. Comics: Spring, 1947 - No. 2, Fall, 1947

	GD	VG	FN	VF	VF/NM	NM-
1-(15¢)	31	62	93	178	259	340
2-(10¢)	27	54	81	152	219	285

PICTURE STORIES FROM THE BIBLE (See Narrative Illustration, the Story of the Comics by M.C. Gaines)
National/All-American/E.C. Comics: 1942 - No. 4, Fall, 1943; 1944-46

	GD	VG	FN	VF	VF/NM	NM-
1-4('42-Fall, '43)-Old Testament (DC)	25	50	75	144	207	270
Complete Old Testament Edition, (12/43-DC, 50¢, 232 pgs.);-1st printing; contains #1-4; 2nd - 8th (1/47) printings exist; later printings by E.C. some with 65¢-c	29	58	87	164	237	310
Complete Old Testament Edition (1945-publ. by Bible Pictures Ltd.)-232 pgs., hardbound, in color with dust jacket	29	58	87	164	237	310

NOTE: *Both Old and New Testaments published in England by Bible Pictures Ltd. in hardback, 1943, in color, 376 pgs. (2 vols.: O.T. 232 pgs. & N.T. 144 pgs.), and were also published by Scarf Press in 1979 (Old Test., $9.95) and in 1980 (New Test., $7.95)*

	GD	VG	FN	VF	VF/NM	NM-
1-3(New Test.; 1944-46, DC)-52 pgs. ea.	19	38	57	107	154	200
The Complete Life of Christ Edition (1945, 25¢, 96 pgs.)-Contains #1&2 of the New Testament Edition	29	58	87	164	237	310
1,2(Old Testament-r in comic book form)(E.C., 1946; 52 pgs.)	19	38	57	107	154	200
1(DC),2(AA),3(EC)(New Testament-r in comic book form)(E.C., 1946; 52 pgs.)	19	38	57	107	154	200
Complete New Testament Edition (1945-E.C., 40¢, 144 pgs.)-Contains #1-3 1946 printing has 50¢-c	29	58	87	164	237	310

NOTE: *Another British series entitled **The Bible Illustrated** from 1947 has recently been discovered, with the same internal artwork. This eight edition series (5-OT, 3-NT) is of particular interest to Classics Ill. collectors because it exactly copied the C.I. logo format. The British publisher was Thorpe & Porter, who in 1951 began publishing the British Classics Ill. series. All editions of The Bible Ill. have new British painted covers. While this market is still new, and not all editions have as yet been found, current market value is about the same as the first U.S. editions of Picture Stories From The Bible.*

PICTURE STORIES FROM WORLD HISTORY
E.C. Comics: Spring, 1947 - No. 2, Summer, 1947 (52, 48 pgs.)

	GD	VG	FN	VF	VF/NM	NM-
1-(15¢)	31	62	93	178	259	340
2-(10¢)	27	54	81	152	219	285

PINHEAD
Marvel Comics (Epic Comics): Dec, 1993 - No. 6, May, 1994 ($2.50)

	GD	VG	FN	VF	VF/NM	NM-
1-($2.95)-Embossed foil-c by Kelley Jones; Intro Pinhead & Disciples (Snakeoil, Hangman, Fan Dancer & Dixie)						3.00
2-6						2.50

PINHEAD & FOODINI (TV)(Also see Foodini & Jingle Dingle Christmas...)
Fawcett Publications: July, 1951 - No. 4, Jan, 1952 (Early TV comic)

	GD	VG	FN	VF	VF/NM	NM-
1-(52 pgs.)-Photo-c; based on TV puppet show	34	68	102	193	279	365
2,3-Photo-c	17	34	51	95	135	175
4	14	28	42	79	110	140

PINHEAD VS. MARSHALL LAW (Law in Hell)
Marvel Comics (Epic): Nov, 1993 - No. 2, Dec, 1993 ($2.95, lim. series)

	GD	VG	FN	VF	VF/NM	NM-
1,2: 1-Embossed red foil-c. 2-Embossed silver foil-c						3.00

PINK DUST
Kitchen Sink Press: 1998 ($3.50, B&W, mature)

	GD	VG	FN	VF	VF/NM	NM-
1-J. O'Barr-s/a						3.50

PINK PANTHER, THE (TV)(See The Inspector & Kite Fun Book)
Gold Key #1-70/Whitman #71-87: April, 1971 - No. 87, Mar, 1984

	GD	VG	FN	VF	VF/NM	NM-
1-The Inspector begins	6	12	18	40	55	70
2-5	3	6	9	18	24	30
6-10	2	4	6	14	18	22
11-30: Warren Tufts-a #16-on	2	4	6	10	12	15
31-60	2	4	6	8	10	12
61-70	1	2	3	5	6	8
71-74,81-83: 81(2/82), 82(3/82), 83(4/82)	1	3	4	6	8	10
75(8/80)-77 (Whitman pre-pack) (scarce)	3	6	9	16	20	24
78(1/81)-80 (Whitman pre-pack) (not as scarce)	2	4	6	10	13	16
84-87(All #90266 on-c, no date or date code): 84(6/83), 85(8/83), 87(3/84)	2	4	6	10	13	16
Mini-comic No. 1(1976)(3-1/4x6-1/2")	1	3	4	6	8	10

NOTE: *Pink Panther began as a movie cartoon. (See Golden Comics Digest #38, 45 and March of Comics #376, 384, 390, 409, 418, 429, 441, 449, 461, 473, 486); #37, 72, 80-85 contain reprints.*

PINK PANTHER SUPER SPECIAL (TV)
Harvey Comics: Oct, 1993 ($2.25, 68 pgs.)

	GD	VG	FN	VF	VF/NM	NM-
V2#1-The Inspector & Wendy Witch stories also						4.00

PINK PANTHER, THE
Harvey Comics: Nov, 1993 - No. 9, July, 1994 ($1.50)

	GD	VG	FN	VF	VF/NM	NM-
V2#1-9						3.00

PINKY & THE BRAIN (See Animaniacs)
DC Comics: July, 1996 - No. 27, Nov, 1998 ($1.75/$1.95/$1.99)

	GD	VG	FN	VF	VF/NM	NM-
1-27, ...Christmas Special (1/96, $1.50)						3.00

PINKY LEE (See Adventures of...)

PINKY THE EGGHEAD
I.W./Super Comics: 1963 (Reprints from Noodnik)

	GD	VG	FN	VF	VF/NM	NM-
I.W. Reprint #1,2(nd)	2	4	6	9	11	14
Super Reprint #14-r/Noodnik Comics #4	2	4	6	9	11	14

PINOCCHIO (See 4-Color #92, 252, 545, 1203, Mickey Mouse Mag. V5#3, Movie Comics under Wonderful Advs. of..., New Advs. of..., Thrilling Comics #2, Walt Disney Showcase, Walt Disney's..., Wonderful Advs. of..., & World's Greatest Stories #2)
Dell Publishing Co.: No. 92, 1945 - No. 1203, Mar, 1962 (Disney)

	GD	VG	FN	VF	VF/NM	NM-
Four Color 92-The Wonderful Adventures of...; 16 pg. Donald Duck story ; entire book by Kelly	53	106	159	420	660	900
Four Color 252 (10/49)-Origin, not by Kelly	12	24	36	84	127	170
Four Color 545 (3/54)-The Wonderful Advs. of...; part-r of 4-Color #92; Disney-movie	8	16	24	58	82	105
Four Color 1203 (3/62)	6	12	18	43	59	75

PINOCCHIO AND THE EMPEROR OF THE NIGHT
Marvel Comics: Mar, 1988 ($1.25, 52 pgs.)

	GD	VG	FN	VF	VF/NM	NM-
1-Adapts film						3.00

PINOCCHIO LEARNS ABOUT KITES (See Kite Fun Book)

PIN-UP PETE (Also see Great Lover Romances & Monty Hall...)

Pitt #6 © Dale Keown

Planetary #5 © WSP

Planet Comics #7 © FH

GD 2.0 | VG 4.0 | FN 6.0 | VF 8.0 | VF/NM 9.0 | NM- 9.2

Toby Press: 1952
1-Jack Sparling pin-ups 19 38 57 107 154 200

PIONEER MARSHAL (See Fawcett Movie Comics)

PIONEER PICTURE STORIES
Street & Smith Publications: Dec, 1941 - No. 9, Dec, 1943
1-The Legless Air Ace begins 31 62 93 175 253 330
2 -True life story of Errol Flynn 16 32 48 89 127 165
3-9 14 28 42 79 110 140

PIONEER WEST ROMANCES (Firehair #1,2,7-11)
Fiction House Magazines: No. 3, Spring, 1950 - No. 6, Winter, 1950-51
3-(52 pgs.)-Firehair continues 21 42 63 118 169 220
4-6 21 42 63 118 169 220

PIPSQUEAK (See The Adventures of...)

PIRACY
E. C. Comics: Oct-Nov, 1954 - No. 7, Oct-Nov, 1955
1-Williamson/Torres-a 26 52 78 195 285 375
2-Williamson/Torres-a 17 34 51 128 184 240
3-7: 5-7-Comics Code symbol on cover 13 26 39 98 144 190
NOTE: *Crandall a-in all; c-2-4. Davis a-1, 2, 6. Evans a-3-7; c-7. Ingels a-3-7. Krigstein a-3-5, 7; c-5, 6. Wood a-1, 2; c-1.*

PIRACY
Gemstone Publishing: March, 1998 - No. 7, Sept, 1998 ($2.50)
1-7: E.C. reprints 2.50
Annual 1 ($10.95) Collects #1-4 11.00
Annual 2 ($7.95) Collects #5-7 8.00

PIRANA (See The Phantom #46 & Thrill-O-Rama #2, 3)

PIRATE CORP$, THE (See Hectic Planet)
Eternity Comics/Slave Labor Graphics: 1987 - No. 4, 1988 ($1.95)
1-4: 1,2-Color. 3,4-B&W 2.25
Special 1 ('89, B&W)-Slave Labor Publ. 2.25

PIRATE CORP$, THE (Volume 2)
Slave Labor Graphics: 1989 - No. 6, 1992 ($1.95)
1-6-Dorkin-s/a 2.25

PIRATE OF THE GULF, THE (See Superior Stories #2)

PIRATES COMICS
Hillman Periodicals: Feb-Mar, 1950 - No. 4, Aug-Sept, 1950 (All 52 pgs.)
1 26 52 78 150 215 280
2-Dave Berg-a 19 38 57 107 154 200
3,4-Berg-a 17 34 51 95 135 175

PIRATES OF DARK WATER, THE (Hanna Barbera)
Marvel Comics: Nov, 1991 - No. 9, Aug, 1992 ($1.95)
1-9: 9-Vess-c 3.00

P.I.'S: MICHAEL MAUSER AND MS. TREE, THE
First Comics: Jan, 1985 - No. 3, May, 1985 ($1.25, limited series)
1-3: Staton-c/a(p) 2.25

PITT, THE (Also see The Draft & The War)
Marvel Comics: Mar, 1988 ($3.25, 52 pgs., one-shot)
1-Ties into Starbrand, D.P.7 3.50

PITT (See Youngblood #4 & Gen 13 #3,#4)
Image Comics #1-9/Full Bleed #1/2,10-on: Jan, 1993 - Present ($1.95, intended as a four part limited series)
1/2-(12/95)-1st Full Bleed issue 4.00
1-Dale Keown-c/a. 1-1st app. The Pitt 4.00
2-13: All Dale Keown-c/a. 3 (Low distribution). 10 (1/96)-Indicia reads "January 1995" 3.00
14-20: 14-Begin $2.50-c, pullout poster 2.50
TPB-(1997, $9.95) r/#1/2, 1-4 10.00
TPB 2-(1999, $11.95) r/#5-9 12.00

PITT CREW
Full Bleed Studios: Aug, 1998 - No. 5, Dec, 1999 ($2.50)
1-5: 1-Richard Pace-s/Ken Lashley-a. 2-4-Scott Lee-a 2.50

PITT IN THE BLOOD
Full Bleed Studios: Aug, 1996 ($2.50, one-shot)
nn-Richard Pace-a/script 2.50

PIXIE & DIXIE & MR. JINKS (TV)(See Jinks, Pixie, and Dixie & Whitman Comic Books)
Dell Publishing Co./Gold Key: July-Sept, 1960 - Feb, 1963 (Hanna-Barbera)
Four Color 1112 9 18 27 63 89 115
Four Color 1196,1264, 01-631-207 (Dell, 7/62) 7 14 21 46 63 80
1(2/63-Gold Key) 8 16 24 53 74 95

PIXIE PUZZLE ROCKET TO ADVENTURELAND
Avon Periodicals: Nov, 1952
1 14 28 42 79 110 140

PIXIES, THE (Advs. of...)(The Mighty Atom and ...#6 on)(See A-1 Comics #16)
Magazine Enterprises: Winter, 1946 - No. 4, Fall?, 1947; No. 5, 1948
1-Mighty Atom 9 18 27 52 66 80
2-5-Mighty Atom 6 12 18 28 34 40
I.W. Reprint #1(1958), 8-(Pee-Wee Pixies), 10-I.W. on cover, Super on inside 2 4 6 8 10 12

PIZZAZZ
Marvel Comics: Oct, 1977 - No. 16, Jan, 1979 (slick-color kids mag. w/puzzles, games, comics)
1-Star Wars photo-c/article; origin Tarzan; KISS photos/article; Iron-On bonus; 2 pg. pin-up calendars thru #8 3 6 9 18 23 28
2-Spider-Man-c; Beatles pin-up calendar 2 4 6 10 13 16
3-8: 3-Close Encounters-s; Bradbury-s. 4-Alice Cooper, Travolta; Charlie's Angels/Fonz/Hulk/Spider-Man-c. 5-Star Trek quiz. 6-Asimov-s. 7-James Bond; Spock/Darth Vader-c. 8-TV Spider-Man photo-c/article 2 4 6 10 13 16
9-14: 9-Shaun Cassidy-c. 10-Sgt. Pepper-c/s. 12-Battlestar Galactica-s; Spider-Man app. 13-TV Hulk-c/s. 14-Meatloaf-c/s 2 4 6 9 11 14
15,16: 15-Battlestar Galactica-s. 16-Movie Superman photo-c/s, Hulk. 2 4 6 10 13 16
NOTE: *Star Wars comics in all (1-6:Chaykin-a, 7-9: DeZuniga-a, 10-13:Simonson/Janson-a. 14-16:Cockrum-a). Tarzan comics, 1pg.-#1-8. 1pg. "Hey Look" by Kurtzman #12-16.*

PLANETARY (See Preview in flip book Gen13 #33)
DC Comics (WildStorm Prod.): Apr, 1999 - Present ($2.50/$2.95)
1-Ellis-s/Cassaday-a/c 1 3 4 6 8 10
2-5 6.00
6-10 5.00
11-15: 12-Fourth Man revealed 4.00
16-21-($2.95) 3.00
...: All Over the World and Other Stories (2000, $14.95) r/#1-6 & Preview 15.00
...: All Over the World and Other Stories-Hardcover (2000, $24.95) r/#1-6 & Preview; with dustjacket 25.00
.../Batman: Night on Earth 1 (8/03, $5.95) Ellis-s/Cassaday-a 6.00
...: Crossing Worlds (2004, $14.95) r/Batman, JLA, and The Authority x-overs 15.00
.../JLA: Terra Occulta (11/02, $5.95) Elseworlds; Ellis-s/Ordway-a 6.00
...: Leaving the 20th Century -HC (2004, $24.95) r/#13-18 25.00
.../The Authority: Ruling the World (8/00, $5.95) Ellis-s/Phil Jimenez-a 6.00
...: The Fourth Man -Hardcover (2001, $24.95) r/#7-12 25.00
...: The Planetary Reader (8/03, $5.95) r/#13-15 6.00

PLANET COMICS
Fiction House Magazines: 1/40 - No. 62, 9/49; No. 63, Wint, 1949-50; No. 64, Spring, 1950; No. 65, 1951(nd); No. 66-68, 1952(nd); No. 69, Wint, 1952-53; No. 70-72, 1953(nd); No. 73, Winter, 1953-54
1-Origin Auro, Lord of Jupiter by Briefer (ends #61); Flint Baker & The Red Comet begin; Eisner/Fine-c 1088 2176 3264 8160 13,330 18,500
2-Lou Fine-c (Scarce) 423 846 1269 2936 4718 6500
3-Eisner-c 300 600 900 1908 3004 4100
4-Gale Allen and the Girl Squadron begins 277 554 831 1731 2666 3600
5,6-(Scarce): 5-Eisner/Fine-c 262 524 786 1638 2519 3400
7-12: 8-Robot-c. 12-The Star Pirate begins 208 416 624 1300 2000 2700
13,14: 13-Reff Ryan begins 154 308 462 963 1482 2000
15-(Scarce)-Mars, God of War begins (11/41); see Jumbo Comics #31 for 1st app. 300 600 900 1892 2946 4000
16-20,22 137 274 411 856 1316 1775
21-The Lost World & Hunt Bowman begin 144 288 432 900 1388 1875
23-26: 26-Space Rangers begin (9/43), end #71 131 262 393 819 1260 1700
27-30 104 208 312 650 1000 1350
31-35: 33-Origin Star Pirates Wonder Boots, reprinted in #52. 35-Mysta of the Moon begins, ends #62 87 174 261 544 835 1125
36-45: 38-1st Mysta of the Moon-c. 41-New origin of "Auro, Lord of Jupiter". 42-Last Gale Allen. 43-Futura begins 79 158 237 494 760 1025
46-60: 48-Robot-c. 53-Used in **SOTI**, pg. 32 62 124 186 388 594 800
61-68,70: 64,70-Robot-c. 65-70-All partial-r of earlier issues. 70-r/stories from #41 48 96 144 293 447 600
69-Used in **POP**, pgs. 101,102 48 96 144 293 447 600

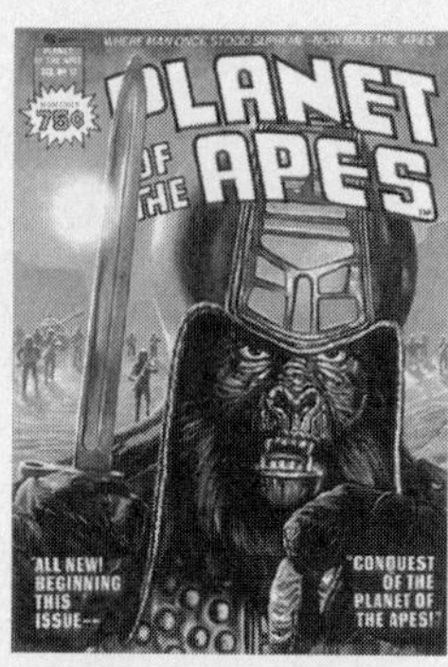

Planet of the Apes #17 © MAR

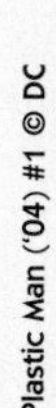
Plastic Man ('04) #1 © DC

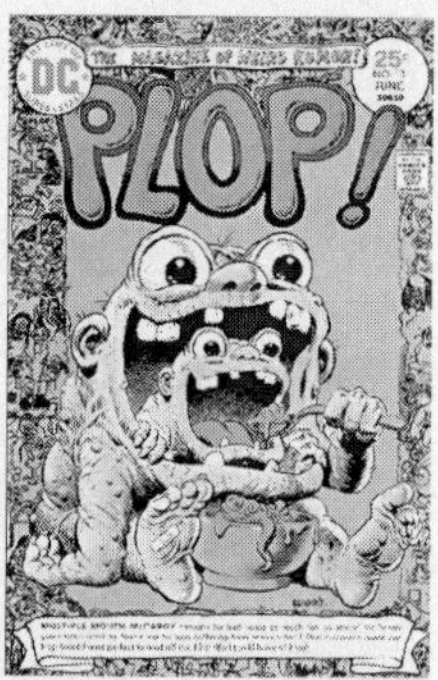

Plop! #13 © DC

	GD 2.0	VG 4.0	FN 6.0	VF 8.0	VF/NM 9.0	NM- 9.2
71-73-No series stories. 71-Space Rangers strip	40	80	120	230	335	440
I.W. Reprint 1,8,9: 1(nd)-r/#70; cover-r from Attack on Planet Mars. 8 (r/#72), 9-r/#73	9	18	27	63	89	115

NOTE: ***Anderson** a-33-38, 40-51 (Star Pirate). **Matt Baker** a-53-59 (Mysta of the Moon). **Celardo** c-12. **Bill Discount** a-71 (Space Rangers). **Elias** c-70. **Evans** a-46-49 (Auro, Lord of Jupiter), 50-64 (Lost World). **Fine** c-2, 5. **Hopper** a-31, 35 (Gale Allen), 41, 42, 48, 49 (Mysta of the Moon). **Ingels** a-24-31 (Lost World), 56-61 (Auro, Lord of Jupiter). **Lubbers** a-44-47 (Space Rangers); c-40, 41. **Moriera** a-43, 44 (Mysta of the Moon). **Renee** a-40-49 (Lost World); c-33, 35, 39. **Tuska** a-30 (Star Pirate). **M. Whitman** a-50-52 (Mysta of the Moon), 53-58 (Star Pirate); c-71-73. **Starr** a-59. **Zolnerwich** c-10. 13-25. Bondage c-53.*

PLANET COMICS
Pacific Comics: 1984 ($5.95)

	GD	VG	FN	VF	VF/NM	NM-
1-Reprints Planet Comics #1(1940)	1	2	3	5	6	8

PLANET COMICS
Blackthorne Publishing: Apr, 1988 - No. 3 ($2.00, color/B&W #3)

	GD	VG	FN	VF	VF/NM	NM-
1-3: New stories. 1-Dave Stevens-c						3.00

PLANET OF THE APES (Magazine) (Also see Adventures on the... & Power Record Comics)
Marvel Comics Group: Aug, 1974 - No. 29, Feb, 1977 (B&W) (Based on movies)

	GD	VG	FN	VF	VF/NM	NM-
1-Ploog-a	4	8	12	24	32	40
2-Ploog-a	3	6	9	16	21	26
3-10	2	4	6	12	16	20
11-20	2	4	6	14	18	22
21-28 (low distribution)	3	6	9	16	21	26
29 (low distribution)	5	10	15	36	48	60

NOTE: ***Alcala** a-7-11, 17-22, 24. **Ploog** a-1-4, 6, 8, 11, 13, 14, 19. **Sutton** a-11, 12, 15, 17, 19, 20, 23, 24, 29. **Tuska** a-1-6.*

PLANET OF THE APES
Adventure Comics: Apr, 1990 - No. 24, 1992 ($2.50, B&W)

	GD	VG	FN	VF	VF/NM	NM-
1-New movie tie-in; comes w/outer-c (3 colors)						4.00
1-Limited serial numbered edition ($5.00)						5.00
1-2nd printing (no outer-c, $2.50)						2.50
2-24						3.00
Annual 1 ($3.50)						4.00
...Urchak's Folly 1-4 ($2.50, mini-series)						3.00

PLANET OF THE APES (The Human War)
Dark Horse Comics: Jun, 2001 - No. 3, Aug, 2001 ($2.99, limited series)

	GD	VG	FN	VF	VF/NM	NM-
1-3-Follows the 2001 movie; Edginton-s						3.00

PLANET OF THE APES
Dark Horse Comics: Sept, 2001 - No. 6, Feb, 2002 ($2.99, ongoing series)

	GD	VG	FN	VF	VF/NM	NM-
1-6: 1-3-Edginton-s. 1-Photo & Wagner covers. 2-Plunkett & photo-c						3.00

PLANET OF VAMPIRES
Seaboard Publications (Atlas): Feb, 1975 - No. 3, July, 1975

	GD	VG	FN	VF	VF/NM	NM-
1-Neal Adams-c(i); 1st Broderick c/a(p); Hama-s	2	4	6	8	10	12
2,3: 2-Neal Adams-c. 3-Heath-c/a	1	2	3	5	7	9

PLANET TERRY
Marvel Comics (Star Comics)/Marvel: April, 1985 - No. 12, March, 1986 (Children's comic)

	GD	VG	FN	VF	VF/NM	NM-
1-12						3.00
1-Variant with "Star Chase" game on last page & inside back-c						10.00

PLASM (See Warriors of Plasm)
Defiant Comics: June, 1993

	GD	VG	FN	VF	VF/NM	NM-
0-Came bound into Diamond Previews V3#6 (6/93); price is for complete Previews with comic still attached						3.00
0-Comic only removed from Previews						2.25

PLASMER
Marvel Comics UK: Nov, 1993 - No. 4, Feb, 1994 ($1.95, limited series)

	GD	VG	FN	VF	VF/NM	NM-
1-($2.50)-Polybagged w/4 trading cards						2.50
2-4: Capt. America & Silver Surfer app.						2.25

PLASTIC FORKS
Marvel Comis (Epic Comics): 1990 - No. 5, 1990 ($4.95, 68 pgs., limited series, mature)

	GD	VG	FN	VF	VF/NM	NM-
Book 1-5: Squarebound						5.00

PLASTIC MAN (Also see Police Comics & Smash Comics #17)
Vital Publ. No. 1,2/Quality Comics No. 3 on: Sum, 1943 - No. 64, Nov, 1956

	GD	VG	FN	VF	VF/NM	NM-
nn(#1)- "In The Game of Death"; Skull-c; Jack Cole-c/a begins; ends-#64?	414	828	1242	2691	4346	6000
nn(#2, 2/44)- "The Gay Nineties Nightmare"	185	370	555	1156	1778	2400
3 (Spr, '46)	123	246	369	769	1185	1600
4 (Sum, '46)	92	184	276	575	888	1200
5 (Aut, '46)	75	150	225	469	722	975
6-10	62	124	186	388	594	800
11-20	55	110	165	340	520	700
21-30: 26-Last non-r issue?	46	92	138	281	428	575
31-40: 40-Used in POP, pg. 91	39	78	117	222	324	425
41-64: 53-Last precode issue. 54-Robot-c	31	62	93	178	259	340
Super Reprint 11,16,18: 11('63)-r/#16. 16-r/#18 & #21; Cole-a. 18('64)-Spirit-r by Eisner from Police #95	5	10	15	36	48	60

NOTE: ***Cole** r-44, 49, 56, 58, 59 at least. **Cuidera** c-32-64i.*

PLASTIC MAN (See DC Special #15 & House of Mystery #160)
National Periodical Publications/DC Comics: 11-12/66 - No. 10, 5-6/68; V4#11, 2-3/76 - No. 20, 10-11/77

	GD	VG	FN	VF	VF/NM	NM-
1-Real 1st app. Silver Age Plastic Man (House of Mystery #160 is actually tryout); Gil Kane-c/a; 12¢ issues begin	10	20	30	70	100	130
2-5: 4-Infantino-c; Mortimer-a	5	10	15	33	44	55
6-10('68): 7-G.A. Plastic Man & Woozy Winks (1st S.A. app.) app.; origin retold. 10-Sparling-a; last 12¢ issue	4	8	12	27	36	45
V4#11('76)-20: 11-20-Fradon-p. 17-Origin retold	1	2	3	5	7	9
...80-Page Giant (2003, $6.95) reprints origin and other stories in 80-Pg. Giant format						7.00
...Special 1 (8/99, $3.95)						4.00

PLASTIC MAN
DC Comics: Nov, 1988 - No. 4, Feb, 1989 ($1.00, mini-series)

	GD	VG	FN	VF	VF/NM	NM-
1-4: 1-Origin; Woozy Winks app.						2.25

PLASTIC MAN
DC Comics: Feb, 2004 - Present ($2.95)

	GD	VG	FN	VF	VF/NM	NM-
1-13-Kyle Baker-s/a in most. 1-Retells origin. 7,12-Scott Morse-s/a. 8-JLA cameo						3.00

PLASTRON CAFE
Mirage Studios: Dec, 1992 - No. 4, July, 1993 ($2.25, B&W)

	GD	VG	FN	VF	VF/NM	NM-
1-4: 1-Teenage Mutant Ninja Turtles app.; Kelly Freas-c. 2-Hildebrandt painted-c. 4-Spaced & Alien Fire stories						2.25

PLAYFUL LITTLE AUDREY (TV)(Also see Little Audrey #25)
Harvey Publications: 6/57 - No. 110, 11/73; No. 111, 8/74 - No. 121, 4/76

	GD	VG	FN	VF	VF/NM	NM-
1	24	48	72	170	260	350
2	12	24	36	86	131	175
3-5	9	18	27	65	93	120
6-10	7	14	21	51	71	90
11-20	6	12	18	38	52	65
21-40	4	8	12	27	36	45
41-60	3	7	10	21	28	35
61-84: 84-Last 12¢ issue	3	6	9	16	21	26
85-99	2	4	6	12	16	20
100-52 pg. Giant	3	6	9	18	24	30
101-103: 52 pg. Giants	3	6	9	16	20	25
104-121	1	3	4	6	8	10
...In 3-D (Spring, 1988, $2.25, Blackthorne #66)						4.00

PLOP! (Also see The Best of DC #60)
National Periodical Publications: Sept-Oct, 1973 - No. 24, Nov-Dec, 1976

	GD	VG	FN	VF	VF/NM	NM-
1-Sergio Aragonés-a begins; Wrightson-a	4	8	12	22	30	38
2-4,6-20	2	4	6	12	16	20
5-Wrightson-a	2	4	6	14	18	22
21-24 (52 pgs.). 23-No Aragonés-a	3	6	9	16	20	24

NOTE: ***Alcala** a-1-3. **Anderson** a-5. **Aragonés** a-1-22, 24. **Ditko** a-16p. **Evans** a-1. **Mayer** a-1. **Orlando** a-21, 22; c-21. **Sekowsky** a-5, 6p. **Toth** a-11. **Wolverton** r-4, 22-24(1 pg.ea.); c-1-12, 14, 17, 18. **Wood** a-14, 16i, 18-24; c-13, 15, 16, 19.*

PLUTO (See Cheerios Premiums, Four Color #537, Mickey Mouse Magazine, Walt Disney Showcase #4, 7, 13, 20, 23, 33 & Wheaties)
Dell Publ. Co.: No. 7, 1942; No. 429, 10/52 - No. 1248, 11-1/61-62 (Disney)

	GD	VG	FN	VF	VF/NM	NM-
Large Feature Comic 7(1942)-Written by Carl Barks, Jack Hannah, & Nick George (Barks' 1st comic book work)	110	220	330	885	1443	2000
Four Color 429 (#1)	10	20	30	73	107	140
Four Color 509	7	14	21	50	68	85
Four Color 595,654,736,853	5	10	15	36	48	60
Four Color 941,1039,1143,1248	5	10	15	33	44	55

POCKET CLASSICS
Academic Inc. Publications: 1984 (B&W, 4 1/4" x 6 3/4", 68 pages)

C1(Black Beauty. C2(The Call of the Wild). C3(Dr. Jekyll and Mr. Hyde). C4(Dracula). C5(Frankenstein). C6(Huckleberry Finn). C7(Moby Dick). C8(The Red Badge of Courage). C9(The Time Machine). C10(Tom Sawyer). C11(Treasure Island). C12(20,000 Leagues Under the Sea). C13(The Great Adventures of Sherlock Holmes). C14(Gulliver's Travels). C15(The Hunchback of Notre Dame). C16(The Invisible Man). C17(Journey to the Center of the Earth). C18(Kidnapped). C19(The Mysterious Island). C20(The Scarlet Letter). C21(The Story of My Life). C22(A Tale of Two Cities). C23(The Three Musketeers). C24(The

Pogo Possum #3 © Oskar Lebeck

Poison Elves Color Special #1 © Drew Hayes

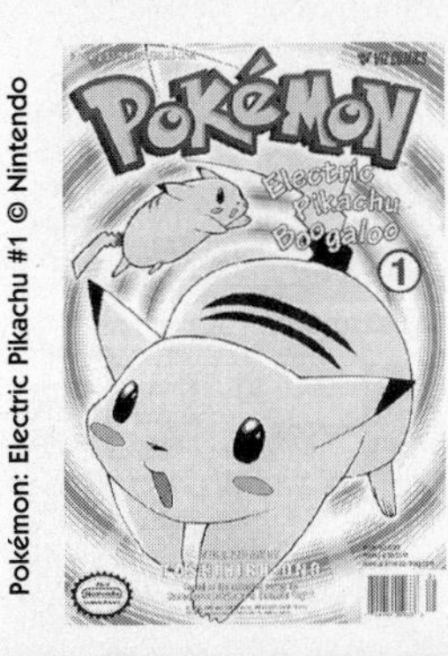

Pokémon: Electric Pikachu #1 © Nintendo

	GD 2.0	VG 4.0	FN 6.0	VF 8.0	VF/NM 9.0	NM- 9.2

War of the Worlds). C25(Around the World in Eighty Days). C26(Captains Courageous). C27(A Connecticut Yankee in King Arthur's Court). C28(Sherlock Holmes - The Hound of the Baskervilles). C29(The House of the Seven Gables). C30(Jane Eyre). C31(The Last of the Mohicans). C32(The Best of O. Henry). C33(The Best of Poe). C34(Two Years Before the Mast). C35(White Fang). C36(Wuthering Heights). C37(Ben Hur). C38(A Christmas Carol). C39(The Food of the Gods). C40(Ivanhoe). C41(The Man in the Iron Mask). C42(The Prince and the Pauper). C43(The Prisoner of Zenda). C44(The Return of the Native). C45(Robinson Crusoe). C46(The Scarlet Pimpernel). C47(The Sea Wolf). C48(The Swiss Family Robinson). C49(Billy Budd). C50(Crime and Punishment). C51(Don Quixote). C52(Great Expectations). C53(Heidi). C54(The Illiad). C55(Lord Jim). C56(The Mutiny on Board H.M.S. Bounty). C57(The Odyssey). C58(Oliver Twist). C59(Pride and Prejudice). C60(The Turn of the Screw) each... 9.00

Shakespeare Series:
S1(As You Like It). S2(Hamlet). S3(Julius Caesar). S4(King Lear). S5(Macbeth). S6(The Merchant of Venice). S7(A Midsummer Night's Dream). S8(Othello). S9(Romeo and Juliet). S10(The Taming of the Shrew). S11(The Tempest). S12(Twelfth Night) each... 9.00

POCKET COMICS (Also see Double Up)
Harvey Publications: Aug, 1941 - No. 4, Jan, 1942 (Pocket size; 100 pgs.) (1st Harvey comic)

	GD	VG	FN	VF	VF/NM	NM-
1-Origin & 1st app. The Black Cat, Cadet Blakey the Spirit of '76, The Red Blazer, The Phantom, Sphinx, & The Zebra; Phantom Ranger, British Agent #99, Spin Hawkins, Satan, Lord of Evil begin (1st app. of each); Simon-c/a in #1-3	96	192	288	600	925	1250
2 (9/41)-Black Cat on-c #2-4	65	130	195	406	623	840
3,4	50	100	150	305	465	625

POE
Cheese Comics: Sept, 1996 - No. 6, Apr, 1997 ($2.00, B&W)
1-6-Jason Asala-s/a 3.00

POE
Sirius Entertainment (Dogstar Press): Oct, 1997 - No. 24 ($2.50/$2.95, B&W)
1-24-Jason Asala-s/a. 20-24 ($2.95) 3.00
... Color Special (12/98, $2.95) Linsner-c 3.00

POGO PARADE (See Dell Giants)

POGO POSSUM (Also see Animal Comics & Special Delivery)
Dell Publishing Co.: No. 105, 4/46 - No. 148, 5/47; 10-12/49 - No. 16, 4-6/54

	GD	VG	FN	VF	VF/NM	NM-
Four Color 105(1946)-Kelly-c/a	60	120	180	502	789	1075
Four Color 148-Kelly-c/a	50	100	150	407	641	875
1-(10-12/49)-Kelly-c/a in all	41	82	123	330	515	700
2	36	72	108	270	423	575
3-5	27	54	81	194	297	400
6-10: 10-Infinity-c	23	46	69	165	253	340
11-16: 11-X-Mas-c	18	36	54	126	193	260

NOTE: *#1-4, 9-13: 52 pgs.; #5-8, 14-16: 36 pgs.*

POINT BLANK
Acme Press (Eclipse): May, 1989 - No. 2, 1989 ($2.95, B&W, magazine)
1,2-European-r 3.00

POINT BLANK (See Wildcats)
DC Comics (WildStorm): Oct, 2002 - No. 5, Feb, 2003 ($2.95, limited series)
1-5-Brubaker-s/Wilson-a/Bisley-c. 1-Variant-c by Wilson; Grifter and John Lynch app. 3.00
TPB (2003, $14.95) r/#1-5 15.00

POISON ELVES (Formerly I, Lusiphur)
Mulehide Graphics: No. 8, 1993- No. 20, 1995 (B&W, magazine/comic size, mature readers)

	GD	VG	FN	VF	VF/NM	NM-
8-Drew Hayes-c/a/scripts.	2	4	6	8	10	12
9-11: 11-1st comic size issue	2	4	6	8	10	12
12,14,16	1	2	3	5	6	8
13,15-(low print)	2	4	6	9	11	14
15-2nd print						4.00
17-20	1	2	3	5	6	8
...Desert of the Third Sin-(1997, $14.95, TPB)-r/#13-18						15.00
...Patrons-($4.95, TPB)-r/#19,20						5.00
...Traumatic Dogs-(1996, $14.95,TPB)-Reprints I, Lusiphur #7, Poison Elves #8-12						15.00

POISON ELVES (See I, Lusiphur)
Sirius Entertainment: June, 1995 - Present ($2.50/$2.95, B&W, mature readers)

	GD	VG	FN	VF	VF/NM	NM-
1-Linsner-c; Drew Hayes-a/scripts in all.						5.00
1-2nd print						2.50
2-25: 12-Purple Marauder-c/app.						3.00
26-45, 47-49						2.50
46,50-79: 61-Fillbäch Brothers-s/a. 74-Art by Crilley (3 pgs.)						3.00
... Baptism By Fire-(2003, $19.95, TPB)-r/#48-59						20.00
... Color Special #1 (12/98, $2.95)						5.00
... Companion (12/02, $3.50) Back-story and character bios						3.50
... FAN Edition #1 mail-in offer; Drew Hayes-c/s/a	1	2	3	5	6	8
... Rogues-(2002, $15.95, TPB)-r/#40-47						16.00
...Salvation-(2001, $19.95, TPB)-r/#26-39						20.00
...Sanctuary-(1999, $14.95, TPB)-r/#1-12						15.00

POISON ELVES: HYENA
Sirius Entertainment: Sept, 2004 - No. 4 ($2.95, B&W, mature readers)
1,2-Keith Davidsen-s/Scott Lewis-a 3.00

POISON ELVES: LUSIPHUR & LIRILITH
Sirius Entertainment: 2001 - No. 4, 2001 ($2.95, B&W, mature readers)
1-4-Drew Hayes-s/Jason Alexander-a 3.00
TPB (2002, $11.95) r/#1-4 12.00

POISON ELVES: PARINTACHIN
Sirius Entertainment: 2001 - No. 3, 2002 ($2.95, B&W, mature readers)
1-3-Drew Hayes-c/Fillbäch Brothers-s/a 3.00
TPB (2003, $8.95) r/#1-3 9.00

POKÉMON (TV) (Also see Magical Pokémon Journey)
Viz Comics: Nov, 1998 - Present ($3.25/$3.50, B&W)

	GD	VG	FN	VF	VF/NM	NM-
...Part 1: The Electric Tale of Pikachu						
1-Toshiro Ono-s/a	1	3	4	6	8	10
1-4 (2nd through current printings)						3.50
2						6.00
3,4						4.00
TPB ($12.95)						13.00
...Part 2: Pikachu Strikes Back						
1						5.00
2-4						4.00
TPB						13.00
...Part 3: Electric Pikachu Boogaloo						
1						4.00
2-4 ($2.95-c)						3.50
TPB						13.00
...Part 4: Surf's Up Pikachu						
1,3,4						4.00
2 ($2.95-c)						3.50
TPB						13.00

NOTE: Multiple printings exist for most issues

POKÉMON ADVENTURES
Viz Comics: Sept, 1999 - No. 4 ($5.95, B&W, magazine-size)
1-4-Includes stickers bound in 6.00

POKÉMON ADVENTURES
Viz Comics: 2000 - Present ($2.95/$4.95, B&W)
Part 2 (2/00-7/00) 1-6-Includes stickers bound in 3.50
Part 3 (8/00-2/01) 1-7 3.50
Part 4 (3/00-6/01) 1-4 5.00
Part 5 (7/01-10/01) 1-4 5.00
Part 6 - 1-4, Part 7 1-5 5.00

POKÉMON: THE FIRST MOVIE
Viz Comics: 1999 ($3.95)
Mewtwo Strikes Back 1-4 4.00
Pikachu's Vacation 4.00

POKÉMON: THE MOVIE 2000
Viz Comics: 2000 ($3.95)
1-Official movie adaption 4.00
Pikachu's Rescue Adventure 4.00
...:The Power of One (mini-series) 1-3 4.00

POLICE ACADEMY (TV)
Marvel Comics: Nov, 1989 - No. 6, Feb, 1990 ($1.00)
1-6: Based on TV cartoon; Post-c/a(p) in all 2.25

POLICE ACTION
Atlas News Co.: Jan, 1954 - No. 7, Nov, 1954

	GD	VG	FN	VF	VF/NM	NM-
1-Violent-a by Robert Q. Sale	21	42	63	118	169	220
2	11	22	33	64	87	110
3-7: 7-Powell-a	10	20	30	58	77	95

NOTE: ***Ayers** a-4, 5. **Colan** a-1. **Forte** a-1, 2. **Mort Lawrence** a-5. **Maneely** a-3; c-1, 5. **Reinman** a-6, 7.*

POLICE ACTION

Police Comics #18 © QUA

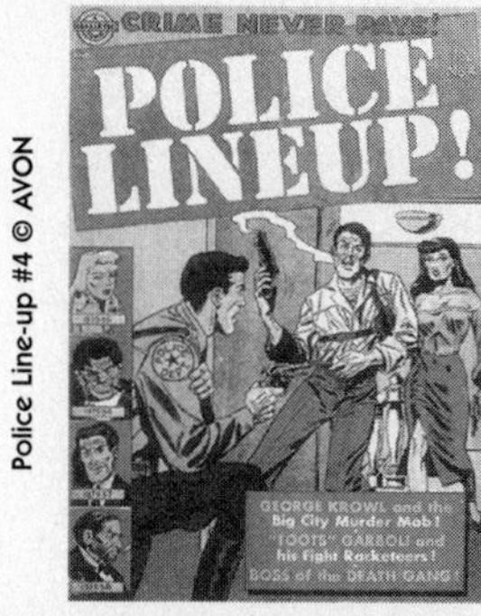

Police Line-up #4 © AVON

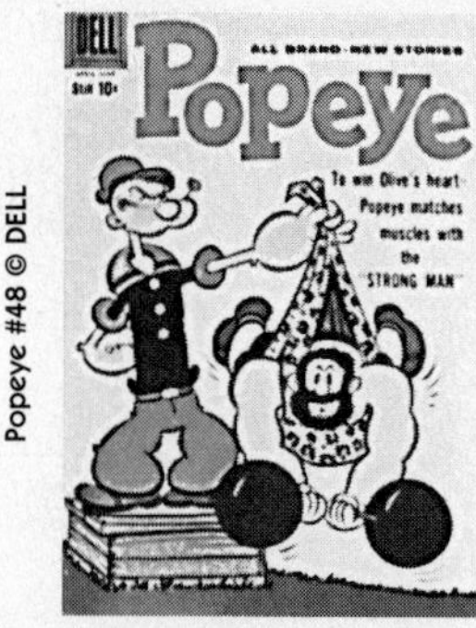

Popeye #48 © DELL

	GD 2.0	VG 4.0	FN 6.0	VF 8.0	VF/NM 9.0	NM- 9.2

Atlas/Seaboard Publ.: Feb, 1975 - No. 3, June, 1975

1-3: 1-Lomax, N.Y.P.D., Luke Malone begin; McWilliams-a. 2-Origin Luke Malone, Manhunter; Ploog-a	1	2	3	5	7	9

NOTE: *Ploog art in all.* ***Sekowsky/McWilliams*** *a-1-3.* ***Thorne*** *c-3.*

POLICE AGAINST CRIME
Premiere Magazines: April, 1954 - No. 9, Aug, 1955

1-Disbrow-a; extreme violence (man's face slashed with knife); Hollingsworth-a	25	50	75	144	207	270
2-Hollingsworth-a	14	28	42	79	110	140
3-9	11	22	33	62	84	105

POLICE BADGE #479 (Formerly Spy Thrillers #1-4)
Atlas Comics (PrPI): No. 5, Sept, 1955

5-Maneely-c/a (6 pgs.); Heck-a	11	22	33	62	84	105

POLICE CASE BOOK (See Giant Comics Editions)

POLICE CASES (See Authentic... & Record Book of...)

POLICE COMICS
Quality Comics Group (Comic Magazines): Aug, 1941 - No. 127, Oct, 1953

1-Origin/1st app. Plastic Man by Jack Cole (r-in DC Special #15), The Human Bomb by Gustavson, & No. 711; intro. Chic Carter by Eisner, The Firebrand by Reed Crandall, The Mouthpiece by Guardineer, Phantom Lady, & The Sword; Firebrand-c 1-4	742	1484	2226	5194	8347	11,500
2-Plastic Man smuggles opium	317	634	951	2061	3331	4600
3	231	462	693	1444	2222	3000
4	196	392	588	1225	1888	2550
5-Plastic Man-c begin; Plastic Man forced to smoke marijuana; Plastic Man covers begin, end #102	188	376	564	1175	1813	2450
6,7	165	330	495	1031	1591	2150
8-Manhunter begins (origin/1st app.) (3/42)	192	384	576	1200	1850	2500
9,10	131	262	393	819	1260	1700
11-The Spirit strip reprints begin by Eisner (origin-strip #1); 1st comic book app. The Spirit & 1st cover app. (9/42)	231	462	693	1444	2222	3000
12-Intro. Ebony	137	274	411	856	1316	1775
13-Intro. Woozy Winks; last Firebrand	131	262	393	819	1260	1700
14-19: 15-Last No. 711; Destiny begins	96	192	288	600	925	1250
20-The Raven x-over in Phantom Lady; features Jack Cole himself	96	192	288	600	925	1250
21,22: 21-Raven & Spider Widow x-over in Phantom Lady (cameo in #22)	83	166	249	519	797	1075
23-30: 23-Last Phantom Lady. 24-26-Flatfoot Burns by Kurtzman in all	77	154	231	481	741	1000
31-41: 37-1st app. Candy by Sahle & begins (12/44). 41-Last Spirit-r by Eisner	54	108	162	329	502	675
42,43-Spirit-r by Eisner/Fine	53	106	159	323	494	665
44-Fine Spirit-r begin, end #88,90,92	53	106	159	323	492	660
45-50: 50-(#50 on-c, #49 on inside, 1/46)	40	80	120	244	372	500
51-60: 58-Last Human Bomb	36	72	108	204	297	390
61-88,90,92: 63-(Some issues have #65 printed on cover, but #63 on inside) Kurtzman-a, 6 pgs. 90,92-Spirit by Fine	27	54	81	154	222	290
89,91,93-No Spirit stories	24	48	72	138	199	260
94-99,101,102: Spirit by Eisner in all; 101-Last Manhunter. 102-Last Spirit & Plastic Man by Jack Cole	34	68	102	196	283	370
100	40	80	120	233	342	450
103-Content change to crime; Ken Shannon & T-Man begin (1st app. of each, 12/50)	28	56	84	158	229	300
104-112,114-127: Crandall-a most issues (not in 104,105,122,125-127). 109-Atomic bomb story. 112-Crandall-a	20	40	60	115	165	215
113-Crandall-c/a(2), 9 pgs. each	22	44	66	123	177	230

NOTE: *Most Spirit stories signed by Eisner are not by him; all are reprints.* ***Cole*** *c-17, 19-21, 24-26, 28-31, 36-38, 40-42, 45-48, 65-68, 69, 73, 75.* ***Crandall*** *Firebrand-1-8. Spirit by* ***Eisner*** *1-41, 94-102; by* ***Eisner/Fine****-42, 43; by* ***Fine****-44-88, 90, 92. 103, 109.* ***Al Bryant*** *c-33, 34.* ***Cole*** *c-17-32, 35-102(most).* ***Crandall*** *c-13, 14.* ***Crandall/Cuidera*** *c-105-127.* ***Eisner*** *c-4i.* ***Gill Fox*** *c-1-3, 4p, 5-12, 15. Bondage c-103, 109, 125.*

POLICE LINE-UP
Avon Periodicals/Realistic Comics #3,4: Aug, 1951 - No. 4, July, 1952 (Painted-c #1-3)

1-Wood-a, 1 pg. plus part-c; spanking panel-r/Saint #5	40	80	120	233	342	450
2-Classic story "The Religious Murder Cult", drugs, perversion; r/Saint #5; c-r/Avon paperback #329	29	58	87	164	237	310
3,4: 3-Kubert-a(r?)/part-c; Kinstler-a (inside-c only)	22	44	66	123	177	230

POLICE TRAP (Public Defender In Action #7 on)
Mainline #1-4/Charlton #5,6: 8-9/54 - No. 4, 2-3/55; No. 5, 7/55 - No. 6, 9/55

1-S&K covers-all issues; Meskin-a; Kirby scripts	31	62	93	178	259	340
2-4	19	38	57	107	154	200
5,6-S&K-c/a	25	50	75	141	203	265

POLICE TRAP
Super Comics: No. 11, 1963; No. 16-18, 1964

Reprint #11,16-18: 11-r/Police Trap #3. 16-r/Justice Traps the Guilty #? 17-r/Inside Crime #3 & r/Justice Traps The Guilty #83; 18-r/Inside Crime #3	2	4	6	10	13	16

POLLY & HER PALS (See Comic Monthly #1)

POLLYANNA (Disney)
Dell Publishing Co.: No. 1129, Aug-Oct, 1960

Four Color 1129-Movie, Haley Mills photo-c	9	18	27	63	89	115

POLLY PIGTAILS (Girls' Fun & Fashion Magazine #44 on)
Parents' Magazine Institute/Polly Pigtails: Jan, 1946 - V4#43, Oct-Nov, 1949

1-Infinity-c; photo-c	12	24	36	69	95	120
2-Photo-c	8	16	24	40	50	60
3-5: 3,4-Photo-c	6	12	18	33	41	48
6-10: 7-Photo-c	6	12	18	29	36	42
11-30: 22-Photo-c	6	12	18	27	33	38
31-43	5	10	15	23	28	32

PONY EXPRESS (See Tales of the...)

PONYTAIL (Teen-age)
Dell Publishing Co./Charlton No. 13 on: 7-9/62 - No. 12, 10-12/65; No. 13, 11/69 - No. 20, 1/71

12-641-209(#1)	4	8	12	27	36	45
2-12	3	6	9	18	24	30
13-20	2	4	6	12	16	20

POP COMICS
Modern Store Publ.: 1955 (36 pgs.; 5x7"; in color) (7¢)

1-Funny animal	6	12	18	28	34	40

POPEYE (See Comic Album #7, 11, 15, Comics Reading Libraries *in the Promotional Comics section*, Eat Right to Work and Win, Giant Comic Album, King Comics, Kite Fun Book, Magic Comics, March of Comics #37,52, 66, 80, 96, 117, 134, 148, 157, 169, 194, 246, 264, 274, 294, 453, 465, 477 & Wow Comics, 1st series)

POPEYE
David McKay Publications: 1937 - 1939 (All by Segar)

Feature Books nn (100 pgs.) (Very Rare)	600	1200	1800	4200	6000	8500
Feature Books 2 (52 pgs.)	85	170	255	531	816	1100
Feature Books 3 (100 pgs.)-r/nn issue with a new-c	79	158	237	494	760	1025
Feature Books 5,10 (76 pgs.)	69	138	207	431	666	900
Feature Books 14 (76 pgs.) (Scarce)	77	154	231	481	741	1000

POPEYE (Strip reprints through 4-Color #70)
Dell #1-65/Gold Key #66-80/King #81-92/Charlton #94-138/Gold Key #139-155/Whitman #156 on: 1941 - 1947; #1, 2-4/48 - #65, 7-9/62; #66, 10/62 - #80, 5/66; #81, 8/66 - #92, 12/67; #94, 2/69 - #138, 1/77; #139, 5/78 - #171, 6/84 (no #93,160,161)

Large Feature Comic 24('41)-Half by Segar	65	130	195	406	628	850
Four Color 25('41)-by Segar	60	120	180	475	763	1050
Large Feature Comic 10('43)	54	108	162	329	502	675
Four Color 17('43),26('43)-by Segar	44	88	132	352	551	750
Four Color 43('44)	32	64	96	240	370	500
Four Color 70('45)-Title: ...& Wimpy	26	52	78	187	296	385
Four Color 113('46-original strips begin),127,145('47),168	15	30	45	105	160	215
1(2-4/48)(Dell)-All new stories continue	29	58	87	206	316	425
2	15	30	45	105	160	215
3-10: 5-Popeye on moon w/rocket-c	12	24	36	87	134	180
11-20	11	22	33	75	110	145
21-40,46: 46-Origin Swee' Pee	9	18	27	63	89	115
41-45,47-50	8	16	24	53	74	95
51-60	7	14	21	46	63	80
61-65 (Last Dell issue)	6	12	18	40	55	70
66,67-Both 84 pgs. (Gold Key)	8	16	24	53	74	95
68-80	4	8	12	28	38	48
81-92,94-97 (no #93): 97-Last 12¢ issue	4	8	12	22	30	38
98,99,101-138	2	4	6	14	18	22
100	3	6	9	19	25	32
139-155: 144-50th Anniversary issue	1	3	4	6	8	10
156,157,162-167(Whitman)(no #160,161).167(3/82)	2	4	6	10	13	16
158(9/80),159(11/80)-pre-pack only	3	6	9	18	24	30
168-171:(All #90069 on-c; pre-pack) 168(6/83). 169(#168 on-c)(8/83). 170(3/84). 171(6/84)	2	4	6	14	18	22

Popular Comics #84 © DELL

Porky Pig Four Color #260 © WB

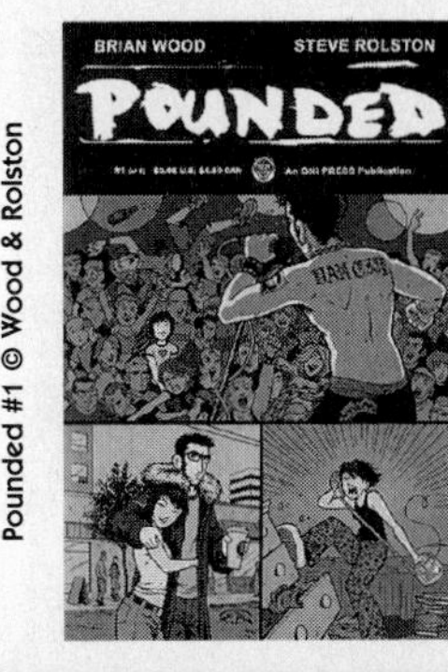

Pounded #1 © Wood & Rolston

NOTE: *Reprints-#145, 147, 149, 151, 153, 155, 157, 163-168(1/3), 170.*

POPEYE
Harvey Comics: Nov, 1993 - No. 7, Aug, 1994 ($1.50)

	GD 2.0	VG 4.0	FN 6.0	VF 8.0	VF/NM 9.0	NM- 9.2
V2#1-7						3.00
...Summer Special V2#1-(10/93, $2.25, 68 pgs.)-Sagendorf-r & others						4.00

POPEYE SPECIAL
Ocean Comics: Summer, 1987 - No. 2, Sept, 1988 ($1.75/$2.00)

	GD 2.0	VG 4.0	FN 6.0	VF 8.0	VF/NM 9.0	NM- 9.2
1,2: 1-Origin						4.00

POPPLES (TV, movie)
Star Comics (Marvel): Dec, 1986 - No. 5, Aug, 1987

	GD 2.0	VG 4.0	FN 6.0	VF 8.0	VF/NM 9.0	NM- 9.2
1-5-Based on toys						4.00

POPPO OF THE POPCORN THEATRE
Fuller Publishing Co. (Publishers Weekly): 10/29/55 - No. 13, 1956 (weekly)

	GD 2.0	VG 4.0	FN 6.0	VF 8.0	VF/NM 9.0	NM- 9.2
1	9	18	27	52	66	80
2-5	7	14	21	35	43	50
6-13	6	12	18	28	34	40

NOTE: *By **Charles Biro**. 10¢ cover, given away by supermarkets such as IGA.*

POP-POP COMICS
R. B. Leffingwell Co.: No date (Circa 1945) (52 pgs.)

	GD 2.0	VG 4.0	FN 6.0	VF 8.0	VF/NM 9.0	NM- 9.2
1-Funny animal	13	26	39	74	102	130

POPULAR COMICS
Dell Publishing Co.: Feb, 1936 - No. 145, July-Sept, 1948

	GD 2.0	VG 4.0	FN 6.0	VF 8.0	VF/NM 9.0	NM- 9.2
1-Dick Tracy (1st comic book app.), Little Orphan Annie, Terry & the Pirates, Gasoline Alley, Don Winslow (1st app.), Harold Teen, Little Joe, Skippy, Moon Mullins, Mutt & Jeff, Tailspin Tommy, Smitty, Smokey Stover, Winnie Winkle & The Gumps begin (all strip-r)	675	1350	2025	4800	-	-
2	230	460	690	1650	-	-
3	175	350	525	1225	-	-
4-6(7/36): 5-Tom Mix begins. 6-1st app. Scribbly	140	280	420	975	-	-
7-10: 8,9-Scribbly & Reglar Fellers app.	110	220	330	775	-	-
11-20: 12-X-Mas-c	82	164	246	472	686	900
21-27: 27-Last Terry & the Pirates, Little Orphan Annie, & Dick Tracy	61	122	183	351	513	675
28-37: 28-Gene Autry app. 31,32-Tim McCoy app. 35-Christmas-c; Tex Ritter app.	48	96	144	276	401	525
38-43: Tarzan in text only. 38-(4/39)-Gang Busters (Radio, 2nd app.) & Zane Grey's Tex Thorne begins? 43-The Masked Pilot app.; 1st non-funny-c?	46	92	138	265	388	510
44,45: 45-Hurricane Kid-c	34	68	102	196	286	375
46-Origin/1st app. Martan, the Marvel Man(12/39)	44	88	132	253	369	485
47-50	33	66	99	190	275	360
51-Origin The Voice (The Invisible Detective) strip begins (5/40)	35	70	105	201	293	385
52-Robot-c	34	68	102	196	286	375
53-59: 55-End of World story	30	60	90	173	254	335
60-Origin/1st app. Professor Supermind and Son (2/41)	32	64	96	184	267	350
61-71: 63-Smilin' Jack begins	25	50	75	144	212	280
72-The Owl & Terry & the Pirates begin (2/42); Smokey Stover reprints begin	41	82	123	236	343	450
73-75	28	56	84	161	236	310
76-78-Capt. Midnight in all (see The Funnies #57)	40	80	120	230	335	440
79-85-Last Owl	26	52	78	150	220	290
86-99: 98-Felix the Cat, Smokey Stover-r begin	18	36	54	103	152	200
100	20	40	60	115	170	225
101-130	11	22	33	63	94	125
131-145: 142-Last Terry & the Pirates	10	20	30	57	84	110

NOTE: *Martan, the Marvel Man c-47-49, 52, 57-59. Professor Supermind c-60-63, 64(1/2), 65, 66. The Voice c-53.*

POPULAR FAIRY TALES (See March of Comics #6, 18)

POPULAR ROMANCE
Better-Standard Publications: No. 5, Dec, 1949 - No. 29, July, 1954

	GD 2.0	VG 4.0	FN 6.0	VF 8.0	VF/NM 9.0	NM- 9.2
5	11	22	33	64	87	110
6-9: 7-Palais-a; lingerie panels	9	18	27	51	62	75
10-Wood-a (2 pgs.)	10	20	30	56	73	90
11,12,14-16,18-21,28,29	8	16	24	40	50	60
13,17-Severin/Elder-a (3&8 pgs.)	8	16	24	46	58	70
22-27-Toth-a	9	18	27	54	70	85

NOTE: *All have photo-c. **Tuska** art in most issues.*

POPULAR TEEN-AGERS (Secrets of Love) (School Day Romances #1-4)
Star Publications: No. 5, Sept, 1950 - No. 23, Nov, 1954

	GD 2.0	VG 4.0	FN 6.0	VF 8.0	VF/NM 9.0	NM- 9.2
5-Toni Gay, Midge Martin & Eve Adams continue from School Day Romances; Ginger Bunn (formerly Ginger Snapp & becomes Honey Bunn #6 on) begins; all features end #8	35	70	105	201	293	385
6-8 (7/51)-Honey Bunn begins; all have L. B. Cole-c; 6-Negligee panels	32	64	96	184	267	350
9-(...Romances; 1st romance issue, 10/51)	21	42	63	121	173	225
10-(...Secrets of Love thru #23)	20	40	60	112	161	210
11,16,18,19,22,23	16	32	48	92	131	170
12,13,17,20,21-Disbrow-a	18	36	54	100	143	185
14-Harrison/Wood-a	24	48	72	135	195	255
15-Wood?, Disbrow-a	19	38	57	107	154	200
Accepted Reprint 5,6 (nd); L.B. Cole-c	9	18	27	54	70	85

NOTE: *All have **L. B. Cole** covers.*

PORKY PIG (See Bugs Bunny &..., Kite Fun Book, Looney Tunes, March of Comics #42, 57, 71, 89, 99, 113, 130, 143, 164, 175, 192, 209, 218, 367, and Super Book #6, 18, 30)

PORKY PIG (...& Bugs Bunny #40-69)
Dell Publishing Co./Gold Key No. 1-93/Whitman No. 94 on: No. 16, 1942 - No. 81, Mar-Apr, 1962; Jan, 1965 - No. 109, June, 1984

	GD 2.0	VG 4.0	FN 6.0	VF 8.0	VF/NM 9.0	NM- 9.2
Four Color 16(#1, 1942)	74	148	222	629	1015	1400
Four Color 48(1944)-Carl Barks-a	86	172	258	706	1128	1550
Four Color 78(1945)	27	54	81	194	297	400
Four Color 112(7/46)	17	34	51	121	186	250
Four Color 156,182,191('49)	12	24	36	86	131	175
Four Color 226,241('49),260,271,277,284,295	10	20	30	73	107	140
Four Color 303,311,322,330: 322-Sci/fi-c/story	8	16	24	53	74	95
Four Color 342,351,360,370,385,399,410,426	6	12	18	40	55	70
25 (11-12/52)-30	5	10	15	33	44	55
31-40	4	8	12	27	36	45
41-60	3	7	10	21	28	35
61-81(3-4/62)	3	6	9	18	23	28
1(1/65-Gold Key)(2nd Series)	6	12	18	38	52	65
2,4,5-r/4-Color 226,284 & 271 in that order	3	7	10	21	28	35
3,6-10: 3-r/Four Color #342	3	6	9	18	23	28
11-30	2	4	6	12	16	20
31-54	2	4	6	10	12	15
55-70	1	3	4	6	8	10
71-93(Gold Key)	1	2	3	5	6	8
94-96	1	2	3	5	7	9
97(9/80),98-pre-pack only (99 known not to exist)	3	6	9	16	21	26
100	2	4	6	10	12	15
101-105: 104(2/82). 105(4/82)	1	3	4	6	8	10
106-109 (All #90140 on-c, no date or date code): 106(7/83), 107(8/83), 108(2/84), 109(6/84) low print run	2	4	6	11	14	18

NOTE: *Reprints-#1-8, 9-35(2/3); 36-46(1/4-1/2), 58, 67, 69-74, 76, 78, 102-109(1/3-1/2).*

PORKY PIG'S DUCK HUNT
Saalfield Publishing Co.: 1938 (12pgs.)(large size)(heavy linen-like paper)

	GD 2.0	VG 4.0	FN 6.0	VF 8.0	VF/NM 9.0	NM- 9.2
2178-1st app. Porky Pig & Daffy Duck by Leon Schlesinger. Illustrated text story book written in verse.1st book ever devoted to these characters. (see Looney Tunes #1 for their 1st comic book app.)	71	141	213	444	685	925

PORTIA PRINZ OF THE GLAMAZONS
Eclipse Comics: Dec, 1986 - No. 6, Oct, 1987 ($2.00, B&W, Baxter paper)

	GD 2.0	VG 4.0	FN 6.0	VF 8.0	VF/NM 9.0	NM- 9.2
1-6						2.25

POSSESSED, THE
DC Comics (Cliffhanger): Sept, 2003 - No. 6, March, 2004 ($2.95, limited series)

	GD 2.0	VG 4.0	FN 6.0	VF 8.0	VF/NM 9.0	NM- 9.2
1-6-Johns & Grimminger-s/Sharp-a						3.00
TPB (2004, $14.95) r/#1-6; promo art and sketch pages						15.00

POST GAZETTE (See Meet the New... in the Promotional Comics section)

POUNDED
Oni Press: Mar, 2002 - No. 3, June, 2002 ($2.95, B&W, limited series)

	GD 2.0	VG 4.0	FN 6.0	VF 8.0	VF/NM 9.0	NM- 9.2
1-3-Brian Wood-s/Steve Rolston-a						3.00
TPB (10/02, $8.95, 8 1/4" x 6") r/#1-3; intro by Kieron Dwyer; sketch pages and pin-ups						9.00

POWDER RIVER RUSTLERS (See Fawcett Movie Comics)

POWER & GLORY (See American Flagg! & Howard Chaykin's American Flagg!
Malibu Comics (Bravura): Feb, 1994 - No. 4, May, 1994 ($2.50, limited series, mature)

	GD 2.0	VG 4.0	FN 6.0	VF 8.0	VF/NM 9.0	NM- 9.2
1A, 1B-By Howard Chaykin; w/Bravura stamp						2.50
1-Newsstand ed. (polybagged w/children's warning on bag), Gold ed., Silver-foil ed., Blue-foil ed.(print run of 10,000), Serigraph ed. (print run of 3,000)($2.95)-Howard Chaykin-c/a begin						3.00

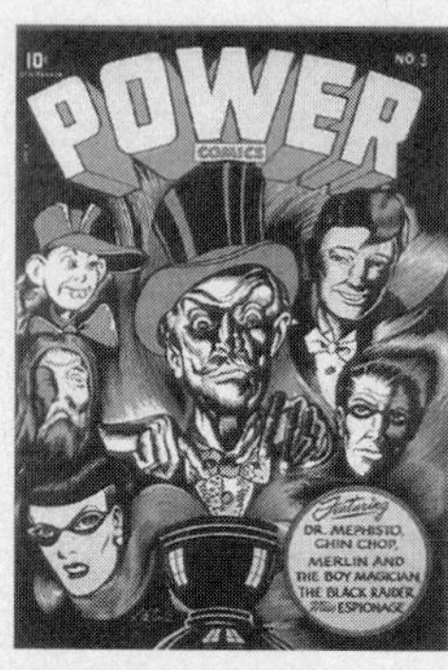

Power Comics #3 © HOKE

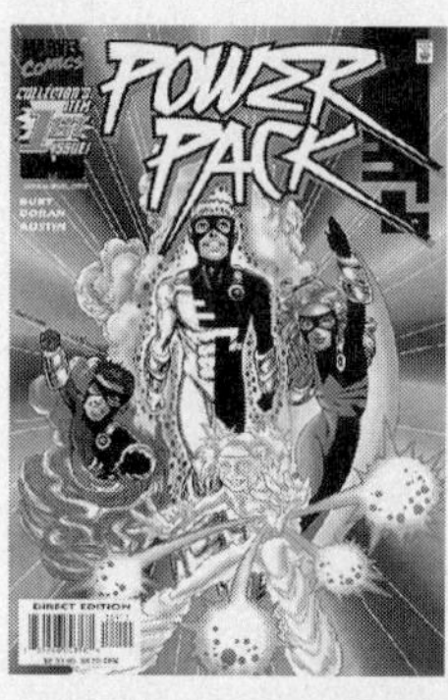

Power Pack V2#1 © MAR

Powerpuff Girls #41 © Cartoon Network

GD VG FN VF VF/NM NM-
2.0 4.0 6.0 8.0 9.0 9.2

2-4-Contains Bravura stamp 2.50
Holiday Special (Win '94, $2.95) 3.00

POWER COMICS
Holyoke Publ. Co./Narrative Publ.: 1944 - No. 4, 1945

1-L. B. Cole-c 148 296 444 925 1425 1925
2-Hitler, Hirohito-c (scarce) 148 296 444 925 1425 1925
3-Classic L.B. Cole-c; Dr. Mephisto begins? 171 342 513 1069 1647 2225
4-L.B. Cole-c; Miss Espionage app. #3,4; Leav-a 148 296 444 925 1425 1925

POWER COMICS
Power Comics Co.: 1977 - No. 5, Dec, 1977 (B&W)

1- "A Boy And His Aardvark" by Dave Sim; first Dave Sim aardvark (not Cerebus)
2 4 6 14 18 22
1-Reprint (3/77, black-c) 1 2 3 5 6 8
2-Cobalt Blue by Gustovich 1 3 4 6 8 10
3-5: 3-Nightwitch. 4-Northern Light. 5-Bluebird 1 3 4 6 8 10

POWER COMICS
Eclipse Comics (Acme Press): Mar, 1988 - No. 4, Sept, 1988 ($2.00, B&W, mini-series)

1-4: Bolland, Gibbons-r in all 2.25

POWER COMPANY, THE
DC Comics: Apr, 2002 - No. 18, Sep, 2003 ($2.50/$2.75)

1-6-Busiek-s/Grummett-a. 6-Green Arrow & Black Canary-c/app. 2.50
7-18: 7:Begin $2.75-c. 8,9-Green Arrow app. 11-Firestorm joins. 15-Batman app. 2.75
...Bork (3/02) Busiek-s/Dwyer-a; Batman & Flash (Barry Allen) app. 2.50
...Josiah Power (3/02) Busiek-s/Giffen-a; Superman app. 2.50
...Manhunter (3/02) Busiek-s/Jurgens-a; Nightwing app. 2.50
...Sapphire (3/02) Busiek-s/Bagley-a; JLA & Kobra app. 2.50
...Skyrocket (3/02) Busiek-s/Staton-a; Green Lantern (Hal Jordan) app. 2.50
...Striker Z (3/02) Busiek-s/Bachs-a; Superboy app. 2.50
...Witchfire (3/02) Busiek-s/Haley-a; Wonder Woman app. 2.50

POWER FACTOR
Wonder Color Comics #1/Pied Piper #2: May, 1987 - No. 2, 1987 ($1.95)

1,2: Super team. 2-Infantino-c 2.25

POWER FACTOR
Innovation Publishing: Oct, 1990 - No. 3, 1991 ($1.95/$2.25)

1-3: 1-R-/1st story + new-a, 2-r/2nd story + new-a. 3-Infantino-a 2.25

POWER GIRL (See All-Star #58, Infinity, Inc., Showcase #97-99)
DC Comics: June, 1988 - No. 4, Sept, 1988 ($1.00, color, limited series)

1-4 3.00

POWERHOUSE PEPPER COMICS (See Gay Comics, Joker Comics & Tessie the Typist)
Marvel Comics (20CC): No. 1, 1943; No. 2, May, 1948 - No. 5, Nov, 1948

1-(60 pgs.)-Wolverton-a in all; c-2,3 185 370 555 1156 1778 2400
2 87 174 261 544 835 1125
3,4 79 158 237 494 760 1025
5-(Scarce) 92 184 276 575 888 1200

POWERLESS
Marvel Comics: Aug, 2004 - No. 6, Jan, 2005 ($2.99, limited series)

1-6-Peter Parker, Matt Murdock and Logan without powers; Gaydos-a 3.00

POWER LINE
Marvel Comics (Epic Comics): May, 1988 - No. 8, Sept, 1989 ($1.25/$1.50)

1-8: 2-Williamson-i. 3-Dr. Zero app. 4-7-Morrow-a. 8-Williamson-i 2.25

POWER LORDS
DC Comics: Dec, 1983 - No. 3, Feb, 1984 (Limited series, Mando paper)

1-3: Based on Revell toys 2.25

POWER MAN (Formerly Hero for Hire; ...& Iron Fist #50 on; see Cage & Giant-Size...)
Marvel Comics Group: No. 17, Feb, 1974 - No. 125, Sept, 1986

17-Luke Cage continues; Iron Man app. 2 4 6 11 14 18
18-20: 18-Last 20¢ issue 2 4 6 8 10 12
21-30 1 2 3 5 6 8
30-(30¢-c variant, limited distribution)(4/76) 2 4 6 8 10 12
31-46: 31-Part Neal Adams-i. 34-Last 25¢ issue. 36-r/Hero For Hire #12.
41-1st app. Thunderbolt. 45-Starlin-c. 1 2 3 4 5 7
31-34-(30¢-c variants, limited distribution)(5-8/76) 1 3 4 6 8 10
44-46-(35¢-c variants, limited distribution)(6-8/77) 1 3 4 6 8 10
47-Barry Smith-a 1 2 3 5 7 9
47-(35¢-c variant, limited distribution)(10/77) 2 4 6 9 11 14
48-50-Byrne-a(p); 48-Power Man/Iron Fist 1st meet. 50-Iron Fist joins Cage
2 4 6 8 10 12

GD VG FN VF VF/NM NM-
2.0 4.0 6.0 8.0 9.0 9.2

51-56,58-65,67-77: 58-Intro El Aguila. 75-Double size. 77-Daredevil app. 4.00
57-New X-Men app. (6/79) 3 6 9 16 20 25
66-2nd app. Sabretooth (see Iron Fist #14) 4 8 12 24 32 40
78,84: 78-3rd app. Sabretooth (cameo under cloak). 84-4th app. Sabretooth
2 4 6 14 18 22
79-83,85-99,101-124: 87-Moon Knight app. 109-The Reaper app. 3.00
100,125-Double size: 100-Origin K'un L'un. 125-Death of Iron Fist 4.00
Annual 1(1976)-Punisher cameo in flashback 2 4 6 10 13 16

NOTE: ***Austin*** *c-102i.* ***Byrne*** *a-48-50; c-102, 104, 106, 107, 112-116.* ***Kane*** *c(p)-24, 25, 28, 48.* ***Miller*** *a-68, 76(2 pgs.); c-66-68, 70-74, 80i.* ***Mooney*** *a-38i, 53i, 55i.* ***Nebres*** *a-76p.* ***Nino*** *a-42i, 43i.* ***Perez*** *a-27.* ***B. Smith*** *a-47i.* ***Tuska*** *a(p)-17, 20, 24, 26, 28, 29, 36, 47. Painted c-75, 100.*

POWER OF PRIME
Malibu Comics (Ultraverse): July, 1995 - No. 4, Nov, 1995 ($2.50, lim. series)

1-4 2.50

POWER OF SHAZAM!, THE (See SHAZAM!)
DC Comics: 1994 (Painted graphic novel) (Prequel to new series)

Hardcover-($19.95)-New origin of Shazam!; Ordway painted-c/a & script
3 6 9 16 20 25
Softcover-($7.50), Softcover-($9.95)-New-c. 2 4 6 8 10 12

POWER OF SHAZAM!, THE
DC Comics: Mar, 1995 - No. 47, Mar, 1999 ($1.50/$1.75/$1.95/$2.50)

1-Jerry Ordway scripts begin 4.00
2-20: 4-Begin $1.75-c. 6:Re-intro of Capt. Nazi. 8-Re-intro of Spy Smasher, Bulletman & Minuteman; Swan-a (7 pgs.). 11-Re-intro of Ibis, Swan-a(2 pgs.). 14-Gil Kane-a(p). 20-Superman-c/app.; "Final Night" 3.00
21-47: 21-Plastic Man-c/app. 22-Batman-c/app. 35,36-X-over w/Starman #39,40. 38-41-Mr. Mind. 43-Bulletman app. 45-JLA-c/app. 2.50
#1,000,000 (11/98) 853rd Century x-over; Ordway-c/s/a 3.00
Annual 1 (1996, $2.95)-Legends of the Dead Earth story; Jerry Ordway-c; Mike Manley-a 4.00

POWER OF STRONGMAN, THE (Also see Strongman)
AC Comics: 1989 ($2.95)

1-Powell G.A.-r 3.00

POWER OF THE ATOM (See Secret Origins #29)
DC Comics: Aug, 1988 - No. 18, Nov, 1989 ($1.00)

1-18: 6-Chronos returns; Byrne-p. 9-JLI app. 2.25

POWER PACHYDERMS
Marvel Comics: Sept, 1989 ($1.25, one-shot)

1-Elephant super-heroes; parody of X-Men, Elektra, & 3 Stooges 2.25

POWER PACK
Marvel Comics Group: Aug, 1984 - No. 62, Feb, 1991

1-($1.00, 52 pgs.)-Origin & 1st app. Power Pack 3.00
2-18,20-26,28,30-45,47-62 2.25
19-(52 pgs.)-Cloak & Dagger, Wolverine app. 3.00
27-Mutant massacre; Wolverine & Sabretooth app. 5.00
29,46: 29-Spider-Man & Hobgoblin app. 46-Punisher app. 2.50
Graphic Novel: Power Pack & Cloak & Dagger: Shelter From the Storm ('89, SC, $7.95) Velluto/Farmer-a 10.00
...Holiday Special 1 (2/92, $2.25, 68 pgs.) 2.25

NOTE: ***Austin*** *scripts-53.* ***Mignola*** *c-20.* ***Morrow*** *a-51.* ***Spiegle*** *a-55i.* ***Williamson*** *a(i)-43, 50, 52.*

POWER PACK (Volume 2)
Marvel Comics: Aug, 2000 - No. 4, Nov, 2000 ($2.99, limited series)

1-4-Doran & Austin-c/a 3.00

POWERPUFF GIRLS, THE (Also see Cartoon Network Starring... #1)
DC Comics: May, 2000 - Present ($1.99/$2.25)

1 4.00
2-55,57: 25-Pin-ups by Allred, Byrne, Baker, Mignola, Hernandez, Warren 2.25
56-($2.95) Bonus pages; Mojo Jojo-c 3.00
...Double Whammy (12/00, $3.95) r/#1,2 & a Dexter's Lab story 4.00
...Movie: The Comic (9/02, $2.95) Movie adaptation; Phil Moy & Chris Cook-a 3.00

POWER RANGERS ZEO (TV)(Saban's...)(Also see Saban's Mighty Morphin Power Rangers)
Image Comics (Extreme Studios): Aug, 1996 ($2.50)

1-Based on TV show 2.50

POWER RECORD COMICS (See the Promotional Comics section)

POWERS
Image Comics: 2000 - No. 37, Feb, 2004 ($2.95)

1-Bendis-s/Oeming-a; murder of Retro Girl 1 3 4 6 8 10

Powers #36 © Jinxworld

Preacher Special: Cassidy: Blood & Whiskey #1 © Ennis & Dillon

Predator: Primal #1 © 20th Century Fox

GD VG FN VF VF/NM NM-
2.0 4.0 6.0 8.0 9.0 9.2

2-6: 6-End of Retro Girl arc. 5.00
7-14: 7-Warren Ellis app. 12-14-Death of Olympia 3.50
15-37: 31-36-Origin of the Powers 3.00
Annual 1 (2001, $3.95) 4.00
....: Anarchy TPB (11/03, $14.95) r/#21-24; interviews, sketchbook, cover gallery 15.00
...Coloring/Activity Book (2001, $1.50, B&W, 8 x 10.5") Oeming-a 2.25
....: Little Deaths TPB (2002, $19.95) r/#7,12-14, Ann. #1, Coloring/Activity Book; sketch pages, cover gallery 20.00
....: Roleplay TPB (2001, $13.95) r/#8-11; sketchbook, cover gallery 14.00
... Scriptbook (2001, $19.95) scripts for #1-11; Oeming sketches 20.00
....: Supergroup TPB (2003, $19.95) r/#15-20; sketchbook, cover gallery 20.00
...: Who Killed Retro Girl TPB (2000, $21.95) r/#1-6; sketchbook, cover gallery, and promotional strips from Comic Shop News 22.00

POWERS
Marvel Comics (Icon): Jul, 2004 - Present ($2.95)

1-6-Bendis-s/Oeming-a 3.00

POWERS THAT BE (Becomes Star Seed No.7 on)
Broadway Comics: Nov, 1995 - No. 6, June, 1996 ($2.50)

1-6: 1-Intro of Fatale & Star Seed. 6-Begin $2.95-c. 3.00
Preview Editions 1-3 (9/95 - 11/95, B&W) 2.50

POW MAGAZINE (Bob Sproul's) (Satire Magazine)
Humor-Vision: Aug, 1966 - No. 3, Feb, 1967 (30¢)

1,2: 2-Jones-a 4 8 12 29 40 50
3-Wrightson-a 6 12 18 38 52 65

PREACHER
DC Comics (Vertigo): Apr, 1995 - No. 66, Oct, 2000 ($2.50, mature)

nn-Preview 2 4 6 12 16 20
1 ($2.95)-Ennis scripts, Dillon-a & Fabry-c in all; 1st app. Jesse, Tulip, & Cassidy
2 4 6 9 11 14
2,3: 2-1st app. Saint of Killers. 1 2 3 5 7 9
4,5 1 2 3 4 5 7
6-10 5.00
11-20: 12-Polybagged w/videogame w/Ennis text. 13-Hunters storyline begins; ends #17. 19-Saint of Killers app.; begin "Crusaders", ends #24 4.00
21-25: 21-24-Saint of Killers app. 25-Origin of Cassidy. 3.00
26-49,52-64: 52-Tulip origin 2.50
50-($3.75) Pin-ups by Jim Lee, Bradstreet, Quesada and Palmiotti 3.75
51-Includes preview of 100 Bullets; Tulip origin 4.00
65,66-($3.75) 65-Almost everyone dies. 66-Final issue 5.00
Alamo (2001, $17.95, TPB) r/#59-66; Fabry-c 18.00
All Hell's a-Coming (2000, $17.95, TPB)-r/#51-58, ...:Tall in the Saddle 18.00
...: Dead or Alive HC (2000, $29.95) Gallery of Glenn Fabry's cover paintings for every Preacher issue; commentary by Fabry & Ennis 30.00
...: Dead or Alive SC (2003, $19.95) 20.00
Dixie Fried (1998, $14.95, TPB)-r/#27-33, Special: Cassidy 15.00
Gone To Texas (1996, $14.95, TPB)-r/#1-7; Fabry-c 15.00
Proud Americans (1997, $14.95, TPB)-r/#18-26; Fabry-c 15.00
Salvation (1999, $14.95, TPB)-r/#41-50; Fabry-c 15.00
Until the End of the World (1996, $14.95, TPB)-r/#8-17; Fabry-c 15.00
War in the Sun (1999, $14.95, TPB)-r/#34-40 15.00

PREACHER SPECIAL: CASSIDY: BLOOD & WHISKEY
DC Comics (Vertigo): 1998 ($5.95, one-shot)

1-Ennis-scripts/Fabry-c /Dillon-a 6.00

PREACHER SPECIAL: ONE MAN'S WAR
DC Comics (Vertigo): Mar, 1998 ($4.95, one-shot)

1-Ennis-scripts/Fabry-c /Snejbjerg-a 5.00

PREACHER SPECIAL: SAINT OF KILLERS
DC Comics (Vertigo): Aug, 1996 - No. 4, Nov, 1996 ($2.50, lim. series, mature)

1-4: Ennis-scripts/Fabry-c. 1,2-Pugh-a. 3,4-Ezquerra-a 3.00
1-Signed & numbered 20.00

PREACHER SPECIAL: THE GOOD OLD BOYS
DC Comics (Vertigo): Aug, 1997 ($4.95, one-shot, mature)

1-Ennis-scripts/Fabry-c /Esquerra-a 5.00

PREACHER SPECIAL: THE STORY OF YOU-KNOW-WHO
DC Comics (Vertigo): Dec, 1996 ($4.95, one-shot, mature)

1-Ennis-scripts/Fabry-c/Case-a 5.00

PREACHER: TALL IN THE SADDLE
DC Comics (Vertigo): 2000 ($5.95, one-shot)

GD VG FN VF VF/NM NM-
2.0 4.0 6.0 8.0 9.0 9.2

1-Ennis-scripts/Fabry-c/Dillon-a; early romance of Tulip and Jesse 6.00

PREDATOR (Also see Aliens Vs. ..., Batman vs. ..., Dark Horse Comics, & Dark Horse Presents)
Dark Horse Comics: June, 1989 - No. 4, Mar, 1990 ($2.25, limited series)

1-Based on movie; 1st app. Predator 1 2 3 4 5 7
1-2nd printing 3.00
2 5.00
3,4 4.00
Trade paperback (1990, $12.95)-r/#1-4 13.00

PREDATOR: (title series) **Dark Horse Comics**

--BAD BLOOD, 12/93 - No. 4, 1994 ($2.50) 1-4 3.00
--BIG GAME, 3/91 - No. 4, 6/91 ($2.50) 1-4: 1-3-Contain 2 Dark Horse trading cards 3.00
--BLOODY SANDS OF TIME, 2/92 - No. 2, 2/92 ($2.50) 1,2-Dan Barry-c/a(p)/scripts 3.00
--CAPTIVE, 4/98 ($2.95, one-shot) 1 3.00
--COLD WAR, 9/91 - No. 4, 12/91 ($2.50) 1-4: All have painted-c 3.00
--DARK RIVER, 7/96 - No.4, 10/96 ($2.95)1-4: Miran Kim-c 3.00
--HELL & HOT WATER, 4/97 - No. 3, 6/97 ($2.95) 1-3 3.00
--HELL COME A WALKIN', 2/98 - No. 2, 3/98 ($2.95) 1,2-In the Civil War 3.00
--HOMEWORLD, 3/99 - No. 4, 6/99 ($2.95) 1-4 3.00
--INVADERS FROM THE FOURTH DIMENSION, 7/94 ($3.95, one-shot, 52 pgs.) 1 4.00
--JUNGLE TALES. 3/95 ($2.95t) 1-r/Dark Horse Comics 3.00
--KINDRED, 12/96 - No. 4, 3/97 ($2.50) 1-4 3.00
--NEMESIS, 12/97 - No. 2, 1/98 ($2.95) 1,2-Predator in Victorian England; Taggart-c 3.00
--PRIMAL, 7/97 - No. 2, 8/97 ($2.95) 1,2 3.00
--RACE WAR (See Dark Horse Presents #67), 2/93 - No. 4,10/93 ($2.50, color)
1-4,0: 1-4-Dorman painted-c #1-4, 0(4/930 3.00
--STRANGE ROUX, 11/96 ($2.95, one-shot) 1 3.00
--XENOGENESIS (Also see Aliens Xenogenesis), 8/99 - No. 4, 11/99 ($2.95)
1,2-Edginton-s 3.00

PREDATOR 2
Dark Horse Comics: Feb, 1991 - No. 2, June, 1991 ($2.50, limited series)

1,2: 1-Adapts movie; both w/trading cards & photo-c 3.00

PREDATOR VS. JUDGE DREDD
Dark Horse Comics: Oct, 1997 - No. 3 ($2.50, limited series)

1-3-Wagner-s/Alcatena-a/Bolland-c 3.00

PREDATOR VS. MAGNUS ROBOT FIGHTER
Dark Horse/Valiant: Oct, 1992 - No. 2, 1993 ($2.95, limited series)
(1st Dark Horse/Valiant x-over)

1,2: (Reg.)-Barry Smith-c; Lee Weeks-a. 2-w/trading cards 3.00
1 (Platinum edition, 11/92)-Barry Smith-c 10.00

PREHISTORIC WORLD (See Classics Illustrated Special Issue)

PREMIERE (See Charlton Premiere)

PRESTO KID, THE (See Red Mask)

PRETTY BOY FLOYD (See On the Spot)

PREZ (See Cancelled Comic Cavalcade, Sandman #54 & Supergirl #10)
National Periodical Publications: Aug-Sept, 1973 - No. 4, Feb-Mar, 1974

1-Origin; Joe Simon scripts 3 6 9 18 24 30
2-4 2 4 6 11 14 18

PRICE, THE (See Eclipse Graphic Album Series)

PRIDE & JOY
DC Comics (Vertigo): July, 1997 - No. 4, Oct, 1997 (2.50, limited series)

1-4-Ennis-s 2.50
TPB (2004, $14.95) r/#1-4 15.00

PRIDE AND THE PASSION, THE
Dell Publishing Co.: No. 824, Aug, 1957

Four Color 824-Movie, Frank Sinatra & Cary Grant photo-c
10 20 30 73 107 140

PRIDE OF THE YANKEES, THE (See Real Heroes & Sport Comics)
Magazine Enterprises: 1949 (The Life of Lou Gehrig)

nn-Photo-c; Ogden Whitney-a 81 162 243 506 778 1050

PRIEST (Also see Asylum)
Maximum Press: Aug, 1996 - No. 2, Oct, 1996 ($2.99)

Prime #4 © MAL

Prince Valiant #4 © KING

Prize Comics #29 © PRIZE

	GD	VG	FN	VF	VF/NM	NM-
	2.0	4.0	6.0	8.0	9.0	9.2

1,2 — 3.00

PRIMAL FORCE
DC Comics: No. 0, Oct, 1994 - No. 14, Dec, 1995 ($1.95/$2.25)

0-14: 0- Teams Red Tornado, Golem, Jack O'Lantern, Meridian & Silver Dragon. 9-begin $2.25-c — 2.25

PRIMAL MAN (See The Crusaders)

PRIMAL RAGE
Sirius Entertainment: 1996 ($2.95)

1-Dark One-c; based of video game — 3.00

PRIME (See Break-Thru, Flood Relief & Ultraforce)
Malibu Comics (Ultraverse): June, 1993 - No. 26, Aug, 1995 ($1.95/$2.50)

1-1st app. Prime; has coupon for Ultraverse Premiere #0 — 3.00
1-With coupon missing — 2.25
1-Full cover holographic edition; 1st of kind w/Hardcase #1 & Strangers #1 — 6.00
1-Ultra 5,000 edition w/silver ink-c — 4.00
2-11,14-26: 2-Polybagged w/card & coupon for U. Premiere #0. 3,4-Prototype app. 4-Direct sale w/o card.4-($2.50)-Newsstand ed. polybagged w/card. 5-($2.50, 48 pgs.)-Rune flip-c/story part B by Barry Smith; see Sludge #1 for 1st app. Rune; 3-pg. Night Man preview. 6-Bill & Chelsea Clinton app. 7-Break-Thru x-over. 8-Mantra app.; 2-pg. origin Freex by Simonson. 10-Firearm app.15-Intro Papa Verite; Perez-c/a. 16-Intro Turbo Charge — 2.50
12-($3.50, 68 pgs.)-Flip book w/Ultraverse Premiere #3; silver foil logo — 3.50
13-($2.95, 52 pgs.)-Variant covers — 3.00
...: Gross and Disgusting 1 (10/94, $3.95)-Boris-c; "Annual" on cover, published monthly in indicia — 4.00
...Month "Ashcan" (8/94, 75¢)-Boris-c — 2.25
... Time: A Prime Collection (1994, $9.95)-r/1-4 — 10.00
...Vs. The Incredible Hulk (1995)-mail away limited edition — 10.00
...Vs. The Incredible Hulk Premium edition — 10.00
...Vs. The Incredible Hulk Super Premium edition — 15.00
NOTE: ***Perez*** *a-15; c-15, 16.*

PRIME (Also see Black September)
Malibu Comics (Ultraverse): Infinity, Sept, 1995 - V2#15, Dec, 1996 ($1.50)

Infinity, V2#1-8: Post Black September storyline. 6-8-Solitaire app. 9-Breyfogle-c/a. 10-12-Ramos-c. 15-Lord Pumpkin app. — 2.25
Infinity Signed Edition (2,000 printed) — 5.00

PRIME/CAPTAIN AMERICA
Malibu Comics: Mar, 1996 ($3.95, one-shot)

1-Norm Breyfogle-a — 4.00

PRIME8: CREATION
Two Morrows Publishing: July, 2001 ($3.95, B&W)

1-Neal Adams-c — 4.00

PRIMER (Comico...)
Comico: Oct (no month), 1982 - No. 6, Feb, 1984 (B&W)

	GD	VG	FN	VF	VF/NM	NM-
1 (52 pgs.)	2	4	6	9	11	14
2-1st app. Grendel & Argent by Wagner	10	20	30	70	100	130
3,4	1	3	4	6	8	10
5-1st Sam Kieth art in comics ('83) & 1st The Maxx	4	8	12	22	30	38
6-Intro & 1st app. Evangeline	2	4	6	10	12	15

PRIMORTALS (Leonard Nimoy's...)

PRIMUS (TV)
Charlton Comics: Feb, 1972 - No. 7, Oct, 1972

	GD	VG	FN	VF	VF/NM	NM-
1-Staton-a in all	2	4	6	12	16	20
2-7: 6-Drug propaganda story	2	4	6	9	11	14

PRINCE NAMOR, THE SUB-MARINER (Also see Namor ...)
Marvel Comics Group: Sept, 1984 - No. 4, Dec, 1984 (Limited-series)

1-4 — 2.50

PRINCESS SALLY (Video game)
Archie Publications: Apr, 1995 - No. 3, June, 1995 ($1.50, limited series)

1-3: Spin-off from Sonic the Hedgehog — 4.00

PRINCE VALIANT (See Ace Comics, Comics Reading Libraries *in the Promotional Comics section*, & King Comics #146, 147)
David McKay Publ./Dell: No. 26, 1941; No. 67, June, 1954 - No. 900, May, 1958

	GD	VG	FN	VF	VF/NM	NM-
Feature Books 26 ('41)-Harold Foster-c/a; newspaper strips reprinted, pgs. 1-28,30-63; color & 68 pgs; Foster cover is only original comic book artwork by him	94	188	282	588	907	1225
Four Color 567 ((6/54)(#1)-By Bob Fuje-Movie, photo-c	12	24	36	87	134	180
Four Color 650 (9/55), 699 (4/56), 719 (8/56),-Fuje-a	8	16	24	58	82	105
Four Color 788 (4/57), 849 (1/58), 900-Fuje-a	8	16	24	55	78	100

PRINCE VALIANT
Marvel Comics: Dec, 1994 - No. 4, Mar, 1995 ($3.95, limited series)

1-4; Kaluta-c in all. — 4.00

PRINCE VANDAL
Triumphant Comics: Nov, 1993 - Apr?, 1994 ($2.50)

1-6: 1,2-Triumphant Unleashed x-over — 2.50

PRIORITY: WHITE HEAT
AC Comics: 1986 - No. 2, 1986 ($1.75, mini-series)

1,2-Bill Black-a — 3.00

PRISCILLA'S POP
Dell Publishing Co.: No. 569, June, 1954 - No. 799, May, 1957

	GD	VG	FN	VF	VF/NM	NM-
Four Color 569 (#1), 630 (5/55), 704 (5/56),799	4	8	12	28	38	48

PRISON BARS (See Behind...)

PRISON BREAK!
Avon Per./Realistic No. 3 on: Sept, 1951 - No. 5, Sept, 1952 (Painted c-3)

	GD	VG	FN	VF	VF/NM	NM-
1-Wood-c & 1 pg.; has-r/Saint #7 retitled Michael Strong Private Eye	43	86	129	262	401	540
2-Wood-c; Kubert-a; Kinstler inside front-c	33	66	99	190	275	360
3-Orlando, Check-a; c-/Avon paperback #179	27	54	81	154	222	290
4,5: 4-Kinstler-c & inside f/c; Lawrence, Lazarus-a. 5-Kinstler-c; Infantino-a	24	48	72	135	195	255

PRISONER, THE (TV)
DC Comics: 1988 - No. 4, 1989 ($3.50, squarebound, mini-series)

1-4 (Books a-d) — 3.50

PRISON RIOT
Avon Periodicals: 1952

	GD	VG	FN	VF	VF/NM	NM-
1-Marijuana Murders-1 pg. text; Kinstler-c; 2 Kubert illos on text pages	30	60	90	170	245	320

PRISON TO PRAISE
Logos International: 1974 (35¢) (Religious, Christian)

	GD	VG	FN	VF	VF/NM	NM-
nn-True Story of Merlin R. Carothers	2	4	6	10	12	15

PRIVATE BUCK
Dell Publishing Co.: No. 21, 1941 - No. 12, 1942

	GD	VG	FN	VF	VF/NM	NM-
Large Feature Comic 21 (#1)(1941)(Series I), 22 (1941)(Series I), 12 (1942)(Series II)	17	34	51	95	135	175

PRIVATEERS
Vanguard Graphics: Aug, 1987 - No. 2, 1987 ($1.50)

1,2 — 2.25

PRIVATE EYE (Cover title: Rocky Jorden...#6-8)
Atlas Comics (MCI): Jan, 1951 - No. 8, March, 1952

	GD	VG	FN	VF	VF/NM	NM-
1-Cover title: Crime Cases... #1-5	22	44	66	123	177	230
2,3-Tuska c/a(3)	14	28	42	79	110	140
4-8	11	22	33	62	84	105

NOTE: ***Henkel*** *a-6(3), 7; c-7.* ***Sinnott*** *a-6.*

PRIVATE EYE (See Mike Shayne...)

PRIVATE SECRETARY
Dell Publishing Co.: Dec-Feb, 1962-63 - No. 2, Mar-May, 1963

	GD	VG	FN	VF	VF/NM	NM-
1	4	8	12	25	33	42
2	3	6	9	19	25	32

PRIVATE STRONG (See The Double Life of...)

PRIZE COMICS (...Western #69 on) (Also see Treasure Comics)
Prize Publications: March, 1940 - No. 68, Feb-Mar, 1948

	GD	VG	FN	VF	VF/NM	NM-
1-Origin Power Nelson, The Futureman & Jupiter, Master Magician; Ted O'Neil, Secret Agent M-11, Jaxon of the Jungle, Bucky Brady & Storm Curtis begin (1st app. of each)	254	508	762	1588	2444	3300
2-The Black Owl begins (1st app.)	112	224	336	700	1075	1450
3,4: 4-Robot-c	94	188	282	588	907	1225
5,6: Dr. Dekkar, Master of Monsters app. in each	87	174	261	544	835	1125
7-(Scarce)-1st app. The Green Lama (12/40); Black Owl by S&K; origin/1st app. Dr. Frost & Frankenstein; Capt. Gallant, The Great Voodini & Twist Turner begin;	192	384	576	1200	1850	2500
8,9-Black Owl & Ted O'Neil by S&K	96	192	288	600	925	1250
10-12,14,15: 11-Origin Bulldog Denny. 14-War-c	71	142	213	444	685	925

Professor Xavier and the X-Men #6 © MAR

Promethea #1 © ABC

Protectors #18 © MAL

	GD 2.0	VG 4.0	FN 6.0	VF 8.0	VF/NM 9.0	NM- 9.2
13-Yank & Doodle begin (8/41, origin/1st app.)	75	150	225	469	722	975
16-20: 16-Spike Mason begins	66	132	198	413	637	860
21-24: 21-War-c. 22-Statue of Liberty jap attack war-c. 23-Uncle Sam patriotic war-c. 24-Lincoln statue patriotic-c	48	96	144	293	447	600
25-30: 25-28 War-c. 26-Liberty Bell-c	33	66	99	190	275	360
31-33: 31-Jap war-c	28	56	84	158	229	300
34-Origin Airmale, Yank & Doodle; The Black Owl joins army, Yank & Doodle's father assumes Black Owl's role	32	64	96	184	267	350
35-36,38-40: 35-Flying Fist & Bingo begin	23	46	69	132	191	250
37-Intro. Stampy, Airmale's sidekick; Hitler-c	40	80	120	230	335	440
41-50: 45-Yank & Doodle learn Black Owl's I.D. (their father). 48-Prince Ra begins	18	36	54	102	146	190
51-62,64,67,68: 53-Transvestism story. 55-No Frankenstein. 57-X-Mas-c. 64-Black Owl retires	15	30	45	86	123	160
63-Simon & Kirby c/a	19	38	57	107	154	200
65,66-Frankenstein-c by Briefer	16	32	48	92	131	170

NOTE: ***Briefer** a 7-on; c-65, 66. **J. Binder** a-16; c-21-29. **Guardineer** a-62. **Kiefer** c-62. **Palais** c-68. **Simon & Kirby** c-63, 75, 83.*

PRIZE COMICS WESTERN (Formerly Prize Comics #1-68)
Prize Publications (Feature): No. 69(V7#2), Apr-May, 1948 - No. 119, Nov-Dec, 1956 (No. 69-84: 52 pgs.)

	GD 2.0	VG 4.0	FN 6.0	VF 8.0	VF/NM 9.0	NM- 9.2
69(V7#2)	15	30	45	85	120	155
70-75: 74-Kurtzman-a (8 pgs.)	13	26	39	74	102	130
76-Randolph Scott photo-c; "Canadian Pacific" movie adaptation	14	28	42	79	110	140
77-Photo-c; Severin/Elder, Mart Bailey-a; "Streets of Laredo" movie adaptation	13	26	39	74	102	130
78-Photo-c; S&K-a, 10 pgs.; Severin, Mart Bailey-a; "Bullet Code", & "Roughshod" movie adaptations	19	38	57	107	154	200
79-Photo-c; Kurtzman-a, 8 pgs.; Severin/Elder, Severin, Mart Bailey-a; "Stage To Chino" movie adaptation w/George O'Brien	19	38	57	107	154	200
80-82-Photo-c; 80,81-Severin/Elder-a(2). 82-1st app. The Preacher by Mart Bailey; Severin/Elder-a(3)	14	28	42	79	110	140
83,84	11	22	33	64	87	110
85-1st app. American Eagle by John Severin & begins (V9#6, 1-2/51)	25	50	75	141	203	265
86,101-105, 109-Severin/Williamson-a	13	26	39	74	102	130
87-99,110,111-Severin/Elder-a(2-3) each	14	28	42	79	110	140
100	15	30	45	83	117	150
106-108,112	10	20	30	56	73	90
113-Williamson/Severin-a(2)/Frazetta?	14	28	42	79	110	140
114-119: Drifter series in all; by Mort Meskin #114-118	9	18	27	52	66	80

NOTE: ***Fass** a-81. **Severin & Elder** c-84-99. **Severin** a-72, 75, 77-79, 83-86, 96, 97, 100-105; c-92,100-109(most), 110-119. **Simon & Kirby** c-75, 83.*

PRIZE MYSTERY
Key Publications: May, 1955 - No. 3, Sept, 1955

	GD 2.0	VG 4.0	FN 6.0	VF 8.0	VF/NM 9.0	NM- 9.2
1	11	22	33	62	84	105
2,3	8	16	24	46	58	70

PRO, THE
Image Comics: July, 2002 ($5.95, squarebound, one-shot)

1-Ennis-s/Conner & Palmiotti-a; prostitute gets super-powers 8.00
1-Second printing with different cover 6.00
Hardcover Edition (10/04, $14.95) oversized reprint plus new 8 pg. story; sketch pages 15.00

PROFESSIONAL FOOTBALL (See Charlton Sport Library)

PROFESSOR COFFIN
Charlton Comics: No. 19, Oct, 1985 - No. 21, Feb, 1986

	GD 2.0	VG 4.0	FN 6.0	VF 8.0	VF/NM 9.0	NM- 9.2
19-21: Wayne Howard-a(r); low print run	1	2	3	5	6	8

PROFESSOR OM
Innovation Publishing: May, 1990 - No. 2, 1990 ($2.50, limited series)

1,2-East Meets West spin-off 2.50

PROFESSOR XAVIER AND THE X-MEN (Also see X-Men, 1st series)
Marvel Comics: Nov, 1995 - No. 18 (99¢)

1-18: Stories featuring the Original X-Men. 2-vs. The Blob. 5-Vs. the Original Brotherhood of Evil Mutants. 10-Vs. The Avengers 2.25

PROJECT, THE
DC Comics (Paradox Press): No. 1,2, 1998? ($5.59)

1,2 6.00

PROJECT A-KO (Manga)
Malibu Comics: Mar, 1994 - No. 4, June, 1994 ($2.95)

1-4-Based on anime film 3.00

PROJECT A-KO 2 (Manga)
CPM Comics: May, 1995 - No. 3, Aug, 1995 ($2.95, limited series)

1-3 3.00

PROJECT A-KO VERSUS THE UNIVERSE (Manga)
CPM Comics: Oct, 1995 - No. 5, June, 1996 ($2.95, limited series, bi-monthly)

1-5 3.00

PROJECT: HERO
Vanguard Graphics (Canadian): Aug, 1987 ($1.50)

1 2.25

PROMETHEA
America's Best Comics: Aug, 1999 - No. 32 ($3.50/$2.95)

1-Alan Moore-s/Williams III & Gray-a; Alex Ross painted-c 3.50
1-Variant-c by Williams III & Gray 3.50
2-30-($2.95): 7-Villarrubia photo-a. 10-"Sex, Stars & Serpents". 26-28-Tom Strong app. 27-Cover swipe of Superman vs. Spider-Man treasury ed. 3.00
Book 1 Hardcover ($24.95, dust jacket) r/#1-6 25.00
Book 1 TPB ($14.95) r/#1-6 15.00
Book 2 Hardcover ($24.95, dust jacket) r/#7-12 25.00
Book 2 TPB ($14.95) r/#7-12 15.00
Book 3 Hardcover ($24.95, dust jacket) r/#13-18 25.00
Book 3 TPB ($14.95) r/#13-18 15.00

PROMETHEUS (VILLAINS) (Leads into JLA #16,17)
DC Comics: Feb, 1998 ($1.95, one-shot)

1-Origin & 1st app.; Morrison-s/Pearson-c 3.00

PROPELLERMAN
Dark Horse Comics: Jan, 1993 - No. 8, Mar, 1994 ($2.95, limited series)

1-8: 2,4,8-Contain 2 trading cards 3.00

PROPHET (See Youngblood #2)
Image Comics (Extreme Studios): Oct, 1993 - No. 10, 1995 ($1.95)

1-($2.50)-Liefeld/Panosian-c/a; 1st app. Mary McCormick; Liefeld scripts in 1-4; #1-3 contain coupons for Prophet #0 2.50
1-Gold foil embossed-c edition rationed to dealers 4.00
2-10: 2-Liefeld-c(p). 3-1st app. Judas. 4-1st app. Omen; Black and White Pt. 3 by Thibert. 4-Alternate-c by Stephen Platt. 5,6-Platt-c/a. 7-(9/94, $2.50)-Platt-c/a. 8-Bloodstrike app. 10-Polybagged w/trading card; Platt-c. 2.50
0-(7/94, $2.50)-San Diego Comic Con ed. (2200 copies) 3.00

PROPHET
Image Comics (Extreme Studios): V2#1, Aug, 1995 - No. 8 ($3.50)

V2#1-8: Dixon scripts in all. 1-4-Platt-a. 1-Boris-c; F. Miller variant-c. 4-Newmen app. 5,6-Wraparound-c 3.50
Annual 1 (9/95, $2.50)-Bagged w/Youngblood gaming card; Quesada-c 2.50
Babewatch Special 1 (12/95, $2.50)-Babewatch tie-in 2.50
1995 San Diego Edition-B&W preview of V2#1. 3.00
TPB-(1996, $12.95) r/#1-7 13.00

PROPHET (Volume 3)
Awesome Comics: Mar, 2000 ($2.99)

1-Flip-c by Jim Lee and Liefeld 3.00

PROPHET/CABLE
Image Comics (Extreme): Jan, 1997 - No. 2, Mar, 1997 ($3.50, limited series)

1,2-Liefeld-c/a: 2-#1 listed on cover 3.50

PROPHET/CHAPEL: SUPER SOLDIERS
Image Comics (Extreme): May, 1996 - No. 2, June, 1996 ($2.50, limited series)

1,2: 1-Two covers exist 2.50
1-San Diego Edition; B&W-c 2.50

PROPOSITION PLAYER
DC Comics (Vertigo): Dec, 1999 - No. 6, May, 2000 ($2.50, limited series)

1-6-Willingham-s/Guinan-a/Bolton-c 2.50
TPB (2003, $14.95) r/#1-6; intro. by James McManus 15.00

PROTECTORS (Also see The Ferret)
Malibu Comics: Sept, 1992 - No. 20, May, 1994 ($1.95-$2.95)

1-20 ($2.50, direct sale)-With poster & diff-c: 1-Origin; has 3/4 outer-c. 3-Polybagged w/Skycap 2.50
1-12 ($1.95, newsstand)-Without poster 2.25

PROTOTYPE (Also see Flood Relief & Ultraforce)

Proximity Effect © TCOW & Spacedog

Psycho #1 © Skywald

The Pulse #1 © MAR

GD	VG	FN	VF	VF/NM	NM-
2.0	4.0	6.0	8.0	9.0	9.2

Malibu Comics (Ultraverse): Aug, 1993 - No. 18, Feb, 1995 ($1.95/$2.50)
1-Holo-c 6.00
1-Ultra Limited silver foil-c 4.00
1-12,0,14-18: 3-($2.50, 48 pgs.)-Rune flip-c/story by B. Smith (3 pgs.). 4-Intro Wrath. 5-Break-Thru & Strangers x-over. 6-Arena cameo. 7,8-Arena-c/story. 12-(7/94). 0-(8/94, $2.50, 44 pgs.), 14(10/94) 2.50
13 (8/94, $3.50)-Flip book(Ultraverse Premiere #6) 3.50
Giant Size 1 (10/94, $2.50, 44 pgs.) 2.50

PROWLER (Also see Revenge of the...)
Eclipse Comics: July, 1987 - No. 4, Oct, 1987 ($1.75)
1-4: Snyder-c/a. 3,4-Origin 2.25

PROWLER, THE
Marvel Comics: Nov, 1994 ($1.75)
1-4: 1-Spider-Man app. 2.25

PROWLER IN "WHITE ZOMBIE", THE
Eclipse Comics: Oct, 1988 ($2.00, B&W, Baxter paper)
1-Adapts Bela Lugosi movie White Zombie 2.25

PROXIMITY EFFECT
Image Comics (Top Cow): Aug, 2004 ($9.99, graphic novel, one shot)
nn-Nakayama-a/Silvestri-c 10.00

PRUDENCE & CAUTION (Also see Dogs of War & Warriors of Plasm)
Defiant: May, 1994 - No. 2, June, 1994 ($3.50/$2.50)(Spanish versions exist)
1-($3.50, 52 pgs.)-Chris Claremont scripts in all 3.50
2-($2.50) 2.50

PRYDE AND WISDOM (Also see Excalibur)
Marvel Comics: Sept, 1996 - No. 3, Nov, 1996 ($1.95, limited series)
1-3: Warren Ellis scripts; Terry Dodson & Karl Story-c/a 2.25

PSCYTHE (Mark Texeira's ...)
Image Comics: Sept, 2004 - No. 2, Oct, 2004 ($3.95, B&W)
1,2-Mark Texeira-s/a; Industry of War back-up by Jordan Raskin 4.00

PSI-FORCE
Marvel Comics Group: Nov, 1986 - No. 32, June, 1989 (75¢/$1.50)
1-25: 11-13-Williamson-i 2.25
26-32 2.50
Annual 1 (10/87) 3.00

PSI-JUDGE ANDERSON
Fleetway Publications (Quality): 1989 - No. 15, 1990 ($1.95, B&W)
1-15 2.50

PSI-LORDS
Valiant: Sept, 1994 - No. 10, June, 1995 ($2.25)
1-($3.50)-Chromium wraparound-c 3.50
1-Gold 5.00
2-10: 3-Chaos Effect Epsilon Pt. 2 2.25

PSYBA-RATS (Also see Showcase '94 #3,4)
DC Comics: Apr, 1995-No. 3, June, 1995 ($2.50, limited series)
1-3 2.50

PSYCHO (Magazine) (Also see Nightmare)
Skywald Publ. Corp.: Jan, 1971 - No. 24, Mar, 1975 (68 pgs.; B&W)
1-All reprints 8 16 24 53 74 95
2-Origin & 1st app. The Heap, series begins 6 12 18 38 52 65
3-Frankenstein series by Adkins begins 5 10 15 33 44 55
4,7,9,10: 4-7-Squarebound. 4-1st Out of Chaos/Satan-c/s 4 8 12 29 40 50
8-(Squarebound)1st app. Edward & Mina Sartyros, the Human Gargoyles 5 10 15 36 48 60
11-18: 13-Cannabalism; 3 pgs of Christopher Lee as Dracula photos. 18-Injury to eye-c. 3 7 10 21 28 35
19-Origin Dracula. 4 8 12 22 30 38
20-24: 20-Severed Head-c. 22-1974 Fall Special; Reese, Wildey-a(r). 24-1975 Winter Special; Dave Sim scripts (1st pro work) 4 8 12 24 32 40
Annual 1 (1972)(68 pgs.) Dracula & the Heap app. 4 8 12 24 32 40
Yearbook (1974-nn)-Everett, Reese-a 3 6 9 19 25 32
NOTE: ***Boris*** *c-3, 5.* ***Buckler*** *a-2, 4, 5.* ***Gene Day*** *a-21, 23, 24.* ***Everett*** *a-3-6.* ***B. Jones*** *a-4.* ***Jeff Jones*** *a-6, 7, 9; c-12.* ***Kaluta*** *a-13.* ***Katz/Buckler*** *a-3.* ***Kim*** *a-24.* ***Morrow*** *a-1.* ***Reese*** *a-5.* ***Dave Sim*** *s-24.* ***Sutton*** *a-3.* ***Wildey*** *a-5.*

PSYCHOANALYSIS
E. C. Comics: Mar-Apr, 1955 - No. 4, Sept-Oct, 1955
1-All Kamen-c/a; not approved by code 19 38 57 143 207 270
2-4-Kamen-c/a in all 13 26 39 98 144 190

PSYCHOANALYSIS
Gemstone Publishing: Oct, 1999 - No. 4, Jan, 2000 ($2.50)
1-4-Reprints E.C. series 2.50
Annual 1 (2000, $10.95) r/#1-4 11.00

PSYCHOBLAST
First Comics: Nov, 1987 - No. 9, July, 1988 ($1.75)
1-9 2.25

PSYCHONAUTS
Marvel Comics (Epic Comics): Oct, 1993 - No. 4, Jan, 1994 ($4.95, lim. series)
1-4: American/Japanese co-produced comic 5.00

PSYLOCKE & ARCHANGEL CRIMSON DAWN
Marvel Comics: Aug, 1997 - No. 4, Nov, 1997 ($2.50, limited series)
1-4-Raab-s/Larroca-a(p) 2.50

P.T. 109 (See Movie Comics)

PUBLIC DEFENDER IN ACTION (Formerly Police Trap)
Charlton Comics: No. 7, Mar, 1956 - No. 12, Oct, 1957
7 10 20 30 60 80 100
8-12 8 16 24 40 50 60

PUBLIC ENEMIES
D. S. Publishing Co.: 1948 - No. 9, June-July, 1949
1-True Crime Stories 26 52 78 150 215 280
2-Used in **SOTI**, pg. 95 23 46 69 130 188 245
3-5: 5-Arrival date of 10/1/48 15 30 45 83 117 150
6,8,9 14 28 42 79 110 140
7-McWilliams-a; injury to eye panel 15 30 45 83 117 150

PUBO
Dark Horse Comics: Dec, 2002 - No. 3, Mar, 2003 ($3.50, B&W, limited series)
1-3-Leland Purvis-s/a 3.50

PUDGY PIG
Charlton Comics: Sept, 1958 - No. 2, Nov, 1958
1,2 3 6 9 19 25 32

PUFFED
Image Comics: Jul, 2003 - No. 3, Sept, 2003 ($2.95, B&W)
1-3-Layman-s/Crosland-a. 1-Two covers by Crosland & Quitely 3.00

PULP FANTASTIC (Vertigo V2K)
DC Comics (Vertigo): Feb, 2000 - No. 3, Apr, 2000 ($2.50, limited series)
1-3-Chaykin & Tischman-s/Burchett-a 2.50

PULP FICTION LIBRARY: MYSTERY IN SPACE
DC Comics: 1999 ($19.95, TPB)
nn-Reprints classic sci-fi stories from Mystery in Space, Strange Adventures, Real Fact Comics and My Greatest Adventure 20.00

PULSE, THE (Also see Alias and Deadline)
Marvel Comics: Apr, 2004 - Present ($2.99)
1-6: 1-5-Bendis-s/Bagley-a; Jessica Jones, Ben Urich, Kat Farrell app. 3-5-Green Goblin app. 6-Brent Anderson-a 3.00
Vol. 1: Thin Air (2004, $13.99) r/#1-5, gallery of cover layouts and sketches 14.00

PUMA BLUES
Aardvark One International/Mirage Studios #21 on: 1986 - No. 26, 1990 ($1.70-$1.75, B&W)
1-19, 21-26: 1-1st & 2nd printings. 25,26-$1.75-c 2.25
20 ($2.25)-By Alan Moore, Miller, Grell, others 3.00
Trade Paperback (12/88, $14.95) 15.00

PUMPKINHEAD: THE RITES OF EXORCISM (Movie)
Dark Horse Comics: 1993 - No. 2, 1993 ($2.50, limited series)
1,2: Based on movie; painted-c by McManus 2.50

PUNCH & JUDY COMICS
Hillman Per.: 1944; No. 2, Fall, 1944 - V3#2, 12/47; V3#3, 6/51 - V3#9, 12/51
V1#1-(60 pgs.) 23 46 69 132 191 250
2 13 26 39 74 102 130
3-12(7/46) 10 20 30 60 80 100
V2#1(8/49),3-9 8 16 24 46 58 70
V2#2,10-12, V3#1-Kirby-a(2) each 24 48 72 135 195 255
V3#2-Kirby-a 22 44 66 123 177 230

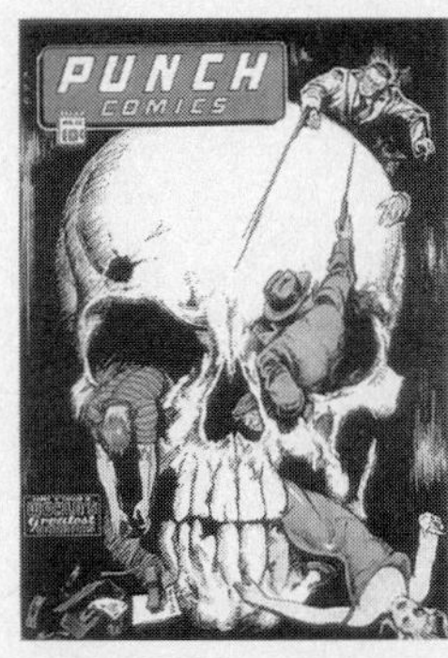

Punisher Official Movie Adaptation #1 © MAR

	GD 2.0	VG 4.0	FN 6.0	VF 8.0	VF/NM 9.0	NM- 9.2
3-9	8	16	24	46	58	70

PUNCH COMICS
Harry 'A' Chesler: 12/41; #2, 2/42; #9, 7/44 - #19, 10/46; #20, 7/47 - #23, 1/48

	GD	VG	FN	VF	VF/NM	NM-
1-Mr. E, The Sky Chief, Hale the Magician, Kitty Kelly begin	131	262	393	819	1260	1700
2-Captain Glory app.	87	174	261	544	835	1125
9-Rocketman & Rocket Girl & The Master Key begin	81	162	243	506	778	1050
10-Sky Chief app.; J. Cole-a; Master Key-r/Scoop #3	62	124	186	388	594	800
11-Origin Master Key-r/Scoop #1; Sky Chief, Little Nemo app.; Jack Cole-a; Fine-*ish* art by Sultan	55	110	165	344	532	720
12-Rocket Boy & Capt. Glory app; classic Skull-c	235	470	705	1469	2260	3050
13-Cover has list of 4 Chesler artists' names on tombstone	62	124	186	388	594	800
14,15,19,21: 21-Hypo needle story	55	110	165	340	520	700
16,17-Gag-c	52	104	156	317	484	650
18-Bondage-c; hypodermic panels	67	134	201	419	647	875
20-Unique cover with bare-breasted women. Rocket Girl-c	96	192	288	600	925	1250
22,23-Little Nemo-not by McCay. 22-Intro Baxter (teenage)(68 pgs.)	30	60	90	170	245	320

PUNCHY AND THE BLACK CROW
Charlton Comics: No. 10, Oct, 1985 - No. 12, Feb, 1986

10-12: Al Fago funny animal-r; low print run 6.00

PUNISHER (See Amazing Spider-Man #129, Blood and Glory, Born, Captain America #241, Classic Punisher, Daredevil #182-184, 257, Daredevil and the..., Ghost Rider V2#5, 6, Marc Spector #8 & 9, Marvel Preview #2, Marvel Super Action, Marvel Tales, Power Pack #46, Spectacular Spider-Man #81-83, 140, 141, 143 & new Strange Tales #13 & 14)

PUNISHER (The...)
Marvel Comics Group: Jan, 1986 - No. 5, May, 1986 (Limited series)

	GD	VG	FN	VF	VF/NM	NM-
1-Double size	2	4	6	11	14	18
2-5	1	3	4	6	8	10
Trade Paperback (1988)-r/#1-5						11.00
Circle of Blood TPB (8/01, $15.95) Zeck-c						16.00

NOTE: *Zeck a-1-4; c-1-5.*

PUNISHER (The...) (Volume 2)
Marvel Comics: July, 1987 - No. 104, July, 1995

	GD	VG	FN	VF	VF/NM	NM-
1	1	3	4	6	8	10
2-9: 8-Portacio/Williams-c/a begins, ends #18. 9-Scarcer, low dist.						6.00
10-Daredevil app; ties in w/Daredevil #257	1	3	4	6	8	10
11-74,76-85,87-89: 13-18-Kingpin app. 19-Stroman-c/a. 20-Portacio-c(p). 24-1st app. Shadowmasters. 25,50:($1.50,52 pgs.). 25-Shadowmasters app. 57-Photo-c; came w/outer-c (newsstand ed. w/o outer-c). 59-Punisher is severely cut & has skin grafts (has black skin). 60-62-Luke Cage app. 62-Punisher back to white skin. 68-Tarantula-c/story. 85-Prequel to Suicide Run Pt. 0. 87,88-Suicide Run Pt. 6 & 9						2.50
75-($2.75, 52 pgs.)-Embossed silver foil-c						3.00
86-($2.95, 52 pgs.)-Embossed & foil stamped-c; Suicide Run part 3						3.00
90-99: 90-bound-in cards. 99-Cringe app.						2.50
100,104: 100-($2.95, 68 pgs.). 104-Last issue						4.00
100-($3.95, 68 pgs.)-Foil cover						5.00
101-103: 102-Bullseye						3.50
"Ashcan" edition (75¢)-Joe Kubert-c						3.00
Annual 1-7 ('88-'94, 68 pgs.) 1-Evolutionary War x-over. 2-Atlantis Attacks x-over; Jim Lee-a(p) (back-up story, 6 pgs.); Moon Knight app. 4-Golden-c(p). 6-Bagged w/card.						3.00
...: A Man Named Frank (1994, $6.95, TPB)						7.00
...and Wolverine in African Saga nn (1989, $5.95, 52 pgs.)-Reprints Punisher War Journal #6 & 7; Jim Lee-c/a(r)						6.00
... Assassin Guild ('88, $6.95, graphic novel)						10.00
Back to School Special 1-3 (11/92-10/94, $2.95, 68 pgs.)						3.00
.../Batman: Deadly Knights (10/94, $4.95)						5.00
.../Black Widow: Spinning Doomsday's Web (1992, $9.95, graphic novel)						12.00
...Bloodlines nn (1991, $5.95, 68 pgs.)						6.00
...: Die Hard in the Big Easy nn ('92, $4.95, 52 pgs.)						5.00
...: Empty Quarter nn ('94, $6.95)						7.00
...G-Force nn (1992, $4.95, 52 pgs.)-Painted-c						5.00
...Holiday Special 1-3 (1/93-1/95,, 52 pgs.,68pgs.)-1-Foil-c						3.00
...Intruder Graphic Novel (1989, $14.95, hardcover)						20.00
...Intruder Graphic Novel (1991, $9.95, softcover)						12.00
...Invades the 'Nam: Final Invasion nn (2/94, $6.95)-J. Kubert-c & chapter break art; reprints The 'Nam #84 & unpublished #85,86						7.00
...Kingdom Gone Graphic Novel (1990, $16.95, hardcover)						20.00
...Meets Archie (8/94, $3.95, 52 pgs.)-Die cut-c; no ads; same contents as Archie Meets The Punisher						5.00
...Movie Special 1 (6/90, $5.95, squarebound, 68 pgs.) painted-c; Brent Anderson-a; contents intended for a 3 issue series which was advertised but not published						6.00
...: No Escape nn (1990, $4.95, 52 pgs.)-New-a						5.00
...Return to Big Nothing Graphic Novel (Epic, 1989, $16.95, hardcover)						25.00
...Return to Big Nothing Graphic Novel (Marvel, 1989, $12.95, softcover)						15.00
...The Prize nn (1990, $4.95, 68 pgs.)-New-a						5.00
Summer Special 1-4(8/91-7/94, 52 pgs.):1-No ads. 2-Bisley-c; Austin-a(i). 3-No ads						3.00

NOTE: ***Austin** c(i)-47, 48. **Cowan** c-39. **Golden** c-50, 85, 86, 100. **Heath** a-26, 27, 89, 90, 91; c-26, 27. **Quesada** c-56p, 62p. **Sienkiewicz** c-Back to School 1.**Stroman** a-76p(9 pgs.). **Williamson** a(i)-25, 60-62i, 64-70, 74, Annual 5; c(i)-62, 65-68.*

PUNISHER (Also see Double Edge)
Marvel Comics: Nov, 1995 - No. 18, Apr, 1997 ($2.95/$1.95/$1.50)

1 ($2.95)-Ostrander scripts begin; foil-c. 3.00
2-18: 7-Vs. S.H.I.E.L.D. 11-"Onslaught." 12-17-X-Cutioner-c/app. 17-Daredevil, Spider-Man-c/app. 2.50

PUNISHER (Marvel Knights)
Marvel Comics: Nov, 1998 - No. 4, Feb, 1999 ($2.99, limited series)

1-4: 1-Wrightson-a; Wrightson & Jusko-c 3.00
1-($6.95) DF Edition; Jae Lee variant-c 7.00

PUNISHER (Marvel Knights) (Volume 3)
Marvel Comics: Apr, 2000 - No. 12, Mar, 2001 ($2.99, limited series)

1-Ennis-s/Dillon & Palmiotti-a/Bradstreet-c 5.00
1-Bradstreet white variant-c 10.00
1-($6.95) DF Edition; Jurgens & Ordway variant-c 7.00
2-Two covers by Bradstreet & Dillon 3.00
3-($3.99) Bagged with Marvel Knights Genesis Edition; Daredevil app. 4.00
4-12: 9-11-The Russian app. 3.00
HC (6/02, $34.95) r/#1-12, Punisher Kills the Marvel Universe, and Marvel Knights Double Shot #1 35.00
.../Painkiller Jane (1/01, $3.50) Jusko-c; Ennis-s/Jusko and Dave Ross-a(p) 3.50
...: Welcome Back Frank TPB (4/01, $19.95) r/#1-12 20.00

PUNISHER (Marvel Knights) (Volume 4)
Marvel Comics: Aug, 2001 - No. 37, Feb, 2004 ($2.99)

1-Ennis-s/Dillon & Palmiotti-a/Bradstreet-c; The Russian app. 4.00
2-Two covers (Dillon & Bradstreet) Spider-Man-c/app. 3.00
3-37: 3-7-Ennis-s/Dillon-a. 9-12-Peyer-s/Gutierrez-a. 13,14-Ennis-s/Dilllon-a. 16,17-Wolverine app.; Robertson-a. 18-23,32-Dillon-a. 24-27-Mandrake-a. 27-Elektra app. 33-37-Spider-Man, Daredevil, & Wolverine app. 36,37-Hulk app. 3.00
...Army of One TPB (2/02, $15.95) r/#1-7; Bradstreet-c 16.00
Vol. 2 HC (2003, $29.95) r/#1-7,13-18; intro. by Mike Millar 30.00
Vol. 3 HC (2004, $29.95) r/#19-27; script pages for #19 30.00
Vol. 3: Business as Usual TPB (2003, $14.99) r/#13-18; Bradstreet-c 15.00
Vol. 4: Full Auto TPB (2003, $17.99) r/#20-26; Bradstreet-c 18.00
Vol. 5: Streets of Laredo TPB (2003, $17.99) r/#19,27-32 18.00
Vol. 6: Confederacy of Dunces TPB (2004, $13.99) r/#33-37 14.00

PUNISHER (Marvel MAX)
Marvel Comics: Mar, 2004 - Present ($2.99)

1-13: 1-Ennis-s/Larosa-a/Bradstreet-c; flashback to his family's murder; Micro app. 6-Micro killed. 7-12-Fernandez-a. 13,14-Braithwaite-a 3.00
Vol. 1: In the Beginning TPB (2004, $14.99) r/#1-6 15.00
Vol. 2: Kitchen Irish TPB (2004, $14.99) r/#7-12 15.00

PUNISHER AND WOLVERINE: DAMAGING EVIDENCE (See Wolverine and...)

PUNISHER ARMORY, THE
Marvel Comics: 7/90 ($1.50); No. 2, 6/91; No. 3, 4/92 - 10/94($1.75/$2.00)

1-10: 1-r/weapons pgs. from War Journal. 1,2-Jim Lee-c. 3-10- All new material. 3-Jusko painted-c 2.50

PUNISHER KILLS THE MARVEL UNIVERSE
Marvel Comics: Nov, 1995 ($5.95, one-shot)

1-Garth Ennis script/Doug Braithwaite-a 7.00
1-2nd printing (3/00) Steve Dillon-c 6.00

PUNISHER MAGAZINE, THE
Marvel Comics: Oct, 1989 - No. 16, Nov, 1990 ($2.25, B&W, Magazine, 52 pgs.)

1-16: 1-r/Punisher #1('86). 2,3-r/Punisher 2-5. 4-16: 4-7-r/Punisher V2#1-8. 4-Chiodo-c. 8-r/Punisher #10 & Daredevil #257; Portacio & Lee-r. 14-r/Punisher War Journal #1,2 w/new Lee-c. 16-r/Punisher W. J. #3,8 3.00

NOTE: ***Chiodo** painted c-4, 7, 16. **Jusko** painted c-6, 8. **Jim Lee** r-8, 14-16; c-14. **Portacio/Williams** r-7-12.*

PUNISHER: OFFICIAL MOVIE ADAPTATION

The Punisher: The End #1 © MAR

Purple Claw #1 © Minoan

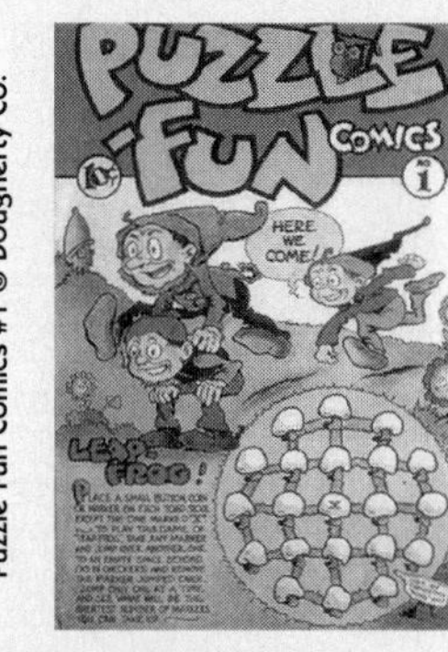

Puzzle Fun Comics #1 © Dougherty Co.

GD 2.0 | VG 4.0 | FN 6.0 | VF 8.0 | VF/NM 9.0 | NM- 9.2

Marvel Comics: May, 2004 - No. 3, May, 2004 ($2.99, limited series)
1-3-Photo-c of Thomas Jane; Milligan-s/Olliffe-a 3.00

PUNISHER: ORIGIN OF MICRO CHIP, THE
Marvel Comics: July, 1993 - No. 2, Aug, 1993 ($1.75, limited series)
1,2 2.25

PUNISHER: P.O.V.
Marvel Comics: 1991 - No. 4, 1991 ($4.95, painted, limited series, 52 pgs.)
1-4: Starlin scripts & Wrightson painted-c/a in all. 2-Nick Fury app. 5.00

PUNISHER: THE END
Marvel Comics: June, 2004 ($4.50, one-shot)
1-Ennis-s/Corben-a/c 4.50

PUNISHER: THE GHOSTS OF INNOCENTS
Marvel Comics: Jan, 1993 - No. 2, Jan, 1993 ($5.95, 52 pgs.)
1,2-Starlin scripts 6.00

PUNISHER: THE MOVIE
Marvel Comics: 2004 ($12.99,TPB)
nn-Reprints Amazing Spider-Man #129; Official Movie Adaptation and Punisher V3 #1 13.00

PUNISHER 2099 (See Punisher War Journal #50)
Marvel Comics: Feb, 1993 - No. 34, Nov, 1995 ($1.25/$1.50/$1.95)
1-24,26-34: 1-Foil stamped-c. 1-Second printing. 13-Spider-Man 2099 x-over; Ron Lim-c(p). 16-bound-in card sheet 2.25
25 ($2.95, 52 pgs.)-Deluxe edition; embossed foil-cover 3.00
25 ($2.25, 52 pgs.) 2.25
(Marvel Knights) #1 (11/04, $2.99) Kirkman-s/Mhan-a/Pat Lee-c 3.00

PUNISHER VS. DAREDEVIL
Marvel Comics: Jun, 2000 ($3.50, one-shot)
1-Reprints Daredevil #183,#184 & #257 3.50

PUNISHER WAR JOURNAL, THE
Marvel Comics: Nov, 1988 - No. 80, July, 1995 ($1.50/$1.75/$1.95)
1-Origin The Punisher; Matt Murdock cameo; Jim Lee inks begin 5.00
2-7: 2,3-Daredevil x-over; Jim Lee-c(i). 4-Jim Lee c/a begins. 6-Two part Wolverine story begins. 7-Wolverine-c, story ends 4.00
8-49,51-60,62,63,65: 13-16,20-22: No Jim Lee-a. 13-Lee-c only. 13-15-Heath-i. 14,15-Spider-Man x-over. 19-Last Jim Lee-c/a.29,30-Ghost Rider app. 31-Andy & Joe Kubert art. 36-Photo-c. 47,48-Nomad/Daredevil-c/stories; see Nomad. 57,58-Daredevil & Ghost Rider-c/stories. 62,63-Suicide Run Pt. 4 & 7.
3.00
50,61,64($2.95, 52 pgs.): 50-Preview of Punisher 2099 (1st app.); embossed-c. 61-Embossed foil cover; Suicide Run Pt. 1. 64-Die-cut-c; Suicide Run Pt. 10 3.00
64-($2.25, 52 pgs.)-Regular cover edition 2.25
66-74,76-80: 66-Bound-in card sheet 2.25
75 ($2.50, 52 pgs.) 2.50
NOTE: ***Golden** c-25-30, 40, 61, 62. **Jusko** painted c-31, 32. **Jim Lee** a-1i-3i, 4p-13p, 17p-19p; c-2i, 3i, 4p-15p, 17p, 18p, 19p. Painted c-40.*

PUNISHER: WAR ZONE, THE
Marvel Comics: Mar, 1992 - No. 41, July, 1995 ($1.75/$1.95)
1-($2.25, 40 pgs.)-Die cut-c; Romita, Jr.-c/a begins 3.00
2-22,24,26,27-41: 8-Last Romita, Jr.-c/a. 19-Wolverine app. 24-Suicide Run Pt. 5. 27-Bound-in card sheet 2.25
23-($2.95, 52 pgs.)-Enbossed foil-c; Suicide Run part 2; Buscema-a(part) 3.00
25-($2.25, 52 pgs.)-Suicide Run part 8; painted-c 2.50
Annual 1,2 ('93, 94, $2.95, 68 pgs.)-1-Bagged w/card; John Buscema-a 3.00
NOTE: ***Golden** c-23. **Romita, Jr.** c/a-1-8.*

PUNISHER: YEAR ONE
Marvel Comics: Dec, 1994 - No. 4, Apr, 1995 ($2.50, limited series)
1-4 2.50

PUNX
Acclaim (Valiant): Nov, 1995 - No. 3, Jan, 1996 ($2.50, unfinished lim. series)
1-3: Giffen story & art in all. 2-Satirizes Scott McCloud's Understanding Comics 2.50
(Manga) Special 1 (3/96, $2.50)-Giffen scripts 2.50

PUPPET COMICS
George W. Dougherty Co.: Spring, 1946 - No. 2, Summer, 1946

	GD	VG	FN	VF	VF/NM	NM-
1-Funny animal in both	13	26	39	74	102	130
2	11	22	33	62	84	105

PUPPETOONS (See George Pal's...)

PUREHEART (See Archie as...)

PURGATORI
Chaos! Comics: Prelude #-1, 5/96 ($1.50, 16 pgs.); 1996 - No. 3 Dec, 1996 ($3.50/$2.95, limited series)
Prelude #-1-Pulido story; Balent-c/a; contains sketches & interviews 2.25
0-(2/01, $2.99) Prelude to "Love Bites"; Rio-c/a 3.00
1/2 (12/00, $2.95) Al Rio-c/a 3.00
1-($3.50)-Wraparound cover; red foil embossed-c; Jim Balent-a 5.00
1-($19.95)-Premium Edition (1000 print run) 20.00
2-($3.00)-Wraparound-c 3.00
2-Variant-c 5.00
...: Heartbreaker 1 (3/02, $2.99) Jolley-s 3.00
...: Love Bites 1 (3/01, $2.99) Turnbull-a/Kaminski-s 3.00
...: Mischief Night 1 (11/01, $2.99) 3.00
...: Re-Imagined 1 (7/02, $2.99) Jolley-s/Neves-a 3.00
...The Dracula Gambit-($2.95) 3.00
...The Dracula Gambit Sketchbook-($2.95) 3.00
...The Vampire's Myth 1-($19.95) Premium Ed. (10,000) 20.00
...Vs. Chastity (7/00, $2.95) Two versions (Alpha and Omega) with different endings; Rio-a 3.00
...Vs. Lady Death (1/01, $2.95) Kaminski-s 3.00
...Vs. Vampirella (4/00, $2.95) Zanier-a; Chastity app. 3.00

PURGATORI
Chaos! Comics: Oct, 1998 - No. 7, Apr, 1999 ($2.95)
1-7-Quinn-s/Rio-c/a. 2-Lady Death-c 3.00

PURGATORI: DARKEST HOUR
Chaos! Comics: Sept, 2001 - No. 2, Oct, 2001 ($2.99, limited series)
1,2 3.00

PURGATORI: EMPIRE
Chaos! Comics: May, 2000 - No. 3, July, 2000 ($2.95, limited series)
1-3-Cleavenger-c 3.00

PURGATORI: GODDESS RISING
Chaos! Comics: July, 1999 - No. 4, Oct, 1999 ($2.95, limited series)
1-4-Deodato-c/a 3.00

PURGATORI: GOD HUNTER
Chaos! Comics: Apr, 2002 - No. 2, May, 2002 ($2.99, limited series)
1,2-Molenaar-a/Jolley-s 3.00

PURGATORI: GOD KILLER
Chaos! Comics: Jun, 2002 - No. 2, July, 2002 ($2.99, limited series)
1,2-Molenaar-a/Jolley-s 3.00

PURGATORI: THE HUNTED
Chaos! Comics: Jun, 2001 - No. 2, Aug, 2001 ($2.99, limited series)
1,2 3.00

PURPLE CLAW, THE (Also see Tales of Horror)
Minoan Publishing Co./Toby Press: Jan, 1953 - No. 3, May, 1953

	GD	VG	FN	VF	VF/NM	NM-
1-Origin; horror/weird stories in all	33	66	99	190	275	360
2,3: 1-3 r-in Tales of Horror #9-11	24	48	72	135	195	255
I.W. Reprint #8-Reprints #1	3	6	9	18	24	30

PUSSYCAT (Magazine)
Marvel Comics Group: Oct, 1968 (B&W reprints from Men's magazines)

	GD	VG	FN	VF	VF/NM	NM-
1-(Scarce)-Ward, Everett, Wood-a; Everett-c	18	36	54	129	197	265

PUZZLE FUN COMICS (Also see Jingle Jangle)
George W. Dougherty Co.: Spring, 1946 - No. 2, Summer, 1946 (52 pgs.)

	GD	VG	FN	VF	VF/NM	NM-
1-Gustavson-a	24	48	72	135	195	255
2	16	32	48	89	127	165

NOTE: *#1 & 2('46) each contain a **George Carlson** cover plus a 6 pg. story "Alec in Fumbleland"; also many puzzles in each.*

PvP (Player vs. Player)
Image Comics: Mar, 2003 - Present ($2.95, B&W, reads sideways)
1-11-Scott Kurtz-s/a. 1-Frank Cho-c. 11-Savage Dragon-c/app. 3.00
...: At Large TPB (7/04, $11.95) r/#1-6 12.00
...: The Dork Ages TPB (2/04, $11.95) r/#1-6 from Dork Storm Press 12.00

QUACK!
Star Reach Productions: July, 1976 - No. 6, 1977? ($1.25, B&W)

	GD	VG	FN	VF	VF/NM	NM-
1-Brunner-c/a on Duckaneer (Howard the Duck clone); Dave Stevens, Gilbert, Shaw-a	2	4	6	8	10	12
1-2nd printing (10/76)						4.00

2-6: 2-Newton the Rabbit Wonder by Aragonés/Leialoha; Gilbert, Shaw-a; Leialoha-c.

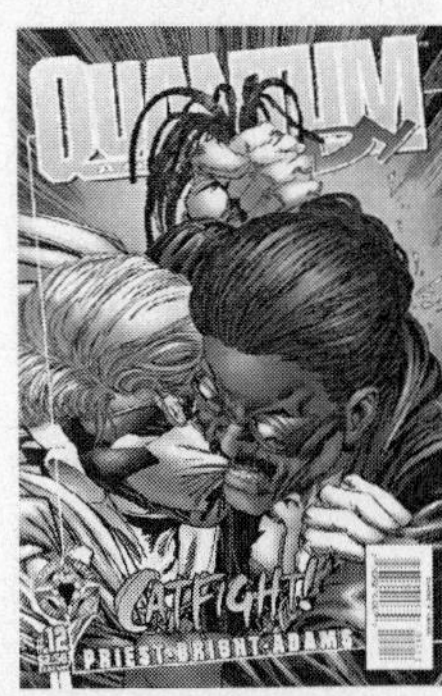

Quantum & Woody #12 © ACC

The Question ('05) #1 © DC

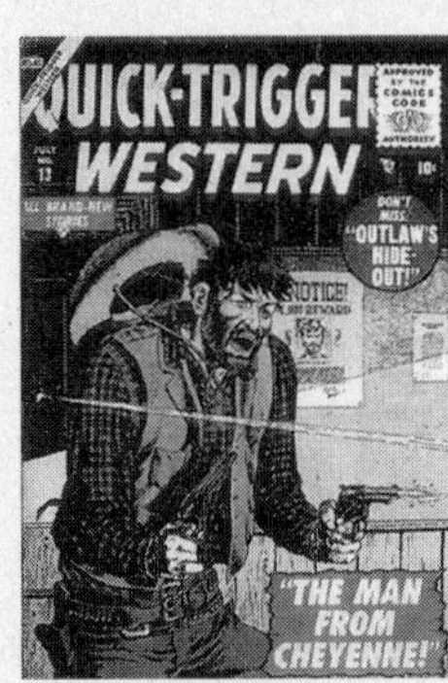

Quick-Trigger Western #13 © MAR

	GD	VG	FN	VF	VF/NM	NM-
	2.0	4.0	6.0	8.0	9.0	9.2

3-The Beavers by Dave Sim begin, end #5; Gilbert, Shaw-a; Sim/Leialoha-c. 6-Brunner-a (Duckeneer); Gilbert-a 1 2 3 5 6 8

QUADRANT
Quadrant Publications: 1983 - No. 8, 1986 (B&W, nudity, adults)

1-Peter Hsu-c/a in all 2 4 6 9 11 14
2-8 1 2 3 5 6 8

QUANTUM & WOODY
Acclaim Comics: June, 1997 - No. 17, No. 32 (9/99), No. 18 - No. 21, Feb, 2000 ($2.50)

1-17: 1-1st app.; two covers. 6-Copycat-c. 9-Troublemakers app. 2.50
32-(9/99); 18-(10/99),19-21 2.50
The Director's Cut TPB ('97, $7.95) r/#1-4 plus extra pages 8.00

QUANTUM LEAP (TV) (See A Nightmare on Elm Street)
Innovation Publishing: Sept, 1991 - No. 12, Jun, 1993 ($2.50, painted-c)

1-12: Based on TV show; all have painted-c. 8-Has photo gallery 3.00
Special Edition 1 (10/92)-r/#1 w/8 extra pgs. of photos & articles 3.00
Time and Space Special 1 (#13) ($2.95)-Foil logo 3.00

QUANTUM TUNNELER, THE
Revolution Studio: Oct, 2001 (no cover price, one-shot)

1-Prequel to "The One" movie; Clayton Henry-a 2.25

QUASAR (See Avengers #302, Captain America #217, Incredible Hulk #234, Marvel Team-Up #113 & Marvel Two-in-One #53)
Marvel Comics: Oct, 1989 - No. 60, Jul, 1994 ($1.00/$1.25, Direct sales #17 on)

1-Origin; formerly Marvel Boy/Marvel Man 3.00
2-49,51-60: 3-Human Torch app. 6-Venom cameo (2 pgs.). 7-Cosmic Spidey. 11-Excalibur x-over. 14-McFarlane-c. 16-($1.50, 52 pgs.). 17-Flash parody (Buried Alien). 20-Fantastic Four app. 23-Ghost Rider x-over. 25-($1.50, 52 pgs.)-New costume Quasar. 26-Infinity Gauntlet x-over; Thanos-c/story. 27-Infinity Gauntlet x-over. 30-Thanos cameo in flashback; last $1.00-c. 31-Begin $1.25-c; D.P. 7 guest stars. 38-40-Infinity War x-overs. 38-Battles Warlock. 39-Thanos-c & cameo. 40-Thanos app. 42-Punisher-c/story. 53-Warlock & Moondragon app. 58-w/bound-in card sheet 2.50
50-($2.95, 52 pgs.)-Holo-grafx foil-c; Silver Surfer, Man-Thing, Ren & Stimpy app. 3.00
Special #1-3 ($1.25, newsstand)-Same as #32-34 2.25

QUEEN & COUNTRY (See Whiteout) (Also see Promotional Comics section for Free Comic Book Day edition)
Oni Press: Mar, 2001 - Present ($2.95/$2.99, B&W)

1-Rucka-s in all. Rolston-a/Sale-c 1 2 3 4 5 7
2-5: 2-4-Rolston-a/Sale-c. 5-Snyder-c/Hurtt-a 4.00
6-24, 26.27: 6,7-Snyder-c/Hurtt-a. 13-15-Alexander-a. 16-20-McNeil-a. 21-24-Hawthorne-a 26.27-Norton-a 3.00
25-($5.99) Rolston-a 6.00
Operation: Blackwall (10/03, $8.95, TPB) r/#13-15; John Rogers intro. 9.00
Operation: Broken Ground (2002, $11.95, TPB) r/#1-4; Ellis intro. 12.00
Operation: Crystal Ball (1/03, $14.95, TPB) r/#8-12; Judd Winick intro. 15.00
Operation: Dandelion HC (8/04, $25.00) r/#21-24; Jamie S. Rich intro. 25.00
Operation: Dandelion (8/04, $11.95, TPB) r/#21-24; Jamie S. Rich intro. 12.00
Operation: Morningstar (9/02, $8.95, TPB) r/#5-7; Stuart Moore intro. 9.00
Operation: Storm Front (3/04, $14.95, TPB) r/#16-20; Geoff Johns intro. 15.00

QUEEN & COUNTRY: DECLASSIFIED
Oni Press: Nov, 2002 - No. 3, Jan, 2003 ($2.95, B&W, limited series)

1-3-Rucka-s/Hurtt-a/Morse-c 3.00
TPB (7/03, $8.95) r/#1-3; intro. by Micah Wright 9.00

QUEEN OF THE WEST, DALE EVANS (TV)(See Dale Evans Comics, Roy Rogers & Western Roundup under Dell Giants)
Dell Publ. Co.: No. 479, 7/53 - No. 22, 1-3/59 (All photo-c; photo back c-4-8,15)

Four Color 479(#1, '53) 24 48 72 170 260 350
Four Color 528(#2, '54) 12 24 36 86 131 175
3,4: 3(4-6/54)-Toth-a. 4-Toth, Manning-a 10 20 30 67 96 125
5-10-Manning-a. 5-Marsh-a 8 16 24 58 82 105
11,19,21-No Manning 21-Tufts-a 6 12 18 43 59 75
12-18,20,22-Manning-a 7 14 21 50 68 85

QUENTIN DURWARD
Dell Publishing Co.: No. 672, Jan, 1956

Four Color 672-Movie, photo-c 8 16 24 55 78 100

QUESTAR ILLUSTRATED SCIENCE FICTION CLASSICS
Golden Press: 1977 (224 pgs.) ($1.95)

11197-Stories by Asimov, Sturgeon, Silverberg & Niven; Starstream-r 4 8 12 22 30 38

	GD	VG	FN	VF	VF/NM	NM-
	2.0	4.0	6.0	8.0	9.0	9.2

QUEST FOR CAMELOT
DC Comics: July, 1998 ($4.95)

1-Movie adaption 5.00

QUEST FOR DREAMS LOST (Also see Word Warriors)
Literacy Volunteers of Chicago: July 4, 1987 ($2.00, B&W, 52 pgs.)(Proceeds donated to help fight illiteracy)

1-Teenage Mutant Ninja Turtles by Eastman/Laird, Trollords, Silent Invasion, The Realm, Wordsmith, Reacto Man, Eb'nn, Aniverse 2.25

QUESTION, THE (See Americomics, Blue Beetle (1967), Charlton Bullseye & Mysterious Suspense)

QUESTION, THE (Also see Showcase '95 #3)
DC Comics: Feb, 1987 - No. 36, Mar, 1990 ($1.50)

1-36: Denny O'Neil scripts in all 2.50
Annual 1 (1988, $2.50) 2.50
Annual 2 (1989, $3.50) 3.50

QUESTION, THE
DC Comics: Jan, 2005 - No. 6 ($2.95, limited series)

1,2-Rick Veitch-s/Tommy Lee Edwards-a 3.00

QUESTION QUARTERLY, THE
DC Comics: Summer, 1990 - No. 5, Spring, 1992 ($2.50, 52pgs.)

1-5 2.50
NOTE: ***Cowan*** *a-1, 2, 4, 5; c-1-3, 5.* ***Mignola*** *a-5i.* ***Quesada*** *a-3-5.*

QUESTION RETURNS, THE
DC Comics: Feb, 1997 ($3.50, one-shot)

1-Brereton-c 3.50

QUESTPROBE
Marvel Comics: 8/84; No. 2, 1/85; No. 3, 11/85 (lim. series)

1-3: 1-The Hulk app. by Romita. 2-Spider-Man; Mooney-a(i). 3-Human Torch & Thing 3.00

QUICK DRAW McGRAW (TV) (Hanna-Barbera)(See Whitman Comic Books)
Dell Publishing Co./Gold Key No. 12 on: No. 1040, 12-2/59-60 - No. 11, 7-9/62; No. 12, 11/62; No. 13, 2/63; No. 14, 4/63; No. 15, 6/69 (1st show aired 9/29/59)

Four Color 1040(#1) 1st app. Quick Draw & Baba Looey, Augie Doggie & Doggie Daddy and Snooper & Blabber 15 30 45 102 156 215
2(4-6/60)-4,6: 2-Augie Doggie & Snooper & Blabber stories (8 pgs. each); pre-dates both of their #1 issues. 4-Augie Doggie & Snooper & Blabber stories. 9 18 27 60 85 110
5-1st Snagglepuss app.; last 10¢ issue 9 18 27 65 93 120
7-11 7 14 21 46 63 80
12,13-Title change to ...Fun-Type Roundup (84pgs.) 9 18 27 65 93 120
14,15: 15-Reprints 6 12 18 40 55 70

QUICK DRAW McGRAW (TV)(See Spotlight #2)
Charlton Comics: Nov, 1970 - No. 8, Jan, 1972 (Hanna-Barbera)

1 6 12 18 40 55 70
2-8 4 8 12 22 30 38

QUICKSILVER (See Avengers)
Marvel Comics: Nov, 1997 - No. 13, Nov, 1998 ($2.99/$1.99)

1-($2.99)-Peyer-s/Casey Jones-a; wraparound-c 3.00
2-11: 2-Two covers-variant by Golden. 4-6-Inhumans app. 2.25
12-($2.99) Siege of Wundagore pt. 4 3.00
13-Magneto-c/app.; last issue 2.25

QUICK-TRIGGER WESTERN (...Action #12; Cowboy Action #5-11)
Atlas Comics (ACI #12/WPI #13-19): No. 12, May, 1956 - No. 19, Sept, 1957

12-Baker-a 17 34 51 95 135 175
13-Williamson-a, 5 pgs. 16 32 48 89 127 165
14-Everett, Crandall, Torres-a; Heath-c 15 30 45 83 117 150
15,16: 15-Torres, Crandall-a. 16-Orlando, Kirby-a 12 24 36 69 95 120
17,18: 18-Baker-a 11 22 33 64 87 110
19 9 18 27 54 70 85
NOTE: ***Ayers*** *a-17.* ***Colan*** *a-16.* ***Maneely*** *a-15, 17; c-15, 18.* ***Morrow*** *a-18.* ***Powell*** *a-14.* ***Severin*** *a-19; c-12, 13, 16, 17, 19.* ***Shores*** *a-16.* ***Tuska*** *a-17.*

QUINCY (See Comics Reading Libraries in the Promotional Comics section)

Q-UNIT
Harris Comics: Dec, 1993 ($2.95)

1-($2.95)-Polybagged w/trading card version 1.2 3.00

RACCOON KIDS, THE (Formerly Movietown Animal Antics)
National Periodical Publications (Arleigh No. 63,64): No. 52, Sept-Oct, 1954 - No. 62, Oct-Nov, 1956; No. 63, Sept, 1957; No. 64, Nov, 1957

The Racing Pettys #1 © STP

Racket Squad in Action #15 © CC

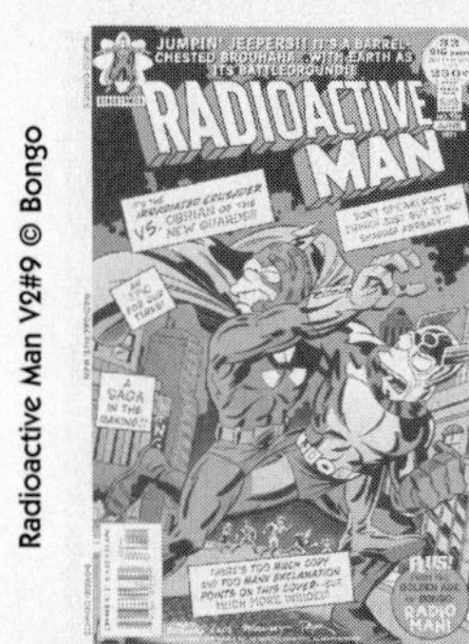

Radioactive Man V2#9 © Bongo

	GD 2.0	VG 4.0	FN 6.0	VF 8.0	VF/NM 9.0	NM- 9.2

52-Doodles Duck by Mayer 15 30 45 83 117 150
53-64: 53-62-Doodles Duck by Mayer 11 22 33 62 84 105
NOTE: *Otto Feuer-a most issues.* ***Rube Grossman****-a most issues.*

RACE FOR THE MOON
Harvey Publications: Mar, 1958 - No. 3, Nov, 1958
1-Powell-a(5); 1/2-pg. S&K-a; cover redrawn from Galaxy Science Fiction pulp (5/53)
15 30 45 86 123 160
2-Kirby/Williamson-c(r)/a(3); Kirby-p 7 more stys 27 54 81 152 219 285
3-Kirby/Williamson-c/a(4); Kirby-p 6 more stys 29 58 87 164 237 310

RACE OF SCORPIONS
Dark Horse Comics: 1990 - No. 2, 1990 ($4.50/$4.95, 52pgs.)
1,2: 1-r/stories from Dark Horse Presents #23-27. 2-($4.95-c) 5.00

RACER-X
Now Comics: 8/88 - No. 11, 8/89; V2#1, 9/89 - V2#10, 1990 ($1.75)
0-Deluxe ($3.50) 3.50
1 (9/88) - 11, V2#1-10 2.25

RACER X (See Speed Racer)
DC Comics (WildStorm): Oct, 2000 - No. 3, Dec, 2000 ($2.95, limited series)
1-3: 1-Tommy Yune-s/Jo Chen-a; 2 covers by Yune. 2,3-Kabala app. 3.50

RACING PETTYS
STP Corp.: 1980 ($2.50, 68 pgs., 10 1/8" x 13 1/4")
1-Bob Kane-a. Kane bio on inside back-c. 10.00

RACK & PAIN
Dark Horse Comics: Mar, 1994 - No. 4, June, 1994 ($2.50, limited series)
1-4: Brian Pulido scripts in all. 1-Greg Capullo-c 3.00

RACK & PAIN: KILLERS
Chaos! Comics: Sept, 1996 - No. 4, Jan, 1997 ($2.95, limited series)
1-4: Reprints Dark Horse series; Jae Lee-c 3.00

RACKET SQUAD IN ACTION
Capitol Stories/Charlton Comics: May-June, 1952 - No. 29, Mar, 1958
1 29 58 87 164 237 310
2-4,6: 3,4,6-Dr. Neff, Ghost Breaker app. 15 30 45 85 120 155
5-Dr. Neff, Ghost Breaker app; headlights-c 23 46 69 130 188 245
7-10: 10-Explosion-c 14 28 42 81 113 145
11-Ditko-c/a 31 62 93 175 253 330
12-Ditko explosion-c (classic); Shuster-a(2) 50 100 150 305 465 625
13-Shuster-c(p)/a. 11 22 33 66 91 115
14-Marijuana story "Shakedown"; Giordano-c 14 28 42 81 113 145
15-28: 15,20,22,23-Giordano-c 10 20 30 60 80 100
29-(15¢, 68 pgs.) 12 24 36 71 98 125

RADIANT LOVE (Formerly Daring Love #1)
Gilmor Magazines: No. 2, Dec, 1953 - No. 6, Aug, 1954
2 9 18 27 54 70 85
3-6 7 14 21 35 43 50

RADICAL DREAMER
Blackball Comics: No. 0, May, 1994 - No. 4, Nov, 1994 ($1.99, bi-monthly) (1st poster format comic)
0-4: 0-2-($1.99, poster format): 0-1st app. Max Wrighter. 3,4-($2.50-c) 3.00

RADICAL DREAMER
Mark's Giant Economy Size Comics: V2#1, June, 1995 - V2#6, Feb, 1996 ($2.95, B&W, limited series)
V2#1-6 3.00
Prime (5/96, $2.95) 3.00
Dreams Cannot Die!-(1996, $20.00, softcover)-Collects V1#0-4 & V2#1-6; intro by Kurt Busiek; afterward by Mark Waid 20.00
Dreams Cannot Die!-(1996, $60.00, hardcover)-Signed & limited edition; collects V1#0-4 & V2#1-6; intro by Kurt Busiek; afterward by Mark Waid 60.00

RADIOACTIVE MAN (Simpsons TV show)
Bongo Comics: 1993 - No. 6, 1994 ($1.95/$2.25, limited series)
1-($2.95)-Glow-in-the-dark-c; bound-in jumbo poster; origin Radioactive Man; (cover dated Nov. 1952) 5.00
2-6: 2-Says #88 on-c & inside & dated May 1962; cover parody of Atlas Kirby monster-c; Superior Squad app.; origin Fallout Boy. 3-($1.95)-Cover "dated" Aug 1972 #216. 4-($2.25)-Cover "dated" Oct 1980 #412; w/trading card. 5-Cover "dated" Jan 1986 #679; w/trading card. 6-(Jan 1995 #1000) 4.00
Colossal #1-($4.95) 7.00
#4 (2001, $2.50) Faux 1953 issue; Murphy Anderson-i (6 pgs.) 2.50
#100 (2000, $2.50) Comic Book Guy-c/app.; faux 1963 issue inside 2.50
#136 (2001, $2.50) Dan DeCarlo-c/a 2.50
#222 (2001, $2.50) Batton Lash-s; Radioactive Man in 1972-style 2.50
#575 (2002, $2.50) Chaykin-c; Radioactive Man in 1984-style 2.50
1963-106 (2002, $2.50) Radioactive Man in 1960s Gold Key-style; Groening-c 2.50
#7 Bongo Super Heroes Starring... (2003, $2.50) Marvel Silver Age-style Superior Squad 2.50
#8 Official Movie Adaptation (2004, $2.99) starring Rainier Wolfcastle and Milhouse 3.00
#9 (#197 on-c) (2004, $2.50) Kirby-esque New Gods spoof; Golden Age Radio Man app. 2.50

RADISKULL & DEVIL DOLL
Image Comics: Nov, 2002 - Present ($2.50/$2.95, B&W, one-shots)
...: Radiskull Hate Christmas (11/02, $2.50) Josh Blaylock & Tim Seeley-s/Mike Norton-a 2.50
...: Radiskull Hate Love (3/03, $2.95) Josh Blaylock & Tim Seeley-s/Jamar Nicholas-a 3.00

RADIX
Image Comics: Dec, 2001 - No. 3, Apr, 2002 ($2.95)
1-3-Ray & Ben Lai-s/a 3.00

RAGAMUFFINS
Eclipse Comics: Jan, 1985 ($1.75, one shot)
1-Eclipse Magazine-r, w/color; Colan-a 2.25

RAGGEDY ANN AND ANDY (See Dell Giants, March of Comics #23 & New Funnies)
Dell Publishing Co.: No. 5, 1942 - No. 533, 2/54; 10-12/64 - No. 4, 3/66
Four Color 5(1942) 47 94 141 376 588 800
Four Color 23(1943) 37 74 111 278 432 585
Four Color 45(1943) 31 62 93 225 355 485
Four Color 72(1945) 27 54 81 194 297 400
1(6/46)-Billy & Bonnie Bee by Frank Thomas 34 68 102 255 403 550
2,3: 3-Egbert Elephant by Dan Noonan begins 19 38 57 138 212 285
4-Kelly-a, 16 pgs. 20 40 60 145 223 300
5,6,8-10 15 30 45 107 164 220
7-Little Black Sambo, Black Mumbo & Black Jumbo only app; Christmas-c
18 36 54 126 193 260
11-20 12 24 36 86 131 175
21-Alice In Wonderland cover/story 15 30 45 107 164 220
22-27,29-39(8/49), Four Color 262(1/50): 34-"...In Candyland"
11 22 33 75 110 145
28-Kelly-c 11 22 33 79 117 155
Four Color 306,354,380,452,533 9 18 27 60 85 110
1(10-12/64-Dell) 5 10 15 33 44 55
2,3(10-12/65), 4(3/66) 4 8 12 22 30 38
NOTE: ***Kelly*** *art ("Animal Mother Goose")-#1-34, 36, 37; c-28. Peterkin Pottle by* ***John Stanley*** *in 32-38.*

RAGGEDY ANN AND ANDY
Gold Key: Dec, 1971 - No. 6, Sept, 1973
1 4 8 12 22 30 38
2-6 3 6 9 16 21 26

RAGGEDY ANN & THE CAMEL WITH THE WRINKLED KNEES (See Dell Jr. Treasury #8)

RAGMAN (See Batman Family #20, The Brave & The Bold #196 & Cancelled Comic Cavalcade)
National Per. Publ./DC Comics No. 5: Aug-Sept, 1976 - No. 5, Jun-Jul, 1977
1-Origin & 1st app. 2 4 6 9 11 14
2-5: 2-Origin ends; Kubert-c. 4-Drug use story 1 2 3 5 6 8
NOTE: ***Kubert*** *a-4, 5; c-1-5.* ***Redondo*** *studios a-1-4.*

RAGMAN (2nd Series)
DC Comics: Oct, 1991 - No. 8, May, 1992 ($1.50, limited series)
1-8: 1-Giffen plots/breakdowns. 3-Origin. 8-Batman-c/story 3.00

RAGMAN: CRY OF THE DEAD
DC Comics: Aug, 1993 - No. 6, Jan, 1994 ($1.75, limited series)
1-6: Joe Kubert-c 3.00

RAGMOP
Image Comics: Sept, 1997 - No. 2 ($2.95, B&W)
1,2-Rob Walton-c/s/a 3.00

RAGS RABBIT (Formerly Babe Ruth Sports #10 or Little Max #10?; also see Harvey Hits #2, Harvey Wiseguys & Tastee Freez)
Harvey Publications: No. 11, June, 1951 - No. 18, March, 1954 (Written & drawn for little folks)
11-(See Nutty Comics #5 for 1st app.) 6 12 18 31 38 45
12-18 5 10 15 24 30 35

RAI (Rai and the Future Force #9-23) (See Magnus #5-8)
Valiant: Mar, 1992 - No. 0, Oct, 1992; No. 9, May, 1993 - No. 33, Jun, 1995 ($1.95/$2.25)

Rampaging Hulk #1 © MAR

Rangers Comics #10 © FH

Ravage 2099 #22 © MAR

GD VG FN VF VF/NM NM-
2.0 4.0 6.0 8.0 9.0 9.2

1-Valiant's 1st original character 2 4 6 9 11 14
2-4,0: 4-Low print run. 0-(11/92)-Origin/1st app. new Rai (Rising Spirit) & 1st full app. & partial origin Bloodshot; also see Eternal Warrior #4; tells future of all characters
1 3 4 6 8 10
5-10: 6,7-Unity x-overs. 7-Death of Rai. 9-($2.50)-Gatefold-c; story cont'd from Magnus #24; Magnus, Eternal Warrior & X-O app. 5.00
11-33: 15-Manowar Armor app. 17-19-Magnus x-over. 21-1st app. The Starwatchers (cameo); trading card. 22-Death of Rai. 26-Chaos Effect Epsilon Pt. 3 2.50
NOTE: ***Layton*** *c-2i, 9i.* ***Miller*** *c-6.* ***Simonson*** *c-7.*

RAIDERS OF THE LOST ARK (Movie)
Marvel Comics Group: Sept, 1981 - No. 3, Nov, 1981 (Movie adaptation)
1-3: 1-r/Marvel Comics Super Special #18 3.00
NOTE: ***Buscema*** *a(p)-1-3; c(p)-1.* ***Simonson*** *a-3i; scripts-1-3.*

RAIL: BROKEN THINGS
Image Comics: Nov, 2001 ($5.95, one-shot)
nn-Dave Dorman-s/a 6.00

RAINBOW BRITE AND THE STAR STEALER
DC Comics: 1985
nn-Movie adaptation 2 4 6 8 10 12

RALPH KINER, HOME RUN KING
Fawcett Publications: 1950 (Pittsburgh Pirates)
nn-Photo-c; life story 60 120 180 375 580 785

RALPH SNART ADVENTURES
Now Comics: June, 1986 - V2#9, 1987; V3#1 - #26, Feb, 1991; V4#1, 1992 - #4, 1992
1-3, V2#1-7,V3#1-23,25,26:1-($1.00, B&W)-1(B&W),V2#1(11/86), B&W), 8,9-color. V3#1(9/88)-Color begins 2.50
V3#24-($2.50)-3-D issue, V4#1-3-Direct sale versions w/cards 2.50
V4#1-3-Newsstand versions w/random cards 2.50
Book 1 1 2 3 5 6 8
3-D Special (11/92, $3.50)-Complete 12-card set w/3-D glasses 3.50

RAMAR OF THE JUNGLE (TV)
Toby Press No. 1/Charlton No. 2 on: 1954 (no month); No. 2, Sept, 1955 - No. 5, Sept, 1956
1-Jon Hall photo-c; last pre-code issue 22 44 66 123 177 230
2-5: 2-Jon Hall photo-c 15 30 45 83 117 150

RAMM
Megaton Comics: May, 1987 - No. 2, Sept, 1987 ($1.50, B&W)
1,2-Both have 1 pg. Youngblood ad by Liefeld 2.25

RAMPAGING HULK (The Hulk #10 on; also see Marvel Treasury Edition)
Marvel Comics Group: Jan, 1977 - No. 9, June, 1978 ($1.00, B&W magazine)
1-Bloodstone story w/Buscema & Nebres-a. Origin re-cap w/Simonson-a; Gargoyle, UFO story; Ken Barr-c 3 6 9 16 20 24
2-Old X-Men app; origin old w/Simonson-a & new X-Men in text w/Cockrum illos; Bloodstone story w/Brown & Nebres-a 2 4 6 11 14 18
3-9: 3-Iron Man app. 4-Gallery of villains w/Giffen-a. 5,6-Hulk vs. Sub-Mariner. 7-Man-Thing story. 8-Original Avengers app. 9-Thor vs. Hulk battle; Shanna the She-Devil story w/DeZuniga-a 2 4 6 9 11 14
NOTE: ***Alcala*** *a-1-3i, 5i, 8i.* ***Buscema*** *a-1.* ***Giffen*** *a-4.* ***Nino*** *a-4i.* ***Simonson*** *a-1-3p.* ***Starlin*** *a-4(w/Nino), 7; c-4, 5, 7.*

RAMPAGING HULK
Marvel Comics: Aug, 1998 - No. 6, Jan, 1999 ($2.99/$1.99)
1-($2.99) Flashback stories of Savage Hulk; Leonardi-a 3.00
2-6-($1.99): 2-Two covers 2.25

RANDOLPH SCOTT (Movie star)(See Crack Western #67, Prize Comics Western #76, Western Hearts #8, Western Love #1 & Western Winners #7)

RANDY O'DONNELL IS THE M@N
Image Comics: May, 2001 - No. 3, Sept, 2001 ($2.95)
1-3-DeFalco & Lim/s&a 3.00

RANGE BUSTERS
Fox Features Syndicate: Sept, 1950 (One shot)
1 (Exist?) 20 40 60 112 161 210

RANGE BUSTERS (Formerly Cowboy Love?; Wyatt Earp, Frontier Marshall #11 on)
Charlton Comics: No. 8, May, 1955 - No. 10, Sept, 1955
8 8 16 24 43 54 65
9,10 6 12 18 28 34 40

RANGELAND LOVE
Atlas Comics (CDS): Dec, 1949 - No. 2, Mar, 1950 (52 pgs.)
1-Robert Taylor & Arlene Dahl photo-c 17 34 51 95 135 175
2-Photo-c 14 28 42 79 110 140

RANGER, THE (See Zane Grey, Four Color #255)

RANGE RIDER, THE (TV)(See Flying A's...)

RANGE ROMANCES
Comic Magazines (Quality Comics): Dec, 1949 - No. 5, Aug, 1950 (#5: 52 pg)
1-Gustavson-c/a 27 54 81 152 219 285
2-Crandall-c/a 27 54 81 152 219 285
3-Crandall, Gustavson-a; photo-c 23 46 69 130 188 245
4-Crandall-a; photo-c 20 40 60 112 161 210
5-Gustavson-a; Crandall-a(p); photo-c 20 40 60 112 161 210

RANGERS COMICS (...of Freedom #1-7)
Fiction House Magazines: 10/41 - No. 67, 10/52; No. 68, Fall, 1952; No. 69, Winter, 1952-53 (Flying stories)
1-Intro. Ranger Girl & The Rangers of Freedom; ends #7, cover app. only #5
300 600 900 1925 3063 4200
2 90 180 270 563 869 1175
3 67 134 201 419 647 875
4,5 60 120 180 375 580 785
6-10: 8-U.S. Rangers begin 48 96 144 293 447 600
11,12-Commando Rangers app. 44 88 132 268 409 550
13-Commando Ranger begins-not same as Commando Rangers
43 86 129 262 401 540
14-20 40 80 120 230 335 440
21-Intro/origin Firehair (begins, 2/45) 40 80 120 239 357 475
22-30: 23-Kazanda begins, ends #28. 28-Tiger Man begins (origin/1st app., 4/46), ends #46. 30-Crusoe Island begins, ends #40 30 60 90 170 245 320
31-40: 33-Hypodermic panels 25 50 75 141 203 265
41-46: 41-Last Werewolf Hunter 21 42 63 118 169 220
47-56- "Eisnerish" Dr. Drew by Grandenetti. 48-Last Glory Forbes. 53-Last 52 pg. issue. 55-Last Sky Rangers 20 40 60 112 161 210
57-60-Straight Dr. Drew by Grandenetti 15 30 45 86 123 160
61-69: 64-Suicide Smith begins. 63-Used in **POP**, pgs. 85, 99. 67-Space Rangers begin, end #69 13 26 39 76 106 135
NOTE: *Bondage, discipline covers, lingerie panels are common. Crusoe Island by* ***Larsen****-#30-36. Firehair by* ***Lubbers****-#30-49. Glory Forbes by* ***Baker****-#36-45, 47; by* ***Whitman****-#34, 35. I Confess in #41-53. Jan of the Jungle in #42-58. King of the Congo in #49-53. Tiger Man by* ***Celardo****-#30-39.* ***M. Anderson*** *a-30?* ***Baker*** *a-36-38, 42, 44.* ***John Celardo*** *a-34, 36-39.* ***Lee Elias*** *a-21-28.* ***Evans*** *a-19, 38-46, 48-52.* ***Hopper*** *a-25, 26.* ***Ingels*** *a-13-16.* ***Larsen*** *a-34.* ***Bob Lubbers*** *a-30-38, 40-44; c-40-45.* ***Moreira*** *a-41-47.* ***Tuska*** *a-16, 17, 19, 22.* ***M. Whitman*** *c-61-66.* ***Zolnerwich*** *c-1-17.*

RANGO (TV)
Dell Publishing Co.: Aug, 1967
1-Photo-c of comedian Tim Conway 4 8 12 22 30 38

RAPHAEL (See Teenage Mutant Ninja Turtles)
Mirage Studios: 1985 ($1.50, 7-1/2x11", B&W w/2 color cover, one-shot)
1-1st Turtles one-shot spin-off; contains 1st drawing of the Turtles as a group from 1983 6.00
1-2nd printing (11/87); new-c & 8 pgs. art 2.25

RASCALS IN PARADISE
Dark Horse Comics: Aug, 1994 - No. 3, Dec, 1994 ($3.95, magazine size)
1-3-Jim Silke-a/story 4.00
Trade paperback-($16.95)-r/#1-3 17.00

RATFINK (See Frantic, Zany, & Ed "Big Daddy" Roth's Ratfink Comix)
Canrom, Inc.: Oct, 1964
1-Woodbridge-a 7 14 21 46 63 80

RAT PATROL, THE (TV)
Dell Publishing Co.: Mar, 1967 - No. 5, Nov, 1967; No. 6, Oct, 1969
1-Christopher George photo-c 8 16 24 58 82 105
2-6: 3-6-Photo-c 5 10 15 36 48 60

RAVAGE 2099 (See Marvel Comics Presents #117)
Marvel Comics: Dec, 1992 - No. 33, Aug, 1995($1.25/$1.50)
1-($1.75)-Gold foil stamped-c; Stan Lee scripts 3.00
1-($1.75)-2nd printing 2.25
2-24,26-33: 5-Last Ryan-c. 6-Last Ryan-a. 14-Punisher 2099 x-over. 15-Ron Lim-c(p). 18-Bound-in card sheet 2.25
25 ($2.25, 52 pgs.) 2.25
25 ($2.95, 52 pgs.)-Silver foil embossed-c 3.00

RAVEN, THE (See Movie Classics)

RAVEN CHRONICLES
Caliber (New Worlds): 1995 - No. 16 ($2.95, B&W)

Rawhide Kid #45 © MAR

Rawhide Kid ('03) #1 © MAR

Razor's Edge #1 © WSP

GD VG FN VF VF/NM NM-
2.0 4.0 6.0 8.0 9.0 9.2

1-16: 10-Flip book w/Wordsmith #6. 15-Flip book w/High Caliber #4 3.00

RAVENS AND RAINBOWS
Pacific Comics: Dec, 1983 (Baxter paper)(Reprints fanzine work in color)

1-Jeff Jones-c/a(r); nudity scenes 3.00

RAWHIDE (TV)
Dell Publishing Co./Gold Key: Sept-Nov, 1959 - June-Aug, 1962; July, 1963 - No. 2, Jan, 1964

	GD	VG	FN	VF	VF/NM	NM-
Four Color 1028 (#1)	25	50	75	179	275	370
Four Color 1097,1160,1202,1261,1269	16	32	48	112	171	230
01-684-208 (8/62, Dell)	14	28	42	97	149	200
1(10071-307) (7/63, Gold Key)	14	28	42	97	149	200
2-(12¢)	13	26	39	90	138	185

NOTE: *All have Clint Eastwood photo-c.* ***Tufts*** *a-1028.*

RAWHIDE KID
Atlas/Marvel Comics (CnPC No. 1-16/AMI No. 17-30): Mar, 1955 - No. 16, Sept, 1957; No. 17, Aug, 1960 - No. 151, May, 1979

	GD	VG	FN	VF	VF/NM	NM-
1-Rawhide Kid, his horse Apache & sidekick Randy begin; Wyatt Earp app.; #1 was not code approved; Maneely splash pg.	90	180	270	563	869	1175
2	40	80	120	239	357	475
3-5	31	62	93	178	259	340
6-10: 7-Williamson-a (4 pgs.)	24	48	72	138	199	260
11-16: 16-Torres-a	20	40	60	112	161	210
17-Origin by Jack Kirby; Kirby-a begins	33	66	99	248	387	525
18-21,24-30	13	26	39	90	138	185
22-Monster-c/story by Kirby/Ayers	16	32	48	112	171	230
23-Origin retold by Jack Kirby	20	40	60	141	216	290
31-35,40: 31,32-Kirby-a. 33-35-Davis-a. 34-Kirby-a. 35-Intro & death of The Raven. 40-Two-Gun Kid x-over.	11	22	33	75	110	145
36,37,39,41,42-No Kirby. 42-1st Larry Lieber issue	10	20	30	70	100	130
38-Red Raven-c/story; Kirby-c (2/64).	12	24	36	84	127	170
43-Kirby-a (beware: pin-up often missing)	12	24	36	84	127	170
44,46: 46-Toth-a. 46-Doc Holliday-c/s	9	18	27	65	93	120
45-Origin retold, 17 pgs.	11	22	33	77	114	150
47-49,51-60	6	12	18	43	59	75
50-Kid Colt x-over; vs. Rawhide Kid	7	14	21	46	63	80
61-70: 64-Kid Colt story. 66-Two-Gun Kid story. 67-Kid Colt story. 70-Last 12¢ issue	5	10	15	33	44	55
71-78,80-83,85	3	6	9	19	25	32
79,84,86,95: 79-Williamson-a(r). 84,86: Kirby-a. 86-Origin-r; Williamson-r/Ringo Kid #13 (4 pgs.)	3	7	10	21	28	35
87-91: 90-Kid Colt app. 91-Last 15¢ issue	3	6	9	18	23	28
92,93 (52 pg.Giants). 92-Kirby-a	4	8	12	25	33	42
94,96-99	3	6	9	16	20	24
100 (6/72)-Origin retold & expanded	3	7	10	21	28	35
101-120: 115-Last new story	2	4	6	11	14	18
121-151	2	4	6	8	10	12
133,134-(30¢-c variants, limited distribution)(5,7/76)	2	4	6	12	16	20
140,141-(35¢-c variants, limited distribution)(7,9/77)	2	4	6	12	16	20
Special 1(9/71, 25¢, 68 pgs.)-All Kirby/Ayers-r	4	8	12	29	40	50

NOTE: ***Ayers*** *a-13, 14, 16.* ***Colan*** *a-5, 35, 37; c-145p, 148p, 149p.* ***Davis*** *a-125r.* ***Everett*** *a-54i, 65, 66, 88, 96i, 148i(r).* ***Gulacy*** *c-147.* ***Heath*** *c-4.* ***G. Kane*** *c-101, 144.* ***Keller*** *a-5, 144r.* ***Kirby*** *a-17-32, 34, 42, 43, 84, 86, 92, 109r, 112r, 137r, Spec. 1; c-17-35, 37, 38, 40, 41, 43-47, 137r.* ***Maneely*** *c-1, 2, 5, 6, 14.* ***Morisi*** *a-13.* ***Morrow/Williamson*** *r-111.* ***Roussos*** *r-146i, 147i, 149-151i.* ***Severin*** *a-16; c-8, 13.* ***Sutton*** *a-93.* ***Torres*** *a-99r.* ***Tuska*** *a-14.* ***Wildey*** *r-146-151(Outlaw Kid).* ***Williamson*** *r-79, 86, 95.*

RAWHIDE KID
Marvel Comics Group: Aug, 1985 - No. 4, Nov, 1985 (Mini-series)

1-4 5.00

RAWHIDE KID
Marvel Comics (MAX): Apr, 2003 - No. 5, June, 2003 ($2.99, limited series)

1-John Severin-a/Ron Zimmerman-s; Dave Johnson-c 3.00
2-5: 3-Dodson-c. 4-Darwyn Cooke-c. 5-J. Scott Campbell-c 3.00
Vol. 1: Slap Leather TPB (2003, $12.99) r/#1-5 13.00

RAY, THE (See Freedom Fighters & Smash Comics #14)
DC Comics: Feb, 1992 - No. 6, July, 1992 ($1.00, mini-series)

1-Sienkiewicz-c; Joe Quesada-a(p) in 1-5 5.00
2-6: 3-6-Quesada-c(p). 6-Quesada layouts only 3.00
...In a Blaze of Power (1994, $12.95)-r/#1-6 w/new Quesada-c 13.00

RAY, THE
DC Comics: May, 1994 - No. 28, Oct, 1996 ($1.75/$1.95/$2.25)

1-Quesada-c(p); Superboy app. 3.00
1-($2.95)-Collectors Edition w/diff. Quesada-c; embossed foil-c 4.00
2-5,0,6-24,26-28: 2-Quesada-c(p); Superboy app. 5-(9/94). 0-(10/94) 2.25
25-($3.50)-Future Flash (Bart Allen)-c/app; double size 3.50
Annual 1 ($3.95, 68 pgs.)-Superman app. 4.00

RAY BRADBURY COMICS
Topps Comics: Feb, 1993 - V4#1, June, 1994 ($2.95)

1-5-Polybagged w/3 trading cards each. 1-All dinosaur issue; Corben-a; Williamson/Torres/Krenkel-r/Weird Science-Fantasy #25. 3-All dinosaur issue; Steacy painted-c; Stout-a 3.00
Special Edition 1 (1994, $2.95)-The Illustrated Man 3.00
...Special: Tales of Horror #1 ($2.50), ...Trilogy of Terror V3#1 (5/94, $2.50), ...Martian Chronicles V4#1 (6/94, $2.50)-Steranko-c 2.50

NOTE: ***Kelley Jones*** *a-Trilogy of Terror V3#1.* ***Kaluta*** *a-Martian Chronicles V4#1.* ***Kurtzman/Matt Wagner*** *c-2.* ***McKean*** *c-4.* ***Mignola*** *a-4.* ***Wood*** *a-Trilogy of Terror V3#1r.*

RAZORLINE
Marvel Comics: Sept, 1993 (75¢, one-shot)

1-Clive Barker super-heroes: Ectokid, Hokum & Hex, Hyperkind & Saint Sinner (all 1st app.) 2.25

RAZOR'S EDGE, THE
DC Comics (WildStorm): Dec, 2004 - Present ($2.95)

1,2-Warblade; Bisley-c/a; Ridley-s 3.00

REAL ADVENTURE COMICS (Action Adventure #2 on)
Gillmor Magazines: Apr, 1955

	GD	VG	FN	VF	VF/NM	NM-
1	8	16	24	43	54	65

REAL ADVENTURES OF JONNY QUEST, THE
Dark Horse Comics: Sept, 1996 - No. 12, Sept, 1997 ($2.95)

1-12 3.00

REAL CLUE CRIME STORIES (Formerly Clue Comics)
Hillman Periodicals: V2#4, June, 1947 - V8#3, May, 1953

	GD	VG	FN	VF	VF/NM	NM-
V2#4(#1)-S&K c/a(3); Dan Barry-a	48	96	144	293	447	600
5-7-S&K c/a(3-4). 7-Iron Lady app.	40	80	120	233	342	450
8-12	12	24	36	69	95	120
V3#1-8,10-12, V4#1-3,5-8,11,12	10	20	30	60	80	100
V3#9-Used in **SOTI**, pg. 102	13	26	39	74	102	130
V4#4-S&K-a	14	28	42	79	110	140
V4#9,10-Krigstein-a	11	22	33	64	87	110
V5#1-5,7,8,10,12	9	18	27	52	66	80
6,9,11(1/54)-Krigstein-a	10	20	30	58	77	95
V6#1-5,8,9,11	8	16	24	46	58	70
6,7,10,12-Krigstein-a. 10-Bondage-c	10	20	30	58	77	95
V7#1-3,5-11, V8#1-3: V7#6-1 pg. Frazetta ad "Prayer" - 1st app.?	8	16	24	46	58	70
4,12-Krigstein-a	10	20	30	58	77	95

NOTE: ***Barry*** *a-9, 10; c-V2#8.* ***Briefer*** *a-V6#6.* ***Fuje*** *a- V2#7(2), 8, 11.* ***Infantino*** *a-V2#8; c-V2#11.* ***Lawrence*** *a-V3#8, V5#7.* ***Powell*** *a-V4#11, 12. V5#4, 5, 7 are 68 pgs.*

REAL EXPERIENCES (Formerly Tiny Tessie)
Atlas Comics (20CC): No. 25, Jan, 1950

	GD	VG	FN	VF	VF/NM	NM-
25-Virginia Mayo photo-c from movie "Red Light"	9	18	27	51	62	75

REAL FACT COMICS
National Periodical Publications: Mar-Apr, 1946 - No. 21, July-Aug, 1949

	GD	VG	FN	VF	VF/NM	NM-
1-S&K-c/a; Harry Houdini story; Just Imagine begins (not by Finlay); Fred Ray-a	60	120	180	375	580	785
2-S&K-a; Rin-Tin-Tin & P. T. Barnum stories	40	80	120	233	342	450
3-H.G. Wells, Lon Chaney stories; 1st DC letter column	37	74	111	209	305	400
4-Virgil Finlay-a on 'Just Imagine' begins, ends #12 (2 pgs. each); Jimmy Stewart & Jack London stories; Joe DiMaggio 1 pg. biography	40	80	120	233	342	450
5-Batman/Robin-c taken from cover of Batman #9; 5 pg. story about creation of Batman & Robin; Tom Mix story	185	370	555	1156	1778	2400
6-Origin & 1st app. Tommy Tomorrow by Weisinger and Sherman (1-2/47); Flag-c; 1st writing by Harlan Ellison (letter column, non-professional); "First Man to Reach Mars" epic-c/story	113	226	339	706	1091	1475
7-(No. 6 on inside)-Roussos-a; D. Fairbanks sty.	20	40	60	112	161	210
8-2nd app. Tommy Tomorrow by Finlay (5-6/47)	62	124	186	388	594	800
9-S&K-a; Glenn Miller, Indianapolis 500 stories	30	60	90	170	245	320
10-Vigilante by Meskin (based on movie serial); 4 pg. Finlay s/f story	29	58	87	164	237	310
11,12: 11-Annie Oakley, G-Men stories; Kinstler-a	16	32	48	89	127	165
13-Dale Evans and Tommy Tomorrow-c/stories	50	100	150	305	465	625
14,17,18: 14-Will Rogers story	15	30	45	85	120	155
15-Nuclear explosion part-c ("Last War on Earth" story); Clyde Beatty story	20	40	60	112	161	210

Real Heroes #2 © PMI

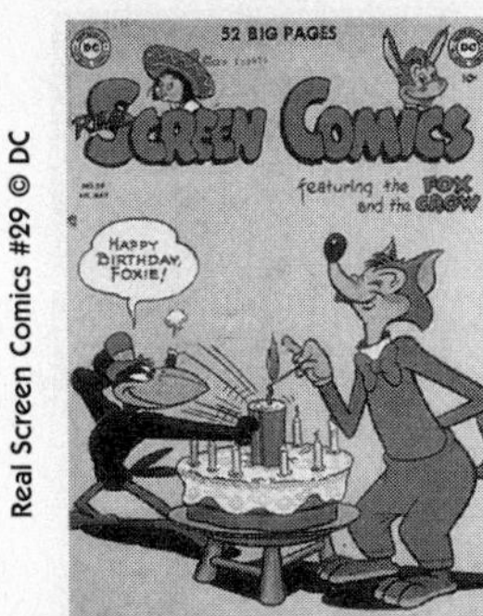

Real Screen Comics #29 © DC

Real Secrets #2 © ACE

	GD 2.0	VG 4.0	FN 6.0	VF 8.0	VF/NM 9.0	NM- 9.2
16-Tommy Tomorrow app.; 1st Planeteers?	46	92	138	281	413	575
19-Sir Arthur Conan Doyle story	17	34	51	95	135	175
20-Kubert-a, 4 pgs; Daniel Boone story	19	38	57	107	154	200
21-Kubert-a, 2 pgs; Kit Carson story	15	30	45	85	120	155

NOTE: ***Barry*** *c-16.* ***Virgil Finlay*** *c-6, 8.* ***Meskin*** *c-10.* ***Roussos*** *a-1-4, 6.*

REAL FUNNIES
Nedor Publishing Co.: Jan, 1943 - No. 3, June, 1943

	GD 2.0	VG 4.0	FN 6.0	VF 8.0	VF/NM 9.0	NM- 9.2
1-Funny animal, humor; Black Terrier app. (clone of The Black Terror)	34	68	102	193	279	365
2,3	17	34	51	95	135	175

REAL GHOSTBUSTERS, THE (Also see Slimer)
Now Comics: Aug, 1988 - No. 32, 1991 ($1.75/$1.95)

	GD 2.0	VG 4.0	FN 6.0	VF 8.0	VF/NM 9.0	NM- 9.2
1-32: 1-Based on Ghostbusters movie. #29-32 exist?						3.00

REAL HEROES COMICS
Parents' Magazine Institute: Sept, 1941 - No. 16, Oct, 1946

	GD 2.0	VG 4.0	FN 6.0	VF 8.0	VF/NM 9.0	NM- 9.2
1-Roosevelt-c/story	34	68	102	193	279	365
2-J. Edgar Hoover-c/story	15	30	45	85	120	155
3-5,7-10: 4-Churchill, Roosevelt stories	13	26	39	76	106	135
6-Lou Gehrig-c/story	21	42	63	118	169	220
11-16: 13-Kiefer-a	9	18	27	54	70	85

REALISTIC ROMANCES
Realistic Comics/Avon Periodicals: July-Aug, 1951 - No. 17, Aug-Sept, 1954 (No #9-14)

	GD 2.0	VG 4.0	FN 6.0	VF 8.0	VF/NM 9.0	NM- 9.2
1-Kinstler-a; c-/Avon paperback #211	23	46	69	130	188	245
2	11	22	33	66	91	115
3,4	11	22	33	62	84	105
5,8-Kinstler-a	11	22	33	64	87	110
6-c-/Diversey Prize Novels #6; Kinstler-a	11	22	33	66	91	115
7-Evans-a?; c-/Avon paperback #360	11	22	33	66	91	115
15,17: 17-Kinstler-c	10	20	30	58	77	95
16-Kinstler marijuana story-r/Romantic Love #6	11	22	33	64	87	110
I.W. Reprint #1,8,9: #1-r/Realistic Romances #4; Astarita-a. 9-r/Women To Love #1	2	4	6	10	13	16

NOTE: ***Astarita*** *a-2-4, 7, 8, 17. Photo c-1, 2. Painted c-3, 4.*

REAL LIFE COMICS
Nedor/Better/Standard Publ./Pictorial Magazine No. 13: Sept, 1941 - No. 59, Sept, 1952

	GD 2.0	VG 4.0	FN 6.0	VF 8.0	VF/NM 9.0	NM- 9.2
1-Uncle Sam-c/story; Daniel Boone story	56	112	168	350	538	725
2	28	56	84	158	229	300
3-Hitler cover	92	184	276	575	888	1200
4,5: 4-Story of American flag "Old Glory"	17	34	51	95	135	175
6-10: 6-Wild Bill Hickok story	16	32	48	89	127	165
11-20: 17-Albert Einstein story	15	30	45	83	117	150
21-23,25,26,28-30: 29-A-Bomb story	11	22	33	66	91	115
24-Story of Baseball (Babe Ruth)	20	40	60	112	161	210
27-Schomburg A-Bomb-c; story of A-Bomb	19	38	57	107	154	200
31-33,35,36,42-44,48,49: 49-Baseball issue	10	20	30	58	77	95
34,37-41,45-47: 34-Jimmy Stewart story. 37-Story of motion pictures; Bing Crosby story. 38-Jane Froman story. 39- "1,000,000 A.D." story. 40-Bob Feller. 41-Jimmie Foxx story ("Jimmy" on-c); "Home Run" Baker story. 45-Story of Olympic games; Burl Ives & Kit Carson story. 46-Douglas Fairbanks Jr. & Sr. story. 47-George Gershwin story	11	22	33	66	91	115
50-Frazetta-a (5 pgs.)	29	58	87	164	237	310
51-Jules Verne "Journey to the Moon" by Evans	20	40	60	112	161	210
52-Frazetta-a (4 pgs.); Severin/Elder-a(2); Evans-a	32	64	96	184	267	350
53-57-Severin/Elder-a. 54-Bat Masterson-c/story	15	30	45	83	117	150
58-Severin/Elder-a(2)	15	30	45	85	120	155
59-1 pg. Frazetta; Severin/Elder-a	15	30	45	83	117	150

NOTE: *Some issues had two titles.* ***Guardineer*** *a-40(2), 44.* ***Meskin*** *a-52.* ***Roussos*** *a-50.* ***Schomburg*** *c-1, 2, 4, 5, 7, 11, 13-21, 23, 24, 26, 28, 30-32, 34-40, 42, 44-47, 55.* ***Tuska*** *a-53. Photo-c 5, 6.*

REAL LIFE SECRETS (Real Secrets #2 on)
Ace Periodicals: Sept, 1949 (one-shot)

	GD 2.0	VG 4.0	FN 6.0	VF 8.0	VF/NM 9.0	NM- 9.2
1-Painted-c	12	24	36	71	98	125

REAL LIFE STORY OF FESS PARKER (Magazine)
Dell Publishing Co.: 1955

	GD 2.0	VG 4.0	FN 6.0	VF 8.0	VF/NM 9.0	NM- 9.2
1	10	20	30	72	104	135

REAL LIFE TALES OF SUSPENSE (See Suspense)

REAL LOVE (Formerly Hap Hazard)
Ace Periodicals (A. A. Wyn): No. 25, April, 1949 - No. 76, Nov, 1956

	GD 2.0	VG 4.0	FN 6.0	VF 8.0	VF/NM 9.0	NM- 9.2
25	13	26	39	74	102	130
26	9	18	27	52	66	80
27-L. B. Cole-a	11	22	33	64	87	110
28-35	8	16	24	43	54	65
36-66: 66-Last pre-code (2/55)	7	14	21	37	46	55
67-76	6	12	18	29	36	42

NOTE: *Photo c-50-76. Painted c-46.*

REALM, THE
Arrow Comics/WeeBee Comics #13/Caliber Press #14 on: Feb, 1986 - No. 21, 1991 ($1.50/$1.95/$2.50, B&W)

	GD 2.0	VG 4.0	FN 6.0	VF 8.0	VF/NM 9.0	NM- 9.2
1-21: 4-1st app. Deadworld (9/86)						2.50
Book 1 ($4.95, B&W)						5.00

REAL McCOYS, THE (TV)
Dell Publ. Co.: No. 1071, 1-3/60 - 5-7/1962 (All have Walter Brennan photo-c)

	GD 2.0	VG 4.0	FN 6.0	VF 8.0	VF/NM 9.0	NM- 9.2
Four Color 1071,1134-Toth-a in both	10	20	30	73	107	140
Four Color 1193,1265	10	20	30	70	100	130
01-689-207 (5-7/62)	9	18	27	63	89	115

REALM OF THE CLAW (Also see Mutant Earth as part of a flipbook)
Image Comics: Oct, 2003 - Present ($2.95)

	GD 2.0	VG 4.0	FN 6.0	VF 8.0	VF/NM 9.0	NM- 9.2
0-(7/03, $5.95) Convention Special; cover has gold-foil title logo						6.00
1,2-Two covers by Yardin						3.00

REAL SCREEN COMICS (#1 titled Real Screen Funnies; TV Screen Cartoons #129-138)
National Periodical Publications: Spring, 1945 - No. 128, May-June, 1959 (#1-40: 52 pgs.)

	GD 2.0	VG 4.0	FN 6.0	VF 8.0	VF/NM 9.0	NM- 9.2
1-The Fox & the Crow, Flippity & Flop, Tito & His Burrito begin	100	200	300	625	963	1300
2	48	96	144	293	447	600
3-5	35	70	105	198	287	375
6-10 (2-3/47)	22	44	66	123	177	230
11-20 (10-11/48): 13-The Crow x-over in Flippity & Flop	17	34	51	95	135	175
21-30 (6-7/50)	13	26	39	74	102	130
31-50	11	22	33	62	84	105
51-99	10	20	30	56	73	90
100	10	20	30	58	77	95
101-128	8	16	24	46	58	70

REAL SECRETS (Formerly Real Life Secrets)
Ace Periodicals: No. 2, Nov, 1950 - No. 5, May, 1950

	GD 2.0	VG 4.0	FN 6.0	VF 8.0	VF/NM 9.0	NM- 9.2
2-Painted-c	10	20	30	56	73	90
3-5: 3-Photo-c	8	16	24	40	50	60

REAL SPORTS COMICS (All Sports Comics #2 on)
Hillman Periodicals: Oct-Nov, 1948 (52 pgs.)

	GD 2.0	VG 4.0	FN 6.0	VF 8.0	VF/NM 9.0	NM- 9.2
1-Powell-a (12 pgs.)	40	80	120	239	357	475

REAL WAR STORIES
Eclipse Comics: July, 1987; No. 2, Jan, 1991 ($2.00, 52 pgs.)

	GD 2.0	VG 4.0	FN 6.0	VF 8.0	VF/NM 9.0	NM- 9.2
1-Bolland-a(p), Bissette-a, Totleben-a(i); Alan Moore scripts (2nd printing exists, 2/88)						3.00
2-($4.95)						5.00

REAL WESTERN HERO (Formerly Wow #1-69; Western Hero #76 on)
Fawcett Publications: No. 70, Sept, 1948 - No. 75, Feb, 1949 (All 52 pgs.)

	GD 2.0	VG 4.0	FN 6.0	VF 8.0	VF/NM 9.0	NM- 9.2
70(#1)-Tom Mix, Monte Hale, Hopalong Cassidy, Young Falcon begin	37	74	111	209	305	400
71-75: 71-Gabby Hayes begins. 71,72-Captain Tootsie by Beck. 75-Big Bow and Little Arrow app.	23	46	69	130	188	245

NOTE: *Painted/photo c-70-73; painted c-74, 75.*

REAL WEST ROMANCES
Crestwood Publishing Co./Prize Publ.: 4-5/49 - V1#6, 3/50; V2#1, Apr-May, 1950 (All 52 pgs. & photo-c)

	GD 2.0	VG 4.0	FN 6.0	VF 8.0	VF/NM 9.0	NM- 9.2
V1#1-S&K-a(p)	26	52	78	147	211	275
2	13	26	39	74	102	130
3-Kirby-a(p) only	14	28	42	79	110	140
4-S&K-a; Whip Wilson, Reno Browne photo-c	20	40	60	112	161	210
5-Audie Murphy, Gale Storm photo-c; S&K-a	18	36	54	100	143	185
6-Produced by S&K, no S&K-a; Robert Preston & Cathy Downs photo-c	14	28	42	79	110	140
V2#1-Kirby-a(p)	11	22	33	64	87	110

NOTE: ***Meskin*** *a-V1#5, 6.* ***Severin/Elder*** *a-V1#3-6, V2#1.* ***Meskin*** *a-V1#6.* ***Leonard Starr*** *a-1-3. Photo-c V1#1-6, V2#1.*

REALWORLDS :...
DC Comics: 2000 ($5.95, one-shots, prestige format)

Batman - Marshall Rogers-a/Golden & Sniegoski-s; Justice League of America -Dematteis-s/Barr-painted art; Superman - Vance-s/García-López & Rubenstein-a; Wonder Woman -

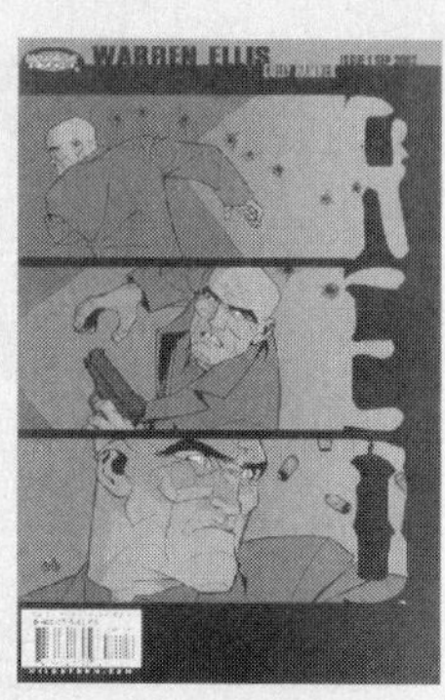

Red #1 © Ellis & Hamner

Red Dragon Comics (2nd) #5 © CN

"Red" Rabbit Comics #1 © Dearfield

GD VG FN VF VF/NM NM-
2.0 4.0 6.0 8.0 9.0 9.2

Hanson & Neuwirth-s/Sam-a 6.00

RE-ANIMATOR IN FULL COLOR
Adventure Comics: Oct, 1991 - No. 3, 1992 ($2.95, mini-series)
1-3: Adapts horror movie. 1-Dorman painted-c 3.00

REAP THE WILD WIND (See Cinema Comics Herald)

REBEL, THE (TV)
Dell Publishing Co.: No. 1076, Feb-Apr, 1960 - No. 1262, Dec-Feb, 1961-62
Four Color 1076 (#1)-Sekowsky-a, photo-c 11 22 33 80 120 160
Four Color 1138 (9-11/60), 1207 (9-11/61), 1262-Photo-c
10 20 30 70 100 130

R.E.B.E.L.S. '94 (Becomes R.E.B.E.L.S. '95 & R.E.B.E.L.S. '96)
DC Comics: No. 0, Oct, 1994 - No. 17, Mar, 1996 ($1.95/$2.25)
0-17: 8-$2.25-c begins. 15-R.E.B.E.L.S '96 begins. 2.25

REBEL SWORD (Manga)
Dark Horse Comics: Oct, 1994 - No. 6, Feb, 1995 ($2.50, B&W)
1-6 2.50

RECORD BOOK OF FAMOUS POLICE CASES
St. John Publishing Co.: 1949 (25¢, 132 pgs.)
nn-Kubert-a(3); r/Son of Sinbad; Baker-c 40 80 120 233 342 450

RED
DC Comics (Homage): Sept, 2003 - No. 3, Feb, 2004 ($2.95, limited series)
1-3-Warren Ellis-s/Cully Hamner-a/c 3.00
Red/Tokyo Storm Warning TPB (2004, $14.95) Flip book r/both series 15.00

RED ARROW
P. L. Publishing Co.: May-June, 1951 - No. 3, Oct, 1951
1 11 22 33 62 84 105
2,3 9 18 27 49 62 75

RED BAND COMICS
Enwil Associates: Nov, 1944 - No. 4, May, 1945
1 40 80 120 230 335 440
2-Origin Bogeyman & Santanas; c-reprint/#1 29 58 87 164 237 310
3,4-Captain Wizard app. in both (1st app.); each has identical contents/cover
27 54 81 154 222 290

REDBLADE
Dark Horse Comics: Apr, 1993 - No. 3, July, 1993 ($2.50, mini-series)
1-3: 1-Double gatefold-c 3.00

RED CIRCLE COMICS (Also see Blazing Comics & Blue Circle Comics)
Rural Home Publications (Enwil): Jan, 1945 - No. 4, April, 1945
1-The Prankster & Red Riot begin 40 80 120 230 335 440
2-Starr-a; The Judge (costumed hero) app. 30 60 90 170 245 320
3,4-Starr-c/a. 3-The Prankster not in costume 23 46 69 132 191 250
4-(Dated 4/45)-Leftover covers to #4 were later restapled over early 1950s coverless comics; variations in the coverless comics used are endless; Woman Outlaws, Dorothy Lamour, Crime Does Not Pay, Sabu, Diary Loves, Love Confessions & Young Love V3#3 known
17 34 51 95 135 175

RED CIRCLE SORCERY (Chilling Adventures in Sorcery #1-5)
Red Circle Prod. (Archie): No. 6, Apr, 1974 - No. 11, Feb, 1975 (All 25¢ iss.)
6,8,9,11: 6-Early Chaykin-a. 7-Pino-a. 8-Only app. The Cobra
2 4 6 8 10 12
7-Bruce Jones-a with Wrightson, Kaluta, Jeff Jones 2 4 6 11 14 18
10-Wood-a(i) 2 4 6 9 11 14
NOTE: ***Chaykin*** *a-6, 10.* ***McWilliams*** *a-10(2 & 3 pgs.).* ***Mooney*** *a-11p.* ***Morrow*** *a-6-8, 9(text illos), 10, 11i; c-6-11.* ***Thorne*** *a-8, 10.* ***Toth*** *a-8, 9.*

RED DOG (See Night Music #7)

RED DRAGON
Comico: June, 1996 ($2.95)
1-Bisley-c 3.00

RED DRAGON COMICS (1st Series) (Formerly Trail Blazers; see Super Magician V5#7, 8)
Street & Smith Publications: No. 5, Jan, 1943 - No. 9, Jan, 1944
5-Origin Red Rover, the Crimson Crimebuster; Rex King, Man of Adventure, Captain Jack Commando, & The Minute Man begin; text origin Red Dragon; Binder-c
100 200 300 625 963 1300
6-Origin The Black Crusader & Red Dragon (3/43); 1st story app. Red Dragon & 1st cover (classic-c) 231 462 693 1444 2222 3000
7-Classic-c 181 362 543 1131 1741 2350

GD VG FN VF VF/NM NM-
2.0 4.0 6.0 8.0 9.0 9.2

8-The Red Knight app. 75 150 225 469 722 975
9-Origin Chuck Magnon, Immortal Man 75 150 225 469 722 975

RED DRAGON COMICS (2nd Series)(See Super Magician V2#8)
Street & Smith Publications: Nov, 1947 - No. 6, Jan, 1949; No. 7, July, 1949
1-Red Dragon begins; Elliman, Nigel app.; Edd Cartier-c/a
92 184 276 575 888 1200
2-Cartier-c 65 130 195 406 623 840
3-1st app. Dr. Neff Ghost Breaker by Powell; Elliman, Nigel app.
55 110 165 336 511 685
4-Cartier c/a 75 150 225 469 722 975
5-7 40 80 120 239 357 475
NOTE: ***Maneely*** *a-5, 7.* ***Powell*** *a-2-7; c-3, 5, 7.*

RED EAGLE
David McKay Publications: No. 16, Aug, 1938
Feature Books 16 26 52 78 147 211 275

REDEYE (See Comics Reading Libraries in the Promotional Comics section)

RED FOX (Formerly Manhunt! #1-14; also see Extra Comics)
Magazine Enterprises: No. 15, 1954
15(A-1 #108)-Undercover Girl story; L.B. Cole-c/a (Red Fox); r-from Manhunt; Powell-a
20 40 60 112 161 210

RED FURY
High Impact Entertainment: 1997 ($2.95, B&W)
1 3.00

RED GOOSE COMIC SELECTIONS (See Comic Selections)

RED HAWK (See A-1 Comics, Bobby Benson's ..#14-16 & Straight Arrow #2)
Magazine Enterprises: No. 90, 1953
A-1 90-Powell-c/a 13 26 39 74 102 130

RED MASK (Formerly Tim Holt; see Best Comics, Blazing Six-Guns)
Magazine Enterprises No. 42-53/Sussex No. 54 (M.E. on-c): No. 42, June-July, 1954 - No. 53, May, 1956; No. 54, Sept, 1957
42-Ghost Rider by Ayers continues, ends #50; Black Phantom continues; 3-D effect c/stories begin 22 44 66 127 184 240
43- 3-D effect-c/stories 20 40 60 112 161 210
44-52: 3-D effect stories only. 47-Last pre-code issue. 50-Last Ghost Rider. 51-The Presto Kid begins by Ayers (1st app.); Presto Kid-c begins; last 3-D effect story.
52-Origin The Presto Kid 18 36 54 100 143 185
53,54-Last Black Phantom; last Presto Kid-c 15 30 45 83 117 150
I.W. Reprint #1 (r-/#52). 2 (nd, r/#51 w/diff.-c). 3, 8 (nd; Kinstler-c); 8-r/Red Mask #52
3 6 9 18 23 28
NOTE: ***Ayers*** *art on Ghost Rider & Presto Kid.* ***Bolle*** *art in all (Red Mask); c-43, 44, 49.* ***Guardineer*** *a-52. Black Phantom in #42-44, 47-50, 53, 54.*

REDMASK OF THE RIO GRANDE
AC Comics: 1990 ($2.50, 28pgs.)(Has photos of movie posters)
1-Bolle-c/a(r); photo inside-c 2.50

RED MOUNTAIN FEATURING QUANTRELL'S RAIDERS (Movie)(Also see Jesse James #28)
Avon Periodicals: 1952
nn-Alan Ladd; Kinstler-c 30 60 90 170 245 320

"RED" RABBIT COMICS
Dearfield Comic/J. Charles Laue Publ. Co.: Jan, 1947 - No. 22, Aug-Sep, 1951
1 14 28 42 79 110 140
2 8 16 24 46 58 70
3-10 7 14 21 37 46 55
11-17,19-22 7 14 21 35 43 50
18-Flying Saucer-c (1/51) 8 16 24 46 58 70

RED RAVEN COMICS (Human Torch #2 on)(Also see X-Men #44 & Sub-Mariner #26, 2nd series)
Timely Comics: August, 1940
1-Origin & 1st app. Red Raven; Comet Pierce & Mercury by Kirby, The Human Top & The Eternal Brain; intro. Magar, the Mystic & only app.; Kirby-c (his 1st signed work)
1088 2176 3264 8160 13,330 18,500

RED ROCKET 7
Dark Horse Comics: Aug, 1997 - No. 7, June, 1998 ($3.95, square format, limited series)
1-7-Mike Allred-c/s/a 4.00

RED RYDER COMICS (Hi Spot #2)(Movies, radio)(See Crackajack Funnies & Super Book of Comics)
Hawley Publ. No. 1/Dell Publishing Co.(K.K.) No. 3 on: 9/40; No. 3, 8/41 - No. 5, 12/41; No.

Red Ryder Comics #11 © DELL

Red Sonja #8 © MAR

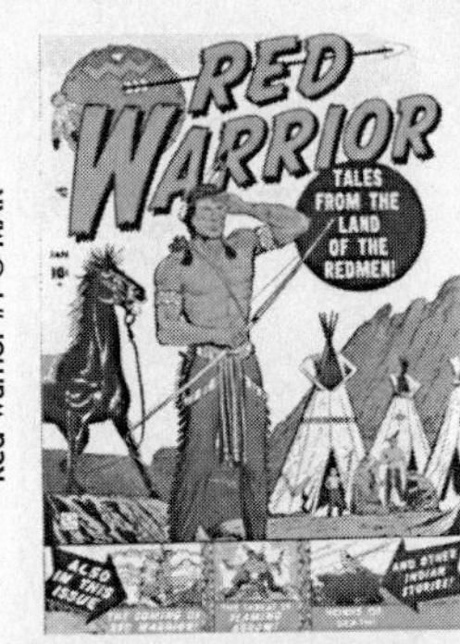

Red Warrior #1 © MAR

GD VG FN VF VF/NM NM-
2.0 4.0 6.0 8.0 9.0 9.2

6, 4/42 - No. 151, 4-6/57

1-Red Ryder, his horse Thunder, Little Beaver & his horse Papoose strip reprints begin by Fred Harman; 1st meeting of Red & Little Beaver; Harman line-drawn-c #1-85 300 600 900 1925 3063 4200
3-(Scarce)-Alley Oop, Capt. Easy, Dan Dunn, Freckles & His Friends, King of the Royal Mtd., Myra North strip-r begin 85 170 255 665 1083 1500
4-6: 6-1st Dell issue (4/42) 41 82 123 305 478 650
7-10 33 66 99 248 387 525
11-20 25 50 75 179 275 370
21-32-Last Alley Oop, Dan Dunn, Capt. Easy, Freckles 17 34 51 121 186 250
33-40 (52 pgs.) 12 24 36 87 134 180
41 (52 pgs.)-Rocky Lane photo back-c; photo back-c begin, end #57 13 26 39 92 141 190
42-46 (52 pgs.): 46-Last Red Ryder strip-r 11 22 33 75 110 145
47-53 (52 pgs.): 47-New stories on Red Ryder begin. 49,52-Harmon photo back-c 9 18 27 65 93 120
54-92: 54-73 (36 pgs.). 59-Harmon photo back-c. 73-Last King of the Royal Mtd; strip-r by Jim Gary. 74-85 (52 pgs.)-Harman line-drawn-c. 86-92 (52 pgs.)-Harman painted-c 8 16 24 53 74 95
93-99,101-106: 94-96 (36 pgs.)-Harman painted-c. 97,98,(36 pgs.)-Harman line-drawn-c. 99,101-106 (36 pgs.)-Jim Bannon Photo-c 7 14 21 46 63 80
100 (36 pgs.)-Bannon photo-c 7 14 21 50 68 85
107-118 (52 pgs.)-Harman line-drawn-c 6 12 18 43 59 75
119-129 (52 pgs.): 119-Painted-c begin, not by Harman, end #151 6 12 18 40 55 70
130-151 (36 pgs.): 145-Title change to Red Ryder Ranch Magazine 149-Title change to Red Ryder Ranch Comics 6 12 18 38 52 65
Four Color 916 (7/58) 6 12 18 38 52 65

NOTE: ***Fred Harman** a-1-99; c-1-98, 107-118. Don Red Barry, Allan Rocky Lane, Wild Bill Elliott & Jim Bannon starred as Red Ryder in the movies. Robert Blake starred as Little Beaver.*

RED RYDER PAINT BOOK
Whitman Publishing Co.: 1941 (8-1/2x11-1/2", 148 pgs.)

nn-Reprints 1940 daily strips 81 162 243 506 778 1050

RED SEAL COMICS (Formerly Carnival Comics, and/or Spotlight Comics?)
Harry 'A' Chesler/Superior Publ. No. 19 on: No. 14, 10/45 - No. 18, 10/46; No. 19, 6/47 - No. 22, 12/47

14-The Black Dwarf begins (continued from Spotlight?); Little Nemo app; bondage/hypo-c; Tuska-a 75 150 225 469 722 975
15-Torture story; funny-c 48 96 144 293 447 600
16-Used in **SOTI**, pg. 181, illo "Outside the forbidden pages of de Sade, you find draining a girl's blood only in children's comics;" drug club story r-later in Crime Reporter #1; Veiled Avenger & Barry Kuda app; Tuska-a; funny-c 63 126 189 394 610 825
17,18,20: Lady Satan, Yankee Girl & Sky Chief app; 17-Tuska-a 48 96 144 293 447 600
19-No Black Dwarf (on-c only); Zor, El Tigre app. 43 86 129 262 401 540
21-Lady Satan & Black Dwarf app. 38 76 114 219 320 420
22-Zor, Rocketman app. (68 pgs.) 38 76 114 219 320 420

REDSKIN (Thrilling Indian Stories)(Famous Western Badmen #13 on)
Youthful Magazines: Sept, 1950 - No. 12, Oct, 1952

1-Walter Johnson-a (7 pgs.) 18 36 54 100 143 185
2 11 22 33 62 84 105
3-12: 3-Daniel Boone story. 6-Geronimo story 10 20 30 56 73 90

NOTE: ***Walter Johnson** c-3, 4. **Palais** a-11. **Wildey** a-5, 11. Bondage c-6, 12.*

RED SONJA (Also see Conan #23, Kull & The Barbarians, Marvel Feature & Savage Sword Of Conan #1)
Marvel Comics Group: 1/77 - No. 15, 5/79; V1#1, 2/83 - V2#2, 3/83; V3#1, 8/83 - V3#4, 2/84; V3#5, 1/85 - V3#13, 5/86

1-Created by Robert E. Howard 2 4 6 10 12 15
2-10: 5-Last 30¢ issue 1 2 3 4 5 7
4,5-(35¢-c variants, limited distribution)(7,9/77) 1 2 3 6 8 10
11-15, V1#1,V2#2: 14-Last 35¢ issue 6.00
V3#1-13: #1-4 ($1.00, 52 pgs.) 3.50

NOTE: ***Brunner** c-12-14. **J. Buscema** a(p)-12, 13, 15; c-V#1. **Nebres** a-V3#3i(part). **N. Redondo** a-8i, V3#2i, 3i. **Simonson** a-V3#1. **Thorne** c/a-1-11.*

RED SONJA: SCAVENGER HUNT
Marvel Comics: Dec, 1995 ($2.95, one-shot)

1 3.00

RED SONJA: THE MOVIE
Marvel Comics Group: Nov, 1985 - No. 2, Dec, 1985 (Limited series)

1,2-Movie adapt-r/Marvel Super Spec. #38 3.00

RED STAR, THE
Image Comics/Archangel Studios: June, 2000 - No. 9, June, 2002 ($2.95)

1-Christian Gossett-s/a(p) 4.00
2-9: 9-Beck-c 3.00
#(7.5) Reprints Wizard #1/2 story with new pages 3.00
Annual 1 (Archangel Studios, 11/02, $3.50) "Run Makita Run" 3.50
TPB (4/01, $24.95, 9x12") Oversized r/#1-4; intro. by Bendis 25.00
Nokgorka TPB (8/02, $24.95, 9x12") Oversized r/#6-9; w/sketch pages 25.00
Wizard 1/2 (mail order) 10.00

RED STAR, THE (Volume 2)
CrossGen Comics #1,2/Archangel Studios #3 on: Feb, 2003 - Present ($2.95/$2.99)

1-5-Christian Gossett-s/a(p) 3.00
Prison of Souls TPB (8/04, $24.95, 9x12") Oversized r/#1-5; w/sketch pages 25.00

RED TORNADO (See All-American #20 & Justice League of America #64)
DC Comics: July, 1985 - No. 4, Oct, 1985 (Limited series)

1-4: Kurt Busiek scripts in all. 1-3-Superman & Batman cameos 3.00

RED WARRIOR
Marvel/Atlas Comics (TCI): Jan, 1951 - No. 6, Dec, 1951

1-Red Warrior & his horse White Wing; Tuska-a 17 34 51 95 135 175
2-Tuska-c 10 20 30 56 73 90
3-6: 4-Origin White Wing. 6-Maneely-c 9 18 27 49 62 75

RED WOLF (See Avengers #80 & Marvel Spotlight #1)
Marvel Comics Group: May, 1972 - No. 9, Sept, 1973

1-(Western hero); Gil Kane/Severin-c; Shores-a 3 6 9 18 24 30
2-9: 2-Kane-c; Shores-a. 6-Tuska-r in back-up. 7-Red Wolf as super hero begins. 9-Origin sidekick, Lobo (wolf) 2 4 6 11 14 18

REESE'S PIECES
Eclipse Comics: Oct, 1985 - No.2, Oct, 1985 ($1.75, Baxter paper)

1,2-B&W-r in color 2.25

REFORM SCHOOL GIRL!
Realistic Comics: 1951

nn-Used in **SOTI**, pg. 358, & cover ill. with caption "Comic books are supposed to be like fairy tales" 162 324 486 1013 1557 2100
(Prices vary widely on this book)

NOTE: *The cover and title originated from a digest-sized book published by Diversey Publishing Co. of Chicago in 1948. The original book "House of Fury", Doubleday, came out in 1941. The girl's real name which appears on the cover of the digest and comic is Marty Collins, Canadian model and ice skating star who posed for this special color photograph for the Diversey novel.*

REGENTS ILLUSTRATED CLASSICS
Prentice Hall Regents, Englewood Cliffs, NJ 07632: 1981 (Plus more recent reprintings) (48 pgs., B&W-a with 14 pgs. of teaching helps)

NOTE: *This series contains Classics Ill. art, and was produced from the same illegal source as **Cassette Books.** But when Twin Circle sued to stop the sale of the Cassette Books, they decided to permit this series to continue. This series was produced as a teaching aid. The 20 title series is divided into four levels based upon number of basic words used therein. There is also a teacher's manual for each level. All of the titles are still available from the publisher for about $5 each retail. The number to call for mail order purchases is (201)767-5937. Almost all of the issues have new covers taken from some interior art panel. Here is a list of the series by Regents ident. no. and the Classics Ill. counterpart.*

16770(CI#24-A2)18333(CI#3-A2)21668(CI#13-A2)32224(CI#21)33051(CI#26)35788(CI#84)37153(CI#16)44460(CI#19-A2)44808(CI#18-A2)52395(CI#4-A2)58627(CI#5-A2)60067(CI#30)68405(CI#23A1)70302(CI#29)78192(CI#7-A2)78193(CI#10-A2)79679(CI#85)92046(CI#1-A2)93062(CI#64)93512(CI#25)

RE: GEX
Awesome-Hyperwerks: Jul, 1998 - No. 0, Dec, 1998; ($2.50)

Preview (7/98) Wizard Con Edition 3.00
0-(12/98) Loeb-s/Liefeld-a/Pat Lee-c, 1-(9/98) Loeb-s/Liefeld-a/c 2.50

REGGIE (Formerly Archie's Rival...; Reggie & Me #19 on)
Archie Publications: No. 15, Sept, 1963 - No. 18, Nov, 1965

15(9/63), 16(10/64), 17(8/65), 18(11/65) 5 10 15 36 48 60

NOTE: *Cover title No. 15 & 16 is Archie's Rival Reggie.*

REGGIE AND ME (Formerly Reggie)
Archie Publ.: No. 19, Aug, 1966 - No. 126, Sept, 1980 (No. 50-68: 52 pgs.)

19-Evilheart app. 4 8 12 25 33 42
20-23-Evilheart app.; with Pureheart #22 3 6 9 19 25 32
24-40(3/70) 2 4 6 14 18 22
41-49(7/71) 2 4 6 10 13 16
50(9/71)-68 (1/74, 52 pgs.) 2 4 6 12 16 20
69-99 1 2 3 5 7 9
100(10/77) 2 4 6 8 10 12
101-126 1 2 3 4 5 7

Reload #1 © Ellis/Gulacy/Palmiotti

Ren & Stimpy Show #38 © Nickelodeon

Resurrection Man #17 © DC

	GD 2.0	VG 4.0	FN 6.0	VF 8.0	VF/NM 9.0	NM- 9.2

REGGIE'S JOKES (See Reggie's Wise Guy Jokes)

REGGIE'S REVENGE!
Archie Comic Publications, Inc.: Spring, 1994 - No. 3 ($2.00, 52 pgs.) (Published semi-annually)

	GD	VG	FN	VF	VF/NM	NM-
1-Bound-in pull-out poster						3.00
2,3						2.25

REGGIE'S WISE GUY JOKES
Archie Publications: Aug, 1968 - No. 55, 1980 (#5-28 are Giants)

	GD	VG	FN	VF	VF/NM	NM-
1	5	10	15	33	44	55
2-4	3	6	9	18	20	24
5-16 (1/71)(68 pg. Giants)	3	6	9	18	24	30
17-28 (52 pg. Giants)	2	4	6	12	16	20
29-40(1/77)	1	2	3	5	7	9
41-55						6.00

REGISTERED NURSE
Charlton Comics: Summer, 1963

	GD	VG	FN	VF	VF/NM	NM-
1-r/Nurse Betsy Crane & Cynthia Doyle	3	6	9	18	23	28

REG'LAR FELLERS
Visual Editions (Standard): No. 5, Nov, 1947 - No. 6, Mar, 1948

	GD	VG	FN	VF	VF/NM	NM-
5,6	9	18	27	49	62	75

REG'LAR FELLERS HEROIC (See Heroic Comics)

REGULATORS
Image Comics: June, 1995 - No. 3, Aug, 1995 ($2.50)

	GD	VG	FN	VF	VF/NM	NM-
1-3: Kurt Busiek scripts						2.50

REID FLEMING, WORLD'S TOUGHEST MILKMAN
Eclipse Comics/ Deep Sea Comics: 8/86; V2#1, 12/86 - V2#3, 12/88; V2#4, 11/89; V2#5, 11/90 (B&W)

	GD	VG	FN	VF	VF/NM	NM-
1 (3rd print, large size, 8/86, $2.50), 1-4th & 5th printings ($2.50)						3.00
V2#1 (10/86, regular size, $2.00), 1-2nd print, 3rd print ($2.00, 2/89)						2.25
2-8 , V2#2-2nd & 3rd printings, V2#4-2nd printing, V2#5 ($2.00)						2.25

REIGN OF THE ZODIAC
DC Comics: Oct, 2003 - No. 8, May, 2004 ($2.75)

	GD	VG	FN	VF	VF/NM	NM-
1-8: 1-6,8-Giffen-s/Doran-a/Harris-c. 7-Byrd-a						2.75

RELATIVE HEROES
DC Comics: Mar, 2000 - No. 6, Aug, 2000 ($2.50, limited series)

	GD	VG	FN	VF	VF/NM	NM-
1-6-Grayson-s/Guichet & Sowd-a. 6-Superman-c/app.						2.50

RELOAD
DC Comics (Homage): May, 2003 - No. 3, Sept, 2003 ($2.95, limited series)

	GD	VG	FN	VF	VF/NM	NM-
1-3-Warren Ellis-s/Paul Gulacy & Jimmy Palmiotti-a						3.00
.../Mek TPB (2004, $14.95, flip book) r/Reload #1-3 & Mek #1-3						15.00

RELUCTANT DRAGON, THE (Walt Disney's...)
Dell Publishing Co.: No. 13, 1940

	GD	VG	FN	VF	VF/NM	NM-
Four Color 13-Contains 2 pgs. of photos from film; 2 pg. foreword to Fantasia by Leopold Stokowski; Donald Duck, Goofy, Baby Weems & Mickey Mouse (as the Sorcerer's Apprentice) app.	150	300	450	1140	1820	2500

REMAINS
IDW Publishing: May, 2004 - No. 5, Sept, 2004 ($3.99)

	GD	VG	FN	VF	VF/NM	NM-
1-5-Steve Niles-s/Kieron Dwyer-a						4.00

REMARKABLE WORLDS OF PROFESSOR PHINEAS B. FUDDLE, THE
DC Comics (Paradox Press): 2000 - No. 4, 2000 ($5.95, limited series)

	GD	VG	FN	VF	VF/NM	NM-
1-4-Boaz Yakin-s/Erez Yakin-a						6.00
TPB (2001, $19.95) r/series						20.00

REMEMBER PEARL HARBOR
Street & Smith Publications: 1942 (68 pgs.) (Illustrated story of the battle)

	GD	VG	FN	VF	VF/NM	NM-
nn-Uncle Sam-c; Jack Binder-a	46	92	138	281	428	575

REN & STIMPY SHOW, THE (TV) (Nicklodeon cartoon characters)
Marvel Comics: Dec, 1992 - No. 44, July, 1996 ($1.75/$1.95)

	GD	VG	FN	VF	VF/NM	NM-
1-($2.25)-Polybagged w/scratch & sniff Ren or Stimpy air fowler (equal numbers of each were made)						6.00
1-2nd & 3rd printing; different dialogue on-c						2.25
2-6: 4-Muddy Mudskipper back-up. 5-Bill Wray painted-c. 6-Spider-Man vs. Powdered Toast Man						4.00
7-17: 12-1st solo back-up story w/Tank & Brenner						2.50
18-44: 18-Powered Toast Man app.						2.50
25 ($2.95) Deluxe edition w/die cut cover						3.00
...Don't Try This at Home (3/94, $12.95, TPB)-r/#9-12						13.00
...Eenteractive Special ('95, $2.95)						3.00
...Holiday Special 1994 (2/95, $2.95, 52 pgs.)						3.00
...Mini Comic (1995)						5.00
...Pick of the Litter nn (1993, $12.95, TPB)-r/#1-4						13.00
...Radio Daze (11/95, $1.95)						2.50
...Running Joke nn (1993, $12.95, TPB)-r/#1-4 plus new-a						13.00
...Seeck Little Monkeys (1/95, $12.95)-r/#17-20						13.00
...Special 2 (7/94, $2.95, 52 pgs.), ...Special 3 (10/94, $2.95, 52 pgs.)-Choose adventure, ...Special: Around the World in a Daze ($2.95), ...Special: Four Swerks (1/95, $2.95, 52 pgs.)-FF #1 cover swipe; cover reads "Four Swerks w/5 pg. coloring book.", ...Special: Powdered Toast Man 1 (4/94, $2.95, 52 pgs.), ...Special: Powdered Toast Man's Cereal Serial (4/95, $2.95), ...Special: Sports (10/95, $2.95)						3.00
...Tastes Like Chicken nn (11/93,$12.95,TPB)-r/#5-8						13.00
...Your Pals (1994, $12.95, TPB)-r/#13-16						13.00

RENFIELD
Caliber Press:1994 - No. 3, 1995 ($2.95, B&W, limited series)

	GD	VG	FN	VF	VF/NM	NM-
1-3						3.00

RENO BROWNE, HOLLYWOOD'S GREATEST COWGIRL (Formerly Margie Comics; Apache Kid #53 on; also see Western Hearts, Western Life Romances & Western Love)
Marvel Comics (MPC): No. 50, April, 1950 - No. 52, Sept, 1950 (52 pgs.)

	GD	VG	FN	VF	VF/NM	NM-
50-Reno Browne photo-c on all	34	68	102	193	279	365
51,52	29	58	87	164	237	310

REPLACEMENT GOD
Amaze Ink: June, 1995 - No. 8 ($2.95, B&W)

	GD	VG	FN	VF	VF/NM	NM-
1-8-Zander Cannon-s/a						3.00

REPLACEMENT GOD
Image Comics: May, 1997 - No. 5 ($2.95, B&W)

	GD	VG	FN	VF	VF/NM	NM-
1-5: 1-Flip book w/"Knute's Escapes", r/original series. 2-Flip book w/"Harris Thermidor". 3-5: 3-Flip book w/"Myth and Legend"						3.00

REPTILICUS (Becomes Reptisaurus #3 on)
Charlton Comics: Aug, 1961 - No. 2, Oct, 1961

	GD	VG	FN	VF	VF/NM	NM-
1 (Movie)	20	40	60	141	216	290
2	10	20	30	75	110	145

REPTISAURUS (Reptilicus #1,2)
Charlton Comics: V2#3, Jan, 1962 - No. 8, Dec, 1962; Summer, 1963

	GD	VG	FN	VF	VF/NM	NM-
V2#3-8: 8-Montes/Bache-c/a	7	14	21	51	71	90
Special Edition 1 (Summer, 1963)	7	14	21	50	68	85

REQUIEM FOR DRACULA
Marvel Comics: Feb, 1993 ($2.00, 52 pgs.)

	GD	VG	FN	VF	VF/NM	NM-
nn-r/Tomb of Dracula #69,70 by Gene Colan						2.25

RESCUERS, THE (See Walt Disney Showcase #40)

RESIDENT EVIL (Based on video game)
Image Comics (WildStorm): Mar, 1998 - No. 5 ($4.95, quarterly magazine)

	GD	VG	FN	VF	VF/NM	NM-
1						7.00
2-5						5.00
...Code: Veronica 1-4 (2002, $14.95) English reprint of Japanese comics						15.00
...Collection One ('99, $14.95, TPB) r/#1-4						15.00

RESIDENT EVIL: FIRE AND ICE
DC Comics (WildStorm): Dec, 2000 - No. 4, May, 2001 ($2.50, limited series)

	GD	VG	FN	VF	VF/NM	NM-
1-4-Bermejo-c						2.50

RESISTANCE, THE
DC Comics (WildStorm): Nov, 2002 - No. 8, June, 2003 ($2.95)

	GD	VG	FN	VF	VF/NM	NM-
1-8-Palmiotti & Gray-s/Santacruz-a						3.00

RESTAURANT AT THE END OF THE UNIVERSE, THE (See Hitchhiker's Guide to the Galaxy & Life, the Universe & Everything)
DC Comics: 1994 - No. 3, 1994 ($6.95, limited series)

	GD	VG	FN	VF	VF/NM	NM-
1-3						7.00

RESTLESS GUN (TV)
Dell Publishing Co.: No. 934, Sept, 1958 - No. 1146, Nov-Jan, 1960-61

	GD	VG	FN	VF	VF/NM	NM-
Four Color 934 (#1)-Photo-c	12	24	36	87	134	180
Four Color 986 (5/59), 1045 (11-1/60), 1089 (3/60), 1146-Wildey-a; all photo-c	9	18	27	65	93	120

RESURRECTION MAN
DC Comics: May, 1997 - No. 27, Aug, 1999 ($2.50)

Return of the Outlaw #6 © TOBY

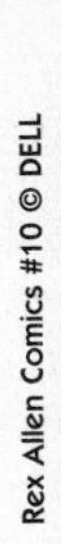
Rex Allen Comics #10 © DELL

Richard Dragon #1 © DC

GD 2.0 | VG 4.0 | FN 6.0 | VF 8.0 | VF/NM 9.0 | NM- 9.2

1-Lenticular disc on cover 5.00
2-5: 2-JLA app. 4.00
6-10: 6-Genesis-x-over. 7-Batman app. 10-Hitman-c/app. 3.00
11-27: 16,17-Supergirl x-over. 18-Deadman & Phantom Stranger-c/app. 21-JLA-c/app. 2.50
#1,000,000 (11/98) 853rd Century x-over 2.50

RETIEF (Keith Laumer's)
Adventure Comics (Malibu): Dec, 1989 - Vol. 2, No.6, ($2.25, B&W)
1-6,Vol. 2, #1-6,Vol. 3 (...of The CDT) #1-6 2.50
...and The Warlords #1-6, ...: Diplomatic Immunity #1 (4/91), ...: Giant Killer #1 (9/91), ...: Crime & Punishment #1 (11/91) 2.50

RETURN FROM WITCH MOUNTAIN (See Walt Disney Showcase #44)

RETURN OF ALISON DARE: LITTLE MISS ADVENTURES, THE (Also see Alison Dare: Little Miss Adventures)
Oni Press: Apr, 2001 - No. 3, Sept, 2001 ($2.95, B&W, limited series)
1-3-J. Torres-s/J.Bone-c/a 3.00

RETURN OF GORGO, THE (Formerly Gorgo's Revenge)
Charlton Comics: No. 2, Aug, 1963; No. 3, Fall, 1964 (12¢)
2,3-Ditko-c/a; based on M.G.M. movie 9 18 27 60 85 110

RETURN OF KONGA, THE (Konga's Revenge #2 on)
Charlton Comics: 1962
nn 8 16 24 55 78 100

RETURN OF MEGATON MAN
Kitchen Sink Press: July, 1988 - No. 3, 1988 ($2.00, limited series)
1-3: Simpson-c/a 2.25

RETURN OF THE OUTLAW
Toby Press (Minoan): Feb, 1953 - No. 11, 1955
1-Billy the Kid 10 20 30 56 73 90
2 7 14 21 35 43 50
3-11 6 12 18 31 38 45

RETURN TO JURASSIC PARK
Topps Comics: Apr, 1995 - No. 9, Feb, 1996 ($2.50/$2.95)
1-9: 3-Begin $2.95-c. 9-Artist's Jam issue 3.00

RETURN TO THE AMALGAM AGE OF COMICS: THE MARVEL COMICS COLLECTION
Marvel Comics: 1997 ($12.95, TPB)
nn-Reprints Amalgam one-shots: Challengers of the Fantastic #1, The Exciting X-Patrol #1, Iron Lantern #1, The Magnetic Men Featuring Magneto #1, Spider-Boy Team-Up #1 & Thorion of the New Asgods #1 13.00

REVEAL
Dark Horse Comics: Nov, 2002 ($6.95, squarebound)
1-Short stories of Dark Horse characters by various; Lone Wolf 2100, Buffy, Spyboy app. 7.00

REVEALING LOVE STORIES (See Fox Giants)

REVEALING ROMANCES
Ace Magazines: Sept, 1949 - No. 6, Aug, 1950
1 13 26 39 74 102 130
2 8 16 24 43 54 65
3-6 7 14 21 37 46 55

REVENGE OF THE PROWLER (Also see The Prowler)
Eclipse Comics: Feb, 1988 - No. 4, June, 1988 ($1.75/$1.95)
1,3,4: 1-$1.75. 3,4-$1.95-c; Snyder III-a(p) 2.25
2 ($2.50)-Contains flexi-disc 2.50

REVENGERS FEATURING MEGALITH
Continuity Comics: Apr, 1985; 1987 - No. 6, 1989 ($2.00, Baxter paper)
1 (1985)-Origin; Neal Adams-c/a, scripts, 1-6 ('87-'89, newsstand) 2.25

REX ALLEN COMICS (Movie star)(Also see Four Color #877 & Western Roundup under Dell Giants)
Dell Publ. Co.: No. 316, Feb, 1951 - No. 31, Dec-Feb, 1958-59 (All-photo-c)
Four Color 316(#1)(52 pgs.)-Rex Allen & his horse Koko begin; Marsh-a 16 32 48 112 171 230
2 (9-11/51, 36 pgs.) 10 20 30 70 100 130
3-10 8 16 24 55 78 100
11-20 7 14 21 46 63 80
21-23,25-31 6 12 18 43 59 75
24-Toth-a 7 14 21 50 68 85
NOTE: *Manning a-20, 27-30. Photo back-c F.C. #316, 2-12, 20, 21.*

REX DEXTER OF MARS (See Mystery Men Comics)
Fox Features Syndicate: Fall, 1940 (68 pgs.)
1-Rex Dexter, Patty O'Day, & Zanzibar (Tuska-a) app.; Briefer-c/a 192 384 576 1200 1850 2500

REX HART (Formerly Blaze Carson; Whip Wilson #9 on)
Timely/Marvel Comics (USA): No. 6, Aug, 1949 - No. 8, Feb, 1950 (All photo-c)
6-Rex Hart & his horse Warrior begin; Black Rider app; Captain Tootsie by Beck 28 56 84 158 229 300
7,8: 18 pg. Thriller in each. 8-Blaze the Wonder Collie app. in text 19 38 57 107 154 200

REX MORGAN, M.D. (Also see Harvey Comics Library)
Argo Publ.: Dec, 1955 - No. 3, Apr?, 1956
1-r/Rex Morgan daily newspaper strips & daily panel-r of "These Women" by D'Alessio & "Timeout" by Jeff Keate 14 28 42 79 110 140
2,3 10 20 30 56 73 90

REX MUNDI (Latin for "King of the World")
Image Comics: No. 0, Aug, 2002 - Present ($2.95)
0-12-Arvid Nelson-s/Eric Johnson-a 3.00
Vol. 1: The Guardian of the Temple TPB (1/04, $14.95) r/#0-5 15.00

REX THE WONDER DOG (See The Adventures of...)

RHUBARB, THE MILLIONAIRE CAT
Dell Publishing Co.: No. 423, Sept-Oct, 1952 - No. 563, June, 1954
Four Color 423 (#1) 6 12 18 43 59 75
Four Color 466(5/53),563 6 12 18 38 52 65

RIB
Dilemma Productions: Oct, 1995 - April, 1996 ($1.95, B&W)
Ashcan, 1 3.00

RIB
Bookmark Productions: 1996 ($2.95, B&W)
1-Sakai-c; Andrew Ford-s/a 3.00

RIB
Caliber Comics: May, 1997 - No. 5, 1998 ($2.95, B&W)
1-5: 1-"Beginnings" pts. 1 & 2 3.00

RIBIT! (Red Sonja imitation)
Comico: Jan, 1989 - No. 4, April?, 1989 ($1.95, limited series)
1-4: Frank Thorne-c/a/scripts 3.00

RIBTICKLER (Also see Fox Giants)
Fox Feature Synd./Green Publ. (1957)/Norlen (1959): 1945 - No. 9, Aug, 1947; 1957; 1959
1-Funny animal 16 32 48 89 127 165
2-(1946) 9 18 27 52 66 80
3-9: 3,7-Cosmo Cat app. 8 16 24 43 54 65
3,7,8 (Green Publ.-1957), 3,7,8 (Norlen Mag.-1959) 3 6 9 18 24 30

RICHARD DRAGON
DC Comics: July, 2004 - Present ($2.50)
1-7: 1-Dixon-s/McDaniel-a/c; Ben Turner app. 2,3-Nightwing app. 4-6-Lady Shiva app. 2.50

RICHARD DRAGON, KUNG-FU FIGHTER (See The Batman Chronicles #5, Brave & the Bold, & The Question)
National Periodical Publ./DC Comics: Apr-May, 1975 - No. 18, Nov-Dec, 1977
1-Intro Richard Dragon, Ben Stanley & O-Sensei; 1st app. Barney Ling; adaptation of Jim Dennis novel "Dragon's Fists" begins, ends #4 2 4 6 11 14 18
2,3: 2-Intro Carolyn Woosan; Starlin/Weiss-c/a; bondage-c. 3-Kirby-a(p); Giordano bondage-c 1 3 4 6 8 10
4-8-Wood inks. 4-Carolyn Woosan dies. 5-1st app. Lady Shiva 1 2 3 4 5 7
9-13,15-18: 9-Ben Stanley becomes Ben Turner; intro Preying Mantis. 16-1st app. Prof Ojo. 18-1st app. Ben Turner as The Bronze Tiger 1 2 3 4 5 7
14-"Spirit of Bruce Lee" 2 4 6 11 14 18
NOTE: ***Buckler** a-14. c-15, 18. **Chua** c-13. **Estrada** a-9, 13-18. **Estrada/Abel** a-10-12. **Estrada/Wood** a-4-8. **Giordano** c-1, 3-11. **Weiss** a-2(partial) c-2i.*

RICHARD THE LION-HEARTED (See Ideal a Classical Comic)

RICHIE RICH (See Harvey Collectors Comics, Harvey Hits, Little Dot, Little Lotta, Little Sad Sack, Million Dollar Digest, Mutt & Jeff, Super Richie, and 3-D Dolly)

RICHIE RICH (...the Poor Little Rich Boy) (See Harvey Hits #3, 9)
Harvey Publ.: Nov, 1960 - #218, Oct, 1982; #219, Oct, 1986 - #254, Jan, 1991
1-(See Little Dot #1 for 1st app.) 150 300 450 1275 2063 2850
2 51 102 153 434 705 975

Richie Rich #1 © HARV

Richie Rich ('91) #1 © HARV

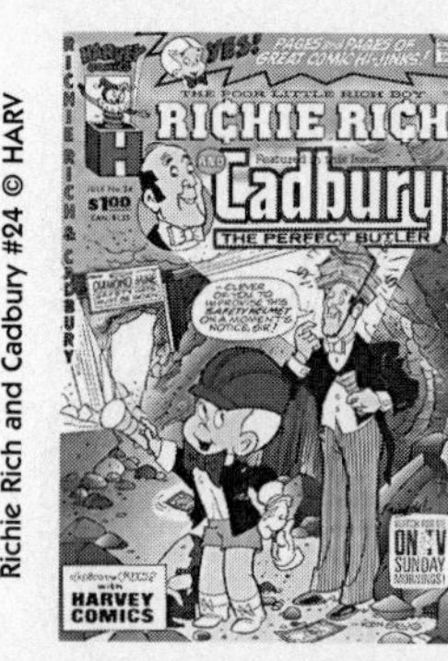

Richie Rich and Cadbury #24 © HARV

	GD 2.0	VG 4.0	FN 6.0	VF 8.0	VF/NM 9.0	NM- 9.2
3-5	34	68	102	255	403	550
6-10: 8-Christmas-c	22	44	66	160	245	330
11-20	14	28	42	102	156	210
21-30	10	20	30	73	107	140
31-40	9	18	27	65	93	120
41-50: 42(10/67)-Flying saucer-c	7	14	21	51	71	90
51-55,57-60: 59-Buck, prototype of Dollar the Dog	6	12	18	40	55	70
56-1st app. Super Richie	7	14	21	50	68	85
61-64,66-80: 71-Nixon & Robert Kennedy caricatures	4	8	12	29	40	50
65-1st app. Dollar the Dog	7	14	21	46	63	80
81-99	3	6	9	19	25	32
100(12/70)-1st app. Irona the robot maid	4	8	12	24	32	40
101-111,117-120	2	4	6	14	18	22
112-116: All 52 pg. Giants	3	6	9	16	20	25
121-140: 137-1st app. Mr. Cheepers	2	4	6	10	12	15
141-160: 145-Infinity-c. 155-3rd app. The Money Monster	2	4	6	8	10	12
161-180	1	3	4	6	8	10
181-199	1	2	3	5	6	8
200	1	3	4	6	8	10
201-218: 210-Stone-Age Riches app	1	2	3	4	5	7
219-254: 237-Last original material						6.00

RICHIE RICH
Harvey Comics: Mar, 1991 - No. 28, Nov, 1994 ($1.00, bi-monthly)

	GD	VG	FN	VF	VF/NM	NM-
1-28: Reprints best of Richie Rich						2.50
Giant Size 1-4 (10/91-10/93, $2.25, 68 pgs.)						3.00

RICHIE RICH ADVENTURE DIGEST MAGAZINE
Harvey Comics: 1992 - No. 7, Sept, 1994 ($1.25, quarterly, digest-size)

	GD	VG	FN	VF	VF/NM	NM-
1-7						4.00

RICHIE RICH AND...
Harvey Comics: Oct, 1987 - No. 11, May, 1990 ($1.00)

	GD	VG	FN	VF	VF/NM	NM-
1-Professor Keenbean						4.00
2-11: 2-Casper. 3-Dollar the Dog. 4-Cadbury. 5 Mayda Munny. 6-Irona. 7-Little Dot. 8-Professor Keenbean. 9-Little Audrey. 10-Mayda Munny. 11-Cadbury						3.00

RICHIE RICH AND BILLY BELLHOPS
Harvey Publications: Oct, 1977 (52 pgs., one-shot)

	GD	VG	FN	VF	VF/NM	NM-
1	2	4	6	10	12	15

RICHIE RICH AND CADBURY
Harvey Publ.: 10/77; #2, 9/78 - #23, 7/82; #24, 7/90 - #29, 1/91 (1-10: 52pgs.)

	GD	VG	FN	VF	VF/NM	NM-
1-(52 pg. Giant)	2	4	6	12	16	20
2-10-(52 pg. Giant)	2	4	6	8	10	12
11-23						6.00
24-29: 24-Begin $1.00-c						4.00

RICHIE RICH AND CASPER
Harvey Publications: Aug, 1974 - No. 45, Sept, 1982

	GD	VG	FN	VF	VF/NM	NM-
1	4	8	12	24	32	40
2-5	2	4	6	14	18	22
6-10: 10-Xmas-c	2	4	6	10	13	16
11-20	1	3	4	6	8	10
21-45: 22-Xmas-c						6.00

RICHIE RICH AND DOLLAR THE DOG (See Richie Rich #65)
Harvey Publications: Sept, 1977 - No. 24, Aug, 1982 (#1-10: 52 pgs.)

	GD	VG	FN	VF	VF/NM	NM-
1-(52 pg. Giant)	2	4	6	12	16	20
2-10-(52 pg. Giant)	2	4	6	8	10	12
11-24						6.00

RICHIE RICH AND DOT
Harvey Publications: Oct, 1974 (one-shot)

	GD	VG	FN	VF	VF/NM	NM-
1	3	6	9	18	23	28

RICHIE RICH AND GLORIA
Harvey Publications: Sept, 1977 - No. 25, Sept, 1982 (#1-11: 52 pgs.)

	GD	VG	FN	VF	VF/NM	NM-
1-(52 pg. Giant)	2	4	6	12	16	20
2-11-(52 pg. Giant)	2	4	6	8	10	12
12-25						6.00

RICHIE RICH AND HIS GIRLFRIENDS
Harvey Publications: April, 1979 - No. 16, Dec, 1982

	GD	VG	FN	VF	VF/NM	NM-
1-(52 pg. Giant)	2	4	6	10	13	16
2-(52 pg. Giant)	1	3	4	6	8	10
3-10	1	2	3	5	6	8
11-16						6.00

RICHIE RICH AND HIS MEAN COUSIN REGGIE
Harvey Publications: April, 1979 - No. 3, 1980 (50¢) (#1,2: 52 pgs.)

	GD	VG	FN	VF	VF/NM	NM-
1	2	4	6	10	13	16
2-3:	1	3	4	6	8	10

NOTE: *No. 4 was advertised, but never released.*

RICHIE RICH AND JACKIE JOKERS (Also see Jackie Jokers)
Harvey Publications: Nov, 1973 - No. 48, Dec, 1982

	GD	VG	FN	VF	VF/NM	NM-
1: 52 pg. Giant; contains material from unpublished Jackie Jokers #5	4	8	12	29	40	50
2,3-(52 pg. Giants). 2-R.R. & Jackie 1st meet	3	6	9	18	23	28
4,5	2	4	6	14	18	22
6-10	2	4	6	10	13	16
11-20,26: 11-1st app. Kool Katz. 26-Star Wars parody	1	3	4	6	8	10
21-25,27-40	1	2	3	4	5	7
41-48						6.00

RICHIE RICH AND PROFESSOR KEENBEAN
Harvey Comics: Sept, 1990 - No. 2, Nov, 1990 ($1.00)

	GD	VG	FN	VF	VF/NM	NM-
1,2						3.00

RICHIE RICH AND THE NEW KIDS ON THE BLOCK
Harvey Publications: Feb, 1991 - No. 3, June, 1991 ($1.25, bi-monthly)

	GD	VG	FN	VF	VF/NM	NM-
1-3: 1,2-New Richie Rich stories						3.00

RICHIE RICH AND TIMMY TIME
Harvey Publications: Sept, 1977 (50¢, 52 pgs, one-shot)

	GD	VG	FN	VF	VF/NM	NM-
1	2	4	6	10	12	15

RICHIE RICH BANK BOOKS
Harvey Publications: Oct, 1972 - No. 59, Sept, 1982

	GD	VG	FN	VF	VF/NM	NM-
1	5	10	15	36	48	60
2-5: 2-2nd app. The Money Monster	3	6	9	18	24	30
6-10	2	4	6	12	16	20
11-20: 18-Super Richie app.	2	4	6	8	10	12
21-30	1	2	3	5	7	9
31-40	1	2	3	4	5	7
41-59						6.00

RICHIE RICH BEST OF THE YEARS
Harvey Publications: Oct, 1977 - No. 6, June, 1980 (128 pgs., digest-size)

	GD	VG	FN	VF	VF/NM	NM-
1(10/77)-Reprints	2	4	6	10	12	15
2-6(11/79-6/80, 95¢). #2(10/78)-Rep.. #3(6/79, 75¢)	1	2	3	5	7	9

RICHIE RICH BIG BOOK
Harvey Publications: Nov, 1992 - No. 2, May, 1993 ($1.50, 52 pgs.)

	GD	VG	FN	VF	VF/NM	NM-
1,2						3.00

RICHIE RICH BIG BUCKS
Harvey Publications: Apr, 1991 - No. 8, July, 1992 ($1.00, bi-monthly)

	GD	VG	FN	VF	VF/NM	NM-
1-8						3.00

RICHIE RICH BILLIONS
Harvey Publications: Oct, 1974 - No. 48, Oct, 1982 (#1-33: 52 pgs.)

	GD	VG	FN	VF	VF/NM	NM-
1	4	8	12	27	36	45
2-5	3	6	9	16	20	25
6-10	2	4	6	11	14	18
11-20	2	4	6	8	10	12
21-33	1	2	3	5	6	8
34-48: 35-Onion app.						6.00

RICHIE RICH CASH
Harvey Publications: Sept, 1974 - No. 47, Aug, 1982

	GD	VG	FN	VF	VF/NM	NM-
1-1st app. Dr. N-R-Gee	4	8	12	24	32	40
2-5	2	4	6	14	18	22
6-10	2	4	6	10	13	16
11-20	1	3	4	6	8	10
21-30	1	2	3	4	5	7
31-47: 33-Dr. Blemish app.						6.00

RICHIE RICH CASH MONEY
Harvey Comics: May, 1992 - No. 2, Aug, 1992 ($1.25)

	GD	VG	FN	VF	VF/NM	NM-
1,2						3.00

RICHIE RICH, CASPER AND WENDY - NATIONAL LEAGUE
Harvey Comics: June, 1976 (50¢)

	GD	VG	FN	VF	VF/NM	NM-
1-Newsstand version of the baseball giveaway	2	4	6	14	18	22

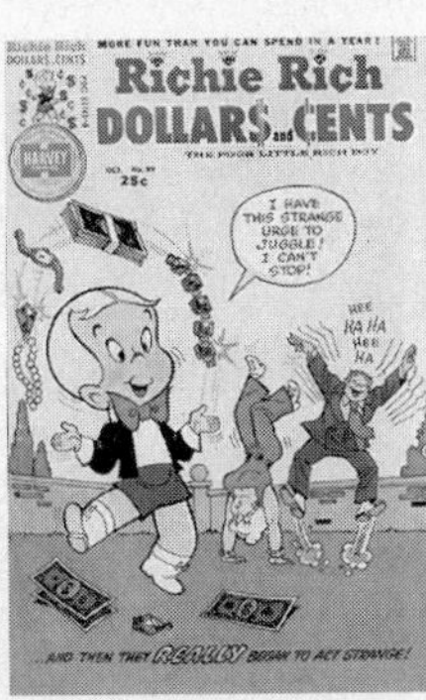

Richie Rich Dollars and Cents #69 © HARV

Richie Rich Gold and Silver #1 © HARV

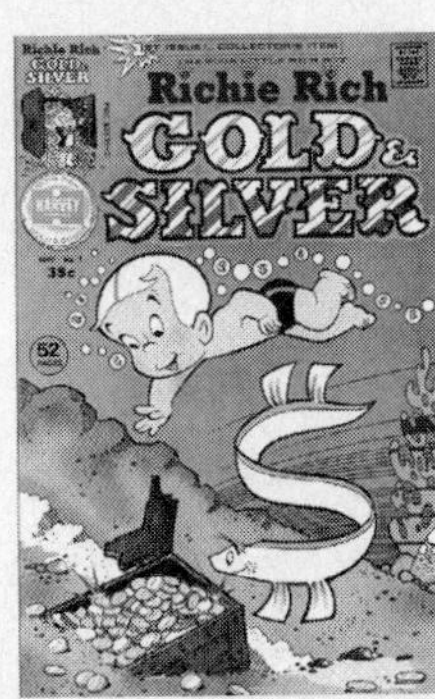

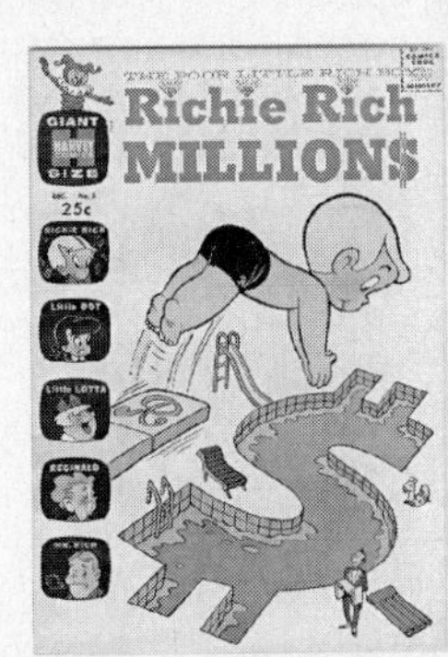

Richie Rich Millions #3 © HARV

RICHIE RICH COLLECTORS COMICS (See Harvey Collectors Comics)

RICHIE RICH DIAMONDS
Harvey Publications: Aug, 1972 - No. 59, Aug, 1982 (#1, 23-45: 52 pgs.)

	GD 2.0	VG 4.0	FN 6.0	VF 8.0	VF/NM 9.0	NM- 9.2
1-(52 pg. Giant)	6	12	18	38	52	65
2-5	3	6	9	18	24	30
6-10	2	4	6	12	16	20
11-22	2	4	6	8	10	12
23-30-(52 pg. Giants)	2	4	6	9	11	14
31-45: 39-r/Origin Little Dot	1	2	3	5	7	9
46-50	1	2	3	4	5	7
51-59						6.00

RICHIE RICH DIGEST
Harvey Publications: Oct, 1986 - No. 42, Oct, 1994 ($1.25/$1.75, digest-size)

	GD 2.0	VG 4.0	FN 6.0	VF 8.0	VF/NM 9.0	NM- 9.2
1	1	3	4	6	8	10
2-10						6.00
11-20						5.00
21-42						4.00

RICHIE RICH DIGEST STORIES (...Magazine #?-on)
Harvey Publications: Oct, 1977 - No., 17, Oct, 1982 (75¢/95¢, digest-size)

	GD 2.0	VG 4.0	FN 6.0	VF 8.0	VF/NM 9.0	NM- 9.2
1-Reprints	2	4	6	10	12	15
2-10: Reprints	1	2	3	5	7	9
11-17: Reprints						6.00

RICHIE RICH DIGEST WINNERS
Harvey Publications: Dec, 1977 - No. 16, Sept, 1982 (75¢/95¢, 132 pgs., digest-size)

	GD 2.0	VG 4.0	FN 6.0	VF 8.0	VF/NM 9.0	NM- 9.2
1	2	4	6	10	12	15
2-5	1	2	3	5	7	9
6-16						6.00

RICHIE RICH DOLLARS & CENTS
Harvey Publications: Aug, 1963 - No. 109, Aug, 1982 (#1-43: 68 pgs.; 44-60, 71-94: 52 pgs.)

	GD 2.0	VG 4.0	FN 6.0	VF 8.0	VF/NM 9.0	NM- 9.2
1: (#1-64 are all reprint issues)	17	34	51	121	186	250
2	10	20	30	67	96	125
3-5: 5-r/1st app. of R.R. from Little Dot #1	7	14	21	51	71	90
6-10	5	10	15	36	48	60
11-20	4	8	12	29	40	50
21-30: 25-r/1st app. Nurse Jenny (Little Lotta #62)	3	7	10	21	28	35
31-43: 43-Last 68 pg. issue	3	6	9	18	23	28
44-60: All 52 pgs.	2	4	6	11	14	18
61-71	1	3	4	6	8	10
72-94: All 52 pgs.	2	4	6	9	11	14
95-99,101-109						6.00
100-Anniversary issue	1	2	3	5	7	9

RICHIE RICH FORTUNES
Harvey Publications: Sept, 1971 - No. 63, July, 1982 (#1-15: 52 pgs.)

	GD 2.0	VG 4.0	FN 6.0	VF 8.0	VF/NM 9.0	NM- 9.2
1	6	12	18	43	59	75
2-5	3	7	10	21	28	35
6-10	2	4	6	14	18	22
11-15: 11-r/1st app. The Onion	2	4	6	10	12	15
16-30	1	2	3	5	7	9
31-40	1	2	3	4	5	7
41-63: 62-Onion app.						6.00

RICHIE RICH GEMS
Harvey Publications: Sept, 1974 - No. 43, Sept, 1982

	GD 2.0	VG 4.0	FN 6.0	VF 8.0	VF/NM 9.0	NM- 9.2
1	4	8	12	24	32	40
2-5	2	4	6	14	18	22
6-10	2	4	6	10	13	16
11-20	1	3	4	6	8	10
21-30	1	2	3	4	5	7
31-43: 36-Dr. Blemish, Onion app. 38-1st app. Stone-Age Riches						6.00

RICHIE RICH GOLD AND SILVER
Harvey Publications: Sept, 1975 - No. 42, Oct, 1982 (#1-27: 52 pgs.)

	GD 2.0	VG 4.0	FN 6.0	VF 8.0	VF/NM 9.0	NM- 9.2
1	3	7	10	21	28	35
2-5	2	4	6	12	16	20
6-10	2	4	6	9	11	14
11-27	1	2	3	5	7	9
28-42: 34-Stone-Age Riches app.						6.00

RICHIE RICH GOLD NUGGETS DIGEST
Harvey Publications: Feb., 1991 - No. 4, June, 1991 ($1.75, digest-size)

	GD 2.0	VG 4.0	FN 6.0	VF 8.0	VF/NM 9.0	NM- 9.2
1-4						3.00

RICHIE RICH HOLIDAY DIGEST MAGAZINE (...Digest #4)
Harvey Publications: Jan, 1980 - #3, Jan, 1982; #4, 3/88; #5, 2/89 (annual)

	GD 2.0	VG 4.0	FN 6.0	VF 8.0	VF/NM 9.0	NM- 9.2
1-X-Mas-c	1	3	4	6	8	10
2-5: 2,3: All X-Mas-c. 4-(3/88, $1.25), 5-(2/89, $1.75)	1	2	3	4	5	7

RICHIE RICH INVENTIONS
Harvey Publications: Oct, 1977 - No. 26, Oct, 1982 (#1-11: 52 pgs.)

	GD 2.0	VG 4.0	FN 6.0	VF 8.0	VF/NM 9.0	NM- 9.2
1	2	4	6	12	16	20
2-5	2	4	6	8	10	12
6-11	1	2	3	5	6	8
12-26						6.00

RICHIE RICH JACKPOTS
Harvey Publications: Oct, 1972 - No. 58, Aug, 1982 (#41-43: 52 pgs.)

	GD 2.0	VG 4.0	FN 6.0	VF 8.0	VF/NM 9.0	NM- 9.2
1	5	10	15	36	48	60
2-5	3	6	9	18	24	30
6-10	2	4	6	12	16	20
11-15,17-20	2	4	6	8	10	12
16-Super Richie app.	2	4	6	10	12	15
21-30	1	2	3	5	7	9
31-40,44-50: 37-Caricatures of Frank Sinatra, Dean Martin, Sammy Davis, Jr. 45-Dr. Blemish app.	1	2	3	4	5	7
41-43 (52 pgs.)	1	3	4	6	8	10
51-58						6.00

RICHIE RICH MILLION DOLLAR DIGEST (...Magazine #?-on)(See Million Dollar Digest)
Harvey Publications: Oct, 1980 - No. 10, Oct, 1982 ($1.50)

	GD 2.0	VG 4.0	FN 6.0	VF 8.0	VF/NM 9.0	NM- 9.2
1	1	3	4	6	8	10
2-10						6.00

RICHIE RICH MILLIONS
Harvey Publ.: 9/61; #2, 9/62 - #113, 10/82 (#1-48: 68 pgs.; 49-64, 85-97: 52 pgs.)

	GD 2.0	VG 4.0	FN 6.0	VF 8.0	VF/NM 9.0	NM- 9.2
1: (#1-3 are all reprint issues)	20	40	60	141	216	290
2	11	22	33	75	110	145
3-10: All other giants are new & reprints. 5-1st 15 pg. Richie Rich story	10	20	30	70	100	130
11-20	6	12	18	43	59	75
21-30	5	10	15	33	44	55
31-48: 31-1st app. The Onion. 48-Last 68 pg. Giant	4	8	12	24	32	40
49-64: 52 pg. Giants	3	6	9	16	20	25
65-67,69-73,75-84	2	4	6	8	10	12
68-1st Super Richie-c (11/74)	2	4	6	12	16	20
74-1st app. Mr. Woody; Super Richie app.	2	4	6	9	11	14
85-97: 52 pg. Giants	2	4	6	9	11	14
98,99	1	2	3	4	5	7
100	1	2	3	5	7	9
101-113						6.00

RICHIE RICH MONEY WORLD
Harvey Publications: Sept, 1972 - No. 59, Sept, 1982

	GD 2.0	VG 4.0	FN 6.0	VF 8.0	VF/NM 9.0	NM- 9.2
1-(52 pg. Giant)-1st app. Mayda Munny	6	12	18	43	59	75
2-Super Richie app.	3	7	10	21	28	35
3-5	3	6	9	18	24	30
6-10: 9,10-Richie Rich mistakenly named Little Lotta on covers	2	4	6	12	16	20
11-20: 16,20-Dr. N-R-Gee	2	4	6	8	10	12
21-30	1	2	3	5	7	9
31-50	1	2	3	4	5	7
51-59						6.00
Digest 1 (2/91, $1.75)						5.00
2-8 (12/93, $1.75)						3.00

RICHIE RICH PROFITS
Harvey Publications: Oct, 1974 - No. 47, Sept, 1982

	GD 2.0	VG 4.0	FN 6.0	VF 8.0	VF/NM 9.0	NM- 9.2
1	4	8	12	24	32	40
2-5	2	4	6	14	18	22
6-10: 10-Origin of Dr. N-R-Gee	2	4	6	10	13	16
11-20: 15-Christmas-c	1	3	4	6	8	10
21-30	1	2	3	4	5	7
31-47						6.00

RICHIE RICH RELICS
Harvey Comics: Jan, 1988 - No.4, Feb, 1989 (75¢/$1.00, reprints)

	GD 2.0	VG 4.0	FN 6.0	VF 8.0	VF/NM 9.0	NM- 9.2
1-4						3.00

RICHIE RICH RICHES
Harvey Publications: July, 1972 - No. 59, Aug, 1982 (#1, 2, 41-45: 52 pgs.)

Richie Rich Success Stories #60 © HARV

Richie Rich Zillionz #1 © HARV

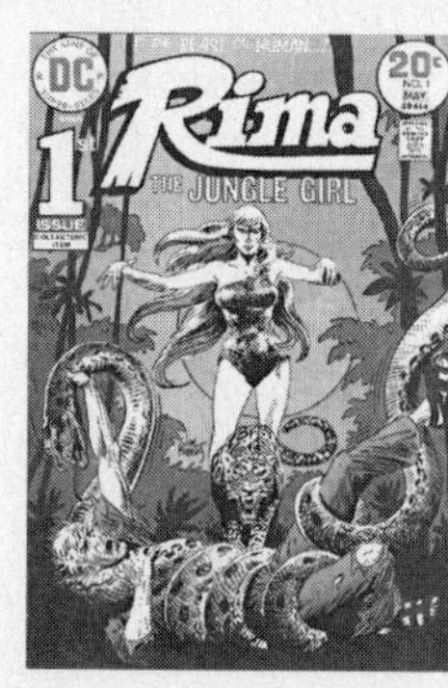

Rima the Jungle Girl #1 © DC

	GD 2.0	VG 4.0	FN 6.0	VF 8.0	VF/NM 9.0	NM- 9.2
1-(52 pg. Giant)-1st app. The Money Monster	6	12	18	43	59	75
2-(52 pg. Giant)	3	7	10	21	28	35
3-5	3	6	9	18	24	30
6-10	2	4	6	12	16	20
11-20: 17-Super Richie app. (3/75)	2	4	6	8	10	12
21-40	1	2	3	5	6	8
41-45: 52 pg. Giants	1	3	4	6	8	10
46-59: 56-Dr. Blemish app.						6.00

RICHIE RICH SUCCESS STORIES
Harvey Publications: Nov, 1964 - No. 105, Sept, 1982 (#1-38: 68 pgs., 39-55, 67-90: 52 pgs.)

	GD 2.0	VG 4.0	FN 6.0	VF 8.0	VF/NM 9.0	NM- 9.2
1	19	38	57	136	198	260
2-5	10	20	30	70	100	130
6-10	6	12	18	43	59	75
11-20	5	10	15	36	48	60
21-30: 27-1st Penny Van Dough (8/69)	4	8	12	27	36	45
31-38: 38-Last 68 pg. Giant	3	7	10	21	28	35
39-55-(52 pgs.): 44-Super Richie app.	2	4	6	14	18	22
56-66	2	4	6	8	10	12
67-90: 52 pgs.	2	4	6	9	11	14
91-105: 91-Onion app. 101-Dr. Blemish app.						6.00

RICHIE RICH SUMMER BONANZA
Harvey Comics: Oct, 1991 ($1.95, one-shot, 68 pgs.)

	GD 2.0	VG 4.0	FN 6.0	VF 8.0	VF/NM 9.0	NM- 9.2
1-Richie Rich, Little Dot, Little Lotta						3.00

RICHIE RICH TREASURE CHEST DIGEST (...Magazine #3)
Harvey Publications: Apr, 1982 - No. 3, Aug, 1982 (95¢, Digest Mag.)
(#4 advertised but not publ.)

	GD 2.0	VG 4.0	FN 6.0	VF 8.0	VF/NM 9.0	NM- 9.2
1	1	2	3	5	7	9
2,3	1	2	3	4	5	7

RICHIE RICH VACATION DIGEST
Harvey Comics: Oct, 1991; Oct, 1992; Oct, 1993 ($1.75, digest-size)

	GD 2.0	VG 4.0	FN 6.0	VF 8.0	VF/NM 9.0	NM- 9.2
1-(10/91), 1-(10/92), 1-(10/93)						4.00

RICHIE RICH VACATIONS DIGEST
Harvey Publ.: 11/77; No. 2, 10/78 - No. 7, 10/81; No. 8, 8/82; (Digest, 132 pgs.)

	GD 2.0	VG 4.0	FN 6.0	VF 8.0	VF/NM 9.0	NM- 9.2
1-Reprints	2	4	6	10	12	15
2-6	1	2	3	5	7	9
7,8						6.00

RICHIE RICH VAULT OF MYSTERY
Harvey Publications: Nov, 1974 - No. 47, Sept, 1982

	GD 2.0	VG 4.0	FN 6.0	VF 8.0	VF/NM 9.0	NM- 9.2
1	4	8	12	24	32	40
2-5	2	4	6	14	18	22
7-10	2	4	6	10	13	16
11-20	1	3	4	6	8	10
21-30	1	2	3	4	5	7
31-47						6.00

RICHIE RICH ZILLIONZ
Harvey Publ.: Oct, 1976 - No. 33, Sept, 1982 (#1-4: 68 pgs.; #5-18: 52 pgs.)

	GD 2.0	VG 4.0	FN 6.0	VF 8.0	VF/NM 9.0	NM- 9.2
1	3	7	10	21	28	35
2-4: 4-Last 68 pg. Giant	2	4	6	12	16	20
5-10	2	4	6	8	10	12
11-18: 18-Last 52 pg. Giant	1	2	3	5	6	8
19-33						6.00

RICK GEARY'S WONDERS AND ODDITIES
Dark Horse Comics: Dec, 1988 ($2.00, B&W, one-shot)

	GD 2.0	VG 4.0	FN 6.0	VF 8.0	VF/NM 9.0	NM- 9.2
1						2.25

RICKY
Standard Comics (Visual Editions): No. 5, Sept, 1953

	GD 2.0	VG 4.0	FN 6.0	VF 8.0	VF/NM 9.0	NM- 9.2
5-Teenage humor	6	12	18	27	33	38

RICKY NELSON (TV)(See Sweethearts V2#42)
Dell Publishing Co.: No. 956, Dec, 1958 - No. 1192, June, 1961 (All photo-c)

	GD 2.0	VG 4.0	FN 6.0	VF 8.0	VF/NM 9.0	NM- 9.2
Four Color 956,998	20	40	60	141	216	290
Four Color 1115	16	32	48	112	171	230
Four Color 1192-Manning-a	16	32	48	112	171	230

RIDE, THE
Image Comics: June, 2004 - No. 2, July, 2004 ($2.95, B&W, anthology)

	GD 2.0	VG 4.0	FN 6.0	VF 8.0	VF/NM 9.0	NM- 9.2
1,2: Hughes-c/Wagner-s. 1-Hamner & Stelfreeze-a. 2-Jeanty & Pearson-a						3.00
...2 For the Road 1 (10/04, $2.95) Dixon-s/Hamner & Gregory-a/Johnson-c						3.00

RIDER, THE (Frontier Trail #6; also see Blazing Sixguns I.W. Reprint #10, 11)
Ajax/Farrell Publ. (Four Star Comic Corp.): Mar, 1957 - No. 5, 1958

	GD 2.0	VG 4.0	FN 6.0	VF 8.0	VF/NM 9.0	NM- 9.2
1-Swift Arrow, Lone Rider begin	13	26	39	74	102	130
2-5	8	16	24	43	54	65

RIDERS OF THE PURPLE SAGE (See Zane Grey & Four Color #372)

RIFLEMAN, THE (TV)
Dell Publ. Co./Gold Key No. 13 on: No. 1009, 7-9/59 - No. 12, 7-9/62; No. 13, 11/62 - No. 20, 10/64

	GD 2.0	VG 4.0	FN 6.0	VF 8.0	VF/NM 9.0	NM- 9.2
Four Color 1009 (#1)	27	54	81	194	297	400
2 (1-3/60)	14	28	42	97	149	200
3-Toth-a (4 pgs.)	14	28	42	97	149	200
4-10: 6-Toth-a (4 pgs.)	12	24	36	86	131	175
11-20	10	20	30	67	96	125

NOTE: ***Warren Tufts** a-2-9. All have Chuck Connors photo-c. Photo back c-13-15.*

RIMA, THE JUNGLE GIRL
National Periodical Publications: Apr-May, 1974 - No. 7, Apr-May, 1975

	GD 2.0	VG 4.0	FN 6.0	VF 8.0	VF/NM 9.0	NM- 9.2
1-Origin, part 1 (#1-5: 20¢; 6,7: 25¢)	2	4	6	10	13	16
2-7: 2-4-Origin, parts 2-4. 7-Origin & only app. Space Marshal	1	2	3	5	6	8

NOTE: ***Kubert** c-1-7. **Nino** a-1-7. **Redondo** a-1-7.*

RING OF BRIGHT WATER (See Movie Classics)

RING OF THE NIBELUNG, THE
DC Comics: 1989 - No. 4, 1990 ($4.95, squarebound, 52 pgs., mature readers)

	GD 2.0	VG 4.0	FN 6.0	VF 8.0	VF/NM 9.0	NM- 9.2
1-4: Adapts novel, Gil Kane-c/a						5.00

RING OF THE NIBELUNG, THE
Dark Horse Comics: Feb, 2000 - Sept, 2001 ($2.95/$2.99/$5.99, limited series)

	GD 2.0	VG 4.0	FN 6.0	VF 8.0	VF/NM 9.0	NM- 9.2
Vol. 1 (The Rhinegold) 1-4: Adapts Wagner; P. Craig Russell-s/a						3.00
Vol. 2,3: Vol. 2 (The Valkyrie) 1-3: 1-(8/00). Vol. 3 (Siegfried) 1-3: 1-(12/00)						3.00
Vol. 4 (The Twilight of the Gods) 1-3: 1-(6/01)						3.00
4-(9/01, $5.99, 64 pgs.) Conclusion with sketch pages						6.00

RINGO KID, THE (2nd Series)
Marvel Comics Group: Jan, 1970 - No. 23, Nov, 1973; No. 24, Nov, 1975 - No. 30, Nov, 1976

	GD 2.0	VG 4.0	FN 6.0	VF 8.0	VF/NM 9.0	NM- 9.2
1-Williamson-a r-from #10, 1956.	3	6	9	18	24	30
2-11: 2-Severin-c. 11-Last 15¢ issue	2	4	6	10	13	16
12 (52 pg. Giant)	3	6	9	16	20	24
13-20: 13-Wildey-r. 20-Williamson-r/#1	2	4	6	8	10	12
21-30	1	2	3	5	7	9
27,28-(30¢-c variant, limited distribution)(5,7/76)	2	4	6	12	16	20

RINGO KID WESTERN, THE (1st Series) (See Wild Western & Western Trails)
Atlas Comics (HPC)/Marvel Comics: Aug, 1954 - No. 21, Sept, 1957

	GD 2.0	VG 4.0	FN 6.0	VF 8.0	VF/NM 9.0	NM- 9.2
1-Origin; The Ringo Kid begins	31	62	93	175	253	330
2-Black Rider app.; origin/1st app. Ringo's Horse Arab	16	32	48	89	127	165
3-5	11	22	33	64	87	110
6-8-Severin-a(3) each	12	24	36	69	95	120
9,11,12,14-21: 12-Orlando-a (4 pgs.)	9	18	27	54	70	85
10,13-Williamson-a (4 pgs.)	10	20	30	58	77	95

NOTE: ***Berg** a-8. **Maneely** a-1-5, 15, 16(text illos only), 17(4), 18, 20, 21; c-1-6, 8, 13, 15-18, 20. **J. Severin** c-10, 11. **Sinnott** a-1. **Wildey** a-16-18.*

RIN TIN TIN (See March of Comics #163,180,195)

RIN TIN TIN (TV) (...& Rusty #21 on; see Western Roundup under Dell Giants)
Dell Publishing Co./Gold Key: Nov, 1952 - No. 38, May-July, 1961; Nov, 1963 (All Photo-c)

	GD 2.0	VG 4.0	FN 6.0	VF 8.0	VF/NM 9.0	NM- 9.2
Four Color 434 (#1)	16	32	48	112	171	230
Four Color 476,523	9	18	27	63	89	115
4(3-5/54)-10	8	16	24	53	74	95
11-20	7	14	21	46	63	80
21-38: 36-Toth-a (4 pgs.)	6	12	18	38	52	65
... & Rusty 1 (11/63-Gold Key)	7	14	21	46	63	80

RIO (Also see Eclipse Monthly)
Comico: June, 1987 ($8.95, 64 pgs.)

	GD 2.0	VG 4.0	FN 6.0	VF 8.0	VF/NM 9.0	NM- 9.2
1-Wildey-c/a						9.00

RIO AT BAY
Dark Horse Comics: July, 1992 - No. 2, Aug, 1992 ($2.95, limited series)

	GD 2.0	VG 4.0	FN 6.0	VF 8.0	VF/NM 9.0	NM- 9.2
1,2-Wildey-c/a						3.00

RIO BRAVO (Movie) (See 4-Color #1018)
Dell Publishing Co.: June, 1959

	GD 2.0	VG 4.0	FN 6.0	VF 8.0	VF/NM 9.0	NM- 9.2
Four Color #1018-Toth-a; John Wayne, Dean Martin, & Ricky Nelson photo-c.	25	50	75	177	271	365

Riot #3 © MAR

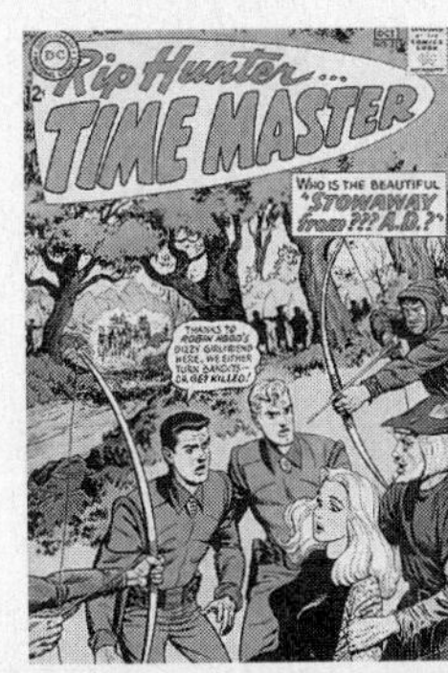

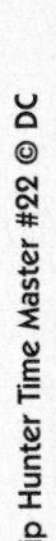
Rip Hunter Time Master #22 © DC

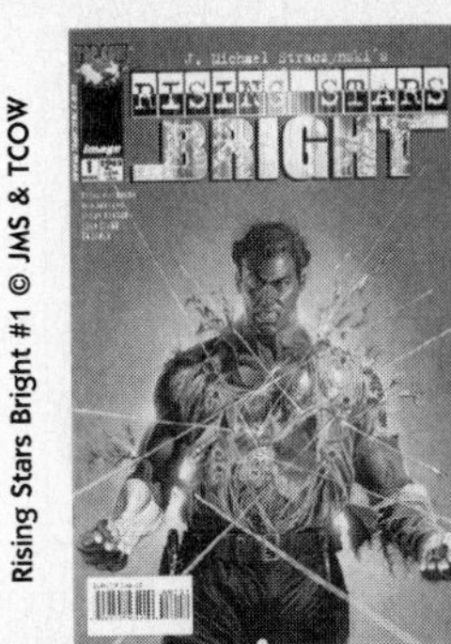

Rising Stars Bright #1 © JMS & TCOW

	GD 2.0	VG 4.0	FN 6.0	VF 8.0	VF/NM 9.0	NM- 9.2

RIO CONCHOS (See Movie Comics)

RIOT (Satire)
Atlas Comics (ACI No. 1-5/WPI No. 6): Apr, 1954 - No. 3, Aug, 1954; No. 4, Feb, 1956 - No. 6, June, 1956

1-Russ Heath-a	31	62	93	178	259	340
2-Li'l Abner satire by Post	23	46	69	130	188	245
3-Last precode (8/54)	20	40	60	112	161	210
4-Infinity-c; Marilyn Monroe "7 Year Itch" movie satire; Mad Rip-off ads	26	52	78	147	211	275
5-Marilyn Monroe, John Wayne parody; part photo-c	27	54	81	153	219	285
6-Lorna of the Jungle satire by Everett; Dennis the Menace satire-c/story; part photo-c	20	40	60	112	161	210

NOTE: ***Berg** a-3. **Burgos** c-1, 2. **Colan** a-1. **Everett** a-1, 4, 6. **Heath** a-1. **Maneely** a-1, 2, 4-6; c-3, 4, 6. **Post** a-1-4. **Reinman** a-2. **Severin** a-4-6.*

RIOT GEAR
Triumphant Comics: Sept, 1993 - No. 11, July, 1994 ($2.50, serially numbered)

1-11: 1-2nd app. Riot Gear. 2-1st app. Rabin. 3,4-Triumphant Unleashed x-over. 3-1st app. Surzar. 4-Death of Captain Tich 2.50
Violent Past 1,2: 1-(2/94, $2.50) 2.50

R.I.P.
TSR, Inc.: 1990 - No. 8, 1991 ($2.95, 44 pgs.)

1-8-Based on TSR game 3.00

RIPCLAW (See Cyberforce)
Image Comics (Top Cow Prod.): Apr, 1995 - No. 3, June, 1995 (Limited series)

1/2-Gold, 1/2-San Diego ed., 1/2-Chicago ed.	1	3	4	6	8	10
1-3: Brandon Peterson-a(p)						3.00
Special 1 (10/95, $2.50)						2.50

RIPCLAW
Image Comics (Top Cow Prod.): V2#1, Dec, 1995 - No. 6, June, 1996 ($2.50)

V2#1-6: 5-Medieval Spawn/Witchblade Preview 2.50

RIPCORD (TV)
Dell Publishing Co.: Mar-May, 1962

Four Color 1294	8	16	24	58	82	105

R.I.P.D.
Dark Horse Comics: Oct, 1999 - No. 4, Jan, 2000 ($2.95, limited series)

1-4 3.00
TPB (2003, $12.95) r/#1-4 13.00

RIPFIRE
Malibu Comics (Ultraverse): No. 0, Apr, 1995 ($2.50, one-shot)

0 2.50

RIP HUNTER TIME MASTER (See Showcase #20, 21, 25, 26 & Time Masters)
National Periodical Publications: Mar-Apr, 1961 - No. 29, Nov-Dec, 1965

1-(3-4/61)	50	100	150	407	641	875
2	27	54	81	194	297	400
3-5: 5-Last 10¢ issue	16	32	48	116	178	240
6,7-Toth-a in each	11	22	33	80	120	160
8-15	9	18	27	65	93	120
16-20: 20-Hitler c/s	7	14	21	51	71	90
21-29: 29-Gil Kane-c	6	12	18	43	59	75

RIP IN TIME (Also see Teenage Mutant Ninja Turtles #5-7)
Fantagor Press: Aug, 1986 - No.5, 1987 ($1.50, B&W)

1-5: Corben-c/a in all 3.00

RIP KIRBY (Also see Harvey Comics Hits #57, & Street Comix)
David McKay Publications: 1948

Feature Books 51,54: Raymond-c; 51-Origin	36	72	108	204	297	390

RIPLEY'S BELIEVE IT OR NOT! (See Ace Comics, All-American Comics, Mystery Comics Digest #1, 4, 7, 10, 13, 16, 19, 22, 25)

RIPLEY'S BELIEVE IT OR NOT!
Harvey Publications: Sept, 1953 - No. 4, March, 1954

1-Powell-a	14	28	42	79	110	140
2-4	10	20	30	56	73	90

RIPLEY'S BELIEVE IT OR NOT! (Continuation of Ripleys'...True Ghost Stories & Ripley's...True War Stories)
Gold Key: No. 4, April, 1967 - No. 94, Feb, 1980

4-Photo-c; McWilliams-a	4	8	12	28	38	48
5-Subtitled "True War Stories"; Evans-a; 1st Jeff Jones-a in comics? (2 pgs.)	4	8	12	28	38	48
6-10: 6-McWilliams-a. 10-Evans-a(2)	4	8	12	24	32	40
11-20: 15-Evans-a	3	6	9	18	24	30
21-30	2	4	6	14	18	22
31-38,40-60	2	4	6	10	13	16
39-Crandall-a	2	4	6	11	14	18
61-73	1	3	4	6	8	10
74,77-83-(52 pgs.)	2	4	6	10	13	16
75,76,84-94	1	2	3	5	6	8
Story Digest Mag. 1(6/70)-4-3/4x6-1/2", 148pp.	6	12	18	40	55	70

NOTE: ***Evanish** art by **Luiz Dominguez** #22-25, 27, 30, 31, 40. **Jeff Jones** a-5(2 pgs.). **McWilliams** a-65, 66, 70, 89. **Orlando** a-8. **Sparling** c-68. Reprints-74, 77-84, 87 (part); 91, 93 (all). **Williamson, Wood** a-80r/#1.*

RIPLEY'S BELIEVE IT OR NOT!
Dark Horse Comics: May, 2002 - No. 4 ($2.99, B&W, limited series)

1-3-Nord-c/a. 1-Stories of Amelia Earhart & D.B. Cooper 3.00

RIPLEY'S BELIEVE IT OR NOT! TRUE GHOST STORIES (Along with Ripley's...True War Stories, the three issues together precede the 1967 series that starts its numbering with #4) (Also see Dan Curtis)
Gold Key: June, 1965 - No. 2, Oct, 1966

1-Williamson, Wood & Evans-a; photo-c	8	16	24	53	74	95
2-Orlando, McWilliams-a; photo-c	5	10	15	33	44	55
Mini-Comic 1(1976-3-1/4x6-1/2")	2	4	6	9	11	14
11186(1977)-Golden Press; ($1.95, 224 pgs.)-All-r	4	8	12	28	38	48
11401(3/79)-Golden Press; ($1.00, 96 pgs.)-All-r	3	6	9	16	21	26

RIPLEY'S BELIEVE IT OR NOT! TRUE WAR STORIES (Along with Ripley's...True Ghost Stories, the three issues together precede the 1967 series that starts its numbering with #4)
Gold Key: Nov, 1965 (Aug, 1965 in indicia)

1-No Williamson-a	4	8	12	28	38	48

RIPLEY'S BELIEVE IT OR NOT! TRUE WEIRD
Ripley Enterprises: June, 1966 - No. 2, Aug, 1966 (B&W Magazine)

1,2-Comic stories & text	3	6	9	18	24	30

RIPTIDE
Image Comics: Sep, 1995 - No. 2, Oct, 1995 ($2.50, limited series)

1,2: Rob Liefeld-c 2.50

RISE OF APOCALYPSE
Marvel Comics: Oct, 1996 - No. 4, Jan, 1997 ($1.95, limited series)

1-4: Adam Pollina-c/a 2.25

RISING STARS
Image Comics(Top Cow): Mar, 1999 - Present ($2.50/$2.99)

Preview-(3/99, $5.00) Straczynski-s						6.00
0-(6/00, $2.50) Gary Frank-a/c						2.50
1/2-(8/01, $2.95) Anderson-c; art & sketch pages by Zanier						3.00
1-Four covers; Keu Cha-c/a	1	2	3	5	7	9
1-($10.00) Gold Editions-four covers						10.00
1-($50.00) Holofoil-c						50.00
2-7: 5-7-Zanier & Lashley-a(p)	1	2	3	5	7	9
8-22: 8-13-Zanier & Lashley-a(p). 14-Immonen-a. 15-Flip book B&W preview of Universe. 15-22-Brent Anderson-a						3.00
Born In Fire TPB (11/00, $19.95) r/#1-8; foreword by Neil Gaiman						20.00
Power TPB (2002, $19.95) r/#9-16						20.00
Prelude-(10/00, $2.95) Cha-a/Lashley-c						3.00
...: Visitations (2002, $8.99) r/#0, 1/2, Preview; new Anderson-c; cover gallery						9.00
Wizard #0-(3/99) Wizard supplement; Straczynski-s						2.25
Wizard #1/2						10.00

RISING STARS BRIGHT
Image Comics(Top Cow): Mar, 2003 - No. 3, May, 2003 ($2.99, limited series)

1-3-Avery-s/Jurgens & Gorder-a/Beck-c 3.00

RIVERDALE HIGH (Archie's... #7,8)
Archie Comics: Aug, 1990 - No. 8, Oct, 1991 ($1.00, bi-monthly)

1 4.00
2-8 3.00

RIVER FEUD (See Zane Grey & Four Color #484)

RIVETS
Dell Publishing Co.: No. 518, Nov, 1953

Four Color 518	4	8	12	24	32	40

RIVETS (A dog)

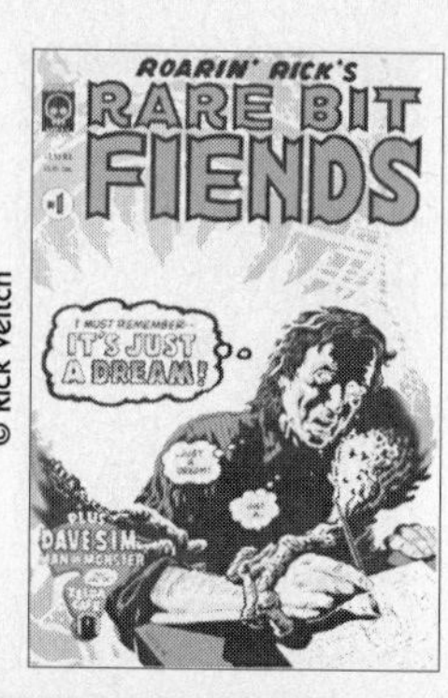

Roarin' Rick's Rare Bit Fiends #1 © Rick Veitch

Robin #126 © DC

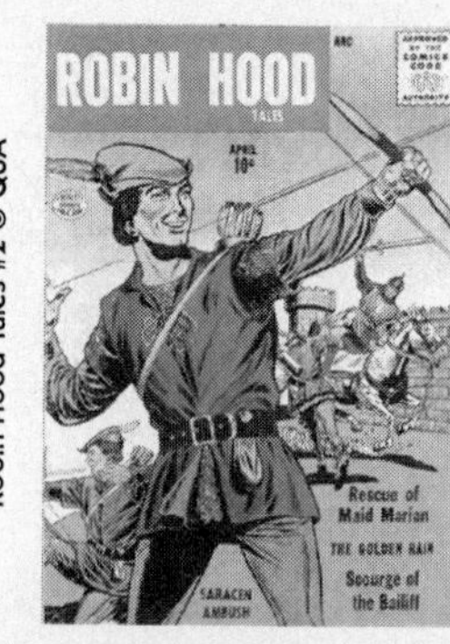

Robin Hood Tales #2 © QUA

GD VG FN VF VF/NM NM-
2.0 4.0 6.0 8.0 9.0 9.2

Argo Publ.: Jan, 1956 - No. 3, May, 1956

1-Reprints Sunday & daily newspaper strips 6 12 18 31 38 45
2,3 5 10 15 22 26 30

ROACHMILL
Blackthorne Publ.: Dec, 1986 - No. 6, Oct, 1987 ($1.75, B&W)

1-6 2.25

ROACHMILL
Dark Horse Comics: May, 1988 - No. 10, Dec, 1990 ($1.75, B&W)

1-10: 10-Contains trading cards 2.25

ROAD RUNNER (See Beep Beep, the...)

ROAD TO PERDITION (Inspired the 2002 Tom Hanks/Paul Newman movie) (Also see On the Road to Perdition)
DC Comics/Paradox Press: 1998, 2002 ($13.95, B&W paperback graphic novel)

nn-(1st printing) Max Allan Collins-s/Richard Piers Rayner-a 30.00
2nd & 3rd printings (2002, $13.95) 14.00
Movie photo cover edition (2002) 14.00

ROADTRIP
Oni Press: Aug, 2000 ($2.95, B&W, one-shot)

1-Reprints Judd Winick's back-up stories from Oni Double Feature #9,10 3.00

ROADWAYS
Cult Press: May, 1994 ($2.75, B&W, limited series)

1 2.75

ROARIN' RICK'S RARE BIT FIENDS
King Hell Press: July, 1994 - No. 21, Aug, 1996 ($2.95, B&W, mature)

1-21: Rick Veitch-c/a/scripts in all. 20-(5/96). 21-(8/96)-Reads Subtleman #1 on cover 3.00
Rabid Eye: The Dream Art of Rick Veitch ($14.95, B&W, TPB)-r/#1-8 & the appendix from #12 15.00
Pocket Universe (6/96, $14.95, B&W, TPB)-Reprints 15.00

ROBERT E. HOWARD'S CONAN THE BARBARIAN
Marvel Comics: 1983 ($2.50, 68 pgs., Baxter paper)

1-r/Savage Tales #2,3 by Smith, c-r/Conan #21 by Smith. 4.00

ROBERT LOUIS STEVENSON'S KIDNAPPED (See Kidnapped)

ROBIN (See Aurora, Birds of Prey, Detective Comics #38, New Teen Titans, Robin II, Robin III, Robin 3000, Star Spangled Comics #65, Teen Titans & Young Justice)

ROBIN (See Batman #457)
DC Comics: Jan, 1991 - No. 5, May, 1991 ($1.00, limited series)

1-Free poster by N. Adams; Bolland-c on all 4.00
1-2nd & 3rd printings (without poster) 2.25
2-5 3.00
2-2nd printing 2.25
Annual 1,2 (1992-93, $2.50, 68 pgs.): 1-Grant/Wagner scripts; Sam Kieth-c. 2-Intro Razorsharp; Jim Balent-c(p) 3.00

ROBIN (See Detective #668)
DC Comics: Nov, 1993 - Present ($1.50/$1.95/$1.99/$2.25)

1-($2.95)-Collector's edition w/foil embossed-c; 1st app. Robin's car, The Redbird; Azrael as Batman app. 4.00
1-Newsstand ed. 2.25
0,2-49,51-66-Regular editions: 3-5-The Spoiler app. 6-The Huntress-c/story cont'd from Showcase '94 #5. 7-Knightquest: The Conclusion w/new Batman (Azrael) vs. Bruce Wayne. 8-KnightsEnd Pt. 5. 9-KnightsEnd Aftermath; Batman-c & app. 10-(9/94)-Zero Hour. 0-(10/94). 11-(11/94). 25-Green Arrow-c/app. 26-Batman app. 27-Contagion Pt. 3; Catwoman-c/app; Penguin & Azrael app. 28-Contagion Pt. 11. 29-Penguin app. 31-Wildcat-c/app. 32-Legacy Pt. 3. 33-Legacy Pt. 7. 35-Final Night. 46-Genesis. 52,53-Cataclysm pt. 7, conclusion. 55-Green Arrow app. 62-64-Flash-c/app. 2.50
14 ($2.50)-Embossed-c; Troika Pt. 4 3.00
50-($2.95)-Lady Shiva & King Snake app. 3.00
67-74,76-78: 67-72-No Man's Land 2.50
75-($2.95) 3.00
79-97: 79-Begin $2.25-c; Green Arrow app. 86-Pander Bros.-a 2.25
98,99-Bruce Wayne: Murderer x-over pt. 6, 11 2.50
100-($3.50) Last Dixon-s 3.50
101-125: 101-Young Justice x-over. 106-Kevin Lau-c. 121,122-Willingham-s/Mays-a. 125-Tim Drake quits 2.25
126-133: 126-Spoiler becomes the new Robin. 129-131-War Games. 132-Robin moves to Bludhaven, Batgirl app. 2.25
#1,000,000 (11/98) 853rd Century x-over 2.50
Annual 3-5: 3-(1994, $2.95)-Elseworlds story. 4-(1995, $2.95)-Year One story. 5-(1996, $2.95)-Legends of the Dead Earth story 3.00
Annual 6 (1997, $3.95)-Pulp Heroes story. 4.00
.../Argent 1 (2/98, $1.95) Argent (Teen Titans) app. 2.25
...Eighty-Page Giant 1 (9/00, $5.95) Chuck Dixon-s/Diego Barreto-a 6.00
...: Flying Solo (2000, $12.95, TPB) r/#1-6, Showcase '94 #5,6 13.00
...Plus 1 (12/96, $2.95) Impulse-c/app.; Waid-s 3.00
...Plus 2 (12/97, $2.95) Fang (Scare Tactics) app. 3.00
...: Unmasked (2004, $12.95, TPB) r/#121-125; Pearson-c 13.00

ROBIN: A HERO REBORN
DC Comics: 1991 ($4.95, squarebound, trade paperback)

nn-r/Batman #455-457 & Robin #1-5; Bolland-c 5.00

ROBIN HOOD (See The Advs. of..., Brave and the Bold, Four Color #413, 669, King Classics, Movie Comics & Power Record Comics)

ROBIN HOOD (...& His Merry Men, The Illustrated Story of...) (See Classic Comics #7 & Classics Giveaways, 12/44)

ROBIN HOOD (Disney)
Dell Publishing Co.: No. 413, Aug, 1952; No. 669, Dec, 1955

Four Color 413-(1st Disney movie Four Color book)(8/52)-Photo-c 11 22 33 80 120 160
Four Color 669 (12/55)-Reprints #413 plus photo-c 7 14 21 46 63 80

ROBIN HOOD (Adventures of... #7, 8)
Magazine Enterprises (Sussex Pub. Co.): No. 52, Nov, 1955 - No. 6, Jun, 1957

52 (#1)-Origin Robin Hood & Sir Gallant of the Round Table 17 34 51 95 135 175
53 (#2), 3-6: 6-Richard Greene photo-c (TV) 13 26 39 74 102 130
I.W. Reprint #1,2,9: 1-r/#3. 2-r/#4. 9-r/#52 (1963) 2 4 6 12 16 20
Super Reprint #10,15: 10-r/#53. 15-r/#5 2 4 6 12 16 20
NOTE: ***Bolle** a-in all; c-52. **Powell** a-6.*

ROBIN HOOD (Not Disney)
Dell Publishing Co.: May-July, 1963 (one-shot)

1 3 6 9 18 24 30

ROBIN HOOD (Disney) (Also see Best of Walt Disney)
Western Publishing Co.: 1973 ($1.50, 8-1/2x11", 52 pgs., cardboard-c)

96151- "Robin Hood", based on movie, 96152- "The Mystery of Sherwood Forest", 96153- "In King Richard's Service", 96154- "The Wizard's Ring" each.... 3 6 9 18 23 28

ROBIN HOOD
Eclipse Comics: July, 1991 - No. 3, Dec, 1991 ($2.50, limited series)

1-3: Timothy Truman layouts 2.50

ROBIN HOOD AND HIS MERRY MEN (Formerly Danger & Adventure)
Charlton Comics: No. 28, Apr, 1956 - No. 38, Aug, 1958

28 10 20 30 56 73 90
29-37 8 16 24 43 54 65
38-Ditko-a (5 pgs.); Rocke-c 14 28 42 79 110 140

ROBIN HOOD TALES (Published by National Periodical #7 on)
Quality Comics Group (Comic Magazines): Feb, 1956 - No. 6, Nov-Dec, 1956

1-All have Baker/Cuidera-c 35 70 105 198 287 375
2-6-Matt Baker-a 34 68 102 193 279 365

ROBIN HOOD TALES (Cont'd from Quality series)(See Brave & the Bold #5)
National Periodical Publ.: No. 7, Jan-Feb, 1957 - No. 14, Mar-Apr, 1958

7-All have Andru/Esposito-c 39 78 117 224 327 430
8-14 34 68 102 193 279 365

ROBINSON CRUSOE (See King Classics & Power Record Comics)
Dell Publishing Co.: Nov-Jan, 1963-64

1 3 6 9 16 21 26

ROBIN II (The Joker's Wild)
DC Comics: Oct, 1991 - No. 4, Dec, 1991 ($1.50, mini-series)

1-(Direct sales, $1.50)-With 4 diff.-c; same hologram on each 3.00
1-(Newsstand, $1.00)-No hologram; 1 version 2.25
1-Collector's set ($10.00)-Contains all 5 versions bagged with hologram trading card inside 12.00
2-(Direct sales, $1.50)-With 3 different-c 2.50
2-4-(Newsstand, $1.00)-1 version of each 2.25
2-Collector's set ($8.00)-Contains all 4 versions bagged with hologram trading card inside 9.00
3-(Direct sale, $1.50)-With 2 different-c 2.50
3-Collector's set ($6.00)-Contains all 3 versions bagged with hologram trading card inside

Robocop #6 © Orion Pict.

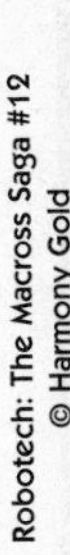
Robotech: The Macross Saga #12 © Harmony Gold

Robotech: Vermillion #1 © Harmony Gold

GD 2.0 | VG 4.0 | FN 6.0 | VF 8.0 | VF/NM 9.0 | NM- 9.2

7.00
4-(Direct sales, $1.50)-Only one version 2.50
4-Collector's set ($4.00)-Contains both versions bagged with Bat-Signal hologram trading card 5.00
Multi-pack (All four issues w/hologram sticker) 8.00
Deluxe Complete Set ($30.00)-Contains all 14 versions of #1-4 plus a new hologram trading card; numbered & limited to 25,000; comes with slipcase & 2 acid free backing boards 35.00

ROBIN III: CRY OF THE HUNTRESS
DC Comics: Dec, 1992 - No. 6, Mar, 1993 (Limited series)
1-6 ($2.50, collector's ed.)-Polybagged w/movement enhanced-c plus mini-poster of newsstand-c by Zeck 3.00
1-6 ($1.25, newsstand ed.): All have Zeck-c 2.25

ROBIN 3000
DC Comics (Elseworlds): 1992 - No. 2, 1992 ($4.95, mini-series, 52 pgs.)
1,2-Foil logo; Russell-c/a 5.00

ROBIN: YEAR ONE
DC Comics: 2000 - No. 4, 2001 ($4.95, square-bound, limited series)
1-4: Earliest days of Robin's career; Javier Pulido-c/a. 2,4-Two-Face app. 5.00
TPB (2002, $14.95) r/#1-4 15.00

ROBOCOP
Marvel Comics: Oct, 1987 ($2.00, B&W, magazine, one-shot)
1-Movie adaptation 4.00

ROBOCOP (Also see Dark Horse Comics)
Marvel Comics: Mar, 1990 - No. 23, Jan, 1992 ($1.50)
1-Based on movie 3.00
2-23 2.50
nn (7/90, $4.95, 52 pgs.)-r/B&W magazine in color; adapts 1st movie 5.00

ROBOCOP (FRANK MILLER'S...) (Also see Promotional Comics section for FCBD Ed.)
Avatar Press: July, 2003 - No. 9 ($3.50, limited series)
1-7-Frank Miller-s/Juan Ryp-a. 1-Three covers by Miller, Ryp, and Barrows. 2-Two covers 3.50

ROBOCOP: MORTAL COILS
Dark Horse Comics: Sept, 1993 - No. 4, Dec, 1993 ($2.50, limited series)
1-4: 1,2-Cago painted-c 2.50

ROBOCOP: PRIME SUSPECT
Dark Horse Comics: Oct, 1992 - No. 4, Jan, 1993 ($2.50, limited series)
1-4: 1,3-Nelson painted-c. 2,4-Bolton painted-c 2.50

ROBOCOP: ROULETTE
Dark Horse Comics: Dec, 1993 - No. 4, 1994 ($2.50, limited series)
1-4: 1,3-Nelson painted-c. 2,4-Bolton painted-c 2.50

ROBOCOP 2
Marvel Comics: Aug, 1990 ($2.25, B&W, magazine, 68 pgs.)
1-Adapts movie sequel 2.50

ROBOCOP 2
Marvel Comics: Aug, 1990; Late Aug, 1990 - #3, Late Sept, 1990 ($1.00, limited series)
nn-(8/90, $4.95, 68 pgs., color)-Same contents as B&W magazine 5.00
1: #1-3 reprint no number issue 3.00
2,3: 2-Guice-c(i) 2.50

ROBOCOP 3
Dark Horse Comics: July, 1993 - No. 3, Nov, 1993 ($2.50, limited series)
1-3: Nelson painted-c; Nguyen-a(p) 2.50

ROBOCOP VERSUS THE TERMINATOR
Dark Horse Comics: Sept, 1992 - No. 4, 1992 (Dec.) ($2.50, limited series)
1-4: Miller scripts & Simonson-c/a in all 3.00
1-Platinum Edition 6.00
NOTE: *All contain a different Robocop cardboard cut-out stand-up.*

ROBO DOJO
DC Comics (WildStorm): Apr, 2002 - No. 6, Sept, 2002 ($2.95, limited series)
1-6-Wolfman-s 3.00

ROBO-HUNTER (Also see Sam Slade...)
Eagle Comics: Apr, 1984 - No. 5, 1984 ($1.00)
1-5-2000 A.D. 2.25

R.O.B.O.T. BATTALION 2050
Eclipse Comics: Mar, 1988 ($2.00, B&W, one-shot)
1 2.25

ROBOT COMICS
Renegade Press: No. 0, June, 1987 ($2.00, B&W, one-shot)
0-Bob Burden story & art 2.25

ROBOTECH
Antarctic Press: Mar, 1997 - No. 11, Nov, 1998 ($2.95)
1-11, Annual 1 (4/98, $2.95) 3.00
...Class Reunion (12/98, $3.95, B&W) 4.00
...Escape (5/98, $2.95, B&W), ...Final Fire (12/98, $2.95, B&W) 3.00

ROBOTECH
DC Comics (WildStorm): No. 0, Feb, 2003 - No. 6, Jul, 2003 ($2.50/$2.95, limited series)
0-Tommy Yune-s; art by Jim Lee, Garza, Bermejo and others; pin-up pages by various 2.50
1-6 ($2.95)-Long Vo-a 3.00
...: From the Stars (2003, $9.95, digest-size) r/#0-6 & Sourcebook 10.00
... Sourcebook (3/03, $2.95) pin-ups and info on characters and mecha; art by various 3.00

ROBOTECH: COVERT-OPS
Antarctic Press: Aug, 1998 - No. 2, Sept, 1998 ($2.95, B&W, limited series)
1,2-Gregory Lane-s/a 3.00

ROBOTECH DEFENDERS
DC Comics: Mar, 1985 - No. 2, Apr, 1985 (Mini-series)
1,2 3.00

ROBOTECH IN 3-D (TV)
Comico: Aug, 1987 ($2.50)
1-Steacy painted-c 4.00

ROBOTECH: INVASION
DC Comics (WildStorm): Feb, 2004 - No. 5, July, 2004 ($2.95, limited series)
1-5-Faerber & Yune-s/Miyazawa & Dogan-a 3.00

ROBOTECH: LOVE AND WAR
DC Comics (WildStorm): Aug, 2003 - No. 6, Jan, 2004 ($2.95, limited series)
1-6-Long Vo & Charles Park-a/Faerber & Yune-s. 2-Variant-c by Warren 3.00

ROBOTECH MASTERS (TV)
Comico: July, 1985 - No. 23, Apr, 1988 ($1.50)
1-23 3.00

ROBOTECH: SENTINELS - RUBICON
Antarctic Press: July, 1998 ($2.95, B&W)
1 3.00

ROBOTECH SPECIAL
Comico: May, 1988 ($2.50, one-shot, 44 pgs.)
1-Steacy wraparound-c; partial photo-c 4.00

ROBOTECH THE GRAPHIC NOVEL
Comico: Aug, 1986 ($5.95, 8-1/2x11", 52 pgs.)
1-Origin SDF-1; intro T.R. Edwards, Steacy-c/a; 2nd printing also exists (12/86) 7.00

ROBOTECH: THE MACROSS SAGA (TV)(Formerly Macross)
Comico: No. 2, Feb, 1985 - No. 36, Feb, 1989 ($1.50)
2-10 4.00
11-36: 12,17-Ken Steacy painted-c. 26-Begin $1.75-c. 35,36-($1.95) 3.00
Volume 1-4 TPB (WildStorm, 2003, $14.95, 5-3/4" x 8-1/4")1-Reprints #2-6 & Macross #1. 2- r/#7-12. 3-r/#13-18. 4-r/#19-24 15.00

ROBOTECH: THE NEW GENERATION
Comico: July, 1985 - No. 25, July, 1988
1-25 3.00

ROBOTECH: VERMILION
Antarctic Press: Mar, 1997 - No. 4, ($2.95, B&W, limited series)
1-4 3.00

ROBOTECH: WINGS OF GIBRALTAR
Antarctic Press: Aug, 1998 - No. 2, Sept, 1998 ($2.95, B&W, limited series)
1,2-Lee Duhig-s/a 3.00

ROBOTIX
Marvel Comics: Feb, 1986 (75¢, one-shot)
1-Based on toy 3.00

ROBOTMEN OF THE LOST PLANET (Also see Space Thrillers)
Avon Periodicals: 1952 (Also see Strange Worlds #19)

Rocket Kelly #3 © FOX

Rock Fantasy Comics #9 © RFC

Rocky Lane Western #8 © FAW

	GD 2.0	VG 4.0	FN 6.0	VF 8.0	VF/NM 9.0	NM- 9.2

1-McCann-a (3 pgs.); Fawcette-a 108 216 324 675 1038 1400

ROB ROY
Dell Publishing Co.: 1954 (Disney-Movie)
Four Color 544-Manning-a, photo-c 9 18 27 63 89 115

ROB ZOMBIE'S SPOOKSHOW INTERNATIONAL
CrossGen Comics/MVCreations: Nov, 2003 - Present ($3.50/$2.95)
1-($3.50) Campbell-c; Rob Zombie-s/Colan, Dwyer & others-a 3.50
2-8-($2.95): 2-Edwards-c 3.00

ROCK, THE (WWF Wrestling)
Chaos! Comics: June, 2001 ($2.99, one-shot)
1-Photo-c; Grant-s/Neves-a 3.00

ROCK & ROLL HIGH SCHOOL
Roger Corman's Cosmic Comics: Oct, 1995 ($2.50)
1-Bob Fingerman scripts 2.50

ROCK AND ROLLO (Formerly TV Teens)
Charlton Comics: V2#14, Oct, 1957 - No. 19, Sept, 1958
V2#14-19 6 12 18 29 36 42

ROCK COMICS
Landgraphic Publ.: Jul/Aug, 1979 ($1.25, tabloid size, 28 pgs.)
1-N. Adams-c; Thor(not Marvel's) story by Adams 2 4 6 14 18 22

ROCKET COMICS
Hillman Periodicals: Mar, 1940 - No. 3, May, 1940
1-Rocket Riley, Red Roberts the Electro Man (origin), The Phantom Ranger, The Steel Shark, The Defender, Buzzard Barnes and his Sky Devils, Lefty Larson, & The Defender, the Man with a Thousand Faces begin (1st app. of each); all have Rocket Riley-c
254 508 762 1588 2444 3300
2,3 125 250 375 781 1203 1625

ROCKETEER, THE (See Eclipse Graphic Album Series, Pacific Presents & Starslayer)

ROCKETEER ADVENTURE MAGAZINE, THE
Comico/Dark Horse Comics No. 3: July, 1988 ($2.00); No. 2, July, 1989 ($2.75); No. 3, Jan, 1995 ($2.95)
1-(7/88, $2.00)-Dave Stevens-c/a in all; Kaluta back-up-a; 1st app. Jonas (character based on The Shadow) 1 2 3 5 7 9
2-(7/89, $2.75)-Stevens/Dorman painted-c 6.00
3-(1/95, $2.95)-Includes pinups by Stevens, Gulacy, Plunkett, & Mignola 3.50
Volume 2-(9/96, $9.95, magazine size TPB)-Reprints #1-3 10.00

ROCKETEER SPECIAL EDITION, THE
Eclipse Comics: Nov, 1984 ($1.50, Baxter paper)(Chapter 5 of Rocketeer serial)
1-Stevens-c/a; Kaluta back-c; pin-ups inside 2 4 6 8 10 12
NOTE: *Originally intended to be published in Pacific Presents.*

ROCKETEER: THE OFFICIAL MOVIE ADAPTATION, THE
W. D. Publications (Disney): 1991
nn-($5.95, 68 pgs.)-Squarebound deluxe edition 6.00
nn-($2.95, 68 pgs.)-Stapled regular edition 3.00
3-D Comic Book (1991, $7.98, 52 pgs.) 8.00

ROCKET KELLY (See The Bouncer, Green Mask #10); becomes Li'l Pan #6)
Fox Feature Syndicate: 1944; Fall, 1945 - No. 5, Oct-Nov, 1946
nn (1944), 1 35 70 105 201 293 385
2-The Puppeteer app. (costumed hero) 26 52 78 147 211 275
3-5: 5-(#5 on cover, #4 inside) 23 46 69 130 188 245

ROCKETMAN (Strange Fantasy #2 on) (See Hello Pal & Scoop Comics)
Ajax/Farrell Publications: June, 1952 (Strange Stories of the Future)
1-Rocketman & Cosmo 40 80 120 239 357 475

ROCKET RACCOON
Marvel Comics: May, 1985 - No. 4, Aug, 1985 (color, limited series)
1-4: Mignola-a 2.25

ROCKET SHIP X
Fox Features Syndicate: September, 1951; 1952
1 62 124 186 388 594 800
1952 (nn, nd, no publ.)-Edited 1951-c (exist?) 40 80 120 233 342 450

ROCKET TO ADVENTURE LAND (See Pixie Puzzle...)

ROCKET TO THE MOON
Avon Periodicals: 1951
nn-Orlando-c/a; adapts Otis Aldebert Kline's "Maza of the Moon"

	GD 2.0	VG 4.0	FN 6.0	VF 8.0	VF/NM 9.0	NM- 9.2

108 216 324 675 1038 1400

ROCK FANTASY COMICS
Rock Fantasy Comics: Dec, 1989 - No. 16?, 1991 ($2.25/$3.00, B&W)(No cover price)
1-Pink Floyd part 1 5.00
1-2nd printing ($3.00-c) 3.00
2,3: 2-Rolling Stones #1. 3-Led Zeppelin #1 4.00
2,3: 2nd printings ($3.00-c, 1/90 & 2/90) 3.00
4-Stevie Nicks Not published
5-Monstrosities of Rock #1; photo back-c 4.00
5-2nd printing ($3.00, 3/90 indicia, 2/90-c) 3.00
6-9,11-15,17,18: 6-Guns n' Roses #1 (1st & 2nd printings, 3/90)-Begin $3.00-c. 7-Sex Pistols #1. 8-Alice Cooper; not published. 9-Van Halen #1; photo back-c. 11-Jimi Hendrix #1; wraparound-c 3.00
10-Kiss #1; photo back-c 2 4 6 8 10 12
16-($5.00, 68 pgs.)-The Great Gig in the Sky(Floyd) 5.00

ROCK HAPPENING (See Bunny and Harvey Pop Comics:...)

ROCK N' ROLL COMICS
Revolutionary Comics: Jun, 1989 - No. 65 ($1.50/$1.95/$2.50, B&W/col. #15 on)
1-Guns N' Roses 1 2 3 5 6 8
1-2nd thru 7th printings. 7th printing (full color w/new-c/a) 2.25
2-Metallica 1 3 4 6 8 10
2-2nd thru 6th printings (6th in color) 2.25
3-Bon Jovi (no reprints) 1 2 3 5 6 8
4-8,10-65: 4-Motley Crue(2nd printing only, 1st destroyed). 5-Def Leppard (2 printings). 6-Rolling Stones(4 printings). 7-The Who (3 printings). 8-Skid Row; not published. 10-Warrant/Whitesnake(2 printings; 1st has 2 diff.-c). 11-Aerosmith (2 printings?). 12-New Kids on the Block(2 printings). 12-3rd printing; rewritten & titled NKOTB Hate Book. 13-Led Zeppelin. 14-Sex Pistols. 15-Poison; 1st color issue. 16-Van Halen. 17-Madonna. 18-Alice Cooper. 19-Public Enemy/2 Live Crew. 20-Queensryche/Tesla. 21-Prince? 22-AC/DC; begin $2.50-c. 23-Living Colour. 24-Anthrax. 29-Ozzy. 45,46-Grateful Dead. 49-Rush. 50,51-Bob Dylan. 56-David Bowie 5.00
9-Kiss 2 4 6 8 10 12
9-2nd & 3rd printings 2.25
NOTE: *Most issues were reprinted except #3. Later reprints are in color. #8 was not released.*

ROCKO'S MODERN LIFE (TV)
Marvel Comics: June, 1994 - No. 7, Dec, 1994 ($1.95) (Nickelodeon cartoon)
1-7 2.25

ROCKY AND HIS FIENDISH FRIENDS (TV)(Bullwinkle)
Gold Key: Oct, 1962 - No. 5, Sept, 1963 (Jay Ward)
1 (25¢, 80 pgs.) 22 44 66 158 242 325
2,3 (25¢, 80 pgs.) 15 30 45 105 160 215
4,5 (Regular size, 12¢) 10 20 30 73 107 140

ROCKY AND HIS FRIENDS (See Kite Fun Book & March of Comics #216 in the Promotional Comics section)

ROCKY AND HIS FRIENDS (TV)
Dell Publishing Co.: No. 1128, 8-10/60 - No.1311,1962 (Jay Ward)
Four Color #1128 (#1) (8-10/60) 34 68 102 255 398 540
Four Color #1152 (12-2/61), 1166, 1208, 1275, 1311('62) 24 48 72 170 260 350

ROCKY HORROR PICTURE SHOW THE COMIC BOOK, THE
Caliber Press: Jul, 1990 - No. 3, Jan, 1991 ($2.95, mini-series, 52 pgs.)
1-3: 1-Adapts cult film plus photos, etc., 1-2nd printing 3.00
...Collection ($4.95) 5.00

ROCKY JONES SPACE RANGER (See Space Adventures #15-18)

ROCKY JORDEN PRIVATE EYE (See Private Eye)

ROCKY LANE WESTERN (Allan Rocky Lane starred in Republic movies & TV for a short time as Allan Lane, Red Ryder & Rocky Lane) (See Black Jack Fawcett Movie Comics, Motion Picture Comics & Six-Gun Heroes)
Fawcett Publications/Charlton No. 56 on: May, 1949 - No. 87, Nov, 1959
1 (36 pgs.)-Rocky, his stallion Black Jack, & Slim Pickens begin; photo-c begin, end #57; photo back-c 100 200 300 625 963 1300
2 (36 pgs.)-Last photo back-c 40 80 120 239 357 475
3-5 (52 pgs.): 4-Captain Tootsie by Beck 31 62 93 175 253 330
6,10 (36 pgs.): 10-Complete western novelette "Badman's Reward" 22 44 66 125 180 235
7-9 (52 pgs.) 24 48 72 135 195 255
11-13,15-17,19,20 (52 pgs.): 15-Black Jack's Hitching Post begins, ends #25. 20-Last Slim Pickens 18 36 54 100 143 185
14,18 (36 pgs.) 15 30 45 85 120 155

Rogue ('04) #1 © DC

ROM #39 © Parker Brothers

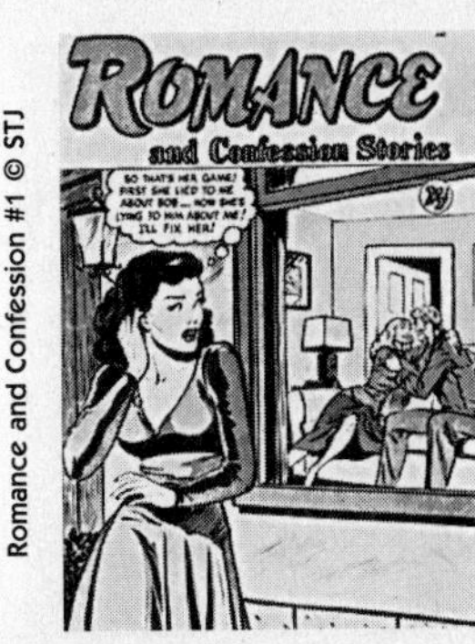

Romance and Confession #1 © STJ

	GD 2.0	VG 4.0	FN 6.0	VF 8.0	VF/NM 9.0	NM- 9.2
21,23,24 (52 pgs.): 21-Dee Dickens begins, ends #55,57,65-68	15	30	45	85	120	155
22,25-28,30 (36 pgs. begin)	14	28	42	81	113	145
29-Classic complete novel "The Land of Missing Men" with hidden land of ancient temple ruins (r-in #65)	20	40	60	112	161	210
31-40	13	26	39	74	102	130
41-54	11	22	33	64	87	110
55-Last Fawcett issue (1/54)	12	24	36	69	95	120
56-1st Charlton issue (2/54)-Photo-c	20	40	60	112	161	210
57,60-Photo-c	12	24	36	69	95	120
58,59,61-64,66-78,80-86: 59-61-Young Falcon app. 64-Slim Pickens app. 66-68: Reprints #30,31,32	10	20	30	58	77	95
65-r/#29, "The Land of Missing Men"	11	22	33	64	87	110
79-Giant Edition (68 pgs.)	12	24	36	69	95	120
87-Last issue	11	22	33	64	87	110

NOTE: *Complete novels in #10, 14, 18, 22, 25, 30-32, 36, 38, 39, 49. Captain Tootsie in #4, 12, 20. Big Bow and Little Arrow in #11, 28, 63. Black Jack's Hitching Post in #15-25, 64, 73.*

ROCKY LANE WESTERN
AC Comics: 1989 ($2.50, B&W, one-shot?)

1-Photo-c; Giordano reprints 4.00
Annual 1 (1991, $2.95, B&W, 44 pgs.)-photo front/back & inside-c; reprints 4.00

ROD CAMERON WESTERN (Movie star)
Fawcett Publications: Feb, 1950 - No. 20, Apr, 1953

	GD	VG	FN	VF	VF/NM	NM-
1-Rod Cameron, his horse War Paint, & Sam The Sheriff begin; photo front/back-c begin	54	108	162	329	502	675
2	29	58	87	164	237	310
3-Novel length story "The Mystery of the Seven Cities of Cibola"	24	48	72	138	199	260
4-10: 9-Last photo back-c	20	40	60	112	161	210
11-19	16	32	48	89	127	165
20-Last issue & photo-c	17	34	51	95	135	175

NOTE: *Novel length stories in No. 1-8, 12-14.*

RODEO RYAN (See A-1 Comics #8)

ROEL
Sirius: Feb, 1997 ($2.95, B&W, one-shot)

1 3.00

ROGAN GOSH
DC Comics (Vertigo): 1994 ($6.95, one-shot)

nn-Peter Milligan scripts 7.00

ROGER DODGER (Also in Exciting Comics #57 on)
Standard Comics: No. 5, Aug, 1952

	GD	VG	FN	VF	VF/NM	NM-
5-Teen-age	6	12	18	28	34	40

ROGER RABBIT (Also see Marvel Graphic Novel)
Disney Comics: June, 1990 - No. 18, Nov, 1991 ($1.50)

1-18-All new stories 3.00
In 3-D 1 (1992, $2.50)-Sold at Wal-Mart?; w/glasses 4.00

ROGER RABBIT'S TOONTOWN
Disney Comics: Aug, 1991 - No. 5, Dec, 1991 ($1.50)

1-5 2.50

ROGER ZELAZNY'S AMBER: THE GUNS OF AVALON
DC Comics: 1996 - No. 3, 1996 ($6.95, limited series)

1-3: Based on novel 7.00

ROG 2000
Pacific Comics: June, 1982 ($2.95, 44 pgs., B&W, one-shot, magazine)

	GD	VG	FN	VF	VF/NM	NM-
nn-Byrne-c/a (r)	2	4	6	8	10	12
2nd printing (7/82)	1	2	3	4	5	7

ROG 2000
Fantagraphics Books: 1987 - No. 2, 1987 ($2.00, limited series)

1,2-Byrne-r 3.00

ROGUE (From X-Men)
Marvel Comics: Jan, 1995 - No. 4, Apr, 1995 ($2.95, limited series)

1-4: 1-Gold foil logo 4.00
TPB-($12.95) r/#1-4 13.00

ROGUE (Volume 2)
Marvel Comics: Sept, 2001 - No. 4, Dec, 2001 ($2.50, limited series)

1-4-Julie Bell painted-c/Lopresti-a; Rogue's early days with X-Men 2.50

ROGUE (From X-Men)
Marvel Comics: Sept, 2004 - Present ($2.99)

1-5: 1-Richards-a. 4-Gambit app. 3.00

ROGUES GALLERY
DC Comics: 1996 ($3.50, one-shot)

1-Pinups of DC villains by various artists 3.50

ROGUES, THE (VILLAINS) (See The Flash)
DC Comics: Feb, 1998 ($1.95, one-shot)

1-Augustyn-s/Pearson-c 2.25

ROGUE TROOPER
Quality Comics/Fleetway Quality #38-on : Oct, 1986 - No. 49, 1991 ($1.25/$1.50/$1.75)

1-49: 6-Double size. 21,22,25-27-Guice-c. 47,48-Alan Moore scripts 2.25

ROLLING STONES: VOODOO LOUNGE
Marvel Comics: 1995 ($6.95, Prestige format, one-shot)

nn-Dave McKean-script/design/art 7.00

ROLY POLY COMIC BOOK
Green Publishing Co.: 1945 - No. 15, 1946 (MLJ reprints)

	GD	VG	FN	VF	VF/NM	NM-
1-Red Rube & Steel Sterling begin; Sahle-c	31	62	93	178	259	340
6-The Blue Circle & The Steel Fist app.	19	38	57	107	154	200
10-Origin Red Rube retold; Steel Sterling story (Zip #41)	28	56	84	158	229	300
11,12: The Black Hood app. in both	19	38	57	107	154	200
14-Classic decapitation-c; the Black Hood app.	39	78	117	230	335	440
15-The Blue Circle & The Steel Fist app.; cover exact swipe from Fox Blue Beetle #1	33	66	99	190	275	360

ROM (Based on the Parker Brothers toy)
Marvel Comics Group: Dec, 1979 - No. 75, Feb, 1986

	GD	VG	FN	VF	VF/NM	NM-
1-Origin/1st app.	2	4	6	8	10	12
2-16,19-23,28-30: 5-Dr. Strange. 13-Saga of the Space Knights begins. 19-X-Men cameo. 23-Powerman & Iron Fist app.						4.00
17,18-X-Men app.	1	2	3	5	7	9
24-27: 24-F.F. cameo; Skrulls, Nova & The New Champions app. 25-Double size. 26,27-Galactus app.						5.00
31-49,51-60: 31,32-Brotherhood of Evil Mutants app. 32-X-Men cameo. 34,35-Sub-Mariner app. 41,42-Dr. Strange app. 56,57-Alpha Flight app. 58,59-Ant-Man app.						2.25
50-Skrulls app. (52 pgs.) Pin-ups by Konkle, Austin						3.00
61-74: 65-West Coast Avengers & Beta Ray Bill app. 65,66-X-Men app.						2.25
75-Last issue						6.00
Annual 1-4: (1982-85, 52 pgs.)						3.00

NOTE: ***Austin** c-3i, 18i, 61i. **Byrne** a-74i; c-56, 57, 74. **Ditko** a-59-75p, Annual 4. **Golden** c-7-12, 19. **Guice** a-61i; c-55, 58, 60p, 70p. **Layton** a-59i, 72i; c-15, 59i, 69. **Miller** c-2p?, 3p, 17p, 18p. **Russell** a(i)-64, 65, 67, 69, 71, 75; c-64, 65i, 66, 71i, 75. **Severin** c-41p. **Sienkiewicz** a-53i; c-46, 47, 52-54, 68, 71p, Annual 2. **Simonson** c-18. **P. Smith** c-59p. **Starlin** c-67. **Zeck** c-50.*

ROMANCE (See True Stories of...)

ROMANCE AND CONFESSION STORIES (See Giant Comics Edition)
St. John Publishing Co.: No date (1949) (25¢, 100 pgs.)

	GD	VG	FN	VF	VF/NM	NM-
1-Baker-c/a; remaindered St. John love comics	40	80	120	239	357	475

ROMANCE DIARY
Marvel Comics (CDS)(CLDS): Dec, 1949 - No. 2, Mar, 1950

	GD	VG	FN	VF	VF/NM	NM-
1,2	15	30	45	83	117	150

ROMANCE OF FLYING, THE
David McKay Publications: 1942

	GD	VG	FN	VF	VF/NM	NM-
Feature Books 33 (nn)-WW II photos	15	30	45	86	123	160

ROMANCES OF MOLLY MANTON (See Molly Manton)

ROMANCES OF NURSE HELEN GRANT, THE
Atlas Comics (VPI): Aug, 1957

	GD	VG	FN	VF	VF/NM	NM-
1	8	16	24	43	54	65

ROMANCES OF THE WEST (Becomes Romantic Affairs #3?)
Marvel Comics (SPC): Nov, 1949 - No. 2, Mar, 1950 (52 pgs.)

	GD	VG	FN	VF	VF/NM	NM-
1-Movie photo-c of Yvonne DeCarlo & Howard Duff (Calamity Jane & Sam Bass)	24	48	72	138	199	260
2-Photo-c	15	30	45	85	120	155

ROMANCE STORIES OF TRUE LOVE (Formerly True Love Problems & Advice Illustrated)
Harvey Publications: No. 45, 5/57 - No. 50, 3/58; No. 51, 9/58 - No. 52, 11/58

	GD	VG	FN	VF	VF/NM	NM-
45-51: 45,46,48-50-Powell-a	6	12	18	31	38	45
52-Matt Baker-a	8	16	24	46	58	70

Romantic Adventures #1 © ACG

Romantic Hearts #7 © STORY

Romantic Secrets #34 © FAW

ROMANCE TALES (Formerly Western Winners #6?)
Marvel Comics (CDS): No. 7, Oct, 1949 - No. 9, Mar, 1950 (7,8: photo-c)

	GD 2.0	VG 4.0	FN 6.0	VF 8.0	VF/NM 9.0	NM- 9.2
7	14	28	42	79	110	140
8,9: 8-Everett-a	10	20	30	56	73	90

ROMANCE TRAIL
National Periodical Publications: July-Aug, 1949 - No. 6, May-June, 1950 (All photo-c & 52 pgs.)

	GD 2.0	VG 4.0	FN 6.0	VF 8.0	VF/NM 9.0	NM- 9.2
1-Kinstler, Toth-a; Jimmy Wakely photo-c	60	120	180	375	580	785
2-Kinstler-a; Jim Bannon photo-c	34	68	102	193	279	365
3-Photo-c; Kinstler, Toth-a	36	72	108	204	297	390
4-Photo-c; Toth-a	26	52	78	147	211	275
5,6: Photo-c on both. 5-Kinstler-a	24	48	72	138	199	260

ROMAN HOLIDAYS, THE (TV)
Gold Key: Feb, 1973 - No. 4, Nov, 1973 (Hanna-Barbera)

	GD 2.0	VG 4.0	FN 6.0	VF 8.0	VF/NM 9.0	NM- 9.2
1	5	10	15	36	48	60
2-4	3	7	10	21	28	35

ROMANTIC ADVENTURES (My... #49-67, covers only)
American Comics Group (B&I Publ. Co.): Mar-Apr, 1949 - No. 67, July, 1956 (Becomes My... #68 on)

	GD 2.0	VG 4.0	FN 6.0	VF 8.0	VF/NM 9.0	NM- 9.2
1	18	36	54	100	143	185
2	10	20	30	58	77	95
3-10	8	16	24	43	54	65
11-20 (4/52)	7	14	21	37	46	55
21-45,51,52: 52-Last Pre-code (2/55)	6	12	18	31	38	45
46-49-3-D effect-c/stories (TrueVision)	11	22	33	64	87	110
50-Classic cover/story "Love of A Lunatic"	10	20	30	58	77	95
53-67	6	12	18	28	34	40

NOTE: *#1-23, 52 pgs.* ***Shelly*** *a-40. Whitney c/art in many issues.*

ROMANTIC AFFAIRS (Formerly Molly Manton's Romances #2 and/or Romances of the West #2 and/or Our Love #2?)
Marvel Comics (SPC): No. 3, Mar, 1950

	GD 2.0	VG 4.0	FN 6.0	VF 8.0	VF/NM 9.0	NM- 9.2
3-Photo-c from Molly Manton's Romances #2	9	18	27	54	70	85

ROMANTIC CONFESSIONS
Hillman Periodicals: Oct, 1949 - V3#1, Apr-May, 1953

	GD 2.0	VG 4.0	FN 6.0	VF 8.0	VF/NM 9.0	NM- 9.2
V1#1-McWilliams-a	16	32	48	89	127	165
2-Briefer-a; negligee panels	10	20	30	56	73	90
3-12	8	16	24	43	54	65
V2#1,2,4-8,10-12: 2-McWilliams-a	7	14	21	37	46	55
3-Krigstein-a	9	18	27	49	62	75
9-One pg. Frazetta ad	7	14	21	37	46	55
V3#1	7	14	21	35	43	50

ROMANTIC HEARTS
Story Comics/Master/Merit Pubs.: Mar, 1951 - No. 10, Oct, 1952; July, 1953 - No. 12, July, 1955

	GD 2.0	VG 4.0	FN 6.0	VF 8.0	VF/NM 9.0	NM- 9.2
1(3/51) (1st Series)	14	28	42	79	110	140
2	8	16	24	46	58	70
3-10: Cameron-a	8	16	24	40	50	60
1(7/53) (2nd Series)-Some say #11 on-c	9	18	27	52	66	80
2	7	14	21	37	46	55
3-12	6	12	18	31	38	45

ROMANTIC LOVE
Avon Periodicals/Realistic (No #14-19): 9-10/49 - #3, 1-2/50; #4, 2-3/51 - #13, 10/52; #20, 3-4/54 - #23, 9-10/54

	GD 2.0	VG 4.0	FN 6.0	VF 8.0	VF/NM 9.0	NM- 9.2
1-c-/Avon paperback #252	25	50	75	144	207	270
2-5: 3-c-/paperback Novel Library #12. 4-c-/paperback Diversey Prize Novel #5. 5-c-/paperback Novel Library #34	15	30	45	85	120	155
6- "Thrill Crazy" marijuana story; c-/Avon paperback #207; Kinstler-a	21	42	63	118	169	220
7,8: 8-Astarita-a(2)	14	28	42	81	113	145
9-12: 9-c-/paperback Novel Library #41; Kinstler-a. 10-c-/Avon paperback #212. 11-c-/paperback Novel Library #17; Kinstler-a. 12-c-/paperback Novel Library #13	15	30	45	85	120	155
13,21-23: 22,23-Kinstler-c	14	28	42	79	110	140
20-Kinstler-c/a	14	28	42	81	113	145
nn(1-3/53)(Realistic-r)	10	20	30	56	73	90

NOTE: ***Astarita*** *a-7, 10, 11, 21. Painted c-1-3, 5, 7-11, 13. Photo c-4, 6.*

ROMANTIC LOVE
Quality Comics Group: 1963-1964

	GD 2.0	VG 4.0	FN 6.0	VF 8.0	VF/NM 9.0	NM- 9.2
I.W. Reprint #2,3,8: 2-r/Romantic Love #2	2	4	6	10	12	15

ROMANTIC MARRIAGE (Cinderella Love #25 on)
Ziff-Davis/St. John No. 18 on (#1-8: 52 pgs.): #1-3 (1950, no months); #4, 5-6/51 - #17, 9/52; #18, 9/53 - #24, 9/54

	GD 2.0	VG 4.0	FN 6.0	VF 8.0	VF/NM 9.0	NM- 9.2
1-Photo-c; Cary Grant/Betsy Drake photo back-c.	21	42	63	118	169	220
2-Painted-c; Anderson-a (also #15)	14	28	42	79	110	140
3-9: 3,4,8,9-Painted-c; 5-7-Photo-c	12	24	36	69	95	120
10-Unusual format; front-c is a painted-c; back-c is a photo-c complete with logo, price, etc.	19	38	57	107	154	200
11-17 13-Photo-c. 15-Signed story by Anderson. 17-(9/52)-Last Z-D issue	11	22	33	62	84	105
18-22,24: 20-Photo-c	11	22	33	62	84	105
23-Baker-c; all stories are reprinted from #15	11	22	33	64	87	110

ROMANTIC PICTURE NOVELETTES
Magazine Enterprises: 1946

	GD 2.0	VG 4.0	FN 6.0	VF 8.0	VF/NM 9.0	NM- 9.2
1-Mary Worth-r; Creig Flessel-c	17	34	51	95	135	175

ROMANTIC SECRETS (Becomes Time For Love)
Fawcett/Charlton Comics No. 5 (10/55) on: Sept, 1949 - No. 39, 4/53; No. 5, 10/55 - No. 52, 11/64 (#1-5: photo-c)

	GD 2.0	VG 4.0	FN 6.0	VF 8.0	VF/NM 9.0	NM- 9.2
1-(52 pg. issues begin, end #?)	16	32	48	89	127	165
2,3	10	20	30	58	77	95
4,9-Evans-a	11	22	33	62	84	105
5-8,10	8	16	24	43	54	65
11-23	8	16	24	40	50	60
24-Evans-a	8	16	24	46	58	70
25-39('53)	7	14	21	37	46	55
5 (Charlton, 2nd Series)(10/55, formerly Negro Romances #4)	10	20	30	56	73	90
6-10	8	16	24	43	54	65
11-20	4	8	12	25	33	42
21-35: Last 10¢ issue?	3	7	10	21	28	35
36-52('64)	3	6	9	18	23	28

NOTE: ***Bailey*** *a-20.* ***Powell*** *a(1st series)-5, 7, 10, 12, 16, 17, 20, 26, 29, 33, 34, 36, 37.* ***Sekowsky*** *a-26. Photo c(1st series)-1-5, 16, 25, 27, 33.* ***Swayze*** *a(1st series)-16, 18, 19, 23, 26-28, 31, 32, 39.*

ROMANTIC STORY (Cowboy Love #28 on)
Fawcett/Charlton Comics No. 23 on: 11/49 - #22, Sum, 1953; #23, 5/54 - #27, 12/54; #28, 8/55 - #130, 11/73

	GD 2.0	VG 4.0	FN 6.0	VF 8.0	VF/NM 9.0	NM- 9.2
1-Photo-c begin, end #24; 52 pgs. begins	18	36	54	100	143	185
2	10	20	30	58	77	95
3-5	9	18	27	52	66	80
6-14	8	16	24	46	58	70
15-Evans-a	9	18	27	52	66	80
16-22(Sum, '53; last Fawcett issue). 21-Toth-a?	7	14	21	37	46	55
23-39: 26,29-Wood swipes	7	14	21	35	43	50
40-(100 pgs.)	11	22	33	64	87	110
41-50	4	8	12	24	32	40
51-80: 57-Hypo needle story	3	6	9	18	23	28
81-99	2	4	6	10	13	16
100	2	4	6	12	16	20
101-130	2	4	6	9	11	14

NOTE: ***Jim Aparo*** *a-94.* ***Powell*** *a-7, 8, 16, 20, 30.* ***Marcus Swayze*** *a-2, 12, 20, 32.*

ROMANTIC THRILLS (See Fox Giants)

ROMANTIC WESTERN
Fawcett Publications: Winter, 1949 - No. 3, June, 1950 (All Photo-c)

	GD 2.0	VG 4.0	FN 6.0	VF 8.0	VF/NM 9.0	NM- 9.2
1	23	46	69	130	188	245
2-(Spr/50)-Williamson, McWilliams-a	21	42	63	118	169	220
3	15	30	45	85	120	155

ROMEO TUBBS (...That Lovable Teenager; formerly My Secret Life)
Fox Feature Syndicate/Green Publ. Co. No. 27: No. 26, 5/50 - No. 28, 7/50; No. 1, 1950; No. 27, 12/52

	GD 2.0	VG 4.0	FN 6.0	VF 8.0	VF/NM 9.0	NM- 9.2
26-Teen-age	11	22	33	64	87	110
28 (7/50)	10	20	30	58	77	95
27 (12/52)-Contains Pedro on inside; Wood-a (exist?)	16	32	48	89	127	165

RONALD McDONALD (TV)
Charlton Press (King Features Synd.): Sept, 1970 - No. 4, March, 1971

	GD 2.0	VG 4.0	FN 6.0	VF 8.0	VF/NM 9.0	NM- 9.2
1	9	18	27	65	93	120
2-4	5	10	15	36	48	60
V2#1,3-Special reprint for McDonald systems; "Not for resale" on cover	6	12	18	43	59	75

RONIN

Rose and Thorn #1 © DC

Route 666 #21 © CRO

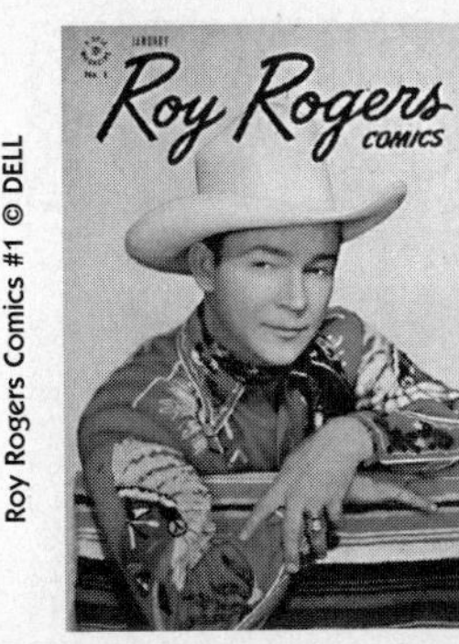

Roy Rogers Comics #1 © DELL

	GD 2.0	VG 4.0	FN 6.0	VF 8.0	VF/NM 9.0	NM- 9.2

DC Comics: July, 1983 - No. 6, Aug, 1984 ($2.50, limited series, 52 pgs.)

	GD	VG	FN	VF	VF/NM	NM-
1-5-Frank Miller-c/a/scripts in all						5.00
6-Scarcer; has fold-out poster.	1	2	3	5	6	8
Trade paperback (1987, $12.95)-Reprints #1-6						13.00

RONNA
Knight Press: Apr, 1997 ($2.95, B&W, one-shot)

	GD	VG	FN	VF	VF/NM	NM-
1-Beau Smith-s						3.00

ROOK (See Eerie Magazine & Warren Presents: The Rook)
Warren Publications: Oct, 1979 - No. 14, April, 1982 (B&W magazine)

	GD	VG	FN	VF	VF/NM	NM-
1-Nino-a/Corben-c; with 8 pg. color insert	2	4	6	14	18	22
2-4,6,7: 2-Voltar by Alcala begins. 3,4-Toth-a	2	4	6	8	10	12
5,8-14: 11-Zorro-s. 12-14-Eagle by Severin	2	4	6	8	10	12

ROOK
Harris Comics: No. 0, Jun, 1995 - No. 4, 1995 ($2.95)

	GD	VG	FN	VF	VF/NM	NM-
0-4: 0-short stories (3) w/preview. 4-Brereton-c.						3.00

ROOKIE COP (Formerly Crime and Justice?)
Charlton Comics: No. 27, Nov, 1955 - No. 33, Aug, 1957

	GD	VG	FN	VF	VF/NM	NM-
27	9	18	27	49	62	75
28-33	6	12	18	31	38	45

ROOM 222 (TV)
Dell Publishing Co.: Jan, 1970; No. 2, May, 1970 - No. 4, Jan, 1971

	GD	VG	FN	VF	VF/NM	NM-
1	6	12	18	43	59	75
2-4: 2,4-Photo-c. 3-Marijuana story. 4 r/#1	4	8	12	25	33	42

ROOTIE KAZOOTIE (TV)(See 3-D-ell)
Dell Publishing Co.: No. 415, Aug, 1952 - No. 6, Oct-Dec, 1954

	GD	VG	FN	VF	VF/NM	NM-
Four Color 415 (#1)	11	22	33	80	120	160
Four Color 459,502(#2,3), 4(4-6/54)-6	8	16	24	58	82	105

ROOTS OF THE SWAMP THING
DC Comics: July, 1986 - No.5, Nov, 1986 ($2.00, Baxter paper, 52 pgs.)

	GD	VG	FN	VF	VF/NM	NM-
1-5: r/Swamp Thing #1-10 by Wrightson & House of Mystery-r. 1-new Wrightson-c (2-5 reprinted covers).						4.00

ROSE (See Bone)
Cartoon Books: Nov, 2000 - No. 3, Feb, 2002 ($5.95, lim. series, square-bound)

	GD	VG	FN	VF	VF/NM	NM-
1-3-Prequel to Bone; Jeff Smith-s/Charles Vess painted-a/c						6.00
HC (2001, $29.95) r/#1-3; new Vess cover painting						30.00
SC (2002, $19.95) r/#1-3; new Vess cover painting						20.00
1-($6.00)-Blood & Glory Edition						6.00

ROSE AND THORN
DC Comics: Feb, 2004 - No. 6, July, 2004 ($2.95, limited series)

	GD	VG	FN	VF	VF/NM	NM-
1-6-Simone-sMelo-a/Hughes-c						3.00

ROSWELL: LITTLE GREEN MAN (See Simpsons Comics #19-22)
Bongo Comics: 1996 - No. 6 ($2.95, quarterly)

	GD	VG	FN	VF	VF/NM	NM-
1-6						3.50
...Walks Among Us ('97, $12.95, TPB) r/ #1-3 & Simpsons flip books						13.00

ROTOGIN: JUNKBOTZ
Image Comics: No. 0, Feb, 2003 - Present ($2.50)

	GD	VG	FN	VF	VF/NM	NM-
0-3-J. Korim-a/c						2.50

ROUNDUP (...Western Crime Stories)
D. S. Publishing Co.: July-Aug, 1948 - No. 5, Mar-Apr, 1949 (All 52 pgs.)

	GD	VG	FN	VF	VF/NM	NM-
1-Kiefer-a	21	42	63	118	169	220
2-5: 2-Marijuana drug mention story	15	30	45	83	117	150

ROUTE 666
CrossGeneration Comics: July, 2002 - No. 22, Jun, 2004 ($2.95)

	GD	VG	FN	VF	VF/NM	NM-
1-22-Bedard-s/Moline-a in most. 5-Richards-a. 15-McCrea-a						3.00
...: Highway to Horror (4/03, $15.95, TPB) r/#1-6						16.00
Vol. 2: Three-Ring Circus (2003, $15.95) r/#7-12						16.00

ROYAL ROY
Marvel Comics (Star Comics): May, 1985 - No.6, Mar, 1986 (Children's book)

	GD	VG	FN	VF	VF/NM	NM-
1-6						4.00

ROY CAMPANELLA, BASEBALL HERO
Fawcett Publications: 1950 (Brooklyn Dodgers)

	GD	VG	FN	VF	VF/NM	NM-
nn-Photo-c; life story	60	120	180	375	580	785

ROY ROGERS (See March of Comics #17, 35, 47, 62, 68, 73, 77, 86, 91, 100, 105, 116, 121, 131, 136, 146, 151, 161, 167, 176, 191, 206, 221, 236, 250)

ROY ROGERS AND TRIGGER
Gold Key: Apr, 1967

	GD	VG	FN	VF	VF/NM	NM-
1-Photo-c; reprints	6	12	18	40	55	70

ROY ROGERS ANNUAL
Wilson Publ. Co., Toronto/Dell: 1947 ("Giant Edition" on-c)(132 pgs., 50¢)

nn-Less than 5 known copies. Front and back cover art are from Roy Rogers #2. Stories reprinted from Roy Rogers #2, Four Color #137 and Four Color #153. (A copy in VG/FN was sold in 1986 for $400, & in 1996 for $1200 & in 2000 for $1500)

ROY ROGERS COMICS (See Western Roundup under Dell Giants)
Dell Publishing Co.: No. 38, 4/44 - No. 177, 12/47 (#38-166: 52 pgs.)

	GD	VG	FN	VF	VF/NM	NM-
Four Color 38 (1944)-49 pg. story; photo front/back-c on all 4-Color issues (1st western comic with photo-c)	200	400	600	1654	2677	3700
Four Color 63 (1945)-Color photos on all four-c	47	94	141	376	588	800
Four Color 86,95 (1945)	35	70	105	263	412	560
Four Color 109 (1946)	29	58	87	206	316	425
Four Color 117,124,137,144	23	46	69	163	249	335
Four Color 153,160,166: 166-48 pg. story	20	40	60	145	223	300
Four Color 177 (36 pgs.)-32 pg. story	20	40	60	141	216	290

ROY ROGERS COMICS (...& Trigger #92(8/55)-on)(Roy starred in Republic movies, radio & TV) (Singing cowboy) (Also see Dale Evans, It Really Happened #8, Queen of the West Dale Evans, & Roy Rogers' Trigger)
Dell Publishing Co.: Jan, 1948 - No. 145, Sept-Oct, 1961 (#1-19: 36 pgs.)

	GD	VG	FN	VF	VF/NM	NM-
1-Roy, his horse Trigger, & Chuck Wagon Charley's Tales begin; photo-c begin, end #145	75	150	225	629	1002	1375
2	30	60	90	218	334	450
3-5	22	44	66	158	242	325
6-10	18	36	54	126	193	260
11-19: 19-Chuck Wagon Charley's Tales ends	14	28	42	102	156	210
20 (52 pgs.)-Trigger feature begins, ends #46	15	30	45	105	160	215
21-30 (52 pgs.)	12	24	36	87	134	180
31-46 (52 pgs.): 37-X-Mas-c	10	20	30	73	107	140
47-56 (36 pgs.): 47-Chuck Wagon Charley's Tales returns, ends #133. 49-X-mas-c. 55-Last photo back-c	8	16	24	55	78	100
57 (52 pgs.)-Heroin drug propaganda story	8	16	24	58	82	105
58-70 (52 pgs.): 58-Heroin drug use/dealing story. 61-X-Mas-c	8	16	24	55	78	100
71-80 (52 pgs.): 73-X-Mas-c	7	14	21	51	70	90
81-91 (36 pgs. #81-on): 85-X-Mas-c	7	14	21	50	68	85
92-99,101-110,112-118: 92-Title changed to Roy Rogers and Trigger (8/55)	7	14	21	46	63	80
100-Trigger feature returns, ends #131	8	16	24	55	78	100
111,119-124-Toth-a	8	16	24	58	82	105
125-131: 125-Toth-a (1 pg.)	6	12	18	43	59	75
132-144-Manning-a. 132-1st Dale Evans-sty by Russ Manning. 138,144-Dale Evans featured	7	14	21	51	71	90
145-Last issue	8	16	24	58	82	105

NOTE: ***Buscema** a-74-108(2 stories each). **Manning** a-123, 124, 132-144. **Marsh** a-110. Photo back-c No. 1-9, 11-35, 38-55.*

ROY ROGERS' TRIGGER
Dell Publishing Co.: No. 329, May, 1951 - No. 17, June-Aug, 1955

	GD	VG	FN	VF	VF/NM	NM-
Four Color 329 (#1)-Painted-c	16	32	48	116	178	240
2 (9-11/51)-Photo-c	13	26	39	92	141	190
3-5: 3-Painted-c begin, end #17, most by S. Savitt	7	14	21	51	71	90
6-17: Title merges with Roy Rogers after #17	6	12	18	40	55	70

ROY ROGERS WESTERN CLASSICS
AC Comics: 1989 -No. 4 ($2.95/$3.95, 44pgs.) (24 pgs. color, 16 pgs. B&W)

	GD	VG	FN	VF	VF/NM	NM-
1-4: 1-Dale Evans-r by Manning, Trigger-r by Buscema; photo covers & interior photos by Roy & Dale. 2-Buscema-r (3); photo-c & B&W photos inside. 3-Dale Evans-r by Manning; Trigger-r by Buscema plus other Buscema-r; photo-c						4.00

RUDOLPH, THE RED-NOSED REINDEER
National Per. Publ.: 1950 - No. 13, Winter, 1962-63 (Issues are not numbered)

	GD	VG	FN	VF	VF/NM	NM-
1950 issue (#1); Grossman-c/a in all	23	46	69	130	188	245
1951-53 issues (3 total)	13	26	39	74	102	130
1954/55, 55/56, 56/57	11	22	33	64	87	110
1957/58, 58/59, 59/60, 60/61, 61/62	8	16	24	53	74	95
1962/63 (rare)(84 pgs.)(shows "Annual" in indicia)	12	24	36	82	124	165

NOTE: *13 total issues published. Has games & puzzles also.*

RUDOLPH, THE RED-NOSED REINDEER (Also see Limited Collectors' Edition C-20, C-24, C-33, C-42, C-50; and All-New Collectors' Edition C-53 & C-60)
National Per. Publ.: Christmas 1972 (Treasury-size)

Rugged Action #4 © ATLAS

Runaways #1 © MAR

Rusty Comics #12 © MAR

GD 2.0 | VG 4.0 | FN 6.0 | VF 8.0 | VF/NM 9.0 | NM- 9.2

nn-Precursor to Limited Collectors' Edition title (scarce)
(implied to be Lim. Coll .Ed. C-20) 25 50 75 177 271 365

RUFF AND REDDY (TV)
Dell Publ. Co.: No. 937, 9/58 - No. 12, 1-3/62 (Hanna-Barbera)(#9 on: 15¢)

Four Color 937(#1)(1st Hanna-Barbera comic book) 14 28 42 97 149 200
Four Color 981,1038 9 18 27 65 93 120
4(1-3/60)-12: 8-Last 10¢ issue 8 16 24 55 78 100

RUGGED ACTION (Strange Stories of Suspense #5 on)
Atlas Comics (CSI): Dec, 1954 - No. 4, June, 1955

1-Brodsky-c 14 28 42 79 110 140
2-4: 2-Last precode (2/55) 10 20 30 56 73 90
NOTE: ***Ayers** a-2, 3. **Maneely** c-2, 3. **Severin** a-2.*

RUGRATS COMIC ADVENTURES (TV)
Nickelodeon Magazines: 1999 - Present ($2.95, magazine size)

1-5, Volume 2: 1-6 3.00

RUINS
Marvel Comics (Alterniverse): July, 1995 - No. 2, Sept, 1995 ($5.00, painted, limited series)

1,2: Phil Sheldon from Marvels; Warren Ellis scripts; acetate-c 5.00

RULAH JUNGLE GODDESS (Formerly Zoot; I Loved #28 on) (Also see All Top Comics & Terrors of the Jungle)
Fox Features Syndicate: No. 17, Aug, 1948 - No. 27, June, 1949

17 98 196 294 613 944 1275
18-Classic girl-fight interior splash 67 134 201 419 647 875
19,20 65 130 195 406 623 840
21-Used in **SOTI**, pg. 388,389 67 134 201 419 642 865
22-Used in **SOTI**, pg. 22,23 65 130 195 406 623 840
23-27 50 100 150 305 465 625
NOTE: ***Kamen** c-17-19, 21, 22.*

RUMBLE GIRLS: SILKY WARRIOR TANSIE
Image Comics: Apr, 2000 - Present ($3.50, B&W)

1-6-Lea Hernandez-s/a. 2-Warren flip-c. 5,6-Warren Ellis short story 3.50

RUNAWAY, THE (See Movie Classics)

RUNAWAYS
Marvel Comics: July, 2003 - No. 18, Nov, 2004 ($2.95/$2.25/$2.99)

1-($2.95) Vaughan-s/Alphona-a/Jo Chen-c 3.00
2-9-($2.50) 2.50
10-18-($2.99) 11,12-Miyazawa-a; Cloak and Dagger app. 16-The mole revealed 3.00
Marvel Age Runaways Vol. 1: Pride and Joy (2004, $7.99, digest size) r/#1-6 8.00
...Vol. 2: Teenage Wasteland (2004, $7.99, digest size) r/#7-12 8.00
...Vol. 3: The Good Die Young (2004, $7.99, digest size) r/#13-18 8.00

RUN BABY RUN
Logos International: 1974 (39¢, Christian religious)

nn-By Tony Tallarico from Nicky Cruz's book 2 4 6 8 10 12

RUN, BUDDY, RUN (TV)
Gold Key: June, 1967 (Photo-c)

1 (10204-706) 3 7 10 21 28 35

RUNE (See Curse of Rune, Sludge & all other Ultraverse titles for previews)
Malibu Comics (Ultraverse): 1994 - No. 9, Apr, 1995 ($1.95)

0-Obtained by sending coupons from 11 comics; came w/Solution #0, poster, temporary tattoo, card 1 2 3 5 6 8
1,2,4-9: 1-Barry Windsor-Smith-c/a/stories begin, ends #6. 5-1st app. of Gemini. 6-Prime & Mantra app. 2.25
1-(1/94)-"Ashcan" edition flip book w/Wrath #1 2.25
1-Ultra 5000 Limited silver foil edition 4.00
3-(3/94, $3.50, 68 pgs.)-Flip book w/Ultraverse Premiere #1 3.50
Giant Size 1 ($2.50, 44 pgs.)-B.Smith story & art. 2.50

RUNE (2nd Series)(Formerly Curse of Rune)(See Ultraverse Unlimited #1)
Malibu Comics (Ultraverse): Infinity, Sept, 1995 - V2#7, Apr, 1996 ($1.50)

Infinity, V2#1-7: Infinity-Black September tie-in; black-c & painted-c exist. 1,3-7-Marvel's Adam Warlock app; regular & painted-c exist. 2-Flip book w/ "Phoenix Resurrection" Pt. 6 2.25
...Vs. Venom 1 (12/95, $3.95) 4.00

RUNE: HEARTS OF DARKNESS
Malibu Comics (Ultraverse): Sept, 1996 - No. 3, Nov, 1996 ($1.50, lim. series)

1-3: Moench scripts & Kyle Hotz-c/a; flip books w/6 pg. Rune story by the Pander Bros. 2.25

RUNE/SILVER SURFER
Marvel Comics/Malibu Comics (Ultraverse): Apr, 1995 ($5.95/$2.95, one-shot)

GD 2.0 | VG 4.0 | FN 6.0 | VF 8.0 | VF/NM 9.0 | NM- 9.2

1 ($5.95, direct market)-BWS-c 6.00
1 ($2.95, newstand)-BWS-c 3.00
1-Collector's limited edition 6.00

RUSE (Also see Archard's Agents)
CrossGeneration Comics: Nov, 2001 - No. 26, Jan, 2004 ($2.95)

1-Waid-s/Guice & Perkins-a 5.00
2-26: 6-Jeff Johnson-a. 11,15-Paul Ryan-a. 12-Last Waid-s 3.00
Enter the Detective Vol. 1 TPB (2002, $15.95) r/#1-6; Guice-c 16.00
...: The Silent Partner Vol. 2 (3/03, $15.95, TPB) r/#7-12 16.00
...: Criminal Intent Vol. 3 ('03, $15.95, TPB) r/#13-18 16.00
Traveler 1,2 ($9.95): Digest-size editions of the TPBs 10.00

RUST
Now Comics: 7/87 - No. 15, 11/88; V2#1, 2/89 - No. 7, 1989 ($1.50/$1.75)

1-15,V2#1-7: 12-(8/88)-5 pg. preview of The Terminator (1st app.) 3.00

RUST
Caliber Comics: 1996/1997 ($2.95, B&W)

1,2 3.00

RUSTLERS, THE (See Zane Grey Four Color 532)

RUSTY, BOY DETECTIVE
Good Comics/Lev Gleason: Mar-April, 1955 - No. 5, Nov, 1955

1-Bob Wood, Carl Hubbell-a begins 9 18 27 49 62 75
2-5 6 12 18 31 38 45

RUSTY COMICS (Formerly Kid Movie Comics; Rusty and Her Family #21, 22; The Kelleys #23 on; see Millie The Model)
Marvel Comics (HPC): No. 12, Apr, 1947 - No. 22, Sept, 1949

12-Mitzi app. 20 40 60 112 161 210
13 11 22 33 64 87 110
14-Wolverton's Powerhouse Pepper (4 pgs.) plus Kurtzman's "Hey Look" 23 46 69 130 188 245
15-17-Kurtzman's "Hey Look" 16 32 48 89 127 165
18,19 10 20 30 60 80 100
20-Kurtzman-a (5 pgs.) 17 34 51 95 135 175
21,22-Kurtzman-a (17 & 22 pgs.) 22 44 66 123 177 230

RUSTY DUGAN (See Holyoke One-Shot #2)

RUSTY RILEY
Dell Publishing Co.: No. 418, Aug, 1952 - No. 554, April, 1954 (Frank Godwin strip reprints)

Four Color 418 (...a Boy, a Horse, and a Dog #1) 6 12 18 38 52 65
Four Color #451(2/53), 486 ('53), 554 4 8 12 29 40 50

RUULE
Beckett Comics: Dec, 2003 - No. 5, Apr, 2004 ($2.99)

1-5-David Mack-c/Mike Hawthorne-a 3.00

RUULE: KISS & TELL
Beckett Comics: Jun, 2004 - Present ($1.99)

1-6: 1-Amano-s/c; Rousseau-a. 4-Maleev-c 2.00

SAARI ("The Jungle Goddess")
P. L. Publishing Co.: November, 1951

1 44 88 132 268 409 550

SABAN POWERHOUSE (TV)
Acclaim Books: 1997 ($4.50, digest size)

1,2-Power Rangers, BeetleBorgs, and others 4.50

SABAN PRESENTS POWER RANGERS TURBO VS. BEETLEBORGS METALLIX (TV)
Acclaim Books: 1997 ($4.50, digest size, one-shot)

nn 4.50

SABAN'S MIGHTY MORPHIN POWER RANGERS
Hamilton Comics: Dec, 1994 - No. 6, May, 1995 ($1.95, limited series)

1-6: 1-w/bound-in Power Ranger Barcode Card 2.25

SABAN'S MIGHTY MORPHIN POWER RANGERS (TV)
Marvel Comics: 1995 - No. 8, 1996 ($1.75)

1-8 2.25

SABAN'S NINJA RANGERS
Hamilton Comics: Dec, 1995 - No. 4, Mar, 1995 ($1.95, limited series)

1-4: Flip book w/Saban's V.R. Troopers 2.25

SABAN'S V.R. TROOPERS (See Saban's Ninja Rangers)

SABLE (Formerly Jon Sable, Freelance; also see Mike Grell's...)

Sabretooth ('04) #1 © MAR

Sabrina, The Teen-Age Witch V2#58 © AP

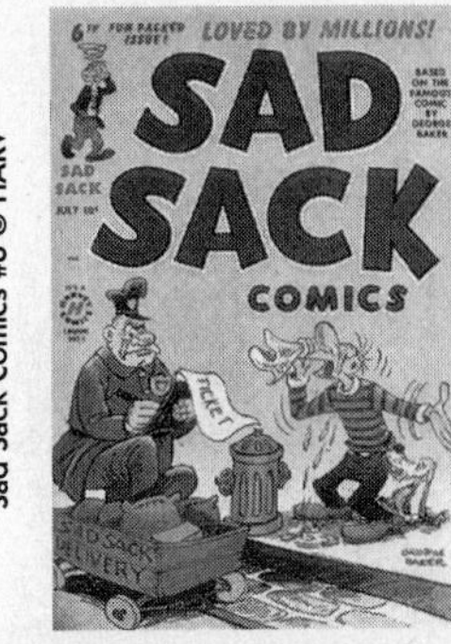

Sad Sack Comics #6 © HARV

First Comics: Mar, 1988 - No. 27, May, 1990 ($1.75/$1.95)

	GD 2.0	VG 4.0	FN 6.0	VF 8.0	VF/NM 9.0	NM- 9.2
1-27: 10-Begin $1.95-c						2.25

SABRE (See Eclipse Graphic Album Series)
Eclipse Comics: Aug, 1982 - No. 14, Aug, 1985 (Baxter paper #4 on)

	GD 2.0	VG 4.0	FN 6.0	VF 8.0	VF/NM 9.0	NM- 9.2
1-14: 1-Sabre & Morrigan Tales begin. 4-6-Incredible Seven origin						2.25

SABRETOOTH (See Iron Fist, Power Man, X-Factor #10 & X-Men)
Marvel Comics: Aug, 1993 - No. 4, Nov, 1993 ($2.95, lim. series, coated paper)

	GD 2.0	VG 4.0	FN 6.0	VF 8.0	VF/NM 9.0	NM- 9.2
1-4: 1-Die-cut-c. 3-Wolverine app.						4.00
...Special 1 "In the Red Zone" (1995, $4.95) Chromium wraparound-c						6.00
V2 #1 (1/98, $5.95, one-shot) Wildchild app.						6.00
Trade paperback (12/94, $12.95) r/#1-4						13.00

SABRETOOTH
Marvel Comics: Dec, 2004 - No. 4, Feb, 2005 ($2.99, limited series)

	GD 2.0	VG 4.0	FN 6.0	VF 8.0	VF/NM 9.0	NM- 9.2
1-4-Sears-a. 3,4-Wendigo app.						3.00

SABRETOOTH AND MYSTIQUE (See Mystique and Sabretooth)

SABRETOOTH CLASSIC
Marvel Comics: May, 1994 - No. 15, July, 1995 ($1.50)

	GD 2.0	VG 4.0	FN 6.0	VF 8.0	VF/NM 9.0	NM- 9.2
1-15: 1-3-r/Power Man & Iron Fist #66,78,84. 4-r/Spec. S-M #116. 9-Uncanny X-Men #212, 10-r/Uncanny X-Men #213. 11-r/ Daredevil #238. 12-r/Classic X-Men #10						3.00

SABRETOOTH: MARY SHELLEY OVERDRIVE
Marvel Comics: Aug, 2002 - No. 4, Nov, 2002 ($2.99, limited series)

	GD 2.0	VG 4.0	FN 6.0	VF 8.0	VF/NM 9.0	NM- 9.2
1-4-Jolley-s; Harris-c						3.00

SABRINA (Volume 2) (Based on animated series)
Archie Publications: Jan, 2000 - Present ($1.79/$1.99/$2.19)

	GD 2.0	VG 4.0	FN 6.0	VF 8.0	VF/NM 9.0	NM- 9.2
1-Teen-age Witch magically reverted to 12 years old						4.00
2-10: 4-Begin $1.99-c						3.00
11-64: 38-Sabrina aged back to 16 years old. 39-Begin $2.19-c. 58-Manga-style begins						2.50

SABRINA'S CHRISTMAS MAGIC (See Archie Giant Series Magazine #196, 207, 220, 231, 243, 455, 467, 479, 491, 503, 515)

SABRINA'S HALLOWEEN SPOOOKTACULAR
Archie Publications: 1993 - 1995 ($2.00, 52 pgs.)

	GD 2.0	VG 4.0	FN 6.0	VF 8.0	VF/NM 9.0	NM- 9.2
1-Neon orange ink-c; bound-in poster	1	2	3	5	6	8
2,3						5.00

SABRINA'S HOLIDAY SPECTACULAR
Archie Publications: 1993 - 1995 ($2.00, 52 pgs.)

	GD 2.0	VG 4.0	FN 6.0	VF 8.0	VF/NM 9.0	NM- 9.2
1	1	2	3	5	6	8
2,3						5.00

SABRINA, THE TEEN-AGE WITCH (TV)(See Archie Giant Series, Archie's Madhouse 22, Archie's TV..., Chilling Advs. In Sorcery, Little Archie #59)
Archie Publications: April, 1971 - No. 77, Jan, 1983 (52 pg.Giants No. 1-17)

	GD 2.0	VG 4.0	FN 6.0	VF 8.0	VF/NM 9.0	NM- 9.2
1-52 pgs. begin, end #17	15	30	45	107	164	220
2-Archie's group x-over	8	16	24	58	82	105
3-5: 3,4-Archie's Group x-over	6	12	18	40	55	70
6-10	5	10	15	36	48	60
11-17(2/74)	4	8	12	27	36	45
18-30	3	6	9	18	24	30
31-40(8/77)	2	4	6	12	16	20
41-60(6/80)	2	4	6	9	11	14
61-70	1	3	4	6	8	10
71-76-low print run	2	4	6	9	11	14
77-Last issue; low print run	2	4	6	12	16	20

SABRINA, THE TEEN-AGE WITCH
Archie Publications: 1996 ($1.50, 32 pgs., one-shot)

	GD 2.0	VG 4.0	FN 6.0	VF 8.0	VF/NM 9.0	NM- 9.2
1-Updated origin						5.00

SABRINA, THE TEEN-AGE WITCH (Continues in Sabrina, Vol. 2)
Archie Publications: May, 1997 - No. 32, Dec, 1999 ($1.50/$1.75/$1.79)

	GD 2.0	VG 4.0	FN 6.0	VF 8.0	VF/NM 9.0	NM- 9.2
1-Photo-c with Melissa Joan Hart	1	2	3	5	6	8
2-10: 9-Begin $1.75-c						5.00
11-20						4.00
21-32: 24-Begin $1.79-c. 28-Sonic the Hedgehog-c/app.						3.00

SABU, "ELEPHANT BOY" (Movie; formerly My Secret Story)
Fox Features Syndicate: No. 30, June, 1950 - No. 2, Aug, 1950

	GD 2.0	VG 4.0	FN 6.0	VF 8.0	VF/NM 9.0	NM- 9.2
30(#1)-Wood-a; photo-c from movie	27	54	81	152	219	285
2-Photo-c from movie; Kamen-a	20	40	60	112	161	210

SACHS & VIOLENS
Marvel Comics (Epic Comics): Nov, 1993 - No. 4, July, 1994 ($2.25, limited series, mature)

	GD 2.0	VG 4.0	FN 6.0	VF 8.0	VF/NM 9.0	NM- 9.2
1-($2.75)-Embossed-c w/bound-in trading card						2.75
1-($3.50)-Platinum edition (1 for each 10 ordered)						4.00
2-4: Perez-c/a; bound-in trading card: 2-(5/94)						2.25

SACRAMENTS, THE
Catechetical Guild Educational Society: Oct, 1955 (25¢)

	GD 2.0	VG 4.0	FN 6.0	VF 8.0	VF/NM 9.0	NM- 9.2
304	5	10	15	22	26	30

SACRED AND THE PROFANE, THE (See Eclipse Graphic Album Series #9 & Epic Illustrated #20)

SADDLE JUSTICE (Happy Houlihans #1,2) (Saddle Romances #9 on)
E. C. Comics: No. 3, Spring, 1948 - No. 8, Sept-Oct, 1949

	GD 2.0	VG 4.0	FN 6.0	VF 8.0	VF/NM 9.0	NM- 9.2
3-The 1st E.C. by Bill Gaines to break away from M. C. Gaines' old Educational Comics format. Craig, Feldstein, H. C. Kiefer, & Stan Asch-a; mentioned in Love and Death	48	96	144	293	447	600
4-1st Graham Ingels-a for E.C.	43	86	129	262	401	540
5-8-Ingels-a in all	40	80	120	239	357	475

NOTE: *Craig and Feldstein art in most issues. Canadian reprints known; see Table of Contents.* ***Craig*** *c-3, 4.* ***Ingels*** *c-5-8. #4 contains a biography of* ***Craig.***

SADDLE ROMANCES (Saddle Justice #3-8; Weird Science #12 on)
E. C. Comics: No. 9, Nov-Dec, 1949 - No. 11, Mar-Apr, 1950

	GD 2.0	VG 4.0	FN 6.0	VF 8.0	VF/NM 9.0	NM- 9.2
9,11: 9-Ingels-c/a. 11-Ingels-a; Feldstein-c	43	86	129	262	401	540
10-Wally Wood's 1st work at E. C.; Ingels-a; Feldstein-c	44	88	132	268	409	550

NOTE: *Canadian reprints known; see Table of Contents.* ***Wood/Harrison*** *a-10, 11.*

SADIE SACK (See Harvey Hits #93)

SAD SACK AND THE SARGE
Harvey Publications: Sept, 1957 - No. 155, June, 1982

	GD 2.0	VG 4.0	FN 6.0	VF 8.0	VF/NM 9.0	NM- 9.2
1	13	26	39	92	141	190
2	7	14	21	51	71	90
3-10	6	12	18	40	55	70
11-20	5	10	15	33	44	55
21-30	3	7	10	21	28	35
31-50	2	4	6	14	18	22
51-70	2	4	6	10	13	16
71-90,97-99	1	3	4	6	8	10
91-96: All 52 pg. Giants	2	4	6	10	13	16
100	2	4	6	8	10	12
101-120	1	2	3	4	5	7
121-155						5.00

SAD SACK COMICS (See Harvey Collector's Comics #16, Little Sad Sack, Tastee Freez Comics #4 & True Comics #55)
Harvey Publications/Lorne-Harvey Publications (Recollections) #288 On: Sept, 1949 - No. 287, Oct, 1982; No. 288, 1992 - No. 293?, 1993

	GD 2.0	VG 4.0	FN 6.0	VF 8.0	VF/NM 9.0	NM- 9.2
1-Infinity-c; Little Dot begins (1st app.); civilian issues begin, end #21; based on comic strip	47	94	141	376	588	800
2-Flying Fool by Powell	24	48	72	174	267	360
3	14	28	42	102	156	210
4-10	11	22	33	77	114	150
11-21	8	16	24	55	78	100
22-("Back In The Army Again" on covers #22-36); "The Specialist" story about Sad Sack's return to Army	9	18	27	60	85	110
23-30	6	12	18	40	55	70
31-50	5	10	15	33	44	55
51-80,100: 62-"The Specialist" reprinted	4	8	12	22	33	38
81-99	3	6	9	18	24	30
101-140	3	6	9	16	20	24
141-170,200	2	4	6	12	16	20
171-199	2	4	6	10	13	16
201-207: 207-Last 12¢ issue	2	4	6	9	11	14
208-222	1	2	3	5	6	8
223-228 (25¢ Giants, 52 pgs.)	2	4	6	9	11	14
229-250	1	3	4	6	8	10
251-285						6.00
286,287-Limited distribution	1	2	3	5	7	9
288,289 ($2.75, 1992): 289-50th anniversary issue						6.00
290-293 ($1.00, 1993, B&W)						3.00
3-D 1 (1/54, 25¢)-Came with 2 pairs of glasses; titled "Harvey 3-D Hits"	18	36	54	126	193	260
...At Home for the Holidays 1 (1993, no-c price)-Publ. by Lorne-Harvey' X-Mas issue						4.00

NOTE: *The Sad Sack Comics comic book was a spin-off from a Sunday Newspaper strip launched through John Wheeler's Bell Syndicate. The previous Sunday page and the first 21 comics depicted the Sad Sack in civvies. Unpopularity caused the Sunday page to be discontinued in the early '50s. Meanwhile Sad Sack returned to the*

Sad Sack Laugh Special #6 © HARV

Saga of the Original Human Torch #2 © MAR

The Saint #4 © AVON

Army, by popular demand, in issue No. 22, remaining there ever since. Incidentally, relatively few of the first 21 issues were ever collected and remain scarce due to this.

SAD SACK FUN AROUND THE WORLD
Harvey Publications: 1974 (no month)

	GD 2.0	VG 4.0	FN 6.0	VF 8.0	VF/NM 9.0	NM- 9.2
1-About Great Britain	2	4	6	12	16	20

SAD SACK GOES HOME
Harvey Publications: 1951 (16 pgs. in color, no cover price)

	GD 2.0	VG 4.0	FN 6.0	VF 8.0	VF/NM 9.0	NM- 9.2
nn-By George Baker	6	12	18	38	52	65

SAD SACK LAUGH SPECIAL
Harvey Publications: Winter, 1958-59 - No. 93, Feb, 1977 (#1-9: 84 pgs.; #10-60: 68 pgs.; #61-76: 52 pgs.)

	GD 2.0	VG 4.0	FN 6.0	VF 8.0	VF/NM 9.0	NM- 9.2
1-Giant 25¢ issues begin	11	22	33	77	114	150
2	6	12	18	43	59	75
3-10	5	10	15	36	48	60
11-30	4	8	12	27	36	45
31-60: 31-1st app. Hi-Fi Tweeter. 60-Last 68 pg. Giant	3	6	9	16	20	25
61-76-(All 52 pg. issues)	2	4	6	11	14	18
77-93	1	2	3	5	6	8

SAD SACK NAVY, GOBS 'N' GALS
Harvey Publications: Aug, 1972 - No. 8, Oct, 1973

	GD 2.0	VG 4.0	FN 6.0	VF 8.0	VF/NM 9.0	NM- 9.2
1: 52 pg. Giant	3	6	9	18	24	30
2-8	2	4	6	10	12	15

SAD SACK'S ARMY LIFE (See Harvey Hits #8, 17, 22, 28, 32, 39, 43, 47, 51, 55, 58, 61, 64, 67, 70)

SAD SACK'S ARMY LIFE (...Parade #1-57, ...Today #58 on)
Harvey Publications: Oct, 1963 - No. 60, Nov, 1975; No. 61, May, 1976

	GD 2.0	VG 4.0	FN 6.0	VF 8.0	VF/NM 9.0	NM- 9.2
1-(68 pg. issues begin)	8	16	24	55	78	100
2-10	4	8	12	29	40	50
11-20	3	7	10	21	28	35
21-34: Last 68 pg. issue	3	6	9	16	20	25
35-51: All 52 pgs.	2	4	6	11	14	18
52-61	1	3	4	6	8	10

SAD SACK'S FUNNY FRIENDS (See Harvey Hits #75)
Harvey Publications: Dec, 1955 - No. 75, Oct, 1969

	GD 2.0	VG 4.0	FN 6.0	VF 8.0	VF/NM 9.0	NM- 9.2
1	11	22	33	77	114	150
2-10	6	12	18	43	59	75
11-20	4	8	12	24	32	40
21-30	3	6	9	18	24	30
31-50	2	4	6	14	18	22
51-75	2	4	6	10	13	16

SAD SACK'S MUTTSY (See Harvey Hits #74, 77, 80, 82, 84, 87, 89, 92, 96, 99, 102, 105, 108, 111, 113, 115, 117, 119, 121)

SAD SACK USA (...Vacation #8)
Harvey Publications: Nov, 1972 - No. 7, Nov, 1973; No. 8, Oct, 1974

	GD 2.0	VG 4.0	FN 6.0	VF 8.0	VF/NM 9.0	NM- 9.2
1	3	6	9	16	20	25
2-8	2	4	6	8	10	12

SAD SACK WITH SARGE & SADIE
Harvey Publications: Sept, 1972 - No. 8, Nov, 1973

	GD 2.0	VG 4.0	FN 6.0	VF 8.0	VF/NM 9.0	NM- 9.2
1-(52 pg. Giant)	3	6	9	16	20	25
2-8	2	4	6	8	10	12

SAD SAD SACK WORLD
Harvey Publ.: Oct, 1964 - No. 46, Dec, 1973 (#1-31: 68 pgs.; #32-38: 52 pgs.)

	GD 2.0	VG 4.0	FN 6.0	VF 8.0	VF/NM 9.0	NM- 9.2
1	7	14	21	51	71	90
2-10	4	8	12	27	36	45
11-20	3	7	10	21	28	35
21-31: 31-Last 68 pg. issue	3	6	9	16	20	25
32-39-(All 52 pgs)	2	4	6	11	14	18
40-46	1	3	4	6	8	10

SAFEST PLACE IN THE WORLD, THE
Dark Horse Comics: 1993 ($2.50, one-shot)

	GD 2.0	VG 4.0	FN 6.0	VF 8.0	VF/NM 9.0	NM- 9.2
1-Steve Ditko-c/a/scripts						2.50

SAFETY-BELT MAN
Sirius Entertainment: June, 1994 - No. 6, 1995 ($2.50, B&W)

	GD 2.0	VG 4.0	FN 6.0	VF 8.0	VF/NM 9.0	NM- 9.2
1-6: 1-Horan-s/Dark One-a/Sprouse-c. 2,3-Warren-c. 4-Linsner back-up story. 5,6-Crilley-a						3.00

SAFETY-BELT MAN ALL HELL
Sirius Entertainment: June, 1996 - No. 6, Mar, 1997 ($2.95, color)

	GD 2.0	VG 4.0	FN 6.0	VF 8.0	VF/NM 9.0	NM- 9.2
1-6-Horan-s/Fillbach Bros.-a						3.00

SAFFIRE
Image Comics: Apr, 2000 - No. 3, Feb, 2001 ($2.95)

	GD 2.0	VG 4.0	FN 6.0	VF 8.0	VF/NM 9.0	NM- 9.2
1-3-Broome-a(p)/c						3.00
Preview-Color & B&W pages						2.25

SAGA OF BIG RED, THE
Omaha World-Herald: Sept, 1976 ($1.25) (In color)

	GD 2.0	VG 4.0	FN 6.0	VF 8.0	VF/NM 9.0	NM- 9.2
nn-by Win Mumma; story of the Nebraska Cornhuskers (sports)						6.00

SAGA OF CRYSTAR, CRYSTAL WARRIOR, THE
Marvel Comics: May, 1983 - No. 11, Feb, 1985 (Remco toy tie-in)

	GD 2.0	VG 4.0	FN 6.0	VF 8.0	VF/NM 9.0	NM- 9.2
1,6: 1-(Baxter paper). 6-Nightcrawler app; Golden-c						4.00
2-5,7-11: 3-Dr. Strange app. 3-11-Golden-c (painted-4,5). 11-Alpha Flight app.						3.00

SAGA OF RA'S AL GHUL, THE
DC Comics: Jan, 1988 - No. 4, Apr, 1988 ($2.50, limited series)

	GD 2.0	VG 4.0	FN 6.0	VF 8.0	VF/NM 9.0	NM- 9.2
1-4-r/N. Adams Batman						6.00

SAGA OF SABAN'S MIGHTY MORPHIN POWER RANGERS (Also see Saban's Mighty Morphin Power Rangers)
Hamilton Comics: 1995 - No. 4, 1995 ($1.95, limited series)

	GD 2.0	VG 4.0	FN 6.0	VF 8.0	VF/NM 9.0	NM- 9.2
1-4						2.25

SAGA OF SEVEN SUNS, THE : VEILED ALLIANCES
DC Comics (WildStorm): 2004 ($24.95, hardcover graphic novel with dustjacket)

	GD 2.0	VG 4.0	FN 6.0	VF 8.0	VF/NM 9.0	NM- 9.2
HC-Kevin J. Anderson-s/Robert Teranishi-a						25.00
SC-(2004, $17.95)						18.00

SAGA OF THE SWAMP THING, THE (See Swamp Thing)

SAGA OF THE ORIGINAL HUMAN TORCH
Marvel Comics: Apr, 1990 - No. 4, July, 1990 ($1.50, limited series)

	GD 2.0	VG 4.0	FN 6.0	VF 8.0	VF/NM 9.0	NM- 9.2
1-4: 1-Origin; Buckler-c/a(p). 3-Hitler-c						2.25

SAGA OF THE SUB-MARINER, THE
Marvel Comics: Nov, 1988 - No. 12, Oct, 1989 ($1.25/$1.50 #5 on, maxi-series)

	GD 2.0	VG 4.0	FN 6.0	VF 8.0	VF/NM 9.0	NM- 9.2
1-12: 9-Original X-Men app.						3.00

SAILOR MOON (Manga)
Mixx Entertainment Inc.: 1998 - Present ($2.95)

	GD 2.0	VG 4.0	FN 6.0	VF 8.0	VF/NM 9.0	NM- 9.2
1	2	4	6	11	14	18
1-(San Diego edition)	2	4	6	12	16	20
2-5	2	4	6	8	10	12
6-25						5.00
26-35						3.00
... Rini's Moon Stick 1						15.00

SAILOR ON THE SEA OF FATE (See First Comics Graphic Novel #11)

SAILOR SWEENEY (Navy Action #1-11, 15 on)
Atlas Comics (CDS): No. 12, July, 1956 - No. 14, Nov, 1956

	GD 2.0	VG 4.0	FN 6.0	VF 8.0	VF/NM 9.0	NM- 9.2
12-14: 12-Shores-a. 13,14-Severin-c	9	18	27	52	66	80

SAINT, THE (Also see Movie Comics(DC) #2 & Silver Streak #18)
Avon Periodicals: Aug, 1947 - No. 12, Mar, 1952

	GD 2.0	VG 4.0	FN 6.0	VF 8.0	VF/NM 9.0	NM- 9.2
1-Kamen bondage-c/a	77	154	231	481	741	1000
2	40	80	120	239	357	475
3-5: 4-Lingerie panels	36	72	108	204	297	390
6-Miss Fury app. by Tarpe Mills (14 pgs.)	44	88	132	268	409	550
7-c-/Avon paperback #118	28	56	84	158	229	300
8,9(12/50): Saint strip-r in #8-12; 9-Kinstler-c	25	50	75	141	203	265
10-Wood-a, 1 pg; c-/Avon paperback #289	25	50	75	141	203	265
11	18	36	54	100	143	185
12-c-/Avon paperback #123	21	42	63	118	169	220

NOTE: *Lucky Dale, Girl Detective in #1,2,4,6.* **Hollingsworth** *a-4, 6. Painted-c 7, 8, 10-12.*

SAINT ANGEL
Image Comics: Mar, 2000 - No. 4, Mar, 2001 ($2.95/$3.95)

	GD 2.0	VG 4.0	FN 6.0	VF 8.0	VF/NM 9.0	NM- 9.2
0-Altstaetter & Napton-s/Altstaetter-a						3.00
1-4-($3.95) Flip book w/Deity. 1-(6/00). 2-(10/00)						4.00

ST. GEORGE
Marvel Comics (Epic Comics): June, 1988 - No.8, Oct, 1989 ($1.25,/$1.50)

	GD 2.0	VG 4.0	FN 6.0	VF 8.0	VF/NM 9.0	NM- 9.2
1-8: Sienkiewicz-c. 3-begin $1.50-c						2.25

SAINT GERMAINE
Caliber Comics: 1997 - No. 8, 1998 ($2.95)

Samson #3 © FOX

San Diego Comic-Con Comics #2 © DH

Sandman #23 © DC

GD VG FN VF VF/NM NM-
2.0 4.0 6.0 8.0 9.0 9.2

1-8: 1,5-Alternate covers 3.00

SAINT SINNER (See Razorline)
Marvel Comics (Razorline): Oct, 1993 - No. 7, Apr, 1994 ($1.75)

1-($2.50)-Foil embossed-c; created by Clive Barker 2.50
2-7: 5-Ectokid x-over 2.25

ST. SWITHIN'S DAY
Trident Comics: Apr, 1990 ($2.50, one-shot)

1-Grant Morrison scripts 3.00

ST. SWITHIN'S DAY
Oni Press: Mar, 1998 ($2.95, B&W, one-shot)

1-Grant Morrison-s/Paul Grist-a 3.00

SALOMÉ (See Night Music #6)

SAM AND MAX, FREELANCE POLICE SPECIAL
Fishwrap Prod./Comico: 1987 ($1.75, B&W); Jan, 1989 ($2.75, 44 pgs.)

1 ($1.75, B&W, Fishwrap) 3.00
2 ($2.75, color, Comico) 2.75

SAM AND TWITCH (See Spawn and Case Files:...)
Image Comics (Todd McFarlane Prod.): Aug, 1999 - No. 26, Feb, 2004 ($2.50)

1-26: 1-19-Bendis-s. 1-14-Medina-a. 15-19-Maleev-a. 20-24-McFarlane-s/Maleev-a 2.50
Book One: Udaku (2000, $21.95, TPB) B&W reprint of #1-8 22.00

SAM HILL PRIVATE EYE
Close-Up (Archie): 1950 - No. 7, 1951

1 17 34 51 95 135 175
2 10 20 30 58 77 95
3-7 10 20 30 56 73 90

SAMMY: TOURIST TRAP
Image Comics: Feb, 2003 - No. 4, May, 2003 ($2.95, B&W, limited series)

1-4-Azad-s/a 3.00
A Very Sammy Day (5/04, $5.95, 5 1/2" x 8") Azad-s/a 6.00

SAM SLADE ROBOHUNTER
Quality Comics: Oct, 1986 - No. 31, 1989 ($1.25/$1.50)

1-31 2.25

SAMSON (1st Series) (Captain Aero #7 on; see Big 3 Comics)
Fox Features Syndicate: Fall, 1940 - No. 6, Sept, 1941 (See Fantastic Comics)

1-Samson begins, ends #6; Powell-a, signed 'Rensie;' Wing Turner by Tuska app; Fine-c?
265 530 795 1656 2553 3450
2-Dr. Fung by Powell; Fine-c? 90 180 270 563 869 1175
3-Navy Jones app.; Joe Simon-c 69 138 207 431 666 900
4-Yarko the Great, Master Magician begins 60 120 180 375 575 775
5,6: 6-Origin The Topper 48 96 144 293 447 600

SAMSON (2nd Series) (Formerly Fantastic Comics #10, 11)
Ajax/Farrell Publications (Four Star): No. 12, April, 1955 - No. 14, Aug, 1955

12-Wonder Boy 31 62 93 175 253 330
13,14: 13-Wonder Boy, Rocket Man 27 54 81 152 219 285

SAMSON (See Mighty Samson)

SAMSON & DELILAH (See A Spectacular Feature Magazine)

SAM STORIES: LEGS
Image Comics: Dec, 1999 ($2.50, one-shot)

1-Sam Kieth-s/a 2.50

SAMUEL BRONSTON'S CIRCUS WORLD (See Circus World under Movie Classics)

SAMURAI (Also see Eclipse Graphic Album Series #14)
Aircel Publications: 1985 - No. 23, 1987 ($1.70, B&W)

1, 14-16-Dale Keown-a 3.00
1-(reprinted),2-12,17-23: 2 (reprinted issue exists) 2.25
13-Dale Keown's 1st published artwork (1987) 5.00

SAMURAI
Warp Graphics: May, 1997 ($2.95, B&W)

1 3.00

SAMURAI CAT
Marvel Comics (Epic Comics): June, 1991 - No. 3, Sept, 1991 ($2.25, limited series)

1-3: 3-Darth Vader-c/story parody 2.25

SAMURAI JACK SPECIAL (TV)
DC Comics: Sept, 2002 ($3.95, one-shot)

1-Adaptation of pilot episode with origin story; Tartakovsky-s 4.00

SAMUREE
Continuity Comics: May, 1987 - No. 9, Jan, 1991

1-9 3.00

SAMUREE
Continuity Comics: V2#1, May, 1993 - V2#4, Jan,1994 ($2.50)

V2#1-4-Embossed-c: 2,4-Adams plot, Nebres-i. 3-Nino-c(i) 2.50

SAMUREE
Acclaim Comics (Windjammer): Oct, 1995 - No. 2, Nov,1995 ($2.50, lim. series)

1,2 2.50

SAN DIEGO COMIC CON COMICS
Dark Horse Comics: 1992 - No.4, 1995 (B&W, promo comic for the San Diego Comic Con)

1-(1992)-Includes various characters published from Dark Horse including Concrete, The Mask, RoboCop and others; 1st app. of Sprint from John Byrne's Next Men; art by Quesada, Byrne, Rude, Burden, Moebius & others; pin-ups by Rude, Dorkin, Allred & others; Chadwick-c 1 2 3 4 5 7
2-(1993)-Intro of Legend imprint; 1st app. of John Byrne's Danger Unlimited, Mike Mignola's Hellboy, Art Adams' Monkeyman & O'Brien; contains stories featuring Concrete, Sin City, Martha Washington & others; Grendel, Madman, & Big Guy pin-ups; Don Martin-c.
1 3 4 6 8 10
3-(1994)-Contains stories featuring Barb Wire, The Mask, The Dirty Pair, & Grendel by Matt Wagner; contains pin-ups of Ghost, Predator & Rascals In Paradise; The Mask-c. 6.00
4-(1995)-Contains Sin City story by Miller (3pg.), Star Wars, The Mask, Tarzan, Foot Soldiers; Sin City & Star Wars flip-c 6.00

SANDMAN, THE (1st Series) (Also see Adventure Comics #40, New York World's Fair & World's Finest #3)
National Periodical Publ.: Winter, 1974; No. 2, Apr-May, 1975 - No. 6, Dec-Jan, 1975-76

1-1st app. Bronze Age Sandman by Simon & Kirby (last S&K collaboration)
6 12 18 38 52 65
2-6: 6-Kirby/Wood-c/a 3 6 9 18 23 28

NOTE: ***Kirby*** *a-1p, 4-6p; c-1-5, 6p.*

SANDMAN (2nd Series) (See Books of Magic, Vertigo Jam & Vertigo Preview)
DC Comics (Vertigo imprint #47 on): Jan, 1989 - No. 75, Mar, 1996 ($1.50-$2.50, mature)

1 ($2.00, 52 pgs.)-1st app. Modern Age Sandman (Morpheus); Neil Gaiman scripts begin; Sam Kieth-a(p) in #1-5; Wesley Dodds (G.A. Sandman) cameo.
4 8 12 24 32 40
2-Cain & Abel app. (from HOM & HOS) 2 4 6 11 14 18
3-5: 3-John Constantine app. 2 4 6 10 12 15
6,7 1 3 4 6 8 10
8-Death-c/story (1st app.)-Regular ed. has Jeanette Kahn publishorial & American Cancer Society ad w/no indicia on inside front-c
2 4 6 14 18 22
8-Limited ed. (600+ copies?); has Karen Berger editorial and next issue teaser on inside covers (has indicia) 5 10 15 36 48 60
9-14: 10-Has explaination about #8 mixup; has bound-in Shocker movie poster. 14-(52 pgs.)-Bound-in Nightbreed fold-out 1 2 3 5 7 9
15-20: 16-Photo-c. 17,18-Kelley Jones-a. 19-Vess-a. 6.00
18-Error version w/1st 3 panels on pg. 1 in blue ink 3 6 9 16 20 25
19-Error version w/pages 18 & 20 facing each other 2 4 6 12 16 20
21,23-27: Seasons of Mist storyline. 22-World Without End preview. 24-Kelley Jones/Russell-a 6.00
22-1st Daniel (Later becomes new Sandman) 2 4 6 8 10 12
28-30 5.00
31-49,51-74: 36-(52 pgs.). 41,44-48-Metallic ink on-c. 48-Cerebus appears as a doll. 54-Re-intro Prez; Death app.; Belushi, Nixon & Wildcat cameos. 57-Metallic ink on c. 65-w/bound-in trading card. 69-Death of Sandman. 70-73-Zulli-a. 74-Jon J. Muth-a. 4.00
50-($2.95, 52 pgs.)-Black-c w/metallic ink by McKean; Russell-a; McFarlane pin-up 5.00
50-($2.95)-Signed & limited (5,000) Treasury Edition with sketch of Neil Gaiman
1 2 3 5 6 8
50-Platinum 20.00
75-($3.95)-Vess-a. 5.00
Special 1 (1991, $3.50, 68 pgs.)-Glow-in-the-dark-c 5.00
...: A Gallery of Dreams ($2.95)-Intro by N. Gaiman 3.00
...: Preludes & Nocturnes ($29.95, HC)-r/#1-8. 30.00
...: The Doll's House (1990, $29.95, HC)-r/#8-16. 30.00
...: Dream Country ($29.95, HC)-r/#17-20. 30.00
...: Season of Mists ($29.95, Leatherbound HC)-r/#21-28. 50.00
...: A Game of You ($29.95, HC)-r/32-37, ...: Fables and Reflections ($29.95, HC)-r/Vertigo Preview #1, Sandman Special #1, #29-31, #38-40 & #50. ...: Brief Lives ($29.95, HC)-r/#41-49. ...: World's End ($29.95, HC)-r/#51-56 30.00

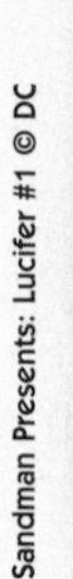
Sandman: Endless Nights HC © DC

Sandman Presents: Lucifer #1 © DC

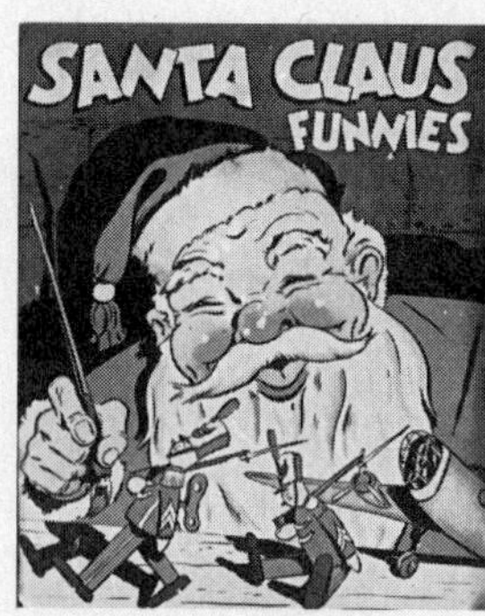

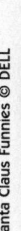

Santa Claus Funnies © DELL

	GD 2.0	VG 4.0	FN 6.0	VF 8.0	VF/NM 9.0	NM- 9.2
...: The Kindly Ones (1996, $34.95, HC)-r/#57-69 & Vertigo Jam #1						35.00
...: The Wake ($29.95, HC)-r/#70-75.						30.00

NOTE: *A new set of hardcover printings with new covers was introduced in 1998-99. Multiple printings exist of softcover collections.* ***Bachalo*** *a-12;* ***Kelley Jones*** *a-17, 18, 22, 23, 26, 27.* ***Vess*** *a-19, 75.*

SANDMAN: ENDLESS NIGHTS
DC Comics (Vertigo): 2003 ($24.95, hardcover, with dust jacket)

	GD 2.0	VG 4.0	FN 6.0	VF 8.0	VF/NM 9.0	NM- 9.2
HC-Neil Gaiman stories of Morpheus and the Endless illustrated by Fabry, Manara, Prado, Quitely, Russell, Sienkiewicz, and Storey; McKean-c						25.00
...Special (11/03, $2.95) Previews hardcover; Dream story w/Prado-a; McKean-c						3.00
SC (2004, $17.95)						18.00

SANDMAN MIDNIGHT THEATRE
DC Comics (Vertigo): Sept, 1995 ($6.95, squarebound, one-shot)

	GD 2.0	VG 4.0	FN 6.0	VF 8.0	VF/NM 9.0	NM- 9.2
nn-Modern Age Sandman (Morpheus) meets G.A. Sandman; Gaiman & Wagner story; McKean-c; Kristiansen-a						7.00

SANDMAN MYSTERY THEATRE (Also see Sandman (2nd Series) #1)
DC Comics (Vertigo): Apr, 1993 - No. 70, Feb, 1999 ($1.95/$2.25/$2.50)

	GD 2.0	VG 4.0	FN 6.0	VF 8.0	VF/NM 9.0	NM- 9.2
1-G.A. Sandman advs. begin; Matt Wagner scripts begin						4.50
2-49: 5-Neon ink logo. 29-32-Hourman app. 38-Ted Knight (G.A. Starman) app. 42-Jim Corrigan (Spectre) app. 45-48-Blackhawk app.						2.50
50-($3.50, 48 pgs.) w/bonus story of S.A. Sandman, Torres-a						3.50
51-70						2.50
Annual 1 (10/94, $3.95, 68 pgs.)-Alex Ross, Bolton & others-a						5.00
...: The Face and the Brute (2004, $19.95) r/#5-12						20.00
...: The Tarantula (1995, $14.95) r/#1-4						15.00

SANDMAN PRESENTS...
DC Comics (Vertigo)

	GD 2.0	VG 4.0	FN 6.0	VF 8.0	VF/NM 9.0	NM- 9.2
Taller Tales TPB (2003, $19.95) r/S.P: The Thessaliad #1-4; Merv Pumpkinhead, Agent...; The Dreaming #55; S.P. Everything You Always...; new McKean-c; intro by Willingham						20.00

SANDMAN PRESENTS: BAST
DC Comics (Vertigo): Mar, 2003 - No. 3, May, 2003 ($2.95, limited series)

	GD 2.0	VG 4.0	FN 6.0	VF 8.0	VF/NM 9.0	NM- 9.2
1-3-Kiernan-s/Bennett-a/McKean-c						3.00

SANDMAN PRESENTS: DEADBOY DETECTIVES (See Sandman #21-28)
DC Comics (Vertigo): Aug, 2001 - No. 4, Nov, 2001 ($2.50, limited series)

	GD 2.0	VG 4.0	FN 6.0	VF 8.0	VF/NM 9.0	NM- 9.2
1-4:Talbot-a/McKean-c/Brubaker-s						2.50

SANDMAN PRESENTS: EVERYTHING YOU ALWAYS WANTED TO KNOW ABOUT DREAMS...BUT WERE AFRAID TO ASK
DC Comics (Vertigo): Jul, 2001 ($3.95, one-shot)

	GD 2.0	VG 4.0	FN 6.0	VF 8.0	VF/NM 9.0	NM- 9.2
1-Short stories by Willingham; art by various; McKean-c						4.00

SANDMAN PRESENTS: LOVE STREET
DC Comics (Vertigo): Jul, 1999 - No. 3, Sept, 1999 ($2.95, limited series)

	GD 2.0	VG 4.0	FN 6.0	VF 8.0	VF/NM 9.0	NM- 9.2
1-3: Teenage Hellblazer in 1968 London; Zulli-a						3.00

SANDMAN PRESENTS: LUCIFER
DC Comics (Vertigo): Mar, 1999 - No. 3, May, 1999 ($2.95, limited series)

	GD 2.0	VG 4.0	FN 6.0	VF 8.0	VF/NM 9.0	NM- 9.2
1-3: Scott Hampton painted-c/a						3.00

SANDMAN PRESENTS: PETREFAX
DC Comics (Vertigo): Mar, 2000 - No. 4, Jun, 2000 ($2.95, limited series)

	GD 2.0	VG 4.0	FN 6.0	VF 8.0	VF/NM 9.0	NM- 9.2
1-4-Carey-s/Leialoha-a						3.00

SANDMAN PRESENTS: THE CORINTHIAN
DC Comics (Vertigo): Dec, 2001 - No. 3, Feb, 2002 ($2.95, limited series)

	GD 2.0	VG 4.0	FN 6.0	VF 8.0	VF/NM 9.0	NM- 9.2
1-3-Macan-s/Zezelj-a/McKean-c						3.00

SANDMAN PRESENTS, THE: THE FURIES
DC Comics (Vertigo): 2002 ($24.95, one-shot)

	GD 2.0	VG 4.0	FN 6.0	VF 8.0	VF/NM 9.0	NM- 9.2
Hardcover-Mike Carey-s/John Bolton-painted art; Lyta Hall's reunion with Daniel						30.00
Softcover-(2003, $17.95)						18.00

SANDMAN PRESENTS, THE: THESSALY: WITCH FOR HIRE
DC Comics (Vertigo): Apr, 2004 - No. 4, July, 2004 ($2.95, limited series)

	GD 2.0	VG 4.0	FN 6.0	VF 8.0	VF/NM 9.0	NM- 9.2
1-4-Willingham-s/McManus-a/McPherson-c						3.00

SANDMAN PRESENTS, THE: THE THESSALIAD
DC Comics (Vertigo): Mar, 2002 - No. 4, Jun, 2002 ($2.95, limited series)

	GD 2.0	VG 4.0	FN 6.0	VF 8.0	VF/NM 9.0	NM- 9.2
1-4-Willingham-s/McManus-a/McKean-c						3.00

SANDMAN, THE: THE DREAM HUNTERS
DC Comics (Vertigo): Oct, 1999 ($29.95/$19.95, one-shot)

	GD 2.0	VG 4.0	FN 6.0	VF 8.0	VF/NM 9.0	NM- 9.2
Hardcover-Neil Gaiman-s/Yoshitaka Amano-painted art						30.00
Softcover-(2000, $19.95) new Amano-c						20.00

SANDSCAPE
Dreamwave Productions: Jan, 2003 - No. 4, May, 2003 ($2.95)

	GD 2.0	VG 4.0	FN 6.0	VF 8.0	VF/NM 9.0	NM- 9.2
1-4: 1-Gatefold wraparound-c						3.00

SANDS OF THE SOUTH PACIFIC
Toby Press: Jan, 1953

	GD 2.0	VG 4.0	FN 6.0	VF 8.0	VF/NM 9.0	NM- 9.2
1	22	44	66	123	177	230

SANTA AND HIS REINDEER (See March of Comics #166)

SANTA AND THE ANGEL (See Dell Junior Treasury #7)
Dell Publishing Co.: Dec, 1949 (Combined w/Santa at the Zoo) (Gollub-a condensed from FC#128)

	GD 2.0	VG 4.0	FN 6.0	VF 8.0	VF/NM 9.0	NM- 9.2
Four Color 259	6	12	18	38	52	65

SANTA AT THE ZOO (See Santa And The Angel)

SANTA CLAUS AROUND THE WORLD (See March of Comics #241 in Promotional Comics section)

SANTA CLAUS CONQUERS THE MARTIANS (See Movie Classics)

SANTA CLAUS FUNNIES (Also see Dell Giants)
Dell Publishing Co.: Dec?, 1942 - No. 1274, Dec, 1961

	GD 2.0	VG 4.0	FN 6.0	VF 8.0	VF/NM 9.0	NM- 9.2
nn(#1)(1942)-Kelly-a	36	72	108	270	423	575
2(12/43)-Kelly-a	25	50	75	181	278	375
Four Color 61(1944)-Kelly-a	25	50	75	177	271	365
Four Color 91(1945)-Kelly-a	19	38	57	134	205	275
Four Color 128('46),175('47)-Kelly-a	15	30	45	107	164	220
Four Color 205,254-Kelly-a	14	28	42	97	149	200
Four Color 302,361,525,607,666,756,867	7	14	21	46	63	80
Four Color 958,1063,1154,1274	6	12	18	43	59	75

NOTE: *Most issues contain only one Kelly story.*

SANTA CLAUS PARADE
Ziff-Davis (Approved Comics)/St. John Publishing Co.: 1951; No. 2, Dec, 1952; No. 3, Jan, 1955 (25¢)

	GD 2.0	VG 4.0	FN 6.0	VF 8.0	VF/NM 9.0	NM- 9.2
nn(1951-Ziff-Davis)-116 pgs. (Xmas Special 1,2)	30	60	90	170	245	320
2(12/52-Ziff-Davis)-100 pgs.; Dave Berg-a	23	46	69	130	188	245
V1#3(1/55-St. John)-100 pgs.; reprints-c/#1	20	40	60	112	161	210

SANTA CLAUS' WORKSHOP (See March of Comics #50,168 in Promotional Comics section)

SANTA IS COMING (See March of Comics #197 in Promotional Comics section)

SANTA IS HERE (See March of Comics #49 in Promotional Comics section)

SANTA'S BUSY CORNER (See March of Comics #31 in Promotional Comics section)

SANTA'S CANDY KITCHEN (See March of Comics #14 in Promotional Comics section)

SANTA'S CHRISTMAS BOOK (See March of Comics #123 in Promotional Comics section)

SANTA'S CHRISTMAS COMICS
Standard Comics (Best Books): Dec, 1952 (100 pgs.)

	GD 2.0	VG 4.0	FN 6.0	VF 8.0	VF/NM 9.0	NM- 9.2
nn-Supermouse, Dizzy Duck, Happy Rabbit, etc.	19	38	57	107	154	200

SANTA'S CHRISTMAS LIST (See March of Comics #255 in Promotional Comics section)

SANTA'S HELPERS (See March of Comics #64, 106, 198 in Promotional Comics section)

SANTA'S LITTLE HELPERS (See March of Comics #270 in Promotional Comics section)

SANTA'S SHOW (See March of Comics #311 in Promotional Comics section)

SANTA'S SLEIGH (See March of Comics #298 in Promotional Comics section)

SANTA'S SURPRISE (See March of Comics #13 in Promotional Comics section)

SANTA'S TINKER TOTS
Charlton Comics: 1958

	GD 2.0	VG 4.0	FN 6.0	VF 8.0	VF/NM 9.0	NM- 9.2
1-Based on "The Tinker Tots Keep Christmas"	4	8	12	24	32	40

SANTA'S TOYLAND (See March of Comics #242 in Promotional Comics section)

SANTA'S TOYS (See March of Comics #12 in Promotional Comics section)

SANTA'S VISIT (See March of Comics #283 in Promotional Comics section)

SANTA THE BARBARIAN
Maximum Press: Dec, 1996 ($2.99, one-shot)

	GD 2.0	VG 4.0	FN 6.0	VF 8.0	VF/NM 9.0	NM- 9.2
1-Fraga/Mhan-s/a						3.00

SANTIAGO (Movie)
Dell Publishing Co.: Sept, 1956 (Alan Ladd photo-c)

	GD 2.0	VG 4.0	FN 6.0	VF 8.0	VF/NM 9.0	NM- 9.2
Four Color 723-Kinstler-a	11	22	33	75	110	145

SARGE SNORKEL (Beetle Bailey)
Charlton Comics: Oct, 1973 - No. 17, Dec, 1976

	GD 2.0	VG 4.0	FN 6.0	VF 8.0	VF/NM 9.0	NM- 9.2
1	2	4	6	12	16	20
2-10	2	4	6	8	10	12

Savage Dragon #100 © Erik Larsen

Savage She-Hulk #4 © MAR

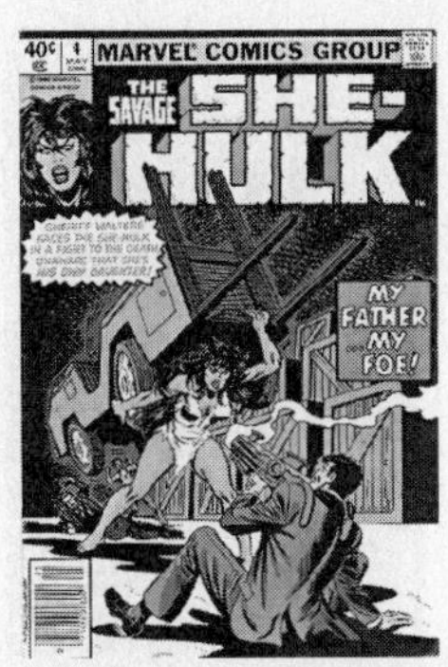

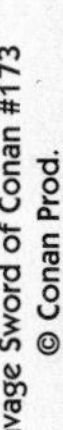
Savage Sword of Conan #173 © Conan Prod.

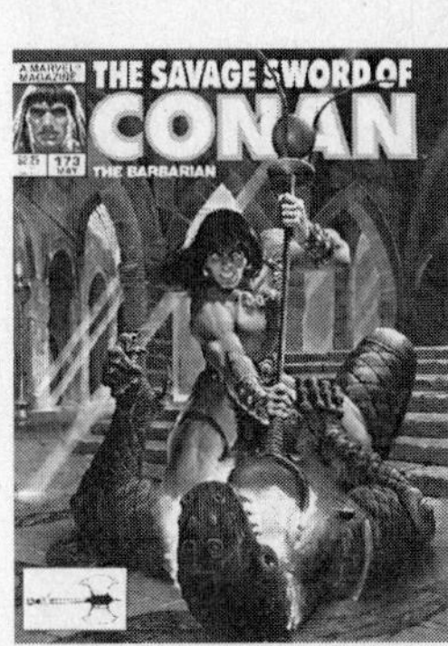

	GD 2.0	VG 4.0	FN 6.0	VF 8.0	VF/NM 9.0	NM- 9.2
11-17	1	2	3	5	7	9

SARGE STEEL (Becomes Secret Agent #9 on; also see Judomaster)
Charlton Comics: Dec, 1964 - No. 8, Mar-Apr, 1966 (All 12¢ issues)

	GD	VG	FN	VF	VF/NM	NM-
1-Origin & 1st app.	4	8	12	29	40	50
2-5,7,8	3	6	9	18	24	30
6-2nd app. Judomaster	4	8	12	24	32	40

SATAN'S SIX
Topps Comics (Kirbyverse): Apr, 1993 - No. 4, July, 1993 ($2.95, lim. series)

1-4: 1-Polybagged w/Kirbychrome trading card; Kirby/McFarlane-c plus 8 pgs. Kirby-a(p); has coupon for Kirbychrome ed. of Secret City Saga #0. 2-4-Polybagged w/3 cards. 4-Teenagents preview 3.00

NOTE: *Ditko a-1. Miller a-1.*

SATAN'S SIX: HELLSPAWN
Topps Comics (Kirbyverse): June, 1994 - No. 3, July, 1994 ($2.50, limited series)

1-3: 1-(6/94)-Indicia incorrectly shows "Vol 1 #2". 2-(6/94) 2.50

SAURIANS: UNNATURAL SELECTION (See Sigil)
CrossGeneration Comics: Feb, 2002 - No. 2, Mar, 2002 ($2.95, limited series)

1,2-Waid-s/DiVito-a 3.00

SAVAGE COMBAT TALES
Atlas/Seaboard Publ.: Feb, 1975 - No. 3, July, 1975

	GD	VG	FN	VF	VF/NM	NM-
1,3: 1-Sgt. Stryker's Death Squad begins (origin); Goodwin-s	1	2	3	5	7	9
2-Toth-a; only app. War Hawk; Goodwin-s	2	4	6	8	10	12

NOTE: *Buckler c-3. McWilliams a-1-3; c-1. Sparling a-1, 3.*

SAVAGE DRAGON, THE (See Megaton #3 & 4)
Image Comics (Highbrow Entertainment): July, 1992 - No. 3, Dec, 1992 ($1.95, lim. series)

1-Erik Larsen-c/a/scripts & bound-in poster in all; 4 cover color variations w/4 different posters; 1st Highbrow Entertainment title 4.00
2-Intro SuperPatriot-c/story (10/92) 3.00
3-Contains coupon for Image Comics #0 3.00
3-With coupon missing 2.25
...Vs. Savage Megaton Man 1 (3/93, $1.95)-Larsen & Simpson-c/a. 3.00
TPB-('93, $9.95) r/#1-3 10.00

SAVAGE DRAGON, THE
Image Comics (Highbrow Entertainment): June, 1993 - Present ($1.95/$2.50)

1-Erik Larsen-c/a/scripts 4.00
2-30: 2-(Wondercon Exclusive): 2-($2.95, 52 pgs.)-Teenage Mutant Ninja Turtles-c/story; flip book features Vanguard #0 (See Megaton for 1st app.). 3-7: Erik Larsen-c/a/scripts. 3-Mighty Man back-up story w/Austin-a(i). 4-Flip book w/Ricochet. 5-Mighty Man flip-c & back-up plus poster. 6-Jae Lee poster. 7-Vanguard poster. 8-Deadly Duo poster by Larsen. 13A (10/94)-Jim Lee-c/a; 1st app. Max Cash (Condition Red). 13B (6/95)-Larsen story. 15-Dragon poster by Larsen. 22-TMNT-c/a; Bisley pin-up. 27-"Wondercon Exclusive" new-c. 28-Maxx-c/app. 29-Wildstar-c/app. 30-Spawn app. 3.00
25 ($3.95)-variant-c exists. 4.00
31-49,51-71: 31-God vs. The Devil; alternate version exists w/o expletives (has "God Is Good" inside Image logo) 33-Birth of Dragon/Rapture's baby. 34,35-Hellboy-c/app. 51-Origin of She-Dragon. 70-Ann Stevens killed 2.50
50-($5.95, 100 pgs.) Kaboom and Mighty Man app.; Matsuda back-c; pin-ups by McFarlane, Simonson, Capullo and others 6.00
72-74: 72-Begin $2.95-c 3.00
75-($5.95) 6.00
76-99,101-106,108-114,116-118: 76-New direction starts. 83,84-Madman-c/app. 84-Atomics app. 97-Dragon returns home; Mighty Man app. 3.00
100-($8.95) Larsen-s/a; inked by various incl. Sienkiewicz, Timm, Austin, Simonson, Royer; plus pin-ups by Timm, Silvestri, Miller, Cho, Art Adams, Pacheco 9.00
107-($3.95) Firebreather, Invincible, Major Damage-c/app.; flip book w/Major Damage 4.00
115-($7.95, 100 pgs.) Wraparound-c; Freak Force app.; Larsen & Englert-a 8.00
...Companion (7/02, $2.95) guide to issues #1-100, character backgrounds 3.00
...Endgame (2/04, $15.95, TPB) r/#47-52 16.00
The Fallen (11/97, $12.95, TPB) r/#7-11, ...Possessed (9/98, $12.95, TPB) r/#12-16, ...Revenge (1998, $12.95, TPB) r/#17-21 13.00
...Gang War (4/00, $16.95, TPB) r/#22-26 17.00
.../Hellboy (10/02, $5.95) r/#34 & #35; Mignola-c 6.00
...Team-Ups (10/98, $19.95, TPB) r/team-ups 20.00
...: Terminated HC (2/03, $28.95) r/#34-40 & #1/2 29.00
...: This Savage World HC (2002, $24.95) r/#76-81; intro. by Larsen 25.00
...: This Savage World SC (2003, $15.95) r/#76-81; intro. by Larsen 16.00
...: Worlds at War SC (2004, $16.95) r/#41-46; intro. by Larsen; sketch pages 17.00

SAVAGE DRAGON ARCHIVES (See Dragon Archives, The)

SAVAGE DRAGONBERT: FULL FRONTAL NERDITY
Image Comics: Oct, 2002 ($5.95, B&W, one-shot)

1-Reprints of the Savage Dragon/Dilbert spoof strips 6.00

SAVAGE DRAGON/DESTROYER DUCK, THE
Image Comics/ Highbrow Entertainment: Nov, 1996 ($3.95, one-shot)

1 4.00

SAVAGE DRAGON: GOD WAR
Image Comics: July, 2004 - No. 3 ($2.95, limited series)

1-Kirkman-s/Englert-a 3.00

SAVAGE DRAGON/MARSHALL LAW
Image Comics: July, 1997 - No. 2, Aug, 1997 ($2.95, B&W, limited series)

1,2-Pat Mills-s, Kevin O'Neill-a 3.00

SAVAGE DRAGON: SEX & VIOLENCE
Image Comics: Aug, 1997 - No. 2, Sept, 1997 ($2.50, limited series)

1,2-T&M Bierbaum-s, Mays, Lupka, Adam Hughes-a 3.00

SAVAGE DRAGON/TEENAGE MUTANT NINJA TURTLES CROSSOVER
Mirage Studios: Sept, 1993 ($2.75, one-shot)

1-Erik Larsen-c(i) only 3.00

SAVAGE DRAGON: THE RED HORIZON
Image Comics/ Highbrow Entertainment: Feb, 1997 - No. 3 ($2.50, lim. series)

1-3 3.00

SAVAGE FISTS OF KUNG FU
Marvel Comics Group: 1975 (Marvel Treasury)

	GD	VG	FN	VF	VF/NM	NM-
1-Iron Fist, Shang Chi, Sons of Tiger; Adams, Starlin-a	3	6	9	18	24	30

SAVAGE HENRY
Vortex Comics: Jan, 1987 - No. 16?, 1990 ($1.75/$2.00, B&W, mature)

1-16 2.50

SAVAGE HULK, THE (Also see Incredible Hulk)
Marvel Comics: Jan, 1996 ($6.95, one-shot)

1-Bisley-c; David, Lobdell, Wagner, Loeb, Gibbons, Messner-Loebs scripts; McKone, Kieth, Ramos & Sale-a. 7.00

SAVAGE RAIDS OF GERONIMO (See Geronimo #4)

SAVAGE RANGE (See Luke Short, Four Color 807)

SAVAGE RETURN OF DRACULA
Marvel Comics: 1992 ($2.00, 52 pgs.)

1-r/Tomb of Dracula #1,2 by Gene Colan 3.00

SAVAGE SHE-HULK, THE (See The Avengers, Marvel Graphic Novel #18 & The Sensational She-Hulk)
Marvel Comics Group: Feb, 1980 - No. 25, Feb, 1982

	GD	VG	FN	VF	VF/NM	NM-
1-Origin & 1st app. She-Hulk	2	4	6	8	10	12
2-5,25: 25-(52 pgs.)						6.00
6-24: 6-She-Hulk vs. Iron Man. 8-Vs. Man-Thing						5.00

NOTE: *Austin a-25i; c-23i-25i. J. Buscema a-1p; c-1, 2p. Golden c-8-11.*

SAVAGE SWORD OF CONAN (The... #41 on; ...The Barbarian #175 on)
Marvel Comics Group: Aug, 1974 - No. 235, July, 1995 ($1.00/$1.25/$2.25, B&W magazine, mature)

	GD	VG	FN	VF	VF/NM	NM-
1-Smith-r; J. Buscema/N. Adams/Krenkel-a; origin Blackmark by Gil Kane (part 1, ends #3); Blackmark's 1st app. in magazine form-r/from paperback) & Red Sonja (3rd app.)	9	18	27	65	93	120
2-Neal Adams-c; Chaykin/N. Adams-a	4	8	12	29	40	50
3-Severin/B. Smith-a; N. Adams-a	3	7	10	21	28	35
4-Neal Adams/Kane-a(r)	3	6	9	16	20	25
5-10: 5-Jeff Jones frontispiece (r)	2	4	6	12	16	20
11-20	2	4	6	10	12	15
21-30	2	4	6	8	10	12
31-50: 34-3 pg. preview of Conan newspaper strip. 35-Cover similar to Savage Tales #1. 45-Red Sonja returns; begin $1.25-c	1	3	4	6	8	10
51-99: 63-Toth frontispiece. 65-Kane-a w/Chaykin/Miller/Simonson/Sherman finishes. 70-Article on movie. 83-Red Sonja-r by Neal Adams from #1	1	2	3	4	5	7
100	1	2	3	5	6	8
101-176: 163-Begin $2.25-c. 169-King Kull story. 171-Soloman Kane by Williamson (i). 172-Red Sonja story						6.00
177-199: 179,187,192-Red Sonja app. 190-193-4 part King Kull story. 196-King Kull story						5.00

Scarab #3 © DC

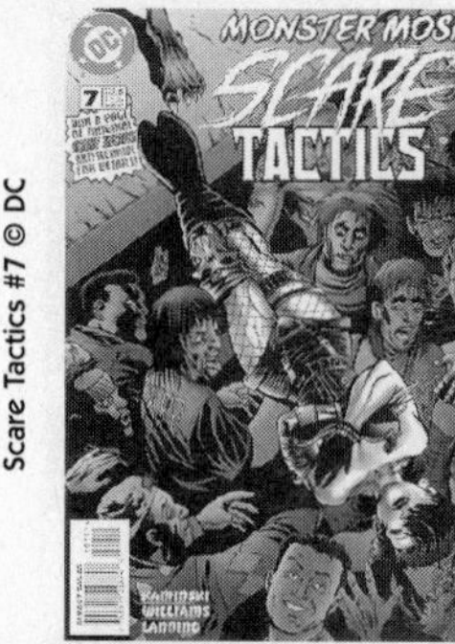

Scare Tactics #7 © DC

Scarlett #14 © DC

	GD 2.0	VG 4.0	FN 6.0	VF 8.0	VF/NM 9.0	NM- 9.2
200-220: 200-New Buscema-a; Robert E. Howard app. with Conan in story. 202-King Kull story. 204-60th anniversary (1932-92). 211-Rafael Kayanan's 1st Conan-a. 214-Sequel to Red Nails by Howard						6.00
221-230	1	2	3	5	6	8
231-234	1	3	4	6	8	10
235-Last issue	2	4	6	10	13	16
Special 1(1975, B&W)-B. Smith-r/Conan #10,13	3	6	9	16	20	25

NOTE: ***N. Adams*** *a-14p, 60, 83p(r).* ***Alcala*** *a-2 ,4, 7, 12, 15-20, 23, 24, 28, 59, 67, 69, 75, 76i, 80i, 82i, 83i, 89, 180i, 184i, 187i, 189i, 216p.* ***Austin*** *a-78i.* ***Boris*** *painted c-1, 4, 5, 7, 9, 10, 12, 15.* ***Brunner*** *a-30; c-8, 30.* ***Buscema*** *a-1-5, 7, 10-12, 15-24, 26-28, 31, 32, 36-43, 45, 47-58p, 60-67p, 70, 71-74p, 76-81p, 87-96p, 98, 99-101p, 190-204p; painted c-40.* ***Chaykin*** *c-31.* ***Chiodo*** *painted c-71, 76, 79, 81, 84, 85, 178.* ***Conrad*** *c-215, 217.* ***Corben*** *a-4, 16, 29.* ***Finlay*** *a-16.* ***Golden*** *a-98, 101; c-98, 101, 105, 106, 117, 124, 150.* ***Kaluta*** *a-11, 18; c-3, 91, 93.* ***Gil Kane*** *a-2, 3, 8, 13r, 29, 47, 64, 65, 67, 85p, 86p.* ***Rafael Kayanan*** *a-211-213, 215, 217.* ***Krenkel*** *a-9, 11, 14, 16, 24.* ***Morrow*** *a-7.* ***Nebres*** *a-93i, 101i, 107, 114.* ***Newton*** *a-6.* ***Nino*** *c/a-6.* ***Redondo*** *painted c-48-50, 52, 56, 57, 85i, 90, 96i.* ***Marie & John Severin*** *a-Special 1.* ***Simonson*** *a-7, 8, 12, 15-17.* ***Barry Smith*** *a-7, 16, 24, 82r, Special 1r.* ***Starlin*** *c-26.* ***Toth*** *a-64.* ***Williamson*** *a(i)-162, 171, 186. No. 8 , 10 & 16 contain a Robert E. Howard Conan adaptation.*

SAVAGE TALES (...Featuring Conan #4 on)(Magazine)
Marvel Comics Group: May, 1971; No. 2, 10/73; No. 3, 2/74 - No. 12, Summer, 1975 (B&W)

	GD 2.0	VG 4.0	FN 6.0	VF 8.0	VF/NM 9.0	NM- 9.2
1-Origin/1st app. The Man-Thing by Morrow; Conan the Barbarian by Barry Smith (1st Conan x-over outside his own title); Femizons by Romita-r/in #3; Ka-Zar story by Buscema	15	30	45	109	167	225
2-B. Smith, Brunner, Morrow, Williamson-a; Wrightson King Kull reprint/ Creatures on the Loose #10	5	10	15	33	44	55
3-B. Smith, Brunner, Steranko, Williamson-a	4	8	12	24	32	40
4,5-N. Adams-c; last Conan (Smith-r/#4) plus Kane/N. Adams-a. 5-Brak the Barbarian begins, ends #8	3	7	10	21	28	35
6-Ka-Zar begins; Williamson-r; N. Adams-c	2	4	6	14	18	22
7-N. Adams-i	2	4	6	10	13	16
8,9,11: 8-Shanna, the She-Devil app. thru #10; Williamson-r	2	4	6	9	11	14
10-Neal Adams-a(i), Williamson-r	2	4	6	10	13	16
...Featuring Ka-Zar Annual 1 (Summer, '75, B&W)(#12 on inside)-Ka-Zar origin by Gil Kane; B. Smith-r/Astonishing Tales	2	4	6	14	18	22

NOTE: ***Boris*** *c-7, 10.* ***Buscema*** *a-5r, 6p, 8p; c-2.* ***Colan*** *a-1p.* ***Fabian*** *c-8.* ***Golden*** *a-1, 4; c-1.* ***Heath*** *a-10p, 11p.* ***Kaluta*** *c-9.* ***Maneely*** *r-2, 4(The Crusader in both).* ***Morrow*** *a-1, 2, Annual 1.* ***Reese*** *a-2.* ***Severin*** *a-1-7.* ***Starlin*** *a-5. Robert E. Howard adaptations-1-4.*

SAVAGE TALES
Marvel Comics Group: Nov, 1985 - No. 8, Dec, 1986 ($1.50, B&W, magazine, mature)

	GD 2.0	VG 4.0	FN 6.0	VF 8.0	VF/NM 9.0	NM- 9.2
1-1st app. The Nam; Golden, Morrow-a						5.00
2-8: 2,7-Morrow-a. 4-2nd Nam story; Golden-a						3.00

SAVANT GARDE (Also see WildC.A.T.S...)
Image Comics/WildStorm Productions: Mar, 1997 - No. 7, Sept, 1997 ($2.50)

	GD 2.0	VG 4.0	FN 6.0	VF 8.0	VF/NM 9.0	NM- 9.2
1-7						2.50

SAVED BY THE BELL (TV)
Harvey Comics: Mar, 1992 - No. 5, May, 1993 ($1.25, limited series)

	GD 2.0	VG 4.0	FN 6.0	VF 8.0	VF/NM 9.0	NM- 9.2
1-5, Holiday Special (3/92), Special 1 (9/92, $1.50)-photo-c, Summer Break 1 (10/92)						2.25

SCAMP (Walt Disney)(See Walt Disney's Comics & Stories #204)
Dell Publ. Co./Gold Key: No. 703, 5/56 - No. 1204, 8-10/61; 11/67 - No. 45, 1/79

	GD 2.0	VG 4.0	FN 6.0	VF 8.0	VF/NM 9.0	NM- 9.2
Four Color 703(#1)	10	20	30	72	104	135
Four Color 777,806('57),833	8	16	24	53	74	95
5(3-5/58)-10(6-8/59)	6	12	18	43	59	75
11-16(12-2/60-61), Four Color 1204(1961)	5	10	15	36	48	60
1(12/67-Gold Key)-Reprints begin	5	10	15	33	44	55
2(3/69)-10	2	4	6	14	18	22
11-20	2	4	6	9	11	14
21-45	1	2	3	4	5	7

NOTE: *New stories-#20(in part), 22-25, 27, 29-31, 34, 36-40, 42-45. New covers-#11, 12, 14, 15, 17-25, 27, 29-31, 34, 36-38.*

SCANDALOUS
Oni Press: Aug, 2004 ($9.95, B&W, 5 1/2" x 8", graphic novel)

	GD 2.0	VG 4.0	FN 6.0	VF 8.0	VF/NM 9.0	NM- 9.2
nn-J. Torres-s/Scott Chantler-a; 1950s Hollywood tale						10.00

SCARAB
DC Comics (Vertigo): Nov, 1993 - No. 8, June, 1994 ($1.95, limited series)

	GD 2.0	VG 4.0	FN 6.0	VF 8.0	VF/NM 9.0	NM- 9.2
1-8-Glenn Fabry painted-c: 1-Silver ink-c. 2-Phantom Stranger app.						2.25

SCAR FACE (See The Crusaders)

SCARECROW OF ROMNEY MARSH, THE (See W. Disney Showcase #53)
Gold Key: April, 1964 - No. 3, Oct, 1965 (Disney TV Show)

	GD 2.0	VG 4.0	FN 6.0	VF 8.0	VF/NM 9.0	NM- 9.2
10112-404 (#1)	4	8	12	29	40	50
2,3	3	7	10	21	28	35

SCARECROW (VILLAINS) (See Batman)

DC Comics: Feb, 1998 ($1.95, one-shot)

	GD 2.0	VG 4.0	FN 6.0	VF 8.0	VF/NM 9.0	NM- 9.2
1-Fegredo-a/Milligan-s/Pearson-c						2.50

SCARE TACTICS
DC Comics: Dec, 1996 - No. 12, Mar, 1998 ($2.25)

	GD 2.0	VG 4.0	FN 6.0	VF 8.0	VF/NM 9.0	NM- 9.2
1-12: 1-1st app.						2.25

SCARLET O'NEIL (See Harvey Comics Hits #59 & Invisible...)

SCARLET CRUSH
Awesome Entertainment: Jan, 1998 - No. 2, Feb, 1998 ($2.50)

	GD 2.0	VG 4.0	FN 6.0	VF 8.0	VF/NM 9.0	NM- 9.2
1-Five covers by Liefeld, Stinsman(wraparound), Churchill, Skroce, and Sprouse; Stinsman-s/a(p)						2.50
1-American Entertainment Ed.; Stinsman-c						5.00
2-Three covers by Stinsman, McGuinness & Peterson						2.50

SCARLET SPIDER
Marvel Comics: Nov, 1995 - No. 2, Jan, 1996 ($1.95, limited series)

	GD 2.0	VG 4.0	FN 6.0	VF 8.0	VF/NM 9.0	NM- 9.2
1,2: Replaces Spider-Man						2.25

SCARLET SPIDER UNLIMITED
Marvel Comics: Nov, 1995 ($3.95, one-shot)

	GD 2.0	VG 4.0	FN 6.0	VF 8.0	VF/NM 9.0	NM- 9.2
1-Replaces Spider-Man Unlimited						4.00

SCARLETT
DC Comics: Jan, 1993 - No. 14, Feb, 1994 (1.75)

	GD 2.0	VG 4.0	FN 6.0	VF 8.0	VF/NM 9.0	NM- 9.2
1-($2.95)						3.00
2-14						2.25

SCARLET TRACES
Dark Horse Comics: Aug, 2003 ($14.95, hardcover, one-shot)

	GD 2.0	VG 4.0	FN 6.0	VF 8.0	VF/NM 9.0	NM- 9.2
nn-Edginton-s/D'Israeli-a						15.00

SCARLET WITCH (See Avengers #16, Vision &... & X-Men #4)
Marvel Comics: Jan, 1994 - No. 4, Apr, 1994 ($1.75, limited series)

	GD 2.0	VG 4.0	FN 6.0	VF 8.0	VF/NM 9.0	NM- 9.2
1-4						2.25

SCARY GODMOTHER (Hardcover story books)
Sirius: 1997 - Present ($19.95, HC with dust jackets, one-shots)

	GD 2.0	VG 4.0	FN 6.0	VF 8.0	VF/NM 9.0	NM- 9.2
Volume 1 (9/97) Jill Thompson-s/a; first app. of Scary Godmother						20.00
Vol. 2 - The Revenge of Jimmy (9/98, $19.95)						20.00
Vol. 3 - The Mystery Date (10/99, $19.95)						20.00
Vol. 4 - The Boo Flu (9/02, $19.95)						20.00

SCARY GODMOTHER
Sirius: 2001 - No. 6, 2002 ($2.95, B&W, limited series)

	GD 2.0	VG 4.0	FN 6.0	VF 8.0	VF/NM 9.0	NM- 9.2
1-6-Jill Thompson-s/a						3.00
...: Activity Book (12/00, $2.95, B&W) Jill Thompson-s/a						3.00
...: Bloody Valentine Special (2/98, $3.95, B&W) Jill Thompson-s/a; pin-ups by Ross, Mignola, Russell						4.00
...: Ghoul's Out For Summer (2002,$14.95, B&W) r/#1-6						15.00
...: Holiday Spooktakular (11/98, $2.95, B&W) Jill Thompson-s/a; pin-ups by Brereton, LaBan, Dorkin, Fingerman						3.00

SCARY GODMOTHER: WILD ABOUT HARRY
Sirius: 2000 - No. 3 ($2.95, B&W, limited series)

	GD 2.0	VG 4.0	FN 6.0	VF 8.0	VF/NM 9.0	NM- 9.2
1-3-Jill Thompson-s/a						3.00
TPB (2001, $9.95) r/series						10.00

SCARY TALES
Charlton Comics: 8/75 - #9, 1/77; #10, 9/77 - #20, 6/79; #21, 8/80 - #46, 10/84

	GD 2.0	VG 4.0	FN 6.0	VF 8.0	VF/NM 9.0	NM- 9.2
1-Origin/1st app. Countess Von Bludd, not in #2	3	6	9	18	24	30
2,4,6,9,10: 4-Sutton-c. 9-Sutton-c/a	2	4	6	8	10	12
3-Sutton painted-c; Ditko-a	2	4	6	10	13	16
5,11-Ditko-c/a.	2	4	6	11	14	18
7,8-Ditko-a	2	4	6	9	11	14
12,15,16,19,21,39-Ditko-a	2	4	6	8	10	12
13,17,20	1	2	3	5	7	9
14,18,30,32-Ditko-c/a	2	4	6	10	12	15
22-29,33-37,39,40: 37,38,40-New-a. 39-Reprints	1	2	3	5	6	8
31,38: 31-Newton-c/a. 38-Mr. Jigsaw app.	1	2	3	5	6	8
41-45-New-a. 41-Ditko-a(3). 42-45-(Low print)	1	2	3	5	7	9
46-Reprints (Low print)	2	4	6	9	11	14
1(Modern Comics reprint, 1977)						4.00

NOTE: ***Adkins*** *a-31i; c-31i.* ***Ditko*** *a-3, 5, 7, 8(2), 11, 12, 14-16r, 18(3)r, 19r, 21r, 30r, 32, 39r, 41(3); c-5, 11, 14, 18, 30, 32.* ***Newton*** *a-31p; c-31p.* ***Powell*** *a-18r.* ***Staton*** *a-1(2 pgs.), 4, 20r; c-1, 20.* ***Sutton*** *a-9; c-4, 9.*

SCATTERBRAIN
Dark Horse Comics: Jun, 1998 - No. 4, Sept, 1998 ($2.95, limited series)

Science Comics #6 © FOX

Scion #25 © CRO

Scooter Girl #1 © Chynna Clugston-Major

	GD 2.0	VG 4.0	FN 6.0	VF 8.0	VF/NM 9.0	NM- 9.2
1-4-Humor anthology by Aragonés, Dorkin, Stevens and others						3.00

SCAVENGERS
Quality Comics: Feb, 1988 - No. 14, 1989 ($1.25/$1.50)

	GD	VG	FN	VF	VF/NM	NM-
1-14: 9-13-Guice-c						2.25

SCAVENGERS
Triumphant Comics: 1993(nd, July) - No. 11, May, 1994 ($2.50, serially numbered)

	GD	VG	FN	VF	VF/NM	NM-
1-9,0,10,11: 5,6-Triumphant Unleashed x-over. 9-(3/94). 0-Retail edition (3/94, $2.50, 36 pgs.). 0-Giveaway edition (3/94, 20 pgs.). 0-Coupon redemption edition. 10-(4/94)						2.50

SCENE OF THE CRIME (Also see Vertigo: Winter's Edge #2)
DC Comics (Vertigo): May, 1999 - No. 4, Aug, 1999 ($2.50, limited series)

	GD	VG	FN	VF	VF/NM	NM-
1-4-Brubaker-s/Lark-a						2.50
...: A Little Piece of Goodnight TPB ('00, $12.95) r/#1-4; Winter's Edge #2						13.00

SCHOOL DAY ROMANCES (...of Teen-Agers #4; Popular Teen-Agers #5 on)
Star Publications: Nov-Dec, 1949 - No. 4, May-June, 1950 (Teenage)

	GD	VG	FN	VF	VF/NM	NM-
1-Toni Gayle (later Toni Gay), Ginger Snapp, Midge Martin & Eve Adams begin	29	58	87	164	237	310
2,3: 3-Jane Powell photo on-c & true life story	21	42	63	118	169	220
4-Ronald Reagan photo on-c; L.B. Cole-c	32	64	96	184	267	350

NOTE: *All have* ***L. B. Cole*** *covers.*

SCHWINN BICYCLE BOOK (...Bike Thrills, 1959)
Schwinn Bicycle Co.: 1949; 1952; 1959 (10¢)

	GD	VG	FN	VF	VF/NM	NM-
1949	6	12	18	28	34	40
1952-Believe It or Not facts; comic format; 36 pgs.	5	10	14	20	24	28
1959	3	6	8	11	13	15

SCIENCE COMICS (1st Series)
Fox Features Syndicate: Feb, 1940 - No. 8, Sept, 1940

	GD	VG	FN	VF	VF/NM	NM-
1-Origin Dynamo (1st app., called Electro in #1), The Eagle (1st app.), & Navy Jones; Marga, The Panther Woman (1st app.), Cosmic Carson & Perisphere Payne, Dr. Doom begin; bondage/hypo-c; Electro-c	430	860	1290	2800	4550	6300
2-Classic Lou Fine Dynamo-c	223	446	669	1394	2147	2900
3-Classic Lou Fine Dynamo-c	185	370	555	1156	1778	2400
4-Kirby-a; Cosmic Carson-c by Joe Simon	162	324	486	1013	1557	2100
5-8: 5,8-Eagle-c. 6,7-Dynamo-c	92	184	276	575	888	1200

NOTE: *Cosmic Carson by* ***Tuska***-*#1-3; by* ***Kirby***-*#4.* ***Lou Fine*** *c-1-3 only.*

SCIENCE COMICS (2nd Series)
Humor Publications (Ace Magazines?): Jan, 1946 - No. 5, 1946

	GD	VG	FN	VF	VF/NM	NM-
1-Palais-c/a in #1-3; A-Bomb-c	20	40	60	112	161	210
2	10	20	30	60	80	100
3-Feldstein-a (6 pgs.)	16	32	48	89	127	165
4,5: 4-Palais-c	9	18	27	51	62	75

SCIENCE COMICS
Ziff-Davis Publ. Co.: May, 1947 (8 pgs. in color)

	GD	VG	FN	VF	VF/NM	NM-
nn-Could be ordered by mail for 10¢; like the nn Amazing Adventures (1950) & Boy Cowboy (1950); used to test the market	40	80	120	233	342	450

SCIENCE COMICS (True Science Illustrated)
Export Publication Ent., Toronto, Canada: Mar, 1951 (Distr. in U.S. by Kable News Co.)

	GD	VG	FN	VF	VF/NM	NM-
1-Science Adventure stories plus some true science features; man on moon story	10	20	30	56	73	90

SCIENCE FICTION SPACE ADVENTURES (See Space Adventures)

SCION (Also see CrossGen Chronicles)
CrossGeneration Comics: July, 2000 - No. 44 ($2.95)

	GD	VG	FN	VF	VF/NM	NM-
1-44: 1-Marz-s/Cheung-a						3.00
...: Conflict of Conscience Vol. 1 TPB (5/01, $19.95) r/#1-7; Adam Hughes-c						20.00
...: Blood For Blood Vol. 2 TPB (2002, $19.95) r/#8-14 & CrossGen Chronicles #2						20.00
...: Divided Loyalties Vol. 3 TPB (2002, $15.95) r/#15-21						16.00
...: Sanctuary Vol. 4 TPB (2003, $15.95) r/#22-27						16.00
Vol. 5: The Far Kingdom (2003, $15.95) r/#28-33						16.00
Vol. 6: The Royal Wedding (2004, $15.95) r/#34-39						16.00
Traveler Vol. 1-3 ($9.95) Digest-sized reprints of TPBs						10.00

SCI-SPY
DC Comics (Vertigo): Apr, 2002 - No. 6, Sept, 2002 ($2.50, limited series)

	GD	VG	FN	VF	VF/NM	NM-
1-6-Moench-s/Gulacy-c/a						2.50

SCI-TECH
DC Comics (WildStorm): Sept, 1999 - No. 4, Dec, 1999 ($2.50, limited series)

	GD	VG	FN	VF	VF/NM	NM-
1-4-Benes-a/Choi & Peterson-s						2.50

SCOOBY DOO (TV)(...Where are you? #1-16,26; ...Mystery Comics #17-25, 27 on)
(See March Of Comics #356, 368, 382, 391 in the Promtional Comics section)
Gold Key: Mar, 1970 - No. 30, Feb, 1975 (Hanna-Barbera)

	GD	VG	FN	VF	VF/NM	NM-
1	14	28	42	97	149	200
2-5	8	16	24	58	82	105
6-10	7	14	21	50	68	85
11-20: 11-Tufts-a	6	12	18	38	52	65
21-30	4	8	12	28	38	48

SCOOBY DOO (TV)
Charlton Comics: Apr, 1975 - No. 11, Dec, 1976 (Hanna-Barbera)

	GD	VG	FN	VF	VF/NM	NM-
1	7	14	21	46	63	80
2-5	4	8	12	28	38	48
6-11	4	8	12	22	30	38
nn-(1976, digest, 68 pgs., B&W)	4	8	12	27	36	45

SCOOBY-DOO (TV)(Newsstand sales only) (See Dynamutt & Laff-A-Lympics)
Marvel Comics Group: Oct, 1977 - No. 9, Feb, 1979 (Hanna-Barbera)

	GD	VG	FN	VF	VF/NM	NM-
1,6-9: 1-Dyno-Mutt begins	3	6	9	19	25	32
1-(35¢-c variant, limited distribution)(10/77)	4	8	12	28	38	48
2-5	3	6	9	16	20	24

SCOOBY-DOO (TV)
Harvey Comics: Sept, 1992 - No. 3, May, 1993 ($1.25)

	GD	VG	FN	VF	VF/NM	NM-
V2#1,2						6.00
Big Book 1,2 (11/92, 4/93, $1.95, 52 pgs.)	1	2	3	4	5	7
Giant Size 1,2 (10/92, 3/93, $2.25, 68 pgs.)	1	2	3	4	5	7

SCOOBY DOO (TV)
Archie Comics: Oct, 1995 -No. 21, June, 1997 ($1.50)

	GD	VG	FN	VF	VF/NM	NM-
1						6.00
2-21: 12-Cover by Scooby Doo creative designer Iwao Takamoto						4.00

SCOOBY DOO (TV)
DC Comics: Aug, 1997 - Present ($1.75/$1.95/$1.99/$2.25)

	GD	VG	FN	VF	VF/NM	NM-
1						6.00
2-10: 5-Begin-$1.95-c						4.00
11-45: 14-Begin $1.99-c						2.50
46-89,91: 63-Begin $2.25-c. 75-With 2 Garbage Pail Kids stickers						2.25
90-($2.95) Bonus stories						3.00
...Spooky Spectacular 1 (10/99, $3.95) Comic Convention story						4.00
...Spooky Spectacular 2000 (10/00, $3.95)						4.00
...Spooky Summer Special 2001 (8/01, $3.95) Staton-a						4.00
...Super Scarefest (8/02, $3.95) r/#20,25,30-32						4.00
Vol. 1: You Meddling Kids (2003, $6.95, digest-size) r/#1-5						7.00
Vol. 2: Ruh-Roh! (2003, $6.95, digest-size) r/#6-10						7.00

SCOOP COMICS (Becomes Yankee Comics #4-7, a digest sized cartoon book not listed in this guide; becomes Snap #9)
Harry 'A' Chesler (Holyoke): November, 1941 - No. 3, Mar, 1943; No. 8, 1944

	GD	VG	FN	VF	VF/NM	NM-
1-Intro. Rocketman & Rocketgirl & begins; origin The Master Key & begins; Dan Hastings begins; Charles Sultan-c/a	131	262	393	819	1260	1700
2-Rocket Boy begins; injury to eye story (reprinted in Spotlight #3); classic-c	142	284	426	888	1369	1850
3-Injury to eye story-r from #2; Rocket Boy	67	134	201	419	647	875
8-Formerly Yankee Comics; becomes Snap	44	88	132	268	409	550

SCOOTER (See Swing With...)

SCOOTER COMICS
Rucker Publ. Ltd. (Canadian): Apr, 1946

	GD	VG	FN	VF	VF/NM	NM-
1-Teen-age/funny animal	11	22	33	63	84	105

SCOOTER GIRL
Oni Press: May, 2003 - No. 6, Feb, 2004 ($2.99, B&W, limited series)

	GD	VG	FN	VF	VF/NM	NM-
1-6-Chynna Clugston-Major-s/a						3.00
TPB (5/04, $14.95, digest size) r/series; sketch pages						15.00

SCORCHED EARTH
Tundra Publishing: Apr, 1991 - No. 6, 1991 ($2.95, stiff-c)

	GD	VG	FN	VF	VF/NM	NM-
1-6						3.00

SCORE, THE
DC Comics (Piranha Press): 1989 - No. 4, 1990 ($4.95, 52 pgs, squarebound, mature)

	GD	VG	FN	VF	VF/NM	NM-
Books One - Four						5.00

SCORPION
Atlas/Seaboard Publ.: Feb, 1975 - No. 3, July, 1975

	GD	VG	FN	VF	VF/NM	NM-
1-Intro.; bondage-c by Chaykin	2	4	6	8	10	12

The Scorpion King #2 © Universal Studios

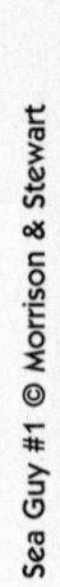
Sea Guy #1 © Morrison & Stewart

Sea Hound #7 © AVON

GD 2.0 | VG 4.0 | FN 6.0 | VF 8.0 | VF/NM 9.0 | NM- 9.2

2-Chaykin-a w/Wrightson, Kaluta, Simonson assists(p) 2 4 6 8 10 12
3-Jim Craig-c/a 1 2 3 5 7 9
NOTE: ***Chaykin** a-1, 2; c-1. **Colon** c-2. **Craig** c/a-3.*

SCORPION KING, THE (Movie)
Dark Horse Comics: March, 2002 - No. 2, Apr, 2002 ($2.99, limited series)
1,2-Photo-c of the Rock; Richards-a 3.00

SCORPIO ROSE
Eclipse Comics: Jan, 1983 - No. 2, Oct, 1983 ($1.25, Baxter paper)
1,2: Dr. Orient back-up story begins. 2-origin. 4.00

SCOTLAND YARD (Inspector Farnsworth of)(Texas Rangers in Action #5 on?)
Charlton Comics Group: June, 1955 - No. 4, Mar, 1956
1-Tothish-a 15 30 45 83 117 150
2-4: 2-Tothish-a 10 20 30 56 73 90

SCOUT (See Eclipse Graphic Album #16, New America & Swords of Texas) (Becomes Scout: War Shaman)
Eclipse Comics: Dec, 1985 - No. 24, Oct, 1987($1.75/$1.25, Baxter paper)
1-15,17,18,20-24: 19-Airboy preview. 10-Bissette-a. 11-Monday, the Eliminator begins. 15-Swords of Texas 2.50
16,19: 16-Scout 3-D Special ($2.50), 16-Scout 2-D Limited Edition, 19-contains flexidisk ($2.50) 3.00
...Handbook 1 (8/87, $1.75, B&W) 2.25
Mount Fire (1989, $14.95, TPB) r/#8-14 15.00

SCOUT: WAR SHAMAN (Formerly Scout)
Eclipse Comics: Mar, 1988 - No. 16, Dec, 1989 ($1.95)
1-16 2.25

SCRATCH
DC Comics: Aug, 2004 - No. 5, Dec, 2004 ($2.50, limited series)
1-5-Sam Kieth-s/a/c; Batman app. 2.50

SCREAM (...Comics) (Andy Comics #20 on)
Humor Publications/Current Books(Ace Magazines): Autumn, 1944 - No. 19, Apr, 1948
1-Teenage humor 17 34 51 95 135 175
2 10 20 30 56 73 90
3-16: 11-Racist humor (Indians). 16-Intro. Lily-Belle 8 16 24 46 58 70
17,19 8 16 24 40 50 60
18-Hypo needle story 8 16 24 46 58 70

SCREAM (Magazine)
Skywald Publ. Corp.: Aug, 1973 - No. 11, Feb, 1975 (68 pgs., B&W) (Painted-c on all)
1-Nosferatu-c/1st app. (series thru #11); Morrow-a. Cthulhu/Necronomicon-s 5 10 15 36 48 60
2,3: 2-(10/73) Lady Satan 1st app. & series begins; Edgar Allan Poe adaptations begin (thru #11); Phantom of the Opera-s. 3-(12/73) Origin Lady Satan 4 8 12 25 33 42
4-1st Cannibal Werewolf and 1st Lunatic Mummy 3 7 10 21 28 35
5,7,8: 5,7-Frankenstein app. 8-Buckler-a; Werewolf-s; Slither-Slime Man-s 3 7 10 21 28 35
6, 9,10: 6-(6/74) Saga of The Victims/ I Am Horror, classic GGA Hewetson series begins (thru #11); Frankenstein 2073-s. 9-Severed head-c; Marcos-a. 9,10-Werewolf-s. 10-Dracula-c/s 4 8 12 24 32 40
11- (1975 Winter Special) "Mr. Poe and the Raven" story 4 8 12 27 36 45
NOTE: ***Buckler** a-8. **Hewetson** s-1-11. **Marcos** a-9. **Miralles** c-2. **Morrow** a-1. **Poe** s-2-11. **Segrelles** a-7; c-1.*

SCREWBALL SQUIRREL
Dark Horse Comics: July, 1995 - No. 3, Sept, 1995 ($2.50, limited series)
1-3: Characters created by Tex Avery 2.50

SCRIBBLY (See All-American Comics, Buzzy, The Funnies, Leave It To Binky & Popular Comics)
National Periodical Publ.: 8-9/48 - No. 13, 8-9/50; No. 14, 10-11/51 - No. 15, 12-1/51-52
1-Sheldon Mayer-c/a in all; 52 pgs. begin 96 192 288 600 925 1250
2 61 122 186 388 594 800
3-5 50 100 150 305 465 625
6-10 40 80 120 230 335 440
11-15: 13-Last 52 pgs. 35 70 105 198 287 375

SCUD: TALES FROM THE VENDING MACHINE
Fireman Press: 1998 - No. 5 ($2.50, B&W)
1-5: 1-Kaniuga-a. 2-Ruben Martinez-a 2.50

SCUD: THE DISPOSABLE ASSASSIN
Fireman Press: Feb, 1994 - No. 19, 1997 ($2.95, B&W)
1 6.00
1-2nd printing in color 2.25
2,3 4.00
4-9 3.00
10-19 2.25
Heavy 3PO ($12.95, TPB) r/#1-4 13.00
Programmed For Damage ($14.95, TPB) r/#5-9 15.00
Solid Gold Bomb ($17.95, TPB) r/#10-15 18.00

SEA DEVILS (See Limited Collectors' Edition #39,45, & Showcase #27-29)
National Periodical Publications: Sept-Oct, 1961 - No. 35, May-June, 1967
1-(9-10/61) 54 108 162 432 679 925
2-Last 10¢ issue 30 60 90 218 334 450
3-Begin 12¢ issues thru #35 19 38 57 136 208 280
4,5 17 34 51 121 186 250
6-10 11 22 33 80 120 160
11,12,14-20 9 18 27 60 85 110
13-Kubert, Colan-a; Joe Kubert app. in story 9 18 27 63 89 115
21-35: 22-Intro. International Sea Devils; origin & 1st app. Capt. X & Man Fish 6 12 18 43 59 75
NOTE: ***Heath** a-Showcase 27-29, 1-10; c-Showcase 27-29, 1-10, 14-16. **Moldoff** a-16i.*

SEA DEVILS (See Tangent Comics/ Sea Devils)

SEADRAGON (Also see the Epsilion Wave)
Elite Comics: May, 1986 - No. 8, 1987 ($1.75)
1-8: 1-1st & 2nd printings exist 2.25

SEAGUY
DC Comics (Vertigo): July, 2004 - No. 3, Sept, 2004 ($2.95, limited series)
1-3-Grant Morrison-s/Cameron Stewart-a/c 3.00

SEA HOUND, THE (Captain Silver's Log Of The...)
Avon Periodicals: 1945 (no month) - No. 2, Sept-Oct, 1945
nn (#1)-29 pg. novel length sty-"The Esmeralda's Treasure" 19 38 57 107 154 200
2 13 26 39 74 102 130

SEA HOUND, THE (Radio)
Capt. Silver Syndicate: No. 3, July, 1949 - No. 4, Sept, 1949
3,4 10 20 30 58 74 90

SEA HUNT (TV)
Dell Publishing Co.: No. 928, 8/58 - No. 1041, 10-12/59; No. 4, 1-3/60 - No. 13, 4-6/62 (All have Lloyd Bridges photo-c)
Four Color 928(#1) 13 26 39 92 141 190
Four Color 994(#2), 4-13: Manning-a #4-6,8-11,13 9 18 27 65 93 120
Four Color 1041(#3)-Toth-a 10 20 30 67 96 125

SEAQUEST (TV)
Nemesis Comics: Mar, 1994 ($2.25)
1-Has 2 diff-c stocks (slick & cardboard); Alcala-i 2.25

SEARCH FOR LOVE
American Comics Group: Feb-Mar, 1950 - No. 2, Apr-May, 1950 (52 pgs.)
1 12 24 36 69 95 120
2 9 18 27 51 63 75

SEARCHERS, THE (Movie)
Dell Publishing Co.: No. 709, 1956
Four Color 709-John Wayne photo-c 28 56 84 199 305 410

SEARCHERS, THE
Caliber Comics: 1996 - No. 4, 1996 ($2.95, B&W)
1-4 3.00

SEARCHERS, THE : APOSTLE OF MERCY
Caliber Comics: 1997 - No. 2, 1997 ($2.95/$3.95, B&W)
1-($2.95) 3.00
2-($3.95) 4.00

SEARS (See Merry Christmas From...)

SEASON'S GREETINGS
Hallmark (King Features): 1935 (6-1/4x5-1/4", 32 pgs. in color)
nn-Cover features Mickey Mouse, Popeye, Jiggs & Skippy. "The Night Before Christmas" told one panel per page, each panel by a famous artist featuring their character. Art by Alex Raymond, Gottfredson, Swinnerton, Segar, Chic Young, Milt Gross, Sullivan (Messmer), Herriman, McManus, Percy Crosby & others (22 artists in all)
Estimated value... 950.00

Second Life of Doctor Mirage #1 © VAL

Secret Missions #1 © STJ

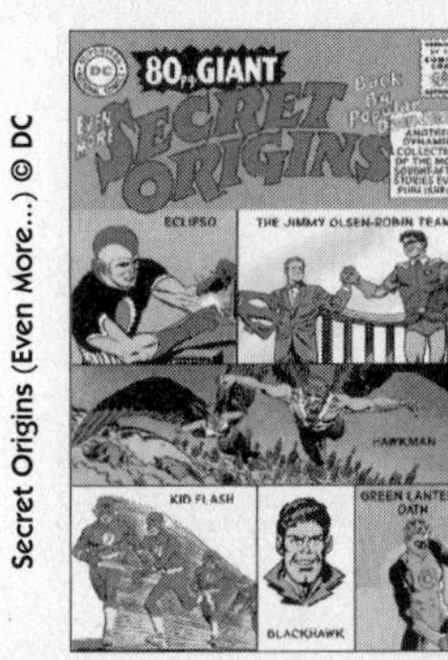

Secret Origins (Even More...) © DC

GD VG FN VF VF/NM NM-
2.0 4.0 6.0 8.0 9.0 9.2

SEBASTIAN O
DC Comics (Vertigo): May, 1993 - No. 3, July, 1993 ($1.95, limited series)

1-3-Grant Morrison scripts; Steve Yeowell-a 2.25
TPB (2004, $9.95) r/#1-3; intro. chronology by Morrison 10.00

SECOND LIFE OF DOCTOR MIRAGE, THE (See Shadowman #16)
Valiant: Nov, 1993 - No. 18, May, 1995 ($2.50)

1-18: 1-With bound-in poster. 5-Shadowman x-over. 7-Bound-in trading card 2.50
1-Gold ink logo edition; no price on-c 3.00

SECRET AGENT (Formerly Sarge Steel)
Charlton Comics: V2#9, Oct, 1966; V2#10, Oct, 1967

V2#9-Sarge Steel part-r begins 3 6 9 19 25 32
10-Tiffany Sinn, CIA app. (from Career Girl Romances #39); Aparo-a
3 6 9 16 20 24

SECRET AGENT (TV) (See Four Color #1231)
Gold Key: Nov, 1966; No. 2, Jan, 1968

1-Photo-c 12 24 36 87 134 180
2-Photo-c 9 18 27 60 85 110

SECRET AGENT X-9 (See Flash Gordon #4 by King)
David McKay Publ.: 1934 (Book 1: 84 pgs.; Book 2: 124 pgs.) (8x7-1/2")

Book 1-Contains reprints of the first 13 weeks of the strip by Alex Raymond; complete except for 2 dailies 44 88 132 268 409 550
Book 2-Contains reprints immediately following contents of Book 1, for 20 weeks by Alex Raymond; complete except for two dailies. Note: Raymond mis-dated the last five strips from 6/34, and while the dating sequence is confusing, the continuity is correct
40 80 120 233 342 450

SECRET AGENT X-9 (See Magic Comics)
Dell Publishing Co.: Dec, 1937 (Not by Raymond)

Feature Books 8 47 94 141 287 436 585

SECRET AGENT Z-2 (See Holyoke One-Shot No. 7)

SECRET CITY SAGA (See Jack Kirby's Secret City Saga)

SECRET DEFENDERS (Also see The Defenders & Fantastic Four #374)
Marvel Comics: Mar, 1993 - No. 25, Mar, 1995 ($1.75/$1.95)

1-($2.50)-Red foil stamped-c; Dr. Strange, Nomad, Wolverine, Spider Woman & Darkhawk begin 3.00
2-11,13-24: 9-New team w/Silver Surfer, Thunderstrike, Dr. Strange & War Machine. 13-Thanos replaces Dr. Strange as leader; leads into Cosmic Powers limited series; 14-Dr. Druid. 15-Bound in card sheet. 18-Giant Man & Iron Fist app. 2.25
12,25: 12-($2.50)-Prismatic foil-c. 25 ($2.50, 52 pgs.) 2.50

SECRET DIARY OF EERIE ADVENTURES
Avon Periodicals: 1953 (25¢ giant, 100 pgs., one-shot)

nn-(Rare)-Kubert-a; Hollingsworth-c; Sid Check back-c
177 354 531 1106 1703 2300

SECRET FILES & ORIGINS GUIDE TO THE DC UNIVERSE
DC Comics: Mar, 2000; Feb, 2002 ($6.95/$4.95)

2000 (3/00, $6.95)-Overview of DC characters; profile pages by various 7.00
2001-2002 (2/02, $4.95) Olivetti-c 5.00

SECRET FILES PRESIDENT LUTHOR
DC Comics: Mar, 2001 ($4.95, one-shot)

1-Short stories & profile pages by various; Harris-c 5.00

SECRET HEARTS
National Periodical Publications (Beverly)(Arleigh No. 50-113):
9-10/49 - No. 6, 7-8/50; No. 7, 12-1/51-52 - No. 153, 7/71

1-Kinstler-a; photo-c begin, end #6 55 110 165 340 520 700
2-Toth-a (1 pg.); Kinstler-a 30 60 90 170 245 320
3,6 (1950) 26 52 78 147 211 275
4,5-Toth-a 27 54 81 152 219 285
7(12-1/51-52) (Rare) 40 80 120 236 351 465
8-10 (1952) 19 38 57 107 154 200
11-20 15 30 45 86 123 160
21-26: 26-Last precode (2-3/55) 13 26 39 76 106 135
27-40 8 16 24 55 78 100
41-50 6 12 18 40 55 70
51-60 5 10 15 36 48 60
61-75,100: 75-Last 10¢ issue 5 10 15 33 44 55
76-99,101-109 4 8 12 25 33 42
110- "Reach for Happiness" serial begins, ends #138 4 8 12 27 36 45
111-119,121-126 3 6 9 18 24 30
120,134-Neal Adams-c 4 8 12 28 38 48
127 (4/68)-Beatles cameo 4 8 12 28 38 48
128-133,135-142: 141,142- "20 Miles to Heartbreak", Chapter 2 & 3 (see Young Love for Chapters 1 & 4); Toth, Colletta-a 3 6 9 18 23 28
143-148,150-152: 144-Morrow-a 2 4 6 14 18 22
149,153: 149-Toth-a. 153-Kirby-i 3 6 9 16 20 24

SECRET ISLAND OF OZ, THE (See First Comics Graphic Novel)

SECRET LOVE (See Fox Giants & Sinister House of...)

SECRET LOVE
Ajax-Farrell/Four Star Comic Corp. No. 2 on: 12/55 - No. 3, 8/56; 4/57 - No. 5, 2/58; No. 6, 6/58

1(12/55-Ajax, 1st series) 10 20 30 56 73 90
2,3 7 14 21 35 43 50
1(4/57-Ajax, 2nd series) 8 16 24 46 58 70
2-6: 5-Bakerish-a 6 12 18 31 38 45

SECRET LOVES
Comic Magazines/Quality Comics Group: Nov, 1949 - No. 6, Sept, 1950

1-Ward-c 25 50 75 141 203 265
2-Ward-c 21 42 63 121 173 225
3-Crandall-a 14 28 42 81 113 145
4,6 11 22 33 62 84 105
5-Suggestive art "Boom Town Babe"; photo-c 14 28 42 81 113 145

SECRET LOVE STORIES (See Fox Giants)

SECRET MISSIONS (Admiral Zacharia's...)
St. John Publishing Co.: February, 1950

1-Joe Kubert-c; stories of U.S. foreign agents 21 42 63 118 169 220

SECRET MYSTERIES (Formerly Crime Mysteries & Crime Smashers)
Ribage/Merit Publications No. 17 on: No. 16, Nov, 1954 - No. 19, July, 1955

16-Horror, Palais-a; Myron Fass-c 28 56 84 158 229 300
17-19-Horror. 17-Fass-c; mis-dated 3/54? 19 38 57 107 154 200

SECRET ORIGINS (1st Series) (See 80 Page Giant #8)
National Periodical Publications: Aug-Oct, 1961 (Annual) (Reprints)

1-Origin Adam Strange (Showcase #17), Green Lantern (Green Lantern #1), Challengers (partial-r/Showcase #6, 6 pgs. Kirby-a), J'onn J'onzz (Det. #225), The Flash (Showcase #4), Green Arrow (1 pg. text), Superman-Batman team (World's Finest #94), Wonder Woman (Wonder Woman #105) 49 98 147 392 609 825
Replica Edition (1998, $4.95) r/entire book and house ads 5.00
Even More Secret Origins (2003, $6.95) reprints origins of Hawkman, Eclipso, Kid Flash, Blackhawks, Green Lantern's oath, and Jimmy Olsen-Robin team in 80 pg. Giant style 7.00

SECRET ORIGINS (2nd Series)
National Periodical Publications: Feb-Mar, 1973 - No. 6, Jan-Feb, 1974; No. 7, Oct-Nov, 1974 (All 20¢ issues) (All origin reprints)

1-Superman(r/1 pg. origin/Action #1, 1st time since G.A.), Batman(Detective #33), Ghost(Flash #88), The Flash(Showcase #4) 5 10 15 33 44 55
2-7: 2-Green Lantern & The Atom(Showcase #22 & 34), Supergirl(Action #252). 3-Wonder Woman(W.W. #1), Wildcat(Sensation #1). 4-Vigilante (Action #42) by Meskin, Kid Eternity(Hit #25). 5-The Spectre by Baily (More Fun #52,53). 6-Blackhawk(Military #1) & Legion of Super-Heroes(Superboy #147). 7-Robin (Detective #38), Aquaman (More Fun #73) 3 6 9 18 24 30
NOTE: ***Infantino*** *a-1.* ***Kane*** *a-2.* ***Kubert*** *a-1.*

SECRET ORIGINS (3rd Series)
DC Comics: 4/86 - No. 50, 8/90 (All origins)(52 pgs. #6 on)(#27 on: $1.50)

1-Origin Superman 6.00
2-6: 2-Blue Beetle. 3-Shazam. 4-Firestorm. 5-Crimson Avenger. 6-Halo/G.A. Batman 3.00
7-9,11,12,14-20,22-26: 7-Green Lantern(Guy Gardner)/G.A. Sandman. 8-Shadow Lass/Doll Man. 9-G.A. Flash/Skyman.11-G.A. Hawkman/Power Girl. 12-Challengers of Unknown/G.A. Fury (2nd modern app.). 14-Suicide Squad; Legends spin-off. 15-Spectre/Deadman. 16-G.A. Hourman/Warlord. 17-Adam Strange story by Carmine infantino; Dr. Occult. 18-G.A. Gr. Lantern/The Creeper. 19-Uncle Sam/The Guardian. 20-Batgirl/G.A. Dr. Mid-Nite. 22-Manhunters. 23-Floronic Man/Guardians of the Universe. 24-Blue Devil/Dr. Fate. 25-LSH/Atom. 26-Black Lightning/Miss America 2.50
10-Phantom Stranger w/Alan Moore scripts; Legends spin-off 2.50
13-Origin Nightwing; Johnny Thunder app. 2.50
21-Jonah Hex/Black Condor 2.50
27-30,36-38,40-49: 27-Zatara/Zatanna. 28-Midnight/Nightshade. 29-Power of the Atom/Mr. America; new 3 pg. Red Tornado story by Mayer (last app. of Scribbly, 8/88). 30-Plastic Man/Elongated Man. 36-Poison Ivy by Neil Gaiman & Mark Buckingham/Green Lantern. 37-Legion Of Substitute Heroes/Doctor Light. 38-Green Arrow/Speedy; Grell scripts. 40-All Ape issue. 41-Rogues Gallery of Flash. 42-Phantom Girl/GrimGhost. 43-Original Hawk &

Secret Six #1 © DC

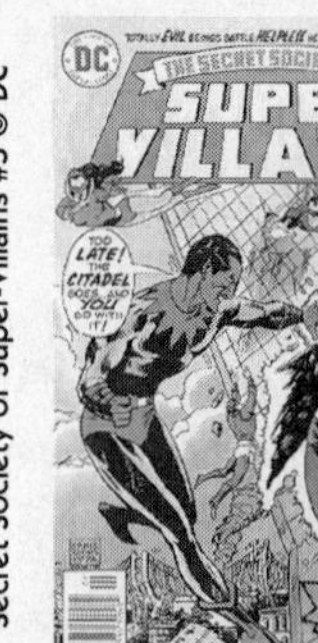

Secret Society of Super-Villains #5 © DC

Secret War #1 © MAR

	GD 2.0	VG 4.0	FN 6.0	VF 8.0	VF/NM 9.0	NM- 9.2
Dove/Cave Carson/Chris KL-99. 44-Batman app.; story based on Det. #40. 45-Blackhawk/El Diablo. 46-JLA/LSH/New Titans. 47-LSH. 48-Ambush Bug/Stanley & His Monster/Rex the Wonder Dog/Trigger Twins. 49-Newsboy Legion/Silent Knight/Bouncing Boy						2.50
31-35,39: 31-JSA. 32-JLA. 33-35-JLI. 39-Animal Man-c/story continued in Animal Man #10; Grant Morrison scripts; Batman app.						3.00
50-($3.95, 100 pgs.)-Batman & Robin in text, Flash of Two Worlds, Johnny Thunder, Dolphin, Black Canary & Space Museum						5.00
Annual 1 (8/87)-Capt. Comet/Doom Patrol						3.00
Annual 2 ('88, $2.00)-Origin Flash II & Flash III						3.00
Annual 3 ('89, $2.95, 84 pgs.)-Teen Titans; 1st app. new Flamebird who replaces original Bat-Girl						3.00
Special 1 (10/89, $2.00)-Batman villains: Penguin, Riddler, & Two-Face; Bolland-c; Sam Kieth-a; Neil Gaiman scripts(2)						3.00

NOTE: ***Art Adams** a-33i(part). **M. Anderson** 8, 19, 21, 25i; c-19(part). **Aparo** c/a-10. **Bissette** c-23. **Bolland** c-7. **Byrne** c/a-Annual 1. **Colan** c/a-5p. **Forte** a-37. **Giffen** a-18p, 44p, 48. **Infantino** a-17, 50p. **Kaluta** c-39. **Gil Kane** a-2, 28; c-2p. **Kirby** c-19(part). **Erik Larsen** a-13. **Mayer** a-29. **Morrow** a-21. **Orlando** a-10. **Perez** a-50i, Annual 3i; c- Annual 3. **Rogers** a-6p. **Russell** a-27i. **Simonson** c-22. **Staton** a-36, 50p. **Steacy** a-35. **Tuska** a-4p, 9p.*

SECRET ORIGINS 80 PAGE GIANT (Young Justice)
DC Comics: Dec, 1998 ($4.95, one-shot)

1-Origin-s of Young Justice members; Ramos-a (Impulse)						5.00

SECRET ORIGINS FEATURING THE JLA
DC Comics: 1999 ($14.95, TPB)

1-Reprints recent origin-s of JLA members; Cassaday-c						15.00

SECRET ORIGINS OF SUPER-HEROES (See DC Special Series #10, 19)

SECRET ORIGINS OF SUPER-VILLAINS 80 PAGE GIANT
DC Comics: Dec, 1999 ($4.95, one-shot)

1-Origin-s of Sinestro, Amazo and others; Gibbons-c						5.00

SECRET ORIGINS OF THE WORLD'S GREATEST SUPER-HEROES
DC Comics: 1989 ($4.95, 148 pgs.)

nn-Reprints Superman, JLA origins; new Batman origin-s; Bolland-c	1	2	3	4	5	7

SECRET ROMANCE
Charlton Comics: Oct, 1968 - No. 41, Nov, 1976; No. 42, Mar, 1979 - No. 48, Feb, 1980

1-Begin 12¢ issues, ends #?	3	6	9	18	23	28
2-10: 9-Reese-a	2	4	6	10	13	16
11-30	2	4	6	8	10	12
31-48	1	2	3	5	7	9

NOTE: *Beyond the Stars app.-No. 9, 11, 12, 14.*

SECRET ROMANCES (Exciting Love Stories)
Superior Publications Ltd.: Apr, 1951 - No. 27, July, 1955

1	15	30	45	86	118	150
2	10	20	30	60	80	100
3-10	8	16	24	46	58	70
11-13,15-18,20-27	7	14	21	37	46	55
14,19-Lingerie panels	8	16	24	40	50	60

SECRET SERVICE (See Kent Blake of the...)

SECRET SIX (See Action Comics Weekly)
National Periodical Publications: Apr-May, 1968 - No. 7, Apr-May, 1969 (12¢)

1-Origin/1st app.	7	14	21	51	71	90
2-7	4	8	12	27	36	45

SECRET SIX (See Tangent Comics/ Secret Six)

SECRET SKULL
IDW Publ.: Aug, 2004 - No. 4 ($3.99)

1-3-Steve Niles-s/Chuck BB-a						4.00

SECRET SOCIETY OF SUPER-VILLAINS
National Per. Publ./DC Comics: May-June, 1976 - No. 15, June-July, 1978

1-Origin; JLA cameo & Capt. Cold app.	2	4	6	11	14	18
2-5,15: 2-Re-intro/origin Capt. Comet; Green Lantern x-over. 5-Green Lantern, Hawkman x-over; Darkseid app. 15-G.A. Atom, Dr. Midnite, & JSA app.	1	3	4	6	8	10
6-14: 9,10-Creeper x-over. 11-Capt. Comet; Orlando-i	1	2	3	5	6	8

SECRET SOCIETY OF SUPER-VILLAINS SPECIAL (See DC Special Series #6)

SECRETS OF HAUNTED HOUSE
National Periodical Publications/DC Comics: 4-5/75 - #5, 12-1/75-76; #6, 6-7/77 - #14, 10-11/78; #15, 8/79 - #46, 3/82

1	5	10	15	33	44	55
2-4	3	6	9	16	20	24
5-Wrightson-c	3	6	9	18	24	30
6-14	2	4	6	10	13	16
15-30	1	3	4	6	8	10
31,44: 31-(12/80) Mr. E series begins (1st app.), ends #41. 44-Wrightson-c	2	4	6	8	10	12
32-(1/81) Origin of Mr. E	1	3	4	6	8	10
33-43,45,46: 34,35-Frankenstein Monster app.	1	2	3	4	5	7

NOTE: ***Aparo** c-7. **Aragones** a-1. **B. Bailey** a-8. **Bissette** a-46. **Buckler** c-32-40p. **Ditko** a-9, 12, 41, 45. **Golden** a-10. **Howard** a-13i. **Kaluta** c-8, 10, 11, 14, 16, 29. **Kubert** c-41, 42. **Sheldon Mayer** a-43p. **McWilliams** a-35. **Nasser** a-24. **Newton** a-30p. **Nino** a-1, 13, 19. **Orlando** c-13, 30, 43, 45i. **N. Redondo** a-4, 5, 29. **Rogers** c-26. **Spiegle** a-31-41. **Wrightson** c-5, 44.*

SECRETS OF HAUNTED HOUSE SPECIAL (See DC Special Series #12)

SECRETS OF LIFE (Movie)
Dell Publishing Co.: 1956 (Disney)

Four Color 749-Photo-c	6	12	18	40	55	70

SECRETS OF LOVE (See Popular Teen-Agers...)

SECRETS OF LOVE AND MARRIAGE
Charlton Comics: V2#1, Aug, 1956 - V2#25, June, 1961

V2#1	5	10	15	33	44	55
V2#2-6	3	7	10	21	28	35
V2#7-9-(All 68 pgs.)	5	10	15	36	48	60
10-25	3	6	9	18	23	28

SECRETS OF MAGIC (See Wisco)

SECRETS OF SINISTER HOUSE (Sinister House of Secret Love #1-4)
National Periodical Publ.: No. 5, June-July, 1972 - No. 18, June-July, 1974

5-(52 pgs.).	5	10	15	33	44	55
6-9: 7-Redondo-a	3	6	9	18	24	30
10-Neal Adams-a(i)	3	7	10	21	28	35
11-18: 15-Redondo-a. 17-Barry-a; early Chaykin 1 pg. strip	2	4	6	11	14	18

NOTE: ***Alcala** a-6, 13, 14. **Glanzman** a-7. **Kaluta** c-6, 7. **Nino** a-8, 11-13. Ambrose Bierce adapt.-#14.*

SECRETS OF THE LEGION OF SUPER-HEROES
DC Comics: Jan, 1981 - No. 3, Mar, 1981 (Limited series)

1-3: 1-Origin of the Legion. 2-Retells origins of Brainiac 5, Shrinking Violet, Sun-Boy, Bouncing Boy, Ultra-Boy, Matter-Eater Lad, Mon-El, Karate Kid & Dream Girl						4.00

SECRETS OF TRUE LOVE
St. John Publishing Co.: Feb, 1958

1	7	14	21	35	43	50

SECRETS OF YOUNG BRIDES
Charlton Comics: No. 5, Sept, 1957 - No. 44, Oct, 1964; July, 1975 - No. 9, Nov, 1976

5	5	10	15	36	48	60
6-10: 8-Negligee panel	4	8	12	24	32	40
11-20	3	7	10	21	28	35
21-30: Last 10¢ issue?	3	6	9	18	24	30
31-44(10/64)	2	4	6	12	16	20
1-(2nd series) (7/75)	2	4	6	14	18	22
2-9	2	4	6	8	10	12

SECRET SQUIRREL (TV)(See Kite Fun Book)
Gold Key: Oct, 1966 (12¢) (Hanna-Barbera)

1-1st Secret Squirrel and Morocco Mole, Squiddly Diddly, Winsome Witch	14	28	42	102	156	210

SECRET STORY ROMANCES (Becomes True Tales of Love)
Atlas Comics (TCI): Nov, 1953 - No. 21, Mar, 1956

1-Everett-a; Jay Scott Pike-c	15	30	45	83	117	150
2	9	18	27	52	66	80
3-11: 11-Last pre-code (2/55)	8	16	24	43	54	65
12-21	7	14	21	37	46	55

NOTE: ***Colletta** a-10, 14, 15, 17, 21; c-10, 14, 17.*

SECRET VOICE, THE (See Great American Comics Presents...)

SECRET WAR
Marvel Comics: Apr, 2004 - No. 5 ($3.99, limited series)

1-Bendis-s/Dell'Otto painted-a/c;						5.00
1-2nd printing with gold logo on white cover and full-color Spider-Man						4.00
1-3rd printing with white cover and B&W sketched Spider-Man						4.00
2,3: 2-Wolverine-c. 3-Capt. America-c						4.00
2-2nd printing with white cover and B&W sketched Wolverine						4.00

SECRET WARS II (Also see Marvel Super Heroes...)
Marvel Comics Group: July, 1985 - No. 9, Mar, 1986 (Maxi-series)

Seeker 3000 #1 © MAR

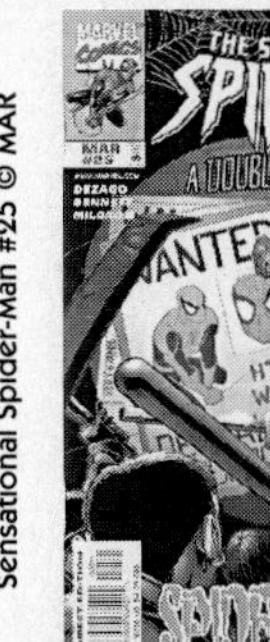

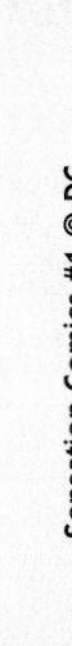
Sensational Spider-Man #25 © MAR

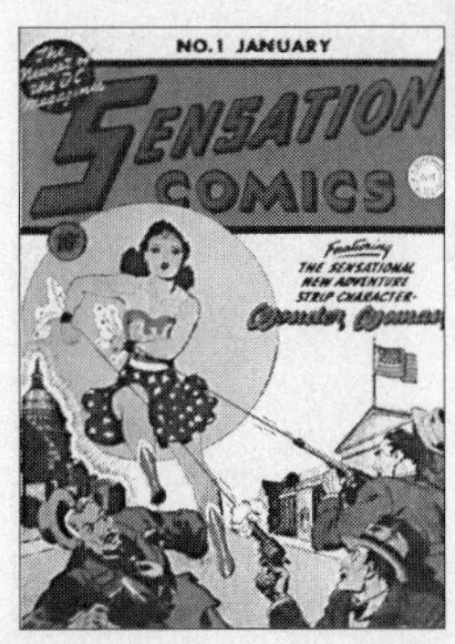

Sensation Comics #1 © DC

	GD	VG	FN	VF	VF/NM	NM-
	2.0	4.0	6.0	8.0	9.0	9.2

GD VG FN VF VF/NM NM- 2.0 4.0 6.0 8.0 9.0 9.2

1,9: 9-(52 pgs.) X-Men app., Spider-Man app. 4.00
2-8: 2,8-X-Men app. 5-1st app. Boom Boom. 5,8-Spider-Man app. 3.00

SECRET WEAPONS
Valiant: Sept, 1993 - No. 21, May, 1995 ($2.25)

1-10,12-21: 3-Reese-a(i). 5-Ninjak app. 9-Bound-in trading card. 12-Bloodshot app. 2.50
11-(Sept. on envelope, Aug on-c, $2.50)-Enclosed in manilla envelope; Bloodshot app; intro new team. 2.50

SECTAURS
Marvel Comics: June, 1985 - No. 8, Sept, 1986 (75¢) (Based on Coleco Toys)

1-8, 1-Giveaway; same-c with "Coleco 1985 Toy Fair Collectors' Edition" 3.00

SECTION ZERO
Image Comics (Gorilla): June, 2000 - No. 3, Sept, 2000 ($2.50)

1-3-Kesel-s/Grummett-a 2.50

SEDUCTION OF THE INNOCENT (Also see New York State Joint Legislative Committee to Study...)
Rinehart & Co., Inc., N. Y.: 1953, 1954 (400 pgs.) (Hardback, $4.00)(Written by Fredric Wertham, M.D.)(Also printed in Canada by Clarke, Irwin & Co. Ltd.)

(1st Version)-with bibliographical note intact (pages 399 & 400)(several copies got out before the comic publishers forced the removal of this page)
55 110 165 340 520 700
Dust jacket only 34 68 102 193 279 365
(1st Version)-without bibliographical note 34 68 102 193 279 365
Dust jacket only 16 32 48 89 127 165
(2nd Version)-Published in England by Kennikat Press, 1954, 399 pgs. has bibliographical page 11 22 33 66 91 115
1972 r-/of 2nd version; 400 pgs. w/bibliography page; Kennikat Press
4 8 12 24 32 40

NOTE: *Material from this book appeared in the November, 1953(Vol.70, pp50-53,214) issue of the* ***Ladies' Home Journal*** *under the title "What Parents Don't Know About Comic Books". With the release of this book, Dr. Wertham reveals seven years of research attempting to link juvenile delinquency to comic books. Many illustrations showing excessive violence, sex, sadism, and torture are shown. This book was used at the Kefauver Senate hearings which led to the Comics Code Authority. Because of the influence this book had on the comic industry and the collector's interest in it, we feel this listing is justified. Also see* ***Parade of Pleasure.***

SEDUCTION OF THE INNOCENT! (Also see Halloween Horror)
Eclipse Comics: Nov, 1985 - 3-D#2, Apr, 1986 ($1.75)

1-6: Double listed under cover title from #7 on 3.00
3-D 1 (10/85, $2.25, 36 pgs.)-contains unpublished Advs. Into Darkness #15 (pre-code); Dave Stevens-c 4.00
2-D 1 (100 copy limited signed & #ed edition)(B&W) 1 2 3 5 6 8
3-D 2 (4/86)-Baker, Toth, Wrightson-c 5.00
2-D 2 (100 copy limited signed & #ed edition)(B&W) 1 2 3 5 7 9
NOTE: ***Anderson*** *r-2, 3.* ***Crandall*** *c/a(r)-1.* ***Meskin*** *c/a(r)-3, 3-D 1.* ***Moreira*** *r-2.* ***Toth*** *a-1-6r; c-4r.* ***Tuska*** *r-6.*

SEEKER
Sky Comics: Apr, 1994 ($2.50, one-shot)

1 2.50

SEEKERS INTO THE MYSTERY
DC Comics (Vertigo): Jan, 1996 - No. 15, Apr, 1997 ($2.50)

1-14: J.M. DeMatteis scripts in all. 1-4-Glenn Barr-a. 5,10-Muth-c/a. 6-9-Zulli-c/a. 11-14-Bolton-c; Jill Thompson-a 2.50
15-($2.95)-Muth-c/a 3.00

SEEKER 3000 (See Marvel Premiere #41)
Marvel Comics: Jun, 1998 - No. 4, Sept, 1998 ($2.99/$2.50, limited series)

1-($2.99)-Set 25 years after 1st app.; wraparound-c 3.00
2-4-($2.50) 2.50
...Premiere 1 (6/98, $1.50) Reprints 1st app. from Marvel Premiere #41; wraparound-c 2.25

SELECT DETECTIVE (Exciting New Mystery Cases)
D. S. Publishing Co.: Aug-Sept, 1948 - No. 3, Dec-Jan, 1948-49

1-Matt Baker-a 30 60 90 170 245 320
2-Baker, McWilliams-a 19 38 57 107 154 200
3 16 32 48 89 127 165

SELF-LOATHING COMICS
Fantagraphics Books: Feb, 1995 ($2.95, B&W)

1,2-Crumb 3.00

SEMPER FI (Tales of the Marine Corp)
Marvel Comics: Dec, 1988- No.9, Aug, 1989 (75¢)

1-9: Severin-c/a 2.25

SENSATIONAL POLICE CASES (Becomes Captain Steve Savage, 2nd Series)
Avon Periodicals: 1952; No. 2, 1954 - No. 4, July-Aug, 1954

nn-(1952, 25¢, 100 pgs.)-Kubert-a?; Check, Larsen, Lawrence & McCann-a; Kinstler-c
40 80 120 233 342 450
2-4: 2-Kirbyish-a (3-4/54). 4-Reprint/Saint #5 15 30 45 83 117 150
I.W. Reprint #5-(1963?, nd)-Reprints Prison Break #5(1952-Realistic); Infantino-a 3 6 9 18 24 30

SENSATIONAL SHE-HULK, THE (She-Hulk #21-23) (See Savage She-Hulk)
Marvel Comics: V2#1, 5/89 - No. 60, Feb, 1994 ($1.50/$1.75, deluxe format)

V2#1-Byrne-c/a(p)/scripts begin, end #8 3.00
2,3,5-8: 3-Spider-Man app. 2.25
4,14-17,21-23: 4-Reintro G.A. Blonde Phantom. 14-17-Howard the Duck app. 21-23-Return of the Blonde Phantom. 22-All Winners Squad app. 2.50
9-13,18-20,24-49,51-60: 25-Thor app. 26-Excalibur app.;Guice-c. 29-Wolverine app. (3 pgs.). 30-Hobgoblin-c & cameo. 31-Byrne-c/a/scripts begin again. 35-Last $1.50-c. 37-Wolverine/Punisher/Spidey-c, but no app. 39-Thing app. 56-War Zone app.; Hulk cameo. 57-Vs. Hulk-c/story. 58-Electro-c/story. 59-Jack O'Lantern app. 2.25
50-($2.95, 52 pgs.)-Embossed green foil-c; Byrne app.; last Byrne-c/a; Austin, Chaykin, Simonson-a; Miller-a(2 pgs.) 3.00
NOTE: ***Dale Keown*** *a(p)-13, 15-22.*

SENSATIONAL SHE-HULK IN CEREMONY, THE
Marvel Comics: 1989 - No. 2, 1989 ($3.95, squarebound, 52 pgs.)

nn-Part 1, nn-Part 2 4.00

SENSATIONAL SPIDER-MAN
Marvel Comics: Apr, 1989 ($5.95, squarebound, 80 pgs.)

1-r/Amazing Spider-Man Annual #14,15 by Miller & Annual #8 by Kirby & Ditko 6.00

SENSATIONAL SPIDER-MAN, THE
Marvel Comics: Jan, 1996 - No. 33, Nov, 1998 ($1.95/$1.99)

0 ($4.95)-Lenticular-c; Jurgens-a/scripts 5.00
1 5.00
1-($2.95) variant-c; polybagged w/cassette 1 2 3 5 6 8
2-5: 2-Kaine & Rhino app. 3-Giant-Man app. 4.00
6-18: 9-Onslaught tie-in; revealed that Peter & Mary Jane's unborn baby is a girl. 11-Revelations. 13-15-Ka-Zar app. 14,15-Hulk app. 3.00
19-24: Living Pharoah app. 22,23-Dr. Strange app. 2.50
25-($2.99) Spiderhunt pt. 1; Normie Osborne kidnapped 4.00
25-Variant-c 1 2 3 5 6 8
26-33: 26-Nauck-a. 27-Double-c with "The Sensational Hornet #1"; Vulture app. 28-Hornet vs. Vulture. 29,30-Black Cat-c/app. 33-Last issue; Gathering of Five concludes 2.50
#(-1) Flashback(7/97) Dezago-s/Wieringo-a 3.00
'96 Annual ($2.95) 3.00

SENSATION COMICS (Sensation Mystery #110 on)
National Per. Publ./All-American: Jan, 1942 - No. 109, May-June, 1952

1-Origin Mr. Terrific(1st app.), Wildcat(1st app.), The Gay Ghost, & Little Boy Blue; Wonder Woman (cont'd from All Star #8), The Black Pirate begin; intro. Justice & Fair Play Club
2575 5150 7725 19,400 31,700 44,000

1-Reprint, Oversize 13-1/2x10". WARNING: This comic is an exact duplicate reprint of the original except for its size. DC published it in 1974 with a second cover titling it as a Famous First Edition. There have been many reported cases of the outer cover being removed and the interior sold as the original edition. The reprint with the new outer cover removed is practically worthless. See Famous First Edition for value.

2-Etta Candy begins 439 878 1317 3073 4937 6800
3-W. Woman gets secretary's job 277 554 831 1731 2666 3600
4-1st app. Stretch Skinner in Wildcat 192 384 576 1200 1850 2500
5-Intro. Justin, Black Pirate's son 154 308 462 963 1482 2000
6-Origin/1st app. Wonder Woman's magic lasso 158 316 474 988 1519 2050
7-10 112 224 336 700 1075 1450
11,12,14-20 100 200 300 625 963 1300
13-Hitler, Tojo, Mussolini-c (as bowling pins) 138 276 414 863 1332 1800
21-30 77 154 231 481 741 1000
31-33 56 112 168 350 538 725
34-Sargon, the Sorcerer begins (10/44), ends #36; begins again #52
60 120 180 375 580 785
35-40: 38-X-Mas-c 52 104 156 317 484 650
41-50: 43-The Whip app. 48 96 144 293 447 600
51-60: 51-Last Black Pirate. 56,57-Sargon by Kubert
44 88 132 268 409 550
61-67,69-80: 63-Last Mr. Terrific. 66-Wildcat by Kubert
40 80 120 244 372 500
68-Origin & 1st app. Huntress (8/47) 46 92 138 281 428 575
81-Used in **SOTI**, pg. 33,34; Krigstein-a 42 84 126 256 391 525
82-93: 83-Last Sargon. 86-The Atom app. 90-Last Wildcat. 91-Streak begins by Alex Toth. 92-Toth-a (2 pgs.) 38 76 114 219 320 420
94-1st all girl issue 50 100 150 305 465 625

Sentinel #4 © MAR

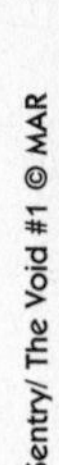

Sentry/ The Void #1 © MAR

Sgt. Bilko's Pvt. Doberman #11 © DC

GD VG FN VF VF/NM NM-
2.0 4.0 6.0 8.0 9.0 9.2

95-99,101-106: 95-Unmasking of Wonder Woman-c/story. 99-1st app. Astra, Girl of the Future, ends #106. 103-Robot-c. 105-Last 52 pgs. 106-Wonder Woman ends
45 90 135 275 418 560
100-(11-12/50) 56 112 168 350 538 725
107-(Scarce, 1-2/52)-1st mystery issue; Johnny Peril by Toth(p), 8 pgs. & begins; continues from Danger Trail #5 (3-4/51)(see Comic Cavalcade #15 for 1st app.)
69 138 207 431 666 900
108-(Scarce)-Johnny Peril by Toth(p) 56 112 168 350 538 725
109-(Scarce)-Johnny Peril by Toth(p) 69 138 207 431 666 900

NOTE: ***Krigstein** a-(Wildcat)-81, 83, 84. **Moldoff** Black Pirate-1-25; Black Pirate not in 34-36, 43-48. **Oskner** c(i)-89-91, 94-106. Wonder Woman by **H. G. Peter**, all issues except #8, 17-19, 21; c-4-7, 9-18, 20-88, 92, 93. **Toth** a-91, 98; c-107. Wonder Woman c-1-106.*

SENSATION COMICS (Also see All Star Comics 1999 crossover titles)
DC Comics: May, 1999 ($1.99, one-shot)

1-Golden Age Wonder Woman and Hawkgirl; Robinson-s 2.25

SENSATION MYSTERY (Formerly Sensation Comics #1-109)
National Periodical Publ.: No. 110, July-Aug, 1952 - No. 116, July-Aug, 1953

110-Johnny Peril continues 44 88 132 268 409 550
111-116-Johnny Peril in all. 116-M. Anderson-a 44 88 132 268 409 550

NOTE: ***M. Anderson** c-110. **Colan** a-114p. **Giunta** a-112. **G. Kane** c(p)-108, 109, 111-115.*

SENSUOUS STREAKER
Marvel Publ.: 1974 (B&W magazine, 68pgs.)

1 3 7 10 21 28 35

SENTINEL
Marvel Comics: June, 2003 - No. 12, April, 2004 ($2.99/$2.50)

1-Sean McKeever-s/Udon Studios-a 3.00
2-12 3.00
Marvel Age Sentinel Vol. 1: Salvage (2004, $7.99, digest size) r/#1-6 8.00
Vol. 2: No Hero (2004, $7.99, digest size) r/#7-12; sketch pages 8.00

SENTINELS OF JUSTICE, THE (See Americomics & Captain Paragon &...)

SENTRY (Also see New Avengers)
Marvel Comics: Sept, 2000 - No. 5, Jan, 2001 ($2.99, limited series)

1-5-Paul Jenkins-s/Jae Lee-a. 3-Spider-Man-c/app. 4-X-Men, FF app. 3.00
.../Fantastic Four (2/01, $2.99) Continues story from #5; Winslade-a 3.00
.../Hulk (2/01, $2.99) Sienkiewicz-c/a 3.00
.../Spider-Man (2/01, $2.99) back story of the Sentry; Leonardi-a 3.00
.../The Void (2/01, $2.99) Conclusion of story; Jae Lee-a 3.00
.../X-Men (2/01, $2.99) Sentry and Archangel; Texeira-a 3.00
TPB (10/01, $24.95) r/#1-5 & all one-shots; Stan Lee interview 25.00

SENTRY SPECIAL
Innovation Publishing: 1991 ($2.75, one-shot)(Hero Alliance spin-off)

1-Lost in Space preview (3 pgs.) 2.75

SERAPHIM
Innovation Publishing: May, 1990 ($2.50, mature readers)

1 2.50

SERGEANT BARNEY BARKER (Becomes G. I. Tales #4 on)
Atlas Comics (MCI): Aug, 1956 - No. 3, Dec, 1956

1-Severin-c/a(4) 20 40 60 112 161 210
2,3: 2-Severin-c/a(4). 3-Severin-c/a(5) 14 28 42 79 110 140

SERGEANT BILKO (Phil Silvers Starring as...) (TV)
National Periodical Publications: May-June, 1957 - No. 18, Mar-Apr, 1960

1-All have Bob Oskner-c 74 148 222 463 714 965
2 40 80 120 233 342 450
3-5 35 70 105 200 290 380
6-18: 11,12,15,17-Photo-c 29 58 87 164 237 310

SGT. BILKO'S PVT. DOBERMAN (TV)
National Periodical Publications: June-July, 1958 - No. 11, Feb-Mar, 1960

1-Bob Oskner c-1-4,7,11 34 68 102 255 403 550
2 20 40 60 141 216 290
3-5: 5-Photo-c 14 28 42 97 149 200
6-11: 6,9-Photo-c 10 20 30 70 100 130

SGT. DICK CARTER OF THE U.S. BORDER PATROL (See Holyoke One-Shot)

SGT. FURY (& His Howling Commandos)(See Fury & Special Marvel Edition)
Marvel Comics Group (BPC earlier issues): May, 1963 - No. 167, Dec, 1981

1-1st app. Sgt. Nick Fury (becomes agent of Shield in Strange Tales #135); Kirby/Ayers-c/a; 1st Dum-Dum Dugan & the Howlers 132 264 396 1122 1811 2500
2-Kirby-a 38 76 114 285 443 600
3-5: 3-Reed Richards x-over. 4-Death of Junior Juniper. 5-1st Baron Strucker app.; Kirby-a 22 44 66 158 242 325
6-10: 8-Baron Zemo, 1st Percival Pinkerton app. 9-Hitler-c & app. 10-1st app. Capt. Savage (the Skipper)(9/64) 13 26 39 92 141 190
11,12,14-20: 14-1st Blitz Squad. 18-Death of Pamela Hawley
8 16 24 55 78 100
13-Captain America & Bucky app.(12/64); 2nd solo Capt. America x-over outside The Avengers; Kirby-a 34 68 102 255 398 540
13-2nd printing (1994) 2 4 6 8 10 12
21-24,26,28-30 6 12 18 40 55 70
25,27: 25-Red Skull app. 27-1st app. Eric Koenig; origin Fury's eye patch
6 12 18 43 59 75
31-33,35-50: 35-Eric Koenig joins Howlers. 43-Bob Hope, Glen Miller app. 44-Flashback on Howlers' 1st mission 4 8 12 24 32 40
34-Origin Howling Commandos 4 8 12 25 33 42
51-60 3 6 9 18 24 32
61-67: 64-Capt. Savage & Raiders x-over; peace symbol-c. 67-Last 12¢ issue; flag-c
3 6 9 16 21 26
68-80: 76-Fury's Father app. in WWI story 3 6 9 16 20 24
81-91: 91-Last 15¢ issue 2 4 6 12 16 20
92-(52 pgs.) 3 6 9 16 21 26
93-99: 98-Deadly Dozen x-over 2 4 6 11 14 18
100-Capt. America, Fantastic 4 cameos; Stan Lee, Martin Goodman & others app.
3 6 9 16 21 26
101-120: 101-Origin retold 2 4 6 10 12 15
121-130: 121-123-r/#19-21 1 3 4 6 8 10
131-167: 167-Reprints (from 1963) 1 2 3 5 6 8
133,134-(30¢-c variants, limited dist.)(5,7/76) 2 4 6 8 10 12
141,142-(35¢-c variants, limited dist.)(7,9/77) 2 4 6 8 10 12
Annual 1(1965, 25¢, 72 pgs.)-r/#4,5 & new-a 15 30 45 107 164 220
Special 2(1966) 6 12 18 40 55 70
Special 3(1967) All new material 4 8 12 27 36 45
Special 4(1968) 3 6 9 19 25 32
Special 5-7(1969-11/71) 3 6 9 16 20 24

NOTE: ***Ayers** a-8, Annual 1. **Ditko** a-15i. **Gil Kane** c-37, 96. **Kirby** a-1-7, 13p, 167p(r). Special 5; c-1-20, 25, 167p. **Severin** a-44-46, 48, 162, 164; inks-49-79, Special 4, 6; c-4i, 5, 6, 44, 46, 110, 149i, 155i, 162-166. **Sutton** a-57p. Reprints in #80, 82, 85, 87, 89, 91, 93, 95, 99, 101, 103, 105, 107, 109, 111, 121-123, 145-155, 167.*

SGT. FURY AND HIS HOWLING DEFENDERS (See The Defenders #147)

SERGEANT PRESTON OF THE YUKON (TV)
Dell Publishing Co.: No. 344, Aug, 1951 - No. 29, Nov-Jan, 1958-59

Four Color 344(#1)-Sergeant Preston & his dog Yukon King begin; painted-c begin, end #18
13 26 39 90 138 185
Four Color 373,397,419('52) 9 18 27 60 85 110
5(11-1/52-53)-10(2-4/54): 6-Bondage-c. 7 14 21 46 63 80
11,12,14-17 6 12 18 40 55 70
13-Origin Sgt. Preston 7 14 21 46 63 80
18-Origin Yukon King; last painted-c 7 14 21 46 63 80
19-29: All photo-c 8 16 24 58 82 105

SGT. ROCK (Formerly Our Army at War; see Brave & the Bold #52 & Showcase #45)
National Periodical Publications/DC Comics: No. 302, Mar, 1977 - No. 422, July, 1988

302 3 7 10 21 28 35
303-310 2 4 6 11 14 18
311-320: 318-Reprints 2 4 6 8 10 12
321-350 1 2 3 5 7 9
329-Whitman variant (scarce) 1 3 4 6 8 10
351-399,401-421 6.00
400,422: 422-1st Joe, Adam, Andy Kubert-a team 1 2 3 5 7 9
Annual 2-4: 2(1982)-Formerly Sgt. Rock's Prize Battle Tales #1. 3(1983). 4(1984)
1 2 3 5 7 9

NOTE: ***Estrada** a-322, 327, 331, 336, 337, 341, 342i. **Glanzman** a-384, 421. **Kubert** a-302, 303, 305r, 306, 328, 351, 356, 368, 373, 422; c-317, 318r, 319-323, 325-333-on, Annual 2, 3. **Severin** a-347. **Spiegle** a-382, Annual 2, 3. **Thorne** a-384. **Toth** a-385r. **Wildey** a-307, 311, 313, 314.*

SGT. ROCK: BETWEEN HELL AND A HARD PLACE
DC Comics (Vertigo): 2003 ($24.95, hardcover one-shot)

HC-Joe Kubert-a/c; Brian Azzarello-s 25.00
SC (2004, $17.95) 18.00

SGT. ROCK SPECIAL (Sgt. Rock #14 on; see DC Special Series #3)
DC Comics: Oct, 1988 - No. 21, Feb, 1992; No. 1, 1992; No. 2, 1994
($2.00, quarterly/monthly, 52 pgs)

1-Reprint begin 1 3 4 6 8 10
2-21: All-r; 5-r/early Sgt. Rock/Our Army at War #81. 7-Tomahawk-r by Thorne. 9-Enemy Ace-r by Kubert. 10-All Rock issue. 11-r/1st Haunted Tank story. 12-All Kubert issue; begins

The Shade #3 © DC

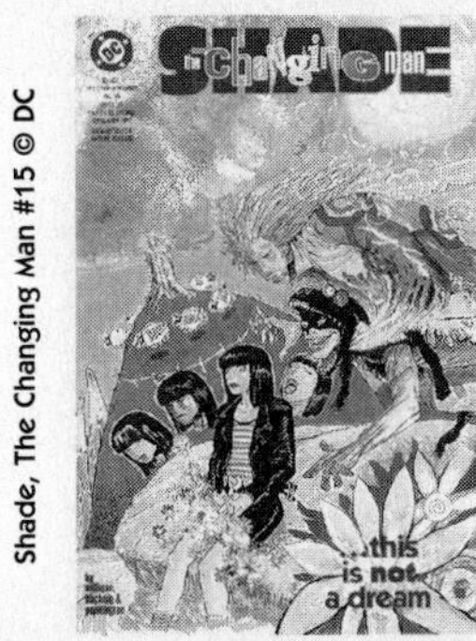

Shade, The Changing Man #15 © DC

The Shadow ('87) #1 © CN

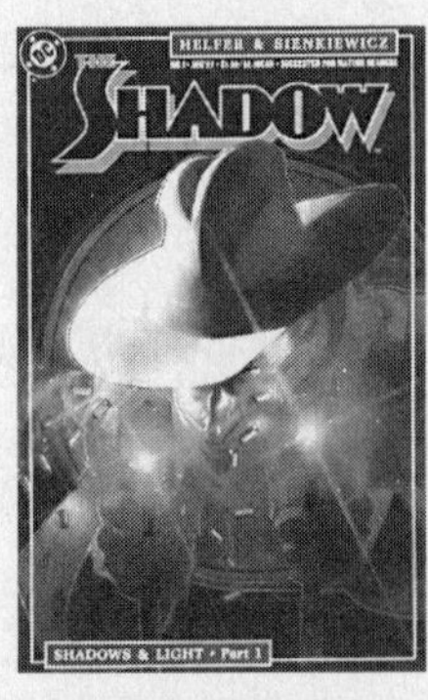

GD 2.0 VG 4.0 FN 6.0 VF 8.0 VF/NM 9.0 NM- 9.2

monthly. 13-Dinosaur story by Heath(r). 14-Enemy Ace-r (22 pgs.) by Adams/Kubert. 15-Enemy Ace (22 pgs.) by Kubert. 16-Iron Major-c/story. 16,17-Enemy Ace-r. 19-r/Batman/Sgt. Rock team-up/B&B #108 by Aparo 6.00
1 (1992, $2.95, 68 pgs.)-Simonson-c; unpubbed Kubert-a; Glanzman, Russell, Pratt, & Wagner-a 5.00
2 (1994, $2.95) Brereton painted-c 4.00
NOTE: ***Neal Adams*** *r-1, 8, 14p.* ***Chaykin*** *a-2; r-3, 9(2pgs.); c-3.* ***Drucker*** *r-6.* ***Glanzman*** *r-20.* ***Golden*** *a-1.* ***Heath*** *a-2; r-5, 9-13, 16, 19, 21.* ***Krigstein*** *r-4, 8.* ***Kubert*** *r-1-17, 20, 21; c-1p, 2, 8, 14-21.* ***Miller*** *r-6p.* ***Severin*** *r-3, 6, 10.* ***Simonson*** *r-2, 4; c-4.* ***Thorne*** *r-7.* ***Toth*** *r-2, 8, 11.* ***Wood*** *r-4.*

SGT. ROCK SPECTACULAR (See DC Special Series #13)

SGT. ROCK'S PRIZE BATTLE TALES (Becomes Sgt. Rock Annual #2 on; see DC Special Series #18 & 80 Page Giant #7)
National Periodical Publications: Winter, 1964 (Giant - 80 pgs., one-shot)
1-Kubert, Heath-r; new Kubert-c 33 66 99 248 387 525
... Replica Edition (2000, $5.95) Reprints entire issue 6.00

SGT. STRYKER'S DEATH SQUAD (See Savage Combat Tales)

SERGIO ARAGONÉS' ACTIONS SPEAK
Dark Horse Comics: Jan, 2001 - No. 6, Jun, 2001 ($2.99, B&W, limited series)
1-6-Aragonés-c/a; wordless one-page cartoons 3.00

SERGIO ARAGONÉS' BLAIR WHICH?
Dark Horse Comics: Dec, 1999 ($2.95, B&W, one-shot)
nn-Aragonés-c/a; Evanier-s. Parody of "Blair Witch Project" movie 3.00

SERGIO ARAGONÉS' BOOGEYMAN
Dark Horse Comics: June, 1998 - No. 4, Sept, 1998 ($2.95, B&W, lim. series)
1-4-Aragonés-c/a 3.00

SERGIO ARAGONÉS DESTROYS DC
DC Comics: June, 1996 ($3.50, one-shot)
1-DC Superhero parody book; Aragonés-c/a; Evanier scripts 3.50

SERGIO ARAGONÉS' DIA DE LOS MUERTOS
Dark Horse Comics: Oct, 1998 ($2.95, one-shot)
1-Aragonés-c/a; Evanier scripts 3.00

SERGIO ARAGONÉS' GROO & RUFFERTO
Dark Horse Comics: Dec, 1998 - No. 4, Mar, 1999 ($2.95, lim. series)
1-3-Aragonés-c/a 3.00

SERGIO ARAGONÉS' GROO: DEATH AND TAXES
Dark Horse Comics: Dec, 2001 - No. 4, Apr, 2002 ($2.99, lim. series)
1-4-Aragonés-c/a; Evanier-s 3.00

SERGIO ARAGONÉS' GROO: MIGHTIER THAN THE SWORD
Dark Horse Comics: Jan, 2000 - No. 4, Apr, 2000 ($2.95, lim. series)
1-4-Aragonés-c/a; Evanier-s 3.00

SERGIO ARAGONÉS' GROO THE WANDERER (See Groo...)

SERGIO ARAGONÉS' LOUDER THAN WORDS
Dark Horse Comics: July, 1997 - No. 6, Dec, 1997 ($2.95, B&W, limited series)
1-6-Aragonés-c/a 3.00

SERGIO ARAGONÉS MASSACRES MARVEL
Marvel Comics: June, 1996 ($3.50, one-shot)
1-Marvel Superhero parody book; Aragonés-c/a; Evanier scripts 3.50

SERGIO ARAGONÉS STOMPS STAR WARS
Marvel Comics: Jan, 2000 ($2.95, one-shot)
1-Star Wars parody; Aragonés-c/a; Evanier scripts 3.00

SERRA ANGEL ON THE WORLDS OF MAGIC THE GATHERING
Acclaim Comics (Armada): Aug, 1996 ($5.95, one-shot)
1 6.00

SEVEN BLOCK
Marvel Comics (Epic Comics): 1990 ($4.50, one-shot, 52 pgs.)
1-Dixon-s/Zaffinoa 4.50
nn-(IDW Publ., 2004, $5.99) reprints #1 6.00

SEVEN DEAD MEN (See Complete Mystery #1)

SEVEN DWARFS (Also see Snow White)
Dell Publishing Co.: No. 227, 1949 (Disney-Movie)
Four Color #227 11 22 33 80 120 160

SEVEN MILES A SECOND
DC Comics (Vertigo Verité): 1996 ($7.95, one-shot)
nn-Wojnarowicz-s/Romberg-a 8.00

SEVEN SAMUROID, THE (See Image Graphic Novel)

SEVEN SEAS COMICS
Universal Phoenix Features/Leader No. 6: Apr, 1946 - No. 6, 1947(no month)
1-South Sea Girl by Matt Baker, Capt. Cutlass begin; Tugboat Tessie by Baker app. 87 174 261 544 835 1125
2-Swashbuckler-c 70 140 210 438 674 910
3,5,6: 3-Six pg. Feldstein-a 65 130 195 406 623 840
4-Classic Baker-c 74 148 222 463 714 965
NOTE: ***Baker*** *a-1-6; c-3-6.*

1776 (See Charlton Classic Library)

7TH VOYAGE OF SINBAD, THE (Movie)
Dell Publishing Co.: Sept, 1958 (photo-c)
Four Color 944-Buscema-a 14 28 42 97 149 200

77 SUNSET STRIP (TV)
Dell Publ. Co./Gold Key: No. 1066, Jan-Mar, 1960 - No. 2, Feb, 1963 (All photo-c)
Four Color 1066-Toth-a 12 24 36 87 134 180
Four Color 1106,1159-Toth-a 10 20 30 72 104 135
Four Color 1211,1263,1291, 01-742-209(7-9/62)-Manning-a in all 10 20 30 67 96 125
1,2: Manning-a. 1(11/62-G.K.) 10 20 30 72 104 135

77TH BENGAL LANCERS, THE (TV)
Dell Publishing Co.: May, 1957
Four Color 791-Photo-c 8 16 24 58 82 105

SEYMOUR, MY SON (See More Seymour)
Archie Publications (Radio Comics): Sept, 1963
1-DeCarlo-a? 4 8 12 22 30 38

SHADE, THE (See Starman)
DC Comics: Apr, 1997 - No. 4, July, 1997 ($2.25, limited series)
1-4-Robinson-s/Harris-c: 1-Gene Ha-a. 2-Williams/Gray-a 3-Blevins-a. 4-Zulli-a 3.00

SHADE, THE CHANGING MAN (See Cancelled Comic Cavalcade)
National Per. Publ./DC Comics: June-July, 1977 - No. 8, Aug-Sept, 1978
1-1st app. Shade; Ditko-c/a in all 2 4 6 9 11 14
2-8 1 2 3 5 6 8

SHADE, THE CHANGING MAN (2nd series) (Also see Suicide Squad #16)
DC Comics (Vertigo imprint #33 on): July, 1990 - No. 70, Apr, 1996 ($1.50-$2.25, mature)
1-($2.50, 52 pgs.)-Peter Milligan scripts in all 4.00
2-41,45-49,51-59: 6-Preview of World Without End. 17-Begin $1.75-c. 33-Metallic ink on-c. 41-Begin $1.95-c 2.25
42-44-John Constantine app. 3.00
50-($2.95, 52 pgs.) 3.50
60-70: 60-begin $2.25-c 2.25
...: The American Scream (2003, $17.95) r/#1-6 18.00
NOTE: ***Bachalo*** *a-1-9, 11-13, 15-21, 23-26, 33-39, 42-45, 47, 49, 50; c-30, 33-41.*

SHADO: SONG OF THE DRAGON (See Green Arrow #63-66)
DC Comics: 1992 - No. 4, 1992 ($4.95, limited series, 52 pgs.)
Book One - Four: Grell scripts; Morrow-a(i) 5.00

SHADOW, THE (See Batman #253, 259 & Marvel Graphic Novel #35)

SHADOW, THE (Pulp, radio)
Archie Comics (Radio Comics): Aug, 1964 - No. 8, Sept, 1965 (All 12¢)
1-Jerrry Siegel scripts in all; Shadow-c. 8 16 24 58 82 105
2-8: 2-App. in super-hero costume on-c only; Reinman-a(backup). 3-Superhero begins; Reinman-a (book-length novel). 3,4,6,7-The Fly 1 pg. strips. 4-8-Reinman-a. 5-8-Siegel scripts. 7-Shield app. 5 10 15 36 48 60

SHADOW, THE
National Periodical Publications: Oct-Nov, 1973 - No. 12, Aug-Sept, 1975
1-Kaluta-a begins 4 8 12 29 40 50
2 3 6 9 16 20 24
3-Kaluta/Wrightson-a 3 6 9 18 23 28
4,6-Kaluta-a ends. 4-Chaykin, Wrightson part-i 2 4 6 12 16 20
5,7-12: 11-The Avenger (pulp character) x-over 1 3 4 6 8 10
NOTE: ***Craig*** *a-10.* ***Cruz*** *a-10-12.* ***Kaluta*** *a-1, 2, 3p, 4, 6; c-1-4, 6, 10-12.* ***Kubert*** *c-9.* ***Robbins*** *a-5, 7-9; c-5, 7, 8.*

SHADOW, THE
DC Comics: May, 1986 - No. 4, Aug, 1986 (limited series)
1-4: Howard Chaykin art in all 3.00

Shadow Comics #1 © CN

Shadow Lady: Dangerous Love #3 © DH

Shadowman V2#13 © ACL

GD 2.0 | VG 4.0 | FN 6.0 | VF 8.0 | VF/NM 9.0 | NM- 9.2

Blood & Judgement ($12.95)-r/1-4 13.00

SHADOW, THE
DC Comics: Aug, 1987 - No. 19, Jan, 1989 ($1.50)

1-19: Andrew Helfer scripts in all. 3.00
Annual 1,2 (12/87, '88,)-2-The Shadow dies; origin retold (story inspired by the movie "Citizen Kane"). 4.00
NOTE: *Kyle Baker a-7i, 8-19, Annual 2. Chaykin c-Annual 1. Helfer scripts in all. Orlando a-Annual 1. Rogers c/a-7. Sienkiewicz c/a-1-6.*

SHADOW, THE (Movie)
Dark Horse Comics: June, 1994 - No. 2, July, 1994 ($2.50, limited series)

1,2-Adaptation from Universal Pictures film 3.00
NOTE: *Kaluta c/a-1, 2.*

SHADOW AND DOC SAVAGE, THE
Dark Horse Comics: July, 1995 - No. 2, Aug, 1995 ($2.95, limited series)

1,2 3.50

SHADOW AND THE MYSTERIOUS 3, THE
Dark Horse Comics: Sept, 1994 ($2.95, one-shot)

1-Kaluta co-scripts. 3.00
NOTE: *Stevens c-1.*

SHADOW CABINET (See Heroes)
DC Comics (Milestone): Jan, 1994 - No. 17, Oct, 1995 ($1.75/$2.50)

0,1-17: 0-($2.50, 52 pgs.)-Silver ink-c; Simonson-c. 1-Byrne-c 2.50

SHADOW COMICS (Pulp, radio)
Street & Smith Publications: Mar, 1940 - V9#5, Aug-Sept, 1949
NOTE: *The Shadow first appeared on radio in 1929 and was featured in pulps beginning in April, 1931, written by Walter Gibson. The early covers of this series were reprinted from the pulp covers.*

V1#1-Shadow, Doc Savage, Bill Barnes, Nick Carter (radio), Frank Merriwell, Iron Munro, the Astonishing Man begin 452 904 1356 3164 5082 7000
2-The Avenger begins, ends #6; Capt. Fury only app. 200 400 600 1250 1925 2600
3(nn-5/40)-Norgil the Magician app.; cover is exact swipe of Shadow pulp from 1/33 138 276 414 863 1332 1800
4,5: 4-The Three Musketeers begins, ends #8. 5-Doc Savage ends 106 212 318 663 1019 1375
6,8,9: 9-Norgil the Magician app. 92 184 276 575 888 1200
7-Origin/1st app. The Hooded Wasp & Wasplet (11/40); series ends V3#8; Hooded Wasp/Wasplet app. on-c thru #9 98 196 294 613 944 1275
10-Origin The Iron Ghost, ends #11; The Dead End Kids begins, ends #14 92 184 276 575 888 1200
11-Origin Hooded Wasp & Wasplet retold 92 184 276 575 888 1200
12-Dead End Kids app. 81 162 243 506 778 1050
V2#1(11/41) 75 150 225 469 722 975
2-(Rare) Giant ant-c; Dead End Kids story 135 270 405 844 1297 1750
3-Origin & 1st app. Supersnipe (3/42); series begins; Little Nemo story 123 246 369 769 1185 1600
4,5: 4,8-Little Nemo story 65 130 195 406 628 850
6-9: 6-Blackstone the Magician story 62 124 186 388 594 800
10,12: 10-Supersnipe app. 60 120 180 375 575 775
11-Classic Devil Kyoti World War 2 sunburst-c 65 130 195 406 623 840
V3#1-5,7-12: 10-Doc Savage begins, not in V5#5, V6#10-12, V8#4 58 116 174 363 557 750
6-Classic underwater-c 62 124 186 388 594 800
V4#1-12 46 92 138 281 428 575
V5#1-12 40 80 120 224 372 500
V6#1-11: 9-Intro. Shadow, Jr. (12/46) 40 80 120 233 342 450
12-Powell-c/a; atom bomb panels 40 80 120 224 372 500
V7#1,2,5,7-9,12: 2,5-Shadow, Jr. app.; Powell-a 40 80 120 224 372 500
3,6,11-Powell-c/a 46 92 138 281 428 575
4-Powell-c/a; Atom bomb panels 48 96 144 293 447 600
10(1/48)-Flying Saucer-c/story (2nd of this theme; see The Spirit 9/28/47); Powell-c/a 56 112 168 350 538 725
V8#1-12-Powell-a. 8-Powell Spider-c/a 46 92 138 281 428 575
V9#1,5-Powell-a 44 88 132 268 409 550
2-4-Powell-c/a 46 92 138 281 428 575
NOTE: *Binder c-V3#1. Powell art in most issues beginning V6#12. Painted c-1-6.*

SHADOWDRAGON
DC Comics: 1995 ($3.50, annual)

Annual 1-Year One story 3.50

SHADOW EMPIRES: FAITH CONQUERS
Dark Horse Comics: Aug, 1994 - No. 4, Nov, 1994 ($2.95, limited series)

1-4 3.00

SHADOWHAWK (See Images of Shadowhawk, New Shadowhawk, Shadowhawk II, Shadowhawk III & Youngblood #2)
Image Comics (Shadowline Ink): Aug, 1992 - No. 4, Mar, 1993; No. 12, Aug, 1994 - No. 18, May, 1995 ($1.95/$2.50)

1-($2.50)-Embossed silver foil stamped-c; Valentino/Liefeld-c; Valentino-c/a/scripts in all; has coupon for Image #0; 1st Shadowline Ink title 4.00
1-With coupon missing 2.25
1-($1.95)-Newsstand version w/o foil stamp 2.25
2-13,0,1418: 2-Shadowhawk poster w/McFarlane-i; brief Spawn app.; wraparound-c w/silver ink highlights. 3-($2.50)-Glow-in-the-dark-c. 4-Savage Dragon-c/story; Valentino/Larsen-c. 5-11-(See Shadowhawk II and III). 12-Cont'd from Shadowhawk III; pull-out poster by Texeira.13-w/ShadowBone poster; WildC.A.T.s app. 0 (10/94)-Liefeld c/a/story; ShadowBart poster. 14-(10/94, $2.50)-The Others app. 16-Supreme app. 17-Spawn app.; story cont'd from Badrock & Co. #6. 18-Shadowhawk dies; Savage Dragon & Brigade app. 2.50
Special 1(12/94, $3.50, 52 pgs.)-Silver Age Shadowhawk flip book 3.50
Gallery (4/94, $1.95) 2.25
Out of the Shadows ($19.95)-r/Youngblood #2, Shadowhawk #1-4, Image Zero #0, Operation: Urban Storm (Never published) 20.00
.../Vampirella (2/95, $4.95)-Pt.2 of x-over (See Vampirella/Shadowhawk for Pt. 1) 5.00
NOTE: *Shadowhawk was originally a four issue limited series. The story continued in Shadowhawk II, Shadowhawk III & then became Shadowhawk again with issue #12.*

SHADOWHAWK II (Follows Shadowhawk #4)
Image Comics (Shadowline Ink): V2#1, May, 1993 - V2#3, Aug, 1993 ($3.50/$1.95/$2.95, limited series)

V2#1 ($3.50)-Cont'd from Shadowhawk #4; die-cut mirricard-c 3.50
2 ($1.95)-Foil embossed logo; reveals identity; gold-c variant exists 2.50
3 ($2.95)-Pop-up-c w/Pact ashcan insert 3.00

SHADOWHAWK III (Follows Shadowhawk II #3)
Image Comics (Shadowline Ink): V3#1, Nov, 1993 - V3#4, Mar, 1994 ($1.95, limited series);

V3#1-4: 1-Cont'd from Shadowhawk II; intro Valentine; gold foil & red foil stamped-c variations. 2-(52 pgs.)-Shadowhawk contracts HIV virus; U.S. Male by M. Anderson (p) in free 16 pg.insert. 4-Continues in Shadowhawk #12 2.50

SHADOWHAWKS OF LEGEND
Image Comics (Shadowline Ink): Nov, 1995 ($4.95, one-shot)

nn-Stories of past Shadowhawks by Kurt Busiek, Beau Smith & Alan Moore 5.00

SHADOW, THE: HELL'S HEAT WAVE (Movie, pulp, radio)
Dark Horse Comics: Apr, 1995 - No. 3, June, 1995 ($2.95, limited series)

1-3: Kaluta story 3.00

SHADOWHUNT SPECIAL
Image Comics (Extreme Studios): Apr, 1996 ($2.50)

1-Retells origin of past Shadowhawks; Valentino script; Chapel app. 2.50

SHADOW, THE: IN THE COILS OF THE LEVIATHAN (Movie, pulp, radio)
Dark Horse Comics: Oct, 1993 - No. 4, Apr, 1994 ($2.95, limited series)

1-4-Kaluta-c & co-scripter 3.00
Trade paperback (10/94, $13.95)-r/1-4 14.00

SHADOW LADY:... (Masakazu Katsura's...)
Dark Horse Comics ($2.50, B&W, limited series, Manga)

Dangerous Love: (Oct, 1998 - No. 7, Apr, 1999) 1-7-Katsura-s/a 2.50
TPB ($17.95) r/#1-7 18.00
The Eyes of a Stranger: (No. 8, May, 1999 - No. 12, Sept, 1999) 8-12 2.50
The Awakening: (No. 13, Oct, 1999 - No. 19, Apr, 2000) 13-19 2.50
Sudden Death: (No. 20, May, 2000 - No. 24) 20-23 2.50

SHADOWLINE SAGA: CRITICAL MASS, A
Marvel Comics (Epic): Jan, 1990 - No. 7, July, 1990 ($4.95, lim. series, 68 pgs)

1-6: Dr. Zero, Powerline, St. George 5.00
7 ($5.95, 84 pgs.)-Morrow-a, Williamson-c(i) 6.00

SHADOWMAN (See X-O Manowar #4)
Valiant/Acclaim Comics (Valiant): May, 1992 - No. 43, Dec, 1995 ($2.50)

1-Partial origin 5.00
2-5: 3-1st app. Sousa the Soul Eater 4.00
6-43: 8-1st app. Master Darque. 16-1st app. Dr. Mirage (8/93). 15-Minor Turok app. 17,18-Archer & Armstrong x-over. 19-Aerosmith-c/story. 23-Dr. Mirage x-over. 24-(4/94). 25-Bound-in trading card. 29-Chaos Effect. 43-Shadowman jumps to his death 2.50
0-($2.50, 4/94)-Regular edition 2.50
0-($3.50)-Wraparound chromium-c edition 3.50
0-Gold 6.00
Yearbook 1 (12/94, $3.95) 4.00

Shang-Chi: Master of Kung Fu #2 © MAR

Shanna the She-Devil #2 © MAR

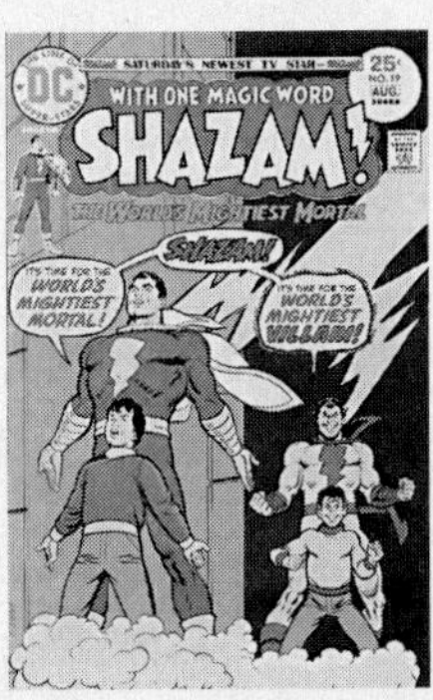

Shazam! #19 © DC

	GD	VG	FN	VF	VF/NM	NM-
	2.0	4.0	6.0	8.0	9.0	9.2

SHADOWMAN (Volume 2)
Acclaim Comics (Valiant Heroes): Mar, 1997 - No. 20 ($2.50, mature)

1-20: 1-1st app. Zero; Garth Ennis scripts begin, end #4. 2-Zero becomes new Shadowman. 4-Origin; Jack Boniface (original Shadowman) rises from the grave. 5-Jamie Delano scripts begin. 9-Copycat-c 2.50
1-Variant painted cover 2.50
#0 Gold 5.00

SHADOWMAN (Volume 3)
Acclaim Comics: July, 1999 - No. 5, Nov, 1999 ($3.95/$2.50)

1-($3.95)-Abnett & Lanning-s/Broome & Benjamin-a 4.00
2-5-($2.50): 3,4-Flip book with Unity 2000 2.50

SHADOWMASTERS
Marvel Comics: Oct, 1989 - No.4, Jan, 1990 ($3.95, squarebound, 52 pgs.)

1-4: Heath-a(i). 1-Jim Lee-c; story cont'd from Punisher 4.00

SHADOW OF THE BATMAN
DC Comics: Dec, 1985 - No. 5, Apr, 1986 ($1.75, limited series)

1-Detective-r (all have wraparound-c) 1 2 3 4 5 7
2,3,5: 3-Penguin-c & cameo. 5-Clayface app. 5.00
4-Joker-c/story 6.00
NOTE: *Austin a(new)-2i, 3i; r-2-4i.* ***Rogers*** *a(new)-1, 2p, 3p, 4, 5; r-1-5p; c-1-5.* ***Simonson*** *a-1r.*

SHADOW OF THE TORTURER, THE
Innovation: July, 1991 - No. 3, 1992 ($2.50, limited series)

1-3: Based on Pocket Books novel 2.50

SHADOW ON THE TRAIL (See Zane Grey & Four Color #604)

SHADOW PLAY (Tales of the Supernatural)
Whitman Publications: June, 1982

1-Painted-c 1 2 3 4 5 7

SHADOW REAVERS
Black Bull Ent.: Oct, 2001 - Present ($2.99)

1-5-Nelson-a; two covers for each issue 3.00
Limited Preview Edition (5/01, no cover price) 2.25

SHADOW RIDERS
Marvel Comics UK, Ltd.: June, 1993 - No. 4, Sept, 1993 ($1.75, limited series)

1-($2.50)-Embossed-c; Cable-c/story 2.50
2-4-Cable app. 2-Ghost Rider app. 2.25

SHADOWS
Image Comics: Feb, 2003 - No. 4, Nov, 2003 ($2.95)

1-4-Jade Dodge-s/Matt Camp-a/c 3.00

SHADOWS & LIGHT
Marvel Comics: Feb, 1998 - No. 3, July, 1998 ($2.99, B&W, quarterly)

1-3: 1-B&W anthology of Marvel characters; Black Widow art by Gene Ha, Hulk by Wrightson, Iron Man by Ditko & Daredevil by Stelfreeze; Stelfreeze painted-c. 2-Weeks, Sharp, Starlin, Thompson-a. 3-Buscema, Grindberg, Giffen, Layton-a 3.00

SHADOW'S FALL
DC Comics (Vertigo): Nov, 1994 - No. 6, Apr, 1995 ($2.95, limited series)

1-6: Van Fleet-c/a in all. 3.00

SHADOWS FROM BEYOND (Formerly Unusual Tales)
Charlton Comics: V2#50, October, 1966

V2#50-Ditko-c 4 8 12 22 30 38

SHADOW SLASHER
Pocket Change Comics: No. 0, 1994 - No. 6, 1995? ($2.50, B&W)

0-6 2.50

SHADOW STATE
Broadway Comics: Dec, 1995 - No. 5, Apr, 1996 ($2.50)

1-5: 1,2-Fatale back-up story; Cockrum-a(p) 2.50
Preview Edition 1,2 (10-11/95, $2.50, B&W) 2.50

SHADOW STRIKES!, THE (Pulp, radio)
DC Comics: Sept, 1989 - No.31, May, 1992 ($1.75)

1-4,7-31: 31-Mignola-c 2.50
5,6-Doc Savage x-over 4.00
Annual 1 (1989, $3.50, 68 pgs.)-Spiegle a; Kaluta-c 3.50

SHADOW WAR OF HAWKMAN
DC Comics: May, 1985 - No. 4, Aug, 1985 (limited series)

1-4 2.25

SHAGGY DOG & THE ABSENT-MINDED PROFESSOR (See Four Color #1199, Movie Comics & Walt Disney Showcase #46)(Disney-Movie)
Dell Publ. Co.: No. 985, May, 1959

Four Color #985 9 18 27 63 89 115

SHALOMAN
Al Wiesner/ Mark 1 Comics: 1989 - Present (B&W)

V1#1-Al Wiesner-s/a in all 4.50
2-9 2.50
V2 #1(The New Adventures)-4,6-10, V3 (The Legend of...) #1-12 2.75
V2 #5 (Color)-Shows Vol 2, No. 4 in indicia 3.00
V4 (The Saga of ...) #1(2004), 2 2.75

SHAMAN'S TEARS (Also see Maggie the Cat)
Image Comics (Creative Fire Studio): 5/93 - No. 2, 8/93; No. 3, 11/94 - No. 0, 1/96 ($2.50/$1.95)

0-2: 0-(DEC-c, 1/96)-Last Issue. 1-(5/93)-Embossed red foil-c; Grell-c/a & scripts in all. 2-Cover unfolds into poster (8/93-c, 7/93 inside) 2.50
3-12: 3-Begin $1.95-c. 5-Re-intro Jon Sable. 12-Re-intro Maggie the Cat (1 pg.) 2.25

SHANG-CHI: MASTER OF KUNG-FU ("Master of Kung Fu" on cover for #1&2)
Marvel Comics: Nov, 2002 - No. 6, Apr, 2003 ($2.99, limited series)

1-6-Moench-s/Gulacy-c/a 3.00
... Vol. 1: The Hellfire Apocalypse TPB (2003, $14.99) r/#1-6 15.00

SHANGRI-LA
Image Comics: Jan, 2004 ($7.95, B&W, square-bound graphic novel)

1-Marc Bryant-s/Shepherd Hendrix-a 8.00

SHANNA, THE SHE-DEVIL (See Savage Tales #8)
Marvel Comics Group: Dec, 1972 - No. 5, Aug, 1973 (All are 20¢ issues)

1-1st app. Shanna; Steranko-c; Tuska-a(p) 3 6 9 19 25 32
2-Steranko-c; heroin drug story 3 6 9 16 20 24
3-5 2 4 6 10 13 16

SHARK FIGHTERS, THE (Movie)
Dell Publishing Co.: Jan, 1957

Four Color 762-Buscema-a; photo-c 9 18 27 63 89 115

SHARKY
Image Comics: Feb, 1998 - No. 4, 1998 ($2.50, bi-monthly)

1-4: 1-Mask app.; Elliot-s/a. Horley painted-c. 3-Three covers by Horley, Bisley, & Horley/Elliot. 4-Two covers (swipe of Avengers #4 and wraparound) 2.50
1-($2.95) "$1,000,000" variant 3.00
2-($2.50) Savage Dragon variant-c 2.50

SHARP COMICS (Slightly large size)
H. C. Blackerby: Winter, 1945-46 - V1#2, Spring, 1946 (52 pgs.)

V1#1-Origin Dick Royce Planetarian 40 80 120 239 357 475
2-Origin The Pioneer; Michael Morgan, Dick Royce, Sir Gallagher, Planetarian, Steve Hagen, Weeny and Pop app. 39 78 117 222 324 425

SHARPY FOX (See Comic Capers & Funny Frolics)
I. W. Enterprises/Super Comics: 1958; 1963

1,2-I.W. Reprint (1958): 2-r/Kiddie Kapers #1 2 4 6 8 10 12
14-Super Reprint (1963) 2 4 6 8 10 12

SHATTER (See Jon Sable #25-30)
First Comics: June, 1985; Dec, 1985 - No. 14, Apr, 1988. ($1.75, Baxter paper/deluxe paper)

1 (6/85)-1st computer generated-a in a comic book (1st printing) 3.00
1-(2nd print.); 1(12/85)-14: computer generated-a & lettering in all 2.25
Special 1 (1988) 2.25

SHATTERED IMAGE
Image Comics (WildStorm Productions): Aug, 1996 - No. 4, Dec, 1996 ($2.50, limited series)

1-4: 1st Image company-wide x-over; Kurt Busiek scripts in all. 1-Tony Daniel-c/a(p). 2-Alex Ross-c/swipe (Kingdom Come) by Ryan Benjamin & Travis Charest 2.50

SHAZAM (See Giant Comics to Color, Limited Collectors' Edition & The Power Of Shazam!)

SHAZAM! (TV)(See World's Finest #253 for story from unpublished #36)
National Periodical Publ./DC Comics: Feb, 1973 - No. 35, May-June, 1978

1-1st revival of original Captain Marvel since G.A. (origin retold), by C.C. Beck; Mary Marvel & Captain Marvel Jr. app.; Superman-c 4 8 12 29 40 50
2-5: 2-Infinity photo-c.; re-intro Mr. Mind & Tawny. 3-Capt. Marvel-r. (10/46). 4-Origin retold; Capt. Marvel-r. (1949). 5-Capt. Marvel Jr. origin retold; Capt. Marvel-r. (1948, 7 pgs.) 2 4 6 11 14 18
6,7,9-11: 6-photo-c; Capt. Marvel-r (1950, 6 pgs.). 9-Mr. Mind app. 10-Last C.C. Beck issue.

Sheena, Queen of the Jungle #15 © FH

She-Hulk ('04) #2 © MAR

Shi: Black White & Red #2 © William Tucci

	GD 2.0	VG 4.0	FN 6.0	VF 8.0	VF/NM 9.0	NM- 9.2
11-Schaffenberger-a begins.	2	4	6	10	12	15
8 (100 pgs.) 8-r/Capt. Marvel Jr. by Raboy; origin/C.M. #80; origin Mary Marvel/C.M.A. #18; origin Mr. Tawny/C.M.A. #79	6	12	18	38	52	65
12-17-(All 100 pgs.). 15-vs. Lex Luthor & Mr. Mind	5	10	15	33	44	55
18-24,26-30: 21-24-All reprints. 26-Sivana app. (10/76). 27-Kid Eternity teams up w/Capt. Marvel. 28-1st S.A. app. of Black Adam. 30-1st DC app. 3 Lt. Marvels	2	4	6	8	10	12
25-1st app. Isis	2	4	6	10	13	16
31-35: 31-1st DC app. Minuteman. 34-Origin Capt. Nazi & Capt. Marvel Jr. retold	2	4	6	10	13	16

NOTE: *Reprints in #1-8, 10, 12-17, 21-24.* **Beck** *a-1-10, 12-17r, 21-24r; c-1, 3-9.* **Nasser** *c-35p.* **Newton** *a-35p.* **Raboy** *a-5r, 8r, 17r.* **Schaffenberger** *a-11, 14-20, 25, 26, 27p, 28, 29-31p, 33i, 35i; c-20, 22, 23, 25, 26i, 27i, 28-33.*

SHAZAM! AND THE SHAZAM FAMILY! ANNUAL
DC Comics: 2002 ($5.95, squarebound, one-shot)

1-Reprints Golden Age stories including 1st Mary Marvel and 1st Black Adam 6.00

SHAZAM!: POWER OF HOPE
DC Comics: Nov, 2000 ($9.95, treasury size, one-shot)

nn-Painted art by Alex Ross; story by Alex Ross and Paul Dini 10.00

SHAZAM: THE NEW BEGINNING
DC Comics: Apr, 1987 - No. 4, July, 1987 (Legends spin-off) (Limited series)

1-4: 1-New origin & 1st modern app. Captain Marvel; Marvel Family cameo. 2-4-Sivana & Black Adam app. 3.00

SHEA THEATRE COMICS
Shea Theatre: No date (1940's) (32 pgs.)

	GD	VG	FN	VF	VF/NM	NM-
nn-Contains Rocket Comics; MLJ cover in one color	10	20	30	58	77	95

SHE-BAT (See Murcielaga, She-Bat & Valeria the She-Bat)

SHEENA (Movie)
Marvel Comics: Dec, 1984 - No. 2, Feb, 1985 (limited series)

1,2-r/Marvel Comics Super Special #34; Tanya Roberts movie 3.00

SHEENA, QUEEN OF THE JUNGLE (See Jerry Iger's Classic..., Jumbo Comics, & 3-D Sheena)
Fiction House Magazines: Spr, 1942; No. 2, Wint, 1942-43; No. 3, Spr, 1943; No. 4, Fall, 1948; No. 5, Sum, 1949; No. 6, Spr, 1950; No. 7-10, 1950(nd); No. 11, Spr, 1951 - No. 18, Wint, 1952-53 (#1-3: 68 pgs.; #4-7: 52 pgs.)

	GD	VG	FN	VF	VF/NM	NM-
1-Sheena begins	262	524	786	1638	2519	3400
2 (Winter, 1942-43)	112	224	336	700	1075	1450
3 (Spring, 1943)	83	166	249	519	797	1075
4,5 (Fall, 1948, Sum, 1949): 4-New logo; cover swipe from Jumbo #20	52	104	156	317	484	650
6,7 (Spring, 1950, 1950)	44	88	132	268	409	550
8-10(1950 - Win/50, 36 pgs.)	40	80	120	241	363	485
11-18: 15-Cover swipe from Jumbo #43. 18-Used in **POP**, pg. 98	36	72	108	204	297	390
I.W. Reprint #9-r/#18; c-r/White Princess #3	5	10	15	36	48	60

NOTE: **Baker** *c-5-10?* **Whitman** *c-11-18(most).*

SHEENA 3-D SPECIAL (Also see Blackthorne 3-D Series #1)
Eclipse Comics: Jan, 1985 ($2.00)

1-Dave Stevens-c 5.00

SHE-HULK (Also see The Savage She-Hulk & The Sensational She-Hulk)
Marvel Comics: May, 2004 - Present ($2.99)

1-4-Bobillo-a/Slott-s/Granov-c. 1-Avengers app. 4-Spider-Man-c/app. 3.00
5-9:Mayhew-c. 9-Pelletier-a 3.00
Vol. 1: Singe Green Female TPB (2004, $14.99) r/#1-6 15.00

SHERIFF BOB DIXON'S CHUCK WAGON (TV) (See Wild Bill Hickok #22)
Avon Periodicals: Nov, 1950

	GD	VG	FN	VF	VF/NM	NM-
1-Kinstler-c/a(3)	14	28	42	79	110	140

SHERIFF OF TOMBSTONE
Charlton Comics: Nov, 1958 - No. 17, Sept, 1961

	GD	VG	FN	VF	VF/NM	NM-
V1#1-Giordano-c; Severin-a	7	14	21	51	71	90
2	4	8	12	27	36	45
3-10	3	6	9	19	25	32
11-17	3	6	9	16	20	25

SHERLOCK HOLMES (See Marvel Preview, New Adventures of..., & Spectacular Stories)

SHERLOCK HOLMES (All New Baffling Adventures of...)(Young Eagle #3 on?)
Charlton Comics: Oct, 1955 - No. 2, Mar, 1956

	GD	VG	FN	VF	VF/NM	NM-
1-Dr. Neff, Ghost Breaker app.	40	80	120	244	372	500
2	38	76	114	219	320	420

SHERLOCK HOLMES (Also see The Joker)
National Periodical Publications: Sept-Oct, 1975

	GD	VG	FN	VF	VF/NM	NM-
1-Cruz-a; Simonson-c	3	6	9	18	23	28

SHERRY THE SHOWGIRL (Showgirls #4)
Atlas Comics: July, 1956 - No. 3, Dec, 1956; No. 5, Apr, 1957 - No. 7, Aug, 1957

	GD	VG	FN	VF	VF/NM	NM-
1-Dan DeCarlo-c/a in all	16	32	48	92	131	170
2	11	22	33	64	87	110
3,5-7	10	20	30	58	77	95

SHE'S JOSIE (See Josie)

SHEVA'S WAR
DC Comics (Helix): Oct, 1998 - No. 5, Feb, 1999 ($2.95, mini-series)

1-5-Christopher Moeller-s/painted-a/c 3.00

SHI (one-shots)
Crusade Comics

...: Akai (2001, $2.99)-Intro. Victoria Cross; Tucci-a/c; J.C. Vaughn-s 3.00
...: Akai Victoria Cross Ed. ($5.95, edition of 2000) variant Tucci-c 6.00
...: C.G.I. (2001, $4.99) preview of unpublished series 5.00
.../ Cyblade: The Battle for the Independents (9/95, $2.95) Tucci-c; Hellboy, Bone app. 3.00
.../ Cyblade: The Battle for the Independents (9/95, $2.95) Silvestri variant-c . 3.00
.../ Daredevil: Honor Thy Mother (1/97, $2.95) Flip book 3.00
...: Judgment Night (200, $3.99) Wolverine app.; Battlebook card and pages; Tucci-a 4.00
...: Kaidan (10/96, $2.95) Two covers; Tucci-c; Jae Lee wraparound-c 3.00
...: Masquerade (3/98, $3.50) Painted art by Lago, Texeira, and others 3.50
...: Nightstalkers (9/97, $3.50) Painted art by Val Mayerik 3.50
...: Rekishi (1/97, $2.95) Character bios and story summaries of Shi: The Way of the Warrior told in Detective Joe Labianca's point of view; Christopher Golden script; Tucci-c; J.G. Jones-a; flip book w/Shi: East Wind Rain preview 3.00
...: The Art of War Tourbook (1998, $4.95) Blank cover for sketches; early Tucci-a inside 5.00
.../ Vampirella (10/97, $2.95) Ellis-s/Lau-a 3.00
... Vs. Tomoe (8/96, $3.95) Tucci-a/scripts; wraparound foil-c 4.00
... Vs. Tomoe (6/96, $5.00. B&W)-Preview Ed.; sold at San Diego Comic Con 5.00

SHI: BLACK, WHITE AND RED
Crusade Comics: Mar, 1998 - No. 2, May, 1998 ($2.95, B&W&Red, mini-series)

1,2-J.G. Jones-painted art 3.00
...- Year of the Dragon Collected Edition (2000, $5.95) r/#1&2 6.00

SHIDIMA
Image Comics: Jan, 2001 - No. 7, Nov, 2002 ($2.95, limited series)

1-7-Prequel to Warlands 3.00
#0-(10/01, $2.25) Short story and sketch pages 2.25

SHI: EAST WIND RAIN
Crusade Comics: Nov, 1997 - No. 2, Feb, 1998 ($3.50, limited series)

1,2-Shi at WW2 Pearl Harbor 3.50

S.H.I.E.L.D. (Nick Fury & His Agents of...) (Also see Nick Fury)
Marvel Comics Group: Feb, 1973 - No. 5, Oct, 1973 (All 20¢ issues)

	GD	VG	FN	VF	VF/NM	NM-
1-All contain reprint stories from Strange Tales #146-155; new Steranko-c	2	4	6	11	14	18
2-New Steranko flag-c	2	4	6	9	11	14
3-5: 3-Kirby/Steranko-c(r). 4-Steranko-c(r)	1	2	3	5	7	9

NOTE: **Buscema** *a-3p(r).* **Kirby** *layouts 1-5; c-3 (w/***Steranko***).* **Steranko** *a-3r, 4r(2).*

SHIELD, THE (Becomes Shield-Steel Sterling #3; #1 titled Lancelot Strong; also see Advs. of the Fly, Double Life of Private Strong, Fly Man, Mighty Comics, The Mighty Crusaders, The Original... & Pep Comics #1)
Archie Enterprises, Inc.: June, 1983 - No. 2, Aug, 1983

1,2: Steel Sterling app. 2-Kanigher-s 4.00
America's 1st Patriotic Comic Book Hero, The Shield (2002, $12.95, TPB) r/Pep Comics #1-5, Shield-Wizard Comics #1; foreward by Robert M. Overstreet 13.00

SHIELD, THE: SPOTLIGHT (TV)
IDW Publishing: Jan, 2004 - No. 5, May, 2004 ($3.99)

1-5-Jeff Marriote-s/Jean Diaz-a/Tommy Lee Edwards-c 4.00
TPB (7/04, $19.99) r/#1-5; Michael Chiklis photo-c 20.00

SHIELD-STEEL STERLING (Formerly The Shield)
Archie Enterprises, Inc.: No. 3, Dec, 1983 (Becomes Steel Sterling No. 4)

3-Nino-a; Steel Sterling by Kanigher & Barreto 3.00

SHIELD WIZARD COMICS (Also see Pep Comics & Top-Notch Comics)
MLJ Magazines: Summer, 1940 - No. 13, Spring, 1944

Shield-Wizard Comics #5 © MLJ

Shinobi #1 © SEGA

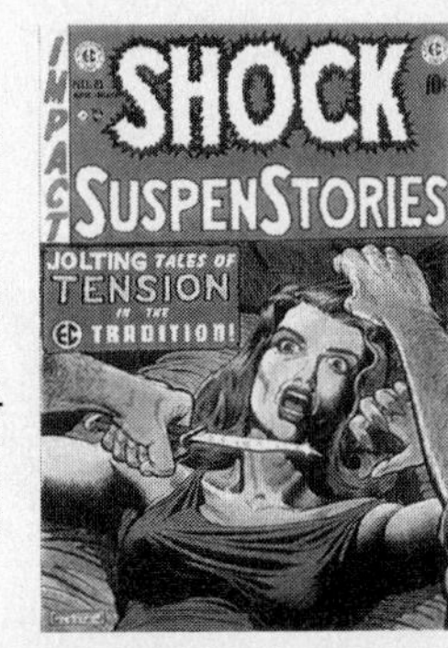

Shock SuspenStories #8 © WMG

GD 2.0 | VG 4.0 | FN 6.0 | VF 8.0 | VF/NM 9.0 | NM- 9.2

1-(V1#5 on inside)-Origin The Shield by Irving Novick & The Wizard by Ed Ashe, Jr; Flag-c 484 968 1452 3388 5444 7500
2-(Winter/40)-Origin The Shield retold; Wizard's sidekick, Roy the Super Boy begins (see Top-Notch #8 for 1st app.) 246 492 738 1538 2369 3200
3,4 150 300 450 938 1444 1950
5-Dusty, the Boy Detective begins 131 262 393 819 1260 1700
6,7: 6-Roy the Super Boy app. 7-Shield dons new costume (Summer, 1942); S & K-c? 127 254 381 794 1222 1650
8-Bondage-c; HItler photo on-c 131 262 393 819 1260 1700
9-13: 9,13-Bondage-c 90 180 270 563 869 1175

NOTE: ***Bob Montana** c-13. **Novick** c-1-6,8-11. **Harry Sahle** c-12.*

SHI: FAN EDITIONS
Crusade Comics: 1997

1-3-Two covers polybagged in FAN #19-21 3.00
1-3-Gold editions 4.00

SHI: HEAVEN AND EARTH
Crusade Comics: June, 1997 - No. 4, Apr, 1998 ($2.95)

1-4 3.00
4-($4.95) Pencil-c variant 5.00
Rising Sun Edition-signed by Tucci in FanClub Starter Pack 4.00
"Tora No Shi" variant-c 3.00

SHI: JU-NEN
Dark Horse Comics: July, 2004 - Present ($2.99, mini-series)

1-Tucci-s/a; origin retold 3.00

SHINING KNIGHT (See Adventure Comics #66)

SHINOBI (Based on Sega video game)
Dark Horse Comics: Aug, 2002 ($2.99, one-shot)

1-Medina-a/c 3.00

SHIP AHOY
Spotlight Publishers: Nov, 1944 (52 pgs.)

1-L. B. Cole-c 20 40 60 112 161 210

SHIP OF FOOLS
Image Comics: Aug, 1997 - No. 3 ($2.95, B&W)

0-3-Glass-s/Oeming-a 3.00

SHI: POISONED PARADISE
Avatar Press: July, 2002 - No. 2, Aug, 2002 ($3.50, limited series)

1,2-Vaughn and Tucci-s/Waller-a; 1-Four covers 3.50

SHIPWRECKED! (Disney-Movie)
Disney Comics: 1990 ($5.95, graphic novel, 68 pgs.)

nn-adaptation; Spiegle-a 6.00

SHI: SEMPO
Avatar Press: Aug, 2003 - No. 2, ($3.50, B&W, limited series)

1,2-Vaughn and Tucci-s/Alves-a; 1-Four covers 3.50

SHI: SENRYAKU
Crusade Comics: Aug, 1995 - No. 3, Nov, 1995 ($2.95, limited series)

1-3: 1-Tucci-c; Quesada, Darrow, Sim, Lee, Smith-a. 2-Tucci-c; Silvestri, Balent, Perez, Mack-a. 3-Jusko-c; Hughes, Ramos, Bell, Moore-a 3.00
1-variant-c (no logo) 4.00
Hardcover ($24.95)-r/#1-3; Frazetta-c. 25.00
Trade Paperback ($13.95)-r/#1-3; Frazetta-c. 14.00

SHI: THE ILLUSTRATED WARRIOR
Crusade Comics: 2002 - No. 7, 2003 ($2.99, B&W)

1-7-Story text with Tucci full page art 3.00

SHI: THE SERIES
Crusade Comics: Aug, 1997 - No. 13 ($2.95, color #1-10, B&W #11)

1-10 3.00
11-13: 11-B&W. 12-Color; Lau-a 3.00
#0 Convention Edition 5.00

SHI: THE WAY OF THE WARRIOR
Crusade Comics: Mar, 1994 - No. 12, Apr, 1997 ($2.50/$2.95)

1/2 4.00
1 2 4 6 8 10 12
1-Commemorative ed., B&W, new-c; given out at 1994 San Diego Comic Con 2 4 6 11 14 18
1-Fan appreciation edition -r/#1 2.25
1-Fan appreciation edition (variant) 6.00
1- 10th Anniversary Edition (2004, $2.99) 3.00
2 5.00
2-Commemorative edition (3,000) 2 4 6 10 13 16
2-Fan appreciation edition -r/#2 2.25
3 4.00
4-7: 4-Silvestri poster. 7-Tomoe app. 2.25
5,6: 5-Silvestri variant-c. 6-Tomoe #1 variant-c 3.00
5-Gold edition 12.00
6,8-12: 6-Fan appreciation edition 2.25
8-Combo Gold edition 6.00
8-Signed Edition-(5000) 3.00
Trade paperback (1995, $12.95)-r/#1-4 13.00
Trade paperback (1995, $14.95)-r/#1-4 revised; Julie Bell-c 15.00

SHI: YEAR OF THE DRAGON
Crusade Comics: 2000 - No. 3, 2000 ($2.99, limited series)

1-3: 1-Two covers; Tucci-a/c; flashback to teen-aged Ana 3.00

SHMOO (See Al Capp's... & Washable Jones &...)

SHOCK (Magazine)
Stanley Publ.: May, 1969 - V3#4, Sept, 1971 (B&W reprints from horror comics, including some pre-code) (No V2#1,3)

V1#1-Cover-r/Weird Tales of the Future #7 by Bernard Baily; r/Weird Chills #1 6 12 18 40 55 70
2-Wolverton-r/Weird Mysteries 5; r-Weird Mysteries #7 used in **SOTI**; cover reprints cover to Weird Chills #1 5 10 15 33 44 55
3,5,6 3 7 10 21 28 35
4-Harrison/Williamson-r/Forbid. Worlds #6 4 8 12 24 32 40
V2#2(5/70), V1#8(7/70), V2#4(9/70)-6(1/71), V3#1-4: V2#4-Cover swipe from Weird Mysteries #6 3 6 9 18 24 30

NOTE: ***Disbrow** r-V2#4; Bondage c-V1#4, V2#6, V3#1.*

SHOCK DETECTIVE CASES (Formerly Crime Fighting Detective)
(Becomes Spook Detective Cases No. 22)
Star Publications: No. 20, Sept, 1952 - No. 21, Nov, 1952

20,21-L.B. Cole-c; based on true crime cases 24 48 72 138 199 260

NOTE: ***Palais** a-20. No. 21-Fox-r.*

SHOCK ILLUSTRATED (...Adult Crime Stories; Magazine format)
E. C. Comics: Sept-Oct, 1955 - No. 3, Spring, 1956 (Adult Entertainment on-c #1,2)(All 25¢)

1-All by Kamen; drugs, prostitution, wife swapping 17 34 51 95 135 175
2-Williamson-a redrawn from Crime SuspenStories #13 plus Ingels, Crandall, Evans & part Torres-i; painted-c 18 36 54 102 146 190
3-Only 100 known copies bound & given away at E.C. office; Crandall, Evans-a; painted-c; shows May, 1956 on-c 104 208 312 650 1000 1350

SHOCKING MYSTERY CASES (Formerly Thrilling Crime Cases)
Star Publications: No. 50, Sept, 1952 - No. 60, Oct, 1954 (All crime reprints?)

50-Disbrow "Frankenstein" story 42 84 126 256 391 525
51-Disbrow-a 28 56 84 158 229 300
52-60: 56-Drug use story 26 52 78 147 211 275

NOTE: ***L. B. Cole** covers on all; a-60(2 pgs.). **Hollingsworth** a-52. **Morisi** a-55.*

SHOCKING TALES DIGEST MAGAZINE
Harvey Publications: Oct, 1981 (95¢)

1-1957-58-r; Powell, Kirby, Nostrand-a 2 4 6 9 11 14

SHOCK ROCKETS
Image Comics (Gorilla): Apr, 2000 - No. 6, Oct, 2000 ($2.50)

1-6-Busiek-s/Immonen & Grawbadger-a. 6-Flip book w/Superstar preview 2.50
...: We Have Ignition TPB (Dark Horse, 8/04, $14.95, 6" x 9") r/#1-6 15.00

SHOCK SUSPENSTORIES
E. C. Comics: Feb-Mar, 1952 - No. 18, Dec-Jan, 1954-55

1-Classic Feldstein electrocution-c 78 156 234 585 855 1125
2 44 88 132 330 483 635
3,4: 4-Used in **SOTI**, pg. 387,388 32 64 96 240 350 460
5-Hanging-c 37 74 111 278 404 530
6-Classic hooded vigilante bondage-c 41 82 123 308 454 600
7-Classic face melting-c 47 94 141 353 514 675
8-Williamson-a 31 62 93 233 344 455
9-11: 9-Injury to eye panel. 10-Junkie story 27 54 81 203 294 385
12- "The Monkey" classic junkie cover/story; anti-drug propaganda issue 34 68 102 255 373 490
13-Frazetta's only solo story for E.C., 7 pgs. 37 74 111 278 404 530
14-Used in Senate Investigation hearings 22 44 66 165 240 315

Showcase #6 © DC

Showcase #34 © DC

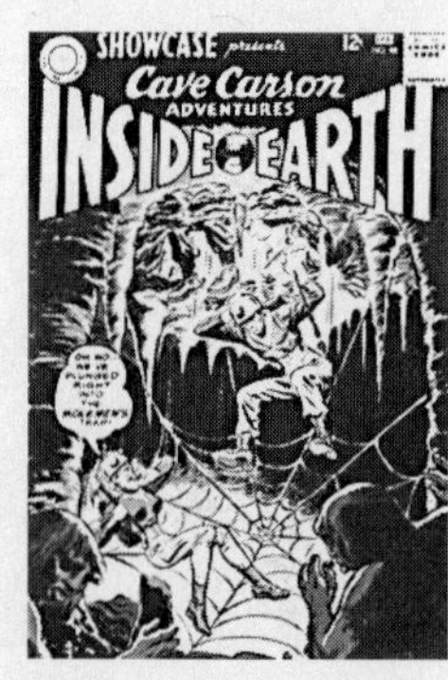

Showcase #48 © DC

GD VG FN VF VF/NM NM-
2.0 4.0 6.0 8.0 9.0 9.2

15-Used in 1954 Reader's Digest article, "For the Kiddies to Read"; Bill Gaines stars in prose story "The EC Caper" 20 40 60 150 218 285
16-18: 16- "Red Dupe" editorial; rape story 19 38 57 143 209 275

NOTE: ***Ray Bradbury** adaptations-1, 7, 9. **Craig** a-11; c-11. **Crandall** a-9-13, 15-18. **Davis** a-1-5. **Evans** a-7, 8, 14-18; c-16-18. **Feldstein** c-1, 7-9, 12. **Ingels** a-1, 2, 6. **Kamen** a-in all; c-10, 13, 15. **Krigstein** a-14, 18. **Orlando** a-1, 3-7, 9, 10, 12, 16, 17. **Wood** a-2-15; c-2-6, 14.*

SHOCK SUSPENSTORIES
Russ Cochran/Gemstone Publishing: Sept, 1992 - No. 18, Dec, 1996 ($1.50/$2.00/$2.50, quarterly)

1-18: 1-3: Reprints with original-c. 17-r/HOF #17 2.50

SHOGUN WARRIORS
Marvel Comics Group: Feb, 1979 - No. 20, Sept, 1980 (Based on Mattel toys of the classic Japanese animation characters) (1-3: 35¢; 4-19: 40¢; 20: 50¢)

1-Raydeen, Combatra, & Dangard Ace begin; Trimpe-a 2 4 6 8 10 12
2-20: 2-Lord Maurkon & Elementals of Evil app.; Rok-Korr app. 6-Shogun vs. Shogun. 7,8-Cerberus. 9-Starchild. 11-Austin-c. 12-Simonson-c. 14-16-Doctor Demonicus. 17-Juggernaut. 19,20-FF x-over 1 2 3 5 6 8
1-3: Reprints 3.00

SHOOK UP (Magazine) (Satire)
Dodsworth Publ. Co.: Nov, 1958

V1#1 4 8 12 29 40 50

SHORT RIBS
Dell Publishing Co.: No. 1333, Apr - June, 1962

Four Color 1333 6 12 18 43 59 75

SHORTSTOP SQUAD (Baseball)
Ultimate Sports Ent. Inc.: 1999 ($3.95, one-shot)

1-Ripken Jr., Larkin, Jeter, Rodriguez app.; Edwards-c/a 4.00

SHORT STORY COMICS (See Hello Pal,...)

SHORTY SHINER (The Five-Foot Fighter in the Ten Gallon Hat)
Dandy Magazine (Charles Biro): June, 1956 - No. 3, Oct, 1956

1 7 14 21 37 46 55
2,3 5 10 15 24 30 35

SHOT CALLERZ
Oni Press: May, 2002 - No. 4, Sept, 2002 ($2.95, B&W, limited series)

1-4-Gary Phillips-s/Brett Weldele-a 3.00

SHOTGUN SLADE (TV)
Dell Publishing Co.: No. 1111, July-Sept, 1960

Four Color 1111-Photo-c 7 14 21 51 71 90

SHOWCASE (See Cancelled Comic Cavalcade & New Talent...)
National Per. Publ./DC Comics: 3-4/56 - No. 93, 9/70; No. 94, 8-9/77 - No. 104, 9/78

1-Fire Fighters; w/Fireman Farrell 262 524 786 2293 3897 5500
2-Kings of the Wild; Kubert-a (animal stories) 81 162 243 689 1120 1550
3-The Frogmen by Russ Heath; Heath greytone-c (early DC example, 7-8/56) 79 158 237 672 1086 1500
4-Origin/1st app. The Flash (1st DC Silver Age hero, Sept-Oct, 1956); Kanigher-s; Infantino & Kubert-c/a; 1st app. Iris West and The Turtle; r/in Secret Origins #1 ('61 & '73); Flash shown reading G.A. Flash Comics #13; back-up story w/Broome-s/Infantino & Kubert-a 1200 2400 3600 13,200 27,600 42,000
5-Manhunters 80 160 240 680 1103 1525
6-Origin/1st app. Challengers of the Unknown by Kirby, partly r/in Secret Origins #1 & Challengers #64,65 (1st S.A. hero team & 1st original concept S.A. series)(1-2/57) 286 572 858 2503 4252 6000
7-Challengers of the Unknown by Kirby (2nd app.) reprinted in Challengers of the Unknown #75 145 290 435 1233 1992 2750
8-The Flash (5-6/57, 2nd app.); origin & 1st app. Captain Cold 820 1640 2460 7503 12,252 17,000
9-Lois Lane (Pre-#1, 7-8/57) (1st Showcase character to win own series) Superman app. on-c 625 1250 1875 4700 7850 11,000
10-Lois Lane; Jor-el cameo; Superman app. on-c 226 452 678 1978 3364 4750
11-Challengers of the Unknown by Kirby (3rd) 139 278 417 1182 1916 2650
12-Challengers of the Unknown by Kirby (4th) 139 278 417 1182 1916 2650
13-The Flash (3rd app.); origin Mr. Element 314 628 942 2873 4887 6900
14-The Flash (4th app.); origin Dr. Alchemy, former Mr. Element (rare in NM) 329 658 987 3010 5130 7250
15-Space Ranger (7-8/58, 1st app.) 157 314 471 1374 2262 3150
16-Space Ranger (9-10/58, 2nd app.) 80 160 240 680 1103 1525
17-(11-12/58)-Adventures on Other Worlds; origin/1st app. Adam Strange by Gardner Fox & Mike Sekowsky 190 380 570 1663 2732 3800

GD VG FN VF VF/NM NM-
2.0 4.0 6.0 8.0 9.0 9.2

18-Adventures on Other Worlds (2nd A. Strange) 100 200 300 850 1375 1900
19-Adam Strange; 1st Adam Strange logo 111 222 333 944 1522 2100
20-Rip Hunter; origin & 1st app. (5-6/59); Moriera-a 84 168 252 714 1157 1600
21-Rip Hunter (7-8/59, 2nd app.); Sekowsky-c/a 47 94 141 376 588 800
22-Origin & 1st app. Silver Age Green Lantern by Gil Kane and John Broome (9-10/59); reprinted in Secret Origins #2 341 682 1023 3120 5310 7500
23-Green Lantern (11-12/59, 2nd app.); nuclear explosion-c 129 258 387 1097 1774 2450
24-Green Lantern (1-2/60, 3rd app.) 129 258 387 1097 1774 2450
25,26-Rip Hunter by Kubert. 25-Grey tone-c 33 66 99 248 387 525
27-Sea Devils (7-8/60, 1st app.); Heath-c/a 71 142 213 604 977 1350
28-Sea Devils (9-10/60, 2nd app.); Heath-c/a 40 80 120 300 468 635
29-Sea Devils; Heath-c/a; grey tone c-27-29 40 80 120 300 468 635
30-Origin Silver Age Aquaman (1-2/61) (see Adventure #260 for 1st S.A. origin) 67 134 201 570 923 1275
31,32-Aquaman 40 80 120 300 468 635
33-Aquaman 41 82 123 308 482 655
34-Origin & 1st app. Silver Age Atom by Gil Kane & Murphy Anderson (9-10/61); reprinted in Secret Origins #2 116 232 348 986 1593 2200
35-The Atom by Gil Kane (2nd); last 10¢ issue 63 126 189 536 868 1200
36-The Atom by Gil Kane (1-2/62, 3rd app.) 50 100 150 413 657 900
37-Metal Men (3-4/62, 1st app.) 56 112 168 476 776 1075
38-Metal Men (5-6/62, 2nd app.) 40 80 120 300 470 640
39-Metal Men (7-8/62, 3rd app.) 31 62 93 228 352 475
40-Metal Men (9-10/62, 4th app.) 29 58 87 206 316 425
41,42-Tommy Tomorrow (parts 1 & 2). 42-Origin 19 38 57 134 205 275
43-Dr. No (James Bond); Nodel-a; originally published as British Classics Illustrated #158A & as #6 in a European Detective series, all with diff. painted-c. This Showcase #43 version is actually censored, deleting all racial skin color and dialogue thought to be racially demeaning (1st DC S.A. movie adaptation)(based on Ian Fleming novel & movie) 41 82 123 318 497 675
44-Tommy Tomorrow 12 24 36 86 131 175
45-Sgt. Rock (7-8/63); pre-dates B&B #52; origin retold; Heath-c 30 60 90 218 334 450
46,47-Tommy Tomorrow 11 22 33 77 114 150
48,49-Cave Carson (3rd tryout series; see B&B) 9 18 27 65 93 120
50,51-I Spy (Danger Trail-r by Infantino), King Farady story (#50 has new 4 pg. story) 8 16 24 58 82 105
52-Cave Carson 8 16 24 58 82 105
53,54-G.I. Joe (11-12/64, 1-2/65); Heath-a 12 24 36 86 131 175
55-Dr. Fate & Hourman (3-4/65); origin of each in text; 1st solo app. G.A. Green Lantern in Silver Age (pre-dates Gr. Lantern #40); 1st S.A. app. Solomon Grundy 26 52 78 184 282 380
56-Dr. Fate & Hourman 15 30 45 107 164 220
57-Enemy Ace by Kubert (7-8/65, 4th app. after Our Army at War #155) 22 44 66 158 242 325
58-Enemy Ace by Kubert (5th app.) 19 38 57 134 205 275
59-Teen Titans (11-12/65, 3rd app.) 12 24 36 87 134 180
60-1st S. A. app. The Spectre; Anderson-a (1-2/66); origin in text 30 60 90 213 327 440
61-The Spectre by Anderson (2nd app.) 15 30 45 109 167 225
62-Origin & 1st app. Inferior Five (5-6/66) 10 20 30 73 107 140
63,65-Inferior Five. 63-Hulk parody. 65-X-Men parody (11-12/66) 7 14 21 46 63 80
64-The Spectre by Anderson (5th app.) 15 30 45 105 160 215
66,67-B'wana Beast 5 10 15 33 44 55
68-Maniaks (1st app., spoof of The Monkees) 5 10 15 33 44 55
69,71-Maniaks. 71-Woody Allen-c/app. 5 10 15 33 44 55
70-Binky (9-10/67)-Tryout issue; 1950's Leave It To Binky reprints with art changes 6 12 18 40 55 70
72-Top Gun (Johnny Thunder-r)-Toth-a 5 10 15 33 44 55
73-Origin/1st app. Creeper; Ditko-c/a (3-4/68) 15 30 45 105 160 215
74-Intro/1st app. Anthro; Post-c/a (5/68) 10 20 30 70 100 130
75-Origin/1st app. Hawk & the Dove; Ditko-c/a 13 26 39 92 141 190
76-1st app. Bat Lash (8/68) 8 16 24 53 74 95
77-1st app. Angel & The Ape (9/68) 8 16 24 53 74 95
78-1st app. Jonny Double (11/68) 5 10 15 33 44 55
79-1st app. Dolphin (12/68); Aqualad origin-r 7 14 21 46 63 80
80-1st S.A. app. Phantom Stranger (1/69); Neal Adams-c 9 18 27 65 93 120
81-Windy & Willy; r/Many Loves of Dobie Gillis #26 with art changes 5 10 15 36 48 60
82-1st app. Nightmaster (5/69) by Grandenetti & Giordano; Kubert-c 8 16 24 53 74 95

Showcase '95 #2 © DC

Shrek #2 © DreamWorks

Shut Up and Die #1 © James Hudnall

GD 2.0 | VG 4.0 | FN 6.0 | VF 8.0 | VF/NM 9.0 | NM- 9.2

83,84-Nightmaster by Wrightson w/Jones/Kaluta ink assist in each; Kubert-c.
83-Last 12¢ issue 84-Origin retold; begin 15¢ 7 14 21 51 71 90
85-87-Firehair; Kubert-a 3 6 9 18 24 30
88-90-Jason's Quest: 90-Manhunter 2070 app. 3 6 9 16 20 25
91-93-Manhunter 2070: 92-Origin. 93-(9/70) Last 15¢ issue
3 6 9 16 20 25
94-Intro/origin new Doom Patrol & Robotman(8-9/77) 2 4 6 11 14 18
95,96-The Doom Patrol. 95-Origin Celsius 1 2 3 5 7 9
97-99-Power Girl; origin-97,98; JSA cameos 1 2 3 5 7 9
100-(52 pgs.)-Most Showcase characters featured 2 4 6 10 12 15
101-103-Hawkman; Adam Strange x-over 1 2 3 5 7 9
104-(52 pgs.)-O.S.S. Spies at War 1 2 3 5 7 9
NOTE: ***Anderson** a-22-24i, 34-36i, 55, 56, 60, 61, 64, 101-103i; c-50i, 51i, 55, 56, 60, 61, 64. **Aparo** c-94-96. **Boring** c-10. **Estrada** a-104. **Fraden** c(p)-30, 31, 33. **Heath** c-3, 27-29. **Infantino** c/a(p)-4, 8, 13, 14; c-50p, 51p. **Gil Kane** a-22-24p, 34-36p; c-17-19, 22-24p(w/**Giella**), 31. **Kane/Anderson** c-34-36. **Kirby** c-11, 12. **Kirby/Stein** c-6, 7. **Kubert** a-2, 4i, 25, 26, 45, 53, 54, 72; c-25, 26, 53, 54, 57, 58, 82-87, 101-104; c-2, 4i. **Moriera** c-5. **Orlando** a-62p, 63p, 97i; c-62, 63, 97i. **Sekowsky** a-65p. **Sparling** a-78. **Staton** a-94, 95-99p, 100; c-97-100p.*

SHOWCASE '93
DC Comics: Jan, 1993 - No. 12, Dec, 1993 ($1.95, limited series, 52 pgs.)

1-12: 1-Begin 4 part Catwoman story & 6 part Blue Devil story; begin Cyborg story; Art Adams/Austin-c. 3-Flash by Travis Charest (p). 6-Azrael in Bat-costume (2 pgs.). 7,8-Knightfall parts 13 & 14. 6-10-Deathstroke app. (6,10-cameo). 9,10-Austin-i. 10-Azrael as Batman in new costume app.; Gulacy-c. 11-Perez-c. 12-Creeper app.; Alan Grant scripts. 3.00

NOTE: ***Chaykin** c-9. **Fabry** c-8. **Giffen** a-12. **Golden** c-3. **Zeck** c-6.*

SHOWCASE '94
DC Comics: Jan, 1994 - No. 12, Dec, 1994 ($1.95, limited series, 52 pgs.)

1-12: 1,2-Joker & Gunfire stories. 1-New Gods. 4-Riddler story. 5-Huntress-c/story w/app. new Batman. 6-Huntress-c/story w/app. Robin; Atom story. 7-Penguin story by Peter David, P. Craig Russell, & Michael T. Gilbert; Penguin-c by Jae Lee. 8,9-Scarface origin story by Alan Grant, John Wagner,& Teddy Kristiansen; Prelude to Zero Hour. 10-Zero Hour tie-in story. 11-Man-Bat. 3.00
NOTE: ***Alan Grant** scripts-3, 4. **Kelley Jones** c-12. **Mignola** c-3. **Nebres** a(i)-2. **Quesada** c-10. **Russell** a-7p. **Simonson** c-5.*

SHOWCASE '95
DC Comics: Jan, 1995 - No. 12, Dec, 1995 ($2.50/$2.95, limited series)

1-4-Supergirl story. 3-Eradicator-c.; The Question story. 4-Thorn c/story 3.00
5-12: 5-Thorn-c/story; begin $2.95-c. 8-Spectre story. 12-The Shade story by James Robinson & Wade Von Grawbadger; Maitresse story by Chris Claremont & Alan Davis 3.00

SHOWCASE '96
DC Comics: Jan, 1996 - No. 12, Dec, 1996 ($2.95, limited series)

1-12: 1-Steve Geppi cameo. 3-Black Canary & Lois Lane-c/story; Deadman story by Jamie Delano & Wade Von Grawbadger, Gary Frank-c. 4-Firebrand & Guardian-c/story; The Shade & Dr. Fate "Times Past" story by James Robinson & Matt Smith begins, ends #5. 6-Superboy-c/app.; Atom app.; Capt. Marvel (Mary Marvel)-c/app. 8-Supergirl by David & Dodson. 11-Scare Tactics app. 11,12-Legion of Super-Heroes vs. Brainiac. 12-Jesse Quick app. 3.00

SHOWGIRLS (Formerly Sherry the Showgirl #3)
Atlas Comics (MPC No. 2): No. 4, 2/57; June, 1957 - No. 2, Aug, 1957

4-(2/57) Dan DeCarlo-c/a begins 10 20 30 58 77 95
1-(6/57) Millie, Sherry, Chili, Pearl & Hazel begin 13 26 39 74 102 130
2 10 20 30 58 77 95

SHREK (Movie)
Dark Horse Comics: Sept, 2003 - No. 3, Dec, 2003 ($2.99, limited series)

1-3-Takes place after 1st movie; Evanier-s/Bachs-a; CGI cover 3.00

SHROUD, THE (See Super-Villain Team-Up #5)
Marvel Comics: Mar, 1994 - No. 4, June, 1994 ($1.75, mini-series)

1-4: 1,2,4-Spider-Man & Scorpion app. 2.25

SHROUD OF MYSTERY
Whitman Publications: June, 1982

1 1 2 3 4 5 7

SHUT UP AND DIE
Image Comics/Halloween: 1998 - No. 3, 1998 ($2.95,B&W, bi-monthly)

1-3: Hudnall-s 3.00

SICK (Sick Special #131) (Magazine) (Satire)
Feature Publ./Headline Publ./Crestwood Publ. Co./Hewfred Publ./ Pyramid Comm./Charlton Publ. No. 109 (4/76) on: Aug, 1960 - No. 134, Fall, 1980

V1#1-Jack Paar photo on-c; Torres-a; Untouchables-s; Ben Hur movie photo-s
16 32 48 114 175 235
2-Torres-a; Elvis app.; Lenny Bruce app. 10 20 30 72 104 135
3-5-Torres-a in all. 3-Khruschev-c; Hitler-s. 4-Newhart-s; Castro-s; John Wayne. 5-JFK/Castro-c; Elvis pin-up; Hitler. 9 18 27 63 89 115
6-Photo-s of Ricky Nelson & Marilyn Monroe; JFK 10 20 30 67 96 125
V2#1,2,4-8 (#7,8,10-14): 1-(#7) Hitler-s; Brando photo-s. 2-(#8) Dick Clark-s. 4-(#10) Untouchables-c; Candid Camera-s. 5-(#11) Nixon-c; Lone Ranger-s; JFK-s. 6-(#12) Beatnik-c/s. 8-(#14) Liz Taylor pin-up, JFK-s; Dobie Gillis-s; Sinatra & Dean Martin photo-s
8 16 24 58 82 105
3-(#9) Marilyn Monroe/JFK-c; Kingston Trio-s 9 18 27 63 89 115
V3#1-7(#15-21): 1-(#15) JFK app.; Liz Tayor/Richard Burton-s. 2-(#16) Ben Casey/ Frankenstein-c/s; Hitler photo-s. 5-(#19) Nixon back-c/s; Sinatra photo-s. 6-(#20) 1st Huckleberry Fink-c 5 10 15 33 44 55
8-(#22) Cassius Clay vs. Liston-s; 1st Civil War Blackouts-/Pvt. Bo Reargard w/ Jack Davis-a 6 12 18 38 52 65
V4#1-5 (#23-27): Civil War Blackouts-/Pvt. Bo Reargard w/ Jack Davis-a in all. 1-(#23) Smokey Bear-c; Tarzan-s. 2-(#24) Goldwater & Paar-s; Castro-s. 3-(#25) Frankenstein-c; Cleopatra/Liz Taylor-s; Steve Reeves photo-s. 4-(#26) James Bond-s; Hitler-s. 5-(#27) Taylor/Burton pin-up; Sinatra, Martin, Andress, Ekberg photo-s
4 8 12 27 36 45
28,31,36,39: 31-Pink Panther movie photo-s; Burke's Law-s. 39-Westerns; Elizabeth Montgomery photo-s; Beat mag-s 3 7 10 21 28 35
29,34,37,38: 29-Beatles-c by Jack Davis. 34-Two pg. Beatles-s & photo pin-up. 37-Playboy parody issue. 38-Addams Family-s 4 8 12 25 33 42
30,32,35,40: 30-Beatles photo pin-up; James Bond photo-s. 32-Ian Fleming-s; LBJ-s; Tarzan-s. 35-Beatles cameo; Three Stooges parody. 40-Tarzan-s; Crosby/Hope-s; Beatles parody
4 8 12 27 36 45
33-Ringo Starr photo-c & spoof on "A Hard Day's Night"; inside-c has Beatles photos
6 12 18 38 52 65
41,50,51,53,54,60: 41-Sports Illustrated parody-c/s. 50-Mod issue; flip-c w/1967 calendar w/Bob Taylor-a. 51-Get Smart-s. 53-Beatles cameo; nudity panels. 54-Monkees-c. 60-TV Daniel Boone-s 3 7 10 21 28 35
42-Fighting American-c revised from Simon/Kirby-c; "Good girl" art by Sparling; profile on Bob Powell; superhero parodies 6 12 18 40 55 70
43-49,52,55-59: 43-Sneaker set begins by Sparling. 45-Has #44 on-c & #45 on inside; TV Westerns-s; Beatles cameo. 46-Hell's Angels-s; NY Mets-s. 47-UFO/Space-c. 49-Men's Adventure mag. parody issue; nudity. 52-LBJ-s. 55-Underground culture special. 56-Alfred E. Neuman-c; inventors issue. 58-Hippie issue-c/s. 59-Hippie-s
3 6 9 18 23 28
61-64,66-69,71,73,75-80: 63-Tiny Tim-c & poster; Monkees-s. 64-Flip-c. 66-Flip-c; Mod Squad-s. 69-Beatles cameo; Peter Sellers photo-s. 71-Flip-c; Clint Eastwood0s. 76-Nixon-s; Marcus Welby-s. 78-Ma Barker-s; Courtship of Eddie's Father-s; Abbie Hoffman-s
3 6 9 16 20 24
65,70,74: 65-Cassius Clay/Brando/J. Wayne-c; Johnny Carson-s. 70-(9/69) John & Yoko-c, 1/2 pg. story. 74-Clay, Agnew, Namath & others as superheroes-c/s; Easy Rider-s; Ghost and Mrs. Muir-s 3 6 9 18 23 28
72-(84 pgs.) Xmas issue w/2 pg. slick color poster; Tarzan-s; 2 pg. Superman & superheroes-s 4 8 12 22 30 38
81-85,87-95,98,99: 81-(2/71) Woody Allen photo-s. 85 Monster Mag. parody-s; Nixon-s w/Ringo & John cameo. 88-Klute photo-s; Nixon paper dolls page. 92-Lily Tomlin; Archie Bunker pin-up. 93-Woody Allen 2 4 6 12 16 20
86,96,97,100: 86-John & Yoko, Tiny Tim-c; Love Story movie photo-s. 96-Kung Fu-c; Mummy-s, Dracula & Frankenstein app. 97-Superman-s; 1974 Calendar; Charlie Brown & Snoopy pin-up. 100-Serpico-s; Cosell-s; Jacques Cousteau-s
2 4 6 14 18 22
101-103,105-114,116,119,120: 101-Three Musketeers-s; Dick Tracy-s. 102-Young Frankenstein-s. 103-Kojak-s; Evel Knievel-s. 105-Towering Inferno-s; Peanuts/Snoopy-s. 106-Cher-c/s. 10 7-Jaws-c/s. 108-Pink Panther-c/s; Archie-s. 109-Adam & Eve-s(nudity). 110-Welcome Back Kotter-s. 111-Sonny & Cher-s. 112-King Kong-c/s. 120-Star Trek-s
2 4 6 10 13 16
104,115,117,118: 104-Muhammad Ali-c/s. 115-Charlie's Angels-s. 117-Bionic Woman & Six Million $ Man-c/s; Cher D'Flower begins by Sparling (nudity). 118-Star Wars-s; Popeye-s
2 4 6 12 16 20
121-125,128,130: 122-Darth Vader-s. 123-Jaws II-s. 128-Superman-c/movie parody. 130-Alien movie-s 2 4 6 11 14 18
126,127: 126-(68 pgs.) Battlestar Galactica-c/s; Star Wars-s; Wonder Woman-s. 127-Mork & Mindy-s; Lord of the Rings-s 2 4 6 14 18 22
131-(1980 Special) Star Wars/Star Trek/Flash Gordon wraparound-c/s; Superman parody; Battlestar Galactica-s 3 6 9 16 20 24
132,133: 132-1980 Election-c/s; Apocalypse Now-s. 133-Star Trek-s; Chips-s; Superheroes page 2 4 6 14 18 22
134 (scarce)(68 pg. Giant)-Star Wars-c; Alien-s; WKRP-s; Mork & Mindy-s; Taxi-s; MASH-s
4 8 12 24 32 40
Annual 1- 7th Annual Yearbook (1967)-Davis-c, 2 pg. glossy poster insert

Silent Hill: Dying Inside #1 © Konami

Silver Age #1 © DC

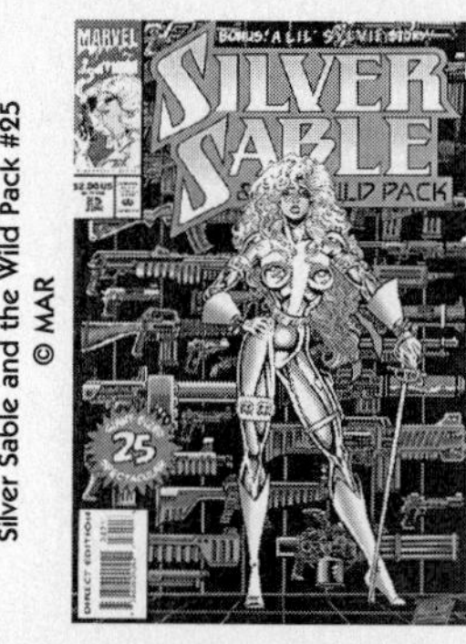

Silver Sable and the Wild Pack #25 © MAR

	GD 2.0	VG 4.0	FN 6.0	VF 8.0	VF/NM 9.0	NM- 9.2
	4	8	12	27	36	45
Annual 2- Birthday Annual (1967)-3 pg. Huckleberry Fink fold out	4	8	12	22	30	38
Annual 3 (1968) "Big Sick Laff-in" on-c (84 pgs.)-w/psychedelic posters; Frankenstein poster	3	7	10	21	28	35
Annual 1969, 1970, 1971	3	6	9	19	25	32
Annual 12,13-(1972,1973, 84 pgs.) 13-Monster-c	3	6	9	19	25	32
Annual 14 (1974, 84 pgs.) Hitler photo-s	3	6	9	19	25	32
Annual 2-4 (1980)	2	4	6	10	13	16
Special 1 (1980) Buck Rogers-c/s; MASH-s	3	6	9	16	20	24
Special 2 (1980) Wraparound Star Wars:Empire Strikes Back-c; Charlie's Angels/Farrah-s; Rocky-s; plus reprints	3	6	9	16	20	24
Yearbook 15(1975, 84 pgs.) Paul Revere-c	3	6	9	18	24	30

NOTE: ***Davis** a-42, 87; c-22, 23, 25, 29, 31, 32. **Powell** a-7, 31, 57. **Simon** a-1-3, 10, 41, 42, 87, 99; c-1, 47, 57, 59, 69, 91, 95-97, 99, 100, 102, 107, 112. **Torres** a-1-3, 29, 31, 47, 49. **Tuska** a-14, 41-43. Civil War Blackouts-23, 24. #42 has biography of Bob Powell.*

SIDEKICKS
Fanboy Ent., Inc.: Jun, 2000 - No. 3, Apr, 2001 ($2.75, B&W, lim. series)

1-3-J.Torres-s/Takesi Miyazawa-a. 3-Variant-c by Wieringo 2.75
...: Super Fun Summer Special (Oni Press, 7/03, $2.99) art by various incl. Wieringo 3.00
...: The Substitute (Oni Press, 7/02, $2.95) 3.00
...: The Transfer Student TPB (Oni Press, 6/02, $8.95, 9" x 6") r/#1-3 9.00
...: The Transfer Student TPB 2nd Ed. (10/03, $11.95, 9" x 6") r/#1-3; The Substitute 12.00

SIDESHOW
Avon Periodicals: 1949 (one-shot)

1-(Rare)-Similar to Bachelor's Diary 35 70 105 198 287 375

SIEGE
Image Comics (WildStorm Prod.): Jan, 1997 - No. 4, Apr, 1997 ($2.50)

1-4 2.50

SIEGEL AND SHUSTER: DATELINE 1930s
Eclipse Comics: Nov, 1984 - No. 2, Sept, 1985 ($1.50/$1.75, Baxter paper #1)

1,2: 1-Unpublished samples of strips from the '30s; includes 'Interplanetary Police'; Shuster-c. 2 ($1.75, B&W)-unpublished strips; Shuster-c 2.50

SIGIL (Also see CrossGen Chronicles)
CrossGeneration Comics: Jul, 2000 - No. 43, Jan, 2004 ($2.95)

1-43: 1-Barbara Kesel-s/Ben & Ray Lai-a. 12-Waid-s begin. 21-Chuck Dixon-s begin 3.00
...: Hostage Planet TPB (4/03, $15.95) r/#21-26 16.00
...: Mark of Power TPB (5/01, $19.95) r/#1-7; Moeller painted-c 20.00
...: The Marked Man Vol. 2 TPB (2002, $19.95) r/#8-14 20.00
...: The Lizard God Vol. 3 TPB (2002, $15.95) r/#15-20 16.00
Vol. 4: Hostage Planet (2003, $15.95) r/#21-26 16.00
Vol. 5: Death Match (2003, $15.95) r/#27-32 16.00

SIGMA
Image Comics (WildStorm Productions): March, 1996 - No. 3, June, 1996 ($2.50, limited series)

1-3: 1-"Fire From Heaven" prelude #2; Coker-a. 2-"Fire From Heaven" pt. 6. 3-"Fire From Heaven" pt. 14. 2.50

SILENT HILL: DYING INSIDE
IDW Publishing: Feb, 2004 - No. 5, June, 2004 ($3.99, limited series)

1-5-Based on the Konami computer game. 1-Templesmith-a; Ashley Wood-c 4.00
TPB (8/04, $19.99) r/#1-5; Ashley Wood-c 20.00

SILENT INVASION, THE
Rengade Press: Apr, 1986 - No.12, Mar, 1988 ($1.70/$2.00, B&W)

1-12-UFO sightings of the '50's 3.00
Book 1- reprints ($7.95) 8.00

SILENT MOBIUS
Viz Select Comics: 1991 - No. 5, 1992 ($4.95, color, squarebound, 44 pgs.)

1-5: Japanese stories translated to English 5.00

SILENT SCREAMERS (Based on the Aztech Toys figures)
Image Comics: Oct, 2000 ($4.95)

Nosferatu Issue - Alex Ross front & back-c 5.00

SILKE
Dark Horse Comics: Jan, 2001 - No. 4, Sept, 2001 ($2.95)

1-4-Tony Daniel-s/a 3.00

SILKEN GHOST
CrossGen Comics: June, 2003 - No. 5, Oct, 2003 ($2.95, limited series)

1-5-Dixon-s/Rosado-a 3.00

GD 2.0 VG 4.0 FN 6.0 VF 8.0 VF/NM 9.0 NM- 9.2

Traveler Vol. 1 (2003, $9.95) digest-sized reprint #1-5 10.00

SILLY PILLY (See Frank Luther's...)

SILLY SYMPHONIES (See Dell Giants)

SILLY TUNES
Timely Comics: Fall, 1945 - No. 7, June, 1947

	GD	VG	FN	VF	VF/NM	NM-
1-Silly Seal, Ziggy Pig begin	21	42	63	118	169	220
2-(2/46)	12	24	36	69	95	120
3-7: 6-New logo	10	20	30	56	73	90

SILVER (See Lone Ranger's Famous Horse...)

SILVER AGE
DC Comics: July, 2000 ($3.95, limited series)

1-Waid-s/Dodson-a; "Silver Age" style x-over; JLA & villains switch bodies 4.00
...: Challengers of the Unknown ($2.50) Joe Kubert-c; vs. Chronos 2.50
...: Dial H For Hero ($2.50) Jim Mooney-c; vs. Martian Manhunter 2.50
...: Doom Patrol ($2.50) Ramona Fradon-c/Peyer-s 2.50
...: Flash ($2.50) Carmine Infantino-c; Kid Flash and Elongated Man app. 2.50
...: Green Lantern ($2.50) Gil Kane-c/Busiek-s/Anderson-a; vs. Sinestro 2.50
...: Justice League of America ($2.50) Ty Templeton-c 2.50
...: Showcase ($2.50) Dick Giordano-c/a; Batgirl, Adam Strange app. 2.50
... Secret Files ($4.95) Intro. Agamemno; short stories & profile pages 5.00
...: Teen Titans ($2.50) Nick Cardy-c; vs. Penguin, Mr. Element, Black Manta 2.50
...: The Brave and the Bold ($2.50) Jim Aparo-c; Batman & Metal Men 2.50
... 80-Page Giant ($5.95) Conclusion of x-over; "lost" Silver Age stories 6.00

SILVERBACK
Comico: 1989 - No. 3, 1990 ($2.50, color, limited series, mature readers)

1-3: Character from Grendel: Matt Wagner-a 3.00

SILVERBLADE
DC Comics: Sept, 1987 - No. 12, Sept, 1988

1-12: Colan-c/a in all 2.25

SILVER CROSS (See Warrior Nun series)
Antarctic Press: Nov, 1997 - No. 3, Mar, 1998 ($2.95)

1-3-Ben Dunn-s/a 3.00

SILVERHAWKS
Star Comics/Marvel Comics #6: Aug, 1987 - No. 6, June, 1988 ($1.00)

1-6 3.00

SILVERHEELS
Pacific Comics: Dec, 1983 - No. 3, May, 1984 ($1.50)

1-3 2.25

SILVER KID WESTERN
Key/Stanmor Publications: Oct, 1954 - No. 5, July, 1955

	GD	VG	FN	VF	VF/NM	NM-
1	10	20	30	56	73	90
2	6	12	18	31	38	45
3-5	6	12	18	28	34	40
I.W. Reprint #1,2-Severin-c: 1-r/#? 2-r/#1	2	4	6	9	11	14

SILVER SABLE AND THE WILD PACK (See Amazing Spider-Man #265)
Marvel Comics: June, 1992 - No. 35, Apr, 1995 ($1.25/$1.50

1-($2.00)-Embossed & foil stamped-c; Spider-Man app. 3.00
2-35: 4,5-Dr. Doom-c/story. 6,7-Deathlok-c/story. 9-Origin Silver Sable. 10-Punisher-c/s. 15-Capt. America-c/s. 16,17-Intruders app. 18,19-Venom-c/s. 19-Siege of Darkness x-over. 23-Daredevil (in new costume) & Deadpool app. 24-Bound-in card sheet. Li'l Sylvie backup story. 25-($2.00, 52 pgs.)-Li'l Sylvie backup story 2.25

SILVER STAR (Also see Jack Kirby's...)
Pacific Comics: Feb, 1983 - No. Jan, 1984 ($1.00)

1-6: 1-1st app. Last of the Viking Heroes. 1-5-Kirby-c/a. 2-Ditko-a 5.00

SILVER STREAK COMICS (Crime Does Not Pay #22 on)
Your Guide Publs. No. 1-7/New Friday Publs. No. 8-17/Comic House Publ./Newsbook Publ.: Dec, 1939 - No. 21, May, 1942; No. 23, 1946; No # 22 (Silver logo-#1-5)

	GD	VG	FN	VF	VF/NM	NM-
1-(Scarce)-Intro The Claw by Cole (r-/in Daredevil #21), Red Reeves, Boy Magician, & Captain Fearless; The Wasp, Mister Midnight begin; Spirit Man app. Silver metallic-c begin, end #5; Claw c-1,2,6-8	1072	2144	3216	7500	12,000	16,500
2-The Claw by Cole; Simon-c/a	386	772	1158	2509	4055	5600
3-1st app. & origin Silver Streak (2nd with lightning speed); Dickie Dean the Boy Inventor, Lance Hale, Ace Powers, Bill Wayne, & The Planet Patrol begin	331	662	993	2152	3476	4800

4-Sky Wolf begins; Silver Streak by Jack Cole (new costume); 1st app. Jackie,

Silver Streak Comics #17 © New Friday Pub.

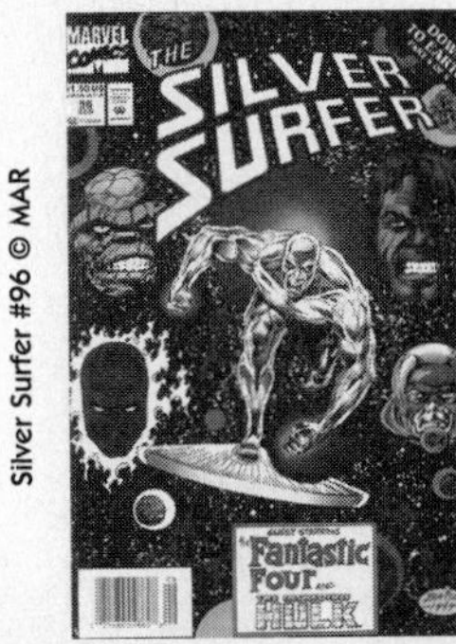

Silver Surfer #96 © MAR

Simpsons Comics #82 © Bongo

GD VG FN VF VF/NM NM-
2.0 4.0 6.0 8.0 9.0 9.2

Lance Hale's sidekick 171 342 513 1069 1647 2225
5-Jack Cole c/a(2) 200 400 600 1250 1925 2600
6-(Scarce, 9/40)-Origin & 1st app. Daredevil (blue & yellow costume) by Jack Binder; The Claw returns; classic Cole Claw-c 1235 2470 3705 9263 15,132 21,000
7-Claw vs. Daredevil (new costume-blue & red) by Jack Cole & 3 other Cole stories (38 pgs.) 761 1522 2283 5327 8564 11,800
8-Claw vs. Daredevil by Cole; last Cole Silver Streak 324 648 972 2106 3403 4700
9-Claw vs. Daredevil by Cole 192 384 576 1200 1850 2500
10-Origin & 1st app. Captain Battle (5/41); Claw vs. Daredevil by Cole; Robot-c 173 346 519 1081 1666 2250
11-Intro. Mercury by Bob Wood, Silver Streak's sidekick; conclusion Claw vs. Daredevil by Rico; in 'Presto Martin,' 2nd pg., newspaper says 'Roussos does it again' 119 238 357 744 1147 1550
12-14: 13-Origin Thun-Dohr 87 174 261 544 835 1125
15, 17-Last Daredevil issue. 81 162 243 506 778 1050
16-Hitler-c 94 188 282 588 907 1225
18-The Saint begins (2/42, 1st app.) by Leslie Charteris (see Movie Comics #2 by DC); The Saint-c 71 142 213 444 685 925
19-21(1942): 20,21 have Wolverton's Scoop Scuttle. 21-Hitler app. in strip on cover 55 110 165 340 520 700
23(1946(An Atomic Comic)-Reprints; bondage-c 46 92 138 281 428 575
nn(11/46)(Newsbook Publ.)-R-/S.S. story from #4-7 plus 2 Captain Fearless stories, all in color; bondage/torture-c 55 110 165 340 520 700
NOTE: ***Binder*** *c-3, 4, 13-15, 17.* ***Jack Cole*** *a-(Daredevil)-#6-10, (Dickie Dean)-#3-10, (Pirate Prince)-#7, (Silver Streak)-#4-8, nn; c-5 (Silver Streak), 6 (Claw), 7, 8 (Daredevil).* ***Everett*** *Red Reed begins #20.* ***Guardineer*** *a-#8-13.* ***Don Rico*** *a-11-17 (Daredevil); c-11, 12, 16.* ***Simon*** *a-3 (Silver Streak).* ***Bob Wood*** *a-9 (Silver Streak); c-9, 10. Captain Battle c-11, 13-15, 17. Claw c-#1, 2, 6-8. Daredevil c-7, 8, 12. Dickie Dean c-19. Ned of the Navy c-20 (war). The Saint c-18. Silver Streak c-5, 9, 10, 16, 23.*

SILVER SURFER (See Fantastic Four, Fantasy Masterpieces V2#1, Fireside Book Series, Marvel Graphic Novel, Marvel Presents #8, Marvel's Greatest Comics & Tales To Astonish #92)

SILVER SURFER, THE (Also see Essential Silver Surfer)
Marvel Comics Group: Aug, 1968 - No. 18, Sept, 1970; June, 1982

1-More detailed origin by John Buscema (p); The Watcher back-up stories begin (origin), end #7; (No. 1-7: 25¢, 68 pgs.) 41 82 123 318 497 675
2 19 38 57 134 205 275
3-1st app. Mephisto 16 32 48 114 175 235
4-Lower distribution; Thor & Loki app. 38 76 114 285 443 600
5-7-Last giant size. 5-The Stranger app.; Fantastic Four app. 6-Brunner inks. 7-(8/69)-Early cameo Frankenstein's monster (see X-Men #40) 11 22 33 77 114 150
8-10: 8-18-(15¢ issues) 9 18 27 60 85 110
11-13,15-18: 15-Silver Surfer vs. Human Torch; Fantastic Four app. 17-Nick Fury app. 18-Vs. The Inhumans; Kirby-c/a 8 16 24 55 78 100
14-Spider-Man x-over 12 24 36 82 124 165
V2#1 (6/82, 52 pgs.)-Byrne-c/a 1 3 4 6 8 10
NOTE: ***Adkins*** *a-8-15i.* ***Brunner*** *a-6i.* ***J. Buscema*** *a-1-17p.* ***Colan*** *a-1-3p.* ***Reinman*** *a-1-4i. #1-14 were reprinted in Fantasy Masterpieces V2#1-14.*

SILVER SURFER (Volume 3) (See Marvel Graphic Novel #38)
Marvel Comics Group: V3#1, July, 1987 - No. 146, Nov, 1998

1-Double size ($1.25) 1 2 3 5 7 9
2-17: 15-Ron Lim-c/a begins (9/88) 4.00
18-33,39-43: 25,31 ($1.50, 52 pgs.). 25-Skrulls app. 32,39-No Ron Lim-c/a. 39-Alan Grant scripts 3.00
34-Thanos returns (cameo); Starlin scripts begin 5.00
35-38: 35-1st full Thanos app. in Silver Surfer (3/90); reintro Drax the Destroyer on last pg. (cameo). 36-Recaps history of Thanos; Capt. Marvel & Warlock app. in recap. 37-1st full app. Drax the Destroyer; Drax-c. 38-Silver Surfer battles Thanos 6.00
44,45,49-Thanos stories (c-44,45) 4.00
46-48: 46-Return of Adam Warlock (2/91); re-intro Gamora & Pip the Troll. 47-Warlock battles Drax. 48-Last Starlin scripts (also #50) 4.00
50-($1.50, 52 pgs.)-Embossed & silver foil-c; Silver Surfer has brief battle w/Thanos; story cont'd in Infinity Gauntlet #1 1 2 3 4 5 7
50-2nd & 3rd printings 2.50
51-59: 51-53: Infinity Gauntlet x-over . 54-57: Infinity Gauntlet x-overs. 54-Rhino app. 55,56-Thanos-c & app. 57-Thanos-c & cameo. 58,59-Infinity Gauntlet x-overs; 58-Ron Lim-c only. 59-Thanos battles Silver Surfer-c/story; Thanos joins 3.00
60-74,76-99,101-124,126-139: 63-Capt. Marvel app. 67-69-Infinity War x-overs. 76-78-Jack of Hearts-c/s. 83-85-Infinity Crusade x-over; 83,84-Thanos cameo. 85-Storm, Wonder Man x-over. 86-Thor-c/s. 87-Dr. Strange & Warlock app. 88-Thanos-c/s. 82 (52 pgs.). 101-Bound in card sheet. 5-FF app. 96-Hulk & FF app. 97-Terrax & Nova app. 106-Doc Doom app. 121-Quasar & Beta Ray Bill app. 123-w/card insert; begin Garney-a. 126-Dr. Strange-c/app. 128-Spider-Man & Daredevil-c/app. 138-Thing-c 2.50
75-($2.50, 52 pgs.)-Embossed foil-c; Lim-c/a 3.00
100 ($2.25, 52 pgs.)-Wraparound-c 2.50
100 ($3.95, 52 pgs.)-Enhanced-c 4.00
125 ($2.95)-Wraparound-c; Vs. Hulk-c/app. 3.00
140-146: 140-142,144,145-Muth-c/a. 143,146-Cowan-a. 146-Last issue 2.50
#(-1) Flashback (7/97) 2.50
Annual 1 (1988, $1.75)-Evolutionary War app.; 1st Ron Lim-a on Silver Surfer (20 pg. back-up story & pin-ups) 5.00
Annual 2-7 ('89-'94, 68 pgs.): 2-Atlantis Attacks. 4-3 pg. origin story; Silver Surfer battles Guardians of the Galaxy. 5-Return of the Defenders, part 3; Lim-c/a (3 pgs. of pin-ups only). 6-Polybagged w/trading card; 1st app. Legacy; card is by Lim/Austin 3.00
Annual '97 ($2.99), .../Thor Annual '98 ($2.99) 3.00
Ashcan (1995, 75¢) reprints part of V1#3; Lim-c 2.25
...Dangerous Artifacts-(1996, $3.95)-Ron Marz scripts; Galactus-c/app. 4.00
Graphic Novel (1988, HC, $14.95) Judgment Day; Lee-s/Buscema-a 15.00
The Enslavers Graphic Novel (1990, $16.95) 17.00
Homecoming Graphic Novel (1991, $12.95, softcover) Starlin-s 15.00
Inner Demons TPB (4/98, $3.50)r/#123,125,126 3.50
...: The First Coming of Galactus nn (11/92, $5.95, 68 pgs.)-Reprints Fantastic Four #48-50 with new Lim-c 6.00
Wizard 1/2 2 4 6 10 12 15
NOTE: ***Austin*** *c(i)-7, 8, 71, 73, 74, 76, 79.* ***Cowan*** *a-143,146.* ***Cully Hamner*** *a-83p.* ***Ron Lim*** *a(p)-15-31, 33-38, 40-55, (56, 57-part-p), 60-65, 73-82, Annual 2, 4; c(p)-15-31, 32-38, 40-84, 86-92, Annual 2, 4-6.* ***Muth*** *c/a-140-142,144,145.* ***M. Rogers*** *a-1-10, 12, 19, 21; c-1-9, 11, 12, 21.*

SILVER SURFER (Volume 4)
Marvel Comics: Sept, 2003 - No. 14, Dec, 2004 ($2.25/$2.99)

1-6: 1-Milx-a; Jusko-c. 2-Jae Lee-c 2.25
7-14-($2.99) 3.00
...Vol. 1: Communion (2004, $14.99) r/#1-6 15.00

SILVER SURFER, THE
Marvel Comics (Epic): Dec, 1988 - No. 2, Jan, 1989 ($1.00, lim. series)

1,2: By Stan Lee scripts & Moebius-c/a 4.00
...: Parable ('98, $5.99) r/#1&2 6.00

SILVER SURFER: LOFTIER THAN MORTALS
Marvel Comics: Oct, 1999 - No. 2, Oct, 1999 ($2.50, limited series)

1,2-Remix of Fantastic Four #57-60; Velluto-a 2.50

SILVER SURFER/SUPERMAN
Marvel Comics: 1996 ($5.95,one-shot)

1-Perez-s/Lim-c/a(p) 6.00

SILVER SURFER VS. DRACULA
Marvel Comics: Feb, 1994 ($1.75, one-shot)

1-r/Tomb of Dracula #50; Everett Vampire-r/Venus #19; Howard the Duck back-up by Brunner; Lim-c(p) 2.25

SILVER SURFER/WARLOCK: RESURRECTION
Marvel Comics: Mar, 1993 - No. 4, June, 1993 ($2.50, limited series)

1-4: Starlin-c/a & scripts 2.50

SILVER SURFER/WEAPON ZERO
Marvel Comics: Apr, 1997 ($2.95, one-shot)

1-"Devil's Reign" pt. 8 3.00

SILVERTIP (Max Brand)
Dell Publishing Co.: No. 491, Aug, 1953 - No. 898, May, 1958

Four Color 491 (#1); all painted-c 9 18 27 65 93 120
Four Color 572,608,637,667,731,789,898-Kinstler-a 6 12 18 38 52 65
Four Color 835 6 12 18 38 52 65

SIMPSONS COMICS (See Bartman, Futurama, Itchy & Scratchy & Radioactive Man)
Bongo Comics Group: 1993 - Present ($1.95/$2.50/$2.99)

1-($2.25)-FF#1-c swipe; pull-out poster; flip book 1 2 3 5 6 8
2-5: 2-Patty & Selma flip-c/sty. 3-Krusty, Agent of K.L.O.W.N. flip-c/story. 4-Infinity-c; flip-c of Busman #1; w/trading card. 5-Wraparound-c w/trading card 5.00
6-40: All Flip books. 6-w/Chief Wiggum's "Crime Comics". 7-w/"McBain Comics". 8-w/"Edna, Queen of the Congo". 9-w/"Barney Gumble". 10-w/"Apu". 11-w/"Homer". 12-w/"White Knuckled War Stories". 13-w/"Jimbo Jones' Wedgie Comics". 14-w/"Grampa". 15-w/"Itchy & Scratchy". 16-w/"Bongo Grab Bag". 17-w/"Headlight Comics". 18-w/"Milhouse". 19,20-w/"Roswell." 21,22-w/"Roswell". 23-w/"Hellfire Comics". 24-w/"Lil' Homey". 36-39-Flip book w/Radioactive Man 4.00
41-49,51-99: 43-Flip book w/Poochie. 52-Dini-s. 77-Dixon-s. 85-Begin $2.99-c 3.00
50-($5.95) Wraparound-c; 80 pgs.; square-bound 1 2 3 4 5 7
100-($6.99) 100 pgs.; square-bound; clip issue of past highlights 7.00
... A Go-Go (1999, $11.95)-r/#32-35; ...Big Bonanza (1998, $11.95)-r/#28-31, ...Extravaganza (1994, $10.00)-r/#1-4; infinity-c, ...On Parade (1998, $11.95)-r/#24-27, ...Simpsorama (1996, $10.95)-r/#11-14 12.00

Simpsons Comics Presents Bart Simpson #12 © Bongo

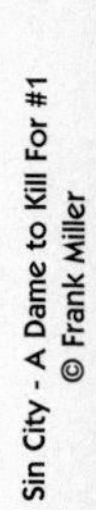
Sin City - A Dame to Kill For #1 © Frank Miller

Sins of Youth: JLA Jr. #1 © DC

GD 2.0 | VG 4.0 | FN 6.0 | VF 8.0 | VF/NM 9.0 | NM- 9.2

Simpsons Classics 1,2 (2004, $3.99, magazine-size) 1-r/#1&2; cover gallery 4.00
Simpsons Comics Belly Buster ('04, $14.95) r/#49,51,53-56 15.00
Simpsons Comics Madness ('03, $14.95) r/#43-48 15.00
Simpsons Comics Royale ('01, $14.95) r/various Bongo issues 15.00

SIMPSONS COMICS AND STORIES
Welsh Publishing Group: 1993 ($2.95, one-shot)
1-(Direct Sale)-Polybagged w/Bartman poster 6.00
1-(Newsstand Edition)-Without poster 4.00

SIMPSONS COMICS PRESENTS BART SIMPSON
Bongo Comics Group: 2000 - Present ($2.50/$2.99, quarterly)
1-20: 7-9-Dan DeCarlo-layouts. 13-Begin $2.99-c. 17-Bartman app. 3.00
The Big Book of Bart Simpson TPB (2002, $12.95) r/#1-4 13.00
The Big Bad Book of Bart Simpson TPB (2003, $12.95) r/#5-8 13.00
The Big Bratty Book of Bart Simpson TPB (2004, $12.95) r/#9-12 13.00

SIMULATORS, THE
Neatly Chiseled Features: 1991 ($2.50, stiff-c)
1-Super hero group 2.50

SINBAD, JR (TV Cartoon)
Dell Publishing Co.: Sept-Nov, 1965 - No. 3, May, 1966

	GD	VG	FN	VF	VF/NM	NM-
1	4	8	12	29	40	50
2,3	3	7	10	21	28	35

SIN CITY (See Dark Horse Presents, A Decade of Dark Horse, & San Diego Comic Con Comics #2,4)
Dark Horse Comics (Legend)
TPB ($15.00) Reprints early DHP stories 15.00
Booze, Broads & Bullets TPB ($15.00) 15.00

SIN CITY: A DAME TO KILL FOR
Dark Horse Comics (Legend): Nov, 1993 - No. 6, May, 1994 ($2.95, B&W, limited series)
1-6: Frank Miller-c/a & story in all. 1-1st app. Dwight. 5.00
Limited Edition Hardcover 85.00
Hardcover 25.00
TPB ($15.00) 15.00

SIN CITY: FAMILY VALUES
Dark Horse Comics (Legend): Oct, 1997 ($10.00, B&W, squarebound, one-shot)
nn-Miller-c/a & story 10.00
Limited Edition Hardcover 75.00

SIN CITY: HELL AND BACK
Dark Horse (Maverick): Jul, 1999 - No. 9 ($2.95/$4.95, B&W, limited series)
1-8-Miller-c/a & story. 7-Color 3.00
9-($4.95) 5.00

SIN CITY: JUST ANOTHER SATURDAY NIGHT
Dark Horse Comics (Legend): Aug, 1997 (Wizard 1/2 offer, B&W, one-shot)
1/2-Miller-c/a & story 1 2 3 5 6 8
nn (10/98, $2.50) r/#1/2 2.50

SIN CITY: LOST, LONELY & LETHAL
Dark Horse Comics (Legend): Dec, 1996 ($2.95, B&W and blue, one-shot)
nn-Miller-c/s/a; w/pin-ups 4.00

SIN CITY: SEX AND VIOLENCE
Dark Horse Comics (Legend): Mar, 1997 ($2.95, B&W and blue, one-shot)
nn-Miller-c/a & story 4.00

SIN CITY: SILENT NIGHT
Dark Horse Comics (Legend): Dec, 1995 ($2.95, B&W, one-shot)
1-Miller-c/a & story; Marv app. 4.00

SIN CITY: THAT YELLOW BASTARD
Dark Horse Comics (Legend): Feb, 1996 - No. 6, July, 1996 ($2.95/$3.50, B&W and yellow, limited series)
1-5: Miller-c/a & story in all. 1-1st app. Hartigan. 5.00
6-($3.50) Error & corrected 5.00
Limited Edition Hardcover 25.00
TPB ($15.00) 15.00

SIN CITY: THE BABE WORE RED AND OTHER STORIES
Dark Horse Comics (Legend): Nov, 1994 ($2.95, B&W and red, one-shot)
1-r/serial run in Previews as well as other stories; Miller-c/a & scripts; Dwight app. 3.00

SIN CITY: THE BIG FAT KILL
Dark Horse Comics (Legend): Nov, 1994 - No. 5, Mar, 1995 ($2.95, B&W, limited series)
1-5-Miller story & art in all; Dwight app. 4.00
Hardcover 25.00
TPB ($15.00) 15.00

SINDBAD (See Capt. Sindbad under Movie Comics, and Fantastic Voyages of Sindbad)

SINGING GUNS (See Fawcett Movie Comics)

SINGLE SERIES (Comics on Parade #30 on)(Also see John Hix...)
United Features Syndicate: 1938 - No. 28, 1942 (All 68 pgs.)

Note: See Individual Alphabetical Listings for prices

1-Captain and the Kids (#1)
2-Broncho Bill (1939) (#1)
3-Ella Cinders (1939)
4-Li'l Abner (1939) (#1)
5-Fritzi Ritz (#1)
6-Jim Hardy by Dick Moores (#1)
7-Frankie Doodle
8-Peter Pat (On sale 7/14/39)
9-Strange As It Seems
10-Little Mary Mixup
11-Mr. and Mrs. Beans
12-Joe Jinks
13-Looy Dot Dope
14-Billy Make Believe
15-How It Began (1939)
16-Illustrated Gags (1940)-Has ad for Captain and the Kids #1 reprint listed below
17-Danny Dingle
18-Li'l Abner (#2 on-c)
19-Broncho Bill (#2 on-c)
20-Tarzan by Hal Foster
21-Ella Cinders (#2 on-c; on sale 3/19/40)
22-Iron Vic
23-Tailspin Tommy by Hal Forrest (#1)
24-Alice in Wonderland (#1)
25-Abbie and Slats
26-Little Mary Mixup (#2 on-c, 1940)
27-Jim Hardy by Dick Moores (1942)
28-Ella Cinders & Abbie and Slats (1942)
1-Captain and the Kids (1939 reprint)-2nd Edition
1-Fritzi Ritz (1939 reprint)-2nd ed.

NOTE: *Some issues given away at the 1939-40 New York World's Fair (#6).*

SINGULARITY 7
IDW Publ.: July, 2004 - No. 4, Oct, 2004 ($3.99, limited series)
1-4-Templesmith-s/a 4.00

SINISTER HOUSE OF SECRET LOVE, THE (Becomes Secrets of Sinister House No. 5 on)
National Periodical Publ.: Oct-Nov, 1971 - No. 4, Apr-May, 1972

	GD	VG	FN	VF	VF/NM	NM-
1 (all 52 pgs.)	16	32	48	116	178	240
2,4: 2-Jeff Jones-c	8	16	24	55	78	100
3-Toth-a	8	16	24	58	82	105

SINS OF YOUTH... (Also see Young Justice: Sins of Youth)
DC Comics: May 2000 ($4.95/$2.50, limited crossover series)
Secret Files 1 ($4.95) Short stories and profile pages; Nauck-c 5.00
...Aquaboy/Lagoon Man; Batboy and Robin; JLA Jr.; Kid Flash/Impulse; Starwoman and the JSA, Superman, Jr./Superboy, Sr.; The Secret/ Deadboy, Wonder Girls ($2.50-c) Old and young heroes switch ages 2.50

SIR CHARLES BARKLEY AND THE REFEREE MURDERS
Hamilton Comics: 1993 ($9.95, 8-1/2" x 11", 52 pgs.)
nn-Photo-c; Sports fantasy comic book fiction (uses real names of NBA superstars). Script by Alan Dean Foster, art by Joe Staton. Comes with bound-in sheet of 35 gummed "Moods of Charles Barkley" stamps. Photo/story on Barkley 2 4 6 8 10 12
Special Edition of 100 copies for charity signed on an affixed book plate by Barkley, Foster & Staton 150.00
Ashcan edition given away to dealers, distributors & promoters (low distribution). Four pages in color, balance of story in b&w 2 4 6 8 10 12

SIREN (Also see Eliminator & Ultraforce)
Malibu Comics (Ultraverse): Sept, 1995 - No. 3, Dec, 1995 ($1.50)
Infinity, 1-3: Infinity-Black-c & painted-c exists. 1-Regular-c & painted-c; War Machine app. 2-Flip book w/Phoenix Resurrection Pt. 3 2.25
Special 1-(2/96, $1.95, 28 pgs.)-Origin Siren; Marvel Comic's Juggernaut-c/app. 2.25

SIREN: SHAPES
Image Comics: May, 1998 - No. 3, Nov, 1998 ($2.95, B&W, limited series)
1-3-J. Torres -s 3.00

SIR LANCELOT (TV)
Dell Publishing Co.: No. 606, Dec, 1954 - No. 775, Mar, 1957

	GD	VG	FN	VF	VF/NM	NM-
Four Color 606 (not TV)	8	16	24	58	82	105
Four Color 775(...and Brian)-Buscema-a; photo-c	11	22	33	77	114	150

SIR WALTER RALEIGH (Movie)
Dell Publishing Co.: May, 1955 (Based on movie "The Virgin Queen")

	GD	VG	FN	VF	VF/NM	NM-
Four Color 644-Photo-c	8	16	24	55	78	100

SISTERHOOD OF STEEL (See Eclipse Graphic Adventure Novel #13)
Marvel Comics (Epic Comics): Dec, 1984 -No. 8, Feb, 1986 ($1.50, Baxter paper, mature)
1-8 3.00

Six-Gun Heroes #5 © FAW

Skeleton Key #30 © Andrew Watson

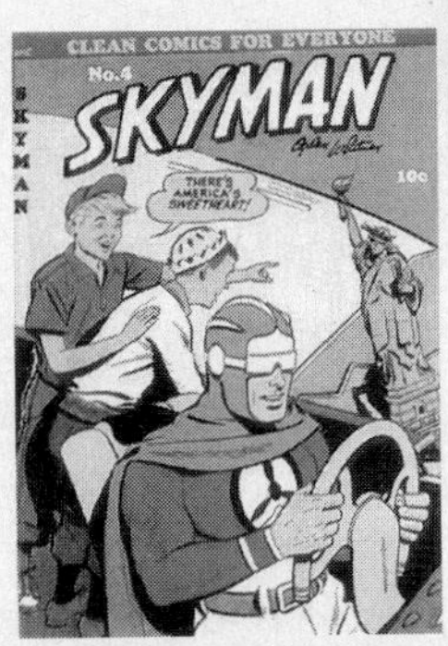

Skyman #4 © CCG

SIX
Image Comics: Aug, 2004 ($5.95, B&W)

	GD 2.0	VG 4.0	FN 6.0	VF 8.0	VF/NM 9.0	NM- 9.2
1-Oeming-s/c; Beavers-a						6.00

6 BLACK HORSES (See Movie Classics)

SIX FROM SIRIUS
Marvel Comics (Epic Comics): July, 1984 - No. 4, Oct, 1984 ($1.50, limited series, mature)

	GD 2.0	VG 4.0	FN 6.0	VF 8.0	VF/NM 9.0	NM- 9.2
1-4: Moench scripts; Gulacy-c/a in all						2.25

SIX FROM SIRIUS II
Marvel Comics (Epic Comics): Feb, 1986 - No. 4, May, 1986 ($1.50, limited series, mature)

	GD 2.0	VG 4.0	FN 6.0	VF 8.0	VF/NM 9.0	NM- 9.2
1-4: Moench scripts; Gulacy-c/a in all						2.25

SIX-GUN HEROES
Fawcett Publications: March, 1950 - No. 23, Nov, 1953 (Photo-c #1-23)

	GD 2.0	VG 4.0	FN 6.0	VF 8.0	VF/NM 9.0	NM- 9.2
1-Rocky Lane, Hopalong Cassidy, Smiley Burnette begin (same date as Smiley Burnette #1)	46	92	138	281	428	575
2	29	58	87	164	237	310
3-5: 5-Lash LaRue begins	20	40	60	112	161	210
6-15	15	30	45	83	117	150
16-22: 17-Last Smiley Burnette. 18-Monte Hale begins	13	26	39	74	102	130
23-Last Fawcett issue	14	28	42	79	110	140

NOTE: *Hopalong Cassidy photo c-1-3. Monte Hale photo c-18. Rocky Lane photo c-4, 5, 7, 9, 11, 13, 15, 17, 20, 21, 23. Lash LaRue photo c-6, 8, 10, 12, 14, 16, 19, 22.*

SIX-GUN HEROES (Cont'd from Fawcett; Gunmasters #84 on) (See Blue Bird)
Charlton Comics: No. 24, Jan, 1954 - No. 83, Mar-Apr, 1965 (All Vol. 4)

	GD 2.0	VG 4.0	FN 6.0	VF 8.0	VF/NM 9.0	NM- 9.2
24-Lash LaRue, Hopalong Cassidy, Rocky Lane & Tex Ritter begin; photo-c	21	42	63	118	169	220
25	11	22	33	64	87	110
26-30: 26-Rod Cameron story. 28-Tom Mix begins?	10	20	30	58	77	95
31-40: 38-Jingles & Wild Bill Hickok (TV)	9	18	27	52	66	80
41-46,48,50	9	18	27	51	62	75
47-Williamson-a, 2 pgs; Torres-a	9	18	27	52	66	80
49-Williamson-a (5 pgs.)	10	20	30	58	77	95
51-56,58-60: 58-Gunmaster app.	4	8	12	29	40	50
57-Origin & 1st app. Gunmaster	6	12	18	38	52	65
61,63-70	3	7	10	21	28	35
62-Origin Gunmaster	4	8	12	27	36	45
71-75,77,78,80-83	3	6	9	16	20	24
76,79: 76-Gunmaster begins. 79-1st app. & origin of Bullet, the Gun-Boy	3	6	9	18	23	28

SIXGUN RANCH (See Luke Short & Four Color #580)

SIX-GUN WESTERN
Atlas Comics (CDS): Jan, 1957 - No. 4, July, 1957

	GD 2.0	VG 4.0	FN 6.0	VF 8.0	VF/NM 9.0	NM- 9.2
1-Crandall-a; two Williamson text illos	21	42	63	118	169	220
2,3-Williamson-a in both	15	30	45	83	117	150
4-Woodbridge-a	10	20	30	60	80	100

NOTE: ***Ayers** a-2, 3. **Maneely** a-1; c-2, 3. **Orlando** a-2. **Pakula** a-2. **Powell** a-3. **Romita** a-1, 4. **Severin** c-1, 4. **Shores** a-2.*

SIX MILLION DOLLAR MAN, THE (TV)
Charlton Comics: 6/76 - No. 4, 12/76; No. 5, 10/77; No. 6, 2/78 - No. 9, 6/78

	GD 2.0	VG 4.0	FN 6.0	VF 8.0	VF/NM 9.0	NM- 9.2
1-Staton-c/a; Lee Majors photo on-c	2	4	6	14	18	22
2-9: 2-Neal Adams-c; Staton-a	2	4	6	10	13	16

SIX MILLION DOLLAR MAN, THE (TV)(Magazine)
Charlton Comics: July, 1976 - No. 7, Nov, 1977 (B&W)

	GD 2.0	VG 4.0	FN 6.0	VF 8.0	VF/NM 9.0	NM- 9.2
1-Neal Adams-c/a	3	6	9	18	23	28
2-Neal Adams-c	2	4	6	14	18	22
3-N. Adams part inks; Chaykin-a	2	4	6	11	14	18
4-7	2	4	6	10	12	15

SIX STRING SAMURAI
Awesome-Hyperwerks: Sept, 1998 ($2.95)

	GD 2.0	VG 4.0	FN 6.0	VF 8.0	VF/NM 9.0	NM- 9.2
1-Stinsman & Fraga-a						3.00

67 SECONDS
Marvel Comics (Epic Comics): 1992 ($15.95, 54 pgs., graphic novel)

	GD 2.0	VG 4.0	FN 6.0	VF 8.0	VF/NM 9.0	NM- 9.2
nn-James Robinson scripts; Steve Yeowell-c/a	2	4	6	11	14	18

SKATEMAN
Pacific Comics: Nov, 1983 (Baxter paper, one-shot)

	GD 2.0	VG 4.0	FN 6.0	VF 8.0	VF/NM 9.0	NM- 9.2
1-Adams-c/a						4.00

SKELETON HAND (...In Secrets of the Supernatural)
American Comics Gr. (B&M Dist. Co.): Sept-Oct, 1952 - No. 6, Jul-Aug, 1953

	GD 2.0	VG 4.0	FN 6.0	VF 8.0	VF/NM 9.0	NM- 9.2
1	44	88	132	268	409	550
2	35	70	105	198	287	375
3-6	28	56	84	158	229	300

SKELETON KEY
Amaze Ink: July, 1995 - No. 30, Jan, 1998 ($1.25/$1.50/$1.75, B&W)

	GD 2.0	VG 4.0	FN 6.0	VF 8.0	VF/NM 9.0	NM- 9.2
1-30						3.00
Special #1 (2/98, $4.95) Unpublished short stories						5.00
Sugar Kat Special (10/98, $2.95) Halloween stories						3.00
Beyond The Threshold TPB (6/96. $11.95)-r/#1-6						12.00
Cats and Dogs TPB ($12.95)-r/#25-30						13.00
The Celestial Calendar TPB ($19.95)-r/#7-18						20.00
Telling Tales TPB ($12.95)-r/#19-24						13.00

SKELETON KEY (Volume 2)
Amaze Ink: 1999 - No. 4, 1999 ($2.95, B&W)

	GD 2.0	VG 4.0	FN 6.0	VF 8.0	VF/NM 9.0	NM- 9.2
1-4-Andrew Watson-s/a						3.00

SKELETON WARRIORS
Marvel Comics: Apr, 1995 - No. 4, July, 1995 ($1.50)

	GD 2.0	VG 4.0	FN 6.0	VF 8.0	VF/NM 9.0	NM- 9.2
1-4: Based on animated series.						2.25

SKIN GRAFT: THE ADVENTURES OF A TATTOOED MAN
DC Comics (Vertigo): July, 1993 - No. 4, Oct, 1993 ($2.50, lim. series, mature)

	GD 2.0	VG 4.0	FN 6.0	VF 8.0	VF/NM 9.0	NM- 9.2
1-4						2.50

SKINWALKER (Also see Promotional Comics section for FCBD Ed.)
Oni Press: May, 2002 - No. 4, Sept, 2002 ($2.95, limited series)

	GD 2.0	VG 4.0	FN 6.0	VF 8.0	VF/NM 9.0	NM- 9.2
1-4-Hurtt & Dela Cruz-a; Talon-c						3.00

SKI PARTY (See Movie Classics)

SKREEMER
DC Comics: May, 1989 - No. 6, Oct, 1989 ($2.00, limited series, mature)

	GD 2.0	VG 4.0	FN 6.0	VF 8.0	VF/NM 9.0	NM- 9.2
1-6: Contains graphic violence; Milligan-s						2.25
TPB (2002, $19.95) r/#1-6						20.00

SKRULL KILL KREW
Marvel Comics: Sept, 1995 - No. 5, Dec, 1995 ($2.95, limited series)

	GD 2.0	VG 4.0	FN 6.0	VF 8.0	VF/NM 9.0	NM- 9.2
1-5: Grant Morrison scripts. 2,3-Cap America app.						3.00

SKUL, THE
Virtual Comics (Byron Preiss Multimedia): Oct, 1996 - No. 3, Dec, 1996 ($2.50, limited series)

	GD 2.0	VG 4.0	FN 6.0	VF 8.0	VF/NM 9.0	NM- 9.2
1-3: Ron Lim & Jimmy Palmiotti-a						2.50

SKULL & BONES
DC Comics: 1992 - No. 3, 1992 ($4.95, limited series, 52 pgs.)

	GD 2.0	VG 4.0	FN 6.0	VF 8.0	VF/NM 9.0	NM- 9.2
Book 1-3: 1-1st app.						5.00

SKULL, THE SLAYER
Marvel Comics Group: Aug, 1975 - No. 8, Nov, 1976 (20¢/25¢)

	GD 2.0	VG 4.0	FN 6.0	VF 8.0	VF/NM 9.0	NM- 9.2
1-Origin & 1st app.; Gil Kane-c	2	4	6	8	10	12
2-8: 2-Gil Kane-c. 5,6-(Regular 25¢-c). 8-Kirby-c	1	2	3	4	5	7
5,6-(30¢-c variants, limited distribution)(5,7/76)	1	3	4	6	8	10

SKY BLAZERS (CBS Radio)
Hawley Publications: Sept, 1940 - No. 2, Nov, 1940

	GD 2.0	VG 4.0	FN 6.0	VF 8.0	VF/NM 9.0	NM- 9.2
1-Sky Pirates, Ace Archer, Flying Aces begin	62	124	186	388	594	800
2-WWII aerial battle-c	40	80	120	233	342	450

SKYMAN (See Big Shot Comics & Sparky Watts)
Columbia Comics Gr.: Fall?, 1941 - No. 2, Fall?, 1942; No. 3, 1948 - No. 4, 1948

	GD 2.0	VG 4.0	FN 6.0	VF 8.0	VF/NM 9.0	NM- 9.2
1-Origin Skyman, The Face, Sparky Watts app.; Whitney-c/a; 3rd story-r from Big Shot #1; Whitney c-1-4	123	246	369	769	1185	1600
2 (1942)-Yankee Doodle	60	120	180	375	580	785
3,4 (1948)	40	80	120	236	351	465

SKYPILOT
Ziff-Davis Publ. Co.: No. 10, 1950(nd) - No. 11, Apr-May, 1951

	GD 2.0	VG 4.0	FN 6.0	VF 8.0	VF/NM 9.0	NM- 9.2
10,11-Frank Borth-a; Saunders painted-c	15	30	45	83	117	150

SKY RANGER (See Johnny Law...)

SKYROCKET
Harry 'A' Chesler: 1944

	GD 2.0	VG 4.0	FN 6.0	VF 8.0	VF/NM 9.0	NM- 9.2
nn-Alias the Dragon, Dr. Vampire, Skyrocket & The Desperado app.; WWII Jap zero-c	33	66	99	190	275	360

SKY SHERIFF (Breeze Lawson...) (Also see Exposed & Outlaws)

Slam-Bang Comics #3 © FAW

Slave Girl Comics #1 © AVON

Smallville #10 © DC

	GD 2.0	VG 4.0	FN 6.0	VF 8.0	VF/NM 9.0	NM- 9.2
D. S. Publishing Co.: Summer, 1948						
1-Edmond Good-c/a	14	28	42	79	110	140
SKY WOLF (Also see Airboy)						
Eclipse Comics: Mar, 1988 - No. 3, Oct, 1988 ($1.25/$1.50/$1.95, lim. series)						
1-3						2.25
SLACKER COMICS						
Slave Labor Graphics: Aug, 1994 - Present ($2.95, B&W, quarterly)						
1-18, 1 (2nd printing)-Reads "2nd print" in indicia						3.00
SLAINE, THE BERSERKER (Slaine the King #21 on)						
Quality: July, 1987 - No. 28, 1989 ($1.25/$1.50)						
1-28						2.25
SLAINE, THE HORNED GOD						
Fleetway: 1998 - No. 3 ($6.99)						
1-3-Reprints series from 2000 A.D.; Bisley-a						7.00
SLAM BANG COMICS (Western Desperado #8)						
Fawcett Publications: Mar, 1940 - No. 7, Sept, 1940 (Combined with Master Comics #7)						
1-Diamond Jack, Mark Swift & The Time Retarder, Lee Granger, Jungle King begin & continue in Master	231	462	693	1444	2222	3000
2	92	184	276	575	888	1200
3-Classic-c	146	292	438	913	1407	1900
4-7: 6-Intro Zoro, the Mystery Man (also in #7)	75	150	225	469	722	975
SLAPSTICK						
Marvel Comics: Nov, 1992 - No. 4, Feb, 1993 ($1.25, limited series)						
1-4: Fry/Austin-c/a. 4-Ghost Rider, D.D., F.F. app.						2.25
SLAPSTICK COMICS						
Comic Magazines Distributors: nd (1946?) (36 pgs.)						
nn-Firetop feature; Post-a(2)	25	50	75	141	203	265
SLASH-D DOUBLECROSS						
St. John Publishing Co.: 1950 (Pocket-size, 132 pgs.)						
nn-Western comics	23	46	69	130	188	245
SLASH MARAUD						
DC Comics: Nov, 1987 - No. 6, Apr, 1988 ($1.75, limited series)						
1-6						2.25
SLAUGHTERMAN						
Comico: Feb, 1983 - No. 2, 1983 ($1.50, B&W)						
1,2						3.00
SLAVE GIRL COMICS (See Malu... & White Princess of the Jungle #2)						
Avon Periodicals/Eternity Comics (1989): Feb, 1949 - No. 2, Apr, 1949 (52 pgs.); Mar, 1989 (B&W, 44 pgs)						
1-Larsen-c/a	92	184	276	575	888	1200
2-Larsen-a	69	138	207	431	666	900
1-(3/89, $2.25, B&W, 44 pgs.)-r/#1						3.00
SLEDGE HAMMER (TV)						
Marvel Comics: Feb, 1988 - No. 2, Mar,1988 ($1.00, limited series)						
1,2						3.00
SLEEPER						
DC Comics (WildStorm): Mar, 2003 - No. 12, Mar, 2004 ($2.95)						
1-12-Brubaker-s/Phillips-c/a. 3-Back-up preview of The Authority: High Stakes pt. 2						3.00
...: All False Moves TPB (2004, $17.95) r/#7-12						18.00
...: Out in the Cold TPB (2004, $17.95) r/#1-6						18.00
SLEEPER: SEASON TWO						
DC Comics (WildStorm): Aug, 2004 - No. 12 ($2.95)						
1-6-Brubaker-s/Phillips-c/a.						3.00
SLEEPING BEAUTY (See Dell Giants & Movie Comics)						
Dell Publishing Co.: No. 973, May, 1959 - No. 984, June, 1959 (Disney)						
Four Color 973 (...and the Prince)	12	24	36	87	134	180
Four Color 984 (...Fairy Godmother's)	10	20	30	70	100	130
SLEEPWALKER						
Marvel Comics: June, 1991 - No. 33, Feb, 1994 ($1.00/$1.25)						
1-1st app. Sleepwalker						3.00
2-33: 4-Williamson-i. 5-Spider-Man-c/stor. 7-Infinity Gauntlet x-over. 8-Vs. Deathlok-c/story. 11-Ghost Rider-c/story. 12-Quesada-c/a(p) 14-Intro Spectra. 15-F.F.-c/story. 17-Darkhawk & Spider-Man x-over. 18-Infinity War x-over; Quesada/Williamson-c. 21,22-Hobgoblin app. 19-($2.00)-Die-cut Sleepwalker mask-c						2.25
25-($2.95, 52 pgs.)-Holo-grafx foil-c; origin						3.00
Holiday Special 1 (1/93, $2.00, 52 pgs.)-Quesada-c(p)						2.25
SLEEPWALKING						
Hall of Heroes: Jan, 1996 ($2.50, B&W)						
1-Kelley Jones-c						2.50
SLEEPY HOLLOW (Movie Adaption)						
DC Comics (Vertigo): 2000 ($7.95, one-shot)						
1-Kelley Jones-a/Seagle-s						8.00
SLEEZE BROTHERS, THE						
Marvel Comics (Epic Comics): Aug, 1989 - No. 6, Jan, 1990 ($1.75, mature)						
1-6: 4-6 (9/89 - 11/89 indicia dates)						2.25
nn-(1991, $3.95, 52 pgs.)						4.00
SLICK CHICK COMICS						
Leader Enterprises: 1947(nd) - No. 3, 1947(nd)						
1-Teenage humor	12	24	36	71	98	125
2,3	9	18	27	52	66	80
SLIDERS (TV)						
Acclaim Comics (Armada): June, 1996 - No. 2, July, 1996 ($2.50, lim. series)						
1,2: D.G. Chichester scripts; Dick Giordano-a.						2.50
SLIDERS: DARKEST HOUR (TV)						
Acclaim Comics (Armada): Oct, 1996 - No. 3, Dec, 1996 ($2.50, limited series)						
1-3						2.50
SLIDERS SPECIAL						
Acclaim Comics (Armada): Nov, 1996 - No 3, Mar, 1997 ($3.95, limited series)						
1-3: 1-Narcotica-Jerry O'Connell-s. 2-Blood and Splendor. 3-Deadly Secrets						4.00
SLIDERS: ULTIMATUM (TV)						
Acclaim Comics (Armada): Sept, 1996 - No. 2, Sept, 1996 ($2.50, lim. series)						
1,2						2.50
SLIMER! (TV cartoon) (Also see the Real Ghostbusters)						
Now Comics: 1989 - No. 19, Feb?, 1991 ($1.75)						
1-19: Based on animated cartoon						3.00
SLIM MORGAN (See Wisco)						
SLINGERS (See Spider-Man: Identity Crisis issues)						
Marvel Comics: Dec, 1998 - No. 12, Nov, 1999 ($2.99/$1.99)						
0-(Wizard #88 supplement) Prelude story						2.25
1-($2.99) Four editions w/different covers for each hero, 16 pages common to all, the other pages from each hero's perspective						3.00
2-12: 2-Two-c. 12-Saltares-a						2.25
SLOW NEWS DAY						
Slave Labor Graphics: July, 2001 - No. 6 ($3.50, B&W)						
1-6-Andi Watson-s/a						3.50
SLUDGE						
Malibu Comics (Ultraverse): Oct, 1993 - No. 12, Dec, 1994 ($2.50/$1.95)						
1-($2.50, 48 pgs.)-Intro/1st app. Sludge; Rune flip-c/story Pt. 1 (1st app., 3 pgs.) by Barry Smith; The Night Man app. (3 pg. preview); The Mighty Magnor 1 pg strip begins by Aragonés (cont. in other titles)						3.00
1-Ultra 5000 Limited silver foil						4.00
2-11: 3-Break-Thru x-over. 4-2 pg. Mantra origin. 8-Bloodstorm app.						2.50
12 ($3.50)-Ultraverse Premiere #8 flip book; Alex Ross poster						3.50
...:Red Xmas (12/94, $2.50, 44 pgs.)						2.50
SLUGGER (Little Wise Guys Starring...)(Also see Daredevil Comics)						
Lev Gleason Publications: April, 1956						
1-Biro-c	7	14	21	35	43	50
SMALL GODS						
Image Comics: Jun, 2004 - Present ($2.95, B&W)						
1-5-Rand-s/Ferreyna-a						3.00
SMALLVILLE (Based on TV series)						
DC Comics: May, 2003 - Present ($3.50/$3.95, bi-monthly)						
1-6-Photo-c. 1-Plunkett-a; interviews with cast; season 1 episode guide begins						3.50
7-11-($3.95) 7-Chloe Chronicles begin; season 2 episode guide begins						4.00
Vol. 1 TPB (2004, $9.95) r/#1-4 & Smallville: The Comic; photo-c						10.00
SMALLVILLE: THE COMIC (Based on TV series)						
DC Comics: Nov, 2002 ($3.95, 64 pages, one-shot)						

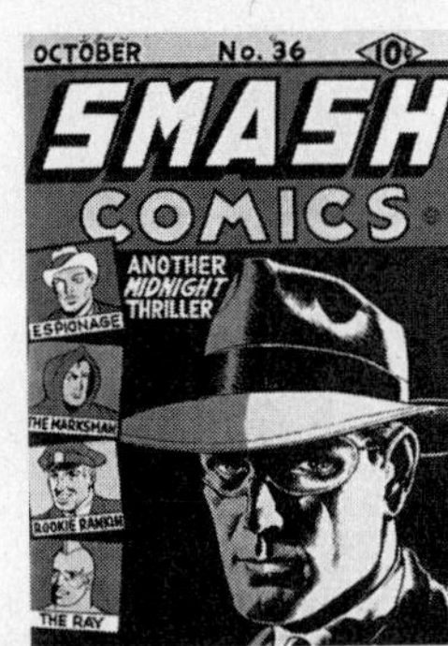

Smash Comics #36 © QUA

Smilin' Jack #2 © DELL

Smurfs #1 © MAR

GD VG FN VF VF/NM NM-
2.0 4.0 6.0 8.0 9.0 9.2

GD VG FN VF VF/NM NM-
2.0 4.0 6.0 8.0 9.0 9.2

1-Photo-c; art by Martinez and Leon; interviews with cast; season 2 preview 4.00

SMASH COMICS (Becomes Lady Luck #86 on)
Quality Comics Group: Aug, 1939 - No. 85, Oct, 1949

1-Origin Hugh Hazard & His Iron Man, Bozo the Robot, Espionage, Starring Black X by Eisner, & Hooded Justice (Invisible Justice #2 on); Chic Carter & Wings Wendall begin; 1st Robot on the cover of a comic book (Bozo) 303 606 909 1970 3185 4400
2-The Lone Star Rider app; Invisible Hood gains power of invisibility; bondage/torture-c 119 238 357 744 1147 1550
3-Captain Cook & Eisner's John Law begin 69 138 207 431 666 900
4,5: 4-Flash Fulton begins 65 130 195 406 628 850
6-12: 12-One pg. Fine-a 56 112 168 350 538 725
13-Magno begins (8/40); last Eisner issue; The Ray app. in full page ad; The Purple Trio begins 58 116 174 363 557 750
14-Intro. The Ray (9/40) by Lou Fine & others 300 600 900 1875 2888 3900
15,16: 16-The Scarlet Seal begins 125 250 375 781 1203 1625
17-Wun Cloo becomes plastic super-hero by Jack Cole (9-months before Plastic Man) 129 258 387 806 1241 1675
18-Midnight by Jack Cole begins (origin & 1st app., 1/41) 162 324 486 1013 1557 2100
19-22: Last Ray by Fine; The Jester begins-#22 87 174 261 544 835 1125
23,24: 24-The Sword app.; last Chic Carter; Wings Wendall dons new costume #24,25 67 134 201 419 647 875
25-Origin/1st app. Wildfire; Rookie Rankin begins 77 154 231 481 741 1000
26-30: 28-Midnight-c begin, end #85 66 132 198 413 637 860
31,32,34: The Ray by Rudy Palais; also #33 55 110 165 344 532 720
33-Origin The Marksman 65 130 195 406 628 850
35-37 51 102 153 311 473 635
38-The Yankee Eagle begins; last Midnight by Jack Cole; classic-c by Cole 96 192 288 600 925 1250
39,40-Last Ray issue 51 102 153 311 473 635
41,44-50 40 80 120 239 357 475
42-Lady Luck begins by Klaus Nordling 125 250 375 781 1203 1625
43-Lady Luck-c (1st & only in Smash) 46 92 138 281 428 575
51-60 31 62 93 177 256 335
61-70 25 50 75 141 203 265
71-85: 79-Midnight battles the Men from Mars-c/s 22 44 66 125 180 235

NOTE: ***Al Bryant** c-54, 63-68. **Cole** a-17-38, 68, 69, 72, 73, 78, 80, 83, 85; c-38, 60-62, 69-84. **Crandall** a-(Ray)-23-29, 35-38; c-36, 39, 40, 42-44, 46. **Fine** a(Ray)-14, 15, 16(w/**Tuska**), 17-22. **Fox** c-24-35. **Fuje** Ray-30. **Gil Fox** a-6-7, 9, 11-13. **Guardineer** a-(The Marksman)-39-?, 49, 52. **Gustavson** a-4-7, 9, 11-13 (The Jester)-22-46; (Magno)-13-21; (Midnight)-39(Cole inks), 49, 52, 63-65. **Kotzky** a-(Espionage)-33-38; c-45, 47-53. **Nordling** a-49, 52, 63-65. **Powell** a-11, 12, (Abdul the Arab)-13-24.Black X c-2, 6, 9, 11, 13, 16. Bozo the Robot c-1, 3, 5, 8, 10, 12, 14, 18, 20, 22, 24, 26. Midnight c-28-85. The Ray c-15, 17, 19, 21, 23, 25, 27. Wings Wendall c-4, 7.*

SMASH COMICS (Also see All Star Comics 1999 crossover titles)
DC Comics: May, 1999 ($1.99, one-shot)

1-Golden Age Doctor Mid-nite and Hourman 2.25

SMASH HIT SPORTS COMICS
Essankay Publications: V2#1, Jan, 1949

V2#1-L.B. Cole-c/a 31 62 93 175 253 330

SMAX (Also see Top Ten)
America's Best Comics: Oct, 2003 - No. 5, May, 2004 ($2.95, limited series)

1-5-Alan Moore-s/Zander Cannon-a 3.00
... Collected Edition (2004, $19.95, HC with dustjacket) r/#1-5 20.00

SMILE COMICS (Also see Gay Comics, Tickle, & Whee)
Modern Store Publ.: 1955 (52 pgs.; 5x7-1/4") (7¢)

1 6 12 18 31 38 45

SMILEY BURNETTE WESTERN (Also see Patches #8 & Six-Gun Heroes)
Fawcett Publ.: March, 1950 - No. 4, Oct, 1950 (All photo front & back-c)

1-Red Eagle begins 46 92 138 281 428 575
2-4 35 70 105 198 287 375

SMILEY (THE PSYCHOTIC BUTTON) (See Evil Ernie)
Chaos! Comics: July, 1998 - Present ($2.95, one-shots)

1-Ivan Reis-a 3.00
... Holiday Special (1/99), ...'s Spring Break (4/99), ...Wrestling Special (5/99) 3.00

SMILIN' JACK (See Famous Feature Stories and Popular Comics) (Also see Super Book of Comics #1&2 and Super-Book of Comics #7&19 in the Promotional Comics section)
Dell Publishing Co.: No. 5, 1940 - No. 8, Oct-Dec, 1949

Four Color 5 55 110 165 432 679 925
Four Color 10 (1940) 46 92 138 370 578 785
Large Feature Comic 12,14,25 (1941) 44 88 132 352 551 750
Four Color 4 (1942) 41 82 123 305 478 650
Four Color 14 (1943) 33 66 99 248 387 525
Four Color 36,58 (1943-44) 25 50 75 177 271 365
Four Color 80 (1945) 16 32 48 116 178 240
Four Color 149 (1947), 1 (1-3/48) 11 22 33 80 120 160
1 (1-3/48) 10 20 30 73 107 140
2 7 14 21 46 63 80
3-8 (10-12/49) 5 10 15 36 48 60

SMILING SPOOK SPUNKY (See Spunky)

SMITTY (See Popular Comics, Super Book #2, 4 & Super Comics)
Dell Publishing Co.: No. 11, 1940 - No. 7, Aug-Oct, 1949; No. 909, Apr, 1958

Four Color 11 (1940) 34 68 102 255 403 550
Large Feature Comic 26 (1941) 35 70 105 201 293 385
Four Color 6 (1942) 23 46 69 165 253 340
Four Color 32 (1943) 17 34 51 121 186 250
Four Color 65 (1945) 14 28 42 97 149 200
Four Color 99 (1946) 12 24 36 84 127 170
Four Color 138 (1947) 10 20 30 73 107 140
1 (2-4/48) 10 20 30 70 100 130
2-(5-7/48) 6 12 18 40 55 70
3,4: 3-(8-10/48), 4-(11-1/48-49) 5 10 15 36 48 60
5-7, Four Color 909 (4/58) 4 8 12 29 40 50

SMOKEY BEAR (TV) (See March Of Comics #234, 362, 372, 383, 407)
Gold Key: Feb, 1970 - No. 13, Mar, 1973

1 4 8 12 22 30 38
2-5 2 4 6 11 14 18
6-13 2 4 6 8 10 12

SMOKEY STOVER (See Popular Comics, Super Book #5,17,29 & Super Comics)
Dell Publishing Co.: No. 7, 1942 - No. 827, Aug, 1957

Four Color 7 (1942)-Reprints 31 62 93 225 355 485
Four Color 35 (1943) 18 36 54 129 197 265
Four Color 64 (1944) 14 28 42 102 156 210
Four Color 229 (1949) 7 14 21 51 71 90
Four Color 730,827 6 12 18 40 55 70

SMOKEY THE BEAR (See Forest Fire for 1st app.)
Dell Publ. Co.: No. 653, 10/55 - No. 1214, 8/61 (See March of Comics #234)

Four Color 653 (#1) 12 24 36 86 131 175
Four Color 708,754,818,932 7 14 21 51 71 90
Four Color 1016,1119,1214 5 10 15 36 48 60

SMOKY (See Movie Classics)

SMURFS (TV)
Marvel Comics: 1982 (Dec) - No. 3, 1983

1-3 1 3 4 6 8 10
...Treasury Edition 1 (64 pgs.)-r/#1-3 3 6 9 18 24 30

SNAFU (Magazine)
Atlas Comics (RCM): Nov, 1955 - V2#2, Mar, 1956 (B&W)

V1#1-Heath/Severin-a; Everett, Maneely-a 13 26 39 76 106 135
V2#1,2-Severin-a 10 20 30 58 77 95

SNAGGLEPUSS (TV)(See Hanna-Barbera Band Wagon, Quick Draw McGraw #5 & Spotlight #4)
Gold Key: Oct, 1962 - No. 4, Sept, 1963 (Hanna-Barbera)

1 10 20 30 72 104 135
2-4 8 16 24 53 74 95

SNAKE PLISSKEN CHRONICLES, (John Carpenter's...)
Hurricane Entertainment: June, 2003 - Present ($2.99)

Preview Issue (8/02, no cover price) B&W preview; John Carpenter interview 2.25
1-4: 1-Three covers; Rodriguez-a 3.00

SNAKES AND LADDERS
Eddie Campbell Comics: 2001 ($5.95, B&W, one-shot)

nn-Alan Moore-s/Eddie Campbell-a 6.00

SNAP (Formerly Scoop #8; becomes Jest #10,11 & Komik Pages #10)
Harry 'A' Chesler: No. 9, 1944

9-Manhunter, The Voice 20 40 60 112 161 210

SNAPPY COMICS
Cima Publ. Co. (Prize Publ.): 1945

1-Airmale app.; 9 pg. Sorcerer's Apprentice adapt; Kiefer-a 34 68 102 193 279 365

Sojourn #11 © CRO

Solar #33 © VAL

Soldier X #10 © MAR

GD VG FN VF VF/NM NM-
2.0 4.0 6.0 8.0 9.0 9.2

SNARKY PARKER (See Life With...)

SNIFFY THE PUP
Standard Publ. (Animated Cartoons): No. 5, Nov, 1949 - No. 18, Sept, 1953

	GD	VG	FN	VF	VF/NM	NM-
5-Two Frazetta text illos	10	20	30	60	80	100
6-10	7	14	21	35	43	50
11-18	6	12	18	28	34	40

SNOOPER AND BLABBER DETECTIVES (TV) (See Whitman Comic Books)
Gold Key: Nov, 1962 - No. 3, May, 1963 (Hanna-Barbera)

	GD	VG	FN	VF	VF/NM	NM-
1	10	20	30	72	104	135
2,3	8	16	24	55	78	100

SNOW WHITE (See Christmas With... (in Promotional Comics section), Mickey Mouse Magazine, Movie Comics & Seven Dwarfs)
Dell Publishing Co.: No. 49, July, 1944 - No. 382, Mar, 1952 (Disney-Movie)

	GD	VG	FN	VF	VF/NM	NM-
Four Color 49 (...& the Seven Dwarfs)	55	110	165	425	675	925
Four Color 382 (1952)-origin; partial reprint of Four Color 49	11	22	33	80	120	160

SNOW WHITE
Marvel Comics: Jan, 1995 ($1.95, one-shot)

1-r/1937 Sunday newspaper pages 2.25

SNOW WHITE AND THE SEVEN DWARFS
Whitman Publications: April, 1982 (60¢)

nn-r/Four Color #49 1 2 3 5 6 8

SNOW WHITE AND THE SEVEN DWARFS GOLDEN ANNIVERSARY
Gladstone: Fall, 1987 ($2.95, magazine size, 52 pgs.)

1-Contains poster 2 4 6 9 11 14

SOAP OPERA LOVE
Charlton Comics: Feb, 1983 - No. 3, June, 1983

1-3-Low print run 3 7 10 21 28 35

SOAP OPERA ROMANCES
Charlton Comics: July, 1982 - No. 5, March, 1983

1-5-Nurse Betsy Crane-r; low print run 3 7 10 21 28 35

SOCK MONKEY
Dark Horse Comics: Sept, 1998 - No. 2, Oct, 1998 ($2.95/$2.99, B&W)

1,2-Tony Millionaire-s/a 4.00
Vol. 2 -(Tony Millionaire's Sock Monkey) July, 1999 - No. 2, Aug, 1999
1,2 3.00
Vol. 3 -(Tony Millionaire's Sock Monkey) Nov, 2000 - No. 2, Dec, 2000
1,2 3.00
Vol. 4 -(Tony Millionaire's Sock Monkey) May, 2003 - No. 2, Aug, 2003
1,2 3.00

SO DARK THE ROSE
CFD Productions: Oct, 1995 ($2.95)

1-Wrightson-c 4.00

SOJOURN
White Cliffs Publ. Co.: Sept, 1977 - No. 2, 1978 ($1.50, B&W & color, tabloid size)

1,2: 1-Tor by Kubert, Eagle by Severin, E. V. Race, Private Investigator by Doug Wildey, T. C. Mars by Aragonés begin plus other strips 2 4 6 8 10 12
NOTE: Most copies came folded. Unfolded copies are worth 50% more.

SOJOURN
CrossGeneration Comics: July, 2001 - No. 34, May, 2004 ($2.95)

Prequel -Ron Marz-s/Greg Land-c/a; preview pages 3.00
1-Ron Marz-s/Greg Land-c/a in most 6.00
2,3 5.00
4-24: 7-Immonen-a. 12-Brigman-a. 17-Lopresti-a. 21-Luke Ross-a 3.25
25-34: 25-$1.00-c. 34-Cariello-a 3.00
...: From the Ashes TPB (2001, $19.95) r/#1-6; Land painted-c 20.00
...: The Dragon's Tale TPB (2002, $15.95) r/#7-12; Jusko painted-c 16.00
...: The Warrior's Tale TPB (2003, $15.95) r/#13-18 16.00
Vol. 4:The Thief's Tale (2003, $15.95) r/#19-24 16.00
Traveler Vol.1,2 ($9.95) digest-sized reprints of TPBs 10.00

SOLAR (...Man of the Atom) (Also see Doctor Solar)
Valiant/Acclaim Comics (Valiant): Sept, 1991 - No. 60, Apr, 1996 ($1.75-$2.50, 44 pgs.)

1-Layton-a(i) on Solar; Barry Windsor-Smith-c/a 1 3 4 6 8 10
2-9: 2-Layton-a(i) on Solar, B. Smith-a. 3-1st app. Harada (11/91). 7-vs. X-O Armor 6.00
10-(6/92, $3.95)-1st app. Eternal Warrior (6 pgs.); black embossed-c; origin & 1st app. Geoff McHenry (Geomancer) 1 3 4 6 8 11
10-($3.95)-2nd printing 4.00
11-15: 11-1st full app. Eternal Warrior. 12,13-Unity x-overs. 14-1st app. Fred Bender (becomes Dr. Eclipse). 15-2nd Dr. Eclipse 3.00
16-60: 17-X-O Manowar app. 23-Solar splits. 29-1st Valiant Vision book. 33-Valiant Vision; bound-in trading card. 38-Chaos Effect Epsilion Pt.1. 46-52-Dan Jurgens-a(p)/scripts w/Giordano-i. 53,54-Jurgens scripts only. 60-Giffen scripts; Jeff Johnson-a(p) 2.50
0-($9.95, trade paperback)-r/Alpha and Omega origin story; polybagged w/poster 10.00
...:Second Death (1994, $9.95)-r/issues #1-4. 10.00
NOTE: *#1-10 all have free 8 pg. insert "Alpha and Omega" which is a 10 chapter Solar origin story. All 10 centerfolds can pieced together to show climax of story.* ***Ditko*** *a-11p, 14p.* ***Giordano*** *a-46, 47, 48, 49, 50, 51, 52i.* ***Johnson*** *a-60p.* ***Jurgens*** *a-46, 47, 48, 49, 50 , 51, 52p.* ***Layton*** *a-1-3i; c-2i, 11i, 17i, 25i.* ***Miller*** *c-12.* ***Quesada*** *c-17p, 20-23p, 29p.* ***Simonson*** *c-13.* ***B. Smith*** *a-1-10; c-1, 3, 5, 7, 19i.* ***Thibert*** *c-22i, 23i.*

SOLAR LORD
Image Comics: Mar, 1999 - No. 7, Sept, 1999 ($2.50)

1-7-Khoo Fuk Lung-s/a 2.50

SOLARMAN (See Pendulum Ill. Originals)
Marvel Comics: Jan, 1989 - No. 2, May, 1990 ($1.00, limited series)

1,2 2.25

SOLAR, MAN OF THE ATOM (Man of the Atom on cover)
Acclaim Comics (Valiant Heroes): Vol. 2, May, 1997 ($3.95, one-shot, 46 pgs)
(1st Valiant Heroes Special Event)

Vol. 2-Reintro Solar; Ninjak cameo; Warren Ellis scripts; Darick Robertson-a 4.00

SOLAR, MAN OF THE ATOM: HELL ON EARTH
Acclaim Comics (Valiant Heroes): Jan, 1998 - No. 4 ($2.50, limited series)

1-4-Priest-s/ Zircher-a(p) 2.50

SOLAR, MAN OF THE ATOM: REVELATIONS
Acclaim Comics (Valiant Heroes): Nov, 1997 ($3.95, one-shot, 46 pgs.)

1-Krueger-s/ Zircher-a(p) 4.00

SOLDIER & MARINE COMICS (Fightin' Army #16 on)
Charlton Comics (Toby Press of Conn. V1#11): No. 11, Dec, 1954 - No. 15, Aug, 1955; V2#9, Dec, 1956

	GD	VG	FN	VF	VF/NM	NM-
V1#11 (12/54)-Bob Powell-a	9	18	27	49	62	75
V1#12(2/55)-15: 12-Photo-c	6	12	18	28	34	40
V2#9(Formerly Never Again; Jerry Drummer V2#10 on)	5	10	15	24	30	35

SOLDIER COMICS
Fawcett Publications: Jan, 1952 - No. 11, Sept, 1953

	GD	VG	FN	VF	VF/NM	NM-
1	13	26	39	74	102	130
2	8	16	24	43	54	65
3-5	8	16	24	40	50	60
6-11: 8-Illo. in **POP**	7	14	21	37	46	55

SOLDIERS OF FORTUNE
American Comics Group (Creston Publ. Corp.): Mar-Apr, 1951 - No. 13, Feb-Mar, 1953

	GD	VG	FN	VF	VF/NM	NM-
1-Capt. Crossbones by Shelly, Ace Carter, Lance Larson begin	24	48	72	135	195	255
2	14	28	42	79	110	140
3-10: 6-Bondage-c	12	24	36	69	95	120
11-13 (War format)	8	16	24	46	58	70

NOTE: ***Shelly*** *a-1-3, 5.* ***Whitney*** *a-6, 8-11, 13; c-1-3, 5, 6.*

SOLDIERS OF FREEDOM
Americomics: 1987 - No. 2, 1987 ($1.75)

1,2 3.00

SOLDIER X (Continued from Cable)
Marvel Comics: Sept, 2002 - No. 12, Aug, 2003 ($2.99/$2.25)

1,10,11,12-($2.99) 1-Kordey-a/Macan-s. 10-Bollers-s/Ranson-a 3.00
2-9-($2.25) 2.25

SOLITAIRE (Also See Prime V2#6-8)
Malibu Comics (Ultraverse): Nov, 1993 - No. 12, Dec, 1994 ($1.95)

1-($2.50)-Collector's edition bagged w/playing card 2.50
1-12: 1-Regular edition w/o playing card. 2,4-Break-Thru x-over. 3-2 pg. origin The Night Man. 4-Gatefold-c. 5-Two pg. origin the Strangers 2.25

SOLO
Marvel Comics: Sept, 1994 - No. 4, Dec, 1994 ($1.75, limited series)

1-4: Spider-Man app. 2.25

SOLO (Movie)
Dark Horse Comics: July, 1996 - No. 2, Aug, 1996 ($2.50, limited series)

Sonic the Hedgehog #64 © SEGA

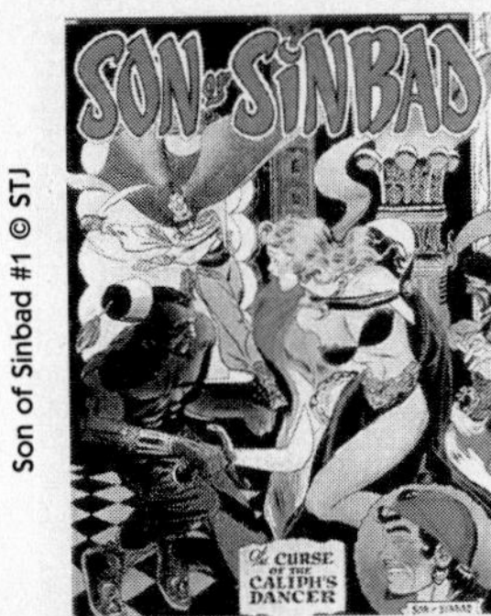

Son of Sinbad #1 © STJ

Soulfire #0 © Aspen MLT

GD 2.0 | VG 4.0 | FN 6.0 | VF 8.0 | VF/NM 9.0 | NM- 9.2

1,2: Adaptation of film; photo-c 2.50

SOLO
DC Comics: Dec, 2004 - Present ($4.95, anthology showcasing individual artists)
1-Tim Sale-a'stories by Sale and various 5.00

SOLO AVENGERS (Becomes Avenger Spotlight #21 on)
Marvel Comics: Dec, 1987 - No. 20, July, 1989 (75¢/$1.00)
1-Jim Lee-a on back-up story 3.00
2-20: 11-Intro Bobcat 2.50

SOLOMON AND SHEBA (Movie)
Dell Publishing Co.: No. 1070, Jan-Mar, 1960
Four Color 1070-Sekowsky-a; photo-c 10 20 30 72 104 135

SOLOMON KANE (Based on the Robert E. Howard character. Also see Blackthorne 3-D Series #60 & Marvel Premiere)
Marvel Comics: Sept, 1985 - No. 6, July, 1986 (Limited series)
1-6: 1-Double size. 3-6-Williamson-a(i) 3.00

SOLUS
CG Entertainment, Inc.: Apr, 2003 - No. 8, Jan, 2004 ($2.95)
1-8: 1-4,6,7-George Pérez-a/c; Barbara Kesel-s. 5-Ryan-a. 8-Kirk-a 3.00
Vol. 1: Genesis (1/04, $15.95) r/#1-6 16.00

SOLUTION, THE
Malibu Comics (Ultraverse): Sept, 1993 - No. 17, Feb, 1995 ($1.95)
1,3-15: 1-Intro Meathook, Deathdance, Black Tiger, Tech. 4-Break-Thru x-over; gatefold-c. 5-2 pg. origin The Strangers. 11-Brereton-c 2.50
1-($2.50)-Newsstand ed. polybagged w/trading card 2.50
1-Ultra 5000 Limited silver foil 4.00
0-Obtained w/Rune #0 by sending coupons from 11 comics 3.00
2-($2.50, 48 pgs.)-Rune flip-c/story by B. Smith; The Mighty Magnor 1 pg. strip by Aragonés 2.50
16 ($3.50)-Flip-c Ultraverse Premiere #10 3.50
17 ($2.50) 2.50

SOMERSET HOLMES (See Eclipse Graphic Novel Series)
Pacific Comics/ Eclipse Comics No. 5, 6: Sept, 1983 - No. 6, Dec, 1984 ($1.50, Baxter paper)
1-6: 1-Brent Anderson-c/a. Cliff Hanger by Williamson in all 3.00

SOMETHING WICKED
Image Comics: Oct, 2003 - Present ($2.95, B&W)
1-3-Jerry Beck-a 3.00

SONG OF THE SOUTH (See Brer Rabbit)

SONIC & KNUCKLES
Archie Comics: Aug, 1995 ($2.00)
1 6.00

SONIC DISRUPTORS
DC Comics: Dec, 1987 - No. 7, July, 1988 ($1.75, unfinished limited series)
1-7 3.00

SONIC'S FRIENDLY NEMESIS KNUCKLES
Archie Publications: July, 1996 - No. 3, Sept, 1996 ($1.50, limited series)
1-3 4.00

SONIC SUPER SPECIAL
Archie Publications: 1997 - Present ($2.00/$2.25/$2.29, 48 pgs)
1-3 4.00
4-6,8-15: 10-Sabrina-c/app. 15-Sin City spoof 3.00
7-(w/Image) Spawn, Maxx, Savage Dragon-c/app.; Valentino-a 3.00

SONIC THE HEDGEHOG (TV, video game)
Archie Comics: No. 0, Feb, 1993 - No. 3, May, 1993 ($1.25, mini-series)
0(2/93),1: Shaw-a(p) & covers on all 3 6 9 18 23 28
2,3 2 4 6 11 14 18
Beginnings TPB (2003, $10.95) r/#0-3 11.00

SONIC THE HEDGEHOG (TV, video game)
Archie Comics: July, 1993 - Present ($1.25/$1.50/$1.75/$1.79/$1.99/$2.19)
1 3 7 10 21 28 35
2,3 2 4 6 14 18 22
4-10: 8-Neon ink-c. 2 4 6 11 14 18
11-20 2 4 6 10 12 15
21-30 ($1.50): 25-Silver ink-c 1 3 4 6 8 10
31-50 1 2 3 4 5 7
51-93 3.50
94-146: 117-Begin $2.19-c 2.25
Triple Trouble Special (10/95, $2.00, 48 pgs.) 4.50

SONIC VS. KNUCKLES "BATTLE ROYAL" SPECIAL
Archie Publications: 1997 ($2.00, one-shot)
1 4.00

SON OF AMBUSH BUG (See Ambush Bug)
DC Comics: July, 1986 - No. 6, Dec, 1986 (75¢)
1-6: Giffen-c/a in all. 5-Bissette-a. 2.25

SON OF BLACK BEAUTY (Also see Black Beauty)
Dell Publishing Co.: No. 510, Oct, 1953 - No. 566, June, 1954
Four Color 510, 566 4 8 12 27 36 45

SON OF FLUBBER (See Movie Comics)

SON OF MUTANT WORLD
Fantagor Press: 1990 - No. 5, 1990? ($2.00, bi-monthly)
1-5: 1-3: Corben-c/a. 4,5 ($1.75, B&W) 3.00

SON OF ORIGINS OF MARVEL COMICS (See Fireside Book Series)

SON OF SATAN (Also see Ghost Rider #1 & Marvel Spotlight #12)
Marvel Comics Group: Dec, 1975 - No. 8, Feb, 1977 (25¢)
1-Mooney-a; Kane-c(p), Starlin splash(p) 3 6 9 18 24 30
2,6-8: 2-Origin The Possessor. 8-Heath-a 2 4 6 10 12 15
3-5-(Regular 25¢ editions)(4-8/76): 5-Russell-p 2 4 6 10 12 15
3-5-(30¢-c variants, limited distribution) 2 4 6 14 18 22

SON OF SINBAD (Also see Abbott & Costello & Daring Adventures)
St. John Publishing Co.: Feb, 1950
1-Kubert-c/a 40 80 120 233 342 450

SON OF SUPERMAN (Elseworlds)
DC Comics: 1999 ($14.95, prestige format, one-shot)
nn-Chaykin & Tischman-s/Williams III & Gray-a 15.00

SON OF TOMAHAWK (See Tomahawk)

SON OF VULCAN (Formerly Mysteries of Unexplored Worlds #1-48; Thunderbolt V3#51 on)
Charlton Comics: V2#49, Nov, 1965 - V2#50, Jan, 1966
V2#49,50: 50-Roy Thomas scripts (1st pro work) 3 6 9 19 25 32

SON OF YUPPIES FROM HELL (See Yuppies From Hell)
Marvel Comics: 1990 ($3.50, B&W, squarebound, 52 pgs.)
nn 3.50

SONS OF KATIE ELDER (See Movie Classics)

SORCERY (See Chilling Adventures in... & Red Circle...)

SORORITY SECRETS
Toby Press: July, 1954
1 9 18 27 52 66 80

SOULFIRE (MICHAEL TURNER PRESENTS:...)
Aspen MLT, Inc.: No. 0, 2004 - Present ($2.50/$2.99)
0-($2.50) Turner-a/c; Loeb-s; intro. to characters & development sketches 2.50
1-($2.99) Two covers 3.00
1-Diamond Previews Exclusive 5.00
2-Two covers 3.00

SOUL OF A SAMURAI
Image Comics: May, 2003 - No. 4, May, 2004 ($5.95, 8 1/4" x 5 3/4", limited series)
1-4-Will Dixon-s/a 6.00

SOULQUEST
Innovation: Apr, 1989 ($3.95, squarebound, 52 pgs.)
1-Blackshard app. 4.00

SOUL SAGA
Image Comics (Top Cow): Feb, 2000 - No. 5, Apr, 2001 ($2.50)
1-5: 1-Madureira-c; Platt & Batt-a 2.50

SOULSEARCHERS AND COMPANY
Claypool Comics: June, 1995 - Present ($2.50, B&W)
1-10: Peter David scripts 5.00
11-25 3.00
26-59 2.50

SOULWIND

Sovereign Seven #18 © Chris Claremont

Space Adventures #12 © CC

Space Circus #4 © Aragonés & Evanier

GD VG FN VF VF/NM NM-
2.0 4.0 6.0 8.0 9.0 9.2

Image Comics: Mar, 1997 - No. 8 ($2.95, B&W, limited series)
1-8: 5-"The Day I Tried To Live" pt. 1 — 3.00
Book Five; The August Ones (Oni Press, 3/01, $8.50) — 8.50
...The Kid From Planet Earth (1997, $9.95, TPB) — 10.00
...The Kid From Planet Earth (Oni Press, 1/00, $8.50, TPB) — 8.50
...The Day I Tried to Live (Oni Press, 4/00, $8.50, TPB) — 8.50
The Complete Soulwind TPB ($29.95, 11/03, 8" x 5 1/2") r/Oni Books #1-5 — 30.00

SOUPY SALES COMIC BOOK (TV)(The Official...)
Archie Publications: 1965
1 — 10 20 30 70 100 130

SOUTHERN KNIGHTS, THE (See Crusaders #1)
Guild Publ/Fictioneer Books: No. 2, 1983 - No. 41, 1993 (B&W)
2-Magazine size — 1 2 3 5 6 8
3-35, 37-41 — 3.00
36-($3.50-c) — 3.50
Dread Halloween Special 1, Primer Special 1 (Spring, 1989, $2.25) — 2.25
Graphic Novels #1-4 — 4.00

SOVEREIGN SEVEN (Also see Showcase '95 #12)
DC Comics: July, 1995 - No. 36, July, 1998 ($1.95) (1st creator-owned mainstream DC comic)
1-1st app. Sovereign Seven (Reflex, Indigo, Cascade, Finale, Cruiser, Network & Rampart); 1st app. Maitresse; Darkseid app.; Chris Claremont-s & Dwayne Turner-c/a begins — 3.00
1-Gold — 8.00
1-Platinum — 40.00
2-25: 2-Wolverine cameo. 4-Neil Gaiman cameo. 5,8-Batman app. 7-Ramirez cameo (from the movie Highlander). 9-Humphrey Bogart cameo from Casablanca. 10-Impulse app; Manoli Wetherell & Neal Conan cameo from Uncanny X-Men #226. 11-Robin app. 16-Final Night. 24-Superman app. 25-Power Girl app. — 2.25
26-36: 26-Begin $2.25-c. 28-Impulse-c/app. — 2.25
Annual 1 (1995, $3.95)-Year One story; Big Barda & Lobo app.; Jeff Johnson-c/a — 4.00
Annual 2 (1996, $2.95)-Legends of the Dead Earth; Leonardi-c/a — 3.50
...Plus 1(2/97, $2.95)-Legion-c/app. — 3.50
TPB-($12.95) r/#1-5, Annual #1 & Showcase '95 #12 — 13.00

SOVIET SUPER SOLDIERS
Marvel Comics: Nov, 1992 ($2.00, one-shot)
1-Marvel's Russian characters; Median & Saltares-a — 2.25

SPACE: ABOVE AND BEYOND (TV)
Topps Comics: Jan, 1996 - No. 3, Mar, 1996 ($2.95, limited series)
1-3: Adaptation of pilot episode; Steacy-c. — 3.00

SPACE: ABOVE AND BEYOND--THE GAUNTLET (TV)
Topps Comics: May, 1996 -No. 2, June, 1996 ($2.95, limited series)
1,2 — 3.00

SPACE ACE (Also see Manhunt!)
Magazine Enterprises: No. 5, 1952
5(A-1 #61)-Guardineer-a — 54 108 162 329 502 675

SPACE ACE: DEFENDER OF THE UNIVERSE (Based on the Don Bluth video game)
CrossGen Comics: Oct, 2003 - No. 6 ($2.95, limited series)
1,2-Kirkman-s/Borges-a — 3.00

SPACE ACTION
Ace Magazines (Junior Books): June, 1952 - No. 3, Oct, 1952
1-Cameron-a in all (1 story) — 75 150 225 469 722 975
2,3 — 55 110 165 336 511 685

SPACE ADVENTURES (War At Sea #22 on)
Capitol Stories/Charlton Comics: 7/52 - No. 21, 8/56; No. 23, 5/58 - No. 59, 11/64; V3#60, 10/67; V1#2, 7/68 - V1#8, 7/69; No. 9, 5/78 - No. 13, 3/79
1 — 52 104 156 317 484 650
2 — 28 56 84 158 229 300
3-5: 4,6-Flying saucer-c/stories — 22 44 66 125 180 235
6-9: 7-Sex change story "Transformation". 8-Robot-c. 9-A-Bomb panel — 20 40 60 112 161 210
10,11-Ditko-c/a. 10-Robot-c. 11-Two Ditko stories — 52 104 156 317 484 650
12-Ditko-c (classic) — 62 124 186 388 594 800
13-(Fox-r, 10-11/54); Blue Beetle-c/story — 16 32 48 92 131 170
14,15,17,18: 14-Blue Beetle-c/story; Fox-r (12-1/54-55, last pre-code). 15,17,18-Rocky Jones-c/s.(TV); 15-Part photo-c — 21 42 63 118 169 220
16-Krigstein-a; Rocky Jones-c/story (TV) — 23 46 69 130 188 245
19 — 15 30 45 83 117 150
20-Reprints Fawcett's "Destination Moon" — 27 54 81 152 219 285
21-(8/56) (no #22)(Becomes War At Sea) — 15 30 45 83 117 150
23-(5/58; formerly Nyoka, The Jungle Girl)-Reprints Fawcett's "Destination Moon" — 24 48 72 135 195 255
24,25,31,32-Ditko-a. 24-Severin-a(signed "LePoer") — 21 42 63 118 169 220
26,27-Ditko-a(4) each. 26,28-Flying saucer-c — 22 44 66 123 177 230
28-30 — 10 20 30 58 77 95
33-Origin/1st app. Capt. Atom by Ditko (3/60) — 39 78 117 293 459 625
34-40,42-All Captain Atom by Ditko — 16 32 48 112 171 230
41,43,45-59: 45-Mercury Man app. — 5 10 15 36 48 60
44-1st app. Mercury Man — 6 12 18 38 52 65
V3#60(#1, 10/67)-Origin & 1st app. Paul Mann & The Saucers From the Future — 6 12 18 38 52 65
2,5,6,8 (1968-69)-Ditko-a: 2-Aparo-c/a — 4 8 12 22 30 38
3,4,7: 4-Aparo-c/a — 3 6 9 18 23 28
9-13(1978-79)-Capt. Atom-r/Space Adventures by Ditko; 9-Reprints origin/1st app. Capt. Atom from #33 — 5.00

NOTE: *Aparo a-V3#60. c-V3#8.* ***Ditko*** *c-12, 31-42.* ***Giordano*** *c-3, 4, 7-9, 18p.* ***Krigstein*** *c-15.* ***Shuster*** *a-11. Issues 13 & 14 have Blue Beetle logos; #15-18 have Rocky Jones logos.*

SPACE ARK
Americomics (AC Comics)/ Apple Comics #3 on: June, 1985 - No. 5, Sept, 1987 ($1.75)
1-5: Funny animal (#1,2-color; #3-5-B&W) — 2.25

SPACE BUSTERS
Ziff-Davis Publ. Co.: Spring, 1952 - No. 2, Fall, 1952
1-Krigstein-a(3); Painted-c by Norman Saunders — 81 162 243 506 778 1050
2-Kinstler-a(2 pgs.); Saunders painted-c — 63 126 189 394 610 825

NOTE: ***Anderson*** *a-2. Bondage c-2.*

SPACE CADET (See Tom Corbett,...)

SPACE CIRCUS
Dark Horse Comics: July, 2000 - No. 4, Oct, 2000 ($2.95, limited series)
1-4-Aragonés-a/Evanier-s — 3.00

SPACE COMICS (Formerly Funny Tunes)
Avon Periodicals: No. 4, Mar-Apr, 1954 - No. 5, May-June, 1954
4,5-Space Mouse, Peter Rabbit, Super Pup (formerly Spotty the Pup), & Merry Mouse continue from Funny Tunes — 8 16 24 40 50 60
I.W. Reprint #8 (nd)-Space Mouse-r — 2 4 6 8 10 12

SPACED
Anthony Smith Publ. #1,2/Unbridled Ambition/Eclipse Comics #10 on: 1982 - No. 13, 1988 ($1.25/$1.50, B&W, quarterly)
1-($1.25-c) — 3.00
2-13, Special Edition (1983, Mimeo) — 2.25

SPACE DETECTIVE
Avon Periodicals: July, 1951 - No. 4, July, 1952
1-Rod Hathway, Space Detective begins, ends #4; Wood-c/a(3)-23 pgs.; "Opium Smugglers of Venus" drug story; Lucky Dale-r/Saint #4 — 110 220 330 688 1057 1425
2-Tales from the Shadow Squad story; Wood/Orlando-c; Wood inside layouts; "Slave Ship of Saturn" story — 83 166 249 519 797 1075
3,4: 3-Kinstler-c. 4-Kinstlerish-a by McCann — 40 80 120 244 372 500
I.W. Reprint #1(Reprints #2), 8(Reprints cover #1 & part Famous Funnies #191) — 4 8 12 27 36 45
I.W. Reprint #9-Exist? — 4 8 12 27 36 45

SPACE EXPLORER (See March of Comics #202)

SPACE FAMILY ROBINSON (TV)(...Lost in Space #15-37, ...Lost in Space On Space Station One #38 on)(See Gold Key Champion)
Gold Key: Dec, 1962 - No. 36, Oct, 1969; No. 37, 10/73 - No. 54, 11/78; No. 55, 3/81 - No. 59, 5/82 (All painted covers)
1-(Low distribution); Spiegle-a in all — 25 50 75 179 275 370
2(3/63)-Family becomes lost in space — 13 26 39 90 138 185
3-5 — 9 18 27 60 85 110
6-10: 6-Captain Venture back-up stories begin — 8 16 24 53 74 95
11-20: 14-(10/65). 15-Title change (1/66) — 6 12 18 38 52 65
21-36: 28-Last 12¢ issue. 36-Captain Venture ends — 4 8 12 27 36 45
37-48: 37-Origin retold — 2 4 6 11 14 18
49-59: Reprints #49,50,55-59 — 2 4 6 8 10 12

NOTE: *The TV show first aired on 9/15/65. Title changed after TV show debuted.*

SPACE FAMILY ROBINSON (See March of Comics #320, 328, 352, 404, 414)

SPACE GHOST (TV) (Also see Golden Comics Digest #2 & Hanna-Barbera Super TV Heroes #3-7)
Gold Key: March, 1967 (Hanna-Barbera) (TV debut was 9/10/66)
1 (10199-703)-Spiegle-a — 33 66 99 248 387 525

Space Ghost #1 © H-B

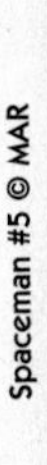

Spaceman #5 © MAR

Sparkle Comics #2 © UFS

SPACE GHOST (TV cartoon)
Comico: Mar, 1987 ($3.50, deluxe format, one-shot) (Hanna-Barbera)

	GD 2.0	VG 4.0	FN 6.0	VF 8.0	VF/NM 9.0	NM- 9.2
1-Steve Rude-c/a	1	2	3	5	6	8

SPACE GHOST (TV cartoon)
DC Comics: Jan, 2005 - No. 5 ($2.95, limited series)

	GD 2.0	VG 4.0	FN 6.0	VF 8.0	VF/NM 9.0	NM- 9.2
1-Alex Ross-c/Ariel Olivetti-a/Joe Kelly-s; origin of Space Ghost						3.00

SPACE GIANTS, THE (TV cartoon)
FBN Publications: 1979 ($1.00, B&W, one-shots)

	GD 2.0	VG 4.0	FN 6.0	VF 8.0	VF/NM 9.0	NM- 9.2
1-Based on Japanese TV series	2	4	6	10	12	15

SPACEHAWK
Dark Horse Comics: 1989 - No. 3, 1990 ($2.00, B&W)

	GD 2.0	VG 4.0	FN 6.0	VF 8.0	VF/NM 9.0	NM- 9.2
1-3-Wolverton-c/a(r) plus new stories by others.						4.00

SPACE JAM
DC Comics: 1996 ($5.95, one-shot, movie adaption)

	GD 2.0	VG 4.0	FN 6.0	VF 8.0	VF/NM 9.0	NM- 9.2
1-Wraparound photo cover of Michael Jordan	1	2	3	5	6	8

SPACE KAT-ETS (...in 3-D)
Power Publishing Co.: Dec, 1953 (25¢, came w/glasses)

	GD 2.0	VG 4.0	FN 6.0	VF 8.0	VF/NM 9.0	NM- 9.2
1	34	68	102	193	279	365

SPACEKNIGHTS
Marvel Comics: Oct, 2000 - No. 5, Feb, 2001 ($2.99, limited series)

	GD 2.0	VG 4.0	FN 6.0	VF 8.0	VF/NM 9.0	NM- 9.2
1-5-Starlin-s/Batista-a						3.00

SPACEMAN (Speed Carter...)
Atlas Comics (CnPC): Sept, 1953 - No. 6, July, 1954

	GD 2.0	VG 4.0	FN 6.0	VF 8.0	VF/NM 9.0	NM- 9.2
1-Grey tone-c	66	132	198	413	637	860
2	43	86	129	262	401	540
3-6: 4-A-Bomb explosion-c	40	80	120	233	342	450

NOTE: ***Everett*** *c-1, 3.* ***Heath*** *a-1.* ***Maneely*** *a-1(3), 2(4), 3(3), 4-6; c-5, 6.* ***Romita*** *a-1.* ***Sekowsky*** *c-4.* ***Sekowsky/Abel*** *a-4(3).* ***Tuska*** *a-5(3).*

SPACE MAN
Dell Publ. Co.: No. 1253, 1-3/62 - No. 8, 3-5/64; No. 9, 7/72 - No. 10, 10/72

	GD 2.0	VG 4.0	FN 6.0	VF 8.0	VF/NM 9.0	NM- 9.2
Four Color 1253 (#1)(1-3/62)(15¢-c)	9	18	27	60	85	110
2,3: 2-(15¢-c). 3-(12¢-c)	5	10	15	36	48	60
4-8-(12¢-c)	4	8	12	27	36	45
9,10-(15¢-c): 9-Reprints #1253. 10-Reprints #2	2	4	6	10	12	15

SPACEMAN (From the Atomics)
Oni Press: July, 2002 ($2.95, one-shot)

	GD 2.0	VG 4.0	FN 6.0	VF 8.0	VF/NM 9.0	NM- 9.2
1-Mike Allred-s/a; Lawrence Marvit additional art						3.00

SPACE MOUSE (Also see Funny Tunes & Space Comics)
Avon Periodicals: April, 1953 - No. 5, Apr-May, 1954

	GD 2.0	VG 4.0	FN 6.0	VF 8.0	VF/NM 9.0	NM- 9.2
1	10	20	30	56	73	90
2	7	14	21	35	43	50
3-5	6	12	18	28	34	40

SPACE MOUSE (Walter Lantz...:#1; see Comic Album #17)
Dell Publishing Co./Gold Key: No. 1132, Aug-Oct, 1960 - No. 5, Nov, 1963 (Walter Lantz)

	GD 2.0	VG 4.0	FN 6.0	VF 8.0	VF/NM 9.0	NM- 9.2
Four Color 1132,1244, 1(11/62)(G.K.)	5	10	15	36	48	60
2-5	4	8	12	29	40	50

SPACE MYSTERIES
I.W. Enterprises: 1964 (Reprints)

	GD 2.0	VG 4.0	FN 6.0	VF 8.0	VF/NM 9.0	NM- 9.2
1-r/Journey Into Unknown Worlds #4 w/new-c	3	6	9	18	23	28
8,9: 9-r/Planet Comics #73	3	6	9	18	23	28

SPACE: 1999 (TV) (Also see Power Record Comics)
Charlton Comics: Nov, 1975 - No. 7, Nov, 1976

	GD 2.0	VG 4.0	FN 6.0	VF 8.0	VF/NM 9.0	NM- 9.2
1-Origin Moonbase Alpha; Staton-c/a	2	4	6	12	16	20
2,7: 2-Staton-a	2	4	6	9	11	14
3-6: All Byrne-a; c-3,5,6	2	4	6	12	16	20

SPACE: 1999 (TV)(Magazine)
Charlton Comics: Nov, 1975 - No. 8, Nov, 1976 (B&W) (#7 shows #6 inside)

	GD 2.0	VG 4.0	FN 6.0	VF 8.0	VF/NM 9.0	NM- 9.2
1-Origin Moonbase Alpha; Morrow-c/a	2	4	6	14	18	22
2-8: 2,3-Morrow-c/a. 4-6-Morrow-c. 5,8-Morrow-a	2	4	6	10	13	16

SPACE PATROL (TV)
Ziff-Davis Publishing Co. (Approved Comics): Summer, 1952 - No. 2, Oct-Nov, 1952 (Painted-c by Norman Saunders)

	GD 2.0	VG 4.0	FN 6.0	VF 8.0	VF/NM 9.0	NM- 9.2
1-Krigstein-a	89	178	267	556	853	1150
2-Krigstein-a(3)	65	130	195	406	623	840

SPACE PIRATES (See Archie Giant Series #533)

SPACE RANGER (See Mystery in Space #92, Showcase #15 & Tales of the Unexpected)

SPACE SQUADRON (In the Days of the Rockets)(Becomes Space Worlds #6)
Marvel/Atlas Comics (ACI): June, 1951 - No. 5, Feb, 1952

	GD 2.0	VG 4.0	FN 6.0	VF 8.0	VF/NM 9.0	NM- 9.2
1-Space team; Brodsky c-1,5	66	132	198	413	637	860
2: Tuska c-2-4	55	110	165	340	520	700
3-5: 3-Capt. Jet Dixon by Tuska(3). 4-Weird advs. begin	46	92	138	281	428	575

SPACE THRILLERS
Avon Periodicals: 1954 (25¢ Giant)

	GD 2.0	VG 4.0	FN 6.0	VF 8.0	VF/NM 9.0	NM- 9.2
nn-(Scarce)-Robotmen of the Lost Planet; contains 3 rebound comics of The Saint & Strange Worlds. Contents could vary	115	230	345	719	1110	1500

SPACE TRIP TO THE MOON (See Space Adventures #23)

SPACE USAGI
Mirage Studios: June, 1992 - No. 3, 1992 ($2.00, B&W, mini-series)
V2#1, Nov, 1993 - V2#3, Jan, 1994 ($2.75)

	GD 2.0	VG 4.0	FN 6.0	VF 8.0	VF/NM 9.0	NM- 9.2
1-3: Stan Sakai-c/a/scripts, V2#1-3						3.00

SPACE USAGI
Dark Horse Comics: Jan, 1996 - No. 3, Mar, 1996 ($2.95, B&W, limited series)

	GD 2.0	VG 4.0	FN 6.0	VF 8.0	VF/NM 9.0	NM- 9.2
1-3: Stan Sakai-c/a/scripts						3.00

SPACE WAR (Fightin' Five #28 on)
Charlton Comics: Oct, 1959 - No. 27, Mar, 1964; No. 28, Mar, 1978 - No. 34, 3/79

	GD 2.0	VG 4.0	FN 6.0	VF 8.0	VF/NM 9.0	NM- 9.2
V1#1-Giordano-c begin, end #3	14	28	42	97	149	200
2,3	8	16	24	55	78	100
4-6,8,10-Ditko-c/a	14	28	42	97	149	200
7,9,11-15: Last 10¢ issue?	6	12	18	40	55	70
16-27 (3/64): 18,19-Robot-c	5	10	15	36	48	60
28(3/78),29-31,33,34-Ditko-c/a(r): 30-Staton, Sutton/Wood-a. 31-Ditko-c/a(3); same-c as Strange Suspense Stories #2 (1968); atom blast-c	1	3	4	6	8	10
32-r/Charlton Premiere V2#2; Sutton-a						5.00

SPACE WESTERN (Formerly Cowboy Western Comics; becomes Cowboy Western Comics #46 on)
Charlton Comics (Capitol Stories): No. 40, Oct, 1952 - No. 45, Aug, 1953

	GD 2.0	VG 4.0	FN 6.0	VF 8.0	VF/NM 9.0	NM- 9.2
40-Intro Spurs Jackson & His Space Vigilantes; flying saucer story	60	120	180	375	575	775
41,43-45: 41-Flying saucer-c. 45-Hitler app.	43	86	129	262	401	540
42-Atom bomb explosion-c	46	92	138	281	428	575

SPACE WORLDS (Formerly Space Squadron #1-5)
Atlas Comics (Male): No. 6, April, 1952

	GD 2.0	VG 4.0	FN 6.0	VF 8.0	VF/NM 9.0	NM- 9.2
6-Sol Brodsky-c	43	86	129	262	401	540

SPAGHETTI WESTERN
Oni Press: June, 2004 ($11.95, digest-size, widescreen, sepia & white)

	GD 2.0	VG 4.0	FN 6.0	VF 8.0	VF/NM 9.0	NM- 9.2
nn-Scott Morse-s/a; outer wraparound-c						12.00

SPANKY & ALFALFA & THE LITTLE RASCALS (See The Little Rascals)

SPANNER'S GALAXY
DC Comics: Dec, 1984 - No. 6, May, 1985 (limited series)

	GD 2.0	VG 4.0	FN 6.0	VF 8.0	VF/NM 9.0	NM- 9.2
1-6: Mandrake-c/a in all.						2.25

SPARKIE, RADIO PIXIE (Radio)(Becomes Big Jon & Sparkie #4)
Ziff-Davis Publ. Co.: Winter, 1951 - No. 3, July-Aug, 1952 (Painted-c)(Sparkie #2,3; #1?)

	GD 2.0	VG 4.0	FN 6.0	VF 8.0	VF/NM 9.0	NM- 9.2
1-Based on children's radio program	29	58	87	167	241	315
2,3: 3-Big Jon and Sparkie on-c only	20	40	60	112	161	210

SPARKLE COMICS
United Features Synd.: Oct-Nov, 1948 - No. 33, Dec-Jan, 1953-54

	GD 2.0	VG 4.0	FN 6.0	VF 8.0	VF/NM 9.0	NM- 9.2
1-Li'l Abner, Nancy, Captain & the Kids, Ella Cinders (#1-3: 52 pgs.)	15	30	45	83	117	150
2	9	18	27	49	62	75
3-10	8	16	24	40	50	60
11-20	6	12	18	33	41	48
21-32	6	12	18	28	34	40
33(2-3/54) 2 pgs. early Peanuts by Schulz	8	16	24	43	54	65

SPARKLE PLENTY (See Harvey Comics Library #2 & Dick Tracy)

SPARKLER COMICS (1st series)
United Feature Comic Group: July, 1940 - No. 2, 1940

	GD 2.0	VG 4.0	FN 6.0	VF 8.0	VF/NM 9.0	NM- 9.2
1-Jim Hardy	40	80	120	235	348	460

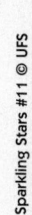

Sparkler Comics #39 © UFS

Sparkling Stars #11 © UFS

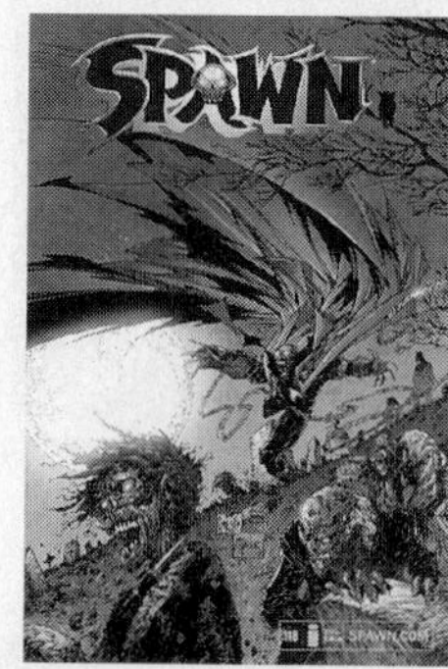
Spawn #118 © TMP

	GD 2.0	VG 4.0	FN 6.0	VF 8.0	VF/NM 9.0	NM- 9.2
2-Frankie Doodle	31	62	93	175	253	330

SPARKLER COMICS (2nd series)(Nancy & Sluggo #121 on)(Cover title becomes Nancy and Sluggo #101? on)
United Features Syndicate: July, 1941 - No. 120, Jan, 1955

	GD 2.0	VG 4.0	FN 6.0	VF 8.0	VF/NM 9.0	NM- 9.2
1-Origin 1st app. Sparkman; Tarzan (by Hogarth in all issues), Captain & the Kids, Ella Cinders, Danny Dingle, Dynamite Dunn, Nancy, Abbie & Slats, Broncho Bill, Frankie Doodle, begin; Spark Man c-1-9,11,12; Hap Hopper c-10,13	246	492	738	1538	2369	3200
2	83	166	249	519	797	1075
3,4	65	130	195	406	628	850
5-9: 9-Spark Man's new costume	60	120	180	375	575	775
10-Origin Spark Man?	60	120	180	375	575	775
11,12-Spark Man war-c. 12-Spark Man's new costume (color change)	48	96	144	293	447	600
13-Hap Hopper war-c	44	88	132	268	409	550
14-Tarzan-c by Hogarth	55	110	165	340	520	700
15,17: 15-Capt & Kids-c. 17-Nancy & Sluggo-c	40	80	120	233	342	450
16,18-Spark Man war-c	45	90	135	275	420	565
19-1st Race Riley and the Commandos-c/s	44	88	132	268	409	550
20-Nancy war-c	40	80	120	233	342	450
21,25,28,31,34,37,39-Tarzan-c by Hogarth	47	94	141	287	436	585
22-24,26,27,29,30: 22-Race Riley & the Commandos strips begin, ends #44	35	70	105	198	287	375
32,33,35,36,38,40	21	42	63	118	169	220
41,43,45,46,48,49	15	30	45	83	117	150
42,44,47,50-Tarzan-c (42,47,50 by Hogarth)	30	60	90	170	245	320
51,52,54-70: 57-Li'l Abner begins (not in #58); Fearless Fosdick app. in #58	14	28	42	79	110	140
53-Tarzan-c by Hogarth	25	50	75	144	207	270
71-80	10	20	30	56	73	90
81,82,84-86: 86 Last Tarzan; lingerie panels	9	18	27	49	62	75
83-Tarzan-c; Li'l Abner ends	12	24	36	71	98	125
87-96,98-99	8	16	24	46	58	70
97-Origin Casey Ruggles by Warren Tufts	13	26	39	74	102	130
100	9	18	27	52	66	80
101-107,109-112,114-119	7	14	21	37	46	55
108,113-Toth-a	9	18	27	52	66	80
120-(10-11/54) 2 pgs. early Peanuts by Schulz	8	16	24	46	58	70

SPARKLING LOVE
Avon Periodicals/Realistic (1953): June, 1950; 1953

	GD 2.0	VG 4.0	FN 6.0	VF 8.0	VF/NM 9.0	NM- 9.2
1(Avon)-Kubert-a; photo-c	24	48	72	135	195	255
nn(1953)-Reprint; Kubert-a	9	18	27	52	66	80

SPARKLING STARS
Holyoke Publishing Co.: June, 1944 - No. 33, March, 1948

	GD 2.0	VG 4.0	FN 6.0	VF 8.0	VF/NM 9.0	NM- 9.2
1-Hell's Angels, FBI, Boxie Weaver, Petey & Pop, & Ali Baba begin	20	40	60	112	161	210
2-Speed Spaulding story	11	22	33	62	84	105
3-Actual FBI case photos & war photos	9	18	27	52	66	80
4-10: 7-X-Mas-c	8	16	24	46	58	70
11-19: 13-Origin/1st app. Jungo the Man-Beast-c/s	8	16	24	40	50	60
20-Intro Fangs the Wolf Boy	8	16	24	46	58	70
21-29,32,33: 29-Bondage-c	8	16	24	40	50	60
31-Sid Greene-a	8	16	24	40	50	60

SPARK MAN (See Sparkler Comics)
Frances M. McQueeny: 1945 (36 pgs., one-shot)

	GD 2.0	VG 4.0	FN 6.0	VF 8.0	VF/NM 9.0	NM- 9.2
1-Origin Spark Man r/Sparkler #1-3; female torture story; cover redrawn from Sparkler #1	34	68	102	193	279	365

SPARKY WATTS (Also see Big Shot Comics & Columbia Comics)
Columbia Comic Corp.: Nov?, 1942 - No. 10, 1949

	GD 2.0	VG 4.0	FN 6.0	VF 8.0	VF/NM 9.0	NM- 9.2
1(1942)-Skyman & The Face app; Hitler-c	67	134	201	419	647	875
2(1943)	30	60	90	170	245	320
3(1944)	21	42	63	121	173	225
4(1944)-Origin	19	38	57	107	154	200
5(1947)-Skyman app.; Boody Rogers-c/a	16	32	48	89	127	165
6,7,9,10: 6(1947),10(1949)	10	20	30	58	77	95
8(1948)-Surrealistic-c	14	28	42	79	110	140

NOTE: *Boody Rogers c-1-8.*

SPARTACUS (Movie)
Dell Publishing Co.: No. 1139, Nov, 1960 (Kirk Douglas photo-c)

	GD 2.0	VG 4.0	FN 6.0	VF 8.0	VF/NM 9.0	NM- 9.2
Four Color 1139-Buscema-a	14	28	42	97	149	200

SPARTAN: WARRIOR SPIRIT (Also see WildC.A.T.S: Covert Action Teams)
Image Comics (WildStorm Productions): July, 1995 - No. 4, Nov, 1995 ($2.50, limited series)

	GD 2.0	VG 4.0	FN 6.0	VF 8.0	VF/NM 9.0	NM- 9.2
1-4: Kurt Busiek scripts; Mike McKone-c/a						2.50

SPAWN (Also see Curse of the Spawn and Sam & Twitch)
Image Comics (Todd McFarlane Prods.): May, 1992 - Present ($1.95/$2.50)

	GD 2.0	VG 4.0	FN 6.0	VF 8.0	VF/NM 9.0	NM- 9.2
1-1st app. Spawn; McFarlane-c/a begins; McFarlane/Steacy-c; 1st Todd McFarlane Productions title.	1	3	4	6	8	10
1-Black & white edition	2	4	6	12	16	20
2,3: 2-1st app. Violator; McFarlane/Steacy-c	1	2	3	5	7	9
4-Contains coupon for Image Comics #0	1	2	3	5	7	9
4-With coupon missing						3.00
4-Newsstand edition w/o poster or coupon						3.00
5-Cerebus cameo (1 pg.) as stuffed animal; Spawn mobile poster #1						6.00
6-8,10: 7-Spawn Mobile poster #2. 8-Alan Moore scripts; Miller poster. 10-Cerebus app.; Dave Sim scripts; 1 pg. cameo app. by Superman						4.00
9-Neil Gaiman scripts; Jim Lee poster; 1st Angela.						6.00
11-17,19,20,22-30: 11-Miller script; Darrow poster. 12-Bloodwulf poster by Liefeld. 14,15-Violator app. 16,17-Grant Morrison scripts; Capullo-c/a(p). 23,24-McFarlane-a/stories. 25-(10/94). 19-(10/94). 20-(11/94)						3.00
18-Grant Morrison script, Capullo-c/a(p); low distr.	1	2	3	5	7	9
21-low distribution	1	2	3	5	7	9
31-49: 31-1st app. The Redeemer; new costume (brief). 32-1st full app. new costume. 38-40,42,44,46,48-Tony Daniel-c/a(p). 38-1st app. Cy-Gor. 40,41-Cy-Gor & Curse app.						4.00
50-($3.95, 48 pgs.)						3.00
51-66: 52-Savage Dragon app. 56-w/ Darkchylde preview. 57-Cy-Gor-c/app. 64-Polybagged w/McFarlane Toys catalog. 65-Photo-c of movie Spawn and McFarlane						3.00
67-97: 81-Billy Kincaid returns. 97-Angela-c/app.						2.50
98,99,101-140-($2.50): 98,99-Angela app.						2.50
100-($4.95) Angela dies; 6 covers by McFarlane, Ross, Miller, Capullo, Wood, Mignola						5.00
Annual 1-Blood & Shadows ('99, $4.95) Ashley Wood-c/a; Jenkins-s						5.00
...Bible-(8/96, $1.95)-Character bios						4.00
Book 1 TPB($9.95) r/#1-5; Book 2-r/#6-9,11; Book 3 -r/#12-15, Book 4- r/#16-20; Book 5-r/#21-25; Book 6- r/#26-30; Book 7-r/#31-34; Book 8-r/#35-38; Book 9-r/#39-42; Book 10-r/#43-47						11.00
Book 11 TPB ($10.95) r/#48-50; Book 12-r/#51-54						11.00
...Simony (5/04, $7.95) English translation of French Spawn story; Briclot-a						8.00

NOTE: ***Capullo** a-16p-18p; c-16p-18p. **Daniel** a-38-40, 42, 44, 46. **McFarlane** a-1-15; c-1-15p. **Thibert** a-16i(part). Posters come with issues 1, 4, 7-9, 11, 12. #25 was released before #19 & 20.*

SPAWN-BATMAN (Also see Batman/Spawn: War Devil under Batman: One-Shots)
Image Comics (Todd McFarlane Productions): 1994 ($3.95, one-shot)

	GD 2.0	VG 4.0	FN 6.0	VF 8.0	VF/NM 9.0	NM- 9.2
1-Miller scripts; McFarlane-c/a						6.00

SPAWN: BLOOD FEUD
Image Comics (Todd McFarlane Prods.): June, 1995 - No. 4, Sept, 1995 ($2.25, lim. series)

	GD 2.0	VG 4.0	FN 6.0	VF 8.0	VF/NM 9.0	NM- 9.2
1-4-Alan Moore scripts, Tony Daniel-a						3.50

SPAWN FAN EDITION
Image Comics (Todd McFarlane Productions): Aug, 1996 - No. 3, Oct, 1996 (Giveaway, 12 pgs.) (Polybagged w/Overstreet's FAN)

	GD 2.0	VG 4.0	FN 6.0	VF 8.0	VF/NM 9.0	NM- 9.2
1-3: Beau Smith scripts; Brad Gorby-a(p). 1-1st app. Nordik, the Norse Hellspawn. 2-1st app. McFallon. 3-1st app. Mercy	1	2	3	5	6	8
1-3-(Gold): All retailer incentives						16.00
1-3-Variant-c	1	2	3	5	6	8
2-(Platinum)-Retailer incentive						25.00

SPAWN: THE DARK AGES
Image Comics (Todd McFarlane Productions): Mar, 1999 - No. 28, Oct, 2001 ($2.50)

	GD 2.0	VG 4.0	FN 6.0	VF 8.0	VF/NM 9.0	NM- 9.2
1-Fabry-c; Holguin-s/Sharp-a; variant-c by McFarlane						2.50
2-28						2.50

SPAWN THE IMPALER
Image Comics (Todd McFarlane Prods.): Oct, 1996 - No. 3, Dec, 1996 ($2.95, limited series)

	GD 2.0	VG 4.0	FN 6.0	VF 8.0	VF/NM 9.0	NM- 9.2
1-3-Mike Grell scripts, painted-a						3.00

SPAWN: THE UNDEAD
Image Comics (Todd McFarlane Prod.): Jun, 1999 - No. 9, Feb, 2000 ($1.95/$2.25)

	GD 2.0	VG 4.0	FN 6.0	VF 8.0	VF/NM 9.0	NM- 9.2
1-9-Dwayne Turner-c/a; Jenkins-s. 7-9-($2.25-c)						2.50

SPAWN/WILDC.A.T.S
Image Comics (WildStorm): Jan, 1996 - No. 4, Apr, 1996 ($2.50, lim. series)

	GD 2.0	VG 4.0	FN 6.0	VF 8.0	VF/NM 9.0	NM- 9.2
1-4: Alan Moore scripts in all.						3.00

SPECIAL AGENT (Steve Saunders...)(Also see True Comics #68)
Parents' Magazine Institute (Commended Comics No. 2): Dec, 1947 - No. 8, Sept, 1949 (Based on true FBI cases)

Special Marvel Edition #15 © MAR

Spectacular Spider-Man #2 © MAR

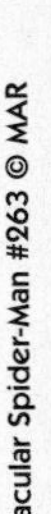
Spectacular Spider-Man #263 © MAR

GD VG FN VF VF/NM NM-
2.0 4.0 6.0 8.0 9.0 9.2

1-J. Edgar Hoover photo on-c 12 24 36 69 95 120
2 8 16 24 40 50 60
3-8 7 14 21 35 43 50

SPECIAL COLLECTORS' EDITION (See Savage Fists of Kung-Fu)

SPECIAL COMICS (Becomes Hangman #2 on)
MLJ Magazines: Winter, 1941-42

1-Origin The Boy Buddies (Shield & Wizard x-over); death of The Comet; origin The Hangman retold; Hangman-c 292 584 876 1825 2813 3800

SPECIAL EDITION (See Gorgo and Reptisaurus)

SPECIAL EDITION COMICS
Fawcett Publications: 1940 (August) (68 pgs., one-shot)

1-1st book devoted entirely to Captain Marvel; C.C. Beck-c/a; only app. of Captain Marvel with belt buckle; Capt. Marvel appears with button-down flap; 1st story (came out before Captain Marvel #1) 839 1678 2517 5873 9437 13,000

NOTE: *Prices vary widely on this book. Since this book is all Captain Marvel stories, it is actually a pre-Captain Marvel #1. There is speculation that this book almost became* ***Captain Marvel #1****. After* ***Special Edition*** *was published, there was an editor change at Fawcett. The new editor commissioned Kirby to do a nn* ***Captain Marvel*** *book early in 1941. This book was followed by a 2nd book several months later. This 2nd book was advertised as a #3 (making Special Edition the #1, & the nn issue the #2). However, the 2nd book did come out as a #2.*

SPECIAL EDITION: SPIDER-MAN VS. THE HULK (See listing under The Amazing Spider-Man)

SPECIAL EDITION X-MEN
Marvel Comics Group: Feb, 1983 ($2.00, one-shot, Baxter paper)

1-r/Giant-Size X-Men #1 plus one new story 2 4 6 8 10 12

SPECIAL MARVEL EDITION (Master of Kung Fu #17 on)
Marvel Comics Group: Jan, 1971 - No. 16, Feb, 1974 (#1-3: 25¢, 68 pgs.; #4: 52 pgs.; #5-16: 20¢, regular ed.)

1-Thor-r by Kirby; 68 pgs. 3 6 9 18 24 30
2-4: Thor-r by Kirby; 2,3-68 pg. Giant. 4-(52 pgs.) 2 4 6 11 14 18
5-14: Sgt. Fury-r; 11-r/Sgt. Fury #13 (Capt. America) 1 3 4 6 8 10
15-Master of Kung Fu (Shang-Chi) begins (1st app., 12/73); Starlin-a; origin/1st app. Nayland Smith & Dr. Petric 9 18 27 65 93 120
16-1st app. Midnight; Starlin-a (2nd Shang-Chi) 4 8 12 29 40 50

NOTE: *Kirby c-10-14.*

SPECIAL MISSIONS (See G.I. Joe...)

SPECIAL WAR SERIES (Attack V4#3 on?)
Charlton Comics: Aug, 1965 - No. 4, Nov, 1965

V4#1-D-Day (also see D-Day listing) 4 8 12 27 36 45
2-Attack! 3 6 9 16 20 25
3-War & Attack (also see War & Attack) 3 6 9 16 20 25
4-Judomaster (intro/1st app.; see Sarge Steel) 8 16 24 55 78 100

SPECIES (Movie)
Dark Horse Comics: June, 1995 - No. 4, Sept, 1995 ($2.50, limited series)

1-4: Adaptation of film 3.00

SPECIES: HUMAN RACE (Movie)
Dark Horse Comics: Nov, 1996 - No. 4, Feb, 1997 ($2.95, limited series)

1-4 3.00

SPECTACULAR ADVENTURES (See Adventures)

SPECTACULAR FEATURE MAGAZINE, A (Formerly My Confessions)
(Spectacular Features Magazine #12)
Fox Feature Syndicate: No. 11, April, 1950

11 (#1)-Samson and Delilah 31 62 93 175 253 330

SPECTACULAR FEATURES MAGAZINE (Formerly A Spectacular Feature Magazine)
Fox Feature Syndicate: No. 12, June, 1950 - No. 3, Aug, 1950

12 (#2)-Iwo Jima; photo flag-c 31 62 93 175 253 330
3-True Crime Cases From Police Files 25 50 75 141 203 265

SPECTACULAR SCARLET SPIDER
Marvel Comics: Nov, 1995 - No. 2, Dec, 1995 ($1.95, limited series)

1,2: Replaces Spectacular Spider-Man 2.25

SPECTACULAR SPIDER-MAN, THE (See Marvel Special Edition and Marvel Treasury Edition)

SPECTACULAR SPIDER-MAN, THE (Magazine)
Marvel Comics Group: July, 1968 - No. 2, Nov, 1968 (35¢)

1-(B&W)-Romita/Mooney 52 pg. story plus updated origin story with Everett-a(i) 11 22 33 80 120 160
1-Variation w/single c-price of 40¢ 11 22 33 80 120 160
2-(Color)-Green Goblin-c & 58 pg. story; Romita painted-c (story reprinted in King Size Spider-Man #9); Romita/Mooney-a 12 24 36 87 134 180

GD VG FN VF VF/NM NM-
2.0 4.0 6.0 8.0 9.0 9.2

SPECTACULAR SPIDER-MAN, THE (Peter Parker...#54-132, 134)
Marvel Comics Group: Dec, 1976 - No. 263, Nov, 1998

1-Origin recap in text; return of Tarantula 5 10 15 36 48 60
2-Kraven the Hunter app. 2 4 6 14 18 22
3-5: 3-Intro Lightmaster. 4-Vulture app. 2 4 6 10 13 16
6-8-Morbius app.; 6-r/Marvel Team-Up #3 w/Morbius 2 4 6 11 14 18
7,8-(35¢-c variants, limited distribution)(6,7/77) 3 6 9 17 22 27
9-20: 9,10-White Tiger app. 11-Last 30¢-c. 17,18-Angel & Iceman app. (from Champions); Ghost Rider cameo in flashback 2 4 6 8 10 12
9-11-(35¢-c variants, limited distribution)(8-10/77) 2 4 6 11 14 18
21,24-26: 21-Scorpion app. 26-Daredevil app. 1 2 3 5 7 9
22,23-Moon Knight app. 1 3 4 6 8 10
27-Miller's 1st art on Daredevil (2/79); also see Captain America #235 4 8 12 24 32 40
28-Miller Daredevil (p) 3 6 9 18 24 30
29-55,57,59: 33-Origin Iguana. 38-Morbius app. 5.00
56-2nd app. Jack O'Lantern (Macendale) & 1st Spidey/Jack O'Lantern battle (7/81) 6.00
58-Byrne-a(p) 6.00
60-Double size; origin retold with new facts revealed 6.00
61-63,65-68,71-74: 65-Kraven the Hunter app. 4.00
64-1st app. Cloak & Dagger (3/82) 2 4 6 10 12 15
69,70-Cloak & Dagger app. 1 2 3 5 6 8
75-Double size 5.00
76-80: 78,79-Punisher cameo 4.00
81,82-Punisher, Cloak & Dagger app. 6.00
83-Origin Punisher retold (10/83) 1 3 4 6 8 10
84,86-89,91-99: 94-96-Cloak & Dagger app. 98-Intro The Spot 4.00
85-Hobgoblin (Ned Leeds) app. (12/83); gains powers of original Green Goblin (see Amazing Spider-Man #238) 1 3 4 6 8 10
90-Spider-Man's new black costume, last panel (ties w/Amazing Spider-Man #252 & Marvel Team-Up #141 for 1st app.) 4.00
100-(3/85)-Double size 5.00
101-115,117,118,120-129: 107-110-Death of Jean DeWolff. 111-Secret Wars II tie-in. 128-Black Cat new costume 3.00
116,119-Sabretooth-c/story 1 3 4 5 6 8
130-132: 30-Hobgoblin app. 131-Six part Kraven tie-in. 132-Kraven tie-in 1 2 3 4 5 7
133-140: 138-1st full app. Tombstone (origin #139). 140-Punisher cameo 3.00
141-143-Punisher app. 5.00
144-146,148-157: 151-Tombstone returns 3.00
147-1st brief app. new Hobgoblin (Macendale), 1 page; continued in Web of Spider-Man #48 2 4 6 8 10 12
158-Spider-Man gets new powers (1st Cosmic Spidey, cont'd in Web of Spider-Man #59) 1 2 3 4 5 7
159-Cosmic Spider-Man app. 6.00
160-170: 161-163-Hobgoblin app. 168-170-Avengers x-over. 169-1st app. The Outlaws 2.50
171-188,190-199: 180,181,183,184-Green Goblin app. 197-199-Original X-Men-c/story 2.50
189-($2.95, 52 pgs.)-Silver hologram on-c; battles Green Goblin; origin Spidey retold; Vess poster w/Spidey & Hobgoblin 4.00
189-(2nd printing)-Gold hologram on-c 3.00
195-(Deluxe ed.)-Polybagged w/"Dirt" magazine #2 & Beastie Boys/Smithereens music cassette 4.00
200-($2.95)-Holo-grafx foil-c; Green Goblin-c/story 3.00
201-219,221,222,224,226-228,230-247: 212-w/card sheet. 203-Maximum Carnage x-over. 204-Begin 4 part death of Tombstone story. 207,208-The Shroud-c/story. 208-Siege of Darkness x-over (#207 is a tie-in). 209-Black Cat back-up. 215,216-Scorpion app. 217-Power & Responsibility Pt. 4. 231-Return of Kaine; Spider-Man corpse discovered. 232-New Doc Octopus app. 233-Carnage-c/app. 235-Dragon Man cameo. 236-Dragon Man-c/app; Lizard app.; Peter Parker regains powers. 238,239-Lizard app. 239-w/card insert. 240-Revelations storyline begins. 241-Flashback 2.50
213-Collectors ed. polybagged w/16 pg. preview & animation cel; foil-c; 1st meeting Spidey & Typhoid Mary 3.00
213-Version polybagged w/Gamepro #7; no-c date, price 2.50
217,219 ($2.95)-Deluxe edition foil-c: flip book 3.00
220 ($2.25, 52 pgs.)-Flip book, Mary Jane reveals pregnancy 3.00
223,229: ($2.50) 229-Spidey quits 3.00
223,225: ($2.95)-223-Die Cut-c. 225-Newsstand ed. 3.00
225,229: ($3.95) 225-Direct Market Holodisk-c (Green Goblin). 229-Acetate-c, Spidey quits 4.00
240-Variant-c 3.00
248,249,251-254,256: 249-Return of Norman Osborn 256-1st app. Prodigy 2.50
250-($3.25) Double gatefold-c 3.25
255-($2.99) Spiderhunt pt. 4 3.00

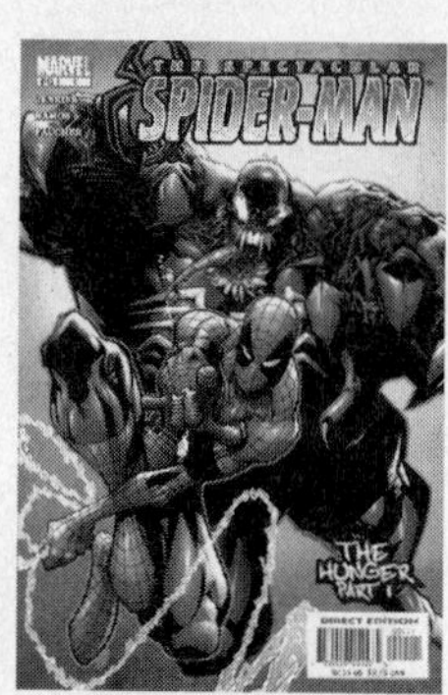

Spectacular Spider-Man ('03) #1 © MAR

The Spectre #6 © DC

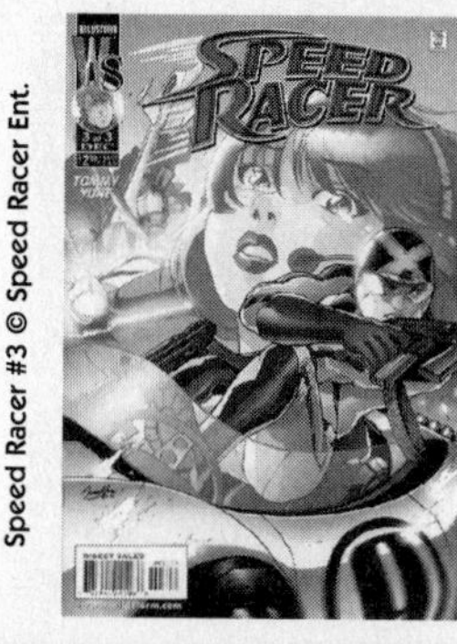

Speed Racer #3 © Speed Racer Ent.

GD VG FN VF VF/NM NM-
2.0 4.0 6.0 8.0 9.0 9.2

257-262: 257-Double cover with "Spectacular Prodigy #1"; battles Jack O'Lantern. 258-Spidey is cleared. 259,260-Green Goblin & Hobgoblin app. 262-Byrne-s 2.50
263-Final issue; Byrne-c; Aunt May returns 4.00
#(-1) Flashback (7/97) 2.50
Annual 1 (1979)-Doc Octopus-c & 46 pg. story 2 4 6 8 10 12
Annual 2 (1980)-Origin/1st app. Rapier 1 2 3 4 5 7
Annual 3-5: ('81-'83) 3-Last Man-Wolf 4.00
Annual 6-14: 8 ('88,$ 1.75)-Evolutionary War x-over; Daydreamer returns Gwen Stacy "clone" back to real self (not Gwen Stacy). 9 ('89, $2.00, 68 pgs.)-Atlantis Attacks. 10 ('90, $2.00, 68 pgs.)-McFarlane-a 11 ('91, $2.00, 68 pgs.)-Iron Man app. 12 ('92, $2.25, 68 pgs.)-Venom solo story cont'd from Amazing Spider-Man Annual #26. 13 ('93, $2.95, 68 pgs.)-Polybagged w/trading card; John Romita, Sr. back-up-a 3.00
Special 1 (1995, $3.95)-Flip book 4.00
NOTE: ***Austin*** *c-21i, Annual 11i.* ***Buckler*** *a-103, 107-111, 116, 117, 119, 122, Annual 1, Annual 10; c-103, 107-111, 113, 116-119, 122, Annual 1.* ***Buscema*** *a-121.* ***Byrne*** *c(p)-17, 43, 58, 101, 102.* ***Giffen*** *a-120p.* ***Hembeck*** *c/a-86p.* ***Larsen*** *c-Annual 11p.* ***Miller*** *c-46p, 48p, 50, 51p, 52p, 54p, 55, 56p, 57, 60.* ***Mooney*** *a-7i, 11i, 21p, 23p, 25p, 26p, 29-34p, 36p, 37p, 39i, 41, 42i, 49p, 50i, 51i, 53p, 54-57i, 59-66i, 68i, 71i, 73-79i, 81-83i, 85i, 87-99i, 102i, 125p, Annual 1i, 2p.* ***Nasser*** *c-37p.* ***Perez*** *c-10.* ***Simonson*** *c-54i.* ***Zeck*** *a-118, 131, 132; c-131, 132.*

SPECTACULAR SPIDER-MAN
Marvel Comics: Sept, 2003 - Present ($2.25)
1-Jenkins-s/Ramos-a/c; Venom-c/app. 3.00
2-21: 2-5-Venom app. 6-9-Dr. Octopus app. 11-13-The Lizard app. 14-Rivera painted-a. 15,16-Capt. America app. 17,18-Ramos-a. 20-Spider-Man gets organic webshooters 21-Caldwell-a; FF, Dr. Strange, Kingpin app. 2.25
Vol. 1: The Hunger TPB (2003, $11.99) r/#1-5 12.00
Vol. 2: Countdown TPB (2004, $11.99) r/#6-10 12.00
Vol. 3: Here There Be Monsters TPB (2004, $9.99) r/#11-14 10.00
Vol. 4: Disassembled TPB (2004, $14.99) r/#15-20 15.00

SPECTACULAR STORIES MAGAZINE (Formerly A Star Presentation)
Fox Feature Syndicate (Hero Books): No. 4, July, 1950; No. 3, Sept, 1950
4-Sherlock Holmes (true crime stories) 40 80 120 233 342 450
3-The St. Valentine's Day Massacre (true crime) 28 56 84 158 229 300

SPECTRE, THE (1st Series) (See Adventure Comics #431-440, More Fun & Showcase)
National Periodical Publ.: Nov-Dec, 1967 - No. 10, May-June, 1969 (All 12¢)
1-(11-12/67)-Anderson-c/a 13 26 39 94 145 195
2-5-Neal Adams-c/a; 3-Wildcat x-over 9 18 27 65 93 120
6-8,10: 6-8-Anderson inks. 7-Hourman app. 6 12 18 43 59 75
9-Wrightson-a 7 14 21 50 68 85

SPECTRE, THE (2nd Series) (See Saga of the Swamp Thing #58, Showcase '95 #8 & Wrath of the...)
DC Comics: Apr, 1987 - No. 31, Oct, 1989 ($1.00, new format)
1-Colan-a begins 4.00
2-32: 9-Nudity panels. 10-Batman cameo. 10,11-Millennium tie-ins 3.00
Annual 1 (1988, $2.00)-Deadman app. 3.00
NOTE: ***Art Adams*** *c-Annual 1.* ***Colan*** *a-1-6.* ***Kaluta*** *c-1-3.* ***Mignola*** *c-7-9.* ***Morrow*** *a-9-15.* ***Sears*** *c/a-22.* ***Vess*** *c-13-15.*

SPECTRE, THE (3rd Series) (Also see Brave and the Bold #72, 75, 116, 180, 199 & Showcase '95 #8)
DC Comics: Dec, 1992 - No. 62, Feb, 1998 ($1.75/$1.95/$2.25/$2.50)
1-($1.95)-Glow-in-the-dark-c; Mandrake-a begins 5.00
2,3 3.00
4-7,9-12,14-20: 10-Kaluta-c. 11-Hildebrandt painted-c. 16-Aparo/K. Jones-a. 19-Snyder III-c. 20-Sienkiewicz-c 2.50
8,13-($2.50)-Glow-in-the-dark-c 3.00
21-62: 22-(9/94)-Superman-c & app. 23-(11/94). 43-Kent Williams-c. 44-Kaluta-c. 47-Final Night x-over. 49-Begin Bolton-c. 51-Batman-c/app. 52-Gianni-c. 54-Corben-c. 60-Harris-c 2.50
#0 (10/94) Released between #22 & #23 2.50
Annual 1 (1995, $3.95)-Year One story 4.00
NOTE: ***Bisley*** *c-27.* ***Fabry*** *c-2.* ***Kelley Jones*** *c-31.* ***Vess*** *c-5.*

SPECTRE, THE (4th Series) (Hal Jordan; also see Day of Judgment #5 and Legends of the DC Universe #33-36)
DC Comics: Mar, 2001 - No. 27, May, 2003 ($2.50/$2.75)
1-DeMatteis-s/Ryan Sook-c/a 3.00
2-27: 3,4-Superman & Batman-c/app. 5-Two-Face-c/app. 20-Begin $2.75-c. 21-Sinestro returns. 24-JLA app. 2.75

SPEEDBALL (See Amazing Spider-Man Annual #12, Marvel Super-Heroes & The New Warriors)
Marvel Comics: Sept, 1988(10/88-inside) - No. 11, July, 1989 (75¢)
1-11: Ditko/Guice a-1-4, c-1; Ditko a-1-10; c-1-11p 2.25

SPEED BUGGY (TV)(Also see Fun-In #12, 15)
Charlton Comics: July, 1975 - No. 9, Nov, 1976 (Hanna-Barbera)
1 3 6 9 18 23 28
2-9 2 4 6 11 14 18

SPEED CARTER SPACEMAN (See Spaceman)

SPEED COMICS (New Speed)(Also see Double Up)
Brookwood Publ./Speed Publ./Harvey Publications No. 14 on:
10/39 - #11, 8/40; #12, 3/41 - #44, 1-2/47 (#14-16: pocket size, 100 pgs.)
1-Origin & 1st app. Shock Gibson; Ted Parrish, the Man with 1000 Faces begins; Powell-a; becomes Champion #2 on?; has earliest? full page panel in comics 331 662 993 2152 3476 4800
2-Powell-a 115 230 345 719 1110 1500
3 67 134 201 419 647 875
4,5: 4-Powell-a? 5-Dinosaur-c 55 110 165 336 511 685
6-11: 7-Mars Mason begins, ends #11 48 96 144 293 447 600
12 (3/41; shows #11 in indicia)-The Wasp begins; Major Colt app. (Capt. Colt #12) 53 106 159 323 494 665
13-Intro. Captain Freedom & Young Defenders; Girl Commandos, Pat Parker (costumed heroine), War Nurse begins; Major Colt app. 60 120 180 375 575 775
14-16 (100 pg. pocket size, 1941): 14-2nd Harvey comic (See Pocket); Shock Gibson dons new costume. 15-Pat Parker dons costume, last in costume #23; no Girl Commandos 71 142 213 444 685 925
17-Black Cat begins (4/42, early app.; see Pocket #1); origin Black Cat-r/Pocket #1; not in #40,41; S&K-c 74 148 222 463 714 965
18-20-S&K-c 59 118 177 369 565 760
21-Hitler, Tojo-c; Kirby-c 71 142 213 444 685 925
22-Kirby-c 59 118 177 369 565 760
23-Origin Girl Commandos; Kirby-c 59 118 177 369 565 760
24-Pat Parker team-up with Girl Commandos; Hitler, Tojo, & Mussolini-c 56 112 168 350 538 725
25-30: 26-Flag-c 48 96 144 293 447 600
31-Schomburg Hitler & Hirohito-c 69 138 207 431 666 900
32-36-Schomburg-c 54 108 162 329 502 675
37,39-42, 44 44 88 132 268 409 550
38-Iwo-Jima Flag-c 46 92 138 281 428 575
43-Robot-c 48 96 144 293 447 600
NOTE: ***Al Avison*** *c-14-16, 30, 43.* ***Briefer*** *a-6, 7.* ***Jon Henri*** *(Kirbyesque) c-17-20.* ***Kubert*** *a-37, 38, 42-44.* ***Kirby/Caseneuve*** *c-21-23.* ***Cecelia Munson*** *a-7-11(Mars Mason).* ***Palais*** *c-37, 39-42.* ***Powell*** *a-1, 2, 4-7, 28, 31, 44.* ***Schomburg*** *c-31-36.* ***Tuska*** *a-3, 6, 7. Bondage c-18, 35. Captain Freedom c-16-24, 25(part), 26-44(w/Black Cat #27, 29, 31, 32-40). Shock Gibson c-1-15.*

SPEED DEMON (Also see Marvel Versus DC #3 & DC Versus Marvel #4)
Marvel Comics (Amalgam): Apr, 1996 ($1.95, one-shot)
1 2.25

SPEED DEMONS (Formerly Frank Merriwell at Yale #1-4?; Submarine Attack #11 on)
Charlton Comics: No. 5, Feb, 1957 - No. 10, 1958
5-10 7 14 21 35 43 50

SPEED FORCE (See The Flash 2nd Series #143-Cobalt Blue)
DC Comics: Nov, 1997 ($3.95, one-shot)
1-Flash & Kid Flash vs. Cobalt Blue; Waid-s/Aparo & Sienkiewicz-a; Flash family stories and pin-ups by various 4.00

SPEED RACER (Also see The New Adventures of...)
Now Comics: July, 1987 - No. 38, Nov, 1990 ($1.75)
1-38, 1-2nd printing 2.50
Special 1 (1988, $2.00) 2.50
Special 2 (1988, $3.50) 3.50

SPEED RACER (Also see Racer X)
DC Comics (WildStorm): Oct, 1999 - No. 3, Dec, 1999 ($2.50, limited series)
1-3-Tommy Yune-s/a; origin of Racer X; debut of the Mach 5 2.50
...: Born To Race (2000, $9.95, TPB) r/series & conceptual art 10.00
...: The Original Manga Vol. 1 ('00, $9.95, TPB) r/1950s B&W manga 10.00

SPEED RACER FEATURING NINJA HIGH SCHOOL
Now Comics: Aug, 1993 - No. 2, 1993 ($2.50, mini-series)
1,2: 1-Polybagged w/card. 2-Exists? 2.50

SPEED RACER: RETURN OF THE GRX
Now Comics: Mar, 1994 - No. 2, Apr, 1994 ($1.95, limited series)
1,2 2.50

SPEED SMITH-THE HOT ROD KING (Also see Hot Rod King)
Ziff-Davis Publishing Co.: Spring, 1952
1-Saunders painted-c 24 48 72 135 195 255

Spellbound #1 © MAR

Spider-Girl #60 © MAR

Spider-Man #44 © MAR

GD 2.0 | VG 4.0 | FN 6.0 | VF 8.0 | VF/NM 9.0 | NM- 9.2

SPEEDY GONZALES
Dell Publishing Co.: No. 1084, Mar, 1960
Four Color 1084 6 12 18 43 59 75

SPEEDY RABBIT (See Television Puppet Show)
Realistic/I. W. Enterprises/Super Comics: nd (1953); 1963
nn (1953)-Realistic Reprint? 2 4 6 10 13 16
I.W. Reprint #1 (2 versions w/diff. c/stories exist)-Peter Cottontail #?
Super Reprint #14(1963) 2 4 6 8 10 12

SPELLBINDERS
Quality: Dec, 1986 - No. 12, Jan, 1988 ($1.25)
1-12: Nemesis the Warlock, Amadeus Wolf 2.25

SPELLBOUND (See The Crusaders)

SPELLBOUND (Tales to Hold You... #1, Stories to Hold You...)
Atlas Comics (ACI 1-15/Male 16-23/BPC 24-34): Mar, 1952 - #23, June, 1954; #24, Oct, 1955 - #34, June, 1957
1-Horror/weird stories in all 67 134 201 419 647 875
2-Edgar A. Poe app. 40 80 120 230 335 440
3-5: 3-Whitney-a; cannibalism story 34 68 102 196 283 370
6-Krigstein-a 34 68 102 196 283 370
7-10: 8-Ayers-a 29 58 87 167 241 315
11-16,18-20: 14-Ed Win-a 24 48 72 138 199 260
17-Krigstein-a 25 50 75 141 203 265
21-23: 23-Last precode (6/54) 20 40 60 112 161 210
24-28,30,31,34: 25-Orlando-a 18 36 54 100 143 185
29-Ditko-a (4 pgs.) 20 40 60 112 161 210
32,33-Torres-a 18 36 54 100 143 185
NOTE: ***Brodsky*** *a-5; c-1, 5-7, 10, 11, 13, 15, 25-27, 32.* ***Colan*** *a-17.* ***Everett*** *a-2, 5, 7, 10, 16, 28, 31; c-2, 8, 9, 14, 17-19, 28, 30.* ***Forgione/Abel*** *a-29.* ***Forte/Fox*** *a-16.* ***Al Hartley*** *a-2.* ***Heath*** *a-2, 4, 8, 9, 12, 14, 16; c-3, 4, 12, 16, 20, 21.* ***Infantino*** *a-15.* ***Keller*** *a-5.* ***Kida*** *a-2, 14.* ***Maneely*** *a-7, 14, 27; c-24, 29, 31.* ***Mooney*** *a-5, 13, 18.* ***Mac Pakula*** *a-22, 32.* ***Post*** *a-8.* ***Powell*** *a-19, 20, 32.* ***Robinson*** *a-1.* ***Romita*** *a-24, 26, 27.* ***R.Q. Sale*** *a-29.* ***Sekowsky*** *a-5.* ***Severin*** *c-29.* ***Sinnott*** *a-8, 16, 17.*

SPELLBOUND
Marvel Comics: Jan, 1988 - Apr, 1988 ($1.50, bi-weekly, Baxter paper)
1-5 2.25
6 ($2.25, 52 pgs.) 2.50

SPELLJAMMER (Also see TSR Worlds Comics Annual)
DC Comics: Sept, 1990 - No. 15, Nov, 1991 ($1.75)
1-15: Based on TSR game. 11-Heck-a. 2.25

SPENCER SPOOK (Formerly Giggle Comics; see Adventures of...)
American Comics Group: No. 100, Mar-Apr, 1955 - No. 101, May-June, 1955
100,101 7 14 21 37 46 55

SPIDER, THE
Eclipse Books: 1991 - Book 3, 1991 ($4.95, 52 pgs., limited series)
Book 1-3-Truman-c/a 5.00

SPIDER-BOY (Also see Marvel Versus DC #3)
Marvel Comics (Amalgam): Apr, 1996 ($1.95)
1-Mike Wieringo-c/a; Karl Kesel story; 1st app. of Bizarnage, Insect Queen, Challengers of the Fantastic, Sue Storm: Agent of S.H.I.E.L. D., & King Lizard 2.25

SPIDER-BOY TEAM-UP
Marvel Comics (Amalgam): June, 1997 ($1.95, one-shot)
1-Karl Kesel & Roger Stern-s/Jo Ladronn-a(p) 2.25

SPIDER-GIRL (See What If #105)
Marvel Comics: Oct, 1998 - Present ($1.99/$2.25)
0-($2.99)-r/1st app. Peter Parker's daughter from What If #105; previews regular series, Avengers-Next and J2 1 2 3 4 5 7
1-DeFalco-s/Olliffe & Williamson-s 1 2 3 4 5 7
2-Two covers 4.00
3-16,18-20: 3-Fantastic Five-c/app. 10,11-Spider-Girl time-travels to meet teenaged Spider-Man 2.50
17-($2.99) Peter Parker suits up 3.00
21-24,26-49,51-59: 21-Begin $2.25-c. 31-Avengers app. 2.25
25-($2.99) Spider-Girl vs. the Savage Six 3.00
50-($3.50) 3.50
59-81-($2.99) 59-Avengers app.; Ben Parker born. 75-May in Black costume 3.00
1999 Annual ($3.99) 4.00
... A Fresh Start (1/99,$5.99, TPB) r/#1&2 6.00
TPB (10/01, $19.95) r/#0-8; new Olliffe-c 20.00
Marvel Age Spider-Girl Vol. 1: Legacy (2004, $7.99, digest size) r/#0-5 8.00

GD 2.0 | VG 4.0 | FN 6.0 | VF 8.0 | VF/NM 9.0 | NM- 9.2

Marvel Age Spider-Girl Vol. 2: Like Father, Like Daughter (2004, $7.99, digest) r/#6-11 8.00

SPIDER-MAN (See Amazing..., Giant-Size..., Marvel Age..., Marvel Knights..., Marvel Tales, Marvel Team-Up, Spectacular..., Spidey Super Stories, Ultimate Marvel Team-Up, Ultimate..., Venom, & Web Of...)

SPIDER-MAN
Marvel Comics: Aug, 1990 - No. 98, Nov, 1998 ($1.75/$1.95/ $1.99)
1-Silver edition, direct sale only (unbagged) 1 2 3 5 6 8
1-Silver bagged edition; direct sale, no price on comic, but $2.00 on plastic bag (125,000 print run) 20.00
1-Regular edition w/Spidey face in UPC area (unbagged); green-c 6.00
1-Regular bagged edition w/Spidey face in UPC area; green cover (125,000) 12.00
1-Newsstand bagged w/UPC code 8.00
1-Gold edition, 2nd printing (unbagged) with Spider-Man in box (400,000-450,000) 5.00
1-Gold 2nd printing w/UPC code; (less than 10,000 print run) intended for Wal-Mart; much scarcer than originally believed 120.00
1-Platinum ed. mailed to retailers only (10,000 print run); has new McFarlane-a & editorial material instead of ads; stiff-c, no cover price 120.00
2-26: 2-McFarlane-c/a/scripts continue. 6,7-Ghost Rider & Hobgoblin app. 8-Wolverine cameo; Wolverine storyline begins. 12-Wolverine storyline ends. 13-Spidey's black costume returns; Morbius app. 14-Morbius app. 15-Erik Larsen-c/a; Beast c/s. 16-X-Force-c/story w/Liefeld assists; continues in X-Force #4; reads sideways; last McFarlane issue. 17-Thanos-c/story; Leonardi/Williamson-c/a. 13,14-Spidey in black costume. 18-Ghost Rider-c/story. 18-23-Sinister Six storyline w/Erik Larsen-c/a/scripts. 19-Hulk & Hobgoblin-c & app. 20-22-Deathlok app. 22,23-Ghost Rider, Hulk, Hobgoblin app. 23-Wrap-around gatefold-c. 24-Infinity War x-over w/Demogoblin & Hobgoblin-c/story. 24-Demogoblin dons new costume & battles Hobgoblin-c/story. 26-($3.50, 52 pgs.)-Silver hologram on-c w/gatefold poster by Ron Lim; Spidey retells his origin. 4.00
26-2nd printing; gold hologram on-c 3.50
27-45: 32-34-Punisher-c/story. 37-Maximum Carnage x-over. 39,40-Electro-c/s (cameo #38). 41-43-Iron Fist-c/stories w/Jae Lee-c/a. 42-Intro Platoon. 44-Hobgoblin app. 3.00
46-49,51-53, 55, 56,58-74,76-81: 46-Begin $1.95-c; bound-in card sheet. 51-Power & Responsibility Pt. 3. 52,53-Venom app. 60-Kaine revealed. 61-Origin Kaine. 65-Mysterio app. 66-Kaine-c/app.; Peter Parker app. 67-Carnage-c/app. 68,69-Hobgoblin-c/app. 72-Onslaught x-over; Spidey vs. Sentinels. 74-Daredevil-c/app. 77-80-Morbius-c/app. 2.50
46-($2.95)-Polybagged; silver ink-c w/16 pg. preview of cartoon series & animation style print; bound-in trading card sheet 3.00
50-($2.50)-Newsstand edition 2.50
50-($3.95)-Collectors edition w/holographic-c 4.00
51-($2.95)-Deluxe edition foil-c; flip book 3.00
54-($2.75, 52 pgs.)-Flip book 2.75
57-($2.50) 2.50
57-($2.95)-Die cut-c 3.00
65-($2.95)-Variant-c; polybagged w/cassette 3.00
75-($2.95)-Wraparound-c; return of the Green Goblin; death of Ben Reilly (who was the clone) 4.00
82-97: 84-Juggernaut app. 91-Double cover with "Dusk #1"; battles the Shocker. 93-Ghost Rider app. 2.50
98-Double cover; final issue 3.00
#(-1) Flashback (7/97) 2.50
Annual '97 ($2.99), '98 ($2.99)-Devil Dinosaur-c/app. 3.00
...and Batman ('95, $5.95) DeMatteis-s; Joker, Carnage app. 6.00
...and Daredevil ('84, $2.00) 1-r/Spectacular Spider-Man #26-28 by Miller 3.00
...: Carnage nn (6/93, $6.95, TPB)-r/Amazing S-M #344,345,359-363; spot varnish-c 7.00
.../Daredevil (10/02, $2.99) Vatche Mavlian-c/a; Brett Matthews-s 3.00
.../Dr. Strange: "The Way to Dusty Death" nn (1992, $6.95, 68 pgs.) 7.00
.../Elektra '98-($2.99) vs. The Silencer 3.00
... Fear Itself Graphic Novel (2/92, $12.95) 18.00
Giant-Sized Spider-Man (12/98, $3.99) r/team-ups 4.00
Holiday Special 1995 ($2.95) 3.00
Identity Crisis (9/98, $19.95, TPB) 20.00
...Legends Vol. 1: Todd McFarlane ('03, $19.95, TPB)-r/Amaz. S-M #298-305 20.00
...Legends Vol. 2: Todd McFarlane ('03, $19.99, TPB)-r/Amaz. S-M #306-314, & Spec. Spider-Man Annual #10 20.00
...Legends Vol. 3: Todd McFarlane ('04, $24.99, TPB)-r/Amaz. S-M #315-323,325,328 25.00
...Legends Vol. 4: Spider-Man & Wolverine ('03, $13.95, TPB) r/Spider-Man & Wolverine #1-4 and Spider-Man/Daredevil #1 14.00
.../Marrow (2/01, $2.99) Garza-a 3.00
..., Punisher, Sabretooth: Designer Genes (1993, $8.95) 9.00
...Return of the Goblin TPB (See Peter Parker: Spider-Man)
...Revelations ('97, $14.99, TPB) r/end of Clone Saga plus 14 new pages by Romita Jr. 15.00
...: Son of the Goblin (2004, $15.99, TPB) r/AS-M#136-137,312 & Spec. S-M #189,200 16.00
Special Edition 1 (12/92-c, 11/92 inside)-The Trial of Venom; ordered thru mail with $5.00 donation or more to UNICEF; embossed metallic ink; came bagged w/bound-in poster; Daredevil app. 1 3 4 6 8 10

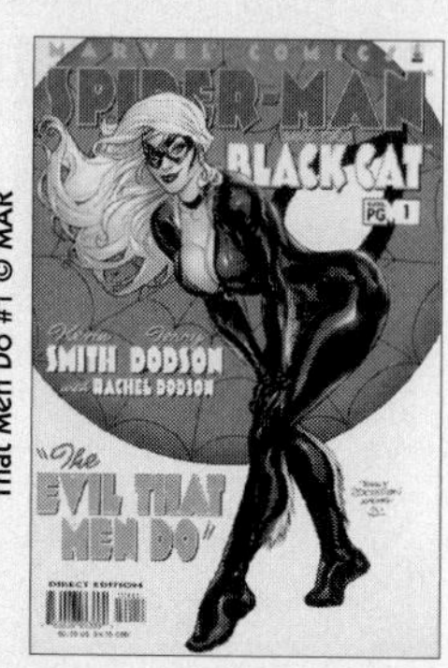

Spider-Man/Black Cat: The Evil That Men Do #1 © MAR

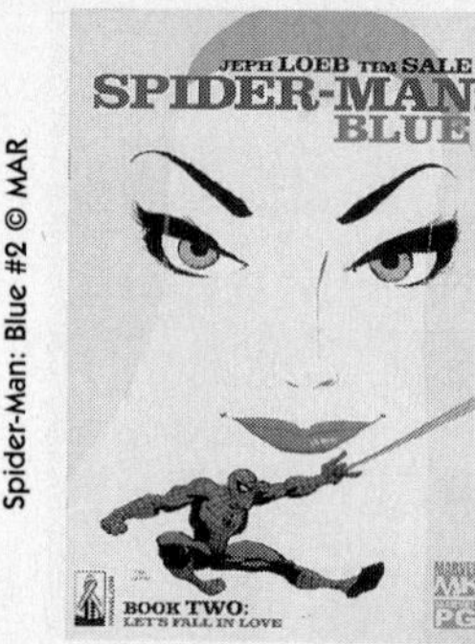

Spider-Man: Blue #2 © MAR

Spider-Man: India #1 © MAR

GD	VG	FN	VF	VF/NM	NM-
2.0	4.0	6.0	8.0	9.0	9.2

Super Special (7/95, $3.95)-Planet of the Symbiotes 4.00
The Best of Spider-Man Vol. 2 (2003, $29.99, HC with dust jacket) r/AS-M V2 #37-45, Peter Parker: S-M #44-47, and S-M's Tangled Web #10,11; Pearson-c 30.00
The Best of Spider-Man Vol. 3 (2004, $29.99, HC with d.j.) r/AS-M V2 #46-58, 500 30.00
The Complete Frank Miller Spider-Man (2002, $29.95, HC) r/Miller-s/a 30.00
The Death of Captain Stacy ($3.50) r/AS-M#88-90 3.50
The Death of Gwen Stacy ($14.95) r/AS-M#96-98,121,122 15.00
...: The Movie ($12.95) adaptation by Stan Lee-s/Alan Davis-a; plus r/Ultimate Spider-Man #8, Peter Parker #35, Tangled Web #10; photo-c 13.00
...: The Official Movie Adaptation ($5.95) Stan Lee-s/Alan Davis-a 6.00
Torment TPB (5/01$15.95) r/#1-5, Spec. S-M #10 16.00
... Vs. Doctor Octopus ($17.95) reprints early battles; Sean Chen-c 18.00
... Vs. Punisher (7/00, $2.99) Michael Lopez-c/a 3.00
...Vs. Venom (1990, $8.95, TPB)-r/Amaz. S-M #300,315-317 w/new McFarlane-c 9.00
...Visionaries (10/01, $19.95, TPB)-r/Amaz. S-M #298-305; McFarlane-a 20.00
...Visionaries: John Romita (8/01, $19.95, TPB)-r/Amaz. S-M #39-42, 50,68,69,108,109; new Romita-c 20.00
Wizard 1/2 ($10.00) Leonardi-a; Green Goblin app. 10.00
NOTE: ***Erik Larsen** c/a-15, 18-23. **M. Rogers/Keith Williams** c/a-27, 28.*

SPIDER-MAN ADVENTURES
Marvel Comics: Dec, 1994 - No. 15, Mar, 1996 ($1.50)
1-15 ($1.50)-Based on animated series 2.25
1-($2.95)-Foil embossed-c 3.00

SPIDER-MAN AND HIS AMAZING FRIENDS (See Marvel Action Universe)
Marvel Comics Group: Dec, 1981 (one-shot)
1-Adapted from NBC TV cartoon show; Green Goblin-c/story; 1st Spidey, Firestar, Iceman team-up; Spiegle-p 5.00

SPIDER-MAN AND THE INCREDIBLE HULK (See listing under Amazing...)

SPIDER-MAN AND THE UNCANNY X-MEN
Marvel Comics: Mar, 1996 ($16.95, trade paperback)
nn-r/Uncanny X-Men #27, Uncanny X-men #35, Amazing Spider-Man #92, Marvel Team-Up Annual #1, Marvel Team-Up #150, & Spectacular Spider-Man #197-199 17.00

SPIDER-MAN & WOLVERINE (See Spider-Man Legends Vol. 4 for TPB reprint)
Marvel Comics: Aug, 2003 - No. 4, Nov, 2003 ($2.99, limited series)
1-4-Matthews-s/Mavlian-a 3.00

SPIDER-MAN AND X-FACTOR
Marvel Comics: May, 1994 - No. 3, July, 1994 ($1.95, limited series)
1-3 2.25

SPIDER-MAN /BADROCK
Maximum Press: Mar, 1997 ($2.99, mini-series)
1A, 1B(#2)-Jurgens-s 3.00

SPIDER-MAN/BLACK CAT: THE EVIL THAT MEN DO
Marvel Comics: Aug, 2002 - No. 4 ($2.99, unfinished limited series)
1-3-Kevin Smith-s/Terry Dodson-c/a 3.00

SPIDER-MAN: BLUE
Marvel Comics: July, 2002 - No. 6, Apr, 2003 ($3.50, limited series)
1-6: Jeph Loeb-s/Tim Sale-a/c; flashback to early MJ and Gwen Stacy 3.50
HC (2003, $21.99, with dust jacket) over-sized r/#1-6; intro. by John Romita 22.00
SC (2004, $14.99) r/#1-6; cover gallery 15.00

SPIDER-MAN: CHAPTER ONE
Marvel Comics: Dec, 1998 - No. 12, Oct, 1999 ($2.50, limited series)
1-Retelling/updating of origin; John Byrne-s/c/a 2.50
1-($6.95) DF Edition w/variant-c by Jae Lee 7.00
2-11: 2-Two covers (one is swipe of ASM #1); Fantastic Four app. 9-Daredevil. 11-Giant-Man-c/app. 2.50
12-($3.50) Battles the Sandman 3.50
0-(5/99) Origins of Vulture, Lizard and Sandman 2.50

SPIDER-MAN CLASSICS
Marvel Comics: Apr, 1993 - No. 16, July, 1994 ($1.25)
1-14,16: 1-r/Amaz. Fantasy #15 & Strange Tales #115. 2-16-r/Amaz. Spider-Man #1-15. 6-Austin-c(i) 2.25
15-($2.95)-Polybagged w/16 pg. insert & animation style print; r/Amazing Spider-Man #14 (1st Green Goblin) 3.00

SPIDER-MAN COLLECTOR'S PREVIEW
Marvel Comics: Dec, 1994 ($1.50, 100 pgs., one-shot)
1-wraparound-c; no comics 3.00

GD	VG	FN	VF	VF/NM	NM-
2.0	4.0	6.0	8.0	9.0	9.2

SPIDER-MAN COMICS MAGAZINE
Marvel Comics Group: Jan, 1987 - No. 13, 1988 ($1.50, digest-size)
1-13-Reprints 6.00

SPIDER-MAN: DEAD MAN'S HAND
Marvel Comics: Apr, 1997 ($2.99, one-shot)
1 3.00

SPIDER-MAN: DEATH AND DESTINY
Marvel Comics: Aug, 2000 - No. 3, Oct, 2000 ($2.99, limited series)
1-3-Aftermath of the death of Capt. Stacy 3.00

SPIDER-MAN/ DOCTOR OCTOPUS: OUT OF REACH
Marvel Comics: Jan, 2004 - No. 5, May, 2004 ($2.99, limited series)
1-5: 1-Keron Grant-a/Colin Mitchell-s 3.00
Marvel Age... TPB (2004, $5.99, digest size) r/#1-5 6.00

SPIDER-MAN/ DOCTOR OCTOPUS: YEAR ONE
Marvel Comics: Aug, 2004 - No. 5 ($2.99, limited series)
1-4-Kaare Andrews-a/Zeb Wells-s 3.00

SPIDER-MAN: FRIENDS AND ENEMIES
Marvel Comics: Jan, 1995 - No. 4, Apr, 1995 ($1.95, limited series)
1-4-Darkhawk, Nova & Speedball app. 2.25

SPIDER-MAN: FUNERAL FOR AN OCTOPUS
Marvel Comics: Mar, 1995 - No. 3, May, 1995 ($1.50, limited series)
1-3 2.25

SPIDER-MAN/ GEN 13
Marvel Comics: Nov, 1996 ($4.95, one-shot)
nn-Peter David-s/Stuart Immonen-a 5.00

SPIDER-MAN: GET KRAVEN
Marvel Comics: Aug, 2002 - No. 6, Jan, 2003 ($2.99/$2.25, limited series)
1-($2.99) McCrea-a/Quesada-c; back-up story w/Rio-a 3.00
2-6-($2.25) 2-Sub-Mariner app. 2.25

SPIDER-MAN: HOBGOBLIN LIVES
Marvel Comics: Jan, 1997 - No. 3, Mar, 1997 ($2.50, limited series)
1-3-Wraparound-c 2.50
TPB (1/98, $14.99) r/#1-3 plus timeline 15.00

SPIDER-MAN: HOT SHOTS
Marvel Comics: Jan, 1996 ($2.95, one-shot)
nn-fold out posters by various, inc. Vess and Ross 3.00

SPIDER-MAN: INDIA
Marvel Comics: Jan, 2005 - Present ($2.99)
1-Pavitr Prabhakar gains spider powers; Kang-a/Seetharaman-s 3.00

SPIDER-MAN: LEGACY OF EVIL
Marvel Comics: June, 1996 ($3.95, one-shot)
1-Kurt Busiek script & Mark Texeira-c/a 4.00

SPIDER-MAN: LEGEND OF THE SPIDER-CLAN (See Marvel Mangaverse for TPB)
Marvel Comics: Dec, 2002 - No. 5, Apr, 2003 ($2.25, limited series)
1-5-Marvel Mangaverse Spider-Man; Kaare Andrews-s/Skottie Young-c/a 2.25

SPIDER-MAN: LIFELINE
Marvel Comics: Apr, 2001 - No. 3, June, 2001 ($2.99, limited series)
1-3-Nicieza-s/Rude-c/a; The Lizard app. 3.00

SPIDER-MAN: MADE MEN
Marvel Comics: Aug, 1998 ($5.99, one-shot)
1-Spider-Man & Daredevil vs. Kingpin 6.00

SPIDER-MAN MAGAZINE
Marvel Comics: 1994 - No. 3, 1994 ($1.95, magazine)
1-3: 1-Contains 4 S-M promo cards & 4 X-Men Ultra Fleer cards; Spider-Man story by Romita, Sr.; X-Men story; puzzles & games. 2-Doc Octopus & X-Men stories 3.00

SPIDER-MAN: MAXIMUM CLONAGE
Marvel Comics: 1995 ($4.95)
Alpha #1-Acetate-c, Omega #1-Chromium-c. 5.00

SPIDER-MAN MEGAZINE
Marvel Comics: Oct, 1994 - No. 6, Mar, 1995 ($2.95, 100 pgs.)
1-6: 1-r/ASM #16,224,225, Marvel Team-Up #1 3.00

SPIDER-MAN: POWER OF TERROR

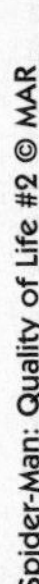

Spider-Man: Quality of Life #2 © MAR

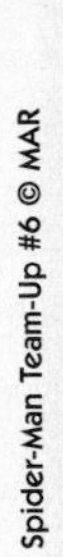

Spider-Man Team-Up #6 © MAR

Spider-Man 2: The Movie © MAR

GD 2.0 | VG 4.0 | FN 6.0 | VF 8.0 | VF/NM 9.0 | NM- 9.2

Marvel Comics: Jan, 1995 - No. 4, Apr, 1995 ($1.95, limited series)
1-4-Silvermane & Deathlok app. 2.25

SPIDER-MAN/PUNISHER: FAMILY PLOT
Marvel Comics: Feb, 1996 - No. 2, Mar, 1996 ($2.95, limited series)
1,2 3.00

SPIDER-MAN: QUALITY OF LIFE
Marvel Comics: Jul, 2002 - No. 4, Oct, 2002 ($2.99, limited series)
1-4-All CGI art by Scott Sava; Rucka-s; Lizard app. 3.00
TPB (2002, $12.99) r/#1-4; a "Making of..." section detailing the CGI process 13.00

SPIDER-MAN: REDEMPTION
Marvel Comics: Sept, 1996 - No. 4, Dec, 1996 ($1.50, limited series)
1-4: DeMatteis scripts; Zeck-a 2.25

SPIDER-MAN: REVENGE OF THE GREEN GOBLIN
Marvel Comics: Oct, 2000 - No. 3, Dec, 2000 ($2.99, limited series)
1-3-Frenz & Olliffe-a; continues in AS-M #25 & PP:S-M #25 3.00

SPIDER-MAN SAGA
Marvel Comics: Nov, 1991 - No. 4, Feb, 1992 ($2.95, limited series)
1-4: Gives history of Spider-Man: text & illustrations 3.00

SPIDER-MAN: SWEET CHARITY
Marvel Comics: Aug, 2002 ($4.95, one-shot)
1-The Scorpion-c/app.; Campbell-c/Zimmerman-s/Robertson-a 5.00

SPIDER-MAN'S TANGLED WEB (Titled **"Tangled Web"** in indicia for #1-4)
Marvel Comics: Jun, 2001 - No. 22, Mar, 2003 ($2.99)
1-3: "The Thousand" on-c; Ennis-s/McCrea-a/Fabry-c 4.00
4-"Severance Package" on-c; Rucka-s/Risso-a; Kingpin-c/app. 5.00
5,6-Flowers for Rhino; Milligan-s/Fegredo-a 3.00
7-10,12,15-20,22: 7-9-Gentlemen's Agreement; Bruce Jones-s/Lee Weeks-a. 10-Andrews-s/a. 12-Fegredo-a. 15-Paul Pope-s/a. 18-Ted McKeever-s/a. 19-Mahfood-a. 20-Haspiel-a 3.00
11,13,21-($3.50) 11-Darwyn Cooke-s/a. 13-Phillips-a. 21-Christmas-s by Cooke & Bone 3.50
14-Azzarello & Scott Levy (WWE's Raven)-s about Crusher Hogan 4.00
TPB (10/01, $15.95) r/#1-6 16.00
Volume 2 TPB (4/02, $14.95) r/#7-11 15.00
Volume 3 TPB (2002, $15.99) r/#12-17; Jason Pearson-c 16.00
Volume 4 TPB (2003, $15.99) r/#18-22; Frank Cho-c 16.00

SPIDER-MAN TEAM-UP
Marvel Comics: Dec, 1995 - No. 7, June, 1996 ($2.95)
1-7: 1-w/ X-Men. 2-w/Silver Surfer. 3-w/Fantastic Four. 4-w/Avengers. 5-Gambit & Howard the Duck-c/app. 7-Thunderbolts-c/app. 3.00

SPIDER-MAN: THE ARACHNIS PROJECT
Marvel Comics: Aug, 1994 - No. 6, Jan, 1995 ($1.75, limited series)
1-6-Venom, Styx, Stone & Jury app. 2.25

SPIDER-MAN: THE CLONE JOURNAL
Marvel Comics: Mar, 1995 ($2.95, one-shot)
1 3.00

SPIDER-MAN: THE FINAL ADVENTURE
Marvel Comics: Nov, 1995 - No. 4, Feb, 1996 ($2.95, limited series)
1-4: 1-Nicieza scripts; foil-c 3.00

SPIDER-MAN: THE JACKAL FILES
Marvel Comics: Aug, 1995 ($1.95, one-shot)
1 2.25

SPIDER-MAN: THE LOST YEARS
Marvel Comics: Aug, 1995-No. 3, Oct, 1995; No. 0, 1996 ($2.95/$3.95,lim. series)
0-(1/96, $3.95)-Reprints. 4.00
1-3-DeMatteis scripts, Romita, Jr.-c/a 3.00
NOTE: ***Romita** c-0i. **Romita, Jr.** a-0r, 1-3p. c-0-3p. **Sharp** a-0r.*

SPIDER-MAN: THE MANGA
Marvel Comics: Dec, 1997 - No. 31, June, 1999 ($3.99/$2.99, B&W, bi-weekly)
1-($3.99)-English translation of Japanese Spider-Man 4.00
2-31-($2.99) 3.00

SPIDER-MAN: THE MUTANT AGENDA
Marvel Comics: No. 0, Feb, 1994; No. 1, Mar, 1994 - No. 3, May, 1994 ($1.75, limited series)
0-(2/94, $1.25, 52 pgs.)-Crosses over w/newspaper strip; has empty pages to paste in newspaper strips; gives origin of Spidey 2.25
1-3: Beast & Hobgoblin app. 1-X-Men app. 2.25

SPIDER-MAN: THE MYSTERIO MANIFESTO (Listed as "Spider-Man and Mysterio" in indicia)
Marvel Comics: Jan, 2001 - No. 3, Mar, 2001 ($2.99, limited series)
1-3-Daredevil-c/app.; Weeks & McLeod-a 3.00

SPIDER-MAN: THE PARKER YEARS
Marvel Comics: Nov, 1995 ($2.50, one-shot)
1 2.50

SPIDER-MAN 2: THE MOVIE
Marvel Comics: Nov, 1995 ($3.50/$12.99, one-shot)
1-($3.50) Movie adaptation; Johnson, Lim & Olliffe-a 3.50
TPB-($12.99) Movie adaptation; r/Amazing Spider-Man #50, Ultimate Spider-Man #14,15 13.00

SPIDER-MAN 2099 (See Amazing Spider-Man #365)
Marvel Comics: Nov, 1992 - No. 46, Aug, 1996 ($1.25/$1.50/$1.95)
1-(stiff-c)-Red foil stamped-c; begins origin of Miguel O'Hara (Spider-Man 2099); Leonardi/Williamson-c/a begins 3.00
1-2nd printing, 2-24,26-40: 2-Origin continued, ends #3. 4-Doom 2099 app. 13-Extra 16 pg. insert on Midnight Sons. 19-Bound-in trading card sheet. 35-Variant-c. 36-Two-c; Jae Lee-a. 37,38-Two-c 2.25
25-($2.25, 52 pgs.)-Newsstand edition 2.25
25-($2.95, 52 pgs.)-Deluxe edition w/embossed foil-c 3.00
41-46: 46-The Vulture app; Mike McKone-a(p)
Annual 1 (1994, $2.95, 68 pgs.) 3.00
Special 1 (1995, $3.95) 4.00
NOTE: ***Chaykin** c-37. **Ron Lim** a(p)-18; c(p)-13, 16, 18. **Kelley Jones** c/a-9. **Leonardi/Williamson** a-1-8, 10-13, 15-17, 19, 20, 22-25; c-1-13, 15, 17-19, 20, 22-25, 35.*

SPIDER-MAN 2099 MEETS SPIDER-MAN
Marvel Comics: 1995 ($5.95, one-shot)
nn-Peter David script; Leonardi/Williamson-c/a. 6.00

SPIDER-MAN UNIVERSE
Marvel Comics: Mar, 2000 - No. 7, Oct, 2000 ($4.95/$3.99, reprints)
1-5-Reprints recent issues from the various Spider-Man titles 5.00
6,7-($3.99) 4.00

SPIDER-MAN UNLIMITED
Marvel Comics: May, 1993 - No. 22, Nov, 1998 ($3.95, quarterly, 68 pgs.)
1-Begin Maximum Carnage storyline, ends; Carnage-c/story 5.00
2-12: 2-Venom & Carnage-c/story; Lim-c/a(p) in #2-6. 10-Vulture app. 4.00
13-22: 13-Begin $2.99-c; Scorpion-c/app. 15-Daniel-c; Puma-c/app. 19-Lizard-c/app. 20-Hannibal King and Lilith app. 21,22-Deodato-a 3.00

SPIDER-MAN UNLIMITED (Based on the TV animated series)
Marvel Comics: Dec, 1999 - No. 5, Apr, 2000 ($2.99/$1.99)
1-($2.99) Venom and Carnage app. 3.00
2-5: 2-($1.99) Green Goblin app. 2.25

SPIDER-MAN UNLIMITED
Marvel Comics: Mar, 2004 - Present ($2.99)
1-6: 1-Short stories by various incl. Miyazawa & Chen-a. 2-Mays-a. 6-Allred-c 3.00

SPIDER-MAN UNMASKED
Marvel Comics: Nov, 1996 ($5.95, one-shot)
nn-Art w/text 6.00

SPIDER-MAN: VENOM AGENDA
Marvel Comics: Jan, 1998 ($2.99, one-shot)
1-Hama-s/Lyle-c/a 3.00

SPIDER-MAN VS. DRACULA
Marvel Comics: Jan, 1994 ($1.75, 52 pgs., one-shot)
1-r/Giant-Size Spider-Man #1 plus new Matt Fox-a 2.25

SPIDER-MAN VS. WOLVERINE
Marvel Comics Group: Feb, 1987; V2#1, 1990 (68 pgs.)
1-Williamson-c/a(i); intro Charlemagne; death of Ned Leeds (old Hobgoblin) 2 4 6 12 16 20
V2#1 (1990, $4.95)-Reprints #1 (2/87) 5.00

SPIDER-MAN: WEB OF DOOM
Marvel Comics: Aug, 1994 - No. 3, Oct, 1994 ($1.75, limited series)
1-3 2.25

SPIDER-MAN: YEAR IN REVIEW
Marvel Comics: Feb, 2000 ($2.99)
1-Text recaps of 1999 issues 3.00

Spider-Woman #1 © MAR

The Spirit #7 © Will Eisner

The Spirit #20 © Will Eisner

GD 2.0 VG 4.0 FN 6.0 VF 8.0 VF/NM 9.0 NM- 9.2

SPIDER REIGN OF THE VAMPIRE KING, THE (Also see The Spider)
Eclipse Books: 1992 - No. 3, 1992 ($4.95, limited series, coated stock, 52 pgs.)
Book One - Three: Truman scripts & painted-c 5.00

SPIDER'S WEB, THE (See G-8 and His Battle Aces)

SPIDER-WOMAN (Also see The Avengers #240, Marvel Spotlight #32, Marvel Super Heroes Secret Wars #7 & Marvel Two-In-One #29)
Marvel Comics Group: April, 1978 - No. 50, June, 1983 (New logo #47 on)
1-New complete origin & mask added 2 4 6 11 14 18
2-5,7-18: 2-Excalibur app. 3,11,12-Brother Grimm app. 13,15-The Shroud-c/s. 16-Sienkiewicz-c 5.00
6,19,20,28,29,32: 6-Morgan LeFay app. 6,19,32-Werewolf by Night-c/s. 20,28,29-Spider-Man app. 32-Miller-c 6.00
21-27,30,31,33-36 5.00
37,38-X-Men x-over: 37-1st app. Siryn of X-Force; origin retold 1 3 4 6 8 10
39-49: 46-Kingpin app. 49-Tigra-c/story 4.00
50-(52 pgs.)-Death of Spider-Woman; photo-c 2 4 6 9 11 14
NOTE: ***Austin** a-37i. **Byrne** c-26p. **Infantino a**-1-19. **Layton** c-19. **Miller** c-32p.*

SPIDER-WOMAN
Marvel Comics: Nov, 1993 - No. 4, Feb, 1994 ($1.75, mini-series)
V2#1-4: 1,2-Origin; U.S. Agent app. 2.25

SPIDER-WOMAN
Marvel Comics: July, 1999 - No. 18, Dec, 2000 ($2.99/$1.99/$2.25)
1-($2.99) Byrne-s/Sears-a 3.00
2-18: 2-11-($1.99). 2-Two covers. 12-Begin $2.25-c. 15-Capt. America-c/app. 2.25

SPIDEY SUPER STORIES (Spider-Man) (Also see Fireside Books)
Marvel/Children's TV Workshop: Oct, 1974 - No. 57, Mar, 1982 (35¢, no ads)
1-Origin (stories simplified for younger readers) 4 8 12 29 40 50
2-Kraven 3 6 9 18 23 28
3-10,15: 6-Iceman. 15-Storm-c/sty 2 4 6 12 16 20
11-14,16-20: 19,20-Kirby-c 2 4 6 11 14 18
21-30: 24-Kirby-c 2 4 6 10 13 16
31-53: 31-Moondragon-c/app.; Dr. Doom app. 33-Hulk. 34-Sub-Mariner. 38-F.F. 39-Thanos-c/story. 44-Vision. 45-Silver Surfer & Dr. Doom app. 2 4 6 9 11 14
54-57: 56-Battles Jack O'Lantern-c/sty (exactly one year after 1st app. in Machine Man #19) 2 4 6 12 16 20

SPIKE AND TYKE (See M.G.M.'s...)

SPIN & MARTY (TV) (Walt Disney's)(See Walt Disney Showcase #32)
Dell Publishing Co. (Mickey Mouse Club): No. 714, June, 1956 - No. 1082, Mar-May, 1960 (All photo-c)
Four Color 714 (#1) 14 28 42 97 149 200
Four Color 767,808 (#2,3) 10 20 30 72 104 135
Four Color 826 (#4)-Annette Funicello photo-c 25 50 75 177 271 365
5(3-5/58) - 9(6-8/59) 9 18 27 63 89 115
Four Color 1026,1082 9 18 27 63 89 115

SPINE-TINGLING TALES (Doctor Spektor Presents...)
Gold Key: May, 1975 - No. 4, Jan, 1976 (All 25¢ issues)
1-1st Tragg-r/Mystery Comics Digest #3 2 4 6 10 12 15
2-4: 2-Origin Ra-Ka-Tep-r/Mystery Comics Digest #1; Dr. Spektor #12. 3-All Durak-r issue; 4-Baron Tibor's 1st app.-r/Mystery Comics Digest #4; painted-c 1 2 3 5 6 8

SPINWORLD
Amaze Ink (Slave Labor Graphics): July, 1997 - No. 4, Jan, 1998 ($2.95/$3.95, B&W, mini-series)
1-3-Brent Anderson-a(p) 3.00
4-($3.95) 4.00

SPIRAL PATH, THE
Eclipse Comics: July, 1986 - No. 2 ($1.75, Baxter paper, limited series)
1,2 2.25

SPIRAL ZONE
DC Comics: Feb, 1988 - No. 4, May, 1988 ($1.00, mini-series)
1-4-Based on Tonka toys 2.25

SPIRIT, THE (Newspaper comics - see Promotional Comics section)

SPIRIT, THE (1st Series)(Also see Police Comics #11)
Quality Comics Group (Vital): 1944 - No. 22, Aug, 1950
nn(#1)- "Wanted Dead or Alive" 81 162 243 506 778 1050

GD 2.0 VG 4.0 FN 6.0 VF 8.0 VF/NM 9.0 NM- 9.2

nn(#2)- "Crime Doesn't Pay" 45 90 135 275 418 560
nn(#3)- "Murder Runs Wild" 40 80 120 233 342 450
4,5: 4-Flatfoot Burns begins, ends #22. 5-Wertham app. 31 62 93 178 259 340
6-10 27 54 81 152 219 285
11 24 48 72 138 199 260
12-17-Eisner-c. 19-Honeybun app. 35 70 105 201 293 385
18-21-Strip-r by Eisner; Eisner-c 40 80 120 239 357 475
22-Used by N.Y. Legis. Comm; classic Eisner-c 56 112 168 350 538 725
Super Reprint #11-r/Quality Spirit #19 by Eisner 3 7 10 21 28 35
Super Reprint #12-r/Spirit #17 by Fine; Sol Brodsky-c 3 7 10 21 28 35

SPIRIT, THE (2nd Series)
Fiction House Magazines: Spring, 1952 - No. 5, 1954
1-Not Eisner 40 80 120 241 363 485
2-Eisner-c/a(2) 40 80 120 236 351 465
3-Eisner/Grandenetti-c 34 68 102 193 279 365
4-Eisner/Grandenetti-c; Eisner-a 35 70 105 198 287 375
5-Eisner-c/a(4) 39 78 117 227 331 435

SPIRIT, THE
Harvey Publications: Oct, 1966 - No. 2, Mar, 1967 (Giant Size, 25¢, 68 pgs.)
1-Eisner-r plus 9 new pgs.(origin Denny Colt, Take 3, plus 2 filler pgs.) (#3 was advertised, but never published) 9 18 27 60 85 110
2-Eisner-r plus 9 new pgs.(origin of the Octopus) 7 14 21 46 63 80

SPIRIT, THE (Underground)
Kitchen Sink Enterprises (Krupp Comics): Jan, 1973 - No. 2, Sept, 1973 (Black & White)
1-New Eisner-c & 4 pgs. new Eisner-a plus-r (titled Crime Convention) 2 4 6 11 14 18
2-New Eisner-c & 4 pgs. new Eisner-a plus-r (titled Meets P'Gell) 2 4 6 14 18 22

SPIRIT, THE (Magazine)
Warren Publ. Co./Krupp Comic Works No. 17 on: 4/74 - No. 16, 10/76; No. 17, Winter, 1977 - No. 41, 6/83 (B&W w/color) (#6-14,16 are squarebound)
1-Eisner-r begin; 8 pg. color insert 4 8 12 24 32 40
2-5: 2-Powder Pouf-s; UFO-s. 4-Silk Satin-s 2 4 6 14 18 22
6-9,11-15: 7-All Ebony issue. 8-Female Foes issue. 8,12-Sand Seref-s. 9-P'Gell & Octupus-s. 12-X-Mas issue 2 4 6 11 14 18
10-Giant Summer Special ($1.50)-Origin 3 6 9 16 20 24
16-Giant Summer Special ($1.50)-Olga Bustle-c/s 2 4 6 12 16 20
17,18(8/78): 17-Lady Luck-r 1 3 4 6 8 10
19-21-New Eisner-a. 20,21-Wood-r (#21-r/A DP on the Moon by Wood). 20-Outer Space-r 1 3 4 6 8 10
22-41: 22,23-Wood-r (#22-r/Mission the Moon by Wood). 28-r/last story (10/5/52). 30-(7/81)-Special Spirit Jam issue w/Caniff, Corben, Bolland, Byrne, Miller, Kurtzman, Rogers, Sienkiewicz-a & 40 others. 36-Begin Spirit Section-r; r/1st story (6/2/40) in color; new Eisner-c/a(18 pgs.)($2.95). 37-r/2nd story in color plus 18 pgs. new Eisner-a. 38-41: r/3rd - 6th stories in color. 41-Lady Luck Mr. Mystic in color 1 2 3 5 7 9
Special 1(1975)-All Eisner-a (mail only, full color) 5 10 15 36 48 60
NOTE: *Covers pencilled/inked by **Eisner** only #1-9,12-16; painted by Eisner & Ken Kelly #10 & 11; painted by Eisner #17-up; one color story reprinted in #1-10. **Austin** a-30i. **Byrne** a-30p. **Miller** a-30p.*

SPIRIT, THE
Kitchen Sink Enterprises: Oct, 1983 - No. 87, Jan, 1992 ($2.00, Baxter paper)
1-60: 1-Origin-r/12/23/45 Spirit Section. 2-r/ 1/20/46-2/10/46. 3-r/2/17/46-3/10/46. 4-r/3/17/46-4/7/46. 11-Last color issue. 54-r/section 2/19/50 4.00
61-87: 85-87-Reprint the Outer Space Spirit stories by Wood. 86-r/A DP on the Moon by Wood from 1952 4.00

SPIRIT JAM
Kitchen Sink Press: Aug, 1998 ($5.95, B&W, oversized, square-bound)
nn-Reprints Spirit (Magazine) #30 by Eisner & 50 others; and "Cerebus Vs. The Spirit" from Cerebus Jam #1 6.00

SPIRIT, THE: THE NEW ADVENTURES
Kitchen Sink Press: 1997 - No. 8, Nov, 1998 ($3.50, anthology)
1-Moore-s/Gibbons-c/a 4.00
2-8: 2-Gaiman-s/Eisner-c. 3-Moore-s/Bolland-c/Moebius back-c. 4-Allred-s/a; Busiek-s/Anderson-a. 5-Chadwick-s/c/a(p); Nyberg-i. 6-S.Hampton & Mandrake-a 3.50

SPIRIT: THE ORIGIN YEARS
Kitchen Sink Press: May, 1992 - No. 10, Dec, 1993 ($2.95, B&W)
1-10: 1-r/sections 6/2/40(origin)-6/23/40 (all 1940s) 3.00

SPIRITMAN (Also see Three Comics)

Spitfire Comics #133 © Malverne Herald

Spoof #1 © MAR

Spooky Spooktown #1 © HARV

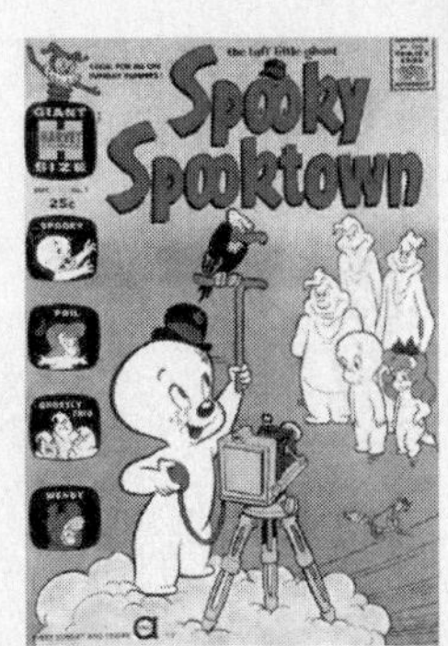

No publisher listed: No date (1944) (10¢)
(Triangle Sales Co. ad on back cover)

	GD 2.0	VG 4.0	FN 6.0	VF 8.0	VF/NM 9.0	NM- 9.2
1-Three 16pg. Spirit sections bound together, (1944, 10¢, 52 pgs.)	21	42	63	121	173	225
2-Two Spirit sections (3/26/44, 4/2/44) bound together; by Lou Fine	19	38	57	107	154	200

SPIRIT OF THE BORDER (See Zane Grey & Four Color #197)

SPIRIT OF THE TAO
Image Comics (Top Cow): Jun, 1998 - No. 15, May, 2000 ($2.50)

	GD 2.0	VG 4.0	FN 6.0	VF 8.0	VF/NM 9.0	NM- 9.2
Preview						5.00
1-14: 1-D-Tron-s/Tan & D-Tron-a						2.50
15-($4.95)						5.00

SPIRIT OF WONDER (Manga)
Dark Horse Comics: Apr, 1996 - No. 5, Aug, 1996 ($2.95, B&W, limited series)

	GD 2.0	VG 4.0	FN 6.0	VF 8.0	VF/NM 9.0	NM- 9.2
1-5						3.00

SPIRIT WORLD (Magazine)
National Periodical Publications: Fall, 1971 (B&W)

	GD 2.0	VG 4.0	FN 6.0	VF 8.0	VF/NM 9.0	NM- 9.2
1-New Kirby-a; Neal Adams-c; poster inside (1/2 price without poster)	7	14	21	50	68	85

SPITFIRE
Malverne Herald (Elliot)(J. R. Mahon): No. 132, 1944 (Aug) - No. 133, 1945
(Female undercover agent)

	GD 2.0	VG 4.0	FN 6.0	VF 8.0	VF/NM 9.0	NM- 9.2
132,133: Both have Classics Gift Box ads on b/c with checklist to #20	26	52	78	147	211	275

SPITFIRE AND THE TROUBLESHOOTERS
Marvel Comics: Oct, 1986 - No. 9, June, 1987 (Codename: Spitfire #10 on)

	GD 2.0	VG 4.0	FN 6.0	VF 8.0	VF/NM 9.0	NM- 9.2
1-3,5-9						2.25
4-McFarlane-a						3.00

SPITFIRE COMICS (Also see Double Up)
Harvey Publications: Aug, 1941 - No. 2, Oct, 1941 (Pocket size; 100 pgs.)

	GD 2.0	VG 4.0	FN 6.0	VF 8.0	VF/NM 9.0	NM- 9.2
1-Origin The Clown, The Fly-Man, The Spitfire & The Magician From Bagdad	79	158	237	494	760	1025
2-(Scarce)	73	146	219	456	703	950

SPLITTING IMAGE
Image Comics: Mar, 1993 - No. 2, 1993 ($1.95)

	GD 2.0	VG 4.0	FN 6.0	VF 8.0	VF/NM 9.0	NM- 9.2
1,2-Simpson-c/a; parody comic						2.25

SPOOF
Marvel Comics Group: Oct, 1970; No. 2, Nov, 1972 - No. 5, May, 1973

	GD 2.0	VG 4.0	FN 6.0	VF 8.0	VF/NM 9.0	NM- 9.2
1-Infinity-c; Dark Shadows-c & parody	3	6	9	16	20	24
2-5: 2-All in the Family. 3-Beatles, Osmond's, Jackson 5, David Cassidy, Nixon & Agnew-c. 5-Rod Serling, Woody Allen, Ted Kennedy-c	2	4	6	10	13	16

SPOOK (Formerly Shock Detective Cases)
Star Publications: No. 22, Jan, 1953 - No. 30, Oct, 1954

	GD 2.0	VG 4.0	FN 6.0	VF 8.0	VF/NM 9.0	NM- 9.2
22-Sgt. Spook-r; acid in face story; hanging-c	40	80	120	236	351	465
23,25,27: 25-Jungle Lil-r. 27-Two Sgt. Spook-r	30	60	90	170	245	320
24-Used in **SOTI**, pgs. 182,183-r/Inside Crime #2; Transvestism story	31	62	93	175	253	330
26,28-30: 26-Disbrow-a. 28,29-Rulah app. 29-Jo-Jo app. 30-Disbrow-c/a(2); only Star-c	30	60	90	170	245	320

NOTE: ***L. B. Cole** covers-all issues except #30; a-28(1 pg.). **Disbrow** a-26(2), 28, 29(2), 30(2); No. 30 r/Blue Bolt Weird Tales #114.*

SPOOK COMICS
Baily Publications/Star: 1946

	GD 2.0	VG 4.0	FN 6.0	VF 8.0	VF/NM 9.0	NM- 9.2
1-Mr. Lucifer story	31	62	93	175	253	330

SPOOKY (The Tuff Little Ghost; see Casper The Friendly Ghost)
Harvey Publications: 11/55 - 139, 11/73; No. 140, 7/74 - No. 155, 3/77; No. 156, 12/77 - No. 158, 4/78; No. 159, 9/78; No. 160, 10/79; No. 161, 9/80

	GD 2.0	VG 4.0	FN 6.0	VF 8.0	VF/NM 9.0	NM- 9.2
1-Nightmare begins (see Casper #19)	41	82	123	330	515	700
2	22	44	66	155	238	320
3-10(1956-57)	13	26	39	92	141	190
11-20(1957-58)	8	16	24	55	78	100
21-40(1958-59)	6	12	18	40	55	70
41-60	5	10	15	33	44	55
61-80,100	4	8	12	22	30	38
81-99	3	6	9	18	24	30
101-120	2	4	6	11	14	18
121-126,133-140	2	4	6	8	10	12
127-132: All 52 pg. Giants	2	4	6	11	14	18
141-161	1	2	3	5	6	8

SPOOKY
Harvey Comics: Nov, 1991 - No. 4, Sept, 1992 ($1.00/$1.25)

	GD 2.0	VG 4.0	FN 6.0	VF 8.0	VF/NM 9.0	NM- 9.2
1						4.00
2-4: 3-Begin $1.25-c						3.00
...Digest 1-3 (10/92, 6/93, 10/93, $1.75, 100 pgs.)-Casper, Wendy, etc.						4.00

SPOOKY HAUNTED HOUSE
Harvey Publications: Oct, 1972 - No. 15, Feb, 1975

	GD 2.0	VG 4.0	FN 6.0	VF 8.0	VF/NM 9.0	NM- 9.2
1	3	7	10	21	28	35
2-5	2	4	6	11	14	18
6-10	2	4	6	8	10	12
11-15	1	2	3	5	7	9

SPOOKY MYSTERIES
Your Guide Publ. Co.: No date (1946) (10¢)

	GD 2.0	VG 4.0	FN 6.0	VF 8.0	VF/NM 9.0	NM- 9.2
1-Mr. Spooky, Super Snooper, Pinky, Girl Detective app.	20	40	60	112	161	210

SPOOKY SPOOKTOWN
Harvey Publ.: 9/61; No. 2, 9/62 - No. 52, 12/73; No. 53, 10/74 - No. 66, 12/76

	GD 2.0	VG 4.0	FN 6.0	VF 8.0	VF/NM 9.0	NM- 9.2
1-Casper, Spooky; 68 pgs. begin	17	34	51	121	186	250
2	10	20	30	67	96	125
3-5	7	14	21	50	68	85
6-10	6	12	18	38	52	65
11-20	4	8	12	25	33	42
21-39: 39-Last 68 pg. issue	3	7	10	21	28	35
40-45: All 52 pgs.	2	4	6	11	14	18
46-66: 61-Hot Stuff/Spooky team-up story	1	2	3	5	7	9

SPORT COMICS (Becomes True Sport Picture Stories #5 on)
Street & Smith Publications: Oct, 1940 (No mo.) - No. 4, Nov, 1941

	GD 2.0	VG 4.0	FN 6.0	VF 8.0	VF/NM 9.0	NM- 9.2
1-Life story of Lou Gehrig	55	110	165	340	520	700
2	32	64	96	184	267	350
3,4	28	56	84	158	229	300

SPORT LIBRARY (See Charlton Sport Library)

SPORTS ACTION (Formerly Sport Stars)
Marvel/Atlas Comics (ACI No. 2,3/SAI No. 4-14): No. 2, Feb, 1950 - No. 14, Sept, 1952

	GD 2.0	VG 4.0	FN 6.0	VF 8.0	VF/NM 9.0	NM- 9.2
2-Powell painted-c; George Gipp life story	42	84	126	256	391	525
1-(nd,no price, no publ., 52pgs, #1 on-c; has same-c as #2; blank inside-c (giveaway?)	23	46	69	130	188	245
3-Everett-a	25	50	75	144	207	270
4-11,14: Weiss-a	22	44	66	127	184	240
12,13: 12-Everett-c. 13-Krigstein-a	24	48	72	138	199	260

NOTE: *Title may have changed after No. 3, to Crime Must Lose No. 4 on, due to publisher change. **Sol Brodsky** c-4-7, 13, 14. **Maneely** c-3, 8-11.*

SPORT STARS
Parents' Magazine Institute (Sport Stars): Feb-Mar, 1946 - No. 4, Aug-Sept, 1946 (Half comic, half photo magazine)

	GD 2.0	VG 4.0	FN 6.0	VF 8.0	VF/NM 9.0	NM- 9.2
1- "How Tarzan Got That Way" story of Johnny Weissmuller	40	80	120	236	351	465
2-Baseball greats	27	54	81	154	222	290
3,4	24	48	72	135	195	255

SPORT STARS (Becomes Sports Action #2 on)
Marvel Comics (ACI): Nov, 1949 (52 pgs.)

	GD 2.0	VG 4.0	FN 6.0	VF 8.0	VF/NM 9.0	NM- 9.2
1-Knute Rockne; painted-c	44	88	132	268	409	550

SPORT THRILLS (Formerly Dick Cole; becomes Jungle Thrills #16)
Star Publications: No. 11, Nov, 1950 - No. 15, Nov, 1951

	GD 2.0	VG 4.0	FN 6.0	VF 8.0	VF/NM 9.0	NM- 9.2
11-Dick Cole begins; Ted Williams & Ty Cobb life stories	31	62	93	175	253	330
12-Joe DiMaggio, Phil Rizzuto stories & photos on-c; L.B. Cole-c/a	25	50	75	141	203	265
13-15-All L. B. Cole-c. 13-Jackie Robinson, Pee Wee Reese stories & photo on-c. 14-Johnny Weissmuller life story	25	50	75	141	203	265
Accepted Reprint #11 (#15 on-c, nd); L.B. Cole-c	9	18	27	54	70	85
Accepted Reprint #12 (nd); L.B. Cole-c; Joe DiMaggio & Phil Rizzuto life stories-r/#12	9	18	27	54	70	85

SPOTLIGHT (TV) (newsstand sales only)
Marvel Comics Group: Sept, 1978 - No. 4, Mar, 1979 (Hanna-Barbera)

	GD 2.0	VG 4.0	FN 6.0	VF 8.0	VF/NM 9.0	NM- 9.2
1-Huckleberry Hound, Yogi Bear; Shaw-a	4	8	12	24	32	40
2,4: 2-Quick Draw McGraw, Augie Doggie, Snooper & Blabber. 4-Magilla Gorilla,						

Spy Cases #14 © MAR

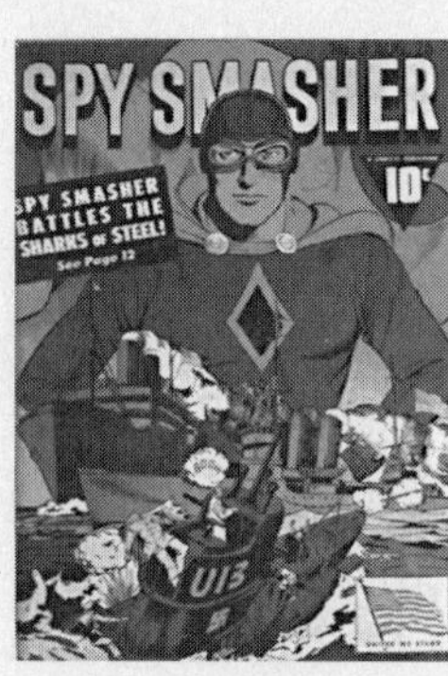

Spy Smasher #6 © FAW

Squadron Supreme TPB © MAR

	GD 2.0	VG 4.0	FN 6.0	VF 8.0	VF/NM 9.0	NM- 9.2
Snagglepuss	3	6	9	18	24	30
3-The Jetsons; Yakky Doodle	4	8	12	24	32	40

SPOTLIGHT COMICS (Becomes Red Seal Comics #14 on?)
Harry 'A' Chesler (Our Army, Inc.): Nov, 1944 - No. 3, 1945

	GD 2.0	VG 4.0	FN 6.0	VF 8.0	VF/NM 9.0	NM- 9.2
1-The Black Dwarf (cont'd in Red Seal?), The Veiled Avenger, & Barry Kuda begin; Tuska-c	75	150	225	469	722	975
2	55	110	165	340	520	700
3-Injury to eye story (reprinted from Scoop #3)	56	112	168	350	538	725

SPOTTY THE PUP (Becomes Super Pup #4, see Television Puppet Show)
Avon Periodicals/Realistic Comics: No. 2, Oct-Nov, 1953 - No. 3, Dec-Jan, 1953-54 (Also see Funny Tunes)

	GD 2.0	VG 4.0	FN 6.0	VF 8.0	VF/NM 9.0	NM- 9.2
2,3	7	14	21	35	43	50
nn (1953, Realistic-r)	4	7	9	14	16	18

SPUNKY (...Junior Cowboy)(...Comics #2 on)
Standard Comics: April, 1949 - No. 7, Nov, 1951

	GD 2.0	VG 4.0	FN 6.0	VF 8.0	VF/NM 9.0	NM- 9.2
1-Text illos by Frazetta	11	22	33	64	87	110
2-Text illos by Frazetta	9	18	27	49	62	75
3-7	6	12	18	31	38	45

SPUNKY THE SMILING SPOOK
Ajax/Farrell (World Famous Comics/Four Star Comic Corp.): Aug, 1957 - No. 4, May, 1958

	GD 2.0	VG 4.0	FN 6.0	VF 8.0	VF/NM 9.0	NM- 9.2
1-Reprints from Frisky Fables	10	20	30	56	73	90
2-4	6	12	18	31	38	45

SPY AND COUNTERSPY (Becomes Spy Hunters #3 on)
American Comics Group: Aug-Sept, 1949 - No. 2, Oct-Nov, 1949 (52 pgs.)

	GD 2.0	VG 4.0	FN 6.0	VF 8.0	VF/NM 9.0	NM- 9.2
1-Origin, 1st app. Jonathan Kent, Counterspy	27	54	81	152	219	285
2	17	34	51	95	135	175

SPYBOY
Dark Horse Comics: Oct, 1999 - No. 17, May, 2001 ($2.50/$2.95/$2.99)

	GD 2.0	VG 4.0	FN 6.0	VF 8.0	VF/NM 9.0	NM- 9.2
1-17: 1-6-Peter David-s/Pop Mhan-a. 7,8-Meglia-a. 9-17-Mhan-a						3.00
13.1-13.3 (4/03-8/03, $2.99), 13.2,13.3-Mhan-a						3.00
... Special (5/02, $4.99) David-s/Mhan-a						5.00

SPYBOY: FINAL EXAM
Dark Horse Comics: May, 2004 - No. 4, Aug, 2004 ($2.99, limited series)

	GD 2.0	VG 4.0	FN 6.0	VF 8.0	VF/NM 9.0	NM- 9.2
1-4-Peter David-s/Pop Mhan-a/c						3.00
TPB (2005, $12.95) r/series						13.00

SPYBOY/ YOUNG JUSTICE
Dark Horse Comics: Feb, 2002 - No. 3, Apr, 2002 ($2.99, limited series)

	GD 2.0	VG 4.0	FN 6.0	VF 8.0	VF/NM 9.0	NM- 9.2
1-3: 1-Peter David-s/Todd Nauck-a/Pop Mhan-c. 2-Mhan-a						3.00

SPY CASES (Formerly The Kellys)
Marvel/Atlas Comics (Hercules Publ.): No. 26, Sept, 1950 - No. 19, Oct, 1953

	GD 2.0	VG 4.0	FN 6.0	VF 8.0	VF/NM 9.0	NM- 9.2
26 (#1)	24	48	72	135	195	255
27(#2),28(#3, 2/51): 27-Everett-a; bondage-c	14	28	42	79	110	140
4(4/51) - 7,9,10	12	24	36	69	95	120
8-A-Bomb-c/story	14	28	42	79	110	140
11-19: 10-14-War format	10	20	30	56	73	90

NOTE: ***Sol Brodsky** c-1-5, 8, 9, 11-14, 17, 18. **Maneely** a-8; c-7, 10. **Tuska** a-7.*

SPY FIGHTERS
Marvel/Atlas Comics (CSI): March, 1951 - No. 15, July, 1953
(Cases from official records)

	GD 2.0	VG 4.0	FN 6.0	VF 8.0	VF/NM 9.0	NM- 9.2
1-Clark Mason begins; Tuska-a; Brodsky-c	25	50	75	144	207	270
2-Tuska-a	14	28	42	79	110	140
3-13: 3-5-Brodsky-c. 7-Heath-c	12	24	36	71	98	125
14,15-Pakula-a(3), Ed Win-a. 15-Brodsky-c	13	26	39	74	102	130

SPY-HUNTERS (Formerly Spy & Counterspy)
American Comics Group: No. 3, Dec-Jan, 1949-50 - No. 24, June-July, 1953 (#3-14: 52 pgs.)

	GD 2.0	VG 4.0	FN 6.0	VF 8.0	VF/NM 9.0	NM- 9.2
3-Jonathan Kent continues, ends #10	24	48	72	135	195	255
4-10: 4,8,10-Starr-a	14	28	42	79	110	140
11-15,17-22,24: 18-War-c begin. 21-War-c/stories begin	10	20	30	58	77	95
16-Williamson-a (9 pgs.)	16	32	48	89	127	165
23-Graphic torture, injury to eye panel	21	42	63	118	169	220

NOTE: ***Drucker** a-12. **Whitney** a-many issues; c-7, 8, 10-12, 15, 16.*

SPYMAN (Top Secret Adventures on cover)
Harvey Publications (Illustrated Humor): Sept, 1966 - No. 3, Feb, 1967 (12¢)

	GD 2.0	VG 4.0	FN 6.0	VF 8.0	VF/NM 9.0	NM- 9.2
1-Origin and 1st app. of Spyman. Steranko-a(p)-1st pro work; 1 pg. Neal Adams ad; Tuska-c/a, Crandall-a(i)	8	16	24	53	74	95
2-Simon-c; Steranko-a(p)	5	10	15	33	44	55
3-Simon-c	4	8	12	29	40	50

SPY SMASHER (See Mighty Midget, Whiz & Xmas Comics) (Also see Crime Smasher)
Fawcett Publications: Fall, 1941 - No. 11, Feb, 1943

	GD 2.0	VG 4.0	FN 6.0	VF 8.0	VF/NM 9.0	NM- 9.2
1-Spy Smasher begins; silver metallic-c	372	744	1116	2418	3909	5400
2-Raboy-c	169	338	507	1056	1628	2200
3,4: 3-Bondage-c. 4-Irvin Steinberg-c	115	230	345	719	1110	1500
5-7: Raboy-a; 6-Raboy-c/a. 7-Part photo-c (movie).	100	200	300	625	963	1300
8,11: War-c	81	162	243	506	778	1050
9-Hitler, Tojo, Mussolini-c.	96	192	288	600	925	1250
10-Hitler-c	92	184	276	575	888	1200

SPY THRILLERS (Police Badge No. 479 #5)
Atlas Comics (PrPI): Nov, 1954 - No. 4, May, 1955

	GD 2.0	VG 4.0	FN 6.0	VF 8.0	VF/NM 9.0	NM- 9.2
1-Brodsky c-1,2	22	44	66	123	177	230
2-Last precode (1/55)	13	26	39	74	102	130
3,4	10	20	30	58	77	95

SQUADRON SUPREME (Also see Marvel Graphic Novel)
Marvel Comics Group: Aug, 1985 - No. 12, Aug, 1986 (Maxi-series)

	GD 2.0	VG 4.0	FN 6.0	VF 8.0	VF/NM 9.0	NM- 9.2
1-Double size						3.00
2-12						2.50
TPB ($24.99) r/#1-12; Alex Ross painted-c; printing inks contain some of the cremated remains of late writer Mark Gruenwald						25.00
TPB-2nd printing ($24.99): Inks contain no ashes						25.00

SQUADRON SUPREME: NEW WORLD ORDER
Marvel Comics: Sept, 1998 ($5.99, one-shot)

	GD 2.0	VG 4.0	FN 6.0	VF 8.0	VF/NM 9.0	NM- 9.2
1-Wraparound-c; Kaminski-s						6.00

SQUALOR
First Comics: Dec, 1989 - Aug, 1990 ($2.75, limited series)

	GD 2.0	VG 4.0	FN 6.0	VF 8.0	VF/NM 9.0	NM- 9.2
1-4: Sutton-a						2.75

SQUEE
Slave Labor Graphics: Apr, 1997 - No. 4, May, 1998 ($2.95, B&W)

	GD 2.0	VG 4.0	FN 6.0	VF 8.0	VF/NM 9.0	NM- 9.2
1-4: Jhonen Vasquez-s/a in all						3.00

SQUEEKS (Also see Boy Comics)
Lev Gleason Publications: Oct, 1953 - No. 5, June, 1954

	GD 2.0	VG 4.0	FN 6.0	VF 8.0	VF/NM 9.0	NM- 9.2
1-Funny animal; Biro-c; Crimebuster's pet monkey "Squeeks" begins	9	18	27	52	66	80
2-Biro-c	6	12	18	28	34	40
3-5: 3-Biro-c	5	10	15	24	30	35

S.R. BISSETTE'S SPIDERBABY COMIX
SpiderBaby Grafix: Aug, 1996 - No. 2 ($3.95, B&W, magazine size)

	GD 2.0	VG 4.0	FN 6.0	VF 8.0	VF/NM 9.0	NM- 9.2
Preview-(8/96, $3.95)-Graphic violence & nudity; Laurel & Hardy app.						4.00
1,2						4.00

S.R. BISSETTE'S TYRANT
SpiderBaby Grafix: Sept, 1994 - No. 4 ($2.95, B&W)

	GD 2.0	VG 4.0	FN 6.0	VF 8.0	VF/NM 9.0	NM- 9.2
1-4						4.00

STAINLESS STEEL RAT
Eagle Comics: Oct, 1985 - No. 6, Mar, 1986 (Limited series)

	GD 2.0	VG 4.0	FN 6.0	VF 8.0	VF/NM 9.0	NM- 9.2
1 (52 pgs.; $2.25-c)						3.00
2-6 ($1.50)						2.25

STALKER (Also see All Star Comics 1999 and crossover issues)
National Periodical Publications: June-July, 1975 - No. 4, Dec-Jan, 1975-76

	GD 2.0	VG 4.0	FN 6.0	VF 8.0	VF/NM 9.0	NM- 9.2
1-Origin & 1st app; Ditko/Wood-c/a	2	4	6	9	11	14
2-4-Ditko/Wood-c/a	1	2	3	5	6	8

STALKERS
Marvel Comics (Epic Comics): Apr, 1990 - No. 12, Mar, 1991 ($1.50)

	GD 2.0	VG 4.0	FN 6.0	VF 8.0	VF/NM 9.0	NM- 9.2
1-12: 1-Chadwick-c						2.25

STAMP COMICS (Stamps... on-c; Thrilling Adventures In...#8)
Youthful Magazines/Stamp Comics, Inc.: Oct, 1951 - No. 7, Oct, 1952

	GD 2.0	VG 4.0	FN 6.0	VF 8.0	VF/NM 9.0	NM- 9.2
1-(15¢) ('Stamps' on indicia No. 1-3,5,7)	30	60	90	173	249	325
2	17	34	51	95	135	175
3-6: 3,4-Kiefer, Wildey-a	15	30	45	83	117	150
7-Roy Krenkel (4 pgs.)	19	38	57	107	154	200

NOTE: *Promotes stamp collecting; gives stories behind various commemorative stamps. No. 2, 10¢ printed over 15¢ c-price. **Kiefer** a-1-7. **Kirkel** a-1-6. **Napoli** a-2-7. **Palais** a-2-4, 7.*

STANLEY & HIS MONSTER (Formerly The Fox & the Crow)

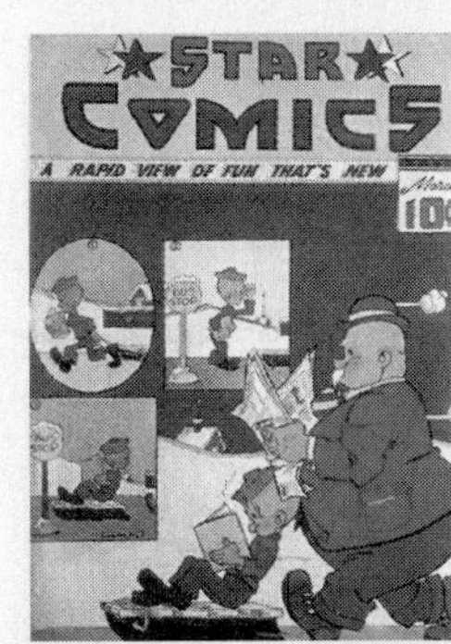

Star Comics V2#2 © CEN

Starjammers #1 © MAR

Starman (2nd) #6 © DC

	GD 2.0	VG 4.0	FN 6.0	VF 8.0	VF/NM 9.0	NM- 9.2

National Periodical Publ.: No. 109, Apr-May, 1968 - No. 112, Oct-Nov, 1968

109-112 3 7 10 21 28 35

STANLEY & HIS MONSTER
DC Comics: Feb, 1993 - No. 4, May, 1993 ($1.50, limited series)

1-4 2.25

STAN SHAW'S BEAUTY & THE BEAST
Dark Horse Comics: Nov, 1993 ($4.95, one-shot)

1 5.00

STAR
Image Comics (Highbrow Entertainment): June, 1995 - No. 4, Oct, 1995 ($2.50, lim. series)

1-4 2.50

STARBLAST
Marvel Comics: Jan, 1994 - No. 4, Apr, 1994 ($1.75, limited series)

1-4: 1-($2.00, 52 pgs.)-Nova, Quasar, Black Bolt; painted-c 2.25

STAR BLAZERS
Comico: Apr, 1987 - No. 4, July, 1987 ($1.75, limited series)

1-4 3.00

STAR BLAZERS
Comico: 1989 ($1.95/$2.50, limited series)

1-5- Steacy wraparound painted-c on all 3.00

STAR BLAZERS (The Magazine of Space Battleship Yamato)
Argo Press: No. 0, Aug, 1995 - No. 3, Dec, 1995 ($2.95)

0-3 3.00

STAR BRAND
Marvel Comics (New Universe): Oct, 1986 - No. 19, May, 1989 (75¢/$1.25)

1-15: 14-begin $1.25-c 2.25
16-19-Byrne story & art; low print run 4.00
Annual 1 (10/87) 2.25

STARCHILD
Tailspin Press: 1992 - No. 12($2.25/$2.50, B&W)

1,2-('92),0(4/93),3-12: 0-Illos by Chadwick, Eisner, Sim, M. Wagner. 3-(7/93). 4-(11/93). 6-(2/94) 3.00

STARCHILD: MYTHOPOLIS
Image Comics: No. 0, July, 1997 - No. 4, Apr, 1998 ($2.95, B&W, limited series)

0-4-James Owen-s/a 3.00

STAR COMICS
Ultem Publ. (Harry `A' Chesler)/Centaur Publications: Feb, 1937 - V2#7 (No. 23), Aug, 1939 (#1-6: large size)

V1#1-Dan Hastings (s/f) begins 185 370 555 1156 1778 2400
2 83 166 249 519 797 1075
3-6 (#6, 9/37): 4,5-Little Nemo-c/stories 71 142 213 444 685 925
7-9: 8-Severed head centerspread; Impy & Little Nemo by Winsor McCay Jr, Popeye app. by Bob Wood; Mickey Mouse & Popeye app. as toys in Santa's bag on-c; X-Mas-c 65 130 195 406 628 850
10 (1st Centaur; 3/38)-Impy by Winsor McCay Jr; Don Marlow by Guardineer begins 87 174 261 544 835 1125
11-1st Jack Cole comic-a, 1 pg. (4/38) 65 130 195 406 628 850
12-15: 12-Riders of the Golden West begins; Little Nemo app. 15-Speed Silvers by Gustavson & The Last Pirate by Burgos begins 55 110 165 340 520 700
16 (12/38)-The Phantom Rider & his horse Thunder begins, ends V2#6 56 112 168 350 538 725
V2#1(#17, 2/39)-Phantom Rider-c (only non-funny-c) 60 120 180 375 575 775
2-7(#18-23): 2-Diana Deane by Tarpe Mills app. 3-Drama of Hollywood by Mills begins. 7-Jungle Queen app. 50 100 150 305 465 625

NOTE: ***Biro*** *c-6, 9, 10.* ***Burgos*** *a-15, 16, V2#1-7.* ***Ken Ernst*** *a-10, 12, 14.* ***Filchock*** *c-15, 18, 22.* ***Gill Fox*** *c-14, 19.* ***Guardineer*** *a-6, 8-14.* ***Gustavson*** *a-13-16, V2#1-7.* ***Winsor McCay*** *c-4, 5.* ***Tarpe Mills*** *a-15, V2#1-7.* ***Schwab*** *c-20, 23.* ***Bob Wood*** *a-10, 12, 13; c-7, 8.*

STAR COMICS MAGAZINE
Marvel Comics (Star Comics): Dec, 1986 - No. 13, 1988 ($1.50, digest-size)

1,9-Spider-Man-c/s 2 4 6 8 10 12
2-8-Heathcliff, Ewoks, Top Dog, Madballs-r in #1-13 1 2 3 5 6 8
10-13 1 3 4 6 8 10

S.T.A.R. CORPS
DC Comics: Nov, 1993 - No. 6, Apr, 1994 ($1.50, limited series)

1-6: 1,2-Austin-c(i). 1-Superman app. 2.25

STAR CROSSED
DC Comics (Helix): June, 1997 - No. 3, Aug, 1997 ($2.50, limited series)

1-3-Matt Howarth-s/a 2.50

STARDUST (See Neil Gaiman and Charles Vess' Stardust)

STAR FEATURE COMICS
I. W. Enterprises: 1963

Reprint #9-Stunt-Man Stetson-r/Feat. Comics #141 2 4 6 10 13 16

STARFIRE (Not the Teen Titans character)
National Periodical Publ./DC Comics: Aug-Sept, 1976 - No. 8, Oct-Nov, 1977

1-Origin (CCA stamp fell off cover art; so it was approved by code) 2 4 6 8 10 12
2-8 1 2 3 4 5 7

STAR HUNTERS (See DC Super Stars #16)
National Periodical Publ./DC Comics: Oct-Nov, 1977 - No. 7, Oct-Nov, 1978

1,7: 1-Newton-a(p). 7-44 pgs. 1 3 4 6 8 10
2-6 6.00

NOTE: ***Buckler*** *a-4-7p; c-1-7p.* ***Layton*** *a-1-5i; c-1-6i.* ***Nasser*** *a-3p.* ***Sutton*** *a-6i.*

STARJAMMERS (See X-Men Spotlight on Starjammers)

STARJAMMERS (Also see Uncanny X-Men)
Marvel Comics: Oct, 1995 - No. 4, Jan, 1996 ($2.95, limited series)

1-4: Foil-c; Ellis scripts 3.00

STARJAMMERS
Marvel Comics: Sept, 2004 - No. 6, Jan, 2005 ($2.99, limited series)

1-6-Kevin J. Anderson-s. 1-Garza-a. 2-6-Lucas-a 3.00

STARK TERROR
Stanley Publications: Dec, 1970 - No. 5, Aug, 1971 (B&W, magazine, 52 pgs.) (1950s Horror reprints, including pre-code)

1-Bondage, torture-c 6 12 18 38 52 65
2-4 (Gillmor/Aragon-r) 4 8 12 22 30 38
5 (ACG-r) 3 6 9 18 24 30

STARLET O'HARA IN HOLLYWOOD (Teen-age) (Also see Cookie)
Standard Comics: Dec, 1948 - No. 4, Sept, 1949

1-Owen Fitzgerald-a in all 25 50 75 144 207 270
2 15 30 45 83 117 150
3,4 12 24 36 71 98 125

STAR-LORD THE SPECIAL EDITION (Also see Marvel Comics Super Special #10, Marvel Premiere & Preview & Marvel Spotlight V2#6,7)
Marvel Comics Group: Feb, 1982 (one-shot, direct sales) (1st Baxter paper comic)

1-Byrne/Austin-a; Austin-c; 8 pgs. of new-a by Golden (p); Dr. Who story by Dave Gibbons; 1st deluxe format comic 6.00

STARLORD
Marvel Comics: Dec, 1996 - No. 3, Feb, 1997 ($2.50, limited series)

1-3-Timothy Zahn-s 2.50

STARLORD MEGAZINE
Marvel Comics: Nov, 1996 ($2.95, one-shot)

1-Reprints w/preview of new series 3.00

STARMAN (1st Series) (Also see Justice League & War of the Gods)
DC Comics: Oct, 1988 - No. 45, Apr, 1992 ($1.00)

1-25,29-45: 1-Origin. 4-Intro The Power Elite. 9,10,34-Batman app. 14-Superman app. 17-Power Girl app. 38-War of the Gods x-over. 42-45-Eclipso-c/stories 2.50
26-1st app. David Knight (G.A.Starman's son). 5.00
27,28: 27-Starman (David Knight) app. 28-Starman disguised as Superman; leads into Superman #50 4.00

STARMAN (2nd Series) (Also see The Golden Age, Showcase 95 #12, Showcase 96 #4,5)
DC Comics : No. 0, Oct, 1994 - No. 80, Aug, 2001 ($1.95/$2.25/$2.50)

0,1: 0-James Robinson scripts, Tony Harris-c/a(p) & Wade Von Grawbadger-a(i) begins; Sins of the Father storyline begins, ends #3; 1st app. new Starman (Jack Knight); reintro of the G.A. Mist & G.A. Shade; 1st app. Nash; David Knight dies 1 2 3 4 5 7
2-7: 2-Reintro Charity from Forbidden Tales of Dark Mansion. 3-Reintro/2nd app. "Blue" Starman (1st app. in 1st Issue Special #12); Will Payton app. (both cameos). 5-David Knight app. 6-The Shade "Times Past" story; Teddy Kristiansen-a. 7-The Black Pirate cameo 5.00
8-17: 8-Begin $2.25-c. 10-1st app. new Mist (Nash). 11-JSA "Times Past" story; Matt Smith-a. 12-16-Sins of the Child. 17-The BlackPirate app. 4.00

Starman: The Mist #1 © DC

Stars and S.T.R.I.P.E. #1 © DC

Starslayer #18 © FC

18-37: 18-G.A. Starman "Times Past" story; Watkiss-a. 19-David Knight app. 20-23-G.A. Sandman app. 24-26-Demon Quest; all 3 covers make-up triptych. 33-36-Batman-c/app. 37-David Knight and deceased JSA members app. 3.00
38-49,51-56: 38-Nash vs. Justice League Europe. 39,40-Crossover w/ Power of Shazam! #35,36; Bulletman app. 42-Demon-c/app. 43-JLA-c/app. 44-Phantom Lady-c/app. 46-Gene Ha-a. 51-Jor-el app. 52,53-Adam Strange-c/app. 2.50
50-($3.95) Gold foil logo on-c; Star Boy (LSH) app. 4.00
57-79: 57-62-Painted covers by Harris and Alex Ross. 72-Death of Ted Knight 2.50
80-($3.95) Final issue; cover by Harris & Robinson 4.00
#1,000,000 (11/98) 853rd Century x-over; Snejbjerg-a 2.50
Annual 1 (1996, $3.50)-Legends of the Dead Earth story; Prince Gavyn & G.A. Starman stories; J.H. Williams III, Bret Blevins, Craig Hamilton-c/a(p) 4.00
Annual 2 (1997, $3.95)-Pulp Heroes story; 4.00
...80 Page Giant (1/99, $4.95) Harris-c 5.00
...Secret Files 1 (4/98, $4.95)-Origin stories and profile pages 5.00
...The Mist (6/98, $1.95) Girlfrenzy; Mary Marvel app. 2.50
A Starry Knight-($17.95, TPB) r/#47-53 18.00
Grand Guingnol-(2004, $19.95, TPB)-r/#61-73 20.00
Infernal Devices-($17.95, TPB) r/#29-35,37,38 18.00
Night and Day-($14.95, TPB)-r/#7-10,12-16 15.00
Sins of the Father-($12.95, TPB)-r/#0-5 13.00
Stars My Destination-(2003, $14.95, TPB)-r/#55-60 15.00
Times Past-($17.95, TPB)-r/stories of other Starmen 18.00

STARMASTERS
Americomics: Mar, 1984 ($1.50, one-shot)
1-Origin The Women of W.O.S.P. & Breed 3.00

STAR PRESENTATION, A (Formerly My Secret Romance #1,2; Spectacular Stories #4 on) (Also see This Is Suspense)
Fox Features Syndicate (Hero Books): No. 3, May, 1950
3-Dr. Jekyll & Mr. Hyde by Wood & Harrison (reprinted in Startling Terror Tales #10); "The Repulsing Dwarf" by Wood; Wood-c 55 110 165 340 520 700

STAR QUEST COMIX (Warren Presents... on cover)
Warren Publications: Oct, 1978 ($1.50, B&W magazine, 84 pgs., square-bound)
1-Corben, Maroto, Neary-a; Ken Kelly-c; Star Wars 2 4 6 10 12 15

STAR RAIDERS (See DC Graphic Novel #1)

STAR RANGER (Cowboy Comics #13 on)
Chesler Publ./Centaur Publ.: Feb, 1937 - No. 12, May, 1938 (Large size: No. 1-6)
1-(1st Western comic)-Ace & Deuce, Air Plunder; Creig Flessel-a 192 384 576 1200 1850 2500
2 87 174 261 544 835 1125
3-6 75 150 225 469 722 975
7-9: 8(12/37)-Christmas-c; Air Patrol, Gold coast app.; Guardineer centerfold 56 112 168 350 538 725
V2#10 (1st Centaur; 3/38) 87 174 261 544 835 1125
11,12 65 130 195 406 628 850
NOTE: ***J. Cole** a-10, 12; c-12. **Ken Ernst** a-11. **Gill Fox** a-8(illo), 9, 10. **Guardineer** a-1, 3, 6, 7, 8(illos), 9, 10, 12. **Gustavson** a-8-10, 12. **Fred Schwab** c-2-11. **Bob Wood** a-8-10.*

STAR RANGER FUNNIES (Formerly Cowboy Comics)
Centaur Publications: V1#15, Oct, 1938 - V2#5, Oct, 1939
V1#15-Lyin Lou, Ermine, Wild West Junior, The Law of Caribou County by Eisner, Cowboy Jake, The Plugged Dummy, Spurs by Gustavson, Red Coat, Two Buckaroos & Trouble Hunters begin 98 196 294 613 944 1275
V2#1 (1/39) 74 148 222 463 712 960
2-5: 2-Night Hawk by Gustavson. 4-Kit Carson app. 62 124 186 388 594 800
NOTE: ***Jack Cole** a-V2#1, 3; c-V2#1. **Filchock** c-V2#2, 3. **Guardineer** a-V2#3. **Gustavson** a-V2#2. **Pinajian** c/a-V2#5.*

STAR REACH (Mature content)
Star Reach Publ.: Apr, 1974 - No. 18 (B&W, #12-15 w/color)
1-(75¢, 52 pgs.) Art by Starlin, Simonson. Chaykin-c/a; origin Death. Cody Starbuck-sty 2 4 6 11 14 18
1-2nd, 3th, and 4th printings ($1.00-$1.50-c) 6.00
2-11: 2-Adams, Giordano-a; 1st Stephanie Starr-c/s. 3-1st Linda Lovecraft. 4-1st Sherlock Duck. 5-1st Gideon Faust by Chaykin. 6-Elric-c. 7-BWS-c. 9-14-Sacred & Profane-c/s by Steacy. 11-Samurai 1 2 3 5 7 9
2-2nd printing 4.00
12-15 (44 pgs.): 12-Zelazny-s. Nasser-a, Brunner-c 2 4 6 8 10 12
16-18-Magazine size: 17-Poe's Raven-c/s 2 4 6 8 10 12
NOTE: ***Adams** c-2. **Bonivert** a-17. **Brunner** a-3,5; c-3,10,12. **Chaykin** a-1,4,5; c-1(1st ed),4,5; back-c-1(2nd,3rd,4th ed). **Gene Day** a-6,8,9,11,15. **Friedrich** s-2,3,8,10. **Gasbarri** a-7. **Gilbert** a-9,12. **Giordano** a-2. **Gould** a-6. **Hirota/Mukaide** s/a-7. **Jones** c-6. **Konz** a-17. **Leialoha** a-3,4,6-i, 13,15; c-13,15. **Lyda** a-6,12-15. **Marrs** a-2-5,7,10,14,15,16,18; c-18; back-c-2. **Mukaide** a-18. **Nasser** a-12. **Nino** a-6; **Russell** a-8,10; c-8. **Dave Sim** s-7; lettering-9. **Simonson** a-1. **Skeates** a-1,2. **Starlin** a-1(x2), 2(x2); back-c-1(1st ed); c-1(2nd,3rd,4th ed). **Barry Smith** c-7. **Staton** a-5,6,7. **Steacy** a-8-14; c-9,11,14,16. **Vosburg** a-2-5,7,10. **Workman** a-2-5,8. Nudity panels in most. Wraparound-c: 3-5,7-11,13-16,18.*

STAR REACH CLASSICS
Eclipse Comics: Mar, 1984 - No. 6, Aug, 1984 ($1.50, Baxter paper)
1-6: 1-Neal Adams-r/Star Reach #1 3.00
NOTE: ***Dave Sim** a-1. **Starlin** a-1.*

STARR FLAGG, UNDERCOVER GIRL (See Undercover...)

STARRIORS
Marvel Comics: Aug, 1984 - Feb, 1985 (Limited series) (Based on Tomy toys)
1-4 3.00

STARS AND S.T.R.I.P.E. (Also see JSA)
DC Comics: July, 1999 - No. 14, Sept, 2000 ($2.95/$2.50)
0-($2.95) Moder and Weston-a; Starman app. 3.00
1-Johns and Robinson-s/Moder-a; origin new Star Spangled Kid 2.50
2-14: 4-Marvel Family app. 9-Seven Soldiers of Victory-c/app. 2.50

STARS AND STRIPES COMICS
Centaur Publications: No. 2, May, 1941 - No. 6, Dec, 1941
2(#1)-The Shark, The Iron Skull, A-Man, The Amazing Man, Mighty Man, Minimidget begin; The Voice & Dash Dartwell, the Human Meteor, Reef Kinkaid app.; Gustavson Flag-c 227 454 681 1419 2185 2950
3-Origin Dr. Synthe; The Black Panther app. 125 250 375 781 1203 1625
4-Origin/1st app. The Stars and Stripes; injury to eye-c 108 216 324 675 1038 1400
5(#5 on cover & inside) 75 150 225 469 722 975
5(#6)-(#5 on cover, #6 on inside) 75 150 225 469 722 975
NOTE: ***Gustavson** c/a-3. **Myron Strauss** c-4, 5(#5), 5(#6).*

STAR SEED (Formerly Powers That Be)
Broadway Comics: No. 7, 1996 - No. 9 ($2.95)
7-9 3.00

STARSHIP TROOPERS
Dark Horse Comics: 1997 - No. 2, 1997 ($2.95, limited series)
1,2-Movie adaption 3.00

STARSHIP TROOPERS: BRUTE CREATIONS
Dark Horse Comics: 1997 ($2.95, one-shot)
1 3.00

STARSHIP TROOPERS: DOMINANT SPECIES
Dark Horse Comics: Aug, 1998 - No. 4, Nov, 1998 ($2.95, limited series)
1-4-Strnad-s/Bolton-c 3.00

STARSHIP TROOPERS: INSECT TOUCH
Dark Horse Comics: 1997 - No. 3, 1997 ($2.95, limited series)
1-3 3.00

STAR SLAMMERS (See Marvel Graphic Novel #6)
Malibu Comics (Bravura): May, 1994 - No. 4, Aug, 1994 ($2.50, unfinished limited series)
1-4: W. Simonson-a/stories; contain Bravura stamps 2.50

STAR SLAMMERS SPECIAL
Dark Horse Comics (Legend): June, 1996 ($2.95, one-shot)
nn-Simonson-c/a/scripts; concludes Bravura limited series. 3.00

STARSLAYER
Pacific Comics/First Comics No. 7 on: Feb, 1982 - No. 6, Apr, 1983; No. 7, Aug, 1983 - No. 34, Nov, 1985
1-Origin & 1st app.; excessive blood & gore; 1 pg. Rocketeer brief app. which continues in #2 5.00
2-Origin/1st full app. the Rocketeer (4/82) by Dave Stevens (Chapter 1 of Rocketeer saga; see Pacific Presents #1,2) 1 2 3 5 6 8
3-Chapter 2 of Rocketeer saga by Stevens 6.00
4,6,7: 7-Grell-a ends 3.00
5-2nd app. Groo the Wanderer by Aragones 1 2 3 4 5 7
8-34: 10-1st app. Grimjack (11/83, ends #17). 18-Starslayer meets Grimjack. 20-The Black Flame begins (9/84, 1st app.), ends #33. 27-Book length Black Flame story 2.50
NOTE: ***Grell** a-1-7; c-1-8. **Stevens** back c-2, 3. **Sutton** a-17p, 20-22p, 24-27p, 29-33p.*

STARSLAYER (The Director's Cut)
Acclaim Comics (Windjammer): June, 1994 - No. 8, Dec, 1995 ($2.50)
1-8: Mike Grell-c/a/scripts 2.50

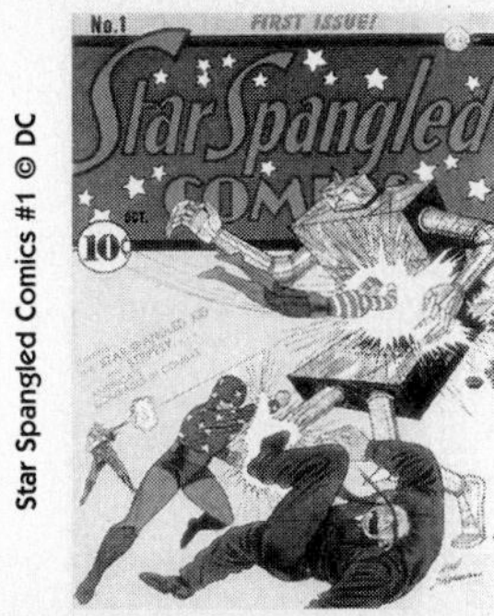

Star Spangled Comics #1 © DC

Star Spangled Comics #125 © DC

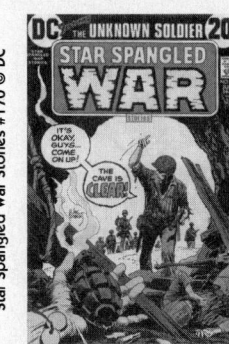

Star Spangled War Stories #170 © DC

STAR SPANGLED COMICS (Star Spangled War Stories #131 on)
National Periodical Publications: Oct, 1941 - No. 130, July, 1952

	GD 2.0	VG 4.0	FN 6.0	VF 8.0	VF/NM 9.0	NM- 9.2
1-Origin/1st app. Tarantula; Captain X of the R.A.F., Star Spangled Kid (see Action #40), Armstrong of the Army begin; Robot-c	503	1006	1509	3521	5661	7800
2	169	338	507	1056	1628	2200
3-5	108	216	324	675	1038	1400
6-Last Armstrong/Army; Penniless Palmer begins	63	126	189	394	610	825
7-(4/42)-Origin/1st app. The Guardian by S&K, & Robotman (by Paul Cassidy & created by Siegel);The Newsboy Legion (1st app.), Robotman & TNT begin; last Captain X	626	1252	1878	4382	7041	9700
8-Origin TNT & Dan the Dyna-Mite	238	476	714	1488	2294	3100
9,10	165	330	495	1031	1591	2150
11-17	123	246	369	769	1185	1600
18-Origin Star Spangled Kid	154	308	462	963	1482	2000
19-Last Tarantula	123	246	369	769	1185	1600
20-Liberty Belle begins (5/43)	133	266	399	831	1278	1725
21-29-Last S&K issue; 23-Last TNT. 25-Robotman by Jimmy Thompson begins. 29-Intro Robbie the Robotdog	104	208	312	650	1000	1350
30-40: 31-S&K-c	58	116	174	363	557	750
41-51: 41,49-Kirby-c. 51-Robot-c by Kirby	53	106	159	323	494	665
52-64: 53 by S&K. 64-Last Newsboy Legion & The Guardian	48	96	144	293	447	600
65-Robin begins with c/app. (2/47); Batman cameo in 1 panel; Robin-c begins, end #95	146	292	438	913	1407	1900
66-Batman cameo in Robin story	83	166	249	519	797	1075
67,68,70-80: 68-Last Liberty Belle? 72-Burnley Robin-c	67	134	201	419	647	875
69-Origin/1st app. Tomahawk by F. Ray; atom bomb story & splash (6/47)	104	208	312	650	1000	1350
81-Origin Merry, Girl of 1000 Gimmicks in Star Spangled Kid story	57	114	171	356	546	735
82,85: 82-Last Robotman? 85-Last Star Spangled Kid?	52	104	156	317	484	650
83-Tomahawk enters the lost valley, a land of dinosaurs; Capt. Compass begins, ends #130	52	104	156	317	484	650
84,87 (Rare): 87-Batman cameo in Robin	77	154	231	481	741	1000
86-Batman cameo in Robin story	58	116	174	363	557	750
88(1/49)-94: Batman-c/stories in all. 91-Federal Men begin, end #93. 94-Manhunters Around the World begin, end #121	60	120	180	375	575	775
95-Batman story; last Robin-c	53	106	159	323	494	665
96,98-Batman cameo in Robin stories. 96-1st Tomahawk-c (also #97-121)	40	80	120	233	342	450
97,99	36	72	108	204	297	390
100 (1/50)-Pre-Bat-Hound tryout in Robin story (pre-dates Batman #92).	40	80	120	241	363	485
101-109,118,119,121: 121-Last Tomahawk-c	34	68	102	193	279	365
110,111,120-Batman cameo in Robin stories. 120-Last 52 pg. issue	35	70	105	200	290	380
112-Batman & Robin story	37	74	111	209	305	400
113-Frazetta-a (10 pgs.)	42	84	126	252	391	525
114-Retells Robin's origin (3/51); Batman & Robin story	44	88	132	268	409	550
115,117-Batman app. in Robin stories	37	74	111	209	305	400
116-Flag-c	37	74	111	209	305	400
122-(11/51)-Ghost Breaker-c/stories begin (origin/1st app.), ends #130 (Ghost Breaker covers #122-130)	40	80	120	244	372	500
123-126,128,129	31	62	93	177	256	335
127-Batman app.	33	66	99	190	275	360
130-Batman cameo in Robin story	35	70	105	200	290	380

NOTE: *Most all issues after #29 signed by Simon & Kirby are not by them.* ***Bill Ely*** *c-122-130.* ***Mortimer*** *c-65-74(most), 76-95(most).* ***Fred Ray*** *c-96-106, 109, 110, 112, 113, 115-120.* ***S&K*** *c-7-31, 33, 34, 36, 37, 39, 40, 48, 49, 50-54, 56-58.* ***Hal Sherman*** *c-1-6.* ***Dick Sprang*** *c-75.*

STAR SPANGLED COMICS (Also see All Star Comics 1999 crossover titles)
DC Comics: May, 1999 ($1.99, one-shot)

	GD 2.0	VG 4.0	FN 6.0	VF 8.0	VF/NM 9.0	NM- 9.2
1-Golden Age Sandman and the Star Spangled Kid						2.25

STAR SPANGLED KID (See Action #40, Leading Comics & Star Spangled Comics)

STAR SPANGLED WAR STORIES (Formerly Star Spangled Comics #1-130; Becomes The Unknown Soldier #205 on) (See Showcase)
National Periodical Publications: No. 131, 8/52 - No. 133, 10/52; No. 3, 11/52 - No. 204, 2-3/77

	GD 2.0	VG 4.0	FN 6.0	VF 8.0	VF/NM 9.0	NM- 9.2
131(#1)	100	200	300	625	963	1300
132	67	134	201	419	647	875
133-Used in **POP**, pg. 94	55	110	165	344	532	720
3-6: 4-Devil Dog Dugan app. 6-Evans-a	40	80	120	239	357	475
7-10	25	50	75	181	278	375
11-20	21	42	63	150	230	310
21-30: 30-Last precode (2/55)	18	36	54	129	197	265
31-33,35-40	12	24	36	87	134	180
34-Krigstein-a	13	26	39	90	138	185
41-44,46-50: 50-1st S.A. issue	12	24	36	84	127	170
45-1st DC grey tone war-c (5/56)	17	34	51	121	160	250
51,52,54-63,65,66, 68-83	10	20	30	67	96	125
53-"Rock Sergeant," 3rd Sgt. Rock prototype; inspired "P.I. & The Sand Fleas" in G.I. Combat #56 (1/57)	14	28	42	100	153	205
64-Pre-Sgt. Rock Easy Co. story (12/57)	12	24	36	84	127	170
67-2 Easy Co. stories without Sgt. Rock	12	24	36	87	134	180
84-Origin Mlle. Marie	18	36	54	126	193	260
85-89-Mlle. Marie in all	11	22	33	77	114	150
90-1st app. "War That Time Forgot" series; dinosaur issue-c/story (4-5/60) (also see Weird War Tales #94 & #99)	35	70	105	263	412	560
91,93-No dinosaur stories	10	20	30	70	100	130
92-2nd dinosaur-c/s	14	28	42	102	156	210
94 (12/60)- "Ghost Ace" story; Baron Von Richter as The Enemy Ace (predates Our Army at War #151)	18	36	54	131	201	270
95-99: Dinosaur-c/s	13	26	39	90	138	185
100-Dinosaur-c/story.	15	30	45	107	164	220
101-115: All dinosaur issues	11	22	33	77	114	150
116-125,127-133,135-137-Last dinosaur story; Heath Birdman-#129,131	10	20	30	70	100	130
126-No dinosaur story	8	16	24	58	82	105
134-Dinosaur story; Neal Adams-a	11	22	33	80	120	160
138-New Enemy Ace-c/stories begin by Joe Kubert (4-5/68), end #150 (also see Our Army at War #151 and Showcase #57)	12	24	36	86	131	175
139-Origin Enemy Ace (7/68)	10	20	30	67	96	125
140-143,145: 145-Last 12¢ issue (6-7/69)	7	14	21	50	68	85
144-Neal Adams/Kubert-a	8	16	24	55	78	100
146-Enemy Ace-c and cameo app.	5	10	15	33	44	55
147,148-New Enemy Ace stories	6	12	18	40	55	70
149,150-Last new Enemy Ace by Kubert. Viking Prince by Kubert	6	12	18	38	52	65
151-1st solo app. Unknown Soldier (6-7/70); Enemy Ace-r begin (from Our Army at War, Showcase & SSWS); end #161	15	30	45	107	164	220
152-Reprints 2nd Enemy Ace app.	5	10	15	33	44	55
153,155-Enemy Ace reprints; early Unknown Soldier stories	4	8	12	25	33	42
154-Origin Unknown Soldier	11	22	33	80	120	160
156-1st Battle Album; Unknown Soldier story; Kubert-c/a	4	8	12	25	33	42
157-Sgt. Rock x-over in Unknown Soldier story.	4	8	12	22	30	38
158-163-(52 pgs.): New Unknown Soldier stories; Kubert-c/a. 161-Last Enemy Ace-r	3	6	9	18	23	28
164-183,200: 181-183-Enemy Ace vs. Balloon Buster serial app; Frank Thorne-a. 200-Enemy Ace back-up	2	4	6	10	13	16
184-199,201-204	2	4	6	8	10	12

NOTE: ***Anderson*** *a-28.* ***Chaykin*** *a-167.* ***Drucker*** *a-59, 61, 64, 66, 67, 73-84.* ***Estrada*** *a-149.* ***John Giunta*** *a-72.* ***Glanzman*** *a-167, 171, 172, 174.* ***Heath*** *a-122, 132, 133; c-67, 122, 132-134.* ***Kaluta*** *a-197i; c-167.* ***G. Kane*** *a-169.* ***Kubert*** *a-6-163(most later issues), 200.* ***Maurer*** *a-160, 165.* ***Severin*** *a-65, 162.* ***S&K*** *c-7-31, 33, 34, 37, 40.* ***Simonson*** *a-170, 172, 174, 180.* ***Sutton*** *a-168.* ***Thorne*** *a-183.* ***Toth*** *a-164.* ***Wildey*** *a-161. Suicide Squad in 110, 116-118, 120, 121, 127.*

STARSTREAM (Adventures in Science Fiction)(See Questar illustrated)
Whitman/Western Publishing Co.: 1976 (79¢, 68 pgs, cardboard-c)

	GD 2.0	VG 4.0	FN 6.0	VF 8.0	VF/NM 9.0	NM- 9.2
1-4: 1-Bolle-a. 2-4-McWilliams & Bolle-a	2	4	6	10	13	16

STARSTRUCK
Marvel Comics (Epic Comics): Feb, 1985 - No. 6, Feb, 1986 ($1.50, mature)

	GD 2.0	VG 4.0	FN 6.0	VF 8.0	VF/NM 9.0	NM- 9.2
1-6: Kaluta-a						3.00

STARSTRUCK
Dark Horse Comics: Aug, 1990 - No. 4, Nov?, 1990 ($2.95, B&W, 52pgs.)

	GD 2.0	VG 4.0	FN 6.0	VF 8.0	VF/NM 9.0	NM- 9.2
1-3:Kaluta-r/Epic series plus new-c/a in all						3.00
4 (68, pgs.)-contains 2 trading cards						3.00

STAR STUDDED
Cambridge House/Superior Publishers: 1945 (25¢, 132 pgs.); 1945 (196 pgs.)

	GD 2.0	VG 4.0	FN 6.0	VF 8.0	VF/NM 9.0	NM- 9.2
nn-Captain Combat by Giunta, Ghost Woman, Commandette, & Red Rogue app.; Infantino-a	33	66	99	190	275	360
nn-The Cadet, Edison Bell, Hoot Gibson, Jungle Lil (196 pgs.); copies vary; Blue Beetle in some	27	54	81	152	219	285

Startling Comics #44 © Nedor

Startling Stories: The Thing - Night Falls on Yancy Street #1 © MAR

STAR TREK
A scientist escapes into Time with a doomsday bomb!

Star Trek #36 © Paramount

GD VG FN VF VF/NM NM-
2.0 4.0 6.0 8.0 9.0 9.2

STARTLING COMICS
Better Publications (Nedor): June, 1940 - No. 53, Sept, 1948

1-Origin Captain Future-Man Of Tomorrow, Mystico (By Sansone), The Wonder Man; The Masked Rider & his horse Pinto begins; Masked Rider formerly in pulps; drug use story 262 524 786 1638 2519 3400
2 -Don Davis, Espionage Ace begins 98 196 294 613 944 1275
3 81 162 243 506 778 1050
4 60 120 180 375 580 785
5-9 51 102 153 311 473 635
10-The Fighting Yank begins (9/41, origin/1st app.) 372 744 1116 2418 3909 5400
11-2nd app. Fighting Yank 115 230 345 719 1110 1500
12-Hitler, Hirohito, Mussolini-c 98 196 294 613 944 1275
13-15 62 124 186 388 594 800
16-Origin The Four Comrades; not in #32,35 65 130 195 406 628 850
17-Last Masked Rider & Mystico 49 98 147 299 455 610
18-Pyroman begins (12/42, origin)(also see America's Best Comics #3 for 1st app., 11/42) 98 196 294 613 944 1275
19 49 98 147 299 455 610
20,21: 20-The Oracle begins (3/43); not in issues 26,28,33,34. 21-Origin The Ape, Oracle's enemy 51 102 153 311 473 635
22-34: 34-Origin The Scarab & only app. 49 98 147 299 455 610
35-Hypodermic syringe attacks Fighting Yank in drug story 51 102 153 311 473 635
36-43: 36-Last Four Comrades. 38-Bondage/torture-c. 40-Last Capt. Future & Oracle. 41-Front Page Peggy begins; A-Bomb-c. 43-Last Pyroman 43 86 129 262 399 535
44,45: 44-Lance Lewis, Space Detective begins; Ingels-c; sci/fi-c begin. 45-Tygra begins (intro/origin, 5/47); Ingels-c/a (splash pg. & inside f/c B&W ad) 67 134 201 419 647 875
46-Classic Ingels-c; Ingels-a 98 196 294 613 944 1275
47,48,50-53: 50,51-Sea-Eagle app. 62 124 186 388 594 800
49-Classic Schomburg Robot-c; last Fighting Yank 372 744 1116 2418 3909 5400

NOTE: ***Ingels** a-44, 45; c-44, 45, 46(wash). **Schomburg (Xela)** c-21-43; 47-53 (airbrush). **Tuska** c-45? Bondage c-16, 21, 37, 46-49. Captain Future c-1-9, 13, 14. Fighting Yank c-10-12, 15-17, 21, 22, 24, 26, 28, 30, 32, 34, 36, 38, 40, 42. Pyroman c-18-20, 23, 25, 27, 29, 31, 33, 35, 37, 39, 41, 43.*

STARTLING STORIES: BANNER
Marvel Comics: July, 2001 - No. 4, Oct, 2001 ($2.99, limited series)

1-4-Hulk story by Azzarello; Corben-c/a 3.00
TPB (11/01, $12.95) r/1-4 13.00

STARTLING STORIES: FANTASTIC FOUR - UNSTABLE MOLECULES (See Fantastic Four - ...)

STARTLING STORIES: THE MEGALOMANIACAL SPIDER-MAN
Marvel Comics: Jun, 2002 ($2.99, one-shot)

1-Spider-Man spoof; Peter Bagge-s/a 3.00

STARTLING STORIES: THE THING
Marvel Comics: 2003 ($3.50, one-shot)

1-Zimmerman-s/Kramer-a; Inhumans and the Hulk app. 3.50

STARTLING STORIES: THE THING - NIGHT FALLS ON YANCY STREET
Marvel Comics: Jun, 2003 - No. 4, Sept, 2003 ($3.50, limited series)

1-4-Dorkin-s/Haspiel-a. 2,3-Frightful Four app. 3.50

STARTLING TERROR TALES
Star Publications: No. 10, May, 1952 - No. 14, Feb, 1953; No. 4, Apr, 1953 - No. 11, 1954

10-(1st Series)-Wood/Harrison-a (r/A Star Presentation #3) Disbrow/Cole-c; becomes 4 different titles after #10; becomes Confessions of Love #11 on, The Horrors #11 on, Terrifying Tales #11 on, Terrors of the Jungle #11 on & continues w/Startling Terror #11 73 146 219 456 703 950
11-(8/52)-L. B. Cole Spider-c; r-Fox's "A Feature Presentation" #5 (blue-c) 131 262 393 819 1260 1700
11-Black-c (variant; believed to be a pressrun change) (Unique) 138 276 414 863 1332 1800
12,14 31 62 93 178 259 340
13-Jo-Jo-r; Disbrow-a 33 66 99 190 275 360
4-9,11(1953-54) (2nd Series): 11-New logo 28 56 84 158 229 300
10-Disbrow-a 35 70 105 200 290 380

NOTE: ***L. B. Cole** covers-all issues. **Palais** a-V2#8r, V2#11r.*

STAR TREK (TV) (See Dan Curtis Giveaways, Dynabrite Comics & Power Record Comics)
Gold Key: 7/67; No. 2, 6/68; No. 3, 12/68; No. 4, 6/69 - No. 61, 3/79

1-Photo-c begin, end #9 41 82 123 305 478 650
1 (rare variation w/photo back-c) 44 88 132 352 551 750
2 24 48 72 170 260 350
2 (rare variation w/photo back-c) 43 86 129 262 401 540
3-5 16 32 48 116 178 240
3 (rare variation w/photo back-c) 25 50 75 181 278 375
6-9 13 26 39 90 138 185
10-20 8 16 24 58 82 105
21-30 7 14 21 46 63 80
31-40 5 10 15 36 48 60
41-61: 52-Drug propaganda story 4 8 12 27 36 45
...the Enterprise Logs nn (8/76)-Golden Press, ($1.95, 224 pgs.)-r/#1-8 plus 7 pgs. by McWilliams (#11185)-Photo-c 5 10 15 36 48 60
...the Enterprise Logs Vol. 2 ('76)-r/#9-17 (#11187)-Photo-c 5 10 15 33 44 55
...the Enterprise Logs Vol. 3 ('77)-r/#18-26 (#11188); McWilliams-a (4 pgs.)-Photo-c 5 10 15 33 44 55
Star Trek Vol. 4 (Winter '77)-Reprints #27,28,30-34,36,38 (#11189) plus 3 pgs. new art 5 10 15 33 44 55
... : The Key Collection (Checker Book Publ. Group, 2004, $22.95) r/#1-8 23.00

NOTE: ***McWilliams** a-38, 40-44, 46-61. #29 reprints #1; #35 reprints #4; #37 reprints #5; #45 reprints #7. The tabloids all have photo covers and blank inside covers. Painted covers #10-44, 46-59.*

STAR TREK
Marvel Comics Group: April, 1980 - No. 18, Feb, 1982

1: 1-3-r/Marvel Super Special; movie adapt. 2 4 6 10 12 15
2-16: 5-Miller-c 1 2 3 5 6 8
17-Low print run 2 4 6 8 10 12
18-Last issue; low print run 2 4 6 11 14 18

NOTE: ***Austin** c-18i. **Buscema** a-13. **Gil Kane** a-15. **Nasser** c/a-7. **Simonson** c-17.*

STAR TREK (Also see Who's Who In Star Trek)
DC Comics: Feb, 1984 - No. 56, Nov, 1988 (75¢, Mando paper)

1-Sutton-a(p) begins 1 3 4 6 8 10
2-5 6.00
6-10: 7-Origin Saavik 5.00
11-20: 19-Walter Koenig story 4.00
21-32 3.50
33-($1.25, 52 pgs.)-20th anniversary issue 4.00
34-49: 37-Painted-c 3.00
50-($1.50, 52 pgs.) 4.00
51-56, Annual 1-3: 1(1985). 2(1986). 3(1988, $1.50) 3.00

NOTE: ***Morrow** a-28, 35, 36, 56. **Orlando** c-8i. **Perez** c-1-3. **Spiegle** a-19. **Starlin** c-24, 25. **Sutton** a-1-6p, 8-18p, 20-27p, 29p, 31-34p, 39-52p, 55p; c-4-6p, 8-22p, 46p.*

STAR TREK
DC Comics: Oct, 1989 - No. 80, Jan, 1996 ($1.50/$1.75/$1.95/$2.50)

1-Capt. Kirk and crew 6.00
2,3 4.00
4-23,25-30: 10-12-The Trial of James T. Kirk. 21-Begin $1.75-c 3.00
24-($2.95, 68 pgs.)-40 pg. epic w/pin-ups 3.50
31-49,51-60 2.50
50-($3.50, 68 pgs.)-Painted-c 3.50
61-74,76-80 2.50
75 ($3.95) 4.00
Annual 1-6('90-'95, 68 pgs.): 1-Morrow-a. 3-Painted-c 4.00
Special 1-3 ('9-'95, 68 pgs.)-1-Sutton-a. 4.00
...: The Ashes of Eden (1995, $14.95, 100 pgs.)-Shatner story 15.00
...Generations (1994, $3.95, 68 pgs.)-Movie adaptation 4.00
...Generations (1994, $5.95, 68 pgs.)-Squarebound 6.00

STAR TREK...(TV)
DC Comics (WildStorm): one-shots

All of Me (4/00, $5.95, prestige format) Lopresti-a 6.00
Enemy Unseen TPB (2001, $17.95) r/Perchance to Dream, Embrace the Wolf, The Killing Shadows; Struzan-c 18.00
Enter the Wolves (2001, $5.95) Crispin & Weinstein-s; Mota-a/c 6.00
New Frontier - Double Time (11/00, $5.95)-Captain Calhoun's USS Excalibur; Peter David-s; Stelfreeze-c 6.00
Other Realities TPB (2001, $14.95) r/All of Me, New Frontier - Double Time, and DS9-N-Vector; Van Fleet-c 15.00
Special (2001, $6.95) Stories from all 4 series by various; Van Fleet-c 7.00

STAR TREK: DEBT OF HONOR
DC Comics: 1992 ($24.95/$14.95, graphic novel)

Hardcover ($24.95) Claremont-s/Hughes-a(p) 25.00
Softvcover ($14.95) 15.00

STAR TREK: DEEP SPACE NINE (TV)
Malibu Comics: Aug, 1993 - No. 32, Jan, 1996 ($2.50)

Star Trek #6 © Paramount

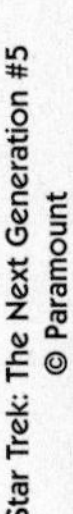
Star Trek: The Next Generation #5 © Paramount

Star Trek Untold Voyages #1 © Paramount

	GD 2.0	VG 4.0	FN 6.0	VF 8.0	VF/NM 9.0	NM- 9.2

1-Direct Sale Edition w/line drawn-c 4.00
1-Newsstand Edition with photo-c 3.00
0-(1/95, $2.95)-Terok Nor 3.00
2-30: 2-Polybagged w/trading card. 9-4 pg. prelude to Hearts & Minds 2.50
31-($3.95) 4.00
32-($3.50) 3.50
Annual 1 (1/95, $3.95, 68 pgs.) 4.00
Special 1 (1995, $3.50) 3.50
Ultimate Annual 1 (12/95, $5.95) 6.00
...:Lightstorm (12/94, $3.50) 3.50

STAR TREK: DEEP SPACE NINE (TV)
Marvel Comics (Paramount Comics): Nov, 1996 - No. 15, Mar, 1998 ($1.95/$1.99)

1-15: 12,13-"Telepathy War" pt. 2,3 2.50

STAR TREK: DEEP SPACE NINE -- N-VECTOR (TV)
DC Comics (WildStorm): Aug, 2000 - No. 4, Nov, 2000 ($2.50, limited series)

1-4-Cypress-a 2.50

STAR TREK DEEP SPACE NINE-THE CELEBRITY SERIES
Malibu Comics: May, 1995 ($2.95)

1-Blood and Honor; Mark Lenard script 3.00
1-Rules of Diplomacy; Aron Eisenberg script 3.00

STAR TREK: DEEP SPACE NINE HEARTS AND MINDS
Malibu Comics: June, 1994 - No. 4, Sept, 1994 ($2.50, limited series)

1-4 2.50
1-Holographic-c 4.00

STAR TREK: DEEP SPACE NINE, THE MAQUIS
Malibu Comics: Feb, 1995 - No. 3, Apr, 1995 ($2.50, limited series)

1-3-Newsstand-c, 1-Photo-c 2.50

STAR TREK: DEEP SPACE NINE/THE NEXT GENERATION
Malibu Comics: Oct, 1994 - No. 2, Nov, 1994 ($2.50, limited series)

1,2: Parts 2 & 4 of x-over with Star Trek: TNG/DS9 from DC Comics 2.50

STAR TREK: DEEP SPACE NINE WORF SPECIAL
Malibu Comics: Dec, 1995 ($3.95, one-shot)

1-Includes pinups 4.00

STAR TREK: DIVIDED WE FALL
DC Comics (WildStorm): July, 2001 - No. 4, Oct, 2001 ($2.95, limited series)

1-4: Ordover & Mack-s; Lenara Kahn, Verad and Odan app. 3.00

STAR TREK EARLY VOYAGES(TV)
Marvel Comics (Paramount Comics): Feb, 1997 - No. 17, Jun, 1998 ($2.95/$1.95/$1.99)

1-($2.95) 3.00
2-17 2.50

STAR TREK: FIRST CONTACT (Movie)
Marvel Comics (Paramount Comics): Nov, 1996 ($5.95, one-shot)

nn-Movie adaption 6.00

STAR TREK: MIRROR MIRROR
Marvel Comics (Paramount Comics): Feb, 1997 ($3.95, one-shot)

1-DeFalco-s 4.00

STAR TREK MOVIE SPECIAL
DC Comics: 1984 (June) - No. 2, 1987 ($1.50); No. 1, 1989 ($2.00, 52 pgs)

nn-(#1)-Adapts Star Trek III; Sutton-p (68 pgs.) 3.00
2-Adapts Star Trek IV; Sutton-a; Chaykin-c. (68 pgs.) 3.00
1 (1989)-Adapts Star Trek V; painted-c 3.00

STAR TREK: OPERATION ASSIMILATION
Marvel Comics (Paramount Comics): Dec, 1996 ($2.95, one-shot)

1 3.00

STAR TREK VI: THE UNDISCOVERED COUNTRY (Movie)
DC Comics: 1992

1-($2.95, regular edition, 68 pgs.)-Adaptation of film 3.00
nn-($5.95, prestige edition)-Has photos of movie not included in regular edition; painted-c by Palmer; photo back-c 6.00

STAR TREK: STARFLEET ACADEMY
Marvel Comics (Paramount Comics): Dec, 1996 - No. 19, Jun, 1998 ($1.95/$1.99)

1-19: Begin new series. 12-"Telepathy War" pt. 1. 18-English and Klingon language editions 2.50

STAR TREK: TELEPATHY WAR
Marvel Comics (Paramount Comics): Nov, 1997 ($2.99, 48 pgs., one-shot)

1-"Telepathy War" x-over pt. 6 3.00

STAR TREK - THE MODALA IMPERATIVE
DC Comics: Late July, 1991 - No. 4, Late Sept, 1991 ($1.75, limited series)

1-4 2.50
TPB ($19.95) r/series and ST:TNG - The Modala Imperative 20.00

STAR TREK: THE NEXT GENERATION (TV)
DC Comics: Feb, 1988 - No. 6, July, 1988 (limited series)

1 ($1.50, 52 pgs.)-Sienkiewicz painted-c 6.00
2-6 ($1.00) 4.00

STAR TREK: THE NEXT GENERATION (TV)
DC Comics: Oct, 1989 -No. 80, 1995 ($1.50/$1.75/$1.95)

1-Capt. Picard and crew from TV show 1 2 3 5 7 9
2,3 5.00
4-10 4.00
11-23,25-49,51-60 3.00
24,50: 24-($2.50, 52 pgs.). 50-($3.50, 68 pgs.)-Painted-c 5.00
61-74,76-80 2.50
75-($3.95, 50 pgs.) 4.00
Annual 1-6 ('90-'95, 68 pgs.) 4.00
Special 1 -3('93-'95, 68 pgs.)-1-Contains 3 stories 4.00
...-The Series Finale (1994, $3.95, 68 pgs.) 4.00

STAR TREK: THE NEXT GENERATION (TV)
DC Comics (WildStorm): one-shots

Embrace the Wolf (6/00, $5.95, prestige format) Golden & Sniegoski-s 6.00
Forgiveness (2001, $24.95, HC) David Brin-s/Scott Hampton painted-a; dust jacket-c 30.00
Forgiveness (2002, $17.95, SC) 18.00
The Gorn Crisis (1/01, $29.95, HC) Kordey painted-a/dust jacket-c 30.00
The Gorn Crisis (1/01, $17.95, SC) Kordey painted-a 18.00

STAR TREK: THE NEXT GENERATION/DEEP SPACE NINE (TV)
DC Comics: Dec, 1994 - No. 2, Jan, 1995 ($2.50, limited series)

1,2-Parts 1 & 3 of x-over with Star Trek: DS9/TNG from Malibu Comics 2.50

STAR TREK: THE NEXT GENERATION - ILL WIND
DC Comics: Nov, 1995 - No. 4, Feb, 1996 ($2.50, limited series)

1-4: Hugh Fleming painted-c on all 2.50

STAR TREK: THE NEXT GENERATION - PERCHANCE TO DREAM
DC Comics/WildStorm: Feb, 2000 - No. 4, May, 2000 ($2.50, limited series)

1-4-Bradstreet-c 2.50

STAR TREK: THE NEXT GENERATION - RIKER
Marvel Comics (Paramount Comics): July, 1998 ($3.50, one-shot)

1-Riker joins the Maquis 3.50

STAR TREK: THE NEXT GENERATION - SHADOWHEART
DC Comics: Dec, 1994 - No. 4, Mar, 1995 ($1.95, limited series)

1-4 2.50

STAR TREK: THE NEXT GENERATION - THE KILLING SHADOWS
DC Comics/WildStorm: Nov, 2000 - No. 4, Feb, 2001 ($2.50, limited series)

1-4-Scott Ciencin-s; Sela app. 2.50

STAR TREK: THE NEXT GENERATION - THE MODALA IMPERATIVE
DC Comics: Early Sept, 1991 - No. 4, Late Oct, 1991 ($1.75, limited series)

1-4 2.50

STAR TREK UNLIMITED
Marvel Comics (Paramount Comics): Nov, 1996 - No. 10, July, 1998 ($2.95/$2.99)

1,2-Stories from original series and Next Generation 4.00
3-10: 3-Begin $2.99-c. 6-"Telepathy War" pt. 4. 7-Q & Trelane swap Kirk & Picard 3.50

STAR TREK UNTOLD VOYAGES
Marvel Comics (Paramount Comics): May, 1998 - No. 5, July, 1998 ($2.50)

1-5-Kirk's crew after the 1st movie 2.50

STAR TREK: VOYAGER
Marvel Comics (Paramount Comics): Nov, 1996 - No. 15, Mar, 1998 ($1.95/$1.99)

1-15: 13-"Telepathy War" pt. 5. 14-Seven of Nine joins crew 3.00

STAR TREK: VOYAGER
DC Comics/WildStorm: one-shots and trade paperbacks

- Elite Force (7/00, $5.95) The Borg app.; Abnett & Lanning-s 6.00
... Encounters With the Unknown TPB (2001, $19.95) reprints 20.00

Star Wars #65 © Lucasfilm Ltd.

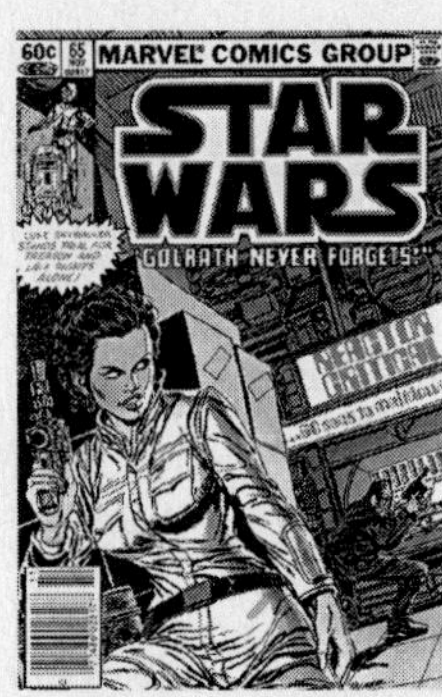

Star Wars: A Valentine Story #1 © Lucasfilm Ltd.

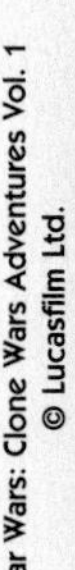
Star Wars: Clone Wars Adventures Vol. 1 © Lucasfilm Ltd.

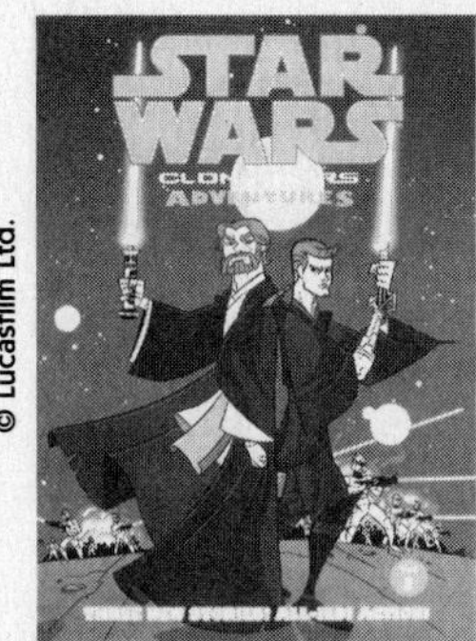

GD VG FN VF VF/NM NM-
2.0 4.0 6.0 8.0 9.0 9.2

GD VG FN VF VF/NM NM-
2.0 4.0 6.0 8.0 9.0 9.2

- False Colors (1/00, $5.95) Photo-c and Jim Lee-c; Jeff Moy-a 6.00

STAR TREK: VOYAGER-- THE PLANET KILLER
DC Comics/WildStorm: Mar, 2001 - No. 3, May, 2001 ($2.95, limited series)
1-3-Voyager vs. the Planet Killer from the ST:TOS episode; Teranishi-a 3.00

STAR TREK: VOYAGER SPLASHDOWN
Marvel Comics (Paramount Comics): Apr, 1998 - No. 4, July, 1998 ($2.50, limited series)
1-4-Voyager crashes on a water planet 3.00

STAR TREK/ X-MEN
Marvel Comics (Paramount Comics): Dec, 1996 ($4.99, one-shot)
1-Kirk's crew & X-Men; art by Silvestri, Tan, Winn & Finch; Lobdell-s 5.00

STAR TREK/ X-MEN: 2ND CONTACT
Marvel Comics (Paramount Comics): May, 1998 ($4.99, 64 pgs., one-shot)
1-Next Gen. crew & X-Men battle Kang, Sentinels & Borg following First Contact movie 5.00
1-Painted wraparound variant cover 5.00

STAR WARS (Movie) (See Classic..., Contemporary Motivators, Dark Horse Comics, The Droids, The Ewoks, Marvel Movie Showcase, Marvel Special Ed.)
Marvel Comics Group: July, 1977 - No. 107, Sept, 1986
1-(Regular 30¢ edition)-Price in square w/UPC code; #1-6 adapt first movie; first issue on sale before movie debuted 6 12 18 40 55 70
1-(35¢-c; limited distribution - 1500 copies?)- Price in square w/UPC code (Prices vary widely on this book. In 2004, a CGC certified 9.2 sold for $4,050, a CGC 9.0 sold for $3,200 and a CGC 7.5 sold for $999.99)
NOTE: *The rare 35¢ edition has the cover price in a square box, and the UPC box in the lower left hand corner has the UPC code lines running through it.*
2-4-(30¢ issues). 4-Battle with Darth Vader 3 7 10 21 28 35
2-4-(35¢ with UPC code; not reprints) 7 14 21 50 68 85
5,6: 5-Begin 35¢-c on all editions. 6-Stevens-a(i). 2 4 6 12 16 20
7-20 2 4 6 8 10 12
21-70: 39-44-The Empire Strikes Back-r by Al Williamson in all. 50-Giant. 68-Reintro Boba Fett. 1 2 3 5 7 9
71-80 1 3 4 6 8 10
81-90: 81-Boba Fett app. 2 4 6 8 10 12
91,93-99: 98-Williamson-a. 2 4 6 10 12 15
92,100-106: 92,100-($1.00, 52 pgs.). 2 4 6 12 16 20
107(low dist.); Portacio-a(i) 6 12 18 40 55 70
1-9: Reprints; has "reprint" in upper lefthand corner of cover or on inside or price and number inside a diamond with no date or UPC on cover; 30¢ and 35¢ issues published 4.00
Annual 1 (12/79, 52 pgs.)-Simonson-c 2 4 6 8 10 12
Annual 2 (11/82, 52 pgs.), 3(12/83, 52 pgs.) 1 3 4 6 8 10
... A Long Time Ago...Vol. 1 TPB (Dark Horse Comics, 6/02, $29.95) r/#1-14 30.00
... A Long Time Ago...Vol. 2 TPB (Dark Horse Comics, 7/02, $29.95) r/#15-28 30.00
... A Long Time Ago...Vol. 3 TPB (Dark Horse Comics, 11/02, $29.95) r/#39-53 30.00
... A Long Time Ago...Vol. 4 TPB (Dark Horse Comics, 1/03, $29.95) r/#54-67 & Ann. 2 30.00
... A Long Time Ago...Vol. 5 TPB (Dark Horse Comics, 3/03, $29.95) r/#68-81 & Ann. 3 30.00
... A Long Time Ago...Vol. 6 TPB (Dark Horse Comics, 5/03, $29.95) r/#82-93 30.00
... A Long Time Ago...Vol. 7 TPB (Dark Horse Comics, 6/03, $29.95) r/#96-107 30.00
***Austin** a-11-15i, 21i, 38; c-12-15i, 21i. **Byrne** c-13p. **Chaykin** a-1-10p; c-1. **Golden** c/a-38. **Miller** c-47p; pin-up-43. **Nebres** c/a-Annual 2i. **Portacio** a-107i. **Sienkiewicz** c-92i, 98. **Simonson** a-16p, 49p, 51-63p, 65p, 66p; c-16, 49-51, 52p, 53-62, Annual 1. **Steacy** painted a-105i, 106i; c-105. **Williamson** a-39-44p, 50p, 98; c-39, 40, 41-44p. Painted c-81, 87, 92, 95, 98, 100, 105.*

STAR WARS (Monthly series)
Dark Horse Comics: Dec, 1998 - Present ($2.50/$2.95/$2.99)
1-12: 1-6-Prelude To Rebellion; Strnad-s. 4-Brereton-c. 7-12-Outlander 3.00
5,6 (Holochrome-c variants) 6.00
13, 17-18-($2.95): 13-18-Emissaries to Malastare; Truman-s 3.00
14-16-($2.50) Schultz-c 3.00
19-67: 19-22-Twilight; Duursema-a. 23-26-Infinity's End. 51-65-Republic 3.00
#0 Another Universe.com Ed.($10.00) r/serialized pages from Pizzazz Magazine; new Dorman painted-c 10.00
... A Valentine Story (2/03, $3.50) Leia & Han Solo on Hoth; Winick-s/Chadwick-a/c 3.50
...: Clone Wars Vol. 1 (2003, $14.95) 15.00
...: Clone Wars Vol. 2 (2003, $14.95) r/#51-53 & Star Wars: Jedi - Shaak Ti 15.00
...: Clone Wars Vol. 3 (2004, $14.95) r/#55-59 15.00
...: Clone Wars Vol. 4 (2004, $16.95) r/#54, 63 & Star Wars: Jedi - Aayla Secura & Dooku 17.00
...: Clone Wars Vol. 5 (2004, $17.95) r/#60-62, 64 & Star Wars: Jedi - Yoda 17.00
...: Rite of Passage (2004, $12.95) r/#42-45 13.00
...: The Stark Hyperspace War (903, $12.95) r/#36-39 13.00

STAR WARS: A NEW HOPE- THE SPECIAL EDITION
Dark Horse Comics: Jan, 1997 - No. 4, Apr, 1997 ($2.95, limited series)
1-4-Dorman-c 4.00

STAR WARS: BOBA FETT
Dark Horse Comics: Dec, 1995 - No. 3 ($3.95) (Originally intended as a one-shot)
1-Kennedy-c/a 6.00
2,3 5.00
Death, Lies, & Treachery TPB (1/98, $12.95) r/#1-3 13.00
... - Agent of Doom (11/00, $2.99) Ostrander-s/Cam Kennedy-a 3.00
Twin Engines of Destruction (1/97, $2.95) 3.00

STAR WARS: BOBA FETT: ENEMY OF THE EMPIRE
Dark Horse Comics: Jan, 1999 - No. 4, Apr, 1999 ($2.95, limited series)
1-4-Recalls 1st meeting of Fett and Vader 3.00

STAR WARS: CHEWBACCA
Dark Horse Comics: Jan, 2000 - No. 4, Apr, 2000 ($2.95, limited series)
1-4-Macan-s/art by various incl. Anderson, Kordey, Gibbons; Phillips-c 3.00

STAR WARS: CLONE WARS ADVENTURES
Dark Horse Comics: 2004 ($6.95, digest-sized)
1,2-Short stories inspired by Clone Wars animated series 7.00

STAR WARS: CRIMSON EMPIRE
Dark Horse Comics: Dec, 1997 - No. 6, May, 1998 ($2.95, limited series)
1-Richardson-s/Gulacy-a 1 2 3 4 5 7
2-6 5.00

STAR WARS: CRIMSON EMPIRE II: COUNCIL OF BLOOD
Dark Horse Comics: Nov, 1998 - No. 6, Apr, 1999 ($2.95, limited series)
1-6-Richardson & Stradley-s/Gulacy-a 3.00

STAR WARS: DARK EMPIRE
Dark Horse Comics: Dec, 1991 - No. 6, Oct, 1992 ($2.95, limited series)
Preview-(99¢) 3.00
1-All have Dorman painted-c 1 2 3 5 7 9
1-3-2nd printing 4.00
2-Low print run 2 4 6 8 10 12
3 6.00
4-6 4.00
Gold Embossed Set (#1-6)-With gold embossed foil logo (price is for set) 90.00
Platinum Embossed Set (#1-6) 120.00
Trade paperback (4/93, 16.95) 17.00
Dark Empire 1 - TPB 3rd printing (2003, $16.95) 17.00
Ltd. Ed. Hardcover ($99.95) Signed & numbered 100.00

STAR WARS: DARK EMPIRE II
Dark Horse Comics: Dec, 1994 - No. 6, May, 1995 ($2.95, limited series)
1-Dave Dorman painted-c 5.00
2-6: Dorman-c in all. 4.00
Platinum Embossed Set (#1-6) 35.00
Trade paperback ($17.95) 18.00

STAR WARS: DARK FORCE RISING
Dark Horse Comics: May, 1997 - No. 6, Oct, 1997 ($2.95, limited series)
1-6 4.00
TPB (2/98, $17.95) r/#1-6 18.00

STAR WARS: DARTH MAUL
Dark Horse Comics: Sept, 2000 - No. 4, Dec, 2000 ($2.95, limited series)
1-4-Photo-c and Struzan painted-c; takes place 6 months before Ep. 1 3.00

STAR WARS: DROIDS (See Dark Horse Comics #17-19)
Dark Horse Comics: Apr, 1994 - #6, Sept, 1994; V2#1, Apr, 1995 - V2#8, Dec, 1995 ($2.50, limited series)
1-($2.95)-Embossed-c 4.00
2-6 , Special 1 (1/95, $2.50), V2#1-8 3.00

STAR WARS: EMPIRE
Dark Horse Comics: Sept, 2002 - Present ($2.99)
1-24: 1-Benjamin-a; takes place weeks before SW: A New Hope. 7-Boba Fett-c. 14-Vader after the destruction of the Death Star. 15-Death of Biggs; Wheatley-a 3.00
... Volume 1 (2003, $12.95, TPB) r/#1-4 13.00
... Volume 2 (2004, $17.95, TPB) r/#8-12,15 18.00
... Volume 3: The Imperial Perspective (2004, $17.95, TPB) r/#13,14,16-19 18.00

STAR WARS: EMPIRE'S END
Dark Horse Comics: Oct, 1995 - No. 2, Nov, 1995 ($2.95, limited series)
1,2-Dorman-c 3.00

STAR WARS: EPISODE 1 THE PHANTOM MENACE
Dark Horse Comics: May, 1999 - No. 4 ($2.95, movie adaptation)

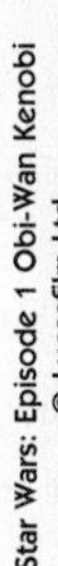

Star Wars: Episode 1 Obi-Wan Kenobi © Lucasfilm Ltd.

Star Wars: Infinities - The Empire Strikes Back #4 © Lucasfilm Ltd.

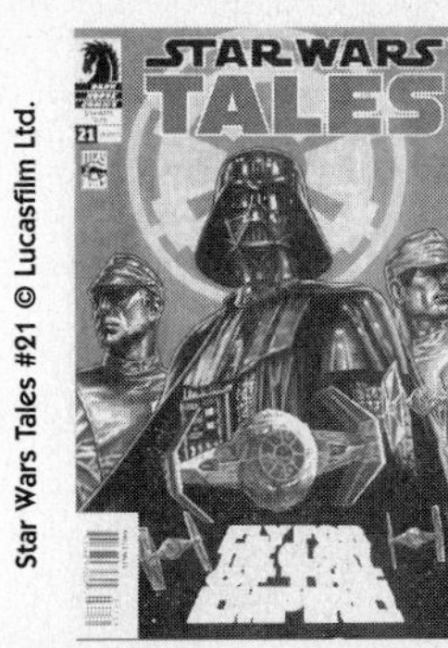
Star Wars Tales #21 © Lucasfilm Ltd.

GD 2.0 | VG 4.0 | FN 6.0 | VF 8.0 | VF/NM 9.0 | NM- 9.2

1-4-Regular and photo-c; Damaggio & Williamson-a 3.00
TPB ($12.95) r/#1-4 13.00
...Anakin Skywalker-Photo-c & Bradstreet-c, ...Obi-Wan Kenobi-Photo-c & Egeland-c, ...Queen Amidala-Photo-c & Bradstreet-c, ...Qui-Gon Jinn-Photo-c & Bradstreet-c 3.00
Gold foil covers; Wizard 1/2 10.00

STAR WARS: EPISODE II - ATTACK OF THE CLONES
Dark Horse Comics: Apr, 2002 - No. 4, May, 2002 ($3.99, movie adaptation)
1-4-Regular and photo-c; Duursema-a 4.00
TPB ($17.95) r/#1-4; Struzan-c 18.00

STAR WARS HANDBOOK
Dark Horse Comics: July, 1998 - Present ($2.95, one-shots)
...X-Wing Rogue Squadron (7/98)-Guidebook to characters and spacecraft 3.00
...Crimson Empire (7/99) Dorman-c 3.00
...Dark Empire (3/00) Dorman-c 3.00

STAR WARS: HEIR TO THE EMPIRE
Dark Horse Comics: Oct, 1995 - No.6, Apr, 1996 ($2.95, limited series)
1-6: Adaptation of Zahn novel 3.00

STAR WARS: INFINITIES - A NEW HOPE
Dark Horse Comics: May, 2001 - No. 4, Oct, 2001 ($2.99, limited series)
1-4: "What If..." the Death Star wasn't destroyed in Episode 4 3.00
TPB (2002, $12.95) r/ #1-4 13.00

STAR WARS: INFINITIES - THE EMPIRE STRIKES BACK
Dark Horse Comics: July, 2002 - No. 4, Oct, 2002 ($2.99, limited series)
1-4: "What If..." Luke died on the ice planet Hoth; Bachalo-c 3.00
TPB (2/03, $12.95) r/ #1-4 13.00

STAR WARS: INFINITIES - RETURN OF THE JEDI
Dark Horse Comics: Nov, 2003 - No. 4, Mar, 2004 ($2.99, limited series)
1- 4:"What If..." ; Benjamin-a 3.00

STAR WARS: JABBA THE HUTT
Dark Horse Comics: Apr, 1995 ($2.50, one-shots)
nn, ...The Betrayal, ...The Dynasty Trap, ...The Hunger of Princess Nampi 3.00

STAR WARS: JANGO FETT - OPEN SEASONS
Dark Horse Comics: Apr, 2002 - No. 4, July, 2002 ($2.99, limited series)
1-Bachs & Fernandez-a 3.00

STAR WARS: JEDI
Dark Horse Comics: Feb, 2003 - Jun, 2004 ($4.99, one-shots)
... - Aayla Secura (8/03) Ostrander-s/Duursema-a 5.00
... - Count Dooku (11/03) Duursema-a 5.00
... - Mace Windu (2/03) Duursema-a 5.00
... - Shaak Ti (5/03) Ostrander-s/Duursema-a 5.00
... - Yoda (6/04) Barlow-s/Hoon-a 5.00

STAR WARS: JEDI ACADEMY - LEVIATHAN
Dark Horse Comics: Oct, 1998 - No. 4, Jan, 1999 ($2.95, limited series)
1-4: 1-Lago-c. 2-4-Chadwick-c 3.00

STAR WARS: JEDI COUNCIL: ACTS OF WAR
Dark Horse Comics: Jun, 2000 - No. 4, Sept, 2000 ($2.95, limited series)
1-4-Stradley-s; set one year before Episode 1 3.00

STAR WARS: JEDI QUEST
Dark Horse Comics: Sept, 2001 - No. 4, Dec, 2001 ($2.99, limited series)
1-4-Anakin's Jedi training; Windham-s/Mhan-a 3.00

STAR WARS: JEDI VS. SITH
Dark Horse Comics: Apr, 2001 - No. 6, Sept, 2001 ($2.99, limited series)
1-6: Macan-s/Bachs-a/Robinson-c 3.00

STAR WARS: MARA JADE
Dark Horse Comics: Aug, 1998 - No. 6, Jan, 1999 ($2.95, limited series)
1-6-Ezquerra-a 3.00

STAR WARS: QUI-GON & OBI-WAN - LAST STAND ON ORD MANTELL
Dark Horse Comics: Dec, 2000 - No. 3, Mar, 2001 ($2.99, limited series)
1-3: 1-Three covers (photo, Tony Daniel, Bachs) Windham-s 3.00

STAR WARS: QUI-GON & OBI-WAN - THE AURORIENT EXPRESS
Dark Horse Comics: Feb, 2002 - No. 2, Mar, 2002 ($2.99, limited series)
1,2-Six years prior to Phantom Menace; Marangon-a 3.00

STAR WARS: RETURN OF THE JEDI (Movie)
Marvel Comics Group: Oct, 1983 - No. 4, Jan, 1984 (limited series)
1-4-Williamson-p in all; r/Marvel Super Special #27 1 3 4 6 8 10
Oversized issue (1983, $2.95, 10-3/4x8-1/4", 68 pgs., cardboard-c)-r/#1-4 2 4 6 10 13 16

STAR WARS: RIVER OF CHAOS
Dark Horse Comics: June, 1995 - No. 4, Sept, 1995 ($2.95, limited series)
1-4: Louise Simonson scripts 3.00

STAR WARS: SHADOWS OF THE EMPIRE
Dark Horse Comics: May, 1996 - No. 6, Oct, 1996 ($2.95, limited series)
1-6: Story details events between The Empire Strikes Back & Return of the Jedi; Russell-a(i). 3.00

STAR WARS: SHADOWS OF THE EMPIRE - EVOLUTION
Dark Horse Comics: Feb, 1998 - No. 5, June, 1998 ($2.95, limited series)
1-5: Perry-s/Fegredo-c. 3.00

STAR WARS: SHADOW STALKER
Dark Horse Comics: Sept, 1997 ($2.95, one-shot)
nn-Windham-a. 3.00

STAR WARS: SPLINTER OF THE MIND'S EYE
Dark Horse Comics: Dec, 1995 - No. 4, June, 1996 ($2.50, limited series)
1-4: Adaption of Alan Dean Foster novel 3.00

STAR WARS: STARFIGHTER
Dark Horse Comics: Jan, 2002 - No. 3, March, 2002 ($2.99, limited series)
1-3-Williams & Gray-c 3.00

STAR WARS: TAG & BINK ARE DEAD
Dark Horse Comics: Oct, 2001 - No. 2, Nov, 2001($2.99, limited series)
1,2-Rubio-s 3.00

STAR WARS TALES
Dark Horse Comics: Sept, 1999 - Present ($4.95/$5.95/$5.99, anthology)
1-4-Short stories by various 5.00
5-21 ($5.95/$5.99-c) Art and photo-c on each 6.00
Volume 1 (1/02, $19.95) r/#1-4 20.00
Volume 2 ('02, $19.95) r/#5-8 20.00
Volume 3 (1/03, $19.95) r/#9-12 20.00
Volume 4 (1/04, $19.95) r/#13-16 20.00

STAR WARS: TALES - A JEDI'S WEAPON (See Promotional Comics section)

STAR WARS: TALES FROM MOS EISLEY
Dark Horse Comics: Mar, 1996 ($2.95, one-shot)
nn-Bret Blevins-a. 3.00

STAR WARS: TALES OF THE JEDI (See Dark Horse Comics #7)
Dark Horse Comics: Oct, 1993 - No. 5, Feb, 1994 ($2.50, limited series)
1-5: All have Dave Dorman painted-c. 3-r/Dark Horse Comics #7-9 w/new coloring & some panels redrawn 3.00
1-5-Gold foil embossed logo; limited # printed-7500 (set) 50.00

STAR WARS: TALES OF THE JEDI-DARK LORDS OF THE SITH
Dark Horse Comics: Oct, 1994 - No. 6, Mar, 1995 ($2.50, limited series)
1-6: 1-Polybagged w/trading card 3.00

STAR WARS: TALES OF THE JEDI-REDEMPTION
Dark Horse Comics: July, 1998 - No. 5, Nov, 1998 ($2.95, limited series)
1-5: 1-Kevin J. Anderson-s/Kordey-c 3.00

STAR WARS: TALES OF THE JEDI-THE FALL OF THE SITH
Dark Horse Comics: June, 1997 - No. 5, Oct, 1997 ($2.95, limited series)
1-5 3.00

STAR WARS: TALES OF THE JEDI-THE FREEDON NADD UPRISING
Dark Horse Comics: Aug, 1994 - No. 2, Nov, 1994 ($2.50, limited series)
1,2 3.00

STAR WARS: TALES OF THE JEDI-THE GOLDEN AGE OF THE SITH
Dark Horse Comics: July, 1996 - No. 5, Feb, 1997 (99¢/$2.95, limited series)
0-(99¢)-Anderson-s 3.00
1-5-Anderson-s 3.00

STAR WARS: TALES OF THE JEDI-THE SITH WAR
Dark Horse Comics: Aug, 1995 - No. 6, Jan, 1996 ($2.50, limited series)
1-6: Anderson scripts 3.00

STAR WARS: THE BOUNTY HUNTERS

Star Wars: Vader's Quest #1 © Lucasfilm Ltd.

Steel #9 © DC

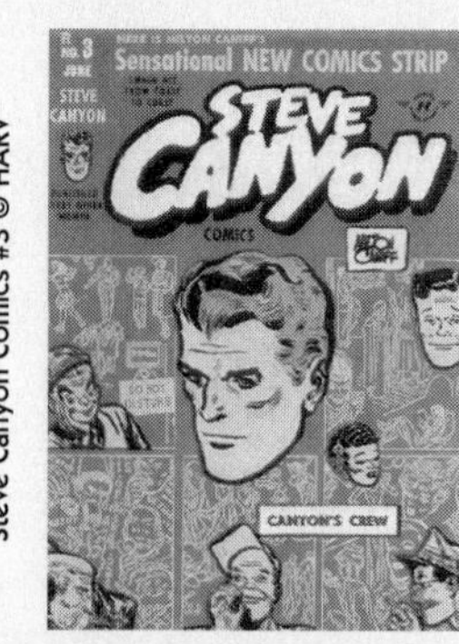

Steve Canyon Comics #3 © HARV

GD VG FN VF VF/NM NM-
2.0 4.0 6.0 8.0 9.0 9.2

GD VG FN VF VF/NM NM-
2.0 4.0 6.0 8.0 9.0 9.2

Dark Horse Comics: July, 1999 - Oct, 1999 ($2.95, one-shots)
...Aurra Sing (7/99), ...Kenix Kil (10/99), ...Scoundrel's Wages (8/99) Lando Calrissian app. 3.00

STAR WARS: THE JABBA TAPE
Dark Horse Comics: Dec, 1998 ($2.95, one-shot)
nn-Wagner-s/Plunkett-a 3.00

STAR WARS: THE LAST COMMAND
Dark Horse Comics: Nov, 1997 - No. 6, July, 1998 ($2.95, limited series)
1-6:Based on the Timothy Zaun novel 4.00

STAR WARS: THE PROTOCOL OFFENSIVE
Dark Horse Comics: Sept, 1997 ($4.95, one-shot)
nn-Anthony Daniels & Ryder Windham-s 5.00

STAR WARS: UNDERWORLD - THE YAVIN VASSILIKA
Dark Horse Comics: Dec, 2000 - No. 5, June, 2001 ($2.99, limited series)
1-5-(Photo and Robinson covers) 3.00

STAR WARS: UNION
Dark Horse Comics: Nov, 1999 - No. 4, Feb, 2000 ($2.95, limited series)
1-4-Wedding of Luke and Mara Jade; Teranishi-a/Stackpole-s 3.00

STAR WARS: VADER'S QUEST
Dark Horse Comics: Feb, 1999 - No. 4, May, 1999 ($2.95, limited series)
1-4-Follows destruction of 1st Death Star; Gibbons-a 3.00

STAR WARS: X-WING ROGUE SQUADRON (Star Wars: X-Wing Rogue Squadron-The Phantom Affair #5-8 appears on cover only)
Dark Horse Comics: July, 1995 - No. 35, Nov, 1998 ($2.95)
1/2 8.00
1-24,26-35: 1-4-Baron scripts. 5-20-Stackpole scripts 3.00
25-($3.95) 4.00
The Phantom Affair TPB ($12.95) r/#5-8 13.00

S.T.A.T.
Majestic Entertainment: Dec, 1993 ($2.25)
1 2.25

STATIC (Also see Eclipse Monthly)
Charlton Comics: No, 11, Oct, 1985 - No. 12, Dec, 1985
11,12-Ditko-c/a; low print run 6.00

STATIC (See Heroes)
DC Comics (Milestone): June, 1993 - No. 45, Mar, 1997 ($1.50/$1.75/$2.50)
1-($2.95)-Collector's Edition; polybagged w/poster & trading card & backing board (direct sales only) 4.00
1-24,26-45: 2-Origin. 8-Shadow War; Simonson silver ink-c. 14-($2.50, 52 pgs.)-Worlds Collide Pt. 14. 27-Kent Williams-c 2.50
25 ($3.95) 4.00
...: Trial by Fire (2000, $9.95) r/#1-4; Leon-c 10.00

STATIC SHOCK!: REBIRTH OF THE COOL (TV)
DC Comics: Jan, 2001 - No. 4, Sept, 2001 ($2.50, limited series)
1-4: McDuffie-s/Leon-c/a 2.50

STATIC-X
Chaos! Comics: Aug, 2002 ($5.99)
1-Polybagged with music CD; metal band as super-heroes; Pulido-s 6.00

STEAMPUNK
DC/WildStorm (Cliffhanger): Apr, 2000 - No. 12, Aug, 2002 ($2.50/$3.50)
Catechism (1/00) Prologue -Kelly-s/Bachalo-a 2.50
1-4,6-11: 4-Four covers by Bachalo, Madureira, Ramos, Campbell 2.50
5,12-($3.50) 3.50
...: Drama Obscura ('03, $14.95) r/#6-12 15.00
...: Manimatron ('01, $14.95) r/#1-5, Catechism, Idiosincratica 15.00

STEED AND MRS. PEEL (TV)(Also see The Avengers)
Eclipse Books/ ACME Press: 1990 - No. 3, 1991 ($4.95, limited series)
Books One - Three: Grant Morrison scripts 5.00

STEEL (Also see JLA)
DC Comics: Feb, 1994 - No. 52, July, 1998 ($1.50/$1.95/$2.50)
1-8,0,9-52: 1-From Reign of the Supermen storyline. 6,7-Worlds Collide Pt. 5 &12. 8-(9/94). 0-(10/94). 9-(11/94). 46-Superboy-c/app. 50-Millennium Giants x-over 2.50
Annual 1 (1994, $2.95)-Elseworlds story 3.00
Annual 2 (1995, $3.95)-Year One story 4.00
...Forging of a Hero TPB (1997, $19.95) r/ early app. 20.00

STEEL: THE OFFICIAL COMIC ADAPTION OF THE WARNER BROS. MOTION PICTURE
DC Comics: 1997 ($4.95, Prestige format, one-shot)
nn-Movie adaption; Bogdanove & Giordano-a 5.00

STEELGRIP STARKEY
Marvel Comics (Epic Comics): June, 1986 - No. 6, July, 1987 ($1.50, limited series, Baxter paper)
1-6 2.25

STEEL STERLING (Formerly Shield-Steel Sterling; see Blue Ribbon, Jackpot, Mighty Comics, Mighty Crusaders, Roly Poly & Zip Comics)
Archie Enterprises, Inc.: No. 4, Jan, 1984 - No. 7, July, 1984
4-7: 4-6-Kanigher-s; Barreto-a. 5,6-Infantino-a. 6-McWilliams-a 4.00

STEEL, THE INDESTRUCTIBLE MAN (See All-Star Squadron #8)
DC Comics: Mar, 1978 - No. 5, Oct-Nov, 1978
1 1 3 4 6 8 10
2-5: 5-44 pgs. 6.00

STEELTOWN ROCKERS
Marvel Comics: Apr, 1987 - No. 6, Sept, 1990 ($1.00, limited series)
1-6: Small town teens form rock band 2.25

STEVE AUSTIN (See Stone Cold Steve Austin)

STEVE CANYON (See Harvey Comics Hits #52)
Dell Publishing Co.: No. 519, 11/53 - No. No. 1033, 9/59 (All Milton Caniff-a except #519, 939, 1033)
Four Color 519 (1, '53) 10 20 30. 70 100 130
Four Color 578 (8/54), 641 (7/55), 737 (10/56), 804 (5/57), 939 (10/58), 1033 (9/59) (photo-c) 6 12 18 43 59 75

STEVE CANYON
Grosset & Dunlap: 1959 (6-3/4x9", 96 pgs., B&W, no text, hardcover)
100100-Reprints 2 stories from strip (1953, 1957) 6 12 18 31 38 45
100100 (softcover edition) 5 10 15 24 30 35

STEVE CANYON COMICS
Harvey Publ.: Feb, 1948 - No. 6, Dec, 1948 (Strip reprints, No. 4,5: 52pgs.)
1-Origin; has biography of Milton Caniff; Powell-a, 2 pgs.; Caniff-a 24 48 72 135 195 255
2-Caniff, Powell-a in #2-6 15 30 45 83 117 150
3-6: 6-Intro Madame Lynx-c/story 14 28 42 79 110 140

STEVE CANYON IN 3-D
Kitchen Sink Press: June, 1986 ($2.25, one-shot)
1-Contains unpublished story from 1954 5.00

STEVE DITKO'S STRANGE AVENGING TALES
Fantagraphics Books: Feb, 1997 ($2.95, B&W)
1-Ditko-c/s/a 3.00

STEVE DONOVAN, WESTERN MARSHAL (TV)
Dell Publishing Co.: No. 675, Feb, 1956 - No. 880, Feb, 1958 (All photo-c)
Four Color 675-Kinstler-a 9 18 27 65 93 120
Four Color 768-Kinstler-a 8 16 24 53 74 95
Four Color 880 6 12 18 38 52 65

STEVE ROPER
Famous Funnies: Apr, 1948 - No. 5, Dec, 1948
1-Contains 1944 daily newspaper-r 12 24 36 71 98 125
2 9 18 27 51 62 75
3-5 8 16 24 40 50 60

STEVE SAUNDERS SPECIAL AGENT (See Special Agent)

STEVE SAVAGE (See Captain...)

STEVE ZODIAC & THE FIRE BALL XL-5 (TV)
Gold Key: Jan, 1964
10108-401 (#1) 9 18 27 65 93 120

STEVIE (Mazie's boy friend)(Also see Flat-Top, Mazie & Mortie)
Mazie (Magazine Publ.): Nov, 1952 - No. 6, Apr, 1954
1-Teenage humor; Stevie, Mortie & Mazie begin 8 16 24 46 58 70
2-6 6 12 18 28 34 40

STEVIE MAZIE'S BOY FRIEND (See Harvey Hits #5)

STEWART THE RAT (See Eclipse Graphic Album Series)

Stone V2#1 © Haberlin & Portacio

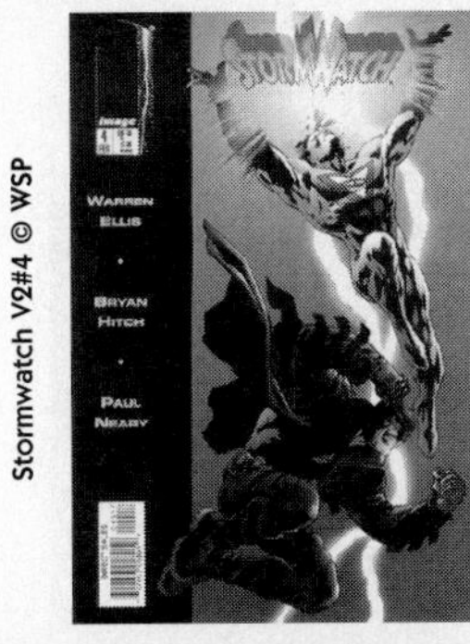

Stormwatch V2#4 © WSP

Straight Arrow #13 © ME

GD VG FN VF VF/NM NM-
2.0 4.0 6.0 8.0 9.0 9.2

ST. GEORGE (See listing under Saint...)

STIG'S INFERNO
Vortex/Eclipse: 1985 - No. 7, Mar, 1987 ($1.95, B&W)

1-7 ($1.95) 2.25
Graphic Album (1988, $6.95, B&W, 100 pgs.) 7.00

STING OF THE GREEN HORNET (See The Green Hornet)
Now Comics: June, 1992 - No. 4, 1992 ($2.50, limited series)

1-4: Butler-c/a 2.50
1-4 ($2.75)-Collectors Ed.; polybagged w/poster 3.00

STOKER'S DRACULA
Marvel Comics: 2004 - No. 4 ($3.99, B&W)

1-Reprints from Dracula Lives! #5-8; Roy Thomas-s/Dick Giordano-a 4.00

STONE
Avalon Studios: Aug, 1998 - No. 4, Apr, 1999 ($2.50, limited series)

1-4-Portacio-a/Haberlin-s 2.50
1-Alternate-c 5.00
2-($14.95) DF Stonechrome Edition 15.00

STONE (Volume 2)
Avalon Studios: Aug, 1999 - No. 4, May, 2000 ($2.50)

1-4-Portacio-a/Haberlin-s 2.50
1-Chrome-c 5.00

STONE COLD STEVE AUSTIN (WWF Wrestling)
Chaos! Comics: Oct, 1999 - No. 4, Feb, 2000 ($2.95)

1-4-Reg. & photo-c; Steven Grant-s 3.00
1-Premium Ed. ($10.00) 10.00
Preview ($5.00) 5.00

STONEY BURKE (TV)
Dell Publishing Co.: June-Aug, 1963 - No. 2, Sept-Nov, 1963

1,2-Jack Lord photo-c on both 3 6 9 19 25 32

STONY CRAIG
Pentagon Publishing Co.: 1946 (No #)

nn-Reprints Bell Syndicate's "Sgt. Stony Craig" newspaper strips
8 16 24 40 50 60

STORIES BY FAMOUS AUTHORS ILLUSTRATED (Fast Fiction #1-5)
Seaboard Publ./Famous Authors Ill.: No. 6, Aug, 1950 - No. 13, Mar, 1951

1-Scarlet Pimpernel-Baroness Orczy 36 72 108 204 297 390
2-Capt. Blood-Raphael Sabatini 35 70 105 198 287 375
3-She, by Haggard 40 80 120 233 342 450
4-The 39 Steps-John Buchan 24 48 72 135 195 255
5-Beau Geste-P. C. Wren 24 48 72 135 195 255

NOTE: *The above five issues are exact reprints of Fast Fiction #1-5 except for the title change and new Kiefer covers on #1 and 2. Kiefer c(r)-3-5. The above 5 issues were released before Famous Authors #6.*

6-Macbeth, by Shakespeare; Kiefer art (8/50); used in **SOTI**, pg. 22,143;
Kiefer-c; 36 pgs. 33 66 99 190 275 360
7-The Window; Kiefer-c/a; 52 pgs. 24 48 72 135 195 255
8-Hamlet, by Shakespeare; Kiefer-c/a; 36 pgs. 29 58 87 164 237 310
9,10: 9-Nicholas Nickleby, by Dickens; G. Schrotter-a; 52 pgs. 10-Romeo & Juliet,
by Shakespeare; Kiefer-c/a; 36 pgs. 24 48 72 135 195 255
11-13: 11-Ben-Hur; Schrotter-a; 52 pgs. 12-La Svengali; Schrotter-a; 36 pgs.
13-Scaramouche; Kiefer-c/a; 36 pgs. 23 46 69 130 188 245

NOTE: *Artwork was prepared/advertised for #14, The Red Badge Of Courage. Gilberton bought out Famous Authors, Ltd. and used that story as C.I. #98. Famous Authors, Ltd. then published the Classics Junior series. The Famous Authors titles were published as part of the regular Classics Ill. Series in Brazil starting in 1952.*

STORIES FROM THE TWILIGHT ZONE
Skylark Pub: Mar, 1979, 68pgs. (B&W comic digest, 5-1/4x7-5/8")

15405-2: Pfevfer-a, 56 pgs, new comics 3 6 9 18 24 30

STORIES OF ROMANCE (Formerly Meet Miss Bliss)
Atlas Comics (LMC): No. 5, Mar, 1956 - No. 13, Aug, 1957

5-Baker-a? 10 20 30 56 73 90
6-10,12,13 7 14 21 35 43 50
11-Baker, Romita-a; Colletta-c/a 8 16 24 46 58 70

NOTE: ***Ann Brewster** a-13. **Colletta** a-9(2), 11; c-5, 11.*

STORM
Marvel Comics: Feb, 1996 - No. 4, May, 1996 ($2.95, limited series)

1-4-Foil-c; Dodson-a(p); Ellis-s: 2-4-Callisto; 3.50

STORMQUEST
Caliber Press (Sky Universe): Nov, 1994 - No. 6, Apr, 1995 ($1.95)

1-6 2.25

STORMWATCH (Also see The Authority)
Image Comics (WildStorm Prod.): May, 1993 - No. 50, Jul, 1997 ($1.95/$2.50)

1-8,0,9-36: 1-Intro StormWatch (Battalion, Diva, Winter, Fuji, & Hellstrike); 1st app. Weatherman; Jim Lee-c & part scripts; Lee plots in all. 1-Gold edition.1-3-Includes coupon for limited edition StormWatch trading card #00 by Lee. 3-1st brief app. Backlash. 0-($2.50)-Polybagged w/card; 1st full app. Backlash. 9-(4/94, $2.50)-Intro Defile. 10-(6/94),11,12-Both (8/94). 13,14-(9/94). 15-(10/94). 21-Reads #1 on-c. 22-Direct Market; Wildstorm Rising Pt. 9, bound-in card. 23-Spartan joins team. 25-(6/94, June 1995 on-c, $2.50). 35-Fire From Heaven Pt. 5. 36-Fire From Heaven Pt. 12 2.50
10-Alternate Portacio-c, see Deathblow #5 2.50
22-($1.95)-Newsstand, Wildstorm Rising Pt. 9 2.50
37-(7/96, $3.50, 38 pgs.)-Weatherman forms new team; 1st app. Jenny Sparks, Jack Hawksmoor & Rose Tattoo; Warren Ellis scripts begin; Justice League #1-c/swipe 3.50
38-49: 44-Three covers. 2.50
50-($4.50) 4.50
Special 1 ,2(1/94, 5/95, $3.50, 52 pgs.) 3.50
Sourcebook 1 (1/94, $2.50) 2.50
Forces of Nature ('99, $14.95, TPB) r/V1 #37-42 15.00
Lightning Strikes ('00, $14.95, TPB) r/V1 #43-47 15.00

STORMWATCH (Also see The Authority)
Image Comics (WildStorm): Oct, 1997 - No. 11, Sept, 1998 ($2.50)

1-Ellis-s/Jimenez-a(p); two covers by Bennett 2.50
1-($3.50)-Voyager Pack bagged w/Gen 13 preview 3.50
2-4: 4-1st app. Midnighter and Apollo 2.50
5-11: 7,8-Freefall app. 9-Gen13 & DV8 app. 2.50
A Finer World ('99, $14.95, TPB) r/V2 #4-9 15.00
Change or Die ('99, $14.95, TPB) r/V1 #48-50 & V2 #1-3 15.00
Final Orbit ('01, $9.95, TPB) r/V2 #10,11 & WildC.A.T.S./Aliens; Hitch-c 10.00

STORMWATCHER
Eclipse Comics (Acme Press): Apr, 1989 - No. 4, Dec, 1989 ($2.00, B&W)

1-4 2.25

STORMWATCH: TEAM ACHILLES
DC Comics (WildStorm): Sept, 2002 - Present ($2.95)

1-8: 1-Two covers by Portacio; Portacio-a/Wright-s. 5,6-The Authority app. 3.00
9-23: 9-Back-up preview of The Authority: High Stakes pt. 1 3.00
TPB (2003, $14.95) r/Wizard Preview and #1-6; Portacio art pages 15.00
Book 2 (2004, $14.95) r/#7-11 & short story from Eye of the Storm Annual 15.00

STORMY (Disney) (Movie)
Dell Publishing Co.: No. 537, Feb, 1954

Four Color 537 (...the Thoroughbred)-on top 2/3 of each page; Pluto story on bottom 1/3
5 10 15 36 48 60

STORY OF JESUS (See Classics Illustrated Special Issue)

STORY OF MANKIND, THE (Movie)
Dell Publishing Co.: No. 851, Jan, 1958

Four Color 851-Vincent Price/Hedy Lamarr photo-c 8 16 24 58 82 105

STORY OF MARTHA WAYNE, THE
Argo Publ.: April, 1956

1-Newspaper strip-r 6 12 18 29 36 42

STORY OF RUTH, THE
Dell Publishing Co.: No. 1144, Nov-Jan, 1961 (Movie)

Four Color #1144-Photo-c 10 20 30 72 104 135

STORY OF THE COMMANDOS, THE (Combined Operations)
Long Island Independent: 1943 (15¢, B&W, 68 pgs.) (Distr. by Gilberton)

nn-All text (no comics); photos & illustrations; ad for Classic Comics on back cover (Rare)
34 68 102 193 279 365

STORY OF THE GLOOMY BUNNY, THE (See March of Comics #9)

STRAIGHT ARROW (Radio)(See Best of the West & Great Western)
Magazine Enterprises: Feb-Mar, 1950 - No. 55, Mar, 1956 (All 36 pgs.)

1-Straight Arrow (alias Steve Adams) & his palomino Fury begin; 1st mention of Sundown Valley & the Secret Cave 46 92 138 281 428 575
2-Red Hawk begins (1st app?) by Powell (origin), ends #55
24 48 72 138 199 260
3-Frazetta-c 31 62 93 178 259 340
4,5: 4-Secret Cave-c 22 44 66 123 177 230
6-10 20 40 60 112 161 210
11-Classic story "The Valley of Time", with an ancient civilization made of gold

Strange #1 © MAR

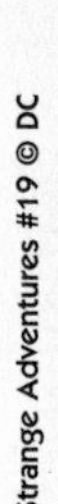
Strange Adventures #19 © DC

Strange Confessions #2 © Z-D

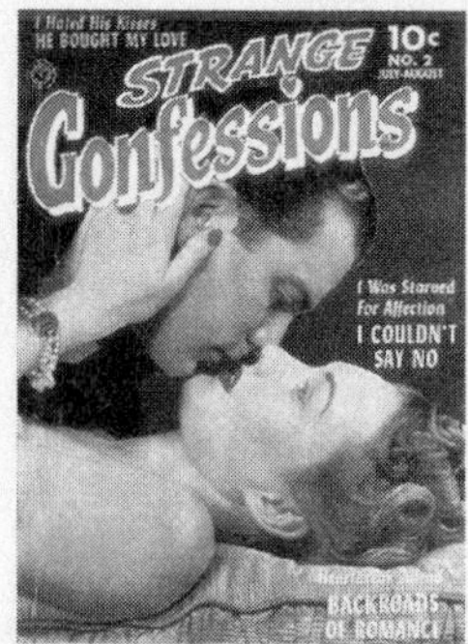

	GD 2.0	VG 4.0	FN 6.0	VF 8.0	VF/NM 9.0	NM- 9.2
	22	44	66	123	177	230
12-19	15	30	45	85	120	155
20-Origin Straight Arrow's Shield	17	34	51	95	135	175
21-Origin Fury	22	44	66	123	177	230
22-Frazetta-c	25	50	75	141	203	265
23,25-30: 25-Secret Cave-c. 28-Red Hawk meets The Vikings	11	22	33	62	84	105
24-Classic story "The Dragons of Doom!" with prehistoric pteradactyls	14	28	42	79	110	140
31-38: 36-Red Hawk drug story by Powell	9	18	27	51	62	75
39-Classic story "The Canyon Beast", with a dinosaur egg hatching a Tyranosaurus Rex	12	24	36	71	98	125
40-Classic story "Secret of The Spanish Specters", with Conquistadors' lost treasure	11	22	33	62	84	105
41,42,44-54: 45-Secret Cave-c	8	16	24	43	54	65
43-Intro & 1st app. Blaze, S. Arrow's Warrior dog	9	18	27	54	70	85
55-Last issue	10	20	30	58	77	95

NOTE: ***Fred Meagher** a 1-55; c-1, 2, 4-21, 23-55. **Powell** a 2-55. **Whitney** a-1. Many issues advertise the radio premiums associated with Straight Arrow.*

STRAIGHT ARROW'S FURY (Also see A-1 Comics)
Magazine Enterprises: No. 119, 1954 (one-shot)

	GD 2.0	VG 4.0	FN 6.0	VF 8.0	VF/NM 9.0	NM- 9.2
A-1 119-Origin; Fred Meagher-c/a	16	32	48	89	127	165

STRANGE (Tales You'll Never Forget)
Ajax-Farrell Publ. (Four Star Comic Corp.): March, 1957 - No. 6, May, 1958

	GD 2.0	VG 4.0	FN 6.0	VF 8.0	VF/NM 9.0	NM- 9.2
1	22	44	66	123	177	230
2-Censored r/Haunted Thrills	11	22	33	66	91	115
3-6	10	20	30	58	77	95

STRANGE (Dr. Strange)
Marvel Comics (Marvel Knghts): Nov, 2004 - Present ($3.50)

	GD 2.0	VG 4.0	FN 6.0	VF 8.0	VF/NM 9.0	NM- 9.2
1,2-Straczynski & Barnes-s/Peterson-a; Dr. Strange's origin retold						3.50

STRANGE ADVENTURES
National Periodical Publications: Aug-Sept, 1950 - No. 244, Oct-Nov, 1973 (No. 1-12: 52 pgs.)

	GD 2.0	VG 4.0	FN 6.0	VF 8.0	VF/NM 9.0	NM- 9.2
1-Adaptation of "Destination Moon"; preview of movie w/photo-c from movie (also see Fawcett Movie Comic #2); adapt. of Edmond Hamilton's "Chris KL-99" in #1-3; Darwin Jones begins	240	480	720	2040	3420	4800
2	113	226	339	961	1556	2150
3,4	76	152	228	646	1048	1450
5-8,10: 7-Origin Kris KL-99	65	130	195	553	897	1240
9-(6/51)-Origin/1st app. Captain Comet (c/story)	153	306	459	1300	2100	2900
11-20: 12,13,17,18-Toth-a. 14-Robot-c	47	94	141	376	588	800
21-30: 28-Atomic explosion panel. 30-Robot-c	38	76	114	285	443	600
31,34-38	34	68	102	255	403	550
32,33-Krigstein-a	35	70	105	263	412	560
39-Ill. in **SOTI** "Treating police contemptuously" (top right)	40	80	120	300	470	640
40-49-Last Capt. Comet; not in 45,47,48	33	66	99	248	392	535
50-53-Last precode issue (2/55)	25	50	75	177	271	365
54-70	18	36	54	126	193	260
71-99	14	28	42	97	149	200
100	16	32	48	112	171	230
101-110: 104-Space Museum begins by Sekowsky	11	22	33	77	114	150
111-116,118,119: 114-Star Hawkins begins, ends #185; Heath-a in Wood E.C. style	10	20	30	73	107	140
117-(6/60)-Origin/1st app. Atomic Knights.	50	100	150	400	625	850
120-2nd app. Atomic Knights	25	50	75	177	271	365
121,122,125,127,128,130,131,133,134: 134-Last 10¢ issue	9	18	27	65	93	120
123,126-3rd & 4th app. Atomic Knights	14	28	42	97	149	200
124-Intro/origin Faceless Creature	10	20	30	73	107	140
129,132,135,138,141,147-Atomic Knights app.	11	22	33	75	110	145
136,137,139,140,143,145,146,148,149,151,152,154,155,157-159: 159-Star Rovers app.; Gil Kane/Anderson-a.	7	14	21	48	63	80
142-2nd app. Faceless Creature	8	16	24	55	78	100
144-Only Atomic Knights-c (by M. Anderson)	11	22	33	80	120	160
150,153,156,160: Atomic Knights in each. 153-(6/63)-3rd app. Faceless Creature; atomic explosion-c. 160-Last Atomic Knights	8	16	24	55	78	100
161-179: 161-Last Space Museum. 163-Star Rovers app. 170-Infinity-c. 177-Intro/origin Immortal Man	5	10	15	36	48	60
180-Origin/1st app. Animal Man	19	38	57	134	205	275
181-183,185-189: 187-Intro/origin The Enchantress	4	8	12	29	40	50
184-2nd app. Animal Man by Gil Kane	12	24	36	84	127	170
190-1st app. Animal Man in costume	15	30	45	107	164	220
191-194,196-200,202-204	4	8	12	27	36	45
195-1st full app. Animal Man	8	16	24	58	82	105
201-Last Animal Man; 2nd full app.	6	12	18	40	55	70
205-(10/67)-Intro/origin Deadman by Infantino & begin series, ends #216	12	24	36	87	134	180
206-Neal Adams-a begins	9	18	27	65	93	120
207-210	9	18	27	60	85	110
211-216: 211-Space Museum-r. 216-(1-2/69)-Deadman story finally concludes in Brave & the Bold #86 (10-11/69); secret message panel by Neal Adams (pg. 13); tribute to Steranko	7	14	21	51	71	90
217-r/origin & 1st app. Adam Strange from Showcase #17, begin-r; Atomic Knights-r begin	3	6	9	16	20	24
218-221,223-225: 218-Last 12¢ issue. 225-Last 15¢ issue	2	4	6	14	18	22
222-New Adam Strange story; Kane/Anderson-a	3	7	10	21	28	36
226,227,230-236-(68-52 pgs.): 226, 227-New Adam Strange text story w/illos by Anderson (8,6 pgs.) 231-Last Atomic Knights-r. 235-JLA-c/s	2	4	6	14	18	22
228,229 (68 pgs.)	3	6	9	18	23	28
237-243	2	4	6	9	11	14
244-Last issue	2	4	6	10	13	16

NOTE: ***Neal Adams** a-206-216; c-207-216, 228, 235. **Anderson** a-8-52, 94, 96, 99, 115, 117, 119-163, 217r, 218r, 222, 223-225r, 226, 229r, 242i(r); c-18, 19, 21, 23, 24, 27, 30, 32-44(most); c/r-157i, 190i, 217-224, 228-231, 233, 235-239, 241-243. **Ditko** a-188, 189. **Drucker** a-42, 43, 45. **Elias** a-212. **Finlay** a-2, 3, 6, 7, 210r, 229r. **Giunta** a-237r. **Heath** a-116. **Infantino** a-10-101, 106-151, 154, 157-163, 180, 190, 218-221r, 223-244p(r); c-50; c(r)-190p, 197, 199-211, 218-221, 223-244. **Kaluta** c-238, 240. **Gil Kane** a-8-116, 124, 125, 130, 138, 146-157, 173-186, 204r, 222r, 227-231r; c(p)-11-17, 25, 154, 157. **Kubert** a-55(2 pgs.), 226; c-219, 220, 225-227, 232, 234. **Moriera** c-26, 28, 29, 71. **Morrow** c-230. **Mortimer** c-8. **Powell** a-4. **Sekowsky** a-71p, 97-162p, 217p(r), 218p(r); c-206, 217-219r. **Simon & Kirby** a-2r (2 pgs) **Sparling** a-201. **Toth** a-8, 12, 13, 17-19. **Wood** a-154i. Atomic Knights in #117, 120, 123, 126, 129, 132, 135, 138, 141, 144, 147, 150, 153, 156, 160. Atomic Knights reprints by **Anderson** in 217-221, 223-231. Chris KL99 in 1-3, 5, 7, 9, 11, 15. Capt. Comet covers-9-14, 17-19, 24, 26, 27, 32-44.*

STRANGE ADVENTURES
DC Comics (Vertigo): Nov, 1999 - No. 4 ($2.50, limited series)

	GD 2.0	VG 4.0	FN 6.0	VF 8.0	VF/NM 9.0	NM- 9.2
1-3: 1-Bolland-c; art by Bolland, Gibbons, Quitely						2.50

STRANGE AS IT SEEMS (See Famous Funnies-A Carnival of Comics, Feature Funnies #1, The John Hix Scrap Book & Peanuts)

STRANGE AS IT SEEMS
United Features Syndicate: 1939

	GD 2.0	VG 4.0	FN 6.0	VF 8.0	VF/NM 9.0	NM- 9.2
Single Series 9, 1, 2	36	72	108	204	297	390

STRANGE ATTRACTORS
RetroGraphix: 1993 - No. 15, Feb, 1997 ($2.50, B&W)

	GD 2.0	VG 4.0	FN 6.0	VF 8.0	VF/NM 9.0	NM- 9.2
1-15: 1-(5/93), 2-(8/93), 3-(11/93), 4-(2/94)						2.50
Volume One-($14.95, trade paperback)-r/#1-7						15.00

STRANGE ATTRACTORS: MOON FEVER
Caliber Comics: Feb, 1997 - No. 3, June, 1997 ($2.95, B&W, mini-series)

	GD 2.0	VG 4.0	FN 6.0	VF 8.0	VF/NM 9.0	NM- 9.2
1-3						3.00

STRANGE COMBAT TALES
Marvel Comics (Epic Comics): Oct, 1993 - No. 4, Jan, 1994 ($2.50, limited series)

	GD 2.0	VG 4.0	FN 6.0	VF 8.0	VF/NM 9.0	NM- 9.2
1-4						2.50

STRANGE CONFESSIONS
Ziff-Davis Publ. Co.: Jan-Mar (Spring on-c), 1952 - No. 4, Fall, 1952 (All have photo-c)

	GD 2.0	VG 4.0	FN 6.0	VF 8.0	VF/NM 9.0	NM- 9.2
1(Scarce)-Kinstler-a	52	104	156	317	484	650
2(Scarce, 7-8/52)	37	74	111	209	305	400
3(Scarce, 9-10/52)-#3 on-c, #2 on inside; Reformatory girl story; photo-c	37	74	111	209	305	400
4(Scarce)	37	74	111	209	305	400

STRANGE DAYS
Eclipse Comics: Oct, 1984 - No. 3, Apr, 1985 ($1.75, Baxter paper)

	GD 2.0	VG 4.0	FN 6.0	VF 8.0	VF/NM 9.0	NM- 9.2
1-3: Freakwave, Johnny Nemo, & Paradax from Vanguard Illustrated; nudity, violence & strong language						2.25

STRANGE DAYS (Movie)
Marvel Comics: Dec, 1995 ($5.95, squarebound, one-shot)

	GD 2.0	VG 4.0	FN 6.0	VF 8.0	VF/NM 9.0	NM- 9.2
1-Adaptation of film						6.00

STRANGE FANTASY (Eerie Tales of Suspense!)(Formerly Rocketman #1)
Ajax-Farrell: Aug, 1952 - No. 14, Oct-Nov, 1954

	GD 2.0	VG 4.0	FN 6.0	VF 8.0	VF/NM 9.0	NM- 9.2
2(#1, 8/52)-Jungle Princess story; Kamenish-a; reprinted from Ellery Queen #1	46	92	138	281	428	575
2(10/52)-No Black Cat or Rulah; Bakerish, Kamenish-a; hypo/meathook-c	40	80	120	235	348	460

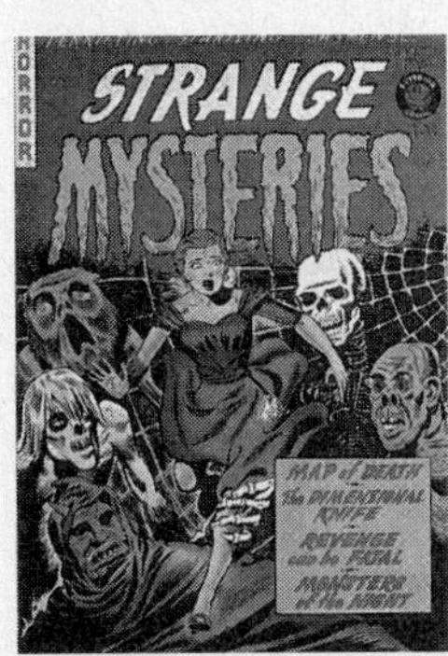

Strange Mysteries #10 © SUPR

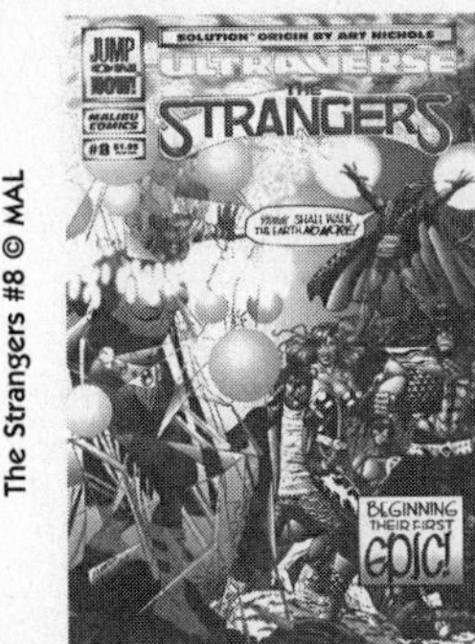

The Strangers #8 © MAL

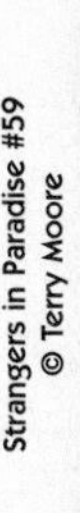

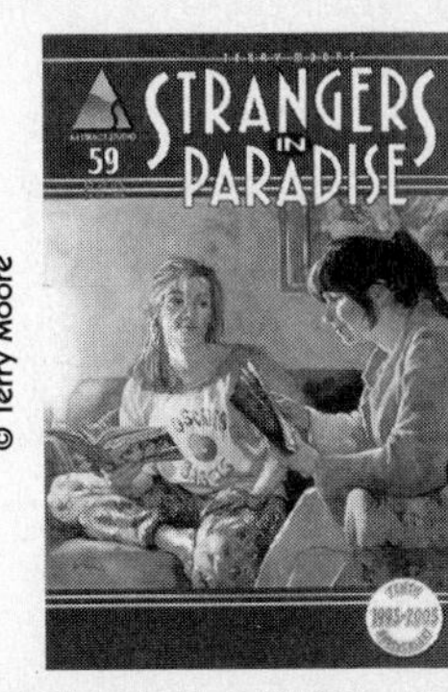

Strangers in Paradise #59 © Terry Moore

GD 2.0 | VG 4.0 | FN 6.0 | VF 8.0 | VF/NM 9.0 | NM- 9.2

3-Rulah story, called Pulah 40 80 120 233 342 450
4-Rocket Man app. (2/53) 38 76 114 219 320 420
5,6,8,10,12,14 27 54 81 152 219 285
7-Madam Satan/Slave story 38 76 114 219 320 420
9(w/Black Cat), 9(w/Boy's Ranch; S&K-a), 9(w/War)(A rebinding of Harvey interiors; not publ. by Ajax) 34 68 102 193 279 365
9-Regular issue; Steve Ditko's 3rd published work (tied with Captain 3D) 44 88 132 268 409 550
11-Jungle story 35 70 105 198 287 375
13-Bondage-c; Rulah (Kolah) story 35 70 105 198 287 375

STRANGE GALAXY
Eerie Publications: V1#8, Feb, 1971 - No. 11, Aug, 1971 (B&W, magazine)

V1#8-Reprints-c/Fantastic V19#3 (2/70) (a pulp) 4 8 12 22 30 38
9-11 3 6 9 18 23 28

STRANGEHAVEN
Abiogenesis Press: June, 1995 - Present ($2.95, B&W)

1-15 3.00

STRANGE JOURNEY
America's Best (Steinway Publ.) (Ajax/Farrell): Sept, 1957 - No. 4, Jun, 1958 (Farrell reprints)

1 20 40 60 112 161 210
2-4: 2-Flying saucer-c. 3-Titanic-c 14 28 42 79 110 140

STRANGE LOVE (See Fox Giants)

STRANGELOVE
Entity Comics: 1995 ($2.50)

1 2.50

STRANGE MYSTERIES
Superior/Dynamic Publications: Sept, 1951 - No. 21, Jan, 1955

1-Kamenish-a & horror stories begin 62 124 186 388 594 800
2 37 74 111 213 312 410
3-5 35 70 105 200 290 380
6-8 30 60 90 170 245 320
9-Bondage 3-D effect-c 35 70 105 201 293 385
10-Used in **SOTI**, pg. 181 27 54 81 152 219 285
11-18 23 46 69 132 191 250
19-r/Journey Into Fear #1; cover is a splash from one story; Baker-r(2) 25 50 75 141 203 265
20,21-Reprints; 20-r/#1 with new-c 18 36 54 100 143 185

STRANGE MYSTERIES
I. W. Enterprises/Super Comics: 1963 - 1964

I.W. Reprint #9; Rulah-r/Spook #28; Disbrow-a 4 8 12 24 32 40
Super Reprint #10-12,15-17(1963-64): 10,11-r/Strange #2,1. 12-r/Tales of Horror #5 (3/53) less-c. 15-r/Dark Mysteries #23. 16-r/The Dead Who Walk. 17-r/Dark Mysteries #22 4 8 12 24 32 40
Super Reprint #18-r/Witchcraft #1; Kubert-a 4 8 12 24 32 40

STRANGE PLANETS
I. W. Enterprises/Super Comics: 1958; 1963-64

I.W. Reprint #1(nd)-Reprints E. C. Incredible S/F #30 plus-c/Strange Worlds #3 7 14 21 50 68 85
I.W. Reprint #9-Orlando/Wood-r/Strange Worlds #4; cover-r from Flying Saucers #1 9 18 27 60 85 110
Super Reprint #10-Wood-r (22 pg.) from Space Detective #1; cover-r/Attack on Planet Mars 9 18 27 60 85 110
Super Reprint #11-Wood-r (25 pg.) from An Earthman on Venus 10 20 30 67 96 125
Super Reprint #12-Orlando-r/Rocket to the Moon 9 18 27 60 85 110
Super Reprint #15-Reprints Journey Into Unknown Worlds #8; Heath, Colan-r 5 10 15 36 48 60
Super Reprint #16-Reprints Avon's Strange Worlds #6; Kinstler, Check-a 6 12 18 38 52 65
Super Reprint #18-r/Great Exploits #1 (Daring Adventures #6); Space Busters, Explorer Joe, The Son of Robin Hood; Krigstein-a 4 8 12 29 40 50

STRANGERS
Image Comics: Mar, 2003 - No. 6, Sept, 2003 ($2.95)

1-6-Randy & Jean-Marc Lofficier-s; two covers. 2-Nexus back-up story 3.00

STRANGERS, THE
Malibu Comics (Ultraverse): June, 1993 - No. 24, May, 1995 ($1.95/$2.50)

1-4,6-12,14-20: 1-1st app. The Strangers; has coupon for Ultraverse Premiere #0; 1st app. the Night Man (not in costume). 2-Polybagged w/trading card. 7-Break-Thru x-over. 8-2 pg. origin Solution. 12-Silver foil logo; wraparound-c. 17-Rafferty app. 2.50
1-With coupon missing 2.25
1-Full cover holographic edition, 1st of kind w/Hardcase #1 & Prime #1 6.00
1-Ultra 5000 limited silver foil 4.00
4-($2.50)-Newsstand edition bagged w/card 2.50
5-($2.50, 52 pgs.)-Rune flip-c/story by B. Smith (3 pgs.); The Mighty Magnor 1 pg. strip by Aragones; 3-pg. Night Man preview 2.50
13-($3.50, 68 pgs.)-Mantra app.; flip book w/Ultraverse Premiere #4 3.50
21-24 ($2.50) 2.50
...:The Pilgrim Conundrum Saga (1/95, $3.95, 68pgs.) 4.00

STRANGERS IN PARADISE
Antarctic Press: Nov, 1993 - No. 3, Feb, 1994 ($2.75, B&W, limited series)

1 6 12 18 38 52 65
1-2nd/3rd prints 1 2 3 5 6 8
2 (2300 printed) 4 8 12 27 36 45
3 3 6 9 18 24 30
Trade paperback (Antarctic Press, $6.95)-Red -c (5000 print run) 10.00
Trade paperback (Abstract Studios, $6.95)-Red-c (2000 print run) 15.00
Trade paperback (Abstract Studios, $6.95, 1st-4th printing)-Blue- 7.00
Hardcover ('98, $29.95) includes first draft pages 30.00
Gold Reprint Series ($2.75) 1-3-r/#1-3 2.75

STRANGERS IN PARADISE
Abstract Studios: Sept, 1994 - No. 14, July, 1996 ($2.75, B&W)

1 2 4 6 10 13 16
1,3- 2nd printings 4.00
2,3: 2-Color dream sequence 1 2 3 5 6 8
4-10 4.00
4-6-2nd printings 2.75
11-14: 14-The Letters of Molly & Poo 3.00
Gold Reprint Series ($2.75) 1-13-r/#1-13 2.75
I Dream Of You ($16.95, TPB) r/#1-9 17.00
It's a Good Life ($8.95, TPB) r/#10-13 9.00

STRANGERS IN PARADISE (Volume Three)
Homage Comics #1-8/Abstract Studios #9-on: Oct, 1996 - Present ($2.75/$2.95, color #1-5, B&W #6-on)

1-Terry Moore-c/s/a in all; dream seq. by Jim Lee-a 4.00
1-Jim Lee variant-c 1 2 3 6 7 8
2-5 3.50
6-16: 6-Return to B&W. 13-15-High school flashback. 16-Xena Warrior Princess parody; two covers 3.00
17-66: 33-Color issue. 46-Molly Lane. 49-Molly & Poo 3.00
...Lyrics and Poems (2/99) 2.75
...Source Book (2003, $2.95) Background on characters & story arcs, checklists 3.00
Brave New World ('02, $8.95, TPB) r/#44,45,47,48 9.00
Child of Rage ($15.95, TPB) r/#31-38 16.00
David's Story (6/04, $8.95, TPB) r/#61-63 9.00
Flower to Flame ('03, $15.95, TPB) r/#55-60 16.00
Heart in Hand ('03, $12.95, TPB) r/#50-54 13.00
High School ('98, $8.95, TPB) r/#13-16 9.00
Immortal Enemies ('98, $14.95, TPB) r/#6-12 15.00
Love Me Tender ($12.95, TPB) r/#1-5 in B&W w/ color Lee seq. 13.00
My Other Life ($14.95, TPB) r/#25-30 15.00
Pocket Book 2 ($17.95, 5 1/2" x 8", TPB) r/#1-17 in B&W 18.00
Sanctuary ($15.95, TPB) r/#17-24 16.00
Tomorrow Now (11/04, $14.95, TPB) r/#64-69 15.00
Tropic of Desire ($12.95, TPB) r/#39-43 13.00
The Complete... : Volume 3 Part 3 HC ('01, $49.95) r/#26-38 50.00

STRANGE SPORTS STORIES (See Brave & the Bold #45-49, DC Special, and DC Super Stars #10)
National Periodical Publications: Sept-Oct, 1973 - No. 6, July-Aug, 1974

1 3 6 9 18 24 30
2-6: 2-Swan/Anderson-a 2 4 6 10 13 16

STRANGE STORIES FROM ANOTHER WORLD (Unknown World #1)
Fawcett Publications: No. 2, Aug, 1952 - No. 5, Feb, 1953

2-Saunders painted-c 51 102 153 311 476 640
3-5-Saunders painted-c 40 80 120 235 348 460

STRANGE STORIES OF SUSPENSE (Rugged Action #1-4)
Atlas Comics (CSI): No. 5, Oct, 1955 - No. 16, Aug, 1957

5(#1) 40 80 120 236 351 465

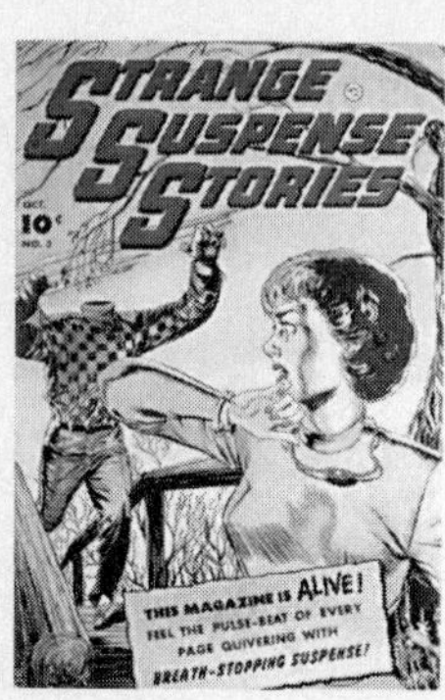

Strange Suspense Stories #3 © FAW

Strange Tales #28 © MAR

Strange Tales #146 © MAR

	GD 2.0	VG 4.0	FN 6.0	VF 8.0	VF/NM 9.0	NM- 9.2
6,9	25	50	75	141	203	265
7-E. C. swipe cover/Vault of Horror #32	26	52	78	147	211	275
8-Morrow/Williamson-a; Pakula-a	27	54	81	152	219	285
10-Crandall, Torres, Meskin-a	26	52	78	147	211	275
11-13: 12-Torres, Pakula-a. 13-E.C. art swipes	21	42	63	118	169	220
14-16: 14-Williamson/Mayo-a. 15-Krigstein-a. 16-Fox, Powell-a	23	46	69	130	188	245

NOTE: ***Everett** a-6, 7, 13; c-8, 9, 11-14. **Heath** a-5. **Maneely** c-5. **Morisi** a-11. **Morrow** a-13. **Powell** a-8. **Severin** c-7. **Wildey** a-14.*

STRANGE STORY (Also see Front Page)
Harvey Publications: June-July, 1946 (52 pgs.)

	GD 2.0	VG 4.0	FN 6.0	VF 8.0	VF/NM 9.0	NM- 9.2
1-The Man in Black Called Fate by Powell	33	66	99	190	275	360

STRANGE SUSPENSE STORIES (Lawbreakers Suspense Stories #10-15; This Is Suspense #23-26; Captain Atom V1#78 on)
Fawcett Publications/Charlton Comics No. 16 on: 6/52 - No. 5, 2/53; No. 16, 1/54 - No. 22, 11/54; No. 27, 10/55 - No. 77, 10/65; V3#1, 10/67 - V1#9, 9/69

	GD 2.0	VG 4.0	FN 6.0	VF 8.0	VF/NM 9.0	NM- 9.2
1-(Fawcett)-Powell, Sekowsky-a	81	162	243	506	778	1050
2-George Evans horror story	48	96	144	293	447	600
3-5 (2/53)-George Evans horror stories	40	80	120	244	372	480
16(1-2/54)-Formerly Lawbreakers S.S.	30	60	90	173	249	325
17,21: 21-Shuster-a	24	48	72	138	199	260
18-E.C. swipe/HOF 7; Ditko-c/a(2)	40	80	120	236	351	465
19-Ditko electric chair-c; Ditko-a	51	102	153	311	473	635
20-Ditko-c/a(2)	40	80	120	236	351	465
22(11/54)-Ditko-c, Shuster-a; last pre-code issue; becomes This Is Suspense	35	70	105	201	293	385
27(10/55)-(Formerly This Is Suspense #26)	15	30	45	83	117	150
28-30,38	10	20	30	60	80	100
31-33,35,37,40-Ditko-c/a(2-3 each)	22	44	66	123	177	230
34-Story of ruthless business man, Wm. B. Gaines; Ditko-c/a	46	92	138	281	428	575
36-(15¢, 68 pgs.); Ditko-a(4)	26	52	78	147	211	275
39,41,52,53-Ditko-a	18	36	54	100	143	185
42-44,46,49,54-60	6	12	18	40	55	70
45,47,48,50,51-Ditko-c/a	14	28	42	97	149	200
61-74	4	8	12	29	40	50
75(6/65)-Reprints origin/1st app. Captain Atom by Ditko from Space Advs. #33; r/Severin-a/Space Advs. #24 (75-77: 12¢ issues)	13	26	39	90	138	185
76,77-Captain Atom-r by Ditko/Space Advs.	7	14	21	50	68	85
V3#1(10/67): 12ç issues begin	4	8	12	22	30	38
V1#2-Ditko-c/a; atom bomb-c	4	8	12	22	30	38
V1#3-9: All 12¢ issues	2	4	6	12	16	20

NOTE: ***Alascia** a-19. **Aparo** a-60, V3#1, 2, 4; c-V1#4, 8. **Baily** a-1-3; c-2, 5. **Evans** c-3, 4. **Giordano** c-16, 17p, 24p, 25p. **Montes/Bache** c-66. **Powell** a-4. **Shuster** a-19, 21. **Marcus Swayze** a-27.*

STRANGE TALES (...Featuring Warlock #178-181; Doctor Strange #169 on)
Atlas (CCPC #1-67/ZPC #68-79/VPI #80-85)/Marvel #86(7/61) on:
June, 1951 - No. 168, May, 1968; No. 169, Sept, 1973 - No. 188, Nov, 1976

	GD 2.0	VG 4.0	FN 6.0	VF 8.0	VF/NM 9.0	NM- 9.2
1-Horror/weird stories begin	312	624	936	2000	3100	4200
2	102	204	306	638	982	1325
3,5: 3-Atom bomb panels	77	154	231	481	741	1000
4-Cosmic eyeball story "The Evil Eye"	81	162	243	506	778	1050
6-9: 6-Heath-c/a. 7-Colan-a	56	112	168	350	538	725
10-Krigstein-a	60	120	180	375	575	775
11-14,16-20	40	80	120	240	360	480
15-Krigstein-a	40	80	120	244	372	500
21,23-27,29-34: 27-Atom bomb panels. 33-Davis-a. 34-Last pre-code issue (2/55)	36	72	108	204	297	390
22-Krigstein, Forte/Fox-a	37	74	111	209	305	400
28-Jack Katz story used in Senate Investigation report, pgs. 7 & 169	37	74	111	209	305	400
35-41,43,44: 37-Vampire story by Colan	20	40	60	141	216	290
42,45,59,61-Krigstein-a; #61 (2/58)	21	42	63	150	230	310
46-57,60: 51-1st S.A. issue. 53,56-Crandall-a. 60-(8/57)	18	36	54	129	197	265
58,64-Williamson-a in each, with Mayo-#58	19	38	57	134	205	275
62,63,65,66: 62-Torres-a. 66-Crandall-a	17	34	51	123	189	255
67-Prototype ish. (Quicksilver)	19	38	57	136	208	280
68,71,72,74,77,80: Ditko/Kirby-a in #67-80	18	36	54	129	197	265
69,70,73,75,76,78,79: 69-Prototype ish. (Prof. X). 70-Prototype ish. (Giant Man). 73-Prototype ish. (Ant-Man). 75-Prototype ish. (Iron Man). 76-Prototype ish. (Human Torch). 78-Prototype ish. (Ant-Man). 79-Prototype ish. (Dr. Strange) (12/60)	23	46	69	163	249	335
81-83,85-88,90,91-Ditko/Kirby-a in all: 86-Robot-c. 90-(11/61)-Atom bomb blast panel	17	34	51	119	182	245
84-Prototype ish. (Magneto)(5/61); has powers like Magneto of X-Men, but two years earlier; Ditko/Kirby-a	21	42	63	150	230	310
89-1st app. Fin Fang Foom (10/61) by Kirby	43	86	129	344	535	725
92-Prototype ish. (Ancient One); last 10¢ issue	18	36	54	129	197	265
93,95,96,98-100: Kirby-a	15	30	45	107	164	220
94-Prototype ish. (The Thing); Kirby-a	18	36	54	129	197	265
97-1st app. Aunt May & Uncle Ben by Ditko (6/62), before Amazing Fantasy #15; (see Tales Of Suspense #7); Kirby-a	38	76	114	285	443	600
101-Human Torch begins by Kirby (10/62); origin recap Fantastic Four & Human Torch; Human Torch-c begin	95	190	285	808	1304	1800
102-1st app. Wizard; robot-c	36	72	108	270	423	575
103-105: 104-1st app. Trapster. 105-2nd Wizard	31	62	93	223	342	460
106,108,109: 106-Fantastic Four guests (3/63)	21	42	63	150	230	310
107-(4/63)-Human Torch/Sub-Mariner battle; 4th S.A. Sub-Mariner app. & 1st x-over outside of Fantastic Four	27	54	81	194	297	400
110-(7/63)-Intro Doctor Strange, Ancient One & Wong by Ditko	111	222	333	944	1522	2100
111-2nd Dr. Strange	34	68	102	255	403	550
112,113	15	30	45	107	164	220
114-Acrobat disguised as Captain America, 1st app. since the G.A.; intro. & 1st app. Victoria Bentley; 3rd Dr. Strange app. & begin series (11/63)	39	78	117	293	459	625
115-Origin Dr. Strange; Human Torch vs. Sandman (Spidey villain; 2nd app. & brief origin); early Spider-Man x-over, 12/63	47	94	141	376	588	800
116-(1/64)-Human Torch battles The Thing; 1st Thing x-over	13	26	39	90	138	185
117,118,120: 120-1st Iceman x-over (from X-Men)	10	20	30	73	107	140
119-Spider-Man x-over (2 panel cameo)	12	24	36	82	124	165
121,122,124,126-134: Thing/Torch team-up in 121-134. 126-Intro Clea. 128-Quicksilver & Scarlet Witch app. (1/65). 130-The Beatles cameo. 134-Last Human Torch; The Watcher-c/story; Wood-a(i)	8	16	24	58	82	105
123-1st app. The Beetle (see Amazing Spider-Man #21 for next app.); 1st Thor x-over (8/64); Loki app.	9	18	27	65	93	120
125-Torch & Thing battle Sub-Mariner (10/64)	9	18	27	65	93	120
135-Col. (formerly Sgt.) Nick Fury becomes Nick Fury Agent of Shield (origin/1st app.) by Kirby (8/65); series begins	14	28	42	97	149	200
136-140: 138-Intro Eternity	6	12	18	40	55	70
141-147,149: 145-Begins alternating-c features w/Nick Fury (odd #'s) & Dr. Strange (even #'s). 146-Last Ditko Dr. Strange who is in consecutive stories since #113; only full Ditko Dr. Strange-c this title. 147-Dr. Strange (by Everett #147-152) continues thru #168, then Dr. Strange #169	5	10	15	33	44	55
148-Origin Ancient One	7	14	21	51	71	90
150(11/66)-John Buscema's 1st work at Marvel	6	12	18	38	52	65
151-Kirby/Steranko-c/a; 1st Marvel work by Steranko	8	16	24	53	74	95
152,153-Kirby/Steranko-a	6	12	18	38	52	65
154-158-Steranko-a/script	6	12	18	38	52	65
159-Origin Nick Fury retold; Intro Val; Captain America-c/story; Steranko-a	7	14	21	46	63	80
160-162-Steranko-a/scripts; Capt. America app.	6	12	18	38	52	65
163-166,168-Steranko-a(p). 168-Last Nick Fury (gets own book next month) & last Dr. Strange who also gets own book	5	10	15	36	48	60
167-Steranko pen/script; classic flag-c	7	14	21	46	63	80
169-1st app. Brother Voodoo(origin in #169,170) & begin series, ends #173.	2	4	6	12	16	20
170-174: 174-Origin Golem	2	4	6	9	11	14
175-177: 177-Brunner-c	1	3	4	6	8	10
178-(2/75)-Warlock by Starlin begins; origin Warlock & Him retold; 1st app. Magus; Starlin-c/a/scripts in #178-181 (all before Warlock #9)	3	6	9	16	20	25
179-181-All Warlock. 179-Intro/1st app. Pip the Troll. 180-Intro Gamora. 181-(8/75)-Warlock story continued in Warlock #9	2	4	6	10	13	16
182-188: 185,186-(Regular 25¢ editions)						6.00
185,186-(30¢-c variants, limited distribution)(5,7/76)	2	4	6	11	14	18
Annual 1(1962)-Reprints from Strange Tales #73,76,78, Tales of Suspense #7,9, Tales to Astonish #1,6,7, & Journey Into Mystery #53,55,59; (1st Marvel annual?)	48	96	144	384	605	825
Annual 2(7/63)-Reprints from Strange Tales #67, Strange Worlds (Atlas) #1-3, World of Fantasy #16; new Human Torch vs. Spider-Man story by Kirby/Ditko (1st Spidey x-over; 4th app.); Kirby-c	66	132	198	561	906	1250

NOTE: ***Briefer** a-17. **Burgos** a-123p. **J. Buscema** a-174p. **Colan** a-7, 11, 20, 37, 53, 169-173p, 188p. **Davis** c-71. **Ditko** a-46, 50, 67-122, 123-125p, 126-146, 175r, 182-188r; c-51, 93, 115, 121, 146. **Everett** a-4, 21, 40-42, 73, 147-152, 164i; c-8, 10, 11, 13, 15, 24, 45, 49-54, 56, 58, 60, 61, 63, 148, 150, 152, 158i. **Forte** a-27, 43, 50, 53, 54, 60. **Heath** a-2, 6; c-6, 18-20. **Kamen** a-45. **G. Kane** c-170-173, 182p. **Kirby** Human Torch-101-105, 108, 109, 114, 120; Nick Fury-135p, 141-143p; (Layouts)-135-153; other **Kirby** a-67-100p; c-68-70, 72-74, 76-92, 94, 95,*

Strange Worlds #7 © AVON

Stray Bullets #1 © David Lapham

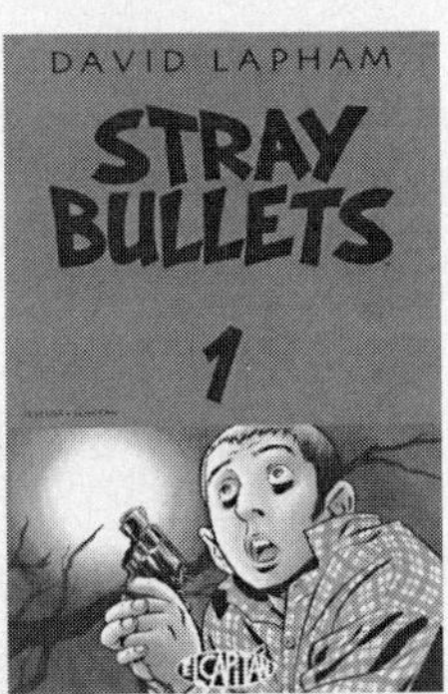

Street Fighter ('03) #2 © Capcom

	GD 2.0	VG 4.0	FN 6.0	VF 8.0	VF/NM 9.0	NM- 9.2

101-114, 116-123, 125-130, 132-135, 136p, 138-145, 147, 149, 151p. ***Kirby/Ayers*** *c-101-106, 108-110.* ***Kirby/Ditko*** *a-80, 88, 121; c-75, 93, 97, 100, 139.* ***Lawrence*** *a-29.* ***Leiber/ Fox*** *a-110-113.* ***Maneely*** *a-3, 7, 37, 42; c-33, 40.* ***Moldoff*** *a-20.* ***Mooney*** *a-174i.* ***Morisi*** *a-53, 56.* ***Morrow*** *a-54.* ***Orlando*** *a-41, 44, 46, 49, 52.* ***Powell*** *a-42, 44, 49, 54, 130-134p; c-131p.* ***Reinman*** *a-11, 50, 74, 88, 91, 95, 104, 106, 112i, 124-127i.* ***Robinson*** *a-17.* ***Romita*** *c-169.* ***Roussos*** *c-201i.* ***R.Q. Sale*** *a-56; c-16.* ***Sekowski*** *a-3, 11.* ***Severin*** *a(i)-136-138; c-137.* ***Starlin*** *a-178, 179, 180p, 181p; c-178-180, 181p.* ***Steranko*** *a-151-161, 162-168p; c-151i, 153, 155, 157, 159, 161, 163, 165, 167.* ***Torres*** *a-53, 62.* ***Tuska*** *a-14, 166p.* ***Whitney*** *a-149.* ***Wildey*** *a-42, 56.* ***Woodbridge*** *a-59. Fantastic Four cameos #101-134. Jack Katz app.-26.*

STRANGE TALES
Marvel Comics Group: Apr, 1987 - No. 19, Oct, 1988

	GD	VG	FN	VF	VF/NM	NM-
V2#1-19						2.25

STRANGE TALES
Marvel Comics: Nov, 1994 ($6.95, one-shot)

	GD	VG	FN	VF	VF/NM	NM-
V3#1-acetate-c						7.00

STRANGE TALES (Anthology; continues stories from Man-Thing #8 and Werewolf By Night #6)
Marvel Comics: Sept, 1998 - No. 2, Oct, 1998 ($4.99)

	GD	VG	FN	VF	VF/NM	NM-
1,2: 1-Silver Surfer app. 2-Two covers						5.00

STRANGE TALES: DARK CORNERS
Marvel Comics: May, 1998 ($3.99, one-shot)

	GD	VG	FN	VF	VF/NM	NM-
1-Anthology; stories by Baron & Maleev, McGregor & Dringenberg, DeMatteis & Badger; Estes painted-c						4.00

STRANGE TALES OF THE UNUSUAL
Atlas Comics (ACI No. 1-4/WPI No. 5-11): Dec, 1955 - No. 11, Aug, 1957

	GD	VG	FN	VF	VF/NM	NM-
1-Powell-a	44	88	132	268	409	550
2	29	58	87	164	237	310
3-Williamson-a (4 pgs.)	30	60	90	170	245	320
4,6,8,11	21	42	63	118	169	220
5-Crandall, Ditko-a	26	52	78	147	211	275
7,9: 7-Kirby, Orlando-a. 9-Krigstein-a	23	46	69	130	188	245
10-Torres, Morrow-a	21	42	63	118	169	220

NOTE: ***Baily*** *a-6.* ***Brodsky*** *c-2-4.* ***Everett*** *a-2, 6; c-6, 9, 11.* ***Heck*** *a-1.* ***Maneely*** *c-1.* ***Orlando*** *a-7.* ***Pakula*** *a-10.* ***Romita*** *a-1.* ***R.Q. Sale*** *a-3.* ***Wildey*** *a-3.*

STRANGE TERRORS
St. John Publishing Co.: June, 1952 - No. 7, Mar, 1953

	GD	VG	FN	VF	VF/NM	NM-
1-Bondage-c; Zombies spelled Zoombies on-c; Fine-*esque* -a	55	110	165	340	520	700
2	34	68	102	193	279	365
3-Kubert-a; painted-c	40	80	120	239	357	475
4-Kubert-a (reprinted in Mystery Tales #18); Ekgren painted-c; Fine-*esque* -a; Jerry Iger caricature	51	102	153	311	476	640
5-Kubert-a; painted-c	40	80	120	239	357	475
6-Giant (25¢, 100 pgs.)(1/53); bondage-c	51	102	153	311	476	640
7-Giant (25¢, 100 pgs.); Kubert-c/a	55	110	165	340	520	700

NOTE: ***Cameron*** *a-6, 7.* ***Morisi*** *a-6.*

STRANGE WORLD OF YOUR DREAMS
Prize Publications: Aug, 1952 - No. 4, Jan-Feb, 1953

	GD	VG	FN	VF	VF/NM	NM-
1-Simon & Kirby-a	62	124	186	388	594	800
2,3-Simon & Kirby-c/a. 2-Meskin-a	50	100	150	305	465	625
4-S&K-c; Meskin-a	40	80	120	241	363	485

STRANGE WORLDS (#18 continued from Avon's Eerie #1-17)
Avon Periodicals: 11/50 - No. 9, 11/52; No. 18, 10-11/54 - No. 22, 9-10/55 (No #11-17)

	GD	VG	FN	VF	VF/NM	NM-
1-Kenton of the Star Patrol by Kubert (r/Eerie #1 from 1947); Crom the Barbarian by John Giunta	119	238	357	744	1147	1550
2-Wood-a; Crom the Barbarian by Giunta; Dara of the Vikings app.; used in **SOTI**, pg. 112; injury to eye panel	110	220	330	688	1057	1425
3-Wood/Orlando-a (Kenton), Wood/Williamson/Frazetta/Krenkel/Orlando-a (7 pgs.); Malu Slave Girl Princess app.; Kinstler-c	208	416	624	1300	2000	2700
4-Wood-c/a (Kenton); Orlando-a; origin The Enchanted Daggar; Sultan-a; classic cover	119	238	357	744	1147	1550
5-Orlando/Wood-a (Kenton); Wood-c	62	124	186	388	594	800
6-Kinstler-a(2); Orlando/Wood-c; Check-a	45	90	135	275	418	560
7-Fawcette & Becker/Alascia-a	40	80	120	236	351	465
8-Kubert, Kinstler, Hollingsworth & Lazarus-a; Lazarus Robot-c	40	80	120	236	351	465
9-Kinstler, Fawcette, Alascia-a	40	80	120	230	335	440
18-(Formerly Eerie #17)-Reprints "Attack on Planet Mars" by Kubert	33	66	99	190	275	360
19-r/Avon's "Robotmen of the Lost Planet"; last pre-code issue; Robot-c	33	66	99	190	275	360
20-War-c/story; Wood-c(r)/U.S. Paratroops #1	10	20	30	58	77	95
21,22-War-c/stories. 22-New logo	9	18	27	51	62	75
I.W. Reprint #5-Kinstler-a(r)/Avon's #9	4	8	12	29	40	50

STRANGE WORLDS
Marvel Comics (MPI No. 1,2/Male No. 3,5): Dec, 1958 - No. 5, Aug, 1959

	GD	VG	FN	VF	VF/NM	NM-
1-Kirby & Ditko-a; flying saucer issue	87	174	261	544	835	1125
2-Ditko-c/a	51	102	153	311	473	635
3-Kirby-a(2)	40	80	120	240	360	480
4-Williamson-a	40	80	120	233	342	450
5-Ditko-a	35	70	105	198	287	375

NOTE: ***Buscema*** *a-3, 4.* ***Ditko*** *a-1-5; c-2..* ***Heck*** *a-2.* ***Kirby*** *a-1, 3.* ***Kirby/Brodsky*** *c-1, 3-5.*

STRAWBERRY SHORTCAKE
Marvel Comics (Star Comics): Jun, 1985 - No. 6, Feb, 1986 (Children's comic)

	GD	VG	FN	VF	VF/NM	NM-
1-6: Howie Post-a						6.00

STRAY
DC Comics (Homage Comics): 2001 ($5.95, prestige format, one-shot)

	GD	VG	FN	VF	VF/NM	NM-
1-Pollina-c/a; Lobdell & Palmiotti-s						6.00

STRAY BULLETS (Also see Promotional Comics section for Free Comic Book Day edition)
El Capitan Books: 1995 - Present ($2.95/$3.50, B&W, mature readers)

	GD	VG	FN	VF	VF/NM	NM-
1-David Lapham-c/a/scripts	2	4	6	8	10	12
2,3						6.00
4-8						3.50
9-21,31,32-($2.95)						3.00
22-30,33-35-($3.50) 22-Includes preview to Murder Me Dead						3.50
Innocence of Nihilism Volume 1 HC ($29.95, hardcover) r/#1-7						30.00
Somewhere Out West Volume 2 HC ($34.95, hardcover) r/#8-14						35.00
Other People Volume 3 HC ($34.95, hardcover) r/#15-22						35.00
Volume 1-3 TPB ($11.95, softcover) 1-r/#1-4. 2-r/#5-8. 3-r/ #9-12						12.00
Volume 4-7 TPB ($14.95) 4- r/#13-16. 5- r/#17-20. 6- r/#21-24. 7-r/#25-28						15.00

NOTE: *Multiple printings of most issues exist & are worth cover price.*

STRAY TOASTERS
Marvel Comics (Epic Comics): Jan, 1988 - No. 4, April, 1989 ($3.50, squarebound, limited series)

	GD	VG	FN	VF	VF/NM	NM-
1-4: Sienkiewicz-c/a/scripts						3.50

STREET COMIX
Street Enterprises/King Features: 1973 (50¢, B&W, 36 pgs.)(20,000 print run)

	GD	VG	FN	VF	VF/NM	NM-
1-Rip Kirby	2	4	6	9	11	14
2-Flash Gordon	2	4	6	11	14	18

STREETFIGHTER
Ocean Comics: Aug, 1986 - No. 4, Spr, 1987 ($1.75, limited series)

	GD	VG	FN	VF	VF/NM	NM-
1-4: 2-Origin begins						3.00

STREET FIGHTER
Malibu Comics: Sept, 1993 - No. 3, Nov, 1993 ($2.95)

	GD	VG	FN	VF	VF/NM	NM-
1-3: 3-Includes poster; Ferret x-over						3.00

STREET FIGHTER
Image Comics: Sept, 2003 - Present ($2.95)

	GD	VG	FN	VF	VF/NM	NM-
1-Back-up story w/Madureira-a; covers by Madureira and Tsang						3.00
2-6,8-11: 2-Two covers by Campbell and Warren; back-up story w/Warren-a						3.00
7-($4.50) Larocca-c						4.50
... Vol. 1 (3/04, $9.99, digest-size) r/main stories from #1-6						10.00

STREET FIGHTER: THE BATTLE FOR SHADALOO
DC Comics/CAP Co. Ltd.: 1995 ($3.95, one-shot)

	GD	VG	FN	VF	VF/NM	NM-
1-Polybagged w/trading card & Tattoo						4.00

STREET FIGHTER II
Tokuma Comics (Viz): Apr, 1994 - No. 8, Nov, 1994 ($2.95, limited series)

	GD	VG	FN	VF	VF/NM	NM-
1-8						3.00

STREET POET RAY
Blackthorne Publ./Marvel Comics: Spring, 1989; 1990 - No. 4, 1990 ($2.95, B&W, squarebound)

	GD	VG	FN	VF	VF/NM	NM-
1 (Blackthorne, $2.00)						3.00
1-4 (Marvel, $2.95, thick-c & paper)						3.00

STREETS
DC Comics: 1993 - No. 3, 1993 ($4.95, limited series, 52 pgs.)

	GD	VG	FN	VF	VF/NM	NM-
Book 1-3-Estes painted-c						5.00

STREET SHARKS
Archie Publications: Jan, 1996 - No. 3, Mar, 1996 ($1.50, limited series)

Stryke Force V2#1 © TCOW

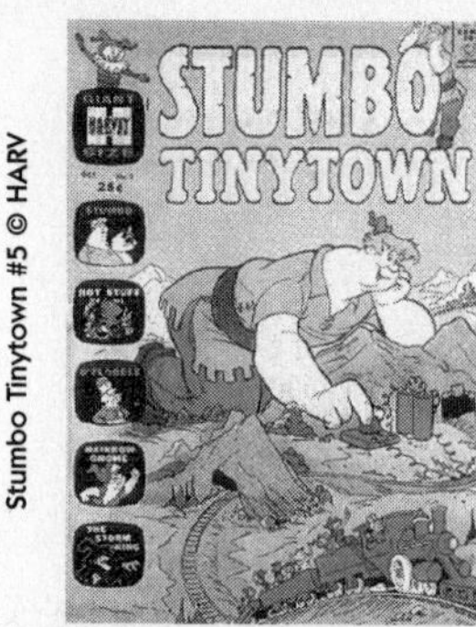

Stumbo Tinytown #5 © HARV

Sub-Mariner #6 © MAR

	GD	VG	FN	VF	VF/NM	NM-
	2.0	4.0	6.0	8.0	9.0	9.2

1-3 2.25

STREET SHARKS
Archie Publications: May, 1996 - No. 6 ($1.50, published 8 times a year)

1-6 2.25

STRICTLY PRIVATE (You're in the Army Now)
Eastern Color Printing Co.: July, 1942 (#1 on sale 6/15/42)

1,2: Private Peter Plink. 2-Says 128 pgs. on-c 24 48 72 135 195 255

STRIKE!
Eclipse Comics: Aug, 1987 - No. 6, Jan, 1988 ($1.75)

1-6, ...Vs. Sgt. Strike Special 1 (5/88, $1.95) 2.25

STRIKEBACK! (The Hunt For Nikita)
Malibu Comics (Bravura): Oct, 1994 - No. 3, Jan, 1995 ($2.95, unfinished limited series)

1-3: Jonathon Peterson script, Kevin Maguire-c/a 3.00
1-Gold foil embossed-c 5.00

STRIKEBACK!
Image Comics (WildStorm Productions): Jan, 1996 - No. 5, May, 1996 ($2.50, limited series)

1-5: Reprints original Bravura series w/additional story & art by Kevin Maguire & Jonathon Peterson; new Maguire-c in all. 4,5-New story & art 2.50

STRIKEFORCE: AMERICA
Comico: Dec, 1995 ($2.95)

V2#1-Polybagged w/gaming card; S. Clark-a(p) 3.00

STRIKEFORCE: MORITURI
Marvel Comics Group: Dec, 1986 - No. 31, July, 1989

1-31: 14-Williamson-i. 13-Double size. 25-Heath-c 2.25

STRIKEFORCE MORITURI: ELECTRIC UNDERTOW
Marvel Comics: Dec, 1989 - No. 5, Mar, 1990 ($3.95, 52 pgs., limited series)

1-5 Squarebound 4.00

STRONG GUY REBORN (See X-Factor)
Marvel Comics: Sept, 1997 ($2.99, one-shot)

1-Dezago-s/Andy Smith, Art Thibert-a 3.00

STRONG MAN (Also see Complimentary Comics & Power of...)
Magazine Enterprises: Mar-Apr, 1955 - No. 4, Sept-Oct, 1955

1(A-1 #130)-Powell-c/a 24 48 72 138 199 260
2-4: (A-1 #132,134,139)-Powell-a. 2-Powell-c 19 38 57 107 154 200

STRONTIUM DOG
Eagle Comics: Dec, 1985 - No. 4, Mar, 1986 ($1.25, limited series)

1-4, Special 1: 4-Moore script. Special 1 (1986)-Moore script 2.25

STRYFE'S STRIKE FILE
Marvel Comics: Jan, 1993 ($1.75, one-shot, no ads)

1-Stroman, Capullo, Andy Kubert, Brandon Peterson-a; silver metallic ink-c; X-Men tie-in to X-Cutioner's Song 3.00
1-Gold metallic ink 2nd printing 2.25

STRYKEFORCE
Image Comics (Top Cow): May, 2004 - No. 5, Oct, 2004 ($2.99)

1-5-Faerber-s/Kirkham-a. 4,5-Preview of HumanKind 3.00

STUCK RUBBER BABY
DC Comics (Paradox Press): 1998 (Graphic novel)

Hardcover ($24.95) 25.00
Softcover ($13.95) 14.00

STUMBO THE GIANT (See Harvey Hits #49,54,57,60,63,66,69,72,78,88 & Hot Stuff #2)

STUMBO TINYTOWN
Harvey Publications: Oct, 1963 - No. 13, Nov, 1966 (All 25¢ giants)

1-Stumbo, Hot Stuff & others begin 15 30 45 107 164 220
2 10 20 30 70 100 130
3-5 8 16 24 53 74 95
6-13 6 12 18 43 59 75

STUNT DAWGS
Harvey Comics: Mar, 1993 ($1.25, one-shot)

1 2.25

STUNTMAN COMICS (Also see Thrills Of Tomorrow)
Harvey Publ.: Apr-May, 1946 - No. 2, June-July, 1946; No. 3, Oct-Nov, 1946

1-Origin Stuntman by S&K reprinted in Black Cat #9; S&K-c
115 230 345 719 1110 1500

	GD	VG	FN	VF	VF/NM	NM-
	2.0	4.0	6.0	8.0	9.0	9.2

2-S&K-c/a; The Duke of Broadway story 69 138 207 431 666 900
3-Small size (5-1/2x8-1/2"; B&W; 32 pgs.); distributed to mail subscribers only; S&K-a; Kid Adonis by S&K reprinted in Green Hornet #37
73 146 219 456 703 950
(Also see All-New #15, Boy Explorers #2, Flash Gordon #5 & Thrills of Tomorrow)

STUPID COMICS (Also see 40 oz. Collected)
Oni Press/Image Comics: July, 2000; Sept, 2002; Oct, 2003 ($2.95, B&W)

1-(Oni Press, 7/00) Jim Mahfood 1 page satire strips reprinted from JAVA magazine 3.00
1,2-(Image Comics, 9/02; 10/03) Jim Mahfood 1 page and 2 page satire strips 3.00

STUPID HEROES
Mirage Studios: Sept, 1993 - No. 3, Dec, 1994 ($2.75, unfinished limited series)

1-3-Laird-c/a & scripts; 2 trading cards bound in 2.75

STUPID, STUPID RAT TAILS (See Bone)
Cartoon Books: Dec, 1999 - No. 3, Feb, 2000 ($2.95, limited series)

1-3-Jeff Smith-a/Tom Sniegoski-s 3.00

STYGMATA
Entity Comics: No. 0, July, 1994 - No. 3, Oct, 1994 ($2.95, B&W, limited series)

0, 1-3: 0,1-Foil-c. 3-Silver foil logo 3.00
Yearbook 1 (1995, $2.95) 3.00

SUBHUMAN
Dark Horse Comics: Nov, 1998 - No. 4, Feb, 1999 ($2.95, limited series)

1-4-Mark Schultz-c 3.00

SUBMARINE ATTACK (Formerly Speed Demons)
Charlton Comics: No. 11, May, 1958 - No. 54, Feb-Mar, 1966

11 4 8 12 29 40 50
12-20 3 7 10 21 28 35
21-30 3 6 9 18 24 30
31-54 3 6 9 16 20 24

NOTE: ***Glanzman*** *c/a-25.* ***Montes/Bache*** *a-38, 40, 41.*

SUB-MARINER (See All-Select, All-Winners, Blonde Phantom, Daring, The Defenders, Fantastic Four #4, Human Torch, The Invaders, Iron Man &..., Marvel Mystery, Marvel Spotlight #27, Men's Adventures, Motion Picture Funnies Weekly, Namora, Namor, The..., Prince Namor, The Sub-Mariner, Saga Of The..., Tales to Astonish #70 & 2nd series, USA & Young Men)

SUB-MARINER, THE (2nd Series)(Sub-Mariner #31 on)
Marvel Comics Group: May, 1968 - No. 72, Sept, 1974 (No. 43: 52 pgs.)

1-Origin Sub-Mariner; story continued from Iron Man & Sub-Mariner #1
17 34 51 121 186 250
2-Triton app. 8 16 24 55 78 100
3-5: 5-1st Tiger Shark (9/68) 6 12 18 43 59 75
6,7,9,10: 6-Tiger Shark-c & 2nd app., cont'd from #5. 7-Photo-c. (1968). 9-1st app. Serpent Crown (origin in #10 & 12) 5 10 15 33 44 55
8-Sub-Mariner vs. Thing 9 18 27 63 89 115
8-2nd printing (1994) 2 4 6 8 10 12
11-13,15: 15-Last 12¢ issue 4 8 12 25 33 42
14-Sub-Mariner vs. G.A. Human Torch; death of Toro (1st modern app. & only app. Toro, 6/69)
5 10 15 36 48 60
16-20: 19-1st Sting Ray (11/69); Stan Lee, Romita, Heck, Thomas, Everett & Kirby cameos. 20-Dr. Doom app. 3 6 9 18 23 28
21,23-33,37-39,41,42: 25-Origin Atlantis. 30-Capt. Marvel x-over. 37-Death of Lady Dorma. 38-Origin retold. 42-Last 15¢ issue. 2 4 6 14 18 22
22,40: 22-Dr. Strange x-over. 40-Spider-Man x-over 3 6 9 16 20 24
34-Prelude (w/#35) to 1st Defenders story; Hulk & Silver Surfer x-over
7 14 21 50 68 85
35-Namor/Hulk/Silver Surfer team-up to battle The Avengers-c/story (3/71); hints at teaming up again 6 12 18 38 52 65
36-Wrightson-a(i) 3 6 9 18 23 28
43-King Size Special (52 pgs.) 3 6 9 18 23 28
44,45-Sub-Mariner vs. Human Torch 3 6 9 16 20 25
46-49,56,62,64-72: 47,48-Dr. Doom app. 49-Cosmic Cube story. 62-1st Tales of Atlantis, ends #66. 64-Hitler cameo. 67-New costume; F.F. x-over. 69-Spider-Man x-over (6 panels)
1 3 4 6 8 10
50-1st app. Nita, Namor's niece (later Namorita in New Warriors)
2 4 6 10 12 15
51-55,57,58,60,61,63-Everett issues: 61-Last artwork by Everett; 1st 4 pgs. completed by Mortimer; pgs. 5-20 by Mooney 2 4 6 9 11 14
59-1st battle with Thor; Everett-a 3 6 9 16 20 25
Special 1 (1/71)-r/Tales to Astonish #70-73 3 6 9 18 24 30
Special 2 (1/72)-(52 pgs.)-r/T.T.A. #74-76; Everett-a 2 4 6 14 18 22

NOTE: ***Bolle*** *a-67i.* ***Buscema*** *a(p)-1-8, 20, 24.* ***Colan*** *a(p)-10, 11, 40, 43, 46-49, Special 1, 2; c(p)-10, 11, 40.* ***Craig*** *a-17i, 19-23i.* ***Everett*** *a-45r, 50-55, 57, 58, 59-61(plot), 63(plot); c-47, 48i, 55, 57-59i, 61, Spec. 2.* ***G. Kane*** *c(p)-42-52, 58, 66, 70, 71.* ***Mooney*** *a-24i, 25i, 32-35i, 39i, 42i, 44i, 45i, 60i, 61i, 65p, 66p, 68i.* ***Severin*** *c/a-38i.*

Sub-Mariner Comics #1 © MAR

Suicide Squad ('03) #1 © DC

Sunfire & Big Hero Six #1 © MAR

	GD 2.0	VG 4.0	FN 6.0	VF 8.0	VF/NM 9.0	NM- 9.2

*Starlin c-59p. **Tuska** a-41p, 42p, 69-71p. **Wrightson** a-36i. #53, 54-r/stories Sub-Mariner Comics #41 & 39.*

SUB-MARINER COMICS (1st Series) (The Sub-Mariner #1, 2, 33-42)(Official True Crime Cases #24 on; Amazing Mysteries #32 on; Best Love #33 on)
Timely/Marvel Comics (TCI 1-7/SePI 8/MPI 9-32/Atlas Comics (CCC 33-42)): Spring, 1941 - No. 23, Sum, 1947; No. 24, Wint, 1947 - No. 31, 4/49; No. 32, 7/49; No. 33, 4/54 - No. 42, 10/55

	GD	VG	FN	VF	VF/NM	NM-
1-The Sub-Mariner by Everett & The Angel begin	2650	5300	7950	21,200	35,600	50,000
2-Everett-a	529	1058	1587	3703	4952	8200
3-Churchill assassination-c; 40 pg. S-M story	423	846	1269	2790	4495	6200
4-Everett-a, 40 pgs.; 1 pg. Wolverton-a	338	676	1014	2197	3549	4900
5-Gabrielle/Klein-c	281	562	843	1756	2703	3650
6-10: 9-Wolverton-a, 3 pgs.; flag-c	242	484	726	1513	2332	3150
11-Classic Schomburg-c	238	476	714	1488	2294	3100
12-15	173	346	519	1081	1666	2250
16-20	140	280	420	875	1350	1825
21-Last Angel; Everett-a	108	216	324	675	1038	1400
22-Young Allies app.	108	216	324	675	1038	1400
23-The Human Torch, Namora x-over (Sum/47); 2nd app. Namora after Marvel Mystery #82	127	254	381	794	1222	1650
24-Namora x-over (3rd app.)	108	216	324	675	1038	1400
25-The Blonde Phantom begins (Spr/48), ends No. 31; Kurtzman-a; Namora x-over; last quarterly issue	131	262	393	819	1260	1700
26-28: 28-Namora cover; Everett-a	108	216	324	675	1038	1400
29-31 (4/49): 29-The Human Torch app. 31-Capt. America app.	108	216	324	675	1038	1400
32 (7/49, Scarce)-Origin Sub-Mariner	162	324	486	1013	1557	2100
33 (4/54)-Origin Sub-Mariner; The Human Torch app.; Namora x-over in Sub-Mariner #33-42	98	196	294	613	944	1275
34,35-Human Torch in each	77	154	231	481	741	1000
36,37,39-41: 36,39-41-Namora app.	75	150	225	469	722	975
38-Origin Sub-Mariner's wings; Namora app.; last pre-code (2/55)	85	170	255	531	816	1100
42-Last issue	87	174	261	544	835	1125

NOTE: *Angel by **Gustavson**-#1, 8. **Brodsky** c-34-36, 42. **Everett** a-1-4, 22-24, 26-42; c-32, 33, 40. **Maneely** a-38; c-37, 39-41. **Rico** c-27-31. **Schomburg** c-1-4, 6, 8-18, 20. **Sekowsky** c-24. 25, 26(w/**Rico**). **Shores** c-21-23, 38. Bondage c-13, 22, 24, 25, 34.*

SUBSPECIES
Eternity Comics: May, 1991 - No. 4, Aug, 1991 ($2.50, limited series)

	GD	VG	FN	VF	VF/NM	NM-
1-4: New stories based on horror movie						2.50

SUBTLE VIOLENTS
CFD Productions: 1991 ($2.50, B&W, mature)

	GD	VG	FN	VF	VF/NM	NM-
1-Linsner-c & story	1	3	4	8	10	12
San Diego Limited Edition	4	8	12	29	40	50

SUE & SALLY SMITH (Formerly My Secret Life)
Charlton Comics: V2#48, Nov, 1962 - No. 54, Nov, 1963 (Flying Nurses)

	GD	VG	FN	VF	VF/NM	NM-
V2#48	3	6	9	18	24	30
49-54	2	4	6	12	16	20

SUGAR & SPIKE (Also see The Best of DC & DC Silver Age Classics)
National Periodical Publications: Apr-May, 1956 - No. 98, Oct-Nov, 1971

	GD	VG	FN	VF	VF/NM	NM-
1 (Scarce)	277	554	831	1731	2666	3600
2	96	192	288	600	925	1250
3-5: 3-Letter column begins	67	134	201	419	647	875
6-10	42	84	126	256	391	525
11-20	38	76	114	219	320	420
21-29: 26-Christmas-c	26	52	78	147	211	275
30-Scribbly & Scribbly, Jr. x-over	27	54	81	152	219	285
31-40	15	30	45	105	160	215
41-60	10	20	30	67	96	125
61-80: 69-1st app. Tornado-Tot-c/story. 72-Origin & 1st app. Bernie the Brain	8	16	24	53	74	95
81-84,86-95: 84-Bernie the Brain apps. as Superman in 1 panel (9/69)	6	12	18	43	59	75
85 (68 pgs.)-r/#72	7	14	21	50	68	85
96 (68 pgs.)	8	16	24	53	74	95
97,98 (52 pgs.)	7	14	21	50	68	85
No. 1 Replica Edition (2002, $2.95) reprint of #1						3.00

NOTE: *All written and drawn by **Sheldon Mayer**.*

SUGAR BOWL COMICS (Teen-age)
Famous Funnies: May, 1948 - No. 5, Jan, 1949

	GD	VG	FN	VF	VF/NM	NM-
1-Toth-c/a	15	30	45	86	123	160
2,4,5	9	18	27	52	66	80
3-Toth-a	10	20	30	58	77	95

SUGARFOOT (TV)
Dell Publishing Co.: No. 907, May, 1958 - No. 1209, Oct-Dec, 1961

	GD	VG	FN	VF	VF/NM	NM-
Four Color 907 (#1)-Toth-a, photo-c	14	28	42	97	149	200
Four Color 992 (5-7/59), Toth-a, photo-c	13	26	39	90	138	185
Four Color 1059 (11-1/60), 1098 (5-7/60), 1147 (11-1/61), 1209-all photo-c	10	20	30	70	100	130

SUICIDE SQUAD (See Brave & the Bold and Doom Patrol & Suicide Squad Spec., Legends #3 & note under Star Spangled War stories)
DC Comics: May, 1987 - No. 66, June, 1992 (Direct sales only #32 on)

	GD	VG	FN	VF	VF/NM	NM-
1-66: 9-Millennium x-over. 10-Batman-c/story. 13-JLI app. (Batman). 16-Re-intro Shade The Changing Man. 23-1st Oracle. 27-34,36,37-Snyder-a. 40-43-"The Phoenix Gambit" Batman storyline. 40-Free Batman/Suicide Squad poster						2.25
Annual 1 (1988, $1.50)-Manhunter x-over						2.25

NOTE: *Chaykin c-1.*

SUICIDE SQUAD (2nd series)
DC Comics: Nov, 2001 - No. 12, Oct, 2002 ($2.50)

	GD	VG	FN	VF	VF/NM	NM-
1-12-Giffen-s/Medina-a; Sgt. Rock app. 4-Heath-a. 10-J. Severin-a. 12-JSA app.						2.50

SUMMER FUN (See Dell Giants)

SUMMER FUN (Formerly Li'l Genius; Holiday Surprise #55)
Charlton Comics: No. 54, Oct, 1966 (Giant)

	GD	VG	FN	VF	VF/NM	NM-
54	4	8	12	27	36	45

SUMMER FUN (Walt Disney's...)
Disney Comics: Summer, 1991 ($2.95, annual, 68 pgs.)

	GD	VG	FN	VF	VF/NM	NM-
1-D. Duck, M. Mouse, Brer Rabbit, Chip 'n' Dale & Pluto, Li'l Bad Wolf, Super Goof, Scamp stories						4.00

SUMMER LOVE (Formerly Brides in Love?)
Charlton Comics: V2#46, Oct, 1965; V2#47, Oct, 1966; V2#48, Nov, 1968

	GD	VG	FN	VF	VF/NM	NM-
V2#46-Beatles-c & 8 pg. story	14	28	42	97	149	200
47-(68 pgs.) Beatles-c & 12 pg. story	11	22	33	77	114	150
48	3	6	9	16	20	24

SUMMER MAGIC (See Movie Comics)

SUNDANCE (See Hotel Deparee...)

SUNDANCE KID (Also see Blazing Six-Guns)
Skywald Publications: June, 1971 - No. 3, Sept, 1971 (52 pgs.)(Pre-code reprints & new-s)

	GD	VG	FN	VF	VF/NM	NM-
1-Durango Kid; Two Kirby Bullseye-r	3	6	9	16	20	24
2,3: 2-Swift Arrow, Durango Kid, Bullseye by S&K; Meskin plus 1 pg. origin. 3-Durango Kid, Billy the Kid, Red Hawk-r	2	4	6	10	13	16

SUNDAY PIX (Christian religious)
David C. Cook Pub/USA Weekly Newsprint Color Comics: V1#1, Mar,1949 - V16#26, July 19, 1964 (7x10", 12 pgs., mail subscription only)

	GD	VG	FN	VF	VF/NM	NM-
V1#1	7	14	21	37	46	55
V1#2-up	5	10	15	24	30	35
V2#1-52 (1950)	5	10	15	22	26	30
V3-V6 (1951-1953)	4	8	12	17	21	24
V7-V11#1-7,23-52 (1954-1959)	2	4	6	12	16	20
V11#8-22 (2/22-5/31/59) H.G. Wells First Men in the Moon serial	2	4	6	14	18	22
V12#1-19,21-52; V13-V15#1,2,9-52; V16#1-26(7/19/64)	2	4	6	10	13	16
V12#20 (5/15/60) 2 page interview with Peanuts' Charles Schulz	4	8	12	27	36	45
V15#3-8 (2/24/63) John Glenn, Christian astronaut	2	4	6	14	18	22

SUN DEVILS
DC Comics: July, 1984 - No. 12, June, 1985 ($1.25, maxi series)

	GD	VG	FN	VF	VF/NM	NM-
1-12: 6-Death of Sun Devil						2.25

SUNDIATA: A LEGEND OF AFRICA
NBM Publishing Inc.: 2002 ($15.95, hardcover with dustjacket)

	GD	VG	FN	VF	VF/NM	NM-
nn-Will Eisner-s/a; adaptation of an African folk tale						16.00

SUN FUN KOMIKS
Sun Publications: 1939 (15¢, B&W & red)

	GD	VG	FN	VF	VF/NM	NM-
1-Satire on comics	33	66	99	190	275	360

SUNFIRE & BIG HERO SIX (See Alpha Flight)
Marvel Comics: Sept, 1998 - No. 3, Nov, 1998 ($2.50, limited series)

Sun Girl #1 © MAR

Superboy #182 © DC

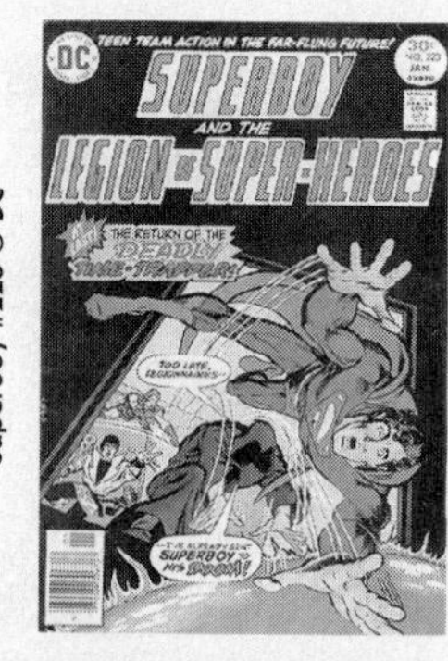

Superboy #223 © DC

GD VG FN VF VF/NM NM-
2.0 4.0 6.0 8.0 9.0 9.2

1-3-Lobdell-s 2.50

SUN GIRL (See The Human Torch & Marvel Mystery Comics #88)
Marvel Comics (CCC): Aug, 1948 - No. 3, Dec, 1948

1-Sun Girl begins; Miss America app. 162 324 486 1013 1557 2100
2,3: 2-The Blonde Phantom begins 115 230 345 719 1110 1500

SUNGLASSES
Verotik: Nov, 1995 - No. 6, Nov, 1996 ($2.95, limited series, mature)

1-5: Nancy Collins scripts; adapt. of "Sunglasses after Dark" 3.00
6-($3.95) 4.00

SUNNY, AMERICA'S SWEETHEART (Formerly Cosmo Cat #1-10)
Fox Features Syndicate: No. 11, Dec, 1947 - No. 14, June, 1948

11-Feldstein-c/a 85 170 255 531 816 1100
12-14-Feldstein-c/a; 14-Lingerie panels 65 130 195 406 628 850
I.W. Reprint #8-Feldstein-a; r/Fox issue 12 24 36 86 131 175

SUN-RUNNERS (Also see Tales of the...)
Pacific Comics/Eclipse Comics/Amazing Comics: 2/84 - No. 3, 5/84; No. 4, 11/84 - No. 7, 1986 (Baxter paper)

1-7: P. Smith-a in #2-4 2.25
Christmas Special 1 (1987, $1.95)-By Amazing 2.25

SUNSET CARSON (Also see Cowboy Western)
Charlton Comics: Feb, 1951 - No. 4, 1951 (No month) (Photo-c on each)

1-Photo/retouched-c (Scarce, all issues) 87 174 261 544 835 1125
2-Kit Carson story; adapts "Kansas Raiders" w/Brian Donlevy, Audie Murphy & Margaret Chapman 62 124 186 388 594 800
3,4 48 96 144 293 447 600

SUNSET PASS (See Zane Grey & 4-Color #230)

SUPER ANIMALS PRESENTS PIDGY & THE MAGIC GLASSES
Star Publications: Dec, 1953 (25¢, came w/glasses)

1-(3-D Comics)-L. B. Cole-c 42 84 126 256 391 525

SUPERBOY (See Adventure, Aurora, DC Comics Presents, DC 100 Page Super Spectacular #15, DC Super Stars, 80 Page Giant #10, More Fun Comics, The New Advs. of... & Superman Family #191, Young Justice)

SUPERBOY (1st Series)(...& the Legion of Super-Heroes with #231)
(Becomes The Legion of Super-Heroes No. 259 on)
National Periodical Publications/DC Comics: Mar-Apr, 1949 - No. 258, Dec, 1979 (#1-16: 52 pgs.)

1-Superman cover; intro in More Fun #101 (1-2/45)
774 1548 2322 5418 8709 12,000
2-Used in **SOTI**, pg. 35-36,226 212 424 636 1325 2038 2750
3 162 324 486 1013 1557 2100
4,5: 5-1st pre-Supergirl tryout (c/story, 11-12/49) 108 216 324 675 1038 1400
6-10: 8-1st Superbaby. 10-1st app. Lana Lang 94 188 282 588 907 1225
11-15 73 146 219 456 703 950
16-20: 20-2nd Jor-El cover 50 100 150 305 465 625
21-26,28-30: 21-Lana Lang app. 40 80 120 239 357 475
27-Low distribution 40 80 120 244 372 500
31-38: 38-Last pre-code issue (1/55) 35 70 105 201 293 385
39-48,50 (7/56) 31 62 93 177 256 335
49 (6/56)-1st app. Metallo (Jor-El's robot) 33 66 99 190 275 360
51-60: 52-1st S.A. issue. 56-Krypto-c 22 44 66 123 177 230
61-67 18 36 54 100 143 185
68-Origin/1st app. original Bizarro (10-11/58) 56 112 168 350 538 725
69-77,79: 76-1st Supermonkey 14 28 42 81 113 145
78-Origin Mr. Mxyzptlk & Superboy's costume 22 44 66 127 184 240
80-1st meeting Superboy/Supergirl (4/60) 20 40 60 112 161 210
81,83-85,87,88: 83-Origin/1st app. Kryptonite Kid 10 20 30 72 104 135
82-1st Bizarro Krypto 11 22 33 75 110 145
86-(1/61)-4th Legion app; Intro Pete Ross 18 36 54 131 201 270
89-(6/61)-1st app. Mon-el; 2nd Phantom Zone 28 56 84 199 305 410
90-92: 90-Pete Ross learns Superboy's I.D. 92-Last 10¢ issue
10 20 30 72 104 135
93-10th Legion app.(12/61); Chameleon Boy app. 11 22 33 75 110 145
94-97,99 8 16 24 58 82 105
98-(7/62)-18th Legion app; origin & 1st app. Ultra Boy; Pete Ross joins Legion
11 22 33 80 120 160
100-(10/62)-Ultra Boy app; 1st app. Phantom Zone villains, Dr. Xadu & Erndine. 2 pg. map of Krypton; origin Superboy retold; r-cover of Superman #1
19 38 57 134 205 275
101-120: 104-Origin Phantom Zone. 115-Atomic bomb-c. 117-Legion app.
7 14 21 51 70 90

GD VG FN VF VF/NM NM-
2.0 4.0 6.0 8.0 9.0 9.2

121-128: 124-(10/65)-1st app. Insect Queen (Lana Lang). 125-Legion cameo. 126-Origin Krypto the Super Dog retold with new facts 7 14 21 46 63 80
129-(80-pg. Giant G-22)-Reprints origin Mon-el 9 18 27 60 85 110
130-137,139,140: 131-Legion statues cameo in Dog Legionnaires story. 132-1st app. Supremo. 133-Superboy meets Robin 6 12 18 38 52 65
138 (80-pg. Giant G-35) 7 14 21 50 68 85
141-146,148-155,157: 145-Superboy's parents regain their youth. 148-Legion app. 157-Last 12¢ issue 4 8 12 27 36 45
147(6/68)-Giant G-47; 1st origin of L.S.H. (Saturn Girl, Lightning Lad, Cosmic Boy); origin Legion of Super-Pets-r/Adv. #293 6 12 18 40 55 70
147 Replica Edition (2003, $6.95) reprints entire issue; cover recreation by Ordway 7.00
156,165,174 (Giants G-59,71,83): 165-r/1st app. Krypto the Superdog from Adventure Comics #210 4 8 12 29 40 50
158-164,166-171,175: 171-1st app. Aquaboy 3 6 9 18 23 28
172,173,176-Legion app.: 172-Origin Yango (Super Ape). 176-Partial photo-c; last 15¢ issue
3 6 9 18 24 30
177-184,186,187 (All 52 pgs.): 182-All new origin of the classic World's Finest team (Superman & Batman) as teenagers (2/72, 22pgs). 184-Origin Dial H for Hero-r
3 6 9 19 25 32
185-Also listed as DC 100 Pg. Super Spectacular #12; Legion-c/story; Teen Titans, Kid Eternity(r/Hit #46), Star Spangled Kid-r(S.S. #55)
(see DC 100 Pg. Super Spectacular #12 for price)
188-190,192,194,196: 188-Origin Karkan. 196-Last Superboy solo story
2 4 6 10 13 16
191,193,195: 191-Origin Sunboy retold; Legion app. 193-Chameleon Boy & Shrinking Violet get new costumes. 195-1st app. Erg-1/Wildfire; Phantom Girl gets new costume
2 4 6 11 14 18
197-Legion series begins; Lightning Lad's new costume
3 7 10 21 28 35
198,199: 198-Element Lad & Princess Projectra get new costumes
2 4 6 14 18 22
200-Bouncing Boy & Duo Damsel marry; J'onn J'onzz cameo
3 6 9 16 21 26
201,204,206,207,209: 201-Re-intro Erg-1 as Wildfire. 204-Supergirl resigns fromLegion. 206-Ferro Lad & Invisible Kid app. 209-Karate Kid gets new costume
2 4 6 11 14 18
202,205-(100 pgs.): 202-Light Lass gets new costume; Mike Grell's 1st comic work-i (5-6/74)
5 10 15 36 48 60
203-Invisible Kid killed by Validus 3 6 9 16 21 26
208,210: 208-(68 pgs.). 208-Legion of Super-Villains app. 210-Origin Karate Kid
3 6 9 16 20 24
211-220: 212-Matter-Eater Lad resigns. 216-1st app. Tyroc, who joins the Legion in #218
2 4 6 9 11 14
221-230,246-249: 226-Intro. Dawnstar. 228-Death of Chemical King
1 3 4 6 8 10
231-245: (Giants). 240-Origin Dawnstar. 242-(52 pgs.). 243-Legion of Substitute Heroes app. 243-245-(44 pgs.). 2 4 6 10 13 16
244,245-(Whitman variants; low print run, no issue# shown on cover)
2 4 6 12 16 20
246-248-(Whitman variants; low ...) 2 4 6 10 12 15
250-258: 253-Intro Blok. 257-Return of Bouncing Boy & Duo Damsel by Ditko
1 2 3 5 6 8
251-258-(Whitman variants; low print run) 2 4 6 8 10 12
Annual 1 (Sum/64, 84 pgs.)-Origin Krypto-r 19 38 57 134 205 275
Spectacular 1 (1980, Giant)-1st comic distributed only through comic stores; mostly-r
1 2 3 5 7 9

NOTE: ***Neal Adams** c-143, 145, 146, 148-155, 157-161, 163, 164, 166-168, 172, 173, 175, 176, 178. **M. Anderson** a-178,179, 245i. **Ditko** a-257p. **Grell** a-202i, 203-219, 220-224p, 235p; c-207-232, 235, 236p, 237, 239p, 240p, 243p, 246, 258. **Nasser** a(p)-222, 225, 226, 230, 231, 233, 236. **Simonson** a-237p. **Starlin** a(p)-239, 250, 251; c-238. **Staton** a-227p, 243-249p, 252-258p; c-247-251p. **Swan/Moldoff** c-109. **Tuska** a-172, 173, 176, 183, 235p. **Wood** inks-153-155, 157-161. Legion app.-172, 173, 176, 177, 183, 184, 188, 190, 191, 193, 195, 197-258.*

SUPERBOY (TV)(2nd Series)(The Adventures of...#19 on)
DC Comics: Feb, 1990 - No. 22, Dec, 1991 ($1.00/$1.25)

1-22: Mooney-a(p) in 1-8,18-20; 1-Photo-c from TV show. 8-Bizarro-c/story; Arthur Adams-a(i). 9-12,14-17-Swan-p 3.00
...Special 1 (1992, $1.75) Swan-a 3.00

SUPERBOY (3rd Series)
DC Comics: Feb, 1994 - No. 100, Jul, 2002 ($1.50/$1.95/$1.99/$2.25)

1-Metropolis Kid from Reign of the Supermen 4.00
2-8,0,9-24,26-76: 6,7-Worlds Collide Pts. 3 & 8. 8-(9/94)-Zero Hour x-over. 0-(10/94). 9-(11/94)-King Shark app. 21-Legion app. 28-Supergirl-c/app. 33-Final Night. 38-41-"Meltdown". 45-Legion-c/app. 47-Green Lantern-c/app. 50-Last Boy on Earth begins. 60-Crosses Hypertime. 68-Demon-c/app. 2.50

Superboy (3rd) #62 © DC

Super Comics #10 © DELL

Super Duck Comics #18 © AP

	GD 2.0	VG 4.0	FN 6.0	VF 8.0	VF/NM 9.0	NM- 9.2
25-($2.95)-New Gods & Female Furies app.; w/pin-ups						3.50
77-99: 77-Begin $2.25-c. 79-Superboy's powers return. 80,81-Titans app. 83-New costume. 85-Batgirl app. 90,91-Our Worlds at War x-over						2.25
100-($3.50) Sienkiewicz-c; Grummett & McCrea-a; Superman cameo						3.50
#1,000,000 (11/98) 853rd Century x-over						2.50
Annual 1 (1994, $2.95, 68 pgs.)-Elseworlds story, Pt. 2 of The Super Seven (see Adventures Of Superman Annual #6)						3.00
Annual 2 (1995, $3.95)-Year One story						4.00
Annual 3 (1996, $2.95)-Legends of the Dead Earth						3.00
Annual 4 (1997, $3.95)-Pulp Heroes story						4.00
...Plus 1 (Jan, 1997, $2.95) w/Capt. Marvel Jr.						3.00
...Plus 2 (Fall, 1997, $2.95) w/Slither (Scare Tactics)						3.00
.../Risk Double-Shot 1 (Feb, 1998, $1.95) w/Risk (Teen Titans)						2.50

SUPERBOY & THE RAVERS
DC Comics: Sept, 1996 - No. 19, March, 1998 ($1.95)

	GD	VG	FN	VF	VF/NM	NM-
1-19: 4-Adam Strange app. 7-Impulse-c/app. 9-Superman-c/app.						2.50

SUPERBOY/ROBIN: WORLD'S FINEST THREE
DC Comics: 1996 - No. 2, 1996 ($4.95, squarebound, limited series)

	GD	VG	FN	VF	VF/NM	NM-
1,2: Superboy & Robin vs. Metallo & Poison Ivy; Karl Kesel & Chuck Dixon scripts; Tom Grummett-c(p)/a(p)						5.00

SUPERBOY'S LEGION (Elseworlds)
DC Comics: 2001 - No. 2, 2001 ($5.95, squarebound, limited series)

	GD	VG	FN	VF	VF/NM	NM-
1,2-31st century Superboy forms Legion; Farmer-s/i; Davis-a(p)/c						6.00

SUPER BRAT (Li'l Genius #5 on)
Toby Press: Jan, 1954 - No. 4, July, 1954

	GD	VG	FN	VF	VF/NM	NM-
1	8	16	24	43	54	65
2-4: 4-Li'l Teevy by Mel Lazarus	5	10	15	24	30	35
I.W. Reprint #1,2,3,7,8('58): 1-r/#1	2	4	6	8	10	12
I.W. (Super) Reprint #10('63)	2	4	6	8	10	12

SUPERCAR (TV)
Gold Key: Nov, 1962 - No. 4, Aug, 1963 (All painted-c)

	GD	VG	FN	VF	VF/NM	NM-
1	23	46	69	165	253	340
2,3	12	24	36	84	127	170
4-Last issue	15	30	45	107	164	220

SUPER CAT (Formerly Frisky Animals; also see Animal Crackers)
Star Publications #56-58/Ajax/Farrell Publ. (Four Star Comic Corp.):
No. 56, Nov, 1953 - No. 58, May, 1954; Aug, 1957 - No. 4, May, 1958

	GD	VG	FN	VF	VF/NM	NM-
56-58-L.B. Cole-c on all	21	42	63	118	169	220
1(1957-Ajax)- "The Adventures of..." c-only	10	20	30	56	73	90
2-4	7	14	21	35	43	50

SUPER CIRCUS (TV)
Cross Publishing Co.: Jan, 1951 - No. 5, Sept, 1951 (Mary Hartline)

	GD	VG	FN	VF	VF/NM	NM-
1-(52 pgs.)-Cast photos on-c	15	30	45	86	123	160
2-Cast photos on-c	10	20	30	58	77	95
3-5	9	18	27	51	62	75

SUPER CIRCUS (TV)
Dell Publ. Co.: No. 542, Mar, 1954 - No. 694, Mar, 1956 (Mary Hartline)

	GD	VG	FN	VF	VF/NM	NM-
Four Color 542: Mary Hartline photo-c	8	16	24	58	82	105
Four Color 592,694: Mary Hartline photo-c	8	16	24	53	74	95

SUPER COMICS
Dell Publishing Co.: May, 1938 - No. 121, Feb-Mar, 1949

	GD	VG	FN	VF	VF/NM	NM-
1-Terry & The Pirates, The Gumps, Dick Tracy, Little Orphan Annie, Little Joe, Gasoline Alley, Smilin' Jack, Smokey Stover, Smitty, Tiny Tim, Moon Mullins, Harold Teen, Winnie Winkle begin	291	582	873	1630	2365	3100
2	108	216	324	605	878	1150
3	94	188	282	526	763	1000
4,5: 4-Dick Tracy-c; also #8-10,17,26(part),31	75	150	225	420	610	800
6-10	60	120	180	336	488	640
11-20: 20-Smilin' Jack-c (also #29,32)	47	94	141	263	382	500
21-29: 21-Magic Morro begins (origin & 1st app., 2/40). 22,27-Ken Ernst-c (also #25?); Magic Morro c-22,25,27,34	38	76	113	213	307	400
30- "Sea Hawk" movie adaptation-c/story with Errol Flynn	39	78	116	218	314	410
31-40: 34-Ken Ernst-c	32	64	96	179	260	340
41-50: 41-Intro Lightning Jim. 43-Terry & The Pirates ends	27	54	81	151	218	285
51-60	20	40	60	112	161	210
61-70: 62-Flag-c. 65-Brenda Starr-r begin? 67-X-Mas-c	18	36	54	101	146	190
71-80	14	28	42	78	114	150
81-99	13	26	39	73	104	135
100	14	28	42	78	112	145
101-115-Last Dick Tracy (moves to own title)	9	18	27	50	73	95
116-121: 116,118-All Smokey Stover. 117-All Gasoline Alley. 119-121-Terry & The Pirates app. in all	8	16	24	45	63	80

SUPER COPS, THE
Red Circle Productions (Archie): July, 1974 (one-shot)

	GD	VG	FN	VF	VF/NM	NM-
1-Morrow-c/a; art by Pino, Hack, Thorne	1	3	4	6	8	10

SUPER COPS
Now Comics: Sept, 1990 - No. 4, Dec?, 1990 ($1.75)

	GD	VG	FN	VF	VF/NM	NM-
1-($2.75, 52 pgs.)-Dave Dorman painted-c (both printings)						2.75
2-4						2.25

SUPER CRACKED (See Cracked)

SUPER DC GIANT (25-50¢, all 68-52 pg. Giants)
National Per. Publ.: No. 13, 9-10/70 - No. 26, 7-8/71; V3#27, Summer, 1976 (No #1-12)

	GD	VG	FN	VF	VF/NM	NM-
S-13-Binky	11	22	33	80	120	160
S-14-Top Guns of the West; Kubert-c; Trigger Twins, Johnny Thunder, Wyoming Kid-r; Moreira-r (9-10/70)	5	10	15	36	48	60
S-15-Western Comics; Kubert-c; Pow Wow Smith, Vigilante, Buffalo Bill-r; new Gil Kane-a (9-10/70)	5	10	15	36	48	60
S-16-Best of the Brave & the Bold; Batman-r & Metamorpho origin-r from Brave & the Bold; Spectre pin-up.	4	8	12	27	36	45
S-17-Love 1970 (scarce)	25	50	75	181	278	375
S-18-Three Mouseketeers; Dizzy Dog, Doodles Duck, Bo Bunny-r; Sheldon Mayer-a	10	20	30	72	104	135
S-19-Jerry Lewis; Neal Adams pin-up	10	20	30	75	110	145
S-20-House of Mystery; N. Adams-c; Kirby-r(3)	7	14	21	50	68	85
S-21-Love 1971 (scarce)	29	58	87	218	334	450
S-22-Top Guns of the West; Kubert-c	4	8	12	24	32	40
S-23-The Unexpected	4	8	12	29	40	50
S-24-Supergirl	4	8	12	29	40	40
S-25-Challengers of the Unknown; all Kirby/Wood-r	3	7	10	22	30	38
S-26-Aquaman (1971)-r/S.A. Aquaman origin story from Showcase #30	3	7	10	22	30	38
27-Strange Flying Saucers Adventures (Sum, 1976)	3	6	9	21	28	35

NOTE: ***Sid Greene** r-27p(2), **Heath** r-27. **G. Kane** a-14r(2), 15, 27r(p). **Kubert** r-16.*

SUPER-DOOPER COMICS
Able Mfg. Co./Harvey: 1946 - No. 8, 1946 (10¢, 32 pgs., paper-c)

	GD	VG	FN	VF	VF/NM	NM-
1-The Clock, Gangbuster app.	22	44	66	127	184	240
2	14	28	42	79	110	140
3,4,6	12	24	36	69	95	120
5-Capt. Freedom	14	28	42	79	110	140
7,8-Shock Gibson. 7-Where's Theres A Will by Ed Wheelan, Steve Case Crime Rover, Penny & Ullysses Jr. 8-Sam Hill app.	14	28	42	79	110	140

SUPER DUCK COMICS (The Cockeyed Wonder) (See Jolly Jingles)
MLJ Mag. No. 1-4(9/45)/Close-Up No. 5 on (Archie): Fall, 1944 - No. 94, Dec, 1960 (Also see Laugh #24)(#1-5 are quarterly)

	GD	VG	FN	VF	VF/NM	NM-
1-Origin; Hitler & Hirohito-c	55	110	165	340	520	700
2-Bill Vigoda-c	25	50	75	141	203	265
3-5: 4-20-Al Fagaly-c (most)	17	34	51	95	135	175
6-10	14	28	42	79	110	140
11-20(6/48)	10	20	30	58	77	95
21,23-40 (10/51)	9	18	27	52	66	80
22-Used in **SOTI**, pg. 35,307,308	10	20	30	56	73	90
41-60 (2/55)	8	16	24	43	54	65
61-94	7	14	21	35	43	50

SUPER DUPER (Formerly Pocket Comics #1-4?)
Harvey Publications: No. 5, 1941 - No. 11, 1941

	GD	VG	FN	VF	VF/NM	NM-
5-Captain Freedom & Shock Gibson app.	33	66	99	190	275	360
8,11	21	42	63	118	169	220

SUPER DUPER COMICS (Formerly Latest Comics?)
F. E. Howard Publ.: No. 3, May-June, 1947

	GD	VG	FN	VF	VF/NM	NM-
3-1st app. Mr. Monster	15	30	45	86	123	160

SUPER FRIENDS (TV) (Also see Best of DC & Limited Collectors' Edition)
National Periodical Publications/DC Comics: Nov, 1976 - No. 47, Aug, 1981 (#14 is 44 pgs.)

	GD	VG	FN	VF	VF/NM	NM-
1-Superman, Batman, Robin, Wonder Woman, Aquaman, Atom, Wendy, Marvin & Wonder Dog begin (1st Super Friends)	4	8	12	24	32	40

Super Friends #18 © DC

Supergirl #79 © DC

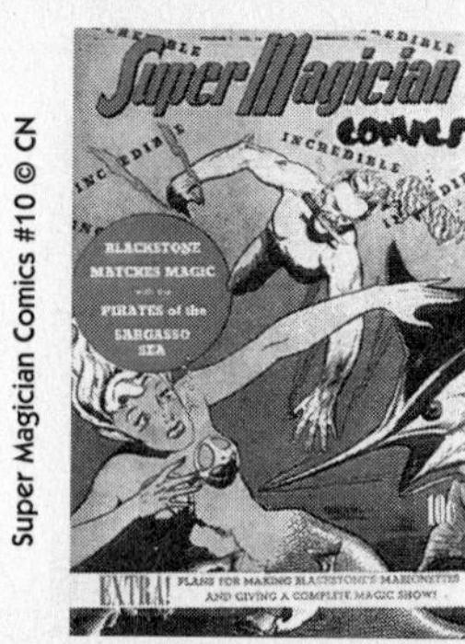

Super Magician Comics #10 © CN

GD VG FN VF VF/NM NM-
2.0 4.0 6.0 8.0 9.0 9.2

2-Penguin-c/sty 2 4 6 12 16 20
3-5 2 4 6 11 14 18
6-10,14: 7-1st app. Wonder Twins & The Seraph. 8-1st app. Jack O'Lantern. 9-1st app. Icemaiden. 14-Origin Wonder Twins 2 4 6 9 11 14
11-13,15-30: 13-1st app. Dr. Mist. 25-1st app. Fire as Green Fury. 28-Bizarro app. 1 3 4 6 8 10
13-16,20-23,25,32-(Whitman variants; low print run, no issue# on cover) 2 4 6 8 10 12
31,47: 31-Black Orchid app. 47-Origin Fire & Green Fury 2 4 6 8 10 12
32-46: 36,43-Plastic Man app. 1 2 3 5 7 9
TBP (2001, $14.95) r/#1,6-9,14,21,27 & L.C.E. C-41; Alex Ross-c 15.00
...: Truth, Justice and Peace TPB (2003, $14.95) r/#10,12,13,25,28,29,31,36,37 15.00
NOTE: *Estrada a-1p, 2p.* ***Orlando*** *a-1p.* ***Staton*** *a-43, 45.*

SUPER FUN
Gillmor Magazines: Jan, 1956 (By A.W. Nugent)
1-Comics, puzzles, cut-outs by A.W. Nugent 6 12 18 31 38 45

SUPER FUNNIES (...Western Funnies #3,4)
Superior Comics Publishers Ltd. (Canada): Dec, 1953 - No. 4, Sept, 1954
1-(3-D, 10¢)-...Presents Dopey Duck; make your own 3-D glasses cut-out inside front-c; did not come w/glasses 39 78 117 222 324 425
2-Horror & crime satire 14 28 42 79 110 140
3-Phantom Ranger-c/s; Geronimo, Billy the Kid app. 9 18 27 49 62 75
4-Phantom Ranger-c/story 9 18 27 49 62 75

SUPERGIRL (See Action, Adventure #281, Brave & the Bold, Crisis on Infinite Earths #7, Daring New Advs. of..., Super DC Giant, Superman Family, & Super-Team Family)

SUPERGIRL
National Periodical Publ.: Nov, 1972 - No. 9, Dec-Jan, 1973-74; No. 10, Sept-Oct, 1974 (1st solo title)(20¢)
1-Zatanna back-up stories begin, end #5 6 12 18 40 55 70
2-4,6,7,9 3 6 9 18 24 30
5,8,10: 5-Zatanna origin-r. 8-JLA x-over; Batman cameo. 10-Prez 3 6 9 19 25 32
NOTE: *Zatanna in #1-5, 7(Guest); Prez app. in #10. #1-10 are 20¢ issues.*

SUPERGIRL (Formerly Daring New Adventures of...)
DC Comics: No. 14, Dec, 1983 - No. 23, Sept, 1984
14-23: 16-Ambush Bug app. 20-JLA & New Teen Titans app. 3.00
...Movie Special (1985)-Adapts movie; Morrow-a; photo back-c 4.00

SUPERGIRL
DC Comics: Feb, 1994 - No. 4, May, 1994 ($1.50, limited series)
1-4: Guice-a(i) 3.00

SUPERGIRL (See Showcase '96 #8)
DC Comics: Sept, 1996 - No. 80, May, 2003 ($1.95/$1.99/$2.25/$2.50)
1-Peter David scripts & Gary Frank-c/a; DC cover logo in upper left is blue 1 2 3 5 6 8
1-2nd printing-DC cover logo in upper left is red 3.00
2,4-9: 4-Gorilla Grodd-c/app. 6-Superman-c/app. 9-Last Frank-a 4.00
3-Final Night, Gorilla Grodd app. 5.00
10-19: 14-Genesis x-over. 16-Power Girl app. 3.50
20-35: 20-Millennium Giants x-over; Superman app. 23-Steel-c/app. 24-Resurrection Man x-over. 25-Comet ID revealed; begin $1.99-c 3.00
36-46: 36,37-Young Justice x-over 2.50
47-49,51-74: 47-Begin $2.25-c. 51-Adopts costume from animated series. 54-Green Lantern app. 59-61-Our Worlds at War x-over. 62-Two-Face-c/app. 66,67-Demon-c/app. 68-74-Mary Marvel app. 70-Nauck-a. 73-Begin $2.50-c 2.50
50-($3.95) Supergirl's final battle with the Carnivore 4.00
75-80: 75-Re-intro. Kara Zor-El; cover swipe of Action #252 by Haynes; Benes-a. 78-Spectre app. 80-Last issue; Romita-c 2.50
#1,000,000 (11/98) 853rd Century x-over 3.00
Annual 1 (1996, $2.95)-Legends of the Dead Earth 3.00
Annual 2 (1997, $3.95)-Pulp Heroes; LSH app.; Chiodo-c 4.00
...: Many Happy Returns TPB (2003, $14.95) r/#75-80; intro. by Peter David 15.00
...Plus (2/97, $2.95) Capt.(Mary) Marvel-c/app.; David-s/Frank-a 3.00
.../Prysm Double-Shot 1 (Feb, 1998, $1.95) w/Prysm (Teen Titans) 2.50
...: Wings (2001, $5.95) Elseworlds; DeMatteis-s/Tolagson-a 6.00
TPB-('98, $14.95) r/Showcase '96 #8 & Supergirl #1-9 15.00

SUPERGIRL/LEX LUTHOR SPECIAL (Supergirl and Team Luthor on-c)
DC Comics: 1993 ($2.50, 68 pgs., one-shot)
1-Pin-ups by Byrne & Thibert 2.50

GD VG FN VF VF/NM NM-
2.0 4.0 6.0 8.0 9.0 9.2

SUPER GOOF (Walt Disney) (See Dynabrite & The Phantom Blot)
Gold Key No. 1-57/Whitman No. 58 on: Oct, 1965 - No. 74, July, 1984
1 5 10 15 36 48 60
2-5 3 6 9 18 24 30
6-10 3 6 9 16 20 24
11-20 2 4 6 9 11 14
21-30 1 3 4 6 8 10
31-50 1 2 3 4 5 7
51-57 6.00
58,59 (Whitman) 1 2 3 4 5 7
60(8/80), 62(11/80) 3-pack only (scarce) 3 6 9 16 20 24
61(9-10/80) 3-pack only (rare) 2 4 6 14 18 22
63-66('81) 1 2 3 5 6 8
67-69: 67(2/82), 68(2-3/82), 69(3/82) 6.00
70-74 (#90180 on-c; pre-pack, nd, nd code): 70(5/83), 71(8/83), 72(5/84), 73(6/84), 74(7/84) 2 4 6 11 14 18
NOTE: *Reprints in #16, 24, 28, 29, 37, 38, 43, 45, 46, 54(1/2), 56-58, 65(1/2), 72(r-#2).*

SUPER GREEN BERET (Tod Holton...)
Lightning Comics (Milson Publ. Co.): Apr, 1967 - No. 2, Jun, 1967
1-(25¢, 68 pgs) 5 10 15 36 48 60
2-(25¢, 68 pgs) 4 8 12 24 32 40

SUPER HEROES (See Giant-Size... & Marvel...)

SUPER HEROES
Dell Publishing Co.: Jan, 1967 - No. 4, June, 1967
1-Origin & 1st app. Fab 4 4 8 12 29 40 50
2-4 3 6 9 19 25 32

SUPER-HEROES BATTLE SUPER-GORILLAS (See DC Special #16)
National Periodical Publications: Winter, 1976 (52 pgs., all reprints, one-shot)
1-Superman, Batman, Flash stories; Infantino-a(p) 2 4 6 10 12 15

SUPER HEROES VERSUS SUPER VILLAINS
Archie Publications (Radio Comics): July, 1966 (no month given)(68 pgs.)
1-Flyman, Black Hood, Web, Shield-r; Reinman-a 7 14 21 46 63 80

SUPERHERO WOMEN, THE - FEATURING THE FABULOUS FEMALES OF MARVEL COMICS (See Fireside Book Series)

SUPERICHIE (Formerly Super Richie)
Harvey Publications: No. 5, Oct, 1976 - No. 18, Jan, 1979 (52 pgs. giants)
5-Origin/1st app. new costumes for Rippy & Crashman 2 4 6 10 13 16
6-18 2 4 6 8 10 12

SUPERIOR STORIES
Nesbit Publishers, Inc.: May-June, 1955 - No. 4, Nov-Dec, 1955
1-The Invisible Man by H.G. Wells 24 48 72 135 195 255
2-4: 2-The Pirate of the Gulf by J.H. Ingrahams. 3-Wreck of the Grosvenor by William Clark Russell. 4-The Texas Rangers by O'Henry 11 22 33 64 87 110
NOTE: ***Morisi*** *c/a in all. Kiwanis stories in #3 & 4. #4 has photo of Gene Autry on-c.*

SUPER MAGIC (Super Magician Comics #2 on)
Street & Smith Publications: May, 1941
V1#1-Blackstone the Magician-c/story; origin/1st app. Rex King (Black Fury); Charles Sultan-c; Blackstone-c begin 154 308 462 963 1482 2000

SUPER MAGICIAN COMICS (Super Magic #1)
Street & Smith Publications: No. 2, Sept, 1941 - V5#8, Feb-Mar, 1947
V1#2-Blackstone the Magician continues; Rex King, Man of Adventure app. 62 124 186 388 594 800
3-Tao-Anwar, Boy Magician begins 40 80 120 236 351 465
4-7,9-12: 4-Origin Transo. 11-Supersnipe app. 39 78 117 222 324 425
8-Abbott & Costello story (1st app?, 11/42) 40 80 120 233 342 450
V2#1-The Shadow app. 40 80 120 239 357 475
2-12: 5-Origin Tigerman. 8-Red Dragon begins 21 42 63 118 169 220
V3#1-12: 5-Origin Mr. Twilight 21 42 63 118 169 220
V4#1-12: 11-Nigel Elliman Ace of Magic begins (3/46) 17 34 51 95 135 175
V5#1-6 17 34 51 95 135 175
7,8-Red Dragon by Edd Cartier-c/a 40 80 120 233 342 450
NOTE: ***Jack Binder*** *c-1-14(most). Red Dragon c-V5#7, 8.*

SUPERMAN (See Action Comics, Advs. of..., All-New Coll. Ed., All-Star Comics, Best of DC, Brave & the Bold, Cosmic Odyssey, DC Comics Presents, Heroes Against Hunger, JLA, The Kents, Krypton Chronicles, Limited Coll. Ed., Man of Steel, Phantom Zone, Power Record Comics, Special Edition, Steel, Super Friends, Superman: The Man of Steel, Superman: The Man of Tomorrow, Taylor's Christmas Tabloid, Three-Dimension Advs., World Of Krypton, World Of Metropolis, World Of Smallville & World's Finest)

Superman #2 © DC

Superman #76 © DC

Superman #300 © DC

GD VG FN VF VF/NM NM-
2.0 4.0 6.0 8.0 9.0 9.2

SUPERMAN (Becomes Adventures of...#424 on)
National Periodical Publ./DC Comics: Summer, 1939 - No. 423, Sept, 1986
(#1-5 are quarterly)

1(nn)-1st four Action stories reprinted; origin Superman by Siegel & Shuster; has a new 2 pg. origin plus 4 pgs. omitted in Action story; see The Comics Magazine #1 & More Fun #14-17 for Superman prototype app.; cover r/splash page from Action #10; 1st pin-up Superman on back-c - 1st pin-up in comics 17,250 34,500 51,750 134,000 217,000 300,000

1-Reprint, Oversize 13-1/2x10". **WARNING:** This comic is an exact duplicate reprint of the original except for its size. DC published it in 1978 with a second cover titling it as a Famous First Edition. There have been many reported cases of the outer cover being removed and the interior sold as the original edition. The reprint with the new outer cover removed is practically worthless. See Famous First Edition for value.

2-All daily strip-r; full pg. ad for N.Y. World's Fair 1147 2294 3441 8603 14,052 19,500
3-2nd story-r from Action #5; 3rd story-r from Action #6 742 1484 2226 5194 8347 11,500
4-2nd mention of Daily Planet (Spr/40); also see Action #23; 2nd & 3rd app. Luthor (red-headed; also see Action #23) 568 1136 1704 3976 6388 8800
5-4th Luthor app. (red hair) 452 904 1356 3164 5082 7000
6,7: 6-1st splash pg. in a Superman comic. 7-1st Perry White? (11-12/40) 303 606 909 1970 3185 4400
8-10: 10-5th app. Luthor (1st bald Luthor, 5-6/41) 300 600 900 1892 2946 4000
11-13,15: 13-Jimmy Olsen & Luthor app. 231 462 693 1444 2222 3000
14-Patriotic Shield-c classic by Fred Ray 328 656 984 2132 3441 4750
16,18-20: 16-1st Lois Lane-c this title (5-6/42); 2nd Lois-c after Action #29 181 362 543 1131 1741 2350
17-Hitler, Hirohito-c 277 554 831 1731 2666 3600
21,22,25: 25-Clark Kent's only military service; Fred Ray's only super-hero story 135 270 405 844 1297 1750
23-Classic periscope-c 158 316 474 988 1519 2050
24-Classic Jack Burnley flag-c 208 416 624 1300 2000 2700
26-Classic war-c 200 400 600 1250 1925 2600
27-29: 27,29-Lois Lane-c. 28-Lois Lane Girl Reporter series begins, ends #40,42 127 254 381 794 1222 1650
28-Overseas edition for Armed Forces; same as reg. #28 127 254 381 794 1222 1650
30-Origin & 1st app. Mr. Mxyztplk (9-10/44)(pronounced "Mix-it-plk") in comic books; name later became Mxyzptlk ("Mix-yez-pit-l-ick"); the character was inspired by a combination of the name of Al Capp's Joe Blyfstyk (the little man with the black cloud over his head) & the devilish antics of Bugs Bunny; he 1st app. in newspapers 3/7/44 246 492 738 1538 2369 3200
31-40: 33-(3-4/45)-3rd app. Mxyztplk. 35,36-Lois Lane-c. 38-Atomic bomb story (1-2/46); delayed because of gov't censorship; Superman shown reading Batman #32 on cover. 40-Mxyztplk-c 106 212 318 663 1019 1375
41-50: 42-Lois Lane-c. 45-Lois Lane as Superwoman (see Action #60 for 1st app.). 46-(5-6/47)-1st app. Superboy this title? 48-1st time Superman travels thru time 85 170 255 531 816 1100
51,52: 51-Lois Lane-c 69 138 207 431 666 900
53-Third telling of Superman origin; 10th anniversary issue ('48); classic origin-c by Boring 292 584 876 1825 2813 3800
54,56-60: 57-Lois Lane as Superwoman-c. 58-Intro Tiny Trix 69 138 207 431 666 900
55-Used in **SOTI**, pg. 33 71 142 213 444 685 925
61-Origin Superman retold; origin Green Kryptonite (1st Kryptonite story); Superman returns to Krypton for 1st time & sees his parents for 1st time since infancy, discovers he's not an Earth man 142 284 426 888 1369 1850
62-70: 62-Orson Welles-c/story. 65-1st Krypton Foes: Mala, Kizo, & U-Ban. 66-2nd Superbaby story. 67-Perry Como-c/story. 68-1st Luthor-c this title (see Action Comics) 67 134 201 419 647 875
71-75: 74-2nd Luthor-c this title. 75-Some have #74 on-c 65 130 195 406 628 850
76-Batman x-over; Superman & Batman learn each other's I.D. for the 1st time (5-6/52) (also see World's Finest #71) 181 362 543 1131 1741 2350
77-81: 78-Last 52 pg. issue. 81-Used in **POP**, pg. 88 62 124 186 388 594 800
82-87,89,90: 89-1st Curt Swan-c in title 55 110 165 340 520 700
88-Prankster, Toyman & Luthor team-up 60 120 180 375 575 775
91-95: 95-Last precode issue (2/55) 48 96 144 293 447 600
96-99: 96-Mr. Mxyztplk-c/story 40 80 120 244 372 500
100 (9-10/55)-Shows cover to #1 on-c 208 416 624 1300 2000 2700
101-105,107-110: 109-1st S.A. issue 40 80 120 239 357 475
106 (7/56)-Retells origin 40 80 120 244 372 500
111-120 37 74 111 209 305 400
121,122,124-127,129: 127-Origin/1st app. Titano. 129-Intro/origin Lori Lemaris, The Mermaid 31 62 93 178 259 340
123-Pre-Supergirl tryout-c/story (8/58). 39 78 117 222 324 425
128-(4/59)-Red Kryptonite used. Bruce Wayne x-over who protects Superman's i.d. (3rd story) 33 66 99 190 275 360
130-(7/59)-2nd app, Krypto, the Superdog with Superman (see Sup.'s Pal Jimmy Olsen #29) (all other previous app. w/Superboy) 33 66 99 190 275 360
131-139: 135-2nd Lori Lemaris app. 139-Lori Lemaris app.; 25 50 75 141 203 265
140-1st Blue Kryptonite & Bizarro Supergirl; origin Bizarro Jr. #1 26 52 78 147 211 275
141-145,148: 142-2nd Batman x-over 20 40 60 115 165 215
146-(7/61)-Superman's life story; back-up hints at Earth II. Classic-c 26 52 78 150 215 280
147(8/61)-7th Legion app; 1st app. Legion of Super-Villains; 1st app. Adult Legion; swipes-c to Adv. #247 25 50 75 141 203 265
149(11/61)-8th Legion app. (cameo); "The Death of Superman" imaginary story; last 10¢ issue 22 44 66 127 184 240
150,151,153,154,157,159,160: 157-Gold Kryptonite used (see Adv. #299); Mon-el app.; Lightning Lad cameo (11/62) 10 20 30 73 107 140
152,155,156,158,162: 152(4/62)-15th Legion app. 155-(8/62)-Legion app; Lightning Man & Cosmic Man, & Adult Legion app. 156,162-Legion app. 158-1st app. Flamebird & Nightwing & Nor-Kan of Kandor(12/62) 11 22 33 75 110 145
161-1st told death of Ma and Pa Kent 11 22 33 75 110 145
161-2nd printing (1987, $1.25)-New DC logo; sold thru So Much Fun Toy Stores (cover title: Superman Classic) 3.00
163-166,168-180: 166-XMas-c. 168-All Luthor issue; JFK tribute/memorial. 169-Bizarro Invasion of Earth-c/story; last Sally Selwyn. 170-Pres. Kennedy story is finally published after delay from #168 due to assassination. 172,173-Legion cameos. 174-Super-Mxyzptlk; Bizarro app. 9 18 27 60 85 110
167-New origin Brainiac & Brainiac 5; intro Tharla (later Luthor's wife) 11 22 33 75 110 145
181,182,184-186,188-192,194-196,198,200: 181-1st 2965 story/series. 182-1st S.A. app. of The Toyman (1/66). 189-Origin/destruction of Krypton II. 7 14 21 51 71 90
183 (Giant G-18) 10 20 30 70 100 130
187,193,197 (Giants G-23,G-31,G-36) 8 16 24 58 82 105
199-1st Superman/Flash race (8/67): also see Flash #175 & World's Finest #198,199 (r-in Limited Coll. Ed. C-48) 26 52 78 187 286 385
201,203-206,208-211,213-216: 213-Brainiac-5 app. 216-Last 12¢ issue 5 10 15 36 48 60
202 (80-pg. Giant G-42)-All Bizarro issue 7 14 21 46 63 80
207,212,217 (Giants G-48,G-54,G-60): 207-30th anniversary Superman (6/68) 7 14 21 46 63 80
218-221,223-226,228-231 4 8 12 29 40 50
222,239(Giants, G-66,G-84) 6 12 18 43 59 75
227,232(Giants, G-72,G-78)-All Krypton issues 6 12 18 40 55 70
233-2nd app. Morgan Edge; Clark Kent switches from newspaper reporter to TV newscaster; all Kryptonite on earth destroyed; classic Neal Adams-c 7 14 21 51 71 90
234-238 4 8 12 27 36 45
240-Kaluta-a; last 15¢ issue 3 7 10 21 28 35
241-244 (All 52 pgs.): 241-New Wonder Woman app. 243-G.A.-r/#38 4 8 12 22 30 38
245-Also listed as DC 100 Pg. Super Spectacular #7; Air Wave, Kid Eternity, Hawkman-r; Atom-r/Atom #3 (see DC 100 Pg. Super Spectacular #7 for price)
246-248,250,251,253 (All 52 pgs.): 246-G.A.-r/#40. 248-World of Krypton story. 251-G.A.-r/#45. 253-Finlay-a, 2 pgs., G.A.-r/#1 4 8 12 22 30 38
249,254-Neal Adams-a. 249-(52 pgs.); origin & 1st app. Terra-Man by Neal Adams (inks) 5 10 15 33 44 55
252-Also listed as DC 100 Pg. Super Spectacular #13; Ray(r/Smash #17), Black Condor, (r/Crack #18), Hawkman(r/Flash #24); Starman-r/Adv. #67; Dr. Fate & Spectre-r/More Fun #57; N. Adams-c (see DC 100 Pg. Super Spectacular #13 for price)
255-271,273-277,279-283: 263-Photo-c. 264-1st app. Steve Lombard. 276-Intro Capt. Thunder. 279-Batman, Batgirl app. 2 4 6 10 12 15
272,278,284-All 100 pgs. G.A.-r in all. 272-r/2nd app. Mr. Mxyztplk from Action #80 5 10 15 33 44 55
285-299: 289-Partial photo-c. 292-Origin Lex Luthor retold 1 2 3 6 8 10
300-(6/76) Superman in the year 2001 3 6 9 19 25 32
301-350: 301,320-Solomon Grundy app. 323-Intro. Atomic Skull. 327-329-(44 pgs.). 327-Kobra app. 330-More facts revealed about I.D. 338-The bottled city of Kandor enlarged. 344-Frankenstein & Dracula app. 6.00
321-323,325-327,329-332,335-345,348,350 (Whitman variants; low print run; no issue # on cover) 1 2 3 5 7 9
351-399: 353-Brief origin. 354,355,357-Superman 2020 stories (354-Debut of Superman III). 356-World of Krypton story (also #360,367,375). 366-Fan letter by Todd McFarlane.

Superman #416 © DC

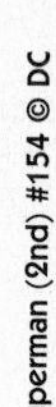

Superman (2nd) #154 © DC

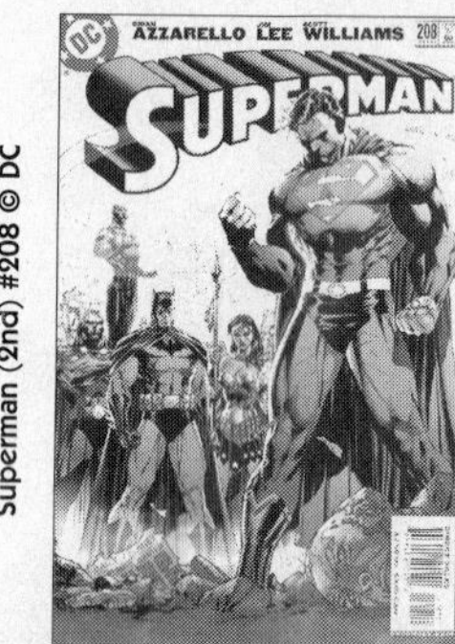

Superman (2nd) #208 © DC

GD 2.0 | VG 4.0 | FN 6.0 | VF 8.0 | VF/NM 9.0 | NM- 9.2

372-Superman 2021 story. 376-Free 16 pg. preview Daring New Advs. of Supergirl. 377-Free 16 pg. preview Masters of the Universe 5.00
400 (10/84, $1.50, 68 pgs.)-Many top artists featured; Chaykin painted cover, Miller back-c; Steranko-s/a (10 pages) 6.00
401-422: 405-Super-Batman story. 408-Nuclear Holocaust-c/story. 411-Special Julius Schwartz tribute issue. 414,415-Crisis x-over. 422-Horror-c 4.00
423-Alan Moore scripts; Perez-a(i); last Earth I Superman story, cont'd in Action #583
1 3 4 6 8 10
Annual 1(10/60, 84 pgs.)-Reprints 1st Supergirl story/Action #252; r/Lois Lane #1; Krypto-r (1st Silver Age DC annual) 86 172 258 733 1193 1650
Annual 2(Win, 1960-61)-Super-villain issue; Brainiac, Titano, Metallo, Bizarro origin-r
41 82 123 318 497 675
Annual 3(Sum, 1961)-Strange Lives of Superman 29 58 87 210 323 435
Annual 4(Win, 1961-62)-11th Legion app; 1st Legion origins (text & pictures); advs. in time, space & on alien worlds 24 48 72 170 260 350
Annual 5(Sum, 1962)-All Krypton issue 19 38 57 134 205 275
Annual 6(Win, 1962-63)-Legion-r/Adv. #247 17 34 51 121 186 250
Annual 7(Sum, 1963)-Origin-r/Superman-Batman team/Adv. 275; r/1955 Superman dailies
13 26 39 92 141 190
Annual 8(Win, 1963-64)-All origins issue 12 24 36 82 124 165
Annual 9(8/64)-Was advertised but came out as 80 Page Giant #1 instead
Annual 9(1983)-Toth/Austin-a 6.00
Annuals 10-12: 10(1984, $1.25)-M. Anderson inks. 11(1985)-Moore scripts. 12(1986)-Bolland-c 4.00
Special 1-3('83-'85): 1-G. Kane-c/a; contains German-r 4.00
The Amazing World of Superman "Official Metropolis Edition" (1973, $2.00, treasury-size)-Origin retold; Wood-r(i) from Superboy #153,161; poster incl. (half price if poster missing)
4 8 12 29 40 50
11195 (2/79, $1.95, 224 pgs.)-Golden Press 4 8 12 24 32 40

NOTE: ***N. Adams*** *a-249i, 254p; c-204-206, 210, 212-215, 219, 231i, 233-237, 240-243, 249-252, 254, 263, 307, 308, 313, 314, 317.* ***Adkins*** *a-323i.* ***Austin*** *c-368i.* ***Wayne Boring*** *art-late 1940's to early 1960's.* ***Buckler*** *a(p)-352, 363, 364, 369; c(p)-324-327, 356, 363, 368, 369, 373, 376, 378.* ***Burnley*** *a-252r; c-19-25, 30, 33, 34, 35p, 38p, 39p, 45p.* ***Fine*** *a-252r.* ***Kaluta*** *a-400.* ***Gil Kane*** *a-272r, 367, 372, 375, Special 2; c-374p, 375p, 377, 381, 382, 384-390, 392, Annual 9, Special 2.* ***Joe Kubert*** *c-216.* ***Morrow*** *a-238.* ***Mortimer*** *a-250r.* ***Perez*** *c-364p.* ***Fred Ray*** *a-25; c-6, 8-18.* ***Starlin*** *c-355.* ***Staton*** *a-354i, 355i.* ***Swan/Moldoff*** *c-149.* ***Williamson*** *a(i)-408-410, 412-416; c-408i, 409i.* ***Wrightson*** *a-400, 416.*

SUPERMAN (2nd Series)
DC Comics: Jan, 1987 - Present (75¢/$1.00/$1.25/$1.50/$1.95/$1.99)

0-(10/94) Zero Hour; released between #93 & #94 2.50
1-Byrne-c/a begins; intro new Metallo 5.00
2-8,10: 3-Legends x-over; Darkseid-c & app. 7-Origin/1st app. Rampage. 8-Legion app. 3.00
9-Joker-c 4.50
11-15,17-20,22-49,51,52,54-56,58-67: 11-1st new Mr. Mxyzptlk. 12-Lori Lemaris revived. 13-1st app. new Toyman. 13,14-Millennium x-over. 20-Doom Patrol app.; Supergirl cameo. 31-Mr. Mxyzptlk app. 37-Newsboy Legion app. 41-Lobo app. 44-Batman storyline, part 1. 45-Free extra 8 pgs. 54-Newsboy Legion story. 63-Aquaman x-over. 67-Last $1.00-c 2.50
16,21: 16-1st app. new Supergirl (4/88). 21-Supergirl-c/story; 1st app. Matrix who becomes new Supergirl 4.00
50-($1.50, 52 pgs.)-Clark Kent proposes to Lois 5.00
50-2nd printing 2.25
53-Clark reveals i.d. to Lois (Cont'd from Action #662) 3.00
53-2nd printing 2.25
57-($1.75, 52 pgs.) 3.00
68-72: 65,66,68-Deathstroke-c/stories. 70-Superman & Robin team-up 2.50
73-Doomsday cameo 5.00
74-Doomsday Pt. 2 (Cont'd from Justice League #69); Superman battles Doomsday 6.00
73,74-2nd printings 2.25
75-($2.50)-Collector's Ed.; Doomsday Pt. 6; Superman dies; polybagged w/poster of funeral, obituary from Daily Planet, postage stamp & armband premiums (direct sales only)
2 4 6 11 14 18
75-Direct sales copy (no upc code, 1st print) 1 2 3 5 6 8
75-Direct sales copy (no upc code, 2nd-4th prints) 2.25
75-Newsstand copy w/upc code 1 2 3 5 6 8
75-Platinum Edition; given away to retailers 55.00
76,77-Funeral For a Friend parts 4 & 8 3.00
78-($1.95)-Collector's Edition with die-cut outer-c & mini poster; Doomsday cameo 3.00
78-($1.50)-Newsstand Edition w/poster and different-c; Doomsday-c & cameo 2.25
79-81,83-89: 83-Funeral for a Friend epilogue; new Batman (Azrael) cameo. 87,88-Bizarro-c/story 2.50
82-($3.50)-Collector's Edition w/all chromium-c; real Superman revealed; Green Lantern x-over from G.L. #46; no ads 6.00
82-($2.00, 44 pgs.)-Regular Edition w/different-c 2.50
90-99: 93-(9/94)-Zero Hour. 94-(11/94). 95-Atom app. 96-Brainiac returns 2.50
100-Death of Clark Kent foil-c 4.00
100-Newsstand 3.00

GD 2.0 | VG 4.0 | FN 6.0 | VF 8.0 | VF/NM 9.0 | NM- 9.2

101-122: 101-Begin $1.95-c; Black Adam app. 105-Green Lantern app. 110-Plastic Man-c/app. 114-Brainiac app; Dwyer-c. 115-Lois leaves Metropolis. 116-(10/96)-1st app. Teen Titans by Jurgens & Perez in 8 pg. preview. 117-Final Night. 118-Wonder Woman app. 119-Legion app. 122-New powers 2.50
123-Collector's Edition w/glow in the dark-c, new costume 6.00
123-Standard ed., new costume 4.00
124-149: 128-Cyborg-c/app. 131-Birth of Lena Luthor. 132-Superman Red/Superman Blue. 134-Millennium Giants. 136,137-Superman 2999. 139-Starlin-a. 140-Grindberg-a 2.50
150-($2.95) Standard Ed.; Brainiac 2.0 app.; Jurgens-s 3.00
150-($3.95) Collector's Ed. w/holo-foil enhanced variant-c 4.00
151-158: 151-Loeb-s begins; Daily Planet reopens 2.25
159-174: 159-$2.25-c begin. 161-Joker-c/app. 162-Aquaman-c/app. 163-Young Justice app. 165-JLA app.; Ramos; Madureira, Liefeld, A. Adams, Wieringo, Churchill-a. 166-Collector's and reg. editions. 167-Return to Krypton. 168-Batman-c/app.(cont'd in Detective #756). 171-173-Our Worlds at War. 173-Sienkiewicz-a (2 pgs.). 174-Adopts black & red "S" logo 2.25
175-($3.50) Joker: Last Laugh x-over; Doomsday-c/app. 3.50
176-189,191-199: 176,180-Churchill-a. 180-Dracula app. 181-Bizarro-c/app. 184-Return to Krypton II. 189-Van Fleet-c. 192,193,195,197-199-New Supergirl app. 2.25
190-($2.25) Regular edition 2.25
190-($3.95) Double-Feature Issue; included reprint of Superman: The 10¢ Adventure 4.00
200-($3.50) Gene Ha-c/art by various; preview art by Yu & Bermejo 3.50
201-Mr Majestic-c/app.; cover swipe of Action #1 2.25
202,203-Godfall parts 3,6; Turner-c; Caldwell-a(p). 203-Jim Lee sketch pages 2.25
204-Jim Lee-c/a begins; Azzarello-s 3.00
204-Diamond Retailer Summit edition with sketch cover 100.00
205-211: 205-Two covers by Jim Lee and Michael Turner. 208-JLA app. 211-Battles Wonder Woman 2.50
#1,000,000 (11/98) 853rd Century x-over; Gene Ha-c 2.25
Annual 1,2: 1 (1987)-No Byrne-a. 2 (1988)-Byrne-a; Newsboy Legion; Guardian returns 4.00
Annual 3-6 ('91-'94 68 pgs.): 1-Armageddon 2001 x-over; Batman app.; Austin-c(i) & part inks. 4-Eclipso app. 6-Elseworlds sty 3.00
Annual 3-2nd & 3rd printings; 3rd has silver ink 2.25
Annual 7 (1995, $3.95, 69 pgs.)-Year One story 4.00
Annual 8 (1996, $2.95)-Legends of the Dead Earth story 3.00
Annual 9 (1997, $3.95)-Pulp Heroes story 4.00
Annual 10 (1998, $2.95)-Ghosts; Wrightson-c 3.00
Annual 11 (1999, $2.95)-JLApe; Art Adams-c 3.00
Annual 12 (2000, $3.50)-Planet DC 3.50
...: Critical Condition ('03, $14.95, TPB) r/2000 Kryptonite poisoning storyline 15.00
...: 80 Page Giant (2/99, $4.95) Jurgens-c 5.00
...: 80 Page Giant 2 (6/99, $4.95) Harris-c 5.00
...: 80 Page Giant 3 (11/00, $5.95) Nowlan-c; art by various 6.00
...: Endgame (2000, $14.95, TPB)-Reprints Y2K and Brainiac story line 15.00
...: Eradication! The Origin of the Eradicator (1996, $12.95, TPB) 13.00
...: Exile (1998, $14.95, TPB)-Reprints space exile following execution of Kryptonian criminals; 1st Eradicator 15.00
...: Godfall HC (2004, $19.95, dustjacket) r/Action #812-813, Advs. of Superman #625-626, Superman #202-203; Caldwell sketch pages; Turner cover gallery; new Turner-c 20.00
... In the Fifties ('02, $19.95, TPB) Intro. by Mark Waid 20.00
... In the Seventies ('00, $19.95, TPB) Intro. by Christopher Reeve 20.00
... No Limits ('00, $14.95, TPB) Reprints early 2000 stories 15.00
...: Our Worlds at War Book 1 ('02, $19.95, TPB) r/1st half of x-over 20.00
...: Our Worlds at War Book 2 ('02, $19.95, TPB) r/2nd half of x-over 20.00
...Plus 1(2/97, $2.95)-Legion of Super-Heroes-c/app. 3.00
...: President Lex TPB (2003, $17.95) r/Luthor's run for the White House; Harris-c 18.00
...: Return to Krypton (2004, $17.95, TPB) r/2001-2002 x-over 18.00
Special 1 (1992, $3.50, 68 pgs.)-Simonson-c/a 5.00
The Death of Clark Kent (1997, $19.95, TPB)-Reprints Man of Steel #43 (1 page), Superman #99 (1 page),#100-102, Action #709 (1 page), #710,711, Advs. of Superman #523-525, Superman:The Man of Tomorrow #1 20.00
The Death of Superman (1993, $4.95, TPB)-Reprints Man of Steel #17-19, Superman #73-75, Advs. of Superman #496,497, Action #683,684, & Justice League #69
1 2 3 5 6 8
The Death of Superman, 2nd & 3rd printings 5.00
The Death of Superman Platinum Edition 15.00
...: The Greatest Stories Ever Told ('04, $19.95, TPB) Ross-c, Uslan intro. 20.00
...: The Man of Steel Vol. 2 ('03, $19.95, TPB) r/Superman #1-3, Action #584-586, Advs. of Superman #424-426 & Who's Who Update '87 20.00
...: The Man of Steel Vol. 3 ('04, $19.95, TPB) r/Superman #4-6, Action #587-589, Advs. of Superman #427-429; intro. by Ordway; new Ordway-c 20.00
The Trial of Superman ('97, $14.95, TPB) reprints story arc 15.00
...: They Saved Luthor's Brain ('00, $14.95) r/ "death" and return of Luthor 15.00
...: 'Til Death Do Us Part ('01, $17.95) reprints; Mahnke-c 18.00

Superman Adventures #25 © DC

Superman/Batman #13 © DC

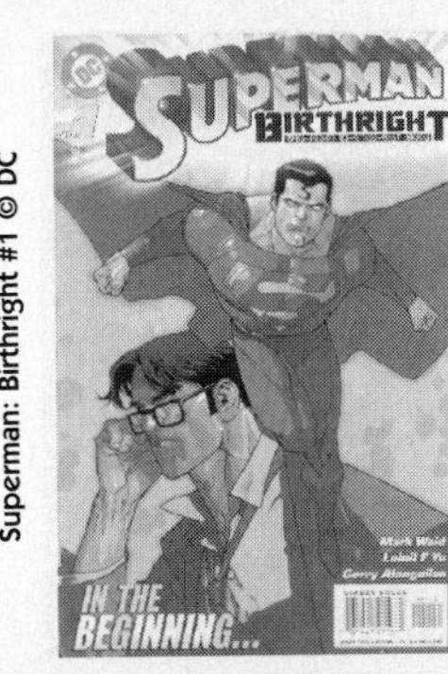

Superman: Birthright #1 © DC

GD VG FN VF VF/NM NM-
2.0 4.0 6.0 8.0 9.0 9.2

...: Time and Time Again (1994, $7.50, TPB)-Reprints 8.00
...: Transformed ('98, $12.95, TPB) r/post Final Night powerless Superman to Electric Superman 13.00
... Vs. The Revenge Squad (1999, $12.95, TPB) 13.00
NOTE: *Austin a(i)-1-3. **Byrne** a-1-16p, 17, 19-21p, 22; c-1-17, 20-22; scripts-1-22. **Guice** c/a-64. **Kirby** c-37p. **Joe Quesada** c-Annual 4. **Russell** c/a-23i. **Simonson** c-69i. #19-21 2nd printings sold in multi-packs.*

SUPERMAN (one-shots)
Daily News Magazine Presents DC Comics' Superman nn-(1987, 8 pgs.)-Supplement to New York Daily News; Perez-c/a 5.00
...: A Nation Divided (1999, $4.95)-Elseworlds Civil War story 5.00
... & Savage Dragon: Chicago (2002, $5.95) Larsen-a; Ross-c 6.00
... & Savage Dragon: Metropolis (11/99, $4.95) Bogdanove-a 5.00
...: At Earth's End (1995, $4.95)-Elseworlds story 5.00
...: Blood of My Ancestors (2003, $6.95)-Gil Kane & John Buscema-a 7.00
...: Distant Fires (1998, $5.95)-Elseworlds; Chaykin-s 6.00
...: Emperor Joker (10/00, $3.50)-Follows Action #769 3.50
...: End of the Century (2/00, $24.95, HC)-Immonen-s/a 25.00
...: End of the Century (2003, $17.95, SC)-Immonen-s/a 18.00
... For Earth (1991, $4.95, 52 pgs, printed on recycled paper)-Ordway wraparound-c 5.00
...IV Movie Special (1987, $2.00)-Movie adaptation; Heck-a 3.00
...Gallery, The 1 (1993, $2.95)-Poster-a 3.00
..., Inc. (1999, $6.95)-Elseworlds Clark as a sports hero; Garcia-Lopez-a 7.00
...: Kal (1995, $5.95)-Elseworlds story 6.00
...: Lex 2000 (1/01, $3.50)-Election night for the Luthor Presidency 3.50
...: Monster (1999, $5.95)-Elseworlds story; Anthony Williams-a 6.00
... Movie Special-(9/83)-Adaptation of Superman III; other versions exist with store logos on bottom 1/3 of-c 4.00
...: Our Worlds at War Secret Files 1-(8/01, $5.95)-Stories & profile pages 6.00
...'s Metropolis-(1996, $5.95, prestige format)-Elseworlds; McKeever-c/a 6.00
...: Speeding Bullets-(1993, $4.95, 52 pgs.)-Elseworlds 5.00
.../Spider-Man-(1995, $3.95)-r/DC and Marvel Presents... 4.00
... 10-Cent Adventure 1 (3/02, 10¢) McDaniel-a; intro. Cir-El Supergirl 2.25
...: The Earth Stealers 1-(1988, $2.95, 52 pgs, prestige format) Byrne script; painted-c 4.00
...: The Earth Stealers 1-2nd printing 3.00
...: The Legacy of Superman #1 (3/93, $2.50, 68 pgs.)-Art Adams-c; Simonson-a 4.00
...: The Last God of Krypton ('99,$4.95) Hildebrandt Bros.-a/Simonson-s 5.00
...: The Odyssey ('99, $4.95) Clark Kent's post-Smallville journey 5.00
...: 3-D (12/98, $3.95)-with glasses 4.00
.../Thundercats (1/04, $5.95) Winick-s/Garza-a; two covers by Garza & McGuinness 6.00
.../Toyman-(1996, $1.95) 2.50
...: True Brit (2004, $24.95, HC w/dust jacket) Elseworlds; Kal-El's rocket lands in England; co-written by John Cleese and Kim Howard Johnson; John Byrne-a 25.00
...: Under A Yellow Sun (1994, $5.95, 68 pgs.)-A Novel by Clark Kent; embossed-c 6.00
... Vs. Darkseid: Apokolips Now! 1 (3/03, $2.95) McKone-a; Kara (Supergirl #75) app. 3.00
...: War of the Worlds (1999, $5.95)-Battles Martians 6.00
...: Where is thy Sting? (2001, $6.95)-McCormack-Sharp-c/a 7.00
...: Y2K (2/00, $4.95)-1st Brainiac 13 app.; Guice-c/a 5.00

SUPERMAN ADVENTURES, THE (Based on animated series)
DC Comics: Oct, 1996 - No. 66, Apr, 2002 ($1.75/$1.95/$1.99)

1-Rick Burchett-c/a begins; Paul Dini script; Lex Luthor app.; silver ink, wraparound-c 3.00
2-20,22: 2-McCloud scripts begin; Metallo-c/app. 3-Brainiac-c/app. 6-Mxyzptlk-c/app. 2.50
21-($3.95) 1st animated Supergirl 5.00
23-66: 23-Begin $1.99-c; Livewire app. 25-Batgirl-c/app. 28-Manley-a. 54-Retells Superman #233 "Kryptonite Nevermore" 58-Ross-c 2.25
Annual 1 (1997, $3.95)-Zatanna and Bruce Wayne app. 4.00
Special 1 (2/98, $2.95) Superman vs. Lobo 3.00
TPB (1998, $7.95) r/#1-6 8.00
... Vol 1: Up, Up and Away (2004, $6.95, digest-size) r/#16,19,22-24; Amancio-a 7.00
... Vol 2: The Never-Ending Battle (2004, $6.95, digest-size) r/#25-29 7.00

SUPERMAN ALIENS 2: GOD WAR (Also see Superman Vs. Aliens)
DC Comics/Dark Horse Comics: May, 2002 - No. 4, Nov, 2002 ($2.99, limited series)

1-4-Bogdanove & Nowlan-a; Darkseid & New Gods app. 3.00
TPB (6/03, $12.95) r/#1-4 13.00

SUPERMAN & BATMAN: GENERATIONS (Elseworlds)
DC Comics: 1999 - No. 4, 1999 ($4.95, limited series)

1-4-Superman & Batman team-up from 1939 to the future; Byrne-c/s/a 5.00
TPB (2000, $14.95) r/series 15.00

SUPERMAN & BATMAN: GENERATIONS II (Elseworlds)
DC Comics: 2001 - No. 4, 2001 ($5.95, limited series)

1-4-Superman, Batman & others team-up from 1942-future; Byrne-c/s/a 6.00
TPB (2003, $19.95) r/series 20.00

SUPERMAN & BATMAN: GENERATIONS III (Elseworlds)
DC Comics: Mar, 2003 - No. 12, Feb, 2004 ($2.95, limited series)

1-12-Superman & Batman through the centuries; Byrne-c/s/a 3.00

SUPERMAN & BATMAN: WORLD'S FUNNEST (Elseworlds)
DC Comics: 2000 ($6.95, square-bound, one-shot)

nn-Mr. Mxyzptlk and Bat-Mite destroy each DC Universe; Dorkin-s/ art by various incl. Ross, Timm, Miller, Allred, Moldoff, Gibbons, Cho, Jimenez 7.00

SUPERMAN & BUGS BUNNY
DC Comics: Jul, 2000 - No. 4, Oct, 2000 ($2.50, limited series)

1-4-JLA & Looney Tunes characters meet 2.50

SUPERMAN/BATMAN
DC Comics: Oct, 2003 - Present ($2.95)

1-Two covers (Superman or Batman in foreground) Loeb-s/McGuinness-a; Metallo app. 5.00
1-2nd printing (Batman cover) 3.00
1-3rd printing; new McGuinness cover 3.00
1-Diamond/Alliance Retailer Summit Edition-variant cover 100.00
2-6: 2,5-Future Superman app. 6-Luthor in battlesuit 3.00
7-Pat Lee-c/a; Superboy & Robin app. 3.00
8-Michael Turner-c/a; intro. new Kara Zor-El 5.00
8-Second printing with sketch cover 3.00
8-Third printing with new Turner cover 3.00
9-13-Michael Turner-c/a; Wonder Woman app. 10,13-Variant-c by Jim Lee 3.00
14,15-Pacheco-a; Lightning Lord, Saturn Queen & Cosmic King app. 3.00
...Public Enemies HC (2004, $19.95) r/#1-6 & Secret Files 2003 20.00
...Secret Files 2003 (11/03, $4.95) Reis-a; pin-ups by various; Loeb/Sale short-s 5.00

SUPERMAN/BATMAN: ALTERNATE HISTORIES
DC Comics: 1996 ($14.95, trade paperback)

nn-Reprints Detective Comics Annual #7, Action Comics Annual #6, Steel Annual #1, Legends of the Dark Knight Annual #4 15.00

SUPERMAN: BIRTHRIGHT
DC Comics: Sept, 2003 - No. 12, Sept, 2004 ($2.95, limited series)

1-12-Waid-s/Leinil Yu-a; retelling of origin and early Superman years 3.00
HC (2004, $29.95, dustjacket) r/series; cover gallery; Waid proposal with Yu concept art 30.00

SUPERMAN: DAY OF DOOM
DC Comics: Jan, 2003 - No. 4, Feb, 2003 ($2.95, weekly limited series)

1-4-Jurgens-s/Jurgens & Sienkiewicz-a 3.00
TPB (2003, $9.95) r/#1-4 10.00

SUPERMAN/DOOMSDAY: HUNTER/PREY
DC Comics: 1994 - No. 3, 1994 ($4.95, limited series, 52 pgs.)

1-3 5.00

SUPERMAN FAMILY, THE (Formerly Superman's Pal Jimmy Olsen)
National Per. Publ./DC Comics: No. 164, Apr-May, 1974 - No. 222, Sept, 1982

	GD 2.0	VG 4.0	FN 6.0	VF 8.0	VF/NM 9.0	NM- 9.2
164-(100 pgs.) Jimmy Olsen, Supergirl, Lois Lane begin	5	10	15	33	44	55
165-169 (100 pgs.)	3	7	10	21	28	35
170-176 (68 pgs.)	2	4	6	14	18	22
177-190 (52 pgs.): 177-181-52 pgs. 182-Marshall Rogers-a; $1.00 issues begin; Krypto begins, ends #192. 183-Nightwing-Flamebird begins, ends #194. 189-Brainiac 5, Mon-el app.	2	4	6	10	12	15
191-193,195-199: 191-Superboy begins, ends #198	1	2	3	5	7	9
194,200: 194-Rogers-a. 200-Book length sty	1	3	4	6	8	10
201-222: 211-Earth II Batman & Catwoman marry	1	2	3	4	5	7

NOTE: ***N. Adams** c-182-185. **Anderson** a-186i. **Buckler** c(p)-190, 191, 209, 210, 215, 217, 220. **Jones** a-191-193. **Gil Kane** c(p)-221, 222. **Mortimer** a(p)-191-193, 199, 201-222. **Orlando** a(i)-186, 187. **Rogers** a-182, 194. **Staton** a-191-194, 196p. **Tuska** a(p)-203, 207-209.*

SUPERMAN/FANTASTIC FOUR
DC Comics/Marvel Comics: 1999 ($9.95, tabloid size, one-shot)

1-Battle Galactus and the Cyborg; wraparound-c by Alex Ross and Dan Jurgens; Jurgens-s/a; Thibert-a 10.00

SUPERMAN FOR ALL SEASONS
DC Comics: 1998 - No, 4, 1998 ($4.95, limited series, prestige format)

1-Loeb-s/Sale-a/c; Superman's first year in Metropolis 6.00
2-4 5.00
Hardcover (1999, $24.95) r/#1-4 25.00

SUPERMAN FOR EARTH (See Superman one-shots)

SUPERMAN FOREVER
DC Comics: Jun, 1998 ($5.95, one-shot)

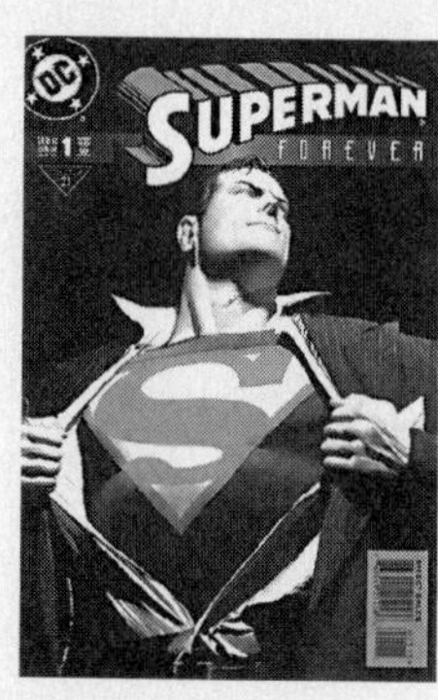

Superman Forever #1 © DC

Superman: Metropolis #1 © DC

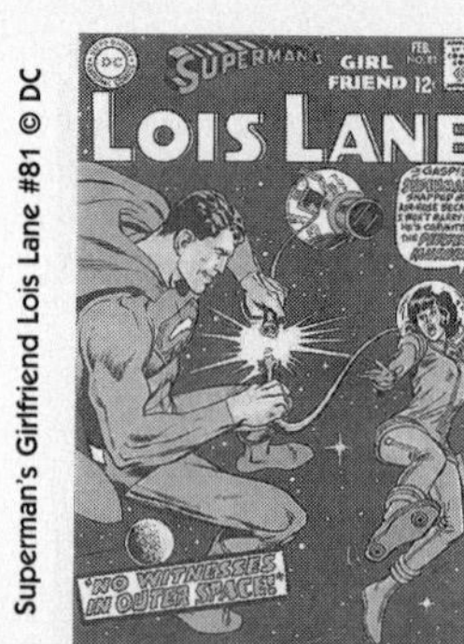

Superman's Girlfriend Lois Lane #81 © DC

	GD 2.0	VG 4.0	FN 6.0	VF 8.0	VF/NM 9.0	NM- 9.2

1-($5.95)-Collector's Edition with a 7-image lenticular-c by Alex Ross; Superman returns to normal; s/a by various 7.00
1-($4.95) Standard Edition with single image Ross-c 5.00

SUPERMAN/GEN13
DC Comics (WildStorm): Jun, 2000 - No. 3, Aug, 2000 ($2.50, limited series)

1-3-Hughes-s/ Bermejo-a; Campbell variant-c for each 2.50
TPB (2001, $9.95) new Bermejo-c; cover gallery 10.00

SUPERMAN: KING OF THE WORLD
DC Comics: June, 1999 ($3.95/$4.95, one-shot)

1-($3.95) Regular Ed. 4.00
1-($4.95) Collectors' Ed. with gold foil enhanced-c 5.00

SUPERMAN: LAST SON OF EARTH
DC Comics: 2000 - No. 2, 2000 ($5.95, limited series, prestige format)

1,2-Elseworlds; baby Clark rockets to Krypton; Gerber-s/Wheatley-a 6.00

SUPERMAN: LAST STAND ON KRYPTON
DC Comics: 2003 ($6.95, one-shot, prestige format)

1-Sequel to Superman: Last Son of Earth; Gerber-s/Wheatley-a 7.00

SUPERMAN: LOIS LANE (Girlfrenzy)
DC Comics: Jun, 1998 ($1.95, one shot)

1-Connor & Palmiotti-a 2.25

SUPERMAN/MADMAN HULLABALOO!
Dark Horse Comics: June, 1997 - No. 3, Aug, 1997 ($2.95, limited series)

1-3-Mike Allred-c/s/a 3.00
TPB (1997, $8.95) 9.00

SUPERMAN: METROPOLIS
DC Comics: Apr, 2003 - No. 12, Mar, 2004 ($2.95, limited series)

1-12-Focus on Jimmy Olsen; Austen-s. 1-6-Zezelj-a. 7-12-Kristiansen-a. 8,9-Creeper app. 3.00

SUPERMAN METROPOLIS SECRET FILES
DC Comics: Jun, 2000 ($4.95, one shot)

1-Short stories, pin-ups and profile pages; Hitch and Neary-c 5.00

SUPERMAN: PEACE ON EARTH
DC Comics: Jan, 1999 ($9.95, Treasury-sized, one-shot)

1-Alex Ross painted-c/a; Paul Dini-s 12.00

SUPERMAN: RED SON
DC Comics: 2003 - No. 3, 2003 ($5.95, limited series, prestige format)

1-Elseworlds; Superman's rocket lands in Russia; Mark Millar-s/Dave Johnson-c/a 10.00
2,3 6.00
TPB (2004, $17.95) r/#1-3; intro. by Tom DeSanto; sketch pages 18.00

SUPERMAN RED/ SUPERMAN BLUE
DC Comics: Feb, 1998 ($4.95, one shot)

1-Polybagged w/3-D glasses and reprint of Superman 3-D (1955); Jurgens-plot/3-D cover; script and art by various 5.00
1-($3.95)-Standard Ed.; comic only, non 3-D cover 4.00

SUPERMAN: SAVE THE PLANET
DC Comics: Oct, 1998 ($2.95, one-shot)

1-($2.95) Regular Ed.; Luthor buys the Daily Planet 3.00
1-($3.95) Collector's Ed. with acetate cover 4.00

SUPERMAN SCRAPBOOK (Has blank pages; contains no comics)

SUPERMAN: SECRET FILES
DC Comics: Jan, 1998; May 1999 ($4.95)

1,2: 1-Retold origin story, "lost" pages & pin-ups 5.00
... & Origins 2004 (8/04) pin-ups by Lee, Turner and others 5.00

SUPERMAN: SECRET IDENTITY
DC Comics: 2004 - No. 4, 2004 ($5.95, squarebound, mini-series)

1-4-Busiek-s/Immonen-a/c 6.00

SUPERMAN'S GIRLFRIEND LOIS LANE (See Action Comics #1, 80 Page Giant #3, 14, Lois Lane, Showcase #9, 10, Superman #28 & Superman Family)

SUPERMAN'S GIRLFRIEND LOIS LANE (See Showcase #9,10)
National Periodical Publ.: Mar-Apr, 1958 - No. 136, Jan-Feb, 1974; No. 137, Sept-Oct, 1974

	GD 2.0	VG 4.0	FN 6.0	VF 8.0	VF/NM 9.0	NM- 9.2
1-(3-4/58)	300	600	900	2625	4463	6300
2	78	156	234	663	1069	1475
3	51	102	153	434	705	975
4,5	44	88	132	352	551	750
6,7	35	70	105	263	412	560
8-10: 9-Pat Boone-c/story	30	60	90	218	334	450
11-13,15-19: 12-(10/59)-Aquaman app.	19	38	57	134	205	275
14-Supergirl x-over; Batman app. on-c only	19	38	57	138	212	285
20-Supergirl-c/sty	18	38	57	138	212	285
21-28: 23-1st app. Lena Thorul, Lex Luthor's sister; 1st Lois as Elastic Lass. 27-Bizarro-c/story	14	28	42	102	156	210
29-Aquaman, Batman, Green Arrow cover app. and cameo; last 10¢ issue	15	30	45	107	164	220
30-32,34-46,48,49	9	18	27	65	93	120
33(5/62)-Mon-el app.	10	20	30	70	100	130
47-Legion app.	10	20	30	70	100	130
50(7/64)-Triplicate Girl, Phantom Girl & Shrinking Violet app.	10	20	30	67	96	125
51-55,57-67,69: 59-Jor-el app.; Batman back-up sty	7	14	21	51	71	90
56-Saturn Girl app.	8	16	24	53	74	95
68-(Giant G-26)	9	18	27	63	89	115
70-Penguin & Catwoman app. (1st S.A. Catwoman, 11/66; also see Detective #369 for 3rd app.); Batman & Robin cameo	25	50	75	181	278	375
71-Batman & Robin cameo (3 panels); Catwoman story cont'd from #70 (2nd app.); see Detective #369 for 3rd app	14	28	42	102	156	210
72,73,75,76,78	6	12	18	40	55	70
74-1st Bizarro Flash (5/67); JLA cameo	6	12	18	43	59	75
77-(Giant G-39)	8	16	24	53	74	95
79-Neal Adams-c or c(i) begin, end #95,108	6	12	18	43	59	75
80-85,87,88,90-92: 92-Last 12¢ issue	4	8	12	28	38	48
86,95 (Giants G-51,G-63)-Both have Neal Adams-c	7	14	21	46	63	80
89,93: 89-Batman x-over; all N. Adams-c. 93-Wonder Woman-c/story	4	8	12	29	40	50
94,96-99,101-103,107-110	4	8	12	22	30	38
100	4	8	12	25	33	42
104-(Giant G-75)	6	12	18	40	55	70
105-Origin/1st app. The Rose & the Thorn.	6	12	18	40	55	70
106-"Black Like Me" sty; Lois changes her skin color to black	6	12	18	38	52	65
111-Justice League-c/s; Morrow-a; last 15¢ issue	4	8	12	25	33	42
112,114-123 (52 pgs.): 122-G.A. Lois Lane-r/Superman #30. 123-G.A. Batman-r/Batman #35 (w/Catwoman)	4	8	12	24	32	40
113-(Giant G-87) Kubert-a (previously unpublished G.A. story)(scarce in NM)	7	14	21	46	63	80
124-135: 130-Last Rose & the Thorn. 132-New Zatanna story	3	6	9	16	20	24
136,137: 136-Wonder Woman x-over	3	6	9	18	23	28
Annual 1(Sum, 1962)-r/L. Lane #12; Aquaman app.	22	44	66	160	245	330
Annual 2(Sum, 1963)	15	30	45	105	160	215

NOTE: ***Buckler*** *a-117-121p.* ***Curt Swan or Kurt Schaffenberger*** *a-1-81(most); c(p)-1-15.*

SUPERMAN: SILVER BANSHEE
DC Comics: Dec, 1998 - No. 2, Jan, 1999 ($2.25, mini-series)

1,2-Brereton-s/c; Chin-a 2.25

SUPERMAN'S NEMESIS: LEX LUTHOR
DC Comics: Mar, 1999 - No. 4, Jun, 1999 ($2.50, mini-series)

1-4-Semeiks-a 2.50

SUPERMAN'S PAL JIMMY OLSEN (Superman Family #164 on)
(See Action Comics #6 for 1st app. & 80 Page Giant)
National Periodical Publ.: Sept-Oct, 1954 - No. 163, Feb-Mar, 1974 (Fourth World #133-148)

	GD 2.0	VG 4.0	FN 6.0	VF 8.0	VF/NM 9.0	NM- 9.2
1	409	818	1227	3742	6371	9000
2	129	258	387	1097	1774	2450
3-Last pre-code issue	70	140	210	595	960	1325
4,5	50	100	150	413	657	900
6-10	38	76	114	285	443	600
11-20: 15-1st S.A. issue	26	52	78	189	290	390
21-30: 29-(6/58) 1st app. Krypto with Superman	17	34	51	121	186	250
31-Origin & 1st app. Elastic Lad (Jimmy Olsen)	15	30	45	109	167	225
32-40: 33-One pg. biography of Jack Larson (TV Jimmy Olsen). 36-Intro Lucy Lane. 37-2nd app. Elastic Lad & 1st cover app.	12	24	36	87	134	180
41-50: 41-1st J.O. Robot. 48-Intro/origin Superman Emergency Squad	10	20	30	73	107	140
51-56: 56-Last 10¢ issue	9	18	27	60	85	110
57-62,64-70: 57-Olsen marries Supergirl. 62-Mon-el & Elastic Lad app. but not as Legionnaires. 70-Element Boy (Lad) app.	7	14	21	46	63	80
63(9/62)-Legion of Super-Villains app.	7	14	21	50	68	85
71,74,75,78,80-84,86,89,90: 86-Jimmy Olsen Robot becomes Congorilla	6	12	18	38	52	65

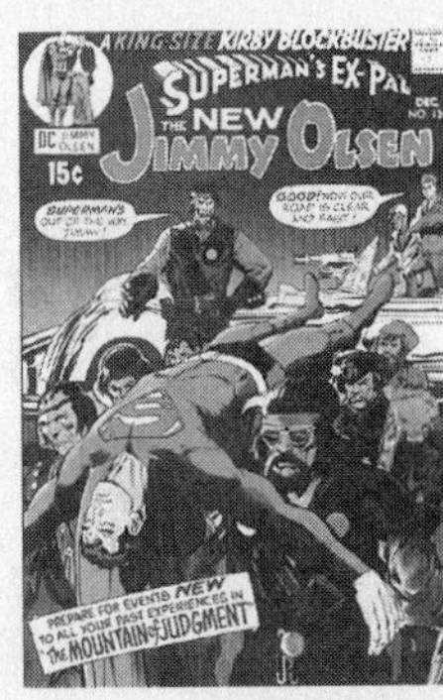
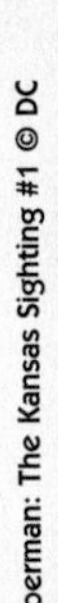
Superman's Pal Jimmy Olsen #134 © DC

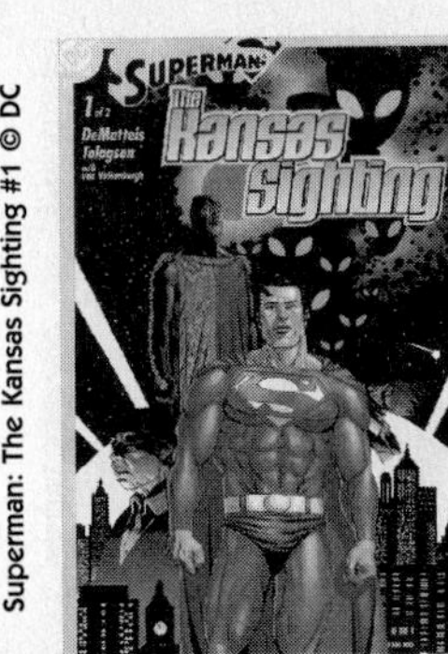
Superman: The Kansas Sighting #1 © DC

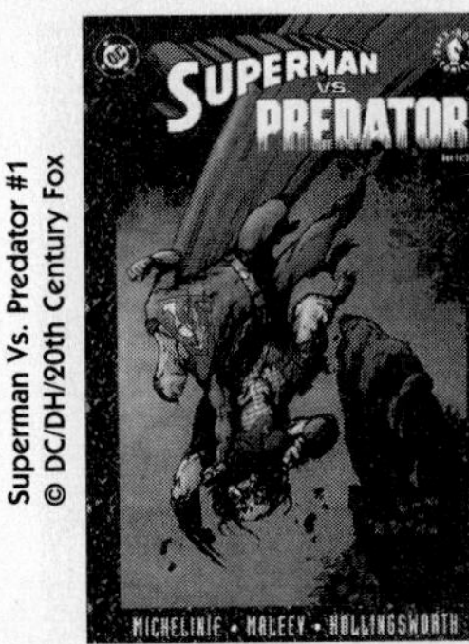
Superman Vs. Predator #1 © DC/DH/20th Century Fox

GD VG FN VF VF/NM NM-
2.0 4.0 6.0 8.0 9.0 9.2

GD VG FN VF VF/NM NM-
2.0 4.0 6.0 8.0 9.0 9.2

72,73,76,77,79,85,87,88: 72(10/63)-Legion app; Elastic Lad (Olsen) joins. 73-Ultra Boy app. 76,85-Legion app. 76-Legion app. 77-Olsen with Colossal Boy's powers & costume; origin Titano retold. 79-(9/64)-Titled The Red-headed Beatle of 1000 B.C. 85-Legion app. 87-Legion of Super-Villains app. 88-Star Boy app. 6 12 18 40 55 70
91-94,96-98 5 10 15 33 44 55
95 (Giant G-25) 8 16 24 53 74 95
99-Olsen w/powers & costumes of Lightning Lad, Sun Boy & Element Lad 5 10 15 36 48 60
100-Legion cameo 6 12 18 38 52 65
101-103,105-112,114-120: 106-Legion app. 110-Infinity-c. 117-Batman & Legion cameo. 120-Last 12¢ issue 4 8 12 24 32 40
104 (Giant G-38) 6 12 18 43 59 75
113,122,131,140 (Giants G-50,G-62,G-74,G-86) 6 12 18 38 52 65
121,123-130,132 3 7 10 21 28 35
133-(10/70)-Jack Kirby story & art begins; re-intro Newsboy Legion; 1st app. Morgan Edge 7 14 21 50 68 85
134-1st app. Darkseid (1 panel, 12/70) 8 16 24 55 78 100
135-2nd app. Darkseid (1 pg. cameo; see New Gods & Forever People); G.A. Guardian app. 5 10 15 36 48 60
136-139: 136-Origin new Guardian. 138-Partial photo-c. 139-Last 15¢ issue 4 8 12 27 36 45
141-150: (25¢,52 pgs.). 141-Photo-c; Newsboy Legion-r by S&K begin; full pg. self-portrait of Jack Kirby; Don Rickles cameo. 149,150-G.A. Plastic Man-r in both; 150-Newsboy Legion app. 4 8 12 24 32 40
151-163 3 6 9 16 20 24

NOTE: *Issues #141-148 contain* ***Simon & Kirby*** *Newsboy Legion reprints from Star Spangled #7, 8, 9, 10, 11, 12, 13, 14 in that order.* ***N. Adams*** *c-109-112, 115, 117, 118, 120, 121, 132, 134-136, 147, 148.* ***Kirby*** *a-133-139p, 141-148p; c-133, 137, 139, 142, 145p.* ***Kirby/N. Adams*** *c-137, 138, 141-144, 146.* ***Curt Swan*** *c-1-14(most)., 140.*

SUPERMAN SPECTACULAR (Also see DC Special Series #5)
DC Comics: 1982 (Magazine size, 52 pgs., square binding)
1-Saga of Superman Red/ Superman Blue; Luthor and Terra-Man app.; Gonzales & Colletta-a 1 3 4 6 8 10

SUPERMAN / TARZAN: SONS OF THE JUNGLE
Dark Horse Comics: Oct, 2001 - No. 3, May, 2002 ($2.99, limited series)
1-3-Elseworlds; Kal-El lands in the jungle; Dixon-s/Meglia-a/Ramos-c 3.00

SUPERMAN: THE DARK SIDE
DC Comics: 1998 - No. 3, 1998 ($4.95, squarebound, mini-series)
1-3: Elseworlds; Kal-El lands on Apokolips 5.00

SUPERMAN: THE DOOMSDAY WARS
DC Comics: 1998 - No. 3, 1999 ($4.95, squarebound, mini-series)
1-3: Superman & JLA vs. Doomsday; Jurgens-s/a(p) 5.00

SUPERMAN: THE KANSAS SIGHTING
DC Comics: 2003 - No. 2, 2003 ($6.95, squarebound, mini-series)
1,2-DeMatteis-s/Tolagson-a 7.00

SUPERMAN: THE MAN OF STEEL (Also see Man of Steel, The)
DC Comics: July, 1991 - No. 134, Mar, 2003 ($1.00/$1.25/$1.50/$1.95/$2.25)
0-(10/94) Zero Hour; released between #37 & #38 2.50
1-($1.75, 52 pgs.)-Painted-c 5.00
2-16: 3-War of the Gods x-over. 5-Reads sideways. 10-Last $1.00-c. 14-Superman & Robin team-up 3.00
17-1st brief app. Doomsday 1 2 3 4 5 7
17,18: 17-2nd printing. 18-2nd & 3rd printings 2.25
18-1st full app. Doomsday 1 2 3 5 7 9
19-Doomsday battle issue (c/story) 6.00
20-22: 20,21-Funeral for a Friend. 22-($1.95)-Collector's Edition w/die-cut outer-c & bound-in poster; Steel-c/story 2.50
22-($1.50)-Newsstand Ed. w/poster & different-c 2.25
23-49,51-99: 30-Regular edition. 32-Bizarro-c/story. 35,36-Worlds Collide Pt. 1 & 10. 37-(9/94)-Zero Hour x-over. 38-(11/94). 48-Aquaman app. 54-Spectre-c/app; Lex Luthor app. 56-Mxyzptlk-c/app. 57-G.A. Flash app. 58-Supergirl app. 59-Parasite-c/app.; Steel app. 60-Reintro Bottled City of Kandor. 62-Final Night. 64-New Gods app. 67-New powers. 75-"Death" of Mxyzptlk. 78,79-Millennium Giants. 80-Golden Age style. 92-JLA app. 98-Metal Men app. 2.50
30-($2.50)-Collector's Edition; polybagged with Superman & Lobo vinyl clings that stick to wraparound-c; Lobo-c/story 3.00
50 ($2.95)-The Trial of Superman 4.00
100-($2.99) New Fortress of Solitude revealed 3.00
100-($3.99) Special edition with fold out cardboard-c 4.00
101,102-101-Batman app. 2.25
103-133: 103-Begin $2.25. 105-Batman-c/app. 111-Return to Krypton. 115-117-Our Worlds at War. 117-Maxima killed. 121-Royal Flush Gang app. 128-Return to Krypton II. 2.25
134-($2.75) Last issue; Steel app.; Bogdanove-c 2.75
#1,000,000 (11/98) 853rd Century x-over; Gene Ha-c 2.50
Annual 1-5 ('92-'96,68 pgs.): 1-Eclipso app.; Joe Quesada-c(p). 2-Intro Edge. 3 -Elseworlds; Mignola-c; Batman app. 4-Year One story. 5-Legends of the Dead Earth story 3.00
Annual 6 (1997, $3.95)-Pulp Heroes story 4.00
...Gallery (1995, $3.50) Pin-ups by various 3.50

SUPERMAN: THE MAN OF TOMORROW
DC Comics: 1995 - No. 15, Fall, 1999 ($1.95, quarterly)
1-15: 1-Lex Luthor app. 3-Lex Luthor-c/app; Joker app. 4-Shazam! app. 5-Wedding of Lex Luthor. 10-Maxima-c/app. 13-JLA-c/app. 2.50
#1,000,000 (11/98) 853rd Century x-over; Gene Ha-c 2.50

SUPERMAN: THE SECRET YEARS
DC Comics: Feb, 1985 - No. 4, May, 1985 (limited series)
1-4-Miller-c on all 3.00

SUPERMAN: THE WEDDING ALBUM
DC Comics: Dec, 1996 ($4.95, 96 pgs, one-shot)
1-Standard Edition-Story & art by past and present Superman creators; gatefold back-c. Byrne-c 5.00
1-Collector's Edition-Embossed cardstock variant-c w/ metallic silver ink and matte and gloss varnishes 5.00
TPB ('97, $14.95) r/Wedding and honeymoon stories 15.00

SUPERMAN 3-D (See Three-Dimension Adventures)

SUPERMAN-TIM (See Promotional Comics section)

SUPERMAN VILLAINS SECRET FILES
DC Comics: Jun, 1998 ($4.95, one shot)
1-Origin stories, "lost" pages & pin-ups 5.00

SUPERMAN VS. ALIENS (Also see Superman Aliens 2: God War)
DC Comics/Dark Horse Comics: July, 1995 - No. 3, Sept, 1995 ($4.95, limited series)
1-3: Jurgens/Nowlan-a 5.00

SUPERMAN VS. MUHAMMAD ALI (See All-New Collectors' Edition C-56)

SUPERMAN VS. PREDATOR
DC Comics/Dark Horse Comics: 2000 - No. 3, 2000 ($4.95, limited series)
1-3-Micheline-s/Maleev-a 5.00
TPB (2001, $14.95) r/series 15.00

SUPERMAN VS. THE AMAZING SPIDER-MAN (Also see Marvel Treasury Edition No. 28)
National Periodical Publications/Marvel Comics Group: 1976 ($2.00, Treasury sized, 100 pgs.)
1-Superman and Spider-Man battle Lex Luthor and Dr. Octopus; Andru/Giordano-a; 1st Marvel/DC x-over. 7 14 21 51 71 90
1-2nd printing; 5000 numbered copies signed by Stan Lee & Carmine Infantino on front cover & sold through mail 13 26 39 90 138 185
nn-(1995, $5.95)-r/#1 6.00

SUPERMAN VS. THE TERMINATOR: DEATH TO THE FUTURE
Dark Horse/DC Comics: Dec, 1999 - No. 4, Mar, 2000 ($2.95, limited series)
1-4-Grant-s/Pugh-a/c: Steel and Supergirl app. 3.00

SUPERMAN/WONDER WOMAN: WHOM GODS DESTROY
DC Comics: 1997 ($4.95, prestige format, limited series)
1-4-Elseworlds; Claremont-s 5.00

SUPERMAN WORKBOOK
National Periodical Publ./Juvenile Group Foundation: 1945 (B&W, reprints, 68 pgs)
nn-Cover-r/Superman #14 154 308 462 963 1482 2000

SUPER MANGA BLAST
Dark Horse Comics: Mar, 2000 - Present ($4.95/$4.99, B&W, anthology)
1-14-Reprints Oh My Goddess, 3X3 Eyes, What's Michael and others 5.00

SUPER MARIO BROS. (Also see Adventures of the..., Blip, Gameboy, and Nintendo Comics System)
Valiant Comics: 1990 - No. 5?, 1991 ($1.95, slick-c) V2#1, 1991 - No. 5, 1991
1-Wildman-a 4.00
2-5, V2#1-5-($1.50) 3.00
Special Edition 1 (1990, $1.95)-Wildman-a 3.00

SUPERMEN OF AMERICA
DC Comics: Mar, 1999 ($3.95/$4.95, one-shot)
1-($3.95) Regular Ed.; Immonen-s/art by various 4.00
1-($4.95) Collectors' Ed. with membership kit 5.00

Super-Mystery Comics #2 © ACE

Superpatriot #1 © IM

Supersnipe Comics #15 © S&S

	GD 2.0	VG 4.0	FN 6.0	VF 8.0	VF/NM 9.0	NM- 9.2

SUPERMEN OF AMERICA (Mini-series)
DC Comics: Mar, 2000 - No. 6, Aug, 2000 ($2.50)

1-6-Nicieza-s/Braithwaite-a						2.50

SUPERMOUSE (...the Big Cheese; see Coo Coo Comics)
Standard Comics/Pines No. 35 on (Literary Ent.): Dec, 1948 - No. 34, Sept, 1955; No. 35, Apr, 1956 - No. 45, Fall, 1958

	GD	VG	FN	VF	VF/NM	NM-
1-Frazetta text illos (3)	30	60	90	170	245	320
2-Frazetta text illos	15	30	45	83	117	150
3,5,6-Text illos by Frazetta in all	13	26	39	74	102	130
4-Two pg. text illos by Frazetta	14	28	42	79	110	140
7-10	8	16	24	43	54	65
11-20: 13-Racist humor (Indians)	7	14	21	35	43	50
21-45	6	12	18	28	34	40
1-Summer Holiday issue (Summer, 1957, 25¢, 100 pgs.)-Pines	14	28	42	79	110	140
2-Giant Summer issue (Summer, 1958, 25¢, 100 pgs.)-Pines; has games, puzzles & stories	10	20	30	56	73	90

SUPER-MYSTERY COMICS
Ace Magazines (Periodical House): July, 1940 - V8#6, July, 1949

	GD	VG	FN	VF	VF/NM	NM-
V1#1-Magno, the Magnetic Man & Vulcan begins (1st app.); Q-13, Corp. Flint, & Sky Smith begin	300	600	900	1933	3117	4300
2	100	200	300	625	963	1300
3-The Black Spider begins (1st app.)	79	158	237	494	760	1025
4-Origin Davy	56	112	168	350	538	725
5-Intro. The Clown & begin series (12/40)	60	120	180	375	580	785
6(2/41)	51	102	153	311	473	635
V2#1(4/41)-Origin Buckskin	49	98	147	299	455	610
2-6(2/42): 6-Vulcan begins again	46	92	138	281	428	575
V3#1(4/42),2: 1-Black Ace begins	40	80	120	241	363	485
3-Intro. The Lancer; Dr. Nemesis & The Sword begin; Kurtzman-c/a(2) (Mr. Risk & Paul Revere Jr.); Robot-c	52	104	156	317	484	650
4-Kurtzman-c/a	45	90	135	275	420	565
5-Kurtzman-a(2); L.B. Cole-a; Mr. Risk app.	50	100	150	305	465	625
6(10/43)-Mr. Risk app.; Kurtzman's Paul Revere Jr.; L.B. Cole-a	50	100	150	305	465	625
V4#1(1/44)-L.B. Cole-a	44	88	132	268	409	550
2-6(4/45): 2,5,6-Mr. Risk app.	33	66	99	190	275	360
V5#1(7/45)-6	33	66	99	190	275	360
V6#1-6: 3-Torture c-story. 4-Last Magno. Mr. Risk app. in #2,4-6. 6-New logo	26	52	78	150	215	280
V7#1-6, V8#1-4,6	24	48	72	135	195	255
V8#5-Meskin, Tuska, Sid Greene-a	24	48	72	135	195	255

NOTE: ***Sid Greene** a-V7#4. **Mooney** c-V1#5, 6, V2#1-6. **Palais** a-V5#3, 4; c-V4#6-V5#4, V6#2, V8#4. Bondage c-V2#5, 6, V3#2, 5. Magno c-V1#1-V3#6, V4#2-V5#5, V6#2. The Sword c-V4#1, 6(w/Magno).*

SUPERNATURAL LAW (Formerly Wolff & Byrd, Counselors of the Macabre)
Exhibit A Press: No. 24, Oct, 1999 - Present ($2.50/$2.95, B&W)

24-35-Batton Lash-s/a. 29-Marie Severin-c. 33-Cerebus spoof						2.50
36-39-($2.95). 37-Frank Cho pin-up and story panels						3.00

SUPERNATURAL LAW SECRETARY MAVIS
Exhibit A Press: 2001 - Present ($2.95/$3.50, B&W)

1-3: 3-DeCarlo-c						3.00
4-($3.50) Jaime Hernandez-c						3.50

SUPERNATURALS
Marvel Comics: Dec, 1998 - No. 4, Dec, 1998 ($3.99, weekly limited series)

1-4-Pulido-s/Balent-c; bound-in Halloween masks						4.00
1-4-With bound-in Ghost Rider mask (1 in 10)						4.00

SUPERNATURAL THRILLERS
Marvel Comics Group: Dec, 1972 - No. 6, Nov, 1973; No. 7, Jun, 1974 - No. 15, Oct, 1975

	GD	VG	FN	VF	VF/NM	NM-
1-It!; Sturgeon adap. (see Astonishing Tales #21)	3	6	9	18	24	30
2-4,6: 2-The Invisible Man; H.G. Wells adapt. 3-The Valley of the Worm; R.E. Howard adapt. 4-Dr. Jekyll & Mr. Hyde; R.L. Stevenson adapt.. 6-The Headless Horseman; last 20¢ issue	2	4	6	11	14	18
5-1st app. The Living Mummy	6	12	18	43	59	75
7-15: 7-The Living Mummy begins	3	6	9	16	20	24

NOTE: ***Brunner** c-11. **Buckler** a-5p. **Ditko** a-8r, 9r. **G. Kane** a-3p; c-3, 9p, 15p. **Mayerik** a-2p, 7, 8, 9p, 10p, 11. **McWilliams** a-14i. **Mortimer** a-4. **Steranko** c-1, 2. **Sutton** a-15. **Tuska** a-6p.*

SUPERPATRIOT (Also see Freak Force & Savage Dragon #2)
Image Comics (Highbrow Entertainment): July, 1993 - No. 4, Dec, 1993 ($1.95, lim. series)

1-4: Dave Johnson-c/a; Larsen scripts; Giffen plots						2.50

SUPERPATRIOT: AMERICA'S FIGHTING FORCE
Image Comics: July, 2002 - No. 4, Oct, 2002 ($2.95, limited series)

	GD 2.0	VG 4.0	FN 6.0	VF 8.0	VF/NM 9.0	NM- 9.2

1-4-Cory Walker-a/c; Savage Dragon app.						3.00

SUPERPATRIOT: LIBERTY & JUSTICE
Image Comics (Highbrow Entertainment): July, 1995 - No. 4, Oct, 1995 ($2.50, lim. series)

1-4: Dave Johnson-c/a. 1-1st app. Liberty & Justice						2.50
TPB (2002, $12.95) r/#1-4; new cover by Dave Johnson; sketch pages						13.00

SUPERPATRIOT: WAR ON TERROR
Image Comics: July, 2004 - No. 4 ($2.95, limited series)

1-Kirkman-s/Su-a						3.00

SUPER POWERS (1st Series)
DC Comics: July, 1984 - No. 5, Nov, 1984

1-5: 1-Joker/Penguin-c/story; Batman app.; all Kirby-c. 5-Kirby c/a						5.00

SUPER POWERS (2nd Series)
DC Comics: Sept, 1985 - No. 6, Feb, 1986

1-6: Kirby-c/a; Capt. Marvel & Firestorm join; Batman cameo; Darkseid storyline in all. 4-Batman cameo. 5,6-Batman app.						5.00

SUPER POWERS (3rd Series)
DC Comics: Sept, 1986 - No. 4, Dec, 1986

1-4: 1-Cyborg joins; 1st app. Samurai from Super Friends TV show. 1-4-Batman cameos; Darkseid storyline in #1-4						4.00

SUPER PUP (Formerly Spotty The Pup) (See Space Comics)
Avon Periodicals: No. 4, Mar-Apr, 1954 - No. 5, 1954

	GD	VG	FN	VF	VF/NM	NM-
4,5: 5-Robot-c	6	12	18	31	38	45

SUPER RABBIT (See All Surprise, Animated Movie Tunes, Comedy Comics, Comic Capers, Ideal Comics, It's A Duck's Life, Movie Tunes & Wisco)
Timely Comics (CmPI): Fall, 1944 - No. 14, Nov, 1948

	GD	VG	FN	VF	VF/NM	NM-
1-Hitler & Hirohito-c; war effort paper recycling PSA by S&K; Ziggy Pig & Silly begin?	71	142	213	444	685	925
2	37	74	111	209	305	400
3-5	23	46	69	132	191	250
6-Origin	25	50	75	144	207	270
7-10: 9-Infinity-c	15	30	45	83	117	150
11-Kurtzman's "Hey Look"	15	30	45	86	123	160
12-14	15	30	45	83	117	150
I.W. Reprint #1,2('58),7,10('63): 1-r/#13. 2-r/#10.	2	4	6	10	13	16

SUPER RICHIE (Superichie #5 on) (See Richie Rich Millions #68)
Harvey Publications: Sept, 1975 - No. 4, Mar, 1976 (All 52 pg. Giants)

	GD	VG	FN	VF	VF/NM	NM-
1	3	6	9	18	23	28
2-4	2	4	6	11	14	18

SUPER SLUGGERS (Baseball)
Ultimate Sports Ent. Inc.: 1999 ($3.95, one-shot)

1-Bonds, Piazza, Caminiti, Griffey Jr. app.; Martinbrough-c/a						4.00

SUPERSNIPE COMICS (Formerly Army & Navy #1-5)
Street & Smith Publications: V1#6, Oct, 1942 - V5#1, Aug-Sept, 1949
(See Shadow Comics V2#3)

	GD	VG	FN	VF	VF/NM	NM-
V1#6-Rex King - Man of Adventure (costumed hero, see Super Magic/Magician) by Jack Binder begins; Supersnipe by George Marcoux continues from Army & Navy #5; Bill Ward-a	108	216	324	675	1038	1400
7,10-12: 10,11-Little Nemo app.	51	102	153	311	476	640
8-Hitler, Tojo, Mussolini in Hell with Devil-c	79	158	237	494	760	1025
9-Doc Savage x-over in Supersnipe; Hitler-c	83	166	249	519	797	1075
V2 #1: Both V2#1(2/44) & V2#2(4/44) have V2#1 on outside-c; Huck Finn by Clare Dwiggins begins, ends V3#5 (rare)	75	150	225	469	722	975
V2#2 (4/44) has V2#1 on outside-c; classic shark-c	45	90	135	275	418	560
3-12	40	80	120	236	351	465
V3#1-12: 8-Bobby Crusoe by Dwiggins begins, ends V3#12. 9-X-Mas-c	35	70	105	201	293	385
V4#1-12, V5#1: V4#10-X-Mas-c	25	50	75	141	203	265

NOTE: ***George Marcoux** c-V1#6-V3#4. Doc Savage app. in some issues.*

SUPER SOLDIER (See Marvel Versus DC #3)
DC Comics (Amalgam): Apr, 1996 ($1.95, one-shot)

1-Mark Waid script & Dave Gibbons-c/a.						2.25

SUPER SOLDIER: MAN OF WAR
DC Comics (Amalgam): June, 1997 ($1.95, one-shot)

1-Waid & Gibbons-s/Gibbons & Palmiotti-c/a.						2.25

SUPER SOLDIERS

Supreme #7 © Rob Liefeld

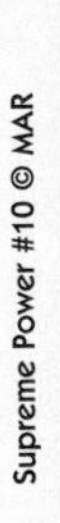
Supreme Power #10 © MAR

Sure-Fire Comics #1 © ACE

	GD 2.0	VG 4.0	FN 6.0	VF 8.0	VF/NM 9.0	NM- 9.2

Marvel Comics UK: Apr, 1993 - No. 8, Nov, 1993 ($1.75)
1-($2.50)-Embossed silver foil logo 2.50
2-8: 5-Capt. America app. 6-Origin; Nick Fury app.; neon ink-c 2.25

SUPERSPOOK (Formerly Frisky Animals on Parade)
Ajax/Farrell Publications: No. 4, June, 1958
4 8 16 24 46 58 70

SUPER SPY (See Wham Comics)
Centaur Publications: Oct, 1940 - No. 2, Nov, 1940 (Reprints)
1-Origin The Sparkler 110 220 330 688 1057 1425
2-The Inner Circle, Dean Denton, Tim Blain, The Drew Ghost, The Night Hawk by Gustavson, & S.S. Swanson by Glanz app. 66 132 198 413 637 860

SUPERSTAR: AS SEEN ON TV
Image Comics (Gorilla): 2001 ($5.95)
1-Busiek-s/Immonen-a 6.00

SUPER STAR HOLIDAY SPECIAL (See DC Special Series #21)

SUPER-TEAM FAMILY
National Periodical Publ./DC Comics: Oct-Nov, 1975 - No. 15, Mar-Apr, 1978
1-Reprints by Neal Adams & Kane/Wood; 68 pgs. begin, ends #4. New Gods app. 2 4 6 14 18 22
2,3: New stories 2 4 6 10 13 16
4-7: Reprints. 4-G.A. JSA-r & Superman/Batman/Robin-r from World's Finest. 5-52 pgs. begin 2 4 6 8 10 12
8-14: 8-10-New Challengers of the Unknown stories. 9-Kirby-a. 11-14: New stories 2 4 6 10 13 16
15-New Gods app. New stories 2 4 6 11 14 18
NOTE: ***Neal Adams** r-1-3. **Brunner** c-3. **Buckler** c-8p. **Tuska** a-7r. **Wood** a-1i(r), 3.*

SUPER TV HEROES (See Hanna-Barbera...)

SUPER-VILLAIN CLASSICS
Marvel Comics Group: May, 1983
1-Galactus -The Origin; Kirby-a 6.00

SUPER-VILLAIN TEAM-UP (See Fantastic Four #6 & Giant-Size...)
Marvel Comics Group: 8/75 - No. 14, 10/77; No. 15, 11/78; No. 16, 5/79; No. 17, 6/80
1-Giant-Size Super-Villain Team-Up #2; Sub-Mariner & Dr. Doom begin, end #10 4 8 12 24 32 40
2-5: 5-1st app. The Shroud 2 4 6 10 12 15
5-(30¢-c variant, limited distribution)(4/76) 2 4 6 14 18 22
6,7-(25¢ editions) 6-(6/76)-F.F., Shroud app. 7-Origin Shroud 1 2 3 5 7 9
6,7-(30¢-c, limited distribution)(6,8/76) 2 4 6 9 11 14
8-17: 9-Avengers app. 11-15-Dr. Doom & Red Skull app. 1 2 3 5 7 9
12-14-(35¢-c variants, limited distribution)(6,8,10/77) 2 4 6 9 11 14
NOTE: ***Buckler** c-4p, 5p, 7p. **Buscema** c-1. **Byrne/Austin** c-14. **Evans** a-1p, 3p. **Everett** a-1p. **Giffen** a-8p, 13p; c-13p. **Kane** c-2p, 9p. **Mooney** a-4i. **Starlin** c-6. **Tuska** r-1p, 15p. **Wood** r-15p.*

SUPER WESTERN COMICS (Also see Buffalo Bill)
Youthful Magazines: Aug, 1950 (One shot)
1-Buffalo Bill begins; Wyatt Earp, Calamity Jane & Sam Slade app; Powell-c/a 14 28 42 79 110 140

SUPER WESTERN FUNNIES (See Super Funnies)

SUPERWORLD COMICS
Hugo Gernsback (Komos Publ.): Apr, 1940 - No. 3, Aug, 1940 (68 pgs.)
1-Origin & 1st app. Hip Knox, Super Hypnotist; Mitey Powers & Buzz Allen, the Invisible Avenger, Little Nemo begin; cover by Frank R. Paul (all have sci/fi-c) (Scarce) 677 1354 2031 4739 7620 10,500
2-Marvo 1-2 Go+, the Super Boy of the Year 2680 (1st app.); Paul-c (Scarce) 400 800 1200 2600 4200 5800
3 (Scarce) 312 624 936 2000 3200 4400

SUPREME (Becomes ...The New Adventures #43-48)(See Youngblood #3)
(Also see Bloodwulf Special, Legend of Supreme, & Trencher #3)
Image Comics (Extreme Studios)/ Awesome Entertainment #49 on:
V2#1, Nov, 1992 - V2#42, Sept, 1996; V3#49 - No. 56, Feb, 1998
V2#1-Liefeld-a(i) & scripts; embossed foil logo 4.00
1-Gold Edition 6.00
2-(3/93)-Liefeld co-plots & inks; 1st app. Grizlock 3.00
3-42: 3-Intro Bloodstrike; 1st app. Khrome. 5-1st app. Thor. 6-1st brief app. The Starguard. 7-1st full app. The Starguard. 10-Black and White Pt 1 (1st app.) by Art Thibert (2 pgs. ea. installment). 25-(5/94)-Platt-c. 11-Coupon #4 for Extreme Prejudice #0; Black and White Pt. 7 by Thibert. 12-(4/94)-Platt-c. 13,14-(6/94). 15 (7/94). 16 (7/94)-Stormwatch app. 18-Kid Supreme Sneak Preview; Pitt app.19,20-Polybagged w/trading card. 20-1st app. Woden & Loki (as a dog); Overkill app. 21-1st app. Loki (in true form). 21-23-Poly-bagged trading card. 32-Lady Supreme cameo. 33-Origin & 1st full app. of Lady Supreme (Probe from the Starguard); Babewatch! tie-in. 37-Intro Loki; Fraga-c. 40-Retells Supreme's past advs. 41-Alan Moore scripts begin; Supreme revised; intro The Supremacy; Jerry Ordway-c (Joe Bennett variant-c exists). 42-New origin w/Rick Veitch-a; intro Radar, The Hound Supreme & The League of Infinity 3.00
28-Variant-c by Quesada & Palmiotti 3.00
(#43-48-**See Supreme: The New Adventures**)
V3#49,51: 49-Begin $2.99-c 3.00
50-($3.95)-Double sized, 2 covers, pin-up gallery 4.00
52a,52b-($3.50) 3.50
53-56: 53-Sprouse-a begins. 56-McGuinness-c 3.00
Annual 1-(1995, $2.95) 3.00
...: The Return TPB (Checker Book Publ., 2003, $24.95) r/#53-56 & Supreme; The Return #1-6; Ross-c; additional sketch pages by Ross 25.00
...: The Story of the Year TPB (Checker Book Publ., 2002, $26.95) r/#41-52; Ross-c 27.00
NOTE: ***Rob Liefeld** a(i)-1, 2; co-plots-2-4; scripts-1, 5, 6. **Ordway** c-41. **Platt** c-12, 25. **Thibert** c(i)-7-9.*

SUPREME: GLORY DAYS
Image Comics (Extreme Studios): Oct, 1994 - No. 2, Dec, 1994 ($2.95/$2.50, limited series)
1,2: 2-Diehard, Roman, Superpatriot, & Glory app. 3.00

SUPREME POWER
Marvel Comics (MAX): Oct, 2003 - Present ($2.99)
1-($2.99) Straczynski-s/Frank-a; Frank-c 3.00
1-($4.99) Special Edition with variant Quesada-c; includes r/early Squadron Supreme apps. 5.00
2-13: 4-Intro. Nighthawk. 6-The Blur debuts. 10-Princess Zarda returns 3.00
Vol. 1: Contact TPB (2004, $14.99) r/#1-6 15.00
Vol. 2: Powers & Principalities TPB (2004, $14.99) r/#7-12 15.00

SUPREME: THE NEW ADVENTURES (Formerly Supreme)
Maximum Press: V3#43, Oct, 1996 - V3#48, May, 1997 ($2.50)
V3#43-48: 43-Alan Moore scripts begin; Joe Bennett-a; Rick Veitch-a (8 pgs.); Dan Jurgens-a (1 pg.); intro Citadel Supreme & Suprematons; 1st Allied Supermen of America 3.00

SUPREME: THE RETURN
Awesome Entertainment: May, 1999 - No. 6, June, 2000 ($2.99)
1-6: Alan Moore-s. 1,2-Sprouse & Gordon-a/c. 2,4-Liefeld-c. 6-Kirby app. 3.00

SURE-FIRE COMICS (Lightning Comics #4 on)
Ace Magazines: June, 1940 - No. 4, Oct, 1940 (Two No. 3's)
V1#1-Origin Flash Lightning & begins; X-The Phantom Fed, Ace McCoy, Buck Steele, Marvo the Magician, The Raven, Whiz Wilson (Time Traveler) begin (all 1st app.); Flash Lightning c-1-4 177 354 531 1106 1703 2300
2 81 162 243 506 778 1050
3(9/40), 3(#4)(10/40)-nn on-c, #3 on inside 60 120 180 375 580 785

SURF 'N' WHEELS
Charlton Comics: Nov, 1969 - No. 6, Sept, 1970
1 4 8 12 24 32 40
2-6 3 6 9 16 20 24

SURGE
Eclipse Comics: July, 1984 - No. 4, Jan, 1985 ($1.50, lim. series, Baxter paper)
1-4 Ties into DNAgents series 2.25

SURPRISE ADVENTURES (Formerly Tormented)
Sterling Comic Group: No. 3, Mar, 1955 - No. 5, July, 1955
3-5: 3,5-Sekowsky-a 8 16 24 46 58 70

SUSIE Q. SMITH
Dell Publishing Co.: No. 323, Mar, 1951 - No. 553, Apr, 1954
Four Color 323 (#1) 5 10 15 36 48 60
Four Color 377, 453 (2/53), 553 4 8 12 27 36 45

SUSPENSE (Radio/TV issues #1-11; Real Life Tales of... #1-4) (Amazing Detective Cases #3 on?)
Marvel/Atlas Comics (CnPC No. 1-10/BFP No. 11-29): Dec, 1949 - No. 29, Apr, 1953 (#1-8, 17-23: 52 pgs.)
1-Powell-a; Peter Lorre, Sidney Greenstreet photo-c from Hammett's "The Verdict" 60 120 180 375 580 785
2-Crime stories; Dennis O'Keefe & Gale Storm photo-c from Universal movie "Abandoned" 35 70 105 201 293 385
3-Change to horror 40 80 120 233 342 450
4,7-10: 7-Dracula-sty 30 60 90 173 249 325
5-Krigstein, Tuska, Everett-a 32 64 96 184 267 350
6-Tuska, Everett, Morisi-a 31 62 93 178 259 340

Suspense Comics #7 © Continental Magazines

Swamp Thing #147 © DC

Sweeney #5 © STD

GD 2.0 | VG 4.0 | FN 6.0 | VF 8.0 | VF/NM 9.0 | NM- 9.2

11-13,15-17,19,20 24 48 72 138 199 260
14-Clasic Heath Hypo-c; A-Bomb panels 35 70 105 201 293 385
18,22-Krigstein-a 25 50 75 144 207 270
21,23,24,26-29: 24-Tuska-a 22 44 66 125 180 235
25-Electric chair-c/story 31 62 93 177 256 335
NOTE: ***Ayers*** *a-20.* ***Briefer*** *a-5, 7, 27.* ***Brodsky*** *c-4, 6-9, 11, 16, 17, 25.* ***Colan*** *a-8(2), 9.* ***Everett*** *a-5, 6(2), 19, 23, 28; c-21-23, 26.* ***Fuje*** *a-29.* ***Heath*** *a-5, 6, 8, 10, 12, 14; c-14, 19, 24.* ***Maneely*** *a-12, 23, 24, 28, 29; c-5, 6p, 10, 13, 15, 18.* ***Mooney*** *a-24, 28.* ***Morisi*** *a-6, 12.* ***Palais*** *a-10.* ***Rico*** *a-7-9.* ***Robinson*** *a-29.* ***Romita*** *a-20(2), 25.* ***Sekowsky*** *a-11, 13, 14.* ***Sinnott*** *a-23, 25.* ***Tuska*** *a-5, 6(2), 12; c-12.* ***Whitney*** *a-15, 16, 22.* ***Ed Win*** *a-27.*

SUSPENSE COMICS
Continental Magazines: Dec, 1943 - No. 12, Sept, 1946
1-The Grey Mask begins; bondage/torture-c; L. B. Cole-a (7 pgs.)
386 772 1158 2509 4055 5600
2-Intro. The Mask; Rico, Giunta, L. B. Cole-a (7 pgs.)
285 570 855 1781 2741 3700
3-L.B. Cole-a; classic Schomburg-c (Scarce) 1800 3600 5400 10,800 15,400 20,000
4-6: 4-L. B. Cole-c begin 219 438 657 1369 2110 2850
7,9,10,12: 9-L.B. Cole eyeball-c 165 330 495 1031 1591 2150
8-Classic L. B. Cole spider-c 386 772 1158 2509 4055 5600
11-Classic Devil-c 314 628 942 2041 3296 4550
NOTE: ***L. B. Cole*** *c-4-12.* ***Fuje*** *a-8.* ***Larsen*** *a-11.* ***Palais*** *a-10, 11. Bondage c-1, 3, 4.*

SUSPENSE DETECTIVE
Fawcett Publications: June, 1952 - No. 5, Mar, 1953
1-Evans-a (11 pgs); Baily-c/a 44 88 132 268 409 550
2-Evans-a (10 pgs.) 29 58 87 164 237 310
3-5 24 48 72 135 195 255
NOTE: ***Baily*** *a-4, 5; c-1-3.* ***Sekowsky*** *a-2, 4, 5; c-5.*

SUSPENSE STORIES (See Strange Suspense Stories)

SUSSEX VAMPIRE, THE (Sherlock Holmes)
Caliber Comics: 1996 ($2.95, 32 pgs., B&W, one-shot)
nn-Adapts Sir Arthur Conan Doyle's story; Warren Ellis scripts 3.00

SUZIE COMICS (Formerly Laugh Comix; see Laugh Comics, Liberty Comics #10, Pep Comics & Top-Notch Comics #28)
Close-Up No. 49,50/MLJ Mag./Archie No. 51 on: No. 49, Spring, 1945 - No. 100, Aug, 1954
49-Ginger begins 24 48 72 135 195 255
50-55: 54-Transvestism story. 55-Woggon-a 15 30 45 83 117 150
56-Katy Keene begins by Woggon 15 30 45 85 120 155
57-65 11 22 33 64 87 110
66-80 10 20 30 60 80 100
81-87,89-99 10 20 30 58 77 95
88,100: 88-Used in **POP**, pgs. 76,77; Bill Woggon draws himself in story.
100-Last Katy Keene 10 20 30 60 80 100
NOTE: ***Al Fagaly*** *c-49-67. Katy Keene app. in 53-82, 85-100.*

SWAMP FOX, THE (TV, Disney)(See Walt Disney Presents #2)
Dell Publishing Co.: No. 1179, Dec, 1960
Four Color 1179-Leslie Nielsen photo-c 10 20 30 70 100 130

SWAMP THING (See Brave & the Bold, Challengers of the Unknown #82, DC Comics Presents #8 & 85, DC Special Series #2, 14, 17, 20, House of Secrets #92, Limited Collectors' Edition C-59, & Roots of the...)

SWAMP THING
National Per. Publ./DC Comics: Oct-Nov, 1972 - No. 24, Aug-Sept, 1976
1-Wrightson-c/a begins; origin 12 24 36 87 134 180
2-1st brief app. Patchwork Man (1 panel) 6 12 18 43 59 75
3-1st full app. Patchwork Man (see House of Secrets #140)
4 8 12 29 40 50
4-6, 4 8 12 27 36 45
7-Batman-c/story 4 8 12 29 40 50
8-10: 10-Last Wrightson issue 3 7 10 21 28 35
11-20: 11-19-Redondo-a. 13-Origin retold (1 pg.) 2 4 6 11 14 18
21-24: 23,24-Swamp Thing reverts back to Dr. Holland. 23-New logo
2 4 6 11 14 18
NOTE: ***J. Jones*** *a-9i(assist).* ***Kaluta*** *a-9i.* ***Redondo*** *c-12-19, 21.* ***Wrightson*** *issues (#1-10) reprinted in DC Special Series #2, 14, 17, 20 & Roots of the Swampthing.*

SWAMP THING (Saga Of The... #1-38,42-45) (See Essential Vertigo:...)
DC Comics (Vertigo imprint #129 on): May, 1982 - No. 171, Oct, 1996
(Direct sales #65 on)
1-Origin retold; Phantom Stranger series begins; ends #13; Yeates-c/a begins 6.00
2-15: 2-Photo-c from movie. 13-Last Yeates-a 4.00
16-19: Bissette-a. 5.00
20-1st Alan Moore issue 2 4 6 14 18 22
21-New origin 2 4 6 11 14 18
22,23,25: 25-John Constantine 1-panel cameo 2 4 6 8 10 12
24-JLA x-over; Last Yeates-c. 2 4 6 9 11 14
26-30 1 2 3 4 5 7
31-33,35,36: 33-r/1st app. from House of Secrets #92 5.00
34 1 2 3 5 6 8
37-1st app. John Constantine (Hellblazer) (6/85) 2 4 6 10 12 15
38-40: John Constantine app. 1 2 3 5 6 8
41-52,54-64: 44-Batman cameo. 44-51-John Constantine app. 46-Crisis x-over; Batman cameo. 49-Spectre app. 50-($1.25, 52 pgs.)-Deadman, Dr. Fate, Demon. 52-Arkham Asylum-c/story; Joker-c/cameo. 58-Spectre preview. 64-Last Moore issue 3.50
53-($1.25, 52 pgs.)-Arkham Asylum; Batman-c/story 4.50
65-83,85-99,101-124,126-149,151-153: 65-Direct sales only begins. 66-Batman & Arkham Asylum story. 70,76-John Constantine x-over; 76-X-over w/Hellblazer #9. 79-Superman-c/story. 85-Jonah Hex app. 102-Preview of World Without End. 116-Photo-c. 129-Metallic ink on-c. 140-Millar scripts begin, end #171 3.00
84-Sandman (Morpheus) cameo. 4.00
100,125,150: 100 ($2.50, 52 pgs.). 125-($2.95, 52 pgs.)-20th anniversary issue. 150 (52 pgs.)-Anniversary issue 3.00
154-171: 154-$2.25-c begins. 165-Curt Swan-a(p). 166,169,171-John Constantine & Phantom Stranger app. 168-Arcane returns 2.50
Annual 1,3-6('82-91): 1-Movie Adaptation; painted-c. 3-New format; Bolland-c. 4-Batman-c/story. 5-Batman cameo; re-intro Brother Power (Geek),1st app. since 1968 4.00
Annual 2 (1985)-Moore scripts; Bissette-a(p); Deadman, Spectre app. 7.00
Annual 7(1993, $3.95)-Children's Crusade 4.00
...A Murder of Crows (2001, $19.95)-r/#43-50; Moore-s 20.00
...: Earth To Earth (2002, $17.95)-r/#51-56; Batman app. 18.00
...Love and Death (1990, $17.95)-r/#28-34 & Annual #2; Totleben painted-c 18.00
...: Regenesis (2004, $17.95, TPB) r/#65-70; Veitch-s 18.00
...: Reunion (2003, $19.95, TPB) r/#57-64; Moore-s 20.00
...: Roots (1998, $7.95) Jon J Muth-s/painted-a/c 8.00
Saga of the Swamp Thing ('87, '89)-r/#21-27 (1st & 2nd print) 13.00
...: The Curse (2000, $19.95, TPB) r/#35-42; Bisley-c 20.00
NOTE: ***Bissette*** *a(p)-16-19, 21-27, 29, 30, 34-36, 39-42, 44, 46, 50, 64; c-17i, 24-32p, 35-37p, 40p, 44p, 46-50p, 51-58, 61, 62, 63p.* ***Kaluta*** *c/a-74.* ***Spiegle*** *a-1-3, 6.* ***Sutton*** *a-98p.* ***Totleben*** *a(i)-10, 16-27, 29, 31, 34-40, 42, 44, 46, 48, 50, 53, 55i; c-25-32i, 33, 35-40i, 42i, 44i, 46-50i, 53, 55i, 59p, 64, 65, 68, 73, 76, 80, 82, 84, 89, 91-100, Annual 4, 5.* ***Vess*** *painted c-121, 129-139, Annual 7.* ***Williamson*** *86i.* ***Wrightson*** *a-18i(r), 33r. John Constantine appears in #37-40, 44-51, 65-67, 70-77, 80-90, 99, 114, 115, 130, 134-138.*

SWAMP THING
DC Comics (Vertigo): May, 2000 - No. 20, Dec, 2001 ($2.50)
1-3-Tefé Holland's return; Vaughan-s/Petersen-a; Hale painted-c. 3.00
4-20: 7-9-Bisley-c. 10-John Constantine-c/app. 10-12-Fabry-c. 13-15-Mack-c 18-Swamp Thing app. 2.50
Preview-16 pg. flip book w/Lucifer Preview 2.25

SWAMP THING
DC Comics (Vertigo): May, 2004 - Present ($2.95)
1-10: 1-Diggle-s/Breccia-a; Constantine app. 2-6-Sargon app. 7,8-Corben-c/a 3.00
...: Bad Seed (2004, $9.95) r/#1-6 10.00

SWAT MALONE (America's Home Run King)
Swat Malone Enterprises: Sept, 1955
V1#1-Hy Fleishman-a 11 22 33 62 84 105

SWEATSHOP
DC Comics: Jun, 2003 - No. 6, Nov, 2003 ($2.95)
1-6-Peter Bagge-s/a; Destefano-a 3.00

SWEENEY (Formerly Buz Sawyer)
Standard Comics: No. 4, June, 1949 - No. 5, Sept, 1949
4,5: 5-Crane-a 9 18 27 49 62 75

SWEE'PEA (Also see Popeye #46)
Dell Publishing Co.: No. 219, Mar, 1949
Four Color 219 10 20 30 70 100 130

SWEET CHILDE
Advantage Graphics Press: 1995 - No. 2, 1995 ($2.95, B&W, mature)
1,2 3.00

SWEETHEART DIARY (Cynthia Doyle #66-on)
Fawcett Publications/Charlton Comics No. 32 on: Wint, 1949; #2, Spr, 1950; #3, 6/50 - #5, 10/50; #6, 1951(nd); #7, 9/51 - #14, 1/53; #32, 10/55; #33, 4/56 - #65, 8/62 (#1-14: photo-c)
1 19 38 57 107 154 200
2 10 20 30 60 80 100
3,4-Wood-a 15 30 45 86 123 160
5-10: 8-Bailey-a 9 18 27 52 66 80
11-14: 13-Swayze-a. 14-Last Fawcett issue 8 16 24 40 50 60
32 (10/55; 1st Charlton issue)(Formerly Cowboy Love #31)

Sweet Love #3 © HARV

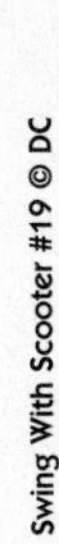
Swing With Scooter #19 © DC

Sword of Dracula #1 © Jason Henderson

	GD 2.0	VG 4.0	FN 6.0	VF 8.0	VF/NM 9.0	NM- 9.2
	8	16	24	43	54	65
33-40: 34-Swayze-a	6	12	18	28	34	40
41-(68 pgs.)	6	12	18	31	38	45
42-60	3	6	9	19	25	32
61-65	3	6	9	18	24	30

SWEETHEARTS (Formerly Captain Midnight)
Fawcett Publications/Charlton No. 122 on: #68, 10/48 - #121, 5/53; #122, 3/54; V2#23, 5/54 - #137, 12/73

	GD 2.0	VG 4.0	FN 6.0	VF 8.0	VF/NM 9.0	NM- 9.2
68-Photo-c begin	17	34	51	98	139	180
69,70	10	20	30	56	73	90
71-80	9	18	27	51	62	75
81-84,86-93,95-99,105	8	16	24	43	54	65
85,94,103,110,117-George Evans-a	9	18	27	52	66	80
100	9	18	27	51	62	75
101,107-Powell-a	8	16	24	46	58	70
102,104,106,108,109,112-116,118	8	16	24	40	50	60
111-1 pg. Ronald Reagan biography	9	18	27	54	70	85
119-Marilyn Monroe & Richard Widmark photo-c (1/54?); also appears in story; part Wood-a	48	96	144	293	447	600
120-Atom Bomb story	11	22	33	62	84	105
121-Liz Taylor/Fernanado Lamas photo-c	21	42	63	121	173	225
122-(1st Charlton? 3/54)-Marijuana story	11	22	33	62	84	105
V2#23 (5/54)-28: 28-Last precode issue (2/55)	7	14	21	37	46	55
29-39,41,43-45,47-50	4	8	12	27	36	45
40-Photo-c; Tommy Sands story	4	8	12	29	40	50
42-Ricky Nelson photo-c/story	9	18	27	65	93	120
46-Jimmy Rodgers photo-c/story	4	8	12	29	40	50
51-60	4	8	12	22	30	38
61-80,100	3	6	9	19	25	32
81-99	3	6	9	18	24	30
101-110	2	4	6	12	16	20
111-137	2	4	6	10	13	16

NOTE: *Photo c-68-121(Fawcett), 40, 42, 46(Charlton).* ***Swayze*** *a(Fawcett)-70-118(most).*

SWEETHEART SCANDALS (See Fox Giants)

SWEETIE PIE
Dell Publishing Co.: No. 1185, May-July, 1961 - No. 1241, Nov-Jan, 1961/62

	GD 2.0	VG 4.0	FN 6.0	VF 8.0	VF/NM 9.0	NM- 9.2
Four Color 1185 (#1)	5	10	15	36	48	60
Four Color 1241	4	8	12	27	36	45

SWEETIE PIE
Ajax-Farrell/Pines (Literary Ent.): Dec, 1955 - No. 15, Fall, 1957

	GD 2.0	VG 4.0	FN 6.0	VF 8.0	VF/NM 9.0	NM- 9.2
1-By Nadine Seltzer	9	18	27	52	66	80
2 (5/56; last Ajax?)	6	12	18	29	36	42
3-15	5	10	15	23	28	32

SWEET LOVE
Home Comics (Harvey): Sept, 1949 - No. 5, May, 1950 (All photo-c)

	GD 2.0	VG 4.0	FN 6.0	VF 8.0	VF/NM 9.0	NM- 9.2
1	10	20	30	60	80	100
2	7	14	21	37	46	55
3,4: 3-Powell-a	6	12	18	31	38	45
5-Kamen, Powell-a	9	18	27	49	62	75

SWEET ROMANCE
Charlton Comics: Oct, 1968

	GD 2.0	VG 4.0	FN 6.0	VF 8.0	VF/NM 9.0	NM- 9.2
1	2	4	6	12	16	22

SWEET SIXTEEN (...Comics and Stories for Girls)
Parents' Magazine Institute: Aug-Sept, 1946 - No. 13, Jan, 1948 (All have movie stars photos on covers)

	GD 2.0	VG 4.0	FN 6.0	VF 8.0	VF/NM 9.0	NM- 9.2
1-Van Johnson's life story; Dorothy Dare, Queen of Hollywood Stunt Artists begins (in all issues); part photo-c	21	42	63	121	173	225
2-Jane Powell, Roddy McDowall "Holiday in Mexico" photo on-c; Alan Ladd story	15	30	45	83	117	150
3,5,6,8-11: 5-Ann Francis photo on-c; Gregory Peck story. 6-Dick Haymes story. 8-Shirley Jones photo on-c. 10-Jean Simmons photo on-c; James Stewart story	10	20	30	60	80	100
4-Elizabeth Taylor photo on-c	21	42	63	121	173	225
7-Ronald Reagan's life story	21	42	63	118	169	220
12-Bob Cummings, Vic Damone story	11	22	33	64	87	110
13-Robert Mitchum's life story	11	22	33	66	91	115

SWEET XVI
Marvel Comics: May, 1991 - No. 5, Sept, 1991($1.00, color)

1-5: Barbara Slate story & art 3.00

SWIFT ARROW (Also see Lone Rider & The Rider)
Ajax/Farrell Publications: Feb-Mar, 1954 - No. 5, Oct-Nov, 1954; Apr, 1957 - No. 3, Sept, 1957

	GD 2.0	VG 4.0	FN 6.0	VF 8.0	VF/NM 9.0	NM- 9.2
1(1954) (1st Series)	17	34	51	98	139	180
2	10	20	30	56	73	90
3-5: 5-Lone Rider story	9	18	27	51	62	75
1 (2nd Series) (Swift Arrow's Gunfighters #4)	9	18	27	52	66	80
2,3: 2-Lone Rider begins	8	16	24	40	50	60

SWIFT ARROW'S GUNFIGHTERS (Formerly Swift Arrow)
Ajax/Farrell Publ. (Four Star Comic Corp.): No. 4, Nov, 1957

	GD 2.0	VG 4.0	FN 6.0	VF 8.0	VF/NM 9.0	NM- 9.2
4	8	16	24	40	50	60

SWING WITH SCOOTER
National Periodical Publ.: June-July, 1966 - No. 35, Aug-Sept, 1971; No. 36, Oct-Nov, 1972

	GD 2.0	VG 4.0	FN 6.0	VF 8.0	VF/NM 9.0	NM- 9.2
1	9	18	27	60	85	110
2,6-10: 9-Alfred E. Newman swipe in last panel	5	10	15	33	44	55
3-5: 3-Batman cameo on-c. 4-Batman cameo inside. 5-JLA cameo	5	10	15	36	48	60
11-13,15-19: 18-Wildcat of JSA 1pg. text. 19-Last 12¢-c	3	7	10	21	28	35
14-Alfred E. Neuman cameo	4	8	12	22	30	38
20 (68 pgs.)	5	10	15	33	44	55
21-23,25-31	3	6	9	18	23	28
24-Frankenstein-c.	3	7	10	21	28	35
32-34 (68 pgs.). 32-Batman cameo. 33-Interview with David Cassidy. 34-Interview with Rick Ely (The Rebels)	4	8	12	29	40	50
35-(52 pgs.). 1 pg. app. Clark Kent and 4 full pgs. of Superman	8	16	24	53	74	95
36-Bat-signal refererence to Batman	3	7	10	21	28	35

NOTE: ***Aragonés*** *a-13 (1pg.), 18(1pg.), 30(2pgs.)* ***Orlando*** *a-1-11; c-1-11, 13. #20, 33, 34: 68 pgs.; #35: 52 pgs.*

SWISS FAMILY ROBINSON (Walt Disney's..; see King Classics & Movie Comics)
Dell Publishing Co.: No. 1156, Dec, 1960

	GD 2.0	VG 4.0	FN 6.0	VF 8.0	VF/NM 9.0	NM- 9.2
Four Color 1156-Movie-photo-c	9	18	27	60	85	110

SWORD & THE DRAGON, THE
Dell Publishing Co.: No. 1118, June, 1960

	GD 2.0	VG 4.0	FN 6.0	VF 8.0	VF/NM 9.0	NM- 9.2
Four Color 1118-Movie, photo-c	9	18	27	63	89	115

SWORD & THE ROSE, THE (Disney)
Dell Publishing Co.: No. 505, Oct, 1953 - No. 682, Feb, 1956

	GD 2.0	VG 4.0	FN 6.0	VF 8.0	VF/NM 9.0	NM- 9.2
Four Color 505-Movie, photo-c	10	20	30	70	100	130
Four Color 682-When Knighthood Was in Flower-Movie, reprint of #505; Renamed the Sword & the Rose for the novel; photo-c	8	16	24	58	82	105

SWORD IN THE STONE, THE (See March of Comics #258 & Movie Comics & Wart and the Wizard)

SWORD OF DAMOCLES
Image Comics (WildStorm Productions): Mar, 1996 - No. 2, Apr, 1996 ($2.50, limited series)

1,2: Warren Ellis scripts. 1-Prelude to "Fire From Heaven" x-over; 1st app. Sword 2.50

SWORD OF DRACULA
Image Comics: Oct, 2003 - No. 6, Sept, 2004 ($2.95, B&W, limited series)

1-6-Tony Harris-c. 1,2-Greg Scott-a 3.00

SWORD OF SORCERY
National Periodical Publications: Feb-Mar, 1973 - No. 5, Nov-Dec, 1973 (20¢)

	GD 2.0	VG 4.0	FN 6.0	VF 8.0	VF/NM 9.0	NM- 9.2
1-Leiber Fafhrd & The Grey Mouser; Chaykin/Neal Adams (Crusty Bunkers) art; Kaluta-c	2	4	6	14	18	22
2,3: 2-Wrightson-c(i); Adams-a(i). 3-Wrightson-i(5 pgs.)	2	4	6	8	10	12
4,5: 5-Starlin-a(p); Conan cameo	1	2	3	5	7	9

NOTE: ***Chaykin*** *a-1-4p; c-2p, 3-5.* ***Kaluta*** *a-3i.* ***Simonson*** *a-3i, 4i, 5p; c-5.*

SWORD OF THE ATOM
DC Comics: Sept, 1983 - No. 4, Dec, 1983 (Limited series)

1-4: Gil Kane-c/a in all 3.00
Special 1-3('84, '85, '88): 1,2-Kane-c/a each 3.00

SWORDS OF TEXAS (See Scout #15)
Eclipse Comics: Oct, 1987 - No. 4, Jan, 1988 ($1.75, color, Baxter paper)

1-4: Scout app. 2.25

SWORDS OF THE SWASHBUCKLERS (See Marvel Graphic Novel)
Marvel Comics (Epic Comics): May, 1985 - No. 12, Jun, 1987 ($1.50; mature)

1-12-Butch Guice-c/a (Cont'd from Marvel G.N.) 2.25

SWORN TO PROTECT
Marvel Comics: Sept, 1995 ($1.95) (Based on card game)

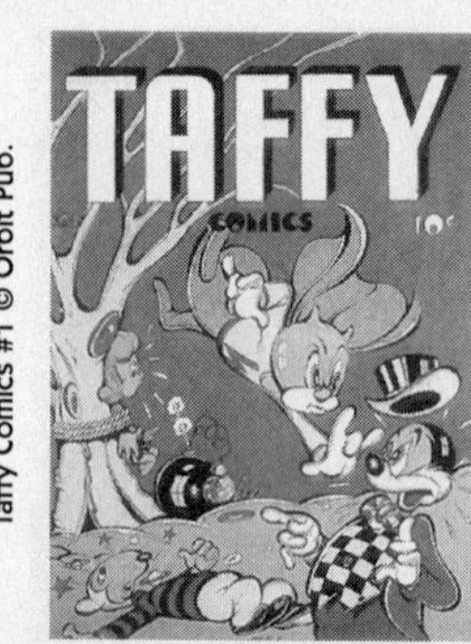

Taffy Comics #1 © Orbit Pub.

Tails #2 © SEGA

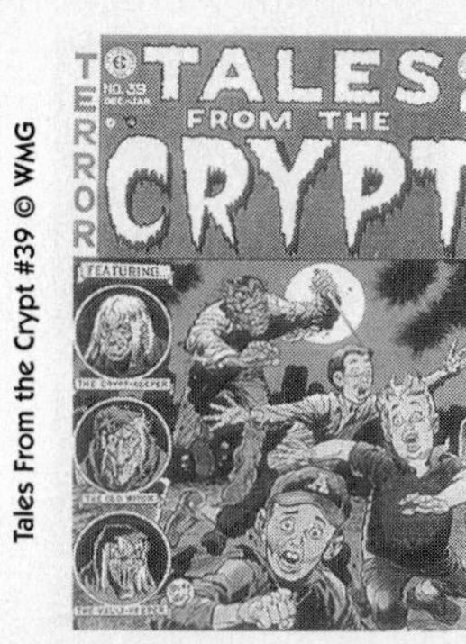

Tales From the Crypt #39 © WMG

GD VG FN VF VF/NM NM-
2.0 4.0 6.0 8.0 9.0 9.2

nn-Overpower Game Guide; Jubilee story 2.25

SYLVIA FAUST
Image Comics: Aug, 2004 - No. 4 ($2.95, limited series)
1,2-Jason Henderson-s/Greg Scott-a/c 3.00

SYN
Dark Horse Comics: Aug, 2003 - No. 5, Feb, 2004 ($2.99, limited series)
1-5-Giffen-s/Titus-a 3.00

SYPHONS
Now Comics: V2#1, May, 1994 - V2#3, 1994 ($2.50, limited series)
V2#1-3: 1-Stardancer, Knightfire, Raze & Brigade begin 2.50
TPB (9/04, $15.95) B&W reprints #1-3; intro. by Tony Caputo 16.00

SYSTEM, THE
DC Comics (Vertigo Verite): May, 1996 - No. 3, July, 1996 ($2.95, lim. series)
1-3: Kuper-c/a 3.00
TPB (1997, $12.95) r/#1-3 13.00

TAFFY COMICS
Rural Home/Orbit Publ.: Mar-Apr, 1945 - No. 12, 1948
1-L.B. Cole-c; origin & 1st app. of Wiggles The Wonderworm plus 7 chapter
WWII funny animal adventures 60 120 180 375 575 775
2-L.B. Cole-c; Wiggles-c/stories in #1-4 31 62 93 178 259 340
3,4,6-12: 6-Perry Como-c/story. 7-Duke Ellington, 2 pgs. 8-Glenn Ford-c/story. 9-Lon
McCallister part photo-c & story. 10-Mort Leav-c. 11-Mickey Rooney-c/story
14 28 42 79 110 140
5-L.B. Cole-c; Van Johnson-c/story 22 44 66 127 184 240

TAILGUNNER JO
DC Comics: Sept, 1988 - No. 6, Jan, 1989 ($1.25)
1-6 2.25

TAILS
Archie Publications; Dec, 1995 - No. 3, Feb, 1996 ($1.50, limited series)
1-3: Based on Sonic, the Hedgehog video game 4.00

TAILSPIN
Spotlight Publishers: November, 1944
nn-Firebird app.; L.B. Cole-c 29 58 87 164 237 310

TAILSPIN TOMMY (Also see Popular Comics)
United Features Syndicate/Service Publ. Co.: 1940; 1946
Single Series 23(1940) 40 80 120 236 331 465
Best Seller (nd, 1946)-Service Publ. Co. 15 30 45 86 123 160

TAINTED
DC Comics (Vertigo): Jan, 1995 ($4.95, one-shot)
1-Jamie Delano scripts; Al Davison-c/a; reads February '95 on-c 5.00

TAKION
DC Comics: June, 1996 - No. 7, Dec, 1996 ($1.75)
1-7: Lopresti-c/a(p). 1-Origin; Green Lantern app. 6-Final Night x-over 2.50

TALENT SHOWCASE (See New Talent Showcase)

TALE OF ONE BAD RAT, THE
Dark Horse Comics: Oct, 1994 - No. 4, Jan, 1995 ($2.95, limited series)
1-4: Bryan Talbot-c/a/scripts 3.00
HC ($69.95, signed and numbered) R/#1-4 70.00

TALES CALCULATED TO DRIVE YOU BATS
Archie Publications: Nov, 1961 - No. 7, Nov, 1962; 1966 (Satire)
1-Only 10¢ issue; has cut-out Werewolf mask (price includes mask)
13 26 39 92 141 190
2-Begin 12¢ issues 8 16 24 53 74 95
3-6: 3-UFO cover 6 12 18 40 55 70
7-Storyline change 6 12 18 38 52 65
1(1966, 25¢, 44 pg. Giant)-r/#1; UFO cover 6 12 18 38 52 65

TALES CALCULATED TO DRIVE YOU MAD
E.C. Publications: Summer, 1997 - No. 8, Winter, 1999 ($3.99/$4.99, satire)
1-6-Full color reprints of Mad: 1-(#1-3), 2-(#4-6), 3-(#7-9), 4-(#10-12)
5-(#13-15), 6-(#16-18) 5.00
7,8-($4.99-c): 7-(#19-21), 8-(#22,23) 5.00

TALES FROM THE AGE OF APOCALYPSE
Marvel Comics: 1996 ($5.95, prestige format, one-shots)
1, ...: Sinister Bloodlines (1997, $5.95) 6.00

TALES FROM THE BOG
Aberration Press: Nov, 1995 - No. 7, Nov, 1997 ($2.95/$3.95, B&W)
1-7 4.00
Alternate #1 (Director's Cut) (1998, $2.95) 3.00

TALES FROM THE BULLY PULPIT
Image Comics: Aug, 2004 ($6.95, square-bound)
1-Teddy Roosevelt and Edison's ghost with a time machine; Cereno-s/MacDonald-a 7.00

TALES FROM THE CRYPT (Formerly The Crypt Of Terror; see Three Dimensional...)
E.C. Comics: No. 20, Oct-Nov, 1950 - No. 46, Feb-Mar, 1955
20-See Crime Patrol #15 for 1st Crypt Keeper 112 224 336 840 1233 1625
21-Kurtzman-r/Haunt of Fear #15(#1) 92 184 276 690 1010 1330
22-Moon Girl costume at costume party, one panel 72 144 216 540 790 1040
23-25: 24-E. A. Poe adaptation 56 112 168 420 615 810
26-30: 26-Wood's 2nd EC-c 45 90 135 338 494 650
31-Williamson-a(1st at E.C.); B&W and color illos. in **POP**; Kamen draws himself,
Gaines & Feldstein; Ingels, Craig & Davis draw themselves in his story
46 92 138 345 503 660
32,35-39: 38-Censored-c 40 80 120 300 433 565
33-Origin The Crypt Keeper 63 126 189 473 687 900
34-Used in **POP**, pg. 83; lingerie panels 41 82 123 308 444 580
40-Used in Senate hearings & in Hartford Cournat anti-comics editorials-1954
40 80 120 300 433 565
41-45: 45-2 pgs. showing E.C. staff 39 78 117 293 427 560
46-Low distribution; pre-advertised cover for unpublished 4th horror title
"Crypt of Terror" used on this book 46 92 138 345 503 660
NOTE: ***Ray Bradbury*** *adaptations-34, 36.* ***Craig*** *a-20, 22-24; c-20.* ***Crandall*** *a-38, 44.* ***Davis*** *a-24-46; c-29-46.* ***Elder*** *a-37, 38.* ***Evans*** *a-32-34, 36, 40, 41, 43, 46.* ***Feldstein*** *a-20-23; c-21-25, 28. Ingels a-in all.* ***Kamen*** *a-20, 22, 25, 27-31, 33-36, 39, 41-45.* ***Krigstein*** *a-40, 42, 45.* ***Kurtzman*** *a-21.* ***Orlando*** *a-27-30, 35, 37, 39, 41-45.* ***Wood*** *a-21, 24, 25; c-26, 27. Canadian reprints known; see Table of Contents.*

TALES FROM THE CRYPT (Magazine)
Eerie Publications: No. 10, July, 1968 (35¢, B&W)
10-Contains Farrell reprints from 1950s 4 8 12 27 36 45

TALES FROM THE CRYPT
Gladstone Publishing: July, 1990 - No. 6, May, 1991 ($1.95/$2.00, 68 pgs.)
1-r/TFTC #33 & Crime S.S. #17; Davis-c(r) 3.00
2-6: 2,3,5,6-Davis-c(r). 4-Begin $2.00-c; Craig-c(r) 3.00

TALES FROM THE CRYPT
Extra-Large Comics (Russ Cochran)/Gemstone Publishing: Jul, 1991 - No. 6 ($3.95, 10 1/4 x13 1/4", 68 pgs.)
1-Davis-c(r); Craig back-c(r); E.C. reprints 4.00
2-6 ($2.00, comic sized) 3.00

TALES FROM THE CRYPT
Russ Cochran: Sept, 1991 - No. 7, July, 1992 ($2.00, 64 pgs.)
1-7 3.00

TALES FROM THE CRYPT
Russ Cochran/Gemstone: Sept, 1992 - No. 30, Dec, 1999 ($1.50, quarterly)
1-4-r/Crypt of Terror #17-19, TFTC #20 w/original-c 3.00
5-30: 5-15 ($2.00)-r/TFTC #21-23 w/original-c. 16-30 ($2.50) 3.00
Annual 1-6('93-'99) 1-r/#1-5. 2- r/#6-10. 3- r/#11-15. 4- r/#16-20. 5-r/#21-25. 6- r/#26-30 14.00

TALES FROM THE GREAT BOOK
Famous Funnies: Feb, 1955 - No. 4, Jan, 1956 (Religious themes)
1-Story of Samson; John Lehti-a in all 9 18 27 52 66 80
2-4: 2-Joshua. 3-Joash the Boy King. 4-David 7 14 21 35 43 50

TALES FROM THE HEART OF AFRICA (The Temporary Natives)
Marvel Comics (Epic Comics): Aug, 1990 ($3.95, 52 pgs.)
1 4.00

TALES FROM THE TOMB (Also see Dell Giants)
Dell Publishing Co.: Oct, 1962 (25¢ giant)
1(02-810-210)-All stories written by John Stanley 13 26 39 104 182 260

TALES FROM THE TOMB (Magazine)
Eerie Publications: V1#6, July, 1969 - V7#3, 1975 (52 pgs.)
V1#6 6 12 18 43 59 75
V1#7,8 5 10 15 36 48 60
V2#1-6: 4-LSD story-r/Weird V3#5. 6-Rulah-r 4 8 12 27 36 45
V3#1-Rulah-r 4 8 12 27 36 45
2-6('71),V4#1-5('72),V5#1-6('73),V6#1-6('74),V7#1-3('75)
4 8 12 24 32 40

Tales of Suspense #15 © MAR

Tales of Suspense #39 © MAR

Tales of Suspense V2#1 © MAR

GD VG FN VF VF/NM NM-
2.0 4.0 6.0 8.0 9.0 9.2

TALES OF ASGARD
Marvel Comics Group: Oct, 1968 (25¢, 68 pgs.); Feb, 1984 ($1.25, 52 pgs.)

1-Reprints Tales of Asgard (Thor) back-up stories from Journey into Mystery #97-106;
new Kirby-c; Kirby-a 5 10 15 33 44 55
V2#1 (2/84)-Thor-r; Simonson-c 3.00

TALES OF EVIL
Atlas/Seaboard Publ.: Feb, 1975 - No. 3, July, 1975 (All 25¢ issues)

1-3: 1-Werewolf w/Sekowsky-a. 2-Intro. The Bog Beast; Sparling-a.
3-Origin The Man-Monster; Buckler-a(p) 1 2 3 6 8 10

NOTE: ***Grandenetti** a-1, 2. **Lieber** c-1. **Sekowsky** a-1. **Sutton** a-2. **Thorne** c-2.*

TALES OF GHOST CASTLE
National Periodical Publications: May-June, 1975 - No. 3, Sept-Oct, 1975 (All 25¢ issues)

1-Redondo-a 3 6 9 16 20 25
2,3: 2-Nino-a. 3-Redondo-a. 2 4 6 9 11 14

TALES OF G.I. JOE
Marvel Comics: Jan, 1988 - No. 15, Mar, 1989

1 ($2.25, 52 pgs.) 3.00
2-15 ($1.50): 1-15-r/G.I. Joe #1-15 2.25

TALES OF HORROR
Toby Press/Minoan Publ. Corp.: June, 1952 - No. 13, Oct, 1954

1 40 80 120 236 351 465
2-Torture scenes 34 68 102 193 279 365
3-13: 9-11-Reprints Purple Claw #1-3 22 44 66 125 180 235
12-Myron Fass-c/a; torture scenes 23 46 69 130 188 245

NOTE: ***Andru** a-5. **Baily** a-5. **Myron Fass** a-2, 3, 12; c-1-3, 12. **Hollingsworth** a-2. **Sparling** a-6, 9; c-9.*

TALES OF JUSTICE
Atlas Comics(MjMC No. 53-66/Male No. 67): No. 53, May, 1955 - No. 67, Aug, 1957

53 16 32 48 89 127 165
54-57: 54-Powell-a 11 22 33 63 84 105
58,59-Krigstein-a 12 24 36 69 95 120
60-63,65: 60-Powell-a 10 20 30 56 73 90
64,66,67: 64,67-Crandall-a. 66-Torres, Orlando-a 10 20 30 58 77 95

NOTE: ***Everett** a-53, 60. **Orlando** a-65, 66. **Severin** a-64; c-58, 60, 65. **Wildey** a-64, 67.*

TALES OF SUSPENSE (Becomes Captain America #100 on)
Atlas (WPI No. 1,2/Male No. 3-12/VPI No. 13-18)/Marvel No. 19 on:
Jan, 1959 - No. 99, Mar, 1968

1-Williamson-a (5 pgs.); Heck-c; #1-4 have sci/fi-c 137 274 411 1165 1883 2600
2,3: 2-Robot-c. 3-Flying saucer-c/story 50 100 150 413 657 900
4-Williamson-a (4 pgs.); Kirby/Everett-c/a 44 88 132 352 551 750
5,6,8,10: 5-Kirby monster-c begin 33 66 99 248 387 525
7-Prototype ish. (Lava Man); 1 panel app. Aunt May (see Str. Tales #97)
37 74 111 278 432 585
9-Prototype ish. (Iron Man) 38 76 114 285 448 610
11,12,15,17-19: 12-Crandall-a. 27 54 81 194 297 400
13-Elektro-c/story 28 56 84 199 305 410
14-Intro/1st app. Colossus-c/sty 33 66 99 248 384 520
16-1st Metallo-c/story (4/61, Iron Man prototype) 32 64 96 240 375 510
20-Colossus-c/story (2nd app.) 28 56 84 199 305 410
21-25: 25-Last 10¢ issue 22 44 66 155 238 320
26,27,29,30,33,34,36-38: 33-(9/62)-Hulk 1st x-over cameo (picture on wall)
18 36 54 129 197 265
28-Prototype ish. (Stone Men) 19 38 57 134 205 275
31-Prototype ish. (Dr. Doom) 22 44 66 155 238 320
32-Prototype ish. (Dr. Strange)(8/62)-Sazzik The Sorcerer app.; "The Man and the Beehive" story, 1 month before TTA #35 (2nd Antman), came out after "The Man in the Ant Hill" in TTA #27 (1/62) (1st Antman)-Characters from both stories were tested to see which got best fan response 31 62 93 225 355 485
35-Prototype issue (The Watcher) 22 44 66 155 238 320
39 (3/63)-Origin/1st app. Iron Man & begin series; 1st Iron Man story has Kirby layouts
409 818 1227 3742 6371 9000
40-2nd app. Iron Man (in new armor) 145 290 435 1233 1992 2750
41-3rd app. Iron Man; Dr. Strange (villain) app. 79 158 237 672 1086 1500
42-45: 45-Intro. & 1st app. Happy & Pepper 47 94 141 376 588 800
46,47: 46-1st app. Crimson Dynamo 36 72 108 270 423 575
48-New Iron Man armor by Ditko 41 82 123 318 497 675
49-1st X-Men x-over (same date as X-Men #3, 1/64); also 1st Avengers x-over (w/o Captain America); 1st Tales of the Watcher back-up story & begins (2nd app. Watcher; see F.F. #13) 50 100 150 413 657 900
50-1st app. Mandarin 24 48 72 170 260 350
51-1st Scarecrow 20 40 60 145 223 300
52-1st app. The Black Widow (4/64) 30 60 90 218 334 450
53-Origin The Watcher; 2nd Black Widow app. 20 40 60 145 223 300
54-56: 56-1st app. Unicorn 14 28 42 102 156 210
57-Origin/1st app. Hawkeye (9/64) 30 60 90 218 334 450
58-Captain America battles Iron Man (10/64)-Classic-c; 2nd Kraven app.
(Cap's 1st app. in this title) 34 68 102 255 403 550
59-Iron Man plus Captain America double feature begins (11/64); 1st S.A. Captain America solo story; intro Jarvis, Avenger's butler; classic-c 34 68 102 255 403 550
60-2nd app. Hawkeye (#64 is 3rd app.) 19 38 57 134 205 275
61,62,64: 62-Origin Mandarin (2/65) 11 22 33 79 117 155
63-1st Silver Age origin Captain America (3/65) 27 54 81 194 297 400
65-G.A. Red Skull in WWII stories(also in #66);-1st Silver-Age Red Skull (5/65).
20 40 60 145 223 300
66-Origin Red Skull 15 30 45 109 167 225
67-70: 69-1st app. Titanium Man. 70-Begin alternating-c features w/Capt. America (even #'s) & Iron Man (odd #'s) 9 18 27 65 93 120
71-75, 77,78,81-98: 75-1st app. Agent 13 later named Sharon Carter. 78-Col. Nick Fury app. 81-Intro the Adaptoid by Kirby (also in #82-84). 88-Mole Man app. in Iron Man story. 92-1st Nick Fury x-over (cameo, as Agent of S.H.I.E.L.D., 8/67). 94-Intro Modok. 95-Capt. America's i.d. revealed. 97-1st Whiplash. 98-1st brief app. new Zemo (son?); #99 is 1st full app. 7 14 21 46 63 80
76-Intro Batroc & Sharon Carter, Agent 13 of S.H.I.E.L.D.
7 14 21 51 71 90
79-Begin 3 part Iron Man Sub-Mariner battle story; Sub-Mariner-c & cameo;
1st app. Cosmic Cube; 1st modern Red Skull 8 16 24 55 78 100
80-Iron Man battles Sub-Mariner story cont'd in Tales to Astonish #82; classic Red Skull-c
8 16 24 55 78 100
99-Captain America story cont'd in Captain America #100; Iron Man story cont'd in Iron Man & Sub-Mariner #1 8 16 24 58 82 105

NOTE: ***Abel** a-73-81i(as Gary Michaels), **J. Buscema** a-1; c-3. **Colan** a-39, 73-99p; c(p)-73, 75, 77, 79, 81, 83, 85-87, 89, 91, 93, 95, 97, 99. **Crandall** a-12. **Davis** a-38. **Ditko** a-1-15, 17-44, 46, 47-49p; c-2, 10i, 13i, 23i. **Kirby/Ditko** a-7; c-10, 13, 22, 28, 34. **Everett** a-8. **Forte** a-5, 9. **Giacoia** a-82. **Heath** a-2, 10. **Gil Kane** a-88p, 89-91; c-88, 89-91p. **Kirby** a(p)-2-4, 6-35, 40, 41, 43, 59-75, 77-86, 92-99; layouts-69-75, 77; c(p)4-28(most), 29-56, 58-72, 74, 76, 78, 80, 82, 84, 86, 92, 94, 96, 98. **Leiber/Fox** a-42, 43, 45, 51. **Reinman** a-26, 44i, 49i, 52i, 53i. **Tuska** a-58, 70-74. **Wood** c/a-71i.*

TALES OF SUSPENSE
Marvel Comics: V2#1, Jan, 1995 ($6.95, one-shot)

V2#1-James Robinson script; acetate-c. 7.00

TALES OF SWORD & SORCERY (See Dagar)

TALES OF TELLOS (See Tellos)
Image Comics: Oct, 2004 - No. 3, ($3.50, anthology)

1,2: 1-Dezago-s; art by Yates & Rousseau; Wieringo-c 3.50

TALES OF TERROR
Toby Press Publications: 1952 (no month)

1-Fawcette-c; Ravielli-a 26 52 78 150 215 280

NOTE: *This title was cancelled due to similarity to the E.C. title.*

TALES OF TERROR (See Movie Classics)

TALES OF TERROR (Magazine)
Eerie Publications: Summer, 1964

1 5 10 15 36 48 60

TALES OF TERROR
Eclipse Comics: July, 1985 - No. 13, July, 1987 ($2.00, Baxter paper, mature)

1-13: 5-1st Lee Weeks-a. 7-Sam Kieth-a. 10-Snyder-a. 12-Vampire story 3.00

TALES OF TERROR (IDW's...)
IDW Publishing: Sept, 2004 ($16.99, hardcover)

1-Anthology of short graphic stories and text stories; incl. 30 Days of Night 17.00

TALES OF TERROR ANNUAL
E.C. Comics: 1951 - No. 3, 1953 (25¢, 132 pgs., 16 stories each)

nn(1951)(Scarce)-Feldstein infinity-c 575 1150 1725 4600 - -
2(1952)-Feldstein-c 215 430 645 1613 2207 2800
3(1953)-Feldstein bondage/torture-c 166 332 498 1245 1703 2160

NOTE: *No. 1 contains three horror and one science fiction comic which came out in 1950. No. 2 contains a horror, crime, and science fiction book which generally had cover dates in 1951, and No. 3 had horror, crime, and shock books that generally appeared in 1952. All E.C. annuals contain four complete books that did not sell on the stands which were rebound in the annual format, minus the covers, and sold from the E.C. office and on the stands in key cities. The contents of each annual may vary in the same year. Crypt Keeper, Vault Keeper, Old Witch app. on all-c.*

TALES OF TERROR ILLUSTRATED (See Terror Illustrated)

TALES OF TEXAS JOHN SLAUGHTER (See Walt Disney Presents, 4-Color #997)

TALES OF THE BEANWORLD
Beanworld Press/Eclipse Comics: Feb, 1985 - No. 19, 1991; No. 20, 1993 - No. 21, 1993

Tales of the Legion of Super-Heroes #315 © DC

Tales of the Mysterious Traveler #10 © CC

Tales of the Vampires #1 © 20th Century Fox

	GD 2.0	VG 4.0	FN 6.0	VF 8.0	VF/NM 9.0	NM- 9.2
($1.50/$2.00, B&W)						
1-21						3.00

TALES OF THE BIZARRO WORLD
DC Comics: 2000 ($14.95, TPB)

	GD 2.0	VG 4.0	FN 6.0	VF 8.0	VF/NM 9.0	NM- 9.2
nn-Reprints early Bizarro stories; new Jaime Hernandez-c						15.00

TALES OF THE DARKNESS
Image Comics (Top Cow): Apr, 1998 - No. 4, Dec, 1998 ($2.95)

	GD 2.0	VG 4.0	FN 6.0	VF 8.0	VF/NM 9.0	NM- 9.2
1-4: 1,2-Portacio-c/a(p). 3,4-Lansing & Nocon-a(p)						3.00
1-American Entertainment Ed.						3.00
#1/2 (1/01, $2.95)						3.00

TALES OF THE GREEN BERET
Dell Publishing Co.: Jan, 1967 - No. 5, Oct, 1969

	GD 2.0	VG 4.0	FN 6.0	VF 8.0	VF/NM 9.0	NM- 9.2
1-Glanzman-a in 1-4 & 5r	4	8	12	24	32	40
2-5: 5-Reprints #1	3	6	9	18	24	30

TALES OF THE GREEN HORNET
Now Comics: Sept, 1990 - No. 2, 1990; V2#1, Jan, 1992 - No.4, Apr, 1992; V3#1, Sept, 1992 - No. 3, Nov, 1992

	GD 2.0	VG 4.0	FN 6.0	VF 8.0	VF/NM 9.0	NM- 9.2
1,2						2.50
V2#1-4 ($1.95)						2.50
V3#1 ($2.75)-Polybagged w/hologram trading card						3.00
V3#2,3 ($2.50)						2.50

TALES OF THE GREEN LANTERN CORPS (See Green Lantern #107)
DC Comics: May, 1981 - No. 3, July, 1981 (Limited series)

	GD 2.0	VG 4.0	FN 6.0	VF 8.0	VF/NM 9.0	NM- 9.2
1-3: 1-Origin of G.L. & the Guardians, Annual 1 (1/85)-Gil Kane-c/a						3.50

TALES OF THE INVISIBLE SCARLET O'NEIL (See Harvey Comics Hits #59)

TALES OF THE KILLERS (Magazine)
World Famous Periodicals: V1#10, Dec, 1970 - V1#11, Feb, 1971 (B&W, 52 pg)

	GD 2.0	VG 4.0	FN 6.0	VF 8.0	VF/NM 9.0	NM- 9.2
V1#10-One pg. Frazetta; r/Crime Does Not Pay	4	8	12	27	36	45
11-similar-c to Crime Does Not Pay #47; contains r/Crime Does Not Pay	4	8	12	22	30	38

TALES OF THE LEGION (Formerly Legion of Super-Heroes)
DC Comics: No. 314, Aug, 1984 - No. 354, Dec, 1987

	GD 2.0	VG 4.0	FN 6.0	VF 8.0	VF/NM 9.0	NM- 9.2
314-354: 326-r-begin						2.50
Annual 4,5 (1986, 1987)-Formerly LSH Annual						3.50

TALES OF THE MARINES (Formerly Devil-Dog Dugan #1-3)
Atlas Comics (OPI): No. 4, Feb, 1957 (Marines At War #5 on)

	GD 2.0	VG 4.0	FN 6.0	VF 8.0	VF/NM 9.0	NM- 9.2
4-Powell-a; Severin-c	8	16	24	43	54	65

TALES OF THE MARVELS
Marvel Comics: 1995/1996 (all acetate, painted-c)

	GD 2.0	VG 4.0	FN 6.0	VF 8.0	VF/NM 9.0	NM- 9.2
...Blockbuster 1 (1995, $5.95, one-shot), ...Inner Demons 1 (1996, $5.95, one shot), ...Wonder Years 1,2 (1995, $4.95, limited series)						6.00

TALES OF THE MARVEL UNIVERSE
Marvel Comics: Feb, 1997 ($2.95, one-shot)

	GD 2.0	VG 4.0	FN 6.0	VF 8.0	VF/NM 9.0	NM- 9.2
1-Anthology; wraparound-c; Thunderbolts, Ka-Zar app.						3.00

TALES OF THE MYSTERIOUS TRAVELER (See Mysterious...)
Charlton Comics: Aug, 1956 - No. 13, June, 1959; V2#14, Oct, 1985 - No. 15, Dec, 1985

	GD 2.0	VG 4.0	FN 6.0	VF 8.0	VF/NM 9.0	NM- 9.2
1-No Ditko-a; Giordano/Alascia-c	47	94	141	287	436	585
2-Ditko-a(1)	40	80	120	240	360	480
3-Ditko-c/a(1)	40	80	120	244	372	500
4-6-Ditko-c/a(3-4 stories each)	48	96	144	293	447	600
7-9-Ditko-a(1-2 each). 8-Rocke-c	40	80	120	236	351	465
10,11-Ditko-c/a(3-4 each)	43	86	129	262	401	540
12	18	36	54	100	143	185
13-Baker-a (r?)	19	38	57	107	154	200
V2#14,15 (1985)-Ditko-c/a-low print run	1	2	3	5	7	9

TALES OF THE NEW TEEN TITANS
DC Comics: June, 1982 - No. 4, Sept, 1982 (Limited series)

	GD 2.0	VG 4.0	FN 6.0	VF 8.0	VF/NM 9.0	NM- 9.2
1-4						4.00

TALES OF THE PONY EXPRESS (TV)
Dell Publishing Co.: No. 829, Aug, 1957 - No. 942, Oct, 1958

	GD 2.0	VG 4.0	FN 6.0	VF 8.0	VF/NM 9.0	NM- 9.2
Four Color 829 (#1)--Painted-c	6	12	18	38	52	65
Four Color 942-Title -Pony Express	6	12	18	38	52	65

TALES OF THE REALM
CrossGen Comics/MVCreations #4-on: Oct, 2003 - No. 5, May, 2004 ($2.95, limited series)

	GD 2.0	VG 4.0	FN 6.0	VF 8.0	VF/NM 9.0	NM- 9.2
1-5-Robert Kirkman-s/Matt Tyree-a						3.00

TALES OF THE SUN RUNNERS
Sirius Comics/Amazing Comics No. 3: V2#1, July, 1986 - V2#3, 1986? ($1.50)

	GD 2.0	VG 4.0	FN 6.0	VF 8.0	VF/NM 9.0	NM- 9.2
V2#1-3, Christmas Special 1(12/86)						2.25

TALES OF THE TEENAGE MUTANT NINJA TURTLES (See Teenage Mutant...)
Mirage Studios: May, 1987 - No. 7, Aug (Apr-c), 1989 (B&W, $1.50)

	GD 2.0	VG 4.0	FN 6.0	VF 8.0	VF/NM 9.0	NM- 9.2
1-7: 2-Title merges w/Teenage Mutant Ninja...						2.25

TALES OF THE TEEN TITANS (Formerly The New Teen Titans)
DC Comics: No. 41, Apr, 1984 - No. 91, July, 1988 (75¢)

	GD 2.0	VG 4.0	FN 6.0	VF 8.0	VF/NM 9.0	NM- 9.2
41,45-49: 46-Aqualad & Aquagirl join						3.00
42-44: The Judas Contract part 1-3 with Deathstroke the Terminator in all; concludes in Annual #3. 44-Dick Grayson becomes Nightwing (3rd to be Nightwing) & joins Titans; Jericho (Deathstroke's son) joins; origin Deathstroke						3.50
50,53-55: 50-Double size; app. Betty Kane (Bat-Girl) out of costume. 53-1st full app. Azrael; Deathstroke cameo. 54,55-Deathstroke-c/stories						3.50
51,52,56-91: 52-1st brief app. Azrael (not same as newer character). 56-Intro Jinx. 57-Neutron app. 59-r/DC Comics Presents #26. 60-91-r/New Teen Titans Baxter series. 68-B. Smith-c. 70-Origin Kole						2.50
Annual 3(1984, $1.25)-Part 4 of The Judas Contract; Deathstroke-c/story; Death of Terra; indicia says Teen Titans Annual; previous annuals listed as New Teen Titans Annual #1,2						4.00
Annual 4-(1986, $1.25)						2.50

TALES OF THE TEXAS RANGERS (See Jace Pearson...)

TALES OF THE TMNT (Also see Teenage Mutant Ninja Turtles)
Mirage Studios: Jan, 2004 - Present ($2.95, B&W)

	GD 2.0	VG 4.0	FN 6.0	VF 8.0	VF/NM 9.0	NM- 9.2
1-6: 1-Brizuela-a						3.00

TALES OF THE UNEXPECTED (Becomes The Unexpected #105 on)(See Adventure #75, Super DC Giant)
National Periodical Publications: Feb-Mar, 1956 - No. 104, Dec-Jan, 1967-68

	GD 2.0	VG 4.0	FN 6.0	VF 8.0	VF/NM 9.0	NM- 9.2
1	92	184	276	782	1266	1750
2	46	92	138	368	572	775
3-5	33	66	99	248	387	525
6-10: 6-1st Silver Age issue	28	56	84	199	305	410
11,14,19,20	18	36	54	126	193	260
12,13,15-18,21-24: All have Kirby-a. 15,17-Grey tone-c. 16-Character named 'Thor' with a magic hammer by Kirby (8/57, unlike later Thor)	23	46	69	165	253	340
25-30	15	30	45	105	160	215
31-39	13	26	39	92	141	190
40-Space Ranger begins (8/59, 3rd ap.), ends #82	91	182	273	774	1250	1725
41,42-Space Ranger stories	36	72	108	270	423	575
43-1st Space Ranger-c this title; grey tone-c	63	126	189	536	868	1200
44-46	25	50	75	181	278	375
47-50	19	38	57	134	205	275
51-60: 54-Dinosaur-c/story	15	30	45	109	167	225
61-67: 67-Last 10¢ issue	13	26	39	90	138	185
68-82: 82-Last Space Ranger	8	16	24	58	82	105
83-90,92-99	6	12	18	40	55	70
91,100: 91-1st Automan (also in #94,97)	6	12	18	43	59	75
101-104	5	10	15	36	48	60

NOTE: ***Neal Adams*** *c-104.* ***Anderson*** *a-50.* ***Brown*** *a-50-82(Space Ranger); c-19, 40, & many Space Ranger-c.* ***Cameron*** *a-24, 27, 29; c-24.* ***Heath*** *a-49.* ***Bob Kane*** *a-24, 48.* ***Kirby*** *a-12, 13, 15-18, 21-24; c-13, 18, 22.* ***Meskin*** *a-15, 18, 26, 27, 35, 66.* ***Moreira*** *a-16, 20, 29, 38, 44, 62, 71; c-38.* ***Roussos*** *c-10.* ***Wildey*** *a-31.*

TALES OF THE VAMPIRES (Also see Buffy the Vampire Slayer and related titles)
Dark Horse Comics: 2003 - No. 5, Apr, 2004 ($2.99, limited series)

	GD 2.0	VG 4.0	FN 6.0	VF 8.0	VF/NM 9.0	NM- 9.2
1-Short stories by Joss Whedon and others. 1-Totleben-c. 3-Powell-c. 4-Edlund-c						3.00
TPB (11/04, $15.95) r/#1-5; afterword by Marv Wolfman						16.00

TALES OF THE WEST (See 3-D...)

TALES OF THE WITCHBLADE
Image Comics (Top Cow Productions): Nov, 1996 - Present ($2.95)

	GD 2.0	VG 4.0	FN 6.0	VF 8.0	VF/NM 9.0	NM- 9.2
1/2	1	2	3	5	7	9
1/2 Gold						15.00
1-Daniel-c/a(p)	1	3	4	6	8	10
1-Variant-c by Turner	2	4	6	10	12	15
1-Platinum Edition						30.00
2,3						6.00
4-6: 6-Green-c						5.00
7-9: 9-Lara Croft-c						3.00
7-Variant-c by Turner	1	2	3	5	6	8
Witchblade: Distinctions (4/01, $14.95, TPB) r/#1-6; Green-c						15.00

Tales To Astonish #6 © MAR

Taleweaver #2 © Agimat, LLC

Tangent Comics/The Batman #1 © DC

GD 2.0 | VG 4.0 | FN 6.0 | VF 8.0 | VF/NM 9.0 | NM- 9.2

TALES OF THE WITCHBLADE COLLECTED EDITION
Image Comics (Top Cow): May, 1998 - Present ($4.95/$5.95, square-bound)

1,2: 1-r/#1,2. 2-($5.95) r/#3,4 — 6.00

TALES OF THE WIZARD OF OZ (See Wizard of OZ, 4-Color #1308)

TALES OF THE ZOMBIE (Magazine)
Marvel Comics Group: Aug, 1973 - No. 10, Mar, 1975 (75¢, B&W)

	GD	VG	FN	VF	VF/NM	NM-
V1#1-Reprint/Menace #5; origin	4	8	12	24	32	40
2,3: 2-Everett biog. & memorial	3	6	9	18	24	30
V2#1(#4)-Photos & text of James Bond movie "Live & Let Die"	3	6	9	16	21	26
5-10: 8-Kaluta-a	3	6	9	16	20	24
Annual 1(Summer,'75)(#11)-B&W; Everett, Buscema-a	3	6	9	18	23	28

NOTE: Brother Voodoo app. 2, 5, 6, 10. ***Alcala*** *a-7-9.* ***Boris*** *c-1-4.* ***Colan*** *a-2r, 6.* ***Heath*** *a-5r.* ***Reese*** *a-2.* ***Tuska*** *a-2r.*

TALES OF THUNDER
Deluxe Comics: Mar, 1985

1-Dynamo, Iron Maiden, Menthor app.; Giffen-a — 2.25

TALES OF VOODOO
Eerie Publications: V1#11, Nov, 1968 - V7#6, Nov, 1974 (Magazine)

	GD	VG	FN	VF	VF/NM	NM-
V1#11	5	10	15	36	48	60
V2#1(3/69)-V2#4(9/69)	4	8	12	25	33	42
V3#1-6('70): 4- "Claws of the Cat" redrawn from Climax #1	3	7	10	21	28	35
V4#1-6('71), V5#1-7('72), V6#1-6('73), V7#1-6('74)	3	7	10	21	28	35
Annual 1	4	8	12	22	30	38

NOTE: *Bondage-c-V1#10, V2#4, V3#4.*

TALES OF WELLS FARGO (TV)(See Western Roundup under Dell Giants)
Dell Publishing Co.: No. 876, Feb, 1958 - No. 1215, Oct-Dec, 1961

	GD	VG	FN	VF	VF/NM	NM-
Four Color 876 (#1)-Photo-c	10	20	30	73	107	140
Four Color 968 (2/59), 1023, 1075 (3/60), 1113 (7-9/60)-All photo-c	10	20	30	70	100	130
Four Color 1167 (3-5/61), 1215-Photo-c	9	18	27	65	93	120

TALESPIN (Also see Cartoon Tales & Disney's Talespin Limited Series)
Disney Comics: June, 1991 - No. 7, Dec, 1991 ($1.50)

1-7 — 2.25

TALES TO ASTONISH (Becomes The Incredible Hulk #102 on)
Atlas (MAP No. 1/ZPC No. 2-14/VPI No. 15-21/Marvel No. 22 on: Jan, 1959 - No. 101, Mar, 1968

	GD	VG	FN	VF	VF/NM	NM-
1-Jack Davis-a; monster-c.	137	274	411	1165	1883	2600
2-Ditko flying saucer-c (Martians); #2-4 have sci/fi-c.	57	114	171	485	780	1075
3,4	44	88	132	352	551	750
5-Prototype issue (Stone Men); Williamson-a (4 pgs.); Kirby monster-c begin	46	92	138	368	572	775
6-Prototype issue (Stone Men)	37	74	111	278	432	585
7-Prototype issue (Toad Men)	37	74	111	278	432	585
8-10	33	66	99	248	387	525
11-14,17-20: 13-Swipes story from Menace #8	27	54	81	194	297	400
15-Prototype issue (Electro)	34	68	102	255	403	550
16-Prototype issue (Stone Men)	29	58	87	210	323	435
21-(7/61)-Hulk prototype	29	58	87	210	323	435
22-26,28-34	20	40	60	145	223	300
27-1st Ant-Man app. (1/62); last 10¢ issue (see Strange Tales #73,78 & Tales of Suspense #32)	318	638	954	2910	4955	7000
35-(9/62)-2nd app. Ant-Man, 1st in costume; begin series & Ant-Man-c	153	306	459	1324	2162	3000
36-3rd app. Ant-Man	71	142	213	604	977	1350
37-40: 38-1st app. Egghead	41	82	123	318	497	675
41-43	32	64	96	240	370	500
44-Origin & 1st app. The Wasp (6/63)	41	82	123	330	515	700
45-48: 48-Origin & 1st app. The Porcupine.	20	40	60	141	216	290
49-Ant-Man becomes Giant Man (11/63)	24	48	72	170	260	350
50,51,53-56,58: 50-Origin/1st app. Human Top (alias Whirlwind). 53-Origin Colossus	12	24	36	87	134	180
52-Origin/1st app. Black Knight (2/64)	15	30	45	107	164	220
57-Early Spider-Man app. (7/64)	27	54	81	194	297	400
59-Giant Man vs. Hulk feature story (9/64); Hulk's 1st app. this title	31	62	93	228	352	475
60-Giant Man & Hulk double feature begins	20	40	60	145	223	300
61-69: 61-All Ditko issue; 1st mailbag. 62-1st app./origin The Leader; new Wasp costume. 63-Origin Leader; 65-New Giant Man costume. 68-New Human Top costume. 69-Last Giant Man.	10	20	30	73	107	140
70-Sub-Mariner & Incredible Hulk begins (8/65)	11	22	33	80	120	160
71-81,83-91,94-99: 72-Begin alternating-c features w/Sub-Mariner (even #'s) & Hulk (odd #'s). 79-Hulk vs. Hercules-c/story. 81-1st app. Boomerang. 90-1st app. The Abomination. 97-X-Men cameo (brief)	6	12	18	40	55	70
82-Iron Man battles Sub-Mariner (1st Iron Man x-over outside The Avengers & TOS); story cont'd from Tales of Suspense #80	7	14	21	50	68	85
92-1st Silver Surfer x-over (outside of Fantastic Four, 6/67); 1 panel cameo only	6	12	18	43	59	75
93-Hulk battles Silver Surfer-c/story (1st full x-over)	11	22	33	77	114	150
100-Hulk battles Sub-Mariner full-length story	7	14	21	50	68	85
101-Hulk story cont'd in Incredible Hulk #102; Sub-Mariner story continued in Iron Man & Sub-Mariner #1	8	16	24	55	78	100

GD 2.0 | VG 4.0 | FN 6.0 | VF 8.0 | VF/NM 9.0 | NM- 9.2

NOTE: ***Ayers*** *c(i)-9-12, 16, 18, 19.* ***Berg*** *a-1.* ***Burgos*** *a-62-64p.* ***Buscema*** *a-85-87p.* ***Colan*** *a(p)-70-76, 78-82, 84, 85, 101; c(p)-71-76, 78, 80, 82, 84, 86, 88, 90.* ***Ditko*** *a-1, 3-48, 50i, 60-67p; c-2, 7i, 8i, 14i, 17i.* ***Everett*** *a-78, 79i, 80-84, 85-90i, 94i, 95, 96; c(i)-79-81, 83, 86, 88.* ***Forte*** *a-6.* ***Kane*** *a-76, 88-91; c-89, 91.* ***Kirby*** *a(p)-1, 5-34-40, 44, 49-51, 68-70, 82, 83; layouts-71-84; c(p)-1, 3-48, 50-70, 72, 73, 75, 77, 78, 79, 81, 85, 90.* ***Kirby/Ditko*** *a-7, 8, 12, 13, 50; c-7, 8, 10, 13.* ***Leiber/Fox*** *a-47, 48, 50, 51.* ***Powell*** *a-65-69p, 73, 74.* ***Reinman*** *a-6, 36, 45, 46, 54i, 56-60i.*

TALES TO ASTONISH (2nd Series)
Marvel Comics Group: Dec, 1979 - No. 14, Jan, 1981

V1#1-Reprints Sub-Mariner #1 by Buscema — 6.00
2-14: Reprints Sub-Mariner #2-14 — 4.00

TALES TO ASTONISH
Marvel Comics: V3#1, Oct, 1994 ($6.95, one-shot)

V3#1-Peter David scripts; acetate, painted-c — 7.00

TALES TO HOLD YOU SPELLBOUND (See Spellbound)

TALES TO OFFEND
Dark Horse Comics: July, 1997 ($2.95, one-shot)

1-Frank Miller-s/a, EC-style cover — 3.50

TALES TOO TERRIBLE TO TELL (Becomes Terrology #10, 11)
New England Comics: Wint, 1989-90 - No. 11, Nov-Dec.1993 ($2.95/$3.50, B&W with card-stock covers)

1-($2.95) Reprints of non-EC pre-code horror; EC-style cover by Bisette — 4.00
2-8-($3.50) Story reprints, history of the pre-code titles and creators; cover galleries (B&W) inside & on back-c (color) — 4.00
9-11-($2.95) 10,11-"Terrology" on cover — 4.00

TALEWEAVER
DC Comics (WildStorm): Nov, 2001 - No. 6, Apr, 2002 ($3.50, limited series)

1-6-Philip Tan-a/Leonard Banaag-s. 2-Variant-c by Anacleto — 3.50

TALKING KOMICS
Belda Record & Publ. Co.: 1947 (20 pgs, slick-c)

	GD	VG	FN	VF	VF/NM	NM-
Each comic contained a record that followed the story - much like the Golden Record sets. Known titles: Chirpy Cricket, Lonesome Octopus, Sleepy Santa, Grumpy Shark, Flying Turtle, Happy Grasshopper with records...	3	6	9	18	24	30

TALLY-HO COMICS
Swappers Quarterly (Baily Publ. Co.): Dec, 1944

	GD	VG	FN	VF	VF/NM	NM-
nn-Frazetta's 1st work as Giunta's assistant; Man in Black horror story; violence; Giunta-c	44	88	132	268	409	550

TALOS OF THE WILDERNESS SEA
DC Comics: Aug, 1987 ($2.00, one-shot)

1 — 2.25

TALULLAH (See Comic Books Series I)

TAMMY, TELL ME TRUE
Dell Publishing Co.: No. 1233, 1961

	GD	VG	FN	VF	VF/NM	NM-
Four Color 1233-Movie	8	16	24	53	74	95

TANGENT COMICS
.../ THE ATOM, DC Comics: Dec, 1997 ($2.95, one-shot)
1-Dan Jurgens-s/Jurgens & Paul Ryan-a — 3.00

.../ THE BATMAN, DC Comics: Sept, 1998 ($1.95, one-shot)
1-Dan Jurgens-s/Klaus Janson-a — 2.25

.../ DOOM PATROL, DC Comics: Dec, 1997 ($2.95, one-shot)
1- Dan Jurgens-s/Sean Chen & Kevin Conrad-a — 3.00

.../ THE FLASH, DC Comics: Dec, 1997 ($2.95, one-shot)
1-Todd Dezago-s/Gary Frank & Cam Smith-a — 3.00

Tank Girl 2 #4 © Deadline Publ.

Target Comics #11 © NOVP

Tarzan #7 © ERB

GD VG FN VF VF/NM NM-
2.0 4.0 6.0 8.0 9.0 9.2

.../ GREEN LANTERN, DC Comics: Dec, '97 ($2.95, one-shot)
1-James Robinson-s/J.H. Williams III & Mick Gray-a 3.00

.../ JLA, DC Comics: Sept, 1998 ($1.95, one-shot)
1-Dan Jurgens-s/Banks & Rapmund-a 2.25

.../ THE JOKER, DC Comics: Dec, 1997 ($2.95, one-shot)
1-Karl Kesel-s/Matt Haley & Tom Simmons-a 3.00

.../ THE JOKER'S WILD, DC Comics: Sept, 1998 ($1.95, one-shot)
1-Kesel & Simmons-s/Phillips & Rodriguez-a 2.25

.../ METAL MEN, DC Comics: Dec, 1997 ($2.95, one-shot)
1-Ron Marz-s/Mike McKone & Mark McKenna-a 3.00

.../ NIGHTWING, DC Comics: Dec, 1997 ($2.95, one-shot)
1-John Ostrander-s/Jan Duursema-a 3.00

.../ NIGHTWING: NIGHTFORCE, DC Comics: Sept, 1998 ($1.95, one-shot)
1-John Ostrander-s/Jan Duursema-a 2.25

.../ POWERGIRL, DC Comics: Sept, 1998 ($1.95, one-shot)
1-Marz-s/Abell & Vines-a 2.25

.../ SEA DEVILS, DC Comics: Dec, 1997 ($2.95, one-shot)
1-Kurt Busiek-s/Vince Giarrano & Tom Palmer-a 3.00

.../ SECRET SIX, DC Comics: Dec, 1997 ($2.95, one-shot)
1-Chuck Dixon-s/Tom Grummett & Lary Stucker-a 3.00

.../ THE SUPERMAN, DC Comics: Sept, 1998 ($1.95, one-shot)
1-Millar-s/Guice-a 2.25

.../ TALES OF THE GREEN LANTERN, DC Comics: Sept, 1998 ($1.95, one-shot)
1-Story & art by various 2.25

.../ THE TRIALS OF THE FLASH, DC Comics: Sept, 1998 ($1.95, one-shot)
1-Dezago-s/Pelletier & Lanning-a 2.25

.../ WONDER WOMAN DC Comics: Sept, 1998 ($1.95, one-shot),
1-Peter David-s/Unzueta & Mendoza-a 2.25

TANGLED WEB (See Spider-Man's Tangled Web)

TANK GIRL
Dark Horse Comics: May, 1991 - No. 4, Aug, 1991 ($2.25, B&W, mini-series)
1-Contains Dark Horse trading cards 6.00
2-4 4.00

TANK GIRL: APOCALYPSE
DC Comics: Nov, 1995 - No. 4, Feb, 1996 ($2.25, limited series)
1-4 3.00

TANK GIRL: MOVIE ADAPTATION
DC Comics: 1995 ($5.95, 68 pgs., one-shot)
nn-Peter Milligan scripts 6.00

TANK GIRL: THE ODYSSEY
DC Comics: May, 1995 - No.4, Oct, 1995 ($2.25, limited series)
1-4: Peter Milligan scripts; Hewlett-a 3.00

TANK GIRL 2
Dark Horse Comics: June, 1993 - No. 4, Sept, 1993 ($2.50, lim. series, mature)
1-4: Jamie Hewlett & Alan Martin-s/a 3.00
TPB (2/95, $17.95) r/#1-4 18.00

TAPPAN'S BURRO (See Zane Grey & 4-Color #449)

TAPPING THE VEIN (Clive Barker's...)
Eclipse Comics: 1989 - No. 5, 1992 ($6.95, squarebound, mature, 68 pgs.)
Book 1-5: 1-Russell-a, Bolton-c. 2-Bolton-a. 4-Die-cut-c 7.00
TPB (2002, $24.95, Checker Book Publ. Group) r/#1-5 25.00

TARANTULA (See Weird Suspense)

TARGET: AIRBOY
Eclipse Comics: Mar, 1988 ($1.95)
1 2.25

TARGET COMICS (...Western Romances #106 on)
Funnies, Inc./Novelty Publications/Star Publ.: Feb, 1940 - V10#3 (#105), Aug-Sept, 1949
V1#1-Origin & 1st app. Manowar, The White Streak by Burgos, & Bulls-Eye Bill by Everett; City Editor (ends #5), High Grass Twins by Jack Cole (ends #4), T-Men by Joe Simon (ends #9), Rip Rory (ends #4), Fantastic Feature Films by Tarpe Mills (ends #39), & Calling 2-R (ends #14) begin; marijuana use story
503 1006 1509 3521 5661 7800
2-Everett-c/a 258 516 774 1613 2482 3350
3,4-Everett, Jack Cole-a 154 308 462 963 1482 2000
5-Origin The White Streak in text; Space Hawk by Wolverton begins (6/40) (see Blue Bolt & Circus) 423 846 1269 2936 4718 6500
6-The Chameleon by Everett begins (7/40, 1st app.); White Streak origin cont'd. in text; early mention of comic collecting in letter column; 1st letter column in comics? (7/40)
200 400 600 1250 1925 2600
7-Wolverton Spacehawk-c/story (Scarce) 503 1006 1509 3521 5661 7800
8-Classic sci-fi cover 154 308 462 963 1482 2000
9,12: 12-(1/41) 142 284 426 888 1369 1850
10-Intro/1st app. The Target (11/40); Simon-c; Spacehawk-s; text piece by Wolverton
208 416 624 1300 2000 2700
11-Origin The Target & The Targeteers 179 358 537 1119 1722 2325
V2#1-Target by Bob Wood; Uncle Sam flag-c 89 178 267 556 853 1150
2-Ten part Treasure Island serial begins; Harold Delay-a; reprinted in Catholic Comics V3#1-10 (see Key Comics #5) 79 158 237 494 760 1025
3-5: 4-Kit Carter, The Cadet begins 62 124 186 388 594 800
6-9: Red Seal with White Streak in #6-10 60 120 180 375 575 775
10-Classic-c 103 206 309 644 992 1340
11,12: 12-10-part Last of the Mohicans serial begins; Delay-a
58 116 174 363 557 750
V3#1-3,5-7,9,10: 10-Last Wolverton issue 56 112 168 350 543 735
4-V for Victory-c 60 120 180 375 575 775
8-Hitler, Tojo, Flag-c; 6-part Gulliver Travels serial begins; Delay-a.
73 146 219 456 703 950
11,12 19 38 57 107 154 200
V4#1-4,7-12: 8-X-Mas-c 13 26 39 74 102 130
5-Classic Statue of Liberty-c 15 30 45 83 117 150
6-Targetoons by Wolverton 15 30 45 83 117 150
V5#1-8 11 22 33 66 91 115
V6#1-4,6-10 11 22 33 64 87 110
5-Tojo-c 14 28 42 79 110 140
V7#1-12 10 20 30 60 80 100
V8#1,3-5,8,9,11,12 10 20 30 58 77 95
2,6,7-Krigstein-a 11 22 33 64 87 110
10-L.B. Cole-c 36 72 108 204 297 390
V9#1,4,6,8,10-L.B. Cole-c 35 70 105 200 290 380
2,3,5,7,9,11, V10#1 10 20 30 58 77 95
12-Classic L.B. Cole-c 39 78 117 222 324 425
V10#2,3-L.B. Cole-c 34 68 102 193 279 365
NOTE: ***Certa** c-V8#9, 11, 12, V9#5, 9, 11, V10#1. **Jack Cole** a-1-8. **Everett** a-1-9; c(signed Blake)-1, 2. **Al Fago** c-V6#8. **Sid Greene** c-V2#9, 12, V3#3. **Walter Johnson** c-V5#6, V6#4. **Tarpe Mills** a-1-4, 6, 8, 11, V3#1. **Rico** a-V7#4, 10, V8#5, 6, V9#3; c-V7#6, 8, 10, V8#2, 4, 6, 7. **Simon** a-1, 2. **Bob Wood** c-V2#2, 3, 5, 6.*

TARGET: THE CORRUPTORS (TV)
Dell Publishing Co.: No. 1306, Mar-May, 1962 - No. 3, Oct-Dec, 1962
(All have photo-c)
Four Color 1306(#1), #2,3 7 14 21 46 63 80

TARGET WESTERN ROMANCES (Formerly Target Comics; becomes Flaming Western Romances #3)
Star Publications: No. 106, Oct-Nov, 1949 - No. 107, Dec-Jan, 1949-50
106(#1)-Silhouette nudity panel; L.B. Cole-c 39 78 117 222 324 425
107(#2)-L.B. Cole-c; lingerie panels 33 66 99 187 271 355

TARGITT
Atlas/Seaboard Publ.: March, 1975 - No. 3, July, 1975
1-3: 1-Origin; Nostrand-a in all. 2-1st in costume. 3-Becomes Man-Stalker
1 2 3 5 7 9

TARZAN (See Aurora, Comics on Parade, Crackajack, DC 100-Page Super Spec., Edgar Rice Burroughs'..., Famous Feature Stories #1, Golden Comics Digest #4, 9, Jeep Comics #1-29, Jungle Tales of..., Limited Collectors' Edition, Popular, Sparkler, Sport Stars #1, Tip Top & Top Comics)

TARZAN
Dell Publishing Co./United Features Synd.: No. 5, 1939 - No. 161, Aug, 1947
Large Feature Comic 5('39)-(Scarce)-By Hal Foster; reprints 1st dailies from 1929
162 324 486 1013 1557 2100
Single Series 20(:40)-By Hal Foster 115 230 345 719 1110 1500
Four Color 134(2/47)-Marsh-c/a 55 110 165 460 743 1025
Four Color 161(8/47)-Marsh-c/a 51 102 153 408 634 860

TARZAN (...of the Apes #138 on)
Dell Publishing Co./Gold Key No. 132 on: 1-2/48 - No. 131, 7-8/62; No. 132, 11/62 - No. 206, 2/72
1-Jesse Marsh-a begins 100 200 300 790 1270 1750
2 46 92 138 368 577 785
3-5 33 66 99 248 387 525
6-10: 6-1st Tantor the Elephant. 7-1st Valley of the Monsters

Tarzan #10 © ERB

Tarzan The Savage Heart #1 © ERB

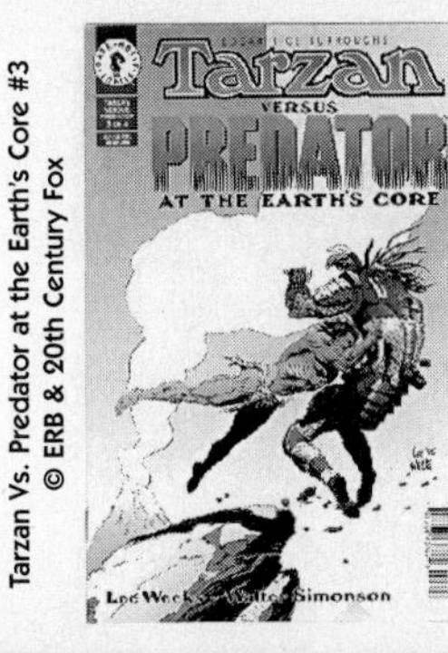

Tarzan Vs. Predator at the Earth's Core #3 © ERB & 20th Century Fox

GD 2.0 | VG 4.0 | FN 6.0 | VF 8.0 | VF/NM 9.0 | NM- 9.2

29 58 87 206 316 425
11-15: 11-Two Against the Jungle begins, ends #24. 13-Lex Barker photo-c begin
24 48 72 170 260 350
16-20 19 38 57 136 208 280
21-24,26-30 15 30 45 107 164 220
25-1st "Brothers of the Spear" episode; series ends #156,160,161,196-206
17 34 51 121 186 250
31-40 12 24 36 82 124 165
41-54: Last Barker photo-c 9 18 27 65 93 120
55-60: 56-Eight pg. Boy story 8 16 24 53 74 95
61,62,64-70 7 14 21 50 68 85
63-Two Tarzan stories, 1 by Manning 7 14 21 51 71 90
71-79 6 12 18 43 59 75
80-99: 80-Gordon Scott photo-c begin 6 12 18 38 52 65
100 6 12 18 43 59 75
101-109 5 10 15 36 48 60
110 (Scarce)-Last photo-c 6 12 18 43 59 75
111-120 5 10 15 33 44 55
121-131: Last Dell issue 4 8 12 29 40 50
132-1st Gold Key issue 5 10 15 36 48 60
133-138,140-154 4 8 12 25 33 42
139-(12/63)-1st app. Korak (Boy); leaves Tarzan & gets own book (1/64)
6 12 18 40 55 70
155-Origin Tarzan 5 10 15 33 44 55
156-161: 157-Banlu, Dog of the Arande begins, ends #159, 195. 169-Leopard Girl app.
4 8 12 22 30 38
162,165,168,171 (TV)-Ron Ely photo covers 4 8 12 24 32 40
163,164,166,167,169,170: 169-Leopard Girl app. 3 7 10 27 28 35
172-199,201-206: 178-Tarzan origin-r/#155; Leopard Girl app., also in #179, 190-193
3 6 9 18 24 30
200 4 8 12 22 30 38
Story Digest 1-(6/70, G.K., 148pp.)(scarce) 9 18 27 60 85 110

NOTE: *#162, 165, 168, 171 are TV issues. #1-153 all have* **Marsh** *art on Tarzan. #154-161, 163, 164, 166, 167, 172-177 all have* **Manning** *art on Tarzan. #178, 202 have* **Manning** *Tarzan reprints. No "Brothers of the Spear" in #1-24, 157-159, 162-195. #39-126, 128-156 all have* **Russ Manning** *art on "Brothers of the Spear". #196-201, 203-205 all have* **Manning** *B.O.T.S. reprints; #25-38, 127 all have Jesse* **Marsh** *art on B.O.T.S. #206 has a Marsh B.O.T.S. reprint.* **Gollub** *c-8-12.* **Marsh** *c-1-7.* **Doug Wildey** *a-162, 179-187. Many issues have front and back photo covers.*

TARZAN (Continuation of Gold Key series)
National Periodical Publications: No. 207, Apr, 1972 - No. 258, Feb, 1977

207-Origin Tarzan by Joe Kubert, part 1; John Carter begins (origin); 52 pg. issues thru #209 5 10 15 36 48 60
208,209-(52 pgs.): 208-210-Parts 2-4 of origin. 209-Last John Carter
3 6 9 18 24 30
210-220: 210-Kubert-a. 211-Hogarth, Kubert-a. 212-214: Adaptations from "Jungle Tales of Tarzan". 213-Beyond the Farthest Star begins, ends #218. 215-218,224,225-All by Kubert. 215-part Foster-r. 219-223: Adapts "The Return of Tarzan" by Kubert
2 4 6 12 16 20
221-229: 221-223-Continues adaptation of "The Return of Tarzan". 226-Manning-a
2 4 6 10 12 15
230-DC 100 Page Super Spectacular; Kubert, Kaluta-a(p); Korak begins, ends #234; Carson of Venus app. 4 8 12 25 33 42
231-235-New Kubert-a.: 231-234-(All 100 pgs.)-Adapts "Tarzan and the Lion Man"; Rex, the Wonder Dog r-#232, 233. 235-(100 pgs.)-Last Kubert issue.
4 8 12 24 32 40
236,237,239-258: 240-243 adapts "Tarzan & the Castaways". 250-256 adapts "Tarzan the Untamed." 252,253-r/#213 1 3 4 6 8 10
238-(68 pgs.) 2 4 6 12 16 20
Comic Digest 1-(Fall, 1972, 50¢, 164 pgs.)(DC)-Digest size; Kubert-c; Manning-a
5 10 15 33 44 55

NOTE: **Anderson** *a-207, 209, 217, 218.* **Chaykin** *a-216.* **Finlay** *a(r)-212.* **Foster** *strip-r #207-209, 211, 212, 221.* **Heath** *a-230i.* **G. Kane** *a(r)-232p, 233p.* **Kubert** *a-207-225, 227-235, 257r, 258r; c-207-249, 253.* **Lopez** *a-250-255p; c-250p, 251, 252, 254.* **Manning** *strip-r 230-235, 238.* **Morrow** *a-208.* **Nino** *a-231-234.* **Sparling** *a-230, 231.* **Starr** *a-233r.*

TARZAN (Lord of the Jungle)
Marvel Comics Group: June, 1977 - No. 29, Oct, 1979

1-New adaptions of Burrough stories; Buscema-a 1 3 4 6 8 10
1-(35¢-c variant, limited distribution)(6/77) 2 4 6 10 12 15
2-29: 2-Origin by John Buscema. 9-Young Tarzan. 12-14-Jungle Tales of Tarzan. 25-29-New stories 5.00
2-5-(35¢-c variants, limited distribution)(7-10/77) 1 2 3 5 6 8
Annual 1-3: 1-(1977). 2-(1978). 3-(1979) 5.00

NOTE: **N. Adams** *c-11i, 12i.* **Alcala** *a-9i, 10i; c-8i, 9i.* **Buckler** *c-25-27p, Annual 3p.* **John Buscema** *a-1-3, 4-18p, Annual 1; c-1-7, 8p, 9p, 10, 11p, 12p, 13, 14-19p, 21p, 22, 23p, 24p, 28p, Annual 1.* **Mooney** *a-22i.* **Nebres** *a-22i.* **Russell** *a-29i.*

TARZAN
Dark Horse Comics: July, 1996 - No. 20, Mar, 1998 ($2.95)

1-20: 1-6-Suydam-c 3.00

TARZAN / CARSON OF VENUS
Dark Horse Comics: May, 1998 - No. 4, Aug, 1998 ($2.95, limited series)

1-4-Darko Macan-s/Igor Korday-a 3.00

TARZAN FAMILY, THE (Formerly Korak, Son of Tarzan)
National Periodical Publications: No. 60, Nov-Dec, 1975 - No. 66, Nov-Dec, 1976

60-62-(68 pgs.): 60-Korak begins; Kaluta-r 2 4 6 10 13 16
63-66 (52 pgs.) 2 4 6 8 10 12

NOTE: *Carson of Venus-r 60-65. New John Carter-62-64, 65r, 66r. New Korak-60-66. Pellucidar feature-66. Foster strip r-60(9/4/32-10/16/32), 62(6/29/32-7/31/32), 63(10/11/31-12/13/31).* **Kaluta** *Carson of Venus-60-65.* **Kubert** *a-61, 64; c-60-64.* **Manning** *strip-r 60-62, 64.* **Morrow** *a-66r.*

TARZAN/JOHN CARTER: WARLORDS OF MARS
Dark Horse Comics: Jan, 1996 - No. 4, June, 1996 ($2.50, limited series)

1-4: Bruce Jones scripts in all. 1,2,4-Bret Blevins-c/a. 2-(4/96)-Indicia reads #3 3.00

TARZAN KING OF THE JUNGLE (See Dell Giant #37, 51)

TARZAN, LORD OF THE JUNGLE
Gold Key: Sept, 1965 (Giant) (25¢, soft paper-c)

1-Marsh-r 9 18 27 65 93 120

TARZAN: LOVE, LIES AND THE LOST CITY (See Tarzan the Warrior)
Malibu Comics: Aug. 10, 1992 - No. 3, Sept, 1992 ($2.50, limited series)

1-($3.95, 68 pgs.)-Flip book format; Simonson & Wagner scripts 4.00
2,3-No Simonson or Wagner scripts 3.00

TARZAN MARCH OF COMICS (See March of Comics #82, 98, 114, 125, 144, 155, 172, 185, 204, 223, 240, 252, 262, 272, 286, 300, 332, 342, 354, 366)

TARZAN OF THE APES
Metropolitan Newspaper Service: 1934? (Hardcover, 4x12", 68 pgs.)

1-Strip reprints 26 52 78 147 211 275

TARZAN OF THE APES
Marvel Comics Group: July, 1984 - No. 2, Aug, 1984 (Movie adaptation)

1,2: Origin-r/Marvel Super Spec. 3.00

TARZAN'S JUNGLE ANNUAL (See Dell Giants)

TARZAN'S JUNGLE WORLD (See Dell Giant #25)

TARZAN: THE BECKONING
Malibu Comics: 1992 - No. 7, 1993 ($2.50, limited series)

1-7 3.00

TARZAN: THE LOST ADVENTURE (See Edgar Rice Burroughs' ...)

TARZAN-THE RIVERS OF BLOOD
Dark Horse Comics: Nov, 1999 - No. 8 ($2.95, limited series)

1-4: Korday-c/a 3.00

TARZAN THE SAVAGE HEART
Dark Horse Comics: Apr, 1999 - No. 4, July, 1999 ($2.95, limited series)

1-4: Grell-c/a 3.00

TARZAN THE WARRIOR (Also see Tarzan: Love, Lies and the Lost City)
Malibu Comics: Mar, 19, 1992 - No. 5, 1992 ($2.50, limited series)

1-5: 1-Bisley painted pack-c (flip book format-c) 3.00
1-2nd printing w/o flip-c by Bisley 2.50

TARZAN VS. PREDATOR AT THE EARTH'S CORE
Dark Horse Comics: Jan, 1996 - No. 4, June, 1996 ($2.50, limited series)

1-4: Lee Weeks-c/a; Walt Simonson scripts 3.00

TASKMASTER
Marvel Comics: Apr, 2002 - No. 4, July, 2002 ($2.99, limited series)

1-4-Udon Studio-s/a. 1-Iron Man app. 3.00

TASMANIAN DEVIL & HIS TASTY FRIENDS
Gold Key: Nov, 1962 (12¢)

1-Bugs Bunny & Elmer Fudd x-over 15 30 45 105 160 215

TATTERED BANNERS
DC Comics (Vertigo): Nov, 1998 - No. 4, Feb, 1999 ($2.95, limited series)

1-4-Grant & Giffen-s/McMahon-a 3.00

TEAM AMERICA (See Captain America #269)
Marvel Comics Group: June, 1982 - No. 12, May, 1983

Team America #8 © MAR

Team One: Stormwatch #1 © WSP

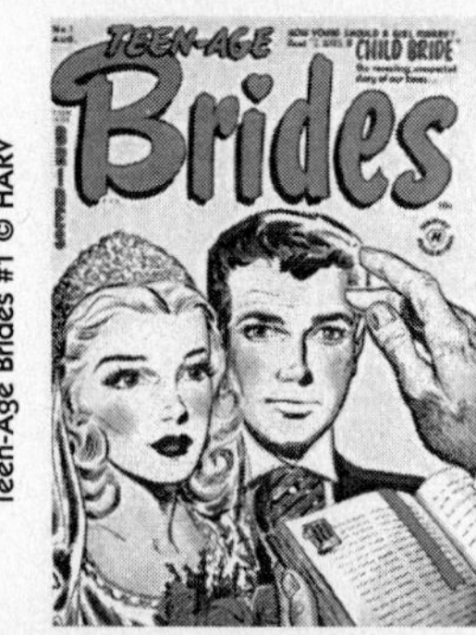

Teen-Age Brides #1 © HARV

GD VG FN VF VF/NM NM-
2.0 4.0 6.0 8.0 9.0 9.2

GD VG FN VF VF/NM NM-
2.0 4.0 6.0 8.0 9.0 9.2

1-12:1-Origin; Ideal Toy motorcycle characters. 9-Iron Man app. 11-Ghost Rider app. 12-Double size 2.25

TEAM ANARCHY
Dagger Comics: Oct, 1993 - No.8, 1994? ($2.50)
1-($2.75)-Red foil logo; intro Team Anarchy 2.75
1-Platinum, 2,3,3-Bronze,3-Gold,3-Silver,4-8 2.75

TEAM HELIX
Marvel Comics: Jan, 1993 - No. 4, Apr, 1993 ($1.75, limited series)
1-4: Teen Super Group. 1,2-Wolverine app. 2.25

TEAM ONE: STORMWATCH (Also see StormWatch)
Image Comics (WildStorm Productions): June, 1995 - No. 2, Aug, 1995 ($2.50, lim. series)
1,2: Steven T. Seagle scripts 2.50

TEAM ONE: WILDC.A.T.S (Also see WildC.A.T.S)
Image Comics (WildStorm Productions): July, 1995 - No. 2, Aug, 1995 ($2.50, limited series)
1,2: James Robinson scripts 2.50

TEAM 7
Image Comics (WildStorm Productions): Oct, 1994 - No.4, Feb, 1995 ($2.50, limited series)
1-4: Dixon scripts in all, 1-Portacio variant-c 2.50

TEAM 7-DEAD RECKONING
Image Comics (WildStorm Productions): Jan, 1996 - No. 4, Apr, 1996 ($2.50, limited series)
1-4: Dixon scripts in all 2.50

TEAM 7-OBJECTIVE HELL
Image Comics (WildStorm Productions): May, 1995 - No. 3, July, 1995 ($1.95/$2.50, limited series)
1-($1.95)-Newstand; Dixon scripts in all; Barry Smith-c 2.25
1-3: 1-($2.50)-Direct Market; Barry Smith-c, bound-in card 2.50

TEAM SUPERMAN
DC Comics: July, 1999 ($2.95, one-shot)
1-Jeanty-a/Stelfreeze-c 3.00
...Secret Files 1 (5/98, $4.95)Origin-s and pin-ups of Superboy, Supergirl and Steel 5.00

TEAM TITANS (See Deathstroke & New Titans Annual #7)
DC Comics: Sept, 1992 - No. 24, Sept, 1994 ($1.75/$1.95)
1-Five different #1s exist w/origins in 1st half & the same 2nd story in each: Kilowat, Mirage, Nightrider w/Netzer/Perez-a, Redwing, & Terra w/part Perez-p; Total Chaos Pt. 3 3.00
2-24: 2-Total Chaos Pt 6. 11-Metallik app. 24-Zero Hour x-over 2.25
Annual 1,2 ('93, '94, $3.50, 68 pgs.): 2-Elseworlds tory 3.50

TEAM X/TEAM 7
Marvel Comics: Nov, 1996 ($4.95, one-shot)
1 5.00

TEAM X 2000
Marvel Comics: Feb, 1999 ($3.50, one-shot)
1-Kevin Lau-a; Bishop vs. Shi'ar Empire 3.50

TEAM YANKEE
First Comics: Jan, 1989 - No. 6, Feb, 1989 ($1.95, weekly limited series)
1-6 2.25

TEAM YOUNGBLOOD (Also see Youngblood)
Image Comics (Extreme Studios): Sept, 1993 - No. 22, Sept, 1995 ($1.95/$2.50)
1-22: 1-9-Liefeld scripts in all: 1,2,4-6,8-Thibert-c(i). 1-1st app. Dutch & Masada. 3-Spawn cameo. 5-1st app. Lynx. 7,8-Coupons 1 & 4 for Extreme Prejudice #0; Black and White Pt. 4 & 8 by Thibert. 8-Coupon #4 for E. P. #0. 9-Liefeld wraparound-c &(p)/a(p) on Pt. I. 16,17-Bagged w/trading card. 21-Angela & Glory-app. 2.50

TECH JACKET
Image Comics: Nov, 2002 - No. 6, Apr, 2003 ($2.95)
1-6-Kirkman-s/Su-a 3.00
Vol. 1: Lost and Found TPB (7/03, $12.95, 7-3/4" x 5-1/4") B&W r/#1-6; intro. by Valentino 13.00

TEDDY ROOSEVELT & HIS ROUGH RIDERS (See Real Heroes #1)
Avon Periodicals: 1950
1-Kinstler-c; Palais-a; Flag-c 19 38 57 107 154 200

TEDDY ROOSEVELT ROUGH RIDER (See Battlefield #22 & Classics Illustrated Special Issue)

TED MCKEEVER'S METROPOL (See Transit)
Marvel Comics (Epic Comics): Mar, 1991 - No. 12, Mar, 1992 ($2.95, limited series)
V1#1-12: Ted McKeever-c/a/scripts 3.50

TED MCKEEVER'S METROPOL A.D.
Marvel Comics (Epic Comics): Oct, 1992 - No. 3, Dec, 1992 ($3.50, limited series)
V2#1-3: Ted McKeever-c/a/scripts 3.50

TEENA
Magazine Enterprises/Standard Comics No. 20 on: No. 11, 1948 - No. 15, 1948; No. 20, Aug, 1949 - No. 22, Oct, 1950
A-1 #11-Teen-age; Ogden Whitney-c 9 18 27 54 70 85
A-1 #12, 15 8 16 24 46 58 70
20-22 (Standard) 6 12 18 31 38 45

TEEN-AGE BRIDES (True Bride's Experiences #8 on)
Harvey/Home Comics: Aug, 1953 - No. 7, Aug, 1954
1-Powell-a 11 22 33 64 87 110
2-Powell-a 8 16 24 46 58 70
3-7: 3,6-Powell-a 8 16 24 40 50 60

TEEN-AGE CONFESSIONS (See Teen Confessions)

TEEN-AGE CONFIDENTIAL CONFESSIONS
Charlton Comics: July, 1960 - No. 22, 1964
1 4 8 12 29 40 50
2-10 3 6 9 18 24 30
11-22 2 4 6 14 18 22

TEEN-AGE DIARY SECRETS (Formerly Blue Ribbon Comics; becomes Diary Secrets #10 on)
St. John Publishing Co.: No. 4, 9/49; nn (#5), 9/49 - No. 7, 11/49; No. 8, 2/50; No. 9, 8/50
4(9/49)-Oversized; part mag., part comic 29 58 87 164 237 310
nn(#5)(no indicia)-Oversized, all comics; contains sty "I Gave Boys the Green Light."
24 48 72 138 199 260
6,8: (Reg. size) -Photo-c; Baker-a(2-3) in each 24 48 72 135 195 255
7,9-Digest size (Pocket Comics); Baker-a(5); both have same contents; diff.-c
26 52 78 150 215 280

TEEN-AGE DOPE SLAVES (See Harvey Comics Library #1)

TEENAGE HOTRODDERS (Top Eliminator #25 on; see Blue Bird)
Charlton Comics: Apr, 1963 - No. 24, July, 1967
1 7 14 21 46 63 80
2-10 4 8 12 24 32 40
11-24 3 6 9 19 25 32

TEEN-AGE LOVE (See Fox Giants)

TEEN-AGE LOVE (Formerly Intimate)
Charlton Comics: V2#4, July, 1958 - No. 96, Dec, 1973
V2#4 5 10 15 33 44 55
5-9 4 8 12 22 30 38
10(9/59)-20 3 6 9 18 24 30
21-35 3 6 9 16 20 25
36-70 2 4 6 12 16 20
71-96: 61&62-Jonnie Love begins (origin) 2 4 6 10 12 15

TEENAGE MUTANT NINJA TURTLES (Also see Anything Goes, Donatello, First Comics Graphic Novel, Gobbledygook, Grimjack #26, Leonardo, Michaelangelo, Raphael & Tales Of The...)
Mirage Studios: 1984 - No. 62, Aug, 1993 ($1.50/$1.75, B&W; all 44-52 pgs.)
1-1st printing (3000 copies)-Origin and 1st app. of the Turtles and Splinter. Only printing to have ad for Gobbledygook #1 & 2; Shredder app. (#1-4: 7-1/2x11") (Prices vary widely on this book. In 2004, a CGC certified 9.2 sold for $1,713, a CGC 8.5 sold for $1,300 and a CGC 7.0 sold for $700)
1-2nd printing (6/84)(15,000 copies) 2 4 6 12 16 20
1-3rd printing (2/85)(36,000 copies) 2 4 6 8 10 12
1-4th printing, new-c (50,000 copies) 5.00
1-5th printing, new-c (8/88-c, 11/88 inside) 4.00
1-Counterfeit. **Note**: Most counterfeit copies have a half inch wide white streak or scratch marks across the center of back cover. Black part of cover is a bluish black instead of a deep black. Inside paper is very white & inside cover is bright white (no value)
2-1st printing (1984; 15,000 copies) 6 12 18 43 59 75
2-2nd printing 1 3 4 6 8 10
2-3rd printing; new Corben-c/a (2/85) 5.00
2-Counterfeit with glossy cover stock (no value).
3-1st printing (1985, 44 pgs.) 4 8 12 29 40 50
3-Variant, 500 copies, given away in NYC. Has 'Laird's Photo' in white rather than light blue
7 14 21 50 68 85
3-2nd printing; contains new back-up story 3.00
4-1st printing (1985, 44 pgs.) 3 7 10 21 28 35
4,5-2nd printing (5/87, 11/87) 2.25
5-Fugitoid begins, ends #7; 1st full color-c (1985) 2 4 6 11 14 18

Teenage Mutant Ninja Turtles #22 © MS

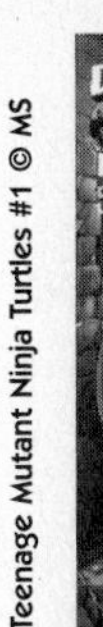

Teenage Mutant Ninja Turtles #1 © MS

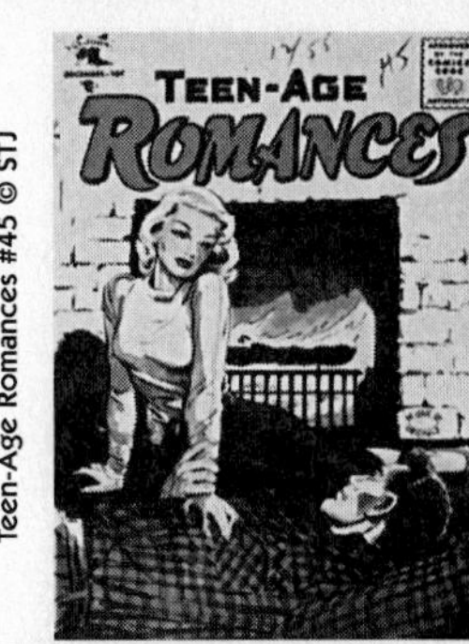

Teen-Age Romances #45 © STJ

	GD 2.0	VG 4.0	FN 6.0	VF 8.0	VF/NM 9.0	NM- 9.2
6-1st printing (1986)	2	4	6	8	10	12
6-2nd printing (4/88-c, 5/88 inside)						2.25
7-4 pg. Eastman/Corben color insert; 1st color TMNT (1986, $1.75-c); Bade Biker back-up story	1	2	3	5	6	8
7-2nd printing (1/89) w/o color insert						2.25
8-Cerebus-c/story with Dave Sim-a (1986)						6.00
9,10: 9 (9/86)-Rip In Time by Corben						5.00
11-15						4.00
16-18: 18-Mark Bode'-a						3.00
18-2nd printing ($2.25, color, 44 pgs.)-New-c						2.50
19-34: 19-Begin $1.75-c. 24-26-Veitch-c/a.						2.50
32-2nd printing ($2.75, 52 pgs., full color)						3.00
35-49,51: 35-Begin $2.00-c.						2.50
50-Features pin-ups by Larsen, McFarlane, Simonson, etc.						3.00
52-62: 52-Begin $2.25-c						2.50
nn (1990, $5.95, B&W)-Movie adaptation						6.00
Book 1,2($1.50, B&W): 2-Corben-c						2.50
...Christmas Special 1 (12/90, $1.75, B&W, 52 pgs.)-Cover title: Michaelangelo Christmas Special; r/Michaelangelo one-shot plus new Raphael story						2.50
...Special (The Maltese Turtle) nn (1/93, $2.95, color, 44 pgs.)						3.00
...Special: "Times" Pipeline nn (9/92, $2.95, color, 44 pgs.)-Mark Bode-c/a						3.00
Hardcover ($100)-r/#1-10 plus one-shots w/dust jackets - limited to 1000 w/letter of authenticity						100.00
Softcover ($40)-r/#1-10						40.00

TEENAGE MUTANT NINJA TURTLES
Mirage Studios: V2#1, Oct, 1993 - V2#13, Oct, 1995 ($2.75)

V2#1-13: 1-Wraparound-c						2.75

TEENAGE MUTANT NINJA TURTLES
Image Comics (Highbrow Ent.): June, 1996 - No. 23, Oct, 1999 ($1.95-$2.95)

1-23: 1-8: Eric Larsen-c(i) on all. 10-Savage Dragon-c/app.						3.00

TEENAGE MUTANT NINJA TURTLES
Mirage Publishing: V4#1, Dec, 2001 - Present ($2.95, B&W)

V4#1-9,11-17-Laird-s/a(i)/Lawson-a(p).						3.00
10-($3.95) Splinter dies						4.00

TEENAGE MUTANT NINJA TURTLES
Dreamwave Productions: June 2003 - Present ($2.95, color)

1-7-Animated style; Peter David-s/Lesean-a						3.00
Vol. 1 TPB (2003, $9.95) r/#1-4; cover gallery and sketch pages						10.00

TEENAGE MUTANT NINJA TURTLES (Adventures)
Archie Publications: Jan, 1996 - No. 3, Mar, 1996 ($1.50, limited series)

1-3						2.50

TEENAGE MUTANT NINJA TURTLES ADVENTURES (TV)
Archie Comics: 8/88 - No. 3, 12/88; 3/89 - No. 72, Oct, 1995 ($1.00/$1.25/$1.50/$1.75)

1-Adapts TV cartoon; not by Eastman/Laird						3.00
2,3,1-5: 2,3 (Mini-series). 1 (2nd on-going series). 5-Begins original stories not based on TV						2.50
1-11: 2nd printings						2.25
6-72: 14-Simpson-a(p). 19-1st Mighty Mutanimals (also in #20, 51-54). 22-Gene Colan-c/a. 50-Poster by Eastman/Laird. 62-w/poster						2.50
nn (1990, $2.50)-Movie adaptation						2.50
nn (Spring, 1991, $2.50, 68 pgs.)-(Meet Archie)						2.50
nn (Sum, 1991, $2.50, 68 pgs.)-(Movie II)-Adapts movie sequel						2.50
...Meet the Conservation Corps 1 (1992, $2.50, 68 pgs.)						2.50
...III The Movie: The Turtles are Back...In Time (1993, $2.50, 68 pgs.)						2.50
Special 1,4,5 (Sum/92, Spr/93, Sum/93, 68 pgs.)-1-Bill Wray-c						2.50
Giant Size Special 6 (Fall/93, $1.95, 52 pgs.)						2.50
Special 7-10 (Win/93-Fall//94, 52 pgs.): 9-Jeff Smith-c						2.50

NOTE: *There are 2nd printings of #1-11 w/B&W inside covers. Originals are color.*

TEENAGE MUTANT NINJA TURTLES CLASSICS DIGEST (TV)
Archie Comics: Aug, 1993 - No. 8, Mar, 1995? ($1.75)

1-8: Reprints TMNT Advs.						3.00

TEENAGE MUTANT NINJA TURTLES/FLAMING CARROT CROSSOVER
Mirage Publishing: Nov, 1993 - No. 4, Feb, 1994 ($2.75, limited series)

1-4: Bob Burden story						3.00

TEENAGE MUTANT NINJA TURTLES PRESENTS: APRIL O'NEIL
Archie Comics: Mar, 1993 - No. 3, June, 1993 ($1.25, limited series)

1-3						2.50

TEENAGE MUTANT NINJA TURTLES PRESENTS: DONATELLO AND LEATHERHEAD
Archie Comics: July, 1993 - No. 3, Sept, 1993 ($1.25, limited series)

1-3						2.50

TEENAGE MUTANT NINJA TURTLES PRESENTS: MERDUDE
Archie Comics: Oct, 1993 - No. 3, Dec, 1993 ($1.25, limited series)

1-3-See Mighty Mutanimals #7 for 1st app. Merdude						2.50

TEENAGE MUTANT NINJA TURTLES/SAVAGE DRAGON CROSSOVER
Mirage Studios: Aug, 1995 ($2.75, one-shot)

1						3.00

TEEN-AGE ROMANCE (Formerly My Own Romance)
Marvel Comics (ZPC): No. 77, Sept, 1960 - No. 86, Mar, 1962

	GD 2.0	VG 4.0	FN 6.0	VF 8.0	VF/NM 9.0	NM- 9.2
77-83	4	8	12	27	36	45
84-86-Kirby-c. 84-Kirby-a(2 pgs.). 85,86-(3 pgs.)	5	10	15	33	44	55

TEEN-AGE ROMANCES
St. John Publ. Co. (Approved Comics): Jan, 1949 - No. 45, Dec, 1955

1-Baker-c/a(1)	40	80	120	239	357	475
2,3: 2-Baker-c/a. 3-Baker-c/a(3)	26	52	78	147	211	275
4,5,7,8-Photo-c; Baker-a(2-3) each	21	42	63	121	173	225
6-Slightly large size; photo-c; part magazine; Baker-a (10/49)	23	46	69	130	188	245
9-Baker-c/a; Kubert-a	27	54	81	154	222	290
10-12,20-Baker-c/a(2-3) each	20	40	60	115	165	215
13-19,21,22-Complete issues by Baker	27	54	81	154	222	290
23-25-Baker-c/a(2-3) each	19	38	57	107	154	200
26,27,33,34,36-40,42: Baker-c/a. 33,40-Signed story by Estrada. 38-Suggestive-c. 42-r/Cinderella Love #9; Last pre-code (3/55)	13	26	39	76	106	135
28-30-No Baker-a	8	16	24	46	58	70
31,32-Baker-c. 31-Estrada-s	11	22	33	64	87	110
35-Baker-c/a (16 pgs.)	14	28	42	81	113	145
41-Baker-c; Infantino-a(r); all stories are Ziff-Davis-r	11	22	33	66	91	115
43-45-Baker-c/a	14	28	42	81	113	145

TEEN-AGE TALK
I.W. Enterprises: 1964

Reprint #1	2	4	6	11	14	18
Reprint #5,8,9: 5-r/Hector #? 9-Punch Comics #?; L.B. Cole-c reprint from School Day Romances #1	2	4	6	10	13	16

TEEN-AGE TEMPTATIONS (Going Steady #10 on)(See True Love Pictorial)
St. John Publishing Co.: Oct, 1952 - No. 9, Aug, 1954

1-Baker-c/a; has story "Reform School Girl" by Estrada	45	90	135	275	420	565
2,4-Baker-c	18	36	54	102	146	190
3,5-7,9-Baker-c/a	25	50	75	141	203	265
8-Teenagers smoke reefers; Baker-c/a	25	50	75	141	203	265

NOTE: ***Estrada** a-1, 3-5.*

TEEN BEAM (Formerly Teen Beat #1)
National Periodical Publications: No. 2, Jan-Feb, 1968

2-Superman cameo; Herman's Hermits, Yardbirds, Simon & Garfunkel, Lovin Spoonful, Young Rascals app.; Orlando, Drucker-a(r); Monkees photo-c;	8	16	24	55	78	100

TEEN BEAT (Becomes Teen Beam #2)
National Periodical Publications: Nov-Dec, 1967

1-Photos & text only; Monkees photo-c; Beatles, Herman's Hermits, Animals, Supremes, Byrds app.	10	20	30	67	96	125

TEEN COMICS (Formerly All Teen; Journey Into Unknown Worlds #36 on)
Marvel Comics (WFP): No. 21, Apr, 1947 - No. 35, May, 1950

21-Kurtzman's "Hey Look"; Patsy Walker, Cindy (1st app.?), Georgie, Margie app.; Syd Shores-a begins, end #23	15	30	45	86	123	160
22,23,25,27,29,31-35: 22-(6/47)-Becomes Hedy Devine #22 (8/47) on?	11	22	33	66	91	115
24,26,28,30-Kurtzman's "Hey Look"	12	24	36	71	98	125

TEEN CONFESSIONS
Charlton Comics: Aug, 1959 - No. 97, Nov, 1976

1	9	18	27	60	85	110
2	5	10	15	33	44	55
3-10	4	8	12	25	33	42
11-30	3	6	9	19	25	32
31-Beatles-c	12	24	36	86	131	175

Teen Titans #13 © DC

Teen Titans (2nd series) Annual #1 © DC

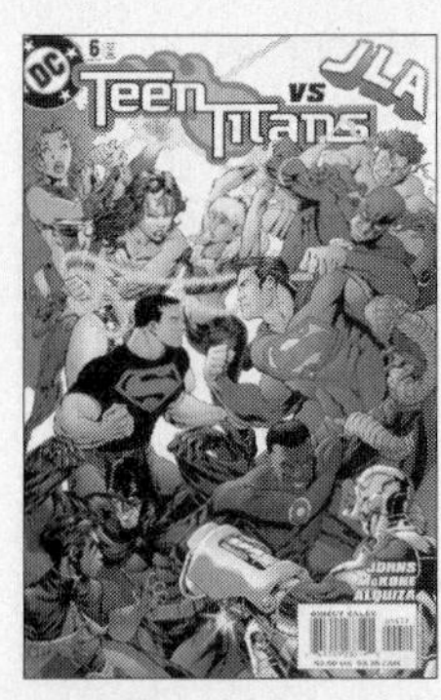

Teen Titans ('03) #6 © DC

GD VG FN VF VF/NM NM-
2.0 4.0 6.0 8.0 9.0 9.2

32-36,38-55 3 6 9 16 20 24
37 (1/66)-Beatles Fan Club story; Beatles-c 12 24 36 86 131 175
56-58,60-97: 89,90-Newton-c 2 4 6 10 13 16
59-Kaluta's 1st pro work? (12/69) 3 6 9 18 24 30

TEENIE WEENIES, THE (America's Favorite Kiddie Comic)
Ziff-Davis Publishing Co.: No. 10, 1950 - No. 11, Apr-May, 1951 (Newspaper reprints)

10,11-Painted-c 20 40 60 112 161 210

TEEN-IN (Tippy Teen)
Tower Comics: Summer, 1968 - No. 4, Fall, 1969

nn(#1, Summer, 1968) 7 14 21 51 71 90
nn(#2, Spring, 1969),3,4 5 10 15 36 48 60

TEEN LIFE (Formerly Young Life)
New Age/Quality Comics Group: No. 3, Winter, 1945 - No. 5, Fall, 1945 (Teenage magazine)

3-June Allyson photo on-c & story 13 26 39 74 102 130
4-Duke Ellington photo on-c & story 11 22 33 62 84 105
5-Van Johnson, Woody Herman & Jackie Robinson articles; Van Johnson & Woody Herman photos on-c 13 26 39 76 106 135

TEEN LOVE STORIES (Magazine)
Warren Publ. Co.: Sept, 1969 - No. 3, Jan, 1970 (68 pgs., photo covers, B&W)

1-Photos & articles plus 36-42 pgs. new comic stories in all; Frazetta-a 6 12 18 40 55 70
2,3: 2-Anti-marijuana story 4 8 12 29 40 50

TEEN ROMANCES
Super Comics: 1964

10,11,15-17-Reprints 2 4 6 9 11 14

TEEN SECRET DIARY (Nurse Betsy Crane #12 on)
Charlton Comics: Oct, 1959 - No. 11, June, 1961; No. 1, 1972

1 6 12 18 38 52 65
2 4 8 12 24 32 40
3-11 3 6 9 19 25 32
1 (1972)(exist?) 3 6 9 16 20 24

TEEN TALK (See Teen)

TEEN TITANS (See Brave & the Bold #54,60, DC Super-Stars #1, Marvel & DC Present, New Teen Titans, New Titans, Official...Index and Showcase #59)
National Periodical Publications/DC Comics: 1-2/66 - No. 43, 1-2/73; No. 44, 11/76 - No. 53, 2/78

1-(1-2/66)-Titans join Peace Corps; Batman, Flash, Aquaman, Wonder Woman cameos 27 54 81 194 297 400
2 12 24 36 86 131 175
3-5: 4-Speedy app. 8 16 24 55 78 100
6-10: 6-Doom Patrol app.; Beast Boy x-over; readers polled on him joining Titans 7 14 21 46 63 80
11-18: 11-Speedy app. 13-X-Mas-c 6 12 18 38 52 65
19-Wood-i; Speedy begins as regular 6 12 18 40 55 70
20-22: All Neal Adams-a. 21-Hawk & Dove app.; last 12¢ issue. 22-Origin Wonder Girl 7 14 21 51 71 90
23-Wonder Girl dons new costume 4 8 12 24 32 40
24-31: 25-Flash, Aquaman, Batman, Green Arrow, Green Lantern, Superman, & Hawk & Dove guests; 1st app. Lilith who joins T.T. West in #50. 29-Hawk & Dove & Ocean Master app. 30-Aquagirl app. 31-Hawk & Dove app.; last 15¢ issue 4 8 12 25 33 42
32-34,40-43 3 6 9 16 21 26
35-39-(52 pgs.): 36,37-Superboy-r. 38-Green Arrow/Speedy-r; Aquaman/Aqualad story. 39-Hawk & Dove-r. 3 6 9 18 24 30
44-(11/76) Dr. Light app.; Mal becomes the Guardian 2 4 6 9 11 14
45,47,49,51,52 2 4 6 9 11 14
46,48: 46-Joker's daughter begins (see Batman Family). 48-Intro Bumblebee; Joker's daughter becomes Harlequin 2 4 6 12 16 20
50-1st revival original Bat-Girl; intro. Teen Titans West 2 4 6 14 18 22
53-Origin retold 2 4 6 10 13 16

*NOTE: **Aparo** a-36. **Buckler** c-46-53. **Cardy** c-1-16. **Kane** a(p)-19, 22-24, 39r. **Tuska** a(p)-31, 36, 38, 39. DC Super-Stars #1 (3/76) was released before #44.*

TEEN TITANS (Also see Titans Beat in the Promotional Comics section)
DC Comics: Oct, 1996 - No. 24, Sept, 1998 ($1.95)

1-Dan Jurgens-c/a(p)/scripts & George Pérez-c/a(i) begin; Atom forms new team (Risk, Argent, Prysm, & Joto); 1st app. Loren Jupiter & Omen; no indicia. 1-3-Origin. 4.00
2-24: 4,5-Robin, Nightwing, Supergirl, Capt. Marvel Jr. app. 12-"Then and Now" begins w/original Teen Titans-c/app. 15-Death of Joto. 17-Capt. Marvel Jr. and Fringe join. 19-Millennium Giants x-over. 23,24-Superman app. 3.00
Annual 1 (1997, $3.95)-Pulp Heroes story 4.00

TEEN TITANS (Also see Titans/Young Justice: Graduation Day)
DC Comics: Sept, 2003 - Present ($2.50)

1-McKone-c/a;Johns-s 4.00
1-Variant-c by Michael Turner 5.00
1-2nd and 3rd printings 2.50
2-Deathstroke app. 5.00
2-2nd printing 2.50
3-15: 4-Impulse becomes Kid Flash. 5-Raven returns. 6-JLA app. 2.50
16-18: 16-Titans go to 31st Century; Legion and Fatal Five app. 17,18-Future Titans app. 2.50
.../Legion Special (11/04, $3.50) (cont'd from #16) Reis-a; leads into 2005 Legion of Super-Heroes series; LSH preview by Waid & Kitson 3.50
#1/2 (Wizard mail offer) origin of Ravager; Reis-a 8.00
.../Outsiders Secret Files 2003 (12/03, $5.95) Reis & Jimenez-a; pin-ups by various 6.00
A Kid's Game TPB (2004, $9.95) r/#1-7; Turner-c from #1; McKone sketch pages 10.00
Family Lost TPB (2004, $9.95) r/#8-12 & #1/2 10.00

TEEN TITANS GO! (Based on Cartoon Network series) (Also see Free Comic Book Day Edition in the Promotional Comics section)
DC Comics: Jan, 2004 - Present ($2.25)

1-12: 1,2-Nauck-a/Bullock-c/J. Torres-s. 6-Thunder & Lightning app. 8-Mad Mod app. 2.25
13-($2.95) Bonus pages with Shazam! rep. 3.00
... Vol 1: Truth, Justice, Pizza! (2004, $6.95, digest-size) r/#1-5 7.00

TEEN TITANS SPOTLIGHT
DC Comics: Aug, 1986 - No. 21, Apr, 1988

1-21: 7-Guice's 1st work at DC. 14-Nightwing; Batman app. 15-Austin-c(i). 18,19-Millennium x-over. 21-($1.00-c)-Original Teen Titans; Spiegle-a 3.00

*Note: **Guice** a-7p, 8p; c-7,8. **Orlando** c/a-11p. **Perez** c-1, 17i, 19. **Sienkiewicz** c-10*

TEEPEE TIM (...Heap Funny Indian Boy)(Formerly Ha Ha Comics)
American Comics Group: No. 100, Feb-Mar, 1955 - No. 102, June-July, 1955

100-102 6 12 18 31 38 45

TEGRA JUNGLE EMPRESS (Zegra Jungle Empress #2 on)
Fox Features Syndicate: August, 1948

1-Blue Beetle, Rocket Kelly app.; used in **SOTI**, pg. 31 56 112 168 350 538 725

TEKKEN FOREVER
Image Comics: Dec, 2001 - No. 4 ($2.95, limited series)

1-Based on the video game 3.00

TEKNO COMIX HANDBOOK
Tekno Comix: May, 1996 ($3.95, one-shot)

1-Guide to the Tekno Universe 4.00

TEKNOPHAGE (See Neil Gaiman's...)

TEKNOPHAGE VERSUS ZEERUS
BIG Entertainment: July, 1996 ($3.25, one-shot)

1-Paul Jenkins script 3.25

TEKWORLD (William Shatner's... on-c only)
Epic Comics (Marvel): Sept, 1992 - Aug, 1994 ($1.75)

1-Based on Shatner's novel, TekWar, set in L.A. in the year 2120 3.00
2-24 2.25

TELEVISION (See TV)

TELEVISION COMICS (Early TV comic)
Standard Comics (Animated Cartoons): No. 5, Feb, 1950 - No. 8, Nov, 1950

5-1st app. Willy Nilly 10 20 30 56 73 90
6-8: 6 has #2 on inside 8 16 24 43 54 65

TELEVISION PUPPET SHOW (Early TV comic) (See Spotty the Pup)
Avon Periodicals: 1950 - No. 2, Nov, 1950

1-1st app. Speedy Rabbit, Spotty The Pup 20 40 60 112 161 210
2 14 28 42 79 110 140

TELEVISION TEENS MOPSY (See TV Teens)

TELL IT TO THE MARINES
Toby Press Publications: Mar, 1952 - No. 15, July, 1955

1-Lover O'Leary and His Liberty Belles (with pin-ups), ends #6; Spike & Bat begin, end #6 20 40 60 112 161 210
2-Madame Cobra-c/story 11 22 33 64 87 110
3-5 9 18 27 49 62 75

The Tenth (2nd) #4 © Tony Daniel

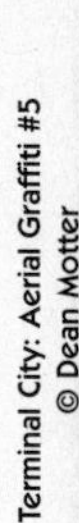
Terminal City: Aerial Graffiti #5 © Dean Motter

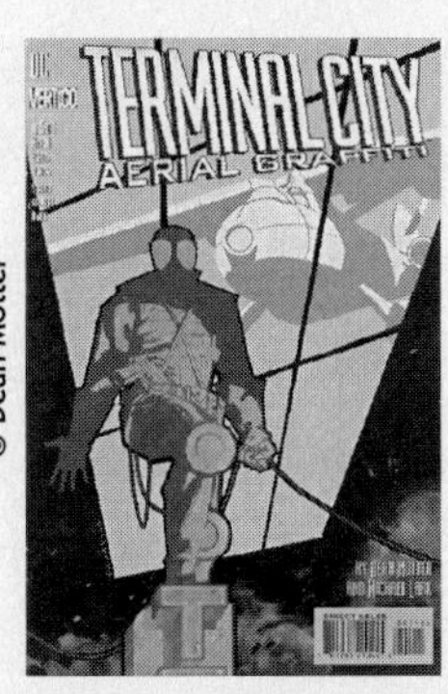

The Terminator ('98) #1 © Canal + DA

	GD 2.0	VG 4.0	FN 6.0	VF 8.0	VF/NM 9.0	NM- 9.2
6-12,14,15: 7-9,14,15-Photo-c	8	16	24	40	50	60
13-John Wayne photo-c	14	28	42	79	110	140
I.W. Reprint #9-r/#1 above	2	4	6	8	10	12
Super Reprint #16(1964)-r/#4 above	2	4	6	8	10	12

TELLOS
Image Comics: May, 1999 - Present ($2.50)

	GD	VG	FN	VF	VF/NM	NM-
1-Dezago-s/Wieringo-a						3.00
1-Variant-c ($7.95)						8.00
2-10: 4-Four covers						2.50
...: Maiden Voyage (3/01, $5.95) Didier Crispeels-a/c						6.00
...: Sons & Moons (2002, $5.95) Nick Cardy-c						6.00
...: The Last Heist (2001, $5.95) Rousseau-a/c						6.00
Prelude ($5.00, AnotherUniverse.com)						5.00
Prologue ($3.95, Dynamic Forces)						4.00
...Collected Edition 1 (12/99, $8.95) r/#1-3						9.00
...: Kindred Spirits (2/01, $17.95) r/#6-10, Section Zero #1 (Scatterjack-s)						18.00
...: Reluctant Heroes (2/01, $17.95) r/#1-5, Prelude, Prologue; sketchbook						18.00

TEMPEST (See Aquaman, 3rd Series)
DC Comics: Nov, 1996 - No. 4, Feb, 1997 ($1.75, limited series)

	GD	VG	FN	VF	VF/NM	NM-
1-4: Formerly Aqualad; Phil Jimenez-c/a/scripts in all						2.25

TEMPUS FUGITIVE
DC Comics: 1990 - No. 4, 1991 ($4.95, squarebound, 52 pgs.)

	GD	VG	FN	VF	VF/NM	NM-
Book 1,2: Ken Steacy painted-c/a & scripts						6.00
Book 3,4-($5.95-c)						6.00
TPB (Dark Horse Comics, 1/97, $17.95)						18.00

TEN COMMANDMENTS (See Moses & the... and Classics Illustrated Special)

TENDER LOVE STORIES
Skywald Publ. Corp.: Feb, 1971 - No. 4, July, 1971 (Pre-code reprints and new stories)

	GD	VG	FN	VF	VF/NM	NM-
1 (All 25¢, 52 pgs.)	3	6	9	19	25	32
2-4	2	4	6	14	18	22

TENDER ROMANCE (Ideal Romance #3 on)
Key Publications (Gilmour Magazines): Dec, 1953 - No. 2, Feb, 1954

	GD	VG	FN	VF	VF/NM	NM-
1-Headlight & lingerie panels; B. Baily-c	18	36	54	100	143	185
2-Bernard Baily-c	10	20	30	58	77	95

TENSE SUSPENSE
Fago Publications: Dec, 1958 - No. 2, Feb, 1959

	GD	VG	FN	VF	VF/NM	NM-
1	10	20	30	56	73	90
2	8	16	24	40	50	60

TEN STORY LOVE (Formerly a pulp magazine with same title)
Ace Periodicals: V29#3, June-July, 1951 - V36#5(#209), Sept, 1956 (#3-6: 52 pgs.)

	GD	VG	FN	VF	VF/NM	NM-
V29#3(#177)-Part comic, part text; painted-c	12	24	36	69	95	120
4-6(1/52)	8	16	24	43	54	65
V30#1(3/52)-6(1/53)	8	16	24	40	50	60
V31#1(2/53),V32#2(4/53)-6(12/53)	7	14	21	37	46	55
V33#1(1/54)-3(5#54, #195), V34#4(7/54, #196)-6(10/54, #198)	7	14	21	35	43	50
V35#1(12/54, #199)-3(4/55, #201)-Last precode	6	12	18	31	38	45
V35#4-6(9/55, #201-204), V36#1(11/55, #205)-3, 5(9/56, #209)	6	12	18	28	34	40
V36#4-L.B. Cole-a	9	18	27	54	70	85

TENTH, THE
Image Comics: Jan, 1997 - No. 4, June, 1997 ($2.50, limited series)

	GD	VG	FN	VF	VF/NM	NM-
1-4-Tony Daniel-c/a, Beau Smith-s						5.00
Abuse of Humanity TPB ($10.95) r/#1-4						11.00
Abuse of Humanity TPB (10/98, $11.95) r/#1-4 & 0(8/97)						12.00

TENTH, THE
Image Comics: Sept, 1997 - No. 14, Jan, 1999 ($2.50)

	GD	VG	FN	VF	VF/NM	NM-
0-(8/97, $5.00) American Ent. Ed.						6.00
1-Tony Daniel-c/a, Beau Smith-s						6.00
2-9: 3,7-Variant-c						4.00
10-14						3.00
...Configuration (8/98) Re-cap and pin-ups						2.50
...Collected Edition 1 ('98, $4.95, square-bound) r/#1,2						5.00
...Special (4/00, $2.95) r/#0 and Wizard #1/2						3.00
Wizard #1/2-Daniel-s/Steve Scott-a						10.00

TENTH, THE (Volume 3) (The Black Embrace)
Image Comics: Mar, 1999 - No. 4, June, 1999 ($2.95)

	GD	VG	FN	VF	VF/NM	NM-
1-4-Daniel-c/a						3.00
TPB (1/00, $12.95) r/#1-4						13.00

TENTH, THE (Volume 4) (Evil's Child)
Image Comics: Sept, 1999 - No. 4, Mar, 2000 ($2.95, limited series)

	GD	VG	FN	VF	VF/NM	NM-
1-4-Daniel-c/a						3.00

TENTH, THE : RESURRECTED
Dark Horse Comics: July, 2001 - No. 4, Feb, 2002 ($2.99, limited series)

	GD	VG	FN	VF	VF/NM	NM-
1-4: 1-Two covers; Daniel-s/c; Romano-a						3.00

10th MUSE
Image Comics (TidalWave Studios): Nov, 2000 - No. 9, Jan, 2002 ($2.95)

	GD	VG	FN	VF	VF/NM	NM-
1-Character based on wrestling's Rena Mero; regular & photo covers						3.00
2-9: 2-Photo and 2 Lashley covers; flip book Dollz preview. 5-Savage Dragon app.; 2 covers by Lashley and Larsen. 6-Tellos x-over						3.00

10th MUSE (Volume 2)
Avatar Press: July, 2002 ($3.50)

	GD	VG	FN	VF	VF/NM	NM-
1-Wolfman-s; Cruz-a. 1-Five homage covers by various						3.50

TEN WHO DARED (Disney)
Dell Publishing Co.: No. 1178, Dec, 1960

	GD	VG	FN	VF	VF/NM	NM-
Four Color 1178-Movie, painted-c; cast member photo on back-c	9	18	27	60	85	110

TERMINAL CITY
DC Comics (Vertigo): July, 1996 - No. 9, Mar, 1997 ($2.50, limited series)

	GD	VG	FN	VF	VF/NM	NM-
1-9: Dean Motter scripts, 7,8-Matt Wagner-c						2.50
TPB ('97, $19.95) r/series						20.00

TERMINAL CITY: AERIAL GRAFFITI
DC Comics (Vertigo): Nov, 1997 - No. 5, Mar, 1998 ($2.50, limited series)

	GD	VG	FN	VF	VF/NM	NM-
1-5: Dean Motter-s/Lark-a/Chiarello-c						2.50

TERMINATOR, THE (See Robocop vs. ... & Rust #12 for 1st app.)
Now Comics: Sept, 1988 - No. 17, 1989 ($1.75, Baxter paper)

	GD	VG	FN	VF	VF/NM	NM-
1-Based on movie	1	3	4	6	8	10
2-5						6.00
6-17: 12-($2.95, 52 pgs.)-Intro. John Connor						3.00
Trade paperback (1989, $9.95)						10.00

TERMINATOR, THE
Dark Horse Comics: Aug, 1990 - No. 4, Nov, 1990 ($2.50, limited series)

	GD	VG	FN	VF	VF/NM	NM-
1-Set 39 years later than the movie						4.00
2-4						3.00

TERMINATOR, THE
Dark Horse Comics: 1998 - No. 4, Dec, 1998 ($2.95, limited series)

	GD	VG	FN	VF	VF/NM	NM-
1-4-Alan Grant-s/Steve Pugh-a/c						3.00
...Special (1998, $2.95) Darrow-c/Grant-s						3.00

TERMINATOR, THE: ALL MY FUTURES PAST
Now Comics: V3#1, Aug, 1990 - V3#2, Sept, 1990 ($1.75, limited series)

	GD	VG	FN	VF	VF/NM	NM-
V3#1,2						3.00

TERMINATOR, THE: ENDGAME
Dark Horse Comics: Sept, 1992 - No. 3, Nov, 1992 ($2.50, limited series)

	GD	VG	FN	VF	VF/NM	NM-
1-3: Guice-a(p); painted-c						3.00

TERMINATOR, THE: HUNTERS AND KILLERS
Dark Horse Comics: Mar, 1992 - No. 3, May, 1992 ($2.50, limited series)

	GD	VG	FN	VF	VF/NM	NM-
1-3						3.00

TERMINATOR, THE: ONE SHOT
Dark Horse Comics: July, 1991 ($5.95, 56 pgs.)

	GD	VG	FN	VF	VF/NM	NM-
nn-Matt Wagner-a; contains stiff pop-up inside						6.00

TERMINATOR, THE: SECONDARY OBJECTIVES
Dark Horse Comics: July, 1991 - No. 4, Oct, 1991 ($2.50, limited series)

	GD	VG	FN	VF	VF/NM	NM-
1-4: Gulacy-c/a(p) in all						3.00

TERMINATOR, THE: THE BURNING EARTH
Now Comics: V2#1, Mar, 1990 - V2#5, July, 1990 ($1.75, limited series)

	GD	VG	FN	VF	VF/NM	NM-
V2#1: Alex Ross painted art (1st published work)	2	4	6	10	12	15
2-5: Ross-c/a in all	1	3	4	6	8	10
Trade paperback (1990, $9.95)-Reprints V2#1-5						12.00
Trade paperback (ibooks, 2003, $17.95)-Digitally remastered reprint						18.00

TERMINATOR, THE: THE DARK YEARS

Terrific Comics #6 © Continental

Terrors of the Jungle #21 © STAR

Terry and the Pirates #3 © NYNS

GD VG FN VF VF/NM NM-
2.0 4.0 6.0 8.0 9.0 9.2

GD VG FN VF VF/NM NM-
2.0 4.0 6.0 8.0 9.0 9.2

Dark Horse Comics: Aug, 1999 - No. 4, Dec, 1999 ($2.95, limited series)

1-4-Alan Grant-s/Mel Rubi-a; Jae Lee-c 3.00

TERMINATOR: THE ENEMY FROM WITHIN, THE
Dark Horse Comics: Nov, 1991 - No. 4, Feb, 1992 ($2.50, limited series)

1-4: All have Simon Bisley painted-c 3.00

TERMINATOR 2: CYBERNETIC DAWN
Malibu: Nov, 1995 - No.4, Feb, 1996; No. 0. Apr, 1996 ($2.50, lim. series)

0 (4/96, $2.95)-Erskine-c/a; flip book w/Terminator 2: Nuclear Twilight 3.00
1-4: Continuation of film. 3.00

TERMINATOR 2: JUDGEMENT DAY
Marvel Comics: Early Sept, 1991 - No. 3, Early Oct, 1991 ($1.00, lim. series)

1-3: Based on movie sequel; 1-3-Same as nn issues 3.00
nn (1991, $4.95, squarebound, 68 pgs.)-Photo-c 5.00
nn (1991, $2.25, B&W, magazine, 68 pgs.) 3.00

TERMINATOR 2: NUCLEAR TWILIGHT
Malibu: Nov, 1995 - No.4, Feb, 1996; No. 0, Apr, 1996 ($2.50, lim. series)

0 (4/96, $2.95)-Erskine-c/a; flip book w/Terminator 2: Cybernetic Dawn 3.00
1-4:Continuation of film. 3.00

TERMINATOR 3: RISE OF THE MACHINES (... BEFORE THE RISE on cover)
Beckett Comics: July, 2003 - No. 6, Jan, 2004 ($5.95, limited series)

1-6: 1,2-Leads into movie; 2 covers on each. 3-6-Movie adaptation 6.00

TERRAFORMERS
Wonder Color Comics: April, 1987 - No. 2, 1987 ($1.95, limited series)

1,2-Kelley Jones-a 2.25

TERRANAUTS
Fantasy General Comics: Aug, 1986 - No. 2, 1986 ($1.75, limited series)

1,2 2.25

TERRA OBSCURA (See Tom Strong)
America's Best Comics: Aug, 2003 - No. 6, Feb, 2004 ($2.95)

1-6-Alan Moore & Peter Hogan-s/Paquette-a 3.00
TPB (2004, $14.95) r/#1-6 15.00

TERRA OBSCURA VOLUME 2 (See Tom Strong)
America's Best Comics: Oct, 2004 - No. 6 ($2.95)

1-4-Alan Moore & Peter Hogan-s/Paquette-a; Tom Strange app. 3.00

TERRARISTS
Marvel Comics (Epic): Nov, 1993 - No. 4, Feb, 1994 ($2.50, limited series)

1-4-Bound-in trading cards in all 2.50

TERRIFIC COMICS (Also see Suspense Comics)
Continental Magazines: Jan, 1944 - No. 6, Nov, 1944

1-Kid Terrific; opium story 328 656 984 2132 3441 4750
2-1st app. The Boomerang by L.B. Cole & Ed Wheelan's "Comics" McCormick,
called the world's #1 comic book fan begins 242 484 726 1513 2332 3150
3-Diana becomes Boomerang's costumed aide; L.B. Cole-c
242 484 726 1513 2332 3150
4-Classic war-c (Scarce) 386 772 1158 2509 4055 5600
5-The Reckoner begins; Boomerang & Diana by L.B. Cole; Classic Schomburg
bondage & hooded vigilante-c (Scarce) 667 1334 2000 3900 5950 8000
6-L.B. Cole-c/a 223 446 669 1394 2147 2900

NOTE: ***L.B. Cole** a-1, 2(2), 3-6. **Fuje** a-5, 6. **Rico** a-2; c-1. **Schomburg** c-2, 5.*

TERRIFIC COMICS (Formerly Horrific; Wonder Boy #17 on)
Mystery Publ.(Comic Media)/(Ajax/Farrell): No. 14, Dec, 1954; No. 16, Mar, 1955 (No #15)

14-Art swipe/Advs. into the Unknown #37; injury-to-eye-c; pg. 2, panel 5 swiped from
Phantom Stranger #4; surrealistic Palais-a; Human Cross story; classic-c
56 112 168 350 538 725
16-Wonder Boy-c/story (last pre-code) 26 52 78 150 215 280

TERRIFYING TALES (Formerly Startling Terror Tales #10)
Star Publications: No. 11, Jan, 1953 - No. 15, Apr, 1954

11-Used in **POP**, pgs. 99,100; all Jo-Jo-r 50 100 150 305 465 625
12-Reprints Jo-Jo #19 entirely; L.B. Cole splash 48 96 144 293 447 600
13-All Rulah-r; classic devil-c 55 110 165 336 511 685
14-All Rulah reprints 44 88 132 268 409 550
15-Rulah, Zago-r; used in **SOTI**-r/Rulah #22 44 88 132 268 409 550

NOTE: *All issues have **L.B. Cole** covers; bondage covers-No. 12-14.*

TERRITORY, THE
Dark Horse Comics: Jan, 1999 - No. 4, Apr, 1999 ($2.95, limited series)

1-4-Delano-s/David Lloyd-c/a 3.00

TERROR ILLUSTRATED (Adult Tales of...)
E.C. Comics: Nov-Dec, 1955 - No. 2, Spring (April on-c), 1956 (Magazine, 25¢)

1-Adult Entertainment on-c 21 42 63 121 173 225
2-Charles Sultan-a 15 30 45 83 117 150

NOTE: ***Craig, Evans, Ingels, Orlando** art in each. **Crandall** c-1, 2.*

TERROR INC. (See A Shadowline Saga #3)
Marvel Comics: July, 1992 - No. 13, July, 1993 ($1.75)

1-8,11-13: 6,7-Punisher-c/story. 13-Ghost Rider app. 2.25
9,10-Wolverine-c/story 3.00

TERRORS OF DRACULA (Magazine)
Modern Day Periodical/Eerie Publ.: Vol. 1 #3, May, 1979 - Vol. 3 #2, Sept, 1981 (B&W)

Vol. 1 #3 (5/79, 1st issue) 4 8 12 22 30 38
#4(8/79), #5(11/79) 3 6 9 18 23 28
Vol. 2 #1-3: 1-(2/80). 2-(5/80). 3-(8/80) 2 4 6 14 18 22
Vol. 3 #1 (5/81), #2 (9/81) 3 6 9 18 23 28

TERRORS OF THE JUNGLE (Formerly Jungle Thrills)
Star Publications: No. 17, 5/52 - No. 21, 2/53; No. 4, 4/53 - No. 10, 9/54

17-Reprints Rulah #21, used in **SOTI**; L.B. Cole bondage-c
48 96 144 293 447 600
18-Jo-Jo-r 37 74 111 209 305 400
19,20(1952)-Jo-Jo-r; Disbrow-a 35 70 105 198 287 375
21-Jungle Jo, Tangi-r; used in **POP**, pg. 100 & color illos.; shrunken heads on-c
39 78 117 222 324 425
4-10: All Disbrow-a. 5-Jo-Jo-r. 8-Rulah, Jo-Jo-r. 9-Jo-Jo-r; Disbrow-a; Tangi
by Orlando10-Rulah-r 39 78 117 222 324 425

NOTE: ***L.B. Cole** c-all; bondage c-17, 19, 21, 5, 7.*

TERROR TALES (See Beware Terror Tales)

TERROR TALES (Magazine)
Eerie Publications: V1#7, 1969 - V6#6, Dec, 1974; V7#1, Apr, 1976 - V10, 1979? (V1-V6: 52 pgs.; V7 on: 68 pgs.)

V1#7 6 12 18 38 52 65
V1#8-11('69): 9-Bondage-c 4 8 12 25 33 42
V2#1-6('70), V3#1-6('71), V4#1-7('72), V5#1-6('73), V6#1-6('74), V7#1,4('76)
(no V7#2), V8#1-3('77) 4 8 12 22 30 38
V7#3-(7/76) LSD story-r/Weird V3#5 4 8 12 22 30 38
V9#2-4, V10 4 8 12 24 32 40

TERRY AND THE PIRATES (See Famous Feature Stories, Merry Christmas From Sears Toyland, Popular Comics, Super Book #3,5,9,16,28, & Super Comics)

TERRY AND THE PIRATES
Dell Publishing Co.: 1939 - 1953 (By Milton Caniff)

Large Feature Comic 2(1939) 79 158 237 494 760 1025
Large Feature Comic 6(1938)-r/1936 dailies 71 142 213 444 685 925
Four Color 9(1940) 50 100 150 407 641 875
Large Feature Comic 27('41), 6('42) 56 112 168 350 613 735
Four Color 44('43) 37 74 111 278 432 585
Four Color 101('45) 26 52 78 189 290 390
Family Album(1942) 20 40 60 112 161 210

TERRY AND THE PIRATES (Formerly Boy Explorers; Long John Silver & the Pirates #30 on) (Daily strip-r) (Two #26's)
Harvey Publications/Charlton No. 26-28: No. 3, 4/47 - No. 26, 4/51; No. 26, 6/55 - No. 28, 10/55

3(#1)-Boy Explorers by S&K; Terry & the Pirates begin by Caniff; 1st app.
The Dragon Lady 40 80 120 239 357 475
4-S&K Boy Explorers 25 50 75 141 203 265
5-11: 11-Man in Black app. by Powell 12 24 36 71 98 125
12-20: 16-Girl threatened with red hot poker 10 20 30 58 77 95
21-26(4/51)-Last Caniff issue & last pre-code issue 10 20 30 56 73 90
26-28('55)(Formerly This Is Suspense)-No Caniff-a 9 18 27 49 62 75

NOTE: ***Powell** a (Tommy Tween)-5-10, 12, 14; 15-17(1/2 to 2 pgs. each).*

TERRY BEARS COMICS (TerryToons, The... #4)
St. John Publishing Co.: June, 1952 - No. 3, Mar, 1953

1-By Paul Terry 10 20 30 56 73 90
2,3 7 14 21 35 43 50

TERRY-TOONS ALBUM (See Giant Comics Edition)

TERRY-TOONS COMICS (1st Series) (Becomes Paul Terry's Comics #85 on; later issues titled "Paul Terry's...")
Timely/Marvel No. 1-59 (8/47)(Becomes Best Western No. 58 on?, Marvel)/

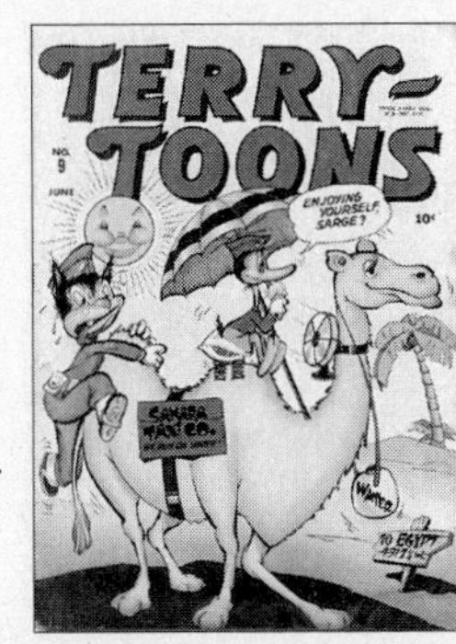

Terry-Toons Comics #9 © MAR

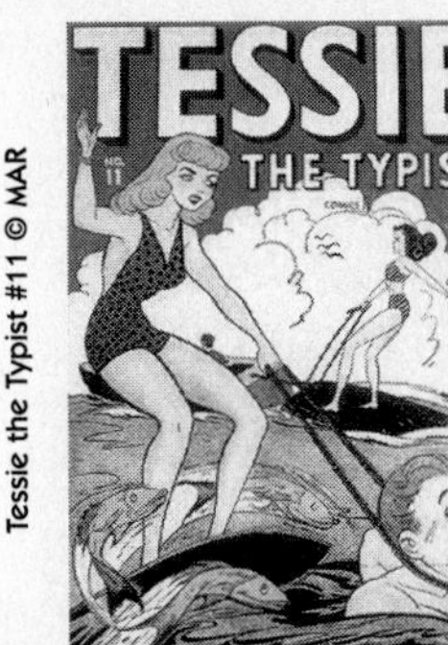

Tessie the Typist #11 © MAR

Tex Ritter Western #1 © FAW

St. John No. 60 (9/47) on: Oct, 1942 - No. 86, May, 1951

	GD 2.0	VG 4.0	FN 6.0	VF 8.0	VF/NM 9.0	NM- 9.2
1 (Scarce)-Features characters that 1st app. on movie screen; Gandy Goose & Sourpuss begin; war-c; Gandy Goose c-1-37	169	338	507	1056	1628	2200
2	62	124	186	388	594	800
3-5	44	88	132	268	409	550
6,8-10: 9,10-World War II gag-c	35	70	105	201	293	385
7-Hitler, Hirohito, Mussolini-c	46	92	138	281	428	575
11-20	22	44	66	123	177	230
21-37	15	30	45	86	123	160
38-Mighty Mouse begins (1st app., 11/45); Mighty Mouse-c begin, end #86; Gandy, Sourpuss welcome Mighty Mouse on-c	123	246	369	769	1185	1600
39-2nd app. Mighty Mouse	40	80	120	244	372	500
40-49: 43-Infinity-c	19	38	57	107	154	200
50-1st app. Heckle & Jeckle (11/46)	40	80	120	239	357	475
51-60: 55-Infinity-c. 60-(9/47)-Atomic explosion panel; 1st St. John issue	12	24	36	71	96	125
61-86: 85,86-Same book as Paul Terry's Comics #85,86 with only a title change; published at same time?	12	24	36	71	98	110

TERRY-TOONS COMICS (2nd Series)
St. John Publishing Co./Pines: June, 1952 - No. 9, Nov, 1953; 1957; 1958

	GD 2.0	VG 4.0	FN 6.0	VF 8.0	VF/NM 9.0	NM- 9.2
1-Gandy Goose & Sourpuss begin by Paul Terry	20	40	60	112	161	210
2	10	20	30	58	77	95
3-9	9	18	27	54	70	85
Giant Summer Fun Book 101,102-(Sum, 1957, Sum, 1958, 25¢, Pines)(TV) CBS Television Presents...; Tom Terrific, Mighty Mouse, Heckle & Jeckle Gandy Goose app.	14	28	42	79	110	140

TERRYTOONS, THE TERRY BEARS (Formerly Terry Bears Comics)
Pines Comics: No. 4, Summer, 1958 (CBS Television Presents...)

	GD 2.0	VG 4.0	FN 6.0	VF 8.0	VF/NM 9.0	NM- 9.2
4	6	12	18	31	38	45

TESSIE THE TYPIST (Tiny Tessie #24; see Comedy Comics, Gay Comics & Joker Comics)
Timely/Marvel Comics (20CC): Summer, 1944 - No. 23, Aug, 1949

	GD 2.0	VG 4.0	FN 6.0	VF 8.0	VF/NM 9.0	NM- 9.2
1-Doc Rockblock & others by Wolverton	65	130	195	406	628	850
2-Wolverton's Powerhouse Pepper	40	80	120	230	335	440
3-(3/45)-No Wolverton	15	30	45	86	123	160
4,5,7,8-Wolverton-a. 4-(Fall/45)	30	60	90	170	245	320
6-Kurtzman's "Hey Look", 2 pgs. Wolverton-a	30	60	90	170	245	320
9-Wolverton's Powerhouse Pepper (8 pgs.) & 1 pg. Kurtzman's "Hey Look"	33	66	99	190	275	360
10-Wolverton's Powerhouse Pepper (4 pgs.)	31	62	93	175	253	330
11-Wolverton's Powerhouse Pepper (8 pgs.)	33	66	99	190	275	360
12-Wolverton's Powerhouse Pepper (4 pgs.) & 1 pg. Kurtzman's "Hey Look"	31	62	93	175	253	330
13-Wolverton's Powerhouse Pepper (4 pgs.)	31	62	93	175	253	330
14,15: 14-Wolverton's Dr. Whackyhack (1 pg.); 1-1/2 pgs. Kurtzman's "Hey Look". 15-Kurtzman's "Hey Look" (3 pgs.) & 3 pgs. Giggles 'n' Grins	23	46	69	132	191	250
16-18-Kurtzman's "Hey Look" (?, 2 & 1 pg.)	16	32	48	89	127	165
19-Annie Oakley story (8 pgs.)	12	24	36	69	95	120
20-23: 20-Anti-Wertham editorial (2/49)	11	22	33	62	84	105

NOTE: *Lana app.-21. Millie The Model app.-13, 15, 17, 21. Rusty app.-10, 11, 13, 15, 17.*

TEXAN, THE (Fightin' Marines #15 on; Fightin' Texan #16 on)
St. John Publishing Co.: Aug, 1948 - No. 15, Oct, 1951

	GD 2.0	VG 4.0	FN 6.0	VF 8.0	VF/NM 9.0	NM- 9.2
1-Buckskin Belle	16	32	48	89	127	165
2	10	20	30	56	73	90
3,10: 10-Oversized issue	9	18	27	52	66	80
4,5,7,15-Baker-c/a	17	34	51	95	135	175
6,9-Baker-c	11	22	33	64	87	110
8,11,13,14-Baker-c/a(2-3) each	18	36	54	100	143	185
12-All Matt Baker-c/a; Peyote story	24	48	72	135	195	255

NOTE: ***Matt Baker** c-4-9, 11-15. **Larsen** a-4-6, 8-10, 15. **Tuska** a-1, 2, 7-9.*

TEXAN, THE (TV)
Dell Publishing Co.: No. 1027, Sept-Nov, 1959 - No. 1096, May-July, 1960

	GD 2.0	VG 4.0	FN 6.0	VF 8.0	VF/NM 9.0	NM- 9.2
Four Color 1027 (#1)-Photo-c	10	20	30	70	100	130
Four Color 1096-Rory Calhoun photo-c	9	18	27	65	93	120

TEXAS JOHN SLAUGHTER (See Walt Disney Presents, 4-Color #997, 1181 & #2)

TEXAS KID (See Two-Gun Western, Wild Western)
Marvel/Atlas Comics (LMC): Jan, 1951 - No. 10, July, 1952

	GD 2.0	VG 4.0	FN 6.0	VF 8.0	VF/NM 9.0	NM- 9.2
1-Origin; Texas Kid (alias Lance Temple) & his horse Thunder begin; Tuska-a	25	50	75	141	203	265
2	13	26	39	74	102	130
3-10	10	20	30	58	77	95

NOTE: ***Maneely** a-1-4; c-1, 3, 5-10.*

TEXAS RANGERS, THE (See Jace Pearson of... and Superior Stories #4)

TEXAS RANGERS IN ACTION (Formerly Captain Gallant or Scotland Yard?)
Charlton Comics: No. 5, Jul, 1956 - No. 79, Aug, 1970 (See Blue Bird Comics)

	GD 2.0	VG 4.0	FN 6.0	VF 8.0	VF/NM 9.0	NM- 9.2
5	8	16	24	46	58	70
6,7,9,10	6	12	18	28	34	40
8-Ditko-a (signed)	10	20	30	56	73	90
11-Williamson-a(5&8 pgs.); Torres/Williamson-a (5 pgs.)	10	20	30	56	73	90
12,14-20	5	10	15	23	28	32
13-Williamson-a (5 pgs); Torres, Morisi-a	8	16	24	43	54	65
21-30	3	6	9	18	23	28
31-59: 32-Both 10¢-c & 15¢-c exist	2	4	6	14	18	22
60-Riley's Rangers begin	3	6	9	16	20	24
61-65,68-70	2	4	6	9	11	14
66,67: 66-1st app. The Man Called Loco. 67-Origin	2	4	6	10	13	16
71-79	1	3	4	6	8	10
76 (Modern Comics-r, 1977)						4.00

TEXAS SLIM (See A-1 Comics)

TEX DAWSON, GUN-SLINGER (Gunslinger #2 on)
Marvel Comics Group: Jan, 1973 (20¢)(Also see Western Kid, 1st series)

	GD 2.0	VG 4.0	FN 6.0	VF 8.0	VF/NM 9.0	NM- 9.2
1-Steranko-c; Williamson-r (4 pgs.); Tex Dawson-r by Romita(3) from 1955; Tuska-r	3	6	9	16	20	25

TEX FARNUM (See Wisco)

TEX FARRELL (...Pride of the Wild West)
D. S. Publishing Co.: Mar-Apr, 1948

	GD 2.0	VG 4.0	FN 6.0	VF 8.0	VF/NM 9.0	NM- 9.2
1-Tex Farrell & his horse Lightning; Shelly-c	16	32	48	89	127	165

TEX GRANGER (Formerly Calling All Boys; see True Comics)
Parents' Magazine Inst./Commended: No. 18, Jun, 1948 - No. 24, Sept, 1949

	GD 2.0	VG 4.0	FN 6.0	VF 8.0	VF/NM 9.0	NM- 9.2
18-Tex Granger & his horse Bullet begin	12	24	36	69	95	120
19	10	20	30	56	73	90
20-24: 22-Wild Bill Hickok story. 23-Vs. Billy the Kid; Tim Holt app.	8	16	24	46	58	70

TEX MORGAN (See Blaze Carson and Wild Western)
Marvel Comics (CCC): Aug, 1948 - No. 9, Feb, 1950

	GD 2.0	VG 4.0	FN 6.0	VF 8.0	VF/NM 9.0	NM- 9.2
1-Tex Morgan, his horse Lightning & sidekick Lobo begin	30	60	90	170	245	320
2	19	38	57	107	154	200
3-6: 3,4-Arizona Annie app.	12	24	36	71	98	125
7-9: All photo-c. 7-Captain Tootsie by Beck. 8-18 pg. story "The Terror of Rimrock Valley"; Diablo app.	19	38	57	107	154	200

NOTE: *Tex Taylor app.-6, 7, 9. **Brodsky** c-6. **Syd Shores** c-2, 5.*

TEX RITTER WESTERN (Movie star; singing cowboy; see Six-Gun Heroes and Western Hero)
Fawcett No. 1-20 (1/54)/Charlton No. 21 on: Oct, 1950 - No. 46, May, 1959 (Photo-c: 1-21)

	GD 2.0	VG 4.0	FN 6.0	VF 8.0	VF/NM 9.0	NM- 9.2
1-Tex Ritter, his stallion White Flash & dog Fury begin; photo front/back-c begin	69	138	207	431	666	900
2	35	70	105	198	287	375
3-5: 5-Last photo back-c	26	52	78	150	215	280
6-10	20	40	60	112	161	210
11-19	14	28	42	81	113	145
20-Last Fawcett issue (1/54)	15	30	45	85	120	155
21-1st Charlton issue; photo-c (3/54)	19	38	57	107	154	200
22-B&W photo back-c begin, end #32	11	22	33	64	87	110
23-30: 23-25-Young Falcon app.	10	20	30	58	77	95
31-38,40-45	9	18	27	52	66	80
39-Williamson-a; Whitman-c (1/58)	10	20	30	58	77	95
46-Last issue	10	20	30	56	73	90

TEX TAYLOR (...The Fighting Cowboy on-c #1, 2)(See Blaze Carson, Kid Colt, Tex Morgan, Wild West, Wild Western, & Wisco)
Marvel Comics (HPC): Sept, 1948 - No. 9, March, 1950

	GD 2.0	VG 4.0	FN 6.0	VF 8.0	VF/NM 9.0	NM- 9.2
1-Tex Taylor & his horse Fury begin	30	60	90	170	245	320
2	16	32	48	89	127	165
3	14	28	42	81	113	145
4-6: All photo-c. 4-Anti-Wertham editorial. 5,6-Blaze Carson app.	17	34	51	95	135	175

7-9: 7-Photo-c;18 pg. Movie-Length Thriller "Trapped in Time's Lost Land!" with sabretoothed tigers, dinosaurs; Diablo app. 8-Photo-c; 18 pg. Movie-Length Thriller "The Mystery of Devil-Tree Plateau!" with dwarf horses, dwarf people & a lost miniature

THB #1 © Paul Pope

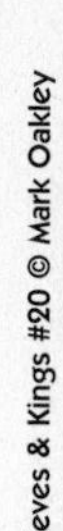

Thieves & Kings #20 © Mark Oakley

30 Days of Night: Return to Barrow #1 © Niles & Templesmith

	GD 2.0	VG 4.0	FN 6.0	VF 8.0	VF/NM 9.0	NM- 9.2
Inca type village; Diablo app. 9-Photo-c; 18 pg. Movie-Length Thriller "Guns Along the Border!" Captain Tootsie by Schreiber; Nimo the Mountain Lion app.	20	40	60	112	161	210

NOTE: *Syd Shores c-1-3.*

THANE OF BAGARTH (Also see Hercules, 1967 series)
Charlton Comics: No. 24, Oct, 1985 - No. 25, Dec, 1985

	GD	VG	FN	VF	VF/NM	NM-
24,25-Low print run						5.00

THANOS
Marvel Comics: Dec, 2003 - No. 12, Sept, 2004 ($2.99)

	GD	VG	FN	VF	VF/NM	NM-
1-12: 1-6-Starlin-s/a(p)/Milgrom-i; Galactus app. 7-12-Giffen-s/Lim-a						3.00
Vol. 4: Epiphany TPB (2004, $14.99) r/#1-6						15.00
Vol. 5: Samaritan TPB (2004, $14.99) r/#7-12						15.00

THANOS QUEST, THE (See Capt. Marvel #25, Infinity Gauntlet, Iron Man #55, Logan's Run, Marvel Feature #12, Marvel Universe: The End, Silver Surfer #34 & Warlock #9)
Marvel Comics: 1990 - No. 2, 1990 ($4.95, squarebound, 52 pgs.)

	GD	VG	FN	VF	VF/NM	NM-
1,2-Both have Starlin scripts & covers (both printings)	1	2	3	4	5	7
1-(3/2000, $3.99) r/material from #1&2						4.00

THAT CHEMICAL REFLEX
CFD Productions: 1994 - No. 3 ($2.50, B&W, mature)

	GD	VG	FN	VF	VF/NM	NM-
1-3: 1-Dan Brereton-c/a						2.50

THAT DARN CAT (See Movie Comics & Walt Disney Showcase #19)

THAT'S MY POP! GOES NUTS FOR FAIR
Bystander Press: 1939 (76 pgs., B&W)

	GD	VG	FN	VF	VF/NM	NM-
nn-by Milt Gross	30	60	90	173	249	325

THAT WILKIN BOY (Meet Bingo...)
Archie Publications: Jan, 1969 - No. 52, Oct, 1982

	GD	VG	FN	VF	VF/NM	NM-
1-1st app. Bingo's Band, Samantha & Tough Teddy	4	8	12	29	40	50
2-5	3	6	9	16	20	25
6-11	2	4	6	11	14	18
12-26-Giants. 12-No # on-c	2	4	6	14	18	22
27-40(1/77)	1	3	4	6	8	10
41-52						5.00

THB
Horse Press: Oct, 1994 - Present ($5.50/$2.50/$2.95, B&W)

	GD	VG	FN	VF	VF/NM	NM-
1 ($5.50) Paul Pope-s/a in all	1	2	3	5	6	8
1 (2nd Printing)-r/#1 w/new material						3.00
2 ($2.50)						5.00
3-5						4.00
69 (1995, no price, low distribution, 12 pgs.)-story reprinted in #1 (2nd Printing)						3.00
Giant THB-($4.95)						5.00
Giant THB 1 V2-(2003, $6.95)						7.00
...M3/THB: Mars' Mightiest Mek #1 (2000, $3.95)						4.00
...6A: Mek-Power #1, 6B: Mek-Power #2, 6C: Mek-Power #3 (2000, $3.95)						4.00
... 6D: Mek-Power #4 (2002, $4.95)						5.00

T.H.E. CAT (TV)
Dell Publishing Co.: Mar, 1967 - No. 4, Oct, 1967 (All have photo-c)

	GD	VG	FN	VF	VF/NM	NM-
1	4	8	12	27	36	45
2-4	3	6	9	19	25	32

THERE'S A NEW WORLD COMING
Spire Christian Comics/Fleming H. Revell Co.: 1973 (35/49¢)

	GD	VG	FN	VF	VF/NM	NM-
nn	1	3	4	6	8	11

THEY ALL KISSED THE BRIDE (See Cinema Comics Herald)

THIEF OF BAGHDAD
Dell Publishing Co.: No. 1229, Oct-Dec, 1961 (one-shot)

	GD	VG	FN	VF	VF/NM	NM-
Four Color 1229-Movie, Crandall/Evans-a, photo-c	8	16	24	55	78	100

THIEVES & KINGS
I Box: 1994 - Present ($2.35, B&W, bi-monthly)

	GD	VG	FN	VF	VF/NM	NM-
1						4.00
1-(2nd printing), 2-42						2.50

THIMK (Magazine) (Satire)
Counterpoint: May, 1958 - No. 6, May, 1959

	GD	VG	FN	VF	VF/NM	NM-
1	9	18	27	52	66	80
2-6	6	12	18	33	41	48

THING!, THE (Blue Beetle #18 on)
Song Hits No. 1,2/Capitol Stories/Charlton: Feb, 1952 - No. 17, Nov, 1954

	GD	VG	FN	VF	VF/NM	NM-
1-Weird/horror stories in all; shrunken head-c	85	170	255	531	816	1100
2,3	56	112	168	350	538	725
4-6,8,10: 5-Severed head-c; headlights	51	102	153	311	476	640
7-Injury to eye-c & inside panel	69	138	207	431	666	900
9-Used in **SOTI**, pg. 388 & illo "Stomping on the face is a form of brutality which modern children learn early"	79	158	237	494	765	1035
11-Necronomicon story; Hansel & Gretel parody; Injury-to-eye panel; Check-a	62	124	186	388	594	800
12-1st published Ditko-c; "Cinderella" parody; lingerie panels. Ditko-a	85	170	255	531	816	1100
13,15-Ditko-c/a(3 & 5)	85	170	255	531	816	1100
14-Extreme violence/torture; Rumpelstiltskin story; Ditko-c/a(4)	87	174	261	544	835	1125
16-Injury to eye panel	31	62	93	175	253	330
17-Ditko-c; classic parody "Through the Looking Glass"; Powell-r/Beware Terror Tales #1 & recolored	75	150	225	469	722	975

NOTE: *Excessive violence, severed heads, injury to eye are common No. 5 on.* ***Al Fago*** *c-4.* ***Forgione*** *c-1i, 2, 6, 8, 9. All* ***Ditko*** *issues #14, 15.*

THING, THE (See Fantastic Four, Marvel Fanfare, Marvel Feature #11,12, Marvel Two-In-One and Startling Stories:...- Night Falls on Yancy Street)
Marvel Comics Group: July, 1983 - No. 36, June, 1986

	GD	VG	FN	VF	VF/NM	NM-
1-Life story of Ben Grimm; Byrne scripts begin						3.00
2-36: 5-Spider-Man, She-Hulk app.						2.25

NOTE: ***Byrne*** *a-2i, 7; c-1, 7, 36i; scripts-1-13, 19-22.* ***Sienkiewicz*** *c-13i.*

THING & SHE-HULK: THE LONG NIGHT (Fantastic Four)
Marvel Comics: May, 2002 ($2.99, one-shot)

	GD	VG	FN	VF	VF/NM	NM-
1-Hitch-c/a(pg. 1-25); Reis-a(pg. 26-39); Dezago-s						3.00

THING, THE (From Another World)
Dark Horse Comics: 1991 - No. 2, 1992 ($2.95, mini-series, stiff-c)

	GD	VG	FN	VF	VF/NM	NM-
1,2-Based on Universal movie; painted-c/a						3.00

THING, THE: FREAKSHOW (Fantastic Four)
Marvel Comics: Aug, 2002 - No. 4, Nov, 2002 ($2.99, limited series)

	GD	VG	FN	VF	VF/NM	NM-
1-4-Geoff Johns-s/Scott Kolins-a						3.00

THING FROM ANOTHER WORLD: CLIMATE OF FEAR, THE
Dark Horse Comics: July, 1992 - No. 4, Dec, 1992 ($2.50, mini-series)

	GD	VG	FN	VF	VF/NM	NM-
1-4: Painted-c						3.00

THING FROM ANOTHER WORLD: ETERNAL VOWS
Dark Horse Comics: Dec, 1993 - No. 4, 1994 ($2.50, mini-series)

	GD	VG	FN	VF	VF/NM	NM-
1-4-Gulacy-c/a						3.00

THIRD WORLD WAR
Fleetway Publ. (Quality): 1990 - No. 6, 1991 ($2.50, thick-c, mature)

	GD	VG	FN	VF	VF/NM	NM-
1-6						2.50

THIRTEEN (...Going on 18)
Dell Publishing Co.: 11-1/61-62 - No. 25, 12/67; No. 26, 7/69 - No. 29, 1/71

	GD	VG	FN	VF	VF/NM	NM-
1	7	14	21	50	68	85
2-10	6	12	18	38	52	65
11-25	4	8	12	29	40	50
26-29-r	4	8	12	27	36	45

NOTE: ***John Stanley*** *script-No. 3-29; art?*

13: ASSASSIN
TSR, Inc.: 1990 - No. 8, 1991 ($2.95, 44 pgs.)

	GD	VG	FN	VF	VF/NM	NM-
1-8: Agent 13; Alcala-a(i); Springer back-up-a						3.00

30 DAYS OF NIGHT
Idea + Design Works: June, 2002 - No. 3, Oct, 2002 ($3.99, limited series)

	GD	VG	FN	VF	VF/NM	NM-
1-Vampires in Alaska; Steve Niles-s/Ben Templesmith-a/Ashley Wood-c						30.00
1-2nd printing						10.00
2						12.00
3						6.00
Annual 2004 (1/04, $4.99) Niles-s/art by Templesmith and others						5.00
TPB (2003, $17.99) r/#1-3, foreward by Clive Barker; script for #1						18.00
The Complete 30 Days of Night (2004, $75.00, oversized hardcover with slipcase) r/#1-3; prequel; script pages for #1-3; original cover and promotional materials						75.00

30 DAYS OF NIGHT: BLOODSUCKER TALES
IDW Publishing: Oct, 2004 - Present ($3.99, limited series)

	GD	VG	FN	VF	VF/NM	NM-
1,2-Niles-s/Chamberlain-a; Fraction-s/Templesmith-a/c						4.00

30 DAYS OF NIGHT: RETURN TO BARROW
IDW Publishing: Mar, 2004 - No. 6, Aug, 2004 ($3.99, limited series)

This Magazine is Haunted #9 © FAW

Thor #160 © MAR

Thor #321 © MAR

	GD 2.0	VG 4.0	FN 6.0	VF 8.0	VF/NM 9.0	NM- 9.2
1-6-Steve Niles-s/Ben Templesmith-a/c						4.00
TPB (2004, $19.99) r/#1-6; cover gallery						20.00

THIRTY SECONDS OVER TOKYO (See American Library)

THIS IS SUSPENSE! (Formerly Strange Suspense Stories; Strange Suspense Stories #27 on)
Charlton Comics: No. 23, Feb, 1955 - No. 26, Aug, 1955

	GD 2.0	VG 4.0	FN 6.0	VF 8.0	VF/NM 9.0	NM- 9.2
23-Wood-a(r)/A Star Presentation #3 "Dr. Jekyll & Mr. Hyde"; last pre-code issue	28	56	84	158	229	300
24-Censored Fawcett-r; Evans-a (r/Suspense Detective #1)	15	30	45	83	117	150
25,26: 26-Marcus Swayze-a	10	20	30	58	77	95

THIS IS THE PAYOFF (See Pay-Off)

THIS IS WAR
Standard Comics: No. 5, July, 1952 - No. 9, May, 1953

	GD 2.0	VG 4.0	FN 6.0	VF 8.0	VF/NM 9.0	NM- 9.2
5-Toth-a	14	28	42	79	110	140
6,9-Toth-a	11	22	33	62	84	105
7,8: 8-Ross Andru-c	8	16	24	46	58	70

THIS IS YOUR LIFE, DONALD DUCK (See Donald Duck..., Four Color #1109)

THIS MAGAZINE IS CRAZY (Crazy #? on)
Charlton Publ. (Humor Magazines): V3#2, July, 1957 - V4#8, Feb, 1959 (25¢, magazine, 68 pgs.)

	GD 2.0	VG 4.0	FN 6.0	VF 8.0	VF/NM 9.0	NM- 9.2
V3#2-V4#7: V4#5-Russian Sputnik-c parody	9	18	27	51	62	75
V4#8-Davis-a (8 pgs.)	9	18	27	54	70	85

THIS MAGAZINE IS HAUNTED (Danger and Adventure #22 on)
Fawcett Publications/Charlton No. 15(2/54) on: Oct, 1951 - No. 14, 12/53; No. 15, 2/54 - V3#21, Nov, 1954

	GD 2.0	VG 4.0	FN 6.0	VF 8.0	VF/NM 9.0	NM- 9.2
1-Evans-a; Dr. Death as host begins	63	126	189	394	610	825
2,5-Evans-a	44	88	132	268	409	550
3,4: 3-Vampire-c/story	36	72	108	204	297	390
6-9,11,12,14	26	52	78	147	211	275
10-Severed head-c	40	80	120	239	357	475
13-Severed head-c/story	39	78	117	230	335	440
15,20: 15-Dick Giordano-c. 20-Cover is swiped from panel in The Thing #16	21	42	63	121	173	225
16,19-Ditko-c. 19-Injury-to-eye panel; story-r/#1	40	80	120	236	351	465
17-Ditko-c/a(4); blood drainage story	46	92	138	281	428	575
18-Ditko-c/a(1 story); E.C. swipe/Haunt of Fear #5; injury-to-eye panel; reprints "Caretaker of the Dead" from Beware Terror Tales & recolored	40	80	120	224	372	500
21-Ditko-c, Evans-r/This Magazine Is Haunted #1	38	76	114	219	320	420

NOTE: ***Baily** a-1, 3, 4, 21r/#1. **Moldoff** c/a-1-13. **Powell** a-3-5, 11, 12, 17. **Shuster** a-18-20. Issues 19-21 have reprints which have been recolored from This Magazine is Haunted #1.*

THIS MAGAZINE IS HAUNTED (2nd Series) (Formerly Zaza the Mystic; Outer Space #17 on)
Charlton Comics: V2#12, July, 1957 - V2#16, May, 1958

	GD 2.0	VG 4.0	FN 6.0	VF 8.0	VF/NM 9.0	NM- 9.2
V2#12-14-Ditko-c/a in all	40	80	120	236	351	465
15-No Ditko-c/a	10	20	30	60	80	100
16-Ditko-a	28	56	84	158	229	300

THIS MAGAZINE IS WILD (See Wild)

THIS WAS YOUR LIFE (Religious)
Jack T. Chick Publ.: 1964 (3 1/2 x 5 1/2", 40 pgs., B&W and red)

	GD 2.0	VG 4.0	FN 6.0	VF 8.0	VF/NM 9.0	NM- 9.2
nn, Another version (5x2 3/4", 26 pgs.)	2	4	6	10	12	15

THOR (See Avengers #1, Giant-Size..., Marvel Collectors Item Classics, Marvel Graphic Novel #33, Marvel Preview, Marvel Spectacular, Marvel Treasury Edition, Special Marvel Edition & Tales of Asgard)

THOR (Journey Into Mystery #1-125, 503-on)(The Mighty Thor #413-490)
Marvel Comics Group: No. 126, Mar, 1966 - No. 502, Sept, 1996

	GD 2.0	VG 4.0	FN 6.0	VF 8.0	VF/NM 9.0	NM- 9.2
126-Thor continues (#125-130 Thor vs. Hercules)	19	38	57	134	205	275
127-130: 127-1st app. Pluto	9	18	27	60	85	110
131-133,135-140: 132-1st app. Ego	7	14	21	51	71	90
134-Intro High Evolutionary	8	16	24	53	74	95
141-150: 146-Inhumans begin (early app.), end #151 (see Fantastic Four #45 for 1st app.). 146,147-Origin The Inhumans. 148,149-Origin Black Bolt in each. 149-Origin Medusa, Crystal, Maximus, Gorgon, Karnak	6	12	18	43	59	75
151-157,159,160	5	10	15	36	48	60
158-Origin-r/#83; 158,159-Origin Dr. Blake (Thor)	9	18	27	60	85	110
161,167,170-179: 179-Last Kirby issue	4	8	12	29	40	50
162,168,169-Origin Galactus; Kirby-a	6	12	18	38	52	65
163,164-2nd & 3th brief app. Warlock (Him)	4	8	12	29	40	50
165-1st full app. Warlock (Him) (6/69, see Fantastic Four #67); last 12¢ issue; Kirby-a	7	14	21	51	71	90
166-2nd full app. Warlock (Him); battles Thor	6	12	18	43	59	75
180,181-Neal Adams-a	5	10	15	33	44	55
182-192: 192-Last 15¢ issue	3	6	9	18	24	30
193-(25¢, 52 pgs.); Silver Surfer x-over	6	12	18	43	59	75
194-199	3	6	9	16	20	24
200	3	6	9	18	24	30
201-206,208-224	2	4	6	9	11	14
207-Rutland, Vermont Halloween x-over	2	4	6	11	14	18
225-Intro. Firelord	2	4	6	11	14	18
226-245	1	3	4	6	8	10
246-250-(Regular 25¢ editions)(4-8/76)	1	3	4	6	8	10
246-250-(30¢-c variants, limited distribution)	2	4	6	10	12	15
251-280: 271-Iron Man x-over. 274-Death of Balder the Brave						6.00
260-264-(35¢-c variants, limited distribution)(6-10/77)	1	2	3	5	7	9
281-299: 294-Origin Asgard & Odin						5.00
300-(12/80)-End of Asgard; origin of Odin & The Destroyer	1	2	3	5	6	8
301-336,338-373,375-381,383: 316-Iron Man x-over. 332,333-Dracula app. 340-Donald Blake returns as Thor. 341-Clark Kent & Lois Lane cameo. 373-X-Factor tie-in						3.00
337-Simonson-c/a begins, ends #382; Beta Ray Bill becomes new Thor	1	2	3	5	7	9
374-Mutant Massacre; X-Factor app.						4.00
382-($1.25)-Anniversary issue; last Simonson-a						4.00
384-Intro. new Thor						4.00
385-399,401-410,413-428: 385-Hulk x-over. 391-Spider-Man x-over; 1st Eric Masterson. 395-Intro Earth Force. 408-Eric Masterson becomes Thor. 427,428-Excalibur x-over						2.50
400,411: 400-($1.75, 68 pgs.)-Origin Loki. 411-Intro New Warriors (appears in costume in last panel); Juggernaut-c/story						4.00
412-1st full app. New Warriors (Marvel Boy, Kid Nova, Namorita, Night Thrasher, Firestar & Speedball)						6.00
429-431,434-443: 429,430-Ghost Rider x-over. 434-Capt. America x-over. 437-Thor vs. Quasar; Hercules app.;Tales of Asgard back-up stories begin. 443-Dr. Strange & Silver Surfer x-over; last $1.00-c						2.50
432,433: 432-(52 pgs.)-Thor's 300th app. (vs. Loki); reprints origin & 1st app. from Journey into Mystery #83. 433-Intro new Thor						3.00
444-449,451-473: 448-Spider-Man-c/story. 455,456-Dr. Strange back-up. 457-Old Thor returns (3 pgs.). 459-Intro Thunderstrike. 460-Starlin scripts begin. 465-Super Skrull app. 466-Drax app. 469,470-Infinity Watch x-over. 472-Intro the Godlings						2.50
450-($2.50, 68 pgs.)-Flip-book format; r/story JIM #87 (1st Loki) plus-c plus a gallery of past-c; gatefold-c						3.00
474,476-481,483-499: 474-Begin $1.50-c; bound-in trading card sheet. 459-Intro Thunderstrike. 460-Starlin scripts begin. 472-Intro the Godlings. 490-The Absorbing Man app. 491-Warren Ellis scripts begins, ends #494; Deodato-c/a begins. 492-Reintro The Enchantress; Beta Ray Bill dies. 495-Wm. Messner-Loebs scripts begin; Isherwood-c/a.						2.50
475 ($2.00, 52 pgs.)-Regular edition						2.50
475 ($2.50, 52 pgs.)-Collectors edition w/foil embossed-c						3.00
482 ($2.95, 84 pgs.)-400th issue						3.00
500 ($2.50)-Double-size; wraparound-c; Deodato-c/a; Dr. Strange app.						5.00
501-Reintro Red Norvell						3.00
502-Onslaught tie-in; Red Norvell, Jane Foster & Hela app.						4.00
Special 2(9/66)-See Journey Into Mystery for 1st annual	9	18	27	60	85	110
Special 2 (2nd printing, 1994)	2	4	6	8	10	12
King Size Special 3(1/71)	3	7	10	21	28	35
Special 4(12/71)-r/Thor #131,132 & JIM #113	3	6	9	16	21	26
Annual 5,6: 5(11/76). 6(10/77)-Guardians of the Galaxy app.	2	4	6	10	12	15
Annual 7,8: 7(1978). 8(1979)-Thor vs. Zeus-c/story	1	3	4	6	8	10
Annual 9-12: 9('81). 10('82). 11('83). 12('84)						6.00
Annual 13-19('85-'94, 68 pgs.):14-Atlantis Attacks. 16-3 pg. origin; Guardians of the Galaxy x-over.18-Polybagged w/card						3.00
...Alone Against the Celestials nn (6/92, $5.95)-r/Thor #387-389						6.00
...Legends Vol. 2: Walter Simonson Book 2 TPB (2003, $24.99) r/#349-355,357-359						25.00
...Legends Vol. 3: Walter Simonson Book 3 TPB (2004, $24.99) r/#360-369						25.00
... Visionaries: Mike Deodato Jr. TPB (2004, $19.99) r/#491-494,498-500						20.00
... Visionaries: Walter Simonson TPB (5/01, $24.95) r/#337-348						25.00
....: Worldengine (8/96, $9.95)-r/#491-494; Deodato-c/a; story & new intermission by Warren Ellis						10.00

NOTE: ***Neal Adams** a-180,181; c-179-181. **Austin** a-342i, 346i; c-312i. **Buscema** a(p)-178, 182-213, 215-226, 231-238, 241-253, 254r, 256-259, 272-278, 283-285, 370, Annual 6, 8, 11i; c(p)-175, 182-196, 198-200, 202-204, 206, 211, 212, 215, 219, 221, 226, 256, 259, 261, 262, 272-278, 283, 289, 370, Annual 6. **Everett** a(i)-143, 170-175; c(i)-171, 172, 174, 176, 241. **Gil Kane** a-318p; c(p)-201, 205, 207-210, 216, 220, 222, 223, 231, 233-240, 242, 243, 318. **Kirby** a(p)-126-177, 179, 194r, 254r; c(p)-126-169, 171-174, 176-178, 249-253, 255, 257, 258, Annual 5, Special 2-4. **Mooney** a(i)-201, 204, 214-216, 218, 322i, 324i, 325i, 327i. **Sienkiewicz** c-332, 333, 335. **Simonson** a-260-271p, 337-354, 357-367, 380, Annual 7p; c-260, 263-271, 337-355, 357-369, 371, 373-382, Annual 7. **Starlin** c-213.*

Thor V2#85 © MAR

Thor: Son of Asgard #1 © MAR

3-D-ell #3 © DELL

GD VG FN VF VF/NM NM-
2.0 4.0 6.0 8.0 9.0 9.2

THOR (Volume 2)
Marvel Comics: July, 1998 - No. 85, Dec, 2004 ($2.99/$1.99/$2.25)

1-($2.99)-Follows Heroes Return; Jurgens-s/Romita Jr. & Janson-a; wraparound-c; battles the Destroyer 5.00
1-Variant-c 1 2 3 5 6 8
1-Rough Cut-($2.99) Features original script and pencil pages 3.00
1-Sketch cover 20.00
2-($1.99) Two covers; Avengers app. 3.00
3-11,13-23: 3-Assumes Jake Olson ID. 4-Namor-c/app. 8-Spider-Man-c/app. 14-Iron Man c/app. 17-Juggernaut-c 2.50
12-($2.99) Wraparound-c; Hercules appears 3.00
12-($10.00) Variant-c by Jusko 10.00
24,26-31,33,34: 24-Begin $2.25-c. 26-Mignola-c/Larsen-a. 29-Andy Kubert-a. 30-Maximum Security x-over; Beta Ray Bill-c/app. 33-Intro. Thor Girl 2.25
25-($2.99) Regular edition 3.00
25-($3.99) Gold foil enhanced cover 4.00
32-($3.50, 100 pgs.) new story plus reprints w/Kirby-a; Simonson-a 3.50
35-($2.99) Thor battles The Gladiator; Andy Kubert-a 3.00
36-49,51-61: 37-Starlin-a. 38,39-BWS-c. 38-42-Immonen-a. 40-Odin killed. 41-Orbik-c. 44-'Nuff Said silent issue. 51-Spider-Man app. 57-Art by various. 58-Davis-a; x-over with Iron Man #64. 60-Brereton-c 2.25
50-($4.95) Raney-c/a; back-ups w/Nuckols-a & Armenta-s/Bennett-a 5.00
62-84: 62-Begin $2.99-c. 64-Loki-c/app. 80-Oeming-s begins; Avengers app. 3.00
85-Last issue; Thor dies; Oeming-s/DiVito-a/Epting-c 3.00
...1999 Annual ($3.50) Jurgens-s/a(p) 3.50
...2000 Annual ($3.50) Jurgens-s/Ordway-a(p); back-up stories 3.50
...2001 Annual ($3.50) Jurgens-s/Grummett-a(p); Lightle-c 3.50
...Across All Worlds (9/01, $19.95, TPB) r/#28-35 20.00
Avengers Disassembled: Thor TPB (2004, $16.99) r/#80-85; afterword by Oeming 17.00
...Resurrection ($5.99, TPB) r/#1,2 6.00
...: The Dark Gods (7/00, $15.95, TPB) r/#9-13 16.00
...Vol. 1: The Death of Odin (7/02, $12.99, TPB) r/#39-44 13.00
...Vol. 2: Lord of Asgard (9/02, $15.99, TPB) r/#45-50 16.00
...Vol. 3: Gods on Earth (2003, $21.99, TPB) r/#51-58, Avengers #63, Iron Man #64, Marvel Double-Shot #1; Beck-c 22.00
...Vol. 4: Spiral (2003, $19.99, TPB) r/#59-67; Brereton-c 20.00
...Vol. 5: The Reigning (2004, $17.99, TPB) r/#68-74 18.00
...Vol. 6: Gods and Men (2004, $13.99, TPB) r/#75-79 14.00

THOR CORPS
Marvel Comics: Sept, 1993 - No. 4, Jan, 1994 ($1.75, limited series)

1-4: 1-Invaders cameo. 2-Invaders app. 3-Spider-Man 2099, Rawhide Kid, Two-Gun Kid & Kid Colt app. 4-Painted-c 2.25

THOR: GODSTORM
Marvel Comics: Nov, 2001 - No. 3, Jan, 2002 ($3.50, limited series)

1-3-Steve Rude-c/a; Busiek-s; Avengers app. 3.50

THORION OF THE NEW ASGODS
Marvel Comics (Amalgam): June, 1997 ($1.95, one-shot)

1-Keith Giffen-s/John Romita Jr.-c/a 2.25

THOR: SON OF ASGARD
Marvel Comics: May, 2004 - Present ($2.99, limited series)

1-10: Teenaged Thor, Sif, and Balder; Tocchini-a. 1-6-Granov-c. 7-10-Jo Chen-c 3.00
... Vol. 1: The Warriors Teen (2004, $7.99, digest-size) r/#1-6 8.00

THOR: THE LEGEND
Marvel Comics: Sept, 1996 ($3.95, one-shot)

nn-Tribute issue 4.00

THOR: VIKINGS
Marvel Comics (MAX): Sept, 2003 - No. 5, Jan, 2004 ($3.50, limited series)

1-5-Garth Ennis-s/Glenn Fabry-a/c 3.50
TPB (2004, $13.99) r/series 14.00

THOSE MAGNIFICENT MEN IN THEIR FLYING MACHINES (See Movie Comics)

THRAX
Event Comics: Nov, 1996 ($2.95, one-shot)

1 3.00

THREE CABALLEROS (Walt Disney's...)
Dell Publishing Co.: No. 71, 1945

Four Color 71-by Walt Kelly, c/a 70 140 210 550 875 1200

THREE CHIPMUNKS, THE (TV) (Also see Alvin)
Dell Publishing Co.: No. 1042, Oct-Dec, 1959

GD VG FN VF VF/NM NM-
2.0 4.0 6.0 8.0 9.0 9.2

Four Color 1042 (#1)-(Alvin, Simon & Theodore) 7 14 21 51 70 90

THREE COMICS (Also see Spiritman)
The Penny King Co.: 1944 (10¢, 52 pgs.) (2 different covers exist)

1,3,4-Lady Luck, Mr. Mystic, The Spirit app. (3 Spirit sections bound together); Lou Fine-a 26 52 78 150 215 280

NOTE: *No. 1 contains Spirit Sections 4/9/44 - 4/23/44, and No. 4 is also from 4/44.*

3-D (NOTE: The prices of all the 3-D comics listed include glasses. Deduct 40-50 percent if glasses are missing, and reduce slightly if glasses are loose.)

3-D ACTION
Atlas Comics (ACI): Jan, 1954 (Oversized, 15¢)(2 pairs of glasses included)

1-Battle Brady; Sol Brodsky-c 39 78 117 222 324 425

3-D ADVENTURE COMICS
Stats, Etc.: Aug, 1986 (one shot)

1-Promo material 4.00

3-D ALIEN TERROR
Eclipse Comics: June, 1986 ($2.50)

1-Old Witch, Crypt-Keeper, Vault Keeper cameo; Morrow, John Pound-a, Yeates-c 6.00
...in 2-D: 100 copies signed, numbered(B&W) 1 3 4 8 10 12

3-D ANIMAL FUN (See Animal Fun)

THREE DAYS IN EUROPE
Oni Press: Nov, 2002 - No. 5, Apr, 2003 ($2.95, B&W, limited series)

1-5-Johnston-s/Hawthorne-a 3.00
TPB (11/03, $14.95, digest-sized) r/#1-5 15.00

3-D BATMAN (Also see Batman 3-D)
National Periodical Publications: 1953 (Reprinted in 1966)

1953-(25¢)-Reprints Batman #42 & 48 (Penguin-c/story); Tommy Tomorrow story; came with pair of 3-D Bat glasses 113 226 339 706 1091 1475
1966-Reprints 1953 issue; new cover by Infantino/Anderson; has inside-c photos of Batman & Robin from TV show (50¢) 40 80 120 230 335 440

3-D CIRCUS
Fiction House Magazines (Real Adventures Publ.): 1953 (25¢, w/glasses)

1 39 78 117 222 324 425

3-D COMICS (See Mighty Mouse, Tor and Western Fighters)

3-D DOLLY
Harvey Publications: December, 1953 (25¢, came with 2 pairs of glasses)

1-Richie Rich story redrawn from his 1st app. in Little Dot #1; shows cover in 3-D on inside 65 130 195 406 628 850

3-D-ELL
Dell Publishing Co.: No. 1, 1953; No. 3, 1953 (3-D comics) (25¢, came w/glasses)

1-Rootie Kazootie (#2 does not exist) 39 78 117 224 327 430
3-Flukey Luke 37 74 112 213 312 410

3-D EXOTIC BEAUTIES
The 3-D Zone: Nov, 1990 ($2.95, 28 pgs.)

1-L.B. Cole-c 1 2 3 5 6 8

3-D FEATURES PRESENTS JET PUP
Dimensions Publications: Oct-Dec (Winter on-c), 1953 (25¢, came w/glasses)

1-Irving Spector-a(2) 39 78 117 222 324 425

3-D FUNNY MOVIES
Comic Media: 1953 (25¢, came w/glasses)

1-Bugsey Bear & Paddy Pelican 39 78 117 222 324 425

THREE-DIMENSION ADVENTURES (Superman)
National Periodical Publications: 1953 (25¢, large size, came w/glasses)

nn-Origin Superman (new art) 113 226 339 706 1091 1475

THREE DIMENSIONAL ALIEN WORLDS (See Alien Worlds)
Pacific Comics: July, 1984 (1st Ray Zone 3-D book)(one-shot)

1-Bolton-a(p); Stevens-a(i); Art Adams 1st published-a(p) 6.00

THREE DIMENSIONAL DNAGENTS (See New DNAgents)

THREE DIMENSIONAL E. C. CLASSICS (Three Dimensional Tales From the Crypt No. 2)
E. C. Comics: Spring, 1954 (Prices include glasses; came with 2 pair)

1-Stories by Wood (Mad #3), Krigstein (W.S. #7), Evans (F.C. #13), & Ingels (CSS #5); Kurtzman-c (rare in high grade due to unstable paper) 90 180 270 563 869 1175

NOTE: *Stories redrawn to 3-D format. Original stories not necessarily by artists listed. CSS: Crime SuspenStories; F.C.: Frontline Combat; W.S.: Weird Science.*

The Three Mouseketeers #9 © DC

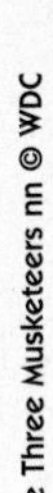
The Three Musketeers nn © WDC

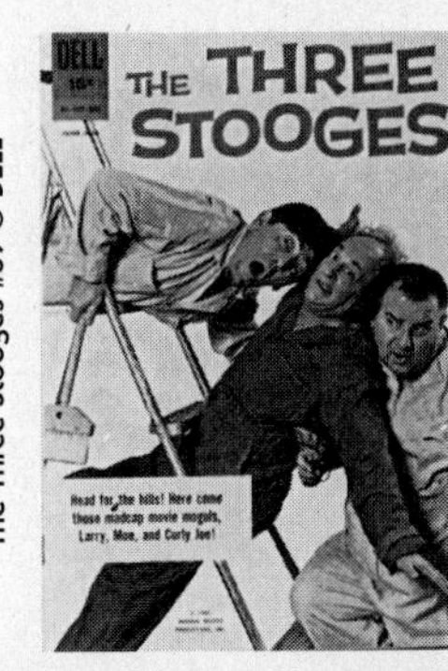

The Three Stooges #39 © DELL

	GD 2.0	VG 4.0	FN 6.0	VF 8.0	VF/NM 9.0	NM- 9.2

THREE DIMENSIONAL TALES FROM THE CRYPT (Formerly Three Dimensional E. C. Classics)(Cover title: ...From the Crypt of Terror)
E. C. Comics: No. 2, Spring, 1954 (Prices include glasses; came with 2 pair)

2-Davis (TFTC #25), Elder (VOH #14), Craig (TFTC #24), & Orlando (TFTC #22) stories; Feldstein-c (rare in high grade) 89 178 267 556 853 1150

NOTE: *Stories redrawn to 3-D format. Original stories not necessarily by artists listed. TFTC: Tales From the Crypt; VOH: Vault of Horror.*

3-D LOVE
Steriographic Publ. (Mikeross Publ.): Dec, 1953 (25¢, came w/glasses)

1 39 78 117 222 324 425

3-D NOODNICK (See Noodnick)

3-D ROMANCE
Steriographic Publ. (Mikeross Publ.): Jan, 1954 (25¢, came w/glasses)

1 39 78 117 222 324 425

3-D SHEENA, JUNGLE QUEEN (Also see Sheena 3-D)
Fiction House Magazines: 1953 (25¢, came w/glasses)

1-Maurice Whitman-c 72 144 216 450 695 940

3-D SUBSTANCE
The 3-D Zone: July, 1990 ($2.95, 28 pgs.)

1-Ditko-c/a(r) 4.00

3-D TALES OF THE WEST
Atlas Comics (CPS): Jan, 1954 (Oversized) (15¢, came with 2 pair of glasses)

1 (3-D)-Sol Brodsky-c 39 78 117 222 324 425

3-D THREE STOOGES (Also see Three Stooges)
Eclipse Comics: Sept, 1986 - No. 2, Nov, 1986; No. 3, Oct, 1987; No. 4, 1989 ($2.50)

1-4: 3-Maurer-r. 4-r-/"Three Missing Links" 5.00
1-3 (2-D) 5.00

3-D WHACK (See Whack)

3-D ZONE, THE
The 3-D Zone (Renegade Press)/Ray Zone: Feb, 1987 - No. 20, 1989 ($2.50)

1,3,4,7-9,11,12,14,15,17,19,20: 1-r/A Star Presentation. 3-Picture Scope Jungle Advs. 4-Electric Fear. 7-Hollywood 3-D Jayne Mansfield photo-c. 8-High Seas 3-D, 9-Redmask-r. 11-Danse Macabre; Matt Fox c/a(r). 12-3-D Presidents. 14-Tyranostar. 15-3-Dementia Comics; Kurtzman-c, Kubert, Maurer-a. 17-Thrilling Love. 19-Cracked Classics. 20-Commander Battle and His Atomic Submarine 6.00
2,5,6,10,13,16,18: 2-Wolverton-r. 5-Krazy Kat-r. 6-Ratfink. 10-Jet 3-D; Powell & Williamson-r. 13-Flash Gordon. 16-Space Vixens; Dave Stevens-c/a. 18-Spacehawk; Wolverton-r 6.00

NOTE: *Davis r-19. Ditko r-19. Elder r-19. Everett r-19. Feldstein r-17. Frazetta r-17. Heath r-19. Kamen r-17. Severin r-19. Ward r-17,19. Wolverton r-2,18,19. Wood r-1,17. Photo c-12*

3 GEEKS, THE (Also see Geeksville)
3 Finger Prints: 1996 - No. 11, Jun, 1999 (B&W)

1,2 -Rich Koslowski-s/a in all 1 2 3 5 6 8
1-(2nd printing) 2.50
3-7, 9-11 2.50
8-(48 pgs.) 4.00
10-Variant-c 3.50
...48 Page Super-Sized Summer Spectacular (7/04, $4.95) 5.00
...Full Circle (7/03, $4.95) Origin story of the 3 Geeks; "Buck Rodinski" app. 5.00
How to Pick Up Girls If You're a Comic Book Geek (color)(7/97) 4.00
When the Hammer Fallls TPB (2001, $14.95) r/#8-11 15.00

300
Dark Horse Comics: May, 1998 - No. 5, Sept, 1998 ($2.95/$3.95, limited series)

1,5: 1-Frank Miller-s/c/a; Spartans vs. Persians war. 5-($3.95-c) 4.00
1-Second printing, 2-4 3.00

3 LITTLE KITTENS
BroadSword Comics: Aug, 2002 - No. 3, Dec, 2002 ($2.95, limited series)

1-3-Jim Balent-s/a; two covers 3.00

3 LITTLE PIGS (Disney)(...and the Wonderful Magic Lamp)
Dell Publishing Co.: No. 218, Mar, 1949

Four Color 218 (#1) 12 24 36 87 134 180

3 LITTLE PIGS, THE (See Walt Disney Showcase #15 & 21)
Gold Key: May, 1964; No. 2, Sept, 1968 (Walt Disney)

1-Reprints Four Color #218 4 8 12 24 32 40
2 3 6 9 16 21 26

THREE MOUSEKETEERS, THE (1st Series)(See Funny Stuff #1)
National Per. Publ.: 3-4/56 - No. 24, 9-10/59; No. 25, 8-9/60 - No. 26, 10-12/60

1 18 36 54 126 193 260
2 10 20 30 70 100 130
3-10: 6,8-Grey tone-c 8 16 24 55 78 100
11-26: 24-Cover says 11/59, inside says 9-10/59 7 14 21 50 68 85

NOTE: *Rube Grossman a-1-26. Sheldon Mayer a-1-8; c-1-7.*

THREE MOUSEKETEERS, THE (2nd Series) (See Super DC Giant)
National Periodical Publications: May-June, 1970 - No. 7, May-June, 1971 (#5-7: 68 pgs.)

1-Mayer-r in all 6 12 18 43 59 75
2-4: 4-Doodles Duck begins (1st app.) 4 8 12 27 36 45
5-7:(68 pgs.). 5-Dodo & the Frog, Bo Bunny begin 6 12 18 40 55 70

THREE MUSKETEERS, THE (Also see Disney's The Three Musketeers)
Gemstone Publishing: 2004 ($3.95, squarebound, one-shot)

nn-Adaptation of the 2004 DVD movie; Petrossi-c/a 4.00

THREE NURSES (Confidential Diary #12-17; Career Girl Romances #24 on)
Charlton Comics: V3#18, May, 1963 - V3#23, Mar, 1964

V3#18-23 3 6 9 18 23 28

THREE RASCALS
I. W. Enterprises: 1958; 1963

I.W. Reprint #1,2,10: 1-(Says Super Comics on inside)-(M.E.'s Clubhouse Rascals) DeCarlo-a. #2-(1958). 10-(1963)-r/#1 2 4 6 8 10 12

THREE RING COMICS
Spotlight Publishers: March, 1945

1-Funny animal 17 34 51 95 135 175

THREE RING COMICS (Also see Captain Wizard & Meteor Comics)
Century Publications: April, 1946

1-Prankster-c; Captain Wizard, Impossible Man, Race Wilkins, King O'Leary, & Dr. Mercy app. 35 70 105 201 293 385

THREE ROCKETEERS (See Blast-Off)

THREE STOOGES (See Comic Album #18, Top Comics, The Little Stooges, March of Comics #232, 248, 268, 280, 292, 304, 316, 336, 373, Movie Classics & Comics & 3-D Three Stooges)

THREE STOOGES
Jubilee No. 1/St. John No. 1 (9/53) on: Feb, 1949 - No. 2, May, 1949; Sept, 1953 - No. 7, Oct, 1954

1-(Scarce, 1949)-Kubert-a; infinity-c 113 226 339 706 1091 1475
2-(Scarce)-Kubert, Maurer-a 79 158 237 494 760 1025
1(9/53)-Hollywood Stunt Girl by Kubert (7 pgs.) 69 138 207 431 666 900
2(3-D, 10/53, 25¢)-Came w/glasses; Stunt Girl story by Kubert 50 100 150 305 465 625
3(3-D, 10/53, 25¢)-Came w/glasses; has 3-D-c 47 94 141 287 436 585
4(3/54)-7(10/54): 4-1st app. Li'l Stooge? 40 80 120 233 342 450

NOTE: *All issues have **Kubert-Maurer** art & **Maurer** covers. 6, 7-Partial photo-c.*

THREE STOOGES
Dell Publishing Co./Gold Key No. 10 (10/62) on: No. 1043, Oct-Dec, 1959 - No. 55, June, 1972

Four Color 1043 (#1) 27 54 81 194 297 400
Four Color 1078,1127,1170,1187 14 28 42 97 149 200
6(9-11/61) - 10: 6-Professor Putter begins; ends #16 11 22 33 80 120 160
11-14,16,18-20 10 20 30 70 100 130
15-Go Around the World in a Daze (movie scenes) 10 20 30 73 107 140
17-The Little Monsters begin (5/64)(1st app.?) 10 20 30 73 107 140
21,23-30 9 18 27 60 85 110
22-Movie scenes from "The Outlaws Is Coming" 9 18 27 65 93 120
31-55 7 14 21 50 68 85

NOTE: *All Four Colors, 6-50, 52-55 have photo-c.*

THREE STOOGES IN 3-D, THE
Eternity Comics: 1991 ($3.95, high quality paper, w/glasses)

1-Reprints Three Stooges by Gold Key; photo-c 5.00

THREE STRIKES
Oni Press: Apr, 2003 - No. 5, Oct, 2003 ($2.99, B&W, limited series)

1-5-Brian Hurtt-a/DeFilippis & Weir-s 3.00
TPB (3/04, $14.95, digest-size) r/#1-5; Ed Brubaker intro. 15.00

3 WORLDS OF GULLIVER
Dell Publishing Co.: No. 1158, July, 1961 (2 issues exist with diff. covers)

Four Color 1158-Movie, photo-c 8 16 24 55 78 100

THRILL COMICS (See Flash Comics, Fawcett)

Thrilling Comics #15 © STD

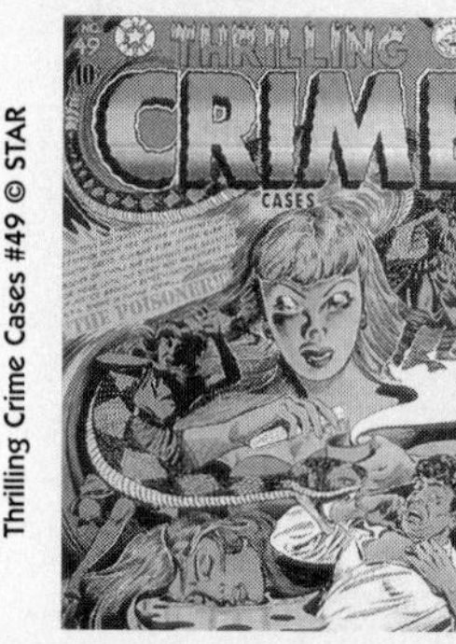

Thrilling Crime Cases #49 © STAR

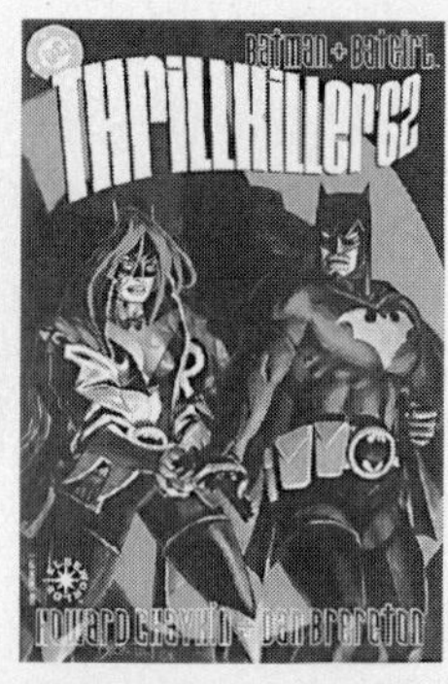

Thrillkiller '62 © DC

GD VG FN VF VF/NM NM-
2.0 4.0 6.0 8.0 9.0 9.2

THRILLER
DC Comics: Nov, 1983 - No. 12, Nov, 1984 ($1.25, Baxter paper)
1-12: 1-Intro Seven Seconds; Von Eeden-c/a begins. 2-Origin. 5,6-Elvis satire 2.25

THRILLING ADVENTURES IN STAMPS COMICS (Formerly Stamp Comics)
Stamp Comics, Inc. (Very Rare): V1#8, Jan, 1953 (25¢, 100 pgs.)
V1#8-Harrison, Wildey, Kiefer, Napoli-a 74 148 222 463 712 960

THRILLING ADVENTURE STORIES (See Tigerman)
Atlas/Seaboard Publ.: Feb, 1975 - No. 2, Aug, 1975 (B&W, 68 pgs.)
1-Tigerman, Kromag the Killer begin; Heath, Thorne-a; Doc Savage movie photos of Ron Ely 2 4 6 14 18 22
2-Heath, Toth, Severin, Simonson-a; Adams-c 3 6 9 19 25 32

THRILLING COMICS
Better Publ./Nedor/Standard Comics: Feb, 1940 - No. 80, April, 1951
1-Origin & 1st app. Dr. Strange (37 pgs.), ends #?; Nickie Norton of the Secret Service begins 300 600 900 1892 2946 4000
2-The Rio Kid, The Woman in Red, Pinocchio begins 131 262 393 819 1260 1700
3-The Ghost & Lone Eagle begin 83 166 249 519 797 1075
4-6,8-10: 5-Dr. Strange changed to Doc Strange 63 126 189 394 610 825
7-Classic-c 81 162 243 506 778 1050
11-18,20 55 110 165 34 520 700
19-Origin & 1st app. The American Crusader (8/41), ends #39,41 62 124 186 388 594 800
21-30: 24-Intro. Mike, Doc Strange's sidekick (1/42). 27-Robot-c. 29-Last Rio Kid 49 98 147 299 455 610
31-40: 36-Commando Cubs begin (7/43, 1st app.) 43 86 129 262 399 535
41-Classic Hitler & Mussolini-c 96 192 288 600 925 1250
42,43,45-51: 45-Hitler pict. on-c 39 78 117 222 324 425
44-Hitler-c 85 170 255 531 816 1100
52-Classic Schomburg hooded bondage-c; the Ghost ends 58 116 174 363 557 750
53-The Phantom Detective begins; The Cavalier app.; no Commando Cubs 39 78 117 222 324 425
54-The Cavalier app.; no Commando Cubs 39 78 117 222 324 425
55-Lone Eagle ends 35 70 105 198 287 375
56-Princess Pantha begins (10/46, 1st app.) 48 96 144 293 447 600
57-66: 61-Ingels-a; The Lone Eagle app. 65-Last Phantom Detective & Commando Cubs. 66-Frazetta text illo 40 80 120 233 342 450
67,70-73: Frazetta-a(5-7 pgs.) in each. 72-Sea Eagle app.; Buck Ranger, Cowboy Detective begins 46 92 138 281 428 575
68,69-Frazetta-a(2), 8 & 6 pgs.; 9 & 7 pgs. 50 100 150 305 465 625
74-Last Princess Pantha; Tara app. 32 64 96 184 267 350
75-78: 75-All western format begins 15 30 45 85 120 155
79-Krigstein-a 16 32 48 89 127 165
80-Severin & Elder, Celardo, Moreira-a 16 32 48 89 127 165

NOTE: *Bondage c-5, 9, 13, 20, 22, 27-30, 38, 41, 52, 54, 70.* **Kinstler** *a-45.* **Leo Morey** *a-7.* **Schomburg** *(sometimes signed as* **Xela***) c-7, 9-19, 36-80 (airbrush 62-71).* **Tuska** *a-62, 63. Woman in Red not in #19, 23, 31-33, 39-45. No. 45 exists as a Canadian reprint but numbered #48. No. 72 exists as a Canadian reprint with no* **Frazetta** *story.American Crusader c-20-24. Buck Ranger c-72-80. Commando Cubs c-37, 39, 41, 43, 45, 47, 49, 51. Doc Strange c-1-19, 25-36, 38, 40, 42, 44, 46, 48, 50, 52-57, 59. Princess Pantha c-58, 60-71.*

THRILLING COMICS (Also see All Star Comics 1999 crossover titles)
DC Comics: May, 1999 ($1.99, one-shot)
1-Golden Age Hawkman and Wildcat; Russ Heath-a 2.25

THRILLING CRIME CASES (Formerly 4Most; becomes Shocking Mystery Cases #50 on)
Star Publications: No. 41, June-July, 1950 - No. 49, July, 1952
41 29 58 87 164 237 310
42-45: 42-L. B. Cole-c/a (1); Chameleon story (Fox-r) 26 52 78 147 211 275
46-48: 47-Used in **POP**, pg. 84 25 50 75 141 203 265
49-(7/52)-Classic L. B. Cole-c 44 88 132 268 409 550

NOTE: **L. B. Cole** *c-all; a-43p, 45p, 46p, 49(2 pgs.).* **Disbrow** *a-48.* **Hollingsworth** *a-48.*

THRILLING ROMANCES
Standard Comics: No. 5, Dec, 1949 - No. 26, June, 1954
5 13 26 39 74 102 130
6,8 9 18 27 51 62 75
7-Severin/Elder-a (7 pgs.) 10 20 30 60 80 100
9,10-Severin/Elder-a; photo-c 9 18 27 54 70 85
11,14-21,26: 12-Tyrone Power/ Susan Hayward photo-c.14-Gene Tierney & Danny Kaye photo-c from movie "On the Riviera". 15-Tony Martin/Janet Leigh photo-c 8 16 24 43 54 65
12-Wood-a (2 pgs.) 11 22 33 62 84 105
13-Severin-a 9 18 27 51 62 75
22-25-Toth-a 10 20 30 56 73 90

NOTE: *All photo-c.* **Celardo** *a-9, 16.* **Colletta** *a-23, 24(2).* **Toth** *text illos-19.* **Tuska** *a-9.*

THRILLING SCIENCE TALES
AC Comics: 1989 - No. 2 ($3.50, 2/3 color, 52 pgs.)
1,2: 1-r/Bob Colt #6(saucer); Frazetta, Guardineer (Space Ace), Wood, Krenkel, Orlando, WIlliamson-r; Kaluta-c. 2-Capt. Video-r by Evans, Capt. Science-r by Wood, Star Pirate-r by Whitman & Mysta of the Moon-r by Moreira 4.00

THRILLING TRUE STORY OF THE BASEBALL...
Fawcett Publications: 1952 (Photo-c, each)
...Giants-photo-c; has Willie Mays rookie photo-biography; Willie Mays, Eddie Stanky & others photos on-c 69 138 207 431 666 900
...Yankees-photo-c; Yogi Berra, Joe DiMaggio, Mickey Mantle & others photos on-c 67 134 201 419 647 875

THRILLING WONDER TALES
AC Comics : 1991 ($2.95, B&W)
1-Includes a Bob Powell Thun'da story 3.00

THRILLKILLER
DC Comics : Jan, 1997 - No. 3, Mar, 1997($2.50, limited series)
1-3-Elseworlds Robin & Batgirl; Chaykin-s/Brereton-c/a 3.00
...'62 ('98, $4.95, one-shot) Sequel; Chaykin-s/Brereton-c/a 5.00
TPB-(See Batman: Thrillkiller)

THRILLOGY
Pacific Comics: Jan, 1984 (One-shot, color)
1-Conrad-c/a 3.00

THRILL-O-RAMA
Harvey Publications (Fun Films): Oct, 1965 - No. 3, Dec, 1966
1-Fate (Man in Black) by Powell app.; Doug Wildey-a(2); Simon-c 6 12 18 40 55 70
2-Pirana begins (see Phantom #46); Williamson 2 pgs.; Fate (Man in Black) app.; Tuska/Simon-c 4 8 12 25 33 42
3-Fate (Man in Black) app.; Sparling-c 3 7 10 21 28 35

THRILLS OF TOMORROW (Formerly Tomb of Terror)
Harvey Publications: No. 17, Oct, 1954 - No. 20, April, 1955
17-Powell-a (horror); r/Witches Tales #7 15 30 45 83 117 150
18-Powell-a (horror); r/Tomb of Terror #1 13 26 39 74 102 130
19,20-Stuntman-c/stories by S&K (r/from Stuntman #1 & 2); 19 has origin & is last pre-code (2/55) 34 68 102 193 279 365

NOTE: **Kirby** *c-19, 20.* **Palais** *a-17.* **Simon** *c-18?*

THROBBING LOVE (See Fox Giants)

THROUGH GATES OF SPLENDOR
Spire Christian Comics (Flemming H. Revell Co.): 1973, 1974 (36 pages) (39-49 cents)
nn 1 3 4 6 8 11

THUMPER (Disney)
Dell Publishing Co.: No, 19, 1942 - No. 243, Sept, 1949
Four Color 19-Walt Disney's...Meets the Seven Dwarfs; reprinted in Silly Symphonies 49 98 147 392 614 835
Four Color 243-...Follows His Nose 12 24 36 84 127 170

THUN'DA (...King of the Congo)
Magazine Enterprises: 1952 - No. 6, 1953
1(A-1 #47)-Origin; Frazetta c/a; only comic done entirely by Frazetta; all Thun'da stories, no Cave Girl 146 292 438 913 1407 1900
2(A-1 #56)-Powell-c/a begins, ends #6; Intro/1st app. Cave Girl in filler strip (also app. in 3-6) 24 48 72 138 199 260
3(A-1 #73), 4(A-1 #78) 17 34 51 98 139 180
5(A-1 #83), 6(A-1 #86) 16 32 48 92 131 170

THUN'DA TALES (See Frank Frazetta's...)

THUNDER AGENTS (See Dynamo, Noman & Tales Of Thunder)
Tower Comics: 11/65 - No. 17, 12/67; No. 18, 9/68, No. 19, 11/68, No. 20, 11/69 (No. 1-16: 68 pgs.; No. 17 on: 52 pgs.)(All are 25¢)
1-Origin & 1st app. Dynamo, Noman, Menthor, & The Thunder Squad; 1st app. The Iron Maiden 20 40 60 141 216 290
2-Death of Egghead; A-bomb blast panel 11 22 33 77 114 150
3-5: 4-Guy Gilbert becomes Lightning who joins Thunder Squad; Iron Maiden app. 8 16 24 58 82 105
6-10: 7-Death of Menthor. 8-Origin & 1st app. The Raven 7 14 21 50 68 85

Thunderbolts #65 © MAR

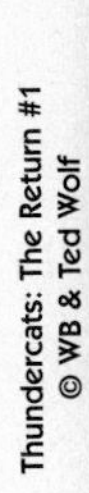
Thundercats: The Return #1 © WB & Ted Wolf

Thunderstrike #8 © MAR

GD VG FN VF VF/NM NM-
2.0 4.0 6.0 8.0 9.0 9.2

11-15: 13-Undersea Agent app.; no Raven story 6 12 18 40 55 70
16-19 6 12 18 40 55 70
20-Special Collectors Edition; all reprints 4 8 12 27 36 45
...Archives Vol. 1 (DC Comics, 2003, $49.95, HC) r/#1-4, restored and recolored 50.00
...Archives Vol. 2 (DC Comics, 2003, $49.95, HC) r/#5-7, Dynamo #1 50.00
...Archives Vol. 3 (DC Comics, 2003, $49.95, HC) r/#8-10, Dynamo #2 50.00
...Archives Vol. 4 (DC Comics, 2004, $49.95, HC) r/#11, Noman #1,2 & Dynamo #3 50.00
NOTE: *Crandall a-1, 4p, 5p, 18, 20r; c-18. Ditko a-6, 7p, 12p, 13?, 14p, 16, 18. Giunta a-6. Kane a-1, 5p, 6p?, 14, 16p; c-14, 15. Reinman a-13. Sekowsky a-6. Tuska a-1p, 7, 8, 10, 13-17, 19. Whitney a-9p, 10, 13, 15, 17, 18; c-17. Wood a-1-11, 15(w/Ditko-12, 18), (inks-#9, 13, 14, 16, 17), 19i, 20r; c-1-8, 9i, 10-13(#10 w/Williamson(p)), 16.*

T.H.U.N.D.E.R. AGENTS (See Blue Ribbon Comics, Hall of Fame Featuring the..., JCP Features & Wally Wood's...)
JC Comics (Archie Publications): May, 1983 - No. 2, Jan, 1984
1,2: 1-New Manna/Blyberg-c/a. 2-Blyberg-c 6.00

THUNDER BIRDS (See Cinema Comics Herald)

THUNDERBOLT (See The Atomic...)

THUNDERBOLT (Peter Cannon...; see Crisis on Infinite Earths & Peter...)
Charlton Comics: Jan, 1966; No. 51, Mar-Apr, 1966 - No. 60, Nov, 1967
1-Origin & 1st app. Thunderbolt 4 8 12 29 40 50
51-(Formerly Son of Vulcan #50) 3 7 10 21 28 35
52-59: 54-Sentinels begin. 59-Last Thunderbolt & Sentinels (back-up story) 2 4 6 14 18 22
60-Prankster app. 3 6 9 16 20 24
57,58 ('77)-Modern Comics-r 4.00
NOTE: *Aparo a-60. Morisi a-1, 51-56, 58; c-1, 51-56, 58, 59.*

THUNDERBOLTS (Also see Incredible Hulk #449)
Marvel Comics: Apr, 1997 - No. 81, Sept, 2003 ($1.95-$2.99)
1-($2.99)-Busiek-s/Bagley-c/a 1 2 3 5 7 9
1-2nd printing; new cover colors 2.50
2-4: 2-Two covers. 4-Intro. Jolt 6.00
5-11: 9-Avengers app. 3.50
12-($2.99)-Avengers and Fantastic Four-c/app. 4.00
13-24: 14-Thunderbolts return to Earth. 21-Hawkeye app. 2.50
25-($2.99) Wraparound-c 3.00
26-38: 26-Manco-a 2.25
39-($2.99) 100 Page Monster; Iron Man reprints 3.00
40-49: 40-Begin $2.25-c; Sandman-c/app. 44-Avengers app. 47-Captain Marvel app. 49-Zircher-a 2.25
50-($2.99) Last Bagley-a; Captain America becomes leader 3.00
51-74,76,77,80,81: 51,52-Zircher-a; Dr. Doom app. 80,81-Spider-Man app. 2.25
75-($3.50) Hawkeye leaves the team; Garcia-a 3.50
78,79-($2.99-c) Velasco-a begins 3.00
Annual '97 ($2.99)-Wraparound-c 3.00
Annual 2000 ($3.50) Breyfogle-a 3.50
...: Distant Rumblings (#-1) (7/97, $1.95) Busiek-s 5.00
First Strikes (1997, $4.99,TPB) r/#1,2 5.00
...: Life Sentences (7/01, $3.50) Adlard-a 3.50
...: Marvel's Most Wanted TPB ('98, $16.99) r/origin stories of original Masters of Evil 17.00
Wizard #0 (bagged with Wizard #89) 2.25

THUNDERBUNNY (See Blue Ribbon Comics #13, Charlton Bullseye & Pep Comics #393)
Red Circle Comics: Jan, 1984 (Direct sale only)
WaRP Graphics: Second series No. 1, 1985 - No. 6, 1985
Apple Comics: No. 7, 1986 - No. 12, 1987
1-Humor/parody; origin Thunderbunny; 2 page pin-up by Anderson 5.00
(2nd series) 1,2-Magazine size 3.00
3-12-Comic size 2.25

THUNDERCATS (TV)
Marvel Comics (Star Comics)/Marvel #22 on: Dec, 1985 - No. 24, June, 1988 (75¢)
1-Mooney-c/a begins 2 4 6 9 11 14
2-20: 2-(65¢ & 75¢ cover exists). 12-Begin $1.00-c. 18-20-Williamson-i 1 2 3 5 7 9
21-24: 23-Williamson-c(i) 1 3 4 6 8 10

THUNDERCATS (TV)
DC Comics (WildStorm): No. 0, Oct, 2002 - No. 5, Feb, 2003 ($2.50/$2.95, limited series)
0-($2.50) J. Scott Campbell-c/a 3.00
1-5-($2.95) 1-McGuinness-a/c; variant cover by Art Adams; rebirth of Mumm-Ra 3.00
.../ Battle of the Planets (7/03, $4.95) Kaare Andrews-s/a; 2 covers by Campbell & Ross 5.00
...: Origins-Heroes & Villains (2/04, $3.50) short stories by various 3.50
...Reclaiming Thundera TPB (2003, $12.95) r/#0-5 13.00
... Sourcebook (1/03, $2.95) pin-ups and info on characters; art by various; A. Adams-c 3.00

THUNDERCATS: DOGS OF WAR
DC Comics (WildStorm): Aug, 2003 - No. 5, Dec, 2003 ($2.95, limited series)
1-5: 1-Two covers by Booth & Pearson; Booth-a/Layman-s. 2-4-Two covers 3.00
TPB (2004, $14.95) r/#1-5 15.00

THUNDERCATS: ENEMY'S PRIDE
DC Comics (WildStorm): Aug, 2004 - No. 5 ($2.95, limited series)
1-5-Vriens-a/Layman-s 3.00

THUNDERCATS: HAMMERHAND'S REVENGE
DC Comics (WildStorm): Dec, 2003 - No. 5, Apr, 2004 ($2.95, limited series)
1-5-Avery-s/D'Anda-a. 2-Variant-c by Warren 3.00
TPB (2004, $14.95) r/#1-5 15.00

THUNDERCATS: THE RETURN
DC Comics (WildStorm): Apr, 2003 - No. 5, Aug, 2003 ($2.95, limited series)
1-5: 1-Two covers by Benes & Cassaday; Gilmore-s 3.00
TPB (2004, $12.95) r/series 13.00

THUNDERGOD
Crusade Entertainment: July, 1996 - No. 3 ($2.95, B&W)
1-3: Christopher Golden scripts; painted-c 3.00

THUNDERGOD
Caliber Comics: 1997 ($2.95, B&W, one-shot)
1 3.00

THUNDER MOUNTAIN (See Zane Grey, Four Color #246)

THUNDERSTRIKE (See Thor #459)
Marvel Comics: June, 1993 - No. 24, July, 1995 ($1.25)
1-($2.95, 52 pgs.)-Holo-grafx lightning patterned foil-c; Bloodaxe returns 3.00
2-24: 2-Juggernaut-c/s. 4-Capt. America app. 4-6-Spider-Man app. 8-bound-in trading card sheet. 18-Bloodaxe app. 24-Death of Thunderstrike 2.25
Marvel Double Feature...Thunderstrike/Code Blue #13 ($2.50)-Same as Thunderstrike #13 w/Code Blue flip book 2.50

TICK, THE (Also see The Chroma-Tick)
New England Comics Press: Jun, 1988 - No. 12, May, 1993 ($1.75/$1.95/$2.25; B&W, over-sized)
Special Edition 1-1st comic book app. serially numbered & limited to 5,000 copies 6 12 18 38 52 65
Special Edition 1-(5/96, $5.95)-Double-c; foil-c; serially numbered (5,001 thru 14,000) & limited to 9,000 copies 6.00
Special Edition 2-Serially numbered and limited to 3000 copies 5 10 15 33 44 55
Special Edition 2-(8/96, $5.95)-Double-c; foil-c; serially numbered (5,001 thru 14,000) & limited to 9,000 copies 1 2 3 5 6 8
1-Regular Edition 1st printing; reprints Special Ed. 1 w/minor changes 4 8 12 27 36 45
1-2nd printing 6.00
1-3rd-5th printing 3.00
2-Reprints Special Ed. 2 w/minor changes 2 4 6 14 18 22
2-8-All reprints 3.00
3-5 ($1.95): 4-1st app. Paul the Samurai 1 3 4 6 8 10
6,8 ($2.25) 5.00
7-1st app. Man-Eating Cow. 6.00
8-Variant with no logo, price, issue number or company logos. 2 4 6 11 14 18
9-12 ($2.75) 4.00
12-Special Edition; card-stock, virgin foil-c; numbered edition 2 4 6 14 18 22
Pseudo-Tick #13 (11/00, $3.50) Continues story from #12 (1993) 4.00
Promo Sampler-(1990)-Tick-c/story 1 2 3 5 6 8

TICK, THE (One shots)
--BIG BACK TO SCHOOL SPECIAL
1-(10/98, $3.50, B&W) Tick and Arthur undercover in high school 3.50
--BIG CRUISE SHIP VACATION SPECIAL
1-(9/00, $3.50, B&W) 3.50
--BIG FATHER'S DAY SPECIAL
1-(6/00, $3.50, B&W) 3.50
--BIG HALLOWEEN SPECIAL
1-(10/99, $3.50, B&W) 3.50
...2000 (10/00, $3.50) 3.50

The Tick and Arthur #1 © Ben Edlund

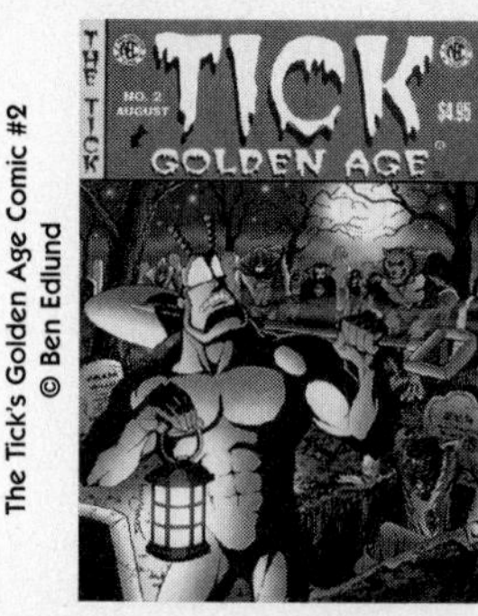

The Tick's Golden Age Comic #2 © Ben Edlund

Tigress #5 © Heroic Publ.

GD 2.0 | VG 4.0 | FN 6.0 | VF 8.0 | VF/NM 9.0 | NM- 9.2

...2001 (9/01, $3.95) 4.00

--BIG MOTHER'S DAY SPECIAL
1-(4/00, $3.50, B&W) 3.50

--BIG RED-N-GREEN CHRISTMAS SPECTACLE
1-(12/01, $3.95) 4.00

--BIG SUMMER ANNUAL
1-(7/99, $3.50, B&W) Chainsaw Vigilante vs. Barry 3.50

--BIG SUMMER FUN SPECIAL
1-(8/98, $3.50, B&W) Tick and Arthur at summer camp 3.50

--BIG TAX TIME TERROR
1-(4/00, $3.50, B&W) 3.50

--BIG YEAR 2000 SPECTACLE
1-(3/00, $3.50, B&W) 3.50

--BIG YULE LOG SPECIAL
2001-(12/00, $3.50, B&W) 3.50

--INCREDIBLE INTERNET COMIC
1-(7/01, $3.95, color) reprints story from New England Comics website 4.00

INTRODUCING THE TICK
1-(4/02, $3.95, color) summary of Tick's life and adventures 4.00

--MASSIVE SUMMER DOUBLE SPECTACLE
1,2-(7,8/00, $3.50, B&W) 3.50

TICK & ARTIE
1-(6/02, $3.50, color) prints strips from Internet comic 3.50
2-(10/02, $3.95) 4.00

TICK'S BACK, THE
0-(8/97, $2.95, B&W) 3.50

TICK'S BIG ROMANTIC ADVENTURE, THE
1-(2/98, $2.95, B&W) Candy box cover with candy map on back 3.50

TICK AND ARTHUR, THE
New England Comics: Feb, 1999 - Present ($3.50, B&W)
1-6-Sean Wang-s/a 3.50

TICK BIG BLUE DESTINY, THE
New England Comics: Oct, 1997 - Present ($2.95)
1-4: 1-"Keen" Ed. 2-Two covers 3.50
1-($4.95) "Wicked Keen" Ed. w/die cut-c 5.00
5-($3.50) 3.50
6-Luny Bin Trilogy Preview #0 (7/98, $1.50) 3.50
7-9: 7-Luny Bin Trilogy begins 3.50

TICK BIG BLUE YULE LOG SPECIAL, THE
New England Comics: Dec, 1997; 1999 ($2.95, B&W)
1-"Jolly" and "Traditional" covers; flip book w/"Arthur Teaches the Tick About Hanukkah" 3.50
...1999 ($3.50) 3.50

TICK, THE : CIRCUS MAXIMUS
New England Comics: Mar, 2000 - No. 4, Jun, 2000 ($3.50, B&W)
1-4-Encyclopedia of characters from Tick comics 3.50
Giant No. 1 (8/03, $14.95) r/#1-4, Redux 15.00
Redux No. 1 (4/01, $3.50) 3.50

TICK, THE - COLOR
New England Comics: Jan, 2001 - Present ($3.95)
1-6: 1-Marc Sandroni-a 4.00

TICK, THE - HEROES OF THE CITY
New England Comics: Feb, 1999 - Present ($3.50, B&W)
1-6-Short stories by various 3.50

TICK KARMA TORNADO (The...)
New England Comics Press: Oct, 1993 - No. 9, Mar, 1995 ($2.75, B&W)
1-($3.25) 4.00
2-9: 2-$2.75-c begins 3.50

TICK'S BIG XMAS TRILOGY, THE
New England Comics: Dec, 2002 - No. 3, Dec, 2002 ($3.95, limited series)
1-3 4.00

TICK'S GOLDEN AGE COMIC, THE
New England Comics: May, 2002 - No. 3, Feb, 2003 ($4.95, Golden Age size)
1-3-Facsimile 1940s-style Tick issue; 2 covers 5.00
Giant Edition TPB (9/03, $12.95) r/#1-3 13.00

GD 2.0 | VG 4.0 | FN 6.0 | VF 8.0 | VF/NM 9.0 | NM- 9.2

TICK'S GIANT CIRCUS OF THE MIGHTY, THE
New England Comics: Summer, 1992 - No. 3, Fall, 1993 ($2.75, B&W, magazine size)
1-(A-O). 2-(P-Z). 3-1993 Update 4.00

TICKLE COMICS (Also see Gay, Smile, & Whee Comics)
Modern Store Publ.: 1955 (7¢, 5x7-1/4", 52 pgs)
1 6 12 18 28 34 40

TICK TOCK TALES
Magazine Enterprises: Jan, 1946 - V3#33, Jan-Feb, 1951
1-Koko & Kola begin 15 30 45 83 117 150
2 9 18 27 51 62 75
3-10 8 16 24 43 54 65
11-33: 19-Flag-c. 23-Muggsy Mouse, The Pixies & Tom-Tom the Jungle Boy app. 24-X-mas-c. 25-The Pixies & Tom-Tom app. 7 14 21 37 46 55

TIGER (Also see Comics Reading Libraries in the Promotional Comics section)
Charlton Press (King Features): Mar, 1970 - No. 6, Jan, 1971 (15¢)
1 3 6 9 16 20 24
2-6 2 4 6 9 11 14

TIGER BOY (See Unearthly Spectaculars)

TIGER GIRL
Gold Key: Sept, 1968 (15¢)
1(10227-809)-Sparling-c/a; Jerry Siegel scripts. Some issues have a pin-up on back cover instead of advertising 4 8 12 29 40 50

TIGERMAN (Also see Thrilling Adventure Stories)
Seaboard Periodicals (Atlas): Apr, 1975 - No. 3, Sept, 1975 (All 25¢ issues)
1-3: 1-Origin; Colan-c. 2,3-Ditko-p in each 1 3 4 6 8 11

TIGER WALKS, A (See Movie Comics)

TIGRA (The Avengers)
Marvel Comics: May, 2002 - No. 4, Aug, 2002 ($2.99, limited series)
1-4-Christina Z-s/Deodato-c/a 3.00

TIGRESS, THE
Hero Graphics: Aug, 1992 - No. 6?, June, 1993 ($3.95/$2.95/$3.95, B&W)
1,6: 1-Tigress vs. Flare. 6-44 pgs. 4.00
2-5: 2-$2.95-c begins 3.00

TILLIE THE TOILER (See Comic Monthly)
Dell Publishing Co.: No. 15, 1941 - No. 237, July, 1949
Four Color 15(1941) 34 68 102 255 398 540
Large Feature Comic 30(1941) 33 66 99 190 275 360
Four Color 8(1942) 33 66 99 190 275 360
Four Color 22(1943) 18 36 54 131 201 270
Four Color 55(1944), 89(1945) 14 28 42 102 156 210
Four Color 106('45),132('46): 132-New stories begin 11 22 33 77 114 150
Four Color 150,176,184 10 20 30 72 104 135
Four Color 195,213,237 8 16 24 55 78 100

TIMBER WOLF (See Action Comics #372, & Legion of Super-Heroes)
DC Comics: Nov, 1992 - No. 5, Mar, 1993 ($1.25, limited series)
1-5 2.50

TIME BANDITS
Marvel Comics Group: Feb, 1982 (one-shot, Giant)
1-Movie adaptation 4.00

TIME BEAVERS (See First Comics Graphic Novel #2)

TIME BREAKERS
DC Comics (Helix): Jan, 1997 - No. 5, May, 1997 ($2.25, limited series)
1-5-Pollack-s 2.50

TIMECOP (Movie)
Dark Horse Comics: Sept, 1994 - No. 2, Nov, 1994 ($2.50, limited series)
1,2-Adaptation of film 2.50

TIME FOR LOVE (Formerly Romantic Secrets)
Charlton Comics: V2#53, Oct, 1966; Oct, 1967 - No. 47, May, 1976
V2#53(10/66) Herman-s Hermits app. 3 7 10 21 28 35
1(10/67) 4 8 12 24 32 40
2(12/67)-10 3 6 9 16 20 24
11-20 2 4 6 11 14 18
21-29 2 4 6 9 11 14
30-(10/72)-Full-length portrait of David Cassidy 3 6 9 18 24 30

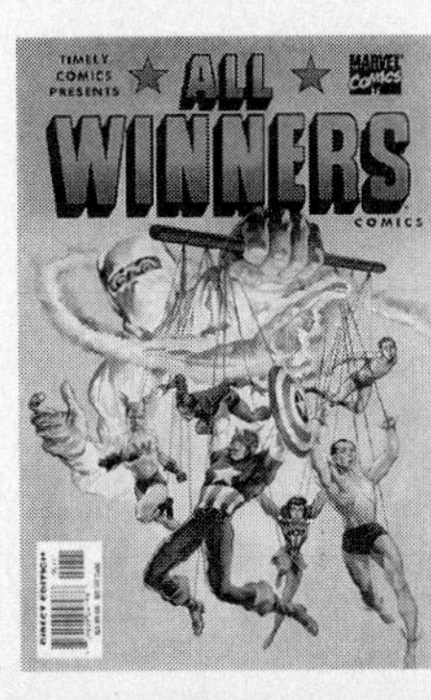

Timely Presents: All Winners #1 © MAR

Timewalker #14 © VAL

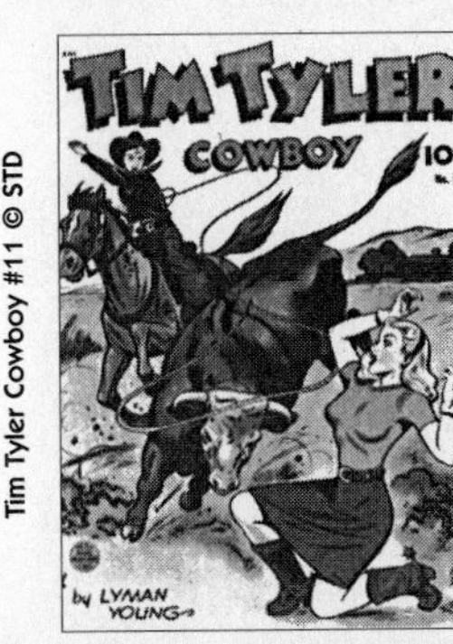

Tim Tyler Cowboy #11 © STD

GD 2.0 | VG 4.0 | FN 6.0 | VF 8.0 | VF/NM 9.0 | NM- 9.2

31-47 2 4 6 8 10 12

TIMELESS TOPIX (See Topix)

TIMELY PRESENTS: ALL WINNERS
Marvel Comics: Dec, 1999 ($3.99)
1-Reprints All Winners Comics #19 (Fall 1946); new Lago-c 4.00

TIMELY PRESENTS: HUMAN TORCH
Marvel Comics: Feb, 1999 ($3.99)
1-Reprints Human Torch Comics #5 (Fall 1941); new Lago-c 4.00

TIME MACHINE, THE
Dell Publishing Co.: No. 1085, Mar, 1960 (H.G. Wells)
Four Color 1085-Movie, Alex Toth-a; Rod Taylor photo-c
16 32 48 112 171 230

TIME MASTERS
DC Comics: Feb, 1990 - No. 8, Sept, 1990 ($1.75, mini-series)
1-8: New Rip Hunter series. 5-Cave Carson, Viking Prince app. 6-Dr. Fate app. 2.25

TIMESLIP COLLECTION
Marvel Comics: Nov, 1998 ($2.99, one-shot)
1-Pin-ups reprinted from Marvel Vision magazine 3.00

TIMESLIP SPECIAL (The Coming of the Avengers)
Marvel Comics: Oct, 1998 ($5.99, one-shot)
1-Alternate world Avengers vs. Odin 6.00

TIMESPIRITS
Marvel Comics (Epic Comics): Oct, 1984 - No. 8, Mar, 1986 ($1.50, Baxter paper, direct sales)
1-8: 4-Williamson-a 2.25

TIME TUNNEL, THE (TV)
Gold Key: Feb, 1967 - No. 2, July, 1967 (12¢)
1-Photo back-c on both issues 8 16 24 55 78 100
2 6 12 18 43 59 75

TIME TWISTERS
Quality Comics: Sept, 1987 - No. 21, 1989 ($1.25/$1.50)
1-21: Alan Moore scripts in 1-4, 6-9, 14 (2 pg.). 14-Bolland-a (2 pg.). 15,16-Guice-c 2.25

TIME 2: THE EPIPHANY (See First Comics Graphic Novel #9)

TIMEWALKER (Also see Archer & Armstrong)
Valiant: Jan, 1994 - No. 15, Oct, 1995 ($2.50)
1-15,0(3/96): 2-"JAN" on-c, February, 1995 in indicia. 2.50
Yearbook 1 (5/95, $2.95) 3.00

TIME WARP (See The Unexpected #210)
DC Comics, Inc.: Oct-Nov, 1979 - No. 5, June-July, 1980 ($1.00, 68 pgs.)
1 2 4 6 9 11 14
2-5 1 3 4 6 8 10
NOTE: ***Aparo*** *a-1.* ***Buckler*** *a-1p.* ***Chaykin*** *a-2.* ***Ditko*** *a-1-4.* ***Kaluta*** *c-1-5.* ***G. Kane*** *a-2.* ***Nasser*** *a-4.* ***Newton*** *a-1-5p.* ***Orlando*** *a-2.* ***Sutton*** *a-1-3.*

TIME WARRIORS: THE BEGINNING
Fantasy General Comics: 1986 (Aug) - No. 2, 1986? ($1.50)
1,2-Alpha Track/Skellon Empire 2.25

TIM HOLT (Movie star) (Becomes Red Mask #42 on; also see Crack Western #72, & Great Western)
Magazine Enterprises: 1948 - No. 41, April-May, 1954 (All 36 pgs.)
1-(A-1 #14)-Line drawn-c w/Tim Holt photo on-c; Tim Holt, His horse Lightning & sidekick Chito begin 67 134 201 419 647 875
2-(A-1 #17)(9-10/48)-Photo-c begin, end #18 38 76 114 219 320 420
3-(A-1 #19)-Photo back-c 30 60 90 170 245 320
4(1-2/49),5: 5-Photo front/back-c 21 42 63 121 173 225
6-(5/49)-1st app. The Calico Kid (alias Rex Fury), his horse Ebony & Sidekick Sing-Song (begin series); photo back-c 35 70 105 201 293 385
7-10: 7-Calico Kid by Ayers. 8-Calico Kid by Guardineer (r-in/Great Western #10). 9-Map of Tim's Home Range 18 36 54 102 146 190
11-The Calico Kid becomes The Ghost Rider (origin & 1st app.) by Dick Ayers (r-in/Great Western I.W. #8); his horse Spectre & sidekick Sing-Song begin series
46 92 138 281 428 575
12-16,18-Last photo-c 15 30 45 83 117 150
17-Frazetta Ghost Rider-c 40 80 120 239 357 475
19,22,24: 19-Last Tim Holt-c; Bolle line-drawn-c begin; Tim Holt photo on covers #19-28,30-41. 22-interior photo-c 12 24 36 71 98 125
20-Tim Holt becomes Redmask (origin); begin series; Redmask-c #20-on
18 36 54 100 143 185
21-Frazetta Ghost Rider/Redmask-c 40 80 120 230 335 440
23-Frazetta Redmask-c 31 62 93 178 259 340
25-1st app. Black Phantom 21 42 63 118 169 220
26-30: 28-Wild Bill Hickok, Bat Masterson team up with Redmask. 29-B&W photo-c
11 22 33 64 87 110
31-33-Ghost Rider ends 10 20 30 60 80 100
34-Tales of the Ghost Rider begins (horror)-Classic "The Flower Women" & "Hard Boiled Harry!" 14 28 42 79 110 140
35-Last Tales of the Ghost Rider 11 22 33 64 87 110
36-The Ghost Rider returns, ends #41; liquid hallucinogenic drug story
12 24 36 71 98 125
37-Ghost Rider classic "To Touch Is to Die!", about Inca treasure
12 24 36 71 98 125
38-The Black Phantom begins (not in #39); classic Ghost Rider "The Phantom Guns of Feather Gap!" 12 24 36 71 98 125
39-41: All 3-D effect c/stories 15 30 45 85 120 155
NOTE: ***Dick Ayers*** *a-7, 9-41.* ***Bolle*** *a-1-41; c-19, 20, 22, 24-28, 30-41.*

TIM McCOY (Formerly Zoo Funnies; Pictorial Love Stories #22 on)
Charlton Comics: No. 16, Oct, 1948 - No. 21, Aug, 1949 (Western Movie Stories)
16-John Wayne, Montgomery Clift app. in "Red River"; photo back-c
44 88 132 268 409 550
17-21: 17-Allan "Rocky" Lane guest stars. 18-Rod Cameron guest stars. 19-Whip Wilson, Andy Clyde guest star; Jesse James story. 20-Jimmy Wakely guest stars. 21-Johnny Mack Brown guest stars 40 80 120 233 342 450

TIMMY
Dell Publishing Co.: No. 715, Aug, 1956 - No. 1022, Aug-Oct, 1959
Four Color 715 (#1) 5 10 15 36 48 60
Four Color 823 (8/57), 923 (8/58), 1022 4 8 12 25 33 42

TIMMY THE TIMID GHOST (Formerly Win-A-Prize?; see Blue Bird)
Charlton Comics: No. 3, 2/56 - No. 44, 10/64; No. 45, 9/66; 10/67 - No. 23, 7/71; V4#24, 9/85 - No. 26, 1/86
3(1956) (1st Series) 11 22 33 66 88 110
4,5 7 14 21 37 46 55
6-10 3 7 10 21 28 35
11,12(4/58,10/58)-(100 pgs.) 7 14 21 50 68 85
13-20 3 6 9 18 24 30
21-45(1966) 2 4 6 12 16 20
1(10/67, 2nd series) 3 6 9 16 20 24
2-10 2 4 6 10 12 15
11-23: 23 (7/71) 1 3 4 8 10 12
24-26 (1985-86): Fago-r (low print run) 6.00

TIM TYLER (See Harvey Comics Hits #54)

TIM TYLER (Also see Comics Reading Libraries in the Promotional Comics section)
Better Publications: 1942
1 15 30 45 83 117 150

TIM TYLER COWBOY
Standard Comics (King Features Synd.): No. 11, Nov, 1948 - No. 18, 1950
11-By Lyman Young 9 18 27 54 70 85
12-18: 13-15-Full length western adventures 7 14 21 37 46 55

TINCAN MAN
Image Comics: Jan, 2000 - No. 3, Mar, 2000 ($2.95, limited series)
1-3-Thornton-s/Dietrich Smith & Pierre Andre-Dery-a 3.00

TINKER BELL (Disney, TV)(See Walt Disney Showcase #37)
Dell Publishing Co.: No. 896, Mar, 1958 - No. 982, Apr-June, 1959
Four Color 896 (#1)-The Adventures of... 10 20 30 70 100 130
Four Color 982-The New Advs. of... 9 18 27 65 93 120

TINY FOLKS FUNNIES
Dell Publishing Co.: No. 60, 1944
Four Color 60 17 34 51 119 182 245

TINY TESSIE (Tessie #1-23; Real Experiences #25)
Marvel Comics (20CC): No. 24, Oct, 1949 (52 pgs.)
24 11 22 33 62 84 105

TINY TIM (Also see Super Comics)
Dell Publishing Co.: No. 4, 1941 - No. 235, July, 1949
Large Feature Comic 4('41) 40 80 120 240 360 480

Tippy's Friends Go-Go and Animal #9 © TC

Tip Top Comics #24 © UFS

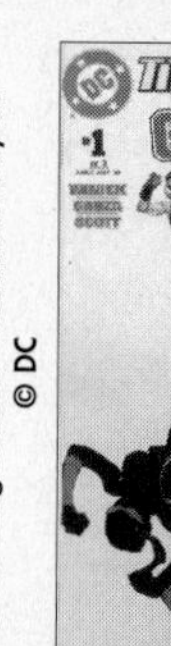

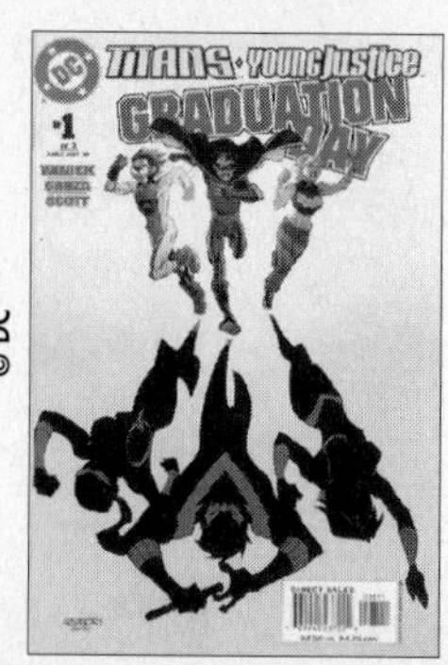

Titans/Young Justice: Graduation Day #1 © DC

	GD 2.0	VG 4.0	FN 6.0	VF 8.0	VF/NM 9.0	NM- 9.2
Four Color 20(1941)	29	58	87	206	316	425
Four Color 42(1943)	18	36	54	126	193	260
Four Color 235	6	12	18	40	55	70

TINY TOT COMICS
E. C. Comics: Mar, 1946 - No. 10, Nov-Dec, 1947 (For younger readers)

	GD 2.0	VG 4.0	FN 6.0	VF 8.0	VF/NM 9.0	NM- 9.2
1(nn)-52 pg. issues begin, end #4	40	80	120	230	335	440
2 (5/46)	22	44	66	125	180	235
3-10: 10-Christmas-c	20	40	60	112	161	210

TINY TOT FUNNIES (Formerly Family Funnies; becomes Junior Funnies)
Harvey Publ. (King Features Synd.): No. 9, June, 1951

	GD 2.0	VG 4.0	FN 6.0	VF 8.0	VF/NM 9.0	NM- 9.2
9-Flash Gordon, Mandrake, Dagwood, Daisy, etc.	8	16	24	43	54	65

TINY TOTS COMICS
Dell Publishing Co.: 1943 (Not reprints)

	GD 2.0	VG 4.0	FN 6.0	VF 8.0	VF/NM 9.0	NM- 9.2
1-Kelly-a(2); fairy tales	40	80	120	235	348	460

TIPPY & CAP STUBBS (See Popular Comics)
Dell Publishing Co.: No. 210, Jan, 1949 - No. 242, Aug, 1949

	GD 2.0	VG 4.0	FN 6.0	VF 8.0	VF/NM 9.0	NM- 9.2
Four Color 210 (#1)	6	12	18	38	52	65
Four Color 242	4	8	12	29	40	50

TIPPY'S FRIENDS GO-GO & ANIMAL
Tower Comics: July, 1966 - No. 15, Oct, 1969 (25¢)

	GD 2.0	VG 4.0	FN 6.0	VF 8.0	VF/NM 9.0	NM- 9.2
1	9	18	27	60	85	110
2-5,7,9-15: 12-15 titled "Tippy's Friend Go-Go"	5	10	15	33	44	55
6-The Monkees photo-c	8	16	24	55	78	100
8-Beatles app. on front/back-c	11	22	33	77	114	150

TIPPY TEEN (See Vicki)
Tower Comics: Nov, 1965 - No. 25, Oct, 1969 (25¢)

	GD 2.0	VG 4.0	FN 6.0	VF 8.0	VF/NM 9.0	NM- 9.2
1	10	20	30	70	100	130
2-4,6-10	6	12	18	38	52	65
5-1 pg. Beatles pin-up	6	12	18	43	59	75
11-20: 16-Twiggy photo-c	5	10	15	36	48	60
21-25	4	8	12	29	40	50
Special Collectors' Editions nn-(1969, 25¢)	5	10	15	36	48	60

TIPPY TERRY
Super/I. W. Enterprises: 1963

	GD 2.0	VG 4.0	FN 6.0	VF 8.0	VF/NM 9.0	NM- 9.2
Super Reprint #14('63)-r/Little Groucho #1	2	4	6	8	10	12
I.W. Reprint #1 (nd)-r/Little Groucho #1	2	4	6	8	10	12

TIP TOP COMICS
United Features #1-187/St. John #188-210/Dell Publishing Co. #211 on:
4/36 - No. 210, 1957; No. 211, 11-1/57-58 - No. 225, 5-7/61

	GD 2.0	VG 4.0	FN 6.0	VF 8.0	VF/NM 9.0	NM- 9.2
1-Tarzan by Hal Foster, Li'l Abner, Broncho Bill, Fritzi Ritz, Ella Cinders, Capt. & The Kids begin; strip-r (1st comic book app. of each)	952	1904	2856	5331	7666	10,000
2	229	458	687	1282	1841	2400
3-Tarzan-c	205	410	615	1148	1649	2150
4	117	234	351	655	940	1225
5-8,10: 7-Photo & biography of Edgar Rice Burroughs. 8-Christmas-c	83	166	249	465	670	875
9-Tarzan-c	105	210	315	588	844	1100
11,13,16,18-Tarzan-c: 11-Has Tarzan pin-up	80	160	240	448	644	840
12,14,15,17,19,20: 20-Christmas-c	65	130	195	364	525	685
21,24,27,30-(10/38)-Tarzan-c	65	130	195	364	525	685
22,23,25,26,28,29	45	90	135	252	364	475
31,35,38,40	40	80	120	230	335	440
32,36-Tarzan-c: 32-1st published Jack Davis-a (cartoon). 36-Kurtzman panel (1st published comic work)	54	108	162	329	502	675
33,34,37,39-Tarzan-c	50	100	150	305	465	625
41-Reprints 1st Tarzan Sunday; Tarzan-c	54	108	162	329	502	675
42,44,46,48,49	35	70	105	198	287	375
43,45,47,50,52-Tarzan-c. 43-Mort Walker panel	40	80	120	236	351	465
51,53	34	68	102	193	279	365
54-Origin Mirror Man & Triple Terror, also featured on cover	40	80	120	230	335	440
55,56,58,60: Last Tarzan by Foster	27	54	81	152	219	285
57,59,61,62-Tarzan by Hogarth	34	68	102	196	283	370
63-80: 65,67-70,72-74,77,78-No Tarzan	17	34	51	95	135	175
81-90	15	30	45	83	117	150
91-99	13	26	39	74	110	130
100	14	28	42	79	110	140
101-140: 110-Gordo story. 111-Li'l Abner app. 118, 132-No Tarzan. 137-Sadie Hawkins Day story	9	18	27	54	70	85
141-170: 145,151-Gordo stories. 157-Last Li'l Abner; lingerie panels	8	16	24	43	54	65
171-188-Tarzan reprints by B. Lubbers in all. 177-Peanuts by Schulz begins?; no Peanuts in #178,179,181-183	8	16	24	46	58	70
189-225-Peanuts (8 pgs.) in most	7	14	21	37	46	55
Bound Volumes (Very Rare) sold at 1939 World's Fair; bound by publisher in pictorial comic boards (also see Comics on Parade)						
Bound issues 1-12	269	538	807	1681	2591	3500
Bound issues 13-24	135	270	405	844	1297	1750
Bound issues 25-36	119	238	357	744	1147	1550

NOTE: *Tarzan by* ***Foster***-#1-40, 44-50; *by* ***Rex Maxon***-#41-43; *by* ***Burne Hogarth***-#57, 59, 62.

TIP TOPPER COMICS
United Features Syndicate: Oct-Nov, 1949 - No. 28, 1954

	GD 2.0	VG 4.0	FN 6.0	VF 8.0	VF/NM 9.0	NM- 9.2
1-Li'l Abner, Abbie & Slats	11	22	33	64	87	110
2	8	16	24	43	54	65
3-5: 5-Fearless Fosdick app.	7	14	21	37	46	55
6-10: 6-Fearless Fosdick app.	7	14	21	35	43	50
11-16	6	12	18	28	34	40
17(6-7/52) (2nd app. of Peanuts by Schulz in comics?) (see United Comics #22 for 5-6/52 app.)	8	16	24	46	58	70
18-26: 18-24,26-Early Peanuts (2 pgs.). 25-Early Peanuts (3 pgs.) 26-Twin Earths	8	16	24	40	50	60
27,28-Twin Earths	7	14	21	37	46	55

NOTE: *Many lingerie panels in Fritzi Ritz stories.*

TITAN A.E.
Dark Horse Comics: May, 2000 - No. 3, July, 2000 ($2.95, limited series)

	NM- 9.2
1-3-Movie prequel; Al Rio-a	3.00

TITANS (Also see Teen Titans, New Teen Titans and New Titans)
DC Comics: Mar, 1999 - No. 50, Apr, 2003 ($2.50/$2.75)

	NM- 9.2
1-Titans re-form; Grayson-s; 2 covers	3.00
2-11,13-24,26-50: 2-Superman-c/app. 9,10,21,22-Deathstroke app. 24-Titans from "Kingdom Come" app. 32-36-Asamiya-c. 44-Begin $2.75-c	2.75
12-($3.50, 48 pages)	3.50
25-($3.95) Titans from "Kingdom Come" app.; Wolfman & Faerber-s; art by Pérez, Cardy, Grumment, Jimenez, Dodson, Pelletier	4.00
Annual 1 ('00, $3.50) Planet DC; intro Bushido	3.50
...Secret Files 1,2 (3/99, 10/00; $4.95) Profile pages & short stories	5.00

TITANS/ LEGION OF SUPER-HEROES: UNIVERSE ABLAZE
DC Comics: 2000 - No. 4, 2000 ($4.95, prestige format, limited series)

	NM- 9.2
1-4-Jurgens-s/a; P. Jimenez-a; teams battle Universo	5.00

TITAN SPECIAL
Dark Horse Comics: June, 1994 ($3.95, one-shot)

	NM- 9.2
1-($3.95, 52 pgs.)	4.00

TITANS: SCISSORS, PAPER, STONE
DC Comics: 1997 ($4.95, one-shot)

	NM- 9.2
1-Manga style Elseworlds; Adam Warren-s/a(p)	5.00

TITANS SELL-OUT SPECIAL
DC Comics: Nov, 1992 ($3.50, 52 pgs., one-shot)

	NM- 9.2
1-Fold-out Nightwing poster; 1st Teeny Titans	3.50

TITANS/ YOUNG JUSTICE: GRADUATION DAY
DC Comics: Early July, 2003 - No. 3, Aug, 2003 ($2.50, limited series)

	NM- 9.2
1,2-Winick-s/Garza-a; leads into Teen Titans and The Outsiders series. 2-Lilith dies	2.50
3-Death of Donna Troy (Wonder Girl)	2.50
TPB (2003, $6.95) r/#1-3; plus previews of Teen Titans and The Outsiders series	7.00

T-MAN (Also see Police Comics #103)
Quality Comics Group: Sept, 1951 - No. 38, Dec, 1956

	GD 2.0	VG 4.0	FN 6.0	VF 8.0	VF/NM 9.0	NM- 9.2
1-Pete Trask, T-Man begins; Jack Cole-a	40	80	120	236	351	465
2-Crandall-c	22	44	66	125	180	235
3,7,8: All Crandall-c	20	40	60	112	161	210
4,5-Crandall-c/a each	21	42	63	121	173	225
6-"The Man Who Could Be Hitler" c/story; Crandall-c.	22	44	66	125	180	235
9,10-Crandall-c	17	34	51	95	135	175
11-Used in **POP**, pg. 95 & color illo.	13	26	39	76	106	135
12,13,15-19,21,22-26: 21- "The Return of Mussolini" c/story. 23-H-Bomb panel. 24-Last pre-code issue (4/55). 25-Not Crandall-a	11	22	33	64	87	110
14-Hitler-c	15	30	45	83	117	150
20-H-Bomb explosion-c/story	15	30	45	83	117	150
27-38	11	22	33	64	87	110

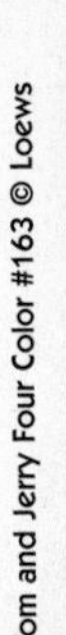

Tokyo Storm Warning #1 © Ellis & Raiz

Tom and Jerry Four Color #163 © Loews

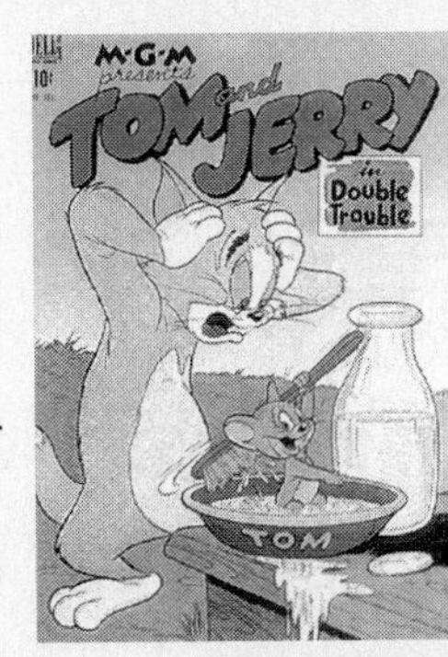

Tomb of Dracula #7 © MAR

	GD 2.0	VG 4.0	FN 6.0	VF 8.0	VF/NM 9.0	NM- 9.2

NOTE: *Anti-communist stories common.* **Crandall** *c-2-10p.* **Cuidera** *c(i)-1-38. Bondage c-15.*

TMNT MUTANT UNIVERSE SOURCEBOOK
Archie Comics: 1992 - No. 3, 1992? ($1.95, 52 pgs.)(Lists characters from A-Z)

1-3: 3-New characters; fold-out poster 2.25

TNT COMICS
Charles Publishing Co.: Feb, 1946 (36 pgs.)

1-Yellowjacket app. 31 62 93 175 253 330

TOBY TYLER (Disney, see Movie Comics)
Dell Publishing Co.: No. 1092, Apr-June, 1960

Four Color 1092-Movie, photo-c 8 16 24 53 74 95

TODAY'S BRIDES
Ajax/Farrell Publishing Co.: Nov, 1955; No. 2, Feb, 1956; No. 3, Sept, 1956; No. 4, Nov, 1956

1 9 18 27 49 62 75
2-4 6 12 18 31 38 45

TODAY'S ROMANCE
Standard Comics: No. 5, March, 1952 - No. 8, Sept, 1952 (All photo-c?)

5-Photo-c 9 18 27 54 70 85
6-Photo-c; Toth-a 10 20 30 56 73 90
7,8 8 16 24 40 50 60

TOE TAGS FEATURING GEORGE A. ROMARO
DC Comics: Dec, 2004 - Present ($2.95)

1-3-Zombie story by George Romaro; Wrightson-c/Castillo-a 3.00

TOKA (Jungle King)
Dell Publishing Co.: Aug-Oct, 1964 - No. 10, Jan, 1967 (Painted-c #1,2)

1 5 10 15 33 44 55
2 3 6 9 18 24 30
3-10 3 6 9 16 20 24

TOKYO STORM WARNING (See Red/Tokyo Storm Warning for TPB)
DC Comics (Cliffhanger): Aug, 2003 - No. 3, Dec, 2003 ($2.95, limited series)

1-3-Warren Ellis-s/James Raiz-a 3.00

TOMAHAWK (Son of... on-c of #131-140; see Star Spangled Comics #69 & World's Finest Comics #65)
National Periodical Publications: Sept-Oct, 1950 - No. 140, May-June, 1972

1-Tomahawk & boy sidekick Dan Hunter begin by Fred Ray
162 324 486 1013 1557 2100
2-Frazetta/Williamson-a (4 pgs.) 65 130 195 406 628 850
3-5 40 80 120 239 357 475
6-10: 7-Last 52 pg. issue 35 70 105 198 287 375
11-20 24 48 72 138 199 260
21-27,30: 30-Last precode (2/55) 20 40 60 112 161 210
28-1st app. Lord Shilling (arch-foe) 21 42 63 118 169 220
29-Frazetta-r/Jimmy Wakely #3 (3 pgs.) 26 52 78 147 211 275
31-40 12 24 36 84 127 170
41-50 10 20 30 72 104 135
51-56,58-60 8 16 24 55 78 100
57-Frazetta-r/Jimmy Wakely #6 (3 pgs.) 10 20 30 72 104 135
61-77: 77-Last 10¢ issue 7 14 21 50 68 85
78-85: 81-1st app. Miss Liberty. 83-Origin Tomahawk's Rangers
6 12 18 38 52 65
86-99: 96-Origin/1st app. The Hood, alias Lady Shilling
4 8 12 27 36 45
100 4 8 12 28 38 48
101-110: 107-Origin/1st app. Thunder-Man 4 8 12 22 30 38
111-115,120,122: 122-Last 12¢ issue 3 7 10 21 28 35
116-119,121,123-130-Neal Adams-c 4 8 12 24 32 40
131-Frazetta-r/Jimmy Wakely #7 (3 pgs.); origin Firehair retold
3 6 9 19 25 32
132-135: 135-Last 15¢ issue 2 4 6 14 18 22
136-138,140 (52 pg. Giants) 3 6 9 18 23 28
139-Frazetta-r/Star Spangled #113 3 6 9 19 25 32

NOTE: **Fred Ray** *c-1, 2, 8, 11, 30, 34, 35, 40-43, 45, 46, 82. Firehair by* **Kubert**-*131-134, 136.* **Maurer** *a-138.* **Severin** *a-135.* **Starr** *a-5.* **Thorne** *a-137, 140.*

TOM AND JERRY (See Comic Album #4, 8, 12, Dell Giant #21, Dell Giants, Golden Comics Digest #1, 5, 8, 13, 15, 18, 22, 25, 28, 35, Kite fun Book & March of Comics #21, 46, 61, 70, 88, 103, 119, 128, 145, 154, 173, 190, 207, 224, 281, 295, 305, 321,333, 345, 361, 365, 388, 400, 444, 451, 463, 480)

TOM AND JERRY (...Comics, early issues) (M.G.M.)
(Formerly Our Gang No. 1-59) (See Dell Giants for annuals)
Dell Publishing Co./Gold Key No. 213-327/Whitman No. 328 on: No. 193, 6/48; No. 60, 7/49 - No. 212, 7-9/62; No. 213, 11/62 - No. 291, 2/75; No. 292, 3/77 - No. 342, 5/82 - No. 344, 6/84

Four Color 193 (#1)-Titled "M.G.M. Presents..." 22 44 66 160 245 330
60-Barney Bear, Benny Burro cont. from Our Gang; Droopy begins
12 24 36 82 124 165
61 10 20 30 70 100 130
62-70: 66-X-Mas-c 8 16 24 58 82 105
71-80: 77,90-X-Mas-c. 79-Spike & Tyke begin 7 14 21 50 68 85
81-99 6 12 18 43 59 75
100 7 14 21 46 63 80
101-120 5 10 15 36 48 60
121-140: 126-X-Mas-c 5 10 15 33 44 55
141-160 4 8 12 28 38 48
161-200 4 8 12 25 33 42
201-212(7-9/62)(Last Dell issue) 4 8 12 22 30 38
213,214-(84 pgs.)-Titled "...Funhouse" 7 14 21 51 71 90
215-240: 215-Titled "...Funhouse" 3 6 9 18 24 30
241-270 2 4 6 12 16 20
271-300: 286- "Tom & Jerry" 2 4 6 9 11 14
301-327 (Gold Key) 1 3 4 6 8 10
328,329 (Whitman) 2 4 6 9 11 14
330(8/80),331(10/80), 332-(3-pack only) 3 6 9 16 21 26
333-341: 339(2/82), 340(2-3/82), 341(4/82) 2 4 6 8 10 12
342-344 (All #90058, no date, date code, 3-pack): 342(6/83), 343(8/83), 344(6/84)
2 4 6 12 16 20
Mouse From T.R.A.P. 1(7/66)-Giant, G. K. 6 12 18 38 52 65
Summer Fun 1(7/67, 68 pgs.)(Gold Key)-Reprints Barks' Droopy from Summer Fun #1
6 12 18 38 52 65

NOTE: *#60-87, 98-121, 268, 277, 289, 302 are 52 pgs.. Reprints-#225, 241, 245, 247, 252, 254, 266, 268, 270, 292-327, 329-342, 344.*

TOM & JERRY
Harvey Comics: Sept, 1991 - No. 18, Aug, 1994 ($1.25)

1-18: 1-Tom & Jerry, Barney Bear-r by Carl Barks 3.00
50th Anniversary Special 1 (10/91, $2.50, 68 pgs.)-Benny the Lonesome Burro-r by Barks (story/a)/Our Gang #9 4.00

TOMB, THE
Oni Press: June, 2004 ($14.95, B&W, digest size, grpahic novel)

nn-Christina Weir & Nunzio DeFilippis-s/Christopher Mitten-a 15.00

TOMB OF DARKNESS (Formerly Beware)
Marvel Comics Group: No. 9, July, 1974 - No. 23, Nov, 1976

9 3 6 9 18 23 28
10-23: 11,16,18-21-Kirby-a. 15,19-Ditko-r. 17-Woodbridge-r/Astonishing #62; Powell-r. 20-Everett Venus-r/Venus #19. 22-r/Tales To Astonish #27; 1st Hank Pym. 23-Everett-r
2 4 6 10 12 15
20,21-(30¢-c variants, limited distribution)(5,7/76) 3 6 9 16 20 24

TOMB OF DRACULA (See Giant-Size Dracula, Dracula Lives, Nightstalkers, Power Record Comics & Requiem for Dracula)
Marvel Comics Group: Apr, 1972 - No. 70, Aug, 1979

1-1st app. Dracula & Frank Drake; Colan-p in all; Neal Adams-c
15 30 45 107 164 220
2 7 14 21 50 68 85
3-6: 3-Intro. Dr. Rachel Van Helsing & Inspector Chelm. 6-Neal Adams-c
6 12 18 38 52 65
7-9 4 8 12 29 40 50
10-1st app. Blade the Vampire Slayer (who app. in 1998 and 2002 movies)
12 24 36 86 131 175
11,12,14-16,20: 3 7 10 21 28 35
12-2nd app. Blade; Brunner-c(p) 6 12 18 38 52 65
13-Origin Blade 7 14 21 50 68 85
17,19: 17-Blade bitten by Dracula. 19-Blade discovers he is immune to vampire's bite. 1st mention of Blade having vampire blood in him 4 8 12 28 38 48
18-Two-part x-over cont'd in Werewolf by Night #15 4 8 12 22 30 38
21,24-Blade app. 3 6 9 18 23 28
22,23,26,27,29 2 4 6 14 18 22
25-1st app. & origin Hannibal King 3 6 9 18 23 28
25-2nd printing (1994) 2 4 6 8 10 12
28-Blade app. on-c & inside as an illusion 3 6 9 18 23 28
30,41,42-45-Blade app. 45-Intro. Deacon Frost, the vampire who bit Blade's mother
3 6 9 16 20 24
31-40 2 4 6 12 16 20
43-45-(30¢-c variants, limited distribution) 3 7 10 21 28 36
46,47-(Regular 25¢ editions)(4-8/76) 2 4 6 8 10 12

Tomb of Terror #9 © HARV

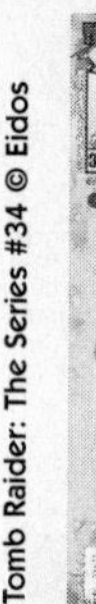

Tomb Raider: The Series #34 © Eidos

Tom Mix Western #8 © FAW

	GD 2.0	VG 4.0	FN 6.0	VF 8.0	VF/NM 9.0	NM- 9.2
46,47-(30¢-c variants, limited distribution)	2	4	6	11	14	18
48,49,51-57,59,60: 57,59,60-(30¢-c)	2	4	6	8	10	12
50-Silver Surfer app.	2	4	6	14	18	22
57,59,60-(35¢-c variants)(6-9/77)	2	4	6	11	14	18
58-All Blade issue (Regular 30¢ edition)	3	6	9	18	23	28
58-(35¢-c variant)(7/77)	4	8	12	25	33	42
61-69	2	4	6	8	10	12
70-Double size	3	6	9	16	20	24

NOTE: ***N. Adams*** *c-1, 6.* ***Colan*** *a-1-70p; c(p)-8, 38-42, 44-56, 58-70.* ***Wrightson*** *c-43.*

TOMB OF DRACULA, THE (Magazine)
Marvel Comics Group: Oct, 1979 - No. 6, Aug, 1980 (B&W)

	GD	VG	FN	VF	VF/NM	NM-
1,3: 1-Colan-a; features on movies "Dracula" and "Love at First Bite" w/photos. 3-Good girl cover-a; Miller-a (2 pg. sketch)	2	4	6	10	12	15
2,6: 2-Ditko-a (36 pgs.); Nosferatu movie feature. 6-Lilith story w/Sienkiewicz-a	1	3	4	6	8	10
4,5: Stephen King interview	2	4	6	11	14	18

NOTE: ***Buscema*** *a-4p, 5p.* ***Chaykin*** *c-5, 6.* ***Colan*** *a(p)-1, 3-6.* ***Miller*** *a-3.* ***Romita*** *a-2p.*

TOMB OF DRACULA
Marvel Comics (Epic Comics): 1991 - No. 4, 1992 ($4.95, 52 pgs., squarebound, mini-series)

	GD	VG	FN	VF	VF/NM	NM-
Book 1-4: Colan/Williamson-a; Colan painted-c						5.00

TOMB OF DRACULA
Marvel Comics: Dec, 2004 - Present ($2.99)

	GD	VG	FN	VF	VF/NM	NM-
1-3-Blade app.; Tolagson-a/Sienkiewicz-c						3.00

TOMB OF LEGEIA (See Movie Classics)

TOMB OF TERROR (Thrills of Tomorrow #17 on)
Harvey Publications: June, 1952 - No. 16, July, 1954

	GD	VG	FN	VF	VF/NM	NM-
1	43	86	129	262	401	540
2	26	52	78	150	215	280
3-Bondage-c; atomic disaster story	27	54	81	154	222	290
4-12: 4-Heart ripped out. 8-12-Nostrand-a	25	50	75	141	203	265
13,14-Special S/F issues. 14-Check-a	35	70	105	201	293	385
15-S/F issue; c-shows face exploding	55	110	165	340	520	700
16-Special S/F issue; Nostrand-a	32	64	96	181	263	345

NOTE: ***Edd Cartier*** *a-13?* ***Elias*** *c-2, 5-16.* ***Kremer*** *a-1, 7; c-1.* ***Nostrand*** *a-8-12, 15r 16.* ***Palais*** *a-2, 3, 5-7.* ***Powell*** *a-1, 3, 5, 9-16.* ***Sparling*** *a-12, 13, 15.*

TOMB RAIDER (one-shots)
Image Comics (Top Cow Prod.)

	GD	VG	FN	VF	VF/NM	NM-
...: Arabian Nights (8/04, $5.99) Avery-s/Tan-a/c						6.00
.../The Darkness Special 1 (2001, TopCowStore.com)-Wohl-s/Tan-a						3.00
Epiphany 1 (8/03, $4.99)-Jurgens-s/Banks-a/Haley-c; preview of Witchblade Animated						5.00
Takeover 1 (1/04, $2.99)-Benefiel-a/Daniel-c						3.00

TOMB RAIDER: JOURNEYS
Image Comics (Top Cow Prod.): Jan, 2002 - No. 12, May, 2003 ($2.50/$2.99)

	GD	VG	FN	VF	VF/NM	NM-
1-12: 1-Avery-s/Drew Johnson-a. 1-Two covers by Johnson & Hughes						3.00

TOMB RAIDER: THE GREATEST TREASURE OF ALL
Image Comics (Top Cow Prod.): 2002

	GD	VG	FN	VF	VF/NM	NM-
Prelude (2002, 16 pgs., no cover price) Jusko-c/a						5.00

TOMB RAIDER: THE SERIES (Also see Witchblade/Tomb Raider)(Also see Promotional Comics section for Free Comic Book Day edition)
Image Comics (Top Cow Prod.): Dec, 1999 - Present ($2.50/$2.99)

	GD	VG	FN	VF	VF/NM	NM-
1-Jurgens-s/Park-a; 3 covers by Park, Finch, Turner						4.00
2-24,26-29,31-47: 21-Black-c w/foil. 31-Mhan-a. 37-Flip book preview of Stryke Force						3.00
25-Michael Turner-c/a; Witchblade app.; Endgame x-over with Witchblade #60 & Evo #1						3.00
30-($4.99) Tony Daniel-a						5.00
#0 (6/01, $2.50) Avery-s/Ching-a/c						2.50
#1/2 (10/01, $2.95) Early days of Lara Croft; Jurgens-s/Lopez-a						3.00
...: Chasing Shangri-La (2002, $12.95, TPB) r/#11-15						13.00
...Gallery (12/00, $2.95) Pin-ups & previous covers by various						3.00
...Magazine (6/01, $4.95) Hughes-c; r/#1,2; Jurgens interview						5.00
...: Mystic Artifacts (2001, $14.95, TPB) r/#5-10						15.00
...: Saga of the Medusa Mask (9/00, $9.95, TPB) r/#1-4; new Park-c						10.00

TOMB RAIDER/WITCHBLADE SPECIAL (Also see Witchblade/Tomb Raider)
Top Cow Prod.: Dec, 1997 (mail-in offer, one-shot)

	GD	VG	FN	VF	VF/NM	NM-
1-Turner-s/a(p); green background cover	1	3	4	6	8	10
1-Variant-c with orange sun background	1	3	4	6	8	10
1-Variant-c with black sides	1	3	4	6	8	10
1-Revisited (12/98, $2.95) reprints #1, Turner-c						3.00
...: Trouble Seekers TPB (2002, $7.95) rep. T.R./W & W/T.R. & W/T.R. 1/2; new Turner-c						8.00

TOMBSTONE TERRITORY
Dell Publishing Co.: No. 1123, Aug, 1960

	GD	VG	FN	VF	VF/NM	NM-
Four Color 1123	10	20	30	70	100	130

TOM CAT (Formerly Bo; Atom The Cat #9 on)
Charlton Comics: No. 4, Apr, 1956 - No. 8, July, 1957

	GD	VG	FN	VF	VF/NM	NM-
4-Al Fago-c/a	8	16	24	46	58	70
5-8	6	12	18	31	38	45

TOM CORBETT, SPACE CADET (TV)
Dell Publishing Co.: No. 378, Jan-Feb, 1952 - No. 11, Sept-Nov, 1954 (All painted covers)

	GD	VG	FN	VF	VF/NM	NM-
Four Color 378 (#1)-McWilliams-a	19	38	57	134	205	275
Four Color 400,421-McWilliams-a	11	22	33	80	120	160
4(11-1/53) - 11	9	18	27	65	93	120

TOM CORBETT SPACE CADET (See March of Comics #102)

TOM CORBETT SPACE CADET (TV)
Prize Publications: V2#1, May-June, 1955 - V2#3, Sept-Oct, 1955

	GD	VG	FN	VF	VF/NM	NM-
V2#1-Robot-c	33	66	99	190	275	360
2,3-Meskin-c	26	52	78	147	211	275

TOM, DICK & HARRIET (See Gold Key Spotlight)

TOM JUDGE: END OF DAYS
Image Comics: Jan, 2003 ($3.99)

	GD	VG	FN	VF	VF/NM	NM-
1-Jenkins-s/Crain-a; flip book wih Evo Preview Edition; Silvestri-c						4.00

TOM LANDRY AND THE DALLAS COWBOYS
Spire Christian Comics/Fleming H. Revell Co.: 1973 (35/49¢)

	GD	VG	FN	VF	VF/NM	NM-
nn-35¢ edition	2	4	6	14	18	22
nn-49¢ edition	2	4	6	10	12	15

TOM MIX WESTERN (Movie, radio star) (Also see The Comics, Crackajack Funnies, Master Comics, 100 Pages Of Comics, Popular Comics, Real Western Hero, Six Gun Heroes, Western Hero & XMas Comics)
Fawcett Publications: Jan, 1948 - No. 61, May, 1953 (1-17: 52 pgs.)

	GD	VG	FN	VF	VF/NM	NM-
1 (Photo-c, 52 pgs.)-Tom Mix & his horse Tony begin; Tumbleweed Jr. begins, ends #52,54,55	100	200	300	625	963	1300
2 (Photo-c)	44	88	132	268	409	550
3-5 (Painted/photo-c): 5-Billy the Kid & Oscar app.	35	70	105	200	290	380
6-8: 6,7 (Painted/photo-c). 8-Kinstler tempera-c	30	60	90	170	245	320
9,10 (Painted/photo-c)-Used in **SOTI**, pgs. 323-325	29	58	87	164	237	310
11-Kinstler oil-c	25	50	75	141	203	265
12 (Painted/photo-c)	22	44	66	125	180	235
13-17 (Painted-c, 52 pgs.)	22	44	66	125	180	235
18,22 (Painted-c, 36 pgs.)	19	38	57	107	154	200
19 (Photo-c, 52 pgs.)	20	40	60	112	161	210
20,21,23 (Painted-c, 52 pgs.)	19	38	57	107	154	200
24,25,27-29 (52 pgs.): 24-Photo-c begin, end #61. 29-Slim Pickens app.	16	32	48	89	127	165
26,30 (36 pgs.)	15	30	45	85	120	155
31-33,35-37,39,40,42 (52 pgs.): 39-Red Eagle app.	15	30	45	83	117	150
34,38 (36 pgs. begin)	13	26	39	76	106	135
41,43-60: 57-(9/52)-Dope smuggling story	10	20	30	58	77	95
61-Last issue	12	24	36	69	95	120

NOTE: *Photo-c from 1930s Tom Mix movies (he died in 1940). Many issues contain ads for Tom Mix, Rocky Lane, Space Patrol and other premiums. Captain Tootsie by* ***C.C. Beck*** *in #6-11, 20.*

TOM MIX WESTERN
AC Comics: 1988 - No. 2, 1989? ($2.95, B&W w/16 pgs. color, 44 pgs.)

	GD	VG	FN	VF	VF/NM	NM-
1-Tom Mix-r/Master #124,128,131,102 plus Billy the Kid-r by Severin; photo front/back/inside-c						3.50
2-($2.50, B&W)-Gabby Hayes-r; photo covers						3.00
...Holiday Album 1 (1990, $3.50, B&W, one-shot, 44 pgs.)-Contains photos & 1950s Tom Mix-r; photo inside-c						4.00

TOMMY OF THE BIG TOP (Thrilling Circus Adventures)
King Features Synd./Standard Comics: No. 10, Sep, 1948 - No. 12, Mar, 1949

	GD	VG	FN	VF	VF/NM	NM-
10-By John Lehti	9	18	27	51	62	75
11,12	6	12	18	29	36	42

TOMMYSAURUS REX
Image Comics: Aug, 2004 ($11.95, B&W, graphic novel)

	GD	VG	FN	VF	VF/NM	NM-
Vol. 1 - Doug TenNapel-s/a						12.00

TOMMY TOMORROW (See Action Comics #127, Real Fact #6, Showcase #41,42,44,46,47 & World's Finest #102)

TOMOE (Also see Shi: The Way Of the Warrior #6)

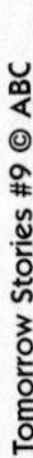
Tomorrow Stories #9 © ABC

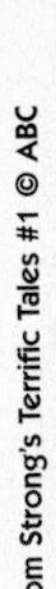
Tom Strong's Terrific Tales #1 © ABC

The Toodles #10 © Z-D

GD 2.0 | VG 4.0 | FN 6.0 | VF 8.0 | VF/NM 9.0 | NM- 9.2

Crusade Comics: July, 1995 - No. 3, June, 1996($2.95)
0-3: 2-B&W Dogs o' War preview. 3-B&W Demon Gun preview 3.00
0 (3/96, $2.95)-variant-c. 3.00
0-Commemorative edition (5,000) 2 4 6 8 10 12
1-Commemorative edition (5,000) 2 4 6 10 12 15
1-($2.95)-FAN Appreciation edition 3.00
TPB (1997, $14.95) r/#0-3 15.00

TOMOE: UNFORGETTABLE FIRE
Crusade Comics: June, 1997 ($2.95, one-shot)
1-Prequel to Shi: The Series 3.00

TOMOE-WITCHBLADE/FIRE SERMON
Crusade Comics: Sept, 1996 ($3.95, one-shot)
1-Tucci-c 5.00
1-($9.95)-Avalon Ed. w/gold foil-c 10.00

TOMOE-WITCHBLADE/MANGA SHI PREVIEW EDITION
Crusade Comics: July, 1996 ($5.00, B&W)
nn-San Diego Preview Edition 5.00

TOMORROW KNIGHTS
Marvel Comics (Epic Comics): June, 1990 - No. 6, Mar, 1991 ($1.50)
1-6: 1-($1.95, 52 pgs.) 2.25

TOMORROW STORIES
America's Best Comics: Oct, 1999 - Present ($3.50/$2.95)
1-Two covers by Ross and Nowlan; Moore-s 3.50
2-12-($2.95) 3.00
Book 1 Hardcover (2002, $24.95) r/#1-6 25.00
Book 2 Hardcover (2004, $24.95) r/#7-12 25.00

TOM SAWYER (See Adventures of... & Famous Stories)

TOM SKINNER-UP FROM HARLEM (See Up From Harlem)

TOM STRONG (Also see Many Worlds of Tesla Strong)
America's Best Comics: June, 1999 - Present ($3.50/$2.95)
1-Two covers by Ross and Sprouse; Moore-s/Sprouse-a 4.00
2-29-($2.95): 4-Art Adams-a (8 pgs.) 13-Fawcett homage w/art by Sprouse, Baker, Heath 20-Origin of Tom Stone. 22-Ordway-a 3.00
...: Book One HC ('00, $24.95) r/#1-7, cover gallery and sketchbook 25.00
...: Book One TPB ('01, $14.95) r/#1-7, cover gallery and sketchbook 15.00
...: Book Two HC ('02, $24.95) r/#8-14, sketchbook 25.00
...: Book Two TPB ('03, $14.95) r/#8-14, sketchbook 15.00
...: Book Three HC ('04, $24.95) r/#15-19, sketchbook 25.00
...: Book Four HC ('04, $24.95) r/#20-25, sketch pages 25.00

TOM STRONG'S TERRIFIC TALES
America's Best Comics: Jan, 2002 - Present ($3.50/$2.95)
1-Short stories; Moore-s; art by Adams, Rivoche, Hernandez, Weiss 3.50
2-12-($2.95) 2-Adams, Ordway, Weiss-a; Adams-c. 4-Rivoche-a. 5-Pearson, Aragonés-a 11-Timm-a 3.00
...: Book One HC ('04, $24.95) r/#1-6, cover gallery and sketch pages 25.00

TOM TERRIFIC! (TV)(See Mighty Mouse Fun Club Magazine #1)
Pines Comics (Paul Terry): Summer, 1957 - No. 6, Fall, 1958
(See Terry Toons Giant Summer Fun Book)
1-1st app.?; CBS Television Presents... 24 48 72 138 199 260
2-6-(scarce) 17 34 51 95 135 175

TOM THUMB
Dell Publishing Co.: No. 972, Jan, 1959
Four Color 972-Movie, George Pal 10 20 30 72 104 135

TOM-TOM, THE JUNGLE BOY (See A-1 Comics & Tick Tock Tales)
Magazine Enterprises: 1947 - No. 3, 1947; Nov, 1957 - No. 3, Mar, 1958
1-Funny animal 11 22 33 64 87 110
2,3(1947): 3-Christmas issue 8 16 24 46 58 70
Tom-Tom & Itchi the Monk 1(11/57) - 3(3/58) 4 8 12 18 22 25
I.W. Reprint No. 1,2,8,10: 1,2,8-r/Koko & Kola #? 2 4 6 8 10 12

TONGUE LASH
Dark Horse Comics: Aug, 1996 - No. 2, Sept, 1996 ($2.95, lim. series, mature)
1,2: Taylor-c/a 3.00

TONGUE LASH II
Dark Horse Comics: Feb, 1999 - No. 2, Mar, 1999 ($2.95, lim. series, mature)
1,2: Taylor-c/a 3.00

TONKA (Disney)
Dell Publishing Co.: No. 966, Jan, 1959
Four Color 966-Movie (Starring Sal Mineo)-photo-c 10 20 30 67 96 125

TONTO (See The Lone Ranger's Companion...)

TONY TRENT (The Face #1,2)
Big Shot/Columbia Comics Group: No. 3, 1948 - No. 4, 1949
3,4: 3-The Face app. by Mart Bailey 19 38 57 107 154 200

TOODLES, THE (The Toodle Twins with #1)
Ziff-Davis (Approved Comics)/Argo: No. 10, July-Aug, 1951; Mar, 1956 (Newspaper-r)
10-Painted-c, some newspaper-r by The Baers 11 22 33 64 87 110
...Twins 1(Argo, 3/56)-Reprints by The Baers 8 16 24 43 54 65

TOO MUCH COFFEE MAN
Adhesive Comics: July, 1993 - No. 10, Dec, 2000 ($2.50, B&W)
1-Shannon Wheeler story & art 2 4 6 10 12 15
2,3 1 2 3 5 7 9
4,5 6.00
6-10 3.00
Full Color Special-nn($2.95),2-(7/97, $3.95) 4.00

TOO MUCH COFFEE MAN SPECIAL
Dark Horse Comics: July, 1997 ($2.95, B&W)
nn-Reprints Dark Horse Presents #92-95 3.00

TOO MUCH HOPELESS SAVAGES
Oni Press: June, 2003 - No. 4, Apr, 2004 ($2.99, B&W, limited series)
1-4-Van Meter-s/Norrie-a 3.00
TPB (8/04, $11.95, digest-size) r/series 12.00

TOOTH AND CLAW
Image Comics: Aug, 1999 - No. 3, Oct, 1999 ($2.95, limited series)
1-3-Mark Pacella-s/a 3.00

TOOTS & CASPER
Dell Publishing Co.: No. 5, 1942
Large Feature Comic 5 19 38 57 107 154 200

TOP ADVENTURE COMICS
I. W. Enterprises: 1964 (Reprints)
1-r/High Adv. (Explorer Joe #2); Krigstein-r 2 4 6 12 16 20
2-Black Dwarf-r/Red Seal #22; Kinstler-c 2 4 6 14 18 22

TOP CAT (TV) (Hanna-Barbera)(See Kite Fun Book)
Dell Publishing Co./Gold Key No. 4 on: 12-2/61-62 - No. 3, 6-8/62; No. 4, 10/62 - No. 31, 9/70
1 (TV show debuted 9/27/61) 16 32 48 112 171 230
2-Augie Doggie back-ups in #1-4 9 18 27 63 89 115
3-5: 3-Last 15¢ issue. 4-Begin 12¢ issues; Yakky Doodle app. in 1 pg. strip. 5-Touché Turtle app. 8 16 24 53 74 95
6-10 6 12 18 40 55 70
11-20 4 8 12 29 40 50
21-31-Reprints 4 8 12 22 30 38

TOP CAT (TV) (Hanna-Barbera)(See TV Stars #4)
Charlton Comics: Nov, 1970 - No. 20, Nov, 1973
1 7 14 21 46 63 80
2-10 4 8 12 24 32 40
11-20 3 6 9 19 25 32
NOTE: *#8 (1/72) went on sale late in 1972 between #14 and #15 with the 1/73 issues.*

TOP COMICS
K. K. Publications/Gold Key: July, 1967 (All reprints)
nn-The Gnome-Mobile (Disney-movie) 2 4 6 12 16 20
1-Beagle Boys (#7), Beep Beep the Road Runner (#5), Bugs Bunny, Chip 'n' Dale, Daffy Duck (#50), Flipper, Huey, Dewey & Louie, Junior Woodchucks, Lassie, The Little Monsters (#71), Moby Duck, Porky Pig (has Gold Key label - says Top Comics on inside), Scamp, Super Goof, Tom & Jerry, Top Cat (#21), Tweety & Sylvester (#7), Walt Disney C&S (#322), Woody Woodpecker known issues; each character given own book 2 4 6 9 11 14
1-Donald Duck (not Barks), Mickey Mouse 2 4 6 12 16 20
1-Flintstones 4 8 12 24 32 40
1-Huckleberry Hound, Yogi Bear (#30) 2 4 6 14 18 22
1-The Jetsons 5 10 15 36 48 60
1-Tarzan of the Apes (#169) 3 6 9 16 21 26
1-Three Stooges (#35) 3 6 9 19 25 32

Top Love Stories #18 © STAR

Topix V10#10 © CG

Top-Notch Comics #5 © AP

	GD 2.0	VG 4.0	FN 6.0	VF 8.0	VF/NM 9.0	NM- 9.2
1-Uncle Scrooge (#70)	3	6	9	18	23	28
1-Zorro (r/G.K. Zorro #7 w/Toth-a; says 2nd printing)	2	4	6	14	18	22
2-Bugs Bunny, Daffy Duck, Mickey Mouse (#114), Porky Pig, Super Goof, Tom & Jerry, Tweety & Sylvester, Walt Disney's C&S (r/#325), Woody Woodpecker	2	4	6	9	11	14
2-Donald Duck (not Barks), Three Stooges, Uncle Scrooge (#71)-Barks-c, Yogi Bear (#30), Zorro (r/#8; Toth-a)	2	4	6	11	14	18
2-Snow White & 7 Dwarfs(6/67)(1944-r)	2	4	6	10	13	16
3-Donald Duck	2	4	6	11	14	18
3-Uncle Scrooge (#72)	2	4	6	12	16	20
3,4-The Flintstones	4	8	12	24	32	40
3,4: 3-Mickey Mouse (r/#115), Tom & Jerry, Woody Woodpecker, Yogi Bear. 4-Mickey Mouse, Woody Woodpecker	2	4	6	9	11	14

NOTE: *Each book in this series is identical to its counterpart except for cover, and came out at same time. The number in parentheses is the original issue it contains.*

TOP COW (Company one-shots)
Image Comics (Top Cow Productions)

... Book of Revelations (7/03, $3.99)-Pin-ups and info; art by various; Gossett-c 4.00
... Convention Sketchbook 2004 (4/04, $3.00, B&W) art by various 3.00
... Productions, Inc./Ballistic Studios Swimsuit Special (5/95, $2.95) 3.00
... Secrets: Special Winter Lingerie Edition 1 (1/96, $2.95) Pin-ups 3.00
... 2001 Preview (no cover price) Preview pages of Tomb Raider; Jusko-a; flip cover & pages of Inferno 2.25

TOP COW CLASSICS IN BLACK AND WHITE
Image Comics (Top Cow): Feb, 2000 - Present ($2.95, B&W reprints)

...: Aphrodite IX #1(9/00) B&W reprint 3.00
...: Ascension #1(4/00) B&W reprint plus time-line of series 3.00
...: Battle of the Planets #1(1/03) B&W reprint plus script and cover gallery 3.00
...: Darkness #1(3/00) B&W reprint plus time-line of series 3.00
...: Fathom #1(5/00) B&W reprint 3.00
...: Magdalena #1(10/02) B&W reprint plus time-line of series 3.00
...: Midnight Nation #1(9/00) B&W preview 3.00
...: Rising Stars #1(7/00) B&W reprint plus cover gallery 3.00
...: Tomb Raider #1(12/00) B&W reprint plus back-story 3.00
...: Witchblade #1(2/00) B&W reprint plus back-story 3.00
...: Witchblade #25(5/01) B&W reprint plus interview with Wohl & Haberlin 3.00

TOP DETECTIVE COMICS
I. W. Enterprises: 1964 (Reprints)

9-r/Young King Cole #14; Dr. Drew (not Grandenetti) 2 4 6 11 14 18

TOP DOG (See Star Comics Magazine, 75¢)
Star Comics (Marvel): Apr, 1985 - No. 14, June, 1987 (Children's book)

1-14: 10-Peter Parker & J. Jonah Jameson cameo 4.00

TOP ELIMINATOR (Teenage Hotrodders #1-24; Drag 'n' Wheels #30 on)
Charlton Comics: No. 25, Sept, 1967 - No. 29, July, 1968

25-29 3 6 9 18 23 28

TOP FLIGHT COMICS: Four Star Publ.: 1947 (Advertised, not published)

TOP FLIGHT COMICS
St. John Publishing Co.: July, 1949

1(7/49, St. John)-Hector the Inspector; funny animal 9 18 27 54 70 85

TOP GUN (See Luke Short, 4-Color #927 & Showcase #72)

TOP GUNS OF THE WEST (See Super DC Giant)

TOPIX (...Comics) (Timeless Topix-early issues) (Also see Men of Battle, Men of Courage & Treasure Chest)(V1-V5#1,V7 on-paper-c)
Catechetical Guild Educational Society: 11/42 - V10#15, 1/28/52 (Weekly - later issues)

	GD	VG	FN	VF	VF/NM	NM-
V1#1(8 pgs.,8x11")	25	50	75	144	207	270
2,3(8 pgs.,8x11")	14	28	42	79	110	140
4-8(16 pgs.,8x11")	11	22	33	64	87	110
V2#1-10(16 pgs.,8x11"): V2#8-Pope Pius XII	10	20	30	58	77	95
V3#1-10(16 pgs.,8x11"): V3#1-(9/44)	10	20	30	56	73	90
V4#1-10: V4#1-(9/45)	9	18	27	49	62	75
V5#1(10/46,52 pgs.,2(11/46),no #3),4(1/47)-9(6/47),10(7/47), no #13,4(10/47), 14(11/47),15(12/47)	8	16	24	40	50	60
11(8/47),12(9/47)-Life of Christ editions	10	20	30	56	73	90
V6#4(1/48),5(2/48),7(3/48),8(4/48),9(5/48),11(7/48)-14 (no #1-3,6,10)	7	14	21	35	43	50
V7#1(9/1/48)-20(6/15/49), 36 pgs.	6	12	18	29	36	42
V8#1(9/19/49)-3,5-11,13-30(5/15/50)	6	12	18	28	34	40
4-Dagwood Splits the Atom(10/10/49)-Magazine format	8	16	24	43	54	65
12-Ingels-a	10	20	30	56	73	90
V9#1(9/25/50)-11,13-30(5/14/51)	6	12	18	27	33	38
12-Special 36 pg. Xmas issue, text illos format	6	12	18	28	34	40
V10#1(10/1/51)-15: 14-Hollingsworth-a	6	12	18	27	33	38

TOP JUNGLE COMICS
I. W. Enterprises: 1964 (Reprint)

1(nd)-Reprints White Princess of the Jungle #3, minus cover; Kintsler-a 3 6 9 18 24 30

TOP LOVE STORIES (Formerly Gasoline Alley #2)
Star Publications: No. 3, 5/51 - No. 19, 3/54

	GD	VG	FN	VF	VF/NM	NM-
3(#1)	24	48	72	138	199	260
4,5,7-9: 8-Wood story	19	38	57	107	154	200
6-Wood-a	25	50	75	144	207	270
10-16,18,19-Disbrow-a	19	38	57	107	154	200
17-Wood art (Fox-r)	20	40	60	115	165	215

NOTE: *All have **L. B. Cole** covers.*

TOP-NOTCH COMICS (...Laugh #28-45; Laugh Comix #46 on)
MLJ Magazines: Dec, 1939 - No. 45, June, 1944

	GD	VG	FN	VF	VF/NM	NM-
1-Origin/1st app. The Wizard; Kardak the Mystic Magician, Swift of the Secret Service (ends #3), Air Patrol, The Westpointer, Manhunters (by J. Cole), Mystic (ends #2) & Scott Rand (ends #3) begin; Wizard covers begin, end #8	581	1162	1743	4067	6534	9000
2-(1/40)-Dick Storm (ends #8), Stacy Knight M.D. (ends #4) begin; Jack Cole-a; 1st app. Nazis swastika on-c	246	492	738	1538	2369	3200
3-Bob Phantom, Scott Rand on Mars begin; J. Cole-a	169	338	507	1056	1628	2200
4-Origin/1st app. Streak Chandler on Mars; Moore of the Mounted only app.; J. Cole-a	150	300	450	938	1444	1950
5-Flag-c; origin/1st app. Galahad; Shanghai Sheridan begins (ends #8); Shield cameo; Novick-a; classic-c	162	324	486	1013	1557	2100
6-Meskin-a	108	216	324	675	1038	1400
7-The Shield x-over in Wizard; The Wizard dons new costume	129	258	387	806	1241	1675
8-Origin/1st app. The Firefly & Roy, the Super Boy (9/40, 2nd costumed boy hero after Robin?; also see Toro in Human Torch #1 (Fall/40)	150	300	450	938	1444	1950
9-Origin & 1st app. The Black Hood; 1st Black Hood-c & logo (10/40); Fran Frazier begins (Scarce)	542	1084	1626	3794	6097	8400
10-2nd app. Black Hood	177	354	531	1106	1703	2300
11-15	108	216	324	675	1038	1400
16-20	94	188	282	588	907	1225
21-30: 23-26-Roy app. 24-No Wizard. 25-Last Bob Phantom. 27-Last Firefly. 28-Suzie, Pokey Oakey begin. 29-Last Kardak	69	138	207	431	666	900
31-44: 33-Dotty & Ditto by Woggon begins (2/43, 1st app.). 44-Black Hood series ends	40	80	120	239	357	475
45-Last issue	46	92	138	281	428	575

NOTE: ***J. Binder** a-1-3. **Meskin** a-2, 3, 6, 15. **Bob Montana** a-30; c-28-31. **Harry Sahle** c-42-45. **Woggon** a-33-40, 42. Bondage c-17, 19. Black Hood also appeared on radio in 1944.Black Hood app. on c-9-34, 41-44. Roy the Super Boy app. on c-8, 9, 11-27. The Wizard app. on c-1-8, 11-13, 15-22, 24, 25, 27. Pokey Oakey app. on c-28-43. Suzie app. on c-44-on.*

TOPPER & NEIL (TV)
Dell Publishing Co.: No. 859, Nov, 1957

Four Color 859 6 12 18 38 52 65

TOPPS COMICS: Four Star Publications: 1947 (Advertised, not published)

TOPS
July, 1949 - No. 2, Sept, 1949 (25¢, 10-1/4x13-1/4", 68 pgs.)
Tops Magazine, Inc. (Lev Gleason): (Large size-magazine format; for the adult reader)

1 (Rare)-Story by Dashiell Hammett; Crandall/Lubbers, Tuska, Dan Barry, Fuje-a; Biro painted-c 115 230 345 719 1110 1500
2 (Rare)-Crandall/Lubbers, Biro, Kida, Fuje, Guardineer-a 108 216 324 675 1038 1400

TOPS COMICS
Consolidated Book Publishers: 1944 (10¢, 132 pgs.)

2000-(Color-c, inside in red shade & some in full color)-Ace Kelly by Rick Yager, Black Orchid, Don on the Farm, Dinky Dinkerton (Rare) 27 54 81 152 219 285

NOTE: *This book is printed in such a way that when the staple is removed, the strips on the left side of the book correspond with the same strips on the right side. Therefore, if strips are removed from the book, each strip can be folded into a complete comic section of its own.*

TOPS COMICS (See Tops in Humor)
Consolidated Book (Lev Gleason): 1944 (7-1/4x5", 32 pgs.)

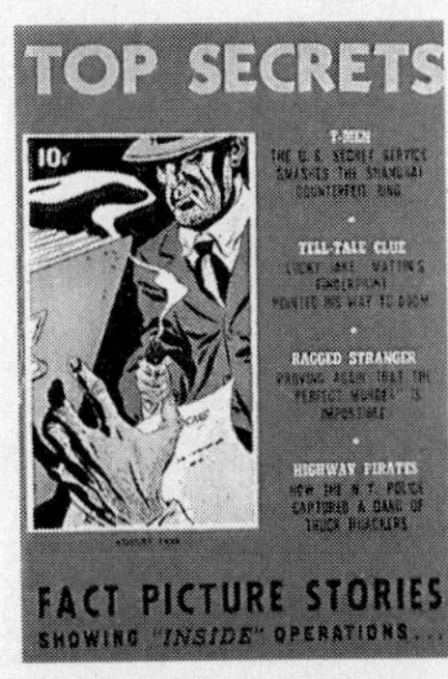

Top Secrets #4 © S&S

Total Justice #3 © DC

A Touch of Silver #1 © Jim Valentino

	GD 2.0	VG 4.0	FN 6.0	VF 8.0	VF/NM 9.0	NM- 9.2
2001-The Jack of Spades (costumed hero)	17	34	51	95	135	175
2002-Rip Raider	10	20	30	56	73	90
2003-Red Birch (gag cartoons)	5	10	14	20	24	28

TOP SECRET
Hillman Publ.: Jan, 1952

	GD	VG	FN	VF	VF/NM	NM-
1	21	42	63	118	169	220

TOP SECRET ADVENTURES (See Spyman)

TOP SECRETS (...of the F.B.I.)
Street & Smith Publications: Nov, 1947 - No. 10, July-Aug, 1949

	GD	VG	FN	VF	VF/NM	NM-
1-Powell-c/a	35	70	105	200	290	380
2-Powell-c/a	26	52	78	147	211	275
3-6,8,10-Powell-a	23	46	69	130	188	245
9-Powell-c/a	24	48	72	135	195	255
7-Used in **SOTI**, pg. 90 & illo. "How to hurt people"; used by N.Y. Legis. Comm.; Powell-c/a	35	70	105	200	290	380

NOTE: ***Powell** c-1-3, 5-10.*

TOPS IN ADVENTURE
Ziff-Davis Publishing Co.: Fall, 1952 (25¢, 132 pgs.)

	GD	VG	FN	VF	VF/NM	NM-
1-Crusader from Mars, The Hawk, Football Thrills, He-Man; Powell-a; painted-c	46	92	138	281	428	575

TOPS IN HUMOR (See Tops Comics?)
Consolidated Book Publ. (Lev Gleason): 1944 (7-1/4x5")

	GD	VG	FN	VF	VF/NM	NM-
2001(#1)-Origin The Jack of Spades, Ace Kelly by Rick Yager, Black Orchid (female crime fighter) app.	17	34	51	95	135	175
2	11	22	33	62	84	105

TOP SPOT COMICS
Top Spot Publ. Co.: 1945

	GD	VG	FN	VF	VF/NM	NM-
1-The Menace, Duke of Darkness app.	36	72	108	204	297	390

TOPSY-TURVY (Teenage)
R. B. Leffingwell Publ.: Apr, 1945

	GD	VG	FN	VF	VF/NM	NM-
1-1st app. Cookie	12	24	36	69	95	120

TOP TEN
America's Best Comics: Sept, 1999 - No. 12, Oct, 2001 ($3.50/$2.95)

	NM-
1-Two covers by Ross and Ha/Cannon; Alan Moore-s/Gene Ha-a	3.50
2-11-($2.95)	3.00
12-($3.50)	3.50
Hardcover ('00, $24.95) Dust jacket with Gene Ha-a; r/#1-7	25.00
Softcover ('00, $14.95) new Gene Ha-c; r/#1-7	15.00
Book 2 HC ('02, $24.95) Dust jacket with Gene Ha-a; r/#8-12	25.00
Book 2 SC ('03, $14.95) new Gene Ha-c; r/#8-12	15.00

TOR (Prehistoric Life on Earth) (Formerly One Million Years Ago)
St. John Publ. Co.: No. 2, Oct, 1953; No. 3, May, 1954 - No. 5, Oct, 1954

	GD	VG	FN	VF	VF/NM	NM-
3-D 2(10/53)-Kubert-c/a	14	28	42	79	110	140
3-D 2(10/53)-Oversized, otherwise same contents	12	24	36	69	95	120
3-D 2(11/53)-Kubert-c/a; has 3-D cover	12	24	36	69	95	120
3-5-Kubert-c/a: 3-Danny Dreams by Toth; Kubert 1 pg. story (w/self portrait)	14	28	42	79	110	140

NOTE: *The two October 3-D's have same contents and **Powell** art; the October & November issues are titled 3-D Comics. All 3-D issues are 25¢ and came with 3-D glasses.*

TOR (See Sojourn)
National Periodical Publications: May-June, 1975 - No. 6, Mar-Apr, 1976

	GD	VG	FN	VF	VF/NM	NM-
1-New origin by Kubert	2	4	6	8	10	12
2-6: 2-Origin-r/St. John #1						6.00

NOTE: ***Kubert** a-1, 2-6r; c-1-6. **Toth** a(p)-3r.*

TOR (3-D)
Eclipse Comics: July, 1986 - No. 2, Aug, 1987 ($2.50)

	GD	VG	FN	VF	VF/NM	NM-
1,2: 1-r/One Million Years Ago. 2-r/Tor 3-D #2						5.00
...2-D: 1,2-Limited signed & numbered editions	1	2	3	4	5	7

TOR
Marvel Comics (Epic Comics/Heavy Hitters): June, 1993 - No. 4, 1993 ($5.95, limited series)

	NM-
1-4: Joe Kubert-c/a/scripts	6.00

TOR BY JOE KUBERT
DC Comics: 2001 - Present ($49.95, hardcover with dust jacket)

	NM-
Volume 1 (2001) r/One Million Years Ago #1 & 3-D Comics #1&2 in flat color; script pages, sketch pages, proposals for TV and newspapers strips; intro. by Roy Thomas	50.00
Volume 2 (2002) r/Tor (St. John) #3-5; Danny Dreams; portfolio section	50.00
Volume 3 (2003) r/Tor (DC '75) #1; (Marvel '93) #1-4; portfolio section	50.00

TORCH OF LIBERTY SPECIAL
Dark Horse Comics (Legend): Jan, 1995 ($2.50, one-shot)

	NM-
1-Byrne scripts	2.50

TORCHY (...Blonde Bombshell) (See Dollman, Military, & Modern)
Quality Comics Group: Nov, 1949 - No. 6, Sept, 1950

	GD	VG	FN	VF	VF/NM	NM-
1-Bill Ward-c, Gil Fox-a	154	308	462	963	1482	2000
2,3-Fox-c/a	67	134	201	419	647	875
4-Fox-c/a(3), Ward-a (9 pgs.)	83	166	249	519	797	1075
5,6-Ward-c/a, 9 pgs; Fox-a(3) each	100	200	300	625	963	1300
Super Reprint #16(1964)-r/#4 with new-c	10	20	30	67	96	125

TO RIVERDALE AND BACK AGAIN (Archie Comics Presents...)
Archie Comics: 1990 ($2.50, 68 pgs.)

	NM-
nn-Byrne-c, Colan-a(p); adapts NBC TV movie	5.00

TORMENTED, THE (Becomes Surprise Adventures #3 on)
Sterling Comics: July, 1954 - No. 2, Sept, 1954

	GD	VG	FN	VF	VF/NM	NM-
1,2: Weird/horror stories	26	52	78	147	211	275

TORNADO TOM (See Mighty Midget Comics)

TORSO (See Jinx: Torso)

TOTAL ECLIPSE
Eclipse Comics: May, 1988 - No. 5, Apr, 1989 ($3.95, 52 pgs., deluxe size)

	NM-
Book 1-5: 3-Intro/1st app. new Black Terror. 4-Many copies have upside down pages and are mis-cut	4.00

TOTAL ECLIPSE
Image Comics: July, 1998 (one-shot)

	NM-
1-McFarlane-c; Eclipse Comics character pin-ups by Image artists	2.25

TOTAL ECLIPSE: THE SERAPHIM OBJECTIVE
Eclipse Comics: Nov, 1988 ($1.95, one-shot, Baxter paper)

	NM-
1-Airboy, Valkyrie, The Heap app.	3.00

TOTAL JUSTICE
DC Comics: Oct, 1996 - No. 3, Nov, 1996 ($2.25, bi-weekly limited series) (Based on toyline)

	NM-
1-3	2.25

TOTAL RECALL (Movie)
DC Comics: 1990 ($2.95, 68 pgs., movie adaptation, one-shot)

	NM-
1-Arnold Schwarzenegger photo-c	3.00

TOTAL WAR (M.A.R.S. Patrol #3 on)
Gold Key: July, 1965 - No. 2, Oct, 1965 (Painted-c)

	GD	VG	FN	VF	VF/NM	NM-
1-Wood-a in both issues	8	16	24	55	78	100
2	6	12	18	43	59	75

TOTEMS (Vertigo V2K)
DC Comics (Vertigo): Feb, 2000 ($5.95, one-shot)

	NM-
1-Swamp Thing, Animal Man, Zatanna, Shade app.; Fegredo-c	6.00

TO THE HEART OF THE STORM
Kitchen Sink Press: 1991 (B&W, graphic novel)

	NM-
Softcover-Will Eisner-s/a/c	15.00
Hardcover ($24.95)	25.00
TPB-(DC Comics, 9/00, $14.95) reprints 1991 edition	15.00

TO THE LAST MAN (See Zane Grey Four Color #616)

TOUCH
DC Comics (Focus): Jun, 2004 - No. 6, Nov, 2004 ($2.50)

	NM-
1-6-J.F. Moore-s/Wes Craig-a	2.50

TOUCH OF SILVER, A
Image Comics: Jan, 1997 - No. 6, Nov, 1997 ($2.95, B&W, bi-monthly)

	NM-
1-6-Valentino-s/a; photo-c: 5-color pgs. w/Round Table	3.00
TPB ($12.95) r/#1-6	13.00

TOUGH KID SQUAD COMICS
Timely Comics (TCI): Mar, 1942

	GD	VG	FN	VF	VF/NM	NM-
1-(Scarce)-Origin & 1st app.The Human Top & The Tough Kid Squad; The Flying Flame app.	968	1936	2904	6776	10,888	15,000

TOWER OF SHADOWS (Creatures on the Loose #10 on)
Marvel Comics Group: Sept, 1969 - No. 9, Jan, 1971

	GD	VG	FN	VF	VF/NM	NM-
1-Classic Romita-c, Steranko, Craig-a(p)	7	14	21	50	68	85
2,3: 2-Neal Adams-a. 3-Barry Smith, Tuska-a	4	8	12	25	33	42
4,6: 4-Marie Severin-c. 6-Wood-a	3	6	9	19	25	32

Toyland Comics #3 © FH

Transformers #8 © Hasbro

Transformers/G.I. Joe #3 © Hasbro

GD 2.0 | VG 4.0 | FN 6.0 | VF 8.0 | VF/NM 9.0 | NM- 9.2

5-B. Smith-a(p), Wood-a; Wood draws himself (1st pg., 1st panel) 3 7 10 21 28 35
7-9: 7-B. Smith-a(p), Wood-a. 8-Wood-a; Wrightson-c. 9-Wrightson-c; Roy Thomas app. 4 8 12 25 33 42
Special 1(12/71, 52 pgs.)-Neal Adams-a; Romita-c 3 7 10 21 28 35
NOTE: *J. Buscema a-1p, 2p, Special 1r. Colan a-3p, 6p, Special 1. J. Craig a(r)-1p. Ditko a-6, 8, 9r, Special 1. Everett a-9(i)r; c-5i. Kirby a-9(p)r. Severin c-5p, 6. Steranko a-1p. Tuska a-3. Wood a-5-8. Issues 1-9 contain new stories with some pre-Marvel age reprints in 6-9. H. P. Lovecraft adaptation-9.*

TOWN & COUNTRY
Publisher?: May, 1940
nn-Origin The Falcon 46 92 138 281 428 575

TOXIC AVENGER (Movie)
Marvel Comics: Apr, 1991 - No. 11, Feb, 1992 ($1.50)
1-11: Based on movie character. 3,10-Photo-c 2.25

TOXIC CRUSADERS (TV)
Marvel Comics: May, 1992 - No. 8, Dec, 1992 ($1.25)
1-8: 1-3,8-Sam Kieth-c; based on USA network cartoon 2.25

TOXIC GUMBO
DC Comics (Vertigo): 1998 ($5.95, one-shot, mature)
1-McKeever-a/Lydia Lunch-s 6.00

TOYBOY
Continuity Comics: Oct, 1986 - No. 7, Mar, 1989 ($2.00, Baxter paper)
1-7 3.00
NOTE: *N. Adams a-1; c-1, 2,5. Golden a-7p; c-6,7. Nebres a(i)-1,2.*

TOYLAND COMICS
Fiction House Magazines: Jan, 1947 - No. 2, Mar, 1947; No. 3, July, 1947
1-Wizard of the Moon begins 31 62 93 175 253 330
2,3-Bob Lubbers-c. 3-Tuska-a 17 34 51 95 135 175
NOTE: *All above contain strips by Al Walker.*

TOY TOWN COMICS
Toytown/Orbit Publ./B. Antin/Swapper Quarterly: 1945 - No. 7, May, 1947
1-Mertie Mouse; L. B. Cole-c/a; funny animal 40 80 120 235 348 460
2-L. B. Cole-a 24 48 72 138 199 260
3-7-L. B. Cole-a. 5-Wiggles the Wonderworm-c 21 42 63 118 169 220

TRAGG AND THE SKY GODS (See Gold Key Spotlight, Mystery Comics Digest #3,9 & Spine Tingling Tales)
Gold Key/Whitman No. 9: June, 1975 - No. 8, Feb, 1977; No. 9, May, 1982 (Painted-c #3-8)
1-Origin 2 4 6 11 14 18
2-8: 4-Sabre-Fang app. 8-Ostellon app. 1 3 4 6 8 10
9-(Whitman, 5/82) r/#1 1 2 3 5 7 9
NOTE: *Santos a-1, 2, 9r; c-3-7. Spiegel a-3-8.*

TRAIL BLAZERS (Red Dragon #5 on)
Street & Smith Publications: 1941; No. 2, Apr, 1942 - No. 4, Oct, 1942 (True stories of American heroes)
1-Life story of Jack Dempsey & Wright Brothers 36 72 108 204 297 390
2-Brooklyn Dodgers-c/story; Ben Franklin story 23 46 69 130 188 245
3,4: 3-Fred Allen, Red Barber, Yankees stories 21 42 63 121 173 225

TRAIL COLT (Also see Extra Comics & Manhunt!)
Magazine Enterprises: 1949 - No. 2, 1949
nn(A-1 #24)-7 pg. Frazetta-a r-in Manhunt #13; Undercover Girl app.; The Red Fox by L. B. Cole; Ingels-c; Whitney-a (Scarce) 40 80 120 233 342 450
2(A-1 #26)-Undercover Girl; Ingels-c; L. B. Cole-a (6 pgs.) 34 68 102 193 279 365

TRAKK: MONSTER HUNTER (Stan Winston's...)
Image Comics: Sept, 2003 - Present ($2.95)
1,2-Two covers by Tan & Bisley; Tan-a 3.00

TRANSFORMERS, THE (TV)(See G.I. Joe and...)
Marvel Comics Group: Sept, 1984 - No. 80, July, 1991 (75¢/$1.00)
1-Based on Hasbro Toys 2 4 6 10 12 15
2-5: 2-Golden-c. 3-Spider-Man (black costume)-c/app. 4-Texeira-c 1 3 4 6 8 10
6-10 6.00
11-49: 21-Intro Aerialbots 4.00
50-60: 53-Jim Lee-c. 54-Intro Micromasters 6.00
61-70: 67-Jim Lee-c 1 3 4 6 8 10
71-77: 75-($1.50, 52 pgs.) (Low print run) 2 4 6 11 14 18
78,79 (Low print run) 3 6 9 18 23 28

GD 2.0 | VG 4.0 | FN 6.0 | VF 8.0 | VF/NM 9.0 | NM- 9.2

80-Last issue 4 8 12 22 30 38
NOTE: *Second and third printings of most early issues (1-9?) exist and are worth less than originals. Was originally planned as a four issue mini-series. Wrightson a-64i(4 pgs.).*

TRANSFORMERS ARMADA (Continues as Transformers Energon with #19) (Also see Promotional Comics section for FCBD Ed.)
Dreamwave Productions: July, 2002 - No. 18, Dec, 2003 ($2.95)
1-Sarracini-s/Raiz-a; wraparound gatefold-c 3.00
2-18 3.00
Vol. 1 TPB (2003, $13.95) r/#1-5 14.00
Vol. 2 TPB (2003, $15.95) r/#6-11 16.00

TRANSFORMERS ARMADA: MORE THAN MEETS THE EYE
Dreamwave Productions: Mar, 2004 - No. 3, May, 2004 ($4.95, limited series)
1-3-Pin-ups with tech info; art by Pat Lee & various 5.00

TRANSFORMERS COMICS MAGAZINE
Marvel Comics: Oct, 1986 - No. 11, 1988 ($1.50, digest size)
1-11: 2-Spider-Man-c/s 4.00

TRANSFORMERS DIGEST
Marvel Comics: Jan, 1987 - No. 10, July, 1988
1,2-Spider-Man-c/s 2 4 6 10 12 15
3-10 2 4 6 8 10 12

TRANSFORMERS ENERGON (Continued from Transformers Armada #18)
Dreamwave Productions: No. 19, Jan, 2004 - Present ($2.95)
19-29-Furman-s 3.00

TRANSFORMERS: GENERATION 1
Dreamwave Productions: Apr, 2002 - No. 6, Oct, 2002 ($2.95)
Preview- 6 pg. story; robot sketch pages; Pat Lee-a 2.00
1-Pat Lee-a; 2 wraparound covers by Lee 4.00
2-6: 2-Optimus Prime reactivated; 2 covers by Pat Lee 3.00
...Vol. 1 HC (2003, $49.95) r/#1-6; black hardcover with red foil lettering and art 50.00
...Vol. 1 TPB (2002, $17.95) r/#1-6 plus six page preview; 8 pg. preview of future issues 18.00

TRANSFORMERS: GENERATION 1 (Volume 2)
Dreamwave Productions: Apr, 2003 - No. 6, Sept, 2003 ($2.95)
1-6: 1-Pat Lee-a; 2 wraparound gatefold covers by Lee 3.00
1-($5.95) Chrome wraparound variant-c 6.00

TRANSFORMERS: GENERATION 1 (Volume 3)
Dreamwave Productions: No. 0, Dec, 2003 - Present ($2.95)
0-10: 0-Pat Lee-a. 1-Figueroa-a; wrapaound-c 3.00

TRANSFORMERS: GENERATION 2
Marvel Comics: Nov, 1993 - No. 12, Oct, 1994 ($1.75)
1-($2.95, 68 pgs.)-Collector's ed. w/bi-fold metallic-c 1 2 3 5 6 8
1-11: 1-Newsstand edition (68 pgs.) 6.00
12-($2.25, 52 pgs.) 1 2 3 5 6 8

TRANSFORMERS/G.I. JOE
Dreamwave Productions: Aug, 2003 - No. 6, Mar, 2004 ($2.95/$5.25)
1-Art & gatefold wraparound-c by Jae Lee; Ney Rieber-s; variant-c by Pat Lee 3.00
1-($5.95) Holofoil wraparound-c by Norton 6.00
2-6-Jae Lee-a/c 3.00
TPB (8/04, $17.95) r/#1-6; cover gallery and sketch pages 18.00

TRANSFORMERS/G.I. JOE: DIVIDED FRONT
Dreamwave Productions: Oct, 2004 - Present ($2.95)
1-Art & gatefold wraparound-c by Pat Lee 3.00

TRANSFORMERS: HEADMASTERS
Marvel Comics Group: July, 1987 - No. 4, Jan, 1988 ($1.00, limited series)
1-Springer, Akin, Garvey-a 4.00
2-4-Springer-c on all 3.00

TRANSFORMERS: MICROMASTERS
Dreamwave Productions: June, 2004 - No. 4 ($2.95, limited series)
1-4-Ruffolo-a; Pat Lee-c 3.00

TRANSFORMERS: MORE THAN MEETS THE EYE
Dreamwave Productions: Apr, 2003 - No. 8, Nov, 2003 ($5.25)
1-8-Pin-ups with tech info on Autobots and Decepticons; art by Pat Lee & various 5.25
Vol. 1 TPB (2004, $24.95) r/#1-4 25.00

TRANSFORMERS SUMMER SPECIAL
Dreamwave Productions: May, 2004 ($4.95)
1-Pat Lee-a; Figueroa-a 5.00

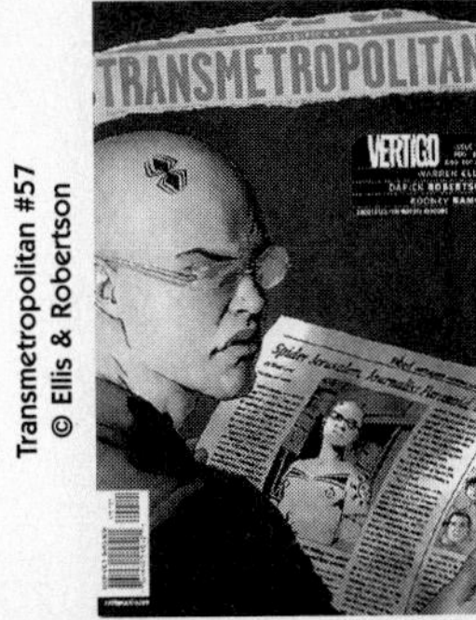

Transmetropolitan #57 © Ellis & Robertson

Treasure Comics #9 © PRIZE

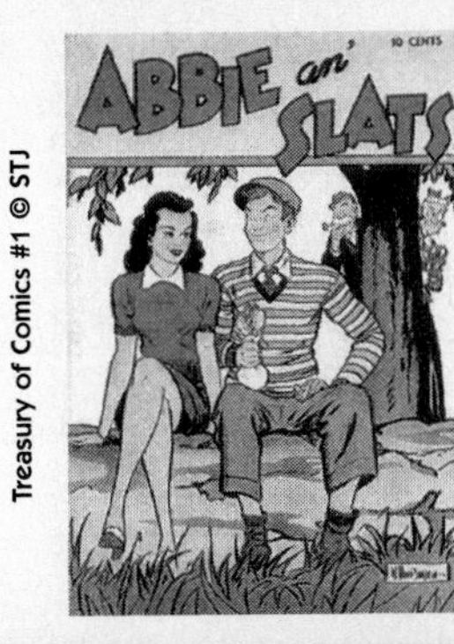

Treasury of Comics #1 © STJ

GD 2.0 | VG 4.0 | FN 6.0 | VF 8.0 | VF/NM 9.0 | NM- 9.2

TRANSFORMERS, THE MOVIE
Marvel Comics Group: Dec, 1986 - No. 3, Feb, 1987 (75¢, limited series)
1-3-Adapts animated movie 3.00

TRANSFORMERS: THE WAR WITHIN
Dreamwave Productions: Oct, 2002 - No. 6, Mar, 2003 ($2.95)
1-6-Furman-s/Figueroa-a. 1-Wraparound gatefold-c 3.00
TPB (2003, $15.95) r/#1-6; plus cover gallery 16.00

TRANSFORMERS UNIVERSE
Marvel Comics Group: Dec, 1986 - No. 4, Mar, 1987 ($1.25, limited series)
1-4-A guide to all characters 4.00

TRANSFORMERS WAR WITHIN: THE AGE OF WRATH
Dreamwave Productions: Sept, 2004 - No. 6 ($2.95, limited series)
1-3-Furman-s/Ng-a 3.00

TRANSFORMERS WAR WITHIN: THE DARK AGES
Dreamwave Productions: Oct, 2003 - No. 6 ($2.95)
1-6: 1-Furman-s/Wildman-a; two covers by Pat Lee & Figueroa 3.00
TPB (2004, $17.95) r/#1-6; plus cover gallery and design sketches 18.00

TRANSIT
Vortex Publ.: March, 1987 - No. 5, Nov, 1987 (B&W)
1-5-Ted McKeever-s/a 1 2 3 5 6 8

TRANSMETROPOLITAN
DC Comics (Vertigo): Sept, 1997 - No. 60, Nov, 2002 ($2.50)
1-Warren Ellis-s/Darick Robertson-a(p) 2 4 6 8 10 12
2,3 1 2 3 4 5 7
4-8 4.00
9-60: 15-Jae Lee-c. 25-27-Jim Lee-c. 37-39-Bradstreet-c 2.50
Back on the Street ('97, $7.95) r/#1-3 8.00
Dirge ('03, $14.95) r/#43-48 15.00
Filth of the City ('01, $5.95) Spider's columns with pin-up art by various 6.00
Gouge Away ('02, $14.95) r/#31-36 15.00
I Hate It Here ('00, $5.95) Spider's columns with pin-up art by various 6.00
Lonely City ('01, $14.95) r/#25-30; intro. by Patrick Stewart 15.00
Lust For Life ('98, $14.95) r/#4-12 15.00
One More Time ('04, $14.95) r/#55-60 15.00
Spider's Thrash ('02, $14.95) r/#37-42; intro. by Darren Aronofsky 15.00
Tales of Human Waste ('04, $9.95) r/Filth of the City, I Hate It Here & story from Vertigo Winter's Edge 2 10.00
The Cure ('03, $14.95) r/#49-54 15.00
The New Scum ('00, $12.95) r/#19-24 & Vertigo: Winter's Edge #3 13.00
Year of the Bastard ('99, $12.95) r/#13-18 13.00

TRANSMUTATION OF IKE GARUDA, THE
Marvel Comics (Epic Comics): July, 1991 - No. 2, 1991 ($3.95, 52 pgs.)
1,2 4.00

TRAPMAN
Phantom Comics: June, 1994 - No. 2, 1994? ($2.95, quarterly, unfinished limited series)
1,2 3.00

TRAPPED!
Periodical House Magazines (Ace): Oct, 1954 - No. 4, April, 1955
1 (All reprints) 10 20 30 56 73 90
2-4: 4-r/Men Against Crime #4 in its entirety 7 14 21 35 43 50
NOTE: ***Colan** a-1, 4. **Sekowsky** a-1.*

TRASH
Trash Publ. Co.: Mar, 1978 - No. 4, Oct, 1978 (B&W, magazine, 52 pgs.)
1,2: 1-Star Wars parody. 2-UFO-c 2 4 6 10 13 16
3-Parodies of KISS, the Beatles, and monsters 2 4 6 14 18 22
4-(84 pgs.)-Parodies of Happy Days, Rocky movies 3 6 9 16 20 24

TRAVELS OF JAIMIE McPHEETERS, THE (TV)
Gold Key: Dec, 1963
1-Kurt Russell photo on-c plus photo back-c 4 8 12 27 36 48

TREASURE CHEST (Catholic Guild; also see Topix)
George A. Pflaum: 3/12/46 - V27#8, July, 1972 (Educational comics)
(Not published during Summer)
V1#1 26 52 78 150 215 280
2-6 (5/21/46): 5-Dr. Styx app. by Baily 12 24 36 71 98 125
V2#1-20 (9/3/46-5/27/47) 10 20 30 56 73 90
V3#1-5,7-20 (1st slick cover) 9 18 27 52 66 80
V3#6-Jules Verne's "Voyage to the Moon" 11 22 33 62 84 105
V4#1-20 (9/9/48-5/31/49) 8 16 24 46 58 70
V5#1-20 (9/6/49-5/31/50) 8 16 24 43 54 65
V6#1-20 (9/14/50-5/31/51) 8 16 24 40 50 60
V7#1-20 (9/13/51-6/5/52) 7 14 21 37 46 55
V8#1-20 (9/11/52-6/4/53) 7 14 21 35 43 50
V9#1-20 ('53-'54), V10#1-20 ('54-'55) 6 12 18 31 38 45
V11('55-'56), V12('56-'57) 6 12 18 28 34 40
V13#1,3-5,7,9-V17#1 ('57-'63) 5 10 15 24 30 35
V13#2,6,8-Ingels-a 7 14 21 50 68 85
V17#2- "This Godless Communism" series begins(not in odd #'d issues); cover shows hammer & sickle over Statue of Liberty; 8 pg. Crandall-a of family life under communism 18 36 54 126 193 260
V17#3,5,7,9,11,13,15,17,19 3 6 9 18 23 28
V17#4,6,14- "This Godless Communism" stories 12 24 36 86 131 175
V17#8-Shows red octopus encompassing Earth, firing squad; 8 pgs. Crandall-a 15 30 45 105 160 215
V17#10- "This Godless Communism" - how Stalin came to power, part I; Crandall-a 14 28 42 97 149 200
V17#12-Stalin in WWII, forced labor, death by exhaustion; Crandall-a 14 28 42 97 149 200
V17#16-Kruschev takes over; de-Stalinization 14 28 42 97 149 200
V17#18-Kruschev's control; murder of revolters, brainwash, space race by Crandall 14 28 42 97 149 200
V17#20-End of series; Kruschev-people are puppets, firing squads hammer & sickle over Statue of Liberty, snake around communist manifesto by Crandall 17 34 51 119 182 245
V18#1-20, V19#11-20, V20#1-20(1964-65): V18#11-Crandall draws himself & 13 other artists on cover 3 6 9 16 20 25
V18#5- "What About Red China?" - describes how communists took over China 7 14 21 51 71 90
V19#1-10- "Red Victim" anti-communist series in all 7 14 21 51 71 90
V21-V25(1965-70)-(two V24#5's 11/7/68 & 11/21/68) (no V24#6) 2 4 6 14 18 22
V26, V27#1-8 (V26,27-68 pgs.) 3 6 9 16 20 25
Summer Edition V1#1-6('66), V2#1-6('67) 3 6 9 18 23 28
NOTE: ***Anderson** a-V18#13. **Borth** a-V7#10-19 (serial), V8#8-17 (serial), V9#1-10 (serial), V13#2, 6, 11, V14-V25 (except V22#1-3, 11-13), Summer Ed. V1#3-6. **Crandall** a-V16#7, 9, 12, 14, 16-18, 20; V17#1, 2, 4-6, 10, 12, 14, 16-18, 20; V18#1, 2, 3(2 pg.), 7, 9-20; V19#4, 11, 13, 16, 19, 20; V20#1, 2, 4, 6, 8-10, 12, 14-16, 18, 20; V21#1-5, 8-11, 13, 16-18; V22#3, 7, 9-11, 14; V23#3, 6, 9, 16, 18; V24#7, 8, 10, 13, 16; V25#8, 16; V27#1-7r, 8r(2 pg.), Summer Ed. V1#3-5, V2#3; c-V16#7, V18#2(part), 7, 11, V19#4, 19, 20, V20#15, V21#5, 9, V22#3, 7, 9, 11, V23#9, 16, V24#13, 16, V25#8, Summer Ed. V1#2 (back c-V1#2-5). **Powell** a-V10#11. V19#11, 15, V10#13, V13#6, 8 all have wraparound covers.*

TREASURE CHEST OF THE WORLD'S BEST COMICS
Superior, Toronto, Canada: 1945 (500 pgs., hard-c)
Contains Blue Beetle, Captain Combat, John Wayne, Dynamic Man, Nemo, Li'l Abner; contents can vary - represents random binding of extra books; Capt. America on-c 89 178 267 556 853 1150

TREASURE COMICS
Prize Publications? (no publisher listed): No date (1943) (50¢, 324 pgs., cardboard-c)
1-(Rare)-Contains rebound Prize Comics #7-11 from 1942 (blank inside-c) 223 446 669 1394 2147 2900

TREASURE COMICS
Prize Publ. (American Boys' Comics): June-July, 1945 - No. 12, Fall, 1947
1-Paul Bunyan & Marco Polo begin; Highwayman & Carrot Topp only app.; Kiefer-a 44 88 132 268 409 550
2-Arabian Knight, Gorilla King, Dr. Styx begin 26 52 78 147 211 275
3,4,9,12: 9-Kiefer-a 19 38 57 107 154 200
5-Marco Polo-c; Krigstein-a 26 52 78 150 215 280
6,11-Krigstein-a; 11-Krigstein-c 24 48 72 138 199 260
7,8-Frazetta-a (5 pgs. each). 7-Capt. Kidd Jr. app. 40 80 120 241 363 485
10-Simon & Kirby-c/a 35 70 105 198 287 375
NOTE: ***Barry** a-9-11; c-12. **Kiefer** a-3, 5, 7; c-2, 6, 7. **Roussos** a-11.*

TREASURE ISLAND (See Classics Illustrated #64, Doc Savage Comics #1, King Classics, Movie Classics & Movie Comics)
Dell Publishing Co.: No. 624, Apr, 1955 (Disney)
Four Color 624-Movie, photo-c 10 20 30 67 96 125

TREASURY OF COMICS
St. John Publishing Co.: 1947; No. 2, July, 1947 - No. 4, Sept, 1947; No. 5, Jan, 1948
nn(#1)-Abbie an' Slats (nn on-c, #1 on inside) 14 28 42 79 110 140
2-Jim Hardy Comics; featuring Windy & Paddles 11 22 33 62 84 105
3-Bill Bumlin 9 18 27 54 70 85

Treehouse of Horror #10 © Bongo

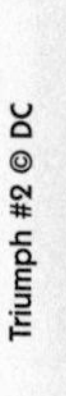
Triumph #2 © DC

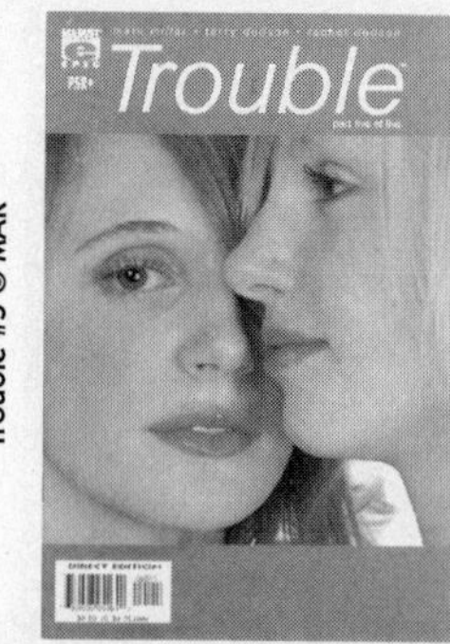

Trouble #5 © MAR

	GD 2.0	VG 4.0	FN 6.0	VF 8.0	VF/NM 9.0	NM- 9.2
4-Abbie an' Slats	11	22	33	62	84	105
5-Jim Hardy Comics #1	11	22	33	63	84	105

TREASURY OF COMICS
St. John Publishing Co.: Mar, 1948 - No. 5, 1948 (Reg. size); 1948-1950 (Over 500 pgs., $1.00)

	GD	VG	FN	VF	VF/NM	NM-
1	20	40	60	112	161	210
2(#2 on-c, #1 on inside)	11	22	33	62	84	105
3-5	10	20	30	56	73	90
1-(1948, 500 pgs., hard-c)-Abbie & Slats, Abbott & Costello, Casper, Little Annie Rooney, Little Audrey, Jim Hardy, Ella Cinders (16 books bound together) (Rare)	108	216	324	675	1038	1400
1(1949, 500 pgs.)-Same format as above	100	200	300	625	963	1300
1(1950, 500 pgs.)-Same format as above; different-c; (also see Little Audrey Yearbook) (Rare)	100	200	300	625	963	1300

TREASURY OF DOGS, A (See Dell Giants)

TREASURY OF HORSES, A (See Dell Giants)

TREEHOUSE OF HORROR (Bart Simpson's...)
Bongo Comics: 1995 - Present ($2.95/$2.50/$3.50/$4.50, annual)

1-(1995, $2.95)-Groening-c; Allred, Robinson & Smith stories 3.50
2-(1996, $2.50)-Stories by Dini & Bagge; infinity-c by Groening 3.00
3-(1997, $2.50)-Dorkin-s/Groening-c 3.00
4-(1998, $2.50)-Lash & Dixon-s/Groening-c 3.00
5-(1999, $3.50)-Thompson-s; Shaw & Aragonés-s/a; TenNapel-s/a 3.50
6-(2000, $4.50)-Mahfood-s/a; DeCarlo-a; Morse-s/a; Kuper-s/a 4.50
7-(2001, $4.50)-Hamill-s/Morrison-a; Ennis-s/McCrea-a; Sakai-s/a; Nixey-s/a; Brereton back-c 4.50
8-(2002, $3.50)-Templeton, Shaw, Barta, Simone, Thompson-s/a 3.50
9-(2003, $4.99)-Lord of the Rings-Brereton-a; Dini, Naifeh, Millidge, Boothby, Noto-s/a 5.00
10-(2004, $4.99)-Monsters of Rock w/Alice Cooper, Gene Simmons, Rob Zombie and Pat Boone; art by Rodriguez, Morrison, Morse, Templeton 5.00

TREKKER (See Dark Horse Presents #6)
Dark Horse Comics: May, 1987 - No. 6, Mar,1988 ($1.50, B&W)

1-6: Sci/Fi stories 2.25
Color Special 1 (1989, $2.95, 52 pgs.) 3.00
Collection ($5.95, B&W) 6.00
Special 1 (6/99, $2.95, color) 3.00

TRENCHCOAT BRIGADE, THE
DC Comics (Vertigo): Mar, 1999 - No. 4, Jun, 1999 ($2.50, limited series)

1-4: Hellblazer, Phantom Stranger, Mister E, Dr. Occult app. 2.50

TRENCHER (See Blackball Comics)
Image Comics: May, 1993 - No. 4, Oct, 1993 ($1.95, unfinished limited series)

1-4: Keith Giffen-c/a/scripts. 3-Supreme-c/story 2.25

TRIBAL FORCE
Mystic Comics: Aug, 1996 ($2.50)

1-Reads "Special Edition" on-c 2.50

TRIB COMIC BOOK, THE
Winnipeg Tribune: Sept. 24, 1977 - Vol. 4, #36, 1980 (8-1/2"x11", 24 pgs., weekly) (155 total issues)

	GD	VG	FN	VF	VF/NM	NM-
V1# 1-Color pages (Sunday strips)-Spiderman, Asterix, Disney's Scamp, Wizard of Id, Doonesbury, Inside Woody Allen, Mary Worth, & others (similar to Spirit sections)	2	4	6	12	14	18
V1#2-15, V2#1-52, V3#1-52, V4#1-33	1	3	4	6	8	10
V4#34-36 (not distributed)	2	4	6	12	16	20

NOTE: *All issues have Spider-Man. Later issues contain Star Trek and Star Wars. 20 strips in ea. The first newspaper to put Sunday pages into a comic book format.*

TRIBE (See WildC.A.T.S #4)
Image Comics/Axis Comics No. 2 on: Apr, 1993; No. 2, Sept, 1993 - No. 3, 1994 ($2.50/$1.95)

1-By Johnson & Stroman; gold foil & embossed on black-c 2.50
1-($2.50)-Ivory Edition; gold foil & embossed on white-c; available only through the creators 2.50
2,3: 2-1st Axis Comics issue. 3-Savage Dragon app. 2.25

TRIBUTE TO STEVEN HUGHES, A
Chaos! Comics: Sept, 2000 ($6.95)

1-Lady Death & Evil Ernie pin-ups by various artists; testimonials 7.00

TRIGGER (See Roy Rogers'...)

TRIGGER
DC Comics (Vertigo): Feb, 2005 - Present ($2.95)

1-Jason Hall-s/John Watkiss-a/c 3.00

TRIGGER TWINS
National Periodical Publications: Mar-Apr, 1973 (20¢, one-shot)

	GD	VG	FN	VF	VF/NM	NM-
1-Trigger Twins & Pow Wow Smith-r/All-Star Western #94,103 & Western Comics #81; Infantino-r(p)	2	4	6	14	18	22

TRINITY (See DC Universe: Trinity)

TRINITY ANGELS
Acclaim Comics (Valiant Heroes): July, 1997 - No. 12, June, 1998 ($2.50)

1-12-Maguire-s/a(p):4-Copycat-c 3.00

TRIPLE GIANT COMICS (See Archie All-Star Specials under Archie Comics)

TRIPLE THREAT
Special Action/Holyoke/Gerona Publ.: Winter, 1945

	GD	VG	FN	VF	VF/NM	NM-
1-Duke of Darkness, King O'Leary	31	62	93	178	259	340

TRIPLE-X
Dark Horse Comics: Dec, 1994 - No. 7, June, 1995 ($3.95, B&W, limited series)

1-7 4.00

TRIUMPH (Also see JLA #28-30, Justice League Task Force & Zero Hour)
DC Comics: June, 1995 - No. 4, Sept, 1995 ($1.75, limited series)

1-4: 3-Hourman, JLA app. 2.25

TRIUMPHANT UNLEASHED
Triumphant Comics: No. 0, Nov, 1993 - No. 1, Nov, 1993 ($2.50, lim. series)

0-Serially numbered, 0-Red logo, 0-White logo (no cover price; giveaway), 1-Cover is negative & reverse of #0-c 2.50

TROLL (Also see Brigade)
Image Comics (Extreme Studios): Dec, 1993 ($2.50, one-shot, 44 pgs.)

1-1st app. Troll; Liefeld scripts; Matsuda-c/a(p) 2.50
Halloween Special (1994, $2.95)-Maxx app. 3.00
...Once A Hero (8/94, $2.50) 2.50

TROLLORDS
Tru Studios/Comico V2#1 on: 2/86 - No. 15, 1988; V2#1, 11/88 - V2#4, 1989 (1-15: $1.50, B&W)

1-15: 1-Both printings. 6-Christmas issue; silver logo 2.50
V2#1-4 ($1.75, color, Comico) 2.50
Special 1 ($1.75, 2/87, color)-Jerry's Big Fun Bk. 2.50

TROLLORDS
Apple Comics: July, 1989 - No. 6, 1990 ($2.25, B&W, limited series)

1-6: 1-"The Big Batman Movie Parody" 2.50

TROLL PATROL
Harvey Comics: Jan, 1993 ($1.95, 52 pgs.)

1 2.25

TROLL II (Also see Brigade)
Image Comics (Extreme Studios): July, 1994 ($3.95, one-shot)

1 4.00

TROUBLE
Marvel Comics (Epic): Sept, 2003 - No. 5, Jan, 2004 ($2.99, limited series)

1-Photo-c; Richard and Ben meet Mary and May; Millar-s/Dodson-a 3.00
1-2nd printing with variant Frank Cho-c 3.00
2-5 3.00

TROUBLED SOULS
Fleetway: 1990 ($9.95, trade paperback)

nn-Garth Ennis scripts & John McCrea painted-c/a. 10.00

TROUBLE MAGNET
DC Comics: Feb, 2000 - No. 4, May, 2000 ($2.50, limited series)

1-4-Windham-s/Plunkett-a 2.50

TROUBLEMAKERS
Acclaim Comics (Valiant Heroes): Apr, 1997 - No. 19, June, 1998 ($2.50)

1-19: Fabian Nicieza scripts in all. 1-1st app. XL, Rebound & Blur; 2 covers. 8-Copycat-c. 12-Shooting of Parker 2.50

TROUBLEMAN
Image Comics (Motown Machineworks): June, 1996 - No. 3, Aug, 1996 ($2.25, lim. series)

1-3 2.25

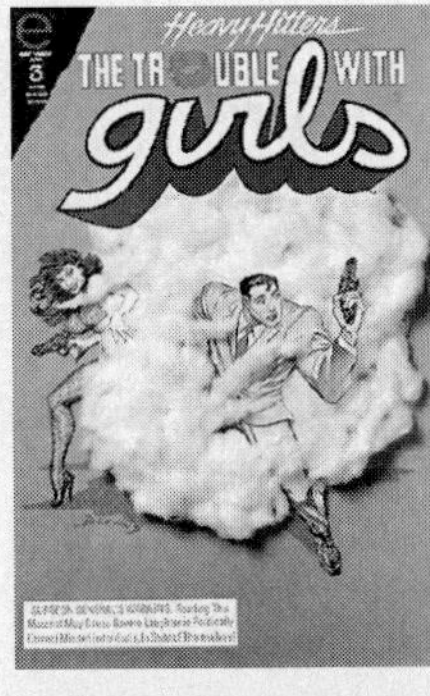

The Trouble With Girls: Night of the Lizard #3 © Gerald Jones

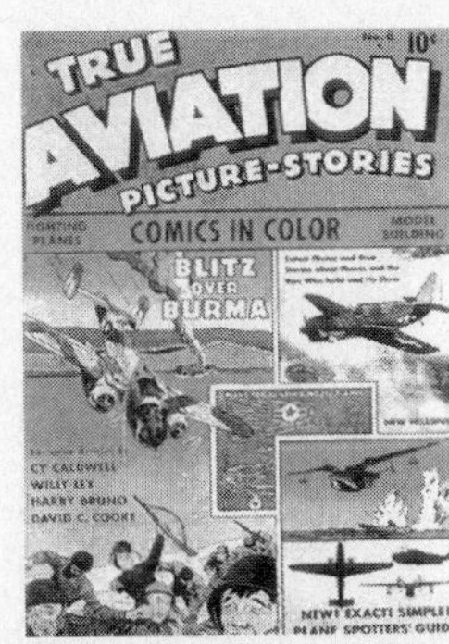

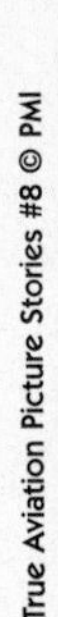
True Aviation Picture Stories #8 © PMI

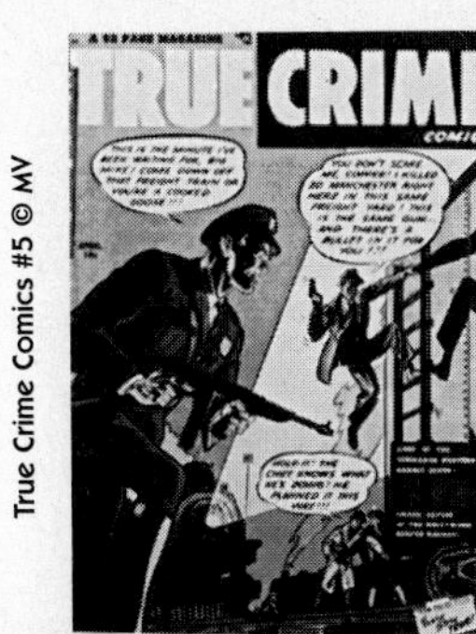

True Crime Comics #5 © MV

TROUBLE SHOOTERS, THE (TV)
Dell Publishing Co.: No. 1108, Jun-Aug, 1960

	GD 2.0	VG 4.0	FN 6.0	VF 8.0	VF/NM 9.0	NM- 9.2
Four Color 1108-Keenan Wynn photo-c	6	12	18	43	59	75

TROUBLE WITH GIRLS, THE
Malibu Comics (Eternity Comics) #7-14/Comico V2#1-4/Eternity V2#5 on: 8/87 - #14, 1988; V2#1, 2/89 - V2#23, 1991? ($1.95, B&W/color)

	GD 2.0	VG 4.0	FN 6.0	VF 8.0	VF/NM 9.0	NM- 9.2
1-14 ($1.95, B&W, Eternity)-Gerard Jones scripts & Tim Hamilton-c/a in all.						2.25
V2#1-23-Jones scripts, Hamilton-c/a.						2.25
Annual 1 (1988, $2.95)						3.00
Christmas Special 1 (12/91, $2.95, B&W, Eternity)-Jones scripts, Hamilton-c/a						3.00
Graphic Novel 1,2 (7/88, B&W)-r/#1-3 & #4-6						8.00

TROUBLE WITH GIRLS, THE: NIGHT OF THE LIZARD
Marvel Comics (Epic Comics/Heavy Hitters): 1993 - No. 4, 1993 ($2.50/$1.95, lim. series)

	GD 2.0	VG 4.0	FN 6.0	VF 8.0	VF/NM 9.0	NM- 9.2
1-Embossed-c; Gerard Jones scripts & Bret Blevins-c/a in all						2.50
2-4: 2-Begin $1.95-c.						2.25

TROUT
Oni Press: Oct, 2001 - No. 2, Feb, 2002 ($2.95, B&W, limited series)

	GD 2.0	VG 4.0	FN 6.0	VF 8.0	VF/NM 9.0	NM- 9.2
1,2-Troy Nixey-s/a						3.00

TRUE ADVENTURES (Formerly True Western)(Men's Adventures #4 on)
Marvel Comics (CCC): No. 3, May, 1950 (52 pgs.)

	GD 2.0	VG 4.0	FN 6.0	VF 8.0	VF/NM 9.0	NM- 9.2
3-Powell, Sekowsky-a; Brodsky-c	17	34	51	95	135	175

TRUE ANIMAL PICTURE STORIES
True Comics Press: Winter, 1947 - No. 2, Spring-Summer, 1947

	GD 2.0	VG 4.0	FN 6.0	VF 8.0	VF/NM 9.0	NM- 9.2
1,2	10	20	30	58	77	95

TRUE AVIATION PICTURE STORIES (Becomes Aviation Adventures & Model Building #16 on)
Parents' Mag. Institute: 1942; No. 2, Jan-Feb, 1943 - No. 15, Sept-Oct, 1946

	GD 2.0	VG 4.0	FN 6.0	VF 8.0	VF/NM 9.0	NM- 9.2
1-(#1 & 2 titled ...Aviation Comics Digest)(not digest size)	15	30	45	83	117	150
2	10	20	30	56	73	90
3-14: 3-10-Plane photos on-c. 11,13-Photo-c	9	18	27	49	62	75
15-(Titled "True Aviation Adventures & Model Building")	8	16	24	46	58	70

TRUE BRIDE'S EXPERIENCES (Formerly Teen-Age Brides)
(True Bride-To-Be Romances No. 17 on)
True Love (Harvey Publications): No. 8, Oct, 1954 - No. 16, Feb, 1956

	GD 2.0	VG 4.0	FN 6.0	VF 8.0	VF/NM 9.0	NM- 9.2
8	9	18	27	49	62	75
9,10: 10-Last pre-code (2/55)	7	14	21	35	43	50
11-15	6	12	18	29	36	42
16-Last issue	7	14	21	35	43	50

NOTE: *Powell a-8-10, 12, 13.*

TRUE BRIDE-TO-BE ROMANCES (Formerly True Bride's Experiences)
Home Comics/True Love (Harvey): No. 17, Apr, 1956 - No. 30, Nov, 1958

	GD 2.0	VG 4.0	FN 6.0	VF 8.0	VF/NM 9.0	NM- 9.2
17-S&K-c, Powell-a	10	20	30	56	73	90
18-20,22,25-28,30	6	12	18	28	34	40
21,23,24,29-Powell-a. 29-Baker-a (1 pg.)	6	12	18	31	38	45

TRUE COMICS (Also see Outstanding American War Heroes)
True Comics/Parents' Magazine Press: April, 1941 - No. 84, Aug, 1950

	GD 2.0	VG 4.0	FN 6.0	VF 8.0	VF/NM 9.0	NM- 9.2
1-Marathon run story; life story Winston Churchill	33	66	99	190	275	360
2-Red Cross story; Everett-a	16	32	48	89	127	165
3-Baseball Hall of Fame story; Chiang Kai-Shek-c/s	19	38	57	107	154	200
4,5: 4-Story of American flag "Old Glory". 5-Life story of Joe Louis	14	28	42	79	110	140
6-Baseball World Series story	17	34	51	95	135	175
7-10: 7-Buffalo Bill story. 10,11-Teddy Roosevelt	10	20	30	60	80	100
11-14,16,18-20: 11-Thomas Edison, Douglas MacArthur stories. 13-Harry Houdini story. 14-Charlie McCarthy story. 18-Story of America begins, ends #26. 19-Eisenhower-c/s	9	18	27	54	70	85
15-Flag-c; Bob Feller story	10	20	30	58	77	95
17-Brooklyn Dodgers story	11	22	33	64	87	110
21-30: 24-Marco Polo story. 28-Origin of Uncle Sam. 29-Beethoven story. 30-Cooper Brothers baseball story	9	18	27	51	62	75
31-Red Grange "Galloping Ghost" story	8	16	24	40	50	60
32-46: 33-Origin/1st app. Steve Saunders, Special Agent of the FBI, series begins. 35-Mark Twain story. 38-General Bradley-c/s. 39-FDR story. 44-Truman story. 46-George Gershwin story	7	14	21	37	46	55
47-Atomic bomb issue (c/story, 3/46)	10	20	30	58	77	95
48-54,56-65: 49-1st app. Secret Warriors. 53-Bobby Riggs story. 58-Jim Jeffries (boxer) story; Harry Houdini story. 59-Bob Hope story; pirates-c/s. 60-Speedway Speed Demon-c/story.	7	14	21	35	43	50
55-(12/46)-1st app. Sad Sack by Baker (1/2 pg.)	9	18	27	51	62	75
66-Will Rogers-c/story	7	14	21	37	46	55
67-1st oversized issue (12/47); Steve Saunders, Special Agent begins	8	16	24	43	54	65
68-70,74-77,79: 68-70,74-77-Features Steve Sanders True FBI advs. 68-Oversized; Admiral Byrd-c/s. 69-Jack Benny story. 74-Amos 'n' Andy story	6	12	18	31	38	45
71-Joe DiMaggio-c/story.	9	18	27	51	62	75
72-Jackie Robinson story; True FBI advs.	8	16	24	40	50	60
73-Walt Disney's life story	9	18	27	51	62	75
78-Stan Musial-c/story; True FBI advs.	8	16	24	40	50	60
80-84 (Scarce)-All distr. to subscribers through mail only; paper-c. 80-Rocket trip to the moon story. 81-Red Grange story	17	34	51	95	135	175

(Prices vary widely on issues 80-84)

NOTE: ***Bob Kane** a-7. **Palais** a-80. **Powell** c/a-80. #80-84 have soft covers and combined with Tex Granger, Jack Armstrong, and Calling All Kids. #68-78 featured true FBI adventures.*

TRUE COMICS AND ADVENTURE STORIES
Parents' Magazine Institute: 1965 (Giant) (25¢)

	GD 2.0	VG 4.0	FN 6.0	VF 8.0	VF/NM 9.0	NM- 9.2
1,2: 1-Fighting Hero of Viet Nam; LBJ on-c	3	6	9	19	25	32

TRUE COMPLETE MYSTERY (Formerly Complete Mystery)
Marvel Comics (PrPl): No. 5, Apr, 1949 - No. 8, Oct, 1949

	GD 2.0	VG 4.0	FN 6.0	VF 8.0	VF/NM 9.0	NM- 9.2
5	27	54	81	152	219	285
6-8: 6-8-Photo-c	21	42	63	118	169	220

TRUE CONFIDENCES
Fawcett Publications: 1949 (Fall) - No. 4, June, 1950 (All photo-c)

	GD 2.0	VG 4.0	FN 6.0	VF 8.0	VF/NM 9.0	NM- 9.2
1-Has ad for Fawcett Love Adventures #1, but publ. as Love Memoirs #1 as Marvel published the title first; Swayze-a	18	36	54	100	143	185
2-4: 3-Swayze-a. 4-Powell-a	11	22	33	64	87	110

TRUE CRIME CASES (...From Official Police Files)
St. John Publishing Co.: 1944 (25¢, 100 pg. Giant)

	GD 2.0	VG 4.0	FN 6.0	VF 8.0	VF/NM 9.0	NM- 9.2
nn-Matt Baker-c	43	86	129	262	401	540

TRUE CRIME COMICS (Also see Complete Book of...)
Magazine Village: No. 2, May, 1947; No. 3, July-Aug, 1948 - No. 6, June-July, 1949; V2#1, Aug-Sept, 1949 (52 pgs.)

	GD 2.0	VG 4.0	FN 6.0	VF 8.0	VF/NM 9.0	NM- 9.2
2-Jack Cole-c/a; used in **SOTI**, pgs. 81,82 plus illo. "A sample of the injury-to-eye motif" & illo. "Dragging living people to death"; used in **POP**, pg. 105; "Murder, Morphine and Me" classic drug propaganda story used by N.Y. Legis. Comm.	146	292	438	913	1407	1900
3-Classic Cole-c/a; drug story with hypo, opium den & with drawing addict	108	216	324	675	1038	1400
4-Jack Cole-c/a; c-taken from a story panel in #3 (r-(2) **SOTI** & **POP** stories/#2?)	94	188	282	588	907	1225
5-Jack Cole-c, Marijuana racket story (Canadian ed. w/cover similar to #3 exists w/out drug story)	62	124	186	388	594	800
6-Not a reprint, original story (Canadian ed. reprints #4 w/different coloring on-c)	50	100	150	305	465	625
V2#1-Used in **SOTI**, pgs. 81,82 & illo. "Dragging living people to death"; Toth, Wood (3 pgs.), Roussos-a; Cole-r from #2	85	170	255	531	816	1100

NOTE: *V2#1 was reprinted in Canada as V2#9 (12/49); same-c & contents minus Wood-a.*

TRUE FAITH
Fleetway: 1990 ($9.95, graphic novel)

	GD 2.0	VG 4.0	FN 6.0	VF 8.0	VF/NM 9.0	NM- 9.2
nn-Garth Ennis scripts	2	4	6	12	16	20
Reprinted by DC/Vertigo ('97, $12.95)						13.00

TRUE GHOST STORIES (See Ripley's...)

TRUE LIFE ROMANCES (...Romance on cover)
Ajax/Farrell Publications: Dec, 1955 - No. 3, Aug, 1956

	GD 2.0	VG 4.0	FN 6.0	VF 8.0	VF/NM 9.0	NM- 9.2
1	10	20	30	60	80	100
2	8	16	24	40	50	60
3-Disbrow-a	8	16	24	46	58	70

TRUE LIFE SECRETS
Romantic Love Stories/Charlton: Mar-April, 1951 - No. 28, Sept, 1955; No. 29, Jan, 1956

	GD 2.0	VG 4.0	FN 6.0	VF 8.0	VF/NM 9.0	NM- 9.2
1-Photo-c begin, end #3?	14	28	42	79	110	140
2	8	16	24	46	58	70
3-19: 12-"I Was An Escort Girl" story	7	14	21	37	46	55
20-29: 25-Last precode(3/55)	6	12	18	31	38	45

TRUE LIFE TALES (Formerly Mitzi's Romances #8?)
Marvel Comics (CCC): No. 8, Oct, 1949 - No. 2, Jan, 1950 (52 pgs.)

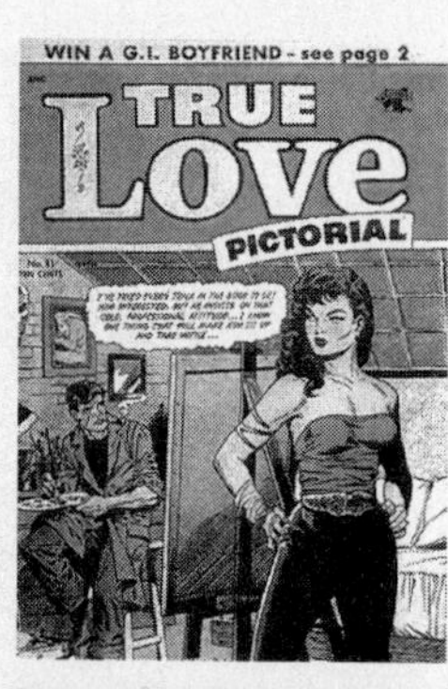

True Love Pictorial #11 © STJ

True Sport Picture Stories V2#7 © S&S

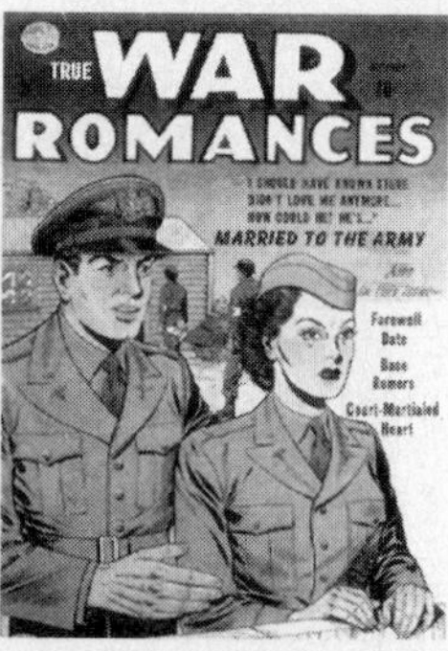

True War Romances #2 © QUA

	GD 2.0	VG 4.0	FN 6.0	VF 8.0	VF/NM 9.0	NM- 9.2
8(#1, 10/49), 2-Both have photo-c	10	20	30	58	77	95

TRUE LOVE
Eclipse Comics: Jan, 1986 - No. 2, Jan, 1986 ($2.00, Baxter paper)

	GD	VG	FN	VF	VF/NM	NM-
1,2-Love stories reprinted from pre-code Standard Comics; Toth-a(p) in both; 1-Dave Stevens-c. 2-Mayo-a						3.00

TRUE LOVE CONFESSIONS
Premier Magazines: May, 1954 - No. 11, Jan, 1956

	GD	VG	FN	VF	VF/NM	NM-
1-Marijuana story	11	22	33	64	87	110
2	7	14	21	37	46	55
3-11	6	12	18	31	38	45

TRUE LOVE PICTORIAL
St. John Publishing Co.: 1952 - No. 11, Aug, 1954

	GD	VG	FN	VF	VF/NM	NM-
1-Only photo-c	17	34	51	95	135	175
2-Baker-c/a	21	42	63	121	173	225
3-5(All 25¢, 100 pgs.): 4-Signed story by Estrada. 5-(4/53)-Formerly Teen-Age Temptations; Kubert-a in #3; Baker-a in #3-5	35	70	105	201	293	385
6,7: Baker-c/a; signed stories by Estrada	19	38	57	107	154	200
8,10,11-Baker-c/a	19	38	57	107	154	200
9-Baker-c	15	30	45	85	120	155

TRUE LOVE PROBLEMS AND ADVICE ILLUSTRATED (Becomes Romance Stories of True Love No. 45 on)
McCombs/Harvey Publ./Home Comics: June, 1949 - No. 6, Apr, 1950; No. 7, Jan, 1951 - No. 44, Mar, 1957

	GD	VG	FN	VF	VF/NM	NM-
V1#1	15	30	45	83	117	150
2	9	18	27	52	66	80
3-10: 7-9-Elias-c	7	14	21	37	46	55
11-13,15-23,25-31: 31-Last pre-code (1/55)	6	12	18	29	36	42
14,24-Rape scene	6	12	18	31	38	45
32-37,39-44	5	10	15	24	30	35
38-S&K-c	9	18	27	49	62	75

NOTE: *Powell a-1, 2, 7-14, 17-25, 28, 29, 33, 40, 41. #3 has True Love... on inside.*

TRUE MOVIE AND TELEVISION (Part teenage magazine)
Toby Press: Aug, 1950 - No. 3, Nov, 1950; No. 4, Mar, 1951 (52 pgs.)(1-3: 10¢)

	GD	VG	FN	VF	VF/NM	NM-
1-Elizabeth Taylor photo-c; Gene Autry, Shirley Temple, Li'l Abner app.	52	104	156	317	484	650
2-(9/50)-Janet Leigh/Liz Taylor/Ava Gardner & others photo-c; Frazetta John Wayne illo from J.Wayne Adv. Comics #2 (4/50)	40	80	120	239	357	475
3-June Allyson photo-c; Montgomery Cliff, Esther Williams, Andrews Sisters app; Li'l Abner featured; Sadie Hawkins' Day	31	62	93	177	256	335
4-Jane Powell photo-c (15¢)	19	38	57	107	154	200

NOTE: *16 pgs. in color, rest movie material in black & white.*

TRUE SECRETS (Formerly Our Love?)
Marvel (IPS)/Atlas Comics (MPI) #4 on: No. 3, Mar, 1950; No. 4, Feb, 1951 - No. 40, Sept, 1956

	GD	VG	FN	VF	VF/NM	NM-
3 (52 pgs.)(IPS one-shot)	14	28	42	79	110	140
4,5,7-10	9	18	27	51	62	75
6,22-Everett-a	10	20	30	60	80	100
11-20	8	16	24	43	54	65
21,23-28: 24-Colletta-c. 28-Last pre-code (2/55)	7	14	21	37	46	55
29-40: 34,36-Colletta-a	7	14	21	35	43	50

TRUE SPORT PICTURE STORIES (Formerly Sport Comics)
Street & Smith Publications: V1#5, Feb, 1942 - V5#2, July-Aug, 1949

	GD	VG	FN	VF	VF/NM	NM-
V1#5-Joe DiMaggio-c/story	37	74	111	209	305	400
6-12 (1942-43): 12-Jack Dempsey story	21	42	63	121	173	225
V2#1-12 (1944-45): 7-Stan Musial-c/story; photo story of the New York Yankees	20	40	60	115	165	215
V3#1-12 (1946-47): 7-Joe DiMaggio, Stan Musial, Bob Feller & others back from the armed service story. 8-Billy Conn vs. Joe Louis-c/story	18	36	54	102	146	190
V4#1-12 (1948-49), V5#1,2	17	34	51	95	135	175

NOTE: *Powell a-V3#10, V4#1-4, 6-8, 10-12; V5#1, 2; c-V3#11, V4#3-7, 9-12. **Ravielli** c-V5#2.*

TRUE STORIES OF ROMANCE
Fawcett Publications: Jan, 1950 - No. 3, May, 1950 (All photo-c)

	GD	VG	FN	VF	VF/NM	NM-
1	13	26	39	76	106	135
2,3: 3-Marcus Swayze-a	9	18	27	54	70	85

TRUE STORY OF JESSE JAMES, THE (See Jesse James, Four Color 757)

TRUE SWEETHEART SECRETS
Fawcett Publications: 5/50; No. 2, 7/50; No. 3, 1951(nd); No. 4, 9/51 - No. 11, 1/53 (All photo-c)

	GD 2.0	VG 4.0	FN 6.0	VF 8.0	VF/NM 9.0	NM- 9.2
1-Photo-c; Debbie Reynolds?	15	30	45	83	117	150
2-Wood-a (11 pgs.)	18	36	54	100	143	185
3-11: 4,5-Powell-a. 8-Marcus Swayze-a. 11-Evans-a	10	20	30	60	80	100

TRUE TALES OF LOVE (Formerly Secret Story Romances)
Atlas Comics (TCI): No. 22, April, 1956 - No. 31, Sept, 1957

	GD	VG	FN	VF	VF/NM	NM-
22	9	18	27	52	66	80
23-24,26-31-Colletta-a in most:	7	14	21	35	43	50
25-Everett-a; Colletta-a	8	16	24	40	50	60

TRUE TALES OF ROMANCE
Fawcett Publications: No. 4, June, 1950

	GD	VG	FN	VF	VF/NM	NM-
4-Photo-c	9	18	27	54	70	85

TRUE 3-D
Harvey Publications: Dec, 1953 - No. 2, Feb, 1954 (25¢)(Both came with 2 pair of glasses)

	GD	VG	FN	VF	VF/NM	NM-
1-Nostrand, Powell-a	6	12	18	43	59	75
2-Powell-a	7	14	21	46	63	80

NOTE: *Many copies of #1 surfaced in 1984.*

TRUE-TO-LIFE ROMANCES (Formerly Guns Against Gangsters)
Star Publ.: #8, 11-12/49; #9, 1-2/50; #3, 4/50 - #5, 9/50; #6, 1/51 - #23, 10/54

	GD	VG	FN	VF	VF/NM	NM-
8(#1, 1949)	25	50	75	141	203	265
9(#2),4-10	18	36	54	100	143	185
3-Janet Leigh/Glenn Ford photo on-c plus true life story of each	20	40	60	112	161	210
11,22,23	15	30	45	86	123	160
12-14,17-21-Disbrow-a	17	34	51	98	139	180
15,16-Wood & Disbrow-a in each	20	40	60	112	161	210

NOTE: ***Kamen** a-13. **Kamen/Feldstein** a-14. All have **L.B. Cole** covers.*

TRUE WAR EXPERIENCES
Harvey Publications: Aug, 1952 - No. 4, Dec, 1952

	GD	VG	FN	VF	VF/NM	NM-
1	10	20	30	70	100	130
2-4	6	12	18	40	55	70

TRUE WAR ROMANCES (Becomes Exotic Romances #22 on)
Quality Comics Group: Sept, 1952 - No. 21, June, 1955

	GD	VG	FN	VF	VF/NM	NM-
1-Photo-c	14	28	42	79	110	140
2	8	16	24	46	58	70
3-10: 9-Whitney-a	8	16	24	40	50	60
11-21: 20-Last precode (4/55). 14-Whitney-a	7	14	21	35	43	50

TRUE WAR STORIES (See Ripley's...)

TRUE WESTERN (True Adventures #3)
Marvel Comics (MMC): Dec, 1949 - No. 2, March, 1950

	GD	VG	FN	VF	VF/NM	NM-
1-Photo-c; Billy The Kid story	17	34	51	98	139	180
2-Alan Ladd photo-c	21	42	63	118	169	220

TRUMP
HMH Publishing Co.: Jan, 1957 - No. 2, Mar, 1957 (50¢, magazine)

	GD	VG	FN	VF	VF/NM	NM-
1-Harvey Kurtzman satire	25	50	75	144	207	270
2-Harvey Kurtzman satire	20	40	60	112	161	210

NOTE: ***Davis, Elder, Heath, Jaffee** art-#1,2; **Wood** a-1. Article by Mel Brooks in #2.*

TRUMPETS WEST (See Luke Short, Four Color #875)

TRUTH ABOUT CRIME (See Fox Giants)

TRUTH ABOUT MOTHER GOOSE (See Mother Goose, Four Color #862)

TRUTH BEHIND THE TRIAL OF CARDINAL MINDSZENTY, THE (See Cardinal Mindszenty in the Promotional Comics section))

TRUTHFUL LOVE (Formerly Youthful Love)
Youthful Magazines: No. 2, July, 1950

	GD	VG	FN	VF	VF/NM	NM-
2-Ingrid Bergman's true life story	11	22	33	62	84	105

TRUTH RED, WHITE & BLACK
Marvel Comics: Jan, 2003 - No. 6 ($3.50, limited series)

	GD	VG	FN	VF	VF/NM	NM-
1-Kyle Baker-a/Robert Morales-s; the testing of Captain America's super-soldier serum						3.50
2-7: 3-Isaiah Bradley 1st dons the Captain America costume						3.50
TPB (2004, $17.99) r/series						18.00

TRY-OUT WINNER BOOK
Marvel Comics: Mar, 1988

	GD	VG	FN	VF	VF/NM	NM-
1-Spider-Man vs. Doc Octopus						5.00

Tug & Buster #7 © Marc Hempel

Turok Dinosaur Hunter #28 © VAL

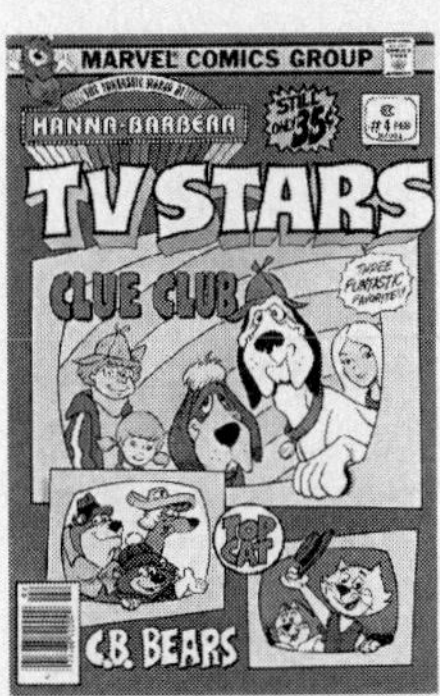

TV Stars #4 © H-B

TSR WORLD (...Annual on cover only)
DC Comics: 1990 ($3.95, 84 pgs.)

	GD 2.0	VG 4.0	FN 6.0	VF 8.0	VF/NM 9.0	NM- 9.2
1-Advanced D&D, ForgottenRealms, Dragonlance & 1st app. Spelljammer						4.00

TSUNAMI GIRL
Image Comics: 1999 - No. 3, 1999 ($2.95)

	GD 2.0	VG 4.0	FN 6.0	VF 8.0	VF/NM 9.0	NM- 9.2
1-3-Sorayama-c/Paniccia-s/a						3.00

TUBBY (See Marge's...)

TUFF GHOSTS STARRING SPOOKY
Harvey Publications: July, 1962 - No. 39, Nov, 1970; No. 40, Sept, 1971 - No. 43, Oct, 1972

	GD 2.0	VG 4.0	FN 6.0	VF 8.0	VF/NM 9.0	NM- 9.2
1-12¢ issues begin	13	26	39	92	141	190
2-5	8	16	24	53	74	95
6-10	6	12	18	38	52	65
11-20	4	8	12	29	40	50
21-30: 29-Hot Stuff/Spooky team-up story	3	6	9	18	24	30
31-39,43	2	4	6	14	18	22
40-42: 52 pg. Giants	3	6	9	16	20	25

TUFFY
Standard Comics: No. 5, July, 1949 - No. 9, Oct, 1950

	GD 2.0	VG 4.0	FN 6.0	VF 8.0	VF/NM 9.0	NM- 9.2
5-All by Sid Hoff	6	12	18	31	38	45
6-9	5	10	15	22	26	30

TUFFY TURTLE
I. W. Enterprises: No date

	GD 2.0	VG 4.0	FN 6.0	VF 8.0	VF/NM 9.0	NM- 9.2
1-Reprint	2	4	6	9	11	14

TUG & BUSTER
Art & Soul Comics: Nov, 1995 - No. 7, Feb, 1998 ($2.95, B&W, bi-monthly)

	GD 2.0	VG 4.0	FN 6.0	VF 8.0	VF/NM 9.0	NM- 9.2
1-7: Marc Hempel-c/a/scripts						3.00
1-(Image Comics, 8/98, $2.95, B&W)						3.00

TUROK
Acclaim Comics: Mar, 1998 - No. 4, Jun, 1998 ($2.50)

	GD 2.0	VG 4.0	FN 6.0	VF 8.0	VF/NM 9.0	NM- 9.2
1-4-Nicieza-s/Kayanan-a						2.50
..., Child of Blood 1 (1/98, $3.95) Nicieza-s/Kayanan-a						4.00
... Evolution 1 (8/02, $2.50) Nicieza-s/Kayanan-a						2.50
..., Redpath 1 (10/97, $3.95) Nicieza-s/Kayanan-a						4.00
... / Shadowman 1 (2/99, $3.95) Priest-s/Broome & Jimenez-a						4.00
...: Spring Break in the Lost Land 1 (7/97, $3.95) Nicieza-s/Kayanan-a						4.00
...: Tales of the Lost Land 1 (4/98, $3.95)						4.00
...: The Empty Souls 1 (4/97, $3.95) Nicieza-s/Kayanan-a; variant-c						4.00

TUROK, DINOSAUR HUNTER (See Magnus Robot Fighter #12 & Archer & Armstrong #2)
Valiant/Acclaim Comics: June, 1993 - No. 47, Aug, 1996 ($2.50)

	GD 2.0	VG 4.0	FN 6.0	VF 8.0	VF/NM 9.0	NM- 9.2
1-($3.50)-Chromium & foil-c						3.50
1-Gold foil-c variant						5.00
0, 2-47: 4-Andar app. 5-Death of Andar. 7-9-Truman/Glanzman-a. 11-Bound-in trading card. 16-Chaos Effect						2.50
Yearbook 1 (1994, $3.95, 52 pgs.)						4.00

TUROK, SON OF STONE (See Dan Curtis, Golden Comics Digest #31 & March of Comics #378, 399, 408)
Dell Publ. Co. #1-29(9/62)/Gold Key #30(12/62)-85(7/73)/Gold Key or Whitman #86(9/73)-125(1/80)/Whitman #126(3/81) on: No. 596, 12/54 - No. 29, 9/62; No. 30, 12/62 - No. 91, 7/74; No. 92, 9/74 - No. 125, 1/80; No. 126, 3/81 - No. 130, 4/82

	GD 2.0	VG 4.0	FN 6.0	VF 8.0	VF/NM 9.0	NM- 9.2
Four Color 596 (12/54)(#1)-1st app./origin Turok & Andar; dinosaur-c. Created by Matthew H. Murphy; written by Alberto Giolitti	50	100	150	419	672	925
Four Color 656 (10/55)(#2)-1st mention of Lanok	32	64	96	240	375	510
3(3-5/56)-5: 3-Cave men	22	44	66	158	242	325
6-10: 8-Dinosaur of the deep; Turok enters Lost Valley; series begins. 9-Paul S. Newman-s (most issues thru end)	15	30	45	109	167	225
11-20: 17-Prehistoric Pygmies	11	22	33	80	120	160
21-29	9	18	27	60	85	110
30-1st Gold Key. 30-33-Painted back-c.	9	18	27	63	89	115
31-Drug use story	9	18	27	60	85	110
32-40	7	14	21	46	63	80
41-50	6	12	18	38	52	65
51-57,59,60	5	10	15	33	44	55
58-Flying Saucer c/story	5	10	15	36	48	60
61-70: 62-12¢ & 15¢ covers. 63,68-Line drawn-c	4	8	12	27	36	45
71-84: 84-Origin & 1st app. Hutec	3	6	9	19	25	32
85-99: 93-r-c/#19 w/changes. 94-r-c/#28 w/changes. 97-r-c/#31 w/changes. 98-r/#58 w/o spaceship & spacemen on-c. 99-r-c/#52 w/changes.	3	6	9	16	21	26
100	3	7	10	21	28	35
101-129: 114,115-(52 pgs.). 129(2/82)	3	6	9	18	24	30
130(4/82)-Last issue	4	8	12	27	36	45
Giant 1(30031-611) (11/66)-Slick-c; r/#10-12 & 16 plus cover to #11	11	22	33	77	114	150
Giant 1-Same as above but with paper-c	12	24	36	84	127	170

NOTE: *Most painted-c; line-drawn #63 & 130.* ***Alberto Gioletti*** *a-24-27, 30-119, 123; painted-c No. 30-129.* ***Sparling*** *a-117, 120-130. Reprints-#36, 54, 57, 75, 112, 114(1/3), 115(1/3), 118, 121, 125, 127(1/3), 128, 129(1/3), 130(1/3), Giant 1. Cover r-93, 94, 97-99, 126(all different from original covers.*

TUROK THE HUNTED
Valiant/Acclaim Comics: Mar, 1995 - No. 2, Apr, 1995 ($2.50, limited series)

	GD 2.0	VG 4.0	FN 6.0	VF 8.0	VF/NM 9.0	NM- 9.2
1,2-Mike Deodato-a(p); price omitted on #1						2.50

TUROK THE HUNTED
Acclaim Comics (Valiant): Feb, 1996 - No. 2, Mar, 1996 ($2.50, limited series)

	GD 2.0	VG 4.0	FN 6.0	VF 8.0	VF/NM 9.0	NM- 9.2
1,2-Mike Grell story						2.50

TUROK, TIMEWALKER
Acclaim Comics (Valiant): Aug, 1997 - No. 2, Sept, 1997 ($2.50, limited series)

	GD 2.0	VG 4.0	FN 6.0	VF 8.0	VF/NM 9.0	NM- 9.2
1,2-Nicieza story						2.50

TUROK 2 (Magazine)
Acclaim Comics: Oct, 1998 ($4.99, magazine size)

	GD 2.0	VG 4.0	FN 6.0	VF 8.0	VF/NM 9.0	NM- 9.2
...Seeds of Evil-Nicieza-s/Broome & Benjamin-a; origin back-up story						5.00
#2 Adon's Curse -Mack painted-c/Broome & Benjamin-a; origin pt. 2						5.00

TUROK 3: SHADOW OF OBLIVION
Acclaim Comics: Sept, 2000 ($4.95, one-shot)

	GD 2.0	VG 4.0	FN 6.0	VF 8.0	VF/NM 9.0	NM- 9.2
1-Includes pin-up gallery						5.00

TURTLE SOUP
Mirage Studios: Sept, 1987 ($2.00, 76 pgs., B&W, one-shot)

	GD 2.0	VG 4.0	FN 6.0	VF 8.0	VF/NM 9.0	NM- 9.2
1-Featuring Teenage Mutant Ninja Turtles						5.00

TURTLE SOUP
Mirage Studios: Nov, 1991 - No. 4, 1992 ($2.50, limited series, coated paper)

	GD 2.0	VG 4.0	FN 6.0	VF 8.0	VF/NM 9.0	NM- 9.2
1-4: Features the Teenage Mutant Ninja Turtles						2.50

TV CASPER & COMPANY
Harvey Publications: Aug, 1963 - No. 46, April, 1974 (25¢ Giants)

	GD 2.0	VG 4.0	FN 6.0	VF 8.0	VF/NM 9.0	NM- 9.2
1- 68 pg. Giants begin; Casper, Little Audrey, Baby Huey, Herman & Catnip, Buzzy the Crow begin	13	26	39	92	141	190
2-5	7	14	21	51	71	90
6-10	5	10	15	36	48	60
11-20	4	8	12	27	36	45
21-31: 31-Last 68 pg. issue	3	6	9	18	24	30
32-46: All 52 pgs.	3	6	9	16	20	25

NOTE: *Many issues contain reprints.*

TV FUNDAY FUNNIES (See Famous TV...)

TV FUNNIES (See New Funnies)

TV FUNTIME (See Little Audrey)

TV LAUGHOUT (See Archie's...)

TV SCREEN CARTOONS (Formerly Real Screen)
National Periodical Publ.: No. 129, July-Aug, 1959 - No. 138, Jan-Feb, 1961

	GD 2.0	VG 4.0	FN 6.0	VF 8.0	VF/NM 9.0	NM- 9.2
129-138 (Scarce)	8	16	24	53	74	95

TV STARS (TV) (Newsstand sales only)
Marvel Comics Group: Aug, 1978 - No. 4, Feb, 1979 (Hanna-Barbera)

	GD 2.0	VG 4.0	FN 6.0	VF 8.0	VF/NM 9.0	NM- 9.2
1-Great Grape Ape app.	3	7	10	21	28	35
2,4: 4-Top Cat app.	3	6	9	18	23	28
3-Toth-c/a; Dave Stevens inks	3	6	9	19	25	32

TV TEENS (Formerly Ozzie & Babs; Rock and Rollo #14 on)
Charlton Comics: V1#14, Feb, 1954 - V2#13, July, 1956

	GD 2.0	VG 4.0	FN 6.0	VF 8.0	VF/NM 9.0	NM- 9.2
V1#14 (#1)-Ozzie & Babs	9	18	27	54	70	85
15 (#2)	6	12	18	29	36	42
V2#3(6/54) - 6-Don Winslow	6	12	18	31	38	45
7-13-Mopsy. 8(7/55)	6	12	18	29	36	42

TWEETY AND SYLVESTER (1st Series) (TV) (Also see Looney Tunes and Merrie Melodies)
Dell Publishing Co.: No. 406, June, 1952 - No. 37, June-Aug, 1962

	GD 2.0	VG 4.0	FN 6.0	VF 8.0	VF/NM 9.0	NM- 9.2
Four Color 406 (#1)	11	22	33	77	114	150
Four Color 489,524	6	12	18	43	59	75
4 (3-5/54) - 20	5	10	15	33	44	55
21-37	4	8	12	27	36	45

(See March of Comics #421, 433, 445, 457, 469, 481)

24: One Shot © 20th Century Fox

Twilight Zone #1 © CBS Ent.

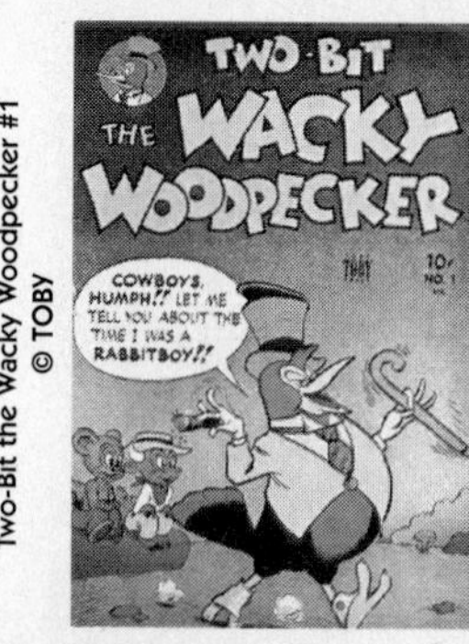

Two-Bit the Wacky Woodpecker #1 © TOBY

TWEETY AND SYLVESTER (2nd Series)(See Kite Fun Book)
Gold Key No. 1-102/Whitman No. 103 on: Nov, 1963; No. 2, Nov, 1965 - No. 121, June, 1984

	GD 2.0	VG 4.0	FN 6.0	VF 8.0	VF/NM 9.0	NM- 9.2
1	5	10	15	33	44	55
2-10	3	7	10	21	28	35
11-30	2	4	6	14	18	22
31-50	2	4	6	10	12	15
51-70	1	3	4	6	8	10
71-102	1	2	3	5	6	8
103,104 (Whitman)	1	3	4	6	8	10
105(9/80),106(10/80),107(12/80) 3-pack only	3	6	9	16	21	26
108-116: 113(2/82),114(2-3/82),115(3/82),116(4/82)	2	4	6	8	10	12
117-121 (All # 90094 on-c; nd, nd code): 117(6/83). 118(7/83). 119(2/84)-r(1/3). 120(5/84). 121(6/84)	2	4	6	11	14	18
Mini Comic No. 1(1976, 3-1/4x6-1/2")	1	3	4	6	8	10

12 O'CLOCK HIGH (TV)
Dell Publishing Co.: Jan-Mar, 1965 - No. 2, Apr-June, 1965 (Photo-c)

	GD 2.0	VG 4.0	FN 6.0	VF 8.0	VF/NM 9.0	NM- 9.2
1	7	14	21	50	68	85
2	6	12	18	38	52	65

2099 A.D.
Marvel Comics: May, 1995 ($3.95, one-shot)

1-Acetate-c by Quesada & Palmiotti 4.00

2099 APOCALYPSE
Marvel Comics: Dec, 1995 ($4.95, one-shot)

1-Chromium wraparound-c; Ellis script 5.00

2099 GENESIS
Marvel Comics: Jan, 1996 ($4.95, one-shot)

1-Chromium wraparound-c; Ellis script 5.00

2099 MANIFEST DESTINY
Marvel Comics: Mar, 1998 ($5.99, one-shot)

1-Origin of Fantastic Four 2099; intro Moon Knight 2099 6.00

2099 UNLIMITED
Marvel Comics: Sept, 1993 - No. 10, 1996 ($3.95, 68 pgs.)

1-10: 1-1st app. Hulk 2099 & begins. 1-3-Spider-Man 2099 app. 9-Joe Kubert-c; Len Wein & Nancy Collins scripts 4.00

2099 WORLD OF DOOM SPECIAL
Marvel Comics: May, 1995 ($2.25, one-shot)

1-Doom's "Contract w/America" 2.25

2099 WORLD OF TOMORROW
Marvel Comics: Sept, 1996 - No. 8, Apr, 1997 ($2.50) (Replaces 2099 titles)

1-8: 1-Wraparound-c. 2-w/bound-in card. 4,5-Phalanx 2.50

21
Image Comics (Top Cow Productions): Feb, 1996 - No. 3, Apr, 1996 ($2.50)

1-3: Len Wein scripts 2.50
1-Variant-c 2.50

21 DOWN
DC Comics (WildStorm): Nov, 2002 - No. 12, Nov, 2003 ($2.95)

1-12: 1-Palmiotti & Gray-s/Saiz-a/Jusko-c 3.00
...: The Conduit (2003, $19.95, TPB) r/#1-7; intro. by Garth Ennis 20.00

24: ONE SHOT (Based on TV series)
IDW Publishing: July, 2004 ($6.99, square-bound)

nn-Jack Bauer's first day on the job at CTU; Vaughn & Haynes-s/Guedes-a 7.00

2020 VISIONS
DC Comics (Vertigo): May, 1997 - No. 12, Apr, 1998 ($2.25, limited series)

1-12-Delano-s: 1-3-Quitely-a. 4-"la tormenta"-Pleece-a 2.25

20,000 LEAGUES UNDER THE SEA (Movie)(See King Classics, Movie Comics & Power Record Comics)
Dell Publishing Co.: No. 614, Feb, 1955 (Disney)

	GD 2.0	VG 4.0	FN 6.0	VF 8.0	VF/NM 9.0	NM- 9.2
Four Color 614-Movie, painted-c	10	20	30	72	104	135

22 BRIDES (See Ash/)
Event Comics: Mar, 1996 - No. 4, Jan, 1997 ($2.95)

1-4: Fabian Nicieza scripts 3.00
2,3-Variant-c 3.00

TWICE TOLD TALES (See Movie Classics)

TWILIGHT
DC Comics: 1990 - No. 3, 1991 ($4.95, 52 pgs, lim. series, squarebound, mature)

1-3: Tommy Tomorrow app; Chaykin scripts, Garcia-Lopez-c/a 5.00

TWILIGHT AVENGER, THE
Elite Comics: July, 1986 - No. 4, 1987 ($1.75, 28 pgs, limited series)

1-4 2.25

TWILIGHT MAN
First Publishing: June, 1989 - No. 4, Sept, 1989 ($2.75, limited series)

1-4 2.75

TWILIGHT ZONE, THE (TV) (See Dan Curtis & Stories From...)
Dell Publishing Co./Gold Key/Whitman No. 92: No. 1173, 3-5/61 - No. 91, 4/79; No. 92, 5/82

	GD 2.0	VG 4.0	FN 6.0	VF 8.0	VF/NM 9.0	NM- 9.2
Four Color 1173 (#1)-Crandall-c/a	23	46	69	165	253	340
Four Color 1288-Crandall/Evans-c/a	13	26	39	90	138	185
01-860-207 (5-7/62-Dell, 15¢)	10	20	30	70	100	130
12-860-210 on-c; 01-860-210 on inside(8-10/62-Dell)-Evans-c/a (3 stories)	10	20	30	70	100	130
1(11/62-Gold Key)-Crandall/Frazetta-a (10 & 11 pgs.); Evans-a	14	28	42	97	149	200
2	9	18	27	60	85	110
3-11: 3(11 pgs.),4(10 pgs.),9-Toth-a	7	14	21	46	63	80
12-15: 12-Williamson-a. 13,15-Crandall-a. 14-Orlando/Crandall/Torres-a	6	12	18	38	52	65
16-20	4	8	12	27	36	45
21-25: 21-Crandall-a(r). 25-Evans/Crandall-a(r); Toth-r/#4; last 12¢ issue	3	7	10	21	28	35
26,27: 26-Flying Saucer-c/story; Crandall, Evans-a(r). 27-Evans-r(2)	3	7	10	21	28	35
28-32: 32-Evans-a(r)	3	6	9	18	24	30
33-51: 43-Celardo-a. 51-Williamson-a	2	4	6	12	16	20
52-70	2	4	6	10	12	15
71-82,85-91: 71-Reprint. 85-Frank Miller-a	2	4	6	8	10	12
83-(52 pgs.)	2	4	6	11	14	18
84-(52 pgs.) Frank Miller's 1st comic book work	3	6	9	18	23	28
92-(Whitman, 5/82) Last issue; r/#1.	2	4	6	9	11	14
Mini Comic #1(1976, 3-1/4x6-1/2")	2	4	6	8	10	12

NOTE: ***Bolle** a-13(w/**McWilliams**), 50, 55, 57, 59, 77, 78, 80, 83, 84. **McWilliams** a-59, 78, 80, 82, 84. **Miller** a-84, 85. **Orlando** a-15, 19, 20, 22, 23. **Sekowsky** a-3. **Simonson** a-50, 54, 55, 83r. **Weiss** a-39, 79r(#39). (See Mystery Comics Digest 3, 6, 9, 12, 15, 18, 21, 24). Reprints-26(1/3), 71, 73, 79, 83, 84, 86, 92. Painted c-1-91.*

TWILIGHT ZONE, THE (TV)
Now Comics: Nov, 1990 ($2.95); Oct, 1991; V2#1, Nov, 1991 - No. 11, Oct, 1992 ($1.95); V3#1, 1993 - No. 4, 1993 ($2.50)

1-(11/90, $2.95, 52 pgs.)-Direct sale edition; Neal Adams-a, Sienkiewicz-c; Harlan Ellison scripts 3.00
1-(11/90, $1.75)-Newsstand ed. w/N. Adams-c 2.50
1-Prestige Format (10/91, $4.95)-Reprints above with extra Harlan Ellison short story 5.00
1-Collector's Edition (10/91, $2.50)-Non-code approved and polybagged; reprints 11/90 issue; gold logo, 1-Reprint ($2.50)-r/direct sale 11/90 version, 1-Reprint ($2.50)-r/newsstand 11/90 version each... 2.50
V2#1-Direct sale & newsstand ed. w/different-c 2.50
V2#2-8,10-11 2.50
V2#9-($2.95)-3-D Special; polybagged w/glasses & hologram on-c 3.00
V2#9-($4.95)-Prestige Edition; contains 2 extra stories & a different hologram on-c; polybagged w/glasses 5.00
V3#1-4, Anniversary Special 1 (1992, $2.50) 2.50
Annual 1 (4/93, $2.50)-No ads 2.50
...Science Fiction Special (3/93, $3.50) 3.50

TWINKLE COMICS
Spotlight Publishers: May, 1945

	GD 2.0	VG 4.0	FN 6.0	VF 8.0	VF/NM 9.0	NM- 9.2
1	25	50	75	141	203	265

TWIST, THE
Dell Publishing Co.: July-Sept, 1962

	GD 2.0	VG 4.0	FN 6.0	VF 8.0	VF/NM 9.0	NM- 9.2
01-864-209-Painted-c	4	8	12	29	40	50

TWISTED TALES (See Eclipse Graphic Album Series #15)
Pacific Comics/Independent Comics Group (Eclipse) #9,10: 11/82 - No. 8, 5/84; No. 9, 11/84; No. 10, 12/84 (Baxter paper)

1-9: 1-B. Jones/Corben-c; Alcala-a; nudity/violence in al. 2-Wrightson-c; Ploog-a 4.00
10-Wrightson painted art; Morrow-a 6.00

NOTE: ***Bolton** painted c-4, 6, 7; a-7. **Conrad** a-1, 3, 5; c-1i, 3, 5. **Guice** a-8. **Wildey** a-3.*

TWO BIT THE WACKY WOODPECKER (See Wacky...)
Toby Press: 1951 - No. 3, May, 1953

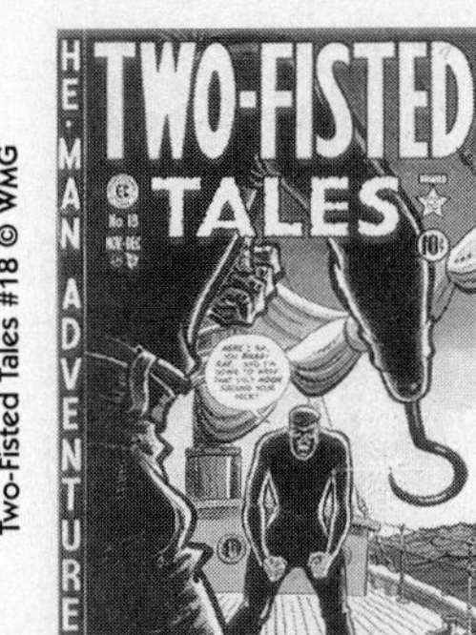

Two-Fisted Tales #18 © WMG

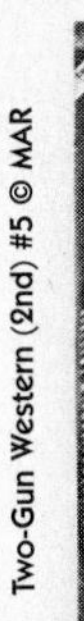
Two-Gun Western (2nd) #5 © MAR

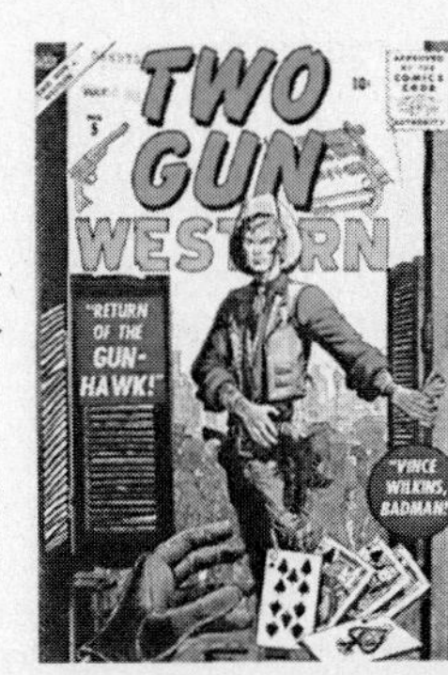

2001: A Space Odyssey #10 © MAR

GD VG FN VF VF/NM NM-
2.0 4.0 6.0 8.0 9.0 9.2

1 10 20 30 56 73 90
2,3 6 12 18 31 38 45

TWO FACES OF TOMORROW, THE
Dark Horse: Aug, 1997 - No. 13, Aug, 1998 ($2.95/$3.95, B&W, lim. series)
1-13: 1-Manga 4.00

TWO-FISTED TALES (Formerly Haunt of Fear #15-17)
E. C. Comics: No. 18, Nov-Dec, 1950 - No. 41, Feb-Mar, 1955
18(#1)-Kurtzman-c 88 176 264 660 968 1275
19-Kurtzman-c 66 132 198 495 728 960
20-Kurtzman-c 42 84 126 315 463 610
21,22-Kurtzman-c 33 66 99 248 364 480
23-25-Kurtzman-c 26 52 78 195 288 380
26-35: 33- "Atom Bomb" by Wood 19 38 57 143 212 280
36-41 15 30 45 113 169 225
Two-Fisted Annual (1952, 25¢, 132 pgs.) 87 174 261 653 902 1150
Two-Fisted Annual (1953, 25¢, 132 pgs.) 69 138 207 518 709 900
NOTE: ***Berg** a-29. **Colan** a-39p. **Craig** a-18, 19, 32. **Crandall** a-35, 36. **Davis** a-20-36, 40; c-30, 34, 35, 41, Annual 2. **Evans** a-34, 40, 41; c-40. **Feldstein** a-18. **Krigstein** a-41. **Kubert** a-32, 33. **Kurtzman** a-18-25; c-18-29, 31, Annual 1. **Severin** a-26, 28, 29, 31, 34-41 (No. 37-39 are all-**Severin** issues); c-36-39. **Severin/Elder** a-19-29, 31, 33, 36. **Wood** a-18-28, 30-35, 41; c-32, 33. Special issues: #26 (ChanJin Reservoir), 31 (Civil War), 35 (Civil War). Canadian reprints known; see Table of Contents. #25-Davis biog. #27-Wood biog. #28-Kurtzman biog.*

TWO-FISTED TALES
Russ Cochran/Gemstone Publishing: Oct, 1992 - No. 24, May, 1998 ($1.50/$2.00/$2.50)
1-24: 1-4r/Two-Fisted Tales #18-21 w/original-c 2.50

TWO-GUN KID (Also see All Western Winners, Best Western, Black Rider, Blaze Carson, Kid Colt, Western Winners, Wild West, & Wild Western)
Marvel/Atlas (MCI No. 1-10/HPC No. 11-59/Marvel No. 60 on): 3/48(No mo.) - No. 10, 11/49; No. 11, 12/53 - No. 59, 4/61; No. 60, 11/62 - No. 92, 3/68; No. 93, 7/70 - No. 136, 4/77
1-Two-Gun Kid & his horse Cyclone begin; The Sheriff begins
108 216 324 675 1038 1400
2 44 88 132 268 409 550
3,4: 3-Annie Oakley app. 37 74 111 209 305 400
5-Pre-Black Rider app. (Wint. 48/49); Anti-Wertham editorial (1st?)
40 80 120 233 342 450
6-10(11/49): 8-Blaze Carson app. 9-Black Rider app.
29 58 87 164 237 310
11(12/53)-Black Rider app.; 1st to have Atlas globe on-c; explains how Kid Colt became an outlaw 23 46 69 130 188 245
12-Black Rider app. 22 44 66 123 177 230
13-20: 14-Opium story 16 32 48 89 127 165
21-24,26-29 15 30 45 85 120 155
25,30: 25-Williamson-a (5 pgs.). 30-Williamson/Torres-a (4 pgs.)
16 32 48 89 127 165
31-33,35,37-40 9 18 27 63 89 115
34-Crandall-a 9 18 27 65 93 120
36,41,42,48-Origin in all 9 18 27 65 93 120
43,44,47 7 14 21 51 71 90
45,46-Davis-a 8 16 24 55 78 100
49,50,52,53-Severin-a(2/3) in each 7 14 21 50 68 85
51-Williamson-a (5 pgs.) 8 16 24 55 78 100
54,55,57,59-Severin-a(3) in each. 59-Kirby-a; last 10¢ issue (4/61)
7 14 21 46 63 80
56 6 12 18 40 55 70
58,60-New origin. 58-Kirby/Ayers-c/a "The Monster of Hidden Valley" cover/story (Kirby monster-c) 7 14 21 46 63 80
60-Edition w/handwritten issue number on cover 8 16 24 58 82 105
61,62-Kirby-a 6 12 18 43 59 75
63-74: 64-Intro. Boom-Boom 4 8 12 29 40 50
75-77-Kirby-a 5 10 15 36 48 60
78-89 3 7 10 21 28 35
90,95-Kirby-a 4 8 12 24 32 40
91,92: 92-Last new story; last 12¢ issue 3 6 9 18 24 30
93,94,96-99 2 4 6 14 18 22
100-Last 15¢-c 3 6 9 16 20 24
101-Origin retold/#58; Kirby-a 3 6 9 16 20 24
102-120-reprints 2 4 6 8 10 12
121-136-reprints. 129-131-(Regular 25¢ editions) 2 4 6 8 10 12
129-131-(30¢-c variants, limited distribution)(4-8/76) 2 4 6 11 14 18
NOTE: ***Ayers** a-26, 27. **Davis** c-45-47. **Drucker** a-23. **Everett** a-82, 91. **Fuje** a-13. **Heath** a-3(2), 4(3), 5(2), 7; c-13, 21, 23, 53. **Keller** a-16, 19, 28. **Kirby** a-54, 55, 57-62, 75-77, 90, 95, 101, 119, 120, 129; c-10, 52, 54-65, 67-72, 74-76, 116. **Maneely** a-20; c-11, 12, 16, 19, 20, 25-28, 30, 35, 49. **Powell** a-38, 102, 104. **Severin** a-9, 29, 51, 55, 57, 99r(3); c-9, 51. **Shores** c-1-8, 11. **Trimpe** c-99. **Tuska** a-11, 12. **Whitney** a-87, 89-91, 98-113, 124, 129; c-87, 89, 91, 113. **Wildey** a-21. **Williamson** a-110r. Kid Colt in #13, 14, 16-21.*

TWO GUN KID: SUNSET RIDERS
Marvel Comics: Nov, 1995 - No. 2, Dec, 1995 ($6.95, squarebound, lim. series)
1,2: Fabian Nicieza scripts in all. 1-painted-c. 7.00

TWO GUN WESTERN (1st Series) (Formerly Casey Crime Photographer #1-4? or My Love #1-4?)
Marvel/Atlas Comics (MPC): No. 5, Nov, 1950 - No. 14, June, 1952
5-The Apache Kid (Intro & origin) & his horse Nightwind begin by Buscema
27 54 81 154 222 290
6-10: 8-Kid Colt, The Texas Kid & his horse Thunder begin?
20 40 60 112 161 210
11-14: 13-Black Rider app. 14 28 42 79 110 140
NOTE: ***Maneely** a-6, 7, 9; c-6, 11-13. **Morrow** a-9. **Romita** a-8. **Wildey** a-8.*

2-GUN WESTERN (2nd Series) (Formerly Billy Buckskin #1-3; Two-Gun Western #5 on)
Atlas Comics (MgPC): No. 4, May, 1956
4-Colan, Ditko, Severin, Sinnott-a; Maneely-c 17 34 51 95 135 175

TWO-GUN WESTERN (Formerly 2-Gun Western)
Atlas Comics (MgPC): No. 5, July, 1956 - No. 12, Sept, 1957
5-Return of the Gun-Hawk-c/story; Black Rider app. 16 32 48 89 127 165
6,7 12 24 36 69 95 120
8,10,12-Crandall-a 13 26 39 74 102 130
9,11-Williamson-a in both (5 pgs. each) 14 28 42 79 110 140
NOTE: ***Ayers** a-9. **Colan** a-5. **Everett** c-12. **Forgione** a-5, 6. **Kirby** a-12. **Maneely** a-6, 8, 12; c-5, 6, 8, 11. **Morrow** a-9, 10. **Powell** a-7, 11. **Severin** c-10. **Sinnott** a-5. **Wildey** a-9.*

TWO MINUTE WARNING
Ultimate Sports Ent.: 2000 - No. 2 ($3.95, cardstock covers)
1,2-NFL players & Teddy Roosevelt battle evil 4.00

TWO MOUSEKETEERS, THE (See 4-Color #475, 603, 642 under M.G.M.'s...;

TWO ON A GUILLOTINE (See Movie Classics)

TWO-STEP
DC Comics (Cliffhanger): Dec, 2003 - No. 3, Jul, 2004 ($2.95, limited series)
1-3-Warren Ellis-s/Amanda Conner-a 3.00

2000 A.D. MONTHLY/PRESENTS (Showcase #25 on)
Eagle Comics/Quality Comics No. 5 on: 4/85 - #6, 9/85; 4/86 - #54, 1991 ($1.25-$1.50, Mando paper)
1-6,1-25:1-4 r/British series featuring Judge Dredd; Alan Moore scripts begin.
1-25 ($1.25)-Reprints from British 2000 AD 2.25
26,27/28, 29/30, 31-54: 27/28, 29/30,31-Guice-c 2.25

2001, A SPACE ODYSSEY (Movie)
Marvel Comics Group: Dec, 1976 - No. 10, Sept, 1977 (30¢)
1-Adaptation of film; Kirby-c/a in all 2 4 6 10 13 16
2-7,9,10 1 2 3 5 6 8
7,9,10-(35¢-c variants, limited distribution)(6-9/77) 2 4 6 8 10 12
8-Origin/1st app. Machine Man (called Mr. Machine) 2 4 6 11 14 18
8-(35¢-c variant, limited distribution)(6,8/77) 3 6 9 17 22 27
...Treasury 1 ('76, 84 pgs.)-All new Kirby-a 3 6 9 16 21 26

2001 NIGHTS
Viz Premiere Comics: 1990 - No. 10, 1991 ($3.75, B&W, lim. series, mature readers, 84 pgs.)
1-10: Japanese sci-fi. 1-Wraparound-c 4.25

2010 (Movie)
Marvel Comics Group: Apr, 1985 - No. 2, May, 1985
1,2-r/Marvel Super Special movie adaptation. 2.25

TYPHOID (Also see Daredevil)
Marvel Comics: Nov, 1995 - No. 4, Feb, 1996 ($3.95, squarebound, lim. series)
1-4: Van Fleet-c/a 4.00

UFO & ALIEN COMIX
Warren Publishing Co.: Jan, 1978 (B&W magazine, 84 pgs., one-shot)
nn-Toth-a, J. Severin-a(r); Pie-s 2 4 6 11 14 18

UFO & OUTER SPACE (Formerly UFO Flying Saucers)
Gold Key: No. 14, June, 1978 - No. 25, Feb, 1980 (All painted covers)
14-Reprints UFO Flying Saucers #3 1 3 4 6 8 10
15,16-Reprints 1 3 4 6 8 10
17-25: 17-20-New material. 23-McWilliams-a. 24-(3 pg.-r). 25-Reprints UFO Flying Saucers #2 w/cover 1 3 4 6 8 10

UFO ENCOUNTERS
Western Publishing Co.: May, 1978 ($1.95, 228 pgs.)

Ultimate Daredevil and Elektra #1 © MAR

Ultimate Fantastic Four #1 © MAR

Ultimate Spider-Man #63 © MAR

	GD 2.0	VG 4.0	FN 6.0	VF 8.0	VF/NM 9.0	NM- 9.2

11192-Reprints UFO Flying Saucers 4 8 12 24 32 40
11404-Vol.1 (128 pgs.)-See UFO Mysteries for Vol.2 3 6 9 19 25 32

UFO FLYING SAUCERS (UFO & Outer Space #14 on)
Gold Key: Oct, 1968 - No. 13, Jan, 1977 (No. 2 on, 36 pgs.)

1(30035-810) (68 pgs.) 5 10 15 33 44 55
2(11/70), 3(11/72), 4(11/74) 2 4 6 14 18 22
5(2/75)-13: Bolle-a #4 on 2 4 6 10 12 15

UFO MYSTERIES
Western Publishing Co.: 1978 ($1.00, reprints, 96 pgs.)

11400-(Vol.2)-Cont'd from UFO Encounters, pgs. 129-224
3 6 9 19 25 32

ULTIMAN GIANT ANNUAL (See Big Bang Comics)
Image Comics: Nov, 2001 ($4.95, B&W, one-shot)

1-Homage to DC 1960's annuals 5.00

ULTIMATE... (Collects 4-issue alternate titles from X-Men Age of Apocalypse crossovers)
Marvel Comics: May, 1995 ($8.95, trade paperbacks, gold foil covers)

Amazing X-Men, Astonishing X-Men, Factor-X, Gambit & the X-Ternals, Generation Next, X-Calibre, X-Man 9.00
Weapon X 10.00

ULTIMATE ADVENTURES
Marvel Comics: Nov, 2002 - No. 6, Dec, 2003 ($2.25)

1-6: 1-Intro. Hawk-Owl; Zimmerman-s/Fegredo-a. 3-Ultimates app. 2.25

ULTIMATE DAREDEVIL AND ELEKTRA
Marvel Comics: Jan, 2003 - No. 4, Mar, 2003 ($2.25, limited series)

1-4-Rucka-s/Larroca-c/a; 1st meeting of Elektra and Matt Murdock 2.25
... Vol.1 TPB (2003, $11.99) r/#1-4, Daredevil Vol. 2 #9; Larroca sketch pages 12.00

ULTIMATE ELEKTRA
Marvel Comics: Oct, 2004 - No. 5 ($2.25, limited series)

1-4-Carey-s/Larroca-c/a. 2-Bullseye app. 2.25

ULTIMATE FANTASTIC FOUR
Marvel Comics: Feb, 2004 - Present ($2.25)

1-Bendis & Millar-s/Adam Kubert-a/Hitch-c 2.25
2-13: 2-Adam Kubert-a/c; intro. Moleman 7-Ellis-s/Immonen-a begin; Dr. Doom app. 13-Kubert-a 2.25
... Vol. 1: The Fantastic (2004, $12.99, TPB) r/#1-6; cover gallery 13.00

ULTIMATE MARVEL MAGAZINE
Marvel Comics: Feb, 2001 - No. 11, 2002 ($3.99, magazine size)

1-11: Reprints of recent stories from the Ultimate titles plus Marvel news and features. 1-Reprints Ultimate Spider-Man #1&2. 11-Lord of the Rings-c 4.00

ULTIMATE MARVEL TEAM-UP (Spider-Man Team-up)
Marvel Comics: Apr, 2001 - No. 16, July, 2002 ($2.99/$2.25)

1-Spider-Man & Wolverine; Bendis-s in all; Matt Wagner-a/c 5.00
2,3-Hulk; Hester-a 3.50
4,5,9-16: 4,5-Iron Man; Allred-a. 9-Fantastic Four; Mahfood-a. 10-Man-Thing; Totleben-a. 11-X-Men; Clugston-Major-a. 12,13-Dr. Strange; McKeever-a.14-Black Widow; Terry Moore-a. 15,16-Shang-Chi; Mays-a 3.00
6-8-Punisher; Sienkiewicz-a. 7,8-Daredevil app. 4.00
TPB (11/01, $14.95) r/#1-5 15.00
HC (8/02, $39.99) r/#1-16 & Ult. Spider-Man Special; Bendis afterword 30.00
...: Vol. 2 TPB (2003, $11.99) r/#9-13; Mahfood-c 12.00
...: Vol. 3 TPB (2003, $12.99) r/#14-16 & Ultimate Spider-Man Super Special; Moore-c 13.00

ULTIMATE NIGHTMARE
Marvel Comics: Oct, 2004 - No. 5 ($2.25, limited series)

1-3: Ellis-s; Ultimates, X-Men, Nick Fury app. 1,2-Hairsine-a/c 2.25

ULTIMATES, THE (Avengers of the Ultimate line)
Marvel Comics: Mar, 2002 - No. 13, Apr, 2004 ($2.25)

1-Intro. Capt. America; Millar-s/Hitch-a & wraparound-c 6.00
2-Intro. Giant-Man and the Wasp 4.00
3-13: 3-1st Capt. America in new costume. 4-Intro. Thor. 5-Ultimates vs. The Hulk. 8-Intro. Hawkeye 3.00
... Volume 1 HC (2004, $29.99) oversized r/series; commentary pages with Millar & Hitch; cover gallery and character design pages; intro. by Joss Whedon 30.00
... Volume 1: Super-Human TPB (8/02, $12.99) r/#1-6 13.00
... Volume 2: Homeland Security TPB (2004, $17.99) r/#7-13 18.00

ULTIMATES 2
Marvel Comics: Feb, 2005 - Present ($2.99)

1-Millar-s/Hitch-a; Giant-Man becomes Ant-Man 3.00

ULTIMATE SIX (Reprinted in Ultimate Spider-Man Vol.5 hardcover)
Marvel Comics: Nov, 2003 - No. 7, June, 2004 ($2.25) (See Ultimate Spider-Man for TPB)

1-The Ultimates & Spider-Man team-up; Bendis-s/Quesada & Hairsine-a; Cassaday-c 5.00
2-7-Hairsine-a; Cassaday-c 2.25

ULTIMATE SPIDER-MAN
Marvel Comics: Oct, 2000 - Present ($2.99/$2.25)

1-Bendis-s/Bagley & Thibert-a; cardstock-c; introduces revised origin and cast separate from regular Spider-continuity 7 14 21 51 71 90
1-Variant white-c (Retailer incentive) 140.00
1-DF Edition 60.00
1-Free Comic Book Day giveaway & Kay Bee Toys variant - (See Promotional Comics section)
2-Cover with Spider-Man on car 3 7 10 21 28 35
2-Cover with Spider-Man swinging past building 3 6 9 21 28 35
3,4: 4-Uncle Ben killed 3 6 9 18 24 30
5-7: 6,7-Green Goblin app. 3 7 10 21 28 35
8-13: 13-Reveals secret to MJ 1 2 3 5 7 9
14-21: 14-Intro. Gwen Stacy & Dr. Octopus 5.00
22-($3.50) Green Goblin returns 3.50
23-32 2.50
33-1st Ultimate Venom-c; intro. Eddie Brock 3.00
34-38-Ultimate Venom 2.50
39-49,51-59: 39-Nick Fury app. 43,44-X-Men app. 46-Prelude to Ultimate Six; Sandman app. 51-53-Elektra app. 54-59-Doctor Octopus app. 2.25
50-($2.99) Intro. Black Cat 3.00
60-Intro. Ultimate Carnage on cover 3.00
61-Intro Ben Reilly; Punisher app. 2.25
62-Gwen Stacy killed by Carnage 3.00
63-69: 63,64-Carnage app. 66,67-Wolverine app. 68,69-Johnny Storm app. 2.25
Collected Edition (1/01, $3.99) r/#1-3 4.00
Hardcover (3/02, $34.95, 7x11", dust jacket) r/#1-13 & Amazing Fantasy #15; sketch pages and Bill Jemas' initial plot and character outlines 35.00
...: Double Trouble TPB (6/02, $17.95) r/#14-21 18.00
...: Learning Curve TPB (12/01, $14.95) r/#8-13 15.00
...: Legacy TPB (2002, $14.99) r/#22-27 15.00
...: Power and Responsibility TPB (4/01, $14.95) r/#1-7 15.00
...Special (7/02, $3.50) art by Bagley and various incl. Romita,Sr., Brereton, Cho, Mack, Sienkiewicz, Phillips, Pearson, Oeming, Mahfood, Russell 3.50
Vol. 6: Venom TPB (2003, $15.99) r/#33-39 16.00
Vol. 7: Irresponsible TPB (2003, $12.99) r/#40-45 13.00
Vol. 8: Cats & Kings TPB (2004, $17.99) r/#47-53 18.00
Vol. 9: Ultimate Six TPB (2004, $17.99) r/#46 & Ultimate Six #1-7 18.00
Vol. 10: Hollywood TPB (2004, $12.99) r/#54-59 13.00
Vol. 11: Carnage TPB (2004, $12.99) r/#60-65 13.00
Volume 2 HC (2003, $29.99, 7x11", dust jacket) r/#14-27; pin-ups & sketch pages 30.00
Volume 3 HC (2003, $29.99, 7x11", dust jacket) r/#28-39 & #1/2; script pages 30.00
Volume 4 HC (2004, $29.99, 7x11", dust jacket) r/#40-45, 47-53; sketch pages 30.00
Volume 5 HC (2004, $29.99, 7x11", dust jacket) r/#46,54-59, Ultimate Six #1-7 30.00
Wizard #1/2 1 3 4 6 8 10

ULTIMATE WAR
Marvel Comics: Feb, 2003 - No. 4, Apr, 2003 ($2.25, limited series)

1-4-Millar-s/Bachalo-c/a; The Ultimates vs. Ultimate X-Men 2.25
Ultimate X-Men Vol. 5: Ultimate War TPB (2003, $10.99) r/#1-4 11.00

ULTIMATE X-MEN (Also see Promotional Comics section for FCBD Ed.)
Marvel Comics: Feb, 2001 - Present ($2.99/$2.25)

1-Millar-s/Adam Kubert & Thibert-a; cardstock-c; introduces revised origin and cast separate from regular X-Men continuity 3 6 9 16 20 25
1-DF Edition 30.00
1-DF Sketch Cover Edition 45.00
2 2 4 6 12 16 20
3-6 2 4 6 9 11 14
7-10 6.00
11-24,26-33: 13-Intro. Gambit. 18,19-Bachalo-a. 23,24-Andrews-a 2.25
25-($3.50) leads into the Ultimate War mini-series; Kubert-a 3.50
34-Spider-Man-c/app.; Bendis-s begin; Finch-a 2.25
35-53: 35-Spider-Man app. 36,37-Daredevil-c/app. 40-Intro. Angel. 42-Intro. Dazzler. 44-Beast dies. 46-Intro. Mr. Sinister. 50-53-Kubert-a; Gambit app. 2.25
...: The Tomorrow People TPB (7/01, $14.95) r/#1-6 15.00
...: Return to Weapon X TPB (4/02, $14.95) r/#7-12 15.00
Vol. 3: World Tour TPB (2002, $17.99) r/#13-20 18.00
Vol. 4: Hellfire and Brimstone TPB (2003, $12.99) r/#21-25 13.00
Vol. 5 (See Ultimate War)

Ultimate X-Men #50 © MAR

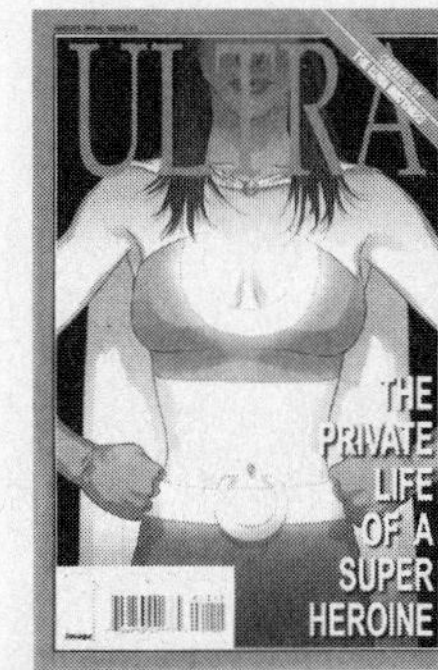

Ultra #1 © Luna Bros. Prods.

Uncanny Tales #1 © MAR

GD 2.0 | VG 4.0 | FN 6.0 | VF 8.0 | VF/NM 9.0 | NM- 9.2

Vol. 6: Return of the King TPB (2003, $16.99) r/#26-33 17.00
Vol. 7: Blockbuster TPB (2004, $12.99) r/#34-39 13.00
Vol. 8: New Mutants TPB (2004, $12.99) r/#40-45 13.00
Vol. 9: The Tempest TPB (2004, $10.99) r/#46-49 11.00
Volume 1 HC (8/02, $34.99, 7x11", dust jacket) r/#1-12 & Giant-Size X-Men #1; sketch pages and Millar and Bendis' initial plot and character outlines 35.00
Volume 2 HC (2003, $29.99, 7x11", dust jacket) r/#13-25; script for #20 30.00
Volume 3 HC (2003, $29.99, 7x11", dust jacket) r/#26-33 & Utimate War #1-4 30.00
Wizard #1/2 2 4 6 10 12 15

ULTRA
Image Comics: Aug, 2004 - No. 8 ($2.95, limited series)

1-4: 1-Intro. Ultra/Pearl Penalosa; Luna Brothers-s/a 3.00

ULTRAFORCE (1st Series) (Also see Avengers/Ultraforce #1)
Malibu Comics (Ultraverse): Aug, 1994 - No. 10, Aug, 1995 ($1.95/$2.50)

0 (9/94, $2.50)-Perez-c/a. 2.50
1-($2.50, 44 pgs.)-Bound-in trading card; team consisting of Prime, Prototype, Hardcase, Pixx, Ghoul, Contrary & Topaz; Gerard Jones scripts begin, ends #6; Perez-c/a begins. 2.50
1-Ultra 5000 Limited Silver Foil Edition 4.00
1-Holographic-c, no price 6.00
2-5: Perez-c/a in all. 2 (10/94, $1.95)-Prime quits, Strangers cameo. 3-Origin of Topaz; Prime rejoins. 5-Pixx dies. 2.50
2 ($2.50)-Florescent logo; limited edition stamp on-c 3.00
6-10: 6-Begin $2.50-c, Perez-c/a. 7-Ghoul story, Steve Erwin-a. 8-Marvel's Black Knight enters the Ultraverse (last seen in Avengers #375); Perez-c/a. 9,10-Black Knight app.; Perez-c. 10-Leads into Ultraforce/Avengers Prelude 2.50
Malibu "Ashcan ": Ultraforce #0A (6/94) 2.50
.../Avengers Prelude 1 (8/95, $2.50)-Perez-c. 2.50
.../Avengers 1 (8/95, $3.95)-Warren Ellis script; Perez-c/a; foil-c 4.00

ULTRAFORCE (2nd Series)(Also see Black September)
Malibu Comics (Ultraverse): Infinity, Sept, 1995 - V2#15, Dec, 1996 ($1.50)

Infinity, V2#1-15: Infinity-Team consists of Marvel's Black Knight, Ghoul, Topaz, Prime & redesigned Prototype; Warren Ellis scripts begin, ends #3; variant-c exists. 1-1st app.Cromwell, Lament & Wreckage. 2-Contains free encore presentation of Ultraforce #1; flip book "Phoenix Resurrection" Pt. 7. 7-Darick Robertson, Jeff Johnson & others-a. 8,9-Intro. Future Ultraforce (Prime, Hellblade, Angel of Destruction, Painkiller & Whipslash); Gary Erskine-c/a. 9-Foxfire app. 10-Len Wein scripts & Deodato Studios-c/a begin. 10-Lament back-up story. 11-Ghoul back-up story by Pander Bros. 12-Ultraforce vs. Maxis (cont'd in Ultraverse Unlimited #2); Exiles & Iron Clad app. 13-Prime leaves; Hardcase returns 2.25
Infinity (2000 signed) 4.00
.../Spider-Man ($3.95)-Marv Wolfman script; Green Goblin app; 2 covers exist. 4.00

ULTRAGIRL
Marvel Comics: Nov, 1996 - No. 3 Mar, 1997($1.50, limited series)

1-3: 1-1st app. 2.25

ULTRA KLUTZ
Onward Comics: 1981; 6/86 - #27, 1/89, #28, 4/90 - #31, 1990? ($1.50/$1.75/$2.00, B&W)

1 (1981)-Re-released after 2nd #1 2.25
1-30: 1-(6/86). 27-Photo back-c 2.25
31-($2.95, 52 pgs.) 3.00

ULTRAMAN
Nemesis Comics: Mar, 1994 - No. 4, Sept, 1994 ($1.75/$1.95)

1-($2.25)-Collector's edition; foil-c; special 3/4 wraparound-c 3.00
1-($1.75)-Newsstand edition 2.50
2-4: 3-$1.95-c begins 2.50
#(-1) (3/93) 2.50

ULTRAMAN TIGA
Dark Horse Comics: Aug, 2003 - No. 10, June, 2004 ($3.99)

1-10-Khoo Fuk Lung-a/Tony Wong-s 4.00

ULTRAVERSE DOUBLE FEATURE
Malibu Comics (Ultraverse): Jan, 1995 ($3.95, one-shot, 68 pgs.)

1-Flip-c featuring Prime & Solitaire. 4.00

ULTRAVERSE ORIGINS
Malibu Comics (Ultraverse): Jan, 1994 (99¢, one-shot)

1-Gatefold-c; 2 pg. origins all characters 2.25
1-Newsstand edition; different-c, no gatefold 2.25

ULTRAVERSE PREMIERE
Malibu Comics (Ultraverse): 1994 (one-shot)

0-Ordered thru mail w/coupons 5.00

ULTRAVERSE UNLIMITED
Malibu Comics (Ultraverse): June, 1996; No. 2, Sept, 1996 ($2.50)

1,2: 1-Adam Warlock returns to the Marvel Universe; Rune-c/app. 2-Black Knight, Reaper & Sierra Blaze return to the Marvel Universe 2.50

ULTRAVERSE YEAR ONE
Malibu Comics (Ultraverse): 1994 ($4.95, one-shot)

nn-In-depth synopsis of the first year's titles & stories. 5.00

ULTRAVERSE YEAR TWO
Malibu Comics (Ultraverse): Aug, 1995 ($4.95, one-shot)

nn-In-depth synopsis of second year's titles & stories 5.00

ULTRAVERSE YEAR ZERO: THE DEATH OF THE SQUAD
Malibu Comics (Ultraverse): Apr, 1995 - No. 4, July, 1995 ($2.95, lim. series)

1-4: 3-Codename: Firearm back-up story. 3.00

UNBIRTHDAY PARTY WITH ALICE IN WONDERLAND (See Alice In Wonderland, Four Color #341)

UNBOUND
Image Comics (Desperado): Jan, 1998 ($2.95, B&W)

1-Pruett-s/Peters-a 3.00

UNCANNY ORIGINS
Marvel Comics: Sept, 1996 - No. 14, Oct, 1997 (99¢)

1-14: 1-Cyclops. 2-Quicksilver. 3-Archangel. 4-Firelord. 5-Hulk. 6-Beast. 7-Venom. 8-Nightcrawler. 9-Storm. 10-Black Cat. 11-Black Knight. 12-Dr. Strange. 13-Daredevil. 14-Iron Fist 2.25

UNCANNY TALES
Atlas Comics (PrPI/PPI): June, 1952 - No. 56, Sept, 1957

1-Heath-a; horror/weird stories begin 89 178 267 556 853 1150
2 48 96 144 293 447 600
3-5 40 80 120 244 372 500
6-Wolvertonish-a by Matt Fox 43 86 129 262 401 540
7-10: 8-Atom bomb story; Tothish-a (by Sekowsky?). 9-Crandall-a 39 78 117 227 331 435
11-20: 17-Atom bomb panels; anti-communist story; Hitler story. 19-Krenkel-a. 20-Robert Q. Sale-c 29 58 87 164 237 310
21-25,27: 25-Nostrand-a? 25 50 75 141 203 265
26-Spider-Man prototype c/story 35 70 105 200 290 380
28-Last precode issue (1/55); Kubert-a; #1-28 contain 2-3 sci/fi stories each 26 52 78 147 211 275
29-41,43-49,51 18 36 54 100 143 185
42,54,56-Krigstein-a 19 38 57 107 154 200
50,53,55-Torres-a 18 36 54 100 143 185
52-Oldest Iron Man prototype (2/57) 20 40 60 112 161 210

NOTE: ***Andru*** *a-15, 27.* ***Ayers*** *a-22.* ***Bailey*** *a-51.* ***Briefer*** *a-19, 20.* ***Brodsky*** *c-1, 3, 4, 6, 8, 12-16, 19.* ***Brodsky/Everett*** *c-9.* ***Cameron*** *a-47.* ***Colan*** *a-11, 16, 17, 52.* ***Drucker*** *a-37, 42, 45.* ***Everett*** *a-2, 9, 12, 32, 36, 39, 48; c-7, 11, 17, 39, 41, 50, 52, 53.* ***Fass*** *a-9, 10, 15, 24. Forte a-18, 27, 34, 52, 53.* ***Heath*** *a-13, 14; c-5, 10, 18.* ***Keller*** *a-3.* ***Lawrence*** *a-14, 17, 19, 23, 27, 28, 35.* ***Maneely*** *a-4, 8, 10, 16, 29, 35; c-2, 22, 26, 33, 38.* ***Moldoff*** *a-23.* ***Morisi*** *a-48, 52.* ***Morrow*** *a-46, 51.* ***Orlando*** *a-49, 50, 53.* ***Powell*** *a-12, 18, 34, 36, 38, 43, 50, 56.* ***Robinson*** *a-3, 13.* ***Reinman*** *a-12.* ***Romita*** *a-10.* ***Roussos*** *a-8.* ***Sale*** *a-47, 53; c-20.* ***Sekowsky*** *a-25.* ***Sinnott*** *a-15, 52.* ***Torres*** *a-53.* ***Tothish****-a by* ***Andru****-27.* ***Wildey*** *a-22, 48.*

UNCANNY TALES
Marvel Comics Group: Dec, 1973 - No. 12, Oct, 1975

1-Crandall-r/Uncanny Tales #9('50s) 3 6 9 18 24 30
2-12: 7,12-Kirby-a 2 4 6 10 13 16

NOTE: ***Ditko*** *reprints-#4, 6-8, 10-12.*

UNCANNY X-MEN, THE (See **X-Men, The,** 1st series, #142-on)

UNCANNY X-MEN AND THE NEW TEEN TITANS (See Marvel and DC Present...)

UNCENSORED MOUSE, THE
Eternity Comics: Apr, 1989 - No. 2, Apr, 1989 ($1.95, B&W)(Came sealed in plastic bag) (Both contain racial stereotyping & violence)

1,2-Early Gottfredson strip-r in each 2 4 6 8 10 13

NOTE: *Both issues contain unauthorized reprints. Series was cancelled.* ***Win Smith*** *r-1, 2.*

UNCLE CHARLIE'S FABLES
Lev Gleason Publ.: Jan, 1952 - No. 5, Sept, 1952 (All have Biro painted-c)

1-Norman Maurer-a; has Biro's picture 16 32 48 89 127 165
2-Fuje-a; Biro photo 10 20 30 56 73 90
3-5 9 18 27 49 62 75

UNCLE DONALD & HIS NEPHEWS DUDE RANCH (See Dell Giant #52)

UNCLE DONALD & HIS NEPHEWS FAMILY FUN (See Dell Giant #38)

UNCLE JOE'S FUNNIES

Uncle Milty #2 © True Cross Pub.

Uncle Scrooge #4 © WDC

Uncle Wiggily Four Color #349 © DELL

GD 2.0 | VG 4.0 | FN 6.0 | VF 8.0 | VF/NM 9.0 | NM- 9.2

Centaur Publications: 1938 (B&W)

1-Games, puzzles & magic tricks, some interior art; Bill Everett-c — 54 108 162 329 502 675

UNCLE MILTY (TV)
Victoria Publications/True Cross: Dec, 1950 - No. 4, July, 1951 (52 pgs.)(Early TV comic)

1-Milton Berle photo on-c of #1,2 — 54 108 162 329 502 675
2 — 35 70 105 201 293 385
3,4 — 30 60 90 173 249 325

UNCLE REMUS & HIS TALES OF BRER RABBIT (See Brer Rabbit, 4-Color #129, 208, 693)

UNCLE SAM
DC Comics (Vertigo): 1997 - No. 2, 1997 ($4.95, limited series)

1,2-Alex Ross painted c/a. Story by Ross and Steve Darnell — 5.00
Hardcover (1998, $17.95) — 18.00
Softcover (2000, $9.95) — 10.00

UNCLE SAM QUARTERLY (Blackhawk #9 on)(See Freedom Fighters)
Quality Comics Group: Autumn, 1941 - No. 8, Fall, 1943 (see National Comics)

1-Origin Uncle Sam; Fine/Eisner-c, chapter headings, 2 pgs. by Eisner; (2 versions: dark cover, no price; light cover with price sticker); Jack Cole-a — 379 758 1137 2464 3982 5500
2-Cameos by The Ray, Black Condor, Quicksilver, The Red Bee, Alias the Spider, Hercules & Neon the Unknown; Eisner, Fine-c/a — 135 270 405 844 1297 1750
3-Tuska-c/a; Eisner-a(2) — 98 196 294 613 944 1275
4 — 87 174 261 544 835 1125
5,7-Hitler, Mussolini & Tojo-c — 104 208 312 650 1000 1350
6,8 — 69 138 207 431 666 900

NOTE: *Kotzky (or Tuska) a-3-8.*

UNCLE SCROOGE (Disney) (Becomes Walt Disney's... #210 on) (See Cartoon Tales, Dell Giants #33, 55, Disney Comic Album, Donald and Scrooge, Dynabrite, Four Color #178, Gladstone Comic Album, Walt Disney's Comics & Stories #98, Walt Disney's ...)
Dell #1-39/Gold Key #40-173/Whitman #174-209: No. 386, 3/52 - No. 39, 8-10/62; No. 40, 12/62 - No. 209, 7/84

Four Color 386(#1)-in "Only a Poor Old Man" by Carl Barks; r-in Uncle Scrooge & Donald Duck #1('65) & The Best of Walt Disney Comics (1974). The very 1st cover app. of Uncle Scrooge — 95 190 285 808 1304 1800
1-(1986)-Reprints F.C. #386; given away with lithograph "Dam Disaster at Money Lake" & as a subscription offer giveaway to Gladstone subscribers — 3 6 9 16 20 24
Four Color 456(#2)-in "Back to the Klondike" by Carl Barks; r-in Best of U.S. & D.D. #1('66) & Gladstone C.A. #4 — 53 106 159 451 726 1000
Four Color 495(#3)-r-in #105 — 43 86 129 344 535 725
4(12-2/53-54)-r-in Gladstone Comic Album #11 — 34 68 102 255 398 540
5-r-in Gladstone Special #2 & Walt Disney Digest #1 — 30 60 90 213 327 440
6-r-in U.S. #106,165,233 & Best of U.S. & D.D. #1('66) — 22 44 66 158 242 325
7-The Seven Cities of Cibola by Barks; r-in #217 & Best of D.D. & U.S. #2 ('67) — 20 40 60 145 223 300
8-10: 8-r-in #111,222. 9-r-in #104,214. 10-r-in #67 — 17 34 51 121 186 250
11-20: 11-r-in #237. 17-r-in #215. 19-r-in Gladstone C.A. #1. 20-r-in #213 — 15 30 45 109 167 225
21-30: 24-X-Mas-c. 26-r-in #211 — 13 26 39 92 141 190
31-35,37-40: 34-r-in #228. 40-X-Mas-c — 11 22 33 80 120 160
36-1st app. Magica De Spell; Number one dime 1st identified by name — 13 26 39 90 138 185
41-60: 48-Magica De Spell-c/story (3/64). 49-Sci/fi-c. 51-Beagle Boys-c/story (8/64) — 10 20 30 70 100 130
61-63,65,66,68-71:71-Last Barks issue w/original story (#71-he only storyboarded the script) — 9 18 27 65 93 120
64-Barks Vietnam War story "Treasure of Marco Polo" banned for reprints by Disney from 1977-1989 because of its Third World revolutionary war theme. It later appeared in the hardcover Carl Barks Library set (4/89) and Walt Disney's Uncle Scrooge Adventures #42 (1/97) — 12 24 36 86 131 175
67,72,73: 67,72,73-Barks-r — 9 18 27 60 85 110
74-84: 74-Barks-r(1pg.). 75-81,83-Not by Barks. 82,84-Barks-r begin — 6 12 18 40 55 70
85-110 — 5 10 15 36 48 60
111-120 — 4 8 12 24 32 40
121-141,143-152,154-157 — 3 7 10 21 28 35
142-Reprints Four Color #456 with-c — 4 8 12 22 30 38
153,158,162-164,166,168-170,178,180: No Barks — 2 4 6 12 16 20
159-160,165,167 — 2 4 6 14 18 22
161(r/#14), 171(r/#11), 177(r/#16),183(r/#6)-Barks-r — 2 4 6 14 18 22
172(1/80),173(2/80)-Gold Key. Barks-a — 3 6 9 16 21 26
174(3/80),175(4/80),176(5/80)-Whitman. Barks-a — 3 7 10 21 28 35
177(6/80),178(7/80) — 4 8 12 22 30 38
179(9/80)(r/#9)-(Very low distribution) — 38 76 114 285 443 600
180(11/80),181(12/80, r/4-Color #495) pre-pack? — 5 10 15 33 44 55
182-195: 184,185,187,188-Barks-a. 182,186,191-194-No Barks. 189(r/#5), 190(r/#4), 195(r/4-Color #386) — 2 4 6 14 18 22
196(4/82),197(5/82): 196(r/#13) — 3 6 9 16 21 26
198-209 (All #90038 on-c; pre-pack; no date or date code): 198(4/83), 199(5/83), 200(6/83), 201(6/83), 202(7/83), 203(7/83), 204(8/83), 205(8/83), 206(4/84), 207(5/83), 208(6/84), 209(7/84). 198-202,204-206: No Barks. 203(r/#12), 207(r/#93,92), 208(r/U.S. #18), 209(r/U.S. #21)-Barks-r — 3 6 9 18 24 30
Uncle Scrooge & Money(G.K.)-Barks-r/from WDC&S #130 (3/67) — 5 10 15 36 48 60
Mini Comic #1(1976)(3-1/4x6-1/2")-r/U.S. #115; Barks-c — 2 4 6 8 10 12

NOTE: *Barks c-Four Color 386, 456, 495, #4-37, 39, 40, 43-71.*

UNCLE SCROOGE & DONALD DUCK
Gold Key: June, 1965 (25¢, paper cover)

1-Reprint of Four Color #386(#1) & lead story from Four Color #29 — 9 18 27 65 93 120

UNCLE SCROOGE COMICS DIGEST
Gladstone Publishing: Dec, 1986 - No. 5, Aug, 1987 ($1.25, Digest-size)

1,3 — 1 2 3 5 6 8
2,4 — 6.00
5 (low print run) — 1 2 3 5 7 9

UNCLE SCROOGE GOES TO DISNEYLAND (See Dell Giants)
Gladstone Publishing Ltd.: Aug, 1985 ($2.50)

1-Reprints Dell Giant w/new-c by Mel Crawford, based on old cover — 2 4 6 8 10 12
...Comics Digest 1 ($1.50, digest size) — 2 4 6 9 11 14

UNCLE SCROOGE IN COLOR
Gladstone Publishing: 1987 ($29.95, Hardcover, 9-1/4"X12-1/4", 96 pgs.)

nn-Reprints "Christmas on Bear Mountain" from Four Color 178 by Barks; Uncle Scrooge's Christmas Carol (published as Donald Duck & the Christmas Carol, A Little Golden Book), reproduced from the original art as adapted by Norman McGary from pencils by Barks; and Uncle Scrooge the Lemonade King, reproduced from the original art, plus Barks' original pencils — 4 8 12 29 40 50
nn-Slipcase edition of 750, signed by Barks, issued at $79.95 — 300.00

UNCLE SCROOGE THE LEMONADE KING
Whitman Publishing Co.: 1960 (A Top Top Tales Book, 6-3/8"x7-5/8", 32 pgs.)

2465-Storybook pencilled by Carl Barks, finished art adapted by Norman McGary — 40 80 120 300 470 640

UNCLE WIGGILY (See March of Comics #19)
Dell Publishing Co.: No. 179, Dec, 1947 - No. 543, Mar, 1954

Four Color 179 (#1)-Walt Kelly-c — 17 34 51 119 182 245
Four Color 221 (3/49)-Part Kelly-c — 10 20 30 73 107 140
Four Color 276 (5/50), 320 (#1, 3/51) — 9 18 27 63 89 115
Four Color 349 (9-10/51), 391 (4-5/52) — 8 16 24 53 74 95
Four Color 428 (10/52), 503 (10/53), 543 — 6 12 18 40 55 70

UNDEAD, THE
Chaos! Comics (Black Label): Feb, 2002 ($4.99, B&W)

1-Pulido-s/Denham-a — 5.00

UNDERCOVER GIRL (Starr Flagg) (See Extra Comics & Manhunt!)
Magazine Enterprises: No. 5, 1952 - No. 7, 1954

5(#1)(A-1 #62)-Fallon of the F.B.I. in all — 40 80 120 233 342 450
6(A-1 #98), 7(A-1 #118)-All have Starr Flagg — 39 78 117 222 324 425

NOTE: *Powell c-6, 7. Whitney a-5-7.*

UNDERDOG (TV)(See Kite Fun Book, March of Comics #426, 438, 467, 479)
Charlton Comics/Gold Key: July, 1970 - No. 10, Jan, 1972; Mar, 1975 - No. 23, Feb, 1979

1 (1st series, Charlton)-1st app. Underdog — 9 18 27 65 93 120
2-10 — 5 10 15 36 48 60
1 (2nd series, Gold Key) — 7 14 21 50 68 85
2-10 — 4 8 12 25 33 42
11-20: 13-1st app. Shack of Solitude — 3 6 9 19 25 32
21-23 — 3 7 10 21 28 35

UNDERDOG

Underworld #4 © DS

Underworld Crime #3 © FAW

Union Jack #1 © MAR

GD 2.0 | VG 4.0 | FN 6.0 | VF 8.0 | VF/NM 9.0 | NM- 9.2

Spotlight Comics: 1987 - No. 3?, 1987 ($1.50)
1-3 4.00

UNDERDOG (Volume 2)
Harvey Comics: Nov, 1993 - No. 5, July, 1994 ($2.25)
1-5 4.00
Summer Special (10/93, $2.25, 68 pgs.) 4.00

UNDERSEA AGENT
Tower Comics: Jan, 1966 - No. 6, Mar, 1967 (25¢, 68 pgs.)
1-Davy Jones, Undersea Agent begins 10 20 30 67 96 125
2-6: 2-Jones gains magnetic powers. 5-Origin & 1st app. of Merman.
6-Kane/Wood-c(r) 7 14 21 46 63 80
NOTE: *Gil Kane a-3-6; c-4, 5. Moldoff a-2i.*

UNDERSEA FIGHTING COMMANDOS (See Fighting Undersea...)
I.W. Enterprises: 1964
I.W. Reprint #1,2('64): 1-r/#? 2-r/#1; Severin-c 2 4 6 10 13 16

UNDERTAKER (World Wrestling Federation)
Chaos! Comics: Feb, 1999 - No. 10, Jan, 2000 ($2.50/$2.95)
Preview (2/99) 2.50
1-10: Reg. and photo covers for each. 1-(4/99) 3.00
1-($6.95) DF Ed.; Brereton painted-c 7.00
...Halloween Special (10/99, $2.95) Reg. & photo-c 3.00
Wizard #0 2.25

UNDERWATER CITY, THE
Dell Publishing Co.: No. 1328, 1961
Four Color 1328-Movie, Evans-a 8 16 24 58 82 105

UNDERWORLD (...True Crime Stories)
D. S. Publishing Co.: Feb-Mar, 1948 - No. 9, June-July, 1949 (52 pgs.)
1-Moldoff (Shelly)-c; excessive violence 44 88 132 268 409 550
2-Moldoff (Shelly)-c; Ma Barker story used in **SOTI**, pg. 95; female electrocution panel;
lingerie art 40 80 120 244 372 500
3-McWilliams-c/a; extreme violence, mutilation 39 78 117 227 331 435
4-Used in Love and Death by Legman; Ingels-a 33 66 99 190 275 360
5-Ingels-a 24 48 72 138 199 260
6-9: 8-Ravielli-a 19 38 57 107 154 200

UNDERWORLD
DC Comics: Dec, 1987 - No. 4, Mar, 1988 ($1.00, limited series, mature)
1-4 2.25

UNDERWORLD (Movie)
IDW Publishing: Sept, 2003 ($6.99, one-shot)
1-Movie adaptation; photo-c 7.00
TPB (7/04, $19.99) r/#1 and Underworld:Red in Tooth and Claw #1-3 20.00

UNDERWORLD CRIME
Fawcett Publications: June, 1952 - No. 9, Oct, 1953
1 33 66 99 190 275 360
2 21 42 63 118 169 220
3-6,8,9 (8,9-exist?) 19 38 57 107 154 200
7-(6/53)-Bondage/torture-c 29 58 87 164 237 310

UNDERWORLD: RED IN TOOTH AND CLAW (Movie)
IDW Publishing: Feb, 2004 - No. 3, Apr, 2004 ($3.99, limited series)
1-3-The early days of the Vampire and Lycan war; Postic & Marinkovich-a 4.00

UNDERWORLD STORY, THE (Movie)
Avon Periodicals: 1950
nn-(Scarce)-Ravielli-c 30 60 90 170 245 320

UNDERWORLD UNLEASHED
DC Comics: Nov, 1995 - No. 3, Jan, 1996 ($2.95, limited series)
1-3: Mark Waid scripts & Howard Porter-c/a(p) 3.50
...: Abyss: Hell's Sentinel 1-($2.95)-Alan Scott, Phantom Stranger, Zatanna app. 3.00
...: Apokolips-Dark Uprising 1 ($1.95) 2.25
...: Batman-Devil's Asylum 1-($2.95)-Batman app. 3.00
...: Patterns of Fear-($2.95) 3.00
TPB (1998, $17.95) r/#1-3 & Abyss-Hell's Sentinel 18.00

UNEARTHLY SPECTACULARS
Harvey Publications: Oct, 1965 - No. 3, Mar, 1967
1-(12¢)-Tiger Boy; Simon-c 4 8 12 29 40 50
2-(25¢ giants)-Jack Q. Frost, Tiger Boy & Three Rocketeers app.; Williamson, Wood, Kane-a;
r-1 story/Thrill-O-Rama #2 5 10 15 36 48 60
3-(25¢ giants)-Jack Q. Frost app.; Williamson/Crandall-a; r-from Alarming Advs. #1,1962
5 10 15 36 48 60
NOTE: ***Crandall** a-3r. **G. Kane** a-2. **Orlando** a-3. **Simon, Sparling, Wood** c-2. **Simon/Kirby** a-3r. **Torres** a-1?. **Wildey** a-1(3). **Williamson** a-2, 3r. **Wood** a-2(2).*

UNEXPECTED, THE (Formerly Tales of the...)
National Per. Publ./DC Comics: No. 105, Feb-Mar, 1968 - No. 222, May, 1982
105-Begin 12¢ cover price 6 12 18 43 59 75
106-113: 113-Last 12¢ issue (6-7/69) 4 8 12 29 40 50
114,115,117,118,120-125 3 7 10 21 28 35
116 (36 pgs.)-Wrightson-a? 4 8 12 22 30 38
119-Wrightson-a, 8pgs.(36 pgs.) 5 10 15 33 44 55
126,127,129-136-(52 pgs.) 3 7 10 21 28 35
128(52 pgs.)-Wrightson-a 5 10 15 33 44 55
137-156 2 4 6 12 16 20
157-162-(100 pgs.) 4 8 12 27 36 45
163-188: 187,188-(44 pgs.) 2 4 6 10 12 15
189,190,192-195 ($1.00, 68 pgs.): 189 on are combined with House of Secrets
& The Witching Hour 2 4 6 10 13 16
191-Rogers-a(p) ($1.00, 68 pgs.) 2 4 6 11 14 18
196-222: 200-Return of Johhny Peril by Tuska. 205-213-Johnny Peril app.
210-Time Warp story. 222-Giffen-a 1 2 3 5 7 9
NOTE: ***Neal Adams** c-110, 112-115, 118, 121, 124. **J. Craig** a-195. **Ditko** a-189, 221p, 222p; c-222. **Drucker** a-107r, 132r. **Giffen** a-219, 222. **Kaluta** c-203, 212. **Kirby** a-127r, 162. **Kubert** c-204, 214-216, 219-221. **Mayer** a-217p, 220, 221p. **Moldoff** a-136r. **Moreira** a-133. **Mortimer** a-212p. **Newton** a-204p. **Orlando** a-202; c-191. **Perez** a-217p. **Redondo** a-155, 166, 195. **Reese** a-145. **Sparling** a-107, 205-209p, 212p. **Spiegle** a-217. **Starlin** c-198. **Toth** a-126r, 127r. **Tuska** a-127, 132, 134, 136, 139, 152, 180, 200p. **Wildey** a-128r, 193. **Wood** a-122i, 133i, 137i, 138i. **Wrightson** a-161r(2 pgs.). Johnny Peril in #106-114, 116, 117, 200, 205-213.*

UNEXPECTED ANNUAL, THE (See DC Special Series #4)

UNIDENTIFIED FLYING ODDBALL (See Walt Disney Showcase #52)

UNION
Image Comics (WildStorm Productions): June, 1993 - No. 0, July, 1994 ($1.95, lim. series)
0-(7/94, $2.50) 2.50
0-Alternate Portacio-c (See Deathblow #5) 5.00
1-($2.50)-Embossed foil-c; Texeira-c/a in all 2.50
1-($1.95)-Newsstand edition w/o foil-c 2.25
2-4: 4-(7/94) 2.50

UNION
Image Comics (WildStorm Prod.): Feb, 1995 - No. 9, Dec, 1995 ($2.50)
1-3,5-9: 3-Savage Dragon app. 6-Fairchild from Gen 13 app. 2.50
4-($1.95, Newsstand)-WildStorm Rising Pt. 3 2.25
4-($2.50, Direct Market)-WildStorm Rising Pt. 3, bound-in card 2.50

UNION: FINAL VENGEANCE
Image Comics (WildStorm Productions): Oct, 1997 ($2.50)
1-Golden-c/Heisler-s 2.50

UNION JACK
Marvel Comics: Dec, 1998 - No. 3, Feb, 1999 ($2.99, limited series)
1-3-Raab-s/Cassaday-s/a 3.00

UNION STATION
Oni Press: Oct, 2003 ($11.95, B&W, graphic novel)
nn-Ande Parks-s/Eduardo Barreto-a 12.00

UNITED COMICS (Formerly Fritzi Ritz #7; has Fritzi Ritz logo)
United Features Syndicate: Aug, 1940; No. 8, 1950 - No. 26, Jan-Feb, 1953
1(68 pgs.)-Fritzi Ritz & Phil Fumble 24 48 72 138 196 260
8-Fritzi Ritz, Abbie & Slats 8 16 24 40 50 60
9-21: 20-Strange As It Seems; Russell Patterson Cheesecake-a
7 14 21 35 43 50
22-(5-6/52) 2 pgs. early Peanuts by Schulz (1st in comics?)
9 18 27 52 66 80
23-26: 23-(7-8/52). 24-(9-10/52). 25-(11-12/52). 26-(1-2/53). All have 2 pgs. early
Peanuts by Schulz 8 16 24 46 58 70
NOTE: *Abbie & Slats reprinted from Tip Top.*

UNITED NATIONS, THE (See Classics Illustrated Special Issue)

UNITED STATES AIR FORCE PRESENTS: THE HIDDEN CREW
U.S. Air Force: 1964 (36 pgs.)
nn-Schaffenberger-a 2 4 6 11 14 18

UNITED STATES FIGHTING AIR FORCE (Also see U.S. Fighting Air Force)
Superior Comics Ltd.: Sept, 1952 - No. 29, Oct, 1956
1 11 22 33 66 88 110

United States Marines #2 © WHW

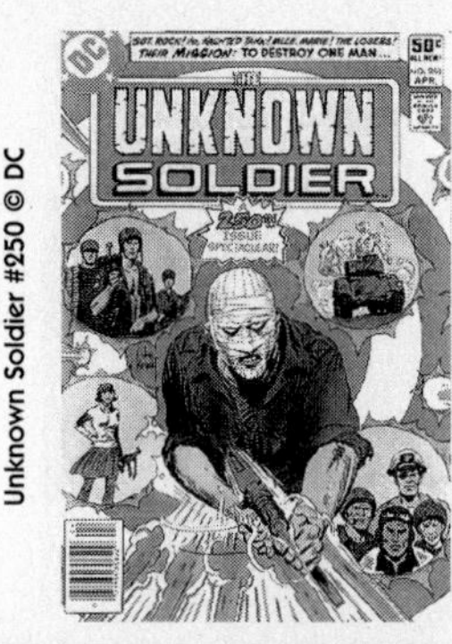

Unknown Soldier #250 © DC

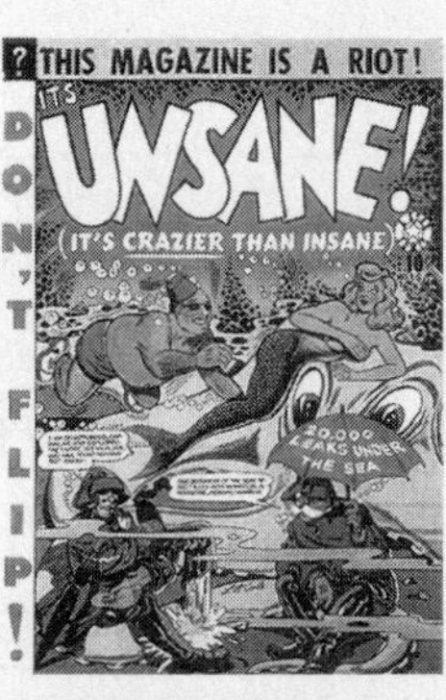

Unsane #15 © STAR

	GD 2.0	VG 4.0	FN 6.0	VF 8.0	VF/NM 9.0	NM- 9.2
2	7	14	21	37	46	55
3-10	6	12	18	31	38	45
11-29	6	12	18	28	34	40

UNITED STATES MARINES
William H. Wise/Life's Romances Publ. Co./Magazine Ent. #5-8/Toby Press #7-11: 1943 - No. 4, 1944; No. 5, 1952 - No. 8, 1952; No. 7 - No. 11, 1953

	GD 2.0	VG 4.0	FN 6.0	VF 8.0	VF/NM 9.0	NM- 9.2
nn-Mart Bailey-a	19	38	57	107	154	200
2-Bailey-a; Tojo classic-c	40	80	120	233	342	450
3-Tojo-c	32	64	96	184	267	350
4	11	22	33	64	87	110
5(A-1 #55)-Bailey-a, 6(A-1 #60), 7(A-1 #68), 8(A-1 #72)	9	18	27	54	70	85
7-11 (Toby)	8	16	24	43	54	65

NOTE: ***Powell*** *a-5-7.*

UNITY
Valiant: No. 0, Aug, 1992 - No. 1, 1992 (Free comics w/limited dist., 20 pgs.)

0 (Blue)-Prequel to Unity x-overs in all Valiant titles; B. Smith-c/a. (Free to everyone that bought all 8 titles that month.) 2.25
0 (Red)-Same as above, but w/red logo (5,000). 3.00
1-Epilogue to Unity x-overs; B. Smith-c/a. (1 copy available for every 8 Valiant books ordered by dealers.) 2.25
1 (Gold), 1-(Platinum)-Promotional copy. 3.00
... : The Lost Chapter 1 (Yearbook) (2/95, $3.95)-"1994" in indicia 4.00

UNITY 2000 (See preludes in Shadowman #3,4 flipbooks)
Acclaim Comics: Nov, 1999 - No. 3, Jan, 2000 ($2.50, unfinished limited series planned for 6 issues)

Preview -B&W plot preview and cover art; paper cover 2.25
1-3-Starlin-a/Shooter-s 2.50

UNIVERSAL MONSTERS
Dark Horse Comics: 1993 ($4.95/$5.95, 52 pgs.)(All adapt original movies)

	GD 2.0	VG 4.0	FN 6.0	VF 8.0	VF/NM 9.0	NM- 9.2
Creature From the Black Lagoon nn-($4.95)-Art Adams/Austin-c/a, Dracula nn-($4.95), Frankenstein nn-($3.95)-Painted-c/a, The Mummy nn-($4.95)-Painted-c	1	2	3	4	5	7

UNIVERSAL PRESENTS DRACULA-THE MUMMY& OTHER STORIES
Dell Publishing Co.: Sept-Nov, 1963 (one-shot, 84 pgs.) (Also see Dell Giants)

	GD 2.0	VG 4.0	FN 6.0	VF 8.0	VF/NM 9.0	NM- 9.2
02-530-311-r/Dracula 12-231-212, The Mummy 12-437-211 & part of Ghost Stories No. 1	15	30	45	120	215	310

UNIVERSAL SOLDIER (Movie)
Now Comics: Sept, 1992 - No. 3, Nov, 1992 (Limited series, polybagged, mature)

1-3 ($2.50, Direct Sales) 1-Movie adapatation; hologram on-c (all direct sales editions have painted-c) 2.50
1-3 ($1.95, Newsstand)-Rewritten & redrawn code approved version; all newsstand editions have photo-c 2.25

UNIVERSE
Image Comics (Top Cow): Sept, 2001 - No. 8, July, 2002 ($2.50)

1-7-Jenkins-s 2.50
8-($4.95) extra short-s by Jenkins; pin-up pages 5.00

UNIVERSE X (See Earth X)
Marvel Comics: Sept, 2000 - No. 12, Sept, 2001 ($3.99/$3.50, limited series)

0-Ross-c/Braithwaite-a/Ross & Krueger-s 4.00
1-12: 5-Funeral of Captain America 3.50
... Beasts (6/00, $3.99) Yeates-a/Ross-c 4.00
... Cap (Capt. America) (2/01, $3.99) Yeates & Totleben-a/Ross-c; Cap dies 4.00
... 4 (Fantastic 4) (10/00, $3.99) Brent Anderson-a/Ross-c 4.00
... Iron Men (9/01, $3.99) Anderson-a/Ross-c; leads into #12 4.00
... Omnibus (6/01, $3.99) Ross B&W sketchbook and character bios 4.00
Sketchbook- Wizard supplement; B&W character sketches and bios 2.25
...Spidey (1/01, $3.99) Romita Sr. flashback-a/Guice-a/Ross-c 4.00
...X (11/01, $3.99) Series conclusion; Braithwaith-a/Ross wraparound-c 4.00
Volume 1 TPB (1/02, $24.95) r/#0-7 & Spidey, 4, & Cap; new Ross-c 25.00
Volume 2 TPB (6/02, $24.95) r/#8-12 &X, Beasts, Iron Men and Omnibus 25.00

UNKNOWN MAN, THE (Movie)
Avon Periodicals: 1951

	GD 2.0	VG 4.0	FN 6.0	VF 8.0	VF/NM 9.0	NM- 9.2
nn-Kinstler-c	29	58	87	164	237	310

UNKNOWN SOLDIER (Formerly Star-Spangled War Stories)
National Periodical Publications/DC Comics: No. 205, Apr-May, 1977 - No. 268, Oct, 1982 (See Our Army at War #168 for 1st app.)

	GD 2.0	VG 4.0	FN 6.0	VF 8.0	VF/NM 9.0	NM- 9.2
205	2	4	6	12	16	20
206-210,220,221,251: 220,221 (44pgs.). 251-Enemy Ace begins	2	4	6	9	11	14
211-218,222-247,250,252-264	1	3	4	6	8	10
219-Miller-a (44 pgs.)	2	4	6	11	14	18
248,249,265-267: 248,249-Origin. 265-267-Enemy Ace vs. Balloon Buster.	1	3	4	6	8	10
268-Death of Unknown Soldier	2	4	6	14	18	22

NOTE: ***Chaykin*** *a-234.* ***Evans*** *a-265-267; c-235.* ***Kubert*** *c-Most.* ***Miller*** *a-219p.* ***Severin*** *a-251-253, 260, 261, 265-267.* ***Simonson*** *a-254-256.* ***Spiegle*** *a-258, 259, 262-264.*

UNKNOWN SOLDIER, THE (Also see Brave &the Bold #146)
DC Comics: Winter, 1988-'89 - No. 12, Dec, 1989 ($1.50, maxi-series, mature)

1-12: 8-Begin $1.75-c 3.00

UNKNOWN SOLDIER
DC Comics (Vertigo): Apr, 1997 - No 4, July, 1997 ($2.50, mini-series)

1-Ennis-s/Plunkett-a/Bradstreet-c in all 6.00
2-4 4.00
TPB (1998, $12.95) r/#1-4 13.00

UNKNOWN WORLD (Strange Stories From Another World #2 on)
Fawcett Publications: June, 1952

	GD 2.0	VG 4.0	FN 6.0	VF 8.0	VF/NM 9.0	NM- 9.2
1-Norman Saunders painted-c	45	90	135	275	418	560

UNKNOWN WORLDS (See Journey Into...)

UNKNOWN WORLDS
American Comics Group/Best Synd. Features: Aug, 1960 - No. 57, Aug, 1967

	GD 2.0	VG 4.0	FN 6.0	VF 8.0	VF/NM 9.0	NM- 9.2
1-Schaffenberger-c	22	44	66	155	238	320
2-Dinosaur-c/story	13	26	39	90	138	185
3-5	11	22	33	77	114	150
6-11: 9-Dinosaur-c/story. 11-Last 10¢ issue	9	18	27	65	93	120
12-19: 12-Begin 12¢ issues?; ends #57	8	16	24	53	74	95
20-Herbie cameo (12-1/62-63)	8	16	24	55	78	100
21-35	6	12	18	40	55	70
36- "The People vs. Hendricks" by Craig; most popular ACG story ever	6	12	18	43	59	75
37-46	5	10	15	36	48	60
47-Williamson-a r-from Adventures Into the Unknown #96, 3 pgs.; Craig-a	6	12	18	38	52	65
48-57: 53-Frankenstein app.	5	10	15	33	44	55

NOTE: ***Ditko*** *a-49, 50p, 54.* ***Forte*** *a-3, 6, 11.* ***Landau*** *a-56(2).* ***Reinman*** *a-3, 9, 13, 20, 22, 23, 36, 38, 54.* ***Whitney*** *c/a-most issues. John Force, Magic Agent app.-35, 36, 48, 50, 52, 54, 56.*

UNKNOWN WORLDS OF FRANK BRUNNER
Eclipse Comics: Aug, 1985 - No. 2, Aug, 1985 ($1.75)

1,2-B&W-r in color 3.50

UNKNOWN WORLDS OF SCIENCE FICTION
Marvel Comics: Jan, 1975 - No. 6, Nov, 1975; 1976 ($1.00, B&W Magazine)

	GD 2.0	VG 4.0	FN 6.0	VF 8.0	VF/NM 9.0	NM- 9.2
1-Williamson/Krenkel/Torres/Frazetta-r/Witzend #1, Neal Adams-r/Phase 1; Brunner & Kaluta-r; Freas/Romita-c	2	4	6	12	16	20
2-6: 5-Kaluta text illos	2	4	6	10	13	16
Special 1(1976,100 pgs.)-Newton painted-c	2	4	6	12	16	20

NOTE: ***Brunner*** *a-2; c-4, 6.* ***Buscema*** *a-Special 1p.* ***Chaykin*** *a-5.* ***Colan*** *a(p)-1, 3, 5, 6.* ***Corben*** *a-4.* ***Kaluta*** *a-2, Special 1(ext illos); c-2.* ***Morrow*** *a-3, 5.* ***Nino*** *a-3, 6, Special 1.* ***Perez*** *a-2, 3. Ray Bradbury interview in #1.*

UNLIMITED ACCESS (Also see Marvel Vs. DC))
Marvel Comics: Dec, 1997 - No. 4, Mar, 1998 ($2.99/$1.99, limited series)

1-Spider-Man, Wonder Woman, Green Lantern & Hulk app. 3.50
2,3-($1.99): 2-X-Men, Legion of Super-Heroes app. 3-Original Avengers vs. original Justice League 2.50
4-($2.99) Amalgam Legion vs. Darkseid & Magneto 3.00

UNSANE (Formerly Mighty Bear #13, 14? or The Outlaws #10-14?)(Satire)
Star Publications: No. 15, June, 1954

	GD 2.0	VG 4.0	FN 6.0	VF 8.0	VF/NM 9.0	NM- 9.2
15-Disbrow-a(2); L. B. Cole-c	39	78	117	222	324	425

UNSEEN, THE
Visual Editions/Standard Comics: No. 5, 1952 - No. 15, July, 1954

	GD 2.0	VG 4.0	FN 6.0	VF 8.0	VF/NM 9.0	NM- 9.2
5-Horror stories in all; Toth-a	40	80	120	239	357	475
6,7,9,10-Jack Katz-a	31	62	93	177	256	335
8,11,13,14	23	46	69	132	191	250
12,15-Toth-a. 12-Tuska-a	31	62	93	177	256	335

NOTE: ***Nick Cardy*** *c-12.* ***Fawcette*** *a-13, 14.* ***Sekowsky*** *a-7, 8(2), 10, 13, 15.*

UNTAMED
Marvel Comics (Epic Comics/Heavy Hitters): June, 1993 - No. 3, Aug, 1993 ($1.95, lim. series)

1-($2.50)-Embossed-c 2.50

Untamed Love #1 © QUA

Unusual Tales #8 © CC

USA Comics #8 © MAR

GD 2.0 | VG 4.0 | FN 6.0 | VF 8.0 | VF/NM 9.0 | NM- 9.2

2,3 — 2.25

UNTAMED LOVE (Also see Frank Frazetta's Untamed Love)
Quality Comics Group (Comic Magazines): Jan, 1950 - No. 5, Sept, 1950

1-Ward-c, Gustavson-a 26 52 78 150 215 280
2,4: 2-5-Photo-c 16 32 48 92 131 170
3,5-Gustavson-a 18 36 54 100 143 185

UNTOLD LEGEND OF CAPTAIN MARVEL, THE
Marvel Comics: Apr, 1997 - No. 3, June, 1997 ($2.50, limited series)

1-3 — 2.50

UNTOLD LEGEND OF THE BATMAN, THE (Also see Promotional section)
DC Comics: July, 1980 - No. 3, Sept, 1980 (Limited series)

1-Origin; Joker-c; Byrne's 1st work at DC — 6.00
2,3 — 4.50
NOTE: *Aparo a-1i, 2, 3. Byrne a-1p.*

UNTOLD ORIGIN OF THE FEMFORCE, THE (Also see Femforce)
AC Comics: 1989 ($4.95, 68 pgs.)

1-Origin Femforce; Bill Black-a(i) & scripts — 6.00

UNTOLD TALES OF CHASTITY
Chaos! Comics: Nov, 2000 ($2.95, one-shot)

1-Origin; Steven Grant-s/Peter Vale-c/a — 3.00
1-Premium Edition with glow in the dark cover — 13.00

UNTOLD TALES OF LADY DEATH
Chaos! Comics: Nov, 2000 ($2.95, one-shot)

1-Origin of Lady Death; Cremator app.; Kaminski-s — 3.00
1-Premium Edition with glow in the dark cover by Steven Hughes — 13.00

UNTOLD TALES OF PURGATORI
Chaos! Comics: Nov, 2000 ($2.95, one-shot)

1-Purgatori in 57 B.C.; Rio-a/Grant-s — 3.00
1-Premium Edition with glow in the dark cover — 13.00

UNTOLD TALES OF SPIDER-MAN (Also see Amazing Fantasy #16-18)
Marvel Comics: Sept, 1995 - No. 25, Sept, 1997 (99¢)

1-Kurt Busiek scripts begin; Pat Olliffe-c/a in all (except #9). — 2.50
2-22, -1(7/97), 23-25: 2-1st app. Batwing. 4-1st app. The Spacemen (Gantry, Orbit, Satellite & Vacuum). 8-1st app. The Headsman; The Enforcers (The Big Man, Montana, The Ox & Fancy Dan) app. 9-Ron Frenz-a. 10-1st app. Commanda. 16-Reintro Mary Jane Watson. 21-X-Men-c/app. 25-Green Goblin — 2.25
...'96-(1996, $1.95, 46 pgs.)-Kurt Busiek scripts; Mike Allred-c/a; Kurt Busiek & Pat Olliffe app. in back-up story; contains pin-ups — 2.25
...'97-(1997, $1.95)-Wraparound-c — 2.25
...: Strange Encounters ('98, $5.99) Dr. Strange app. — 6.00

UNTOUCHABLES, THE (TV)
Dell Publishing Co.: No. 1237, 10-12/61 - No. 4, 8-10/62 (All have Robert Stack photo-c)

Four Color 1237(#1) 24 48 72 170 260 350
Four Color 1286 17 34 51 119 182 245
01-879-207, 12-879-210(01879-210 on inside) 10 20 30 73 107 140

UNTOUCHABLES
Caliber Comics: Aug, 1997 - No. 4 ($2.95, B&W)

1-4: 1-Pruett-s; variant covers by Kaluta & Showman — 3.00

UNUSUAL TALES (Blue Beetle & Shadows From Beyond #50 on)
Charlton Comics: Nov, 1955 - No. 49, Mar-Apr, 1965

1 30 60 90 170 245 320
2 15 30 45 85 120 155
3-5 11 22 33 64 87 110
6-Ditko-c only 15 30 45 83 117 150
7,8-Ditko-c/a. 8-Robot-c 27 54 81 154 222 290
9-Ditko-c/a (20 pgs.) 30 60 90 170 245 320
10-Ditko-c/a(4) 32 64 96 181 263 345
11-(3/58, 68 pgs.)-Ditko-a(4) 30 60 90 170 245 320
12,14-Ditko-a 19 38 57 107 154 200
13,16-20 7 14 21 46 63 80
15-Ditko-c/a 23 46 69 130 188 245
21,24,28 5 10 15 36 48 60
22,23,25-27,29-Ditko-a 10 20 30 73 107 140
30-49 4 8 12 27 36 45
NOTE: *Colan a-11. Ditko c-22, 23, 25-27, 31(part).*

UP FROM HARLEM (Tom Skinner...)
Spire Christian Comics (Fleming H. Revell Co.): 1973 (35/49¢)

nn 1 3 4 6 8 11

UP-TO-DATE COMICS
King Features Syndicate: No date (1938) (36 pgs.; B&W cover) (10¢)

nn-Popeye & Henry cover; The Phantom, Jungle Jim & Flash Gordon by Raymond, The Katzenjammer Kids, Curley Harper & others. Note: Variations in content exist.
26 52 78 150 215 280

UP YOUR NOSE AND OUT YOUR EAR (Satire)
Klevart Enterprises: Apr, 1972 - No. 2, June, 1972 (52 pgs., magazine)

V1#1,2 2 4 6 11 14 18

URBAN
Moving Target Entertainment: 1994 ($1.75, B&W)

1 — 2.25

URTH 4 (Also see Earth 4)
Continuity Comics: May, 1989 - No. 4, Dec, 1990 ($2.00, deluxe format)

1-4: Ms. Mystic characters. 2-Neal Adams-c(i) — 2.25

URZA-MISHRA WAR ON THE WORLD OF MAGIC THE GATHERING
Acclaim Comics (Armada): 1996 - No. 2, 1996 ($5.95, limited series)

1,2 — 6.00

U.S. (See Uncle Sam)

USA COMICS
Timely Comics (USA): Aug, 1941 - No. 17, Fall, 1945

1-Origin Major Liberty (called Mr. Liberty #1), Rockman by Wolverton, & The Whizzer by Avison; The Defender with sidekick Rusty & Jack Frost begin; The Young Avenger only app.; S&K-c plus 1 pg. art 1147 2294 3441 8603 14,052 19,500
2-Origin Captain Terror & The Vagabond; last Wolverton Rockman; Hitler-c
379 758 1137 2464 3982 5500
3-No Whizzer 300 600 900 1892 2946 4000
4-Last Rockman, Major Liberty, Defender, Jack Frost, & Capt. Terror; Corporal Dix app.
254 508 762 1588 2444 3300
5-Origin American Avenger & Roko the Amazing; The Blue Blade, The Black Widow & Victory Boys, Gypo the Gypsy Giant & Hills of Horror only app.; Sergeant Dix begins; no Whizzer; Hitler, Mussolini & Tojo-c 246 492 738 1538 2369 3200
6-Captain America (ends #17), The Destroyer, Jap Buster Johnson, Jeep Jones begin; Terror Squad only app. 300 600 900 1925 3063 4200
7-Captain Daring, Disk-Eyes the Detective by Wolverton app.; origin & only app. Marvel Boy (3/43); Secret Stamp begins; no Whizzer, Sergeant Dix; classic Schomburg-c
300 600 900 1925 3063 4200
8,10: 10-The Thunderbird only app. 204 408 612 1275 1963 2650
9-Last Secret Stamp; Hitler-c; classic-c 235 470 705 1469 2260 3050
11,12: 11-No Jeep Jones 162 324 486 1013 1557 2100
13-17: 13-No Whizzer; Jeep Jones ends. 15-No Destroyer; Jap Buster Johnson ends
119 238 357 744 1147 1550
NOTE: *Brodsky c-14. Gabrielle c-4. Schomburg c-6, 7, 10, 12, 13, 15-17. Shores a-1, 4; c-9, 11. Ed Win a-4. Cover features: 1-The Defender; 2, 3-Captain Terror; 4-Major Liberty; 5-Victory Boys; 6-17-Captain America & Bucky.*

U.S. AGENT (See Jeff Jordan...)

U.S. AGENT (See Captain America #354)
Marvel Comics: June, 1993 - No. 4, Sept, 1993 ($1.75, limited series)

1-4 — 2.25

U.S. AGENT
Marvel Comics: Aug, 2001 - No. 3, Oct, 2001 ($2.99, limited series)

1-3: Ordway-s/a(p)/c. 2,3-Captain America app. — 3.00

USAGI YOJIMBO (See Albedo, Doomsday Squad #3 & Space Usagi)
Fantagraphics Books: July, 1987 - No. 38 ($2.00/$2.25, B&W)

1 1 2 3 5 7 9
1,8,10-2nd printings — 2.25
2-9 — 4.00
10,11: 10-Leonardo app. (TMNT). 11-Aragonés-a — 6.00
12-29 — 3.00
30-38: 30-Begin $2.25-c — 3.00
Color Special 1 (11/89, $2.95, 68 pgs.)-new & r — 3.50
Color Special 2 (10/91, $3.50) — 3.50
Color Special #3 (10/92, $3.50)-Jeff Smith's Bone promo on inside-c — 3.50
Summer Special 1 (1986, B&W, $2.75)-r/early Albedo issues — 3.00

USAGI YOJIMBO
Mirage Studios: V2#1, Mar, 1993 - No. 16, 1994 ($2.75)

V2#1-16: 1-Teenage Mutant Ninja Turtles app. — 3.00

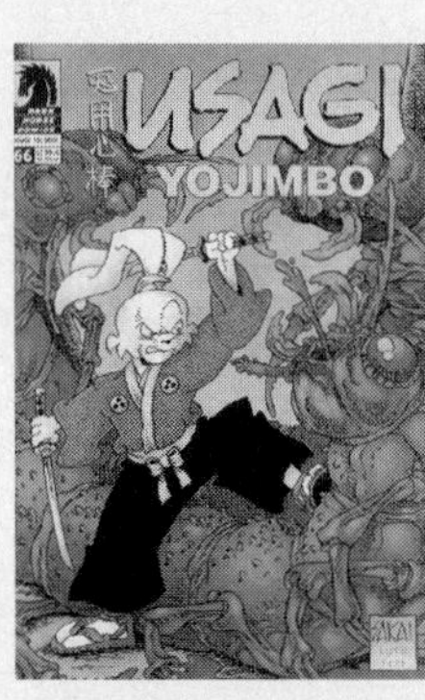

Usagi Yojimbo V3#66 © Stan Sakai

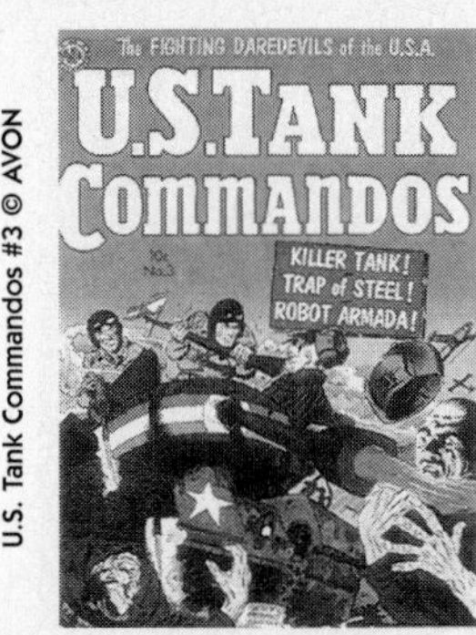

U.S. Tank Commandos #3 © AVON

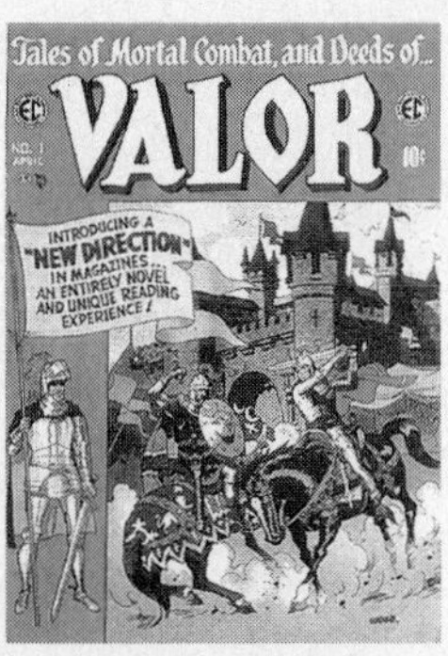

Valor #1 © WMG

	GD 2.0	VG 4.0	FN 6.0	VF 8.0	VF/NM 9.0	NM- 9.2

USAGI YOJIMBO
Dark Horse Comics: V3#1, Apr, 1996 - Present ($2.95/$2.99, B&W)

V3#1-78: Stan Sakai-c/a						3.00
Color Special #4 (7/97, $2.95) "Green Persimmon"						3.00
Daisho TPB ('98, $14.95) r/Mirage series #7-14						15.00
Demon Mask TPB ('01, $15.95)						16.00
Grasscutter TPB ('99, $16.95) r/#13-22						17.00
Gray Shadows TPB ('00, $14.95) r/#23-30						15.00
Seasons TPB ('99, $14.95) r/#7-12						15.00
Shades of Death TPB ('97, $14.95) r/Mirage series #1-6						15.00
The Brink of Life and Death TPB ('98, $14.95) r/Mirage series #13,15,16 & Dark Horse series #1-6						15.00
The Shrouded Moon TPB (1/03, $15.95) r/#46-52						16.00

U.S. AIR FORCE COMICS (Army Attack #38 on)
Charlton Comics: Oct, 1958 - No. 37, Mar-Apr, 1965

1	7	14	21	46	63	80
2	4	8	12	24	32	40
3-10	3	6	9	19	25	32
11-20	3	6	9	18	24	30
21-37	3	6	9	16	20	25

NOTE: ***Glanzman** c/a-9, 10, 12. **Montes/Bache** a-33.*

USA IS READY
Dell Publishing Co.: 1941 (68 pgs., one-shot)

1-War propaganda	40	80	120	239	357	475

U.S. BORDER PATROL COMICS (Sgt. Dick Carter of the...) (See Holyoke One Shot)

USER
DC Comics (Vertigo): 2001 - No. 3, 2001 ($5.95, limited series)

1-3-Devin Grayson-s; Sean Phillips & John Bolton-a						6.00

U.S. FIGHTING AIR FORCE (Also see United States Fighting Air Force)
I. W. Enterprises: No date (1960s?)

1,9(nd): 1-r/United States Fighting...#?. 9-r/#1	2	4	6	9	11	14

U.S. FIGHTING MEN
Super Comics: 1963 - 1964 (Reprints)

10-r/With the U.S. Paratroops #4(Avon)	2	4	6	10	13	16
11,12,15-18: 11-r/Monty Hall #10. 12,16,17,18-r/U.S. Fighting Air Force #10,3,?&? 15-r/Man Comics #11	2	4	6	10	13	16

U.S. JONES (Also see Wonderworld Comics #28)
Fox Features Syndicate: Nov, 1941 - No. 2, Jan, 1942

1-U.S. Jones & The Topper begin; Nazi-c	125	250	375	781	1203	1625
2-Nazi-c	85	170	255	531	816	1100

U.S. MARINES
Charlton Comics: Fall, 1964 (12¢, one-shot)

1-1st app. Capt. Dude; Glanzman-a	3	7	10	21	28	35

U.S. MARINES IN ACTION
Avon Periodicals: Aug, 1952 - No. 3, Dec, 1952

1-Louis Ravielli-c/a	9	18	27	54	70	85
2,3: 3-Kinstler-c	7	14	21	37	46	55

U.S. 1
Marvel Comics Group: May, 1983 - No. 12, Oct, 1984 (7,8: painted-c)

1-12: 2-Sienkiewicz-c. 3-12-Michael Golden-c						2.25

U.S. PARATROOPS (See With the...)

U.S. PARATROOPS
I. W. Enterprises: 1964?

1,8: 1-r/With the U.S. Paratroops #1; Wood-c. 8-r/With the U.S. Paratroops #6; Kinstler-c	2	4	6	10	13	16

U.S. TANK COMMANDOS
Avon Periodicals: June, 1952 - No. 4, Mar, 1953

1-Kinstler-c	10	20	30	58	77	95
2-4: Kinstler-c	8	16	24	43	54	65
I.W. Reprint #1,8: 1-r/#1. 8-r/#3	2	4	6	10	13	16

NOTE: ***Kinstler** a-I.W. #1; c-1-4, I.W. #1, 8.*

U.S. WAR MACHINE (Also see Iron Man and War Machine)
Marvel Comics (MAX): Nov, 2001 - No. 12, Jan, 2002 ($1.50, B&W, weekly limited series)

1-12-Chuck Austen-s/a/c						2.25
TPB (12/01, $14.95) r/#1-12						15.00

U.S. WAR MACHINE 2.0
Marvel Comics (MAX): Sept, 2003 - No. 3, Sept, 2003 ($2.99, weekly, limited series)

1-3-Austen-s/Christian Moore-CGI art						3.00

"V" (TV)
DC Comics: Feb, 1985 - No. 18, July, 1986

1-Based on TV movie & series (Sci/Fi)						3.00
2-18: 17,18-Denys Cowan-c/a						2.25

VACATION COMICS (Also see A-1 Comics)
Magazine Enterprises: No. 16, 1948 (one-shot)

A-1 16-The Pixies, Tom Tom, Flying Fredd & Koko & Kola	6	12	18	31	38	45

VACATION DIGEST
Harvey Comics: Sept, 1987 ($1.25, digest size)

1	1	2	3	5	6	8

VACATION IN DISNEYLAND (Also see Dell Giants)
Dell Publishing Co./Gold Key (1965): Aug-Oct, 1959; May, 1965 (Walt Disney)

Four Color 1025-Barks-a	19	38	57	134	205	275
1(30024-508)(G.K., 5/65, 25¢)-r/Dell Giant #30 & cover to #1 ('58); celebrates Disneyland's 10th anniversary	6	12	18	40	55	70

VACATION PARADE (See Dell Giants)

VALERIA THE SHE BAT
Continuity Comics: May, 1993 - No. 5, Nov, 1993

1-Premium; acetate-c; N. Adams-a/scripts; given as gift to retailers	1	2	3	5	6	8
5 (11/93)-Embossed-c; N. Adams-a/scripts						3.00

NOTE: *Due to lack of continuity, #2-4 do not exist.*

VALERIA THE SHE BAT
Acclaim Comics (Windjammer): Sept, 1995 - No.2, Oct, 1995 ($2.50, limited series)

1,2						2.50

VALKYRIE (See Airboy)
Eclipse Comics: May,1987 - No. 3, July, 1987 ($1.75, limited series)

1-3: 2-Holly becomes new Black Angel						2.50

VALKYRIE
Marvel Comics: Jan, 1997 ($2.95, one-shot)

1-w/pin-ups						3.00

VALKYRIE!
Eclipse Comics: July, 1988 - No. 3, Sept, 1988 ($1.95, limited series)

1-3						2.25

VALLEY OF THE DINOSAURS (TV)
Charlton Comics: Apr, 1975 - No. 11, Dec, 1976 (Hanna-Barbara)

1-W. Howard-i	2	4	6	14	18	22
2,4-11: 2-W. Howard-i	2	4	6	8	10	12
3-Byrne text illos (early work, 7/75)	2	4	6	10	13	16

VALLEY OF THE DINOSAURS (Volume 2)
Harvey Comics: Oct, 1993 ($1.50, giant-sized)

1-Reprints						3.00

VALLEY OF GWANGI (See Movie Classics)

VALOR
E. C. Comics: Mar-Apr, 1955 - No. 5, Nov-Dec, 1955

1-Williamson/Torres-a; Wood-c/a	26	52	78	195	288	380
2-Williamson-c/a; Wood-a	21	42	63	158	234	310
3,4: 3-Williamson, Crandall-a. 4-Wood-c	16	32	48	120	175	230
5-Wood-c/a; Williamson/Evans-a	14	28	42	105	158	210

NOTE: ***Crandall** a-3, 4. **Ingels** a-1, 2, 4, 5. **Krigstein** a-1-5. **Orlando** a-3, 4; c-3. **Wood** a-1, 2, 5; c-1, 4, 5.*

VALOR
Gemstone Publishing: Oct, 1998 - No. 5, Feb, 1999 ($2.50)

1-5-Reprints						2.50

VALOR (Also see Legion of Super-Heroes & Legionnaires)
DC Comics: Nov, 1992 - No. 23, Sept, 1994 ($1.25/$1.50)

1-22: 1-Eclipso The Darkness Within aftermath. 2-Vs. Supergirl. 4-Vs. Lobo. 12-Lobo cameo. 14-Legionnaires, JLA app. 17-Austin-c(i); death of Valor. 18-22-Build-up to Zero Hour						2.25
23-Zero Hour tie-in						3.00

VALOR THUNDERSTAR AND HIS FIREFLIES
Now Comics: Dec, 1986 ($1.50)

Vampirella #13 © WP

Vampirella ('92) #1 © Harris

Vampirella (The New Monthly) #9 © Harris

GD 2.0 | VG 4.0 | FN 6.0 | VF 8.0 | VF/NM 9.0 | NM- 9.2

1-Ordway-c(p) 2.25

VAMPI (Vampirella's...)
Harris Publications (Anarchy Studios): Aug, 2000 - No. 25, Feb, 2003 ($2.95/$2.99)

Limited Edition Preview Book (5/00) Preview pages & sketchbook 3.00
1-(8/00, $2.95) Lau-a(p)/Conway-s 3.00
1-Platinum Edition 20.00
2-25: 17-Barberi-a 3.00
2-25-Deluxe Edition variants ($9.95): 4-Finch-c. 5-Wieringo-c. 6-Cha-c 10.00
...Digital 1 (11/01, $2.95) CGI art; Haberlin-s 3.00
...Digital Preview (Anarchy Studios, 7/01, $2.95) preview of CGI art 3.00
Switchblade Kiss HC (2001, $24.95) r/#1-6 25.00
Vicious Preview Ed. (Apr, 2003, $1.99) Flip book w/ Xin: Journey of the Monkey King Preview Ed. 2.25
Wizard #1/2 (mail order, $9.95) includes sketch pages 10.00

VAMPIRE BITES
Brainstorm Comics: May, 1995 - No. 2, Sept, 1996 ($2.95, B&W)

1,2:1-Color pin-up 3.00

VAMPIRE LESTAT, THE
Innovation Publishing: Jan, 1990 - No. 12, 1991 ($2.50, painted limited series)

1-Adapts novel; Bolton painted-c on all 2 4 6 11 14 18
1-2nd printing (has UPC code, 1st prints don't) 3.00
1-3rd & 4th printings 2.50
2-1st printing 1 2 3 5 6 8
2-2nd & 3rd printings 2.50
3-5 5.00
3-6,9-2nd printings 2.50
6-12 3.00

VAMPIRELLA (Magazine)(See Warren Presents)
Warren Publishing Co./Harris Publications #113: Sept, 1969 - No. 112, Feb, 1983; No. 113, Jan, 1988? (B&W)

1-Intro. Vampirella in original costume & wings; Frazetta-c/intro. page; Adams-a; Crandall-a 41 82 123 305 478 650
2-1st app. Vampirella's cousin Evily-c/s; 1st/only app. Draculina, Vampirella's blonde twin sister 14 28 42 97 149 200
3 (Low distribution) 36 72 108 270 423 575
4,6 11 22 33 75 110 145
5,7,9: 5,7-Frazetta-c. 9-Barry Smith-a; Boris/Wood-c 11 22 33 77 114 150
8-Vampirella begins by Tom Sutton as serious strip (early issues-gag line) 11 22 33 80 120 160
10-No Vampi story; Brunner, Adams, Wood-a 6 12 18 43 59 75
11-Origin & 1st app. Pendragon; Frazetta-c 7 14 21 51 71 90
12-Vampi by Gonzales begins 7 14 21 51 71 90
13-15: 14-1st Maroto-a; Ploog-a 7 14 21 51 71 90
16,22,25: 16-1st full Dracula-c/app. 22-Color insert preview of Maroto's Dracula. 25-Vampi on cocaine-s 7 14 21 46 63 80
17,18,20,21,23,24: 17-Tomb of the Gods begins by Maroto, ends #22. 18-22-Dracula-s 7 14 21 46 63 80
19 (1973 Annual) Creation of Vampi text bio 8 16 24 55 78 100
26,28,34-36,39,40: All have 8 pg. color inserts. 28-Board game inside covers. 34,35-1st Fleur the Witch Woman. 39,40-Color Dracula-s. 40-Wrightson bio 4 8 12 29 40 50
27 (1974 Annual) New color Vampi-s; mostly-r 5 10 15 36 48 60
29,38,45: 38-2nd Vampi as Cleopatra/Blood Red Queen of Hearts; 1st Mayo-a. 4 8 12 29 40 50
30-32: 30-Intro. Pantha; Corben-a(color). 31-Origin Luana, the Beast Girl. 32-Jones-a 4 8 12 29 40 50
33-Wrightson ends; Pantha ends 4 8 12 29 40 50
36,37: 36-1st Vampi as Cleopatra/Blood Red Queen of Hearts. 37-(1975 Annual) 5 10 15 33 44 55
41-44,47,48: 41-Dracula-s 4 8 12 24 32 40
46-(10/75) Origin-r from Annual 1 4 8 12 28 38 48
49-1st Blind Priestess; The Blood Red Queen of Hearts storyline begins; Poe-s 4 8 12 24 32 40
50-Spirit cameo by Eisner; 40 pg. Vampi-s; Pantha & Fleur app.; Jones-a 4 8 12 24 32 40
51-53,56,57,59-62,65,66,68,75,79,80,82-86,88,89: 60-62,65,66-The Blood Red Queen of Hearts app. 60-1st Blind Priestess-c 3 6 9 18 23 28
54,55,63,81,87: 54-Vampi-s (42 pgs.); 8 pg. color Corben-a. 55-All Gonzales-a(r). 63-10 pgs. Wrightson-a 3 6 9 18 23 28
58,70,72: 58-(92 pgs.) 70-Rook app. 3 7 10 21 28 35
64,73: 64-(100 pg. Giant) All Mayo-a; 70 pg. Vampi-s. 73-69 pg. Vampi-s; Mayo-a 4 8 12 22 30 38
67,69,71,74,76-78-All Barbara Leigh photo-c 3 7 10 21 28 35
90-99: 90-Toth-a. 91-All-r; Gonzales-a. 93-Cassandra St. Knight begins, ends #103; new Pantha series begins, ends #108 3 6 9 18 23 28
100 (96 pg. r-special)-Origin reprinted from Ann. 1; mostly reprints; Vampirella appears topless in new 21 pg. story 7 14 21 51 71 90
101-104,106,107: All lower print run. 101,102-The Blood Red Queen of Hearts app. 107-All Maroto reprint-a issue 5 10 15 33 44 55
105,108-110: 108-Torpedo series by Toth begins; Vampi nudity splash page. 110-(100 pg. Summer Spectacular) 5 10 15 33 44 55
111,112: Low print run. 111-Giant Collector's Edition ($2.50) 112-(84 pgs.) last Warren issue 6 12 18 43 59 75
113 (1988)-1st Harris Issue; very low print run 29 58 87 206 316 425
Annual 1(1972)-New definitive origin of Vampirella by Gonzales; reprints by Neal Adams (from #1), Wood (from #9) 27 54 81 194 297 400
Special 1 (1977) Softcover (color, large-square bound)-Only available thru mail order 15 30 45 109 167 225
Special 1 (1977) Hardcover (color, large-square bound)-Only available through mail order (scarce)(500 produced, signed & #'d) 35 70 105 263 412 560
#1 1969 Commemorative Edition (2001, $4.95) reprints entire #1 5.00
...Crimson Chronicles Vol. 1 (2004, $19.95, TPB) reprints stories from #1-10 20.00

NOTE: ***Ackerman** s-1-3. **Neal Adams** a-1, 10p, 19p(r/#10), 44(1 pg.), Annual 1. **Alcala** a-78, 90, 93i. **Bodé/Todd** c-3. **Bodé/Jones** c-4. **Boris/Wood** c-9. **Brunner** a-10, 12(1 pg.). **Corben** a-30, 31, 33, 36, 54; c-30, 31, 33, 54. **Crandall** a-1, 19(r/#1). **Frazetta** c-1, 5, 7, 11, 31. **Heath** a-58, 61, 67, 76-78, 83. **Infantino** a-57-62. **Jones** a-5, 9, 12, 27, 32 (color), 33(2 pg.), 34, 50i, 83r. **Ken Kelly** c-6, 38, 39, 40(back-c), 46, 70, 95. **Nebres** a-84, 88-90, 92-96. **Nino** a-59i, 61i, 67, 76, 85, 90. **Ploog** a-14. **Barry Smith** a-9. **Starlin** a-78. **Sutton** a-1-5, 7-11, Annual 1. **Toth** a-90i, 108, 110. **Wood** a-9, 10, 12, 19(r/#12), 27r, Annual 1; c-9(partial). **Wrightson** a-33(w/**Jones**), 40(Bio cameo) 63r. All reprint issues-19, 74, 83, 91, 105, 107, 109, 111. Annuals from 1973 on are included in regular numbering. Later annuals are same format as regular issues. Color inserts (8 pgs.) in 22, 25-28, 30-35, 39, 40, 45, 46, 49, 54, 55, 67, 72. 16 pg color insert in #36.*

VAMPIRELLA (Also see Cain/... & Vengeance of...)
Harris Publications: Nov, 1992 - No. 5, Nov, 1993 ($2.95)

0-Bagged 5.00
0-Gold 3 6 9 18 24 30
1-Jim Balent inks in #1-3; Adam Hughes c-1-3 2 4 6 12 16 20
1-2nd printing 5.00
1-(11/97) Commemorative Edition 3.00
2 2 4 6 10 12 15
3-5: 4-Snyder III-c. 5-Brereton painted-c 1 2 3 5 6 8
Trade paperback nn (10/93, $5.95)-r/#1-4; Jusko-c 1 2 3 4 5 7

NOTE: *Issues 1-5 contain certificates for free **Dave Stevens** Vampirella poster.*

VAMPIRELLA (THE NEW MONTHLY)
Harris Publications: Nov, 1997 - No. 26, Apr, 2000 ($2.95)

1-3-"Ascending Evil" -Morrison & Millar-s/Conner & Palmiotti-a. 1-Three covers by Quesada/Palmiotti, Conner, and Conner/Palmiotti 3.00
1-3-($9.95) Jae Lee variant covers 10.00
1-($24.95) Platinum Ed.w/Quesada-c 25.00
4-6-"Holy War"-Small & Stull-a, 4-Linsner variant-c 3.00
7-9-"Queen's Gambit"-Shi app. 7-Two covers. 8-Pantha-c/app. 3.00
7-($9.95) Conner variant-c 10.00
10-12-"Hell on Earth"; Small-a/Coney-s. 12-New costume 3.00
10-Jae Lee variant-c 1 3 4 6 8 10
13-15-"World's End" Zircher-p; Pantha back-up, Texeira-a 3.00
16,17: 16-Pantha-c;Texeira-a; Vampi back-up story. 17-(Pantha #2) 3.00
18-20-"Rebirth": Jae Lee-c on all. 18-Loeb-s/Sale-a. 19-Alan Davis-a. 20-Bruce Timm-a 3.00
18-20-($9.95) Variant covers: 18-Sale. 19-Davis. 20-Timm 12.00
21-26: 21,22-Dangerous Games; Small-a. 23-Lady Death-c/app.; Cleavenger-a. 24,25-Lau-a. 26-Lady Death & Pantha-c/app.; Cleavenger-a. 3.00
0-(1/99) also variant-c with Pantha #0; same contents 3.00
TPB ($7.50) r/#1-3 "Ascending Evil" 8.00
Ascending Evil Ashcan (8/97, $1.00) 2.25
Hell on Earth Ashcan (7/98, $1.00) 2.25
The End Ashcan (3/00, $6.00) 6.00
...30th Anniversary Celebration Preview (7/99) B&W preview of #18-20 10.00

VAMPIRELLA
Harris Publications: June, 2001 - No. 22, Aug, 2003 ($2.95/$2.99)

1-Four covers (Mayhew w/foil logo, Campbell, Anacleto, Jae Lee) Mayhew-a; Mark Millar-s 3.00
2-22: 2-Two covers (Mayhew & Chiodo). 3-Timm var-c. 4-Horn var-c. 7-10-Dawn Brown-a; Pantha back-up w/Texeira-a. 15-22-Conner-c 3.00
Giant-Size Ashcan (5/01, $5.95) B&W preview art and Mayhew interview 6.00
...: Halloween Trick & Treat (10/04, $4.95) stories & art by various; three covers 5.00
... : Nowheresville Preview Edition (3/01, $2.95)- previews Mayhew art and photo models 3.00
...Nowheresville TPB (1/02, $12.95) r/#1-3 with cover gallery 13.00

VAMPIRELLA & PANTHA SHOWCASE

Vampirella Comics Magazine #2 © Harris

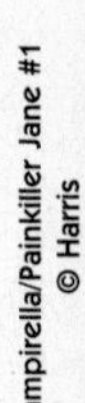

Vampirella/Painkiller Jane #1 © Harris

Vampirella Retro #1 © Harris

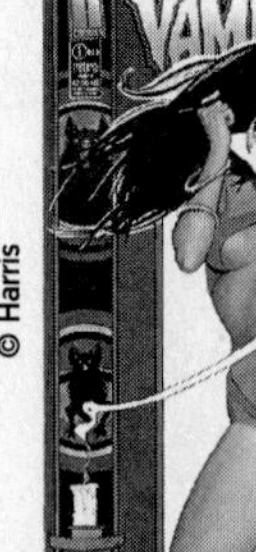

GD 2.0 | VG 4.0 | FN 6.0 | VF 8.0 | VF/NM 9.0 | NM- 9.2

Harris Publications: Jan, 1997 ($1.50, one-shot)

1-Millar-s/Texeira-c/a; flip book w/"Blood Lust"; Robinson-s/Jusko-c/a 3.00

VAMPIRELLA & THE BLOOD RED QUEEN OF HEARTS
Harris Publications: Sept, 1996 ($9.95, 96 pgs., B&W, squarebound, one-shot)

nn-r/Vampirella #49,60-62,65,66,101,102; John Bolton-c; Michael Bair back-c 1 3 4 6 8 10

VAMPIRELLA: BLOODLUST
Harris Publications: July, 1997 - No. 2, Aug, 1997 ($4.95, limited series)

1,2-Robinson-s/Jusko-painted c/a 5.00

VAMPIRELLA CLASSIC
Harris Publications: Feb, 1995 - No. 5, Nov, 1995 ($2.95, limited series)

1-5: Reprints Archie Goodwin stories. 3.00

VAMPIRELLA COMICS MAGAZINE
Harris Publications: Oct, 2003 - Present ($3.95/$9.95, magazine-sized)

1-6-($3.95) 1-Texiera-c; b&w and color stories, Alan Moore interview; reviews. 2-KISS interview. 4-Chiodo-c. 6-Brereton-c 4.00
1-6-($9.95) 1-Three covers (Model Photo cover, Palmiotti-c, Wheatley Frankenstein-c) 10.00

VAMPIRELLA: CROSSOVER GALLERY
Harris Publications: Sept, 1997 ($2.95, one-shot)

1-Wraparound-c by Campbell, pinups by Jae Lee, Mack, Allred, Art Adams, Quesada & Palmiotti and others 3.00

VAMPIRELLA: DEATH & DESTRUCTION
Harris Publications: July, 1996 - No. 3, Sept, 1996 ($2.95, limited series)

1-3: Amanda Conner-a(p) in all. 1-Tucci-c. 2-Hughes-c. 3-Jusko-c 3.00
1-($9.95)-Limited Edition; Beachum-c 10.00

VAMPIRELLA/DRACULA & PANTHA SHOWCASE
Harris Publications: Aug, 1997 ($1.50, one-shot)

1-Ellis, Robinson, and Moore-s; flip book w/"Pantha" 3.00

VAMPIRELLA/DRACULA: THE CENTENNIAL
Harris Publications: Oct, 1997 ($5.95, one-shot)

1-Ellis, Robinson, and Moore-s; Beachum, Frank/Smith, and Mack/Mays-a Bolton-painted-c 6.00

VAMPIRELLA: JULIE STRAIN SPECIAL
Harris Publications: Sept, 2000 ($3.95, one-shot)

1-Photo-c w/yellow background; interview and photo gallery 4.00
1-Limited Edition ($9.95); cover photo w/black background 10.00

VAMPIRELLA/LADY DEATH (Also see Lady Death/Vampirella)
Harris Publications: Feb, 1999 ($3.50, one-shot)

1-Small-a/Nelson painted-c 3.50
1-Valentine Edition ($9.95); pencil-c by Small 10.00

VAMPIRELLA: LEGENDARY TALES
Harris Publications: May, 2000 - No. 2, June, 2000 ($2.95, B&W)

1,2-Reprints from magazine; Cleavenger painted-c 3.00
1,2-($9.95) Variant painted-c by Mike Mayhew 10.00

VAMPIRELLA LIVES
Harris Publications: Dec, 1996 - No. 3, Feb, 1997 ($3.50/$2.95, limited series)

1-Die cut-c; Quesada & Palmiotti-c, Ellis-s/Conner-a 3.50
1-Deluxe Ed.-photo-c 3.50
2,3-($2.95)-Two editions (1 photo-c): 3-J. Scott Campbell-c 3.00

VAMPIRELLA: MORNING IN AMERICA
Harris Publications/Dark Horse Comics: 1991 - No. 4, 1992 ($3.95, B&W, lim. series, 52 pgs.)

1,2-All have Kaluta painted-c 1 2 3 5 6 8
3,4 1 3 4 6 8 10

VAMPIRELLA OF DRAKULON
Harris Publications: Jan, 1996 - No. 5, Sept, 1996 ($2.95)

0-5: All reprints. 0-Jim Silke-c. 3-Polybagged w/card. 4-Texeira-c 3.00

VAMPIRELLA/PAINKILLER JANE
Harris Publications: May, 1998 ($3.50, one-shot)

1-Waid & Augustyn-s/Leonardi & Palmiotti-a 3.50
1-($9.95) Variant-c 10.00

VAMPIRELLA PIN-UP SPECIAL
Harris Publications: Oct, 1995 ($2.95, one-shot)

1-Hughes-c, pin-ups by various 5.00
1-Variant-c 5.00

VAMPIRELLA: RETRO
Harris Publications: Mar, 1998 - No. 3, May, 1998 ($2.50, B&W, limited series)

1-3: Reprints; Silke painted covers 3.00

VAMPIRELLA: SAD WINGS OF DESTINY
Harris Publications: Sept, 1996 ($3.95, one-shot)

1-Jusko-c 4.00

VAMPIRELLA/SHADOWHAWK: CREATURES OF THE NIGHT (Also see Shadowhawk)
Harris Publications: 1995 ($4.95, one-shot)

1 5.00

VAMPIRELLA/SHI (See Shi/Vampirella)
Harris Publications: Oct, 1997 ($2.95, one-shot)

1-Ellis-s 3.00
1-Chromium-c 6.00

VAMPIRELLA: SILVER ANNIVERSARY COLLECTION
Harris Publications: Jan, 1997 - No. 4 Apr, 1997 ($2.50, limited series)

1-4: Two editions: Bad Girl by Beachum, Good Girl by Silke 3.00

VAMPIRELLA'S SUMMER NIGHTS
Harris Publications: 1992 (one-shot)

1-Art Adams infinity cover; centerfold by Stelfreeze 3 7 10 21 28 35

VAMPIRELLA STRIKES
Harris Publications: Sept, 1995 - No. 8, Dec, 1996 ($2.95, limited series)

1-8: 1-Photo-c. 2-Deodato-c; polybagged w/card. 5-Eudaemon-c/app; wraparound-c; alternate-c exists. 6-(6/96)-Mark Millar script; Texeira-c; alternate-c exists. 7-Flip book 3.00
1-Newsstand Edition; diff. photo-c., 1-Limited Ed.; diff. photo-c 3.00
Annual 1-(12/96, $2.95) Delano-s; two covers 3.00

VAMPIRELLA: 25TH ANNIVERSARY SPECIAL
Harris Publications: Oct, 1996 ($5.95, squarebound, one-shot)

nn-Reintro The Blood Red Queen of Hearts; James Robinson, Grant Morrison & Warren Ellis scripts; Mark Texeira, Michael Bair & Amanda Conner-a(p); Frank Frazetta-c 6.00
nn-($6.95)-Silver Edition 7.00

VAMPIRELLA VS. HEMORRHAGE
Harris Publications: Apr, 1997($3.50)

1 3.50

VAMPIRELLA VS. PANTHA
Harris Publications: Mar, 1997 ($3.50)

1-Two covers; Millar-s/Texeira-c/a 3.50

VAMPIRELLA/WETWORKS (See Wetworks/Vampirella)
Harris Publications: June, 1997 ($2.95, one-shot)

1 3.00
1-($9.95) Alternate Edition; cardstock-c 10.00

VAMPIRELLA/WITCHBLADE
Harris Publications: 2003 ($2.99, one-shot)

1-Brian Wood-s/Steve Pugh-a; 3 covers by Texeira, Conner and Pugh 3.00
...: Union of the Damned (10/04, $2.99, one-shot) Sharp-a; three covers 3.00

VAMPIRE'S CHRISTMAS, THE
Image Comics: Oct, 2003 ($5.95, over-sized graphic novel)

nn-Linsner-s/a; Dubisch-painted-a 6.00

VAMPIRE TALES
Marvel Comics Group: Aug, 1973 - No. 11, June, 1975 (75¢, B&W, magazine)

1-Morbius, the Living Vampire begins by Pablo Marcos (1st solo Morbius series & 5th Morbius app.) 5 10 15 36 48 60
2-Intro. Satana; Steranko-r 4 8 12 27 36 45
3,5,6: 3-Satana app. 5-Origin Morbius. 6-1st Lilith app. 3 7 10 21 28 35
4,7 3 6 9 18 23 28
8-1st solo Blade story (see Tomb of Dracula) 4 8 12 27 36 45
9-Blade app. 4 8 12 22 30 38
10,11 3 6 9 18 23 28
Annual 1(10/75)-Heath-r/#9 3 6 9 18 23 28

NOTE: ***Alcala** a-6, 8, 9i. **Boris** c-4, 6. **Chaykin** a-7. **Everett** a-1r. **Gulacy** a-7p. **Heath** a-9. **Infantino** a-3r. **Gil Kane** a-4, 5r.*

VAMPIRE VERSES, THE
CFD Productions: Aug, 1995 - No. 4, 1995 ($2.95, B&W, mature)

1-4 3.00

Vamps: Hollywood & Vein #3 © DC

Vanguard #6 © IM

Vault of Horror #24 © WMG

GD 2.0 | VG 4.0 | FN 6.0 | VF 8.0 | VF/NM 9.0 | NM- 9.2

VAMPI VICIOUS
Harris Publications (Anarchy Studios): Aug, 2003 - No. 3, Nov, 2003 ($2.99)

1-3: 1-McKeever-s/Dogan-a; 3 covers by Dogan, Lau & Noto. 3-Kau-a 3.00

VAMPI VICIOUS CIRCLE
Harris Publications (Anarchy Studios): Jun, 2004 - No. 3, Sept, 2004 ($2.99/$9.95)

1-3: B. Clay Moore-s 3.00
1-3-($9.95) Limited Edition w/variant-c. 1-Noto-c. 2-Norton-c. 3-Lucas-c 10.00

VAMPI VS. XIN
Harris Publications (Anarchy Studios): Oct, 2004 - No. 2 ($2.99)

1-Faerber-s/Lau-a; two covers 3.00

VAMPS
DC Comics (Vertigo): Aug, 1994 - No. 6, Jan, 1995 ($1.95, lim. series, mature)

1-6-Bolland-c 3.00
Trade paperback ($9.95)-r/#1-6 10.00

VAMPS: HOLLYWOOD & VEIN
DC Comics (Vertigo): Feb, 1996 - No. 6, July, 1996 ($2.25, lim. series, mature)

1-6: Winslade-c 2.50

VAMPS: PUMPKIN TIME
DC Comics (Vertigo): Dec, 1998 - No. 3, Feb, 1999 ($2.50, lim. series, mature)

1-3: Quitely-c 2.50

VANGUARD (...Outpost: Earth) (See Megaton)
Megaton Comics: 1987 ($1.50)

1-Erik Larsen-c(p) 3.00

VANGUARD (See Savage Dragon #2)
Image Comics (Highbrow Entertainment): Oct, 1993 - No.6, 1994 ($1.95)

1-6: 1-Wraparound gatefold-c; Erik Larsen back-up-a; Supreme x-over. 3-(12/93)-Indicia says December 1994. 4-Berzerker back-up. 5-Angel Medina-a(p) 3.00

VANGUARD (See Savage Dragon #2)
Image Comics: Aug, 1996 - No.4, Feb, 1997 ($2.95, B&W, limited series)

1-4 3.00

VANGUARD: ETHEREAL WARRIORS
Image Comics: Aug, 2000 ($5.95, B&W)

1-Fosco & Larsen-a 6.00

VANGUARD ILLUSTRATED
Pacific Comics: Nov, 1983 - No. 11, Oct, 1984 (Baxter paper)(Direct sales only)

1-6,8-11: 1,7-Nudity scenes. 2-1st app. Stargrazers (see Legends of the Stargrazers; Dave Stevens-c 3.00
7-1st app. Mr. Monster (r-in Mr. Monster #1) 5.00
NOTE: ***Evans*** *a-7.* ***Kaluta*** *c-5, 7p.* ***Perez*** *a-6; c-6.* ***Rude*** *a-1-4; c-4.* ***Williamson*** *c-3.*

VANGUARD: STRANGE VISITORS
Image Comics: Oct, 1996 - No.4, Feb, 1997 ($2.95, B&W, limited series)

1-4: 3-Supreme-c/app. 3.00

VAN HELSING: FROM BENEATH THE RUE MORGUE (Based on the 2004 movie)
Dark Horse Comics: Apr, 2004 ($2.99, one-shot)

1-Hugh Jackman photo-c; Dysart-s/Alexander-a 3.00

VANITY (See Pacific Presents #3)
Pacific Comics: Jun, 1984 - No. 2, Aug, 1984 ($1.50, direct sales)

1,2: Origin 2.25

VARIETY COMICS (The Spice of Comics)
Rural Home Publ./Croyden Publ. Co.: 1944 - No. 2, 1945; No. 3, 1946

1-Origin Captain Valiant 22 44 66 123 177 230
2-Captain Valiant 13 26 39 74 102 130
3(1946-Croyden)-Captain Valiant 11 22 33 62 84 105

VARIETY COMICS (See Fox Giants)

VARIOGENESIS
Dagger Comics Group: June, 1994 ($3.50)

0 3.50

VARSITY
Parents' Magazine Institute: 1945

1 8 16 24 46 58 70

VAULT OF EVIL
Marvel Comics Group: Feb, 1973 - No. 23, Nov, 1975

1 (1950s reprints begin) 3 6 9 16 21 26
2-23: 3,4-Brunner-c. 11-Kirby-a 2 4 6 10 13 16
NOTE: ***Ditko*** *a-14r, 15r, 20-22r.* ***Drucker*** *a-10r(Mystic #52), 13r(Uncanny Tales #42).* ***Everett*** *a-11r(Menace #2), 13r(Menace #4); c-10.* ***Heath*** *a-5r.* ***Gil Kane*** *c-1, 6.* ***Kirby*** *a-11.* ***Krigstein*** *a-20r(Uncanny Tales #54).* ***Reinman*** *r-1.* ***Tuska*** *a-6r.*

VAULT OF HORROR (Formerly War Against Crime #1-11)
E. C. Comics: No. 12, Apr-May, 1950 - No. 40, Dec-Jan, 1954-55

12 (Scarce)-ties w/Crypt Of Terror as 1st horror comic
462 924 1386 3465 5083 6700
13-Morphine story 97 194 291 728 1064 1400
14 87 174 261 653 957 1260
15- "Terror in the Swamp" is same story w/minor changes as "The Thing in the Swamp" from Haunt of Fear #15 74 148 222 555 815 1075
16, 57 114 171 428 627 825
17-Classic werewolf-c 61 122 183 458 672 885
18,19 45 90 135 338 494 650
20-25: 22-Frankenstein-c & adaptation. 23-Used in **POP**, pg. 84; Davis-a(2). 24-Craig biography 37 74 111 278 407 535
26-B&W & color illos in **POP** 37 74 111 278 407 535
27-36: 30-Dismemberment-c. 31-Ray Bradbury biog. 32-Censored-c. 35-X-Mas-c. 36- "Pipe Dream" classic opium addict story by Krigstein; "Twin Bill" cited in articles by T.E. Murphy, Wertham 30 60 90 225 328 430
37-1st app. Drusilla, a Vampirella look alike; Williamson-a
31 62 93 233 339 445
38-39: 39-Bondage-c 29 58 87 218 317 415
40-Low distribution 37 74 111 278 407 535
NOTE: ***Craig*** *art in all but No. 13 & 33; c-12-40.* ***Crandall*** *a-33, 34, 39.* ***Davis*** *a-17-38.* ***Evans*** *a-27, 28, 30, 32, 33.* ***Feldstein*** *a-12-16.* ***Ingels*** *a-13-20, 22-40.* ***Kamen*** *a-15-22, 25, 29, 35.* ***Krigstein*** *a-36, 38-40.* ***Kurtzman*** *a-12, 13.* ***Orlando*** *a-24, 31, 40.* ***Wood*** *a-12-14. #22, 29 & 31 have Ray Bradbury adaptations. #16 & 17 have H. P. Lovecraft adaptations.*

VAULT OF HORROR, THE
Gladstone Publ.: Aug, 1990 - No. 6, June, 1991 ($1.95, 68 pgs.)(#4 on: $2.00)

1-Craig-c(r); all contain EC reprints 4.00
2-6: 2,4-6-Craig-c(r). 3-Ingels-c(r) 3.00

VAULT OF HORROR
Russ Cochran/Gemstone Publishing: Sept, 1991 - No. 5, May, 1992 ($2.00); Oct, 1992 - No. 29, Oct, 1999 ($1.50/$2.00/$2.50)

1-29: E.C reprints. 1-4r/VOH #12-15 w/original-c 3.00

V...-COMICS (Morse code for "V" - 3 dots, 1 dash)
Fox Features Syndicate: Jan, 1942 - No. 2, Mar-Apr, 1942

1-Origin V-Man & the Boys; The Banshee & The Black Fury, The Queen of Evil, & V-Agents begin; Nazi-c 125 250 375 781 1203 1625
2-Nazi bondage/torture-c 90 180 270 563 869 1175

VECTOR
Now Comics: 1986 - No. 4, 1986? ($1.50, 1st color comic by Now Comics)

1-4: Computer-generated art 2.25

VECTOR (Formerly titled Edge #1-12)
CG Entertainment, Inc.: May, 2003 ($7.95, digest size TPB)

13-Reprints from various CrossGen titles 8.00

VEGAS KNIGHTS
Pioneer Comics: 1989 ($1.95, one-shot)

1 2.25

VEILS
DC Comics (Vertigo): 1999 ($24.95, one-shot)

Hardcover-($24.95) Painted art and photography; McGreal-s 25.00
Softcover ($14.95) 15.00

VELOCITY (Also see Cyberforce)
Image Comics (Top Cow Productions): Nov, 1995 - No. 3, Jan, 1996 ($2.50, limited series)

1-3: Kurt Busiek scripts in all. 2-Savage Dragon-c/app. 3.00

VENGEANCE OF VAMPIRELLA (Becomes Vampirella: Death & Destruction)
Harris Comics: Apr, 1994 - No. 25, Apr, 1996 ($2.95)

1-($3.50)-Quesada/Palmiotti "bloodfoil" wraparound cover 6.00
1-2nd printing; blue foil-c 3.00
1-Gold 18.00
2-8: 8-Polybagged w/trading card 4.00
9-25: 10-w/coupon for Hyde -25 poster. 11,19-Polybagged w/ trading card. 25-Quesada & Palmiotti red foil-c 3.00
...: Bloodshed (1995, $6.95) 7.00

Venom #1 © MAR

Venus #6 © MAR

Vertigo Pop! London #4 © Milligan & Bond

GD VG FN VF VF/NM NM-
2.0 4.0 6.0 8.0 9.0 9.2

VENGEANCE OF VAMPIRELLA: THE MYSTERY WALK
Harris Comics: Nov, 1995 ($2.95, one-shot)

0 3.00

VENGEANCE SQUAD
Charlton Comics: July, 1975 - No. 6, May, 1976 (#1-3 are 25¢ issues)

1-Mike Mauser, Private Eye begins by Staton 2 4 6 8 10 12
2-6: Morisi-a in all 1 2 3 4 5 7
5,6 (Modern Comics-r, 1977) 4.00

VENOM
Marvel Comics: June, 2003 - No. 18, Nov, 2004 ($2.25)

1-7-Herrera-a/Way-s. 6,7-Wolverine app. 2.25
8-18-($2.99): 8-10-Wolverine-c/app.; Kieth-c. 11-Fantastic Four app. 3.00
... Vol. 1: Shiver (2004, $13.99, TPB) r/#1-5 14.00
... Vol. 2: Run (2004, $19.99, TPB) r/#6-13 20.00
... Vol. 3: Twist (2004, $13.99, TPB) r/#14-18 14.00

VENOM: Marvel Comics (Also see Amazing Spider-Man #298-300)

... ALONG CAME A SPIDER, 1/96 - No. 4, 4/96 ($2.95)-Spider-Man & Carnage app. 3.00
... CARNAGE UNLEASHED, 4/95 - No. 4, 7/95 ($2.95) 3.00
... DEATHTRAP: THE VAULT, 3/93 ($6.95) r/Avengers: Deathtrap: The Vault 7.00
... FUNERAL PYRE, 8/93- No. 3, 10/93 ($2.95)-#1-Holo-grafx foil-c; Punisher app. in all 3.00

VENOM: LETHAL PROTECTOR
Marvel Comics: Feb, 1993 - No. 6, July, 1993 ($2.95, limited series)

1-Red holo-grafx foil-c; Bagley-c/a in all 5.00
1-Gold variant sold to retailers 15.00
1-Black-c (at least 23 copies have been authenticated by CGC since 2000)
11 22 33 77 114 150

NOTE: Counterfeit copies of the black-c exist and are valueless

2-6: Spider-Man app. in all 3.00
... LICENSE TO KILL,6/97 - No. 3, 8/97 ($1.95) 2.25
... NIGHTS OF VENGEANCE, 8/94 - No. 4, 11/94 ($2.95), #1-Red foil-c 3.00
... ON TRIAL, 3/97 - No. 3, 5/97 ($1.95) 2.25
... SEED OF DARKNESS, 7/97 ($1.95) #(-1) Flashback 2.25
... SEPARATION ANXIETY,12/94- No. 4, 3/95 ($2.95) #1-Embossed-c 3.00
... SIGN OF THE BOSS,3/97 - No. 2, 10/97 ($1.99) 2.25
... SINNER TAKES ALL, 8/95 - No. 5, 10/95 ($2.95) 3.00
... SUPER SPECIAL, 8/95($3.95) #1-Flip book 4.00
... THE ENEMY WITHIN, 2/94 - No. 3, 4/94 ($2.95)-Demogoblin & Morbius app.
1-Glow-in-the-dark-c 3.00
... THE FINALE, 11/97 - No. 3, 1/98 ($1.99) 2.25
... THE HUNGER, 8/96- No. 4, 11/96 ($1.95) 2.25
... THE HUNTED, 5/96-No. 3, 7/96 ($2.95) 3.00
... THE MACE, 5/94 - No. 3, 7/94 ($2.95)-#1-Embossed-c 3.00
... THE MADNESS, 11/93- No. 3, 1/94 ($2.95)-Kelley Jones-c/a(p).
1-Embossed-c; Juggernaut app. 3.00
... TOOTH AND CLAW, 12/96 - No. 3, 2/97 ($1.95)-Wolverine-c/app. 2.25
... VS. CARNAGE, 9/04 - No. 4, 12/04 ($2.99)-Milligan-s/Crain-a; Spider-Man app. 3.00

VENTURE
AC Comics (Americomics): Aug, 1986 - No. 3, 1986? ($1.75)

1-3: 1-3-Bolt. 1-Astron. 2-Femforce. 3-Fazers 2.25

VENTURE
Image Comics: Jan, 2003 - No. 4, Sept, 2003 ($2.95)

1-4-Faerber-s/Igle-a 3.00

VENUS (See Marvel Spotlight #2 & Weird Wonder Tales)
Marvel/Atlas Comics (CMC 1-9/LCC 10-19): Aug, 1948 - No. 19, Apr, 1952 (Also see Marvel Mystery #91)

1-Venus & Hedy Devine begin; 1st app. Venus; Kurtzman's "Hey Look"
127 254 381 794 1222 1650
2 73 146 219 456 703 950
3,5 60 120 180 375 575 775
4-Kurtzman's "Hey Look" 60 120 180 375 580 785
6-9: 6-Loki app. 7,8-Painted-c. 9-Begin 52 pgs.; book-length feature "Whom the Gods Destroy!" 55 110 165 336 511 685
10-S/F-horror issues begin (7/50) 74 148 222 463 712 960

GD VG FN VF VF/NM NM-
2.0 4.0 6.0 8.0 9.0 9.2

11-S/F end of the world (11/50) 85 170 255 531 816 1100
12-Colan-a 50 100 150 305 465 625
13-19-Venus by Everett, 2-3 stories each; covers-#13,15-19; 14-Everett part cover (Venus).
17-Bondage-c 77 154 231 481 741 1000

NOTE: ***Berg*** *s/f story-13.* ***Everett*** *c-13, 14(part; Venus only), 15-19.* ***Heath*** *s/f story-11.* ***Maneely*** *s/f story 10(3pg.), 16.* ***Morisi*** *a-19.* ***Syd Shores*** *c-6.*

VENUS WARS, THE (Manga)
Dark Horse Comics: Apr, 1991 - No.14, May, 1992 ($2.25, B&W)

1-14: 1-3 Contain 2 Dark Horse trading cards. 1,3,7,10-(44 pgs.) 2.50

VERI BEST SURE FIRE COMICS
Holyoke Publishing Co.: No date (circa 1945) (Reprints Holyoke one-shots)

1-Captain Aero, Alias X, Miss Victory, Commandos of the Devil Dogs, Red Cross, Hammerhead Hawley, Capt. Aero's Sky Scouts, Flagman app.; same-c as Veri Best Sure Shot #1 40 80 120 233 342 450

VERI BEST SURE SHOT COMICS
Holyoke Publishing Co.: No date (circa 1945) (Reprints Holyoke one-shots)

1-Capt. Aero, Miss Victory by Quinlan, Alias X, The Red Cross, Flagman, Commandos of the Devil Dogs, Hammerhead Hawley, Capt. Aero's Sky Scouts; same-c as Veri Best Sure Fire #1 40 80 120 233 342 450

VERMILLION
DC Comics (Helix): Oct, 1996 - No. 12, Sept, 1997 ($2.25/$2.50)

1-12: 1-4: Lucius Shepard scripts. 4,12-Kaluta-c 2.50

VERONICA (Also see Archie's Girls, Betty &...)
Archie Comics: Apr, 1989 - Present

1-(75¢-c) 6.00
2-10: 2-(75¢-c) 4.00
11-38 3.00
39-Love Showdown pt. 4, Cheryl Blossom 5.00
40-70: 34-Neon ink-c 3.00
71-158: 134-Begin $2.19-c. 152,155-Cheryl Blossom app. 2.25

VERONICA'S PASSPORT DIGEST MAGAZINE (Becomes Veronica's Digest Magazine #3 on)
Archie Comics: Nov, 1992 - No. 6 ($1.50/$1.79, digest size)

1 5.00
2-6 3.00

VERONICA'S SUMMER SPECIAL (See Archie Giant Series Magazine #615, 625)

VERTICAL
DC Comics (Vertigo): 2003 ($4.95, 3-1/4" wide pages, one-shot)

1-Seagle-s/Allred & Bond-a; odd format 1/2 width pages with some 20" long spreads 5.00

VERTIGO GALLERY, THE: DREAMS AND NIGHTMARES
DC Comics (Vertigo): 1995 ($3.50, one-shot)

1-Pin-ups of Vertigo characters by Sienkiewicz, Toth, Van Fleet & others; McKean-c 4.00

VERTIGO JAM
DC Comics (Vertigo): Aug, 1993 ($3.95, one-shot, 68 pgs.)(Painted-c by Fabry)

1-Sandman by Neil Gaiman, Hellblazer, Animal Man, Doom Patrol, Swamp Thing, Kid Eternity & Shade the Changing Man 5.00

VERTIGO POP! BANGKOK
DC Comics (Vertigo): July, 2003 - No. 4, Oct, 2003 ($2.95, limited series)

1-4-Camuncoli-c/a; Jonathan Vankin-s 3.00

VERTIGO POP! LONDON
DC Comics (Vertigo): Jan, 2003 - No. 4, Apr, 2003 ($2.95, limited series)

1-4-Philip Bond-c/a; Peter Milligan-s 3.00

VERTIGO POP! TOKYO
DC Comics (Vertigo): Sept, 2002 - No. 4, Dec, 2002 ($2.95, limited series)

1-4-Seth Fisher-c/a; Jonathan Vankin-s 3.00

VERTIGO PREVIEW
DC Comics (Vertigo): 1992 (75¢, one-shot, 36 pgs.)

1-Vertigo previews; Sandman story by Neil Gaiman 2.25

VERTIGO RAVE
DC Comics (Vertigo): Fall, 1994 (99¢, one-shot)

1-Vertigo previews 2.25

VERTIGO SECRET FILES
DC Comics (Vertigo): Aug, 2000 ($4.95)

...: Hellblazer 1 (8/00, $4.95) Background info and story summaries 5.00
...: Swamp Thing 1 (11/00, $4.95) Backstories and origins; Hale-c 5.00

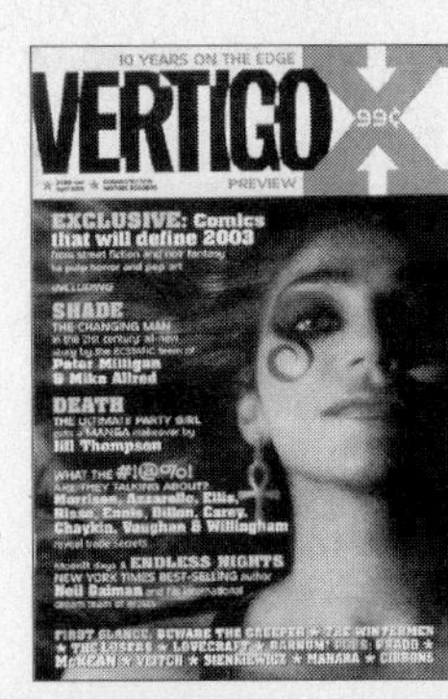

Vertigo X Anniversary Preview © DC

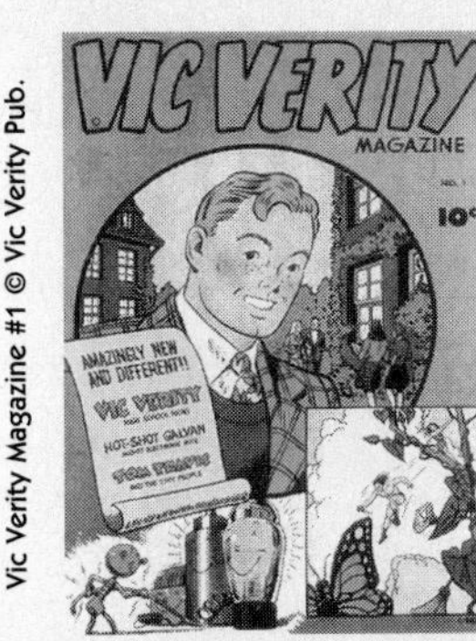

Vic Verity Magazine #1 © Vic Verity Pub.

Vigilante #23 © DC

GD 2.0 | VG 4.0 | FN 6.0 | VF 8.0 | VF/NM 9.0 | NM- 9.2

VERTIGO VERITE: THE UNSEEN HAND
DC Comics (Vertigo): Sept, 1996 - No. 4, Dec, 1996 ($2.50, limited series)
1-4: Terry LaBan scripts in all 2.50

VERTIGO VISIONS
DC Comics (Vertigo): June, 1993 - Present (one-shots)
Dr. Occult 1 (7/94, $3.95) 4.00
Dr. Thirteen 1 (9/98, $5.95) Howarth-s 6.00
Prez 1 (7/95, $3.95) 4.00
The Geek 1 (6/93, $3.95) 4.00
The Eaters ($4.95, 1995)-Milligan story. 5.00
The Phantom Stranger 1 (10/93, $3.50) 3.50
Tomahawk 1 (7/98, $4.95) Pollack-s 5.00

VERTIGO WINTER'S EDGE
DC Comics (Vertigo): 1998, 1999 ($7.95/$6.95, square-bound, annual)
1-Winter stories by Vertigo creators; Desire story by Gaiman/Bolton; Bolland wraparound-c 8.00
2,3-($6.95)-Winter stories: 2-Allred-c. 3-Bond-c; Desire by Gaiman/Zulli 7.00

VERTIGO X ANNIVERSARY PREVIEW
DC Comics (Vertigo): 2003 (99¢, one-shot, 48 pgs.)
1-Previews of upcoming titles and interviews; Endless Nights, Shade, The Originals 2.25

VERY BEST OF DENNIS THE MENACE, THE
Fawcett Publ.: July, 1979 - No. 2, Apr, 1980 (95¢/$1.00, digest-size, 132 pgs.)
1,2-Reprints 1 3 4 6 8 10

VERY BEST OF DENNIS THE MENACE, THE
Marvel Comics Group: Apr, 1982 - No. 3, Aug, 1982 ($1.25, digest-size)
1-3: Reprints 1 2 3 5 7 9
1,2-Mistakenly printed with DC logo on cover 2 4 6 9 11 14
NOTE: *Hank Ketcham c-all. A few thousand of #1 & 2 were printed with DC emblem.*

VERY VICKY
Meet Danny Ocean: 1993? - No. 8, 1995 ($2.50, B&W)
1-8, ...: Calling All Hillbillies (1995, $2.50) 2.50

VEXT
DC Comics: Mar, 1999 - No. 6, Aug, 1999 ($2.50, limited series)
1-6-Giffen-s. 1-Superman app. 2.50

V FOR VENDETTA
DC Comics: Sept, 1988 - No. 10, May, 1989 ($2.00, maxi-series)
1-10: Alan Moore scripts in all 3.00
Trade paperback (1990, $14.95) 15.00

VIC BRIDGES FAZERS SKETCHBOOK AND FACT FILE
AC Comics: Nov, 1986 ($1.75)
1 3.00

VIC FLINT(Crime Buster...)(See Authentic Police Cases #10-14 & Fugitives From Justice #2)
St. John Publ. Co.: Aug, 1948 - No. 5, Apr, 1949 (Newspaper reprints; NEA Service)
1 14 28 42 79 110 140
2 10 20 30 56 73 90
3-5 9 18 27 49 62 75

VIC FLINT (Crime Buster...)
Argo Publ.: Feb, 1956 - No. 2, May, 1956 (Newspaper reprints)
1,2 9 18 27 49 62 75

VIC JORDAN (Also see Big Shot Comics #32)
Civil Service Publ.: April, 1945
1-1944 daily newspaper-r 14 28 42 79 110 140

VICKI (Humor)
Atlas/Seaboard Publ.: Feb, 1975 - No. 4, Aug, 1975 (No. 1,2: 68 pgs.)
1,2-(68 pgs.)-Reprints Tippy Teen; Good Girl art 3 6 9 19 25 32
3,4 (Low print) 3 6 9 19 25 32

VICKI VALENTINE (...Summer Special #1)
Renegade Press: July, 1985 - No. 4, July, 1986 ($1.70, B&W)
1-4: Woggon, Rausch-a; all have paper dolls. 2-Christmas issue 3.00

VICKY
Ace Magazine: Oct, 1948 - No. 5, June, 1949
nn(10/48)-Teenage humor 7 14 21 37 46 55
4(12/48), nn(2/49), 4(4/49), 5(6/49): 5-Dotty app. 6 12 18 31 38 45

VIC TORRY & HIS FLYING SAUCER (Also see Mr. Monster's...#5)
Fawcett Publications: 1950 (one-shot)
nn-Book-length saucer story by Powell; photo/painted-c 67 134 201 419 647 875

GD 2.0 | VG 4.0 | FN 6.0 | VF 8.0 | VF/NM 9.0 | NM- 9.2

VICTORY
Topps Comics: June, 1994 ($2.50, unfinished limited series)
1-Kurt Busiek script; Giffen-c/a; Rob Liefeld variant-c exists 2.50

VICTORY
Image Comics: May, 2003 - No. 4, Feb, 2004 ($2.95, limited series)
1-4: 1-Two covers; Francisco-a 3.00

VICTORY (Volume 2)
Image Comics: Aug, 2004 - No. 4 ($2.95, limited series)
1-2: 1-Three covers; Francisco-a 3.00

VICTORY COMICS
Hillman Periodicals: Aug, 1941 - No. 4, Dec, 1941 (#1 by Funnies, Inc.)
1-The Conqueror by Bill Everett, The Crusader, & Bomber Burns begin; Conqueror's origin in text; Everett-c 300 600 900 1892 2946 4000
2-Everett-c/a 129 258 387 806 1241 1675
3,4 85 170 255 531 816 1100

VIC VERITY MAGAZINE
Vic Verity Publ: 1945; No. 2, Jan?, 1947 - No. 7, Sept, 1946 (A comic book)
1-C. C. Beck-c/a 22 44 66 125 180 235
2-Beck-c 13 26 39 74 102 130
3-7: 6-Beck-a. 7-Beck-c 11 22 33 64 87 110

VIDEO JACK
Marvel Comics (Epic Comics): Nov, 1987 - No. 6, Nov, 1988 ($1.25)
1-5 2.25
6-Neal Adams, Keith Giffen, Wrightson, others-a 4.00

VIETNAM JOURNAL
Apple Comics: Nov, 1987 - No. 16, Apr, 1991 ($1.75/$1.95, B&W)
1-16: Don Lomax-c/a/scripts in all, 1-2nd print 3.00
...: Indian Country Vol. 1 (1990, $12.95)-r/#1-4 plus one new story 13.00

VIETNAM JOURNAL: VALLEY OF DEATH
Apple Comics: June, 1994 - No. 2, Aug, 1994 ($2.75, B&W, limited series)
1,2: By Don Lomax 4.00

VIGILANTE, THE (Also see New Teen Titans #23 & Annual V2#2)
DC Comics: Oct, 1983 - No. 50, Feb, 1988 ($1.25, Baxter paper)
1-Origin 3.00
2-16,19-49: 3-Cyborg app. 4-1st app. The Exterminator; Newton-a(p). 6,7-Origin. 20,21-Nightwing app. 35-Origin Mad Bomber. 47-Batman-c/s 2.50
17,18-Alan Moore scripts 4.00
50-Ken Steacy painted-c 3.00
Annual nn, 2 ('85, '86) 2.50

VIGILANTE: CITY LIGHTS, PRAIRIE JUSTICE (Also see Action Comics #42, Justice League of America #78, Leading Comics & World's Finest #244)
DC Comics: Nov, 1995 - No. 4, Feb, 1996 ($2.50, limited series)
1-4: James Robinson scripts in all 2.50

VIGILANTES, THE
Dell Publishing Co.: No. 839, Sept, 1957
Four Color 839-Movie 8 16 24 58 82 105

VIGILANTE 8: SECOND OFFENSE
Chaos! Comics: Dec, 1999 ($2.95, one-shot)
1-Based on video game 3.00

VIKINGS, THE (Movie)
Dell Publishing Co.: No. 910, May, 1958
Four Color 910-Buscema-a, Kirk Douglas photo-c 10 20 30 67 96 125

VILLAINS AND VIGILANTES
Eclipse Comics: Dec, 1986 - No. 4, May, 1987 ($1.50/$1.75, limited series, Baxter paper)
1-4: Based on role-playing game. 2-4 ($1.75-c) 2.25

VILLAINY OF DOCTOR DOOM, THE
Marvel Comics: 1999 ($17.95, TPB)
nn-Reprints early battle with the Fantastic Four 18.00

VINTAGE MAGNUS (...Robot Fighter)
Valiant: Jan, 1992 - No. 4, Apr, 1992 ($2.25, limited series)

Violator #1 © TMP

The Vision #4 © MAR

Voltron: Defender of the Universe #0 © WEP

GD VG FN VF VF/NM NM-
2.0 4.0 6.0 8.0 9.0 9.2

1-4: 1-Layton-c; r/origin from Magnus R.F. #22 2.25

VIOLATOR (Also see Spawn #2)
Image Comics (Todd McFarlane Productions): May, 1994 - No. 3, Aug, 1994 ($1.95, limited series)
1-Alan Moore scripts in all 5.00
2,3: Bart Sears-c(p)/a(p) 4.00

VIOLATOR VS. BADROCK
Image Comics (Extreme Studios): May, 1995 - No. 4, Aug, 1995 ($2.50, limited series)
1-4: Alan Moore scripts in all. 1-1st app Celestine; variant-c (3?) 2.50

VIOLENT MESSIAHS (...: Lamenting Pain on cover for #9-12, numbered as #1-4)
Image Comics: June, 2000 - Present ($2.95)
1-Two covers by Travis Smith and Medina 4.00
1-Tower Records variant edition 5.00
2-8: 5-Flip book sketchbook 3.00
9-12-Lamenting Pain; 2 covers on each 3.00
...: Genesis (12/01, $5.95) r/'97 B&W issue, Wizard 1/2 prologue 6.00
...: The Book of Job TPB (7/02, $24.95) r/#1-8; Foreward by Gossett 25.00

VIP (TV)
TV Comics: 2000 ($2.95, unfinished series)
1-Based on the Pamela Lee TV show; photo-c 3.00

VIPER (TV)
DC Comics: Aug, 1994 - No. 4, Nov, 1994 ($1.95, limited series)
1-4-Adaptation of television show 2.25

VIRGINIAN, THE (TV)
Gold Key: June, 1963
1(10060-306)-Part photo-c of James Drury plus photo back-c
5 10 15 33 44 55

VIRTUA FIGHTER (Video Game)
Marvel Comics: Aug, 1995 (2.95, one-shot)
1-Sega Saturn game 3.00

VIRUS
Dark Horse Comics: 1993 - No. 4, 1993 ($2.50, limited series)
1-4: Ploog-c 2.50

VISION, THE
Marvel Comics: Nov, 1994 - No. 4, Feb, 1995 ($1.75, limited series)
1-4 2.25

VISION, THE (AVENGERS ICONS: ...)
Marvel Comics: Oct, 2002 - No. 4, Jan, 2003 ($2.99, limited series)
1-4-Geoff Johns-s/Ivan Reis-a 3.00

VISION AND THE SCARLET WITCH, THE (See Marvel Fanfare)
Marvel Comics Group: Nov, 1982 - No. 4, Feb, 1983 (Limited series)
1-4: 2-Nuklo & Future Man app. 3.00

VISION AND THE SCARLET WITCH, THE
Marvel Comics Group: Oct, 1985 - No. 12, Sept, 1986 (Maxi-series)
V2#1-12: 1-Origin; 1st app. in Avengers #57. 2-West Coast Avengers x-over 2.50

VISIONARIES
Marvel Comics (Star)/Marvel Comics #3 on: Nov, 1987 - No. 6, Sept, 1988
1-6 2.50

VISIONS
Vision Publications: 1979 - No. 5, 1983 (B&W, fanzine)
1-Flaming Carrot begins(1st app?); N. Adams-c 4 8 12 25 33 42
2-N. Adams, Rogers-a; Gulacy back-c; signed & numbered to 2000
3 6 9 19 25 32
3-Williamson-c(p); Steranko back-c 2 4 6 12 16 20
4-Flaming Carrot-c & info. 2 4 6 12 16 20
5-1 pg. Flaming Carrot 1 3 4 6 8 10
NOTE: ***Eisner** a-4. **Miller** a-4. **Starlin** a-3. **Williamson** a-5. After #4, Visions became an annual publication of The Atlanta Fantasy Fair.*

VISITOR, THE
Valiant/Acclaim Comics (Valiant): Apr, 1995 - No. 13, Nov, 1995 ($2.50)
1-13: 8-Harbinger revealed. 13-Visitor revealed to be Sting from Harbinger 2.50

VISITOR VS. THE VALIANT UNIVERSE, THE
Valiant: Feb, 1995 - No. 2, Mar, 1995 ($2.95, limited series)
1,2 3.00

GD VG FN VF VF/NM NM-
2.0 4.0 6.0 8.0 9.0 9.2

VOGUE (Also see Youngblood)
Image Comics (Extreme Studios): Oct, 1995 - No.3, Jan, 1996 ($2.50, limited series)
1-3: 1-Liefeld-c, 1-Variant-c 2.50

VOID INDIGO (Also see Marvel Graphic Novel)
Marvel Comics (Epic Comics): 11/84 - No. 2, 3/85 ($1.50, direct sales, unfinished series, mature)
1,2: Cont'd from Marvel G.N.; graphic sex & violence 2.25

VOLCANIC REVOLVER
Oni Press: Dec, 1998 - No. 3, Mar, 1999 ($2.95, B&W, limited series)
1-3: Scott Morse-s/a 3.00
TPB (12/99, $9.95, digest size) r/#1-3 and Oni Double Feature #7 prologue 10.00

VOLTRON (TV)
Modern Publishing: 1985 - No. 3, 1985 (75¢, limited series)
1-3: Ayers-a in all 4.00

VOLTRON: DEFENDER OF THE UNIVERSE (TV)
Image Comics: No. 0, May, 2003 - No. 5, Sept, 2003 ($2.50)
0-Jolley-s/Brooks-a; character pin-ups with background info 2.50
1-5-($2.95) 1-Three covers by Norton, Brooks and Andrews; Norton-a 3.00
...: Revelations TPB (2004, $11.95, digest-sized) r/#1-5; cover gallery 12.00

VOLTRON: DEFENDER OF THE UNIVERSE (TV)
Image Comics: Jan, 2004 - Present ($2.95)
1-10: 1-Jolley-s; wraparound-c 3.00

VOODA (Jungle Princess) (Formerly Voodoo)
Ajax-Farrell (Four Star Publications): No. 20, April, 1955 - No. 22, Aug, 1955
20-Baker-c/a (r/Seven Seas #6) 40 80 120 233 342 450
21,22-Baker-a plus Kamen/Baker story, Kimbo Boy of Jungle, & Baker-c(p) in all.
22-Censored Jo-Jo-r (name Powaa) 36 72 108 204 297 390
NOTE: *#20-22 each contain one heavily censored-r of South Sea Girl by **Baker** from Seven Seas Comics with name changed to Vooda. #20-r/Seven Seas #6; #21-r/#4; #22-r/#3.*

VOODOO (Weird Fantastic Tales) (Vooda #20 on)
Ajax-Farrell (Four Star Publ.): May, 1952 - No. 19, Jan-Feb, 1955
1-South Sea Girl-r by Baker 57 114 171 356 546 735
2-Rulah story-r plus South Sea Girl from Seven Seas #2 by Baker (name changed from Alani to El'nee) 46 92 138 281 428 575
3-Bakerish-a; man stabbed in face 40 80 120 230 335 440
4,8-Baker-r. 8-Severed head panels 40 80 120 230 335 440
5-7,9,10: 5-Nazi death camp story (flaying alive). 6-Severed head panels
32 64 96 184 267 350
11-18: 14-Zombies take over America. 15-Opium drug story-r/Ellery Queen #3. 16-Post nuclear world story.17-Electric chair panels
28 56 84 158 229 300
19-Bondage-c; Baker-r(2)/Seven Seas #5 w/minor changes & #1, heavily modified; last pre-code; contents & covers change to jungle theme
36 72 108 204 297 390
Annual 1(1952, 25¢, 100 pgs.)-Baker-a (scarce) 94 188 282 588 907 1225

VOODOO
Image Comics (WildStorm): Nov, 1997 - No. 4, Mar, 1998 ($2.50, lim. series)
1-4:Alan Moore-s in all; Hughes-c. 2-4-Rio-a 2.50
1-Platinum Ed 10.00
Dancing on the Dark TPB ('99, $9.95) r/#1-4 10.00
...-Zealot: Skin Trade (8/95, $4.95) 5.00

VOODOO (See Tales of...)

VOODOOM
Oni Press: June, 2000 ($4.95, B&W)
1-Scott Morse-s/Jim Mahfood-a 5.00

VORTEX
Vortex Publs.: Nov, 1982 - No. 15, 1988 (No month) ($1.50/$1.75, B&W)
1 ($1.95)-Peter Hsu-a; Ken Steacy-c; nudity 1 2 3 5 7 9
2,12: 2-1st app. Mister X (on-c only). 12-Sam Kieth-a 6.00
3-11,13-15 3.00

VORTEX
Comico: 1991 - No. 2? ($2.50, limited series)
1,2: Heroes from The Elementals 2.50

VORTEX
Entity Comics: 1996 ($2.95)
1,1b: 1b-Kaniuga-c 3.00

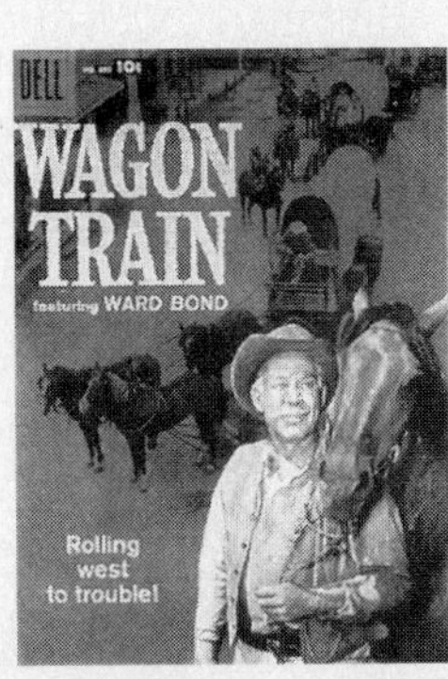

Wagon Train Four Color #895 © Revere

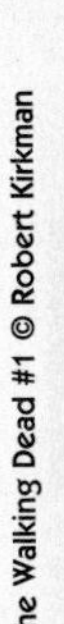

The Walking Dead #1 © Robert Kirkman

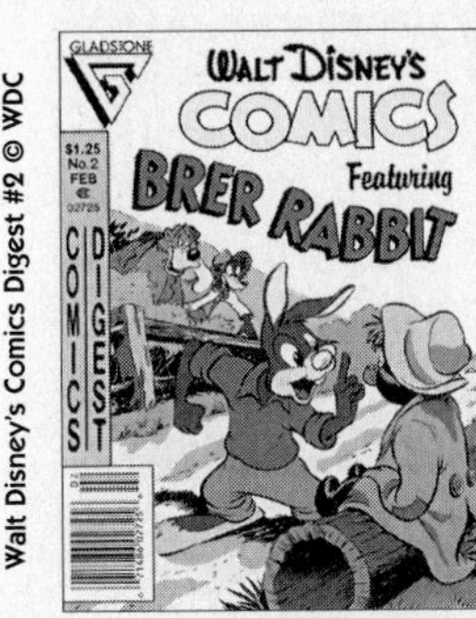

Walt Disney's Comics Digest #2 © WDC

	GD 2.0	VG 4.0	FN 6.0	VF 8.0	VF/NM 9.0	NM- 9.2

VOYAGE TO THE BOTTOM OF THE SEA (Movie, TV)
Dell Publishing Co./Gold Key: No. 1230, Sept-Nov, 1961; Dec, 1964 - #16, Apr, 1970 (Painted-c)

	GD	VG	FN	VF	VF/NM	NM-
Four Color 1230 (1961)	12	24	36	84	127	170
10133-412(#1, 12/64)(Gold Key)	9	18	27	60	85	110
2(7/65) - 5: Photo back-c, 1-5	6	12	18	43	59	75
6-14	5	10	15	36	48	60
15,16-Reprints	3	7	10	21	28	35

VOYAGE TO THE DEEP
Dell Publishing Co.: Sept-Nov, 1962 - No. 4, Nov-Jan, 1964 (Painted-c)

	GD	VG	FN	VF	VF/NM	NM-
1	6	12	18	43	59	75
2-4	4	8	12	28	38	48

WACKO
Ideal Publ. Corp.: Sept, 1980 - No. 3, Oct, 1981 (84 pgs., B&W, magazine)

	GD	VG	FN	VF	VF/NM	NM-
1-3	2	4	6	8	10	12

WACKY ADVENTURES OF CRACKY (Also see Gold Key Spotlight)
Gold Key: Dec, 1972 - No. 12, Sept, 1975

	GD	VG	FN	VF	VF/NM	NM-
1	3	6	9	16	20	24
2	2	4	6	10	12	15
3-12	1	3	4	6	8	10

(See March of Comics #405, 424, 436, 448)

WACKY DUCK (...Comics #3-6; formerly Dopey Duck; Justice Comics #7 on) (See Film Funnies)
Marvel Comics (NPP): No. 3, Fall, 1946 - No. 6, Summer, 1947; Aug, 1948 - No. 2, Oct, 1948

	GD	VG	FN	VF	VF/NM	NM-
3	22	44	66	127	184	240
4-Infinity-c	20	40	60	115	165	215
5,6(1947)-Becomes Justice comics	17	34	51	95	135	175
1(1948)	15	30	45	83	117	150
2(1948)	12	24	36	71	98	125
I.W. Reprint #1,2,7('58): 1-r/Wacky Duck #6	2	4	6	10	13	16
Super Reprint #10(I.W. on-c, Super-inside)	2	4	6	10	13	16

WACKY QUACKY (See Wisco)

WACKY RACES (TV)
Gold Key: Aug, 1969 - No. 7, Apr, 1972 (Hanna-Barbera)

	GD	VG	FN	VF	VF/NM	NM-
1	6	12	18	43	59	75
2-7	4	8	12	25	33	42

WACKY SQUIRREL (Also see Dark Horse Presents)
Dark Horse Comics: Oct, 1987 - No. 4, 1988 ($1.75, B&W)

	NM-
1-4: 4-Superman parody	2.25
Halloween Adventure Special 1 (1987, $2.00)	2.25
Summer Fun Special 1 (1988, $2.00)	2.25

WACKY WITCH (Also see Gold Key Spotlight)
Gold Key: March, 1971 - No. 21, Dec, 1975

	GD	VG	FN	VF	VF/NM	NM-
1	4	8	12	28	38	48
2	3	6	9	16	20	24
3-10	2	4	6	10	13	16
11-21	1	3	4	6	8	10

(See March of Comics #374, 398, 410, 422, 434, 446, 458, 470, 482)

WACKY WOODPECKER (See Two Bit the...)
I. W. Enterprises/Super Comics: 1958; 1963

	GD	VG	FN	VF	VF/NM	NM-
I.W. Reprint #1,2,7 (nd-reprints Two Bit...): 7-r/Two-Bit, the Wacky Woodpecker #1.	2	4	6	9	11	14
Super Reprint #10('63): 10-r/Two-Bit, The Wacky Woodpecker #?	2	4	6	9	11	14

WAGON TRAIN (1st Series) (TV) (See Western Roundup under Dell Giants)
Dell Publishing Co.: No. 895, Mar, 1958 - No. 13, Apr-June, 1962 (All photo-c)

	GD	VG	FN	VF	VF/NM	NM-
Four Color 895 (#1)	12	24	36	87	134	180
Four Color 971(#2),1019(#3)	8	16	24	55	78	100
4(1-3/60),6-13	7	14	21	50	68	85
5-Toth-a	8	16	24	53	74	95

WAGON TRAIN (2nd Series)(TV)
Gold Key: Jan, 1964 - No. 4, Oct, 1964 (All front & back photo-c)

	GD	VG	FN	VF	VF/NM	NM-
1-Tufts-a in all	7	14	21	46	63	80
2-4	5	10	15	36	48	60

WAHOO MORRIS
Image Comics: Mar, 2000 ($3.50, B&W)

	NM-
1-Craig Taillefer-s/a	3.50

WAITING PLACE, THE
Slave Labor Graphics: Apr, 1997 - No. 6, Sept, 1997 ($2.95)

	NM-
1-6-Sean McKeever-s	3.00
Vol. 2 - 1(11/99), 2-11	3.00
12-($4.95)	5.00

WAITING ROOM WILLIE (See Sad Case of...)

WAKE THE DEAD
IDW Publ.: Sept, 2003 - No. 5, Mar, 2004 ($3.99, limited series)

	NM-
1-5-Steve Niles-s/Chee-a	4.00
TPB (6/04, $19.99) r/series; intro. by Michael Dougherty; embossed die cut cover	20.00

WALKING DEAD, THE
Image Comics: Oct, 2003 - Present ($2.95, B&W)

	NM-
1-13-Robert Kirkman-s. 1-6-Tony Moore-a. 7-12-Charlie Adlard-a	3.00
...Vol. 1: Days Gone Bye (5/04, $9.95, TPB) r/#1-4	10.00
...Vol. 2: Miles Behind Us (10/04, $12.95, TPB) r/#7-12	13.00

WALLY (Teen-age)
Gold Key: Dec, 1962 - No. 4, Sept, 1963

	GD	VG	FN	VF	VF/NM	NM-
1	4	8	12	25	33	42
2-4	3	6	9	19	25	32

WALLY THE WIZARD
Marvel Comics (Star Comics): Apr, 1985 - No. 12, Mar, 1986 (Children's comic)

	NM-
1-12: Bob Bolling a-1,3; c-1,9,11,12	4.00
1-Variant with "Star Chase" game on last page and inside back-c	8.00

WALLY WOOD'S T.H.U.N.D.E.R. AGENTS (See Thunder Agents)
Deluxe Comics: Nov, 1984 - No. 5, Oct, 1986 ($2.00, 52 pgs.)

	NM-
1-5: 5-Jerry Ordway-c/a in Wood style	5.00

NOTE: ***Anderson** a-2i, 3i. **Buckler** a-4. **Ditko** a-3, 4. **Giffen** a-1p-4p. **Perez** a-1p, 2, 4; c-1-4.*

WALT DISNEY CHRISTMAS PARADE (Also see Christmas Parade)
Whitman Publ. Co. (Golden Press): Wint, 1977 ($1.95, cardboard-c, 224 pgs.)

	GD	VG	FN	VF	VF/NM	NM-
11191-Barks-r/Christmas in Disneyland #1, Dell Christmas Parade #9 & Dell Giant #53	4	8	12	27	36	45

WALT DISNEY COMICS DIGEST
Gold Key: June, 1968 - No. 57, Feb, 1976 (50¢, digest size)

	GD	VG	FN	VF	VF/NM	NM-
1-Reprints Uncle Scrooge #5; 192 pgs.	9	18	27	63	89	115
2-4-Barks-r	6	12	18	43	59	75
5-Daisy Duck by Barks (8 pgs.); last published story by Barks (art only) plus 21 pg. Scrooge-r by Barks	9	18	27	65	93	120
6-13-All Barks-r	4	8	12	27	36	45
14,15	3	6	9	18	24	30
16-Reprints Donald Duck #26 by Barks	4	8	12	25	33	42
17-20-Barks-r	3	7	10	21	28	35
21-31,33,35-37-Barks-r; 24-Toth Zorro	3	6	9	18	24	30
32,41,45,47-49	2	4	6	12	16	20
34,38,39: 34-Reprints 4-Color #318. 38-Reprints Christmas in Disneyland #1. 39-Two Barks-r/WDC&S #272, 4-Color #1073 plus Toth Zorro-r	3	6	9	18	24	30
40-Mickey Mouse-r by Gottfredson	2	4	6	14	18	22
42,43-Barks-r	2	4	6	14	18	22
44-(Has Gold Key emblem, 50¢)-Reprints 1st story of 4-Color #29,256,275,282	6	12	18	40	55	70
44-Republished in 1976 by Whitman; not identical to original; a bit smaller, blank back-c, 69¢	3	6	9	18	24	30
46,50,52-Barks-r. 52-Barks-r/WDC&S #161,132	2	4	6	12	16	20
51-Reprints 4-Color #71	3	6	9	18	24	30
53-55: 53-Reprints Dell Giant #30. 54-Reprints Donald Duck Beach Party #2. 55-Reprints Dell Giant #49	2	4	6	11	14	18
56-r/Uncle Scrooge #32 (Barks)	2	4	6	14	18	22
57-r/Mickey Mouse Almanac('57) & two Barks stories	2	4	6	12	16	20

NOTE: ***Toth** a-52r. #1-10, 196 pgs.; #11-41, 164 pgs.; #42 on, 132 pgs. Old issues were being reprinted & distributed by Whitman in 1976.*

WALT DISNEY GIANT (Disney)
Bruce Hamilton Company (Gladstone): Sept, 1995 - No. 7, Sept, 1996 ($2.25, bi-monthly, 48 pgs.)

	NM-
1-7: 1-Scrooge McDuck in the Yukon; Rosa-c/a/scripts plus r/F.C. #218. 2-Uncle Scrooge-r by Barks plus 17 pg. text story. 3-Donald the Mighty Duck; Rosa-c; Barks & Rosa-r. 4-Mickey and Goofy; new-a (story actually stars Goofy. Mickey Mouse by Caesar Ferioli; Donald Duck by Giorgio Cavazzano (1st in U.S.). 6-Uncle Scrooge & the Jr. Woodchucks; new-a and Barks-r. 7-Uncle Scrooge-r by Barks plus new-a	3.00

NOTE: *Series was initially solicited as Uncle Walt's Collectory. Issue #8 was advertised, but later cancelled.*

Walt Disney's Christmas Parade #2 © WDC

Walt Disney's Comics and Stories (V3#1)#25 © WDC

Walt Disney's Comics and Stories #120 © WDC

WALT DISNEY PAINT BOOK SERIES
Whitman Publ. Co.: No dates; circa 1975 (Beware! Has 1930s copyright dates) (79¢-c, 52pgs. B&W, treasury-sized) (Coloring books, text stories & comics-r)

	GD 2.0	VG 4.0	FN 6.0	VF 8.0	VF/NM 9.0	NM- 9.2
#2052 (Whitman #886-r) Mickey Mouse & Donald Duck Gag Book	4	8	12	25	33	42
#2053 (Whitman #677-r)	4	8	12	25	33	42
#2054 (Whitman #670-r) Donald-c	4	8	12	28	38	48
#2055 (Whitman #627-r) Mickey-c	4	8	12	25	33	42
#2056 (Whitman #660-r) Buckey Bug-c	4	8	12	22	30	38
#2057 (Whitman #887-r) Mickey & Donald-c	4	8	12	25	33	42

WALT DISNEY PRESENTS (TV)(Disney)
Dell Publishing Co.: No. 997, 6-8/59 - No. 6, 12-2/1960-61; No. 1181, 4-5/61 (All photo-c)

	GD 2.0	VG 4.0	FN 6.0	VF 8.0	VF/NM 9.0	NM- 9.2
Four Color 997 (#1)	9	18	27	60	85	110
2(12-2/60)-The Swamp Fox(origin), Elfego Baca, Texas John Slaughter (Disney TV show) begin	6	12	18	40	55	70
3-6: 5-Swamp Fox by Warren Tufts	6	12	18	38	52	65
Four Color 1181-Texas John Slaughter	8	16	24	58	82	105

WALT DISNEY'S CHRISTMAS PARADE (Also see Christmas Parade)
Gladstone: Winter, 1988; No. 2, Winter, 1989 ($2.95, 100 pgs.)

	GD 2.0	VG 4.0	FN 6.0	VF 8.0	VF/NM 9.0	NM- 9.2
1-Barks-r/painted-c	2	4	6	8	10	12
2-Barks-r	1	2	3	5	7	9

WALT DISNEY'S CHRISTMAS PARADE
Gemstone Publishing: Dec, 2003; 2004 ($8.95, prestige format)

	GD 2.0	VG 4.0	FN 6.0	VF 8.0	VF/NM 9.0	NM- 9.2
1,2: 1-Reprints and 3 new European holiday stories. 2-All reprints						9.00

WALT DISNEY'S COMICS AND STORIES (Cont. of Mickey Mouse Magazine) (#1-30 contain Donald Duck newspaper reprints) (Titled "Comics And Stories" #264 to #?; titled "Walt Disney's Comics And Stories" #511 on)
Dell Publishing Co./Gold Key #264-473/Whitman #474-510/Gladstone #511-547/ Disney Comics #548-585/Gladstone #586-633/Gemstone Publishing #634 on:
10/40 - #263, 8/62; #264, 10/62 - #510, 7/84; #511, 10/86 - #633, 2/99; #634, 7/03 - Present

NOTE: The whole number can always be found at the bottom of the title page in the lower left-hand or right hand panel.

	GD 2.0	VG 4.0	FN 6.0	VF 8.0	VF/NM 9.0	NM- 9.2
1(V1#1-c; V2#1-indicia)-Donald Duck strip-r by Al Taliaferro & Gottfredson's Mickey Mouse begin	1600	3200	4800	11,000	18,000	25,000
2	571	1142	1713	3712	6356	9000
3	214	428	642	1391	2196	3000
4-X-Mas-c; 1st Huey, Dewey & Louie-c this title (See Mickey Mouse Magazine V4#2 for 1st-c ever)	157	314	471	1021	1611	2200
4-Special promotional, complimentary issue; cover same except one corner was blanked out & boxed in to identify the giveaway (not a paste-over). This special pressing was probably sent out to former subscribers to Mickey Mouse Mag. whose subscriptions had expired. (Very rare-5 known copies)	257	514	771	1671	2636	3600
5-Goofy-c	118	236	354	767	1209	1650
6-10: 8-Only Clarabelle Cow-c. 9-Taliaferro-c (1st)	93	186	279	605	953	1300
11-14: 11-Huey, Dewey & Louie-c/app.	75	150	225	488	769	1050
15-17: 15-The 3 Little Kittens (17 pgs.). 16-The 3 Little Pigs (29 pgs.); X-Mas-c. 17-The Ugly Duckling (4 pgs.)	70	140	210	455	715	975
18-21	59	118	177	384	605	825
22-30: 22-Flag-c. 24-The Flying Gauchito (1st original comic book story done for WDC&S). 27-Jose Carioca by Carl Buettner (2nd original story in WDC&S)	47	94	141	306	483	660
31-New Donald Duck stories by Carl Barks begin (See F.C. #9 for 1st Barks Donald Duck)	300	600	900	1950	3175	4400
32-Barks-a	139	278	417	904	1427	1950
33-Barks-a; infinity-c	96	192	288	624	987	1350
34-Gremlins by Walt Kelly begin, end #41; Barks-a	78	156	234	507	804	1100
35,36-Barks-a	71	142	213	462	731	1000
37-Donald Duck by Jack Hannah	37	74	111	241	383	525
38-40-Barks-a. 39-X-Mas-c. 40,41-Gremlins by Kelly	48	96	144	312	494	675
41-50-Barks-a. 43-Seven Dwarfs-c app. (4/44). 45-50-Nazis in Gottfredson's Mickey Mouse Stories	38	76	114	247	394	540
51-60-Barks-a. 51-X-Mas-c. 52-Li'l Bad Wolf begins, ends #203 (not in #55). 58-Kelly flag-c	25	50	75	181	278	375
61-70: Barks-a. 61-Dumbo story. 63,64-Pinocchio stories. 63-Cover swipe from New Funnies #94. 64-X-Mas-c. 65-Pluto story. 66-Infinity-c. 67,68-Mickey Mouse Sunday-r by Bill Wright	22	44	66	158	242	325
71-80: Barks-a. 75-77-Brer Rabbit stories, no Mickey Mouse. 76-X-Mas-c	17	34	51	121	186	250
81-87,89,90: Barks-a. 82-Goofy-c. 82-84-Bongo stories. 86-90-Goofy & Agnes app. 89-Chip 'n' Dale story	15	30	45	105	160	215
88-1st app. Gladstone Gander by Barks (1/48)	19	38	57	134	205	275
91-97,99: Barks-a. 95-1st WDC&S Barks-c. 96-No Mickey Mouse; Little Toot begins, ends #97. 99-X-Mas-c	13	26	39	90	138	185
98-1st Uncle Scrooge app. in WDC&S (11/48)	25	50	75	177	271	365
100-(1/49)-Barks-a	15	30	45	109	167	225
101-110-Barks-a. 107-Taliaferro-c; Donald acquires super powers	12	24	36	84	127	170
111,114,117-All Barks-a	10	20	30	73	107	140
112-Drug (ether) issue (Donald Duck)	10	20	30	73	107	140
113,115,116,118-123: No Barks. 116-Dumbo x-over. 121-Grandma Duck begins, ends #168; not in #135,142,146,155	7	14	21	46	63	80
124,126-130-All Barks-a. 124-X-Mas-c	9	18	27	60	85	110
125-1st app. Junior Woodchucks (2/51); Barks-a	12	24	36	84	127	170
131,133,135-137,139-All Barks-a	9	18	27	60	85	110
132-Barks-a(2) (D. Duck & Grandma Duck)	9	18	27	63	89	115
134-Intro. & 1st app. The Beagle Boys (11/51)	16	32	48	112	171	230
138-Classic Scrooge money story	12	24	36	87	134	180
140-(5/52)-1st app. Gyro Gearloose by Barks; 2nd Barks Uncle Scrooge-c; 3rd Uncle Scrooge cover app.	16	32	48	112	171	230
141-150-All Barks-a. 143-Little Hiawatha begins, ends #151,159	7	14	21	50	68	85
151-170-All Barks-a	6	12	18	43	59	75
171-199-All Barks-a	6	12	18	38	52	65
200	6	12	18	43	59	75
201-240: All Barks-a. 204-Chip 'n' Dale & Scamp begin	5	10	15	36	48	60
241-283: Barks-a. 241-Dumbo x-over. 247-Gyro Gearloose begins, ends #274. 256-Ludwig Von Drake begins, ends #274	5	10	15	33	44	55
284,285,287,290,295,296,309-311-Not by Barks	3	6	9	16	20	25
286,288,291-294,297,298,308-All Barks stories; 293-Grandma Duck's Farm Friends. 297-Gyro Gearloose. 298-Daisy Duck's Diary-r	3	6	9	19	25	32
289-Annette-c & back-c & story; Barks-s	4	8	12	24	32	40
299-307-All contain early Barks-r (#43-117). 305-Gyro Gearloose	3	7	10	21	28	35
312-Last Barks issue with original story	3	7	10	21	28	35
313-315,317-327,329-334,336-341	2	4	6	14	18	22
316-Last issue published during life of Walt Disney	2	4	6	14	18	22
328,335,342-350-Barks-r	2	4	6	14	18	22
351-360-With posters inside; Barks reprints (2 versions of each with & without posters)	4	8	12	27	36	45
351-360-Without posters…	2	4	6	14	18	22
361-400-Barks-r	2	4	6	14	18	22
401-429-Barks-r	2	4	6	12	16	20
430,433,437,438,441,444,445,466-No Barks	1	3	4	6	8	10
431,432,434-436,439,440,442,443-Barks-r	2	4	6	9	11	14
446-465,467-473-Barks-r	1	3	4	6	8	10
474(3/80),475-478 (Whitman)	2	4	6	11	14	18
479(8/80),481(10/80)-484(1/81) pre-pack only	4	8	12	29	40	50
480 (8-12/80)-(Very low distribution)	10	20	30	72	104	135
485-499: 494-r/WDC&S #98	2	4	6	11	14	18
500-510 (All #90011 on-c; pre-packs): 500(4/83), 501(5/83), 502&503(7/83), 504-506(all 8/83), 507(4/84), 508(5/84), 509(6/84), 510(7/84). 506-No Barks	2	4	6	12	16	20
511-Donald Duck by Daan Jippes (1st in U.S.; in all through #518); Gyro Gearloose Barks-r begins (in most through #547); Wuzzles by Disney Studio (1st by Gladstone)	3	6	9	18	24	30
512,513	2	4	6	10	13	16
514-516,520	1	2	3	5	7	9
517-519,521,522,525,527,529,530,532-546: 518-Infinity-c. 522-r/1st app. Huey, Dewey & Louie from D. Duck Sunday. 535-546-Barks-r. 537-1st Donald Duck by William Van Horn in WDC&S. 541-545-52 pgs. 546,547-68 pgs. 546-Kelly-r. 547-Rosa-a						5.00
523,524,526,528,531,547: Rosa-s/a in all. 523-1st Rosa 10 pager	2	4	6	9	11	14
548-($1.50, 6/90)-1st Disney issue; new-a; no M. Mouse						6.00
549,551-570,572,573,577-579,581,584 ($1.50): 549-Barks-r begin, ends #585, not in #555, 556, & 564. 551-r/1 story from F.C. #29. 556,578-r/Mickey Mouse Cheerios Premium by Dick Moores. 562,563,568-570, 572, 581-Gottfredson strip-r. 570-Valentine issue; has Mickey/Minnie centerfold. 584-Taliaferro strip-r						4.00
550 ($2.25, 52 pgs.)-Donald Duck by Barks; previously printed only in The Netherlands (1st time in U.S.); r/Chip 'n Dale & Scamp from #204						5.00
571-($2.95, 68 pgs)-r/Donald Duck's Atomic Bomb by Barks from 1947 Cheerios premium						6.00
574-576,580,582,583 ($2.95, 68 pgs.): 574-r/1st Pinocchio Sunday strip (1939-40). 575-Gottfredson-r, Pinocchio-r/WDC&S #64. 580-r/Donald Duck's 1st app. from Silly Symphony strip 12/16/34 by Taliaferro; Gottfredson strip-r begin; not in #584 & 600.						

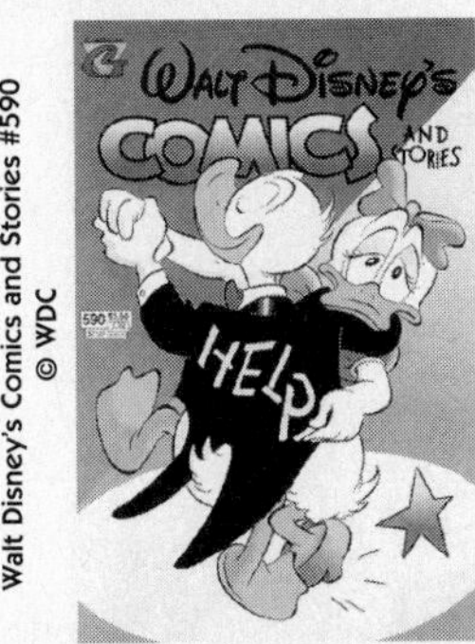

Walt Disney's Comics and Stories #590 © WDC

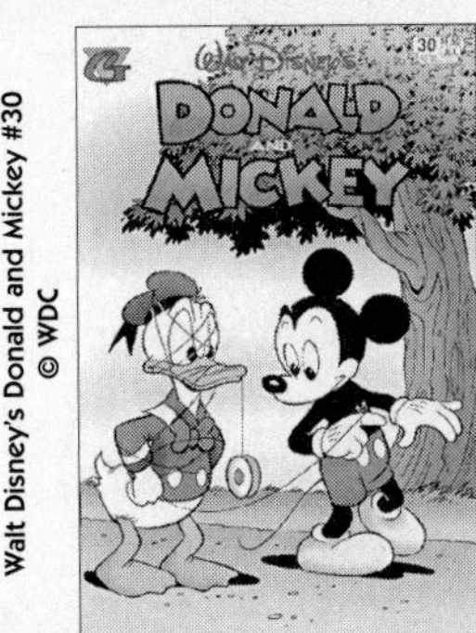

Walt Disney's Donald and Mickey #30 © WDC

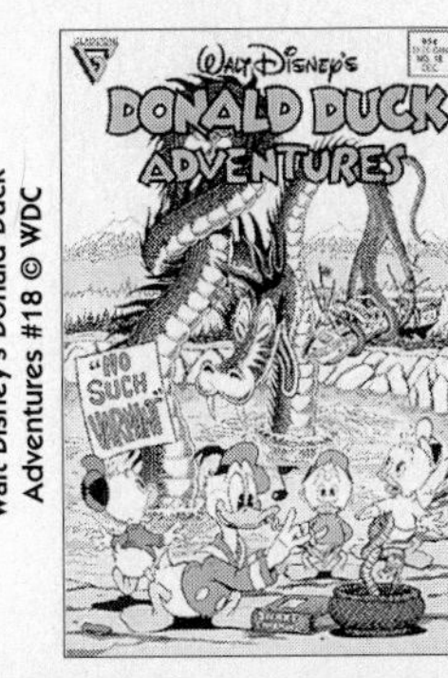

Walt Disney's Donald Duck Adventures #18 © WDC

GD 2.0 | VG 4.0 | FN 6.0 | VF 8.0 | VF/NM 9.0 | NM- 9.2

582,583-r/Mickey Mouse on Sky Island from WDC&S #1,2 5.00
585 ($2.50, 52 pgs.)-r/#140; Barks-r/WDC&S #140 5.00
586,587: 586-Gladstone issues begin again; begin $1.50-c; Gottfredson-r begins (not in #600). 587-Donald Duck by William Van Horn begins 4.00
588-597: 588,591-599-Donald Duck by William Van Horn 3.00
598,599 ($1.95, 36 pgs.): 598-r/1st drawings of Mickey Mouse by Ub Iwerks 3.00
600 ($2.95, 48 pgs.)-L.B. Cole-c(r)/WDC&S #1; Barks-r/WDC&S #32 plus Rosa, Jippes, Van Horn-r and new Rosa centerspread 4.00
601-611 ($5.95, 64 pgs., squarebound, bi-monthly): 601-Barks-c, r/Mickey Mouse V1#1, Rosa-a/scripts. 602-Rosa-c. 604-Taliaferro strip-r/1st Silly Symphony Sundays from 1932. 604,605-Jippes-a. 605-Walt Kelly-c; Gottfredson "Mickey Mouse Outwits the Phantom Blot" r/F.C. #16 6.00
612-633 ($6.95): 633-(2/99) Last Gladstone issue 7.00
634-651: 634-(7/03) First Gemstone issue; William Van Horn-c 7.00
NOTE: *(#1-38, 68 pgs.; #39-42, 60 pgs.; #43-57, 61-134, 143-168, 446, 447, 52 pgs.; #58-60, 135-142, 169-540, 36 pgs.)*

NOTE: **Barks** *art in all issues #31 on, except where noted; c-95, 96, 104, 108, 109, 130-172, 174-178, 183, 198-200, 204, 206-209, 212-216, 218, 220, 226, 228-233, 235-238, 240-243, 247, 250, 253, 256, 260, 261, 276-283, 288-292, 295-298, 301, 303, 304, 306, 307, 309, 310, 313-316, 319, 321, 322, 324, 326, 328, 329, 331, 332, 334, 341, 342, 350, 351, 527r, 530r, 540(never before published), 546r, 557-586r(most), 596p, 601p.* **Kelly** *a-24p, 34-41, 43; r-522-524, 546, 547, 582, 583; covers(most)-34-118, 531r, 537r, 541r-543r, 562r, 571r, 605r. Walt Disney's Comics & Stories featured Mickey Mouse serials which were in practically every issue from #1 through #394 and #511 to date. The titles of the serials, along with the issues they are in, are listed in previous editions of this price guide.* **Floyd Gottfredson** *Mickey Mouse serials in issues #1-14, 18-66, 69-74, 78-100, 128, 562, 563, 568-572, 582, 583, 586-599 , 601-603 , 605-present , plus "Service with a Smile" in #13; "Mickey Mouse in a Warplant" (3 pgs.), and "Pluto Catches a Nazi Spy" (4 pgs.) in #62; "Mystery Next Door", #93; "Sunken Treasure", #94; "Aunt Marissa", #95 (r in #575); "Gangland", #98 (r in #562); "Thanksgiving Dinner", #99 (r in #567); and "The Talking Dog", #100 (r in #563); "Morty's Escapade," #128. "The Brave Little Tailor", #580; "Introducing Mickey Mouse Movies ", #581; Circus Roustabout, #585; "Rumplewatt the Giant", #604. Mickey Mouse by* **Paul Murry** *#152-547 except 155-57 (***Dick Moore***), 327-29 (***Tony Strobl***), 348-50 (***Jack Manning***), 533 (***Bill Wright***).* **Don Rosa** *story/a-523, 524, 526, 528, 531, 547, 601-present.* **Al Taliaferro** *Silly Symphonies in #5-"Three Little Pigs"; #13-"Birds of a Feather"; #14-"The Boarding School Mystery"; #15-"Cookieland" and "Three Little Kittens"; #16-"The Practical Pig"; #17-"The Ugly Duckling"; "The Wise Little Hen" in #580; and "Ambrose the Robber Kitten"; #19-"Penguin Isle"; and "Bucky Bug" in #20-23, 25, 26, 28 (one continuous story from 1932-34; first 2 pgs. not Taliaferro).* **Gottfredson** *strip r-562, 563, 568-572, 581, 585, 586, 590.* **Taliaferro** *strip r-584, 580.* **Van Horn** *a-537, 545, 561, 574, 587, 588, 591-present.*

WALT DISNEY'S COMICS DIGEST
Gladstone: Dec, 1986 - No. 7, Sept, 1987
1 1 2 3 5 6 8
2-7 6.00

WALT DISNEY'S COMICS PENNY PINCHER
Gladstone: May, 1997 - No. 4, Aug, 1997 (99¢, limited series)
1-4 2.25

WALT DISNEY'S DONALD AND MICKEY (Formerly Walt Disney's Mickey and Donald)
Gladstone (Bruce Hamilton Co.): No. 19, Sept, 1993 - No. 30, 1995 ($1.50, 36 & 68 pgs.)
19,21-24,26-30: New & reprints. 19,21,23,24-Barks-r. 19,26-Murry-r. 22-Barks "Omelet" story r/WDC&S #146. 27-Mickey Mouse story by Caesar Ferioli (1st U.S work). 29-Rosa-c; Mickey Mouse story actually starring Goofy (does not include Mickey except on title page.) 4.00
20,25-($2.95, 68 pgs.): 20-Barks, Gottfredson-r 5.00
NOTE: *Donald Duck stories were all reprints.*

WALT DISNEY'S DONALD DUCK ADVENTURES (D.D. Adv. #1-3)
Gladstone: 11/87-No. 20, 4/90 (1st Series); No. 21,8/93-No. 48, 2/98(3rd Series)
1 1 2 3 4 5 7
2-r/F.C. #308 3.00
3,4,6,7,9-11,13,15-18: 3-r/F.C. #223. 4-r/F.C. #62. 9-r/F.C. #159, "Ghost of the Grotto". 11-r/F.C. #159, "Adventure Down Under." 16-r/F.C. #291; Rosa-c. 18-r/FC #318; Rosa-c 3.00
5,8-Don Rosa-c/a 5.00
12($1.50, 52pgs)-Rosa-c/a w/Barks poster 6.00
14-r/F.C. #29, "Mummy's Ring" 4.00
19($1.95, 68 pgs.)-Barks-r/F.C. #199 (1 pg.) 3.00
20($1.95, 68 pgs.)-Barks-r/F.C. #189 & cover-r; William Van Horn-a 3.00
21,22: 21-r/D.D. #46. 22-r/F.C. #282 3.00
23-25,27,29,31,32-($1.50, 36 pgs.): 21,23,29-Rosa-c. 23-Intro/1st app. Andold Wild Duck by Marco Rota. 24-Van Horn-a. 27-1st Pat Block-a, "Mystery of Widow's Gap." 31,32-Block-c 2.50
26,28($2.95, 68 pgs.): 26-Barks-r/F.C. #108, "Terror of the River". 28-Barks-r/F.C. #199, "Sheriff of Bullet Valley" 4.00
30($2.95, 68 pgs.)-r/F.C. #367, Barks' "Christmas for Shacktown" 4.00
33($1.95, 68 pgs.)-r/F.C. #408, Barks' "The Golden Helmet;"Van Horn-c 3.00
34-43: 34-Resume $1.50-c. 34,35,37-Block-a/scripts. 38-Van Horn-c/a 2.50
44-48-($1.95-c) 2.50
NOTE: **Barks** *a-1-22r, 26r, 28r, 33r, 36r; c-3r, 8r, 10r, 14r, 20r.* **Block** *a-27, 30, 34, 35, 37; c-27, 30-32, 34, 35, 37; c-27, 30, 31, 32, 34, 35, 37.* **Rosa** *a-5, 8, 12, 43; c-13, 16, 18, 21, 23, 43.*

WALT DISNEY'S DONALD DUCK ADVENTURES (2nd Series)
Disney Comics: June, 1990 - No. 38, July, 1993 ($1.50)
1-Rosa-a & scripts 5.00
2-21,23,25,27-33,35,36,38: 2-Barks-r/WDC&S #35; William Van Horn-a begins, ends #20. 9-Barks-r/F.C. #178. 9,11,14,17-No Van Horn-a. 11-Mad #1 cover parody. 14-Barks-r. 17-Barks-r. 21-r/FC #203 by Barks. 29-r/MOC #20 by Barks 3.00
22,24,26,34,37: 22-Rosa-a (10 pgs.) & scripts. 24-Rosa-a & scripts. 26-r/March of Comics #41 by Barks. 34-Rosa-c/a. 37-Rosa-a; Barks-r 4.00
NOTE: **Barks** *r-2, 4, 9(F.C. #178), 14(D.D. #45), 17, 21, 26, 27, 29 , 35, 36(D.D #60)-38.* **Taliaferro** *a-34r, 36r.*

WALT DISNEY'S DONALD DUCK ADVENTURES (Take-Along Comic)
Gemstone Publishing: July, 2003 - Present ($7.95, 5" x 7-1/2")
1-9-Mickey Mouse & Uncle Scrooge app. 9-Christmas-c 8.00

WALT DISNEY'S DONALD DUCK AND FRIENDS
Gemstone Publishing: No. 308, Oct, 2003 - Present ($2.95)
308-322: 308-Numbering resumes from Gladstone Donald Duck series; Halloween-c 3.00

WALT DISNEY'S DONALD DUCK AND MICKEY MOUSE (Formerly Walt Disney's Donald and Mickey)
Gladstone (Bruce Hamilton Company): Sept, 1995 - No. 7, Sept, 1996 ($1.50, 32 pgs.)
1-7: 1-Barks-r and new Mickey Mouse stories in all. 5,6-Mickey Mouse stories by Caesar Ferioli. 7-New Donald Duck and Mickey Mouse x-over story; Barks-r/WDC&S #51 2.25
NOTE: *Issue #8 was advertised, but cancelled.*

WALT DISNEY SHOWCASE
Gold Key: Oct, 1970 - No. 54, Jan, 1980 (No. 44-48: 68pgs., 49-54: 52pgs.)

	GD 2.0	VG 4.0	FN 6.0	VF 8.0	VF/NM 9.0	NM- 9.2
1-Boatniks (Movie)-Photo-c	3	7	10	21	28	35
2-Moby Duck	3	6	9	16	20	24
3,4,7: 3-Bongo & Lumpjaw-r. 4,7-Pluto-r	2	4	6	11	14	18
5-$1,000,000 Duck (Movie)-Photo-c	3	6	9	18	23	28
6-Bedknobs & Broomsticks (Movie)	3	6	9	18	23	28
8-Daisy & Donald	2	4	6	12	16	20
9- 101 Dalmatians (cartoon feat.); r/F.C. #1183	3	6	9	19	25	32
10-Napoleon & Samantha (Movie)-Photo-c	3	6	9	18	23	28
11-Moby Duck-r	2	4	6	11	14	18
12-Dumbo-r/Four Color #668	2	4	6	12	16	20
13-Pluto-r	2	4	6	11	14	18
14-World's Greatest Athlete (Movie)-Photo-c	3	6	9	18	23	28
15- 3 Little Pigs-r	2	4	6	12	16	20
16-Aristocats (cartoon feature); r/Aristocats #1	3	6	9	18	23	28
17-Mary Poppins; r/M.P. #10136-501-Photo-c	3	6	9	18	23	28
18-Gyro Gearloose; Barks-r/F.C. #1047,1184	3	7	10	21	28	35
19-That Darn Cat; r/That Darn Cat #10171-602-Hayley Mills photo-c	3	6	9	18	23	28
20,23-Pluto-r	2	4	6	12	16	20
21-Li'l Bad Wolf & The Three Little Pigs	2	4	6	11	14	18
22-Unbirthday Party with Alice in Wonderland; r/Four Color #341	3	6	9	16	20	24
24-26: 24-Herbie Rides Again (Movie); sequel to "The Love Bug"; photo-c. 25-Old Yeller (Movie); r/F.C. #869; Photo-c. 26-Lt. Robin Crusoe USN (Movie); r/Lt. Robin Crusoe USN #10191-601; photo-c	2	4	6	12	16	20
27-Island at the Top of the World (Movie)-Photo-c	3	6	9	16	20	24
28-Brer Rabbit, Bucky Bug-r/WDC&S #58	2	4	6	12	16	20
29-Escape to Witch Mountain (Movie)-Photo-c	3	6	9	16	20	24
30-Magica De Spell; Barks-r/Uncle Scrooge #36 & WDC&S #258	4	8	12	25	33	42
31-Bambi (cartoon feature); r/Four Color #186	2	4	6	14	18	22
32-Spin & Marty-r/F.C. #1026; Mickey Mouse Club (TV)-Photo-c	3	6	9	16	20	24
33-40: 33-Pluto-r/F.C. #1143. 34-Paul Revere's Ride with Johnny Tremain (TV); r/F.C. #822. 35-Goofy-r/F.C. #952. 36-Peter Pan-r/F.C. #442. 37-Tinker Bell & Jiminy Cricket-r/F.C. #982,989. 38,39-Mickey & the Sleuth, Parts 1 & 2. 40-The Rescuers (cartoon feature)	2	4	6	10	13	16
41-Herbie Goes to Monte Carlo (Movie); sequel to "Herbie Rides Again"; photo-c	2	4	6	11	14	18
42-Mickey & the Sleuth	2	4	6	10	13	16
43-Pete's Dragon (Movie)-Photo-c	2	4	6	14	18	22
44-Return From Witch Mountain (new) & In Search of the Castaways-r (Movies)-Photo-c; 68 pg. giants begin	3	6	9	16	20	24
45-The Jungle Book (Movie); r/#30033-803	3	6	9	19	25	32
46-48: 46-The Cat From Outer Space (Movie)(new), & The Shaggy Dog (Movie)-r/F.C. #985; photo-c. 47-Mickey Mouse Surprise Party-r. 48-The Wonderful Advs. of Pinocchio-r/F.C. #1203; last 68 pg. issue	2	4	6	11	14	18

49-54: 49-North Avenue Irregulars (Movie); Zorro-r/Zorro #11; 52 pgs. begin; photo-c. 50-Bedknobs & Broomsticks-r/#6; Mooncussers-r/World of Adv. #1; photo-c. 51-101 Dalmatians-r. 52-Unidentified Flying Oddball (Movie); r/Picnic Party #8; photo-c.

Walt Disney's Mickey and Donald #11 © WDC

Walt Disney's Uncle Scrooge #335 © WDC

Wambi, Jungle Boy #10 © FH

GD VG FN VF VF/NM NM-
2.0 4.0 6.0 8.0 9.0 9.2

53-The Scarecrow-r (TV). 54-The Black Hole (Movie)-Photo-c (predates Black Hole #1)
2 4 6 10 13 16

WALT DISNEY'S MAGAZINE (TV)(Formerly Walt Disney's Mickey Mouse Club Magazine) (50¢, bi-monthly)
Western Publishing Co.: V2#4, June, 1957 - V4#6, Oct, 1959

V2#4-Stories & articles on the Mouseketeers, Zorro, & Goofy and other Disney characters & people 7 14 21 51 71 90
V2#5, V2#6(10/57) 7 14 21 46 63 80
V3#1(12/57), V3#3-5 6 12 18 40 55 70
V3#2-Annette Funicello photo-c 12 24 36 86 131 175
V3#6(10/58)-TV Zorro photo-c 9 18 27 60 85 110
V4#1(12/58) - V4#2-4,6(10/59) 6 12 18 40 55 70
V4#5-Annette Funicello photo-c, w/ 2-photo articles 12 24 36 86 131 175
NOTE: *V2#4-V3#6 were 11-1/2x8-1/2", 48 pgs.; V4#1 on were 10x8", 52 pgs. (Peak circulation of 400,000).*

WALT DISNEY'S MERRY CHRISTMAS (See Dell Giant #39)

WALT DISNEY'S MICKEY AND DONALD (M & D #1,2)(Becomes Walt Disney's Donald & Mickey #19 on)
Gladstone: Mar, 1988 - No. 18, May, 1990 (95¢)

1-Don Rosa-a; r/1949 Firestone giveaway 6.00
2-8: 3-Infinity-c. 4-8-Barks-r 3.00
9-15: 9-r/1948 Firestone giveaway; X-Mas-c 3.00
16($1.50, 52 pgs.)-r/FC #157 5.00
17-(68 pgs.) Barks M.M.-r/FC #79 plus Barks D.D.-r; Rosa-a; x-mas-c 6.00
18($1.95, 68 pgs.)-Gottfredson-r/WDC&S #13,72-74; Kelly-c(r); Barks-r 5.00
NOTE: ***Barks** reprints in 1-15, 17, 18. **Kelly** c-13r, 14 (r/Walt Disney's C&S #58), 18r.*

WALT DISNEY'S MICKEY MOUSE ADVENTURES (Take-Along Comic)
Gemstone Publishing: Aug, 2004 - Present ($7.95, 5" x 7-1/2")

1-Goofy, Donald Duck & Uncle Scrooge app. 8.00

WALT DISNEY'S MICKEY MOUSE AND FRIENDS
Gemstone Publishing: No. 257, Oct, 2003 - Present ($2.95)

257-271: 257-Numbering resumes from Gladstone Mickey Mouse series; Halloween-c 3.00

WALT DISNEY'S MICKEY MOUSE CLUB MAGAZINE (TV)(Becomes Walt Disney's Magazine)
Western Publishing Co.: Winter, 1956 - V2#3, Apr, 1957 (11-1/2x8-1/2", quarterly, 48 pgs.)

V1#1 16 32 48 112 171 230
2-4 9 18 27 63 89 115
V2#1,2 7 14 21 51 71 90
3-Annette photo-c 14 28 42 97 149 200
Annual(1956)-Two different issues; ($1.50-Whitman); 120 pgs., cardboard covers, 11-3/4x8-3/4"; reprints 16 32 48 112 171 230
Annual(1957)-Same as above 13 26 39 90 138 185

WALT DISNEY'S PINOCCHIO SPECIAL
Gladstone: Spring, 1990 ($1.00)

1-50th anniversary edition; Kelly-r/F.C. #92 3.00

WALT DISNEY'S THE ADVENTUROUS UNCLE SCROOGE MCDUCK
Gladstone: Jan, 1998 - No. 2, Mar, 1998 ($1.95)

1,2: 1-Barks-a(r). 2-Rosa-a(r) 2.50

WALT DISNEY'S THE JUNGLE BOOK
W.D. Publications (Disney Comics): 1990 ($5.95, graphic novel, 68 pgs.)

nn-Movie adaptation; movie rereleased in 1990 6.00
nn-($2.95, 68 pgs.)-Comic edition; wraparound-c 3.00

WALT DISNEY'S UNCLE SCROOGE (Formerly Uncle Scrooge #1-209)
Gladstone #210-242/Disney Comics #243-280/Gladstone #281-318/Gemstone #319 on: No. 210, 10/86 - No. 242, 4/90; No. 243, 6/90 - No. 318, 2/99; No. 319, 7/03 - Present

210-1st Gladstone issue; r/WDC&S #134 (1st Beagle Boys)
2 4 6 10 13 16
211-218: 216-New story ("Go Slowly Sands of Time") plotted and partly scripted by Barks. 217-r/U.S. #7, "Seven Cities of Cibola" 2 4 6 10 12 15
219-"Son Of The Sun" by Rosa 3 6 9 16 20 25
220-Don Rosa-a/scripts 1 2 3 5 6 8
221-223,225,228-234,236-240 4.00
224,226,227,235: 224-Rosa-c/a. 226,227-Rosa-a. 235-Rosa-a/scripts 5.00
241-($1.95, 68 pgs.)-Rosa finishes over Barks-r 6.00
242-($1.95, 68 pgs.)-Barks-r; Rosa-a(1 pg.) 6.00
243-249,251-260,264-275,277-280,282-284-($1.50): 243-1st by Disney Comics. 274-All Barks issue. 275-Contains centerspread by Rosa. 279-All Barks issue; Rosa-c. 283-r/WDC&S #98 3.00
250-($2.25, 52 pgs.)-Barks-r; wraparound-c 4.00
261-263,276-Don Rosa-c/a 5.00
281-Gladstone issues start again; Rosa-c 6.00
285-The Life and Times of Scrooge McDuck Pt. 1; Rosa-c/a/scripts
1 3 4 6 8 10
286-293: The Life and Times of Scrooge McDuck Pt. 2-8; Rosa-c/a/scripts. 293-($1.95, 36 pgs.)-The Life and Times of Scrooge McDuck Pt. 9 6.00
294-299, 301-308-($1.50, 32 pgs.): 294-296-The Life and Times of Scrooge McDuck Pt. 10-12. 297-The Life and Times of Uncle Scrooge Pt. 0; Rosa-c/a/scripts 3.00
300-($2.25, 48 pgs.)-Rosa-c; Barks-r/WDC&S #104 and U.S. #216; r/U.S. #220; includes new centerfold. 4.00
309-318-($6.95) 318-(2/99) Last Gladstone issue 7.00
319-336: 319-(7/03) First Gemstone issue; The Dutchman's Secret by Don Rosa 7.00
NOTE: ***Barks** r-210-218, 220-223, 224(2pg.), 225-234, 236-242, 245, 246, 250-253, 255, 256, 258, 261(2 pg.), 265, 267, 268, 270(2), 272-284, 299-present; c(r)-210, 212, 221, 228, 229, 232, 233, 284. scripts-287, 293. **Rosa** a-219, 220, 224, 226, 227, 235, 261-263, 268, 275-277, 285-289; c-219, 224, 231, 261-263, 276, 278-281, 285-289; scripts-219, 220, 224, 235, 261-263, 268, 276, 285-289.*

WALT DISNEY'S UNCLE SCROOGE ADVENTURES (U. Scrooge Advs. #1-3)
Gladstone Publishing: Nov, 1987 - No. 21, May, 1990; No. 22, Sept, 1993 - No. 54, Feb, 1998

1-Barks-r begin, ends #26 1 2 3 5 6 8
2-4 4.00
5,9,14: 5-Rosa-c/a; no Barks-r. 9,14-Rosa-a 5.00
6-8,10-13,15-19: 10-r/U.S. #18(all Barks) 3.00
20,21 ($1.95, 68 pgs.) 20-Rosa-c/a. 21-Rosa-a 5.00
22 ($1.50)-Rosa-c; r/U.S. #26 5.00
23-($2.95, 68 pgs.)-Vs. The Phantom Blot-r/P.B. #3; Barks-r 4.00
24-26,29,31,32,34-36: 24,25,29,31,32-Rosa-c. 25-r/U.S. #21 2.50
27-Guardians of the Lost Library - Rosa-c/a/story; origin of Junior Woodchuck Guidebook 3.00
28-($2.95, 68 pgs.)-r/U.S. #13 w/restored missing panels 4.00
30-($2.95, 68 pgs.)-r/U.S. #12; Rosa-c 4.00
33-($2.95, 64 pgs.)-New Barks story 3.00
37-54 2.50
NOTE: ***Barks** r-1-4, 6-8, 10-13, 15-21, 23, 22, 24; c(r)-15, 16, 17, 21. **Rosa** a-5, 9, 14, 20, 21, 27, 51; c-5, 13, 14, 17(finishes), 20, 22, 24, 25, 27, 28, 51; scripts-5, 9, 14, 27.*

WALT DISNEY'S UNCLE SCROOGE AND DONALD DUCK
Gladstone: Jan, 1998 - No. 2, Mar, 1998 ($1.95)

1,2: 1-Rosa-a(r) 2.50

WALT DISNEY'S UNCLE SCROOGE ADVENTURES IN COLOR
Gladstone Publ.: Dec, 1995 - Present ($8.95/$9.95, squarebound, 56 issue limited series) (Polybagged w/card) (Series chronologically reprints all the stories written & drawn by Carl Barks)

1-56: 1-(12/95)-r/FC #386. 15-(12/96)-r/US #15. 16-(12/96)-r/US #16. 18-(1/97)-r/US #18 10.00

WALT DISNEY'S VACATION PARADE
Gemstone Publishing: 2004 ($8.95, squarebound, one-shot)

1-Reprints stories from Dell Giant Comics Vacation Parade 1 (July 1950) 9.00

WALT DISNEY'S WHEATIES PREMIUMS (See Wheaties in the Promotional section)

WALTER (Campaign of Terror) (Also see The Mask)
Dark Horse Comics: Feb, 1996 - No. 4, May, 1996 ($2.50, limited series)

1-4 2.50

WALTER LANTZ ANDY PANDA (Also see Andy Panda)
Gold Key: Aug, 1973 - No. 23, Jan, 1978 (Walter Lantz)

1-Reprints 3 6 9 16 20 24
2-10-All reprints 2 4 6 10 12 15
11-23: 15,17-19,22-Reprints 1 2 3 5 7 9

WALT KELLY'S...
Eclipse Comics: Dec, 1987; Apr, 1988 ($1.75/$2.50, Baxter paper)

...Christmas Classics 1 (12/87)-Kelly-r/Peter Wheat & Santa Claus Funnies, ...Springtime Tales 1 (4/88, $2.50)-Kelly-r 2.50

WALTONS, THE (See Kite Fun Book)

WALT SCOTT (See Little People)

WALT SCOTT'S CHRISTMAS STORIES (See Christmas Stories, 4-Color #959, 1062)

WAMBI, JUNGLE BOY (See Jungle Comics)
Fiction House Magazines: Spr, 1942; No. 2, Win, 1942-43; No. 3, Spr, 1943; No. 4, Fall, 1948; No. 5, Sum, 1949; No. 6, Spr, 1950; No. 7-10, 1950(nd); No. 11, Spr, 1951 - No. 18, Win, 1952-53 (#1-3: 68 pgs.)

1-Wambi, the Jungle Boy begins 92 184 276 575 888 1200
2 (1942)-Kiefer-c 50 100 150 305 466 625
3 (1943)-Kiefer-c/a 40 80 120 230 335 440
4 (1948)-Origin in text 24 48 72 138 199 260

Wanted #2 © Millar & Jones

Wanted Comics #33 © Toytown

War Against Crime #2 © WMG

	GD 2.0	VG 4.0	FN 6.0	VF 8.0	VF/NM 9.0	NM- 9.2
5 (Fall, 1949, 36 pgs.)-Kiefer-c/a	20	40	60	115	165	215
6-10: 7-(52 pgs.)-New logo	19	38	57	107	154	200
11-18	13	26	39	74	102	130
I.W. Reprint #8('64)-r/#12 with new-c	3	6	9	16	20	25

NOTE: ***Alex Blum*** *c-8.* ***Kiefer*** *c-1-5.* ***Whitman*** *c-11-18.*

WANDERERS (See Adventure Comics #375, 376)
DC Comics: June, 1988 - No. 13, Apr, 1989 ($1.25) (Legion of Super-Heroes spin off)

	GD	VG	FN	VF	VF/NM	NM-
1-13: 1,2-Steacy-c. 3-Legion app.						2.25

WANDERING STAR
Pen & Ink Comics/Sirius Entertainment No. 12 on: 1993 - No. 21, Mar, 1997 ($2.50/$2.75, B&W)

	GD	VG	FN	VF	VF/NM	NM-
1-1st printing; Teri Sue Wood c/a/scripts in all	1	2	3	5	6	8
1-2nd and 3rd printings						2.75
2-1st printing.						4.00
2-21: 2-2nd printing. 12-(1/96)-1st Sirius issue						2.75
Trade paperback ($11.95)-r/1-7; 1st printing of 1000, signed and #'d						18.00
Trade paperback-2nd printing, 2000 signed						15.00
TPB Volume 2,3 (11/98, 12/98, $14.95) 2-r/#8-14, 3-r/#15-21						15.00

WANTED
Image Comics (Top Cow): Dec, 2003 - No. 6 ($2.99)

	GD	VG	FN	VF	VF/NM	NM-
1-Three covers; Mark Millar-s/J.G. Jones-a; intro Wesley Gibson						3.00
1,2-Death Row Edition; r/#1,2 with extra sketch pages and deleted panels						3.00
2-5: 2-Cameos of DC villains						3.00
...Dossier (5/04, $2.99) Pin-ups and character info; art by Jones, Romita Jr. & others						3.00

WANTED COMICS
Toytown Publications/Patches/Orbit Publ.: No. 9, Sept-Oct, 1947 - No. 53, April, 1953 (#9-33: 52 pgs.)

	GD	VG	FN	VF	VF/NM	NM-
9-True crime cases; radio's Mr. D. A. app.	23	46	69	132	191	250
10,11: 10-Giunta-a; radio's Mr. D. A. app.	14	28	42	81	113	145
12-Used in **SOTI**, pg. 277	15	30	45	83	117	150
13-Heroin drug propaganda story	13	26	39	74	102	130
14-Marijuana drug mention story (2 pgs.)	11	22	33	66	91	115
15-17,19,20	10	20	30	60	80	100
18-Marijuana story, "Satan's Cigarettes"; r-in #45 & retitled	24	48	72	135	195	255
21,22: 21-Krigstein-a. 22-Extreme violence	11	22	33	62	84	105
23,25-34,36-38,40-44,46-48,53	9	18	27	51	62	75
24-Krigstein-a; "The Dope King", marijuana mention story	11	22	33	66	91	115
35-Used in **SOTI**, pg. 160	11	22	33	64	87	110
39-Drug propaganda story "The Horror Weed"	15	30	45	85	120	155
45-Marijuana story from #18	10	20	30	60	80	100
49-Has unstable pink-c that fades easily; rare in mint condition	10	20	30	56	73	90
50-Has unstable pink-c like #49; surrealist-c by Buscema; horror stories	14	28	42	81	113	145
51- "Holiday of Horror" junkie story; drug-c	12	24	36	69	95	120
52-Classic "Cult of Killers" opium use story	12	24	36	69	95	120

NOTE: ***Buscema*** *c-50, 51.* ***Lawrence*** *and* ***Leav*** *c/a most issues.* ***Syd Shores*** *c/a-48; c-37. Issues 9-46 have wanted criminals with their descriptions & drawn picture on cover.*

WANTED: DEAD OR ALIVE (TV)
Dell Publishing Co.: No. 1102, May-July, 1960 - No. 1164, Mar-May, 1961

	GD	VG	FN	VF	VF/NM	NM-
Four Color 1102 (#1)-Steve McQueen photo-c	14	28	42	97	149	200
Four Color 1164-Steve McQueen photo-c	11	22	33	75	110	145

WANTED, THE WORLD'S MOST DANGEROUS VILLAINS (See DC Special)
National Periodical Publ.: July-Aug, 1972 - No. 9, Aug-Sept, 1973 (All reprints & 20¢ issues)

	GD	VG	FN	VF	VF/NM	NM-
1-Batman, Green Lantern (story r-from G.L. #1), & Green Arrow	4	8	12	24	32	40
2-Batman/Joker/Penguin-c/story r-from Batman #25; plus Flash story (r-from Flash #121)	3	6	9	18	24	30
3-9: 3-Dr. Fate(r/More Fun #65), Hawkman(r/Flash #100), & Vigilante(r/Action #69). 4-Green Lantern(r/All-American #61) & Kid Eternity(r/Kid Eternity #15). 5-Dollman/Green Lantern. 6-Burnley Starman; Wildcat/Sargon. 7-Johnny Quick(r/More Fun #76), Hawkman(r/Flash #90), Hourman by Baily(r/Adv. #72). 8-Dr. Fate/Flash(r/Flash #114). 9-S&K Sandman/Superman	3	6	9	16	20	24

NOTE: ***B. Bailey*** *a-7r.* ***Infantino*** *a-2r.* ***Kane*** *r-1, 5.* ***Kubert*** *r-3i, 6, 7.* ***Meskin*** *r-3, 7.* ***Reinman*** *r-4, 6.*

WAR (See Fightin' Marines #122)
Charlton Comics: Jul, 1975 - No. 9, Nov, 1976; No. 10, Sept, 1978 - No. 49, 1984

	GD	VG	FN	VF	VF/NM	NM-
1-Boyette painted-c	2	4	6	11	14	18
2-10	1	3	4	6	8	10
11-20	1	2	3	4	5	7
21-40						6.00
41-49 (lower print run): 47-Reprints	1	2	3	4	5	7
7,9 (Modern Comics-r, 1977)						4.00

WAR, THE (See The Draft & The Pitt)
Marvel Comics: 1989 - No. 4, 1990 ($3.50, squarebound, 52 pgs.)

	GD	VG	FN	VF	VF/NM	NM-
1-4: Characters from New Universe						3.50

WAR ACTION (Korean War)
Atlas Comics (CPS): April, 1952 - No. 14, June, 1953

	GD	VG	FN	VF	VF/NM	NM-
1	21	42	63	118	169	220
2	11	22	33	64	87	110
3-10,14: 7-Pakula-a	9	18	27	54	70	85
11-13-Krigstein-a	10	20	30	58	77	95

NOTE: ***Brodsky*** *c-1-4.* ***Heath*** *a-1; c-7, 14.* ***Keller*** *a-6.* ***Maneely*** *a-1.* ***Tuska*** *a-2, 8.*

WAR ADVENTURES
Atlas Comics (HPC): Jan, 1952 - No. 13, Feb, 1953

	GD	VG	FN	VF	VF/NM	NM-
1-Tuska-a	17	34	51	95	135	175
2	10	20	30	56	73	90
3-7,9-13: 3-Pakula-a. 7-Maneely-c	9	18	27	51	62	75
8-Krigstein-a	10	20	30	56	73	90

NOTE: ***Brodsky*** *c-1-3, 6, 8, 11, 12.* ***Heath*** *a-5, 7, 10; c-4, 5, 9, 13.* ***Robinson*** *a-3; c-10.*

WAR ADVENTURES ON THE BATTLEFIELD (See Battlefield)

WAR AGAINST CRIME! (Becomes Vault of Horror #12 on)
E. C. Comics: Spring, 1948 - No. 11, Feb-Mar, 1950

	GD	VG	FN	VF	VF/NM	NM-
1-Real Stories From Police Records on-c #1-9	75	150	225	469	722	975
2,3	44	88	132	268	409	550
4-9	40	80	120	240	360	480
10-1st Vault Keeper app. & 1st Vault of Horror	197	394	591	1478	2164	2850
11-2nd Vault Keeper app.; 1st horror-c	116	232	348	870	1273	1675

NOTE: *All have* ***Johnny Craig*** *covers.* ***Feldstein*** *a-4, 7-9.* ***Harrison/Wood*** *a-11.* ***Ingels*** *a-1, 2, 8.* ***Palais*** *a-8. Changes to horror with #10.*

WAR AGAINST CRIME
Gemstone Publishing: Apr, 2000 - No. 11, Feb, 2001 ($2.50)

	GD	VG	FN	VF	VF/NM	NM-
1-11: E.C. reprints						2.50

WAR AND ATTACK (Also see Special War Series #3)
Charlton Comics: Fall, 1964; V2#54, June, 1966 - V2#63, Dec, 1967

	GD	VG	FN	VF	VF/NM	NM-
1-Wood-a (25 pgs.)	5	10	15	36	48	60
V2#54(6/66)-#63 (Formerly Fightin' Air Force)	3	6	9	16	20	25

NOTE: ***Montes/Bache*** *a-55, 56, 60, 63.*

WAR AT SEA (Formerly Space Adventures)
Charlton Comics: No. 22, Nov, 1957 - No. 42, June, 1961

	GD	VG	FN	VF	VF/NM	NM-
22	6	12	18	31	38	45
23-30	5	10	15	23	28	32
31-42	3	6	9	18	23	28

WAR BATTLES
Harvey Publications: Feb, 1952 - No. 9, Dec, 1953

	GD	VG	FN	VF	VF/NM	NM-
1-Powell-a; Elias-c	10	20	30	73	107	140
2-Powell-a	6	12	18	40	55	70
3-5,7-9: 3,7-Powell-a	6	12	18	38	52	65
6-Nostrand-a	7	14	21	46	63	80

WAR BIRDS
Fiction House Magazines: 1952(nd) - No. 3, Winter, 1952-53

	GD	VG	FN	VF	VF/NM	NM-
1	16	32	48	92	131	170
2,3	10	20	30	56	73	90

WARBLADE: ENDANGERED SPECIES (Also see WildC.A.T.S: Covert Action Teams)
Image Comics (WildStorm Productions): Jan, 1995 - No. 4, Apr, 1995 ($2.50, limited series)

	GD	VG	FN	VF	VF/NM	NM-
1-4: 1-Gatefold wraparound-c						2.50

WARCHILD
Maximum Press: Jan. 1995 - No. 4, Aug, 1995 ($2.50)

	GD	VG	FN	VF	VF/NM	NM-
1-4-Rob Liefeld-c/a/scripts						2.50
1-4: Variant-c						3.00
Trade paperback (1/96, $12.95)-r/#1-4.						13.00

WAR COMBAT (Becomes Combat Casey #6 on)
Atlas Comics (LBI No. 1/SAI No. 2-5): March, 1952 - No. 5, Nov, 1952

	GD	VG	FN	VF	VF/NM	NM-
1	15	30	45	86	123	160
2	9	18	27	54	70	85
3-5	8	16	24	46	58	70

War Comics #26 © EC

War Heroes #10 © DELL

Warlock ('99) #2 © MAR

NOTE: ***Berg*** *a-2, 4, 5.* ***Brodsky*** *c-1, 2, 4, 5.* ***Henkel*** *a-5.* ***Maneely*** *a-1, 4; c-3.*

WAR COMICS (War Stories #5 on)(See Key Ring Comics)
Dell Publishing Co.: May, 1940 (No month given) - No. 4, Sept, 1941

	GD 2.0	VG 4.0	FN 6.0	VF 8.0	VF/NM 9.0	NM- 9.2
1-Sikandur the Robot Master, Sky Hawk, Scoop Mason, War Correspondent begin; McWilliams-c; 1st war comic	58	116	174	363	557	750
2-Origin Greg Gilday (5/41)	35	70	105	201	293	385
3-Joan becomes Greg Gilday's aide	24	48	72	135	195	255
4-Origin Night Devils	25	50	75	141	203	265

WAR COMICS
Marvel/Atlas (USA No. 1-41/JPI No. 42-49): Dec, 1950 - No. 49, Sept, 1957

	GD 2.0	VG 4.0	FN 6.0	VF 8.0	VF/NM 9.0	NM- 9.2
1	26	52	78	150	215	280
2	14	28	42	79	110	140
3-10	11	22	33	64	87	110
11-Flame thrower w/burning bodies on-c	13	26	39	74	102	130
12-20	10	20	30	56	73	90
21,23-32: 26-Valley Forge story. 32-Last pre-code issue (2/55)	8	16	24	46	58	70
22-Krigstein-a	10	20	30	56	73	90
33-37,39-42,44,45,47,48	8	16	24	46	58	70
38-Kubert/Moskowitz-a	9	18	27	52	66	80
43,49-Torres-a. 43-Severin/Elder E.C. swipe from Two-Fisted Tales #31	9	18	27	52	66	80
46-Crandall-a	9	18	27	52	66	80

NOTE: ***Colan*** *a-4, 36, 48, 49.* ***Drucker*** *a-37, 43, 48.* ***Everett*** *a-17.* ***Heath*** *a-7-9, 16, 19, 25, 36; c-11, 16, 19, 23, 25, 26, 29-32, 36.* ***G. Kane*** *a-19.* ***Lawrence*** *a-36.* ***Maneely*** *a-7, 9, 14, 20; c-6, 27, 37.* ***Orlando*** *a-42, 48.* ***Pakula*** *a-26.* ***Ravielli*** *a-27.* ***Reinman*** *a-11, 16, 26.* ***Robinson*** *a-15; c-13.* ***Severin*** *a-26, 27; c-48.*

WAR DANCER (Also see Charlemagne, Doctor Chaos #2 & Warriors of Plasm)
Defiant: Feb, 1994 - No. 6, July, 1994 ($2.50)

	NM- 9.2
1-3,5,6: 1-Intro War Dancer; Weiss-c/a begins. 1-3-Weiss-a(p). 6-Pre-Schism issue	2.50
4-($3.25, 52 pgs.)-Charlemagne app.	3.25

WAR DOGS OF THE U.S. ARMY
Avon Periodicals: 1952

	GD 2.0	VG 4.0	FN 6.0	VF 8.0	VF/NM 9.0	NM- 9.2
1-Kinstler-c/a	15	30	45	83	117	150

WARFRONT
Harvey Publications: 9/51 - #35, 11/58; #36, 10/65; #39, 2/67

	GD 2.0	VG 4.0	FN 6.0	VF 8.0	VF/NM 9.0	NM- 9.2
1-Korean War	12	24	36	82	124	165
2	7	14	21	46	63	80
3-10	6	12	18	38	52	65
11,12,14,16-20	5	10	15	33	44	55
13,15,22-Nostrand-a	7	14	21	46	63	80
21,23-27,31-33,35	5	10	15	33	44	55
28-30,34-Kirby-c	7	14	21	50	68	85
36-(12/66)-Dynamite Joe begins, ends #39; Williamson-a	6	12	18	38	52	65
37-Wood-a (17 pgs.)	6	12	18	38	52	65
38,39-Wood-a, 2-3 pgs.; Lone Tiger app.	5	10	15	33	44	55

NOTE: ***Powell*** *a-1-6, 9-11, 14, 17, 20, 23, 25-28, 30, 31, 34, 36.* ***Powell/Nostrand*** *a-12, 13, 15.* ***Simon*** *c-36?, 38.*

WAR FURY
Comic Media/Harwell (Allen Hardy Assoc.): Sept, 1952 - No. 4, Mar, 1953

	GD 2.0	VG 4.0	FN 6.0	VF 8.0	VF/NM 9.0	NM- 9.2
1-Heck-c/a in all; Palais-a; bullet hole in forehead-c; all issues are very violent; soldier using flame thrower on enemy	25	50	75	144	207	270
2-4: 4-Morisi-a	13	26	39	76	106	135

WAR GODS OF THE DEEP (See Movie Classics)

WARHAWKS
TSR, Inc.: 1990 - No. 10, 1991 ($2.95, 44 pgs.)

	NM- 9.2
1-10-Based on TSR game, Spiegle a-1-6	3.00

WARHEADS
Marvel Comics UK: June, 1992 - No. 14, Aug, 1993 ($1.75)

	NM- 9.2
1-Wolverine-c/story; indicia says #2 by mistake	3.00
2-14: 2-Nick Fury app. 3-Iron Man-c/story. 4,5-X-Force. 5-Liger vs. Cable. 6,7-Death's Head II app. (#6 is cameo)	2.25

WAR HEROES (See Marine War Heroes)

WAR HEROES
Dell Publishing Co.: 7-9/42 (no month); No. 2, 10-12/42 - No. 11, 3/45 (Published quarterly)

	GD 2.0	VG 4.0	FN 6.0	VF 8.0	VF/NM 9.0	NM- 9.2
1-General Douglas MacArthur-c	26	52	78	150	215	280
2	15	30	45	83	117	150
3,5: 3-Pro-Russian back-c	11	22	33	66	91	115
4-Disney's Gremlins app.	19	38	57	107	154	200
6-11: 6-Tothish-a by Discount	10	20	30	58	77	95

NOTE: *No. 1 was to be released in July, but was delayed. Painted c-4, 6-9.*

WAR HEROES
Ace Magazines: May, 1952 - No. 8, Apr, 1953

	GD 2.0	VG 4.0	FN 6.0	VF 8.0	VF/NM 9.0	NM- 9.2
1	11	22	33	64	87	110
2-Lou Cameron-a	8	16	24	43	54	65
3-8: 6,7-Cameron-a	7	14	21	37	46	55

WAR HEROES (Also see Blue Bird Comics)
Charlton Comics: Feb, 1963 - No. 27, Nov, 1967

	GD 2.0	VG 4.0	FN 6.0	VF 8.0	VF/NM 9.0	NM- 9.2
1,2: 2-John F. Kennedy story	4	8	12	27	36	45
3-10	3	6	9	18	24	30
11-26	2	4	6	14	18	22
27-1st Devils Brigade by Glanzman	3	6	9	18	24	30

NOTE: ***Montes/Bache*** *a-3-7, 21, 25, 27; c-3-7.*

WAR IS HELL
Marvel Comics Group: Jan, 1973 - No. 15, Oct, 1975

	GD 2.0	VG 4.0	FN 6.0	VF 8.0	VF/NM 9.0	NM- 9.2
1-Williamson-a(r), 5 pgs.; Ayers-a	3	6	9	18	23	28
2-8-Reprints. 6-(11/73). 7-(6/74). 7,8-Kirby-a	2	4	6	9	11	14
9-Intro Death	5	10	15	36	48	60
10-15-Death app.	3	6	9	18	23	28

NOTE: ***Bolle*** *a-3r.* ***Powell*** *a-1.* ***Woodbridge*** *a-1. Sgt. Fury reprints-7, 8.*

WARLANDS
Image Comics: Aug, 1999 - No. 12, Feb, 2001 ($2.50)

	NM- 9.2
1-9,11,12-Pat Lee-a(p)/Adrian Tsang-s	2.50
10-($2.95) Flip book w/Shidima preview	3.00
... Chronicles 1,2 (2/00, 7/00; $7.95) 1-r/#1-3. 2-r/#4-6	8.00
...Darklyte TPB (8/01, $14.95) r/#0,1/2,1-6 w/cover gallery; new Lee-c	15.00
...Epilogue: Three Stories (3/01, $5.95) includes r/Wizard #1/2 & AE #0	6.00
Another Universe #0	3.00
Wizard #1/2	5.00

WARLANDS: THE AGE OF ICE (Volume 2)
Image Comics: July, 2001 - No. 9, Nov, 2002 ($2.95)

	NM- 9.2
#0-(2/02, $2.25)	2.25
#1/2 (4/02, $2.25)	2.25
1-9: 2-Flip book preview of Banished Knights	3.00
TPB (2003, $15.95) r/#1-9	16.00

WARLANDS: DARK TIDE RISING (Volume 3)
Image Comics: Dec, 2002 - No. 6, May, 2003 ($2.95)

	NM- 9.2
1-6: 1-Wraparound gatefold-c	3.00

WARLOCK (The Power of...)(Also see Avengers Annual #7, Fantastic Four #66, 67, Incredible Hulk #178, Infinity Crusade, Infinity Gauntlet, Infinity War, Marvel Premiere #1, Marvel Two-In-One Annual #2, Silver Surfer V3#46, Strange Tales #178-181 & Thor #165)
Marvel Comics Group: Aug, 1972 - No. 8, Oct, 1973; No. 9, Oct, 1975 - No. 15, Nov, 1976

	GD 2.0	VG 4.0	FN 6.0	VF 8.0	VF/NM 9.0	NM- 9.2
1-Origin by Kane	6	12	18	38	52	65
2,3	3	6	9	19	25	32
4-8: 4-Death of Eddie Roberts	2	4	6	11	14	18
9-Starlin's 2nd Thanos saga begins, ends #15; new costume Warlock; Thanos cameo only; story cont'd from Strange Tales #178-181; Starlin-c/a in #9-15	3	6	9	18	23	28
10-Origin Thanos & Gamora; recaps events from Capt. Marvel #25-34. Thanos vs.The Magus-c/story	3	7	10	21	28	35
11-Thanos app.; Warlock dies	2	4	6	14	18	22
12-14: (Regular 25¢ edition) 14-Origin Star Thief; last 25¢ issue	2	4	6	10	13	16
12-14-(30¢-c, limited distribution)	3	6	9	16	20	24
15-Thanos-c/story	2	4	6	11	14	18

NOTE: ***Buscema*** *a-2p; c-8p.* ***G. Kane*** *a-1p, 3-5p; c-1p, 2, 3, 4p, 5p, 7p.* ***Starlin*** *a-9-14p, 15; c-9, 10, 11p, 12p, 13-15.* ***Sutton*** *a-1-8i.*

WARLOCK (...Special Edition on-c)
Marvel Comics Group: Dec, 1982 - No. 6, May, 1983 ($2.00, slick paper, 52 pgs.)

	NM- 9.2
1-Warlock-r/Strange Tales #178-180.	4.00
2-6: 2-r/Str. Tales #180,181 & Warlock #9. 3-r/Warlock #10-12(Thanos origin recap). 4-r/Warlock #12-15. 5-r/Warlock #15, Marvel Team-Up #55 & Avengers Ann. #7. 6-r/2nd half Avengers Annual #7 & Marvel Two-in-One Annual #2	4.00
Special Edition #1(12/83)	4.00

NOTE: ***Byrne*** *a-5r.* ***Starlin*** *a-1-6r; c-1-6(new). Direct sale only.*

WARLOCK
Marvel Comics: V2#1, May, 1992 - No. 6, Oct, 1992 ($2.50, limited series)

Warlord #3 © DC

War of the Gods #1 © DC

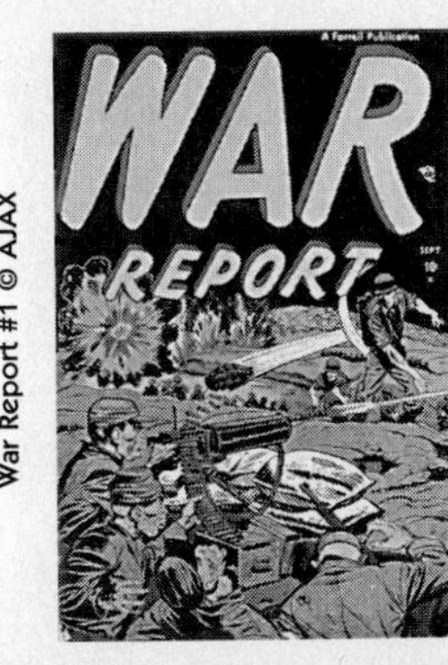

War Report #1 © AJAX

GD 2.0 | VG 4.0 | FN 6.0 | VF 8.0 | VF/NM 9.0 | NM- 9.2

GD 2.0 | VG 4.0 | FN 6.0 | VF 8.0 | VF/NM 9.0 | NM- 9.2

V2#1-6: 1-Reprints 1982 reprint series w/Thanos 2.50

WARLOCK
Marvel Comics: Nov, 1998 - No. 4, Feb, 1999 ($2.99, limited series)

1-4-Warlock vs. Drax 3.00

WARLOCK (M-Tech)
Marvel Comics: Oct, 1999 - No. 9, June, 2000 ($1.99/$2.50)

1-5: 1-Quesada-c. 2-Two covers 2.50
6-9: 6-Begin $2.50-c. 8-Avengers app. 2.50

WARLOCK
Marvel Comics: Nov, 2004 - Present ($2.99)

1-3-Adlard-a/Williams-c 3.00

WARLOCK AND THE INFINITY WATCH (Also see Infinity Gauntlet)
Marvel Comics: Feb, 1992 - No. 42, July, 1995 ($1.75) (Sequel to Infinity Gauntlet)

1-Starlin-scripts begin; brief origin recap; sequel to Infinity Gauntlet 3.00
2,3: 2-Reintro Moondragon 2.50
4-24,26: 7-Reintro The Magus; Moondragon app.; Thanos cameo on last 2 pgs. 8,9-Thanos battles Gamora-c/story. 8-Magus & Moondragon app. 10-Thanos-c/story; Magus app. 13-Hulk x-over. 21-Drax vs. Thor 2.25
25-($2.95, 52 pgs.)-Die-cut & embossed double-c; Thor & Thanos app. 3.00
28-42: 28-$1.95-c begins; bound-in card sheet 2.25
NOTE: *Austin c/a-1-4i, 7i. **Leonardi** a(p)-3, 4. **Medina** c/a(p)-1, 2, 5; 6, 9, 10, 14, 15, 20. **Williams** a(i)-8, 12, 13, 16-19.*

WARLOCK CHRONICLES
Marvel Comics: June, 1993 - No. 8, Feb, 1994 ($2.00, limited series)

1-($2.95)-Holo-grafx foil & embossed-c; origin retold; Starlin scripts begin; Keith Williams-a(i) in all 3.00
2-8: 3-Thanos & Mephisto-c/story. 4-Vs. Magus-c/s. 8-Contains free 16 pg. Razorline insert 2.25

WARLOCK 5
Aircel Pub.: 11/86 - No. 22, 5/89; V2#1, June, 1989 - V2#5, 1989 ($1.70, B&W)

1-5,7-11-Gordon Derry-s/Denis Beauvais-a thru #11. 5-Green Cyborg on-c. 5-Misnumbered as #6 (no #6); Blue Girl on-c. 2.25
12-22-Barry Blair-s/a. 18-$1.95-c begins 3.00
V2#1-5 ($2.00, B&W)-All issues by Barry Blair 2.25
Compilation 1,2: 1-r/#1-5 (1988, $5.95); 2-r/#6-9 6.00

WARLORD (See 1st Issue Special #8)
National Periodical Publications/DC Comics #123 on: 1-2/76; No.2, 3-4/76; No.3, 10-11/76 - No. 133, Win, 1988-89

	GD	VG	FN	VF	VF/NM	NM-
1-Story cont'd. from 1st Issue Special #8	3	6	9	18	24	30
2-Intro. Machiste	2	4	6	10	12	15
3-5	1	3	4	6	8	10
6-10: 6-Intro Mariah. 7-Origin Machiste. 9-Dons new costume	1	2	3	4	5	7

11-20: 11-Origin-r. 12-Intro Aton. 15-Tara returns; Warlord has son 5.00
21-36,40,41: 27-New facts about origin. 28-1st app. Wizard World. 32-Intro Shakira. 40-Warlord gets new costume 4.00

	GD	VG	FN	VF	VF/NM	NM-
22-Whitman variant edition	1	2	3	5	6	8

37-39: 37,38-Origin Omac by Starlin. 38-Intro Jennifer Morgan, Warlord's daughter. 39-Omac ends. 5.00
42-48: 42-47-Omac back-up series. 48-(52 pgs.)-1st app. Arak; contains free 14 pg. Arak Son of Thunder; Claw The Unconquered app. 4.00
49-62,64-99,101-130,132: 49-Claw The Unconquered app. 50-Death of Aton. 51-Reprints #1. 55-Arion Lord of Atlantis begins, ends #62. 91-Origin w/new facts. 114,115-Legends x-over. 125-Death of Tara 3.00
63-The Barren Earth begins; free 16pg. Masters of the Universe preview 4.00
100-($1.25, 52 pgs.). 4.00
131-1st DC work by Rob Liefeld (9/88) 5.00
133-($1.50, 52 pgs.) 4.00
Remco Toy Giveaway (2-3/4x4") 5.00
Annual 1-6 ('82-'87): 1-Grell-c,/a(p). 6-New Gods app. 4.00
NOTE: ***Grell** a-1-15, 16-50p, 51r, 52p, 59p, Annual 1p; c-1-70, 100-104, 112, 116, 117, Annual 1, 5. **Wayne Howard** a-64i. **Starlin** a-37-39p.*

WARLORD
DC Comics: Jan, 1992 - No. 6, June, 1992 ($1.75, limited series)

1-6: Grell-c & scripts in all 2.25

WARLORDS (See DC Graphic Novel #2)

WAR MAN
Marvel Comics (Epic Comics): Nov, 1993 - No. 2, Dec, 1993 ($2.50, lim. series)

1,2 2.50

WAR MACHINE (Also see Iron Man #281,282 & Marvel Comics Presents #152)
Marvel Comics: Apr, 1994 - No. 25, Apr, 1996 ($1.50)

"Ashcan" edition (nd, 75¢, B&W, 16 pgs.) 2.25
1-($2.00, 52 pgs.)-Newsstand edition; Cable app. 2.25
1-($2.95, 52 pgs.)-Collectors ed.; embossed foil-c 3.00
2-14, 16-25: 2-Bound-in trading card sheet; Cable app. 2,3-Deathlok app. 8-red logo 2.25
8-($2.95)-Polybagged w/16 pg. Marvel Action Hour preview & acetate print; yellow logo 3.00
15 ($2.50)-Flip book 2.50

WAR OF THE GODS
DC Comics: Sept, 1991 - No. 4, Dec, 1991 ($1.75, limited series)

1-4: Perez layouts, scripts & covers. 1-Contains free mini posters (Robin, Deathstroke). 2-4-Direct sale versions include 4 pin-ups printed on cover stock plus different-c 2.25

WAR OF THE WORLDS, THE
Caliber: 1996 - No. 5 ($2.95, B&W, 32 pgs.)(Based on H. G. Wells novel)

1-5: 1-Randy Zimmerman scripts begin 3.00

WARP
First Comics: Mar, 1983 - No. 19, Feb, 1985 ($1.00/$1.25, Mando paper)

1-Sargon-Mistress of War app.; Brunner-c/a thru #9 2.25
2-19: 2-Faceless Ones begin. 10-New Warp advs., & Outrider begin 2.25
Special 1-3: 1(7/83, 36 pgs.)-Origin Chaos-Prince of Madness; origin of Warp Universe begins, ends #3. 2(1/84)-Lord Cumulus vs. Sargon Mistress of War ($1.00). 3(6/84)-Chaos-Prince of Madness 2.25

WAR PARTY
Lightning Comics: Oct, 1994 (2.95, B&W)

1-1st app. Deathmark 3.00

WARPATH (Indians on the...)
Key Publications/Stanmor: Nov, 1954 - No. 3, Apr, 1955

	GD	VG	FN	VF	VF/NM	NM-
1	11	22	33	66	88	110
2,3	8	16	24	40	50	60

WARPED
Empire Entertainment (Solson): Jun, 1990 - No. 2, Oct-Nov, 1990 (B&W mag)

1,2 2.25

WARP GRAPHICS ANNUAL
WaRP Graphics: Dec, 1985; 1988 ($2.50)

1-Elfquest, Blood of the Innocent, Thunderbunny & Myth Adventures 5.00
1 (1988) 4.00

WARREN PRESENTS
Warren Publications: Jan, 1979 - No. 14, Nov, 1981(B&W magazine)

	GD	VG	FN	VF	VF/NM	NM-
1-Eerie, Creepy, & Vampirella-r; Ring of the Warlords; Merlin-s; Dax-s; Sanjulian-c	3	6	9	16	20	24
2-6(10/79): 2-The Rook. 3-Alien Invasions Comix. 4-Movie Aliens. 5-Dracula '79. 6-Strange Stories of Vampires Comix	2	4	6	9	11	14
8(10/80)-r/1st app. Pantha from Vamp. #30	2	4	6	11	14	18
9(11/80) Empire Encounters Comix	2	4	6	10	13	16
13(10/81),14(11/81):13-Sword and Sorcery Comix	2	4	6	14	18	22
(#7,10,11,12 may not exist, or may be a Special below)						
Special-Alien Collectors Edition (1979)	2	4	6	14	18	22
Special-Close Encounters of the Third Kind (1978)	2	4	6	9	11	14
Special-Lord of the Rings (6/79)	3	7	10	21	28	35
Special-Meteor (1/80)	2	4	6	9	11	14
Special-Moonraker/James Bond (10/79)	2	4	6	9	11	14
Special-Star Wars (1977)	3	7	10	21	28	35

WAR REPORT
Ajax/Farrell Publications (Excellent Publ.): Sept, 1952 - No. 5, May, 1953

	GD	VG	FN	VF	VF/NM	NM-
1	12	24	36	69	95	120
2-Flame thrower w/burning bodies on-c	10	20	30	56	73	90
3-5: 4-Used in **POP**, pg. 94	8	16	24	40	50	60

WARRIOR (Wrestling star)
Ultimate Creations: May, 1996 - No. 4, 1997 ($2.95)

1-4: Warrior scripts; Callahan-c/a. 3-Wraparound-c. 4-Warrior #3 in indicia; pin-ups 3.00
1-Variant-c. 5.00

WARRIOR COMICS
H.C. Blackerby: 1945 (1930s DC reprints)

	GD	VG	FN	VF	VF/NM	NM-
1-Wing Brady, The Iron Man, Mark Markon	23	46	69	132	191	250

WARRIOR OF WAVERLY STREET, THE
Dark Horse Comics: Nov, 1996 - No. 2, Dec, 1996 ($2.95, mini-series)

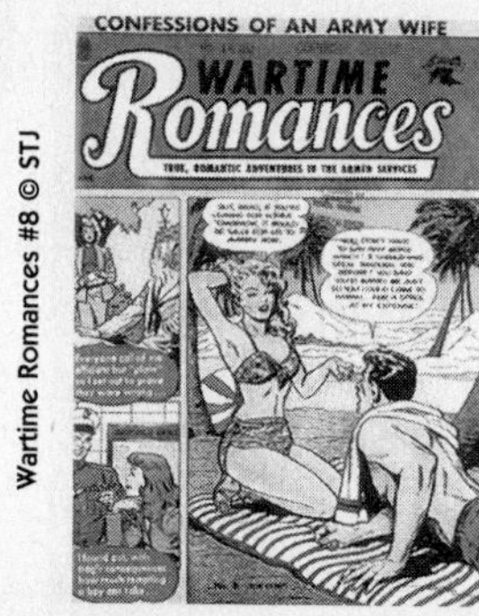

Wartime Romances #8 © STJ

Watchmen #2 © DC

Weapon X #25 © MAR

GD 2.0 | VG 4.0 | FN 6.0 | VF 8.0 | VF/NM 9.0 | NM- 9.2

1,2-Darrow-c 3.00

WARRIORS
CFD Productions: 1993 (B&W, one-shot)
1-Linsner, Dark One-a 2 4 6 11 14 18

WARRIORS OF PLASM (Also see Plasm)
Defiant: Aug, 1993 - No. 13, Aug, 1995 ($2.95/$2.50)
1-4: Shooter-scripts; Lapham-c/a: 1-1st app. Glory. 4-Bound-in fold-out poster 3.00
5-7,10-13: 5-Begin $2.50-c. 13-Schism issue 2.50
8,9-($2.75, 44 pgs.) 2.75
The Collected Edition (2/94, $9.95)-r/Plasm #0, WOP #1-4 & Splatterball 10.00

WAR ROMANCES (See True...)

WAR SHIPS
Dell Publishing Co.: 1942 (36 pgs.)(Similar to Large Feature Comics)
nn-Cover by McWilliams; contains photos & drawings of U.S. war ships
19 38 57 107 154 200

WARSTONE
Devil's Due Publishing: Apr, 2004 ($4.95, one-shot)
1-Josh Blaylock-s/Matt & Mike Cossin-a 5.00

WAR STORIES (Formerly War Comics)
Dell Publ. Co.: No. 5, 1942(nd); No. 6, Aug-Oct, 1942 - No. 8, Feb-Apr, 1943
5-Origin The Whistler 27 54 81 154 222 290
6-8: 6-8-Night Devils app. 8-Painted-c 20 40 60 112 161 210

WAR STORIES (Korea)
Ajax/Farrell Publications (Excellent Publ.): Sept, 1952 - No. 5, May, 1953
1 11 22 33 64 87 110
2 7 14 21 37 46 55
3-5 7 14 21 35 43 50

WAR STORIES (See Star Spangled...)

WAR STORY
DC Comics (Vertigo): Nov, 2001 - Present ($4.95, series of World War II one-shots)
...: Archangel (4/03) Ennis-s/Erskine-a 5.00
...: Condors (3/03) Ennis-s/Ezquerra-a 5.00
...: D-Day Dodgers (12/01) Ennis-s/Higgins-a 5.00
...: J For Jenny (2/03) Ennis-s/Lloyd-a 5.00
...: Johann's Tiger (11/01) Ennis-s/Weston-a 5.00
...: Nightingale (2/02) Ennis-s/Lloyd-a 5.00
...: Screaming Eagles (1/02) Ennis-s/Gibbons-a 5.00
...: The Reivers (1/03) Ennis-s/Kennedy-a 5.00
Vol. 1 (2004, $19.95) r/Johann's Tiger, D-Day Dodgers, Screaming Eagles, Nightingale 20.00

WARSTRIKE
Malibu Comics (Ultraverse): May, 1994 - No. 7, Nov, 1995 ($1.95)
1-7: 1-Simonson-c 2.25
1-Ultra 5000 Limited silver foil 4.00
Giant Size 1 (12/94, 2.50, 44pgs.)-Prelude to Godwheel 2.50

WART AND THE WIZARD (See The Sword & the Stone under Movie Comics)
Gold Key: Feb, 1964 (Walt Disney)(Characters from Sword in the Stone movie)
1 (10102-402) 5 10 15 36 48 60

WARTIME ROMANCES
St. John Publishing Co.: July, 1951 - No. 18, Nov, 1953
1-All Baker-c/a 35 70 105 198 287 375
2-All Baker-c/a 24 48 72 135 195 255
3,4-All Baker-c/a 22 44 66 125 180 235
5-8-Baker-c/a(2-3) each 20 40 60 112 161 210
9,11,12,16,18: Baker-c/a each. 9-Two signed stories by Estrada
15 30 45 86 123 160
10,13-15,17-Baker-c only 10 20 30 56 73 90

WAR VICTORY ADVENTURES (#1 titled War Victory Comics)
U.S. Treasury Dept./War Victory/Harvey Publ.: Summer, 1942 - No. 3, Winter, 1943-44 (5¢)
1-(Promotion of Savings Bonds)-Featuring America's greatest comic art by top syndicated cartoonists; Blondie, Joe Palooka, Green Hornet, Dick Tracy, Superman, Gumps, etc.; (36 pgs.); all profits were contributed to U.S.O. & Army/Navy relief funds
40 80 120 239 357 475
2-Battle of Stalingrad story; Powell-a (8/43); flag-c 22 44 66 125 180 235
3-Capt. Red Cross-c & text only; Powell-a 20 40 60 112 161 210

WAR WAGON, THE (See Movie Classics)

WAR WINGS
Charlton Comics: Oct, 1968
1 3 6 9 16 20 24

WARWORLD!
Dark Horse Comics: Feb, 1989 ($1.75, B&W, one-shot)
1-Gary Davis sci/fi art in Moebius style 2.25

WARZONE
Entity Comics: 1995 ($2.95, B&W)
1-3 3.00

WASHABLE JONES AND THE SHMOO (Also see Al Capp's Shmoo)
Toby Press: June, 1953
1- "Super-Shmoo" 21 42 63 118 169 220

WASH TUBBS (See The Comics, Crackajack Funnies)
Dell Publishing Co.: No. 11, 1942 - No. 53, 1944
Four Color 11 (#1) 31 62 93 228 352 475
Four Color 28 (1943) 22 44 66 158 242 325
Four Color 53 16 32 48 114 175 235

WASTELAND
DC Comics: Dec, 1987 - No. 18, May, 1989 ($1.75-$2.00 #13 on, mature)
1-5(4/88), 5(5/88), 6(5/88)-18: 13,15-Orlando-a 2.25
NOTE: *Orlando a-12, 13, 15. Truman a-10; c-13.*

WATCHMEN
DC Comics: Sept, 1986 - No. 12, Oct, 1987 (maxi-series)
1-Alan Moore scripts & Dave Gibbons-c/a in all 1 2 3 4 5 7
2-12 5.00
Hardcover Collection-Slip-cased-r/#1-12 w/new material; produced by Graphitti Designs 70.00
Trade paperback (1987, $14.95)-r/#1-12 18.00

WATER BIRDS AND THE OLYMPIC ELK (Disney)
Dell Publishing Co.: No. 700, Apr, 1956
Four Color 700-Movie 6 12 18 43 59 75

WATERLOO SUNSET
Image Comics: July, 2004 ($6.95, B&W, graphic novel)
1-Stephenson-s/Goring-a 7.00

WATERWORLD: CHILDREN OF LEVIATHAN
Acclaim Comics: Aug, 1997 - No. 4, Nov, 1997 ($2.50, mini-series)
1-4 2.50

WAY OF THE RAT (Also see Promotional Comics section for FCBD Ed.)
CrossGeneration Comics: Jun, 2002 - No. 24, June, 2004 ($2.95)
1-24: 1-Dixon-s/ Jeff Johnson-a. 5-Whigham-a. 9,14-Luke Ross-a 3.00
...: The Walls of Zhumar Vol. 1 (1/03, $15.95) r/#1-6 16.00
Vol. 2: The Dragon's Wake (2003, $15.95) r/#7-12 16.00

WEAPON X
Marvel Comics: Apr, 1994 ($12.95, one-shot)
nn-r/Marvel Comics Presents #72-84 13.00

WEAPON X
Marvel Comics: Mar, 1995 - No. 4, June, 1995 ($1.95)
1-Age of Apocalypse 4.00
2-4 2.50

WEAPON X
Marvel Comics: Nov, 2002 - No. 28, Nov, 2004 ($2.25/$2.99)
1-7: 1-Sabretooth-c/app.; Tieri-s/Jeanty-a 2.25
8-28: 8-Begin $2.99-c. 14-Invaders app. 15-Chamber joins. 16-18,21-25-Wolverine app. 3.00
Vol. 1: The Draft TPB (2003, $21.99) r/#1-5, #1/2 & The Draft one-shots 22.00
Vol. 2: The Underground TPB (2003, $19.99) r/#6-13 20.00
Wizard #1/2 (2002) 5.00

WEAPON X: THE DRAFT (Leads into 2002 Weapon X series)
Marvel Comics: Oct, 2002 ($2.25, one-shots)
...Kane 1- JH Williams-c/Raimondi-a 2.25
...Marrow 1- JH Williams-c/Badeaux-a 2.25
...Sauron 1- JH Williams-c/Kerschl-a; Emma Frost app. 2.25
...Wild Child 1- JH Williams-c/Van Sciver-a; Aurora (Alpha Flight) app. 2.25
...Zero 1- JH Williams-c/Plunkett-a; Wolverine app. 2.25

WEAPON ZERO
Image Comics (Top Cow Productions): No. T-4(#1), June, 1995 - No. T-0(#5), Dec, 1995 ($2.50, limited series)

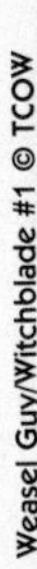
Weasel Guy/Witchblade #1 © TCOW

Web of Horror #3 © Major Mag.

Web of Spider-Man #8 © MAR

GD VG FN VF VF/NM NM-
2.0 4.0 6.0 8.0 9.0 9.2

T-4(#1): Walt Simonson scripts in all. 5.00
T-3(#2) - T-1(#4) 4.00
T-0(#5) 3.00

WEAPON ZERO
Image Comics (Top Cow Productions): V2#1, Mar, 1996 - No. 15, Dec, 1997 ($2.50)
V2#1-Walt Simonson scripts. 3.00
2-14: 8-Begin Top Cow. 10-Devil's Reign 2.50
15-($3.50) Benitez-a 3.50

WEAPON ZERO/SILVER SURFER
Image Comics/Marvel Comics: Jan, 1997($2.95, one-shot)
1-Devil's Reign Pt. 1 3.00

WEASELGUY: ROAD TRIP
Image Comics: Sept, 1999 - No. 2 ($3.50, limited series)
1,2-Steve Buccellato-s/a 3.50
1-Variant-c by Bachalo 5.00

WEASELGUY/WITCHBLADE
Hyperwerks: July, 1998 ($2.95, one-shot)
1-Steve Buccellato-s/a; covers by Matsuda and Altstaetter 3.00

WEASEL PATROL SPECIAL, THE (Also see Fusion #17)
Eclipse Comics: Apr, 1989 ($2.00, B&W, one-shot)
1-Funny animal 2.25

WEAVEWORLD
Marvel Comics (Epic): Dec, 1991 - No. 3, 1992 ($4.95, lim. series, 68 pgs.)
1-3: Clive Barker adaptation 5.00

WEB, THE (Also see Mighty Comics & Mighty Crusaders)
DC Comics (Impact Comics): Sept, 1991 - No. 14, Oct, 1992 ($1.00)
1-14: 5-The Fly x-over 9-Trading card inside 2.25
Annual 1 (1992, $2.50, 68 pgs.)-With Trading card 2.50
NOTE: ***Gil Kane** c-5, 9, 10, 12-14. **Bill Wray** a(i)-1-9, 10(part).*

WEB OF EVIL
Comic Magazines/Quality Comics Group: Nov, 1952 - No. 21, Dec, 1954
1-Used in **SOTI**, pg. 388. Jack Cole-a; morphine use story 58 116 174 363 557 750
2-4,6,7: 2,3-Jack Cole-a. 4,6,7-Jack Cole-c/a 40 80 120 244 372 500
5-Electrocution-c/story; Jack Cole-c/a 46 92 138 281 428 575
8-11-Jack Cole-a 40 80 120 230 335 440
12,13,15,16,19-21 25 50 75 144 207 270
14-Part Crandall-c; Old Witch swipe 26 52 78 150 215 280
17-Opium drug propaganda story 26 52 78 147 211 275
18-Acid-in-face story 26 52 78 150 215 280
NOTE: ***Jack Cole** a(2 each)-2, 6, 8, 9. **Cuidera** c-1-21i. **Ravielli** a-13.*

WEB OF HORROR
Major Magazines: Dec, 1969 - No. 3, Apr, 1970 (Magazine)
1-Jeff Jones painted-c; Wrightson-a, Kaluta-a 8 16 24 55 78 100
2-Jones painted-c; Wrightson-a(2), Kaluta-a 7 14 21 46 63 80
3-Wrightson-c/a (1st published-c); Brunner, Kaluta, Bruce Jones-a 7 14 21 46 63 80

WEB OF MYSTERY
Ace Magazines (A. A. Wyn): Feb, 1951 - No. 29, Sept, 1955
1 55 110 165 340 520 700
2-Bakerish-a 32 64 96 184 267 350
3-10: 4-Colan-a 29 58 87 164 237 310
11-18,20-26: 12-John Chilly's 1st cover art. 13-Surrealistic-c. 20-r/The Beyond #1 25 50 75 141 203 265
19-Reprints Challenge of the Unknown #6 used in N.Y. Legislative Committee 25 50 75 141 203 265
27-Bakerish-a(r/The Beyond #2); last pre-code ish 23 46 69 132 191 250
28,29: 28-All-r 18 36 54 102 146 190
NOTE: *This series was to appear as "Creepy Stories", but title was changed before publication. **Cameron** a-6, 8, 11-13, 17-20, 22, 24, 25, 27; c-8, 13, 17. **Palais** a-28r. **Sekowsky** a-1-3, 7, 8, 11, 14, 21, 29. **Tothish** a-by **Bill Discount** #16. 29-all-r, 19-28-partial-r.*

WEB OF SCARLET SPIDER
Marvel Comics: Oct, 1995 - No. 4, Jan, 1996 ($1.95, limited series)
1-4: Replaces "Web of Spider-Man" 2.25

WEB OF SPIDER-MAN (Replaces Marvel Team-Up)
Marvel Comics Group: Apr, 1985 - No. 129, Sept, 1995
1-Painted-c (5th app. black costume?) 2 4 6 10 12 15
2,3 5.00
4-8: 7-Hulk x-over; Wolverine splash 4.00
9-13: 10-Dominic Fortune guest stars; painted-c 4.00
14-17,19-28: 19-Intro Humbug & Solo 3.00
18-1st app. Venom (behind the scenes, 9/86) 3.00
29-Wolverine, new Hobgoblin (Macendale) app. 1 2 3 5 6 8
30-Origin recap The Rose & Hobgoblin I (entire book is flashback story); Punisher & Wolverine cameo 4.00
31,32-Six part Kraven storyline begins 5.00
33-37,39-47,49: 36-1st app. Tombstone 3.00
38-Hobgoblin app.; begin $1.00-c 4.00
48-Origin Hobgoblin II(Demogoblin) cont'd from Spectacular Spider-Man #147; Kingpin app. 1 2 3 5 7 9
50-($1.50, 52 pgs.) 3.50
51-58 2.50
59-Cosmic Spidey cont'd from Spect. Spider-Man 3.50
60-89,91-99,101-106: 66,67-Green Goblin (Norman Osborn) app. as a super-hero. 69,70-Hulk x-over. 74-76-Austin-c(i). 76-Fantastic Four x-over. 78-Cloak & Dagger app. 81-Origin/1st app. Bloodshed. 84-Begin 6 part Rose & Hobgoblin II storyline; last $1.00-c. 86-Demon leaves Hobgoblin; 1st Demogoblin. 93-Gives brief history of Hobgoblin. 93,94-Hobgoblin (Macendale) Reborn-c/story, parts 1,2; MoonKnight app. 94-Venom cameo. 95-Begin 4 part x-over w/Spirits of Venom w/Ghost Rider/Blaze/Spidey vs. Venom & Demogoblin (cont'd in Ghost Rider/Blaze #5,6). 96-Spirits of Venom part 3; painted-c. 101,103-Maximum Carnage x-over. 103-Venom & Carnage app. 104-106-Nightwatch back-up stories 2.50
90-($2.95, 52 pgs.)-Polybagged w/silver hologram-c, gatefold poster showing Spider-Man & Spider-Man 2099 (Williamson-i) 3.50
90-2nd printing; gold hologram-c 3.00
100-($2.95, 52 pgs.)-Holo-grafx foil-c; intro new Spider-Armor 4.00
107-111: 107-Intro Sandstorm; Sand & Quicksand app. 2.50
112-116, 118, 119, 121-124, 126-128: 112-Begin $1.50-c; bound-in trading card sheet. 113-Regular Ed.; Gambit & Black Cat app. 118-1st solo clone story; Venom app. 2.25
113-($2.95)-Collector's ed. polybagged w/foil-c; 16 pg. preview of Spider-Man cartoon & animation cel 3.00
117-($1.50)-Flip book; Power & Responsibility Pt.1 2.25
117-($2.95)-Collector's edition; foil-c; flip book 3.00
119-($6.45)-Direct market edition; polybagged w/ Marvel Milestone Amazing Spider-Man #150 & coupon for Amazing Spider-Man #396, Spider-Man #53, & Spectacular Spider-Man #219. 7.00
120 ($2.25)-Flip book w/ preview of the Ultimate Spider-Man 2.50
125 ($3.95)-Holodisk-c; Gwen Stacy clone 4.00
125,129: 25 ($2.95)-Newsstand. 129-Last issue 3.00
Annual 1 (1985) 3.00
Annual 2 (1986)-New Mutants; Art Adams-a 1 2 3 5 6 8
Annual 3-10 ('87-'94, 68 pgs.): 4-Evolutionary War x-over. 5-Atlantis Attacks; Captain Universe by Ditko (p) & Silver Sable stories; F.F. app. 6-Punisher back-up plus Capt. Universe by Ditko; G. Kane-a. 7-Origins of Hobgoblin I, Hobgoblin II, Green Goblin I & II & Venom; Larsen/Austin-c. 8-Part 3 of Venom story; New Warriors x-over; Black Cat back-up sty. 9-Bagged w/card 3.00
Super Special 1 (1995, $3.95)-flip book 4.00
NOTE: ***Art Adams** a-Annual 2. **Byrne** c-3-6. **Chaykin** c-10. **Mignola** a-Annual 2. **Vess** c-1, 8, Annual 1, 2. **Zeck** a-6i, 31, 32; c-31, 32.*

WEBSPINNERS: TALES OF SPIDER-MAN
Marvel Comics: Jan, 1999 - No. 18, Jun, 2000 ($2.99/$2.50)
1-DeMatteis-s/Zulli-a; back-up story w/Romita Sr. art 3.00
1-($6.95) DF Edition 7.00
2,3: 2-Two covers 2.50
4-11,13-18: 4,5-Giffen-a; Silver Surfer-c/app. 7-9-Kelly-s/Sears and Smith-a. 10,11-Jenkins-s/Sean Phillips-a 2.50
12-($3.50) J.G. Jones-c/a; Jenkins-s 3.50

WEDDING BELLS
Quality Comics Group: Feb, 1954 - No. 19, Nov, 1956
1-Whitney-a 15 30 45 86 123 160
2 10 20 30 56 73 90
3-9: 8-Last precode (4/55) 8 16 24 40 50 60
10-Ward-a (9 pgs.) 14 28 42 79 110 140
11-14,17 7 14 21 35 43 50
15-Baker-c 8 16 24 43 54 65
16-Baker-c/a 10 20 30 56 73 90
18,19-Baker-a each 8 16 24 46 58 70

WEDDING OF DRACULA
Marvel Comics: Jan, 1993 ($2.00, 52 pgs.)
1-Reprints Tomb of Dracula #30,45,46 2.25

Weird Comics #2 © FOX

Weird Fantasy #16(#1) © WMG

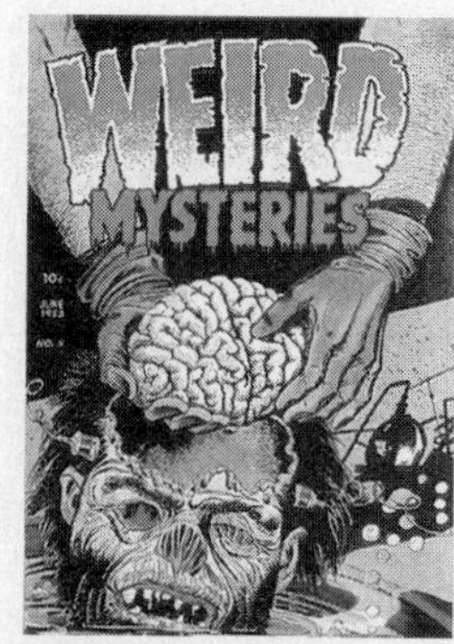

Weird Mysteries #5 © Gilmore

GD VG FN VF VF/NM NM-
2.0 4.0 6.0 8.0 9.0 9.2

GD VG FN VF VF/NM NM-
2.0 4.0 6.0 8.0 9.0 9.2

WEEKENDER, THE (Illustrated...)
Rucker Pub. Co.: V1#1, Sept, 1945? - V1#4, Nov, 1945; V2#1, Jan, 1946 - V2#3, Aug, 1946 (52 pgs.)

V1#1-4: 1-Same-c as Zip Comics #45, inside-c and back-c blank; Steel Sterling, Senor Banana, Red Rube and Ginger. 2-Capt. Victory on-c. 3-Super hero-c; Mr. E, Dan Hastings, Sky Chief and the Echo. 4-Same-c as Punch Comics #10 (9/44); r/Hale the Magician (7 pgs.) & r/Mr. E (8 pgs.-Lou Fine? or Gustavson?) plus 3 humor strips & many B&W photos & r/newspaper articles plus cheesecake photos of Hollywood stars
17 34 51 95 135 175
V2#1-Same-c as Dynamic Comics #11; 36 pgs. comics, 16 in newspaper format with photos; partial Dynamic Comics reprints; 4 pgs. of cels from the Disney film Pinocchio; Little Nemo story by Winsor McCay, Jr.; Jack Cole-a 19 38 57 107 154 200
V2#2,3: 2-Same-c as Dynamic Comics #9 by Raboy; Dan Hastings (Tuska), Rocket Boy, The Echo, Lucky Coyne. 3-Humor-c by Boddington?; Dynamic Man, Ima Slooth, Master Key, Dynamic Boy, Captain Glory 17 34 51 95 135 175

WEIRD
Eerie Publications: V1#10, 1/66 - V8#6, 12/74; V9#1, 1/75 - V14#3, Nov, 1981 (Magazine) (V1-V8: 52 pgs.; V9 on: 68 pgs.)

V1#10(#1)-Intro. Morris the Caretaker of Weird (ends V2#10); Burgos-a
7 14 21 50 68 85
11,12 4 8 12 29 40 50
V2#1-4(10/67), V3#1(1/68), V2#6(4/68)-V2#7,9,10(12/68)
4 8 12 29 40 50
V2#8-r/Ditko's 1st story/Fantastic Fears #5 6 12 18 38 52 65
V3#1(2/69)-V3#4 4 8 12 25 33 42
V3#5(12/69)-Rulah reprint; "Rulah" changed to "Pulah", LSD story reprinted in Horror Tales V4#4, Tales From the Tomb V2#4, & 20 4 8 12 25 33 42
V4#1-6('70), V5#1-6('71), V6#1-7('72), V7#1-7('73), V8#1-3, V8#4(8/74), V8#4(10/74), (V8#5 does not exist), V8#6('74), V9#1-4(1/75-'76), V10#1-3('77), V11#1-4('78), V12#1(2/79)-V14#3(11/81) 4 8 12 25 33 42

NOTE: *There are two V8#4 issues (8/74 & 10/74). V9#4 (12/76) has a cover swipe from Horror Tales V5#1 (2/73). There are two V13#3 issues (6/80 & 9/80).*

WEIRD
DC Comics (Paradox Press): Sum, 1997 - Present ($2.99, B&W, magazine)

1-4: 4-Mike Tyson-c 3.00

WEIRD, THE
DC Comics: Apr, 1988 - No. 4, July, 1988 ($1.50, limited series)

1-4: Wrightson-c/a in all 3.00

WEIRD ADVENTURES
P. L. Publishing Co. (Canada): May-June, 1951 - No. 3, Sept-Oct, 1951

1- "The She-Wolf Killer" by Matt Baker (6 pgs.) 55 110 165 340 520 700
2-Bondage/hypodermic panel 44 88 132 268 409 550
3-Male bondage/torture-c; severed head story 40 80 120 233 342 450

WEIRD ADVENTURES
Ziff-Davis Publishing Co.: No. 10, July-Aug, 1951

10-Painted-c 40 80 120 233 342 450

WEIRD CHILLS
Key Publications: July, 1954 - No. 3, Nov, 1954

1-Wolverton-r/Weird Mysteries No. 4; blood transfusion-c by Baily
83 166 249 519 797 1075
2-Extremely violent injury to eye-c by Baily; Hitler story
75 150 225 469 722 975
3-Bondage E.C. swipe-c by Baily 48 96 144 293 447 600

WEIRD COMICS
Fox Features Syndicate: Apr, 1940 - No. 20, Jan, 1942

1-The Birdman, Thor, God of Thunder (ends #5), The Sorceress of Zoom, Blast Bennett, Typhon, Voodoo Man, & Dr. Mortal begin; George Tuska bondage-c
465 930 1395 3255 5228 7200
2-Lou Fine-c 231 462 693 1444 2222 3000
3,4: 3-Simon-c. 4-Torture-c 121 242 363 756 1166 1575
5-Intro. Dart & sidekick Ace (8/40) (ends #20); bondage/hypo-c
127 254 381 794 1222 1650
6,7-Dynamite Thor app. in each. 6-Super hero covers begin
98 196 294 613 944 1275
8-Dynamo, the Eagle (11/40, early app.; see Science #1) & sidekick Buddy & Marga, the Panther Woman begin 96 192 288 600 925 1250
9,10: 10-Navy Jones app. 77 154 231 481 741 1000
11-19: 16-Flag-c. 17-Origin The Black Rider. 60 120 180 375 575 775
20-Origin The Rapier; Swoop Curtis app; Churchill & Hitler-c
71 142 213 444 685 925

NOTE *Cover features: Sorceress of Zoom-4; Dr. Mortal-5; Dart & Ace-6-13, 15; Eagle-14, 16-20.*

WEIRD FANTASY (Formerly A Moon, A Girl, Romance; becomes Weird Science-Fantasy #23 on)
E. C. Comics: No. 13, May-June, 1950 - No. 22, Nov-Dec, 1953

13(#1) (1950) 193 386 579 1448 2124 2800
14-Necronomicon story; Cosmic Ray Bomb explosion-c/story by Feldstein; Feldstein & Gaines star 90 180 270 675 988 1300
15,16: 16-Used in **SOTI**, pg. 144 60 120 180 450 660 870
17 (1951) 50 100 150 375 550 725
6-10: 6-Robot-c 41 82 123 308 452 595
11-13 (1952): 12-E.C. artists cameo. 13-Anti-Wertham "Cosmic Correspondence"
34 68 102 255 373 490
14-Frazetta/Williamson(1st team-up at E.C.)/Krenkel-a (7 pgs.); Orlando draws E.C. staff
47 94 141 353 517 680
15-Williamson/Evans-a(3), 4,3,&7 pgs. 34 68 102 255 373 490
16-19-Williamson/Krenkel-a in all. 18-Williamson/Feldstein-c
32 64 96 240 350 460
20-Frazetta/Williamson-a (7 pgs.) 35 70 105 263 384 505
21-Frazetta/Williamson-c & Williamson/Krenkel-a 47 94 141 353 517 680
22-Bradbury adaptation 25 50 75 188 274 360

NOTE: ***Ray Bradbury** adaptations-13, 17-20, 22. **Crandall** a-22. **Elder** a-17. **Feldstein** a-13(#1)-8; c-13(#1)-18 (#18 w/**Williamson**), 20. **Harrison/Wood** a-13. **Kamen** a-13(#1)-16, 18-22. **Krigstein** a-22. **Kurtzman** a-13(#1)-17(#5), 6. **Orlando** a-9-22 (2 stories in #16); c-19, 22. **Severin/Elder** a-18-21. **Wood** a-13(#1)-14, 17(2 stories ea. in #10-13). Ray Bradbury adaptations in #17-19, 22. Canadian reprints exist; see Table of Contents.*

WEIRD FANTASY
Russ Cochran/Gemstone Publ.: Oct, 1992 - No. 22, Jan, 1998 ($1.50/$2.00/$2.50)

1-22: 1,2: 1,2-r/Weird Fantasy #13,14; Feldstein-c. 3-5-r/Weird Fantasy #15-17 3.00

WEIRD HORRORS (Nightmare #10 on)
St. John Publishing Co.: June, 1952 - No. 9, Oct, 1953

1-Tuska-a 56 112 168 350 538 725
2,3: 3-Hashish story 37 74 111 209 305 400
4,5 31 62 93 178 259 340
6-Ekgren-c; atomic bomb story 48 96 144 293 447 600
7-Ekgren-c; Kubert, Cameron-a 50 100 150 305 465 625
8,9-Kubert-c/a 40 80 120 241 363 485

NOTE: ***Cameron** a-7, 9. **Finesque** a-1-5. **Forgione** a-6. **Morisi** a-3. Bondage c-8.*

WEIRD MYSTERIES
Gillmore Publications: Oct, 1952 - No. 12, Sept, 1954

1-Partial Wolverton-c swiped from splash page "Flight to the Future" in Weird Tales of the Future #2; "Eternity" has an Ingels swipe 85 170 255 531 816 1100
2- "Robot Woman" by Wolverton; Bernard Baily-c reprinted in Mister Mystery #18; acid in face panel 113 226 339 706 1091 1475
3,6: Both have decapitation-c 58 116 174 363 557 750
4- "The Man Who Never Smiled" (3 pgs.) by Wolverton; Classic B. Baily skull-c
106 212 318 663 1019 1375
5-Wolverton story "Swamp Monster" (6 pgs.). Classic exposed brain-c
112 224 336 700 1075 1450
7-Used in **SOTI**, illo "Indeed", illo "Sex and blood" 81 162 243 506 778 1050
8-Wolverton-c panel-r/#5; used in a '54 Readers Digest anti-comics article by T. E. Murphy entitled "For the Kiddies to Read" 56 112 168 350 538 725
9-Excessive violence, gore & torture 54 108 162 329 502 675
10-Silhouetted nudity panel 48 96 144 293 447 600
11,12: 12-r/Mr. Mystery #8(2), Weird Mysteries #3 & Weird Tales of the Future #6
44 88 132 268 409 550

NOTE: ***Baily** c-2-12. Anti-Wertham column in #5. #1-12 all have 'The Ghoul Teacher' (host).*

WEIRD MYSTERIES (Magazine)
Pastime Publications: Mar-Apr, 1959 (35¢, B&W, 68 pgs.)

1-Torres-a; E. C. swipe from Tales From the Crypt #46 by Tuska "The Ragman"
9 18 27 51 62 75

WEIRD MYSTERY TALES (See DC 100 Page Super Spectacular)

WEIRD MYSTERY TALES (See Cancelled Comic Cavalcade)
National Periodical Publications: July-Aug, 1972 - No. 24, Nov, 1975

1-Kirby-a; Wrightson splash pg. 6 12 18 38 52 65
2-Titanic-c/s 3 7 10 21 28 35
3,21: 21-Wrightson-c 3 6 9 16 20 25
4-10 2 4 6 11 14 18
11-20,22-24 2 4 6 9 11 14

NOTE: ***Alcala** a-5, 10, 13, 14. **Aparo** c-4. **Bailey** a-8. **Bolle** a-8?. **Howard** a-4. **Kaluta** a-4, 24; c-1. **G. Kane** a-10. **Kirby** a-1, 2p, 3p. **Nino** a-5, 6, 9, 13, 16, 21. **Redondo** a-9, 17. **Sparling** c-6. **Starlin** a-3?, 4. **Wood** a-23.*

WEIRD ROMANCE (Seduction of the Innocent #9)
Eclipse Comics: Feb, 1988 ($2.00, B&W)

1-Pre-code horror-r; Lou Cameron-r(2) 2.25

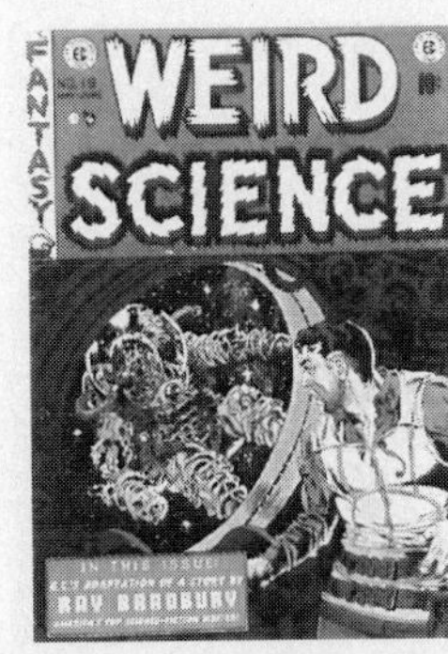

Weird Science #19 © WMG

Weird Tales of the Future #7 © S.P.M.

Weird War Tales #21 © DC

	GD 2.0	VG 4.0	FN 6.0	VF 8.0	VF/NM 9.0	NM- 9.2

WEIRD SCIENCE (Formerly Saddle Romances) (Becomes Weird Science-Fantasy #23 on)
E. C. Comics: No. 12, May-June, 1950 - No. 22, Nov-Dec, 1953

12(#1) (1950)-"Lost in the Microcosm" classic-c/story by Kurtzman; "Dream of Doom" stars Gaines & E.C. artists 193 386 579 1448 2124 2800
13-Flying saucers over Washington-c/story, 2 years before the actual event 88 176 264 660 968 1275
14-Robot, End of the World-c/story by Feldstein 84 168 252 630 928 1225
15-War of Worlds-c/story (1950) 78 156 234 585 855 1125
5-Atomic explosion-c 59 118 177 443 649 855
6-10: 9-Wood's 1st EC-c 48 96 144 360 528 695
11-14 (1952) 34 68 102 255 373 490
15-18-Williamson/Krenkel-a in each; 15-Williamson-a. 17-Used in **POP**, pgs. 81,82. 18-Bill Gaines doll app. in story 36 72 108 270 395 520
19,20-Williamson/Frazetta-a (7 pgs. each). 19-Used in **SOTI**, illo "A young girl on her wedding night stabs her sleeping husband to death with a hatpin..." 46 92 138 345 505 665
21-Williamson/Frazetta-a (6 pgs.); Wood draws E.C. staff; Gaines & Feldstein app. in story 46 92 138 345 505 665
22-Williamson/Frazetta/Krenkel-a (8 pgs.); Wood draws himself in his story (last pg. & panel) 46 92 138 345 505 665

NOTE: ***Elder** a-14, 19. **Evans** a-22. **Feldstein** a-12(#1)-8; c-12(#1)-8, 11. **Ingels** a-15. **Kamen** a-12(#1)-13, 15-18, 20, 21. **Kurtzman** a-12(#1)-7. **Orlando** a-10-22. **Wood** a-12(#1), 13(#2), 5-22 (#9, 10, 12, 13 all have 2 **Wood** stories); c-9, 10, 12-22. Canadian reprints exist; see Table of Contents. Ray Bradbury adaptations in #17-20.*

WEIRD SCIENCE
Gladstone Publishing: Sept, 1990 - No. 4, Mar, 1991 ($1.95/$2.00, 68 pgs.)

1-4: Wood-c(r); all reprints in each 3.00

WEIRD SCIENCE
Russ Cochran/Gemstone Publishing: Sept, 1992 - No. 22, Dec, 1997 ($1.50/$2.00/$2.50)

1-22: 1,2: r/Weird Science #12,13 w/original-c. ,4-r/#14,15. 5-7-w/original-c 3.00

WEIRD SCIENCE-FANTASY (Formerly Weird Science & Weird Fantasy)
(Becomes Incredible Science Fiction #30)
E. C. Comics: No. 23 Mar, 1954 - No. 29, May-June, 1955 (#23,24: 15¢)

23-Williamson, Wood-a; Bradbury adaptation 33 66 99 248 362 475
24-Williamson & Wood-a; Harlan Ellison's 1st professional story, "Upheaval!", later adapted into a short story as "Mealtime", and then into a TV episode of Voyage to the Bottom of the Sea as "The Price of Doom" 33 66 99 248 362 475
25-Williamson-c; Williamson/Torres/Krenkel-a plus Wood-a; Bradbury adaptation; cover price back to 10¢ 36 72 108 270 395 520
26-Flying Saucer Report; Wood, Crandall-a; A-bomb panels 34 68 102 255 373 490
27-Adam Link/I Robot series begins? 33 66 99 248 362 475
28-Williamson/Krenkel/Torres-a; Wood-a 34 68 102 255 373 490
29-Frazetta-c; Williamson/Krenkel & Wood-a; last pre-code issue; new logo 69 138 207 518 759 1000

NOTE: ***Crandall** a-26, 27, 29. **Evans** a-26. **Feldstein** c-24, 26, 28. **Kamen** a-27, 28. **Krigstein** a-23-25. **Orlando** a-in all. **Wood** a-in all; c-23, 27. The cover to #29 was originally intended for Famous Funnies #217 (Buck Rogers), but was rejected for being "too violent."*

WEIRD SCIENCE-FANTASY
Russ Cochran/Gemstone Publishing: Nov, 1992 - No. 7, May , 1994 ($1.50/$2.00/$2.50)

1-7: 1,2: r/Weird Science-Fantasy #23,24. 3-7 r/#25-29 3.00

WEIRD SCIENCE-FANTASY ANNUAL
E. C. Comics: 1952, 1953 (Sold thru the E. C. office & on the stands in some major cities) (25¢, 132 pgs.)

1952-Feldstein-c 215 430 645 1612 2206 2800
1953-Feldstein-c 138 276 414 1035 1418 1800

NOTE: *The 1952 annual contains books cover-dated in 1951 & 1952, and the 1953 annual from 1952 & 1953. Contents of each annual may vary in same year.*

WEIRD SECRET ORIGINS
DC Comics: Oct, 2004 ($5.95, square-bound, one-shot)

nn-Reprints origins of Dr. Fate, Spectre, Congorilla, Metamorpho, Animal Man & others 6.00

WEIRD SUSPENSE
Atlas/Seaboard Publ.: Feb, 1975 - No. 3, July, 1975

1-3: 1-Tarantula begins. 3-Freidrich-s 1 2 3 5 7 9

NOTE: ***Boyette** a-1-3. **Buckler** c-1, 3.*

WEIRD SUSPENSE STORIES (Canadian reprints of Crime SuspenStories #1-3; see Table of Contents)

WEIRD TALES ILLUSTRATED
Millennium Publications: 1992 - No. 2, 1992 ($2.95, high quality paper)

1,2-Bolton painted-c. 1-Adapts E.A. Poe & Harlan Ellison stories. 2-E.A. Poe & H.P. Lovecraft adaptations 3.50
1-($4.95, 52 pgs.)-Deluxe edition w/Tim Vigil-a not in regular #1; stiff-c; Bolton painted-c 5.00

WEIRD TALES OF THE FUTURE
S.P.M. Publ. No. 1-4/Aragon Publ. No. 5-8: Mar, 1952 - No. 8, July-Aug, 1953

1-Andru-a(2); Wolverton partial-c 104 208 312 650 1000 1350
2,3-Wolverton-c/a(3) each. 2- "Jumpin Jupiter" satire by Wolverton begins, ends #5 138 276 414 863 1332 1800
4- "Jumpin Jupiter" satire, partial Wolverton-c 121 242 363 756 1166 1575
5-Wolverton-c/a(2); "Jumpin Jupiter" satire 138 276 414 863 1332 1800
6-Bernard Baily-c 55 110 165 340 520 700
7- "The Mind Movers" from the art to Wolverton's "Brain Bats of Venus" from Mr. Mystery #7 which was cut apart, pasted up, partially redrawn, and rewritten by Harry Kantor, the editor; Baily-c 117 234 351 731 1128 1525
8-Reprints Weird Mysteries #1(10/52) minus cover; gory cover showing heart ripped out, by B. Baily 75 150 225 469 722 975

WEIRD TALES OF THE MACABRE (Magazine)
Atlas/Seaboard Publ.: Jan, 1975 - No. 2, Mar, 1975 (75¢, B&W)

1-Jeff Jones painted-c; Boyette-a 2 4 6 12 18 22
2-Boris Vallejo painted-c; Severin-a 3 6 9 18 24 30

WEIRD TERROR (Also see Horrific)
Allen Hardy Associates (Comic Media): Sept, 1952 - No. 13, Sept, 1954

1- "Portrait of Death", adapted from Lovecraft's "Pickman's Model"; lingerie panels, Hitler story 56 112 168 350 538 725
2,3: 2-Text on Marquis DeSade, Torture, Demonology, & St. Elmo's Fire. 3-Extreme violence, whipping, torture; article on sin eating, dowsing 47 94 141 287 436 585
4-Dismemberment, decapitation, article on human flesh for sale, Devil, whipping 47 94 141 287 436 585
5-Article on body snatching, mutilation; cannibalism story 40 80 120 244 372 500
6-Dismemberment, decapitation, man hit by lightning 43 86 129 262 399 535
7-Body burning in fireplace-c 40 80 120 244 372 500
8,11: 8-Decapitation story; Ambrose Bierce adapt. 11-End of the world story w/atomic blast panels; Tothish-a by Bill Discount 41 82 123 250 380 510
9,10,13: 13-Severed head panels 37 74 111 209 305 400
12-Discount-a 37 74 111 209 305 400

NOTE: ***Don Heck** a-most issues; c-1-13. **Landau** a-6. **Morisi** a-2-5, 7, 9, 12. **Palais** a-1, 5, 6, 8(2), 10, 12. **Powell** a-10. **Ravielli** a-11, 20.*

WEIRD THRILLERS
Ziff-Davis Publ. Co. (Approved Comics): Sept-Oct, 1951 - No. 5, Oct-Nov, 1952 (#2-5: painted-c)

1-Rondo Hatton photo-c 87 174 261 544 835 1125
2-Toth, Anderson, Colan-a 63 126 189 394 610 825
3-Two Powell, Tuska-a; classic-c 85 170 255 531 816 1100
4-Kubert, Tuska-a 60 120 180 375 575 775
5-Powell-a 55 110 165 340 520 700

NOTE: ***M. Anderson** a-2, 3. **Roussos** a-4. #2, 3 reprinted in Nightmare #10 & 13; #4, 5 reprinted in Amazing Ghost Stories #16 & #15.*

WEIRD VAMPIRE TALES (Comic magazine)
Modern Day Periodical Pub.: V3 #1, Apr, 1979 - V5 #3, Mar, 1982 (B&W)

V3 #1 (4/79) First issue, no V1 or V2 4 8 12 24 32 40
V3 #2-4 3 6 9 18 24 30
V4 #2 (4/80), V4 #3 (7/80) (no V4 #1) 3 6 9 16 20 25
V5 #1 (1/81), V5 #2 (two issues, 4/81 & 8/81) 3 6 9 16 20 25
V5 #3 (3/82) Last issue; low print 3 7 10 21 28 35

WEIRD WAR TALES
National Periodical Publ./DC Comics: Sept-Oct, 1971 - No. 124, June, 1983 (#1-5: 52 pgs.)

1-Kubert-a in #1-4,7; c-1-7 23 46 69 165 253 340
2,3-Drucker-a: 2-Crandall-a. 3-Heath-a 10 20 30 70 100 130
4,5: 5-Toth-a; Heath-a 7 14 21 51 71 90
6,7,9,10: 6,10-Toth-a. 7-Heath-a 5 10 15 36 48 60
8-Neal Adams-c/a(i) 6 12 18 43 59 75
11-20 3 6 9 18 24 30
21-35 2 4 6 12 16 20
36-(68 pgs.)-Crandall & Kubert-r/#2; Heath-r/#3; Kubert-c 3 6 9 16 20 24
37-50: 38,39-Kubert-c 2 4 6 8 10 12
51-63: 58-Hitler-c/app. 60-Hindenburg-c/s 1 3 4 6 8 10
64-Frank Miller-a (1st DC work) 3 6 9 18 24 30
65-67,69-89,91,92: 89-Nazi Apes-c/s. 1 2 3 4 5 7
68-Frank Miller-a (2nd DC work) 2 4 6 14 18 22
90-Hitler app. 1 2 3 5 6 8
93-Intro/origin Creature Commandos 1 2 3 5 7 9

	GD 2.0	VG 4.0	FN 6.0	VF 8.0	VF/NM 9.0	NM- 9.2

Weird Wonder Tales #20 © MAR

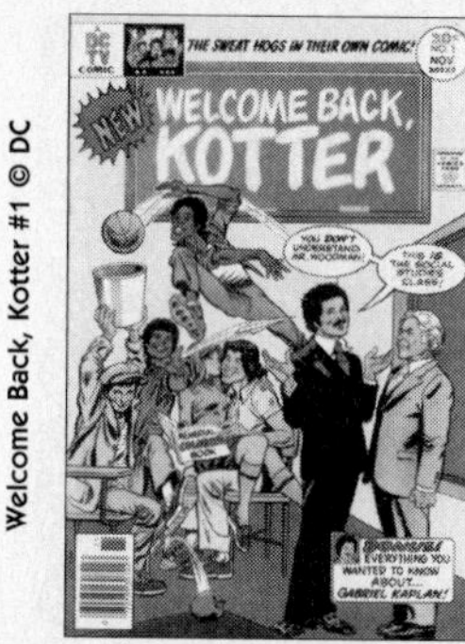

Welcome Back, Kotter #1 © DC

Werewolf By Night V2#2 © MAR

	GD 2.0	VG 4.0	FN 6.0	VF 8.0	VF/NM 9.0	NM- 9.2
94-Return of War that Time Forgot; dinosaur-c/s	1	3	4	6	8	10
95,96,98,102-123: 98-Sphinx-c. 102-Creature Commandos battle Hitler. 110-Origin/1st app. Medusa. 123-1st app. Captain Spaceman	1	2	3	4	5	7
97,99,100,101,124: 99-War that Time Forgot. 100-Creature Commandos in War that Time Forgot. 101-Intro/origin G.I. Robot	1	2	3	5	6	8

NOTE: ***Chaykin*** *a-76, 82.* ***Ditko*** *a-95, 99, 104-106.* ***Evans*** *c-73, 74, 83, 85.* ***Kane*** *c-116, 118.* ***Kubert*** *c-55, 58, 60, 62, 72, 75-81, 87, 88, 90-96, 100, 103, 104, 106, 107.* ***Newton*** *a-122.* ***Starlin*** *c-89.* ***Sutton*** *a-91, 92, 103.* ***Creature Commandos*** *-93, 97, 100, 102, 105, 108-112, 114, 116-119, 121, 124.* ***G.I. Robot*** *- 101, 108, 111, 113, 116-118, 120, 122.* ***War That Time Forgot*** *- 94, 99, 100, 103, 106, 109, 120.*

WEIRD WAR TALES
DC Comics (Vertigo): June, 1997 - No. 4, Sept, 1997 ($2.50)

	GD	VG	FN	VF	VF/NM	NM-
1-4-Anthology by various						3.00

WEIRD WAR TALES
DC Comics (Vertigo): April, 2000 ($4.95, one-shot)

	GD	VG	FN	VF	VF/NM	NM-
1-Anthology by various; last Biukovic-a						5.00

WEIRD WESTERN TALES (Formerly All-Star Western)
National Per. Publ./DC Comics: No. 12, June-July, 1972 - No. 70, Aug, 1980

	GD	VG	FN	VF	VF/NM	NM-
12-(52 pgs.)-3rd app. Jonah Hex; Bat Lash, Pow Wow Smith reprints; El Diablo by Neal Adams/Wrightson	12	24	36	86	131	175
13-Jonah Hex-c & 4th app.; Neal Adams-a	9	18	27	60	85	110
14-Toth-a	6	12	18	43	59	75
15-Adams-c/a; no Jonah Hex	4	8	12	24	32	40
16,17,19,20	4	8	12	24	32	40
18,29: 18-1st all Jonah Hex issue (7-8/73) & begins. 29-Origin Jonah Hex	5	10	15	33	44	55
21-28,30: Jonah Hex in all	3	6	9	16	20	25
31-38: Jonah Hex in all. 38-Last Jonah Hex	2	4	6	12	16	20
39-Origin/1st app. Scalphunter & begins	2	4	6	11	14	18
40-47,50-69: 64-Bat Lash-c/story	1	2	3	5	6	8
48,49: (44 pgs.)-1st & 2nd app. Cinnamon	1	2	3	5	7	9
70-Last issue	2	4	6	8	10	12

NOTE: ***Alcala*** *a-16, 17.* ***Evans*** *inks-39-48; c-39i, 40, 47.* ***G. Kane*** *a-15, 20.* ***Kubert*** *c-12, 33.* ***Starlin*** *c-44, 45.* ***Wildey*** *a-26. 48 & 49 are 44 pgs..*

WEIRD WESTERN TALES
DC Comics (Vertigo): Apr, 2001 - No. 4, Jul, 2001 ($2.50, limited series)

	GD	VG	FN	VF	VF/NM	NM-
1-4-Anthology by various						2.50

WEIRD WONDER TALES
Marvel Comics Group: Dec, 1973 - No. 22, May, 1977

	GD	VG	FN	VF	VF/NM	NM-
1-Wolverton-r/Mystic #6 (Eye of Doom)	3	6	9	18	23	28
2-10	2	4	6	10	13	16
11-22: 16-18-Venus-r by Everett from Venus #19,18 & 17. 19-22-r/Dr. Droom (re-named Dr. Druid) by Kirby. 22-New art by Byrne	2	4	6	9	11	14
15-17-(30¢-c variants, limited distribution)(4-8/76)	2	4	6	13	17	21

NOTE: *All 1950s & early 1960s reprints.* ***Check*** *r-1.* ***Colan*** *r-17.* ***Ditko*** *r-4, 5, 10-13, 19-21.* ***Drucker*** *r-12, 20.* ***Everett*** *r-3(Spellbound #16), 6(Astonishing #10), 9(Adv. Into Mystery #5).* ***Heath*** *a-13r.* ***Heck*** *a-10r, 14r.* ***Gil Kane*** *c-1, 2, 10.* ***Kirby*** *r-4, 6, 10, 11, 13, 15-22; c-17, 19, 20.* ***Krigstein*** *r-19.* ***Kubert*** *r-22.* ***Maneely*** *r-8.* ***Mooney*** *r-7p.* ***Powell*** *r-3, 7.* ***Torres*** *r-7.* ***Wildey*** *r-2, 7.*

WEIRD WORLDS (See Adventures Into...)

WEIRD WORLDS (Magazine)
Eerie Publications: V1#10(12/70), V2#1(2/71) - No. 4, Aug, 1971 (52 pgs.)

	GD	VG	FN	VF	VF/NM	NM-
V1#10-Sci-fi/horror	4	8	12	25	33	42
V2#1-4	3	6	9	19	25	32

WEIRD WORLDS (Also see Ironwolf: Fires of the Revolution)
National Periodical Publications: Aug-Sept, 1972 - No. 9, Jan-Feb, 1974; No. 10, Oct-Nov, 1974 (All 20¢ issues)

	GD	VG	FN	VF	VF/NM	NM-
1-Edgar Rice Burrough's John Carter Warlord of Mars & David Innes begin (1st DC app.); Kubert-c	2	4	6	14	18	22
2-4: 2-Infantino/Orlando-c. 3-Murphy Anderson-c. 4-Kaluta-a	2	4	6	9	11	14
5-7: .5-Kaluta-c. 7-Last John Carter.	1	3	4	6	8	10
8-10: 8-Iron Wolf begins by Chaykin (1st app.)	1	2	3	5	7	9

NOTE: ***Neal Adams*** *a-2i, 3i. John Carter by* ***Andersonin*** *#1-3.* ***Chaykin*** *c-7, 8.* ***Kaluta*** *a-4; c-4-6, 10.* ***Orlando*** *a-4i; c-2, 3, 4i.* ***Wrightson*** *a-2i, 4i.*

WELCOME BACK, KOTTER (TV) (See Limited Collectors' Edition #57 for unpublished #11)
National Periodical Publ./DC Comics: Nov, 1976 - No. 10, Mar-Apr, 1978

	GD	VG	FN	VF	VF/NM	NM-
1-Sparling-a(p)	3	6	9	16	20	25
2-10: 3-Estrada-a	2	4	6	9	11	14

WELCOME SANTA (See March of Comics #63,183)

WELCOME TO THE LITTLE SHOP OF HORRORS
Roger Corman's Cosmic Comics: May, 1995 -No. 3, July, 1995 ($2.50, limited series)

	GD 2.0	VG 4.0	FN 6.0	VF 8.0	VF/NM 9.0	NM- 9.2
1-3						2.50

WELLS FARGO (See Tales of...)

WENDY AND THE NEW KIDS ON THE BLOCK
Harvey Comics: Mar, 1991 - No. 3, July, 1991 ($1.25)

	GD	VG	FN	VF	VF/NM	NM-
1-3						2.25

WENDY DIGEST
Harvey Comics: Oct, 1990 - No. 5, Mar, 1992 ($1.75, digest size)

	GD	VG	FN	VF	VF/NM	NM-
1-5						4.00

WENDY PARKER COMICS
Atlas Comics (OMC): July, 1953 - No. 8, July, 1954

	GD	VG	FN	VF	VF/NM	NM-
1	10	20	30	60	80	100
2	8	16	24	43	54	65
3-8	7	14	21	37	46	55

WENDY, THE GOOD LITTLE WITCH (TV)
Harvey Publ.: 8/60 - #82, 11/73; #83, 8/74 - #93, 4/76; #94, 9/90 - #97, 12/90

	GD	VG	FN	VF	VF/NM	NM-
1-Wendy & Casper the Friendly Ghost begin	26	52	78	184	282	380
2	13	26	39	92	141	190
3-5	10	20	30	70	100	130
6-10	7	14	21	51	71	90
11-20	6	12	18	38	52	65
21-30	4	8	12	28	38	48
31-50	3	6	9	19	25	32
51-64,66-69	2	4	6	12	16	20
65 (2/71)-Wendy origin.	3	6	9	18	24	30
70-74: All 52 pg. Giants	3	6	9	18	23	28
75-93	2	4	6	9	11	14
94-97 (1990, $1.00-c): 94-Has #194 on-c						4.00

(See Casper the Friendly Ghost #20 & Harvey Hits #7, 16, 21, 23, 27, 30, 33)

WENDY THE GOOD LITTLE WITCH (2nd Series)
Harvey Comics: Apr, 1991 - No. 15, Aug, 1994 ($1.00/$1.25 #7-11/$1.50 #12-15)

	GD	VG	FN	VF	VF/NM	NM-
1-15-Reprints Wendy & Casper stories. 12-Bunny app.						3.00

WENDY WITCH WORLD
Harvey Publications: 10/61; No. 2, 9/62 - No. 52, 12/73; No. 53, 9/74

	GD	VG	FN	VF	VF/NM	NM-
1-(25¢, 68 pg. Giants begin)	14	28	42	97	149	200
2-5	8	16	24	55	78	100
6-10	6	12	18	40	55	70
11-20	5	10	15	33	44	55
21-30	4	8	12	24	32	40
31-39: 39-Last 68 pg. issue	3	6	9	18	24	30
40-45: 52 pg. issues	2	4	6	12	16	20
46-53	2	4	6	9	11	14

WEREWOLF (Super Hero) (Also see Dracula & Frankenstein)
Dell Publishing Co.: Dec, 1966 - No. 3, April, 1967

	GD	VG	FN	VF	VF/NM	NM-
1-1st app.	4	8	12	25	33	42
2,3	2	4	6	14	18	22

WEREWOLF BY NIGHT (See Giant-Size..., Marvel Spotlight #2-4 & Power Record Comics)
Marvel Comics Group: Sept, 1972 - No. 43, Mar, 1977

	GD	VG	FN	VF	VF/NM	NM-
1-Ploog-a cont'd. from Marvel Spotlight #4	10	20	30	70	100	130
2	5	10	15	33	44	55
3-5	4	8	12	24	32	40
6-10	3	6	9	16	21	26
11-14,16-20	2	4	6	11	14	18
15-New origin Werewolf; Dracula-c/story cont'd from Tomb of Dracula #18; classic Ploog-c	3	6	9	18	24	30
21-31	2	4	6	8	10	12
32-Origin & 1st app. Moon Knight (8/75)	10	20	30	67	96	125
33-2nd app. Moon Knight	5	10	15	33	44	55
34,36,38-43: 35-Starlin/Wrightson-c	1	3	4	6	8	10
37-Moon Knight app; part Wrightson-c	1	2	3	10	12	15
38,39-(30¢-c variants, limited distribution)(5,7/76)	2	4	6	14	18	22

NOTE: ***Bolle*** *a-6i.* ***G. Kane*** *a-11p, 12p; c-21, 22, 24-30, 34p.* ***Mooney*** *a-7i.* ***Ploog*** *1-4p, 5, 6p, 7p, 13-16p; c-5-8, 13-16.* ***Reinman*** *a-8i.* ***Sutton*** *a(i)-9, 11, 16, 35.*

WEREWOLF BY NIGHT (Vol. 2, continues in Strange Tales #1 (9/98))
Marvel Comics Group: Feb, 1998 - No. 6, July, 1998 ($2.99)

	GD	VG	FN	VF	VF/NM	NM-
1-6-Manco-a: 2-Two covers. 6-Ghost Rider-c/app.						3.00

WEREWOLVES & VAMPIRES (Magazine)
Charlton Comics: 1962 (One Shot)

	GD	VG	FN	VF	VF/NM	NM-
1	8	16	24	58	82	105

West Coast Avengers Annual #4 © MAR

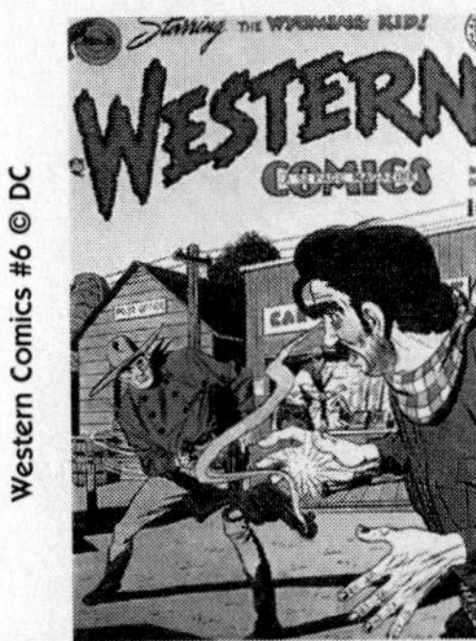

Western Comics #6 © DC

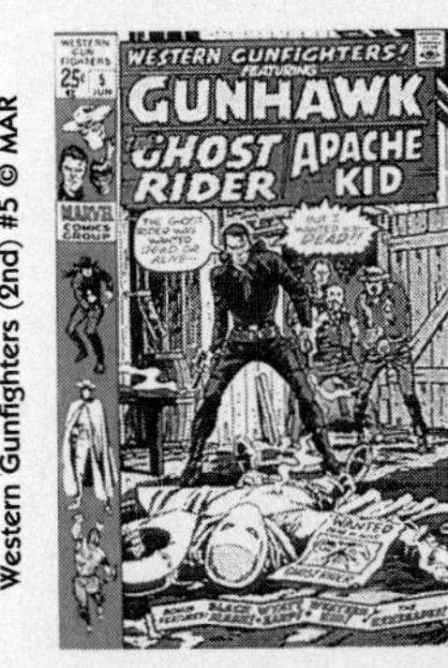

Western Gunfighters (2nd) #5 © MAR

GD	VG	FN	VF	VF/NM	NM-
2.0	4.0	6.0	8.0	9.0	9.2

WEST COAST AVENGERS
Marvel Comics Group: Sept, 1984 - No. 4, Dec, 1984 (lim. series, Mando paper)
1-Origin & 1st app. W.C. Avengers (Hawkeye, Iron Man, Mockingbird & Tigra) 4.00
2-4 3.00

WEST COAST AVENGERS (Becomes Avengers West Coast #48 on)
Marvel Comics Group: Oct, 1985 - No. 47, Aug, 1989
V2#1-41 3.00
42-47: 42-Byrne-a(p)/scripts begin. 46-Byrne-c; 1st app. Great Lakes Avengers 3.00
Annual 1-3 (1986-1988): 3-Evolutionary War app. 3.00
Annual 4 (1989, $2.00)-Atlantis Attacks; Byrne/Austin-a 3.00

WESTERN ACTION
I. W. Enterprises: No. 7, 1964
7-Reprints Cow Puncher #? by Avon 2 4 6 9 11 14

WESTERN ACTION
Atlas/Seaboard Publ.: Feb, 1975
1-Kid Cody by Wildey & The Comanche Kid stories; intro. The Renegade
1 3 4 6 8 10

WESTERN ACTION THRILLERS
Dell Publishers: Apr, 1937 (10¢, square binding; 100 pgs.)
1-Buffalo Bill, The Texas Kid, Laramie Joe, Two-Gun Thompson, & Wild West Bill app.
85 170 255 531 816 1100

WESTERN ADVENTURES COMICS (Western Love Trails #7 on)
Ace Magazines: Oct, 1948 - No. 6, Aug, 1949
nn(#1)-Sheriff Sal, The Cross-Draw Kid, Sam Bass begin
24 48 72 135 195 255
nn(#2)(12/48) 13 26 39 74 102 130
nn(#3)(2/49)-Used in **SOTI**, pgs. 30,31 13 26 39 76 106 135
4-6 11 22 33 64 87 110

WESTERN BANDITS
Avon Periodicals: 1952 (Painted-c)
1-Butch Cassidy, The Daltons by Larsen; Kinstler-a; c-part-r/paperback Avon Western Novel #1 17 34 51 95 135 175

WESTERN BANDIT TRAILS (See Approved Comics)
St. John Publishing Co.: Jan, 1949 - No. 3, July, 1949
1-Tuska-a; Baker-c; Blue Monk, Ventrilo app. 26 52 78 150 215 280
2-Baker-c 20 40 60 112 161 210
3-Baker-c/a; Tuska-a 24 48 72 135 195 255

WESTERN COMICS (See Super DC Giant #15)
National Per. Publ: Jan-Feb, 1948 - No. 85, Jan-Feb, 1961 (1-27: 52pgs.)
1-Wyoming Kid & his horse Racer, The Vigilante in "Jesse James Rides Again" (Meskin-a), Cowboy Marshal, Rodeo Rick begin 81 162 243 506 778 1050
2 40 80 120 233 342 450
3,4-Last Vigilante 37 74 111 209 305 400
5-Nighthawk & his horse Nightwind begin (not in #6); Captain Tootsie by Beck
31 62 93 175 253 330
6,7,9,10 24 48 72 135 195 255
8-Origin Wyoming Kid; 2 pg. pin-ups of rodeo queens
36 72 108 204 297 390
11-20 20 40 60 112 161 210
21-40: 24-Starr-a. 27-Last 52 pgs. 28-Flag-c 15 30 45 85 120 155
41,42,44-49: 49-Last precode issue (2/55) 14 28 42 81 113 145
43-Pow Wow Smith begins, ends #85 15 30 45 83 117 150
50-60 12 24 36 69 95 120
61-85-Last Wyoming Kid. 77-Origin Matt Savage Trail Boss. 82-1st app. Fleetfoot, Pow Wow's girlfriend 10 20 30 58 77 95
NOTE: ***G. Kane, Infantino*** *art in most.* ***Meskin*** *a-1-4.* ***Moreira*** *a-28-39.* ***Post*** *a-3-5.*

WESTERN CRIME BUSTERS
Trojan Magazines: Sept, 1950 - No. 10, Mar-Apr, 1952
1-Six-Gun Smith, Wilma West, K-Bar-Kate, & Fighting Bob Dale begin; headlight-a
37 74 111 209 305 400
2 20 40 60 115 165 215
3-5: 3-Myron Fass-c 19 38 57 107 154 200
6-Wood-a 35 70 105 201 293 385
7-Six-Gun Smith by Wood 35 70 105 201 293 385
8 19 38 57 107 154 200
9-Tex Gordon & Wilma West by Wood; Lariat Lucy app.
34 68 102 196 283 370
10-Wood-a 31 62 93 177 256 335

WESTERN CRIME CASES (Formerly Indian Warriors #7,8; becomes The Outlaws #10 on)
Star Publications: No. 9, Dec, 1951
9-White Rider & Super Horse; L. B. Cole-c 22 44 66 123 177 230

WESTERNER, THE (Wild Bill Pecos)
"Wanted" Comic Group/Toytown/Patches: No. 14, June, 1948 - No. 41, Dec, 1951 (#14-31: 52 pgs.)
14 15 30 45 83 117 150
15-17,19-21: 19-Meskin-a 9 18 27 51 62 75
18,22-25-Krigstein-a 10 20 30 60 80 100
26(4/50)-Origin & 1st app. Calamity Kate, series ends #32; Krigstein-a
14 28 42 79 110 140
27-Krigstein-a(2) 13 26 39 74 102 130
28-41: 33-Quest app. 37-Lobo, the Wolf Boy begins 7 14 21 37 46 55
NOTE: ***Mort Lawrence*** *a-20-27, 29, 37, 39; c-19, 22-24, 26, 27.* ***Leav*** *c-14-18, 20, 31.* ***Syd Shores*** *a-39; c-34, 35, 37-41.*

WESTERNER, THE
Super Comics: 1964
Super Reprint 15-17: 15-r/Oklahoma Kid #? 16-r/Crack West. #65; Severin-c; Crandall-r. 17-r/Blazing Western #2; Severin-c 2 4 6 9 11 14

WESTERN FIGHTERS
Hillman Periodicals/Star Publ.: Apr-May, 1948 - V4#7, Mar-Apr, 1953 (#1-V3#2: 52 pgs.)
V1#1-Simon & Kirby-c 37 74 111 209 305 400
2-Not Kirby-a 12 24 36 71 98 125
3-Fuje-c 10 20 30 60 80 100
4-Krigstein, Ingels, Fuje-a 11 22 33 66 91 115
5,6,8,9,12 8 16 24 46 58 70
7,10-Krigstein-a 10 20 30 58 77 95
11-Williamson/Frazetta-a 31 62 93 175 253 330
V2#1-Krigstein-a 10 20 30 58 77 95
2-12: 4-Berg-a 7 14 21 37 46 55
V3#1-11,V4#1,4-7 7 14 21 35 43 50
12,V4#2,3-Krigstein-a 10 20 30 58 77 95
3-D 1(12/53, 25¢, Star Publ.)-Came w/glasses; L. B. Cole-c
39 78 117 222 324 425
NOTE: ***Kinstlerish*** *a-V2#6, 8, 9, 12; V3#2, 5-7, 11, 12; V4#1(plus cover).* ***McWilliams*** *a-11.* ***Powell*** *a-V2#2.* ***Reinman*** *a-1-12, V4#3.* ***Rowich*** *c-5, 6i.* ***Starr*** *a-5.*

WESTERN FRONTIER
P. L. Publishers: Apr-May, 1951 - No. 7, 1952
1 13 26 39 74 102 130
2 8 16 24 43 54 65
3-7 7 14 21 35 43 50

WESTERN GUNFIGHTERS (1st Series) (Apache Kid #11-19)
Atlas Comics (CPS): No. 20, June, 1956 - No. 27, Aug, 1957
20 13 26 39 74 102 130
21-Crandall-a 13 26 39 74 102 130
22-Wood & Powell-a 19 38 57 107 154 200
23,24: 23-Williamson-a. 24-Toth-a 13 26 39 74 102 130
25-27 10 20 30 56 73 90
NOTE: ***Berg*** *a-20.* ***Colan*** *a-20, 26, 27.* ***Crandall*** *a-21.* ***Heath*** *a-25.* ***Maneely*** *a-24, 25; c-22, 23, 25.* ***Morisi*** *a-24.* ***Morrow*** *a-26.* ***Pakula*** *a-23.* ***Severin*** *c-20, 27.* ***Torres*** *a-26.* ***Woodbridge*** *a-27.*

WESTERN GUNFIGHTERS (2nd Series)
Marvel Comics Group: Aug, 1970 - No. 33, Nov, 1975 (#1-6: 25¢, 68 pgs.)
1-Ghost Rider begins; Fort Rango, Renegades & Gunhawk app.
6 12 18 38 52 65
2,3,5,6: 2-Origin Nightwind (Apache Kid's horse) 3 6 9 19 25 32
4-Barry Smith-a 4 8 12 25 33 42
7-(52 pgs) Origin Ghost Rider retold 3 6 9 18 24 30
8-14: 10-Origin Black Rider. 12-Origin Matt Slade 2 4 6 12 16 20
15-20 2 4 6 9 11 14
21-33 2 4 6 8 10 12
NOTE: ***Baker*** *r-2, 3.* ***Colan*** *r-2.* ***Drucker*** *r-3.* ***Everett*** *a-6i.* ***G. Kane*** *c-29, 31.* ***Kirby*** *a-1p(r), 5, 10-12; c-19, 21.* ***Kubert*** *r-2.* ***Maneely*** *r-2, 10.* ***Morrow*** *r-29.* ***Severin*** *c-10.* ***Shores*** *a-3, 4.* ***Barry Smith*** *a-4.* ***Steranko*** *c-14.* ***Sutton*** *a-1, 2i, 5, 4.* ***Torres*** *r-26('57).* ***Wildey*** *r-8, 9.* ***Williamson*** *r-2, 18.* ***Woodbridge*** *r-27('57). Renegades in #4, 5; Ghost Rider in #1-7.*

WESTERN HEARTS
Standard Comics: Dec, 1949 - No. 10, Mar, 1952 (All photo-c)
1-Severin-a; Whip Wilson & Reno Browne photo-c 24 48 72 138 199 260
2-Beverly Tyler & Jerome Courtland photo-c from movie "Palomino"; Williamson/Frazetta-a (2 pgs.) 24 48 72 138 199 260
3-Rex Allen photo-c 14 28 42 81 113 145

Western Hearts #2 © STD

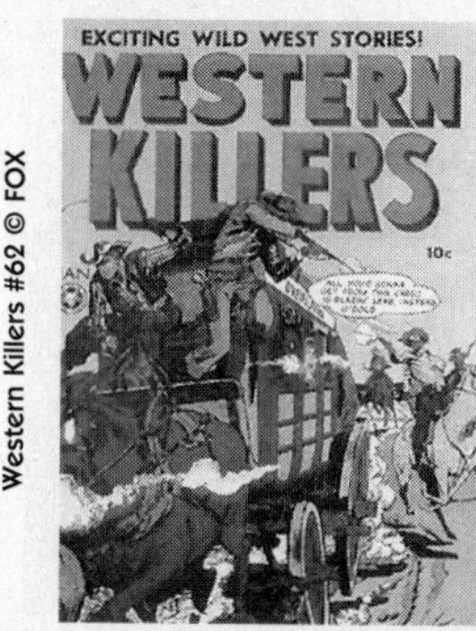

Western Killers #62 © FOX

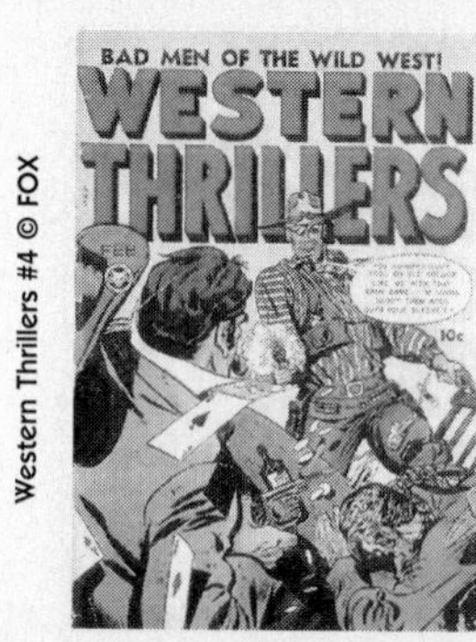

Western Thrillers #4 © FOX

	GD 2.0	VG 4.0	FN 6.0	VF 8.0	VF/NM 9.0	NM- 9.2

4-7,10-Severin & Elder, Al Carreno-a. 5-Ray Milland & Hedy Lamarr photo-c from movie "Copper Canyon". 6-Fred MacMurray & Irene Dunn photo-c from movie "Never a Dull Moment". 7-Jock Mahoney photo-c. 10-Bill Williams & Jane Nigh photo-c
14 28 42 79 110 140
8-Randolph Scott & Janis Carter photo-c from "Santa Fe"; Severin & Elder-a
14 28 42 81 113 145
9-Whip Wilson & Reno Browne photo-c; Severin & Elder-a
15 30 45 86 123 160

WESTERN HERO (Wow Comics #1-69; Real Western Hero #70-75)
Fawcett Publications: No. 76, Mar, 1949 - No. 112, Mar, 1952

76(#1, 52 pgs.)-Tom Mix, Hopalong Cassidy, Monte Hale, Gabby Hayes, Young Falcon (ends #78,80), & Big Bow and Little Arrow (ends #102,105) begin; painted-c begin
31 62 93 175 253 330
77 (52 pgs.) 18 36 54 100 143 185
78,80-82 (52 pgs.): 81-Capt. Tootsie by Beck 17 34 51 95 135 175
79,83 (36 pgs.): 83-Last painted-c 15 30 45 83 117 150
84-86,88-90 (52 pgs.): 84-Photo-c begin, end #112. 86-Last Hopalong Cassidy
15 30 45 86 120 155
87,91,95,99 (36 pgs.): 87-Bill Boyd begins, ends #95
13 26 39 76 106 135
92-94,96-98,101 (52 pgs.): 96-Tex Ritter begins. 101-Red Eagle app.
14 28 42 81 113 145
100 (52 pgs.) 15 30 45 85 120 155
102-111: 102-Begin 36 pg. issues 13 26 39 76 106 135
112-Last issue 14 28 42 81 113 145
NOTE: *1/2 to 1 pg. Rocky Lane (Carnation) in 80-83, 86, 88, 97. Photo covers feature Hopalong Cassidy #84, 86, 89; Tom Mix #85, 87, 90, 92, 94, 97; Monte Hale #88, 91, 93, 95, 98, 100, 104, 107, 110; Tex Ritter #96, 99, 101, 105, 108, 111; Gabby Hayes #103.*

WESTERN KID (1st Series)
Atlas Comics (CPC): Dec, 1954 - No. 17, Aug, 1957

1-Origin; The Western Kid (Tex Dawson), his stallion Whirlwind & dog Lightning begin
21 42 63 118 169 220
2 (2/55)-Last pre-code 11 22 33 64 87 110
3-8 10 20 30 56 73 90
9,10-Williamson-a in both (4 pgs. each) 10 20 30 58 77 95
11-17 8 16 24 46 58 70
NOTE: ***Ayers** a-6, 7. **Maneely** c-2-7, 10, 14. **Romita** a-1-17; c-1, 12. **Severin** c-17.*

WESTERN KID, THE (2nd Series)
Marvel Comics Group: Dec, 1971 - No. 5, Aug, 1972 (All 20¢ issues)

1-Reprints; Romita-c/a(3) 3 6 9 18 23 28
2,4,5: 2-Romita-a; Severin-c. 4-Everett-r 2 4 6 10 13 16
3-Williamson-a 2 4 6 12 16 20

WESTERN KILLERS
Fox Features Syndicate: nn, July?, 1948; No. 60, Sept, 1948 - No. 64, May, 1949; No. 6, July, 1949

nn(#59?)(nd, F&J Trading Co.)-Range Busters; formerly Blue Beetle #57?
25 50 75 141 203 265
60 (#1, 9/48)-Extreme violence; lingerie panel 27 54 81 152 219 285
61-Jack Cole, Starr-a 22 44 66 125 180 235
62-64, 6 (#6-exist?) 20 40 60 112 161 210

WESTERN LIFE ROMANCES (My Friend Irma #3 on?)
Marvel Comics (IPP): Dec, 1949 - No. 2, Mar, 1950 (52 pgs.)

1-Whip Wilson & Reno Browne photo-c 21 42 63 118 169 220
2-Audie Murphy & Gale Storm photo-c 17 34 51 95 135 175

WESTERN LOVE
Prize Publ.: July-Aug, 1949 - No. 5, Mar-Apr, 1950 (All photo-c & 52 pgs.)

1-S&K-a; Randolph Scott photo-c from movie "Canadian Pacific" (see Prize Comics #76)
31 62 93 175 253 330
2,5-S&K-a: 2-Whip Wilson & Reno Browne photo-c. 5-Dale Robertson photo-c 24 48 72 135 195 255
3,4: 3-Reno Browne? photo-c 15 30 45 86 123 160
NOTE: ***Meskin** & **Severin/Elder** a-2-5.*

WESTERN LOVE TRAILS (Formerly Western Adventures)
Ace Magazines (A. A. Wyn): No. 7, Nov, 1949 - No. 9, Mar, 1950

7 12 24 36 69 95 120
8,9 10 20 30 56 73 90

WESTERN MARSHAL (See Steve Donovan...)
Dell Publishing Co.: No. 534, 2-4/54 - No. 640, 7/55 (Based on Ernest Haycox's "Trailtown")

Four Color 534 (#1)-Kinstler-a 7 14 21 50 68 85
Four Color 591 (10/54), 613 (2/55), 640-All Kinstler-a 6 12 18 43 59 75

	GD 2.0	VG 4.0	FN 6.0	VF 8.0	VF/NM 9.0	NM- 9.2

WESTERN OUTLAWS (Junior Comics #9-16; My Secret Life #22 on)
Fox Features Syndicate: No. 17, Sept, 1948 - No. 21, May, 1949

17-Kamen-a; Iger shop-a in all; 1 pg. "Death and the Devil Pills" r-in Ghostly Weird #122
36 72 108 204 297 390
18-21 21 42 63 118 169 220

WESTERN OUTLAWS
Atlas Comics (ACI No. 1-14/WPI No. 15-21): Feb, 1954 - No. 21, Aug, 1957

1-Heath, Powell-a; Maneely hanging-c 23 46 69 130 188 245
2 12 24 36 69 95 120
3-10: 7-Violent-a by R.Q. Sale 10 20 30 56 73 90
11,14-Williamson-a in both (6 pgs. each) 11 22 33 62 84 105
12,18,20,21: Severin covers 9 18 27 52 66 80
13,15: 13-Baker-a. 15-Torres-a 10 20 30 56 73 90
16-Williamson text illo 9 18 27 52 66 80
17,19-Crandall-a. 17-Williamson text illo 10 20 30 56 73 90
NOTE: ***Ayers** a-7, 10, 18, 20. **Bolle** a-21. **Colan** a-5, 10, 11, 17. **Drucker** a-11. **Everett** a-9, 10. **Heath** a-1; c-3, 4, 8, 16. **Kubert** a-9p. **Maneely** a-13, 16, 17, 19; c-1, 5, 7, 9, 10, 12, 13. **Morisi** a-18. **Powell** a-3, 16. **Romita** a-7, 13. **Severin** a-8, 16, 19; c-17, 18, 20, 21. **Tuska** a-6, 15.*

WESTERN OUTLAWS & SHERIFFS (Formerly Best Western)
Marvel/Atlas Comics (IPC): No. 60, Dec, 1949 - No. 73, June, 1952

60 (52 pgs.) 24 48 72 138 199 260
61-65: 61-Photo-c 19 38 57 107 154 200
66-Story contains 5 hangings 19 38 57 107 154 200
68-72 14 28 42 79 110 140
67-Cannibalism story 19 38 57 107 154 200
73-Black Rider story; Everett-c 16 32 48 89 127 165
NOTE: ***Maneely** a-62, 67; c-62, 69-73. **Robinson** a-68. **Sinnott** a-70. **Tuska** a-69-71.*

WESTERN PICTURE STORIES (1st Western comic)
Comics Magazine Company: Feb, 1937 - No. 4, June, 1937

1-Will Eisner-a 185 370 555 1156 1778 2400
2-Will Eisner-a 100 200 300 625 963 1300
3,4: 3-Eisner-a. 4-Caveman Cowboy story 83 166 249 519 797 1075

WESTERN PICTURE STORIES (See Giant Comics Edition #6, 11)

WESTERN ROMANCES (See Target...)

WESTERN ROUGH RIDERS
Gillmor Magazines No. 1,4 (Stanmor Publ.): Nov, 1954 - No. 4, May, 1955

1 9 18 27 49 62 75
2-4 7 14 21 35 43 50

WESTERN ROUNDUP (See Dell Giants & Fox Giants)

WESTERN TALES (Formerly Witches...)
Harvey Publications: No. 31, Oct, 1955 - No. 33, July-Sept, 1956

31,32-All S&K-a; Davy Crockett app. in each 21 42 63 118 169 220
33-S&K-a; Jim Bowie app. 20 40 60 112 161 210
NOTE: *#32 & 33 contain Boy's Ranch reprints. **Kirby** c-31.*

WESTERN TALES OF BLACK RIDER (Formerly Black Rider; Gunsmoke Western #32 on)
Atlas Comics (CPS): No. 28, May, 1955 - No. 31, Nov, 1955

28 (#1): The Spider (a villain) dies 21 42 63 118 169 220
29-31 14 28 42 79 110 140
NOTE: ***Lawrence** a-30. **Maneely** c-28-30. **Severin** a-28. **Shores** c-31.*

WESTERN TEAM-UP
Marvel Comics Group: Nov, 1973 (20¢)

1-Origin & 1st app. The Dakota Kid; Rawhide Kid-r; Gunsmoke Kid-r by Jack Davis
4 8 12 24 32 40

WESTERN THRILLERS (My Past Confessions #7 on)
Fox Features Syndicate/M.S. Distr. No. 52: Aug, 1948 - No. 6, June, 1949; No. 52, 1954?

1- "Velvet Rose" (Kamenish-a); "Two-Gun Sal", "Striker Sisters" (all women outlaws issue); Brodsky-c 48 96 144 293 447 600
2 22 44 66 125 180 235
3-6: 4,5-Bakerish-a; 5-Butch Cassidy app. 20 40 60 112 161 210
52-(Reprint, M.S. Dist.)-1954? No date given (becomes My Love Secret #53)
8 16 24 46 58 70

WESTERN THRILLERS (Cowboy Action #5 on)
Atlas Comics (ACI): Nov, 1954 - No. 4, Feb, 1955 (All-r/Western Outlaws & Sheriffs)

1 16 32 48 89 127 165
2-4 10 20 30 56 73 90
NOTE: ***Heath** c-3. **Maneely** a-1; c-2. **Powell** a-4. **Robinson** a-4. **Romita** c-4. **Tuska** a-2.*

WESTERN TRAILS (Ringo Kid Starring in...)
Atlas Comics (SAI): May, 1957 - No. 2, July, 1957

Western True Crime #16 © MAR

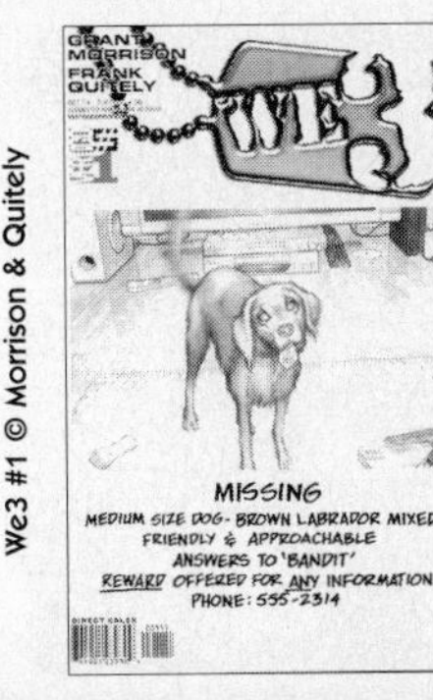

We3 #1 © Morrison & Quitely

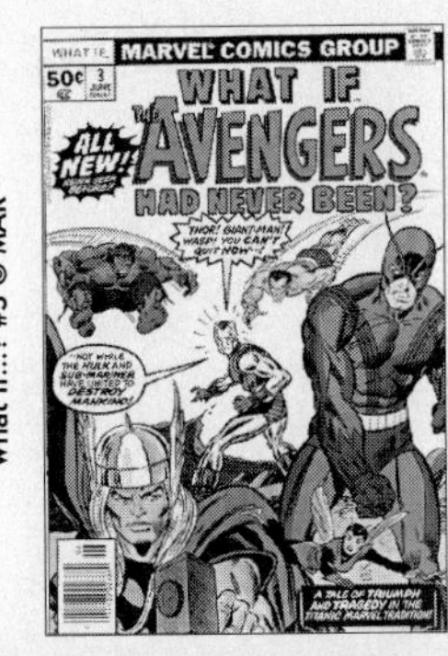

What If...? #3 © MAR

	GD 2.0	VG 4.0	FN 6.0	VF 8.0	VF/NM 9.0	NM- 9.2
1-Ringo Kid app.; Severin-c	14	28	42	79	110	140
2-Severin-c	9	18	27	52	66	80

NOTE: *Bolle a-1, 2.* ***Maneely*** *a-1, 2.* ***Severin*** *c-1, 2.*

WESTERN TRUE CRIME (Becomes My Confessions)
Fox Features Syndicate: No. 15, Aug, 1948 - No. 6, June, 1949

	GD 2.0	VG 4.0	FN 6.0	VF 8.0	VF/NM 9.0	NM- 9.2
15(#1)-Kamen-a; formerly Zoot #14 (5/48)?	33	66	99	190	275	360
16(#2)-Kamenish-a; headlight panels, violence	24	48	72	135	195	255
3-Kamen-a	25	50	75	144	207	270
4-6: 4-Johnny Craig-a	16	32	48	89	127	165

WESTERN WINNERS (Formerly All-Western Winners; becomes Black Rider #8 on & Romance Tales #7 on?)
Marvel Comics (CDS): No. 5, June, 1949 - No. 7, Dec, 1949

	GD 2.0	VG 4.0	FN 6.0	VF 8.0	VF/NM 9.0	NM- 9.2
5-Two-Gun Kid, Kid Colt, Black Rider; Shores-c	34	68	102	193	279	365
6-Two-Gun Kid, Black Rider, Heath Kid Colt story; Captain Tootsie by C.C. Beck	29	58	87	164	237	310
7-Randolph Scott Photo-c w/true stories about the West	29	58	87	164	237	310

WEST OF THE PECOS (See Zane Grey, 4-Color #222)

WESTWARD HO, THE WAGONS (Disney)
Dell Publishing Co.: No. 738, Sept, 1956 (Movie)

	GD 2.0	VG 4.0	FN 6.0	VF 8.0	VF/NM 9.0	NM- 9.2
Four Color 738-Fess Parker photo-c	11	22	33	75	110	145

WE3
DC Comics (Vertigo): Oct, 2004 - No. 3 ($2.95, limited series)

1,2-Grant Morrison-s/Frank Quitely-a 3.00

WETWORKS (See WildC.A.T.S: Covert Action Teams #2)
Image Comics (WildStorm): June, 1994 - No. 43, Aug, 1998 ($1.95/$2.50)

1-"July" on-c; gatefold wraparound-c; Portacio/Williams-c/a 3.00
1-Chicago Comicon edition 6.00
1-(2/98, $4.95) "3-D Edition" w/glasses 5.00
2-4 2.50
2-Alternate Portacio-c, see Deathblow #5 6.00
5-7,9-24: 5-($2.50). 13-Portacio-c. 16,17-Fire From Heaven Pts. 4 & 11 2.50
8 ($1.95)-Newstand, Wildstorm Rising Pt. 7 2.25
8 ($2.50)-Direct Market, Wildstorm Rising Pt. 7 2.50
25-($3.95) 4.00
26-43: 32-Variant-c by Pat Lee & Charest. 39,40-Stormwatch app. 42-Gen 13 app. 2.50
Sourcebook 1 (10/94, $2.50)-Text & illustrations (no comics) 2.50
Voyager Pack (8/97, $3.50)- #32 w/Phantom Guard preview 3.50

WETWORKS/VAMPIRELLA (See Vampirella/Wetworks)
Image Comics (WildStorm Productions): July, 1997 ($2.95, one-shot)

1-Gil Kane-c 3.00

WHACK (Satire)
St. John Publishing Co. (Jubilee Publ.): Oct, 1953 - No. 3, May, 1954

	GD 2.0	VG 4.0	FN 6.0	VF 8.0	VF/NM 9.0	NM- 9.2
1-(3-D, 25¢)-Kubert-a; Maurer-c; came w/glasses	33	66	99	190	275	360
2,3-Kubert-a in each. 2-Bing Crosby on-c; Mighty Mouse & Steve Canyon parodies. 3-Li'l Orphan Annie parody; Maurer-c	17	34	51	95	135	175

WHACKY (See Wacky)

WHAM COMICS (See Super Spy)
Centaur Publications: Nov, 1940 - No. 2, Dec, 1940

	GD 2.0	VG 4.0	FN 6.0	VF 8.0	VF/NM 9.0	NM- 9.2
1-The Sparkler, The Phantom Rider, Craig Carter and his Magic Ring, Detecto, Copper Slug, Speed Silvers by Gustavson, Speed Centaur & Jon Linton (s/f) begin	162	324	486	1013	1557	2100
2-Origin Blue Fire & Solarman; The Buzzard app.	108	216	324	675	1038	1400

WHAM-O GIANT COMICS
Wham-O Mfg. Co. : April, 1967 (98¢, newspaper size, one-shot)(Six issue subscription was advertised)

	GD 2.0	VG 4.0	FN 6.0	VF 8.0	VF/NM 9.0	NM- 9.2
1-Radian & Goody Bumpkin by Wood; 1 pg. Stanley-a; Fine, Tufts-a; flying saucer reports; wraparound-c	8	16	24	58	81	105

WHAT IF? (1st Series) (What If? Featuring... #13 & #?-33)
Marvel Comics Group: Feb, 1977 - No. 47, Oct, 1984; June, 1988 (All 52 pgs.)

	GD 2.0	VG 4.0	FN 6.0	VF 8.0	VF/NM 9.0	NM- 9.2
1-Brief origin Spider-Man, Fantastic Four	3	6	9	18	24	30
2-Origin The Hulk retold	2	4	6	9	11	14
3-5: 3-Avengers. 4-Invaders. 5-Capt. America	1	3	4	6	8	10
6-10,13,17: 8-Daredevil; Spidey parody. 9-Origins Venus, Marvel Boy, Human Robot, 3-D Man. 13-Conan app.; John Buscema-c/a(p). 17-Ghost Rider & Son of Satan app.	1	2	3	5	7	9
11,12,14-16: 11-Marvel Bullpen as F.F.						6.00
18-26,29: 18-Dr. Strange. 19-Spider-Man. 22-Origin Dr. Doom retold						5.00
27-X-Men app.; Miller-c	2	4	6	12	16	20
28-Daredevil by Miller; Ghost Rider app.	2	4	6	9	11	14
30-"What If...Spider-Man's Clone Had Lived?"	1	2	3	5	7	9
31-Begin $1.00-c; featuring Wolverine & the Hulk; X-Men app.; death of Hulk, Wolverine & Magneto	2	4	6	14	18	22
32-34,36-47: 32,36-Byrne-a. 34-Marvel crew each draw themselves. 37-Old X-Men & Silver Surfer app. 39-Thor battles Conan						4.00
35-What if Elektra had lived?; Miller/Austin-a.	1	2	3	5	6	8
Special 1 ($1.50, 6/88)-Iron Man, F.F., Thor app.						3.00

NOTE: ***Austin*** *a-27p, 32i, 34, 35i; c-35i, 36i.* ***J. Buscema*** *a-13p, 15p; c-10, 13p, 23p.* ***Byrne*** *a-32i, 36; c-36p.* ***Colan*** *a-21p; c-17p, 18p, 21p.* ***Ditko*** *a-35, Special 1.* ***Golden*** *c-29, 40-42.* ***Guice*** *a-40p.* ***Gil Kane*** *a-3p, 24p; c(p)-2-4, 7, 8.* ***Kirby*** *a-11p; c-9p, 11p.* ***Layton*** *a-32i, 33i; c-30, 32p, 33i, 34.* ***Mignola*** *c-39i.* ***Miller*** *a-28p, 32i, 34(1), 35p; c-27, 28p.* ***Mooney*** *a-8i, 30i.* ***Perez*** *a-15p.* ***Robbins*** *a-4p.* ***Sienkiewicz*** *c-43-46.* ***Simonson*** *a-15p, 32i.* ***Starlin*** *a-32i.* ***Stevens*** *a-8, 16i(part).* ***Sutton*** *a-2i, 18p, 28.* ***Tuska*** *a-5p.* ***Weiss*** *a-37p.*

WHAT IF...? (2nd Series)
Marvel Comics: V2#1, July, 1989 - No. 114, Nov, 1998 ($1.25/$1.50)

V2#1-...The Avengers Had Lost the Evol. War 4.00
2-5: 2-Daredevil, Punisher app. 3.00
6-X-Men app. 4.00
7-Wolverine app.; Liefeld-c/a(1st on Wolvie?) 5.00
8,10,11,13-15,17-30: 10-Punisher app. 11-Fantastic Four app.; McFarlane-c(i).13-Prof. X; Jim Lee-c. 14-Capt. Marvel; Lim/Austin-c.15-F.F.; Capullo-c/a(p). 17-Spider-Man/Kraven. 18-F.F. 19-Vision. 20,21-Spider-Man. 22-Silver Surfer by Lim/Austin-c/a 23-X-Men. 24-Wolverine; Punisher app. 25-(52 pgs.)-Wolverine app. 26-Punisher app. 27-Namor/F.F. 28,29-Capt. America. 29-Swipes cover to Avengers #4. 30-(52 pgs.)-F.F. 3.00
9,12-X-Men 3.50
16-Wolverine battles Conan; Red Sonja app.; X-Men cameo 4.00
31-104: 31-Cosmic Spider-Man & Venom app.; Hobgoblin cameo. 32,33-Phoenix; X-Men app. 35-Fantastic Five (w/Spidey). 36-Avengers vs. Guardians of the Galaxy. 37-Wolverine; Thibert-c(i). 38-Thor; Rogers-p(part). 40-Storm; X-Men app. 41-(52 pgs.)-Avengers vs. Galactus. 42-Spider-Man. 43-Wolverine. 44-Venom/Punisher. 45-Ghost Rider. 46-Cable. 47-Magneto. 49-Infinity Gauntlet w/Silver Surfer & Thanos. 50-(52 pgs.)-Foil embossed-c; "What If Hulk Had Killed Wolverine" 52-Dr. Doom. 54-Death's Head. 57-Punisher as Shield. 58-"What if Punisher Had Killed Spider-Man" w/cover similar to Amazing S-M #129. 59-...Wolverine led Alpha Flight. 60-X-Men Wedding Album. 61-bound-in card sheet. 61,86,88-Spider-Man. 74,77,81,84,85-X-Men. 76-Last app. Watcher in title. 78-Bisley-c. 80-Hulk. 87-Sabretooth. 89-Fantastic Four. 90-Cyclops & Havok. 91-The Hulk. 93-Wolverine. 94-Juggernaut. 95-Ghost Rider. 97-Black Knight. 100-($2.99, double-sized) Gambit and Rogue, Fantastic Four 3.00

	GD 2.0	VG 4.0	FN 6.0	VF 8.0	VF/NM 9.0	NM- 9.2
105-Spider-Girl debut; Sienkiewicz-a	2	4	6	12	16	20

106-114: 106-Gambit. 108-Avengers. 111-Wolverine. 114-Secret Wars 2.25
#(-1) Flashback (7/97) 3.00

'WHAT'S NEW? - THE COLLECTED ADVENTURES OF PHIL & DIXIE'
Palliard Press: Oct, 1991 - No. 2, 1991 ($5.95, mostly color, sq.-bound, 52 pgs.)

1,2-By Phil Foglio 6.00

WHAT THE- -?!
Marvel Comics: Aug, 1988 - No. 26, 1993 ($1.25/$1.50/$2.50, semi-annual #5 on)

1-All contain parodies 3.00
2-24: 3-X-Men parody; Todd McFarlane-a. 5-Punisher/Wolverine parody; Jim Lee-a. 6-Punisher, Wolverine, Alpha Flight. 9-Wolverine. 16-EC back-c parody. 17-Wolverine/Punisher parody. 18-Star Trek parody w/Wolverine. 19-Punisher, Wolverine, Ghost Rider. 21-Weapon X parody. 22-Punisher/Wolverine parody 2.25
25-Summer Special 1 (1993, $2.50)-X-Men parody 2.50
26-Fall Special ($2.50, 68 pgs.)-Spider-Ham 2099-c/story; origin Silver Surfer; Hulk & Doomsday parody; indica reads "Winter Special." 2.50

NOTE: ***Austin*** *a-6i.* ***Byrne*** *a-2, 6, 10; c-2, 6-8, 10, 12, 13.* ***Golden*** *a-22.* ***Dale Keown*** *a-8p(8 pgs.).* ***McFarlane*** *a-3.* ***Rogers*** *c-15i, 16p.* ***Severin*** *a-2.* ***Staton*** *a-21p.* ***Williamson*** *a-2i.*

WHEE COMICS (Also see Gay, Smile & Tickle Comics)
Modern Store Publications: 1955 (7¢, 5x7-1/4", 52 pgs.)

	GD 2.0	VG 4.0	FN 6.0	VF 8.0	VF/NM 9.0	NM- 9.2
1-Funny animal	6	12	18	28	34	40

WHEEDIES (See Panic #11 -EC Comics)

WHEELIE AND THE CHOPPER BUNCH (TV)
Charlton Comics: July, 1975 - No. 7, July, 1976 (Hanna-Barbera)

	GD 2.0	VG 4.0	FN 6.0	VF 8.0	VF/NM 9.0	NM- 9.2
1-3: 1-Byrne text illo (see Nightmare for 1st art); Staton-a. 2-Byrne-a. 2,3-Mike Zeck text illos. 3-Staton-a; Byrne-c/a	3	6	9	18	24	30
4-7-Staton-a	2	4	6	12	16	20

WHEN KNIGHTHOOD WAS IN FLOWER (See The Sword & the Rose, 4-Color #505, 682)

WHEN SCHOOL IS OUT (See Wisco in Promotional Comics section)

WHERE CREATURES ROAM
Marvel Comics Group: July, 1970 - No. 8, Sept, 1971

Where in the World is Carmen Sandiego #4 © DC

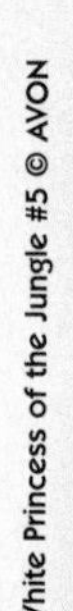
White Princess of the Jungle #5 © AVON

Whiz Comics #2(#3) © FAW

	GD 2.0	VG 4.0	FN 6.0	VF 8.0	VF/NM 9.0	NM- 9.2
1-Kirby/Ayers-c/a(r)	4	8	12	22	30	38
2-8-Kirby-c/a(r)	3	6	9	16	20	25

NOTE: *Ditko r-1-6, 7. **Heck** r-2, 5. All contain pre super-hero reprints.*

WHERE IN THE WORLD IS CARMEN SANDIEGO (TV)
DC Comics: June, 1996 - No. 4, Dec, 1996 ($1.75)

1-4: Adaptation of TV show 2.25

WHERE MONSTERS DWELL
Marvel Comics Group: Jan, 1970 - No. 38, Oct, 1975

1-Kirby/Ditko-r; all contain pre super-hero-r	4	8	12	24	32	40
2-10: 4-Crandall-a(r)	3	6	9	16	21	26
11,13-20: 11-Last 15¢ issue. 18,20-Starlin-c	2	4	6	12	16	20
12-Giant issue (52 pgs.)	3	6	9	19	25	32
21-37	2	4	6	10	13	16
38-Williamson-r/World of Suspense #3	2	4	6	12	16	20

NOTE: ***Colan** r-12. **Ditko** a(r)-4, 6, 8, 10, 12, 17-19, 23-25, 37. **Kirby** r-1-3, 5-16, 18-27, 30-32, 34-36, 38; c-12? **Reinman** a-3r, 4r, 12r. **Severin** c-15.*

WHERE'S HUDDLES? (TV) (See Fun-In #9)
Gold Key: Jan, 1971 - No. 3, Dec, 1971 (Hanna-Barbera)

1	4	8	12	22	30	38
2,3: 3-r/most #1	2	4	6	12	16	20

WHIP WILSON (Movie star) (Formerly Rex Hart; Gunhawk #12 on; see Western Hearts, Western Life Romances, Western Love)
Marvel Comics: No. 9, April, 1950 - No. 11, Sept, 1950 (#9,10: 52 pgs.)

9-Photo-c; Whip Wilson & his horse Bullet begin; origin Bullet; issue #23 listed on splash page; cover changed to #9	60	120	180	375	580	785
10,11: Both have photo-c. 11-36 pgs.	37	74	111	209	305	400
I.W. Reprint #1(1964)-Kinstler-c; r-Marvel #11	3	6	9	19	25	32

WHIRLWIND COMICS (Also see Cyclone Comics)
Nita Publication: June, 1940 - No. 3, Sept, 1940

1-Origin & 1st app. Cyclone; Cyclone-c	200	400	600	1250	1925	2600
2,3: Cyclone-c	104	208	312	650	1000	1350

WHIRLYBIRDS (TV)
Dell Publishing Co.: No. 1124, Aug, 1960 - No. 1216, Oct-Dec, 1961

Four Color 1124 (#1)-Photo-c	10	20	30	70	100	130
Four Color 1216-Photo-c	9	18	27	65	93	120

WHISKEY DICKEL, INTERNATIONAL COWGIRL
Image Comics: Aug, 2003 ($12.95, softcover, B&W)

nn-Mark Ricketts-s/Mike Hawthorne-a; pin-up by various incl. Oeming, Thompson, Mack 13.00

WHISPER (Female Ninja)
Capital Comics: Dec, 1983 - No. 2, 1984 ($1.75, Baxter paper)

1,2: 1-Origin; Golden-c, Special (11/85, $2.50) 2.50

WHISPER (Vol. 2)
First Comics: Jun, 1986 - No. 37, June, 1990 ($1.25/$1.75/$1.95)

1-37 2.25

WHITE CHIEF OF THE PAWNEE INDIANS
Avon Periodicals: 1951

nn-Kit West app.; Kinstler-c	17	34	51	95	135	175

WHITE EAGLE INDIAN CHIEF (See Indian Chief)

WHITE FANG
Disney Comics: 1990 ($5.95, 68 pgs.)

nn-Graphic novel adapting new Disney movie 6.00

WHITE INDIAN
Magazine Enterprises: No. 11, July, 1953 - No. 15, 1954

11(A-1 94), 12(A-1 101), 13(A-1 104)-Frazetta-r(Dan Brand) in all from Durango Kid. 11-Powell-c	24	48	72	135	195	255
14(A-1 117), 15(A-1 135)-Check-a; Torres-a-#15	12	24	36	71	98	125

NOTE: *#11 contains reprints from Durango Kid #1-4; #12 from #5, 9, 10, 11; #13 from #7, 12, 13, 16. #14 & 15 contain all new stories.*

WHITEOUT (Also see Queen & Country)
Oni Press: July, 1998 - No. 4, Nov, 1998 ($2.95, B&W, limited series)

1-4: 1-Matt Wagner-c. 2-Mignola-c. 3-Gibbons-c 3.00
TPB (5/99, $10.95) r/#1-4; Miller-c 11.00

WHITEOUT: MELT
Oni Press: Sept, 1999 - No. 4, Feb, 2000 ($2.95, B&W, limited series)

1-4-Greg Rucka-s/Steve Lieber-a 3.00

WHITE PRINCESS OF THE JUNGLE (Also see Jungle Adventures & Top Jungle Comics)
Avon Periodicals: July, 1951 - No. 5, Nov, 1952

1-Origin of White Princess (Taanda) & Capt'n Courage (r); Kinstler-c	55	110	165	340	520	700
2-Reprints origin of Malu, Slave Girl Princess from Avon's Slave Girl Comics #1 w/Malu changed to Zora; Kinstler-c/a(2)	40	80	120	239	357	475
3-Origin Blue Gorilla; Kinstler-c/a	37	74	112	213	312	410
4-Jack Barnum, White Hunter app.; r/Sheena #9	32	64	96	184	267	350
5-Blue Gorilla by McCann?; Kinstler inside-c; Fawcette/Alascia-a(3)	35	70	105	198	287	375

WHITE RIDER AND SUPER HORSE (Formerly Humdinger V2#2; Indian Warriors #7 on; also see Blue Bolt #1, 4Most & Western Crime Cases)
Novelty-Star Publications/Accepted Publ.: No. 4, 9/50 - No. 6, 3/51

4-6-Adapts "The Last of the Mohicans". 4(#1)-(9/50)-Says #11 on inside	17	34	51	95	135	175
Accepted Reprint #5(r/#5),6 (nd); L.B. Cole-c	9	18	27	52	66	80

NOTE: *All have **L. B. Cole** covers.*

WHITE WILDERNESS (Disney)
Dell Publishing Co.: No. 943, Oct, 1958

Four Color 943-Movie	8	16	24	53	74	95

WHITMAN COMIC BOOK, A
Whitman Publishing Co.: Sept., 1962 (136 pgs.; 7-3/4x5-3/4; hardcover) (B&W)

1-3,5,7: 1-Yogi Bear. 2-Huckleberry Hound. 3-Mr. Jinks and Pixie & Dixie. 5-Augie Doggie & Loopy de Loop. 7-Bugs Bunny-r from #47,51,53,54 & 55	8	16	24	53	74	95
4,6: 4-The Flintstones. 6-Snooper & Blabber Fearless Detectives/Quick Draw McGraw of the Wild West	8	16	24	58	82	105
8-Donald Duck-reprints most of WDC&S #209-213. Includes 5 Barks stories, 1 complete Mickey Mouse serial by Paul Murry & 1 Mickey Mouse serial missing the 1st episode	9	18	27	65	93	120

NOTE: *Hanna-Barbera #1-6(TV), reprints of British tabloid comics. Dell reprints-#7,8.*

WHIZ COMICS (Formerly Flash & Thrill Comics #1)(See 5 Cent Comics)
Fawcett Publications: No. 2, Feb, 1940 - No. 155, June, 1953

1-(nn on cover, #2 inside)-Origin & 1st newsstand app. Captain Marvel (formerly Captain Thunder) by C. C. Beck (created by Bill Parker), Spy Smasher, Golden Arrow, Ibis the Invincible, Dan Dare, Scoop Smith, Sivana, & Lance O'Casey begin	7000	14,000	21,000	40,000	64,000	88,000

(The only Mint copy sold in 1995 for $176,000 cash)

1-Reprint, oversize 13-1/2x10". **WARNING**: This comic is an exact duplicate reprint (except for dropping "Gangway for Captain Marvel" from-c) of the original except for its size. DC published it in 1974 with a second cover titling it as a Famous First Edition. There have been many reported cases of the outer cover being removed and the interior sold as the original edition. The reprint with the new outer cover removed is practically worthless. See Famous First Edition for value.

2-(3/40, nn on cover, #3 inside); cover to Flash #1 redrawn, pg. 12, panel 4; Spy Smasher reveals I.D. to Eve	452	904	1356	3164	5082	7000
3-(4/40, #3 on-c, #4 inside)-1st app. Beautia	317	634	951	2061	3331	4600
4-(5/40, #4 on cover, #5 inside)-Brief origin Capt. Marvel retold	292	584	876	1825	2813	3800
5-Captain Marvel wears button-down flap on splash page only	246	492	738	1538	2369	3200
6-10: 7-Dr. Voodoo begins (by Raboy-#9-22)	185	370	555	1156	1778	2400
11-14: 12-Capt. Marvel does not wear cape	127	254	381	794	1222	1650
15-Origin Sivana; Dr. Voodoo by Raboy	137	274	411	856	1316	1775
16-18-Spy Smasher battles Captain Marvel	131	262	393	819	1260	1700
19,20	87	174	261	544	835	1125
21-(9/41)-Origin & 1st cover app. Lt. Marvels, the 1st team in Fawcett comics. In this issue, Capt. Death similar to Ditko's later Dr. Strange	90	180	270	563	869	1175
22-24: 23-Only Dr. Voodoo by Tuska	69	138	207	431	666	900
25-(12/41)-Captain Nazi jumps from Master Comics #21 to take on Capt. Marvel solo after being beaten by Capt. Marvel/Bulletman team, causing the creation of Capt. Marvel Jr.; 1st app./origin of Capt. Marvel Jr. (part II of trilogy origin by CC. Beck & Mac Raboy); Captain Marvel sends Jr. back to Master #22 to aid Bulletman against Capt. Nazi; origin Old Shazam in text	542	1084	1626	3794	6097	8400
26-30	62	124	186	388	594	800
31,32: 32-1st app. The Trolls; Hitler/Mussolini satire by Beck	55	110	165	336	511	685
33-Spy Smasher, Captain Marvel x-over on cover and inside	62	124	186	388	594	800
34,36-40: 37-The Trolls app. by Swayze	40	80	120	239	357	475
35-Captain Marvel & Spy Smasher-c	50	100	150	305	465	625
41-50: 43-Spy Smasher, Ibis, Golden Arrow x-over in Capt. Marvel. 44-Flag-c. 47-Origin recap (1 pg.)	37	74	111	209	305	400

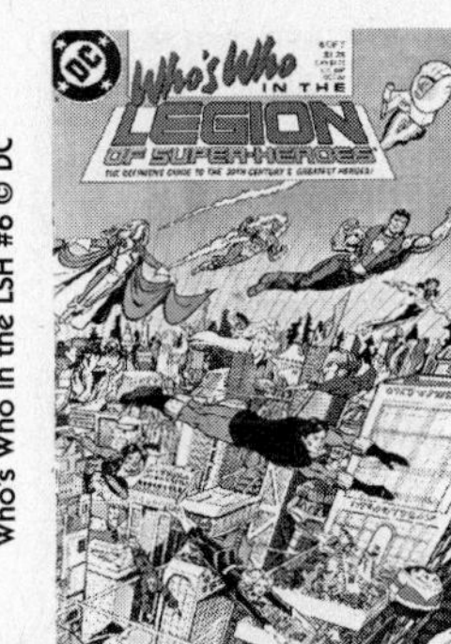

Who's Who in the LSH #6 © DC

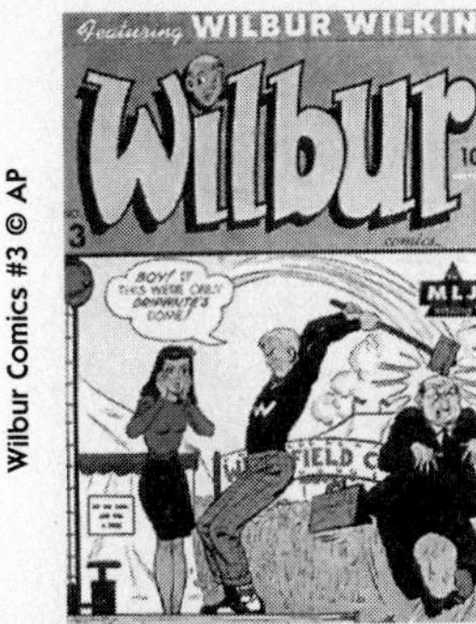

Wilbur Comics #3 © AP

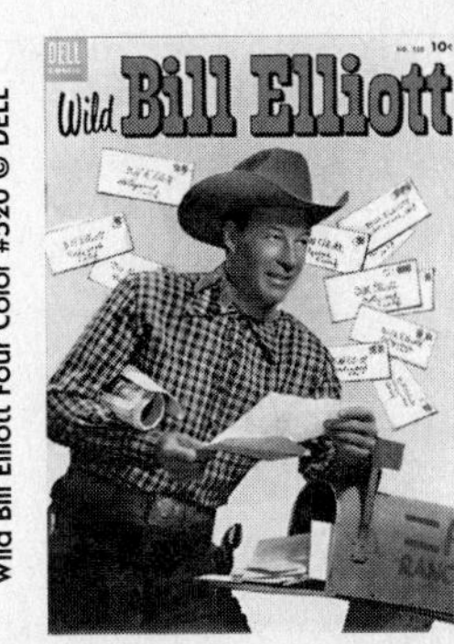

Wild Bill Elliott Four Color #520 © DELL

GD VG FN VF VF/NM NM-
2.0 4.0 6.0 8.0 9.0 9.2

51-60: 52-Capt. Marvel x-over in Ibis. 57-Spy Smasher, Golden Arrow, Ibis cameo
30 60 90 173 249 325
61-70 28 56 84 158 229 300
71,77-80 26 52 78 147 211 275
72-76-Two Captain Marvel stories in each; 76-Spy Smasher becomes Crime Smasher
26 52 78 150 215 280
81-99: 86-Captain Marvel battles Sivana Family; robot-c. 91-Infinity-c
26 52 78 147 211 275
100-(8/48)-Anniversary issue 30 60 90 170 245 320
101-106: 102-Commando Yank app. 106-Bulletman app.
25 50 75 141 203 265
107-149: 107-Capitol Building photo-c. 108-Brooklyn Bridge photo-c. 112-Photo-c. 139-Infinity-c. 140-Flag-c. 142-Used in **POP**, pg. 89
25 50 75 141 203 265
150-152-(Low dist.) 27 54 81 152 219 285
153-155-(Scarce):154,155-1st/2nd Dr. Death stories 35 70 105 198 287 375
NOTE: **C.C. Beck** *Captain Marvel-No. 25(part).* **Krigstein** *Golden Arrow-No. 75, 78, 91, 95, 96, 98-100.* **Mac Raboy** *Dr. Voodoo-No. 9-22. Captain Marvel-No. 25(part).* **M.Swayze** *a-37, 38, 59; c-38.* **Schaffenberger** *c-138-155(most).* **Wolverton** *1/2 pg. "Culture Corner"-No. 65-67, 68(2 1/2 pgs), 70-85, 87-96, 98-100, 102-109, 112-121, 123, 125, 126, 128-131, 133, 134, 136, 142, 143, 146.*

WHIZ KIDS (Also see Big Bang Comics)
Image Comics: Apr, 2003 ($4.95, B&W, one-shot)
1-Galahad, Cyclone, Thunder Girl and Moray app.; Jeff Austin-a 5.00

WHOA, NELLIE (Also see Love & Rockets)
Fantagraphics Books: July, 1996 - No. 3, Sept, 1996 ($2.95, B&W, lim. series)
1-3: Jamie Hernandez-c/a/scripts 3.00

WHODUNIT
D.S. Publishing Co.: Aug-Sept, 1948 - No. 3, Dec-Jan, 1948-49 (#1,2: 52 pgs.)
1-Baker-a (7 pgs.) 26 52 78 147 211 275
2,3-Detective mysteries 13 26 39 74 102 130

WHODUNNIT?
Eclipse Comics: June, 1986 - No. 3, Apr, 1987 ($2.00, limited series)
1-3: Spiegle-a. 2-Gulacy-c 2.25

WHO FRAMED ROGER RABBIT (See Marvel Graphic Novel)

WHO IS NEXT?
Standard Comics: No. 5, Jan, 1953
5-Toth, Sekowsky, Andru-a; crime stories 21 42 63 118 169 220

WHO IS THE CROOKED MAN?
Crusade: Sept, 1996 ($3.50, B&W, 40 pgs.)
1-Intro The Martyr, Scarlet 7 & Garrison 3.50

WHO'S MINDING THE MINT? (See Movie Classics)

WHO'S WHO IN STAR TREK
DC Comics: Mar, 1987 - #2, Apr, 1987 ($1.50, limited series)
1,2 6.00
NOTE: **Byrne** *a-1, 2.* **Chaykin** *c-1, 2.* **Morrow** *a-1, 2.* **McFarlane** *a-2.* **Perez** *a-1, 2.* **Sutton** *a-1, 2.*

WHO'S WHO IN THE LEGION OF SUPER-HEROES
DC Comics: Apr, 1987 - No. 7, Nov, 1988 ($1.25, limited series)
1-7 4.00

WHO'S WHO: THE DEFINITIVE DIRECTORY OF THE DC UNIVERSE
DC Comics: Mar, 1985 - No. 26, Apr, 1987 (Maxi-series, no ads)
1-DC heroes from A-Z 4.00
2-26: All have 1-2 pgs-a by most DC artists 4.00
NOTE: **Art Adams** *a-4, 11, 18, 20.* **Anderson** *a-1-5, 7-12, 14, 15, 19, 21, 23-25.* **Aparo** *a-2, 3, 9, 10, 12, 13, 14, 15, 17, 18, 21, 23.* **Byrne** *a-4, 7, 14, 16, 18i, 19, 22i, 24; c-22.* **Cowan** *a-3-5, 8, 10-13, 16-18, 22-25.* **Ditko** *a-19-22.* **Evans** *a-20.* **Giffen** *a-1, 3,-6, 8, 13, 15, 17, 18, 23.* **Grell** *a-6, 9, 14, 20, 23, 25, 26.* **Infantino** *a-1-10, 12, 15, 17-22, 24, 25.* **Kaluta** *a-14, 21.* **Gil Kane** *a-1-11, 13, 14, 16, 19, 21-23, 25.* **Kirby** *a-2-6, 8-18, 20, 22, 25.* **Kubert** *a-2, 3, 7-11, 19, 20, 25.* **Erik Larsen** *a-24.* **McFarlane** *a-10-12, 17, 19, 25, 26.* **Morrow** *a-4, 7, 25, 26.* **Orlando** *a-1, 4, 10, 11, 21i.* **Perez** *a-1-5, 8-19, 22-26; c-1-4, 13-18.* **Rogers** *a-1, 2, 5-7, 11, 12, 15, 24.* **Starlin** *a-13, 14, 16.* **Stevens** *a-4, 7, 18.*

WHO'S WHO UPDATE '87
DC Comics: Aug, 1987 - No. 5, Dec, 1987 ($1.25, limited series)
1-5: Contains art by most DC artists 3.00
NOTE: **Giffen** *a-1.* **McFarlane** *a-1-4; c-4.* **Perez** *a-1-4.*

WHO'S WHO UPDATE '88
DC Comics: Aug, 1988 - No. 4, Nov, 1988 ($1.25, limited series)
1-4: Contains art by most DC artists 3.00
NOTE: **Giffen** *a-1.* **Erik Larsen** *a-1.*

WICKED, THE
Avalon Studios: Dec, 1999 - No. 7, Aug, 2000 ($2.95)
Preview-(7/99, $5.00, B&W) 5.00
1-7-Anacleto-c/Martinez-a 3.00
...: Medusa's Tale (11/00, $3.95, one shot) story plus pin-up gallery 4.00
...: Vol. 1: Omnibus (2003, $19.95) r/#0-8; Drew-c 20.00

WICKED WEST, THE
Image Comics: Oct, 2004 ($9.95, graphic novel, one-shot)
1-Neil Vokes-a/Todd Livingston & Robert Tinnell-s; vampires in the Wild West 10.00

WILBUR COMICS (Teen-age) (Also see Laugh Comics, Laugh Comix, Liberty Comics #10 & Zip Comics)
MLJ Magazines/Archie Publ. No. 8, Spring, 1946 on: Sum', 1944 - No. 87, 11/59; No. 88, 9/63; No. 89, 10/64; No. 90, 10/65 (No. 1-46: 52 pgs.) (#1-11 are quarterly)
1 50 100 150 305 465 625
2(Fall, 1944) 29 58 87 164 237 310
3,4(Wint, '44-45; Spr, '45) 21 42 63 118 169 220
5-1st app. Katy Keene (Sum, '45) & begin series; Wilbur story same as Archie story in Archie #1 except Wilbur replaces Archie 89 178 267 556 853 1150
6-10: 10-(Fall, 1946) 24 48 72 135 195 255
11-20 15 30 45 83 117 150
21-30: 30-(4/50) 10 20 30 58 77 95
31-50 8 16 24 46 58 70
51-70 8 16 24 40 50 60
71-90: 88-Last 10¢ issue (9/63) 4 8 12 29 40 50
NOTE: *Katy Keene in No. 5-56, 58-61, 63-69.* **Al Fagaly** *c-6-9, 12-24 at least.* **Vigoda** *c-2.*

WILD
Atlas Comics (IPC): Feb, 1954 - No. 5, Aug, 1954
1 27 54 81 154 222 290
2 16 32 48 89 127 165
3-5 14 28 42 79 110 140
NOTE: **Berg** *a-5; c-4.* **Burgos** *c-3.* **Colan** *a-4.* **Everett** *a-1-3.* **Heath** *a-2, 3, 5.* **Maneely** *a-1-3, 5; c-1, 5.* **Post** *a-2, 5.* **Ed Win** *a-1, 3.*

WILD (This Magazine Is...) (Satire)
Dell Publishing Co.: Jan, 1968 - No. 3, 1968 (Magazine, 52 pgs.)
1-3 3 6 9 16 20 24

WILD ANIMALS
Pacific Comics: Dec, 1982 ($1.00, one-shot, direct sales)
1-Funny animal; Sergio Aragones-a; Shaw-c/a 4.00

WILD BILL ELLIOTT (Also see Western Roundup under Dell Giants)
Dell Publishing Co.: No. 278, 5/50 - No. 643, 7/55 (No #11,12) (All photo-c)
Four Color 278(#1, 52pgs.)-Titled "Bill Elliott"; Bill & his horse Stormy begin; photo front/back-c begin 14 28 42 102 156 210
2 (11/50), 3 (52 pgs.) 9 18 27 60 85 110
4-10(10-12/52) 7 14 21 46 63 80
Four Color 472(6/53),520(12/53)-Last photo back-c 6 12 18 38 52 65
13(4-6/54) - 17(4-6/55) 5 10 15 36 48 60
Four Color 643 (7/55) 5 10 15 33 44 55

WILD BILL HICKOK (Also see Blazing Sixguns)
Avon Periodicals: Sept-Oct, 1949 - No. 28, May-June, 1956
1-Ingels-c 24 48 72 138 199 260
2-Painted-c; Kit West app. 12 24 36 71 98 125
3-5-Painted-c (4-Cover by Howard Winfield) 9 18 27 52 66 80
6-10,12: 8-10-Painted-c. 12-Kinsler-c? 9 18 27 52 66 80
11,13,14-Kinstler-c/a (#11-c & inside-f/c art only) 10 20 30 56 73 90
15,17,18,20: 18-Kit West story. 20-Kit West by Larsen
8 16 24 43 54 65
16-Kamen-a; r-3 stories/King of the Badmen of Deadwood
8 16 24 46 58 70
19-Meskin-a 8 16 24 43 54 65
21-Reprints 2 stories/Chief Crazy Horse 8 16 24 40 50 60
22-McCann-a?; r/Sheriff Bob Dixon's... 8 16 24 40 50 60
23-27: 23-Kinstler-c. 24-27-Kinstler-c/a(r) (24,25-r?) 8 16 24 40 50 60
28-Kinstler-c/a (new); r-/Last of the Comanches 8 16 24 43 54 65
I.W. Reprint #1-r/#2; Kinstler-c 2 4 6 10 13 16
Super Reprint #10-12: 10-r/#18. 11-r/#?. 12-r/#8 2 4 6 10 13 16
NOTE: *#23, 25 contain numerous editing deletions in both art and script due to code.* **Kinstler** *c-6, 7, 11-14, 17, 18, 20-22, 24-28.* **Howard Larsen** *a-1, 2, 4, 5, 6(3), 7-9, 11, 12, 17, 18, 20-24, 26.* **Meskin** *a-7.* **Reinman** *a-6, 17.*

WILD BILL HICKOK AND JINGLES (TV)(Formerly Cowboy Western) (Also see Blue Bird)
Charlton Comics: No. 68, Aug, 1958 - No. 75, Dec, 1959
68,69-Williamson-a (all are 10¢ issues) 11 22 33 62 84 105

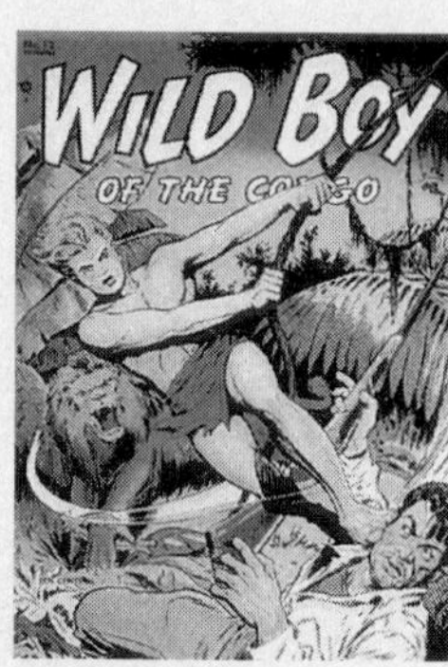

Wild Boy of the Congo #12 © Z-D

WildC.A.T.S. #16 © WSP

Wildcore #7 © WSP

70-Two pgs. Williamson-a 8 16 24 43 54 65
71-75 (#76, exist?) 6 12 18 28 34 40

WILD BILL PECOS WESTERN (Also see The Westerner)
AC Comics: 1989 ($3.50, 1/2 color/1/2 B&W, 52 pgs.)

1-Syd Shores-c/a(r)/Westerner; photo back-c 4.00

WILD BOY OF THE CONGO (Also see Approved Comics)
Ziff-Davis No. 10-12,4-8/St. John No. 9,11 on: No. 10, 2-3/51 - No. 12, 8-9/51; No. 4, 10-11/51 - No. 9, 10/53; No. 11-#15,6/55 (No #10, 1953)

10(#1)(2-3/51)-Origin; bondage-c by Saunders (painted); used in **SOTI**, pg. 189; painted-c begin, end #9 24 48 72 138 199 260
11(4-5/51),12(8-9/51)-Norman Saunders painted-c 13 26 39 74 102 130
4(10-11/51)-Saunders painted bondage-c 13 26 39 74 102 130
5(Winter,'51)-Saunders painted-c 11 22 33 64 87 110
6,8,9(10/53): 6-Saunders-c. 6-9-Painted-c 11 22 33 64 87 110
7(8-9/52)-Kinstler-a 13 26 39 74 102 130
11-13-Baker-c. 11-r/#7 w/new Baker-c; Kinstler-a (2 pgs.) 14 28 42 79 110 140
14(4/55)-Baker-c; r-#12('51) 14 28 42 79 110 140
15(6/55) 10 20 30 58 77 95

WILDCAT (See Sensation Comics #1)

WILDC.A.T.S ADVENTURES (TV cartoon)
Image Comics (WildStorm): Sept, 1994 - No. 10, June, 1995 ($1.95/$2.50)

1-10 2.50
Sourcebook 1 (1/95, $2.95) 3.00

WILDC.A.T.S: COVERT ACTION TEAMS
Image Comics (WildStorm Productions): Aug, 1992 - No. 4, Mar, 1993; No. 5, Nov, 1993 - No. 50, June, 1998 ($1.95/$2.50)

1-1st app; Jim Lee/Williams-c/a & Lee scripts begin; contains 2 trading cards (Two diff versions of cards inside); 1st WildStorm Productions title 4.50
1-All gold foil signed edition 12.00
1-All gold foil unsigned edition 8.00
1-Newsstand edition w/o cards 3.00
1-"3-D Special"(8/97, $4.95) w/3-D glasses; variant-c by Jim Lee. 5.00
2-($2.50)-Prism foil stamped-c; contains coupon for Image Comics #0 & 4 pg. preview to Portacio's Wetworks (back-up) 4.50
2-With coupon missing 2.25
2-Direct sale misprint w/o foil-c 3.00
2-Newsstand ed., no prism or coupon 2.25
3-Lee/Liefeld-c (1/93-c, 12/92 inside) 3.50
4-($2.50)-Polybagged w/Topps trading card; 1st app. Tribe by Johnson & Stroman; Youngblood cameo 3.50
4-Variant w/red card 6.00
5-7-Jim Lee/Williams-c/a; Lee script 3.00
8-X-Men's Jean Grey & Scott Summers cameo 4.00
9-12: 10-1st app. Huntsman & Soldier; Claremont scripts begin, ends #13. 11-1st app. Savant, Tapestry & Mr. Majestic. 3.00
11-Alternate Portacio-c, see Deathblow #5 5.00
13-19,21-24: 15-James Robinson scripts begin, ends #20. 15,16-Black Razor story. 21-Alan Moore scripts begin, end #34; intro Tao & Ladytron; new WildC.A.T.S team forms (Mr. Majestic, Savant, Condition Red (Max Cash), Tao & Ladytron). 22-Maguire-a 3.00
20-($2.50)-Direct Market, WildStorm Rising Pt. 2 w/bound-in card 3.00
20-($1.95)-Newsstand, WildStorm Rising Part 2 2.25
25-($4.95)-Alan Moore script; wraparound foil-c. 5.00
26-49: 29-(5/96)-Fire From Heaven Pt 7; reads Apr on-c. 30-(6/96)-Fire From Heaven Pt. 13; Spartan revealed to have transplanted personality of John Colt (from Team One: WildC.A.T.S). 31-(9/96)-Grifter rejoins team; Ladytron dies 2.50
40-($3.50)Voyager Pack bagged w/Divine Right preview 6.00
50-($3.50) Stories by Robinson/Lee, Choi & Peterson/Benes, and Moore/Charest; Charest sketchbook; Lee wraparound-c 4.00
50-Chromium cover 6.00
Annual 1 (2/98, $2.95) Robinson-s 3.00
Compendium (1993, $9.95)-r/#1-4; bagged w/#0 10.00
Sourcebook 1 (9/93, $2.50)-Foil embossed-c 2.50
Sourcebook 1-($1.95)-Newsstand ed. w/o foil embossed-c 2.25
Sourcebook 2 (11/94, $2.50)-wraparound-c 2.50
Special 1 (11/93, $3.50, 52 pgs.)-1st Travis Charest WildC.A.T.S-a 3.50
...A Gathering of Eagles (5/97, $9.95, TPB) r/#10-12 10.00
.../ Cyberforce: Killer Instinct TPB (2004, $14.95) r/#5-7 & Cyberforce V2 #1-3 15.00
...Gang War ('98, $16.95, TPB) r/#28-34 17.00
...Homecoming (8/98, $19.95, TPB) r/#21-27 20.00

WILDCATS
DC Comics (WildStorm): Mar, 1999 - No. 28, Dec, 2001 ($2.50)

1-Charest-a; six covers by Lee, Adams, Bisley, Campbell, Madureira and Ramos; Lobdell-s 3.00
1-($6.95) DF Edition; variant cover by Ramos 7.00
2-28: 2-Voodoo cover. 3-Bachalo variant-c. 5-Hitch-a/variant-c. 7-Meglia-a. 8-Phillips-a begins. 17-J.G. Jones-c. 18,19-Jim Lee-c. 20,21-Dillon-a 2.50
Annual 2000 (12/00, $3.50) Bermejo-a; Devil's Night x-over 3.50
...: Battery Park ('03, $17.95, TPB) r/#20-28; Phillips-c 18.00
... Ladytron (10/00, $5.95) Origin; Casey-s/Canete-a 6.00
... Mosaic (2/00, $3.95) Tuska-a (10 pg. back-up story) 4.00
...: Serial Boxes ('01, $14.95, TPB) r/#14-19; Phillips-c 15.00
...: Street Smart ('00, $24.95, HC) r/#1-6; Charest-c 25.00
...: Street Smart ('02, $14.95, SC) r/#1-6; Charest-c 15.00
...: Vicious Circles ('00, $14.95, TPB) r/#8-13; Phillips-c 15.00

WILDC.A.T.S/ ALIENS
Image Comics/Dark Horse: Aug, 1998 ($4.95, one-shot)

1-Ellis-s/Sprouse-a/c; Aliens invade Skywatch; Stormwatch app.; death of Winter; destruction of Skywatch 1 2 3 5 6 8
1-Variant-c by Gil Kane 1 3 4 6 8 10

WILDC.A.T.S: SAVANT GARDE FAN EDITION
Image Comics/WildStorm Productions: Feb, 1997 - No. 3, Apr, 1997 (Giveaway, 8 pgs.) (Polybagged w/Overstreet's FAN)

1-3: Barbara Kesel-s/Christian Uche-a(p) 3.00
1-3-(Gold): All retailer incentives 10.00

WILDC.A.T.S TRILOGY
Image Comics (WildStorm Productions): June, 1993 - No. 3, Dec, 1993 ($1.95, lim. series)

1-($2.50)-1st app. Gen 13 (Fairchild, Burnout, Grunge, Freefall) Multi-color foil-c; Jae Lee-c/a in all 5.00
1-($1.95)-Newsstand ed. w/o foil-c 2.25
2,3-($1.95)-Jae Lee-c/a 2.25

WILDCATS VERSION 3.0
DC Comics (WildStorm): Oct, 2002 - No. 24, Oct, 2004 ($2.95)

1-24: 1-Casey-s/Nguyen-a; two covers by Nguyen and Rian Hughes and Nguyen. 8-Back-up preview of The Authority: High Stakes pt. 3 3.00
...: Brand Building TPB (2003, $14.95) r/#1-6 15.00
...: Full Disclosure TPB (2004, $14.95) r/#7-12 15.00

WILDC.A.T.S/ X-MEN: THE GOLDEN AGE (See also X-Men/WildC.A.T.S.: The Dark Age)
Image Comics (WildStorm Productions): Feb, 1997 ($4.50, one-shot)

1-Lobdell-s/Charest-a; Two covers (Charest, Jim Lee) 5.00
1-"3-D" Edition ($6.50) w/glasses 7.00

WILDC.A.T.S/ X-MEN: THE MODERN AGE
Image Comics (WildStorm Productions): Aug, 1997 ($4.50, one-shot)

1-Robinson-s/Hughes-a; Two covers (Hughes, Paul Smith) 5.00
1-"3-D" Edition ($6.50) w/glasses 7.00

WILDC.A.T.S/ X-MEN: THE SILVER AGE
Image Comics (WildStorm Productions): June, 1997 ($4.50, one-shot)

1-Lobdell-s/Jim Lee-a; Two covers(Neal Adams, Jim Lee) 5.00
1-"3-D" Edition ($6.50) w/glasses 7.00

WILDCORE
Image Comics (WildStorm Prods.): Nov, 1997 - No. 10, Dec, 1998 ($2.50)

1-10: 1-Two covers (Booth/McWeeney, Charest) 2.50
1-($3.50)-Voyager Pack w/DV8 preview 3.50
1-Chromium-c 5.00

WILD DOG
DC Comics: Sept, 1987 - No. 4, Dec, 1987 (75¢, limited series)

1-4 2.50
Special 1 (1989, $2.50, 52 pgs.) 2.50

WILDERNESS TREK (See Zane Grey, Four Color 333)

WILDFIRE (See Zane Grey, FourColor 433)

WILDFLOWER
Sirius Entertainment/Neko Press: 1996 - Present (B&W)

1-5-('96, $2.50) Billy Martinez-s/a 2.50
... Beginnings TPB (Neko Press, 2003, $14.99) r/#1-5 15.00
... Dark Euphoria 1 (2004, $2.99) Kiethan Jones-a/c; Martinez-s 3.00
... Dark Euphoria 1 (2004, $3.99) w/alternate-c by Martinez 4.00
... Tribal Screams 1-4 (12/00 - 2/03, $2.99) 3.00
... Tribal Screams 1 ($4.99) w/alternate-c by Dark One 5.00

Wild Girl #1 © DC

Wildstar #4 © IM

Wild Western #10 © MAR

	GD 2.0	VG 4.0	FN 6.0	VF 8.0	VF/NM 9.0	NM- 9.2
... Y2K (16 pgs, edition of 2000) each contains an original Martinez sketch						10.00

WILD FRONTIER (Cheyenne Kid #8 on)
Charlton Comics: Oct, 1955 - No. 7, Apr, 1957

	GD 2.0	VG 4.0	FN 6.0	VF 8.0	VF/NM 9.0	NM- 9.2
1-Davy Crockett	10	20	30	56	73	90
2-6-Davy Crockett in all	7	14	21	37	46	55
7-Origin & 1st app. Cheyenne Kid	9	18	27	51	62	75

WILD GIRL
DC Comics (WildStorm): Jan, 2005 - No. 6 ($2.95)

	GD 2.0	VG 4.0	FN 6.0	VF 8.0	VF/NM 9.0	NM- 9.2
1,2-Leah Moore & John Reppion-s/Shawn McManus-a/c						3.00

WILDGUARD: CASTING CALL
Image Comics: Sept, 2003 - No. 6, Feb, 2004 ($2.95)

	GD 2.0	VG 4.0	FN 6.0	VF 8.0	VF/NM 9.0	NM- 9.2
1-6: 1-Nauck-s/a; two covers by Nauck and McGuinness. 2-Wieringo var-c. 6-Noto var-c						3.00

WILDSTAR (Also see The Dragon & The Savage Dragon)
Image Comics (Highbrow Entertainment): Sept, 1995 - No. 3, Jan, 1996 ($2.50, lim. series)

	GD 2.0	VG 4.0	FN 6.0	VF 8.0	VF/NM 9.0	NM- 9.2
1-3: Al Gordon scripts; Jerry Ordway-c/a						2.50

WILDSTAR: SKY ZERO
Image Comics (Highbrow Entertainment): Mar, 1993 - No. 4, Nov, 1993 ($1.95, lim. series)

	GD 2.0	VG 4.0	FN 6.0	VF 8.0	VF/NM 9.0	NM- 9.2
1-4: 1-($2.50)-Embossed-c w/silver ink; Ordway-c/a in all						2.50
1-($1.95)-Newsstand ed. w/silver ink-c, not embossed						2.50
1-Gold variant						6.00

WILD STARS
Little Rocket Productions: July, 2001 - Present ($2.95, B&W)

	GD 2.0	VG 4.0	FN 6.0	VF 8.0	VF/NM 9.0	NM- 9.2
Vol. 3: #1-6-Brunner-c; Tierney-s. 1,2-Brewer-a. 3-6-Simons-a						3.00
7-($5.95) Simons-a						6.00

WILDSTORM
Image Comics/DC Comics (WildStorm Publishing): 1994-2001 (one-shots)

	GD 2.0	VG 4.0	FN 6.0	VF 8.0	VF/NM 9.0	NM- 9.2
...Annual 2000 (12/00, $3.50) Devil's Night x-over; Moy-a						3.50
...Chamber of Horrors (10/95, $3.50)-Bisley-c						3.50
...Fine Arts: The Gallery Collection (12/98, $19.95) Lee-c						20.00
...Halloween 1 (10/97, $2.50) Warner-c						2.50
...Rarities 1(12/94, $4.95, 52 pgs.)-r/Gen 13 1/2 & other stories						5.00
...Summer Special 1 (2001, $5.95) Short stories by various; Hughes-c						6.00
...Swimsuit Special 1 (12/94, $2.95), ...Swimsuit Special 2 (1995, $2.50)						3.00
...Swimsuit Special '97 #1 (7/97, $2.50)						2.50
...Thunderbook 1 (10/00, $6.95) Short stories by various incl. Hughes, Moy						7.00
...Ultimate Sports 1 (8/97, $2.50)						2.50
...Universe Sourcebook (5/95, $2.50)						2.50

WILDSTORM!
Image Comics (WildStorm Publishing): Aug, 1995 - No. 4, Nov, 1995 ($2.50, B&W/color, anthology)

	GD 2.0	VG 4.0	FN 6.0	VF 8.0	VF/NM 9.0	NM- 9.2
1-4: 1-Simonson-a						2.50

WILDSTORM RISING
Image Comics (WildStorm Publishing): May, 1995 - No.2, June, 1995 ($1.95/$2.50)

	GD 2.0	VG 4.0	FN 6.0	VF 8.0	VF/NM 9.0	NM- 9.2
1-($2.50)-Direct Market, WildStorm Rising Pt. 1 w/bound-in card						2.50
1-($1.95)-Newstand, WildStorm Rising Pt. 1						2.25
2-($2.50)-Direct Market, WildStorm Rising Pt. 10 w/bound-in card; continues in WildC.A.T.S #21.						2.50
2-($1.95)-Newstand, WildStorm Rising Pt. 10						2.25
Trade paperback (1996, $19.95)-Collects x-over; B. Smith-c						20.00

WILDSTORM SPOTLIGHT
Image Comics (WildStorm Publishing): Feb, 1997 - No. 4 ($2.50)

	GD 2.0	VG 4.0	FN 6.0	VF 8.0	VF/NM 9.0	NM- 9.2
1-4: 1-Alan Moore-s						2.50

WILDSTORM UNIVERSE '97
Image Comics (WildStorm Publishing): Dec, 1996 - No. 3 ($2.50, limited series)

	GD 2.0	VG 4.0	FN 6.0	VF 8.0	VF/NM 9.0	NM- 9.2
1-3: 1-Wraparound-c. 3-Gary Frank-c						2.50

WILDTHING
Marvel Comics UK: Apr, 1993 - No. 7, Oct, 1993 ($1.75)

	GD 2.0	VG 4.0	FN 6.0	VF 8.0	VF/NM 9.0	NM- 9.2
1-($2.50)-Embossed-c; Venom & Carnage cameo						2.50
2-7: 2-Spider-Man & Venom. 6-Mysterio app.						2.25

WILD THING (Wolverine's daughter in the M2 universe)
Marvel Comics: Oct, 1999 - No. 5, Feb, 2000 ($1.99)

	GD 2.0	VG 4.0	FN 6.0	VF 8.0	VF/NM 9.0	NM- 9.2
1-5: 1-Lim-a in all. 2-Two covers						2.25
Wizard #0 supplement; battles the Hulk						2.25

WILDTIMES
DC Comics (WildStorm Productions): Aug, 1999 ($2.50, one-shots)

	GD 2.0	VG 4.0	FN 6.0	VF 8.0	VF/NM 9.0	NM- 9.2
...Deathblow #1 -set in 1899; Edwards-a; Jonah Hex app., ...DV8 #1 -set in 1944; Altieri-s/p; Sgt. Rock app., ...Gen13 #1 -set in 1969; Casey-s/Johnson-a; Teen Titans app., ...Grifter #1 -set in 1923; Paul Smith-a, ...Wetworks #1 -Waid-s/Lopresti-a; Superman app.						2.50
...WildC.A.T.s #0 -Wizard supplement; Charest-c						2.25

WILD WEST (Wild Western #3 on)
Marvel Comics (WFP): Spring, 1948 - No. 2, July, 1948

	GD 2.0	VG 4.0	FN 6.0	VF 8.0	VF/NM 9.0	NM- 9.2
1-Two-Gun Kid, Arizona Annie, & Tex Taylor begin; Shores-c	36	72	108	204	297	390
2-Captain Tootsie by Beck; Shores-c	24	48	72	135	195	255

WILD WEST (Black Fury #1-57)
Charlton Comics: V2#58, Nov, 1966

	GD 2.0	VG 4.0	FN 6.0	VF 8.0	VF/NM 9.0	NM- 9.2
V2#58	2	4	6	12	16	20

WILD WEST C.O.W.-BOYS OF MOO MESA (TV)
Archie Comics: Dec, 1992 - No. 3, Feb, 1993 (limited series)
V2#1, Mar, 1993 - No. 3, July, 1993 ($1.25)

	GD 2.0	VG 4.0	FN 6.0	VF 8.0	VF/NM 9.0	NM- 9.2
1-3,V2#1-3						2.25

WILD WESTERN (Formerly Wild West #1,2)
Marvel/Atlas (WFP): No. 3, 9/48 - No. 57, 9/57 (3-11: 52 pgs, 12-on: 36 pgs)

	GD 2.0	VG 4.0	FN 6.0	VF 8.0	VF/NM 9.0	NM- 9.2
3(#1)-Tex Morgan begins; Two-Gun Kid, Tex Taylor, & Arizona Annie continue from Wild West	29	58	87	164	237	310
4-Last Arizona Annie; Captain Tootsie by Beck; Kid Colt app.	21	42	63	118	169	220
5-2nd app. Black Rider (1/49); Blaze Carson, Captain Tootsie (by Beck) app.	24	48	72	135	195	255
6-8: 6-Blaze Carson app; anti-Wertham editorial	15	30	45	86	123	160
9-Photo-c; Black Rider begins, ends #19	20	40	60	112	161	210
10-Charles Starrett photo-c	23	46	69	130	188	245
11-(Last 52 pg. issue)	15	30	45	86	123	160
12-14,16-19: All Black Rider-c/stories. 12-14-The Prairie Kid & his horse Fury app.	15	30	45	83	117	150
15-Red Larabee, Gunhawk (origin), his horse Blaze, & Apache Kid begin, end #22; Black Rider-c/story	15	30	45	85	120	155
20-30: 20-Kid Colt-c begin. 24-Has 2 Kid Colt stories. 26-1st app. The Ringo Kid? (2/53); 4 pg. story. 30-Katz-a	12	24	36	71	98	125
31-40	10	20	30	56	73	90
41-47,49-51,53,57	9	18	27	49	62	75
48-Williamson/Torres-a (4 pgs); Drucker-a	10	20	30	58	77	95
52-Crandall-a	10	20	30	58	77	95
54,55-Williamson-a in both (5 & 4 pgs.), #54 with Mayo plus 2 text illos	10	20	30	58	77	95
56-Baker-a?	9	18	27	49	62	75

NOTE: *Annie Oakley in #46, 47. Apache Kid in #15-22, 39. Arizona Kid in #21, 23. Arrowhead in #34-39. Black Rider in #5, 9-19, 33-44. Fighting Texan in #17. Kid Colt in #4-6, 9-11, 20-47, 52, 54-56. Outlaw Kid in #43. Red Hawkins in #13, 14. Ringo Kid in #26, 39, 41, 43, 44, 46, 47, 50, 52-56. Tex Morgan in #3, 4, 6, 9, 11. Tex Taylor in #3-6, 9, 11. Texas Kid in #23-25. Two-Gun Kid in #3-6, 9, 11, 12, 33-39, 41. Wyatt Earp in #47.* **Ayers** *a-41, 42.* **Berg** *a-26; c-24.* **Colan** *a-49.* **Forte** *a-28, 30.* **Al Hartley** *a-16.* **Heath** *a-4, 5, 8; c-34, 44.* **Keller** *a-24, 26(2), 29-40, 44-46, 48, 52.* **Maneely** *a-10, 12, 15, 16, 28, 35, 38, 40-45; c-18-22, 33, 35, 36, 38, 39, 41, 42, 45.* **Morisi** *a-23, 52.* **Pakula** *a-42, 52.* **Powell** *a-51.* **Romita** *a-24(2).* **Severin** *a-46, 47; c-48.* **Shores** *a-3, 5, 30, 31, 33, 35, 36, 38, 41; c-3-5.* **Sinnott** *a-34-39.* **Wildey** *a-43. Bondage c-19.*

WILD WESTERN ACTION (Also see The Bravados)
Skywald Publ. Corp.: Mar, 1971 - No. 3, June, 1971 (25¢, reprints, 52 pgs.)

	GD 2.0	VG 4.0	FN 6.0	VF 8.0	VF/NM 9.0	NM- 9.2
1-Durango Kid, Straight Arrow-r; with all references to "Straight" in story relettered to "Swift"; Bravados begin; Shores-a (new)	3	6	9	16	20	24
2,3: 2-Billy Nevada, Durango Kid. 3-Red Mask, Durango Kid	2	4	6	10	13	16

WILD WESTERN ROUNDUP
Red Top/Decker Publications/I. W. Enterprises: Oct, 1957; 1960-'61

	GD 2.0	VG 4.0	FN 6.0	VF 8.0	VF/NM 9.0	NM- 9.2
1(1957)-Kid Cowboy-r	5	10	14	20	24	28
I.W. Reprint #1('60-61)-r/#1 by Red Top	2	4	6	9	11	14

WILD WEST RODEO
Star Publications: 1953 (15¢)

	GD 2.0	VG 4.0	FN 6.0	VF 8.0	VF/NM 9.0	NM- 9.2
1-A comic book coloring book with regular full color cover & B&W inside	8	16	24	46	58	70

WILD WILD WEST, THE (TV)
Gold Key: June, 1966 - No. 7, Oct, 1969 (All have Robert Conrad photo-c)

	GD 2.0	VG 4.0	FN 6.0	VF 8.0	VF/NM 9.0	NM- 9.2
1-McWilliams-a	14	28	42	97	149	200
1-Variant edition with photo back-c (scarce)	15	30	45	107	164	220
2-McWilliams-a	10	20	30	73	107	140
2-Variant edition with photo back-c (scarce)	11	22	33	80	120	160

Willie the Wise-Guy #1 © MAR

Will To Power #2 © DH

Wings Comics #26 © FH

	GD 2.0	VG 4.0	FN 6.0	VF 8.0	VF/NM 9.0	NM- 9.2
3-7	9	18	27	63	89	115

WILD, WILD WEST, THE (TV)
Millennium Publications: Oct, 1990 - No. 4, Jan?, 1991 ($2.95, limited series)

	GD	VG	FN	VF	VF/NM	NM-
1-4-Based on TV show						3.00

WILKIN BOY (See That...)

WILL EISNER READER
Kitchen Sink Press: 1991 ($9.95, B&W, 8 1/2" x 11", TPB)

	GD	VG	FN	VF	VF/NM	NM-
nn-Reprints stories from Will Eisner's Quarterly; Eisner-s/a/c						10.00
nn-(DC Comics, 10/00, $9.95)						10.00

WILLIE COMICS (Formerly Ideal #1-4; Crime Cases #24 on; Li'l Willie #20 & 21) (See Gay Comics, Laugh, Millie The Model & Wisco)
Marvel Comics (MgPC): #5, Fall, 1946 - #19, 4/49; #22, 1/50 - #23, 5/50 (No #20 & 21)

	GD	VG	FN	VF	VF/NM	NM-
5(#1)-George, Margie, Nellie the Nurse & Willie begin	21	42	63	121	173	225
6,8,9	12	24	36	69	95	120
7(1),10,11-Kurtzman's "Hey Look"	12	24	36	71	98	125
12,14-18,22,23	11	22	33	64	87	110
13,19-Kurtzman's "Hey Look" (#19-last by Kurtzman?)	11	22	33	66	91	115

NOTE: *Cindy app. in #17. Jeanie app. in #17. Little Lizzie app. in #22.*

WILLIE MAYS (See The Amazing...)

WILLIE THE PENGUIN
Standard Comics: Apr, 1951 - No. 6, Apr, 1952

	GD	VG	FN	VF	VF/NM	NM-
1-Funny animal	9	18	27	49	65	75
2-6	6	12	18	28	34	40

WILLIE THE WISE-GUY (Also see Cartoon Kids)
Atlas Comics (NPP): Sept, 1957

	GD	VG	FN	VF	VF/NM	NM-
1-Kida, Maneely-a	9	18	27	49	62	75

WILLOW
Marvel Comics: Aug, 1988 - No. 3, Oct, 1988 ($1.00)

	GD	VG	FN	VF	VF/NM	NM-
1-3-R/Marvel Graphic Novel #36 (movie adaptation)						3.00

WILL ROGERS WESTERN (Formerly My Great Love #1-4; see Blazing & True Comics #66)
Fox Features Syndicate: No. 5, June, 1950 - No. 2, Aug, 1950

	GD	VG	FN	VF	VF/NM	NM-
5(#1)	36	72	108	204	297	390
2: Photo-c	31	62	93	175	253	330

WILL TO POWER (Also see Comic's Greatest World)
Dark Horse Comics: June, 1994 - No. 12, Aug, 1994 ($1.00, weekly limited series, 20 pgs.)

	GD	VG	FN	VF	VF/NM	NM-
1-12: 12-Vortex kills Titan.						2.25

NOTE: ***Mignola** c-10-12. **Sears** c-1-3.*

WILL-YUM!
Dell Publishing Co.: No. 676, Feb, 1956 - No. 902, May, 1958

	GD	VG	FN	VF	VF/NM	NM-
Four Color 676 (#1), 765 (1/57), 902	4	8	12	27	36	45

WIN A PRIZE COMICS (Timmy The Timid Ghost #3 on?)
Charlton Comics: Feb, 1955 - No. 2, Apr, 1955

	GD	VG	FN	VF	VF/NM	NM-
V1#1-S&K-a; Poe adapt; E.C. War swipe	69	138	207	431	666	900
2-S&K-a	50	100	150	305	465	625

WINDY & WILLY
National Periodical Publications: May-June, 1969 - No. 4, Nov-Dec, 1969

	GD	VG	FN	VF	VF/NM	NM-
1- r/Dobie Gillis with some art changes begin	4	8	12	28	38	48
2-4	3	6	9	18	23	28

WINGS COMICS
Fiction House Mag.: 9/40 - No. 109, 9/49; No. 110, Wint, 1949-50; No. 111, Spring, 1950; No. 112, 1950(nd); No. 113 - No. 115, 1950(nd); No. 116, 1952(nd); No. 117, Fall, 1952 - No. 122, Wint, 1953-54; No. 123 - No. 124, 1954(nd)

	GD	VG	FN	VF	VF/NM	NM-
1-Skull Squad, Clipper Kirk, Suicide Smith, Jane Martin, War Nurse, Phantom Falcons, Greasemonkey Griffin, Parachute Patrol & Powder Burns begin	254	508	762	1588	2444	3300
2	98	196	294	613	944	1275
3-5	67	134	201	419	647	875
6-10: 8-Indicia shows #7 (#8 on cover)	55	110	165	340	520	700
11-15	49	98	147	299	455	610
16-Origin & 1st app. Captain Wings & begin series	54	108	162	329	502	675
17-20	40	80	120	244	372	500
21-30	40	80	120	233	342	450
31-40	35	70	105	201	293	385
41-50	29	58	87	164	237	310
51-60: 60-Last Skull Squad	27	54	81	152	219	285
61-67: 66-Ghost Patrol begins (becomes Ghost Squadron #71 on), ends #112?	23	46	69	132	191	250
68,69: 68-Clipper Kirk becomes The Phantom Falcon-origin, Part 1; part 2 in #69	23	46	69	132	191	250
70-72: 70-1st app. The Phantom Falcon in costume, origin-Part 3; Capt. Wings battles Col. Kamikaze in all	22	44	66	127	184	240
73-99: 80-Phantom Falcon by Larsen. 99-King of the Congo begins?	22	44	66	127	184	240
100-(12/48)	24	48	72	138	199	260
101-124: 111-Last Jane Martin. 112-Flying Saucer-c/story (1950). 115-Used in **POP**, pg. 89	18	36	54	102	146	190

NOTE: *Bondage covers are common. Captain Wings battles Sky Hag-#75, 76; ...Mr. Atlantis-#85-92; ...Mr. Pupin(Red Agent)-#98-103. Capt. Wings by **Elias**-#52-64, 68, 69; by **Lubbers**-#29-32, 70-111; by **Renee**-#33-46. **Evans** a-85-106, 108-111(Jane Martin); text illos-72-84. **Larsen** a-52, 59, 64, 73-77. Jane Martin by **Fran Hopper**-#68-84; Suicide Smith by **John Celardo**-#72, 74, 76, 80-104; by **Hollingsworth**-#68-70, 105-109, 111; Ghost Squadron by **Astarita**-#67-79; by **Maurice Whitman**-#80-111. King of the Congo by **Moreira**-#99, 100. Skull Squad by **M. Baker**-#52-60; Clipper Kirk by **Baker**-#60, 61; by **Colan**-#53; by **Ingels**-(some issues?). Phantom Falcon by **Larsen**-#73-84. **Elias** c-58-72. **Fawcette** c-3-12, 16, 17, 19, 22-33. **Lubbers** c-74-109. **Tuska** a-5. **Whitman** c-110-124. **Zolnerwich** c-15, 21.*

WINGS OF THE EAGLES, THE
Dell Publishing Co.: No. 790, Apr, 1957 (10¢ & 15¢ editions exist)

	GD	VG	FN	VF	VF/NM	NM-
Four Color 790-Movie; John Wayne photo-c; Toth-a	16	32	48	112	171	230

WINKY DINK (Adventures of...)
Pines Comics: No. 75, Mar, 1957 (one-shot)

	GD	VG	FN	VF	VF/NM	NM-
75-Marv Levy-c/a	6	12	18	31	38	45

WINKY DINK (TV)
Dell Publishing Co.: No. 663, Nov, 1955

	GD	VG	FN	VF	VF/NM	NM-
Four Color 663 (#1)	9	18	27	65	93	120

WINNIE-THE-POOH (Also see Dynabrite Comics)
Gold Key No. 1-17/Whitman No. 18 on: January, 1977 - No. 33, July, 1984 (Walt Disney) (Winnie-The-Pooh began as Edward Bear in 1926 by Milne)

	GD	VG	FN	VF	VF/NM	NM-
1-New art	3	6	9	18	23	28
2-5: 5-New material	2	4	6	10	13	16
6-17: 12-up-New material	2	4	6	8	10	12
18,19(Whitman)	2	4	6	10	13	16
20,21('80) pre-pack only	3	6	9	16	21	26
22('80) (scarcer) pre-pack only	4	8	12	22	30	38
23-28: 27(2/82), 28(4/82)	2	4	6	10	13	16
29-33 (#90299 on-c, no date or date code; pre-pack): 29(4/82), 30(5/83), 31(8/83), 32(4/84), 33(7/84)	2	4	6	14	18	22

WINNIE WINKLE (See Popular Comics & Super Comics)
Dell Publishing Co.: 1941 - No. 7, Sept-Nov, 1949

	GD	VG	FN	VF	VF/NM	NM-
Large Feature Comic 2 (1941)	26	52	78	150	215	280
Four Color 94 (1945)	13	26	39	90	138	185
Four Color 174	9	18	27	60	85	110
1(3-5/48)-Contains daily & Sunday newspaper-r from 1939-1941	8	16	24	55	78	100
2 (6-8/48)	6	12	18	38	52	65
3-7	4	8	12	29	40	50

WINTERWORLD
Eclipse Comics: Sept, 1987 - No. 3, Mar, 1988 ($1.75, limited series)

	GD	VG	FN	VF	VF/NM	NM-
1-3						2.25

WISE GUYS (See Harvey...)

WISE LITTLE HEN, THE
David McKay Publ./Whitman: 1934 ,1935(48 pgs.); 1937 (Story book)

	GD	VG	FN	VF	VF/NM	NM-
nn-(1934 edition w/dust jacket)(48 pgs. with color, 8-3/4x9-3/4") -Debut of Donald Duck (see Advs. of Mickey Mouse); Donald app. on cover with Wise Little Hen & Practical Pig; painted cover; same artist as the B&W's from Silly Symphony Cartoon, The Wise Little Hen (1934) (McKay)						
Book w/dust jacket	233	466	699	1282	2041	2800
Dust jacket only	55	110	165	325	500	675
nn-(1935 edition w/dust jacket), same as 1934 ed.	139	278	417	765	1183	1600
888 (1937)(9-1/2x13", 12 pgs.)(Whitman) Donald Duck app.	35	70	105	198	287	375

WISE SON: THE WHITE WOLF
DC Comics (Milestone): Nov, 1996 - No. 4, Feb, 1997 ($2.50, limited series)

	GD	VG	FN	VF	VF/NM	NM-
1-4: Ho Che Anderson-c/a						2.50

WIT AND WISDOM OF WATERGATE (Humor magazine)
Marvel Comics: 1973, 76 pgs., squarebound

Witchblade #25 © TCOW

Witches #1 © MAR

The Witching #1 © DC

	GD 2.0	VG 4.0	FN 6.0	VF 8.0	VF/NM 9.0	NM- 9.2
1-Low print run	4	8	12	24	32	40

WITCHBLADE (Also see Cyblade/Shi, Tales Of The..., & Top Cow Classics)
Image Comics (Top Cow Productions): Nov, 1995 - Present ($2.50/$2.99)

	GD 2.0	VG 4.0	FN 6.0	VF 8.0	VF/NM 9.0	NM- 9.2
0	1	2	3	5	6	8
1/2-Mike Turner/Marc Silvestri-c.	4	8	12	24	32	40
1/2 Gold Ed., 1/2 Chromium-c	4	8	12	24	32	40
1/2-(Vol. 2, 11/02, $2.99) Wohl-s/Ching-a/c						3.00
1-Mike Turner-a(p)	4	8	12	24	32	40
1,2-American Ent. Encore Ed.	1	2	3	4	5	7
2,3	2	4	6	12	16	20
4,5	2	4	6	10	13	16
6-9: 8-Wraparound-c. 9-Tony Daniel-a(p)	1	2	3	5	7	9
9-Sunset variant-c	2	4	6	8	10	12
9-DF variant-c	2	4	6	12	16	20
10-Flip book w/Darkness #0, 1st app. the Darkness	2	4	6	8	10	12
10-Variant-c	2	4	6	10	12	15
10-Gold logo	3	6	9	18	24	30
10-($3.95) Dynamic Forces alternate-c	1	2	3	5	6	8
11-15						5.00
16-19: 18,19-"Family Ties" Darkness x-over pt. 1,4						4.00
18-Face to face variant-c, 18-American Ent. Ed., 19-AE Gold Ed.	1	2	3	5	6	8
20-25: 24-Pearson, Green-a. 25-($2.95) Turner-a(p)						3.00
25 (Prism variant)						30.00
25 (Special)						15.00
26-39: 26-Green-a begins						2.50
27 (Variant)						10.00
40-49,51-53: 40-Begin Jenkins & Veitch-s/Keu Cha-a. 47-Zulli-c/a						2.50
40-Pittsburgh Convention Preview edition; B&W preview of #40						3.00
41-eWanted Chrome-c edition						5.00
49-Gold logo	1	2	3	5	6	8
50-($4.95) Darkness app.; Ching-a; B&W preview of Universe						5.00
54-59: 54-Black outer-c with gold foil logo; Wohl-s/Manapul-a						2.50
55-Variant Battle of the Planets Convention cover						3.00
60-74,76-80: 60-($2.99) Endgame x-over with Tomb Raider #25 & Evo #1. 64,65-Magdalena app. 71-Kirk-a. 77-Land-c. 80-Four covers						3.00
75-($4.99) Manapul-a						5.00
...: Animated (8/03, $2.99) Magdalena & Darkness app.; Dini-s/Bone, Bullock, Cooke-a/c						3.00
...: Blood Oath (8/04, $4.99) Sara teams with Phenix & Sibilla; Roux-a						5.00
...: Blood Relations TPB (2003, $12.99) r/#54-58						13.00
.../Darkchylde (7/00, $2.50) Green-s/a(p)						2.50
.../Dark Minds (6/04, $9.99) new story plus r/Dark Minds/Witchblade #1						10.00
.../Darkness: Family Ties Collected Edition (10/98, $9.95) r/#18,19 and Darkness #9,10						10.00
.../Darkness Special (12/99, $3.95) Green-c/a						4.00
...: Demon 1 (2003, $6.99) Mark Millar-s/Jae Lee-c/a						7.00
...: Distinctions (See Tales of the Witchblade)						
... Gallery (11/00, $2.95) Profile pages and pin-ups by various; Turner-c						3.00
Infinity (5/99, $3.50) Lobdell-s/Pollina-c/a						3.50
.../Lady Death (11/01, $4.95) Manapul-c/a						5.00
...: Prevailing TPB (2000, $14.95) r/#20-25; new Turner-c						15.00
...: Revelations TPB (2000, $24.95) r/#9-17; new Turner-c						25.00
.../Tomb Raider #1/2 (7/00, $2.95) Covers by Turner and Cha						3.00
Wizard #500						10.00
.../Wolverine (6/04, $2.99) Basaldua-c/a; Claremont-s						3.00

WITCHBLADE/ALIENS/THE DARKNESS/PREDATOR
Dark Horse Comics/Top Cow Productions: Nov, 2000 ($2.99)

	GD 2.0	VG 4.0	FN 6.0	VF 8.0	VF/NM 9.0	NM- 9.2
1-3-Mel Rubi-a						3.00

WITCHBLADE COLLECTED EDITION
Image Comics (Top Cow Productions): July, 1996 - No. 8 ($4.95/$6.95, squarebound, limited series)

	GD 2.0	VG 4.0	FN 6.0	VF 8.0	VF/NM 9.0	NM- 9.2
1-7-($4.95): Two issues reprinted in each						5.00
8-($6.95) r/#15-17						7.00
...Slipcase (10/96, $10.95)-Packaged w/ Coll. Ed. #1-4						11.00

WITCHBLADE: DESTINY'S CHILD
Image Comics (Top Cow): Jun, 2000 - No. 3, Sept, 2000 ($2.95, lim. series)

	GD 2.0	VG 4.0	FN 6.0	VF 8.0	VF/NM 9.0	NM- 9.2
1-3: 1-Boller-a/Keu Cha-c						3.00

WITCHBLADE/ ELEKTRA
Image Comics (Top Cow Productions): Mar, 1997 ($2.95)

	GD 2.0	VG 4.0	FN 6.0	VF 8.0	VF/NM 9.0	NM- 9.2
1-Devil's Reign Pt. 6						3.00

WITCHBLADE: OBAKEMONO
Image Comics (Top Cow Productions): 2002 ($9.95, one-shot graphic novel)

	GD 2.0	VG 4.0	FN 6.0	VF 8.0	VF/NM 9.0	NM- 9.2
1-Fiona Avery-s/Billy Tan-a; forward by Straczynski						10.00

WITCHBLADE/ TOMB RAIDER SPECIAL (Also see Tomb Raider/...)
Image Comics (Top Cow Productions): Dec, 1998 ($2.95)

	GD 2.0	VG 4.0	FN 6.0	VF 8.0	VF/NM 9.0	NM- 9.2
1-Based on video game character; Turner-a(p)						3.00
1-Silvestri variant-c						5.00
1-Turner bikini variant-c						10.00
1-Prism-c						12.00
Wizard 1/2 -Turner-s						10.00

WITCHCRAFT (See Strange Mysteries, Super Reprint #18)
Avon Periodicals: Mar-Apr, 1952 - No. 6, Mar, 1953

	GD 2.0	VG 4.0	FN 6.0	VF 8.0	VF/NM 9.0	NM- 9.2
1-Kubert-a; 1 pg. Check-a	69	138	207	431	666	900
2-Kubert & Check-a	52	104	156	317	484	650
3,6: 3-Lawrence-a; Kinstler inside-c	40	80	120	244	372	500
4-People cooked alive c/story	45	90	135	275	420	565
5-Kelly Freas painted-c	51	102	153	311	473	635

NOTE: ***Hollingsworth** a-4-6; c-4, 6. **McCann** a-3?*

WITCHCRAFT
DC Comics (Vertigo): June, 1994 - No. 3, Aug, 1994 ($2.95, limited series)

	GD 2.0	VG 4.0	FN 6.0	VF 8.0	VF/NM 9.0	NM- 9.2
1-3: James Robinson scripts & Kaluta-c in all						4.00
1-Platinum Edition						8.00
Trade paperback-(1996, $14.95)-r/#1-3; Kaluta-c						15.00

WITCHCRAFT: LA TERREUR
DC Comics (Vertigo): Apr, 1998 - No. 3, Jun, 1998 ($2.50, limited series)

	GD 2.0	VG 4.0	FN 6.0	VF 8.0	VF/NM 9.0	NM- 9.2
1-3: Robinson-s/Zulli & Locke-a; interlocking cover images						2.50

WITCHES
Marvel Comics: Aug, 2004 - No. 4, Sept, 2004 ($2.99, limited series)

	GD 2.0	VG 4.0	FN 6.0	VF 8.0	VF/NM 9.0	NM- 9.2
1-4: 1,2-Deodato, Jr-a; Dr. Strange app. 3,4-Conrad-a						3.00
... Vol. 1: The Gathering (2004, $9.99) r/series						10.00

WITCHES TALES (Witches Western Tales #29,30)
Witches Tales/Harvey Publications: Jan, 1951 - No. 28, Dec, 1954 (date misprinted as 4/55)

	GD 2.0	VG 4.0	FN 6.0	VF 8.0	VF/NM 9.0	NM- 9.2
1-Powell-a (1 pg.)	55	110	165	340	520	700
2-Eye injury panel	35	70	105	198	287	375
3-7,9,10	26	52	78	150	215	280
8-Eye injury panels	27	54	81	154	272	290
11-13,15,16: 12-Acid in face story	23	46	69	130	188	245
14,17-Powell/Nostrand-a. 17-Atomic disaster story	25	50	75	144	207	270
18-Nostrand-a; E.C. swipe/Shock S.S.	25	50	75	144	207	270
19-Nostrand-a; E.C. swipe/ "Glutton"; Devil-c	27	54	81	154	222	290
20-24-Nostrand-a. 21-E.C. swipe; rape story. 23-Wood E.C. swipes/Two-Fisted Tales #34	25	50	75	144	207	270
25-Nostrand-a; E.C. swipe/Mad Barber; decapitation-c	35	70	105	198	287	375
26-28: 27-r/#6 with diff.-c. 28-r/#8 with diff.-c	18	36	54	102	146	190

NOTE: ***Check** a-24. **Elias** c-8, 10, 16-27. **Kremer** a-18; c-25. **Nostrand** a-17-25; 14, 17(w/**Powell**). **Palais** a-1, 2, 4(2), 5(2), 7-9, 12, 14, 15, 17. **Powell** a-3-7, 10, 11, 19-27. Bondage-c 1, 3, 5, 6, 8, 9.*

WITCHES TALES (Magazine)
Eerie Publications: V1#7, July, 1969 - V7#1, Feb, 1975 (B&W, 52 pgs.)

	GD 2.0	VG 4.0	FN 6.0	VF 8.0	VF/NM 9.0	NM- 9.2
V1#7(7/69)	5	10	15	36	48	60
V1#8(9/69), 9(11/69)	5	10	15	36	48	60
V2#1-6('70), V3#1-6('71)	4	8	12	24	32	40
V4#1-6('72), V5#1-6('73), V6#1-6('74), V7#1	3	7	10	21	28	35

NOTE: *Ajax/Farrell reprints in early issues.*

WITCHES' WESTERN TALES (Formerly Witches Tales)(Western Tales #31 on)
Harvey Publications: No. 29, Feb, 1955 - No. 30, Apr, 1955

	GD 2.0	VG 4.0	FN 6.0	VF 8.0	VF/NM 9.0	NM- 9.2
29,30-Featuring Clay Duncan & Boys' Ranch; S&K-r/from Boys' Ranch including-c. 29-Last pre-code	21	42	63	118	169	220

WITCHFINDER, THE
Image Comics (Liar): Sept, 1999 - No. 3, Jan, 2000 ($2.95)

	GD 2.0	VG 4.0	FN 6.0	VF 8.0	VF/NM 9.0	NM- 9.2
1-3-Romano-a/Sharon & Matthew Scott-plot						3.00

WITCH HUNTER
Malibu Comics (Ultraverse): Apr, 1996 ($2.50, one-shot)

	GD 2.0	VG 4.0	FN 6.0	VF 8.0	VF/NM 9.0	NM- 9.2
1						2.50

WITCHING, THE
DC Comics (Vertigo): Aug, 2004 - Present ($2.95)

	GD 2.0	VG 4.0	FN 6.0	VF 8.0	VF/NM 9.0	NM- 9.2
1-6-Vankin-s/Gallagher-a/McPherson-c. 1,2-Lucifer app.						3.00

WITCHING HOUR ("The ..." in later issues)
National Periodical Publ./DC Comics: Feb-Mar, 1969 - No. 85, Oct, 1978

The Witching Hour #2 © Loeb & Bachalo

Wolverine (mini-series) #3 © MAR

Wolverine #125 © MAR

	GD 2.0	VG 4.0	FN 6.0	VF 8.0	VF/NM 9.0	NM- 9.2
1-Toth-a, plus Neal Adams-a (2 pgs.)	12	24	36	84	127	170
2,6: 6-Toth-a	6	12	18	40	55	70
3,5-Wrightson-a; Toth-p. 3-Last 12¢ issue	6	12	18	43	59	75
4,7-12: Toth-a in all. 8-Toth, Neal Adams-a	4	8	12	27	36	45
13-Neal Adams-c/a, 2pgs.	4	8	12	29	40	50
14-Williamson/Garzon, Jones-a; N. Adams-c	5	10	15	33	44	55
15	3	6	9	16	21	26
16-21-(52 pg. Giants)	3	6	9	19	25	32
22-37,39,40	2	4	6	11	14	18
38-(100 pgs.)	5	10	15	33	44	55
41-60	2	4	6	9	11	14
61-83,85	1	3	4	6	8	10
84-(44 pgs.)	2	4	6	8	10	12

NOTE: *Combined with The Unexpected with #189.* ***Neal Adams*** *c-7-11, 13, 14.* ***Alcala*** *a-24, 27, 33, 41, 43.* ***Anderson*** *a-9, 38.* ***Cardy*** *c-4, 5.* ***Kaluta*** *a-7.* ***Kane*** *a-12p.* ***Morrow*** *a-10, 13, 15, 16.* ***Nino*** *a-31, 40, 45, 47.* ***Redondo*** *a-20, 23, 24, 34, 65; c-53.* ***Reese*** *a-23.* ***Sparling*** *a-1.* ***Toth*** *a-1, 3-12, 38r.* ***Tuska*** *a-11, 12.* ***Wood*** *a-15.*

WITCHING HOUR, THE
DC Comics (Vertigo): 1999 - No. 3, 2000 ($5.95, limited series)

	GD 2.0	VG 4.0	FN 6.0	VF 8.0	VF/NM 9.0	NM- 9.2
1-3-Bachalo & Thibert-c/a; Loeb & Bachalo-s						6.00
Hardcover (2000, $29.95) r/#1-3; embossed cover						30.00
Softcover (2003, $19.95) r/#1-3						20.00

WITHIN OUR REACH
Star Reach Productions: 1991 ($7.95, 84 pgs.)

	GD 2.0	VG 4.0	FN 6.0	VF 8.0	VF/NM 9.0	NM- 9.2
nn-Spider-Man, Concrete by Chadwick, Gift of the Magi by Russell; X-mas stories; Chadwick-c; Spidey back-c						8.00

WITH THE MARINES ON THE BATTLEFRONTS OF THE WORLD
Toby Press: 1953 (no month) - No. 2, Mar, 1954 (Photo covers)

	GD 2.0	VG 4.0	FN 6.0	VF 8.0	VF/NM 9.0	NM- 9.2
1-John Wayne story	30	60	90	173	249	325
2-Monty Hall in #1,2	9	18	27	54	70	85

WITH THE U.S. PARATROOPS BEHIND ENEMY LINES (Also see U.S. Paratroops...; #2-6 titled U.S. Paratroops...)
Avon Periodicals: 1951 - No. 6, Dec, 1952

	GD 2.0	VG 4.0	FN 6.0	VF 8.0	VF/NM 9.0	NM- 9.2
1-Wood-c & inside f/c	17	34	51	95	135	175
2-Kinstler-c & inside f/c only	10	20	30	56	73	90
3-6: 6-Kinstler-c & inside f/c only	9	18	27	52	66	80

NOTE: ***Kinstler*** *c-2, 4-6.*

WITNESS, THE (Also see Amazing Mysteries, Captain America #71, Ideal #4, Marvel Mystery #92 & Mystic #7)
Marvel Comics (MjMe): Sept, 1948

	GD 2.0	VG 4.0	FN 6.0	VF 8.0	VF/NM 9.0	NM- 9.2
1(Scarce)-Rico-c?	185	370	555	1156	1778	2400

WITTY COMICS
Irwin H. Rubin Publ./Chicago Nite Life News No. 2: 1945 - No. 2, 1945

	GD 2.0	VG 4.0	FN 6.0	VF 8.0	VF/NM 9.0	NM- 9.2
1-The Pioneer, Junior Patrol; Jap war-c	30	60	90	170	245	320
2-The Pioneer, Junior Patrol	15	30	45	83	117	150

WIZARD OF FOURTH STREET, THE
Dark Horse Comics: Dec, 1987 - No. 2, 1988 ($1.75, B&W, limited series)

	GD 2.0	VG 4.0	FN 6.0	VF 8.0	VF/NM 9.0	NM- 9.2
1,2: Adapts novel by S/F author Simon Hawke						2.25

WIZARD OF OZ (See Classics Illustrated Jr. 535, Dell Jr. Treasury No. 5, First Comics Graphic Novel, Marvelous..., & Marvel Treasury of Oz)
Dell Publishing Co.: No. 1308, Mar-May, 1962 (TV)

	GD 2.0	VG 4.0	FN 6.0	VF 8.0	VF/NM 9.0	NM- 9.2
Four Color 1308	13	26	39	90	138	185

WIZARD'S TALE, THE
Image Comics (Homage Comics): 1997 ($19.95, squarebound, one-shot)

	GD 2.0	VG 4.0	FN 6.0	VF 8.0	VF/NM 9.0	NM- 9.2
nn-Kurt Busiek-s/David Wenzel-painted-a/c						20.00

WOLF & RED
Dark Horse Comics: Apr, 1995 - No. 3, June, 1995 ($2.50, limited series)

	GD 2.0	VG 4.0	FN 6.0	VF 8.0	VF/NM 9.0	NM- 9.2
1-3: Characters created by Tex Avery						2.50

WOLFF & BYRD, COUNSELORS OF THE MACABRE (Becomes Supernatural Law with issue #24)
Exhibit A Press: May, 1994 - No. 23, Aug, 1999 ($2.50, B&W)

	GD 2.0	VG 4.0	FN 6.0	VF 8.0	VF/NM 9.0	NM- 9.2
1-23-Batton Lash-s/a						2.50

WOLF GAL (See Al Capp's...)

WOLFMAN, THE (See Movie Classics)

WOLFPACK
Marvel Comics: Feb, 1988 ($7.95); Aug, 1988 - No. 12, July, 1989 (Lim. series)

	GD 2.0	VG 4.0	FN 6.0	VF 8.0	VF/NM 9.0	NM- 9.2
1-1st app./origin (Marvel Graphic Novel #31)						8.00
1-12						2.25

WOLVERINE (See Alpha Flight, Daredevil #196, 249, Ghost Rider; Wolverine; Punisher, Havok &..., Incredible Hulk #180, Incredible Hulk &..., Kitty Pryde And..., Marvel Comics Presents, Power Pack, Punisher and..., Spider-Man vs... & X-Men #94)

WOLVERINE (See Incredible Hulk #180 for 1st app.)
Marvel Comics Group: Sept, 1982 - No. 4, Dec, 1982 (limited series)

	GD 2.0	VG 4.0	FN 6.0	VF 8.0	VF/NM 9.0	NM- 9.2
1-Frank Miller-c/a(p) in all	6	12	18	38	52	65
2-4	4	8	12	29	40	50
Trade paperback 1(7/87, $4.95)-Reprints #1-4 with new Miller-c.	2	4	6	11	14	18
Trade paperback nn (2nd printing, $9.95)-r/#1-4	2	4	6	8	10	12

WOLVERINE
Marvel Comics: Nov, 1988 - No. 189, June, 2003 ($1.50/$1.75/$1.95/$1.99/$2.25)

	GD 2.0	VG 4.0	FN 6.0	VF 8.0	VF/NM 9.0	NM- 9.2
1	4	8	12	27	36	45
2	2	4	6	14	18	22
3-5: 4-BWS back-c	2	4	6	10	13	16
6-9: 6-McFarlane back-c. 7,8-Hulk app.	1	3	4	6	8	10
10-1st battle with Sabretooth (before Wolverine had his claws)	3	6	9	18	24	30
11-16: 11-New costume	1	2	3	5	6	8
17-20: 17-Byrne-c/a(p) begins, ends #23	1	2	3	4	5	7
21-30: 24,25,27-Jim Lee-c. 26-Begin $1.75-c						5.00
31-40,44,47						4.00
41-Sabretooth claims to be Wolverine's father; Cable cameo						6.00
41-Gold 2nd printing ($1.75)						2.50
42-Sabretooth, Cable & Nick Fury app.; Sabretooth proven not to be Wolverine's father	1	2	3	5	6	8
42-Gold ink 2nd printing ($1.75)						2.50
43-Sabretooth cameo (2 panels); saga ends						5.00
45,46-Sabretooth-c/stories						5.00
48-51: 48,49-Sabretooth app. 48-Begin 3 part Weapon X sequel. 50-(64 pgs.)-Die cut-c; Wolverine back to old yellow costume; Forge, Cyclops, Jubilee, Jean Grey & Nick Fury app. 51-Sabretooth-c & app.						4.00
52-74,76-80: 54-Shatterstar (from X-Force) app. 55-Gambit, Jubilee, Sunfire-c/story. 55-57,73-Gambit app. 57-Mariko Yashida dies (Late 7/92). 58,59-Terror, Inc. x-over. 60-64-Sabretooth storyline (60,62,64-c)						4.00
75-($3.95, 68 pgs.)-Wolverine hologram on-c						5.00
81-84,86: 81-bound-in card sheet						3.00
85-($2.50)-Newsstand edition						3.00
85-($3.50)-Collectors edition						5.00
87-90 ($1.95)-Deluxe edition						3.00
87-90 ($1.50)-Regular edition						2.50
91-99,101-114: 91-Return from "Age of Apocalypse," 93-Juggernaut app. 94-Gen X app. 101-104-Elektra app. 104-Origin of Onslaught. 105-Onslaught x-over. 110-Shaman-c/app. 114-Alternate-c						3.00
100 ($3.95)-Hologram-c; Wolverine loses humanity	1	2	3	5	7	9
100 ($2.95)-Regular-c.						4.00
115-124: 115- Operation Zero Tolerance						2.50
125-($2.99) Wraparound-c; Viper secret						3.00
125-($6.95) Jae Lee variant-c						7.00
126-144: 126,127-Sabretooth-c/app. 128-Sabretooth & Shadowcat app.; Platt-a. 129-Wendigo-c/app. 131-Initial printing contained lettering error. 133-Begin Larsen-s/ Matsuda-a. 138-Galactus-c/app. 139-Cable app.; Yu-a. 142,143-Alpha Flight app.						2.50
145-($2.99) 25th Anniversary issue; Hulk and Sabretooth app.						3.00
145-($3.99) Foil enhanced cover (also see Promotional section for Nabisco mail-in ed.)						4.00
146-149: 147-Apocalypse: The Twelve; Angel-c/app. 149-Nova-c/app.						2.50
150-($2.99) Steve Skroce-s/a						3.00
151-174,176-182,184-189: 151-Begin $2.25-c. 154,155-Liefeld-s/a. 156-Churchill-a. 159-Chen-a begins. 160-Sabretooth app. 163-Texeira-a(p). 167-BWS-c. 172,173-Alpha Flight app. 176-Colossus app. 185,186-Punisher app.						2.50
175,183-($3.50) 175-Sabretooth app.						3.50
#(-1) Flashback (7/97) Logan meets Col. Fury; Nord-a						2.50
Annual nn (1990, $4.50, squarebound, 52 pgs.)-The Jungle Adventure; Simonson scripts; Mignola-c/a						5.00
Annual 2 (12/90, $4.95, squarebound, 52 pgs.)-Bloodlust						5.00
Annual nn (#3, 8/91, $5.95, 68 pgs.)-Rahne of Terror; Cable & The New Mutants app.; Andy Kubert-c/a (2nd print exists)						6.00
Annual '95 (1995, $3.95)						4.00
Annual '96 (1996, $2.95)- Wraparound-c; Silver Samurai, Yukio, and Red Ronin app.						3.00
Annual '97 ($2.99) - Wraparound-c						3.00
Annual 1999, 2000 ($3.50) : 1999-Deadpool app.						3.50
Annual 2001 ($2.99) - Tieri-s; JH Williams-c						3.00
...Battles The Incredible Hulk nn (1989, $4.95, squarebound, 52 pg.) r/Incr. Hulk #180,181						5.00

Wolverine V3#20 © MAR

Wolverine/Doop #1 © MAR

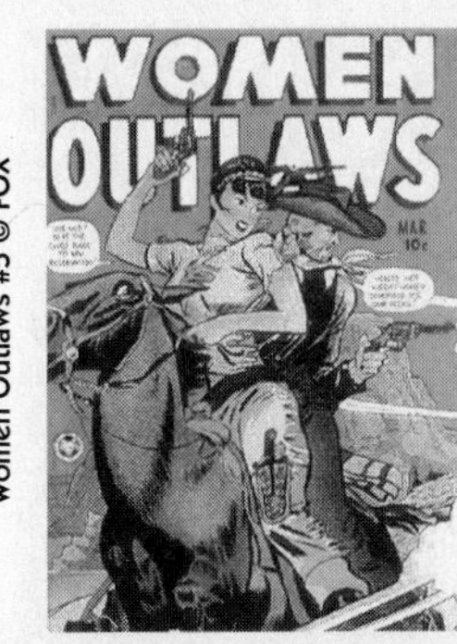

Women Outlaws #5 © FOX

GD VG FN VF VF/NM NM-
2.0 4.0 6.0 8.0 9.0 9.2

Best of Wolverine Vol. 1 HC (2004, $29.99) oversized reprints of Hulk #181, mini-series #1-4, Capt. America Ann, #8, Uncanny X-Men #205 & Marvel Comics Presents #72-84 30.00
...Black Rio (11/98, $5.99)-Casey-s/Oscar Jimenez-a 6.00
...Blood Debt TPB (7/01, $12.95)-r/#150-153; Skroce-c 13.00
...Blood Hungry nn (1993, $6.95, 68 pgs.)-Kieth-r/Marvel Comics Presents #85-92 w/ new Kieth-c 7.00
...: Bloody Choices nn (1993, $7.95, 68 pgs.)-r/Graphic Novel; Nick Fury app. 8.00
... Cable Guts and Glory (10/99, $5.99) Platt-a 6.00
.../Deadpool: Weapon X TPB (7/02, $21.99)-r/#162-166 & Deadpool #57-60 22.00
... Doombringer (11/97, $5.99)-Silver Samurai-c/app. 6.00
... Evilution (9/94, $5.95) 6.00
...: Global Jeopardy 1 (12/93, $2.95, one-shot)-Embossed-c; Sub-Mariner, Zabu, Ka-Zar, Shanna & Wolverine app.; produced in cooperation with World Wildlife Fund 3.00
...:Inner Fury nn (1992, $5.95, 52 pgs.)-Sienkiewicz-c/a 6.00
...: Judgment Night (2000, $3.99) Shi app.; Battlebook 4.00
...: Killing (9/93)-Kent Williams-a 6.00
...: Knight of Terra (1995, $6.95)-Ostrander script 7.00
... Legends Vol. 2: Meltdown (2003, $19.99) r/Havok & Wolverine: Meltdown #1-4 20.00
... Legends Vol. 3 (2003, $12.99) r/#181-186 13.00
... Legends Vol. 4,5: 4-(See Wolverine: Xisle). 5-(See Wolverine: Snikt!)
... Legends Vol. 6: Marc Silvestri Book 1 (2004, $19.99) r/#31-34, 41-42, 48-50 20.00
.../ Nick Fury: The Scorpio Connection Hardcover (1989, $16.95) 25.00
.../ Nick Fury: The Scorpio Connection Softcover(1990, $12.95) 15.00
...: Not Dead Yet (12/98, $14.95, TPB)-r/#119-122 15.00
...: Save The Tiger 1 (7/92, $2.95, 84 pgs.)-Reprints Wolverine stories from Marvel Comics Presents #1-10 w/new Kieth-c 3.00
...Scorpio Rising ($5.95, prestige format, one-shot) 6.00
.../Shi: Dark Night of Judgment (Crusade Comics, 2000, $2.99) Tucci-a 3.00
...Triumphs And Tragedies-(1995, $16.95, trade paperback)-r/Uncanny X-Men #109,172,173, Wolverine limited series #4, & Wolverine #41,42,75 17.00
...Typhoid's Kiss (6/94, $6.95)-r/Wolverine stories from Marvel Comics Presents #109-116 7.00
...Vs. Spider-Man 1 (3/95, $2.50) -r/Marvel Comics Presents #48-50 2.50
.../Witchblade 1 (3/97, $2.95) Devil's Reign Pt. 5 4.00
Wizard #1/2 (1997) Joe Phillips-a(p) 10.00

NOTE: ***Austin** c-3i. **Bolton** c(back)-5. **Buscema** a-1-16,25,27p; c-1-10. **Byrne** a-17-22p, 23; c-1(back), 17-22, 23p. **Colan** a-24. **Andy Kubert** c/a-51. **Jim Lee** c-24, 25, 27. **Silvestri** a(p)-31-43, 45, 46, 48-50, 52, 53, 55-57; c-31-42p, 43, 45p, 46p, 48, 49p, 50p, 52p, 53p, 55-57p. **Stroman** a-44p; c-60p. **Williamson** a-1i, 3-8i; c(i)-1, 3-6.*

WOLVERINE (Volume 3)
Marvel Comics: July, 2003 - Present ($2.25)

1-Rucka-s/Robertson-a 3.00
2-19: 6-Nightcrawler app. 13-16-Sabretooth app. 2.25
20-Millar-s/Romita, Jr.-a begin, Elektra app. 3.00
21,22: 21-Elektra-c/app. 2.25
...Vol. 1: The Brotherhood (2003, $12.99) r/#1-6 13.00
...Vol. 2: Coyote Crossing (2004, $11.99) r/#7-11 12.00

WOLVERINE AND THE PUNISHER: DAMAGING EVIDENCE
Marvel Comics: Oct, 1993 - No. 3, Dec, 1993 ($2.00, limited series)

1-3: 2,3-Indicia says "The Punisher and Wolverine…" 2.50

WOLVERINE/CAPTAIN AMERICA
Marvel Comics: Apr, 2004 - No. 4, Apr, 2004 ($2.99, limited series)

1-4-Derenick-a/c 3.00

WOLVERINE: DAYS OF FUTURE PAST
Marvel Comics: Dec, 1997 - No. 3, Feb, 1998 ($2.50, limited series)

1-3: J.F. Moore-s/Bennett-a 2.50

WOLVERINE/DOOP (Also see X-Force and X-Statix)(Reprinted in X-Statix Vol. 2)
Marvel Comics: July, 2003 - No. 2, July, 2003 ($2.99, limited series)

1,2-Peter Milligan-s/Darwyn Cooke & J. Bone-a 3.00

WOLVERINE/GAMBIT: VICTIMS
Marvel Comics: Sept, 1995 - No. 4, Dec, 1995 ($2.95, limited series)

1-4: Jeph Loeb scripts & Tim Sale-a; foil-c 4.00

WOLVERINE/HULK
Marvel Comics: Apr, 2002 - No. 4, July, 2002 ($3.50, limited series)

1-4-Sam Kieth-s/a/c 3.50
Wolverine Legends Vol. 1: Wolverine/Hulk (2003, $9.99, TPB) r/#1-4 10.00

WOLVERINE: NETSUKE
Marvel Comics: Nov, 2002 - No. 4, Feb, 2003 ($3.99, limited series)

1-4-George Pratt-s/painted-a 4.00

WOLVERINE/PUNISHER
Marvel Comics: May, 2004 - No. 5, Sept, 2004 ($2.99, limited series)

1-5: Milligan-s/Weeks-a 3.00
... Vol. 1 TPB (2004, $13.99) r/series 14.00

WOLVERINE/PUNISHER REVELATIONS (Marvel Knights)
Marvel Comics: Jun, 1999 - No. 4, Sept, 1999 ($2.95, limited series)

1-4: Pat Lee-a(p) 4.00
...: Revelation (4/00, $14.95, TPB) r/#1-4 15.00

WOLVERINE SAGA
Marvel Comics: Sept, 1989 - No. 4, Mid-Dec, 1989 ($3.95, lim. series, 52 pgs.)

1-Gives history; Liefeld/Austin-c (front & back) 5.00
2-4: 2-Romita, Jr./Austin-c. 4-Kaluta-c 5.00

WOLVERINE: SNIKT!
Marvel Comics: July, 2003 - No. 5, Nov, 2003 ($2.99, limited series)

1-5-Manga-style; Tsutomu Nihei-s/a 3.00
Wolverine Legends Vol. 5: Snikt! TPB (2003, $13.99) r/#1-5 14.00

WOLVERINE: THE END
Marvel Comics: Jan, 2004 - No. 6 ($2.99, limited series)

1-5-Jenkins-s/Castellini-a 3.00
1-Wizard World Texas variant-c 20.00

WOLVERINE: THE ORIGIN
Marvel Comics: Nov, 2001 - No. 6, July, 2002 ($3.50, limited series)

1-Origin of Logan; Jenkins-s/Andy Kubert-a; Quesada-c 40.00
1-DF edition 60.00
2 15.00
3 9.00
4-6 5.00
HC (3/02, $34.95) r/#1-6; dust jacket; sketch pages and treatments 35.00
SC (2002, $14.95) r/#1-6; afterwords by Jemas and Quesada 15.00

WOLVERINE: XISLE
Marvel Comics: June, 2003 - No. 5, June, 2003 ($2.50, weekly limited series)

1-5-Bruce Jones-s/Jorge Lucas-a 2.50
Wolverine Legends Vol. 4 TPB (2003, $13.99) r/ #1-5 14.00

WOMEN IN LOVE (A Feature Presentation #5)
Fox Features Synd./Hero Books: Aug, 1949 - No. 4, Feb, 1950

1 32 64 96 184 267 350
2-Kamen/Feldstein-c 26 52 78 150 215 280
3 18 36 54 100 143 185
4-Wood-a 21 42 63 118 169 220

WOMEN IN LOVE (Thrilling Romances for Adults)
Ziff-Davis Publishing Co.: Winter, 1952 (25¢, 100 pgs.)

nn-(Scarce)-Kinstler-a; painted-c 54 108 162 329 502 675

WOMEN OUTLAWS (My Love Memories #9 on)(Also see Red Circle)
Fox Features Syndicate: July, 1948 - No. 8, Sept, 1949

1-Used in **SOTI**, illo "Giving children an image of American womanhood"; negligee panels 75 150 225 469 722 975
2,3: 3-Kamenish-a 59 118 177 369 565 760
4-8 47 94 141 287 436 585
nn(nd)-Contains Cody of the Pony Express; same cover as #7 35 70 105 198 287 375

WOMEN TO LOVE
Realistic: No date (1953)

nn-(Scarce)-Reprints Complete Romance #1; c-/Avon paperback #165 40 80 120 233 342 450

WONDER BOY (Formerly Terrific Comics) (See Blue Bolt, Bomber Comics & Samson)
Ajax/Farrell Publ.: No. 17, May, 1955 - No. 18, July, 1955 (Code approved)

17-Phantom Lady app. Bakerish-c/a 46 92 138 281 428 575
18-Phantom Lady app. 40 80 120 233 342 450

NOTE: *Phantom Lady not by Matt Baker.*

WONDER COMICS (Wonderworld #3 on)
Fox Features Syndicate: May, 1939 - No. 2, June, 1939 (68 pgs.)

1-(Scarce)-Wonder Man only app. by Will Eisner; Dr. Fung (by Powell), K-51 begins; Bob Kane-a; Eisner-c 1324 2648 3972 9930 16,215 22,500
2-(Scarce)-Yarko the Great, Master Magician (see Samson) by Eisner begins; 'Spark' Stevens by Bob Kane, Patty O'Day, Tex Mason app. Lou Fine's 1st-c; Fine-a (2 pgs.); Yarko-c (Wonder Man-c #1) 452 904 1356 3164 5082 7000

WONDER COMICS
Great/Nedor/Better Publications: May, 1944 - No. 20, Oct, 1948

Wonder Comics #17 © BP

Wonder Woman #1 © DC

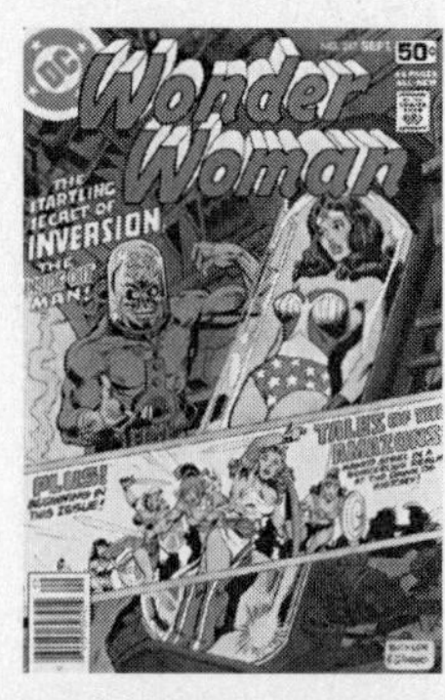

Wonder Woman #247 © DC

	GD 2.0	VG 4.0	FN 6.0	VF 8.0	VF/NM 9.0	NM- 9.2
1-The Grim Reaper & Spectro, the Mind Reader begin; Hitler/Hirohito bondage-c	146	292	438	913	1407	1900
2-Origin The Grim Reaper; Super Sleuths begin, end #8,17	69	138	207	431	666	900
3-5: 3-Indicia reads "Vol. 1, #2"	62	124	186	388	594	800
6-10: 6-Flag-c. 8-Last Spectro. 9-Wonderman begins	51	102	153	311	473	635
11-14: 11-Dick Devens, King of Futuria begins, ends #14. 11,12-Ingels-c & splash pg. 14-Bondage-c	60	120	180	375	575	775
15-Tara begins (origin), ends #20	69	138	207	431	666	900
16,18: 16-Spectro app.; last Grim Reaper. 18-The Silver Knight begins	60	120	180	375	575	775
17-Wonderman with Frazetta panels; Jill Trent with all Frazetta inks	62	124	186	388	594	800
19-Frazetta panels	60	120	180	375	575	775
20-Most of Silver Knight by Frazetta	71	142	213	444	685	925

NOTE: ***Ingels*** *c-11, 12.* ***Roussos*** *a-19.* ***Schomburg (Xela)*** *c-1-10; (airbrush)-13-20. Bondage c-12, 13, 15. Cover features: Grim Reaper #1-8; Wonder Man #9-15; Tara #16-20.*

WONDER DUCK (See Wisco)
Marvel Comics (CDS): Sept, 1949 - No. 3, Mar, 1950

	GD 2.0	VG 4.0	FN 6.0	VF 8.0	VF/NM 9.0	NM- 9.2
1-Funny animal	16	32	48	92	131	170
2,3	10	20	30	60	80	100

WONDERFUL ADVENTURES OF PINOCCHIO, THE (See Movie Comics & Walt Disney Showcase #48)
Whitman Publishing Co.: April, 1982 (Walt Disney)

	GD 2.0	VG 4.0	FN 6.0	VF 8.0	VF/NM 9.0	NM- 9.2
nn-(#3 Continuation of Movie Comics?); r/FC #92						6.00

WONDERFUL WORLD OF DISNEY, THE (Walt Disney)
Whitman Publishing Co.: 1978 (Digest, 116 pgs.)

	GD 2.0	VG 4.0	FN 6.0	VF 8.0	VF/NM 9.0	NM- 9.2
1-Barks-a (reprints)	3	6	9	18	24	30
2 (no date)	2	4	6	12	16	20

WONDERFUL WORLD OF THE BROTHERS GRIMM (See Movie Comics)

WONDERLAND: CHILDREN OF THE FUTURE AGE
Image Comics: 2004 ($6.95, squarebound, graphic novel)

	GD 2.0	VG 4.0	FN 6.0	VF 8.0	VF/NM 9.0	NM- 9.2
1-Derek Watson-s/Kit Wallis-a						7.00

WONDERLAND COMICS
Feature Publications/Prize: Summer, 1945 - No. 9, Feb-Mar, 1947

	GD 2.0	VG 4.0	FN 6.0	VF 8.0	VF/NM 9.0	NM- 9.2
1-Alex in Wonderland begins; Howard Post-c	20	40	60	112	161	210
2-Howard Post-c/a(2)	11	22	33	62	84	105
3-9: 3,4-Post-c	10	20	30	56	73	90

WONDER MAN (See The Avengers #9, 151)
Marvel Comics Group: Mar, 1986 ($1.25, one-shot, 52 pgs.)

	GD 2.0	VG 4.0	FN 6.0	VF 8.0	VF/NM 9.0	NM- 9.2
1						3.00

WONDER MAN
Marvel Comics Group: Sept, 1991 - No. 29, Jan, 1994 ($1.00)

	GD 2.0	VG 4.0	FN 6.0	VF 8.0	VF/NM 9.0	NM- 9.2
1-29: 1-Free fold out poster by Johnson/Austin. 1-3-Johnson/Austin-c/a. 2-Avengers West Coast x-over. 4 Austin-c(i)						2.25
Annual 1 (1992, $2.25)-Immonen-a (10 pgs.)						2.50
Annual 2 (1993, $2.25)-Bagged w/trading card						2.50

WONDERS OF ALADDIN, THE
Dell Publishing Co.: No. 1255, Feb-Apr, 1962

	GD 2.0	VG 4.0	FN 6.0	VF 8.0	VF/NM 9.0	NM- 9.2
Four Color 1255-Movie	8	16	24	53	74	95

WONDER WOMAN (See Adventure Comics #459, All-Star Comics, Brave & the Bold, DC Comics Presents, JLA, Justice League of America, Legend of..., Power Record Comics, Sensation Comics, Super Friends and World's Finest Comics #244)

WONDER WOMAN
National Periodical Publications/All-American Publ./DC Comics:
Summer, 1942 - No. 329, Feb, 1986

	GD 2.0	VG 4.0	FN 6.0	VF 8.0	VF/NM 9.0	NM- 9.2
1-Origin Wonder Woman retold (more detailed than All-Star #8); H. G. Peter-c/a begins	2200	4400	6600	16,500	27,000	37,500

1-Reprint, Oversize 13-1/2x10". **WARNING:** This comic is an exact reprint of the original except for its size. DC published it in 1974 with a second cover titling it as a Famous First Edition. There have been many reported cases of the outer cover being removed and the interior sold as the original edition. The reprint with the new outer cover removed is practically worthless. See Famous First Edition for value.

	GD 2.0	VG 4.0	FN 6.0	VF 8.0	VF/NM 9.0	NM- 9.2
2-Origin/1st app. Mars; Duke of Deception app.	414	828	1242	2691	4346	6000
3	231	462	693	1444	2222	3000
4,5: 5-1st Dr. Psycho app.	177	354	531	1106	1703	2300
6-9: 6-1st Cheetah app.	138	276	414	863	1332	1800
10-Invasion from Saturn classic sci-fi-c/s	150	300	450	938	1444	1950
11-20	112	224	336	700	1075	1450
21-30: 23-Story from Wonder Woman's childhood	89	178	267	556	853	1150
31-33,35-40: 38-Last H.G. Peter-c	62	124	186	388	594	800
34-Robot-c	65	130	195	406	628	850
41-44,46-49: 49-Used in **SOTI**, pgs. 234,236; last 52 pg. issue	51	102	153	311	476	640
45-Origin retold	94	188	282	588	907	1225
50-(44 pgs.)-Used in **POP**, pg. 97	51	102	153	311	476	640
51-60: 60-New logo	40	80	120	235	348	460
61-72: 62-Origin of W.W. i.d. 64-Story about 3-D movies. 70-1st Angle Man app. 72-Last pre-code (2/55)	37	74	111	209	305	400
73-90: 80-Origin The Invisible Plane. 85-1st S.A. issue. 89-Flying saucer-c/story	33	66	99	190	275	360
91-94,96,97,99: 97-Last H. G. Peter-a	27	54	81	152	219	285
95-A-Bomb-c	28	56	84	158	229	300
98-New origin & new art team (Andru & Esposito) begin (5/58); origin W.W. id w/new facts	30	60	90	173	249	325
100-(8/58)	30	60	90	173	249	325
101-104,106,108-110	23	46	69	132	191	250
105-(Scarce, 4/59)-W. W.'s secret origin; W. W. appears as girl (no costume yet) (called Wonder Girl - see DC Super-Stars #1)	100	200	300	625	963	1300
107-1st advs. of Wonder Girl; 1st Merboy; tells how Wonder Woman won her costume	33	66	99	190	275	360
111-120	19	38	57	107	154	200
121-126: 121-1st app. Wonder Woman Family. 122-1st app. Wonder Tot. 126-Last 10¢ issue	15	30	45	86	123	160
127-130: 128-Origin The Invisible Plane retold. 129-2nd app. Wonder Woman Family (#133 is 3rd app.)	10	20	30	67	96	125
131-150: 132-Flying saucer-c	8	16	24	55	78	100
151-155,157,158,160-170 (1967): 151-Wonder Girl solo issue	7	14	21	46	63	80
156-(8/65)-Early mention of a comic book shop & comic collecting; mentions DCs selling for $100 a copy	7	14	21	51	71	90
159-Origin retold (1/66); 1st S.A. origin?	9	18	27	65	93	120
171-176	5	10	15	36	48	60
177-W. Woman/Supergirl battle	7	14	21	50	68	85
178-1st new W. Woman	7	14	21	51	71	90
179-Wears no costume to issue #203.	6	12	18	38	52	65
180-195: 180-Death of Steve Trevor. 195-Wood inks	4	8	12	27	36	45
196 (52 pgs.)-Origin-r/All-Star #8 (6 out of 9 pgs.)	4	8	12	29	40	50
197,198 (52 pgs.)-Reprints	4	8	12	29	40	50
199-Jeff Jones painted-c; 52 pgs.	6	12	18	43	59	75
200 (5-6/72)-Jeff Jones-c; 52 pgs.	7	14	21	50	68	85
201,202-Catwoman app. 202-Fafhrd & The Grey Mouser debut.	3	6	9	19	25	32
203,205-210,212: 212-The Cavalier app.	2	4	6	14	18	22
204-Return to old costume; death of I Ching.	3	6	9	18	23	28
211,214-(100 pgs.)	6	12	18	43	59	75
213,215,216,218-220: 220-N. Adams assist	2	4	6	12	16	20
217: (68 pgs.)	3	6	9	19	25	32
221,222,224-227,229,230,233-236,238-240	2	4	6	9	11	14
223,228,231,232,237,241,248: 223-Steve Trevor revived as Steve Howard & learns W.W.'s I.D. 228-Both Wonder Women team up & new World War II stories begin, end #243. 231,232: JSA app. 237-Origin retold. 241-Intro Bouncer; Spectre app. 248-Steve Trevor Howard dies (44 pgs.)	2	4	6	10	13	16
242-246,252-266,269,270: 243-Both W. Women team-up again. 269-Last Wood a(i) for DC? (7/80)	1	2	3	5	6	8
247,249-251,271: 247,249 (44 pgs.). 249-Hawkgirl app. 250-Origin/1st app. Orana, the new W. Woman. 251-Orana dies. 271-Huntress & 3rd Life of Steve Trevor begin	1	2	3	5	7	9
250-252,255-262,264-(Whitman variants, low print run, no issue # on cover)	2	4	6	10	13	16
267,268-Re-intro Animal Man (5/80 & 6/80)	1	3	4	6	8	10
272-280,284-286,289,290,294-299,301-325						5.00
281-283: Joker-c/stories in Huntress back-ups	1	2	3	5	7	9
287,288,291-293: 287-New Teen Titans x-over. 288-New costume & logo. 291-293-Three part epic with Super-Heroines						6.00
300-($1.50, 76 pgs.)-Anniv. issue; Giffen-a; New Teen Titans, Bronze Age Sandman, JLA & G.A. Wonder Woman app.; 1st app. Lyta Trevor who becomes Fury in All-Star Squadron #25; G.A. Wonder Woman & Steve Trevor revealed as married						6.00
326-328						6.00
329 (Double size)-S.A. W.W. & Steve Trevor wed	2	4	6	8	10	12

NOTE: ***Andru/Esposito*** *c-66-160(most).* ***Buckler*** *a-300.* ***Colan*** *a-288-305p; c-288-290p.* ***Giffen*** *a-300p.* ***Grell*** *c-217.* ***Kaluta*** *c-297.* ***Gil Kane*** *c-294p, 303-305, 307, 312, 314.* ***Miller*** *c-298p.* ***Morrow*** *c-233.* ***Nasser*** *a-232p; c-231p, 232p.* ***Bob Oskner*** *c(i)-39-65(most).* ***Perez*** *c-283p, 284p.* ***Spiegle*** *a-312.* ***Staton*** *a(p)-241, 271-287, 289,*

Wonder Woman (2nd) #204 © DC

Wonderworld Comics #24 © FOX

Woody Woodpecker ('91) #1 © Walter Lantz

290, 294-299; c(p)-241, 245, 246. Huntress back-up stories 271-287, 289, 290, 294-299, 301-321.

WONDER WOMAN
DC Comics: Feb, 1987 - Present (75¢/$1.00/$1.25/$1.95/$1.99/$2.25)

	GD 2.0	VG 4.0	FN 6.0	VF 8.0	VF/NM 9.0	NM- 9.2
0-(10/94) Zero Hour; released between #90 & #91	1	2	3	5	6	8
1-New origin; Perez-c/a begins	1	2	3	4	5	7
2-5						5.00
6-20: 9-Origin Cheetah. 12,13-Millennium x-over. 18,26-Free 16 pg. story						4.00
21-49: 24-Last Perez-a; scripts continue thru #62						3.00
50-($1.50, 52 pgs.)-New Titans, Justice League						4.00
51-62: Perez scripts. 60-Vs. Lobo; last Perez-c. 62-Last $1.00-c						3.00
63-New direction & Bolland-c begin; Deathstroke story continued fromW. W. Special #1						4.00
64-84						2.50
85-1st Deodato-a; ends #100	2	4	6	8	10	12
86-88: 88-Superman-c & app.						5.00
89-97: 90-(9/94)-1st Artemis. 91-(11/94). 93-Hawkman app. 96-Joker-c						4.00
98,99						3.00
100 ($2.95, Newsstand)-Death of Artemis; Bolland-c ends.						4.00
100 ($3.95, Direct Market)-Death of Artemis; foil-c.						6.00
101-119, 121-125: 101-Begin $1.95-c; Byrne-c/a/scripts begin. 101-104-Darkseid app. 105-Phantom Stranger cameo. 106-108-Phantom Stranger & Demon app. 107,108-Arion app. 111-1st app. new Wonder Girl. 111,112-Vs.Doomsday. 112-Superman app. 113-Wonder Girl-c/app; Sugar & Spike app.						2.50
120 ($2.95)-Perez-c						3.00
126-149: 128-Hippolyta becomes new W.W. 130-133-Flash (Jay Garrick) & JSA app. 136-Diana returns to W.W. role; last Byrne issue. 137-Priest-s. 139-Luke-s/Paquette-a begin; Hughes-c thru #146						2.50
150-($2.95) Hughes-c/Clark-a; Zauriel app.						3.00
151-158-Hughes-c. 153-Superboy app.						2.25
159-163: 159-Begin $2.25-c. 160,161-Clayface app. 162,163-Aquaman app.						2.25
164-171: Phil Jimenez-s/a begin; Hughes-c; Batman app. 168,169-Pérez co-plot 169-Wraparound-c.170-Lois Lane-c/app.						2.25
172-Our Worlds at War; Hippolyta killed						3.00
173,174: 173-Our Worlds at War; Darkseid app. 174-Every DC heroine app.						2.25
175-($3.50) Joker: Last Laugh; JLA app.; Jim Lee-c						3.50
176-199: 177-Paradise Island returns. 179-Jimenez-c. 184,185-Hippolyta-c/app.; Hughes-c 186-Cheetah app. 189-Simonson-s/Ordway-a begin. 190-Diana's new look. 195-Rucka-s/Drew Johnson-a begin. 197-Flash-c/app. 198,199-Noto-c						2.25
200-($3.95) back-up stories in 1940s and 1960s styles; pin-ups by various						4.00
201-210: 203,204-Batman-c/app. 204-Matt Wagner-c						2.25
#1,000,000 (11/98) 853rd Century x-over; Deodato-c						3.00
Annual 1,2: 1 ('88, $1.50)-Art Adams-a. 2 ('89, $2.00, 68 pgs.)-All women artists issue; Perez-c(i)/a.						4.00
Annual 3 (1992, $2.50, 68 pgs.)-Quesada-c(p)						3.00
Annual 4 (1995, $3.50)-Year One						3.50
Annual 5 (1996, $2.95)-Legends of the Dead Earth story; Byrne scripts; Cockrum-a						3.00
Annual 6 (1997, $3.95)-Pulp Heroes						4.00
Annual 7,8 ('98,'99, $2.95)-7-Ghosts; Wrightson-c. 8-JLApe, A.Adams-c						3.00
...: Challenge of the Gods TPB ('04, $19.95) r/#8-14; Pérez-s/a						20.00
...Donna Troy (6/98, $1.95) Girlfrenzy; Jimenez-a						2.50
...: Down To Earth TPB (2004, $14.95) r/#195-200; Greg Land-c						15.00
... 80-Page Giant 1 (2002, $4.95) reprints in format of 1960s' 80-Page Giants						5.00
Gallery (1996, $3.50)-Bolland-c; pin-ups by various						4.00
...: Gods and Mortals TPB ('04, $19.95) r/#1-7; Pérez-a						20.00
...: Gods of Gotham TPB ('01, $5.95) r/#164-167; Jimenez-s/a						6.00
Lifelines TPB ('98, $9.95) r/#106-112; Byrne-c/a						10.00
...: Our Worlds at War (10/01, $2.95) History of the Amazons; Jae Lee-c						3.00
...: Paradise Found TPB ('03, $14.95) r/#171-177, Secret Files #3; Jimenez-s/a						15.00
...: Paradise Lost TPB ('02, $14.95) r/#164-170; Jimenez-s/a						15.00
Plus 1 (1/97, $2.95)-Jesse Quick-c/app.						3.00
Second Genesis TPB (1997, $9.95)-r/#101-105						10.00
Secret Files 1-3 (3/98, 7/99, 5/02; $4.95)						5.00
Special 1 (1992, $1.75, 52 pgs.)-Deathstroke-c/story continued in Wonder Woman #63						4.00
...: The Blue Amazon (2003, $6.95) Elseworlds; McKeever-a						7.00
The Challenge Of Artemis TPB (1996, $9.95)-r/#94-100; Deodato-c/a						10.00
...: The Once and Future Story (1998, $4.95) Trina Robbins-s/Doran & Guice-a						5.00

NOTE: ***Art Adams*** *a-Annual 1.* ***Byrne*** *c/a 101-107.* ***Bolton*** *a-Annual 1.* ***Deodato*** *a-85-100.* ***Perez*** *a-Annual 1; c-Annual 1(i).* ***Quesada*** *c(p)-Annual 3.*

WONDER WOMAN: AMAZONIA
DC Comics: 1997 ($7.95, Graphic Album format, one shot)

	GD 2.0	VG 4.0	FN 6.0	VF 8.0	VF/NM 9.0	NM- 9.2
1-Elseworlds; Messner-Loebs-s/Winslade-a						8.00

WONDER WOMAN SPECTACULAR (See DC Special Series #9)

WONDER WOMAN: SPIRIT OF TRUTH
DC Comics: Nov, 2001 ($9.95, treasury size, one-shot)

	GD 2.0	VG 4.0	FN 6.0	VF 8.0	VF/NM 9.0	NM- 9.2
nn-Painted art by Alex Ross; story by Alex Ross and Paul Dini						10.00

WONDER WOMAN: THE HIKETEIA
DC Comics: 2002 ($24.95, hardcover, one-shot)

	GD 2.0	VG 4.0	FN 6.0	VF 8.0	VF/NM 9.0	NM- 9.2
nn-Wonder Woman battles Batman; Greg Rucka-s/J.G. Jones-a						25.00
Softcover (2003, $17.95)						18.00

WONDERWORLD COMICS (Formerly Wonder Comics)
Fox Features Syndicate: No. 3, July, 1939 - No. 33, Jan, 1942

	GD 2.0	VG 4.0	FN 6.0	VF 8.0	VF/NM 9.0	NM- 9.2
3-Intro The Flame by Fine; Dr. Fung (Powell-a), K-51 (Powell-a?), & Yarko the Great, Master Magician (Eisner-a) continues; Eisner/Fine-c	658	1316	1974	4606	7403	10,200
4-Lou Fine-c	317	634	951	2061	3331	4600
5,6,9,10: Lou Fine-c	181	362	543	1131	1741	2350
7-Classic Lou Fine-c	300	600	900	1925	3063	4200
8-Classic Lou Fine-c	262	524	786	1638	2519	3400
11-Origin The Flame	138	276	414	863	1332	1800
12-15:13-Dr. Fung ends; last Fine-c	115	230	345	719	1110	1500
16-20	85	170	255	531	816	1100
21-Origin The Black Lion & Cub	77	154	231	481	741	1000
22-27: 22,25-Dr. Fung app.	62	124	186	388	594	800
28-Origin & 1st app. U.S. Jones (8/41); Lu-Nar, the Moon Man begins	83	166	249	519	802	1085
29,31,33	50	100	150	305	465	625
30-Intro & Origin Flame Girl	90	180	270	563	869	1175
32-Hitler-c	71	142	213	444	685	925

NOTE: *Spies at War by* ***Eisner*** *in #13, 17. Yarko by* ***Eisner*** *in #3-11.* ***Eisner*** *text illos-3.* ***Lou Fine*** *a-3-11; c-3-13, 15; text illos-4.* ***Nordling*** *a-4-14.* ***Powell*** *a-3-12.* ***Tuska*** *a-5-9. Bondage-c 14, 15, 28, 31, 32. Cover features: The Flame-#3, 5-31; U.S. Jones-#32, 33.*

WONDERWORLDS
Innovation Publishing: 1992 ($3.50, squarebound, 100 pgs.)

	GD 2.0	VG 4.0	FN 6.0	VF 8.0	VF/NM 9.0	NM- 9.2
1-Rebound super-hero comics, contents may vary; Hero Alliance, Terraformers, etc.						3.50

WOODSY OWL (See March of Comics #395)
Gold Key: Nov, 1973 - No. 10, Feb, 1976

	GD 2.0	VG 4.0	FN 6.0	VF 8.0	VF/NM 9.0	NM- 9.2
1	2	4	6	14	18	22
2-10	2	4	6	8	10	12

WOODY WOODPECKER (Walter Lantz... #73 on?)(See Dell Giants for annuals)
(Also see The Funnies, Jolly Jingles, Kite Fun Book, New Funnies)
Dell Publishing Co./Gold Key No. 73-187/Whitman No. 188 on:
No. 169, 10/47 - No. 72, 5-7/62; No. 73, 10/62 - No. 201, 3/84 (nn 192)

	GD 2.0	VG 4.0	FN 6.0	VF 8.0	VF/NM 9.0	NM- 9.2
Four Color 169(#1)-Drug turns Woody into a Mr. Hyde	18	36	54	131	201	270
Four Color 188	12	24	36	86	131	175
Four Color 202,232,249,264,288	9	18	27	65	93	120
Four Color 305,336,350	7	14	21	46	63	80
Four Color 364,374,390,405,416,431('52)	6	12	18	38	52	65
16 (12-1/52-53) - 30('55)	4	8	12	29	40	50
31-50	4	8	12	22	30	38
51-72 (Last Dell)	3	6	9	18	24	30
73-75 (Giants, 84 pgs., Gold Key)	6	12	18	38	52	65
76-80	3	6	9	16	21	26
81-103: 103-Last 12¢ issue	2	4	6	14	18	22
104-120	2	4	6	12	16	20
121-140	2	4	6	10	12	15
141-160	1	3	4	6	8	10
161-187	1	2	3	5	7	9
188,189 (Whitman)	2	4	6	9	11	14
190(9/80),191(11/80)-pre-pack only	3	6	9	16	20	24
(No #192)						
193-197: 196(2/82), 197(4/82)	2	4	6	11	14	18
198-201 (All #90062 on-c, no date or date code, pre-pack): 198(6/83), 199(7/83), 200(8/83), 201(3/84)	2	4	6	12	16	20
Christmas Parade 1(11/68-Giant)(G.K.)	5	10	15	33	44	55
Summer Fun 1(6/66-G.K.)(84 pgs.)	6	12	18	38	52	65
nn (1971, 60¢, 100 pgs.) B&W one page gags	2	4	6	14	18	22

NOTE: *15¢ Canadian editions of the 12¢ issues exist. Reprints-No. 92, 102, 103, 105, 106, 124, 125, 152, 153, 157, 162, 165, 194(1/3)-200(1/3).*

WOODY WOODPECKER (See Comic Album #5,9,13, Dell Giant #24, 40, 54, Dell Giants, The Funnies, Golden Comics Digest #1, 3, 5, 8, 15, 16, 20, 24, 32, 37, 44, March of Comics #16, 34, 85, 93, 109, 124, 139, 158, 177, 184, 203, 222, 239, 249, 261, 420, 454, 466, 478, New Funnies & Super Book #12, 24)

WOODY WOODPECKER
Harvey Comics: Sept, 1991 - No. 15, Aug, 1994 ($1.25)

	GD 2.0	VG 4.0	FN 6.0	VF 8.0	VF/NM 9.0	NM- 9.2
1-15: 1-r/W.W. #53						2.50

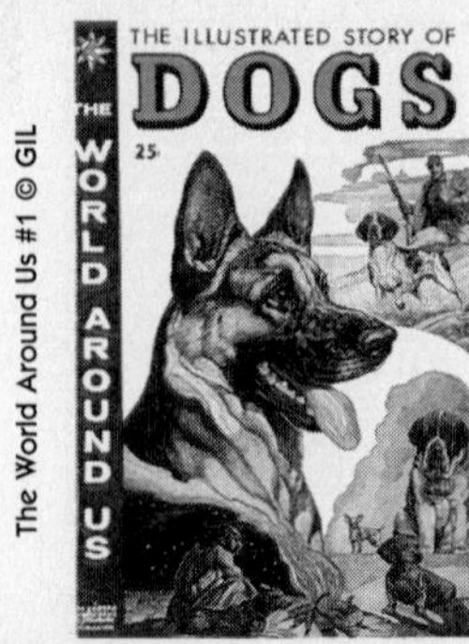

The World Around Us #1 © GIL

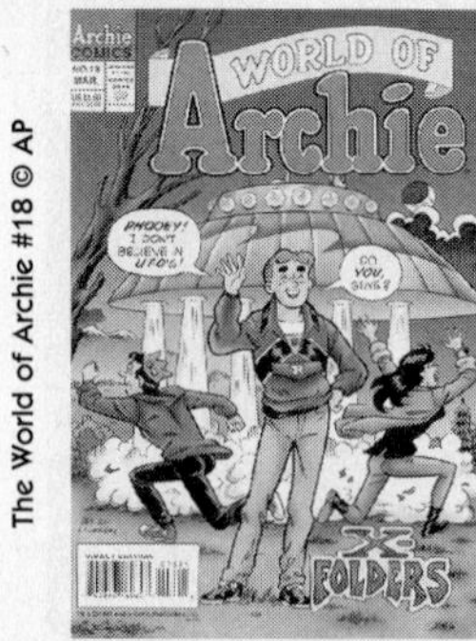

The World of Archie #18 © AP

World of Mystery #6 © MAR

GD VG FN VF VF/NM NM-
2.0 4.0 6.0 8.0 9.0 9.2

50th Anniversary Special 1 (10/91, $2.50, 68 pgs.) 3.00

WOODY WOODPECKER AND FRIENDS
Harvey Comics: Dec, 1991 - No. 4, 1992 ($1.25)
1-4 2.50

WORDSMITH (1st Series)
Renegade Press: Aug, 1985 - No. 12, Jan, 1988 ($1.70/$2.00, B&W, bi-monthly)
1-12: R. G. Taylor-c/a 3.00

WORDSMITH (2nd Series)
Caliber: 1996 - No. 9, 1997 ($2.95, B&W, limited series)
1-9: Reprints in all. 1-Contains 3 pg. sketchbook. 6-Flip book w/Raven Chronicles #10 3.00

WORD WARRIORS (Also see Quest for Dreams Lost)
Literacy Volunteers of Chicago: 1987 ($1.50, B&W)(Proceeds donated to help literacy)
1-Jon Sable by Grell, Ms. Tree, Streetwolf; Chaykin-c 3.00

WORLD AROUND US, THE (Illustrated Story of...)
Gilberton Publishers (Classics Illustrated): Sep, 1958 -No. 36, Oct, 1961 (25¢)
1-Dogs; Evans-a 9 18 27 51 62 75
2-4: 2-Indians; Check-a. 3-Horses; L. B. Cole-c. 4-Railroads; L. B. Cole-a (5 pgs.)
8 16 24 46 58 70
5-Space; Ingels-a 10 20 30 56 73 90
6-The F.B.I.; Disbrow, Evans, Ingels-a 10 20 30 56 73 90
7-Pirates; Disbrow, Ingels, Kinstler-a 9 18 27 52 66 80
8-Flight; Evans, Ingels, Crandall-a 9 18 27 52 66 80
9-Army; Disbrow, Ingels, Orlando-a 8 16 24 46 58 70
10-13: 10-Navy; Disbrow, Kinstler-a. 11-Marine Corps. 12-Coast Guard; Ingels-a (9 pgs.).
13-Air Force; L.B. Cole-c 8 16 24 46 58 70
14-French Revolution; Crandall, Evans, Kinstler-a 10 20 30 56 73 90
15-Prehistoric Animals; Al Williamson-a, 6 & 10 pgs. plus Morrow-a
10 20 30 58 77 95
16-18: 16-Crusades; Kinstler-a. 17-Festivals; Evans, Crandall-a. 18-Great Scientists;
Crandall, Evans, Torres, Williamson, Morrow-a 9 18 27 52 66 80
19-Jungle; Crandall, Williamson, Morrow-a 10 20 30 58 77 95
20-Communications; Crandall, Evans, Torres-a 10 20 30 56 73 90
21-American Presidents; Crandall/Evans, Morrow-a 10 20 30 56 73 90
22-Boating; Morrow-a 8 16 24 43 54 65
23-Great Explorers; Crandall, Evans-a 9 18 27 52 66 80
24-Ghosts; Morrow, Evans-a 10 20 30 56 73 90
25-Magic; Evans, Morrow-a 10 20 30 56 73 90
26-The Civil War 11 22 33 63 84 105
27-Mountains (High Advs.); Crandall/Evans, Morrow, Torres-a
9 18 27 52 66 80
28-Whaling; Crandall, Evans, Morrow, Torres, Wildey-a; L.B. Cole-c
9 18 27 52 66 80
29-Vikings; Crandall, Evans, Torres, Morrow-a 10 20 30 58 77 95
30-Undersea Adventure; Crandall/Evans, Kirby, Morrow, Torres-a
10 20 30 56 73 90
31-Hunting; Crandall/Evans, Ingels, Kinstler, Kirby-a 9 18 27 52 66 80
32,33: 32-For Gold & Glory; Morrow, Kirby, Crandall, Evans-a. 33-Famous Teens;
Torres, Crandall, Evans-a 9 18 27 52 66 80
34-36: 34-Fishing; Crandall/Evans-a. 35-Spies; Kirby, Morrow?, Evans-a.
36-Fight for Life (Medicine); Kirby-a 9 18 27 52 66 80

NOTE: See Classics Illustrated Special Edition. Another *World Around Us* issue entitled *The Sea* had been prepared in 1962 but was never published in the U.S. It was published in the British/European *World Around Us* series. Those series then continued with seven additional WAU titles not in the U.S. series.

WORLD BELOW, THE
Dark Horse Comics: Mar, 1999 - No. 4, Jun, 1999 ($2.50, limited series)
1-4-Paul Chadwick-s/c/a 2.50

WORLD BELOW, THE: DEEPER AND STRANGER
Dark Horse Comics: Dec, 1999 - No. 4, Mar, 2000 ($2.95, B&W)
1-4-Paul Chadwick-s/c/a 3.00

WORLD CLASS COMICS
Image Comics: Aug, 2002 ($4.95, B&W)
1-Characters from Big Bang Comics 5.00

WORLD FAMOUS HEROES MAGAZINE
Comic Corp. of America (Centaur): Oct, 1941 - No. 4, Apr, 1942 (comic book)
1-Gustavson-c; Lubbers, Glanzman-a; Davy Crockett, Paul Revere, Lewis & Clark,
John Paul Jones stories; Flag-c 119 238 357 744 1147 1550
2-Lou Gehrig life story; Lubbers-a 50 100 150 305 465 625
3,4-Lubbers-a. 4-Wild Bill Hickok story; 2 pg. Marlene Dietrich story
46 92 138 281 428 575

WORLD FAMOUS STORIES
Croyden Publishers: 1945
1-Ali Baba, Hansel & Gretel, Rip Van Winkle, Mid-Summer Night's Dream
14 28 42 79 110 140

WORLD IS HIS PARISH, THE
George A. Pflaum: 1953 (15¢)
nn-The story of Pope Pius XII 6 12 18 28 34 40

WORLD OF ADVENTURE (Walt Disney's...)(TV)
Gold Key: Apr, 1963 - No. 3, Oct, 1963 (12¢)
1-Disney TV characters; Savage Sam, Johnny Shiloh, Capt. Nemo, The Mooncussers
4 8 12 25 33 42
2,3 3 6 9 16 21 26

WORLD OF ARCHIE, THE (See Archie Giant Series Mag. #148, 151, 156, 160, 165, 171, 177, 182, 188, 193, 200, 208, 213, 225, 232, 237, 244, 249, 456, 461, 468, 473, 480, 485, 492, 497, 504, 509, 516, 521, 532, 543, 554, 565, 574, 587, 599, 612, 627)

WORLD OF ARCHIE
Archie Comics: Aug, 1992 - No. 22 ($1.25/$1.50)
1 4.00
2-15: 9-Neon ink-c 3.00
16-22 2.50

WORLD OF FANTASY
Atlas Comics (CPC No. 1-15/ZPC No. 16-19): May, 1956 - No. 19, Aug, 1959
1 46 92 138 281 428 575
2-Williamson-a (4 pgs.) 33 66 99 190 275 360
3-Sid Check, Roussos-a 29 58 87 164 237 310
4-7 22 44 66 125 180 235
8-Matt Fox, Orlando, Berg-a 24 48 72 135 195 255
9-Krigstein-a 23 46 69 130 188 245
10-15: 11-Torres-a 18 36 54 100 143 185
16-Williamson-a (4 pgs.); Ditko, Kirby-a 25 50 75 144 207 270
17-19-Ditko, Kirby-a 25 50 75 144 207 270

NOTE: ***Ayers*** *a-3.* ***B. Baily*** *a-4.* ***Berg*** *a-5, 6, 8.* ***Brodsky*** *c-3.* ***Check*** *a-3.* ***Ditko*** *a-17, 19.* ***Everett*** *a-2; c-4-7, 9, 12, 13.* ***Forte*** *a-4.* ***Infantino*** *a-14.* ***Kirby*** *c-15, 17-19.* ***Krigstein*** *a-9.* ***Maneely*** *c-2, 14.* ***Mooney*** *a-14.* ***Morrow*** *a-7.* ***Orlando*** *a-8, 13, 14.* ***Pakula*** *a-9.* ***Powell*** *a-4, 6.* ***R.Q. Sale*** *a-3, 9.* ***Severin*** *c-1.*

WORLD OF GIANT COMICS, THE (See Archie All-Star Specials under Archie Comics)

WORLD OF GINGER FOX, THE (Also see Ginger Fox)
Comico: Nov, 1986 ($6.95, 8 1/2 x 11", 68 pgs., mature)
Graphic Novel ($6.95) 7.00
Hardcover ($27.95) 28.00

WORLD OF JUGHEAD, THE (See Archie Giant Series Mag. #9, 14, 19, 24, 30, 136, 143, 149, 152, 157, 161, 166, 172, 178, 183, 189, 194, 202, 209, 215, 227, 233, 239, 245, 251, 457, 463, 469, 475, 481, 487, 493, 499, 505, 511, 517, 523, 531, 542, 553, 564, 577, 590, 602)

WORLD OF KRYPTON, THE (World of...#3) (See Superman #248)
DC Comics, Inc.: 7/79 - No. 3, 9/79; 12/87 - No. 4, 3/88 (Both are lim. series)
1-3 (1979, 40¢; 1st comic book mini-series): 1-Jor-El marries Lara. 3-Baby Superman
sent to Earth; Krypton explodes; Mon-el app. 5.00
1-4 (75¢)-Byrne scripts; Byrne/Simonson-c 3.00

WORLD OF METROPOLIS, THE
DC Comics: Aug, 1988 - No. 4, July, 1988 ($1.00, limited series)
1-4: Byrne scripts 3.00

WORLD OF MYSTERY
Atlas Comics (GPI): June, 1956 - No. 7, July, 1957
1-Torres, Orlando-a; Powell-a? 46 92 138 281 428 575
2-Woodish-a 20 40 60 112 161 210
3-Torres, Davis, Ditko-a 25 50 75 141 203 265
4-Pakula, Powell-a 25 50 75 141 203 265
5,7: 5-Orlando-a 20 40 60 112 161 210
6-Williamson/Mayo-a (4 pgs.); Ditko-a; Crandall text illo
25 50 75 141 203 265

NOTE: ***Brodsky*** *c-2.* ***Colan*** *a-7.* ***Everett*** *c-1, 3.* ***Pakula*** *a-4, 6.* ***Romita*** *a-2.* ***Severin*** *c-7.*

WORLD OF SMALLVILLE
DC Comics: Apr, 1988 - No. 4, July, 1988 (75¢, limited series)
1-4: Byrne scripts 3.00

WORLD OF SUSPENSE
Atlas News Co.: Apr, 1956 - No. 8, July, 1957
1 40 80 120 239 357 475
2-Ditko-a (4 pgs.) 24 48 72 138 199 260
3,7-Williamson-a in both (4 pgs.); #7-with Mayo 24 48 72 135 195 255

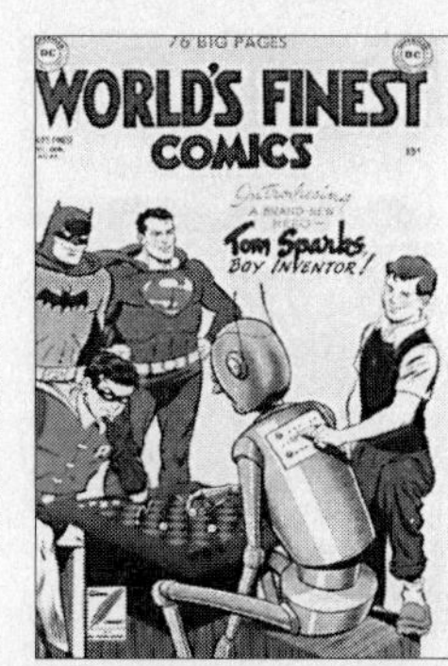

World's Finest Comics #49 © DC

World's Finest Comics #90 © DC

World's Finest Comics #210 © DC

	GD 2.0	VG 4.0	FN 6.0	VF 8.0	VF/NM 9.0	NM- 9.2

4-6,8 20 40 60 112 161 210

NOTE: ***Berg** a-6. **Cameron** a-2. **Ditko** a-2. **Drucker** a-1. **Everett** a-1, 5; c-6. **Heck** a-5. **Maneely** a-1; c-1-3. **Orlando** a-5. **Powell** a-6. **Reinman** a-4. **Roussos** a-6. **Shores** a-1.*

WORLD OF WHEELS (Formerly Dragstrip Hotrodders)
Charlton Comics: No. 17, Oct, 1967 - No. 32, June, 1970

17-20-Features Ken King 3 7 10 21 28 35
21-32-Features Ken King 3 6 9 18 23 28
Modern Comics Reprint 23(1978) 5.00

WORLD OF WOOD
Eclipse Comics: 1986 - No. 4, 1987; No. 5, 2/89 ($1.75, limited series)

1-4:1-Dave Stevens-c. 2-Wood/Stevens-c 4.00
5 ($2.00, B&W)-r/Avon's Flying Saucers 5.00

WORLD'S BEST COMICS (World's Finest Comics #2 on)
National Per. Publications (100 pgs.): Spring, 1941 (Cardboard-c)(DC's 6th annual format comic)

1-The Batman, Superman, Crimson Avenger, Johnny Thunder, The King, Young Dr. Davis, Zatara, Lando, Man of Magic, & Red, White & Blue begin; Superman, Batman & Robin covers begin (inside-c is blank); Fred Ray-c; 15¢ cover price
1429 2858 4287 10,080 16,290 22,500

WORLD'S BEST COMICS: GOLDEN AGE SAMPLER
DC Comics: 2003 (99¢, one-shot, samples from DC Archive editions)

1-Golden Age reprints from Superman #6, Batman #5, Sensation #11, Police #11 2.25

WORLD'S BEST COMICS: SILVER AGE SAMPLER
DC Comics: 2004 (99¢, one-shot, samples from DC Archive editions)

1-Silver Age reprints from Justice League #4, Adventure #247, Our Army at War #81 2.25

WORLDS BEYOND (Stories of Weird Adventure)(Worlds of Fear #2 on)
Fawcett Publications: Nov, 1951

1-Powell, Bailey-a; Moldoff-c 45 90 135 275 418 560

WORLDS COLLIDE
DC Comics: July, 1994 ($2.50, one-shot)

1-($2.50, 52 pgs.)-Milestone & Superman titles x-over 2.50
1-($3.95, 52 pgs.)-Polybagged w/vinyl clings 4.00

WORLD'S FAIR COMICS (See New York...)

WORLD'S FINEST (Also see Legends of The World's Finest)
DC Comics: 1990 - No. 3, 1990 ($3.95, squarebound, limited series, 52 pgs.)

1-3: Batman & Superman team-up against The Joker and Lex Luthor; Dave Gibbons scripts & Steve Rude-c/a. 2,3-Joker/Luthor painted-c by Steve Rude 5.00
TPB-($19.95) r/#1-3 20.00

WORLD'S FINEST COMICS (Formerly World's Best Comics #1)
National Periodical Publ./DC Comics: No. 2, Sum, 1941 - No. 323, Jan, 1986 (#1-17 have cardboard covers) (#2-9 have 100 pgs.)

2 (100 pgs.)-Superman, Batman & Robin covers continue from World's Best; (cover price 15¢ #2-70) 432 864 1296 3024 4862 6700
3-The Sandman begins; last Johnny Thunder; origin & 1st app. The Scarecrow
327 654 981 2126 3438 4750
4-Hop Harrigan app.; last Young Dr. Davis 262 524 786 1638 2519 3400
5-Intro. TNT & Dan the Dyna-Mite; last King & Crimson Avenger
262 524 786 1638 2519 3400
6-Star Spangled Kid begins (Sum/42); Aquaman app.; S&K Sandman with Sandy in new costume begins, ends #7 192 384 576 1200 1850 2500
7-Green Arrow begins (Fall/42); last Lando & Red, White & Blue; S&K art
192 384 576 1200 1850 2500
8-Boy Commandos begin (by Simon(p) #12); last The King; includes "Minute Man Answers the Call" promo 181 362 543 1131 1741 2350
9-Batman cameo in Star Spangled Kid; S&K-a; last 100 pg. issue; Hitler, Mussolini, Tojo-c 204 408 612 1275 1963 2650
10-S&K-a; 76 pg. issues begin 169 338 507 1056 1628 2200
11-17: 17-Last cardboard cover issue 138 276 414 863 1332 1800
18-20: 18-Paper covers begin; last Star Spangled Kid. 20-Last quarterly issue
121 242 363 756 1166 1575
21-30: 21-Begin bi-monthly. 30-Johnny Everyman app.
87 174 261 544 835 1125
31-40: 33-35-Tomahawk app. 77 154 231 481 741 1000
41-50: 41-Boy Commandos end. 42-Intro The Wyoming Kid & begins (9-10/49), ends #63. 43-Full Steam Foley begins, ends #48. 48-Last square binding. 49-Tom Sparks, Boy Inventor begins; robot-c 60 120 180 375 575 775
51-60: 51-Zatara ends. 54-Last 76 pg. issue. 59-Manhunters Around the World begins (7-8/52), ends #62 56 112 168 350 543 735
61-64: 61-Joker story. 63-Capt. Compass app. 55 110 165 343 527 710
65-Origin Superman; Tomahawk begins (7-8/53), ends #101
79 158 237 494 765 1035
66-70-(15¢ issues, scarce)-Last 15¢, 68pg. issue 55 110 165 343 527 710
71-(10¢ issue, scarce)-Superman & Batman begin as team (7-8/54); were in separate stories until now; Superman & Batman exchange identities; 10¢ issues begin
119 238 357 744 1147 1550
72,73-(10¢ issue, scarce) 66 132 198 495 773 1050
74-Last pre-code issue 50 100 150 375 588 800
75-(1st code approved, 3-4/55) 48 96 144 360 560 760
76-80: 77-Superman loses powers & Batman obtains them
47 94 141 287 436 585
81-90: 84-1st S.A. issue. 88-1st Joker/Luthor team-up. 89-2nd Batmen of All Nations (aka Club of Heroes). 90-Batwoman's 1st app. in World's Finest (10/57, 3rd app. anywhere) plus-c app. 29 58 87 210 323 435
91-93,95-99: 96-99-Kirby Green Arrow. 99-Robot-c 22 44 66 155 238 320
94-Origin Superman/Batman team retold 53 106 159 424 662 900
100 (3/59) 36 72 108 270 428 585
101-110: 102-Tommy Tomorrow begins, ends #124 15 30 45 109 160 210
111-121: 111-1st app. The Clock King. 113-Intro. Miss Arrowette in Green Arrow; 1st Bat-Mite/Mr. Mxyzptlk team-up (11/60). 117-Batwoman-c. 121-Last 10¢ issue
12 24 36 86 131 175
122-128: 123-2nd Bat-Mite/Mr. Mxyzptlk team-up (2/62). 125-Aquaman begins (5/62), ends #139 (Aquaman #1 is dated 1-2/62) 10 20 30 67 96 125
129-Joker/Luthor team-up-c/story 11 22 33 77 114 150
130-142: 135-Last Dick Sprang story. 140-Last Green Arrow. 142-Origin The Composite Superman (villain); Legion app. 8 16 24 53 74 95
143-150: 143-1st Mailbag. 144-Clayface/Brainiac team-up; last Clayface until Action #443
6 12 18 43 59 75
151-153,155,157-160: 156-Intro of Bizarro Batman. 157-2nd Super Sons story; last app. Kathy Kane (Bat-Woman) until Batman Family #10
6 12 18 38 52 65
154-1st Super Sons story; last Bat-Woman in costume until Batman Family #10.
6 12 18 43 59 75
156-1st Bizarro Batman; Joker-c/story 10 20 30 73 107 140
161,170 (80-Pg. Giants G-28,G-40) 7 14 21 46 63 80
162-165,167,168,171,172: 168,172-Adult Legion app.
4 8 12 29 40 50
166-Joker-c/story 5 10 15 36 48 60
169-3rd app. new Batgirl(9/67)(cover and 1 panel cameo); 3rd Bat-Mite/Mr. Mxyzptlk team-up 5 10 15 33 44 55
173-('68)-1st S.A. app. Two-Face as Batman becomes Two-Face in story
9 18 27 65 93 120
174-Adams-c 5 10 15 33 44 55
175,176-Neal Adams-c/a; both reprint J'onn J'onzz origin/Detective #225,226
5 10 15 36 48 60
177-Joker/Luthor team-up-c/story 5 10 15 33 44 55
178,180,182,183,185,186: Adams-c on all. 182-Silent Knight-r/Brave & Bold #6. 185-Last 12¢ issue. 186-Johnny Quick-r 4 8 12 25 33 42
179-(80 Page Giant G-52) -Adams-c; r/#94 6 12 18 40 55 70
181,184,187: 187-Green Arrow origin-r by Kirby (Adv. #256)
4 8 12 22 30 38
188,197:(Giants G-64,G-76; 64 pages) 6 12 18 38 52 65
189-196: 190-193-Robin-r 3 6 9 18 24 30
198,199-3rd Superman/Flash race (see Flash #175 & Superman #199). 199-Adams-c 9 18 27 63 89 115
200-Adams-c 3 7 10 21 28 35
201-203: 203-Last 15¢ issue. 3 6 9 16 21 26
204,205-(52 pgs.) Adams-c: 204-Wonder Woman app. 205-Shining Knight-r (6 pgs.) by Frazetta/Adv. #153; Teen Titans x-over 3 6 9 18 24 30
206 (Giant G-88, 64 pgs.) 5 10 15 33 44 55
207,212-(52 pgs.) 3 6 9 18 24 30
208-211(25¢-c) Adams-c: 208-(52 pgs.) Origin Robotman-r/Det. #138. 209-211-(52 pgs.) 3 6 9 19 25 32
213,214,216-222,229: 217-Metamorpho begins, ends #220; Batman/Superman team-ups resume. 229-r/origin Superman-Batman team 2 4 6 10 13 16
215-Intro. Batman Jr. & Superman Jr. 3 6 9 18 24 30
223-228-(100 pgs.). 223-N. Adams-r. 223-Deadman origin. 226-N. Adams, S&K, Toth-r; Manhunter part origin-r/Det. #225,226. 227-Deadman app.
4 8 12 29 40 50
230-(68 pgs.) 3 6 9 18 23 28
231-243,247,248: 242-Super Sons. 248-Last Vigilante
2 4 6 8 10 12
244-246-Adams-c: 244-$1.00, 84 pg. issues begin; Green Arrow, Black Canary,

World's Finest Comics #258 © DC

Worlds Unknown #5 © MAR

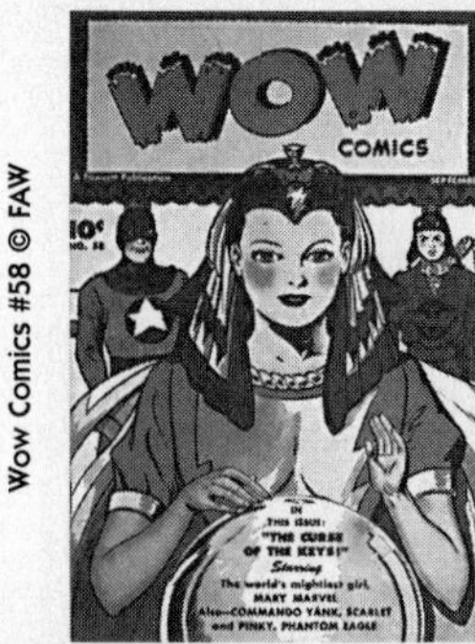

Wow Comics #58 © FAW

GD 2.0 | VG 4.0 | FN 6.0 | VF 8.0 | VF/NM 9.0 | NM- 9.2

Wonder Woman, Vigilante begin; 246-Death of Stuff in Vigilante; origin Vigilante retold 2 4 6 12 16 20
249-252 (84 pgs.) Ditko-a: 249-The Creeper begins by Ditko, 84 pgs. 250-The Creeper origin retold by Ditko. 252-Last 84 pg. issue 2 4 6 12 16 20
253-257,259-265: 253-Capt. Marvel begins; 68 pgs. begin, end #265. 255-Last Creeper. 256-Hawkman begins. 257-Black Lightning begins. 263-Super Sons. 264-Clay Face app. 2 4 6 8 10 12
258-Adams-c 2 4 6 9 11 14
266-270,272-282-(52 pgs.). 267-Challengers of the Unknown app.; 3 Lt. Marvels return. 268-Capt. Marvel Jr. origin retold. 274-Zatanna begins. 279, 280-Capt. Marvel Jr. & Kid Eternity learn they are brothers 1 3 4 6 8 10
271-(52pgs.) Origin Superman/Batman team retold 2 4 6 8 10 12
283-299: 284-Legion app. 1 2 3 4 5 7
300-($1.25, 52pgs.)-Justice League of America, New Teen Titans & The Outsiders app.; Perez-a (3 pgs.) 1 2 3 5 6 8
301-322: 304-Origin Null and Void. 309,319-Free 16 pg. story in each (309-Flash Force 2000, 319-Mask preview) 3.00
323-Last issue 6.00

NOTE: ***Neal Adams** a-230ir; c-174-176, 178-180, 182, 183, 185, 186, 199-205, 208-211, 244-246, 258. **Austin** a-244-246i. **Burnley** a-8, 10; c-7-9, 11-14, 15p?, 16-18p, 20-31p. **Colan** a-274p, 297, 299. **Ditko** a-249-255. **Giffen** a-322; c-284p, 322. **G. Kane** a-38, 174r, 282, 283; c-281, 282, 289. **Kirby** a-187. **Kubert** Zatara-40-44. **Miller** c-285p. **Mooney** c-134. **Morrow** a-245-248. **Mortimer** c-16-21, 26-71. **Nasser** a(p)-244-246, 259, 260. **Newton** a-253-281p. **Orlando** a-224r. **Perez** a-300i; c-271, 276, 277p, 278p. **Fred Ray** c-1-5. **Fred Ray/Robinson** c-13-16. **Robinson** a-5, 6, 9-11, 13?, 14-16; c-6. **Rogers** a-259p. **Roussos** a-212r. **Simonson** c-291. **Spiegle** a-275-278, 284. **Staton** a-262p, 273p. **Swan/Moldoff** c-126. **Swan/Mortimer** c-79-82. **Toth** a-228r. **Tuska** a-230r, 250p, 252p, 254p, 257p, 283p, 284p, 308p. Boy Commandos by **Infantino** #39-41.*

WORLD'S FINEST COMICS DIGEST (See DC Special Series #23)

WORLD'S FINEST: OUR WORLDS AT WAR
DC Comics: Oct, 2001 ($2.95, one-shot)

1-Concludes the Our Worlds at War x-over; Jae Lee-c; art by various 3.00

WORLD'S GREATEST ATHLETE (See Walt Disney Showcase #14)

WORLD'S GREATEST SONGS
Atlas Comics (Male): Sept, 1954

1-(Scarce)-Heath & Harry Anderson-a; Eddie Fisher life story plus-c; gives lyrics to Frank Sinatra song "Young at Heart" 40 80 120 233 342 450

WORLD'S GREATEST STORIES
Jubilee Publications: Jan, 1949 - No. 2, May, 1949

1-Alice in Wonderland; Lewis Carroll adapt. 35 70 105 200 290 380
2-Pinocchio 33 66 99 190 275 360

WORLDS OF FEAR (Stories of Weird Adventure)(Formerly Worlds Beyond #1)
Fawcett Publications: V1#2, Jan, 1952 - V2#10, June, 1953

V1#2 46 92 138 281 428 575
3-Evans-a 40 80 120 240 360 480
4-6(9/52) 38 76 114 219 320 420
V2#7-9 35 70 105 198 287 375
10-Saunders painted-c; man with no eyes surrounded by eyeballs-c plus eyes ripped out story 77 154 231 481 741 1000

NOTE: ***Moldoff** c-2-8. **Powell** a-2, 4, 5. **Sekowsky** a-4, 5.*

WORLDS UNKNOWN
Marvel Comics Group: May, 1973 - No. 8, Aug, 1974

1-r/from Astonishing #54; Torres, Reese-a 2 4 6 14 18 22
2-8 2 4 6 10 12 15

NOTE: ***Adkins/Mooney** a-5. **Buscema** c/a-4p. W. **Howard** c/a-3i. **Kane** a(p)-1,2; c(p)-5, 6, 8. **Sutton** a-2. **Tuska** a(p)-7, 8; c-7p. No. 7, 8 has Golden Voyage of Sinbad movie adaptation.*

WORLD WAR STORIES
Dell Publishing Co.: Apr-June, 1965 - No. 3, Dec, 1965

1-Glanzman-a in all 5 10 15 33 44 55
2,3 3 6 9 19 25 32

WORLD WAR II (See Classics Illustrated Special Issue)

WORLD WAR II: 1946
Antarctic Press: Oct, 1998 - No. 2 ($3.95, B&W)

1,2-Nomura-s/a 4.00

WORLD WAR III
Ace Periodicals: Mar, 1953 - No. 2, May, 1953

1-(Scarce)-Atomic bomb blast-c; Cameron-a 75 150 225 469 722 975
2-Used in **POP**, pg. 78 & B&W & color illos; Cameron-a 56 112 168 350 538 725

WORLDWATCH
Wild and Wooly Press: June, 2004 - Present ($2.95)

1,2-Austen-s/Derenick-a. 1-B&W. 2-Color 3.00

WORLD WITHOUT END
DC Comics: 1990 - No. 6, 1991 ($2.50, limited series, mature, stiff-c)

1-6: Horror/fantasy; all painted-c/a 2.50

WORLD WRESTLING FEDERATION BATTLEMANIA
Valiant: 1991 - No. 5?, 1991 ($2.50, magazine size, 68 pgs.)

1-5: 5-Includes 2 free pull-out posters 4.00

WORST FROM MAD, THE (Annual)
E. C. Comics: 1958 - No. 12, 1969 (Each annual cover is reprinted from the cover of the Mad issues being reprinted)(Value is 1/2 if bonus is missing)

nn(1958)-Bonus; record labels & travel stickers; 1st Mad annual; r/Mad #29-34 43 86 129 262 399 535
2(1959)-Bonus is small 33¹/3 rpm record entitled "Meet the Staff of Mad"; r/Mad #35-40 43 86 129 262 399 525
3(1960)-Has 20x30" campaign poster "Alfred E. Neuman for President"; r/Mad #41-46 20 40 60 145 223 300
4(1961)-Sunday comics section; r/Mad #47-54 19 38 57 134 205 275
5(1962)-Has 33-1/3 record; r/Mad #55-62 28 56 84 199 305 410
6(1963)-Has 33-1/3 record; r/Mad #63-70 28 56 84 199 305 410
7(1964)-Mad protest signs; r/Mad #71-76 11 22 33 79 117 155
8(1965)-Build a Mad Zeppelin 13 26 39 90 138 185
9(1966)-33-1/3 rpm record; Beatles on-c 19 38 57 134 205 275
10(1967)-Mad bumper sticker 8 16 24 55 78 160
11(1968)-Mad cover window stickers 8 16 24 53 74 95
12(1969)-Mad picture postcards; Orlando-a 8 16 24 53 74 95

NOTE: *Covers: **Bob Clarke**-#8. **Mingo**-#7, 9-12.*

WOTALIFE COMICS (Formerly Nutty Life #2; Phantom Lady #13 on)
Fox Features Syndicate/Norlen Mag.: No. 3, Aug-Sept, 1946 - No. 12, July, 1947; 1959

3-Cosmo Cat, Li'l Pan, others begin 10 20 30 60 80 100
4-12-Cosmo Cat, Li'l Pan in all 9 18 27 51 62 75
1(1959-Norlen)-Atomic Rabbit, Atomic Mouse; reprints cover to #6; reprints entire book? 8 16 24 40 50 60

WOTALIFE COMICS
Green Publications: 1957 - No. 5, 1957

1 7 14 21 35 43 50
2-5 5 10 15 22 26 30

WOW COMICS
Henle Publishing Co.: July, 1936 - No. 4, Nov, 1936 (52 pgs., magazine size)

1-Buck Jones in "The Phantom Rider" (1st app. in comics), Fu Manchu; Capt. Scott Dalton begins; Eisner-a; Briefer-c 285 570 855 1781 2741 3700
2-Ken Maynard, Fu Manchu, Popeye by Segar plus article on Popeye; Eisner-a 200 400 600 1250 1925 2600
3-Eisner-c/a(3); Popeye by Segar, Fu Manchu, Hiram Hick by Bob Kane, Space Limited app.; Jimmy Dempsey talks about Popeye's punch; Bob Ripley Believe it or Not begins; Briefer-a 185 370 555 1156 1778 2400
4-Flash Gordon by Raymond, Mandrake, Popeye by Segar, Tillie The Toiler, Fu Manchu, Hiram Hick by Bob Kane; Eisner-a(3); Briefer-c/a 231 462 693 1444 2222 3000

WOW COMICS (Real Western Hero #70 on)(See XMas Comics)
Fawcett Publ.: Winter, 1940-41; No. 2, Summer, 1941 - No. 69, Fall, 1948

nn(#1)-Origin Mr. Scarlet by S&K; Atom Blake, Boy Wizard, Jim Dolan, & Rick O'Shay begin; Diamond Jack, The White Rajah, & Shipwreck Roberts, only app.; 1st mention of Gotham City in comics; the cover was printed on unstable paper stock and is rarely found in fine or mint condition; blank inside-c; bondage-c by Beck 1265 2530 3795 9488 15,494 21,500
2 (Scarce)-The Hunchback begins 246 492 738 1538 2369 3200
3 (Fall, 1941) 117 234 351 731 1128 1525
4-Origin & 1st app. Pinky 121 242 363 756 1166 1575
5 79 158 237 494 760 1025
6-Origin & 1st app. The Phantom Eagle (7/15/42); Commando Yank begins 79 158 237 494 760 1025
7,8,10: 10-Swayze-c/a on Mary Marvel 62 124 186 388 594 800
9 (1/6/43)-Capt. Marvel, Capt. Marvel Jr., Shazam app.; Scarlet & Pinky x-over; Mary Marvel-c/stories begin (cameo #9) 135 270 405 844 1297 1750
11-17,19,20: 15-Flag-c 48 96 144 293 447 600
18-1st app. Uncle Marvel (10/43); infinity-c 50 100 150 305 465 625
21-30: 23-Robot-c. 28-Pinky x-over in Mary Marvel 31 62 93 178 259 340
31-40: 32-68-Phantom Eagle by Swayze 22 44 66 123 177 230
41-50 20 40 60 115 165 215
51-58: Last Mary Marvel 19 38 57 107 154 200

Wrath of the Spectre #1 © DC

Wyatt Earp #3 © MAR

Xena Vs. Callisto #1 © Universal TV

GD VG FN VF VF/NM NM-
2.0 4.0 6.0 8.0 9.0 9.2

59-69: 59-Ozzie (teenage) begins. 62-Flying Saucer gag-c (1/48). 65-69-Tom Mix stories (cont'd in Real Western Hero) 17 34 51 95 135 175

NOTE: *Cover features: Mr. Scarlet-#1-5; Commando Yank-#6, 7, (w/Mr. Scarlet #8); Mary Marvel-#9-56, (w/Commando Yank-#46-50), (w/Mr. Scarlet & Commando Yank-#51), (w/Mr. Scarlet & Pinky #53), (w/Phantom Eagle #54, 56), (w/Commando Yank & Phantom Eagle #58); Ozzie-#59-69.*

WRATH (Also see Prototype #4)
Malibu Comics: Jan, 1994 - No. 9, Nov, 1995 ($1.95)

1-9: 2-Mantra x-over. 3-Intro/1st app. Slayer. 4,5-Freex app. 8-Mantra & Warstrike app. 9-Prime app. 2.25
1-Ultra 5000 Limited silver foil 4.00
Giant Size 1 (2.50, 44 pgs.) 2.50

WRATH OF THE SPECTRE, THE
DC Comics: May, 1988 - No. 4, Aug, 1988 ($2.50, limited series)

1-3: Aparo-r/Adventure #431-440 4.00
4-New stories 5.00

WRECK OF GROSVENOR (See Superior Stories #3)

WRETCH, THE
Caliber: 1996 ($2.95, B&W)

1-Phillip Hester-a/scripts 3.00

WRETCH, THE
Amaze Ink: 1997 - No. 4, 1998 ($2.95, B&W)

1-4-Phillip Hester-a/scripts 3.00
... Vol. 1: Everyday Doomsday (4/03, $13.95) 14.00

WRINGLE WRANGLE (Disney)
Dell Publishing Co.: No. 821, July, 1957

Four Color 821-Based on movie "Westward Ho, the Wagons"; Marsh-a; Fess Parker photo-c 9 18 27 65 93 120

WULF THE BARBARIAN
Atlas/Seaboard Publ.: Feb, 1975 - No. 4, Sept, 1975

1,2: 1-Origin; Janson-a. 2-Intro. Berithe the Swordswoman; Janson-a w/Neal Adams, Wood, Reese-a assists 2 4 6 8 10 12
3,4: 3-Skeates-s. 4-Friedrich-s 1 2 3 5 7 9

WYATT EARP
Atlas Comics/Marvel No. 23 on (IPC): Nov, 1955 - #29, June, 1960; #30, Oct, 1972 - #34, June, 1973

1 22 44 66 125 180 235
2-Williamson-a (4 pgs.) 14 28 42 79 110 140
3-6,8-11: 3-Black Bart app. 8-Wild Bill Hickok app. 11 22 33 62 84 105
7,12-Williamson-a, 4 pgs. ea.; #12 with Mayo 11 22 33 62 84 105
13-20: 17-1st app. Wyatt's deputy, Grizzly Grant 10 20 30 56 73 90
21-Davis-c 9 18 27 52 66 80
22-24,26-29: 22-Ringo Kid app. 23-Kid From Texas app. 29-Last 10¢ issue 8 16 24 43 54 65
25-Davis-a 8 16 24 46 58 70
30-Williamson-r (1972) 2 4 6 12 16 20
31-34-Reprints. 32-Torres-a(r) 2 4 6 10 13 16

NOTE: ***Ayers** a-8, 10(2), 17, 20(4). **Berg** a-9. **Everett** c-6. **Kirby** c-25, 29. **Maneely** a-1; c-1-4, 8, 12, 17, 20. **Maurer** a-2(2), 3(4), 4(4), 8(4). **Severin** a-4, 9(4), 10; c-2, 9, 10, 14. **Wildey** a-5, 17, 24, 28.*

WYATT EARP (TV) (Hugh O'Brian Famous Marshal)
Dell Publishing Co.: No. 860, Nov, 1957 - No. 13, Dec-Feb, 1960-61 (Hugh O'Brian photo-c)

Four Color 860 (#1)-Manning-a 11 22 33 80 120 160
Four Color 890,921(6/58)-All Manning-a 9 18 27 60 85 110
4 (9-11/58) - 12-Manning-a. 5-Photo back-c 6 12 18 43 59 75
13-Toth-a 7 14 21 46 63 80

WYATT EARP FRONTIER MARSHAL (Formerly Range Busters) (Also see Blue Bird)
Charlton Comics: No. 12, Jan, 1956 - No. 72, Dec, 1967

12 9 18 27 49 62 75
13-19 6 12 18 31 38 45
20-(68 pgs.)-Williamson-a(4), 8,5,5,& 7 pgs. 10 20 30 56 73 90
21-30 3 6 9 18 24 30
31-50 2 4 6 12 16 20
51-72 (1967) 2 4 6 9 11 14

WYNONNA EARP
Image Comics (WildStorm Productions): Dec, 1996 - No. 5, Apr, 1997 ($2.50)

1-5-Smith-s/Chin-a 2.50

WYNONNA EARP: HOME ON THE STRANGE
IDW Publishing: Dec, 2003 - No. 3, Feb, 2004 ($3.99)

1-3-Smith-s/Ferreira-a 4.00

X (Comics' Greatest World: X #1 only) (Also see Comics' Greatest World & Dark Horse Comics #8)
Dark Horse Comics: Feb, 1994 - No. 25, Apr, 1996 ($2.00/$2.50)

1-25: 3-Pit Bulls x-over. 8 -Ghost-c & app. 18-Miller-c.; Predator app. 19-22-Miller-c. 2.50
Hero Illustrated Special #1,2 (1994, $1.00, 20 pgs.) 2.25
One Shot to the Head (1994, $2.50, 36 pgs.)-Miller-c. 2.50

NOTE: ***Miller** c-18-22. **Quesada** c-6. **Russell** a-6.*

XANADU COLOR SPECIAL
Eclipse Comics: Dec, 1988 ($2.00, one-shot)

1-Continued from Thoughts & Images 2.25

XAVIER INSTITUTE ALUMNI YEARBOOK (See X-Men titles)
Marvel Comics: Dec, 1996 ($5.95, square-bound, one-shot)

1-Text w/art by various 6.00

X-BABIES
Marvel Comics: (one-shots)

...: Murderama (8/98, $2.95) J.J. Kirby-a 3.50
...: Reborn (1/00, $3.50) J.J. Kirby-a 3.50

X-CALIBRE
Marvel Comics: Mar, 1995 - No. 4, July, 1995 ($1.95, limited series)

1-4-Age of Apocalypse 2.25

XENA: WARRIOR PRINCESS (TV)
Topps Comics: Aug, 1997 - No. 0, Oct, 1997 ($2.95)

1-Two stories by various; J. Scott Campbell-c 1 3 4 6 8 10
1,2-Photo-c 1 3 4 6 8 10
2-Stevens-c 6.00
0-(10/97)-Lopresti-c, 0-(10/97)-Photo-c 1 2 3 5 6 8
...First Appearance Collection ('97, $9.95) r/Hercules the Legendary Journeys #3-5 and 5-page story from TV Guide 10.00

XENA: WARRIOR PRINCESS (TV)
Dark Horse Comics: Sept, 1999 - No. 14, Oct, 2000 ($2.95/$2.99)

1-14: 1-Mignola-c and photo-c. 2,3-Bradstreet-c & photo-c 3.00

XENA: WARRIOR PRINCESS AND THE ORIGINAL OLYMPICS (TV)
Topps Comics: Jun, 1998 - No. 3, Aug, 1998 ($2.95, limited series)

1-3-Regular and Photo-c; Lim-a/T&M Bierbaum-s 3.00

XENA: WARRIOR PRINCESS-BLOODLINES (TV)
Topps Comics: May, 1998 - No. 2, June, 1998 ($2.95, limited series)

1,2-Lopresti-s/c/a. 2-Reg. and photo-c 3.00
1-Bath photo-c, 1-American Ent. Ed. 4.00

XENA: WARRIOR PRINCESS / JOXER: WARRIOR PRINCE (TV)
Topps Comics: Nov, 1997 - No. 3, Jan, 1998 ($2.95, limited series)

1-3-Regular and Photo-c; Lim-a/T&M Bierbaum-s 3.00

XENA: WARRIOR PRINCESS-THE DRAGON'S TEETH (TV)
Topps Comics: Dec, 1997 - No. 3, Feb, 1998 ($2.95, limited series)

1-3-Regular and Photo-c; Teranishi-a/Thomas-s 3.00

XENA: WARRIOR PRINCESS-THE ORPHEUS TRILOGY (TV)
Topps Comics: Mar, 1998 - No. 3, May, 1998 ($2.95, limited series)

1-3-Regular and Photo-c; Teranishi-a/T&M Bierbaum-s 3.00

XENA: WARRIOR PRINCESS VS. CALLISTO (TV)
Topps Comics: Feb, 1998 - No. 3, Apr, 1998 ($2.95, limited series)

1-3-Regular and Photo-c; Morgan-a/Thomas-s 3.00

XENOBROOD
DC Comics: No. 0, Oct, 1994 - No. 6, Apr, 1995 ($1.50, limited series)

0-6: 0-Indicia says "Xenobroods" 2.25

XENON
Eclipse Comics: Dec, 1987 - No. 23, Nov. 1, 1988 ($1.50, B&W, bi-weekly)

1-23 2.25

XENOTECH
Mirage Studios: Sept, 1993 - No. 3, Dec, 1994 ($2.75)

1-3: Bound with 2 trading cards. 2-(10/94) 2.75

XENOZOIC TALES (Also see Cadillacs & Dinosaurs, Death Rattle #8)
Kitchen Sink Press: Feb, 1986 - No. 14, Oct, 1996

1-Mark Schultz-s/a in all 1 3 4 6 8 10

X-Factor V2#1 © MAR

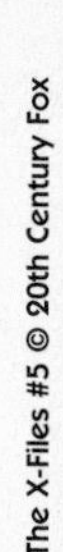
The X-Files #5 © 20th Century Fox

X-Force #73 © MAR

	GD	VG	FN	VF	VF/NM	NM-
	2.0	4.0	6.0	8.0	9.0	9.2

1(2nd printing)(1/89) 3.00
2-14 5.00
Volume 1 ($14.95) r/#1-6 & Death Rattle #8 15.00
Volume 2 (5/03, $14.95, TPB) B&W r/#7-14; intro by Frank Cho 15.00

XENYA
Sanctuary Press: Apr, 1994 - No. 3 ($2.95)

1-3: 1-Hildebrandt-c; intro Xenya 3.00

XERO
DC Comics: May, 1997 - No. 12, Apr, 1998 ($1.75)

1-7 2.50
8-12 2.25

X-FACTOR (Also see The Avengers #263, Fantastic Four #286 and Mutant X)
Marvel Comics Group: Feb, 1986 - No. 149, Sept, 1998

1-($1.25, 52 pgs)-Story recaps 1st app. from Avengers #263; story cont'd from F.F. #286; return of original X-Men (now X-Factor); Guice/Layton-a; Baby Nathan app. (2nd after X-Men #201) 6.00
2-4 4.00
5-1st brief app. Apocalypse (2 pages) 4.00
6-1st full app. Apocalypse 1 3 4 6 8 10
7-10: 10-Sabretooth app. (11/86, 3 pgs.) cont'd in X-Men #212; 1st app. in an X-Men comic book 4.00
11-22: 13-Baby Nathan app. in flashback. 14-Cyclops vs. The Master Mold. 15-Intro wingless Angel 3.00
23-1st brief app. Archangel (2 pages) 1 2 3 4 5 7
24-1st full app. Archangel (now in Uncanny X-Men); Fall Of The Mutants begins; origin Apocalypse 1 2 3 5 7 9
25,26: Fall Of The Mutants; 26-New outfits 3.00
27-39,41-83,87-91,93-99,101: 35-Origin Cyclops. 38,50-(52 pgs.): 50-Liefeld/McFarlane-c. 51-53-Sabretooth app. 52-Liefeld-c(p). 54-Intro Crimson; Silvestri-c/a(p). 60-X-Tinction Agenda x-over; New Mutants (w/Cable) x-over in #60-62; Wolverine in #62. 60-Gold ink 2nd printing. 61,62-X-Tinction Agenda. 62-Jim Lee-c. 63-Portacio/Thibert-c/a(p) begins, ends #69. 65-68-Lee co-plots. 65-The Apocalypse Files begins, ends #68. 66,67-Baby Nathan app. 67-Inhumans app. 68-Baby Nathan is sent into future to save his life. 69,70-X-Men(w/Wolverine) x-over. 71-New team begins (Havok, Polaris, Strong Guy, Wolfsbane & Madrox); Stroman-c/a begins. 71-2nd printing ($1.25). 75-(52 pgs.). 77-Cannonball (of X-Force) app. 87-Quesada-c/a(p) in monthly comic begins,ends #92. 88-1st app. Random 2.50
40-Rob Liefeld-c/a (4/89, 1st at Marvel?) 3.00
84-86 -Jae Lee a(p); 85,86-Jae Lee-c. Polybagged with trading card in each; X-Cutioner's Song x-overs. 3.00
92-($3.50, 68 pgs.)-Wraparound-c by Quesada w/Havok hologram on-c; begin X-Men 30th anniversary issues; Quesada-a. 5.00
92-2nd printing 2.25
100-($2.95, 52 pgs.)-Embossed foil-c; Multiple Man dies. 5.00
100-($1.75, 52 pgs.)-Regular edition 2.25
102-105,107: 102-bound-in card sheet 2.25
106-($2.00)-Newsstand edition 2.25
106-($2.95)-Collectors edition 3.00
108-124,126-148: 112-Return from Age of Apocalypse. 115-card insert. 119-123-Sabretooth app. 123-Hound app. 124-w/Onslaught Update. 126-Onslaught x-over; Beast vs. Dark Beast 128-w/card insert; return of Multiple Man. 130-Assassination of Grayson Creed. 146,148-Moder-a 2.25
125-($2.95)-"Onslaught"; Post app.; return of Havok 4.00
149-Last issue 3.00
#(-1) Flashback (7/97) Matsuda-a 2.25
Annual 1-9: 1-(10/86-'94, 68 pgs.) 3-Evolutionary War x-over. 4-Atlantis Attacks; Byrne/Simonson-a;Byrne-c. 5-Fantastic Four, New Mutants x-over; Keown 2 pg. pin-up. 6-New Warriors app.; 5th app. X-Force cont'd from X-Men Annual #15. 7-1st Quesada-a(p) on X-Factor plus-c(p). 8-Bagged w/trading card. 9-Austin-a(i) 3.00
...Prisoner of Love (1990, $4.95, 52 pgs.)-Starlin scripts; Guice-a 5.00

NOTE: ***Art Adams*** *a-41p, 42p.* ***Buckler*** *a-50p.* ***Liefeld*** *a-40; c-40, 50i, 52p.* ***McFarlane*** *c-50i.* ***Mignola*** *c-70.* ***Brandon Peterson*** *a-78p(part).* ***Whilce Portacio*** *c/a(p)-63-69.* ***Quesada*** *a(p)-87-92, Annual 7. c(p)-78, 79, 82, Annual 7.* ***Simonson*** *c/a-10, 11, 13-15, 17-19, 21, 23-31, 33, 34, 36-39; c-12, 16.* ***Paul Smith*** *a-44-48; c-43.* ***Stroman*** *a(p)-71-75, 77, 78(part), 80, 81; c(p)-71-77, 80, 81, 84.* ***Zeck*** *c-2.*

X-FACTOR (Volume 2)
Marvel Comics: June, 2002 - No. 4, Oct, 2002 ($2.50)

1-4: Jensen-s/Ranson-a. 1-Phillips-c. 2,3-Edwards-c 2.50

X-51 (Machine Man)
Marvel Comics: Sept, 1999 - No. 12, Jul, 2000 ($1.99/$2.50)

1-7: 1-Joe Bennett-a. 2-Two covers 2.50
8-12: 8-Begin $2.50-c 2.50
Wizard #0 2.25

X-FILES, THE (TV)
Topps Comics: Jan, 1995 - No. 41, July, 1998 ($2.50)

-2(9/96)-Black-c; r/X-Files Magazine #1&2 1 3 4 6 8 10
-1(9/96)-Silver-c; r/Hero Illustrated Giveaway 1 3 4 6 8 10
0-($3.95)-Adapts pilot episode 4.00
0-"Mulder" variant-c 1 2 3 5 6 8
0-"Scully" variant-c 1 2 3 5 6 8
1/2-W/certificate 3 6 9 16 20 25
1-New stories based on the TV show; direct market & newsstand editions; Miran Kim-c on all 3 6 9 18 24 30
2 2 4 6 11 14 18
3,4 1 2 3 5 6 8
5-10 4.00
11-41: 11-Begin $2.95-c. 21-W/bound-in card. 40,41-Reg. & photo-c 3.00
Annual 1,2 ($3.95) 4.00
Afterflight TPB ($5.95) Art by Thompson, Saviuk, Kim 6.00
Collection 1 TPB ($19.95)-r/#1-6. 20.00
Collection 2 TPB ($19.95)-r/#7-12, Annual #1. 20.00
...Fight the Future ('98, $5.95) Movie adaptation 6.00
Hero Illustrated Giveaway 2 4 6 10 12 15
Special Edition 1-5 ($4.95)-r/#1-3, 4-6, 7-9, 10-12, 13, Annual 1 5.00
Star Wars Galaxy Magazine Giveaway (B&W) 1 3 4 6 8 10
Trade paperback ($19.95) 20.00

X-FILES COMICS DIGEST, THE
Topps Comics: Dec, 1995 - No. 3 ($3.50, quarterly, digest-size)

1-3: 1,2: New X-Files stories w/Ray Bradbury Comics-r 4.00

NOTE: ***Adlard*** *a-1, 2.* ***Jack Davis*** *a-2r.* ***Russell*** *a-1r.*

X-FILES, THE: GROUND ZERO (TV)
Topps Comics: Nov, 1997 - No. 4, March, 1998 ($2.95, limited series)

1-4-Adaptation of the Kevin J. Anderson novel 3.00

X-FILES, THE: SEASON ONE (TV)
Topps Comics: July, 1997 - July, 1998 ($4.95, adaptations of TV episodes)

1,2,Squeeze, Conduit, Ice, Space, Fire, Beyond the Sea, Shadows 5.00

X-FORCE (Becomes X-Statix) (Also see The New Mutants #100)
Marvel Comics: Aug, 1991 - No. 129, Aug, 2002 ($1.00-$2.25)

1-($1.50, 52 pgs.)-Polybagged with 1 of 5 diff. Marvel Universe trading cards inside (1 each); 6th app. of X-Force; Liefeld-c/a begins 4.00
1-1st printing with Cable trading card inside 5.00
1-2nd printing; metallic ink-c (no bag or card) 2.25
2-4: 2-Deadpool-c/story. 3-New Brotherhood of Evil Mutants app. 4-Spider-Man x-over; cont'd from Spider-Man #16; reads sideways 3.00
5-10: 6-Last $1.00-c. 7,9-Weapon X back-ups. 8-Intro The Wild Pack (Cable, Kane, Domino, Hammer, G.W. Bridge, & Grizzly); Liefeld-c/a (4); Mignola-a. 10-Weapon X full-length story (part 3). 11-1st Weapon Prime; Deadpool-c/story 3.00
11-15,19-24,26-33: 15-Cable leaves X-Force 2.50
16-18-Polybagged w/trading card in each; X-Cutioner's Song x-overs 3.00
25-($3.50, 52 pgs.)-Wraparound-c w/Cable hologram on-c; Cable returns 4.00
34-37,39-45: 34-bound-in card sheet 2.50
38,40-43: 38-($2.00)-Newsstand edition. 40-43 ($1.95)-Deluxe edition 2.25
38-($2.95)-Collectors edition (prismatic) 5.00
44-49,51-67: 44-Return from Age of Apocalypse. 45-Sabretooth app. 49-Sebastian Shaw app. 52-Blob app., Onslaught cameo. 55-Vs. S.H.I.E.L.D. 56-Deadpool app. 57-Mr. Sinister & X-Man-c/app. 57,58-Onslaught x-over. 59-W/card insert; return of Longshot. 60-Dr. Strange 2.50
50 ($3.95)-Gatefold wrap-around foil-c 4.00
50 ($3.95)-Liefeld variant-c 5.00
68-74: 68-Operation Zero Tolerance 2.50
75,100-($2.99): 75-Cannonball-c/app. 3.00
76-99,101,102: 81-Pollina poster. 95-Magneto-c. 102-Ellis-s/Portacio-a 2.25
103-115: 103-Begin $2.25-c; Portacio-a thru #106. 115-Death of old team 2.25
116-New team debuts; Allred-c/a; Milligan-s; no Comics Code stamp on-c 4.00
117-129: 117-Intro. Mr. Sensitive. 120-Wolverine-c/app. 123-'Nuff Said issue. 124-Darwyn Cooke-a/c. 128-Death of U-Go Girl. 129-Fegredo-a 2.25
#(-1) Flashback (7/97) story of John Proudstar; Pollina-a 2.25
Annual 1-3 ('92-'94, 68 pgs.)-1-1st Greg Capullo-a(p) on X-Force. 2-Polybagged w/trading card; intro X-Treme & Neurtap 3.00
...And Cable '95 (12/95, $3.95)-Impossible Man app. 4.00
...And Cable '96, ...'97 ('96, 7/97) -'96-Wraparound-c 3.00
...And Spider-Man: Sabotage nn (11/92, $6.95)-Reprints X-Force #3,4 & Spider-Man #16 7.00
.../ Champions '98 ($3.50) 3.50
Annual 99 ($3.50) 3.50

X-Man #1 © MAR

X-Men #15 © MAR

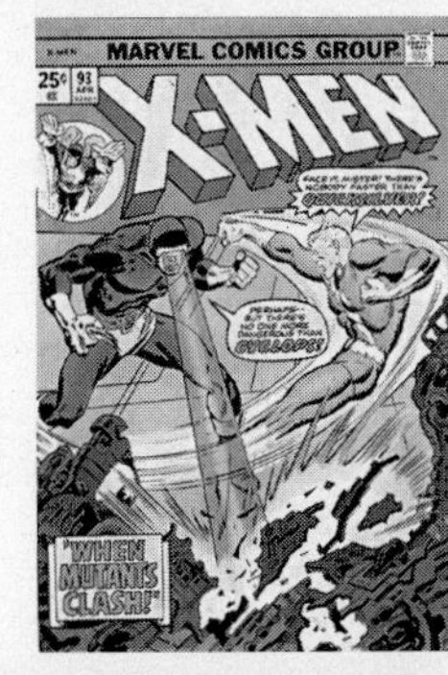

X-Men #93 © MAR

GD	VG	FN	VF	VF/NM	NM-
2.0	4.0	6.0	8.0	9.0	9.2

...: Famous, Mutant & Mortal HC (2003, $29.99) oversized r/#116-129; foreward by Milligan; gallery of covers and pin-ups; script for #123 30.00
...New Beginnings TPB (10/01, $14.95) r/#116-120 15.00
...Rough Cut ($2.99) Pencil pages and script for #102 3.00
...Youngblood (8/96, $4.95)-Platt-c 5.00
NOTE: ***Capullo** a(p)-15-25, Annual 1; c(p)-14-27. **Rob Liefeld** a-1-7, 9p; c-1-9, 11p; plots-1-12. **Mignola** a-8p.*

X-FORCE
Marvel Comics: Oct, 2004 - Present ($2.99)
1-4-Liefeld-c/a; Nicieza-s 3.00

X-FORCE MEGAZINE
Marvel Comics: Nov, 1996 ($3.95, one-shot)
1-Reprints 4.00

XIMOS: VIOLENT PAST
Triumphant Comics: Mar, 1994 - No. 2, Mar, 1994 ($2.50, limited series)
1,2 2.50

XIN: JOURNEY OF THE MONKEY KING
Anarchy Studios: May, 2003 - No. 3, July, 2003 ($2.99)
Preview Edition (Apr, 2003, $1.99) Flip book w/ Vampi Vicious Preview Edition 2.25
1-3-Kevin Lau-a. 1-Three covers by Lau, Park and Nauck. 2-Three covers 3.00

XIN: LEGEND OF THE MONKEY KING
Anarchy Studios: Nov, 2002 - No. 3, Jan, 2003 ($2.99)
Preview Edition (Summer 2002, Diamond Dateline supplement) 2.25
1-3-Kevin Lau-a. 1-Two covers by Lau & Madureira. 2-Two covers by Lau & Oeming 3.00
TPB (10/03, $12.95) r/#1-3; cover gallery and sketch pages 13.00

X-MAN (Also see X-Men Omega & X-Men Prime)
Marvel Comics: Mar, 1995 - No. 75, May, 2001 ($1.95/$1.99/$2.25)
1-Age of Apocalypse 5.00
1-2nd print 2.25
2-4,25: 25-($2.99)-Wraparound-c 3.00
5-24, 26-28: 5-Post Age of Apocalypse stories begin. 5-7-Madelyne Pryor app. 10-Professor X app. 12-vs. Excalibur. 13-Marauders, Cable app. 14-Vs. Cable; Onslaught app. 15-17-Vs. Holocaust. 17-w/Onslaught Update. 18-Onslaught x-over; X-Force-c/app; Marauders app. 19-Onslaught x-over. 20-Abomination-c/app.; w/card insert. 23-Bishop app. 24-Spider-Man, Morbius-c/app. 27-Re-appearance of Aurora(Alpha Flight) 2.50
29-49,51-62: 29-Operation Zero Tolerance. 37,38-Spider-Man-c/app. 56-Spider-Man app. 2.50
50-($2.99) Crossover with Generation X #50 3.00
63-74: 63-Ellis & Grant-s/Olivetti-a begins. 64-Begin $2.25-c 2.25
75 ($2.99) Final issue; Alcatena-a 3.00
#(-1) Flashback (7/97) 2.25
...'96, ...'97-($2.95)-Wraparound-c; '96-Age of Apocalypse 3.00
...: All Saints' Day ('97, $5.99) Dodson-a 6.00
.../Hulk '98 ($2.99) Wraparound-c; Thanos app. 3.00

XMAS COMICS
Fawcett Publications: 12?/1941 - No. 2, 12?/1942; (50¢, 324 pgs.)
No. 7, 12?/1947 (25¢, 132 pgs.)(#3-6 do not exist)
1-Contains Whiz #21, Capt. Marvel #3, Bulletman #2, Wow #3, & Master #18; Raboy back-c. Not rebound, remaindered comics; printed at same time as originals 386 772 1158 2509 4055 5600
2-Capt. Marvel, Bulletman, Spy Smasher 154 308 462 963 1482 2000
7-Funny animals (Hoppy, Billy the Kid & Oscar) 62 124 186 388 594 800

XMAS COMICS
Fawcett Publications: No. 4, Dec, 1949 - No. 7, Dec, 1952 (50¢, 196 pgs.)
4-Contains Whiz, Master, Tom Mix, Captain Marvel, Nyoka, Capt. Video, Bob Colt, Monte Hale, Hot Rod Comics, & Battle Stories. Not rebound, remaindered comics; printed at the same time as originals. Stocking on cover is made of green or red felt 67 134 201 419 647 875
5-7-Same as above. 5- Red felt on-c. 7-Bill Boyd app.; stocking on cover is made of green felt (novelty cover) 55 110 165 336 511 685

X-MEN, THE (See Adventures of Cyclops and Phoenix, Amazing Adventures, Archangel, Brotherhood, Capt. America #172, Classic X-Men, Exiles, Further Adventures of Cyclops & Phoenix, Gambit, Giant-Size..., Heroes For Hope..., Kitty Pryde & Wolverine, Marvel & DC Present, Marvel Collector's Edition:..., Marvel Fanfare, Marvel Graphic Novel, Marvel Super Heroes, Marvel Team-Up, Marvel Triple Action, The Marvel X-Men Collection, New Mutants, Nightcrawler, Official Marvel Index To..., Rogue, Special Edition..., Ultimate..., Uncanny..., Wolverine, X-Factor, X-Force, X-Terminators)

X-MEN, THE (1st series)(Becomes Uncanny X-Men at #142)(The X-Men #1-93; X-Men #94-141) (The Uncanny X-Men on-c only #114-141)
Marvel Comics Group: Sept, 1963 - No. 66, Mar, 1970; No. 67, Dec, 1970 - No. 141, Jan, 1981
1-Origin/1st app. X-Men (Angel, Beast, Cyclops, Iceman & Marvel Girl); 1st app. Magneto & Professor X 650 1300 1950 6000 10,000 13,000
2-1st app. The Vanisher 153 306 459 1300 2100 2900
3-1st app. The Blob (1/64) 79 158 237 672 1086 1500
4-1st Quicksilver & Scarlet Witch & Brotherhood of the Evil Mutants (3/64); 1st app. Toad; 2nd app. Magneto 82 164 246 697 1124 1550
5-Magneto & Evil Mutants-c/story 55 110 165 468 759 1050
6,7: 6-Sub-Mariner app. 7-Magneto app. 50 100 150 407 641 875
8,9,11: 8-1st Unus the Untouchable. 9-Early Avengers app. (1/65); 1st Lucifer. 11-1st app. The Stranger. 41 82 123 305 478 650
10-1st S.A. app. Ka-Zar & Zabu the sabertooth (3/65) 36 72 108 270 423 575
12-Origin Prof. X; Origin/1st app. Juggernaut 44 88 132 352 551 750
13-Juggernaut and Human Torch app. 31 62 93 225 355 485
14,15: 14-1st app. Sentinels. 15-Origin Beast 32 64 96 240 370 500
16-20: 19-1st app. The Mimic (4/66) 18 36 54 131 201 270
21-27,29,30: 27-Re-enter The Mimic (r-in #75); Spider-Man cameo 13 26 39 92 141 190
28-1st app. The Banshee (1/67)(r-in #76) 20 40 60 145 223 300
28-2nd printing (1994) 2 4 6 8 10 12
31-34,36,37,39: 34-Adkins-c/a. 39-New costumes 11 22 33 77 114 150
35-Spider-Man x-over (8/67)(r-in #83); 1st app. Changeling 23 46 69 165 253 340
38,40: 38-Origins of the X-Men series begins, ends #57. 40-(1/68) 1st app. Frankenstein's monster at Marvel 11 22 33 80 120 160
41-49: 42-Death of Prof. X (Changeling disguised as). 44-1st S.A. app. G.A. Red Raven. 49-Steranko-c; 1st Polaris 10 20 30 67 96 125
50,51-Steranko-c/a 10 20 30 70 100 130
52 9 18 27 60 85 110
53-Barry Smith-c/a (his 1st comic book work) 10 20 30 70 100 130
54,55-B. Smith-c. 54-1st app. Alex Summers who later becomes Havok. 55-Summers discovers he has mutant powers 10 20 30 72 104 135
56,57,59-63,65-Neal Adams-a(p). 56-Intro Havok w/o costume. 60-1st Sauron. 65-Return of Professor X. 10 20 30 70 100 130
58-1st app. Havok in costume; N. Adams-a(p) 12 24 36 86 131 175
62,63-2nd printings (1994) 2 4 6 8 10 12
64-1st app. Sunfire 10 20 30 67 96 125
66-Last new story w/original X-Men; battles Hulk 10 20 30 73 107 140
67-93: 67-Reprints begin, end #93. 67-70,72: (52 pgs.). 71-Last 15¢ issue. 73-86-r/#25-38 w/new-c. 83-Spider-Man-c/story. 87-93-r/#39-45 with covers 7 14 21 50 68 85
94 (8/75)-New X-Men begin (see Giant-Size X-Men for 1st app.); Colossus, Nightcrawler, Thunderbird, Storm, Wolverine, & Banshee join; Angel, Marvel Girl & Iceman resign 53 106 159 451 726 1000
95-Death of Thunderbird 14 28 42 97 149 200
96,97 9 18 27 60 85 110
98,99-(Regular 25¢ edition)(4,6/76) 8 16 24 58 82 105
98,99-(30¢-c variants, limited distribution) 15 30 45 109 167 225
100-Old vs. New X-Men; part origin Phoenix; last 25¢ issue (8/76) 10 20 30 70 100 130
100-(30¢-c variant, limited distribution) 18 36 54 126 193 260
101-Phoenix origin concludes 11 22 33 77 114 150
102-104: 102-Origin Storm. 104-1st brief app. Starjammers; Magneto-c/story 6 12 18 43 59 75
105-107-(Regular 30¢ editions). 106-(8/77)Old vs. New X-Men. 107-1st full app. Starjammers; last 30¢ issue 6 12 18 43 59 75
105-107-(35¢-c variants, limited distribution) 9 18 27 65 93 120
108-Byrne-a begins (see Marvel Team-Up #53) 7 14 21 46 63 80
109-1st app. Weapon Alpha (becomes Vindicator) 6 12 18 40 55 70
110,111: 110-Phoenix joins 4 8 12 29 40 50
112-116 4 8 12 29 40 50
117-119: 117-Origin Professor X 4 8 12 24 32 40
120-1st app. Alpha Flight, story line begins (4/79); 1st app. Vindicator (formerly Weapon Alpha); last 35¢ issue 6 12 18 40 55 70
121-1st full Alpha Flight story 6 12 18 38 52 65
122-128: 123-Spider-Man x-over. 124-Colossus becomes Proletarian 3 7 10 21 28 35
129-Intro Kitty Pryde (1/80); last Banshee; Dark Phoenix saga begins; intro. Emma Frost (White Queen) 4 8 12 29 40 50
130-1st app. The Dazzler by Byrne (2/80) 3 7 10 21 28 35
131-135: 131-Dazzler app.; 1st White Queen-c. 133-Wolverine app. 134-Phoenix becomes Dark Phoenix 3 7 10 21 28 35
136,138: 138-Dazzler app.; Cyclops leaves 3 6 9 18 23 28
137-Giant; death of Phoenix 3 7 10 21 28 35
139-Alpha Flight app.; Kitty Pryde joins; new costume for Wolverine 3 7 10 21 28 35

The Uncanny X-Men #226 © MAR

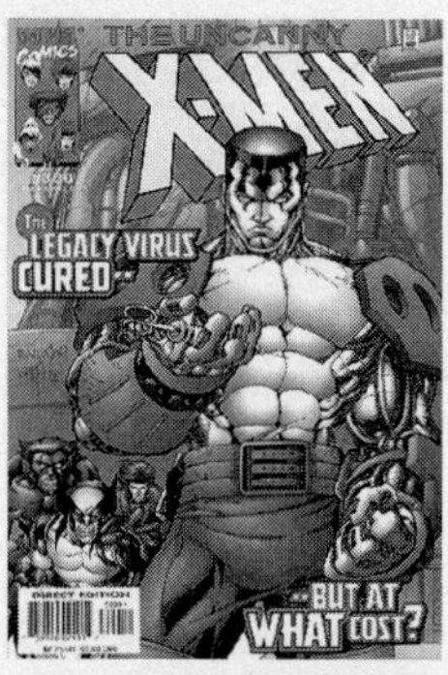

The Uncanny X-Men #390 © MAR

The Uncanny X-Men #451 © MAR

GD VG FN VF VF/NM NM-
2.0 4.0 6.0 8.0 9.0 9.2

140-Alpha Flight app. 3 7 10 21 28 35
141-Intro Future X-Men & The New Brotherhood of Evil Mutants; 1st app. Rachel (Phoenix II); Death of Franklin Richards 4 8 12 24 32 40

X-MEN: Titled THE UNCANNY X-MEN #142, Feb, 1981 - Present

142-Rachel app.; deaths of alt. future Wolverine, Storm & Colossus 5 10 15 33 44 55
143-Last Byrne issue 3 7 10 21 28 35
144-150: 144-Man-Thing app. 145-Old X-Men app. 148-Spider-Woman, Dazzler app. 150-Double size 2 4 6 9 11 14
151-157,159-161,163,164: 161-Origin Magneto. 163-Origin Binary. 164-1st app. Binary as Carol Danvers 1 3 4 6 8 10
158-1st app. Rogue in X-Men (6/82, see Avengers Annual #10) 2 4 6 11 14 18
162-Wolverine solo story 2 4 6 9 11 14
165-Paul Smith-c/a begins, ends #175 1 3 4 6 8 10
166-170: 166-Double size; Paul Smith-a. 167-New Mutants app. (3/83); same date as New Mutants #1; 1st meeting w/X-Men; ties into N.M. #3,4; Starjammers app.; contains skin "Tattooz" decals. 168-1st brief app. Madelyne Pryor (last page) in X-Men (see Avengers Annual #10) 1 2 3 5 7 9
171-Rogue joins X-Men; Simonson-c/a 2 4 6 10 13 16
172-174: 172,173-Two part Wolverine solo story. 173-Two cover variations, blue & black. 174-Phoenix cameo 1 2 3 5 6 8
175-(52 pgs.)-Anniversary issue; Phoenix returns 1 3 4 6 8 10
176-185,187-192,194-199: 181-Sunfire app. 182-Rogue solo story. 184-1st app. Forge (8/84). 190,191-Spider-Man & Avengers x-over. 195-Power Pack x-over 1 2 3 4 5 7
186,193: 186-Double-size; Barry Smith/Austin-a. 193-Double size; 100th app. New X-Men; 1st app. Warpath in costume (see New Mutants #16) 1 2 3 5 6 8
200-(12/85, $1.25, 52 pgs.) 1 2 3 5 6 8
201-(1/86)-1st app. Cable? (as baby Nathan; see X-Factor #1); 1st Whilce Portacio-c/a(i) on X-Men (guest artist) 3 6 9 16 20 25
202-204,206-209: 204-Nightcrawler solo story; 2nd Portacio-a(i) on X-Men. 207-Wolverine/Phoenix story 1 2 3 4 5 7
205-Wolverine solo story by Barry Smith 2 4 6 9 11 14
210,211-Mutant Massacre begins 3 6 9 16 20 24
212,213-Wolverine vs. Sabretooth (Mutant Mass.) 3 6 9 18 23 28
214-221,223,224: 219-Havok joins (7/87); brief app. Sabretooth 1 2 3 4 5 7
222-Wolverine battles Sabretooth-c/story 3 6 9 16 20 24
225-242: 225-227: Fall Of The Mutants. 226-Double size. 240-Sabretooth app. 242-Double size, X-Factor app., Inferno tie-in 1 2 3 4 5 7
243,245-247: 245-Rob Liefeld-a(p) 1 2 3 4 5 7
244-1st app. Jubilee 3 6 9 18 24 30
248-1st Jim Lee art on X-Men (1989) 2 4 6 14 18 22
248-2nd printing (1992, $1.25) 2.50
249-252: 252-Lee-c 1 2 3 4 5 7
253-255: 253-All new X-Men begin. 254-Lee-c 1 2 3 4 5 7
256,257-Jim Lee-c/a begins 1 2 3 5 7 9
258-Wolverine solo story; Lee-c/a 1 2 3 5 7 9
259-Silvestri-c/a; no Lee-a 1 2 3 4 5 7
260-265-No Lee-a. 260,261,264-Lee-c 1 2 3 4 5 7
266-1st full app. Gambit (see Ann. #14)-No Lee-a 4 8 12 27 36 45
267-Jim Lee-c/a resumes; 2nd full Gambit app. 2 4 6 10 13 16
268-Capt. America, Black Widow & Wolverine team-up; Lee-a 2 4 6 11 14 18
268,270: 268-2nd printing. 270-Gold 2nd printing 2.50
269,273-275: 269-Lee-a. 273-New Mutants (Cable) & X-Factor x-over; Golden, Byrne & Lee part pencils. 275-(52 pgs.)-Tri-fold-c by Jim Lee (p); Prof. X 1 2 3 4 5 7
270-X-Tinction Agenda begins 1 2 3 5 6 8
271,272-X-Tinction Agenda 1 2 3 5 6 8
275-Gold 2nd printing 2.50
276-280: 277-Last Lee-c/a. 280-X-Factor x-over 6.00
281-(10/91)-New team begins (Storm, Archangel, Colossus, Iceman & Marvel Girl); Whilce Portacio-c/a begins; Byrne scripts begin; wraparound-c (white logo) 1 2 3 4 5 7
281-2nd printing with red metallic ink logo w/o UPC box ($1.00-c); does not say 2nd printing inside 2.50
282-1st brief app. Bishop (cover & 1 page) 2 4 6 8 10 12
282-Gold ink 2nd printing ($1.00-c) 2.50
283-1st full app. Bishop (12/91) 2 4 6 8 10 12
284-299: 284-Last $1.00-c. 286,287-Lee plots. 287-Bishop joins team. 288-Lee/Portacio plots. 290-Last Portacio-c/a. 294-Peterson-a(p) begins (#292 is 1st Peterson-c). 294-296 ($1.50)-Bagged w/trading card in each; X-Cutioner's Song x-overs; Peterson/Austin-c/a on all 4.00
300-($3.95, 68 pgs.)-Holo-grafx foil-c; Magneto app. 6.00
301-303,305-309,311 3.00
303,307-Gold Edition 1 2 3 5 6 8
304-($3.95, 68 pgs.)-Wraparound-c with Magneto hologram on-c; 30th anniversary issue; Jae Lee-a (4 pgs.) 6.00
310-($1.95)-Bound-in trading card sheet 3.00
312-$1.50-c begins; bound-in card sheet; 1st Madureira 4.00
313-321 3.00
316,317-($2.95)-Foil enhanced editions 4.00
318-321-($1.95)-Deluxe editions 3.00
322-Onslaught 5.00
323,324,326-346: 323-Return from Age of Apocalypse. 328-Sabretooth-c. 329,330-Dr. Strange app. 331-White Queen-c/app. 334-Juggernaut app.; w/Onslaught Update. 335-Onslaught, Avengers, Apocalypse, & X-Man app. 336-Onslaught. 338-Archangel's wings return to normal. 339-Havok vs. Cyclops; Spider-Man app. 341-Gladiator-c/app. 342-Deathbird cameo; two covers. 343,344-Phalanx 2.50
325-($3.95)-Anniversary issue; gatefold-c 5.00
342-Variant-c 1 3 4 6 8 10
347-349:347-Begin $1.99-c. 349-"Operation Zero Tolerance" 2.50
350-($3.99, 48 pgs.) Prismatic etched foil gatefold wraparound-c; Trial of Gambit; Seagle-s begin 1 2 3 5 6 8
351-359: 353-Bachalo-a begins. 354-Regular-c. 355-Alpha Flight-c/app. 356-Original X-Men-c 2.50
354-Dark Phoenix variant-c 4.00
360-($2.99) 35th Anniv. issue; Pacheco-c 3.00
360-($3.99) Etched Holo-foil enhanced-c 4.00
360-($6.95) DF Edition with Jae Lee variant-c 7.00
361-374: 361-Gambit returns; Skroce-a. 362-Hunt for Xavier pt. 1; Bachelo-a. 364-Yu-a. 366-Magneto-c. 369-Juggernaut-c 2.50
375-($2.99) Autopsy of Wolverine 3.00
376-379: 376,377-Apocalypse: The Twelve 2.25
380-($2.99) Polybagged with X-Men Revolution Genesis Edition preview 3.00
381,382,384-389,391-393: 381-Begin $2.25-c; Claremont-s. 387-Maximum Security 2.25
383-($2.99) 3.00
390-Colossus dies to cure the Legacy Virus 3.00
394-New look X-Men begins; Casey-s/Churchill-c/a 3.00
395-399-Poptopia. 398-Phillips & Wood-a 2.25
400-($3.50) Art by Ashley Wood, Eddie Campbell, Hamner, Phillips, Pulido and Matt Smith; wraparound-c by Wood 3.50
401-415: 401-'Nuff Said issue; Garney-a. 404,405,407-409,413-415-Phillips-a 2.25
416-421: 416-Asamiya-a begins. 421-Garney-a 2.25
422-($3.50) Alpha Flight app.; Garney-a 3.50
423-(25¢-c) Holy War pt. 1; Garney-a/Philip Tan-c 2.25
424-449,452-453: 425,426,429,430-Tan-a. 428-Birth of Nightcrawler. 437-Larroca-a begins. 444-New team, new costumes; Claremont-s/Davis-a begins. 448,449-Coipel-a 2.25
450,451-X-23 app.; Davis-a 2.25
#(-1) Flashback (7/97) Ladronn-c/Hitch & Neary-a 2.50
Special 1(12/70)-Kirby-c/a; origin The Stranger 10 20 30 67 96 125
Special 2(11/71, 52 pgs.) 7 14 21 50 68 85
Annual 3(1979, 52 pgs.)-New story; Miller/Austin-c; Wolverine still in old yellow costume 4 8 12 22 30 38
Annual 4(1980, 52 pgs.)-Dr. Strange guest stars 2 4 6 10 12 15
Annual 5(1981, 52 pgs.) 1 2 3 5 7 9
Annual 6-8('82-'84 52 pgs.)-6-Dracula app. 6.00
Annual 9,10('85, '86)-9-New Mutants x-over cont'd from New Mutants Special Ed. #1; Art Adams-a. 10-Art Adams-a 1 2 3 5 7 9
Annual 11-13:('87-'89, 68 pgs.): 12-Evolutionary War; A.Adams-a(p). 13-Atlantis Attacks 4.00
Annual 14(1990, $2.00, 68 pgs.)-1st app. Gambit (minor app., 5 pgs.); Fantastic Four, New Mutants (Cable) & X-Factor x-over; Art Adams-c/a(p) 3 6 9 16 20 25
Annual 15 (1991, $2.00, 68 pgs.)-4 pg. origin; New Mutants x-over; 4 pg. Wolverine solo back-up story; 4th app. X-Force cont'd from New Warriors Annual #1 4.00
Annual 16-18 ('92-'94, 68 pgs.)-16-Jae Lee-c/a(p). 17-Bagged w/card 3.00
Annual '95-(11/95, $3.95)-Wraparound-c 4.00
Annual '96,'97-Wraparound-c 3.00
.../Fantastic Four Annual '98 ($2.99) Casey-s 3.00
Annual '99 ($3.50) Jubilee app. 3.50
Annual 2000 ($3.50) Cable app.; Ribic-a 3.50
Annual 2001 ($3.50, printed wide-ways) Ashley Wood-c/a; Casey-s 3.50
...At The State Fair of Texas (1983, 36 pgs., one-shot); Supplement to the Dallas Times Herald 2 4 6 10 12 15
...: The Dark Phoenix Saga TPB 1st printing (1984, $12.95) 40.00
...: The Dark Phoenix Saga TPB 2nd-5th printings 30.00

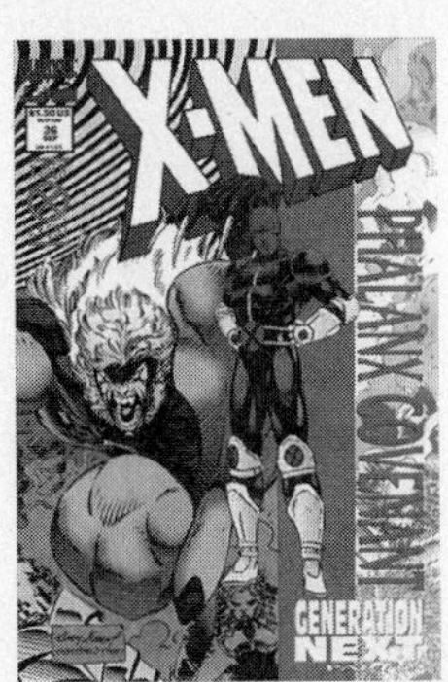

X-Men (2nd series) #36 © MAR

X-Men (2nd series) #115 © MAR

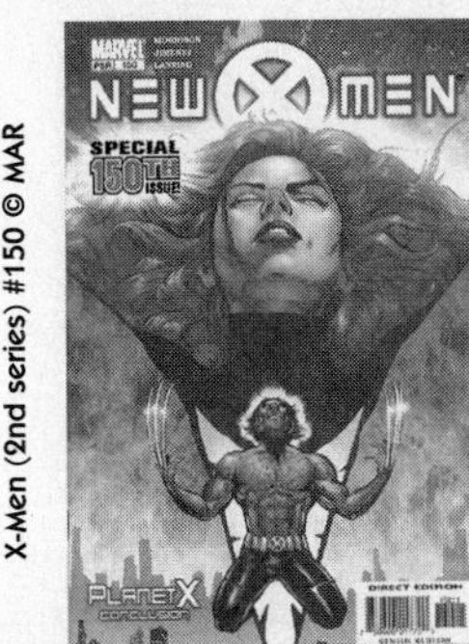

X-Men (2nd series) #150 © MAR

GD VG FN VF VF/NM NM-
2.0 4.0 6.0 8.0 9.0 9.2

GD VG FN VF VF/NM NM-
2.0 4.0 6.0 8.0 9.0 9.2

...: The Dark Phoenix Saga TPB 6th-10th printings 20.00

... Days of Future Past TPB (2004, $19.99) r/#138-143 & Annual #4 20.00

...From The Ashes TPB (1990, $14.95) r/#168-176 15.00

...:God Loves, Man Kills ($6.95)-r/Marvel Graphic Novel #5 7.00

...:God Loves, Man Kills - Special Edition (2003, $4.99)-reprint with new Hughes-c 5.00

...In The Days of Future Past TPB (1989, $3.95, 52 pgs.) 4.00

...Old Soldiers TPB (2004, $19.99) r/#213,215 & Ann. #11; New Mutants Ann. #2&3 20.00

...Poptopia TPB (10/01, $15.95) r/#394-399 16.00

Vignettes TPB (9/01, $17.95) r/Claremont & Bolton Classic X-Men #1-13 18.00

... Vol. 1: Hope TPB (2003, $12.99) r/#410-415; Harris-c 13.00

... Vol. 2: Dominant Species TPB (2003, $11.99) r/#416-420; Asamiya-c 12.00

... Vol. 3: Holy War TPB (2003, $17.99) r/#421-427 18.00

... Vol. 4: The Draco TPB (2004, $15.99) r/#428-434 16.00

... Vol. 5: She Lies with Angels TPB (2004, $11.99) r/#437-441 12.00

... Vol. 6: Bright New Mourning TPB (2004, $14.99) r/#435,436,442,443 & (New) X-Men #155,156; Larroca sketch covers 15.00

... - The New Age Vol. 1: The End of History (2004, $12.99) r/#444-449 13.00

NOTE: ***Art Adams*** *a-Annual 9, 10p, 12p, 14p; c-218p.* ***Neal Adams*** *a-56-63p, 65p; c-56-63.* ***Adkins*** *a-34, 35p; c-31, 34, 35.* ***Austin*** *a-108i, 109i, 111-117i, 119-143i, 186i, 204i, 228i, 294-297i, Annual 3i, 7i, 9i, 13; c-109-111i, 114-122i, 123, 124-141i, 142, 143, 196i, 204i, 228i, 294-297i, Annual 3i.* ***J. Buscema*** *c-42, 43, 45.* ***Buscema/Tuska*** *a-45.* ***Byrne*** *a(p)-108, 109, 111-143, 273; c(p)-113-116, 127, 129, 131-141.* ***Capullo*** *c-14.* ***Ditko*** *r-86, 89-91, 93.* ***Everett*** *c-73.* ***Golden*** *a-273, Annual 7p.* ***Guice*** *a-216p, 217p.* ***G. Kane*** *c(p)-33, 74-76, 79, 80, 94, 95.* ***Kirby*** *a(p)-1-17 (#12-17, 67r-layouts); c(p)-1-17, 25, 30 (18, 26-parts).* ***Layton*** *a-105i; c-112i, 113i.* ***Jim Lee*** *a(p)-248, 256-258, 267-277; c(p)-252, 254, 256-261, 264, 267, 270, 275-277, 286.* ***Perez*** *a-Annual 3p; c(p)-112, 128, Annual 3.* ***Peterson*** *a(p)-294-300, 304(part); c(p)-294-299.* ***Whilce Portacio*** *a(p)-281-286, 289, 290; a(i)-267; c-281-285p, 289p, 290; c(i)-267.* ***Romita, Jr.*** *a-300; c-300.* ***Roussos*** *a-84i.* ***Simonson*** *a-171p; c-171, 217.* ***B. Smith*** *a-53, 186p, 198p, 205, 214; c-53-55, 186p, 198, 205, 212, 214, 216.* ***Paul Smith*** *a(p)-165-170, 172-175, 278; c-165-170, 172-175, 278.* ***Sparling*** *a-78p.* ***Steranko*** *a-50p, 51p; c-49-51.* ***Sutton*** *a-106i.* ***Art Thibert*** *a(i)-281-286; c(i)-281, 282, 284, 285.* ***Toth*** *a-12p, 67p(r).* ***Tuska*** *a-40-42i, 43-46p, 88i(r); c-39-41, 77p, 78p.* ***Williamson*** *a-202i, 203i, 211i; c-202i, 203i, 206i.* ***Wood*** *c-14i.*

UNCANNY X-MEN AND THE NEW TEEN TITANS (See Marvel and DC Present...)

X-MEN (2nd Series)
Marvel Comics: Oct, 1991 - Present ($1.00/$1.25/$1.95/$1.99)

1 a-d ($1.50, 52 pgs.)-Jim Lee-c/a begins, ends #11; new team begins (Cyclops, Beast, Wolverine, Gambit, Psylocke & Rogue); new Uncanny X-Men & Magneto app.; four different covers exist 4.00

1 e ($3.95)-Double gate-fold-c consisting of all four covers from 1a-d by Jim Lee; contains all pin-ups from #1a-d plus inside-c foldout poster; no ads; printed on coated stock 5.00

2-7: 4-Wolverine back to old yellow costume (same date as Wolverine #50); last $1.00-c. 5-Byrne scripts. 6-Sabretooth-c/story 5.00

8-10: 8-Gambit vs. Bishop-c/story; last Lee-a; Ghost Rider cameo cont'd in Ghost Rider #26. 9-Wolverine vs. Ghost Rider; cont'd/G.R. #26. 10-Return of Longshot 4.00

11-13,17-24,26-29,31: 12,13-Art Thibert-c/a. 28,29-Sabretooth app. 3.00

11-Silver ink 2nd printing; came with X-Men board game 2 4 6 10 12 15

14-16-($1.50)-Polybagged with trading card in each; X-Cutioner's Song x-overs; 14-Andy Kubert-c/a begins 3.00

25-($3.50, 52 pgs.)-Wraparound-c with Gambit hologram on-c; Professor X erases Magneto's mind 2 4 6 8 10 12

25-30th anniversary issue w/B&W-c with Magneto in color & Magneto hologram & no price on-c 2 4 6 10 12 15

25-Gold 30.00

30-($1.95)-Wedding issue w/bound-in trading card sheet 5.00

32-37: 32-Begin $1.50-c; bound-in card sheet. 33-Gambit & Sabretooth-c/story 3.00

36,37-($2.95)-Collectors editions (foil-c) 5.00

38-44,46-49,51-53, 55-65: 42,43- Paul Smith-a. 46,49,53-56-Onslaught app. 51-Waid scripts begin, end #56. 54-(Reg. edition)-Onslaught revealed as Professor X. 55,56-Onslaught x-over; Avengers, FF & Sentinels app. 56-Dr. Doom app. 57-Xavier taken into custody; Byrne-c/swipe (X-Men,1st Series #138). 59-Hercules-c/app. 61-Juggernaut-c/app. 62-Re-intro. Shang Chi; two covers. 63-Kingpin cameo. 64- Kingpin app. 2.50

45-($3.95)-Annual issue; gatefold-c 5.00

50-($2.95)-Vs. Onslaught, wraparound-c. 4.00

50-($3.95)-Vs. Onslaught, wraparound foil-c. 5.00

50-($2.95)-Variant gold-c. 4 8 12 24 32 40

50-($2.95)-Variant silver-c. 1 2 3 5 6 8

54-(Limited edition)-Embossed variant-c; Onslaught revealed as Professor X 3 6 9 18 24 30

66-69,71-74,76-79: 66-Operation Zero Tolerance. 76-Origin of Maggott 2.50

70-($2.99, 48 pgs.)-Joe Kelly-s begin, new members join 3.00

75-($2.99, 48 pgs.) vs. N'Garai; wraparound-c 3.00

80-($3.99) 35th Anniv. issue; holo-foil-c 5.00

80-($2.99) Regular-c 3.00

80-($6.95) Dynamic Forces Ed.; Quesada-c 7.00

81-93,95: 82-Hunt for Xavier pt. 2. 85-Davis-a. 86-Origin of Joseph. 87-Magneto War ends. 88-Juggernaut app. 2.50

94-($2.99) Contains preview of X-Men: Hidden Years 3.00

96-99: 96,97-Apocalypse: The Twelve 2.50

100-($2.99) Art Adams-c; begin Claremont-s/Yu-a 3.00

100-DF alternate-c 1 3 4 6 8 10

101-105,107,108,110-114: 101-Begin $2.25-c. 107-Maximum Security x-over; Bishop-c/app. 108-Moira MacTaggart dies; Senator Kelly shot. 111-Magneto-c. 112,113-Eve of Destruction 2.25

106-($2.99) X-Men battle Domina 3.00

109-($3.50, 100 pgs.) new and reprinted Christmas-themed stories 3.50

114-Title change to "New X-Men," Morrison-s/Quitely-c/a begins 4.00

115-Two covers (Quitely & BWS) 3.00

116-125,127-149: 116-Emma Frost joins. 117,118-Van Sciver-a. 121,122,135-Quitely-a. 127-Leon & Sienkiewicz-a. 128-Kordey-a. 132,139-141-Jimenez-a. 136-138-Quitely-a 142-Sabretooth app.; Bachalo-c/a thru #145. 146-Magneto returns; Jimenez-a 2.25

126-($3.25) Quitely-a; defeat of Cassanova 3.25

150-($3.50) Jean Grey dies again; last Jimenez-a 3.50

151-156: 151-154-Silvestri-c/a 2.25

157-164: 157-X-Men Reload begins 2.25

#(-1) Flashback (7/97); origin of Magneto 2.50

Annual 1-3 ('92-'94, $2.25-$2.95, 68 pgs.) 1-Lee-c & layouts; #2-Bagged w/card 4.00

Special '95 ($3.95) 4.00

... '96,...'97-Wraparound-c 3.00

.../ Dr. Doom '98 Annual ($2.99) Lopresti-a 3.00

... Annual '99 ($3.50) Adam Kubert-c 3.50

Annual 2000 ($3.50) Art Adams-c/Claremont-s/Eaton-a 3.50

...2001 Annual ($3.50) Morrison-s/Yu-a; issue printed sideways 3.50

Animation Special Graphic Novel (12/90, $10.95) adapts animated series 11.00

Ashcan #1 (1994, 75¢) Introduces new team members 2.25

Ashcan (75¢ Ashcan Edition) (1994) 2.25

... Archives Sketchbook (12/00, $2.99) Early B&W character design sketches by various incl. Lee, Davis, Yu, Pacheco, BWS, Art Adams, Liefeld 3.00

...: Declassified (10/00, $3.50) Profile pin-ups by various; Jae Lee-c 3.50

...:Fatal Attractions ('94, $17.95)-r/x-Factor #92, X-Force #25, Uncanny X-Men #304, X-Men #25, Wolverine #75, & Excalibur #71 18.00

...Millennial Visions (8/00, $3.99) Various artists interpret future X-Men 4.00

...Millennial Visions 2 (1/02, $3.50) Various artists interpret future X-Men 3.50

New X-Men: E is for Extinction TPB (11/01, $12.95) r/#114-117 13.00

New X-Men: Imperial TPB (7/02, $19.99) r/#118-126; Quitely-c 20.00

New X-Men: New Worlds TPB (2002, $14.99) r/#127-133; Quitely-c 15.00

New X-Men: Riot at Xavier's TPB (2003, $11.99) r/#134-138; Quitely-c 12.00

New X-Men: Vol. 5: Assault on Weapon Plus TPB (2003, $14.99) r/#139-145 15.00

New X-Men: Vol. 6: Planet X TPB (2004, $12.99) r/#146-150 13.00

New X-Men: Vol. 7: Here Comes Tomorrow TPB (2004, $10.99) r/#151-154 11.00

New X-Men: Volume 1 HC (2002, $29.99) oversized r/#114-126 & 2001 Annual 30.00

New X-Men: Volume 2 HC (2003, $29.99) oversized r/#127-141; sketch & script pages 30.00

New X-Men: Volume 3 HC (2004, $29.99) oversized r/#142-154; sketch & script pages 30.00

...Pizza Hut Mini-comics-(See Marvel Collector's Edition: X-Men in Promotional Comics section)

...Premium Edition #1 (1993)-Cover says "Toys 'R' Us Limited Edition X-Men" 2.25

...:Rarities (1995, $5.95)-Reprints 6.00

...:Road Trippin' ('99, $24.95, TPB) r/X-Men road trips 25.00

...:The Coming of Bishop ('95, $12.95)-r/Uncanny X-Men #282-285, 287,288 13.00

...:The Magneto War (3/99, $2.99) Davis-a 3.00

...:The Rise of Apocalypse ('98, $16.99)-r/Rise Of Apocalypse #1-4, X-Factor #5,6 17.00

... Visionaries: Chris Claremont ('98, $24.95)-r/Claremont-s; art by Byrne, BWS, Jim Lee 25.00

... Visionaries: Jim Lee ('02, $29.99)-r/Jim Lee-a from various issues between Uncanny X-Men #248 & 286; r/Classic X-Men #39 and X-Men Annual #1 30.00

... Visionaries: Joe Madureira (7/00, $17.95)-r/Uncanny X-Men #325,326,329,330,341-343; new Madureira-c 18.00

...: Zero Tolerance ('00, $24.95, TPB) r/crossover series 25.00

NOTE: ***Jim Lee*** *a-1-11p; c-1-6p, 7, 8, 9p, 10, 11p.* ***Art Thibert*** *a-6-9i, 12, 13; c-6i, 12, 13.*

X-MEN ADVENTURES (TV)
Marvel Comics: Nov, 1992 - No. 15, Jan, 1994 ($1.25)(Based on animated series)

1-Wolverine, Cyclops, Jubilee, Rogue, Gambit 3.00

2-15: 3-Magneto-c/story. 6-Sabretooth-c/story. 7-Cable-c/story. 10-Archangel guest star. 11-Cable-c/story. 15-($1.75, 52 pgs.) 2.50

X-MEN ADVENTURES II (TV)
Marvel Comics: Feb, 1994 - No. 13, Feb, 1995 ($1.25/$1.50)(Based on 2nd TV season)

1-13: 4-Bound-in trading card sheet. 5-Alpha Flight app. 2.50

...Captive Hearts/Slave Island (TPB, $4.95)-r/X-Men Adventures #5-8 5.00

...The Irresistible Force, The Muir Island Saga (5.95, 10/94, TPB) r/X-Men Advs. #9-12 6.00

X-MEN ADVENTURES III (TV)(See Adventures of the X-Men)
Marvel Comics: Mar, 1995 - No. 13, Mar, 1996 ($1.50) (Based on 3rd TV season)

X-Men: Children of the Atom #1 © MAR

X-Men: Hidden Years #2 © MAR

X-Men: The End #1 © MAR

	GD 2.0	VG 4.0	FN 6.0	VF 8.0	VF/NM 9.0	NM- 9.2

1-13 2.50

X-MEN ALPHA
Marvel Comics: 1994 ($3.95, one-shot)
nn-Age of Apocalypse; wraparound chromium-c 1 2 3 5 6 8
nn ($49.95)-Gold logo 50.00

X-MEN/ALPHA FLIGHT
Marvel Comics Group: Dec, 1985 - No. 2, Dec, 1985 ($1.50, limited series)
1,2: 1-Intro The Berserkers; Paul Smith-a 5.00

X-MEN/ALPHA FLIGHT
Marvel Comics Group: May, 1998 - No. 2, June, 1998 ($2.99, limited series)
1,2-Flashback to early meeting; Raab-s/Cassaday-s/a 3.00

X-MEN AND THE MICRONAUTS, THE
Marvel Comics Group: Jan, 1984 - No. 4, Apr, 1984 (Limited series)
1-4: Guice-c/a(p) in all 4.00

X-MEN ARCHIVES
Marvel Comics: Jan, 1995 - No. 4, Apr, 1995 ($2.25, limited series)
1-4: Reprints Legion stories from New Mutants. 4-Magneto app. 2.25

X-MEN ARCHIVES FEATURING CAPTAIN BRITAIN
Marvel Comics: July, 1995 - No. 7, 1996 ($2.95, limited series)
1-7: Reprints early Capt. Britain stories 3.00

X-MEN BLACK SUN (See Black Sun:...)

X-MEN BOOKS OF ASKANI
Marvel Comics: 1995 ($2.95, one-shot)
1-Painted pin-ups w/text 3.00

X-MEN: CHILDREN OF THE ATOM
Marvel Comics: Nov, 1999 - No. 6 ($2.99, limited series)
1-6-Casey-s; X-Men before issue #1. 1-3-Rude-c/a. 4-Paul Smith-a/Rude-c. 5,6-Essad Ribic-c/a 3.00
TPB (11/01, $16.95) r/series; sketch pages; Casey intro. 17.00

X-MEN CHRONICLES
Marvel Comics: Mar, 1995 - No. 2, June, 1995 ($3.95, limited series)
1,2: Age of Apocalypse x-over. 1-wraparound-c 5.00

X-MEN: CLANDESTINE
Marvel Comics: Oct, 1996 - No. 2, Nov, 1996 ($2.95, limited series, 48 pgs.)
1,2: Alan Davis-c(p)/a(p)/scripts & Mark Farmer-c(i)/a(i) in all; wraparound-c 3.00

X-MEN CLASSIC (Formerly Classic X-Men)
Marvel Comics: No. 46, Apr, 1990 - No. 110, Aug, 1995 ($1.25/$1.50)
46-110: Reprints from X-Men. 54-(52 pgs.). 57,60-63,65-Russell-c(i); 62-r/X-Men #158(Rogue). 66-r/#162(Wolverine). 69-Begins-r of Paul Smith issues (#165 on). 70,79,90,97(52 pgs.). 70-r/X-Men #166. 90-r/#186. 100-($1.50). 104-r/X-Men #200 2.50

X-MEN CLASSICS
Marvel Comics Group: Dec, 1983 - No. 3, Feb, 1984 ($2.00, Baxter paper)
1-3: X-Men-r by Neal Adams 6.00
NOTE: *Zeck c-1-3.*

X-MEN: EARTHFALL
Marvel Comics: Sept, 1996 ($2.95, one-shot)
1-r/Uncanny X-Men #232-234; wraparound-c 3.00

X-MEN: EVOLUTION (Based on the animated series)
Marvel Comics: Feb, 2002 - No. 9, Sept, 2002 ($2.25)
1-9: 1-8-Grayson-s/Udon-a. 9-Farber-s/J.J.Kirby-a 2.25
TPB (7/02, $8.99) r/#1-4 9.00
Vol. 2 TPB (2003, $11.99) r/#5-9; Asamiya-c 12.00

X-MEN FIRSTS
Marvel Comics: Feb, 1996 ($4.95, one-shot)
1-r/Avengers Annual #10, Uncanny X-Men #266, #221; Incredible Hulk #181 5.00

X-MEN FOREVER
Marvel Comics: Jan, 2001 - No. 6, June, 2001 ($3.50, limited series)
1-6-Jean Grey, Iceman, Mystique, Toad, Juggernaut app.; Maguire-a 3.50

X-MEN: HELLFIRE CLUB
Marvel Comics: Jan, 2000 - No. 4, Apr, 2000 ($2.50, limited series)
1-4-Origin of the Hellfire Club 2.50

X-MEN: HIDDEN YEARS
Marvel Comics: Dec, 1999 - No. 22, Sept. 2001 ($3.50/$2.50)
1-New adventures from pre-#94 era; Byrne-s/a(p) 3.50
2-4,6-11,13-22-($2.50): 2-Two covers. 3-Ka-Zar app. 8,9-FF-c/app. 2.50
5-($2.75) 2.75
12-($3.50) Magneto-c/app. 3.50

X-MEN: LIBERATORS
Marvel Comics: Nov, 1998 - No. 4, Feb, 1999 ($2.99, limited series)
1-4-Wolverine, Nightcrawler & Colossus; P. Jimenez 3.00

X-MEN LOST TALES
Marvel Comics: 1997 ($2.99)
1,2-r/Classic X-Men back-up stories 3.00

X-MEN OMEGA
Marvel Comics: June, 1995 ($3.95, one-shot)
nn-Age of Apocalypse finale 1 3 4 6 8 10
nn-($49.95)-Gold edition 50.00

X-MEN: PHOENIX
Marvel Comics: Dec, 1999 - No. 3, Mar, 2000 ($2.50, limited series)
1-3: 1-Apocalypse app. 2.50

X-MEN: PHOENIX - LEGACY OF FIRE
Marvel Comics: July, 2003 - No. 3, Sep, 2003 ($2.99, limited series)
1-3-Manga-style; Ryan Kinnard-s/a/c; intro page art by Adam Warren 3.00

X-MEN PRIME
Marvel Comics: July, 1995 ($4.95, one-shot)
nn-Post Age of Apocalyse begins 1 3 4 6 8 10

X-MEN RARITIES
Marvel Comics: 1995 ($5.95, one-shot)
nn-Reprints hard-to-find stories 6.00

X-MEN ROAD TO ONSLAUGHT
Marvel Comics: Oct, 1996 ($2.50, one-shot)
nn-Retells Onslaught Saga 2.50

X-MEN: RONIN
Marvel Comics: May, 2003 - No. 5, July, 2003 ($2.99, limited series)
1-5-Manga-style X-Men; Torres-s/Nakatsuka-a 3.00

X-MEN: SEARCH FOR CYCLOPS
Marvel Comics: Oct, 2000 - No. 4, Mar, 2001 ($2.99, limited series)
1-4-Two covers (Raney, Pollina); Raney-a 3.00

X-MEN SPOTLIGHT ON... STARJAMMERS (Also see X-Men #104)
Marvel Comics: 1990 - No. 2, 1990 ($4.50, 52 pgs.)
1,2: Features Starjammers 4.50

X-MEN SURVIVAL GUIDE TO THE MANSION
Marvel Comics: Aug, 1993 ($6.95, spiralbound)
1 7.00

X-MEN: THE EARLY YEARS
Marvel Comics: May, 1994 - No. 17, Sept, 1995 ($1.50/$2.50)
1-16: r/X-Men #1-8 w/new-c 2.25
17-$2.50-c; r/X-Men #17,18 2.50

X-MEN: THE END
Marvel Comics: Oct, 2004 - No. 6 ($2.99, limited series)
1-5-Claremont-s/Chen-a/Land-c 3.00

X-MEN: THE MANGA
Marvel Comics: Mar, 1998 - No. 26, June, 1999 ($2.99, B&W)
1-26-English version of Japanese X-Men comics: 23,24-Randy Green-c 3.00

X-MEN: THE MOVIE
Marvel Comics: Aug, 2000; Sept, 2000
Adaptation (9/00, $5.95) Macchio-s/Williams & Lanning-a 6.00
Adaptation TPB (9/00, $14.95) Movie adaptation and key reprints of main characters; four photo covers (movie X, Magneto, Rogue, Wolverine) 15.00
Prequel: Magneto (8/00, $5.95) Texeira & Palmiotti-a; art & photo covers 6.00
Prequel: Rogue (8/00, $5.95) Evans & Nikolakakis-a; art & photo covers 6.00
Prequel: Wolverine (8/00, $5.95) Waller & McKenna-a; art & photo covers 6.00
TPB X-Men: Beginnings (8/00, $14.95) reprints 3 prequels w/photo-c 15.00

X-MEN 2: THE MOVIE
Marvel Comics: 2003

X-Men 2 Prequel: Wolverine #1 © MAR

X-O Manowar #57 © Acclaim

X-Statix #21 © MAR

GD 2.0 | VG 4.0 | FN 6.0 | VF 8.0 | VF/NM 9.0 | NM- 9.2

Adaptation (6/03, $3.50) Movie adaptation; photo-c; Austen-s/Zircher-a 3.50
Adaptation TPB (2003, $12.99) Movie adaptation & r/Prequels Nightcrawler & Wolverine 13.00
Prequel: Nightcrawler (5/03, $3.50) Kerschl-a; photo cover 3.50
Prequel: Wolverine (5/03, $3.50) Mandrake-a; photo cover; Sabretooth app. 3.50

X-MEN: THE ULTRA COLLECTION
Marvel Comics: Dec, 1994 - No. 5, Apr, 1995 ($2.95, limited series)

1-5: Pin-ups; no scripts 3.00

X-MEN: THE WEDDING ALBUM
Marvel Comics: 1994 ($2.95, magazine size, one-shot)

1-Wedding of Scott Summers & Jean Grey 3.00

X-MEN TRUE FRIENDS
Marvel Comics: Sept, 1999 - No. 3, Nov, 1999 ($2.99, limited series)

1-3-Claremont-s/Leonardi-a 3.00

X-MEN 2099 (Also see 2099: World of Tomorrow)
Marvel Comics: Oct, 1993 - No. 35, Aug, 1996 ($1.25/$1.50/$1.95)

1-($1.75)-Foil-c; Ron Lim/Adam Kubert-a begins 3.00
1-2nd printing ($1.75) 2.25
1-Gold edition (15,000 made); sold thru Diamond for $19.40 20.00
2-24,26-35: 3-Death of Tina; Lim-c/a(p) in #1-8. 8-Bound-in trading card sheet. 35-Nostromo (from X-Nation) app; storyline cont'd in 2099: World of Tomorrow 2.25
25-($2.50)-Double sized 2.50
Special 1 ($3.95) 4.00
...: Oasis ($5.95, one-shot) -Hildebrandt Bros.-c/a 6.00

X-MEN ULTRA III PREVIEW
Marvel Comics: 1995 ($2.95)

nn-Kubert-a 3.00

X-MEN UNIVERSE
Marvel Comics: Dec, 1999 - Present ($4.99/$3.99)

1-8-Reprints stories from recent X-Men titles 5.00
9-15-($3.99) 4.00

X-MEN UNIVERSE: PAST, PRESENT AND FUTURE
Marvel Comics: Feb, 1999 ($2.99, one-shot)

1-Previews 1999 X-Men events; background info 3.00

X-MEN UNLIMITED
Marvel Comics: 1993 - No. 50, Sept, 2003 ($3.95/$2.99, 68 pgs.)

1-Chris Bachalo-c/a; Quesada-a. 5.00
2-11: 2-Origin of Magneto script. 3-Sabretooth-c/story. 10-Dark Beast vs. Beast; Mark Waid script. 11-Magneto & Rogue 4.00
12-33: 12-Begin $2.99-c; Onslaught x-over; Juggernaut-c/app. 19-Caliafore-a. 20-Generation X app. 27-Origin Thunderbird. 29-Maximum Security x-over; Bishop-c/app. 30-Mahfood-a. 31-Stelfreeze-c/a. 32-Dazzler; Thompson-c/a 33-Kaluta-c 3.00
34-37,39,40-42-($3.50) 34-Von Eeden-a. 35-Finch, Conner, Maguire-a. 36-Chiodo-c/a; Larroca, Totleben-a. 39-Bachalo-c; Pearson-a. 41-Bachalo-c; X-Statix app. 3.50
38-($2.25) Kitty Pryde; Robertson-a 2.25
43-50-($2.50) 43-Sienkiewicz-c/a; Paul Smith-a. 45-Noto-c. 46-Bisley-a. 47-Warren-s/Mays-a. 48-Wolverine story w/Isanove painted-a 2.50
X-Men Legends Vol. 4: Hated and Feared TPB (2003, $19.99) r/stories by various 20.00
NOTE: ***Bachalo*** *c/a-1.* ***Quesada*** *a-1.* ***Waid*** *scripts-10*

X-MEN UNLIMITED
Marvel Comics: Apr, 2004 - Present ($2.99)

1-5-Pat Lee-c; short stories by various. 2-District X preview; Granov-a 3.00

X-MEN VS. DRACULA
Marvel Comics: Dec, 1993 ($1.75)

1-r/X-Men Annual #6; Austin-c(i) 2.25

X-MEN VS. THE AVENGERS, THE
Marvel Comics Group: Apr, 1987 - No. 4, July, 1987 ($1.50, limited series, Baxter paper)

1 4.00
2-4 3.00

X-MEN VS. THE BROOD, THE
Marvel Comics Group: Sept, 1996 - No. 2, Oct, 1996 ($2.95, limited series)

1,2-Wraparound-c; Ostrander-s/Hitch-a(p) 3.00
TPB('97, $16.99) reprints X-Men/Brood: Day of Wrath #1,2 & Uncanny X-Men #232-234 17.00

X-MEN VISIONARIES
Marvel Comics: 1995,1996,2000 (trade paperbacks)

nn-($8.95) Reprints X-Men stories; Adam & Andy Kubert-a 9.00
...2: The Neal Adams Collection (1996) r/X-Men #56-63,65 30.00

GD 2.0 | VG 4.0 | FN 6.0 | VF 8.0 | VF/NM 9.0 | NM- 9.2

...2: The Neal Adams Col. (2nd printing, 2000, $24.95) new Adams-c 25.00

X-MEN/WILDC.A.T.S.: THE DARK AGE (See also WildC.A.T.S./X-Men...)
Marvel Comics: 1998 ($4.50, one-shot)

1-Two covers (Broome & Golden); Ellis-s 4.50

X-NATION 2099
Marvel Comics: Mar, 1996 - No. 6, Aug, 1996 ($1.95)

1-($3.95)-Humberto Ramos-a(p); wraparound, foil-c 4.00
2-6: 2,3-Ramos-a. 4-Exodus-c/app. 6-Reed Richards app 2.25

X-O MANOWAR (1st Series)
Valiant/Acclaim Comics (Valiant) No. 43 on: Feb, 1992 - No. 68, Sept, 1996 ($1.95/$2.25/$2.50, high quality)

0-(8/93, $3.50)-Wraparound embossed chromium-c by Quesada; Solar app.; origin Aric (X-O Manowar) 3.50
0-Gold variant 5.00
1-Intro/1st app. & partial origin of Aric (X-O Manowar); Barry Smith/Layton-a
1 2 3 5 6 8
2-4: 2-B. Smith/Layton-c. 3-Layton-c(i). 4-1st app. Shadowman 6.00
5-15: 5-B. Smith-c. 6-Begin $2.25-c; Ditko-a(p). 7,8-Unity x-overs. 7-Miller-c. 8-Simonson-c. 12-1st app. Randy Calder. 14,15-Turok-c/stories 3.00
15-Hot pink logo variant; came with Ultra Pro Rigid Comic Sleeves box; no price on cover 4.00
16-24,26-43: 20-Serial number contest insert. 27-29-Turok x-over. 28-Bound-in trading card. 30-1st app. new "good skin"; Solar app. 33-Chaos Effect Delta Pt. 3. 42-Shadowman app.; includes X-O Manowar Birthquake! Prequel 2.50
25-($3.50)-Has 16 pg. Armorines #0 bound-in w/origin 3.50
44-68: 44-Begin $2.50-c. 50-X, 50-O, 51, 52, 63-Bart Sears-c/a/scripts. 68-Revealed that Aric's past stories were premonitions of his future 2.50
Trade paperback nn (1993, $9.95)-Polybagged with copy of X-O Database #1 inside 10.00
Yearbook 1 (4/95, $2.95) 3.00
NOTE: ***Layton*** *a-1i, 2i(part); c-1, 2i, 3i, 6i, 21i.* ***Reese*** *a-4i(part); c-26i.*

X-O MANOWAR (2nd Series)(Also see Iron Man/X-O Manowar: Heavy Metal)
Acclaim Comics (Valiant Heroes): V2#1, Oct, 1996 - No. 21, Jun, 1998 ($2.50)

V2#1-21: 1-Mark Waid & Brian Augustyn scripts begin; 1st app. Donavon Wylie; Rand Banion dies; painted variant-c exists. 2-Donavon Wylie becomes new X-O Manowar. 7-9-Augustyn-s. 10-Copycat-c 2.50

X-O MANOWAR FAN EDITION
Acclaim Comics (Valiant Heroes): Feb, 1997 (Overstreet's FAN giveaway)

1-Reintro the Armorines & the Hard Corps; 1st app. Citadel; Augustyn scripts; McKone-c/a 4.00

X-O MANOWAR/IRON MAN: IN HEAVY METAL (See Iron Man/X-O Manowar: Heavy Metal)
Acclaim Comics (Valiant Heroes): Sept, 1996 ($2.50, one-shot)
(1st Marvel/Valiant x-over)

1-Pt 1 of X-O Manowar/Iron Man x-over; Arnim Zola app.; Nicieza scripts; Andy Smith-a 2.50

XOMBI
DC Comics (Milestone): Jan, 1994 - No. 21, Feb, 1996 ($1.75/$2.50)

0-($1.95)-Shadow War x-over; Simonson silver ink varnish-c 2.50
1-21: 1-John Byrne-c 2.50
1-Platinum 8.00

X-PATROL
Marvel Comics (Amalgam): Apr, 1996 ($1.95, one-shot)

1-Cruz-a(p) 2.25

XSE
Marvel Comics: Nov, 1996 - No. 4, Feb, 1997 ($1.95, limited series)

1-4: 1-Bishop & Shard app. 2.25
1-Variant-c 3.00

X-STATIX
Marvel Comics: Sept, 2002 - No. 26, Oct, 2004 ($2.99/$2.25)

1-($2.99)Allred-a/c; intro. Venus Dee Milo; back-up w/Cooke-a 3.00
2-9-($2.25) 4-Quitely-c. 5-Pope-c/a 2.25
10-26: 10-Begin $2.99-c; Bond-a; U-Go Girl flashback. 13,14-Spider-Man app. 21-25-Avengers app. 26-Team dies 3.00
... Vol. 1: Good Omens TPB (2003, $11.99) r/#1-5 12.00
... Vol. 2: Good Guys & Bad Guys TPB (2003, $15.99) r/#6-10 & Wolverine/Doop #1&2 16.00
... Vol. 3: Back From the Dead TPB (2004, $19.99) r/#11-18 20.00
... Vol. 4: X-Statix Vs. the Avengers TPB (2004, $19.99) r/#19-26; pin-ups 20.00

X-TERMINATORS
Marvel Comics: Oct, 1988 - No. 4, Jan, 1989 ($1.00, limited series)

X-Treme X-Men #25 © MAR

Yankee Comics #1 © CHES

Yellowjacket Comics #3 © Frank Comunale

	GD 2.0	VG 4.0	FN 6.0	VF 8.0	VF/NM 9.0	NM- 9.2

1-1st app.; X-Men/X-Factor tie-in; Williamson-i 3.00
2-4 2.25

X, THE MAN WITH THE X-RAY EYES (See Movie Comics)

X-TREME X-MEN (Also see Mekanix)
Marvel Comics: July, 2001 - No. 46, Jun, 2004 ($2.99/$3.50)

1-Claremont-s/Larroca-c/a 4.00
2-24: 2-Two covers (Larroca & Pacheco); Psylocke killed 3.00
25-35, 40-46: 25-30-God Loves, Man Kills II; Stryker app.; Kordey-a 3.00
36-39-($3.50) 3.50
Annual 2001 ($4.95) issue opens longways 5.00
... Vol. 1: Destiny TPB (2002, $19.95) r/#1-9 20.00
... Vol. 2: Invasion TPB (2003, $19.99) r/#10-18 20.00
... Vol. 3: Schism TPB (2003, $16.99) r/#19-23; X-Treme X-Posé #1&2 17.00
... Vol. 4: Mekanix TPB (2003, $16.99) r/Mekanix #1-6 17.00
... Vol. 5: God Loves Man Kills TPB (2003, $19.99) r/#25-30 20.00
... Vol. 6: Intifada TPB (2004, $16.99) r/#24,31-35 17.00
... Vol. 7: Storm the Arena TPB (2004, $16.99) r/#36-39 17.00
... Vol. 8: Prisoner of Fire TPB (2004, $19.99) r/#40-46 and Annual 2001 20.00

X-TREME X-MEN: SAVAGE LAND
Marvel Comics: Nov, 2001 - No. 4, Feb, 2002 ($2.99, limited series)

1-4-Claremont-s/Sharpe-c/a; Beast app. 3.00

X-TREME X-POSE
Marvel Comics: Jan, 2003 - No. 2, Feb, 2003 ($2.99, limited series)

1,2-Claremont-s/Ranson-a/Migliari-c 3.00

X-UNIVERSE
Marvel Comics: May, 1995 - No. 2, June, 1995 ($3.50, limited series)

1,2: Age of Apocalypse 5.00

X-VENTURE (Super Heroes)
Victory Magazines Corp.: July, 1947 - No. 2, Nov, 1947

1-Atom Wizard, Mystery Shadow, Lester Trumble begin
112 224 336 700 1075 1450
2 56 112 168 350 538 725

XYR (See Eclipse Graphic Album Series #21)

YAK YAK
Dell Publishing Co.: No. 1186, May-July, 1961 - No. 1348, Apr-June, 1962

Four Color 1186 (#1)- Jack Davis-c/a; 2 versions, one minus 3pgs.
10 20 30 70 100 130
Four Color 1348 (#2)-Davis c/a 9 18 27 65 93 120

YAKKY DOODLE & CHOPPER (TV) (See Dell Giant #44)
Gold Key: Dec, 1962 (Hanna-Barbera)

1 9 18 27 63 89 115

YANG (See House of Yang)
Charlton Comics: Nov, 1973 - No. 13, May, 1976; V14#15, Sept, 1985 - No. 17, Jan, 1986 (No V14#14, series resumes with #15)

1-Origin; Sattler-a begins; slavery-s 2 4 6 12 16 20
2-13(1976) 1 2 3 6 9 10
15-17(1986): 15-Reprints #1 (Low print run) 6.00
3,10,11(Modern Comics-r, 1977) 4.00

YANKEE COMICS
Harry 'A' Chesler: Sept, 1941 - No. 7, 1942?

1-Origin The Echo, The Enchanted Dagger, Yankee Doodle Jones, The Firebrand, & The Scarlet Sentry; Black Satan app.; Yankee Doodle Jones app. on all covers
173 346 519 1081 1666 2250
2-Origin Johnny Rebel; Major Victory app.; Barry Kuda begins
79 158 237 494 760 1025
3,4: 4-(3/42) 60 120 180 375 580 785
4 (nd, 1940s; 7-1/4x5", 68 pgs, distr. to the service)-Foxy Grandpa, Tom, Dick & Harry, Impy, Ace & Deuce, Dot & Dash, Ima Slooth by Jack Cole (Remington Morse publ.)
10 20 30 56 73 90
5-7 (nd; 10¢, 7-1/4x5", 68 pgs.)(Remington Morse publ.)-urges readers to send their copies to servicemen. 9 18 27 51 62 75

YANKEE DOODLE THE SPIRIT OF LIBERTY
Spire Publications: 1984 (no price, 36 pgs)

nn-Al Hartley-s/c/a 1 3 4 6 8 10

YANKS IN BATTLE
Quality Comics Group: Sept, 1956 - No. 4, Dec, 1956; 1963

1-Cuidera-c(i) 10 20 30 56 73 90
2-4: Cuidera-c(i) 7 14 21 37 46 55
I.W. Reprint #3(1963)-r/#?; exist? 2 4 6 10 12 15

YARDBIRDS, THE (G. I. Joe's Sidekicks)
Ziff-Davis Publishing Co.: Summer, 1952

1-By Bob Oskner 10 20 30 58 77 95

YARN MAN (See Megaton Man)
Kitchen Sink : Oct, 1989 ($2.00, B&W, one-shot)

1-Donald Simpson-c/a/scripts 2.25

YARNS OF YELLOWSTONE
World Color Press: 1972 (50¢, 36 pgs.)

nn-Illustrated by Bill Chapman 2 4 6 9 11 14

YEAH!
DC Comics (Homage): Oct, 1999 - No. 9, Jun, 2000 ($2.95)

1-Bagge-s/Hernandez-a 3.00
2-9: 2-Editorial page contains adult language 3.00

YELLOW CLAW (Also see Giant Size Master of Kung Fu)
Atlas Comics (MjMC): Oct, 1956 - No. 4, Apr, 1957

1-Origin by Joe Maneely 96 192 288 600 925 1250
2-Kirby-a 77 154 231 481 741 1000
3,4-Kirby-a; 4-Kirby/Severin-a 74 148 222 463 712 960
NOTE: ***Everett** c-3. **Maneely** c-1. **Reinman** a-2i, 3. **Severin** c-2, 4.*

YELLOWJACKET COMICS (Jack in the Box #11 on)(See TNT Comics)
E. Levy/Frank Comunale/Charlton: Sept, 1944 - No. 10, June, 1946

1-Intro & origin Yellowjacket; Diana, the Huntress begins; E.A. Poe's "The Black Cat" adaptation 67 134 201 419 647 875
2-Yellowjacket-c begin, end #10 40 80 120 244 372 500
3,5 40 80 120 239 357 475
4-E.A. Poe's "Fall of the House Of Usher" adaptation; Palais-a
40 80 120 244 372 500
6 49 98 147 299 455 610
7-Classic skull-c 98 196 294 613 944 1275
8-10: 1,3,4,6-10-Have stories narrated by old witch in "Tales of Terror" (1st horror series?)
47 94 141 287 436 585

YELLOWSTONE KELLY (Movie)
Dell Publishing Co.: No. 1056, Nov-Jan, 1959/60

Four Color 1056-Clint Walker photo-c 7 14 21 46 63 80

YELLOW SUBMARINE (See Movie Comics)

YIN FEI THE CHINESE NINJA
Leung's Publications: 1988 - No. 8, 1990 ($1.80/$2.00, 52 pgs.)

1-8 2.25

YOGI BEAR (See Dell Giant #41, Golden Comics Digest, Kite Fun Book, March of Comics #253, 265, 279, 291, 309, 319, 337, 344, Movie Comics under "Hey There It's..." & Whitman Comic Books)

YOGI BEAR (TV) (Hanna-Barbera) (See Four Color #990)
Dell Publishing Co./Gold Key No. 10 on: No. 1067, 12-2/59-60 - No. 9, 7-9/62; No. 10, 10/62 - No. 42, 10/70

Four Color 1067 (#1)-TV show debuted 1/30/61 12 24 36 87 134 180
Four Color 1104,1162 (5-7/61) 9 18 27 60 85 110
4(8-9/61) - 6(12-1/61-62) 7 14 21 46 63 80
Four Color 1271(11/61) 7 14 21 46 63 80
Four Color 1349(1/62)-Photo-c 10 20 30 72 104 135
7(2-3/62) - 9(7-9/62)-Last Dell 7 14 21 46 63 80
10(10/62-G.K.), 11(1/63)-titled "Yogi Bear Jellystone Jollies" (80 pgs.); 11-X-Mas-c
8 16 24 58 82 105
12(4/63), 14-20 6 12 18 38 52 65
13(7/63, 68 pgs.)-Surprise Party 8 16 24 58 82 105
21-30 4 8 12 24 32 40
31-42 3 6 9 19 25 32

YOGI BEAR (TV)
Charlton Comics: Nov, 1970 - No. 35, Jan, 1976 (Hanna-Barbera)

1 5 10 15 36 48 60
2-6,8-10 3 6 9 18 24 30
7-Summer Fun (Giant, 52 pgs.) 5 10 15 36 48 60
11-20 3 6 9 18 23 28
21-35: 28-31-partial-r 2 4 6 12 16 20
Digest (nn, 1972, 75¢-c, B&W, 100 pgs.) (scarce) 4 8 12 22 30 38

YOGI BEAR (TV)(See The Flintstones, 3rd series & Spotlight #1)

Young Allies Comics #13 © MAR

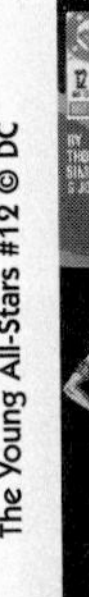
The Young All-Stars #12 © DC

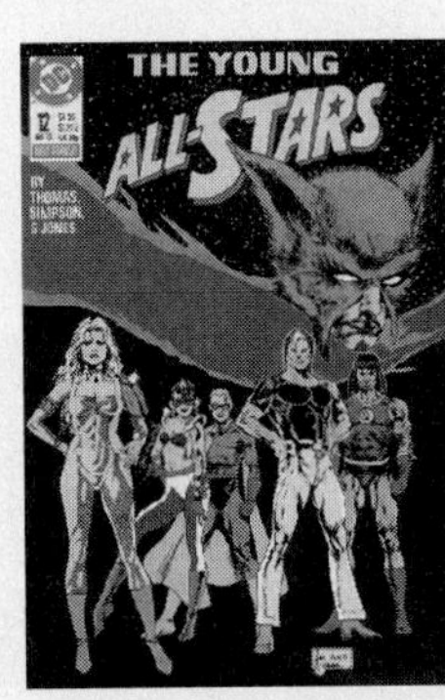

Young Heroes in Love #6 © DC

	GD 2.0	VG 4.0	FN 6.0	VF 8.0	VF/NM 9.0	NM- 9.2

Marvel Comics Group: Nov, 1977 - No. 9, Mar, 1979 (Hanna-Barbera)

	GD	VG	FN	VF	VF/NM	NM-
1,7-9: 1-Flintstones begin (Newsstand sales only)	3	6	9	18	24	30
2-6	2	4	6	12	16	20

YOGI BEAR (TV)
Harvey Comics: Sept, 1992 - No. 6, Mar, 1994 ($1.25/$1.50) (Hanna-Barbera)

V2#1-6 3.00
...Big Book V2#1,2 ($1.95, 52 pgs): 1-(11/92). 2-(3/93) 3.00
...Giant Size V2#1,2 ($2.25, 68 pgs.): 1-(10/92). 2-(4/93) 3.00

YOGI BEAR'S EASTER PARADE (See The Funtastic World of Hanna-Barbera #2)

YOGI BERRA (Baseball hero)
Fawcett Publications: 1951 (Yankee catcher)

	GD	VG	FN	VF	VF/NM	NM-
nn-Photo-c (scarce)	71	142	213	444	685	925

YOSEMITE SAM (...& Bugs Bunny) (TV)
Gold Key/Whitman: Dec, 1970 - No. 81, Feb, 1984

	GD	VG	FN	VF	VF/NM	NM-
1	5	10	15	36	48	60
2-10	3	6	9	18	23	28
11-20	2	4	6	11	14	18
21-30	2	4	6	9	11	14
31-50	1	3	4	6	8	10
51-65 (Gold Key)	1	2	3	5	6	8
66,67 (Whitman)	2	4	6	8	10	12
68(9/80), 69(10/80), 70(12/80) 3-pack only	3	6	9	16	20	26
71-78: 76(2/82), 77(3/82), 78(4/82)	2	4	6	9	11	14
79-81 (All #90263 on-c, no date or date code; 3-pack): 79(7/83). 80(8/83). 81(2/84)-(1/3-r)	2	4	6	14	18	22

(See March of Comics #363, 380, 392)

YOUNG ALLIES COMICS (All-Winners #21; see Kid Komics #2)
Timely Comics (USA 1-7/NPI 8,9/YAI 10-20): Sum, 1941 - No. 20, Oct, 1946

	GD	VG	FN	VF	VF/NM	NM-
1-Origin/1st app. The Young Allies (Bucky, Toro, others); 1st meeting of Captain America & Human Torch; Red Skull-c & app.; S&K-c/splash; Hitler-c; Note: the cover was altered after its preview in Human Torch #5. Stalin was shown with Hitler but was removed due to Russia becoming an ally	1353	2706	4059	10,148	16,574	23,000
2-(Winter, 1941)-Captain America & Human Torch app.; Simon & Kirby-c	379	758	1137	2464	3982	5500
3-Fathertime, Captain America & Human Torch app.; Remember Pearl Harbor issue (Spring, 1942); Stan Lee scripts; Vs. Japs-c/full-length story	296	592	888	1850	2850	3850
4-The Vagabond & Red Skull, Capt. America, Human Torch app. Classic Red Skull-c	393	786	1179	2555	4128	5700
5-Captain America & Human Torch app.	192	384	576	1200	1850	2500
6,7,10: 10-Origin Tommy Tyme & Clock of Ages; ends #19	135	270	405	844	1297	1750
8-Classic Schomburg WW2 bondage-c	142	284	426	888	1369	1850
9-Hitler, Tojo, Mussolini-c.	154	308	462	963	1482	2000
11-20: 12-Classic decapitation story	102	204	306	638	982	1325

NOTE: ***Brodsky** c-15. **Gabrielle** a-3; c-3, 4. **S&K** c-1, 2. **Schomburg** c-5-13, 16-19. **Shores** c-20.*

YOUNG ALL-STARS
DC Comics: June, 1987 - No. 31, Nov, 1989 ($1.00, deluxe format)

1-31: 1-1st app. Iron Munro & The Flying Fox. 8,9-Millennium tie-ins 2.25
Annual 1 (1988, $2.00) 2.25

YOUNGBLOOD (See Brigade #4, Megaton Explosion & Team Youngblood)
Image Comics (Extreme Studios): Apr, 1992 - No. 4, Feb, 1993 ($2.50, lim. series); No. 6, June, 1994 (No #5) - No. 10, Dec, 1994 ($1.95/$2.50)

1-Liefeld-c/a/scripts in all; flip book format with 2 trading cards; 1st Image/Extreme Studios title. 5.00
1,2-2nd printing 2.50
2-(JUN-c, July 1992 indicia)-1st app. Shadowhawk in solo back-up story; 2 trading cards inside; flip book format; 1st app. Prophet, Kirby, Berzerkers, Darkthorn 2.50
3,0,4,5: 3-(OCT-c, August 1992 indicia)-Contains 2 trading cards inside (flip book); 1st app. Supreme in back-up story; 1st app. Showdown. 0-(12/92, $1.95)-Contains 2 trading cards; 2 cover variations exist, green or beige logo; w/Image #0 coupon. 4-(2/93)-Glow-in-the-dark cover w/2 trading cards; 2nd app. Dale Keown's The Pitt; Bloodstrike app. 5-Flip book w/Brigade #4 2.50
6-($3.50, 52 pgs.)-Wraparound-c 3.50
7-10: 7, 8-Liefeld-c(p)/a(p)/story. 8,9-(9/94) 9-Valentino story & art 2.50
Battlezone 1 (May-c, 4/93 inside, $1.95)-Arsenal book; Liefeld-c(p) 2.50
Battlezone 2 (7/94, $2.95)-Wraparound-c 3.00
Yearbook 1 (7/93, $2.50)-Fold out panel; 1st app. Tyrax & Kanan 2.50
...Super Special (Winter '97, $2.99) Sprouse -a 3.00
TPB (1996, $16.95)-r/Team Youngblood #8-10 & Youngblood #6-8,10 17.00

	GD 2.0	VG 4.0	FN 6.0	VF 8.0	VF/NM 9.0	NM- 9.2

YOUNGBLOOD
Image Comics (Extreme Studios)/Maximum Press No. 14: V2#1, Sept, 1995 - No. 14, Dec, 1996 ($2.50)

V2#1-10,14: Roger Cruz-a in all. 4-Extreme Destroyer Pt. 4 w/gaming card. 5-Variant-c exists. 6-Angela & Glory. 7-Shadowhunt Pt. 3; Shadowhawk app. 8,10-Thor (from Supreme) app. 10-(7/96). 14-(12/96)-1st Maximum Press issue 2.50

YOUNGBLOOD (Volume 3)
Awesome/ Awesome-Hyperwerks #2 on: Feb, 1998 - No. 2, Aug, 1998 ($2.50)

1-Alan Moore-s/Skroce & Stucker-a; 12 diff. covers 2.50
1-Gold foil-c; 1+ Alter Ego Gold Foil 5.00
1-Blue foil-c Orlando Con Ed. 10.00
2-(8/98) Skroce & Liefeld covers 2.50

YOUNGBLOOD: STRIKEFILE
Image Comics (Extreme Studios): Apr, 1993 - No. 11, Feb, 1995 ($1.95/$2.50/$2.95)

1-10: 1-($1.95)-Flip book w/Jae Lee-c/a & Liefeld-c/a in #1-3; 1st app. The Allies,Giger, & Glory. 3-Thibert-i asisst. 4-Liefeld-c(p); no Lee-a. 5-Liefeld-c(p). 8-Platt-c 3.00
NOTE: *Youngblood: Strikefile began as a four issue limited series.*

YOUNGBLOOD/X-FORCE
Image Comics (Extreme Studios): July, 1996 ($4.95, one-shot)

1-Cruz-a(p); two covers exist 5.00

YOUNG BRIDES (True Love Secrets)
Feature/Prize Publ.: Sept-Oct, 1952 - No. 30, Nov-Dec, 1956 (Photo-c: 1-4)

	GD	VG	FN	VF	VF/NM	NM-
V1#1-Simon & Kirby-a	35	70	105	198	287	375
2-S&K-a	19	38	57	107	154	200
3-6-S&K-a	17	34	51	98	139	180
V2#1,3-7,10-12 (#7-18)-S&K-a	16	32	48	92	131	170
2,8,9-No S&K-a	8	16	24	40	50	60
V3#1-3(#19-21)-Last precode (3-4/55)	7	14	21	37	46	55
4,6(#22,24), V4#1,3(#25,27)	6	12	18	31	38	45
V3#5(#23)-Meskin-c	7	14	21	35	43	50
V4#2(#26)-All S&K issue	15	30	45	83	117	150
V4#4(#28)-S&K-a	11	22	33	66	91	115
V4#5,6(#29,30)	7	14	21	37	46	55

YOUNG DR. MASTERS (See The Adventures of Young Dr. Masters)

YOUNG DOCTORS, THE
Charlton Comics: Jan, 1963 - No. 6, Nov, 1963

	GD	VG	FN	VF	VF/NM	NM-
V1#1	4	8	12	25	33	42
2-6	3	6	9	16	20	24

YOUNG EAGLE
Fawcett Publications/Charlton: 12/50 - No. 10, 6/52; No. 3, 7/56 - No. 5, 4/57 (Photo-c: 1-10)

	GD	VG	FN	VF	VF/NM	NM-
1-Intro Young Eagle	19	38	57	107	154	200
2-Complete picture novelette "The Mystery of Thunder Canyon"	10	20	30	56	73	90
3-9	9	18	27	49	62	75
10-Origin Thunder, Young Eagle's Horse	8	16	24	43	54	65
3-5(Charlton)-Formerly Sherlock Holmes?	6	12	18	31	38	45

YOUNG HEARTS
Marvel Comics (SPC): Nov, 1949 - No. 2, Feb, 1950

	GD	VG	FN	VF	VF/NM	NM-
1-Photo-c	13	26	39	75	106	135
2-Colleen Townsend photo-c from movie	9	18	27	52	66	80

YOUNG HEARTS IN LOVE
Super Comics: 1964

	GD	VG	FN	VF	VF/NM	NM-
17,18: 17-r/Young Love V5#6 (4-5/62)	2	4	6	11	14	18

YOUNG HEROES (Formerly Forbidden Worlds #34)
American Comics Group (Titan): No. 35, Feb-Mar, 1955 - No. 37, Jun-Jul, 1955

	GD	VG	FN	VF	VF/NM	NM-
35-37-Frontier Scout	10	20	30	56	73	90

YOUNG HEROES IN LOVE
DC Comics: June, 1997 - No. 17; #1,000,000, Nov, 1998 ($1.75/$1.95/$2.50)

1-1st app. Young Heroes; Madan-a 3.00
2-17: 3-Superman-c/app. 7-Begin $1.95-c 2.50
#1,000,000 (11/98, $2.50) 853 Century x-over 2.50

YOUNG INDIANA JONES CHRONICLES, THE
Dark Horse Comics: Feb, 1992 - No. 12, Feb, 1993 ($2.50)

1-12: Dan Barry scripts in all 2.50
NOTE: ***Dan Barry** a(p)-1, 2, 5, 6, 10; c-1-10. **Morrow** a-3, 4, 5p, 6p. **Springer** a-1i, 2i.*

YOUNG INDIANA JONES CHRONICLES, THE

Young Justice #47 © DC

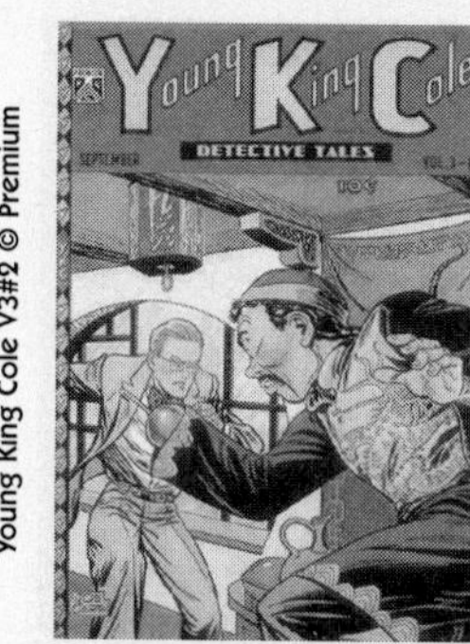

Young King Cole V3#2 © Premium

Young Men #28 © MAR

	GD 2.0	VG 4.0	FN 6.0	VF 8.0	VF/NM 9.0	NM- 9.2

Hollywood Comics (Disney): 1992 ($3.95, squarebound, 68 pgs.)

Issue	GD 2.0	VG 4.0	FN 6.0	VF 8.0	VF/NM 9.0	NM- 9.2
1-3: 1-r/YIJC #1,2 by D. Horse. 2-r/#3,4. 3-r/#5,6						4.00

YOUNG JUSTICE (Also see Teen Titans and Titans/Young Justice)
DC Comics: Sept, 1998 - No. 55, May, 2003 ($2.50/$2.75)

Issue	GD 2.0	VG 4.0	FN 6.0	VF 8.0	VF/NM 9.0	NM- 9.2
1-Robin, Superboy & Impulse team-up; David-s/Nauck-a						4.00
2,3: 3-Mxyzptlk app.						3.00
4-20: 4-Wonder Girl, Arrowette and the Secret join. 6-JLA app. 13-Supergirl x-over. 20-Sins of Youth aftermath						3.00
21-49: 25-Empress ID revealed. 28,29-Forever People app. 32-Empress origin. 35,36-Our Worlds at War x-over. 38-Joker: Last Laugh. 41-The Ray joins. 42-Spectre-c/app. 44,45-World Without YJ x-over pt. 1,5; Ramos-c. 48-Begin $2.75-c						2.75
50-($3.95) Wonder Twins,CM3 and other various DC teen heroes app.						4.00
51-55: 53,54-Darkseid app. 55-Last issue; leads into Titans/Young Justice mini-series						2.75
#1,000,000 (11/98) 853 Century x-over						2.50
...: A League of Their Own (2000, $14.95, TPB) r/#1-7, Secret Files #1						15.00
...: 80-Page Giant (5/99, $4.95) Ramos-c; stories and art by various						5.00
...: In No Man's Land (7/99, $3.95) McDaniel-c						4.00
...: Our Worlds at War (8/01, $2.95) Jae Lee-c; Linear Men app.						3.00
...: Secret Files (1/99, $4.95) Origin-s & pin-ups						5.00
...: The Secret (6/98, $1.95) Girlfrenzy; Nauck-a						2.50

YOUNG JUSTICE: SINS OF YOUTH (Also see Sins of Youth x-over issues and Sins of Youth: Secret Files)
DC Comics: May, 2000 - No. 2, May, 2000 ($3.95, limited series)

Issue	GD 2.0	VG 4.0	FN 6.0	VF 8.0	VF/NM 9.0	NM- 9.2
1,2-Young Justice, JLA & JSA swap ages; David-s/Nauck-a						4.00
TPB (2000, $19.95) r/#1,2 & all x-over issues)						20.00

YOUNG KING COLE (...Detective Tales)(Becomes Criminals on the Run)
Premium Group/Novelty Press: Fall, 1945 - V3#12, July, 1948

Issue	GD 2.0	VG 4.0	FN 6.0	VF 8.0	VF/NM 9.0	NM- 9.2
V1#1-Toni Gayle begins	34	68	102	196	283	370
2	16	32	48	92	131	170
3-4	15	30	45	83	117	150
V2#1-7(8-9/46-7/47): 6,7-Certa-c	11	22	33	62	84	105
V3#1,3-6,8,9,12: 3-Certa-c. 5-McWilliams-c/a. 8,9-Harmon-c	10	20	30	60	80	100
2-L.B. Cole-a; Certa-c	17	34	51	95	135	175
7-L.B. Cole-c/a	23	46	69	132	191	250
10,11-L.B. Cole-c	20	40	60	112	161	210

YOUNG LAWYERS, THE (TV)
Dell Publishing Co.: Jan, 1971 - No. 2, Apr, 1971

Issue	GD 2.0	VG 4.0	FN 6.0	VF 8.0	VF/NM 9.0	NM- 9.2
1	3	6	9	18	24	30
2	2	4	6	12	16	20

YOUNG LIFE (Teen Life #3 on)
New Age Publ./Quality Comics Group: Summer, 1945 - No. 2, Fall, 1945

Issue	GD 2.0	VG 4.0	FN 6.0	VF 8.0	VF/NM 9.0	NM- 9.2
1-Skip Homeier, Louis Prima stories	15	30	45	86	123	160
2-Frank Sinatra photo on-c plus story	17	34	51	98	139	180

YOUNG LOVE (Sister title to Young Romance)
Prize(Feature)Publ.(Crestwood): 2-3/49 - No. 73, 12-1/56-57; V3#5, 2-3/60 - V7#1, 6-7/63

Issue	GD 2.0	VG 4.0	FN 6.0	VF 8.0	VF/NM 9.0	NM- 9.2
V1#1-S&K-c/a(2)	44	88	132	268	409	550
2-Photo-c begin; S&K-a	26	52	78	147	211	275
3-S&K-a	19	38	57	107	154	200
4-5-Minor S&K-a	12	24	36	71	98	125
V2#1(#7)-S&K-a(2)	19	38	57	107	154	200
2-5(#8-11)-Minor S&K-a	11	22	33	62	84	105
6,8(#12,14)-S&K-c only. 14-S&K 1 pg. art	12	24	36	69	95	120
7,9-12(#13,15-18)-S&K-c/a	18	36	54	102	146	190
V3#1-4(#19-22)-S&K-c/a	16	32	48	92	131	170
5-7,9-12(#23-25,27-30)-Photo-c resume; S&K-a	15	30	45	83	117	150
8(#26)-No S&K-a	8	16	24	40	50	60
V4#1,6(#31,36)-S&K-a	14	28	42	79	110	140
2-5,7-12(#32-35,37-42)-Minor S&K-a	11	22	33	62	84	105
V5#1-12(#43-54), V6#1-9(#55-63)-Last precode; S&K-a in some	7	14	21	37	46	55
V6#10-12(#64-66)	4	8	12	27	36	45
V7#1-7(#67-73)	4	8	12	24	32	40
V3#5(2-3/60),6(4-5/60)(Formerly All For Love)	4	8	12	24	32	40
V4#1(6-7/60)-6(4-5/61)	4	8	12	22	30	38
V5#1(6-7/61)-6(4-5/62)	4	8	12	22	30	38
V6#1(6-7/62)-6(4-5/63), V7#1	3	7	10	21	28	35

NOTE: **Meskin** *a-14(2), 27, 42.* **Powell** *a-V4#6.* **Severin/Elder** *a-V1#3. S&K art not in #53, 57, 58, 61, 63-65. Photo-c most V3#5-V5#11.*

YOUNG LOVE
National Periodical Publ.(Arleigh Publ. Corp #49-61)/DC Comics: #39, 9-10/63 - #120, Wint./75-76; #121, 10/76 - #126, 7/77

Issue	GD 2.0	VG 4.0	FN 6.0	VF 8.0	VF/NM 9.0	NM- 9.2
39	6	12	18	38	52	65
40-50	4	8	12	25	33	42
51-68,70	4	8	12	22	30	38
69-(80 pg. Giant)(8-9/68)	6	12	18	43	59	75
71,72,74-77,80	3	6	9	19	25	32
73,78,79-Toth-a	3	7	10	21	28	35
81-99: 88-96-(52 pg. Giants)	3	6	9	18	24	30
100	3	6	9	19	25	32
101-106,115-120	3	6	9	16	20	24
107 (100 pgs.)	9	18	27	60	85	110
108-114 (100 pgs.)	8	16	24	53	74	95
121-126 (52 pgs.)	4	8	12	28	38	48

NOTE: **Bolle** *a-117.* **Colan** *a-107r.* **Nasser** *a-123, 124.* **Orlando** *a-122.* **Simonson** *c-125.* **Toth** *a-73, 78, 79, 122-125r.* **Wood** *a-109r(4 pgs.).*

YOUNG LOVER ROMANCES (Formerly & becomes Great Lover...)
Toby Press: No. 4, June, 1952 - No. 5, Aug, 1952

Issue	GD 2.0	VG 4.0	FN 6.0	VF 8.0	VF/NM 9.0	NM- 9.2
4,5-Photo-c	8	16	24	40	50	60

YOUNG LOVERS (My Secret Life #19 on)(Formerly Brenda Starr?)
Charlton Comics: No. 16, July, 1956 - No. 18, May, 1957

Issue	GD 2.0	VG 4.0	FN 6.0	VF 8.0	VF/NM 9.0	NM- 9.2
16,17('56): 16-Marcus Swayze-a	8	16	24	46	58	70
18-Elvis Presley picture-c, text story (biography)(Scarce)	60	120	180	375	580	785

YOUNG MARRIAGE
Fawcett Publications: June, 1950

Issue	GD 2.0	VG 4.0	FN 6.0	VF 8.0	VF/NM 9.0	NM- 9.2
1-Powell-a; photo-c	13	26	39	74	102	130

YOUNG MEN (Formerly Cowboy Romances)(...on the Battlefield #12-20(4/53); ...In Action #21)
Marvel/Atlas Comics (IPC): No. 4, 6/50 - No. 11, 10/51; No. 12, 12/51 - No. 28, 6/54

Issue	GD 2.0	VG 4.0	FN 6.0	VF 8.0	VF/NM 9.0	NM- 9.2
4-(52 pgs.)	20	40	60	112	161	210
5-11	13	26	39	74	102	130
12-23: 12-20-War format. 21-23-Hot Rod issues starring Flash Foster	12	24	36	71	98	125
24-(12/53)-Origin Captain America, Human Torch, & Sub-Mariner which are revived thru #28; Red Skull app.	292	584	876	1825	2813	3800
25-28: 25-Romita-c/a (see Men's Advs.). 27-Death of Golden Age Red Skull	112	224	336	700	1075	1450
25-2nd printing (1994)	2	4	6	8	10	12

NOTE: **Berg** *a-7, 14, 17, 18, 20; c-17?* **Brodsky** *c-4-9, 13, 14, 16, 17, 21-25.* **Burgos** *c-26-28.* **Colan** *a-14, 15.* **Everett** *a-18-20.* **Heath** *a-13, 14.* **Maneely** *c-10, 12, 15.* **Pakula** *a-14, 15.* **Robinson** *c-18. Captain America by* **Romita**-*#24?, 25, 26?, 27, 28. Human Torch by* **Burgos**-*#25, 27, 28. Sub-Mariner by* **Everett**-*#24-28.*

YOUNG REBELS, THE (TV)
Dell Publishing Co.: Jan, 1971

Issue	GD 2.0	VG 4.0	FN 6.0	VF 8.0	VF/NM 9.0	NM- 9.2
1-Photo-c	3	6	9	16	20	24

YOUNG ROMANCE COMICS (The 1st romance comic)
Prize/Headline (Feature Publ.) (Crestwood): Sept-Oct, 1947 - V16#4, June-July, 1963 (#1-33: 52 pgs.)

Issue	GD 2.0	VG 4.0	FN 6.0	VF 8.0	VF/NM 9.0	NM- 9.2
V1#1-S&K-c/a(2)	48	96	144	293	447	600
2-S&K-c/a(2-3)	32	64	96	184	267	350
3-6-S&K-c/a(2-3) each	28	56	84	158	229	300
V2#1-6(#7-12)-S&K-c/a(2-3) each	25	50	75	144	207	270
V3#1-3(#13-15): V3#1-Photo-c begin; S&K-a	17	34	51	98	139	180
4-12(#16-24)-Photo-c; S&K-a	17	34	51	98	139	180
V4#1-11(#25-35)-S&K-a	16	32	48	92	131	170
12(#36)-S&K, Toth-a	18	36	54	100	143	185
V5#1-12(#37-48), V6#4-12(#52-60)-S&K-a	16	32	48	92	131	170
V6#1-3(#49-51)-No S&K-a	9	18	27	51	62	75
V7#1-11(#61-71)-S&K-a in most	14	28	42	79	110	140
V7#12(#72), V8#1-3(#73-75)-Last precode (12-1/54-55)-No S&K-a	8	16	24	40	50	60
V8#4(#76, 4-5/55), 5(#77)-No S&K-a	7	14	21	35	43	50
V8#6-8(#78-80, 12-1/55-56)-S&K-a	11	22	33	62	84	105
V9#3,5,6(#81, 2-3/56, 83,84)-S&K-a	11	22	33	62	84	105
4, V10#1(#82,85)-All S&K-a	11	22	33	66	91	115
V10#2-6(#86-90, 10-11/57)-S&K-a	8	16	24	58	82	105
V11#1,2,5,6(#91,92,95,96)-S&K-a	8	16	24	58	82	105
3,4(#93,94), V12#2,4,5(#98,100,101)-No S&K	4	8	12	27	36	45
V12#1,3,6(#97,99,102)-S&K-a	8	16	24	58	82	105
V13#1(#103)-Powell-a; S&K's last-a for Crestwood	8	16	24	58	82	105
2,4-6(#104-108)	4	8	12	24	32	40
V13#3(#105, 4-5/60)-Elvis Presley-c app. only	6	12	18	38	52	65

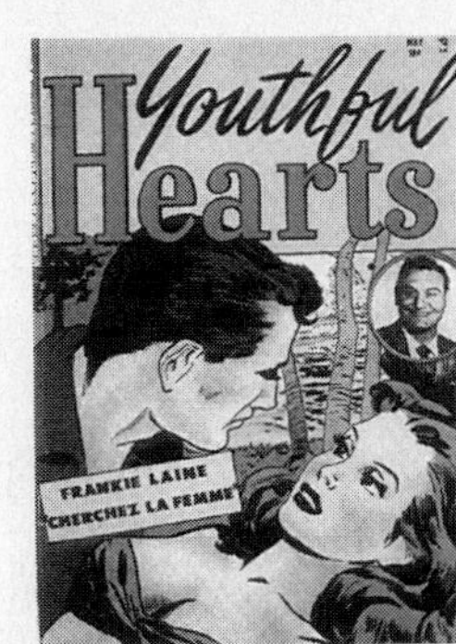

Youthful Hearts #1 © YM

Y: The Last Man #3 © Vaughan & Guerra

Zago, Jungle Prince #4 © FOX

	GD 2.0	VG 4.0	FN 6.0	VF 8.0	VF/NM 9.0	NM- 9.2
V14#1-6, V15#1-6, V16#1-4(#109-124)	3	7	10	21	28	35

NOTE: *Meskin a-16, 24(2), 33, 47, 50.* ***Robinson/Meskin*** *a-6.* ***Leonard Starr*** *a-11. Photo c-13-32, 34-65. Issues 1-3 say "Designed for the More* ***Adult*** *Readers of* ***Comics****" on cover.*

YOUNG ROMANCE COMICS (Continued from Prize series)
National Periodical Publ.(Arleigh Publ. Corp. No. 127): No. 125, Aug-Sept, 1963 - No. 208, Nov-Dec, 1975

	GD	VG	FN	VF	VF/NM	NM-
125	8	16	24	55	78	100
126-140	5	10	15	33	44	55
141-153,156-162,165-169	4	8	12	24	32	40
154-Neal Adams-c	5	10	15	36	48	60
155-1st publ. Aragonés-s (no art)	5	10	15	33	44	55
163,164-Toth-a	4	8	12	29	40	50
170-172 (68 pg. Giants): 170-Michell from Young Love ends; Lily Martin, the Swinger begins	5	10	15	33	44	55
173-183 (52 pgs.)	4	8	12	27	36	45
184-196	3	6	9	18	23	28
197-204-(100 pgs.)	8	16	24	53	74	95
205-208	3	6	9	16	20	25

YOUNG ZEN: CITY OF DEATH
Entity Comics: Late 1994 ($3.25, B&W)

1 — 3.25

YOUNG ZEN INTERGALACTIC NINJA (Also see Zen...)
Entity Comics: 1993 - No. 3, 1994 ($3.50/$2.95, B&W)

1-($3.50)-Polybagged w/Sam Keith chromium trading card; gold foil logo — 3.50
2,3-($2.95)-Gold foil logo — 3.00

YOUR DREAMS (See Strange World of...)

YOU'RE UNDER ARREST (Manga)
Dark Horse Comics: Dec, 1995 - No. 8, July, 1996 ($2.95, limited series)

1-8 — 3.00

YOUR UNITED STATES
Lloyd Jacquet Studios: 1946

	GD	VG	FN	VF	VF/NM	NM-
nn-Used in **SOTI**, pg. 309,310; Sid Greene-a	24	48	72	135	195	255

YOUTHFUL HEARTS (Daring Confessions #4 on)
Youthful Magazines: May, 1952 - No. 3, Sept, 1952

	GD	VG	FN	VF	VF/NM	NM-
1- "Monkey on Her Back" swipes E.C. drug story/Shock SuspenStories #12; Frankie Laine photo on-c; Doug Wildey-a in al	30	60	90	170	245	320
2,3: 2-Vic Damone photo on-c. 3-Johnny Raye photo on-c	21	42	63	118	169	220

YOUTHFUL LOVE (Truthful Love #2)
Youthful Magazines: May, 1950

	GD	VG	FN	VF	VF/NM	NM-
1	12	24	36	71	98	125

YOUTHFUL ROMANCES
Pix-Parade #1-14/Ribage #15 on: 8-9/49 - No. 5, 4/50; No. 6, 2/51; No. 7, 5/51 - #14, 10/52; #15, 1/53 - #18, 7/53; No. 5, 9/53 - No. 9, 8/54

	GD	VG	FN	VF	VF/NM	NM-
1-(1st series)-Titled Youthful Love-Romances	27	54	81	154	222	290
2-Walter Johnson c-1-4	16	32	48	89	127	165
3-5	13	26	39	74	102	130
6,7,9-14(10/52, Pix-Parade; becomes Daring Love #15). 10(1/52)-Mel Torme photo-c/story. 12-Tony Bennett photo-c, 8pg. story & text bio.13-Richard Hayes (singer) photo-c/story; Bob & Ray photo/text story.	11	22	33	66	91	115
8-Frank Sinatra photo/text story; Wood-c/a	19	38	57	107	154	200
15-18 (Ribage)-All have photos on-c. 15-Spike Jones photo-c/story. 16-Tony Bavaar photo-c	11	22	33	62	84	105
5(9/53, Ribage)-Les Paul & Mary Ford photo-c/story; Charlton Heston photo/text story	10	20	30	58	77	95
6-9: 6-Bobby Wayne (singer) photo-c/story; Debbie Reynolds photo/text story. 7(2/54)-Tony Martin photo-c/story; Cyd Charise photo/text story. 8(5/54)-Gordon McCrae photo-c/story. (8/54)-Ralph Flanagan (band leader) photo-c/story; Audrey Hepburn photo/text story	9	18	27	52	66	80

Y: THE LAST MAN
DC Comics (Vertigo): Sept, 2002 - Present ($2.95)

	GD	VG	FN	VF	VF/NM	NM-
1-Intro. Yorick Brown; Vaughan-s/Guerra-a/J.G. Jones-c	2	4	6	8	10	12
2	1	2	3	5	6	8
3-5						6.00
6-29: 16,17-Chadwick-a. 21,22-Parlov-a						3.00
... - Cycles TPB (2003, $12.95) r/#6-10; sketch pages by Guerra						13.00
... - One Small Step TPB (2004, $12.95) r/#11-17						13.00
... - Safeword TPB (2004, $12.95) r/#18-23						13.00
... - Unmanned TPB (2002, $12.95) r/#1-5						13.00

Y2K: THE COMIC
New England Comics Press: Oct, 1999 ($3.95, one-shot)

1-Y2K scenarios and survival tips — 4.00

YUPPIES FROM HELL (Also see Son of...)
Marvel Comics: 1989 ($2.95, B&W, one-shot, direct sales, 52 pgs.)

1-Satire — 3.00

ZAGO, JUNGLE PRINCE (My Story #5 on)
Fox Features Syndicate: Sept, 1948 - No. 4, Mar, 1949

	GD	VG	FN	VF	VF/NM	NM-
1-Blue Beetle app.; partial-r/Atomic #4 (Toni Luck)	60	120	180	375	580	785
2,3-Kamen-a	48	96	144	293	447	600
4-Baker-c	40	80	120	239	357	475

ZANE GREY'S STORIES OF THE WEST
Dell Publishing Co./Gold Key 11/64: No. 197, 9/48 - No. 996, 5-7/59; 11/64 (All painted-c)

	GD	VG	FN	VF	VF/NM	NM-
Four Color 197(#1)(9/48)	13	26	39	90	138	185
Four Color 222,230,236('49)	8	16	24	58	82	105
Four Color 246,255,270,301,314,333,346	6	12	18	40	55	70
Four Color 357,372,395,412,433,449,467,484	5	10	15	36	48	60
Four Color 511-Kinstler-a; Kubert-a	6	12	18	40	55	70
Four Color 532,555,583,604,616,632(5/55)	5	10	15	36	48	60
27(9-11/55) - 39(9-11/58)	5	10	15	36	48	60
Four Color 996(5-7/59)	5	10	15	36	48	60
10131-411-(11/64-G.K.)-Nevada; r/4-Color #996	4	8	12	24	32	40

ZANY (Magazine)(Satire)(See Frantic & Ratfink)
Candor Publ. Co.: Sept, 1958 - No. 4, May, 1959

	GD	VG	FN	VF	VF/NM	NM-
1-Bill Everett-c	10	20	30	60	80	100
2-4: 4-Everett-c	8	16	24	43	54	65

ZATANNA (See Adv. Comics #413, JLA #161, Supergirl #1, World's Finest Comics #274)
DC Comics: July, 1993 - No. 4, Oct, 1993 ($1.95, limited series)

1-4 — 2.25
...: Everyday Magic (2003, $5.95, one-shot) Dini-s/Mays-a/Bolland-c; Constantine app. — 6.00
Special 1(1987, $2.00)-Gray Morrow-c/a — 3.00

ZAZA, THE MYSTIC (Formerly Charlie Chan; This Magazine Is Haunted V2#12 on)
Charlton Comics: No. 10, Apr, 1956 - No. 11, Sept, 1956

	GD	VG	FN	VF	VF/NM	NM-
10,11	12	24	36	71	98	125

ZEALOT (Also see WildC.A.T.S: Covert Action Teams)
Image Comics: Aug, 1995 - No. 3, Nov, 1995 ($2.50, limited series)

1-3 — 2.50

ZEGRA JUNGLE EMPRESS (Formerly Tegra)(My Love Life #6 on)
Fox Features Syndicate: No. 2, Oct, 1948 - No. 5, April, 1949

	GD	VG	FN	VF	VF/NM	NM-
2	62	124	186	388	594	800
3-5	48	96	144	293	447	600

ZEN (Intergalactic Ninja)
Zen Comics Publishing: No. 0, Apr, 2003 - No. 4, Aug, 2003 ($2.95)

0-4-Bill Maus-a/Steve Stern-s. 0-Wraparound-c — 3.00

ZEN INTERGALACTIC NINJA
No Publisher: 1987 -1993 ($1.75/$2.00, B&W)

	GD	VG	FN	VF	VF/NM	NM-
1	2	4	6	11	14	18
2-6: Copyright-Stern & Cote	1	3	4	6	8	10
V2#1-4-($2.00)						3.00
V3#1-5-($2.95)						3.00
... :Christmas Special 1 (1992, $2.95)						3.00
... :Earth Day Special 1 (1993, $2.95)						3.00

ZEN, INTERGALACTIC NINJA (mini-series)
Zen Comics/Archie Comics: Sept, 1992 - No. 3, 1992 ($1.25)(Formerly a B&W comic by Zen Comics)

1-3: 1-Origin Zen; contains mini-poster — 3.00

ZEN INTERGALACTIC NINJA
Entity Comics: No. 0, June-July, 1993 - No. 3, 1994 ($2.95, B&W, limited series)

0-Gold foil stamped-c; photo-c of Zen model — 3.00
1-3: Gold foil stamped-c; Bill Maus-c/a — 3.00
0-(1993, $3.50, color)-Chromium-c by Jae Lee — 3.50
...Sourcebook 1-(1993, $3.50) — 3.50
...Sourcebook '94-(1994, $3.50) — 3.50

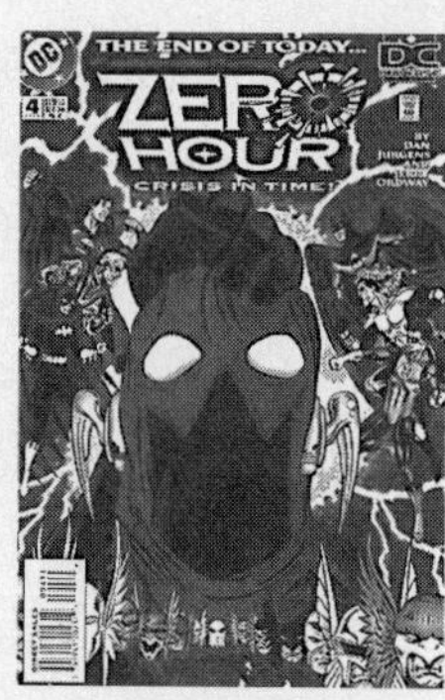

Zero Hour #4(#1) © DC

Zip Comics #18 © MLJ

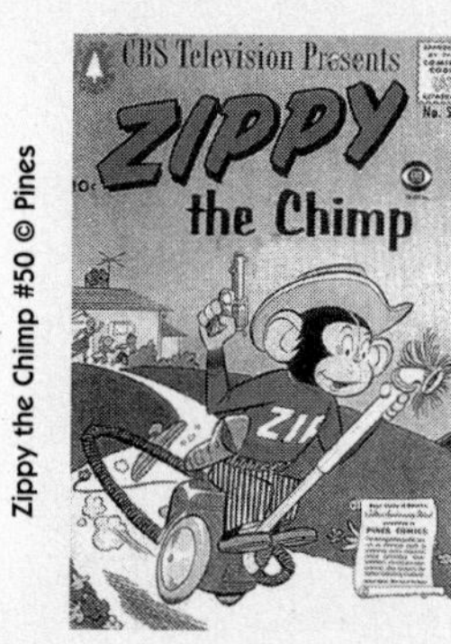

Zippy the Chimp #50 © Pines

	GD 2.0	VG 4.0	FN 6.0	VF 8.0	VF/NM 9.0	NM- 9.2

ZEN INTERGALACTIC NINJA: APRIL FOOL'S SPECIAL
Parody Press: 1994 ($2.50, B&W)

1-w/flip story of Renn Intergalactic Chihuahua 3.00

ZEN INTERGALACTIC NINJA COLOR
Entity Comics: 1994 - No. 7, 1995 ($2.25)

1-($3.95)-Chromium die cut-c 4.00
1, 0-($2.25)-Newsstand; Jae Lee-c; r/...All New Color Special #0 3.00
2-($2.50)-Flip book 3.00
2-($3.50)-Flip book, polybagged w/chromium trading card 3.50
3-7 3.00
Summer Special (1994, $2.95) 3.00
Yearbook: Hazardous Duty 1 (1995) 3.00
Zen-isms 1 (1995, 2.95) 3.00
Ashcan-Tour of the Universe-(no price) w/flip cover 3.00

ZEN INTERGALACTIC NINJA COMMEMORATIVE EDITION
Zen Comics Publishing: 1997 ($5.95, color)

1-Stern-s/Cote-a 6.00

ZEN INTERGALACTIC NINJA MILESTONE
Entity Comics: 1994 - No. 3, 1994 ($2.95, limited series)

1-3: Gold foil logo; r/Defend the Earth 3.00

ZEN INTERGALATIC NINJA SPRING SPECTACULAR
Entity Comics: 1994 ($2.95, B&W, one-shot)

1-Gold foil logo 3.00

ZEN INTERGALACTIC NINJA STARQUEST
Entity Comics: 1994 - No. 6, 1995 ($2.95, B&W)

1-6: Gold foil logo 3.00

ZEN, INTERGALACTIC NINJA: THE HUNTED
Entity Comics: 1993 - No. 3, 1994 ($2.95, B&W, limited series)

1-3: Newsstand Edition; foil logo 3.00
1-($3.50)-Polybagged w/chromium card by Kieth; foil logo 3.50

ZERO GIRL
DC Comics (Homage): Feb, 2001 - No. 5, Jun, 2001 ($2.95, limited series)

1-5-Sam Kieth-s/a 3.00
TPB (2001, $14.95) r/#1-5; intro. by Alan Moore 15.00

ZERO GIRL: FULL CIRCLE
DC Comics (Homage): Jan, 2003 - No. 5, May, 2003 ($2.95, limited series)

1-5-Sam Kieth-s/a 3.00
TPB (2003, $17.95) r/#1-5 18.00

ZERO HOUR: CRISIS IN TIME (Also see Showcase '94 #8-10)
DC Comics: No. 4(#1), Sept, 1994 - No. 0(#5), Oct, 1994 ($1.50, limited series)

4(#1)-0(#5) 4.00
"Ashcan"-(1994, free, B&W, 8 pgs.) several versions exist 2.25
TPB ('94, $9.95) 10.00

ZERO PATROL, THE
Continuity Comics: Nov, 1984 - No. 2 ($1.50); 1987 - No. 5, May, 1989 ($2.00)

1,2: Neal Adams-c/a; Megalith begins 4.00
1-5 (#1,2-reprints above, 1987) 3.00

ZERO TOLERANCE
First Comics: Oct, 1990 - No. 4, Jan, 1991 ($2.25, limited series)

1-4: Tim Vigil-c/a(p) (his 1st color limited series) 3.00

ZERO ZERO
Fantagraphics: Mar, 1995 -No. 27 ($3.95/$4.95, B&W, anthology, mature)

1-7,9-15,17-25 5.00
8,16 6.00
26-($4.95) Bagge-c 5.00

ZIGGY PIG-SILLY SEAL COMICS (See Animal Fun, Animated Movie-Tunes, Comic Capers, Krazy Komics, Silly Tunes & Super Rabbit)
Timely Comics (CmPL): Fall, 1944 - No. 6, Fall, 1946

	GD	VG	FN	VF	VF/NM	NM-
1-Vs. the Japs	27	54	81	152	219	285
2	13	26	39	76	106	135
3-5	11	22	33	66	91	115
6-Infinity-c	14	28	42	81	113	145
I.W. Reprint #1(1958)-r/Krazy Komics	2	4	6	10	13	16
I.W. Reprint #2,7,8	2	4	6	10	13	16

ZIP COMICS
MLJ Magazines: Feb, 1940 - No. 47, Summer, 1944 (#1-7?: 68 pgs.)

	GD	VG	FN	VF	VF/NM	NM-
1-Origin Kalathar the Giant Man, The Scarlet Avenger, & Steel Sterling; Mr. Satan (by Edd Ashe), Nevada Jones (masked hero) & Zambini, the Miracle Man, War Eagle, Captain Valor begins	503	1006	1509	3521	5661	7800
2-Nevada Jones adds mask & horse Blaze	238	476	714	1488	2294	3100
3-Biro robot-c	189	378	567	1181	1816	2450
4,5-Biro WW2-c	156	312	468	975	1500	2025
6-8-Biro-c	135	270	405	844	1297	1750
9-Last Kalathar & Mr. Satan; classic-c	152	304	456	950	1463	1975
10-Inferno, the Flame Breather begins, ends #13	144	288	432	900	1388	1875
11,12: 11-Inferno without costume	106	212	318	663	1019	1375
13-Electrocution-c	115	230	345	719	1110	1500
14,16,19	100	200	300	625	963	1300
15-Classic spider-c	123	246	369	769	1185	1600
17-Last Scarlet Avenger; women in bondage being cooked alive-c by Biro	115	230	345	719	1110	1500
18-Wilbur begins (9/41, 1st app.)	115	230	345	719	1110	1500
20-Origin & 1st app. Black Jack (11/41); Hitler-c	169	338	507	1056	1628	2200
21,23-26: 25-Last Nevada Jones. 26-Black Witch begins; last Captain Valor; "Remember Pearl Harbor!" cover caption	92	184	276	575	888	1200
22-Classic-c	135	270	405	844	1297	1750
27-Intro. Web (7/42) plus-c app.	154	308	462	963	1482	2000
28-Origin Web	135	270	405	844	1297	1750
29,30: 29-The Hyena app.	63	126	189	394	610	825
31,33-38: 34-1st Applejack app. 35-Last Zambini, Black Jack. 38-Last Web issue	50	100	150	305	465	625
32-Classic skeleton Nazi WW2-c	63	126	189	394	610	825
39-Red Rube begins (origin, 8/43)	50	100	150	305	465	625
40-46: 45-Wilbur ends	43	86	129	262	401	540
47-Last issue; scarce	46	92	138	281	428	575

NOTE: ***Biro*** *a-5, 9, 17; c-3-17.* ***Meskin*** *a-1-3, 5-7, 9, 10, 12, 13, 15, 16 at least.* ***Montana*** *c-29, 30, 32-35.* ***Novick*** *c-18-28, 31.* ***Sahle*** *c-37, 38, 40-46. Bondage c-8, 9, 33, 34. Cover features: Steel Sterling-1-43, 47; (w/Blackjack-20-27 & Web-27-35), 28-39; (w/Red Rube-40-43); Red Rube-44-47.*

ZIP-JET (Hero)
St. John Publishing Co.: Feb, 1953 - No. 2, Apr-May, 1953

	GD	VG	FN	VF	VF/NM	NM-
1-Rocketman-r from Punch Comics; #1-c from splash in Punch #10	75	150	225	469	722	975
2	50	100	150	305	465	625

ZIPPY THE CHIMP (CBS TV Presents...)
Pines (Literary Ent.): No. 50, March, 1957; No. 51, Aug, 1957

	GD	VG	FN	VF	VF/NM	NM-
50,51	8	16	24	40	50	60

ZODY, THE MOD ROB
Gold Key: July, 1970

	GD	VG	FN	VF	VF/NM	NM-
1	3	6	9	18	24	30

ZOMBIE WORLD (one-shots)
Dark Horse Comics

... :Eat Your Heart Out (4/98, $2.95) Kelley Jones-c/s/a 3.00
... :Home For The Holidays (12/97, $2.95) 3.00

ZOMBIE WORLD: CHAMPION OF THE WORMS
Dark Horse Comics: Sept, 1997 - No. 3, Nov, 1997 ($2.95, limited series)

1-3-Mignola & McEown-c/s/a 3.00

ZOMBIE WORLD: DEAD END
Dark Horse Comics: Jan, 1998 - No. 2, Feb, 1998 ($2.95, limited series)

1,2-Stephen Blue-c/s/a 3.00

ZOMBIE WORLD: TREE OF DEATH
Dark Horse Comics: Jun, 1999 - No. 4, Oct, 1999 ($2.95, limited series)

1-4-Mills-s/Deadstock-a 3.00

ZOMBIE WORLD: WINTER'S DREGS
Dark Horse Comics: May, 1998 - No. 4, Aug, 1998 ($2.95, limited series)

1-4-Fingerman-s/Edwards-a 3.00

ZONE (Also see Dark Horse Presents)
Dark Horse Comics: 1990 ($1.95, B&W)

1-Character from Dark Horse Presents 2.00

ZONE CONTINUUM, THE
Caliber Press: 1994 ($2.95, B&W)

1 3.00

ZOO ANIMALS
Star Publications: No. 8, 1954 (15¢, 36 pgs.)

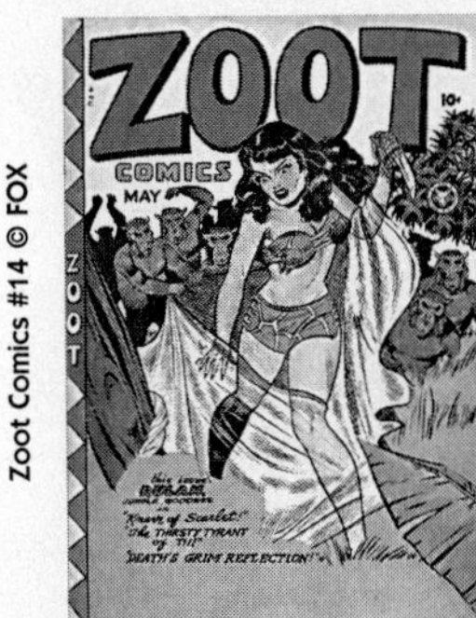

Zoot Comics #14 © FOX

Zorro #7 © Johnston McCulley

Zot! #34 © Scott McCloud

	GD 2.0	VG 4.0	FN 6.0	VF 8.0	VF/NM 9.0	NM- 9.2
8-(B&W for coloring)	7	14	21	35	43	50
ZOO FUNNIES (Tim McCoy #16 on)						
Charlton Comics/Children Comics Publ.: Nov, 1945 - No. 15, 1947						
101(#1)(11/45, 1st Charlton comic book)-Funny animal; Al Fago-c	22	44	66	123	177	230
2(12/45, 52 pgs.) Classic-c	15	30	45	83	117	150
3-5	11	22	33	62	84	105
6-15: 8-Diana the Huntress app.	9	18	27	52	66	80
ZOO FUNNIES (Becomes Nyoka, The Jungle Girl #14 on?)						
Capitol Stories/Charlton Comics: July, 1953 - No. 13, Sept, 1955; Dec, 1984						
1-1st app.? Timothy The Ghost; Fago-c/a	11	22	33	66	91	115
2	8	16	24	43	54	65
3-7	7	14	21	37	46	55
8-13-Nyoka app.	9	18	27	54	70	85
1(1984) (Low print run)						6.00
ZOONIVERSE						
Eclipse Comics: 8/86 - No. 6, 6/87 ($1.25/$1.75, limited series, Mando paper)						
1-6						2.25
ZOO PARADE (TV)						
Dell Publishing Co.: #662, 1955 (Marlin Perkins)						
Four Color 662	6	12	18	40	55	70
ZOOM COMICS						
Carlton Publishing Co.: Dec, 1945 (one-shot)						
nn-Dr. Mercy, Satannas, from Red Band Comics; Capt. Milksop origin retold	40	80	120	239	357	475
ZOOT (Rulah Jungle Goddess #17 on)						
Fox Features Syndicate: nd (1946) - No. 16, July, 1948 (Two #13s & 14s)						
nn-Funny animal only	21	42	63	121	173	225
2-The Jaguar app.	20	40	60	112	161	210
3(Fall, 1946) - 6-Funny animals & teen-age	11	22	33	64	87	110
7-(6/47)-Rulah, Jungle Goddess (origin/1st app.)	96	192	288	600	925	1250
8-10	66	132	198	413	637	860
11-Kamen bondage-c	70	140	210	438	674	910
12-Injury-to-eye panels, torture scene	48	96	144	293	447	600
13(2/48)	48	96	144	293	447	600
14(3/48)-Used in **SOTI**, pg. 104, "One picture showing a girl nailed by her wrists to trees with blood flowing from the wounds, might be taken straight from an ill. ed. of the Marquis deSade"	62	124	186	388	599	810
13(4/48),14(5/48)-Western True Crime #15 on?	48	96	144	293	447	600
15,16	48	96	144	293	447	600
ZORRO (Walt Disney with #882)(TV)(See Eclipse Graphic Album)						
Dell Publishing Co.: May, 1949 - No. 15, Sept-Nov, 1961 (Photo-c 882 on)						
(Zorro first appeared in a pulp story Aug 19, 1919)						
Four Color 228 (#1)	23	46	69	165	253	340

	GD 2.0	VG 4.0	FN 6.0	VF 8.0	VF/NM 9.0	NM- 9.2
Four Color 425,617,732	13	26	39	92	141	190
Four Color 497,538,574-Kinstler-a	14	18	42	97	149	200
Four Color 882-Photo-c begin;1st TV Disney; Toth-a	17	34	51	123	189	255
Four Color 920,933,960,976-Toth-a in all	13	26	39	92	141	190
Four Color 1003('59)-Toth-a	13	26	39	92	141	190
Four Color 1037-Annette Funicello photo-c	16	32	48	114	175	235
8(12-2/59-60)	10	20	30	67	96	125
9-Toth-a	10	20	30	72	104	135
10,11,13-15-Last photo-c	9	18	27	63	89	115
12-Toth-a; last 10¢ issue	10	20	30	72	104	135
NOTE: *Warren Tufts a-4-Color 1037, 8, 9, 10, 13.*						
ZORRO (Walt Disney)(TV)						
Gold Key: Jan, 1966 - No. 9, Mar, 1968 (All photo-c)						
1-Toth-a	9	18	27	65	93	120
2,4,5,7-9-Toth-a. 5-r/F.C. #1003 by Toth	6	12	18	38	52	65
3,6-Tufts-a	5	10	15	36	48	60
NOTE: *#1-9 are reprinted from Dell issues.* ***Tufts*** *a-3, 4. #1-r/F.C. #882. #2-r/F.C. #960. #3-r/#12-c & #8 inside. #4-r/#9-c & insides. #6-r/#11(all); #7-r/#14-c. #8-r/F.C. #933 inside & back-c & #976-c. #9-r/F.C. #920.*						
ZORRO (TV)						
Marvel Comics: Dec, 1990 - No. 12, Nov, 1991 ($1.00)						
1-12: Based on TV show. 12-Toth-c						3.00
ZORRO (Also see Mask of Zorro)						
Topps Comics: Nov, 1993 - No. 11, Nov, 1994 ($2.50/$2.95)						
0-(11/93, $1.00, 20 pgs.)-Painted-c; collector's ed.						2.25
1,4,6-9,11: 1-Miller-c. 4-Mike Grell-c. 6-Mignola-c. 7-Lady Rawhide-c by Gulacy. 8-Perez-c. 10-Julie Bell-c. 11-Lady Rawhide-c						3.00
2-Lady Rawhide-app. (not in costume)						5.00
3-1st app. Lady Rawhide in costume, 3-Lady Rawhide-c by Adam Hughes	1	2	3	5	6	8
5-Lady Rawhide app.						4.00
10-($2.95)-Lady Rawhide-c/app.						3.00
The Lady Wears Red (12/98, $12.95, TPB) r/#1-3						13.00
Zorro's Renegades (2/99, $14.95, TPB) r/#4-8						15.00
ZOT!						
Eclipse Comics: 4/84 - No. 10, 7/85; No. 11, 1/87 - No. 36 7/91 ($1.50, Baxter-p)						
1						5.00
2,3						4.00
4-10: 4-Origin. 10-Last color issue						3.00
10 1/2 (6/86, 25¢, Not Available Comics) Ashcan; art by Feazell & Scott McCloud						4.00
11-14,15-35-($2.00-c) B&W issues						3.00
14 1/2 (Adventures of Zot! in Dimension 10 1/2)(7/87) Antisocialman app.						3.00
36-($2.95-c) B&W						4.00
Z-2 COMICS (Secret Agent...)(See Holyoke One-Shot #7)						
ZULU (See Movie Classics)						

BEDROCK CITY
COMIC COMPANY
TM
Horror headquarters
TALES OF HORROR IN OTHER WORLDS!
TOMB OF TERROR
NEVER HAS A STORY BURST WITH THE TERROR OF
BREAK-UP!
WEIRD MYSTERIES
STRANGE SUSPENSE STORIES
operator--YOU'VE GOT TO GET THROUGH--he's innocent!
10¢
You'll find extreme *shock values* on-line at
www.bedrockcity.com
Check out our giant *head*quarters at:
6517 Westheimer (at Hillcroft)
Houston, Texas 77057
Phone (713) 780-0675 Fax (713) 780-2366
And our other *skull-smashing* stores:
4683 FM 1960 W.
Houston, Texas 77069
Phone (281) 444-9763
106 W. Bay Area Blvd.
Webster, Texas 77598
Phone (281) 557-2748

Here we go rearing our ugly heads again. Yes, we've got those comics that the illus-trious Doctor Wertham claimed were a mindless pursuit at best, if not the foundation for a career in San Quentin.

Well, our frontal lobes might be barbecued, but we at Bedrock City steadfastly maintain that good taste is a (gray) matter of opinion!

Bedrock City
comics connoisseurs

Tomb of Terror #15 ©Harvey Publications, Weird Mysteries #5 ©Gilmore Publications, Strange Suspense Stories #19 ©Charlton Comics Group

BUYING ALL COMICS

with 10 and 12¢ cover prices

TOP PRICES PAID!

IMMEDIATE CASH PAYMENT

**Stop Throwing Away
Those Old Comic Books!**

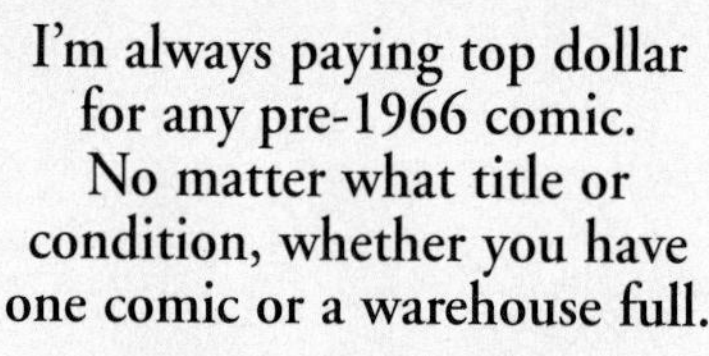
I'm always paying top dollar
for any pre-1966 comic.
No matter what title or
condition, whether you have
one comic or a warehouse full.

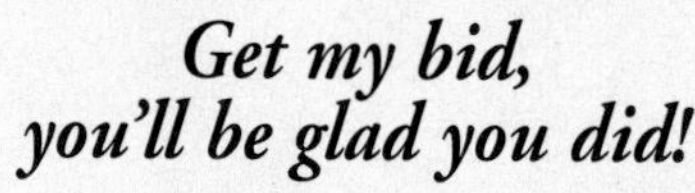
***Get my bid,
you'll be glad you did!***

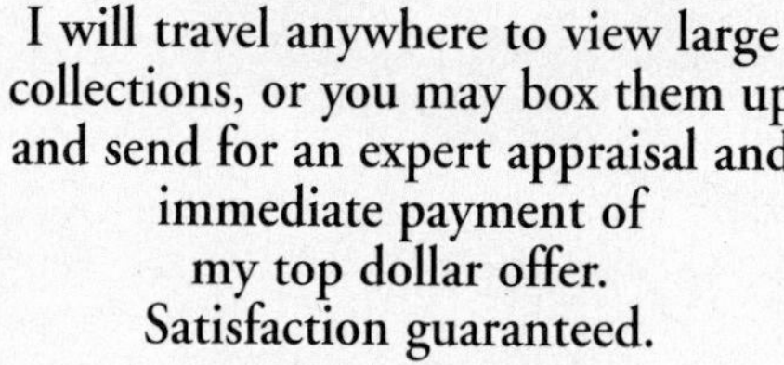
I will travel anywhere to view large
collections, or you may box them up
and send for an expert appraisal and
immediate payment of
my top dollar offer.
Satisfaction guaranteed.

**For a quick reply
Send a List
of What You Have
or Call Toll Free**

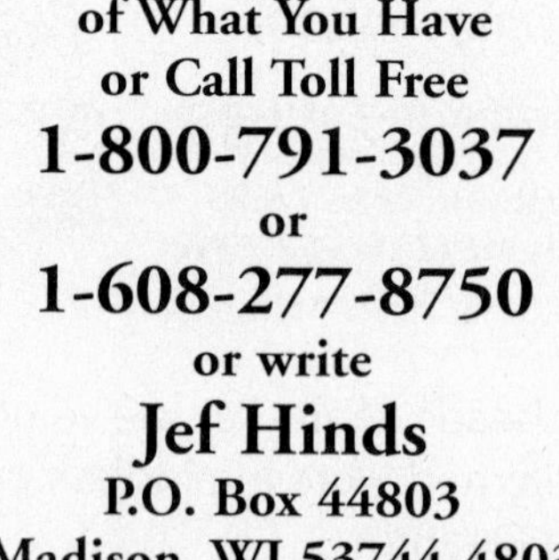
1-800-791-3037
or
1-608-277-8750
or write
Jef Hinds
P.O. Box 44803
Madison, WI 53744-4803

www.jhcomics.com

SHOWCASE NEW ENGLAND

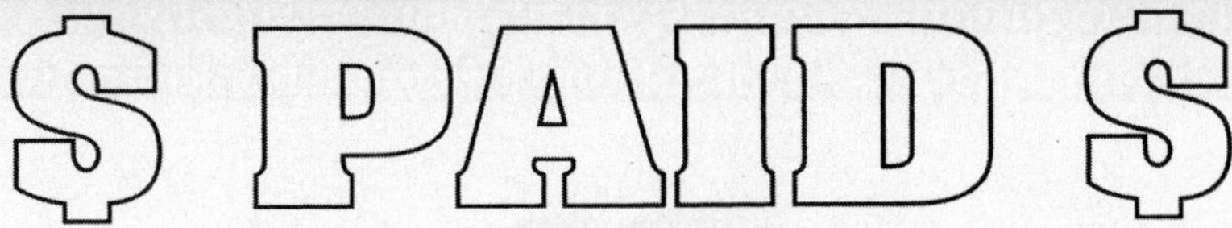

$700,000 PAID in Florida

$460,000 PAID in California

$375,000 PAID in New York, NY

$220,000 PAID in Georgia

$125,000 PAID in New Jersey

We pay amounts from

$1,000 to $50,000

EVERY WEEK

for books we need.

Call today for immediate, no nonsense response!

BOOKS SHOWN BY APPOINTMENT ONLY • WEEKDAYS 9:30 a.m. - 5:30 p.m. E.S.T.
CALL DANIEL GREENHALGH TODAY

CBG Customer Service Award Winner Seven Consecutive Years
Member AACBC Authenticity, Certification, & Grading Committee
Christie's Five Consecutive Years Sotheby's Five Consecutive Years
Senior Advisor to Overstreet Price Guide 1995, 1996, 1997, 1998, 1999, 2000, 2001, 2002, 2003, 2004

67 Gail Drive • Northford, CT 06472 • (203) 484-4579 • Fax (203) 484-4837 • Email: comics@showcasene.com

Looking to polish up your collection of prestigious panelists like *Kirby, Buscema, Kane, Romita,* or *Infantino*? Seeking an elusive Silver Key in sparkling condition? It's time to get your beaming butt to Bedrock City Comics!

In addition to offering Golden, Atomic, Bronze, and Modern Age comics, we've forged a sterling reputation as a Silver Age shangri-la!

Bedrock City
comics connoisseurs

TV COMICS.COM
30's
40's
50's
60's
70's
TvComics
We BUY Comics pre 1973
eBay ID: TvComics

WANTED

VINTAGE MOVIE POSTERS & LOBBY CARDS

FROM 1900 TO 1976

IF YOU HAVE QUALITY POSTERS FOR SALE, WE WOULD LIKE TO PURCHASE THEM FOR CASH! NO TRADE OFFERS. NO CONSIGNMENTS. JUST CASH.

STEPHEN FISHLER

873 Broadway, Suite 201, New York, NY 10003
Toll-Free (800) 229-6387 or call (212) 260-4147 • Fax (212) 260-4304
stephen@metropoliscomics.com • www.metropoliscomics.com

WANTED

COMIC BOOK

ART

COMIC STRIP ART

BEFORE YOU SELL YOUR ART, CALL ME. I CAN AND WILL PAY YOU MORE.

STEPHEN FISHLER

873 Broadway, Suite 201, New York, NY 10003
Toll-Free (800) 229-6387 or call (212) 260-4147 • Fax (212) 260-4304
stephen@metropoliscomics.com • www.metropoliscomics.com

Batman and Wonder Woman Collectors
We buy pre 1975 Batman comics and memorabilia and Wonder Woman comics and memorabilia from all eras.
P.O. Box 604925
Flushing, NY 11360-4925
e-mail: batt90@aol.com
wwali@aol.com
© DC Comics 2001

COMIC SHOP LOCATOR SERVICE
COMICS
888-COMIC-BOOK
888-266-4226

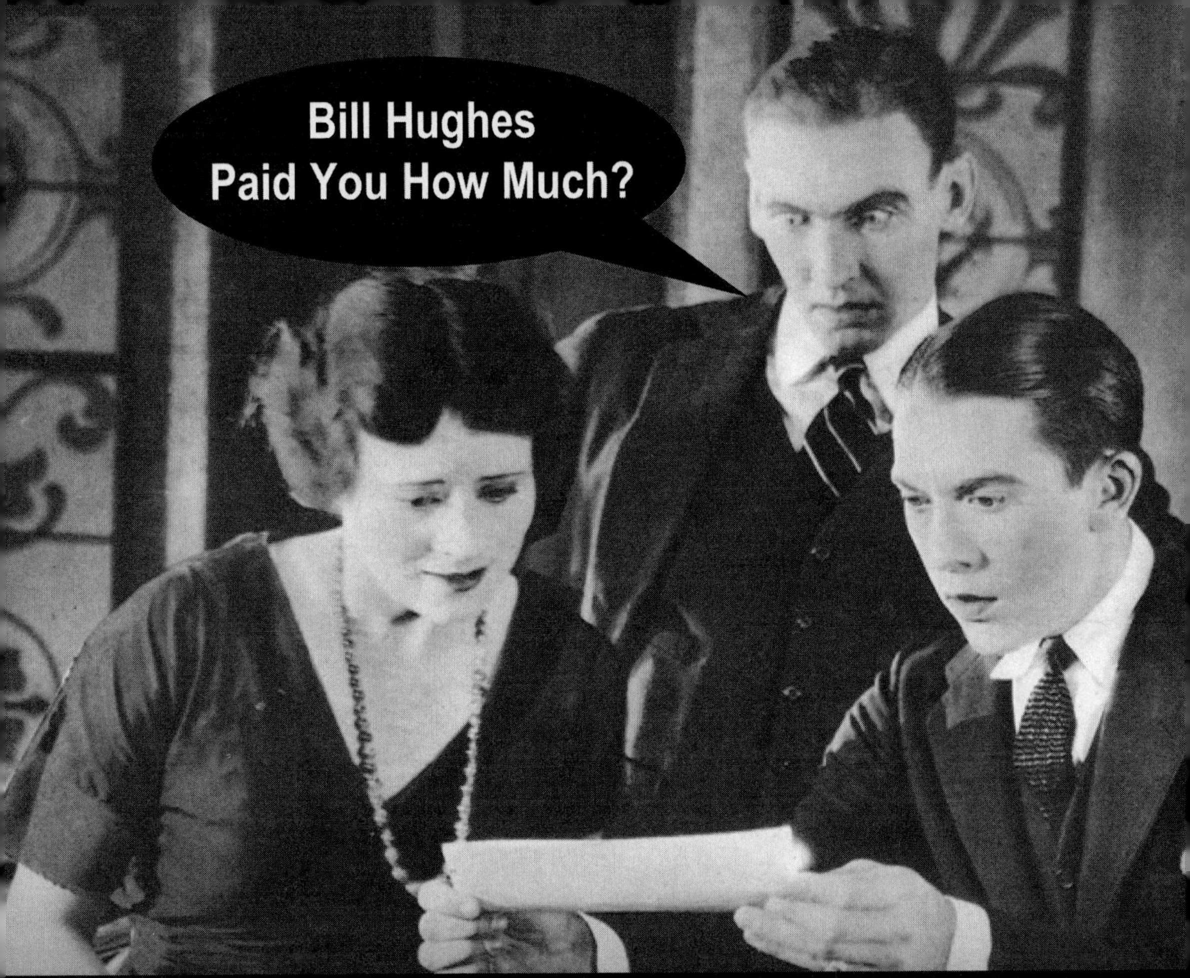

THESE DIDN'T HAPPEN WITHOUT YOUR HELP.

The Overstreet Comic Book Price Guide doesn't happen by magic. A network of advisors – made up of experienced dealers, collectors and comics historians – gives us input for every edition we publish. If you spot an error or omission in this edition or any of our publications, let us know!

Write to us at Gemstone Publishing Inc., 1966 Greenspring Dr., Timonium, MD 21093. Or e-mail **feedback@gemstonepub.com**.

We want your help!

J&S COMICS 732-988-5717

168 WEST SYVANIA AVE.

NEPTUNE CITY, NJ 07753
JANDSCOMICS@AOL.COM

CGC BUYING PRICES!

By now you've probably seen lots of ads offering vague percentages of Guide, like "50% to 500%." Or perhaps an offer of $1,000,000 or more for a book that no one owns, like Actions Comics #1 CGC graded 9.6. Well, we're going to give you an offer you can actually use - firm Buying Prices for CGC books that people actually own. This is just a very small sample of the books we buy. You may send any books listed below for immediate payment (Universal grades only, with off-white or better pages). If you don't see your books listed, email or mail your list for an immediate offer. We will also pay 50% to 80% of the listed prices for NON CGC graded books in the listed grades (books must be strictly graded). This list focuses mostly on late Silver Age and Bronze Age books in high grade, but we also pay great prices for Golden Age, early Silver Age, and lower grade books.

PRICES BELOW ARE WHAT WE PAY FOR CGC BOOKS IN THE LISTED GRADE

	8.5	9.0	9.2	9.4	9.6	9.8
Amazing Spider-Man #14	$1,400	$2,300	$3,500	$4,800	$9,000	$17,000
Amazing Spider-Man #50	425	650	1,000	1,400	2,400	4,500
Amazing Spider-Man #100	115	180	280	400	800	1,500
Amazing #121,122	130	200	300	425	900	1,700
Amazing Spider-Man #129	225	350	500	1,000	2,200	4,000
Captain America #100	190	285	450	625	1,200	2,000
Captain Marvel #1	75	115	160	230	450	900
Daredevil #168	40	55	75	100	225	500
Defenders #1	65	90	125	175	300	600
Fantastic Four #48	500	900	1,400	1,900	3,400	5,500
Fantastic Four #112	75	110	160	230	500	1,000
Giant-Size X-Men #1	550	750	1,000	1,500	2,800	5,000
Incredible Hulk #181	600	800	1,200	1,800	4,000	7,000
Iron Fist #14	60	90	115	150	240	450
Iron Man #1	225	325	500	700	1,400	2,400
Marvel Spotlight #2,5	100	140	200	280	550	1,000
Silver Surfer #1,4	250	400	600	800	1,500	2,500
Sub-Mariner #1	100	160	250	350	600	1,000
Ultimate Spider-Man #1	30	45	60	80	140	250
Werewolf By Night #32	60	85	120	180	320	600
X-Men #31-66 (any)	55	80	110	150	260	500
X-Men #94	500	700	900	1,350	2,500	4,800
All-Star Western #10	225	350	500	700	1,300	2,300
Batman #200,234	90	140	200	280	500	900
Flash #123	800	1,250	2,000	3,000	5,000	9,000
Flash #137	275	400	600	850	1,600	3,000
G. Lantern #59	120	190	260	350	600	1,000
G. Lantern #76	175	275	400	550	1,000	2,000
G. Lantern #77-86 (any)	35	55	80	105	200	375
House of Secrets #92	300	450	600	800	1,500	2,500

Business Card Ads

THE OVERSTREET COMIC BOOK PRICE GUIDE BUSINESS CARD ADS are a great way to advertise in the Guide! Simply send us your business card and we'll reduce it and run it as is. Have your ad seen by thousands of serious comic book collectors for an entire year! If you are a comic book or collectible dealer, retail establishment, mail-order house, etc., you can reach potential customers throughout the United States and around the world in our **BUSINESS CARDS ADS**!

For more information, contact our Advertising Dept.
Gemstone Publishing, Inc. 1966 Greenspring Drive, Suite 400, Timonium, MD 21093.
Call (888) 375-9800 Ext. 410, or fax (410) 252-4582, or e-mail **ads@gemstonepub.com**.

Business Card Ads

BUY • SELL • TRADE • CONSIGN
Specializing in
SERIOUS COLLECTOR'S WANT LISTS
DELL • GOLD KEY • CHARLTON • DC
MARVEL • CLASSICS • MAGAZINES
FANZINES • POCKET BOOKS & MORE!
156 Imperial Ave. Winnipeg MB R2M 0K8
GREG HARDER 204•237•4428
FAX 204•233•5047

Rare Comics, Original Art, Fine Collectibles

P.O. Box 5035
Mesa, AZ 85211

Robert Letscher II
ebay: KeyComics
Phone/Fax: (480) 890-0055
KeyComics@hotmail.com

LOWEST PRICES ON THE WEB...

- Top 5 Online Selection!
- FREE SHIPPING w/ $30 order!
- Prompt, courteous service!
- Secure, easy-to-use website!

...AND WE MEAN IT!

www.HouseofComics.com
back issues 1936 - present
info@houseofcomics.com
(510) 849-2094

OLD COMIC BOOKS FOR SALE
Wide selection, 1940s to 1970s, all publishers
MAGAZINES FOR SALE
Monster, Horror, Sci-fi, Comic, Humor, more
Hardcopy paper catalogs available for $1.00 each or view website. Request "32-page Old Comic Catalog" with $1.00 or request "22-page Magazine Catalog" with $1.00. (Outside US send $4.00 per catalog or $5.00 for both)
Low prices, accurate grades, great service, 100,000 in stock
www.MightyMags.com e-mail MightyMagsCom@aol.com
MightyMags.com, PO Box 7086, Clearwater, FL 33758-7086

BASEMENT COMICS
ALBERT M. STOLTZ, Jr.
1329 Superior Street • Havre de Grace, MD 21078
Home 410-939-8271 • Cell 443-831-2761
eMail **basmntcomx@aol.com**
www.basementcomix.com

SILVER AGE Comics
QUEENS
22-55 31ST STREET
ASTORIA, NY 11105
800.278.9691 OR 718.721.9691
FAX 718.728.9691
GUS@SILVERAGECOMICS.COM
MANHATTAN
47 W 8TH STREET
NY, NY 10011
646.654.7054
SILVERAGECOMICS2@NYC.RR.COM

BATMAN
WONDER WOMAN
COLLECTORS
E-mail: batt90@aol.com
wwali@aol.com

COLLECTORS
P.O. Box 604925
Flushing, NY 11360-4925

The 8th Annual Virginia
VINTAGE COMICS
& Collectibles Show
September 24, 2005 10 til 5
Salem Civic Center
Roanoke Blvd. Salem, VA
Interstate 81, Exit 141
1-540-789-7056

Business Card Ads

$250,000 SEARCH
FOR OLD COMIC BOOKS!!

For 30 years we have paid top prices
for Comic Books From 1033-1073.
Call 607-648-4025, or send Want Lists to:
Rick Semowich
56 John Smith Rd.
Binghamton, N.Y. 13901

$60,000 COMIC BOOKS
FOR SALE!!

GOLD, SILVER, and BRONZE age Comic Books
All priced at www.comicbook-warehouse.com,
Or send want lists to:
Rick Semowich
56 John Smith Rd.
Binghamton, N.Y. 13901

Visit our on-line catalogue at:
www.socalcomics.com

Visit our store at:
8280 Clairemont Mesa Bl. #124
San Diego, CA 92111
858-715-8669
socalcom@aol.com

Buying and selling
Golden Age to Modern
comic books
for plenty of years!!

We Want Your Help!
The Overstreet Comic Book Price Guide and **Hake's Price Guide To Character Toys** need your contributions! If you see something we've missed in **The Overstreet Comic Book Price Guide**, if you have comic character collectibles not included in **Hake's Price Guide To Character Toys**, we want to know about it!

Conact us at: feedback@gemstonepub.com

Directory Listings

(PAID ADVERTISING - STORE LISTINGS)

You can have your store listed here for very reasonable rates. Send for details for next year's Guide. The following list of stores have paid to be included in this list. We cannot assume any responsibility in your dealings with these shops. This list is provided for your information only. When planning trips, it would be advisable to make appointments in advance. Remember, to get your shop included in the next edition, contact us for rates.

Gemstone Publishing, Inc., 1966 Greenspring Dr., Suite 400, Timonium, MD 21093.
PHONE: 888-375-9800 or 410-560-5806
FAX: 410-252-4582
E-MAIL: ads@gemstonepub.com

Items stocked by these shops are noted at the end of each listing and are coded as follows:

(a) Golden Age Comics
(b) Silver Age Comics
(c) Bronze Age Comics
(d) New Comics & Magazines
(e) Back issue magazines
(f) Comic Supplies
(g) Collectible Card Games
(h) Role Playing Games
(i) Gaming Supplies
(j) Manga
(k) Anime
(l) Underground Comics
(m) Original Comic Art
(n) Pulps
(o) Big Little Books
(p) Books - Used
(q) Books - New
(r) Comic Related Posters
(s) Movie Posters
(t) Trading Cards
(u) Statues/Mini-busts, etc.
(v) Premiums (Rings, Decoders, etc.)
(w) Action Figures
(x) Other Toys
(y) Records/CDs
(z) VHS/DVD
(1) Doctor Who Items
(2) Simpsons Items
(3) Star Trek Items
(4) Star Wars Items
(5) HeroClix

ARIZONA

Key Comics: Discount Back-Issues
P.O. Box 5035
Mesa, AZ 85211
PH: (480) 890-0055
E-Mail: keycomics@hotmail.com
(a,b,c,d,e,m)

All About Books and Comics
5060 N. Central Ave.
Phoenix, AZ 85012
PH: (602) 277-0757
FAX: (602) 678-0065
E-Mail: alan@allaboutcomics.com
www.allaboutcomics.com
(a-l,r,u,w,x,2-5)

Samurai Comics
5024 N. 7th St.
Phoenix, AZ 85014
PH: (602) 265-8886
E-Mail: mike@samuraicomics.com
www.samuraicomics.com
(a-l,r,t,u,w,x,z,2,4,5)

ARKANSAS

Alternate Worlds Cards & Comics
3812 Central Ave., Suite G
Hot Springs, AR 71913
PH: (501) 525-8999
www.altworlds.com
E-Mail: frodo@altworlds.com
(b-d,f-k,t,u,w,2-5)

Vintage Stock
4505 W. Walnut Su. 5
Rogers, AR 72764
PH: (479) 936-5881
FAX: (479) 936-5884
E-Mail: rogers@vintagestock.com
(a-l,n-u,w,x,z,2-5)

Vintage Stock
2940 W. Sunset Suite B
Springdale, AR 72764
PH: (479) 756-1367
FAX: (479) 756-2749
E-Mail: springdale@vintagestock.com
(a-l,n-u,w,x,z,2-5)

CALIFORNIA

Bunky Brothers
1243 Broadway Ave
Burlingame, CA 94010
PH: (909) 941-6402
FAX: (650) 347 2305
bunky@BunkyBrothers.com
www.bunkybrothers.com

Terry's Comics
Buying All 10¢ & 12¢ original priced comics
P.O. Box 746
Atwood, CA 92811-0746
PH: (714) 288-8993 or
Hotline: (800) 938-0325
FAX: (714) 288-8992
E-Mail: info@terryscomics.com
www.terryscomics.com
(a,b,d-h,m,n,q)

HouseOfComics.com
The Bay Area's Back Issue Specialist --1936-present
(Website and By Appointment Only)
1700 Shattuck Avenue, #23
Berkeley, CA 94709
PH: (510) 849-2094
E-Mail: info@houseofcomics.com
www.houseofcomics.com
(a-c,m)

Warehouse Auctions Center
Fred McSurley
826 Calle Plano
Camarillo, CA 93012
PH: (805) 383-6288 x103
fredscrypt@hotmail.com

Crush Comics
2869 Castro Valley Blvd.
Castro Valley, CA 94546
PH: (510) 581-4779
E-Mail: crushcomics@yahoo.com
(b-d,f,g,i-k,r,t,u,w,x,2,4,5)

Collectors Ink
2593 Highway 32
Chico, CA 95973
PH: (530) 345-0958
E-Mail: bev@collectorsink.com
www.collectorsink.com
(a-g,i-l,o-r,t,u,w,z,1-5)

Flying Colors Comics & Other Cool Stuff
Joe Field
2980 Treat Blvd
Oak Grove Plaza
Concord, CA 94518
PH: (925) 825-5410
E-Mail: coolstuff@flyingcolorscomics.com
http://flyingcolorscomics.com
(a-g,j,r,t,u,w,x,2,4,5)

High-Quality Comics
1106 2nd St., #110
Encinitas, CA 92024
PH: (800) 682-3936
FAX: (760) 723-7269
E-Mail: customerservice@HighQualityComics.com
Web: www.HighQualityComics.com
(a-f,l,m,p-s,u,w,x,2-4)

Treasure Island Comics
40819 Fremont Blvd.
Fremont, CA 94538
PH: (510) 770-1168
FAX: (510) 770-1168
E-Mail: a@treasureislandcomics.com
Web: www.treasureislandcomics.com
(b-g,r,u,w,x,5)

Geoffrey's Comics
15900 Crenshaw Blvd.; Ste. B
Gardena, CA 90249
PH: (888) 538-3198
FAX: (310) 538-1114
eBay: Geoffrey_comics
(a-g,i-n,r,t,u,w,z,5)

Back Issue Comics
695 E. Lewelling
Hayward, CA 94541
PH: (510) 276-5262
(a,b,c,e,p,t,x,z)

Amazing Comics & Cards
5555 Stearns Street, Suite 103
Long Beach, CA 90815
PH: (562) 493.4427
FAX: (562) 493.3738
www.amazingcomics.com

Comic Collector Shop
167 E. El Camino Real
Mountain View, CA 95117
PH: (650) 965-8272
FAX: (650) 965-9753
E-Mail: phil@comiccollectorshop.com
Web: www.comiccollectorshop.com
(a-o,r,t,u,w,2-5)

Lee's Comics
1020-F N. Rengstorff Ave.
Mountain View, CA 94043
PH: (650) 965-1800
E-Mail: Lee@LCOMICS.com
www.LCOMICS.com
(a-z,1-5)

A-1 Comics
Brian Peets
5800 Madison Ave.
Sacramento, CA 95841
PH: (916) 331-9203
FAX: (916) 331-2141
E-Mail: A1comics@a-1comics.com
www.a-1comics.com
(a-k,m-o,r-u,w,x,z,2-5)

San Diego Comics
6937 El Cajon Blvd.
San Diego, CA 92115
PH: (619) 698-1177
RockofEasy@aol.com
www.san-diego-comics.com
(a,b,c,d,e,p)

Amazing Adventures
3800 Noriega St.
San Francisco, CA 94122
PH: (415) 661-1344
FAX: (415) 661-1694
E-Mail: orders@
amazing-adventures.com
Web:
www.amazing-adventures.com

Captain Nemo Games & Comics
563 Higuera St.
San Luis Obispo, CA 93401
PH: (805) 544-NEMO
FAX: (805) 544-1866
E-Mail: CaptainNemo
@CaptainNemo.biz
www.CaptainNemo.biz
(b,d-l,p,r-u,w,z,2-5)

Lee's Comics
2222 S. El Camino Real
San Mateo, CA 94403
PH: (650) 571-1489
E-Mail: mark@LCOMICS.com
www.LCOMICS.com
(a-z,1-5)

Metro Entertainment
6 West Anapamu
Santa Barbara, CA 93101
PH: (805) 963-2168
FAX: (805) 963-6698
E-Mail: metrocomix@aol.com
www.metroautographs.com
(a-l,r,t,u,w,x,z,2-5)

Colossus Comics
Visit Our Online Store
Santa Clara, CA 95050
PH: (408) 802-8424
steve@colossuscomics.com
www.colossuscomics.com
ebay ID: smortensen
(a-e,w,4)

Hi De Ho Comics & Books with Pictures
525 Santa Monica Blvd.
Santa Monica, CA 90401-2409
PH: (310) 394-2820
E-Mail: info@hideho.com
www.hideho.com
(a-g,i-u,w-z,2-5)

Earth-2 Comics
15017 Ventura Blvd.
Sherman Oaks, CA 91403
PH: (818) 386-9590
FAX: (818) 386-9568
E-Mail: earth2@sbcglobal.net
earth2comics.com
(a-f,p,q,r,u,w,5)

COLORADO

All C's Collectibles, Inc.
1113 S. Abilene St. #104
Aurora, CO 80012
PH: (303) 751-6882
E-Mail: ALLCS@qwest.net
(a-g,i,l,r-u,w,x,3-5)

RTS Unlimited Inc.
P. O. Box 150412
Lakewood, CO 80215-0412
PH: (303) 403-1840
FAX: (303) 403-1837
E-Mail:
rtsunlimited@earthlink.net
www.rtsunlimited.com
(a,b,c,e,f,l,m)

CONNECTICUT

Showcase New England
Dan Greenhalgh
67 Gail Drive
Northford, CT 06472
PH: (203) 484-4579
FAX: (203) 484-4837
comics@showcasene.com

Wonderland Comics
112 Main Street Ste. 15
Putnam, CT 06260
PH: (860) 963-1027
FAX: (860) 935-0000
E-Mail:
wonderlandcomics@aol.com
www.wonderlandcomics.com
(a-j,l,r,s,u,w,x,1-5)

DJ's Comics
1171 North Colony Road
Wallingford, CT 06492
PH: (203) 294-1576
E-Mail: see website
www.djscomics.com
(b-i,r,u,w,x,z,2-5)

FLORIDA

The Comics Club, Inc.
714 W. Lumsden Road
Brandon, FL 33511
PH: (813) 653-4111
E-Mail: mail@comicsclub.com
www.comicsclub.com
(a-j,r,s,t,u,w,x,2,5)

Emerald City Comics & Collectables, Inc.
2475-L McMullen Booth Rd.
Clearwater, FL 33759
PH: (727) 797-0664
www.EmeraldCityComics.com
(a-j,r,t-x,z,2-5)

Pedigree Comics, Inc.
13678 Plaza Mayor Drive
Delray Beach, FL 33446
PH: (561) 496-7667
FAX: (561) 496-7667
E-Mail: DougSchmell
@pedigreecomics.com
www.pedigreecomics.com

Samuel Frazer
11005 Lakeland Circle
Ft. Myers, FL 33913
PH: (239) 768-0649
Sfrazer457@aol.com
www.thefunnycomics.com

Tate's Comics + Toys + Videos & More
4566 North University Drive
Lauderhill, FL 33351
PH: (954) 748-0181
emailus@tatescomics.com
www.tatescomics.com
(b-m,q-u,w,x,z,1-5)

Phil's Comic Shoppe
6512 W. Atlantic Blvd.
Margate, FL 33063
PH: (954) 977-6947
E-Mail:
philscomix@worldnet.att.net
http://home.att.net/
~philscomix/indexphil.html
(b-f,m,5)

CGC
P.O. Box 4738
Sarasota, FL 34230
PH: (877) NM-Comic
FAX: (941) 360-2558
www.scgccomics.com

Emerald City Comics & Collectables, Inc.
9249 Seminole Blvd.
Seminole, FL 33772
PH: (727) 398-2665
E-Mail: CowardlyLion
@EmeraldCityComics.com
Web:
www.EmeraldCityComics.com
(a-k,q,r,t-x,z,1-5)

David T. Alexander
P.O. Box 273086
Tampa, FL 33618
PH: (813) 968-1805
FAX: (813) 264-6226
E-Mail:
davidt@cultureandthrills.com
Web:
www.cultureandthrills.com

Demolition Comics.com
4049 S. Dale Mabry Hwy
Tampa, FL 33611
PH: (813) 832-2692
FAX: (813) 681-9071
E-Mail:
demolitioncomics@aol.com
Web:
www.demolitioncomics.com
(a-l,r-u,w,x,y(records),z,1-5)

GEORGIA

Oxford Comics
2855 Piedmont Road
Atlanta, GA 30305
PH: (404) 233-8682
FAX: (404) 233-7520
(a-z,1-5)

Comic Company
1058 Mistletoe Rd.
Decatur, GA 30033
PH: (404) 248-9846
E-Mail:mail@comiccompany.com
www.comiccompany.com
(a-l,r,u,w,x,5)

Comic Books, ETC!
1105 Parkside Lane, Ste #1212
Woodstock, GA 30189
PH: (770) 592-4747
FAX: (770) 592-0447
E-Mail:
info@comicbooksetc.com
www.comicbooksetc.com
(a-f,j,r,s,u,w,x,z,2-4)

ILLINOIS

Yesterday
1143 West Addison St.
Chicago, IL 60613
PH: (773) 248-8087
(a,b,d,e,f,g,h,i,k,l,m,r,s,t)

he Paper Escape
205 West First Street
Dixon, IL 61021
PH: (815) 284-7567
E-Mail: paperescape
@paperescape.com
www.paperescape.com
(c-k,p,q,r,t,u,w,x,z,3-5)

Tomorrow is Yesterday, Inc.
5600 N. 2nd St.
Loves Park, IL 61111
PH: (815) 633-0330
FAX: (815) 633-3977
E-Mail: info@
tomorrowisyesterday.com
www.tomorrowisyesterday.com
(a-r,s-z,1-5)

M&M Comics
13617 Southwest Hwy.
Orland Park, IL 60462
PH: (708) 349-2486
service@mmcomics.com

Mellow Blue Planet
2212 5th Ave.
Rock Island, IL 61201-8908
PH/FAX: (309) 283-1653
E-Mail: mellowblueplanet
@hotmail.com
(a,b,c)

Unicorn Comics & Cards
216 S. Villa Ave.
Villa Park, IL 60181
PH: (630) 279-5777
(a-g,n-z,1-5)

Fat Tony's Comics, Inc.
110 Washington
Woodstock, IL 60098
PH: (816) 334-0445
FAX: (816) 334-0449
E-Mail:
fattonyscomicsinc@yahoo.com

INDIANA

Books Comics & Things
2212 Maplecrest Rd.
Fort Wayne, IN 46815-7628
PH: (260) 446-0025
FAX: (260) 446-0030
E-Mail: bct@bctcomics.com
www.bctcomics.com
(a-d,f-l,r,t,u,w,x,5)

Books Comics & Things
5936 W. Jefferson Blvd.
Fort Wayne, IN 46804
PH: (260) 431-4999
FAX: (260) 431-1105
E-Mail: bct@bctcomics.com
www.bctcomics.com
(a-d,f-l,r,t,u,w,x,5)

Comic Carnival
7225 N. Keystone Avenue
Suite B
Indianapolis, IN 46240
PH: (317) 253-8882
www.ComicCarnival.com
(a-l,n-u,w,x,z,2-5)

Comic Carnival East
9729 East Washington St.
Indianapolis, IN 46229
PH: (317) 898-5050
www.ComicCarnival.com
(a-l,r,t-z,2-5)

Comic Carnival Southport Center
7311 U.S. 31 South
Indianapolis, IN 46227
PH: (317) 889-8899
www.ComicCarnival.com
(a-d,f-k,r,t,x,2-5)

Comic Carnival West
3837 N. High School Rd.
Indianapolis, IN 46254
PH: (317) 293-4386
(a-z,1-5)

IOWA

Majestic Comics, Ltd.
7100 NE 16th Ct.
Ankeny, IA 50021
PH: (515) 480-4451
E-Mail:majcomic@mchsi.com
majcomic.home.mchsi.com
(a,b,d,f,g)

Oak Leaf Collectibles
23 5th St. SW
Mason City, IA 50401
PH: (641) 424-0333
FAX: (641) 424-0175
E-Mail:MikeT@dustcatchers.com
www.dustcatchers.com
(a-k,o,r,t,u,w-z,2-5)

KANSAS

Vintage Stock
8416 W. 135th St.
Overland Park, KS 66223
PH: (913) 681-1999
FAX: (913) 681-6033
E-Mail: op-135th
@vintagestock.com
(a-l,n-u,w,x,z,2-5)

Vintage Stock
9200 Metcalf Ave. #2
Overland Park, KS 66212
PH: (913) 648-8999
FAX: (913) 648-8995
E-Mail: op-metcalf
@vintagestock.com
(a-l,n-u,w,x,z,2-5)

B-Bop Comics & Games
5336 W. 95th St.
Prairie Village, KS 66207
PH: (913) 383-1777
(a-g,i-n,r-u,w-z,4,5)

Prairie Dog Comics
7130 West Maple, Suite 150
Wichita, KS 67209
PH: (316) 942-3456
FAX: (316) 942-0702
(a-z,1-5)

KENTUCKY

Comic Book World, Inc.
7130 Turfway Rd.
Florence, KY 41042
PH: (859) 371-9562
FAX: (859) 371-6925
E-Mail: comicbw@one.net
Web:www.comicbookworld.com
(a-l,n,r,t,u,w,z,2,5)

Comic Book World, Inc.
6905 Shepherdsville Rd.
Louisville, KY 40219
PH: (502) 964-5500
FAX: (502) 964-5500
E-Mail: comicbw@one.net
Web:www.comicbookworld.com
(a-j,l,n,r,u,5)

Leroy Harper
P.O. Box 212
West Paducah, KY 42086
PH: (270) 744-0732
lhcomics@hotmail.com

LOUISIANA

B.T. & S.J. Giles
P. O. Box 271
Keithville, LA 71047
PH: (318) 925-6654
(a-c,n-p)

MAINE

Top Shelf Comics
25 Central St.
Bangor, ME 04401
PH: (207) 947-4939
E-Mail: topshelf@tcomics.com
www.tcomics.com
(a-f)

MARYLAND

Geppi's Comic World
1116 N. Rolling Road
Baltimore, MD 21228
PH: (410) 788-0900
FAX: (410) 455-9806
E-Mail:
gdoug@diamondcomics.com
(c,d,f,g,i,j,k,t,u,w,x,z,1-5)

E. Gerber
1720 Belmont Ave.
Suite C
Baltimore, MD 21244

Esquire Comics.com
Mark S. Zaid, ESQ.
P.O. Box 3422492
Bethesda, MD 20827-2492
PH: (202) 498-0011
E-Mail:
esquirecomics@aol.com
www.esquirecomics.com
(b-k,r,u,w,4,5)

Alternate Worlds
Yorktowne Plaza
72 Cranbrook Road
Cockeysville, MD 21030
PH: (410) 666-3290
(b-k,r,u,w,4,5)

Liberty Books & Comics
7315 Baltimore Ave.
College Park, MD 20740
PH: (301) 699-0498
(a-c,h,m,n,p,q)

Comics To Astonish Inc.
9400 Snowden River Pkwy.
Columbia, MD 21045
PH: (410) 381-2732
E-Mail: comics2u@aol.com
www.comicstoastonish.com
(a-k,m,r,t,u,w,z,2,3,5)

Basement Comics
Albert M. Stoltz, Jr.
1329 Superior St.
Havre De Grace, MD 21078
PH: (410) 939-8271
Cell: (443) 831-2761
E-Mail:
basemntcomx@aol.com
www.basementcomix.com

Cards, Comics & Collectibles
100-A Chartley Drive
Reisterstown, MD 21136
PH: (410) 526-7410
FAX: (410) 526-4006
E-Mail: cardscomicscollectibles
@yahoo.com
(a-j,r,t-x,2-5)

Diamond Comic Distributors
1966 Greenspring Drive
Timonium, MD 21093
PH: (800) 45-COMIC

Diamond Select Toys
1966 Greenspring Drive
Suite 402
Timonium, MD 21093

Hake's Americana
1966 Greenspring Drive
Suite 400
Timonium, MD 21093
PH: (866) 404-9800
www.hakes.com

Collectors Insurance Agency
Dan Walker
P.O. Box 1200-OPG
Westminster, MD 21158
PH: (888) 837-9537
FAX: (410) 876-9233
info@insurecollectibles.com
www.collectinsure.com

MASSACHUSETTS

New England Comics
131 Harvard Avenue
Allston, MA 02134
PH: (617) 783-1848
www.newenglandcomics.com
(a-d,f-k,r,t,u,w,x,z,2-5)

New England Comics
744 Crescent St.
East Crossing Plaza
Brockton, MA 02402
PH: (508) 559-5068
www.newenglandcomics.com
(a-d,f-k,r,t,u,w,x,z,2-5)

New England Comics
316 Harvard St.
Coolidge Corner
Brookline, MA 02146
PH: (617) 566-0115
www.newenglandcomics.com
(a-d,f-k,r,t,u,w,x,z,2-5)

New England Comics
14A Eliot Street
Harvard Square
Cambridge, MA 02138
PH: (617) 354-5352
www.newenglandcomics.com
(a-d,f-k,r,t,u,w,x,z,2-5)

Gary Dolgoff
116 Pleasant St.
Easthampton, MA 01027
PH: (413) 529-0326
FAX: (413) 529-9824
gary@garydolgoffcomics.com
www.garydolgoffcomics.com

Jerry Weist
18 Edgemoor Rd.
Gloucester, MA 10930
PH: (978) 283-1419
jerryweist@adelphia.net

New England Comics
95 Pleasant St.
Malden Center
Malden, MA 02148
PH: (781) 322-2404
www.newenglandcomics.com
(a-d,f-k,r,t,u,w,x,z,2-5)

New England Comics
732 Washington Street
Norwood Center
Norwood, MA 02062
PH: (781) 769-4552
www.newenglandcomics.com
(a-d,f-k,r,t,u,w,x,z,2-5)

New England Comics
1511 Hancock St.
Quincy Center
Quincy, MA 02169
PH: (617) 770-1848
www.newenglandcomics.com
(a-d,f-k,r,t,u,w,x,z,2-5)

Bill Cole Enterprises Inc.
P.O. Box 60, Dept. 01
Randolph, MA 02368-0060
PH: (781) 986-2653
FAX: (781) 986-2656
bcemylar@cwbusiness.com
www.bcemylar.com

Harrison's Comics and Collectibles
252 Essex Street
Salem, MA 01970
PH: (978) 741-0786
FAX: (978) 741-0737
E-Mail:
harrisonscomics@hotmail.com
www.harrisonscomics.com
(a-l,o-u,w,x,z,1-5)

The Outer Limits
463 Moody St.
Waltham, MA 02453
PH: (781) 891-0444
E-Mail: eouterlimits@aol.com
(a-z,1-5)

SuperWorld Comics.com
Ted Vanliew
P.O. Box 20924
Worcester, MA 01602
PH: (508) 754-0792
lvanliew@aol.com
Superworldcomics.com

MICHIGAN

Comics North
425 N. Main Street
Cheboygan, MI 49721
PH: (231) 627-3740
www.comicsnorth.cjb.net
(b-f,h-k,r,s,w,z,1,3,4)

Amazing Book-Store
3718 Richfield Rd.
Flint, MI 48506
PH: (810) 736-3025
E-Mail: CDSei1@aol.com
(a-f,j-l,u,5)

Tardy's Collector's Corner, Inc.
2009 Eastern Ave. S.E.
Grand Rapids, MI 49507
PH: (616) 247-7828
(a-f,l,n,r,u,w)

Harley Yee Rare Comics
P.O. Box 51758
Livonia, MI 48151
PH: (734) 421-7921
FAX: (734) 421-7928
E-Mail: harleycomx@aol.com
Web:www.harleyyeecomics.com
(a,b,c,i,m,n,o)

Motor City Comics
19785 W. 12 Mile Rd.
PMB 231
Southfield, MI 48076
PH: (248) 426-8059
www.motorcitycomics.com

MINNESOTA

Nostalgia Zone, Inc.
3149 1/2 Hennepin Ave. South
Minneapolis, MN 55408
PH: (612) 822-2806
FAX: (612) 822-2805
E-Mail:
orders@nostalgiazone.com
www.nostalgiazone.com
(a-c,e,f,j-o)

MISSISSIPPI

Golden Age Comics & Games
Patrick Marchbanks
P.O. Box 8822
Gulfport, MS 39506
PH: (228) 860-0256
FAX: (228) 896-5472
goldenagecbc@aol.com

Ken Stribling
P.O. Box 16004
Jackson, MS 39236-6004
PH: (601) 977-5254
kenstrib@was.net

Action Island
579 Highway 51
Ridgeland, MS 39157
PH: (601) 856-1789
E-Mail:
kstribling@jam.rr.com
www.actionisland.com
(a-g,j,k,p-s,u,w,x,z,4,5)

MISSOURI

Vintage Stock
3128 S. Main St.
Joplin, MO 64804
PH: (417) 782-2778
FAX: (417) 627-0875
E-Mail: joplin
@vintagestock.com
(a-l,n-u,w,x,z,2-5)

B-Bop Comics & Games
3940 Main St. (at Westport Rd.)
Kansas City, MO 64111
PH: (816) 753-2267
(a-m,r,t,u,w,x,z,2-5)

Friendly Frank's Comic Cavern
5404 NW 64th St.
Kansas City, MO 64151
PH: (816) 746-4569
(a-o,r,t,u,w,x,z,2-5)

Action Island
579 Highway 51
Ridgeland, MS 39157
PH: (417) 882-2283
FAX: (417) 882-9789
E-Mail: springfield
@vintagestock.com
(a-l,n-u,w,x,z,2-5)

Vintage Stock
2856 S. Glenstone
Springfield, MO 65804
PH: (417) 882-2283
FAX: (417) 882-9789
E-Mail: springfield
@vintagestock.com
(a-l,n-u,w,x,z,2-5)

Vintage Stock
2631 N. Kansas Expressway
Springfield, MO 65803
PH: (417) 866-7227
FAX: (417) 866-7244
E-Mail: springfield2
@vintagestock.com
(a-l,n-u,w,x,z,2-5)

NEBRASKA

Tenthpenny
601 N. Fort Crook Rd.
Bellevue, NE 68005
PH: (402) 933-6598
E-Mail: dave@tenthpenny.com
www.tenthpenny.com
(a-m,p,q,r,t,u,w,x,z,2-5)

Robert Beerbohm Comic Art
P.O. Box 507
Fremont, NE 68026-0507
PH: (402) 727-4071
E-Mail:
Robert@BLBComics.com
(a,b,c,e,l,m,n,o,r,s,t,v,1,2,3,4)

Krypton Comics
2912 S. 84th St.
Omaha, NE 68124
PH: (402) 391-4131
E-Mail:
dean@krypton.coxatwork.com
(a-k,r,u,w,x,z,2-5)

NEVADA

Silver Cactus Comics I
480 N. Nellis Blvd. #C1A
Las Vegas, NV 89110
PH: (702) 438-4408
FAX: (702) 438-5208
(a-k,m,r-z,2-5)

Silver Cactus Comics II
4410 N. Rancho Dr.
Las Vegas, NV 89130
PH: (702) 396-8840
www.silvercactuscomics.com
(a-k,m,r-z,2-5)

NEW HAMPSHIRE

Rare Books & Comics
James F. Payette
P.O. Box 750
Bethlehem, NH 03574
PH: (603) 869-2097
FAX: (603) 869-3475
E-Mail: JimPayette@msn.com
(a-c,e,n,o,p)

NEW JERSEY

NeatStuffCollectilbes.com
Michael Carbonaro
66 Grand Avenue
Englewood, NJ 07631
PH: (718) 326-2713
E-Mail: neatstuffcollectibles
@yahoo.com

ZAPP! Comics
3710 Rt. 9 South
Freehold Raceway Mall
Freehold, NJ 07728
PH: (732) 866-6655
E-Mail: zappcomics@aol.com
(a-g,i,j,r,t,u,w,x,z,2,4,5)

Dewey's Comic City
13 Park Avenue
Madison, NJ 07940
PH: (973) 593-0042
E-Mail: dewey@
deweyscomiccity.com
www.deweyscomiccity.com
(b-j,m,t,w,5)

JC Comics
Joe Conzolo
579 Rt. 22 West
North Plainfield, NJ 07060
PH: (908) 591-1829
jcrx@comcast.net

J&S Comics
Jim Walsh
98 Madison Avenue
Red Bank, NJ 07701
PH: (732) 988-5717
jandscomics@aol.com
www.jscomics.com

All-Star Auctions
Joe & Nadia Mannarino
122 West End Avenue
Ridgewood, NJ 07450
PH: (201) 652-1305
allstarauctions
@mindspring.com

ZAPP! Comics
Ben Lichtenstein
(A&P Center) 574 Valley Road
Wayne, NJ 07470
PH: (973) 628-4500
FAX: (973) 628-1771
zappcomics@aol.com
(a-g,i,j,r,t,u,w,x,z,2,4,5)

JHV Associates
(By Appointment Only)
P. O. Box 317
Woodbury Heights, NJ 08097
PH: (856) 845-4010
FAX: (856) 845-3977
JHVassoc@hotmail.com
(a,b,n,s)

NEW MEXICO

Howard's Rare Comics
8019 Menaul Blvd. N.E.
Albuquerque, NM 87111
PH: (505) 489-6258
E-Mail: hmrockman@juno.com
www.howardscomics.com
(a,b,c,e,f,n,o)

NEW YORK

Silver Age Comics
22-55 31 St.
Astoria, NY 11105
PH: (718) 721-9691
PH: (800) 278-9691
FAX: (718) 728-9691
gus@silveragecomics.com
www.silveragecomics.com
(a-g,j-o,r,t,u,w,x,z,2-4)

Excellent Adventures Comics
110 Milton Ave. (Rt. #50)
Ballston Spa, NY 12020
PH: (518) 884-9498
(a-g,i,n,o,r,u,v,w,3,4,5)

Pinocchio Collectibles
1814 McDonald Ave.
Brooklyn, NY 11223
PH: (718) 645-2573
PH: (718) 256-7832
(b-g)

Conrad Eschenberg
Route 1, Box 204-A
Cold Spring, NY 10516
PH: (914) 265-2649
comicart@pcrealm.net
www.comicsnart@pcrealm.net

HighGradeComics.com
17 Bethany Drive
Commack, NY 11725
PH: (631) 543-1917
FAX: (631) 864-1921
E-Mail: BobStorms@
HighGradeComics.com
www.HighGradeComics.com
(a,b,c)

Tomorrows Treasures
Richard Munchin
P.O. Box 925
Commack, NY 11725
PH/FAX: (631) 543-5737
E-Mail: comics@
tomorrowstreasures.com
www.tomorrowstreasures.com

Comiclink.com
10 Cutter Mill Road
Suite 303
Great Neck NY 11021
PH: (516) 466-2770
buysell@comiclink.com
www.comiclink.com

Comicollectors.net
Marnin Rosenberg
P.O. Box 2047
Great Neck, NY 11022
PH: (516) 466-8147
www.comiccollectors.net
www.collectorsassemble.com

Ravenswood Inc.
8451 Seneca Turnpike
New Hartford, NY 13413
PH: (315) 735-3699
E-Mail:
ravens@dreamscape.com
(a-j,p-u,w,x,z)

Metropolis
873 Broadway
Suite 201
New York, NY 10003
PH: (800) 229-6387
FAX: (212) 260-4304
E-Mail: buying@
metropoliscomics.com
www.metropoliscomics.com

Midtown Comics
200 West 40th Street
New York, NY 10018
PH: (800) 411-3341
gerry@midtowncomics.com
www.midtowncomics.com

Nuff Said Collectibles
320 E. 65th St.
New York, NY 10021
PH: (212) 861-1697
E-Mail: randy@
nuffsaidcollectibles.com
www.nuffsaidcollectibles.com
(q,u,w,x,2,3,4)

Silver Age Comics
47 West 8th Street
New York, NY 10011
PH: (646) 654-7054
E-Mail: silveragecomics2@
NYC.RR.com
www.silveragecomics.com
(a-g,j-o,r,t,u,w,x,z,2-4)

Bags Unlimited
7 Canal St.
Rochester, NY 14608
PH: (585) 436-9006
FAX: (585) 328-8526

Amazing Comics and Collectibles
12 Gillette Ave.
Sayville, NY 11782
PH: (631) 567-8069
E-Mail: info@amazingco.com
www.amazingco.com
(a-g,r,t,u,w,x)

American Legends
1107 Central Park Ave.
Scarsdale, NY 10583
PH: (914) 725-2225
www.amerlegends.com
(a,b,d-g,i,t,w,x,3,4,5)

Four Color Comics
Rob Rogovin
P.O. Box 1399
Scarsdale, NY 10583
PH: (914) 722-4696
keybooks@aol.com

NORTH CAROLINA

Comics Express at Consoltec
135 East Main Avenue
Taylorsville, NC 28681
PH: (828) 635-5422
E-Mail:
info@comicbookexpress.com
www.comicbookexpress.com
(d,f,q,w)

OHIO

Comic Book World, Inc.
4016 Harrison Avenue
Cincinnati, OH 45211
PH: (513) 661-6300
FAX: (513) 661-6300
E-Mail: comicbw@one.net
www.comicbookworld.com
(a-j,l,r,u,5)

Bookery Fantasy
16 West Main St.
Fairborn, OH 45324
PH: (937) 879-1408
E-Mail:bookeryfan@aol.com
www.bookeryfantasy.com
(a-u,w-z,1-5)

Parker's Records & Comics
1222 Suite C Rt. 28
Milford, OH 45150
PH: (513) 575-3665
FAX: (513) 575-3665
E-Mail: dkparker39@fuse.net
www.parkersrc.com
(a-l,n,r,t,u,w,z,2,5)

Mike Burkey
P.O Box 455
Ravenna, OH 44266
PH: (330) 296-5621
MikeBurkey@aol.com

Funnie Farm Bookstore
328 N. Dixie Drive
Vandalia, OH 45377
PH: (937) 898-2794
E-Mail:
pdbroida@earthlink.net
(a-d,f,g,h,i,o,r,t,w)

OKLAHOMA

Vintage Stock
2409 W. Kenosha #129
Broken Arrow, OK 74012
PH: (918) 251-6162
FAX: (918) 251-6948
E-Mail: brokenarrow
@vintagestock.com
(a-l,n-u,w,x,z,2-5)

New World Comics + Games
6219 N. Meridian
Oklahoma City, OK 73112
PH: (405) 721-7634
FAX: (405) 721-7634
(a-j,r,u,w,x,1-5)

Comic Empire of Tulsa
3122 S. Mingo
Tulsa, OK 74146
PH: (918) 664-5808
(a-d,m,n,p-t)

Vintage Stock
6808 S. Memorial #320
Tulsa, OK 74133
PH: (918) 254-8281
FAX: (918) 254-8940
E-Mail: tulsa
@vintagestock.com
(a-l,n-u,w,x,z,2-5)

Vintage Stock
5353 E. 41st
Tulsa, OK 74135
PH: (918) 665-1656
FAX: (918) 665-1415
E-Mail: tulsa2
@vintagestock.com
(a-l,n-u,w,x,z,2-5)

Want List Comics
(Appointment Only)
P.O. Box 701932
Tulsa, OK 74170-1932
PH: (918) 299-0440
E-Mail: WLC777@cox.net
(a,b,c,m,o,s,t,x)

OREGON

Emerald City Comics
770 E 13th
Eugene, OR 97401
PH: (541) 345-2568
(c,d,f-l,w,z,5)

Nostalgia Collectibles
527 Willamette Street
Eugene, OR 97401
PH: (541) 484-9202
E-Mail: darrell7g@comcast.net
(a-x,1-5)

Beyond Comics
322 East Main
Medford, OR 97501
PH: (800) 428-9543
(a-d,f-i,5)

PENNSYLVANIA

Dreamscape Comics
302 West Broad Street
Bethlehem, PA 18018
PH: (610) 867-1178
www.dreamscapecomics.com
(a-l,n-u,w-z,1,3-5)

The Comic Store
28 McGovern Ave.
Lancaster, PA 17602
PH: (717) 397-8737
FAX: (717) 397-8903
E-Mail:
comicstore@juno.com
www.comicstorepa.com
(b-l,p-r,t,u,w,2-5)

Tropic Comics & Collectibles
John Chruscinski
15 Chesapeake St.
Lyndora, PA 16045
Zepp68@bellsouth.net

Flynn's Comics
Jerry Flynn
212 Chestnut Lane
North Wales, PA 19454-1304
PH: (215) 646-2722
purchasing@flynncomics.com
www.flynncomics.com

Duncan Comics, Books, & Accessories
1047 Perry Highway
Pittsburgh, PA 15237
PH: (412) 635-0886
www.duncancomics.com
(a-g,i,n,p,q,r,t,u,w,x,1-5)

Eide's Entertainment
1121 Penn Ave.
Pittsburgh, PA 15222
PH: (412) 261-0900
FAX: (412) 261-3102
E-Mail: eides@eides.com
www.eides.com
(a-g, j-z,1-5)

Dave's American Comics
Buying All 10¢ & 12¢
original priced comics
P.O. Box 8198
Radnor, PA 19087-8198
PH: (610) 275-8817 or
Hotline: (800) 938-0325
FAX: (714) 288-8992
E-Mail:
daveamerican@earthlink.net
www.terryscomics.com
(a,b,d-h,m,n,q)

Comic Swap, Inc.
110 South Fraser Street
State College, PA 16801
PH: (814) 234-6005
E-Mail:
comicswap.inc@verizon.net
(c,d,f-k,r,u,w,5)

Comic Store West
984 Loucks Rd.
Maple Village 2
York, PA 17474
PH: (717) 845-9198
E-Mail: comicswest@aol.com
(d,f,h,t)

RHODE ISLAND

The Time Capsule
537 Pontiac Ave.
Cranston, RI 02910
PH: (401) 781-5017
E-Mail: ryeremian@aol.com
(a-z,1-5)

Shadowland Comics and Collectables
2025 Smith St.
North Providence, RI 02911
PH: (401) 349-4611
FAX: (401) 349-4611
E-Mail: gina.ckri@verizon.net
www.shadowlandscomics.com
(a-g,i,j,l,p,r-u,w,x,z,2-5)

SOUTH CAROLINA

Planet Comics
2704 N. Main St.
Anderson, SC 29621
PH: (864) 261-3578
E-Mail:
service@planetcomics.net
Web: www.planetcomics.net
(a-l,r,u,w,z,1-5)

Heroes and Dragons
1563-B Broad River Rd.
Columbia, SC 29210
PH: (803) 731-4376
HDweb@bellsouth.net
www.heroesanddragons.com

TENNESSEE

Casiberia
Patrick Shipley
650 Industrial Blvd.
Sale Creek, TN 37373
PH: (423) 332-4700 Ext. 210
FAX: (423) 332-7248
http://www.casiberia.com

TEXAS

Lone Star Comics
511 E. Abram St.
Arlington, TX 76010
PH: (817) 860-7827
FAX: (817) 860-2769
E-Mail:
lonestar@lonestarcomics.com
www.mycomicshop.com/
overstreet
(a-j,n,q,r,t-x,1-5)

Classics Incorporated
Matt Nelson
P.O. Box 600263
Dallas, TX 75360
PH: (214) 459-1866
Spectre52@aol.com

Remember When
2431 Valwood Pkwy
Dallas, TX 75234
PH: (972) 243-3439
FAX: (972) 243-1858
E-Mail:
rememberwh@aol.com
www.remembershop.com
(a-f,m,r,s,t,1-4)

Titan Comics
3701 W. Northwest Hwy #125
Dallas, TX 75220
PH: (214) 350-4420
FAX: (214) 956-0560
E-Mail: comix99999@aol.com
www.titancomics.com
(a-f,r,u)

Bill Hughes' Vintage Collectables
P.O. Box 270244
Flower Mound, TX 75027
PH: (972) 539-9190
FAX:(973) 432-4070
Whughes199@yahoo.com
www.vintagecollectables.net

Bedrock City Comic Co.
6517 Westheimer
Houston, TX 77057
PH: (713) 780-0675
www.bedrockcity.com
(a-g,j-o,r-x,z,1-5)

Bedrock City Comic Co.
4683 FM1960 West
Houston, TX 77069
PH: (281) 444-9763
www.bedrockcity.com
(a-g,j-o,r-x,z,1-5)

Bedrock City Comic Co.
10910 Old Katy Rd.
Houston, TX 77043
PH: (713) 365-0063
www.bedrockcity.com
(c-g,j-m,r-x,z,1-5)

Third Planet Sci-Fi Super Store
2718 Southwest Freeway
Houston, TX 77098
PH: (713) 528-1067
FAX: (713) 528-1067 x3
E-Mail: 3planet
@third-planet.com
www.third-planet.com
(a-z,1-5)

Ground Zero Comics
1700 SSE Loop 323, #302
Tyler, TX 75701
PH: (903) 566-1185
Web:
www.groundzerocomics.com
(b-k,r,t,w,3,4,5)

Bedrock City Comic Co.
106 W. Bay Area Blvd.
Webster, TX 77598
PH: (281) 557-2748
www.bedrockcity.com
(a-g,j-o,r-x,z,1-5)

VIRGINIA

Comic & Card Collectorama
2008 Mt. Vernon Avenue
Alexandria, VA 22301
(Greater D.C. area)
E-Mail: collectram@aol.com
(a-f,j,o,p,r,s,t,v,x,1,3,4)

Trilogy Shop
700 E. Little Creek Rd.
Norfolk, VA 23518
PH: (757) 587-2540
FAX: (757) 587-5637
E-Mail:
trilogy2@trilogycomics.com
www.trilogycomics.com

B & D Comic Shop
802 Elm Avenue SW
Roanoke, VA 24016
PH: (504) 342-6642
FAX: (504) 342-6694
E-Mail:
bdcomics1@verizon.net
www.bdcomics.com
(c,d,e,f,g,h,i,q,r,t,5)

Nova Comics
6324 Springfield Plaza
Springfield, VA 22150
PH: (703) 912-6682
FAX: (703) 237-2290
E-Mail:
novacomics@verizon.net
(a-c,f,g,i,r,t)

Trilogy Comics
5773 Princess Anne Rd.
Virginia Beach, VA 23462
PH: (757) 490-2205
E-Mail:
trilogy1@trilogycomics.com
www.trilogycomics.com

WASHINGTON

PGC Mint
Mark Wilson
PO Box 340
Castle Rock, WA 98611
PH: (360) 274-9163
FAX: (360) 274-2270
pgcmintsales@aol.com
www.pgcmint.com

Steve Sibra Vintage Comic Books
P.O. Box 1161
Edwards, WA 98020
PH: (206) 542-7699
E-Mail: herm2pipes@aol.com

Fantasy Masterpieces Paper Art Restoration
P.O. Box 881
Kelso, WA 98626
PH: (360) 577-0351
www.fantasymasterpieces.com

Golden Age Collectibles Ltd.
1501 Pike Place Market
401 Lower Level
Seattle, WA 98101
PH: (206) 622-9799

WISCONSIN

Westfield Comics
8608 University Green
PO Box 620470
Middleton, WI 53562-0470
www.westfieldcomics.com

John Hauser Comics
P.O. Box 510673
New Berlin, WI 53151
PH: (262) 789-1863
E-Mail: JMHComics@aol.com
www.JMHComics.com
(a,b,c,e,l,m,n,o,p)

CANADA

ALBERTA

Redd Skull Comics & CD's
720A Edmonton Trail, NE
Calgary, Alberta T2E 3J4
PH: (403) 226-6800
E-Mail:
reddskullcomics@shaw.ca
www.reddskull.com
(a-k,r,u-z,2,4,5)

BRITISH COLUMBIA

Golden Age Collectibles Ltd.
830 Granville Street
Vancouver, B.C., V6Z 1K3
PH: (604) 683-2819

MANITOBA

Doug Sulipa's Comic World
Box 21986
Steinbach, MB., R5G 1B5
PH: (204) 346-3674
FAX: (204) 346-1632
E-Mail: cworld@mts.net
www.dougcomicworld.com

The Collector's Slave
156 Imperial Ave.
Winnipeg, MB., R2M 0K8
PH: (204) 237-4428
FAX: (204) 233-5047
(a-c,e,l,o,1-5)

ONTARIO

The Comic Cave
25 Perth Street
Brockville, ONT K6V 5C3
PH: (613) 345-4349
(b,c,d,f,g,h,i,u,w,5)

Goblin's Den
Roy Brack
3437 Pinesmoke Cr.
Mississauga, ONT L4Y 3L4
Canada
PH: (905) 848-0559
goblinsden@home.com

Paradise Comics
Peter Dixon
3278 Yonge St.
Toronto ONT. M4N 2L6
Canada
PH: (416) 487-9807
info@paradisecomics.com
www.torontocomiccon.com

Pendragon Comics
3759 Lakeshore Boulevard
West
Toronto, ONT M8W 1R1
Canada
PH: (416) 253-6974
batdude@sympatico.ca

3RD Quadrant Comics
226 Queen St. W., Basement
Toronto, ON M5V 1Z6
PH: (416) 974-9211
E-Mail:
idamahn@yahoo.com
www.3rdquadrantcomics.com

QUEBEC

Heroes Comics
1116 Cure LaBelle
Laval, QC H7V 2V5
PH: (450) 686-9155
E-Mail: heroes@dsuper.net
(a-d,f,g,i,k,m,o,q-t,w,x)

ENGLAND

Silver Acre Comics
P.O. Box 114
Chester CH4 8WQ
England UK
PH: 01244680048
FAX: 01244680686
International phone:
+441244680048
sales@silveracre.com
www.silveracre.com

Vault Auctions Ltd.
P.O. Box 257
South Norwood London
SE25 6JN England
PH: +44 (0) 1342-300-900
FAX: +44 (0) 1342 322-900
contact@vaultautions.com
www.vaultauctions.com

INTERNET

Koop's Comics
PH: (301) 752-6857
E-Mail:
dr.koop@koopscomics.com
www.koopscomics.com

WB Auction Services
Brian Block
We sell everything!
E-Mail:
wbmainoffice@yahoo.com

(PAID ADVERTISING - STORE LISTINGS)

You can have your store listed here for very reasonable rates. Send for details for next year's Guide. The following list of stores have paid to be included in this list. We cannot assume any responsibility in your dealings with these shops. This list is provided for your information only. When planning trips, it would be advisable to make appointments in advance. Remember, to get your shop included in the next edition, contact us for rates.

Gemstone Publishing, Inc., 1966 Greenspring Dr., Suite 400, Timonium, MD 21093.
PHONE: 888-375-9800 or 410-560-5806
FAX: 410-252-4582
E-MAIL: ads@gemstonepub.com

Items stocked by these shops are noted at the end of each listing and are coded as follows:

(a) Golden Age Comics
(b) Silver Age Comics
(c) Bronze Age Comics
(d) New Comics & Magazines
(e) Back issue magazines
(f) Comic Supplies
(g) Collectible Card Games
(h) Role Playing Games
(i) Gaming Supplies
(j) Manga
(k) Anime
(l) Underground Comics
(m) Original Comic Art
(n) Pulps
(o) Big Little Books
(p) Books - Used
(q) Books - New
(r) Comic Related Posters
(s) Movie Posters
(t) Trading Cards
(u) Statues/Mini-busts, etc.
(v) Premiums (Rings, Decoders, etc.)
(w) Action Figures
(x) Other Toys
(y) Records/CDs
(z) VHS/DVD
(1) Doctor Who Items
(2) Simpsons Items
(3) Star Trek Items
(4) Star Wars Items
(5) HeroClix

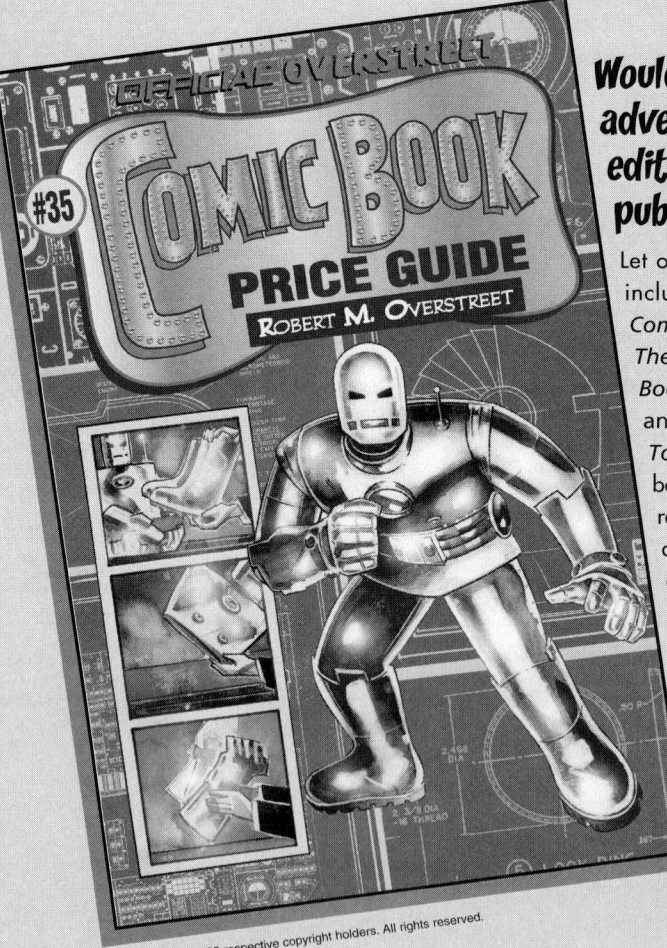

Glossary

a - Story art; **a(i)** - Story art inks; **a(p)** -

Story art pencils; **a(r)** - Story art reprint.

ADULT MATERIAL - Contains story and/or art for "mature" readers. Re: sex, violence, strong language.

ADZINE - A magazine primarily devoted to the advertising of comic books and collectibles as its first publishing priority as opposed to written articles.

ALLENTOWN COLLECTION - A collection discovered in 1987-88 just outside Allentown, Pennsylvania. The Allentown collection consisted of 135 Golden Age comics, characterized by high grade and superior paper quality.

ANNUAL - (1) A book that is published yearly; (2) Can also refer to some square bound comics.

ARRIVAL DATE - The date written (often in pencil) or stamped on the cover of comics by either the local wholesaler, newsstand owner, or distributor. The date precedes the cover date by approximately 15 to 75 days, and may vary considerably from one locale to another or from one year to another.

ASHCAN - A publisher's in-house facsimile of a proposed new title. Most ashcans have black and white covers stapled to an existing coverless comic on the inside; other ashcans are totally black and white. In modern parlance, it can also refer to promotional or sold comics, often smaller than standard comic size and usually in black and white, released by publishers to advertise the forthcoming arrival of a new title or story.

ATOM AGE - Comics published from 1946-1956.

B&W - Black and white art.

BACK-UP FEATURE - A story or character that usually appears after the main feature in a comic book; often not featured on the cover.

BAD GIRL ART - A term popularized in the early '90s to describe an attitude as well as a style of art that portrays women in a sexual and often action-oriented way.

BAXTER PAPER - A high quality, heavy, white paper used in the printing of some comics.

BC - Abbreviation for Back Cover.

BI-MONTHLY - Published every two months.

BI-WEEKLY - Published every two weeks.

BONDAGE COVER - Usually denotes a female in bondage.

BOUND COPY - A comic that has been bound into a book. The process requires that the spine be trimmed and sometimes sewn into a book-like binding.

BRITISH ISSUE - A comic printed for distribution in Great Britain; these copies sometimes have the price listed in pence or pounds instead of cents or dollars.

BRITTLENESS - A severe condition of paper deterioration where paper loses its flexibility and thus chips and/or flakes easily.

BRONZE AGE - Comics published from 1970 to 1984.

BROWNING - (1) The aging of paper characterized by the ever-increasing level of oxidation characterized by darkening; (2) The level of paper deterioration one step more severe than tanning and one step before brittleness.

c - Cover art; **c(i)** - Cover inks; **c(p)** - Cover pencils; **c(r)** - Cover reprint.

CAMEO - The brief appearance of one character in the strip of another.

CANADIAN ISSUE - A comic printed for distribution in Canada; these copies sometimes have no advertising.

CCA - Abbreviation for **Comics Code Authority**.

CCA SEAL - An emblem that was placed on the cover of all CCA approved comics beginning in April-May, 1955.

CENTER CREASE - See **Subscription Copy**.

CENTERFOLD or CENTER SPREAD - The two folded pages in the center of a comic book at the terminal end of the staples.

CERTIFIED GRADING - A process provided by a professional grading service that certifies a given grade for a comic and seals the book in a protective **Slab**.

CF - Abbreviation for **Centerfold**.

CFO - Abbreviation for Centerfold Out.

CGC - Abbreviation for the certified comic book grading company, Comics Guaranty, LLC.

CIRCULATION COPY - See **Subscription Copy**.

CIRCULATION FOLD - See **Subscription Fold**.

CLASSIC COVER - A cover considered by collectors to be highly desirable because of its subject matter, artwork, historical importance, etc.

CLEANING - A process in which dirt and dust is removed.

COLOR TOUCH - A restoration

process by which colored ink is used to hide color flecks, color flakes, and larger areas of missing color. Short for Color Touch-Up.

COLORIST - An artist who paints the color guides for comics. Many modern colorists use computer technology.

COMIC BOOK DEALER - (1) A seller of comic books; (2) One who makes a living buying and selling comic books.

COMIC BOOK REPAIR - When a tear, loose staple or centerfold has been mended without changing or adding to the original finish of the book. Repair may involve tape, glue or nylon gossamer, and is easily detected; it is considered a defect.

COMICS CODE AUTHORITY - A voluntary organization comprised of comic book publishers formed in 1954 to review (and possibly censor) comic books before they were printed and distributed. The emblem of the CCA is a white stamp in the upper right hand corner of comics dated after February 1955. The term "post-Code" refers to the time after this practice started, or approximately 1955 to the present.

COMPLETE RUN - All issues of a given title.

CON - A convention or public gathering of fans.

CONDITION - The state of preservation of a comic book, often inaccurately used interchangeably with Grade.

COPPER AGE - Comics published from 1984 to 1992.

COSMIC AEROPLANE COLLECTION - A collection from Salt Lake City, Utah discovered by Cosmic Aeroplane Books, characterized by the moderate to high grade copies of 1930s-40s comics with pencil check marks in the margins of inside pages. It is thought that these comics were kept by a commercial illustration school and the check marks were placed beside panels that instructors wanted students to draw.

COSTUMED HERO - A costumed crime fighter with "developed" human powers instead of super powers.

COUPON CUT or COUPON MISSING - A coupon has been neatly removed with scissors or razor blade from the interior or exterior of the comic as opposed to having been ripped out.

COVER GLOSS - The reflective quality of the cover inks.

COVER TRIMMED - Cover has been reduced in size by neatly cutting away rough or damaged edges.

COVERLESS - A comic with no cover attached. There is a niche demand for coverless comics, particularly in the case of hard-to-find key books otherwise impossible to locate intact. See Remainders.

C/P - Abbreviation for Cleaned and Pressed.

CREASE - A fold which causes ink removal, usually resulting in a white line. See Corner Crease and Reading Crease.

CROSSOVER - A story where one character appears prominently in the story of another character. See X-Over.

CVR - Abbreviation for Cover.

DEALER - See Comic Book Dealer.

DEACIDIFICATION - Several different processes that reduce acidity in paper.

DEBUT - The first time that a character appears anywhere.

DEFECT - Any fault or flaw that detracts from perfection.

DENVER COLLECTION - A collection consisting primarily of early 1940s high grade number one issues bought at auction in Pennsylvania by a Denver, Colorado dealer.

DIE-CUT COVER - A comic book cover with areas or edges precut by a printer to a special shape or to create a desired effect.

DISTRIBUTOR STRIPES - Color brushed or sprayed on the edges of comic book stacks by the distributor/wholesaler to code them for expedient exchange at the sales racks. Typical colors are red, orange, yellow, green, blue, and purple. Distributor stripes are not a defect.

DOUBLE - A duplicate copy of the same comic book.

DOUBLE COVER - When two covers are stapled to the comic interior instead of the usual one; the exterior cover often protects the interior cover from wear and damage. This is considered a desirable situation by some collectors and may increase collector value; this is not considered a defect.

DRUG PROPAGANDA STORY - A comic that makes an editorial stand about drug use.

DRUG USE STORY - A comic that shows the actual use of drugs: needle use, tripping, harmful effects, etc.

DUOTONE - Printed with black and one other color of ink. This process was common in comics printed in the 1930s.

DUST SHADOW - Darker, usually linear area at the edge of some comics stored in stacks. Some portion of the cover was not covered by the comic immediately above it and it was exposed to settling dust particles. Also see Oxidation Shadow and Sun Shadow.

EDGAR CHURCH COLLECTION - See **Mile High Collection**.

EMBOSSED COVER - A comic book cover with a pattern, shape or image pressed into the cover from the inside, creating a raised area.

ENCAPSULATION - Refers to the process of sealing certified comics in a protective plastic enclosure. Also see "slabbing."

EYE APPEAL - A term which refers to the overall look of a comic book when held at approximately arm's length. A comic may have nice eye appeal yet still possess defects which reduce grade.

FANZINE - An amateur fan publication.

FC - Abbreviation for Front Cover.

FILE COPY - A high grade comic originating from the publisher's file; contrary to what some might believe, not all file copies are in Gem Mint condition. An arrival date on the cover of a comic does not indicate that it is a file copy, though a copyright date may.

FIRST APPEARANCE - See **Debut**.

FLASHBACK - When a previous story is recalled.

FOIL COVER - A comic book cover that has had a thin metallic foil hot stamped on it. Many of these "gimmick" covers date from the early '90s, and might include chromium, prism and hologram covers as well.

FOUR COLOR - Series of comics produced by Dell, characterized by hundreds of different features; named after the four color process of printing. See **One Shot**.

FOUR COLOR PROCESS - The process of printing with the three primary colors (red, yellow, and blue) plus black.

FUMETTI - Illustration system in which individual frames of a film are colored and used for individual panels to make a comic book story. The most famous example is DC's *Movie Comics* #1-6 from 1939.

GATEFOLD COVER - A double-width fold-out cover.

GENRE - Categories of comic book subject matter; e.g. Science Fiction, Super-Hero, Romance, Funny Animal, Teenage Humor, Crime, War, Western, Mystery, Horror, etc.

GIVEAWAY - Type of comic book intended to be given away as a premium or promotional device instead of being sold.

GLASSES ATTACHED - In 3-D comics, the special blue and red cellophane and cardboard glasses are still attached to the comic.

GLASSES DETACHED - In 3-D comics, the special blue and red cellophane and cardboard glasses are not still attached to the comic; obviously less desirable than **Glasses Attached**.

GOLDEN AGE - Comics published from 1938 (*Action Comics* #1) to 1945.

GOOD GIRL ART - Refers to a style of art, usually from the 1930s-50s, that portrays women in a sexually implicit way.

GREY-TONE COVER - A cover art style in which pencil or charcoal underlies the normal line drawing, used to enhance the effects of light and shadow, thus producing a richer quality. These covers, prized by most collectors, are sometimes referred to as **Painted Covers** but are not actually painted.

HB - Abbreviation for Hardback.

HEADLIGHTS - Forward illumation devices installed on all automobiles and many other vehicles...OK, OK, it's a euphemism for a comic book cover prominently featuring a woman's breasts in a provocative way. Also see **Bondage Cover** for another collecting euphemism that has long since outlived its appropriateness in these politically correct times.

HOT STAMPING - The process of pressing foil, prism paper and/or inks on cover stock.

HRN - Abbreviation for Highest Reorder Number. This refers to a method used by collectors of Gilberton's *Classic Comics* and *Classics Illustrated* series to distinguish first editions from later printings.

ILLO - Abbreviation for Illustration.

IMPAINT - Another term for **Color Touch**.

INDICIA - Publishing and title information usually located at the bottom of the first page or the bottom of the inside front cover. In rare cases and in some pre-1938 comics, it was sometimes located on internal pages.

INFINITY COVER - Shows a scene that repeats itself to infinity.

INKER - Artist that does the inking.

INTRO - Same as **Debut**.

INVESTMENT GRADE COPY - (1) Comic of sufficiently high grade and demand to be viewed by collectors as instantly liquid should the need arise to sell; (2) A comic in VF or better condition; (3) A comic purchased primarily to realize a profit.

ISSUE NUMBER - The actual edition number of a given title.

ISH - Short for Issue.

JLA - Abbreviation for Justice League of America.

JSA - Abbreviations for Justice

Society of America.

KEY, KEY BOOK or KEY ISSUE - An issue that contains a first appearance, origin, or other historically or artistically important feature considered especially desirable by collectors.

LAMONT LARSON - Pedigreed collection of high grade 1940s comics with the initials or name of its original owner, Lamont Larson.

LENTICULAR COVERS or "FLICKER" COVERS - A comic book cover overlayed with a ridged plastic sheet such that the special artwork underneath appears to move when the cover is tilted at different angles perpendicular to the ridges.

LETTER COL or LETTER COLUMN - A feature in a comic book that prints and sometimes responds to letters written by its readers.

LINE DRAWN COVER - A cover published in the traditional way where pencil sketches are overdrawn with india ink and then colored. See also **Grey-Tone Cover**, **Photo Cover**, and **Painted Cover**.

LOGO - The title of a strip or comic book as it appears on the cover or title page.

LSH - Abbreviation for Legion of Super-Heroes.

MAGIC LIGHTNING COLLECTION - A collection of high grade 1950s comics from the San Francisco area.

MARVEL CHIPPING - A bindery (trimming/cutting) defect that results in a series of chips and tears at the top, bottom, and right edges of the cover, caused when the cutting blade of an industrial paper trimmer becomes dull. It was dubbed Marvel Chipping because it can be found quite often on Marvel comics from the late '50s and early '60s but can also occur with any company's comic books from the late 1940s through the middle 1960s.

MILE HIGH COLLECTION - High grade collection of over 22,000 comics discovered in Denver, Colorado in 1977, originally owned by Mr. Edgar Church. Comics from this collection are now famous for extremely white pages, fresh smell, and beautiful cover ink reflectivity.

MODERN AGE - A catch-all term applied to comics published since 1992.

MYLAR™ - An inert, very hard, space-age plastic used to make high quality protective bags and sleeves for comic book storage. "Mylar" is a trademark of the DuPont Co.

ND - Abbreviation for **No Date**.

NN - Abbreviation for **No Number**.

NO DATE - When there is no date given on the cover or indicia page.

NO NUMBER - No issue number is given on the cover or indicia page; these are usually first issues or one-shots.

N.Y. LEGIS. COMM. - New York Legislative Committee to Study the Publication of Comics (1951).

ONE-SHOT - When only one issue is published of a title, or when a series is published where each issue is a different title (e.g. Dell's *Four Color Comics*).

ORIGIN - When the story of a character's creation is given.

OVER GUIDE - When a comic book is priced at a value over Guide list.

OXIDATION SHADOW - Darker, usually linear area at the edge of some comics stored in stacks. Some portion of the cover was not covered by the comic immediately above it, and it was exposed to the air. Also see **Dust Shadow** and **Sun Shadow**.

p - Art pencils.

PAINTED COVER - (1) Cover taken from an actual painting instead of a line drawing; (2) Inaccurate name for a grey-toned cover.

PANELOLOGIST - One who researches comic books and/or comic strips.

PANNAPICTAGRAPHIST - One possible term for someone who collects comic books; can you figure out why it hasn't exactly taken off in common parlance?

PAPER COVER - Comic book cover made from the same newsprint as the interior pages. These books are extremely rare in high grade.

PARADE OF PLEASURE - A book about the censorship of comics.

PB - Abbreviation for Paperback.

PEDIGREE - A book from a famous and usually high grade collection - e.g. Allentown, Lamont Larson, Edgar Church/Mile High, Denver, San Francisco, Cosmic Aeroplane, etc. Beware of non-pedigree collections being promoted as pedigree books; only outstanding high grade collections similar to those listed qualify.

PENCILER - Artist that does the pencils...you're figuring out some of these definitions without us by now, aren't you?

PERFECT BINDING - Pages are glued to the cover as opposed to being stapled to the cover, resulting in a flat binded side. Also known as **Square Back or Square Bound**.

PG - Abbreviation for Page.

PHOTO COVER - Comic book cover featuring a photographic image instead of a line drawing or painting.

PLATINUM AGE - Comics published from 1883 to 1938.

POLYPROPALENE - A type of plastic used in the manufacture of comic book bags; now considered harmful to paper and not recommended for long term storage of comics.

POP - Abbreviation for the anti-comic book volume, *Parade of Pleasure*.

POST-CODE - Describes comics published after February 1955 and usually displaying the CCA stamp in the upper right-hand corner.

POUGHKEEPSIE - Refers to a large collection of Dell Comics file copies believed to have originated from the warehouse of Western Publishing in Poughkeepsie, NY.

PP - Abbreviation for Pages.

PRE-CODE - Describes comics published before the Comics Code Authority seal began appearing on covers in 1955.

PRE-HERO DC - A term used to describe *More Fun* #1-51 (pre-Spectre), *Adventure* #1-39 (pre-Sandman), and *Detective* #1-26 (pre-Batman). The term is actually inaccurate because technically there were "heroes" in the above books.

PRE-HERO MARVEL - A term used to describe *Strange Tales* #1-100 (pre-Human Torch), *Journey Into Mystery* #1-82 (pre-Thor), *Tales To Astonish* #1-35 (pre-Ant Man), and *Tales Of Suspense* #1-38 (pre-Iron Man).

PROVENANCE - When the owner of a book is known and is stated for the purpose of authenticating and documenting the history of the book. Example: A book from the Stan Lee or Forrest Ackerman collection would be an example of a value-adding provenance.

PULP - Cheaply produced magazine made from low grade newsprint. The term comes from the wood pulp that was used in the paper manufacturing process.

QUARTERLY - Published every three months (four times a year).

R - Abbreviation for Reprint.

RARE - 10-20 copies estimated to exist.

RAT CHEW - Damage caused by the gnawing of rats and mice. Just where are you storing your comics anyway?

RBCC - Abbreviation for Rockets Blast Comic Collector, one of the first and most prominent adzines instrumental in developing the early comic book market.

READING COPY - A comic that is in FAIR to GOOD condition and is often used for research; the condition has been sufficiently reduced to the point where general handling will not degrade it further.

READING CREASE - Book-length, vertical front cover crease at staples, caused by bending the cover over the staples. Square-bounds receive these creases just by opening the cover too far to the left.

REILLY, TOM - A large high grade collection of 1939-1945 comics with 5000+ books.

REPRINT COMICS - In earlier decades, comic books that contained newspaper strip reprints; modern reprint comics usually contain stories originally featured in older comic books.

RESTORATION - Any attempt, whether professional or amateur, to enhance the appearance of an aging or damaged comic book. These procedures may include any or all of the following techniques: recoloring, adding missing paper, stain, ink, dirt or tape removal, whitening, pressing out wrinkles, staple replacement, trimming, re-glossing, etc. Amateur work can lower the value of a book, and even professional restoration has now gained a certain negative aura in the modern marketplace from some quarters. In all cases, except for some simple cleaning procedures, a restored book can never be worth the same as an unrestored book in the same condition.

REVIVAL - An issue that begins republishing a comic book character after a period of dormancy.

ROCKFORD - A high grade collection of 1940s comics with 2000+ books from Rockford, IL.

ROLLED SPINE - A spine condition caused by folding back pages while reading.

ROUND BOUND - Standard saddle stitch binding typical of most comics.

RUN - A group of comics of one title where most or all of the issues are present. See Complete Run.

S&K - Abbreviation for the legendary creative team of Joe Simon and Jack Kirby, creators of Marvel Comics' Captain America.

SADDLE STITCH - The staple binding of magazines and comic books.

SAN FRANCISCO COLLECTION - (see Reilly, Tom)

SCARCE - 20-100 copies estimated to exist.

SEDUCTION OF THE INNOCENT - An inflammatory book written by Dr. Frederic Wertham and published in 1953; Wertham asserted that comics were responsible for rampant juvenile deliquency in American youth.

SET - (1) A complete run of a given title; (2) A grouping of comics for sale.

SEMI-MONTHLY - Published twice

a month, but not necessarily Bi-Weekly.

SEWN SPINE - A comic with many spine perforations where binders' thread held it into a bound volume. This is considered a defect.

SF - Abbreviation for Science Fiction (the other commonly used term, "sci-fi," is often considered derogatory or indicative of more "low-brow" rather than "literary" science fiction, i.e. "sci-fi television."

SILVER AGE - Comics published from 1956 to 1970.

SILVER PROOF - A black and white actual size print on thick glossy paper hand-painted by an artist to indicate colors to the engraver.

SLAB - Colloquial term for the plastic enclosure used by grading certification companies to seal in certified comics.

SLABBING - Colloquial term for the process of encapsulating certified comics in a plastic enclosure.

SOTI - Abbreviation for Seduction of the Innocent.

SPINE - The left-hand edge of the comic that has been folded and stapled.

SPINE ROLL - A condition where the left edge of the comic book curves toward the front or back, caused by folding back each page as the comic was read.

SPLASH PAGE - A Splash Panel that takes up the entire page.

SPLASH PANEL - (1) The first panel of a comic book story, usually larger than other panels and usually containing the title and credits of the story; (2) An oversized interior panel.

SQUARE BACK or SQUARE BOUND - See Perfect Binding.

STORE STAMP - Store name (and sometimes address and telephone number) stamped in ink via rubber stamp and stamp pad.

SUBSCRIPTION COPY - A comic sent through the mail directly from the publisher or publisher's agent. Most are folded in half, causing a subscription crease or fold running down the center of the comic from top to bottom; this is considered a defect.

SUBSCRIPTION CREASE - See Subscription Copy.

SUBSCRIPTION FOLD - See Subscription Copy. Differs from a Subscription Crease in that no ink is missing as a result of the fold.

SUN SHADOW - Darker, usually linear area at the edge of some comics stored in stacks. Some portion of the cover was not covered by the comic immediately above it, and it suffered prolonged exposure to light. A serious defect, unlike a Dust Shadow, which can sometimes be removed. Also see Oxidation Shadow.

SUPER-HERO - A costumed crime fighter with powers beyond those of mortal man.

SUPER-VILLAIN - A costumed criminal with powers beyond those of mortal man; the antithesis of Super-Hero.

SWIPE - A panel, sequence, or story obviously borrowed from previously published material.

TEXT ILLO. - A drawing or small panel in a text story that almost never has a dialogue balloon.

TEXT PAGE - A page with no panels or drawings.

TEXT STORY - A story with few if any illustrations commonly used as filler material during the first three decades of comics.

3-D COMIC - Comic art that is drawn and printed in two color layers, producing a 3-D effect when viewed through special glasses.

3-D EFFECT COMIC - Comic art that is drawn to appear as if in 3-D but isn't.

TITLE - The name of the comic book.

TITLE PAGE - First page of a story showing the title of the story and possibly the creative credits and indicia.

TTA - Abbreviation for *Tales to Astonish*.

UK - Abbreviation for British edition (United Kingdom).

UNDER GUIDE - When a comic book is priced at a value less than Guide list.

UPGRADE - To obtain another copy of the same comic book in a higher grade.

VARIANT COVER - A different cover image used on the same issue.

VERY RARE - 1 to 10 copies estimated to exist.

VICTORIAN AGE - Comics published from 1828 to 1883.

WANT LIST - A listing of comics needed by a collector, or a list of comics that a collector is interested in purchasing.

WAREHOUSE COPY - Originating from a publisher's warehouse; similar to file copy.

WHITE MOUNTAIN COLLECTION - A collection of high grade 1950s and 1960s comics which originated in New England.

X-OVER - Short for Crossover.

ZINE - Short for Fanzine.

Enduring Duo: Wolfman and Pérez

TEEN TITANS AT 25, Crisis at 20

by J.C. Vaughn

The legendary creative duos in comics include two teams – Joe Simon and Jack Kirby, and Stan Lee and Jack Kirby – for whom it is generally safe to mention only their last names. Others may well someday be added to this pantheon and still others probably already belong to it, but while Simon & Kirby helped define the 1940s and 1950s and Lee & Kirby certainly defined the 1960s, another team defined the 1980s and in many ways helped set the groundwork for the superhero comics we have today.

Writer Marv Wolfman and artist George Pérez, who this year celebrate the 25th anniversary of *New Teen Titans* and the 20th anniversary of *Crisis on Infinite Earths*, have impacted the superhero genre as have few other pairs of creators. Though both worked extensively with other partners before and since those efforts, there is undeniably something compelling and special about that period and their collaborative labors.

Wolfman, a writer or writer-editor by trade, had briefly risen to the Editor-in-Chief spot at Marvel and he'd also had a lengthy run on *Tomb of Dracula*, during which he created the characters Blade and Hannibal King. Pérez had worked on many Marvel titles, but was most famous for his work on *The Avengers*.

Both Wolfman and Pérez had come to DC after recent stints at Marvel. When Wolfman landed there at the end of 1979, he and editor Len Wein pitched DC's Jenette Kahn on bringing back the Teen Titans.

"When Len and I pitched Titans to Jenette her first thought was that book failed twice and she didn't like the previous incarnation at all. Why, she asked, did we think the new version would do well. We said we'd do it better. That is actually what we said. She said fine and let us go ahead," he said. He then recruited Pérez.

"At that point I was still drawing *The Avengers* for Marvel. This would be either late in 1979 or early in 1980. Marv had already gone over to DC and it was he who approached me about doing some work over there. Specifically, a new version of *The Teen Titans*," Pérez said.

DC Comics Presents #26 featured the preview of New Teen Titans

"To be honest, I wasn't particularly interested in doing a new Titans book, although the thought of doing work for DC – I had only worked for Marvel at that point – really intrigued me. I agreed to draw *New Teen Titans* with the provision that I'd be allowed to do a fill-in issue or two of *Justice League Of America*, which was the book I really wanted to do at that time, a logical follow-up to *Avengers* in my mind," he said.

"Len was the original editor," Wolfman said. "He and I had been best friends since we were very young teenagers and we'd gone back and forth as to who edited whom. Len was a DC editor when I went to DC and he was the only one I wanted to work with on the title. Len believed, as I do, to hire the best folks and then leave them alone. In the very beginning he urged me to add a sorcerer to the group - he wanted a magic character in the Titans and I didn't. I came up with Raven to meet him half way and she quickly became my favorite character. Other than that, Len also worked on cover designs and copy editing. He didn't feel the need to get too involved with story content and he let George and me go off and pretty much do the book on our own."

"Len's contributions as the book's editor and champion cannot, however, be ever overvalued," Pérez said. "He was as much of an integral part of the series' initial success as Marv, me and [inker] Romeo Tanghal."

Pérez said he thinks that when the powers at DC at the time saw his initial designs for the new characters Cyborg, Raven and Starfire coupled with Marv's outline for the first story arc, their confidence in the series' potential rose.

At that point, the company took the then-unusual step of including a promotional or teaser comic within the pages of *DC Comics Presents* #26. The title was a Superman team-up series, like *Marvel Team-Up* was for Spider-Man, and it was a good bet as a place to grab other readers.

"That meant that DC was really backing up its faith in the comic with financial risk. The cover price for *DC Comics Presents* #26 remained the same although the printing cost for the *Titans* insert no doubt raised the per unit cost considerably. It was an unheard-of bargain for the fans, but a gamble for the company," Pérez said. "Thankfully, the gamble paid off, much to my surprise."

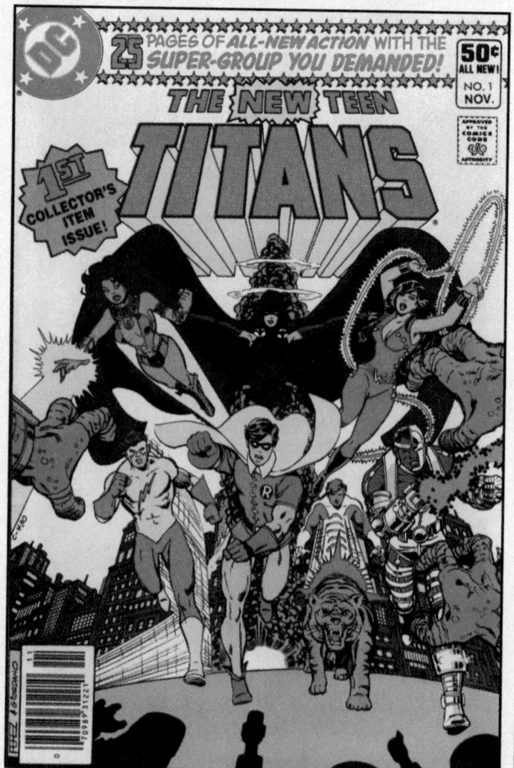

New Teen Titans #1 was a huge success.

The results, at least for the first issue, weren't surprising.

"The book went through the roof in the first issue and then fell in sales for the next four," Wolfman said. "Then with issue #6 it zoomed up and never went down. We were surprised because DC hadn't had a success in years and we weren't sure that no matter how good the book was that readers of that time period would look at a DC title. Fortunately they did and that began the process of helping to rebuild the company."

No one was more surprised than George Pérez at the success of *New Teen Titans*.

"I didn't expect it to last beyond six issues. I only took it on as a stepping stone towards *JLA*. Even after I did get the regular gig on *JLA* after the unexpected death of Dick Dillin, I found that *Titans* was going to be where my future would be mapped out," he said.

New Teen Titans quickly became a runaway success. In many stores, it ran neck-and-neck with the Chris Claremont – John Byrne era of *Uncanny X-Men* in sales. There have been many who speculated as to why it was so successful, but there are not set answers.

"I'd like to think what we did was combine the strengths of DC and Marvel rather than just being a DC comic or a Marvel comic," Wolfman said. "We had Marvel action and character combined with DC plotting and inventiveness. I think George and I developed characters that people liked and we kept surprising them with it. We also created dozens of characters to populate the book, something that's hardly done anymore. Many modern writers just recycle old villains instead of keeping things fresh and new."

Initially the duo worked in "Marvel style," where the agreed upon plot (and sometimes a panel breakdown) is supplied by the writer first. The story is then illustrated, and then the writer adds the dialogue.

"I would add little tweaks here and there, but the details were already put in place by Marv, and I followed them pretty closely," Pérez said.

"By issue 8, the pivotal "A Day In the Lives..." story, I was far more involved in the plotting aspects of the series. I had gotten to love the characters by this point and wanted to be involved more in the characters' development. That issue really galvanized the inner souls of the Titans for me, and I was really dedicated to their future from then on," he said. "Eventually, the working relationship with Marv and me evolved to the point that we no longer had written plots. He and I would talk the stories out and I would draw it from memory, which was a whole lot better then. Marv would then script from my notes accompanying the art. It was a unique and creatively satisfying working experience that I've never been able to duplicate anywhere else.

In its success, *New Teen Titans* spawned a mini-series, several annuals, and a more deluxe version of the series, which was printed on Baxter paper, which was definitely a step up from traditional newsprint. Since nostalgia basically runs on a 20-year cycle, it's not surprising that there is some degree of interest being paid to the work, but nostalgia alone doesn't explain the depth of the affinity that some feel for the series. The affection seems to carry over to the creators of DC's current hit, *Teen Titans*, as well. Pérez said he thinks it's the sense of family and unity of purpose that Wolfman and he instilled in the characters.

"They were young heroes, teens as the title insisted, who had to cope with not only unearthly and sinister menaces, but also the day-to-day traumas and challenges of just simply adapting to the growing pressures of young adulthood," he said. "We dealt with peer pressure, drugs, runaways, parental conflicts, romance, alienation, pretty much what much of the young readership could identify with. And Marv always insisted on respecting his readers. We didn't condescend and we didn't pander. The Titans were written with respect for its audience."

With *New Teen Titans* a firmly established hit, Wolfman and Pérez were handed the assignment to combine the many realities of the DC Universe into one new reality, *Crisis On Infinite Earths*. Gone would be Earth-I and Earth-II with their older and younger sets of heroes and the Justice League – Justice Society crossovers. Gone also would be some popular characters. The decision behind the story, let alone the story itself, was bound to create controversy. Why hand it to a popular duo, who at least theoretically had a lot to lose if it went south?

"I think the *Titans* proved you could do a regular series at DC with strong characters and stories and that people who previously would never have looked at a DC book would follow it. *Crisis* was more of an industry wide phenomenon in that it, for better or worse, completely revolutionized event comics programming," Wolfman said.

"The stories were less character-driven due to the enormous cast, although it was amazing how Marv still managed to get some great emotional moments into such an epic," Pérez said. "Initially, like *Titans* I was not as involved in the plotting, but would get more involved in that process when the story grew a bit too unwieldy for Marv to coordinate on his own. That's when years of a symbiotic working relationship proved to be quite handy."

"Nobody had done it before," Wolfman said, "and now, right to today's *Identity Crisis*, the concepts underlying George's and my *Crisis* are still being done."

Last year George Pérez completed the epic Marvel/DC crossover *JLA/Avengers*. Marv Wolfman wrote for the hit *Teen Titans* cartoon show and finished writing a *Crisis* novel containing a large amount of new material that fits into the original *Crisis* storyline (at press time it is due for April 2005 publication). Wolfman and Pérez together aren't finished either.

In 1987 they had started a lengthy New Teen Titans graphic novel, *Teen Titans: Game*, during their original run on the series. Due to a variety of circumstances, it was never finished. This year they announced they're getting together to finish

Teen Titans: Game, an original graphic novel began by Wolfman and Pérez in 1987, is being completed and should be scheduled soon.

Marge Henderson Buell's Little Lulu reaches two important milestones in 2005: the 70th anniversary of her first publication and the 60th anniversary of her first comic book. Gemstone Publishing's staff dug into publisher Robert Overstreet's vault to find these previously unseen cover concepts by famed Lulu writer/illustrator John Stanley.

From her first appearance in *The Saturday Evening Post* to the long-running HBO Family cartoon series, Little Lulu has been a dearly loved character for legions of fans spanning seven decades. Whether in single-panel gags, comic books, comic strips or on the small screen, Marge Henderson Buell's most famous creation has charmed fans since 1935.

Buell, a pioneering early female cartoonist, was a well-established illustrator when she created Little Lulu, a precocious (or exasperating) child who would stop at nothing to get what she wanted. The single-panel cartoons soon became one of the most popular features in the august publication, vaulting Lulu (and Buell) into a long-term national spokesperson role with Kleenex tissues.

The gag panels, even with their popularity, afforded little room for the characterization that was to so captivate the character's fans. Many of the best-loved elements were added when Buell licensed Little Lulu for cartoons and other products. She reportedly retained approval rights on most or all of the projects. The "other products" included comic books, of course.

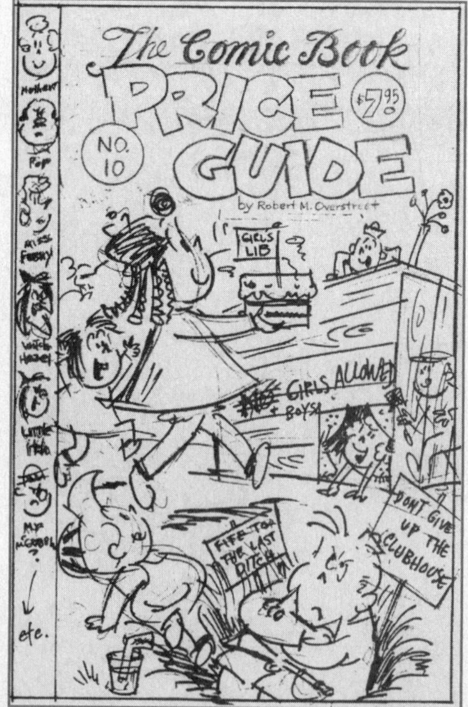

While the cover of one edition of The Official Overstreet Comic Book Price Guide #35 features a John Stanley recreation of Little Lulu, this concept art reveals one of three takes the legendary creator proposed to Guide author Robert Overstreet years ago.

John Stanley became the guiding force in Little Lulu's fictional life beginning with Dell's *Four Color* #74, the first issue featuring "Marge's Little Lulu" in 1945. Stanley wrote and illustrated the first adventures, and then was eventually joined by artist Irv Tripp.

In the long-lived Stanley/Tripp era, Stanley wrote the comic and provided layouts. Trip furnished the finished artwork. Whereas Stanley's solo efforts were distinctly reminiscent of Buell's own work, Tripp's influence presented Lulu and her supporting cast in a somewhat more cartoony style.

When Buell stopped drawing Lulu for *The Saturday Evening Post* in 1947, the little girl was really just getting started. The duo of Stanley and Tripp worked together for more than a decade, producing some of the most widely respected comics for children ever published.

Following the Lulu appearances in *Four Color* – 10 in all – *Marge's Little Lulu* became its own title and ran 268 issues (the latter 61 of them simply as *Little Lulu*), spawning the spin-off *Marge's Tubby*, as well as appearances in *Golden Comics Digest*,

Lulu at 70 (and 60)

by J.C. Vaughn

John Stanley's creative sensibilities are widely credited with giving Lulu and her supporting cast the characteristics generations of fans have come to know and love.

March of Comics and a few specials.

Although the comic would end in 1984, there are still new fans discovering Little Lulu every day. The cartoon show on HBO Family has featured the voices of actresses Tracey Ullman (in the early episodes) and Jane Woods (in the later ones) as Lulu in its 52 episodes since 1995. Another Rainbow presented a hardbound collection of the comics beginning in 1984, and in 2004 Dark Horse Comics began reprinting the entire series in 200-page, 6" x 9" trade paperback format.

The John Stanley-illustrated Little Lulu cover edition of The Overstreet Comic Book Price Guide #35 is available at comic book specialty stores.

"While I'm extremely glad we have these wonderful concept illustrations to look at, I'm saddened that John Stanley is no longer with us to carry them out," Overstreet said. "As comic book fans, though, we're fortunate that we can still enjoy his work."

Jack Kirby and Don Heck's cover for Tales of Suspense #39 introduced Iron Man to the world. With an Iron Man film in the works and a forty-two-year track record in comics – and with appearances in comics and video games – it seemed like an opportune time to figure out whether the clothes made the man just as the man had made the clothes. It also seemed like a great time to figure out what makes Iron Man cool.

Created by the Stan Lee, illustrated by Jack Kirby and Don Heck, Iron Man was the superhero guise of Tony Stark, a wealthy industrialist and weapons inventor who is captured by the enemy. In the original version it happened in southeast Asia during the conflict in Vietnam. Successive versions have tried to make that more ambiguous or more timely, based on world events. Regardless of when and where, Stark capitalized on his chances and created the Iron Man armor. For many years it actually kept him alive in addition to being his foremost weapon other than his own mind.

"What makes Iron Man so cool is that inside that awesome armored suit is a very complex character. Tony Stark is a genius, a billionaire, and a playboy. On the surface he's the guy we all envy, but – and there's always a 'but' in a Stan Lee creation – he's got all sort of problems," said Tim Rassbach, who launched www.ironmanarmory.com, one of the first Iron Man fan sites on the internet, in 1996.

"A very cool thing about most early Marvel characters was that Stan and company usually found a way to justify that hokiest of comic book conventionalisms, the costume," said former Marvel Comics Editor-in-Chief Jim Shooter. "Thor was wearing Asgardian street clothes. The Fantastic Four needed special 'unstable molecule' suits because of the nature of their powers. Spider-Man started out in show biz as a masked performer. Iron Man made the most sense of all. His 'costume' was the source of his power – and, I must say, if I were going off to battle Ultimo, the Mandarin, or even Paste-Pot Pete, I'd prefer to be wearing armor."

"Iron Man is cool because of the juxtaposition of a man with a weak heart, a frail condition being encased a walking iron lung that became a Cold War superhero," said artist John K. Snyder III, who

MAN:

HEAVY METAL

by J.C. Vaughn

recreated the cover of *Tales of Suspense* #39 as one of the covers for this edition of *The Official Overstreet Comic Book Price Guide*.

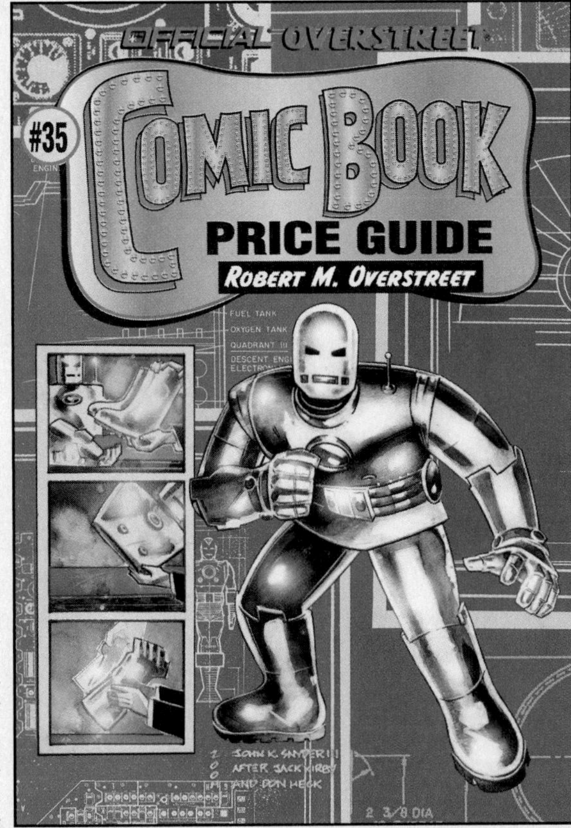

That March 1963 issue featured the first appearance of Iron Man and dropped readers into the world of brilliant inventor Tony Stark. He was someone who appeared to have everything – money, fame, power, an incredible intellect to go with his dashing and debonair appearance. Yet, as readers quickly discovered, there was always some downside to his life.

"Sure, he travels the world, inventing great things, romancing beautiful babes, and suits up and battles all manner of costumed villains in a fantastic battle suit as Iron Man, but his life is troubled," Rassbach said. "He can't get close to anyone for fear of them learning his secret. While his business mind and engineering acumen have brought him great wealth, he is forever fighting off covetous corporate raiders. And over the years he's had a number of major health problems, from his original bum heart to alcoholism to a disintegrating nervous system in later years. On top of all of that, many of his struggles are aggravated by his very role as Iron Man. Yet, if it wasn't for the armor, he'd be dead."

Ah, the armor. The clothes that make the man (and in this case, which were made by the man). Where Captain America has had the smallest of changes in more than six decades and other peers have had one or two alterations over the years, perhaps the only constants in the 42-year history of the character has been the changes in the armor. They started early and have continued since.

Iron Man's first clunky gray/silver armor, assembled on the fly under desperate conditions, quickly gave way to the same basic structure in gold in just his second appearance. The famous gold armor can been seen on the classic cover to *The*

Avengers #1, but by the equally famous image on the front of *The Avengers* #4, the first of his red-and-gold costumes can be seen. From that point, it's been a steady progression of designs. Some of them occurred as major story elements, some simply because an artist just wanted to draw something different. Some even had specialty functions, like the Stealth Armor, the Space Armor or the Hulk-Buster Armor.

The David Michelinie/John Romita, Jr./Bob Layton era of the original series featured a sustained component of specialty armors, and the Len Kaminski/Kevin Hopgood also had its own take. Sean Chen, who as artist kicked off the third volume of *Iron Man*, put a modern echo on the *Avengers* #4-era armor, while George Tuska, Gene Colan and other artists all put their stamp on the character's visual appearance. It is this fluidity that found unique life in Snyder's cover.

"I wanted to emphasize the Tin Woodsman/Iron Giant feel, the '50s/60s visual component of the character in the rendering, but through the blueprints in the background emphasize that Iron Man is an ever-evolving character, that he progresses as the technology progresses," he said.

A VERY BRIEF ARMOR CHECKLIST

First Tony Stark/Iron Man	Tales of Suspense #39
First Gold Armor	Tales of Suspense #40
First Red and Gold Armor	Tales of Suspense #48
First Bolted Mask	Tales of Suspense #54
First "Nose" Mask	Iron Man #68
New Armor / No Nose	Iron Man #85
First Space Armor	Iron Man #142
First Stealth Armor	Iron Man #152
New Red and Gold Armor	Iron Man #231
First War Machine Armor	Iron Man #281
Hulk-Buster Armor	Iron Man #304
First Prometheum Armor	Iron Man Vol. 2 #1
First "Heroes Return" Armor	Iron Man Vol. 3 #1
S.K.I.N. Armor	Iron Man Vol. 3 #44

The Tales of Suspense #39 re-creation cover edition of The Overstreet Comic Book Price Guide #35 is available at comic book specialty stores.

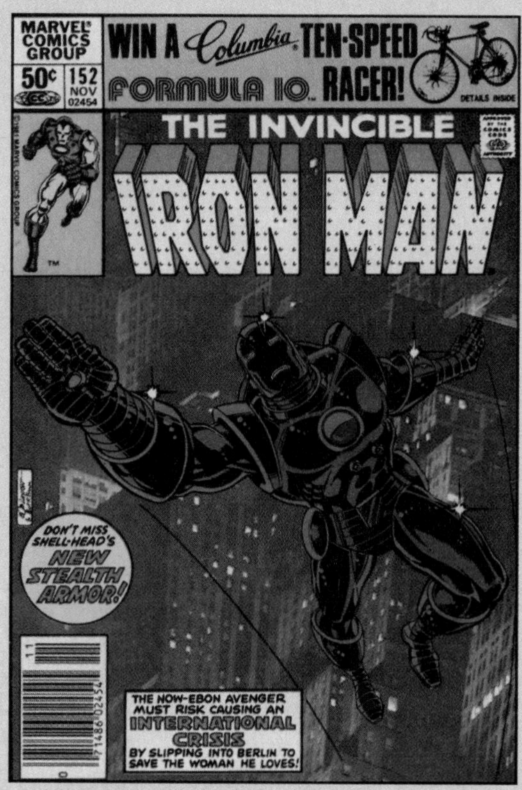

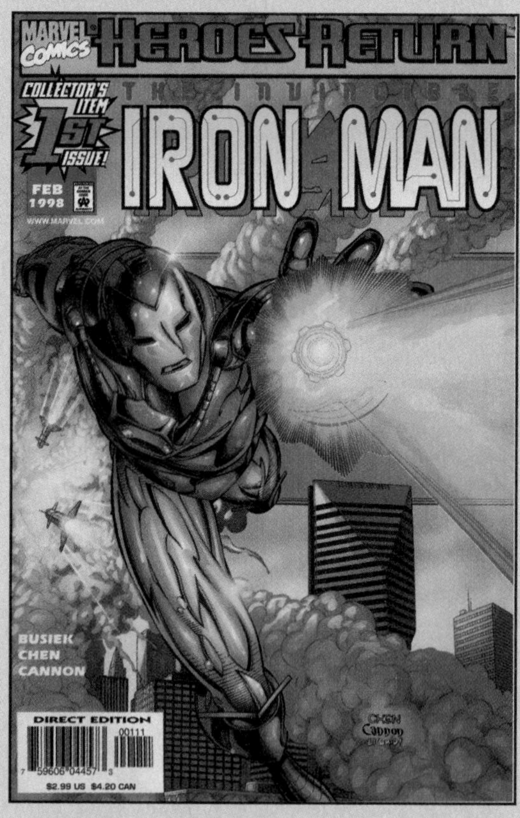

While the stories and concepts have been largely timeless, from the very beginning Iron Man's armor has conveyed a sense of style tied very closely to the era in which the illustration was done. Whether Bob Layton's Stealth armor (above, right), Sean Chen's modern-retro nod to the Avengers #4 era armor (right), the original clunky machine (two pages previous) or John K. Snyder III's recreation of same (previous page), the armor has always reflected its time.

COMICS IN THE SCHOOLS – 1926:

The Lost Comic Book History of THE LONE STAR STATE

by Weldon Adams

One of the biggest topics for comic book publishers in recent years has been the effort to get comics into schools. That doesn't mean kids bringing them to schools and taking a peak when the teacher's not looking. The goal today is getting them into official school curriculums and using them as tools to help teach and encourage reading. Just like they've been doing in Texas since 1926.

In terms of an educational model, the significance of Texas History Movies is difficult to overstate. Though collectors can rightly categorize its various editions as Platinum Age, Golden Age, Silver Age and Bronze Age comics, this series has an even more important standing. It was the very first comic book used as an officially issued classroom textbook. Likewise, it was part of a pioneering, corporately sponsored educational campaign revolving around comics used as textbooks. There has not been an education program like it since then, though don't expect that to be true much longer.

Just, as some fellow Texans would point out, remember who was first.

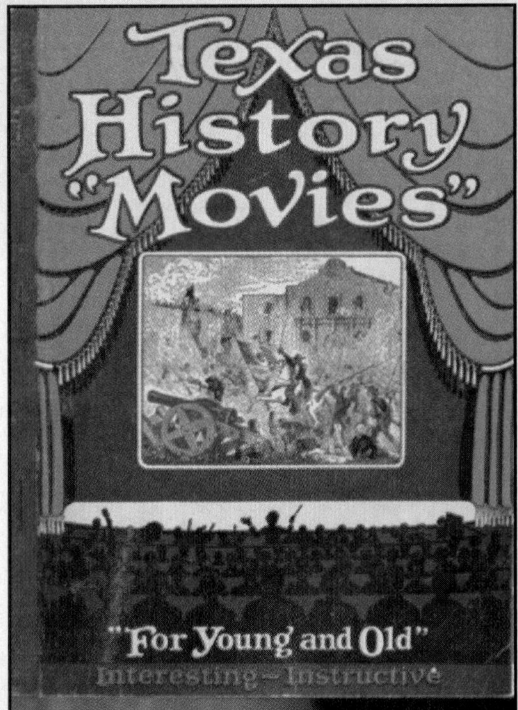

Kids have been getting into trouble for bringing comic books into classrooms since probably the creation of the first true comic book. In recent history, some teachers themselves have purposefully brought comic books to the classroom to use them as teaching aids. But the crossover of comic books to textbooks has a much stronger link and goes farther back than many suspected.

It was the fall of 1926, a time when newspaper comic strips were very popular. The Director of News & Telegraph for the *Dallas Morning News*, E.B. Doran, had an idea for a new comic strip. His concept was to tell the history of the state of Texas in daily comic strip form. He recruited staff artist Jack Patton to draw the series and staff writer John Rosenfield, Jr. to supply the text.

[Texas]

TEXAS—your state and ours— is at once a land of romance and of realization; of romance because of those sturdy pioneers who more than a century ago left the older sections of America to come into a new land, to brave the terrors and the dangers of a frontier to carve out of an uncharted wilderness the splendid empire we know as Texas today; of realization because of the vast progress that has been made since those first pioneers came, the natural resources that have been developed, the homes erected, the farms tilled, the factories built, the accumulation of the vast wealth of this state—the accomplishment of no less than a commercial miracle.

Prompted by a desire to be of service to the pupils of the public schools of Texas and to have some small part in helping impress upon them the remarkable past of their state, its today, and its future, offering unlimited opportunities to every person in Texas, the Magnolia Petroleum Company has had prepared and printed for distribution to the schools of Texas the booklet, "Texas History Movies."

The Magnolia Petroleum Company is itself a pioneer, for its immediate predecessors erected the first oil refinery in Texas at Corsicana in 1896 and the next in Beaumont in 1901.

So with a sincere hope that this booklet will be enjoyed by every pupil in Texas and that it may help impress them how truly wonderful Texas really is and how boundless is its future, we dedicate the "Texas History Movies" to them with every sincere good wish for each pupil in every public school of our great state.

Magnolia Petroleum Company
Producers — Refiners — Distributors
— *of* —
Magnolia Gasoline — Socony Motor Oils
DALLAS
Stations throughout the Southwest

SOMETHING TELLS ME THAT THIS IS THE LAST OF SPAIN IN MEXICO

WITHOUT A BATTLE BARRADOS SURRENDERED TO RETURN TO SPAIN WITH HIS TROOPS.

The series title, *Texas History Movies*, was given by Dr. J. F. Kimball, Superintendent of Schools in Dallas at the time. This shows there was an involvement with and consideration of the educational impact of the strip from the very beginning. And as misleading as the title may be by modern standards, at the time comic strips were sometimes referred to as 'movies in print'. This is a reference to the way that several panels in a row can look like single frames of a movie reel.

The series ran Monday through Saturday from October 5, 1926 until June 8, 1927. The strip took a summer break, but with the beginning of the next school year *Texas History Movies* was back in the paper from October 8, 1927 until the series ended on June 9, 1928. The break period coincided with summer break for public schools. It is evident that teachers were using this newspaper strip in the classrooms, and it perhaps corresponds that the strip never appeared in the Sunday editions of the paper.

These 428 strips chronicled the history of the state of Texas from the Spanish exploration of the New World in 1530 to Texas' reconstruction following the Civil War and on up through 1885. In the words of the creators, "Here the cartoons end abruptly, not because there was nothing else worth telling, but because the things that happened after that make dull pictures; albeit, fascinating reading."

In 1928, the P.L. Turner Company acquired the copyright from The *Dallas Morning News* and published a collection of the strips in a large hardback format. The hardcover volume of *Texas History Movies* measured 9 1/2 inches across and 12 1/2 inches tall. It collected all 428 strips and was 1/2 inch thick. The four panel strips were presented two on a page in a basic 9-panel grid. The top three panels and the first panel of the middle row were one strip. The center panel had the description line for both strips. And the last panel of the middle row started the second strip. The cover art featured the interior of a movie theatre showing a scene from the battle of the Alamo.

In that same year, the Magnolia Petroleum Company recognized the educational potential of the collection and sponsored a smaller digest size version with a cardstock cover. Reportedly, millions of copies of this version were distributed free of charge as a history textbook to students throughout the

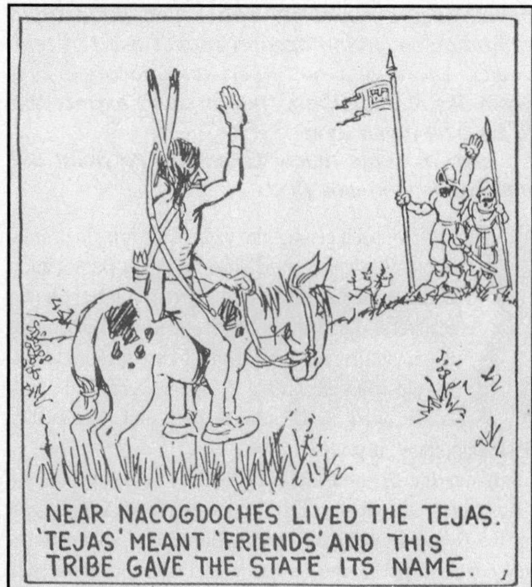
NEAR NACOGDOCHES LIVED THE TEJAS. 'TEJAS' MEANT 'FRIENDS' AND THIS TRIBE GAVE THE STATE ITS NAME.
1

state of Texas. This 5 1/4" by 7" version had only 64 pages with 124 strips, but sported the same "Movie Theatre" cover.

There is a second edition of this version that was produced some years later. The two versions are almost identical except for some minor differences. The second edition has a square-bound blue taped spine. The second edition is on a thinner paper stock also, so it is noticeably thinner than the first printing version.

The back cover is different also. The second edition has an ad featuring four round signs showing the various trade logos these companies were using at the time. But the biggest and most telling difference is that the interior of the second edition refers to both Mobilgas and Magnolia Petroleum as being "A Socony-Vacuum Company" (Socony was shorthand for Standard Oil Company of New York). The Socony Oil Company merged with the Vacuum Oil Company to form "Socony-Vacuum" in 1931. Therefore, this second edition could not have been printed before 1931. Therefore it seems likely that the second edition was published in 1932.

In 1935 Magnolia Petroleum once again sponsored bringing *Texas History Movies* back to the classrooms in a new horizontal format. Reprinted several times from 1935 to 1936, these horizontal versions had various covers. The first horizontal edition featured a covered wagon image on the primarily white cover. And there were at least two other covers featured on reprint editions. Both used a red and blue cover theme.

The horizontal editions were paperbacks that measured 9 inches wide by only 6 inches tall. However, there was also at least one 1935 hardcover horizontal edition. This had a green cover with the covered wagon art. The horizontal editions collect only 101 strips from the original 428, but have an additional 23 strips in a section titled "*Part Two* - The Industrial Development of Texas." These newly commissioned strips were by Jack Patton as well and have never appeared in any other editions of the book. The format for this edition was four panels across the top half of the page with the descriptive line underneath. The bottom half was a purely textual piece running approximately 160 words to the page for 125 pages. The credits for the text piece merely say "Text by One of the Foremost Historians of the State."

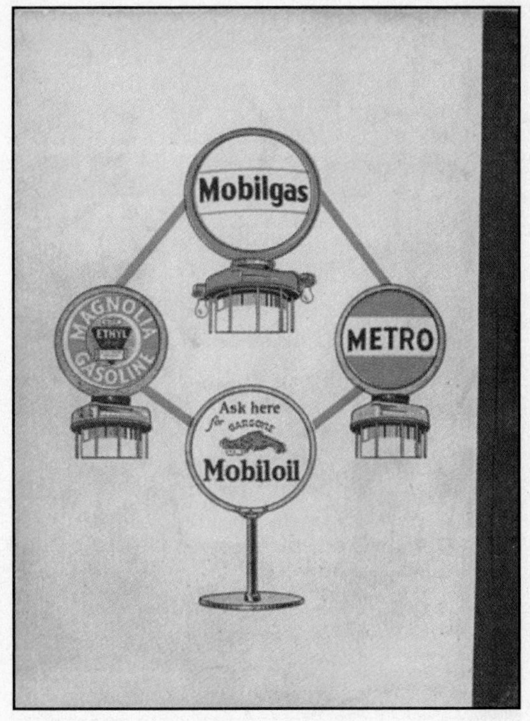

The Magnolia Petroleum Company itself has quite a bit of history in the state of Texas. One of its ancestor companies erected the first oil refinery in Texas at Corsicana in 1896, shortly after the period chronicled in *Texas History Movies* itself. Later known as Mobil Oil, their mascot of a red Pegasus became a familiar site in the Dallas skyline, and it was even included in the last panel in the expanded section of the 1935

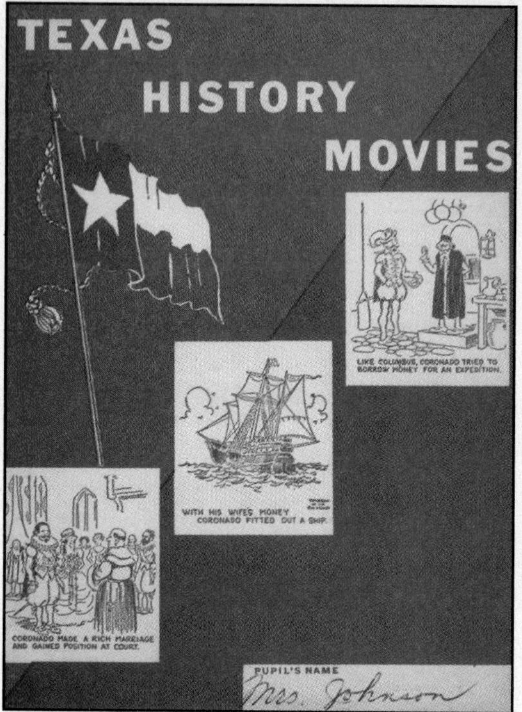

horizontal edition.

In 1936, there was a "Centennial Edition" of the large format book published by the Turner Company to celebrate the anniversary centennial of Texas becoming a Republic. The Centennial Edition has a solid blue hardback cover and this time included several text sections in the front of the book that are not presented in any other edition including the text section from the horizontal editions. Also included in the Centennial Edition were three Texas history plays by Jan Isbelle Fortune, "1685 - The Cavalier from France," "1716 - The Rose Window of San Jose," and "1744 - The Massacre at San Saba."

In 1943, Magnolia Petroleum sponsored a large size format edition of the work. This has an orange cover on the book itself and a red, white and blue dust jacket featuring a photo of the Alamo and seven individual panels from the series. The contents matched the 1928 P.L. Turner edition containing all 428 strips.

That same year, Magnolia Petroleum purchased the copyright to the booklet editions from The Turner Co. and again reprinted the horizontal editions and distributed them to schools throughout the state. The Turner Co., however, retained the publication rights to the larger hardback format books.

In 1954, while a Senate committee in Washington, D.C. was deciding that comic books were leading children to juvenile delinquency, the Texas school systems were reissuing a *Texas History Movies* reprint as a classroom textbook to school children throughout the state. This time the Magnolia Petroleum Company reverted to the digest paperback format measuring 5-1/2" wide by 7" tall. At 128 pages, this edition collects 248 of the newspaper strips running them two to a page just as the hardcover edition did. This edition stayed in print for several years and had various similar covers. At least one version, although noted as copyright 1956, has had the text in the last panel changed to read: "And Texas has reached the estate of 1959." This indicates that the book was still reprinted and used in classrooms until that time.

Each time Magnolia Petroleum changed the format of the work, it seemed to include more and more of the original 428 strips. However by 1961, it had become clear to the successors to Magnolia Petroleum, Socony-Mobil Oil Co., that some of the contents of the book had become quite controversial, as racial issues were a charged topic of those times. They did still recognize the historical value of the work, however. It was at this time that Socony-Mobil Oil Co. donated their copyright on the booklet editions to the Texas State Historical Association.

In 1963, The Turner Co. combined the larger *Texas History Movies* book with a volume of readings in Texas history by Dallas teacher/author Bertha Mae Cox. The edition, titled *Let's Read About Texas*, was soon out of print, however. It is not known if this edition was distributed as a textbook.

In 1970, The Turner Co. was acquired by Graphic Ideas, Inc. They hired Texas history teacher O.O. Mitchell, Jr. to contribute new text pieces to accompany 400 of the original strips in a new large format hardback edition. The cover of this edition noted creators Patton and Mitchell only, and it featured cover artwork of a strip of movie film across the bottom. It is not known if this edition was distributed as a textbook.

In 1974, the *Houston Chronicle* approached the Texas State Historical Association about reprinting *Texas History Movies* as part of an educational program. The TSHA put together a board of advisors to examine the work. Anything that the board deemed offensive in the artwork or text was deleted, altered, or newly created work was substituted. Some panels were presented out of order with new text which completely changed the original meaning. Individual panels and at least two entire strips were substituted by an artist not nearly as talented as Mr. Patton. The booklet the TSHA produced was titled *Texas History Illustrated* and they published 100,000 copies. This edition had only 55 pages and reproduced the equivalent of only 102 strips. These strips were mainly taken from the 1935 editions. It is evident that they merely reprinted the format of the 1935 edition at two original pages per page of the new volume.

In 1986 the TSHA again republished their work, but this time they reverted to the series original title, *Texas History Movies*. This edition had a red and white cover with one panel from the series featuring Travis at the Alamo.

Also in 1986, in celebration of the Texas Sesquicentennial, Spaulding E. Jones and Pepper Jones Martinez reprinted the original 1928 large format book with all 428 strips. There was an exact replica of the 1928 original hardcover edition and a limited edition exact replica version as well. The limited edition version was offered at $250.00 per copy. These large format books were not used in classrooms as they were intended only for historical reference.

At this time, Pepper Jones Martinez, Inc. also published a new horizontal version of the book. Utilizing a staff of ten prominent Texas historians and advisors, they attempted to revise the work by making it "more accurate historically and more relevant to today's attitudes and values." Like the TSHA attempt to sanitize the work before them, PJM and their board cut the strips up, rearranged them and sometimes redrew panels and one entire strip. They did, however try to keep it to a minimum. The three noted art changes include: a drawing of a Mexican Governor, unlucky at love, kicking a cat that had been altered to show him kicking a soldier's helmet instead, two new panels concerning Santa Anna's destruction of Gail Borden's newspaper press as he stormed through the capitol at Harrisburg, and several new panels concerning the legend of Emily Morgan, the "Yellow Rose of Texas." The PJM board primarily chose to simply leave out offending or non-crucial panels and strips. Sometimes four panels from four different strips were combined to create a more succinct passage, but the spirit of the original artwork was still intact. This edition of the book has 153 pages and more or less reprints 152 of the original 428 strips.

The 1986 PJM large hardback and long-digest format reprint book garnered publicity in many newspapers and magazines in Texas. And it apparently made friends in unusual places. Several copies of the long-digest format have been seen with a "Complements of Hochheim Prairie Insurance Companies" sticker on the inside fly page and back covers. It is evident that this company was using the PJM version as a premium or gift for signing up.

Given the number of clients that a statewide insurance company must have and the finite number of copies of the 1986 edition print run, it is obvious that they would one day run out. The book must have been a useful premium for the company because in 1996 they created and published their own version of a cartoon history of the state in an almost exact format. Published in 1996 by Heritage Publishing in Dallas *Texas Cultural Heritage - An Illustrated History* was an original work commissioned and produced for Hochheim Prairie Insurance Companies. A three-page introduction tells an interesting story of the creation of the Hochheim Prairie Insurance Company. And a two-page foreword by publisher Rod Dockery goes to great lengths to explain the ethnic diversity necessary to the creation of the state. The artwork in this book is by Raul Castro. While not as talented as Jack Patton, it is obvious that Castro was doing his best to emulate the look and feel of the previous work while still being an original presentation. All in all, a worthwhile effort and much superior than the new artwork created for the TSHA edition. The text sections for this book were written by Caleb Pirtle III and are very good. His closing remarks include this phrase: "They irrigated the land with their blood and their sweat. When adversity confronted them, they were too determined to run, too stubborn to quit." That captures the spirit of the Texas founding fathers very well.

Overall, *Texas History Movies* presented the history of Texas in a fun, exciting and informative manner. The artwork

itself is some of the best of the time. Expressive and detailed, it is capable of ranging from slapstick to serious in only four panels daily. To make the work resonate with 1926 audiences, the creators purposefully used then-current slang and colloquialisms. For example, one strip features a covered wagon heading to Texas (then known as New Phillipenas) with "*New Phillipenas or Bust*" scrawled on the side. In the original introduction to the hardcover edition, creators Patton and Rosenfield wrote, "The authors of the series directed every effort to keeping the stories humorous, human, vivid and real."

Due to the proclivities of the time during which the work was published however, it is not as politically correct of a historical presentation as is taught in schools today. It is important to note that the work does not make any specific group of people out to be evil, lazy or stupid. Although there are specific instances that depict Negro slaves, Mexicans, and American Indians in a harsh light, there are also many more instances that depict Anglos and even Texas' founding fathers just as harshly.

In the introduction to the 1970 large format reprint edition, Mr. Mitchell had this to say:

"Names out of the past become active, living people with problems, pride, pain and susceptibility to mistakes which make men of all ages brothers. Though Texas heroes are often portrayed bigger than life, *Texas History Movies* also shows them to be quite human in their reactions to events in their day-to-day lives—and not always too heroic in their decisions."

In the daily series, one strip notes Jim Bowie's character as being peaceful, sociable, generous with his friends and brave. The very next day reports he traded with pirates at Galveston, bought slaves and smuggled them into Louisiana,

and used his wife's position as daughter of the Lt. Governor of Texas and Coahuila to his financial advantage. Although satirical and humorous, the series was fair and honest at the same time. And Texas has always been a land proud of its history and heritage, warts and all.

It is interesting to note that both the Centennial edition and the Sesquicentennial editions of the book celebrated Texas becoming an independent republic in 1836. Indeed in 1986 the Texas Sesquicentennial was a statewide event. However, nine years later, the 150th anniversary of Texas becoming a State of the Union passed with hardly a ripple.

Texas History Movies was used in classrooms every few years from 1928 until 1959. In 1963, 1974 and 1986 it showed up in classrooms again, although as a reference book and not issued as a textbook. And the collected works were reprinted to help celebrate both the Texas Republic Centennial and Sesquicentennial.

Those educated in Texas schools with the work remember it fondly. Famed editorial cartoonist Ben Sargent of *Austin Statesman* credits the book as having an influence on his interest in Texas history and cartooning as well. Cartoonist and comic book writer Michael H. Price credits his introduction to *Texas History Movies* in the 1950s school system of Amarillo as being crucial to his learning to cartoon in the first place, and underground creator Jack Jackson readily admits that it's easy to see the influences of the series in his *The Secret of San Saba*.

Collecting *Texas History Movies* books is both challenging and rewarding. The pre-1943 editions all have a combination of events that severely limit the number of books that have survived to the next century. They were (primarily) soft cover books that were issued into the care of school children. In addition, these editions had to survive the paper drives of WWII. The post-1943 editions up through 1959 still have the problem of being soft cover books issued to school children, with wear and tear of entire school years on them, so getting them in top condition is always a challenge.

Another difficulty for collectors is the original one-state-only distribution of these books. While the 1986 editions are fairly plentiful, finding any of the others is difficult even in Texas. Out of state, it used to be basically impossible, though eBay has improved the odds slightly.

Serious enthusiasts will likely find the long-digest format of 1935/1943 and the standard digests from the 1950s to be the most desirable. This is because the long-digest format contains an additional 23 strips that have never been reprinted in any other editions. The 1950's editions contain 248 of the original 428 strips. Although the 1950's editions are slightly more plentiful, they contain twice as many strips. To have a copy of all 451 individual strips, a collector would have to have a copy of one of the large hardback editions *and* one of the long-digest formats.

All in all, this work is of great historical value not just for recognizing comic strips as an educational media, but also as a wonderful window into both Texas history and the history of education in the state of Texas.

Weldon Adams, who recently became an Overstreet Advisor, is a native Texan and nearly life-long comic book collector. He has worked in the retail, distribution, manufacturing, production and marketing ends of the business.

TIMELINE

1926	Original comic strips begin appearing in the *Dallas Morning News*
1928	Series ended it run as a newspaper strip.
1928	Original Hardcover edition
1928	64 Pg. Digest format. "Movie Theater" cover Saddle stitched/taped.
1932	Pg. Digest format. "Movie Theatre" cover (c. 1932) Hardback horizontal edition w/ green cover. Standard Horizontal edition contents w/ green "Covered Wagon" cover
1935	Paperback horizontal edition w/ white "Covered Wagon" cover
	Paperback horizontal edition w/ Red & Blue "2 Panel + Flag" cover "Centennial Edition" in honor of Texas Republic Centennial. (Includes text sections appearing nowhere else; Dust jacket features 7 individual panels and photo of Alamo.)
1943	Paperback horizontal edition w/ Red & Blue "2 Panel + Flag" cover
1954	Digest sized paperback.
1956	Digest sized paperback.
1974	Texas History Illustrated
1986	Replica Edition of original 1928 hardcover edition.

COMIC BOOK CERTIFICATION: AN OVERVIEW OF COMICS GUARANTY, LLC

by Steve Borock

Comics Guaranty, LLC (CGC) opened for business in January of 2000 and quickly became an integral part of the way buyers and sellers do business; this is particularly true of internet transactions. CGC is an expert and impartial third-party grading service, one of three independent companies operating under the umbrella of the Certified Collectibles Group, LLC (CCG). As with the other CCG companies, Numismatic Guaranty Corporation (NGC) and Sportscard Guaranty, LLC (SGC), CGC employs the brightest and most ethical individuals in the comics field. These are persons fully qualified to grade comics while checking for authenticity and detecting restoration that can affect a book's value. This critical information is defined on the CGC label, which is then encapsulated in CGC's inner well along with the book. Such a level of protection, and the confidence it affords to both buyer and seller, have long since revolutionized the coin and card fields. Now, with the establishment of CGC, this protection is available to the comic book and magazine enthusiast.

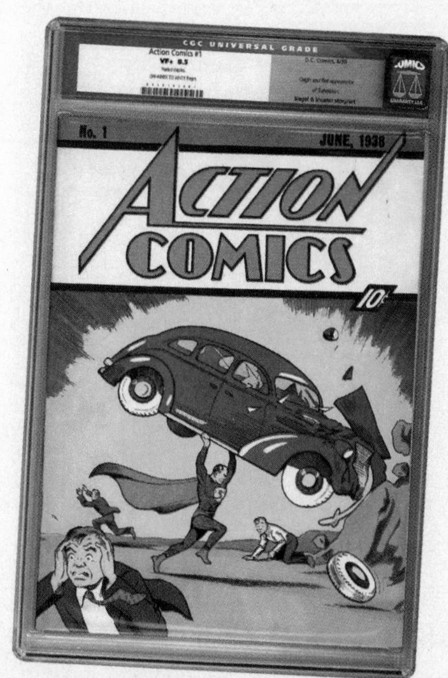

Initially, the CGC principals consulted many of the most respected individuals in our hobby, and based on their recommendations they selected the initial team of graders. Once the core grading team was in place, CGC began the development of its revolutionary tamper-evident holder. This proved to be quite a technical challenge - many designs were rejected before the perfect combination of materials and design was found. A significant amount of time, energy and capital went into perfecting our current holder.

No less challenging was the establishment of a uniform grad-

ing standard that would meet the expectations of knowledgeable buyers and sellers. While everyone seemed to agree that the Overstreet reference was the foundation of this standard, there were a number of subjective interpretations of its published definitions. CGC understood from our inception that this was just a starting point; it was still necessary to take a consensus from the day-to-day experience of the nation's top dealers and collectors. This was achieved by inviting 50 of the hobby's top experts to undertake a grueling, hours long grading test. From this, CGC developed a median standard that reflects the collective knowledge of these prominent figures.

Many thousands of comics and magazines are submitted each month to CGC by persons who have confidence in our consistency and integrity as a grading service. It's likely that little thought is given by these submitters to the exact process by which their comics are graded and encapsulated, since they're pleased with the value received. In actual fact, the process involves numerous steps within several specialized departments, all of which have as their ultimate role the expeditious processing of a "raw" (uncertified) comic into one which is accurately graded and sonically sealed inside a CGC holder. It's quite a team effort, and you're invited to follow along as we trace the progress of a comic through the process of certification at CGC.

SUBMITTING COMICS TO CGC

Typically, comics received by CGC are submitted through one of our authorized member-dealers, each of whom has passed a thorough background check by CGC's Accounting and Customer Service departments. This ensures that a customer's comic is in reliable hands when it's being prepared for shipment to CGC's offices in Florida. The value of such a precaution is self-evident, but it also relieves the collector or investor from having to provide personal and financial information which he or she may wish to keep confidential. Another option for individuals who wish to submit comics directly to CGC is to become a member of the Certified Collectors Society. Such membership provides for direct submission to any one of the three companies comprising the Certified Collectibles Group, as well as offering numerous other benefits.

Pre-printed submission invoices are provided to all of CGC's authorized member-dealers. The member-dealer who handles a customer's submission keeps the bottom copy of each invoice as a record of the comics being sent to CGC. Included on the invoice is the submitter's declaration of each book's value. This is important information to have in the unlikely event of a package being lost while in transit. Comics are typically sent to CGC's offices by registered post or through an insured express company.

THE COMICS ARE RECEIVED

CGC's Receiving Department opens the newly arrived packages each morning and immediately verifies that the number of books in each package matches the number shown on the invoice. Once this is done, a more detailed comparison is made to ensure that their invoice descriptions correspond to the actual comics. This information is entered into a computer, and the comics will henceforth be traceable at all stages of the grading process by their invoice number and their line number within that invoice. Each book is placed within protective Mylar that has affixed to it a label bearing the invoice and line item numbers, information which is duplicated on the label in a bar-coded inscription for quick reading by the computer. Before any grading is performed, each book is examined by CGC's Restoration Detection Expert. If any form of restoration work is detected, he enters this information into the computer so that it will be available to the grading team.

THE GRADING PROCESS

After being examined by the Restoration Detection Expert, a book then passes to a pre-grader, who counts the number of pages and enters into the computer any peculiarities or flaws that may affect grading. Some examples of this would be "a tear on third page," "a corner crease – does not break color," "a 1/2 inch spine split," and so forth. He then enters this information, if necessary, into the "Graders Notes" field and assigns his grading opinion. When the next grader examines the comic, he is not able to see the first person's assigned grade, so as to not influence his own evaluation. After determining his own grade for the comic, he can then view the "Graders Notes" entered by the previous grader, and he may add to this commentary if he believes more remarks are in order. This same process is repeated as the comic passes to the Grading Finalizer. He makes a final restoration check before determining his own grade, at which time he then reviews the grades and notes entered by the previous graders. If all grades are in agreement or are very close, he will then assign the book's final grade. The comic is then forwarded to the Encapsulation Department for sealing. If there is disagreement among the graders, a discussion will ensue until a final determination is made and the book forwarded.

ENCAPSULATING THE COMICS

After each comic has been graded and the necessary numbers and text entered into their respective data fields, all the comics on a particular invoice are taken from the Grading Department into the Encapsulation Department. Here, appropriately color-coded labels are printed out bearing the appropriate descriptive text, including each book's grade and identification number. This last item is extremely important, as it serves to make each certified comic unique and is also an important deterrent to the counterfeiting of CGC's valued product. All of the above information is duplicated in a bar code, which appears underneath the written text on the comic's label.

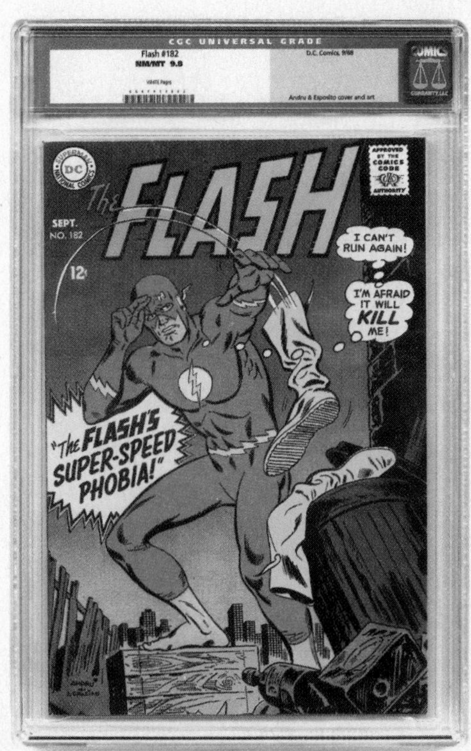

The newly-printed labels are stacked in the same sequence as the comics to be encapsulated with them, ensuring that each book and its label match one another. The comic is now ready to be fitted inside an archival-quality interior

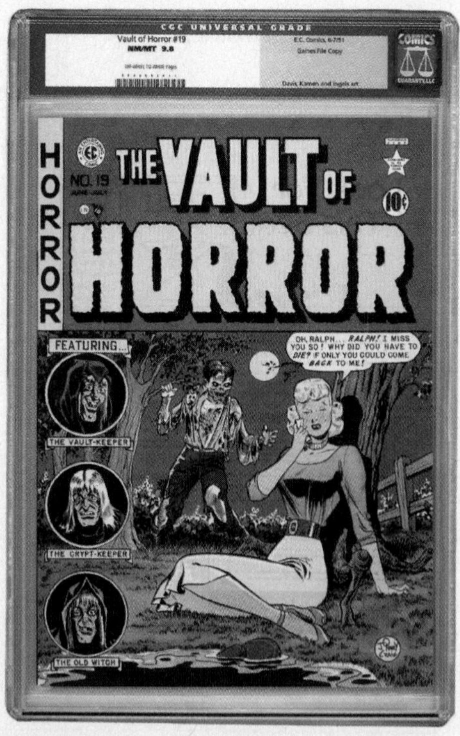

well, which is then sealed within a transparent capsule, along with the book's color-coded label. This is accomplished through a combination of compression and ultrasonic vibration. The result is a newly-encapsulated CGC comic, ready to be shipped to its proud owner.

THE COMICS ARE SHIPPED

After encapsulation, all comics are returned briefly to the Grading Department for a quality control inspection. Here, they are examined to make certain that their labels are correct for both the grade and its accompanying descriptive information. The quality control person also inspects each book for any flaws in its holder, such as scuffs or nicks. While these are quite rare, CGC is careful to make certain that the comics it certifies are not only accurately graded but attractively presented as well.

When all the comics have been inspected, they're either held in CGC's vault for in-person pick-up by the submitter or delivered to our Shipping Department for packaging. As in all steps of the grading process, the comics are counted and their labels checked against the original hand-written or typed invoice to make certain that no mistakes have occurred. A Shipping Department employee then verifies the method of transport as selected by the submitter on the invoice and prepares the comics for delivery.

No matter whether the U. S. Postal Service or some private carrier is used, the method of packaging is essentially the same. The encapsulated comics are placed vertically inside boxes made of very sturdy cardboard, and these boxes contain a row of dividers so that the capsules don't come into contact with one another. A shipping copy of the submitter's invoice is included before the box is sealed and heavy tape is used to prevent accidental or unauthorized opening of the box while it's in transit.

THE CGC LABEL

Comic books certified by CGC bear color-coded labels that have different meanings. Whenever purchasing a CGC-certified comic, be certain to note not just the book's grade but also its label category. A Universal label is denoted by the color blue and indicates that a book was not found to have any qualifying defects or signs of restoration. The above description also applies to CGC's red Modern label, now discontinued. There is one exception to this policy: At CGC's discretion, comics having a very minor amount of glue and/or color touch-up may still qualify for a Universal label provided that they were from 1950 or earlier and that such restoration is noted underneath the assigned grade.

As its name implies, the Restored label, identified by the color purple, is used for books found to have restoration work performed on them. The grade assigned is based on the book's appearance, with the restoration noted. A distinction is made between Amateur and Professional restoration, this judgment being based on the materials used. Since the degree of work performed is also significant with restored books, there are a total of seven possible descriptions under the Restored label. Each description is prefaced with the word Apparent, followed by Slight, Moderate or Extensive in combination with the final descriptors Amateur or Professional. Examples of Restored labels might read Apparent Moderate Professional or Apparent Slight Amateur, both descriptions then being followed by the book's grade. Finally, comics which have had no restoration other than a trimming of their covers or edges are labeled as simply Apparent, followed by their grade.

The Qualified label is green, and this indicates that one qualifying defect is present on a book. An example of such a qualifying feature would be a missing Marvel Value Stamp that does not affect the story. While such a book technically may grade Fair 1.0, it may appear to grade Near Mint+ 9.6. In such instances, assigning a grade of just 1.0 does not fully represent the value of the comic to a collector. Through use of the green Qualified label, a comic buyer is able to make an informed decision as to what he is purchasing in terms of its overall desirability. Because of the complexity involved, green labels are assigned quite seldom and then only when considered absolutely necessary. In addition, comic books that have a signature and that do not fall under the Signature Series label get the Qualified label. This is the most common use for the Qualified label. This shows what the grade of the book would have been if the signature was not present.

CGC's Signature Series label is yellow, and this is used when CGC's policy of determining that a signature is authentic has been met. The yellow label includes the grade before a comic was signed, who signed it, and when it was signed. If appropriate and when known, a Signature Series label may state at which venue a book was signed.

In October, 2003 CGC began to certify comic book related magazines. The certification process and label system for magazines is exactly the same as for comic books. Some examples of the comic book related magazines CGC certifies are *MAD Magazine, Vampirella, Creepy, Eerie* and *Famous Monsters of Filmland.*

COMPLETE CENSUS OF CERTIFIED BOOKS

CGC also offers the CGC Census on the CGC website. The census is a full listing of all comic books and magazines certified by CGC along with the grade awarded and label type. Any comic book enthusiast will have a lot of fun going through this free information to find out how rare their comic books are in relation to other certified copies.

A PROVEN STANDARD OF INTEGRITY

CGC employees are not allowed to engage in the commercial buying or selling of comics. In this way, CGC can remain completely impartial, having no vested interest other than a devotion to serving clients through accurate and consistent grading.

For more information on comic book certification and CGC's many services, please visit our website at www.CGCcomics.com.

PUBLISHER SPOTLIGHT:

In 1986, Dark Horse Comics launched its first title, *Dark Horse Presents*. The anthology title would go on to become a force in comics entertainment for more than a decade, but more importantly, its success spawned a line of comic books and other products that in many ways reflects the diversity of the marketplace. With single-issue comic books, collected editions, posters, lithographs, lunch boxes, action figures, PVC figures, statues, cigarette lighters, coasters, and poker sets, the company has firmly set itself in the big picture world of popular culture, and they're working to expose more readers to comics.

Last year, Pulitzer Prize winner Michael Chabon partnered with the company to produce comic books based on the characters in his best-selling novel *The Amazing Adventures of Kavalier and Clay*, and this year sees the release of the Frank Miller/Robert Rodriguez film collaboration based on Miller's *Sin City* comics.

Between 1986 and those events, Dark Horse grew itself from an upstart to a fixture in the marketplace with strong insights into creator rights, manga, the back-and-forth relationship between comics and film, and even team-ups.

Creator Rights

"Dark Horse was instrumental in setting the modern industry standard for creator's rights," said Mike Richardson, Publisher of Dark Horse Comics. "While publishers such as Mike Fredrick's Star Reach had published creator-owned work previously, we were the first company to actually pay them industry rates at the same time. This practice allowed creators to actually make a living while working for 'independents.' As a result, Frank Miller's defection in 1990 started a trend that began with the major mainstream talent and ended up with the new superstars leaving the 'Big Two.' I know of the cause and effect because I was in the middle of both movements."

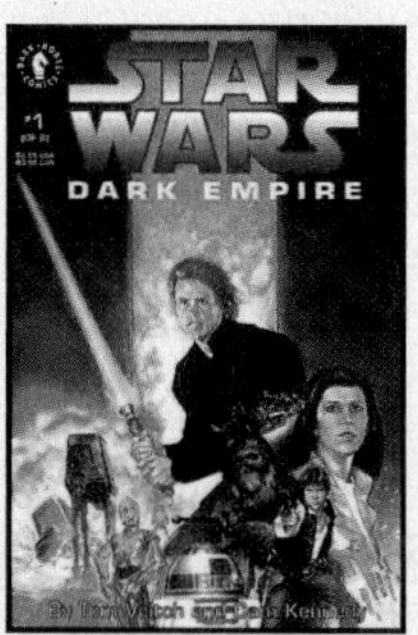

Richardson said that as a result, Marvel and DC were forced to rethink their creator contracts and change many of their practices, and he points to the benefits associated with exclusive contracts both companies now offer selected creators in order to keep their talent.

As a result, Dark Horse has published a virtual 'Hall of Fame' list of creators, including Will Eisner, Jack Kirby, Harvey Kurtzman, Frank Miller, Steve Ditko, Russ Manning, Al Williamson, Mike Mignolia, Barry Smith, Peter Bagge, Paul Chadwick, Dave Stevens, Joe Kubert, Bill Elder, Adam Hughes, Art Adams, John Byrne, Doug Wildey, H. R. Giger, Walt Simonson, Burne Hogarth, Olivia, Schuiten, Frank Frazetta, Dave Gibbons, Matt Wagner, Irving Tripp, John Bolton, Tardi, Brian Bolland, Druillet, Matt Wagner, Moebius, Otomo, John Stanley, Koike, Chris Claremont, Michael Chabon, Mike Kaluta, Mac Raboy, Steve Rude, Geof Darrow, Dan Barry, Gene Colan, Osamu Tezuka, Billy Tucci, and many others.

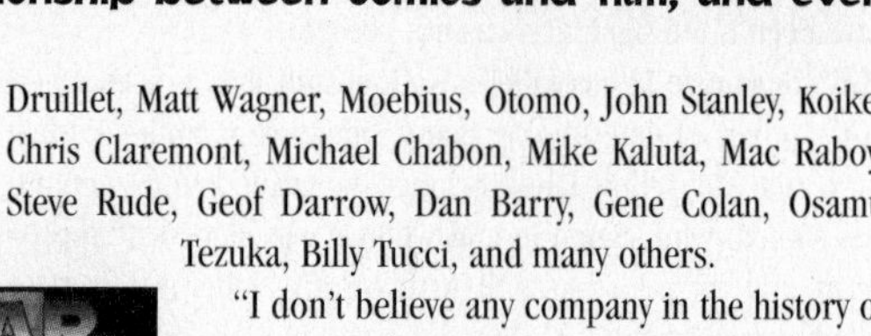

"I don't believe any company in the history of comics has a better pedigree than Dark Horse," Richardson said.

Manga In America

Many different comics companies have published reprinted or repackaged Japanese comics, manga, in the United States. Eclipse, Marvel, DC, and others have published at least some manga titles, but Dark Horse began a dedicated manga line in 1987 which continues to this day.

"I have, over the last seventeen years, made continual trips to Japan to solidify our relationship with the major Japanese talent," Richardson said. "No other company in this country has the track record of titles and talent from Japan that Dark Horse has. I would point to Otomo's *Akira*, Shirow's *Ghost In the Shell*, Koike's *Lone Wolf & Cub*, and Nightow's *Trigun*, just to name a few. Long after the current manga craze is over, we will be publishing, and succeeding, with the best manga."

Film, Television & Comics

Much the way that many filmgoers don't know that Marvel's *Blade* comes from the pages of *Tomb of Dracula*,

DARK HORSE COMICS

by J.C. Vaughn

many don't know the comic book origins of Jim Carrey's breakout hit, *The Mask*. This hasn't slowed the company down though. Dark Horse has transformed a significant number of its comic titles into films and other media. The company has set up 49 film and television projects in the last eleven years, and actually produced 15 of them. Likewise, Richardson said, Dark Horse has also done well going the opposite directions, with comics properties that started out as films or television programs, such as *Star Wars*, *Aliens*, *Predator*, *Terminator*, *Buffy The Vampire Slayer*, *Angel*, and others.

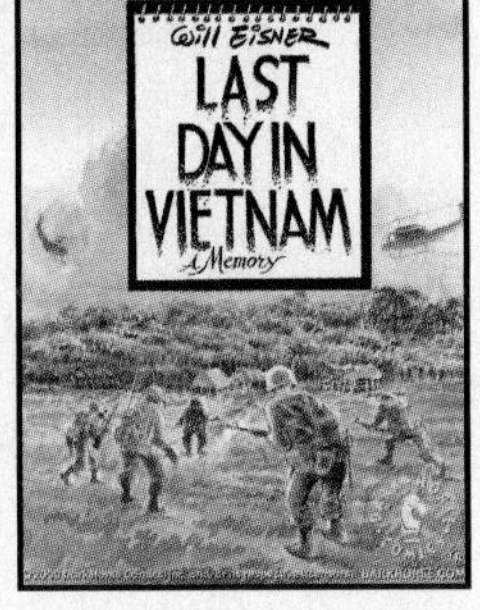

"The comic series based on the *Aliens* motion picture changed movie comics forever," Richardson said. "Rather than relying on the movie logo on the cover to sell copies, or resorting to an adaptation of the movie, Dark Horse created a movie sequel in comic book form. The approach resulted in the hottest comic of the year. Dark Horse followed this success with series based on *Predator*, *Terminator*, and the smash hit, *Aliens Versus Predator*. Compare movie-based comics before and after *Aliens*; the change is dramatic. *Aliens* was the reason."

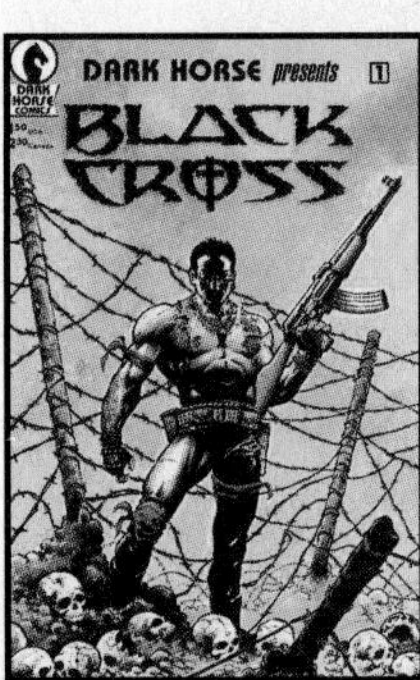

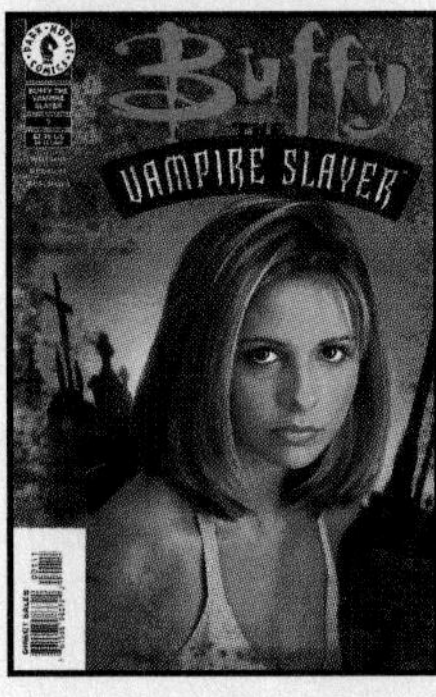

Team-Ups

In addition to teaming up their own characters or licensed properties, Dark Horse has also become known for crossovers with other companies, particularly its semi-regular ventures with DC. *Superman vs. Aliens* and *Batman vs. Predator*, for instance, scored critically in addition to selling well. They've teamed the Mask and the Joker, pitted Robocop against Terminator, and set Magnus Robot Fighter against Predator, just to name a few.

"Has any company in history published another company's characters on a regular basis?" Richardson asked.

Mike Richardson's Brief Dark Horse Timeline

1986 Dark Horse Comics' initial publication, *Dark Horse Presents*, hits comic shops in July. The comic, featuring Paul Chadwick's *Concrete*, is a hit, selling over 50,000 copies. The new company revolutionizes creator rights by not only allowing creators to retain copyright on their work, but earn page rates comparable to Marvel's and DC's at the same time.

1988 Dark Horse re-invents "movie comics" by creating a sequel to the *Aliens* motion picture. The series sells millions and licensed comics will never be the same.

1990 Dark Horse launches *Aliens Versus Predator*, the most successful licensed comic series in the history of the Direct Market.

1990 Frank Miller and Geof Darrow reject offers from Marvel and DC and bring *Hard Boiled* to Dark Horse. Miller, with Dave Gibbons, also brings Dark Horse *Give Me Liberty*. It is the first time major creators have turned down the "Big Two" in favor of an "Independent." The success of these two series leads to the migration of top talent – John Byrne, Walt Simonson, Chris Claremont, Mike Mignola – away from the majors and lays the foundation for other independent imprints such as Image.

1991 Frank Miller begins *Sin City*.

1992 Dark Horse is able to secure the comic book rights to *Star Wars* from Lucasfilm. The company's first series, *Dark Empire*, by Tom Veitch and Cam Kennedy, is a smash hit.

1993 Mike Mignola begins *Hellboy*.

1994 Two Dark Horse properties turned to film, *The Mask* and *TimeCop*, finish number one at the box office.

2000 Dark Horse begins publishing the complete *Lone Wolf and Cub*, by Kazuo Koike and Goseki Kojima. The series runs over 8,000 pages and is published in twenty-eight monthly volumes. The publisher's experimental price and format help create excitement and an industry best seller.

2004 Dark Horse begins publishing *The Escapist*, taken from the pages of Michael Chabon's Pulitzer Prize-winning novel, *The Amazing Adventures of Kavalier and Clay*. The *Hellboy* movie opens at number one at the box office.

BATMAN AND ROBIN
IN THE CHEETAH CAPER
BLB #2031 - 1969. © DC

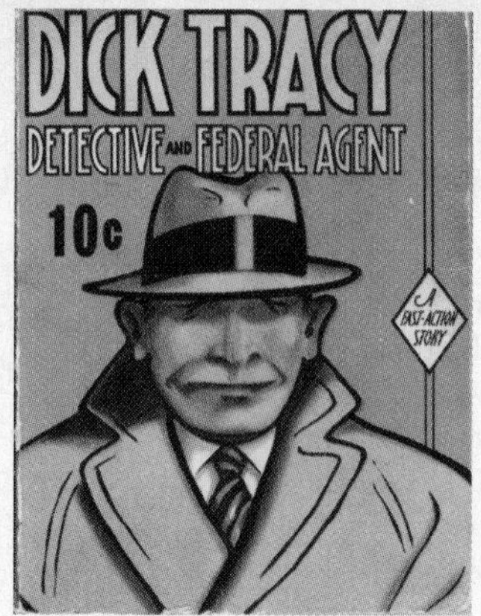

DICK TRACY DETECTIVE AND
FEDERAL AGENT
BLB #6833 - 1936. © NYNS

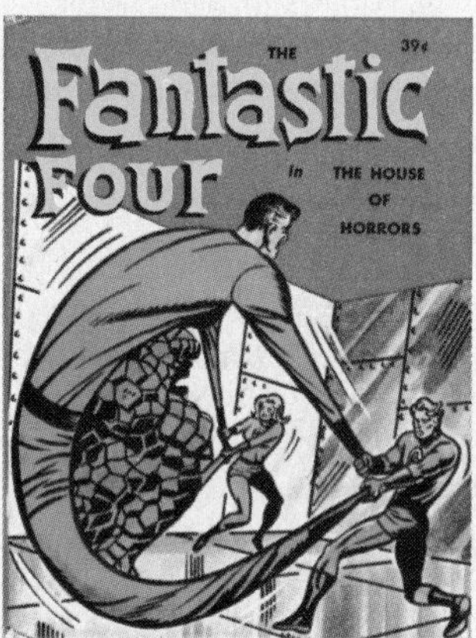

FANTASTIC FOUR IN THE
HOUSE OF HORRORS
BLB #2019 - 1968. © MAR

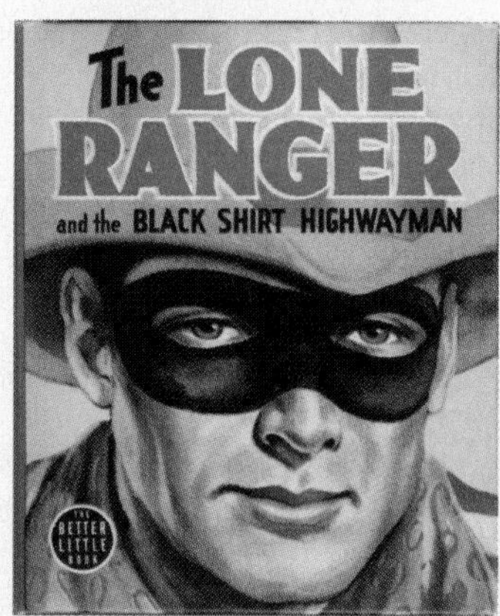

THE LONE RANGER AND THE
BLACK SHIRT HIGHWAYMAN
BLB #1450 - 1939. © Lone Ranger, Inc.

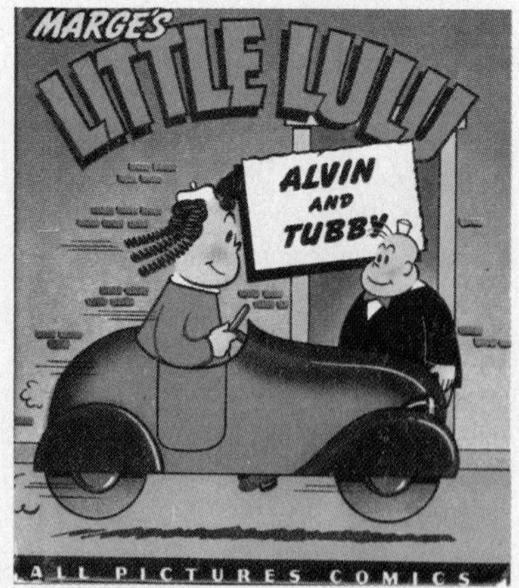

MARGE'S LITTLE LULU
ALVIN AND TUBBY
BLB #1429 - 1947. © Marjorie Buell

BIG LITTLE MOTHER GOOSE
BLB #725 - 1934. © WHIT

LITTLE ORPHAN ANNIE AND HER BIG LITTLE KIT
BLB #3048 - 1937. © WHIT

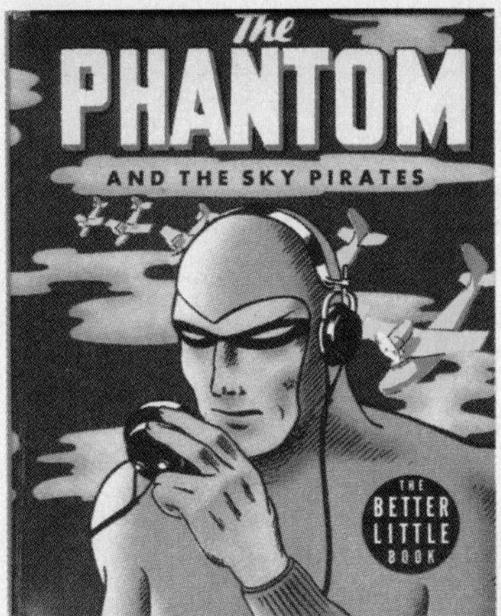

THE PHANTOM AND THE SKY PIRATES
BLB #1468 - 1945. © WHIT

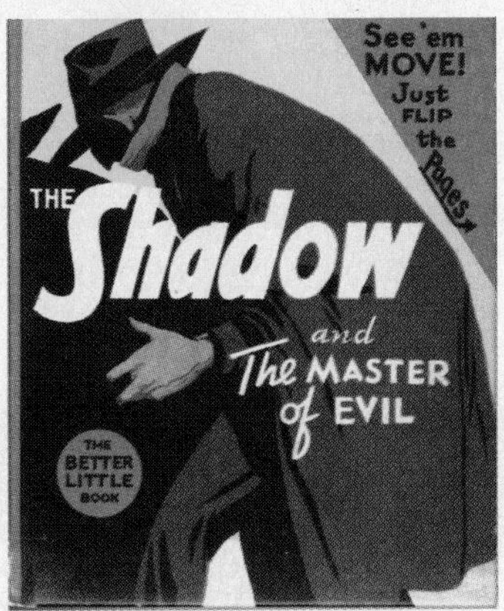

THE SHADOW AND THE MASTER OF EVIL
BLB #1443 - 1941. © WHIT

MY LIFE AND TIMES (BY SHIRLEY TEMPLE)
BLB #1441 - 1937. © WHIT

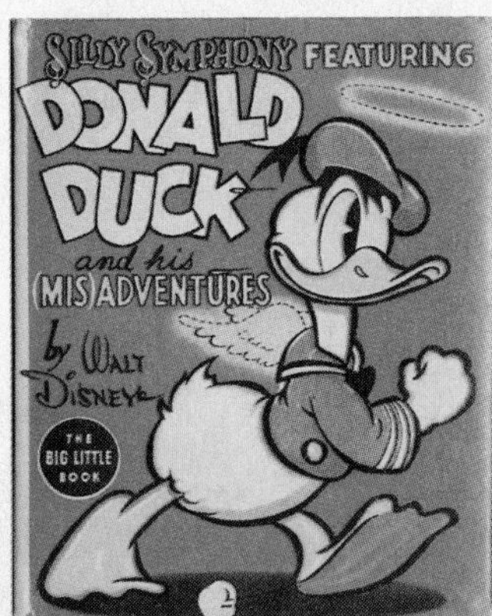

SILLY SYMPHONY FEATURING DONALD DUCK AND HIS (MIS) ADVENTURES
BLB #1441 - 1937. © WDC

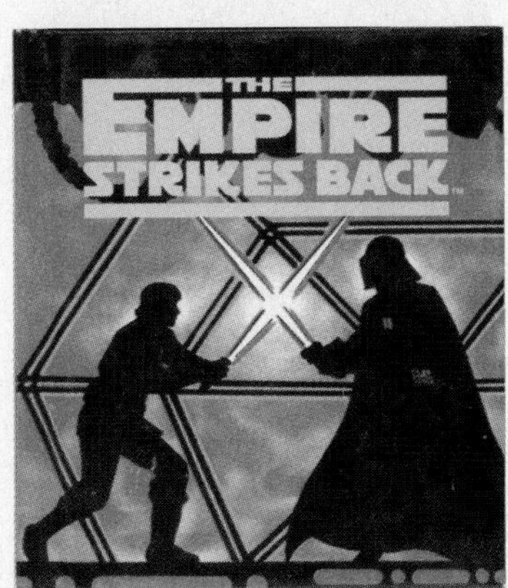

STAR WARS: THE EMPIRE STRIKES BACK
1997. © Lucasfilm Ltd.

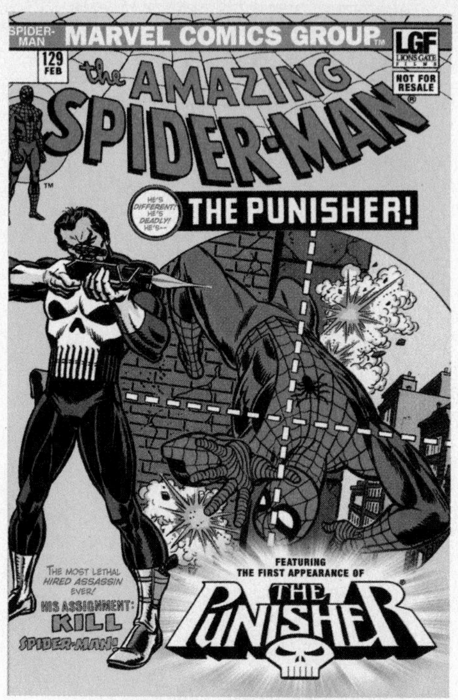

AMAZING SPIDER-MAN #129
June 2004.
Punisher movie promo comic. © MAR

CAPTAIN MARVEL AND THE LIEUTENANTS OF SAFETY #3
1951. © FAW

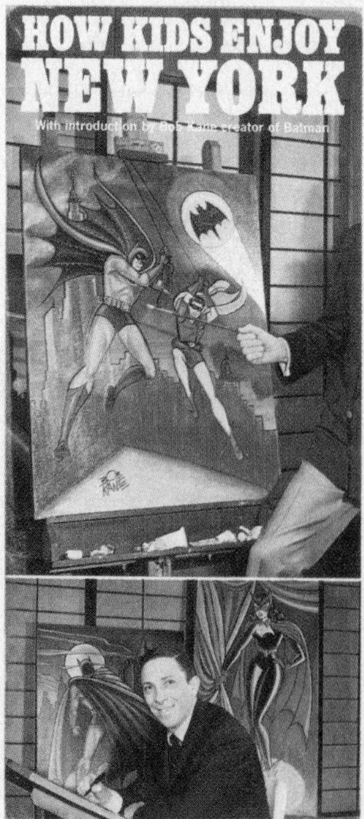

HOW KIDS ENJOY NEW YORK
1966. © DC

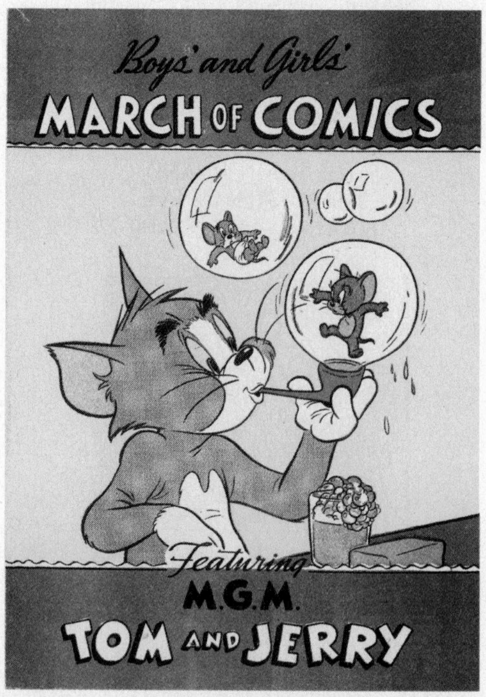

MARCH OF COMICS #71
1951. © K.K. Publications

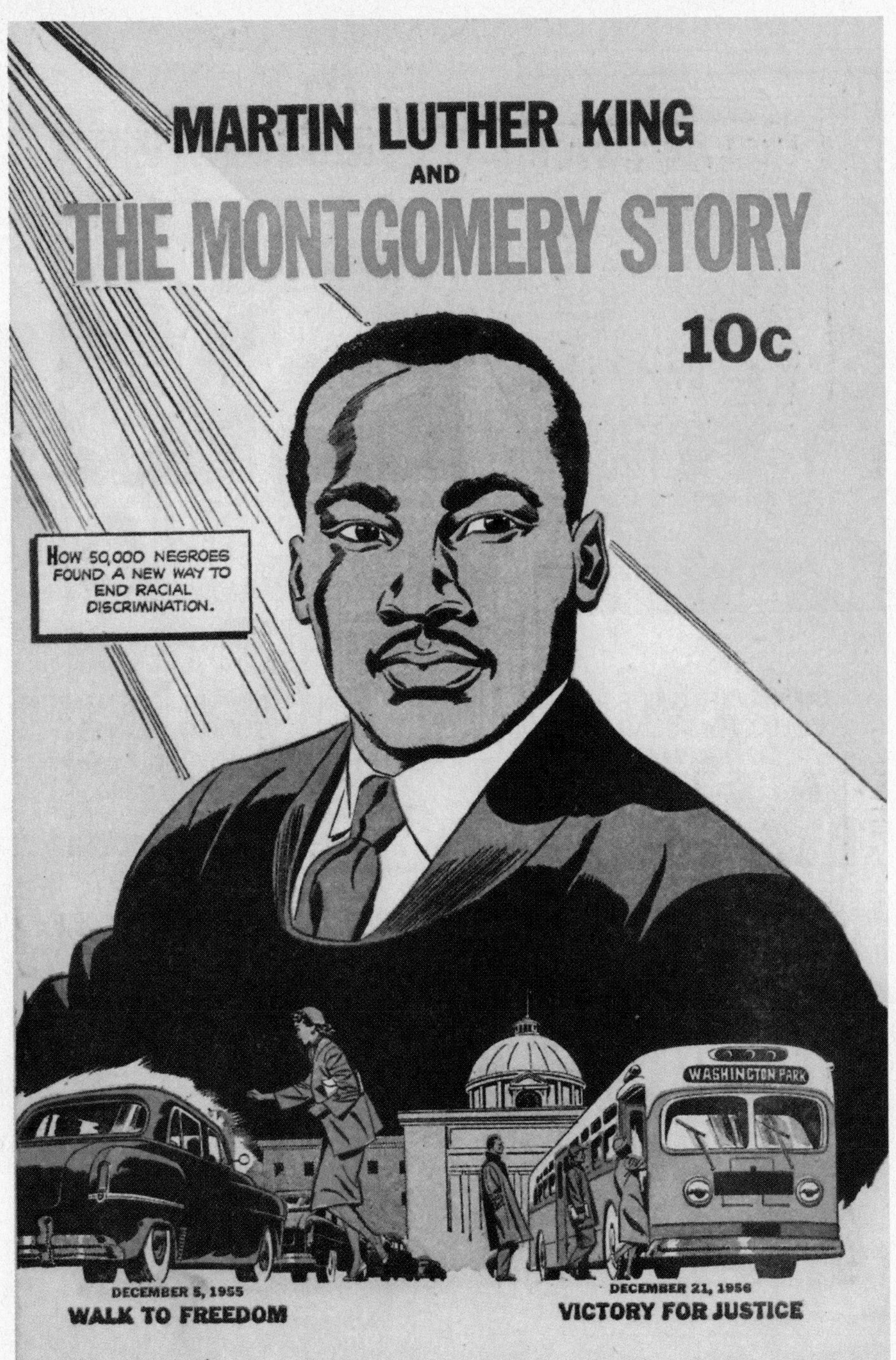

MARTIN LUTHER KING
AND THE MONTGOMERY STORY
1956. Five copies known.
© Fellowship Reconciliation

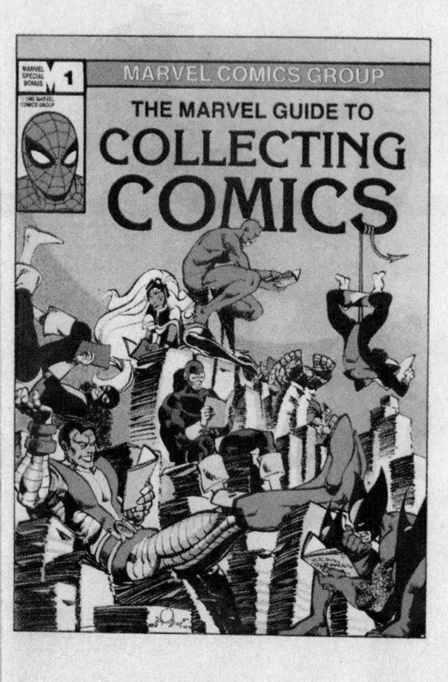

THE MARVEL GUIDE TO
COLLECTING COMICS
1982. © MAR

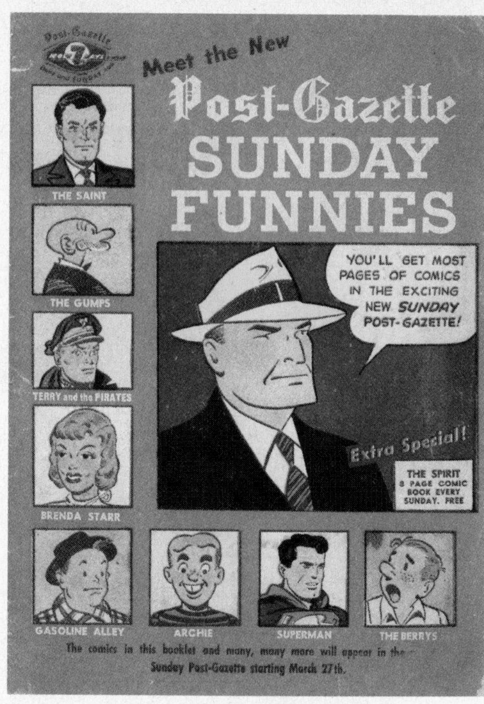

MEET THE NEW POST-GAZETTE
SUNDAY FUNNIES
1949. © Pittsburgh Post Gazette

THE PERSONAL STORY
OF MR. PEANUT
1956. © Planters Nut & Chocolate Co.

ON THE AIR
1947. © NBC Network

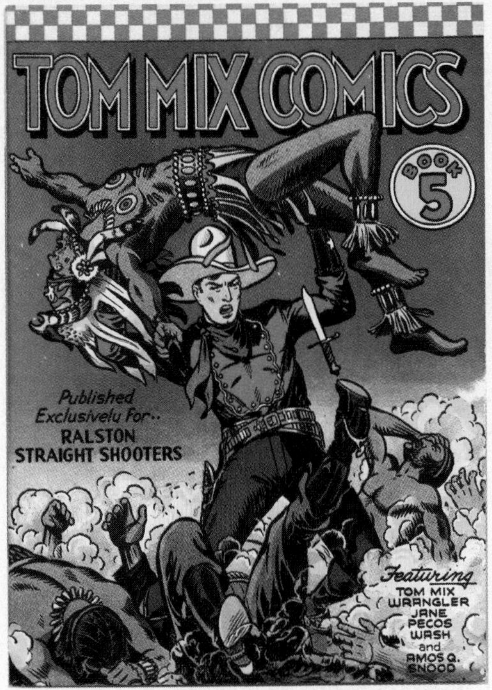

TOM MIX COMICS #5
March 1934. © Ralston-Purina Co.

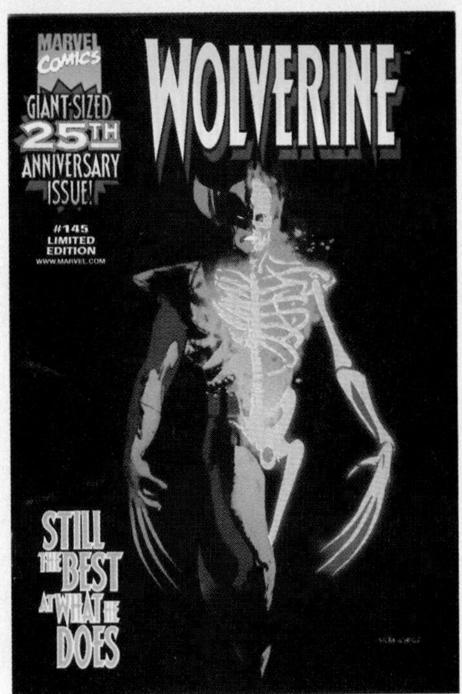

WOLVERINE #145
1999. Nabisco mail-in offer.
© MAR

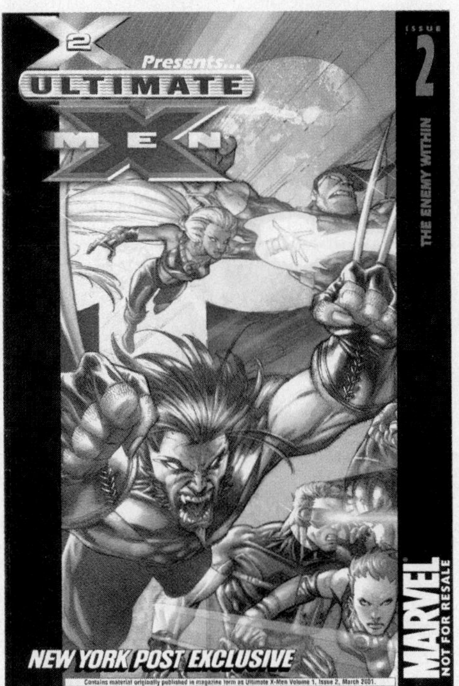

ULTIMATE X-MEN #2
2003. New York Post Exclusive.
© MAR

YALTA TO KOREA
1952. © M. Phillip Corp.

THE BLOODY (BOSTON) MASSACRE
BY PAUL REVERE
1770 (Courtesy of the Philip G. Straus Collection)

"AMUSEMENT FOR JOHN BULL..."
from The European Magazine
1783

"THE CORSICAN MUNCHAUSEN....HUMMING THE LADS OF PARIS" from the London Strand,
December 4, 1813

"A CONSULTATION AT THE MEDICAL BOARD"
from The Pasquin or General Satirist
1821

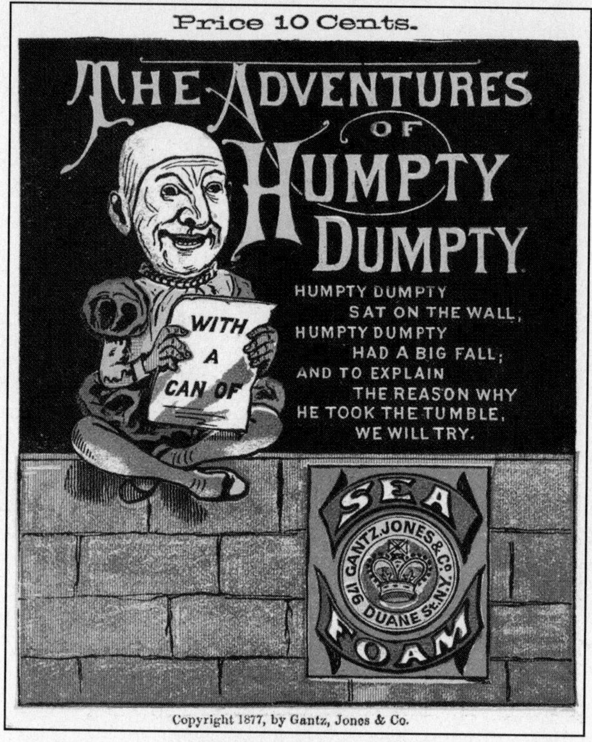

THE ADVENTURES OF
HUMPTY DUMPTY
1877. © Gantz, Jones and Co.

BARKER'S "KOMIC" PICTURE SOUVENIR
1892. © Barker, Moore & Mein Medicine Co.

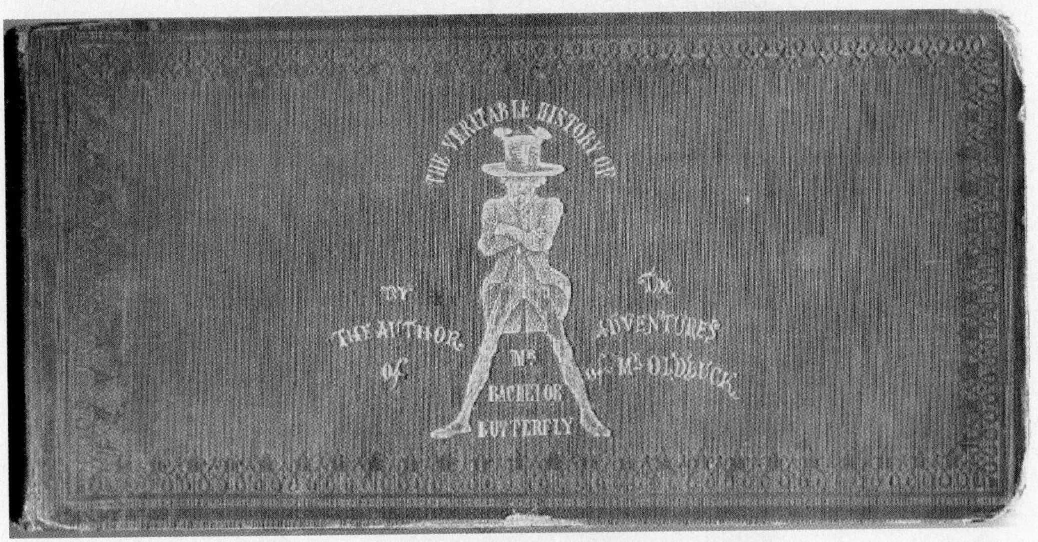

THE VERITABLE HISTORY OF
MR. BACHELOR BUTTERFLY
1845. © D. Bogue, London

THE COMICAL ADVENTURES OF
BEAU OGLEBY
(HISTORY OF MR. OGLEBY)
c. 1843. © Tilt & Bogue, London

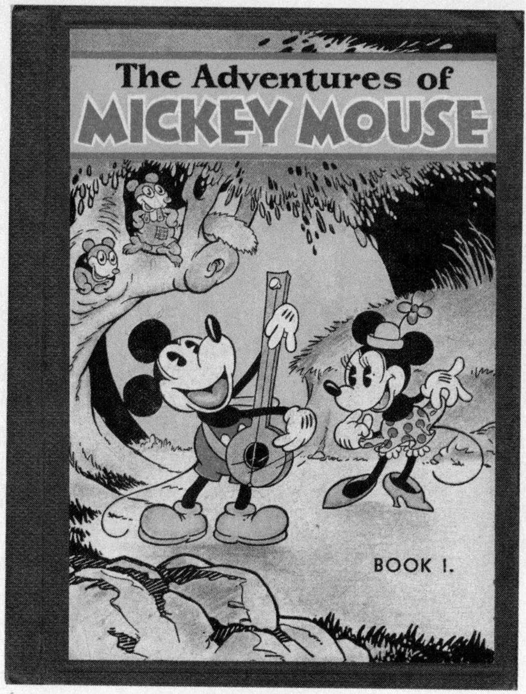

THE ADVENTURES OF
MICKEY MOUSE BOOK I
1931. © Dave McKay Co. Inc.

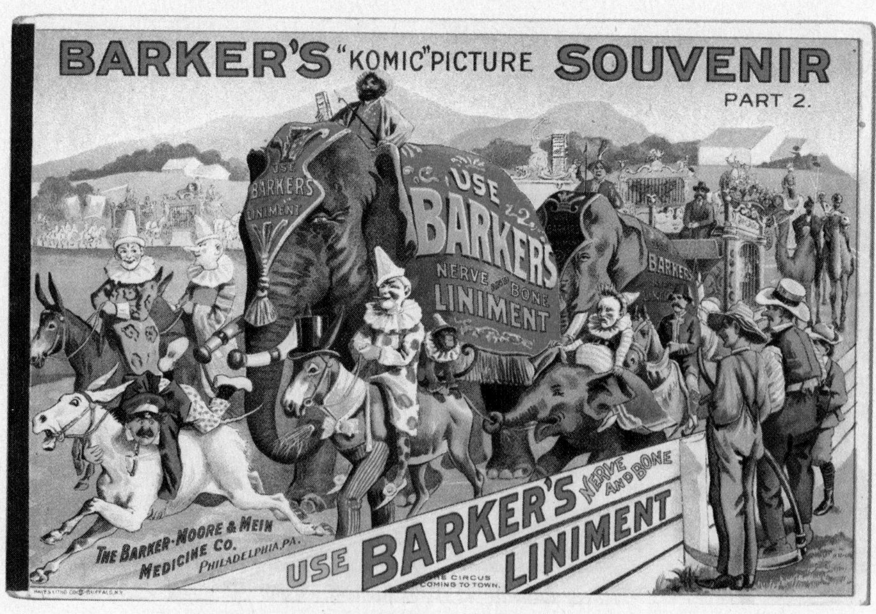

BARKER'S "KOMIC" PICTURE SOUVENIR PART 2
c. 1901-1903. © Barker, Moore & Mein Medicine Co.

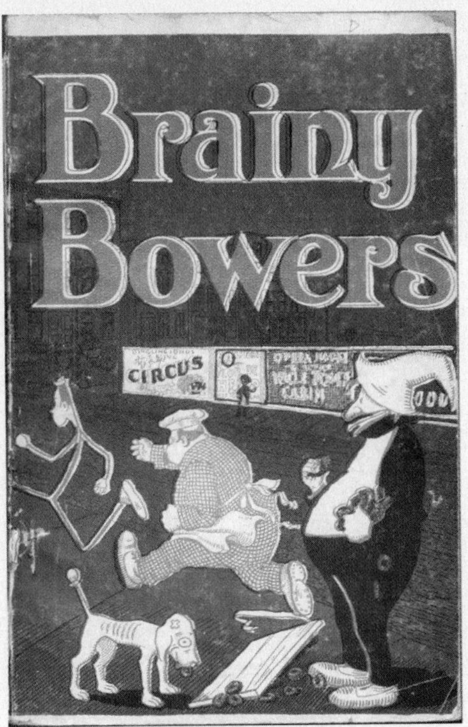

BRAINY BOWERS
AND DROWSY DUGAN
1905. © Star Publishing Co.

BRINGING UP FATHER #8
1924. © Cupples & Leon Co.

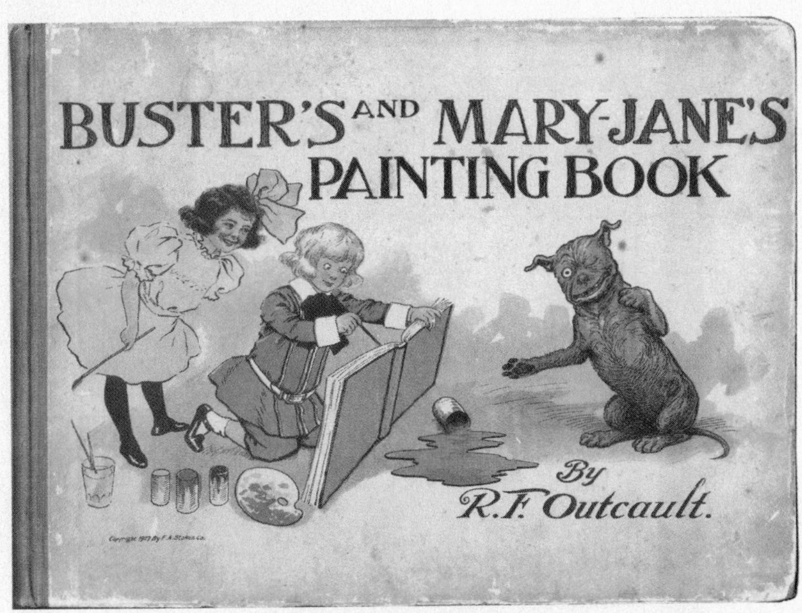

BUSTER'S AND MARY-JANE'S
PAINTING BOOK
1907. © Frederick A. Stokes Co.

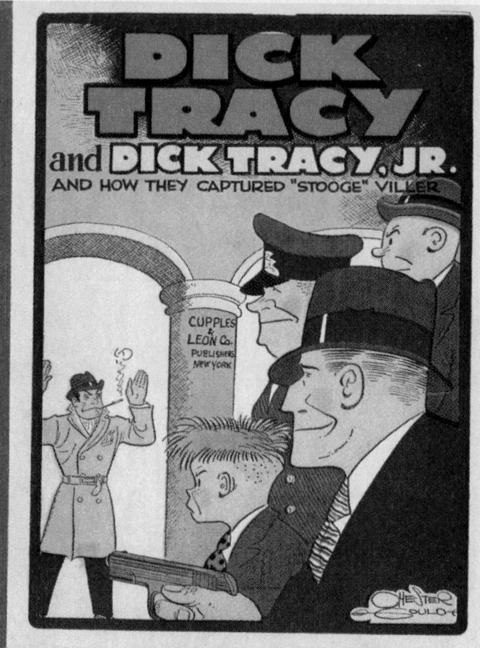

DICK TRACY AND DICK TRACY JR.
AND HOW THEY CAPTURED
"STOOGE" VILLER
1933. © Cupples & Leon Co.

JUDGE'S LIBRARY #183
June 1904 © Judge Publishing

THE NEBBS
1928 © Cupples & Leon Co.

OLD GOLD
CIGARETTE
c.1920s

TILLIE THE TOILER #4
1929. © Cupples & Leon Co.

PECK'S BAD BOY AND
HIS COUNTRY COUSIN CYNTHIA
1907. © Charles C. Thompson Co.

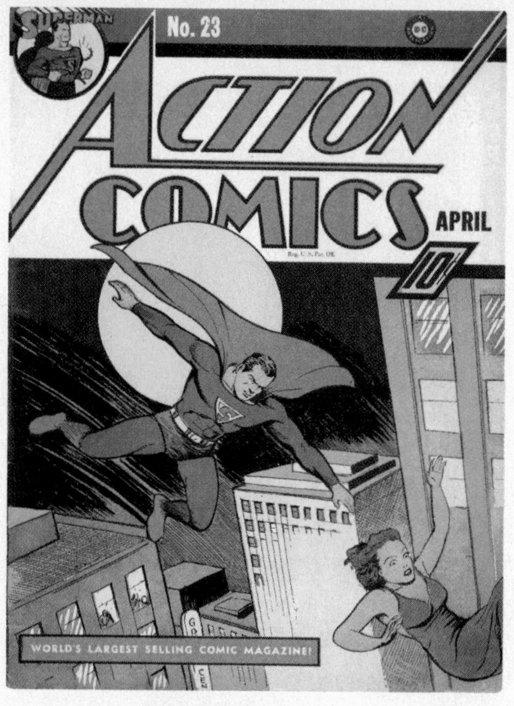

ACTION COMICS #23
April 1940. © DC

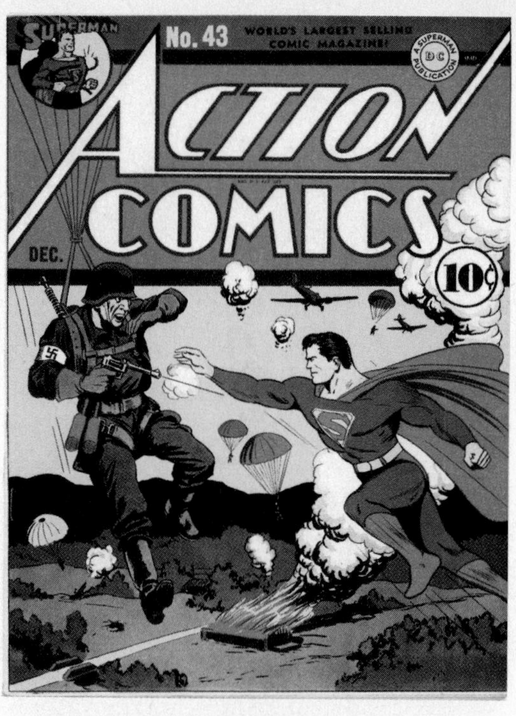

ACTION COMICS #43
December 1941. © DC

THE ADVENTURES OF
DETECTIVE ACE KING
1933. © Humor Publ. Corp.

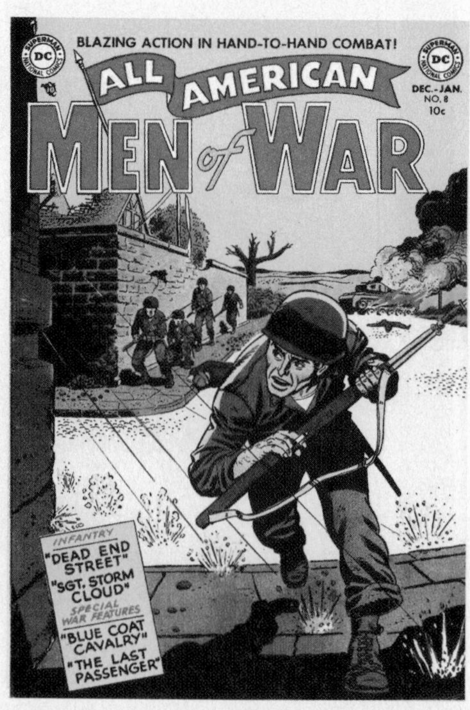

ALL AMERICAN MEN OF WAR #23
December 1953-January 1954. © DC

ALL SELECT COMICS #8
Summer 1945. © MAR

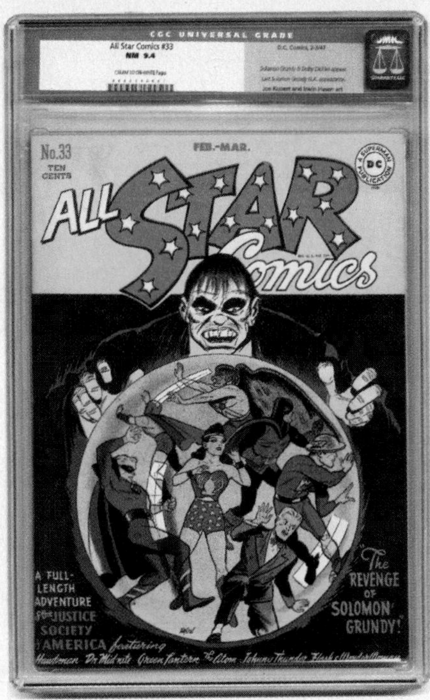

ALL STAR COMICS #33
February-March 1947. © DC

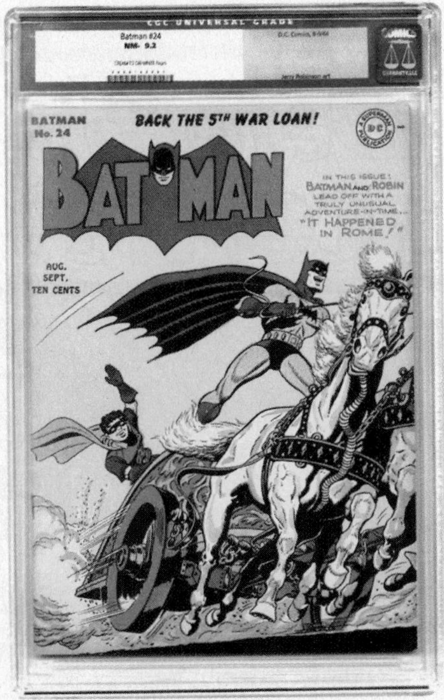

BATMAN #24
August-September 1944. © DC

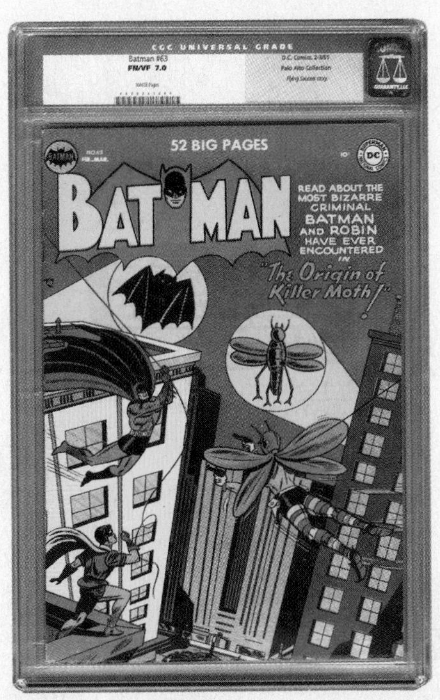

BATMAN #63
February-March 1951. © DC

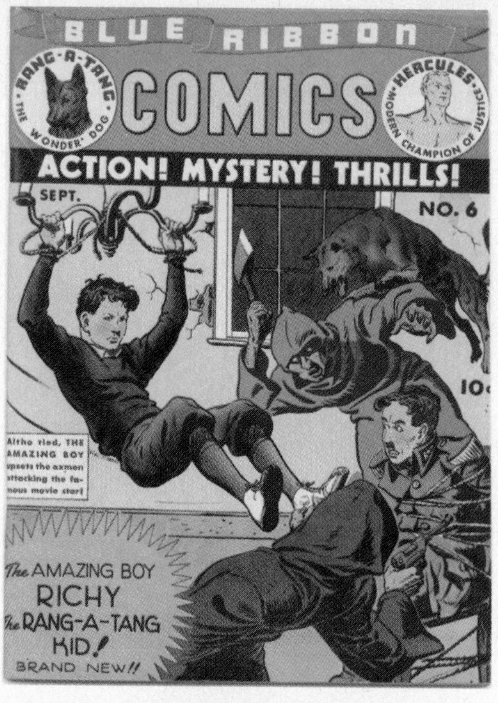

BLUE RIBBON COMICS #6
September 1940. © MLJ

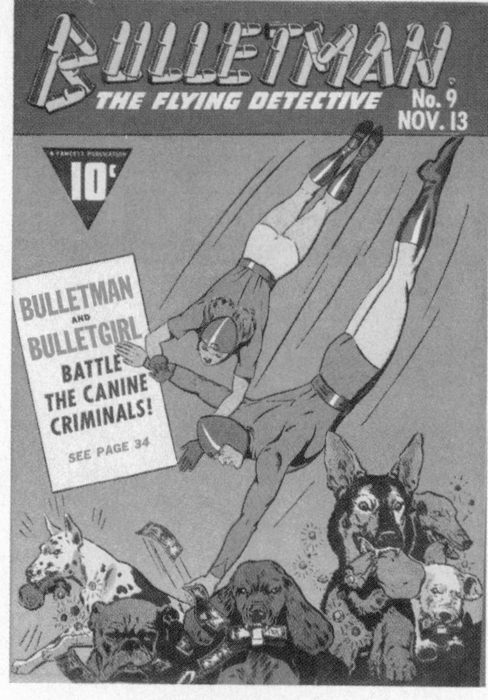

BULLETMAN #9
November 1942. © FAW

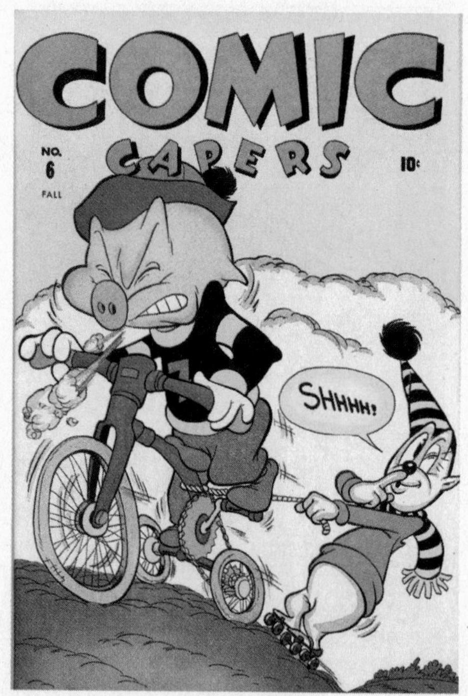

COMIC CAPERS #6
Fall 1946. © MAR

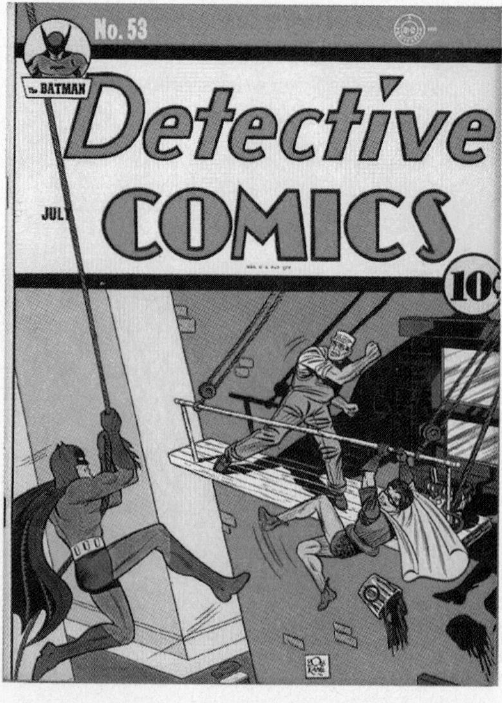

DETECTIVE COMICS #53
July 1941. © DC

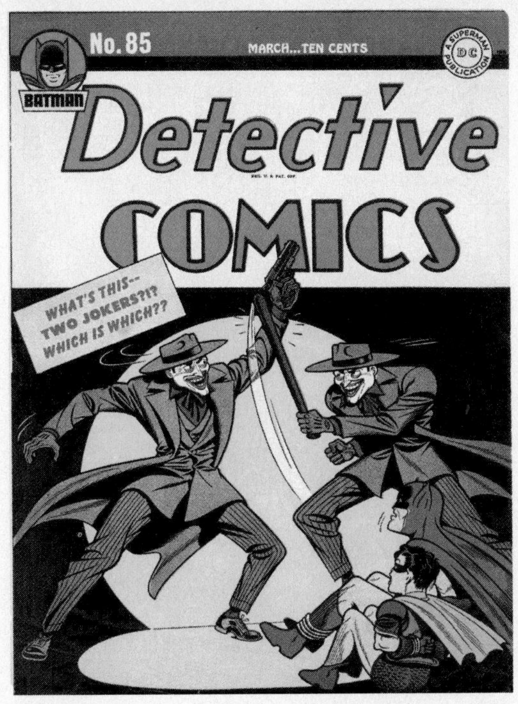

DETECTIVE COMICS #85
March 1944. © DC

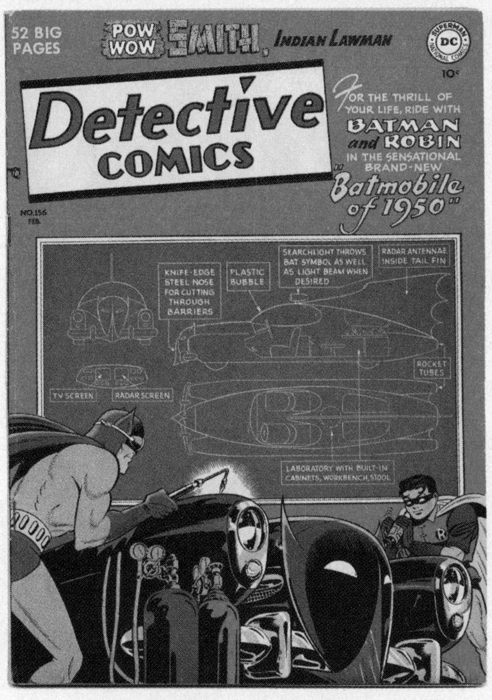

DETECTIVE COMICS #156
February 1950. © DC

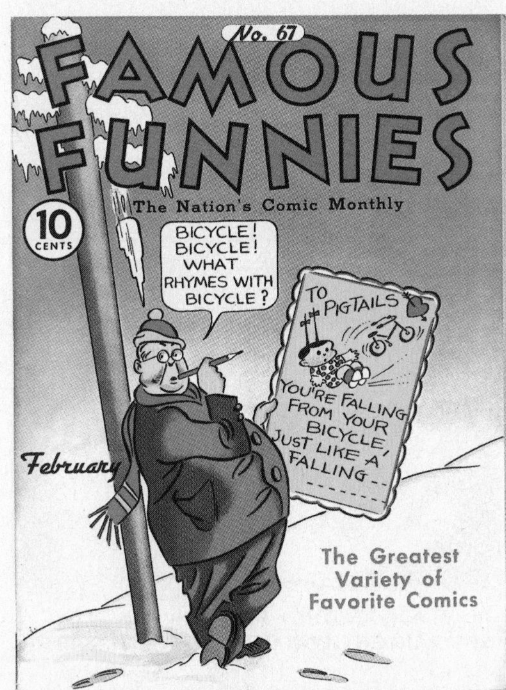

FAMOUS FUNNIES #67
February 1940. © EAS

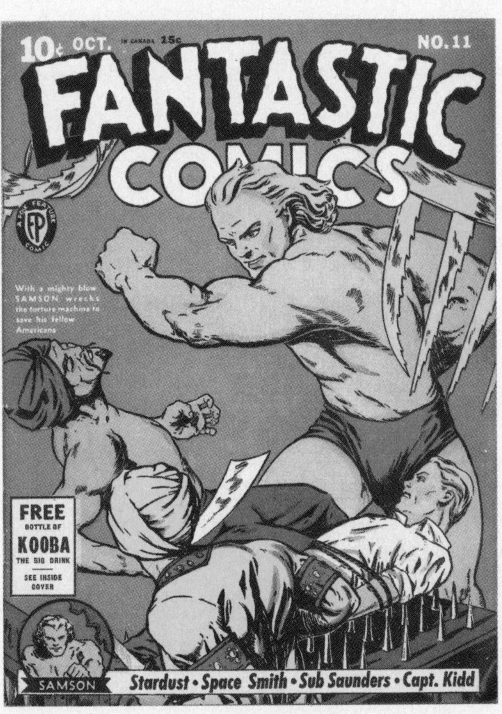

FANTASTIC COMICS #11
October 1940. © FOX

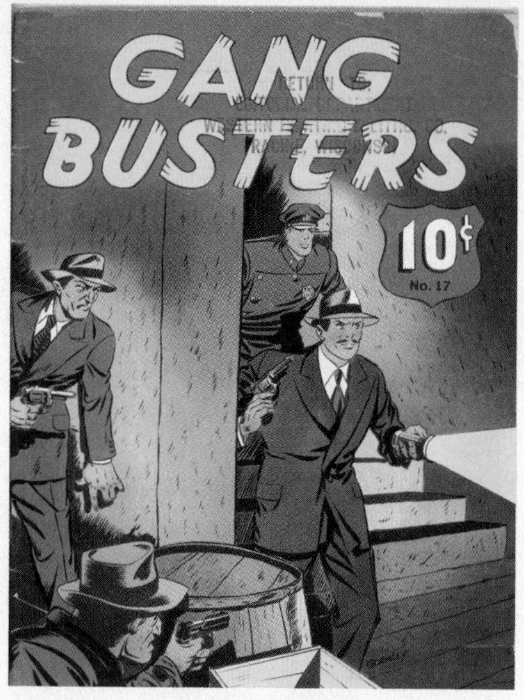

FEATURE BOOK #17
1938. © DMP

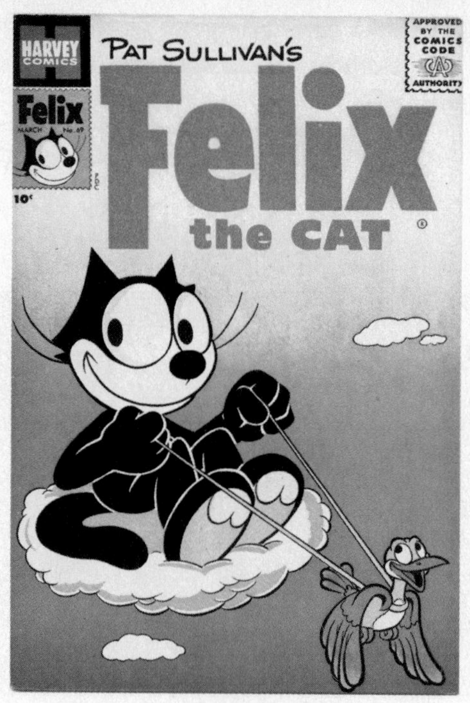

FELIX THE CAT #69
March 1956. © HARV

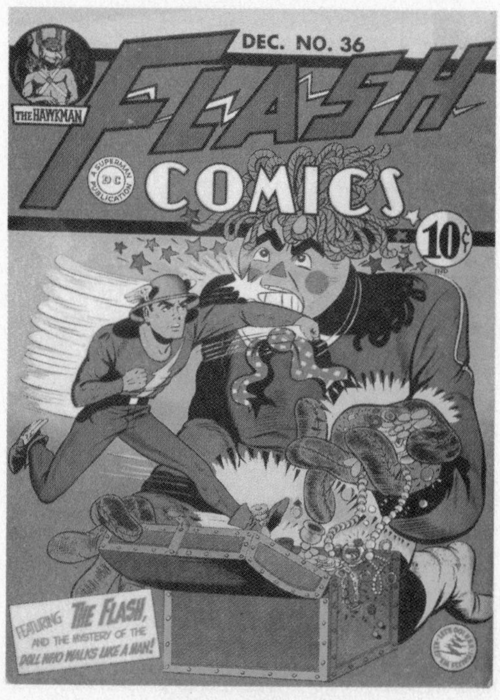

FLASH COMICS #36
December 1942. © DC

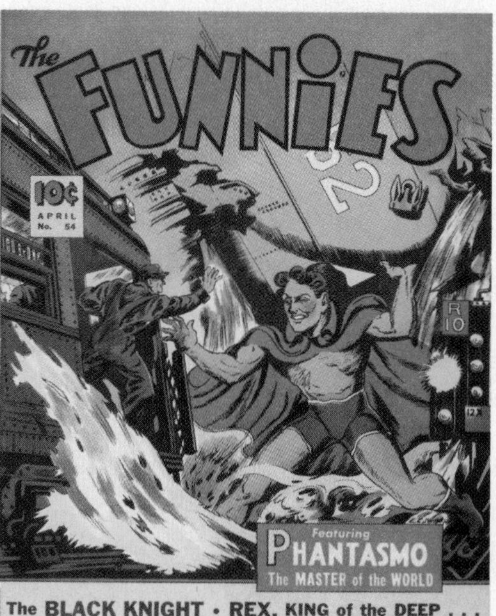

THE FUNNIES #54
April 1941. © DELL

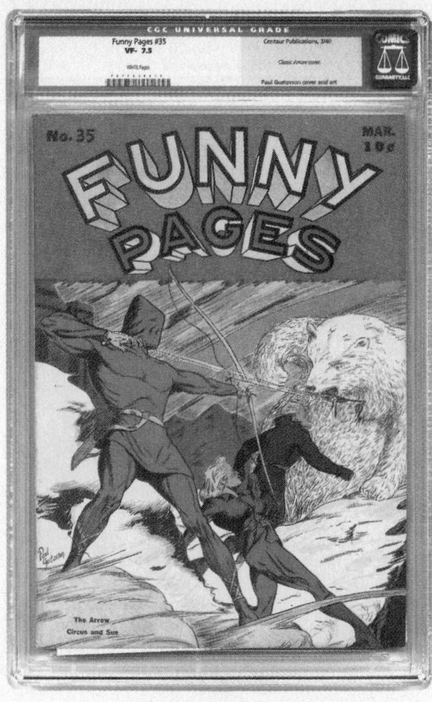

FUNNY PAGES #35
March 1940. © CEN

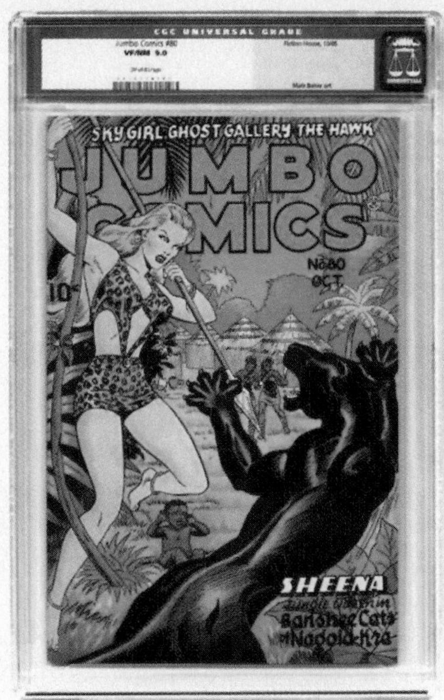

JUMBO COMICS #80
October1945. © FH

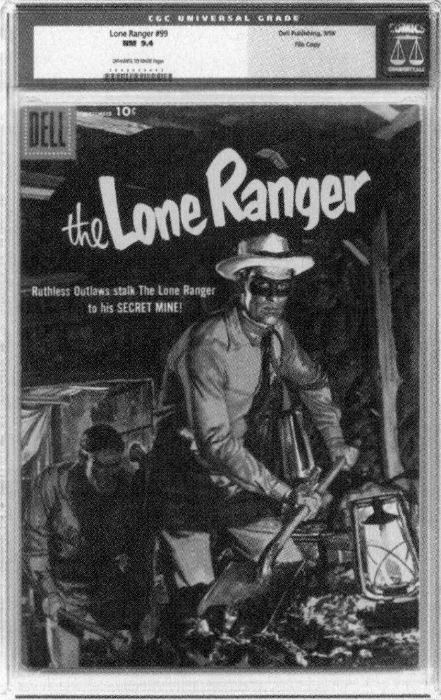

THE LONE RANGER #99
April 1956. © DELL

MR. DISTRICT ATTORNEY #13
January-February 1950. © DC

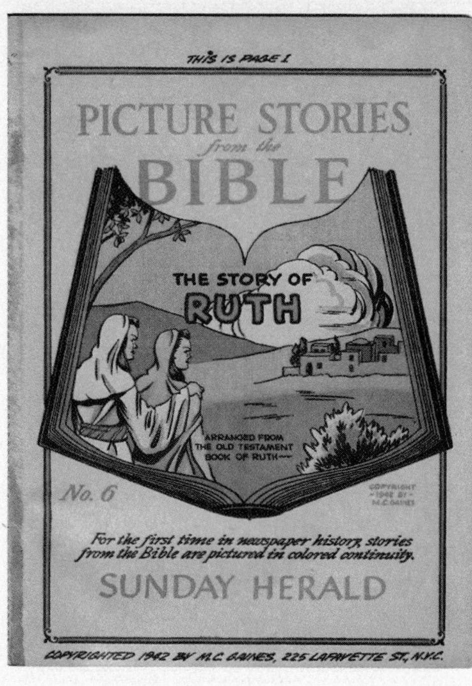

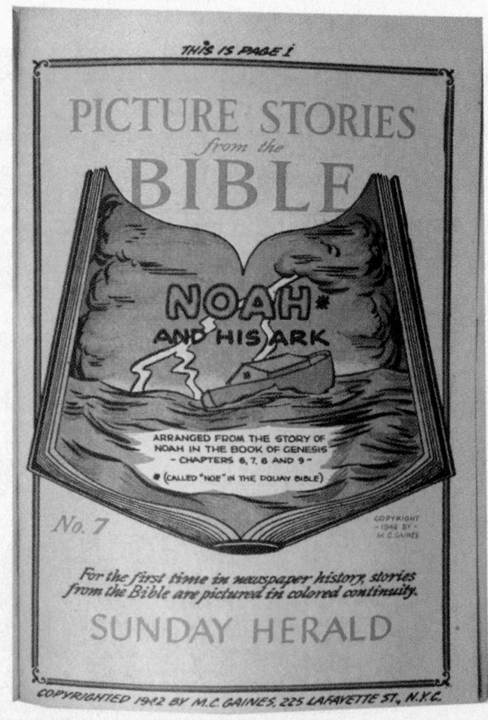

NARRATIVE ILLUSTRATION
THE STORY OF THE COMICS
Summer 1942. Very rare (7 copies known) with several different inserts of Picture Stories from the Bible. Examples known include "The Story of Saul", "Noah and His Ark", and "The Story of Ruth".
© M.C. Gaines

PUNCH COMICS #12
January 1945. © CHES

REAL LIFE COMICS #3
March 1942. © Nedor

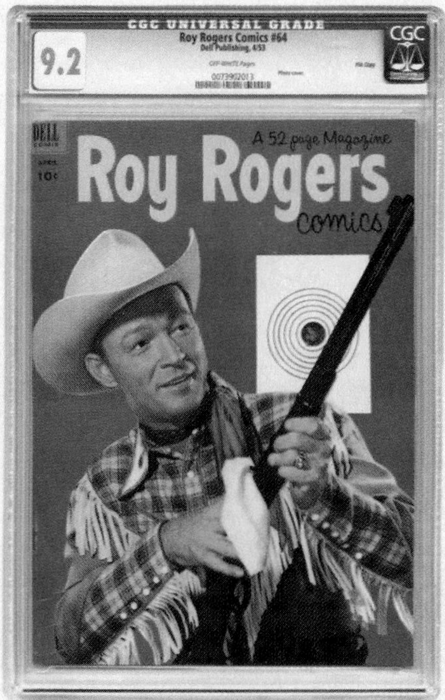

ROY ROGERS COMICS #64
April 1953. © DELL

SPACE ACTION #2
August 1952. © ACE

SPARKLER COMICS #11
June 1942. © UFS

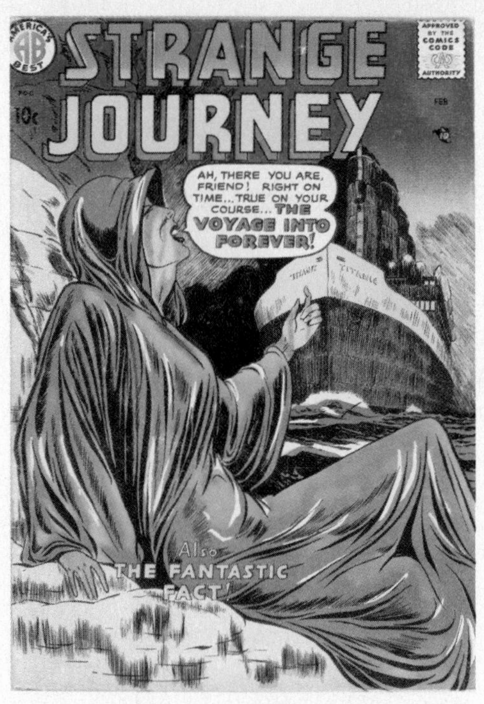

STRANGE JOURNEY #3
February 1958. © America's Best

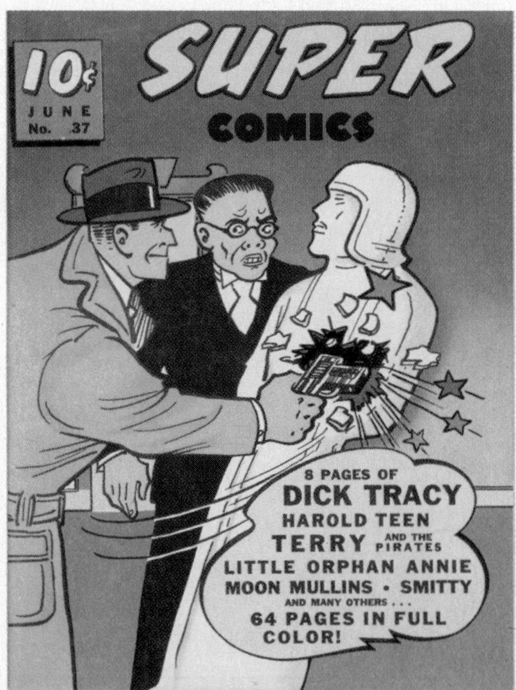

SUPER COMICS #37
June 1941. © DELL

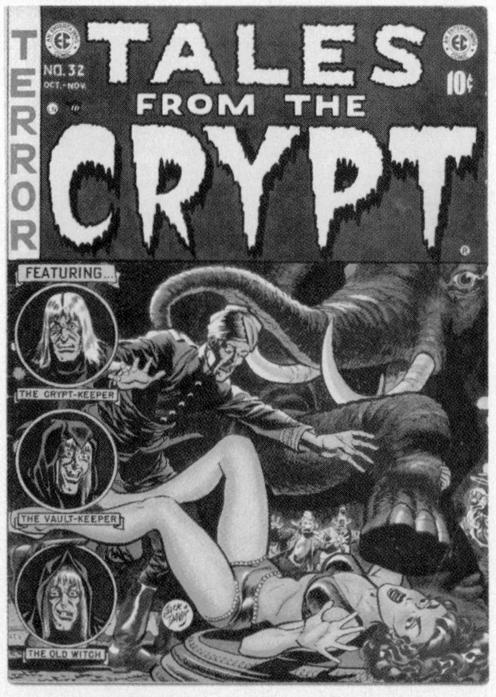

TALES FROM THE CRYPT #32
October-November 1952. © WMG

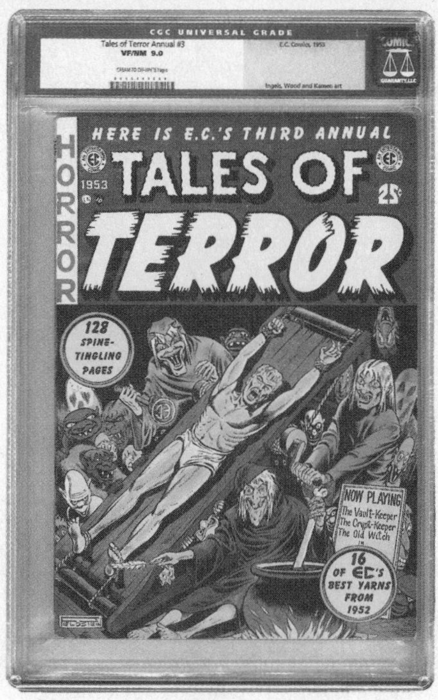

TALES OF TERROR ANNUAL #3
1953. © WMG

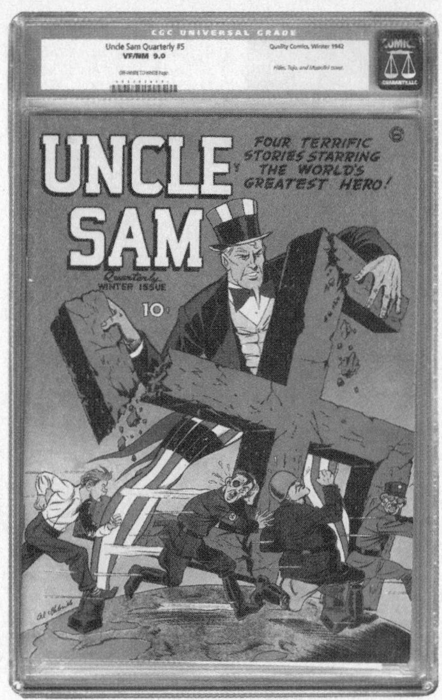

UNCLE SAM QUARTERLY #5
Winter 1942. © QUA

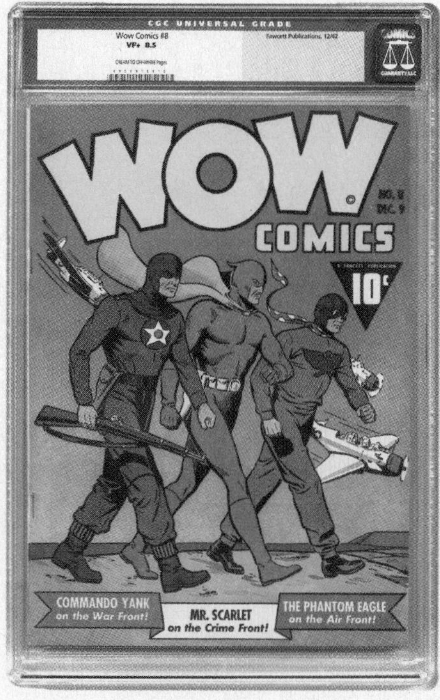

WOW COMICS #8
December 1942. © FAW

YOUNG ALLIES #4
Summer 1942. © MAR

AVENGERS COMICS #2
November 1963. Curator pedigree. © MAR

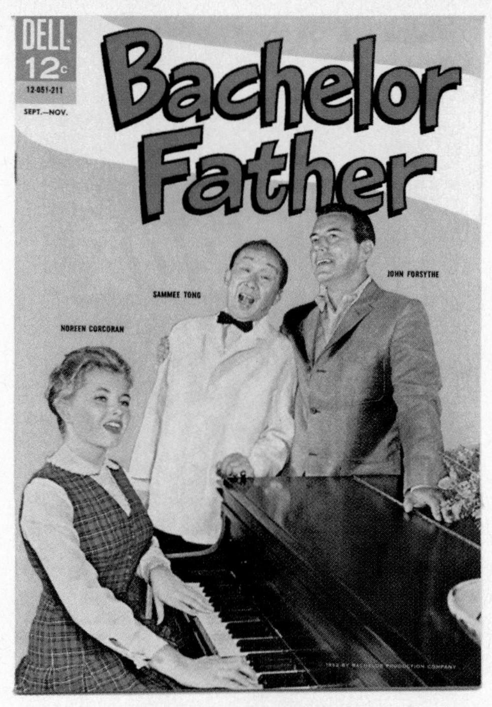

BACHELOR FATHER #2
September-November 1962. © DELL

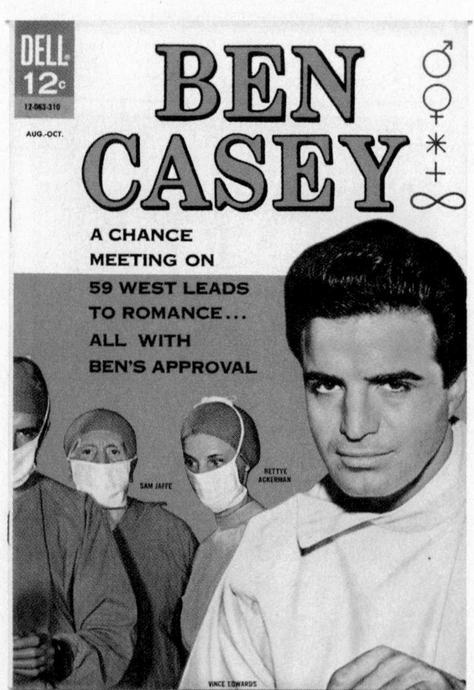

BEN CASEY #2
August-October 1962. © DELL

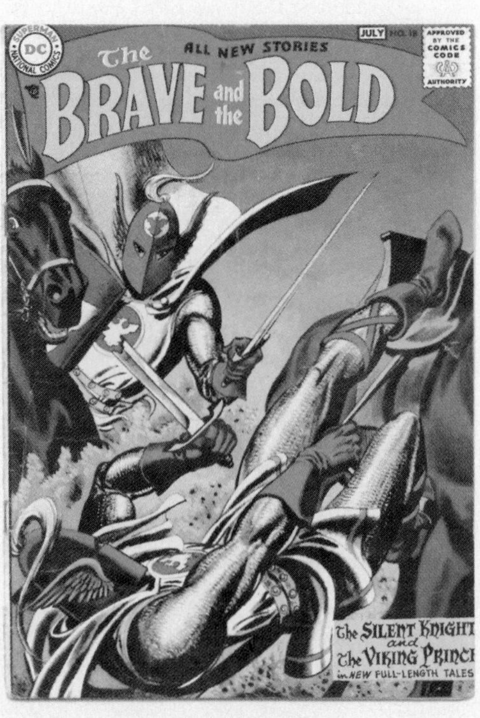

BRAVE AND THE BOLD #18
June-July 1958. © DC

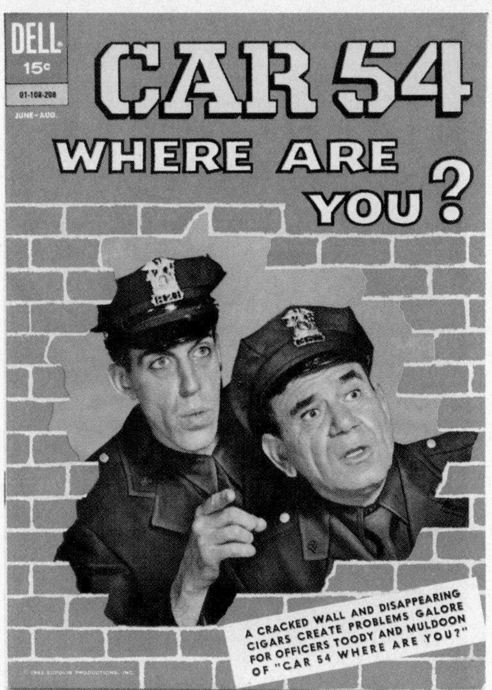

CAR 54 WHERE ARE YOU? #2
August 1962. © DELL

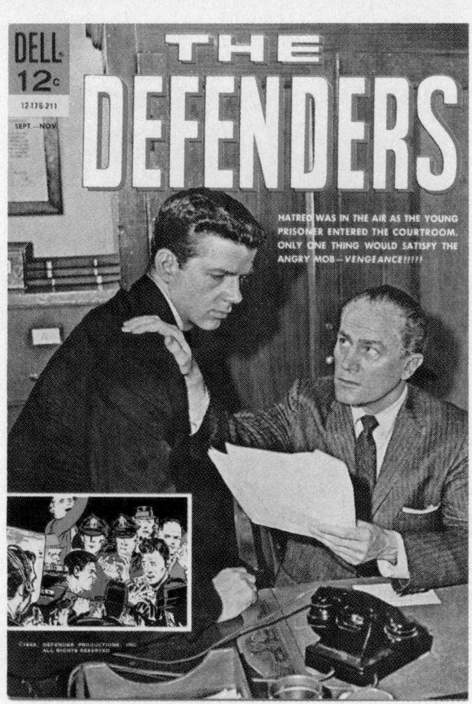

THE DEFENDERS #1
September-November 1962. © DELL

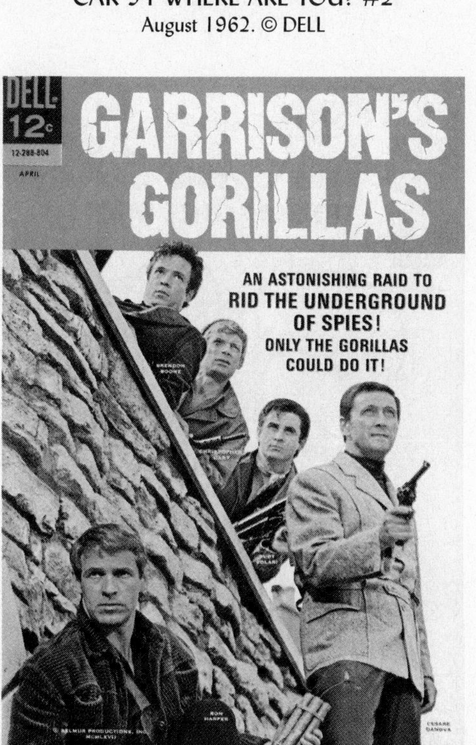

GARRISON'S GORILLAS #3
April 1968. © DELL

GREEN LANTERN #52
April 1967. © DC

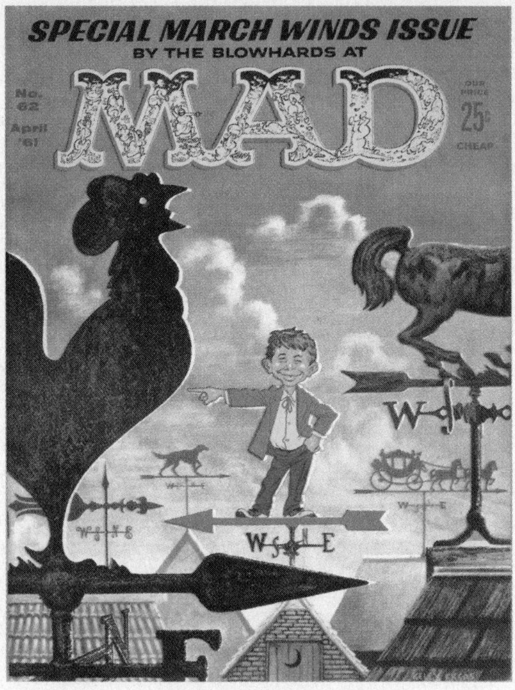

MAD MAGAZINE #62
April 1961. Gaines file copy. © EC

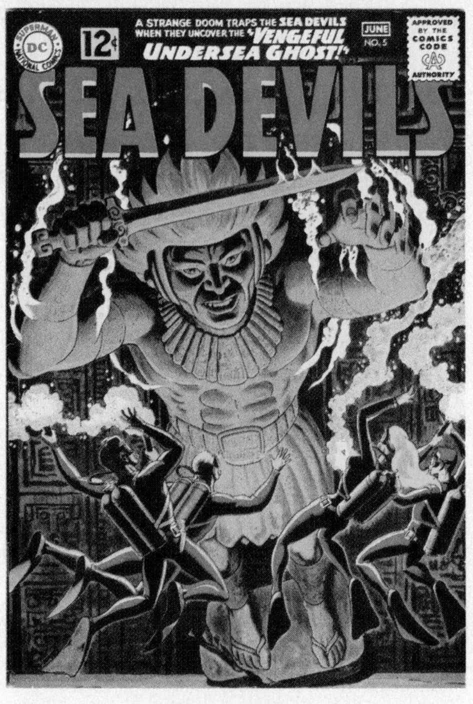

SEA DEVILS #5
May-June 1962. © DC

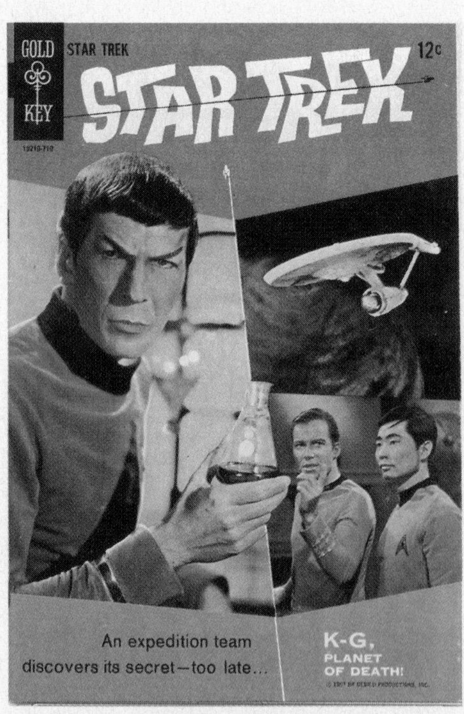

STAR TREK #1
July 1967. Pacific Coast pedigree. © Paramount

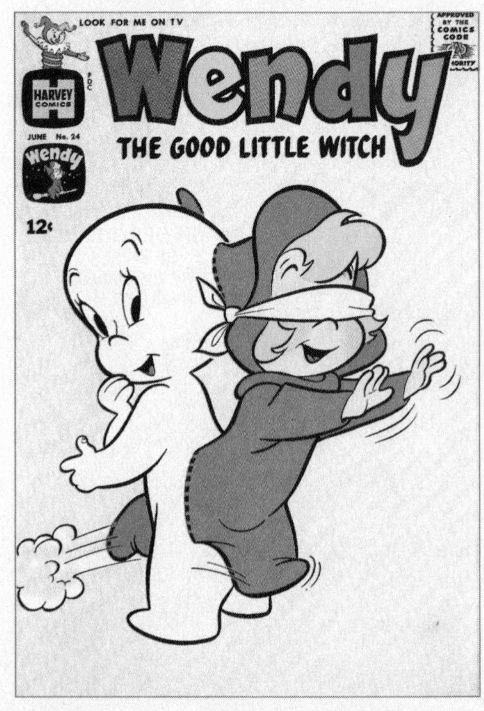

WENDY THE GOOD LITTLE WITCH #24
June 1964. © HARV

X-MEN #2
November 1963. Pacific Coast pedigree. © MAR

AMAZING SPIDER-MAN #135
August 1974. Highest certified copy. © MAR

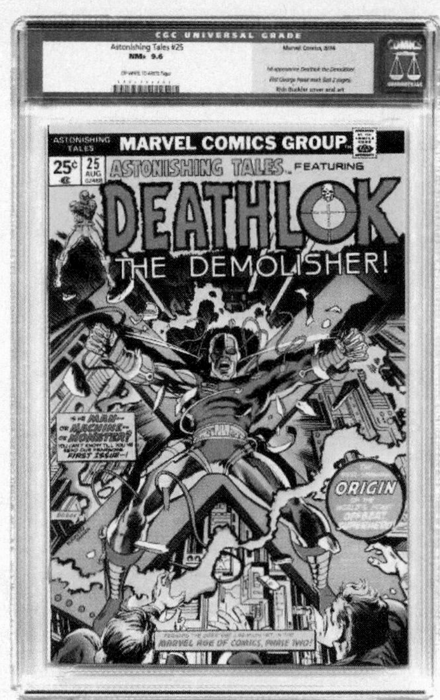

ASTONISHING TALES #25
August 1974. © MAR

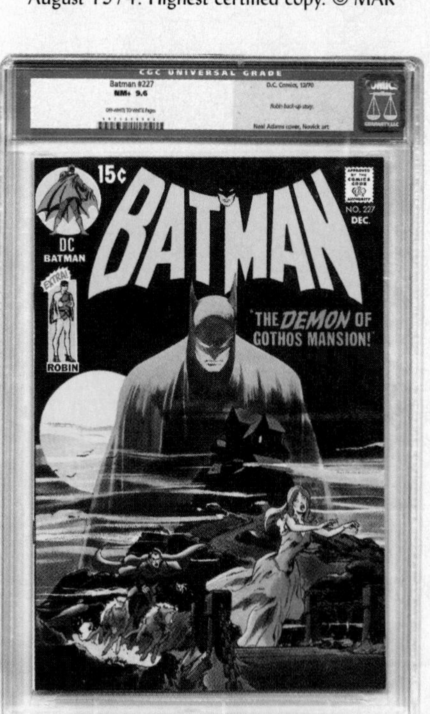

BATMAN #227
December1970. © DC

CAPTAIN AMERICA #156
December1972. © MAR

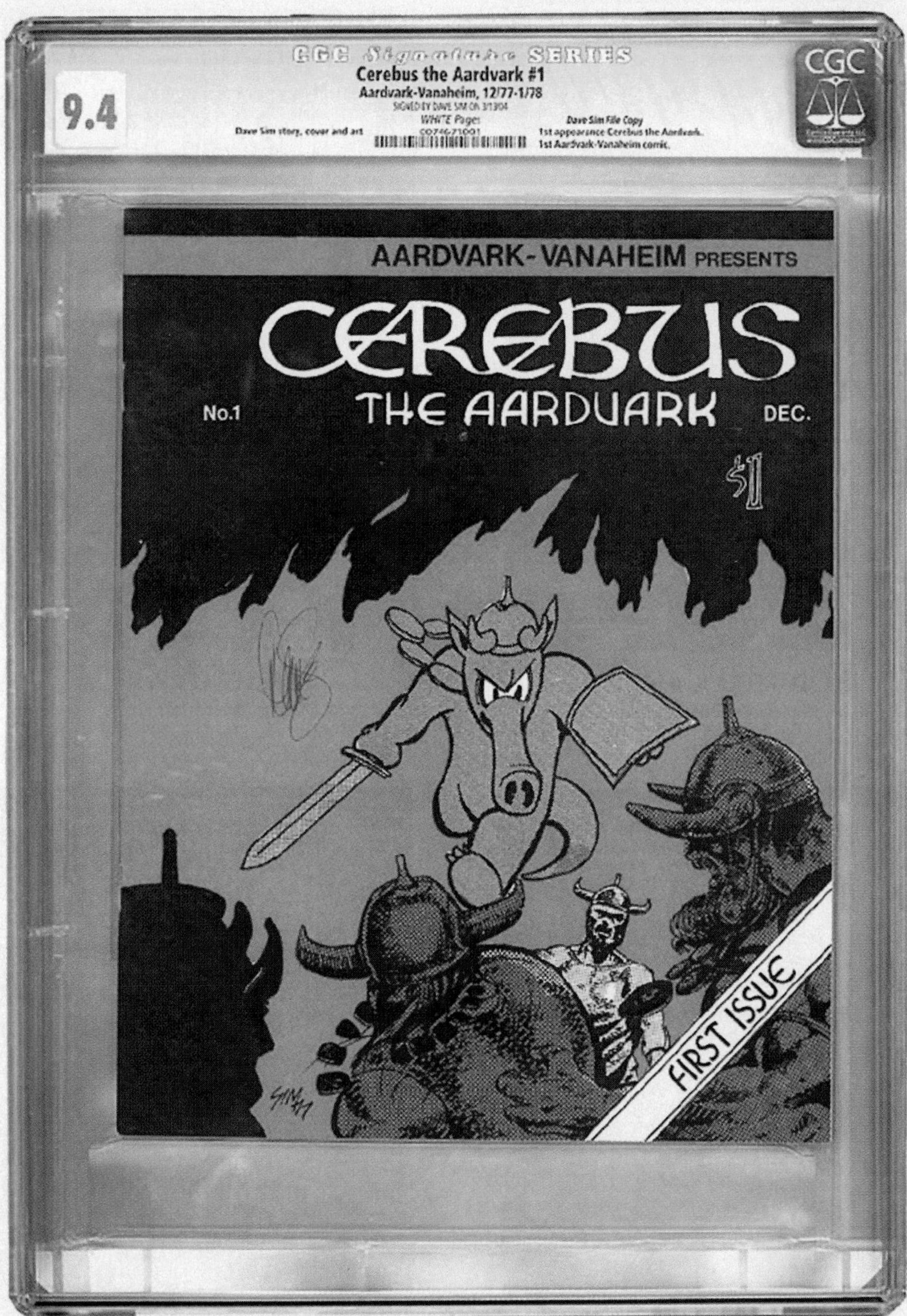

CEREBUS THE AARDVARK #1
December 1977-January 1978. Dave Sim file copy.

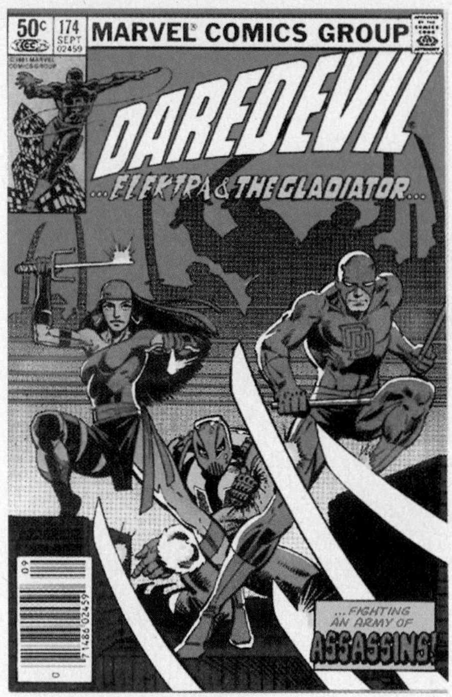

DAREDEVIL #174
September1981. © MAR

FOREVER PEOPLE #1
February-March 1971. © DC

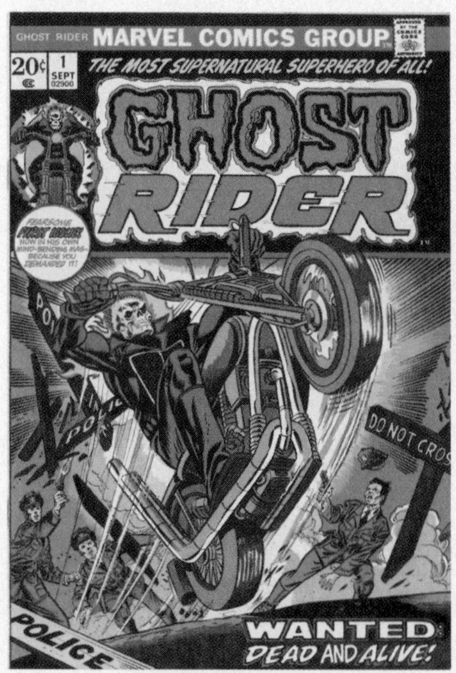

GHOST RIDER #1
September 1973. © MAR

HOUSE OF SECRETS #92
June-July1971. © DC

LITTLE LULU #260
September 1980. Highest certified copy.
© Marjorie Buell

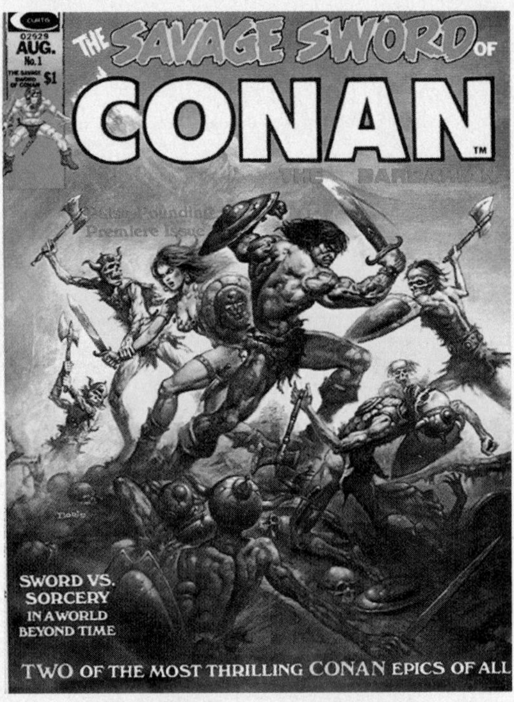

SAVAGE SWORD OF CONAN #1
August 1974. © Conan Prod.

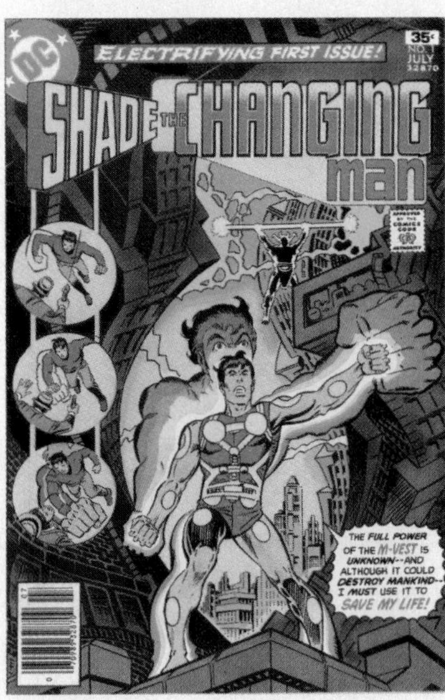

SHADE, THE CHANGING MAN #1
June-July 1977. © DC

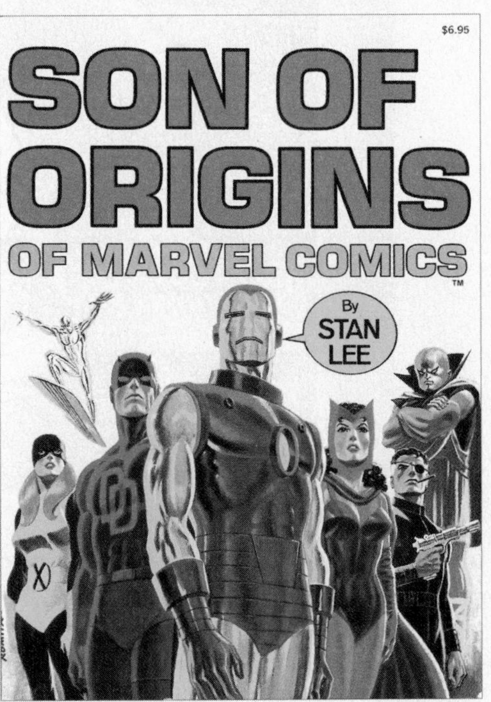

SON OF ORIGINS OF MARVEL COMICS
1975. © MAR

STAR WARS #1
35¢ price variant. July1977.
Highest certified copy.

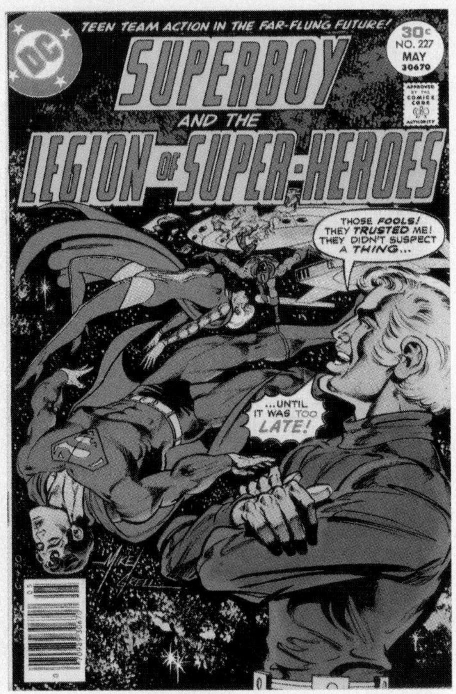

SUPERBOY #227
May 1977. © DC

TOMB OF DRACULA #10
July 1973. © MAR

WEIRD MYSTERY TALES #2
September-October 1972. © DC

X-MEN #98
April 1976. © MAR

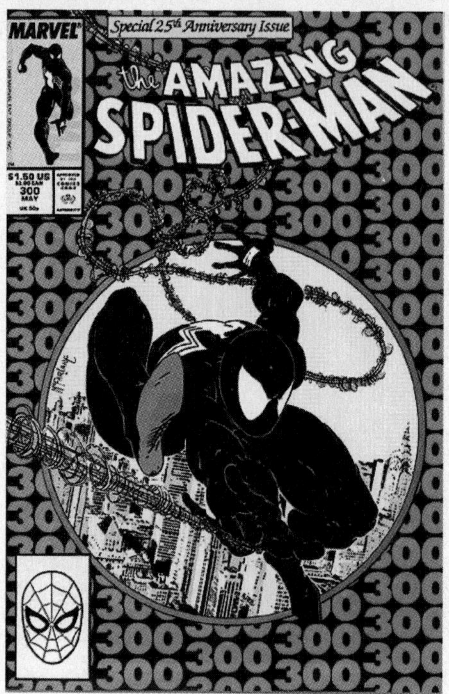

AMAZING SPIDER-MAN #300
May 1988. © MAR

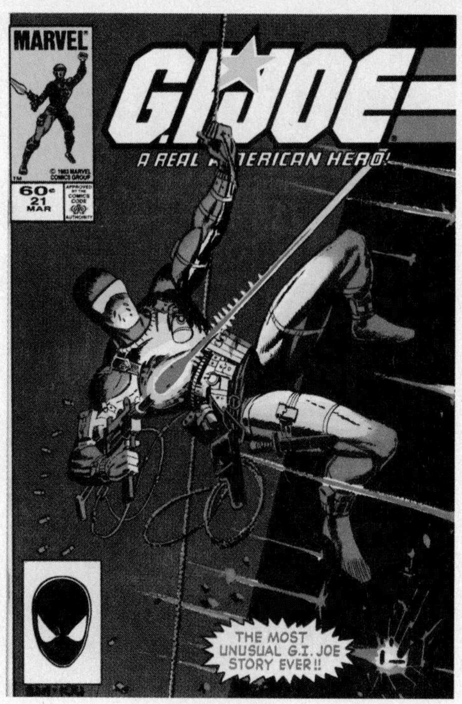

G.I. JOE,
A REAL AMERICAN HERO #21
March 1984. © Hasbro

MIRACLEMAN #1
August 1985. © ECL

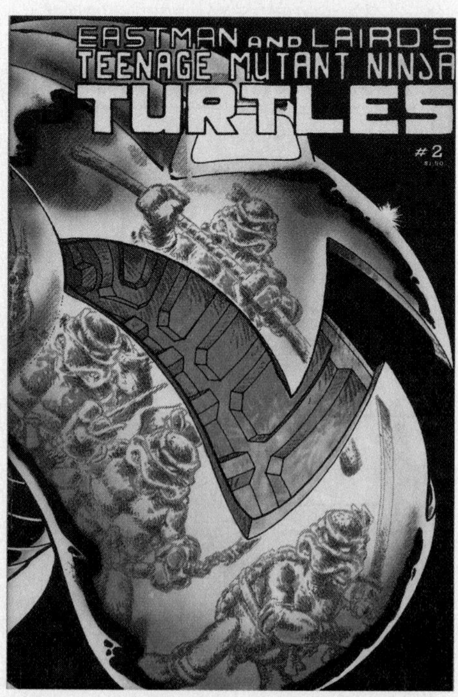

TEENAGE MUTANT NINJA TURTLES #2
1984. © Mirage Studios

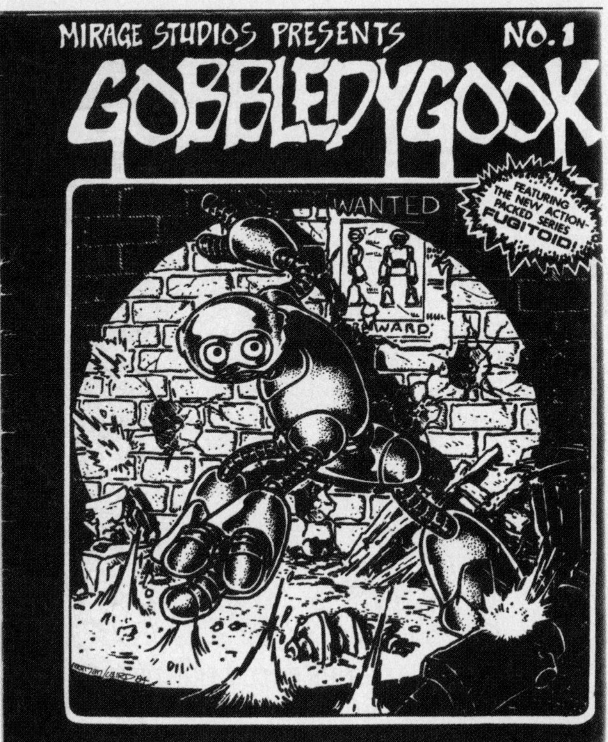

GOBBLEDYGOOK #1
1984. © Mirage Studios

Beware of counterfeit copies, first appearance of Fugitoid and first advertisement for Teenage Mutant Ninja Turtles #1 on the back cover.

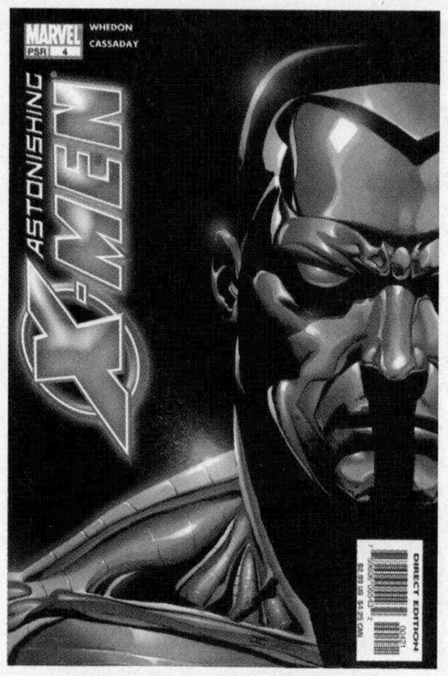

ASTONISHING X-MEN #4
Colossus variant cover. October 2004. © MAR

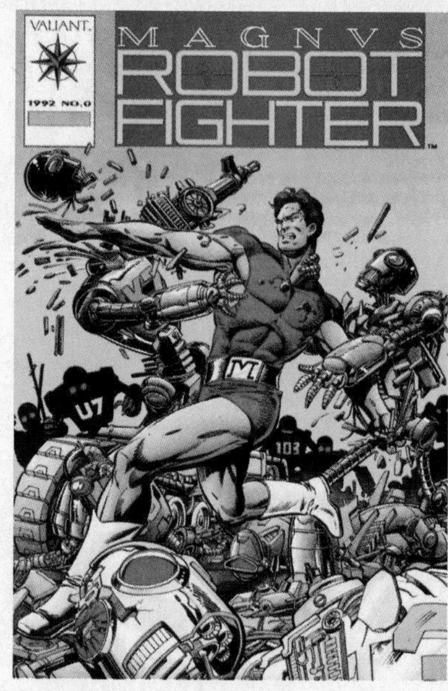

MAGNUS ROBOT FIGHTER #0
Mail-order edition. 1992. © VAL

SHI: JU-NEN #1
ANNA SUI EDITION
Crusade Fine Arts limited edition of
Dark Horse issue. July 2004. © William Tucci

SUPERMAN/BATMAN #8
CGC Signature Series. May 2004. © DC

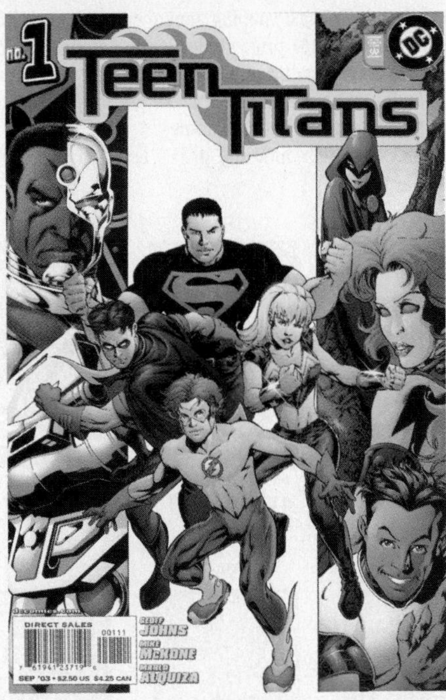

TEEN TITANS #1
1st printing with Mike McKone cover.
September 2003. © DC

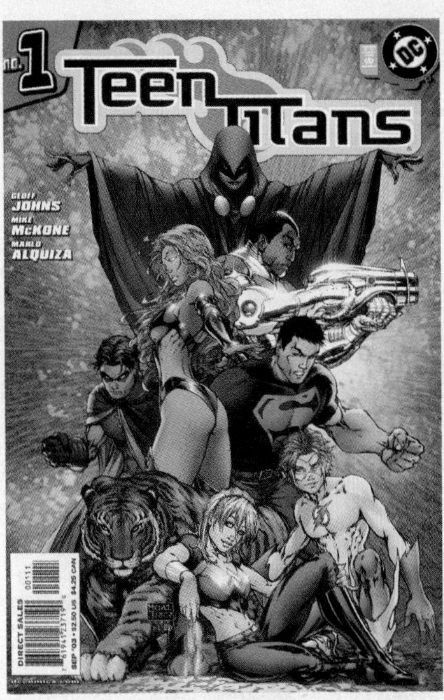

TEEN TITANS #1
1st printing with Michael Turner cover.
September 2003. © DC

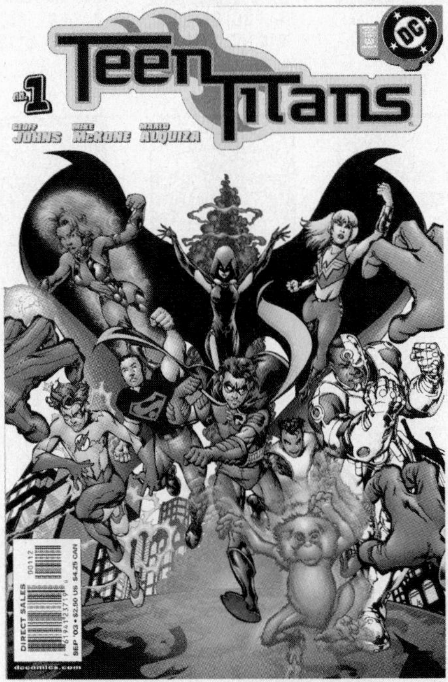

TEEN TITANS #1
2nd printing with Mike McKone cover.
Same cover used for 3rd printing.
September 2003. © DC

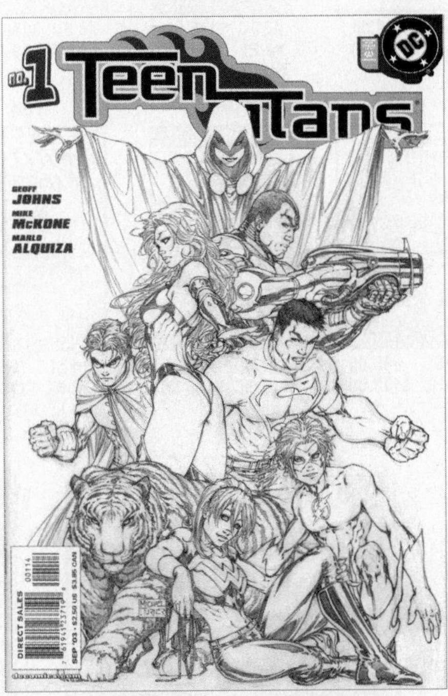

TEEN TITANS #1
4th printing with Michael Turner sketch cover.
September 2003. © DC

Overstreet Price Guide Back Issues

The Overstreet® Comic Book Price Guide has held the record for being the longest running annual comic book publication. We are now celebrating our 35th anniversary, and the demand for the Overstreet® price guides is very strong. Collectors have created a legitimate market for them, and they continue to bring record prices each year. Collectors also have a record of comic book prices going back further than any other source in comic fandom. The prices listed below are for NM condition only, with GD-25% and FN-50% of the NM value. Canadian editions exist for a couple of the early issues.

Special thanks to Robert Rogovin of Four Color Comics for his assistance in researching the prices listed in this section. Abbreviations: SC-softcover, HC-hardcover, L-leather bound.

1970
#1 White SC
$1800.00

1970
#1 Blue SC
(2nd Printing)
$1500.00

1972
#2 SC $650.00
#2 HC $1100.00

1973
#3 SC $300.00
#3 HC $950.00

1974
#4 SC $165.00
#4 HC $475.00

1975
#5 SC $155.00
#5 HC $260.00

1976
#6 SC $105.00
#6 HC $155.00

1977
#7 SC $145.00
#7 HC $230.00

1978
#8 SC $130.00
#8 HC $180.00

1979
#9 SC $130.00
#9 HC $180.00

1980
#10 SC $140.00
#10 HC $190.00

1981
#11 SC $85.00
#11 HC $115.00

1982
#12 SC $85.00
#12 HC $115.00

1983
#13 SC $85.00
#13 HC $115.00

1984
#14 SC $55.00
#14 HC $110.00
#14 L $170.00

1985
#15 SC $55.00
#15 HC $80.00
#15 L $160.00

1986
#16 SC $60.00
#16 HC $85.00
#16 L $170.00

1987
#17 SC $55.00
#17 HC $110.00
#17 L $160.00

1988
#18 SC $45.00
#18 HC $65.00
#18 L $160.00

1989
#19 SC $50.00
#19 HC $60.00
#19 L $170.00

1990
#20 SC $32.00
#20 HC $50.00
#20 L $135.00

1991
#21 SC $35.00
#21 HC $55.00
#21 L $145.00

1992
#22 SC $32.00
#22 HC $50.00

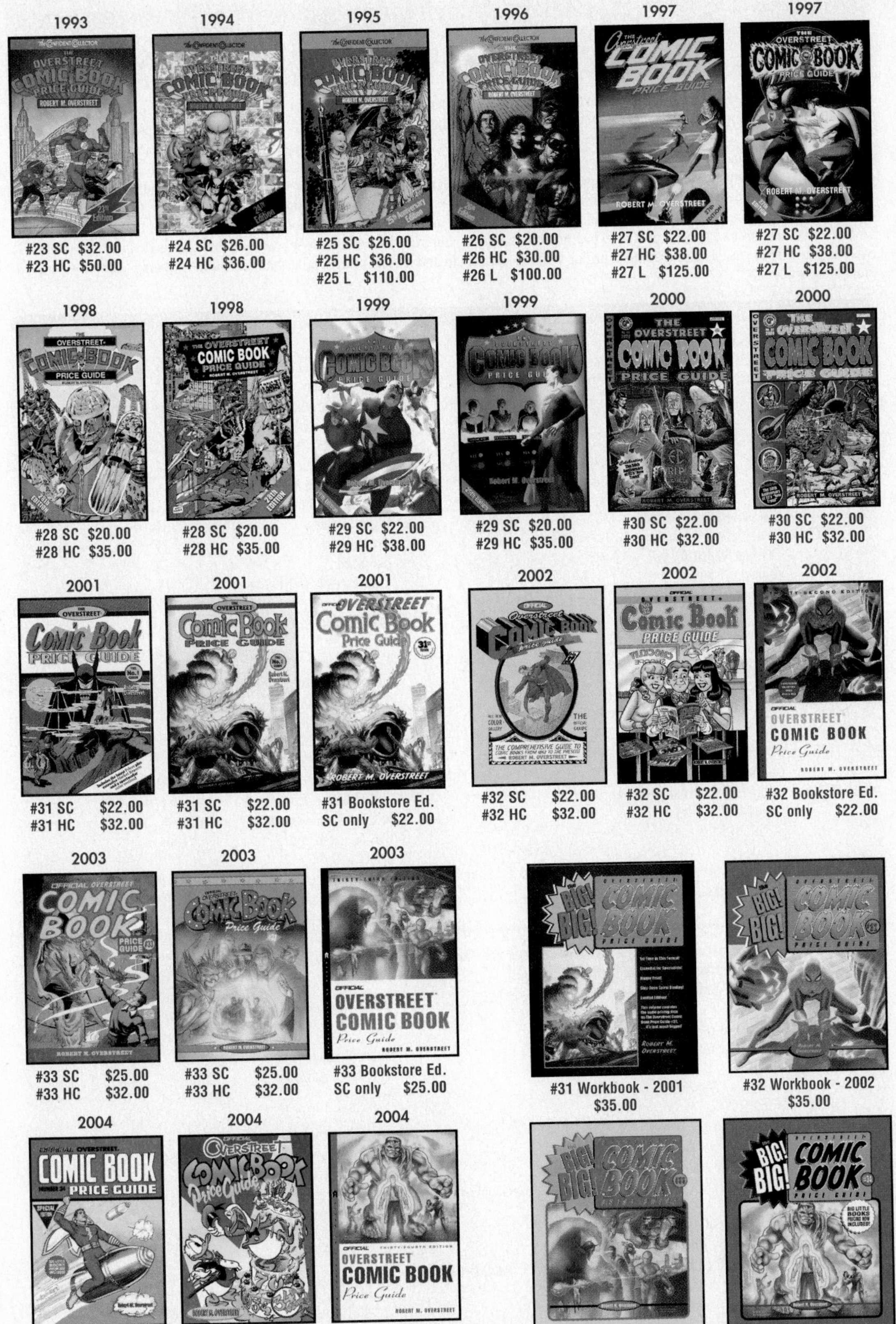

1993 — #23 SC $32.00 / #23 HC $50.00

1994 — #24 SC $26.00 / #24 HC $36.00

1995 — #25 SC $26.00 / #25 HC $36.00 / #25 L $110.00

1996 — #26 SC $20.00 / #26 HC $30.00 / #26 L $100.00

1997 — #27 SC $22.00 / #27 HC $38.00 / #27 L $125.00

1997 — #27 SC $22.00 / #27 HC $38.00 / #27 L $125.00

1998 — #28 SC $20.00 / #28 HC $35.00

1998 — #28 SC $20.00 / #28 HC $35.00

1999 — #29 SC $22.00 / #29 HC $38.00

1999 — #29 SC $20.00 / #29 HC $35.00

2000 — #30 SC $22.00 / #30 HC $32.00

2000 — #30 SC $22.00 / #30 HC $32.00

2001 — #31 SC $22.00 / #31 HC $32.00

2001 — #31 SC $22.00 / #31 HC $32.00

2001 — #31 Bookstore Ed. SC only $22.00

2002 — #32 SC $22.00 / #32 HC $32.00

2002 — #32 SC $22.00 / #32 HC $32.00

2002 — #32 Bookstore Ed. SC only $22.00

2003 — #33 SC $25.00 / #33 HC $32.00

2003 — #33 SC $25.00 / #33 HC $32.00

2003 — #33 Bookstore Ed. SC only $25.00

#31 Workbook - 2001 $35.00

#32 Workbook - 2002 $35.00

2004 — #34 SC $25.00 / #34 HC $32.00

2004 — #34 SC $25.00 / #34 HC $32.00

2004 — #34 Bookstore Ed. SC only $25.00

#33 Workbook - 2003 $37.00

#34 Workbook - 2004 $37.00

Feature Article Index

Over the years, the **Overstreet Comic Book Price Guide** has grown into much more than a simple catalog of values. Almost since the very beginning, Bob has worked hard to make sure that the book reflects the latest information about the hobby, and this has resulted in some fascinating in-depth articles about aspects of the industry and the rich history of comics. Sadly, many of you may never have read a lot of these articles, or even knew they existed.

These two pages contain a comprehensive index to every feature article ever published in the **Overstreet Comic Book Price Guide**. From interviews with legendary creators to exhaustively researched retrospectives, it's all here. Enjoy this look back at the Overstreet legacy, and remember, many of these editions are still available through Gemstone and your local comic book dealer.

Note: The first three editions of the Guide had no feature articles, but from #4 on, a tradition was born that has carried through to the very volume you hold in your hands. This index begins with the 4th edition and lists all articles published up to and including last year's 34th edition of the guide.

ED.	YR.	TITLE	AUTHOR(S)	PGS.
#4	1974	Secrets Behind ALL-STAR COMICS(More Than You May Want to Know)	Jerry Bails	26-37
#5	1975	Edgar Rice Burroughs and the Comics	Kevin B. Hancer	33-38
#6	1976	An Interview with Will Eisner, Creator of the Spirit	Jerry DeFuccio	31-37
		Good Girl Art - An Introduction: Why it Was and What it Was	prod. by the American Comic Book Co. (Carl Macek)	38-43
		The Archives of the Comic Book Price Guide	Landon Chesney (comic strip)	44-45
#7	1977	Esoteric Comics: The Ultimate Collectable	prod. by the American Comic Book Co. (Carl Macek in consultation with Scott Shaw)	A-30-35
		Carl Barks - From Burbank to Calisota	E. B. Boatner	A-37-57
#8	1978	Confessions of a Former Comic Book Artist	Jay Disbrow	A-31-38
		The Man Behind Torchy	Bill Ward	A-40-53
		Women in Comics	Carl Macek in collaboration with Art Amsie	A-54-75
		Tarpe Mills - An Appreciation	Trina Robbins	A-76
#9	1979	For Those Who Know How to Look	Carl Macek	A-35-42
		Good Lord! choke... gasp... It's EC!	E. B. Boatner	A-43-76
#10	1980	The Origin of Marvel Comics	George Olshevsky	A-46-73
#11	1981	Anaglyphs - A Survey of the 3-D Comic Books	Ray Zone	A-44-53
		L. B. Cole: The Man Behind the Mask: (and Captain Aero and Catman and...)	E. B. Boatner	A-55-72
#12	1982	Norman Mingo and Alfred: The World's Greatest Facelift	Jerry DeFuccio	A-45-57
		The Pop Hollinger Story: The First Comic Book Collector/Dealer	Tim Hessee	A-58-66
#13	1983	Great Old Time Radio Premiums	"Little" Jimmy Dempsey	A-62-63
		Reminiscences of a Comic Book Editor	Jack Schiff and Gene Reed	A-64-70
		DC Before Superman	Gary M. Carter and Ken Lane Carter	A-72-86
#14	1984	Katy WHO?...Never Heard of it...	Barbara A. Rausch	A-52-56
		Congratulations Katy Keene	(various comic book and cartoon creators)	A-57-59
		Katy Keene - The Overstreet Connection	Craig Leavitt	A-67-78
#15	1985	Charles Clarence Beck: The World's Second Mightiest Mortal	Jerry DeFuccio	A-78-88
		Mr. Mind and the Monster Society of Evil	C. C. Beck	A-89-93
#16	1986	Twenty-Five Years? I Don't Believe It!	Stan Lee	A-82-84
		Marvel and Me	Jim Shooter	A-85-96
#17	1987	The Man Behind the Cover - Ron Dias	staff	A-84
		The Enduring Magic of Disney Comics	Thomas Andrae (with Bruce Hamilton)	A-85-99
		Walt Disney's Snow White and the Seven: Dwarfs - Fifty Years of Collectibles	Terry Taylor	A-101-111
#18	1988	The Man Behind the Cover - L. B. Cole	Christopher Irons	A-77
		Of Supermen and Kids With Dreams: An Interview with Jerry Siegel and Joe Shuster	Thomas Andrae	A-79-98
#19	1989	Origins of the Dark Knight: A Conversation with Batman Artists	Thomas Andrae, Bob Kane and Jerry Robinson	A-72-93
#20	1990	In a League of Their Own !	Harry B. Thomas	A-77-93
		The Silver Age...The Beginning: A Comparative Chronology of the First Silver Age Comic Books	Gary M. Carter	A-94-107
#21	1991	Archie Comic Publications: The Mirth of a Legend	Scott D. Fulop	A-77-78
		1941: Comic Books Go To War!:	Harry B. Thomas	A-79-98

		Those fabulous comics of World War II	and Gary M. Carter	
#22	1992	Spider-Man - An Amazing Success Story	Steve Saffel	A-77-86
		Journey Into the Unknown World of Atlas Fantasy	Gary M. Carter & Pat S. Calhoun	A-87-103
#23	1993	Green Lantern's Light! A History by...	Thomas Andrae with Keif Fromm	A-71-79
		Silver Sagas of the Scarlet Speedster: Whirlwind Adventures of the Fastest Man Alive! 1956-1960	Gary M. Carter	A-80-86
#24	1994	Three Uncanny Decades of X-Men!	John Townsend, Ph.D.	A-146-156
		Living on Borrowed Time! A Nostalgic Look at the Early Years of DC's Challengers of the Unknown!	Pat S. Calhoun & Gary M. Carter	A-157-164
#25	1995	The Mystery of the 12 Missing ECs	Bruce Hamilton	A-99-106
		100 Years - A Century of Comics	Pat S. Calhoun	A-107-123
#26	1996	The American Comic Book: 1897-1932 The Formative Years - The Platinum Age	Richard D. Olson, Ph.D.	pp. 1-2
		The American Comic Book: 1933-Present The Modern Comic Book	Richard D. Olson, Ph.D.	pp. 10-11
		The Golden Age and Beyond A Short History of Comic Book Fandom & Comic Book Collecting in America	Jerry Weist Sotheby's Comic Book Consultant	652-667
#27	1997	Gotham Knights - A Conversation	Arnold T. Blumberg with Jerry Robinson	A-25-27
		Strange Adventures - A Conversation with Murphy Anderson	Scott Braden	A-30-32
		The American Comic Book: 1897-1932 The Beginning: The Platinum Age	Robert L. Beerbohm	pp. 1-15
		The American Comic Book: 1933-Present The Golden Age and Beyond: The Modern Comic Book	Richard D. Olson, Ph.D.	23-24
#28	1998	Friends of Lulu Sounds Off on Comics	Jackie Estrada	79-81
		The World of Tomorrow : How Comics of the Past Portrayed the 1990s	Arnold T. Blumberg	82-88
		Invasion of the Giant (and Not So Giant) Robots!	Arnold T. Blumberg	83-87
		Built to Last	J. C. Vaughn and Scott Braden	89-102
		The American Comic Book: 1897-1932 In the Beginning: The Platinum Age:	J. C. Vaughn	201-203
		The American Comic Book: 1933-Present The Golden Age & Beyond: The Modern Comic Book (Revised)	Richard D. Olson, Ph.D.	211-212
#29	1999	Special Feature: Grading - The Next Revolution for Comic Books	Bruce Hamilton	17-21
		Avenues of Collecting: A Walk Through the Comic Book Neighborhood	J. C. Vaughn	91-94
		Just Another Justice League?	J. C. Vaughn	95-100
		Legiondary Adventures	Mark Huesman	101-106
		One For All and All For One:	Arnold T. Blumberg	107-112
		A Brief History of Super-Teams: Top Ten Greatest Super-Teams	Benn Ray	108-112
#30	2000	History with a Twist	Arnold T. Blumberg	18-22
		EC, MAD and Beyond: Al Feldstein	J. C. Vaughn	24-28
		Flights to EC and Beyond with Al Williamson	J. C. Vaughn	36-39
		Bob's Bizarre Tales	Bob Overstreet	42-63
		The Marketing of a Medium	Arnold T. Blumberg	195-198
		New Discoveries Beyond the Platinum Age	Beerbohm & Olson	226-234
		The Golden Age & Beyond: Origins of the Modern Comic Book	Beerbohm & Olson	242-249
#31	2001	Why The Fantastic Four Made It To Forty	Arnold T. Blumberg	20-24
		Sixty Years of Wonder Woman	Charles S. Novinskie	26-29
		Brownie Points	Arnold T. Blumberg	30-32
		Re-Creations in a Flash (Murphy Anderson profile)	Arnold T. Blumberg	39-40
		Extraordinary! (John K. Snyder III profile)	J.C. Vaughn	42-44
		Bendis! (Brian Michael Bendis profile)	J.C. Vaughn	46-48
#32	2002	Superman: Patriotic Covers Through the Years	Arnold T. Blumberg	40-43
		Spidey Goes Hollywood	Arnold T. Blumberg	44-46
		Archie at 60	J. C. Vaughn	47-49
#33	2003	A Brief History of the Justice Society	J. C. Vaughn	850-852
		Mutant Movie Stars: The "New" X-Men Storm the Silver Screen	Arnold T. Blumberg	854-856
		Through Waves and Flame: The Elemental Entrance of the Sub-Mariner	Arnold T. Blumberg	858-860
		Variant Watch: Ultimate Spider-Man #1	J. C. Vaughn	862-863
		Comic Book Ages: Starting the Discussion	J. C. Vaughn & Arnold T. Blumberg	866-867
#34	2004	Comic Book Ages: Defining Eras	Arnold T. Blumberg & J. C. Vaughn	948-951
		70 Years and Still Quacking	J. C. Vaughn	952-955
		Going Green: The Best of the Hulk	Arnold T. Blumberg	956-959
		(Joe) Simon Says	J. C. Vaughn	960-963
		Comic Book Charities: Lifelines of the Industry	Dale Moore	964-966

Overstreet Advisors

WELDON ADAMS
Comics Historian
Fort Worth, TX

DAVID T. ALEXANDER
David Alexander Comics
Tampa, FL

TYLER ALEXANDER
David Alexander Comics
Tampa, FL

LON ALLEN
Heritage Comics Auctions
Dallas, TX

DAVE ANDERSON
Want List Comics
Tulsa, OK

STEPHEN BARRINGTON
Collector
Chickasaw, AL

ROBERT BEERBOHM
Robert Beerbohm Comic Art
Fremont, NE

JON BERK
Collector
Hartford, CT

BRIAN BLOCK
WB Auction Services
Adamstown, PA

STEVE BOROCK
Primary Grader
Comics Guaranty, LLC

MICHAEL BROWNING
Collector
Delbarton, WV

MICHAEL CARBONARO
Neatstuffcollectibles.com
Englewood, NJ

GARY CARTER
Collector
Coronado, CA

JOHN CHRUSCINSKI
Tropic Comics
Lyndora, PA

GARY COLABUONO
Dealer/Collector
Elk Grove Village, IL

BILL COLE
Bill Cole Enterprises, Inc.
Randolph, MA

TIM COLLINS
RTS Unlimited, Inc.
Lakewood, CO

JACK COPLEY
Graham Crackers Comics
Naperville, IL

PETER DIXON
Paradise Comics
Toronto, ONT

GARY DOLGOFF
Gary Dolgoff Comics
Easthampton, MA

BRUCE ELLSWORTH
Dealer
Tampa, FL

CONRAD ESCHENBERG
Collector/Dealer
Cold Spring, NY

MICHAEL EURY
Author
Lake Oswego, OR

RICHARD EVANS
Bedrock City Comics
Houston, TX

D'ARCY FARRELL
Pendragon Comics
Toronto, ONT

STEPHEN FISHLER
Metropolis Collectibles, Inc.
New York, NY

DAN FOGEL
Hippy Comix, Inc.
El Sobrante, CA

CHRIS FOSS
Heroes & Dragons
Columbia, SC

STEVEN GENTNER
Golden Age Specialist
Portland, OR

STEVE GEPPI
Diamond Int. Galleries
Timonium, MD

Overstreet Advisors

MICHAEL GOLDMAN
Motor City Comics
Farmington Hills, MI

TOM GORDON
Gemstone Publishing
Timonium, MD

JAMIE GRAHAM
Graham Crackers
Chicago, IL

DANIEL GREENHALGH
Showcase New England
Northford, CT

ERIC J. GROVES
Dealer/Collector
Oklahoma City, OK

ROBERT HALL
Collector
Harrisburg, PA

JIM HALPERIN
Heritage Comics Auctions
Dallas, TX

BRUCE HAMILTON
Collector
Prescott, AZ

MARK HASPEL
Grader
Comics Guaranty, LLC

JOHN HAUSER
Dealer/Collector
New Berlin, WI

GREG HOLLAND
Collector
Malverne, AR

BILL HUGHES
Dealer/Collector
Flower Mound, TX

ROB HUGHES
Arch Angels
Manhattan Beach, CA

WILLIAM INSIGNARES
Demolition Comics
Tampa, FL

ED JASTER
Heritage Comics Auctions
Dallas, TX

PHIL LEVINE
Dealer/Collector
Three Bridges, NJ

PAUL LITCH
Modern Age Specialist
Comics Guaranty, LLC

LARRY LOWERY
Big Little Books Specialist
Danville, CA

NADIA MANNARINO
All Star Auctions
Ridgewood, NJ

PATRICK MARCHBANKS
Golden Age Comics & Games
Gulfport, MS

HARRY MATETSKY
Collector
Middletown, NJ

JON McCLURE
Dealer/Collector
Durango, CO

TODD MCDEVITT
New Dimension Comics
Cranberry Township, PA

MIKE McKENZIE
Alternate Worlds
Cockeysville, MD

FRED McSURLEY
Warehouse Auction Centers
Camarillo, CA

PETER MEROLO
Collector
Sedona, AZ

DALE MOORE
Comics4Kids
Bonney Lake, WA

STEVE MORTENSEN
Colossus Comics
Santa Clara, CA

MICHAEL NAIMAN
Silver Age Specialist
San Diego, CA

MARC NATHAN
Cards, Comics & Collectibles
Reisterstown,MD

JOSHUA NATHANSON
ComicLink
Great Neck, NY

Overstreet Advisors

MATT NELSON
Classics Incorporated
Dallas, TX

CHARLIE NOVINSKIE
Silver Age Specialist
Clifton, CO

RICHARD OLSON
Collector/Academician
Poplarville, MS

TERRY O'NEILL
Terry's Comics
Orange, CA

GEORGE PANTELA
GPAnalysis for Comics
Hampton, Victoria, Australia

JIM PAYETTE
Golden Age Specialist
Bethlehem, NH

CHRIS PEDRIN
Pedrin Conservatory
Redwood City, CA

JOHN PETTY
Heritage Comics Auctions
Dallas, TX

JIM PITTS
Surf City Comix
Mountain View, CA

RON PUSSELL
Redbeard's Book Den
Crystal Bay, NV

JO ANN REISLER
Collector
Vienna, VA

TODD REZNIK
Pacific Comic Exchange
Palos Verdes Peninsula, CA

DAVE ROBIE
Big Little Books Specialist
Lancaster, PA

ROBERT ROGOVIN
Four Color Comics
Scarsdale, NY

MARNIN ROSENBERG
Collectors Assemble
Great Neck, NY

ROBERT ROTER
Pacific Comic Exchange
Palos Verdes Peninsula, CA

CHUCK ROZANSKI
Mile High Comics
Denver, CO

MATT SCHIFFMAN
Bronze Age Specialist
Aloha, OR

DOUG SCHMELL
Pedigree Comics, Inc.
Wellington,FL

JOHN SNYDER
Diamond Int. Galleries
Timonium, MD

TONY STARKS
Silver Age Specialist
Evansville, IN

AL STOLTZ
Basement Comics
Havre de Grace, MD

KEN STRIBLING
Action Island
Jackson, MS

DOUG SULIPA
"Everything 1960-1996"
Manitoba, Canada

MICHAEL TIERNEY
The Comic Book Store
Little Rock, AR

TED VAN LIEW
Superworld Comics
Worcester, MA

JOE VERENEAULT
JHV Associates
Woodbury Heights, NJ

BOB WAYNE
DC Comics
New York City, NY

JERRY WEIST
Sotheby's
Gloucester, MA

HARLEY YEE
Dealer/Collector
Detroit, MI

VINCENT ZURZOLO, JR.
Metropolis Collectibles, Inc.
New York, NY

Advertisers' Index

A

B

C

D

E

F

G

H

HOUSE OF COLLECTIBLES

THE OFFICIAL PRICE GUIDE TO

DISNEY COLLECTIBLES

TED HAKE

The Official Price Guide to Disney Collectibles by noted collectibles expert Ted Hake is the proverbial "must have" book for every Disneyana enthusiast. Whether it's classic Disney animated features such as *Aladdin, Bambi, Beauty and the Beast, Cinderella* or *Snow White and the Seven Dwarfs*, Disney/Pixar collaborations like *A Bug's Life, Finding Nemo*, or *Toy Story*, live action releases such *Bedknobs and Broomsticks, The Black Hole, Herbie the Love Bug* or *Mary Poppins*, or TV series like *Duck Tales, The Hardy Boys*, or *Mickey Mouse Club*, it's in this book!

Every single Disneyana item listed in this volume is also pictured in full color and evaluated. So whether it's a wonderful memory from the opening of Disneyland or a newly cherished toy from the latest theatrical release ***The Official Price Guide to Disney Collectibles*** *is the most comprehensive Disneyana reference ever!*

NEARLY 10,000 ITEMS! MORE THAN 125 SECTIONS!
Covers all the greats from A Bug's Life to Zorro!
Thousands of the rarest Mickey Mouse collectibles!
Includes The Incredibles and all things Disney!

ON SALE SUMMER 2005!

Walt Disney's
Donald Duck
Adventures
BIG
Disney
Thrills
in a Small
package
3
Walt Disney's
Donald Duck
Adventures
Walt Disney's
Donald Duck
Adventures
2
Sometimes the most excitement takes up the least amount of space. That's certainly the case with *Donald Duck Adventures*, the first of Gemstone Publishing's squarebound "Take-Along" comic books, published bimonthly.
©2004 Disney Enterprises, Inc.

You love 'em
we want 'em
DETECTIVE DAN
JUNIOR MEMBER
CLUB
CAPTAIN BATTLE
SILVER STREAK COMICS
BOYS' BRIGADE
JONES CADETS
PINBACKS
We buy cloisonné, vintage,
and Disney pinbacks
in HIGH GRADE.
The market has never been
hotter for these beauties.
Call
Joshua M. Geppi
PIN TRADING
SCROOGE
2000
Toll Free (888)355-9800 x451
E-mail gejosh@diamondgalleries.com
2000
Disneyland

NOSTALGIC AUCTIONS
He sold with us because we have the lowest commission rates in the industry!
He came to us because of our 20 years experience!
She came to us because we give immediate cash!
They came to us because we deal exclusively with comics & original art!
He liked that we promote our auctions with a full color catalog!
He refused to get wholesale for his art. He got retail because he came to us!
These are just some of the reasons people come to the comic book & original art experts at Nostalgic Auctions. We look forward to helping you realize the most money when selling your comic related collectibles.
Nostalgic Auctions
PO Box 98
Marshfield, MA 02059
1-800-770-0855
comics@nostalgicauctions.com
http://www.nostalgicauctions.com
All characters ©2005 respective copyright holders. All rights reserved.
CGC Comics Guaranty, LLC
CHARTER MEMBER DEALER